P9-DTM-413

M·A·N·U·F·A·C·T·U·R·I·N·G USA

Industry Analyses,
Statistics, and Leading Companies

ISSN 1044-7024

M·A·N·U·F·A·C·T·U·R·I·N·G USA

Industry Analyses, Statistics, and Leading Companies

Fifth Edition

- A comprehensive guide to economic activity in 458 manufacturing industries
- Provides unique analysis and synthesis of federal statistics
- Includes more than 21,000 top manufacturing corporations taken from *Ward's Business Directory of U.S. Private and Public Companies*

Volume 1
SIC 2011 - 3299

Arsen J. Darnay, Editor

DETROIT · NEW YORK · TORONTO · LONDON

Arsen J. Darnay, *Editor*

Editorial Code and Data, Inc. Staff

Kenneth Muth, *Data Processing*
Nancy Ratliff, *Data Entry*
Marlita A. Reddy, *Research*

Gale Research Inc. Staff

Kristin Hart, *Editorial Coordinator*
Lynn Osborn, *Assistant Editorial Coordinator*

Mary Beth Trimper, *Production Director*
Shanna Heilveil, *Production Assistant*
Tracey Rowens, *Art Director*
Sherrell Hobbs, *Desktop Publisher*

Manufacturing USA: Industry Analyses, Statistics, and Leading Companies is published by Gale Research Inc. under license from Information Access Company. *Ward's Business Directory* is a trademark of Information Access Company.

Ward's Business Directory™ utilizes an intensive research approach. Information on companies listed in the directory was gathered from annual reports, questionnaires, banks, trade commissions, newsletters, government documents, and telephone interviews. When sales data are unavailable from private companies, *Ward's* offers an estimate based on several considerations. Estimates are so noted with an asterisk (*).

ISBN 0-8103-6453-0 (Vol. 1)
ISBN 0-8103-6454-9 (Vol. 2)
ISSN 1044-7024

Printed in the United States of America
Published in the United States by Gale Research

Contents

Volume I

Volume II

Highlights

Manufacturing USA: Industry Analyses, Statistics, and Leading Companies (MUSA) presents comprehensive information on industrial activity over a span of 17 years in two volumes. This fifth edition of an award winning title (American Library Association, RASD *Outstanding Reference Source*), features preanalyzed statistical data on industry performance and company participation, illustrated with graphics and fully indexed. Highlights include—

- Detailed information on 458 manufacturing industries—as defined in the 1987 revisions of the Standard Industrial Classification (SIC) system.

- Most current data available on industrial activity at this level of detail and across the span of all manufacturing, including, for the first time, results of the 1992 Economic Census.

- 17 year data series (1982-1998), including projections.

- Statistical data series on establishments, employment, compensation, production, and capital expenditures from 1982 to 1994 and projections to 1998.

- Graphic illustration of trends in shipments and employment.

- Precalculated ratios for 20 important industrial measurements, compared with the average of all manufacturing industries, and indexed for easy assessment.

- More than 21,000 company listings, arranged by sales volume. Up to 75 companies are listed per industry, showing name, address, telephone, name of the chief executive officer, sales volume, and employment.

- Updated occupational data for each industry (1994), showing major occupations employed by the industry and trends in employment to the year 2005.

- More detailed and updated (1992) product breakdowns showing the products or product groups that make up each 4-digit SIC industry.

- Materials consumption tables for each industry, showing quantities of materials purchased and their costs, updated to 1992.

- Comprehensive, updated (1992) state-level data on each industry, illustrated with state and regional maps.

Preface

Manufacturing: The Big Picture

Continuing with this, the 5th, edition, a long enough data series is available to provide a general overview of the U.S. manufacturing sector. This will serve as the "big picture" of which the individual SIC chapters are distinct views. Most importantly, with the completion of the 1992 Economic Census, highly reliable data are available for three benchmark years, covering a 15 year span.

Data presented in this section are thus drawn from the 1982, 1987, and 1992 summaries of manufacturing. All three years were Economic Census years, representing a 100 per sample of all U.S. manufacturing (or as close to it as these things get).

The General State of Manufacturing

The health of the U.S. manufacturing sector is still hotly debated—even as competitive pressures from Japan and elsewhere have lessened somewhat: the strong yen, weak European economies, and Germany's preoccupations with reunification have been contributing factors. The statistical picture presented here supports, albeit not very dramatically, media claims that manufacturing is declining. Manufacturing is not declining; it is maturing. But there seems to be a lot of life left in the Old Gray Mare. Here are some statistics:

- Manufacturing was a smaller part of Gross Domestic Product (GDP) in 1992 than it was ten years earlier, but manufacturing has grown in output and employment. This suggests that other sectors of the economy have been expanding more rapidly.

- Manufacturing—along with agriculture, forestry, mining, and construction—are basic economic activities. All other sectors depend upon these. Therefore, the expansion of the services sector is in a very real sense *enabled* by the productivity of these basic sectors.

- More people worked in manufacturing in 1992 than in 1982; there has been no erosion of employment in the manufacturing sector. However, manufacturing employment, as a percentage of the entire workforce, has declined by a percentage point.

- Manufacturing output has grown—but at a lower rate than GDP. Output per employee increased by 55.1 percent in the period; compensation has increased by 66.5 percent.

- As shown by growth in capital investment (56.2 percent) and growth in value added per employee (80.6), technology is playing an increasingly important role in manufacturing.

Indicators of Manufacturing

Establishments. *Correcting the impression left by the last few years, the new Economic Census shows that establishment counts are* **up** *and growth in small establishments is up strongly, suggesting a new vigor in enterprise formation.* Total number of establishments increased from a 1982 level of nearly 309,000 to 371,000 in 1992. Total establishment counts increased by 20.2 percent; small establishments increased by 22.7 percent; large establishments (20 or more employees) increased by 15.1 percent. Company counts are also up from 278,000 in 1982 to 337,000 in 1992 (21.3 percent).

Employment. *Manufacturing employment is keeping up with total employment but growing more sluggishly*. Manufacturing employed nearly 16.97 million people in 1992. While total employment in the manufacturing sector has risen since 1982 by 1.46 million, manufacturing employment as a percent of the labor force has dropped slightly from 16.1 percent in 1982 to 14.8 percent in 1992 (nonagricultural payrolls). In the period 1982 to 1992, the total labor force rose by 19.0 percent and manufacturing employment rose by 9.4 percent.

Production employment in the 1982-1992 period increased at a much lower rate (6.6 percent) than employment of administrative, sales, and technical forces (16.1 percent), suggesting that automation is continuing to reduce the need for factory production jobs.

Compensation. *Compensation levels are up. Growth in compensation is greater for administrative, sales, and technical forces than for production workers.* Compensation in the 1982 to 1992 period (shown in tabular format below) indicates that wages and salaries have increased at a slightly lower level then value of shipments, with salaries rising faster than wages.

Employee Compensation, 1982, 1987, 1992

Annual Earnings - $	*1982*	*1987*	*1992*	*82-92 %*
All Employees	19,138	24,167	29,117	52.1
Admin/tech/sales employees	24,947	32,292	39,946	60.1
Production workers	16,698	20,534	24,167	44.7

Performance. *Manufacturing shipments are a declining percent of GDP. Productivity is increasing*. Measured as a percent of GDP, manufacturing shipments represented 56.2 percent in 1982 and 49.8 percent in 1992. Costs have grown less sharply than shipments. Value added in manufacturing is up most in this period, supported by a strong level of capital investment.

Manufacturing Performance, 1982, 1987, 1992

In Millions of Dollars and Percent	*1982*	*1987*	*1992*	*82-92 %*
Value of Shipments	1,769,777	2,475,970	3,004,862	69.8
Cost of Materials	1,042,259	1,319,211	1,572,561	50.9
Value Added in Manufacturing	721,286	1,165,897	1,425,207	97.6
Capital Investment	66,062	78,653	103,210	56.2

Productivity. *Productivity in manufacturing is up by any measure. Productivity appears to be reflected in a shift of skill from plant floor to engineering departments*. Output per employee has risen faster than compensation. The capital (tooling) available to each employee has increased. Production employment has risen 6.6 percent compared with all employment in manufacturing (9.4 percent) and with administrative, sales, and technical employment (up 16.1 percent), suggesting that production workers are decreasing as a percentage of all manufacturing employment. Some of their functions, clearly, are being taken over by technical and communications employees working in engineering and administrative departments.

Manufacturing Productivity Measures, 1982, 1987, 1992

In Dollars and Percent	*1982*	*1987*	*1992*	*82-92 %*
Shipments per Employee (all)	114,109	139,741	177,038	55.1
Value added per Employee	46,506	65,802	83,969	80.6
Capital Investment per Empl.	4,259	4,439	6,081	42.8
Shipments per Prod. Worker	162,033	202,227	257,966	59.2
Value Added per Prod. Worker	66,038	95,226	122,353	85.3
Capital per Prod. Worker	6,048	6,424	8,861	46.5

Introduction

Manufacturing USA: Industry Analyses, Statistics, and Leading Companies (MUSA) presents statistics on 458 U.S. manufacturing industries drawn from a variety of federal sources and combined with information on leading public and private corporations obtained from *Ward's Business Directory of U.S. Private and Public Companies.*

MUSA represents a unique synthesis of relevant data from the *Census of Manufactures*, the *Annual Survey of Manufactures*, the *County Business Patterns* data series, the *U.S. Industrial Outlook*, the *Benchmark Input-Output Accounts for the U.S. Economy, 1982*, and the *Industry-Occupation Matrix* produced by the U.S. Department of Labor. Data on leading private and public corporations are drawn from *Ward's*, as mentioned above. Together, these materials, in preanalyzed presentation, provide a one-stop and well-indexed access to the most recently available data on manufacturing in the United States.

Features

In its first edition, *MUSA* was cited as an *Outstanding Reference Source* by the American Library Association's Reference and Adult Services Division (RASD). The fifth edition of *MUSA* retains the award-winning features of the first edition—detailed industry profiles, illustrated with graphics and maps, combining the most recent governmental data with information on corporations, and arranged so that significance can be instantly recognized. Projections are now also provided. New features include—

- Updated Census data from 1982 through 1994, including all new detail data from the 1992 Economic Census.

- Projections for the 1995-1998 period. Data for these years are projected by the editors for most of the industry series.

- 17-year continuous series. With updates and projections, *MUSA* now presents a continuous 17-year series from 1982 through 1998.

- Updated industry ratios. Industry ratios are now based on 1994 (the last Census survey data available).

- Updated occupational data for 1994 with projections to the year 2005. In the last edition, data for 1992 were shown projected to 2005.

'The Most Current Data Available'

MUSA reports the most current data available at the time of the book's preparation. The objective is to present *hard* information—data based on actual survey by authoritative bodies—for all manufacturing industries on a *comparable* basis. A few industries may collect more recent information through their industry associations or other bodies. Similarly, estimates are published on this or that industry based on the analyses and guesses of knowledgeable individuals. These data are rarely in the same format as the Federal data and are not available for a large cross section of industry. Therefore, the data in *MUSA* are, indeed, the most current at this level of detail and spanning the entirety of manufacturing activity. It is meant to serve as the foundation on which others can base their own projections.

In addition to presenting current survey data, the editors also provide projected data for most categories from 1995 through 1998—continuing the popular feature introduced in the 4th edition. The methodology used to make these projections is discussed in the next chapter.

Scope and Coverage

MUSA presents statistical data on 458 manufacturing industries nationally and in all 50 states (when the industry is present). Data are presented, in addition, on more than 2,000 products/materials, approximately 400 occupational groupings employed in manufacturing, and more than 21,000 public and private companies. The industry count is down by one in this edition because data for *SIC 2067 - Chewing gum* is no longer being collected by the Bureau of the Census.

Data are shown for the years 1982 to 1994 from the Economic Census surveys (1982, 1987, 1992) and from the *Annual Survey of Manufacturing* (*ASM*) for other years. Occupational data are presented for 1994 (updated from 1992) and projected (by the Department of Labor) to the year 2005 (the same year as in the last edition). Input-Output data for 1982 are taken from the latest I-O study (released in 1991). Corporate data are drawn from the 1996 edition of the *Ward's Business Directory*.

Where possible, data are projected through 1998. A special discussion of the methods used to obtain projections is included in the next chapter.

MUSA follows the 1987 classification conventions published by the Office of Management and Budget (*Standard Industrial Classification Manual: 1987*).

The SIC convention divides economic activity hierarchically into major industry groups (2-digit code), industry groups (3-digit), and industries (4-digit). Most data presented in *MUSA* are shown at the 4-digit industry level. Exceptions are occupational data (presented in 3-digit aggregation or in groups of 3-digit industries) and more detailed product information drawn from 5-digit product class codes and 7-digit product codes.

Organization and Content

MUSA is now divided into two volumes, as follows:

- **Volume I** — covers *SICs 2011 - Meatpacking plants* through *SIC 3299 - Nonmetallic mineral products*. The *User's Guide* is placed in Volume I.

- **Volume II** — covers *SICs 3312 - Blast furnaces and steel mills* through *SIC 3999 - Miscellaneous manufacturing industries, nec*. Indexes are placed in Volume II.

Within each volume, *MUSA* is organized by industry. Within each industry, data are presented in nine tables and two graphics as follows:

1	Trends Graphic	Graphs showing shipments and employment.
2	General Statistics	National statistics.
3	Indices of Change	National data in index format.
4	Selected Ratios	Twenty ratios for the industry.
5	Leading Companies	Up to 75 companies in this industry.
6	Materials Consumed	Purchases of materials and products by quantity and cost.
7	Product Share Details	Product categories within industry in percent of total.
8	Inputs and Outputs	Economic sectors that sell to and buy from industry.
9	Occupations Employed	Occupations employed by 3-digit industry group.
10	Maps	States and regions where industry is active.
11	Industry Data by State	State level statistics.

Each industry begins on a new page. The order of graphics and tables is invariable. In a few instances, tables are split between pages.

The four indexes (found in Volume II) are:

- Standard Industrial Classification (SIC) Code Index
- Product Index
- Company Index
- Occupation Index

The SIC Index is in two parts. The first part is arranged in SIC code sequence followed by the name of the industry and the page number on which it begins; the second part is arranged alphabetically by industry name.

For detailed information on *MUSA*'s industry profiles and indexes, please consult the *Overview of Content and Sources*—found in both volumes.

Comments and Suggestions Are Welcome

Comments on or suggestions for improvement of the usefulness, format, and coverage of *MUSA* are always welcome. Although every effort is made to maintain accuracy, errors may occasionally occur; the editor will be grateful if these are called to his attention. Please contact the editor below with comments and suggestions or, to have technical questions answered, call the editor directly at ECDI at (313) 961-2926.

Editor
Manufacturing USA: Industry Analyses, Statistics, and Leading Companies
Gale Research
835 Penobscot Building
Detroit, MI 48226-4094
Phone:(313) 961-2242
(800) 347-GALE
Fax: (313) 961-6815

Overview of Content and Sources

The 1987 SIC Structure

Data in *MUSA* are ordered in conformity with the 1987 Standard Industrial Classification (SIC) system. This version of the SIC structure is now well entrenched. In relation to the older 1982 SIC system, the user should note five cases:

Case 1. The industry has not changed in any way in the move from the 1982 to the 1987 system; neither SIC number nor the components have changed. In these cases, *MUSA* presents data from 1982 forward to the most currently available year.

Case 2. The industry components have not changed but the SIC number has. Treatment of the industry is the same as in Case 1, but the industry designation is the 1987 SIC.

Case 3. The industry components have changed. However, the Department of Commerce (DOC) has restated the data for earlier years so that a complete series is available. *MUSA* presents these data as reported.

Case 4. The industry SIC *number* has not changed, the industry components *have* changed, and DOC has *not* restated the numbers for earlier years. In these cases, *MUSA* presents historical data, from 1982 to 1986, based on the 1977 components of the SIC. From 1987 forward, the new components are assumed. These industries show an asterisk (*) next to the year 1987, and the source note explains the situation. In these cases, also, the graphic illustrating shipments and employment will have a broken line to show discontinuity of data. This treatment was adopted to show as much historical data as possible, indicative of general trends, even if detailed comparison between early and later years is ill advised.

Case 5. The industry was new at the time of the 1987 SIC structure's unveiling; DOC does not report data earlier than 1987. In this case, the time series begins in 1987.

Recent Change - SIC 2067. A recent change, reflected for the first time in this, the 5th edition, is the elimination of *SIC 2067 - Chewing gum*. In the 1992 Economic Census, the Bureau of the Census did not report data for this industry. Product-level data were collected but were reported as part of *SIC 2064 - Candy & other confectionery products*. This change will undoubtedly be formalized in the next edition of the SIC Manual.

As a consequence of this change, *SIC 2067* has been removed, and *MUSA* now features 458 industries.

Industry Profiles

Each industry profile contains the tables and graphics listed in the *Introduction*. A detailed discussion of each graphic display and table follows; the meaning of each data element is explained, and the sources from which the data were obtained are cited.

1. Trends Graphics: Shipments and Employment

At the beginning of each industry profile, two graphs are presented showing industry shipments and employment plotted for the years 1982 to 1998 (or an earlier date) on logarithmic scale. The curves are provided primarily to give the user an at-a-glance assessment of important trends in the industry. The logarithmic scale ensures that the shipment trends and employment trends can be compared visually despite different magnitudes and denominations of the data (millions of dollars for shipments and thousands of employees for employment); in this mode of presentation, if two curves have the same slope, the values are growing or declining at the same rate. If the values fall within a single cycle (1 to 9, 10 to 90, etc.), a single cycle is shown; if the values bridge two cycles, both are shown.

The data graphed are derived from the first table, *General Statistics*. As many years are plotted as are available. If data gaps appear in the series, missing points are calculated using a least-squares curve fitting algorithm.

In the case of a few industries, data discontinuities are present in the general statistics; data for the 1982-1986 period are not strictly comparable to the data for 1987 and later. In such cases, the line of the graph is interrupted between 1986 and 1987 to show this discontinuity.

Those portions of curves based on projections by the editors are shown in a dotted-line format.

2. General Statistics

This table shows national statistics for the industry for the years 1982-1998 under five groupings: Companies, Establishments, Employment, Compensation, and Production. The last four groupings are further subdivided, as described below.

Data for 1982, 1987, and 1992 are from Economic Census held in each of those years. Data for other years, through and including 1994, are from the *Annual Survey of*

Manufactures (*ASM*). Establishment counts in the *ASM* years are from the *County Business Patterns* for those years; exceptions are the years 1983 and 1984; establishment data for these years are extrapolations of data from the 1982 and 1985 values. New industries created in the 1987 SIC reclassification will not show data earlier than 1987. In the case of some industries, an asterisk appears next to the year 1987. This indicates that data for earlier years are not directly comparable with data for 1987 and later years due to the reclassification of the subcomponents of the industry.

Please note that data from the *U.S. Industrial Outlook* are no longer part of *MUSA*. In its ill-advised downsizing, the Federal government has seen fit to replace this useful publication with another that lacks the necessary numbers in the necessary detail.

Data for the period 1995-1998 are projected by the editors. A discussion of the methods of projection is presented below. Projected data are followed by the letter P.

Company counts are available only from the full *Census of Manufactures* conducted every five years. Data for the 1992 Economic Census add the third data point on company counts for the first time in this edition.

Establishment data are provided for 1982 through 1993; projections are shown thereafter. Establishments counts in the Census years (1982, 1987, 1992) are from the Economic Census. In other years, values are from the *County Business Patterns*. Establishment counts are typically higher than company counts because many companies operate from more than one facility. Total establishments are shown together with establishments that employ 20 or more people. Comparing the number of large establishments with total establishments will tell the user whether the industry is populated by relatively small operations or is dominated by large facilities. Values shown are absolute numbers of establishments.

The **Employment** grouping is subdivided into total employment, shown in 1,000 employees (thus a value of 134.9 means that the industry employs 134,900 people), production workers (in thousands), and production hours worked (in millions of hours). Dividing hours worked by production workers produces hours worked by a production worker in the year. This value is precalculated for the user in the table of Selected Ratios. A value of around 1,940 hours indicates full-time employment—on average; obviously such aggregate data hide the finer details of day-to-day industrial operation: the presence of part-time workers, overtime clocked, etc.

The **Compensation** grouping shows the industry's total payroll (in millions of dollars) and wages (in dollars per hour). The payroll value includes all forms of compensation subject to federal taxes, including wages, salaries, commissions, bonuses, etc. The *Census of Manufactures* provides payroll and wage data as aggregates. The wages per hour were calculated by dividing the Census wage aggregate by the total hours worked in production.

The interested user can reverse this calculation ($/hour times hours will produce wages-in-the-aggregate). Additional calculations can be used to determine the salaries of those employees who are not production workers. The procedure is to calculate aggregate wages and to deduct the result from payroll to obtain salaries paid; next, salaried employees can be calculated by deducting production workers from total employment; finally, salaries paid divided by salaried employment will produce the average annual salary of the administrative/technical work force in the industry.

The **Production** grouping shows cost of materials, value added in manufacturing, value of shipments, and capital investments, all in millions of dollars; thus a value of 0.9 means that the actual value is $900,000.

Cost of materials includes cost of raw materials, fuels, freight, and contract work associated with production and excludes costs of services (e.g., advertising, insurance), overhead, depreciation, rents, royalties, and capital expenditures.

Value Added by Manufacture represents Value of Shipments less cost of materials, supplies, containers, fuel, purchased electrical power, and contract work plus income for services rendered. The result is adjusted by adding the difference between the cost and sales price of the merchandise by merchandising operations plus net change in finished goods and work-in-process inventories between the beginning and the end of the year. Value Added is a good measure of *net* value of production because it avoids the duplications inherent in the Value of Shipments measure (below).

Value of Shipments is the net selling value of products leaving production plants in an industry. In industries where two or more production stages for a product are included under the same SIC, the Value of Shipments measure will tend to overstate the economic importance of the industry. Value of Shipments, however, corresponds to the sales volume of the industry.

The Capital Investments column shows capital expenditures for equipment and structures made by the industry provided that these expenditures are depreciated rather than expensed in the year of acquisition.

3. Indices of Change

The data presented in the *General Statistics* table are restated as indices in the *Indices of Change* table. The purpose of the table is to show the user rapidly how different categories of the industry have changed since 1992.

The year 1992 is used as the base and is therefore shown as 100 in every category. The values in the years 1982-1991 and 1993-1998 are then expressed in relation to the 1992 value. For example, Shipments in 1992 were $50,434.4 million for *SIC 2011, Meat packing plants*. This value is taken as the base for the Shipments column of the *Indices of Change* table. Shipments in 1988 in that industry were $47,333.2 million. That value, divided by $50,434.4 and multiplied by 100 is 94, which is the index for Shipments in 1988.

Thus, for the years 1982-1991 and 1993-1998, values of 100 indicate no change in relation to the 1992 base year; values above 100 mean better and values below 100 indicate worse performance—all relative to the 1992 base. Note, however, that these are *indices* rather than compounded annual rates of growth or decline. Note, also, that the base used in the last edition was 1987. The most recent full Economic Census year is always used as the index reference.

Indexes based on projections by the editors are followed by a P.

4. Selected Ratios

To understand an industry, analysts calculate ratios of various kinds so that the absolute numbers can be placed in a more global perspective. Twenty important industrial ratios are precalculated for the user in the *Selected Ratios* table. Additionally, the same ratios are also provided for the average of all manufacturing industries; an index, comparing the two categories, is also provided.

The ratios are calculated for the most recent complete year available; that year is usually 1994. In calculations using establishments, projected 1994 values are used because 1994 establishment counts were unavailable.

The categories—''Employees per Establishment,'' ''Hours per Production Worker,'' ''Shipments per Production Worker,'' etc.—represent a division between the first and the second element (Total Employees divided by Total Establishments); the exception is ''Wages per Hour,'' which is reproduced without calculation from the *General Statistics* table.

The first column of values represents the **Average of All Manufacturing**. These ratios are calculated by (1) adding all categories for manufacturing and (2) following the method for ratio calculation described above.

The second column of values shows the ratios for the **Analyzed Industry**, i.e., the industry currently under consideration.

The third column is an **Index** comparing the Analyzed Industry to the Average of All Manufacturing Industries. The index is useful for determining quickly and consistently how the Analyzed Industry stands in relation to all manufacturing. Index values of 100 mean that the Analyzed Industry, within a given ratio, is identical to the average of all 458 manufacturing industries. An index value of 500 means that the Analyzed Industry is five times the average—for instance, that it has five times as many employees per establishment or pays five times as much. An index value of 50 would indicate that the Analyzed Industry is half of the average of all industries (50%). Similarly, an index of 105 means 5% above average and 95 indicates 5% below. The best use of these index values is discussed further in the "User's Guide" (Volume I).

5. Leading Companies

The table of *Leading Companies* shows up to 75 companies that participate in the industry. The listings are sorted in descending order of sales and show the company name, address, name of the Chief Executive Officer, telephone, company type, sales (in millions of dollars) and employment (in thousands of employees). The number of companies shown, their total sales, and total employment are summed at the top of the table for the user's convenience.

The data are from the *Ward's Business Directory of U.S. Private and Public Companies* for 1996, Volumes 1, 2, and 3. Public and private corporations, divisions, subsidiaries, joint ventures, and corporate groups are shown. Thus a listing for an industry may show the parent company as well as important divisions and subsidiaries of the same company (usually in a different location).

While this method of presentation has the disadvantage of duplication (the sales of a parent corporation include the sales of any divisions listed separately), it has the advantage of providing the user with information on major components of an enterprise at different locations. In any event, the user should *not* assume that the sum of the sales (or employment) shown in the *Leading Companies* table represents the total sales (or employment) of an industry. The Shipments column of the *General Statistics* table is a better guide to industry sales.

The company's type (private, public, division, etc.) is shown on the table under the column headed "Co Type," thus providing the user with a means of roughly determining the total "net" sales (or employment) represented in the table; this can be accomplished by adding the values and then deducting values corresponding to divisions and subsidiaries of parent organizations also shown in the table. The code used is as follows:

P	Public corporation
R	Private corporation
S	Subsidiary
D	Division
J	Joint venture
G	Corporate group

An asterisk (*) placed behind the sales volume indicates an estimate; the absence of an asterisk indicates that the sales value has been obtained from annual reports, other formal submissions to regulatory bodies, or from the corporation. The symbol "<" appears in front of some employment values to indicate that the actual value is "less than" the value shown. Thus the value of "<0.1" means that the company employs fewer than 100 people.

6. Materials Consumed

The *Materials Consumed* table is a completely updated table drawn from the 1992 Economic Census; it reports the quantities of materials and products (e.g., containers, packaging) used by the industry. The delivered cost of the materials, in millions of dollars, is also shown. Data are not available for all industries. Where data are missing, the table header is reproduced with the notation that data are not available.

A number of symbols are used to indicate why data are omitted or their basis. (D) means that data are withheld to avoid disclosure of competitive data; "na" is used when data are "not available." (S) means that data are withheld because statistical norms were not met; (X) stands for "not applicable;" (Z) means that less than half of the unit quantity is consumed; "nec" means "not elsewhere classified," and "nsk" abbreviates "not specified by kind." A single asterisk (*) shows instances where 10-19 percent of the data were estimated; two asterisks (**) show a 20-29 percent estimate.

7. Product Share Details

The table of *Product Share Details* shows what products the industry makes and what percentile of total shipments these products represent. The data are new, reporting updated 1992 results for the first time. The source is the 1992 Economic Census.

The products shown come primarily from the industry under consideration but include the same products if manufactured under another SIC classification; shipment data based on *products* is not always identical to shipment data based on *industry*—because no one industry makes only products that are classified under its SIC. The volume of such inter-industry transfers is relatively small; thus applying product share percentages to Shipment data (to determine, say, the dollar volume of a particular product shipped) will yield reasonably good (but not precise) results.

The table combines data based on products and product classes (an aggregation of products). This method avoids the need for presenting very extensive tables while allowing details to be shown when appropriate. In many product categories, the ''product-level'' is very finely subdivided—into canned beans by size of container, for instance—so that reproducing all products would make *Manufacturing USA* unmanageably bulky. In other instances, the ''product class'' does not provide sufficient detail for a reasonable overview of the industry's product mix. Decisions on which level to use were made item by item with the aim of presenting a good overall picture of the industry's product array. Once again, in this 5th edition, detail has been expanded. *Product tables are the most detailed ever published in MUSA*.

In some tables, the first item represents the overall category and is shown as 100%. The sum of the following product/product class entries will be 100; sums slightly above or below 100 are due to rounding. Note, however, that the values of *indented* subcategories are summed in the main heading above them.

In some instances, the symbol (D) will appear instead of a value; the symbol appears when data are withheld to prevent disclosure of competitive information. The abbreviation ''nsk'' stands for ''not specified by kind.''

8. Inputs and Outputs

One of the more useful tools for tracing economic activity from industry to industry and from one economic sector to another is an economic data structure known as the input-output table. For this reason, *MUSA* provides an extract from the *Benchmark Study of the U.S. Economy, 1982*, published in the fall of 1991 by the Department of Commerce. Input-Output studies are expensive, complex enterprises; consequently, such data are published infrequently and at a substantial lag in time; nevertheless, these data show the fundamental structural relationships between economic activities and are a useful if imprecise adjunct to market, developmental, locational, and other analyses.

The table of *Inputs and Outputs* is an *extraction* because it records only those transactions between manufacturing industries and other sectors of the economy that represent at least one tenth of one percent of total inputs to an industry or outputs from an industry. All lesser transactions are suppressed in order to conserve space.

The table is in two parts. The first part (column 1) shows economic sectors or industries that supply an industry with goods and services; the second part (column 2) shows economic sectors or industries that purchase the outputs of the industry. (Since some of the economic units shown are not ''industries''—for instance State and Local Government—the term ''sector'' is used to denote such economic entities.) Within each part, the sector/industry is shown first followed by a percentile of input or output; the final entry categorizes the sector/industry by type (Manufacturing, Wholesale or Retail Trade, Services, Utilities, etc.).

The Input-Output accounts are based on the 1977 SIC structure which was in force in 1982. For presentation in *MUSA*, data have been associated with the 1987 SIC structure as closely as possible; the user, however, must keep in mind that two different schemes of classification have been coordinated; for this reason, some distortions are likely.

The sectors/industries in each part of the table are sorted in descending order of importance: the largest supplying and purchasing sectors/industries will be placed at the top of the table. If the percentile is the same, the data are shown in sector order following the SIC classification (from agriculture down to government); if the sector is also the same, sorting is alphabetically by name of activity.

The user should note the following when using this table:

- Most industries buy from and sell to themselves. These transactions may at times be the largest inputs and one of the larger outputs of an industry. The reason for this phenomenon is simply that a 4-digit industry is very often *many* specialized industries that supply each other in a cascade of components.

- Not all inputs to an industry are shown—only those that account for 0.1 percent or more of inputs. The user may know an industry that uses large amounts of electricity—yet the table does not show ''Electric service utilities'' as an input. The reason, most likely, is that electric power is too small a proportion of purchases in relation to other raw material obtained.

- The magnitude of certain inputs may be surprising and difficult to explain without detailed knowledge of an industry. For instance, ''Real estate'' is a major input into industries that produce tobacco products—because acquisition of appropriate land for growing tobacco is an important aspect of that industry's activity.

- Some of the output categories used in the Input-Output study hide the ultimate user. Examples are ''Exports'' and ''Gross private fixed investment''; it is not always possible to know which element of the economy made the investment. This limitation derives from the manner in which the Input-Output accounts are organized by the Department of Commerce.

- The input and output ratios are not likely to be accurate for industries where there has been dramatic change (technological or other) since the early 1980s.

9. Occupations Employed by Industry Group

Manufacturing USA presents data on 200 occupation categories employed by manufacturing industries; since most of these categories combine two or three occupations, nearly 460 occupations are covered. The information presented is an extract from the *Industry-Occupation Matrix* produced by the Bureau of Labor Statistics (BLS), Department of Labor.

The table on *Occupations Employed* presents an extract; showing the entire matrix would have required too much space. Thus only those occupations are included that represent 1% or more of total employment in an industry. The advantage of this method is that the data are kept manageable while *most* of an industry's employment is defined by occupation. The disadvantage is that certain occupations, although employed by an industry, do not make the ''cutoff'' of 1% of total employment.

The data are shown for 1994 (updated from 1992) in percent of Total Employment for an industry group (3-digit industry level or groupings of 3-digit industries). Also shown is the Bureau of Labor Statistics' projection of the anticipated growth or decline of the occupation to the year 2005. This value is reported as a percent change to 2005; a value of 5.5, for instance, means that overall employment, in the industry group, will increase 5.5% between 1992 and 2005; a negative value indicates a corresponding decline. Note that these are *not* rates of annual change. The last update by BLS of this database moved the starting point from 1992 to 1994 but did not move the target year. In the last edition of *MUSA* projections to 2005 were reported but from a 1992 base.

BLS does not provide occupational data at the 4-digit SIC level. Consequently, the same table of *Occupations Employed* is reproduced for each industry which is in the same 3-digit grouping. This approach has been adopted so that the user will find the occupations associated with a 4-digit industry with other data on that industry.

The user should note the following:

- As already stated, the occupations shown are a subset of total occupations employed: those that account for 1% or more of employment in the industry group.

- Since the data are for *groups*, some occupations listed will appear out of place in a particular 4-digit industry; that is because those occupations are employed by a related 4-digit industry in the same group.

- Growth or decline indicated for an occupation within an industry group does not mean that the occupation is growing or declining overall. Also, changes introduced by BLS between editions of this series can be quite drastic. An occupation that grew by several percentage points in an industry two years ago is shown suddenly declining to the year 2005 now.

10. Map Graphics

The geographical presentation of data begins with two maps titled *Location by State* and *Regional Concentration*. In the first map, all states in which the industry is present are shaded. In the second, the industry's concentration is shown by Census region. The two maps, together, tell the user at a glance where the industry is active and which regions rank first, second, and third in value of shipments or in number of establishments; establishment counts are used for ranking in those industries where shipment data are withheld (the (D) symbol) for the majority of states. In the case of some industries, only one or two regions are shaded because the industry is concentrated in a few states. The data for ranking are taken from the table on *Industry Data by State* which immediately follows the maps.

The regional boundaries are those of the Census Regions and are named, from left to right and top to bottom as follows:

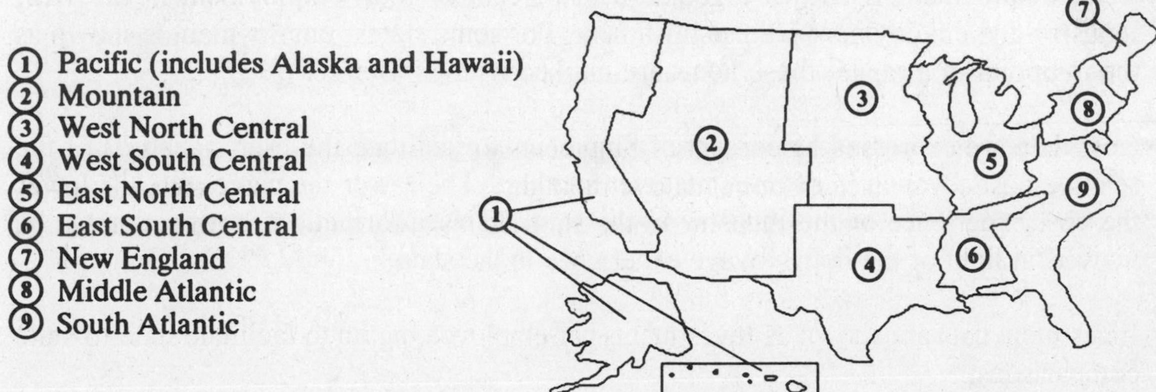

In the case of the Pacific region, all parts of the region are shaded (including Alaska and Hawaii), even if the basis for the ranking is the industry's predominance in California (the usual case).

Although regional data are only graphed and not reported in a separate table, the table of *Industry Data by State* provides all the necessary information for constructing a regional table.

11. Industry Data by State

The table on *Industry Data by State* provides ten data elements for each state in which the industry is active. The data are updated in this edition. They come from the 1992 Economic Census, the most recently available *complete* data set on states. Even in this series, certain data elements are suppressed by the Bureau of the Census to prevent disclosure of competitive information. This may come about in instances where only a few operations are present in the state or they are operated by a small number of companies. The states are shown in descending order of shipments. The categories of Establishments, Shipments, Total Employment, and Wages are identical to those in the table of *General Statistics*. In addition, six elements of information are provided so that the user can more easily compare the size, performance, and characteristics of the industry from one state to the next:

- Shipments are expressed in millions of dollars and as a percent of the total U.S. shipments for the industry. This is useful for determining the relative importance of the state in the industry as a whole. Shipments per Establishment are also provided; this measure gives an insight into the relative size of the factories in the state.

- Total employment is shown together with percent of total employment in the U.S. industry and employment per establishment. For some states, employment is shown as the midpoint of a range; these items are marked with an asterisk (*).

- Cost data are expressed as percent of Shipments to facilitate the user's analysis of the relative cost advantages of one state over another. The lower the percentile, the lower the cost experience of the industry in the state. This information, however, must be viewed in light of the hourly wage experience in the state.

- Investment data are shown as Investments per employee, again to facilitate state-to-state comparisons.

The symbol (D) is used when data are withheld to prevent disclosure. Dashes are used to indicate that the corresponding data element cannot be calculated because some part of the ratio is missing or withheld.

Projected Data Series

Beginning with the 4th edition of *MUSA*, sufficient data points became available to permit the projection of data to the current year and beyond. For this reason, and as a service to the busy user of the book, the editors have introduced a new feature—trend projections of available data.

How Projections Were Made

Projections are based on a curve-fitting algorithm using the least-squares method. In essence, the algorithm calculates a trend line for the data using existing data points. Extensions of the trend line are used to predict future years of data. The method is illustrated in the chart below. It shows actual data values plotted for 1982 through 1994 and the least-squares trend line drawn to overlay the points. The trend line is extended through 1998. The values for 1995 through 1998 represent the ''trend'' of the earlier years.

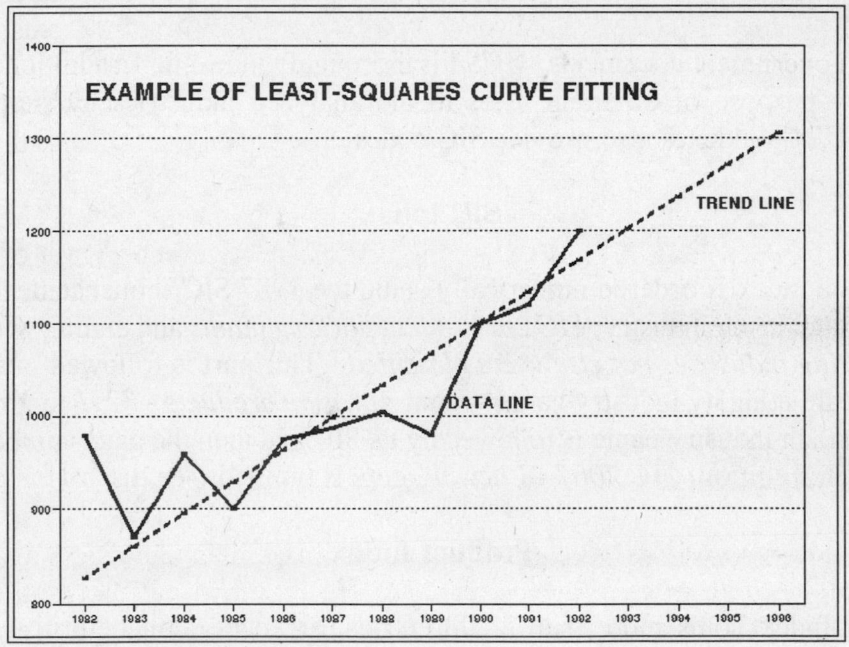

What Values Were Projected

In this edition, every category (column) reported under General Statistics has been subject to projection. In those cases where a coherent series exists from 1982 to the present, the entire series was used. In those cases where the industry definition underwent a change in 1987, trends are calculated from 1987 forward.

Cost of Materials and Value Added by Manufacturer were calculated using the 1994 ratio of costs or value added to shipments in 1994 and then applying that ratio to other years using the projected shipments values for those years. Costs and value added were treated in this manner because averaging these data for a long period (1982-1992, for example) would not properly reflect cost savings and productivity changes achieved most recently. Therefore the use of a ratio, based on the most recent survey year, seemed more appropriate.

Limitations of Projections

Projections are simply means of detecting trends—that may or may not hold in the future. The projections in *MUSA*, therefore, are not as reliable as actual survey data. Most analysts trying to project the future routinely turn to trend projection. In this edition of *MUSA*, the work of doing the projections has been done for the user in advance.

Indexes

Unlike most government documents, *MUSA* is thoroughly indexed. In addition to fulfilling their primary purpose of directing users to the analyzed industries by supplying page numbers, *MUSA*'s indexes also provide SIC codes.

SIC Index

Part one of the index is ordered numerically using the 1987 SIC sequence beginning with the first manufacturing industry, *SIC 2011 - Meat packing plants* and ending with *SIC 3999 - Manufacturing industries not elsewhere classified*. This part is followed immeditely by an alphabetical listing by industry name—from *Abrasive products - 3291* to *Yarn spinning mills - 2281*; each industry name is followed by its SIC and then the page number on which it begins. In this edition, *SIC 2067 - Chewing gum* is omitted (see discussion above).

Product Index

The Product Index holds more than 2,200 entries, arranged alphabetically, identifying products, materials, and chemicals manufactured in the United States. The names were largely, but not exclusively, obtained from the actual product names as published by the *Census of Manufactures*. Additional keywords have been added when the Federal terminology was too technical or obscure. Each product name is followed by one or more SIC codes indicating in which industry or industries the product is manufactured. The references are arranged in SIC order and do not necessarily indicate, by their arrangement, which industry is the predominant supplier of the product.

Company Index

This index shows more than 21,000 company names arranged in alphabetical order; company names that begin with a numeral (3M, etc.) precede company names that begin with the letter A. Company names are followed by page references and a listing of SICs (within brackets).

Occupation Index

The Occupation index shows nearly 460 occupations under 200 occupational groupings. This index does not attempt to refer the user to *every* industry in which an occupation occurs; that approach would render the index unwieldy. ''Inspectors, testers, and graders,'' for instance, are employed in 121 3-digit industries, ''Bookkeeping clerks'' in 75, etc. Rather than to make the index unmanageable, the total number of 3-digit industries employing the occupation is shown, in parentheses, following the name of the occupation; thereafter, the top ten (or fewer) industry groups are shown in their order of importance; the most important group (that which employs the largest number) is shown first.

The user should note, again, that—

- Occupations are reported by 3-digit industry group; a reference to industry 372, for instance, means that the user can find the occupation under *SIC 3721 - Aircraft*; *3724 - Aircraft and engine parts*; and *3728 - Aircraft equipment, not elsewhere classified.*

- Only those occupations are included which represent at least 1% of employment in a 3-digit industry group. As an example, ''Librarians, professional'' are employed by manufacturing companies and at a growing rate; but as highly specialized professionals among others, their numbers do not reach the ''reporting threshold'' used in *Manufacturing USA*.

User's Guide

Manufacturing USA: Industry Analyses, Statistics, and Leading Companies (MUSA) provides the user with a wealth of data and a framework for doing many kinds of assessments and analyses the nature of which will depend on the user's need and specific context. All the possible uses of *MUSA* cannot even be touched upon, much less fully described. The intent is to provide a selection of examples, by category.

The chapter is divided into two parts. The first deals with using *MUSA* as a *reference tool*; the second discusses using *MUSA* as a *research tool.*

Using *MUSA* as a Reference Tool

MUSA is a convenient ''look-up'' tool for the reference librarian, information specialist, provider of technical assistance, consultant, or other kind of ''hand holder'' who needs to respond instantly to a telephone query from a client or constituent—someone who needs a quick answer *now*. Some illustrative examples follow.

Finding the SIC

A typical example of such a request is to identify the SIC associated with a product or company. The caller may begin by saying something like this: ''We have to provide our SIC number on this government procurement. I need to know what SIC my company falls into. We make components for plumbing systems.'' Under *Plumbing* in the Product Index, the SICs 3261, 3431, and 3432 are referenced. A quick look in the SIC Index shows that the three industries are—

3261 - Vitreous plumbing fixtures
3431 - Enameled iron & metal sanitary ware
3432 - Plumbing fittings & brass goods

A question or two determines that the company makes metal rather than china components. A look at the Product Share tables of 3431 and 3432 shows that 3431 is more closely associated with toilets and 3432 with bath tubs, showers, and sinks. After brief discussion, the reference librarian and caller agree that the company participates about equally in both SICs.

Often, of course, the solution requires finding out more from the caller. The company may turn out to make gaskets that are sold primarily to manufacturers of plumbing goods . . . and thus the SIC turns out to be *3053 - Gaskets, packing and sealing devices*.

The particular merit of *MUSA* in such a context is that it permits looking at actual product detail and at company information for better pinpointing the SIC than is possible by looking at the SIC Manual.

Providing Magnitude Information

MUSA is a convenient resource for answering questions on how big an industry is or what the wages in an industry might be. The question: ''How big is the computer industry?'' can be answered rapidly by finding *Computers* in the Product Index, noting that all related products are in four SICs, 3571, 3572, 3575, and 3577. Adding the shipments for all four provides the answer. Employment information is available on the same tables. And the Ratios tables can be used to tell the caller that wages in these high-tech industries range from 6% to 23% higher than the average for all manufacturing.

Eyeballing a Trend

The Trends Graphics and the Indices of Change table permit the reference librarian to provide quick yet accurate answers to journalistic queries or exploratory questions by colleagues about the general trend in an industry. The caller, for instance, may be doing a story on communications equipment and want to insert a comparison with computers for contrast.

The Product index guides the user to *SIC 3663 - Radio and TV communications equipment* and *SIC 3571 - Electronic computers*. Both are recently reclassified industries. Data are available from 1987 forward. They show that radio/TV had strong growth but computers experienced a much flatter rate of increase and a sharper decrease in employment.

Another journalist, comparing motorcycles and guided missiles, for instance, will see a different picture—an industry that has seen fairly sharp decline due to Japanese competition but is recovering (motorcycles) and another with an enviable history of growth that has recently experienced a turn-down due to public sector budget problems (guided missiles and space vehicles) and, more recently still, a resumption of growth.

One of the merits of *MUSA* as a tool for on-the-spot reference work is that the user can obtain such comparisons rapidly and easily without doing analytical work.

Answering Locational Questions

The combined use of indexes, map graphics, the State table, and the Company table can help the reference librarian respond quickly and effectively to questions like "Does somebody manufacture plumbing fixtures in Minnesota or Wisconsin?" A look at the maps for *SIC 3432 - Plumbing fittings & brass goods* shows that Wisconsin does but Minnesota does not.

This answer can be double-checked by looking at the Leading Companies table. On that table, indeed, three companies are shown to be operating in Wisconsin: Kohler, URC, and Frost.

Finding Companies by Product

The Product Index, used in conjunction with the Leading Companies tables, gives the reference librarian a handy facility for finding companies that make some kind of product. A caller, for instance, may be looking for a minimum of three bidders who can provide metal stampings in Michigan. The Product Index (under *Metal stampings* or *Stampings, metal*) points to SIC 3469. The Leading Companies table provides a list of 11 companies with addresses in Michigan. Some of these, of course, may not do external contract work. A little discussion with the caller, however, will rapidly establish which names may be meaningful. Addresses and telephone numbers—together with useful qualifying data on sales and employment size—can be passed on as an added bonus.

Guiding Job Seekers

MUSA provides a painless means of matching occupations to industries and companies—provided, of course, that the occupations fall into the Manufacturing category and are employed in reasonable numbers. The caller, planning a job hunting campaign, calls to find out who she might contact. She has worked for a cab company as a part-time dispatcher and wants a permanent job. She is in the Dallas-Fort Worth area and cannot move. The Occupation Index, under *Dispatchers*, identifies Industry Group 327 as the only major employer of this specialty in manufacturing.

Within *MUSA*, Industry Group 327 explodes into five 4-digit SIC industries in the concrete block and brick, other concrete products, ready-mix concrete, lime, and gypsum businesses. A scan of these five industries provides references to one company in Dallas and two in Fort Worth, complete with addresses and telephone numbers: a reasonable start for the caller in her campaign.

Using *MUSA* as a Research Tool

Scope and Limitations

Be it said at the outset that *MUSA*, however useful, is no more the *only* reference needed for serious analysis than any other compilation of economic data. It is not well suited for macro-economic studies of the national or international economy—it is too detailed for that. It is also limited for doing narrowly focused market analysis; an example might be an exploration of gasoline engines under 10 horsepower—it is not detailed enough for that.

The best use of *MUSA* is in the intermediate range—studies and analyses of larger product groupings and aggregates such as are undertaken continuously by smaller corporations and divisions of large companies; many different kinds of analyses conducted by governmental agencies engaged in resource management, human resources, environmental control, economic development, and technical assistance; strategic analyis and planning carried out by corporations, states, and regional bodies; broad-based market research and sales planning done by corporate staffs and, on their behalf, by consultants and advertising agencies; early-stage locational planning; trends and ratio analysis conducted by litigants, labor unions, and interest groups; early-phase merger and acquisition work, especially strategic orientation and screening; and many similar activities, not least academic research.

Special difficulties are involved with those industries that, because of their relatively small size, are grouped together under industries labelled *nec*, ''not elsewhere classified.'' An extreme example of that, for instance, is *SIC 3999 - Manufacturing industries, nec* which combines 15 very distinct industries including fire extinguishers, amusement machines, furs, umbrellas, tobacco pipes, and others. Within other *nec* industries, similarly, often large, vital, and more or less unrelated activities are lumped together. When dealing with industries with SIC numbers that end in a 9, the user is well advised to study carefully the Product Share Details table (which reveals the heterogeneity of the activities included) before using the aggregate data for that 4-digit SIC in analysis.

However useful in revealing overall patterns, the Inputs and Outputs tables issued in 1991 reflect relatively old data (1982). Nonetheless, Input-Output data continue to be used in certain kinds of analyses because they reveal important relationships between industrial activities. These relationships do *not* change very rapidly in time—the economy has far too much inertia to shift fundamental linkages significantly. But the *ratios* change much more rapidly. An industry that, in 1982, for instance, imported 35% of its product may still be importing a significant amount—but the ratio, in 1992, may be 39% or 25%.

Brief examples of using *MUSA* in different types of research and analysis follow.

Market Analysis, Strategy, and Planning

MUSA is well suited for trends assessment, competitive analysis, self-evaluation, and the exploration of vertical integration strategies or the inverse.

Trends Assessment. Trends assessment is simplified for the user by the provision of graphics and indices of change. A good example is provided by *SIC 3751 - Motorcycles, bicycles and parts*. The Trends graphic for shipments provides an instant picture of both the slide in shipments between 1983 and 1986 and a turn-about in 1987-88 culminating in an upturn that lasts until 1994. The actual change is shown under the Shipments category of the General Statistics table; the data suggest that the industry has bottomed-out in the 1986-1988 period but shows signs of growth thereafter. The Indices of Change table shows the same data normalized to a base of 100 in 1992. Wages, which had been sliding, have also grown—as has employment.

Competitive Analysis. While the table of Leading Companies does not show an exhaustive listing of participants in each industry, significant players will rarely be missing. In the example about motorcycles, for instance, a close study of the leading companies participating in SIC 3751 shows that Kawasaki Motors is present in the US market with a manufacturing facility in Lincoln, Nebraska, and that its sales are now $436 million, up from an estimated $71 million two years ago (see 4th edition).

The user conducting competitive analysis would, of course, have knowledge of the industry in sufficient detail to add significantly to the brief analysis begun above—because the posture and activities of other participants would be known to him or her.

Self-Evaluation. Whether the user is a state agency engaged in economic development work or a corporate analyst exploring strategic options, *MUSA* provides data in a convenient format for evaluating the agency's or corporation's performance against industry performance overall or in a particular state. The Selected Ratios table, for instance, provides pre-calculated ratios the user can compare to those developed for his or her company. The State table provides similar information at the state level. If the average cost per employee, for instance, is $33,070 in an industry—and the user's company experiences an average cost of $58,000/employee, such a finding may well serve to flag the issue for a closer look—especially if the company has consistently higher costs at its various locations as well.

Exploring vertical integration or suppliers. The Inputs and Outputs table provides an excellent means for exploring operations that might be brought into a corporation (through acquisition or internal development) or farmed out to others at lower ultimate cost.

A straightforward case might be that of a publisher considering vertical integration and exploring candidates in the *Book printing - SIC 2732*, *Bookbinding - SIC 2789*, and *Typesetting - SIC 2791* industries which—together—account for 36.7% of inputs to *Book publishing - SIC 2731*. Conversely, the same publisher, with an in-house typesetting operation, may wish to find external candidates to take over this function, at lower cost. In such a case, *MUSA* is helpful in locating nearby candidates (Leading Companies table) and in analyzing the general materials cost and wage patterns in the targeted industries (General Statistics and Industry Data by State tables). In other cases, *MUSA* can be used to identify less obvious linkages between an industry and those on which it depends.

Economic Development

A fundamental concern of those responsible for promoting economic development in an area is the potential fit between local industry and industries that might be induced to move into the state, region, or community.

MUSA provides an excellent framework for screening industries, locating suppliers, for developing state and regional profiles of industry, and other economic development tasks. The primary tools provided are the Industry Data by State and the Materials Consumed tables—and, of course, all tables and graphics on those industries targeted for a closer look. Two examples follow.

Targeting Development Effort. An example of the use of these tables might be a community in Indiana with a sawmill wishing to help the sawmill expand by attracting one or more well-fitting enterprises—a case of targeting development effort.

A browse through the 2400 SIC industries identifies *SIC 2431 - Millwork* as a healthy industry which is a major buyer of lumber, as shown in its Materials Consumed table. As shown by its Product Share Details table, *Millwork* makes windows and doors. *Millwork* also consumes substantial amounts of plywood, supplied by *SIC 2436 - Softwood veneer and plywood*, itself a consumer of sawmill products. From these observations, a broad plan can be formulated to attract both a window manufacturer and a plywood producer.

The table of Industry Data by State for *Millwork* shows that the industry in Indiana has higher costs and neighboring Illinois, lower costs than neighboring Michigan, but lower wages than either. A marketing effort, therefore, directed toward neighboring states, might appear to be a reasonable first step. The table of Leading Companies, finally, provides an initial list of people to contact. The same analysis, of course, would be applied to *Veneer and plywood*.

Helping Local Industry. The economic development professional can use *MUSA* as a tool for helping local industry find alternative suppliers or markets by using the book to trace "forward" and "backward" through a chain of linked industries. The Inputs and Outputs table, for instance, may pinpoint the fact that a local company participates in an industry which is a major exporter—but the local company has never considered exporting. The economic development professional can contact state, regional, or federal agencies that help in promoting exports and thus aid the local company in finding new outlets.

Locational Analysis

Companies thinking of expansion can use *MUSA* effectively for screening locations as a first step in their locational analysis. *MUSA* provides a convenient means of quickly assessing proximity to markets, the labor situation, cost patterns of candidate areas, and the presence or absence of appropriate suppliers.

In this effort, the State map helps in gaining an overview of the location of an industry; the map showing regional concentration can be used to pinpoint areas where, for instance, a critical mass of important suppliers is present. The Industry Data by State table is useful in many ways. The analyst can, for instance, use the table to—

- Compare wages per hour state to state.
- Evaluate costs (expressed as a percentage of shipments) to find the states with the lowest cost experience; the cost column, of course, is really a *composite* value integrating such factors as the actual cost of materials (which may be due to proximity to raw materials and energy sources) as well as distance from markets (because costs include transportation).
- Determine the relative size of plants in a state based on shipments or employment.
- Get some feel for the technological level of the industry in the state by examining investment per employee.

The table of Leading Companies, used in conjunction with other data, can be especially helpful in locational studies because regional divisions and subsidiaries of large corporations are listed together with the parent organization. The relocating or expanding company can thus identify both potential competitors and suppliers in the area in which it anticipates settling.

Diversification, Mergers and Acquisitions

MUSA provides some useful facilities for the early stages of a diversification program—selecting target industries, developing criteria, studying the environment, and identifying candidates for initial contact.

Selecting Target Industries. An example of this process, using *MUSA*, may be that of a company that produces All-Terrain Vehicles (ATVs) and wishes to diversify into other products that use gasoline engines. The selection process, step-by-step, may take this form:

1. A look at the company's own industry (found by looking for *ATVs* in the Product Index) shows that its SIC is *SIC 3799 - Transportation equipment, nec*. This is an industry that combines diverse but related elements. Thus the first step is to examine the components of the industry by looking at the Product Share Details table. The other industries included in this SIC are *golf carts*, *snowmobiles*, and *trailers*. The company already manufactures a line of trailers; but golf carts and snowmobiles can be placed on the list of potentials.

2. An examination of *SIC 3519 - Internal combustion engines* is undertaken to identify other industries that may have characteristics similar to ATVs. The outputs column of that industry's Inputs and Outputs table shows three possible fits—all heavily dependent on engines: *SIC 3523 - Farm machinery & equipment*, *SIC 3524 - Lawn & garden equipment*, and *SIC 3732 - Boat building and repairing*.

3. A look, in turn, at each of these industries shows that farm machinery has had a lackluster history in recent years; lawn and garden equipment has grown; boats have shown significant growth until 1988 followed by a dip; recently there has been growth again.

4. Within the lawn and garden industry, the Product Share Details table helps to narrow the focus to riding lawn mowers, garden tractors, and snow equipment (about 38% of industry shipments); these products are most similar to ATVs in size of transaction, technology, and the company's own production know-how. Within the boat building and repairing industry, the company targets the larger inboard motorboats for the same reason.

Developing Criteria. In addition to the company's own criteria for acquisitions (size of property, location, return, etc.), *MUSA's* Ratios tables and State data can be used to develop additional criteria to help evaluate candidates.

Studying the Environment. *MUSA* provides data for early-phase evaluations—how the industry has done during recent years, where it is located, the levels of investment that may be necessary in an unfamiliar industry, etc. Detailed investigation of candidates in their own locations will be helped by the ''big picture'' perspective *MUSA* provides quickly and easily.

Identifying Candidates. The Leading Companies tables in *MUSA* serve as an excellent first step in building up a list of potential candidates for acquisition: the tables show the companies' location, size, and type. This permits the user to select candidates that meet size and locational criteria. Even companies that may not meet the buyer's criteria may be excellent sources of referral—easily obtained because current telephone numbers are provided.

Employment Analysis

The occupational data in *MUSA* are shown by 3-digit industry group—somewhat of a limitation; at the same time, they show projections of growth or decline to the year 2005, which is useful in planning corporate, governmental, and educational activities.

Analyzing Trends. Some occupations are declining in virtually all listed manufacturing groups (e.g., *Electronic assemblers*); some are growing in some industries while declining in others. *Computer programmers*, for instance, display the following growth and decline rates:

4.2	Periodicals
-7.2	Book printing and publishing
-28.2	Measuring devices
-43.0	Computers and office equipment

Establishing such trends in an occupation begins with finding the occupation in the Occupation Index and then examining the growth trends in the referenced industry groups.

Planning Recruitment/Training Efforts. Data such as those shown above can be used in planning recruiting and training efforts. A company in the aerospace industry, for instance, detecting a steep decline in the employment of some skilled occupation elsewhere, can target recruitment efforts toward that industry.

Competing for Scarce Skills. The example, above, dealing with computer programmers, shows that the demand for this occupation in Book printing and publishing will be the highest of all the industry groups. A participant in this industry can use *MUSA* for detecting this trend and preparing strategies to attract programmers from the Computer industry.

Technology Assessment

An industry's level of technology can be determined, roughly, by using *MUSA's* Ratios tables and other data. A full technology assessment, obviously, must go well beyond the kinds of evaluations possible using these data—but *MUSA* provides a good start. An example is presented comparing three industries:

SIC 2431 - Millwork (primarily windows and doors)
SIC 2732 - Book printing
SIC 3571 - Electronic computers

The following table, drawn from the Ratios tables of the respective industries, shows some relevant index values; a value of 100 means that the industry's ratio is the same as the national average for all manufacturing; above 100 means higher; below 100 means lower.

Industry	*Investment per Employee*	*Cost per Employee*	*Payroll per Employee*	*Shipments per Prod. Worker*	*Value Added per Prod. Worker*
SIC 2431 - Millwork	29	72	78	56	49
SIC 2732 - Books	93	39	95	47	60
SIC 3571 - Computers	130	240	151	572	517

The index for Investment per employee shows computers to be substantially higher than millwork; such a differential can usually be interpreted as showing the level of tooling for the industry, the cost of each "work place."

Cost per employee is a good guide to the cost of the "raw materials" on which the industry works. In the case of millwork, these materials are variously prepared lumber; in book printing it is primarily paper and, in lower proportions, inks, lithographic plates, and other materials; in computers, the "raw materials" will tend to be assemblies, semiconductors, and other advanced aggregates. A high cost per employee, therefore, can *usually* be interpreted to mean relatively high level of technology. However, there are instances (*SIC 2011 - Meat packing plants*) where the cost index may be very high because the primary input material, even though unprocessed, is very expensive (livestock).

Payroll per employee tends to indicate the level of technical skill required for (and/or the degree of unionization of) the industry's work. It appears from the example above that book printing pays somewhat more than millwork but substantially less than computers. The difference *may* be due to the degree of unionization in the two industries. The high payroll/employee index in computers clearly reflects advanced technical skill in the employed occupations.

Shipments per production worker are higher in millwork than in book printing. This index combines at least three factors of which the technological level of the industry is one. Others are the market demand for the product and the production stage occupied by the industry. Book printing, for instance, ships roughly 47% of its output to *SIC 2731 - Book publishing* and 18% to *SIC 2721 - Periodicals*; it may be an industry with a few large, powerful customers; millwork sells to the construction sector and will have many smaller customers.

The Value added per production worker index is a good measure of labor productivity and hence of technological level.

Conclusion

The discussion, above, was presented to illustrate some uses of *Manufacturing USA: Industry Analyses, Statistics, and Leading Companies*. Many other analyses and evaluations are possible using the data in *MUSA*. Comments on this "User's Guide," including suggestions on other cases that should be illustrated in future editions, are welcome.

Abbreviations, Codes, and Symbols

U.S. State Postal Codes

AK	Alaska	MT	Montana
AL	Alabama	NC	North Carolina
AR	Arkansas	ND	North Dakota
AZ	Arizona	NE	Nebraska
CA	California	NH	New Hampshire
CO	Colorado	NJ	New Jersey
CT	Connecticut	NM	New Mexico
CZ	Canal Zone	NV	Nevada
DC	District of Columbia	NY	New York
DE	Delaware	OH	Ohio
FL	Florida	OK	Oklahoma
GA	Georgia	OR	Oregon
GU	Guam	PA	Pennsylvania
HI	Hawaii	PR	Puerto Rico
IA	Iowa	RI	Rhode Island
ID	Idaho	SC	South Carolina
IL	Illinois	SD	South Dakota
IN	Indiana	TN	Tennessee
KS	Kansas	TX	Texas
KY	Kentucky	UT	Utah
LA	Louisiana	VA	Virginia
MA	Massachusetts	VI	Virgin Islands
MD	Maryland	VT	Vermont
ME	Maine	WA	Washington
MI	Michigan	WI	Wisconsin
MN	Minnesota	WV	West Virginia
MO	Missouri	WY	Wyoming
MS	Mississippi		

M·A·N·U·F·A·C·T·U·R·I·N·G USA

Industry Analyses,

Statistics, and Leading Companies

2011 - MEAT PACKING PLANTS

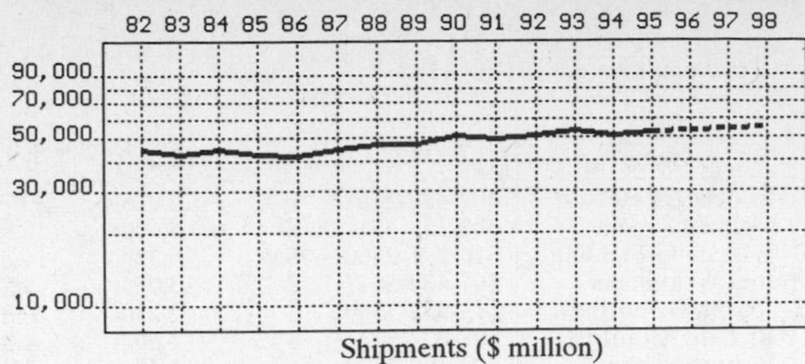

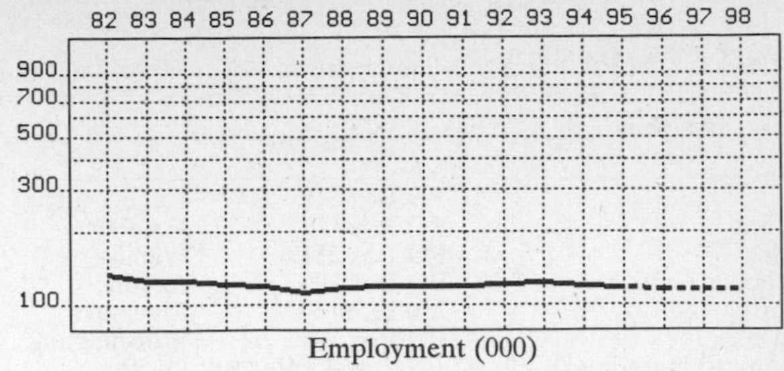

GENERAL STATISTICS

Year	Companies	Establishments: Total	Establishments: with 20 or more employees	Employment: Total (000)	Employment: Production Workers (000)	Employment: Production Hours (Mil)	Compensation: Payroll ($ mil)	Compensation: Wages ($/hr)	Production ($ million): Cost of Materials	Production ($ million): Value Added by Manufacture	Production ($ million): Value of Shipments	Production ($ million): Capital Invest.
1982	1,659	1,780	668	134.9	108.9	220.2	2,549.3	9.06	39,048.6	5,824.6	44,853.6	290.0
1983		1,716	653	126.4	102.4	213.8	2,401.2	8.60	37,507.7	5,327.1	42,774.6	278.0
1984		1,652	638	124.9	102.0	211.2	2,327.8	8.36	38,738.3	5,527.9	44,277.7	273.4
1985		1,588	623	122.2	98.7	201.4	2,252.9	8.48	36,637.2	5,859.4	42,553.5	249.9
1986		1,533	603	119.0	96.0	200.4	2,211.0	8.29	36,680.2	5,692.8	42,384.5	258.9
1987	1,359	1,434	503	113.2	93.0	195.9	2,141.2	8.27	39,796.2	5,221.2	44,990.8	246.1
1988		1,359	491	117.8	97.8	205.4	2,226.5	8.30	41,700.6	5,700.1	47,333.2	272.0
1989		1,290	488	120.3	98.4	209.0	2,225.7	8.16	41,122.4	5,457.0	46,542.0	365.8
1990		1,295	465	119.2	100.1	210.9	2,256.4	8.26	44,462.7	6,666.5	51,069.2	393.7
1991		1,277	453	120.8	103.3	220.4	2,374.6	8.32	43,311.9	5,957.6	49,326.2	423.0
1992	1,297	1,387	431	122.4	105.5	228.5	2,452.8	8.56	43,586.4	6,928.0	50,434.4	343.2
1993		1,367	429	124.4	107.3	232.0	2,541.6	8.64	45,735.8	7,634.2	53,240.3	289.8
1994		1,191P	376P	119.5	102.2	228.0	2,597.1	9.13	42,045.7	8,350.0	50,443.7	328.6
1995		1,148P	352P	117.7P	102.2P	225.1P	2,428.7P	8.52P	43,925.8P	8,723.4P	52,699.3P	365.5P
1996		1,105P	327P	117.1P	102.3P	226.7P	2,439.8P	8.53P	44,611.5P	8,859.6P	53,522.0P	373.6P
1997		1,061P	302P	116.5P	102.5P	228.4P	2,451.0P	8.53P	45,297.3P	8,995.7P	54,344.7P	381.8P
1998		1,018P	278P	115.9P	102.6P	230.0P	2,462.1P	8.54P	45,983.0P	9,131.9P	55,167.5P	389.9P

Sources: 1982, 1987, 1992 *Economic Census*; *Annual Survey of Manufactures*, 83-86, 88-91, 93-94. Establishment counts for non-Census years are from *County Business Patterns*; establishment values for 83-84 are extrapolations. 'P's show projections by the editors. Industries reclassified in 87 will not have data for prior years.

INDICES OF CHANGE

Year	Companies	Establishments: Total	Establishments: with 20 or more employees	Employment: Total (000)	Employment: Production Workers (000)	Employment: Production Hours (Mil)	Compensation: Payroll ($ mil)	Compensation: Wages ($/hr)	Production ($ million): Cost of Materials	Production ($ million): Value Added by Manufacture	Production ($ million): Value of Shipments	Production ($ million): Capital Invest.
1982	128	128	155	110	103	96	104	106	90	84	89	84
1983		124	152	103	97	94	98	100	86	77	85	81
1984		119	148	102	97	92	95	98	89	80	88	80
1985		114	145	100	94	88	92	99	84	85	84	73
1986		111	140	97	91	88	90	97	84	82	84	75
1987	105	103	117	92	88	86	87	97	91	75	89	72
1988		98	114	96	93	90	91	97	96	82	94	79
1989		93	113	98	93	91	91	95	94	79	92	107
1990		93	108	97	95	92	92	96	102	96	101	115
1991		92	105	99	98	96	97	97	99	86	98	123
1992	100	100	100	100	100	100	100	100	100	100	100	100
1993		99	100	102	102	102	104	101	105	110	106	84
1994		86P	87P	98	97	100	106	107	96	121	100	96
1995		83P	82P	96P	97P	99P	99P	100P	101P	126P	104P	106P
1996		80P	76P	96P	97P	99P	99P	100P	102P	128P	106P	109P
1997		77P	70P	95P	97P	100P	100P	100P	104P	130P	108P	111P
1998		73P	64P	95P	97P	101P	100P	100P	105P	132P	109P	114P

Sources: Same as General Statistics. Values reflect change from the base year, 1992. Values above 100 mean greater than 92, values below 100 mean less than 92, and a value of 100 in the 82-91 or 93-98 period means same as 92. 'P's mark projections by the editors.

SELECTED RATIOS

For 1994	Avg. of All Manufact.	Analyzed Industry	Index
Employees per Establishment	49	100	205
Payroll per Establishment	1,500,273	2,179,884	145
Payroll per Employee	30,620	21,733	71
Production Workers per Establishment	34	86	250
Wages per Establishment	853,319	1,747,231	205
Wages per Production Worker	24,861	20,368	82
Hours per Production Worker	2,056	2,231	109
Wages per Hour	12.09	9.13	76
Value Added per Establishment	4,602,255	7,008,597	152
Value Added per Employee	93,930	69,874	74

For 1994	Avg. of All Manufact.	Analyzed Industry	Index
Value Added per Production Worker	134,084	81,703	61
Cost per Establishment	5,045,178	35,291,182	700
Cost per Employee	102,970	351,847	342
Cost per Production Worker	146,988	411,406	280
Shipments per Establishment	9,576,895	42,340,068	442
Shipments per Employee	195,460	422,123	216
Shipments per Production Worker	279,017	493,578	177
Investment per Establishment	321,011	275,811	86
Investment per Employee	6,552	2,750	42
Investment per Production Worker	9,352	3,215	34

Sources: Same as General Statistics. The 'Average of All Manufacturing' column represents the average of all manufacturing industries reported for the most recent complete year available. The Index shows the relationship between the Average and the Analyzed Industry. For example, 100 means that they are equal; 500 that the Analyzed Industry is five times the average; 50 means that the Analyzed Industry is half the national average. The abbreviation 'na' is used to show that data are 'not available'.

LEADING COMPANIES

Number shown: **75** Total sales ($ mil): **43,303** Total employment (000): **124.6**

Company Name	Address				CEO Name	Phone	Co. Type	Sales ($ mil)	Empl. (000)
IBP Inc	PO Box 515	Dakota City	NE	68731	Robert L Peterson	402-494-2061	P	12,075	30.7
Monfort Inc	PO Box G	Greeley	CO	80632	Michael Sanem	303-353-2311	S	5,600*	15.0
Excel Corp	PO Box 2519	Wichita	KS	67201	William G Fielding	316-291-2500	S	5,320	14.2
Hormel Foods Corp	PO Box 800	Austin	MN	55912	Joel W Johnson	507-437-5611	P	3,065	9.5
John Morrell and Co	250 E 5th St	Cincinnati	OH	45202	Joseph B Sebring	513-852-3500	S	2,240	6.0
Monfort Pork Inc	PO Box 369	Worthington	MN	56187	Richard Montfort	507-372-2121	S	1,600*	4.3
Beef America Operating	14748 W Center Rd	Omaha	NE	68144	Robert Norton	402-330-1899	R	1,420	2.2
Farmland Foods Inc	PO Box 7527	Kansas City	MO	64116	George Grazier	816-891-1200	S	960	3.0
National Beef Packing LP	PO Box 978	Liberal	KS	67905	John Miller	316-624-1851	R	820*	2.2
Thorn Apple Valley Inc	18700 W 10 Mile Rd	Southfield	MI	48075	Henry S Dorfman	313-552-0700	P	772	3.4
Packerland Packing Co	PO Box 2300	Green Bay	WI	54305	Rich Vesta	414-468-4000	S	600	2.0
Wilson Foods Corp	2601 NW Expwy	Oklahoma City	OK	73112	John Haynes	405-879-5500	S	520*	3.0
ConAgra Fresh Meats Co	PO Box G	Greeley	CO	80632	Alan Glueck	303-353-2311	S	510*	1.4
EA Miller Inc	PO Box EA	Hyrum	UT	84319	Ted Miller	801-245-6456	S	500	1.3
GFI America Inc	2815 Blaisdell Av S	Minneapolis	MN	55408	Robert Goldberger	612-872-6262	R	500*	0.4
Sun Land Beef Co	PO Box H	Tolleson	AZ	85353	Harvey Dietrich	602-936-7177	R	400	0.6
Clougherty Packing Co	PO Box 58870	Los Angeles	CA	90058	J D Clougherty	213-583-4621	R	350	1.1
Smithfield Packing Company Inc	PO Box 447	Smithfield	VA	23430	Joseph W Luter III	804-357-4321	S	310*	1.9
Fresh Mark Superior Inc	PO Box 8440	Canton	OH	44711	Neil Genshaft	216-832-7491	R	270*	1.1
Lundy Packing Co	PO Box 49	Clinton	NC	28328	A Fetterman	919-592-2104	R	260*	0.7
Sam Kane Beef Processors Inc	PO Box 9254	Corpus Christi	TX	78469	Jerry Kane	512-241-5000	R	250	0.4
Bryan Foods Inc	PO Box 1177	West Point	MS	39773	Roger Loeffelbein	601-494-3741	S	230*	2.2
Green Bay Dressed Beef Inc	520 Lawrence St	Green Bay	WI	54308	Don Garsow	414-437-4311	S	230*	0.6
Washington Beef Inc	PO Box 9344	Yakima	WA	98909	John Kincaid	509-248-3350	R	230*	0.5
Bessin Corp	207 S Water Mkt W	Chicago	IL	60608	Sheldon Sternberg	312-738-2100	R	220*	0.6
Johnsonville Foods Co	PO Box 786	Sheboygan	WI	53082	RC Stayer	414-459-6800	R	220*	0.6
Emge Packing Co	W Red Bank Rd	Fort Branch	IN	47648	Warren Mirtsching	812-753-3214	D	200	0.4
Rymer Foods Inc	4600 S Packers Av	Chicago	IL	60609	John L Patten	312-927-7777	P	162	1.2
Goodmark Foods Inc	6131 Falls of Neuse	Raleigh	NC	27609	Ron E Doggett	919-790-9940	P	160	0.9
Granite State Packing Company	PO Box 5220	Manchester	NH	03108	Irwin Muskat	603-669-3300	R	160*	0.5
Cattleman's Meat Co	1825 Scott St	Detroit	MI	48207	David Rohtbart	313-833-2700	S	138	0.4
Rose Packing Company Inc	65 S Barrington Rd	Barrington	IL	60010	WR Rose	708-381-5700	R	130	0.6
JH Routh Packing Co	PO Box 2253	Sandusky	OH	44871	Tom Routh	419-626-2251	R	125	0.3
Patrick Cudahy Inc	3500 E Barnard Av	Cudahy	WI	53110	Roger Kapella	414-744-2000	S	120	0.7
Greater Omaha Packing Co	5100 S 26th St	Omaha	NE	68107	Penny Davis	402-731-3480	R	110*	0.3
John F Martin and Sons Inc	PO Box 137	Stevens	PA	17578	Lester Martin	717-336-2804	R	110*	0.3
Transhumance Corp	1655 DaVinci Court	Davis	CA	95616	Dennis Breen	916-758-3091	R	100	0.3
Gibbon Meat Packing Inc	PO Box 730	Gibbon	NE	68840	Wesley J Hodge	308-468-5771	R	93*	0.3
Kenosha Beef International Ltd	PO Box 639	Kenosha	WI	53141	Charles Vignieri	414-859-2272	R	91*	0.6
Field Packing Co	PO Box 766	Owensboro	KY	42302	Sam Wise	502-926-2324	S	90*	0.5
Decker Food Co	3200 W Kingsley Rd	Garland	TX	75041		214-278-6192	S	87	0.4
Harris Ranch Beef Co	PO Box 220	Selma	CA	93662	David E Wood	209-233-4116	D	83*	0.5
Parks Sausage Co	PO Box 854	Baltimore	MD	21203	RV Haysbert Sr	410-664-5050	R	82*	0.2
Seaboard Farms of Minnesota	PO Box 1059	Albert Lea	MN	56007	Mark Campbell	507-377-4200	S	81*	1.0
Smithfield Packing Co	2602 W Bernan Av	Kinston	NC	28501	J Oliver	919-522-4777	D	81*	0.5
Federal Beef Processors Inc	2817 Blaisdell Av S	Minneapolis	MN	55408	Robert Goldberger	612-870-8078	S	80	0.3
Vernon Calhoun Packing Co	PO Box 709	Palestine	TX	75802	Vernon Calhoun	903-729-2165	R	80	0.3
Ito Ham USA Inc	3190 Corporate Pl	Hayward	CA	94545	Kinichi Ito	510-887-1612	S	74*	0.2
Pine Valley Meats Inc	PO Box 256	Norwalk	WI	54648	Ron Plueger	608-823-7445	R	74*	0.2
Provimi Veal Corp	PO Box 1608	Waukesha	WI	53187	Aat Groenevelt	414-784-8520	R	74	0.2
Martins Abattoir Wholesale Inc	Rte 1	Godwin	NC	28344	Carlton Martin	919-567-6102	R	68	0.2
Ada Beef Company Inc	1010 Grand River	Ada	MI	49301	Orie Vander Boon	616-949-2350	R	64	0.2
Abbyland Foods Inc	PO Box 69	Abbotsford	WI	54405	H Schraufnagel	715-223-6386	R	63	0.2
Esskay Inc	PO Box 587	Riderwood	MD	21139	Robin W Bissell	410-823-2100	S	62	<0.1
RL Ziegler Company Inc	PO Box 1640	Tuscaloosa	AL	35403	WL Stephens	205-758-3621	R	62	0.5
Alpine Packing Co	9900 Lower Sacr	Stockton	CA	95210	Dennis J Bava	209-477-2691	R	58	0.1
Brown Packing Company Inc	PO Box 130	Gaffney	SC	29342	Walter E Brown	803-489-5723	R	56*	0.2
Colonial Beef Co	3333 S 3rd St	Philadelphia	PA	19148	Ron Davis	215-467-0900	R	56*	0.2
Hoffman Brothers Packing	2731 S Soto St	Los Angeles	CA	90023	J Hoffman	213-267-4600	R	56*	0.2
Cimpl Packing Co	PO Box 80	Yankton	SD	57078	Tom Rosen	605-665-1665	R	55*	0.2
Curtis Packing Co	2416 Randolph Av	Greensboro	NC	27406	Douglas B Curtis	910-275-7684	R	55	0.1
Sioux Preme Packing Co	PO Box 177	Sioux Center	IA	51250	Stan G Lammers	712-722-2555	R	55*	0.1
Owens Country Sausage Inc	PO Box 830249	Richardson	TX	75083	Stewart Owens	214-235-7181	S	50	0.4
Rocco Further Processing Inc	PO Box 750	Timberville	VA	22853	Tad Pritchett	703-896-7041	S	50*	0.5
Travis Meats Inc	PO Box 670	Powell	TN	37849	WS Travis	615-938-9051	R	48	0.2
Gordon Bryans County Farm	PO Box 1267	Calhoun	GA	30701	Kenneth R Bobay	706-625-2275	D	42*	0.4
Braunfels Meats Inc	PO Box 311385	New Braunfels	TX	78131	Bill Campbell	210-625-7627	R	41	0.2
Ohio Packing Co	PO Box 30961	Gahanna	OH	43230	Jim Boyd	614-239-1600	R	41	0.3
Peet Packing Co	PO Box 187	Chesaning	MI	48616	Roger Smigiel	517-845-3021	R	39	0.3
Dubuque Foods Inc	2040 Kerper Blv	Dubuque	IA	52001	Alan Byers	319-588-5400	S	39*	0.2
Beltex Corp	3801 N Grove	Fort Worth	TX	76106	Eric Nauwelaers	817-624-1136	R	37*	0.1
Denver Lamb Co	PO Box 16361	Denver	CO	80216	V Averch	303-296-1795	R	37*	0.1
Lay Packing Co	400 E Jackson Av	Knoxville	TN	37901	Joe Lay Jr	615-546-2511	R	37	0.2
Thomson Packing Company Inc	PO Box 3013	De Pere	WI	54115	Thomas Thomson	414-336-0501	R	37*	0.1
DL Lee and Sons Inc	PO Box 206	Alma	GA	31510	W David Lee	912-632-4406	R	36	0.2

Source: *Ward's Business Directory of U.S. Private and Public Companies*, Volumes 1 and 2, 1996. The company type code used is as follows: P - Public, R - Private, S - Subsidiary, D - Division, J - Joint Venture, A - Affiliate, G - Group. Sales are in millions of dollars, employees are in thousands. An asterisk (*) indicates an estimated sales volume. The symbol < stands for 'less than'. Company names and addresses are truncated, in some cases, to fit into the available space.

MATERIALS CONSUMED

Material		Quantity	Delivered Cost ($ million)
Materials, ingredients, containers, and supplies		(X)	41,036.4
Cattle slaughtered (number of head)	1,000	31,068.3	25,650.8
Cattle slaughtered (live weight)	mil lb	35,747.9	(X)
Calves slaughtered (number of head)	1,000	578.1	243.8
Calves slaughtered (live weight)	mil lb	174.5	(X)
Hogs slaughtered (number of head)	1,000	86,308.4	9,677.0
Hogs slaughtered (live weight)	mil lb	21,511.9	(X)
Sheep and lambs slaughtered (number of head)	1,000	3,568.5	288.8
Sheep and lambs slaughtered (live weight)	mil lb	549.2**	(X)
Fresh and frozen beef	mil lb	585.3	481.5
Fresh and frozen veal	mil lb	17.2**	15.6
Fresh and frozen pork	mil lb	701.7*	433.4
Other fresh and frozen red meats	mil lb	31.8	27.1
Meat materials for sausage and canning not separable by species	mil lb	42.7	17.4
Processed pork (cured, smoked, etc.)	mil lb	34.0	28.9
Other purchased meat materials (cured beef, cured lamb, etc.)	mil lb	20.9	24.8
Poultry; live, fresh, frozen, or prepared		(X)	57.1
Hides, skins, and pelts		(X)	23.0
Spices and curing materials		(X)	69.7
Animal and collagen casings		(X)	23.2
Packaging paper and plastics film, coated and laminated		(X)	239.8
Paperboard containers, boxes, and corrugated paperboard		(X)	317.9
Synthetic casings, including cellulosic and fibrous reinforced		(X)	49.0
All other materials and components, parts, containers, and supplies		(X)	566.8
Materials, ingredients, containers, and supplies, nsk		(X)	2,800.6

Source: 1992 *Economic Census*. Explanation of symbols used: (D): Withheld to avoid disclosure of competitive data; na: Not available; (S): Withheld because statistical norms were not met; (X): Not applicable; (Z): Less than half the unit shown; nec: Not elsewhere classified; nsk: Not specified by kind; - : zero; * : 10-19 percent estimated; ** : 20-29 percent estimated.

PRODUCT SHARE DETAILS

Product or Product Class	% Share
Fresh and frozen meat from animals slaughtered in this plant	100.00
Fresh and frozen beef, made from animals slaughtered in this plant	57.46
Fresh and frozen whole carcass and half carcass beef	21.08
Fresh and frozen primal cuts	4.69
Fresh and frozen subprimal and fabricated cuts packaged in plastics (boxed beef)	56.89
Other fresh and frozen subprimal and fabricated cuts	0.63
Fresh and frozen boneless beef, including hamburger	12.14
Fresh and frozen variety meats (edible organs)	2.81
Other fresh and frozen edible beef, including corned beef	0.30
Beef, not canned or made into sausage, nsk	1.46
Fresh and frozen veal	0.60
Fresh and frozen lamb and mutton	0.72
Fresh and frozen pork	20.59
Lard	0.20
Pork, processed or cured (not canned or made into sausage)	4.37
Sausages and similar products (not canned)	3.67
Fresh sausage (pork sausage, breakfast links, etc.)	43.82
Dry or semidry salami, cervelat, pepperoni, summer sausage, pork roll, etc.	9.96
Frankfurters, including wieners, not canned	20.92
Other sausage, smoked or cooked (bologna, liverwurst, Polish sausage, packaged luncheon meats, minced roll, etc.)	22.51
Jellied goods and similar preparations (headcheese, meat loaves, scrapple, puddings, chili con carne, etc.)	1.15
Sausages and similar products (not canned), nsk	1.65
Canned meats (except dog, cat, and baby food)	(D)
Hides, skins, and pelts	4.26
Miscellaneous byproducts of meat packing plants	(D)
Fresh and frozen meat from animals slaughtered in this plant, nsk	5.99

Source: 1992 *Economic Census*. The values shown are percent of total shipments in an industry. Values of indented subcategories are summed in the main heading. The symbol (D) appears when data are withheld to prevent disclosure of competitive information. The abbreviation nsk stands for 'not specified by kind' and nec for 'not elsewhere classified'.

INPUTS AND OUTPUTS FOR MEAT PACKING PLANTS

Economic Sector or Industry Providing Inputs	%	Sector	Economic Sector or Industry Buying Outputs	%	Sector
Meat animals	78.7	Agric.	Personal consumption expenditures	46.6	
Meat packing plants	5.9	Manufg.	Eating & drinking places	20.2	Trade
Imports	4.5	Foreign	Sausages & other prepared meats	14.0	Manufg.
Advertising	3.0	Services	Meat packing plants	6.4	Manufg.
Wholesale trade	2.2	Trade	Exports	4.1	Foreign
Paperboard containers & boxes	0.8	Manufg.	Leather tanning & finishing	1.6	Manufg.
Sausages & other prepared meats	0.6	Manufg.	Hospitals	1.1	Services
Motor freight transportation & warehousing	0.6	Util.	S/L Govt. purch., elem. & secondary education	0.7	S/L Govt
Electric services (utilities)	0.5	Util.	Frozen specialties	0.6	Manufg.
Metal cans	0.3	Manufg.	Shortening & cooking oils	0.6	Manufg.
Gas production & distribution (utilities)	0.3	Util.	Change in business inventories	0.6	In House
Food preparations, nec	0.2	Manufg.	S/L Govt. purch., health & hospitals	0.5	S/L Govt
Miscellaneous plastics products	0.2	Manufg.	Residential care	0.4	Services
Banking	0.2	Fin/R.E.	Federal Government enterprises nec	0.4	Gov't
Cyclic crudes and organics	0.1	Manufg.	Canned specialties	0.3	Manufg.
Petroleum refining	0.1	Manufg.	S/L Govt. purch., correction	0.3	S/L Govt
Soap & other detergents	0.1	Manufg.	S/L Govt. purch., higher education	0.3	S/L Govt
Communications, except radio & TV	0.1	Util.	Drugs	0.2	Manufg.
Water transportation	0.1	Util.	Nursing & personal care facilities	0.2	Services
Equipment rental & leasing services	0.1	Services	Social services, nec	0.2	Services

Source: Benchmark Input-Output Accounts for the U.S. Economy, 1982, U.S. Department of Commerce, Washington, D.C., July 1991. Data, as reported in the source, are organized by the 1977 SIC structure in use in 1982 but have been matched, as closely as is possible, to the 1987 SIC structure used in this book.

OCCUPATIONS EMPLOYED BY SIC 201 - MEAT PRODUCTS

Occupation	% of Total 1994	Change to 2005	Occupation	% of Total 1994	Change to 2005
Meat, poultry, & fish cutters & trimmers, hand	26.4	29.2	Industrial machinery mechanics	1.8	27.8
Butchers & meatcutters	13.8	-2.2	Inspectors, testers, & graders, precision	1.7	16.2
Assemblers, fabricators, & hand workers nec	4.9	16.2	Cutting & slicing machine setters, operators	1.7	56.9
Hand packers & packagers	4.7	-0.4	Machine operators nec	1.6	2.5
Packaging & filling machine operators	4.4	-7.0	Freight, stock, & material movers, hand	1.6	-7.0
Helpers, laborers, & material movers nec	3.9	16.2	Maintenance repairers, general utility	1.6	4.6
Blue collar worker supervisors	3.5	15.6	Industrial truck & tractor operators	1.3	16.2
Machine feeders & offbearers	3.0	27.9	Crushing & mixing machine operators	1.3	4.6
Truck drivers light & heavy	2.1	19.8	General managers & top executives	1.1	10.3
Janitors & cleaners, incl maids	1.9	-7.0			

Source: Industry-Occupation Matrix, Bureau of Labor Statistics. These data relate to one or more 3-digit SIC industry groups rather than to a single 4-digit SIC. The change reported for each occupation to the year 2005 is a percent of growth or decline as estimated by the Bureau of Labor Statistics. The abbreviation nec stands for 'not elsewhere classified'.

LOCATION BY STATE AND REGIONAL CONCENTRATION

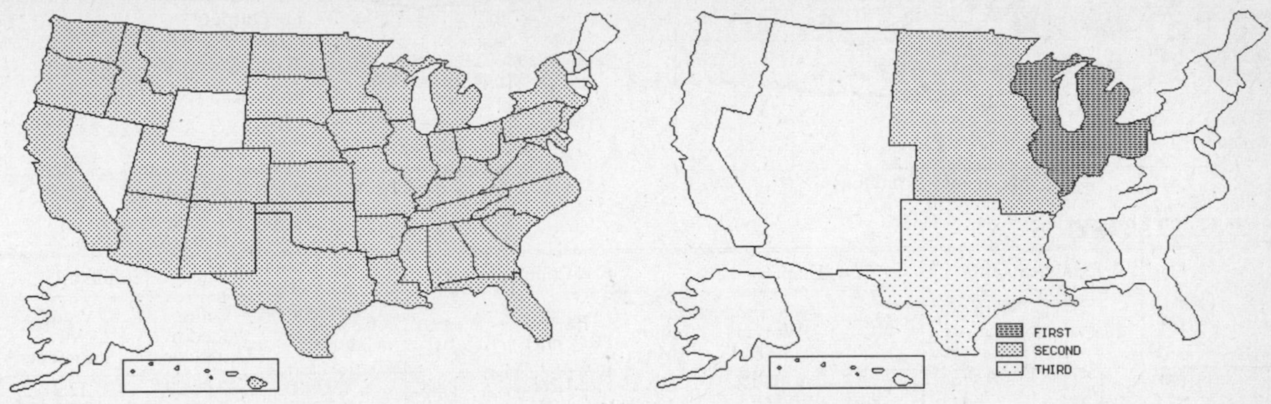

INDUSTRY DATA BY STATE

State	Establish-ments	Shipments			Employment				Cost as % of Shipments	Investment per Employee ($)
		Total ($ mil)	% of U.S.	Per Establ.	Total Number	% of U.S.	Per Establ.	Wages ($/hour)		
Nebraska	48	8,345.8	16.5	173.9	13,700	11.2	285	8.65	85.9	1,190
Kansas	44	6,254.2	12.4	142.1	12,300	10.0	280	8.00	93.0	1,203
Iowa	63	6,111.8	12.1	97.0	16,900	13.8	268	8.56	85.1	1,763
Texas	109	5,700.5	11.3	52.3	11,900	9.7	109	7.84	90.5	2,849
Colorado	40	2,809.6	5.6	70.2	5,100	4.2	127	9.11	91.0	2,843
Illinois	82	2,623.9	5.2	32.0	7,000	5.7	85	8.63	88.2	1,200
Minnesota	30	2,566.9	5.1	85.6	5,600	4.6	187	10.24	73.9	1,839
Pennsylvania	68	1,642.4	3.3	24.2	4,300	3.5	63	10.63	86.7	5,605
Wisconsin	46	1,584.2	3.1	34.4	3,100	2.5	67	9.21	81.0	2,484
California	73	1,338.9	2.7	18.3	3,500	2.9	48	9.27	88.3	7,829
South Dakota	16	1,266.3	2.5	79.1	3,800	3.1	238	9.47	77.5	1,079
Washington	23	1,131.0	2.2	49.2	1,900	1.6	83	8.08	93.0	-
Indiana	42	829.6	1.6	19.8	3,400	2.8	81	9.41	87.5	1,853
Michigan	46	829.2	1.6	18.0	2,300	1.9	50	8.64	87.6	-
Ohio	57	770.3	1.5	13.5	2,800	2.3	49	10.79	78.1	3,643
North Carolina	32	639.5	1.3	20.0	2,900	2.4	91	8.79	81.4	-
Kentucky	28	522.4	1.0	18.7	2,200	1.8	79	9.09	84.3	1,409
Georgia	35	468.5	0.9	13.4	2,100	1.7	60	7.20	84.7	2,190
Missouri	49	463.4	0.9	9.5	1,700	1.4	35	7.84	93.7	1,176
Tennessee	26	250.2	0.5	9.6	1,000	0.8	38	7.75	68.3	2,700
Alabama	26	118.0	0.2	4.5	700	0.6	27	8.25	60.7	-
New York	41	90.8	0.2	2.2	400	0.3	10	8.17	80.4	1,500
Florida	24	84.1	0.2	3.5	400	0.3	17	6.86	90.0	1,250
Oregon	20	79.7	0.2	4.0	300	0.2	15	10.20	81.9	-
New Jersey	14	76.2	0.2	5.4	300	0.2	21	11.60	76.9	1,000
Maryland	11	57.0	0.1	5.2	300	0.2	27	7.00	84.2	-
Hawaii	6	23.5	0.0	3.9	200	0.2	33	8.33	81.7	-
Montana	23	16.4	0.0	0.7	100	0.1	4	5.50	88.4	-
West Virginia	16	10.0	0.0	0.6	100	0.1	6	5.50	88.0	1,000
Oklahoma	42	(D)	-	-	375 *	0.3	9	-	-	-
South Carolina	27	(D)	-	-	1,750 *	1.4	65	-	-	-
Mississippi	25	(D)	-	-	3,750 *	3.1	150	-	-	-
Arkansas	22	(D)	-	-	375 *	0.3	17	-	-	-
Virginia	22	(D)	-	-	3,750 *	3.1	170	-	-	293
Louisiana	17	(D)	-	-	375 *	0.3	22	-	-	800
Utah	17	(D)	-	-	1,750 *	1.4	103	-	-	-
Idaho	13	(D)	-	-	750 *	0.6	58	-	-	-
Arizona	12	(D)	-	-	750 *	0.6	63	-	-	933
New Mexico	10	(D)	-	-	375 *	0.3	38	-	-	533
North Dakota	10	(D)	-	-	375 *	0.3	38	-	-	-

Source: 1992 *Economic Census*. The states are in descending order of shipments or establishments (if shipment data are missing for the majority). The symbol (D) appears when data are withheld to prevent disclosure of competitive information. States marked with (D) are sorted by number of establishments. A dash (-) indicates that the data element cannot be calculated; * indicates the midpoint of a range.

2013 - SAUSAGES AND OTHER PREPARED MEATS

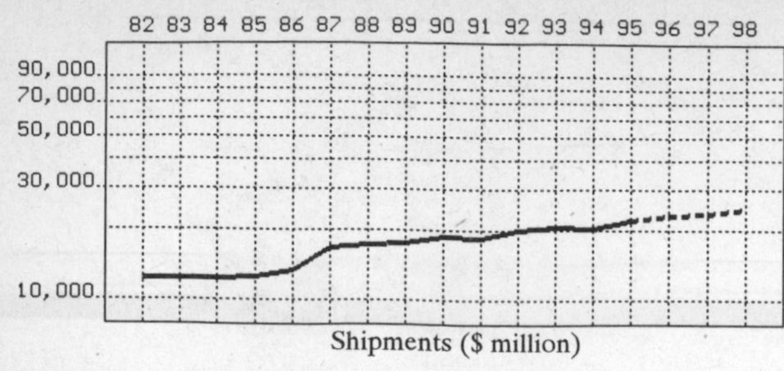

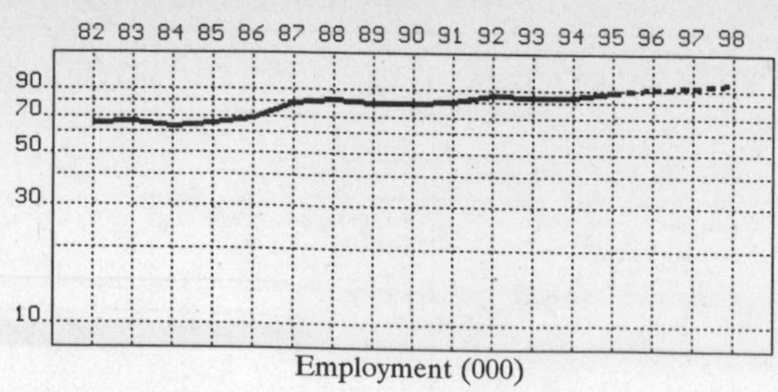

GENERAL STATISTICS

Year	Companies	Establishments: Total	Establishments: with 20 or more employees	Employment: Total (000)	Employment: Production Workers (000)	Employment: Production Hours (Mil)	Compensation: Payroll ($ mil)	Compensation: Wages ($/hr)	Production ($ million): Cost of Materials	Production ($ million): Value Added by Manufacture	Production ($ million): Value of Shipments	Production ($ million): Capital Invest.
1982	1,194	1,311	614	65.5	49.8	98.1	1,206.2	8.68	9,379.1	2,900.9	12,277.5	175.5
1983		1,274	602	65.7	50.1	100.3	1,231.9	8.50	9,323.5	3,072.6	12,365.7	157.5
1984		1,237	590	62.9	48.3	95.5	1,185.1	8.55	9,003.2	3,379.4	12,360.8	173.2
1985		1,199	577	64.6	49.4	98.3	1,237.2	8.66	8,737.3	3,705.1	12,405.7	210.6
1986		1,157	570	68.5	52.5	104.5	1,327.1	8.69	9,524.1	3,844.5	13,354.2	232.4
1987	1,203	1,344	651	79.1	59.8	121.7	1,618.8	8.87	12,136.6	4,475.7	16,622.6	252.5
1988		1,263	639	81.5	61.9	127.0	1,692.2	8.89	12,464.8	4,824.1	17,257.8	261.2
1989		1,200	633	78.7	61.5	126.2	1,747.5	8.91	12,553.0	5,040.2	17,515.5	304.5
1990		1,173	613	78.8	61.2	129.4	1,839.7	9.10	13,485.1	5,315.7	18,779.7	363.9
1991		1,153	583	79.6	59.0	126.0	1,833.4	9.31	13,270.5	5,045.6	18,361.3	326.3
1992	1,129	1,264	623	85.5	65.7	139.9	2,026.3	9.67	14,455.0	5,491.3	19,972.4	379.7
1993		1,236	600	84.2	65.4	139.6	2,005.6	9.77	15,225.3	5,511.7	20,700.7	413.2
1994		1,198P	616P	84.8	67.0	142.6	2,059.4	9.90	14,441.3	5,835.7	20,257.1	370.5
1995		1,193P	617P	89.3P	69.2P	149.1P	2,204.5P	9.84P	15,740.6P	6,360.8P	22,079.7P	429.9P
1996		1,187P	618P	91.3P	70.9P	153.4P	2,288.5P	9.96P	16,326.6P	6,597.6P	22,901.7P	451.6P
1997		1,182P	619P	93.3P	72.5P	157.7P	2,372.5P	10.07P	16,912.7P	6,834.4P	23,723.7P	473.2P
1998		1,176P	621P	95.3P	74.1P	161.9P	2,456.6P	10.19P	17,498.7P	7,071.2P	24,545.8P	494.8P

Sources: 1982, 1987, 1992 *Economic Census*; *Annual Survey of Manufactures*, 83-86, 88-91, 93-94. Establishment counts for non-Census years are from *County Business Patterns*; establishment values for 83-84 are extrapolations. 'P's show projections by the editors. Industries reclassified in 87 will not have data for prior years.

INDICES OF CHANGE

Year	Companies	Establishments: Total	Establishments: with 20 or more employees	Employment: Total (000)	Employment: Production Workers (000)	Employment: Production Hours (Mil)	Compensation: Payroll ($ mil)	Compensation: Wages ($/hr)	Production ($ million): Cost of Materials	Production ($ million): Value Added by Manufacture	Production ($ million): Value of Shipments	Production ($ million): Capital Invest.
1982	106	104	99	77	76	70	60	90	65	53	61	46
1983		101	97	77	76	72	61	88	65	56	62	41
1984		98	95	74	74	68	58	88	62	62	62	46
1985		95	93	76	75	70	61	90	60	67	62	55
1986		92	91	80	80	75	65	90	66	70	67	61
1987	107	106	104	93	91	87	80	92	84	82	83	66
1988		100	103	95	94	91	84	92	86	88	86	69
1989		95	102	92	94	90	86	92	87	92	88	80
1990		93	98	92	93	92	91	94	93	97	94	96
1991		91	94	93	90	90	90	96	92	92	92	86
1992	100	100	100	100	100	100	100	100	100	100	100	100
1993		98	96	98	100	100	99	101	105	100	104	109
1994		95P	99P	99	102	102	102	102	100	106	101	98
1995		94P	99P	104P	105P	107P	109P	102P	109P	116P	111P	113P
1996		94P	99P	107P	108P	110P	113P	103P	113P	120P	115P	119P
1997		93P	99P	109P	110P	113P	117P	104P	117P	124P	119P	125P
1998		93P	100P	112P	113P	116P	121P	105P	121P	129P	123P	130P

Sources: Same as General Statistics. Values reflect change from the base year, 1992. Values above 100 mean greater than 92, values below 100 mean less than 92, and a value of 100 in the 82-91 or 93-98 period means same as 92. 'P's mark projections by the editors.

SELECTED RATIOS

For 1994	Avg. of All Manufact.	Analyzed Industry	Index
Employees per Establishment	49	71	144
Payroll per Establishment	1,500,273	1,718,706	115
Payroll per Employee	30,620	24,285	79
Production Workers per Establishment	34	56	163
Wages per Establishment	853,319	1,178,191	138
Wages per Production Worker	24,861	21,071	85
Hours per Production Worker	2,056	2,128	104
Wages per Hour	12.09	9.90	82
Value Added per Establishment	4,602,255	4,870,278	106
Value Added per Employee	93,930	68,817	73

For 1994	Avg. of All Manufact.	Analyzed Industry	Index
Value Added per Production Worker	134,084	87,100	65
Cost per Establishment	5,045,178	12,052,221	239
Cost per Employee	102,970	170,298	165
Cost per Production Worker	146,988	215,542	147
Shipments per Establishment	9,576,895	16,905,891	177
Shipments per Employee	195,460	238,881	122
Shipments per Production Worker	279,017	302,345	108
Investment per Establishment	321,011	309,207	96
Investment per Employee	6,552	4,369	67
Investment per Production Worker	9,352	5,530	59

Sources: Same as General Statistics. The 'Average of All Manufacturing' column represents the average of all manufacturing industries reported for the most recent complete year available. The Index shows the relationship between the Average and the Analyzed Industry. For example, 100 means that they are equal; 500 that the Analyzed Industry is five times the average; 50 means that the Analyzed Industry is half the national average. The abbreviation 'na' is used to show that data are 'not available'.

LEADING COMPANIES Number shown: **75** Total sales ($ mil): **21,414** Total employment (000): **175.7**

Company Name	Address				CEO Name	Phone	Co. Type	Sales ($ mil)	Empl. (000)
Sara Lee Corp	3 1st National Plz	Chicago	IL	60602	John H Bryan	312-726-2600	P	15,536	146.0
Smithfield Foods Inc	501 N Church St	Smithfield	VA	23430	Joseph W Luter III	804-357-4321	P	1,447	8.0
Foodbrands America Inc	2601 NW Expy	Oklahoma City	OK	73112	RR Devening	405-879-5500	P	751	2.2
Hatfield Quality Meats Inc	PO Box 902	Hatfield	PA	19440	Claire Clemens	215-368-2500	R	240*	1.2
Sara Lee Corp	8000 Ctrview Pkwy	Cordova	TN	38018	Jerry Laner	901-753-1600	D	240	1.5
Gwaltney of Smithfield Ltd	PO Box 489	Smithfield	VA	23431	Larry Seekford	804-357-3131	S	220	1.4
Jordan's Meats Inc	PO Box 588	Portland	ME	04112	Bruce Dunphy	207-772-5411	R	195	0.5
OSI Industries Inc	1225 Corporate	Aurora	IL	60507	David Brooke	708-851-6600	R	160*	0.8
Supreme Beef Processors Inc	5219 2nd Av	Dallas	TX	75210	Steven Spiritas	214-428-1761	R	150	0.4
ESI Meats Inc	PO Box 157	Bristol	IN	46507	CB Baugher	219-848-7661	S	110*	0.6
Sugar Creek Packing Co	2101 Kenskill Av	Wash Ct House	OH	43160	JG Richardson	614-335-7440	R	110	0.5
Carando	PO Box 491	Springfield	MA	01102	George Grazier	413-781-5620	D	100	0.4
Gallo Salame	2411 Baumann Av	San Lorenzo	CA	94580	Phil Francis	510-276-1300	D	100	0.5
Tennessee Dressed Beef	PO Box 23031	Nashville	TN	37202	RN Hall	615-742-5800	R	100	0.2
Vienna Sausage Mfg Co	2501 N Damen Av	Chicago	IL	60647	James Eisenberg	312-278-7800	R	95	0.8
DPM of Arkansas	PO Box 200	Booneville	AR	72927	Mike Middleton	501-675-4555	D	75*	0.4
Goodmark Inc	519 Kaiser Dr	Folcroft	PA	19032	Tom Chapley	215-586-2800	S	74*	0.5
Doughtie's Foods Inc	2410 Wesley St	Portsmouth	VA	23707	Vernon W Mules	804-393-6007	P	73	0.3
Kunzler and Company Inc	PO Box 4747	Lancaster	PA	17604	C C Kunzler Jr	717-299-6301	R	70	0.2
Pierre Frozen Foods Inc	9990 Princeton Rd	Cincinnati	OH	45246	Michael Hudson	513-874-8741	S	68*	0.7
FB Purnell Sausage Company	PO Box 366	Simpsonville	KY	40067	AD Purnell	502-722-5626	R	60*	0.3
Kayem Foods Inc	75 Arlington St	Chelsea	MA	02150	R Monkiewicz	617-889-1600	R	60*	0.3
Cloverdale Foods Company Inc	PO Box 667	Mandan	ND	58554	Don Russell	701-663-9511	R	59	0.4
Land O'Frost of Arkansas	PO Box 9158	Searcy	AR	72143	Charles Niemenski	501-268-2473	S	58*	0.8
Plum Rose Inc	PO Box 160	Elkhart	IN	46515	Martin Groane	219-295-8190	R	52*	0.1
Quality Foods LP	300 Atlantic Av	Camden	NJ	08104	David Cohen	609-964-8902	R	50*	0.3
Quik-to-Fix Food Products	PO Box 462368	Garland	TX	75046	Mike Reyes	214-272-5521	D	50*	0.6
Armour Swift-Eckrich Inc	PO Box 10718	El Paso	TX	79997	Bryan Green	915-779-3072	D	45*	0.2
Bert Packing Co	170 N Green St	Chicago	IL	60607	Allan Bridgford	312-733-0300	D	45	0.2
Bridgford Foods of Illinois	170 N Green St	Chicago	IL	60607	Alan Bridgford Jr	312-733-0300	D	45	0.3
Dold Foods Inc	PO Box 4339	Wichita	KS	67204	JA Nuyten	316-838-9101	S	45	0.3
Advance Food Co	201 S Raleigh Rd	Enid	OK	73701	Paul Allen	405-237-6656	R	41*	0.3
Alphin Brothers Inc	Rt 4	Dunn	NC	28334	JC Alphin Jr	919-892-8751	R	40*	<0.1
Devro Inc	PO Box 858	Somerville	NJ	08876	Colin Tait	908-218-4400	S	40	0.2
JC Potter Sausage Co	PO Box 689	Durant	OK	74702	Thomas G Potter	405-924-2414	R	40	0.2
Vincent Giordano Corp	2600 Washington	Philadelphia	PA	19146	Guy Giordano	215-467-6629	R	40	<0.1
Carl Buddig and Company Inc	950 W 175th St	Homewood	IL	60430	William Buddig	708-798-0900	R	35*	0.3
C and F Packing Company Inc	1350 Greenleaf Rd	Elk Grove Vill	IL	60007	Joe Freda	708-228-6300	R	30	0.1
Otto and Sons Inc	711 Industrial Dr	West Chicago	IL	60185	Tom Kennedy	708-231-9090	S	30*	0.2
Medford's Foods Inc	PO Box 540	Chester	PA	19016	William Medford	215-874-5000	R	28*	0.2
Webber Farms	Hwy 36 W	Cynthiana	KY	41031	Carl Glass	606-234-5154	D	27*	0.2
Provena Foods Inc	5010 Eucalyptus	Chino	CA	91710	John D Determan	909-627-1082	P	26	0.1
Appert's Food Inc	900 S Hwy 10	St Cloud	MN	56304	Tim Appert	612-251-3200	R	25	0.1
Best Provision Company Inc	144 Avon Av	Newark	NJ	07108	Paul Dolinko	201-242-5000	R	25	<0.1
Boyle's Famous Corned Beef	416 E 3rd St	Kansas City	MO	64106	Viola P Boyle	816-221-6283	R	25	0.2
Elm Hill Meats Inc	PO Box 429	Lenoir City	TN	37771	HW Wampler	615-986-8005	R	24	0.2
North Side Packing Co	2200 Rivers Edge	Arnold	PA	15066	R G Hofmann II	412-335-5800	R	24	0.2
Joseph Kirschner	193 Riverside Dr	Augusta	ME	04332	Bill McCall	207-623-3544	D	22*	0.2
Koegel Meats Inc	3400 W Bristol Rd	Flint	MI	48507	John C Koegel	313-238-3685	R	21	0.1
Odom's Tenn Pride Sausage Co	1201 Neelys Bend	Madison	TN	37115	Larry D Odom	615-868-1360	R	20	0.1
Dewied International	5010 East IH 10	San Antonio	TX	78219	Jack R de Wied	210-661-6161	R	19	<0.1
John Hofmeister and Son Inc	2386 S Blue Island	Chicago	IL	60608	EJ Hofmeister	312-847-0700	R	19	<0.1
EW Knauss and Son Inc	625 E Broad St	Quakertown	PA	18951	DT Knauss	215-536-4220	R	18	<0.1
Lennon Foods Inc	PO Box 681-128	Yakima	WA	98907	Kennth Eakes	206-624-2270	R	18	<0.1
Alle Processing Corp	5620 59th St	Maspeth	NY	11378	S Weinstock	718-894-2000	R	17*	0.1
Seitz Foods Inc	PO Box 247	St Joseph	MO	64502	Rick Benward	816-238-1771	S	17*	0.2
Wolfson Casing Corp	700 S Fulton Av	Mount Vernon	NY	10550	Monte Wolfson	914-668-9000	R	17	0.2
Cher-Make Sausage Co	PO Box 1267	Manitowoc	WI	54221	AT Chermak	414-683-5980	R	15	0.1
Formico Food Co	PO Box 100247	Ft Lauderdale	FL	33310	Dominic Dejulio	305-772-3310	R	15	<0.1
Fred Usinger Inc	1030 Old World	Milwaukee	WI	53203	FD Usinger	414-276-9100	R	15	0.2
Hansel 'N Gretel Brand Inc	79-36 Cooper Av	Glendale	NY	11385	Milton S Rattner	718-326-0041	R	15	0.1
J and B Sausage Company Inc	PO Box 7	Waelder	TX	78959	D Janecka	512-665-7511	R	15*	0.1
John McKenzie Packing	PO Box 4059	S Burlington	VT	05406	MaryAlice McKenzie	802-864-4585	R	15*	<0.1
Stevison Ham Co	PO Box 219	Portland	TN	37148	Michael Stevison	615-325-4161	R	15	<0.1
Evergood Sausage Co	1389 Underwood	San Francisco	CA	94124	Harlan Miller	415-822-4660	R	14	<0.1
Tennessee Valley Ham Co	PO Box 1146	Paris	TN	38242	Dan Murphey	901-642-9740	R	14*	<0.1
Sigman Meat Company Inc	6000 W 54th Av	Arvada	CO	80002	D Thompson	303-424-5531	R	13*	0.1
Vie de France Corp	85 S Bragg St	Alexandria	VA	22312	Stanislaus Vilgrain	703-750-9600	P	13	0.1
Allen Clark Inc	PO Drawer 3	Paxinos	PA	17860	Allen Clark	717-648-6851	R	12	<0.1
David Berg and Co	2501 N Damen Av	Chicago	IL	60647	Jim Eisenberg	312-278-5195	S	12*	0.1
Dean Sausage Company Inc	PO Drawer 750	Attalla	AL	35954	Marsue D Lancaster	205-538-6082	R	12	0.1
Green Tree Packing Co	65 Central Av	Passaic	NJ	07055	DP Waters	201-473-1305	R	12*	<0.1
Silver Star Meats Inc	1720 Middletown	McKees Rocks	PA	15136	Richard Rzaca	412-771-5539	R	12	<0.1
Sparrer Sausage Company Inc	4325 W Ogden Av	Chicago	IL	60623	Brian Graves	312-762-3334	R	12*	<0.1
Continental-Capri Inc	250 Jackson St	Englewood	NJ	07631	F Mazza	201-568-7100	R	11*	<0.1

Source: *Ward's Business Directory of U.S. Private and Public Companies*, Volumes 1 and 2, 1996. The company type code used is as follows: P - Public, R - Private, S - Subsidiary, D - Division, J - Joint Venture, A - Affiliate, G - Group. Sales are in millions of dollars, employees are in thousands. An asterisk (*) indicates an estimated sales volume. The symbol < stands for 'less than'. Company names and addresses are truncated, in some cases, to fit into the available space.

MATERIALS CONSUMED

Material		Quantity	Delivered Cost ($ million)
Materials, ingredients, containers, and supplies		(X)	12,723.5
Fresh and frozen beef	mil lb	4,061.7	4,236.3
Fresh and frozen veal	mil lb	159.0	150.7
Fresh and frozen pork	mil lb	4,385.8	2,950.5
Other fresh and frozen red meats	mil lb	69.8**	31.9
Meat materials for sausage and canning not separable by species	mil lb	921.6*	612.0
Processed pork (cured, smoked, etc.)	mil lb	506.5	422.6
Other purchased meat materials (cured beef, cured lamb, etc.)	mil lb	65.7	47.8
Poultry; live, fresh, frozen, or prepared		(X)	402.3
Spices and curing materials		(X)	246.8
Hides, skins, and pelts		(X)	46.9
Animal and collagen casings		(X)	101.8
Synthetic casings, including cellulosic and fibrous reinforced		(X)	169.6
Paperboard containers, boxes, and corrugated paperboard		(X)	290.4
Packaging paper and plastics film, coated and laminated		(X)	301.5
All other materials and components, parts, containers, and supplies		(X)	914.7
Materials, ingredients, containers, and supplies, nsk		(X)	1,797.6

Source: 1992 *Economic Census*. Explanation of symbols used: (D): Withheld to avoid disclosure of competitive data; na: Not available; (S): Withheld because statistical norms were not met; (X): Not applicable; (Z): Less than half the unit shown; nec: Not elsewhere classified; nsk: Not specified by kind; - : zero; * : 10-19 percent estimated; ** : 20-29 percent estimated.

PRODUCT SHARE DETAILS

Product or Product Class	% Share
Sausage and other prepared meats	100.00
Pork, processed or cured, including frozen, not canned or made into sausage	19.71
Sweet-pickled or dry-cured pork, (not smoked, cooked, canned, or made into sausage)	4.01
Dry salt pork	0.51
Smoked pork hams and picnics, except canned	40.73
Smoked pork slab bacon, except canned	0.59
Smoked pork sliced bacon, except canned	27.13
Other smoked pork	3.96
Boiled ham, barbecue pork, and other cooked pork, including frozen, except canned meats and sausages	18.69
Pork, processed or cured, including frozen, nsk	4.37
Sausage and similar products, except canned	32.43
Fresh sausage (pork sausage, breakfast links, etc.), except canned	14.60
Dry or semidry sausage and similar products (salami, cervelat, pepperoni, summer sausage, pork roll, etc.), except canned	16.43
Frankfurters, including wieners, except canned	22.07
Other sausage, smoked or cooked (bologna, liverwurst, Polish sausage, packed luncheon meats, minced roll, smoked pork sausage, etc.), except canned	41.41
Jellied goods and similar preparations, except canned (headcheese, meat loaves, scrapple, puddings, chili con carne, etc.)	1.06
Sausage and similar products, not canned, nsk	4.43
Canned meats (except dog, cat, and baby food), containing 20 percent or more meat	4.93
Other processed, frozen, or cooked meats	32.51
Frozen ground meat patties (processed, frozen, or cooked)	27.83
Frozen portion control meats (processed, frozen, or cooked)	17.93
Pork rind pellets, including pork cracklings (processed, frozen, or cooked)	(D)
Other processed, frozen, or cooked meats, corned beef, frozen primal and fabricated cuts, frozen variety meats, etc.	49.29
Collagen sausage casings (processed, frozen, or cooked)	(D)
Other processed, frozen, or cooked meats, nsk	3.09
Sausage and other prepared meats, nsk	10.43

Source: 1992 *Economic Census*. The values shown are percent of total shipments in an industry. Values of indented subcategories are summed in the main heading. The symbol (D) appears when data are withheld to prevent disclosure of competitive information. The abbreviation nsk stands for 'not specified by kind' and nec for 'not elsewhere classified'.

INPUTS AND OUTPUTS FOR SAUSAGES & OTHER PREPARED MEATS

Economic Sector or Industry Providing Inputs	%	Sector	Economic Sector or Industry Buying Outputs	%	Sector
Meat packing plants	56.6	Manufg.	Personal consumption expenditures	79.4	
Wholesale trade	10.6	Trade	Eating & drinking places	11.4	Trade
Imports	5.7	Foreign	Sausages & other prepared meats	2.0	Manufg.
Sausages & other prepared meats	3.9	Manufg.	Meat packing plants	1.4	Manufg.
Commercial printing	3.8	Manufg.	S/L Govt. purch., elem. & secondary education	1.1	S/L Govt
Advertising	2.8	Services	Hospitals	0.6	Services
Meat animals	2.3	Agric.	Exports	0.6	Foreign
Motor freight transportation & warehousing	2.0	Util.	Change in business inventories	0.6	In House
Metal cans	1.5	Manufg.	Canned specialties	0.4	Manufg.
Paperboard containers & boxes	1.5	Manufg.	Residential care	0.4	Services
Food preparations, nec	1.4	Manufg.	S/L Govt. purch., health & hospitals	0.3	S/L Govt
Poultry dressing plants	1.2	Manufg.	S/L Govt. purch., higher education	0.3	S/L Govt
Miscellaneous plastics products	1.1	Manufg.	Frozen specialties	0.2	Manufg.
Electric services (utilities)	1.1	Util.	Nursing & personal care facilities	0.2	Services
Gas production & distribution (utilities)	0.6	Util.	Social services, nec	0.2	Services
Petroleum refining	0.3	Manufg.	Federal Government enterprises nec	0.2	Gov't
Communications, except radio & TV	0.3	Util.	Federal Government purchases, national defense	0.2	Fed Govt
Equipment rental & leasing services	0.3	Services	S/L Govt. purch., correction	0.2	S/L Govt
Maintenance of nonfarm buildings nec	0.2	Constr.			
Paper coating & glazing	0.2	Manufg.			

Continued on next page.

INPUTS AND OUTPUTS FOR SAUSAGES & OTHER PREPARED MEATS - Continued

Economic Sector or Industry Providing Inputs	%	Sector	Economic Sector or Industry Buying Outputs	%	Sector
Railroads & related services	0.2	Util.			
Eating & drinking places	0.2	Trade			
Banking	0.2	Fin/R.E.			
Real estate	0.2	Fin/R.E.			
Royalties	0.2	Fin/R.E.			
Bags, except textile	0.1	Manufg.			
Cyclic crudes and organics	0.1	Manufg.			
Soap & other detergents	0.1	Manufg.			
Air transportation	0.1	Util.			
Security & commodity brokers	0.1	Fin/R.E.			
U.S. Postal Service	0.1	Gov't			

Source: Benchmark Input-Output Accounts for the U.S. Economy, 1982, U.S. Department of Commerce, Washington, D.C., July 1991. Data, as reported in the source, are organized by the 1977 SIC structure in use in 1982 but have been matched, as closely as is possible, to the 1987 SIC structure used in this book.

OCCUPATIONS EMPLOYED BY SIC 201 - MEAT PRODUCTS

Occupation	% of Total 1994	Change to 2005	Occupation	% of Total 1994	Change to 2005
Meat, poultry, & fish cutters & trimmers, hand	26.4	29.2	Industrial machinery mechanics	1.8	27.8
Butchers & meatcutters	13.8	-2.2	Inspectors, testers, & graders, precision	1.7	16.2
Assemblers, fabricators, & hand workers nec	4.9	16.2	Cutting & slicing machine setters, operators	1.7	56.9
Hand packers & packagers	4.7	-0.4	Machine operators nec	1.6	2.5
Packaging & filling machine operators	4.4	-7.0	Freight, stock, & material movers, hand	1.6	-7.0
Helpers, laborers, & material movers nec	3.9	16.2	Maintenance repairers, general utility	1.6	4.6
Blue collar worker supervisors	3.5	15.6	Industrial truck & tractor operators	1.3	16.2
Machine feeders & offbearers	3.0	27.9	Crushing & mixing machine operators	1.3	4.6
Truck drivers light & heavy	2.1	19.8	General managers & top executives	1.1	10.3
Janitors & cleaners, incl maids	1.9	-7.0			

Source: Industry-Occupation Matrix, Bureau of Labor Statistics. These data relate to one or more 3-digit SIC industry groups rather than to a single 4-digit SIC. The change reported for each occupation to the year 2005 is a percent of growth or decline as estimated by the Bureau of Labor Statistics. The abbreviation nec stands for 'not elsewhere classified'.

LOCATION BY STATE AND REGIONAL CONCENTRATION

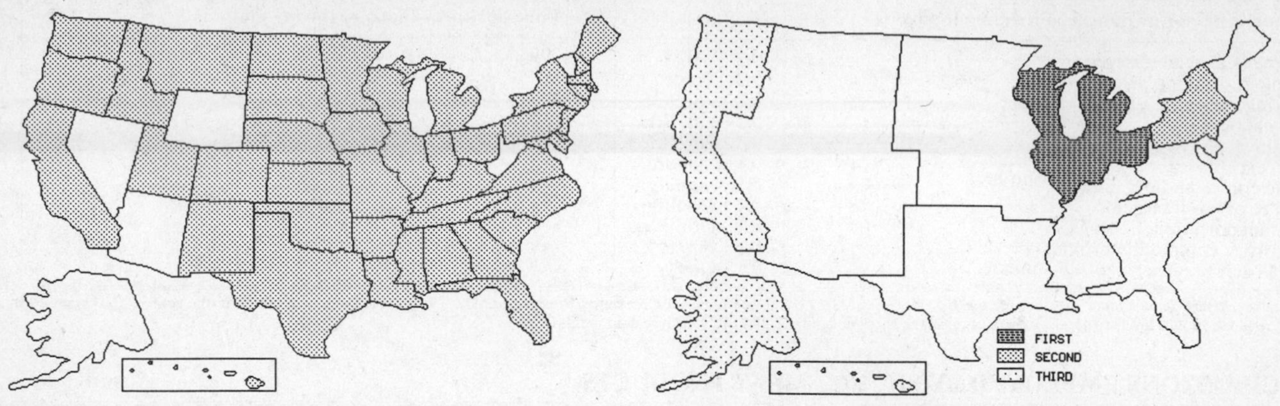

INDUSTRY DATA BY STATE

State	Establish-ments	Shipments			Employment				Cost as % of Shipments	Investment per Employee ($)
		Total ($ mil)	% of U.S.	Per Establ.	Total Number	% of U.S.	Per Establ.	Wages ($/hour)		
Wisconsin	43	2,153.1	10.8	50.1	6,700	7.8	156	11.94	62.8	4,552
Texas	81	1,661.4	8.3	20.5	6,600	7.7	81	8.96	79.8	5,212
California	129	1,382.3	6.9	10.7	5,500	6.4	43	10.09	66.2	3,491
Illinois	85	1,362.4	6.8	16.0	5,700	6.7	67	11.21	67.0	6,877
Iowa	29	1,305.7	6.5	45.0	4,300	5.0	148	11.85	78.8	6,884
Pennsylvania	75	1,287.1	6.4	17.2	4,800	5.6	64	9.97	72.9	2,958
Ohio	41	913.6	4.6	22.3	3,700	4.3	90	9.07	80.1	4,243
North Carolina	48	539.2	2.7	11.2	3,000	3.5	63	7.76	73.1	-
New York	88	536.5	2.7	6.1	2,200	2.6	25	11.88	71.8	3,682
Georgia	36	536.1	2.7	14.9	2,700	3.2	75	8.04	73.3	3,333
Missouri	32	503.7	2.5	15.7	2,500	2.9	78	8.57	79.7	7,760
Florida	33	491.1	2.5	14.9	2,400	2.8	73	9.36	77.3	3,958
New Jersey	41	469.8	2.4	11.5	2,100	2.5	51	10.77	69.9	2,571
Indiana	19	451.4	2.3	23.8	1,600	1.9	84	10.52	75.5	3,500
Nebraska	30	442.8	2.2	14.8	2,300	2.7	77	7.44	80.9	2,043
Tennessee	25	398.2	2.0	15.9	1,800	2.1	72	9.70	65.0	1,722
Oklahoma	13	338.4	1.7	26.0	1,200	1.4	92	8.67	78.5	7,333
Minnesota	22	330.8	1.7	15.0	1,600	1.9	73	8.26	79.4	2,750
Massachusetts	31	285.6	1.4	9.2	1,400	1.6	45	10.06	74.0	2,571
Oregon	21	233.4	1.2	11.1	1,400	1.6	67	7.43	55.3	2,857
Washington	19	202.9	1.0	10.7	900	1.1	47	8.67	65.0	5,333
Maryland	20	179.4	0.9	9.0	1,300	1.5	65	9.32	65.2	-
Louisiana	25	118.0	0.6	4.7	500	0.6	20	7.00	80.8	-
Utah	7	91.4	0.5	13.1	200	0.2	29	7.25	83.6	2,000
Alabama	12	82.2	0.4	6.8	700	0.8	58	7.18	73.6	-
Connecticut	15	57.2	0.3	3.8	300	0.4	20	8.80	65.7	-
Hawaii	15	25.3	0.1	1.7	200	0.2	13	6.67	68.8	2,500
Rhode Island	8	23.2	0.1	2.9	100	0.1	13	12.50	65.9	6,000
Montana	9	22.3	0.1	2.5	200	0.2	22	8.33	64.1	-
Michigan	40	(D)	-	-	3,750 *	4.4	94	-	-	2,667
Colorado	25	(D)	-	-	1,750 *	2.0	70	-	-	-
Virginia	25	(D)	-	-	3,750 *	4.4	150	-	-	1,520
Kansas	23	(D)	-	-	1,750 *	2.0	76	-	-	-
Kentucky	21	(D)	-	-	1,750 *	2.0	83	-	-	-
Mississippi	11	(D)	-	-	750 *	0.9	68	-	-	-
South Carolina	9	(D)	-	-	1,750 *	2.0	194	-	-	-
Maine	7	(D)	-	-	375 *	0.4	54	-	-	-
Arkansas	6	(D)	-	-	1,750 *	2.0	292	-	-	-
Idaho	5	(D)	-	-	750 *	0.9	150	-	-	-
North Dakota	5	(D)	-	-	375 *	0.4	75	-	-	-
Delaware	4	(D)	-	-	175 *	0.2	44	-	-	-
New Hampshire	4	(D)	-	-	375 *	0.4	94	-	-	-
New Mexico	4	(D)	-	-	375 *	0.4	94	-	-	-
South Dakota	2	(D)	-	-	375 *	0.4	188	-	-	-

Source: 1992 *Economic Census*. The states are in descending order of shipments or establishments (if shipment data are missing for the majority). The symbol (D) appears when data are withheld to prevent disclosure of competitive information. States marked with (D) are sorted by number of establishments. A dash (-) indicates that the data element cannot be calculated; * indicates the midpoint of a range.

2015 - POULTRY SLAUGHTERING & PROCESSING

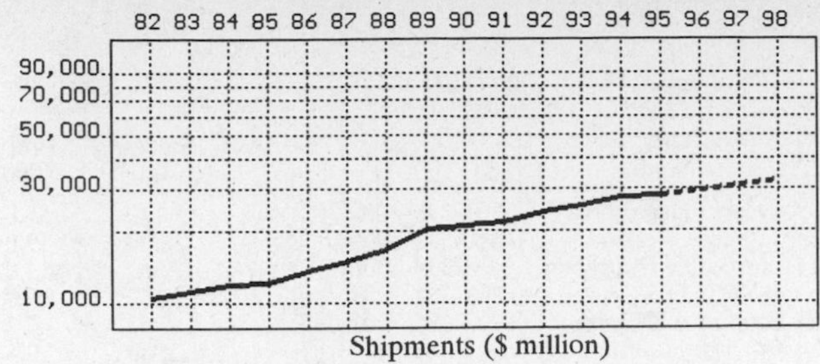

Shipments ($ million)

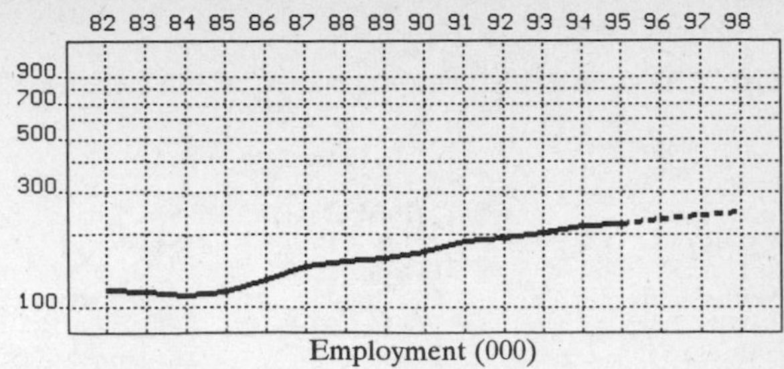

Employment (000)

GENERAL STATISTICS

Year	Companies	Establishments: Total	Establishments: with 20 or more employees	Employment: Total (000)	Production Workers (000)	Production Hours (Mil)	Compensation: Payroll ($ mil)	Compensation: Wages ($/hr)	Cost of Materials	Value Added by Manufacture	Value of Shipments	Capital Invest.
1982		532	401	117.7	106.2	199.6	1,237.1	5.06	8,170.5	2,276.8	10,471.1	231.1
1983				116.2	104.4	197.5	1,274.4	5.28	8,571.1	2,679.3	11,251.6	172.7
1984				112.2	100.5	190.6	1,298.5	5.60	9,024.5	2,918.6	11,939.4	168.2
1985				116.5	105.0	199.7	1,391.9	5.73	8,803.4	3,394.8	12,179.0	256.0
1986				129.7	115.4	216.4	1,595.3	6.01	9,555.6	3,994.4	13,528.9	364.2
1987	283	463	381	147.7	131.5	253.0	1,919.4	6.16	10,835.4	4,118.4	14,912.4	387.4
1988		472	388	155.7	139.0	271.4	2,131.3	6.37	12,013.2	4,636.6	16,597.8	347.8
1989		460	376	158.5	147.1	286.5	2,313.5	6.53	14,409.1	5,886.2	20,282.9	499.8
1990		472	384	170.9	157.6	313.9	2,596.8	6.63	14,507.7	6,452.3	20,927.6	497.6
1991		493	395	189.6	168.0	323.9	2,817.1	6.96	15,237.4	6,472.5	21,703.4	586.6
1992	372	591	432	193.8	172.8	341.5	3,091.5	7.37	17,066.7	6,656.5	23,757.1	466.4
1993		548	417	205.3	184.3	367.0	3,312.2	7.40	17,899.1	7,668.9	25,501.2	554.8
1994				216.0	193.2	394.4	3,605.3	7.49	19,136.8	8,324.2	27,414.9	594.3
1995				220.5P	198.1P	397.4P	3,669.7P	7.80P	19,595.1P	8,523.5P	28,071.4P	650.3P
1996				229.7P	206.3P	415.1P	3,879.8P	8.00P	20,626.5P	8,972.2P	29,549.0P	686.8P
1997				238.9P	214.5P	432.8P	4,089.9P	8.21P	21,657.9P	9,420.9P	31,026.6P	723.4P
1998				248.1P	222.8P	450.5P	4,300.1P	8.42P	22,689.4P	9,869.5P	32,504.2P	760.0P

Sources: 1982, 1987, 1992 *Economic Census*; *Annual Survey of Manufactures*, 83-86, 88-91, 93-94. Establishment counts for non-Census years are from *County Business Patterns*; establishment values for 83-84 are extrapolations. 'P's show projections by the editors. Industries reclassified in 87 will not have data for prior years.

INDICES OF CHANGE

Year	Companies	Establishments: Total	Establishments: with 20 or more employees	Employment: Total (000)	Production Workers (000)	Production Hours (Mil)	Compensation: Payroll ($ mil)	Compensation: Wages ($/hr)	Cost of Materials	Value Added by Manufacture	Value of Shipments	Capital Invest.
1982		90	93	61	61	58	40	69	48	34	44	50
1983				60	60	58	41	72	50	40	47	37
1984				58	58	56	42	76	53	44	50	36
1985				60	61	58	45	78	52	51	51	55
1986				67	67	63	52	82	56	60	57	78
1987	76	78	88	76	76	74	62	84	63	62	63	83
1988		80	90	80	80	79	69	86	70	70	70	75
1989		78	87	82	85	84	75	89	84	88	85	107
1990		80	89	88	91	92	84	90	85	97	88	107
1991		83	91	98	97	95	91	94	89	97	91	126
1992	100	100	100	100	100	100	100	100	100	100	100	100
1993		93	97	106	107	107	107	100	105	115	107	119
1994				111	112	115	117	102	112	125	115	127
1995				114P	115P	116P	119P	106P	115P	128P	118P	139P
1996				119P	119P	122P	125P	109P	121P	135P	124P	147P
1997				123P	124P	127P	132P	111P	127P	142P	131P	155P
1998				128P	129P	132P	139P	114P	133P	148P	137P	163P

Sources: Same as General Statistics. Values reflect change from the base year, 1992. Values above 100 mean greater than 92, values below 100 mean less than 92, and a value of 100 in the 82-91 or 93-98 period means same as 92. 'P's mark projections by the editors.

SELECTED RATIOS

For 1992	Avg. of All Manufact.	Analyzed Industry	Index
Employees per Establishment	46	328	718
Payroll per Establishment	1,332,320	5,230,964	393
Payroll per Employee	29,181	15,952	55
Production Workers per Establishment	31	292	931
Wages per Establishment	734,496	4,258,638	580
Wages per Production Worker	23,390	14,565	62
Hours per Production Worker	2,025	1,976	98
Wages per Hour	11.55	7.37	64
Value Added per Establishment	3,842,210	11,263,113	293
Value Added per Employee	84,153	34,347	41

For 1992	Avg. of All Manufact.	Analyzed Industry	Index
Value Added per Production Worker	122,353	38,521	31
Cost per Establishment	4,239,462	28,877,665	681
Cost per Employee	92,853	88,063	95
Cost per Production Worker	135,003	98,766	73
Shipments per Establishment	8,100,800	40,198,139	496
Shipments per Employee	177,425	122,586	69
Shipments per Production Worker	257,966	137,483	53
Investment per Establishment	278,244	789,171	284
Investment per Employee	6,094	2,407	39
Investment per Production Worker	8,861	2,699	30

Sources: Same as General Statistics. The 'Average of All Manufacturing' column represents the average of all manufacturing industries reported for the most recent complete year available. The Index shows the relationship between the Average and the Analyzed Industry. For example, 100 means that they are equal; 500 that the Analyzed Industry is five times the average; 50 means that the Analyzed Industry is half the national average. The abbreviation 'na' is used to show that data are 'not available'.

LEADING COMPANIES

Number shown: 75 Total sales ($ mil): 21,857 Total employment (000): 215.0

Company Name	Address				CEO Name	Phone	Co. Type	Sales ($ mil)	Empl. (000)
Tyson Foods Inc	2210 W Oaklawn Dr	Springdale	AR	72764	Leland E Tollett	501-290-4000	P	5,110	55.8
Perdue Farms Inc	PO Box 1537	Salisbury	MD	21802	James A Perdue	410-543-3000	R	2,000	19.0
Gold Kist Inc	PO Box 2210	Atlanta	GA	30301	Harold O Chitwood	404-393-5000	R	1,561	14.0
Foster Poultry Farms Inc	PO Box 457	Livingston	CA	95334	Robert Fox	209-394-7901	R	1,160	7.0
Pilgrim's Pride Corp	PO Box 93	Pittsburg	TX	75686	Lonnie A Pilgrim	903-856-7901	P	993	7.2
ConAgra Poultry Co	PO Box 1997	El Dorado	AR	71731	George Haefner	501-863-1600	S	940*	10.5
Hudson Foods Inc	1225 Hudson Rd	Rogers	AR	72756	James T Hudson	501-636-1100	P	921	8.6
WLR Foods Inc	PO Box 7000	Broadway	VA	22815	James L Keeler	703-896-7001	P	727	8.8
Purdue Inc	PO Box 158	Showell	MD	21862	Frank Purdue	410-352-5411	R	530	3.2
Michael Foods Inc	5353 Wayzata Blv	Minneapolis	MN	55416	Gregg A Ostrander	612-546-1500	P	506	2.7
Golden Poultry Company Inc	PO Box 2210	Atlanta	GA	30301	K N Whitmire	404-393-5000	P	447	4.6
Bil Mar Foods	8300 96th Av	Zeeland	MI	49464	George Chivari	616-875-7711	S	410	2.5
Sanderson Farms Inc	PO Box 988	Laurel	MS	39441	Joe F Sanderson Jr	601-649-4030	P	372	3.8
Wampler-Longacre Chicken Inc	PO Box 275	Broadway	VA	22815	Gene Misner	703-896-7000	S	370*	4.0
Fieldale Farms Corp	PO Box 558	Baldwin	GA	30511	Joseph S Hatfield	706-778-5100	R	360	4.0
Cagle's Inc	2000 Hills Av NW	Atlanta	GA	30318	J Douglas Cagle	404-355-2820	P	350	4.0
OK Industries Inc	PO Box 1119	Fort Smith	AR	72902	Randall W Goins	501-783-4186	R	270*	3.0
Townsends Inc	PO Box 468	Millsboro	DE	19966	Coleman Townsend	302-934-3000	R	270*	3.0
Simmons Industries Inc	PO Box 430	Siloam Springs	AR	72761	Lynch Butler	501-524-8151	R	250*	3.0
Wampler-Longacre Inc	PO Box 7275	Broadway	VA	22815	James L Mason	703-867-4000	S	250*	2.8
Allen Family Foods Inc	126 N Shipley St	Seaford	DE	19973	CC Allen III	302-629-9136	R	225	2.0
BC Rogers Poultry Inc	PO Box A	Morton	MS	39117	John M Rogers	601-732-8911	R	220	3.8
Peterson Farms	PO Box 248	Decatur	AR	72722	Vic Evans	501-752-3211	R	185	2.0
Jerome Foods Inc	34 N 7th St	Barron	WI	54812	Jerry Jerome	715-537-3131	R	180	2.0
Tysons in Nashville	100 E Cassady St	Nashville	AR	71852	Paul Britt	501-845-1455	D	160*	1.7
George's Inc	PO Drawer G	Springdale	AR	72765	Gary George	501-751-4686	R	130*	1.5
Plantation Foods Inc	PO Box 20788	Waco	TX	76702	Roane Lacy Jr	817-799-6211	R	130	1.5
Gold'n Plump Poultry	PO Box 1106	St Cloud	MN	56302	Michael Helgeson	612-251-3570	R	120	1.5
Longmont Foods	PO Box 1479	Longmont	CO	80502	Michael Strear	303-776-6611	S	120	1.2
Butterball Turkey Co	411 N Main St	Carthage	MO	64836	T Howe	417-358-5914	S	100*	0.8
Case Farms Inc	PO Box 308	Morganton	NC	28655	Thomas Shelton	704-438-6900	R	100	0.5
House of Raeford Farms Inc	PO Box 100	Raeford	NC	28376	E Marvin Johnson	910-875-5161	S	100	1.1
Peco Foods Inc	3701 Kauloosa Av	Tuscaloosa	AL	35403	Denny Hickman	205-345-3955	R	100	1.4
Sanderson Farms Inc	PO Box 1329	Collins	MS	39428	Dan Nicovich	601-649-4030	D	100*	1.0
Jack Frost Inc	309 Lincoln SE	St Cloud	MN	56301	Chuck Kucharik	612-251-3570	S	96*	1.2
Rocco Turkeys Inc	PO Box 158	Dayton	VA	22821	Jim Darazsdi	703-879-2521	S	95	1.2
Brakebush Brothers Inc	Rte 2	Westfield	WI	53964	W C Brakebush	608-296-2121	R	83	0.5
Seaboard Farms of Chattanooga	PO Box 991	Chattanooga	TN	37401	Marvin Green	615-756-2471	S	82	0.7
Maple Leaf Farms Inc	PO Box 308	Milford	IN	46542	Terry Tucker	219-658-4121	R	80	1.0
West Central Turkeys Inc	PO Box T	Pelican Rapids	MN	56572	Rick Rogers	218-863-3131	R	76	0.8
George's Processing Inc	PO Drawer G	Springdale	AR	72765	Gary George	501-751-4686	S	74	0.5
Mott's of Mississippi	PO Box 708	Water Valley	MS	38965	Bobby Glaub	601-473-1771	D	74*	1.2
Tip Top Poultry Inc	PO Box 6338	Marietta	GA	30065	Robin Burruss	404-973-8070	R	72*	0.8
Cagle's Inc	PO Box 376	Collinsville	AL	35961	R Adrian	205-524-2147	D	70*	0.8
Tony Downs Foods Co	PO Box 28	St James	MN	56081	Richard A Down	507-375-3111	R	70	0.7
Choctaw Maid Farms Inc	PO Box 577	Carthage	MS	39051	Tami Etheridge	601-267-5601	R	63	1.5
Mar-Jac Processing Inc	PO Box 1017	Gainesville	GA	30503	Doug Carnes	404-536-0561	S	63*	0.7
Sylvest Farms Inc	PO Box 250050	Montgomery	AL	36125	Harold Sylvest	205-281-0400	R	62	0.8
Sonstegard Foods Inc	707 E 41st St	Sioux Falls	SD	57105	PO Sonstegard	605-338-4642	R	60	0.3
Southland Foods Inc	PO Drawer 1440	Enterprise	AL	36331	Thomas Smith	205-897-3435	S	60	0.9
Sunny Fresh Foods-Minnesota	206 W 4th St	Monticello	MN	55362	Jim Bassett	612-295-5666	D	60	0.3
Farmers Pride Inc	PO Box 39	Fredericksburg	PA	17026	Bruno Schmalhofer	717-865-6626	R	55	0.5
North Arkansas Poultry Co	PO Box 1510	Rogers	AR	72756	Rick Millsap	501-636-5152	S	54	0.6
Burnett Poultry Co	PO Box 606	Jamestown	TN	38556	James W Burnett	615-879-8146	R	49*	0.3
Dutch Quality House	PO Box 2397	Gainesville	GA	30503	Elton Maddix	404-534-2294	D	47	0.3
Piedmont Poultry Processing Inc	555 Grove St	Herndon	VA	22070	Jamal Barzinji	703-471-9494	S	47*	0.5
Fircrest Farms	PO Box 8	Creswell	OR	97426	Leo Ciccolo	503-895-2161	D	45	0.5
Mid-State Farms Inc	PO Box 524	Siler City	NC	27344	Ralph Seabreeze	919-742-4102	S	45*	0.5
Sanderson Farms Inc	PO Box 765	Hazlehurst	MS	39083	Marvin Hefner	601-894-3721	D	42*	0.6
Pennfield Farms	Rte 22	Fredericksburg	PA	17026	A D Chivinski	717-865-2153	D	40	0.4
Henningsen Foods Inc	2 Corporate Pk Dr	White Plains	NY	10604	Gilbert B Eckhoff	914-694-1000	S	37	0.3
Tyson's of Rogers	PO Box 2018	Rogers	AR	72757	Frank Richert	501-636-1620	D	37	0.3
National Foods Inc	600 Food Center Dr	Bronx	NY	10474	Harvey Potkin	718-842-5000	D	35	0.3
Estherville Foods Inc	PO Box 158	Estherville	IA	51334	Dennis L Tyrrell	712-362-3527	S	34*	0.2
Iowa Turkey Products Inc	PO Box 339	Postville	IA	52162	Thomas Dietrick	319-864-7676	R	31	0.4
Watson Quality Turkey Inc	PO Box 215	Blackwood	NJ	08012	Albert O Watson	609-227-0594	R	30	0.2
National Egg Products	351 Ronthor Rd	Social Circle	GA	30279	Johnny Jacobs	404-464-2652	D	28	0.1
Draper Valley Farms Inc	1000 Jason Ln	Mount Vernon	WA	98273	Jim Koplowitz	206-424-7947	R	27*	0.3
Georges Farms Inc	PO Box G	Springdale	AR	72765	Gary George	501-751-4686	S	27*	0.3
Hudson Foods Inc	PO Box 430	Corydon	IN	47112	Dave Hiner	812-738-3219	D	27*	0.4
Keystone Foods Corp	PO Box 1436	Reidsville	NC	27320	Pete McHugh	919-342-6601	D	27	0.3
Cutler Egg Products Inc	PO Box 489	Abbeville	AL	36310	CC Cutler	205-585-2268	R	25	0.2
Northern Pride Inc	PO Box 598	Thief River Fls	MN	56701	Russel Christianson	218-681-1201	R	23*	0.2
Echo Lake Farm Produce	PO Box 279	Burlington	WI	53105	Jerry Warntjes	414-763-9551	R	20	0.2
Gentrys Poultry Co	Rte 1	Ward	SC	29166	W M Gentry Jr	803-445-2161	R	19	0.2

Source: Ward's Business Directory of U.S. Private and Public Companies, Volumes 1 and 2, 1996. The company type code used is as follows: P - Public, R - Private, S - Subsidiary, D - Division, J - Joint Venture, A - Affiliate, G - Group. Sales are in millions of dollars, employees are in thousands. An asterisk (*) indicates an estimated sales volume. The symbol < stands for 'less than'. Company names and addresses are truncated, in some cases, to fit into the available space.

MATERIALS CONSUMED

Material		Quantity	Delivered Cost ($ million)
Materials, ingredients, containers, and supplies		(X)	16,174.6
Young chickens slaughtered (including commercial broilers)	mil lb	26,037.5	7,450.7
Hens (or fowl) and other chickens slaughtered	mil lb	903.9**	181.1
Turkeys slaughtered	mil lb	5,468.4	2,046.0
Other poultry and small game slaughtered (including ducks, geese, rabbits, etc.)		(X)	32.3
Dressed poultry purchased for processing (cooking, smoking, canning, etc.)	mil lb	4,515.4*	2,980.0
Shell eggs	1,000.cases (30 doz)	34,162.4	368.3
Paperboard containers, boxes, and corrugated paperboard		(X)	388.7
Packaging paper and plastics film, coated and laminated		(X)	185.3
Bags; plastics, foil, and coated paper		(X)	134.1
Metal cans, can lids and ends		(X)	9.5
All other materials and components, parts, containers, and supplies		(X)	1,206.3
Materials, ingredients, containers, and supplies, nsk		(X)	1,192.2

Source: 1992 *Economic Census*. Explanation of symbols used: (D): Withheld to avoid disclosure of competitive data; na: Not available; (S): Withheld because statistical norms were not met; (X): Not applicable; (Z): Less than half the unit shown; nec: Not elsewhere classified; nsk: Not specified by kind; - : zero; * : 10-19 percent estimated; ** : 20-29 percent estimated.

PRODUCT SHARE DETAILS

Product or Product Class	% Share
Poultry and egg processing	100.00
Young chickens (usually under 20 weeks of age), whole or parts	52.28
Wet ice pack broilers and fryers (usually under 20 weeks of age), bulk	41.76
Dry ice pack broilers and fryers (usually under 20 weeks of age), bulk	7.80
Tray pack (consumer packaged) broilers and fryers (usually under 20 weeks of age), chilled	24.78
Other broilers and fryers (usually under 20 weeks of age), including frozen	20.83
Roasters and capons (usually under 20 weeks of age), including frozen	1.65
Young chickens (usually under 20 weeks of age) whole or parts, nsk	3.17
Hens and/or fowl (including frozen), whole or parts	0.45
Egg producing hens and/or fowl (including frozen), whole or parts	60.51
Breeder hens and/or fowl (including frozen), whole or parts	39.21
Hens and/or fowl (including frozen whole or parts), nsk	0.38
Turkeys (including frozen), whole or parts	12.29
Fryer-roaster turkeys (usually under 16 weeks of age), whole, including frozen	6.28
Young turkeys (mature) (usually 4 to 7 months of age), whole, including frozen	38.84
Old turkeys (breeders) (usually over 12 months of age), whole, including frozen	1.18
Turkey parts, including ground turkey, turkey cutlets, etc. (including frozen)	47.02
Turkeys (including frozen, whole or parts), nsk	6.67
Other poultry and small game (including frozen), whole or parts	0.32
Processed poultry and small game (except soups) containing 20 percent or more poultry or meat	27.21
Canned poultry, 10 oz or less (except soups), containing 20 percent or more poultry	(D)
Canned poultry, 40.1 oz to 60 oz sizes (except soups), containing 20 percent or more poultry	(D)
Canned poultry, greater than 60 oz sizes (except soups), containing 20 percent or more poultry	0.38
Cooked or smoked turkey, including frozen (except frankfurters, hams, and luncheon meats), containing 20 percent or more poultry	21.36
Cooked or smoked chicken, including frozen (except frankfurters, hams, and luncheon meats), containing 20 percent or more poultry	43.68
Cooked or smoked poultry frankfurters (including wieners), including frozen, containing 20 percent or more poultry	3.14
Cooked or smoked poultry hams and luncheon meats, including frozen, containing 20 percent or more poultry	14.44
Other cooked or smoked poultry, including frozen, containing 20 percent or more poultry	1.75
Other processed poultry and small game (dehydrated, raw-boned, etc.), including frozen, containing 20 percent or more poultry	12.16
Processed poultry and small game (except soups) containing 20 percent or more poultry or meat, nsk	1.72
Liquid, dried, and frozen eggs	3.18
Dried egg whites	10.85
Dried egg yolks	5.21
Dried eggs, whole	8.52
Dried eggs, mixed	4.69
Frozen or liquid egg whites	35.30
Frozen or liquid egg yolks	4.97
Frozen or liquid eggs, whole	14.51
Frozen or liquid eggs, mixed	9.22
Liquid, dried, and frozen eggs, nsk	6.71
Poultry and egg processing, nsk	4.27

Source: 1992 *Economic Census*. The values shown are percent of total shipments in an industry. Values of indented subcategories are summed in the main heading. The symbol (D) appears when data are withheld to prevent disclosure of competitive information. The abbreviation nsk stands for 'not specified by kind' and nec for 'not elsewhere classified'.

INPUTS AND OUTPUTS FOR POULTRY DRESSING PLANTS

Economic Sector or Industry Providing Inputs	%	Sector	Economic Sector or Industry Buying Outputs	%	Sector
Poultry & eggs	79.2	Agric.	Personal consumption expenditures	62.5	
Poultry dressing plants	4.8	Manufg.	Eating & drinking places	13.0	Trade
Paperboard containers & boxes	2.5	Manufg.	Poultry & egg processing	5.3	Manufg.
Electric services (utilities)	1.9	Util.	Exports	4.7	Foreign
Wholesale trade	1.8	Trade	Poultry dressing plants	4.3	Manufg.
Advertising	1.2	Services	Frozen specialties	2.5	Manufg.
Imports	0.9	Foreign	Sausages & other prepared meats	1.3	Manufg.
Gas production & distribution (utilities)	0.7	Util.	Prepared feeds, nec	1.0	Manufg.
Commercial printing	0.6	Manufg.	Hospitals	0.8	Services
Cyclic crudes and organics	0.6	Manufg.	Artificial trees & flowers	0.5	Manufg.
Petroleum refining	0.6	Manufg.	Canned specialties	0.5	Manufg.

Continued on next page.

INPUTS AND OUTPUTS FOR POULTRY DRESSING PLANTS - Continued

Economic Sector or Industry Providing Inputs	%	Sector	Economic Sector or Industry Buying Outputs	%	Sector
Motor freight transportation & warehousing	0.6	Util.	Dog, cat, & other pet food	0.4	Manufg.
Communications, except radio & TV	0.4	Util.	S/L Govt. purch., health & hospitals	0.4	S/L Govt
Maintenance of nonfarm buildings nec	0.3	Constr.	Forestry products	0.3	Agric.
Eating & drinking places	0.3	Trade	Residential care	0.3	Services
Banking	0.3	Fin/R.E.	S/L Govt. purch., elem. & secondary education	0.3	S/L Govt
Paper coating & glazing	0.2	Manufg.	S/L Govt. purch., higher education	0.3	S/L Govt
Soap & other detergents	0.2	Manufg.	Meat packing plants	0.2	Manufg.
Air transportation	0.2	Util.	Nursing & personal care facilities	0.2	Services
Equipment rental & leasing services	0.2	Services	Social services, nec	0.2	Services
Miscellaneous livestock	0.1	Agric.	Federal Government enterprises nec	0.2	Gov't
Accounting, auditing & bookkeeping	0.1	Services	Change in business inventories	0.2	In House
Legal services	0.1	Services	S/L Govt. purch., correction	0.2	S/L Govt
Management & consulting services & labs	0.1	Services			
State & local government enterprises, nec	0.1	Gov't			

Source: Benchmark Input-Output Accounts for the U.S. Economy, 1982, U.S. Department of Commerce, Washington, D.C., July 1991. Data, as reported in the source, are organized by the 1977 SIC structure in use in 1982 but have been matched, as closely as is possible, to the 1987 SIC structure used in this book.

OCCUPATIONS EMPLOYED BY SIC 201 - MEAT PRODUCTS

Occupation	% of Total 1994	Change to 2005	Occupation	% of Total 1994	Change to 2005
Meat, poultry, & fish cutters & trimmers, hand	26.4	29.2	Industrial machinery mechanics	1.8	27.8
Butchers & meatcutters	13.8	-2.2	Inspectors, testers, & graders, precision	1.7	16.2
Assemblers, fabricators, & hand workers nec	4.9	16.2	Cutting & slicing machine setters, operators	1.7	56.9
Hand packers & packagers	4.7	-0.4	Machine operators nec	1.6	2.5
Packaging & filling machine operators	4.4	-7.0	Freight, stock, & material movers, hand	1.6	-7.0
Helpers, laborers, & material movers nec	3.9	16.2	Maintenance repairers, general utility	1.6	4.6
Blue collar worker supervisors	3.5	15.6	Industrial truck & tractor operators	1.3	16.2
Machine feeders & offbearers	3.0	27.9	Crushing & mixing machine operators	1.3	4.6
Truck drivers light & heavy	2.1	19.8	General managers & top executives	1.1	10.3
Janitors & cleaners, incl maids	1.9	-7.0			

Source: Industry-Occupation Matrix, Bureau of Labor Statistics. These data relate to one or more 3-digit SIC industry groups rather than to a single 4-digit SIC. The change reported for each occupation to the year 2005 is a percent of growth or decline as estimated by the Bureau of Labor Statistics. The abbreviation nec stands for 'not elsewhere classified'.

LOCATION BY STATE AND REGIONAL CONCENTRATION

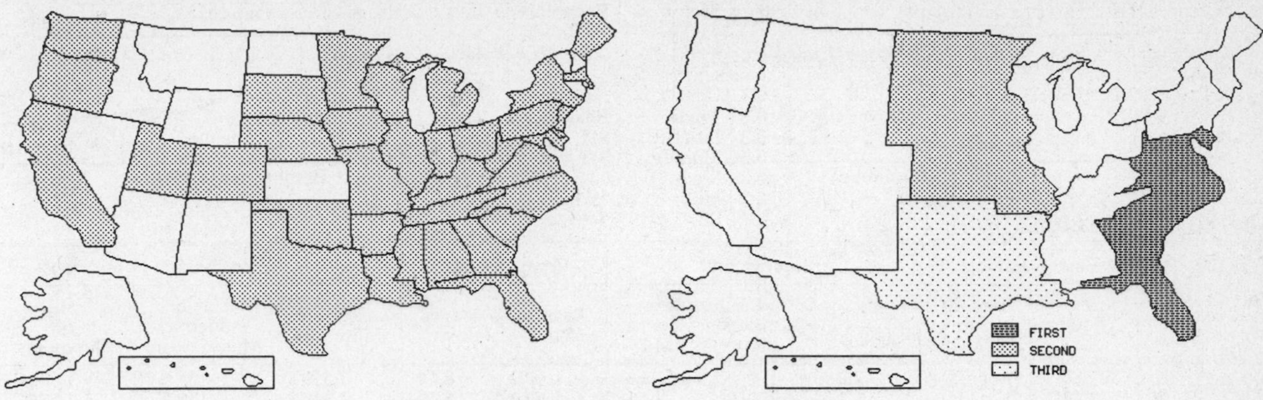

INDUSTRY DATA BY STATE

State	Establish-ments	Shipments			Employment				Cost as % of Shipments	Investment per Employee ($)
		Total ($ mil)	% of U.S.	Per Establ.	Total Number	% of U.S.	Per Establ.	Wages ($/hour)		
Arkansas	47	3,655.4	15.4	77.8	29,100	15.0	619	7.05	75.0	2,770
Georgia	49	2,298.0	9.7	46.9	21,200	10.9	433	7.46	70.3	2,377
North Carolina	29	2,206.5	9.3	76.1	18,200	9.4	628	6.81	70.1	1,956
Alabama	37	2,001.8	8.4	54.1	20,100	10.4	543	6.91	73.5	1,771
Virginia	17	1,315.9	5.5	77.4	9,200	4.7	541	7.31	71.0	1,652
Mississippi	26	1,152.6	4.9	44.3	11,100	5.7	427	6.21	73.2	2,027
Missouri	29	1,149.1	4.8	39.6	8,500	4.4	293	7.46	68.9	3,024
Texas	20	1,146.3	4.8	57.3	9,300	4.8	465	7.34	78.4	2,172
California	41	1,129.8	4.8	27.6	8,900	4.6	217	8.98	74.8	1,056
Minnesota	27	811.6	3.4	30.1	6,500	3.4	241	7.77	69.0	1,785
Pennsylvania	28	719.2	3.0	25.7	5,400	2.8	193	8.71	76.4	1,556
Tennessee	11	621.5	2.6	56.5	4,100	2.1	373	7.38	73.5	1,439
Delaware	8	593.4	2.5	74.2	5,100	2.6	638	7.30	74.9	3,176
Iowa	19	542.6	2.3	28.6	3,100	1.6	163	8.43	71.5	1,645
Maryland	10	404.0	1.7	40.4	3,300	1.7	330	6.37	74.4	2,424
New Jersey	16	351.5	1.5	22.0	2,200	1.1	138	7.26	76.0	3,091
Indiana	11	323.9	1.4	29.4	2,700	1.4	245	6.95	62.7	2,333
Wisconsin	9	319.1	1.3	35.5	2,600	1.3	289	8.27	69.8	6,115
Florida	16	275.0	1.2	17.2	2,900	1.5	181	7.73	89.3	6,310
South Carolina	12	274.0	1.2	22.8	1,800	0.9	150	7.47	56.0	2,444
Illinois	11	201.9	0.8	18.4	1,300	0.7	118	9.89	56.8	2,154
Ohio	19	200.1	0.8	10.5	1,400	0.7	74	6.85	73.1	1,714
Nebraska	7	179.5	0.8	25.6	1,800	0.9	257	9.90	78.8	4,778
Washington	8	139.7	0.6	17.5	900	0.5	113	8.94	79.7	-
Oregon	6	97.7	0.4	16.3	1,000	0.5	167	9.00	74.0	-
New York	21	61.0	0.3	2.9	600	0.3	29	9.40	63.0	1,333
Massachusetts	4	45.6	0.2	11.4	400	0.2	100	7.29	74.8	2,000
Michigan	10	(D)	-	-	1,750 *	0.9	175	-	-	-
Oklahoma	6	(D)	-	-	1,750 *	0.9	292	-	-	-
Colorado	5	(D)	-	-	1,750 *	0.9	350	-	-	-
Louisiana	5	(D)	-	-	1,750 *	0.9	350	-	-	-
Kentucky	4	(D)	-	-	750 *	0.4	188	-	-	-
South Dakota	3	(D)	-	-	375 *	0.2	125	-	-	-
West Virginia	3	(D)	-	-	1,750 *	0.9	583	-	-	-
Maine	2	(D)	-	-	375 *	0.2	188	-	-	-
Utah	2	(D)	-	-	750 *	0.4	375	-	-	-

Source: 1992 *Economic Census*. The states are in descending order of shipments or establishments (if shipment data are missing for the majority). The symbol (D) appears when data are withheld to prevent disclosure of competitive information. States marked with (D) are sorted by number of establishments. A dash (-) indicates that the data element cannot be calculated; * indicates the midpoint of a range.

2021 - CREAMERY BUTTER

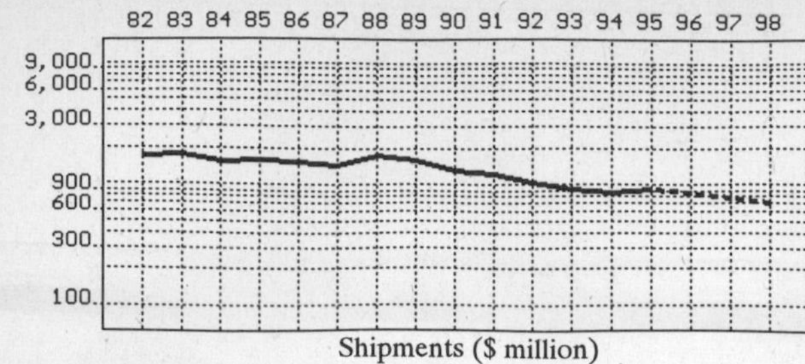

Shipments ($ million)

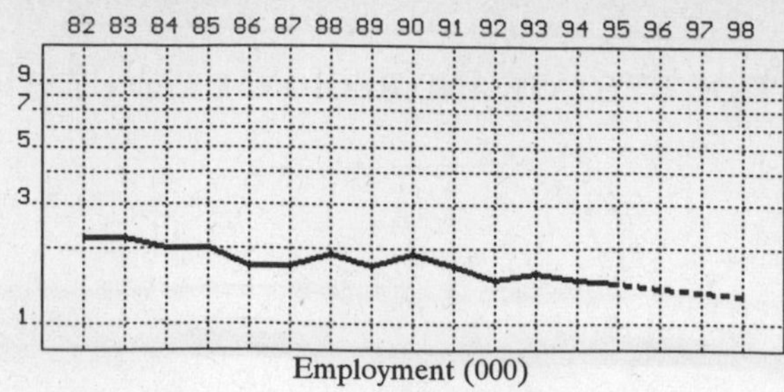

Employment (000)

GENERAL STATISTICS

Year	Com- panies	Establishments: Total	Establishments: with 20 or more employees	Employment: Total (000)	Production Workers (000)	Production Hours (Mil)	Compensation: Payroll ($ mil)	Compensation: Wages ($/hr)	Production ($ million): Cost of Materials	Value Added by Manufacture	Value of Shipments	Capital Invest.
1982	61	74	35	2.2	1.7	3.5	40.2	8.14	1,556.1	135.6	1,686.8	8.4
1983		70	34	2.2	1.7	3.5	43.2	8.49	1,610.8	131.2	1,736.7	4.0
1984		66	33	2.0	1.6	3.4	41.5	8.85	1,478.7	83.3	1,563.8	7.9
1985		62	32	2.0	1.7	3.3	40.9	9.42	1,478.0	97.6	1,571.0	10.5
1986		59	30	1.7	1.4	2.9	40.1	9.86	1,430.1	89.4	1,531.2	8.0
1987	44	49	26	1.7	1.3	2.8	38.9	9.79	1,291.3	133.6	1,420.4	9.7
1988		47	26	1.9	1.5	2.9	43.5	10.66	1,487.6	280.7	1,764.7	9.7
1989		47	24	1.7	1.3	2.8	42.4	10.57	1,331.5	239.7	1,570.4	13.6
1990		46	24	1.9	1.2	2.6	41.5	10.65	1,105.4	207.5	1,307.5	16.5
1991		48	26	1.7	1.2	2.6	44.9	11.62	1,095.8	135.4	1,231.1	17.4
1992	31	32	17	1.5	1.1	2.4	42.4	12.04	883.7	148.4	1,034.0	9.1
1993		36	17	1.6	1.1	2.4	45.0	12.58	736.3	184.3	921.4	12.4
1994		30P	17P	1.5	1.0	2.1	43.0	12.62	710.3	158.4	871.8	7.3
1995		27P	15P	1.4P	0.9P	2.1P	43.9P	13.06P	752.7P	167.8P	923.8P	13.5P
1996		23P	13P	1.4P	0.9P	2.0P	44.2P	13.44P	697.1P	155.5P	855.7P	13.9P
1997		20P	12P	1.3P	0.8P	1.8P	44.5P	13.82P	641.6P	143.1P	787.5P	14.4P
1998		16P	10P	1.3P	0.8P	1.7P	44.7P	14.20P	586.1P	130.7P	719.4P	14.8P

Sources: 1982, 1987, 1992 *Economic Census*; *Annual Survey of Manufactures*, 83-86, 88-91, 93-94. Establishment counts for non-Census years are from *County Business Patterns*; establishment values for 83-84 are extrapolations. 'P's show projections by the editors. Industries reclassified in 87 will not have data for prior years.

INDICES OF CHANGE

Year	Com- panies	Establishments: Total	Establishments: with 20 or more employees	Employment: Total (000)	Production Workers (000)	Production Hours (Mil)	Compensation: Payroll ($ mil)	Compensation: Wages ($/hr)	Production ($ million): Cost of Materials	Value Added by Manufacture	Value of Shipments	Capital Invest.
1982	197	231	206	147	155	146	95	68	176	91	163	92
1983		219	200	147	155	146	102	71	182	88	168	44
1984		206	194	133	145	142	98	74	167	56	151	87
1985		194	188	133	155	137	96	78	167	66	152	115
1986		184	176	113	127	121	95	82	162	60	148	88
1987	142	153	153	113	118	117	92	81	146	90	137	107
1988		147	153	127	136	121	103	89	168	189	171	107
1989		147	141	113	118	117	100	88	151	162	152	149
1990		144	141	127	109	108	98	88	125	140	126	181
1991		150	153	113	109	108	106	97	124	91	119	191
1992	100	100	100	100	100	100	100	100	100	100	100	100
1993		113	100	107	100	100	106	104	83	124	89	136
1994		94P	98P	100	91	87	101	105	80	107	84	80
1995		83P	88P	96P	86P	86P	104P	108P	85P	113P	89P	148P
1996		72P	79P	93P	80P	82P	104P	112P	79P	105P	83P	153P
1997		61P	69P	89P	75P	77P	105P	115P	73P	96P	76P	158P
1998		50P	60P	85P	69P	72P	106P	118P	66P	88P	70P	163P

Sources: Same as General Statistics. Values reflect change from the base year, 1992. Values above 100 mean greater than 92, values below 100 mean less than 92, and a value of 100 in the 82-91 or 93-98 period means same as 92. 'P's mark projections by the editors.

SELECTED RATIOS

For 1994	Avg. of All Manufact.	Analyzed Industry	Index	For 1994	Avg. of All Manufact.	Analyzed Industry	Index
Employees per Establishment	49	50	101	Value Added per Production Worker	134,084	158,400	118
Payroll per Establishment	1,500,273	1,424,699	95	Cost per Establishment	5,045,178	23,534,036	466
Payroll per Employee	30,620	28,667	94	Cost per Employee	102,970	473,533	460
Production Workers per Establishment	34	33	97	Cost per Production Worker	146,988	710,300	483
Wages per Establishment	853,319	878,078	103	Shipments per Establishment	9,576,895	28,884,940	302
Wages per Production Worker	24,861	26,502	107	Shipments per Employee	195,460	581,200	297
Hours per Production Worker	2,056	2,100	102	Shipments per Production Worker	279,017	871,800	312
Wages per Hour	12.09	12.62	104	Investment per Establishment	321,011	241,867	75
Value Added per Establishment	4,602,255	5,248,193	114	Investment per Employee	6,552	4,867	74
Value Added per Employee	93,930	105,600	112	Investment per Production Worker	9,352	7,300	78

Sources: Same as General Statistics. The 'Average of All Manufacturing' column represents the average of all manufacturing industries reported for the most recent complete year available. The Index shows the relationship between the Average and the Analyzed Industry. For example, 100 means that they are equal; 500 that the Analyzed Industry is five times the average; 50 means that the Analyzed Industry is half the national average. The abbreviation 'na' is used to show that data are 'not available'.

LEADING COMPANIES

Number shown: **9** Total sales ($ mil): **5,524** Total employment (000): **10.4**

Company Name	Address				CEO Name	Phone	Co. Type	Sales ($ mil)	Empl. (000)
Land O'Lakes Inc	PO Box 116	Minneapolis	MN	55440	Jack Gherty	612-481-2222	R	2,733	5.0
Mid-America Dairymen Inc	3253 E Chestnut	Springfield	MO	65802	Gary Hanman	417-865-7100	R	2,500	5.0
Grassland Dairy Products Inc	PO Box 160	Greenwood	WI	54437	Dallas L Wuethrich	715-267-6182	R	120	0.1
Berkshire Foods Inc	4600 S Packers Av	Chicago	IL	60609	T Grzywacz	312-254-2424	R	53*	0.1
Plainview Milk Product Coop	130 2nd St SW	Plainview	MN	55964	Dennis Breuer	507-534-3872	R	50	<0.1
Mid-America Dairymen Inc	PO Box 868	Willows	CA	95988	Ivan Strickler	916-934-4671	D	24	<0.1
Ramey Farms Coop Creamery	Rte 3	Foley	MN	56329	Norman Zabloski	612-355-2313	R	19	<0.1
Madison Dairy Produce	PO Box 389	Madison	WI	53701	F C Steinhauer	608-256-5561	R	13	<0.1
St Albans Cooperative Creamery	140 Federal St	St Albans	VT	05478	Leon Berthiaume	802-524-6581	R	11*	<0.1

Source: *Ward's Business Directory of U.S. Private and Public Companies*, Volumes 1 and 2, 1996. The company type code used is as follows: P - Public, R - Private, S - Subsidiary, D - Division, J - Joint Venture, A - Affiliate, G - Group. Sales are in millions of dollars, employees are in thousands. An asterisk (*) indicates an estimated sales volume. The symbol < stands for 'less than'. Company names and addresses are truncated, in some cases, to fit into the available space.

MATERIALS CONSUMED

Material		Quantity	Delivered Cost ($ million)
Materials, ingredients, containers, and supplies		(X)	846.9
Whole milk	mil cwt	7.3	87.9
Cream	mil cwt	(S)	571.8
Butter	mil lb	56.9	45.1
Condensed and evaporated milk	mil lb	(S)	1.4
Packaging paper and plastics film, coated and laminated		(X)	6.2
Plastics containers		(X)	5.0
Paperboard containers, boxes, and corrugated paperboard		(X)	13.0
All other materials and components, parts, containers, and supplies		(X)	107.5
Materials, ingredients, containers, and supplies, nsk		(X)	8.9

Source: 1992 *Economic Census*. Explanation of symbols used: (D): Withheld to avoid disclosure of competitive data; na: Not available; (S): Withheld because statistical norms were not met; (X): Not applicable; (Z): Less than half the unit shown; nec: Not elsewhere classified; nsk: Not specified by kind; - : zero; * : 10-19 percent estimated; ** : 20-29 percent estimated.

PRODUCT SHARE DETAILS

Product or Product Class	% Share	Product or Product Class	% Share
Creamery butter	100.00	3 lb or less)	41.41
Creamery butter, shipped in bulk (containers more than 3 lb)	54.93	Creamery butter, anhydrous butterfat	(D)
Creamery butter, shipped in consumer packages (containers		Creamery butter, nsk, for non-administrative record establishments	(D)

Source: 1992 *Economic Census*. The values shown are percent of total shipments in an industry. Values of indented subcategories are summed in the main heading. The symbol (D) appears when data are withheld to prevent disclosure of competitive information. The abbreviation nsk stands for 'not specified by kind' and nec for 'not elsewhere classified'.

INPUTS AND OUTPUTS FOR CREAMERY BUTTER

Economic Sector or Industry Providing Inputs	%	Sector	Economic Sector or Industry Buying Outputs	%	Sector
Fluid milk	63.1	Manufg.	Personal consumption expenditures	36.9	
Dairy farm products	22.7	Agric.	Eating & drinking places	23.3	Trade
Wholesale trade	6.2	Trade	Federal Government purchases, nondefense	13.1	Fed Govt
Commercial printing	0.8	Manufg.	Commodity Credit Corporation	11.6	Gov't
Paperboard containers & boxes	0.8	Manufg.	Exports	5.3	Foreign
Motor freight transportation & warehousing	0.8	Util.	Hospitals	1.6	Services
Gas production & distribution (utilities)	0.7	Util.	Child day care services	1.0	Services
Miscellaneous plastics products	0.6	Manufg.	S/L Govt. purch., health & hospitals	0.8	S/L Govt
Paper coating & glazing	0.6	Manufg.	Food preparations, nec	0.7	Manufg.
Petroleum refining	0.5	Manufg.	Fluid milk	0.5	Manufg.
Advertising	0.4	Services	Federal Government enterprises nec	0.5	Gov't
Creamery butter	0.3	Manufg.	Change in business inventories	0.5	In House
Air transportation	0.3	Util.	Canned specialties	0.4	Manufg.
Electric services (utilities)	0.3	Util.	Cookies & crackers	0.4	Manufg.
Banking	0.2	Fin/R.E.	Frozen specialties	0.4	Manufg.
Noncomparable imports	0.2	Foreign	Residential care	0.4	Services
Soap & other detergents	0.1	Manufg.	S/L Govt. purch., higher education	0.4	S/L Govt
U.S. Postal Service	0.1	Gov't	Creamery butter	0.3	Manufg.
Imports	0.1	Foreign	Nursing & personal care facilities	0.3	Services
			S/L Govt. purch., correction	0.3	S/L Govt
			Bread, cake, & related products	0.2	Manufg.
			Ice cream & frozen desserts	0.2	Manufg.
			Social services, nec	0.2	Services
			S/L Govt. purch., other education & libraries	0.2	S/L Govt
			Cheese, natural & processed	0.1	Manufg.
			Amusement & recreation services nec	0.1	Services

Source: Benchmark Input-Output Accounts for the U.S. Economy, 1982, U.S. Department of Commerce, Washington, D.C., July 1991. Data, as reported in the source, are organized by the 1977 SIC structure in use in 1982 but have been matched, as closely as is possible, to the 1987 SIC structure used in this book.

OCCUPATIONS EMPLOYED BY SIC 202 - DAIRY PRODUCTS

Occupation	% of Total 1994	Change to 2005	Occupation	% of Total 1994	Change to 2005
Dairy processing equipment workers	9.1	-1.7	Industrial truck & tractor operators	2.2	-11.3
Packaging & filling machine operators	8.1	33.1	Traffic, shipping, & receiving clerks	2.1	-14.6
Truck drivers light & heavy	7.5	-8.5	Maintenance repairers, general utility	2.0	-20.1
Driver/sales workers	5.8	-42.3	General managers & top executives	1.7	-15.8
Helpers, laborers, & material movers nec	4.3	-11.3	Bookkeeping, accounting, & auditing clerks	1.7	-33.4
Blue collar worker supervisors	4.1	-15.0	Machine feeders & offbearers	1.6	-20.1
Precision food & tobacco workers nec	4.0	6.5	Science & mathematics technicians	1.5	-11.3
Machine operators nec	3.7	-21.8	General office clerks	1.4	-24.3
Hand packers & packagers	3.5	-23.9	Inspectors, testers, & graders, precision	1.2	-11.2
Freight, stock, & material movers, hand	3.4	-29.0	Industrial production managers	1.2	-11.2
Industrial machinery mechanics	2.6	-2.4	Secretaries, ex legal & medical	1.1	-19.2
Sales & related workers nec	2.2	-11.3			

Source: Industry-Occupation Matrix, Bureau of Labor Statistics. These data relate to one or more 3-digit SIC industry groups rather than to a single 4-digit SIC. The change reported for each occupation to the year 2005 is a percent of growth or decline as estimated by the Bureau of Labor Statistics. The abbreviation nec stands for 'not elsewhere classified'.

LOCATION BY STATE AND REGIONAL CONCENTRATION

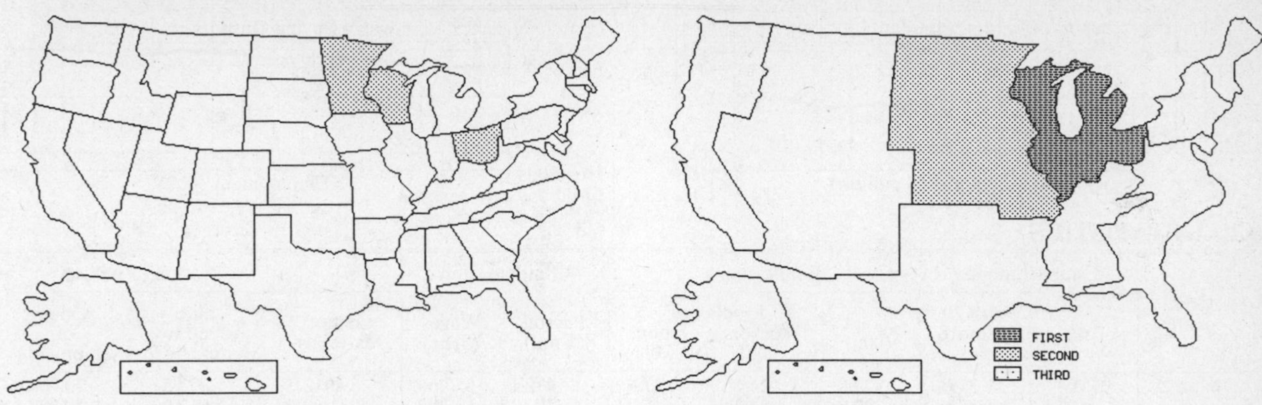

INDUSTRY DATA BY STATE

State	Establish-ments	Shipments			Employment				Cost as % of Shipments	Investment per Employee ($)
		Total ($ mil)	% of U.S.	Per Establ.	Total Number	% of U.S.	Per Establ.	Wages ($/hour)		
Wisconsin	10	491.9	47.6	49.2	700	46.7	70	12.70	86.5	4,143
Minnesota	4	(D)	-	-	175 *	11.7	44	-	-	-
Ohio	2	(D)	-	-	175 *	11.7	88	-	-	-

Source: 1992 *Economic Census*. The states are in descending order of shipments or establishments (if shipment data are missing for the majority). The symbol (D) appears when data are withheld to prevent disclosure of competitive information. States marked with (D) are sorted by number of establishments. A dash (-) indicates that the data element cannot be calculated; * indicates the midpoint of a range.

2022 - CHEESE, NATURAL & PROCESSED

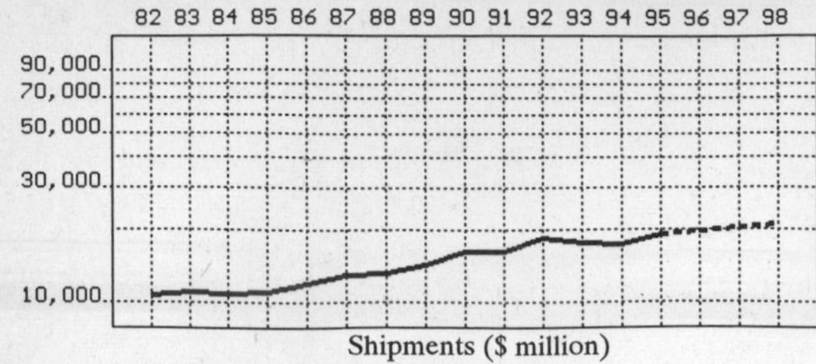

Shipments ($ million)

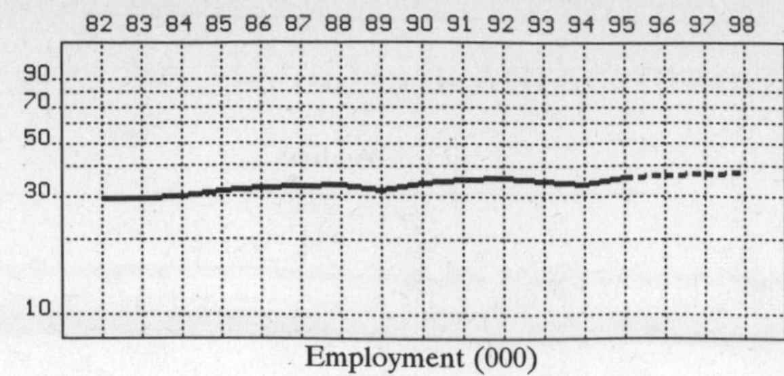

Employment (000)

GENERAL STATISTICS

Year	Companies	Establishments		Employment			Compensation		Production ($ million)			
		Total	with 20 or more employees	Total (000)	Production Workers (000)	Production Hours (Mil)	Payroll ($ mil)	Wages ($/hr)	Cost of Materials	Value Added by Manufacture	Value of Shipments	Capital Invest.
1982	575	704	319	29.6	24.1	47.4	472.1	7.66	9,012.7	1,777.3	10,762.8	161.2
1983		694	322	29.8	24.2	47.0	491.1	7.97	8,930.7	1,957.3	10,907.4	147.4
1984		684	325	30.0	24.4	47.8	519.5	8.32	8,879.3	1,947.9	10,837.0	121.8
1985		674	329	31.5	25.7	49.8	562.2	8.54	9,144.3	1,910.3	11,060.2	133.3
1986		648	323	32.3	25.9	51.8	603.0	8.81	9,537.2	2,306.6	11,892.1	140.1
1987	507	643	310	33.0	27.0	52.6	657.4	9.70	10,315.1	2,622.9	12,947.5	146.1
1988		600	307	33.8	28.1	56.0	689.1	9.70	10,555.6	2,575.7	13,134.7	135.0
1989		593	306	32.0	26.7	53.9	692.8	9.91	11,630.0	2,761.8	14,317.4	169.1
1990		570	301	34.6	28.2	57.8	766.5	10.14	13,369.3	2,850.6	16,155.8	272.1
1991		572	314	35.0	27.9	56.8	788.8	10.41	12,758.7	3,612.6	16,379.7	187.6
1992	418	576	314	36.3	29.2	61.4	883.2	10.71	13,880.9	4,472.4	18,351.7	261.8
1993		572	310	34.7	28.1	59.2	861.2	11.01	13,656.8	3,863.3	17,519.9	262.3
1994		536P	305P	33.6	27.0	56.2	860.4	11.38	13,841.8	3,528.4	17,401.8	279.5
1995		522P	303P	36.2P	29.2P	61.5P	937.4P	11.70P	15,056.4P	3,838.0P	18,928.7P	274.2P
1996		508P	302P	36.6P	29.6P	62.6P	974.1P	12.00P	15,619.3P	3,981.5P	19,636.5P	286.8P
1997		494P	300P	37.1P	30.0P	63.7P	1,010.8P	12.31P	16,182.3P	4,125.0P	20,344.2P	299.4P
1998		480P	299P	37.6P	30.3P	64.8P	1,047.4P	12.61P	16,745.3P	4,268.5P	21,052.0P	312.0P

Sources: 1982, 1987, 1992 *Economic Census*; *Annual Survey of Manufactures*, 83-86, 88-91, 93-94. Establishment counts for non-Census years are from *County Business Patterns*; establishment values for 83-84 are extrapolations. 'P's show projections by the editors. Industries reclassified in 87 will not have data for prior years.

INDICES OF CHANGE

Year	Companies	Establishments		Employment			Compensation		Production ($ million)			
		Total	with 20 or more employees	Total (000)	Production Workers (000)	Production Hours (Mil)	Payroll ($ mil)	Wages ($/hr)	Cost of Materials	Value Added by Manufacture	Value of Shipments	Capital Invest.
1982	138	122	102	82	83	77	53	72	65	40	59	62
1983		120	103	82	83	77	56	74	64	44	59	56
1984		119	104	83	84	78	59	78	64	44	59	47
1985		117	105	87	88	81	64	80	66	43	60	51
1986		113	103	89	89	84	68	82	69	52	65	54
1987	121	112	99	91	92	86	74	91	74	59	71	56
1988		104	98	93	96	91	78	91	76	58	72	52
1989		103	97	88	91	88	78	93	84	62	78	65
1990		99	96	95	97	94	87	95	96	64	88	104
1991		99	100	96	96	93	89	97	92	81	89	72
1992	100	100	100	100	100	100	100	100	100	100	100	100
1993		99	99	96	96	96	98	103	98	86	95	100
1994		93P	97P	93	92	92	97	106	100	79	95	107
1995		91P	97P	100P	100P	100P	106P	109P	108P	86P	103P	105P
1996		88P	96P	101P	101P	102P	110P	112P	113P	89P	107P	110P
1997		86P	96P	102P	103P	104P	114P	115P	117P	92P	111P	114P
1998		83P	95P	104P	104P	106P	119P	118P	121P	95P	115P	119P

Sources: Same as General Statistics. Values reflect change from the base year, 1992. Values above 100 mean greater than 92, values below 100 mean less than 92, and a value of 100 in the 82-91 or 93-98 period means same as 92. 'P's mark projections by the editors.

SELECTED RATIOS

For 1994	Avg. of All Manufact.	Analyzed Industry	Index	For 1994	Avg. of All Manufact.	Analyzed Industry	Index
Employees per Establishment	49	63	128	Value Added per Production Worker	134,084	130,681	97
Payroll per Establishment	1,500,273	1,605,224	107	Cost per Establishment	5,045,178	25,824,254	512
Payroll per Employee	30,620	25,607	84	Cost per Employee	102,970	411,958	400
Production Workers per Establishment	34	50	147	Cost per Production Worker	146,988	512,659	349
Wages per Establishment	853,319	1,193,201	140	Shipments per Establishment	9,576,895	32,466,045	339
Wages per Production Worker	24,861	23,687	95	Shipments per Employee	195,460	517,911	265
Hours per Production Worker	2,056	2,081	101	Shipments per Production Worker	279,017	644,511	231
Wages per Hour	12.09	11.38	94	Investment per Establishment	321,011	521,455	162
Value Added per Establishment	4,602,255	6,582,836	143	Investment per Employee	6,552	8,318	127
Value Added per Employee	93,930	105,012	112	Investment per Production Worker	9,352	10,352	111

Sources: Same as General Statistics. The 'Average of All Manufacturing' column represents the average of all manufacturing industries reported for the most recent complete year available. The Index shows the relationship between the Average and the Analyzed Industry. For example, 100 means that they are equal; 500 that the Analyzed Industry is five times the average; 50 means that the Analyzed Industry is half the national average. The abbreviation 'na' is used to show that data are 'not available'.

LEADING COMPANIES

Number shown: **68** Total sales ($ mil): **4,597** Total employment (000): **15.6**

Company Name	Address				CEO Name	Phone	Co. Type	Sales ($ mil)	Empl. (000)
Leprino Foods Co	PO Box 173400	Denver	CO	80217	James Leprino	303-480-2600	R	590*	2.5
Beatrice Cheese Inc	770 N Springdale	Waukesha	WI	53186	Robert H Burns	414-782-2750	S	560*	2.4
Sorrento Cheese Company Inc	2375 S Park Av	Buffalo	NY	14220	Paul Bensabat	716-823-6262	S	400	1.1
Western Dairymen Cooperative	1140 S 3200 W	Salt Lake City	UT	84104	Lee Mortensen	801-977-3000	R	390*	0.8
Stella Foods Inc	PO Box 19024	Green Bay	WI	54307	Dean Metropolis	414-494-2228	R	230*	1.0
Masters Gallery Foods Inc	PO Box 170	Plymouth	WI	53073	Bernard V Golbach	414-893-8431	R	200	0.1
First District Association	PO Box 842	Litchfield	MN	55355	David Peterson	612-693-3236	R	180	0.2
Pace Dairy Foods Co	2700 Val High Dr	Rochester	MN	55901	Jim Lehman	507-288-6315	S	160	0.4
Zausner Foods Corp	400 S Custer St	New Holland	PA	17557	Jim Williams	717-354-4411	S	130*	0.4
Alto Dairy Cooperative	N 3545 County EE	Waupun	WI	53963	Larry Lemmenes	414-346-2215	R	100	0.5
Dorman Roth Foods Inc	14 Empire Blv	Moonachie	NJ	07074	Richard Dietterich	201-462-0100	S	100*	0.5
Simplot Dairy Products	PO Box 37	Arpin	WI	54410	Marco Meyer	715-652-2177	R	100	0.3
Golden Cheese of California	1138 W Rincon St	Corona	CA	91720	Donald Bradford	909-737-9260	R	91	0.2
Brewster Dairy Inc	PO Box 98	Brewster	OH	44613	F Leeman	216-767-3492	R	90	0.2
Fromageries Bel Inc	2050 Center Av	Fort Lee	NJ	07024	Patrick Robbe	201-592-6601	S	81	0.4
Cabot Creamery Cooperative Inc	PO Box 128	Cabot	VT	05647	Richard Stammer	802-563-2231	S	70	0.2
Friendship Food Products Inc	4900 Maspeth Av	Maspeth	NY	11378	M Schanback	718-381-4000	R	65	0.2
F and A Cheese Corp	PO Box 430	Upland	CA	91786	Frank Terranova Jr	909-985-0955	R	60*	0.1
Bongrain Cheese USA	400 S Custer Av	New Holland	PA	17557	Jim Williams	717-355-8500	S	59	0.3
Kaukauna Cheese Wisconsin LP	PO Box 1974	Kaukauna	WI	54130	Robert Gilbert	414-788-3524	R	56	0.3
Le Sueur Cheese Co	P O Box 107	Le Sueur	MN	56058	Mark Davis	612-665-3353	R	56	<0.1
Raskas Foods Inc	165 N Meramec Av	St Louis	MO	63105	Heschel Raskas	314-727-9992	R	56	0.3
F and A Dairy Products Inc	PO Box 278	Dresser	WI	54009	Jeffrey Terranova	715-755-3485	R	50	<0.1
Heluva Good Cheese Inc	PO Box C	Sodus	NY	14551	John S Yancey	315-483-6971	S	47	0.2
Big Stone Cheese Factory Inc	PO Box 8	Big Stone City	SD	57216	Russ Thielke	605-862-8131	S	41*	0.2
Olympia Cheese Co	3145 Hogum Bay	Lacey	WA	98516	Hernan Etcheto	206-491-5330	R	35	0.1
Hilmar Cheese Company Inc	PO Box 910	Hilmar	CA	95324	John Jeter	209-667-6076	R	32*	0.1
Suprema Specialties Inc	PO Box 280	Paterson	NJ	07543	Mark Cocchiola	201-684-2900	P	32	0.1
Ellsworth Cooperative Creamery	PO Box 610	Ellsworth	WI	54011	Ken McMahon	715-273-4311	R	31*	<0.1
Alto Dairy Cooperative	307 N Clark St	Black Creek	WI	54106	Larry Lemmenes	414-984-3331	D	30	<0.1
Lucille Farms Products	PO Box 125	Swanton	VT	05488	Gennaro Falivene	802-868-7301	R	30*	<0.1
Old Fashioned Foods Inc	650 Furnace St	Mayville	WI	53050	Gary Youso	414-387-4444	R	29*	0.1
Stauffer Cheese Inc	PO Box 68	Blue Mounds	WI	53517	Gerhard Simon	608-437-5598	R	27*	0.1
Miceli Dairy Products Co	2721 E 90th St	Cleveland	OH	44104	Joseph D Miceli	216-791-6222	R	24	0.1
Jerome Cheese Co	PO Box 485	Jerome	ID	83338	Mark Davis	208-324-8806	R	23*	0.1
Minerva Cheese Factory Inc	PO Box 60	Minerva	OH	44657	Phil Mueller	216-868-4196	R	22	<0.1
Bel Cheese	PO Box 156	Leitchfield	KY	42755	JP Plessis	502-259-4071	D	20	0.2
Cucino Classica Italiana Inc	1935 Swarthmore	Lakewood	NJ	08701	Angelo Dominoini	908-363-3800	R	20	<0.1
Wisconsin Cheeseman Inc	Hwy 151	Sun Prairie	WI	53590	Merlin D Sanderson	608-837-5166	R	20	0.3
Valley Queen Cheese Factory	PO Drawer 351	Milbank	SD	57252	Alfred Gonzenbach	605-432-4563	R	18	<0.1
MGF Associates LP	PO Box 727	Orland	CA	95963	John R Ohring	916-865-9601	R	17*	<0.1
Nelson-Ricks Creamery Co	314 W 3rd S	Salt Lake City	UT	84101	Calvin L Nelson	801-364-3607	R	17	<0.1
Avanti Foods Co	PO Box 456	Walnut	IL	61376	Tony Zueger	815-379-2155	R	15	<0.1
Baker Cheese Factory Inc	5279 County Rd	St Cloud	WI	53079	Richard Baker	414-477-7871	R	15	<0.1
Calabro Cheese Corp	580 Coe Av	East Haven	CT	06512	Joseph Calabro	203-469-1311	R	15*	<0.1
Holmes Cheese Co	9444 State Rte 39	Millersburg	OH	44654	Robert J Ramseyer	216-674-6451	R	15	<0.1
Berner Cheese Corp	2034 E Factory Rd	Dakota	IL	61018	S Kneubuehl	815-563-4222	R	14*	<0.1
Farmdale Creamery Inc	1049 W Baseline St	San Bernardino	CA	92411	Norman Shotts	909-889-3002	R	14	<0.1
Colonna Brothers Inc	PO Box 808	North Bergen	NJ	07047	Peter Colonna	201-864-1115	R	12	<0.1
Star Valley Cheese Inc	PO Box 436	Thayne	WY	83127	Morris Farinella	307-883-2446	R	11*	<0.1
Kolb-Lena Cheese Co	3990 N Sunnyside	Lena	IL	61048	Jim Williams	815-369-4577	S	10	<0.1
Nauvoo Cheese Co	1095 Young St	Nauvoo	IL	62354	Heschel Raskas	217-453-2213	S	10*	<0.1
Roth Kasa USA Ltd	PO Box 319	Monroe	WI	53566	Steve McKeon	608-328-2122	R	9*	<0.1
Sun-Re Cheese Corp	178 Lenker Av	Sunbury	PA	17801	P Rescigno	717-286-1511	R	9*	<0.1
Williams Cheese Company Inc	998 N Huron Rd	Linwood	MI	48634	Jim Williams	517-697-4492	R	9	<0.1
4 C Foods Corp	580 Fountain Av	Brooklyn	NY	11208	John Celauro	718-272-4242	R	7	0.2
Alpine Alpa Cheese Factory Inc	1504 US Rte 62	Wilmot	OH	44689	Alice Grossniklaus	216-359-5454	R	6	<0.1
Galaxy Foods Co	244 Viscount Row	Orlando	FL	32809	Angelo S Morini	407-855-5500	P	6	<0.1
Mancuso Cheese Co	612 Mills Rd	Joliet	IL	60433	DJ Mancuso	815-722-2475	R	5*	<0.1
Welcome Dairy Inc	Rte 2	Colby	WI	54421	Terry Eggebrecht	715-223-2874	R	5	<0.1
McClendon's Dairy Products Inc	PO Box 36	Uniontown	AL	36786	WD McClendon	205-628-3311	R	5	<0.1
Sargento Food Services Corp	1 Persnickety	Plymouth	WI	53073	Laurence Gentine	414-893-8484	S	4*	<0.1
Kutters Cheese Factory	857 Main Rd	Corfu	NY	14036	Joan F Miner	716-599-3693	R	3	<0.1
Mozzarella Co	2944 Elm St	Dallas	TX	75226	Paula Lambert	214-741-4072	R	3	<0.1
Vella Cheese Company Inc	PO Box 191	Sonoma	CA	95476	Ignazio Vella	707-938-3232	R	3	<0.1
Taylor Cheese Corp	PO Box 639	Weyauwega	WI	54983	James Taylor	414-867-2337	R	2	<0.1
Marin French Cheese Company	7500 Red Hill Rd	Petaluma	CA	94952	George F Hardy	707-762-6001	R	1	<0.1
Cloverleaf Cheese Inc	W 10911 County N	Stanley	WI	54768	William Marten	715-669-3145	R	1	<0.1

Source: *Ward's Business Directory of U.S. Private and Public Companies*, Volumes 1 and 2, 1996. The company type code used is as follows: P - Public, R - Private, S - Subsidiary, D - Division, J - Joint Venture, A - Affiliate, G - Group. Sales are in millions of dollars, employees are in thousands. An asterisk (*) indicates an estimated sales volume. The symbol < stands for 'less than'. Company names and addresses are truncated, in some cases, to fit into the available space.

MATERIALS CONSUMED

Material		Quantity	Delivered Cost ($ million)
Materials, ingredients, containers, and supplies		(X)	13,105.5
Whole milk	mil cwt	506.8*	6,517.0
Fluid skim milk	mil cwt	2.1	38.7
Cream	mil cwt	(S)	89.5
Butter	mil lb	7.3	8.1
Condensed and evaporated milk	mil lb	141.6*	75.2
Dry milk	mil lb	121.8	112.2
Natural cheese, other than cottage cheese	mil lb	2,557.5	3,391.8
Fats and oils, all types (purchased as such)	mil lb	349.1	96.3
High fructose corn syrup (HFCS)(in terms of solids)	mil lb	(D)	(D)
Crystalline fructose (dry fructose)	mil lb	(D)	(D)
Dextrose and corn syrup, including corn syrup solids (in terms of dry weight)	mil lb	(D)	(D)
Sugar, cane and beet (in terms of sugar solids)	1,000 s tons	10.5**	3.8
Whey, liquid, concentrated, dried; and modified whey products	mil lb	387.1*	80.5
Casein and caseinates	mil lb	59.1	118.5
Chocolate (compounds, cocoa, chocolate liquor, coatings, chocolate flavoring, etc.)	mil lb	1.6	1.2
Flavorings (natural, imitation, etc.), except chocolate		(X)	109.0
Plastics resins consumed in the form of granules, pellets, powders, liquids, etc.	mil lb	1.3	0.4
Packaging paper and plastics film, coated and laminated		(X)	130.6
Bags; plastics, foil, and coated paper		(X)	96.7
Plastics products consumed in the form of sheets, rods, tubes, film, and other shapes		(X)	17.8
Glass containers		(X)	(D)
Plastics containers		(X)	27.0
Paperboard containers, boxes, and corrugated paperboard		(X)	163.2
Metal cans, can lids and ends		(X)	47.9
All other materials and components, parts, containers, and supplies		(X)	1,084.6
Materials, ingredients, containers, and supplies, nsk		(X)	862.2

Source: 1992 *Economic Census*. Explanation of symbols used: (D): Withheld to avoid disclosure of competitive data; na: Not available; (S): Withheld because statistical norms were not met; (X): Not applicable; (Z): Less than half the unit shown; nec: Not elsewhere classified; nsk: Not specified by kind; - : zero; * : 10-19 percent estimated; ** : 20-29 percent estimated.

PRODUCT SHARE DETAILS

Product or Product Class	% Share
Cheese, natural and processed	100.00
Natural cheese, except cottage cheese (cheddar, brick, grated, cream, swiss, italian, etc.)	63.54
Natural cheese, except cottage cheese (cheddar, brick, grated, cream, swiss, italian, etc.), shipped in consumer packages or containers (3 lb or less)	31.19
Natural cheese, except cottage cheese (cheddar, brick, grated, cream, swiss, italian, etc.), shipped in packages or containers of more than 3 lb or in bulk	68.43
Natural cheese, except cottage cheese (cheddar, brick, grated, cream, swiss, italian, etc.), nsk	0.38
Process cheese and related products	31.93
Process cheese, shipped in consumer packages or containers (3 lb or less)	42.98
Process cheese, shipped in packages or containers of more than 3 lb or in bulk	34.12
Cheese food	8.76
Cheese spread	10.28
Other related cheese products, including flavored cheese dips	3.51
Process cheese and related products, nsk	0.35
Cheese substitutes	1.98
Products substituting for natural cheese	58.94
Products substituting for process cheese or related products	41.06
Cheese, natural and processed, nsk	2.55

Source: 1992 *Economic Census*. The values shown are percent of total shipments in an industry. Values of indented subcategories are summed in the main heading. The symbol (D) appears when data are withheld to prevent disclosure of competitive information. The abbreviation nsk stands for 'not specified by kind' and nec for 'not elsewhere classified'.

INPUTS AND OUTPUTS FOR CHEESE, NATURAL & PROCESSED

Economic Sector or Industry Providing Inputs	%	Sector	Economic Sector or Industry Buying Outputs	%	Sector
Dairy farm products	49.8	Agric.	Personal consumption expenditures	39.4	
Cheese, natural & processed	15.7	Manufg.	Eating & drinking places	30.9	Trade
Fluid milk	10.8	Manufg.	Cheese, natural & processed	15.0	Manufg.
Wholesale trade	4.6	Trade	Federal Government purchases, nondefense	8.7	Fed Govt
Imports	3.8	Foreign	Frozen specialties	1.7	Manufg.
Commercial printing	2.0	Manufg.	Commodity Credit Corporation	0.9	Gov't
Condensed & evaporated milk	1.7	Manufg.	Exports	0.8	Foreign
Paper coating & glazing	1.6	Manufg.	Change in business inventories	0.7	In House
Paperboard containers & boxes	1.5	Manufg.	Federal Government enterprises nec	0.4	Gov't
Advertising	1.1	Services	Hospitals	0.3	Services
Gas production & distribution (utilities)	0.7	Util.	Food preparations, nec	0.2	Manufg.
Electric services (utilities)	0.6	Util.	Child day care services	0.2	Services
Cyclic crudes and organics	0.5	Manufg.	Nursing & personal care facilities	0.1	Services
Metal foil & leaf	0.5	Manufg.	Residential care	0.1	Services
Miscellaneous plastics products	0.5	Manufg.	S/L Govt. purch., correction	0.1	S/L Govt
Noncomparable imports	0.5	Foreign	S/L Govt. purch., elem. & secondary education	0.1	S/L Govt
Vegetable oil mills, nec	0.4	Manufg.	S/L Govt. purch., health & hospitals	0.1	S/L Govt
Motor freight transportation & warehousing	0.4	Util.	S/L Govt. purch., higher education	0.1	S/L Govt

Continued on next page.

INPUTS AND OUTPUTS FOR CHEESE, NATURAL & PROCESSED - Continued

Economic Sector or Industry Providing Inputs	%	Sector	Economic Sector or Industry Buying Outputs	%	Sector
Business services nec	0.4	Services			
Petroleum refining	0.3	Manufg.			
Banking	0.3	Fin/R.E.			
Food preparations, nec	0.2	Manufg.			
Maintenance of nonfarm buildings nec	0.1	Constr.			
Metal cans	0.1	Manufg.			
Soap & other detergents	0.1	Manufg.			
Communications, except radio & TV	0.1	Util.			
Railroads & related services	0.1	Util.			
Eating & drinking places	0.1	Trade			
Real estate	0.1	Fin/R.E.			

Source: Benchmark Input-Output Accounts for the U.S. Economy, 1982, U.S. Department of Commerce, Washington, D.C., July 1991. Data, as reported in the source, are organized by the 1977 SIC structure in use in 1982 but have been matched, as closely as is possible, to the 1987 SIC structure used in this book.

OCCUPATIONS EMPLOYED BY SIC 202 - DAIRY PRODUCTS

Occupation	% of Total 1994	Change to 2005	Occupation	% of Total 1994	Change to 2005
Dairy processing equipment workers	9.1	-1.7	Industrial truck & tractor operators	2.2	-11.3
Packaging & filling machine operators	8.1	33.1	Traffic, shipping, & receiving clerks	2.1	-14.6
Truck drivers light & heavy	7.5	-8.5	Maintenance repairers, general utility	2.0	-20.1
Driver/sales workers	5.8	-42.3	General managers & top executives	1.7	-15.8
Helpers, laborers, & material movers nec	4.3	-11.3	Bookkeeping, accounting, & auditing clerks	1.7	-33.4
Blue collar worker supervisors	4.1	-15.0	Machine feeders & offbearers	1.6	-20.1
Precision food & tobacco workers nec	4.0	6.5	Science & mathematics technicians	1.5	-11.3
Machine operators nec	3.7	-21.8	General office clerks	1.4	-24.3
Hand packers & packagers	3.5	-23.9	Inspectors, testers, & graders, precision	1.2	-11.2
Freight, stock, & material movers, hand	3.4	-29.0	Industrial production managers	1.2	-11.2
Industrial machinery mechanics	2.6	-2.4	Secretaries, ex legal & medical	1.1	-19.2
Sales & related workers nec	2.2	-11.3			

Source: Industry-Occupation Matrix, Bureau of Labor Statistics. These data relate to one or more 3-digit SIC industry groups rather than to a single 4-digit SIC. The change reported for each occupation to the year 2005 is a percent of growth or decline as estimated by the Bureau of Labor Statistics. The abbreviation nec stands for 'not elsewhere classified'.

LOCATION BY STATE AND REGIONAL CONCENTRATION

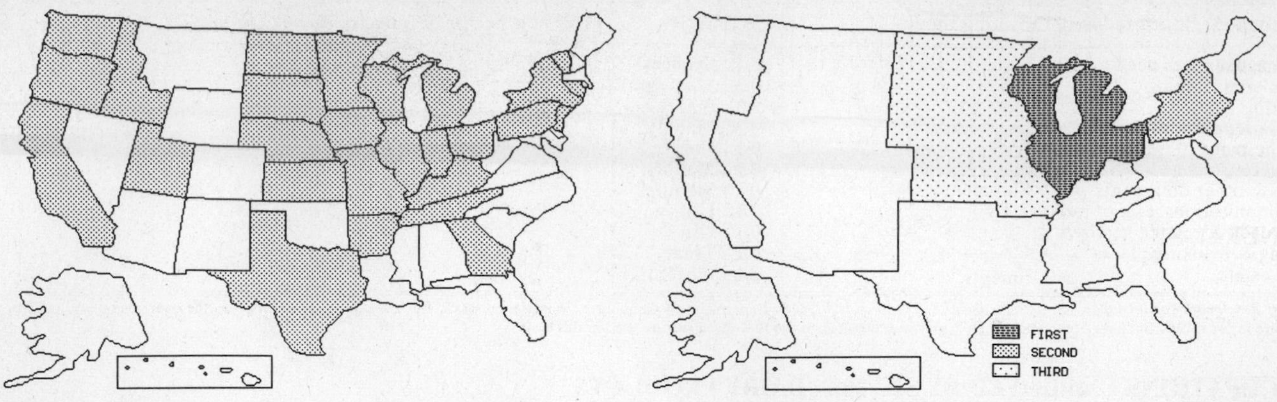

INDUSTRY DATA BY STATE

State	Establish-ments	Shipments			Employment				Cost as % of Shipments	Investment per Employee ($)
		Total ($ mil)	% of U.S.	Per Establ.	Total Number	% of U.S.	Per Establ.	Wages ($/hour)		
Wisconsin	204	6,037.2	32.9	29.6	12,100	33.3	59	10.07	81.0	6,198
Minnesota	27	2,048.5	11.2	75.9	3,300	9.1	122	11.30	72.7	7,667
Illinois	25	1,733.9	9.4	69.4	2,600	7.2	104	14.88	50.3	9,500
Missouri	13	1,624.8	8.9	125.0	2,500	6.9	192	13.02	67.4	5,160
California	44	1,398.7	7.6	31.8	3,200	8.8	73	11.30	75.1	11,187
New York	35	1,023.2	5.6	29.2	2,400	6.6	69	11.08	84.2	12,667
Utah	11	504.7	2.8	45.9	1,200	3.3	109	10.47	68.4	7,000
Pennsylvania	31	502.9	2.7	16.2	1,200	3.3	39	9.57	75.7	7,917
Iowa	13	498.8	2.7	38.4	1,100	3.0	85	7.91	83.7	-
Idaho	14	386.6	2.1	27.6	700	1.9	50	9.23	85.4	12,571
Ohio	20	282.0	1.5	14.1	800	2.2	40	11.00	83.5	3,875
Vermont	12	261.0	1.4	21.7	700	1.9	58	9.27	86.0	4,429
South Dakota	11	221.8	1.2	20.2	500	1.4	45	8.60	82.8	6,600
New Jersey	18	196.1	1.1	10.9	500	1.4	28	10.00	79.4	5,200
Washington	8	123.4	0.7	15.4	300	0.8	38	9.20	72.5	-
Michigan	9	(D)	-	-	375 *	1.0	42	-	-	-
Texas	9	(D)	-	-	375 *	1.0	42	-	-	-
North Dakota	7	(D)	-	-	175 *	0.5	25	-	-	-
Oregon	6	(D)	-	-	375 *	1.0	63	-	-	-
Indiana	5	(D)	-	-	375 *	1.0	75	-	-	-
Kansas	5	(D)	-	-	175 *	0.5	35	-	-	1,143
Nebraska	5	(D)	-	-	375 *	1.0	75	-	-	-
Connecticut	4	(D)	-	-	175 *	0.5	44	-	-	-
Kentucky	4	(D)	-	-	375 *	1.0	94	-	-	-
Tennessee	4	(D)	-	-	175 *	0.5	44	-	-	-
Arkansas	3	(D)	-	-	175 *	0.5	58	-	-	-
Georgia	3	(D)	-	-	175 *	0.5	58	-	-	-

Source: 1992 *Economic Census*. The states are in descending order of shipments or establishments (if shipment data are missing for the majority). The symbol (D) appears when data are withheld to prevent disclosure of competitive information. States marked with (D) are sorted by number of establishments. A dash (-) indicates that the data element cannot be calculated; * indicates the midpoint of a range.

2023 - DRY, CONDENSED, EVAPORATED PRODUCTS

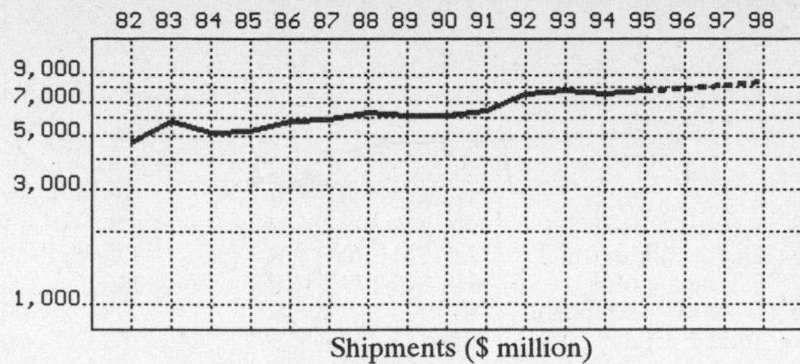

Shipments ($ million)

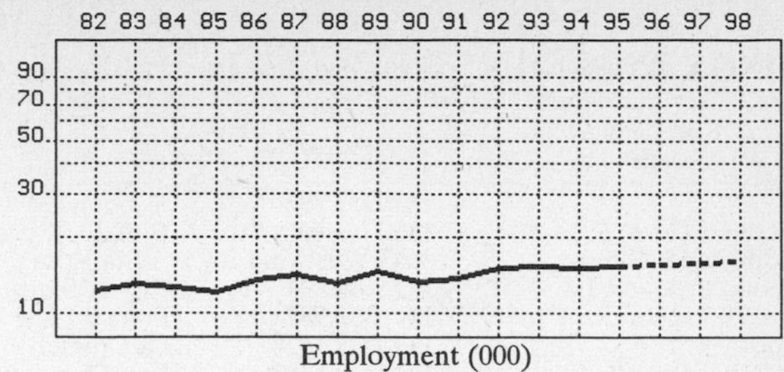

Employment (000)

GENERAL STATISTICS

Year	Companies	Establishments: Total	Establishments: with 20 or more employees	Employment: Total (000)	Production Workers (000)	Production Hours (Mil)	Compensation: Payroll ($ mil)	Compensation: Wages ($/hr)	Production: Cost of Materials	Value Added by Manufacture	Value of Shipments	Capital Invest.
1982	132	204	125	12.2	8.6	18.4	258.7	9.10	3,296.7	1,447.6	4,730.7	98.8
1983		198	123	13.1	8.9	19.7	304.5	9.72	4,059.7	1,736.2	5,745.9	114.9
1984		192	121	12.7	8.6	19.1	294.6	9.95	3,386.4	1,814.1	5,212.7	87.4
1985		186	119	12.0	7.9	18.1	315.5	10.22	3,689.8	1,628.0	5,287.9	
1986		182	108	13.5	8.9	18.5	357.0	10.59	3,577.9	2,254.5	5,807.2	120.7
1987	123	186	115	14.1	8.7	18.0	399.3	11.47	3,463.0	2,391.6	5,856.7	109.6
1988		182	119	13.0	9.3	18.8	377.9	11.70	3,682.9	2,577.9	6,245.5	107.7
1989		179	117	14.6	8.8	18.5	375.4	11.72	3,467.0	2,593.5	6,052.1	153.8
1990		173	113	13.2	8.5	18.1	348.5	11.93	3,509.7	2,670.2	6,135.3	117.2
1991		177	112	13.6	9.2	19.1	405.9	12.46	3,434.4	2,879.6	6,343.5	162.5
1992	153	214	134	15.2	9.9	21.6	451.6	12.61	4,172.4	3,379.5	7,541.0	188.5
1993		214	139	15.3	10.1	21.8	458.6	13.03	4,212.8	3,479.8	7,671.6	134.8
1994		192P	125P	15.1	9.5	20.5	474.9	13.07	4,258.5	3,196.1	7,446.4	178.7
1995		192P	125P	15.3P	9.8P	20.6P	483.5P	13.68P	4,386.1P	3,291.9P	7,669.5P	
1996		193P	126P	15.6P	9.9P	20.8P	499.6P	14.02P	4,509.4P	3,384.4P	7,885.2P	
1997		193P	127P	15.8P	10.0P	21.0P	515.6P	14.35P	4,632.8P	3,477.0P	8,100.9P	
1998		193P	127P	16.0P	10.1P	21.2P	531.7P	14.68P	4,756.1P	3,569.6P	8,316.6P	

Sources: 1982, 1987, 1992 *Economic Census*; *Annual Survey of Manufactures*, 83-86, 88-91, 93-94. Establishment counts for non-Census years are from *County Business Patterns*; establishment values for 83-84 are extrapolations. 'P's show projections by the editors. Industries reclassified in 87 will not have data for prior years.

INDICES OF CHANGE

Year	Companies	Establishments: Total	Establishments: with 20 or more employees	Employment: Total (000)	Production Workers (000)	Production Hours (Mil)	Compensation: Payroll ($ mil)	Compensation: Wages ($/hr)	Production: Cost of Materials	Value Added by Manufacture	Value of Shipments	Capital Invest.
1982	86	95	93	80	87	85	57	72	79	43	63	52
1983		93	92	86	90	91	67	77	97	51	76	61
1984		90	90	84	87	88	65	79	81	54	69	46
1985		87	89	79	80	84	70	81	88	48	70	
1986		85	81	89	90	86	79	84	86	67	77	64
1987	80	87	86	93	88	83	88	91	83	71	78	58
1988		85	89	86	94	87	84	93	88	76	83	57
1989		84	87	96	89	86	83	93	83	77	80	82
1990		81	84	87	86	84	77	95	84	79	81	62
1991		83	84	89	93	88	90	99	82	85	84	86
1992	100	100	100	100	100	100	100	100	100	100	100	100
1993		100	104	101	102	101	102	103	101	103	102	72
1994		90P	93P	99	96	95	105	104	102	95	99	95
1995		90P	94P	101P	99P	95P	107P	109P	105P	97P	102P	
1996		90P	94P	102P	100P	96P	111P	111P	108P	100P	105P	
1997		90P	95P	104P	101P	97P	114P	114P	111P	103P	107P	
1998		90P	95P	105P	102P	98P	118P	116P	114P	106P	110P	

Sources: Same as General Statistics. Values reflect change from the base year, 1992. Values above 100 mean greater than 92, values below 100 mean less than 92, and a value of 100 in the 82-91 or 93-98 period means same as 92. 'P's mark projections by the editors.

SELECTED RATIOS

For 1994	Avg. of All Manufact.	Analyzed Industry	Index
Employees per Establishment	49	79	160
Payroll per Establishment	1,500,273	2,470,903	165
Payroll per Employee	30,620	31,450	103
Production Workers per Establishment	34	49	144
Wages per Establishment	853,319	1,394,065	163
Wages per Production Worker	24,861	28,204	113
Hours per Production Worker	2,056	2,158	105
Wages per Hour	12.09	13.07	108
Value Added per Establishment	4,602,255	16,629,294	361
Value Added per Employee	93,930	211,662	225

For 1994	Avg. of All Manufact.	Analyzed Industry	Index
Value Added per Production Worker	134,084	336,432	251
Cost per Establishment	5,045,178	22,156,957	439
Cost per Employee	102,970	282,020	274
Cost per Production Worker	146,988	448,263	305
Shipments per Establishment	9,576,895	38,743,587	405
Shipments per Employee	195,460	493,139	252
Shipments per Production Worker	279,017	783,832	281
Investment per Establishment	321,011	929,775	290
Investment per Employee	6,552	11,834	181
Investment per Production Worker	9,352	18,811	201

Sources: Same as General Statistics. The 'Average of All Manufacturing' column represents the average of all manufacturing industries reported for the most recent complete year available. The Index shows the relationship between the Average and the Analyzed Industry. For example, 100 means that they are equal; 500 that the Analyzed Industry is five times the average; 50 means that the Analyzed Industry is half the national average. The abbreviation 'na' is used to show that data are 'not available'.

LEADING COMPANIES

Number shown: **25** Total sales ($ mil): **3,705** Total employment (000): **14.3**

Company Name	Address				CEO Name	Phone	Co. Type	Sales ($ mil)	Empl. (000)
Pet Inc	PO Box 392	St Louis	MO	63166	Miles L Marsh	314-622-7700	P	1,582	5.7
Rich Products Corp	1150 Niagara St	Buffalo	NY	14213	Robert E Rich Jr	716-878-8000	R	1,020	5.1
Milk Products Holdings	3645 Westwind Blv	Santa Rosa	CA	95403	David Pilkington	707-524-6700	R	130*	0.5
Presto Food Products Inc	PO Box 584	City of Industry	CA	91747	L Bruce Coffey	818-810-1775	R	130	0.5
Waterford Food Products Inc	PO Box 987	Fond du Lac	WI	54936	David B Leonhardt	414-922-0600	S	95	0.3
DMV Inc	PO Box 1628	La Crosse	WI	54602	John F Lyche	608-781-2345	S	87	<0.1
Land O'Lakes Inc	PO Box 1087	Eau Claire	WI	54702	Rod Olson	715-835-2221	D	75	0.2
O-AT-KA Milk Products Coop	PO Box 718	Batavia	NY	14021	Herb Binsack	716-343-0536	R	71*	0.1
Milnot Co	100 S 4th St	St Louis	MO	63102	Michael Osborne	314-436-7667	R	67	0.2
Davisco International Inc	PO Box 69	Le Sueur	MN	56058	Mark Davis	612-665-8811	R	61	0.2
Dean Foods Co	PO Box 359	Pecatonica	IL	61063	J Gartman	815-239-2631	D	50*	0.1
Guida-Seibert Dairy Co	433 Park St	New Britain	CT	06051	Bernie Guida	203-224-2404	R	50*	0.2
Diehl Inc	24 N Clinton St	Defiance	OH	43512	John P Speiser	419-782-5010	R	40	0.1
Gehl's Guernsey Farms Inc	PO Box 1004	Germantown	WI	53022	John P Gehl	414-251-8570	R	40	<0.1
Maple Island Inc	PO Box 439	Stillwater	MN	55082	WD O'Brien	612-439-2200	R	39*	0.2
Armour Food Ingredients	606 W Main St	Springfield	KY	40069	Bob Goodlett	606-336-3922	D	36	0.1
Erie Foods International Inc	PO Box 648	Erie	IL	61250	DR Reisenbigler	309-659-2233	R	30	<0.1
Ready Foods Products Inc	10975 Dutton Rd	Philadelphia	PA	19154	Stewart Goldsmith	215-824-2800	S	21*	0.1
Wyeth-Ayerst Nutritional Inc	PO Box 2109	Georgia	VT	05468	C Rosenquist	802-527-0521	S	20	0.3
Dairymen Inc	PO Box 667	Franklinton	LA	70438	Bob Shipley	504-839-4481	D	15	<0.1
Armour-Freeborn Foods	PO Box 1186	Albert Lea	MN	56007	Jon Hedlund	507-373-4739	S	13	<0.1
Land O'Lakes Inc	PO Box 116	Minneapolis	MN	55440	Mike Fronk	612-481-2222	D	13	<0.1
American Casein Co	109 Elbow Ln	Burlington	NJ	08016	Richard L Shipley	609-387-3130	R	10	<0.1
Jackson-Mitchell Inc	PO Box 5425	Santa Barbara	CA	93150	Robert D Jackson	805-565-1538	R	10*	<0.1
Snoqualmie Gourmet Ice Cream	2100 196th St SW	Lynnwood	WA	98036	MK Lewis	206-771-0944	R	1	<0.1

Source: *Ward's Business Directory of U.S. Private and Public Companies*, Volumes 1 and 2, 1996. The company type code used is as follows: P - Public, R - Private, S - Subsidiary, D - Division, J - Joint Venture, A - Affiliate, G - Group. Sales are in millions of dollars, employees are in thousands. An asterisk (*) indicates an estimated sales volume. The symbol < stands for 'less than'. Company names and addresses are truncated, in some cases, to fit into the available space.

MATERIALS CONSUMED

Material		Quantity	Delivered Cost ($ million)
Materials, ingredients, containers, and supplies		(X)	3,759.2
Whole milk	mil cwt	129.2	1,559.0
Fluid skim milk	mil cwt	(S)	85.8
Cream	mil cwt	2.6	116.0
Butter	mil lb	(D)	(D)
Condensed and evaporated milk	mil lb	313.3*	125.8
Dry milk	mil lb	283.7	236.4
Natural cheese, other than cottage cheese	mil lb	79.6*	46.1
Fats and oils, all types (purchased as such)	mil lb	235.4*	78.5
High fructose corn syrup (HFCS)(in terms of solids)	mil lb	113.4**	13.8
Crystalline fructose (dry fructose)	mil lb	6.6	1.6
Dextrose and corn syrup, including corn syrup solids (in terms of dry weight)	mil lb	208.6	31.3
Sugar, cane and beet (in terms of sugar solids)	1,000 s tons	153.4	71.4
Whey, liquid, concentrated, dried; and modified whey products	mil lb	1,095.5*	133.7
Casein and caseinates	mil lb	95.9	150.4
Chocolate (compounds, cocoa, chocolate liquor, coatings, chocolate flavoring, etc.)	mil lb	26.9	17.4
Flavorings (natural, imitation, etc.), except chocolate		(X)	55.0
Plastics resins consumed in the form of granules, pellets, powders, liquids, etc.	mil lb	(D)	(D)
Packaging paper and plastics film, coated and laminated		(X)	30.1
Bags; plastics, foil, and coated paper		(X)	24.6
Plastics products consumed in the form of sheets, rods, tubes, film, and other shapes		(X)	11.6
Glass containers		(X)	23.3
Plastics containers		(X)	30.0
Paperboard containers, boxes, and corrugated paperboard		(X)	87.8
Metal cans, can lids and ends		(X)	192.8
All other materials and components, parts, containers, and supplies		(X)	461.5
Materials, ingredients, containers, and supplies, nsk		(X)	118.9

Source: 1992 *Economic Census*. Explanation of symbols used: (D): Withheld to avoid disclosure of competitive data; na: Not available; (S): Withheld because statistical norms were not met; (X): Not applicable; (Z): Less than half the unit shown; nec: Not elsewhere classified; nsk: Not specified by kind; - : zero; * : 10-19 percent estimated; ** : 20-29 percent estimated.

PRODUCT SHARE DETAILS

Product or Product Class	% Share
Dry, condensed, and evaporated milk products	100.00
Dry milk products and mixtures	38.98
Nonfat dry milk, shipped in consumer-type packages (containers 3 lb or less)	3.27
Infants' formula, dry milk type, shipped in consumer-type packages (containers 3 lb or less)	14.21
Other dry milk products (instant chocolate milk, weight control products, whole milk powder, malted milk, etc.), shipped in consumer-type packages (containers 3 lb or less)	20.35
Dry whole milk, food grade (bakeries, confectioners, meat packers, etc.), shipped in bulk (containers more than 3 lb)	6.09
Nonfat dry milk, food grade (bakeries, confectioners, meat packers, etc.), shipped in bulk (containers more than 3 lb)	26.94
Dry whey, food grade (bakeries, confectioners, meat packers, etc.), shipped in bulk (containers more than 3 lb)	10.96
Modified dry whey products (lactose, milk albumin, etc.), food grade (bakeries, confectioners, meat packers, etc.), shipped in bulk (containers more than 3 lb)	5.83
Other food grade dry milk products, shipped in bulk (containers more than 3 lb)	7.76
Feed grade dry milk products and mixtures (dry milk, dry buttermilk, dry whey, etc.), shipped in bulk (containers more than 3 lb)	3.60
Dry milk products and mixtures, nsk	0.99
Canned milk products (consumer-type cans), except substitutes	16.29
Canned evaporated milk (consumer-type cans), except substitutes	27.43
Canned condensed milk (consumer-type cans), except substitutes	12.94
Canned milk-based dietary supplements, weight control products (consumer-type cans), except substitutes	(D)
Canned milk-based infants' formula, liquid (consumer-type cans), except substitutes	51.44
Other canned milk products, including canned whole milk (consumer-type cans)	(D)
Concentrated milk products shipped in bulk (barrels, drums, and tanks), except substitutes	12.24
Concentrated milk products shipped in bulk (barrels, drums, and tanks), except substitutes, feed grade, including concentrated whey and buttermilk	6.72
Concentrated whey (in terms of solids) shipped in bulk (barrels, drums, and tanks), except substitutes, food grade (except ice cream and ice cream mixes)	14.21
All other concentrated milk products shipped in bulk (drums, barrels, and tanks), except substitutes, food grade (except ice cream and ice cream mixes)	78.76
Concentrated milk products shipped in bulk (barrels, drums, and tanks), except substitutes, nsk	0.31
Ice cream mixes and related products	10.07
Ice cream mix	36.05
Ice milk mix	15.92
Sherbet mix	1.02
Frozen yogurt mix	21.76
Milkshake mix	16.07
Other milk-based mixes	6.94
Ice cream mixes and related products, nsk	2.25
Dairy product substitutes	21.22
Coffee whitener dry dairy substitutes	20.79
Infants' formula dry dairy substitutes	9.21
Sour cream dry dairy substitutes	0.50
Other dry dairy substitutes, including whipped topping, etc.	6.07
Canned liquid infants' formula dairy substitutes	(D)
Other canned dairy product substitutes, including dietary supplements and weight control products	(D)
Dry, condensed, and evaporated milk products, nsk	1.19

Source: 1992 *Economic Census*. The values shown are percent of total shipments in an industry. Values of indented subcategories are summed in the main heading. The symbol (D) appears when data are withheld to prevent disclosure of competitive information. The abbreviation nsk stands for 'not specified by kind' and nec for 'not elsewhere classified'.

INPUTS AND OUTPUTS FOR CONDENSED & EVAPORATED MILK

Economic Sector or Industry Providing Inputs	%	Sector	Economic Sector or Industry Buying Outputs	%	Sector
Dairy farm products	43.3	Agric.	Personal consumption expenditures	40.9	
Fluid milk	11.7	Manufg.	Federal Government purchases, nondefense	8.7	Fed Govt
Condensed & evaporated milk	10.8	Manufg.	Eating & drinking places	8.6	Trade
Metal cans	4.4	Manufg.	Condensed & evaporated milk	7.2	Manufg.
Wholesale trade	4.2	Trade	Commodity Credit Corporation	6.6	Gov't
Paper coating & glazing	3.2	Manufg.	Fluid milk	6.0	Manufg.
Advertising	2.9	Services	Exports	5.6	Foreign
Gas production & distribution (utilities)	2.0	Util.	Ice cream & frozen desserts	4.8	Manufg.
Paperboard containers & boxes	1.7	Manufg.	Cheese, natural & processed	3.2	Manufg.
Miscellaneous plastics products	1.6	Manufg.	Confectionery products	2.4	Manufg.
Vegetable oil mills, nec	1.5	Manufg.	Chocolate & cocoa products	2.2	Manufg.
Sugar	1.3	Manufg.	Bread, cake, & related products	1.1	Manufg.
Imports	1.3	Foreign	Change in business inventories	0.5	In House
Pumps & compressors	1.2	Manufg.	Child day care services	0.4	Services
Banking	1.2	Fin/R.E.	Poultry & eggs	0.2	Agric.
Commercial printing	1.1	Manufg.	Cookies & crackers	0.2	Manufg.
Glass containers	0.9	Manufg.	Hospitals	0.2	Services
Electric services (utilities)	0.9	Util.	Federal Government purchases, national defense	0.2	Fed Govt
Motor freight transportation & warehousing	0.5	Util.	S/L Govt. purch., higher education	0.2	S/L Govt
Petroleum refining	0.4	Manufg.	Nursing & personal care facilities	0.1	Services
Chocolate & cocoa products	0.3	Manufg.	Residential care	0.1	Services
Noncomparable imports	0.3	Foreign	Federal Government enterprises nec	0.1	Gov't
Maintenance of nonfarm buildings nec	0.2	Constr.	S/L Govt. purch., correction	0.1	S/L Govt
Flavoring extracts & syrups, nec	0.2	Manufg.			
Food preparations, nec	0.2	Manufg.			
Communications, except radio & TV	0.2	Util.			
Railroads & related services	0.2	Util.			
Eating & drinking places	0.2	Trade			
Royalties	0.2	Fin/R.E.			
Soap & other detergents	0.1	Manufg.			
Water transportation	0.1	Util.			
Credit agencies other than banks	0.1	Fin/R.E.			
Equipment rental & leasing services	0.1	Services			
State & local government enterprises, nec	0.1	Gov't			

Source: Benchmark Input-Output Accounts for the U.S. Economy, 1982, U.S. Department of Commerce, Washington, D.C., July 1991. Data, as reported in the source, are organized by the 1977 SIC structure in use in 1982 but have been matched, as closely as is possible, to the 1987 SIC structure used in this book.

OCCUPATIONS EMPLOYED BY SIC 202 - DAIRY PRODUCTS

Occupation	% of Total 1994	Change to 2005	Occupation	% of Total 1994	Change to 2005
Dairy processing equipment workers	9.1	-1.7	Industrial truck & tractor operators	2.2	-11.3
Packaging & filling machine operators	8.1	33.1	Traffic, shipping, & receiving clerks	2.1	-14.6
Truck drivers light & heavy	7.5	-8.5	Maintenance repairers, general utility	2.0	-20.1
Driver/sales workers	5.8	-42.3	General managers & top executives	1.7	-15.8
Helpers, laborers, & material movers nec	4.3	-11.3	Bookkeeping, accounting, & auditing clerks	1.7	-33.4
Blue collar worker supervisors	4.1	-15.0	Machine feeders & offbearers	1.6	-20.1
Precision food & tobacco workers nec	4.0	6.5	Science & mathematics technicians	1.5	-11.3
Machine operators nec	3.7	-21.8	General office clerks	1.4	-24.3
Hand packers & packagers	3.5	-23.9	Inspectors, testers, & graders, precision	1.2	-11.2
Freight, stock, & material movers, hand	3.4	-29.0	Industrial production managers	1.2	-11.2
Industrial machinery mechanics	2.6	-2.4	Secretaries, ex legal & medical	1.1	-19.2
Sales & related workers nec	2.2	-11.3			

Source: Industry-Occupation Matrix, Bureau of Labor Statistics. These data relate to one or more 3-digit SIC industry groups rather than to a single 4-digit SIC. The change reported for each occupation to the year 2005 is a percent of growth or decline as estimated by the Bureau of Labor Statistics. The abbreviation nec stands for 'not elsewhere classified'.

LOCATION BY STATE AND REGIONAL CONCENTRATION

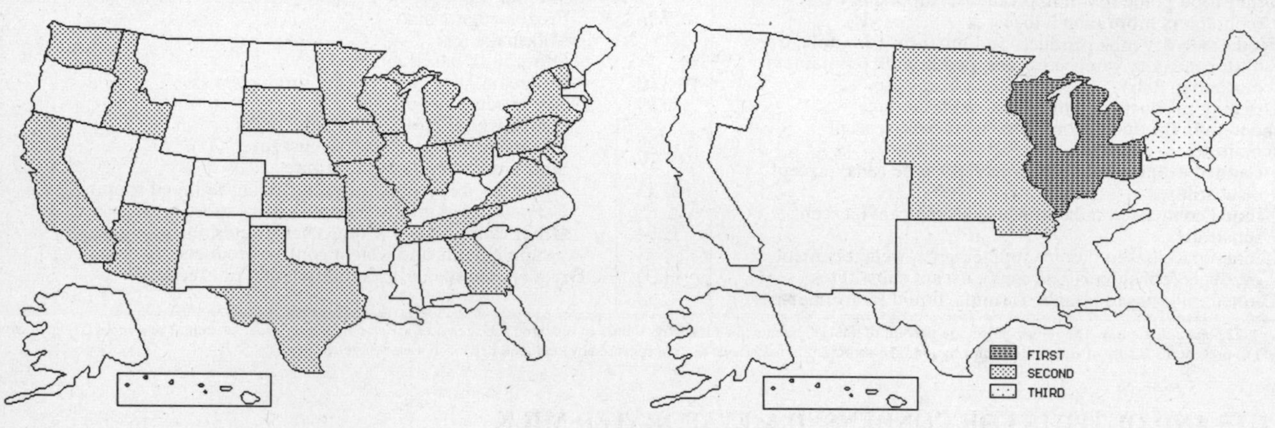

INDUSTRY DATA BY STATE

State	Establish-ments	Shipments: Total ($ mil)	Shipments: % of U.S.	Shipments: Per Establ.	Employment: Total Number	Employment: % of U.S.	Employment: Per Establ.	Employment: Wages ($/hour)	Cost as % of Shipments	Investment per Employee ($)
Michigan	10	1,203.6	16.0	120.4	1,500	9.9	150	16.58	29.8	18,467
Wisconsin	36	850.3	11.3	23.6	2,100	13.8	58	12.27	65.8	5,857
Ohio	10	436.0	5.8	43.6	1,000	6.6	100	12.00	48.3	-
Illinois	17	428.9	5.7	25.2	1,000	6.6	59	11.06	50.2	-
Minnesota	23	421.7	5.6	18.3	1,500	9.9	65	12.20	57.6	5,467
New York	15	226.8	3.0	15.1	400	2.6	27	11.67	69.3	13,250
Tennessee	4	90.1	1.2	22.5	300	2.0	75	11.00	59.6	-
California	18	(D)	-	-	750 *	4.9	42	-	-	-
Pennsylvania	10	(D)	-	-	375 *	2.5	38	-	-	-
Missouri	8	(D)	-	-	375 *	2.5	47	-	-	-
Iowa	7	(D)	-	-	750 *	4.9	107	-	-	12,533
New Jersey	7	(D)	-	-	375 *	2.5	54	-	-	-
South Dakota	4	(D)	-	-	175 *	1.2	44	-	-	-
Georgia	3	(D)	-	-	175 *	1.2	58	-	-	-
Idaho	3	(D)	-	-	175 *	1.2	58	-	-	-
Indiana	3	(D)	-	-	1,750 *	11.5	583	-	-	-
Maryland	3	(D)	-	-	175 *	1.2	58	-	-	-
Washington	3	(D)	-	-	175 *	1.2	58	-	-	-
Kansas	2	(D)	-	-	175 *	1.2	88	-	-	-
Texas	2	(D)	-	-	175 *	1.2	88	-	-	-
Vermont	2	(D)	-	-	375 *	2.5	188	-	-	-
Virginia	2	(D)	-	-	750 *	4.9	375	-	-	-
Arizona	1	(D)	-	-	375 *	2.5	375	-	-	-

Source: 1992 *Economic Census*. The states are in descending order of shipments or establishments (if shipment data are missing for the majority). The symbol (D) appears when data are withheld to prevent disclosure of competitive information. States marked with (D) are sorted by number of establishments. A dash (-) indicates that the data element cannot be calculated; * indicates the midpoint of a range.

2024 - ICE CREAM & FROZEN DESSERTS

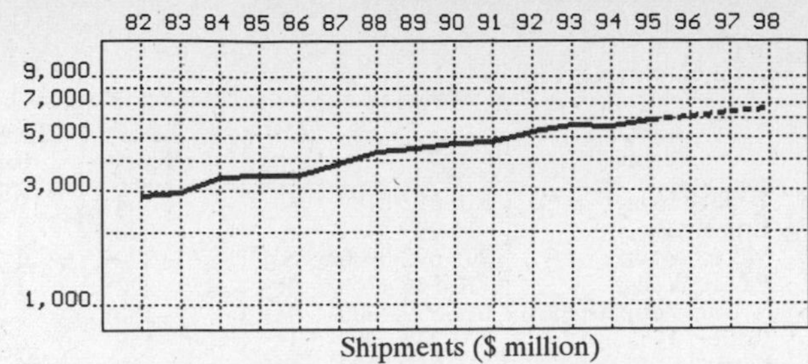

Shipments ($ million)

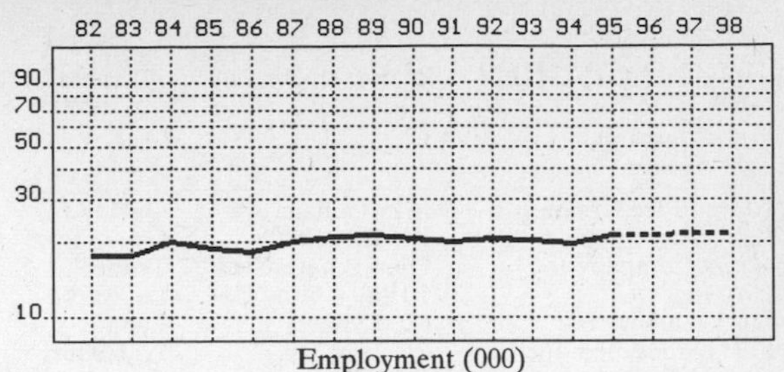

Employment (000)

GENERAL STATISTICS

Year	Com-panies	Establishments		Employment			Compensation		Production ($ million)			
		Total	with 20 or more employees	Total (000)	Production Workers (000)	Production Hours (Mil)	Payroll ($ mil)	Wages ($/hr)	Cost of Materials	Value Added by Manufacture	Value of Shipments	Capital Invest.
1982	482	552	219	17.8	11.1	20.9	313.5	8.48	1,949.0	910.4	2,855.1	79.9
1983		551	220	17.7	9.5	19.7	349.7	8.83	2,104.3	876.6	2,963.4	75.5
1984		550	221	20.0	12.2	23.1	367.2	8.68	2,437.7	1,007.2	3,435.7	84.0
1985		549	221	18.9	11.7	21.5	384.7	9.29	2,443.4	1,040.8	3,476.9	
1986		544	223	18.2	11.7	22.3	383.2	9.82	2,386.5	1,074.8	3,459.0	105.4
1987	467	540	211	20.3	13.8	26.9	439.9	9.99	2,661.3	1,269.3	3,914.5	137.1
1988		518	212	21.2	14.1	28.6	463.8	9.85	2,841.3	1,463.5	4,297.3	158.5
1989		505	201	21.4	13.5	27.2	453.8	10.00	2,947.8	1,518.2	4,474.4	148.0
1990		470	198	20.7	13.0	26.7	493.5	10.38	2,969.3	1,725.5	4,660.2	140.9
1991		446	184	20.2	12.9	27.9	514.9	10.62	3,196.2	1,571.1	4,761.2	161.3
1992	411	456	177	20.9	13.7	28.8	558.2	11.28	3,210.5	2,096.5	5,290.6	188.1
1993		457	188	20.4	13.9	28.7	574.5	11.59	3,245.3	2,363.3	5,608.1	180.3
1994		440P	180P	19.7	13.5	28.5	573.2	12.22	3,137.4	2,414.4	5,566.2	175.1
1995		429P	176P	21.3P	14.5P	30.9P	608.1P	12.07P	3,322.3P	2,556.7P	5,894.2P	
1996		418P	172P	21.5P	14.8P	31.7P	630.5P	12.35P	3,457.7P	2,660.9P	6,134.5P	
1997		406P	167P	21.7P	15.0P	32.5P	652.9P	12.64P	3,593.1P	2,765.1P	6,374.7P	
1998		395P	163P	21.9P	15.3P	33.2P	675.2P	12.92P	3,728.5P	2,869.3P	6,615.0P	

Sources: 1982, 1987, 1992 *Economic Census*; *Annual Survey of Manufactures*, 83-86, 88-91, 93-94. Establishment counts for non-Census years are from *County Business Patterns*; establishment values for 83-84 are extrapolations. 'P's show projections by the editors. Industries reclassified in 87 will not have data for prior years.

INDICES OF CHANGE

Year	Com-panies	Establishments		Employment			Compensation		Production ($ million)			
		Total	with 20 or more employees	Total (000)	Production Workers (000)	Production Hours (Mil)	Payroll ($ mil)	Wages ($/hr)	Cost of Materials	Value Added by Manufacture	Value of Shipments	Capital Invest.
1982	117	121	124	85	81	73	56	75	61	43	54	42
1983		121	124	85	69	68	63	78	66	42	56	40
1984		121	125	96	89	80	66	77	76	48	65	45
1985		120	125	90	85	75	69	82	76	50	66	
1986		119	126	87	85	77	69	87	74	51	65	56
1987	114	118	119	97	101	93	79	89	83	61	74	73
1988		114	120	101	103	99	83	87	89	70	81	84
1989		111	114	102	99	94	81	89	92	72	85	79
1990		103	112	99	95	93	88	92	92	82	88	75
1991		98	104	97	94	97	92	94	100	75	90	86
1992	100	100	100	100	100	100	100	100	100	100	100	100
1993		100	106	98	101	100	103	103	101	113	106	96
1994		96P	102P	94	99	99	103	108	98	115	105	93
1995		94P	99P	102P	106P	107P	109P	107P	103P	122P	111P	
1996		92P	97P	103P	108P	110P	113P	110P	108P	127P	116P	
1997		89P	95P	104P	110P	113P	117P	112P	112P	132P	120P	
1998		87P	92P	105P	112P	115P	121P	115P	116P	137P	125P	

Sources: Same as General Statistics. Values reflect change from the base year, 1992. Values above 100 mean greater than 92, values below 100 mean less than 92, and a value of 100 in the 82-91 or 93-98 period means same as 92. 'P's mark projections by the editors.

SELECTED RATIOS

For 1994	Avg. of All Manufact.	Analyzed Industry	Index
Employees per Establishment	49	45	91
Payroll per Establishment	1,500,273	1,303,805	87
Payroll per Employee	30,620	29,096	95
Production Workers per Establishment	34	31	89
Wages per Establishment	853,319	792,177	93
Wages per Production Worker	24,861	25,798	104
Hours per Production Worker	2,056	2,111	103
Wages per Hour	12.09	12.22	101
Value Added per Establishment	4,602,255	5,491,811	119
Value Added per Employee	93,930	122,558	130

For 1994	Avg. of All Manufact.	Analyzed Industry	Index
Value Added per Production Worker	134,084	178,844	133
Cost per Establishment	5,045,178	7,136,352	141
Cost per Employee	102,970	159,259	155
Cost per Production Worker	146,988	232,400	158
Shipments per Establishment	9,576,895	12,660,918	132
Shipments per Employee	195,460	282,548	145
Shipments per Production Worker	279,017	412,311	148
Investment per Establishment	321,011	398,284	124
Investment per Employee	6,552	8,888	136
Investment per Production Worker	9,352	12,970	139

Sources: Same as General Statistics. The 'Average of All Manufacturing' column represents the average of all manufacturing industries reported for the most recent complete year available. The Index shows the relationship between the Average and the Analyzed Industry. For example, 100 means that they are equal; 500 that the Analyzed Industry is five times the average; 50 means that the Analyzed Industry is half the national average. The abbreviation 'na' is used to show that data are 'not available'.

LEADING COMPANIES

Number shown: **59** Total sales ($ mil): **2,803** Total employment (000): **12.5**

Company Name	Address				CEO Name	Phone	Co. Type	Sales ($ mil)	Empl. (000)
Dreyer's Grand Ice Cream Inc	5929 College Av	Oakland	CA	94618	T Gary Rogers	510-652-8187	P	564	2.1
Good Humor Ice Cream	PO Box 19007	Green Bay	WI	54307	Eric Walsh	414-499-5151	S	320	1.3
Haagen-Dazs Company Inc	Glen Pointe Ctr E	Teaneck	NJ	07666	Mike Paxton	201-692-0900	S	320•	1.6
Wells Dairy Inc	1 Blue Bunny Dr	Le Mars	IA	51031	Fay R Wells	712-546-4163	R	220•	1.0
West Lynn Creamery Inc	626 Lynnway	Lynn	MA	01905	Arthur Pappathanasi	617-599-1300	R	150•	0.7
Ben and Jerry's Homemade Inc	PO Box 240	Waterbury	VT	05676	Robert Holland Jr	802-244-6957	P	149	0.5
Pepperidge Farm Inc	Boot Rd	Downingtown	PA	19335	Patrick O'Donnell	215-269-2500	D	90	0.4
Kinnett Dairies Inc	PO Box 351	Columbus	GA	31994	John R Kinnett Jr	706-571-6111	R	77•	0.4
Eskimo Pie Corp	901 Moorefield Pk	Richmond	VA	23236	David V Clark	804-560-8400	P	71	0.2
Yarnell Ice Cream Company Inc	PO Box 78	Searcy	AR	72143	A Rogers Yarnell II	501-268-2414	R	66•	0.3
Londons Farm Dairy Inc	2136 Pine Grove	Port Huron	MI	48060	Sharon Spradling	810-984-5111	R	65	0.2
Creamland Dairies Inc	PO Box 25067	Albuquerque	NM	87125	Barry J Beaman	505-247-0724	S	61	0.3
Barber Ice Cream Company Inc	126 Barber Ct	Birmingham	AL	35209	WP Langston	205-942-2351	S	46•	0.4
Bresler's Industries Inc	999 E Touhy Av	Des Plaines	IL	60018	David Lasky	708-298-1100	R	45	<0.1
High's Ice Cream Inc	9090 Wh Btm	Laurel	MD	20723	Jack Sherman	301-776-7727	R	45	0.2
Lakeside Dairy	1200 W Russell St	Sioux Falls	SD	57104	Larry Groves	605-336-1958	D	40	0.2
Vandervoort Dairy Foods Co	900 S Main St	Fort Worth	TX	76104	Gary Sturgill	817-332-7551	S	39•	0.2
Kohler Mix Specialties Inc	4041 Hwy 61	Wh Bear Lk	MN	55110	Cliff Kohler	612-426-1633	S	35	<0.1
Frozfruit Corp	14805 San Pedro St	Gardena	CA	90248	William O'Brien	310-217-1034	R	33	0.2
Grant's Dairy Inc	562 Union St	Bangor	ME	04401	Benjamin E Grant	207-942-4601	R	30	0.1
Flav-O-Rich Inc	PO Box 2620	Greensboro	NC	27402	Will Wright	919-299-0221	D	27	0.1
Brigham's Inc	30 Mill St	Arlington	MA	02174	Robert Therlait	617-648-9000	R	25	0.1
Stonyfield Farm Inc	10 Burton Dr	Londonderry	NH	03053	Gary Hirshberg	603-437-4040	R	25	0.1
Vitafreze Frozen Confections Co	1210 66th St	Sacramento	CA	95819	Donald Hansen	916-444-7200	S	24•	<0.1
Stroh's Ice Cream Co	1000 Maple St	Detroit	MI	48207	Phil Roselli	313-568-5100	R	20	<0.1
Klinke Brothers Ice Cream Co	2450 Scaper Cove	Memphis	TN	38114	John Klink	901-743-8250	R	17•	<0.1
Umpqua Dairy Products Co	PO Box 1306	Roseburg	OR	97470	D B Feldkamp	503-672-2638	R	17	<0.1
Sunshine Farms Dairy	123 N Gateway Blvd	Elyria	OH	44035	Roger McVetta	216-322-6301	D	15	0.1
Coastal Dairy Products	PO Box 324	Wilson	NC	27894	RJ Barnes	919-243-6161	R	15	0.1
Schrafft's Ice Cream Ltd	2000 Richmond Ter	Staten Island	NY	10302	J La Sauvage	718-448-2000	R	13•	<0.1
Atkins Inc	15510 Creek Way	Noblesville	IN	46060	T K Atkins Jr	317-773-3330	R	12•	<0.1
Tom McClain Co	15020 N 74th St	Scottsdale	AZ	85260	Tom McClain	602-948-8191	R	12	<0.1
Mister Cookie Face Inc	170 N Overland Av	Lakewood	NJ	08701	Frank Konemund	908-370-5533	S	11•	<0.1
Arctic Ice Cream Novelties LP	1901 23rd Av S	Seattle	WA	98144	Bill Dinslore	206-324-0414	R	10	<0.1
Fairview Dairy Inc	3200 Graham Av	Windber	PA	15963	JE Greubel	814-467-5537	R	9	0.3
Reinhold's Ice Cream Co	800 Fulton St	Pittsburgh	PA	15233	Robert Mandell	412-321-7600	R	8•	<0.1
Sugar Creek Foods	PO Box 747	Russellville	AR	72811	Fred J Fullerton	501-968-1005	R	8	<0.1
Cedar Crest Specialties Inc	7359 Hwy 60	Cedarburg	WI	53012	Ken Kohlwey	414-377-7252	R	7•	<0.1
International Yogurt Co	5858 NE 87th Av	Portland	OR	97220	John N Hanna	503-256-3754	P	7	<0.1
Chalet Desserts Inc	1693 Sabre St	Hayward	CA	94545	Gordon Everett	510-783-8300	R	6	<0.1
Frozen Desserts Inc	135 Walton St	Portland	ME	04103	Robert Drape	207-772-2827	R	6	<0.1
Asael Farr and Sons Co	PO Box 1167	Ogden	UT	84402	Dexter D Farr	801-393-8629	R	5	<0.1
Faith Dairy Inc	3509 E 72nd St	Tacoma	WA	98443	Jay Mensonides	206-531-3398	R	5•	<0.1
AC Petersen Farms Inc	240 Park Rd	West Hartford	CT	06119	Allen C Petersen	203-233-3651	R	4	0.1
Horstmann Mix and Cream Co	30-11 12th St	Long Island Ct	NY	11102	W J Horstmann	718-932-4735	R	4	<0.1
Zurheide Ice Cream Company	PO Box 1318	Sheboygan	WI	53082	John A Zurheide	414-458-4581	R	4	<0.1
Double Rainbow	275 S Van Ness Av	San Francisco	CA	94103	Michael Sachar	415-861-5858	R	3	<0.1
Sauk Rapids Dairy Inc	11 2nd Av N	Sauk Rapids	MN	56379	Dennis Larson	612-252-2025	R	3•	<0.1
Dolly Madison	3835 E 48th Av	Denver	CO	80216	EP Tepper	303-355-1668	R	3	<0.1
Mooresville Ice Cream Company	PO Box 118	Mooresville	NC	28115	HE Millsaps Jr	704-664-5456	R	2	<0.1
Nelson's Ice Cream Inc	651 Walnut St	Royersford	PA	19468	DA Nelson	610-948-3000	R	2	<0.1
Robin Rose America Inc	215 Rose Av	Venice	CA	90291	Robin Rose	310-392-4921	R	2	<0.1
Champ Products Inc	3175 Commercial	Northbrook	IL	60062	David Milazzo	708-498-9560	R	1	<0.1
Ciao Bella Gelato Co	262 Mott St	New York	NY	10012	Frederick W Pearce	212-226-7668	R	1	<0.1
Dankens Inc	2414 SW Andover	Seattle	WA	98106	Dan Samson	206-932-4774	R	1	<0.1
Hey Ice Cream	424 1st St	Dixon	IL	61021	Martin A Hey	815-288-4242	R	1	<0.1
Treat Ice Cream Co	11 S 19th St	San Jose	CA	95116	Al Mauseth	408-292-9321	R	1	<0.1
Heisler's Cloverleaf Dairy Inc	RD 1	Tamaqua	PA	18252	Leonard Ostergard	717-668-3399	R	1•	<0.1
Justin's Ice Cream Company Inc	505 S Main St	San Antonio	TX	78204	Justin V Arecchi	210-222-2707	R	0	<0.1

Source: *Ward's Business Directory of U.S. Private and Public Companies*, Volumes 1 and 2, 1996. The company type code used is as follows: P - Public, R - Private, S - Subsidiary, D - Division, J - Joint Venture, A - Affiliate, G - Group. Sales are in millions of dollars, employees are in thousands. An asterisk (*) indicates an estimated sales volume. The symbol < stands for 'less than'. Company names and addresses are truncated, in some cases, to fit into the available space.

MATERIALS CONSUMED

Material		Quantity	Delivered Cost ($ million)
Materials, ingredients, containers, and supplies		(X)	2,661.3
Whole milk	mil cwt	22.1*	295.0
Fluid skim milk	mil cwt	(S)	59.8
Cream	mil cwt	5.3	321.1
Butter	mil lb	1.9	1.7
Condensed and evaporated milk	mil lb	261.8	123.9
Dry milk	mil lb	85.4	57.7
Ice cream mixes	mil gal	47.5	123.6
Sherbet mixes	mil gal	3.9	8.1
Ice milk mixes	mil gal	5.1	13.9
Frozen yogurt mixes	mil gal	4.1*	9.2
Fats and oils, all types (purchased as such)	mil lb	6.3	3.2
High fructose corn syrup (HFCS)(in terms of solids)	mil lb	284.4*	46.2
Crystalline fructose (dry fructose)	mil lb	1.9	0.3
Dextrose and corn syrup, including corn syrup solids (in terms of dry weight)	mil lb	269.1*	32.8
Sugar, cane and beet (in terms of sugar solids)	1,000 s tons	236.5	92.0
Whey, liquid, concentrated, dried; and modified whey products	mil lb	71.0**	20.4
Casein and caseinates	mil lb	0.8	0.8
Chocolate (compounds, cocoa, chocolate liquor, coatings, chocolate flavoring, etc.)	mil lb	108.0	95.1
Flavorings (natural, imitation, etc.), except chocolate		(X)	284.6
Plastics resins consumed in the form of granules, pellets, powders, liquids, etc.	mil lb	62.6*	16.1
Packaging paper and plastics film, coated and laminated		(X)	69.9
Bags; plastics, foil, and coated paper		(X)	30.3
Plastics products consumed in the form of sheets, rods, tubes, film, and other shapes		(X)	6.6
Plastics containers		(X)	32.3
Paperboard containers, boxes, and corrugated paperboard		(X)	338.5
All other materials and components, parts, containers, and supplies		(X)	355.4
Materials, ingredients, containers, and supplies, nsk		(X)	222.7

Source: 1992 *Economic Census*. Explanation of symbols used: (D): Withheld to avoid disclosure of competitive data; na: Not available; (S): Withheld because statistical norms were not met; (X): Not applicable; (Z): Less than half the unit shown; nec: Not elsewhere classified; nsk: Not specified by kind; - : zero; * : 10-19 percent estimated; ** : 20-29 percent estimated.

PRODUCT SHARE DETAILS

Product or Product Class	% Share	Product or Product Class	% Share
Ice cream and frozen desserts	100.00	Ice milk, novelty forms	2.01
Ice cream, including custards, shipped in bulk (containers 3 gal or more)	9.56	Frozen yogurt	5.59
Ice cream, including custards, shipped in consumer sizes (containers less than 3 gal), except novelty forms	42.69	Water ices containing no real fruit or fruit juice	3.16
Ice cream, including custards, novelty forms	21.57	Ices containing some real fruit or fruit juice	1.55
Ice milk, shipped in bulk (containers 3 gal or more)	0.21	Mellorine and similar frozen desserts containing fats other than butterfat (including tofu-type)	0.53
Ice milk, shipped in consumer sizes (containers less than 3 gal), except novelty forms	4.02	Sherbet, shipped in bulk (containers 3 gal or more)	0.34
		Sherbet, shipped in all other sizes, including novelty forms	1.73
		Other frozen desserts (frozen pudding, etc.)	2.58

Source: 1992 *Economic Census*. The values shown are percent of total shipments in an industry. Values of indented subcategories are summed in the main heading. The symbol (D) appears when data are withheld to prevent disclosure of competitive information. The abbreviation nsk stands for 'not specified by kind' and nec for 'not elsewhere classified'.

INPUTS AND OUTPUTS FOR ICE CREAM & FROZEN DESSERTS

Economic Sector or Industry Providing Inputs	%	Sector	Economic Sector or Industry Buying Outputs	%	Sector
Fluid milk	26.2	Manufg.	Personal consumption expenditures	56.1	
Condensed & evaporated milk	12.1	Manufg.	Eating & drinking places	31.7	Trade
Paperboard containers & boxes	10.0	Manufg.	S/L Govt. purch., elem. & secondary education	3.5	S/L Govt
Wholesale trade	7.4	Trade	Hospitals	2.1	Services
Dairy farm products	6.8	Agric.	S/L Govt. purch., health & hospitals	1.0	S/L Govt
Food preparations, nec	5.0	Manufg.	S/L Govt. purch., higher education	0.9	S/L Govt
Sugar	4.7	Manufg.	Child day care services	0.7	Services
Electric services (utilities)	2.7	Util.	S/L Govt. purch., correction	0.7	S/L Govt
Flavoring extracts & syrups, nec	2.6	Manufg.	Motion pictures	0.6	Services
Paper coating & glazing	2.3	Manufg.	Change in business inventories	0.6	In House
Chocolate & cocoa products	2.2	Manufg.	Residential care	0.4	Services
Advertising	1.9	Services	Federal Government enterprises nec	0.4	Gov't
Cookies & crackers	1.7	Manufg.	Nursing & personal care facilities	0.3	Services
Tree nuts	1.1	Agric.	Amusement & recreation services nec	0.2	Services
Miscellaneous plastics products	1.1	Manufg.	Elementary & secondary schools	0.2	Services
Wood products, nec	1.1	Manufg.	Social services, nec	0.2	Services
Wet corn milling	1.0	Manufg.	Exports	0.2	Foreign
Equipment rental & leasing services	1.0	Services			
Petroleum refining	0.9	Manufg.			
Motor freight transportation & warehousing	0.9	Util.			
Communications, except radio & TV	0.5	Util.			

Continued on next page.

INPUTS AND OUTPUTS FOR ICE CREAM & FROZEN DESSERTS - Continued

Economic Sector or Industry Providing Inputs	%	Sector	Economic Sector or Industry Buying Outputs	%	Sector
Railroads & related services	0.5	Util.			
Chemical preparations, nec	0.4	Manufg.			
Cyclic crudes and organics	0.4	Manufg.			
Gas production & distribution (utilities)	0.4	Util.			
Maintenance of nonfarm buildings nec	0.3	Constr.			
Eating & drinking places	0.3	Trade			
Banking	0.3	Fin/R.E.			
Real estate	0.3	Fin/R.E.			
U.S. Postal Service	0.3	Gov't			
Creamery butter	0.2	Manufg.			
Industrial gases	0.2	Manufg.			
Air transportation	0.2	Util.			
Water transportation	0.2	Util.			
State & local government enterprises, nec	0.2	Gov't			
Food products machinery	0.1	Manufg.			
Ice cream & frozen desserts	0.1	Manufg.			
Metal cans	0.1	Manufg.			
Metal foil & leaf	0.1	Manufg.			
Soap & other detergents	0.1	Manufg.			
Royalties	0.1	Fin/R.E.			
Accounting, auditing & bookkeeping	0.1	Services			
Automotive rental & leasing, without drivers	0.1	Services			
Computer & data processing services	0.1	Services			
Electrical repair shops	0.1	Services			
Legal services	0.1	Services			
Management & consulting services & labs	0.1	Services			
Miscellaneous repair shops	0.1	Services			

Source: Benchmark Input-Output Accounts for the U.S. Economy, 1982, U.S. Department of Commerce, Washington, D.C., July 1991. Data, as reported in the source, are organized by the 1977 SIC structure in use in 1982 but have been matched, as closely as is possible, to the 1987 SIC structure used in this book.

OCCUPATIONS EMPLOYED BY SIC 202 - DAIRY PRODUCTS

Occupation	% of Total 1994	Change to 2005	Occupation	% of Total 1994	Change to 2005
Dairy processing equipment workers	9.1	-1.7	Industrial truck & tractor operators	2.2	-11.3
Packaging & filling machine operators	8.1	33.1	Traffic, shipping, & receiving clerks	2.1	-14.6
Truck drivers light & heavy	7.5	-8.5	Maintenance repairers, general utility	2.0	-20.1
Driver/sales workers	5.8	-42.3	General managers & top executives	1.7	-15.8
Helpers, laborers, & material movers nec	4.3	-11.3	Bookkeeping, accounting, & auditing clerks	1.7	-33.4
Blue collar worker supervisors	4.1	-15.0	Machine feeders & offbearers	1.6	-20.1
Precision food & tobacco workers nec	4.0	6.5	Science & mathematics technicians	1.5	-11.3
Machine operators nec	3.7	-21.8	General office clerks	1.4	-24.3
Hand packers & packagers	3.5	-23.9	Inspectors, testers, & graders, precision	1.2	-11.2
Freight, stock, & material movers, hand	3.4	-29.0	Industrial production managers	1.2	-11.2
Industrial machinery mechanics	2.6	-2.4	Secretaries, ex legal & medical	1.1	-19.2
Sales & related workers nec	2.2	-11.3			

Source: Industry-Occupation Matrix, Bureau of Labor Statistics. These data relate to one or more 3-digit SIC industry groups rather than to a single 4-digit SIC. The change reported for each occupation to the year 2005 is a percent of growth or decline as estimated by the Bureau of Labor Statistics. The abbreviation nec stands for 'not elsewhere classified'.

LOCATION BY STATE AND REGIONAL CONCENTRATION

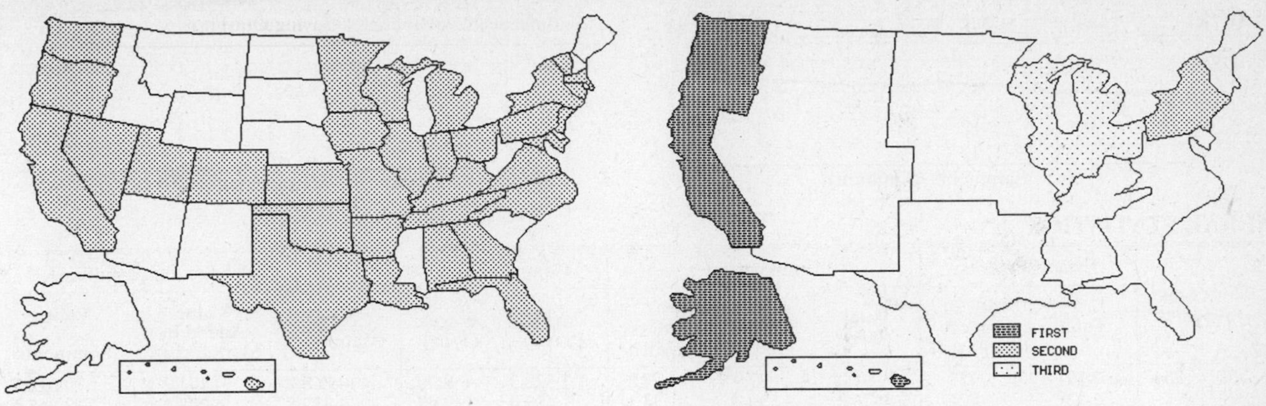

INDUSTRY DATA BY STATE

State	Establish-ments	Shipments			Employment				Cost as % of Shipments	Investment per Employee ($)
		Total ($ mil)	% of U.S.	Per Establ.	Total Number	% of U.S.	Per Establ.	Wages ($/hour)		
California	70	955.5	18.1	13.6	2,800	13.4	40	13.55	57.1	8,036
Pennsylvania	37	382.8	7.2	10.3	1,600	7.7	43	11.70	66.4	14,063
Texas	14	280.9	5.3	20.1	1,600	7.7	114	9.05	55.8	6,625
New York	32	229.9	4.3	7.2	1,400	6.7	44	9.84	62.1	4,429
Indiana	13	170.0	3.2	13.1	400	1.9	31	10.86	56.8	12,500
Maryland	9	148.4	2.8	16.5	600	2.9	67	12.63	61.3	4,167
North Carolina	11	146.2	2.8	13.3	500	2.4	45	9.57	72.5	-
Wisconsin	14	71.6	1.4	5.1	400	1.9	29	10.67	60.6	3,750
Florida	13	43.7	0.8	3.4	300	1.4	23	10.50	91.5	7,667
Tennessee	5	40.9	0.8	8.2	300	1.4	60	8.67	83.6	2,333
Utah	7	26.3	0.5	3.8	200	1.0	29	9.50	69.6	3,000
Hawaii	8	12.6	0.2	1.6	200	1.0	25	13.00	58.7	-
Massachusetts	29	(D)	-	-	1,750 *	8.4	60	-	-	-
Ohio	23	(D)	-	-	750 *	3.6	33	-	-	7,867
New Jersey	19	(D)	-	-	375 *	1.8	20	-	-	-
Washington	15	(D)	-	-	375 *	1.8	25	-	-	6,667
Illinois	14	(D)	-	-	1,750 *	8.4	125	-	-	8,571
Connecticut	13	(D)	-	-	375 *	1.8	29	-	-	-
Michigan	13	(D)	-	-	375 *	1.8	29	-	-	-
Iowa	9	(D)	-	-	750 *	3.6	83	-	-	-
Colorado	7	(D)	-	-	175 *	0.8	25	-	-	-
Missouri	7	(D)	-	-	375 *	1.8	54	-	-	-
Alabama	5	(D)	-	-	750 *	3.6	150	-	-	-
Minnesota	5	(D)	-	-	750 *	3.6	150	-	-	-
Oklahoma	5	(D)	-	-	375 *	1.8	75	-	-	-
Virginia	5	(D)	-	-	175 *	0.8	35	-	-	-
Arkansas	4	(D)	-	-	375 *	1.8	94	-	-	-
Georgia	4	(D)	-	-	750 *	3.6	188	-	-	4,933
Louisiana	4	(D)	-	-	175 *	0.8	44	-	-	-
Vermont	4	(D)	-	-	375 *	1.8	94	-	-	-
Kansas	3	(D)	-	-	175 *	0.8	58	-	-	-
Kentucky	2	(D)	-	-	175 *	0.8	88	-	-	-
Nevada	2	(D)	-	-	375 *	1.8	188	-	-	-
Oregon	2	(D)	-	-	175 *	0.8	88	-	-	-

Source: 1992 *Economic Census*. The states are in descending order of shipments or establishments (if shipment data are missing for the majority). The symbol (D) appears when data are withheld to prevent disclosure of competitive information. States marked with (D) are sorted by number of establishments. A dash (-) indicates that the data element cannot be calculated; * indicates the midpoint of a range.

2026 - FLUID MILK

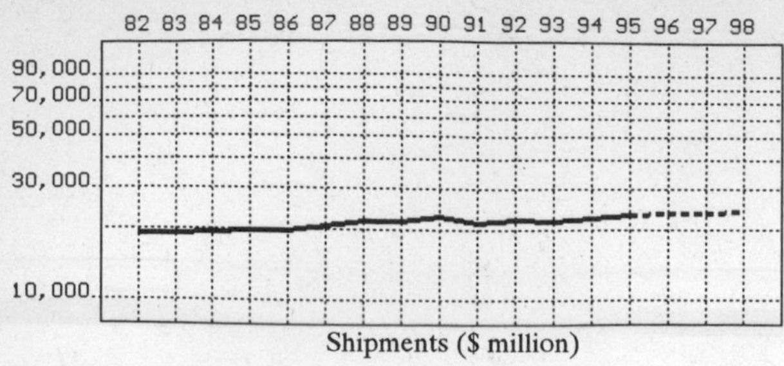

Shipments ($ million)

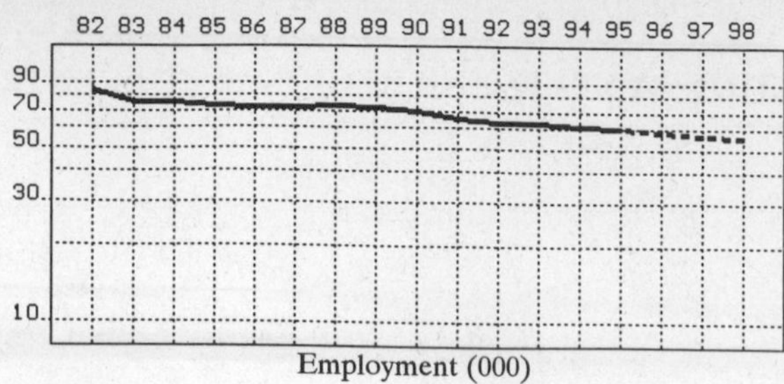

Employment (000)

GENERAL STATISTICS

Year	Companies	Establishments: Total	Establishments: with 20 or more employees	Employment: Total (000)	Production Workers (000)	Production Hours (Mil)	Compensation: Payroll ($ mil)	Compensation: Wages ($/hr)	Production ($ million): Cost of Materials	Value Added by Manufacture	Value of Shipments	Capital Invest.
1982	854	1,191	752	84.0	37.9	77.8	1,522.5	8.90	14,868.2	4,171.2	19,027.7	367.3
1983		1,128	721	76.3	36.3	74.1	1,468.9	9.48	14,472.5	4,398.0	18,865.4	258.3
1984		1,065	690	75.8	37.1	74.6	1,525.5	9.62	14,800.1	4,550.2	19,351.8	265.3
1985		1,001	658	73.2	36.1	74.3	1,572.3	10.15	14,731.3	4,952.5	19,679.2	322.3
1986		936	628	71.4	34.8	71.9	1,590.2	10.42	14,279.2	5,192.6	19,473.7	297.8
1987	654	946	626	72.4	36.2	74.2	1,681.3	10.63	15,189.6	5,426.2	20,590.5	341.7
1988		894	591	73.0	37.1	76.6	1,777.7	10.98	15,745.7	5,758.9	21,502.2	380.3
1989		850	582	71.2	36.1	74.5	1,820.3	11.49	16,215.4	5,454.0	21,630.2	418.8
1990		803	559	69.3	34.0	71.6	1,831.8	12.08	16,921.5	5,779.9	22,703.6	340.4
1991		779	538	65.5	32.3	69.5	1,840.1	12.47	15,476.5	5,656.1	21,137.1	325.8
1992	525	746	506	63.4	32.5	70.8	1,841.1	12.63	15,973.8	5,965.6	21,926.9	362.5
1993		722	494	63.2	32.9	71.3	1,832.9	12.69	15,734.6	6,065.3	21,806.0	335.6
1994		651P	464P	61.6	30.9	68.8	1,850.4	12.72	16,394.1	6,088.1	22,474.3	358.2
1995		610P	441P	60.1P	31.5P	69.3P	1,953.3P	13.49P	16,774.6P	6,229.4P	22,995.9P	370.8P
1996		568P	419P	58.6P	31.0P	68.8P	1,988.9P	13.83P	17,005.3P	6,315.1P	23,312.1P	375.8P
1997		527P	396P	57.0P	30.5P	68.2P	2,024.4P	14.17P	17,236.0P	6,400.7P	23,628.4P	380.7P
1998		485P	373P	55.5P	30.0P	67.7P	2,060.0P	14.51P	17,466.6P	6,486.4P	23,944.6P	385.6P

Sources: 1982, 1987, 1992 *Economic Census*; *Annual Survey of Manufactures*, 83-86, 88-91, 93-94. Establishment counts for non-Census years are from *County Business Patterns*; establishment values for 83-84 are extrapolations. 'P's show projections by the editors. Industries reclassified in 87 will not have data for prior years.

INDICES OF CHANGE

Year	Companies	Establishments: Total	Establishments: with 20 or more employees	Employment: Total (000)	Production Workers (000)	Production Hours (Mil)	Compensation: Payroll ($ mil)	Compensation: Wages ($/hr)	Production ($ million): Cost of Materials	Value Added by Manufacture	Value of Shipments	Capital Invest.
1982	163	160	149	132	117	110	83	70	93	70	87	101
1983		151	142	120	112	105	80	75	91	74	86	71
1984		143	136	120	114	105	83	76	93	76	88	73
1985		134	130	115	111	105	85	80	92	83	90	89
1986		125	124	113	107	102	86	83	89	87	89	82
1987	125	127	124	114	111	105	91	84	95	91	94	94
1988		120	117	115	114	108	97	87	99	97	98	105
1989		114	115	112	111	105	99	91	102	91	99	116
1990		108	110	109	105	101	99	96	106	97	104	94
1991		104	106	103	99	98	100	99	97	95	96	90
1992	100	100	100	100	100	100	100	100	100	100	100	100
1993		97	98	100	101	101	100	100	99	102	99	93
1994		87P	92P	97	95	97	101	101	103	102	102	99
1995		82P	87P	95P	97P	98P	106P	107P	105P	104P	105P	102P
1996		76P	83P	92P	95P	97P	108P	109P	106P	106P	106P	104P
1997		71P	78P	90P	94P	96P	110P	112P	108P	107P	108P	105P
1998		65P	74P	88P	92P	96P	112P	115P	109P	109P	109P	106P

Sources: Same as General Statistics. Values reflect change from the base year, 1992. Values above 100 mean greater than 92, values below 100 mean less than 92, and a value of 100 in the 82-91 or 93-98 period means same as 92. 'P's mark projections by the editors.

SELECTED RATIOS

For 1994	Avg. of All Manufact.	Analyzed Industry	Index
Employees per Establishment	49	95	193
Payroll per Establishment	1,500,273	2,841,008	189
Payroll per Employee	30,620	30,039	98
Production Workers per Establishment	34	47	138
Wages per Establishment	853,319	1,343,638	157
Wages per Production Worker	24,861	28,322	114
Hours per Production Worker	2,056	2,227	108
Wages per Hour	12.09	12.72	105
Value Added per Establishment	4,602,255	9,347,352	203
Value Added per Employee	93,930	98,833	105

For 1994	Avg. of All Manufact.	Analyzed Industry	Index
Value Added per Production Worker	134,084	197,026	147
Cost per Establishment	5,045,178	25,170,647	499
Cost per Employee	102,970	266,138	258
Cost per Production Worker	146,988	530,553	361
Shipments per Establishment	9,576,895	34,505,869	360
Shipments per Employee	195,460	364,843	187
Shipments per Production Worker	279,017	727,324	261
Investment per Establishment	321,011	549,962	171
Investment per Employee	6,552	5,815	89
Investment per Production Worker	9,352	11,592	124

Sources: Same as General Statistics. The 'Average of All Manufacturing' column represents the average of all manufacturing industries reported for the most recent complete year available. The Index shows the relationship between the Average and the Analyzed Industry. For example, 100 means that they are equal; 500 that the Analyzed Industry is five times the average; 50 means that the Analyzed Industry is half the national average. The abbreviation 'na' is used to show that data are 'not available'.

LEADING COMPANIES Number shown: **75** Total sales ($ mil): **18,806** Total employment (000): **86.0**

Company Name	Address				CEO Name	Phone	Co. Type	Sales ($ mil)	Empl. (000)
Borden Inc	180 E Broad St	Columbus	OH	43215	CR Kidder	614-225-4000	P	5,626	32.4
Dean Foods Co	3600 N River Rd	Franklin Park	IL	60131	Howard M Dean	312-625-6200	P	2,431	12.1
Wessanen USA Inc	1 Daily Way	Verona	PA	15147	Richard A Thorne	412-826-6676	S	950	4.5
Dairymen Inc	10140 Linn Station	Louisville	KY	40223	James E Muller	502-426-6455	R	680*	3.2
Flav-O-Rich Inc	10140 Linn Station	Louisville	KY	40223	Steve G Conerly	502-426-6455	S	530*	2.5
California Cooperative Creamery	PO Box 871	Petaluma	CA	94953	Alfonse Bono	707-763-1931	R	500	0.4
Safeway Inc	2800 Ygnacio Val	Walnut Creek	CA	94598	Steve Armstrong	510-944-4616	D	450	2.0
Dannon Company Inc	120 White Plains Rd	Tarrytown	NY	10591	Patrick Gournay	914-697-9700	S	405	0.6
Michigan Milk Producers Assoc	PO Box 8002	Novi	MI	48376	Walt Wosje	810-474-6672	R	400	0.3
Dairy Enterprises Inc	750 Union Av	Union	NJ	07083	James Schreiben	908-851-5180	R	375	0.8
HP Hood Inc	500 Rutherford Av	Boston	MA	02129	Robert Keller	617-242-0600	S	370*	1.8
Swiss Valley Farms Co	PO Box 4493	Davenport	IA	52808	Carl Zurborg	319-391-3341	R	300	0.7
Roberts Dairy Co	PO Box 1435	Omaha	NE	68101	Ron Richardson	402-344-4321	J	250	0.5
San Joaquin Valley	PO Box 2198	Los Banos	CA	93635	Paul Caetana	209-826-4901	R	250	0.1
Tuscan Dairy Farms Inc	750 Union Av	Union	NJ	07083	James Schreiben	908-851-5180	S	250	0.6
Upstate Milk Cooperatives Inc	7115 W Main St	Le Roy	NY	14482	Bob Hall	716-768-2247	R	230	0.7
Golden Guernsey Dairy Coop	2100 N Mayfair Rd	Milwaukee	WI	53226	Joe W Weis	414-476-5611	R	220	0.3
Marigold Foods Inc	2929 University S	Minneapolis	MN	55414	James Green	612-331-3775	S	210*	1.0
United Dairy Farmers Inc	3955 Montgomery	Cincinnati	OH	45212	Robert Lindner Jr	513-396-8700	R	210	3.0
Golden Gallon Inc	PO Box 180603	Chattanooga	TN	37406	Ron Durham	615-899-3800	R	180*	0.9
Hiland Dairy Co	1133 E Kearney St	Springfield	MO	65802	Lynn Oller	417-862-9311	J	180*	0.9
Garelick Farms Inc	PO Box 289	Franklin	MA	02038	PM Bernon	508-528-9000	R	170*	0.8
Valley	PO Box 218	Mt Crawford	VA	22841	Fred H Scott	703-434-7328	R	163	0.5
Danish Creamery Association	PO Box 11865	Fresno	CA	93775	Jim A Gomes	209-233-5154	R	150*	0.1
Mayfield Dairy Farms Inc	PO Box 310	Athens	TN	37371	Howard Dean	615-745-2151	S	150	1.0
Barber Dairies Inc	36 Barber Ct	Birmingham	AL	35209	WP Langston	205-942-2351	R	140	1.0
Barber Pure Milk Co	36 Barber Ct	Birmingham	AL	35209	WP Langston	205-942-2351	D	140*	0.7
Berkeley Farms Inc	PO Box 8465	Emeryville	CA	94662	John Sabatte	510-420-5600	R	130	0.5
TG Lee Foods Inc	315 N Bumby Av	Orlando	FL	32802	Darryl Mahan	407-894-4941	S	120*	0.6
Tillamook Cty Creamery	PO Box 313	Tillamook	OR	97141	Harold Schild	503-842-4481	R	115	0.3
Reiter Dairy Inc	1415 W Waterloo	Akron	OH	44314	Rollin S Reiter	216-745-1123	S	110	0.5
Cass-Clay Creamery Inc	PO Box 2947	Fargo	ND	58108	Don Ommodt	701-232-1566	R	100	0.5
McArthur Dairy Inc	500 Sawgrass Corp	Sunrise	FL	33325	Richard Hills	305-846-1234	S	100*	0.5
Turner Dairies Inc	653 Turner Ln	Covington	TN	38019	PA Turner	901-476-2643	R	100	0.6
Anderson Erickson Dairy Co	2420 University Av	Des Moines	IA	50317	JW Erickson	515-265-2521	R	85*	0.4
Fairmont-Zarda Dairy	3805 Van Brunt	Kansas City	MO	64128	Marty Duffner	816-921-7370	D	81	0.3
Instantwhip Foods Inc	PO Box 333	Columbus	OH	43216	CJ Smith	614-488-2536	R	80*	0.4
Purity Dairies Inc	360 Murfreesboro	Nashville	TN	37210	F Miles Ezell Jr	615-244-1900	R	80*	0.4
Johanna Dairies Inc	PO Box 272	Flemington	NJ	08822	Robert Faechina	908-788-2200	S	74	0.4
Broughton Foods Co	PO Box 656	Marietta	OH	45750	Samuel R Cook	614-373-4121	P	74	0.4
New England Dairies Inc	255 Homestead Av	Hartford	CT	06112	Frank A Starvel	203-241-2700	R	73	0.3
Gustafsons Dairy Inc	PO Box 338	Green Cv Spgs	FL	32043	Edwin S Gustafson	904-284-3750	R	70*	0.3
Sinton Dairy Foods Company	PO Box 578	Co Springs	CO	80901	John Haberkorn	719-633-3821	R	70	0.3
Steuben Foods Inc	155-04 Liberty Av	Jamaica	NY	11433	Kenneth Schlossberg	718-291-3333	R	70	0.2
Green Spring Dairy Inc	2701 Loch Raven	Baltimore	MD	21218	GF Blanchfield	410-235-4477	S	67*	0.3
Bareman Dairy Inc	234 Charles Dr	Holland	MI	49424	S Bareman	616-396-0306	R	65*	0.2
Friendship Dairies Inc	County Roads 20	Friendship	NY	14739	Joseph Murgolo	716-973-3031	S	65	0.2
H Meyer Dairy Co	John & Elliott St	Cincinnati	OH	45215	David R Meyer	513-948-8811	R	60	0.2
Maplehurst Farms Inc	PO Box 41106	Indianapolis	IN	46241	Ralph Dischler	317-244-2481	R	60	0.3
Sani-Dairy	408 Franklin St	Johnstown	PA	15901	Daniel A Kresko	814-533-2500	D	60	0.3
Smith Brothers Farms Inc	27441 68th Av	Kent	WA	98032	Dan P Smith	206-852-1000	R	60	0.3
Louis Trauth Dairy Inc	PO Box 1770	Newport	KY	41071	David E Trauth	606-431-7553	R	56*	0.2
Southern Belle Dairy Co	PO Box D	Somerset	KY	42502	MP Shearer	606-679-1131	R	55	0.3
Oberlin Farms Dairy Inc	3068 W 106th St	Cleveland	OH	44111	R Dzurec	216-671-2300	R	53	0.2
Galliker Dairy Company Inc	PO Box 159	Johnstown	PA	15907	Louis G Galliker	814-266-8702	R	52*	0.2
Flav-O-Rich Inc	PO Box 560	Wilkesboro	NC	28697	Ed Kubale	910-838-3125	D	50*	0.3
Goshen Dairy Inc	1026 Cookson SE	New Philad	OH	44663	William Bichsel Jr	216-339-1959	R	50	0.2
Roberts Dairy Co	PO Box 4866	Des Moines	IA	50306	R Richardson	515-243-6211	D	46	0.2
Coleman Dairy Inc	PO Box 4178	Little Rock	AR	72214	WC Coleman	501-565-1551	R	43	0.3
Meadow Gold Dairies of Hawaii	925 Cedar St	Honolulu	HI	96814	Jay Wilson	808-949-6161	S	42*	0.3
Meadow Brook Dairy Corp	2365 Buffalo Rd	Erie	PA	16510	William J Riley	814-899-3191	R	40	0.1
Oakhurst Dairy	364 Forest Av	Portland	ME	04101	Stanley T Bennett II	207-772-7468	R	38	0.2
Lansing Dairy Inc	PO Box 10210	Lansing	MI	48901	Greg McNeil	517-485-7263	S	36	0.2
Miller Corp	PO Box 267	Cambridge City	IN	47327	John Miller	317-478-4101	R	33	0.2
Holland Dairies Inc	300 Main St	Holland	IN	47541	Earl Carter	812-536-2310	R	32*	0.2
Alpenrose Dairy Inc	PO Box 25030	Portland	OR	97225	Carl Cadonau	503-244-1133	R	31*	0.2
Carolina Dairy Corp	2731 S Memorial Dr	Greenville	NC	27834	Thomas L Edwards	919-756-1185	R	31*	0.2
Elmhurst Milk and Cream Co	155-25 Styler Rd	Jamaica	NY	11433	Henry Schwartz	718-526-3442	R	31	0.2
Foremost Dairies-Hawaii	2277 Kamehameha	Honolulu	HI	96819		808-841-5831	R	31*	0.2
Weeks	330 N State St	Concord	NH	03301	David A French	603-225-3379	D	31*	0.2
East Side Jersey Dairy Inc	PO Box 151540	Anderson	IN	46015	Douglas Banning	317-649-1261	S	30	0.2
Schnuck's Midstate Dairy	6040 N Lindberg	Hazelwood	MO	63042	Dale Parsons	314-731-1150	D	30	0.1
UC Milk Company Inc	PO Box M	Madisonville	KY	42431	William M Corum	502-821-7221	R	29	0.2
Hastings Coop Creamery Co	PO Box 217	Hastings	MN	55033	John T Cook	612-437-9414	R	29*	<0.1
George Benz and Sons Inc	5th & Minnesota St	St Paul	MN	55101	George Benz	612-224-1351	R	28*	0.1

Source: *Ward's Business Directory of U.S. Private and Public Companies*, Volumes 1 and 2, 1996. The company type code used is as follows: P - Public, R - Private, S - Subsidiary, D - Division, J - Joint Venture, A - Affiliate, G - Group. Sales are in millions of dollars, employees are in thousands. An asterisk (*) indicates an estimated sales volume. The symbol < stands for 'less than'. Company names and addresses are truncated, in some cases, to fit into the available space.

MATERIALS CONSUMED

Material		Quantity	Delivered Cost ($ million)
Materials, ingredients, containers, and supplies		(X)	13,843.7
Whole milk	mil cwt	631.6	9,263.1
Fluid skim milk	mil cwt	14.4*	220.2
Cream	mil cwt	4.7	265.8
Butter	mil lb	(S)	24.5
Condensed and evaporated milk	mil lb	215.4	80.9
Dry milk	mil lb	143.2**	115.8
Natural cheese, other than cottage cheese	mil lb	10.1*	11.5
Ice cream mixes	mil gal	20.0*	46.4
Sherbet mixes	mil gal	3.5	5.5
Ice milk mixes	mil gal	5.5*	10.8
Frozen yogurt mixes	mil gal	2.1*	5.3
Fats and oils, all types (purchased as such)	mil lb	70.1*	25.1
High fructose corn syrup (HFCS)(in terms of solids)	mil lb	737.6*	88.1
Crystalline fructose (dry fructose)	mil lb	18.7*	3.2
Dextrose and corn syrup, including corn syrup solids (in terms of dry weight)	mil lb	153.7*	21.3
Sugar, cane and beet (in terms of sugar solids)	1,000 s tons	185.7	68.5
Whey, liquid, concentrated, dried; and modified whey products	mil lb	105.2**	40.0
Casein and caseinates	mil lb	(S)	7.2
Chocolate (compounds, cocoa, chocolate liquor, coatings, chocolate flavoring, etc.)	mil lb	73.1*	55.0
Flavorings (natural, imitation, etc.), except chocolate		(X)	272.8
Plastics resins consumed in the form of granules, pellets, powders, liquids, etc.	mil lb	514.3*	176.8
Packaging paper and plastics film, coated and laminated		(X)	139.9
Bags; plastics, foil, and coated paper		(X)	23.2
Plastics products consumed in the form of sheets, rods, tubes, film, and other shapes		(X)	27.0
Glass containers		(X)	4.1
Plastics containers		(X)	337.3
Paperboard containers, boxes, and corrugated paperboard		(X)	504.3
Metal cans, can lids and ends		(X)	22.2
All other materials and components, parts, containers, and supplies		(X)	856.1
Materials, ingredients, containers, and supplies, nsk		(X)	1,121.9

Source: 1992 *Economic Census*. Explanation of symbols used: (D): Withheld to avoid disclosure of competitive data; na: Not available; (S): Withheld because statistical norms were not met; (X): Not applicable; (Z): Less than half the unit shown; nec: Not elsewhere classified; nsk: Not specified by kind; - : zero; * : 10-19 percent estimated; ** : 20-29 percent estimated.

PRODUCT SHARE DETAILS

Product or Product Class	% Share
Fluid milk	100.00
Bulk fluid milk and cream	16.32
Fluid whole milk, bulk sales	52.71
Fluid skim milk, bulk sales	4.53
Fluid cream and buttermilk, bulk sales	34.25
Other bulk fluid milk and cream (eggnog, lowfat, etc.)	4.60
Bulk fluid milk and cream, nsk	3.91
Packaged fluid milk and related products, including cartons, bottles, cans, and dispenser cans	63.17
Fluid whole milk, packaged (including U.H.T.)	37.85
Low fat milk, packaged (including U.H.T.)	38.70
Skim milk, packaged (including U.H.T.)	10.13
Heavy cream, packaged (whipping cream containing 36 percent butterfat or more)	1.73
Light cream, packaged (coffee cream containing less than 36 percent butterfat)	0.70
Sour cream, unflavored, packaged	3.16
Half and half, packaged	2.56
Whipped topping, butterfat base, packaged	0.62
Packaged fluid milk and related products, including cartons, bottles, cans, and dispenser cans, nsk	4.55
Cottage cheese (including bakers', pot, and farmers' cheese)	4.14
Yogurt, except frozen	5.37
Perishable dairy product substitutes	1.28
Perishable dairy product substitute flavored dips	12.12
Perishable whipped topping, nonbutterfat base (including pressure can type)	19.88
Perishable dairy product substitute coffee whiteners	25.71
Perishable sour cream substitutes	5.45
Perishable substitute dairy flavored drinks (chocolate drink, etc.)	16.02
Other perishable dairy product substitutes	19.34
Perishable dairy product substitutes, nsk	1.43
Other packaged milk products, not elsewhere classified	4.77
Flavored sour cream dips	7.78
Flavored milks (chocolate milk, etc.)	56.09
Other milk products (eggnog, buttermilk, acidophilus milk, reconstituted milk, etc.)	34.50
Other packaged milk products, nec, nsk	1.62
Fluid milk, nsk	4.93

Source: 1992 *Economic Census*. The values shown are percent of total shipments in an industry. Values of indented subcategories are summed in the main heading. The symbol (D) appears when data are withheld to prevent disclosure of competitive information. The abbreviation nsk stands for 'not specified by kind' and nec for 'not elsewhere classified'.

INPUTS AND OUTPUTS FOR FLUID MILK

Economic Sector or Industry Providing Inputs	%	Sector	Economic Sector or Industry Buying Outputs	%	Sector
Dairy farm products	60.8	Agric.	Personal consumption expenditures	53.6	
Fluid milk	14.0	Manufg.	Fluid milk	11.2	Manufg.
Paperboard containers & boxes	4.0	Manufg.	Eating & drinking places	8.7	Trade
Advertising	3.9	Services	Creamery butter	6.0	Manufg.
Wholesale trade	2.4	Trade	Cheese, natural & processed	5.6	Manufg.
Condensed & evaporated milk	2.1	Manufg.	S/L Govt. purch., elem. & secondary education	4.4	S/L Govt
Miscellaneous plastics products	1.8	Manufg.	Ice cream & frozen desserts	2.9	Manufg.
Electric services (utilities)	1.2	Util.	Condensed & evaporated milk	2.2	Manufg.
Food preparations, nec	1.0	Manufg.	Hospitals	1.3	Services
Meat animals	0.8	Agric.	Residential care	0.6	Services
Sugar	0.8	Manufg.	S/L Govt. purch., health & hospitals	0.6	S/L Govt
Metal barrels, drums, & pails	0.7	Manufg.	Change in business inventories	0.4	In House
Plastics materials & resins	0.7	Manufg.	S/L Govt. purch., higher education	0.4	S/L Govt
Gas production & distribution (utilities)	0.6	Util.	Elementary & secondary schools	0.3	Services
Petroleum refining	0.4	Manufg.	Nursing & personal care facilities	0.3	Services
U.S. Postal Service	0.4	Gov't	Social services, nec	0.3	Services
Communications, except radio & TV	0.3	Util.	S/L Govt. purch., correction	0.3	S/L Govt
Motor freight transportation & warehousing	0.3	Util.	Exports	0.2	Foreign
Banking	0.3	Fin/R.E.	Child day care services	0.1	Services
Equipment rental & leasing services	0.3	Services	Federal Government enterprises nec	0.1	Gov't
Maintenance of nonfarm buildings nec	0.2	Constr.			
Ball & roller bearings	0.2	Manufg.			
Chocolate & cocoa products	0.2	Manufg.			
Metal cans	0.2	Manufg.			
Eating & drinking places	0.2	Trade			
Soap & other detergents	0.1	Manufg.			
Real estate	0.1	Fin/R.E.			
State & local government enterprises, nec	0.1	Gov't			

Source: Benchmark Input-Output Accounts for the U.S. Economy, 1982, U.S. Department of Commerce, Washington, D.C., July 1991. Data, as reported in the source, are organized by the 1977 SIC structure in use in 1982 but have been matched, as closely as is possible, to the 1987 SIC structure used in this book.

OCCUPATIONS EMPLOYED BY SIC 202 - DAIRY PRODUCTS

Occupation	% of Total 1994	Change to 2005	Occupation	% of Total 1994	Change to 2005
Dairy processing equipment workers	9.1	-1.7	Industrial truck & tractor operators	2.2	-11.3
Packaging & filling machine operators	8.1	33.1	Traffic, shipping, & receiving clerks	2.1	-14.6
Truck drivers light & heavy	7.5	-8.5	Maintenance repairers, general utility	2.0	-20.1
Driver/sales workers	5.8	-42.3	General managers & top executives	1.7	-15.8
Helpers, laborers, & material movers nec	4.3	-11.3	Bookkeeping, accounting, & auditing clerks	1.7	-33.4
Blue collar worker supervisors	4.1	-15.0	Machine feeders & offbearers	1.6	-20.1
Precision food & tobacco workers nec	4.0	6.5	Science & mathematics technicians	1.5	-11.3
Machine operators nec	3.7	-21.8	General office clerks	1.4	-24.3
Hand packers & packagers	3.5	-23.9	Inspectors, testers, & graders, precision	1.2	-11.2
Freight, stock, & material movers, hand	3.4	-29.0	Industrial production managers	1.2	-11.2
Industrial machinery mechanics	2.6	-2.4	Secretaries, ex legal & medical	1.1	-19.2
Sales & related workers nec	2.2	-11.3			

Source: Industry-Occupation Matrix, Bureau of Labor Statistics. These data relate to one or more 3-digit SIC industry groups rather than to a single 4-digit SIC. The change reported for each occupation to the year 2005 is a percent of growth or decline as estimated by the Bureau of Labor Statistics. The abbreviation nec stands for 'not elsewhere classified'.

LOCATION BY STATE AND REGIONAL CONCENTRATION

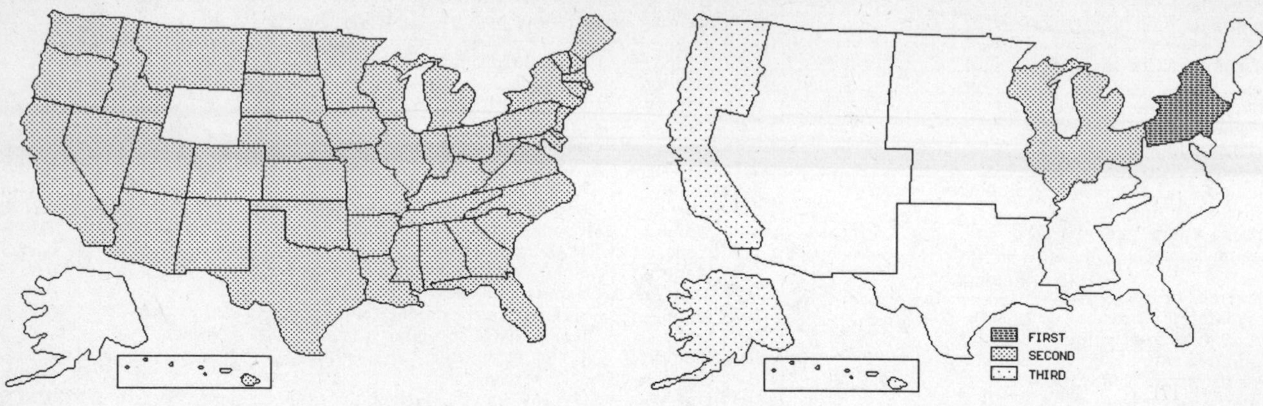

INDUSTRY DATA BY STATE

State	Establish-ments	Shipments			Employment				Cost as % of Shipments	Investment per Employee ($)
		Total ($ mil)	% of U.S.	Per Establ.	Total Number	% of U.S.	Per Establ.	Wages ($/hour)		
California	59	3,312.1	15.1	56.1	6,700	10.6	114	16.36	73.5	8,090
New York	61	1,343.6	6.1	22.0	3,700	5.8	61	12.57	82.3	7,054
Texas	36	1,290.3	5.9	35.8	4,200	6.6	117	10.31	73.8	6,929
Ohio	31	1,243.4	5.7	40.1	3,000	4.7	97	12.64	66.4	8,600
Pennsylvania	59	1,231.0	5.6	20.9	4,100	6.5	69	12.19	73.2	5,537
New Jersey	14	961.5	4.4	68.7	2,100	3.3	150	15.83	75.7	5,095
Florida	20	867.7	4.0	43.4	2,400	3.8	120	10.85	69.2	5,542
Michigan	24	855.4	3.9	35.6	2,400	3.8	100	13.10	70.4	8,667
Illinois	28	754.7	3.4	27.0	1,800	2.8	64	13.80	71.6	5,500
Wisconsin	22	751.8	3.4	34.2	1,200	1.9	55	13.11	77.3	6,167
Massachusetts	19	695.8	3.2	36.6	2,500	3.9	132	14.73	71.3	7,200
Kentucky	12	551.1	2.5	45.9	1,600	2.5	133	10.78	74.5	6,500
Tennessee	8	539.3	2.5	67.4	1,600	2.5	200	9.67	58.3	6,313
North Carolina	14	493.9	2.3	35.3	1,500	2.4	107	8.71	72.8	4,933
Indiana	14	432.7	2.0	30.9	1,500	2.4	107	10.79	75.3	-
Iowa	14	430.8	2.0	30.8	1,100	1.7	79	12.64	68.8	4,364
Minnesota	40	428.2	2.0	10.7	1,200	1.9	30	13.54	72.0	4,917
Maryland	12	400.3	1.8	33.4	1,100	1.7	92	14.27	73.1	3,727
Oregon	22	398.9	1.8	18.1	1,100	1.7	50	14.64	75.5	6,091
Virginia	13	396.4	1.8	30.5	1,400	2.2	108	12.94	70.3	-
Washington	18	368.8	1.7	20.5	900	1.4	50	15.38	73.1	2,667
Arizona	9	328.5	1.5	36.5	800	1.3	89	12.80	72.0	3,000
Alabama	11	319.0	1.5	29.0	1,600	2.5	145	8.73	73.3	3,438
Missouri	9	312.9	1.4	34.8	1,100	1.7	122	12.00	82.8	-
Georgia	11	213.8	1.0	19.4	900	1.4	82	12.30	79.0	2,667
Utah	7	161.7	0.7	23.1	500	0.8	71	10.00	72.6	-
Connecticut	8	142.6	0.7	17.8	600	0.9	75	11.00	72.2	6,167
Arkansas	7	139.6	0.6	19.9	700	1.1	100	10.20	73.9	2,429
Maine	7	128.4	0.6	18.3	400	0.6	57	17.33	70.8	5,000
Hawaii	7	110.2	0.5	15.7	400	0.6	57	12.50	60.7	-
Montana	8	98.9	0.5	12.4	400	0.6	50	15.00	72.1	-
New Hampshire	7	86.1	0.4	12.3	300	0.5	43	9.00	79.1	3,333
Kansas	4	67.8	0.3	17.0	200	0.3	50	9.50	80.2	-
Louisiana	13	(D)	-	-	1,750 *	2.8	135	-	-	1,600
Vermont	13	(D)	-	-	750 *	1.2	58	-	-	-
Colorado	12	(D)	-	-	1,750 *	2.8	146	-	-	2,571
Idaho	8	(D)	-	-	375 *	0.6	47	-	-	-
Nebraska	8	(D)	-	-	750 *	1.2	94	-	-	2,400
Oklahoma	8	(D)	-	-	750 *	1.2	94	-	-	-
Mississippi	7	(D)	-	-	750 *	1.2	107	-	-	-
North Dakota	7	(D)	-	-	375 *	0.6	54	-	-	-
South Carolina	7	(D)	-	-	750 *	1.2	107	-	-	-
South Dakota	6	(D)	-	-	375 *	0.6	63	-	-	-
Delaware	4	(D)	-	-	175 *	0.3	44	-	-	-
West Virginia	4	(D)	-	-	175 *	0.3	44	-	-	-
New Mexico	3	(D)	-	-	375 *	0.6	125	-	-	-
Nevada	2	(D)	-	-	375 *	0.6	188	-	-	-

Source: 1992 *Economic Census*. The states are in descending order of shipments or establishments (if shipment data are missing for the majority). The symbol (D) appears when data are withheld to prevent disclosure of competitive information. States marked with (D) are sorted by number of establishments. A dash (-) indicates that the data element cannot be calculated; * indicates the midpoint of a range.

2032 - CANNED SPECIALTIES

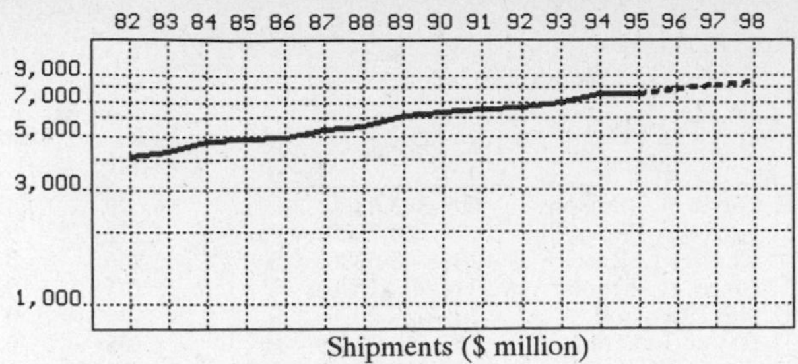

Shipments ($ million)

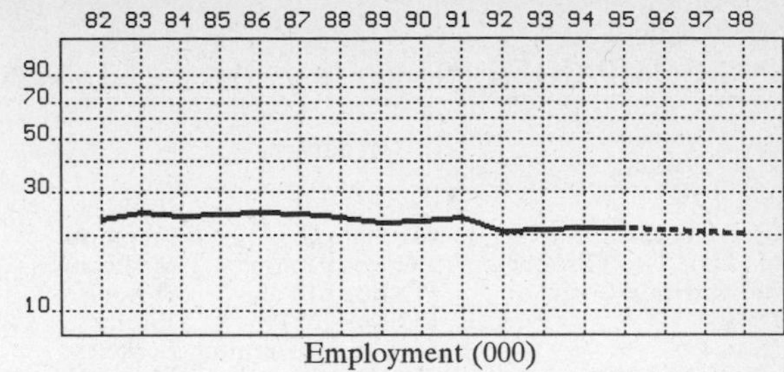

Employment (000)

GENERAL STATISTICS

Year	Com-panies	Establishments		Employment			Compensation		Production ($ million)			
		Total	with 20 or more employees	Total (000)	Production Workers (000)	Production Hours (Mil)	Payroll ($ mil)	Wages ($/hr)	Cost of Materials	Value Added by Manufacture	Value of Shipments	Capital Invest.
1982	171	198	88	23.4	19.0	37.0	392.4	8.04	2,372.0	1,769.3	4,140.8	154.3
1983		195	90	24.8	20.3	40.0	443.8	8.45	2,410.0	1,958.4	4,370.1	79.1
1984		192	92	24.1	19.6	37.9	451.6	9.18	2,631.0	2,158.9	4,784.0	101.4
1985		189	94	24.2	19.7	37.0	476.9	9.92	2,638.4	2,161.2	4,801.7	113.6
1986		184	86	24.7	19.6	38.6	513.2	9.93	2,629.9	2,326.3	4,957.6	178.8
1987	188	211	86	24.5	19.5	38.1	524.8	10.37	2,700.4	2,652.4	5,350.1	144.8
1988		201	84	23.5	18.7	37.7	552.6	11.07	2,863.6	2,687.9	5,551.3	125.0
1989		211	83	22.7	19.0	38.2	560.6	11.25	3,015.1	3,043.1	6,047.5	175.5
1990		202	90	22.9	19.6	39.5	577.0	11.13	3,054.7	3,272.3	6,322.3	251.0
1991		209	88	23.9	19.9	38.9	577.2	11.41	3,068.1	3,408.1	6,474.5	278.6
1992	201	220	76	21.0	17.2	35.5	561.0	12.04	3,057.2	3,617.5	6,662.7	274.7
1993		219	80	21.2	17.4	35.7	575.7	12.39	3,172.4	3,809.1	6,977.6	191.2
1994		219P	80P	21.3	17.5	36.5	597.0	12.40	3,192.1	4,252.7	7,444.6	199.6
1995		221P	79P	21.4P	17.7P	36.7P	630.6P	13.08P	3,242.1P	4,319.3P	7,561.1P	258.9P
1996		224P	78P	21.1P	17.5P	36.6P	646.0P	13.44P	3,357.1P	4,472.5P	7,829.4P	270.9P
1997		226P	77P	20.8P	17.4P	36.4P	661.3P	13.80P	3,472.1P	4,625.7P	8,097.6P	283.0P
1998		229P	76P	20.5P	17.2P	36.3P	676.6P	14.16P	3,587.1P	4,779.0P	8,365.9P	295.1P

Sources: 1982, 1987, 1992 *Economic Census*; *Annual Survey of Manufactures*, 83-86, 88-91, 93-94. Establishment counts for non-Census years are from *County Business Patterns*; establishment values for 83-84 are extrapolations. 'P's show projections by the editors. Industries reclassified in 87 will not have data for prior years.

INDICES OF CHANGE

Year	Com-panies	Establishments		Employment			Compensation		Production ($ million)			
		Total	with 20 or more employees	Total (000)	Production Workers (000)	Production Hours (Mil)	Payroll ($ mil)	Wages ($/hr)	Cost of Materials	Value Added by Manufacture	Value of Shipments	Capital Invest.
1982	85	90	116	111	110	104	70	67	78	49	62	56
1983		89	118	118	118	113	79	70	79	54	66	29
1984		87	121	115	114	107	80	76	86	60	72	37
1985		86	124	115	115	104	85	82	86	60	72	41
1986		84	113	118	114	109	91	82	86	64	74	65
1987	94	96	113	117	113	107	94	86	88	73	80	53
1988		91	111	112	109	106	99	92	94	74	83	46
1989		96	109	108	110	108	100	93	99	84	91	64
1990		92	118	109	114	111	103	92	100	90	95	91
1991		95	116	114	116	110	103	95	100	94	97	101
1992	100	100	100	100	100	100	100	100	100	100	100	100
1993		100	105	101	101	101	103	103	104	105	105	70
1994		99P	106P	101	102	103	106	103	104	118	112	73
1995		101P	104P	102P	103P	103P	112P	109P	106P	119P	113P	94P
1996		102P	103P	100P	102P	103P	115P	112P	110P	124P	118P	99P
1997		103P	102P	99P	101P	103P	118P	115P	114P	128P	122P	103P
1998		104P	101P	98P	100P	102P	121P	118P	117P	132P	126P	107P

Sources: Same as General Statistics. Values reflect change from the base year, 1992. Values above 100 mean greater than 92, values below 100 mean less than 92, and a value of 100 in the 82-91 or 93-98 period means same as 92. 'P's mark projections by the editors.

SELECTED RATIOS

For 1994	Avg. of All Manufact.	Analyzed Industry	Index	For 1994	Avg. of All Manufact.	Analyzed Industry	Index
Employees per Establishment	49	97	199	Value Added per Production Worker	134,084	243,011	181
Payroll per Establishment	1,500,273	2,729,237	182	Cost per Establishment	5,045,178	14,592,963	289
Payroll per Employee	30,620	28,028	92	Cost per Employee	102,970	149,864	146
Production Workers per Establishment	34	80	233	Cost per Production Worker	146,988	182,406	124
Wages per Establishment	853,319	2,069,100	242	Shipments per Establishment	9,576,895	34,033,636	355
Wages per Production Worker	24,861	25,863	104	Shipments per Employee	195,460	349,512	179
Hours per Production Worker	2,056	2,086	101	Shipments per Production Worker	279,017	425,406	152
Wages per Hour	12.09	12.40	103	Investment per Establishment	321,011	912,489	284
Value Added per Establishment	4,602,255	19,441,588	422	Investment per Employee	6,552	9,371	143
Value Added per Employee	93,930	199,657	213	Investment per Production Worker	9,352	11,406	122

Sources: Same as General Statistics. The 'Average of All Manufacturing' column represents the average of all manufacturing industries reported for the most recent complete year available. The Index shows the relationship between the Average and the Analyzed Industry. For example, 100 means that they are equal; 500 that the Analyzed Industry is five times the average; 50 means that the Analyzed Industry is half the national average. The abbreviation 'na' is used to show that data are 'not available'.

LEADING COMPANIES Number shown: **34** Total sales ($ mil): **9,294** Total employment (000): **59.5**

Company Name	Address				CEO Name	Phone	Co. Type	Sales ($ mil)	Empl. (000)
Campbell Soup Co	Campbell Pl	Camden	NJ	08103	David W Johnson	609-342-4800	P	6,690	44.4
Gerber Products Co	445 State St	Fremont	MI	49412	Alfred A Piergallini	616-928-2000	P	1,172	9.2
American Home Food Products	5 Giralda Farms	Madison	NJ	07940	Charles LaRosa	201-660-6300	S	866	3.0
Beech-Nut Nutrition Corp	PO Box 618	St Louis	MO	63188	James A Nichols	314-982-1000	S	145	0.6
Real Fresh Inc	PO Box 1551	Visalia	CA	93279	Jim Hopwood	209-627-2070	S	35	0.1
Vanee Foods Co	5418 W McDermott	Berkeley	IL	60163	A Van Eekeren	708-449-7300	R	35*	0.2
Dean Pickle & Specialty	1430 Western Av	Plymouth	IN	46563	Gary Edgecomb	219-936-4061	S	33	0.2
Golden Harvest Foods Inc	1301 39th St N	Fargo	ND	58102	Bob Campanale	701-282-2300	S	30*	0.2
Venice Maid Foods	PO Box 1505	Vineland	NJ	08360	Dale Guhr	609-691-2100	D	30	0.2
Border Foods Inc	PO Box 751	Deming	NM	88031	M Steinman	505-546-8863	R	25	<0.1
Shelf Stable Foods Inc	10825 Kenwood Rd	Cincinnati	OH	45242	John McQuay	513-794-9800	S	25*	0.2
Juanita's Foods	PO Box 847	Wilmington	CA	90748	George De La Torre	310-834-5339	R	23	<0.1
Bunker Hill Foods	PO Drawer 1048	Bedford	VA	24523	LH Peterson	703-586-8274	D	23	0.2
Sparta Foods Inc	2570 Kasota Av	St Paul	MN	55108	Joel Bahuel	612-646-1888	P	16	0.1
Stagg Foods Inc	12750 Ctr Court Dr	Cerritos	CA	90701	C L Hirsch Jr	310-865-2200	R	15*	0.1
Kelly Foods Inc	513 Airways Blv	Jackson	TN	38301	AC Koch	901-424-2255	R	13*	<0.1
Stokes Canning Co	PO Box 16787	Denver	CO	80216	G Robert Page	303-292-4018	R	13	0.1
Earth's Best Inc	4840 Pearl E Cir	Boulder	CO	80301	Jay G Shoemaker	303-449-3780	R	12	<0.1
Millcrest Products Corp	4667 E Date Av	Fresno	CA	93725	Allan Andrews	209-445-1745	S	12	0.1
HKS Marketing	420 Kent Av	Brooklyn	NY	11211	David Herzog	718-384-2400	R	10	<0.1
Kedem Food Products Co	420 Kent Av	Brooklyn	NY	11211	David Herzog	718-384-2400	S	10	<0.1
Stegner Food Products Co	PO Box 58643	Cincinnati	OH	45258	EJ Stegner	513-922-1125	R	10	<0.1
Ebro Foods Inc	181 S Water Mkt St	Chicago	IL	60608	Venaida Abreu	312-666-5876	R	8*	<0.1
El Molino Foods Inc	2570 W 8th Av	Denver	CO	80204	Alan McCullick	303-623-7870	R	8	<0.1
Suter Company Inc	PO Box 188	Sycamore	IL	60178	George B Suter	815-895-9186	R	8	<0.1
Pastorelli Food Products Inc	162 N Sangamon St	Chicago	IL	60607	Leandro Pastorelli	312-666-2041	R	7	<0.1
Amigos Canning Company Inc	PO Box 37347	San Antonio	TX	78237	RE Velasco Jr	210-434-0433	R	6	<0.1
Foell Packing Co	3117 W 47th St	Chicago	IL	60632	AW Johnson	312-523-5220	R	5	<0.1
Grandma Brown's Beans Inc	PO Box 230	Mexico	NY	13114	Sandra L Brown	315-963-7221	R	5	<0.1
Ray's Brand Products Inc	PO Box 1000	Springfield	IL	62705	Melvin Workman	217-523-9417	D	2	<0.1
Growing Healthy Inc	7615 G Tri	Eden Prairie	MN	55344	Julia Knight	612-942-5655	R	1	<0.1
Rocky Mountain Food Factory	2825 S Raritan St	Englewood	CO	80110	M D Rosario	303-761-3330	R	1	<0.1
Uncle Dave's Kitchens Inc	PO Box 2034	S Londonderry	VT	05155	Lynne M Andreen	802-824-3600	R	1	<0.1
Arizona Catus Ranch	PO Box 8	Green Valley	AZ	85622	Natalie McGee	602-625-4419	R	0*	<0.1

Source: *Ward's Business Directory of U.S. Private and Public Companies*, Volumes 1 and 2, 1996. The company type code used is as follows: P - Public, R - Private, S - Subsidiary, D - Division, J - Joint Venture, A - Affiliate, G - Group. Sales are in millions of dollars, employees are in thousands. An asterisk (*) indicates an estimated sales volume. The symbol < stands for 'less than'. Company names and addresses are truncated, in some cases, to fit into the available space.

MATERIALS CONSUMED

Material		Quantity	Delivered Cost ($ million)
Materials, ingredients, containers, and supplies		(X)	2,900.4
Fresh apples	1,000 s tons	(D)	(D)
Fresh apricots	1,000 s tons	(D)	(D)
Fresh peaches	1,000 s tons	64.9	17.8
Fresh pears	1,000 s tons	(D)	(D)
Fresh pineapples	1,000 s tons	(D)	(D)
Other fresh fruits	1,000 s tons	(S)	4.6
Fresh green peas	1,000 s tons	12.1**	6.2
White potatoes	1,000 s tons	89.8	16.2
Fresh mushrooms	mil lb	(D)	(D)
Fresh tomatoes	1,000 s tons	137.7	34.5
Fresh sweet corn	1,000 s tons	(D)	(D)
Fresh green (snap) or wax beans	1,000 s tons	35.1**	7.8
Other fresh vegetables	1,000 s tons	191.6*	61.9
Sugar, cane and beet (in terms of sugar solids)	1,000 s tons	46.3**	23.9
High fructose corn syrup (HFCS)(in terms of solids)	mil lb	100.3	13.9
Crystalline fructose (dry fructose)	mil lb	(D)	(D)
Dextrose and corn syrup, including corn syrup solids (in terms of dry weight)	mil lb	90.1*	16.2
Fresh, frozen, and prepared meats	mil lb	181.6	194.1
Dressed poultry purchased for processing (cooking, smoking, canning, etc.)	mil lb	90.7	137.0
Dried fruits	1,000 s tons	(D)	(D)
Dried beans	1,000 s tons	227.1	121.1
Concentrated fruit juices	mil gal	3.2	25.9
Frozen fruits (for further processing)	mil lb	(D)	(D)
Frozen vegetables (for further processing)	mil lb	183.0	100.9
Tomato paste (24 percent NTSS equivalent)	mil lb	287.8	155.3
Wheat flour	1,000 cwt	2,077.7	19.9
Fats and oils, all types (purchased as such)	mil lb	120.0	41.1
Printed labels		(X)	54.7
Flexible packaging materials		(X)	39.8
Paperboard containers, boxes, and corrugated paperboard		(X)	83.2
Metal cans, can lids and ends		(X)	650.1
Glass containers		(X)	139.3
All other materials and components, parts, containers, and supplies		(X)	752.4
Materials, ingredients, containers, and supplies, nsk		(X)	93.4

Source: 1992 *Economic Census*. Explanation of symbols used: (D): Withheld to avoid disclosure of competitive data; na: Not available; (S): Withheld because statistical norms were not met; (X): Not applicable; (Z): Less than half the unit shown; nec: Not elsewhere classified; nsk: Not specified by kind; - : zero; * : 10-19 percent estimated; ** : 20-29 percent estimated.

PRODUCT SHARE DETAILS

Product or Product Class	% Share
Canned specialties	100.00
Canned baby foods, except cereal and biscuits	(D)
Canned baby foods, except cereal and biscuits	(D)
Canned soups, except frozen or seafood	34.80
Canned dry beans	19.61
Canned dry beans with pork, 7.1 oz to 13 oz (8 oz short, 8 oz tall, No. 1 picnic, etc.)	(D)
Canned dry beans with pork, 13.1 oz to 22 oz (No. 300, No. 303, No. 2, etc.)	22.91
Canned dry beans with pork, 22.1 oz to 27 oz (jumbo, etc.)	(D)
Canned dry beans with pork, 27.1 oz to 40 oz (No. 2-1/2 quart glass, etc.)	3.94
Canned dry beans with pork, less than 7.1 oz or more than 40 oz	6.03
Canned dry beans with sauce, vegetarian style, including baked, 13.1 oz to 18 oz (No. 300, No. 303, etc.)	5.26
Canned dry beans with sauce, vegetarian style, including baked, other sizes	4.45
All other canned dry beans, including chili con carne containing less than 20 percent meat, 13.1 oz to 18 oz (No. 300, No. 303, etc.)	30.75
All other canned dry beans, including chili con carne containing less than 20 percent meat, all other sizes	13.36
Canned dry beans, nsk	0.03
Other canned specialties and canned nationality foods	(D)
Canned spaghetti with or without meat	(D)
Canned chinese foods (bean sprouts, chop suey, etc.)	(D)
Canned mincemeat	(D)
Canned spanish foods (mexican rice, tortillas, enchiladas, etc.)	11.59
Canned ravioli	18.75
Canned macaroni (except spaghetti) with or without meat	(D)
Canned gravy	(D)
Other canned specialties, including canned puddings (other than canned meats)	35.36
Other canned specialties and canned nationality foods, nsk	0.09
Canned specialties, nsk	3.33

Source: 1992 *Economic Census*. The values shown are percent of total shipments in an industry. Values of indented subcategories are summed in the main heading. The symbol (D) appears when data are withheld to prevent disclosure of competitive information. The abbreviation nsk stands for 'not specified by kind' and nec for 'not elsewhere classified'.

INPUTS AND OUTPUTS FOR CANNED SPECIALTIES

Economic Sector or Industry Providing Inputs	%	Sector	Economic Sector or Industry Buying Outputs	%	Sector
Metal cans	23.7	Manufg.	Personal consumption expenditures	90.1	
Wholesale trade	13.1	Trade	Eating & drinking places	4.0	Trade
Glass containers	7.8	Manufg.	Exports	1.9	Foreign
Advertising	6.1	Services	S/L Govt. purch., elem. & secondary education	1.3	S/L Govt
Dehydrated food products	5.9	Manufg.	Hospitals	0.7	Services
Canned fruits & vegetables	4.2	Manufg.	Canned specialties	0.4	Manufg.
Meat packing plants	4.2	Manufg.	S/L Govt. purch., health & hospitals	0.4	S/L Govt
Paperboard containers & boxes	2.9	Manufg.	Nursing & personal care facilities	0.3	Services
Sausages & other prepared meats	2.6	Manufg.	Residential care	0.3	Services
Crowns & closures	2.3	Manufg.	Social services, nec	0.2	Services
Motor freight transportation & warehousing	2.1	Util.	S/L Govt. purch., correction	0.1	S/L Govt
Frozen fruits, fruit juices & vegetables	1.9	Manufg.	S/L Govt. purch., higher education	0.1	S/L Govt
Vegetables	1.8	Agric.			
Poultry dressing plants	1.7	Manufg.			
Gas production & distribution (utilities)	1.7	Util.			
Commercial printing	1.6	Manufg.			
Greenhouse & nursery products	1.1	Agric.			
Sugar	1.1	Manufg.			
Shortening & cooking oils	1.0	Manufg.			
Electric services (utilities)	1.0	Util.			
Imports	1.0	Foreign			
Petroleum refining	0.8	Manufg.			
Cyclic crudes and organics	0.7	Manufg.			
Flour & other grain mill products	0.7	Manufg.			
Fruits	0.6	Agric.			
Canned specialties	0.6	Manufg.			
Paper coating & glazing	0.5	Manufg.			
Railroads & related services	0.5	Util.			
Miscellaneous crops	0.4	Agric.			
Banking	0.4	Fin/R.E.			
Maintenance of nonfarm buildings nec	0.3	Constr.			
Creamery butter	0.3	Manufg.			
Soap & other detergents	0.3	Manufg.			
Communications, except radio & TV	0.3	Util.			
Equipment rental & leasing services	0.3	Services			
U.S. Postal Service	0.3	Gov't			
Bags, except textile	0.2	Manufg.			
Rice milling	0.2	Manufg.			
Vegetable oil mills, nec	0.2	Manufg.			
Eating & drinking places	0.2	Trade			
Real estate	0.2	Fin/R.E.			
Detective & protective services	0.2	Services			
State & local government enterprises, nec	0.2	Gov't			
Coal	0.1	Mining			
Cheese, natural & processed	0.1	Manufg.			
Chemical preparations, nec	0.1	Manufg.			
Air transportation	0.1	Util.			
Sanitary services, steam supply, irrigation	0.1	Util.			
Water transportation	0.1	Util.			
Credit agencies other than banks	0.1	Fin/R.E.			
Insurance carriers	0.1	Fin/R.E.			
Laundry, dry cleaning, shoe repair	0.1	Services			
Noncomparable imports	0.1	Foreign			

Source: Benchmark Input-Output Accounts for the U.S. Economy, 1982, U.S. Department of Commerce, Washington, D.C., July 1991. Data, as reported in the source, are organized by the 1977 SIC structure in use in 1982 but have been matched, as closely as is possible, to the 1987 SIC structure used in this book.

OCCUPATIONS EMPLOYED BY SIC 203 - PRESERVED FRUITS AND VEGETABLES

Occupation	% of Total 1994	Change to 2005	Occupation	% of Total 1994	Change to 2005
Cannery workers	21.2	6.7	Maintenance repairers, general utility	1.9	-4.0
Packaging & filling machine operators	6.8	6.7	Janitors & cleaners, incl maids	1.8	-14.6
Helpers, laborers, & material movers nec	5.1	6.7	Freight, stock, & material movers, hand	1.7	-14.6
Industrial machinery mechanics	4.5	49.4	Crushing & mixing machine operators	1.4	6.7
Industrial truck & tractor operators	4.5	6.7	Truck drivers light & heavy	1.3	10.0
Blue collar worker supervisors	4.1	3.7	General managers & top executives	1.3	1.2
Hand packers & packagers	3.9	-8.5	Vehicle washers & equipment cleaners	1.1	-1.6
Assemblers, fabricators, & hand workers nec	3.4	6.7	Industrial production managers	1.1	6.7
Agricultural workers nec	2.5	6.7	Sales & related workers nec	1.1	6.7
Cooking, roasting machine operators	2.3	17.4	Bookkeeping, accounting, & auditing clerks	1.0	-20.0
Precision food & tobacco workers nec	2.2	17.4	Traffic, shipping, & receiving clerks	1.0	2.6
Machine operators nec	2.2	-5.9	Secretaries, ex legal & medical	1.0	-2.9
Machine feeders & offbearers	2.1	17.3			

Source: Industry-Occupation Matrix, Bureau of Labor Statistics. These data relate to one or more 3-digit SIC industry groups rather than to a single 4-digit SIC. The change reported for each occupation to the year 2005 is a percent of growth or decline as estimated by the Bureau of Labor Statistics. The abbreviation nec stands for 'not elsewhere classified'.

LOCATION BY STATE AND REGIONAL CONCENTRATION

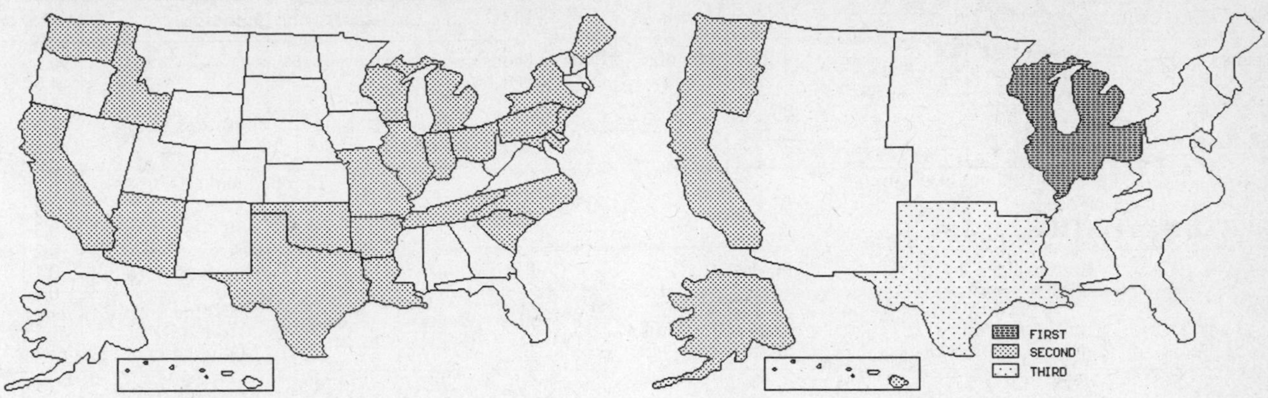

INDUSTRY DATA BY STATE

State	Establish-ments	Shipments			Employment				Cost as % of Shipments	Investment per Employee ($)
		Total ($ mil)	% of U.S.	Per Establ.	Total Number	% of U.S.	Per Establ.	Wages ($/hour)		
Pennsylvania	7	1,016.4	15.3	145.2	3,500	16.7	500	14.11	39.5	23,114
California	31	763.0	11.5	24.6	3,400	16.2	110	12.11	43.6	5,147
Michigan	11	366.5	5.5	33.3	1,100	5.2	100	12.20	43.7	-
Illinois	14	167.4	2.5	12.0	700	3.3	50	9.00	42.5	7,714
New York	8	119.1	1.8	14.9	800	3.8	100	12.11	46.9	-
Louisiana	4	28.0	0.4	7.0	200	1.0	50	9.00	52.5	-
Missouri	8	27.9	0.4	3.5	200	1.0	25	6.00	45.9	-
Texas	18	(D)	-	-	1,750 *	8.3	97	-	-	-
Washington	9	(D)	-	-	750 *	3.6	83	-	-	-
Ohio	7	(D)	-	-	3,750 *	17.9	536	-	-	-
New Jersey	6	(D)	-	-	750 *	3.6	125	-	-	-
Arkansas	5	(D)	-	-	750 *	3.6	150	-	-	-
Indiana	5	(D)	-	-	750 *	3.6	150	-	-	-
Oklahoma	5	(D)	-	-	175 *	0.8	35	-	-	-
Tennessee	5	(D)	-	-	750 *	3.6	150	-	-	-
North Carolina	4	(D)	-	-	1,750 *	8.3	438	-	-	-
Wisconsin	4	(D)	-	-	175 *	0.8	44	-	-	-
Arizona	3	(D)	-	-	375 *	1.8	125	-	-	-
South Carolina	3	(D)	-	-	175 *	0.8	58	-	-	-
Idaho	2	(D)	-	-	750 *	3.6	375	-	-	-
Maine	2	(D)	-	-	175 *	0.8	88	-	-	-
Maryland	2	(D)	-	-	175 *	0.8	88	-	-	-

Source: 1992 *Economic Census*. The states are in descending order of shipments or establishments (if shipment data are missing for the majority). The symbol (D) appears when data are withheld to prevent disclosure of competitive information. States marked with (D) are sorted by number of establishments. A dash (-) indicates that the data element cannot be calculated; * indicates the midpoint of a range.

2033 - CANNED FRUITS VEGETABLES

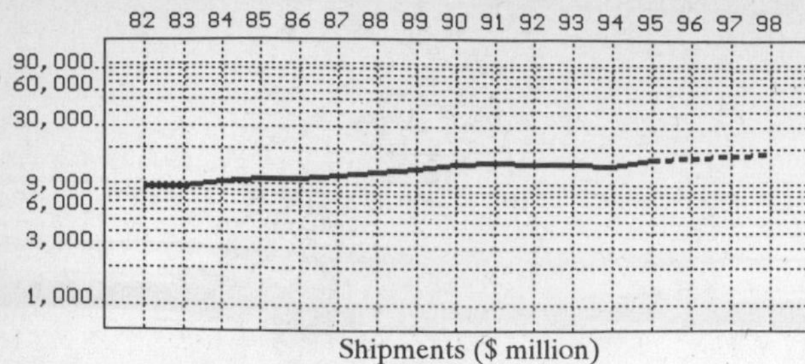

Shipments ($ million)

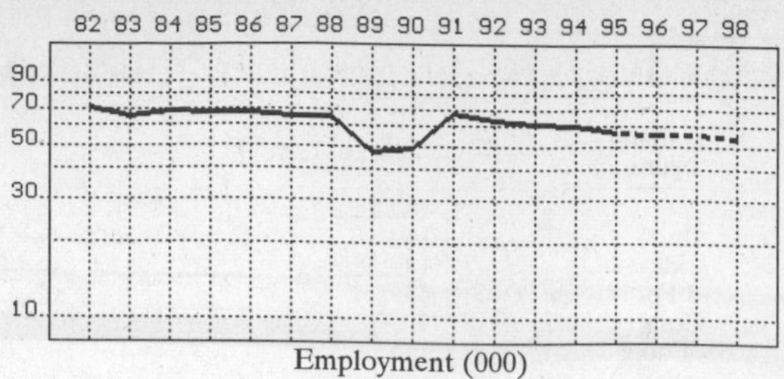

Employment (000)

GENERAL STATISTICS

Year	Companies	Establishments		Employment			Compensation		Production ($ million)			
		Total	with 20 or more employees	Total (000)	Production Workers (000)	Production Hours (Mil)	Payroll ($ mil)	Wages ($/hr)	Cost of Materials	Value Added by Manufacture	Value of Shipments	Capital Invest.
1982	514	715	451	70.5	60.7	113.6	1,040.1	7.24	5,768.1	3,552.7	9,283.4	264.1
1983		696	430	65.2	55.6	103.9	1,007.9	7.48	5,641.4	3,660.8	9,358.1	267.7
1984		677	409	69.0	58.5	109.3	1,134.1	7.82	6,353.0	4,129.8	10,389.6	242.4
1985		657	388	67.6	57.3	105.4	1,132.5	8.04	6,440.2	4,448.3	10,998.7	264.1
1986		645	395	67.4	57.4	102.0	1,105.2	8.08	6,022.7	5,184.8	11,170.7	240.0
1987	471	647	417	65.6	55.9	104.4	1,162.8	8.43	6,465.9	5,440.1	11,889.5	257.9
1988		634	370	64.4	55.2	105.1	1,219.6	8.87	7,080.5	5,789.1	12,872.7	320.7
1989		605	371	47.7	57.1	110.9	1,289.8	8.99	7,757.2	5,899.4	13,605.2	351.5
1990		598	364	48.3	58.2	113.4	1,407.9	9.38	8,362.7	6,405.2	14,697.9	433.6
1991		606	357	67.3	57.2	114.3	1,484.4	9.74	8,759.9	6,858.8	15,579.1	490.2
1992	502	683	397	63.7	53.2	109.3	1,466.7	10.08	8,032.5	6,959.4	15,065.5	445.1
1993		671	350	61.3	51.0	102.6	1,430.9	10.40	7,922.3	6,749.9	14,657.8	404.1
1994		618P	346P	60.1	50.6	101.8	1,437.9	10.60	8,096.0	6,424.1	14,480.9	350.6
1995		613P	339P	56.8P	52.1P	106.6P	1,548.5P	10.86P	9,181.8P	7,285.6P	16,422.9P	455.2P
1996		607P	332P	55.9P	51.5P	106.4P	1,590.3P	11.15P	9,485.6P	7,526.7P	16,966.3P	472.6P
1997		602P	325P	55.0P	50.9P	106.3P	1,632.2P	11.43P	9,789.4P	7,767.8P	17,509.7P	490.0P
1998		597P	318P	54.1P	50.4P	106.2P	1,674.1P	11.72P	10,093.2P	8,008.8P	18,053.1P	507.5P

Sources: 1982, 1987, 1992 *Economic Census*; *Annual Survey of Manufactures*, 83-86, 88-91, 93-94. Establishment counts for non-Census years are from *County Business Patterns*; establishment values for 83-84 are extrapolations. 'P's show projections by the editors. Industries reclassified in 87 will not have data for prior years.

INDICES OF CHANGE

Year	Companies	Establishments		Employment			Compensation		Production ($ million)			
		Total	with 20 or more employees	Total (000)	Production Workers (000)	Production Hours (Mil)	Payroll ($ mil)	Wages ($/hr)	Cost of Materials	Value Added by Manufacture	Value of Shipments	Capital Invest.
1982	102	105	114	111	114	104	71	72	72	51	62	59
1983		102	108	102	105	95	69	74	70	53	62	60
1984		99	103	108	110	100	77	78	79	59	69	54
1985		96	98	106	108	96	77	80	80	64	73	59
1986		94	99	106	108	93	75	80	75	75	74	54
1987	94	95	105	103	105	96	79	84	80	78	79	58
1988		93	93	101	104	96	83	88	88	83	85	72
1989		89	93	75	107	101	88	89	97	85	90	79
1990		88	92	76	109	104	96	93	104	92	98	97
1991		89	90	106	108	105	101	97	109	99	103	110
1992	100	100	100	100	100	100	100	100	100	100	100	100
1993		98	88	96	96	94	98	103	99	97	97	91
1994		91P	87P	94	95	93	98	105	101	92	96	79
1995		90P	85P	89P	98P	97P	106P	108P	114P	105P	109P	102P
1996		89P	84P	88P	97P	97P	108P	111P	118P	108P	113P	106P
1997		88P	82P	86P	96P	97P	111P	113P	122P	112P	116P	110P
1998		87P	80P	85P	95P	97P	114P	116P	126P	115P	120P	114P

Sources: Same as General Statistics. Values reflect change from the base year, 1992. Values above 100 mean greater than 92, values below 100 mean less than 92, and a value of 100 in the 82-91 or 93-98 period means same as 92. 'P's mark projections by the editors.

SELECTED RATIOS

For 1994	Avg. of All Manufact.	Analyzed Industry	Index
Employees per Establishment	49	97	198
Payroll per Establishment	1,500,273	2,326,129	155
Payroll per Employee	30,620	23,925	78
Production Workers per Establishment	34	82	238
Wages per Establishment	853,319	1,745,656	205
Wages per Production Worker	24,861	21,326	86
Hours per Production Worker	2,056	2,012	98
Wages per Hour	12.09	10.60	88
Value Added per Establishment	4,602,255	10,392,436	226
Value Added per Employee	93,930	106,890	114

For 1994	Avg. of All Manufact.	Analyzed Industry	Index
Value Added per Production Worker	134,084	126,958	95
Cost per Establishment	5,045,178	13,097,113	260
Cost per Employee	102,970	134,709	131
Cost per Production Worker	146,988	160,000	109
Shipments per Establishment	9,576,895	23,426,134	245
Shipments per Employee	195,460	240,947	123
Shipments per Production Worker	279,017	286,184	103
Investment per Establishment	321,011	567,175	177
Investment per Employee	6,552	5,834	89
Investment per Production Worker	9,352	6,929	74

Sources: Same as General Statistics. The 'Average of All Manufacturing' column represents the average of all manufacturing industries reported for the most recent complete year available. The Index shows the relationship between the Average and the Analyzed Industry. For example, 100 means that they are equal; 500 that the Analyzed Industry is five times the average; 50 means that the Analyzed Industry is half the national average. The abbreviation 'na' is used to show that data are 'not available'.

LEADING COMPANIES Number shown: **75** Total sales ($ mil): **20,026** Total employment (000): **126.7**

Company Name	Address				CEO Name	Phone	Co. Type	Sales ($ mil)	Empl. (000)
HJ Heinz Co	PO Box 57	Pittsburgh	PA	15230	A JF O'Reilly	412-456-5700	P	7,047	35.7
Hunt-Wesson Inc	1645 W Valencia Dr	Fullerton	CA	92633	Albert J Crosson	714-680-1000	S	2,000	9.0
Del Monte Foods	PO Box 3575	San Francisco	CA	94119	R W D'Ornellas	415-247-3000	R	1,600	17.3
Dole Packaged Foods Co	5795 Lindero	Westlake Vil	CA	91362	Peter Nolan	818-874-4000	D	1,410*	9.0
Ocean Spray Cranberries Inc	1 Ocean Spray Dr	Lakeville	MA	02349	Jack Lewellyn	508-946-1000	R	1,000	2.0
Curtice Burns Foods Inc	PO Box 681	Rochester	NY	14603	Roy A Meyers	716-383-1850	P	829	6.8
Tri Valley Growers	PO Box 7114	San Francisco	CA	94120	James J Saras	415-445-1600	R	821	12.0
JM Smucker Co	1 Strawberry Ln	Orrville	OH	44667	Paul H Smucker	216-682-3000	P	511	2.6
Welch Foods Inc	#3 Concord Farms	Concord	MA	01742	Everett N Baldwin	508-371-1000	S	460	1.3
Santomo Partners	11292 N Alpine Rd	Stockton	CA	95212	Dean Cortopassi	209-948-0792	R	310*	2.0
Comstock Michigan Fruit	PO Box 20670	Rochester	NY	14602	Dennis Mullen	716-383-1070	D	294	1.7
Seneca Foods Corp	1162 Pittsford	Pittsford	NY	14534	Kraig H Kayser	716-385-9500	P	290	3.1
National Fruit Product Company	PO Box 2040	Winchester	VA	22604	Frank Armstrong III	703-662-3401	R	250*	1.6
Seneca Foods Corp	418 E Conde St	Janesville	WI	53546	Michael H Haney	608-757-6000	D	250	1.1
Larsen Co	PO Box 19027	Green Bay	WI	54307	Jeffrey P Shaw	414-435-5301	S	200	0.9
S and W Fine Foods Inc	PO Box 5580	San Ramon	CA	94583	Norman L Correia	510-866-4500	S	200	0.4
Agripac Inc	PO Box 5346	Salem	OR	97304	Jim Dishon	503-363-9255	R	150	0.6
Stanislaus Food Products Co	PO Box 3951	Modesto	CA	95352	Robert Ilse	209-522-7201	S	140*	0.9
Bruce Foods Corp	PO Drawer 1030	New Iberia	LA	70562	JS Brown III	318-365-8101	R	130*	0.8
Maui Land and Pineapple	PO Box 187	Kahului	HI	96732	J W Hartley Jr	808-877-3351	P	126	1.5
Friday Canning Corp	PO Box 129	New Richmond	WI	54017	FC Friday	715-246-2241	S	120	2.5
Lakeside Foods Inc	PO Box 1327	Manitowoc	WI	54221	JD Quick	414-684-3356	R	120	0.6
Cherry Growers Inc	PO Box 509	Traverse City	MI	49685	T Morrison	616-276-9241	R	110*	0.8
ABA Holding Co	1 Rossmore Dr	Jamesburg	NJ	08831	Abbas Bayat	609-395-2900	R	100*	0.4
Bama Food Products	3900 Vanderbilt Rd	Birmingham	AL	35217		205-841-0491	D	85	0.2
Maui Pineapple Company Ltd	PO Box 187	Kahului	HI	96732	Douglas R Schenk	808-877-3351	S	81	1.5
Sun Garden Packing Co	PO Box 6180	San Jose	CA	95150	Richard Dinapoli	408-283-8200	R	80	1.2
La Choy Food Products Co	901 Stryker St	Archbold	OH	43502	Jeffrey Wilson	419-445-8015	D	78*	0.5
Fremont Co	802 N Front St	Fremont	OH	43420	Richard L Smith	419-334-8995	R	65*	0.5
Escalon Packers Inc	PO Box 8	Escalon	CA	95320	Chris Ronson	209-838-7341	S	58	0.3
American Fine Foods Inc	PO Box 460	Payette	ID	83661	Tony Moss	208-642-9061	S	55*	0.3
Pacific Coast Producers	PO Box 1600	Lodi	CA	95240	Larry Clay	209-367-8800	R	51	0.3
Cliffstar Corp	1 Cliffstar Av	Dunkirk	NY	14048	Stanley Star	716-366-6100	R	50	0.4
La Victoria Foods Inc	PO Box 3884	City of Industry	CA	91744	RC Tanklage	818-333-0787	R	50*	0.6
Redwing Co	PO Box 49009	San Jose	CA	95161		408-259-4800	S	47*	0.3
Truitt Brothers Inc	PO Box 309	Salem	OR	97308	David J Truitt	503-362-3674	R	42	0.1
Ingomar Packing Co	PO Box 1448	Los Banos	CA	93635	Greg Pruett	209-826-9494	R	40	<0.1
Clement Pappas and Co	W Parsonage Rd	Seabrook	NJ	08302	Dean C Pappas	609-455-1000	R	39*	0.3
Omni International Trading Inc	121 S 8th St	Minneapolis	MN	55402	Dan Bubalo	612-338-4128	R	36	0.2
Juice Bowl Products Inc	PO Box 1048	Lakeland	FL	33802	A Bayat	813-665-5515	S	35*	0.2
Brooks Foods	PO Box 157	Mount Summit	IN	47361	E W Hermenet	317-836-4801	D	31	0.2
Giorgio Foods Inc	PO Box 96	Temple	PA	19560	J Majewske	610-926-2139	R	30	0.3
Oconomowoc Canning Co	PO Box 248	Oconomowoc	WI	53066	John McCormick	414-567-9151	S	29*	0.1
Reedsburg Foods Corp	PO Box 270	Reedsburg	WI	53959	Steve Burmester	608-524-2346	R	29*	<0.1
Red Giant Foods Inc	PO Box 495	Elwood	IN	46036	Brian Reichart	317-552-3386	S	28*	0.2
Moody Dunbar Inc	PO Box 68	Limestone	TN	37681	SK Dunbar	615-257-2111	R	27	0.2
Daily Juice Products	1 Daily Way	Verona	PA	15147	David Bober	412-828-9020	D	25	0.3
Mullins Food Products	2200 S 25th Av	Broadview	IL	60153	JF Mullins	708-344-3224	R	25	0.2
S Martinelli and Co	PO Box 1868	Watsonville	CA	95077	Steven Martinelli	408-724-1126	R	25*	0.2
SEW Friel Co	Rte 301	Queenstown	MD	21658	SE Friel Jr	410-827-8811	R	25	0.3
Cherokee Products Co	PO Box 98	Haddock	GA	31033	GA Bloodworth Jr	912-932-5211	R	20	0.2
Fiesta-Jimenez Co	4000 Dan Morton	Dallas	TX	75236		214-283-7200	D	20	0.2
Jasper Wyman and Son Inc	PO Box 100	Milbridge	ME	04658	Edward R Flanagan	207-546-2311	R	20	0.1
Odwalla Inc	3500 Coast Hwy 1	Davenport	CA	95017	Greg A Steltenpohl	408-425-4557	P	18	0.4
Agrigold Joint Venture	PO Box 1630	Corona	CA	91718	Reid J Neu	909-272-2600	R	18	<0.1
Artichoke Industries Inc	PO Box 1307	Castroville	CA	95012	Tony Leonardini	408-633-2423	R	18	0.1
Vita-Pakt Citrus Products Co	PO Box 309	Covina	CA	91723	William P Robinett	818-332-1101	R	18*	0.1
Crosby Fruit Products Company	11751 Pacific Av	Fontana	CA	92335	JM Crosby	909-685-1700	R	17	0.1
Old Dutch Mustard Company	98 Cutter Mill Rd	Great Neck	NY	11021	Paul Santich	516-466-0522	R	17	0.1
Owatonna Canning Co	PO Box 447	Owatonna	MN	55060	Stephens J Lange	507-451-7670	R	17	0.4
Seneca-Kennett Foods	PO Box K	Kennett Square	PA	19348	Richard O Mayo	215-444-5820	S	17*	<0.1
Hirzel Canning Co	411 Lemoyne Rd	Toledo	OH	43619	Karl Hirzel	419-693-0531	R	16	0.1
JMS Specialty Foods Inc	PO Box 345	Ripon	WI	54971	Don S Jorgensen	414-748-2858	S	16*	0.1
Orchard Food Products	PO Box 2129	Woburn	MA	01888	Steven Rohtstein	617-935-8400	D	16	0.1
KYD Inc	PO Box 29669	Honolulu	HI	96820	Christopher Johnson	808-545-4554	D	15*	0.1
Mayer Brothers Apple Products	1540 Seneca Creek	West Seneca	NY	14224	John Mayer	716-668-1787	R	14	<0.1
Mushroom Cooperative Co	PO Box 389	Kennett Square	PA	19348	Dennis Newhard	610-444-1400	R	14	<0.1
Speaco Foods Inc	2400 Nicholson Av	Kansas City	MO	64120	Jack Cole	816-483-1700	R	14*	<0.1
Bison Canning Company Inc	PO Box 152	Angola	NY	14006	Robert J Drago	716-549-0076	R	13*	<0.1
Cromers Inc	PO Box 163	Columbia	SC	29202	James Cromer	803-779-2290	R	13*	<0.1
Diana Fruit Company Inc	PO Box 268	Santa Clara	CA	95052	Eugene C Acronico	408-727-9631	R	13	0.2
MH Zeigler and Sons Inc	1513 N Broad St	Lansdale	PA	19446	Joseph Zeigler	215-855-5161	R	12	<0.1
New Era Canning Co	PO Box 68	New Era	MI	49446	Rick Ray	616-861-2151	R	12	<0.1
Olympic Foods Inc	W 5625 Thorpe Rd	Spokane	WA	99204	Chuck Killion	509-455-8059	R	12*	<0.1
Tropical Preserving Co	1712 Newton St	Los Angeles	CA	90021	Ronald Randall	213-748-5108	R	11*	<0.1

Source: *Ward's Business Directory of U.S. Private and Public Companies*, Volumes 1 and 2, 1996. The company type code used is as follows: P - Public, R - Private, S - Subsidiary, D - Division, J - Joint Venture, A - Affiliate, G - Group. Sales are in millions of dollars, employees are in thousands. An asterisk (*) indicates an estimated sales volume. The symbol < stands for 'less than'. Company names and addresses are truncated, in some cases, to fit into the available space.

MATERIALS CONSUMED

Material		Quantity	Delivered Cost ($ million)
Materials, ingredients, containers, and supplies		(X)	7,293.9
Fresh oranges	1,000 s tons	1,635.0	282.7
Fresh apples	1,000 s tons	1,194.8	176.5
Fresh apricots	1,000 s tons	46.5	12.7
Fresh grapes	1,000 s tons	511.1	93.7
Fresh peaches	1,000 s tons	559.9	132.1
Fresh pears	1,000 s tons	428.2	95.7
Fresh pineapples	1,000 s tons	351.0	57.6
Fresh grapefruit	1,000 s tons	(D)	(D)
Other fresh fruits	1,000 s tons	385.7	186.9
Fresh green peas	1,000 s tons	303.4	79.9
White potatoes	1,000 s tons	118.7	14.7
Fresh mushrooms	mil lb	133.3	94.5
Fresh tomatoes	1,000 s tons	8,220.2	520.0
Fresh sweet corn	1,000 s tons	1,864.7	143.0
Fresh green (snap) or wax beans	1,000 s tons	528.3	86.7
Other fresh vegetables	1,000 s tons	811.2*	143.1
Sugar, cane and beet (in terms of sugar solids)	1,000 s tons	138.8	65.7
High fructose corn syrup (HFCS)(in terms of solids)	mil lb	870.7	119.5
Crystalline fructose (dry fructose)	mil lb	77.5	11.8
Dextrose and corn syrup, including corn syrup solids (in terms of dry weight)	mil lb	651.5	71.2
Fresh, frozen, and prepared meats	mil lb	1,157.3	33.7
Dressed poultry purchased for processing (cooking, smoking, canning, etc.)	mil lb	(D)	(D)
Dried fruits	1,000 s tons	13.7	16.1
Dried beans	1,000 s tons	49.7**	26.5
Concentrated fruit juices	mil gal	140.6*	635.1
Frozen fruits (for further processing)	mil lb	198.6	116.2
Frozen vegetables (for further processing)	mil lb	55.9	22.7
Tomato paste (24 percent NTSS equivalent)	mil lb	567.6	229.2
Wheat flour	1,000 cwt	(D)	(D)
Fats and oils, all types (purchased as such)	mil lb	95.2*	28.9
Printed labels		(X)	87.7
Flexible packaging materials		(X)	99.2
Paperboard containers, boxes, and corrugated paperboard		(X)	311.3
Metal cans, can lids and ends		(X)	1,221.1
Glass containers		(X)	531.1
All other materials and components, parts, containers, and supplies		(X)	1,202.8
Materials, ingredients, containers, and supplies, nsk		(X)	305.4

Source: 1992 *Economic Census*. Explanation of symbols used: (D): Withheld to avoid disclosure of competitive data; na: Not available; (S): Withheld because statistical norms were not met; (X): Not applicable; (Z): Less than half the unit shown; nec: Not elsewhere classified; nsk: Not specified by kind; - : zero; * : 10-19 percent estimated; ** : 20-29 percent estimated.

PRODUCT SHARE DETAILS

Product or Product Class	% Share
Canned fruits and vegetables	100.00
Canned fruits, except baby foods	15.63
Canned apples	3.17
Canned applesauce	14.83
Canned apricots	2.00
Canned cherries, red pitted	0.52
Canned cherries, sweet	0.81
Canned cranberries and cranberry sauce	(D)
Canned fruit cocktail	11.92
Canned fruits for salads, including mixed fruits other than fruit cocktail	4.19
Canned olives, ripe and green ripe, including stuffed (drained net weight)	11.95
Canned peaches, including spiced	21.20
Canned pears, including spiced	8.66
Canned pineapple (all styles)	6.40
Other canned fruit	(D)
Canned apple pie mixes	1.16
Canned cherry pie mixes	2.90
Canned peach pie mixes	0.35
Other canned fruit pie mixes	2.03
Canned fruits, except baby foods, nsk	0.54
Canned vegetables, except hominy and mushrooms	17.76
Canned green lima beans	0.82
Canned green and wax beans (including blue lake)	16.02
Canned carrots	1.54
Canned vegetable combinations (mixed vegetables, succotash, carrots and peas, vegetable salad, etc.)	4.42
Canned green peas	9.45
Other canned peas (blackeye, crowder, purple hull, field, etc.)	0.77
Canned pumpkin and squash, including pie mix	(D)
Canned spinach	1.87
Canned sweet potatoes, including pie mix	3.25
Canned white potatoes	1.81
Canned sauerkraut	1.74
Canned asparagus	3.22
Canned beets	2.55
Canned sweet corn, whole kernel	19.12
Canned sweet corn, cream style	4.33
Canned tomatoes, including stewed	19.99
Other canned vegetables, except hominy and mushrooms	(D)
Canned vegetables, except hominy and mushrooms, nsk	0.32
Canned hominy and mushrooms	1.33
Canned hominy	13.12
Canned mushrooms	86.88
Canned vegetable juices	2.70
Canned tomato juice, including combinations containing 70 percent tomato juice or more	95.58
Other canned vegetable juices	4.35
Canned vegetable juices, nsk	0.07
Catsup and other canned tomato sauces, pastes, etc.	24.20
Canned tomato sauce, except pulp, puree, and paste, 7.1 oz to 10 oz (8 oz tall, etc.)	4.19
Canned tomato sauce, except pulp, puree, and paste, other sizes	6.16
Canned catsup, 14 oz to 32 oz	13.22
Canned catsup, all other sizes, including individual serving sizes	12.59
Canned spaghetti, pizza, and marinara sauces, with or without other added ingredients, including those with less than 20 percent meat	35.82
Canned chili sauce	2.15
Canned barbecue sauce	7.19
Canned tomato paste	15.68
Canned tomato pulp and puree	2.33

Continued on next page.

PRODUCT SHARE DETAILS - Continued

Product or Product Class	% Share	Product or Product Class	% Share
Catsup and other tomato sauces, pastes, etc., nsk	0.68	Canned orange juice, single strength	54.67
Canned jams, jellies, and preserves	6.08	Canned grapefruit juice, single strength	5.48
Canned strawberry jams and preserves, pure	27.29	Canned prune juice, single strength	1.36
Canned raspberry jams and preserves, pure	16.93	Other canned whole fruit juices and mixtures of whole fruit juices	15.37
Other canned jams and preserves, pure	5.00	Canned nectars, single strength	0.23
Canned grape jelly, pure	16.66	Fruit juices, concentrated, hot pack	6.33
Other canned jellies, pure	10.93	Canned fruit juices, nectars, and concentrates, nsk	1.90
Canned imitation jellies, jams, and preserves	4.73	Fresh fruit juices and nectars, single strength	7.99
Canned marmalades	2.35	Fresh orange juices and nectars, single strength	44.54
Canned fruit butter	6.22	Other fresh juices amd nectars, single strength	34.74
Canned maraschino cherries, excluding glace and candied	6.33	Concentrated fruit juice, except for fountain use	19.47
Jams, jellies, and preserves, nsk	3.55	Fresh fruit juices and nectars, single strength, nsk	1.24
Canned fruit juices, nectars, and concentrates	21.88	Canned fruits and vegetables, nsk	2.44
Canned apple juice, single strength	14.66		

Source: 1992 *Economic Census*. The values shown are percent of total shipments in an industry. Values of indented subcategories are summed in the main heading. The symbol (D) appears when data are withheld to prevent disclosure of competitive information. The abbreviation nsk stands for 'not specified by kind' and nec for 'not elsewhere classified'.

INPUTS AND OUTPUTS FOR CANNED FRUITS & VEGETABLES

Economic Sector or Industry Providing Inputs	%	Sector	Economic Sector or Industry Buying Outputs	%	Sector
Imports	17.7	Foreign	Personal consumption expenditures	71.4	
Metal cans	17.4	Manufg.	Eating & drinking places	10.7	Trade
Wholesale trade	10.3	Trade	Canned fruits & vegetables	4.3	Manufg.
Fruits	8.3	Agric.	Exports	3.0	Foreign
Vegetables	7.4	Agric.	S/L Govt. purch., elem. & secondary education	1.8	S/L Govt
Canned fruits & vegetables	6.3	Manufg.	Hospitals	1.4	Services
Glass containers	5.6	Manufg.	Change in business inventories	1.2	In House
Motor freight transportation & warehousing	3.8	Util.	Bottled & canned soft drinks	1.1	Manufg.
Paperboard containers & boxes	2.0	Manufg.	Canned specialties	1.0	Manufg.
Gas production & distribution (utilities)	1.8	Util.	Nursing & personal care facilities	0.7	Services
Sugar	1.6	Manufg.	S/L Govt. purch., health & hospitals	0.7	S/L Govt
Advertising	1.6	Services	Residential care	0.4	Services
Flavoring extracts & syrups, nec	1.3	Manufg.	S/L Govt. purch., higher education	0.4	S/L Govt
Frozen fruits, fruit juices & vegetables	1.1	Manufg.	Flavoring extracts & syrups, nec	0.3	Manufg.
Electric services (utilities)	1.1	Util.	Frozen specialties	0.3	Manufg.
Commercial printing	0.9	Manufg.	Social services, nec	0.3	Services
Crowns & closures	0.9	Manufg.	S/L Govt. purch., correction	0.3	S/L Govt
Greenhouse & nursery products	0.8	Agric.	Child day care services	0.2	Services
Wet corn milling	0.8	Manufg.	Federal Government enterprises nec	0.2	Gov't
Dehydrated food products	0.7	Manufg.			
Petroleum refining	0.7	Manufg.			
Railroads & related services	0.6	Util.			
Equipment rental & leasing services	0.6	Services			
Paper coating & glazing	0.5	Manufg.			
Miscellaneous crops	0.3	Agric.			
Maintenance of nonfarm buildings nec	0.3	Constr.			
Food preparations, nec	0.3	Manufg.			
Shortening & cooking oils	0.3	Manufg.			
Communications, except radio & TV	0.3	Util.			
Water transportation	0.3	Util.			
Eating & drinking places	0.3	Trade			
Banking	0.3	Fin/R.E.			
State & local government enterprises, nec	0.3	Gov't			
Bags, except textile	0.2	Manufg.			
Wood pallets & skids	0.2	Manufg.			
Air transportation	0.2	Util.			
Sanitary services, steam supply, irrigation	0.2	Util.			
Real estate	0.2	Fin/R.E.			
U.S. Postal Service	0.2	Gov't			
Cyclic crudes and organics	0.1	Manufg.			
Die-cut paper & board	0.1	Manufg.			
Food products machinery	0.1	Manufg.			
Lubricating oils & greases	0.1	Manufg.			
Meat packing plants	0.1	Manufg.			
Insurance carriers	0.1	Fin/R.E.			
Legal services	0.1	Services			
Management & consulting services & labs	0.1	Services			

Source: Benchmark Input-Output Accounts for the U.S. Economy, 1982, U.S. Department of Commerce, Washington, D.C., July 1991. Data, as reported in the source, are organized by the 1977 SIC structure in use in 1982 but have been matched, as closely as is possible, to the 1987 SIC structure used in this book.

OCCUPATIONS EMPLOYED BY SIC 203 - PRESERVED FRUITS AND VEGETABLES

Occupation	% of Total 1994	Change to 2005	Occupation	% of Total 1994	Change to 2005
Cannery workers	21.2	6.7	Maintenance repairers, general utility	1.9	-4.0
Packaging & filling machine operators	6.8	6.7	Janitors & cleaners, incl maids	1.8	-14.6
Helpers, laborers, & material movers nec	5.1	6.7	Freight, stock, & material movers, hand	1.7	-14.6
Industrial machinery mechanics	4.5	49.4	Crushing & mixing machine operators	1.4	6.7
Industrial truck & tractor operators	4.5	6.7	Truck drivers light & heavy	1.3	10.0
Blue collar worker supervisors	4.1	3.7	General managers & top executives	1.3	1.2
Hand packers & packagers	3.9	-8.5	Vehicle washers & equipment cleaners	1.1	-1.6
Assemblers, fabricators, & hand workers nec	3.4	6.7	Industrial production managers	1.1	6.7
Agricultural workers nec	2.5	6.7	Sales & related workers nec	1.1	6.7
Cooking, roasting machine operators	2.3	17.4	Bookkeeping, accounting, & auditing clerks	1.0	-20.0
Precision food & tobacco workers nec	2.2	17.4	Traffic, shipping, & receiving clerks	1.0	2.6
Machine operators nec	2.2	-5.9	Secretaries, ex legal & medical	1.0	-2.9
Machine feeders & offbearers	2.1	17.3			

Source: *Industry-Occupation Matrix*, Bureau of Labor Statistics. These data relate to one or more 3-digit SIC industry groups rather than to a single 4-digit SIC. The change reported for each occupation to the year 2005 is a percent of growth or decline as estimated by the Bureau of Labor Statistics. The abbreviation nec stands for 'not elsewhere classified'.

LOCATION BY STATE AND REGIONAL CONCENTRATION

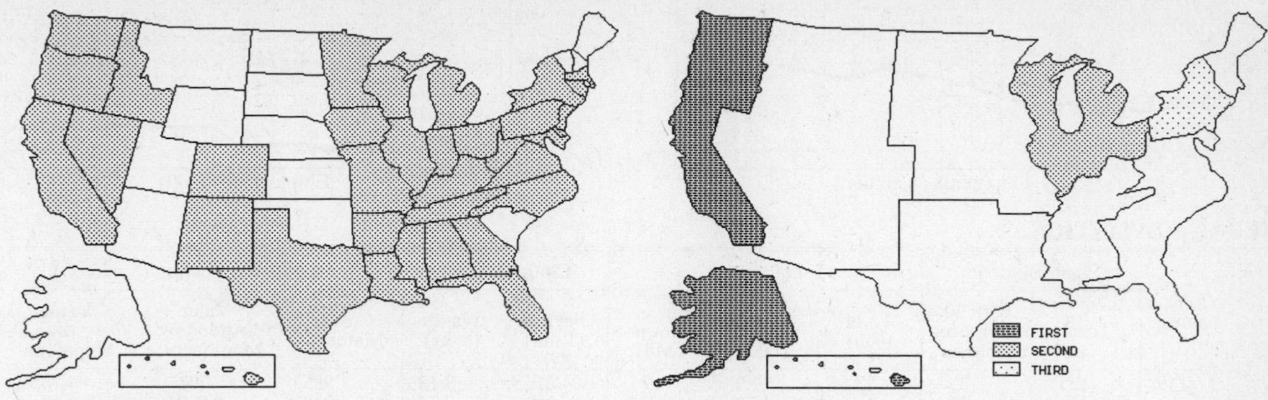

INDUSTRY DATA BY STATE

State	Establish-ments	Shipments			Employment				Cost as % of Shipments	Investment per Employee ($)
		Total ($ mil)	% of U.S.	Per Establ.	Total Number	% of U.S.	Per Establ.	Wages ($/hour)		
California	120	4,233.5	28.1	35.3	18,700	29.4	156	11.37	56.8	6,727
New York	50	1,393.4	9.2	27.9	3,200	5.0	64	10.05	43.6	8,781
Ohio	30	858.3	5.7	28.6	2,900	4.6	97	12.50	42.5	5,138
Wisconsin	56	826.4	5.5	14.8	5,100	8.0	91	8.56	57.0	4,098
Pennsylvania	23	763.0	5.1	33.2	3,300	5.2	143	9.34	55.9	16,970
Michigan	32	564.9	3.7	17.7	2,700	4.2	84	8.57	57.6	4,037
Washington	33	557.5	3.7	16.9	3,400	5.3	103	9.07	50.2	5,441
Texas	25	405.0	2.7	16.2	2,000	3.1	80	8.67	50.3	5,300
Minnesota	20	374.0	2.5	18.7	2,300	3.6	115	8.86	51.4	7,913
New Jersey	14	359.6	2.4	25.7	1,300	2.0	93	11.38	68.2	5,308
Illinois	24	342.8	2.3	14.3	1,700	2.7	71	9.97	54.9	5,824
Massachusetts	7	311.7	2.1	44.5	900	1.4	129	10.25	55.3	-
Indiana	14	301.4	2.0	21.5	1,000	1.6	71	10.56	54.4	20,500
Hawaii	10	194.6	1.3	19.5	1,300	2.0	130	9.16	49.2	1,615
Oregon	28	182.6	1.2	6.5	1,500	2.4	54	9.04	66.1	5,333
Virginia	10	128.6	0.9	12.9	1,000	1.6	100	8.56	54.4	2,200
North Carolina	12	83.1	0.6	6.9	700	1.1	58	8.00	64.5	3,143
Delaware	5	82.0	0.5	16.4	900	1.4	180	6.71	60.2	-
Georgia	6	37.9	0.3	6.3	300	0.5	50	6.83	63.3	2,667
Maryland	14	29.3	0.2	2.1	200	0.3	14	9.50	60.4	4,500
Colorado	16	23.0	0.2	1.4	200	0.3	13	7.25	44.8	1,500
Florida	33	(D)	-	-	3,750 *	5.9	114	-	-	8,720
Missouri	13	(D)	-	-	175 *	0.3	13	-	-	-
Arkansas	9	(D)	-	-	750 *	1.2	83	-	-	-
Tennessee	8	(D)	-	-	375 *	0.6	47	-	-	-
Connecticut	7	(D)	-	-	375 *	0.6	54	-	-	4,000
Iowa	7	(D)	-	-	750 *	1.2	107	-	-	-
Kentucky	7	(D)	-	-	375 *	0.6	54	-	-	11,467
Louisiana	7	(D)	-	-	375 *	0.6	54	-	-	-
Idaho	5	(D)	-	-	750 *	1.2	150	-	-	-
Mississippi	3	(D)	-	-	750 *	1.2	250	-	-	-
New Mexico	3	(D)	-	-	175 *	0.3	58	-	-	-
Alabama	2	(D)	-	-	175 *	0.3	88	-	-	-
Nevada	2	(D)	-	-	175 *	0.3	88	-	-	-
West Virginia	2	(D)	-	-	175 *	0.3	88	-	-	-

Source: 1992 *Economic Census*. The states are in descending order of shipments or establishments (if shipment data are missing for the majority). The symbol (D) appears when data are withheld to prevent disclosure of competitive information. States marked with (D) are sorted by number of establishments. A dash (-) indicates that the data element cannot be calculated; * indicates the midpoint of a range.

2034 - DRIED & DEHYDRATED FRUITS VEGETABLES

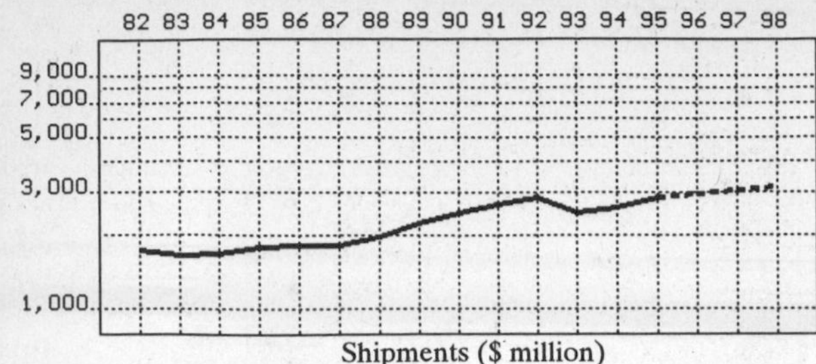

Shipments ($ million)

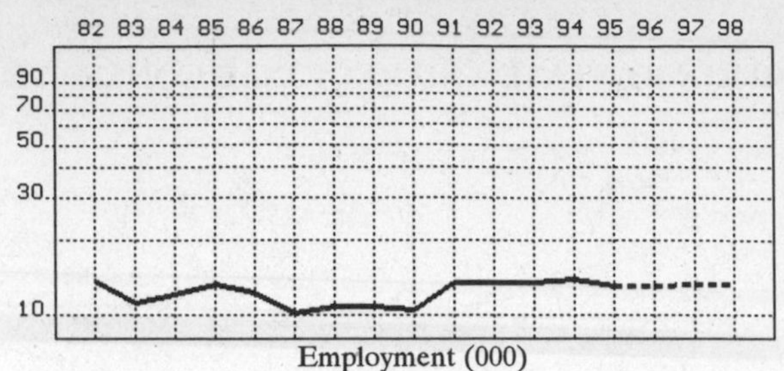

Employment (000)

GENERAL STATISTICS

Year	Com-panies	Establishments		Employment			Compensation		Production ($ million)			
		Total	with 20 or more employees	Total (000)	Production Workers (000)	Production Hours (Mil)	Payroll ($ mil)	Wages ($/hr)	Cost of Materials	Value Added by Manufacture	Value of Shipments	Capital Invest.
1982	119	151	85	13.6	11.2	19.1	216.9	8.18	985.0	792.3	1,745.1	51.7
1983		146	80	11.0	8.8	17.3	210.0	8.76	945.4	697.0	1,646.9	44.0
1984		141	75	11.9	9.7	17.8	216.4	8.60	932.6	685.6	1,686.4	54.9
1985		135	70	13.2	11.0	20.2	242.8	8.66	973.5	839.9	1,788.0	61.4
1986		144	70	12.2	9.9	17.4	221.9	8.82	922.4	859.7	1,816.9	47.1
1987	109	131	68	10.1	8.4	15.4	190.6	8.94	923.8	932.3	1,819.6	48.2
1988		133	64	10.8	9.1	16.7	207.9	8.95	1,032.2	890.6	1,971.4	60.7
1989		140	67	10.8	11.1	20.4	263.4	8.96	1,178.2	1,131.7	2,235.2	125.0
1990		138	68	10.5	11.7	22.8	298.1	8.99	1,372.3	1,124.9	2,453.7	98.6
1991		141	73	13.4	11.0	21.4	316.7	10.27	1,394.8	1,353.2	2,708.3	117.9
1992	124	155	84	13.5	11.3	21.9	320.8	10.25	1,317.9	1,515.0	2,853.1	91.7
1993		150	68	13.5	11.3	21.4	320.4	10.43	1,218.1	1,252.8	2,471.4	81.3
1994		144P	68P	14.0	11.7	22.2	337.7	10.68	1,425.4	1,239.9	2,601.4	148.9
1995		144P	68P	12.9P	11.6P	22.4P	341.1P	10.62P	1,558.9P	1,356.0P	2,845.1P	128.0P
1996		144P	67P	13.0P	11.7P	22.8P	352.9P	10.81P	1,614.2P	1,404.2P	2,946.1P	135.0P
1997		145P	66P	13.1P	11.9P	23.2P	364.6P	11.01P	1,669.6P	1,452.3P	3,047.0P	142.0P
1998		145P	66P	13.2P	12.0P	23.7P	376.4P	11.20P	1,724.9P	1,500.4P	3,148.0P	148.9P

Sources: 1982, 1987, 1992 *Economic Census*; *Annual Survey of Manufactures*, 83-86, 88-91, 93-94. Establishment counts for non-Census years are from *County Business Patterns*; establishment values for 83-84 are extrapolations. 'P's show projections by the editors. Industries reclassified in 87 will not have data for prior years.

INDICES OF CHANGE

Year	Com-panies	Establishments		Employment			Compensation		Production ($ million)			
		Total	with 20 or more employees	Total (000)	Production Workers (000)	Production Hours (Mil)	Payroll ($ mil)	Wages ($/hr)	Cost of Materials	Value Added by Manufacture	Value of Shipments	Capital Invest.
1982	96	97	101	101	99	87	68	80	75	52	61	56
1983		94	95	81	78	79	65	85	72	46	58	48
1984		91	89	88	86	81	67	84	71	45	59	60
1985		87	83	98	97	92	76	84	74	55	63	67
1986		93	83	90	88	79	69	86	70	57	64	51
1987	88	85	81	75	74	70	59	87	70	62	64	53
1988		86	76	80	81	76	65	87	78	59	69	66
1989		90	80	80	98	93	82	87	89	75	78	136
1990		89	81	78	104	104	93	88	104	74	86	108
1991		91	87	99	97	98	99	100	106	89	95	129
1992	100	100	100	100	100	100	100	100	100	100	100	100
1993		97	81	100	100	98	100	102	92	83	87	89
1994		93P	81P	104	104	101	105	104	108	82	91	162
1995		93P	81P	96P	102P	102P	106P	104P	118P	90P	100P	140P
1996		93P	80P	97P	104P	104P	110P	105P	122P	93P	103P	147P
1997		93P	79P	97P	105P	106P	114P	107P	127P	96P	107P	155P
1998		93P	78P	98P	106P	108P	117P	109P	131P	99P	110P	162P

Sources: Same as General Statistics. Values reflect change from the base year, 1992. Values above 100 mean greater than 92, values below 100 mean less than 92, and a value of 100 in the 82-91 or 93-98 period means same as 92. 'P's mark projections by the editors.

SELECTED RATIOS

For 1994	Avg. of All Manufact.	Analyzed Industry	Index	For 1994	Avg. of All Manufact.	Analyzed Industry	Index
Employees per Establishment	49	97	199	Value Added per Production Worker	134,084	105,974	79
Payroll per Establishment	1,500,273	2,348,599	157	Cost per Establishment	5,045,178	9,913,214	196
Payroll per Employee	30,620	24,121	79	Cost per Employee	102,970	101,814	99
Production Workers per Establishment	34	81	237	Cost per Production Worker	146,988	121,829	83
Wages per Establishment	853,319	1,648,929	193	Shipments per Establishment	9,576,895	18,091,928	189
Wages per Production Worker	24,861	20,265	82	Shipments per Employee	195,460	185,814	95
Hours per Production Worker	2,056	1,897	92	Shipments per Production Worker	279,017	222,342	80
Wages per Hour	12.09	10.68	88	Investment per Establishment	321,011	1,035,553	323
Value Added per Establishment	4,602,255	8,623,119	187	Investment per Employee	6,552	10,636	162
Value Added per Employee	93,930	88,564	94	Investment per Production Worker	9,352	12,726	136

Sources: Same as General Statistics. The 'Average of All Manufacturing' column represents the average of all manufacturing industries reported for the most recent complete year available. The Index shows the relationship between the Average and the Analyzed Industry. For example, 100 means that they are equal; 500 that the Analyzed Industry is five times the average; 50 means that the Analyzed Industry is half the national average. The abbreviation 'na' is used to show that data are 'not available'.

LEADING COMPANIES

Number shown: **36** Total sales ($ mil): **3,020** Total employment (000): **14.3**

Company Name	Address				CEO Name	Phone	Co. Type	Sales ($ mil)	Empl. (000)
Sun-Diamond Growers	5568 Gibraltar Dr	Pleasanton	CA	94588	Larry Busboom	510-463-8200	R	600	1.8
Basic American Foods	2999 Oak Rd	Walnut Creek	CA	94596	Larry Ledin	510-472-4000	S	490	2.5
Basic American Inc	600 Montgomery St	San Francisco	CA	94111	George Hume	415-705-5100	R	490	2.5
Dole Dried Fruit and Nut Co	PO Box 2562	Fresno	CA	93745	Jon Rodacy	209-499-6600	D	300*	0.5
Basic Vegetable Products LP	705 E Whitmore	Modesto	CA	95358	Dennis Wittchow	209-538-1071	R	200	1.0
Gilroy Foods Inc	1350 Pacheco Pass	Gilroy	CA	95020	Van Turnstall	408-847-1414	S	200	1.1
Sun-Maid Growers of California	13525 S Bethel Av	Kingsburg	CA	93631	Barry F Kriebel	209-896-8000	S	190	0.7
Nonpareil Corp	40 N 400 W	Blackfoot	ID	83221	Chris T Abend	208-785-5880	R	91*	0.7
Rogers Foods Inc	PO Drawer R	Turlock	CA	95381	James F Palo	209-667-2777	S	80	0.5
Yorkshire Dried Fruit and Nuts	PO Box 11944	Fresno	CA	93776	Jeffrey P Helfer	209-233-1181	S	55*	0.3
Mayfair Packing Company Inc	PO Box 5879	San Jose	CA	95150	James S Meleham	408-280-2300	R	40	0.4
Oregon Freeze Dry Inc	PO Box 1048	Albany	OR	97321	H Aschkenasy	503-926-6001	R	39*	0.2
Vacu-Dry Co	PO Box 2418	Sebastopol	CA	95473	Donal Sugrue	707-829-4600	P	28	0.3
Stockpot Soups Inc	18211 NE 68th St	Redmond	WA	98052	Kevin Fortun	206-885-0779	R	25	0.2
Oregon Potato Co	PO Box 169	Boardman	OR	97818	David Landon	503-481-2715	R	20	0.2
Enoch Packing Company Inc	PO Box 339	Del Rey	CA	93616	Charles J Enoch	209-888-2151	R	18*	0.1
Tule River Cooperative Dryer	PO Box 4477	Woodville	CA	93258	Guido Lombardi	209-784-3396	R	18	0.1
Central California Raisin Packing	PO Box 220	Del Rey	CA	93616	Dan Milinovich	209-888-2195	R	17*	<0.1
Chooljian Brothers Packing Co	PO Box 395	Sanger	CA	93657	Leo Chooljian	209-875-5501	R	17*	<0.1
Graceland Fruit Cooperative	1881 Forrester Rd	Frankfort	MI	49635	Don Nugent	616-352-9741	R	16	0.1
Crystals International Inc	600 ML King	Plant City	FL	33566	William G Carr	813-754-2691	R	15	0.1
Idaho Pacific Corp	PO Box 478	Ririe	ID	83443	R G Zirkelbach	208-538-6971	R	15	0.1
Garry Packing Inc	PO Box 249	Del Rey	CA	93616	James W Garry	209-888-2126	R	10	0.4
Sanofi Bio-Industries	421 Commer St	Anaheim	CA	92803	Fabienne Saadane	714-533-4558	S	10	<0.1
Nile Spice Foods Inc	2203 Airport Way S	Seattle	WA	98134	Nadim Spahi	206-281-7292	R	6*	<0.1
Northwest Pea and Bean	PO Box 11973	Spokane	WA	99211	Don J Driscoll	509-534-3821	R	6*	<0.1
New Meridian Inc	201 W Babb Rd	Eaton	IN	47338	David Brand	317-396-3344	R	5	<0.1
Bernard Fine Foods Inc	PO Box 610490	San Jose	CA	95161	HL Epstein	408-292-9067	R	3*	<0.1
Major Products Company Inc	66 Industrial Av	Little Ferry	NJ	07643	Daniel De Rose	201-641-5555	R	3	<0.1
MC Snack Inc	5355 Mira Sorrento	San Diego	CA	92121	Masafumi Yoshida	619-546-8900	S	3*	<0.1
Tastee Apple Inc	60810 County Rd 9	Newcomerstown	OH	43832	John Hackenbracht	614-498-8316	R	3	<0.1
Timber Crest Farms	4791 Dry Creek Rd	Healdsburg	CA	95448	RE Waltenspiel	707-433-8251	R	3	0.1
Bordo Products Co	125 Moen Av	Cranford	NJ	07016		908-272-0550	R	2	<0.1
Covaldo Inc	51392 Harrison St	Coachella	CA	92236	C Anderson Stocks	619-398-3551	R	1*	<0.1
Innovative Foods Inc	179 Starlite St	S San Francisco	CA	94080	E Hirschberg	415-871-8912	R	1*	<0.1
California Sun Dry Foods	951 Mariners Island	San Mateo	CA	94404	Franklin Conlan	415-341-0118	R	1*	<0.1

Source: *Ward's Business Directory of U.S. Private and Public Companies*, Volumes 1 and 2, 1996. The company type code used is as follows: P - Public, R - Private, S - Subsidiary, D - Division, J - Joint Venture, A - Affiliate, G - Group. Sales are in millions of dollars, employees are in thousands. An asterisk (*) indicates an estimated sales volume. The symbol < stands for 'less than'. Company names and addresses are truncated, in some cases, to fit into the available space.

MATERIALS CONSUMED

Material		Quantity	Delivered Cost ($ million)
Materials, ingredients, containers, and supplies		(X)	1,212.4
Cucumbers	1,000 s tons	(D)	
Fresh fruits	1,000 s tons	167.6**	40.9
Dried fruits	1,000 s tons	363.8	382.8
Corn syrup	mil lb	(D)	(D)
Sugar, cane and beet (in terms of sugar solids)	1,000 s tons	28.1	13.7
Packaging paper and plastics film, coated and laminated		(X)	34.4
Bags; plastics, foil, and coated paper		(X)	28.1
Paperboard containers, boxes, and corrugated paperboard		(X)	84.4
All other materials and components, parts, containers, and supplies		(X)	414.9
Materials, ingredients, containers, and supplies, nsk		(X)	45.8

Source: 1992 *Economic Census*. Explanation of symbols used: (D): Withheld to avoid disclosure of competitive data; na: Not available; (S): Withheld because statistical norms were not met; (X): Not applicable; (Z): Less than half the unit shown; nec: Not elsewhere classified; nsk: Not specified by kind; - : zero; * : 10-19 percent estimated; ** : 20-29 percent estimated.

PRODUCT SHARE DETAILS

Product or Product Class	% Share	Product or Product Class	% Share
Dried and dehydrated fruits, vegetables, and soups	100.00	fruit flour, meal, and powder	11.26
Soup mixes, including oriental, dried and dehydrated, and freeze-dried	21.27	Dried and dehydrated potatoes (except potato flour), not packaged with other ingredients	22.16
Dried and dehydrated fruits and vegetables (including freeze-dried)	76.26	Onions, dried and dehydrated	9.90
Raisins, dried and dehydrated	20.44	Other dried and dehydrated vegetables and vegetable flours, including potato flour	18.07
Prunes, dried and dehydrated	14.36	Dried and dehydrated fruits and vegetables (including freeze-dried), nsk	0.37
Apples, dried and dehydrated	3.44	Dried and dehydrated fruits, vegetables, and soups, nsk	2.48
Other dried and dehydrated fruits and fruit peels, including			

Source: 1992 *Economic Census*. The values shown are percent of total shipments in an industry. Values of indented subcategories are summed in the main heading. The symbol (D) appears when data are withheld to prevent disclosure of competitive information. The abbreviation nsk stands for 'not specified by kind' and nec for 'not elsewhere classified'.

INPUTS AND OUTPUTS FOR DEHYDRATED FOOD PRODUCTS

Economic Sector or Industry Providing Inputs	%	Sector	Economic Sector or Industry Buying Outputs	%	Sector
Dehydrated food products	28.4	Manufg.	Personal consumption expenditures	53.0	
Vegetables	13.2	Agric.	Dehydrated food products	13.4	Manufg.
Wholesale trade	10.8	Trade	Exports	10.8	Foreign
Imports	7.9	Foreign	Canned specialties	5.9	Manufg.
Paperboard containers & boxes	5.0	Manufg.	Eating & drinking places	5.6	Trade
Advertising	5.0	Services	Cereal breakfast foods	2.8	Manufg.
Motor freight transportation & warehousing	4.2	Util.	Canned fruits & vegetables	1.9	Manufg.
Commercial printing	3.4	Manufg.	Food preparations, nec	1.3	Manufg.
Gas production & distribution (utilities)	3.2	Util.	Change in business inventories	1.2	In House
Business services nec	2.8	Services	Child day care services	0.8	Services
Metal foil & leaf	1.9	Manufg.	Hospitals	0.7	Services
Electric services (utilities)	1.9	Util.	S/L Govt. purch., elem. & secondary education	0.5	S/L Govt
Fruits	1.7	Agric.	S/L Govt. purch., higher education	0.4	S/L Govt
Petroleum refining	1.2	Manufg.	S/L Govt. purch., correction	0.3	S/L Govt
Paper coating & glazing	1.0	Manufg.	S/L Govt. purch., health & hospitals	0.3	S/L Govt
Sugar	0.7	Manufg.	Confectionery products	0.2	Manufg.
Railroads & related services	0.7	Util.	Nursing & personal care facilities	0.2	Services
Cyclic crudes and organics	0.5	Manufg.	Residential care	0.2	Services
Food preparations, nec	0.4	Manufg.	Social services, nec	0.1	Services
Miscellaneous plastics products	0.4	Manufg.	Federal Government enterprises nec	0.1	Gov't
Eating & drinking places	0.4	Trade			
Maintenance of nonfarm buildings nec	0.3	Constr.			
Flavoring extracts & syrups, nec	0.3	Manufg.			
Rice milling	0.3	Manufg.			
Communications, except radio & TV	0.3	Util.			
Banking	0.3	Fin/R.E.			
State & local government enterprises, nec	0.3	Gov't			
Food products machinery	0.2	Manufg.			
Sanitary services, steam supply, irrigation	0.2	Util.			
Real estate	0.2	Fin/R.E.			
Management & consulting services & labs	0.2	Services			
Lubricating oils & greases	0.1	Manufg.			
Soap & other detergents	0.1	Manufg.			
Water transportation	0.1	Util.			
Insurance carriers	0.1	Fin/R.E.			
Accounting, auditing & bookkeeping	0.1	Services			
Equipment rental & leasing services	0.1	Services			
Laundry, dry cleaning, shoe repair	0.1	Services			
Legal services	0.1	Services			
Noncomparable imports	0.1	Foreign			

Source: Benchmark Input-Output Accounts for the U.S. Economy, 1982, U.S. Department of Commerce, Washington, D.C., July 1991. Data, as reported in the source, are organized by the 1977 SIC structure in use in 1982 but have been matched, as closely as is possible, to the 1987 SIC structure used in this book.

OCCUPATIONS EMPLOYED BY SIC 203 - PRESERVED FRUITS AND VEGETABLES

Occupation	% of Total 1994	Change to 2005	Occupation	% of Total 1994	Change to 2005
Cannery workers	21.2	6.7	Maintenance repairers, general utility	1.9	-4.0
Packaging & filling machine operators	6.8	6.7	Janitors & cleaners, incl maids	1.8	-14.6
Helpers, laborers, & material movers nec	5.1	6.7	Freight, stock, & material movers, hand	1.7	-14.6
Industrial machinery mechanics	4.5	49.4	Crushing & mixing machine operators	1.4	6.7
Industrial truck & tractor operators	4.5	6.7	Truck drivers light & heavy	1.3	10.0
Blue collar worker supervisors	4.1	3.7	General managers & top executives	1.3	1.2
Hand packers & packagers	3.9	-8.5	Vehicle washers & equipment cleaners	1.1	-1.6
Assemblers, fabricators, & hand workers nec	3.4	6.7	Industrial production managers	1.1	6.7
Agricultural workers nec	2.5	6.7	Sales & related workers nec	1.1	6.7
Cooking, roasting machine operators	2.3	17.4	Bookkeeping, accounting, & auditing clerks	1.0	-20.0
Precision food & tobacco workers nec	2.2	17.4	Traffic, shipping, & receiving clerks	1.0	2.6
Machine operators nec	2.2	-5.9	Secretaries, ex legal & medical	1.0	-2.9
Machine feeders & offbearers	2.1	17.3			

Source: *Industry-Occupation Matrix*, Bureau of Labor Statistics. These data relate to one or more 3-digit SIC industry groups rather than to a single 4-digit SIC. The change reported for each occupation to the year 2005 is a percent of growth or decline as estimated by the Bureau of Labor Statistics. The abbreviation nec stands for 'not elsewhere classified'.

LOCATION BY STATE AND REGIONAL CONCENTRATION

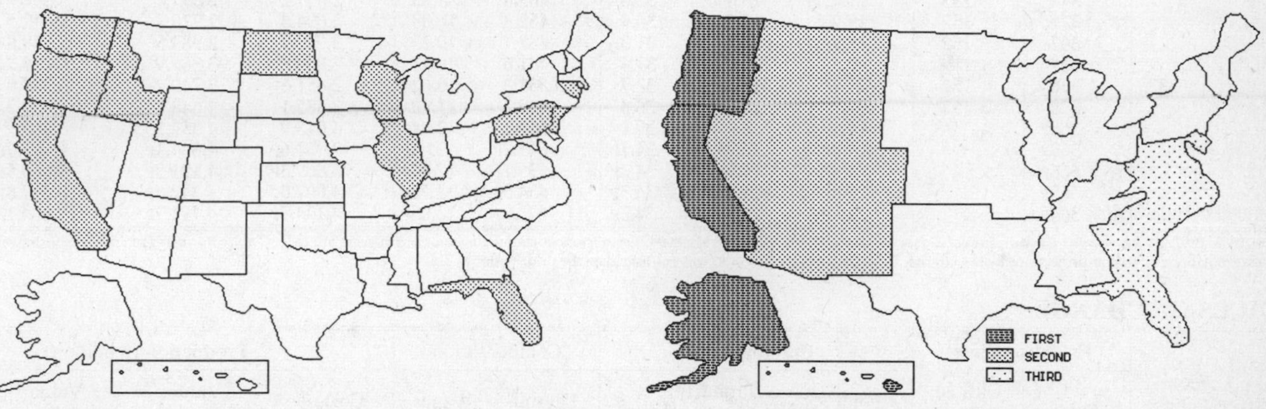

INDUSTRY DATA BY STATE

State	Establish-ments	Shipments			Employment				Cost as % of Shipments	Investment per Employee ($)
		Total ($ mil)	% of U.S.	Per Establ.	Total Number	% of U.S.	Per Establ.	Wages ($/hour)		
California	74	1,518.7	53.2	20.5	7,200	53.3	97	10.03	53.9	6,111
Idaho	11	422.3	14.8	38.4	2,900	21.5	264	8.42	39.9	6,172
Washington	12	83.2	2.9	6.9	600	4.4	50	9.22	55.3	4,333
Oregon	7	18.5	0.6	2.6	200	1.5	29	7.33	36.8	-
Florida	6	18.0	0.6	3.0	100	0.7	17	10.50	47.8	-
New Jersey	4	(D)	-	-	750 *	5.6	188	-	-	-
Illinois	2	(D)	-	-	750 *	5.6	375	-	-	-
North Dakota	2	(D)	-	-	175 *	1.3	88	-	-	-
Wisconsin	2	(D)	-	-	175 *	1.3	88	-	-	-
Connecticut	1	(D)	-	-	175 *	1.3	175	-	-	-
Pennsylvania	1	(D)	-	-	375 *	2.8	375	-	-	-

Source: 1992 *Economic Census*. The states are in descending order of shipments or establishments (if shipment data are missing for the majority). The symbol (D) appears when data are withheld to prevent disclosure of competitive information. States marked with (D) are sorted by number of establishments. A dash (-) indicates that the data element cannot be calculated; * indicates the midpoint of a range.

2035 - PICKLES, SAUCES & SALAD DRESSINGS

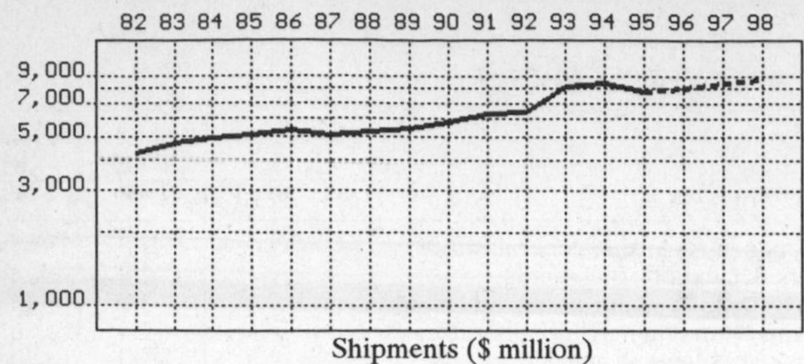

Shipments ($ million)

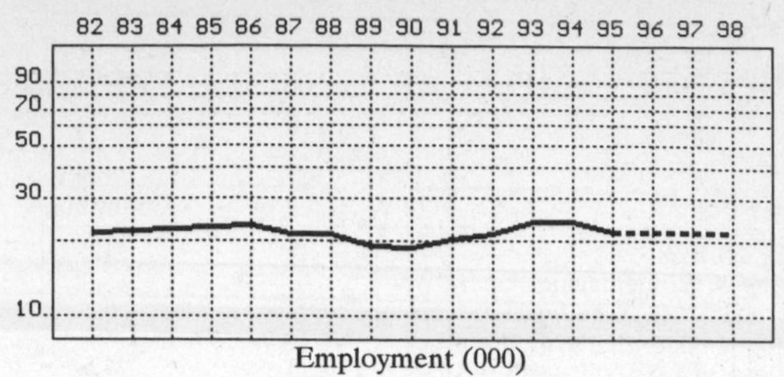

Employment (000)

GENERAL STATISTICS

Year	Companies	Establishments: Total	Establishments: with 20 or more employees	Employment: Total (000)	Production Workers (000)	Production Hours (Mil)	Compensation: Payroll ($ mil)	Compensation: Wages ($/hr)	Production ($ million): Cost of Materials	Value Added by Manufacture	Value of Shipments	Capital Invest.
1982	327	376	156	22.0	17.4	33.3	371.5	7.83	2,532.7	1,736.9	4,268.8	67.5
1983		378		22.2	17.3	33.3	383.6	8.10	2,672.5	2,039.6	4,698.4	61.8
1984		380		22.6	17.9	34.3	416.9	8.44	2,995.5	1,894.2	4,896.3	96.4
1985		381		22.9	18.1	34.2	439.3	8.96	2,998.0	2,115.6	5,123.2	129.5
1986		375	146	23.1	18.1	34.5	471.3	9.45	2,884.1	2,473.2	5,353.2	147.0
1987	349	382	162	21.5	16.6	32.6	451.8	9.51	2,506.8	2,544.8	5,050.3	221.0
1988		373	153	21.4	16.6	32.6	463.8	9.85	2,637.2	2,657.4	5,292.9	165.6
1989		371	152	19.2	15.6	30.9	462.8	10.08	2,694.3	2,720.7	5,412.5	139.2
1990		362	162	18.9	15.7	31.3	488.7	10.23	2,770.7	2,984.5	5,749.8	145.3
1991		369	159	20.5	15.9	31.4	481.6	10.43	2,850.8	3,365.9	6,220.7	210.5
1992	332	376	152	21.4	16.3	32.7	531.3	10.62	2,651.3	3,749.2	6,398.0	158.8
1993		370	152	24.1	18.7	36.6	625.2	11.83	3,485.1	4,648.3	8,130.3	161.3
1994		368P		24.1	18.4	37.1	653.1	12.04	4,015.9	4,352.2	8,365.9	156.6
1995		367P		21.8P	16.9P	34.1P	615.8P	12.07P	3,731.6P	4,044.1P	7,773.7P	198.5P
1996		366P		21.8P	16.9P	34.2P	635.1P	12.40P	3,869.3P	4,193.3P	8,060.5P	206.4P
1997		365P		21.8P	16.8P	34.3P	654.5P	12.72P	4,007.0P	4,342.5P	8,347.3P	214.3P
1998		364P		21.8P	16.8P	34.3P	673.9P	13.05P	4,144.7P	4,491.7P	8,634.1P	222.2P

Sources: 1982, 1987, 1992 *Economic Census*; *Annual Survey of Manufactures*, 83-86, 88-91, 93-94. Establishment counts for non-Census years are from *County Business Patterns*; establishment values for 83-84 are extrapolations. 'P's show projections by the editors. Industries reclassified in 87 will not have data for prior years.

INDICES OF CHANGE

Year	Companies	Establishments: Total	Establishments: with 20 or more employees	Employment: Total (000)	Production Workers (000)	Production Hours (Mil)	Compensation: Payroll ($ mil)	Compensation: Wages ($/hr)	Production ($ million): Cost of Materials	Value Added by Manufacture	Value of Shipments	Capital Invest.
1982	98	100	103	103	107	102	70	74	96	46	67	43
1983		101		104	106	102	72	76	101	54	73	39
1984		101		106	110	105	78	79	113	51	77	61
1985		101		107	111	105	83	84	113	56	80	82
1986		100	96	108	111	106	89	89	109	66	84	93
1987	105	102	107	100	102	100	85	90	95	68	79	139
1988		99	101	100	102	100	87	93	99	71	83	104
1989		99	100	90	96	94	87	95	102	73	85	88
1990		96	107	88	96	96	92	96	105	80	90	91
1991		98	105	96	98	96	91	98	108	90	97	133
1992	100	100	100	100	100	100	100	100	100	100	100	100
1993		98	100	113	115	112	118	111	131	124	127	102
1994		98P		113	113	113	123	113	151	116	131	99
1995		98P		102P	104P	104P	116P	114P	141P	108P	122P	125P
1996		97P		102P	103P	104P	120P	117P	146P	112P	126P	130P
1997		97P		102P	103P	105P	123P	120P	151P	116P	130P	135P
1998		97P		102P	103P	105P	127P	123P	156P	120P	135P	140P

Sources: Same as General Statistics. Values reflect change from the base year, 1992. Values above 100 mean greater than 92, values below 100 mean less than 92, and a value of 100 in the 82-91 or 93-98 period means same as 92. 'P's mark projections by the editors.

SELECTED RATIOS

For 1994	Avg. of All Manufact.	Analyzed Industry	Index
Employees per Establishment	49	65	134
Payroll per Establishment	1,500,273	1,774,144	118
Payroll per Employee	30,620	27,100	89
Production Workers per Establishment	34	50	146
Wages per Establishment	853,319	1,213,416	142
Wages per Production Worker	24,861	24,276	98
Hours per Production Worker	2,056	2,016	98
Wages per Hour	12.09	12.04	100
Value Added per Establishment	4,602,255	11,822,736	257
Value Added per Employee	93,930	180,589	192

For 1994	Avg. of All Manufact.	Analyzed Industry	Index
Value Added per Production Worker	134,084	236,533	176
Cost per Establishment	5,045,178	10,909,178	216
Cost per Employee	102,970	166,635	162
Cost per Production Worker	146,988	218,255	148
Shipments per Establishment	9,576,895	22,725,938	237
Shipments per Employee	195,460	347,133	178
Shipments per Production Worker	279,017	454,668	163
Investment per Establishment	321,011	425,403	133
Investment per Employee	6,552	6,498	99
Investment per Production Worker	9,352	8,511	91

Sources: Same as General Statistics. The 'Average of All Manufacturing' column represents the average of all manufacturing industries reported for the most recent complete year available. The Index shows the relationship between the Average and the Analyzed Industry. For example, 100 means that they are equal; 500 that the Analyzed Industry is five times the average; 50 means that the Analyzed Industry is half the national average. The abbreviation 'na' is used to show that data are 'not available'.

LEADING COMPANIES Number shown: **57** Total sales ($ mil): **2,145** Total employment (000): **13.3**

Company Name	Address				CEO Name	Phone	Co. Type	Sales ($ mil)	Empl. (000)
Lancaster Colony Corp	37 W Broad St	Columbus	OH	43215	John B Gerlach	614-224-7141	P	722	5.6
Nalley's Fine Foods	3303 S 35th St	Tacoma	WA	98411	Patrick Lindenbach	206-383-1621	D	173	1.0
Pace Foods Ltd	PO Box 12636	San Antonio	TX	78212	C Goldsbury	210-224-2211	R	140*	0.5
Thomas J Lipton Co	PO Box 90	Independence	MO	64051	Edward Kerins	816-833-1700	D	120*	0.4
Charles F Cates and Sons Inc	PO Box 158	Faison	NC	28341	W Hennessee Jr	919-267-4711	S	95	0.9
E McIlhenny and Sons Corp	Hwy 329	Avery Island	LA	70513	EM Simmons	318-365-8175	R	85	0.2
Aunt Jane's Foods	55 E Sanborn St	Croswell	MI	48422	David Schindler	313-679-2555	S	60*	0.2
Mount Olive Pickle Company	PO Box 609	Mount Olive	NC	28365	William H Bryan	919-658-2535	R	51	0.3
WB Roddenbery Company Inc	PO Box 60	Cairo	GA	31728	Jim Greisinger	912-377-2102	S	50*	0.4
Paramount Foods Inc	PO Box 32150	Louisville	KY	40232	F Miller Owings	502-969-9363	R	45	0.4
Rod's Food Products Inc	PO Box 1315	City of Industry	CA	91749	Bill James	818-912-1671	S	45*	0.2
Kikkoman Foods Inc	PO Box 69	Walworth	WI	53184	K Hayashi	414-275-6181	S	37*	0.1
Baumer Foods Inc	PO Box 19166	New Orleans	LA	70179	AA Baumer Jr	504-482-5761	R	30	0.2
Henri's Food Products Company	2730 W S Spring	Milwaukee	WI	53209	A J Costigan	414-461-7760	R	30	0.2
Hudson Industries Inc	PO Box 847	Troy	AL	36081	R Paul Hudson	205-566-6274	R	29*	0.2
Randolph Pickle Corp	4401 W 44th Pl	Chicago	IL	60632	Gary Newman	312-927-7700	R	27	<0.1
Litehouse Corp	PO Box 1969	Sandpoint	ID	83864	E W Hawkins Jr	208-263-7569	R	25	0.2
T Marzetti Co	1105 Schrock Rd	Columbus	OH	43229	Larry Noble	614-846-2232	S	25*	0.2
Steinfeld's Products Co	10001 N Rivergate	Portland	OR	97203	Ray Steinfeld Jr	503-286-8241	R	24	0.2
Plochman Inc	2743 W 36th Pl	Chicago	IL	60632	C M Plochman III	312-254-8989	R	22*	0.2
Martin Gillet and Company Inc	6801 Eastern Av	Baltimore	MD	21224	Joseph J Katz	410-633-6000	R	19	0.2
Pacific Choice Brands Inc	4667 E Date Av	Fresno	CA	93725	Alan Andrews	209-237-5583	R	19	0.2
Western Dressing Inc	2215 Sanders Rd	Northbrook	IL	60062	Walt Grineski	708-480-2923	D	18*	<0.1
Piggie Park Enterprises Inc	PO Box 6847	West Columbia	SC	29171	Lloyd M Bessinger	803-791-5887	R	17	0.2
Eggo Foods	PO Box 360869	Milpitas	CA	95035	Larry Snyder	408-263-7540	D	15*	<0.1
Minn-Dak Growers Ltd	PO Box 13276	Grand Forks	ND	58208	Harris Peterson	701-746-7453	R	15	<0.1
MA Gedney Co	PO Box 8	Chaska	MN	55318	G Tuttle	612-448-2612	R	15*	0.1
Olds Products Company Inc	625 N Sacramento	Chicago	IL	60612	RO Remien	312-722-3300	R	15	<0.1
Paradise Products Corp	58 5th Av	Hawthorne	NJ	07506	David Lax	201-423-2601	R	15	<0.1
Piknik Products Company Inc	PO Box 9388	Montgomery	AL	36195	H Loeb Jr	205-265-1567	R	15*	0.1
Tulkoff Products Company Inc	1101 S Conkling St	Baltimore	MD	21224	Sandy Smiley	410-327-6585	R	15*	<0.1
Louisiana Fish Fry Products Ltd	5267 Plank Rd	Baton Rouge	LA	70805	Cliff Pizzolato	504-356-2905	R	13	0.1
Lee Kum Kee Inc	304 S Date Av	Alhambra	CA	91803	David Lee	818-282-0337	R	12	<0.1
Vincent Food Industries Inc	135 S La Salle St	Chicago	IL	60603	Burton J Vincent	312-782-1838	R	12	<0.1
Gilette Food Flavorings Inc	751 Rahway Av	Union	NJ	07083	Vytas Maceikonis	908-688-0500	R	11	<0.1
Spring Glen Fresh Foods Inc	PO Box 518	Ephrata	PA	17522	John Wareheime	717-733-2201	S	10	0.2
Acadiana Pepper Co	PO Box 844	St Martinville	LA	70582	Chriss Carlson	318-394-5538	R	9	<0.1
Gold Pure Food Products Inc	1 Brooklyn Rd	Hempstead	NY	11550	Steven Gold	516-483-5600	R	9	<0.1
Kruger and Sons Inc	22958 Saklan Rd	Hayward	CA	94545	Dennis Kruger	510-782-2636	R	7	<0.1
Sona and Hollen Foods Inc	3712 Cerritos Av	Los Alamitos	CA	90720	John Kidde	310-431-1379	R	7	<0.1
WFI Corp	1209 W St George	Linden	NJ	07036	Paul Berko	908-925-9494	R	5	<0.1
Flamm Pickle and Packing	PO Box 500	Eau Claire	MI	49111	Gina Flamm	616-461-6916	R	4	<0.1
Food Traditions	RR 2	Northumberl	PA	17857	Marlon Grimes	717-473-8720	R	4	<0.1
JG Van Holten and Son Inc	PO Box 66	Waterloo	WI	53594	James D Byrnes	414-478-2144	R	4	<0.1
Marie's Dressings Inc	PO Box 67	Enumclaw	WA	98022	Larry R Parker	206-825-2625	R	4	<0.1
Ralph Sechler and Son Inc	PO Box 152	St Joe	IN	46785	David Sechler	219-337-5461	R	4	<0.1
US Enterprise Corp	30560 San Antonio	Hayward	CA	94544	David H Hall	510-487-8877	R	4	<0.1
Johnny's Enterprises Inc	319 E 25th St	Tacoma	WA	98421	John E Meaker	206-383-4597	R	3	<0.1
San-J International Inc	2880 Sprouse Dr	Richmond	VA	23231	Stephen Zoller	804-226-8333	S	3	<0.1
House of Tsang Ltd	185 Berry St	San Francisco	CA	94107	David Tsang	415-243-9760	S	2	<0.1
Panola Pepper Corp	Rte 2	Lk Providence	LA	71254	Grady Brown	318-559-1774	R	2	<0.1
Cook's Gourmet Foods Inc	5821 Wilderness	Riverside	CA	92504	Thomas Harris Sr	909-352-5700	S	1*	<0.1
Arcobasso Foods Inc	8014 N Broadway	St Louis	MO	63147	Tom Newsham	314-381-8083	R	1	<0.1
Fisherman's Wharf Foods Co	1401 Elwood St	Los Angeles	CA	90021	Nick Abood	213-746-1541	R	1*	<0.1
JL Gourmand Inc	115 S Royal St	Alexandria	VA	22314	Jonna L Cullen	703-836-1670	R	1	<0.1
Signature Foods Corp	4040 Nine	Alpharetta	GA	30201	Jeffrey C Gray	404-475-3523	R	0*	<0.1
Helen's Tropical Exotics Inc	3316 Hamilton Blv	Atlanta	GA	30354	Hartmut Willinsky	404-762-7767	S	0	<0.1

Source: *Ward's Business Directory of U.S. Private and Public Companies*, Volumes 1 and 2, 1996. The company type code used is as follows: P - Public, R - Private, S - Subsidiary, D - Division, J - Joint Venture, A - Affiliate, G - Group. Sales are in millions of dollars, employees are in thousands. An asterisk (*) indicates an estimated sales volume. The symbol < stands for 'less than'. Company names and addresses are truncated, in some cases, to fit into the available space.

MATERIALS CONSUMED

Material		Quantity	Delivered Cost ($ million)
Materials, ingredients, containers, and supplies		(X)	2,517.1
Cucumbers	1,000 s tons	772.4*	181.4
Other fresh vegetables	1,000 s tons	269.8*	86.6
Fresh fruits	1,000 s tons	41.9*	10.1
Dried fruits	1,000 s tons	1.8*	1.3
Corn syrup	mil lb	323.4	42.9
Sugar, cane and beet (in terms of sugar solids)	1,000 s tons	63.1	32.0
Fats and oils, all types (purchased as such)	mil lb	1,967.5	419.1
Packaging paper and plastics film, coated and laminated		(X)	35.9
Bags; plastics, foil, and coated paper		(X)	25.0
Glass containers		(X)	359.4
Paperboard containers, boxes, and corrugated paperboard		(X)	68.5
All other materials and components, parts, containers, and supplies		(X)	1,120.9
Materials, ingredients, containers, and supplies, nsk		(X)	134.0

Source: 1992 *Economic Census*. Explanation of symbols used: (D): Withheld to avoid disclosure of competitive data; na: Not available; (S): Withheld because statistical norms were not met; (X): Not applicable; (Z): Less than half the unit shown; nec: Not elsewhere classified; nsk: Not specified by kind; - : zero; * : 10-19 percent estimated; ** : 20-29 percent estimated.

PRODUCT SHARE DETAILS

Product or Product Class	% Share
Pickles, sauces, and salad dressings	100.00
Pickles and other pickled products	18.48
Finished dill cucumber pickles	41.61
Finished sour cucumber pickles	3.19
Finished sweet cucumber pickles	16.04
Refrigerated finished cucumber pickles, including overnight, half sour, artificially acidified, etc.	7.08
Other finished pickles and pickled products (mushrooms, peppers, onions, etc.)	13.47
Finished horseradish (excluding sauce)	1.62
Finished relishes	8.09
Finished sauerkraut	0.70
Other finished pickled products	3.07
Unfinished pickles (salt stock)	1.47
Unfinished brined cherries	1.52
Other bulk unfinished pickled products, such as mushrooms, sauerkraut, etc.	2.04
Pickles and other pickled products, nsk	0.08
Prepared sauces (except tomato)	26.86
Prepared mustard	18.47
Other prepared sauces, except tomato (Worcestershire, soy, horseradish, meat, vegetable, seafood, etc.)	80.52
Prepared sauces (except tomato), nsk	1.01
Mayonnaise, salad dressings, and sandwich spreads	51.13
Spoon-type salad dressing	25.51
Spoon-type mayonnaise	26.93
Other spoon-type dressing, including sandwich spreads, refrigerated dressings, and all other semisolid-type dressing	20.19
Pourable salad dressing (including reduced calorie, cheese, vinegar and oil, etc.)	27.08
Mayonnaise, salad dressings, and sandwich spreads, nsk	0.28
Pickles, sauces, and salad dressings, nsk	3.53

Source: 1992 *Economic Census*. The values shown are percent of total shipments in an industry. Values of indented subcategories are summed in the main heading. The symbol (D) appears when data are withheld to prevent disclosure of competitive information. The abbreviation nsk stands for 'not specified by kind' and nec for 'not elsewhere classified'.

INPUTS AND OUTPUTS FOR PICKLES, SAUCES, & SALAD DRESSINGS

Economic Sector or Industry Providing Inputs	%	Sector	Economic Sector or Industry Buying Outputs	%	Sector
Shortening & cooking oils	18.9	Manufg.	Personal consumption expenditures	74.3	
Glass containers	13.4	Manufg.	Eating & drinking places	20.2	Trade
Miscellaneous plastics products	9.6	Manufg.	Exports	1.7	Foreign
Wholesale trade	7.6	Trade	S/L Govt. purch., elem. & secondary education	1.1	S/L Govt
Advertising	6.3	Services	Hospitals	0.5	Services
Imports	5.7	Foreign	Pickles, sauces, & salad dressings	0.3	Manufg.
Commercial printing	5.3	Manufg.	Federal Government enterprises nec	0.3	Gov't
Vegetables	4.8	Agric.	S/L Govt. purch., health & hospitals	0.3	S/L Govt
Motor freight transportation & warehousing	3.6	Util.	S/L Govt. purch., higher education	0.3	S/L Govt
Crowns & closures	3.4	Manufg.	Residential care	0.2	Services
Sanitary services, steam supply, irrigation	2.5	Util.	S/L Govt. purch., correction	0.2	S/L Govt
Miscellaneous crops	2.1	Agric.	Nursing & personal care facilities	0.1	Services
Paperboard containers & boxes	2.0	Manufg.	Social services, nec	0.1	Services
Sugar	2.0	Manufg.	Change in business inventories	0.1	In House
Poultry & egg processing	1.6	Manufg.			
Food preparations, nec	1.4	Manufg.			
Wet corn milling	1.2	Manufg.			
Electric services (utilities)	0.9	Util.			
Gas production & distribution (utilities)	0.6	Util.			
Pickles, sauces, & salad dressings	0.5	Manufg.			
Railroads & related services	0.5	Util.			
Fruits	0.4	Agric.			
Petroleum refining	0.4	Manufg.			
Banking	0.4	Fin/R.E.			
Chemical preparations, nec	0.3	Manufg.			
Equipment rental & leasing services	0.3	Services			
Noncomparable imports	0.3	Foreign			

Continued on next page.

INPUTS AND OUTPUTS FOR PICKLES, SAUCES, & SALAD DRESSINGS - Continued

Economic Sector or Industry Providing Inputs	%	Sector	Economic Sector or Industry Buying Outputs	%	Sector
Maintenance of nonfarm buildings nec	0.2	Constr.			
Metal cans	0.2	Manufg.			
Communications, except radio & TV	0.2	Util.			
Water transportation	0.2	Util.			
Eating & drinking places	0.2	Trade			
Real estate	0.2	Fin/R.E.			
Business/professional associations	0.2	Services			
Cyclic crudes and organics	0.1	Manufg.			
Food products machinery	0.1	Manufg.			
Soap & other detergents	0.1	Manufg.			
Credit agencies other than banks	0.1	Fin/R.E.			
Insurance carriers	0.1	Fin/R.E.			
Computer & data processing services	0.1	Services			
Electrical repair shops	0.1	Services			
Laundry, dry cleaning, shoe repair	0.1	Services			
Miscellaneous repair shops	0.1	Services			
U.S. Postal Service	0.1	Gov't			

Source: Benchmark Input-Output Accounts for the U.S. Economy, 1982, U.S. Department of Commerce, Washington, D.C., July 1991. Data, as reported in the source, are organized by the 1977 SIC structure in use in 1982 but have been matched, as closely as is possible, to the 1987 SIC structure used in this book.

OCCUPATIONS EMPLOYED BY SIC 203 - PRESERVED FRUITS AND VEGETABLES

Occupation	% of Total 1994	Change to 2005	Occupation	% of Total 1994	Change to 2005
Cannery workers	21.2	6.7	Maintenance repairers, general utility	1.9	-4.0
Packaging & filling machine operators	6.8	6.7	Janitors & cleaners, incl maids	1.8	-14.6
Helpers, laborers, & material movers nec	5.1	6.7	Freight, stock, & material movers, hand	1.7	-14.6
Industrial machinery mechanics	4.5	49.4	Crushing & mixing machine operators	1.4	6.7
Industrial truck & tractor operators	4.5	6.7	Truck drivers light & heavy	1.3	10.0
Blue collar worker supervisors	4.1	3.7	General managers & top executives	1.3	1.2
Hand packers & packagers	3.9	-8.5	Vehicle washers & equipment cleaners	1.1	-1.6
Assemblers, fabricators, & hand workers nec	3.4	6.7	Industrial production managers	1.1	6.7
Agricultural workers nec	2.5	6.7	Sales & related workers nec	1.1	6.7
Cooking, roasting machine operators	2.3	17.4	Bookkeeping, accounting, & auditing clerks	1.0	-20.0
Precision food & tobacco workers nec	2.2	17.4	Traffic, shipping, & receiving clerks	1.0	2.6
Machine operators nec	2.2	-5.9	Secretaries, ex legal & medical	1.0	-2.9
Machine feeders & offbearers	2.1	17.3			

Source: Industry-Occupation Matrix, Bureau of Labor Statistics. These data relate to one or more 3-digit SIC industry groups rather than to a single 4-digit SIC. The change reported for each occupation to the year 2005 is a percent of growth or decline as estimated by the Bureau of Labor Statistics. The abbreviation nec stands for 'not elsewhere classified'.

LOCATION BY STATE AND REGIONAL CONCENTRATION

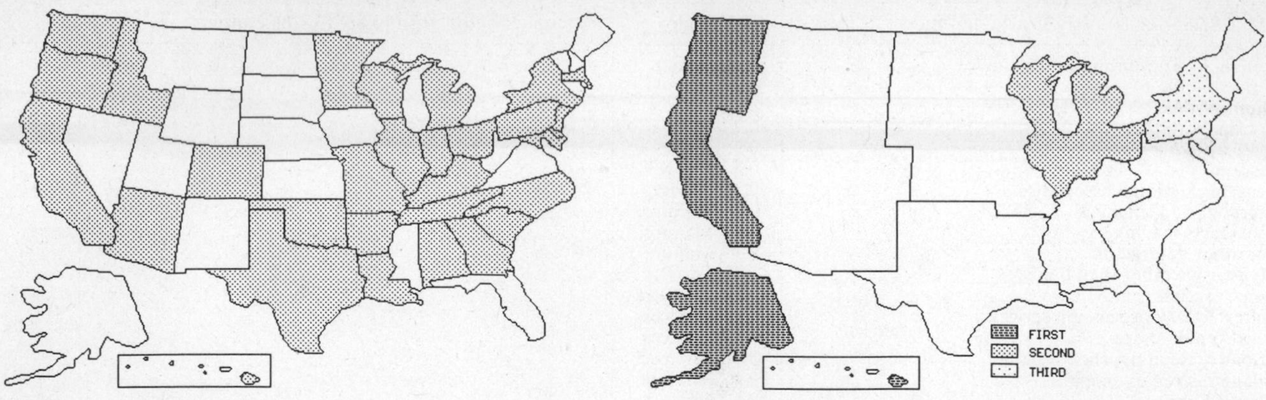

INDUSTRY DATA BY STATE

State	Establish-ments	Shipments			Employment				Cost as % of Shipments	Investment per Employee ($)
		Total ($ mil)	% of U.S.	Per Establ.	Total Number	% of U.S.	Per Establ.	Wages ($/hour)		
California	58	1,115.6	17.4	19.2	3,100	14.5	53	12.06	35.1	6,516
Illinois	20	540.8	8.5	27.0	1,700	7.9	85	11.72	46.8	4,941
Georgia	9	438.5	6.9	48.7	1,400	6.5	156	11.60	41.2	3,786
Michigan	19	320.6	5.0	16.9	1,800	8.4	95	8.82	44.9	5,000
New Jersey	10	240.0	3.8	24.0	400	1.9	40	13.14	33.0	3,500
New York	30	178.4	2.8	5.9	700	3.3	23	8.00	40.3	3,143
Louisiana	12	168.0	2.6	14.0	700	3.3	58	8.56	42.1	4,429
North Carolina	8	133.3	2.1	16.7	900	4.2	113	7.27	42.2	2,111
Indiana	7	127.7	2.0	18.2	800	3.7	114	8.54	52.2	4,750
Maryland	4	98.9	1.5	24.7	500	2.3	125	9.17	65.1	3,400
Oregon	10	55.0	0.9	5.5	400	1.9	40	10.40	49.1	2,250
Hawaii	16	19.2	0.3	1.2	100	0.5	6	7.00	49.0	4,000
Texas	28	(D)	-	-	1,750 *	8.2	63	-	-	7,714
Pennsylvania	19	(D)	-	-	750 *	3.5	39	-	-	-
Wisconsin	12	(D)	-	-	1,750 *	8.2	146	-	-	11,143
Missouri	11	(D)	-	-	750 *	3.5	68	-	-	-
Ohio	11	(D)	-	-	750 *	3.5	68	-	-	-
Massachusetts	8	(D)	-	-	375 *	1.8	47	-	-	-
Washington	8	(D)	-	-	175 *	0.8	22	-	-	-
Arizona	6	(D)	-	-	175 *	0.8	29	-	-	-
Colorado	5	(D)	-	-	375 *	1.8	75	-	-	-
Minnesota	5	(D)	-	-	175 *	0.8	35	-	-	-
South Carolina	5	(D)	-	-	175 *	0.8	35	-	-	-
Arkansas	4	(D)	-	-	375 *	1.8	94	-	-	-
Tennessee	4	(D)	-	-	375 *	1.8	94	-	-	-
Alabama	3	(D)	-	-	375 *	1.8	125	-	-	-
Idaho	3	(D)	-	-	175 *	0.8	58	-	-	-
Oklahoma	3	(D)	-	-	175 *	0.8	58	-	-	-
Kentucky	2	(D)	-	-	375 *	1.8	188	-	-	-
Delaware	1	(D)	-	-	375 *	1.8	375	-	-	-

Source: 1992 *Economic Census*. The states are in descending order of shipments or establishments (if shipment data are missing for the majority). The symbol (D) appears when data are withheld to prevent disclosure of competitive information. States marked with (D) are sorted by number of establishments. A dash (-) indicates that the data element cannot be calculated; * indicates the midpoint of a range.

2037 - FROZEN FRUITS AND VEGETABLES

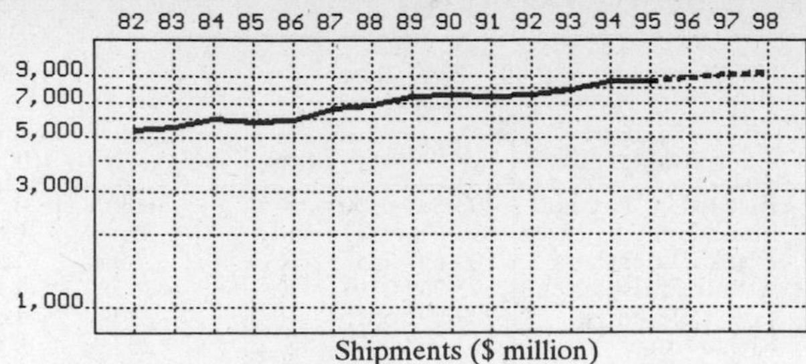

Shipments ($ million)

Employment (000)

GENERAL STATISTICS

Year	Companies	Establishments		Employment			Compensation		Production ($ million)			
		Total	with 20 or more employees	Total (000)	Production Workers (000)	Production Hours (Mil)	Payroll ($ mil)	Wages ($/hr)	Cost of Materials	Value Added by Manufacture	Value of Shipments	Capital Invest.
1982	195	264	199	47.7	41.5	77.1	643.5	6.57	2,970.1	2,408.6	5,374.6	235.7
1983		260	190	47.3	40.9	74.4	681.2	6.98	3,185.7	2,393.4	5,560.8	176.3
1984		256	181	46.9	41.2	76.4	693.4	7.07	3,470.8	2,555.7	5,968.9	189.8
1985		253	173	46.1	40.2	73.3	698.6	7.35	3,435.3	2,355.1	5,802.5	213.5
1986		252	177	46.4	40.1	70.7	701.0	7.45	3,218.6	2,648.6	5,885.7	196.4
1987	194	258	193	49.8	42.8	78.4	786.8	7.54	3,669.5	2,986.8	6,606.2	175.2
1988		244	175	48.5	41.2	76.1	773.5	7.48	3,777.9	3,072.5	6,814.9	235.7
1989		245	179	46.6	39.9	74.4	810.5	7.98	4,299.0	3,089.7	7,422.6	283.9
1990		238	170	46.4	39.2	74.7	817.0	8.06	4,618.9	2,921.6	7,473.6	349.9
1991		240	179	46.0	39.8	76.7	836.3	8.19	4,573.6	2,827.0	7,395.7	298.2
1992	182	255	201	48.0	41.5	79.1	917.6	8.57	4,613.4	2,910.4	7,535.0	254.8
1993		255	189	48.4	41.2	79.7	936.2	8.55	4,643.7	3,170.7	7,875.7	313.2
1994		243P	183P	47.7	41.0	79.3	979.7	9.08	4,735.4	3,799.7	8,482.1	249.0
1995		242P	182P	47.6P	40.6P	78.7P	977.2P	9.03P	4,759.4P	3,819.0P	8,525.1P	309.1P
1996		241P	182P	47.7P	40.5P	79.0P	1,003.9P	9.21P	4,898.2P	3,930.3P	8,773.7P	318.4P
1997		240P	182P	47.7P	40.5P	79.4P	1,030.6P	9.40P	5,037.0P	4,041.7P	9,022.4P	327.7P
1998		238P	182P	47.7P	40.5P	79.7P	1,057.3P	9.58P	5,175.9P	4,153.1P	9,271.1P	337.1P

Sources: 1982, 1987, 1992 *Economic Census*; *Annual Survey of Manufactures*, 83-86, 88-91, 93-94. Establishment counts for non-Census years are from *County Business Patterns*; establishment values for 83-84 are extrapolations. 'P's show projections by the editors. Industries reclassified in 87 will not have data for prior years.

INDICES OF CHANGE

Year	Companies	Establishments		Employment			Compensation		Production ($ million)			
		Total	with 20 or more employees	Total (000)	Production Workers (000)	Production Hours (Mil)	Payroll ($ mil)	Wages ($/hr)	Cost of Materials	Value Added by Manufacture	Value of Shipments	Capital Invest.
1982	107	104	99	99	100	97	70	77	64	83	71	93
1983		102	95	99	99	94	74	81	69	82	74	69
1984		100	90	98	99	97	76	82	75	88	79	74
1985		99	86	96	97	93	76	86	74	81	77	84
1986		99	88	97	97	89	76	87	70	91	78	77
1987	107	101	96	104	103	99	86	88	80	103	88	69
1988		96	87	101	99	96	84	87	82	106	90	93
1989		96	89	97	96	94	88	93	93	106	99	111
1990		93	85	97	94	94	89	94	100	100	99	137
1991		94	89	96	96	97	91	96	99	97	98	117
1992	100	100	100	100	100	100	100	100	100	100	100	100
1993		100	94	101	99	101	102	100	101	109	105	123
1994		95P	91P	99	99	100	107	106	103	131	113	98
1995		95P	91P	99P	98P	99P	107P	105P	103P	131P	113P	121P
1996		94P	91P	99P	98P	100P	109P	108P	106P	135P	116P	125P
1997		94P	91P	99P	98P	100P	112P	110P	109P	139P	120P	129P
1998		93P	91P	99P	98P	101P	115P	112P	112P	143P	123P	132P

Sources: Same as General Statistics. Values reflect change from the base year, 1992. Values above 100 mean greater than 92, values below 100 mean less than 92, and a value of 100 in the 82-91 or 93-98 period means same as 92. 'P's mark projections by the editors.

SELECTED RATIOS

For 1994	Avg. of All Manufact.	Analyzed Industry	Index	For 1994	Avg. of All Manufact.	Analyzed Industry	Index
Employees per Establishment	49	196	400	Value Added per Production Worker	134,084	92,676	69
Payroll per Establishment	1,500,273	4,025,914	268	Cost per Establishment	5,045,178	19,459,336	386
Payroll per Employee	30,620	20,539	67	Cost per Employee	102,970	99,275	96
Production Workers per Establishment	34	168	491	Cost per Production Worker	146,988	115,498	79
Wages per Establishment	853,319	2,958,901	347	Shipments per Establishment	9,576,895	34,855,775	364
Wages per Production Worker	24,861	17,562	71	Shipments per Employee	195,460	177,822	91
Hours per Production Worker	2,056	1,934	94	Shipments per Production Worker	279,017	206,880	74
Wages per Hour	12.09	9.08	75	Investment per Establishment	321,011	1,023,224	319
Value Added per Establishment	4,602,255	15,614,233	339	Investment per Employee	6,552	5,220	80
Value Added per Employee	93,930	79,658	85	Investment per Production Worker	9,352	6,073	65

Sources: Same as General Statistics. The 'Average of All Manufacturing' column represents the average of all manufacturing industries reported for the most recent complete year available. The Index shows the relationship between the Average and the Analyzed Industry. For example, 100 means that they are equal; 500 that the Analyzed Industry is five times the average; 50 means that the Analyzed Industry is half the national average. The abbreviation 'na' is used to show that data are 'not available'.

LEADING COMPANIES Number shown: **59** Total sales ($ mil): **4,063** Total employment (000): **25.0**

Company Name	Address				CEO Name	Phone	Co. Type	Sales ($ mil)	Empl. (000)
Ore-Ida Foods Inc	PO Box 10	Boise	ID	83707	Richard H Wamhoff	208-383-6100	S	840•	4.5
Citrus World Inc	PO Box 1111	Lake Wales	FL	33859	Frank Hunt	813-676-1411	R	330	0.8
Tree Top Inc	PO Box 248	Selah	WA	98942	Frank Elsner	509-697-7251	R	280	1.5
Norpac Foods Inc	PO Box 458	Stayton	OR	97383	Arthur Christiansen	503-769-2101	R	237	1.6
Ruiz Food Products Inc	501 S Alta Av	Dinuba	CA	93618	Tom Colesberry	209-591-5510	R	220•	1.2
McCain Citrus Inc	1821 S Kilbourn	Chicago	IL	60623	Richard Lan	312-762-9000	S	200	0.4
Sunkist Growers Inc	PO Box 3720	Ontario	CA	91761	W G Anderson	909-983-9811	D	175	0.5
Dean Foods Vegetable Co	PO Box 1510	Watsonville	CA	95077	Byron Johnson	408-728-2281	S	170	0.9
Twin City Foods Inc	PO Box 699	Stanwood	WA	98292	Arne Lervick	206-629-2111	R	150•	1.5
Seneca Foods Corp	3736 S Main St	Marion	NY	14505	Steven E Klus	315-926-4284	D	140	1.2
Southern Frozen Foods	PO Box 306	Montezuma	GA	31063	Thomas A Collins	912-472-8101	D	93	0.8
Orange-co Inc	PO Box 2158	Bartow	FL	33830	Ben Hill Griffin III	813-533-0551	P	90	0.5
Orange-co of Florida Inc	PO Box 2158	Bartow	FL	33820	Ben H Griffin III	813-533-0551	S	90	0.5
Indian River Foods Inc	PO Box 13090	Fort Pierce	FL	34979	Dan Dempsey	407-464-5770	S	85	0.3
Patterson Frozen Foods Inc	PO Box 114	Patterson	CA	95363	John Ielmini	209-892-2611	R	80	0.8
National Frozen Foods Corp	PO Box 9366	Seattle	WA	98109	SJ McCaffray	206-322-8900	R	78	0.5
California Farm Products	PO Box 2730	Watsonville	CA	95077	J Burke	408-722-8181	D	72•	0.4
Flavorland Foods Inc	PO Box 157	Forest Grove	OR	97116	Mark Frandsen	503-357-7124	S	45	0.6
Smith Frozen Foods Inc	PO Box 68	Weston	OR	97886	Gordon H Smith	503-566-3515	R	45	0.4
Healthy Roman Foods Inc	8111 LBJ Fwy	Dallas	TX	75251	Garry R Grant	214-437-9907	P	39	1.5
Golden Gem Growers Inc	PO Drawer 9	Umatilla	FL	32784	JF Nelson Jr	904-669-2101	R	38	0.3
Berry Groves Inc	PO Box 5609	Winter Haven	FL	33880	JM Berry Sr	813-324-4988	S	35	0.5
Kerr Concentrates Inc	2340 Hyacinth NE	Salem	OR	97303	Gary Slangan	503-378-0493	S	32•	0.3
Agvest Inc	26001 Miles Rd	Cleveland	OH	44128	Barry Schneider	216-464-3737	R	28•	0.2
Natural Country Farms Inc	PO Box 300	Ellington	CT	06029	Benedict Moser	203-872-8346	R	28	0.2
Coloma Frozen Foods Inc	PO Box 520	Coloma	MI	49038	Alton Wendzel	616-849-0500	R	27	0.2
Holly Hill Fruit Products Inc	PO Box 708	Davenport	FL	33837	LW McKnight	813-422-1131	R	25	0.3
Magic Valley Foods Inc	PO Box 475	Rupert	ID	83350	Roger Jones	208-436-3126	R	25•	0.3
Paramount Citrus Association	PO Box 8599	Mission Hills	CA	91346	Mark Riedel	818-361-1171	S	25	<0.1
Silver Springs Citrus Cooperative	PO Box 771046	Winter Garden	FL	34777	Terry Summer	407-656-1122	R	25•	0.2
Zeropack Co	PO Box 2777	Winchester	VA	22064	Eddie Robbins	703-662-3885	R	25	0.3
Berry Citrus Products Inc	PO Box 459	La Belle	FL	33935	JM Berry	813-675-2769	S	23	0.3
World Citrus West Inc	PO Box 927	Fullerton	CA	92632	Steve Caruso	714-870-6171	S	23•	<0.1
Clermont Inc	PO Box 604	Hillsboro	OR	97123	Wayne Somers	503-648-8544	R	21	0.1
Delagra Corp	PO Box 126	Bridgeville	DE	19933	Charles West	302-337-8206	R	21	0.1
Hi-Country Foods Corp	PO Box 338	Selah	WA	98942	OB Harlan	509-697-7292	R	20•	0.1
Sun Pac Foods Inc	PO Box 9365	Winter Haven	FL	33883	Hugh C Folkard	813-533-0808	R	19•	0.1
Brooklyn Bottling of Milton	PO Box 808	Milton	NY	12547	Eric Miller	914-795-2171	R	15	<0.1
Smeltzer Orchard Co	6032 Joyfield Rd	Frankfort	MI	49635	JH Brian	616-882-4421	R	15	0.1
Alcoma Packing Company Inc	PO Box 231	Lake Wales	FL	33859	JC Updike	813-696-1487	R	14•	<0.1
Yakima Valley Grape Producers	401 Av B	Grandview	WA	98930	Leland Anderson	509-882-1223	R	13•	<0.1
American Fruit Processors	10725 Sutter Av	Pacoima	CA	91331	Fred G Farago	818-899-9574	R	12•	<0.1
Washington Frontier Juice Inc	Rte 3	Prosser	WA	99350	Hiro Kawaguchi	509-786-3900	R	12•	<0.1
Valley Foods Inc	PO Box C	Lindsay	CA	93247	Philip LoBue	209-562-5169	R	10	<0.1
Slush Puppie Corp	1950 Radcliff Dr	Cincinnati	OH	45204	Will Radcliff	513-244-2400	R	9•	<0.1
Symons Frozen Foods Inc	619 Goodrich Rd	Centralia	WA	98531	AE Symons Jr	206-736-1321	R	9	<0.1
Citrus Service Inc	PO Box 7770218	Winter Garden	FL	34777	Bert E Roper	407-656-3233	R	8	<0.1
Paris Food Corp	1632 Carman St	Camden	NJ	08105	Sam Rudderow	609-964-0915	R	8•	<0.1
JG Townsend Jr and Company	PO Box 430	Georgetown	DE	19947	Paul Townsend	302-856-2525	R	7•	<0.1
Merrill Blueberry Farms Inc	PO Box 149	Ellsworth	ME	04605	Delmont N Merrill	207-667-2541	R	7	<0.1
Western Idaho Potato Processing	428 1st St S	Nampa	ID	83651	CJ Marshall	208-466-7805	R	6	0.1
Colorado Frozen Foods Inc	PO Box 31	Rocky Ford	CO	81067	Steven Hyde	719-254-3373	R	5	0.1
BC Cook and Sons Enterprises	PO Box 1597	Haines City	FL	33845	Bud Cook	813-422-1121	R	4•	<0.1
Whiteford Packing Co	2419 Whiteford Rd	Whiteford	MD	21160	Peter S Tutalo	410-452-8133	R	4	<0.1
Nutri-Fruit Inc	PO Box 338	Sumner	WA	98390	Charles C Jarrett	206-643-4489	R	3	<0.1
GM Allen and Son Inc	PO Box 454	Blue Hill	ME	04614	W Allen	207-469-7060	R	1•	0.2
Josef Seidel Co	1311 Woods Rd	Germantown	NY	12526	SJ Seidel	518-537-6227	R	1	<0.1
Pyramid Juice Co	PO Box 1303	Ashland	OR	97520	Larry Friedman	503-482-2292	R	1	<0.1
Orchards Hawaii Inc	55 S Wakea Av	Kahului	HI	96732	Peter Baldwin	808-877-0061	R	0	<0.1

Source: *Ward's Business Directory of U.S. Private and Public Companies*, Volumes 1 and 2, 1996. The company type code used is as follows: P - Public, R - Private, S - Subsidiary, D - Division, J - Joint Venture, A - Affiliate, G - Group. Sales are in millions of dollars, employees are in thousands. An asterisk (*) indicates an estimated sales volume. The symbol < stands for 'less than'. Company names and addresses are truncated, in some cases, to fit into the available space.

MATERIALS CONSUMED

Material		Quantity	Delivered Cost ($ million)
Materials, ingredients, containers, and supplies		(X)	4,246.7
Fresh oranges	1,000 s tons	3,051.2**	643.1
Fresh apples	1,000 s tons	279.9	65.6
Fresh strawberries	1,000 s tons	117.1	80.1
Other fresh fruits	1,000 s tons	863.6	233.7
Fresh green peas	1,000 s tons	188.5	47.6
White potatoes	1,000 s tons	6,678.6	651.7
Fresh sweet corn	1,000 s tons	896.9	62.8
Fresh green (snap) or wax beans	1,000 s tons	188.6	43.0
Other fresh vegetables	1,000 s tons	1,106.5**	293.5
Frozen fruits (for further processing)	mil lb	190.9	164.1
Frozen vegetables (for further processing)	mil lb	491.3**	194.5
Cheese, natural and process, including (imitation cheese and cheese substitutes)	mil lb	17.3	26.1
Sugar, cane and beet (in terms of sugar solids)	1,000 s tons	63.2	30.5
Wheat flour	1,000 cwt	(S)	9.6
Fats and oils, all types (purchased as such)	mil lb	422.1*	116.7
Tomato paste (24 percent NTSS equivalent)	mil lb	0.8	0.3
Poultry; live, fresh, frozen, or prepared	mil lb	2.4	3.0
Meat; fresh, frozen, or prepared	mil lb	2.6	3.0
Aluminum foil packaging products, converted or rolls and sheets		(X)	7.5
Packaging paper and plastics film, coated and laminated		(X)	72.2
Bags; plastics, foil, and coated paper		(X)	19.7
Paperboard containers, boxes, and corrugated paperboard		(X)	265.5
Metal cans, can lids and ends		(X)	105.2
All other materials and components, parts, containers, and supplies		(X)	963.7
Materials, ingredients, containers, and supplies, nsk		(X)	144.0

Source: 1992 *Economic Census.* Explanation of symbols used: (D): Withheld to avoid disclosure of competitive data; na: Not available; (S): Withheld because statistical norms were not met; (X): Not applicable; (Z): Less than half the unit shown; nec: Not elsewhere classified; nsk: Not specified by kind; - : zero; * : 10-19 percent estimated; ** : 20-29 percent estimated.

PRODUCT SHARE DETAILS

Product or Product Class	% Share
Frozen fruits and vegetables	100.00
Frozen fruits, juices, ades, drinks, and cocktails	38.62
Frozen strawberries	6.38
Frozen red sour cherries	1.84
Frozen apples and applesauce	3.44
Frozen berries (including blueberries, raspberries, blackberries, etc.)	3.28
Other frozen fruits	6.03
Frozen concentrated orange juice, consumer and institutional, 6 oz or less	4.23
Frozen concentrated orange juice, consumer and institutional, 6.1 oz to 12 oz	17.98
Frozen concentrated orange juice, consumer and institutional, 12.1 oz to 24 oz	4.64
Frozen concentrated orange juice, consumer and institutional, 24.1 oz or more	4.97
Frozen concentrated orange juice, bulk	21.65
Frozen concentrated grape juice, 4.1 oz to 7 oz	0.62
Frozen concentrated grape juice, 10.1 oz to 13 oz	1.09
Frozen concentrated grape juice, other sizes	0.88
Frozen concentrated grapefruit juice	4.72
Other frozen fruit and berry juices, concentrated	9.56
Frozen concentrated lemonade, 4.1 oz to 7 oz	(D)
Frozen concentrated lemonade, 10.1 oz to 13 oz.	3.06
Frozen concentrated lemonade, other sizes	1.15
All other frozen concentrated ades, drinks, and cocktails	2.96
Frozen citrus pulp	1.07
Frozen fruits, juices, ades, drinks, and cocktails, nsk	(D)
Frozen vegetables	59.59
Frozen asparagus	0.50
Frozen green, regular, and french-cut beans	3.64
Frozen lima beans (baby, emerald, and fordhook)	0.92
Frozen broccoli	2.05
Frozen brussels sprouts	0.48
Frozen carrots	1.77
Frozen cauliflower	1.05
Frozen green peas	3.48
Frozen spinach	1.17
Frozen vegetable combinations (succotash, peas and carrots, mixed vegetables, vegetables with pasta, etc.)	8.74
Frozen french-fried potatoes	41.67
Other frozen potato products (patties, puffs, etc.)	9.84
Frozen sweet cut yellow corn	5.21
Frozen sweet cob yellow corn	3.35
Frozen southern greens (collards, kale, mustard, and turnip)	0.48
Frozen onions (rings, dices, chopped, etc.)	5.53
Other frozen vegetables	9.97
Frozen vegetables, nsk	0.16
Frozen fruits and vegetables, nsk	1.79

Source: 1992 *Economic Census.* The values shown are percent of total shipments in an industry. Values of indented subcategories are summed in the main heading. The symbol (D) appears when data are withheld to prevent disclosure of competitive information. The abbreviation nsk stands for 'not specified by kind' and nec for 'not elsewhere classified'.

INPUTS AND OUTPUTS FOR FROZEN FRUITS, FRUIT JUICES & VEGETABLES

Economic Sector or Industry Providing Inputs	%	Sector	Economic Sector or Industry Buying Outputs	%	Sector
Vegetables	13.2	Agric.	Personal consumption expenditures	63.8	
Fruits	12.9	Agric.	Eating & drinking places	15.0	Trade
Wholesale trade	12.8	Trade	Exports	5.6	Foreign
Frozen fruits, fruit juices & vegetables	6.7	Manufg.	Frozen fruits, fruit juices & vegetables	4.9	Manufg.
Metal foil & leaf	6.4	Manufg.	Frozen specialties	2.3	Manufg.
Miscellaneous plastics products	6.3	Manufg.	Change in business inventories	1.9	In House
Motor freight transportation & warehousing	5.7	Util.	Canned fruits & vegetables	1.5	Manufg.
Paperboard containers & boxes	5.0	Manufg.	Hospitals	1.1	Services
Advertising	4.9	Services	Canned specialties	0.9	Manufg.
Metal cans	3.6	Manufg.	Nursing & personal care facilities	0.6	Services
Electric services (utilities)	2.8	Util.	S/L Govt. purch., health & hospitals	0.5	S/L Govt
Imports	2.4	Foreign	S/L Govt. purch., higher education	0.4	S/L Govt
Cyclic crudes and organics	2.2	Manufg.	Residential care	0.3	Services
Shortening & cooking oils	2.1	Manufg.	S/L Govt. purch., correction	0.3	S/L Govt
Gas production & distribution (utilities)	2.0	Util.	Federal Government enterprises nec	0.2	Gov't
Petroleum refining	0.9	Manufg.	S/L Govt. purch., elem. & secondary education	0.2	S/L Govt
Paper coating & glazing	0.8	Manufg.	Social services, nec	0.1	Services
Railroads & related services	0.7	Util.			
Sugar	0.6	Manufg.			
Equipment rental & leasing services	0.6	Services			
Commercial printing	0.5	Manufg.			
Miscellaneous crops	0.4	Agric.			
Bags, except textile	0.4	Manufg.			
Water transportation	0.4	Util.			
Maintenance of nonfarm buildings nec	0.3	Constr.			
Flavoring extracts & syrups, nec	0.3	Manufg.			
Food preparations, nec	0.3	Manufg.			
Industrial inorganic chemicals, nec	0.3	Manufg.			
Communications, except radio & TV	0.3	Util.			
Eating & drinking places	0.3	Trade			
Banking	0.3	Fin/R.E.			
Chemical preparations, nec	0.2	Manufg.			
Air transportation	0.2	Util.			
Sanitary services, steam supply, irrigation	0.2	Util.			
Real estate	0.2	Fin/R.E.			
State & local government enterprises, nec	0.2	Gov't			
Lubricating oils & greases	0.1	Manufg.			
Rubber & plastics hose & belting	0.1	Manufg.			
Water supply & sewage systems	0.1	Util.			
Insurance carriers	0.1	Fin/R.E.			
Computer & data processing services	0.1	Services			
Electrical repair shops	0.1	Services			
Management & consulting services & labs	0.1	Services			

Source: Benchmark Input-Output Accounts for the U.S. Economy, 1982, U.S. Department of Commerce, Washington, D.C., July 1991. Data, as reported in the source, are organized by the 1977 SIC structure in use in 1982 but have been matched, as closely as is possible, to the 1987 SIC structure used in this book.

OCCUPATIONS EMPLOYED BY SIC 203 - PRESERVED FRUITS AND VEGETABLES

Occupation	% of Total 1994	Change to 2005	Occupation	% of Total 1994	Change to 2005
Cannery workers	21.2	6.7	Maintenance repairers, general utility	1.9	-4.0
Packaging & filling machine operators	6.8	6.7	Janitors & cleaners, incl maids	1.8	-14.6
Helpers, laborers, & material movers nec	5.1	6.7	Freight, stock, & material movers, hand	1.7	-14.6
Industrial machinery mechanics	4.5	49.4	Crushing & mixing machine operators	1.4	6.7
Industrial truck & tractor operators	4.5	6.7	Truck drivers light & heavy	1.3	10.0
Blue collar worker supervisors	4.1	3.7	General managers & top executives	1.3	1.2
Hand packers & packagers	3.9	-8.5	Vehicle washers & equipment cleaners	1.1	-1.6
Assemblers, fabricators, & hand workers nec	3.4	6.7	Industrial production managers	1.1	6.7
Agricultural workers nec	2.5	6.7	Sales & related workers nec	1.1	6.7
Cooking, roasting machine operators	2.3	17.4	Bookkeeping, accounting, & auditing clerks	1.0	-20.0
Precision food & tobacco workers nec	2.2	17.4	Traffic, shipping, & receiving clerks	1.0	2.6
Machine operators nec	2.2	-5.9	Secretaries, ex legal & medical	1.0	-2.9
Machine feeders & offbearers	2.1	17.3			

Source: Industry-Occupation Matrix, Bureau of Labor Statistics. These data relate to one or more 3-digit SIC industry groups rather than to a single 4-digit SIC. The change reported for each occupation to the year 2005 is a percent of growth or decline as estimated by the Bureau of Labor Statistics. The abbreviation nec stands for 'not elsewhere classified'.

LOCATION BY STATE AND REGIONAL CONCENTRATION

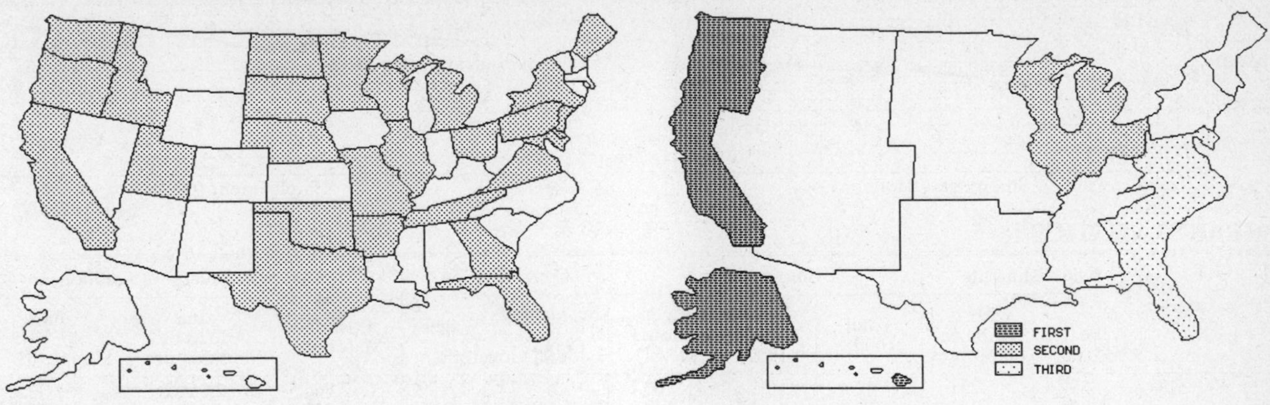

INDUSTRY DATA BY STATE

State	Establish-ments	Shipments			Employment				Cost as % of Shipments	Investment per Employee ($)
		Total ($ mil)	% of U.S.	Per Establ.	Total Number	% of U.S.	Per Establ.	Wages ($/hour)		
Florida	29	1,759.0	23.3	60.7	5,300	11.0	183	8.85	81.2	8,396
California	44	1,114.4	14.8	25.3	8,600	17.9	195	8.11	57.8	3,558
Washington	32	1,086.5	14.4	34.0	6,300	13.1	197	9.93	52.8	5,524
Oregon	27	890.6	11.8	33.0	7,200	15.0	267	8.16	54.0	4,708
Idaho	12	818.8	10.9	68.2	6,500	13.5	542	8.61	53.4	5,462
Wisconsin	10	390.7	5.2	39.1	2,500	5.2	250	8.83	30.0	9,160
New York	11	278.0	3.7	25.3	1,000	2.1	91	9.69	54.2	4,300
Michigan	14	103.2	1.4	7.4	800	1.7	57	8.73	63.9	8,125
Minnesota	4	96.6	1.3	24.2	900	1.9	225	7.33	50.7	-
Texas	6	69.6	0.9	11.6	1,300	2.7	217	5.78	51.3	-
Maine	11	(D)	-	-	1,750 *	3.6	159	-	-	-
Illinois	7	(D)	-	-	750 *	1.6	107	-	-	-
Ohio	6	(D)	-	-	175 *	0.4	29	-	-	2,286
Pennsylvania	5	(D)	-	-	375 *	0.8	75	-	-	-
New Jersey	4	(D)	-	-	375 *	0.8	94	-	-	267
Nebraska	3	(D)	-	-	750 *	1.6	250	-	-	400
Utah	3	(D)	-	-	175 *	0.4	58	-	-	-
Arkansas	2	(D)	-	-	175 *	0.4	88	-	-	-
Delaware	2	(D)	-	-	175 *	0.4	88	-	-	-
Maryland	2	(D)	-	-	175 *	0.4	88	-	-	-
Missouri	2	(D)	-	-	175 *	0.4	88	-	-	-
Oklahoma	2	(D)	-	-	750 *	1.6	375	-	-	-
Georgia	1	(D)	-	-	1,750 *	3.6	1,750	-	-	-
North Dakota	1	(D)	-	-	375 *	0.8	375	-	-	-
South Dakota	1	(D)	-	-	175 *	0.4	175	-	-	-
Tennessee	1	(D)	-	-	750 *	1.6	750	-	-	-
Virginia	1	(D)	-	-	175 *	0.4	175	-	-	-

Source: 1992 *Economic Census*. The states are in descending order of shipments or establishments (if shipment data are missing for the majority). The symbol (D) appears when data are withheld to prevent disclosure of competitive information. States marked with (D) are sorted by number of establishments. A dash (-) indicates that the data element cannot be calculated; * indicates the midpoint of a range.

2038 - FROZEN SPECIALTIES

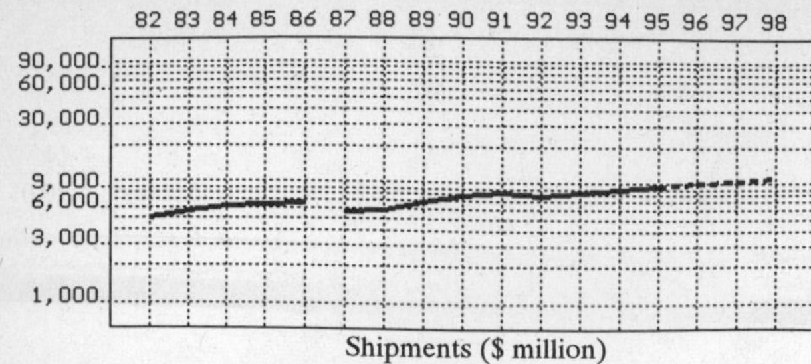

Shipments ($ million)

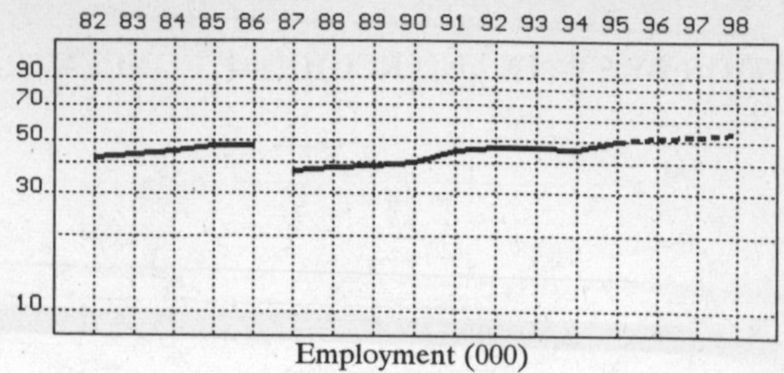

Employment (000)

GENERAL STATISTICS

Year	Companies	Establishments		Employment			Compensation		Production ($ million)			
		Total	with 20 or more employees	Total (000)	Production Workers (000)	Production Hours (Mil)	Payroll ($ mil)	Wages ($/hr)	Cost of Materials	Value Added by Manufacture	Value of Shipments	Capital Invest.
1982	319	389	251	42.4	32.6	63.1	650.7	6.79	2,966.5	2,066.2	5,033.9	160.5
1983		379	245	43.9	34.4	68.0	710.8	7.15	3,252.0	2,433.0	5,678.7	157.8
1984		369	239	44.5	35.7	71.3	748.8	7.45	3,614.5	2,717.9	6,332.7	206.0
1985		359	232	47.0	36.8	69.9	791.3	7.87	3,518.8	2,985.1	6,507.6	224.4
1986		348	224	46.8	37.1	71.0	851.9	8.34	3,359.9	3,342.9	6,701.2	205.8
1987*	247	285	181	37.5	30.1	58.6	668.3	7.87	2,845.6	2,803.0	5,617.0	178.1
1988		279	178	38.0	30.6	60.7	680.6	7.75	2,985.8	2,808.3	5,798.2	188.1
1989		285	179	38.9	33.7	63.8	789.8	8.55	3,532.0	3,374.2	6,904.6	145.6
1990		277	166	40.1	36.3	67.5	852.5	8.79	4,085.2	3,710.4	7,797.0	230.3
1991		280	168	44.9	36.7	72.2	876.1	8.68	4,198.0	4,229.6	8,427.8	224.9
1992	308	363	203	46.7	38.3	73.4	971.5	9.18	3,808.9	4,075.9	7,885.7	249.7
1993		353	208	46.4	38.0	72.5	992.7	9.43	4,090.7	4,184.9	8,272.4	274.8
1994		356P	200P	46.1	38.4	72.7	991.4	9.66	4,321.7	4,540.1	8,863.8	258.4
1995		369P	205P	49.3P	41.1P	77.9P	1,088.1P	9.96P	4,640.5P	4,875.0P	9,517.6P	288.5P
1996		382P	209P	50.9P	42.4P	80.2P	1,140.4P	10.23P	4,864.9P	5,110.8P	9,978.0P	304.0P
1997		395P	213P	52.4P	43.7P	82.5P	1,192.6P	10.50P	5,089.4P	5,346.6P	10,438.3P	319.5P
1998		408P	218P	54.0P	45.0P	84.7P	1,244.9P	10.77P	5,313.9P	5,582.4P	10,898.7P	335.0P

Sources: 1982, 1987, 1992 *Economic Census*; *Annual Survey of Manufactures*, 83-86, 88-91, 93-94. Establishment counts are from *County Business Patterns* for non-Census years; establishment counts for 83-84 are extrapolations. * indicates that industry content changed in 87; earlier years use 77 SICs. 'P's mark projections.

INDICES OF CHANGE

Year	Companies	Establishments		Employment			Compensation		Production ($ million)			
		Total	with 20 or more employees	Total (000)	Production Workers (000)	Production Hours (Mil)	Payroll ($ mil)	Wages ($/hr)	Cost of Materials	Value Added by Manufacture	Value of Shipments	Capital Invest.
1982	104	107	124	91	85	86	67	74	78	51	64	64
1983		104	121	94	90	93	73	78	85	60	72	63
1984		102	118	95	93	97	77	81	95	67	80	82
1985		99	114	101	96	95	81	86	92	73	83	90
1986		96	110	100	97	97	88	91	88	82	85	82
1987*	80	79	89	80	79	80	69	86	75	69	71	71
1988		77	88	81	80	83	70	84	78	69	74	75
1989		79	88	83	88	87	81	93	93	83	88	58
1990		76	82	86	95	92	88	96	107	91	99	92
1991		77	83	96	96	98	90	95	110	104	107	90
1992	100	100	100	100	100	100	100	100	100	100	100	100
1993		97	102	99	99	99	102	103	107	103	105	110
1994		98P	99P	99	100	99	102	105	113	111	112	103
1995		102P	101P	106P	107P	106P	112P	108P	122P	120P	121P	116P
1996		105P	103P	109P	111P	109P	117P	111P	128P	125P	127P	122P
1997		109P	105P	112P	114P	112P	123P	114P	134P	131P	132P	128P
1998		112P	107P	116P	118P	115P	128P	117P	140P	137P	138P	134P

Sources: Same as General Statistics. Values reflect change from the base year, 1992. Values above 100 mean greater than 92, values below 100 mean less than 92, and a value of 100 in the 82-91 or 93-98 period means same as 92. * indicates that industry content changed in 87. Data for earlier years are in 77 SIC format.

SELECTED RATIOS

For 1994	Avg. of All Manufact.	Analyzed Industry	Index	For 1994	Avg. of All Manufact.	Analyzed Industry	Index
Employees per Establishment	49	130	265	Value Added per Production Worker	134,084	118,232	88
Payroll per Establishment	1,500,273	2,788,188	186	Cost per Establishment	5,045,178	12,154,239	241
Payroll per Employee	30,620	21,505	70	Cost per Employee	102,970	93,746	91
Production Workers per Establishment	34	108	315	Cost per Production Worker	146,988	112,544	77
Wages per Establishment	853,319	1,975,080	231	Shipments per Establishment	9,576,895	24,928,325	260
Wages per Production Worker	24,861	18,289	74	Shipments per Employee	195,460	192,273	98
Hours per Production Worker	2,056	1,893	92	Shipments per Production Worker	279,017	230,828	83
Wages per Hour	12.09	9.66	80	Investment per Establishment	321,011	726,718	226
Value Added per Establishment	4,602,255	12,768,461	277	Investment per Employee	6,552	5,605	86
Value Added per Employee	93,930	98,484	105	Investment per Production Worker	9,352	6,729	72

Sources: Same as General Statistics. The 'Average of All Manufacturing' column represents the average of all manufacturing industries reported for the most recent complete year available. The Index shows the relationship between the Average and the Analyzed Industry. For example, 100 means that they are equal; 500 that the Analyzed Industry is five times the average; 50 means that the Analyzed Industry is half the national average. The abbreviation 'na' is used to show that data are 'not available'.

LEADING COMPANIES Number shown: **51** Total sales ($ mil): **7,378** Total employment (000): **56.4**

Company Name	Address				CEO Name	Phone	Co. Type	Sales ($ mil)	Empl. (000)
JR Simplot Co	PO Box 27	Boise	ID	83707	Steve Beebe	208-336-2110	R	2,000	10.0
ConAgra Consumer	5 ConAgra Dr	Omaha	NE	68102	Jim Smith	402-595-6000	S	1,400	7.5
Stouffer Corp	29800 Bainbridge	Solon	OH	44139	Joseph Weller	216-248-3600	S	1,210	21.0
McCain USA Inc	10600 Higgins Rd	Rosemont	IL	60018	Michael McCain	708-297-3381	S	550*	1.6
Stouffer Foods Corp	5750 Harper Rd	Solon	OH	44139	C Wayne Partin	216-248-3600	S	490	4.0
Doskocil Specialty Brands Co	PO Box 5647	Riverside	CA	92517	Robert S Wright	909-782-7800	D	220	1.0
Design Foods	3709 E 1st St	Fort Worth	TX	76111	Doug Higgins	817-831-0981	D	200*	0.9
McCain Foods Inc	10600 Higgins Rd	Rosemont	IL	60018	Bill Voss	708-297-3260	S	140*	1.2
Kerry Ingredients	352 E Grand Av	Beloit	WI	53511	Jack Warner	608-365-5561	S	130*	0.6
Sara Lee Bakery North America	224 S Michigan Av	Chicago	IL	60604	Judith Spriese	312-986-7800	D	120*	1.0
H and M Food Systems Co	6350 Browning Ct	N Richland Hls	TX	76180	Doug Higgins	817-656-5507	S	98*	0.8
Overhill Farms	PO Box 6017	Inglewood	CA	90312	Edward Marek	310-641-3680	R	90	0.9
Sanderson Farms Inc	PO Box 97149	Jackson	MS	39288	Russ McPherson	601-939-9790	D	55	0.3
Culinary Foods Inc	4201 S Ashland Av	Chicago	IL	60609	Howard Davis	312-650-4000	R	50*	0.5
Preferred Meal Systems Inc	1699 E Woodfield	Schaumburg	IL	60173	D Krpan	708-517-5757	R	50	0.4
State Fair Foods Inc	PO Box 561223	Dallas	TX	75356	Jim Hooks	214-630-1500	S	49*	0.4
Better Baked Foods Inc	PO Box 432	North East	PA	16428	R Mikytuck	814-725-8778	R	38	0.4
Request Foods Inc	PO Box 2577	Holland	MI	49422	Jack Dewitt	616-786-0900	R	35	0.3
Rodriguez Festive Foods Inc	PO Box 4369	Fort Worth	TX	76106	Rudy Rodriguez	817-626-3961	R	30*	0.4
Ateeco Inc	600 E Center St	Shenandoah	PA	17976	Thomas F Twardzik	717-462-2745	R	29	0.3
Celentano Brothers Inc	225 Bloomfield Av	Verona	NJ	07044	Dominic Celentano	201-239-8444	R	28	0.1
Delimex	1445 30th St	San Diego	CA	92154	Oscar Ancira	619-575-9433	R	27	0.4
El Encanto Inc	PO Box 293	Albuquerque	NM	87103	Jacqueline Baca	505-243-2722	R	24*	0.2
Nancy's Specialty Foods	205 Constitution Dr	Menlo Park	CA	94025	Nancy Mueller	415-326-5115	R	24	0.2
Wholesome and Hearty Foods	975 E Sandy Blv	Portland	OR	97214	Paul F Wenner	503-238-0109	P	24	0.1
Little Lady Foods Inc	2323 Pratt Blv	Elk Grove Vill	IL	60007	John T Geocaris	708-806-1440	R	20	0.1
Arden International Kitchens Inc	21150 Hamburg Av	Lakeville	MN	55044	R Stephen Tanner	612-469-2000	P	20	0.2
McCain Ellio's Foods Inc	11 Gregg St	Lodi	NJ	07644	Tim Dricoll	201-368-0600	S	18*	0.2
Natalina Foods Inc	3940 Congress Pkwy	Richfield	OH	44286	Kirk Davis	216-659-9733	D	18*	0.2
Dadco Diversified Inc	PO Box 1107	Eau Claire	WI	54701	Mark Donnelly	715-834-3418	R	17*	0.2
Logan International Ltd	901 Washington St	Metolius	OR	97741	Dennis Logan	503-546-5111	R	15	<0.1
Oh Boy Corp	PO Box 923490	Sylmar	CA	91392	Pietro Vitale	818-361-1128	R	15*	0.1
Old Fashion Kitchen Inc	1045 Towbin Av	Lakewood	NJ	08701	Al Bonugli	908-364-4100	R	15*	0.1
Reames Foods Inc	PO Box 71159	Des Moines	IA	50325	David Hammerberg	515-223-6186	S	15	0.1
Tommy's Foods Inc	2030 E Walnut Av	Fullerton	CA	92631	Kathrine Manville	714-879-6666	R	15	0.1
International Food and Beverage	30152 Avntura	R S Margari	CA	92688	Mike Hogarty	714-858-8800	R	12	<0.1
Leon's Texas Cuisine Inc	PO Box 550700	Dallas	TX	75355	Bob L Clements	214-494-1555	R	12*	0.1
Dadco Food Products Inc	PO Box 1107	Eau Claire	WI	54702	Mark Donnelly	715-834-3418	S	11*	0.2
Proferas Pizza Bakery Inc	1130 Moosic St	Scranton	PA	18505	AW Swantek	717-342-4181	R	11	0.1
Palermo's Villa Inc	808 W Maple St	Milwaukee	WI	53204	Giacomo Fallucca Jr	414-643-0919	R	10	<0.1
Jason Pharmaceuticals Inc	11445 Cronhill Dr	Owings Mills	MD	21117	James W Vitale	410-581-8042	R	8	<0.1
DeWafelbakkers	PO Box 13570	N Little Rock	AR	72113	Chuck Meyer	501-791-3320	R	7*	<0.1
Foods C'est Bon Ltd	PO Box 1957	Kenner	LA	70063	Jack Hines	504-466-2159	R	6*	<0.1
Panhandle Foods Inc	1980 Smith Twn	Burgettstown	PA	15021	William Dugas	412-947-2216	R	6	<0.1
Kineret Foods Corp	24 Jericho Tpk	Jericho	NY	11753	JB Krupnick	516-333-2626	R	4	<0.1
Mount Rose Ravioli	157 Gazza Blv	E Farmingdale	NY	11735	Sam Minuto	516-694-6940	R	4	<0.1
Luigino's Inc	PO Box 16630	Duluth	MN	55812	Jeno F Paulucci	218-723-5555	R	3*	<0.1
Matador Processors Inc	PO Box 2200	Blanchard	OK	73010	Betty Wood	405-485-3567	R	3	<0.1
Lucia's Pizza Inc	1106 S Kirkwood	Kirkwood	MO	63122	John Tumminello	314-822-1855	R	2	<0.1
Campobello Foods	10819 E Hwy 40	Independence	MO	64055	Vince Totta	816-358-2011	R	1*	<0.1
My Own Meals Inc	PO Box 334	Deerfield	IL	60015	Mary Anne Jackson	708-948-1118	R	1*	<0.1

Source: *Ward's Business Directory of U.S. Private and Public Companies*, Volumes 1 and 2, 1996. The company type code used is as follows: P - Public, R - Private, S - Subsidiary, D - Division, J - Joint Venture, A - Affiliate, G - Group. Sales are in millions of dollars, employees are in thousands. An asterisk (*) indicates an estimated sales volume. The symbol < stands for 'less than'. Company names and addresses are truncated, in some cases, to fit into the available space.

MATERIALS CONSUMED

Material		Quantity	Delivered Cost ($ million)
Materials, ingredients, containers, and supplies		(X)	3,427.4
Fresh oranges	1,000 s tons	(D)	(D)
Fresh apples	1,000 s tons	(D)	(D)
Other fresh fruits	1,000 s tons	(D)	(D)
Fresh green peas	1,000 s tons	(D)	(D)
White potatoes	1,000 s tons	(D)	(D)
Fresh sweet corn	1,000 s tons	42.3	13.4
Other fresh vegetables	1,000 s tons	(D)	(D)
Frozen fruits (for further processing)	1,000 s tons	1,081.5	237.7
Frozen vegetables (for further processing)	mil lb	36.0	23.5
Cheese, natural and process, including (imitation cheese and cheese substitutes)	mil lb	402.1	171.2
Sugar, cane and beet (in terms of sugar solids)	mil lb	349.1	417.4
Wheat flour	1,000 s tons	32.5	18.9
Fats and oils, all types (purchased as such)	1,000 cwt	10,218.6	138.2
Tomato paste (24 percent NTSS equivalent)	mil lb	259.0	76.7
Poultry; live, fresh, frozen, or prepared	mil lb	176.2	67.3
Meat; fresh, frozen, or prepared	mil lb	505.9	367.9
Aluminum foil packaging products, converted or rolls and sheets	mil lb	438.3	527.2
Packaging paper and plastics film, coated and laminated		(X)	13.6
Bags; plastics, foil, and coated paper		(X)	83.9
Paperboard containers, boxes, and corrugated paperboard		(X)	34.2
Metal cans, can lids and ends		(X)	375.7
All other materials and components, parts, containers, and supplies		(X)	9.1
Materials, ingredients, containers, and supplies, nsk		(X)	683.7
		(X)	154.5

Source: 1992 *Economic Census*. Explanation of symbols used: (D): Withheld to avoid disclosure of competitive data; na: Not available; (S): Withheld because statistical norms were not met; (X): Not applicable; (Z): Less than half the unit shown; nec: Not elsewhere classified; nsk: Not specified by kind; - : zero; * : 10-19 percent estimated; ** : 20-29 percent estimated.

PRODUCT SHARE DETAILS

Product or Product Class	% Share
Frozen specialties, nec	100.00
Frozen dinners (beef, pork, and poultry pies, and nationality foods)	73.89
Frozen dinners with red-meat entree	9.23
Frozen dinners with poultry entree	12.28
Frozen dinners with pasta entree	4.07
Frozen dinners with other entree	3.30
Frozen entrees and side dishes (except rice dishes and nationality foods), with pasta products as major ingredient	6.89
Frozen entrees and side dishes (except rice dishes and nationality foods), with other products as major ingredient	12.09
Frozen beef and pork pies	1.00
Frozen poultry pies	(D)
Frozen enchiladas	1.02
Frozen tortillas	4.34
Frozen tamales	1.54
Frozen pizza	26.70
Frozen chow mein	(D)
Frozen chop suey	(D)
Frozen egg rolls	1.63
All other frozen nationality foods	12.83
Frozen dinners: beef, pork, and poultry pies; and nationality foods, nsk	0.16
Other frozen specialties, nec	23.03
Frozen whipped topping (dairy product substitute, dairy or nondairy base)	26.84
Other frozen dairy product substitutes, except mellorine and similar products	0.81
Frozen waffles, pancakes, and french toast	28.49
Other frozen specialties, except seafood, including soups, etc.	43.00
Other frozen specialties, nec, nsk	0.86
Frozen specialties, nec, nsk	3.08

Source: 1992 *Economic Census*. The values shown are percent of total shipments in an industry. Values of indented subcategories are summed in the main heading. The symbol (D) appears when data are withheld to prevent disclosure of competitive information. The abbreviation nsk stands for 'not specified by kind' and nec for 'not elsewhere classified'.

INPUTS AND OUTPUTS FOR FROZEN SPECIALTIES

Economic Sector or Industry Providing Inputs	%	Sector
Wholesale trade	10.8	Trade
Paperboard containers & boxes	8.8	Manufg.
Miscellaneous plastics products	8.3	Manufg.
Meat packing plants	7.9	Manufg.
Poultry dressing plants	6.8	Manufg.
Cheese, natural & processed	5.6	Manufg.
Advertising	4.8	Services
Frozen fruits, fruit juices & vegetables	3.9	Manufg.
Wet corn milling	3.7	Manufg.
Shortening & cooking oils	3.0	Manufg.
Flour & other grain mill products	2.8	Manufg.
Cyclic crudes and organics	2.5	Manufg.
Metal foil & leaf	2.5	Manufg.
Electric services (utilities)	2.4	Util.
Cottonseed oil mills	2.3	Manufg.
Motor freight transportation & warehousing	2.1	Util.

Economic Sector or Industry Buying Outputs	%	Sector
Personal consumption expenditures	95.9	
Eating & drinking places	1.8	Trade
Change in business inventories	1.0	In House
Exports	0.6	Foreign
Frozen specialties	0.2	Manufg.
Air transportation	0.1	Util.
Hospitals	0.1	Services

Continued on next page.

INPUTS AND OUTPUTS FOR FROZEN SPECIALTIES - Continued

Economic Sector or Industry Providing Inputs	%	Sector	Economic Sector or Industry Buying Outputs	%	Sector
Vegetable oil mills, nec	1.9	Manufg.			
Paper coating & glazing	1.4	Manufg.			
Sugar	1.4	Manufg.			
Bread, cake, & related products	1.1	Manufg.			
Canned fruits & vegetables	1.1	Manufg.			
Sausages & other prepared meats	1.1	Manufg.			
Railroads & related services	1.1	Util.			
Food preparations, nec	0.8	Manufg.			
Bags, except textile	0.7	Manufg.			
Gas production & distribution (utilities)	0.7	Util.			
Equipment rental & leasing services	0.7	Services			
Commercial printing	0.6	Manufg.			
Petroleum refining	0.6	Manufg.			
Poultry & egg processing	0.6	Manufg.			
Communications, except radio & TV	0.4	Util.			
Real estate	0.4	Fin/R.E.			
Vegetables	0.3	Agric.			
Maintenance of nonfarm buildings nec	0.3	Constr.			
Creamery butter	0.3	Manufg.			
Flavoring extracts & syrups, nec	0.3	Manufg.			
Frozen specialties	0.3	Manufg.			
Industrial inorganic chemicals, nec	0.3	Manufg.			
Soybean oil mills	0.3	Manufg.			
Water transportation	0.3	Util.			
Eating & drinking places	0.3	Trade			
Banking	0.3	Fin/R.E.			
Detective & protective services	0.3	Services			
Fruits	0.2	Agric.			
Chemical preparations, nec	0.2	Manufg.			
Metal cans	0.2	Manufg.			
Pumps & compressors	0.2	Manufg.			
Rice milling	0.2	Manufg.			
Rubber & plastics hose & belting	0.2	Manufg.			
Miscellaneous repair shops	0.2	Services			
State & local government enterprises, nec	0.2	Gov't			
Fluid milk	0.1	Manufg.			
Lubricating oils & greases	0.1	Manufg.			
Sanitary services, steam supply, irrigation	0.1	Util.			
Insurance carriers	0.1	Fin/R.E.			
Computer & data processing services	0.1	Services			
Laundry, dry cleaning, shoe repair	0.1	Services			
Management & consulting services & labs	0.1	Services			
U.S. Postal Service	0.1	Gov't			

Source: Benchmark Input-Output Accounts for the U.S. Economy, 1982, U.S. Department of Commerce, Washington, D.C., July 1991. Data, as reported in the source, are organized by the 1977 SIC structure in use in 1982 but have been matched, as closely as is possible, to the 1987 SIC structure used in this book.

OCCUPATIONS EMPLOYED BY SIC 203 - PRESERVED FRUITS AND VEGETABLES

Occupation	% of Total 1994	Change to 2005	Occupation	% of Total 1994	Change to 2005
Cannery workers	21.2	6.7	Maintenance repairers, general utility	1.9	-4.0
Packaging & filling machine operators	6.8	6.7	Janitors & cleaners, incl maids	1.8	-14.6
Helpers, laborers, & material movers nec	5.1	6.7	Freight, stock, & material movers, hand	1.7	-14.6
Industrial machinery mechanics	4.5	49.4	Crushing & mixing machine operators	1.4	6.7
Industrial truck & tractor operators	4.5	6.7	Truck drivers light & heavy	1.3	10.0
Blue collar worker supervisors	4.1	3.7	General managers & top executives	1.3	1.2
Hand packers & packagers	3.9	-8.5	Vehicle washers & equipment cleaners	1.1	-1.6
Assemblers, fabricators, & hand workers nec	3.4	6.7	Industrial production managers	1.1	6.7
Agricultural workers nec	2.5	6.7	Sales & related workers nec	1.1	6.7
Cooking, roasting machine operators	2.3	17.4	Bookkeeping, accounting, & auditing clerks	1.0	-20.0
Precision food & tobacco workers nec	2.2	17.4	Traffic, shipping, & receiving clerks	1.0	2.6
Machine operators nec	2.2	-5.9	Secretaries, ex legal & medical	1.0	-2.9
Machine feeders & offbearers	2.1	17.3			

Source: Industry-Occupation Matrix, Bureau of Labor Statistics. These data relate to one or more 3-digit SIC industry groups rather than to a single 4-digit SIC. The change reported for each occupation to the year 2005 is a percent of growth or decline as estimated by the Bureau of Labor Statistics. The abbreviation nec stands for 'not elsewhere classified'.

LOCATION BY STATE AND REGIONAL CONCENTRATION

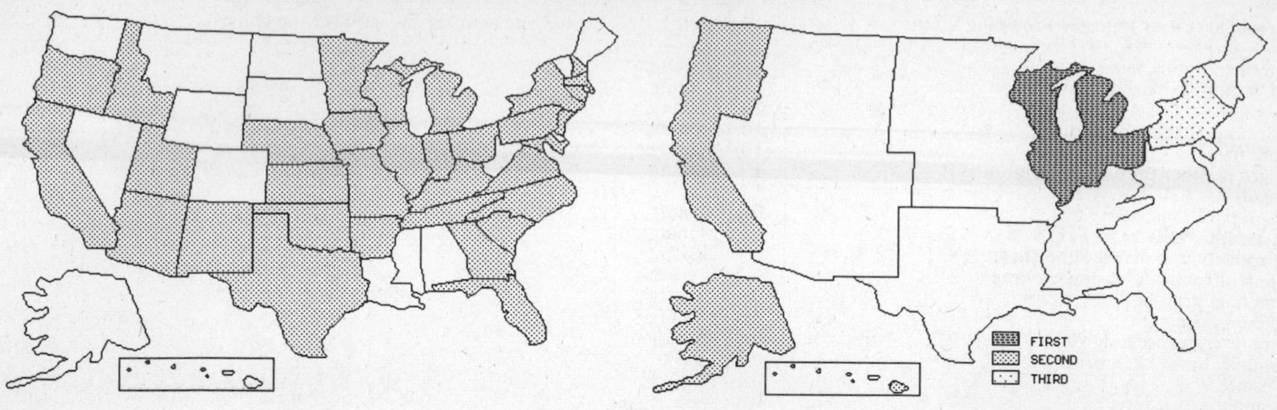

INDUSTRY DATA BY STATE

State	Establish-ments	Shipments			Employment				Cost as % of Shipments	Investment per Employee ($)
		Total ($ mil)	% of U.S.	Per Establ.	Total Number	% of U.S.	Per Establ.	Wages ($/hour)		
California	62	1,058.7	13.4	17.1	7,700	16.5	124	7.64	44.2	3,390
Ohio	12	840.3	10.7	70.0	4,800	10.3	400	11.22	57.3	6,792
Arkansas	4	625.2	7.9	156.3	3,500	7.5	875	8.05	50.4	-
Minnesota	17	426.6	5.4	25.1	2,300	4.9	135	7.29	40.0	6,304
New York	27	389.3	4.9	14.4	2,200	4.7	81	9.68	41.9	3,955
Wisconsin	16	362.7	4.6	22.7	1,600	3.4	100	9.42	41.3	-
Illinois	29	348.5	4.4	12.0	2,500	5.4	86	7.70	53.5	2,800
Pennsylvania	21	264.7	3.4	12.6	2,100	4.5	100	8.55	41.6	4,143
Texas	20	242.7	3.1	12.1	2,600	5.6	130	8.00	47.5	-
New Jersey	17	229.3	2.9	13.5	1,100	2.4	65	10.20	38.1	3,273
Oregon	8	163.3	2.1	20.4	800	1.7	100	9.77	43.2	5,000
Iowa	5	123.1	1.6	24.6	700	1.5	140	10.38	59.3	2,571
Connecticut	8	115.9	1.5	14.5	600	1.3	75	9.25	49.1	-
Indiana	6	79.6	1.0	13.3	400	0.9	67	9.50	48.9	-
Massachusetts	10	36.6	0.5	3.7	300	0.6	30	15.00	52.7	4,333
Florida	8	31.1	0.4	3.9	200	0.4	25	9.33	54.7	4,000
Michigan	11	(D)	-	-	375 *	0.8	34	-	-	2,133
Missouri	11	(D)	-	-	750 *	1.6	68	-	-	-
Utah	7	(D)	-	-	1,750 *	3.7	250	-	-	-
Tennessee	6	(D)	-	-	750 *	1.6	125	-	-	-
Oklahoma	5	(D)	-	-	750 *	1.6	150	-	-	-
Virginia	5	(D)	-	-	1,750 *	3.7	350	-	-	-
Georgia	4	(D)	-	-	750 *	1.6	188	-	-	-
Idaho	3	(D)	-	-	375 *	0.8	125	-	-	-
Kansas	3	(D)	-	-	1,750 *	3.7	583	-	-	-
Maryland	3	(D)	-	-	1,750 *	3.7	583	-	-	-
Arizona	2	(D)	-	-	175 *	0.4	88	-	-	-
Nebraska	2	(D)	-	-	1,750 *	3.7	875	-	-	-
North Carolina	2	(D)	-	-	375 *	0.8	188	-	-	-
South Carolina	2	(D)	-	-	1,750 *	3.7	875	-	-	-
Kentucky	1	(D)	-	-	750 *	1.6	750	-	-	-
New Hampshire	1	(D)	-	-	175 *	0.4	175	-	-	-
New Mexico	1	(D)	-	-	175 *	0.4	175	-	-	-

Source: 1992 *Economic Census*. The states are in descending order of shipments or establishments (if shipment data are missing for the majority). The symbol (D) appears when data are withheld to prevent disclosure of competitive information. States marked with (D) are sorted by number of establishments. A dash (-) indicates that the data element cannot be calculated; * indicates the midpoint of a range.

2041 - FLOUR & OTHER GRAIN MILL PRODUCTS

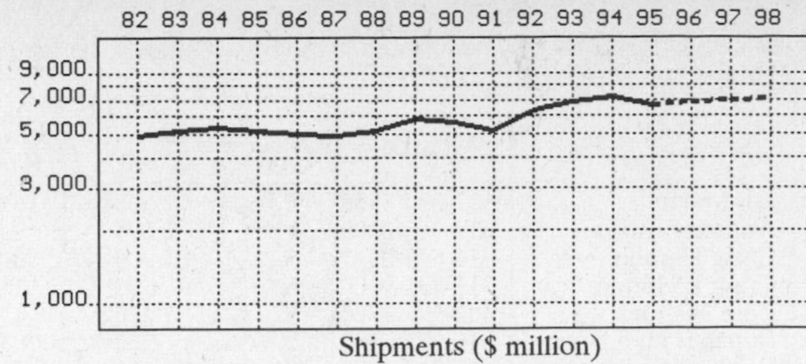

Shipments ($ million)

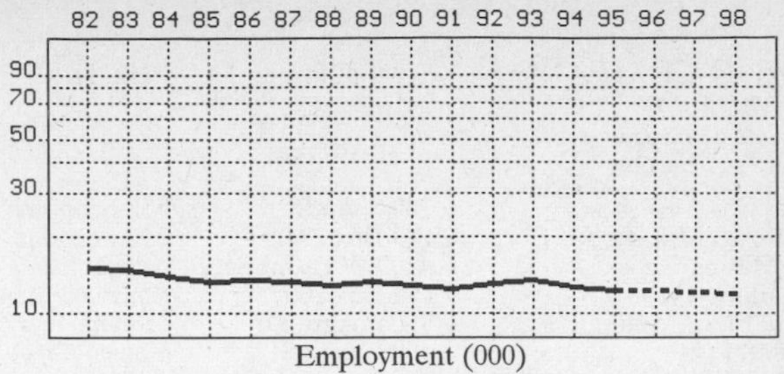

Employment (000)

GENERAL STATISTICS

Year	Companies	Establishments: Total	Establishments: with 20 or more employees	Employment: Total (000)	Employment: Production Workers (000)	Employment: Production Hours (Mil)	Compensation: Payroll ($ mil)	Compensation: Wages ($/hr)	Production ($ million): Cost of Materials	Production ($ million): Value Added by Manufacture	Production ($ million): Value of Shipments	Production ($ million): Capital Invest.
1982	251	360	174	15.1	11.4	24.2	323.0	9.64	3,825.5	1,094.3	4,932.8	90.6
1983		357	175	14.7	10.9	24.2	335.4	9.81	4,012.1	1,198.4	5,228.6	64.6
1984		354	176	13.9	10.3	22.3	335.5	10.51	4,108.5	1,208.0	5,305.7	68.7
1985		352	176	13.3	9.8	21.0	331.5	10.96	4,039.0	1,159.4	5,204.6	82.7
1986		357	177	13.5	9.9	21.4	348.7	11.28	3,642.5	1,345.9	5,003.1	62.8
1987	240	358	165	13.3	9.9	21.4	354.6	11.50	3,657.0	1,336.7	4,984.8	79.5
1988		353	170	12.8	9.6	21.3	351.0	11.71	3,781.4	1,439.4	5,205.0	130.3
1989		353	170	13.2	9.0	20.0	339.6	11.58	4,362.6	1,420.3	5,776.5	92.4
1990		348	169	12.8	9.1	19.9	351.0	12.08	4,348.0	1,251.3	5,624.7	114.2
1991		344	165	12.4	9.2	20.4	362.0	12.18	3,806.2	1,394.4	5,207.1	152.1
1992	230	365	172	13.1	9.5	21.5	408.9	12.87	4,675.3	1,624.5	6,294.4	253.5
1993		359	175	13.4	9.9	22.1	420.8	13.08	4,990.7	1,885.2	6,837.2	119.7
1994		354P	169P	12.7	9.2	21.3	397.0	12.68	5,186.8	1,908.0	7,089.1	95.9
1995		354P	168P	12.3P	8.8P	20.2P	406.3P	13.43P	4,850.5P	1,784.3P	6,629.4P	160.9P
1996		354P	168P	12.2P	8.7P	20.0P	413.1P	13.70P	4,958.9P	1,824.2P	6,777.7P	168.5P
1997		353P	167P	12.0P	8.6P	19.8P	420.0P	13.97P	5,067.4P	1,864.1P	6,925.9P	176.0P
1998		353P	167P	11.8P	8.4P	19.6P	426.8P	14.24P	5,175.8P	1,904.0P	7,074.1P	183.5P

Sources: 1982, 1987, 1992 *Economic Census*; *Annual Survey of Manufactures*, 83-86, 88-91, 93-94. Establishment counts for non-Census years are from *County Business Patterns*; establishment values for 83-84 are extrapolations. 'P's show projections by the editors. Industries reclassified in 87 will not have data for prior years.

INDICES OF CHANGE

Year	Companies	Establishments: Total	Establishments: with 20 or more employees	Employment: Total (000)	Employment: Production Workers (000)	Employment: Production Hours (Mil)	Compensation: Payroll ($ mil)	Compensation: Wages ($/hr)	Production ($ million): Cost of Materials	Production ($ million): Value Added by Manufacture	Production ($ million): Value of Shipments	Production ($ million): Capital Invest.
1982	109	99	101	115	120	113	79	75	82	67	78	36
1983		98	102	112	115	113	82	76	86	74	83	25
1984		97	102	106	108	104	82	82	88	74	84	27
1985		96	102	102	103	98	81	85	86	71	83	33
1986		98	103	103	104	100	85	88	78	83	79	25
1987	104	98	96	102	104	100	87	89	78	82	79	31
1988		97	99	98	101	99	86	91	81	89	83	51
1989		97	99	101	95	93	83	90	93	87	92	36
1990		95	98	98	96	93	86	94	93	77	89	45
1991		94	96	95	97	95	89	95	81	86	83	60
1992	100	100	100	100	100	100	100	100	100	100	100	100
1993		98	102	102	104	103	103	102	107	116	109	47
1994		97P	98P	97	97	99	97	99	111	117	113	38
1995		97P	98P	94P	93P	94P	99P	104P	104P	110P	105P	63P
1996		97P	98P	93P	92P	93P	101P	106P	106P	112P	108P	66P
1997		97P	97P	92P	90P	92P	103P	109P	108P	115P	110P	69P
1998		97P	97P	90P	89P	91P	104P	111P	111P	117P	112P	72P

Sources: Same as General Statistics. Values reflect change from the base year, 1992. Values above 100 mean greater than 92, values below 100 mean less than 92, and a value of 100 in the 82-91 or 93-98 period means same as 92. 'P's mark projections by the editors.

SELECTED RATIOS

For 1994	Avg. of All Manufact.	Analyzed Industry	Index
Employees per Establishment	49	36	73
Payroll per Establishment	1,500,273	1,121,613	75
Payroll per Employee	30,620	31,260	102
Production Workers per Establishment	34	26	76
Wages per Establishment	853,319	763,047	89
Wages per Production Worker	24,861	29,357	118
Hours per Production Worker	2,056	2,315	113
Wages per Hour	12.09	12.68	105
Value Added per Establishment	4,602,255	5,390,523	117
Value Added per Employee	93,930	150,236	160

For 1994	Avg. of All Manufact.	Analyzed Industry	Index
Value Added per Production Worker	134,084	207,391	155
Cost per Establishment	5,045,178	14,653,859	290
Cost per Employee	102,970	408,409	397
Cost per Production Worker	146,988	563,783	384
Shipments per Establishment	9,576,895	20,028,278	209
Shipments per Employee	195,460	558,197	286
Shipments per Production Worker	279,017	770,554	276
Investment per Establishment	321,011	270,939	84
Investment per Employee	6,552	7,551	115
Investment per Production Worker	9,352	10,424	111

Sources: Same as General Statistics. The 'Average of All Manufacturing' column represents the average of all manufacturing industries reported for the most recent complete year available. The Index shows the relationship between the Average and the Analyzed Industry. For example, 100 means that they are equal; 500 that the Analyzed Industry is five times the average; 50 means that the Analyzed Industry is half the national average. The abbreviation 'na' is used to show that data are 'not available'.

LEADING COMPANIES Number shown: **55** Total sales ($ mil): **9,446** Total employment (000): **31.8**

Company Name	Address				CEO Name	Phone	Co. Type	Sales ($ mil)	Empl. (000)
Pillsbury Co	200 S 6th St	Minneapolis	MN	55402	Ian Martin	612-330-4966	S	2,900•	16.0
International MultiFoods Corp	PO Box 2942	Minneapolis	MN	55402	Anthony Luiso	612-340-3300	P	2,295	7.5
Krause Milling Co	4200 W Burnham St	Milwaukee	WI	53215	Craig Hamlin	414-645-0411	S	1,200	<0.1
ADM Milling Co	PO Box 7007	Shawnee Msn	KS	66207	Craig L Hamlin	913-491-9400	S	890•	1.1
ConAgra Flour Milling Co	9 ConAgra Dr	Omaha	NE	68102	Tom Manuel	402-595-7300	S	470	1.8
Bartlett and Co	4800 Main St	Kansas City	MO	64112	James B Hebenstrit	816-753-6300	R	260•	0.6
Bay State Milling Co	100 Congress St	Quincy	MA	02169	Brian G Rothwell	617-328-4400	S	150•	0.4
Trinitas Corp	100 Congress St	Quincy	MA	02169	B J Rothwell II	617-328-4400	R	150•	0.4
Lauhoff Grain Co	PO Box 571	Danville	IL	61834	Richard Pittelkow	217-442-1800	S	130•	0.3
Azteca Milling Co	PO Box 141	Edinburg	TX	78540	Eduardo Livas	210-383-4911	R	100	0.4
Illinois Cereal Mills Inc	PO Box 550	Paris	IL	61944	JW Hasler	217-465-5331	R	100	0.3
Hawaiian Flour Mills Inc	PO Box 855	Honolulu	HI	96808	Alan Yoshikami	808-527-3222	R	68•	0.1
Interstate Milling Co	PO Box 31155	Charlotte	NC	28231	Dennis Tucker	704-332-3165	D	62•	<0.1
Star of West Mill Inc	121 E Tuscola St	Frankenmuth	MI	48734	Richard Krafft	517-652-9971	R	60	0.1
Amber Milling Co	PO Box 64594	St Paul	MN	55164	Garry A Pistoria	612-641-6457	D	52	<0.1
Siemer Milling Co	PO Box 670	Teutopolis	IL	62467	Richard C Siemer	217-857-3131	R	40	0.1
Wilkins-Rogers Inc	PO Box 308	Ellicott City	MD	21041	S H Rogers Jr	410-465-5800	R	35	0.2
Southeastern Mills Inc	PO Box 908	Rome	GA	30161	V Grizzard Jr	706-291-6528	R	34•	0.2
Illinois Cereal Mills Inc	1730 W Michigan St	Indianapolis	IN	46222	Allan Russell	317-632-2347	D	33•	<0.1
JR Short Milling Co	500 W Madison St	Chicago	IL	60606	JR Short Jr	312-559-5450	R	31	0.2
Kerr Pacific Corp	811 SW Front St	Portland	OR	97204	E Randolf Labbe	503-221-1301	R	31	0.2
Morrison Milling Co	PO Box 719	Denton	TX	76201	EW Morrison Jr	817-387-6111	R	27•	0.2
Archer Daniels Midland Co	PO Drawer 400	Dodge City	KS	67801	Ken Bailey	316-227-8101	S	20•	<0.1
Bartlett Milling Co	PO Box 831	Statesville	NC	28677	GE Bure	704-872-9581	S	20•	0.1
King Milling Co	PO Box 99	Lowell	MI	49331	K Doyle	616-897-9264	R	20	<0.1
Roman Meal Milling Co	4014 15th Av NW	Fargo	ND	58102	Rich Axlund	701-282-9656	R	20	<0.1
Archer Daniels Midland Co	1701 Armour Rd	N Kansas City	MO	64116	Ted Bownik	816-221-7272	D	16	0.1
Knappen Milling Company Inc	110 S Water St	Augusta	MI	49012	CB Knappen III	616-731-4141	R	15•	<0.1
Stafford County Flour Mills Co	PO Box 7	Hudson	KS	67545	Alvin A Brensing	316-458-4121	R	15	<0.1
Hopkinsville Milling Company	PO Box 669	Hopkinsville	KY	42241	Haywood Strader	502-886-1231	R	14•	<0.1
Midstate Mills Inc	PO Box 349	Newton	NC	28658	B Drum	704-464-1611	R	14•	0.2
Roush Products Company Inc	PO Box 427	Cedar Rapids	IA	52406	Vincent Noce	319-365-9423	S	13	<0.1
House Autry Mills Inc	635 Houses Mill Rd	Newton Grove	NC	28366	Richard M Justice	919-594-0802	R	12	0.1
Acme-Evans Co	854 Bethel Av	Beech Grove	IN	46107	Marvin Baker	317-783-3321	D	11	<0.1
Sands, Taylor and Wood Co	Box 1010	Norwich	VT	05055	Frank Sands	802-649-3881	R	11	<0.1
Capitol Milling Co	PO Box 2796	Los Angeles	CA	90051	SN Loew Jr	213-628-8235	R	10	<0.1
H Nagel and Son Co	2478 Central Pkwy	Cincinnati	OH	45214	William Nagel	513-665-4550	R	10	<0.1
Mennel Milling of Illinois	PO Box 255	Mount Olive	IL	62069	Mark Miller	217-999-2161	S	10•	<0.1
Pendleton Flour Mills	PO Box 1427	Pendleton	OR	97801	Anthony J Flagg	503-276-6511	D	10	<0.1
Wall-Rogalsky Milling Co	416 N Main St	McPherson	KS	67460	J Brent Wall	316-241-2410	R	10	<0.1
Williams Brothers Co	162 N Water St	Kent	OH	44240	C A Williams III	216-673-2941	R	10•	<0.1
Inland Mills Co	1925 E Grand Av	Des Moines	IA	50316	Tony Warner	515-266-2156	D	9	<0.1
Spangler's Flour Mills Inc	PO Box 175	Mount Joy	PA	17552	B Flattery	717-653-1403	S	9	<0.1
Nokomis Mill	3501 Hiawatha Av	Minneapolis	MN	55406	Larry Glerum	612-729-8383	D	8	<0.1
Lacey Milling Co	PO Box 1193	Hanford	CA	93230	CX Lendrum	209-584-6634	R	7	<0.1
Walnut Acres Inc	PO Box 8	Penns Creek	PA	17862	Robert Anderson	717-837-0601	R	7	0.1
Birkett Mills	PO Box 440	Penn Yan	NY	14527	Wayne W Wagner	315-536-3311	R	6	<0.1
Quality Ingredients Corp	PO Box 306	Chester	NJ	07930	Thomas Schmidt	908-879-2227	R	6•	<0.1
Allen Brothers Milling Company	PO Box 1437	Columbia	SC	29202	EJ Edgerton Jr	803-779-2460	R	5	<0.1
McIntosh Farm Service Co	350 State St	McIntosh	MN	56556	Robert Kringlen	218-563-3735	R	3	<0.1
Base Inc	5307 E Pine St	Tulsa	OK	74115	P M-Chapman	918-835-3702	R	2	<0.1
Shenandoah Mills Inc	PO Box 369	Lebanon	TN	37087	Dale Nunnery	615-444-0841	R	2	<0.1
Antigo Flour and Feed Co	602 5th Av	Antigo	WI	54409	Jacob V Hunter	715-623-5333	R	1	<0.1
Quinoa Corp	PO Box 1039	Torrance	CA	90505	David Schnorr	310-530-8666	R	1	<0.1
Fowler's Milling Co	12500 Fowler's Mill	Chardon	OH	44024	Richard C Erickson	216-286-2024	R	0	<0.1

Source: *Ward's Business Directory of U.S. Private and Public Companies*, Volumes 1 and 2, 1996. The company type code used is as follows: P - Public, R - Private, S - Subsidiary, D - Division, J - Joint Venture, A - Affiliate, G - Group. Sales are in millions of dollars, employees are in thousands. An asterisk (*) indicates an estimated sales volume. The symbol < stands for 'less than'. Company names and addresses are truncated, in some cases, to fit into the available space.

MATERIALS CONSUMED

Material		Quantity	Delivered Cost ($ million)
Materials, ingredients, containers, and supplies		(X)	4,323.3
Wheat	mil bushels	875.9	3,177.8
Corn	mil bushels	133.9	287.7
Barley	mil bushels	(S)	8.8
Oats	mil bushels	32.6	58.0
Other	mil bushels	12.4**	43.8
Wheat flour	1,000 cwt	23,336.2	146.9
Sugar, cane and beet (in terms of sugar solids)	1,000 s tons	97.9*	30.6
Fats and oils	mil lb	(S)	39.6
Packaging paper and plastics film, coated and laminated		(X)	36.1
Bags; plastics, foil, and coated paper		(X)	14.2
Bags; uncoated paper and multiwall		(X)	49.2
Bags, textile (burlap, cotton, polypropylene, etc.)		(X)	3.7
Paperboard containers, boxes, and corrugated paperboard		(X)	16.5
All other materials and components, parts, containers, and supplies		(X)	225.2
Materials, ingredients, containers, and supplies, nsk		(X)	185.1

Source: 1992 *Economic Census*. Explanation of symbols used: (D): Withheld to avoid disclosure of competitive data; na: Not available; (S): Withheld because statistical norms were not met; (X): Not applicable; (Z): Less than half the unit shown; nec: Not elsewhere classified; nsk: Not specified by kind; - : zero; * : 10-19 percent estimated; ** : 20-29 percent estimated.

PRODUCT SHARE DETAILS

Product or Product Class	% Share
Flour and other grain mill products	100.00
Wheat flour, except flour mixes	67.68
Commercial dollar exports, all white flour types	3.55
All other exports of white flour, such as those under Public Law 480,	(D)
Bakers' and institutional white bread-type flours, domestic shipments in bulk cars or trucks	42.28
Bakers' and institutional white bread-type flours, domestic shipments in containers, including tote bins	10.53
Bakers' and institutional soft wheat flour (bakery, restaurant, etc.), domestic shipments in bulk cars or trucks	9.74
Bakers' and institutional soft wheat flour (bakery, restaurant, etc.), domestic shipments in containers, including tote bins	2.01
Family white flour, other than self-rising, domestic shipments in containers less than 25 lb	12.24
Family white flour, other than self-rising, domestic shipments in containers 25 lb or more	2.34
Self-rising family white flour, domestic shipments	2.62
Domestic shipments of white flour shipped to blenders or other processors for use in food products (mixes, refrigerated doughs, soups, etc.)	3.36
Domestic shipments of white flour shipped to blenders or other processors for use in nonfood products (pet food, industrial, etc.)	0.38
Whole wheat flour	1.49
Durum flour and semolina	7.04
Bulgur flour	(D)
Other wheat flour, including farina	1.10
Wheat flour, except flour mixes, nsk	0.01
Wheat mill products other than flour	7.98
Wheat mill feed	93.43
Wheat mill products, other than flour and mill feed, including wheat germ, wheat bran, etc.	6.57
Corn mill products	12.52
Whole cornmeal for human consumption	7.28
Degermed cornmeal for human consumption	8.60
Corn grits and hominy, except for brewers' use, for human consumption	(D)
Corn grits and flakes for brewers' use, for human consumption	4.86
Hominy feed, cornmeal, and other byproducts of dry corn milling (for animal feed)	15.62
Corn flour	24.95
Other corn mill products for human consumption	24.84
Other corn mill products, not for human consumption	(D)
Flour mixes, and refrigerated and frozen doughs and batters made in flour mills	5.58
Pancake and waffle mixes	19.02
Cake mixes, including gingerbread	4.37
Biscuit mixes	14.51
Piecrust mixes	(D)
Doughnuts and other sweet yeast goods mixes	(D)
Bread and bread-type roll mixes	13.41
Other prepared flour mixes, including cookie mixes	46.37
Other refrigerated doughs and batters, including pizza, coffeecake, pancake, etc.	0.38
Frozen bread and bread-type roll dough	(D)
Frozen cookie dough	(D)
Other frozen doughs and batters, including pizza, coffeecake, pancake, etc.	(D)
Other grain mill products	2.80
Rye, oat, buckwheat, and other flour	36.56
Other mill feed (oats, rye, buckwheat, etc.)	63.44
Flour and other grain mill products, nsk	3.44

Source: 1992 *Economic Census*. The values shown are percent of total shipments in an industry. Values of indented subcategories are summed in the main heading. The symbol (D) appears when data are withheld to prevent disclosure of competitive information. The abbreviation nsk stands for 'not specified by kind' and nec for 'not elsewhere classified'.

INPUTS AND OUTPUTS FOR FLOUR & OTHER GRAIN MILL PRODUCTS

Economic Sector or Industry Providing Inputs	%	Sector	Economic Sector or Industry Buying Outputs	%	Sector
Food grains	55.6	Agric.	Bread, cake, & related products	26.3	Manufg.
Wholesale trade	12.2	Trade	Personal consumption expenditures	22.2	
Railroads & related services	6.2	Util.	Prepared feeds, nec	10.3	Manufg.
Feed grains	4.7	Agric.	Exports	6.5	Foreign
Advertising	2.3	Services	Cookies & crackers	6.2	Manufg.
Flour & other grain mill products	2.2	Manufg.	Macaroni & spaghetti	4.9	Manufg.
Electric services (utilities)	2.0	Util.	Blended & prepared flour	3.5	Manufg.
Motor freight transportation & warehousing	2.0	Util.	Eating & drinking places	3.3	Trade
Water transportation	2.0	Util.	Flour & other grain mill products	1.9	Manufg.
Sugar	1.1	Manufg.	Frozen specialties	1.9	Manufg.
Imports	1.1	Foreign	Food preparations, nec	1.8	Manufg.
Bags, except textile	1.0	Manufg.	Poultry & eggs	1.7	Agric.
Miscellaneous crops	0.7	Agric.	Cereal breakfast foods	1.7	Manufg.
Paperboard containers & boxes	0.7	Manufg.	Dairy farm products	1.4	Agric.
Vegetable oil mills, nec	0.6	Manufg.	Dog, cat, & other pet food	1.3	Manufg.
Flavoring extracts & syrups, nec	0.4	Manufg.	Malt beverages	1.2	Manufg.
Textile bags	0.4	Manufg.	Meat animals	1.0	Agric.
Gas production & distribution (utilities)	0.4	Util.	Commodity Credit Corporation	0.9	Gov't
Banking	0.4	Fin/R.E.	Miscellaneous livestock	0.5	Agric.
Eating & drinking places	0.3	Trade	Canned specialties	0.4	Manufg.
Petroleum refining	0.2	Manufg.	Child day care services	0.4	Services
Air transportation	0.2	Util.	Residential care	0.1	Services
Communications, except radio & TV	0.2	Util.			
Equipment rental & leasing services	0.2	Services			
Maintenance of nonfarm buildings nec	0.1	Constr.			
Paper coating & glazing	0.1	Manufg.			
Royalties	0.1	Fin/R.E.			
Hotels & lodging places	0.1	Services			
Legal services	0.1	Services			
Management & consulting services & labs	0.1	Services			
State & local government enterprises, nec	0.1	Gov't			
U.S. Postal Service	0.1	Gov't			
Noncomparable imports	0.1	Foreign			

Source: Benchmark Input-Output Accounts for the U.S. Economy, 1982, U.S. Department of Commerce, Washington, D.C., July 1991. Data, as reported in the source, are organized by the 1977 SIC structure in use in 1982 but have been matched, as closely as is possible, to the 1987 SIC structure used in this book.

OCCUPATIONS EMPLOYED BY SIC 204 - GRAIN MILL PRODUCTS AND FATS AND OILS

Occupation	% of Total 1994	Change to 2005	Occupation	% of Total 1994	Change to 2005
Packaging & filling machine operators	8.2	-5.4	General office clerks	2.0	-10.3
Truck drivers light & heavy	6.0	8.4	Secretaries, ex legal & medical	1.9	-4.3
Crushing & mixing machine operators	5.7	-5.4	Separating & still machine operators	1.9	5.1
Blue collar worker supervisors	5.5	0.1	Machine feeders & offbearers	1.8	-5.3
Helpers, laborers, & material movers nec	4.7	5.1	Machine operators nec	1.8	-7.3
Industrial machinery mechanics	3.7	15.7	Bookkeeping, accounting, & auditing clerks	1.7	-21.1
Freight, stock, & material movers, hand	3.4	-15.9	Industrial production managers	1.7	5.1
Industrial truck & tractor operators	3.2	5.1	Science & mathematics technicians	1.5	5.2
Sales & related workers nec	2.6	5.2	Material moving equipment operators nec	1.5	5.1
General managers & top executives	2.5	-0.3	Janitors & cleaners, incl maids	1.4	-15.9
Maintenance repairers, general utility	2.4	-5.4	Inspectors, testers, & graders, precision	1.2	5.2
Hand packers & packagers	2.2	-9.9	Agricultural workers nec	1.1	5.2
Extruding & forming machine workers	2.1	-26.4	Plant & system operators nec	1.0	39.3
Precision food & tobacco workers nec	2.1	5.1	Traffic, shipping, & receiving clerks	1.0	1.2
Cooking, roasting machine operators	2.0	11.4			

Source: Industry-Occupation Matrix, Bureau of Labor Statistics. These data relate to one or more 3-digit SIC industry groups rather than to a single 4-digit SIC. The change reported for each occupation to the year 2005 is a percent of growth or decline as estimated by the Bureau of Labor Statistics. The abbreviation nec stands for 'not elsewhere classified'.

LOCATION BY STATE AND REGIONAL CONCENTRATION

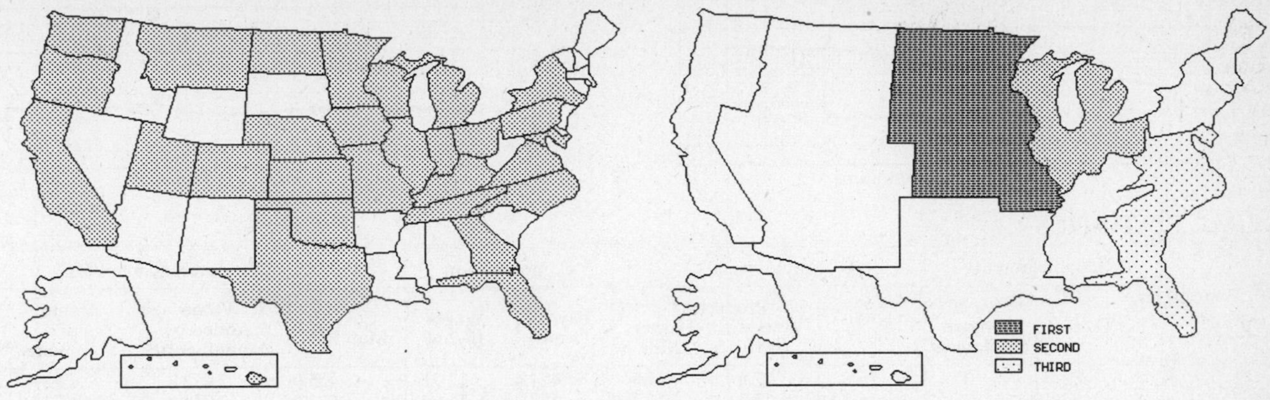

INDUSTRY DATA BY STATE

State	Establish-ments	Shipments			Employment				Cost as % of Shipments	Investment per Employee ($)
		Total ($ mil)	% of U.S.	Per Establ.	Total Number	% of U.S.	Per Establ.	Wages ($/hour)		
New York	20	574.0	9.1	28.7	900	6.9	45	15.76	78.6	-
Kansas	22	477.7	7.6	21.7	900	6.9	41	11.25	77.5	6,222
Minnesota	18	465.2	7.4	25.8	700	5.3	39	14.43	81.4	7,571
Missouri	13	432.3	6.9	33.3	700	5.3	54	15.70	66.2	10,714
Texas	18	428.7	6.8	23.8	1,600	12.2	89	9.79	68.7	14,125
California	29	390.6	6.2	13.5	600	4.6	21	14.70	74.2	86,167
Tennessee	9	343.4	5.5	38.2	500	3.8	56	10.20	62.4	5,600
Ohio	11	235.9	3.7	21.4	400	3.1	36	15.17	81.1	7,000
Iowa	9	213.8	3.4	23.8	600	4.6	67	14.11	63.7	8,333
Michigan	11	203.3	3.2	18.5	700	5.3	64	15.30	65.9	4,286
Nebraska	6	197.8	3.1	33.0	400	3.1	67	15.14	75.1	-
Indiana	14	187.2	3.0	13.4	400	3.1	29	12.17	77.0	5,250
North Carolina	23	178.8	2.8	7.8	600	4.6	26	9.00	81.2	4,000
Pennsylvania	26	136.7	2.2	5.3	200	1.5	8	11.25	83.2	8,500
Florida	5	110.9	1.8	22.2	100	0.8	20	15.50	80.1	4,000
Utah	9	109.0	1.7	12.1	300	2.3	33	13.50	76.8	2,000
Oregon	3	108.2	1.7	36.1	100	0.8	33	14.00	85.8	-
Virginia	12	71.2	1.1	5.9	100	0.8	8	10.00	69.8	-
Kentucky	5	25.3	0.4	5.1	100	0.8	20	10.00	62.5	-
Illinois	14	(D)	-	-	750 *	5.7	54	-	-	13,067
Washington	10	(D)	-	-	175 *	1.3	18	-	-	-
Georgia	8	(D)	-	-	375 *	2.9	47	-	-	-
Wisconsin	8	(D)	-	-	175 *	1.3	22	-	-	3,429
Colorado	6	(D)	-	-	175 *	1.3	29	-	-	-
Oklahoma	5	(D)	-	-	375 *	2.9	75	-	-	-
Maryland	3	(D)	-	-	175 *	1.3	58	-	-	-
Montana	3	(D)	-	-	175 *	1.3	58	-	-	-
North Dakota	2	(D)	-	-	175 *	1.3	88	-	-	-
Hawaii	1	(D)	-	-	175 *	1.3	175	-	-	-

Source: 1992 *Economic Census*. The states are in descending order of shipments or establishments (if shipment data are missing for the majority). The symbol (D) appears when data are withheld to prevent disclosure of competitive information. States marked with (D) are sorted by number of establishments. A dash (-) indicates that the data element cannot be calculated; * indicates the midpoint of a range.

2043 - CEREAL BREAKFAST FOODS

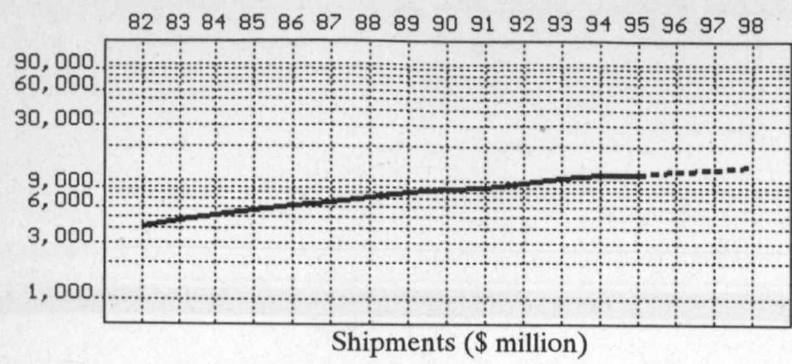

Shipments ($ million)

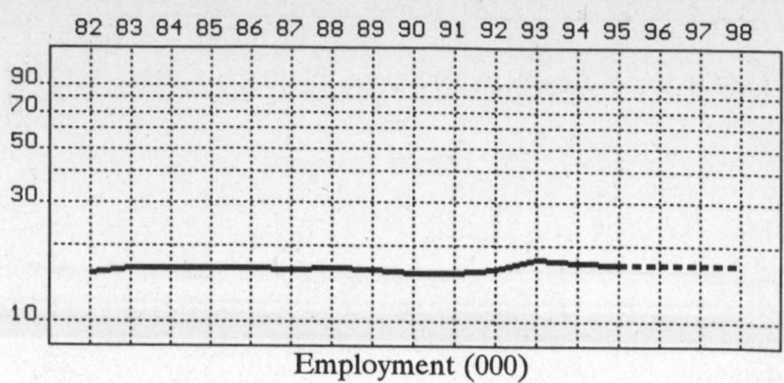

Employment (000)

GENERAL STATISTICS

Year	Com-panies	Establishments		Employment			Compensation		Production ($ million)			
		Total	with 20 or more employees	Total (000)	Production Workers (000)	Production Hours (Mil)	Payroll ($ mil)	Wages ($/hr)	Cost of Materials	Value Added by Manufacture	Value of Shipments	Capital Invest.
1982	32	52	37	15.6	12.8	25.5	424.4	12.91	1,475.0	2,622.8	4,131.9	165.4
1983		52	37	16.3	13.3	26.7	483.0	14.09	1,502.0	3,069.3	4,571.9	176.7
1984		52	37	16.2	13.2	26.8	525.9	15.49	1,636.2	3,478.6	5,107.2	189.3
1985		52	38	16.3	13.3	27.3	563.1	16.38	1,721.2	3,994.7	5,718.1	228.3
1986		49	33	16.4	13.3	27.8	585.1	16.72	1,681.4	4,513.1	6,167.6	270.1
1987	33	53	34	16.0	13.1	28.4	598.9	16.85	1,669.8	4,904.5	6,565.7	333.4
1988		56	35	16.4	13.7	30.4	654.6	17.29	1,823.3	5,463.8	7,274.4	394.5
1989		55	35	16.0	13.2	30.2	665.1	17.62	2,150.4	5,754.1	7,912.3	483.1
1990		57	36	15.7	13.1	29.0	384.0	18.84	2,371.4	6,325.3	8,704.6	396.8
1991		62	40	15.7	12.7	27.1	707.1	20.62	2,371.5	6,580.7	8,954.4	297.9
1992	42	65	42	16.1	13.1	29.7	745.3	20.12	2,470.9	7,338.1	9,798.6	396.6
1993		65	40	17.6	14.4	31.6	761.8	19.26	2,835.0	7,762.6	10,615.0	396.4
1994		64P	39P	17.1	14.1	31.1	765.2	19.61	2,770.1	8,720.8	11,506.5	339.1
1995		66P	40P	16.7P	13.7P	31.4P	774.6P	21.30P	2,809.4P	8,844.6P	11,669.8P	450.7P
1996		67P	40P	16.8P	13.8P	31.8P	798.8P	21.87P	2,954.1P	9,300.0P	12,270.7P	470.3P
1997		68P	40P	16.9P	13.9P	32.2P	823.1P	22.43P	3,098.7P	9,755.4P	12,871.5P	490.0P
1998		70P	41P	16.9P	13.9P	32.6P	847.3P	22.99P	3,243.4P	10,210.8P	13,472.4P	509.7P

Sources: 1982, 1987, 1992 *Economic Census*; *Annual Survey of Manufactures*, 83-86, 88-91, 93-94. Establishment counts for non-Census years are from *County Business Patterns*; establishment values for 83-84 are extrapolations. 'P's show projections by the editors. Industries reclassified in 87 will not have data for prior years.

INDICES OF CHANGE

Year	Com-panies	Establishments		Employment			Compensation		Production ($ million)			
		Total	with 20 or more employees	Total (000)	Production Workers (000)	Production Hours (Mil)	Payroll ($ mil)	Wages ($/hr)	Cost of Materials	Value Added by Manufacture	Value of Shipments	Capital Invest.
1982	76	80	88	97	98	86	57	64	60	36	42	42
1983		80	88	101	102	90	65	70	61	42	47	45
1984		80	88	101	101	90	71	77	66	47	52	48
1985		80	90	101	102	92	76	81	70	54	58	58
1986		75	79	102	102	94	79	83	68	62	63	68
1987	79	82	81	99	100	96	80	84	68	67	67	84
1988		86	83	102	105	102	88	86	74	74	74	99
1989		85	83	99	101	102	89	88	87	78	81	122
1990		88	86	98	100	98	52	94	96	86	89	100
1991		95	95	98	97	91	95	102	96	90	91	75
1992	100	100	100	100	100	100	100	100	100	100	100	100
1993		100	95	109	110	106	102	96	115	106	108	100
1994		99P	93P	106	108	105	103	97	112	119	117	86
1995		101P	94P	104P	105P	106P	104P	106P	114P	121P	119P	114P
1996		103P	95P	104P	105P	107P	107P	109P	120P	127P	125P	119P
1997		105P	96P	105P	106P	108P	110P	111P	125P	133P	131P	124P
1998		107P	96P	105P	106P	110P	114P	114P	131P	139P	137P	129P

Sources: Same as General Statistics. Values reflect change from the base year, 1992. Values above 100 mean greater than 92, values below 100 mean less than 92, and a value of 100 in the 82-91 or 93-98 period means same as 92. 'P's mark projections by the editors.

SELECTED RATIOS

For 1994	Avg. of All Manufact.	Analyzed Industry	Index
Employees per Establishment	49	266	542
Payroll per Establishment	1,500,273	11,885,903	792
Payroll per Employee	30,620	44,749	146
Production Workers per Establishment	34	219	638
Wages per Establishment	853,319	9,473,167	1,110
Wages per Production Worker	24,861	43,253	174
Hours per Production Worker	2,056	2,206	107
Wages per Hour	12.09	19.61	162
Value Added per Establishment	4,602,255	135,460,767	2,943
Value Added per Employee	93,930	509,988	543

For 1994	Avg. of All Manufact.	Analyzed Industry	Index
Value Added per Production Worker	134,084	618,496	461
Cost per Establishment	5,045,178	43,028,148	853
Cost per Employee	102,970	161,994	157
Cost per Production Worker	146,988	196,461	134
Shipments per Establishment	9,576,895	178,731,231	1,866
Shipments per Employee	195,460	672,895	344
Shipments per Production Worker	279,017	816,064	292
Investment per Establishment	321,011	5,267,263	1,641
Investment per Employee	6,552	19,830	303
Investment per Production Worker	9,352	24,050	257

Sources: Same as General Statistics. The 'Average of All Manufacturing' column represents the average of all manufacturing industries reported for the most recent complete year available. The Index shows the relationship between the Average and the Analyzed Industry. For example, 100 means that they are equal; 500 that the Analyzed Industry is five times the average; 50 means that the Analyzed Industry is half the national average. The abbreviation 'na' is used to show that data are 'not available'.

LEADING COMPANIES

Number shown: **14** Total sales ($ mil): **25,959** Total employment (000): **180.7**

Company Name	Address				CEO Name	Phone	Co. Type	Sales ($ mil)	Empl. (000)
General Mills Inc	PO Box 1113	Minneapolis	MN	55440	HB Atwater Jr	612-540-2311	P	8,517	125.7
Kellogg Co	PO Box 3599	Battle Creek	MI	49016	Arnold G Langbo	616-961-2000	P	6,562	16.0
Quaker Oats Co	PO Box 049001	Chicago	IL	60604	W D Smithburg	312-222-7111	P	5,955	20.0
Kellogg USA Inc	PO Box 3599	Battle Creek	MI	49016	Arnold G Langbo	616-961-2000	S	2,240*	5.8
Quaker Oats Co	PO Box 049001	Chicago	IL	60604	Dave Bere'	312-222-7111	D	1,573	5.5
Ralcorp Holdings Inc	901 Chouteau Av	St Louis	MO	63102	Richard A Pearce	314-982-1000	P	987	7.1
National Oats	1515 H Av NE	Cedar Rapids	IA	52402	Michael Kirby	319-364-9161	D	82	0.4
Grain Millers of Iowa Inc	PO Box 399	St Ansgar	IA	50472	Shirley Kitteson	515-736-4801	R	13	<0.1
Little Crow Foods	PO Box 1038	Warsaw	IN	46580	Dennis M Fuller	219-267-7141	R	8*	<0.1
US Mills Inc	200 Reservior St	Needham	MA	02194	Charles T Verde	617-444-0440	R	8*	<0.1
Grist Mill Co	PO Box 430	Lakeville	MN	55044	Thomas T Tatoian	612-469-4981	D	7*	<0.1
New Morning Inc	42 Davis Rd	Acton	MA	01720	Gene Fialkoff	508-263-1201	R	6	<0.1
Healthy Times Inc	461 Vernon Way	El Cajon	CA	92020	Richard Prescott	619-593-2229	R	2	<0.1
Wholly Cow Foods	PO Box 252	Cloverdale	OR	97112	Steve Kulju	503-392-4277	R	0	<0.1

Source: *Ward's Business Directory of U.S. Private and Public Companies*, Volumes 1 and 2, 1996. The company type code used is as follows: P - Public, R - Private, S - Subsidiary, D - Division, J - Joint Venture, A - Affiliate, G - Group. Sales are in millions of dollars, employees are in thousands. An asterisk (*) indicates an estimated sales volume. The symbol < stands for 'less than'. Company names and addresses are truncated, in some cases, to fit into the available space.

MATERIALS CONSUMED

Material		Quantity	Delivered Cost ($ million)
Materials, ingredients, containers, and supplies		(X)	1,966.5
Wheat	mil bushels	18.5	76.3
Oats	mil bushels	(S)	78.2
Corn	mil bushels	(D)	(D)
Barley	mil bushels	18.1	2.4
Rice, rough	mil lb	297.3	54.5
Other grains	mil bushels	(S)	1.2
Corn grits	mil bushels	523.7	51.4
Corn meal and flakes	1,000 cwt	(D)	(D)
Wheat flour	1,000 cwt	(S)	33.5
Flour, other than wheat	1,000 cwt	(S)	60.7
Prepared four mixes	1,000 cwt	(D)	(D)
White sugar, cane and beet, in terms of sugar solids	1,000 s tons	511.5	238.1
Brown sugar, cane and beet, in terms of sugar solids	1,000 s tons	19.8*	11.8
Fats and oils	mil lb	133.6	38.8
Raisins	1,000 cwt	787.8	70.8
Dried fruits except raisins	1,000 cwt	133.1	28.1
Nut meats, dried or dehydrated	1,000 cwt	63.6	7.7
Nuts and nut meats, raw	1,000 cwt	234.5	38.9
Packaging paper and plastics film, coated and laminated		(X)	103.2
Bags; plastics, foil, and coated paper		(X)	59.6
Bags; uncoated paper and multiwall		(X)	(D)
Paperboard containers, boxes, and corrugated paperboard		(X)	451.0
All other materials and components, parts, containers, and supplies		(X)	502.6
Materials, ingredients, containers, and supplies, nsk		(X)	6.5

Source: 1992 *Economic Census*. Explanation of symbols used: (D): Withheld to avoid disclosure of competitive data; na: Not available; (S): Withheld because statistical norms were not met; (X): Not applicable; (Z): Less than half the unit shown; nec: Not elsewhere classified; nsk: Not specified by kind; - : zero; * : 10-19 percent estimated; ** : 20-29 percent estimated.

PRODUCT SHARE DETAILS

Product or Product Class	% Share
Cereal breakfast foods	100.00
Ready to serve cereal breakfast foods, except infant cereals	93.25
Corn flakes and other corn breakfast foods (except infant cereals), with fruits and/or nuts	19.27
Wheat flakes and other wheat breakfast foods (except infant cereals), with fruits and/or nuts	24.78
Oat breakfast foods (except infant cereals), with fruit and/or nuts	17.98
Rice breakfast foods (except infant cereals), with fruits and/or nuts	9.38
Breakfast preparations of other grains and mixed grains (except infant cereals), with fruits and/or nuts	28.59
Other cereal breakfast foods	6.36

Product or Product Class	% Share
Infants' cereals, all types	(D)
Instant hot cereals, all types of grains (mix with hot water and eat type)	(D)
Farina and other wheat foods intended to be cooked before serving, except instant and infants' cereals	19.03
Rolled oats and oatmeal intended to be cooked before serving, except instant and infants' cereals	34.10
Cereal preparations of other grains and mixed grains intended to be cooked before serving, except instant and infants' cereals	1.96
Other cereal breakfast foods, nsk	0.69
Cereal breakfast foods, nsk	0.39

Source: 1992 *Economic Census*. The values shown are percent of total shipments in an industry. Values of indented subcategories are summed in the main heading. The symbol (D) appears when data are withheld to prevent disclosure of competitive information. The abbreviation nsk stands for 'not specified by kind' and nec for 'not elsewhere classified'.

INPUTS AND OUTPUTS FOR CEREAL BREAKFAST FOODS

Economic Sector or Industry Providing Inputs	%	Sector	Economic Sector or Industry Buying Outputs	%	Sector
Advertising	16.3	Services	Personal consumption expenditures	93.5	
Paperboard containers & boxes	14.3	Manufg.	Exports	1.4	Foreign
Wholesale trade	11.6	Trade	Eating & drinking places	1.2	Trade
Sugar	8.3	Manufg.	Residential care	0.7	Services
Food grains	5.3	Agric.	Child day care services	0.6	Services
Flour & other grain mill products	4.4	Manufg.	Hospitals	0.5	Services
Dehydrated food products	4.2	Manufg.	Social services, nec	0.4	Services
Feed grains	3.1	Agric.	Federal Government purchases, national defense	0.4	Fed Govt
Tree nuts	2.5	Agric.	S/L Govt. purch., health & hospitals	0.4	S/L Govt
Hotels & lodging places	2.5	Services	Nursing & personal care facilities	0.3	Services
Rice milling	2.4	Manufg.	S/L Govt. purch., higher education	0.2	S/L Govt
Paper coating & glazing	2.0	Manufg.	S/L Govt. purch., correction	0.1	S/L Govt
Electric services (utilities)	2.0	Util.			
Railroads & related services	1.7	Util.			
Gas production & distribution (utilities)	1.5	Util.			
Motor freight transportation & warehousing	1.5	Util.			
Vegetable oil mills, nec	1.4	Manufg.			
Bags, except textile	1.0	Manufg.			
Metal foil & leaf	1.0	Manufg.			
Wet corn milling	1.0	Manufg.			
Royalties	1.0	Fin/R.E.			
Maintenance of nonfarm buildings nec	0.8	Constr.			
Metal cans	0.8	Manufg.			
Banking	0.8	Fin/R.E.			
Petroleum refining	0.7	Manufg.			
Imports	0.6	Foreign			
Eating & drinking places	0.5	Trade			
Detective & protective services	0.5	Services			
Miscellaneous plastics products	0.4	Manufg.			
Drugs	0.3	Manufg.			
Food products machinery	0.3	Manufg.			
Air transportation	0.3	Util.			
Communications, except radio & TV	0.3	Util.			
Water transportation	0.3	Util.			
Business/professional associations	0.3	Services			
Blended & prepared flour	0.2	Manufg.			
Insurance carriers	0.2	Fin/R.E.			
Real estate	0.2	Fin/R.E.			
Legal services	0.2	Services			
Management & consulting services & labs	0.2	Services			
Miscellancous repair shops	0.2	Services			
Services to dwellings & other buildings	0.2	Services			
State & local government enterprises, nec	0.2	Gov't			
Coal	0.1	Mining			
Cyclic crudes and organics	0.1	Manufg.			
Accounting, auditing & bookkeeping	0.1	Services			
Computer & data processing services	0.1	Services			
U.S. Postal Service	0.1	Gov't			

Source: Benchmark Input-Output Accounts for the U.S. Economy, 1982, U.S. Department of Commerce, Washington, D.C., July 1991. Data, as reported in the source, are organized by the 1977 SIC structure in use in 1982 but have been matched, as closely as is possible, to the 1987 SIC structure used in this book.

OCCUPATIONS EMPLOYED BY SIC 204 - GRAIN MILL PRODUCTS AND FATS AND OILS

Occupation	% of Total 1994	Change to 2005	Occupation	% of Total 1994	Change to 2005
Packaging & filling machine operators	8.2	-5.4	General office clerks	2.0	-10.3
Truck drivers light & heavy	6.0	8.4	Secretaries, ex legal & medical	1.9	-4.3
Crushing & mixing machine operators	5.7	-5.4	Separating & still machine operators	1.9	5.1
Blue collar worker supervisors	5.5	0.1	Machine feeders & offbearers	1.8	-5.3
Helpers, laborers, & material movers nec	4.7	5.1	Machine operators nec	1.8	-7.3
Industrial machinery mechanics	3.7	15.7	Bookkeeping, accounting, & auditing clerks	1.7	-21.1
Freight, stock, & material movers, hand	3.4	-15.9	Industrial production managers	1.7	5.1
Industrial truck & tractor operators	3.2	5.1	Science & mathematics technicians	1.5	5.2
Sales & related workers nec	2.6	5.2	Material moving equipment operators nec	1.5	5.1
General managers & top executives	2.5	-0.3	Janitors & cleaners, incl maids	1.4	-15.9
Maintenance repairers, general utility	2.4	-5.4	Inspectors, testers, & graders, precision	1.2	5.2
Hand packers & packagers	2.2	-9.9	Agricultural workers nec	1.1	5.2
Extruding & forming machine workers	2.1	-26.4	Plant & system operators nec	1.0	39.3
Precision food & tobacco workers nec	2.1	5.1	Traffic, shipping, & receiving clerks	1.0	1.2
Cooking, roasting machine operators	2.0	11.4			

Source: Industry-Occupation Matrix, Bureau of Labor Statistics. These data relate to one or more 3-digit SIC industry groups rather than to a single 4-digit SIC. The change reported for each occupation to the year 2005 is a percent of growth or decline as estimated by the Bureau of Labor Statistics. The abbreviation nec stands for 'not elsewhere classified'.

LOCATION BY STATE AND REGIONAL CONCENTRATION

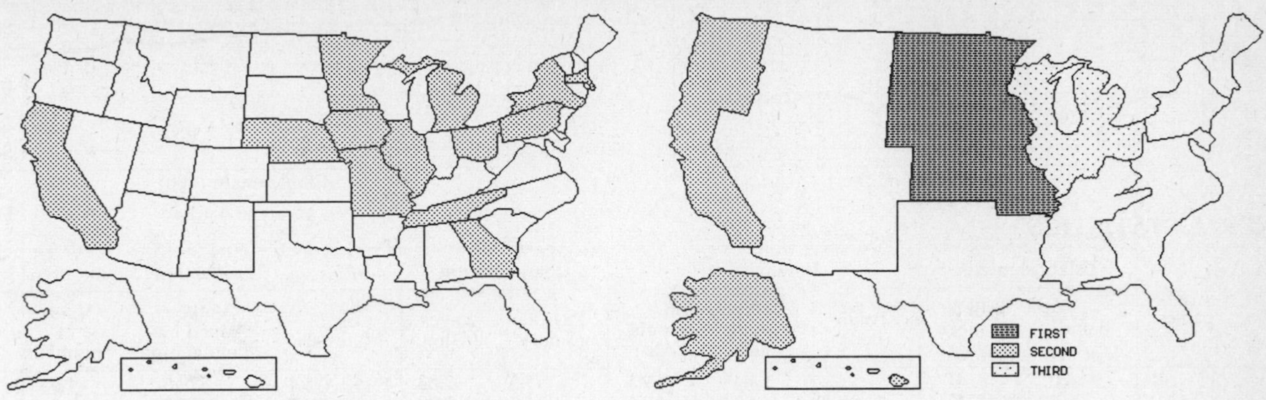

INDUSTRY DATA BY STATE

State	Establish-ments	Shipments			Employment				Cost as % of Shipments	Investment per Employee ($)
		Total ($ mil)	% of U.S.	Per Establ.	Total Number	% of U.S.	Per Establ.	Wages ($/hour)		
Michigan	3	2,301.7	23.5	767.2	3,900	24.2	1,300	20.56	23.0	-
Illinois	4	1,182.0	12.1	295.5	1,900	11.8	475	19.74	21.7	-
California	11	(D)	-	-	1,750 *	10.9	159	-	-	-
Minnesota	7	(D)	-	-	750 *	4.7	107	-	-	-
New York	4	(D)	-	-	750 *	4.7	188	-	-	14,800
Ohio	4	(D)	-	-	1,750 *	10.9	438	-	-	-
Pennsylvania	4	(D)	-	-	1,750 *	10.9	438	-	-	-
Iowa	3	(D)	-	-	1,750 *	10.9	583	-	-	-
Nebraska	3	(D)	-	-	750 *	4.7	250	-	-	-
Massachusetts	2	(D)	-	-	175 *	1.1	88	-	-	-
Tennessee	2	(D)	-	-	750 *	4.7	375	-	-	-
Georgia	1	(D)	-	-	175 *	1.1	175	-	-	-
Missouri	1	(D)	-	-	750 *	4.7	750	-	-	-

Source: 1992 *Economic Census*. The states are in descending order of shipments or establishments (if shipment data are missing for the majority). The symbol (D) appears when data are withheld to prevent disclosure of competitive information. States marked with (D) are sorted by number of establishments. A dash (-) indicates that the data element cannot be calculated; * indicates the midpoint of a range.

2044 - RICE MILLING

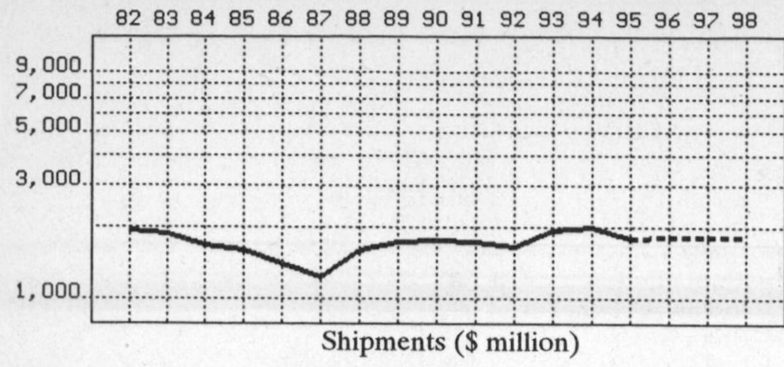

Shipments ($ million)

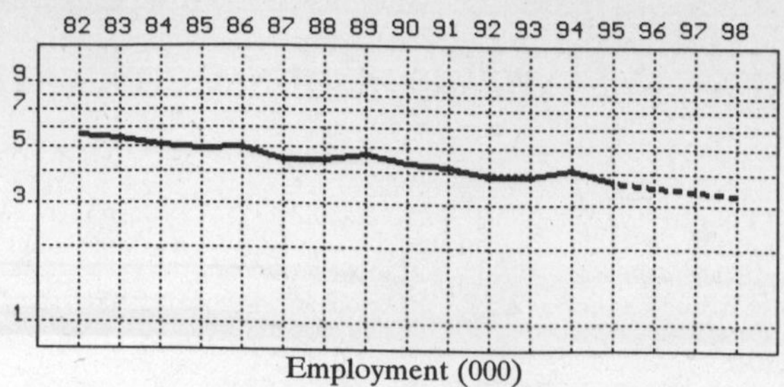

Employment (000)

GENERAL STATISTICS

Year	Com-panies	Establishments		Employment			Compensation		Production ($ million)			
		Total	with 20 or more employees	Total (000)	Production Workers (000)	Production Hours (Mil)	Payroll ($ mil)	Wages ($/hr)	Cost of Materials	Value Added by Manufacture	Value of Shipments	Capital Invest.
1982	50	68	44	5.6	4.4	9.1	95.5	7.03	1,498.4	379.6	1,933.9	41.0
1983		67	42	5.4	4.1	8.5	94.3	7.28	1,394.9	456.3	1,868.0	20.7
1984		66	40	5.1	3.7	7.8	95.6	7.68	1,287.2	397.8	1,689.5	24.6
1985		64	39	4.9	3.5	7.2	97.6	8.44	1,187.1	388.8	1,581.4	
1986		62	40	5.0	3.9	8.2	99.2	8.11	1,032.7	368.8	1,412.7	52.9
1987	48	63	35	4.5	3.5	7.3	89.1	8.27	822.4	466.7	1,234.9	48.9
1988		60	39	4.5	3.5	7.7	97.9	8.44	1,163.6	398.4	1,603.4	38.4
1989		59	39	4.7	3.7	7.9	97.1	8.39	1,203.0	553.4	1,743.0	27.0
1990		60	38	4.3	3.5	7.7	95.7	8.44	1,180.7	592.5	1,771.7	23.2
1991		58	36	4.2	3.4	7.5	96.8	8.80	1,267.9	450.9	1,739.2	25.2
1992	44	53	33	3.9	3.1	6.7	94.4	9.79	1,204.4	437.0	1,650.7	23.5
1993		58	36	3.9	3.2	7.0	97.9	9.66	1,393.9	602.6	1,944.3	39.7
1994		54P	34P	4.1	3.3	7.1	105.8	10.15	1,417.4	602.6	2,004.1	38.6
1995		53P	33P	3.7P	3.0P	6.8P	99.5P	10.07P	1,270.3P	540.1P	1,796.2P	
1996		52P	32P	3.5P	3.0P	6.6P	99.9P	10.30P	1,279.5P	544.0P	1,809.1P	
1997		51P	32P	3.4P	2.9P	6.5P	100.3P	10.52P	1,288.6P	547.8P	1,822.0P	
1998		50P	31P	3.3P	2.8P	6.4P	100.7P	10.75P	1,297.7P	551.7P	1,834.9P	

Sources: 1982, 1987, 1992 *Economic Census*; *Annual Survey of Manufactures*, 83-86, 88-91, 93-94. Establishment counts for non-Census years are from *County Business Patterns*; establishment values for 83-84 are extrapolations. 'P's show projections by the editors. Industries reclassified in 87 will not have data for prior years.

INDICES OF CHANGE

Year	Com-panies	Establishments		Employment			Compensation		Production ($ million)			
		Total	with 20 or more employees	Total (000)	Production Workers (000)	Production Hours (Mil)	Payroll ($ mil)	Wages ($/hr)	Cost of Materials	Value Added by Manufacture	Value of Shipments	Capital Invest.
1982	114	128	133	144	142	136	101	72	124	87	117	174
1983		126	127	138	132	127	100	74	116	104	113	88
1984		125	121	131	119	116	101	78	107	91	102	105
1985		121	118	126	113	107	103	86	99	89	96	
1986		117	121	128	126	122	105	83	86	84	86	225
1987	109	119	106	115	113	109	94	84	68	107	75	208
1988		113	118	115	113	115	104	86	97	91	97	163
1989		111	118	121	119	118	103	86	100	127	106	115
1990		113	115	110	113	115	101	86	98	136	107	99
1991		109	109	108	110	112	103	90	105	103	105	107
1992	100	100	100	100	100	100	100	100	100	100	100	100
1993		109	109	100	103	104	104	99	116	138	118	169
1994		102P	103P	105	106	106	112	104	118	138	121	164
1995		100P	100P	94P	98P	101P	105P	103P	105P	124P	109P	
1996		98P	98P	91P	96P	99P	106P	105P	106P	124P	110P	
1997		96P	96P	87P	93P	97P	106P	107P	107P	125P	110P	
1998		94P	94P	84P	91P	95P	107P	110P	108P	126P	111P	

Sources: Same as General Statistics. Values reflect change from the base year, 1992. Values above 100 mean greater than 92, values below 100 mean less than 92, and a value of 100 in the 82-91 or 93-98 period means same as 92. 'P's mark projections by the editors.

SELECTED RATIOS

For 1994	Avg. of All Manufact.	Analyzed Industry	Index
Employees per Establishment	49	76	155
Payroll per Establishment	1,500,273	1,954,324	130
Payroll per Employee	30,620	25,805	84
Production Workers per Establishment	34	61	178
Wages per Establishment	853,319	1,331,175	156
Wages per Production Worker	24,861	21,838	88
Hours per Production Worker	2,056	2,152	105
Wages per Hour	12.09	10.15	84
Value Added per Establishment	4,602,255	11,131,150	242
Value Added per Employee	93,930	146,976	156

For 1994	Avg. of All Manufact.	Analyzed Industry	Index
Value Added per Production Worker	134,084	182,606	136
Cost per Establishment	5,045,178	26,182,032	519
Cost per Employee	102,970	345,707	336
Cost per Production Worker	146,988	429,515	292
Shipments per Establishment	9,576,895	37,019,479	387
Shipments per Employee	195,460	488,805	250
Shipments per Production Worker	279,017	607,303	218
Investment per Establishment	321,011	713,014	222
Investment per Employee	6,552	9,415	144
Investment per Production Worker	9,352	11,697	125

Sources: Same as General Statistics. The 'Average of All Manufacturing' column represents the average of all manufacturing industries reported for the most recent complete year available. The Index shows the relationship between the Average and the Analyzed Industry. For example, 100 means that they are equal; 500 that the Analyzed Industry is five times the average; 50 means that the Analyzed Industry is half the national average. The abbreviation 'na' is used to show that data are 'not available'.

LEADING COMPANIES

Number shown: **15** Total sales ($ mil): **1,746** Total employment (000): **5.2**

Company Name	Address				CEO Name	Phone	Co. Type	Sales ($ mil)	Empl. (000)
Riceland Foods Inc	PO Box 927	Stuttgart	AR	72160	Richard E Bell	501-673-5500	R	687	1.9
ERLY Industries Inc	10990 Wilshire Blv	Los Angeles	CA	90024	Gerald D Murphy	213-879-1480	P	335	0.8
American Rice Inc	PO Box 2587	Houston	TX	77252	Douglass A Murphy	713-873-8800	P	214	0.6
Producers Rice Mill Inc	PO Box 461	Stuttgart	AR	72160	Keith Glover	501-673-4444	R	196	0.5
Riviana Foods Inc	PO Box 2636	Houston	TX	77252	Joseph A Hafner Jr	713-529-3251	R	170	0.8
Liberty Rice Mill Inc	PO Box 218	Kaplan	LA	70548	Brian Kaplan	318-643-7176	R	30	0.1
Pacific International Rice Mills	PO Box 652	Woodland	CA	95695	Louis Werner	916-666-1691	D	27	<0.1
Pacific Grain Products Inc	PO Box 2060	Woodland	CA	95776	Al Aragona	916-662-5056	R	23	0.1
ADM Milling Co	PO Box 368	Weiner	AR	72479	Mike Gray	501-684-7444	D	20*	0.1
Cormier Rice Milling Company	PO Box 152	De Witt	AR	72042	H W Cormier Jr	501-946-3561	R	12	<0.1
Dore Rice Mill	PO Box 461	Crowley	LA	70527	J Elliot Dore	318-783-3372	D	12*	<0.1
Supreme Rice Mill Inc	PO Box 490	Crowley	LA	70527	WA Dore	318-783-5222	R	12	<0.1
Affiliated Rice Milling Inc	PO Box 1446	Alvin	TX	77512	Robert McCann	713-331-6176	S	7	<0.1
Seaberg Rice Co	PO Box 100	Dayton	TX	77535	R Seaberg	409-258-2627	R	1*	<0.1
Specialty Rice Marketing Inc	PO Box 880	Brinkley	AR	72021	Lehman Fowler	501-734-1234	R	1	<0.1

Source: *Ward's Business Directory of U.S. Private and Public Companies*, Volumes 1 and 2, 1996. The company type code used is as follows: P - Public, R - Private, S - Subsidiary, D - Division, J - Joint Venture, A - Affiliate, G - Group. Sales are in millions of dollars, employees are in thousands. An asterisk (*) indicates an estimated sales volume. The symbol < stands for 'less than'. Company names and addresses are truncated, in some cases, to fit into the available space.

MATERIALS CONSUMED

Material		Quantity	Delivered Cost ($ million)
Materials, ingredients, containers, and supplies		(X)	1,117.7
Rice, rough	mil lb	13,455.5	795.8
Calcium carbonate		(X)	(D)
Bags, textile (burlap, cotton, polypropylene, etc.)		(X)	22.0
Bags; plastics, foil, and coated paper		(X)	2.8
Bags; uncoated paper and multiwall		(X)	4.3
Packaging paper and plastics film, coated and laminated		(X)	14.5
All other materials and components, parts, containers, and supplies		(X)	(D)
Materials, ingredients, containers, and supplies, nsk		(X)	19.7

Source: 1992 *Economic Census*. Explanation of symbols used: (D): Withheld to avoid disclosure of competitive data; na: Not available; (S): Withheld because statistical norms were not met; (X): Not applicable; (Z): Less than half the unit shown; nec: Not elsewhere classified; nsk: Not specified by kind; - : zero; * : 10-19 percent estimated; ** : 20-29 percent estimated.

PRODUCT SHARE DETAILS

Product or Product Class	% Share	Product or Product Class	% Share
Rice milling	100.00	other containers	32.55
Head rice not packaged with other ingredients, packed in bags of 100 lb or more	36.71	Milled rice second heads	3.46
Head rice not packaged with other ingredients, packed in containers of 3 lb or less	15.49	Milled rice screenings and brewers' rice	2.22
Head rice not packaged with other ingredients, packed in all		Milled rice bran	1.46
		Milled rice sharps and other residues and byproducts	1.12
		All other milled rice, including rice flour	5.69

Source: 1992 *Economic Census*. The values shown are percent of total shipments in an industry. Values of indented subcategories are summed in the main heading. The symbol (D) appears when data are withheld to prevent disclosure of competitive information. The abbreviation nsk stands for 'not specified by kind' and nec for 'not elsewhere classified'.

INPUTS AND OUTPUTS FOR RICE MILLING

Economic Sector or Industry Providing Inputs	%	Sector	Economic Sector or Industry Buying Outputs	%	Sector
Food grains	64.9	Agric.	Exports	52.9	Foreign
Wholesale trade	11.7	Trade	Personal consumption expenditures	30.8	
Railroads & related services	6.6	Util.	Malt beverages	3.6	Manufg.
Water transportation	2.3	Util.	Prepared feeds, nec	3.0	Manufg.
Advertising	2.3	Services	Eating & drinking places	2.5	Trade
Electric services (utilities)	1.6	Util.	Cereal breakfast foods	2.1	Manufg.
Motor freight transportation & warehousing	1.5	Util.	Poultry & eggs	1.1	Agric.
Hotels & lodging places	1.5	Services	Dairy farm products	0.9	Agric.
Paperboard containers & boxes	1.2	Manufg.	Meat animals	0.7	Agric.
Gas production & distribution (utilities)	1.1	Util.	Miscellaneous livestock	0.3	Agric.
Imports	0.8	Foreign	Dog, cat, & other pet food	0.3	Manufg.
Noncomparable imports	0.7	Foreign	Commodity Credit Corporation	0.3	Gov't
Banking	0.6	Fin/R.E.	Canned specialties	0.2	Manufg.
Petroleum refining	0.4	Manufg.	Dehydrated food products	0.2	Manufg.

Continued on next page.

INPUTS AND OUTPUTS FOR RICE MILLING - Continued

Economic Sector or Industry Providing Inputs	%	Sector	Economic Sector or Industry Buying Outputs	%	Sector
Rice milling	0.2	Manufg.	Frozen specialties	0.2	Manufg.
Air transportation	0.2	Util.	Rice milling	0.2	Manufg.
Eating & drinking places	0.2	Trade	Residential care	0.1	Services
Equipment rental & leasing services	0.2	Services	Social services, nec	0.1	Services
Bags, except textile	0.1	Manufg.			
Paper coating & glazing	0.1	Manufg.			
Communications, except radio & TV	0.1	Util.			
Royalties	0.1	Fin/R.E.			
Miscellaneous repair shops	0.1	Services			

Source: Benchmark Input-Output Accounts for the U.S. Economy, 1982, U.S. Department of Commerce, Washington, D.C., July 1991. Data, as reported in the source, are organized by the 1977 SIC structure in use in 1982 but have been matched, as closely as is possible, to the 1987 SIC structure used in this book.

OCCUPATIONS EMPLOYED BY SIC 204 - GRAIN MILL PRODUCTS AND FATS AND OILS

Occupation	% of Total 1994	Change to 2005	Occupation	% of Total 1994	Change to 2005
Packaging & filling machine operators	8.2	-5.4	General office clerks	2.0	-10.3
Truck drivers light & heavy	6.0	8.4	Secretaries, ex legal & medical	1.9	-4.3
Crushing & mixing machine operators	5.7	-5.4	Separating & still machine operators	1.9	5.1
Blue collar worker supervisors	5.5	0.1	Machine feeders & offbearers	1.8	-5.3
Helpers, laborers, & material movers nec	4.7	5.1	Machine operators nec	1.8	-7.3
Industrial machinery mechanics	3.7	15.7	Bookkeeping, accounting, & auditing clerks	1.7	-21.1
Freight, stock, & material movers, hand	3.4	-15.9	Industrial production managers	1.7	5.1
Industrial truck & tractor operators	3.2	5.1	Science & mathematics technicians	1.5	5.2
Sales & related workers nec	2.6	5.2	Material moving equipment operators nec	1.5	5.1
General managers & top executives	2.5	-0.3	Janitors & cleaners, incl maids	1.4	-15.9
Maintenance repairers, general utility	2.4	-5.4	Inspectors, testers, & graders, precision	1.2	5.2
Hand packers & packagers	2.2	-9.9	Agricultural workers nec	1.1	5.2
Extruding & forming machine workers	2.1	-26.4	Plant & system operators nec	1.0	39.3
Precision food & tobacco workers nec	2.1	5.1	Traffic, shipping, & receiving clerks	1.0	1.2
Cooking, roasting machine operators	2.0	11.4			

Source: Industry-Occupation Matrix, Bureau of Labor Statistics. These data relate to one or more 3-digit SIC industry groups rather than to a single 4-digit SIC. The change reported for each occupation to the year 2005 is a percent of growth or decline as estimated by the Bureau of Labor Statistics. The abbreviation nec stands for 'not elsewhere classified'.

LOCATION BY STATE AND REGIONAL CONCENTRATION

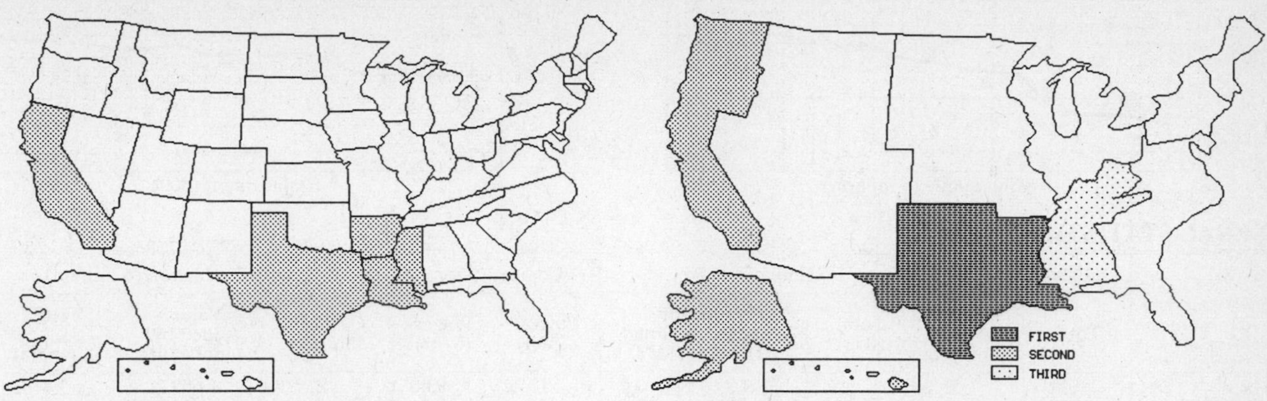

INDUSTRY DATA BY STATE

State	Establish-ments	Shipments			Employment				Cost as % of Shipments	Investment per Employee ($)
		Total ($ mil)	% of U.S.	Per Establ.	Total Number	% of U.S.	Per Establ.	Wages ($/hour)		
Arkansas	15	599.7	36.3	40.0	1,500	38.5	100	8.24	81.8	6,533
Texas	8	307.7	18.6	38.5	500	12.8	63	11.22	75.6	-
California	11	283.4	17.2	25.8	700	17.9	64	12.91	68.0	-
Louisiana	8	241.4	14.6	30.2	600	15.4	75	9.00	71.2	3,833
Mississippi	3	(D)	-	-	375 *	9.6	125	-	-	-

Source: 1992 *Economic Census*. The states are in descending order of shipments or establishments (if shipment data are missing for the majority). The symbol (D) appears when data are withheld to prevent disclosure of competitive information. States marked with (D) are sorted by number of establishments. A dash (-) indicates that the data element cannot be calculated; * indicates the midpoint of a range.

2045 - PREPARED FLOUR MIXES AND DOUGHS

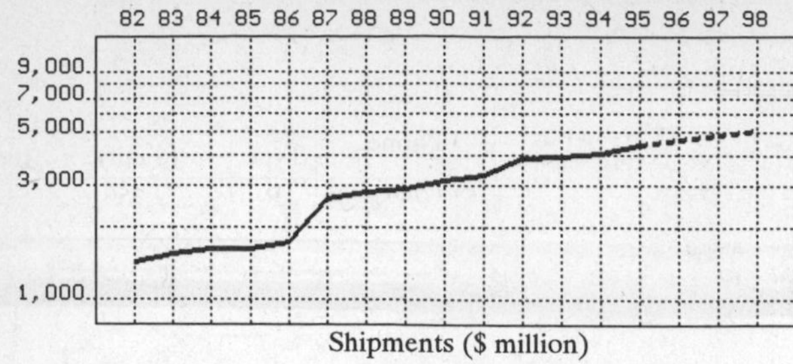

Shipments ($ million)

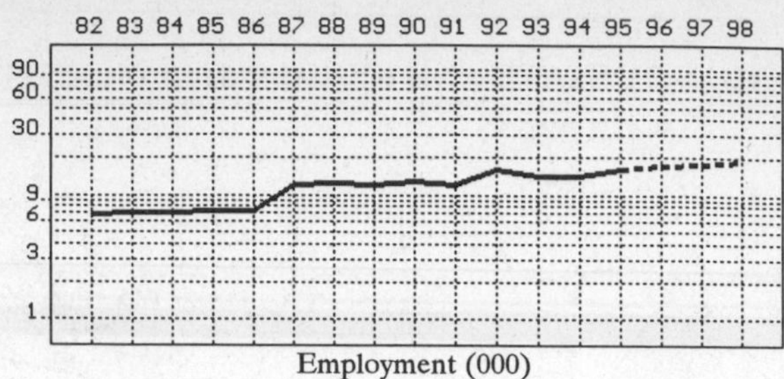

Employment (000)

GENERAL STATISTICS

Year	Com-panies	Establishments		Employment			Compensation		Production ($ million)			
		Total	with 20 or more employees	Total (000)	Production Workers (000)	Production Hours (Mil)	Payroll ($ mil)	Wages ($/hr)	Cost of Materials	Value Added by Manufacture	Value of Shipments	Capital Invest.
1982	91	111	55	6.8	4.8	9.0	131.2	9.00	829.3	609.2	1,419.1	28.7
1983		110	58	7.1	4.9	9.5	150.4	9.73	893.2	630.2	1,538.3	78.2
1984		109	61	7.0	5.0	9.6	149.8	9.89	936.0	720.0	1,642.0	93.0
1985		109	64	7.3	5.1	9.9	160.2	10.35	936.9	700.1	1,634.6	
1986		110	64	7.4	5.2	10.0	166.8	10.67	951.6	764.0	1,713.7	61.6
1987	118	149	97	12.1	8.2	16.5	275.9	9.50	1,339.6	1,278.8	2,625.1	66.1
1988		148	88	12.4	8.4	17.2	290.2	9.80	1,418.4	1,400.5	2,802.9	67.3
1989		146	90	12.0	8.4	17.7	311.2	10.61	1,640.1	1,287.1	2,912.0	101.1
1990		143	91	12.6	8.4	17.6	313.3	11.19	1,669.3	1,496.7	3,155.5	108.3
1991		149	89	12.1	8.4	17.3	337.1	11.77	1,628.3	1,691.7	3,302.0	103.6
1992	156	209	122	15.8	11.8	24.4	429.2	11.32	2,040.3	1,821.7	3,865.7	160.6
1993		219	128	14.1	10.2	22.1	436.2	11.91	2,014.5	1,941.4	3,948.3	105.5
1994		203P	124P	14.2	10.6	22.6	422.5	11.75	2,159.1	1,896.8	4,048.7	117.8
1995		212P	131P	16.2P	11.7P	25.0P	473.1P	12.10P	2,340.5P	2,056.2P	4,388.9P	
1996		221P	137P	17.0P	12.3P	26.3P	501.4P	12.31P	2,472.1P	2,171.7P	4,635.6P	
1997		230P	143P	17.7P	12.8P	27.6P	529.8P	12.53P	2,603.6P	2,287.3P	4,882.2P	
1998		239P	149P	18.5P	13.4P	29.0P	558.1P	12.75P	2,735.2P	2,402.9P	5,128.9P	

Sources: 1982, 1987, 1992 *Economic Census*; *Annual Survey of Manufactures*, 83-86, 88-91, 93-94. Establishment counts for non-Census years are from *County Business Patterns*; establishment values for 83-84 are extrapolations. 'P's show projections by the editors. Industries reclassified in 87 will not have data for prior years.

INDICES OF CHANGE

Year	Com-panies	Establishments		Employment			Compensation		Production ($ million)			
		Total	with 20 or more employees	Total (000)	Production Workers (000)	Production Hours (Mil)	Payroll ($ mil)	Wages ($/hr)	Cost of Materials	Value Added by Manufacture	Value of Shipments	Capital Invest.
1982	58	53	45	43	41	37	31	80	41	33	37	18
1983		53	48	45	42	39	35	86	44	35	40	49
1984		52	50	44	42	39	35	87	46	40	42	58
1985		52	52	46	43	41	37	91	46	38	42	
1986		53	52	47	44	41	39	94	47	42	44	38
1987	76	71	80	77	69	68	64	84	66	70	68	41
1988		71	72	78	71	70	68	87	70	77	73	42
1989		70	74	76	71	73	73	94	80	71	75	63
1990		68	75	80	71	72	73	99	82	82	82	67
1991		71	73	77	71	71	79	104	80	93	85	65
1992	100	100	100	100	100	100	100	100	100	100	100	100
1993		105	105	89	86	91	102	105	99	107	102	66
1994		97P	102P	90	90	93	98	104	106	104	105	73
1995		101P	107P	103P	99P	102P	110P	107P	115P	113P	114P	
1996		106P	112P	107P	104P	108P	117P	109P	121P	119P	120P	
1997		110P	117P	112P	109P	113P	123P	111P	128P	126P	126P	
1998		115P	122P	117P	114P	119P	130P	113P	134P	132P	133P	

Sources: Same as General Statistics. Values reflect change from the base year, 1992. Values above 100 mean greater than 92, values below 100 mean less than 92, and a value of 100 in the 82-91 or 93-98 period means same as 92. 'P's mark projections by the editors.

SELECTED RATIOS

For 1994	Avg. of All Manufact.	Analyzed Industry	Index
Employees per Establishment	49	70	143
Payroll per Establishment	1,500,273	2,085,639	139
Payroll per Employee	30,620	29,754	97
Production Workers per Establishment	34	52	152
Wages per Establishment	853,319	1,310,868	154
Wages per Production Worker	24,861	25,052	101
Hours per Production Worker	2,056	2,132	104
Wages per Hour	12.09	11.75	97
Value Added per Establishment	4,602,255	9,363,411	203
Value Added per Employee	93,930	133,577	142

For 1994	Avg. of All Manufact.	Analyzed Industry	Index
Value Added per Production Worker	134,084	178,943	133
Cost per Establishment	5,045,178	10,658,235	211
Cost per Employee	102,970	152,049	148
Cost per Production Worker	146,988	203,689	139
Shipments per Establishment	9,576,895	19,986,103	209
Shipments per Employee	195,460	285,120	146
Shipments per Production Worker	279,017	381,953	137
Investment per Establishment	321,011	581,511	181
Investment per Employee	6,552	8,296	127
Investment per Production Worker	9,352	11,113	119

Sources: Same as General Statistics. The 'Average of All Manufacturing' column represents the average of all manufacturing industries reported for the most recent complete year available. The Index shows the relationship between the Average and the Analyzed Industry. For example, 100 means that they are equal; 500 that the Analyzed Industry is five times the average; 50 means that the Analyzed Industry is half the national average. The abbreviation 'na' is used to show that data are 'not available'.

LEADING COMPANIES

Number shown: **16** Total sales ($ mil): **1,113** Total employment (000): **4.2**

Company Name	Address				CEO Name	Phone	Co. Type	Sales ($ mil)	Empl. (000)
Dawn Food Products Inc	2021 Micor Dr	Jackson	MI	49203	RL Jones	517-789-4400	R	350	1.2
Gilster-Mary Lee Corp	1037 State St	Chester	IL	62233	Don Welge	618-826-2361	R	290*	1.4
Cereal Foods Processors Inc	2001 Shawn Msn	Mission Woods	KS	66205	FL Merrill	913-262-1121	R	240	0.4
JW Allen and Co	555 Allendale Dr	Wheeling	IL	60090	JW Allen Jr	708-459-5400	R	60	0.2
Caravan Products Inc	100 Adams Dr	Totowa	NJ	07512	Alexander Weber	201-256-8886	R	49*	0.3
International MultiFoods Corp	Multifoods Twr	Minneapolis	MN	55402	Bob Wallace	612-340-3300	D	27	0.1
Roman Meal Co	2101 S Tacoma Way	Tacoma	WA	98409	William L Matthaei	206-475-0964	R	19	0.1
ADM Arkady	100 Paniplus Rdwy	Olathe	KS	66061	G Degnan	913-782-8800	D	15	0.1
April Hill Inc	PO Box 7157	Grand Rapids	MI	49510	Rob Folkert	616-245-0595	D	15	<0.1
Langlois Co	10810 W S Sevaine	Mira Loma	CA	91752	RW Langlois	909-360-3900	R	11	<0.1
Rich Products Corp	PO Box 245	Buffalo	NY	14240	Dennis P Lanning	716-878-8000	D	11	<0.1
Virga Pizza Crust of Virginia Inc	4005 Victory Blv	Portsmouth	VA	23701	JJ Virga	804-488-4493	R	11	0.2
Amendt Corp	PO Box 722	Monroe	MI	48161	Gary O Campbell	313-242-2411	R	8	<0.1
Modern Products Inc	3015 W Vera Av	Milwaukee	WI	53209	AA Palermo	414-352-3333	R	5	<0.1
Northwest Spec Baking	PO Box 25240	Portland	OR	97225	Scott MacCaskill	503-643-2351	R	2	<0.1
Hol N One Donut	2210 Pacific Av N	Seattle	WA	98103	Eilif Kuhnle	206-633-3330	R	0	<0.1

Source: *Ward's Business Directory of U.S. Private and Public Companies*, Volumes 1 and 2, 1996. The company type code used is as follows: P - Public, R - Private, S - Subsidiary, D - Division, J - Joint Venture, A - Affiliate, G - Group. Sales are in millions of dollars, employees are in thousands. An asterisk (*) indicates an estimated sales volume. The symbol < stands for 'less than'. Company names and addresses are truncated, in some cases, to fit into the available space.

MATERIALS CONSUMED

Material		Quantity	Delivered Cost ($ million)
Materials, ingredients, containers, and supplies		(X)	1,858.5
Wheat	mil bushels	(D)	(D)
Oats	mil bushels	(S)	0.5
Other grains	mil bushels	(D)	(D)
Corn grits	mil bushels	(D)	(D)
Corn meal and flakes	1,000 cwt	13.8	1.3
Wheat flour	1,000 cwt	20,397.8	465.1
Flour, other than wheat	1,000 cwt	2,400.5	245.4
Prepared four mixes	1,000 cwt	1,400.6	11.8
White sugar, cane and beet, in terms of sugar solids	1,000 s tons	263.0	130.2
Brown sugar, cane and beet, in terms of sugar solids	1,000 s tons	6.0	2.6
Fats and oils	mil lb	315.6	103.9
Raisins	1,000 cwt	(S)	4.3
Dried fruits except raisins	1,000 cwt	(D)	(D)
Nut meats, dried or dehydrated	1,000 cwt	(D)	(D)
Nuts and nut meats, raw	1,000 cwt	14.3	2.5
Packaging paper and plastics film, coated and laminated		(X)	44.0
Bags; plastics, foil, and coated paper		(X)	5.9
Bags; uncoated paper and multiwall		(X)	12.5
Paperboard containers, boxes, and corrugated paperboard		(X)	179.4
All other materials and components, parts, containers, and supplies		(X)	449.7
Materials, ingredients, containers, and supplies, nsk		(X)	142.2

Source: 1992 *Economic Census*. Explanation of symbols used: (D): Withheld to avoid disclosure of competitive data; na: Not available; (S): Withheld because statistical norms were not met; (X): Not applicable; (Z): Less than half the unit shown; nec: Not elsewhere classified; nsk: Not specified by kind; - : zero; * : 10-19 percent estimated; ** : 20-29 percent estimated.

PRODUCT SHARE DETAILS

Product or Product Class	% Share	Product or Product Class	% Share
Flour mixes, doughs, and batters	100.00	Other prepared flour mixes, including cookie mixes	11.83
Pancake and waffle mixes	4.26	Other refrigerated doughs and batters, including pizza, coffeecake, pancake, etc.	4.16
Cake mixes, including gingerbread	16.15	Frozen bread and bread-type roll dough	11.50
Biscuit mixes	3.52	Frozen cookie dough	3.85
Pie crust mixes	0.51	Other frozen doughs and batters	14.74
Doughnuts and other sweet yeast goods mixes	8.69		
Bread and bread-type roll mixes	3.30		

Source: 1992 *Economic Census*. The values shown are percent of total shipments in an industry. Values of indented subcategories are summed in the main heading. The symbol (D) appears when data are withheld to prevent disclosure of competitive information. The abbreviation nsk stands for 'not specified by kind' and nec for 'not elsewhere classified'.

INPUTS AND OUTPUTS FOR BLENDED & PREPARED FLOUR

Economic Sector or Industry Providing Inputs	%	Sector	Economic Sector or Industry Buying Outputs	%	Sector
Flour & other grain mill products	19.0	Manufg.	Personal consumption expenditures	83.2	
Sugar	13.2	Manufg.	Bread, cake, & related products	6.0	Manufg.
Paperboard containers & boxes	12.0	Manufg.	Eating & drinking places	5.1	Trade
Wholesale trade	7.9	Trade	Commodity Credit Corporation	1.8	Gov't
Advertising	7.0	Services	Change in business inventories	1.2	In House
Vegetable oil mills, nec	6.9	Manufg.	Exports	0.5	Foreign
Poultry & egg processing	6.6	Manufg.	S/L Govt. purch., higher education	0.4	S/L Govt
Wet corn milling	4.7	Manufg.	Hospitals	0.3	Services
Railroads & related services	2.6	Util.	S/L Govt. purch., correction	0.3	S/L Govt
Hotels & lodging places	2.1	Services	Cookies & crackers	0.2	Manufg.
Motor freight transportation & warehousing	2.0	Util.	S/L Govt. purch., elem. & secondary education	0.2	S/L Govt
Flavoring extracts & syrups, nec	1.6	Manufg.	Blended & prepared flour	0.1	Manufg.
Paper coating & glazing	1.3	Manufg.	Cereal breakfast foods	0.1	Manufg.
Cyclic crudes and organics	1.1	Manufg.	Nursing & personal care facilities	0.1	Services
Metal foil & leaf	1.1	Manufg.	Federal Government enterprises nec	0.1	Gov't
Electric services (utilities)	0.9	Util.	S/L Govt. purch., health & hospitals	0.1	S/L Govt
Bags, except textile	0.6	Manufg.			
Miscellaneous plastics products	0.6	Manufg.			
Banking	0.6	Fin/R.E.			
Industrial gases	0.5	Manufg.			
Equipment rental & leasing services	0.5	Services			
Communications, except radio & TV	0.4	Util.			
Gas production & distribution (utilities)	0.4	Util.			
Eating & drinking places	0.4	Trade			
Royalties	0.4	Fin/R.E.			
Electrical repair shops	0.4	Services			
Blended & prepared flour	0.3	Manufg.			
Soybean oil mills	0.3	Manufg.			
Air transportation	0.3	Util.			
Sanitary services, steam supply, irrigation	0.3	Util.			
Water transportation	0.3	Util.			
Real estate	0.3	Fin/R.E.			
Maintenance of nonfarm buildings nec	0.2	Constr.			
Bread, cake, & related products	0.2	Manufg.			
Food preparations, nec	0.2	Manufg.			
Petroleum refining	0.2	Manufg.			
U.S. Postal Service	0.2	Gov't			
Industrial inorganic chemicals, nec	0.1	Manufg.			
Insurance carriers	0.1	Fin/R.E.			
Accounting, auditing & bookkeeping	0.1	Services			
Legal services	0.1	Services			
Management & consulting services & labs	0.1	Services			
Miscellaneous repair shops	0.1	Services			

Source: Benchmark Input-Output Accounts for the U.S. Economy, 1982, U.S. Department of Commerce, Washington, D.C., July 1991. Data, as reported in the source, are organized by the 1977 SIC structure in use in 1982 but have been matched, as closely as is possible, to the 1987 SIC structure used in this book.

OCCUPATIONS EMPLOYED BY SIC 204 - GRAIN MILL PRODUCTS AND FATS AND OILS

Occupation	% of Total 1994	Change to 2005	Occupation	% of Total 1994	Change to 2005
Packaging & filling machine operators	8.2	-5.4	General office clerks	2.0	-10.3
Truck drivers light & heavy	6.0	8.4	Secretaries, ex legal & medical	1.9	-4.3
Crushing & mixing machine operators	5.7	-5.4	Separating & still machine operators	1.9	5.1
Blue collar worker supervisors	5.5	0.1	Machine feeders & offbearers	1.8	-5.3
Helpers, laborers, & material movers nec	4.7	5.1	Machine operators nec	1.8	-7.3
Industrial machinery mechanics	3.7	15.7	Bookkeeping, accounting, & auditing clerks	1.7	-21.1
Freight, stock, & material movers, hand	3.4	-15.9	Industrial production managers	1.7	5.1
Industrial truck & tractor operators	3.2	5.1	Science & mathematics technicians	1.5	5.2
Sales & related workers nec	2.6	5.2	Material moving equipment operators nec	1.5	5.1
General managers & top executives	2.5	-0.3	Janitors & cleaners, incl maids	1.4	-15.9
Maintenance repairers, general utility	2.4	-5.4	Inspectors, testers, & graders, precision	1.2	5.2
Hand packers & packagers	2.2	-9.9	Agricultural workers nec	1.1	5.2
Extruding & forming machine workers	2.1	-26.4	Plant & system operators nec	1.0	39.3
Precision food & tobacco workers nec	2.1	5.1	Traffic, shipping, & receiving clerks	1.0	1.2
Cooking, roasting machine operators	2.0	11.4			

Source: Industry-Occupation Matrix, Bureau of Labor Statistics. These data relate to one or more 3-digit SIC industry groups rather than to a single 4-digit SIC. The change reported for each occupation to the year 2005 is a percent of growth or decline as estimated by the Bureau of Labor Statistics. The abbreviation nec stands for 'not elsewhere classified'.

LOCATION BY STATE AND REGIONAL CONCENTRATION

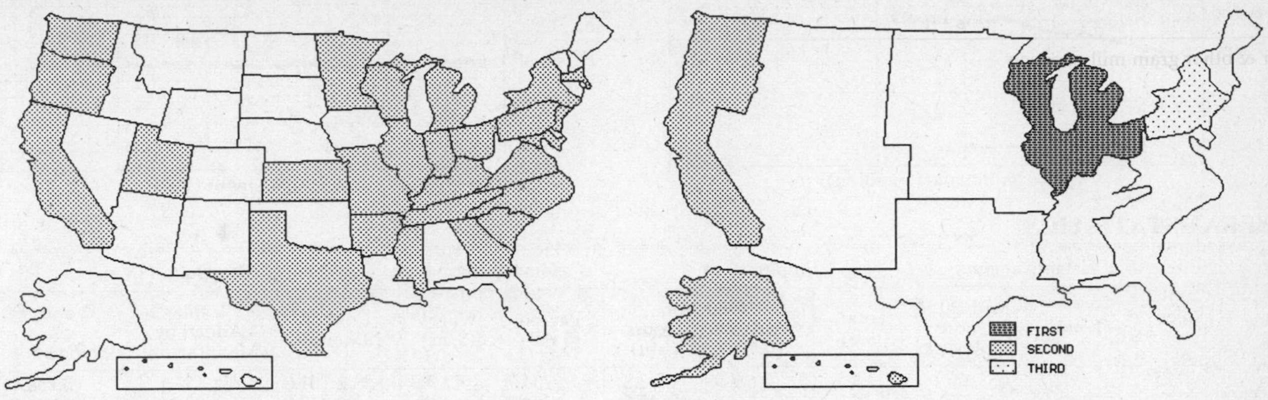

INDUSTRY DATA BY STATE

State	Establish-ments	Shipments			Employment				Cost as % of Shipments	Investment per Employee ($)
		Total ($ mil)	% of U.S.	Per Establ.	Total Number	% of U.S.	Per Establ.	Wages ($/hour)		
Illinois	19	558.5	14.4	29.4	2,000	12.7	105	9.97	55.1	14,200
Texas	10	299.8	7.8	30.0	700	4.4	70	14.18	35.2	-
Ohio	11	227.8	5.9	20.7	700	4.4	64	11.33	51.5	11,143
Washington	7	186.6	4.8	26.7	700	4.4	100	10.87	66.0	-
California	23	177.0	4.6	7.7	1,000	6.3	43	13.62	41.2	11,100
Georgia	7	169.4	4.4	24.2	900	5.7	129	10.92	51.7	5,000
Michigan	8	98.3	2.5	12.3	400	2.5	50	9.83	48.7	4,500
New Jersey	6	79.7	2.1	13.3	400	2.5	67	9.25	55.7	-
Oregon	8	69.7	1.8	8.7	300	1.9	38	8.50	62.4	3,333
Minnesota	8	39.2	1.0	4.9	400	2.5	50	9.60	63.0	7,500
New York	15	(D)	-	-	750 *	4.7	50	-	-	-
Pennsylvania	7	(D)	-	-	375 *	2.4	54	-	-	-
Kansas	6	(D)	-	-	375 *	2.4	63	-	-	-
Missouri	6	(D)	-	-	1,750 *	11.1	292	-	-	-
Tennessee	6	(D)	-	-	1,750 *	11.1	292	-	-	-
Indiana	5	(D)	-	-	750 *	4.7	150	-	-	-
Kentucky	5	(D)	-	-	750 *	4.7	150	-	-	-
Maryland	5	(D)	-	-	175 *	1.1	35	-	-	2,857
Wisconsin	5	(D)	-	-	750 *	4.7	150	-	-	-
Arkansas	4	(D)	-	-	175 *	1.1	44	-	-	-
North Carolina	4	(D)	-	-	175 *	1.1	44	-	-	-
Mississippi	3	(D)	-	-	175 *	1.1	58	-	-	-
Massachusetts	2	(D)	-	-	175 *	1.1	88	-	-	-
South Carolina	2	(D)	-	-	175 *	1.1	88	-	-	-
Utah	2	(D)	-	-	175 *	1.1	88	-	-	-
Virginia	2	(D)	-	-	375 *	2.4	188	-	-	-

Source: 1992 *Economic Census*. The states are in descending order of shipments or establishments (if shipment data are missing for the majority). The symbol (D) appears when data are withheld to prevent disclosure of competitive information. States marked with (D) are sorted by number of establishments. A dash (-) indicates that the data element cannot be calculated; * indicates the midpoint of a range.

2046 - WET CORN MILLING

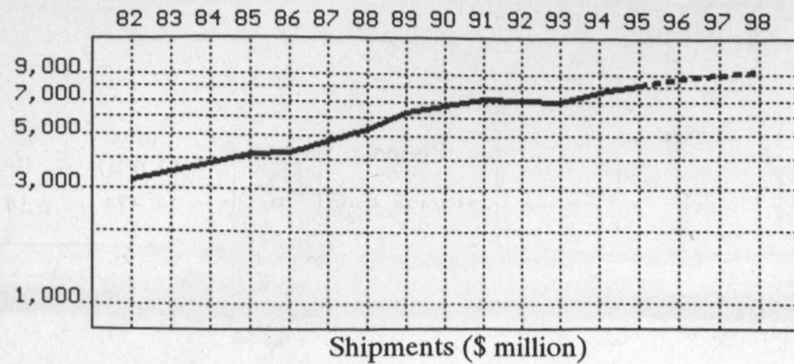

Shipments ($ million)

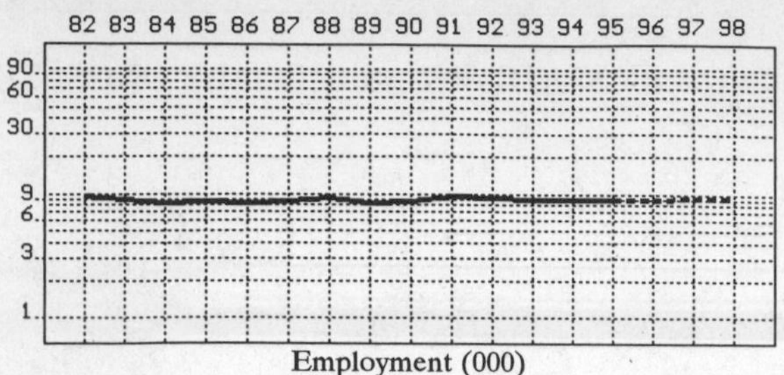

Employment (000)

GENERAL STATISTICS

Year	Companies	Establishments Total	Establishments with 20 or more employees	Employment Total (000)	Production Workers (000)	Production Hours (Mil)	Compensation Payroll ($ mil)	Compensation Wages ($/hr)	Cost of Materials	Value Added by Manufacture	Value of Shipments	Capital Invest.
1982	25	42	27	9.5	6.7	13.8	254.7	12.36	2,101.0	1,157.4	3,268.4	326.2
1983		45	28	8.9	6.3	13.5	254.0	12.68	2,279.9	1,224.1	3,501.2	131.3
1984		48	29	8.4	5.9	12.5	247.9	13.38	2,803.4	1,020.3	3,814.8	179.3
1985		51	31	8.7	6.1	13.0	266.5	13.65	2,826.4	1,363.4	4,189.7	450.9
1986		51	30	8.3	5.6	12.2	263.2	13.74	2,778.7	1,472.8	4,273.5	340.5
1987	32	60	35	8.6	5.9	12.9	298.9	14.95	2,694.4	2,074.5	4,788.9	281.9
1988		59	37	9.2	6.0	13.4	351.1	14.51	3,230.7	2,120.2	5,312.5	383.2
1989		55	34	8.3	6.0	13.5	359.4	14.35	3,745.8	2,554.7	6,287.9	283.9
1990		54	33	8.6	6.0	13.7	355.6	15.01	3,860.1	2,867.7	6,696.4	290.4
1991		50	33	9.7	6.2	14.5	386.6	14.98	3,867.5	3,265.9	7,114.1	369.5
1992	28	51	34	9.2	6.1	14.7	371.3	15.90	3,742.3	3,257.5	7,045.2	409.2
1993		54	34	9.0	6.1	13.9	364.4	16.41	3,644.3	3,262.4	6,886.2	441.9
1994		57P	36P	9.0	6.2	13.9	372.8	16.60	4,426.5	3,209.5	7,623.2	546.4
1995		58P	37P	9.0P	6.0P	14.2P	409.7P	16.81P	4,750.2P	3,444.2P	8,180.7P	473.9P
1996		58P	38P	9.1P	6.0P	14.4P	422.7P	17.14P	4,977.0P	3,608.7P	8,571.3P	492.8P
1997		59P	38P	9.1P	6.0P	14.5P	435.6P	17.47P	5,203.8P	3,773.1P	8,961.9P	511.8P
1998		60P	39P	9.1P	6.0P	14.6P	448.6P	17.80P	5,430.7P	3,937.6P	9,352.5P	530.8P

Sources: 1982, 1987, 1992 *Economic Census*; *Annual Survey of Manufactures*, 83-86, 88-91, 93-94. Establishment counts for non-Census years are from *County Business Patterns*; establishment values for 83-84 are extrapolations. 'P's show projections by the editors. Industries reclassified in 87 will not have data for prior years.

INDICES OF CHANGE

Year	Companies	Establishments Total	Establishments with 20 or more employees	Employment Total (000)	Production Workers (000)	Production Hours (Mil)	Compensation Payroll ($ mil)	Compensation Wages ($/hr)	Cost of Materials	Value Added by Manufacture	Value of Shipments	Capital Invest.
1982	89	82	79	103	110	94	69	78	56	36	46	80
1983		88	82	97	103	92	68	80	61	38	50	32
1984		94	85	91	97	85	67	84	75	31	54	44
1985		100	91	95	100	88	72	86	76	42	59	110
1986		100	88	90	92	83	71	86	74	45	61	83
1987	114	118	103	93	97	88	81	94	72	64	68	69
1988		116	109	100	98	91	95	91	86	65	75	94
1989		108	100	90	98	92	97	90	100	78	89	69
1990		106	97	93	98	93	96	94	103	88	95	71
1991		98	97	105	102	99	104	94	103	100	101	90
1992	100	100	100	100	100	100	100	100	100	100	100	100
1993		106	100	98	100	95	98	103	97	100	98	108
1994		111P	107P	98	102	95	100	104	118	99	108	134
1995		113P	108P	98P	98P	97P	110P	106P	127P	106P	116P	116P
1996		114P	110P	98P	98P	98P	114P	108P	133P	111P	122P	120P
1997		116P	112P	99P	98P	98P	117P	110P	139P	116P	127P	125P
1998		118P	114P	99P	98P	99P	121P	112P	145P	121P	133P	130P

Sources: Same as General Statistics. Values reflect change from the base year, 1992. Values above 100 mean greater than 92, values below 100 mean less than 92, and a value of 100 in the 82-91 or 93-98 period means same as 92. 'P's mark projections by the editors.

SELECTED RATIOS

For 1994	Avg. of All Manufact.	Analyzed Industry	Index
Employees per Establishment	49	158	323
Payroll per Establishment	1,500,273	6,563,030	437
Payroll per Employee	30,620	41,422	135
Production Workers per Establishment	34	109	318
Wages per Establishment	853,319	4,062,107	476
Wages per Production Worker	24,861	37,216	150
Hours per Production Worker	2,056	2,242	109
Wages per Hour	12.09	16.60	137
Value Added per Establishment	4,602,255	56,502,267	1,228
Value Added per Employee	93,930	356,611	380

For 1994	Avg. of All Manufact.	Analyzed Industry	Index
Value Added per Production Worker	134,084	517,661	386
Cost per Establishment	5,045,178	77,927,181	1,545
Cost per Employee	102,970	491,833	478
Cost per Production Worker	146,988	713,952	486
Shipments per Establishment	9,576,895	134,204,108	1,401
Shipments per Employee	195,460	847,022	433
Shipments per Production Worker	279,017	1,229,548	441
Investment per Establishment	321,011	9,619,205	2,997
Investment per Employee	6,552	60,711	927
Investment per Production Worker	9,352	88,129	942

Sources: Same as General Statistics. The 'Average of All Manufacturing' column represents the average of all manufacturing industries reported for the most recent complete year available. The Index shows the relationship between the Average and the Analyzed Industry. For example, 100 means that they are equal; 500 that the Analyzed Industry is five times the average; 50 means that the Analyzed Industry is half the national average. The abbreviation 'na' is used to show that data are 'not available'.

LEADING COMPANIES

Number shown: **13** Total sales ($ mil): **15,785** Total employment (000): **22.0**

Company Name	Address				CEO Name	Phone	Co. Type	Sales ($ mil)	Empl. (000)
Archer Daniels Midland Co	PO Box 1470	Decatur	IL	62525	Dwayne O Andreas	217-424-5200	P	11,374	14.0
AE Staley Manufacturing Co	2200 E El Dorado	Decatur	IL	62525	Larry G Pillard	217-423-4411	S	1,140*	2.3
CPC International Inc	PO Box 8000 Intlz	Englewood Clfs	NJ	07632	Bernard H Kastory	201-894-4000	D	1,097	1.5
Corn Products Co	PO Box 345	Argo	IL	60501	Samuel C Scott	708-563-2400	S	760	0.5
American Maize-Products Co	250 Harbor Dr	Stamford	CT	06902	Patric J McLaughlin	203-356-9000	P	604	2.0
American Maize-Products Co	1100 Indianapolis	Hammond	IN	46320	Patrick McLaughlin	219-659-2000	D	353	0.8
Minnesota Corn Processors Inc	400 W Main St	Marshall	MN	56258	Rich Jurgenson	507-537-0577	R	270*	0.3
Penford Products Co	1001 1st St SW	Cedar Rapids	IA	52404	HT Reed	319-398-3700	D	110	0.3
Cornnuts Inc	PO Box 6759	Oakland	CA	94603	Joe Heaney	510-523-3949	R	40	0.2
Manildra Milling Corp	4210 Shawn Msn	Shawnee Msn	KS	66205	John T Stout Jr	913-362-0777	S	14	<0.1
Western Polymer Corp	32 Rd R SE	Moses Lake	WA	98837	J Townsend	509-765-1803	R	10*	<0.1
Anderson Custom Processing Inc	121 Lindbergh Dr	Little Falls	MN	56345	Glen B Anderson	612-632-2338	R	8*	<0.1
Mississippi Blending Co	900 Hope St	Stamford	CT	06907	Charles Carvette	203-324-8838	R	4	<0.1

Source: *Ward's Business Directory of U.S. Private and Public Companies*, Volumes 1 and 2, 1996. The company type code used is as follows: P - Public, R - Private, S - Subsidiary, D - Division, J - Joint Venture, A - Affiliate, G - Group. Sales are in millions of dollars, employees are in thousands. An asterisk (*) indicates an estimated sales volume. The symbol < stands for 'less than'. Company names and addresses are truncated, in some cases, to fit into the available space.

MATERIALS CONSUMED

Material		Quantity	Delivered Cost ($ million)
Materials, ingredients, containers, and supplies		(X)	3,184.0
Rice, rough	mil lb	(D)	(D)
Corn	mil bushels	1,303.1	2,587.7
Sorghum	mil bushels	(D)	(D)
Calcium carbonate		(X)	(D)
Enzymes		(X)	60.9
Acids, organic		(X)	42.1
Bags, textile (burlap, cotton, polypropylene, etc.)		(X)	(D)
Bags; plastics, foil, and coated paper		(X)	(D)
Bags; uncoated paper and multiwall		(X)	24.0
Packaging paper and plastics film, coated and laminated		(X)	4.2
All other materials and components, parts, containers, and supplies		(X)	404.5
Materials, ingredients, containers, and supplies, nsk		(X)	10.6

Source: 1992 *Economic Census*. Explanation of symbols used: (D): Withheld to avoid disclosure of competitive data; na: Not available; (S): Withheld because statistical norms were not met; (X): Not applicable; (Z): Less than half the unit shown; nec: Not elsewhere classified; nsk: Not specified by kind; - : zero; * : 10-19 percent estimated; ** : 20-29 percent estimated.

PRODUCT SHARE DETAILS

Product or Product Class	% Share	Product or Product Class	% Share
Wet corn milling	100.00	Other modified starch and dextrin (potato, rice, wheat, etc.)	(D)
Corn sweeteners	45.37	Other not modified starch and dextrin	(D)
Glucose syrup sweeteners, type I (20 up to 38 dextrose equivalent)	3.51	Manufactured starch, nsk	0.37
Glucose syrup sweeteners, type II (38 up to 58)	11.03	Corn oil	12.49
Glucose syrup sweeteners, type III (58 up to 90)	4.63	Crude corn oil	30.00
Glucose syrup sweeteners, type IV (90 or more)	(D)	Once-refined corn oil, after alkali or caustic wash	2.15
Glucose syrup solids	2.64	Fully-refined corn oil, including margarine oil	63.83
Dextrose monohydrate and dextrose anhydrous sweeteners	(D)	Once-refined corn oil, purchased and deodorized only	4.02
High fructose corn syrup (HFCS) sweeteners, 20 up to 50 percent fructose	23.82	Wet process corn byproducts	21.25
HFCS sweeteners, 50 percent or more fructose	41.18	Wet process corn gluten feed	48.37
Manufactured starch	20.35	Wet process corn gluten meal	25.83
Modified corn starch and dextrin	66.79	Wet process gluten (except corn), including wheat, rice, potato, etc.	(D)
Not modified corn starch and dextrin	25.34	Other wet process corn byproducts	(D)
		Wet corn milling, nsk	0.53

Source: 1992 *Economic Census*. The values shown are percent of total shipments in an industry. Values of indented subcategories are summed in the main heading. The symbol (D) appears when data are withheld to prevent disclosure of competitive information. The abbreviation nsk stands for 'not specified by kind' and nec for 'not elsewhere classified'.

INPUTS AND OUTPUTS FOR WET CORN MILLING

Economic Sector or Industry Providing Inputs	%	Sector	Economic Sector or Industry Buying Outputs	%	Sector
Feed grains	38.2	Agric.	Exports	17.5	Foreign
Wholesale trade	12.3	Trade	Bottled & canned soft drinks	11.9	Manufg.
Wet corn milling	11.6	Manufg.	Personal consumption expenditures	10.8	
Gas production & distribution (utilities)	5.5	Util.	Wet corn milling	9.0	Manufg.
Railroads & related services	4.5	Util.	Flavoring extracts & syrups, nec	8.2	Manufg.
Electric services (utilities)	4.4	Util.	Paper mills, except building paper	5.8	Manufg.
Motor freight transportation & warehousing	3.8	Util.	Bread, cake, & related products	3.9	Manufg.
Advertising	3.7	Services	Frozen specialties	3.6	Manufg.
Coal	2.0	Mining	Prepared feeds, nec	3.6	Manufg.
Paperboard containers & boxes	1.9	Manufg.	Confectionery products	3.4	Manufg.
Hotels & lodging places	1.4	Services	Shortening & cooking oils	3.2	Manufg.
Imports	1.2	Foreign	Agricultural chemicals, nec	2.2	Manufg.
Petroleum refining	1.1	Manufg.	Canned fruits & vegetables	1.9	Manufg.
Water transportation	1.0	Util.	Dog, cat, & other pet food	1.4	Manufg.
Commercial printing	0.9	Manufg.	Soybean oil mills	1.4	Manufg.
State & local government enterprises, nec	0.8	Gov't	Blended & prepared flour	1.3	Manufg.
Miscellaneous crops	0.6	Agric.	Paperboard mills	1.2	Manufg.
Banking	0.5	Fin/R.E.	Food preparations, nec	1.1	Manufg.
Food products machinery	0.4	Manufg.	Pickles, sauces, & salad dressings	1.0	Manufg.
Equipment rental & leasing services	0.4	Services	Adhesives & sealants	0.9	Manufg.
Water supply & sewage systems	0.3	Util.	Chewing gum	0.7	Manufg.
Miscellaneous repair shops	0.3	Services	Drugs	0.7	Manufg.
Maintenance of nonfarm buildings nec	0.2	Constr.	Ice cream & frozen desserts	0.7	Manufg.
Air transportation	0.2	Util.	Cookies & crackers	0.6	Manufg.
Communications, except radio & TV	0.2	Util.	Cereal breakfast foods	0.5	Manufg.
Eating & drinking places	0.2	Trade	Poultry & eggs	0.4	Agric.
Royalties	0.2	Fin/R.E.	Paper coating & glazing	0.4	Manufg.
Noncomparable imports	0.2	Foreign	Dairy farm products	0.3	Agric.
Sanitary services, steam supply, irrigation	0.1	Util.	Chocolate & cocoa products	0.3	Manufg.
Insurance carriers	0.1	Fin/R.E.	Meat animals	0.2	Agric.
Security & commodity brokers	0.1	Fin/R.E.	Miscellaneous livestock	0.2	Agric.
Automotive rental & leasing, without drivers	0.1	Services	Chemical preparations, nec	0.2	Manufg.
Computer & data processing services	0.1	Services	Malt beverages	0.2	Manufg.
Detective & protective services	0.1	Services	Mineral wool	0.2	Manufg.
U.S. Postal Service	0.1	Gov't	Pulp mills	0.2	Manufg.
			Wines, brandy, & brandy spirits	0.2	Manufg.
			Building paper & board mills	0.1	Manufg.
			Soap & other detergents	0.1	Manufg.

Source: Benchmark Input-Output Accounts for the U.S. Economy, 1982, U.S. Department of Commerce, Washington, D.C., July 1991. Data, as reported in the source, are organized by the 1977 SIC structure in use in 1982 but have been matched, as closely as is possible, to the 1987 SIC structure used in this book.

OCCUPATIONS EMPLOYED BY SIC 204 - GRAIN MILL PRODUCTS AND FATS AND OILS

Occupation	% of Total 1994	Change to 2005	Occupation	% of Total 1994	Change to 2005
Packaging & filling machine operators	8.2	-5.4	General office clerks	2.0	-10.3
Truck drivers light & heavy	6.0	8.4	Secretaries, ex legal & medical	1.9	-4.3
Crushing & mixing machine operators	5.7	-5.4	Separating & still machine operators	1.9	5.1
Blue collar worker supervisors	5.5	0.1	Machine feeders & offbearers	1.8	-5.3
Helpers, laborers, & material movers nec	4.7	5.1	Machine operators nec	1.8	-7.3
Industrial machinery mechanics	3.7	15.7	Bookkeeping, accounting, & auditing clerks	1.7	-21.1
Freight, stock, & material movers, hand	3.4	-15.9	Industrial production managers	1.7	5.1
Industrial truck & tractor operators	3.2	5.1	Science & mathematics technicians	1.5	5.2
Sales & related workers nec	2.6	5.2	Material moving equipment operators nec	1.5	5.1
General managers & top executives	2.5	-0.3	Janitors & cleaners, incl maids	1.4	-15.9
Maintenance repairers, general utility	2.4	-5.4	Inspectors, testers, & graders, precision	1.2	5.2
Hand packers & packagers	2.2	-9.9	Agricultural workers nec	1.1	5.2
Extruding & forming machine workers	2.1	-26.4	Plant & system operators nec	1.0	39.3
Precision food & tobacco workers nec	2.1	5.1	Traffic, shipping, & receiving clerks	1.0	1.2
Cooking, roasting machine operators	2.0	11.4			

Source: Industry-Occupation Matrix, Bureau of Labor Statistics. These data relate to one or more 3-digit SIC industry groups rather than to a single 4-digit SIC. The change reported for each occupation to the year 2005 is a percent of growth or decline as estimated by the Bureau of Labor Statistics. The abbreviation nec stands for 'not elsewhere classified'.

LOCATION BY STATE AND REGIONAL CONCENTRATION

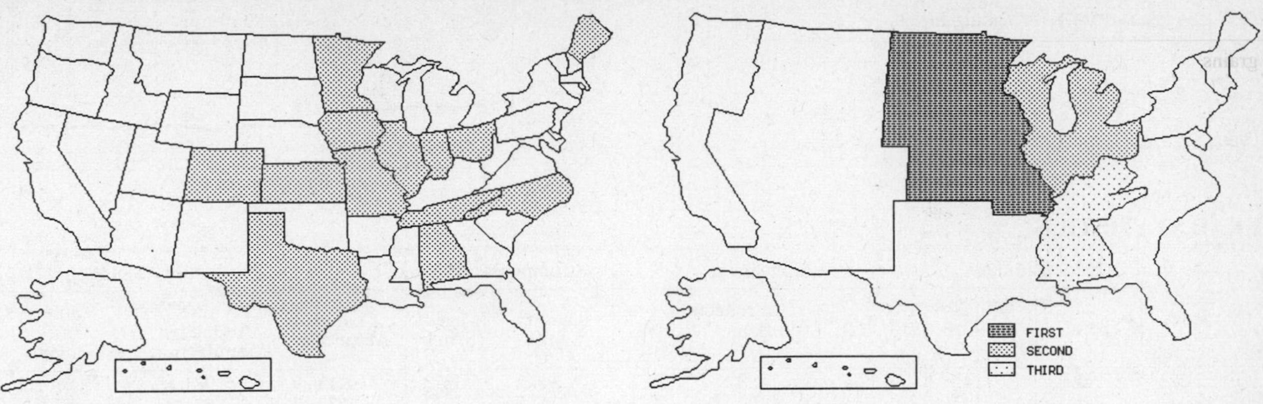

INDUSTRY DATA BY STATE

State	Establish-ments	Shipments			Employment				Cost as % of Shipments	Investment per Employee ($)
		Total ($ mil)	% of U.S.	Per Establ.	Total Number	% of U.S.	Per Establ.	Wages ($/hour)		
Iowa	8	2,399.9	34.1	300.0	3,000	32.6	375	18.00	54.9	46,933
Illinois	6	1,932.1	27.4	322.0	2,000	21.7	333	17.15	57.0	49,500
Indiana	4	834.7	11.8	208.7	1,700	18.5	425	15.29	38.7	28,118
Minnesota	4	(D)	-	-	175 *	1.9	44	-	-	-
Ohio	3	(D)	-	-	375 *	4.1	125	-	-	-
Tennessee	3	(D)	-	-	750 *	8.2	250	-	-	-
Texas	3	(D)	-	-	175 *	1.9	58	-	-	-
Alabama	2	(D)	-	-	175 *	1.9	88	-	-	-
Colorado	2	(D)	-	-	175 *	1.9	88	-	-	-
Kansas	2	(D)	-	-	375 *	4.1	188	-	-	-
Maine	2	(D)	-	-	175 *	1.9	88	-	-	-
Missouri	1	(D)	-	-	175 *	1.9	175	-	-	-
North Carolina	1	(D)	-	-	175 *	1.9	175	-	-	-

Source: 1992 *Economic Census*. The states are in descending order of shipments or establishments (if shipment data are missing for the majority). The symbol (D) appears when data are withheld to prevent disclosure of competitive information. States marked with (D) are sorted by number of establishments. A dash (-) indicates that the data element cannot be calculated; * indicates the midpoint of a range.

2047 - DOG & CAT FOOD

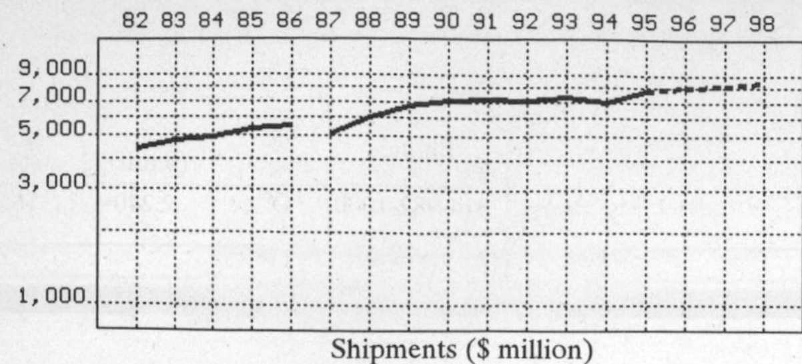

Shipments ($ million)

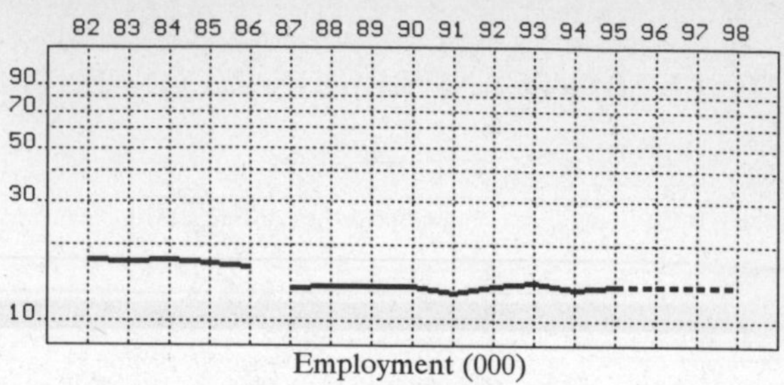

Employment (000)

GENERAL STATISTICS

Year	Com-panies	Establishments		Employment			Compensation		Production ($ million)			
		Total	with 20 or more employees	Total (000)	Production Workers (000)	Production Hours (Mil)	Payroll ($ mil)	Wages ($/hr)	Cost of Materials	Value Added by Manufacture	Value of Shipments	Capital Invest.
1982	222	285	142	17.4	12.8	25.7	340.2	8.78	2,136.9	2,281.4	4,402.2	101.7
1983		280	143	17.1	12.6	25.0	342.5	9.17	2,323.5	2,431.7	4,775.9	66.4
1984		275	144	17.3	12.8	24.9	366.6	9.59	2,296.2	2,626.5	4,913.7	78.5
1985		269	145	16.7	12.0	23.5	386.1	10.40	2,248.5	3,073.7	5,306.2	97.8
1986		258	139	16.2	11.7	23.7	412.9	11.27	2,361.0	3,143.4	5,478.2	112.9
1987*	130	186	101	13.4	9.9	20.5	365.8	11.91	2,296.8	2,741.5	5,069.3	108.2
1988		186	113	13.7	10.1	20.9	384.6	12.17	2,911.0	3,088.4	5,956.4	143.9
1989		179	106	13.7	9.8	20.1	395.1	13.11	3,149.2	3,577.6	6,703.3	144.2
1990		169	106	13.8	9.5	20.0	395.4	13.11	3,210.5	3,842.2	7,015.0	167.9
1991		164	101	12.8	9.6	20.6	405.0	13.17	3,467.3	3,619.8	7,097.4	167.7
1992	102	161	105	13.8	10.5	22.4	455.6	13.46	3,295.5	3,729.9	7,023.9	179.8
1993		169	103	14.1	10.7	23.5	477.6	13.77	3,591.7	3,643.0	7,245.3	141.4
1994		157P	103P	13.3	9.8	22.1	454.4	13.71	3,465.2	3,477.5	6,938.2	191.2
1995		153P	102P	13.6P	10.2P	23.0P	485.1P	14.21P	3,862.2P	3,875.9P	7,733.1P	191.7P
1996		149P	102P	13.6P	10.3P	23.3P	500.3P	14.47P	3,984.5P	3,998.7P	7,978.0P	199.7P
1997		144P	101P	13.6P	10.3P	23.7P	515.4P	14.73P	4,106.8P	4,121.4P	8,222.9P	207.8P
1998		140P	101P	13.6P	10.4P	24.1P	530.6P	14.99P	4,229.1P	4,244.2P	8,467.8P	215.8P

Sources: 1982, 1987, 1992 *Economic Census*; *Annual Survey of Manufactures*, 83-86, 88-91, 93-94. Establishment counts are from *County Business Patterns* for non-Census years; establishment counts for 83-84 are extrapolations. * indicates that industry content changed in 87; earlier years use 77 SICs. 'P's mark projections.

INDICES OF CHANGE

Year	Com-panies	Establishments		Employment			Compensation		Production ($ million)			
		Total	with 20 or more employees	Total (000)	Production Workers (000)	Production Hours (Mil)	Payroll ($ mil)	Wages ($/hr)	Cost of Materials	Value Added by Manufacture	Value of Shipments	Capital Invest.
1982	218	177	135	126	122	115	75	65	65	61	63	57
1983		174	136	124	120	112	75	68	71	65	68	37
1984		171	137	125	122	111	80	71	70	70	70	44
1985		167	138	121	114	105	85	77	68	82	76	54
1986		160	132	117	111	106	91	84	72	84	78	63
1987*	127	116	96	97	94	92	80	88	70	74	72	60
1988		116	108	99	96	93	84	90	88	83	85	80
1989		111	101	99	93	90	87	97	96	96	95	80
1990		105	101	100	90	89	87	97	97	103	100	93
1991		102	96	93	91	92	89	98	105	97	101	93
1992	100	100	100	100	100	100	100	100	100	100	100	100
1993		105	98	102	102	105	105	102	109	98	103	79
1994		97P	98P	96	93	99	100	102	105	93	99	106
1995		95P	97P	99P	97P	103P	106P	106P	117P	104P	110P	107P
1996		92P	97P	99P	98P	104P	110P	108P	121P	107P	114P	111P
1997		90P	96P	99P	98P	106P	113P	109P	125P	110P	117P	116P
1998		87P	96P	99P	99P	108P	116P	111P	128P	114P	121P	120P

Sources: Same as General Statistics. Values reflect change from the base year, 1992. Values above 100 mean greater than 92, values below 100 mean less than 92, and a value of 100 in the 82-91 or 93-98 period means same as 92. * indicates that industry content changed in 87. Data for earlier years are in 77 SIC format.

SELECTED RATIOS

For 1994	Avg. of All Manufact.	Analyzed Industry	Index
Employees per Establishment	49	85	173
Payroll per Establishment	1,500,273	2,896,903	193
Payroll per Employee	30,620	34,165	112
Production Workers per Establishment	34	62	182
Wages per Establishment	853,319	1,931,637	226
Wages per Production Worker	24,861	30,917	124
Hours per Production Worker	2,056	2,255	110
Wages per Hour	12.09	13.71	113
Value Added per Establishment	4,602,255	22,169,854	482
Value Added per Employee	93,930	261,466	278

For 1994	Avg. of All Manufact.	Analyzed Industry	Index
Value Added per Production Worker	134,084	354,847	265
Cost per Establishment	5,045,178	22,091,439	438
Cost per Employee	102,970	260,541	253
Cost per Production Worker	146,988	353,592	241
Shipments per Establishment	9,576,895	44,232,605	462
Shipments per Employee	195,460	521,669	267
Shipments per Production Worker	279,017	707,980	254
Investment per Establishment	321,011	1,218,944	380
Investment per Employee	6,552	14,376	219
Investment per Production Worker	9,352	19,510	209

Sources: Same as General Statistics. The 'Average of All Manufacturing' column represents the average of all manufacturing industries reported for the most recent complete year available. The Index shows the relationship between the Average and the Analyzed Industry. For example, 100 means that they are equal; 500 that the Analyzed Industry is five times the average; 50 means that the Analyzed Industry is half the national average. The abbreviation 'na' is used to show that data are 'not available'.

LEADING COMPANIES

Number shown: **27** Total sales ($ mil): **4,549** Total employment (000): **27.8**

Company Name	Address				CEO Name	Phone	Co. Type	Sales ($ mil)	Empl. (000)
Ralston Purina Co	Checkerboard Sq	St Louis	MO	63164	W Patrick McGinnis	314-982-1000	D	2,240*	16.4
Hartz Mountain Corp	700 FE Rodgers	Harrison	NJ	07029	David D Lovitz	201-481-4800	R	850	4.5
Quaker Oats Co	PO Box 9001	Chicago	IL	60604	Douglas Mills	312-222-7111	D	538	1.8
ALPO Petfoods Inc	PO Box 25100	Lehigh Valley	PA	18002	Larry Wheeler	215-395-3301	S	240	1.3
Kal Kan Foods Inc	PO Box 58853	Vernon	CA	90058	Michael Murphy	213-587-3663	S	220*	1.2
Doane Products Co	PO Box 879	Joplin	MO	64802	Bob Robinson	417-624-6166	R	140	1.0
Pet Life Foods Inc	PO Box 5260	Woodridge	IL	60517	John Donahue	708-789-5757	R	50	0.1
Pet Products Plus Inc	1600 Heritage	St Charles	MO	63303	Stan Howton	314-926-0003	S	41*	0.1
Allied Foods Inc	PO Box 93326	Atlanta	GA	30318		404-351-2400	R	40*	0.2
Ralston Purina Co	4555 York St	Denver	CO	80216	CL Mulder	303-295-0818	D	31	0.2
Deep Run Packing Company Inc	PO Box 247	Dublin	PA	18917	Gene W Fickes	215-249-3543	R	20	<0.1
Star Milling Co	PO Box 728	Perris	CA	92572	Richard Cramer	909-657-3143	R	19*	<0.1
Doane Products Co	PO Box 879	Joplin	MO	64802	Bob Robinson	417-624-6166	D	18	0.1
Benco Pet Foods Inc	PO Box 151	Zanesville	OH	43702	Dante Benincasa	614-454-8575	S	13*	0.1
Strongheart Products Co	PO Box 943	Frontenac	KS	66763	Kurt Terlip	316-231-0011	R	13	<0.1
Cadillac Foods	9130 G Morgan	Pennsauken	NJ	08110	Don Green Jr	609-662-7412	D	12	<0.1
Mardel Laboratories Inc	1958 Brandon Ct	Glendale H	IL	60139	Jan Mulholland	708-351-0606	R	12*	<0.1
Petrx Inc	1958 Brandon Ct	Glendale H	IL	60139	Jan Mulholland	708-351-0606	S	12*	<0.1
Nature's Recipe Pet Foods	341 Bonnie Cir	Corona	CA	91720	Jeffrey P Bennett	909-278-4280	R	10*	<0.1
Natural Life Pet Products Inc	1601 W McKay St	Frontenac	KS	66763	Kurt Terlip	316-231-7711	R	9*	<0.1
Freeport Roller Mills Inc	PO Box 7	Freeport	MN	56331	Al Beste	612-836-2145	R	5	<0.1
Barr Enterprises Inc	7276 W Chickadee	Greenwood	WI	54437	Steve Denk	715-267-6335	R	3	<0.1
Consolidated Pet Foods Inc	1840 14th St	Santa Monica	CA	90404	HR Brahms	310-393-9393	R	3	<0.1
EJ Houle Inc	55 SW 2nd St	Forest Lake	MN	55025	Gregory Houle	612-464-3326	R	3	<0.1
Martin's Feed Mills Inc	PO Box 46	New Paris	IN	46553	John H Martin	219-831-2121	R	3*	<0.1
Pretty Bird International Inc	PO Box 177	Stacy	MN	55079	Michael Massie	612-462-1799	R	3*	<0.1
Thompson's Pet Pasta Products	PO Box 5037	Kansas City	KS	66119	R C Thompson	913-281-0500	R	1	<0.1

Source: *Ward's Business Directory of U.S. Private and Public Companies*, Volumes 1 and 2, 1996. The company type code used is as follows: P - Public, R - Private, S - Subsidiary, D - Division, J - Joint Venture, A - Affiliate, G - Group. Sales are in millions of dollars, employees are in thousands. An asterisk (*) indicates an estimated sales volume. The symbol < stands for 'less than'. Company names and addresses are truncated, in some cases, to fit into the available space.

MATERIALS CONSUMED

Material		Quantity	Delivered Cost ($ million)
Materials, ingredients, containers, and supplies		(X)	2,538.6
Wheat	1,000 s tons	238.3	27.2
Field corn, whole grain	mil lb	(S)	168.7
Oats	1,000 s tons	(D)	(D)
Barley	1,000 s tons	4.7	1.2
Sorghum	1,000 s tons	36.7	5.4
Wheat flour	1,000 cwt	3,375.5	27.4
Wheat millfeed and screenings	1,000 s tons	360.4*	34.8
Soybean millfeed and screenings	1,000 s tons	37.7	7.7
Other millfeed and screenings	1,000 s tons	(D)	(D)
Hominy feed and meal	1,000 s tons	28.1	3.9
Corn meal	1,000 cwt	594.7*	7.3
Corn gluten feed and meal	1,000 s tons	334.3*	80.5
Alfalfa meal, excluding alfalfa hay	1,000 s tons	10.5	1.6
Sugar, cane and beet (in terms of sugar solids)	1,000 s tons	(S)	5.8
Molasses	1,000 s tons	2.6	0.3
Cottonseed cake and meal	1,000 s tons	(D)	(D)
Fats and oils	1,000 s tons	272.1*	92.8
Meat meal and tankage	1,000 s tons	941.3*	194.8
Poultry feather and byproducts meal	1,000 s tons	320.0	118.4
Fish meal and solubles (dry weight equivalent)	1,000 s tons	116.8	50.6
Brewers' and distillers' grains	1,000 s tons	111.7	21.5
Soybean cake and meal	1,000 s tons	(S)	150.3
Calcium	1,000 s tons	(S)	4.6
Phosphorus, elemental (technical)	1,000 s tons	15.2**	11.9
Salt	1,000 s tons	49.0	4.8
Other minerals, except trace minerals	1,000 s tons	20.2**	8.7
Vitamins		(X)	24.6
Drugs and antibiotics		(X)	0.4
Other microingredients, including trace minerals		(X)	47.6
Paperboard containers, boxes, and corrugated paperboard		(X)	117.5
Packaging paper and plastics film, coated and laminated		(X)	36.3
Bags, textile (burlap, cotton, polyporpylene, etc.)		(X)	(D)
Bags; plastics, foil, and coated paper		(X)	88.8
Bags; uncoated paper and multiwall		(X)	90.8
Metal cans, can lids and ends		(X)	291.8
All other materials and components, parts, containers, and supplies		(X)	660.0
Materials, ingredients, containers, and supplies, nsk		(X)	122.0

Source: 1992 *Economic Census*. Explanation of symbols used: (D): Withheld to avoid disclosure of competitive data; na: Not available; (S): Withheld because statistical norms were not met; (X): Not applicable; (Z): Less than half the unit shown; nec: Not elsewhere classified; nsk: Not specified by kind; - : zero; * : 10-19 percent estimated; ** : 20-29 percent estimated.

PRODUCT SHARE DETAILS

Product or Product Class	% Share	Product or Product Class	% Share
Dog and cat food	100.00	Canned cat food, fish base	32.04
Dog food	61.74	Canned cat food, meat base	18.05
Canned ration-type dog food	6.65	Other canned cat food (ration meal base)	1.95
Other canned dog food	21.61	Dry cat food	42.89
Dry and semimoist dog food, in packages less than 25 lb	28.50	Semimoist cat food	4.59
Dry and semimoist dog food, in packages 25 lb or more	42.52	Cat food, nsk	0.48
Dog food, nsk	0.72	Dog and cat food, nsk	2.30
Cat food	35.96		

Source: 1992 *Economic Census*. The values shown are percent of total shipments in an industry. Values of indented subcategories are summed in the main heading. The symbol (D) appears when data are withheld to prevent disclosure of competitive information. The abbreviation nsk stands for 'not specified by kind' and nec for 'not elsewhere classified'.

INPUTS AND OUTPUTS FOR DOG, CAT, & OTHER PET FOOD

Economic Sector or Industry Providing Inputs	%	Sector	Economic Sector or Industry Buying Outputs	%	Sector
Metal cans	12.1	Manufg.	Personal consumption expenditures	90.8	
Advertising	10.3	Services	Exports	3.3	Foreign
Wholesale trade	9.1	Trade	Miscellaneous livestock	3.1	Agric.
Animal & marine fats & oils	7.8	Manufg.	S/L Govt. purch., other general government	1.2	S/L Govt
Soybean oil mills	7.7	Manufg.	Change in business inventories	0.7	In House
Paperboard containers & boxes	5.2	Manufg.	Management & consulting services & labs	0.6	Services
Feed grains	4.7	Agric.	Dog, cat, & other pet food	0.1	Manufg.
Bags, except textile	3.9	Manufg.			
Drugs	2.8	Manufg.			
Miscellaneous plastics products	2.8	Manufg.			
Miscellaneous livestock	2.6	Agric.			
Flour & other grain mill products	2.5	Manufg.			
Commercial printing	2.4	Manufg.			
Hotels & lodging places	2.2	Services			
Motor freight transportation & warehousing	1.9	Util.			
Wet corn milling	1.8	Manufg.			
Electric services (utilities)	1.7	Util.			
Food grains	1.6	Agric.			
Imports	1.6	Foreign			
Poultry dressing plants	1.5	Manufg.			
Gas production & distribution (utilities)	1.3	Util.			
Railroads & related services	1.3	Util.			
Cyclic crudes and organics	0.9	Manufg.			
Miscellaneous crops	0.7	Agric.			
Banking	0.7	Fin/R.E.			
Royalties	0.6	Fin/R.E.			
Maintenance of nonfarm buildings nec	0.4	Constr.			
Meat packing plants	0.4	Manufg.			
Petroleum refining	0.4	Manufg.			
Prepared feeds, nec	0.4	Manufg.			
Communications, except radio & TV	0.4	Util.			
Dog, cat, & other pet food	0.3	Manufg.			
Malt	0.3	Manufg.			
Vegetable oil mills, nec	0.3	Manufg.			
Air transportation	0.3	Util.			
Sanitary services, steam supply, irrigation	0.3	Util.			
Water transportation	0.3	Util.			
Eating & drinking places	0.3	Trade			
Chemical preparations, nec	0.2	Manufg.			
Food products machinery	0.2	Manufg.			
Malt beverages	0.2	Manufg.			
Rice milling	0.2	Manufg.			
Textile bags	0.2	Manufg.			
Equipment rental & leasing services	0.2	Services			
Cottonseed oil mills	0.1	Manufg.			
Frozen fruits, fruit juices & vegetables	0.1	Manufg.			
Industrial inorganic chemicals, nec	0.1	Manufg.			
Polishes & sanitation goods	0.1	Manufg.			
Insurance carriers	0.1	Fin/R.E.			
Legal services	0.1	Services			
Management & consulting services & labs	0.1	Services			
Miscellaneous repair shops	0.1	Services			
U.S. Postal Service	0.1	Gov't			

Source: Benchmark Input-Output Accounts for the U.S. Economy, 1982, U.S. Department of Commerce, Washington, D.C., July 1991. Data, as reported in the source, are organized by the 1977 SIC structure in use in 1982 but have been matched, as closely as is possible, to the 1987 SIC structure used in this book.

OCCUPATIONS EMPLOYED BY SIC 204 - GRAIN MILL PRODUCTS AND FATS AND OILS

Occupation	% of Total 1994	Change to 2005	Occupation	% of Total 1994	Change to 2005
Packaging & filling machine operators	8.2	-5.4	General office clerks	2.0	-10.3
Truck drivers light & heavy	6.0	8.4	Secretaries, ex legal & medical	1.9	-4.3
Crushing & mixing machine operators	5.7	-5.4	Separating & still machine operators	1.9	5.1
Blue collar worker supervisors	5.5	0.1	Machine feeders & offbearers	1.8	-5.3
Helpers, laborers, & material movers nec	4.7	5.1	Machine operators nec	1.8	-7.3
Industrial machinery mechanics	3.7	15.7	Bookkeeping, accounting, & auditing clerks	1.7	-21.1
Freight, stock, & material movers, hand	3.4	-15.9	Industrial production managers	1.7	5.1
Industrial truck & tractor operators	3.2	5.1	Science & mathematics technicians	1.5	5.2
Sales & related workers nec	2.6	5.2	Material moving equipment operators nec	1.5	5.1
General managers & top executives	2.5	-0.3	Janitors & cleaners, incl maids	1.4	-15.9
Maintenance repairers, general utility	2.4	-5.4	Inspectors, testers, & graders, precision	1.2	5.2
Hand packers & packagers	2.2	-9.9	Agricultural workers nec	1.1	5.2
Extruding & forming machine workers	2.1	-26.4	Plant & system operators nec	1.0	39.3
Precision food & tobacco workers nec	2.1	5.1	Traffic, shipping, & receiving clerks	1.0	1.2
Cooking, roasting machine operators	2.0	11.4			

Source: Industry-Occupation Matrix, Bureau of Labor Statistics. These data relate to one or more 3-digit SIC industry groups rather than to a single 4-digit SIC. The change reported for each occupation to the year 2005 is a percent of growth or decline as estimated by the Bureau of Labor Statistics. The abbreviation nec stands for 'not elsewhere classified'.

LOCATION BY STATE AND REGIONAL CONCENTRATION

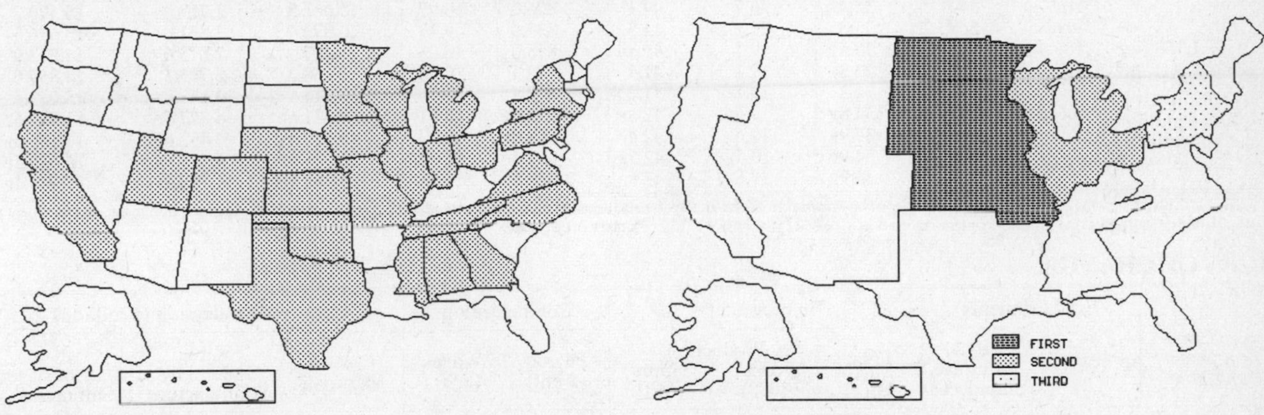

INDUSTRY DATA BY STATE

State	Establish-ments	Shipments: Total ($ mil)	Shipments: % of U.S.	Shipments: Per Establ.	Employment: Total Number	Employment: % of U.S.	Employment: Per Establ.	Employment: Wages ($/hour)	Cost as % of Shipments	Investment per Employee ($)
New York	6	684.9	9.8	114.1	800	5.8	133	16.85	40.4	18,000
Kansas	10	548.8	7.8	54.9	1,300	9.4	130	15.73	35.5	-
Ohio	10	517.6	7.4	51.8	900	6.5	90	15.19	48.4	11,000
Missouri	11	514.6	7.3	46.8	1,000	7.2	91	12.69	38.9	-
California	15	512.5	7.3	34.2	1,300	9.4	87	14.00	46.0	6,231
Pennsylvania	8	450.8	6.4	56.3	1,600	11.6	200	13.39	53.8	8,625
Minnesota	8	93.0	1.3	11.6	300	2.2	38	10.17	44.0	4,000
Tennessee	4	58.3	0.8	14.6	200	1.4	50	13.00	58.0	-
Indiana	4	45.6	0.6	11.4	200	1.4	50	10.33	56.1	-
Texas	11	(D)	-	-	750 *	5.4	68	-	-	7,333
Wisconsin	8	(D)	-	-	375 *	2.7	47	-	-	-
Michigan	6	(D)	-	-	175 *	1.3	29	-	-	-
Iowa	5	(D)	-	-	750 *	5.4	150	-	-	-
Alabama	4	(D)	-	-	375 *	2.7	94	-	-	-
Illinois	4	(D)	-	-	750 *	5.4	188	-	-	-
North Carolina	4	(D)	-	-	175 *	1.3	44	-	-	-
Virginia	4	(D)	-	-	175 *	1.3	44	-	-	10,857
Georgia	3	(D)	-	-	175 *	1.3	58	-	-	-
Mississippi	3	(D)	-	-	375 *	2.7	125	-	-	-
Nebraska	3	(D)	-	-	750 *	5.4	250	-	-	-
Utah	3	(D)	-	-	375 *	2.7	125	-	-	-
Colorado	2	(D)	-	-	375 *	2.7	188	-	-	-
New Jersey	2	(D)	-	-	175 *	1.3	88	-	-	-
Oklahoma	2	(D)	-	-	175 *	1.3	88	-	-	-

Source: 1992 *Economic Census*. The states are in descending order of shipments or establishments (if shipment data are missing for the majority). The symbol (D) appears when data are withheld to prevent disclosure of competitive information. States marked with (D) are sorted by number of establishments. A dash (-) indicates that the data element cannot be calculated; * indicates the midpoint of a range.

2048 - PREPARED FEEDS, NEC

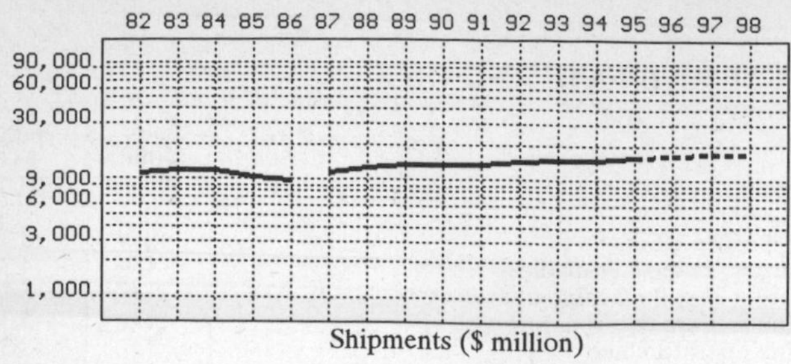

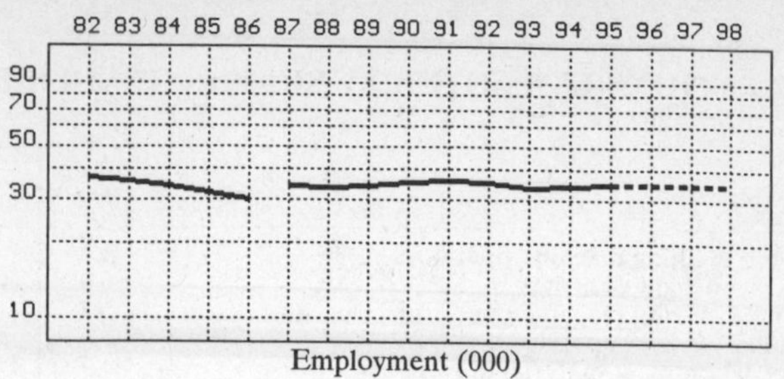

GENERAL STATISTICS

Year	Com-panies	Establishments: Total	Establishments: with 20 or more employees	Employment: Total (000)	Employment: Production Workers (000)	Employment: Production Hours (Mil)	Compensation: Payroll ($ mil)	Compensation: Wages ($/hr)	Production ($ million): Cost of Materials	Production ($ million): Value Added by Manufacture	Production ($ million): Value of Shipments	Production ($ million): Capital Invest.
1982	1,245	1,827	585	37.5	21.7	45.2	617.4	7.25	9,099.7	2,188.4	11,298.1	130.5
1983		1,784	577	36.3	21.3	43.6	627.1	7.66	9,525.9	2,256.0	11,765.9	130.7
1984		1,741	569	34.5	19.4	39.6	620.0	8.18	9,494.3	2,385.8	11,902.6	156.6
1985		1,699	562	32.0	17.6	35.9	595.8	8.63	8,105.0	2,276.2	10,409.8	141.8
1986		1,662	541	30.0	16.0	33.7	595.6	8.74	7,535.8	2,137.1	9,673.7	127.1
1987*	1,182	1,738	545	34.5	19.5	40.8	720.4	8.55	8,854.5	2,616.2	11,468.2	153.7
1988		1,681	577	33.4	19.3	40.3	710.2	8.52	10,046.5	2,806.8	12,790.6	139.7
1989		1,627	545	34.5	19.7	42.0	766.6	9.00	10,801.2	2,762.3	13,538.8	228.5
1990		1,616	544	35.4	20.7	44.1	806.0	8.97	10,662.5	2,919.0	13,570.2	215.7
1991		1,609	569	35.8	21.1	44.3	831.0	9.49	10,872.4	2,831.0	13,696.5	161.7
1992	1,160	1,714	569	35.5	19.7	41.5	875.0	10.05	11,487.7	2,875.6	14,373.9	183.6
1993		1,713	580	33.8	19.1	41.4	872.1	10.06	11,068.3	3,783.1	14,857.0	154.4
1994		1,667P	577P	34.2	19.1	41.2	892.4	10.06	10,911.5	4,148.8	15,063.6	223.2
1995		1,666P	581P	34.8P	19.6P	42.3P	935.8P	10.51P	11,381.6P	4,327.5P	15,712.6P	202.5P
1996		1,665P	586P	34.9P	19.6P	42.4P	964.0P	10.77P	11,710.4P	4,452.6P	16,166.5P	206.9P
1997		1,664P	590P	34.9P	19.5P	42.5P	992.1P	11.04P	12,039.3P	4,577.6P	16,620.5P	211.3P
1998		1,663P	594P	34.9P	19.5P	42.6P	1,020.3P	11.30P	12,368.1P	4,702.6P	17,074.4P	215.7P

Sources: 1982, 1987, 1992 *Economic Census*; *Annual Survey of Manufactures*, 83-86, 88-91, 93-94. Establishment counts are from *County Business Patterns* for non-Census years; establishment counts for 83-84 are extrapolations. * indicates that industry content changed in 87; earlier years use 77 SICs. 'P's mark projections.

INDICES OF CHANGE

Year	Com-panies	Establishments: Total	Establishments: with 20 or more employees	Employment: Total (000)	Employment: Production Workers (000)	Employment: Production Hours (Mil)	Compensation: Payroll ($ mil)	Compensation: Wages ($/hr)	Production ($ million): Cost of Materials	Production ($ million): Value Added by Manufacture	Production ($ million): Value of Shipments	Production ($ million): Capital Invest.
1982	107	107	103	106	110	109	71	72	79	76	79	71
1983		104	101	102	108	105	72	76	83	78	82	71
1984		102	100	97	98	95	71	81	83	83	83	85
1985		99	99	90	89	87	68	86	71	79	72	77
1986		97	95	85	81	81	68	87	66	74	67	69
1987*	102	101	96	97	99	98	82	85	77	91	80	84
1988		98	101	94	98	97	81	85	87	98	89	76
1989		95	96	97	100	101	88	90	94	96	94	124
1990		94	96	100	105	106	92	89	93	102	94	117
1991		94	100	101	107	107	95	94	95	98	95	88
1992	100	100	100	100	100	100	100	100	100	100	100	100
1993		100	102	95	97	100	100	100	96	132	103	84
1994		97P	101P	96	97	99	102	100	95	144	105	122
1995		97P	102P	98P	99P	102P	107P	105P	99P	150P	109P	110P
1996		97P	103P	98P	99P	102P	110P	107P	102P	155P	112P	113P
1997		97P	104P	98P	99P	102P	113P	110P	105P	159P	116P	115P
1998		97P	104P	98P	99P	103P	117P	112P	108P	164P	119P	117P

Sources: Same as General Statistics. Values reflect change from the base year, 1992. Values above 100 mean greater than 92, values below 100 mean less than 92, and a value of 100 in the 82-91 or 93-98 period means same as 92. * indicates that industry content changed in 87. Data for earlier years are in 77 SIC format.

SELECTED RATIOS

For 1994	Avg. of All Manufact.	Analyzed Industry	Index	For 1994	Avg. of All Manufact.	Analyzed Industry	Index
Employees per Establishment	49	21	42	Value Added per Production Worker	134,084	217,215	162
Payroll per Establishment	1,500,273	535,241	36	Cost per Establishment	5,045,178	6,544,469	130
Payroll per Employee	30,620	26,094	85	Cost per Employee	102,970	319,050	310
Production Workers per Establishment	34	11	33	Cost per Production Worker	146,988	571,283	389
Wages per Establishment	853,319	248,591	29	Shipments per Establishment	9,576,895	9,034,804	94
Wages per Production Worker	24,861	21,700	87	Shipments per Employee	195,460	440,456	225
Hours per Production Worker	2,056	2,157	105	Shipments per Production Worker	279,017	788,670	283
Wages per Hour	12.09	10.06	83	Investment per Establishment	321,011	133,870	42
Value Added per Establishment	4,602,255	2,488,356	54	Investment per Employee	6,552	6,526	100
Value Added per Employee	93,930	121,310	129	Investment per Production Worker	9,352	11,686	125

Sources: Same as General Statistics. The 'Average of All Manufacturing' column represents the average of all manufacturing industries reported for the most recent complete year available. The Index shows the relationship between the Average and the Analyzed Industry. For example, 100 means that they are equal; 500 that the Analyzed Industry is five times the average; 50 means that the Analyzed Industry is half the national average. The abbreviation 'na' is used to show that data are 'not available'.

LEADING COMPANIES

Number shown: **75** Total sales ($ mil): **34,582** Total employment (000): **161.9**

Company Name	Address				CEO Name	Phone	Co. Type	Sales ($ mil)	Empl. (000)
ConAgra Inc	1 ConAgra Dr	Omaha	NE	68102	Philip B Fletcher	402-595-4000	P	23,512	87.3
Ralston Purina Co	Checkerboard Sq	St Louis	MO	63164	William P Stiritz	314-982-1000	P	5,759	54.1
Moorman Manufacturing Co	Box C1	Quincy	IL	62305	Thomas McKenna	217-222-7100	R	800	3.5
SmithKline Beecham	1600 Paoli Pike	West Chester	PA	19380	Ignace Goethals	215-251-7400	D	602	3.0
Novus International Inc	530 Maryville Ctr	St Louis	MO	63141	R Michael Hickey	314-576-8886	R	300	0.1
Master Mix Feeds	PO Box 2508	Fort Wayne	IN	46801	John A Muse	219-479-5000	S	275	0.8
Alabama Farmers Cooperative	PO Box 2227	Decatur	AL	35609	John Anderson	205-353-6843	R	250	0.6
Hubbard Milling Co	PO Box 8500	Mankato	MN	56002	Rick Confer	507-388-9400	R	250	1.2
Pennfield Corp	PO Box 4366	Lancaster	PA	17604	Donald E Horn	717-299-2561	R	140	0.7
Archer Daniels Midland Co	PO Box 1470	Decatur	IL	62525	John Alley	217-424-5200	D	120*	0.2
Blue Seal Feeds Inc	PO Box 8	Lawrence	MA	01842	Norman Van Ord	508-686-4131	S	100*	0.5
Bioproducts Inc	320 Springside Dr	Fairlawn	OH	44333	R Michael Hickey	216-526-5522	S	95	0.3
Triple F Inc	10104 Douglas Av	Des Moines	IA	50322	WF Fox	515-254-1200	R	95*	0.5
OH Kruse Grain	PO Box 51493	Ontario	CA	91761	Kevin Kruse	909-983-1771	R	93*	0.3
Milk Specialties Co	PO Box 278	Dundee	IL	60118	George Gill	708-426-3411	R	85	0.2
Golden Technologies Company	15165 W 44th Av	Golden	CO	80403	Dean Rulis	303-384-1700	S	84*	0.5
Kent Feeds Inc	PO Box 749	Muscatine	IA	52761	Jack May	319-264-4211	S	70	0.5
Farmers Coop Elevator Co	PO Box 108	Cottonwood	MN	56229	James Duncan	507-423-5412	R	66*	<0.1
Georgia Proteins Inc	4990 Leland Dr	Cumming	GA	30131	John Hald	404-887-6148	S	65	0.1
NutriBasics LP	115 Executive Dr	Highland	IL	62249	Dan Rose	618-654-4424	J	65*	0.2
Manna Pro Corp	7711 Carondelet	St Louis	MO	63105	LR Chapman	314-746-1700	R	61	0.3
Walnut Grove Products	201 Linn	Atlantic	IA	50022	Ray Underwood	712-243-1030	D	60	0.5
Pennfield Corp	14040 Industrial Rd	Omaha	NE	68144	Andy Winstrom	402-330-6000	D	59*	0.3
ConAgra Feed Co	980 Molly Pond Rd	Augusta	GA	30901	George Thames	706-722-6081	S	58	0.1
Grist Mill Co	21340 Hayes Av	Lakeville	MN	55044	Glen S Bolander	612-469-4981	P	56	0.5
Vita Plus Corp	PO Box 9126	Madison	WI	53715	Robert S Tramburg	608-256-1988	R	55	0.1
Furst-McNess Co	120 E Clark St	Freeport	IL	61032	FE Furst	815-235-6151	R	53	0.4
Harvest Land Cooperative	PO Box 278	Morgan	MN	56266	Myron Weelborg	507-249-3196	R	53*	0.1
Kaytee Products Inc	PO Box 230	Chilton	WI	53014	W D Engler Jr	414-849-2321	R	53*	0.3
Texas Farm Products Co	PO Box 630009	Nacogdoches	TX	75963	MS Wright III	409-564-3711	R	50	0.4
Yoder Inc	PO Box 310	Kalona	IA	52247	Phil G Yoder	319-683-2201	R	50	0.2
United Feeds Inc	PO Box 108	Sheridan	IN	46069	John B Swisher	317-758-4495	R	49*	0.2
Ursa Farmers Cooperative	202 W Maple St	Ursa	IL	62376	Gerald Jenkins	217-964-2111	R	45	<0.1
Agri-Bio Corp	PO Box 897	Gainesville	GA	30503		404-536-0111	S	40	<0.1
Altair Corp	350 Barclay Blv	Lincolnshire	IL	60069	G Brainin	708-634-9540	S	40	0.4
Producers Cooperative Feed Mill	PO Box 2229	Monroe	NC	28110	Samuel O Starnes	704-283-7555	R	40	<0.1
Prince Manufacturing Co	PO Box 1009	Quincy	IL	62306	C Davis	217-222-8854	S	37	0.1
Effingham Equity	PO Box 488	Effingham	IL	62401	Harry Fehrenbacher	217-342-4101	R	36*	0.2
Kemin Industries Inc	PO Box 70	Des Moines	IA	50301	RW Nelson	515-266-2111	R	35	0.1
Merrick's Inc	2415 Parview Rd	Middleton	WI	53562	William Merrick III	608-831-3440	R	35	0.1
Purina Mills Inc Circleville	901 South Ct	Circleville	OH	43113	John Prince	614-474-2155	D	35*	<0.1
FM Browns Sons Inc	205 Woodrow Av	Sinking Spring	PA	19608	Franklin Brown Sr	215-678-4567	R	33*	<0.1
Stillwater Milling Co	PO Box 2407	Stillwater	OK	74076	H Cudd	405-372-3445	R	32	0.1
Quali Tech Inc	318 Lake Hazeltine	Chaska	MN	55318	Del Ploen	612-448-5151	R	30	<0.1
Keith Smith Company Inc	PO Drawer A	Hot Springs	AR	71902	James Smith II	501-321-9990	R	29*	0.1
Good Life Feed Additives	PO Box 687	Effingham	IL	62401	Richard W Worman	217-342-3986	D	28	<0.1
PharmTech Ltd	PO Box 3600	Des Moines	IA	50322	Leroy Hanson	515-254-1290	S	26	<0.1
Buckeye Feed Mills Inc	PO Box 505	Dalton	OH	44618	TM Stults II	216-828-2251	R	25	<0.1
Coast Grain Company Inc	5355 E Airport Dr	Ontario	CA	91761	R W-Gewelber	909-390-9766	R	25	0.2
Farm Service Elevator Co	PO Box 933	Willmar	MN	56201	Virgil Stangeland	612-235-1080	R	25*	<0.1
Four Paws Products Ltd	50 Wireless Blv	Hauppauge	NY	11788	Allen Simon	516-434-1100	R	25	0.1
Hess and Clark Inc	7th & Orange St	Ashland	OH	44805	BL Bookmeyer	419-289-9129	S	25	0.1
Hunt and Behrens Inc	PO Box 2040	Petaluma	CA	94953	EH Behrens	707-762-4594	R	25	<0.1
Scope Industries	233 Wilshire Blv	Santa Monica	CA	90401	Meyer Luskin	310-458-1574	P	23	0.2
Jasper Farmers Elevator	PO Box 266	Jasper	MN	56144	Ben Fuller	507-348-3911	R	23	<0.1
Eight in One Pet Products Inc	2100 Pacific St	Hauppauge	NY	11788	Howard Stern	516-232-1200	R	21*	0.1
Kay Dee Feed Company Inc	1919 Grand Av	Sioux City	IA	51107	Royal Lohry	712-277-2011	R	21*	<0.1
Farmers Elevator Co	8th & Dwelle Sts	Lake City	MN	55041	Greg Schwanbeck	612-345-3328	R	21	<0.1
Diamond Pacific Product Co	PO Box 758	Perris	CA	92370	W R Cramer Jr	909-657-5121	R	20	<0.1
Flint River Mills Inc	PO Box 278	Bainbridge	GA	31717	Loyd Poitevint	912-246-2232	R	20	0.1
Form A Feed Inc	PO Box 9	Stewart	MN	55385	Steve Nelson	612-562-2413	R	20	0.1
Hintzsche Feed and Grain Inc	PO Box 807	Maple Park	IL	60520	Ken Hintzsche	708-557-2406	R	20	<0.1
John A Vanden Bosch Co	PO Box 19	Zeeland	MI	49464	W Vanden Bosch	616-772-2179	R	20	<0.1
JS West Milling Company Inc	PO Box 1041	Modesto	CA	95353	D Gary West	209-577-3221	R	20	0.1
Modesto Tallow Company Inc	PO Box 1036	Modesto	CA	95353	CL Tocalino	209-522-7224	R	20	0.1
Mountaire Feeds Inc	PO Box 5391	N Little Rock	AR	72119	Dee Ann Landreth	501-376-6751	S	20	0.1
Yeager and Sullivan Inc	PO Box 11	Camden	IN	46917	Charles Yeager	219-967-4145	R	20	<0.1
K and L Feed Mill Corp	PO Box 52	North Franklin	CT	06254	John Lombardi Jr	203-642-7555	R	19	<0.1
Agri-King Inc	PO Box 208	Fulton	IL	61252	C Curley	815-589-2525	R	19	0.2
Grange Cooperative	PO Box 3637	Central Point	OR	97502	J Hudson	503-664-1261	R	18	<0.1
Farmers Cooperative Co	PO Box 337	Hubbard	IA	50122	Dennis Erickson	515-864-2266	R	17	<0.1
Morgan Grain and Feed Co	PO Box 248	Morgan	MN	56266	Richard A Potter	507-249-3157	R	17*	<0.1
Pro-Edge Ltd	1568 N Main St	Sioux Center	IA	51250	Jan Schuiteman	712-722-3506	R	17	0.2
BioZyme Inc	PO Box 4428	St Joseph	MO	64504	M Ehlert	816-238-3326	R	16	0.1
Cole Grain Co	PO Box 1289	Muskogee	OK	74401	Don Mauery	918-687-7565	R	16*	<0.1

Source: *Ward's Business Directory of U.S. Private and Public Companies*, Volumes 1 and 2, 1996. The company type code used is as follows: P - Public, R - Private, S - Subsidiary, D - Division, J - Joint Venture, A - Affiliate, G - Group. Sales are in millions of dollars, employees are in thousands. An asterisk (*) indicates an estimated sales volume. The symbol < stands for 'less than'. Company names and addresses are truncated, in some cases, to fit into the available space.

MATERIALS CONSUMED

Material		Quantity	Delivered Cost ($ million)
Materials, ingredients, containers, and supplies		(X)	10,434.5
Wheat	1,000 s tons	835.4	74.6
Field corn, whole grain	mil lb	(S)	2,147.6
Oats	1,000 s tons	573.6	72.1
Barley	1,000 s tons	707.5*	79.4
Sorghum	1,000 s tons	1,075.5	103.0
Wheat flour	1,000 cwt	8,555.5*	48.2
Wheat millfeed and screenings	1,000 s tons	3,326.2	337.0
Soybean millfeed and screenings	1,000 s tons	1,210.1*	170.6
Other millfeed and screenings	1,000 s tons	2,254.0**	195.1
Hominy feed and meal	1,000 s tons	134.6*	14.5
Corn meal	1,000 cwt	(D)	(D)
Corn gluten feed and meal	1,000 s tons	(D)	(D)
Alfalfa meal, excluding alfalfa hay	1,000 s tons	298.9*	36.4
Sugar, cane and beet (in terms of sugar solids)	1,000 s tons	19.6*	7.7
Molasses	1,000 s tons	(S)	75.3
Cottonseed cake and meal	1,000 s tons	1,068.7	129.6
Fats and oils	1,000 s tons	1,106.7	291.8
Meat meal and tankage	1,000 s tons	1,307.2	308.0
Poultry feather and byproducts meal	1,000 s tons	754.5	179.2
Fish meal and solubles (dry weight equivalent)	1,000 s tons	315.6	106.3
Brewers' and distillers' grains	1,000 s tons	501.3	70.2
Soybean cake and meal	1,000 s tons	8,751.6	1,644.7
Calcium	1,000 s tons	(S)	59.8
Phosphorus, elemental (technical)	1,000 s tons	689.9	161.6
Salt	1,000 s tons	(S)	26.3
Other minerals, except trace minerals	1,000 s tons	(S)	177.2
Vitamins		(X)	273.7
Drugs and antibiotics		(X)	331.8
Other microingredients, including trace minerals		(X)	285.1
Paperboard containers, boxes, and corrugated paperboard		(X)	8.1
Packaging paper and plastics film, coated and laminated		(X)	7.9
Bags, textile (burlap, cotton, polyporpylene, etc.)		(X)	8.1
Bags; plastics, foil, and coated paper		(X)	15.5
Bags; uncoated paper and multiwall		(X)	79.1
Metal cans, can lids and ends		(X)	4.0
All other materials and components, parts, containers, and supplies		(X)	662.9
Materials, ingredients, containers, and supplies, nsk		(X)	2,108.7

Source: 1992 *Economic Census*. Explanation of symbols used: (D): Withheld to avoid disclosure of competitive data; na: Not available; (S): Withheld because statistical norms were not met; (X): Not applicable; (Z): Less than half the unit shown; nec: Not elsewhere classified; nsk: Not specified by kind; - : zero; * : 10-19 percent estimated; ** : 20-29 percent estimated.

PRODUCT SHARE DETAILS

Product or Product Class	% Share	Product or Product Class	% Share
Prepared feeds, nec	100.00	Other poultry complete feed (duck, etc.)	3.65
Chicken and turkey feed, supplements, concentrates, and premixes	36.81	Other poultry feed supplements and concentrates (duck, etc.)	(D)
Complete chicken feed, starter-growers	11.68	Other poultry feed premixes (feed-base) (duck, etc.)	(D)
Complete chicken feed, layer-breeders	13.89	Horse and mule complete feed	48.86
Complete chicken feed, broilers	52.41	Other livestock (sheep, etc.) complete feed	13.58
Complete turkey feed	9.38	Horse and mule feed supplements and concentrates	2.21
Chicken feed supplements and concentrates, starter-growers	0.39	Other livestock (sheep, etc.) feed supplements and concentrates	8.17
Chicken feed supplements and concentrates, layer-breeders	1.23	Horse and mule feed premixes (feed-base)	0.39
Chicken feed supplements and concentrates, broilers	2.72	Other livestock (sheep, etc.) feed premixes (feed-base)	4.06
Turkey feed supplements and concentrates	0.14	Other poultry and livestock feed, nsk	6.49
Chicken feed premixes (feed-base), starter-growers	(D)	Other prepared animal feed, including feeding materials and adjuncts	3.50
Chicken feed premixes (feed-base), layer-breeders	0.57	Grain animal feed (ground, rolled, pulverized, chopped, or crimped), excluding cornmeal	22.91
Chicken feed premixes (feed-base), broilers	0.31	Mineral mixture animal feed, including oyster shells prepared for feed use	33.76
Turkey feed premixes (feed-base)	(D)	Dehydrated alfalfa meal animal feed	6.51
Chicken and turkey feed, supplements, concentrates, and premixes, nsk	6.84	Sun cured and cubed alfalfa meal animal feed	5.01
Dairy cattle feed, complete	10.95	Other prepared animal feed	21.81
Dairy cattle feed supplements, concentrates, and premixes	5.11	Other prepared animal feeds, including feeding materials and adjuncts, nsk	10.06
Dairy cattle feed supplements and concentrates	78.41	Specialty feed	5.63
Dairy cattle feed premixes (feed-base)	18.84	Fresh and frozen meat of horses and other animals for animal feed	8.16
Dairy cattle feed supplements, concentrates, and premixes, nsk	2.74	Other specialty pet food, except dog and cat	20.99
Swine feed, complete	4.08	Specialty laboratory feed (mouse, guinea pig, etc.)	4.74
Swine feed supplements, concentrates, and premixes	8.89	Specialty fur animal (mink, fox, etc.) feed	0.33
Swine feed supplements and concentrates	76.76	Specialty bird (wild, tame, pigeon, game) feed	19.13
Swine feed premixes (feed-base)	20.89	Specialty rabbit feed	5.02
Swine feed supplements, concentrates, and premixes, nsk	2.34	Specialty fish feed	22.36
Beef cattle feed, complete	3.95	Other specialty feed	12.38
Beef cattle feed supplements, concentrates, and premixes	4.69	Specialty feeds, nsk	6.89
Beef cattle feed supplements and concentrates	83.80	Prepared feeds, nec, nsk	12.55
Beef cattle feed premixes (feed-base)	15.14		
Beef cattle feed supplements, concentrates, and premixes, nsk	1.08		
Other poultry and livestock feed	3.85		

Source: 1992 *Economic Census*. The values shown are percent of total shipments in an industry. Values of indented subcategories are summed in the main heading. The symbol (D) appears when data are withheld to prevent disclosure of competitive information. The abbreviation nsk stands for 'not specified by kind' and nec for 'not elsewhere classified'.

INPUTS AND OUTPUTS FOR PREPARED FEEDS, NEC

Economic Sector or Industry Providing Inputs	%	Sector	Economic Sector or Industry Buying Outputs	%	Sector
Prepared feeds, nec	23.9	Manufg.	Poultry & eggs	30.4	Agric.
Soybean oil mills	17.1	Manufg.	Meat animals	27.9	Agric.
Feed grains	11.4	Agric.	Prepared feeds, nec	23.6	Manufg.
Drugs	8.1	Manufg.	Dairy farm products	12.9	Agric.
Wholesale trade	7.1	Trade	Exports	1.8	Foreign
Animal & marine fats & oils	4.2	Manufg.	Personal consumption expenditures	0.9	
Flour & other grain mill products	3.5	Manufg.	Forestry products	0.8	Agric.
Motor freight transportation & warehousing	3.0	Util.	Drugs	0.5	Manufg.
Cyclic crudes and organics	2.9	Manufg.	Miscellaneous livestock	0.4	Agric.
Railroads & related services	2.4	Util.	Management & consulting services & labs	0.3	Services
Advertising	1.3	Services	Agricultural, forestry, & fishery services	0.1	Agric.
Cottonseed oil mills	1.2	Manufg.			
Banking	0.9	Fin/R.E.			
Food grains	0.8	Agric.			
Sugar	0.8	Manufg.			
Wet corn milling	0.8	Manufg.			
Petroleum refining	0.7	Manufg.			
Poultry dressing plants	0.7	Manufg.			
Electric services (utilities)	0.7	Util.			
Bags, except textile	0.6	Manufg.			
Water transportation	0.6	Util.			
Malt beverages	0.4	Manufg.			
Rice milling	0.4	Manufg.			
Imports	0.4	Foreign			
Distilled liquor, except brandy	0.3	Manufg.			
Industrial inorganic chemicals, nec	0.3	Manufg.			
Nitrogenous & phosphatic fertilizers	0.3	Manufg.			
Vegetable oil mills, nec	0.3	Manufg.			
Gas production & distribution (utilities)	0.3	Util.			
Miscellaneous crops	0.2	Agric.			
Chemical & fertilizer mineral	0.2	Mining			
Chemical preparations, nec	0.2	Manufg.			
Food preparations, nec	0.2	Manufg.			
Pipe, valves, & pipe fittings	0.2	Manufg.			

Continued on next page.

INPUTS AND OUTPUTS FOR PREPARED FEEDS, NEC - Continued

Economic Sector or Industry Providing Inputs	%	Sector	Economic Sector or Industry Buying Outputs	%	Sector
Textile goods, nec	0.2	Manufg.			
Communications, except radio & TV	0.2	Util.			
Eating & drinking places	0.2	Trade			
Business services nec	0.2	Services			
Detective & protective services	0.2	Services			
U.S. Postal Service	0.2	Gov't			
Malt	0.1	Manufg.			
Rubber & plastics hose & belting	0.1	Manufg.			
Textile bags	0.1	Manufg.			
Sanitary services, steam supply, irrigation	0.1	Util.			
Automotive rental & leasing, without drivers	0.1	Services			
Equipment rental & leasing services	0.1	Services			

Source: Benchmark Input-Output Accounts for the U.S. Economy, 1982, U.S. Department of Commerce, Washington, D.C., July 1991. Data, as reported in the source, are organized by the 1977 SIC structure in use in 1982 but have been matched, as closely as is possible, to the 1987 SIC structure used in this book.

OCCUPATIONS EMPLOYED BY SIC 204 - GRAIN MILL PRODUCTS AND FATS AND OILS

Occupation	% of Total 1994	Change to 2005	Occupation	% of Total 1994	Change to 2005
Packaging & filling machine operators	8.2	-5.4	General office clerks	2.0	-10.3
Truck drivers light & heavy	6.0	8.4	Secretaries, ex legal & medical	1.9	-4.3
Crushing & mixing machine operators	5.7	-5.4	Separating & still machine operators	1.9	5.1
Blue collar worker supervisors	5.5	0.1	Machine feeders & offbearers	1.8	-5.3
Helpers, laborers, & material movers nec	4.7	5.1	Machine operators nec	1.8	-7.3
Industrial machinery mechanics	3.7	15.7	Bookkeeping, accounting, & auditing clerks	1.7	-21.1
Freight, stock, & material movers, hand	3.4	-15.9	Industrial production managers	1.7	5.1
Industrial truck & tractor operators	3.2	5.1	Science & mathematics technicians	1.5	5.2
Sales & related workers nec	2.6	5.2	Material moving equipment operators nec	1.5	5.1
General managers & top executives	2.5	-0.3	Janitors & cleaners, incl maids	1.4	-15.9
Maintenance repairers, general utility	2.4	-5.4	Inspectors, testers, & graders, precision	1.2	5.2
Hand packers & packagers	2.2	-9.9	Agricultural workers nec	1.1	5.2
Extruding & forming machine workers	2.1	-26.4	Plant & system operators nec	1.0	39.3
Precision food & tobacco workers nec	2.1	5.1	Traffic, shipping, & receiving clerks	1.0	1.2
Cooking, roasting machine operators	2.0	11.4			

Source: Industry-Occupation Matrix, Bureau of Labor Statistics. These data relate to one or more 3-digit SIC industry groups rather than to a single 4-digit SIC. The change reported for each occupation to the year 2005 is a percent of growth or decline as estimated by the Bureau of Labor Statistics. The abbreviation nec stands for 'not elsewhere classified'.

LOCATION BY STATE AND REGIONAL CONCENTRATION

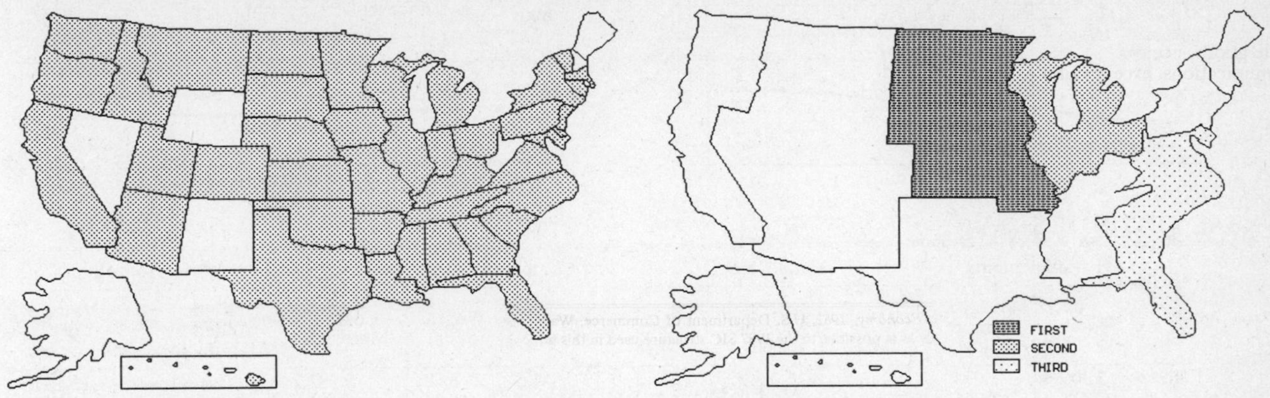

INDUSTRY DATA BY STATE

State	Establish-ments	Shipments			Employment				Cost as % of Shipments	Investment per Employee ($)
		Total ($ mil)	% of U.S.	Per Establ.	Total Number	% of U.S.	Per Establ.	Wages ($/hour)		
California	110	1,161.8	8.1	10.6	2,200	6.2	20	10.97	83.0	3,409
Iowa	117	1,012.4	7.0	8.7	3,100	8.7	26	11.40	74.4	5,516
Texas	102	979.1	6.8	9.6	2,700	7.6	26	8.51	79.4	5,111
Arkansas	56	925.7	6.4	16.5	1,200	3.4	21	9.82	93.2	3,667
Georgia	59	856.1	6.0	14.5	1,400	3.9	24	9.67	89.5	3,857
North Carolina	72	813.0	5.7	11.3	1,300	3.7	18	9.73	83.9	7,692
Illinois	83	737.4	5.1	8.9	2,700	7.6	33	11.46	76.6	3,222
Alabama	46	675.9	4.7	14.7	1,000	2.8	22	9.38	91.7	3,700
Pennsylvania	89	598.1	4.2	6.7	1,600	4.5	18	9.86	79.7	5,188
Missouri	56	516.6	3.6	9.2	1,300	3.7	23	9.47	77.5	3,231
Wisconsin	85	457.4	3.2	5.4	1,600	4.5	19	10.00	67.0	2,938
Indiana	47	420.9	2.9	9.0	1,000	2.8	21	11.55	71.4	4,900
Minnesota	68	399.8	2.8	5.9	1,100	3.1	16	11.38	71.1	6,727
Nebraska	79	378.0	2.6	4.8	1,300	3.7	16	9.63	66.4	3,308
Ohio	51	338.8	2.4	6.6	1,100	3.1	22	9.27	74.1	5,000
Kansas	57	333.1	2.3	5.8	1,000	2.8	18	9.67	79.7	4,800
Oklahoma	38	313.6	2.2	8.3	900	2.5	24	8.70	73.1	4,778
New York	49	286.6	2.0	5.8	900	2.5	18	10.78	76.3	-
Virginia	30	232.4	1.6	7.7	600	1.7	20	10.86	82.5	11,000
Maryland	12	228.4	1.6	19.0	300	0.8	25	9.40	92.7	1,000
Tennessee	26	223.3	1.6	8.6	600	1.7	23	10.25	89.5	4,667
Florida	35	212.4	1.5	6.1	500	1.4	14	8.67	79.2	11,800
Washington	33	203.7	1.4	6.2	600	1.7	18	8.56	79.1	3,500
Mississippi	29	185.5	1.3	6.4	400	1.1	14	6.88	81.9	15,250
Oregon	20	152.2	1.1	7.6	400	1.1	20	11.80	76.5	3,500
Colorado	34	130.3	0.9	3.8	400	1.1	12	9.00	77.4	3,500
Kentucky	27	124.0	0.9	4.6	400	1.1	15	11.00	74.0	-
Michigan	26	111.8	0.8	4.3	300	0.8	12	8.75	74.5	5,333
Louisiana	22	110.9	0.8	5.0	300	0.8	14	7.75	78.8	-
Vermont	6	95.0	0.7	15.8	300	0.8	50	12.33	75.5	-
South Carolina	14	87.0	0.6	6.2	300	0.8	21	11.50	89.9	-
Utah	17	82.4	0.6	4.8	300	0.8	18	10.67	71.8	1,667
New Jersey	6	39.3	0.3	6.6	200	0.6	33	11.33	60.8	6,000
Idaho	11	35.1	0.2	3.2	200	0.6	18	12.50	60.1	-
Massachusetts	6	24.0	0.2	4.0	100	0.3	17	13.00	78.8	-
Montana	18	(D)	-	-	175 *	0.5	10	-	-	5,714
South Dakota	17	(D)	-	-	375 *	1.1	22	-	-	-
North Dakota	14	(D)	-	-	175 *	0.5	13	-	-	-
Arizona	11	(D)	-	-	375 *	1.1	34	-	-	7,733
Connecticut	6	(D)	-	-	375 *	1.1	63	-	-	-
Delaware	5	(D)	-	-	175 *	0.5	35	-	-	-
Hawaii	3	(D)	-	-	175 *	0.5	58	-	-	-

Source: 1992 *Economic Census*. The states are in descending order of shipments or establishments (if shipment data are missing for the majority). The symbol (D) appears when data are withheld to prevent disclosure of competitive information. States marked with (D) are sorted by number of establishments. A dash (-) indicates that the data element cannot be calculated; * indicates the midpoint of a range.

2051 - BREAD & OTHER BAKERY PRODUCTS

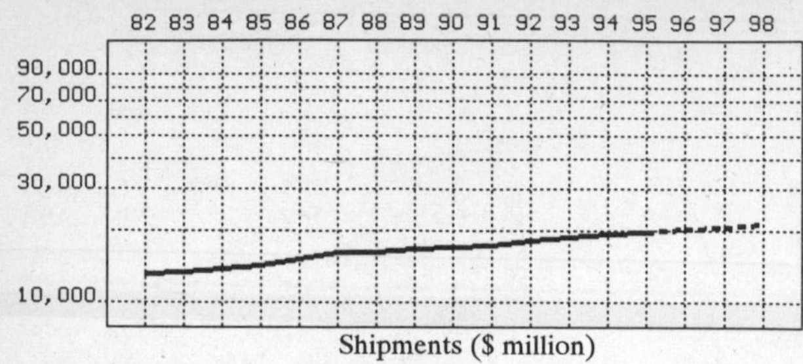

Shipments ($ million)

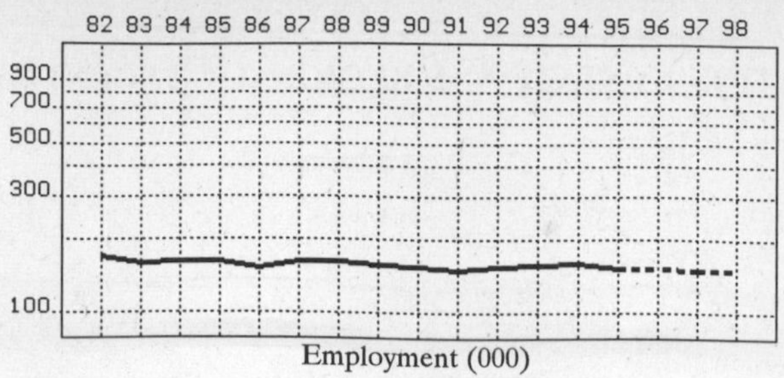

Employment (000)

GENERAL STATISTICS

Year	Companies	Establishments		Employment			Compensation		Production ($ million)			
		Total	with 20 or more employees	Total (000)	Production Workers (000)	Production Hours (Mil)	Payroll ($ mil)	Wages ($/hr)	Cost of Materials	Value Added by Manufacture	Value of Shipments	Capital Invest.
1982	1,869	2,305	1,074	170.7	88.9	175.1	3,249.6	8.68	5,282.7	7,861.1	13,143.3	382.4
1983		2,311	1,066	160.9	85.2	166.1	3,249.7	9.34	5,274.5	8,020.1	13,293.4	284.2
1984		2,317	1,058	162.1	84.8	164.2	3,366.5	9.56	5,403.1	8,304.8	13,701.5	408.4
1985		2,323	1,051	162.1	82.7	159.9	3,515.4	10.16	5,576.8	8,810.8	14,388.5	378.0
1986		2,228	1,031	153.4	81.9	159.9	3,371.2	10.40	5,565.9	9,585.8	15,148.2	408.7
1987	1,947	2,357	1,031	161.6	86.5	168.9	3,556.0	10.15	5,670.6	10,532.9	16,202.1	519.3
1988		2,259	1,005	162.8	86.4	171.8	3,676.4	10.22	5,899.6	10,466.3	16,362.2	446.3
1989		2,136	998	158.2	82.0	161.6	3,702.3	11.14	6,327.3	10,258.9	16,580.1	483.8
1990		2,027	968	154.8	82.4	161.5	3,763.3	11.69	6,549.3	10,475.5	17,019.2	541.5
1991		2,012	970	150.2	83.0	164.9	3,833.7	11.63	6,484.5	10,800.7	17,278.6	515.9
1992	2,180	2,539	946	155.1	88.3	172.1	4,061.6	11.82	6,680.1	11,462.0	18,142.5	514.4
1993		2,377	986	157.9	89.7	173.9	4,204.1	12.34	6,984.5	11,677.8	18,658.4	510.7
1994		2,240P	943P	159.0	88.6	177.9	4,262.7	12.29	7,155.1	12,177.7	19,328.5	592.1
1995		2,236P	931P	153.4P	86.6P	171.3P	4,274.7P	12.79P	7,303.8P	12,430.7P	19,730.1P	593.5P
1996		2,232P	920P	152.6P	86.8P	171.8P	4,359.9P	13.08P	7,496.0P	12,757.8P	20,249.3P	612.5P
1997		2,228P	909P	151.7P	87.0P	172.4P	4,445.2P	13.38P	7,688.2P	13,085.0P	20,768.5P	631.5P
1998		2,224P	898P	150.9P	87.2P	172.9P	4,530.4P	13.67P	7,880.4P	13,412.1P	21,287.7P	650.5P

Sources: 1982, 1987, 1992 *Economic Census*; *Annual Survey of Manufactures*, 83-86, 88-91, 93-94. Establishment counts for non-Census years are from *County Business Patterns*; establishment values for 83-84 are extrapolations. 'P's show projections by the editors. Industries reclassified in 87 will not have data for prior years.

INDICES OF CHANGE

Year	Companies	Establishments		Employment			Compensation		Production ($ million)			
		Total	with 20 or more employees	Total (000)	Production Workers (000)	Production Hours (Mil)	Payroll ($ mil)	Wages ($/hr)	Cost of Materials	Value Added by Manufacture	Value of Shipments	Capital Invest.
1982	86	91	114	110	101	102	80	73	79	69	72	74
1983		91	113	104	96	97	80	79	79	70	73	55
1984		91	112	105	96	95	83	81	81	72	76	79
1985		91	111	105	94	93	87	86	83	77	79	73
1986		88	109	99	93	93	83	88	83	84	83	79
1987	89	93	109	104	98	98	88	86	85	92	89	101
1988		89	106	105	98	100	91	86	88	91	90	87
1989		84	105	102	93	94	91	94	95	90	91	94
1990		80	102	100	93	94	93	99	98	91	94	105
1991		79	103	97	94	96	94	98	97	94	95	100
1992	100	100	100	100	100	100	100	100	100	100	100	100
1993		94	104	102	102	101	104	104	105	102	103	99
1994		88P	100P	103	100	103	105	104	107	106	107	115
1995		88P	98P	99P	98P	100P	105P	108P	109P	108P	109P	115P
1996		88P	97P	98P	98P	100P	107P	111P	112P	111P	112P	119P
1997		88P	96P	98P	99P	100P	109P	113P	115P	114P	114P	123P
1998		88P	95P	97P	99P	100P	112P	116P	118P	117P	117P	126P

Sources: Same as General Statistics. Values reflect change from the base year, 1992. Values above 100 mean greater than 92, values below 100 mean less than 92, and a value of 100 in the 82-91 or 93-98 period means same as 92. 'P's mark projections by the editors.

SELECTED RATIOS

For 1994	Avg. of All Manufact.	Analyzed Industry	Index
Employees per Establishment	49	71	145
Payroll per Establishment	1,500,273	1,903,081	127
Payroll per Employee	30,620	26,809	88
Production Workers per Establishment	34	40	115
Wages per Establishment	853,319	976,114	114
Wages per Production Worker	24,861	24,677	99
Hours per Production Worker	2,056	2,008	98
Wages per Hour	12.09	12.29	102
Value Added per Establishment	4,602,255	5,436,731	118
Value Added per Employee	93,930	76,589	82

For 1994	Avg. of All Manufact.	Analyzed Industry	Index
Value Added per Production Worker	134,084	137,446	103
Cost per Establishment	5,045,178	3,194,392	63
Cost per Employee	102,970	45,001	44
Cost per Production Worker	146,988	80,757	55
Shipments per Establishment	9,576,895	8,629,203	90
Shipments per Employee	195,460	121,563	62
Shipments per Production Worker	279,017	218,155	78
Investment per Establishment	321,011	264,343	82
Investment per Employee	6,552	3,724	57
Investment per Production Worker	9,352	6,683	71

Sources: Same as General Statistics. The 'Average of All Manufacturing' column represents the average of all manufacturing industries reported for the most recent complete year available. The Index shows the relationship between the Average and the Analyzed Industry. For example, 100 means that they are equal; 500 that the Analyzed Industry is five times the average; 50 means that the Analyzed Industry is half the national average. The abbreviation 'na' is used to show that data are 'not available'.

LEADING COMPANIES

Number shown: **75** Total sales ($ mil): **20,644** Total employment (000): **203.2**

Company Name	Address				CEO Name	Phone	Co. Type	Sales ($ mil)	Empl. (000)
Grand Metropolitan Inc	200 S 6th St	Minneapolis	MN	55402	Ian Martin	612-330-4966	S	6,980*	60.0
Continental Baking Co	Checkerboard Sq	St Louis	MO	63164	Robert W Bracken	314-982-1000	S	1,997	21.3
Campbell Taggart Inc	8400 Maryland Av	Saint Louis	MO	63105	D S Leavenworth	314-259-7000	S	1,600	19.3
Interstate Bakeries Corp	PO Box 419627	Kansas City	MO	64141	Charles A Sullivan	816-561-6600	P	1,143	14.0
Interstate Brands Corp	PO Box 419627	Kansas City	MO	64141	Charles A Sullivan	816-561-6600	S	1,143	14.0
Flowers Industries Inc	PO Box 1338	Thomasville	GA	31799	Amos R McMullian	912-226-9110	P	990	7.8
Interstate Brands Corp	PO Box 419627	Kansas City	MO	64141	HL Shetler	816-561-6600	D	726	4.6
McKee Foods Corp	PO Box 750	Collegedale	TN	37315	Ellsworth McKee	615-238-7111	R	580	4.0
Metz Baking Co	PO Box 448	Sioux City	IA	51102	Henry J Metz	712-255-7611	R	480*	7.0
Interstate Brands Corp	PO Box 419627	Kansas City	MO	64141	Robert P Morgan	816-561-6600	D	400	4.6
Stroehmann Bakeries Inc	PO Box 976	Horsham	PA	19044	David C Collins	215-672-8010	S	350*	4.2
Interstate Brands Corp	PO Box 419627	Kansas City	MO	64141	Frank A Fiorini	816-561-6600	D	325	4.7
Merico Inc	8400 Maryland Av	St Louis	MO	63105	Michael D Kafoure	314-259-7000	S	300	0.8
Merita Bakeries	PO Box 668648	Charlotte	NC	28266	R Dennis O'Connor	704-394-1181	D	290*	3.5
Country Home Bakery Inc	PO Box 2327	Bridgeport	CT	06608	Doris Zilnsky	203-333-2151	R	160	1.3
Charles Freihofer Baking Co	522 Washington Av	Albany	NY	12203	Peter Rollins	518-463-2221	S	150	1.5
Tasty Baking Co	2801 Hunting Pk	Philadelphia	PA	19129	Carl S Watts	215-221-8500	P	142	1.1
Harrison Baking Co	840 Jersey St	Harrison	NJ	07029	Morton Pechter	201-483-3374	S	140*	0.5
Newly Weds Foods Inc	4140 W Fullerton	Chicago	IL	60639	Charles T Angell	312-489-7000	R	140	0.5
Krispy Kreme Doughnut Corp	PO Box 83	Winston-Salem	NC	27102	J A McAleer Jr	910-725-2981	R	135	3.0
Schmidt Baking Company Inc	7801 Fitch Ln	Baltimore	MD	21236	C Peter Smith	410-668-8200	R	120*	1.2
United States Bakery Inc	PO Box 14769	Portland	OR	97214	M Robert Albers	503-232-2191	R	118	1.4
Mrs Baird's Bakeries Inc	PO Box 937	Fort Worth	TX	76101	Allen Baird	817-293-6230	R	110*	1.1
Alfred Nickles Bakery Inc	26 N Main St	Navarre	OH	44662	Ernest A Nickles	216-879-5635	R	100*	2.0
San Francisco French Bread Co	7801 Edgewater Dr	Oakland	CA	94621	Bill Grove	510-568-5511	S	100	1.0
Hostess Cake	6007 S Andrews Pl	Los Angeles	CA	90047	Fred Martich	213-753-3521	D	91	0.9
Klosterman Baking Company Inc	4760 Paddock Rd	Cincinnati	OH	45229	K Klosterman Jr	513-242-1004	R	75	0.9
Fresh Start Bakeries	PO Box 9939	Brea	CA	92622	Craig Olson	714-256-8900	S	70*	0.5
Heinemann's Bakeries Inc	3925 W 43rd St	Chicago	IL	60632	V V Graham Jr	312-523-5000	R	66	0.7
Holsum	3400 MacArthur Dr	Alexandria	LA	71303	Don Stephens	318-448-6600	D	63*	0.9
Alpha Baking Co	4545 W Lyndale St	Chicago	IL	60639	Michael Marcucci	312-489-5400	R	62	0.6
Smith's Bakery Inc	PO Box 70137	Mobile	AL	36607	John C Johnson	205-476-1611	R	61	0.6
H and S Bakery Inc	603 S Bond St	Baltimore	MD	21231	John Paterakis Sr	410-276-7254	R	60	0.3
Palmetto Baking Co	272 Broughton SE	Orangeburg	SC	29116	Sherman Strider	803-534-3535	S	60	0.5
Awrey Bakeries Inc	12301 Farmington	Livonia	MI	48150	Robert C Awrey	313-522-1100	R	55	0.5
Grocers Baking Co	210 28th St SE	Grand Rapids	MI	49548	Rodney A Folkert	616-245-9127	R	50	0.7
Lucks Co	PO Box 24266	Seattle	WA	98124	W Lucks	206-622-4608	R	50*	0.2
Storck Baking Company Inc	PO Box 389	Parkersburg	WV	26102	SS Ross	304-485-5441	R	50	0.3
Flowers Baking of Thomasville	PO Box 1219	Thomasville	GA	31799	Terrell Kirkland	912-226-5331	S	45	0.2
Svenhard's Swedish Bakery Inc	335 Adeline St	Oakland	CA	94607	Ron Svenhard	510-834-5035	R	45*	0.4
Fornaca Family Bakery Inc	2069 Alder Grove	Escondido	CA	92029	Ron Fornaca	619-233-7364	S	41	0.3
Bama Pie Ltd	PO Box 4829	Tulsa	OK	74159	P M-Chapman	918-592-0778	R	40	0.4
Kilpatrick's Bakeries Inc	PO Box 2093	Oakland	CA	94606	Robert Majors	510-436-5350	S	40	0.5
Penny Curtiss Baking Co	PO Box 486	Syracuse	NY	13211	David A Adamsen	315-454-3241	R	40	0.3
Richter's Bakery Inc	PO Box 1039	San Antonio	TX	78294	Herman J Richter	210-225-5811	R	40*	0.4
Butternut Bread Bakeries	747 W 5th St	Cincinnati	OH	45203	Fred Crowfoot	513-721-0212	D	39*	0.5
Gonnella Baking Co	2002 W Erie St	Chicago	IL	60612	Robert Gonnella	312-733-2020	R	38	0.3
Flowers Distributors Co	PO Box 3637	Baton Rouge	LA	70821	R A Spaulding	504-381-9699	S	38*	0.3
RDO Specialty Foods	PO Box 6004	Fargo	ND	58108	Richard Blajsczak	701-282-2300	D	38*	0.2
Indianapolis Bakery	6801 English Av	Indianapolis	IN	46219	Jack Rosenberger	317-322-5015	D	35*	0.4
Sweet Street Desserts	722 Hiesters Ln	Reading	PA	19605	Sandy Solomon	610-921-8113	R	35*	0.4
Giant Food Bakery	930 King St	Silver Spring	MD	20910	David Larson	301-341-4322	D	32*	0.5
Golden State Foods Corp	1525-A O Cov	Conyers	GA	30208	David Gilbert	404-483-0711	D	31*	0.3
Pitaria Products Co	4501 W District	Chicago	IL	60632	John Scales	312-847-2250	D	31*	0.3
Plantation Baking Company Inc	1400 Skokie Hwy	Lake Bluff	IL	60044		708-689-8400	S	31	0.3
Flowers Baking of Jacksonville	PO Box 12579	Jacksonville	FL	32209	Ray McDaniel	904-354-3771	S	30	0.2
Jessie Lord Inc	21100 S Western	Torrance	CA	90501	Judith Bork	310-533-6010	S	30	0.2
Rhodes International Inc	PO Box 25487	Salt Lake City	UT	84125	Ken Farnsworth Jr	801-972-0122	R	30*	0.3
Snyder's Bakery Inc	110 N Fancher Rd	Spokane	WA	99212	Bob Albers	509-535-7726	S	30	0.3
Purity Baking Co	PO Box 1338	Decatur	IL	62525		217-429-4318	S	27	0.4
Flowers Baking of Tyler	PO Box 360	Tyler	TX	75710	Steve Green	903-595-2421	S	25	0.3
Hawaii Baking Company Inc	PO Box 29609	Honolulu	HI	96820	Joseph R Trifari	808-488-6871	R	25*	0.2
Ideal Baking Company Inc	PO Box 2577	Batesville	AR	72501	E L Cochran Sr	501-793-6851	R	25	0.3
L Karp and Sons Inc	1301 Estes Av	Elk Grove Vill	IL	60007	Jack L Karp	708-593-5700	R	24	0.7
Flowers Baking of Lynchburg	PO Box 3307	Lynchburg	VA	24503	Jackie Forrest	804-528-0441	S	22	0.2
Gardner Baking	3401 E Washington	Madison	WI	53704	Robert Thompson	608-244-4747	D	22	0.4
Ottenberg's Bakers Inc	655 Taylor St NE	Washington	DC	20017	Lee Ottenberg	202-529-5800	R	22	0.2
Pechter Baking Company Inc	800 Pacific St	Brooklyn	NY	11238	H Field	718-638-6100	R	21	0.3
Rotellas Italian Bakery Inc	6949 S 108th St	Omaha	NE	68138	Louis J Rotella Sr	402-592-6600	R	20*	0.2
Butter Krust Baking Co	249 N 11th St	Sunbury	PA	17801	James G Apple	717-286-5845	R	20	0.3
Atlanta Baking Company Inc	PO Box 4996	Atlanta	GA	30302	Jerry Parmer	404-653-9700	S	20	0.5
Bishop Baking Co	PO Box 3720	Cleveland	TN	37320	Jean Veazey	615-472-1561	R	20*	0.2
Capital Bakers	PO Box 4469	Harrisburg	PA	17111	T Maurer	717-564-1891	D	20	<0.1
City Market Bakery	6 Town Plz	Durango	CO	81301	Tim Sparks	303-247-3962	D	20*	0.2
JJ Cassone Bakery Inc	202 S Regent St	Port Chester	NY	10573	Rocky T Cassone	914-939-1568	R	20*	0.2

Source: *Ward's Business Directory of U.S. Private and Public Companies*, Volumes 1 and 2, 1996. The company type code used is as follows: P - Public, R - Private, S - Subsidiary, D - Division, J - Joint Venture, A - Affiliate, G - Group. Sales are in millions of dollars, employees are in thousands. An asterisk (*) indicates an estimated sales volume. The symbol < stands for 'less than'. Company names and addresses are truncated, in some cases, to fit into the available space.

MATERIALS CONSUMED

Material		Quantity	Delivered Cost ($ million)
Materials, ingredients, containers, and supplies		(X)	4,506.3
White bread-type wheat flour (except prepared mixes)	mil lb	9,299.8	992.5
Cake-type wheat flour (except prepared mixes)	mil lb	424.9	48.4
Cookie and cracker-type wheat flour (except prepared mixes)	mil lb	150.9*	15.7
Wheat gluten	mil lb	242.7	93.0
Other wheat flour, including whole wheat, and clear flour (except prepared mixes)	mil lb	999.9**	128.0
Prepared doughnut mixes, cake and yeast types	mil lb	244.1*	77.4
Prepared bread mixes, including franchise mixes	mil lb	263.9	59.2
Prepared cake mixes	mil lb	78.6	28.2
Other prepared mixes, including sweetgoods	mil lb	77.8	30.6
Sugar, cane and beet (in terms of sugar solids)	1,000 s tons	505.2	232.8
Glucose syrup (corn syrup), conventional or regular (in terms of solids)	mil lb	268.8	42.1
High fructose corn syrup (HFCS)(in terms of solids)	mil lb	735.4*	108.6
Other natural sweeteners, including dextrose, honey, molasses, etc.	mil lb	224.5	62.3
Artificial sweeteners (in terms of solids)	mil lb	5.2*	1.7
100 percent vegetable shortening	mil lb	549.6*	162.1
Animal and blends of animal and vegetable shortening	mil lb	97.8	25.8
Lard	mil lb	10.4**	2.3
Other fats and oils (cooking oils, butter, margarine, puff paste, etc.)	mil lb	237.6	92.8
Compressed yeast	mil lb	290.3*	106.7
Active dry yeast	mil lb	83.4*	31.0
Frozen fruits	mil lb	69.8	52.0
Dried fruits and nuts, including raisins	1,000 cwt	841.1*	111.8
Glace, candied and crystallized fruits, fruit peel, nuts, and other vegetable substances	mil lb	12.7*	9.6
Jams, jellies and preserves, including fruit butter and maraschino cherries	mil lb	26.2	16.6
Liquid, dried, and frozen eggs (in terms of dry weight equivalent)	mil lb	135.3*	72.0
Cheese, process	mil lb	31.5*	23.1
Milk and milk replacers, including dry milk, dry whey, blends, soy whey, and others	mil lb	124.3**	57.4
Chocolate (compounds, cocoa, chocolate liquor, coatings, chocolate flavoring, etc.)	mil lb	79.0	46.0
Aluminum foil packaging products, converted or rolls and sheets		(X)	22.3
Packaging paper and plastics film, coated and laminated		(X)	131.8
Bags; plastics, foil, and coated paper		(X)	243.8
Bags; uncoated paper and multiwall		(X)	13.5
Paperboard containers, boxes, and corrugated paperboard		(X)	247.5
All other materials and components, parts, containers, and supplies		(X)	631.7
Materials, ingredients, containers, and supplies, nsk		(X)	486.0

Source: 1992 *Economic Census*. Explanation of symbols used: (D): Withheld to avoid disclosure of competitive data; na: Not available; (S): Withheld because statistical norms were not met; (X): Not applicable; (Z): Less than half the unit shown; nec: Not elsewhere classified; nsk: Not specified by kind; - : zero; * : 10-19 percent estimated; ** : 20-29 percent estimated.

PRODUCT SHARE DETAILS

Product or Product Class	% Share
Bread, cake, and related products	100.00
Bread: white, wheat, and rye (including frozen)	41.03
White pan bread, except frozen	48.24
Frozen white pan bread	0.11
White hearth bread, except frozen (including French, Italian, etc.)	13.40
Frozen white hearth bread (including French, Italian, etc.)	2.86
Whole wheat, cracked wheat, multigrain, and other dark wheat breads, except frozen	21.13
Frozen whole wheat, cracked wheat, multigrain, and other dark wheat breads	0.80
Rye bread (including pumpernickel), except frozen	4.41
Frozen rye bread (including pumpernickel)	0.11
Other variety breads (raisin, potato, salt-rising, salt-free, canned, etc.), except frozen	7.02
Other frozen variety breads (raisin, potato, salt-rising, salt-free, canned, etc.)	0.45
Bread: white, wheat, and rye (including frozen), nsk	1.47
Rolls, bread-type	27.68
Hamburger and wiener rolls, except frozen	47.33
Frozen hamburger and wiener rolls	1.96
Brown and serve rolls, except frozen	5.10
Frozen brown and serve rolls	0.12
English muffins, except frozen	8.93
Frozen english muffins	0.24
Hearth rolls, except frozen	4.85
Frozen hearth rolls	0.51
Bagels, except frozen	2.17
Frozen bagels	6.61
Croissants, except frozen	0.43
Frozen croissants	3.52
Other bread-type rolls (kaiser except hearth-type, parkerhouse, etc., except frozen)	8.08
Other frozen bread-type rolls (kaiser except hearth-type, parkerhouse, etc.)	1.38
Bread stuffing, croutons, and bread crumbs (plain and seasoned)	8.10
Rolls, bread-type, nsk	0.65
Sweet yeast goods	5.76
Yeast-raised doughnuts, except frozen	18.95
All other sweet yeast goods, except frozen (including sweet rolls and coffeecake)	79.56
Sweet yeast goods, nsk	1.49
Soft cakes	12.95
Soft snack cakes, except frozen	76.10
Soft fruit cakes, holiday-type, except frozen	3.71
All other soft cakes, except frozen (including pound, layer, sheet, cheese, etc.)	19.45
Soft cakes, nsk	0.73
Pies (fruit, cream, and custard)	2.85
Snack pies (fruit, cream, and custard), except frozen	59.80
All other pies (fruit, custard, and cream types, etc.), except frozen	39.76
Pies (fruit, cream, and custard), nsk	0.46
Pastries (except frozen), all types of baking powder leavened only	0.99
Doughnuts, cake-type (except frozen) (baking powder leavened)	3.42
Bread, cake, and related products, nsk	5.33

Source: 1992 *Economic Census*. The values shown are percent of total shipments in an industry. Values of indented subcategories are summed in the main heading. The symbol (D) appears when data are withheld to prevent disclosure of competitive information. The abbreviation nsk stands for 'not specified by kind' and nec for 'not elsewhere classified'.

INPUTS AND OUTPUTS FOR BREAD, CAKE, & RELATED PRODUCTS

Economic Sector or Industry Providing Inputs	%	Sector
Flour & other grain mill products	21.0	Manufg.
Advertising	7.6	Services
Wholesale trade	6.8	Trade
Accounting, auditing & bookkeeping	5.8	Services
Shortening & cooking oils	4.1	Manufg.
Paper coating & glazing	3.9	Manufg.
Paperboard containers & boxes	3.5	Manufg.
Sugar	3.2	Manufg.
Petroleum refining	2.7	Manufg.
Imports	2.7	Foreign
Food preparations, nec	2.4	Manufg.
Electric services (utilities)	2.3	Util.
Blended & prepared flour	2.2	Manufg.
Wet corn milling	2.1	Manufg.
Gas production & distribution (utilities)	2.0	Util.
Bags, except textile	1.9	Manufg.
Railroads & related services	1.8	Util.
Motor freight transportation & warehousing	1.6	Util.
Banking	1.6	Fin/R.E.
Tree nuts	1.3	Agric.
U.S. Postal Service	1.3	Gov't
Miscellaneous plastics products	1.1	Manufg.
Condensed & evaporated milk	1.0	Manufg.
Eating & drinking places	1.0	Trade
Noncomparable imports	1.0	Foreign
Chocolate & cocoa products	0.9	Manufg.
Communications, except radio & TV	0.9	Util.
Real estate	0.9	Fin/R.E.
Poultry & egg processing	0.8	Manufg.
Metal foil & leaf	0.7	Manufg.
Equipment rental & leasing services	0.7	Services
Business services nec	0.6	Services
Maintenance of nonfarm buildings nec	0.5	Constr.
Royalties	0.5	Fin/R.E.
Automotive rental & leasing, without drivers	0.5	Services
Cyclic crudes and organics	0.4	Manufg.
Meat packing plants	0.4	Manufg.
Air transportation	0.4	Util.
Sanitary services, steam supply, irrigation	0.4	Util.
Automotive repair shops & services	0.4	Services
Business/professional associations	0.4	Services
Food products machinery	0.3	Manufg.
Lubricating oils & greases	0.3	Manufg.
Water transportation	0.3	Util.
Insurance carriers	0.3	Fin/R.E.
Legal services	0.3	Services
Management & consulting services & labs	0.3	Services
Miscellaneous repair shops	0.3	Services
Industrial inorganic chemicals, nec	0.2	Manufg.
Machinery, except electrical, nec	0.2	Manufg.
Retail trade, except eating & drinking	0.2	Trade
Computer & data processing services	0.2	Services
Fabricated rubber products, nec	0.1	Manufg.
Tires & inner tubes	0.1	Manufg.
Engineering, architectural, & surveying services	0.1	Services
Hotels & lodging places	0.1	Services
State & local government enterprises, nec	0.1	Gov't

Economic Sector or Industry Buying Outputs	%	Sector
Personal consumption expenditures	74.3	
Eating & drinking places	19.0	Trade
S/L Govt. purch., elem. & secondary education	1.4	S/L Govt
Hospitals	0.7	Services
Child day care services	0.4	Services
Residential care	0.4	Services
Exports	0.4	Foreign
Change in business inventories	0.4	In House
S/L Govt. purch., health & hospitals	0.4	S/L Govt
Motion pictures	0.3	Services
Federal Government enterprises nec	0.3	Gov't
S/L Govt. purch., higher education	0.3	S/L Govt
Food preparations, nec	0.2	Manufg.
Frozen specialties	0.2	Manufg.
Air transportation	0.2	Util.
Nursing & personal care facilities	0.2	Services
Social services, nec	0.2	Services
S/L Govt. purch., correction	0.2	S/L Govt

Source: Benchmark Input-Output Accounts for the U.S. Economy, 1982, U.S. Department of Commerce, Washington, D.C., July 1991. Data, as reported in the source, are organized by the 1977 SIC structure in use in 1982 but have been matched, as closely as is possible, to the 1987 SIC structure used in this book.

OCCUPATIONS EMPLOYED BY SIC 205 - BAKERY PRODUCTS

Occupation	% of Total 1994	Change to 2005	Occupation	% of Total 1994	Change to 2005
Bakers, manufacturing	13.7	8.5	Sales & related workers nec	1.9	-8.4
Driver/sales workers	7.9	-40.5	Traffic, shipping, & receiving clerks	1.8	-11.9
Hand packers & packagers	7.6	-21.5	Assemblers, fabricators, & hand workers nec	1.7	-8.4
Packaging & filling machine operators	7.1	37.3	Cashiers	1.5	-8.4
Helpers, laborers, & material movers nec	6.8	-8.4	Machine operators nec	1.5	-19.3
Blue collar worker supervisors	4.4	-13.4	Marketing & sales worker supervisors	1.5	-8.4
Janitors & cleaners, incl maids	4.1	-26.7	General managers & top executives	1.4	-13.1
Truck drivers light & heavy	3.7	-5.6	Machine feeders & offbearers	1.4	-17.6
Precision food & tobacco workers nec	2.9	0.7	Food preparation & service workers nec	1.4	9.9
Industrial machinery mechanics	2.4	0.7	Maintenance repairers, general utility	1.3	-17.6
Salespersons, retail	2.3	-8.4	General office clerks	1.2	-21.9
Freight, stock, & material movers, hand	2.0	-26.8	Crushing & mixing machine operators	1.1	-8.4
Cooking, roasting machine operators	1.9	-17.6			

Source: *Industry-Occupation Matrix*, Bureau of Labor Statistics. These data relate to one or more 3-digit SIC industry groups rather than to a single 4-digit SIC. The change reported for each occupation to the year 2005 is a percent of growth or decline as estimated by the Bureau of Labor Statistics. The abbreviation nec stands for 'not elsewhere classified'.

LOCATION BY STATE AND REGIONAL CONCENTRATION

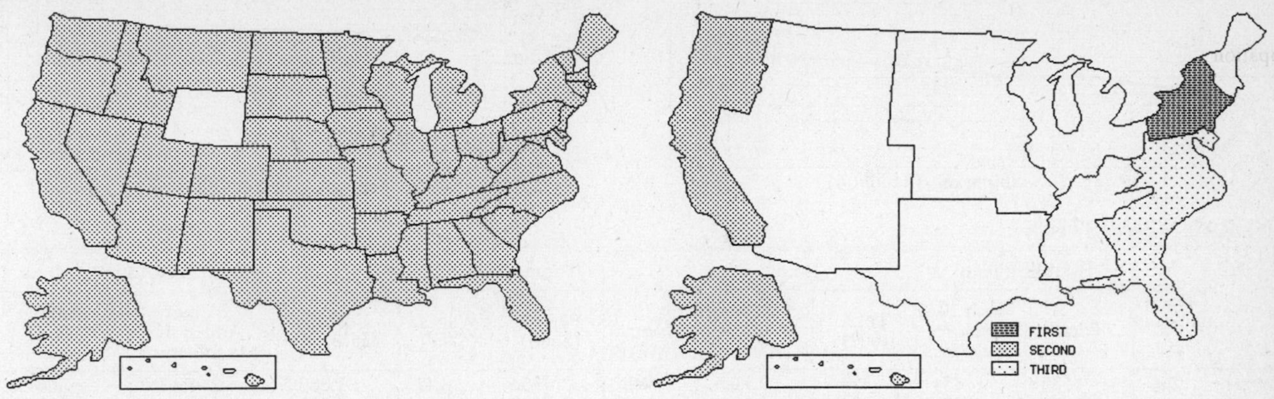

INDUSTRY DATA BY STATE

State	Establish-ments	Shipments			Employment				Cost as % of Shipments	Investment per Employee ($)
		Total ($ mil)	% of U.S.	Per Establ.	Total Number	% of U.S.	Per Establ.	Wages ($/hour)		
California	336	2,113.5	11.6	6.3	18,300	11.8	54	13.10	34.6	4,372
New York	359	1,514.3	8.3	4.2	11,600	7.5	32	12.13	31.7	3,534
Pennsylvania	165	1,239.6	6.8	7.5	9,500	6.1	58	11.31	29.8	3,095
Illinois	97	1,088.9	6.0	11.2	9,400	6.1	97	12.70	37.5	2,670
Texas	112	1,087.4	6.0	9.7	9,400	6.1	84	11.54	40.5	6,011
Tennessee	38	1,069.4	5.9	28.1	9,200	5.9	242	10.64	45.4	-
Ohio	82	830.3	4.6	10.1	6,200	4.0	76	12.96	38.9	1,919
Florida	126	594.5	3.3	4.7	5,000	3.2	40	10.64	37.2	3,960
Georgia	39	583.7	3.2	15.0	4,700	3.0	121	11.91	35.8	1,872
New Jersey	118	524.6	2.9	4.4	3,700	2.4	31	12.07	35.5	5,946
Indiana	35	455.6	2.5	13.0	4,200	2.7	120	12.86	38.8	2,119
Maryland	56	441.0	2.4	7.9	2,500	1.6	45	10.72	31.4	3,640
Michigan	75	435.7	2.4	5.8	4,500	2.9	60	10.60	38.5	2,467
North Carolina	45	430.1	2.4	9.6	5,000	3.2	111	9.78	40.2	1,360
Massachusetts	113	427.1	2.4	3.8	3,900	2.5	35	11.60	36.3	3,000
Washington	56	378.6	2.1	6.8	2,800	1.8	50	13.76	39.2	2,750
Oregon	42	278.3	1.5	6.6	2,200	1.4	52	13.27	39.1	-
Wisconsin	51	264.2	1.5	5.2	3,000	1.9	59	9.84	39.2	-
Missouri	37	256.7	1.4	6.9	2,600	1.7	70	12.65	40.8	2,962
Minnesota	37	243.5	1.3	6.6	2,700	1.7	73	10.79	42.5	1,778
Kentucky	17	233.8	1.3	13.8	2,200	1.4	129	10.59	49.5	1,864
Iowa	20	179.1	1.0	9.0	1,800	1.2	90	11.84	47.9	1,833
Arizona	31	165.2	0.9	5.3	1,500	1.0	48	14.06	35.0	3,333
West Virginia	13	163.8	0.9	12.6	1,100	0.7	85	8.29	30.6	2,727
Oklahoma	8	146.0	0.8	18.3	1,000	0.6	125	14.40	37.5	-
Arkansas	14	130.5	0.7	9.3	1,400	0.9	100	11.29	39.5	1,714
Utah	28	115.9	0.6	4.1	1,000	0.6	36	11.85	32.5	-
Hawaii	29	70.0	0.4	2.4	900	0.6	31	11.91	38.6	1,444
Vermont	16	32.1	0.2	2.0	400	0.3	25	9.00	47.7	-
Nevada	13	19.3	0.1	1.5	300	0.2	23	7.75	33.7	1,000
Virginia	51	(D)	-	-	3,750 *	2.4	74	-	-	-
Colorado	42	(D)	-	-	1,750 *	1.1	42	-	-	1,600
Connecticut	36	(D)	-	-	1,750 *	1.1	49	-	-	-
Louisiana	23	(D)	-	-	1,750 *	1.1	76	-	-	-
Alabama	22	(D)	-	-	3,750 *	2.4	170	-	-	-
Rhode Island	21	(D)	-	-	750 *	0.5	36	-	-	2,133
Kansas	19	(D)	-	-	1,750 *	1.1	92	-	-	-
Maine	18	(D)	-	-	1,750 *	1.1	97	-	-	-
New Mexico	12	(D)	-	-	750 *	0.5	63	-	-	-
South Carolina	12	(D)	-	-	1,750 *	1.1	146	-	-	-
Mississippi	11	(D)	-	-	750 *	0.5	68	-	-	-
Nebraska	11	(D)	-	-	1,750 *	1.1	159	-	-	-
North Dakota	8	(D)	-	-	375 *	0.2	47	-	-	-
Delaware	7	(D)	-	-	175 *	0.1	25	-	-	-
Montana	7	(D)	-	-	375 *	0.2	54	-	-	-
South Dakota	6	(D)	-	-	375 *	0.2	63	-	-	-
Idaho	5	(D)	-	-	375 *	0.2	75	-	-	-
D.C.	4	(D)	-	-	175 *	0.1	44	-	-	-
Alaska	3	(D)	-	-	175 *	0.1	58	-	-	-

Source: 1992 *Economic Census*. The states are in descending order of shipments or establishments (if shipment data are missing for the majority). The symbol (D) appears when data are withheld to prevent disclosure of competitive information. States marked with (D) are sorted by number of establishments. A dash (-) indicates that the data element cannot be calculated; * indicates the midpoint of a range.

2052 - COOKIES & CRACKERS

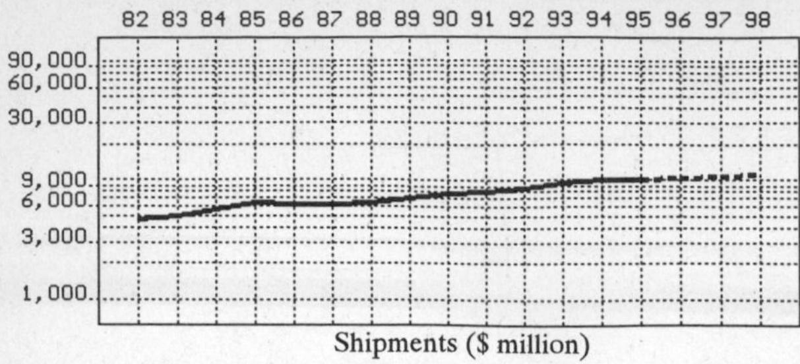

Shipments ($ million)

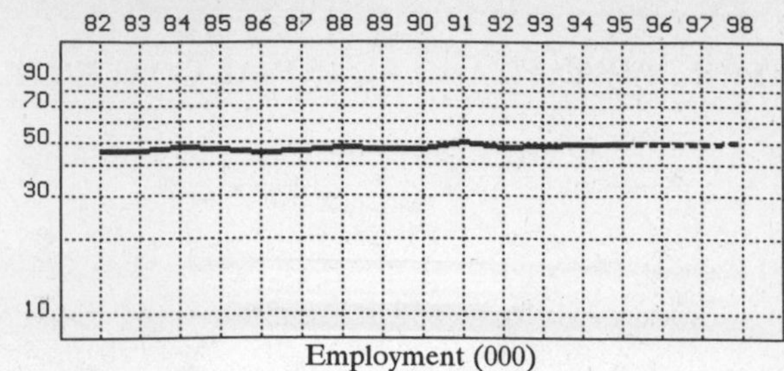

Employment (000)

GENERAL STATISTICS

Year	Companies	Establishments		Employment			Compensation		Production ($ million)			
		Total	with 20 or more employees	Total (000)	Production Workers (000)	Production Hours (Mil)	Payroll ($ mil)	Wages ($/hr)	Cost of Materials	Value Added by Manufacture	Value of Shipments	Capital Invest.
1982	296	358	187	45.6	35.0	66.8	796.5	8.42	1,880.2	2,789.3	4,664.9	107.8
1983		358	190	45.7	34.7	66.9	858.8	9.14	1,928.6	2,988.8	4,914.8	103.6
1984		358	193	47.1	36.0	72.0	929.2	9.07	2,230.4	3,460.9	5,685.2	176.2
1985		357	195	46.7	35.2	71.5	962.8	9.31	2,288.6	4,183.8	6,445.9	208.4
1986		348	193	45.0	33.2	66.6	1,019.7	10.38	2,202.9	3,968.1	6,177.4	163.3
1987	316	380	191	45.4	33.9	65.2	1,009.8	10.78	2,241.0	4,100.7	6,309.1	185.1
1988		362	194	47.0	34.3	63.6	1,051.9	11.46	2,411.6	4,109.2	6,498.6	202.2
1989		378	191	46.3	35.5	68.8	1,127.4	10.91	2,842.3	4,290.6	7,099.9	240.6
1990		361	193	46.7	35.3	70.3	1,181.2	13.82	3,005.0	4,823.1	7,803.5	255.5
1991		368	194	49.3	36.2	72.2	1,246.5	11.52	3,055.1	4,990.5	8,021.7	406.6
1992	374	441	212	47.2	35.1	71.9	1,250.3	11.84	3,151.0	5,523.4	8,687.5	310.3
1993		451	216	48.0	36.2	73.4	1,285.1	12.18	3,410.5	6,045.2	9,441.9	314.2
1994		421P	207P	48.7	37.7	75.3	1,334.6	12.29	3,512.4	6,629.6	10,093.5	385.2
1995		427P	209P	48.5P	36.4P	73.3P	1,386.3P	13.28P	3,475.5P	6,560.0P	9,987.5P	392.6P
1996		434P	211P	48.7P	36.5P	73.8P	1,429.9P	13.63P	3,620.8P	6,834.2P	10,405.0P	415.0P
1997		441P	213P	48.9P	36.7P	74.3P	1,473.5P	13.98P	3,766.1P	7,108.4P	10,822.5P	437.5P
1998		448P	215P	49.2P	36.8P	74.9P	1,517.1P	14.32P	3,911.4P	7,382.6P	11,240.0P	459.9P

Sources: 1982, 1987, 1992 *Economic Census*; *Annual Survey of Manufactures*, 83-86, 88-91, 93-94. Establishment counts for non-Census years are from *County Business Patterns*; establishment values for 83-84 are extrapolations. 'P's show projections by the editors. Industries reclassified in 87 will not have data for prior years.

INDICES OF CHANGE

Year	Companies	Establishments		Employment			Compensation		Production ($ million)			
		Total	with 20 or more employees	Total (000)	Production Workers (000)	Production Hours (Mil)	Payroll ($ mil)	Wages ($/hr)	Cost of Materials	Value Added by Manufacture	Value of Shipments	Capital Invest.
1982	79	81	88	97	100	93	64	71	60	50	54	35
1983		81	90	97	99	93	69	77	61	54	57	33
1984		81	91	100	103	100	74	77	71	63	65	57
1985		81	92	99	100	99	77	79	73	76	74	67
1986		79	91	95	95	93	82	88	70	72	71	53
1987	84	86	90	96	97	91	81	91	71	74	73	60
1988		82	92	100	98	88	84	97	77	74	75	65
1989		86	90	98	101	96	90	92	90	78	82	78
1990		82	91	99	101	98	94	117	95	87	90	82
1991		83	92	104	103	100	100	97	97	90	92	131
1992	100	100	100	100	100	100	100	100	100	100	100	100
1993		102	102	102	103	102	103	103	108	109	109	101
1994		95P	98P	103	107	105	107	104	111	120	116	124
1995		97P	99P	103P	104P	102P	111P	112P	110P	119P	115P	127P
1996		98P	99P	103P	104P	103P	114P	115P	115P	124P	120P	134P
1997		100P	100P	104P	105P	103P	118P	118P	120P	129P	125P	141P
1998		101P	101P	104P	105P	104P	121P	121P	124P	134P	129P	148P

Sources: Same as General Statistics. Values reflect change from the base year, 1992. Values above 100 mean greater than 92, values below 100 mean less than 92, and a value of 100 in the 82-91 or 93-98 period means same as 92. 'P's mark projections by the editors.

SELECTED RATIOS

For 1994	Avg. of All Manufact.	Analyzed Industry	Index
Employees per Establishment	49	116	236
Payroll per Establishment	1,500,273	3,173,269	212
Payroll per Employee	30,620	27,405	89
Production Workers per Establishment	34	90	261
Wages per Establishment	853,319	2,200,405	258
Wages per Production Worker	24,861	24,547	99
Hours per Production Worker	2,056	1,997	97
Wages per Hour	12.09	12.29	102
Value Added per Establishment	4,602,255	15,763,153	343
Value Added per Employee	93,930	136,131	145

For 1994	Avg. of All Manufact.	Analyzed Industry	Index
Value Added per Production Worker	134,084	175,851	131
Cost per Establishment	5,045,178	8,351,409	166
Cost per Employee	102,970	72,123	70
Cost per Production Worker	146,988	93,167	63
Shipments per Establishment	9,576,895	23,999,243	251
Shipments per Employee	195,460	207,259	106
Shipments per Production Worker	279,017	267,732	96
Investment per Establishment	321,011	915,887	285
Investment per Employee	6,552	7,910	121
Investment per Production Worker	9,352	10,218	109

Sources: Same as General Statistics. The 'Average of All Manufacturing' column represents the average of all manufacturing industries reported for the most recent complete year available. The Index shows the relationship between the Average and the Analyzed Industry. For example, 100 means that they are equal; 500 that the Analyzed Industry is five times the average; 50 means that the Analyzed Industry is half the national average. The abbreviation 'na' is used to show that data are 'not available'.

LEADING COMPANIES

Number shown: **63** Total sales ($ mil): **2,743** Total employment (000): **23.2**

Company Name	Address				CEO Name	Phone	Co. Type	Sales ($ mil)	Empl. (000)
Lance Inc	PO Box 32368	Charlotte	NC	28232	PA Stroup III	704-554-1421	P	473	5.5
Consolidated Biscuit Corp	PO Box 847	McComb	OH	45858	James Appold	419-293-2911	R	400*	2.6
Interbake Foods Inc	2821 Emerywood	Richmond	VA	23230	Ray A Baxter	804-755-7107	S	400	3.0
Eagle Snacks Inc	8115 Preston Rd	Dallas	TX	75225	D S Leavenworth	214-265-5100	S	240*	1.6
J and J Snack Foods Corp	6000 Central Hwy	Pennsauken	NJ	08109	Gerald B Shreiber	609-665-9533	P	174	1.7
Delicious/Frookie Company Inc	270 River Rd	Des Plaines	IL	60018	Phillip Rooth	708-699-5990	R	100	<0.1
Roskam Baking Co	PO Box 2485	Grand Rapids	MI	49501	Robert O Roskam	616-771-9100	R	70*	0.5
Midwest Biscuit Co	PO Box 888	Burlington	IA	52601	Gary Martin	319-754-6551	S	65	0.6
Holland American Wafer Co	3300 R B Chaffee	Grand Rapids	MI	49508	S Vanderheide	616-243-0191	R	62*	0.4
Bake-Line Products Inc	1 Bakeline Plz	Des Plaines	IL	60016	TE Kallen	708-699-1000	S	60*	0.5
DF Stauffer Biscuit Company	PO Box 1426	York	PA	17405	Yosunobu Narihiro	717-843-9016	R	60	0.5
Mrs Alison's Cookie Company	1780 Burns Av	St Louis	MO	63132	JE Elliott	314-429-2111	R	47	0.4
Stella D'oro Biscuit Company	184 W 237th St	Bronx	NY	10463	Harold J Lees	212-549-3700	S	47*	0.3
Ripon Foods Inc	PO Box 348	Ripon	WI	54971	Edward Bumby	414-748-3151	R	44	0.5
Crackin Good Bakers Inc	PO Box 370	Valdosta	GA	31603	LW Harris	912-242-7850	S	40	0.5
B Manischewitz Co	1 Manischewitz Plz	Jersey City	NJ	07302	Robert Kroll	201-333-3700	R	35*	0.2
Roush Gourmet Foods	PO Box 5790	Cedar Rapids	IA	52406	John Sheafer	319-363-9853	R	31*	0.2
Evans Food Products Co	4118 S Halsted	Chicago	IL	60609	Alex Silva	312-254-7400	R	24	0.2
Pretzels Inc	PO Box 503	Bluffton	IN	46714	Bill Huggins	219-824-4838	R	22*	0.1
Boca Foods Inc	400 S 2nd St	Harrison	NJ	07029	Edward Reisman	201-483-1100	R	20	0.2
Century Cookie Co	400 S 2nd St	Harrison	NJ	07029	Edward Reisman	201-483-1100	D	20	0.2
Colonial Cake Company Inc	PO Box 18303	San Antonio	TX	78218	Richard Richter	210-661-2361	S	20	0.4
J and J Snack Foods Corp	5353 Downey Rd	Vernon	CA	90058	John Schiavo	213-581-0171	D	20	0.3
Rudolph Foods Co	PO Box 509	Lima	OH	45802	John E Rudolph	419-648-3611	R	20	0.3
Specialty Bakers Inc	450 S State Rd	Marysville	PA	17053	John Piotrowski	717-957-2131	R	19*	0.1
Silver Lake Cookie Co	141 Freeman Av	Islip	NY	11751	Joseph Vitarelli	516-581-4000	R	18	0.4
Fleetwood Snacks Inc	18 W Poplar St	Fleetwood	PA	19522	GF Randolph Plass	610-944-7623	R	17	0.2
Stella D'oro Biscuit of California	PO Box 1876	San Leandro	CA	94577	Nick Calarco	510-357-2300	D	15*	0.1
Willmar Cookie and Nut	PO Box 88	Willmar	MN	56201	Mike Mickelson	612-235-0600	R	14	0.2
Turnbull Cone Baking Co	PO Box 6248	Chattanooga	TN	37401	W Turnbull	615-265-4551	R	13	0.1
Keystone Pretzel Bakery	124 W Airport Rd	Lititz	PA	17543	Glen Hyneman	717-560-1882	D	11	<0.1
Vesper Corp	124 W Airport Rd	Lititz	PA	17543	George Phillips	717-560-1882	R	11*	<0.1
Ellison Bakery Inc	PO Box 9087	Fort Wayne	IN	46899	Robert E Ellis Jr	219-747-6136	R	10	0.1
Sesmark Foods Inc	PO Box 5764	Rockford	IL	61125	K Miyagawa	815-874-8202	R	10*	<0.1
Richmond Baking Company Inc	PO Box 698	Richmond	IN	47374	JR Quigg	317-962-8535	R	8	<0.1
Tom Sturgis Pretzels Inc	325 Lancaster Pk W	Shillington	PA	19607	Thomas D Sturgis	215-775-0335	R	8	<0.1
Amorous Andi's	8350 Alban Rd	Springfield	VA	22150	Peter Ewens	703-912-5000	R	7*	<0.1
Davis Cookie Company Inc	PO Box 430	Rimersburg	PA	16248	David Davis	814-473-3125	R	7*	<0.1
La Tempesta Bakery Confections	439 Littlefield Av	S San Francisco	CA	94080	Bonnie Tempesta	415-873-8944	R	7	<0.1
Maurice Lenell Cooky Co	4474 N Harlem Av	Chicago	IL	60656	Sonny Cohen	708-456-6500	R	7	0.1
Byrd Cookie Co	PO Box 13086	Savannah	GA	31416	Benny Curl	912-355-1716	R	6	<0.1
Derby Cone Company Inc	PO Box 99157	Louisville	KY	40299	G G Buttermann Jr	502-491-1220	R	6	<0.1
Diamond Bakery Company Ltd	PO Box 17760	Honolulu	HI	96817	Paul Ishii	808-847-3551	R	6*	<0.1
Little Dutch Boy Bakeries Inc	PO Box 240	Draper	UT	84020	Frank Bakker	801-571-3800	R	6	<0.1
Bremner Inc	824 6th Av SE	Minneapolis	MN	55414	Lynn Mortenson	612-331-5908	D	5*	<0.1
Bud's Best Cookies Inc	2070 Parkway Office	Hoover	AL	35244	Albert L Cason	205-987-4840	R	5*	<0.1
Fort Biscuit Co	PO Box 1059	Fort Smith	AR	72902	Phillip J White	501-783-4490	R	5	<0.1
Pure Food Specialties Inc	2929 S 25th Av	Broadview	IL	60153	Elliott Pure	708-344-8884	R	5	<0.1
Bader's Dutch Biscuit Company	7224 1st Av S	Seattle	WA	98134	Stephanie Chilton	206-764-1001	R	4	<0.1
Pinahs Company Inc	N8W22100 Johnson	Waukesha	WI	53186	Carl Pinahs	414-547-2447	R	4	<0.1
Mom's Best Cookies Inc	6995 Venture Cir	Orlando	FL	32807	C Van Vliet	407-678-8769	D	3	<0.1
Bremner Biscuit Co	4600 Joliet St	Denver	CO	80239	EG Bremner Jr	303-371-8180	R	2	<0.1
Readi-Bake Inc	PO Box 7189	Grand Rapids	MI	49510	Eugene Kilburg	616-246-1540	S	2	<0.1
East Shore Specialty Foods Inc	PO Box 138	Nashotah	WI	53058	Jeri Mesching	414-367-8988	R	1	<0.1
Golden Walnut Specialty Foods	3840 Swanson Ct	Gurnee	IL	60031	Frederick C Came	708-244-8050	D	1*	<0.1
GH Bent Co	7 Pleasant St	Milton	MA	02186	Eugene Pierotti	617-698-5945	R	1	<0.1
Peggy Lawton Kitchens Inc	255 Washington St	East Walpole	MA	02032	LD Wolf	508-668-1215	R	1	<0.1
Short Order Fortune	PO Box 6051	Bellevue	WA	98008	Melissa Handler	206-641-3644	R	1*	<0.1
Cookie-Grams of Georgia	PO Box 1304	Forest Park	GA	30050	Greg Fievet	404-363-4438	R	1*	<0.1
Gourmet Goodies Inc	8847 Commerce Pk	Indianapolis	IN	46268	Kim Harvey	317-872-3663	R	1*	<0.1
Fortunately Yours	326 Vista Dr	Gahanna	OH	43230	Rhonda L Lashen	614-337-1889	R	0	<0.1
Mrs Barry's Kona Cookies	75-5744 Alii Dr	Kailua Kona	HI	96740	Hansung Barry	808-329-6055	R	0	<0.1
Tell City Pretzel Co	632 Main St	Tell City	IN	47586	Craig Kendall	812-547-4631	R	0*	<0.1

Source: *Ward's Business Directory of U.S. Private and Public Companies*, Volumes 1 and 2, 1996. The company type code used is as follows: P - Public, R - Private, S - Subsidiary, D - Division, J - Joint Venture, A - Affiliate, G - Group. Sales are in millions of dollars, employees are in thousands. An asterisk (*) indicates an estimated sales volume. The symbol < stands for 'less than'. Company names and addresses are truncated, in some cases, to fit into the available space.

MATERIALS CONSUMED

Material		Quantity	Delivered Cost ($ million)
Materials, ingredients, containers, and supplies		(X)	2,419.4
White bread-type wheat flour (except prepared mixes)	mil lb	325.4	34.7
Cake-type wheat flour (except prepared mixes)	mil lb	212.4	22.6
Cookie and cracker-type wheat flour (except prepared mixes)	mil lb	2,758.4	278.6
Wheat gluten	mil lb	2.5*	1.6
Other wheat flour, including whole wheat, and clear flour (except prepared mixes)	mil lb	262.3	27.9
Prepared bread mixes, including franchise mixes	mil lb	20.7	2.4
Prepared cake mixes	mil lb	6.6*	0.8
Other prepared mixes, including sweetgoods	mil lb	8.0*	4.5
Sugar, cane and beet (in terms of sugar solids)	1,000 s tons	395.3	199.4
Glucose syrup (corn syrup), conventional or regular (in terms of solids)	mil lb	83.2	10.7
High fructose corn syrup (HFCS)(in terms of solids)	mil lb	118.5	17.0
Other natural sweeteners, including dextrose, honey, molasses, blends of corn sweeteners and sugar	mil lb	137.9	39.2
Artificial sweeteners (in terms of solids)	mil lb	15.3**	3.0
100 percent vegetable shortening	mil lb	700.8	199.6
Animal and blends of animal and vegetable shortening	mil lb	16.1	4.1
Lard	mil lb	6.4	1.7
Other fats and oils (cooking oils, butter, margarine, puff paste, etc.)	mil lb	107.8*	37.5
Compressed yeast	mil lb	(S)	3.7
Active dry yeast	mil lb	3.7	2.2
Frozen fruits	mil lb	1.2	0.9
Dried fruits and nuts, including raisins	1,000 cwt	726.5*	95.0
Glace, candied and crystallized fruits, fruit peel, nuts, and other vegetable substances	mil lb	2.4*	2.5
Jams, jellies and preserves, including fruit butter and maraschino cherries	mil lb	39.1	36.1
Liquid, dried, and frozen eggs (in terms of dry weight equivalent)	mil lb	15.8*	13.3
Cheese, process	mil lb	31.8	49.0
Milk and milk replacers, including dry milk, dry whey, blends, soy whey, and others	mil lb	(S)	15.9
Chocolate (compounds, cocoa, chocolate liquor, coatings, chocolate flavoring, etc.)	mil lb	159.8	126.1
Aluminum foil packaging products, converted or rolls and sheets		(X)	10.3
Packaging paper and plastics film, coated and laminated		(X)	219.1
Bags; plastics, foil, and coated paper		(X)	46.3
Bags; uncoated paper and multiwall		(X)	15.0
Paperboard containers, boxes, and corrugated paperboard		(X)	354.9
All other materials and components, parts, containers, and supplies		(X)	441.3
Materials, ingredients, containers, and supplies, nsk		(X)	102.2

Source: 1992 *Economic Census*. Explanation of symbols used: (D): Withheld to avoid disclosure of competitive data; na: Not available; (S): Withheld because statistical norms were not met; (X): Not applicable; (Z): Less than half the unit shown; nec: Not elsewhere classified; nsk: Not specified by kind; - : zero; * : 10-19 percent estimated; ** : 20-29 percent estimated.

PRODUCT SHARE DETAILS

Product or Product Class	% Share	Product or Product Class	% Share
Cookies and crackers	100.00	Sandwich cookies, made from cookies made in this plant	19.69
Crackers, pretzels, biscuits, and related products	42.94	Marshmallow cookies	0.93
Graham crackers	5.71	Creme-filled cookies	2.96
Saltine crackers	18.05	Chocolate chip cookies	15.47
Cracker meal and crumbs	0.93	Oatmeal cookies	4.80
Cracker sandwiches made from crackers produced in this plant	12.59	Other cookies and wafers, excluding wafers for making ice cream sandwiches	45.25
Pretzels	13.79	Toaster pastries	5.71
Other crackers and related products (sponge, sprayed, low-sugar biscuits, melba toast, unsalted soda, taco shells, etc.)	48.49	Wafers for making ice cream sandwiches	(D)
Crackers, pretzels, biscuits, and related products, nsk	0.45	Ice cream cones and cups	3.33
Cookies, wafers, and ice cream cones and cups (except frozen)	55.57	Cookies, wafers, and ice cream cones and cups except frozen, nsk	(D)
		Cookies and crackers, nsk	1.49

Source: 1992 *Economic Census*. The values shown are percent of total shipments in an industry. Values of indented subcategories are summed in the main heading. The symbol (D) appears when data are withheld to prevent disclosure of competitive information. The abbreviation nsk stands for 'not specified by kind' and nec for 'not elsewhere classified'.

INPUTS AND OUTPUTS FOR COOKIES & CRACKERS

Economic Sector or Industry Providing Inputs	%	Sector	Economic Sector or Industry Buying Outputs	%	Sector
Flour & other grain mill products	14.5	Manufg.	Personal consumption expenditures	88.9	
Paperboard containers & boxes	11.6	Manufg.	Eating & drinking places	5.9	Trade
Wholesale trade	9.1	Trade	Residential care	0.9	Services
Shortening & cooking oils	7.7	Manufg.	Ice cream & frozen desserts	0.8	Manufg.
Sugar	7.7	Manufg.	Hospitals	0.5	Services
Advertising	5.9	Services	Social services, nec	0.5	Services
Paper coating & glazing	5.5	Manufg.	Change in business inventories	0.5	In House
Miscellaneous plastics products	3.3	Manufg.	S/L Govt. purch., health & hospitals	0.4	S/L Govt
Chocolate & cocoa products	3.2	Manufg.	S/L Govt. purch., elem. & secondary education	0.3	S/L Govt
Bags, except textile	2.7	Manufg.	Cookies & crackers	0.2	Manufg.

Continued on next page.

INPUTS AND OUTPUTS FOR COOKIES & CRACKERS - Continued

Economic Sector or Industry Providing Inputs	%	Sector	Economic Sector or Industry Buying Outputs	%	Sector
Business services nec	2.4	Services	Food preparations, nec	0.2	Manufg.
Gas production & distribution (utilities)	2.0	Util.	S/L Govt. purch., correction	0.2	S/L Govt
Meat packing plants	1.9	Manufg.	S/L Govt. purch., higher education	0.2	S/L Govt
Electric services (utilities)	1.9	Util.	Motion pictures	0.1	Services
Motor freight transportation & warehousing	1.8	Util.	Nursing & personal care facilities	0.1	Services
Railroads & related services	1.5	Util.			
Flavoring extracts & syrups, nec	1.0	Manufg.			
Industrial gases	1.0	Manufg.			
Wet corn milling	1.0	Manufg.			
Automotive repair shops & services	0.9	Services			
Food preparations, nec	0.8	Manufg.			
Noncomparable imports	0.8	Foreign			
Cyclic crudes and organics	0.7	Manufg.			
Eating & drinking places	0.7	Trade			
Communications, except radio & TV	0.6	Util.			
Banking	0.6	Fin/R.E.			
Equipment rental & leasing services	0.6	Services			
Metal foil & leaf	0.5	Manufg.			
Soybean oil mills	0.5	Manufg.			
Condensed & evaporated milk	0.4	Manufg.			
Cookies & crackers	0.4	Manufg.			
Creamery butter	0.4	Manufg.			
Food products machinery	0.4	Manufg.			
Petroleum refining	0.4	Manufg.			
Royalties	0.4	Fin/R.E.			
Maintenance of nonfarm buildings nec	0.3	Constr.			
Industrial inorganic chemicals, nec	0.3	Manufg.			
Poultry & egg processing	0.3	Manufg.			
Real estate	0.3	Fin/R.E.			
State & local government enterprises, nec	0.3	Gov't			
U.S. Postal Service	0.3	Gov't			
Blended & prepared flour	0.2	Manufg.			
Lubricating oils & greases	0.2	Manufg.			
Sanitary services, steam supply, irrigation	0.2	Util.			
Water transportation	0.2	Util.			
Credit agencies other than banks	0.2	Fin/R.E.			
Insurance carriers	0.2	Fin/R.E.			
Accounting, auditing & bookkeeping	0.2	Services			
Computer & data processing services	0.2	Services			
Legal services	0.2	Services			
Management & consulting services & labs	0.2	Services			
Miscellaneous repair shops	0.2	Services			
Machinery, except electrical, nec	0.1	Manufg.			

Source: Benchmark Input-Output Accounts for the U.S. Economy, 1982, U.S. Department of Commerce, Washington, D.C., July 1991. Data, as reported in the source, are organized by the 1977 SIC structure in use in 1982 but have been matched, as closely as is possible, to the 1987 SIC structure used in this book.

OCCUPATIONS EMPLOYED BY SIC 205 - BAKERY PRODUCTS

Occupation	% of Total 1994	Change to 2005	Occupation	% of Total 1994	Change to 2005
Bakers, manufacturing	13.7	8.5	Sales & related workers nec	1.9	-8.4
Driver/sales workers	7.9	-40.5	Traffic, shipping, & receiving clerks	1.8	-11.9
Hand packers & packagers	7.6	-21.5	Assemblers, fabricators, & hand workers nec	1.7	-8.4
Packaging & filling machine operators	7.1	37.3	Cashiers	1.5	-8.4
Helpers, laborers, & material movers nec	6.8	-8.4	Machine operators nec	1.5	-19.3
Blue collar worker supervisors	4.4	-13.4	Marketing & sales worker supervisors	1.5	-8.4
Janitors & cleaners, incl maids	4.1	-26.7	General managers & top executives	1.4	-13.1
Truck drivers light & heavy	3.7	-5.6	Machine feeders & offbearers	1.4	-17.6
Precision food & tobacco workers nec	2.9	0.7	Food preparation & service workers nec	1.4	9.9
Industrial machinery mechanics	2.4	0.7	Maintenance repairers, general utility	1.3	-17.6
Salespersons, retail	2.3	-8.4	General office clerks	1.2	-21.9
Freight, stock, & material movers, hand	2.0	-26.8	Crushing & mixing machine operators	1.1	-8.4
Cooking, roasting machine operators	1.9	-17.6			

Source: Industry-Occupation Matrix, Bureau of Labor Statistics. These data relate to one or more 3-digit SIC industry groups rather than to a single 4-digit SIC. The change reported for each occupation to the year 2005 is a percent of growth or decline as estimated by the Bureau of Labor Statistics. The abbreviation nec stands for 'not elsewhere classified'.

LOCATION BY STATE AND REGIONAL CONCENTRATION

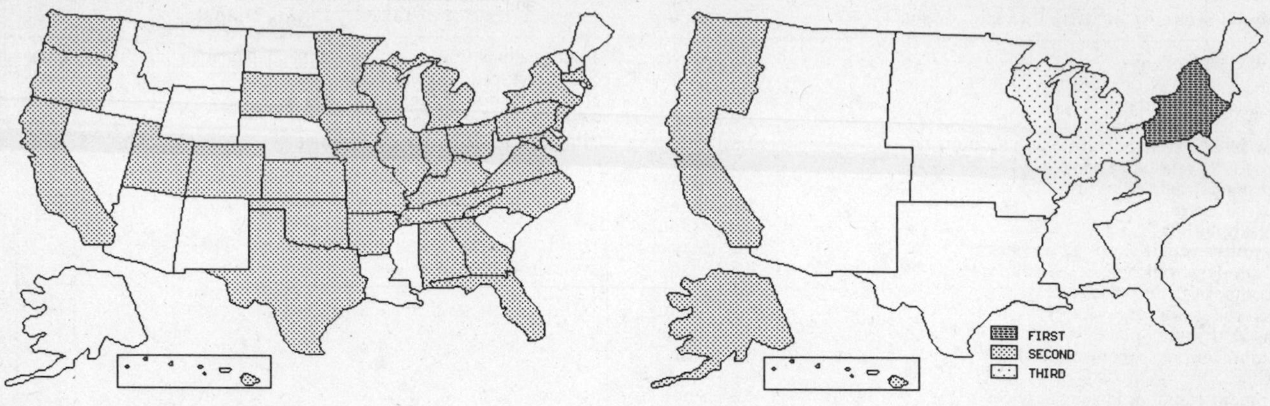

INDUSTRY DATA BY STATE

State	Establish-ments	Shipments			Employment				Cost as % of Shipments	Investment per Employee ($)
		Total ($ mil)	% of U.S.	Per Establ.	Total Number	% of U.S.	Per Establ.	Wages ($/hour)		
Illinois	24	1,437.7	16.5	59.9	4,600	9.7	192	12.39	34.9	6,848
Georgia	14	993.1	11.4	70.9	4,000	8.5	286	13.62	34.5	4,475
Pennsylvania	57	872.0	10.0	15.3	5,200	11.0	91	12.58	35.8	12,346
Ohio	17	753.9	8.7	44.3	3,200	6.8	188	12.79	32.1	2,969
California	72	602.1	6.9	8.4	3,500	7.4	49	11.86	43.3	5,229
New Jersey	23	592.6	6.8	25.8	3,500	7.4	152	14.17	36.2	-
Kentucky	5	301.5	3.5	60.3	1,500	3.2	300	9.84	38.5	3,867
New York	45	208.4	2.4	4.6	1,800	3.8	40	9.00	37.1	2,056
Texas	21	173.9	2.0	8.3	1,700	3.6	81	10.90	39.9	-
Florida	17	165.2	1.9	9.7	1,000	2.1	59	8.71	41.9	-
Indiana	8	76.0	0.9	9.5	600	1.3	75	9.00	47.1	-
Washington	15	32.2	0.4	2.1	400	0.8	27	10.20	43.8	3,000
Massachusetts	8	18.8	0.2	2.3	200	0.4	25	14.00	48.9	2,000
Hawaii	10	10.5	0.1	1.0	200	0.4	20	6.00	42.9	1,500
Michigan	10	(D)	-	-	1,750 *	3.7	175	-	-	-
Missouri	10	(D)	-	-	750 *	1.6	75	-	-	2,400
North Carolina	8	(D)	-	-	7,500 *	15.9	938	-	-	-
Oregon	8	(D)	-	-	750 *	1.6	94	-	-	-
Wisconsin	8	(D)	-	-	750 *	1.6	94	-	-	8,267
Iowa	6	(D)	-	-	750 *	1.6	125	-	-	-
Tennessee	5	(D)	-	-	750 *	1.6	150	-	-	-
Virginia	5	(D)	-	-	1,750 *	3.7	350	-	-	-
Maryland	4	(D)	-	-	175 *	0.4	44	-	-	-
Oklahoma	4	(D)	-	-	750 *	1.6	188	-	-	-
Arkansas	3	(D)	-	-	175 *	0.4	58	-	-	-
Kansas	3	(D)	-	-	750 *	1.6	250	-	-	-
Minnesota	3	(D)	-	-	175 *	0.4	58	-	-	1,714
Utah	3	(D)	-	-	750 *	1.6	250	-	-	-
Alabama	2	(D)	-	-	175 *	0.4	88	-	-	-
Colorado	2	(D)	-	-	750 *	1.6	375	-	-	-
South Dakota	1	(D)	-	-	375 *	0.8	375	-	-	-

Source: 1992 *Economic Census*. The states are in descending order of shipments or establishments (if shipment data are missing for the majority). The symbol (D) appears when data are withheld to prevent disclosure of competitive information. States marked with (D) are sorted by number of establishments. A dash (-) indicates that the data element cannot be calculated; * indicates the midpoint of a range.

2053 - FROZEN BAKERY PRODUCTS EXCEPT BREAD

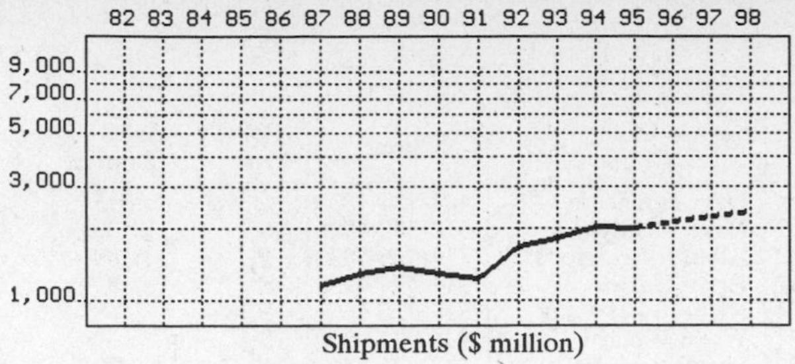

Shipments ($ million)

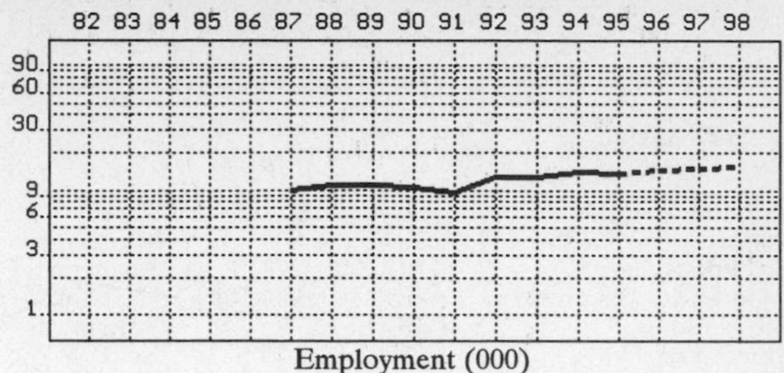

Employment (000)

GENERAL STATISTICS

Year	Com-panies	Establishments: Total	Establishments: with 20 or more employees	Employment: Total (000)	Employment: Production Workers (000)	Employment: Production Hours (Mil)	Compensation: Payroll ($ mil)	Compensation: Wages ($/hr)	Production ($ million): Cost of Materials	Production ($ million): Value Added by Manufacture	Production ($ million): Value of Shipments	Production ($ million): Capital Invest.
1982												
1983												
1984												
1985												
1986												
1987	103	114	66	9.9	7.5	14.2	195.0	9.31	565.4	600.1	1,165.4	31.8
1988		133	73	10.7	8.1	15.3	208.0	9.08	620.4	679.4	1,296.0	36.9
1989		139	78	10.7	8.2	16.6	205.2	8.83	635.7	751.9	1,386.0	26.4
1990		129	72	10.6	7.9	16.2	199.0	8.56	623.9	672.4	1,298.6	30.5
1991		130	72	9.4	7.3	14.9	198.6	8.86	566.1	660.4	1,238.3	25.9
1992	160	172	101	12.7	9.8	20.4	288.2	9.66	762.6	919.2	1,671.4	37.1
1993		171	104	13.0	10.2	21.1	293.3	9.53	806.0	1,007.0	1,809.6	38.6
1994		175P	104P	14.0	11.4	24.1	346.4	10.15	920.1	1,131.9	2,048.7	61.3
1995		184P	110P	13.8P	11.0P	23.7P	334.7P	9.83P	898.5P	1,105.4P	2,000.7P	49.1P
1996		193P	116P	14.3P	11.5P	24.9P	355.3P	9.96P	949.6P	1,168.2P	2,114.4P	51.9P
1997		201P	122P	14.9P	12.0P	26.2P	376.0P	10.09P	1,000.6P	1,231.0P	2,228.0P	54.8P
1998		210P	128P	15.4P	12.5P	27.5P	396.6P	10.22P	1,051.7P	1,293.8P	2,341.7P	57.7P

Sources: 1982, 1987, 1992 *Economic Census*; *Annual Survey of Manufactures*, 83-86, 88-91, 93-94. Establishment counts for non-Census years are from *County Business Patterns*; establishment values for 83-84 are extrapolations. 'P's show projections by the editors. Industries reclassified in 87 will not have data for prior years.

INDICES OF CHANGE

Year	Com-panies	Establishments: Total	Establishments: with 20 or more employees	Employment: Total (000)	Employment: Production Workers (000)	Employment: Production Hours (Mil)	Compensation: Payroll ($ mil)	Compensation: Wages ($/hr)	Production ($ million): Cost of Materials	Production ($ million): Value Added by Manufacture	Production ($ million): Value of Shipments	Production ($ million): Capital Invest.
1982												
1983												
1984												
1985												
1986												
1987	64	66	65	78	77	70	68	96	74	65	70	86
1988		77	72	84	83	75	72	94	81	74	78	99
1989		81	77	84	84	81	71	91	83	82	83	71
1990		75	71	83	81	79	69	89	82	73	78	82
1991		76	71	74	74	73	69	92	74	72	74	70
1992	100	100	100	100	100	100	100	100	100	100	100	100
1993		99	103	102	104	103	102	99	106	110	108	104
1994		102P	103P	110	116	118	120	105	121	123	123	165
1995		107P	109P	109P	113P	116P	116P	102P	118P	120P	120P	132P
1996		112P	115P	113P	118P	122P	123P	103P	125P	127P	127P	140P
1997		117P	121P	117P	123P	129P	130P	104P	131P	134P	133P	148P
1998		122P	126P	121P	128P	135P	138P	106P	138P	141P	140P	156P

Sources: Same as General Statistics. Values reflect change from the base year, 1992. Values above 100 mean greater than 92, values below 100 mean less than 92, and a value of 100 in the 82-91 or 93-98 period means same as 92. 'P's mark projections by the editors.

SELECTED RATIOS

For 1994	Avg. of All Manufact.	Analyzed Industry	Index	For 1994	Avg. of All Manufact.	Analyzed Industry	Index
Employees per Establishment	49	80	163	Value Added per Production Worker	134,084	99,289	74
Payroll per Establishment	1,500,273	1,974,593	132	Cost per Establishment	5,045,178	5,244,870	104
Payroll per Employee	30,620	24,743	81	Cost per Employee	102,970	65,721	64
Production Workers per Establishment	34	65	189	Cost per Production Worker	146,988	80,711	55
Wages per Establishment	853,319	1,394,385	163	Shipments per Establishment	9,576,895	11,678,257	122
Wages per Production Worker	24,861	21,457	86	Shipments per Employee	195,460	146,336	75
Hours per Production Worker	2,056	2,114	103	Shipments per Production Worker	279,017	179,711	64
Wages per Hour	12.09	10.15	84	Investment per Establishment	321,011	349,430	109
Value Added per Establishment	4,602,255	6,452,199	140	Investment per Employee	6,552	4,379	67
Value Added per Employee	93,930	80,850	86	Investment per Production Worker	9,352	5,377	57

Sources: Same as General Statistics. The 'Average of All Manufacturing' column represents the average of all manufacturing industries reported for the most recent complete year available. The Index shows the relationship between the Average and the Analyzed Industry. For example, 100 means that they are equal; 500 that the Analyzed Industry is five times the average; 50 means that the Analyzed Industry is half the national average. The abbreviation 'na' is used to show that data are 'not available'.

LEADING COMPANIES

Number shown: 22 Total sales ($ mil): **848** Total employment (000): **6.3**

Company Name	Address				CEO Name	Phone	Co. Type	Sales ($ mil)	Empl. (000)
Flowers Indust Specialty	5087E S Royal	Tucker	GA	30084	Gary Harrison	404-934-4800	D	225	2.0
Pillsbury Bakeries	200 S 6th St	Minneapolis	MN	55402	Mike McGlynn	612-330-4966	S	130*	0.5
Bridgford Foods Corp	PO Box 3773	Anaheim	CA	92803	Allan L Bridgford	714-526-5533	P	109	0.7
Hazelwood Farms Bakeries Inc	8840 Pershall Rd	Hazelwood	MO	63042	Brent Baxter	314-595-4150	S	87*	0.8
Mrs Smith's Inc	PO Box 298	Pottstown	PA	19464	Richard F Troyak	610-326-2600	S	68*	0.5
Plush Pippin Corp	21331 88th Pl S	Kent	WA	98031	Wynn Willard	206-872-7300	S	39*	0.2
WesCap Holdings LP	2 Gateway Ctr	Pittsburgh	PA	15222	Dick Kennedy	412-471-3707	R	32*	0.3
Rich Products Corp	PO Box 2055	Winchester	VA	22601	T Tierney	703-667-1955	D	29*	0.2
Pies Inc	300 Lake Hazeltine	Chaska	MN	55318	Neil Jansen	612-448-2150	S	21	0.2
Bridgford Foods Corp	PO Box 152808	Dallas	TX	75315	Joe Dealcuaz	214-428-1535	D	16*	0.1
Eli's Chicago Finest Inc	6510 W Dakin St	Chicago	IL	60634	Marc S Schulman	312-736-3417	R	13	0.1
Cookietree Bakeries	4122 S 500 W	Salt Lake City	UT	84123	Greg Schenk	801-268-2253	R	12*	0.1
Main Street Muffins Inc	170 Muffin Ln	Cuyahoga Falls	OH	44223	Steven L Marks	216-929-0000	R	12*	<0.1
James Skinner Baking Co	PO Box 6306	Omaha	NE	68106	Lyn Juric	402-558-7428	R	11	0.2
Gourmet Concepts International	1651 Montreal Cir	Tucker	GA	30084	Hartmut Willinsky	404-491-2100	R	10*	0.1
Bavarian Specialty Foods	22417 S Vermont	Torrance	CA	90502	Gary Lowman	310-212-6199	D	8	0.1
Dressels Bakeries Inc	6630 S Ashland Av	Chicago	IL	60636	Thierry Joulin	312-434-5300	S	6*	<0.1
Rhino Foods Inc	79 Industrial Pkwy	Burlington	VT	05401	Ted Castle	802-862-0252	R	6	<0.1
Evans Bakery Inc	PO Box 284	Cozad	NE	69130	Gale E Evans	308-784-2409	R	5	<0.1
Bubbles Baking Co	15215 Keswick St	Van Nuys	CA	91405	Torbin Jenson	818-786-1700	R	4*	<0.1
Jana's Classics Inc	19552 SW 90th Ct	Tualatin	OR	97062	Jana Taylor	503-691-1600	R	4	<0.1
Nancy's Pies Inc	337 2nd St	Rock Island	IL	61201	George H Coin	309-793-0161	R	1*	<0.1

Source: *Ward's Business Directory of U.S. Private and Public Companies*, Volumes 1 and 2, 1996. The company type code used is as follows: P - Public, R - Private, S - Subsidiary, D - Division, J - Joint Venture, A - Affiliate, G - Group. Sales are in millions of dollars, employees are in thousands. An asterisk (*) indicates an estimated sales volume. The symbol < stands for 'less than'. Company names and addresses are truncated, in some cases, to fit into the available space.

MATERIALS CONSUMED

Material		Quantity	Delivered Cost ($ million)
Materials, ingredients, containers, and supplies		(X)	710.6
White bread-type wheat flour (except prepared mixes)	mil lb	187.2**	20.8
Cake-type wheat flour (except prepared mixes)	mil lb	67.7**	7.2
Cookie and cracker-type wheat flour (except prepared mixes)	mil lb	8.4**	1.1
Wheat gluten	mil lb	1.1	0.6
Other wheat flour, including whole wheat, and clear flour (except prepared mixes)	mil lb	96.0	10.2
Prepared doughnut mixes, cake and yeast types	mil lb	37.8	11.7
Prepared bread mixes, including franchise mixes	mil lb	(D)	(D)
Prepared cake mixes	mil lb	10.7*	4.9
Other prepared mixes, including sweetgoods	mil lb	(S)	3.0
Sugar, cane and beet (in terms of sugar solids)	1,000 s tons	77.0*	46.6
Glucose syrup (corn syrup), conventional or regular (in terms of solids)	mil lb	39.7	5.3
High fructose corn syrup (HFCS)(in terms of solids)	mil lb	30.1*	4.1
Other natural sweeteners, including dextrose, honey, molasses, blends of corn sweeteners and sugar	mil lb	12.0	3.4
Artificial sweeteners (in terms of solids)	mil lb	(D)	(D)
100 percent vegetable shortening	mil lb	99.3*	34.1
Animal and blends of animal and vegetable shortening	mil lb	5.2	1.6
Lard	mil lb	11.9	2.7
Other fats and oils (cooking oils, butter, margarine, puff paste, etc.)	mil lb	48.1	18.0
Compressed yeast	mil lb	9.6	5.2
Active dry yeast	mil lb	2.8	1.2
Frozen fruits	mil lb	132.2*	75.5
Dried fruits and nuts, including raisins	1,000 cwt	116.3*	20.1
Glace, candied and crystallized fruits, fruit peel, nuts, and other vegetable substances	mil lb	(D)	(D)
Jams, jellies and preserves, including fruit butter and maraschino cherries	mil lb	7.1	4.3
Liquid, dried, and frozen eggs (in terms of dry weight equivalent)	mil lb	39.7*	21.8
Cheese, process	mil lb	19.4*	17.3
Milk and milk replacers, including dry milk, dry whey, blends, soy whey, and others	mil lb	33.7	18.5
Chocolate (compounds, cocoa, chocolate liquor, coatings, chocolate flavoring, etc.)	mil lb	10.7**	10.2
Aluminum foil packaging products, converted or rolls and sheets		(X)	34.7
Packaging paper and plastics film, coated and laminated		(X)	16.9
Bags; plastics, foil, and coated paper		(X)	4.0
Bags; uncoated paper and multiwall		(X)	0.3
Paperboard containers, boxes, and corrugated paperboard		(X)	70.8
All other materials and components, parts, containers, and supplies		(X)	111.5
Materials, ingredients, containers, and supplies, nsk		(X)	107.4

Source: 1992 *Economic Census*. Explanation of symbols used: (D): Withheld to avoid disclosure of competitive data; na: Not available; (S): Withheld because statistical norms were not met; (X): Not applicable; (Z): Less than half the unit shown; nec: Not elsewhere classified; nsk: Not specified by kind; - : zero; * : 10-19 percent estimated; ** : 20-29 percent estimated.

PRODUCT SHARE DETAILS

Product or Product Class	% Share	Product or Product Class	% Share
Frozen bakery products	100.00	Frozen pies	37.80
Frozen yeast-raised doughnuts	3.09	Frozen doughnuts, cake-type (baking powder leavened)	3.58
All other frozen sweet yeast goods, including sweet rolls and coffeecake	5.84	Frozen pastries, all types of baking powder leavened only (cream puffs, eclairs, lady fingers, french pastry, puff pastry, etc)	9.66
Frozen soft cakes, including pound, layer, sheet, fruit, cheese, etc.	23.60	All other frozen bakery products	13.81

Source: 1992 *Economic Census*. The values shown are percent of total shipments in an industry. Values of indented subcategories are summed in the main heading. The symbol (D) appears when data are withheld to prevent disclosure of competitive information. The abbreviation nsk stands for 'not specified by kind' and nec for 'not elsewhere classified'.

INPUTS AND OUTPUTS FOR BREAD, CAKE, & RELATED PRODUCTS

Economic Sector or Industry Providing Inputs	%	Sector	Economic Sector or Industry Buying Outputs	%	Sector
Flour & other grain mill products	21.0	Manufg.	Personal consumption expenditures	74.3	
Advertising	7.6	Services	Eating & drinking places	19.0	Trade
Wholesale trade	6.8	Trade	S/L Govt. purch., elem. & secondary education	1.4	S/L Govt
Accounting, auditing & bookkeeping	5.8	Services	Hospitals	0.7	Services
Shortening & cooking oils	4.1	Manufg.	Child day care services	0.4	Services
Paper coating & glazing	3.9	Manufg.	Residential care	0.4	Services
Paperboard containers & boxes	3.5	Manufg.	Exports	0.4	Foreign
Sugar	3.2	Manufg.	Change in business inventories	0.4	In House
Petroleum refining	2.7	Manufg.	S/L Govt. purch., health & hospitals	0.4	S/L Govt
Imports	2.7	Foreign	Motion pictures	0.3	Services
Food preparations, nec	2.4	Manufg.	Federal Government enterprises nec	0.3	Gov't
Electric services (utilities)	2.3	Util.	S/L Govt. purch., higher education	0.3	S/L Govt
Blended & prepared flour	2.2	Manufg.	Food preparations, nec	0.2	Manufg.
Wet corn milling	2.1	Manufg.	Frozen specialties	0.2	Manufg.
Gas production & distribution (utilities)	2.0	Util.	Air transportation	0.2	Util.
Bags, except textile	1.9	Manufg.	Nursing & personal care facilities	0.2	Services
Railroads & related services	1.8	Util.	Social services, nec	0.2	Services
Motor freight transportation & warehousing	1.6	Util.	S/L Govt. purch., correction	0.2	S/L Govt
Banking	1.6	Fin/R.E.			
Tree nuts	1.3	Agric.			
U.S. Postal Service	1.3	Gov't			
Miscellaneous plastics products	1.1	Manufg.			
Condensed & evaporated milk	1.0	Manufg.			
Eating & drinking places	1.0	Trade			
Noncomparable imports	1.0	Foreign			
Chocolate & cocoa products	0.9	Manufg.			
Communications, except radio & TV	0.9	Util.			
Real estate	0.9	Fin/R.E.			
Poultry & egg processing	0.8	Manufg.			
Metal foil & leaf	0.7	Manufg.			
Equipment rental & leasing services	0.7	Services			
Business services nec	0.6	Services			
Maintenance of nonfarm buildings nec	0.5	Constr.			
Royalties	0.5	Fin/R.E.			
Automotive rental & leasing, without drivers	0.5	Services			
Cyclic crudes and organics	0.4	Manufg.			
Meat packing plants	0.4	Manufg.			
Air transportation	0.4	Util.			
Sanitary services, steam supply, irrigation	0.4	Util.			
Automotive repair shops & services	0.4	Services			
Business/professional associations	0.4	Services			
Food products machinery	0.3	Manufg.			
Lubricating oils & greases	0.3	Manufg.			
Water transportation	0.3	Util.			
Insurance carriers	0.3	Fin/R.E.			
Legal services	0.3	Services			
Management & consulting services & labs	0.3	Services			
Miscellaneous repair shops	0.3	Services			
Industrial inorganic chemicals, nec	0.2	Manufg.			
Machinery, except electrical, nec	0.2	Manufg.			
Retail trade, except eating & drinking	0.2	Trade			
Computer & data processing services	0.2	Services			
Fabricated rubber products, nec	0.1	Manufg.			
Tires & inner tubes	0.1	Manufg.			
Engineering, architectural, & surveying services	0.1	Services			
Hotels & lodging places	0.1	Services			
State & local government enterprises, nec	0.1	Gov't			

Source: Benchmark Input-Output Accounts for the U.S. Economy, 1982, U.S. Department of Commerce, Washington, D.C., July 1991. Data, as reported in the source, are organized by the 1977 SIC structure in use in 1982 but have been matched, as closely as is possible, to the 1987 SIC structure used in this book.

OCCUPATIONS EMPLOYED BY SIC 205 - BAKERY PRODUCTS

Occupation	% of Total 1994	Change to 2005	Occupation	% of Total 1994	Change to 2005
Bakers, manufacturing	13.7	8.5	Sales & related workers nec	1.9	-8.4
Driver/sales workers	7.9	-40.5	Traffic, shipping, & receiving clerks	1.8	-11.9
Hand packers & packagers	7.6	-21.5	Assemblers, fabricators, & hand workers nec	1.7	-8.4
Packaging & filling machine operators	7.1	37.3	Cashiers	1.5	-8.4
Helpers, laborers, & material movers nec	6.8	-8.4	Machine operators nec	1.5	-19.3
Blue collar worker supervisors	4.4	-13.4	Marketing & sales worker supervisors	1.5	-8.4
Janitors & cleaners, incl maids	4.1	-26.7	General managers & top executives	1.4	-13.1
Truck drivers light & heavy	3.7	-5.6	Machine feeders & offbearers	1.4	-17.6
Precision food & tobacco workers nec	2.9	0.7	Food preparation & service workers nec	1.4	9.9
Industrial machinery mechanics	2.4	0.7	Maintenance repairers, general utility	1.3	-17.6
Salespersons, retail	2.3	-8.4	General office clerks	1.2	-21.9
Freight, stock, & material movers, hand	2.0	-26.8	Crushing & mixing machine operators	1.1	-8.4
Cooking, roasting machine operators	1.9	-17.6			

Source: Industry-Occupation Matrix, Bureau of Labor Statistics. These data relate to one or more 3-digit SIC industry groups rather than to a single 4-digit SIC. The change reported for each occupation to the year 2005 is a percent of growth or decline as estimated by the Bureau of Labor Statistics. The abbreviation nec stands for 'not elsewhere classified'.

LOCATION BY STATE AND REGIONAL CONCENTRATION

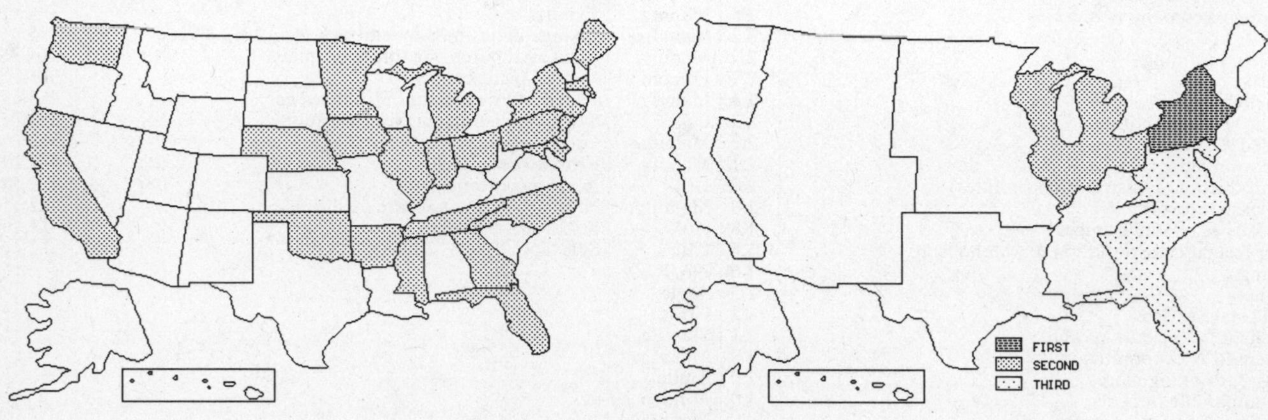

INDUSTRY DATA BY STATE

State	Establish-ments	Shipments Total ($ mil)	Shipments % of U.S.	Shipments Per Establ.	Employment Total Number	Employment % of U.S.	Employment Per Establ.	Employment Wages ($/hour)	Cost as % of Shipments	Investment per Employee ($)
Pennsylvania	16	354.9	21.2	22.2	2,000	15.7	125	12.26	39.6	3,750
Georgia	8	124.6	7.5	15.6	700	5.5	88	10.25	43.5	3,714
California	16	124.1	7.4	7.8	1,200	9.4	75	7.09	50.9	4,000
Indiana	8	66.2	4.0	8.3	600	4.7	75	9.00	56.9	-
New York	19	45.3	2.7	2.4	400	3.1	21	7.00	45.9	2,000
Illinois	9	36.0	2.2	4.0	400	3.1	44	10.00	45.6	1,000
Washington	5	34.3	2.1	6.9	200	1.6	40	9.67	50.7	7,000
Ohio	7	33.0	2.0	4.7	300	2.4	43	7.75	39.4	667
Massachusetts	11	24.6	1.5	2.2	300	2.4	27	7.67	42.3	1,667
Florida	7	16.4	1.0	2.3	200	1.6	29	6.75	40.2	-
New Jersey	7	9.7	0.6	1.4	100	0.8	14	7.00	47.4	-
Michigan	7	(D)	-	-	1,750 *	13.8	250	-	-	-
Minnesota	6	(D)	-	-	750 *	5.9	125	-	-	4,000
Maine	4	(D)	-	-	175 *	1.4	44	-	-	-
North Carolina	4	(D)	-	-	750 *	5.9	188	-	-	-
Maryland	3	(D)	-	-	175 *	1.4	58	-	-	-
Nebraska	3	(D)	-	-	175 *	1.4	58	-	-	-
Oklahoma	3	(D)	-	-	375 *	3.0	125	-	-	-
Arkansas	2	(D)	-	-	175 *	1.4	88	-	-	-
Iowa	2	(D)	-	-	750 *	5.9	375	-	-	-
Mississippi	1	(D)	-	-	750 *	5.9	750	-	-	-
Tennessee	1	(D)	-	-	175 *	1.4	175	-	-	-

Source: 1992 *Economic Census*. The states are in descending order of shipments or establishments (if shipment data are missing for the majority). The symbol (D) appears when data are withheld to prevent disclosure of competitive information. States marked with (D) are sorted by number of establishments. A dash (-) indicates that the data element cannot be calculated; * indicates the midpoint of a range.

2061 - CANE SUGAR EXCEPT REFINING

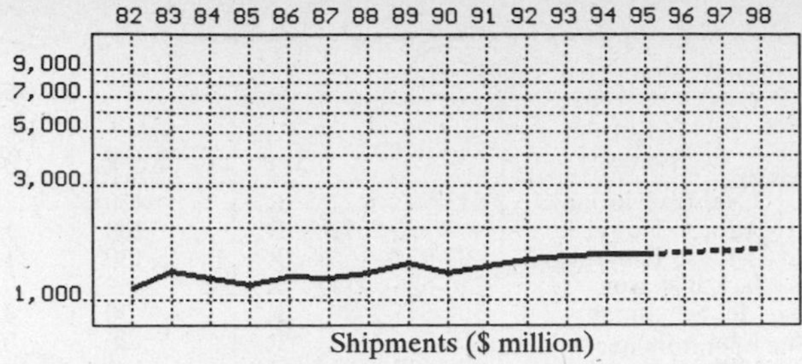

Shipments ($ million)

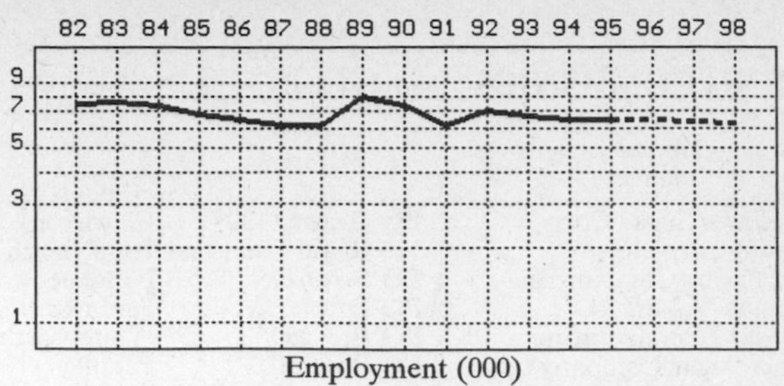

Employment (000)

GENERAL STATISTICS

Year	Com-panies	Establishments: Total	Establishments: with 20 or more employees	Employment: Total (000)	Employment: Production Workers (000)	Employment: Production Hours (Mil)	Compensation: Payroll ($ mil)	Compensation: Wages ($/hr)	Production ($ million): Cost of Materials	Production ($ million): Value Added by Manufacture	Production ($ million): Value of Shipments	Production ($ million): Capital Invest.
1982	43	51	44	7.5	5.8	13.1	133.8	7.67	755.8	297.7	1,113.9	89.6
1983		50	43	7.6	6.1	13.0	141.1	8.17	837.8	478.4	1,311.6	41.9
1984		49	42	7.4	5.8	12.8	143.2	8.31	791.2	449.8	1,232.5	48.7
1985		48	40	6.8	5.4	11.6	141.4	9.21	772.3	451.7	1,168.6	49.3
1986		50	40	6.4	5.0	11.3	141.3	9.35	789.6	429.6	1,244.0	34.0
1987	32	40	40	6.2	4.8	11.0	143.3	9.85	792.1	504.2	1,239.4	46.2
1988		52	43	6.2	4.8	11.0	148.7	10.17	815.1	493.6	1,287.1	36.0
1989		43	41	7.9	4.8	10.7	152.2	10.49	894.1	520.8	1,436.0	62.6
1990		43	41	7.3	4.6	10.2	156.2	11.00	785.0	502.0	1,295.6	82.3
1991		44	41	6.2	4.7	10.4	162.8	11.35	888.6	554.2	1,374.4	32.4
1992	37	45	41	7.0	5.1	11.7	175.8	10.96	887.6	561.9	1,459.8	59.3
1993		47	41	6.7	5.0	11.6	177.8	11.14	892.1	673.0	1,519.1	52.7
1994		43P	40P	6.4	4.7	10.9	185.9	12.03	889.1	662.4	1,562.7	42.2
1995		43P	40P	6.5P	4.4P	10.3P	182.2P	12.36P	876.3P	652.9P	1,540.2P	47.3P
1996		42P	40P	6.4P	4.3P	10.1P	186.2P	12.70P	893.7P	665.8P	1,570.8P	46.6P
1997		42P	40P	6.3P	4.2P	10.0P	190.2P	13.04P	911.1P	678.8P	1,601.3P	45.9P
1998		41P	40P	6.3P	4.1P	9.8P	194.2P	13.38P	928.4P	691.7P	1,631.8P	45.2P

Sources: 1982, 1987, 1992 *Economic Census*; *Annual Survey of Manufactures*, 83-86, 88-91, 93-94. Establishment counts for non-Census years are from *County Business Patterns*; establishment values for 83-84 are extrapolations. 'P's show projections by the editors. Industries reclassified in 87 will not have data for prior years.

INDICES OF CHANGE

Year	Com-panies	Establishments: Total	Establishments: with 20 or more employees	Employment: Total (000)	Employment: Production Workers (000)	Employment: Production Hours (Mil)	Compensation: Payroll ($ mil)	Compensation: Wages ($/hr)	Production ($ million): Cost of Materials	Production ($ million): Value Added by Manufacture	Production ($ million): Value of Shipments	Production ($ million): Capital Invest.
1982	116	113	107	107	114	112	76	70	85	53	76	151
1983		111	105	109	120	111	80	75	94	85	90	71
1984		109	102	106	114	109	81	76	89	80	84	82
1985		107	98	97	106	99	80	84	87	80	80	83
1986		111	98	91	98	97	80	85	89	76	85	57
1987	86	89	98	89	94	94	82	90	89	90	85	78
1988		116	105	89	94	94	85	93	92	88	88	61
1989		96	100	113	94	91	87	96	101	93	98	106
1990		96	100	104	90	87	89	100	88	89	89	139
1991		98	100	89	92	89	93	104	100	99	94	55
1992	100	100	100	100	100	100	100	100	100	100	100	100
1993		104	100	96	98	99	101	102	101	120	104	89
1994		96P	98P	91	92	93	106	110	100	118	107	71
1995		95P	98P	92P	87P	88P	104P	113P	99P	116P	106P	80P
1996		94P	98P	92P	85P	87P	106P	116P	101P	118P	108P	79P
1997		92P	97P	91P	83P	85P	108P	119P	103P	121P	110P	77P
1998		91P	97P	90P	81P	84P	110P	122P	105P	123P	112P	76P

Sources: Same as General Statistics. Values reflect change from the base year, 1992. Values above 100 mean greater than 92, values below 100 mean less than 92, and a value of 100 in the 82-91 or 93-98 period means same as 92. 'P's mark projections by the editors.

SELECTED RATIOS

For 1994	Avg. of All Manufact.	Analyzed Industry	Index
Employees per Establishment	49	148	302
Payroll per Establishment	1,500,273	4,299,019	287
Payroll per Employee	30,620	29,047	95
Production Workers per Establishment	34	109	317
Wages per Establishment	853,319	3,032,369	355
Wages per Production Worker	24,861	27,899	112
Hours per Production Worker	2,056	2,319	113
Wages per Hour	12.09	12.03	99
Value Added per Establishment	4,602,255	15,318,290	333
Value Added per Employee	93,930	103,500	110

For 1994	Avg. of All Manufact.	Analyzed Industry	Index
Value Added per Production Worker	134,084	140,936	105
Cost per Establishment	5,045,178	20,560,827	408
Cost per Employee	102,970	138,922	135
Cost per Production Worker	146,988	189,170	129
Shipments per Establishment	9,576,895	36,138,122	377
Shipments per Employee	195,460	244,172	125
Shipments per Production Worker	279,017	332,489	119
Investment per Establishment	321,011	975,893	304
Investment per Employee	6,552	6,594	101
Investment per Production Worker	9,352	8,979	96

Sources: Same as General Statistics. The 'Average of All Manufacturing' column represents the average of all manufacturing industries reported for the most recent complete year available. The Index shows the relationship between the Average and the Analyzed Industry. For example, 100 means that they are equal; 500 that the Analyzed Industry is five times the average; 50 means that the Analyzed Industry is half the national average. The abbreviation 'na' is used to show that data are 'not available'.

LEADING COMPANIES

Number shown: **15** Total sales ($ mil): **1,007** Total employment (000): **11.0**

Company Name	Address				CEO Name	Phone	Co. Type	Sales ($ mil)	Empl. (000)
United States Sugar Corp	PO Drawer 1207	Clewiston	FL	33440	J Nelson Fairbanks	813-983-8121	R	430•	2.7
Okleelanta Corp	316 Royal Poinciana	Palm Beach	FL	33480	Alfonso Fanjul Jr	407-996-9072	R	200	5.0
Osceola Farms Company Inc	PO Box 679	Pahokee	FL	33476	Alfonso Fanjul	407-924-7156	R	130	1.0
Rio Grande Val Sugar	PO Drawer A	Santa Rosa	TX	78593	Jack P Nelson	210-636-1411	R	63	0.6
Cora-Texas Manufacturing	PO Box 280	White Castle	LA	70788	Mel Schudmak	504-545-3679	R	30	0.1
Hamakua Sugar Company Inc	PO Box 250	Paauilo	HI	96776	John T Goss	808-776-1511	R	25	0.4
Waialua Sugar Company Inc	PO Box 665	Waialua	HI	96791	Michael F O'Brien	808-637-3521	S	22	0.4
Cajun Sugar Cooperative Inc	PO Box 13940	New Iberia	LA	70562	Felix Blanchard	318-365-3401	R	20	<0.1
Louisiana Sugar Cane Coop	6092 Resweber Hwy	St Martinville	LA	70582	Jackie Theriot	318-394-3255	R	20•	0.1
Iberia Sugar Cooperative Inc	PO Box 11108	New Iberia	LA	70562	Malcolm Viator	318-364-0628	R	16	<0.1
Savoie Industries Inc	PO Box 69	Belle Rose	LA	70341	Patrick Cancienne	504-473-9293	R	15	0.1
MA Patout and Son Ltd	3512 J Patout Burns	Jeanerette	LA	70544	William S Patout III	318-276-4592	R	13•	0.1
St James Sugar Cooperative Inc	PO Box 67	St James	LA	70086	F Neil Bolton	504-265-4056	R	10•	<0.1
Glenwood Cooperative Inc	PO Box 545	Napoleonville	LA	70390	R Blanchard	504-369-2941	R	8•	<0.1
Caire and Graugnard	PO Box 7	Edgard	LA	70049	JB Graugnard	504-497-3351	R	5	0.2

Source: *Ward's Business Directory of U.S. Private and Public Companies*, Volumes 1 and 2, 1996. The company type code used is as follows: P - Public, R - Private, S - Subsidiary, D - Division, J - Joint Venture, A - Affiliate, G - Group. Sales are in millions of dollars, employees are in thousands. An asterisk (•) indicates an estimated sales volume. The symbol < stands for 'less than'. Company names and addresses are truncated, in some cases, to fit into the available space.

MATERIALS CONSUMED

Material		Quantity	Delivered Cost ($ million)
Materials, ingredients, containers, and supplies		(X)	838.6
Sugar cane	1,000 s tons	23,984.2	771.7
All other materials and components, parts, containers, and supplies		(X)	63.0
Materials, ingredients, containers, and supplies, nsk		(X)	3.8

Source: 1992 *Economic Census*. Explanation of symbols used: (D): Withheld to avoid disclosure of competitive data; na: Not available; (S): Withheld because statistical norms were not met; (X): Not applicable; (Z): Less than half the unit shown; nec: Not elsewhere classified; nsk: Not specified by kind; - : zero; * : 10-19 percent estimated; ** : 20-29 percent estimated.

PRODUCT SHARE DETAILS

Product or Product Class	% Share	Product or Product Class	% Share
Raw cane sugar	100.00	Sugarcane molasses and syrup, including cane blackstrap	4.84
Raw cane sugar	93.83		

Source: 1992 *Economic Census*. The values shown are percent of total shipments in an industry. Values of indented subcategories are summed in the main heading. The symbol (D) appears when data are withheld to prevent disclosure of competitive information. The abbreviation nsk stands for 'not specified by kind' and nec for 'not elsewhere classified'.

INPUTS AND OUTPUTS FOR SUGAR

Economic Sector or Industry Providing Inputs	%	Sector	Economic Sector or Industry Buying Outputs	%	Sector
Sugar	32.7	Manufg.	Sugar	27.3	Manufg.
Sugar crops	26.4	Agric.	Personal consumption expenditures	19.9	
Imports	18.3	Foreign	Bottled & canned soft drinks	8.8	Manufg.
Wholesale trade	4.5	Trade	Confectionery products	4.3	Manufg.
Gas production & distribution (utilities)	4.2	Util.	Flavoring extracts & syrups, nec	4.3	Manufg.
Motor freight transportation & warehousing	2.7	Util.	Eating & drinking places	3.5	Trade
Paperboard containers & boxes	1.5	Manufg.	Bread, cake, & related products	2.7	Manufg.
Petroleum refining	1.1	Manufg.	Food preparations, nec	2.6	Manufg.
Railroads & related services	1.0	Util.	Chocolate & cocoa products	2.3	Manufg.
Water transportation	1.0	Util.	Cookies & crackers	2.2	Manufg.
Miscellaneous plastics products	0.9	Manufg.	Cereal breakfast foods	2.1	Manufg.
Commercial printing	0.6	Manufg.	Federal Government purchases, nondefense	2.1	Fed Govt
Cyclic crudes and organics	0.6	Manufg.	Canned fruits & vegetables	1.8	Manufg.
Electric services (utilities)	0.6	Util.	Exports	1.8	Foreign
Advertising	0.6	Services	Blended & prepared flour	1.7	Manufg.
Banking	0.4	Fin/R.E.	Fluid milk	1.7	Manufg.
Water supply & sewage systems	0.3	Util.	Prepared feeds, nec	1.6	Manufg.
Coal	0.2	Mining	Ice cream & frozen desserts	1.5	Manufg.
Maintenance of nonfarm buildings nec	0.2	Constr.	Meat animals	1.1	Agric.
Communications, except radio & TV	0.2	Util.	Frozen specialties	0.7	Manufg.
Eating & drinking places	0.2	Trade	Pickles, sauces, & salad dressings	0.7	Manufg.
Equipment rental & leasing services	0.2	Services	Dairy farm products	0.6	Agric.
Sanitary services, steam supply, irrigation	0.1	Util.	Condensed & evaporated milk	0.6	Manufg.

Continued on next page.

INPUTS AND OUTPUTS FOR SUGAR - Continued

Economic Sector or Industry Providing Inputs	%	Sector	Economic Sector or Industry Buying Outputs	%	Sector
Miscellaneous repair shops	0.1	Services	Flour & other grain mill products	0.6	Manufg.
			Malt beverages	0.6	Manufg.
			Chewing gum	0.5	Manufg.
			Canned specialties	0.4	Manufg.
			Frozen fruits, fruit juices & vegetables	0.4	Manufg.
			S/L Govt. purch., elem. & secondary education	0.4	S/L Govt
			Hospitals	0.2	Services
			Dehydrated food products	0.1	Manufg.
			Residential care	0.1	Services
			S/L Govt. purch., health & hospitals	0.1	S/L Govt

Source: Benchmark Input-Output Accounts for the U.S. Economy, 1982, U.S. Department of Commerce, Washington, D.C., July 1991. Data, as reported in the source, are organized by the 1977 SIC structure in use in 1982 but have been matched, as closely as is possible, to the 1987 SIC structure used in this book.

OCCUPATIONS EMPLOYED BY SIC 206 - SUGAR AND CONFECTIONERY PRODUCTS

Occupation	% of Total 1994	Change to 2005	Occupation	% of Total 1994	Change to 2005
Packaging & filling machine operators	12.1	31.8	Cooking, roasting machine operators	2.0	-17.6
Hand packers & packagers	8.9	-24.7	Industrial truck & tractor operators	1.9	-12.1
Precision food & tobacco workers nec	8.4	0.7	General managers & top executives	1.5	-16.6
Helpers, laborers, & material movers nec	6.9	-12.1	Salespersons, retail	1.5	-12.1
Blue collar worker supervisors	4.4	-14.1	Agricultural workers nec	1.4	-12.1
Industrial machinery mechanics	4.0	-3.3	Machine operators nec	1.4	-22.5
Freight, stock, & material movers, hand	3.1	-29.7	Secretaries, ex legal & medical	1.3	-20.0
Janitors & cleaners, incl maids	3.1	-29.7	Assemblers, fabricators, & hand workers nec	1.2	-12.0
Extruding & forming machine workers	3.0	-12.1	Truck drivers light & heavy	1.1	-9.4
Maintenance repairers, general utility	2.3	-20.9	Traffic, shipping, & receiving clerks	1.1	-15.4
Machine feeders & offbearers	2.2	-20.9	Electricians	1.0	-17.5

Source: Industry-Occupation Matrix, Bureau of Labor Statistics. These data relate to one or more 3-digit SIC industry groups rather than to a single 4-digit SIC. The change reported for each occupation to the year 2005 is a percent of growth or decline as estimated by the Bureau of Labor Statistics. The abbreviation nec stands for 'not elsewhere classified'.

LOCATION BY STATE AND REGIONAL CONCENTRATION

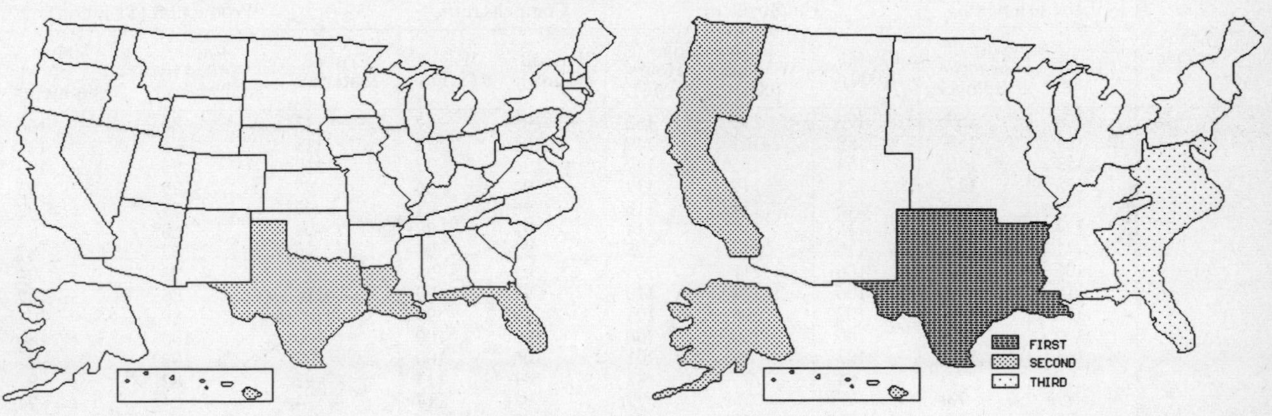

INDUSTRY DATA BY STATE

State	Establish-ments	Shipments			Employment				Cost as % of Shipments	Investment per Employee ($)
		Total ($ mil)	% of U.S.	Per Establ.	Total Number	% of U.S.	Per Establ.	Wages ($/hour)		
Florida	7	777.2	53.2	111.0	2,400	34.3	343	13.29	63.5	8,750
Louisiana	25	365.0	25.0	14.6	1,700	24.3	68	8.71	69.5	11,941
Hawaii	11	(D)	-	-	1,750 *	25.0	159	-	-	-
Texas	1	(D)	-	-	750 *	10.7	750	-	-	-

Source: 1992 *Economic Census*. The states are in descending order of shipments or establishments (if shipment data are missing for the majority). The symbol (D) appears when data are withheld to prevent disclosure of competitive information. States marked with (D) are sorted by number of establishments. A dash (-) indicates that the data element cannot be calculated; * indicates the midpoint of a range.

2062 - CANE SUGAR REFINING

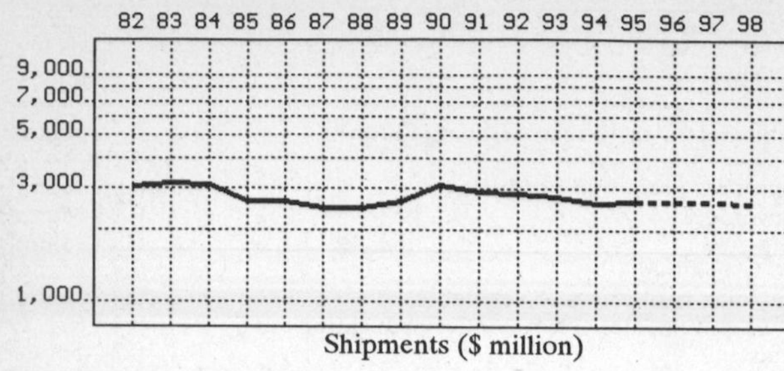

Shipments ($ million)

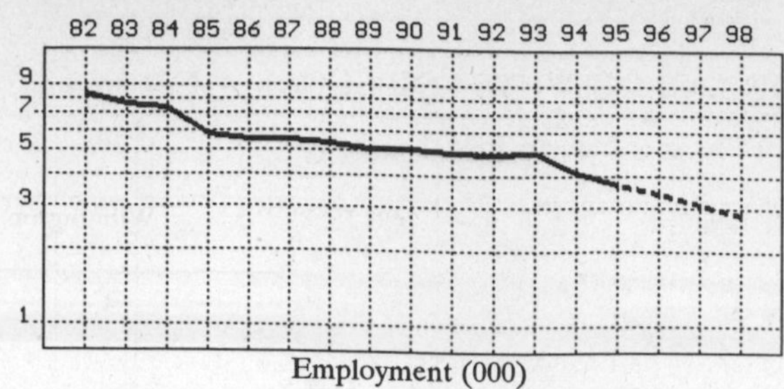

Employment (000)

GENERAL STATISTICS

Year	Companies	Establishments		Employment			Compensation		Production ($ million)			
		Total	with 20 or more employees	Total (000)	Production Workers (000)	Production Hours (Mil)	Payroll ($ mil)	Wages ($/hr)	Cost of Materials	Value Added by Manufacture	Value of Shipments	Capital Invest.
1982	19	30	25	8.3	6.2	12.8	197.2	10.90	2,424.9	622.4	3,040.3	69.2
1983		28	23	7.6	5.8	11.8	195.1	11.98	2,512.6	631.3	3,145.1	51.9
1984		26	21	7.4	5.6	11.6	198.1	12.59	2,538.3	536.4	3,081.0	69.5
1985		23	19	5.8	4.3	9.4	175.8	14.13	2,029.4	583.5	2,616.4	41.0
1986		23	18	5.5	4.1	9.2	179.3	14.45	2,063.8	551.2	2,604.9	34.9
1987	14	21	16	5.5	4.2	9.0	177.4	14.49	2,002.8	445.4	2,460.2	32.7
1988		24	15	5.3	4.1	8.3	171.7	15.71	2,058.4	422.2	2,458.4	33.1
1989		18	15	5.1	4.0	8.3	170.7	16.04	2,124.5	534.9	2,641.9	42.3
1990		20	15	5.1	4.1	8.7	181.5	16.41	2,438.8	659.7	3,075.3	45.0
1991		20	15	4.9	3.9	8.3	186.0	16.24	2,284.4	654.9	2,925.9	50.3
1992	12	17	15	4.8	3.6	7.9	187.5	16.38	2,138.2	737.2	2,822.9	56.3
1993		20	15	4.9	3.5	8.0	198.0	16.34	1,994.5	757.1	2,769.5	31.9
1994		16P	12P	4.1	2.7	6.5	188.9	18.75	1,969.0	607.4	2,592.7	78.2
1995		15P	11P	3.7P	2.7P	6.3P	183.3P	18.64P	2,013.2P	621.0P	2,650.9P	47.4P
1996		14P	10P	3.4P	2.5P	5.8P	183.0P	19.17P	1,998.4P	616.5P	2,631.4P	47.1P
1997		13P	9P	3.1P	2.2P	5.4P	182.7P	19.69P	1,983.6P	611.9P	2,612.0P	46.9P
1998		12P	8P	2.8P	2.0P	5.0P	182.5P	20.22P	1,968.8P	607.4P	2,592.5P	46.7P

Sources: 1982, 1987, 1992 *Economic Census*; *Annual Survey of Manufactures*, 83-86, 88-91, 93-94. Establishment counts for non-Census years are from *County Business Patterns*; establishment values for 83-84 are extrapolations. 'P's show projections by the editors. Industries reclassified in 87 will not have data for prior years.

INDICES OF CHANGE

Year	Companies	Establishments		Employment			Compensation		Production ($ million)			
		Total	with 20 or more employees	Total (000)	Production Workers (000)	Production Hours (Mil)	Payroll ($ mil)	Wages ($/hr)	Cost of Materials	Value Added by Manufacture	Value of Shipments	Capital Invest.
1982	158	176	167	173	172	162	105	67	113	84	108	123
1983		165	153	158	161	149	104	73	118	86	111	92
1984		153	140	154	156	147	106	77	119	73	109	123
1985		135	127	121	119	119	94	86	95	79	93	73
1986		135	120	115	114	116	96	88	97	75	92	62
1987	117	124	107	115	117	114	95	88	94	60	87	58
1988		141	100	110	114	105	92	96	96	57	87	59
1989		106	100	106	111	105	91	98	99	73	94	75
1990		118	100	106	114	110	97	100	114	89	109	80
1991		118	100	102	108	105	99	99	107	89	104	89
1992	100	100	100	100	100	100	100	100	100	100	100	100
1993		118	100	102	97	101	106	100	93	103	98	57
1994		95P	79P	85	75	82	101	114	92	82	92	139
1995		89P	73P	77P	75P	79P	98P	114P	94P	84P	94P	84P
1996		84P	67P	71P	69P	74P	98P	117P	93P	84P	93P	84P
1997		78P	62P	64P	62P	69P	97P	120P	93P	83P	93P	83P
1998		72P	56P	58P	56P	63P	97P	123P	92P	82P	92P	83P

Sources: Same as General Statistics. Values reflect change from the base year, 1992. Values above 100 mean greater than 92, values below 100 mean less than 92, and a value of 100 in the 82-91 or 93-98 period means same as 92. 'P's mark projections by the editors.

SELECTED RATIOS

For 1994	Avg. of All Manufact.	Analyzed Industry	Index
Employees per Establishment	49	253	517
Payroll per Establishment	1,500,273	11,673,596	778
Payroll per Employee	30,620	46,073	150
Production Workers per Establishment	34	167	486
Wages per Establishment	853,319	7,531,601	883
Wages per Production Worker	24,861	45,139	182
Hours per Production Worker	2,056	2,407	117
Wages per Hour	12.09	18.75	155
Value Added per Establishment	4,602,255	37,535,955	816
Value Added per Employee	93,930	148,146	158

For 1994	Avg. of All Manufact.	Analyzed Industry	Index
Value Added per Production Worker	134,084	224,963	168
Cost per Establishment	5,045,178	121,679,775	2,412
Cost per Employee	102,970	480,244	466
Cost per Production Worker	146,988	729,259	496
Shipments per Establishment	9,576,895	160,223,034	1,673
Shipments per Employee	195,460	632,366	324
Shipments per Production Worker	279,017	960,259	344
Investment per Establishment	321,011	4,832,584	1,505
Investment per Employee	6,552	19,073	291
Investment per Production Worker	9,352	28,963	310

Sources: Same as General Statistics. The 'Average of All Manufacturing' column represents the average of all manufacturing industries reported for the most recent complete year available. The Index shows the relationship between the Average and the Analyzed Industry. For example, 100 means that they are equal; 500 that the Analyzed Industry is five times the average; 50 means that the Analyzed Industry is half the national average. The abbreviation 'na' is used to show that data are 'not available'.

LEADING COMPANIES

Number shown: 9 Total sales ($ mil): **4,361** Total employment (000): **14.3**

Company Name	Address				CEO Name	Phone	Co. Type	Sales ($ mil)	Empl. (000)
Tate and Lyle Inc	1403 Foulk Rd	Wilmington	DE	19803		302-478-4773	S	1,280*	8.0
Savannah Foods and Industries	PO Box 339	Savannah	GA	31402	W W Sprague Jr	912-234-1261	P	1,074	2.1
Domino Sugar Corp	1114 Av of the	New York	NY	10036	Ed Makin	212-789-9700	S	690*	1.7
Imperial Holly Corp	PO Box 9	Sugar Land	TX	77487	James C Kempner	713-491-9181	P	587	1.5
Refined Sugars Inc	1 Federal St	Yonkers	NY	10702	Gregory J Hoskins	914-963-2400	R	450	<0.1
Colonial Sugars Inc	PO Box 3360	Gramercy	LA	70052	Jean de Chazal	504-869-5521	S	200*	0.4
Griffin Entities Inc	PO Box 1928	Muskogee	OK	74401	John W Griffin	918-687-6311	R	64	0.4
Caldwell Sugar Cooperative Inc	PO Box 5538	Thibodaux	LA	70302	Roland Talbot	504-447-4023	R	13	0.1
Griffin Food Co	PO Box 1928	Muskogee	OK	74402	John W Griffin	918-687-6311	S	3*	<0.1

Source: *Ward's Business Directory of U.S. Private and Public Companies*, Volumes 1 and 2, 1996. The company type code used is as follows: P - Public, R - Private, S - Subsidiary, D - Division, J - Joint Venture, A - Affiliate, G - Group. Sales are in millions of dollars, employees are in thousands. An asterisk (*) indicates an estimated sales volume. The symbol < stands for 'less than'. Company names and addresses are truncated, in some cases, to fit into the available space.

MATERIALS CONSUMED

Material		Quantity	Delivered Cost ($ million)
Materials, ingredients, containers, and supplies		(X)	2,059.8
Raw cane sugar (converted to 96 degree basis)	1,000 s tons	4,664.3*	1,869.9
Paperboard containers, boxes, and corrugated paperboard		(X)	(D)
Packaging paper and plastics film, coated and laminated		(X)	32.1
Bags; plastics, foil, and coated paper		(X)	(D)
Bags; uncoated paper and multiwall		(X)	(D)
All other materials and components, parts, containers, and supplies		(X)	115.8
Materials, ingredients, containers, and supplies, nsk		(X)	4.6

Source: 1992 *Economic Census*. Explanation of symbols used: (D): Withheld to avoid disclosure of competitive data; na: Not available; (S): Withheld because statistical norms were not met; (X): Not applicable; (Z): Less than half the unit shown; nec: Not elsewhere classified; nsk: Not specified by kind; - : zero; * : 10-19 percent estimated; ** : 20-29 percent estimated.

PRODUCT SHARE DETAILS

Product or Product Class	% Share	Product or Product Class	% Share
Cane sugar refining	100.00	Soft or brown, containers of 10 lb or less	2.78
Granulated, small paper packets	1.02	Soft or brown, containers of more than 10 lb	2.48
Granulated, cartons and sacks of 25 lb or less	32.33	Liquid sugar or sugar syrup, sucrose type	5.55
Granulated, bags and other containers more than 25 lb	21.95	Liquid sugar or sugar syrup, invert and/or partially invert type	1.55
Granulated, shipped in rail cars, trucks, or bins	23.94	Other cane sugar refining products and byproducts, including refiners' blackstrap and syrup	1.25
Confectioners' powdered, containers 10 lb or less	2.34		
Confectioners' powdered, containers of more than 10 lb	4.30		

Source: 1992 *Economic Census*. The values shown are percent of total shipments in an industry. Values of indented subcategories are summed in the main heading. The symbol (D) appears when data are withheld to prevent disclosure of competitive information. The abbreviation nsk stands for 'not specified by kind' and nec for 'not elsewhere classified'.

INPUTS AND OUTPUTS FOR SUGAR

Economic Sector or Industry Providing Inputs	%	Sector	Economic Sector or Industry Buying Outputs	%	Sector
Sugar	32.7	Manufg.	Sugar	27.3	Manufg.
Sugar crops	26.4	Agric.	Personal consumption expenditures	19.9	
Imports	18.3	Foreign	Bottled & canned soft drinks	8.8	Manufg.
Wholesale trade	4.5	Trade	Confectionery products	4.3	Manufg.
Gas production & distribution (utilities)	4.2	Util.	Flavoring extracts & syrups, nec	4.3	Manufg.
Motor freight transportation & warehousing	2.7	Util.	Eating & drinking places	3.5	Trade
Paperboard containers & boxes	1.5	Manufg.	Bread, cake, & related products	2.7	Manufg.
Petroleum refining	1.1	Manufg.	Food preparations, nec	2.6	Manufg.
Railroads & related services	1.0	Util.	Chocolate & cocoa products	2.3	Manufg.
Water transportation	1.0	Util.	Cookies & crackers	2.2	Manufg.
Miscellaneous plastics products	0.9	Manufg.	Cereal breakfast foods	2.1	Manufg.
Commercial printing	0.6	Manufg.	Federal Government purchases, nondefense	2.1	Fed Govt
Cyclic crudes and organics	0.6	Manufg.	Canned fruits & vegetables	1.8	Manufg.
Electric services (utilities)	0.6	Util.	Exports	1.8	Foreign
Advertising	0.6	Services	Blended & prepared flour	1.7	Manufg.
Banking	0.4	Fin/R.E.	Fluid milk	1.7	Manufg.
Water supply & sewage systems	0.3	Util.	Prepared feeds, nec	1.6	Manufg.
Coal	0.2	Mining	Ice cream & frozen desserts	1.5	Manufg.
Maintenance of nonfarm buildings nec	0.2	Constr.	Meat animals	1.1	Agric.
Communications, except radio & TV	0.2	Util.	Frozen specialties	0.7	Manufg.

Continued on next page.

INPUTS AND OUTPUTS FOR SUGAR - Continued

Economic Sector or Industry Providing Inputs	%	Sector	Economic Sector or Industry Buying Outputs	%	Sector
Eating & drinking places	0.2	Trade	Pickles, sauces, & salad dressings	0.7	Manufg.
Equipment rental & leasing services	0.2	Services	Dairy farm products	0.6	Agric.
Sanitary services, steam supply, irrigation	0.1	Util.	Condensed & evaporated milk	0.6	Manufg.
Miscellaneous repair shops	0.1	Services	Flour & other grain mill products	0.6	Manufg.
			Malt beverages	0.6	Manufg.
			Chewing gum	0.5	Manufg.
			Canned specialties	0.4	Manufg.
			Frozen fruits, fruit juices & vegetables	0.4	Manufg.
			S/L Govt. purch., elem. & secondary education	0.4	S/L Govt
			Hospitals	0.2	Services
			Dehydrated food products	0.1	Manufg.
			Residential care	0.1	Services
			S/L Govt. purch., health & hospitals	0.1	S/L Govt

Source: Benchmark Input-Output Accounts for the U.S. Economy, 1982, U.S. Department of Commerce, Washington, D.C., July 1991. Data, as reported in the source, are organized by the 1977 SIC structure in use in 1982 but have been matched, as closely as is possible, to the 1987 SIC structure used in this book.

OCCUPATIONS EMPLOYED BY SIC 206 - SUGAR AND CONFECTIONERY PRODUCTS

Occupation	% of Total 1994	Change to 2005	Occupation	% of Total 1994	Change to 2005
Packaging & filling machine operators	12.1	31.8	Cooking, roasting machine operators	2.0	-17.6
Hand packers & packagers	8.9	-24.7	Industrial truck & tractor operators	1.9	-12.1
Precision food & tobacco workers nec	8.4	0.7	General managers & top executives	1.5	-16.6
Helpers, laborers, & material movers nec	6.9	-12.1	Salespersons, retail	1.5	-12.1
Blue collar worker supervisors	4.4	-14.1	Agricultural workers nec	1.4	-12.1
Industrial machinery mechanics	4.0	-3.3	Machine operators nec	1.4	-22.5
Freight, stock, & material movers, hand	3.1	-29.7	Secretaries, ex legal & medical	1.3	-20.0
Janitors & cleaners, incl maids	3.1	-29.7	Assemblers, fabricators, & hand workers nec	1.2	-12.0
Extruding & forming machine workers	3.0	-12.1	Truck drivers light & heavy	1.1	-9.4
Maintenance repairers, general utility	2.3	-20.9	Traffic, shipping, & receiving clerks	1.1	-15.4
Machine feeders & offbearers	2.2	-20.9	Electricians	1.0	-17.5

Source: Industry-Occupation Matrix, Bureau of Labor Statistics. These data relate to one or more 3-digit SIC industry groups rather than to a single 4-digit SIC. The change reported for each occupation to the year 2005 is a percent of growth or decline as estimated by the Bureau of Labor Statistics. The abbreviation nec stands for 'not elsewhere classified'.

LOCATION BY STATE AND REGIONAL CONCENTRATION

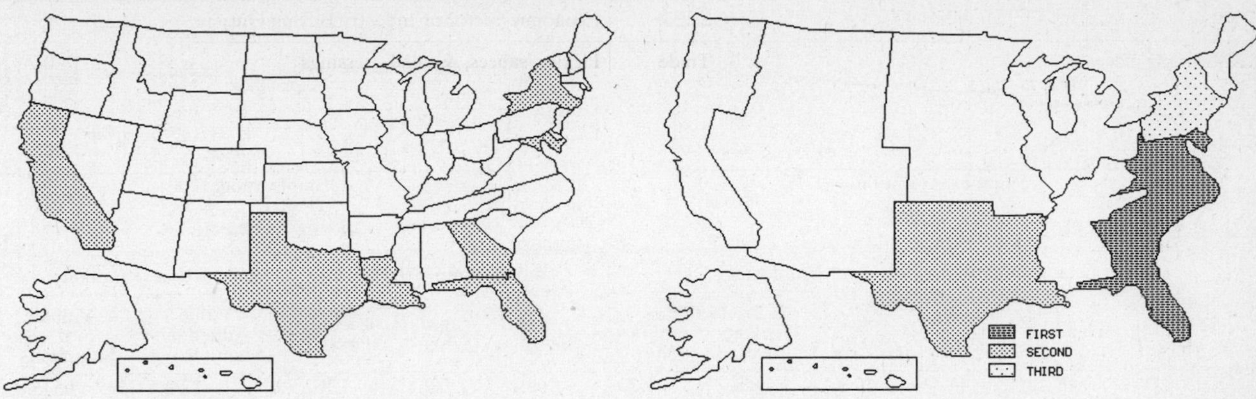

INDUSTRY DATA BY STATE

State	Establish-ments	Shipments			Employment				Cost as % of Shipments	Investment per Employee ($)
		Total ($ mil)	% of U.S.	Per Establ.	Total Number	% of U.S.	Per Establ.	Wages ($/hour)		
Louisiana	3	587.6	20.8	195.9	1,000	20.8	333	14.59	72.5	-
Florida	3	(D)	-	-	175 *	3.6	58	-	-	10,286
Georgia	2	(D)	-	-	750 *	15.6	375	-	-	-
New York	2	(D)	-	-	750 *	15.6	375	-	-	-
California	1	(D)	-	-	750 *	15.6	750	-	-	-
Maryland	1	(D)	-	-	750 *	15.6	750	-	-	-
Texas	1	(D)	-	-	750 *	15.6	750	-	-	-

Source: 1992 *Economic Census*. The states are in descending order of shipments or establishments (if shipment data are missing for the majority). The symbol (D) appears when data are withheld to prevent disclosure of competitive information. States marked with (D) are sorted by number of establishments. A dash (-) indicates that the data element cannot be calculated; * indicates the midpoint of a range.

2063 - BEET SUGAR

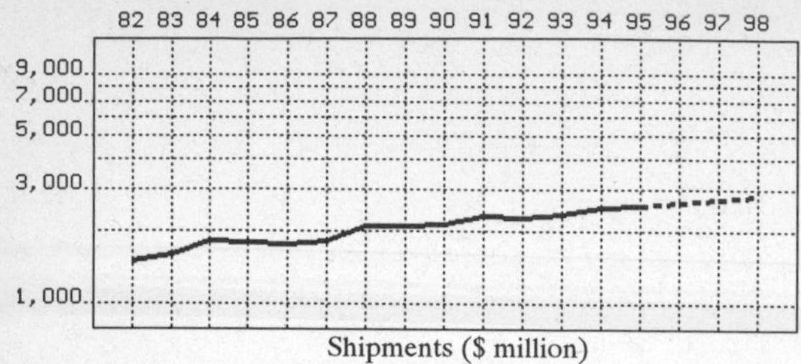

Shipments ($ million)

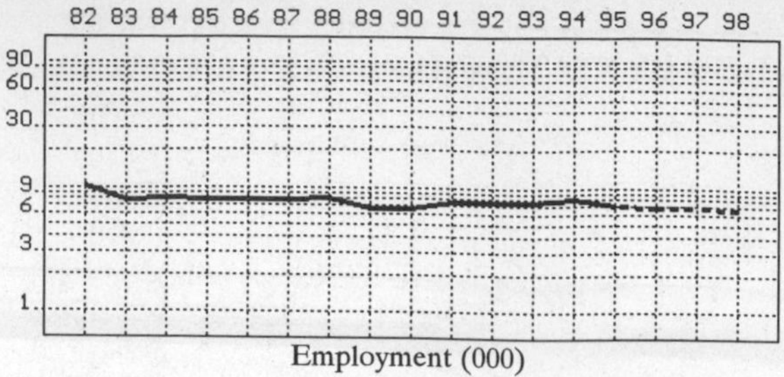

Employment (000)

GENERAL STATISTICS

Year	Companies	Establishments		Employment			Compensation		Production ($ million)			
		Total	with 20 or more employees	Total (000)	Production Workers (000)	Production Hours (Mil)	Payroll ($ mil)	Wages ($/hr)	Cost of Materials	Value Added by Manufacture	Value of Shipments	Capital Invest.
1982	14	48	44	10.3	8.8	17.3	169.4	7.88	1,102.5	432.2	1,515.8	32.8
1983		47	42	7.8	6.6	14.3	155.1	8.71	1,087.1	530.9	1,584.7	27.9
1984		46	40	8.2	7.0	14.7	168.4	9.16	1,232.1	659.6	1,835.1	62.5
1985		46	37	7.9	6.6	14.7	180.6	9.71	1,203.3	524.3	1,788.8	85.3
1986		46	39	7.9	6.5	14.6	186.2	9.96	1,145.6	665.3	1,757.7	88.3
1987	14	42	38	7.9	6.6	14.4	190.1	10.49	1,277.0	613.2	1,831.5	42.5
1988		42	38	8.0	6.7	14.4	195.8	10.60	1,365.8	685.2	2,093.4	46.4
1989		40	36	6.7	6.9	14.2	193.9	11.12	1,295.4	798.1	2,096.8	60.5
1990		38	36	6.7	6.5	14.1	197.6	11.22	1,342.2	828.8	2,139.9	55.0
1991		37	36	7.6	6.5	13.9	209.5	11.69	1,534.7	791.2	2,330.7	108.1
1992	13	40	37	7.6	6.6	14.3	220.2	12.13	1,559.3	799.7	2,282.0	96.5
1993		39	37	7.6	6.6	14.1	227.5	13.10	1,603.8	765.3	2,359.1	127.2
1994		36P	35P	8.1	7.1	15.7	241.6	12.61	1,732.1	752.9	2,516.0	117.7
1995		35P	34P	7.1P	6.4P	14.1P	238.0P	13.39P	1,762.9P	766.3P	2,560.7P	117.8P
1996		34P	33P	6.9P	6.3P	14.0P	244.1P	13.78P	1,817.1P	789.8P	2,639.4P	124.2P
1997		33P	33P	6.8P	6.3P	13.9P	250.2P	14.17P	1,871.2P	813.4P	2,718.1P	130.6P
1998		32P	32P	6.7P	6.2P	13.8P	256.4P	14.56P	1,925.4P	836.9P	2,796.7P	137.0P

Sources: 1982, 1987, 1992 *Economic Census*; *Annual Survey of Manufactures*, 83-86, 88-91, 93-94. Establishment counts for non-Census years are from *County Business Patterns*; establishment values for 83-84 are extrapolations. 'P's show projections by the editors. Industries reclassified in 87 will not have data for prior years.

INDICES OF CHANGE

Year	Companies	Establishments		Employment			Compensation		Production ($ million)			
		Total	with 20 or more employees	Total (000)	Production Workers (000)	Production Hours (Mil)	Payroll ($ mil)	Wages ($/hr)	Cost of Materials	Value Added by Manufacture	Value of Shipments	Capital Invest.
1982	108	120	119	136	133	121	77	65	71	54	66	34
1983		117	114	103	100	100	70	72	70	66	69	29
1984		115	108	108	106	103	76	76	79	82	80	65
1985		115	100	104	100	103	82	80	77	66	78	88
1986		115	105	104	98	102	85	82	73	83	77	92
1987	108	105	103	104	100	101	86	86	82	77	80	44
1988		105	103	105	102	101	89	87	88	86	92	48
1989		100	97	88	105	99	88	92	83	100	92	63
1990		95	97	88	98	99	90	92	86	104	94	57
1991		93	97	100	98	97	95	96	98	99	102	112
1992	100	100	100	100	100	100	100	100	100	100	100	100
1993		98	100	100	100	99	103	108	103	96	103	132
1994		90P	94P	107	108	110	110	104	111	94	110	122
1995		88P	92P	93P	97P	98P	108P	110P	113P	96P	112P	122P
1996		85P	90P	91P	96P	98P	111P	114P	117P	99P	116P	129P
1997		83P	89P	90P	95P	97P	114P	117P	120P	102P	119P	135P
1998		80P	87P	88P	94P	97P	116P	120P	123P	105P	123P	142P

Sources: Same as General Statistics. Values reflect change from the base year, 1992. Values above 100 mean greater than 92, values below 100 mean less than 92, and a value of 100 in the 82-91 or 93-98 period means same as 92. 'P's mark projections by the editors.

SELECTED RATIOS

For 1994	Avg. of All Manufact.	Analyzed Industry	Index	For 1994	Avg. of All Manufact.	Analyzed Industry	Index
Employees per Establishment	49	224	457	Value Added per Production Worker	134,084	106,042	79
Payroll per Establishment	1,500,273	6,682,984	445	Cost per Establishment	5,045,178	47,912,238	950
Payroll per Employee	30,620	29,827	97	Cost per Employee	102,970	213,840	208
Production Workers per Establishment	34	196	572	Cost per Production Worker	146,988	243,958	166
Wages per Establishment	853,319	5,476,313	642	Shipments per Establishment	9,576,895	69,595,977	727
Wages per Production Worker	24,861	27,884	112	Shipments per Employee	195,460	310,617	159
Hours per Production Worker	2,056	2,211	108	Shipments per Production Worker	279,017	354,366	127
Wages per Hour	12.09	12.61	104	Investment per Establishment	321,011	3,255,742	1,014
Value Added per Establishment	4,602,255	20,826,236	453	Investment per Employee	6,552	14,531	222
Value Added per Employee	93,930	92,951	99	Investment per Production Worker	9,352	16,577	177

Sources: Same as General Statistics. The 'Average of All Manufacturing' column represents the average of all manufacturing industries reported for the most recent complete year available. The Index shows the relationship between the Average and the Analyzed Industry. For example, 100 means that they are equal; 500 that the Analyzed Industry is five times the average; 50 means that the Analyzed Industry is half the national average. The abbreviation 'na' is used to show that data are 'not available'.

LEADING COMPANIES

Number shown: **12** Total sales ($ mil): **4,007** Total employment (000): **22.0**

Company Name	Address				CEO Name	Phone	Co. Type	Sales ($ mil)	Empl. (000)
Valhi Inc	5430 LBJ Fwy	Dallas	TX	75240	Harold C Simmons	214-233-1700	P	812	3.1
Contran Corp	5430 LBJ Fwy	Dallas	TX	75240	Harold C Simmons	214-233-1700	R	781	7.5
Holly Sugar Corp	PO Box 1052	Co Springs	CO	80901	Roger W Hill	719-471-0123	S	460*	1.2
Amalgamated Sugar Co	PO Box 1520	Ogden	UT	84402	Allan M Lipman Jr	801-399-3431	S	431	2.2
Spreckels Industries Inc	4234 Hacienda Dr	Pleasanton	CA	94588	Bart A Brown Jr	510-460-0840	P	379	2.2
Michigan Sugar Co	PO Box 1348	Saginaw	MI	48605	David H Roche	517-799-7300	S	350*	0.7
American Crystal Sugar Co	101 N 3rd St	Moorhead	MN	56560	Joseph Famalette	218-236-4400	R	320*	2.0
Spreckels Sugar Company Inc	PO Box 8025	Pleasanton	CA	94588	David E Dennehy	510-463-3400	S	205	1.1
Minn-Dak Farmers Cooperative	7525 Red River Rd	Wahpeton	ND	58075	LD Steward	701-642-8411	R	93	0.5
Monitor Sugar Co	2600 S Euclid Av	Bay City	MI	48707	Robert L Hetzler	517-686-0161	S	75*	0.7
S Min Beet Sugar	PO Box 500	Renville	MN	56284	Irvin Zitterkopf	612-329-8305	R	69	0.5
Holly Sugar Corp	PO Box 700	Torrington	WY	82240	Alan Hutsinpiller	307-532-7141	D	32	0.4

Source: *Ward's Business Directory of U.S. Private and Public Companies*, Volumes 1 and 2, 1996. The company type code used is as follows: P - Public, R - Private, S - Subsidiary, D - Division, J - Joint Venture, A - Affiliate, G - Group. Sales are in millions of dollars, employees are in thousands. An asterisk (*) indicates an estimated sales volume. The symbol < stands for 'less than'. Company names and addresses are truncated, in some cases, to fit into the available space.

MATERIALS CONSUMED

Material		Quantity	Delivered Cost ($ million)
Materials, ingredients, containers, and supplies		(X)	1,390.3
Sugar beets	1,000 s tons	27,617.7	1,188.1
Paperboard containers, boxes, and corrugated paperboard		(X)	7.6
Packaging paper and plastics film, coated and laminated		(X)	7.2
Bags; plastics, foil, and coated paper		(X)	(D)
Bags; uncoated paper and multiwall		(X)	(D)
All other materials and components, parts, containers, and supplies		(X)	178.5

Source: 1992 *Economic Census*. Explanation of symbols used: (D): Withheld to avoid disclosure of competitive data; na: Not available; (S): Withheld because statistical norms were not met; (X): Not applicable; (Z): Less than half the unit shown; nec: Not elsewhere classified; nsk: Not specified by kind; - : zero; * : 10-19 percent estimated; ** : 20-29 percent estimated.

PRODUCT SHARE DETAILS

Product or Product Class	% Share	Product or Product Class	% Share
Beet sugar	100.00	Liquid beet sugar or sugar syrup, sucrose type	4.81
Granulated, in individual services	16.91	Whole, straighthouse or discard beet sugar molasses	2.88
Granulated, in bags and other containers of more than 25 lb	19.29	Molasses beet sugar pulp, bulk	2.03
Granulated, shipped in rail cars, trucks, or bins	43.12	Molasses beet sugar pulp, pelletized	5.42
Confectioners' powdered beet sugar	3.49	All other beet sugar pulp, including raw beet sugar, dried and other beet pulp (plain)	0.68
Soft or brown beet sugar	1.14		

Source: 1992 *Economic Census*. The values shown are percent of total shipments in an industry. Values of indented subcategories are summed in the main heading. The symbol (D) appears when data are withheld to prevent disclosure of competitive information. The abbreviation nsk stands for 'not specified by kind' and nec for 'not elsewhere classified'.

INPUTS AND OUTPUTS FOR SUGAR

Economic Sector or Industry Providing Inputs	%	Sector	Economic Sector or Industry Buying Outputs	%	Sector
Sugar	32.7	Manufg.	Sugar	27.3	Manufg.
Sugar crops	26.4	Agric.	Personal consumption expenditures	19.9	
Imports	18.3	Foreign	Bottled & canned soft drinks	8.8	Manufg.
Wholesale trade	4.5	Trade	Confectionery products	4.3	Manufg.
Gas production & distribution (utilities)	4.2	Util.	Flavoring extracts & syrups, nec	4.3	Manufg.
Motor freight transportation & warehousing	2.7	Util.	Eating & drinking places	3.5	Trade
Paperboard containers & boxes	1.5	Manufg.	Bread, cake, & related products	2.7	Manufg.
Petroleum refining	1.1	Manufg.	Food preparations, nec	2.6	Manufg.
Railroads & related services	1.0	Util.	Chocolate & cocoa products	2.3	Manufg.
Water transportation	1.0	Util.	Cookies & crackers	2.2	Manufg.
Miscellaneous plastics products	0.9	Manufg.	Cereal breakfast foods	2.1	Manufg.
Commercial printing	0.6	Manufg.	Federal Government purchases, nondefense	2.1	Fed Govt
Cyclic crudes and organics	0.6	Manufg.	Canned fruits & vegetables	1.8	Manufg.
Electric services (utilities)	0.6	Util.	Exports	1.8	Foreign
Advertising	0.6	Services	Blended & prepared flour	1.7	Manufg.
Banking	0.4	Fin/R.E.	Fluid milk	1.7	Manufg.
Water supply & sewage systems	0.3	Util.	Prepared feeds, nec	1.6	Manufg.
Coal	0.2	Mining	Ice cream & frozen desserts	1.5	Manufg.
Maintenance of nonfarm buildings nec	0.2	Constr.	Meat animals	1.1	Agric.

Continued on next page.

INPUTS AND OUTPUTS FOR SUGAR - Continued

Economic Sector or Industry Providing Inputs	%	Sector	Economic Sector or Industry Buying Outputs	%	Sector
Communications, except radio & TV	0.2	Util.	Frozen specialties	0.7	Manufg.
Eating & drinking places	0.2	Trade	Pickles, sauces, & salad dressings	0.7	Manufg.
Equipment rental & leasing services	0.2	Services	Dairy farm products	0.6	Agric.
Sanitary services, steam supply, irrigation	0.1	Util.	Condensed & evaporated milk	0.6	Manufg.
Miscellaneous repair shops	0.1	Services	Flour & other grain mill products	0.6	Manufg.
			Malt beverages	0.6	Manufg.
			Chewing gum	0.5	Manufg.
			Canned specialties	0.4	Manufg.
			Frozen fruits, fruit juices & vegetables	0.4	Manufg.
			S/L Govt. purch., elem. & secondary education	0.4	S/L Govt
			Hospitals	0.2	Services
			Dehydrated food products	0.1	Manufg.
			Residential care	0.1	Services
			S/L Govt. purch., health & hospitals	0.1	S/L Govt

Source: Benchmark Input-Output Accounts for the U.S. Economy, 1982, U.S. Department of Commerce, Washington, D.C., July 1991. Data, as reported in the source, are organized by the 1977 SIC structure in use in 1982 but have been matched, as closely as is possible, to the 1987 SIC structure used in this book.

OCCUPATIONS EMPLOYED BY SIC 206 - SUGAR AND CONFECTIONERY PRODUCTS

Occupation	% of Total 1994	Change to 2005	Occupation	% of Total 1994	Change to 2005
Packaging & filling machine operators	12.1	31.8	Cooking, roasting machine operators	2.0	-17.6
Hand packers & packagers	8.9	-24.7	Industrial truck & tractor operators	1.9	-12.1
Precision food & tobacco workers nec	8.4	0.7	General managers & top executives	1.5	-16.6
Helpers, laborers, & material movers nec	6.9	-12.1	Salespersons, retail	1.5	-12.1
Blue collar worker supervisors	4.4	-14.1	Agricultural workers nec	1.4	-12.1
Industrial machinery mechanics	4.0	-3.3	Machine operators nec	1.4	-22.5
Freight, stock, & material movers, hand	3.1	-29.7	Secretaries, ex legal & medical	1.3	-20.0
Janitors & cleaners, incl maids	3.1	-29.7	Assemblers, fabricators, & hand workers nec	1.2	-12.0
Extruding & forming machine workers	3.0	-12.1	Truck drivers light & heavy	1.1	-9.4
Maintenance repairers, general utility	2.3	-20.9	Traffic, shipping, & receiving clerks	1.1	-15.4
Machine feeders & offbearers	2.2	-20.9	Electricians	1.0	-17.5

Source: Industry-Occupation Matrix, Bureau of Labor Statistics. These data relate to one or more 3-digit SIC industry groups rather than to a single 4-digit SIC. The change reported for each occupation to the year 2005 is a percent of growth or decline as estimated by the Bureau of Labor Statistics. The abbreviation nec stands for 'not elsewhere classified'.

LOCATION BY STATE AND REGIONAL CONCENTRATION

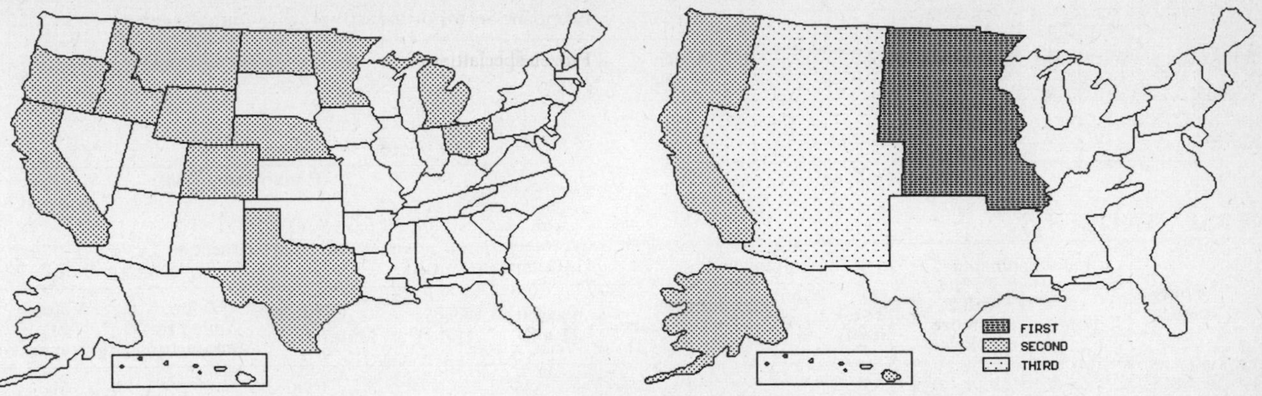

INDUSTRY DATA BY STATE

State	Establish-ments	Shipments			Employment				Cost as % of Shipments	Investment per Employee ($)
		Total ($ mil)	% of U.S.	Per Establ.	Total Number	% of U.S.	Per Establ.	Wages ($/hour)		
California	9	(D)	-	-	1,750 *	23.0	194	-	-	-
Michigan	5	(D)	-	-	750 *	9.9	150	-	-	-
Minnesota	4	(D)	-	-	1,750 *	23.0	438	-	-	-
North Dakota	4	(D)	-	-	750 *	9.9	188	-	-	-
Idaho	3	(D)	-	-	1,750 *	23.0	583	-	-	-
Nebraska	3	(D)	-	-	375 *	4.9	125	-	-	-
Wyoming	3	(D)	-	-	375 *	4.9	125	-	-	-
Colorado	2	(D)	-	-	175 *	2.3	88	-	-	-
Montana	2	(D)	-	-	375 *	4.9	188	-	-	-
Ohio	1	(D)	-	-	175 *	2.3	175	-	-	-
Oregon	1	(D)	-	-	375 *	4.9	375	-	-	-
Texas	1	(D)	-	-	175 *	2.3	175	-	-	-

Source: 1992 *Economic Census*. The states are in descending order of shipments or establishments (if shipment data are missing for the majority). The symbol (D) appears when data are withheld to prevent disclosure of competitive information. States marked with (D) are sorted by number of establishments. A dash (-) indicates that the data element cannot be calculated; * indicates the midpoint of a range.

2064 - CANDY & OTHER CONFECTIONERY PRODUCTS

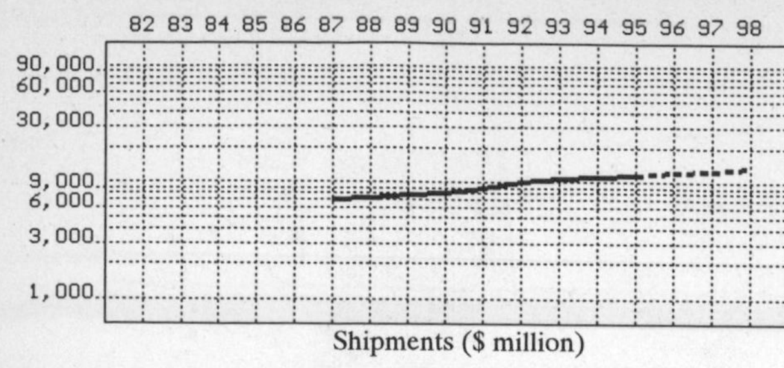

Shipments ($ million)

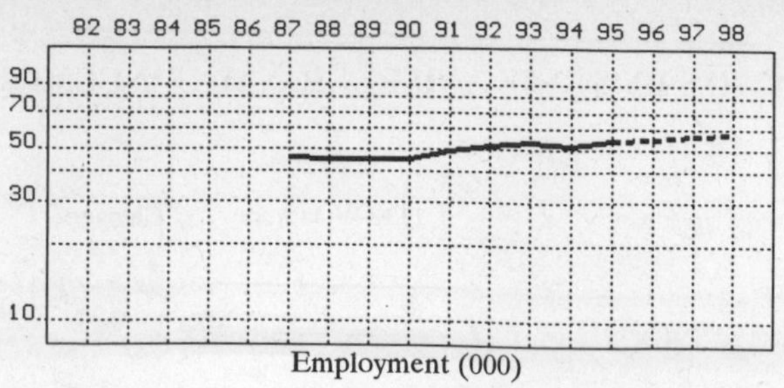

Employment (000)

GENERAL STATISTICS

Year	Com-panies	Establishments: Total	Establishments: with 20 or more employees	Employment: Total (000)	Employment: Production Workers (000)	Employment: Production Hours (Mil)	Compensation: Payroll ($ mil)	Compensation: Wages ($/hr)	Production ($ million): Cost of Materials	Production ($ million): Value Added by Manufacture	Production ($ million): Value of Shipments	Production ($ million): Capital Invest.
1982												
1983												
1984												
1985												
1986												
1987	624	685	295	45.8	37.0	68.3	899.5	9.27	3,165.6	3,837.7	6,979.8	233.2
1988		640	305	44.7	36.3	68.1	922.0	9.48	3,258.8	4,219.3	7,419.1	225.6
1989		636	305	45.0	40.0	71.7	995.7	9.86	3,535.0	4,401.4	7,863.5	262.4
1990		629	292	44.7	39.5	75.6	1,072.6	9.95	3,646.7	4,354.9	7,991.8	296.5
1991		659	292	49.1	39.3	75.0	1,120.8	10.31	3,722.3	4,999.4	8,745.6	217.2
1992	705	759	298	51.5	41.0	79.5	1,262.7	10.60	3,903.3	6,348.9	10,207.1	378.7
1993		741	304	52.8	41.9	82.0	1,317.9	11.14	4,283.4	6,378.1	10,669.6	411.4
1994		740P	299P	51.2	40.7	82.8	1,347.3	11.29	4,402.6	6,504.2	10,910.6	354.3
1995		755P	299P	53.6P	42.5P	85.8P	1,436.8P	11.58P	4,684.9P	6,921.2P	11,610.1P	407.0P
1996		770P	299P	54.8P	43.2P	88.1P	1,507.8P	11.88P	4,932.5P	7,287.1P	12,223.9P	431.4P
1997		786P	299P	56.0P	43.8P	90.4P	1,578.8P	12.17P	5,180.2P	7,652.9P	12,837.6P	455.8P
1998		801P	299P	57.2P	44.5P	92.7P	1,649.8P	12.47P	5,427.8P	8,018.8P	13,451.3P	480.1P

Sources: 1982, 1987, 1992 *Economic Census*; *Annual Survey of Manufactures*, 83-86, 88-91, 93-94. Establishment counts for non-Census years are from *County Business Patterns*; establishment values for 83-84 are extrapolations. 'P's show projections by the editors. Industries reclassified in 87 will not have data for prior years.

INDICES OF CHANGE

Year	Com-panies	Establishments: Total	Establishments: with 20 or more employees	Employment: Total (000)	Employment: Production Workers (000)	Employment: Production Hours (Mil)	Compensation: Payroll ($ mil)	Compensation: Wages ($/hr)	Production ($ million): Cost of Matcrials	Production ($ million): Value Added by Manufacture	Production ($ million): Value of Shipments	Production ($ million): Capital Invest.
1982												
1983												
1984												
1985												
1986												
1987	89	90	99	89	90	86	71	87	81	60	68	62
1988		84	102	87	89	86	73	89	83	66	73	60
1989		84	102	87	98	90	79	93	91	69	77	69
1990		83	98	87	96	95	85	94	93	69	78	78
1991		87	98	95	96	94	89	97	95	79	86	57
1992	100	100	100	100	100	100	100	100	100	100	100	100
1993		98	102	103	102	103	104	105	110	100	105	109
1994		97P	100P	99	99	104	107	107	113	102	107	94
1995		99P	100P	104P	104P	108P	114P	109P	120P	109P	114P	107P
1996		101P	100P	106P	105P	111P	119P	112P	126P	115P	120P	114P
1997		104P	100P	109P	107P	114P	125P	115P	133P	121P	126P	120P
1998		106P	100P	111P	109P	117P	131P	118P	139P	126P	132P	127P

Sources: Same as General Statistics. Values reflect change from the base year, 1992. Values above 100 mean greater than 92, values below 100 mean less than 92, and a value of 100 in the 82-91 or 93-98 period means same as 92. 'P's mark projections by the editors.

SELECTED RATIOS

For 1994	Avg. of All Manufact.	Analyzed Industry	Index
Employees per Establishment	49	69	141
Payroll per Establishment	1,500,273	1,821,379	121
Payroll per Employee	30,620	26,314	86
Production Workers per Establishment	34	55	160
Wages per Establishment	853,319	1,263,747	148
Wages per Production Worker	24,861	22,968	92
Hours per Production Worker	2,056	2,034	99
Wages per Hour	12.09	11.29	93
Value Added per Establishment	4,602,255	8,792,854	191
Value Added per Employee	93,930	127,035	135

For 1994	Avg. of All Manufact.	Analyzed Industry	Index
Value Added per Production Worker	134,084	159,808	119
Cost per Establishment	5,045,178	5,951,757	118
Cost per Employee	102,970	85,988	84
Cost per Production Worker	146,988	108,172	74
Shipments per Establishment	9,576,895	14,749,749	154
Shipments per Employee	195,460	213,098	109
Shipments per Production Worker	279,017	268,074	96
Investment per Establishment	321,011	478,969	149
Investment per Employee	6,552	6,920	106
Investment per Production Worker	9,352	8,705	93

Sources: Same as General Statistics. The 'Average of All Manufacturing' column represents the average of all manufacturing industries reported for the most recent complete year available. The Index shows the relationship between the Average and the Analyzed Industry. For example, 100 means that they are equal; 500 that the Analyzed Industry is five times the average; 50 means that the Analyzed Industry is half the national average. The abbreviation 'na' is used to show that data are 'not available'.

LEADING COMPANIES Number shown: **75** Total sales ($ mil): **2,671** Total employment (000): **24.2**

Company Name	Address				CEO Name	Phone	Co. Type	Sales ($ mil)	Empl. (000)
Archibald Candy Corp	1137 W Jackson	Chicago	IL	60607	R M Peritz Sr	312-243-2700	S	350	3.5
Russell Stover Candies Inc	1000 Walnut St	Kansas City	MO	64106	Thomas S Ward	816-842-9240	R	300	3.0
Tootsie Roll Industries Inc	7401 S Cicero Av	Chicago	IL	60629	Melvin J Gordon	312-838-3400	P	297	1.7
Farley Foods USA	2945 W 31st St	Chicago	IL	60623	William Ellis	312-254-0900	R	250	2.0
See's Candy Shops Inc	210 El Camino Real	S San Francisco	CA	94080	Charles N Huggins	415-583-7307	S	200	1.2
Brach and Brock Confections Inc	PO Box 22427	Chattanooga	TN	37422	Paul K Brock	615-899-1100	P	102	0.8
Comet Confectionery Inc	RD 2	St Albans	VT	05478	Rudy Pachl	802-524-9711	S	65	0.2
Grist Mill Co	PO Box 430	Lakeville	MN	55044	Michael J Cannon	612-469-4981	D	52	0.3
Ferrara Pan Candy Co	7301 W Harrison St	Forest Park	IL	60130	Salvatore Ferrara II	708-366-0500	R	45	0.4
Dahlgren and Company Inc	PO Box 609	Crookston	MN	56716	Kelly Engelstad	218-281-2985	S	40	0.1
Spangler Candy Co	PO Box 71	Bryan	OH	43506	C Gregory Spangler	419-636-4221	R	40	0.4
American Candy Co	PO Box 11708	Richmond	VA	23230	James Rogula	804-287-3330	S	36	0.6
Louis Sherry Inc	169 Lackawanna	Parsippany	NJ	07054	Steven Silk	201-335-1000	S	35*	0.3
Standard Candy Company Inc	PO Box 101025	Nashville	TN	37224	J W Spradley Jr	615-889-6360	R	35	0.3
School House Candy Co	1005 Main St	Pawtucket	RI	02860	Harris N Rosen	401-726-4500	R	29	0.5
Lincoln Snacks Co	2015 W Main St	Stamford	CT	06902	C Alan MacDonald	203-363-5265	P	28	<0.1
Just Born Inc	PO Box 1158	Bethlehem	PA	18016	IB Born	215-867-7568	R	27*	0.3
Andes Candies Inc	1400 E Wisconsin St	Delavan	WI	53115	Mike Coltart	414-728-9121	R	25*	0.3
Ben Myerson Candy Co	928 Towne Av	Los Angeles	CA	90021	James P Myerson	213-623-6266	R	25	0.3
Herman Goelitz Candy Company	2400 N Watney Way	Fairfield	CA	94533	H G Rowland Sr	707-428-2800	R	25	0.2
Kidd and Company Inc	308 N Martin St	Ligonier	IN	46767	Charles Kidd	219-894-3131	R	25*	0.3
Necco Stark Candy Co	PO Box 65	Pewaukee	WI	53072	Dominick Antonellis	414-691-0600	S	25	0.2
New England Confectionery Co	254 Massachusetts	Cambridge	MA	02139	DM Antonellis	617-876-4700	S	25	0.4
Finnfoods	500 N Field Dr	Lake Forest	IL	60045	Bob Clouston	708-735-7813	D	23	0.1
Bob's Candies Inc	PO Box 3170	Albany	GA	31708	Greg McCormack	912-430-8300	R	21	0.5
Golden Stream Quality Foods	11899 Exit 5 Pkwy	Fishers	IN	46038	Stephen A Farber	317-845-5534	R	21	0.1
Morley Candy Makers Company	PO Box 463237	Mount Clemens	MI	48046	Thomas M Morley	313-468-4300	R	21*	0.2
Brown and Haley	PO Box 1596	Tacoma	WA	98401	Fred T Haley	206-593-3000	R	20*	0.3
Ce De Candy Inc	1091 Lousons Rd	Union	NJ	07083	Edward Dee	908-964-0660	R	20*	0.1
Lindt and Sprungli USA	1 Fine Chocolate Pl	Stratham	NH	03885	Lee Mizusawa	603-778-8100	S	20	<0.1
Pennsylvania Dutch Company	408 N Baltimore	Mt Holly Sprgs	PA	17065	LA Warrell	717-486-3496	R	18	0.3
Premiere Candy Co	PO Box 969	Hammond	IN	46325	Bud Foster	219-932-2400	R	18*	0.4
Falcon Candy Co	PO Box 3875	Philadelphia	PA	19146	Pat Branca	215-985-0774	R	17*	0.2
Pearson Candy Co	PO Box 64459	St Paul	MN	55164	Larry L Hassler	612-698-0356	R	17*	0.2
Pez Candy Inc	PO Box 541	Orange	CT	06477	S McWhinnie	203-795-0531	R	16	0.2
Zachary Confections Inc	PO Box 219	Frankfort	IN	46041	John Zachary Jr	317-659-4751	R	15	0.2
Gorant Candies Inc	PO Box 9068	Youngstown	OH	44513	Robert Portman	216-726-8821	R	14*	0.8
Sweet Candy Co	PO Box 2008	Salt Lake City	UT	84110	RA Sweet	801-363-6707	R	14	0.1
Joel Inc	PO Box 488	Elizabethtown	PA	17022	David Deck	717-367-2441	R	13	0.1
F and F Laboratories Inc	3501 W 48th Pl	Chicago	IL	60632	B Fox	312-927-3737	R	13	0.2
HB Hunter Co	PO Box 1599	Norfolk	VA	23501	JR Newell Jr	804-855-0000	R	13	<0.1
Pez Manufacturing Corp	35 Prindle Hill Rd	Orange	CT	06477	Scott McWhinnie	203-795-0531	S	13*	0.1
Beacon Sweets Inc	PO Box 329	Mooresville	NC	28115	Andy Cohen	704-664-4300	R	12	0.2
Price Candy Company Inc	8300 Undergr	Kansas City	MO	64161	John L Hendrich	816-455-6000	D	12	0.2
Simon Candy Co	PO Box 448	Elizabethtown	PA	17022	David B Deck	717-367-2441	S	12	0.1
Idaho Candy Co	PO Box 1217	Boise	ID	83701	John W Wagers	208-342-5505	R	11	<0.1
Chocolate House Inc	PO Box 21890	Milwaukee	WI	53221	Allen W McKie	414-281-7800	R	10*	0.1
FB Washburn Candy Corp	PO Box 3277	Brockton	MA	02404	L Gilson	508-588-0820	R	10*	<0.1
Goetze's Candy Company Inc	3900 E Monument	Baltimore	MD	21205	Spaulding Goetz	410-342-2010	R	10*	0.1
Henry Heide Inc	14 Terminal Rd	New Brunswick	NJ	08903	Philip E Heide	908-846-2400	R	10	0.2
Leader Candies Inc	132 Harrison Pl	Brooklyn	NY	11237	Howard Kastin	718-366-6900	R	10*	0.1
Pangburn Candy Corp	PO Box 901016	Fort Worth	TX	76101	Jmaes Harrison	817-332-8856	R	10	0.2
Scott's Inc	301 Broadway Dr	Sun Prairie	WI	53590	Steve Holt	608-837-8020	S	10	0.1
Square Shooter Candy Co	207 S 9th St	Edwardsville	KS	66113	Bob Simon	913-422-7222	R	10	<0.1
Melster Candies Inc	Madison St	Cambridge	WI	53523	LA Warrell	608-423-3221	S	9*	0.1
Home of the Hebert Candies Inc	PO Box 39	Shrewsbury	MA	01545	R Hebert	508-845-8051	R	8	0.2
Palmer Candy Co	PO Box 326	Sioux City	IA	51102	MB Palmer	712-258-5543	R	8	<0.1
Van Duyn Chocolates	PO Box 10384	Portland	OR	97210	Sean Gilronan	503-227-1927	D	8	<0.1
Adams and Brooks Inc	1915 S Hoover St	Los Angeles	CA	90007	JE Brooks	213-749-3226	R	7	0.1
Banner Candy Mfg Corp	14 Vanderventer	Ft Washington	NY	11050	Peter Stone	516-883-4000	R	7	<0.1
Bradley Candy Mfg Co	211 Babb Dr	Lebanon	TN	37087	Jack P Bradley	615-444-8586	R	7*	0.1
Chiodo Candy Co	2923 Adeline St	Oakland	CA	94608	LJ Chiodo	510-451-5585	R	7*	<0.1
Coast Novelty Manufacturing Co	4064 Glencoe Av	Venice	CA	90292	Robert M Murdock	310-823-0911	R	7	0.1
Davidson of Dundee Inc	PO Box 800	Dundee	FL	33838	Glen Davidson	813-439-1698	R	7	<0.1
Gardner Candies Inc	PO Box E	Tyrone	PA	16686	David J Black	814-684-3925	R	6	0.3
Gilliam Candy Company Inc	PO Box 1060	Paducah	KY	42002	Brian Duwe	502-443-6532	R	6*	<0.1
Golden Harvest Products Inc	3421 Merriam Ln	Overland Park	KS	66203	Kert Rabe	913-831-3800	R	6*	<0.1
Judson-Atkinson Candies	PO Box 830046	San Antonio	TX	78283	BE Atkinson	210-227-5201	R	6*	0.1
Lundeen Inc	1350 Atlantic St	Union City	CA	94587	Ivette Morales	510-487-1696	R	6*	<0.1
Allen Wertz Candies	PO Box 1168	Chino	CA	91708	Gino Marinelli	909-613-0030	R	5	<0.1
Arway Confections Inc	3323 W Newport	Chicago	IL	60618	James Resnick	312-267-5770	R	5	<0.1
Glauber's Fine Candies Inc	1020 Register Av	Baltimore	MD	21239	Kenneth R Glauber	410-377-6800	R	5	<0.1
Hawaiian Candies and Nuts Ltd	707 Waiakamilo Rd	Honolulu	HI	96817	Patrick Arakaki	808-841-3344	R	5	<0.1
Mary Sue Candies Inc	707 S Caton Av	Baltimore	MD	21229	Mark E Berman	410-945-7450	R	5	<0.1
Old Dominion Peanut Inc	208 W 24th St	Norfolk	VA	23517	T Brown	804-622-1633	R	5*	<0.1

Source: *Ward's Business Directory of U.S. Private and Public Companies*, Volumes 1 and 2, 1996. The company type code used is as follows: P - Public, R - Private, S - Subsidiary, D - Division, J - Joint Venture, A - Affiliate, G - Group. Sales are in millions of dollars, employees are in thousands. An asterisk (*) indicates an estimated sales volume. The symbol < stands for 'less than'. Company names and addresses are truncated, in some cases, to fit into the available space.

MATERIALS CONSUMED

Material		Quantity	Delivered Cost ($ million)
Materials, ingredients, containers, and supplies		(X)	3,473.0
Nuts, in shell (including peanuts)	mil lb	(D)	(D)
Nutmeats, including peanuts, processed	mil lb	186.2	195.5
Nutmeats, raw	mil lb	41.7	54.5
Fresh and dried fruits	mil lb	61.3	43.6
Milk and milk products		(X)	212.0
High fructose corn syrup (HFCS)(in terms of solids)	mil lb	161.8	28.2
Crystalline fructose (dry fructose)	mil lb	2.8**	0.9
Dextrose and corn syrup, including corn syrup solids (in terms of dry weight)	mil lb	1,165.7	146.0
Sugar substitutes (mannitol, sorbitol, etc.)	1,000 s tons	49.2	45.8
Sugar, cane and beet (in terms of sugar solids)	1,000 s tons	1,047.1	461.5
Fats and oils, including shortening	1,000 s tons	197.4	95.0
Chocolate coatings	1,000 s tons	171.2	222.3
Unsweetened chocolate (chocolate liquor)	1,000 s tons	35.5	79.8
Cocoa beans	1,000 s tons	(D)	(D)
Cocoa, pressed cake and powder	1,000 s tons	11.1	9.9
Cocoa butter	mil lb	61.2	97.5
Chewing gum base including chicle		(X)	(D)
Essential oils and flavors, synthetic		(X)	107.5
Packaging paper and plastics film, coated and laminated		(X)	343.3
Aluminum foil packaging products, converted or rolls and sheets		(X)	50.8
Paperboard containers, boxes, and corrugated paperboard		(X)	324.1
Plastics containers		(X)	29.1
Glass containers		(X)	6.6
Metal cans, can lids and ends		(X)	11.5
All other materials and components, parts, containers, and supplies		(X)	397.6
Materials, ingredients, containers, and supplies, nsk		(X)	307.7

Source: 1992 *Economic Census*. Explanation of symbols used: (D): Withheld to avoid disclosure of competitive data; na: Not available; (S): Withheld because statistical norms were not met; (X): Not applicable; (Z): Less than half the unit shown; nec: Not elsewhere classified; nsk: Not specified by kind; - : zero; * : 10-19 percent estimated; ** : 20-29 percent estimated.

PRODUCT SHARE DETAILS

Product or Product Class	% Share	Product or Product Class	% Share
Candy and other confectionery products	100.00	Cough drops, except pharmaceutical type	36.02
Chocolate and chocolate-type confectionery products made from purchased chocolate	57.63	Glace, candied, and crystallized fruits, fruit peels, nuts, and other vegetable substances	60.19
Nonchocolate-type confectionery products, including bar goods, granola bars, package goods, specialties, etc.	37.59	Other confectionery-type products, nsk	3.79
Other confectionery-type products	0.84	Candy and other confectionery products, nsk	3.84

Source: 1992 *Economic Census*. The values shown are percent of total shipments in an industry. Values of indented subcategories are summed in the main heading. The symbol (D) appears when data are withheld to prevent disclosure of competitive information. The abbreviation nsk stands for 'not specified by kind' and nec for 'not elsewhere classified'.

INPUTS AND OUTPUTS FOR CONFECTIONERY PRODUCTS

Economic Sector or Industry Providing Inputs	%	Sector	Economic Sector or Industry Buying Outputs	%	Sector
Confectionery products	12.4	Manufg.	Personal consumption expenditures	82.8	
Chocolate & cocoa products	9.4	Manufg.	Confectionery products	7.3	Manufg.
Oil bearing crops	9.3	Agric.	Eating & drinking places	3.9	Trade
Wholesale trade	9.3	Trade	Exports	2.4	Foreign
Sugar	6.5	Manufg.	Change in business inventories	1.8	In House
Paperboard containers & boxes	5.2	Manufg.	Chocolate & cocoa products	0.3	Manufg.
Imports	5.2	Foreign	S/L Govt. purch., higher education	0.3	S/L Govt
Tree nuts	5.0	Agric.	Motion pictures	0.2	Services
Advertising	2.9	Services	S/L Govt. purch., correction	0.2	S/L Govt
Condensed & evaporated milk	2.7	Manufg.	Hospitals	0.1	Services
Noncomparable imports	2.6	Foreign	Federal Government purchases, national defense	0.1	Fed Govt
Wet corn milling	2.4	Manufg.			
Paper coating & glazing	2.3	Manufg.			
Motor freight transportation & warehousing	1.6	Util.			
Business services nec	1.6	Services			
Electric services (utilities)	1.5	Util.			
Flavoring extracts & syrups, nec	1.3	Manufg.			
Fruits	1.1	Agric.			
Bags, except textile	1.1	Manufg.			
Food preparations, nec	1.1	Manufg.			
Metal foil & leaf	1.1	Manufg.			
Miscellaneous plastics products	1.1	Manufg.			
Cyclic crudes and organics	1.0	Manufg.			
Metal cans	1.0	Manufg.			
Shortening & cooking oils	1.0	Manufg.			

Continued on next page.

INPUTS AND OUTPUTS FOR CONFECTIONERY PRODUCTS - Continued

Economic Sector or Industry Providing Inputs	%	Sector	Economic Sector or Industry Buying Outputs	%	Sector
Banking	0.9	Fin/R.E.			
Glass containers	0.8	Manufg.			
Railroads & related services	0.8	Util.			
Gas production & distribution (utilities)	0.7	Util.			
Maintenance of nonfarm buildings nec	0.4	Constr.			
Commercial printing	0.4	Manufg.			
Communications, except radio & TV	0.4	Util.			
Eating & drinking places	0.4	Trade			
Air transportation	0.3	Util.			
Water transportation	0.3	Util.			
Real estate	0.3	Fin/R.E.			
U.S. Postal Service	0.3	Gov't			
Chemical preparations, nec	0.2	Manufg.			
Crowns & closures	0.2	Manufg.			
Machinery, except electrical, nec	0.2	Manufg.			
Petroleum refining	0.2	Manufg.			
Poultry & egg processing	0.2	Manufg.			
Sanitary services, steam supply, irrigation	0.2	Util.			
Automotive repair shops & services	0.2	Services			
Equipment rental & leasing services	0.2	Services			
Management & consulting services & labs	0.2	Services			
Miscellaneous repair shops	0.2	Services			
Dehydrated food products	0.1	Manufg.			
Fabricated rubber products, nec	0.1	Manufg.			
Lubricating oils & greases	0.1	Manufg.			
Pipe, valves, & pipe fittings	0.1	Manufg.			
Royalties	0.1	Fin/R.E.			
Accounting, auditing & bookkeeping	0.1	Services			
Business/professional associations	0.1	Services			
Legal services	0.1	Services			

Source: Benchmark Input-Output Accounts for the U.S. Economy, 1982, U.S. Department of Commerce, Washington, D.C., July 1991. Data, as reported in the source, are organized by the 1977 SIC structure in use in 1982 but have been matched, as closely as is possible, to the 1987 SIC structure used in this book.

OCCUPATIONS EMPLOYED BY SIC 206 - SUGAR AND CONFECTIONERY PRODUCTS

Occupation	% of Total 1994	Change to 2005	Occupation	% of Total 1994	Change to 2005
Packaging & filling machine operators	12.1	31.8	Cooking, roasting machine operators	2.0	-17.6
Hand packers & packagers	8.9	-24.7	Industrial truck & tractor operators	1.9	-12.1
Precision food & tobacco workers nec	8.4	0.7	General managers & top executives	1.5	-16.6
Helpers, laborers, & material movers nec	6.9	-12.1	Salespersons, retail	1.5	-12.1
Blue collar worker supervisors	4.4	-14.1	Agricultural workers nec	1.4	-12.1
Industrial machinery mechanics	4.0	-3.3	Machine operators nec	1.4	-22.5
Freight, stock, & material movers, hand	3.1	-29.7	Secretaries, ex legal & medical	1.3	-20.0
Janitors & cleaners, incl maids	3.1	-29.7	Assemblers, fabricators, & hand workers nec	1.2	-12.0
Extruding & forming machine workers	3.0	-12.1	Truck drivers light & heavy	1.1	-9.4
Maintenance repairers, general utility	2.3	-20.9	Traffic, shipping, & receiving clerks	1.1	-15.4
Machine feeders & offbearers	2.2	-20.9	Electricians	1.0	-17.5

Source: Industry-Occupation Matrix, Bureau of Labor Statistics. These data relate to one or more 3-digit SIC industry groups rather than to a single 4-digit SIC. The change reported for each occupation to the year 2005 is a percent of growth or decline as estimated by the Bureau of Labor Statistics. The abbreviation nec stands for 'not elsewhere classified'.

LOCATION BY STATE AND REGIONAL CONCENTRATION

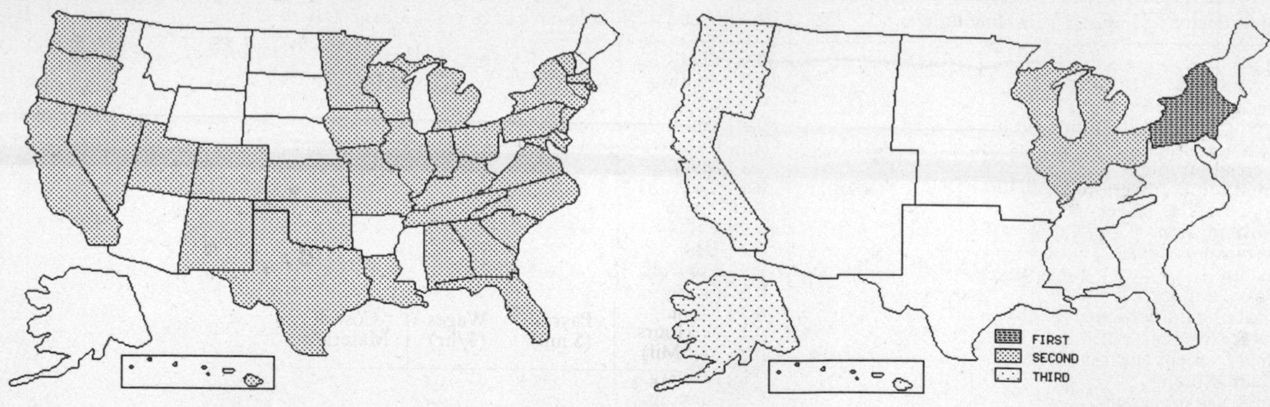

INDUSTRY DATA BY STATE

State	Establish-ments	Shipments			Employment				Cost as % of Shipments	Investment per Employee ($)
		Total ($ mil)	% of U.S.	Per Establ.	Total Number	% of U.S.	Per Establ.	Wages ($/hour)		
Illinois	65	3,012.9	29.5	46.4	12,200	23.7	188	11.56	38.4	10,566
Pennsylvania	83	1,425.0	14.0	17.2	7,800	15.1	94	10.75	37.7	-
Tennessee	15	767.2	7.5	51.1	2,700	5.2	180	10.91	32.7	20,037
California	80	730.1	7.2	9.1	4,000	7.8	50	11.31	41.8	5,100
New Jersey	30	617.1	6.0	20.6	1,800	3.5	60	16.65	42.2	18,556
New York	53	222.6	2.2	4.2	2,200	4.3	42	8.81	49.7	3,773
Massachusetts	19	157.4	1.5	8.3	1,300	2.5	68	9.78	40.3	3,308
Minnesota	14	157.3	1.5	11.2	1,200	2.3	86	9.39	32.2	-
Ohio	35	151.2	1.5	4.3	1,400	2.7	40	9.00	42.1	3,500
Washington	22	62.6	0.6	2.8	600	1.2	27	8.75	39.0	2,000
Hawaii	12	61.0	0.6	5.1	400	0.8	33	7.67	66.2	-
Florida	21	55.4	0.5	2.6	400	0.8	19	7.57	48.7	2,750
Kansas	6	12.2	0.1	2.0	100	0.2	17	14.00	48.4	-
Texas	49	(D)	-	-	1,750 *	3.4	36	-	-	-
Wisconsin	22	(D)	-	-	750 *	1.5	34	-	-	-
Oregon	20	(D)	-	-	175 *	0.3	9	-	-	-
Utah	19	(D)	-	-	750 *	1.5	39	-	-	-
Michigan	17	(D)	-	-	1,750 *	3.4	103	-	-	-
Georgia	15	(D)	-	-	1,750 *	3.4	117	-	-	2,057
Louisiana	13	(D)	-	-	375 *	0.7	29	-	-	3,733
Virginia	13	(D)	-	-	1,750 *	3.4	135	-	-	-
Indiana	12	(D)	-	-	1,750 *	3.4	146	-	-	2,286
Missouri	12	(D)	-	-	1,750 *	3.4	146	-	-	-
Kentucky	11	(D)	-	-	175 *	0.3	16	-	-	-
Colorado	10	(D)	-	-	1,750 *	3.4	175	-	-	-
North Carolina	10	(D)	-	-	175 *	0.3	18	-	-	-
Connecticut	8	(D)	-	-	750 *	1.5	94	-	-	-
Maryland	8	(D)	-	-	375 *	0.7	47	-	-	-
Vermont	7	(D)	-	-	175 *	0.3	25	-	-	-
Nevada	6	(D)	-	-	750 *	1.5	125	-	-	-
Iowa	5	(D)	-	-	750 *	1.5	150	-	-	-
Alabama	4	(D)	-	-	375 *	0.7	94	-	-	-
New Mexico	4	(D)	-	-	175 *	0.3	44	-	-	-
Oklahoma	3	(D)	-	-	375 *	0.7	125	-	-	-
South Carolina	3	(D)	-	-	750 *	1.5	250	-	-	-
Rhode Island	1	(D)	-	-	375 *	0.7	375	-	-	-

Source: 1992 *Economic Census*. The states are in descending order of shipments or establishments (if shipment data are missing for the majority). The symbol (D) appears when data are withheld to prevent disclosure of competitive information. States marked with (D) are sorted by number of establishments. A dash (-) indicates that the data element cannot be calculated; * indicates the midpoint of a range.

2066 - CHOCOLATE & COCOA PRODUCTS

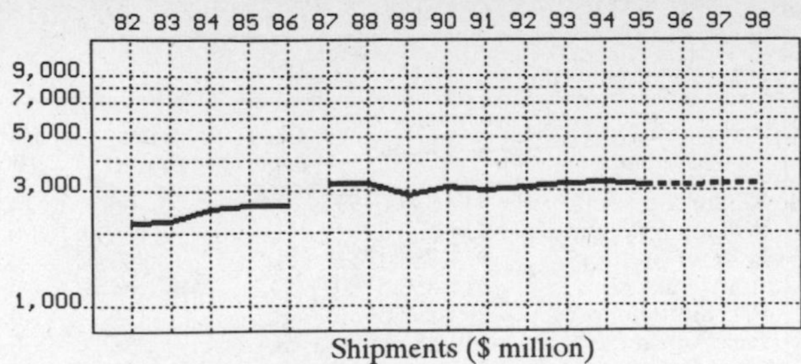

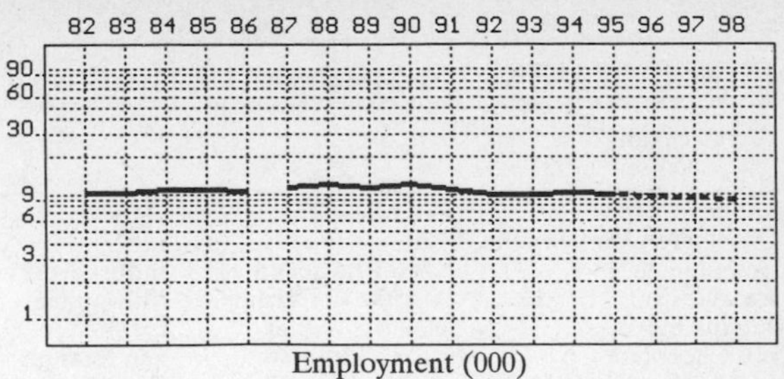

GENERAL STATISTICS

Year	Companies	Establishments		Employment			Compensation		Production ($ million)			
		Total	with 20 or more employees	Total (000)	Production Workers (000)	Production Hours (Mil)	Payroll ($ mil)	Wages ($/hr)	Cost of Materials	Value Added by Manufacture	Value of Shipments	Capital Invest.
1982	77	86	29	10.1	7.9	16.2	205.7	9.04	1,217.1	1,006.7	2,217.4	53.8
1983		98	32	10.1	7.9	16.6	221.2	9.62	1,165.2	1,071.0	2,258.8	62.7
1984		110	35	10.7	8.4	17.3	236.1	9.79	1,459.4	1,052.0	2,484.4	70.1
1985		122	39	10.8	8.6	17.1	251.5	10.30	1,459.8	1,136.8	2,595.6	
1986		121	36	10.5	8.2	15.8	263.6	11.31	1,496.3	1,088.9	2,586.7	85.1
1987*	173	186	53	11.0	8.5	16.3	283.3	11.71	1,677.4	1,523.0	3,181.4	74.9
1988		186	59	11.8	9.1	17.3	309.9	11.77	1,731.8	1,467.5	3,212.6	94.4
1989		196	62	11.2	7.9	15.5	295.9	12.58	1,587.4	1,278.0	2,843.1	130.1
1990		186	64	12.0	8.2	16.0	320.5	12.74	1,654.7	1,418.1	3,061.3	129.1
1991		193	59	10.9	7.8	15.5	319.7	12.70	1,513.9	1,501.6	3,013.0	132.8
1992	146	156	32	9.9	7.1	13.9	323.3	14.35	1,632.3	1,475.3	3,106.4	261.9
1993		154	40	10.0	7.1	14.4	334.4	14.47	1,658.1	1,556.0	3,203.2	125.5
1994		157P	39P	10.1	7.1	14.4	341.7	14.31	1,646.3	1,571.7	3,232.8	111.3
1995		151P	36P	9.8P	6.6P	13.6P	348.9P	15.06P	1,610.9P	1,537.9P	3,163.2P	175.9P
1996		145P	32P	9.5P	6.4P	13.2P	356.2P	15.50P	1,617.3P	1,544.0P	3,175.8P	185.5P
1997		140P	29P	9.3P	6.1P	12.9P	363.5P	15.94P	1,623.6P	1,550.1P	3,188.3P	195.1P
1998		134P	25P	9.0P	5.8P	12.5P	370.8P	16.38P	1,630.0P	1,556.2P	3,200.9P	204.8P

Sources: 1982, 1987, 1992 *Economic Census*; *Annual Survey of Manufactures*, 83-86, 88-91, 93-94. Establishment counts are from *County Business Patterns* for non-Census years; establishment counts for 83-84 are extrapolations. * indicates that industry content changed in 87; earlier years use 77 SICs. 'P's mark projections.

INDICES OF CHANGE

Year	Companies	Establishments		Employment			Compensation		Production ($ million)			
		Total	with 20 or more employees	Total (000)	Production Workers (000)	Production Hours (Mil)	Payroll ($ mil)	Wages ($/hr)	Cost of Materials	Value Added by Manufacture	Value of Shipments	Capital Invest.
1982	53	55	91	102	111	117	64	63	75	68	71	21
1983		63	100	102	111	119	68	67	71	73	73	24
1984		71	109	108	118	124	73	68	89	71	80	27
1985		78	122	109	121	123	78	72	89	77	84	
1986		78	113	106	115	114	82	79	92	74	83	32
1987*	118	119	166	111	120	117	88	82	103	103	102	29
1988		119	184	119	128	124	96	82	106	99	103	36
1989		126	194	113	111	112	92	88	97	87	92	50
1990		119	200	121	115	115	99	89	101	96	99	49
1991		124	184	110	110	112	99	89	93	102	97	51
1992	100	100	100	100	100	100	100	100	100	100	100	100
1993		99	125	101	100	104	103	101	102	105	103	48
1994		101P	122P	102	100	104	106	100	101	107	104	42
1995		97P	111P	99P	94P	98P	108P	105P	99P	104P	102P	67P
1996		93P	100P	96P	90P	95P	110P	108P	99P	105P	102P	71P
1997		90P	90P	94P	86P	92P	112P	111P	99P	105P	103P	75P
1998		86P	79P	91P	82P	90P	115P	114P	100P	105P	103P	78P

Sources: Same as General Statistics. Values reflect change from the base year, 1992. Values above 100 mean greater than 92, values below 100 mean less than 92, and a value of 100 in the 82-91 or 93-98 period means same as 92. * indicates that industry content changed in 87. Data for earlier years are in 77 SIC format.

SELECTED RATIOS

For 1994	Avg. of All Manufact.	Analyzed Industry	Index	For 1994	Avg. of All Manufact.	Analyzed Industry	Index
Employees per Establishment	49	64	131	Value Added per Production Worker	134,084	221,366	165
Payroll per Establishment	1,500,273	2,178,415	145	Cost per Establishment	5,045,178	10,495,537	208
Payroll per Employee	30,620	33,832	110	Cost per Employee	102,970	163,000	158
Production Workers per Establishment	34	45	132	Cost per Production Worker	146,988	231,873	158
Wages per Establishment	853,319	1,313,705	154	Shipments per Establishment	9,576,895	20,609,836	215
Wages per Production Worker	24,861	29,023	117	Shipments per Employee	195,460	320,079	164
Hours per Production Worker	2,056	2,028	99	Shipments per Production Worker	279,017	455,324	163
Wages per Hour	12.09	14.31	118	Investment per Establishment	321,011	709,563	221
Value Added per Establishment	4,602,255	10,019,945	218	Investment per Employee	6,552	11,020	168
Value Added per Employee	93,930	155,614	166	Investment per Production Worker	9,352	15,676	168

Sources: Same as General Statistics. The 'Average of All Manufacturing' column represents the average of all manufacturing industries reported for the most recent complete year available. The Index shows the relationship between the Average and the Analyzed Industry. For example, 100 means that they are equal; 500 that the Analyzed Industry is five times the average; 50 means that the Analyzed Industry is half the national average. The abbreviation 'na' is used to show that data are 'not available'.

LEADING COMPANIES

Number shown: **25** Total sales ($ mil): **4,144** Total employment (000): **17.1**

Company Name	Address				CEO Name	Phone	Co. Type	Sales ($ mil)	Empl. (000)
Hershey Foods Corp	PO Box 810	Hershey	PA	17033	Kenneth L Wolfe	717-534-6799	P	3,606	14.0
Wilbur Chocolate Company Inc	20 N Broad St	Lititz	PA	17543	William Shaughnessy	717-626-1131	S	105	0.3
Shade Foods Inc	400 Prairie Village	Indust Apt	KS	66031	H Peter Stettler	913-780-1212	S	90	0.3
WR Grace and Co	12500 W Carmen	Milwaukee	WI	53225	John Timson	414-358-5700	D	64	0.4
Lyons-Magnus Inc	1636 S 2nd St	Fresno	CA	93702	R E Smittcamp	209-268-5966	R	52	0.4
Ghirardelli Chocolate Co	1111 139th Av	San Leandro	CA	94578	Jack Anton	510-483-6970	R	36	0.1
Guittard Chocolate Corp	10 Guittard Rd	Burlingame	CA	94010	Gary Guittard	415-697-4427	R	32	0.2
Madelaine Chocolate Novelties	PO Box 166	Rockaway Bch	NY	11693	Jacob Gold	718-945-1500	R	25	0.3
Merckens Chocolate Co	150 Oakland St	Mansfield	MA	02048	Frank O'Korn	508-339-8921	S	24•	0.2
Van-Leer Chocolate Co	110 Hoboken Av	Jersey City	NJ	07303	Theodore Van Leer	201-798-8080	R	19•	0.1
E D and F Man Cocoa Products	600 Ellis Rd	Glassboro	NJ	08028	Frank Donadio	609-881-4000	D	16•	0.1
Geoffrey Boehm Chocolates Inc	91 43rd St	Pittsburgh	PA	15201	Jeffrey Edwards	412-687-3370	R	14•	<0.1
Rocky Mountain Chocolate	265 Turner Dr	Durango	CO	81301	Franklin E Crail	303-259-0554	P	9	0.2
Gayle's Chocolates Inc	417 S Washington	Royal Oak	MI	48067	Gayle Harte	810-398-0001	R	8•	<0.1
Van Rian Corp	PO Box 10384	Portland	OR	97210	Sean Gilronan	503-227-1927	R	8	<0.1
Harry London's Candies Inc	1281 S Main St	North Canton	OH	44720	C Waggoner	216-494-0833	R	6	0.1
Lou-retta's Custom Chocolates	3764 Harlem Rd	Cheektowaga	NY	14215	Loretta Kaminsky	716-834-7111	R	6•	<0.1
Storck USA LP	500 N Michigan Av	Chicago	IL	60611	Richard Harshman	312-467-5700	R	6•	<0.1
Burnham and Brady Inc	34 Burnside Av	East Hartford	CT	06108	Harriet Sessa	203-528-9271	R	5•	<0.1
Five H Island Foods Inc	PO Box 19160	Honolulu	HI	96817	Tom Horiuchi	808-848-2067	R	4•	<0.1
Nog Inc	PO Box 162	Dunkirk	NY	14048	B H Ritenburg III	716-366-3322	R	3	<0.1
Omanhene Cocoa Bean Co	PO Box 22	Milwaukee	WI	53201	Steven C Wallace	414-225-5501	R	2•	<0.1
Tell Chocolate Corp	PO Box 060650	Staten Island	NY	10306	Robert Ricci	718-266-4651	R	2	<0.1
Crowley Candy Company Inc	4609 Magazine St	New Orleans	LA	70115	Gary E Crowley	504-899-1549	R	1	<0.1
Behr's Chocolates Inc	624 Douglas Av	Altamonte Sp	FL	32714	Glenn Behr	407-682-3003	R	1•	<0.1

Source: *Ward's Business Directory of U.S. Private and Public Companies*, Volumes 1 and 2, 1996. The company type code used is as follows: P - Public, R - Private, S - Subsidiary, D - Division, J - Joint Venture, A - Affiliate, G - Group. Sales are in millions of dollars, employees are in thousands. An asterisk (•) indicates an estimated sales volume. The symbol < stands for 'less than'. Company names and addresses are truncated, in some cases, to fit into the available space.

MATERIALS CONSUMED

Material		Quantity	Delivered Cost ($ million)
Materials, ingredients, containers, and supplies		(X)	1,534.6
Nuts, in shell (including peanuts)	mil lb	(D)	(D)
Nutmeats, including peanuts, processed	mil lb	5.2*	6.1
Nutmeats, raw	mil lb	(D)	(D)
Milk and milk products		(X)	172.4
High fructose corn syrup (HFCS)(in terms of solids)	mil lb	66.2	8.2
Dextrose and corn syrup, including corn syrup solids (in terms of dry weight)	mil lb	75.1	9.3
Sugar substitutes (mannitol, sorbitol, etc.)	1,000 s tons	(S)	1.2
Sugar, cane and beet (in terms of sugar solids)	1,000 s tons	537.2	212.8
Fats and oils, including shortening	1,000 s tons	87.2	39.0
Chocolate coatings	1,000 s tons	29.1	29.4
Unsweetened chocolate (chocolate liquor)	1,000 s tons	68.8	75.8
Cocoa beans	1,000 s tons	310.2	368.4
Cocoa, pressed cake and powder	1,000 s tons	65.7	48.3
Cocoa butter	mil lb	111.3	168.4
Essential oils and flavors, synthetic		(X)	15.8
Packaging paper and plastics film, coated and laminated		(X)	57.1
Aluminum foil packaging products, converted or rolls and sheets		(X)	(D)
Paperboard containers, boxes, and corrugated paperboard		(X)	42.1
Plastics containers		(X)	20.3
Glass containers		(X)	(D)
Metal cans, can lids and ends		(X)	16.4
All other materials and components, parts, containers, and supplies		(X)	129.9
Materials, ingredients, containers, and supplies, nsk		(X)	45.8

Source: 1992 *Economic Census*. Explanation of symbols used: (D): Withheld to avoid disclosure of competitive data; na: Not available; (S): Withheld because statistical norms were not met; (X): Not applicable; (Z): Less than half the unit shown; nec: Not elsewhere classified; nsk: Not specified by kind; - : zero; * : 10-19 percent estimated; ** : 20-29 percent estimated.

PRODUCT SHARE DETAILS

Product or Product Class	% Share	Product or Product Class	% Share
Chocolate and cocoa products	100.00	Other unsweetened powdered cocoa products	14.59
Chocolate coatings	19.07	Other sweetened (or mixed with other substances) powdered cocoa products, in cans or packages of 2 1/2 lb or less	9.61
Sweet chocolate coatings	15.44	Other sweetened (or mixed with other substances) powdered cocoa products, in other containers and in bulk (barrels, drums, bags)	4.52
Milk chocolate coatings	38.97	Cocoa butter	(D)
Liquor chocolate coatings	16.12	Chocolate liquor base syrup, in cans or packages of 16 oz or less	(D)
Confectionery coatings, including ice cream coating (made chiefly from cocoa powder and fats other than cocoa butter)	27.97	Chocolate liquor base syrup, in other containers or in bulk	13.42
Chocolate coatings, nsk	1.51	Cocoa powder base chocolate syrup	5.25
Chocolate and chocolate-type confectionery products made from cocoa beans ground in the same establishment	48.39	Other chocolate and cocoa products, nsk	0.48
Other chocolate and cocoa products	30.52	Chocolate and cocoa products, nsk	2.02
Other unsweetened chocolate products, except coatings	1.78		
Other sweetened chocolate products, except coatings	42.85		

Source: 1992 *Economic Census*. The values shown are percent of total shipments in an industry. Values of indented subcategories are summed in the main heading. The symbol (D) appears when data are withheld to prevent disclosure of competitive information. The abbreviation nsk stands for 'not specified by kind' and nec for 'not elsewhere classified'.

INPUTS AND OUTPUTS FOR CHOCOLATE & COCOA PRODUCTS

Economic Sector or Industry Providing Inputs	%	Sector	Economic Sector or Industry Buying Outputs	%	Sector
Noncomparable imports	17.7	Foreign	Personal consumption expenditures	44.9	
Imports	16.9	Foreign	Confectionery products	24.1	Manufg.
Chocolate & cocoa products	9.4	Manufg.	Chocolate & cocoa products	10.5	Manufg.
Wholesale trade	7.9	Trade	Cookies & crackers	3.5	Manufg.
Sugar	7.8	Manufg.	Eating & drinking places	3.3	Trade
Metal cans	6.0	Manufg.	Bread, cake, & related products	3.0	Manufg.
Condensed & evaporated milk	5.9	Manufg.	Ice cream & frozen desserts	2.6	Manufg.
Motor freight transportation & warehousing	3.1	Util.	Food preparations, nec	2.2	Manufg.
Business services nec	3.0	Services	Fluid milk	2.0	Manufg.
Shortening & cooking oils	2.4	Manufg.	Change in business inventories	1.5	In House
Advertising	2.4	Services	Exports	1.1	Foreign
Miscellaneous plastics products	2.2	Manufg.	Condensed & evaporated milk	0.6	Manufg.
Paperboard containers & boxes	2.1	Manufg.	S/L Govt. purch., elem. & secondary education	0.3	S/L Govt
Confectionery products	1.4	Manufg.	Hospitals	0.2	Services
Paper coating & glazing	1.2	Manufg.			
Electric services (utilities)	1.1	Util.			
Metal foil & leaf	1.0	Manufg.			
Commercial printing	0.7	Manufg.			
Water transportation	0.7	Util.			
Banking	0.7	Fin/R.E.			
Bags, except textile	0.6	Manufg.			
Wet corn milling	0.5	Manufg.			
Gas production & distribution (utilities)	0.5	Util.			
Tree nuts	0.4	Agric.			
Railroads & related services	0.4	Util.			
Maintenance of nonfarm buildings nec	0.3	Constr.			
Food preparations, nec	0.3	Manufg.			
Chemical preparations, nec	0.2	Manufg.			
Cyclic crudes and organics	0.2	Manufg.			
Food products machinery	0.2	Manufg.			
Petroleum refining	0.2	Manufg.			
Communications, except radio & TV	0.2	Util.			
Eating & drinking places	0.2	Trade			
Equipment rental & leasing services	0.2	Services			
Royalties	0.1	Fin/R.E.			
Automotive repair shops & services	0.1	Services			
U.S. Postal Service	0.1	Gov't			

Source: Benchmark Input-Output Accounts for the U.S. Economy, 1982, U.S. Department of Commerce, Washington, D.C., July 1991. Data, as reported in the source, are organized by the 1977 SIC structure in use in 1982 but have been matched, as closely as is possible, to the 1987 SIC structure used in this book.

OCCUPATIONS EMPLOYED BY SIC 206 - SUGAR AND CONFECTIONERY PRODUCTS

Occupation	% of Total 1994	Change to 2005	Occupation	% of Total 1994	Change to 2005
Packaging & filling machine operators	12.1	31.8	Cooking, roasting machine operators	2.0	-17.6
Hand packers & packagers	8.9	-24.7	Industrial truck & tractor operators	1.9	-12.1
Precision food & tobacco workers nec	8.4	0.7	General managers & top executives	1.5	-16.6
Helpers, laborers, & material movers nec	6.9	-12.1	Salespersons, retail	1.5	-12.1
Blue collar worker supervisors	4.4	-14.1	Agricultural workers nec	1.4	-12.1
Industrial machinery mechanics	4.0	-3.3	Machine operators nec	1.4	-22.5
Freight, stock, & material movers, hand	3.1	-29.7	Secretaries, ex legal & medical	1.3	-20.0
Janitors & cleaners, incl maids	3.1	-29.7	Assemblers, fabricators, & hand workers nec	1.2	-12.0
Extruding & forming machine workers	3.0	-12.1	Truck drivers light & heavy	1.1	-9.4
Maintenance repairers, general utility	2.3	-20.9	Traffic, shipping, & receiving clerks	1.1	-15.4
Machine feeders & offbearers	2.2	-20.9	Electricians	1.0	-17.5

Source: Industry-Occupation Matrix, Bureau of Labor Statistics. These data relate to one or more 3-digit SIC industry groups rather than to a single 4-digit SIC. The change reported for each occupation to the year 2005 is a percent of growth or decline as estimated by the Bureau of Labor Statistics. The abbreviation nec stands for 'not elsewhere classified'.

LOCATION BY STATE AND REGIONAL CONCENTRATION

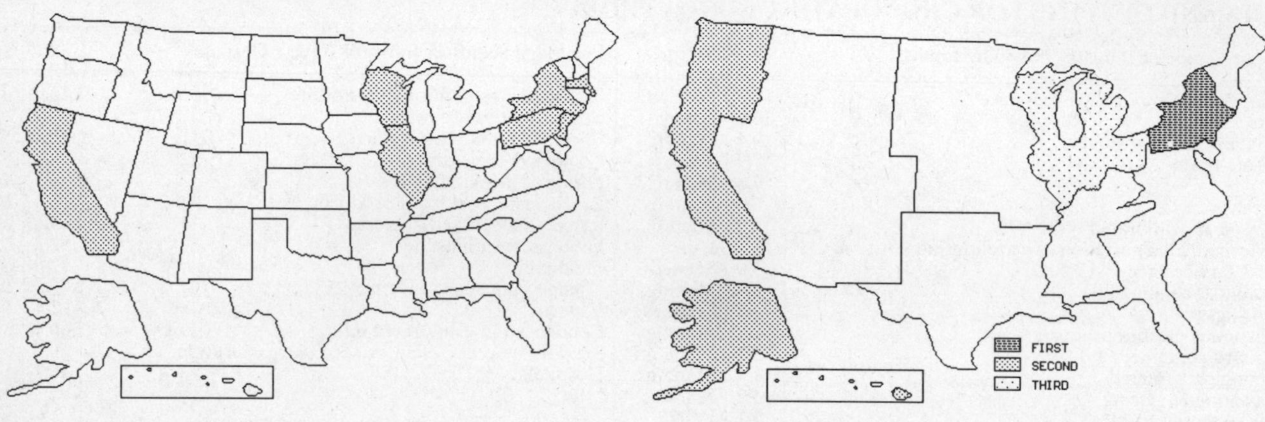

INDUSTRY DATA BY STATE

State	Establish-ments	Shipments Total ($ mil)	Shipments % of U.S.	Shipments Per Establ.	Employment Total Number	Employment % of U.S.	Employment Per Establ.	Employment Wages ($/hour)	Cost as % of Shipments	Investment per Employee ($)
California	22	496.1	16.0	22.5	1,200	12.1	55	14.16	39.2	11,000
Wisconsin	10	425.1	13.7	42.5	1,200	12.1	120	11.27	45.4	-
New York	21	(D)	-	-	1,750 *	17.7	83	-	-	-
Pennsylvania	21	(D)	-	-	7,500 *	75.8	357	-	-	-
New Jersey	9	(D)	-	-	375 *	3.8	42	-	-	-
Massachusetts	6	(D)	-	-	175 *	1.8	29	-	-	-
Illinois	5	(D)	-	-	175 *	1.8	35	-	-	-

Source: 1992 *Economic Census*. The states are in descending order of shipments or establishments (if shipment data are missing for the majority). The symbol (D) appears when data are withheld to prevent disclosure of competitive information. States marked with (D) are sorted by number of establishments. A dash (-) indicates that the data element cannot be calculated; * indicates the midpoint of a range.

2068 - SALTED & ROASTED NUTS & SEEDS

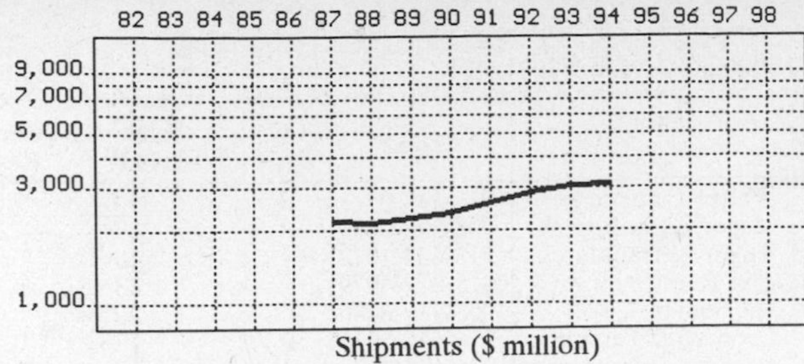

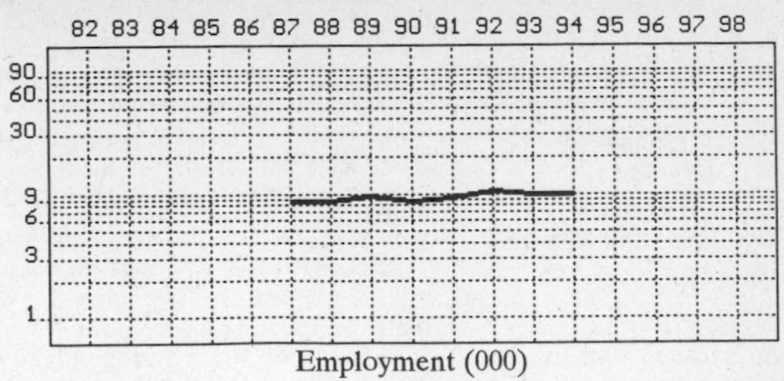

GENERAL STATISTICS

Year	Com-panies	Establishments		Employment			Compensation		Production ($ million)			
		Total	with 20 or more employees	Total (000)	Production Workers (000)	Production Hours (Mil)	Payroll ($ mil)	Wages ($/hr)	Cost of Materials	Value Added by Manufacture	Value of Shipments	Capital Invest.
1982												
1983												
1984												
1985												
1986												
1987	79	88	65	8.8	6.9	13.4	172.1	8.60	1,291.2	866.8	2,178.0	28.0
1988		91	65	8.7	6.9	14.0	182.4	8.96	1,311.2	828.3	2,129.6	36.0
1989		89	61	9.5								
1990		87	61	8.7	7.0	13.9	200.2	9.25	1,405.5	985.9	2,373.0	34.1
1991		90	59	9.3								
1992	102	112	69	10.4	8.1	16.2	233.4	8.83	1,837.3	1,028.0	2,834.4	44.7
1993		104	62	10.0	7.7	16.2	233.9	9.07	1,937.8	1,235.5	3,043.9	70.5
1994		107P	63P	9.8	7.9	16.7	240.1	9.35	1,944.5	1,152.8	3,098.3	75.5
1995		111P	63P					8.13P				
1996		114P	63P					8.39P				
1997		117P	62P					8.64P				
1998		120P	62P					8.89P				

Sources: 1982, 1987, 1992 *Economic Census*; *Annual Survey of Manufactures*, 83-86, 88-91, 93-94. Establishment counts for non-Census years are from *County Business Patterns*; establishment values for 83-84 are extrapolations. 'P's show projections by the editors. Industries reclassified in 87 will not have data for prior years.

INDICES OF CHANGE

Year	Com-panies	Establishments		Employment			Compensation		Production ($ million)			
		Total	with 20 or more employees	Total (000)	Production Workers (000)	Production Hours (Mil)	Payroll ($ mil)	Wages ($/hr)	Cost of Materials	Value Added by Manufacture	Value of Shipments	Capital Invest.
1982												
1983												
1984												
1985												
1986												
1987	77	79	94	85	85	83	74	97	70	84	77	63
1988		81	94	84	85	86	78	101	71	81	75	81
1989		79	88	91								
1990		78	88	84	86	86	86	105	76	96	84	76
1991		80	86	89								
1992	100	100	100	100	100	100	100	100	100	100	100	100
1993		93	90	96	95	100	100	103	105	120	107	158
1994		96P	91P	94	98	103	103	106	106	112	109	169
1995		99P	91P					92P				
1996		102P	91P					95P				
1997		105P	90P					98P				
1998		108P	90P					101P				

Sources: Same as General Statistics. Values reflect change from the base year, 1992. Values above 100 mean greater than 92, values below 100 mean less than 92, and a value of 100 in the 82-91 or 93-98 period means same as 92. 'P's mark projections by the editors.

SELECTED RATIOS

For 1994	Avg. of All Manufact.	Analyzed Industry	Index
Employees per Establishment	49	91	186
Payroll per Establishment	1,500,273	2,234,973	149
Payroll per Employee	30,620	24,500	80
Production Workers per Establishment	34	74	214
Wages per Establishment	853,319	1,453,477	170
Wages per Production Worker	24,861	19,765	80
Hours per Production Worker	2,056	2,114	103
Wages per Hour	12.09	9.35	77
Value Added per Establishment	4,602,255	10,730,851	233
Value Added per Employee	93,930	117,633	125

For 1994	Avg. of All Manufact.	Analyzed Industry	Index
Value Added per Production Worker	134,084	145,924	109
Cost per Establishment	5,045,178	18,100,399	359
Cost per Employee	102,970	198,418	193
Cost per Production Worker	146,988	246,139	167
Shipments per Establishment	9,576,895	28,840,559	301
Shipments per Employee	195,460	316,153	162
Shipments per Production Worker	279,017	392,190	141
Investment per Establishment	321,011	702,793	219
Investment per Employee	6,552	7,704	118
Investment per Production Worker	9,352	9,557	102

Sources: Same as General Statistics. The 'Average of All Manufacturing' column represents the average of all manufacturing industries reported for the most recent complete year available. The Index shows the relationship between the Average and the Analyzed Industry. For example, 100 means that they are equal; 500 that the Analyzed Industry is five times the average; 50 means that the Analyzed Industry is half the national average. The abbreviation 'na' is used to show that data are 'not available'.

LEADING COMPANIES

Number shown: **20** Total sales ($ mil): **909** Total employment (000): **5.0**

Company Name	Address				CEO Name	Phone	Co. Type	Sales ($ mil)	Empl. (000)
Blue Diamond Growers	1802 C St	Sacramento	CA	95814	Walter F Payne	916-442-0771	R	450	2.0
John B Sanfilippo and Son Inc	2299 Busse Rd	Elk Grove Vill	IL	60007	Jasper B Sanfilippo	708-593-2300	P	209	1.3
Fisher Nut Co	6250 Ctr Hill Av	Cincinnati	OH	45224	Roger Schrankler	513-634-1042	S	48*	0.3
Azar Nut Co	1800 Northwestern	El Paso	TX	79912	Tim Ratliffe	915-877-4079	R	43	0.3
Sun-Diamond Growers	16500 W 103rd St	Lemont	IL	60439	EA Squier	708-739-3000	D	20	0.1
Fairmont Snacks Group Inc	6133 Rockside Rd	Independence	OH	44131	Leonard P Tannen	216-642-3336	R	17	0.2
Peterson Nut Co	6133 Rockside Rd	Independence	OH	44131	Leonard P Tannen	216-642-3336	S	17	0.2
AL Bazzini Company Inc	339 Greenwich St	New York	NY	10013	Rocco Damato	212-334-1280	R	16	<0.1
David and Sons Inc	8064 Chivvis Dr	St Louis	MO	63123	Ed Schmalkuche	314-832-7575	S	16	0.1
South Georgia Pecan Co	PO Box 5366	Valdosta	GA	31603	JP Worn	912-244-1321	R	13	<0.1
Kar Nut Products Co	1525 Wanda St	Ferndale	MI	48220	Ernest L Nicolay Jr	313-541-7870	R	12	<0.1
Universal Blanchers	PO Drawer 727	Blakely	GA	31723	John W Bowen	912-723-4181	R	12	0.1
Ellis Pecan Co	PO Box 4373	Fort Worth	TX	76106	Brian Hammons	817-624-7216	S	8	<0.1
Chicago Almond Inc	2901 Oakland Av	Elkhart	IN	46517	James D Brodie	219-522-2877	R	7*	<0.1
Beer Nuts Inc	PO Box 1549	Bloomington	IL	61702	RO Shirk	309-827-8580	R	5	<0.1
Priester Pecan Company Inc	PO Drawer 381	Fort Deposit	AL	36032	NT Ellis	205-227-4301	R	5	<0.1
Superior Nut Company Inc	225 O'Brien	Cambridge	MA	02141	Harry Hintlian	617-876-3808	R	5*	<0.1
Jensen Manufacturing Co	9525 Brasher St	Pico Rivera	CA	90660	Barry Levin	213-234-7683	R	3*	<0.1
Reeves Peanut Company Inc	PO Box 565	Eufaula	AL	36027	Ben C Reeves	205-687-2756	R	2*	<0.1
Nature's Select Inc	1608 Cooper St	Jackson	MI	49202	Peter T Assaly	517-784-0700	R	1	<0.1

Source: *Ward's Business Directory of U.S. Private and Public Companies*, Volumes 1 and 2, 1996. The company type code used is as follows: P - Public, R - Private, S - Subsidiary, D - Division, J - Joint Venture, A - Affiliate, G - Group. Sales are in millions of dollars, employees are in thousands. An asterisk (*) indicates an estimated sales volume. The symbol < stands for 'less than'. Company names and addresses are truncated, in some cases, to fit into the available space.

MATERIALS CONSUMED

Material		Quantity	Delivered Cost ($ million)
Materials, ingredients, containers, and supplies		(X)	1,762.5
Nuts, in shell (including peanuts)	mil lb	1,122.4	635.7
Nutmeats, including peanuts, processed	mil lb	150.9	125.7
Nutmeats, raw	mil lb	590.9	661.3
Fresh and dried fruits	mil lb	13.6*	13.1
Sugar, cane and beet (in terms of sugar solids)	1,000 s tons	19.0	8.4
Fats and oils, including shortening	1,000 s tons	46.4	16.8
Packaging paper and plastics film, coated and laminated		(X)	41.3
Paperboard containers, boxes, and corrugated paperboard		(X)	53.9
Plastics containers		(X)	5.8
Glass containers		(X)	13.3
Metal cans, can lids and ends		(X)	29.4
All other materials and components, parts, containers, and supplies		(X)	116.7
Materials, ingredients, containers, and supplies, nsk		(X)	41.2

Source: 1992 *Economic Census*. Explanation of symbols used: (D): Withheld to avoid disclosure of competitive data; na: Not available; (S): Withheld because statistical norms were not met; (X): Not applicable; (Z): Less than half the unit shown; nec: Not elsewhere classified; nsk: Not specified by kind; - : zero; * : 10-19 percent estimated; ** : 20-29 percent estimated.

PRODUCT SHARE DETAILS

Product or Product Class	% Share	Product or Product Class	% Share
Nuts and seeds	100.00	Other canned nuts, canned separately or with 3 varieties or less	6.60
Peanuts, shipped separately, sold in bulk	13.76	Other packaged peanuts, shipped separately	7.61
Mixed nuts, including 4 varieties or more, sold in bulk	0.65	Other packaged mixed nuts, including 4 varieties or more	2.65
Other nuts, shipped separately or with 3 varieties or less, sold in bulk	16.75	Other packaged nuts, packaged separately or with 3 varieties or less	29.90
Canned peanuts, shipped separately	10.43	Seeds (sunflower, pumpkin, etc.)	4.56
Canned mixed nuts, including 4 varieties or more	5.52		

Source: 1992 *Economic Census*. The values shown are percent of total shipments in an industry. Values of indented subcategories are summed in the main heading. The symbol (D) appears when data are withheld to prevent disclosure of competitive information. The abbreviation nsk stands for 'not specified by kind' and nec for 'not elsewhere classified'.

INPUTS AND OUTPUTS FOR FOOD PREPARATIONS, NEC

Economic Sector or Industry Providing Inputs	%	Sector
Miscellaneous plastics products	11.8	Manufg.
Wholesale trade	11.6	Trade
Imports	8.7	Foreign
Cyclic crudes and organics	5.8	Manufg.
Noncomparable imports	4.0	Foreign
Paper coating & glazing	3.9	Manufg.
Oil bearing crops	3.8	Agric.
Paperboard containers & boxes	3.8	Manufg.
Vegetables	3.6	Agric.
Advertising	3.2	Services
Motor freight transportation & warehousing	2.9	Util.
Shortening & cooking oils	2.8	Manufg.
Glass containers	2.5	Manufg.
Sugar	2.2	Manufg.
Commercial printing	2.1	Manufg.
Bags, except textile	1.9	Manufg.
Miscellaneous livestock	1.2	Agric.
Metal cans	1.2	Manufg.
Electric services (utilities)	1.2	Util.
Miscellaneous crops	1.1	Agric.
Metal foil & leaf	1.1	Manufg.
Gas production & distribution (utilities)	1.1	Util.
Flour & other grain mill products	1.0	Manufg.
Forestry products	0.9	Agric.
Feed grains	0.8	Agric.
Eating & drinking places	0.8	Trade
Chemical preparations, nec	0.7	Manufg.
Cottonseed oil mills	0.7	Manufg.
Industrial inorganic chemicals, nec	0.7	Manufg.
Railroads & related services	0.7	Util.
Water transportation	0.7	Util.
Business services nec	0.7	Services
Chocolate & cocoa products	0.5	Manufg.
Food preparations, nec	0.5	Manufg.
Wet corn milling	0.5	Manufg.
Banking	0.5	Fin/R.E.
Bread, cake, & related products	0.4	Manufg.
Crowns & closures	0.4	Manufg.
Dehydrated food products	0.4	Manufg.
Communications, except radio & TV	0.4	Util.
Electrical repair shops	0.4	Services
Maintenance of nonfarm buildings nec	0.3	Constr.
Cheese, natural & processed	0.3	Manufg.
Flavoring extracts & syrups, nec	0.3	Manufg.
Petroleum refining	0.3	Manufg.
Real estate	0.3	Fin/R.E.
Equipment rental & leasing services	0.3	Services
Legal services	0.3	Services
Management & consulting services & labs	0.3	Services
U.S. Postal Service	0.3	Gov't
Sugar crops	0.2	Agric.
Creamery butter	0.2	Manufg.
Soybean oil mills	0.2	Manufg.
Air transportation	0.2	Util.
Sanitary services, steam supply, irrigation	0.2	Util.
Royalties	0.2	Fin/R.E.
Accounting, auditing & bookkeeping	0.2	Services
Detective & protective services	0.2	Services
State & local government enterprises, nec	0.2	Gov't
Alkalies & chlorine	0.1	Manufg.
Bottled & canned soft drinks	0.1	Manufg.
Food products machinery	0.1	Manufg.
Lubricating oils & greases	0.1	Manufg.
Machinery, except electrical, nec	0.1	Manufg.
Poultry & egg processing	0.1	Manufg.
Water supply & sewage systems	0.1	Util.
Business/professional associations	0.1	Services
Miscellaneous repair shops	0.1	Services

Economic Sector or Industry Buying Outputs	%	Sector
Personal consumption expenditures	75.9	
Eating & drinking places	10.8	Trade
Exports	1.6	Foreign
Bread, cake, & related products	1.1	Manufg.
Fluid milk	1.1	Manufg.
Sausages & other prepared meats	1.1	Manufg.
Change in business inventories	1.1	In House
Ice cream & frozen desserts	0.8	Manufg.
Meat packing plants	0.6	Manufg.
Motion pictures	0.6	Services
Hospitals	0.5	Services
Federal Government purchases, nondefense	0.5	Fed Govt
Confectionery products	0.4	Manufg.
Residential care	0.4	Services
Food preparations, nec	0.3	Manufg.
Pickles, sauces, & salad dressings	0.3	Manufg.
Canned fruits & vegetables	0.2	Manufg.
Frozen specialties	0.2	Manufg.
Prepared feeds, nec	0.2	Manufg.
Nursing & personal care facilities	0.2	Services
Social services, nec	0.2	Services
S/L Govt. purch., elem. & secondary education	0.2	S/L Govt
S/L Govt. purch., health & hospitals	0.2	S/L Govt
S/L Govt. purch., higher education	0.2	S/L Govt
Cheese, natural & processed	0.1	Manufg.
Cookies & crackers	0.1	Manufg.
Federal Government enterprises nec	0.1	Gov't
Federal Government purchases, national defense	0.1	Fed Govt

Source: Benchmark Input-Output Accounts for the U.S. Economy, 1982, U.S. Department of Commerce, Washington, D.C., July 1991. Data, as reported in the source, are organized by the 1977 SIC structure in use in 1982 but have been matched, as closely as is possible, to the 1987 SIC structure used in this book.

OCCUPATIONS EMPLOYED BY SIC 206 - SUGAR AND CONFECTIONERY PRODUCTS

Occupation	% of Total 1994	Change to 2005	Occupation	% of Total 1994	Change to 2005
Packaging & filling machine operators	12.1	31.8	Cooking, roasting machine operators	2.0	-17.6
Hand packers & packagers	8.9	-24.7	Industrial truck & tractor operators	1.9	-12.1
Precision food & tobacco workers nec	8.4	0.7	General managers & top executives	1.5	-16.6
Helpers, laborers, & material movers nec	6.9	-12.1	Salespersons, retail	1.5	-12.1
Blue collar worker supervisors	4.4	-14.1	Agricultural workers nec	1.4	-12.1
Industrial machinery mechanics	4.0	-3.3	Machine operators nec	1.4	-22.5
Freight, stock, & material movers, hand	3.1	-29.7	Secretaries, ex legal & medical	1.3	-20.0
Janitors & cleaners, incl maids	3.1	-29.7	Assemblers, fabricators, & hand workers nec	1.2	-12.0
Extruding & forming machine workers	3.0	-12.1	Truck drivers light & heavy	1.1	-9.4
Maintenance repairers, general utility	2.3	-20.9	Traffic, shipping, & receiving clerks	1.1	-15.4
Machine feeders & offbearers	2.2	-20.9	Electricians	1.0	-17.5

Source: Industry-Occupation Matrix, Bureau of Labor Statistics. These data relate to one or more 3-digit SIC industry groups rather than to a single 4-digit SIC. The change reported for each occupation to the year 2005 is a percent of growth or decline as estimated by the Bureau of Labor Statistics. The abbreviation nec stands for 'not elsewhere classified'.

LOCATION BY STATE AND REGIONAL CONCENTRATION

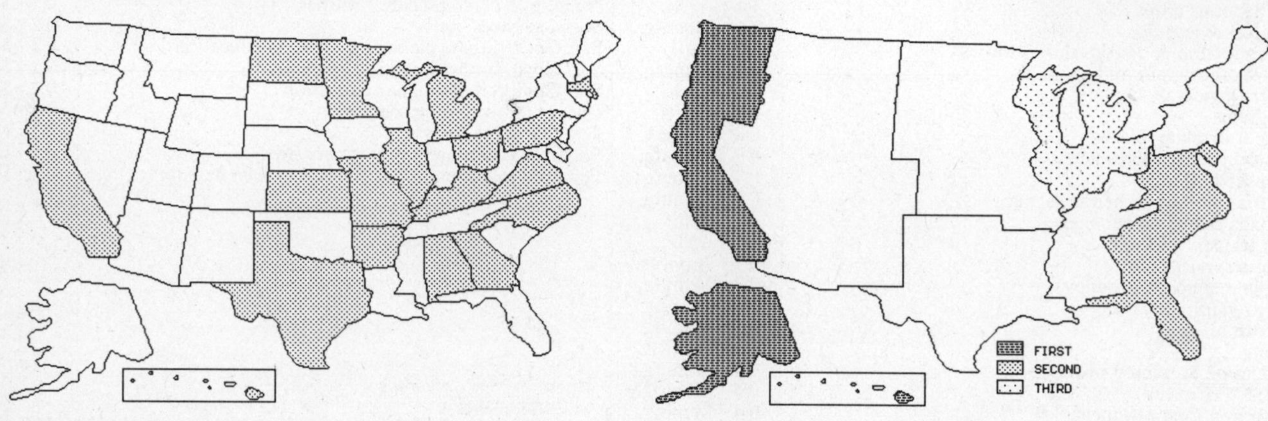

INDUSTRY DATA BY STATE

State	Establish-ments	Shipments Total ($ mil)	Shipments % of U.S.	Shipments Per Establ.	Employment Total Number	Employment % of U.S.	Employment Per Establ.	Wages ($/hour)	Cost as % of Shipments	Investment per Employee ($)
California	23	1,028.6	36.3	44.7	3,700	35.6	161	8.11	57.5	4,108
Georgia	10	366.8	12.9	36.7	1,500	14.4	150	9.48	78.2	3,733
North Carolina	6	207.8	7.3	34.6	700	6.7	117	8.25	57.8	3,143
Minnesota	4	96.4	3.4	24.1	500	4.8	125	10.29	62.7	1,600
Ohio	3	18.9	0.7	6.3	100	1.0	33	13.00	62.4	-
Michigan	6	18.1	0.6	3.0	200	1.9	33	7.00	43.6	1,500
Illinois	7	(D)	-	-	375 *	3.6	54	-	-	-
Texas	5	(D)	-	-	375 *	3.6	75	-	-	-
Virginia	5	(D)	-	-	750 *	7.2	150	-	-	-
Hawaii	4	(D)	-	-	750 *	7.2	188	-	-	1,733
Massachusetts	4	(D)	-	-	375 *	3.6	94	-	-	4,800
Pennsylvania	4	(D)	-	-	175 *	1.7	44	-	-	-
North Dakota	3	(D)	-	-	175 *	1.7	58	-	-	1,714
Alabama	2	(D)	-	-	175 *	1.7	88	-	-	-
Kansas	2	(D)	-	-	175 *	1.7	88	-	-	-
Kentucky	2	(D)	-	-	175 *	1.7	88	-	-	-
Arkansas	1	(D)	-	-	375 *	3.6	375	-	-	-
Missouri	1	(D)	-	-	175 *	1.7	175	-	-	-

Source: 1992 *Economic Census*. The states are in descending order of shipments or establishments (if shipment data are missing for the majority). The symbol (D) appears when data are withheld to prevent disclosure of competitive information. States marked with (D) are sorted by number of establishments. A dash (-) indicates that the data element cannot be calculated; * indicates the midpoint of a range.

2074 - COTTONSEED OIL MILLS

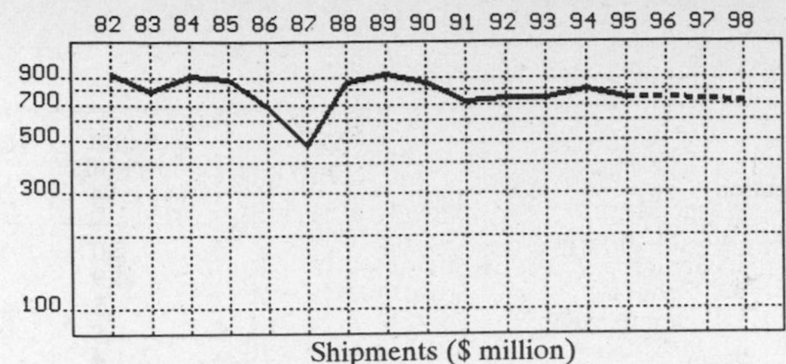

Shipments ($ million)

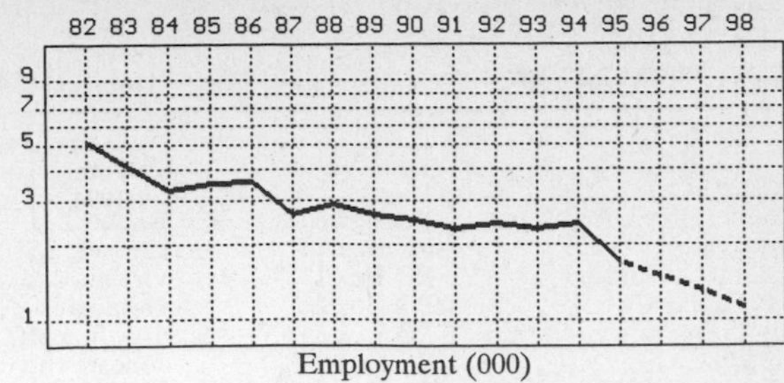

Employment (000)

GENERAL STATISTICS

Year	Companies	Establishments: Total	Establishments: with 20 or more employees	Employment: Total (000)	Employment: Production Workers (000)	Employment: Production Hours (Mil)	Compensation: Payroll ($ mil)	Compensation: Wages ($/hr)	Production ($ million): Cost of Materials	Production ($ million): Value Added by Manufacture	Production ($ million): Value of Shipments	Production ($ million): Capital Invest.
1982	47	77	60	5.2	4.3	9.7	76.2	5.62	715.0	202.9	933.3	59.6
1983		72	57	4.1	3.3	7.4	65.2	6.04	572.9	229.9	791.4	16.9
1984		67	54	3.3	2.6	6.0	57.9	6.57	727.0	197.2	906.2	23.2
1985		62	50	3.5	2.7	6.6	64.5	6.71	640.2	219.3	880.8	22.0
1986		60	51	3.6	2.8	6.2	61.2	6.50	487.6	177.4	678.0	17.9
1987	31	52	40	2.6	2.0	4.5	44.8	6.62	378.8	106.9	470.7	12.2
1988		52	38	2.9	2.3	5.3	58.2	7.64	628.6	264.7	851.6	19.2
1989		46	37	2.6	2.5	5.6	59.7	7.48	714.5	210.1	938.7	28.8
1990		45	35	2.5	2.3	4.9	52.8	7.53	619.6	185.0	850.5	24.8
1991		45	33	2.3	1.8	4.0	43.8	7.47	483.8	198.4	716.3	27.4
1992	22	45	35	2.4	1.9	4.3	49.6	7.88	510.8	211.4	737.8	12.0
1993		42	27	2.3	1.8	4.1	48.8	8.27	529.5	214.6	743.7	21.8
1994		35P	24P	2.4	1.9	4.4	52.5	7.77	614.3	200.9	803.8	69.8
1995		32P	21P	1.7P	1.4P	3.1P	44.2P	8.41P	565.4P	184.9P	739.8P	30.7P
1996		28P	19P	1.5P	1.3P	2.8P	42.4P	8.60P	559.7P	183.0P	732.3P	31.2P
1997		25P	16P	1.3P	1.1P	2.4P	40.7P	8.79P	553.9P	181.2P	724.8P	31.7P
1998		22P	13P	1.1P	0.9P	2.1P	38.9P	8.98P	548.2P	179.3P	717.3P	32.2P

Sources: 1982, 1987, 1992 *Economic Census*; *Annual Survey of Manufactures*, 83-86, 88-91, 93-94. Establishment counts for non-Census years are from *County Business Patterns*; establishment values for 83-84 are extrapolations. 'P's show projections by the editors. Industries reclassified in 87 will not have data for prior years.

INDICES OF CHANGE

Year	Companies	Establishments: Total	Establishments: with 20 or more employees	Employment: Total (000)	Employment: Production Workers (000)	Employment: Production Hours (Mil)	Compensation: Payroll ($ mil)	Compensation: Wages ($/hr)	Production ($ million): Cost of Materials	Production ($ million): Value Added by Manufacture	Production ($ million): Value of Shipments	Production ($ million): Capital Invest.
1982	214	171	171	217	226	226	154	71	140	96	126	497
1983		160	163	171	174	172	131	77	112	109	107	141
1984		149	154	137	137	140	117	83	142	93	123	193
1985		138	143	146	142	153	130	85	125	104	119	183
1986		133	146	150	147	144	123	82	95	84	92	149
1987	141	116	114	108	105	105	90	84	74	51	64	102
1988		116	109	121	121	123	117	97	123	125	115	160
1989		102	106	108	132	130	120	95	140	99	127	240
1990		100	100	104	121	114	106	96	121	88	115	207
1991		100	94	96	95	93	88	95	95	94	97	228
1992	100	100	100	100	100	100	100	100	100	100	100	100
1993		93	77	96	95	95	98	105	104	102	101	182
1994		77P	69P	100	100	102	106	99	120	95	109	582
1995		70P	61P	71P	74P	73P	89P	107P	111P	87P	100P	256P
1996		63P	53P	63P	66P	65P	86P	109P	110P	87P	99P	260P
1997		56P	45P	55P	58P	57P	82P	112P	108P	86P	98P	264P
1998		49P	36P	47P	50P	48P	78P	114P	107P	85P	97P	268P

Sources: Same as General Statistics. Values reflect change from the base year, 1992. Values above 100 mean greater than 92, values below 100 mean less than 92, and a value of 100 in the 82-91 or 93-98 period means same as 92. 'P's mark projections by the editors.

SELECTED RATIOS

For 1994	Avg. of All Manufact.	Analyzed Industry	Index	For 1994	Avg. of All Manufact.	Analyzed Industry	Index
Employees per Establishment	49	69	141	Value Added per Production Worker	134,084	105,737	79
Payroll per Establishment	1,500,273	1,510,462	101	Cost per Establishment	5,045,178	17,673,845	350
Payroll per Employee	30,620	21,875	71	Cost per Employee	102,970	255,958	249
Production Workers per Establishment	34	55	159	Cost per Production Worker	146,988	323,316	220
Wages per Establishment	853,319	983,613	115	Shipments per Establishment	9,576,895	23,125,894	241
Wages per Production Worker	24,861	17,994	72	Shipments per Employee	195,460	334,917	171
Hours per Production Worker	2,056	2,316	113	Shipments per Production Worker	279,017	423,053	152
Wages per Hour	12.09	7.77	64	Investment per Establishment	321,011	2,008,195	626
Value Added per Establishment	4,602,255	5,780,035	126	Investment per Employee	6,552	29,083	444
Value Added per Employee	93,930	83,708	89	Investment per Production Worker	9,352	36,737	393

Sources: Same as General Statistics. The 'Average of All Manufacturing' column represents the average of all manufacturing industries reported for the most recent complete year available. The Index shows the relationship between the Average and the Analyzed Industry. For example, 100 means that they are equal; 500 that the Analyzed Industry is five times the average; 50 means that the Analyzed Industry is half the national average. The abbreviation 'na' is used to show that data are 'not available'.

LEADING COMPANIES

Number shown: **10** Total sales ($ mil): **427** Total employment (000): **1.8**

Company Name	Address				CEO Name	Phone	Co. Type	Sales ($ mil)	Empl. (000)
Plains Cooperative Oil Mill Inc	PO Box 841	Lubbock	TX	79408	Wayne Martin	806-747-3434	R	105	0.3
Chickasha Cotton Oil Co	PO Box 2710	Chandler	AZ	85244	Ernest C Inmon Jr	602-963-3300	S	93	0.6
Yazoo Valley Oil Mill Inc	PO Box 1320	Greenwood	MS	38930	TS Shuler	601-453-4312	R	85	0.4
Osceola Products Co	PO Box 217	Osceola	AR	72370	SW Cooper	501-563-6541	R	50	0.2
Producers Cooperative Oil Mill	PO Box 26907	Oklahoma City	OK	73126	TW Detamore	405-232-7555	R	38	0.1
Delta Oil Mill	PO Box 29	Jonestown	MS	38639	EL McMurchy	601-358-4481	R	21*	0.1
Helena Cotton Oil Company Inc	PO Box 569	Helena	AR	72342	Billy Clark	501-338-8381	R	20	<0.1
Liberal Hull Company Inc	PO Box 2725	Liberal	KS	67905	Tom Manning	316-624-2211	S	7*	<0.1
Union Oil Mill Inc	PO Box 97	West Monroe	LA	71294	TS Shuler	318-387-2402	R	6	<0.1
Louisville Fertilizer Gin Co	106 W Broad St	Louisville	GA	30434	Don H Evans Jr	912-625-7212	R	2*	<0.1

Source: *Ward's Business Directory of U.S. Private and Public Companies*, Volumes 1 and 2, 1996. The company type code used is as follows: P - Public, R - Private, S - Subsidiary, D - Division, J - Joint Venture, A - Affiliate, G - Group. Sales are in millions of dollars, employees are in thousands. An asterisk (*) indicates an estimated sales volume. The symbol < stands for 'less than'. Company names and addresses are truncated, in some cases, to fit into the available space.

MATERIALS CONSUMED

Material		Quantity	Delivered Cost ($ million)
Materials, ingredients, containers, and supplies		(X)	421.4
Cottonseed seeds, nuts, and beans	1,000 s tons	3,618.9	354.1
Crude cottonseed oil	mil lb	(D)	(D)
Once-refined cottonseed oil	mil lb	(D)	(D)
All other materials and components, parts, containers, and supplies		(X)	28.9
Materials, ingredients, containers, and supplies, nsk		(X)	26.7

Source: 1992 *Economic Census*. Explanation of symbols used: (D): Withheld to avoid disclosure of competitive data; na: Not available; (S): Withheld because statistical norms were not met; (X): Not applicable; (Z): Less than half the unit shown; nec: Not elsewhere classified; nsk: Not specified by kind; - : zero; * : 10-19 percent estimated; ** : 20-29 percent estimated.

PRODUCT SHARE DETAILS

Product or Product Class	% Share	Product or Product Class	% Share
Cottonseed oil mills	100.00	Cottonseed cake and meal	57.84
Cottonseed oil, crude	14.93	Cottonseed hulls	(D)
Cottonseed oil, once-refined (after alkali or caustic wash but before deodorizing or use in end products)	23.89	Other cottonseed byproducts	(D)
Cotton linters	7.64	Cottonseed oil, once-refined, purchased and deodorized only	31.64
Cottonseed cake and meal and other byproducts	50.71	Cottonseed oil mills, nsk	2.82

Source: 1992 *Economic Census*. The values shown are percent of total shipments in an industry. Values of indented subcategories are summed in the main heading. The symbol (D) appears when data are withheld to prevent disclosure of competitive information. The abbreviation nsk stands for 'not specified by kind' and nec for 'not elsewhere classified'.

INPUTS AND OUTPUTS FOR COTTONSEED OIL MILLS

Economic Sector or Industry Providing Inputs	%	Sector	Economic Sector or Industry Buying Outputs	%	Sector
Cotton	63.1	Agric.	Exports	23.2	Foreign
Wholesale trade	12.8	Trade	Prepared feeds, nec	20.0	Manufg.
Electric services (utilities)	5.2	Util.	Shortening & cooking oils	10.8	Manufg.
Miscellaneous plastics products	3.2	Manufg.	Frozen specialties	8.8	Manufg.
Gas production & distribution (utilities)	2.9	Util.	Food preparations, nec	6.7	Manufg.
Cottonseed oil mills	1.9	Manufg.	Poultry & eggs	5.6	Agric.
Motor freight transportation & warehousing	1.8	Util.	Meat animals	5.0	Agric.
Advertising	1.8	Services	Paints & allied products	4.7	Manufg.
Railroads & related services	0.9	Util.	Pulp mills	3.5	Manufg.
Banking	0.6	Fin/R.E.	Surgical appliances & supplies	2.7	Manufg.
Imports	0.6	Foreign	Paper mills, except building paper	2.0	Manufg.
Oil bearing crops	0.5	Agric.	Cottonseed oil mills	1.7	Manufg.
Miscellaneous repair shops	0.5	Services	Mattresses & bedsprings	1.7	Manufg.
Eating & drinking places	0.4	Trade	Dairy farm products	1.2	Agric.
Paperboard containers & boxes	0.3	Manufg.	Miscellaneous livestock	1.0	Agric.
Cyclic crudes and organics	0.2	Manufg.	Upholstered household furniture	1.0	Manufg.
Communications, except radio & TV	0.2	Util.	Dog, cat, & other pet food	0.3	Manufg.
Computer & data processing services	0.2	Services	Padding & upholstery filling	0.3	Manufg.
Detective & protective services	0.2	Services			
U.S. Postal Service	0.2	Gov't			
Maintenance of nonfarm buildings nec	0.1	Constr.			
Glass containers	0.1	Manufg.			
Metal cans	0.1	Manufg.			
Air transportation	0.1	Util.			
Sanitary services, steam supply, irrigation	0.1	Util.			
Equipment rental & leasing services	0.1	Services			
Legal services	0.1	Services			
Management & consulting services & labs	0.1	Services			

Source: Benchmark Input-Output Accounts for the U.S. Economy, 1982, U.S. Department of Commerce, Washington, D.C., July 1991. Data, as reported in the source, are organized by the 1977 SIC structure in use in 1982 but have been matched, as closely as is possible, to the 1987 SIC structure used in this book.

OCCUPATIONS EMPLOYED BY SIC 207 - GRAIN MILL PRODUCTS AND FATS AND OILS

Occupation	% of Total 1994	Change to 2005	Occupation	% of Total 1994	Change to 2005
Packaging & filling machine operators	8.2	-5.4	General office clerks	2.0	-10.3
Truck drivers light & heavy	6.0	8.4	Secretaries, ex legal & medical	1.9	-4.3
Crushing & mixing machine operators	5.7	-5.4	Separating & still machine operators	1.9	5.1
Blue collar worker supervisors	5.5	0.1	Machine feeders & offbearers	1.8	-5.3
Helpers, laborers, & material movers nec	4.7	5.1	Machine operators nec	1.8	-7.3
Industrial machinery mechanics	3.7	15.7	Bookkeeping, accounting, & auditing clerks	1.7	-21.1
Freight, stock, & material movers, hand	3.4	-15.9	Industrial production managers	1.7	5.1
Industrial truck & tractor operators	3.2	5.1	Science & mathematics technicians	1.5	5.2
Sales & related workers nec	2.6	5.2	Material moving equipment operators nec	1.5	5.1
General managers & top executives	2.5	-0.3	Janitors & cleaners, incl maids	1.4	-15.9
Maintenance repairers, general utility	2.4	-5.4	Inspectors, testers, & graders, precision	1.2	5.2
Hand packers & packagers	2.2	-9.9	Agricultural workers nec	1.1	5.2
Extruding & forming machine workers	2.1	-26.4	Plant & system operators nec	1.0	39.3
Precision food & tobacco workers nec	2.1	5.1	Traffic, shipping, & receiving clerks	1.0	1.2
Cooking, roasting machine operators	2.0	11.4			

Source: Industry-Occupation Matrix, Bureau of Labor Statistics. These data relate to one or more 3-digit SIC industry groups rather than to a single 4-digit SIC. The change reported for each occupation to the year 2005 is a percent of growth or decline as estimated by the Bureau of Labor Statistics. The abbreviation nec stands for 'not elsewhere classified'.

LOCATION BY STATE AND REGIONAL CONCENTRATION

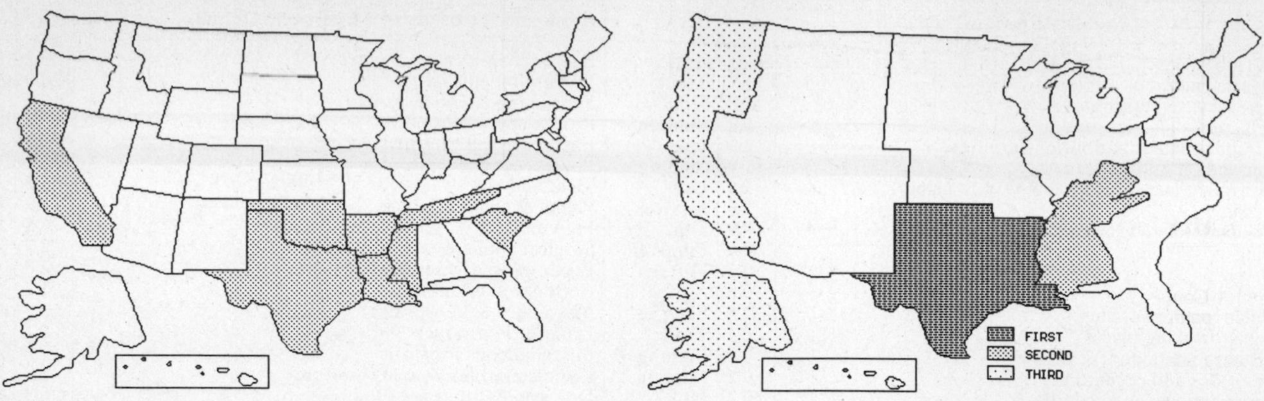

INDUSTRY DATA BY STATE

State	Establish-ments	Shipments			Employment				Cost as % of Shipments	Investment per Employee ($)
		Total ($ mil)	% of U.S.	Per Establ.	Total Number	% of U.S.	Per Establ.	Wages ($/hour)		
Texas	12	243.9	33.1	20.3	800	33.3	67	8.21	74.3	5,375
Mississippi	10	104.4	14.2	10.4	500	20.8	50	6.11	69.0	3,600
Arkansas	4	83.5	11.3	20.9	300	12.5	75	7.83	77.1	9,000
California	3	(D)	-	-	175 *	7.3	58	-	-	-
Louisiana	3	(D)	-	-	175 *	7.3	58	-	-	-
Oklahoma	2	(D)	-	-	175 *	7.3	88	-	-	-
South Carolina	2	(D)	-	-	175 *	7.3	88	-	-	-
Tennessee	1	(D)	-	-	175 *	7.3	175	-	-	-

Source: 1992 *Economic Census*. The states are in descending order of shipments or establishments (if shipment data are missing for the majority). The symbol (D) appears when data are withheld to prevent disclosure of competitive information. States marked with (D) are sorted by number of establishments. A dash (-) indicates that the data element cannot be calculated; * indicates the midpoint of a range.

2075 - SOYBEAN OIL MILLS

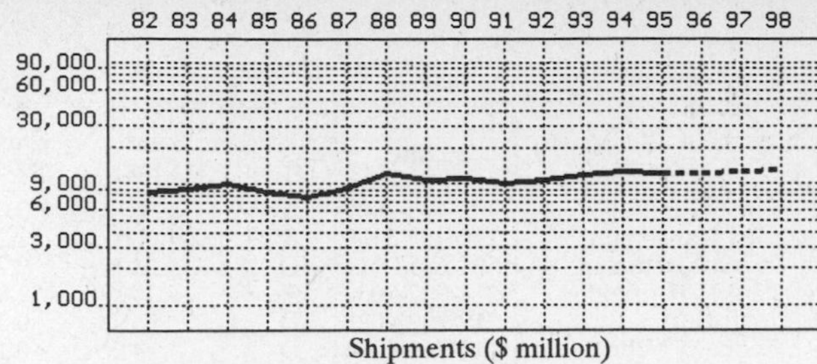

Shipments ($ million)

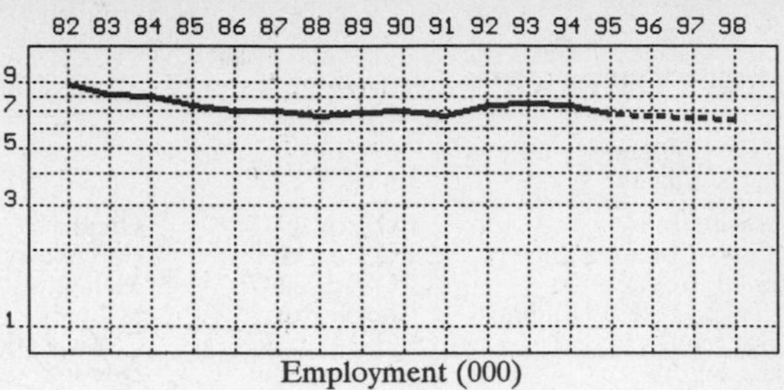

Employment (000)

GENERAL STATISTICS

Year	Companies	Establishments		Employment			Compensation		Production ($ million)			
		Total	with 20 or more employees	Total (000)	Production Workers (000)	Production Hours (Mil)	Payroll ($ mil)	Wages ($/hr)	Cost of Materials	Value Added by Manufacture	Value of Shipments	Capital Invest.
1982	34	114	84	8.9	6.2	13.4	188.7	9.19	7,896.8	678.2	8,603.6	113.4
1983		119	83	8.1	5.6	12.1	180.6	9.91	8,362.2	888.1	9,059.8	79.5
1984		124	82	7.9	5.3	11.0	186.6	10.72	9,067.3	651.6	9,988.2	96.5
1985		129	81	7.3	4.8	10.1	168.8	10.97	7,911.7	711.7	8,629.4	109.5
1986		127	80	7.0	4.6	9.4	166.6	11.32	7,104.6	676.7	7,815.5	93.3
1987	47	106	73	7.0	4.8	10.1	172.5	11.11	8,103.3	1,011.5	9,074.1	90.7
1988		117	74	6.7	4.5	9.8	176.5	11.64	10,885.4	1,411.4	12,140.3	126.4
1989		109	69	6.9	4.1	8.9	167.9	12.03	9,313.7	1,231.4	10,723.6	99.1
1990		106	69	7.0	4.8	10.3	199.2	12.37	9,516.2	1,519.0	10,966.3	166.0
1991		105	70	6.7	4.6	10.0	197.2	12.56	8,832.5	1,186.5	9,965.0	207.9
1992	42	99	70	7.4	5.1	11.1	225.3	12.89	9,372.5	1,273.8	10,650.6	123.2
1993		98	71	7.5	5.2	11.2	230.7	12.82	10,153.0	1,537.2	11,705.1	146.7
1994		98P	66P	7.4	5.1	11.2	239.8	13.33	10,605.9	1,864.1	12,496.2	137.0
1995		96P	64P	6.8P	4.6P	10.0P	225.3P	13.75P	10,277.0P	1,806.3P	12,108.7P	162.0P
1996		94P	63P	6.7P	4.5P	9.9P	230.0P	14.06P	10,515.7P	1,848.2P	12,389.9P	167.7P
1997		91P	61P	6.6P	4.5P	9.8P	234.8P	14.37P	10,754.4P	1,890.2P	12,671.2P	173.3P
1998		89P	59P	6.5P	4.4P	9.7P	239.5P	14.67P	10,993.1P	1,932.2P	12,952.4P	179.0P

Sources: 1982, 1987, 1992 *Economic Census*; *Annual Survey of Manufactures*, 83-86, 88-91, 93-94. Establishment counts for non-Census years are from *County Business Patterns*; establishment values for 83-84 are extrapolations. 'P's show projections by the editors. Industries reclassified in 87 will not have data for prior years.

INDICES OF CHANGE

Year	Companies	Establishments		Employment			Compensation		Production ($ million)			
		Total	with 20 or more employees	Total (000)	Production Workers (000)	Production Hours (Mil)	Payroll ($ mil)	Wages ($/hr)	Cost of Materials	Value Added by Manufacture	Value of Shipments	Capital Invest.
1982	81	115	120	120	122	121	84	71	84	53	81	92
1983		120	119	109	110	109	80	77	89	70	85	65
1984		125	117	107	104	99	83	83	97	51	94	78
1985		130	116	99	94	91	75	85	84	56	81	89
1986		128	114	95	90	85	74	88	76	53	73	76
1987	112	107	104	95	94	91	77	86	86	79	85	74
1988		118	106	91	88	88	78	90	116	111	114	103
1989		110	99	93	80	80	75	93	99	97	101	80
1990		107	99	95	94	93	88	96	102	119	103	135
1991		106	100	91	90	90	88	97	94	93	94	169
1992	100	100	100	100	100	100	100	100	100	100	100	100
1993		99	101	101	102	101	102	99	108	121	110	119
1994		99P	94P	100	100	101	106	103	113	146	117	111
1995		97P	92P	91P	90P	90P	100P	107P	110P	142P	114P	131P
1996		94P	89P	90P	89P	89P	102P	109P	112P	145P	116P	136P
1997		92P	87P	89P	88P	88P	104P	111P	115P	148P	119P	141P
1998		90P	85P	88P	86P	88P	106P	114P	117P	152P	122P	145P

Sources: Same as General Statistics. Values reflect change from the base year, 1992. Values above 100 mean greater than 92, values below 100 mean less than 92, and a value of 100 in the 82-91 or 93-98 period means same as 92. 'P's mark projections by the editors.

SELECTED RATIOS

For 1994	Avg. of All Manufact.	Analyzed Industry	Index
Employees per Establishment	49	75	154
Payroll per Establishment	1,500,273	2,445,804	163
Payroll per Employee	30,620	32,405	106
Production Workers per Establishment	34	52	152
Wages per Establishment	853,319	1,522,722	178
Wages per Production Worker	24,861	29,274	118
Hours per Production Worker	2,056	2,196	107
Wages per Hour	12.09	13.33	110
Value Added per Establishment	4,602,255	19,012,610	413
Value Added per Employee	93,930	251,905	268

For 1994	Avg. of All Manufact.	Analyzed Industry	Index
Value Added per Production Worker	134,084	365,510	273
Cost per Establishment	5,045,178	108,173,296	2,144
Cost per Employee	102,970	1,433,230	1,392
Cost per Production Worker	146,988	2,079,588	1,415
Shipments per Establishment	9,576,895	127,453,129	1,331
Shipments per Employee	195,460	1,688,676	864
Shipments per Production Worker	279,017	2,450,235	878
Investment per Establishment	321,011	1,397,311	435
Investment per Employee	6,552	18,514	283
Investment per Production Worker	9,352	26,863	287

Sources: Same as General Statistics. The 'Average of All Manufacturing' column represents the average of all manufacturing industries reported for the most recent complete year available. The Index shows the relationship between the Average and the Analyzed Industry. For example, 100 means that they are equal; 500 that the Analyzed Industry is five times the average; 50 means that the Analyzed Industry is half the national average. The abbreviation 'na' is used to show that data are 'not available'.

LEADING COMPANIES

Number shown: **11** Total sales ($ mil): **3,209** Total employment (000): **6.8**

Company Name	Address				CEO Name	Phone	Co. Type	Sales ($ mil)	Empl. (000)
Ag Processing Inc	PO Box 2047	Omaha	NE	68103	James Lindsay	402-496-7809	R	1,377	3.0
Central Soya Company Inc	PO Box 1400	Fort Wayne	IN	46801	Carl Hausmann	219-425-5100	R	1,000	1.2
Honeymead Products Co	PO Box 3247	Mankato	MN	56002	Merritt Petersen	507-625-7911	D	380	0.2
Protein Techn Intern Holdings	Checkerboard Sq	St Louis	MO	63164	Paul H Hatfield	314-982-1000	S	294	1.8
Cargill Soybean	PO Box 2817	Cedar Rapids	IA	52406	John Bill	319-399-4025	D	65	0.2
Ag Processing Inc	800 Diagonal St	Dawson	MN	56232	Leonard Miller	612-769-4386	D	41*	<0.1
Cargill Inc	PO Box 2309	Fayetteville	NC	28302	Walker Humphries	910-433-4900	D	24	<0.1
Ag Processing Inc Sergeant Bluff	PO Box 200	Sergeant Bluff	IA	51054	Jeff Rodgers	712-943-4282	D	10	<0.1
Southern Soya Corp	PO Box 727	Estill	SC	29918	Thomas L Harper	803-625-2711	R	8*	<0.1
ADM Protein Specialties	4666 Faries Pkwy	Decatur	IL	62526	Larry Cunningham	217-424-5200	D	5*	<0.1
American Lecithin Company Inc	PO Box 1908	Danbury	CT	06813	Randall E Zigmont	203-790-2700	S	5	<0.1

Source: *Ward's Business Directory of U.S. Private and Public Companies*, Volumes 1 and 2, 1996. The company type code used is as follows: P - Public, R - Private, S - Subsidiary, D - Division, J - Joint Venture, A - Affiliate, G - Group. Sales are in millions of dollars, employees are in thousands. An asterisk (*) indicates an estimated sales volume. The symbol < stands for 'less than'. Company names and addresses are truncated, in some cases, to fit into the available space.

MATERIALS CONSUMED

Material		Quantity	Delivered Cost ($ million)
Materials, ingredients, containers, and supplies		(X)	8,743.4
Soybean seeds, nuts, and beans	1,000 s tons	34,984.7	6,939.3
Crude soybean oil	mil lb	5,461.7	1,060.2
Paper and paperboard containers, including shipping sacks and other paper packaging supplies		(X)	23.4
All other materials and components, parts, containers, and supplies		(X)	666.4
Materials, ingredients, containers, and supplies, nsk		(X)	54.1

Source: 1992 *Economic Census*. Explanation of symbols used: (D): Withheld to avoid disclosure of competitive data; na: Not available; (S): Withheld because statistical norms were not met; (X): Not applicable; (Z): Less than half the unit shown; nec: Not elsewhere classified; nsk: Not specified by kind; - : zero; * : 10-19 percent estimated; ** : 20-29 percent estimated.

PRODUCT SHARE DETAILS

Product or Product Class	% Share
Soybean oil mills	100.00
Soybean oil	27.70
Crude soybean oil, degummed	54.34
Crude soybean oil, not degummed	32.93
Soybean oil, once-refined (after alkali or caustic wash but before deodorizing or use in end products)	12.12
Soybean oil processed for inedible purposes (acid refined, etc.)	0.45
Soybean oil, nsk	0.16
Soybean cake, meal, and other byproducts	71.77
Soybean cake and meal	78.20
Soy flour and grits	1.99
Soybean lecithin	0.65
Soybean millfeed (hullmeal)	1.86
Other soybean products, including isolates and concentrates	4.07
Soybean oil, once-refined, purchased and deodorized only	13.20
Soybean cake, meal, and other byproducts, nsk	0.03
Soybean oil mills, nsk	0.53

Source: 1992 *Economic Census*. The values shown are percent of total shipments in an industry. Values of indented subcategories are summed in the main heading. The symbol (D) appears when data are withheld to prevent disclosure of competitive information. The abbreviation nsk stands for 'not specified by kind' and nec for 'not elsewhere classified'.

INPUTS AND OUTPUTS FOR SOYBEAN OIL MILLS

Economic Sector or Industry Providing Inputs	%	Sector	Economic Sector or Industry Buying Outputs	%	Sector
Oil bearing crops	72.3	Agric.	Prepared feeds, nec	31.5	Manufg.
Wholesale trade	11.3	Trade	Exports	22.9	Foreign
Soybean oil mills	5.1	Manufg.	Shortening & cooking oils	20.7	Manufg.
Gas production & distribution (utilities)	1.6	Util.	Poultry & eggs	6.5	Agric.
Miscellaneous crops	1.3	Agric.	Meat animals	5.7	Agric.
Railroads & related services	1.3	Util.	Soybean oil mills	5.3	Manufg.
Motor freight transportation & warehousing	1.1	Util.	Dog, cat, & other pet food	2.5	Manufg.
Electric services (utilities)	1.0	Util.	Dairy farm products	1.5	Agric.
Water transportation	0.7	Util.	Miscellaneous livestock	1.1	Agric.
Wet corn milling	0.6	Manufg.	Personal consumption expenditures	0.7	
Advertising	0.6	Services	Paints & allied products	0.4	Manufg.
Banking	0.5	Fin/R.E.	Plastics materials & resins	0.3	Manufg.
Miscellaneous plastics products	0.3	Manufg.	Food preparations, nec	0.2	Manufg.
Petroleum refining	0.3	Manufg.	Cookies & crackers	0.1	Manufg.
Cotton	0.2	Agric.	Flavoring extracts & syrups, nec	0.1	Manufg.
Miscellaneous repair shops	0.2	Services	Frozen specialties	0.1	Manufg.
Cyclic crudes and organics	0.1	Manufg.			
Paperboard containers & boxes	0.1	Manufg.			
Soap & other detergents	0.1	Manufg.			

Source: Benchmark Input-Output Accounts for the U.S. Economy, 1982, U.S. Department of Commerce, Washington, D.C., July 1991. Data, as reported in the source, are organized by the 1977 SIC structure in use in 1982 but have been matched, as closely as is possible, to the 1987 SIC structure used in this book.

OCCUPATIONS EMPLOYED BY SIC 207 - GRAIN MILL PRODUCTS AND FATS AND OILS

Occupation	% of Total 1994	Change to 2005	Occupation	% of Total 1994	Change to 2005
Packaging & filling machine operators	8.2	-5.4	General office clerks	2.0	-10.3
Truck drivers light & heavy	6.0	8.4	Secretaries, ex legal & medical	1.9	-4.3
Crushing & mixing machine operators	5.7	-5.4	Separating & still machine operators	1.9	5.1
Blue collar worker supervisors	5.5	0.1	Machine feeders & offbearers	1.8	-5.3
Helpers, laborers, & material movers nec	4.7	5.1	Machine operators nec	1.8	-7.3
Industrial machinery mechanics	3.7	15.7	Bookkeeping, accounting, & auditing clerks	1.7	-21.1
Freight, stock, & material movers, hand	3.4	-15.9	Industrial production managers	1.7	5.1
Industrial truck & tractor operators	3.2	5.1	Science & mathematics technicians	1.5	5.2
Sales & related workers nec	2.6	5.2	Material moving equipment operators nec	1.5	5.1
General managers & top executives	2.5	-0.3	Janitors & cleaners, incl maids	1.4	-15.9
Maintenance repairers, general utility	2.4	-5.4	Inspectors, testers, & graders, precision	1.2	5.2
Hand packers & packagers	2.2	-9.9	Agricultural workers nec	1.1	5.2
Extruding & forming machine workers	2.1	-26.4	Plant & system operators nec	1.0	39.3
Precision food & tobacco workers nec	2.1	5.1	Traffic, shipping, & receiving clerks	1.0	1.2
Cooking, roasting machine operators	2.0	11.4			

Source: Industry-Occupation Matrix, Bureau of Labor Statistics. These data relate to one or more 3-digit SIC industry groups rather than to a single 4-digit SIC. The change reported for each occupation to the year 2005 is a percent of growth or decline as estimated by the Bureau of Labor Statistics. The abbreviation nec stands for 'not elsewhere classified'.

LOCATION BY STATE AND REGIONAL CONCENTRATION

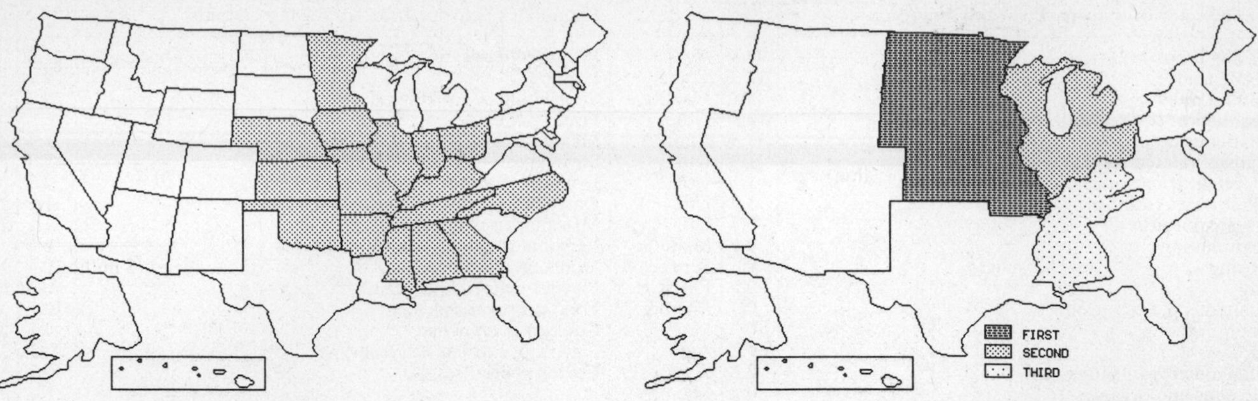

INDUSTRY DATA BY STATE

State	Establish-ments	Shipments			Employment				Cost as % of Shipments	Investment per Employee ($)
		Total ($ mil)	% of U.S.	Per Establ.	Total Number	% of U.S.	Per Establ.	Wages ($/hour)		
Illinois	16	2,590.4	24.3	161.9	2,300	31.1	144	13.03	85.9	17,652
Iowa	12	1,679.0	15.8	139.9	700	9.5	58	13.20	89.6	-
Minnesota	5	699.9	6.6	140.0	400	5.4	80	13.60	87.1	4,250
Ohio	5	672.2	6.3	134.4	400	5.4	80	13.67	89.1	-
Indiana	5	658.8	6.2	131.8	600	8.1	120	14.25	87.3	-
Tennessee	3	373.6	3.5	124.5	600	8.1	200	15.40	79.2	-
Kansas	6	(D)	-	-	375 *	5.1	63	-	-	6,400
Georgia	4	(D)	-	-	175 *	2.4	44	-	-	-
Nebraska	4	(D)	-	-	175 *	2.4	44	-	-	-
Mississippi	3	(D)	-	-	175 *	2.4	58	-	-	-
Missouri	3	(D)	-	-	175 *	2.4	58	-	-	-
North Carolina	3	(D)	-	-	175 *	2.4	58	-	-	-
Alabama	2	(D)	-	-	175 *	2.4	88	-	-	-
Arkansas	2	(D)	-	-	175 *	2.4	88	-	-	-
Kentucky	1	(D)	-	-	175 *	2.4	175	-	-	-
Oklahoma	1	(D)	-	-	175 *	2.4	175	-	-	-

Source: 1992 *Economic Census*. The states are in descending order of shipments or establishments (if shipment data are missing for the majority). The symbol (D) appears when data are withheld to prevent disclosure of competitive information. States marked with (D) are sorted by number of establishments. A dash (-) indicates that the data element cannot be calculated; * indicates the midpoint of a range.

2076 - VEGETABLE OIL MILLS

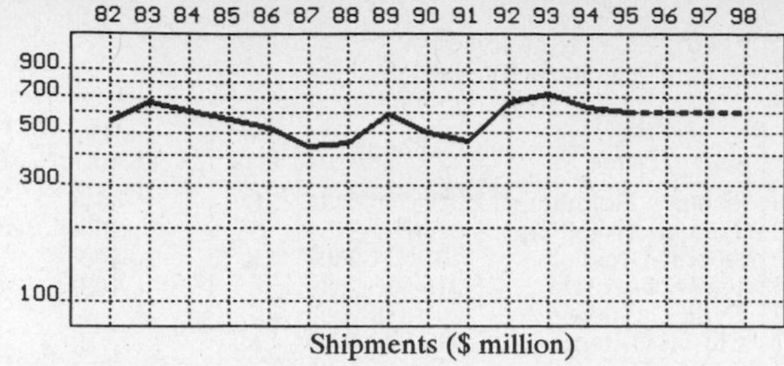

Shipments ($ million)

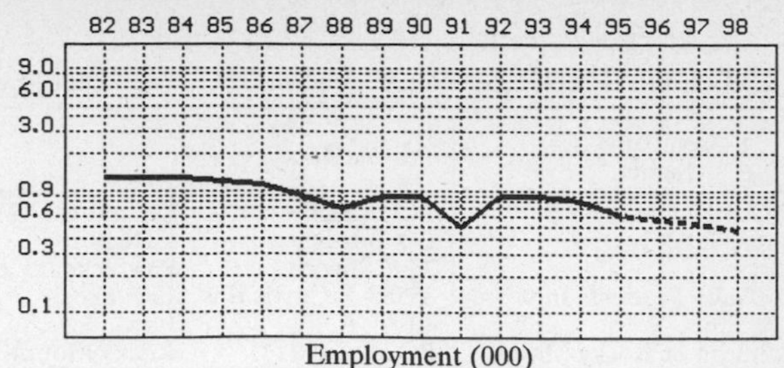

Employment (000)

GENERAL STATISTICS

Year	Companies	Establishments: Total	Establishments: with 20 or more employees	Employment: Total (000)	Employment: Production Workers (000)	Employment: Production Hours (Mil)	Compensation: Payroll ($ mil)	Compensation: Wages ($/hr)	Production ($ million): Cost of Materials	Production ($ million): Value Added by Manufacture	Production ($ million): Value of Shipments	Production ($ million): Capital Invest.
1982	26	29	15	1.3	0.9	1.8	22.3	8.22	467.0	80.0	556.9	66.9
1983		27	14	1.3	1.0	2.1	24.2	7.67	543.0	134.0	659.0	58.4
1984		25	13	1.3	1.0	2.1	21.9	7.33	546.6	53.1	616.7	44.0
1985		22	12	1.2	0.9	1.8	21.4	8.06	507.3	43.1	566.0	
1986		22	13	1.1	0.8	1.7	20.4	7.35	426.4	110.4	524.5	1.3
1987	20	23	15	0.9	0.5	1.1	19.9	10.36	353.3	82.7	431.5	4.9
1988		23	15	0.7	0.5	1.0	15.6	9.70	397.3	64.5	448.9	4.9
1989		24	14	0.9	0.5	1.1	16.8	9.09	447.4	128.8	591.3	34.8
1990		29	15	0.9	0.5	1.1	16.6	8.64	405.9	98.6	490.4	5.9
1991		25	14	0.5	0.3	0.6	13.0	12.17	316.0	120.0	455.1	6.5
1992	18	26	14	0.9	0.6	1.2	26.2	12.67	532.3	133.8	666.2	10.4
1993		27	16	0.9	0.6	1.4	27.5	11.79	603.8	139.8	721.1	8.1
1994		25P	15P	0.8	0.5	1.1	24.2	12.36	522.7	80.7	630.0	6.0
1995		25P	15P	0.6P	0.3P	0.8P	21.1P	12.74P	492.1P	76.0P	593.1P	
1996		25P	15P	0.6P	0.3P	0.7P	21.2P	13.18P	495.3P	76.5P	597.0P	
1997		25P	15P	0.5P	0.2P	0.6P	21.2P	13.62P	498.5P	77.0P	600.9P	
1998		26P	15P	0.5P	0.2P	0.5P	21.3P	14.07P	501.8P	77.5P	604.8P	

Sources: 1982, 1987, 1992 *Economic Census*; *Annual Survey of Manufactures*, 83-86, 88-91, 93-94. Establishment counts for non-Census years are from *County Business Patterns*; establishment values for 83-84 are extrapolations. 'P's show projections by the editors. Industries reclassified in 87 will not have data for prior years.

INDICES OF CHANGE

Year	Companies	Establishments: Total	Establishments: with 20 or more employees	Employment: Total (000)	Employment: Production Workers (000)	Employment: Production Hours (Mil)	Compensation: Payroll ($ mil)	Compensation: Wages ($/hr)	Production ($ million): Cost of Materials	Production ($ million): Value Added by Manufacture	Production ($ million): Value of Shipments	Production ($ million): Capital Invest.
1982	144	112	107	144	150	150	85	65	88	60	84	643
1983		104	100	144	167	175	92	61	102	100	99	562
1984		96	93	144	167	175	84	58	103	40	93	423
1985		85	86	133	150	150	82	64	95	32	85	
1986		85	93	122	133	142	78	58	80	83	79	13
1987	111	88	107	100	83	92	76	82	66	62	65	47
1988		88	107	78	83	83	60	77	75	48	67	47
1989		92	100	100	83	92	64	72	84	96	89	335
1990		112	107	100	83	92	63	68	76	74	74	57
1991		96	100	56	50	50	50	96	59	90	68	63
1992	100	100	100	100	100	100	100	100	100	100	100	100
1993		104	114	100	100	117	105	93	113	104	108	78
1994		98P	107P	89	83	92	92	98	98	60	95	58
1995		98P	108P	70P	56P	64P	81P	101P	92P	57P	89P	
1996		98P	109P	64P	49P	57P	81P	104P	93P	57P	90P	
1997		98P	110P	59P	41P	50P	81P	108P	94P	58P	90P	
1998		98P	111P	53P	33P	42P	81P	111P	94P	58P	91P	

Sources: Same as General Statistics. Values reflect change from the base year, 1992. Values above 100 mean greater than 92, values below 100 mean less than 92, and a value of 100 in the 82-91 or 93-98 period means same as 92. 'P's mark projections by the editors.

SELECTED RATIOS

For 1994	Avg. of All Manufact.	Analyzed Industry	Index
Employees per Establishment	49	32	64
Payroll per Establishment	1,500,273	952,983	64
Payroll per Employee	30,620	30,250	99
Production Workers per Establishment	34	20	57
Wages per Establishment	853,319	535,403	63
Wages per Production Worker	24,861	27,192	109
Hours per Production Worker	2,056	2,200	107
Wages per Hour	12.09	12.36	102
Value Added per Establishment	4,602,255	3,177,924	69
Value Added per Employee	93,930	100,875	107

For 1994	Avg. of All Manufact.	Analyzed Industry	Index
Value Added per Production Worker	134,084	161,400	120
Cost per Establishment	5,045,178	20,583,652	408
Cost per Employee	102,970	653,375	635
Cost per Production Worker	146,988	1,045,400	711
Shipments per Establishment	9,576,895	24,809,069	259
Shipments per Employee	195,460	787,500	403
Shipments per Production Worker	279,017	1,260,000	452
Investment per Establishment	321,011	236,277	74
Investment per Employee	6,552	7,500	114
Investment per Production Worker	9,352	12,000	128

Sources: Same as General Statistics. The 'Average of All Manufacturing' column represents the average of all manufacturing industries reported for the most recent complete year available. The Index shows the relationship between the Average and the Analyzed Industry. For example, 100 means that they are equal; 500 that the Analyzed Industry is five times the average; 50 means that the Analyzed Industry is half the national average. The abbreviation 'na' is used to show that data are 'not available'.

LEADING COMPANIES

Number shown: **6** Total sales ($ mil): **572** Total employment (000): **1.6**

Company Name	Address				CEO Name	Phone	Co. Type	Sales ($ mil)	Empl. (000)
Capital City Products	PO Box 569	Columbus	OH	43216	Tommie Holmberg	614-299-3131	D	150*	0.6
Karlshamns USA Inc	PO Box 569	Columbus	OH	43216	Tommie Holmberg	614-299-3131	S	150	0.6
Colfax Inc	38 Colfax St	Pawtucket	RI	02860	Abbott Dressler	401-724-3800	R	100*	0.2
SVO Specialty Products Inc	35585-B Curtis Blv	Eastlake	OH	44095	R W Schoenfeld	216-942-0680	S	100	<0.1
CasChem Inc	40 Av A	Bayonne	NJ	07002	Cyrill C Baldwin Jr	201-858-7900	S	64	0.2
New Southern of Rocky Mount	PO Box 109	Rocky Mount	NC	27802	Clifton O Barnes	919-977-1000	R	8	<0.1

Source: *Ward's Business Directory of U.S. Private and Public Companies*, Volumes 1 and 2, 1996. The company type code used is as follows: P - Public, R - Private, S - Subsidiary, D - Division, J - Joint Venture, A - Affiliate, G - Group. Sales are in millions of dollars, employees are in thousands. An asterisk (*) indicates an estimated sales volume. The symbol < stands for 'less than'. Company names and addresses are truncated, in some cases, to fit into the available space.

MATERIALS CONSUMED

Material		Quantity	Delivered Cost ($ million)
Materials, ingredients, containers, and supplies		(X)	485.0
Flaxseed seeds, nuts, and beans	1,000 s tons	(D)	(D)
Sunflower seeds, nuts, and beans	1,000 s tons	1,002.1	183.8
Peanut seeds, nuts, and beans	1,000 s tons	(D)	(D)
Other seeds, nuts, and beans (excluding cottonseed, sunflower, soybean, flaxseed, and peanuts)	1,000 s tons	(X)	(D)
All other materials and components, parts, containers, and supplies		(X)	181.3
Materials, ingredients, containers, and supplies, nsk		(X)	5.9

Source: 1992 *Economic Census*. Explanation of symbols used: (D): Withheld to avoid disclosure of competitive data; na: Not available; (S): Withheld because statistical norms were not met; (X): Not applicable; (Z): Less than half the unit shown; nec: Not elsewhere classified; nsk: Not specified by kind; - : zero; * : 10-19 percent estimated; ** : 20-29 percent estimated.

PRODUCT SHARE DETAILS

Product or Product Class	% Share
Vegetable oil mills, nec	100.00
Linseed oil	10.66
Linseed oil, crude	(D)
Linseed oil, processed (refined, blown, heat treated, or chemically modified)	(D)
Linseed oil, nsk	4.28
Vegetable oils, nec	62.40
Coconut oil, once-refined (after alkali or caustic wash but before deodorizing or use in end products)	13.56
Peanut oil, crude	16.04
Peanut oil, once-refined (after alkali or caustic wash but before deodorizing or use in end products)	4.73
Sunflower seed oil, crude	(D)
Sunflower seed oil, once-refined (after alkali or caustic wash but before deodorizing or use in end products)	(D)
Other crude vegetable oils, including safflower, castor, tung, etc.	4.08
Once-refined palm oil (after alkali or caustic wash but before deodorizing)	(D)
Other once-refined vegetable oils, including safflower, castor, tung, etc.	14.29
Other vegetable oils processed for inedible purposes (tung oil, dehydrated castor oil, etc.)	(D)
Vegetable oils, nec, nsk	0.11
Other vegetable oil mill products, nec	24.99
Linseed cake and meal	(D)
Peanut cake and meal	15.14
Sunflower seed cake and meal	22.01
Other oil seed cake and meal	2.25
Palm oil, once-refined, purchased and deodorized only	2.84
Coconut oil, once-refined, purchased and deodorized only	8.86
Peanut oil, once-refined, purchased and deodorized only	16.32
Sunflower oil, once-refined, purchased and deodorized only	(D)
Other oils, once-refined, except cottonseed, soybean, linseed, peanut, or sunflower, purchased and deodorized only	12.24
Vegetable oil mills, nec, nsk	1.95

Source: 1992 *Economic Census*. The values shown are percent of total shipments in an industry. Values of indented subcategories are summed in the main heading. The symbol (D) appears when data are withheld to prevent disclosure of competitive information. The abbreviation nsk stands for 'not specified by kind' and nec for 'not elsewhere classified'.

INPUTS AND OUTPUTS FOR VEGETABLE OIL MILLS, NEC

Economic Sector or Industry Providing Inputs	%	Sector	Economic Sector or Industry Buying Outputs	%	Sector
Imports	50.0	Foreign	Shortening & cooking oils	24.5	Manufg.
Oil bearing crops	30.2	Agric.	Exports	11.3	Foreign
Wholesale trade	6.4	Trade	Frozen specialties	7.1	Manufg.
Motor freight transportation & warehousing	2.2	Util.	Blended & prepared flour	6.9	Manufg.
Paperboard containers & boxes	1.1	Manufg.	Soap & other detergents	6.0	Manufg.
Electric services (utilities)	1.1	Util.	Condensed & evaporated milk	5.9	Manufg.
Advertising	1.1	Services	Prepared feeds, nec	5.3	Manufg.
Gas production & distribution (utilities)	1.0	Util.	Cheese, natural & processed	4.2	Manufg.
Minerals, ground or treated	0.7	Manufg.	Paints & allied products	3.7	Manufg.
Railroads & related services	0.7	Util.	Toilet preparations	3.4	Manufg.
Petroleum refining	0.6	Manufg.	Cereal breakfast foods	2.9	Manufg.
Sanitary services, steam supply, irrigation	0.6	Util.	Commodity Credit Corporation	2.8	Gov't

Continued on next page.

INPUTS AND OUTPUTS FOR VEGETABLE OIL MILLS, NEC - Continued

Economic Sector or Industry Providing Inputs	%	Sector	Economic Sector or Industry Buying Outputs	%	Sector
Banking	0.5	Fin/R.E.	Flour & other grain mill products	2.6	Manufg.
Vegetable oil mills, nec	0.4	Manufg.	Federal Government purchases, nondefense	2.6	Fed Govt
Communications, except radio & TV	0.4	Util.	Chemical preparations, nec	2.0	Manufg.
Water transportation	0.4	Util.	Synthetic rubber	1.7	Manufg.
Clay, ceramic, & refractory minerals	0.3	Mining	Surface active agents	1.2	Manufg.
Security & commodity brokers	0.3	Fin/R.E.	Dog, cat, & other pet food	0.9	Manufg.
Cyclic crudes and organics	0.2	Manufg.	Flavoring extracts & syrups, nec	0.8	Manufg.
Miscellaneous repair shops	0.2	Services	Canned specialties	0.7	Manufg.
Noncomparable imports	0.2	Foreign	Plastics materials & resins	0.6	Manufg.
Coal	0.1	Mining	Meat animals	0.4	Agric.
Food products machinery	0.1	Manufg.	Poultry & eggs	0.4	Agric.
Eating & drinking places	0.1	Trade	Fluid milk	0.4	Manufg.
Equipment rental & leasing services	0.1	Services	Organic fibers, noncellulosic	0.4	Manufg.
			Polishes & sanitation goods	0.4	Manufg.
			Vegetable oil mills, nec	0.3	Manufg.
			Lubricating oils & greases	0.2	Manufg.
			Dairy farm products	0.1	Agric.
			Asbestos products	0.1	Manufg.

Source: Benchmark Input-Output Accounts for the U.S. Economy, 1982, U.S. Department of Commerce, Washington, D.C., July 1991. Data, as reported in the source, are organized by the 1977 SIC structure in use in 1982 but have been matched, as closely as is possible, to the 1987 SIC structure used in this book.

OCCUPATIONS EMPLOYED BY SIC 207 - GRAIN MILL PRODUCTS AND FATS AND OILS

Occupation	% of Total 1994	Change to 2005	Occupation	% of Total 1994	Change to 2005
Packaging & filling machine operators	8.2	-5.4	General office clerks	2.0	-10.3
Truck drivers light & heavy	6.0	8.4	Secretaries, ex legal & medical	1.9	-4.3
Crushing & mixing machine operators	5.7	-5.4	Separating & still machine operators	1.9	5.1
Blue collar worker supervisors	5.5	0.1	Machine feeders & offbearers	1.8	-5.3
Helpers, laborers, & material movers nec	4.7	5.1	Machine operators nec	1.8	-7.3
Industrial machinery mechanics	3.7	15.7	Bookkeeping, accounting, & auditing clerks	1.7	-21.1
Freight, stock, & material movers, hand	3.4	-15.9	Industrial production managers	1.7	5.1
Industrial truck & tractor operators	3.2	5.1	Science & mathematics technicians	1.5	5.2
Sales & related workers nec	2.6	5.2	Material moving equipment operators nec	1.5	5.1
General managers & top executives	2.5	-0.3	Janitors & cleaners, incl maids	1.4	-15.9
Maintenance repairers, general utility	2.4	-5.4	Inspectors, testers, & graders, precision	1.2	5.2
Hand packers & packagers	2.2	-9.9	Agricultural workers nec	1.1	5.2
Extruding & forming machine workers	2.1	-26.4	Plant & system operators nec	1.0	39.3
Precision food & tobacco workers nec	2.1	5.1	Traffic, shipping, & receiving clerks	1.0	1.2
Cooking, roasting machine operators	2.0	11.4			

Source: Industry-Occupation Matrix, Bureau of Labor Statistics. These data relate to one or more 3-digit SIC industry groups rather than to a single 4-digit SIC. The change reported for each occupation to the year 2005 is a percent of growth or decline as estimated by the Bureau of Labor Statistics. The abbreviation nec stands for 'not elsewhere classified'.

LOCATION BY STATE AND REGIONAL CONCENTRATION

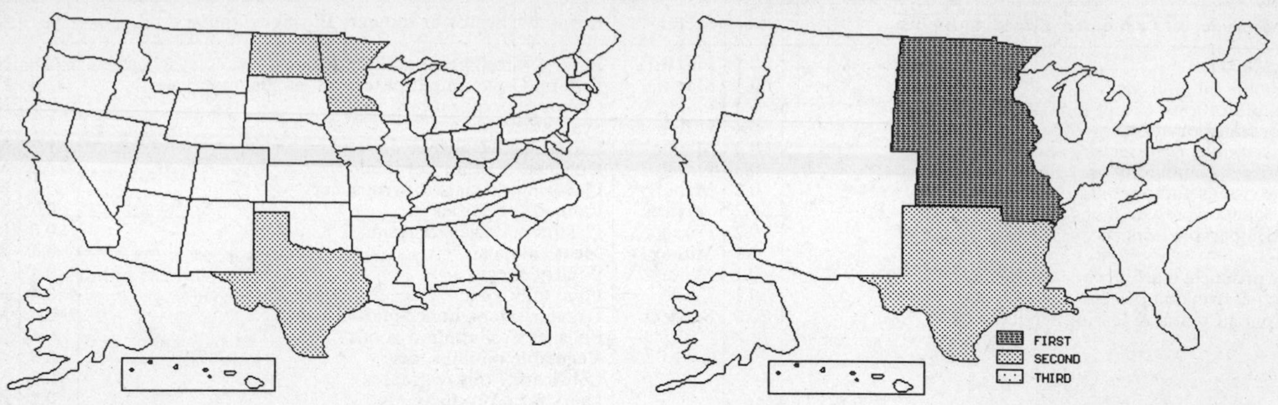

INDUSTRY DATA BY STATE

State	Establish-ments	Shipments			Employment				Cost as % of Shipments	Investment per Employee ($)
		Total ($ mil)	% of U.S.	Per Establ.	Total Number	% of U.S.	Per Establ.	Wages ($/hour)		
North Dakota	3	(D)	-	-	175 *	19.4	58	-	-	-
Minnesota	2	(D)	-	-	175 *	19.4	88	-	-	-
Texas	2	(D)	-	-	175 *	19.4	88	-	-	-

Source: 1992 *Economic Census*. The states are in descending order of shipments or establishments (if shipment data are missing for the majority). The symbol (D) appears when data are withheld to prevent disclosure of competitive information. States marked with (D) are sorted by number of establishments. A dash (-) indicates that the data element cannot be calculated; * indicates the midpoint of a range.

2077 - ANIMAL & MARINE FATS & OILS

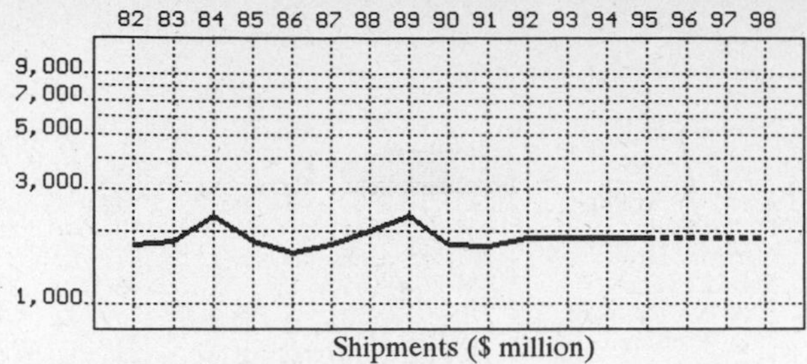

Shipments ($ million)

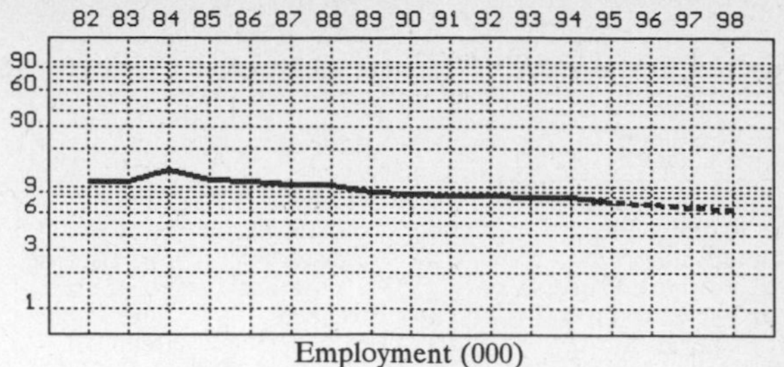

Employment (000)

GENERAL STATISTICS

Year	Com-panies	Establishments		Employment			Compensation		Production ($ million)			
		Total	with 20 or more employees	Total (000)	Production Workers (000)	Production Hours (Mil)	Payroll ($ mil)	Wages ($/hr)	Cost of Materials	Value Added by Manufacture	Value of Shipments	Capital Invest.
1982	270	386	189	10.8	7.2	15.5	215.1	8.25	1,188.5	562.6	1,752.5	56.5
1983		370	184	10.7	7.1	15.1	215.6	8.35	1,202.6	630.1	1,817.7	58.7
1984		354	179	13.7	9.2	15.7	253.6	8.69	1,599.1	730.0	2,323.2	76.2
1985		337	174	11.1	6.9	13.0	233.9	9.41	1,189.2	609.6	1,820.2	
1986		318	160	10.8	5.9	11.2	223.6	10.21	989.6	635.9	1,632.8	41.3
1987	194	305	154	10.3	6.2	12.8	215.7	8.71	1,022.9	752.9	1,763.4	60.4
1988		302	161	10.2	6.0	12.9	231.0	8.87	1,313.1	725.5	2,024.1	102.2
1989		288	152	9.0	5.8	12.5	230.9	9.49	1,463.0	832.7	2,297.9	57.1
1990		280	153	8.7	4.8	10.4	208.0	9.41	1,056.6	715.4	1,776.2	45.2
1991		276	146	8.5	4.9	10.6	208.4	10.20	1,000.3	718.0	1,725.3	40.1
1992	159	268	137	8.5	5.5	12.6	220.3	10.36	1,094.6	755.4	1,858.2	70.3
1993		258	139	8.2	5.4	12.6	222.6	10.11	1,089.1	815.4	1,875.4	70.1
1994		238P	131P	8.0	5.4	12.7	225.7	10.82	1,099.2	764.6	1,857.9	71.4
1995		227P	126P	7.4P	4.5P	10.9P	218.5P	10.70P	1,107.0P	770.0P	1,871.0P	
1996		215P	121P	7.1P	4.3P	10.7P	217.8P	10.88P	1,105.7P	769.1P	1,868.8P	
1997		204P	117P	6.7P	4.1P	10.4P	217.1P	11.06P	1,104.4P	768.2P	1,866.6P	
1998		193P	112P	6.4P	3.8P	10.1P	216.4P	11.24P	1,103.1P	767.3P	1,864.4P	

Sources: 1982, 1987, 1992 *Economic Census*; *Annual Survey of Manufactures*, 83-86, 88-91, 93-94. Establishment counts for non-Census years are from *County Business Patterns*; establishment values for 83-84 are extrapolations. 'P's show projections by the editors. Industries reclassified in 87 will not have data for prior years.

INDICES OF CHANGE

Year	Com-panies	Establishments		Employment			Compensation		Production ($ million)			
		Total	with 20 or more employees	Total (000)	Production Workers (000)	Production Hours (Mil)	Payroll ($ mil)	Wages ($/hr)	Cost of Materials	Value Added by Manufacture	Value of Shipments	Capital Invest.
1982	170	144	138	127	131	123	98	80	109	74	94	80
1983		138	134	126	129	120	98	81	110	83	98	83
1984		132	131	161	167	125	115	84	146	97	125	108
1985		126	127	131	125	103	106	91	109	81	98	
1986		119	117	127	107	89	101	99	90	84	88	59
1987	122	114	112	121	113	102	98	84	93	100	95	86
1988		113	118	120	109	102	105	86	120	96	109	145
1989		107	111	106	105	99	105	92	134	110	124	81
1990		104	112	102	87	83	94	91	97	95	96	64
1991		103	107	100	89	84	95	98	91	95	93	57
1992	100	100	100	100	100	100	100	100	100	100	100	100
1993		96	101	96	98	100	101	98	99	108	101	100
1994		89P	95P	94	98	101	102	104	100	101	100	102
1995		85P	92P	88P	82P	87P	99P	103P	101P	102P	101P	
1996		80P	89P	84P	78P	85P	99P	105P	101P	102P	101P	
1997		76P	85P	79P	74P	82P	99P	107P	101P	102P	100P	
1998		72P	82P	75P	70P	80P	98P	108P	101P	102P	100P	

Sources: Same as General Statistics. Values reflect change from the base year, 1992. Values above 100 mean greater than 92, values below 100 mean less than 92, and a value of 100 in the 82-91 or 93-98 period means same as 92. 'P's mark projections by the editors.

SELECTED RATIOS

For 1994	Avg. of All Manufact.	Analyzed Industry	Index	For 1994	Avg. of All Manufact.	Analyzed Industry	Index
Employees per Establishment	49	34	69	Value Added per Production Worker	134,084	141,593	106
Payroll per Establishment	1,500,273	948,440	63	Cost per Establishment	5,045,178	4,619,076	92
Payroll per Employee	30,620	28,213	92	Cost per Employee	102,970	137,400	133
Production Workers per Establishment	34	23	66	Cost per Production Worker	146,988	203,556	138
Wages per Establishment	853,319	577,443	68	Shipments per Establishment	9,576,895	7,807,297	82
Wages per Production Worker	24,861	25,447	102	Shipments per Employee	195,460	232,237	119
Hours per Production Worker	2,056	2,352	114	Shipments per Production Worker	279,017	344,056	123
Wages per Hour	12.09	10.82	89	Investment per Establishment	321,011	300,038	93
Value Added per Establishment	4,602,255	3,213,014	70	Investment per Employee	6,552	8,925	136
Value Added per Employee	93,930	95,575	102	Investment per Production Worker	9,352	13,222	141

Sources: Same as General Statistics. The 'Average of All Manufacturing' column represents the average of all manufacturing industries reported for the most recent complete year available. The Index shows the relationship between the Average and the Analyzed Industry. For example, 100 means that they are equal; 500 that the Analyzed Industry is five times the average; 50 means that the Analyzed Industry is half the national average. The abbreviation 'na' is used to show that data are 'not available'.

LEADING COMPANIES

Number shown: **21** Total sales ($ mil): **903** Total employment (000): **3.3**

Company Name	Address				CEO Name	Phone	Co. Type	Sales ($ mil)	Empl. (000)
Darling International Inc	251 O'Connor	Irving	TX	75038	Frank W Miller	214-717-0300	P	354	1.5
American Proteins Inc	575 Colonial Pk Dr	Roswell	GA	30075	Dallas Gay	404-641-7845	R	170	0.5
Daybrook Holdings Inc	161 Madison Av	Morristown	NJ	07960	Gregory Holt	201-538-6766	R	87*	0.3
Carolina&Southern Processing	5533 S York Rd	Gastonia	NC	28052	David Evans	704-864-9941	S	42*	0.1
Cape Fear Feed Products Co	PO Box 1659	Fayetteville	NC	28302	Charles Atkinson	910-483-0473	S	36	0.1
Beaufort Fisheries Inc	PO Box 240	Beaufort	NC	28516	Jule Whetley	919-728-3144	R	35*	0.1
Griffin Industries Inc	4221 Alexandria Pk	Cold Spring	KY	41076	Dennis Griffin	606-781-2010	R	35*	0.1
Coast Packing Co	PO Box 58918	Vernon	CA	90058	Ron Gustafson	213-587-8141	R	30	<0.1
Standard Tallow Corp	1215 Harrison Av	Kearny	NJ	07032	Burton Levy	201-997-7550	R	21	<0.1
Baker Commodities Inc	PO Box 58368	Seattle	WA	98188	Bill Hamon	206-243-7387	D	15*	<0.1
Inland Products Inc	PO Box 926	Columbus	OH	43216	GH Baas	614-444-1127	R	15*	0.1
Tampa Soap and Chemical	1001 Orient Rd	Tampa	FL	33619	Bob Huffman	813-626-1135	D	14	<0.1
Standard Rendering Co	PO Box 578	Russellville	AR	72801	Bill Donnell	501-968-2567	S	12*	<0.1
Neatsfoot Oil Refineries Corp	E Ontario & Bath	Philadelphia	PA	19134	Alan S Berg	215-739-1291	R	10	<0.1
Animal By-Products Corp	PO Box 106	New Carlisle	IN	46552	Maurice Cocquyt Jr	219-654-3141	R	5*	<0.1
Werner G Smith Inc	1730 Train Av	Cleveland	OH	44113	W Meckes Jr	216-861-3676	R	5	<0.1
Florin Tallow Co	PO Box 699	Dixon	CA	95620	Gary Essex	916-441-5811	S	5	<0.1
Maricopa By-Products Inc	3602 W Elwood St	Phoenix	AZ	85041	James W Gieszl	602-275-3402	R	4*	<0.1
West Coast Rendering	4105 Bandini Blv	Vernon	CA	90023	David Brownstein	213-261-4176	R	4*	<0.1
Eugene Chemical	PO Box 244	Harrisburg	OR	97446	J Demergasso	503-995-6025	R	3*	<0.1
California Protein Products Inc	3300 Bandini Blv	Vernon	CA	90023	Harold Murph	213-263-9544	R	1	<0.1

Source: *Ward's Business Directory of U.S. Private and Public Companies*, Volumes 1 and 2, 1996. The company type code used is as follows: P - Public, R - Private, S - Subsidiary, D - Division, J - Joint Venture, A - Affiliate, G - Group. Sales are in millions of dollars, employees are in thousands. An asterisk (*) indicates an estimated sales volume. The symbol < stands for 'less than'. Company names and addresses are truncated, in some cases, to fit into the available space.

MATERIALS CONSUMED

Material	Quantity	Delivered Cost ($ million)
Materials, ingredients, containers, and supplies	(X)	897.4
Paper and paperboard containers, including shipping sacks and other paper packaging supplies	(X)	0.2
Plastics containers	(X)	0.3
Metal containers	(X)	0.2
All other materials and components, parts, containers, and supplies	(X)	570.4
Materials, ingredients, containers, and supplies, nsk	(X)	326.3

Source: 1992 *Economic Census*. Explanation of symbols used: (D): Withheld to avoid disclosure of competitive data; na: Not available; (S): Withheld because statistical norms were not met; (X): Not applicable; (Z): Less than half the unit shown; nec: Not elsewhere classified; nsk: Not specified by kind; - : zero; * : 10-19 percent estimated; ** : 20-29 percent estimated.

PRODUCT SHARE DETAILS

Product or Product Class	% Share
Animal and marine fats and oils	100.00
Animal and marine grease and inedible tallow	34.55
Animal and marine inedible tallow, including inedible animal stearin	75.26
Animal and marine grease, other than wool grease	22.47
Grease and inedible tallow, nsk	2.25
Animal and marine feed and fertilizer byproducts	52.38
Animal and marine meat and bonemeal feed and fertilizer byproducts	45.47
Animal and marine dry rendered tankage feed and fertilizer byproducts	4.41
Animal and marine feather meal feed and fertilizer byproducts	4.76
Other feed and fertilizer byproducts, including dried blood, poultry fat and byproducts, meal, and raw products for pet food	35.72
Feed and fertilizer byproducts, nsk	9.65
Animal and marine oil mill products	7.29
Foots (animal, vegetable, and fish), and acidulated soap stock	13.58
Animal oil mill products, including all other animal oils, except fatty acids	22.24
Fish and marine animal oil	14.27
Fish scrap and meal	33.32
Other fish and marine animal oil products	9.99
Animal and marine oil mill products, nsk	6.55
Animal and marine fats and oils, nsk	5.78

Source: 1992 *Economic Census*. The values shown are percent of total shipments in an industry. Values of indented subcategories are summed in the main heading. The symbol (D) appears when data are withheld to prevent disclosure of competitive information. The abbreviation nsk stands for 'not specified by kind' and nec for 'not elsewhere classified'.

INPUTS AND OUTPUTS FOR ANIMAL & MARINE FATS & OILS

Economic Sector or Industry Providing Inputs	%	Sector	Economic Sector or Industry Buying Outputs	%	Sector
Animal & marine fats & oils	35.1	Manufg.	Exports	25.3	Foreign
Miscellaneous plastics products	16.2	Manufg.	Animal & marine fats & oils	24.2	Manufg.
Wholesale trade	10.1	Trade	Prepared feeds, nec	23.3	Manufg.
Commercial fishing	7.1	Agric.	Dog, cat, & other pet food	7.8	Manufg.
Scrap	6.4	Scrap	Poultry & eggs	4.8	Agric.
Gas production & distribution (utilities)	3.8	Util.	Chemical preparations, nec	4.3	Manufg.
Motor freight transportation & warehousing	3.6	Util.	Soap & other detergents	2.2	Manufg.
Imports	3.2	Foreign	Toilet preparations	2.1	Manufg.
Petroleum refining	2.5	Manufg.	Miscellaneous livestock	1.3	Agric.
Electric services (utilities)	2.4	Util.	Meat animals	1.2	Agric.
Advertising	2.1	Services	Lubricating oils & greases	0.7	Manufg.
Meat packing plants	1.8	Manufg.	Leather tanning & finishing	0.6	Manufg.
Railroads & related services	0.6	Util.	Fertilizers, mixing only	0.4	Manufg.
Banking	0.5	Fin/R.E.	Printing ink	0.4	Manufg.
Communications, except radio & TV	0.4	Util.	Surface active agents	0.4	Manufg.
Water transportation	0.3	Util.	Adhesives & sealants	0.3	Manufg.
Miscellaneous repair shops	0.3	Services	Drugs	0.2	Manufg.
Maintenance of nonfarm buildings nec	0.2	Constr.	Petroleum refining	0.2	Manufg.
Food products machinery	0.2	Manufg.			
Minerals, ground or treated	0.2	Manufg.			
Air transportation	0.2	Util.			
Eating & drinking places	0.2	Trade			
Computer & data processing services	0.2	Services			
Detective & protective services	0.2	Services			
Real estate	0.1	Fin/R.E.			
Equipment rental & leasing services	0.1	Services			
State & local government enterprises, nec	0.1	Gov't			
U.S. Postal Service	0.1	Gov't			
Noncomparable imports	0.1	Foreign			

Source: Benchmark Input-Output Accounts for the U.S. Economy, 1982, U.S. Department of Commerce, Washington, D.C., July 1991. Data, as reported in the source, are organized by the 1977 SIC structure in use in 1982 but have been matched, as closely as is possible, to the 1987 SIC structure used in this book.

OCCUPATIONS EMPLOYED BY SIC 207 - GRAIN MILL PRODUCTS AND FATS AND OILS

Occupation	% of Total 1994	Change to 2005	Occupation	% of Total 1994	Change to 2005
Packaging & filling machine operators	8.2	-5.4	General office clerks	2.0	-10.3
Truck drivers light & heavy	6.0	8.4	Secretaries, ex legal & medical	1.9	-4.3
Crushing & mixing machine operators	5.7	-5.4	Separating & still machine operators	1.9	5.1
Blue collar worker supervisors	5.5	0.1	Machine feeders & offbearers	1.8	-5.3
Helpers, laborers, & material movers nec	4.7	5.1	Machine operators nec	1.8	-7.3
Industrial machinery mechanics	3.7	15.7	Bookkeeping, accounting, & auditing clerks	1.7	-21.1
Freight, stock, & material movers, hand	3.4	-15.9	Industrial production managers	1.7	5.1
Industrial truck & tractor operators	3.2	5.1	Science & mathematics technicians	1.5	5.2
Sales & related workers nec	2.6	5.2	Material moving equipment operators nec	1.5	5.1
General managers & top executives	2.5	-0.3	Janitors & cleaners, incl maids	1.4	-15.9
Maintenance repairers, general utility	2.4	-5.4	Inspectors, testers, & graders, precision	1.2	5.2
Hand packers & packagers	2.2	-9.9	Agricultural workers nec	1.1	5.2
Extruding & forming machine workers	2.1	-26.4	Plant & system operators nec	1.0	39.3
Precision food & tobacco workers nec	2.1	5.1	Traffic, shipping, & receiving clerks	1.0	1.2
Cooking, roasting machine operators	2.0	11.4			

Source: Industry-Occupation Matrix, Bureau of Labor Statistics. These data relate to one or more 3-digit SIC industry groups rather than to a single 4-digit SIC. The change reported for each occupation to the year 2005 is a percent of growth or decline as estimated by the Bureau of Labor Statistics. The abbreviation nec stands for 'not elsewhere classified'.

LOCATION BY STATE AND REGIONAL CONCENTRATION

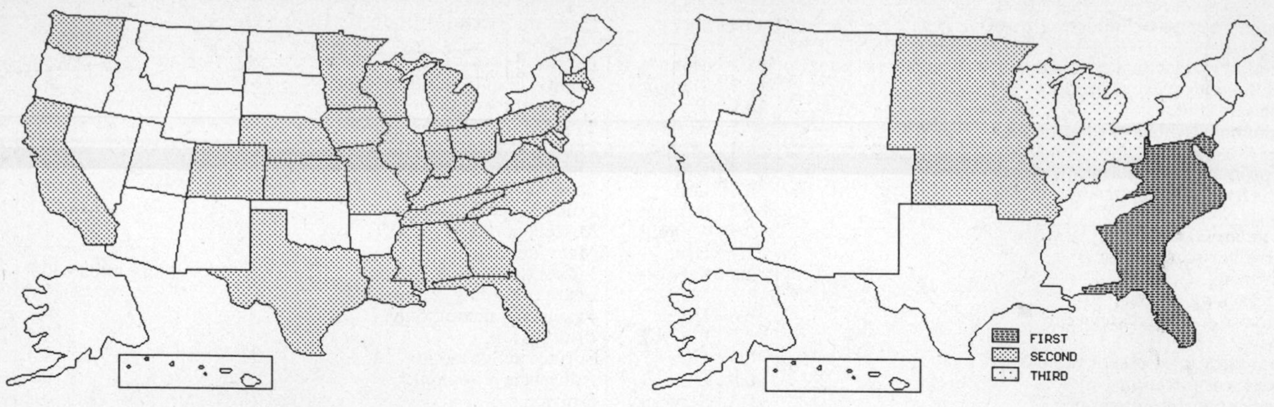

INDUSTRY DATA BY STATE

State	Establish-ments	Shipments			Employment				Cost as % of Shipments	Investment per Employee ($)
		Total ($ mil)	% of U.S.	Per Establ.	Total Number	% of U.S.	Per Establ.	Wages ($/hour)		
California	21	141.6	7.6	6.7	700	8.2	33	11.67	59.2	8,143
North Carolina	13	98.3	5.3	7.6	600	7.1	46	10.75	60.3	-
Alabama	7	73.4	4.0	10.5	200	2.4	29	8.33	65.3	12,500
Louisiana	7	64.9	3.5	9.3	500	5.9	71	13.43	35.6	-
Florida	8	50.3	2.7	6.3	300	3.5	38	8.33	49.1	8,333
Nebraska	12	50.3	2.7	4.2	300	3.5	25	9.60	64.0	-
Missouri	4	45.7	2.5	11.4	100	1.2	25	11.50	67.0	2,000
Washington	7	44.3	2.4	6.3	300	3.5	43	11.00	53.3	4,333
Ohio	7	40.9	2.2	5.8	200	2.4	29	12.00	50.9	-
Massachusetts	3	25.1	1.4	8.4	200	2.4	67	7.00	55.0	3,000
Texas	26	(D)	-	-	750 *	8.8	29	-	-	-
Iowa	12	(D)	-	-	375 *	4.4	31	-	-	4,267
Georgia	11	(D)	-	-	375 *	4.4	34	-	-	25,867
Virginia	11	(D)	-	-	375 *	4.4	34	-	-	4,000
Illinois	10	(D)	-	-	175 *	2.1	18	-	-	-
Indiana	10	(D)	-	-	375 *	4.4	38	-	-	-
Minnesota	10	(D)	-	-	375 *	4.4	38	-	-	14,400
Colorado	7	(D)	-	-	175 *	2.1	25	-	-	-
Kansas	7	(D)	-	-	175 *	2.1	25	-	-	-
Pennsylvania	7	(D)	-	-	175 *	2.1	25	-	-	-
Tennessee	7	(D)	-	-	175 *	2.1	25	-	-	-
Mississippi	6	(D)	-	-	175 *	2.1	29	-	-	-
Wisconsin	5	(D)	-	-	175 *	2.1	35	-	-	-
Kentucky	4	(D)	-	-	175 *	2.1	44	-	-	-
Michigan	4	(D)	-	-	175 *	2.1	44	-	-	-
Maryland	3	(D)	-	-	175 *	2.1	58	-	-	-
New Jersey	2	(D)	-	-	375 *	4.4	188	-	-	-

Source: 1992 *Economic Census*. The states are in descending order of shipments or establishments (if shipment data are missing for the majority). The symbol (D) appears when data are withheld to prevent disclosure of competitive information. States marked with (D) are sorted by number of establishments. A dash (-) indicates that the data element cannot be calculated; * indicates the midpoint of a range.

2079 - EDIBLE FAT, NEC

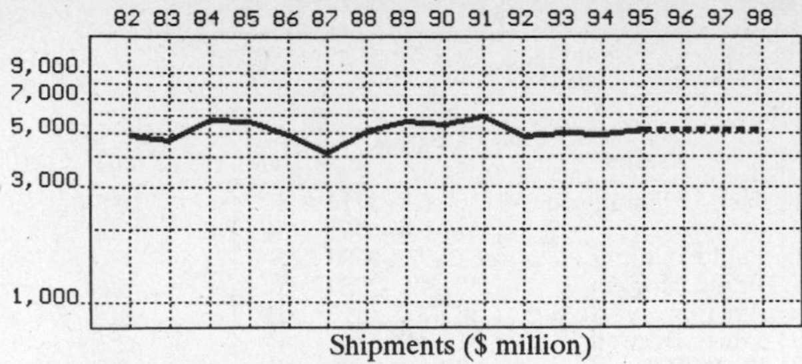

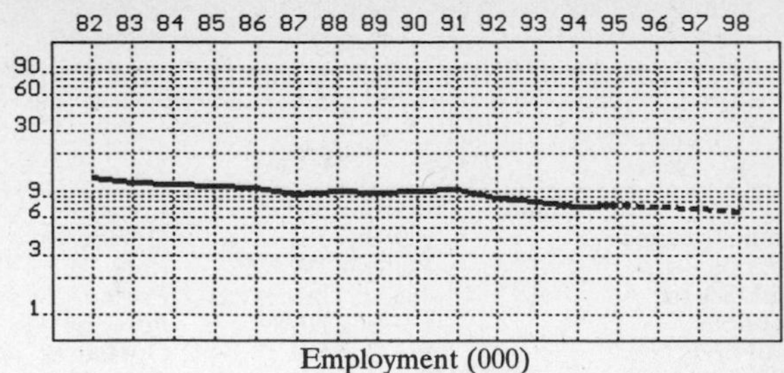

GENERAL STATISTICS

Year	Companies	Establishments: Total	Establishments: with 20 or more employees	Employment: Total (000)	Production Workers (000)	Production Hours (Mil)	Compensation: Payroll ($ mil)	Compensation: Wages ($/hr)	Cost of Materials	Value Added by Manufacture	Value of Shipments	Capital Invest.
1982	79	118	85	12.5	8.7	17.6	272.0	9.88	3,643.3	1,261.7	4,905.6	96.5
1983		116	83	11.6	8.1	16.6	270.9	10.33	3,580.1	1,199.6	4,745.0	84.7
1984		114	81	11.4	8.2	16.6	271.2	10.56	4,444.8	1,291.3	5,716.9	77.2
1985		112	78	10.7	7.5	15.3	264.8	11.04	4,368.1	1,190.4	5,608.4	100.3
1986		115	85	10.4	7.2	14.5	262.7	11.51	3,631.3	1,290.0	4,951.0	82.0
1987	66	100	74	9.3	6.6	13.7	253.3	12.22	2,886.3	1,260.1	4,151.1	86.2
1988		101	75	9.9	7.0	14.2	274.1	12.38	3,637.3	1,454.1	5,052.1	78.6
1989		94	70	9.5	7.5	15.0	288.2	11.93	4,055.6	1,542.9	5,642.9	65.4
1990		104	73	10.0	7.1	14.2	273.9	11.89	3,822.5	1,600.3	5,415.8	85.0
1991		105	72	10.2	7.1	14.5	281.1	12.06	4,278.8	1,592.0	5,873.8	94.4
1992	72	102	66	8.7	6.1	12.9	257.1	12.41	3,446.4	1,384.7	4,830.4	107.0
1993		106	72	8.2	5.8	12.0	254.7	12.73	3,616.7	1,404.1	5,022.7	88.4
1994		98P	66P	7.5	5.5	11.5	245.1	13.35	3,609.7	1,390.4	4,987.5	77.7
1995		96P	65P	7.7P	5.6P	11.6P	259.4P	13.40P	3,767.9P	1,451.3P	5,206.1P	86.1P
1996		95P	63P	7.4P	5.4P	11.2P	258.4P	13.64P	3,774.1P	1,453.7P	5,214.6P	86.1P
1997		93P	62P	7.0P	5.1P	10.7P	257.3P	13.88P	3,780.2P	1,456.1P	5,223.1P	86.0P
1998		92P	60P	6.7P	4.9P	10.3P	256.3P	14.12P	3,786.4P	1,458.5P	5,231.6P	86.0P

Sources: 1982, 1987, 1992 *Economic Census*; *Annual Survey of Manufactures*, 83-86, 88-91, 93-94. Establishment counts for non-Census years are from *County Business Patterns*; establishment values for 83-84 are extrapolations. 'P's show projections by the editors. Industries reclassified in 87 will not have data for prior years.

INDICES OF CHANGE

Year	Companies	Establishments: Total	Establishments: with 20 or more employees	Employment: Total (000)	Production Workers (000)	Production Hours (Mil)	Compensation: Payroll ($ mil)	Compensation: Wages ($/hr)	Cost of Materials	Value Added by Manufacture	Value of Shipments	Capital Invest.
1982	110	116	129	144	143	136	106	80	106	91	102	90
1983		114	126	133	133	129	105	83	104	87	98	79
1984		112	123	131	134	129	105	85	129	93	118	72
1985		110	118	123	123	119	103	89	127	86	116	94
1986		113	129	120	118	112	102	93	105	93	102	77
1987	92	98	112	107	108	106	99	98	84	91	86	81
1988		99	114	114	115	110	107	100	106	105	105	73
1989		92	106	109	123	116	112	96	118	111	117	61
1990		102	111	115	116	110	107	96	111	116	112	79
1991		103	109	117	116	112	109	97	124	115	122	88
1992	100	100	100	100	100	100	100	100	100	100	100	100
1993		104	109	94	95	93	99	103	105	101	104	83
1994		96P	101P	86	90	89	95	108	105	100	103	73
1995		94P	98P	88P	92P	90P	101P	108P	109P	105P	108P	80P
1996		93P	96P	85P	88P	87P	101P	110P	110P	105P	108P	80P
1997		91P	94P	81P	84P	83P	100P	112P	110P	105P	108P	80P
1998		90P	92P	77P	81P	80P	100P	114P	110P	105P	108P	80P

Sources: Same as General Statistics. Values reflect change from the base year, 1992. Values above 100 mean greater than 92, values below 100 mean less than 92, and a value of 100 in the 82-91 or 93-98 period means same as 92. 'P's mark projections by the editors.

SELECTED RATIOS

For 1994	Avg. of All Manufact.	Analyzed Industry	Index
Employees per Establishment	49	77	157
Payroll per Establishment	1,500,273	2,510,335	167
Payroll per Employee	30,620	32,680	107
Production Workers per Establishment	34	56	164
Wages per Establishment	853,319	1,572,416	184
Wages per Production Worker	24,861	27,914	112
Hours per Production Worker	2,056	2,091	102
Wages per Hour	12.09	13.35	110
Value Added per Establishment	4,602,255	14,240,596	309
Value Added per Employee	93,930	185,387	197

For 1994	Avg. of All Manufact.	Analyzed Industry	Index
Value Added per Production Worker	134,084	252,800	189
Cost per Establishment	5,045,178	36,970,857	733
Cost per Employee	102,970	481,293	467
Cost per Production Worker	146,988	656,309	447
Shipments per Establishment	9,576,895	51,082,402	533
Shipments per Employee	195,460	665,000	340
Shipments per Production Worker	279,017	906,818	325
Investment per Establishment	321,011	795,810	248
Investment per Employee	6,552	10,360	158
Investment per Production Worker	9,352	14,127	151

Sources: Same as General Statistics. The 'Average of All Manufacturing' column represents the average of all manufacturing industries reported for the most recent complete year available. The Index shows the relationship between the Average and the Analyzed Industry. For example, 100 means that they are equal; 500 that the Analyzed Industry is five times the average; 50 means that the Analyzed Industry is half the national average. The abbreviation 'na' is used to show that data are 'not available'.

LEADING COMPANIES

Number shown: 13 Total sales ($ mil): **461** Total employment (000): **1.7**

Company Name	Address				CEO Name	Phone	Co. Type	Sales ($ mil)	Empl. (000)
Golden Foods/Golden Brands	PO Box 398	Louisville	KY	40201	Jack V Thompson	502-636-3712	R	100	0.1
Schad Industries Inc	PO Box 591	Opelousas	LA	70570		318-948-6561	R	70*	0.2
Bunge Foods Corp	PO Box 192	Kankakee	IL	60901	Paul Friedman	815-933-0600	S	65	0.6
Giurlani USA Inc	4652 E Date Av	Fresno	CA	93725	Frank Morgan	209-498-2920	R	50	<0.1
Gregg's Foods	PO Box 20789	Portland	OR	97220	Art Lowery	503-255-5512	D	40	0.1
Lou Ana Foods	PO Box 591	Opelousas	LA	70570	James Boswell	318-948-6561	D	35*	0.1
Osceola Foods Inc	PO Box 368	Osceola	AR	72370	Shelby Massey	501-563-2601	R	32	0.1
Purity Inc	1800 NW 70th Av	Miami	FL	33126	Carlos Fernandez	305-592-3600	R	24	0.1
HRR Enterprises	2129 W Pershing Rd	Chicago	IL	60609	W Dan Tarpley	312-376-7735	S	16	<0.1
Holsum Foods	919 14th St	Albert Lea	MN	56007	D Kallemeyh	507-373-2431	D	15	0.1
Food Oils Corp	145 Grand St	Carlstadt	NJ	07072	Juan Sieho	201-935-7888	S	8	<0.1
Technical Oil Products Inc	190 19th Av	Paterson	NJ	07504	Alan S Geisler	201-684-4441	R	5	<0.1
Base 10 Inc	PO Box 685	Waialua	HI	96791	Dana G Gray	808-637-5620	R	1	<0.1

Source: *Ward's Business Directory of U.S. Private and Public Companies*, Volumes 1 and 2, 1996. The company type code used is as follows: P - Public, R - Private, S - Subsidiary, D - Division, J - Joint Venture, A - Affiliate, G - Group. Sales are in millions of dollars, employees are in thousands. An asterisk (*) indicates an estimated sales volume. The symbol < stands for 'less than'. Company names and addresses are truncated, in some cases, to fit into the available space.

MATERIALS CONSUMED

Material		Quantity	Delivered Cost ($ million)
Materials, ingredients, containers, and supplies		(X)	3,178.5
Tallow and stearin, edible	mil lb	(S)	53.3
Lard	mil lb	(S)	49.4
Crude cottonseed oil	mil lb	1,037.2	193.6
Once-refined cottonseed oil	mil lb	195.1	47.8
Fully-refined cottonseed oil	mil lb	77.9	22.0
Crude soybean oil	mil lb	3,705.3	740.5
Once-refined soybean oil	mil lb	552.7	127.9
Fully-refined soybean oil	mil lb	2,150.8	547.0
Crude corn oil	mil lb	158.1	45.9
Once-refined corn oil	mil lb	46.2	15.8
Fully-refined corn oil	mil lb	292.6	98.9
Other crude oil	mil lb	673.1	170.7
Other once-refined oil	mil lb	42.9	11.6
Other fully-refined oil	mil lb	395.0	111.3
Paper and paperboard containers, including shipping sacks and other paper packaging supplies		(X)	137.5
Plastics containers		(X)	205.0
Glass containers		(X)	6.1
Metal containers		(X)	16.6
All other materials and components, parts, containers, and supplies		(X)	484.9
Materials, ingredients, containers, and supplies, nsk		(X)	92.7

Source: 1992 *Economic Census*. Explanation of symbols used: (D): Withheld to avoid disclosure of competitive data; na: Not available; (S): Withheld because statistical norms were not met; (X): Not applicable; (Z): Less than half the unit shown; nec: Not elsewhere classified; nsk: Not specified by kind; - : zero; * : 10-19 percent estimated; ** : 20-29 percent estimated.

PRODUCT SHARE DETAILS

Product or Product Class	% Share
Edible fats and oils, nec	100.00
Shortening and cooking oils (edible)	72.78
Baking or frying fats (shortening), 100 percent vegetable oil (edible)	43.57
Baking or frying fats (shortening), 100 percent animal fat or blends of vegetable oil and animal fat (edible)	8.54
Edible hydrogenated oils other than baking or frying fats (for confectionery fats, mellorine fats, whipped topping, etc.)	3.18
Partially hydrogenated edible soybean cooking or salad oil (fully-refined and deodorized at the same establishment)	29.85
Other edible soybean cooking or salad oil (fully-refined and deodorized at the same establishment)	0.89
Edible cottonseed cooking or salad oil (fully-refined and deodorized at the same establishment)	0.88
Edible mixtures of vegetable cooking or salad oil (fully-refined and deodorized at the same establishment)	0.42
All other edible cooking or salad oil (fully-refined and deodorized at the same establishment)	10.62
Edible vegetable oil winter stearin	(D)
Edible canola oil used for margarine	(D)
Other edible oils used for margarine	(D)
All other fully-refined edible shortening and cooking oils, except corn	0.29
Shortening and cooking oils, nsk	0.23
Margarine, including butter blends	26.52
Edible fats and oils, nec, nsk	0.70

Source: 1992 *Economic Census*. The values shown are percent of total shipments in an industry. Values of indented subcategories are summed in the main heading. The symbol (D) appears when data are withheld to prevent disclosure of competitive information. The abbreviation nsk stands for 'not specified by kind' and nec for 'not elsewhere classified'.

INPUTS AND OUTPUTS FOR ANIMAL & MARINE FATS & OILS

Economic Sector or Industry Providing Inputs	%	Sector	Economic Sector or Industry Buying Outputs	%	Sector
Animal & marine fats & oils	35.1	Manufg.	Exports	25.3	Foreign
Miscellaneous plastics products	16.2	Manufg.	Animal & marine fats & oils	24.2	Manufg.
Wholesale trade	10.1	Trade	Prepared feeds, nec	23.3	Manufg.
Commercial fishing	7.1	Agric.	Dog, cat, & other pet food	7.8	Manufg.
Scrap	6.4	Scrap	Poultry & eggs	4.8	Agric.
Gas production & distribution (utilities)	3.8	Util.	Chemical preparations, nec	4.3	Manufg.
Motor freight transportation & warehousing	3.6	Util.	Soap & other detergents	2.2	Manufg.
Imports	3.2	Foreign	Toilet preparations	2.1	Manufg.
Petroleum refining	2.5	Manufg.	Miscellaneous livestock	1.3	Agric.
Electric services (utilities)	2.4	Util.	Meat animals	1.2	Agric.
Advertising	2.1	Services	Lubricating oils & greases	0.7	Manufg.
Meat packing plants	1.8	Manufg.	Leather tanning & finishing	0.6	Manufg.
Railroads & related services	0.6	Util.	Fertilizers, mixing only	0.4	Manufg.
Banking	0.5	Fin/R.E.	Printing ink	0.4	Manufg.
Communications, except radio & TV	0.4	Util.	Surface active agents	0.4	Manufg.
Water transportation	0.3	Util.	Adhesives & sealants	0.3	Manufg.
Miscellaneous repair shops	0.3	Services	Drugs	0.2	Manufg.
Maintenance of nonfarm buildings nec	0.2	Constr.	Petroleum refining	0.2	Manufg.
Food products machinery	0.2	Manufg.			
Minerals, ground or treated	0.2	Manufg.			
Air transportation	0.2	Util.			
Eating & drinking places	0.2	Trade			
Computer & data processing services	0.2	Services			
Detective & protective services	0.2	Services			
Real estate	0.1	Fin/R.E.			
Equipment rental & leasing services	0.1	Services			
State & local government enterprises, nec	0.1	Gov't			
U.S. Postal Service	0.1	Gov't			
Noncomparable imports	0.1	Foreign			

Source: Benchmark Input-Output Accounts for the U.S. Economy, 1982, U.S. Department of Commerce, Washington, D.C., July 1991. Data, as reported in the source, are organized by the 1977 SIC structure in use in 1982 but have been matched, as closely as is possible, to the 1987 SIC structure used in this book.

OCCUPATIONS EMPLOYED BY SIC 207 - GRAIN MILL PRODUCTS AND FATS AND OILS

Occupation	% of Total 1994	Change to 2005	Occupation	% of Total 1994	Change to 2005
Packaging & filling machine operators	8.2	-5.4	General office clerks	2.0	-10.3
Truck drivers light & heavy	6.0	8.4	Secretaries, ex legal & medical	1.9	-4.3
Crushing & mixing machine operators	5.7	-5.4	Separating & still machine operators	1.9	5.1
Blue collar worker supervisors	5.5	0.1	Machine feeders & offbearers	1.8	-5.3
Helpers, laborers, & material movers nec	4.7	5.1	Machine operators nec	1.8	-7.3
Industrial machinery mechanics	3.7	15.7	Bookkeeping, accounting, & auditing clerks	1.7	-21.1
Freight, stock, & material movers, hand	3.4	-15.9	Industrial production managers	1.7	5.1
Industrial truck & tractor operators	3.2	5.1	Science & mathematics technicians	1.5	5.2
Sales & related workers nec	2.6	5.2	Material moving equipment operators nec	1.5	5.1
General managers & top executives	2.5	-0.3	Janitors & cleaners, incl maids	1.4	-15.9
Maintenance repairers, general utility	2.4	-5.4	Inspectors, testers, & graders, precision	1.2	5.2
Hand packers & packagers	2.2	-9.9	Agricultural workers nec	1.1	5.2
Extruding & forming machine workers	2.1	-26.4	Plant & system operators nec	1.0	39.3
Precision food & tobacco workers nec	2.1	5.1	Traffic, shipping, & receiving clerks	1.0	1.2
Cooking, roasting machine operators	2.0	11.4			

Source: Industry-Occupation Matrix, Bureau of Labor Statistics. These data relate to one or more 3-digit SIC industry groups rather than to a single 4-digit SIC. The change reported for each occupation to the year 2005 is a percent of growth or decline as estimated by the Bureau of Labor Statistics. The abbreviation nec stands for 'not elsewhere classified'.

LOCATION BY STATE AND REGIONAL CONCENTRATION

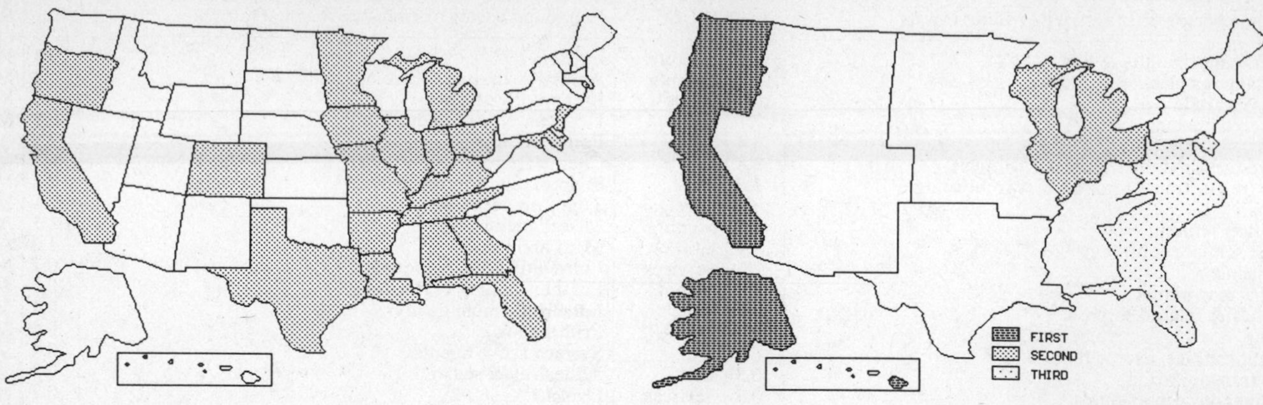

INDUSTRY DATA BY STATE

State	Establish-ments	Shipments			Employment				Cost as % of Shipments	Investment per Employee ($)
		Total ($ mil)	% of U.S.	Per Establ.	Total Number	% of U.S.	Per Establ.	Wages ($/hour)		
Illinois	10	613.4	12.7	61.3	1,300	14.9	130	13.28	80.6	9,769
California	21	611.2	12.7	29.1	1,200	13.8	57	15.50	60.0	7,250
Ohio	6	467.9	9.7	78.0	900	10.3	150	15.00	57.9	9,000
Texas	6	406.3	8.4	67.7	800	9.2	133	11.38	67.2	5,875
Tennessee	3	381.7	7.9	127.2	400	4.6	133	12.00	73.7	-
New Jersey	6	248.3	5.1	41.4	400	4.6	67	11.67	67.9	-
Georgia	6	199.7	4.1	33.3	500	5.7	83	12.37	74.5	-
Florida	4	(D)	-	-	175 *	2.0	44	-	-	-
Missouri	4	(D)	-	-	175 *	2.0	44	-	-	-
Iowa	3	(D)	-	-	175 *	2.0	58	-	-	-
Arkansas	2	(D)	-	-	375 *	4.3	188	-	-	-
Colorado	2	(D)	-	-	175 *	2.0	88	-	-	-
Kentucky	2	(D)	-	-	175 *	2.0	88	-	-	-
Maryland	2	(D)	-	-	375 *	4.3	188	-	-	-
Michigan	2	(D)	-	-	175 *	2.0	88	-	-	-
Oregon	2	(D)	-	-	175 *	2.0	88	-	-	-
Alabama	1	(D)	-	-	375 *	4.3	375	-	-	-
Indiana	1	(D)	-	-	175 *	2.0	175	-	-	116,000
Louisiana	1	(D)	-	-	175 *	2.0	175	-	-	-
Minnesota	1	(D)	-	-	175 *	2.0	175	-	-	-
Rhode Island	1	(D)	-	-	175 *	2.0	175	-	-	-

Source: 1992 *Economic Census*. The states are in descending order of shipments or establishments (if shipment data are missing for the majority). The symbol (D) appears when data are withheld to prevent disclosure of competitive information. States marked with (D) are sorted by number of establishments. A dash (-) indicates that the data element cannot be calculated; * indicates the midpoint of a range.

2082 - MALT BEVERAGES

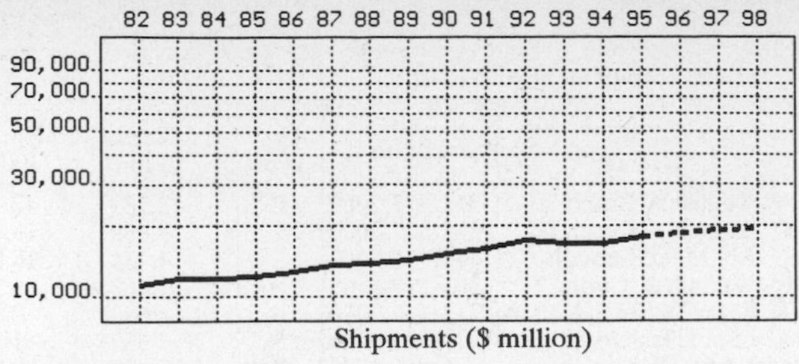

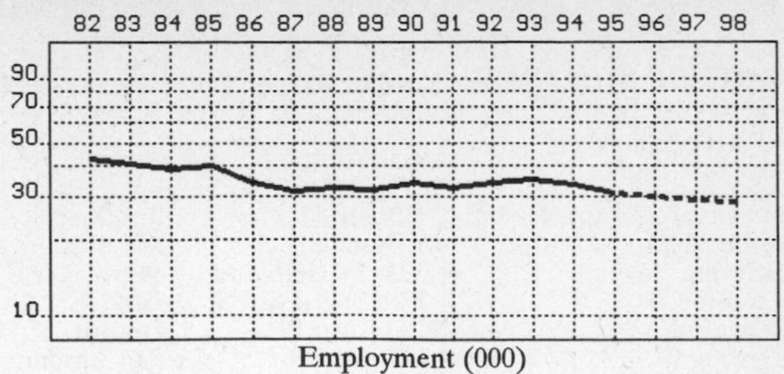

GENERAL STATISTICS

Year	Com-panies	Establishments Total	Establishments with 20 or more employees	Employment Total (000)	Production Workers (000)	Production Hours (Mil)	Compensation Payroll ($ mil)	Compensation Wages ($/hr)	Cost of Materials	Value Added by Manufacture	Value of Shipments	Capital Invest.
1982	67	109	74	43.0	29.5	57.5	1,307.9	15.37	6,669.7	4,534.8	11,183.2	665.0
1983		109	72	40.7	28.5	55.1	1,302.6	16.19	6,443.2	5,324.6	11,797.5	599.8
1984		109	70	38.8	27.4	51.8	1,313.6	17.99	6,485.0	5,393.7	11,868.2	594.1
1985		110	67	40.3	27.0	52.6	1,357.8	18.10	6,529.1	5,681.1	12,215.8	372.2
1986		119	66	34.0	24.8	50.5	1,255.1	17.64	6,502.5	6,184.5	12,677.9	578.3
1987	91	134	64	31.9	22.7	44.7	1,355.4	20.76	6,311.8	7,284.8	13,618.6	473.6
1988		139	68	32.4	23.2	42.7	1,316.6	21.20	6,414.0	7,450.8	13,870.7	570.3
1989		150	71	32.0	23.3	43.8	1,364.6	21.26	6,555.0	7,783.3	14,321.2	601.8
1990		154	81	34.0	23.5	44.3	1,425.1	21.34	6,988.5	8,192.8	15,186.2	542.8
1991		177	85	32.4	23.5	43.1	1,445.8	22.30	6,885.8	9,036.7	15,924.9	649.0
1992	160	194	75	34.5	25.1	45.9	1,566.7	22.89	7,179.8	10,189.3	17,340.2	565.0
1993		215	91	35.3	25.3	46.5	1,596.3	22.71	7,125.3	9,543.2	16,656.3	479.3
1994		205P	83P	33.5	23.6	46.6	1,565.9	23.01	6,941.8	9,847.2	16,794.8	563.5
1995		215P	84P	30.8P	22.4P	41.4P	1,576.5P	24.62P	7,370.1P	10,454.8P	17,831.1P	541.1P
1996		224P	86P	30.1P	22.0P	40.4P	1,602.0P	25.27P	7,589.7P	10,766.3P	18,362.4P	538.7P
1997		234P	87P	29.4P	21.6P	39.5P	1,627.5P	25.92P	7,809.4P	11,077.9P	18,893.7P	536.3P
1998		243P	89P	28.7P	21.2P	38.5P	1,653.0P	26.57P	8,029.0P	11,389.4P	19,425.0P	533.9P

Sources: 1982, 1987, 1992 *Economic Census*; *Annual Survey of Manufactures*, 83-86, 88-91, 93-94. Establishment counts for non-Census years are from *County Business Patterns*; establishment values for 83-84 are extrapolations. 'P's show projections by the editors. Industries reclassified in 87 will not have data for prior years.

INDICES OF CHANGE

Year	Com-panies	Establishments Total	Establishments with 20 or more employees	Employment Total (000)	Production Workers (000)	Production Hours (Mil)	Compensation Payroll ($ mil)	Compensation Wages ($/hr)	Cost of Materials	Value Added by Manufacture	Value of Shipments	Capital Invest.
1982	42	56	99	125	118	125	83	67	93	45	64	118
1983		56	96	118	114	120	83	71	90	52	68	106
1984		56	93	112	109	113	84	79	90	53	68	105
1985		57	89	117	108	115	87	79	91	56	70	66
1986		61	88	99	99	110	80	77	91	61	73	102
1987	57	69	85	92	90	97	87	91	88	71	79	84
1988		72	91	94	92	93	84	93	89	73	80	101
1989		77	95	93	93	95	87	93	91	76	83	107
1990		79	108	99	94	97	91	93	97	80	88	96
1991		91	113	94	94	94	92	97	96	89	92	115
1992	100	100	100	100	100	100	100	100	100	100	100	100
1993		111	121	102	101	101	102	99	99	94	96	85
1994		106P	111P	97	94	102	100	101	97	97	97	100
1995		111P	112P	89P	89P	90P	101P	108P	103P	103P	103P	96P
1996		116P	114P	87P	88P	88P	102P	110P	106P	106P	106P	95P
1997		120P	116P	85P	86P	86P	104P	113P	109P	109P	109P	95P
1998		125P	118P	83P	84P	84P	106P	116P	112P	112P	112P	94P

Sources: Same as General Statistics. Values reflect change from the base year, 1992. Values above 100 mean greater than 92, values below 100 mean less than 92, and a value of 100 in the 82-91 or 93-98 period means same as 92. 'P's mark projections by the editors.

SELECTED RATIOS

For 1994	Avg. of All Manufact.	Analyzed Industry	Index
Employees per Establishment	49	163	333
Payroll per Establishment	1,500,273	7,631,768	509
Payroll per Employee	30,620	46,743	153
Production Workers per Establishment	34	115	335
Wages per Establishment	853,319	5,225,931	612
Wages per Production Worker	24,861	45,435	183
Hours per Production Worker	2,056	1,975	96
Wages per Hour	12.09	23.01	190
Value Added per Establishment	4,602,255	47,992,556	1,043
Value Added per Employee	93,930	293,946	313

For 1994	Avg. of All Manufact.	Analyzed Industry	Index
Value Added per Production Worker	134,084	417,254	311
Cost per Establishment	5,045,178	33,832,432	671
Cost per Employee	102,970	207,218	201
Cost per Production Worker	146,988	294,144	200
Shipments per Establishment	9,576,895	81,853,257	855
Shipments per Employee	195,460	501,337	256
Shipments per Production Worker	279,017	711,644	255
Investment per Establishment	321,011	2,746,345	856
Investment per Employee	6,552	16,821	257
Investment per Production Worker	9,352	23,877	255

Sources: Same as General Statistics. The 'Average of All Manufacturing' column represents the average of all manufacturing industries reported for the most recent complete year available. The Index shows the relationship between the Average and the Analyzed Industry. For example, 100 means that they are equal; 500 that the Analyzed Industry is five times the average; 50 means that the Analyzed Industry is half the national average. The abbreviation 'na' is used to show that data are 'not available'.

LEADING COMPANIES

Number shown: **64** Total sales ($ mil): **30,111** Total employment (000): **82.9**

Company Name	Address				CEO Name	Phone	Co. Type	Sales ($ mil)	Empl. (000)
Anheuser-Busch Companies Inc	1 Busch Pl	St Louis	MO	63118	August A Busch III	314-577-2000	P	13,733	42.6
Anheuser-Busch Inc	1 Busch Pl	St Louis	MO	63118	August A Busch III	314-577-2000	S	8,669	15.0
Miller Brewing Co	3939 W Highland	Milwaukee	WI	53208	J N MacDonough	414-931-2000	S	4,154	10.0
Adolph Coors Co	12th St & Ford St	Golden	CO	80401	William K Coors	303-279-6565	P	1,663	6.3
Stroh Brewery Co	100 River Pl	Detroit	MI	48207	Peter W Stroh	313-446-2000	R	680	2.7
Pabst Brewing Co	PO Box 1661	San Antonio	TX	78296	Lutz E Issleib	210-226-0231	S	330*	1.3
Genesee Corp	PO Box 762	Rochester	NY	14603	John L Wehle Jr	716-546-1030	P	137	0.8
Genesee Brewing Company Inc	445 St Paul St	Rochester	NY	14605	John Wehle Jr	716-546-1030	S	114	0.5
Rainier Brewing Co	PO Box 24828	Seattle	WA	98124	Steven Sarich	206-622-2600	D	83*	0.3
Pearl Brewing Co	PO Box 1661	San Antonio	TX	78296	Lutz E Issleib	210-226-0231	S	77*	0.3
Pittsburgh Brewing Co	3340 Liberty Av	Pittsburgh	PA	15201	Micheal D Graham	412-682-7400	R	55	0.4
Dock Street Brewing Co	225 City Line Av	Bala Cynwyd	PA	19004	Jeffrey Ware	215-668-1480	R	51*	0.2
David Michael and Co	10801 Decatur Rd	Philadelphia	PA	19154	Edward Rosenbaum	215-632-3100	R	38	0.2
Matt Brewing Company Inc	811 Edward St	Utica	NY	13503	FX Matt II	315-732-3181	R	35	0.2
Sierra Nevada Brewing Co	1075 E 20th St	Chico	CA	95928	Ken Grossman	916-893-3520	R	26	<0.1
Minnesota Brewing Co	882 W 7th St	St Paul	MN	55102	Dick McMahon	612-228-9173	P	25	0.2
Redhook Ale Brewery Inc	3400 Phinney Av N	Seattle	WA	98103	Paul Shipman	206-548-8000	R	25*	0.1
Evansville Brewing Co	1301 W Lloyd	Evansville	IN	47710	Mark Mattingly	812-425-7101	R	23	0.1
Olde Towne Tavern	3 Russell Av	Gaithersburg	MD	20877	Chris Covell	301-948-4200	R	19*	<0.1
Lion Inc	700 N Pennsylvania	Wilkes-Barre	PA	18705	Charles Lawson	717-823-8801	R	15*	0.1
Breckinridge Brewery Denver	2220 Blake St	Denver	CO	80205	Richard Squire	303-297-3644	R	13	<0.1
Hart Brewing Co	91 S RBrougham	Seattle	WA	98134	George Hancock	206-682-8322	R	13	0.2
Jacob Leinenkugel Brewing	PO Box 368	Chippewa Falls	WI	54729	Leonard Goldstein	715-723-5558	S	13*	<0.1
Pete's Brewing Co	514 High St	Palo Alto	CA	94301	Mark F Bozzini	415-328-7383	R	12	<0.1
Wynkoop Brewing Co	1634 18th St	Denver	CO	80202	John Hickenlooper	303-297-2700	R	11*	0.1
Anchor Brewing Co	1705 Mariposa St	San Francisco	CA	94107	Fritz Maytag	415-863-8350	R	10*	<0.1
BC Marketing Concepts Inc	506 Columbia St	Hood River	OR	97031	Irene M Firmat	503-386-2281	R	9	<0.1
Bridgeport Brewing Company	1313 NW Marshall	Portland	OR	97209	Richard Ponzi	503-241-7179	R	8	<0.1
Jones Brewing Co	254 2nd St	Smithton	PA	15479	G M Podlucky Jr	412-872-6626	R	6	<0.1
Celis Brewery Inc	PO Box 141636	Austin	TX	78714	Christine Celis	512-835-0884	R	4*	<0.1
Eastern Brewing Corp	334 N Washington	Hammonton	NJ	08037	J Penza Sr	609-561-2700	R	4	<0.1
Mendocino Brewing Company	PO Box 400	Hopland	CA	95449	Michael Laybourn	707-744-1015	P	3	<0.1
Brewski Brewing Co	9355 Culver Blv	Culver City	CA	90232	Sandy Saemann	310-202-9400	R	3*	<0.1
Hops Extract Corporation	305 N 2nd Av	Yakima	WA	98902	G Savory	509-248-1530	R	3	<0.1
Jacques Bobbe and Associates	212 Sausalito Blv	Casselberry	FL	32707	Jacques Bobbe	407-767-8869	R	3	<0.1
Rocky's Brewing Co	2880 Wilderness Pl	Boulder	CO	80301	Gina Day	303-444-8448	R	3	<0.1
Massachusetts Bay Brewing Co	306 Northern Av	Boston	MA	02210	Richard Doyle	617-574-9551	R	3	<0.1
Yakima Brewing and Malting Co	PO Box 9158	Yakima	WA	98909	Herbert L Grant	509-575-1900	R	3	<0.1
Sprecher Brewing Company Inc	701 W Glendale	Glendale	WI	53209	Randal Sprecher	414-964-2739	R	2	<0.1
Alaskan Brewing&Bottling Co	5429 Shaune Dr	Juneau	AK	99801	Geoffrey Larson	907-780-5866	R	2	<0.1
Boulevard Brewing Co	2501 Southwest Blv	Kansas City	MO	64108	John McDonald	816-474-7095	R	2	<0.1
Portland Brewing Co	3015 NW Industrial	Portland	OR	97210	Tony Adams	503-222-7150	P	2	<0.1
Kennebunkport Brewing Co	86 Newbury St	Portland	ME	04101	Fred Forsley	207-761-0807	R	2	<0.1
North Coast Brewing Company	444 N Main St	Fort Bragg	CA	95437	Mark Ruedrich	707-964-2739	R	2	<0.1
Widmer Brewing Co	929 N Russell St	Portland	OR	97227	Kurt Widmer	503-281-2437	R	2*	<0.1
Zip City Brewing Co	3 W 18th St	New York	NY	10011	Kirby Shyer	212-366-6333	R	2	<0.1
Catamount Brewing Co	PO Box 457	Wh Riv Jnc	VT	05001	Steve Mason	802-296-2248	R	2	<0.1
Wild Goose Brewery	20 Washington St	Cambridge	MD	21613	James W Lutz	410-221-1121	R	2	<0.1
Frankenmuth Brewery Inc	425 S Main St	Frankenmuth	MI	48734	Randall E Heine	517-652-6183	R	2	<0.1
DL Geary Brewing Co	38 Evergreen Dr	Portland	ME	04103	David L Geary	207-878-2337	R	1	<0.1
Otter Creek Brewing Inc	74 Exchange St	Middlebury	VT	05753	Lawrence Miller	802-388-0727	R	1	<0.1
Bohannon Brewing Co	134 2nd Av N	Nashville	TN	37201	Lindsay Bohannon	615-242-8223	R	1	<0.1
Hale's Ales Ltd	4301 Leary NW	Seattle	WA	98107	Mike Hale	206-827-4359	R	1*	<0.1
Hartford Brewery Ltd	35 Pearl St	Hartford	CT	06103	Philip Hopkins	203-246-2337	R	1	<0.1
James Page Brewing Co	1300 Quincy St	Minneapolis	MN	55413	James Page	612-781-8247	R	1	<0.1
Lakeview Brewery LP	1830 N Besly Ct	Chicago	IL	60622	Stephen Dinehart	312-252-2739	R	1	<0.1
New Haven Brewing Co	458 Grand Av	New Haven	CT	06513	Blair Potts	203-772-2739	R	1*	<0.1
Saint Arnold Brewing Co	2522 Fairway Pk Dr	Houston	TX	77092	J Kevin Bartol	713-686-9494	R	1*	<0.1
S and P Co	PO Box 992	Corte Madera	CA	94925	William Bitting	415-332-0550	R	1*	<0.1
Tabernash Brewing Co	205 Denargo Mkt	Denver	CO	80216	Eric Warner	303-293-2337	R	1	<0.1
KMT Management Inc	6861 Main St	Williamsville	NY	14221	Kevin Townsell	716-828-0004	R	1	<0.1
Maritime Pacific Brewing Co	1514 NW Leary	Seattle	WA	98107	George A Hancock	206-782-6181	R	1	<0.1
Stoudt's Brewing Inc	Rte 272	Adamstown	PA	19501	Carol Stoudt	717-484-4387	R	1*	<0.1
Lakefront Brewery Inc	818A E Chambers	Milwaukee	WI	53212	Russ Klisch	414-372-8800	R	1	<0.1

Source: *Ward's Business Directory of U.S. Private and Public Companies*, Volumes 1 and 2, 1996. The company type code used is as follows: P - Public, R - Private, S - Subsidiary, D - Division, J - Joint Venture, A - Affiliate, G - Group. Sales are in millions of dollars, employees are in thousands. An asterisk (*) indicates an estimated sales volume. The symbol < stands for 'less than'. Company names and addresses are truncated, in some cases, to fit into the available space.

MATERIALS CONSUMED

Material		Quantity	Delivered Cost ($ million)
Materials, ingredients, containers, and supplies		(X)	6,864.3
Barley	mil bushels	15.5	69.3
Corn, purchased as grain	mil bushels	(D)	(D)
Corn grits	1,000 cwt	7,043.6	66.2
Corn meal and flakes	1,000 cwt	(D)	(D)
Malt	1,000 cwt	50,252.1	721.1
Dextrose and corn syrup, including corn syrup solids (in terms of dry weight)	mil lb	605.4	68.5
High fructose corn syrup (HFCS)(in terms of solids)	mil lb	(D)	(D)
Sugar, cane and beet (in terms of sugar solids)	1,000 s tons	(D)	(D)
Paperboard containers, boxes, and corrugated paperboard		(X)	563.5
Glass containers, excluding those capitalized		(X)	1,470.0
Metal cans, can lids and ends		(X)	2,815.1
All other materials and components, parts, containers, and supplies		(X)	987.4
Materials, ingredients, containers, and supplies, nsk		(X)	55.3

Source: 1992 *Economic Census*. Explanation of symbols used: (D): Withheld to avoid disclosure of competitive data; na: Not available; (S): Withheld because statistical norms were not met; (X): Not applicable; (Z): Less than half the unit shown; nec: Not elsewhere classified; nsk: Not specified by kind; - : zero; * : 10-19 percent estimated; ** : 20-29 percent estimated.

PRODUCT SHARE DETAILS

Product or Product Class	% Share
Malt beverages	100.00
Canned beer and ale case goods	61.47
Canned beer and ale case goods, 12 oz cans	89.57
Canned beer and ale case goods, 16 oz cans	8.24
Canned beer and ale case goods, other can sizes	2.18
Canned beer and ale case goods, nsk	0.01
Bottled beer and ale case goods	28.10
Bottled beer case goods in returnable bottles less than 12 oz	0.23
In returnable 12 oz bottles	23.25
In returnable 32 oz bottles	(D)
In all other returnable bottle sizes	0.34
In nonreturnable bottles less than 12 oz	2.20
In nonreturnable 12 oz bottles	59.66
In nonreturnable 32 oz bottles	3.46
In all other nonreturnable bottle sizes	(D)
Bottled ale case goods	0.87
Beer and ale in barrels and kegs	5.93
Beer and ale in 1/2 barrel size	88.92
Beer and ale in other barrel sizes	11.07
All other malt beverages and brewing products	3.77
Malt liquors, in either cans or bottles	79.85
Dry brewers' spent grains	2.94
Wet brewers' spent grains (dry weight equivalent or actual weight of dry grains employed in the manufacture)	7.08
All other malt beverages and brewery products (porter, stout, etc., bulk transfers, malt extracts, malt syrup)	10.00
Malt beverages, nsk	0.72

Source: 1992 *Economic Census*. The values shown are percent of total shipments in an industry. Values of indented subcategories are summed in the main heading. The symbol (D) appears when data are withheld to prevent disclosure of competitive information. The abbreviation nsk stands for 'not specified by kind' and nec for 'not elsewhere classified'.

INPUTS AND OUTPUTS FOR MALT BEVERAGES

Economic Sector or Industry Providing Inputs	%	Sector	Economic Sector or Industry Buying Outputs	%	Sector
Metal cans	31.5	Manufg.	Personal consumption expenditures	77.3	
Glass containers	15.8	Manufg.	Eating & drinking places	20.1	Trade
Malt	7.6	Manufg.	Exports	0.7	Foreign
Advertising	7.4	Services	Prepared feeds, nec	0.4	Manufg.
Imports	6.8	Foreign	S/L Govt. purch., higher education	0.4	S/L Govt
Paperboard containers & boxes	3.6	Manufg.	Malt beverages	0.3	Manufg.
Wholesale trade	3.6	Trade	Air transportation	0.2	Util.
Commercial printing	1.9	Manufg.	Federal Government enterprises nec	0.2	Gov't
Miscellaneous crops	1.7	Agric.	Racing (including track operations)	0.1	Services
Motor freight transportation & warehousing	1.7	Util.			
Electric services (utilities)	1.5	Util.			
Gas production & distribution (utilities)	1.4	Util.			
Banking	1.3	Fin/R.E.			
Railroads & related services	1.2	Util.			
Feed grains	1.0	Agric.			
Crowns & closures	1.0	Manufg.			
Engineering, architectural, & surveying services	0.9	Services			
Rice milling	0.8	Manufg.			
Flour & other grain mill products	0.7	Manufg.			
Petroleum refining	0.7	Manufg.			
State & local government enterprises, nec	0.6	Gov't			
Malt beverages	0.5	Manufg.			
Sugar	0.5	Manufg.			
Insurance carriers	0.5	Fin/R.E.			
Maintenance of nonfarm buildings nec	0.4	Constr.			
Metal foil & leaf	0.4	Manufg.			
Miscellaneous plastics products	0.4	Manufg.			
Eating & drinking places	0.3	Trade			
Coal	0.2	Mining			
Food products machinery	0.2	Manufg.			

Continued on next page.

INPUTS AND OUTPUTS FOR MALT BEVERAGES - Continued

Economic Sector or Industry Providing Inputs	%	Sector	Economic Sector or Industry Buying Outputs	%	Sector
Pipe, valves, & pipe fittings	0.2	Manufg.			
Soap & other detergents	0.2	Manufg.			
Air transportation	0.2	Util.			
Communications, except radio & TV	0.2	Util.			
Water transportation	0.2	Util.			
Real estate	0.2	Fin/R.E.			
Equipment rental & leasing services	0.2	Services			
Miscellaneous repair shops	0.2	Services			
Pumps & compressors	0.1	Manufg.			
Sanitary services, steam supply, irrigation	0.1	Util.			
U.S. Postal Service	0.1	Gov't			

Source: Benchmark Input-Output Accounts for the U.S. Economy, 1982, U.S. Department of Commerce, Washington, D.C., July 1991. Data, as reported in the source, are organized by the 1977 SIC structure in use in 1982 but have been matched, as closely as is possible, to the 1987 SIC structure used in this book.

OCCUPATIONS EMPLOYED BY SIC 208 - BEVERAGES

Occupation	% of Total 1994	Change to 2005	Occupation	% of Total 1994	Change to 2005
Packaging & filling machine operators	11.6	-48.1	Salespersons, retail	1.9	-4.1
Driver/sales workers	7.8	-28.1	Marketing & sales worker supervisors	1.9	-20.1
Sales & related workers nec	6.5	-20.1	Marketing, advertising, & PR managers	1.9	-20.1
Truck drivers light & heavy	5.5	-17.6	General office clerks	1.6	-31.9
Industrial truck & tractor operators	5.2	-20.1	Bookkeeping, accounting, & auditing clerks	1.6	-40.1
Industrial machinery mechanics	3.6	-12.1	Industrial production managers	1.4	-20.2
Helpers, laborers, & material movers nec	3.3	-20.1	Separating & still machine operators	1.4	-12.1
Hand packers & packagers	2.7	-31.5	Maintenance repairers, general utility	1.3	-28.1
Freight, stock, & material movers, hand	2.7	-36.1	Managers & administrators nec	1.2	-20.2
Secretaries, ex legal & medical	2.5	-27.3	Management support workers nec	1.2	-20.1
General managers & top executives	2.2	-24.2	Precision food & tobacco workers nec	1.1	-20.2
Coin & vending machine servicers & repairers	2.0	-36.1	Science & mathematics technicians	1.0	-20.2
Agricultural workers nec	2.0	-20.1	Traffic, shipping, & receiving clerks	1.0	-23.1

Source: Industry-Occupation Matrix, Bureau of Labor Statistics. These data relate to one or more 3-digit SIC industry groups rather than to a single 4-digit SIC. The change reported for each occupation to the year 2005 is a percent of growth or decline as estimated by the Bureau of Labor Statistics. The abbreviation nec stands for 'not elsewhere classified'.

LOCATION BY STATE AND REGIONAL CONCENTRATION

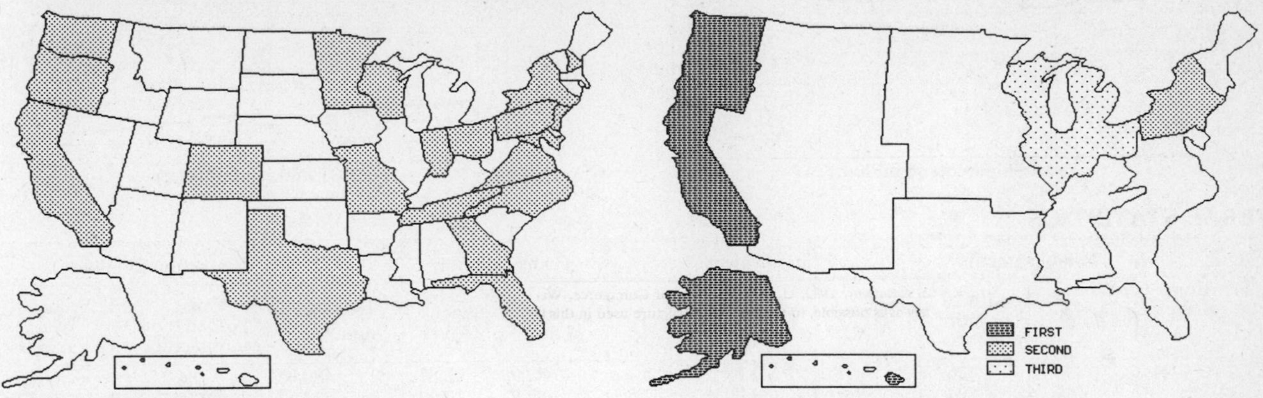

INDUSTRY DATA BY STATE

State	Establish- ments	Shipments Total ($ mil)	Shipments % of U.S.	Shipments Per Establ.	Employment Total Number	Employment % of U.S.	Employment Per Establ.	Employment Wages ($/hour)	Cost as % of Shipments	Investment per Employee ($)
Texas	8	1,987.3	11.5	248.4	2,800	8.1	350	23.91	44.7	12,286
New York	9	1,246.5	7.2	138.5	2,700	7.8	300	21.91	46.8	12,741
Wisconsin	11	1,076.0	6.2	97.8	2,800	8.1	255	20.91	47.8	6,679
Pennsylvania	15	313.5	1.8	20.9	1,300	3.8	87	18.75	62.1	5,692
Oregon	11	102.8	0.6	9.3	400	1.2	36	16.25	49.7	12,250
California	35	(D)	-	-	3,750 *	10.9	107	-	-	11,973
Washington	14	(D)	-	-	750 *	2.2	54	-	-	8,000
Colorado	13	(D)	-	-	7,500 *	21.7	577	-	-	-
Ohio	6	(D)	-	-	1,750 *	5.1	292	-	-	-
Minnesota	5	(D)	-	-	375 *	1.1	75	-	-	-
Virginia	5	(D)	-	-	1,750 *	5.1	350	-	-	-
Florida	4	(D)	-	-	1,750 *	5.1	438	-	-	-
Indiana	4	(D)	-	-	175 *	0.5	44	-	-	-
Missouri	4	(D)	-	-	3,750 *	10.9	938	-	-	-
New Jersey	4	(D)	-	-	1,750 *	5.1	438	-	-	-
North Carolina	3	(D)	-	-	1,750 *	5.1	583	-	-	-
Georgia	2	(D)	-	-	750 *	2.2	375	-	-	-
New Hampshire	2	(D)	-	-	750 *	2.2	375	-	-	-
Tennessee	2	(D)	-	-	375 *	1.1	188	-	-	-
Maryland	1	(D)	-	-	375 *	1.1	375	-	-	-

Source: 1992 *Economic Census.* The states are in descending order of shipments or establishments (if shipment data are missing for the majority). The symbol (D) appears when data are withheld to prevent disclosure of competitive information. States marked with (D) are sorted by number of establishments. A dash (-) indicates that the data element cannot be calculated; * indicates the midpoint of a range.

2083 - MALT

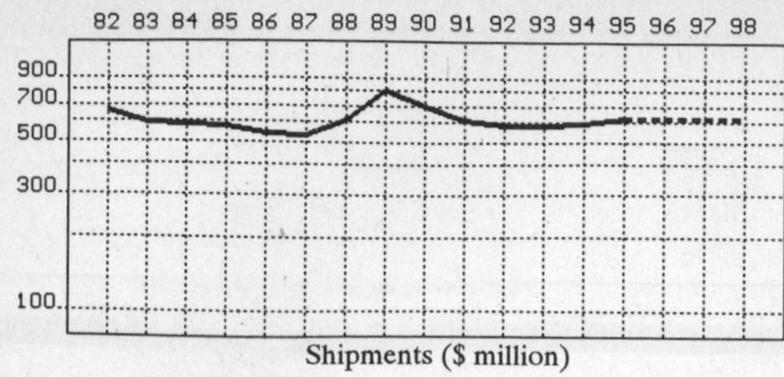

Shipments ($ million)

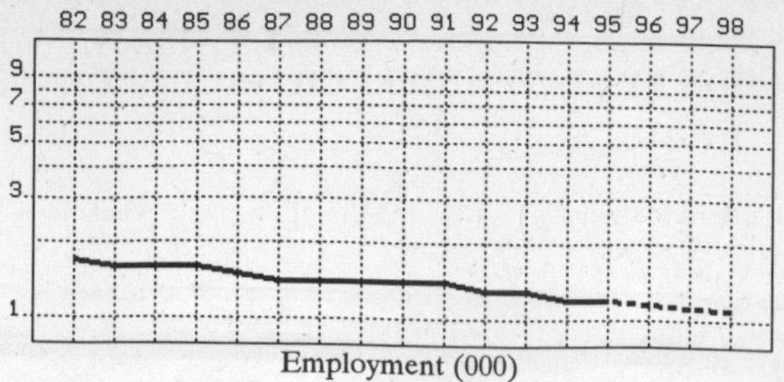

Employment (000)

GENERAL STATISTICS

Year	Companies	Establishments: Total	Establishments: with 20 or more employees	Employment: Total (000)	Employment: Production Workers (000)	Employment: Production Hours (Mil)	Compensation: Payroll ($ mil)	Compensation: Wages ($/hr)	Production ($ million): Cost of Materials	Production ($ million): Value Added by Manufacture	Production ($ million): Value of Shipments	Production ($ million): Capital Invest.
1982	24	36	26	1.7	1.3	2.7	42.9	11.81	480.0	166.2	661.5	29.5
1983		35	24	1.6	1.2	2.5	42.9	12.48	414.5	135.7	587.1	54.8
1984		34	22	1.6	1.2	2.4	45.0	13.71	435.3	162.2	586.7	20.6
1985		33	21	1.6	1.2	2.3	43.7	13.91	393.4	161.8	571.3	29.1
1986		31	19	1.5	1.1	2.2	41.0	13.45	368.1	162.5	538.6	13.5
1987	15	27	19	1.4	1.1	2.2	44.2	14.59	368.0	153.6	530.9	13.8
1988		29	19	1.4	1.0	2.1	42.8	14.38	456.1	178.0	613.2	28.7
1989		29	19	1.4	1.1	2.3	45.9	14.70	565.6	254.6	798.1	15.4
1990		28	20	1.4	1.0	2.1	45.2	16.05	494.9	170.8	700.4	17.4
1991		28	18	1.4	1.0	2.0	46.0	16.50	435.9	179.7	610.3	18.5
1992	16	26	18	1.3	0.9	1.8	44.4	16.94	387.3	175.9	575.8	27.1
1993		27	18	1.3	0.9	1.8	44.7	16.89	399.0	184.2	576.4	39.3
1994		25P	16P	1.2	0.8	1.7	43.9	17.24	417.5	165.6	589.7	73.4
1995		24P	16P	1.2P	0.8P	1.7P	45.2P	17.92P	437.3P	173.5P	617.7P	36.6P
1996		23P	15P	1.2P	0.8P	1.6P	45.3P	18.36P	438.0P	173.7P	618.7P	37.6P
1997		22P	14P	1.1P	0.7P	1.5P	45.5P	18.81P	438.7P	174.0P	619.7P	38.7P
1998		21P	14P	1.1P	0.7P	1.5P	45.7P	19.25P	439.4P	174.3P	620.7P	39.7P

Sources: 1982, 1987, 1992 *Economic Census*; *Annual Survey of Manufactures*, 83-86, 88-91, 93-94. Establishment counts for non-Census years are from *County Business Patterns*; establishment values for 83-84 are extrapolations. 'P's show projections by the editors. Industries reclassified in 87 will not have data for prior years.

INDICES OF CHANGE

Year	Companies	Establishments: Total	Establishments: with 20 or more employees	Employment: Total (000)	Employment: Production Workers (000)	Employment: Production Hours (Mil)	Compensation: Payroll ($ mil)	Compensation: Wages ($/hr)	Production ($ million): Cost of Materials	Production ($ million): Value Added by Manufacture	Production ($ million): Value of Shipments	Production ($ million): Capital Invest.
1982	150	138	144	131	144	150	97	70	124	94	115	109
1983		135	133	123	133	139	97	74	107	77	102	202
1984		131	122	123	133	133	101	81	112	92	102	76
1985		127	117	123	133	128	98	82	102	92	99	107
1986		119	106	115	122	122	92	79	95	92	94	50
1987	94	104	106	108	122	122	100	86	95	87	92	51
1988		112	106	108	111	117	96	85	118	101	106	106
1989		112	106	108	122	128	103	87	146	145	139	57
1990		108	111	108	111	117	102	95	128	97	122	64
1991		108	100	108	111	111	104	97	113	102	106	68
1992	100	100	100	100	100	100	100	100	100	100	100	100
1993		104	100	100	100	100	101	100	103	105	100	145
1994		94P	90P	92	89	94	99	102	108	94	102	271
1995		91P	87P	92P	90P	93P	102P	106P	113P	99P	107P	135P
1996		88P	84P	89P	86P	89P	102P	108P	113P	99P	107P	139P
1997		84P	80P	87P	82P	85P	102P	111P	113P	99P	108P	143P
1998		81P	77P	84P	78P	81P	103P	114P	113P	99P	108P	147P

Sources: Same as General Statistics. Values reflect change from the base year, 1992. Values above 100 mean greater than 92, values below 100 mean less than 92, and a value of 100 in the 82-91 or 93-98 period means same as 92. 'P's mark projections by the editors.

SELECTED RATIOS

For 1994	Avg. of All Manufact.	Analyzed Industry	Index
Employees per Establishment	49	49	100
Payroll per Establishment	1,500,273	1,788,519	119
Payroll per Employee	30,620	36,583	119
Production Workers per Establishment	34	33	95
Wages per Establishment	853,319	1,194,030	140
Wages per Production Worker	24,861	36,635	147
Hours per Production Worker	2,056	2,125	103
Wages per Hour	12.09	17.24	143
Value Added per Establishment	4,602,255	6,746,667	147
Value Added per Employee	93,930	138,000	147

For 1994	Avg. of All Manufact.	Analyzed Industry	Index
Value Added per Production Worker	134,084	207,000	154
Cost per Establishment	5,045,178	17,009,259	337
Cost per Employee	102,970	347,917	338
Cost per Production Worker	146,988	521,875	355
Shipments per Establishment	9,576,895	24,024,815	251
Shipments per Employee	195,460	491,417	251
Shipments per Production Worker	279,017	737,125	264
Investment per Establishment	321,011	2,990,370	932
Investment per Employee	6,552	61,167	934
Investment per Production Worker	9,352	91,750	981

Sources: Same as General Statistics. The 'Average of All Manufacturing' column represents the average of all manufacturing industries reported for the most recent complete year available. The Index shows the relationship between the Average and the Analyzed Industry. For example, 100 means that they are equal; 500 that the Analyzed Industry is five times the average; 50 means that the Analyzed Industry is half the national average. The abbreviation 'na' is used to show that data are 'not available'.

LEADING COMPANIES

Number shown: **9** Total sales ($ mil): **279** Total employment (000): **0.8**

Company Name	Address				CEO Name	Phone	Co. Type	Sales ($ mil)	Empl. (000)
Great Western Malting Co	PO Box 1529	Vancouver	WA	98668	Stewart Reeder	206-693-3661	S	100	0.3
Froedtert Malt Corp	PO Box 712	Milwaukee	WI	53201	Gabriel Pujol	414-671-1166	R	70	0.2
Schreier Malting Co	PO Box 59	Sheboygan	WI	53082	TR Testwuide	414-458-6126	R	34	<0.1
Rahr Malting Co	PO Box 15186	Minneapolis	MN	55415	John Alsip	612-332-5161	R	31*	0.2
Minnesota Malting Co	918 N 7th St	Cannon Falls	MN	55009	RD Mensing	507-263-3911	R	20	<0.1
Froedtert Malt Corp Winona	PO Box 497	Winona	MN	55987	Robert Cabelka	507-454-1535	D	15	<0.1
ADM Malting Co	PO Box 15666	Minneapolis	MN	55415	Tim Malm	612-371-3480	S	7*	<0.1
New England Brewing Co	13 Marshall St	Norwalk	CT	06854	Marcia L King	203-866-1339	R	1	<0.1
Northwestern Extract Co	3590 N 126th St	Brookfield	WI	53005	William Peter	414-781-6670	R	1	<0.1

Source: *Ward's Business Directory of U.S. Private and Public Companies*, Volumes 1 and 2, 1996. The company type code used is as follows: P - Public, R - Private, S - Subsidiary, D - Division, J - Joint Venture, A - Affiliate, G - Group. Sales are in millions of dollars, employees are in thousands. An asterisk (*) indicates an estimated sales volume. The symbol < stands for 'less than'. Company names and addresses are truncated, in some cases, to fit into the available space.

MATERIALS CONSUMED

Material		Quantity	Delivered Cost ($ million)
Materials, ingredients, containers, and supplies		(X)	345.5
Barley	mil bushels	128.9	326.9
All other materials and components, parts, containers, and supplies		(X)	12.6
Materials, ingredients, containers, and supplies, nsk		(X)	6.1

Source: 1992 *Economic Census*. Explanation of symbols used: (D): Withheld to avoid disclosure of competitive data; na: Not available; (S): Withheld because statistical norms were not met; (X): Not applicable; (Z): Less than half the unit shown; nec: Not elsewhere classified; nsk: Not specified by kind; - : zero; * : 10-19 percent estimated; ** : 20-29 percent estimated.

PRODUCT SHARE DETAILS

Product or Product Class	% Share	Product or Product Class	% Share
Malt	100.00		

Source: 1992 *Economic Census*. The values shown are percent of total shipments in an industry. Values of indented subcategories are summed in the main heading. The symbol (D) appears when data are withheld to prevent disclosure of competitive information. The abbreviation nsk stands for 'not specified by kind' and nec for 'not elsewhere classified'.

INPUTS AND OUTPUTS FOR MALT

Economic Sector or Industry Providing Inputs	%	Sector	Economic Sector or Industry Buying Outputs	%	Sector
Feed grains	48.2	Agric.	Malt beverages	90.8	Manufg.
Wholesale trade	14.8	Trade	Exports	2.9	Foreign
Motor freight transportation & warehousing	8.6	Util.	Prepared feeds, nec	2.2	Manufg.
Gas production & distribution (utilities)	5.2	Util.	Distilled liquor, except brandy	2.0	Manufg.
Electric services (utilities)	4.7	Util.	Dog, cat, & other pet food	1.0	Manufg.
Railroads & related services	3.7	Util.	Flavoring extracts & syrups, nec	0.7	Manufg.
Advertising	3.6	Services	Malt	0.4	Manufg.
Banking	2.3	Fin/R.E.			
Imports	2.3	Foreign			
Petroleum refining	1.2	Manufg.			
Water transportation	0.9	Util.			
Malt	0.5	Manufg.			
Miscellaneous repair shops	0.4	Services			
State & local government enterprises, nec	0.3	Gov't			
Coal	0.2	Mining			
Paperboard containers & boxes	0.2	Manufg.			
Sanitary services, steam supply, irrigation	0.2	Util.			
Automotive rental & leasing, without drivers	0.2	Services			
Automotive repair shops & services	0.2	Services			
Computer & data processing services	0.2	Services			
Noncomparable imports	0.2	Foreign			
Pipe, valves, & pipe fittings	0.1	Manufg.			
Soap & other detergents	0.1	Manufg.			
Air transportation	0.1	Util.			
Communications, except radio & TV	0.1	Util.			
Water supply & sewage systems	0.1	Util.			
Eating & drinking places	0.1	Trade			
Insurance carriers	0.1	Fin/R.E.			
Real estate	0.1	Fin/R.E.			

Source: *Benchmark Input-Output Accounts for the U.S. Economy, 1982*, U.S. Department of Commerce, Washington, D.C., July 1991. Data, as reported in the source, are organized by the 1977 SIC structure in use in 1982 but have been matched, as closely as is possible, to the 1987 SIC structure used in this book.

OCCUPATIONS EMPLOYED BY SIC 208 - BEVERAGES

Occupation	% of Total 1994	Change to 2005	Occupation	% of Total 1994	Change to 2005
Packaging & filling machine operators	11.6	-48.1	Salespersons, retail	1.9	-4.1
Driver/sales workers	7.8	-28.1	Marketing & sales worker supervisors	1.9	-20.1
Sales & related workers nec	6.5	-20.1	Marketing, advertising, & PR managers	1.9	-20.1
Truck drivers light & heavy	5.5	-17.6	General office clerks	1.6	-31.9
Industrial truck & tractor operators	5.2	-20.1	Bookkeeping, accounting, & auditing clerks	1.6	-40.1
Industrial machinery mechanics	3.6	-12.1	Industrial production managers	1.4	-20.2
Helpers, laborers, & material movers nec	3.3	-20.1	Separating & still machine operators	1.4	-12.1
Hand packers & packagers	2.7	-31.5	Maintenance repairers, general utility	1.3	-28.1
Freight, stock, & material movers, hand	2.7	-36.1	Managers & administrators nec	1.2	-20.2
Secretaries, ex legal & medical	2.5	-27.3	Management support workers nec	1.2	-20.1
General managers & top executives	2.2	-24.2	Precision food & tobacco workers nec	1.1	-20.2
Coin & vending machine servicers & repairers	2.0	-36.1	Science & mathematics technicians	1.0	-20.2
Agricultural workers nec	2.0	-20.1	Traffic, shipping, & receiving clerks	1.0	-23.1

Source: Industry-Occupation Matrix, Bureau of Labor Statistics. These data relate to one or more 3-digit SIC industry groups rather than to a single 4-digit SIC. The change reported for each occupation to the year 2005 is a percent of growth or decline as estimated by the Bureau of Labor Statistics. The abbreviation nec stands for 'not elsewhere classified'.

LOCATION BY STATE AND REGIONAL CONCENTRATION

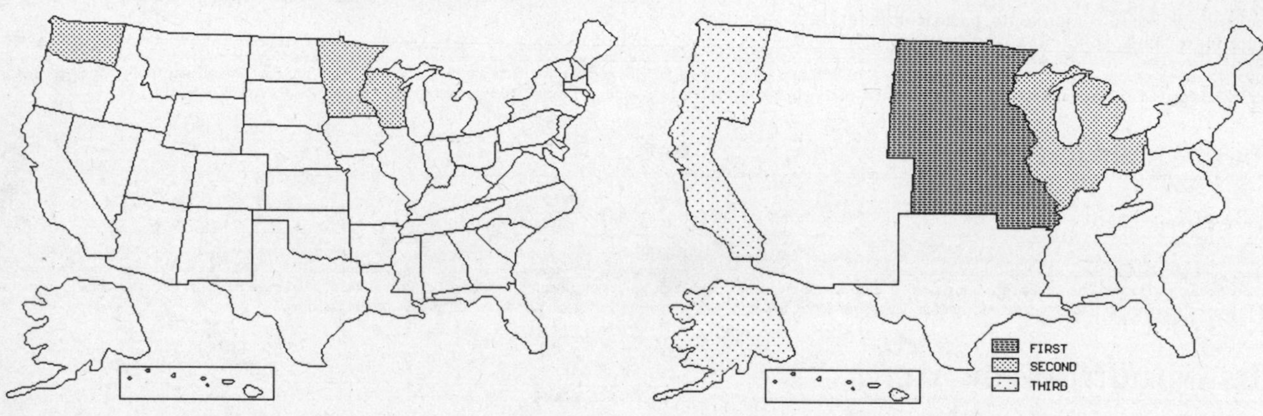

INDUSTRY DATA BY STATE

State	Establish-ments	Shipments			Employment				Cost as % of Shipments	Investment per Employee ($)
		Total ($ mil)	% of U.S.	Per Establ.	Total Number	% of U.S.	Per Establ.	Wages ($/hour)		
Wisconsin	7	240.0	41.7	34.3	500	38.5	71	18.86	67.0	15,200
Minnesota	8	160.5	27.9	20.1	300	23.1	38	15.00	63.7	43,000
Washington	1	(D)	-	-	175 *	13.5	175	-	-	-

Source: 1992 *Economic Census*. The states are in descending order of shipments or establishments (if shipment data are missing for the majority). The symbol (D) appears when data are withheld to prevent disclosure of competitive information. States marked with (D) are sorted by number of establishments. A dash (-) indicates that the data element cannot be calculated; * indicates the midpoint of a range.

2084 - WINES BRANDY & BRANDY SPIRITS

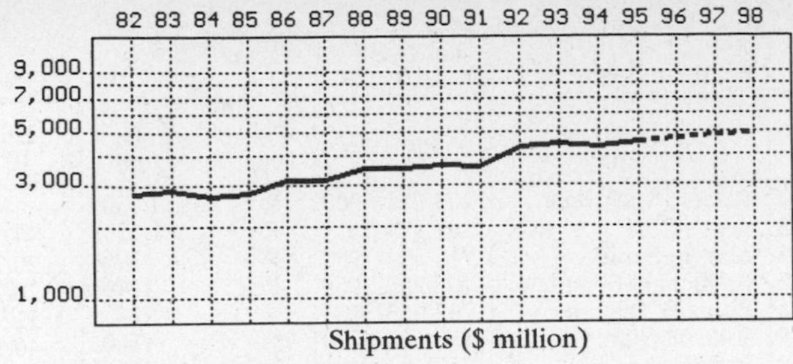

Shipments ($ million)

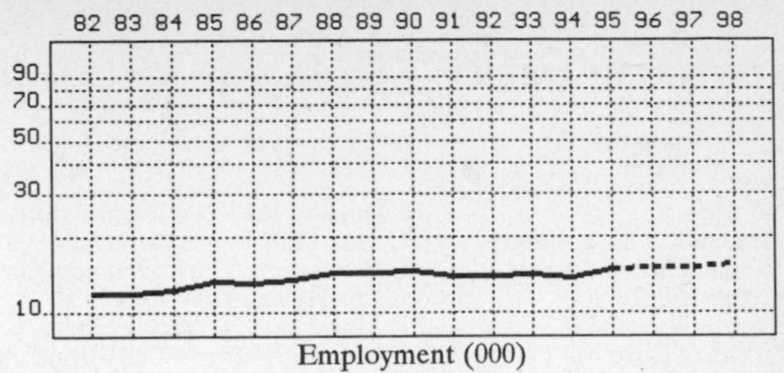

Employment (000)

GENERAL STATISTICS

Year	Com-panies	Establishments		Employment			Compensation		Production ($ million)			
		Total	with 20 or more employees	Total (000)	Production Workers (000)	Production Hours (Mil)	Payroll ($ mil)	Wages ($/hr)	Cost of Materials	Value Added by Manufacture	Value of Shipments	Capital Invest.
1982	324	366	103	11.8	6.8	12.8	245.8	9.80	1,762.9	996.7	2,785.7	136.8
1983		387	105	11.8	6.7	12.6	257.8	10.44	1,711.1	1,058.2	2,836.6	97.7
1984		408	107	12.2	7.0	13.2	274.2	10.20	1,627.6	1,080.7	2,694.8	93.4
1985		429	108	13.2	7.1	13.5	296.6	10.28	1,674.1	1,063.1	2,763.4	112.1
1986		456	106	13.1	7.0	13.2	318.1	11.06	1,896.4	1,234.1	3,162.6	112.1
1987	457	508	108	13.5	7.0	12.7	329.3	11.32	1,831.2	1,350.8	3,178.9	99.9
1988		513	132	14.3	7.4	13.5	372.9	11.69	2,032.8	1,710.0	3,528.4	104.3
1989		505	136	14.5	7.1	13.1	385.1	11.97	1,909.6	1,772.0	3,539.2	123.4
1990		521	140	14.6	7.1	13.1	400.8	11.95	1,872.5	1,810.1	3,657.8	108.2
1991		527	139	13.9	6.8	12.7	378.3	12.13	1,884.5	1,797.6	3,585.8	96.9
1992	514	553	136	14.0	6.5	12.6	425.9	12.68	2,394.0	2,088.7	4,301.0	114.7
1993		559	153	14.1	6.6	12.8	436.3	12.80	2,520.4	2,118.6	4,514.1	146.1
1994		593P	153P	13.7	6.6	12.9	437.4	13.53	2,325.2	2,022.7	4,300.8	151.0
1995		610P	158P	14.8P	6.7P	12.9P	470.5P	13.53P	2,441.6P	2,124.0P	4,516.1P	129.8P
1996		628P	162P	15.0P	6.7P	12.8P	487.6P	13.82P	2,524.0P	2,195.6P	4,668.4P	131.9P
1997		646P	167P	15.2P	6.7P	12.8P	504.7P	14.10P	2,606.3P	2,267.2P	4,820.7P	134.0P
1998		664P	171P	15.4P	6.7P	12.8P	521.8P	14.39P	2,688.6P	2,338.9P	4,973.1P	136.1P

Sources: 1982, 1987, 1992 *Economic Census*; *Annual Survey of Manufactures*, 83-86, 88-91, 93-94. Establishment counts for non-Census years are from *County Business Patterns*; establishment values for 83-84 are extrapolations. 'P's show projections by the editors. Industries reclassified in 87 will not have data for prior years.

INDICES OF CHANGE

Year	Com-panies	Establishments		Employment			Compensation		Production ($ million)			
		Total	with 20 or more employees	Total (000)	Production Workers (000)	Production Hours (Mil)	Payroll ($ mil)	Wages ($/hr)	Cost of Materials	Value Added by Manufacture	Value of Shipments	Capital Invest.
1982	63	66	76	84	105	102	58	77	74	48	65	119
1983		70	77	84	103	100	61	82	71	51	66	85
1984		74	79	87	108	105	64	80	68	52	63	81
1985		78	79	94	109	107	70	81	70	51	64	98
1986		82	78	94	108	105	75	87	79	59	74	98
1987	89	92	79	96	108	101	77	89	76	65	74	87
1988		93	97	102	114	107	88	92	85	82	82	91
1989		91	100	104	109	104	90	94	80	85	82	108
1990		94	103	104	109	104	94	94	78	87	85	94
1991		95	102	99	105	101	89	96	79	86	83	84
1992	100	100	100	100	100	100	100	100	100	100	100	100
1993		101	113	101	102	102	102	101	105	101	105	127
1994		107P	112P	98	102	102	103	107	97	97	100	132
1995		110P	116P	106P	104P	102P	110P	107P	102P	102P	105P	113P
1996		114P	119P	107P	103P	102P	114P	109P	105P	105P	109P	115P
1997		117P	123P	109P	103P	102P	119P	111P	109P	109P	112P	117P
1998		120P	126P	110P	103P	102P	123P	113P	112P	112P	116P	119P

Sources: Same as General Statistics. Values reflect change from the base year, 1992. Values above 100 mean greater than 92, values below 100 mean less than 92, and a value of 100 in the 82-91 or 93-98 period means same as 92. 'P's mark projections by the editors.

SELECTED RATIOS

For 1994	Avg. of All Manufact.	Analyzed Industry	Index
Employees per Establishment	49	23	47
Payroll per Establishment	1,500,273	737,964	49
Payroll per Employee	30,620	31,927	104
Production Workers per Establishment	34	11	32
Wages per Establishment	853,319	294,472	35
Wages per Production Worker	24,861	26,445	106
Hours per Production Worker	2,056	1,955	95
Wages per Hour	12.09	13.53	112
Value Added per Establishment	4,602,255	3,412,618	74
Value Added per Employee	93,930	147,642	157

For 1994	Avg. of All Manufact.	Analyzed Industry	Index
Value Added per Production Worker	134,084	306,470	229
Cost per Establishment	5,045,178	3,922,984	78
Cost per Employee	102,970	169,723	165
Cost per Production Worker	146,988	352,303	240
Shipments per Establishment	9,576,895	7,256,136	76
Shipments per Employee	195,460	313,927	161
Shipments per Production Worker	279,017	651,636	234
Investment per Establishment	321,011	254,761	79
Investment per Employee	6,552	11,022	168
Investment per Production Worker	9,352	22,879	245

Sources: Same as General Statistics. The 'Average of All Manufacturing' column represents the average of all manufacturing industries reported for the most recent complete year available. The Index shows the relationship between the Average and the Analyzed Industry. For example, 100 means that they are equal; 500 that the Analyzed Industry is five times the average; 50 means that the Analyzed Industry is half the national average. The abbreviation 'na' is used to show that data are 'not available'.

LEADING COMPANIES

Number shown: 75 Total sales ($ mil): **4,665** Total employment (000): **15.6**

Company Name	Address				CEO Name	Phone	Co. Type	Sales ($ mil)	Empl. (000)
Heublein Inc	16 Munson Rd	Farmington	CT	06032	Robert M Fureck	203-231-5000	S	1,700*	2.5
Ernest and Julio Gallo Winery	PO Box 1130	Modesto	CA	95353		209-579-3111	R	1,150*	5.0
Canandaigua Wine Company Inc	116 Buffalo St	Canandaigua	NY	14424	Marvin Sands	716-394-7900	P	306	1.1
Robert Mondavi Corp	7801 St Helena Hwy	Oakville	CA	94562	R Michael Mondavi	707-259-9463	P	146	0.6
Sutter Home Winery Inc	PO Box 248	St Helena	CA	94574	Louis B Trinchero	707-963-3104	R	145	0.3
Banfi Products Corp	1111 Cedar Swamp	Old Brookville	NY	11545	John Mariani	516-626-9200	R	100	0.2
Fetzer Vineyards	5801 Christie Av	Emeryville	CA	94608	Paul Dolan	510-653-7400	D	100*	0.3
Wine World Estates	PO Box 111	St Helena	CA	94574	Walt Klenz	707-963-7115	S	100*	0.5
Stimson Lane Wine	PO Box 1976	Woodinville	WA	98072	Allen C Shoup	206-488-1133	S	89	0.6
F Korbel and Bros Inc	13250 River Rd	Guerneville	CA	95446	Gary B Heck	707-887-2294	R	80	0.3
SS Pierce Co	20 3rd Av	Somerville	MA	02143	Harvey Allen	617-776-6700	S	50	0.2
Sebastiani Vineyards Inc	PO Box AA	Sonoma	CA	95476	Don Sebastiani	707-938-5532	R	44	0.3
Bronco Wine Co	PO Box 789	Ceres	CA	95307	Fred Franzia	209-538-3131	R	43*	0.2
Chateau Ste Michelle	PO Box 1976	Woodinville	WA	98072	Allen Shoup	206-488-1133	S	43*	0.2
Columbia Crest Winery	PO Box 231	Paterson	WA	99345	Allen Shoup	509-875-2061	S	40	0.3
Freixenet Sonoma Caves Inc	PO Box 1427	Sonoma	CA	95476	Pedro Ferrer	707-996-7256	S	35	<0.1
Domaine Chandon Inc	PO Box 2470	Yountville	CA	94599	C Edwin Farver	707-944-8844	S	33	0.2
Wine Alliance	PO Box 948	Healdsburg	CA	95448	Jon Moramarco	707-433-8268	S	32*	0.2
Klein Family Vintners	PO Box 368	Windsor	CA	95492	Thomas B Klein	707-433-6511	R	30	0.3
Rodney Strong Vineyards	PO Box 368	Windsor	CA	95492	Al Nirenstein	707-433-6511	S	30*	0.3
Vie-Del Co	PO Box 2896	Fresno	CA	93745	Dianne S Nury	209-834-2525	R	25	0.1
Louis M Martini Corp	PO Box 112	St Helena	CA	94574	Carolyn Martini	707-963-2736	R	22	<0.1
C Mondavi and Sons	PO Box 191	St Helena	CA	94574	Peter Mondavi Sr	707-963-2761	R	20	0.1
Chateau St Jean	PO Box 293	Kenwood	CA	95452	Doug Walker	707-833-4134	S	18	<0.1
Clos du Bois Wines	PO Box 940	Geyserville	CA	95441	Jon Moramarco Jr	707-857-1651	D	16	0.1
Widmer's Wine Cellars Inc	1 Lake Niagara Ln	Naples	NY	14512	Charles E Hetterich	716-374-6311	S	15	0.1
Weibel Inc	PO Box 3398	Fremont	CA	94539	Fred E Weibel Jr	510-656-2340	R	14*	<0.1
Kenwood Vineyards	PO Box 447	Kenwood	CA	95452	John Sheela	707-833-5891	R	13	<0.1
Simi Winery Inc	PO Box 698	Healdsburg	CA	95448	Zelma R Long	707-433-6981	S	11*	<0.1
Trefethen Vineyards Winery Inc	PO Box 2460	Napa	CA	94558	Janet Trefethen	707-255-7700	R	11	<0.1
Gibson Wine Company Inc	1720 Academy	Sanger	CA	93657	Kim Spruance	209-875-2505	R	10	<0.1
Hogue Cellars Ltd	PO Box 31	Prosser	WA	99350	Gary Hogue	509-786-4557	R	10	<0.1
Raymond Vineyard and Cellar	849 Zinfandel Ln	St Helena	CA	94574	Roy Raymond Jr	707-963-3141	S	9	<0.1
Takara Sake USA	708 Addison St	Berkeley	CA	94710	Kosei Yamamoto	510-540-8250	S	9	<0.1
Columbia Winery	PO Box 1248	Woodinville	WA	98072	Don Baty	206-488-2776	R	8*	<0.1
Hess Collection Winery	PO Box 4140	Napa	CA	94558	Donald Hess	707-255-1144	R	8*	<0.1
Thornton Winery	PO Box 9008	Temecula	CA	92589	John H Byrne	909-699-0099	R	7	0.1
Ariel Vineyards	PO Box 3437	Napa	CA	94558	Barry Gnekow	707-258-8048	R	6	<0.1
Belvedere Winery	1440 Grove St	Healdsburg	CA	95448	Edward R Schrufer	707-433-8236	R	6	<0.1
Napa Valley Cooperative Winery	401 St Helena Av	St Helena	CA	94574	Douglas Stanton	707-963-2335	R	6	<0.1
Beverage Source Inc	1887 N Mooney	Tulare	CA	93274	Richard McCombs	209-688-1766	S	5*	<0.1
Buena Vista Winery Inc	PO Box 182	Sonoma	CA	95476	Harry Parsley	707-252-7117	S	5	<0.1
Matanzas Creek Winery	6097 Bennett Val	Santa Rosa	CA	95404	Sandra P MacIver	707-528-6464	R	5	<0.1
Merryvale Vineyards	1000 Main St	St Helena	CA	94574	Jack Schlatter	707-963-2225	J	5	<0.1
Pine Ridge Winery	5901 Silverado Trail	Napa	CA	94558	Gary Andrus	707-253-7500	R	5*	<0.1
Piper Sonoma	PO Box 309	Healdsburg	CA	95448	Bernard LaBorie	707-433-8843	S	5	<0.1
Silver Oak Wine Cellars	PO Box 414	Oakville	CA	94562	Justin Meyer	707-944-8808	R	5	<0.1
Gundlach-Bundschu Winery	PO Box 1	Vineburg	CA	95487	Jim Bundschu	707-938-5277	R	5	<0.1
Ingleside Plantation Inc	PO Box 1038	Oak Grove	VA	22443	Douglas Flemer	804-224-8687	R	5	0.1
Kunde Enterprises Inc	PO Box 639	Kenwood	CA	95452	Pete Schneider	707-833-5501	R	4	<0.1
Grape Links Wine Productions	134 Lystra Ct	Santa Rosa	CA	95403	Michael Houlihan	707-524-8000	R	4	<0.1
Kohnan Inc	1 Executive Way	Napa	CA	94558	Sakae Higo	707-258-6160	R	4	<0.1
Markham Vineyards	PO Box 636	St Helena	CA	94574	Bryan Del Bondio	707-963-5292	R	4*	<0.1
St Julian Wine Co	PO Box 127	Paw Paw	MI	49079	David Braganini	616-657-5568	R	4*	<0.1
Unibev	311 10th St	Golden	CO	80401	Vinny Prattico	303-279-6565	D	4*	<0.1
Vichon Vineyards	PO Box 363	Oakville	CA	94562	Karen Culler	707-944-2811	D	4	<0.1
L Foppiano Wine Co	PO Box 606	Healdsburg	CA	95448	LJ Foppiano	707-433-7272	R	4	<0.1
Ste Chapelle Inc	14068 Sunny Slope	Caldwell	ID	83605	Richard Symms	208-459-7222	R	3	<0.1
California Wine Co	155 Cherry Creek	Cloverdale	CA	95425	John Merritt Jr	707-894-4295	R	3	<0.1
Fess Parker Winery and Vineyard	PO Box 908	Los Olivos	CA	93441	Fess G Parker Jr	805-688-1545	S	3	<0.1
Firestone Vineyard	PO Box 244	Los Olivos	CA	93441	AB Firestone	805-688-3940	R	3*	<0.1
Freemark Abbey Winery	PO Box 410	St Helena	CA	94574	Charles A Carpy	707-963-9694	R	3*	<0.1
Frog's Leap Winery	PO Box 189	Rutherford	CA	94573	John Williams	707-963-4704	R	3*	<0.1
Glenora Wine Cellars Inc	5435 Rte 14	Dundee	NY	14837	E Pierce	607-243-5511	R	3*	<0.1
Ingleside Plantation Winery	PO Box 1038	Oak Grove	VA	22443	Douglas Flemer	804-224-8687	S	3	<0.1
Joseph Cerniglia Winery Inc	RFD 1	Proctorsville	VT	05153	Joseph Cerniglia	802-226-7575	R	3	<0.1
Parker Station Inc	PO Box 908	Los Olivos	CA	93441	Fess G Parker Jr	805-688-1545	R	3	<0.1
Prince Michel Vineyards	HCR 4	Leon	VA	22725	Gale Sysock	703-547-3707	S	3*	<0.1
Silverado Vineyards	6121 Silverado Trail	Napa	CA	94558	Ron Miller	707-257-1770	R	3	<0.1
Viansa Winery and Marketplace	25200 Arnold Dr	Sonoma	CA	95476	Sam Sebastiani	707-935-4700	R	3	<0.1
Flora Springs Wine Co	1978 Zinfandel Ln	St Helena	CA	94574	John A Komes	707-963-5711	R	2	<0.1
Benmarl Wine Company Ltd	156 Highland Av	Marlboro	NY	12542	Mark Miller	914-236-4265	R	2*	<0.1
Bully Hill Vineyards Inc	8843 GHT Mem	Hammondsport	NY	14840	Walter S Taylor	607-868-3610	R	2	<0.1
Cain Cellars Inc	3800 Langtry Rd	St Helena	CA	94574	Nancy Meadlock	707-963-1616	R	2	<0.1
Caymus Vineyards	PO Box 268	Rutherford	CA	94573	Chuck Wagner	707-963-4204	R	2	<0.1

Source: *Ward's Business Directory of U.S. Private and Public Companies*, Volumes 1 and 2, 1996. The company type code used is as follows: P - Public, R - Private, S - Subsidiary, D - Division, J - Joint Venture, A - Affiliate, G - Group. Sales are in millions of dollars, employees are in thousands. An asterisk (*) indicates an estimated sales volume. The symbol < stands for 'less than'. Company names and addresses are truncated, in some cases, to fit into the available space.

MATERIALS CONSUMED

Material		Quantity	Delivered Cost ($ million)
Materials, ingredients, containers, and supplies		(X)	2,207.3
Fresh grapes	1,000 s tons	3,031.0	778.8
Purchased wines used for blending	mil wine gal	239.0	352.4
Purchased wines used for other purposes	mil wine gal	(S)	13.2
Glass containers used for wine and brandy manufacture	1,000 gross	11,377.0	393.4
Paperboard boxes and containers used for wine and brandy manufacture		(X)	36.7
All other materials and components, parts, containers, and supplies		(X)	472.6
Materials, ingredients, containers, and supplies, nsk		(X)	160.3

Source: 1992 *Economic Census*. Explanation of symbols used: (D): Withheld to avoid disclosure of competitive data; na: Not available; (S): Withheld because statistical norms were not met; (X): Not applicable; (Z): Less than half the unit shown; nec: Not elsewhere classified; nsk: Not specified by kind; - : zero; * : 10-19 percent estimated; ** : 20-29 percent estimated.

PRODUCT SHARE DETAILS

Product or Product Class	% Share	Product or Product Class	% Share
Wines, brandy, and brandy spirits	100.00	artificially carbonated)	8.39
White grape wines, 14 percent or less	36.27	Vermouth	0.47
Red grape wines, 14 percent or less	18.74	Wine coolers	6.35
Rose grape wines, 14 percent or less	9.04	Other specialty wines	2.60
Other fruit and berry wines, 14 percent or less	0.86	Beverage brandy, neutral fruit spirits, and neutral brandy, excluding neutral citrus residue brandy	5.50
Dessert wines (excluding specialties)	5.36		
Effervescent wines, including sparkling wines (naturally and			

Source: 1992 *Economic Census*. The values shown are percent of total shipments in an industry. Values of indented subcategories are summed in the main heading. The symbol (D) appears when data are withheld to prevent disclosure of competitive information. The abbreviation nsk stands for 'not specified by kind' and nec for 'not elsewhere classified'.

INPUTS AND OUTPUTS FOR WINES, BRANDY, & BRANDY SPIRITS

Economic Sector or Industry Providing Inputs	%	Sector	Economic Sector or Industry Buying Outputs	%	Sector
Imports	36.8	Foreign	Personal consumption expenditures	70.5	
Fruits	13.9	Agric.	Eating & drinking places	11.6	Trade
Glass containers	10.7	Manufg.	Retail trade, except eating & drinking	8.5	Trade
Wholesale trade	10.6	Trade	Wines, brandy, & brandy spirits	6.9	Manufg.
Wines, brandy, & brandy spirits	10.0	Manufg.	Air transportation	1.1	Util.
Advertising	4.8	Services	Exports	0.7	Foreign
Commercial printing	3.0	Manufg.			
Motor freight transportation & warehousing	2.3	Util.			
Banking	1.1	Fin/R.E.			
Crowns & closures	0.8	Manufg.			
Paperboard containers & boxes	0.8	Manufg.			
Electric services (utilities)	0.7	Util.			
Gas production & distribution (utilities)	0.5	Util.			
Railroads & related services	0.4	Util.			
Wet corn milling	0.2	Manufg.			
Air transportation	0.2	Util.			
Communications, except radio & TV	0.2	Util.			
Water transportation	0.2	Util.			
Eating & drinking places	0.2	Trade			
Insurance carriers	0.2	Fin/R.E.			
Equipment rental & leasing services	0.2	Services			
Noncomparable imports	0.2	Foreign			
Maintenance of nonfarm buildings nec	0.1	Constr.			
Food products machinery	0.1	Manufg.			
Petroleum refining	0.1	Manufg.			
Pipe, valves, & pipe fittings	0.1	Manufg.			
Real estate	0.1	Fin/R.E.			

Source: *Benchmark Input-Output Accounts for the U.S. Economy, 1982*, U.S. Department of Commerce, Washington, D.C., July 1991. Data, as reported in the source, are organized by the 1977 SIC structure in use in 1982 but have been matched, as closely as is possible, to the 1987 SIC structure used in this book.

OCCUPATIONS EMPLOYED BY SIC 208 - BEVERAGES

Occupation	% of Total 1994	Change to 2005	Occupation	% of Total 1994	Change to 2005
Packaging & filling machine operators	11.6	-48.1	Salespersons, retail	1.9	-4.1
Driver/sales workers	7.8	-28.1	Marketing & sales worker supervisors	1.9	-20.1
Sales & related workers nec	6.5	-20.1	Marketing, advertising, & PR managers	1.9	-20.1
Truck drivers light & heavy	5.5	-17.6	General office clerks	1.6	-31.9
Industrial truck & tractor operators	5.2	-20.1	Bookkeeping, accounting, & auditing clerks	1.6	-40.1
Industrial machinery mechanics	3.6	-12.1	Industrial production managers	1.4	-20.2
Helpers, laborers, & material movers nec	3.3	-20.1	Separating & still machine operators	1.4	-12.1
Hand packers & packagers	2.7	-31.5	Maintenance repairers, general utility	1.3	-28.1
Freight, stock, & material movers, hand	2.7	-36.1	Managers & administrators nec	1.2	-20.2
Secretaries, ex legal & medical	2.5	-27.3	Management support workers nec	1.2	-20.1
General managers & top executives	2.2	-24.2	Precision food & tobacco workers nec	1.1	-20.2
Coin & vending machine servicers & repairers	2.0	-36.1	Science & mathematics technicians	1.0	-20.2
Agricultural workers nec	2.0	-20.1	Traffic, shipping, & receiving clerks	1.0	-23.1

Source: *Industry-Occupation Matrix*, Bureau of Labor Statistics. These data relate to one or more 3-digit SIC industry groups rather than to a single 4-digit SIC. The change reported for each occupation to the year 2005 is a percent of growth or decline as estimated by the Bureau of Labor Statistics. The abbreviation nec stands for 'not elsewhere classified'.

LOCATION BY STATE AND REGIONAL CONCENTRATION

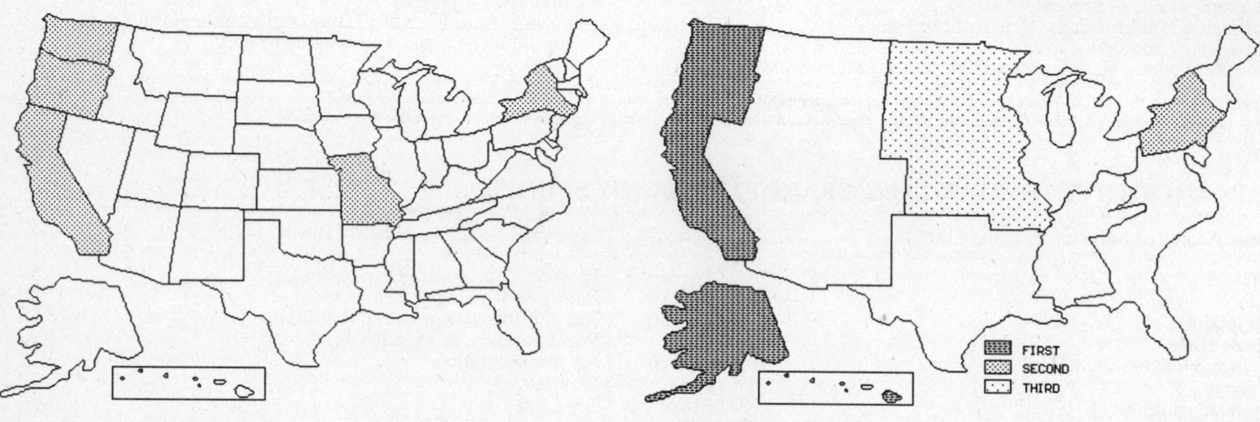

INDUSTRY DATA BY STATE

State	Establish-ments	Shipments: Total ($ mil)	Shipments: % of U.S.	Shipments: Per Establ.	Employment: Total Number	Employment: % of U.S.	Employment: Per Establ.	Employment: Wages ($/hour)	Cost as % of Shipments	Investment per Employee ($)
California	329	3,664.3	85.2	11.1	11,800	84.3	36	13.22	54.1	8,763
New York	31	381.9	8.9	12.3	800	5.7	26	10.27	75.1	4,125
Washington	28	89.8	2.1	3.2	300	2.1	11	9.50	42.5	13,000
Oregon	32	(D)	-	-	175 *	1.3	5	-	-	-
Missouri	14	(D)	-	-	175 *	1.3	13	-	-	-

Source: 1992 *Economic Census*. The states are in descending order of shipments or establishments (if shipment data are missing for the majority). The symbol (D) appears when data are withheld to prevent disclosure of competitive information. States marked with (D) are sorted by number of establishments. A dash (-) indicates that the data element cannot be calculated; * indicates the midpoint of a range.

2085 - DISTILLED & BLENDED LIQUORS

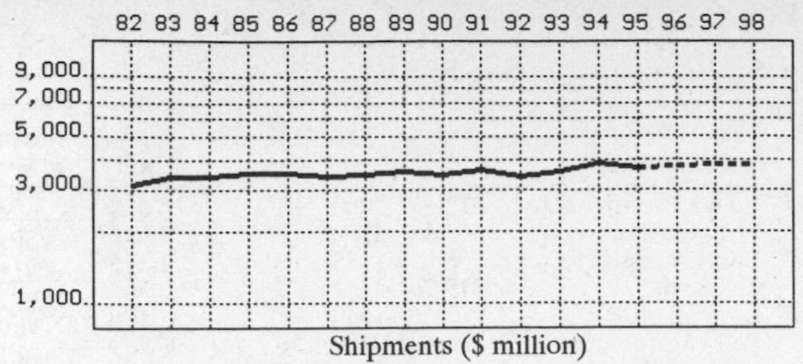

Shipments ($ million)

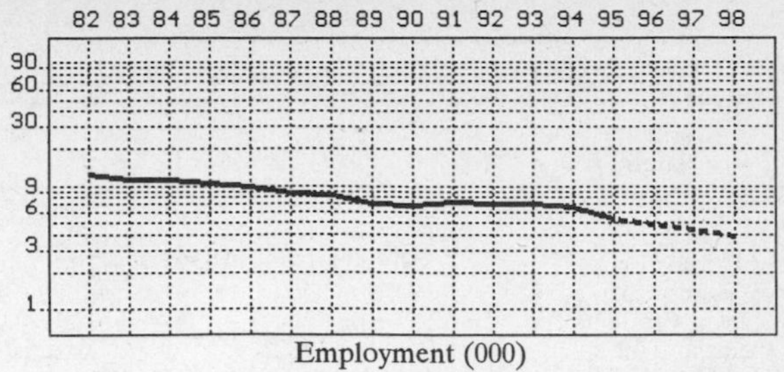

Employment (000)

GENERAL STATISTICS

Year	Com-panies	Establishments		Employment			Compensation		Production ($ million)			
		Total	with 20 or more employees	Total (000)	Production Workers (000)	Production Hours (Mil)	Payroll ($ mil)	Wages ($/hr)	Cost of Materials	Value Added by Manufacture	Value of Shipments	Capital Invest.
1982	71	104	75	12.2	8.9	18.0	263.8	10.15	1,700.5	1,460.1	3,126.1	90.0
1983		98	71	11.3	8.2	16.9	261.1	10.91	1,839.3	1,534.7	3,396.7	87.2
1984		92	67	11.3	7.8	16.0	268.1	11.56	1,744.9	1,685.2	3,404.9	48.1
1985		85	64	10.5	7.4	15.1	267.6	12.03	1,846.1	1,690.9	3,494.8	37.3
1986		81	64	9.9	6.8	13.8	261.4	12.54	1,730.2	1,845.3	3,504.3	41.4
1987	47	71	56	8.8	6.3	12.4	240.2	13.05	1,499.9	2,054.8	3,441.2	43.9
1988		74	57	8.3	5.9	11.5	237.1	13.55	1,413.1	2,038.8	3,468.8	33.4
1989		63	50	7.1	5.3	10.8	225.8	13.74	1,423.9	2,163.9	3,601.9	37.6
1990		62	49	6.9	5.2	11.0	235.4	13.78	1,587.0	1,888.3	3,473.5	36.4
1991		64	45	7.4	5.2	10.6	236.7	14.23	1,545.2	2,147.4	3,656.0	59.1
1992	43	65	48	7.1	5.1	10.5	243.9	15.05	1,446.9	1,945.6	3,394.1	56.3
1993		62	47	7.0	5.1	10.4	245.1	15.49	1,472.1	2,112.9	3,568.8	42.1
1994		51P	40P	6.6	4.7	10.1	240.1	15.43	1,649.9	2,208.5	3,887.5	39.7
1995		47P	37P	5.4P	3.9P	8.1P	229.8P	16.21P	1,580.2P	2,115.2P	3,723.3P	33.1P
1996		43P	34P	4.9P	3.6P	7.5P	227.2P	16.64P	1,594.1P	2,133.8P	3,756.1P	30.6P
1997		40P	32P	4.4P	3.2P	6.8P	224.5P	17.07P	1,608.0P	2,152.5P	3,788.9P	28.2P
1998		36P	29P	3.9P	2.9P	6.1P	221.9P	17.50P	1,622.0P	2,171.1P	3,821.7P	25.7P

Sources: 1982, 1987, 1992 *Economic Census*; *Annual Survey of Manufactures*, 83-86, 88-91, 93-94. Establishment counts for non-Census years are from *County Business Patterns*; establishment values for 83-84 are extrapolations. 'P's show projections by the editors. Industries reclassified in 87 will not have data for prior years.

INDICES OF CHANGE

Year	Com-panies	Establishments		Employment			Compensation		Production ($ million)			
		Total	with 20 or more employees	Total (000)	Production Workers (000)	Production Hours (Mil)	Payroll ($ mil)	Wages ($/hr)	Cost of Materials	Value Added by Manufacture	Value of Shipments	Capital Invest.
1982	165	160	156	172	175	171	108	67	118	75	92	160
1983		151	148	159	161	161	107	72	127	79	100	155
1984		142	140	159	153	152	110	77	121	87	100	85
1985		131	133	148	145	144	110	80	128	87	103	66
1986		125	133	139	133	131	107	83	120	95	103	74
1987	109	109	117	124	124	118	98	87	104	106	101	78
1988		114	119	117	116	110	97	90	98	105	102	59
1989		97	104	100	104	103	93	91	98	111	106	67
1990		95	102	97	102	105	97	92	110	97	102	65
1991		98	94	104	102	101	97	95	107	110	108	105
1992	100	100	100	100	100	100	100	100	100	100	100	100
1993		95	98	99	100	99	100	103	102	109	105	75
1994		79P	83P	93	92	96	98	103	114	114	115	71
1995		73P	77P	76P	77P	78P	94P	108P	109P	109P	110P	59P
1996		67P	72P	69P	70P	71P	93P	111P	110P	110P	111P	54P
1997		61P	66P	62P	63P	65P	92P	113P	111P	111P	112P	50P
1998		55P	60P	55P	56P	58P	91P	116P	112P	112P	113P	46P

Sources: Same as General Statistics. Values reflect change from the base year, 1992. Values above 100 mean greater than 92, values below 100 mean less than 92, and a value of 100 in the 82-91 or 93-98 period means same as 92. 'P's mark projections by the editors.

SELECTED RATIOS

For 1994	Avg. of All Manufact.	Analyzed Industry	Index	For 1994	Avg. of All Manufact.	Analyzed Industry	Index
Employees per Establishment	49	129	263	Value Added per Production Worker	134,084	469,894	350
Payroll per Establishment	1,500,273	4,682,801	312	Cost per Establishment	5,045,178	32,178,901	638
Payroll per Employee	30,620	36,379	119	Cost per Employee	102,970	249,985	243
Production Workers per Establishment	34	92	267	Cost per Production Worker	146,988	351,043	239
Wages per Establishment	853,319	3,039,491	356	Shipments per Establishment	9,576,895	75,820,035	792
Wages per Production Worker	24,861	33,158	133	Shipments per Employee	195,460	589,015	301
Hours per Production Worker	2,056	2,149	105	Shipments per Production Worker	279,017	827,128	296
Wages per Hour	12.09	15.43	128	Investment per Establishment	321,011	774,291	241
Value Added per Establishment	4,602,255	43,073,582	936	Investment per Employee	6,552	6,015	92
Value Added per Employee	93,930	334,621	356	Investment per Production Worker	9,352	8,447	90

Sources: Same as General Statistics. The 'Average of All Manufacturing' column represents the average of all manufacturing industries reported for the most recent complete year available. The Index shows the relationship between the Average and the Analyzed Industry. For example, 100 means that they are equal; 500 that the Analyzed Industry is five times the average; 50 means that the Analyzed Industry is half the national average. The abbreviation 'na' is used to show that data are 'not available'.

LEADING COMPANIES

Number shown: **19** Total sales ($ mil): **8,725** Total employment (000): **27.7**

Company Name	Address				CEO Name	Phone	Co. Type	Sales ($ mil)	Empl. (000)
Joseph E Seagram and Sons Inc	375 Park Av	New York	NY	10152	Edgar Bronfman Jr	212-572-7000	S	4,650*	16.0
Brown-Forman Corp	PO Box 1080	Louisville	KY	40201	W Lyons Brown Jr	502-585-1100	P	1,692	6.7
Jim Beam Brands Co	510 Lake Cook Rd	Deerfield	IL	60015	Barry M Berish	708-948-8888	S	1,195	1.5
Grain Processing Corp	PO Box 349	Muscatine	IA	52761	GA Kent	319-264-4211	S	300	0.8
Midwest Grain Products Inc	PO Box 130	Atchison	KS	66002	L M Seaberg	913-367-1480	P	186	0.5
Sazerac Company Inc	PO Box 52821	New Orleans	LA	70152	Peter Bordeaux	504-831-9450	R	150	0.4
Heaven Hill Distilleries Inc	1064 Loretto Rd	Bardstown	KY	40004	George Shapira	502-348-3921	R	87*	0.3
Jack Daniel's Distillery	PO Box 199	Lynchburg	TN	37352	Lyons Brown	615-759-4221	D	77*	0.4
Todhunter International Inc	PO Drawer 4057	W Palm Beach	FL	33402	AK Pincourt	407-655-8977	P	76	0.4
Consolidated Distilled Prod	3247 S Kedzie Av	Chicago	IL	60623	Greg Mauloff	312-927-4161	D	63	0.2
Chatam International Inc	2633 Trenton Av	Philadelphia	PA	19125	Norton Cooper	215-425-9300	R	60	0.1
Boulevard Distillers	PO Box 180	Lawrenceburg	KY	40342	John Senter	502-839-4544	S	58*	0.2
Majestic Distilling Co	PO Box 7372	Baltimore	MD	21227	Sidney H Cohen	410-242-0200	R	50	<0.1
Laird and Co	1 Laird Rd	Scobeyville	NJ	07724	LW Laird	908-542-0312	R	40	<0.1
David Sherman Corp	5050 Kemper Av	St Louis	MO	63139	Donn Lux	314-772-2626	R	20*	<0.1
George A Dickel Co	PO Box 490	Tullahoma	TN	37388	Jennings D Backus	615-857-3124	S	7	<0.1
Skyy Spirits Inc	1626 Union St	San Francisco	CA	94123	Maurice Kanbar	415-931-2000	R	7*	<0.1
McCormick Distilling Company	1 McCormick Ln	Weston	MO	64098		816-386-2276	R	5*	<0.1
Clear Creek Distillery Ltd	1430 NW 23rd Av	Portland	OR	97210	Steve McCarthy	503-248-9470	R	2	<0.1

Source: *Ward's Business Directory of U.S. Private and Public Companies*, Volumes 1 and 2, 1996. The company type code used is as follows: P - Public, R - Private, S - Subsidiary, D - Division, J - Joint Venture, A - Affiliate, G - Group. Sales are in millions of dollars, employees are in thousands. An asterisk (*) indicates an estimated sales volume. The symbol < stands for 'less than'. Company names and addresses are truncated, in some cases, to fit into the available space.

MATERIALS CONSUMED

Material		Quantity	Delivered Cost ($ million)
Materials, ingredients, containers, and supplies		(X)	1,196.1
Corn, purchased as grain	mil bushels	18.2*	37.3
Malt	1,000 cwt	494.3	8.0
Cooperage used in grain distilling	millions	492.8	39.1
All other materials, ingredients, and supplies consumed in distilling operations		(X)	58.3
Neutral spirits used in the processing of whiskey	mil tax gal	14.7	11.0
Neutral spirits used in the processing of vodka	mil tax gal	78.7*	86.3
Neutral spirits used in the processing of gin	mil tax gal	31.4	24.6
Neutral spirits used in the processing of other liquor	mil tax gal	23.9	106.2
Aged whiskey used in the processing and bottling of distilled liquors	mil tax gal	44.4	154.4
Paperboard boxes and containers used in the processing and bottling of distilled liquors		(X)	23.5
Plastics containers		(X)	26.5
Glass containers used in the processing and bottling of distilled liquors		(X)	313.3
All other materials and components, parts, containers, and supplies		(X)	291.9
Materials, ingredients, containers, and supplies, nsk		(X)	15.7

Source: 1992 *Economic Census*. Explanation of symbols used: (D): Withheld to avoid disclosure of competitive data; na: Not available; (S): Withheld because statistical norms were not met; (X): Not applicable; (Z): Less than half the unit shown; nec: Not elsewhere classified; nsk: Not specified by kind; - : zero; * : 10-19 percent estimated; ** : 20-29 percent estimated.

PRODUCT SHARE DETAILS

Product or Product Class	% Share
Distilled and blended liquors	100.00
Distilled liquor, except brandy	19.77
Distilled whiskey, raw (bourbon, rye, etc.)	26.20
Distilled vodka (including original and continuous distillation and/or processing operations)	16.24
Other distilled liquors, including rum, gin, and cane neutral spirits	24.39
Distillers' dried grains, dark and light, and dried solubles	33.02
Distilled liquor, except brandy, nsk	0.16
Bottled liquor, except brandy	79.38
Bottled unprocessed whiskey	13.26
Bottled blends of whiskey without neutral spirits	8.60
Bottled blends of whiskey with neutral spirits	2.72
Other bottled whiskey	16.25
Bottled gin	7.06
Bottled cordials, liqueurs	15.77
Bottled cocktails and similar compounds	(D)
Bottled vodka	13.61
Bottled rum	2.16
Other bottled liquors (excluding bottled in bond)	4.39
Bottled in bond liquors	(D)
Bottled liquor, except brandy, nsk	0.07
Distilled and blended liquors, nsk	0.86

Source: 1992 *Economic Census*. The values shown are percent of total shipments in an industry. Values of indented subcategories are summed in the main heading. The symbol (D) appears when data are withheld to prevent disclosure of competitive information. The abbreviation nsk stands for 'not specified by kind' and nec for 'not elsewhere classified'.

INPUTS AND OUTPUTS FOR DISTILLED LIQUOR, EXCEPT BRANDY

Economic Sector or Industry Providing Inputs	%	Sector	Economic Sector or Industry Buying Outputs	%	Sector
Imports	37.4	Foreign	Personal consumption expenditures	47.7	
Distilled liquor, except brandy	12.4	Manufg.	Eating & drinking places	34.2	Trade
Glass containers	11.8	Manufg.	Retail trade, except eating & drinking	7.2	Trade
Wholesale trade	10.0	Trade	Distilled liquor, except brandy	5.6	Manufg.
Advertising	8.0	Services	Exports	1.0	Foreign
Commercial printing	3.3	Manufg.	Prepared feeds, nec	0.5	Manufg.
Wood containers	2.2	Manufg.	Air transportation	0.5	Util.
Motor freight transportation & warehousing	1.7	Util.	Wholesale trade	0.4	Trade
Feed grains	1.6	Agric.	Federal Government enterprises nec	0.3	Gov't
Miscellaneous plastics products	1.3	Manufg.			
Banking	1.3	Fin/R.E.			
Insurance carriers	1.3	Fin/R.E.			
Gas production & distribution (utilities)	0.9	Util.			
Crowns & closures	0.5	Manufg.			
Pumps & compressors	0.5	Manufg.			
Electric services (utilities)	0.5	Util.			
Malt	0.4	Manufg.			
Petroleum refining	0.4	Manufg.			
Paper coating & glazing	0.3	Manufg.			
Paperboard containers & boxes	0.3	Manufg.			
Rubber & plastics hose & belting	0.3	Manufg.			
Railroads & related services	0.3	Util.			
Equipment rental & leasing services	0.3	Services			
Food grains	0.2	Agric.			
Metal foil & leaf	0.2	Manufg.			
Eating & drinking places	0.2	Trade			
Noncomparable imports	0.2	Foreign			
Maintenance of nonfarm buildings nec	0.1	Constr.			
Air transportation	0.1	Util.			
Communications, except radio & TV	0.1	Util.			
Water transportation	0.1	Util.			
Security & commodity brokers	0.1	Fin/R.E.			

Source: Benchmark Input-Output Accounts for the U.S. Economy, 1982, U.S. Department of Commerce, Washington, D.C., July 1991. Data, as reported in the source, are organized by the 1977 SIC structure in use in 1982 but have been matched, as closely as is possible, to the 1987 SIC structure used in this book.

OCCUPATIONS EMPLOYED BY SIC 208 - BEVERAGES

Occupation	% of Total 1994	Change to 2005	Occupation	% of Total 1994	Change to 2005
Packaging & filling machine operators	11.6	-48.1	Salespersons, retail	1.9	-4.1
Driver/sales workers	7.8	-28.1	Marketing & sales worker supervisors	1.9	-20.1
Sales & related workers nec	6.5	-20.1	Marketing, advertising, & PR managers	1.9	-20.1
Truck drivers light & heavy	5.5	-17.6	General office clerks	1.6	-31.9
Industrial truck & tractor operators	5.2	-20.1	Bookkeeping, accounting, & auditing clerks	1.6	-40.1
Industrial machinery mechanics	3.6	-12.1	Industrial production managers	1.4	-20.2
Helpers, laborers, & material movers nec	3.3	-20.1	Separating & still machine operators	1.4	-12.1
Hand packers & packagers	2.7	-31.5	Maintenance repairers, general utility	1.3	-28.1
Freight, stock, & material movers, hand	2.7	-36.1	Managers & administrators nec	1.2	-20.2
Secretaries, ex legal & medical	2.5	-27.3	Management support workers nec	1.2	-20.1
General managers & top executives	2.2	-24.2	Precision food & tobacco workers nec	1.1	-20.2
Coin & vending machine servicers & repairers	2.0	-36.1	Science & mathematics technicians	1.0	-20.2
Agricultural workers nec	2.0	-20.1	Traffic, shipping, & receiving clerks	1.0	-23.1

Source: Industry-Occupation Matrix, Bureau of Labor Statistics. These data relate to one or more 3-digit SIC industry groups rather than to a single 4-digit SIC. The change reported for each occupation to the year 2005 is a percent of growth or decline as estimated by the Bureau of Labor Statistics. The abbreviation nec stands for 'not elsewhere classified'.

LOCATION BY STATE AND REGIONAL CONCENTRATION

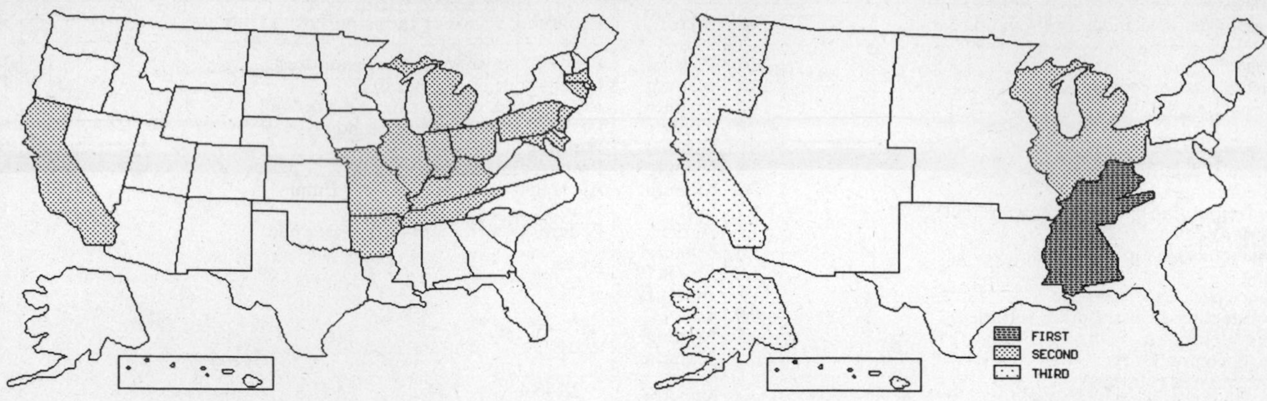

INDUSTRY DATA BY STATE

State	Establish-ments	Shipments			Employment				Cost as % of Shipments	Investment per Employee ($)
		Total ($ mil)	% of U.S.	Per Establ.	Total Number	% of U.S.	Per Establ.	Wages ($/hour)		
Kentucky	18	1,169.2	34.4	65.0	2,700	38.0	150	13.59	45.5	8,407
Maryland	5	111.4	3.3	22.3	600	8.5	120	17.00	68.7	-
California	5	(D)	-	-	375 *	5.3	75	-	-	-
New Jersey	4	(D)	-	-	175 *	2.5	44	-	-	-
Missouri	3	(D)	-	-	175 *	2.5	58	-	-	-
Tennessee	3	(D)	-	-	375 *	5.3	125	-	-	-
Illinois	2	(D)	-	-	175 *	2.5	88	-	-	-
Indiana	2	(D)	-	-	750 *	10.6	375	-	-	-
Ohio	2	(D)	-	-	375 *	5.3	188	-	-	-
Arkansas	1	(D)	-	-	175 *	2.5	175	-	-	-
Connecticut	1	(D)	-	-	175 *	2.5	175	-	-	-
Massachusetts	1	(D)	-	-	175 *	2.5	175	-	-	-
Michigan	1	(D)	-	-	375 *	5.3	375	-	-	-
Pennsylvania	1	(D)	-	-	175 *	2.5	175	-	-	-

Source: 1992 *Economic Census*. The states are in descending order of shipments or establishments (if shipment data are missing for the majority). The symbol (D) appears when data are withheld to prevent disclosure of competitive information. States marked with (D) are sorted by number of establishments. A dash (-) indicates that the data element cannot be calculated; * indicates the midpoint of a range.

2086 - BOTTLED & CANNED SOFT DRINKS

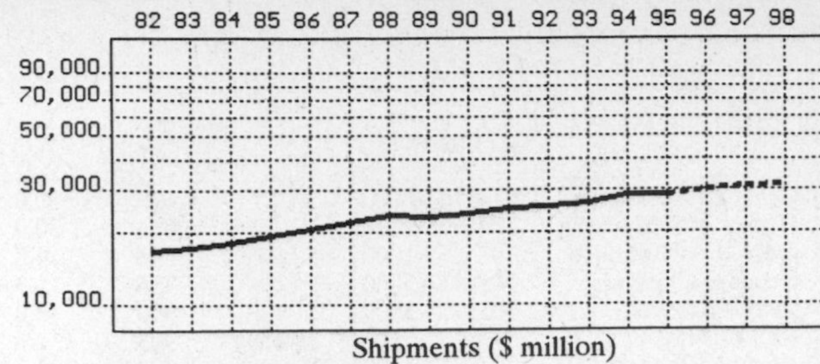

Shipments ($ million)

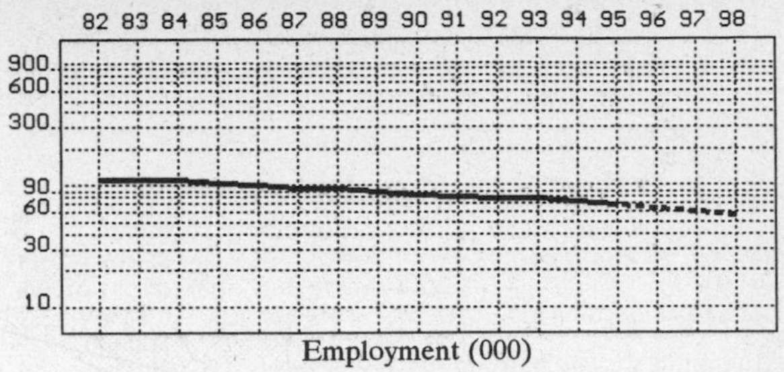

Employment (000)

GENERAL STATISTICS

Year	Companies	Establishments: Total	Establishments: with 20 or more employees	Employment: Total (000)	Employment: Production Workers (000)	Employment: Production Hours (Mil)	Compensation: Payroll ($ mil)	Compensation: Wages ($/hr)	Production ($ million): Cost of Materials	Production ($ million): Value Added by Manufacture	Production ($ million): Value of Shipments	Production ($ million): Capital Invest.
1982	1,236	1,626	1,095	113.8	42.4	85.2	2,146.4	7.84	9,981.3	6,856.1	16,807.5	649.5
1983		1,555	1,057	112.3	41.5	85.1	2,244.8	8.24	10,248.5	7,086.1	17,320.8	680.5
1984		1,484	1,019	110.4	39.8	81.7	2,282.8	8.51	10,941.1	7,141.8	18,052.0	694.1
1985		1,414	980	105.8	37.2	77.8	2,344.8	9.10	11,830.7	7,587.2	19,358.2	720.8
1986		1,335	927	102.0	35.5	73.5	2,348.1	9.77	12,483.1	8,215.4	20,686.8	560.7
1987	818	1,190	787	95.6	35.4	71.5	2,276.7	10.45	13,461.0	8,573.7	22,006.0	569.2
1988		1,135	761	94.6	35.2	71.8	2,361.8	10.78	14,250.9	9,122.4	23,310.3	567.7
1989		1,027	697	88.7	33.4	67.7	2,190.5	10.98	14,146.0	8,898.4	23,002.1	507.8
1990		941	635	82.7	32.0	65.7	2,132.0	11.48	14,772.2	9,075.1	23,847.5	460.0
1991		913	623	81.7	31.9	66.8	2,210.3	11.85	15,644.3	9,554.8	25,191.1	548.5
1992	637	926	572	77.1	30.5	65.0	2,162.8	11.91	15,853.4	9,586.4	25,416.9	698.5
1993		886	560	78.6	31.6	68.1	2,228.1	11.66	15,779.6	10,228.4	25,997.6	616.2
1994		722P	458P	73.4	29.0	62.6	2,212.9	12.89	16,757.7	11,647.3	28,334.3	773.8
1995		648P	404P	68.1P	27.6P	59.4P	2,199.9P	13.24P	16,957.7P	11,786.3P	28,672.4P	606.0P
1996		574P	350P	64.5P	26.6P	57.6P	2,193.9P	13.64P	17,499.8P	12,163.1P	29,589.0P	604.2P
1997		500P	296P	60.9P	25.5P	55.7P	2,188.0P	14.04P	18,041.9P	12,539.9P	30,505.6P	602.3P
1998		426P	242P	57.2P	24.5P	53.8P	2,182.0P	14.44P	18,584.0P	12,916.6P	31,422.2P	600.5P

Sources: 1982, 1987, 1992 *Economic Census*; *Annual Survey of Manufactures*, 83-86, 88-91, 93-94. Establishment counts for non-Census years are from *County Business Patterns*; establishment values for 83-84 are extrapolations. 'P's show projections by the editors. Industries reclassified in 87 will not have data for prior years.

INDICES OF CHANGE

Year	Companies	Establishments: Total	Establishments: with 20 or more employees	Employment: Total (000)	Employment: Production Workers (000)	Employment: Production Hours (Mil)	Compensation: Payroll ($ mil)	Compensation: Wages ($/hr)	Production ($ million): Cost of Materials	Production ($ million): Value Added by Manufacture	Production ($ million): Value of Shipments	Production ($ million): Capital Invest.
1982	194	176	191	148	139	131	99	66	63	72	66	93
1983		168	185	146	136	131	104	69	65	74	68	97
1984		160	178	143	130	126	106	71	69	74	71	99
1985		153	171	137	122	120	108	76	75	79	76	103
1986		144	162	132	116	113	109	82	79	86	81	80
1987	128	129	138	124	116	110	105	88	85	89	87	81
1988		123	133	123	115	110	109	91	90	95	92	81
1989		111	122	115	110	104	101	92	89	93	90	73
1990		102	111	107	105	101	99	96	93	95	94	66
1991		99	109	106	105	103	102	99	99	100	99	79
1992	100	100	100	100	100	100	100	100	100	100	100	100
1993		96	98	102	104	105	103	98	100	107	102	88
1994		78P	80P	95	95	96	102	108	106	121	111	111
1995		70P	71P	88P	91P	91P	102P	111P	107P	123P	113P	87P
1996		62P	61P	84P	87P	89P	101P	115P	110P	127P	116P	86P
1997		54P	52P	79P	84P	86P	101P	118P	114P	131P	120P	86P
1998		46P	42P	74P	80P	83P	101P	121P	117P	135P	124P	86P

Sources: Same as General Statistics. Values reflect change from the base year, 1992. Values above 100 mean greater than 92, values below 100 mean less than 92, and a value of 100 in the 82-91 or 93-98 period means same as 92. 'P's mark projections by the editors.

SELECTED RATIOS

For 1994	Avg. of All Manufact.	Analyzed Industry	Index
Employees per Establishment	49	102	207
Payroll per Establishment	1,500,273	3,064,251	204
Payroll per Employee	30,620	30,149	98
Production Workers per Establishment	34	40	117
Wages per Establishment	853,319	1,117,351	131
Wages per Production Worker	24,861	27,825	112
Hours per Production Worker	2,056	2,159	105
Wages per Hour	12.09	12.89	107
Value Added per Establishment	4,602,255	16,128,271	350
Value Added per Employee	93,930	158,683	169

For 1994	Avg. of All Manufact.	Analyzed Industry	Index
Value Added per Production Worker	134,084	401,631	300
Cost per Establishment	5,045,178	23,204,754	460
Cost per Employee	102,970	228,307	222
Cost per Production Worker	146,988	577,852	393
Shipments per Establishment	9,576,895	39,235,126	410
Shipments per Employee	195,460	386,026	197
Shipments per Production Worker	279,017	977,045	350
Investment per Establishment	321,011	1,071,498	334
Investment per Employee	6,552	10,542	161
Investment per Production Worker	9,352	26,683	285

Sources: Same as General Statistics. The 'Average of All Manufacturing' column represents the average of all manufacturing industries reported for the most recent complete year available. The Index shows the relationship between the Average and the Analyzed Industry. For example, 100 means that they are equal; 500 that the Analyzed Industry is five times the average; 50 means that the Analyzed Industry is half the national average. The abbreviation 'na' is used to show that data are 'not available'.

LEADING COMPANIES Number shown: 75 Total sales ($ mil): 29,527 Total employment (000): 134.0

Company Name	Address				CEO Name	Phone	Co. Type	Sales ($ mil)	Empl. (000)
Pepsi-Cola Co	1 Pepsi Way	Somers	NY	10589	Craig E Weatherup	914-767-6000	S	8,638	30.0
Coca-Cola Enterprises Inc	1 Coca-Colaz NW	Atlanta	GA	30313	Henry A Schimberg	404-676-2100	P	6,011	30.0
Pepsi-Cola General Bottlers Inc	3501 Algonquin Rd	Rolling Mdws	IL	60008	Gerald A McGuire	708-253-1000	S	1,256	4.8
Whitman Corp	3501 Algonquin Rd	Rolling Mdws	IL	60008	Bruce S Chelberg	708-818-5000	P	1,256	15.3
Florida Coca-Cola Bottling Co	3350 Pembroke Rd	Hollywood	FL	33021	Jerry Graves	305-985-5000	S	950	3.0
Gatorade	5625 E 14th St	Oakland	CA	94621	Tim Olsem	510-261-5800	D	905	2.6
Coca-Cola Bottling Consolidated	PO Box 31487	Charlotte	NC	28231	J Frank Harrison III	704-551-4400	P	724	4.7
Coca-Cola Bottling United	PO Box 2006	Birmingham	AL	35201	Claude Nielsen	205-841-2653	R	520	2.2
Snapple Beverage Corp	1500 Hemsted Tpk	East Meadow	NY	11554	Leonard Marsh	516-222-0022	P	516	0.2
Coca-Cola Bottling	1334 S Central Av	Los Angeles	CA	90021	Gary Schroeder	213-746-5555	S	510*	2.5
Coca-Cola Bottling of New York	20 Horseneck Ln	Greenwich	CT	06830	James Maloney	203-625-4000	R	460	3.0
Arrowhead Mountain	601 E P Grande	Monterey Park	CA	91754	Dimitrios Smyrnios	213-888-8000	S	430	1.8
WB Bottling Corp	3220 E 26th St	Vernon	CA	90023	Barton S Brodkin	213-268-7779	R	364	1.8
National Beverage Corp	PO Box 16720	Ft Lauderdale	FL	33318	Nick A Caporella	305-581-0922	P	348	1.0
Dr Pepper Bottling of Texas	PO Box 655024	Dallas	TX	75265	Jim Turner	214-579-1024	S	310	1.3
Dr Pepper Bottling Holdings Inc	PO Box 655024	Dallas	TX	75265	Jim Turner	214-579-1024	R	310	1.3
All-American Bottling Corp	15 N Robinson St	Oklahoma City	OK	73102	Steve Browne	405-232-1158	R	290*	1.3
Abarta Inc	1000 RIDC Plz	Pittsburgh	PA	15238	John F Bitzer Jr	412-963-6226	R	280	1.2
Delta Beverage Group Inc	2221 Democrat Rd	Memphis	TN	38132	Ken Keiser	901-344-7100	R	280*	1.2
Coca-Cola Bottling	PO Box 2008	Dallas	TX	75221	David Van Houten	214-357-1781	S	270	1.4
Coca-Cola Bottling of Ohio	1560 Triplett Blv	Akron	OH	44306	Claude Clements	216-784-2653	S	260*	0.7
Phil Coca-Cola	725 E Erie Av	Philadelphia	PA	19134	J Bruce Llewellyn	215-427-4500	R	255	0.9
McKesson Water Products Co	3280 E Foothill	Pasadena	CA	91107	Charles Norris	818-487-6660	S	240	1.1
Shasta Beverages Inc	26901 Indrial Blvd	Hayward	CA	94545	Nick Caporella	510-783-3200	S	230	0.6
Hornell Brewing Company Inc	4501 Glenwood Rd	Brooklyn	NY	11203	John Ferolito	718-284-1200	R	200	0.1
Coca-Cola Bottling	9000 Marshall Dr	Lenexa	KS	66215	Pete Ciacco	913-492-8100	D	192	0.9
Swire Pacific Holdings Inc	875 S Temple St W	Salt Lake City	UT	84101	Craig Taylor	801-530-5300	S	180	1.1
Midwest Coca-Cola Bottling Co	2750 Eagandale	St Paul	MN	55121	Paul Gunderson	612-454-5460	D	165	1.0
Coca-Cola Enterprises Inc	5723 Mdlebrk Pk	Knoxville	TN	37921	Tony Ellis	615-558-3300	D	160*	0.8
Keystone Coca-Cola Bottling	300 Oak St	Pittston	PA	18640		717-655-2874	S	150	1.1
Mid-Continent Bottlers Inc	4500 Westown Pkwy	W Des Moines	IA	50265	B Trebilcock	515-224-7877	R	126	0.6
Southeast Atlantic Corp	PO Box 17999	Jacksonville	FL	32245	Robert H Paul III	904-739-1000	R	125	0.7
Southwest Canners Inc	PO Drawer 809	Portales	NM	88130	Kenneth G Abbott	505-356-6623	R	120	<0.1
Deer Park Spring Water Inc	190 Jony Dr	Carlstadt	NJ	07072	Kim Jeffrey	201-804-6060	S	110*	0.5
Rochester Coca-Cola	123 Upper Falls	Rochester	NY	14605	George Keim	716-546-3900	R	110*	0.5
Sparkletts Drinking Water Corp	3280 E Foothill	Pasadena	CA	91107	Charlie Norris	818-585-1000	S	100	1.0
Wichita Coca-Cola Bottling Co	PO Box 365	Wichita	KS	67201	R D Richardson	316-682-1553	R	100*	0.4
Southwest Canners of Texas Inc	617 Industrial Dr	Nacogdoches	TX	75961	RA Drake	409-569-9737	S	93*	<0.1
Warrenton Products Inc	PO Box 309	Warrenton	MO	63383	Raymond E Baker	314-456-3492	R	88	<0.1
Gulf States Canners Inc	Clinton Industrial	Clinton	MS	39056	Albert Clark	601-924-0511	R	87*	0.1
Noel Corp	1001 S 1st St	Yakima	WA	98901	Rodger Noel	509-248-4545	R	86	0.5
Columbus Seven-Up	950 Stelzer Rd	Columbus	OH	43219	Michael Straw	614-237-4201	D	83*	0.4
Magnolia Coca-Cola Bottling Co	PO Box 27000	El Paso	TX	79926	Bill Neslage	915-593-2653	R	83*	0.4
Coca-Cola Bottling of St Louis	19 Worthington Dr	Maryland H	MO	63043	David Huelsmann	314-878-0800	D	82*	0.4
Coca-Cola Bottling Indianapolis	PO Box 24036	Speedway	IN	46224	Tony Stroinski	317-240-6670	R	73	0.5
Roanoke Coca-Cola Bottling Inc	235 Shenendoah	Roanoke	VA	24016	Donald Doolittle	703-343-8041	S	73*	0.5
Klarbrunn Inc	860 West St	Watertown	WI	53094	Barbara Parish	414-262-6300	S	71*	0.3
Wis-Pak Inc	860 West St	Watertown	WI	53094	Barbara Parish	414-262-6300	R	71*	0.3
Pepsi-Cola Northwest	PO Box C-14117	Seattle	WA	98144	Keith Riemer	206-323-2932	D	70*	1.2
Pepcom Industries Inc	800 East Gate Blv	Garden City	NY	11530	Richard Poillon	516-228-8200	R	65*	0.5
Carolina Canners Inc	PO Box 929	Cheraw	SC	29520	Brantley T Burnett	803-537-5281	R	63*	0.3
Coca-Cola Bottling of Arkansas	7000 Interstate 30	Little Rock	AR	72209	Mike Hagan	501-569-2700	S	60*	0.3
Kalil Bottling Co	PO Box 26888	Tucson	AZ	85726	George Kalil	602-624-1788	R	58	0.4
Royal Crown Company Inc	6917 Collins Av	Miami Beach	FL	33141	John C Carson	305-866-3281	S	53*	0.2
Durham Coca-Cola Bottling Co	PO Box 2627	Durham	NC	27705	M Hagar Rand	919-383-1531	R	51	0.4
Choice USA Beverages	PO Box 2669	Gastonia	NC	28053	JP Falls Sr	704-865-1242	R	47*	0.2
Meridian Coca-Cola Bottling Co	PO Box 5207	Meridian	MS	39302	Hardy P Graham	601-483-5272	R	47*	0.2
Coca-Cola Cleveland	25000 Miles Rd	Cleveland	OH	44146	Rick Horn	216-690-2653	D	46*	0.2
Marion Pepsi-Cola Bottling Co	Old Rte 13 W	Marion	IL	62959	HL Crisp II	618-997-1377	R	45	0.4
AJ Canfield Co	50 E 89th Pl	Chicago	IL	60619	AJ Canfield III	312-483-7000	R	44	0.3
Pepsi-Cola Chicago	650 W 51st St	Chicago	IL	60609	Cole McCombs	312-536-4900	D	44	0.8
Carolina Coca-Cola Bottling Co	PO Box 1150	Sumter	SC	29151	WS Heath	803-773-3336	R	41*	0.2
Canada Dry of Delaware Valley	5300 Whitaker Av	Philadelphia	PA	19124	Thomas J Dooley	215-533-1500	R	40	0.3
Pepsi-Cola Buffalo	2770 Walden Av	Buffalo	NY	14225	Irwin Pastor	716-684-4900	R	40	0.2
Premium Beverage Packers Inc	1090 Spring St	Wyomissing	PA	19610	Jeff D Hettinger	215-376-6131	R	40	0.2
Portland Bottling Co	1321 NE Couch St	Portland	OR	97232	Robert C Cole Jr	503-230-7777	R	36	0.2
Suntory Water Group Inc	280 Interstate N	Atlanta	GA	30339	James M Stevens	404-933-1400	S	36	0.3
Concord Beverage Co	Concord Industrial	Concordville	PA	19331	Harold Honickman	215-459-9220	R	35*	0.2
Fremont Beverages Inc	PO Box 58	Worland	WY	82401	Newell Sargeant	307-347-4231	R	35*	0.2
Nor-Cal Beverage Company Inc	2286 Stone Blv	W Sacramento	CA	95691	G Deary	916-372-0600	R	35	0.3
Seltzer and Rydholm Inc	PO Box 1090	Auburn	ME	04211	Goerge Cotton	207-784-5791	R	32	0.3
Coca-Cola Bottling of Memphis	499 S Hollywood	Memphis	TN	38111	John B Beal	901-454-8700	S	31	0.5
Crystal Geyser Water Co	PO Box 304	Calistoga	CA	94515	Leo Soong	707-942-0500	R	31*	0.1
Hansen Beverage Co	2401 E Katella Av	Anaheim	CA	92806	Harold C Taber Jr	714-634-4200	S	30	<0.1
Hansen Natural Corp	2401 E Katella Av	Anaheim	CA	92806	Rodney C Sacks	714-634-4200	P	30	<0.1

Source: *Ward's Business Directory of U.S. Private and Public Companies*, Volumes 1 and 2, 1996. The company type code used is as follows: P - Public, R - Private, S - Subsidiary, D - Division, J - Joint Venture, A - Affiliate, G - Group. Sales are in millions of dollars, employees are in thousands. An asterisk (*) indicates an estimated sales volume. The symbol < stands for 'less than'. Company names and addresses are truncated, in some cases, to fit into the available space.

MATERIALS CONSUMED

Material		Quantity	Delivered Cost ($ million)
Materials, ingredients, containers, and supplies		(X)	14,351.9
Sugar, cane and beet (in terms of sugar solids)	1,000 s tons	(S)	26.3
Up to 50% fructose corn syrup, in terms of solids	mil lb	1,408.3	217.0
50% or more fructose corn syrup, in terms of solids	mil lb	6,140.2	962.4
Other natural sweeteners, including dextrose, honey, molasses, blends of corn sweeteners and sugar	mil lb	234.5	45.0
Artificial sweeteners (in terms of solids)	mil lb	343.0*	25.5
Concentrated liquid beverage bases (finished drink basis), with some juice content	mil cases	391.9	262.3
Other concentrated liquid beverage bases (finished drink basis)	mil cases	5,224.1*	3,399.9
Syrup beverage bases (finished drink basis)	mil cases	(S)	705.8
Concentrated fruit juices	mil gal	37.7**	270.8
Plastics wrappings, trays, carriers, etc., including preforms		(X)	273.6
Paperboard containers, boxes, and corrugated paperboard		(X)	361.2
Plastics bottles and cans		(X)	1,153.1
Refillable glass containers with or without paperboard wrapping		(X)	72.5
Nonrefillable glass containers with or without paperboard wrapping or plastic shielding		(X)	717.6
Metal cans, can lids and ends		(X)	3,342.6
All other materials and components, parts, containers, and supplies		(X)	1,183.1
Materials, ingredients, containers, and supplies, nsk		(X)	1,333.2

Source: 1992 *Economic Census*. Explanation of symbols used: (D): Withheld to avoid disclosure of competitive data; na: Not available; (S): Withheld because statistical norms were not met; (X): Not applicable; (Z): Less than half the unit shown; nec: Not elsewhere classified; nsk: Not specified by kind; - : zero; * : 10-19 percent estimated; ** : 20-29 percent estimated.

PRODUCT SHARE DETAILS

Product or Product Class	% Share
Bottled and canned soft drinks	100.00
Bottled carbonated soft drinks	31.36
Total bottled carbonated soft drinks in refillable glass bottles (regular and diet)	8.03
Total bottled carbonated soft drinks in non-refillable glass bottles (regular and diet)	28.77
Total bottled carbonated soft drinks in plastics bottles (regular and diet)	63.00
Bottled carbonated soft drinks, nsk	0.10
Canned carbonated soft drinks	41.82
Soft drink flavoring syrup sold in bulk	4.43
Soft drink flavoring syrup sold in bulk, postmix	78.93
Soft drink flavoring syrup sold in bulk, premix	13.65
Soft drink flavoring syrup sold in bulk, nsk	7.42
Noncarbonated soft drinks	16.40
Noncarbonated fruit drinks, cocktails, and ades containing some real juice, 16.9 oz (1/2 liter) container or less, except concentrates	15.02
Noncarbonated fruit drinks, cocktails, and ades containing some real juice, in other size containers (cartons, bottles, cans, etc.), except concentrates	49.05
Noncarbonated fruit drinks, cocktails, and ades concentrates containing some real juice	5.29
Noncarbonated fruit drinks, cocktails, and ades, containing no real juice, 16.9 oz (1/2 liter) container or less, except concentrates	3.43
Noncarbonated fruit drinks, cocktails, and ades, containing no real juice, in other size containers (cartons, bottles, cans, etc.), except concentrates	5.43
Noncarbonated fruit drinks, cocktails, and ades concentrates containing no real juice	0.40
Canned iced tea (noncarbonated), with or without flavorings	2.56
All other noncarbonated soft drinks	12.31
Bottled water (noncarbonated), processed or pasteurized; except natural spring, artificially carbonated, mineral, distilled, and sterile	4.95
Noncarbonated soft drinks, nsk	1.57
Bottled and canned soft drinks, nsk	5.99

Source: 1992 *Economic Census*. The values shown are percent of total shipments in an industry. Values of indented subcategories are summed in the main heading. The symbol (D) appears when data are withheld to prevent disclosure of competitive information. The abbreviation nsk stands for 'not specified by kind' and nec for 'not elsewhere classified'.

INPUTS AND OUTPUTS FOR BOTTLED & CANNED SOFT DRINKS

Economic Sector or Industry Providing Inputs	%	Sector	Economic Sector or Industry Buying Outputs	%	Sector
Metal cans	23.0	Manufg.	Personal consumption expenditures	91.1	
Flavoring extracts & syrups, nec	16.7	Manufg.	Eating & drinking places	6.1	Trade
Glass containers	7.8	Manufg.	Bottled & canned soft drinks	0.6	Manufg.
Wholesale trade	7.4	Trade	Change in business inventories	0.5	In House
Advertising	6.4	Services	Exports	0.4	Foreign
Sugar	6.0	Manufg.	Hospitals	0.3	Services
Miscellaneous plastics products	4.9	Manufg.	Motion pictures	0.2	Services
Wet corn milling	3.9	Manufg.	S/L Govt. purch., elem. & secondary education	0.2	S/L Govt
Paperboard containers & boxes	2.1	Manufg.	S/L Govt. purch., health & hospitals	0.1	S/L Govt
Crowns & closures	1.9	Manufg.			
Communications, except radio & TV	1.6	Util.			
Motor freight transportation & warehousing	1.4	Util.			
Maintenance of nonfarm buildings nec	1.3	Constr.			
Canned fruits & vegetables	1.2	Manufg.			
Banking	1.2	Fin/R.E.			
Miscellaneous repair shops	1.2	Services			
Electric services (utilities)	1.1	Util.			
Bottled & canned soft drinks	0.9	Manufg.			
Petroleum refining	0.7	Manufg.			
Railroads & related services	0.7	Util.			

Continued on next page.

INPUTS AND OUTPUTS FOR BOTTLED & CANNED SOFT DRINKS - Continued

Economic Sector or Industry Providing Inputs	%	Sector	Economic Sector or Industry Buying Outputs	%	Sector
Eating & drinking places	0.6	Trade			
Equipment rental & leasing services	0.6	Services			
Commercial printing	0.5	Manufg.			
Cyclic crudes and organics	0.5	Manufg.			
Computer & data processing services	0.5	Services			
Imports	0.5	Foreign			
Gas production & distribution (utilities)	0.4	Util.			
Real estate	0.4	Fin/R.E.			
Air transportation	0.3	Util.			
U.S. Postal Service	0.3	Gov't			
Food products machinery	0.2	Manufg.			
Pipe, valves, & pipe fittings	0.2	Manufg.			
Rubber & plastics hose & belting	0.2	Manufg.			
Soap & other detergents	0.2	Manufg.			
Water transportation	0.2	Util.			
Accounting, auditing & bookkeeping	0.2	Services			
Legal services	0.2	Services			
Management & consulting services & labs	0.2	Services			
Coal	0.1	Mining			
Lubricating oils & greases	0.1	Manufg.			
Machinery, except electrical, nec	0.1	Manufg.			
Insurance carriers	0.1	Fin/R.E.			
Royalties	0.1	Fin/R.E.			
Electrical repair shops	0.1	Services			

Source: Benchmark Input-Output Accounts for the U.S. Economy, 1982, U.S. Department of Commerce, Washington, D.C., July 1991. Data, as reported in the source, are organized by the 1977 SIC structure in use in 1982 but have been matched, as closely as is possible, to the 1987 SIC structure used in this book.

OCCUPATIONS EMPLOYED BY SIC 208 - BEVERAGES

Occupation	% of Total 1994	Change to 2005	Occupation	% of Total 1994	Change to 2005
Packaging & filling machine operators	11.6	-48.1	Salespersons, retail	1.9	-4.1
Driver/sales workers	7.8	-28.1	Marketing & sales worker supervisors	1.9	-20.1
Sales & related workers nec	6.5	-20.1	Marketing, advertising, & PR managers	1.9	-20.1
Truck drivers light & heavy	5.5	-17.6	General office clerks	1.6	-31.9
Industrial truck & tractor operators	5.2	-20.1	Bookkeeping, accounting, & auditing clerks	1.6	-40.1
Industrial machinery mechanics	3.6	-12.1	Industrial production managers	1.4	-20.2
Helpers, laborers, & material movers nec	3.3	-20.1	Separating & still machine operators	1.4	-12.1
Hand packers & packagers	2.7	-31.5	Maintenance repairers, general utility	1.3	-28.1
Freight, stock, & material movers, hand	2.7	-36.1	Managers & administrators nec	1.2	-20.2
Secretaries, ex legal & medical	2.5	-27.3	Management support workers nec	1.2	-20.1
General managers & top executives	2.2	-24.2	Precision food & tobacco workers nec	1.1	-20.2
Coin & vending machine servicers & repairers	2.0	-36.1	Science & mathematics technicians	1.0	-20.2
Agricultural workers nec	2.0	-20.1	Traffic, shipping, & receiving clerks	1.0	-23.1

Source: Industry-Occupation Matrix, Bureau of Labor Statistics. These data relate to one or more 3-digit SIC industry groups rather than to a single 4-digit SIC. The change reported for each occupation to the year 2005 is a percent of growth or decline as estimated by the Bureau of Labor Statistics. The abbreviation nec stands for 'not elsewhere classified'.

LOCATION BY STATE AND REGIONAL CONCENTRATION

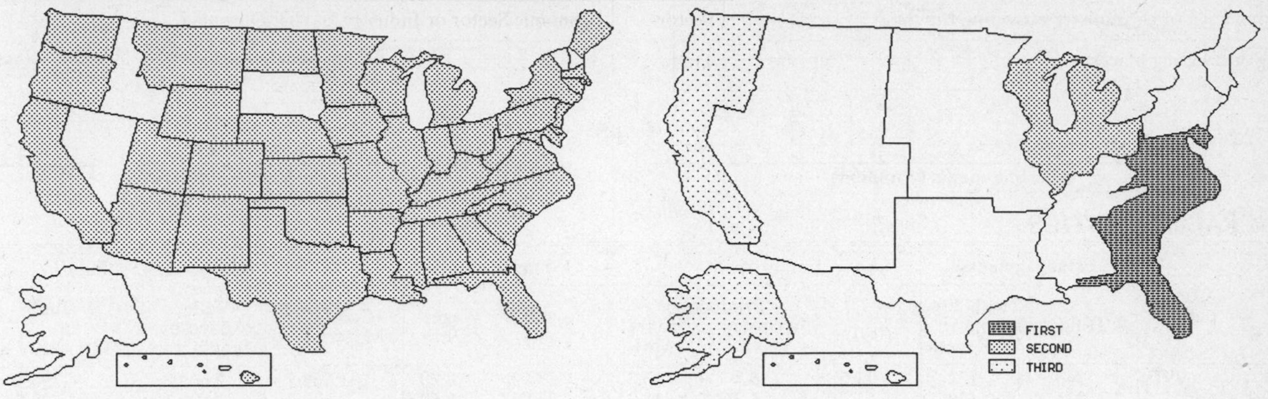

INDUSTRY DATA BY STATE

State	Establish-ments	Shipments			Employment				Cost as % of Shipments	Investment per Employee ($)
		Total ($ mil)	% of U.S.	Per Establ.	Total Number	% of U.S.	Per Establ.	Wages ($/hour)		
California	97	2,878.6	11.3	29.7	6,800	8.8	70	12.87	58.4	15,206
Texas	58	2,128.8	8.4	36.7	7,100	9.2	122	11.10	63.6	5,873
Florida	47	1,674.8	6.6	35.6	5,100	6.6	109	12.36	57.7	-
New York	56	1,489.1	5.9	26.6	4,200	5.4	75	14.73	66.6	8,048
Illinois	32	1,235.5	4.9	38.6	3,200	4.2	100	11.30	58.4	12,594
Michigan	26	1,013.9	4.0	39.0	1,900	2.5	73	13.08	58.4	8,684
Pennsylvania	45	1,011.5	4.0	22.5	3,500	4.5	78	10.97	59.4	13,143
New Jersey	27	975.1	3.8	36.1	2,300	3.0	85	15.91	53.4	6,696
Indiana	24	885.2	3.5	36.9	1,900	2.5	79	11.82	58.1	11,526
Tennessee	19	813.4	3.2	42.8	2,800	3.6	147	9.68	56.7	-
Ohio	31	813.0	3.2	26.2	3,500	4.5	113	11.96	77.0	8,600
Georgia	21	735.8	2.9	35.0	1,700	2.2	81	11.93	64.2	-
Wisconsin	24	602.1	2.4	25.1	1,000	1.3	42	13.23	65.8	-
Maryland	17	581.8	2.3	34.2	2,000	2.6	118	10.54	64.6	8,200
Washington	16	579.9	2.3	36.2	1,300	1.7	81	14.38	62.9	23,846
Missouri	22	578.8	2.3	26.3	1,800	2.3	82	13.17	58.2	-
Massachusetts	25	533.5	2.1	21.3	1,300	1.7	52	14.50	71.6	6,846
Minnesota	19	472.9	1.9	24.9	1,300	1.7	68	12.08	65.8	-
Louisiana	15	447.6	1.8	29.8	2,200	2.9	147	8.07	60.3	9,955
Arizona	19	425.3	1.7	22.4	1,300	1.7	68	10.00	58.5	6,538
Iowa	12	335.4	1.3	28.0	1,200	1.6	100	13.00	56.6	10,167
Oregon	14	265.0	1.0	18.9	900	1.2	64	12.00	76.4	6,889
Kentucky	21	226.6	0.9	10.8	1,400	1.8	67	9.29	72.2	9,857
Nebraska	5	138.8	0.5	27.8	500	0.6	100	10.33	65.6	2,400
Hawaii	7	134.2	0.5	19.2	500	0.6	71	12.00	68.6	-
Maine	5	95.0	0.4	19.0	300	0.4	60	10.33	59.7	10,333
Connecticut	12	88.0	0.3	7.3	400	0.5	33	14.00	65.2	-
Montana	9	46.2	0.2	5.1	300	0.4	33	8.50	75.3	6,667
North Carolina	32	(D)	-	-	1,750 *	2.3	55	-	-	7,657
Virginia	23	(D)	-	-	1,750 *	2.3	76	-	-	7,657
Oklahoma	20	(D)	-	-	1,750 *	2.3	88	-	-	-
Colorado	19	(D)	-	-	1,750 *	2.3	92	-	-	3,486
South Carolina	14	(D)	-	-	1,750 *	2.3	125	-	-	-
Mississippi	13	(D)	-	-	1,750 *	2.3	135	-	-	-
Alabama	11	(D)	-	-	1,750 *	2.3	159	-	-	-
Arkansas	11	(D)	-	-	750 *	1.0	68	-	-	7,733
Kansas	10	(D)	-	-	750 *	1.0	75	-	-	7,867
Utah	7	(D)	-	-	750 *	1.0	107	-	-	7,467
Rhode Island	6	(D)	-	-	375 *	0.5	63	-	-	-
New Mexico	5	(D)	-	-	175 *	0.2	35	-	-	-
North Dakota	4	(D)	-	-	175 *	0.2	44	-	-	-
West Virginia	4	(D)	-	-	175 *	0.2	44	-	-	-
Wyoming	2	(D)	-	-	175 *	0.2	88	-	-	-
Delaware	1	(D)	-	-	175 *	0.2	175	-	-	-

Source: 1992 *Economic Census*. The states are in descending order of shipments or establishments (if shipment data are missing for the majority). The symbol (D) appears when data are withheld to prevent disclosure of competitive information. States marked with (D) are sorted by number of establishments. A dash (-) indicates that the data element cannot be calculated; * indicates the midpoint of a range.

2087 - FLAVORING EXTRACTS ETC., NEC

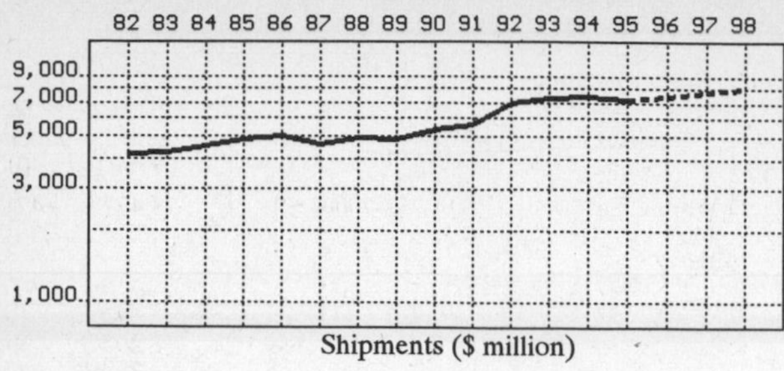

Shipments ($ million)

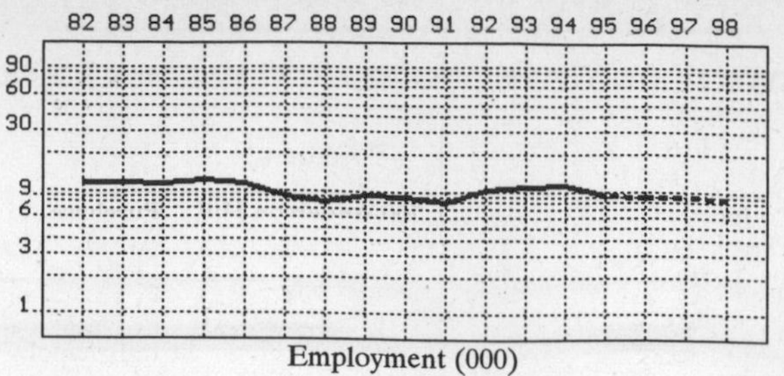

Employment (000)

GENERAL STATISTICS

Year	Com-panies	Establishments		Employment			Compensation		Production ($ million)			
		Total	with 20 or more employees	Total (000)	Production Workers (000)	Production Hours (Mil)	Payroll ($ mil)	Wages ($/hr)	Cost of Materials	Value Added by Manufacture	Value of Shipments	Capital Invest.
1982	297	343	131	11.6	6.5	13.3	237.3	8.20	1,569.3	2,669.8	4,236.8	57.1
1983		331	129	11.7	6.7	13.2	244.2	8.60	1,605.7	2,698.1	4,289.1	39.8
1984		319	127	11.4	6.7	13.8	276.6	9.93	1,772.7	2,824.9	4,573.9	77.3
1985		306	126	12.0	7.3	15.8	314.0	9.74	1,750.4	3,108.4	4,840.3	66.3
1986		302	128	11.3	6.7	14.8	325.2	10.85	1,741.9	3,310.2	5,016.7	60.2
1987	237	280	99	9.0	4.8	9.8	253.7	11.27	1,368.4	3,285.0	4,646.4	51.9
1988		266	101	8.0	4.5	9.7	220.6	11.47	1,422.2	3,509.4	4,930.9	50.9
1989		264	101	9.2	4.6	9.5	244.4	12.06	1,323.8	3,543.3	4,870.8	51.3
1990		266	100	9.0	4.5	9.7	260.7	12.69	1,472.5	3,896.9	5,332.5	49.9
1991		271	102	8.1	4.6	9.9	274.7	13.19	1,514.4	4,123.0	5,642.0	72.9
1992	264	300	123	10.3	5.8	12.2	341.1	12.92	1,651.9	5,269.7	6,911.4	75.6
1993		299	115	10.7	6.0	13.6	375.8	13.07	1,710.9	5,497.3	7,248.7	64.3
1994		263P	101P	11.0	6.4	13.9	372.3	12.28	1,893.4	5,517.4	7,440.2	119.7
1995		258P	99P	9.1P	5.0P	11.1P	344.3P	14.08P	1,826.3P	5,321.8P	7,176.5P	83.2P
1996		253P	97P	9.0P	4.9P	11.0P	352.3P	14.49P	1,891.5P	5,511.8P	7,432.7P	85.9P
1997		248P	95P	8.8P	4.8P	10.8P	360.4P	14.89P	1,956.7P	5,701.8P	7,688.9P	88.6P
1998		243P	93P	8.7P	4.7P	10.7P	368.5P	15.30P	2,021.9P	5,891.8P	7,945.1P	91.3P

Sources: 1982, 1987, 1992 *Economic Census*; *Annual Survey of Manufactures*, 83-86, 88-91, 93-94. Establishment counts for non-Census years are from *County Business Patterns*; establishment values for 83-84 are extrapolations. 'P's show projections by the editors. Industries reclassified in 87 will not have data for prior years.

INDICES OF CHANGE

Year	Com-panies	Establishments		Employment			Compensation		Production ($ million)			
		Total	with 20 or more employees	Total (000)	Production Workers (000)	Production Hours (Mil)	Payroll ($ mil)	Wages ($/hr)	Cost of Materials	Value Added by Manufacture	Value of Shipments	Capital Invest.
1982	113	114	107	113	112	109	70	63	95	51	61	76
1983		110	105	114	116	108	72	67	97	51	62	53
1984		106	103	111	116	113	81	77	107	54	66	102
1985		102	102	117	126	130	92	75	106	59	70	88
1986		101	104	110	116	121	95	84	105	63	73	80
1987	90	93	80	87	83	80	74	87	83	62	67	69
1988		89	82	78	78	80	65	89	86	67	71	67
1989		88	82	89	79	78	72	93	80	67	70	68
1990		89	81	87	78	80	76	98	89	74	77	66
1991		90	83	79	79	81	81	102	92	78	82	96
1992	100	100	100	100	100	100	100	100	100	100	100	100
1993		100	93	104	103	111	110	101	104	104	105	85
1994		88P	82P	107	110	114	109	95	115	105	108	158
1995		86P	81P	89P	86P	91P	101P	109P	111P	101P	104P	110P
1996		84P	79P	87P	84P	90P	103P	112P	115P	105P	108P	114P
1997		83P	77P	86P	82P	89P	106P	115P	118P	108P	111P	117P
1998		81P	75P	84P	80P	87P	108P	118P	122P	112P	115P	121P

Sources: Same as General Statistics. Values reflect change from the base year, 1992. Values above 100 mean greater than 92, values below 100 mean less than 92, and a value of 100 in the 82-91 or 93-98 period means same as 92. 'P's mark projections by the editors.

SELECTED RATIOS

For 1994	Avg. of All Manufact.	Analyzed Industry	Index
Employees per Establishment	49	42	85
Payroll per Establishment	1,500,273	1,414,774	94
Payroll per Employee	30,620	33,845	111
Production Workers per Establishment	34	24	71
Wages per Establishment	853,319	648,645	76
Wages per Production Worker	24,861	26,671	107
Hours per Production Worker	2,056	2,172	106
Wages per Hour	12.09	12.28	102
Value Added per Establishment	4,602,255	20,966,628	456
Value Added per Employee	93,930	501,582	534

For 1994	Avg. of All Manufact.	Analyzed Industry	Index
Value Added per Production Worker	134,084	862,094	643
Cost per Establishment	5,045,178	7,195,094	143
Cost per Employee	102,970	172,127	167
Cost per Production Worker	146,988	295,844	201
Shipments per Establishment	9,576,895	28,273,445	295
Shipments per Employee	195,460	676,382	346
Shipments per Production Worker	279,017	1,162,531	417
Investment per Establishment	321,011	454,871	142
Investment per Employee	6,552	10,882	166
Investment per Production Worker	9,352	18,703	200

Sources: Same as General Statistics. The 'Average of All Manufacturing' column represents the average of all manufacturing industries reported for the most recent complete year available. The Index shows the relationship between the Average and the Analyzed Industry. For example, 100 means that they are equal; 500 that the Analyzed Industry is five times the average; 50 means that the Analyzed Industry is half the national average. The abbreviation 'na' is used to show that data are 'not available'.

LEADING COMPANIES Number shown: **50** Total sales ($ mil): **47,798** Total employment (000): **530.4**

Company Name	Address				CEO Name	Phone	Co. Type	Sales ($ mil)	Empl. (000)
PepsiCo Inc	700 Anderson Hill	Purchase	NY	10577	D Wayne Calloway	914-253-2000	P	28,472	471.0
Coca-Cola Co	PO Drawer 1734	Atlanta	GA	30301	Roberto C Goizueta	404-676-2121	P	16,172	34.0
Dr Pepper/Seven-Up Companies	PO Box 655086	Dallas	TX	75265	John R Albers	214-360-7000	P	707	1.0
CFC Holdings Corp	1000 Corporate Dr	Ft Lauderdale	FL	33334	John Carson	305-351-5600	S	610*	9.0
RC/Arby's Corp	1000 Corporate Dr	Ft Lauderdale	FL	33334	John Carson	305-351-5600	S	610*	9.0
Universal Flavor Corp	5600 W Raymond St	Indianapolis	IN	46241	Frank J Listi Jr	317-243-3521	S	263	1.0
Tastemaker	1199 Edison Dr	Cincinnati	OH	45216	Michael E Davis	513-948-8000	J	210	1.1
Quest International	10 Painters Mill Rd	Owings Mills	MD	21117	Joe Dunne	410-363-2550	S	100	0.3
Kalama Chemical Inc	1110 B of Ca	Seattle	WA	98164	Bob Kirchner	206-682-7890	S	70	0.2
Jel Sert Co	Hwy 59 & Conde St	West Chicago	IL	60185	CT Wegner IV	708-231-7590	R	50	0.4
Robertet Inc	125 Bauer Dr	Oakland	NJ	07436	Peter Lombardo	201-337-7100	S	47*	0.2
Fantasy-BlankeBaer	PO Box 87140	Carol Stream	IL	60188	Jim Hieserman	708-462-5000	D	40*	<0.1
MacAndrews and Forbes Corp	3rd & Jefferson St	Camden	NJ	08104	Stephen Taub	609-964-8840	S	36*	0.2
Sanofi Bio-Industries Inc	8 Neshaminy	Trevose	PA	19053	Paul Murphy	215-638-7801	D	34*	0.3
Consolidated Flavor Corp	231 Rock Indrial Dr	Bridgeton	MO	63044	Philip Dressel	314-291-5444	R	33	0.1
Fries and Fries Inc	1199 Edison Dr	Cincinnati	OH	45216	Michael E Davis	513-948-8000	S	33*	0.5
Guernsey Dell Inc	4300 S Morgan St	Chicago	IL	60609	Steve Schickler	312-927-4000	R	30	0.1
Richardson Foods Corp	10 State St	Fairport	NY	14450	Bruce MacCleod	716-388-2200	S	29	0.2
Flavorite Laboratories Inc	5980 Hurt Rd	Horn Lake	MS	38637	John F Garner	601-393-3610	R	25	0.2
Meer Corp	PO Box 9006	North Bergen	NJ	07047		201-861-9500	D	25	0.2
Robertet Flavors Inc	640 Montrose Av	South Plainfield	NJ	07080	Peter Lombardo	908-561-2181	S	24	<0.1
Virginia Dare Extract Company	882 3rd Av	Brooklyn	NY	11232	Howard Smith	718-788-1776	R	23	0.2
DD Williamson and Company	1901 Payne St	Louisville	KY	40206	Theodore H Nixon	502-895-2438	R	22	0.2
Edlong Corp	225 Scott St	Elk Grove Vill	IL	60007	Eugene L Rondenet	708-439-9230	R	22*	<0.1
Fidco Inc	201 Housatonic Av	New Milford	CT	06776	Sam Lee	203-350-7600	S	17*	0.3
Sethness Products Co	PO Box 597963	Chicago	IL	60659	CB Sethness	708-329-2080	R	15	<0.1
Nielsen-Massey Vanillas Inc	1550 Shields Dr	Waukegan	IL	60085	Camilla Nielson	708-578-1550	R	13	<0.1
Mother Murphys Laboratories	PO Box 16846	Greensboro	NC	27416	KL Murphy Sr	919-273-1737	R	9	<0.1
Beck Flavors	PO Box 22509	St Louis	MO	63147	Charley Beck	314-436-3133	R	7	<0.1
Angostura International Ltd	20 Commerce Dr	Cranford	NJ	07016	Tyler Phillips	908-272-2200	D	6	<0.1
Dohler America Inc	561 Jersey Av	New Brunswick	NJ	08901	Allan Himmelstein	908-247-2555	S	4	<0.1
Flavtek Inc	1960 Hawkins Cir	Los Angeles	CA	90001	C Chow	213-588-5880	R	4	<0.1
Bar None Inc	1302 Santa Fe Dr	Tustin	CA	92680	JF Underwood	714-259-8450	R	3*	<0.1
Barq's Inc	601 Poydras St	New Orleans	LA	70130	John E Koerner	504-524-5142	R	3*	<0.1
Kosto Food Products Co	1325 N Old Rand	Wauconda	IL	60084	Don Colby	708-487-2600	R	3	<0.1
Monarch Company Inc	1100 Johnson Ferry	Atlanta	GA	30342	Mark Armstrong	404-252-4511	R	3*	<0.1
RH Bauman and Company Inc	9258 Deering Av	Chatsworth	CA	91311	Russell H Bauman	818-709-1093	R	3	<0.1
Sea Breeze Fruit Flavors Inc	441 Rte 202	Towaco	NJ	07082	Steven Sanders	201-334-7777	R	3*	<0.1
Kloss Manufacturing Company	PO Box 1149	Allentown	PA	18105	Richard C Kloss	215-435-9071	R	3	<0.1
Fruitcrown Products Corp	250 Adams Blv	Farmingdale	NY	11735	Eugene Jugenburg	516-694-5800	R	2	<0.1
Nedlog Co	90 E Marquardt Dr	Wheeling	IL	60090	G Golden	708-541-0924	R	2	<0.1
Products Enterprises Inc	PO Box 209	Hanover	PA	17331	S A Conway Jr	717-637-1700	R	2	<0.1
Vanlaw Food Products Inc	951 S Cypress St	La Habra	CA	90631	MO Jones	714-870-9091	R	2*	<0.1
W and G Flavors Inc	951 Fell St	Baltimore	MD	21231	J Wayne Wheeler	410-675-5878	R	2	<0.1
Delaware Punch Co	601 Poydras	New Orleans	LA	70130	JE Koerner III	504-524-5142	R	1	<0.1
Cook Flavoring Co	3319 Pacific Av	Tacoma	WA	98408	Ray Lochhead	206-472-1361	R	1*	<0.1
Fee Brothers Inc	453 Portland Av	Rochester	NY	14605	JC Fee	716-544-9530	R	1	<0.1
JE Siebel Son's	4055 W Peterson	Chicago	IL	60646	Ronald Siebel	312-463-3400	D	1	<0.1
Lorann Oils Inc	PO Box 22009	Lansing	MI	48909	John Grettenberger	517-882-0215	R	1	<0.1
Dilijan Products Inc	PO Box 145	Ringoes	NJ	08551	Corinne Kachigian	908-806-6048	R	1	<0.1

Source: *Ward's Business Directory of U.S. Private and Public Companies*, Volumes 1 and 2, 1996. The company type code used is as follows: P - Public, R - Private, S - Subsidiary, D - Division, J - Joint Venture, A - Affiliate, G - Group. Sales are in millions of dollars, employees are in thousands. An asterisk (*) indicates an estimated sales volume. The symbol < stands for 'less than'. Company names and addresses are truncated, in some cases, to fit into the available space.

MATERIALS CONSUMED

Material		Quantity	Delivered Cost ($ million)
Materials, ingredients, containers, and supplies		(X)	1,543.3
Sugar, cane and beet (in terms of sugar solids)	1,000 s tons	146.3*	72.6
Up to 50% fructose corn syrup, in terms of solids	mil lb	208.9	32.3
50% or more fructose corn syrup, in terms of solids	mil lb	(D)	(D)
Other natural sweeteners, including dextrose, honey, molasses, blends of corn sweeteners and sugar	mil lb	73.6	9.8
Artificial sweeteners (in terms of solids)	mil lb	2,027.7	128.1
Concentrated liquid beverage bases (finished drink basis), with some juice content	mil cases	6.1	9.4
Other concentrated liquid beverage bases (finished drink basis)	mil cases	3.1	117.2
Syrup beverage bases (finished drink basis)	mil cases	(D)	(D)
Concentrated fruit juices	mil gal	4.2	34.9
Plastics wrappings, trays, carriers, etc., including preforms		(X)	3.0
Paperboard containers, boxes, and corrugated paperboard		(X)	57.3
Plastics bottles and cans		(X)	39.0
Refillable glass containers with or without paperboard wrapping		(X)	1.2
Nonrefillable glass containers with or without paperboard wrapping or plastic shielding		(X)	15.5
Metal cans, can lids and ends		(X)	17.3
All other materials and components, parts, containers, and supplies		(X)	664.7
Materials, ingredients, containers, and supplies, nsk		(X)	151.9

Source: 1992 *Economic Census*. Explanation of symbols used: (D): Withheld to avoid disclosure of competitive data; na: Not available; (S): Withheld because statistical norms were not met; (X): Not applicable; (Z): Less than half the unit shown; nec: Not elsewhere classified; nsk: Not specified by kind; - : zero; * : 10-19 percent estimated; ** : 20-29 percent estimated.

PRODUCT SHARE DETAILS

Product or Product Class	% Share
Flavoring extracts and syrups, nec	100.00
Flavoring extracts, emulsions, and other liquid flavors	7.57
Natural or true flavoring extracts, emulsions, and other liquid flavors, in containers 8 oz or less	20.61
Natural or true flavoring extracts, emulsions, and other liquid flavors, in containers more than 8 oz	39.46
Imitation flavoring extracts, emulsions, and other liquid flavors	31.58
Flavoring extracts, emulsions, and other liquid flavors, nsk	8.37
Liquid beverage bases not for use by soft drink bottlers	2.34
Cocktail mix beverage bases not for use by soft drink bottlers	29.03
Other liquid beverage bases not for use by soft drink bottlers	57.12
Liquid beverage bases not for use by soft drink bottlers, nsk	13.85
Liquid beverage bases for use by soft drink bottlers	43.77
Liquid beverage base concentrates with some juice content, for sale to soft drink bottlers	7.13
Other liquid beverage base concentrates, for sale to soft drink bottlers	(D)
Liquid beverage base syrups, for sale to soft drink bottlers	7.54
Liquid beverage base concentrates with some juice content, for sale to trade or nonbottler distributors	0.74
Other liquid beverage base concentrates, for sale to trade or nonbottler distributors	(D)
Liquid beverage base syrups, for sale to trade or nonbottler distributors	1.43
Liquid beverage bases for use by soft drink bottlers, nsk	0.34
Other flavoring agents (except chocolate syrups)	39.75
Soft drink (effervescent and noneffervescent) flavoring powders, tablets, and pastes	7.00
Other flavoring powders, tablets, and paste, including dry mix cocktails	35.53
Flavoring syrups for fountain, ice cream, and home beverage use; excluding liquid beverage bases, soft drinks in bulk, and chocolate syrups	(D)
Fruit, crushed or whole, for fountain and ice cream flavoring agent use	5.98
Food colorings, except synthetic	3.87
Concentrated fruit juice products (not frozen or hot pack), for fountain flavoring agent use	2.25
Other flavoring agents (except chocolate syrups), nsk	(D)
Flavoring extracts and syrups, nec, nsk	6.56

Source: 1992 *Economic Census*. The values shown are percent of total shipments in an industry. Values of indented subcategories are summed in the main heading. The symbol (D) appears when data are withheld to prevent disclosure of competitive information. The abbreviation nsk stands for 'not specified by kind' and nec for 'not elsewhere classified'.

INPUTS AND OUTPUTS FOR FLAVORING EXTRACTS & SYRUPS, NEC

Economic Sector or Industry Providing Inputs	%	Sector	Economic Sector or Industry Buying Outputs	%	Sector
Advertising	17.7	Services	Bottled & canned soft drinks	34.5	Manufg.
Flavoring extracts & syrups, nec	16.3	Manufg.	Personal consumption expenditures	25.5	
Sugar	10.5	Manufg.	Eating & drinking places	15.5	Trade
Wholesale trade	9.5	Trade	Flavoring extracts & syrups, nec	9.4	Manufg.
Wet corn milling	9.4	Manufg.	Exports	5.3	Foreign
Imports	8.6	Foreign	Canned fruits & vegetables	2.0	Manufg.
Chemical preparations, nec	3.9	Manufg.	Confectionery products	1.2	Manufg.
Noncomparable imports	2.8	Foreign	Ice cream & frozen desserts	1.1	Manufg.
Metal cans	2.3	Manufg.	Chewing gum	1.0	Manufg.
Commercial printing	2.1	Manufg.	Change in business inventories	0.9	In House
Motor freight transportation & warehousing	1.8	Util.	Food preparations, nec	0.5	Manufg.
Railroads & related services	1.4	Util.	Cookies & crackers	0.4	Manufg.
Banking	1.3	Fin/R.E.	Blended & prepared flour	0.3	Manufg.
Cyclic crudes and organics	1.2	Manufg.	Flour & other grain mill products	0.3	Manufg.
Canned fruits & vegetables	1.0	Manufg.	Frozen fruits, fruit juices & vegetables	0.2	Manufg.
Miscellaneous plastics products	1.0	Manufg.	Frozen specialties	0.2	Manufg.
Paperboard containers & boxes	1.0	Manufg.	Hospitals	0.2	Services
Water transportation	0.6	Util.	Federal Government enterprises nec	0.2	Gov't

Continued on next page.

INPUTS AND OUTPUTS FOR FLAVORING EXTRACTS & SYRUPS, NEC - Continued

Economic Sector or Industry Providing Inputs	%	Sector	Economic Sector or Industry Buying Outputs	%	Sector
Crowns & closures	0.5	Manufg.	S/L Govt. purch., correction	0.2	S/L Govt
Industrial gases	0.5	Manufg.	S/L Govt. purch., higher education	0.2	S/L Govt
Electric services (utilities)	0.5	Util.	Condensed & evaporated milk	0.1	Manufg.
Gas production & distribution (utilities)	0.5	Util.	Amusement & recreation services nec	0.1	Services
Petroleum refining	0.4	Manufg.	Motion pictures	0.1	Services
Soybean oil mills	0.4	Manufg.			
Bottled & canned soft drinks	0.3	Manufg.			
Drugs	0.3	Manufg.			
Vegetable oil mills, nec	0.3	Manufg.			
Royalties	0.3	Fin/R.E.			
Miscellaneous crops	0.2	Agric.			
Maintenance of nonfarm buildings nec	0.2	Constr.			
Food preparations, nec	0.2	Manufg.			
Glass containers	0.2	Manufg.			
Malt	0.2	Manufg.			
Air transportation	0.2	Util.			
Communications, except radio & TV	0.2	Util.			
Eating & drinking places	0.2	Trade			
Distilled liquor, except brandy	0.1	Manufg.			
Food products machinery	0.1	Manufg.			
Industrial inorganic chemicals, nec	0.1	Manufg.			
Soap & other detergents	0.1	Manufg.			
Insurance carriers	0.1	Fin/R.E.			
Real estate	0.1	Fin/R.E.			
Equipment rental & leasing services	0.1	Services			
Miscellaneous repair shops	0.1	Services			

Source: Benchmark Input-Output Accounts for the U.S. Economy, 1982, U.S. Department of Commerce, Washington, D.C., July 1991. Data, as reported in the source, are organized by the 1977 SIC structure in use in 1982 but have been matched, as closely as is possible, to the 1987 SIC structure used in this book.

OCCUPATIONS EMPLOYED BY SIC 208 - BEVERAGES

Occupation	% of Total 1994	Change to 2005	Occupation	% of Total 1994	Change to 2005
Packaging & filling machine operators	11.6	-48.1	Salespersons, retail	1.9	-4.1
Driver/sales workers	7.8	-28.1	Marketing & sales worker supervisors	1.9	-20.1
Sales & related workers nec	6.5	-20.1	Marketing, advertising, & PR managers	1.9	-20.1
Truck drivers light & heavy	5.5	-17.6	General office clerks	1.6	-31.9
Industrial truck & tractor operators	5.2	-20.1	Bookkeeping, accounting, & auditing clerks	1.6	-40.1
Industrial machinery mechanics	3.6	-12.1	Industrial production managers	1.4	-20.2
Helpers, laborers, & material movers nec	3.3	-20.1	Separating & still machine operators	1.4	-12.1
Hand packers & packagers	2.7	-31.5	Maintenance repairers, general utility	1.3	-28.1
Freight, stock, & material movers, hand	2.7	-36.1	Managers & administrators nec	1.2	-20.2
Secretaries, ex legal & medical	2.5	-27.3	Management support workers nec	1.2	-20.1
General managers & top executives	2.2	-24.2	Precision food & tobacco workers nec	1.1	-20.2
Coin & vending machine servicers & repairers	2.0	-36.1	Science & mathematics technicians	1.0	-20.2
Agricultural workers nec	2.0	-20.1	Traffic, shipping, & receiving clerks	1.0	-23.1

Source: Industry-Occupation Matrix, Bureau of Labor Statistics. These data relate to one or more 3-digit SIC industry groups rather than to a single 4-digit SIC. The change reported for each occupation to the year 2005 is a percent of growth or decline as estimated by the Bureau of Labor Statistics. The abbreviation nec stands for 'not elsewhere classified'.

LOCATION BY STATE AND REGIONAL CONCENTRATION

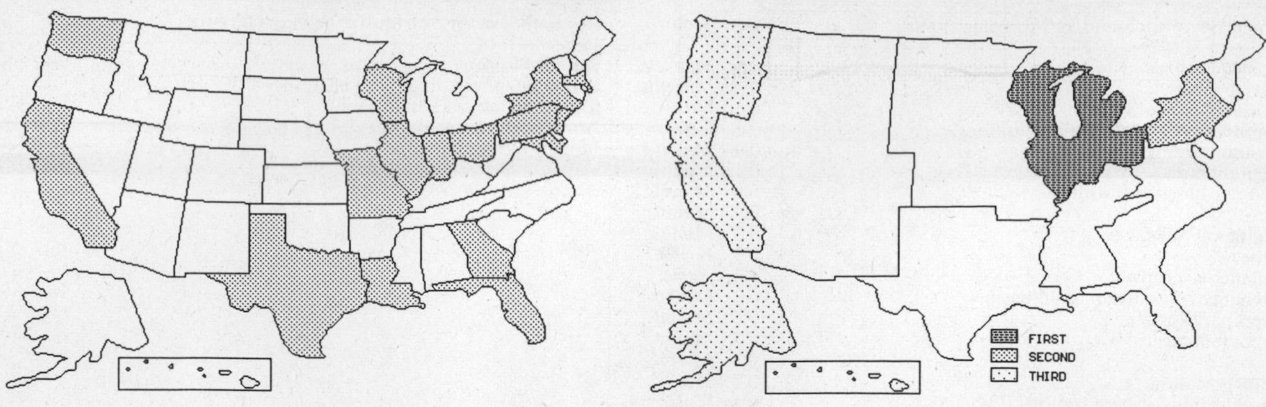

INDUSTRY DATA BY STATE

State	Establish-ments	Shipments			Employment				Cost as % of Shipments	Investment per Employee ($)
		Total ($ mil)	% of U.S.	Per Establ.	Total Number	% of U.S.	Per Establ.	Wages ($/hour)		
Illinois	28	1,114.6	16.1	39.8	1,900	18.4	68	13.29	29.6	8,316
Ohio	20	791.8	11.5	39.6	1,100	10.7	55	13.46	19.7	-
California	47	671.5	9.7	14.3	1,300	12.6	28	12.00	34.8	5,769
Pennsylvania	13	120.1	1.7	9.2	400	3.9	31	15.20	54.0	14,000
Wisconsin	13	51.2	0.7	3.9	100	1.0	8	10.00	43.4	-
New Jersey	27	(D)	-	-	750 *	7.3	28	-	-	-
New York	20	(D)	-	-	375 *	3.6	19	-	-	-
Missouri	16	(D)	-	-	375 *	3.6	23	-	-	-
Texas	16	(D)	-	-	750 *	7.3	47	-	-	6,933
Florida	15	(D)	-	-	375 *	3.6	25	-	-	-
Maryland	8	(D)	-	-	375 *	3.6	47	-	-	5,333
Georgia	6	(D)	-	-	375 *	3.6	63	-	-	-
Massachusetts	5	(D)	-	-	175 *	1.7	35	-	-	-
Indiana	4	(D)	-	-	750 *	7.3	188	-	-	-
Louisiana	4	(D)	-	-	175 *	1.7	44	-	-	-
Washington	3	(D)	-	-	175 *	1.7	58	-	-	-

Source: 1992 *Economic Census*. The states are in descending order of shipments or establishments (if shipment data are missing for the majority). The symbol (D) appears when data are withheld to prevent disclosure of competitive information. States marked with (D) are sorted by number of establishments. A dash (-) indicates that the data element cannot be calculated; * indicates the midpoint of a range.

2091 - CANNED & CURED FISH & SEAFOODS

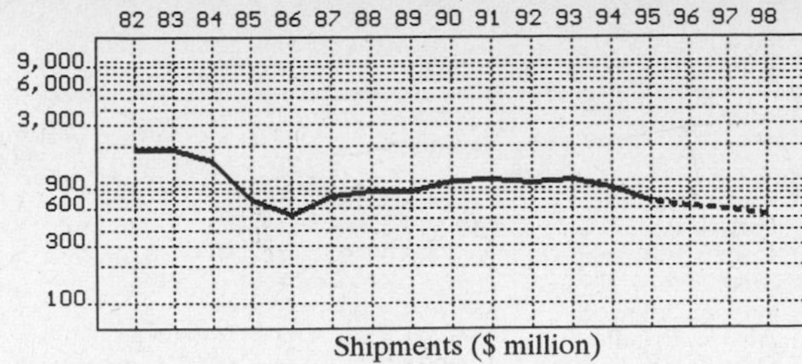

Shipments ($ million)

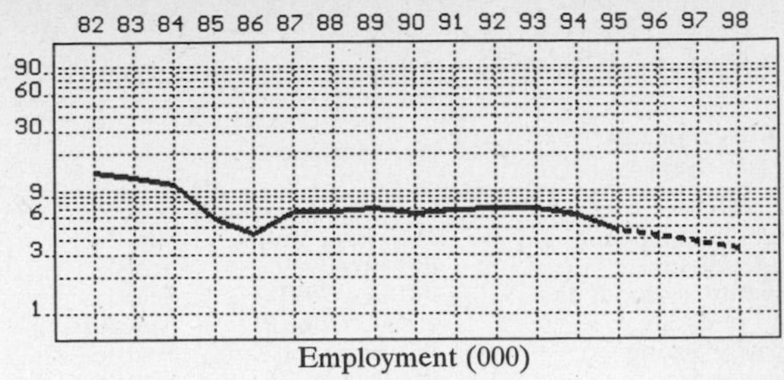

Employment (000)

GENERAL STATISTICS

Year	Com-panies	Establishments		Employment			Compensation		Production ($ million)			
		Total	with 20 or more employees	Total (000)	Production Workers (000)	Production Hours (Mil)	Payroll ($ mil)	Wages ($/hr)	Cost of Materials	Value Added by Manufacture	Value of Shipments	Capital Invest.
1982	170	204	107	13.9	12.1	21.1	194.9	7.14	1,235.3	613.4	1,849.1	20.5
1983		199	98	12.6	10.7	19.5	199.2	7.76	1,211.5	620.7	1,836.8	20.6
1984		194	89	11.4	9.8	20.9	183.9	6.54	1,028.9	479.9	1,506.9	11.0
1985		190	80	5.8	5.0	9.1	84.5	6.55	471.6	227.4	697.0	11.6
1986		183	73	4.4	3.7	6.5	71.4	7.62	354.2	186.1	539.7	14.8
1987	154	175	81	6.7	5.4	9.2	99.8	7.60	482.4	283.3	767.0	14.4
1988		187	83	6.6	5.4	9.3	101.3	7.26	533.7	313.1	844.1	13.1
1989		171	77	7.1	5.2	9.7	108.5	7.66	594.1	241.2	837.8	16.8
1990		172	73	6.5	5.7	10.3	122.8	7.82	695.2	303.2	998.2	33.1
1991		175	76	6.9	5.4	10.5	134.2	8.03	678.2	350.4	1,029.2	26.5
1992	143	158	61	7.0	5.5	10.3	132.7	8.52	606.5	362.0	968.4	20.1
1993		149	54	7.2	5.7	10.4	142.4	9.13	655.7	388.2	1,043.9	45.1
1994		152P	56P	6.2	5.1	9.7	116.3	7.45	560.8	335.6	896.6	43.8
1995		148P	52P	4.7P	3.5P	6.5P	103.2P	8.45P	427.7P	256.0P	683.9P	37.1P
1996		143P	49P	4.2P	3.0P	5.7P	99.4P	8.57P	393.9P	235.7P	629.7P	39.2P
1997		139P	45P	3.8P	2.6P	4.9P	95.5P	8.69P	360.0P	215.5P	575.6P	41.3P
1998		135P	42P	3.3P	2.2P	4.1P	91.7P	8.80P	326.2P	195.2P	521.5P	43.4P

Sources: 1982, 1987, 1992 *Economic Census*; *Annual Survey of Manufactures*, 83-86, 88-91, 93-94. Establishment counts for non-Census years are from *County Business Patterns*; establishment values for 83-84 are extrapolations. 'P's show projections by the editors. Industries reclassified in 87 will not have data for prior years.

INDICES OF CHANGE

Year	Com-panies	Establishments		Employment			Compensation		Production ($ million)			
		Total	with 20 or more employees	Total (000)	Production Workers (000)	Production Hours (Mil)	Payroll ($ mil)	Wages ($/hr)	Cost of Materials	Value Added by Manufacture	Value of Shipments	Capital Invest.
1982	119	129	175	199	220	205	147	84	204	169	191	102
1983		126	161	180	195	189	150	91	200	171	190	102
1984		123	146	163	178	203	139	77	170	133	156	55
1985		120	131	83	91	88	64	77	78	63	72	58
1986		116	120	63	67	63	54	89	58	51	56	74
1987	108	111	133	96	98	89	75	89	80	78	79	72
1988		118	136	94	98	90	76	85	88	86	87	65
1989		108	126	101	95	94	82	90	98	67	87	84
1990		109	120	93	104	100	93	92	115	84	103	165
1991		111	125	99	98	102	101	94	112	97	106	132
1992	100	100	100	100	100	100	100	100	100	100	100	100
1993		94	89	103	104	101	107	107	108	107	108	224
1994		96P	92P	89	93	94	88	87	92	93	93	218
1995		94P	86P	67P	63P	63P	78P	99P	71P	71P	71P	185P
1996		91P	80P	60P	55P	55P	75P	101P	65P	65P	65P	195P
1997		88P	74P	54P	47P	48P	72P	102P	59P	60P	59P	206P
1998		85P	68P	47P	39P	40P	69P	103P	54P	54P	54P	216P

Sources: Same as General Statistics. Values reflect change from the base year, 1992. Values above 100 mean greater than 92, values below 100 mean less than 92, and a value of 100 in the 82-91 or 93-98 period means same as 92. 'P's mark projections by the editors.

SELECTED RATIOS

For 1994	Avg. of All Manufact.	Analyzed Industry	Index
Employees per Establishment	49	41	83
Payroll per Establishment	1,500,273	765,132	51
Payroll per Employee	30,620	18,758	61
Production Workers per Establishment	34	34	98
Wages per Establishment	853,319	475,428	56
Wages per Production Worker	24,861	14,170	57
Hours per Production Worker	2,056	1,902	93
Wages per Hour	12.09	7.45	62
Value Added per Establishment	4,602,255	2,207,895	48
Value Added per Employee	93,930	54,129	58

For 1994	Avg. of All Manufact.	Analyzed Industry	Index
Value Added per Production Worker	134,084	65,804	49
Cost per Establishment	5,045,178	3,689,474	73
Cost per Employee	102,970	90,452	88
Cost per Production Worker	146,988	109,961	75
Shipments per Establishment	9,576,895	5,898,684	62
Shipments per Employee	195,460	144,613	74
Shipments per Production Worker	279,017	175,804	63
Investment per Establishment	321,011	288,158	90
Investment per Employee	6,552	7,065	108
Investment per Production Worker	9,352	8,588	92

Sources: Same as General Statistics. The 'Average of All Manufacturing' column represents the average of all manufacturing industries reported for the most recent complete year available. The Index shows the relationship between the Average and the Analyzed Industry. For example, 100 means that they are equal; 500 that the Analyzed Industry is five times the average; 50 means that the Analyzed Industry is half the national average. The abbreviation 'na' is used to show that data are 'not available'.

LEADING COMPANIES

Number shown: **27** Total sales ($ mil): **2,033** Total employment (000): **14.0**

Company Name	Address				CEO Name	Phone	Co. Type	Sales ($ mil)	Empl. (000)
Trident Seafoods Corp	5303 Shilshole Av N	Seattle	WA	98107	Chuck Bundrant	206-783-3818	R	540*	4.0
Van Camp Seafood Company	4510 Executive	San Diego	CA	92121	Patrick Rose	619-597-4200	R	440	2.7
Icicle Seafoods Inc	PO Box 79003	Seattle	WA	98119	Robert F Brophy	206-282-0988	R	240	2.5
Ocean Beauty Seafoods Inc	PO Box 70739	Seattle	WA	98107	Mike Selby	206-285-6800	R	200	0.4
Star-Kist Foods Inc	1 Riverfront Pl	Newport	KY	41071	William Johnson	606-655-5700	S	200*	1.5
Wards Cove Packing Co	PO Box C-5030	Seattle	WA	98105	Alec W Brindle	206-323-3200	R	100	0.2
Queen Fisheries	PO Box 70226	Seattle	WA	98107	Odin E Bendicksen	206-284-7571	R	48	0.5
Stinson Seafood Co	HCR 60	Prospect Hbr	ME	04669	R J Klingaman	207-963-7331	R	39	0.7
Morey Fish Co	PO Box 248	Motley	MN	56466	Stephen Frank	218-352-6345	R	34	0.1
Port Clyde Canning Co	PO Box 188	Rockland	ME	04841	Charles Crowe	207-594-4412	S	21	0.1
Noon Hour Food Products	660 W Randolph	Chicago	IL	60661	Paul A Buhl	312-782-1177	R	19	<0.1
Annette Island Packing Co	PO Box 70547	Seattle	WA	98107	Patrick J Kelly	206-545-6840	R	15	<0.1
Cape May Canners Inc	PO Box 158	Cape May	NJ	08204	Peter A LaMonica	609-465-4551	R	15	0.1
Los Angeles Smoking	778 Kohler St	Los Angeles	CA	90021	Delford B McGee	213-622-0724	R	15	0.1
Southern Shell Fish Company	PO Box 97	Harvey	LA	70059	R Skrmetta	504-341-5631	R	15	0.1
Vita Food Products Inc	2222 W Lake St	Chicago	IL	60612	Stephen D Rubin	312-738-4500	R	15	0.1
Manischewitz Food Prod Corp	214 N Delsea Dr	Vineland	NJ	08360	Cletus Beckel	609-692-6350	S	13*	<0.1
Washington Crab Producers Inc	PO Box 1488	Westport	WA	98595	Mike Brown	206-268-9161	R	12*	0.3
L Ray Packing Co	Rte 1	Milbridge	ME	04658	Ivan Ray	207-546-2355	R	11	<0.1
Nelson Crab Inc	PO Box 520	Tokeland	WA	98590	C Nelson	206-267-2911	R	10*	<0.1
JH Miles and Company Inc	PO Box 178	Norfolk	VA	23501	John R Miles	804-622-9264	R	9	<0.1
Ducktrap River Fish Farm Inc	57 Little River Dr	Belfast	ME	04915	Desmond Fitzgerald	207-338-6280	R	8	0.1
Lyon Food Products Inc	2301 Nevada Av N	Golden Valley	MN	55427	Dean Terry	612-544-4484	S	8*	<0.1
Cossack Caviar Inc	6900 191st Pl NE	Arlington	WA	98223	GD Shaw	206-435-6600	R	4*	<0.1
Abbots of New England	PO Box 609	New London	CT	06320	John Laundon	203-437-2105	R	1*	<0.1
Siberian Salmon Egg Co	6900 191st Pl NE	Arlington	WA	98223	GD Shaw	206-435-6600	D	1	<0.1
Carolyn Collins Caviar Co	925 W Jackson Blv	Chicago	IL	60607	Carolyn M Collins	312-226-0342	R	1	<0.1

Source: *Ward's Business Directory of U.S. Private and Public Companies*, Volumes 1 and 2, 1996. The company type code used is as follows: P - Public, R - Private, S - Subsidiary, D - Division, J - Joint Venture, A - Affiliate, G - Group. Sales are in millions of dollars, employees are in thousands. An asterisk (*) indicates an estimated sales volume. The symbol < stands for 'less than'. Company names and addresses are truncated, in some cases, to fit into the available space.

MATERIALS CONSUMED

Material		Quantity	Delivered Cost ($ million)
Materials, ingredients, containers, and supplies		(X)	556.1
Tuna	1,000 s tons	(D)	(D)
Salmon	1,000 s tons	119.1*	156.0
Sardines	1,000 s tons	31.4*	5.2
Ground fish (cod, cusk, haddock, hake, Atlantic Ocean perch, Atlantic pollock, and whiting)	1,000 s tons	8.4	4.9
Flounder		(X)	(D)
Other fin fish		(X)	43.5
Shrimp		(X)	(D)
Crabs		(X)	0.1
Oysters		(X)	(D)
Clams		(X)	45.4
Other shellfish		(X)	(D)
Frozen fish blocks	1,000 s tons	3.4	23.3
Fats and oils, all types (purchased as such)	mil lb	(S)	7.5
Paperboard containers, boxes, and corrugated paperboard		(X)	9.5
Packaging paper and plastics film, coated and laminated		(X)	3.0
Metal cans, can lids and ends		(X)	54.4
All other materials and components, parts, containers, and supplies		(X)	60.1
Materials, ingredients, containers, and supplies, nsk		(X)	50.1

Source: 1992 *Economic Census*. Explanation of symbols used: (D): Withheld to avoid disclosure of competitive data; na: Not available; (S): Withheld because statistical norms were not met; (X): Not applicable; (Z): Less than half the unit shown; nec: Not elsewhere classified; nsk: Not specified by kind; - : zero; * : 10-19 percent estimated; ** : 20-29 percent estimated.

PRODUCT SHARE DETAILS

Product or Product Class	% Share
Canned and cured fish and other seafoods	100.00
Canned tuna (except soups, stews, and chowders)	14.39
Canned salmon (except soups, stews, and chowders)	30.94
Canned sardines (except soups, stews, and chowders)	(D)
Canned clams (except soups, stews, and chowders)	7.69
Canned shrimp (except soups, stews, and chowders)	2.70
Other canned fish and other seafood (including gefilte fish, fish roe, fishcakes, surimi-based products, etc., except soups, stews, and chowders)	6.20
Canned seafood soups, stews, and chowders (clam chowder, oyster stew, turtle soup, etc.)	13.08
Smoked salmon	7.12
Other smoked fish (herring, whitefish, chub, cisco, etc.)	5.34
Salted and pickled fish (including sun-dried)	2.75
Other cured seafood, except fish	(D)

Source: 1992 *Economic Census*. The values shown are percent of total shipments in an industry. Values of indented subcategories are summed in the main heading. The symbol (D) appears when data are withheld to prevent disclosure of competitive information. The abbreviation nsk stands for 'not specified by kind' and nec for 'not elsewhere classified'.

INPUTS AND OUTPUTS FOR CANNED & CURED SEAFOODS

Economic Sector or Industry Providing Inputs	%	Sector	Economic Sector or Industry Buying Outputs	%	Sector
Imports	51.1	Foreign	Personal consumption expenditures	69.8	
Commercial fishing	26.5	Agric.	Eating & drinking places	14.5	Trade
Metal cans	6.0	Manufg.	Exports	9.2	Foreign
Wholesale trade	5.1	Trade	S/L Govt. purch., elem. & secondary education	1.7	S/L Govt
Commercial printing	1.8	Manufg.	Nursing & personal care facilities	1.0	Services
Advertising	1.1	Services	Hospitals	0.8	Services
Paperboard containers & boxes	0.9	Manufg.	Federal Government purchases, national defense	0.6	Fed Govt
Shortening & cooking oils	0.7	Manufg.	S/L Govt. purch., health & hospitals	0.5	S/L Govt
Electric services (utilities)	0.7	Util.	Canned & cured seafoods	0.4	Manufg.
Petroleum refining	0.6	Manufg.	S/L Govt. purch., higher education	0.3	S/L Govt
Sanitary services, steam supply, irrigation	0.5	Util.	Motion pictures	0.2	Services
Canned & cured seafoods	0.4	Manufg.	Residential care	0.2	Services
Miscellaneous plastics products	0.4	Manufg.	Federal Government enterprises nec	0.2	Gov't
Gas production & distribution (utilities)	0.3	Util.	S/L Govt. purch., correction	0.2	S/L Govt
Eating & drinking places	0.3	Trade	Social services, nec	0.1	Services
Banking	0.3	Fin/R.E.			
Air transportation	0.2	Util.			
Communications, except radio & TV	0.2	Util.			
Motor freight transportation & warehousing	0.2	Util.			
Real estate	0.2	Fin/R.E.			
Noncomparable imports	0.2	Foreign			
Maintenance of nonfarm buildings nec	0.1	Constr.			
Water transportation	0.1	Util.			
Credit agencies other than banks	0.1	Fin/R.E.			
Detective & protective services	0.1	Services			
Management & consulting services & labs	0.1	Services			
U.S. Postal Service	0.1	Gov't			

Source: Benchmark Input-Output Accounts for the U.S. Economy, 1982, U.S. Department of Commerce, Washington, D.C., July 1991. Data, as reported in the source, are organized by the 1977 SIC structure in use in 1982 but have been matched, as closely as is possible, to the 1987 SIC structure used in this book.

OCCUPATIONS EMPLOYED BY SIC 209 - MISCELLANEOUS FOODS AND KINDRED PRODUCTS

Occupation	% of Total 1994	Change to 2005	Occupation	% of Total 1994	Change to 2005
Cannery workers	10.4	26.3	Machine feeders & offbearers	1.9	3.3
Packaging & filling machine operators	8.7	26.3	Industrial truck & tractor operators	1.9	14.8
Hand packers & packagers	8.0	-1.6	Janitors & cleaners, incl maids	1.7	-8.2
Helpers, laborers, & material movers nec	6.7	14.8	Bakers, manufacturing	1.7	35.9
Meat, poultry, & fish cutters & trimmers, hand	5.8	14.8	Maintenance repairers, general utility	1.5	3.3
Cooking, roasting machine operators	3.4	26.3	Inspectors, testers, & graders, precision	1.5	14.8
Truck drivers light & heavy	3.2	18.3	Agricultural workers nec	1.3	14.8
Driver/sales workers	2.8	3.3	Industrial production managers	1.3	14.8
General managers & top executives	2.2	8.9	Bookkeeping, accounting, & auditing clerks	1.2	-13.9
Industrial machinery mechanics	2.2	26.2	Traffic, shipping, & receiving clerks	1.2	10.5
Precision food & tobacco workers nec	2.2	14.8	Secretaries, ex legal & medical	1.2	4.5
Freight, stock, & material movers, hand	2.1	-8.2	Extruding & forming machine workers	1.2	26.3
Crushing & mixing machine operators	2.0	14.8	Butchers & meatcutters	1.2	27.4
Assemblers, fabricators, & hand workers nec	2.0	14.8	General office clerks	1.1	-2.1
Sales & related workers nec	1.9	14.8			

Source: Industry-Occupation Matrix, Bureau of Labor Statistics. These data relate to one or more 3-digit SIC industry groups rather than to a single 4-digit SIC. The change reported for each occupation to the year 2005 is a percent of growth or decline as estimated by the Bureau of Labor Statistics. The abbreviation nec stands for 'not elsewhere classified'.

LOCATION BY STATE AND REGIONAL CONCENTRATION

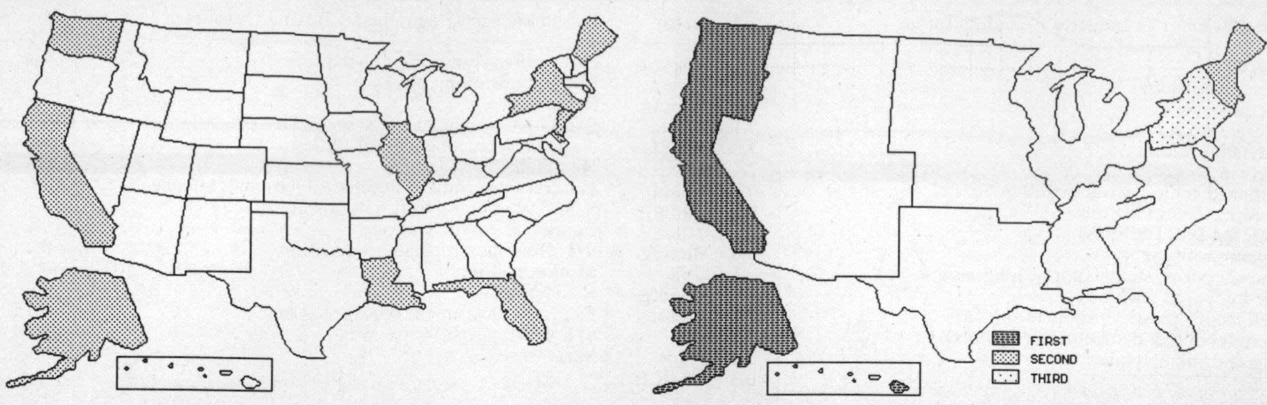

INDUSTRY DATA BY STATE

State	Establish-ments	Shipments Total ($ mil)	Shipments % of U.S.	Shipments Per Establ.	Employment Total Number	Employment % of U.S.	Employment Per Establ.	Wages ($/hour)	Cost as % of Shipments	Investment per Employee ($)
California	17	253.0	26.1	14.9	1,700	24.3	100	10.03	62.7	2,471
Alaska	21	194.9	20.1	9.3	1,000	14.3	48	7.80	66.6	2,600
Washington	29	98.5	10.2	3.4	1,000	14.3	34	9.00	64.8	-
New Jersey	8	89.0	9.2	11.1	700	10.0	88	8.63	55.6	6,571
New York	5	77.8	8.0	15.6	300	4.3	60	10.25	65.2	1,667
Maine	16	48.1	5.0	3.0	900	12.9	56	6.50	47.8	1,000
Louisiana	8	23.6	2.4	3.0	100	1.4	13	6.50	65.7	-
Florida	7	(D)	-	-	175 *	2.5	25	-	-	-
Delaware	3	(D)	-	-	750 *	10.7	250	-	-	-
Illinois	2	(D)	-	-	175 *	2.5	88	-	-	-

Source: 1992 *Economic Census*. The states are in descending order of shipments or establishments (if shipment data are missing for the majority). The symbol (D) appears when data are withheld to prevent disclosure of competitive information. States marked with (D) are sorted by number of establishments. A dash (-) indicates that the data element cannot be calculated; * indicates the midpoint of a range.

2092 - FRESH OR FROZEN PREPARED FISH

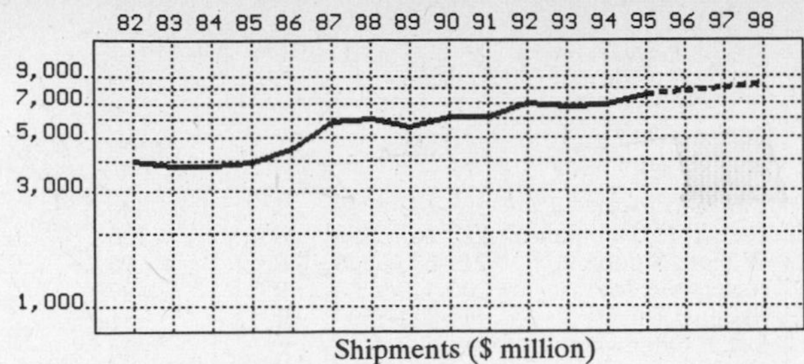

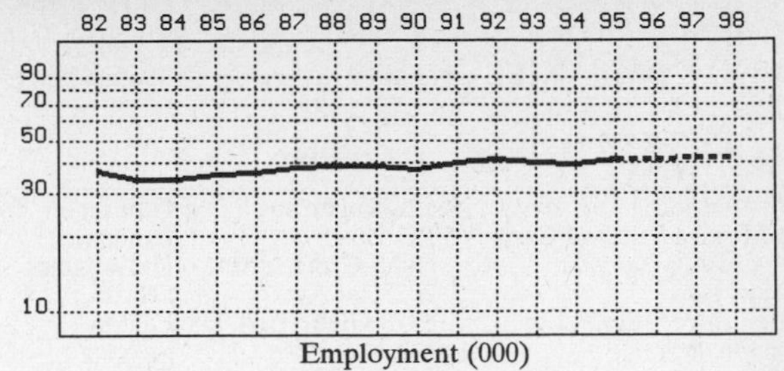

GENERAL STATISTICS

Year	Companies	Establishments		Employment			Compensation		Production ($ million)			
		Total	with 20 or more employees	Total (000)	Production Workers (000)	Production Hours (Mil)	Payroll ($ mil)	Wages ($/hr)	Cost of Materials	Value Added by Manufacture	Value of Shipments	Capital Invest.
1982	697	783	433	37.5	32.5	55.5	408.6	5.47	3,040.0	966.7	4,009.1	62.2
1983		743	405	34.3	29.5	51.5	398.4	5.51	2,846.5	936.5	3,789.5	42.2
1984		703	377	34.1	28.8	49.4	396.8	5.63	2,802.7	962.6	3,773.9	56.1
1985		662	350	36.0	30.6	53.7	410.7	5.35	2,866.1	1,070.1	3,946.9	58.9
1986		641	325	36.6	30.6	53.3	461.0	6.20	3,236.4	1,252.8	4,490.2	58.4
1987	576	644	358	38.3	32.5	58.2	531.3	6.56	4,214.7	1,537.1	5,752.0	105.0
1988		635	332	39.4	32.9	58.3	571.7	6.91	4,413.7	1,557.4	5,970.0	75.3
1989		609	325	38.9	31.5	58.2	588.2	7.10	3,952.0	1,614.2	5,552.1	138.5
1990		617	315	37.8	34.2	65.7	651.4	6.79	4,306.4	1,776.9	6,087.7	217.1
1991		622	333	39.9	33.6	64.0	672.4	7.10	4,166.9	1,932.2	6,079.1	112.0
1992	599	684	366	41.3	34.2	67.0	761.1	7.77	4,671.4	2,325.1	6,995.7	149.6
1993		690	353	40.1	33.0	61.0	723.5	8.17	4,290.8	2,390.8	6,700.5	113.0
1994		614P	316P	39.7	32.8	63.5	752.9	8.05	4,497.9	2,349.1	6,847.7	137.8
1995		605P	310P	41.3P	34.2P	66.9P	808.7P	8.37P	4,897.4P	2,557.8P	7,455.9P	167.1P
1996		597P	304P	41.8P	34.5P	68.1P	843.7P	8.61P	5,091.8P	2,659.3P	7,751.9P	176.4P
1997		588P	298P	42.2P	34.8P	69.4P	878.8P	8.85P	5,286.2P	2,760.8P	8,047.9P	185.7P
1998		579P	292P	42.7P	35.1P	70.6P	913.8P	9.10P	5,480.6P	2,862.3P	8,343.8P	195.0P

Sources: 1982, 1987, 1992 *Economic Census*; *Annual Survey of Manufactures*, 83-86, 88-91, 93-94. Establishment counts for non-Census years are from *County Business Patterns*; establishment values for 83-84 are extrapolations. 'P's show projections by the editors. Industries reclassified in 87 will not have data for prior years.

INDICES OF CHANGE

Year	Companies	Establishments		Employment			Compensation		Production ($ million)			
		Total	with 20 or more employees	Total (000)	Production Workers (000)	Production Hours (Mil)	Payroll ($ mil)	Wages ($/hr)	Cost of Materials	Value Added by Manufacture	Value of Shipments	Capital Invest.
1982	116	114	118	91	95	83	54	70	65	42	57	42
1983		109	111	83	86	77	52	71	61	40	54	28
1984		103	103	83	84	74	52	72	60	41	54	37
1985		97	96	87	89	80	54	69	61	46	56	39
1986		94	89	89	89	80	61	80	69	54	64	39
1987	96	94	98	93	95	87	70	84	90	66	82	70
1988		93	91	95	96	87	75	89	94	67	85	50
1989		89	89	94	92	87	77	91	85	69	79	93
1990		90	86	92	100	98	86	87	92	76	87	145
1991		91	91	97	98	96	88	91	89	83	87	75
1992	100	100	100	100	100	100	100	100	100	100	100	100
1993		101	96	97	96	91	95	105	92	103	96	76
1994		90P	86P	96	96	95	99	104	96	101	98	92
1995		88P	85P	100P	100P	100P	106P	108P	105P	110P	107P	112P
1996		87P	83P	101P	101P	102P	111P	111P	109P	114P	111P	118P
1997		86P	81P	102P	102P	104P	115P	114P	113P	119P	115P	124P
1998		85P	80P	103P	103P	105P	120P	117P	117P	123P	119P	130P

Sources: Same as General Statistics. Values reflect change from the base year, 1992. Values above 100 mean greater than 92, values below 100 mean less than 92, and a value of 100 in the 82-91 or 93-98 period means same as 92. 'P's mark projections by the editors.

SELECTED RATIOS

For 1994	Avg. of All Manufact.	Analyzed Industry	Index
Employees per Establishment	49	65	132
Payroll per Establishment	1,500,273	1,226,797	82
Payroll per Employee	30,620	18,965	62
Production Workers per Establishment	34	53	156
Wages per Establishment	853,319	832,923	98
Wages per Production Worker	24,861	15,585	63
Hours per Production Worker	2,056	1,936	94
Wages per Hour	12.09	8.05	67
Value Added per Establishment	4,602,255	3,827,690	83
Value Added per Employee	93,930	59,171	63

For 1994	Avg. of All Manufact.	Analyzed Industry	Index
Value Added per Production Worker	134,084	71,619	53
Cost per Establishment	5,045,178	7,329,006	145
Cost per Employee	102,970	113,297	110
Cost per Production Worker	146,988	137,131	93
Shipments per Establishment	9,576,895	11,157,837	117
Shipments per Employee	195,460	172,486	88
Shipments per Production Worker	279,017	208,771	75
Investment per Establishment	321,011	224,535	70
Investment per Employee	6,552	3,471	53
Investment per Production Worker	9,352	4,201	45

Sources: Same as General Statistics. The 'Average of All Manufacturing' column represents the average of all manufacturing industries reported for the most recent complete year available. The Index shows the relationship between the Average and the Analyzed Industry. For example, 100 means that they are equal; 500 that the Analyzed Industry is five times the average; 50 means that the Analyzed Industry is half the national average. The abbreviation 'na' is used to show that data are 'not available'.

LEADING COMPANIES Number shown: **59** Total sales ($ mil): **1,798** Total employment (000): **10.6**

Company Name	Address				CEO Name	Phone	Co. Type	Sales ($ mil)	Empl. (000)
Gorton's Seafood	128 Roger St	Gloucester	MA	01930	S H Warhover	508-283-3000	S	400	1.0
King and Prince Seafood Corp	PO Box 899	Brunswick	GA	31521	Robert P Brubaker	912-265-5155	R	120	0.8
Ore-Cal Corp	634 S Crocker St	Los Angeles	CA	90021	William Shinbane	213-680-9540	R	90	0.1
Oceantrawl Inc	2025 1st Av	Seattle	WA	98121	Assen Nicolov	206-448-9200	R	87•	0.5
Sea Watch International Ltd	8978 Glebe Park Dr	Easton	MD	21601	Michael Burns	410-822-7500	S	81	0.5
Bee Gee Shrimp	PO Box 3709	Lakeland	FL	33802	Lee F Odenwald	813-687-4411	D	76	0.5
Unisea Inc	PO Box 97019	Redmond	WA	98073	JR Pace	206-881-8181	R	76•	0.5
Louis Kemp Seafood Co	3931 W 1st St	Duluth	MN	55807	Roland Chambers	218-628-0365	D	61•	0.4
Farm Fresh Catfish Co	PO Box 85	Hollandale	MS	38748	Don Haynes	601-827-2204	S	60	0.6
National Sea Products Inc	PO Box 839	Portsmouth	NH	03801	Arne Pettersson	603-431-5835	S	59	0.2
Royal Seafoods Inc	PO Box 19032	Seattle	WA	98109	Stuart Looney	206-285-8900	R	57	0.4
Kitchens of the Oceans Inc	104 SE 5th Ct	Deerfield Bch	FL	33441	BA Margus	305-421-2192	R	50	0.3
Point Adams Fishing Co	PO Box 162	Hammond	OR	97121	Dean Bugatto	503-861-2226	S	45•	0.3
Iceland Seafood Corp	PO Box K	Camp Hill	PA	17011	Hal Carper	717-761-2600	R	35•	0.3
America's Catch Inc	PO Box 584	Itta Bena	MS	38941	Solon Scott III	601-254-7207	R	30	0.2
Bon Secour Fisheries Inc	PO Box 60	Bon Secour	AL	36511	John R Nelson	205-949-7411	R	30•	0.2
RCV Seafood Corp	PO Box 85	Morattico	VA	22523	Weston F Conley Jr	804-462-5101	R	30•	<0.1
United Shellfish Inc	PO Box 146	Grasonville	MD	21638	Dave Messenger	410-827-8171	S	28	0.1
Chesapeake Fish Company Inc	535 Harbor Ln	San Diego	CA	92101	Nick Vitalich	619-238-0526	R	25	<0.1
Seattle Seafoods Inc	PO Box C-70718	Seattle	WA	98107	Judy Macias	206-285-9191	S	25	0.1
Mermaid Seafoods Inc	115 Mason St	Greenwich	CT	06830	Erna Reingold	203-622-1666	R	22	<0.1
Sugiyo USA	PO Box 1017	Anacortes	WA	98221	M Takahashi	206-742-7122	S	22•	0.2
Olympic Fish Co	1520 W Marine	Everett	WA	98201	Jeff H Buske	206-258-0407	R	20	0.1
Seafood Producers Cooperative	2875 Roeder Av	Bellingham	WA	98225	Barry S Lester	360-733-0120	R	20	0.3
Pick Fisheries Inc	702 W Fulton St	Chicago	IL	60661	Gerald Lesser	312-226-4700	S	19	<0.1
Sau-Sea Foods Inc	1000 Saw Mill River	Yonkers	NY	10702	Abraham Kaplan	914-969-5922	R	18	0.1
Simmons Farm Raised Catfish	2628 Erickson Rd	Yazoo City	MS	39194	Harry Simmons Jr	601-746-5687	R	18•	0.1
Deals Seafood Company Inc	212 E Madison Av	Magnolia	NJ	08049	G Ralph Deal	609-783-8700	R	15	0.3
Luther L Smith and Son Fish	PO Box 67	Atlantic	NC	28511	William E Smith	919-225-3341	R	15	<0.1
Metompkin Bay Oyster Co	11 Dock St	Crisfield	MD	21817	Casey I Todd	410-968-0660	R	15•	0.1
Ocean Foods of Astoria Inc	PO Box 626	Astoria	OR	97103	Tim Horgan	503-325-2421	R	15•	0.1
Lafitte Frozen Foods Corp	1020 Caroline St	Lafitte	LA	70067	Edward Lee	504-689-2041	R	12•	0.1
All Alaskan Seafoods Inc	130 Nickerson St	Seattle	WA	98109	Lloyd Cannon	206-285-8200	R	10•	<0.1
CF Gollott and Son Seafood	PO Box 1191	Biloxi	MS	39533	A C Gollott Sr	601-392-2747	R	10	0.2
Viking Seafoods Inc	50 Crystal St	Malden	MA	02148	Jim Covelluzzi	617-321-6050	R	10•	0.1
Wiegardt Brothers Inc	PO Box 309	Ocean Park	WA	98640	Lee J Wiegardt	206-665-4111	R	10	0.1
Eastern Shore Seafood	PO Box 38	Mappsville	VA	23407	Rick Myers	804-824-5651	R	8	0.3
North Pacific Processors Inc	PO Box 31179	Seattle	WA	98103	Akio Shiokawa	206-632-9900	S	8•	<0.1
Riverside Seafoods Inc	2520 Wilson St	Two Rivers	WI	54241	Mark A Kornely	414-793-4511	R	8	<0.1
Sea Harvest Packing Co	PO Box 818	Brunswick	GA	31521	Charles Wells	912-264-3212	D	6	<0.1
Chinook Packing Co	PO Box 206	Chinook	WA	98614	Terry Krager	206-777-8272	R	5	<0.1
Ecrevisse Acadienne USA	228 St Charles Av	New Orleans	LA	70130	Charles S Williams	504-524-3660	J	5	0.1
Indian Ridge Canning Company	PO Box 550	Houma	LA	70361	Richard G Fakier	504-594-3361	R	5	<0.1
Navillus Seafood Co	5221 Lorain Av	Cleveland	OH	44102	Sean Sullivan	216-631-3474	R	5	<0.1
Sea Garden Seafoods Inc	PO Box 87	Valona	GA	31332	JL Amason	912-832-4437	R	4	<0.1
Texas Pack Inc	PO Box 1643	Port Isabel	TX	78578	William Zimmerman	210-943-5461	R	4	0.2
Bayou Land Seafood	1008 Berard	Breaux Bridge	LA	70517	Roy J Robin	318-667-6118	R	4	0.1
Associated Seafood Co	1504 State Hwy 105	Aberdeen	WA	98520	Edwin Sherwood	206-648-2226	R	3•	<0.1
JM Clayton Co	PO Box 321	Cambridge	MD	21613	John C Brooks Jr	410-228-1661	R	3	<0.1
Victory Seafood Processors Inc	208 W Elina St	Abbeville	LA	70510	Jason G Guidry	318-893-9029	R	3•	0.1
RA Fayard Seafood Company	PO Box 343	Biloxi	MS	39533	Robert A Fayard III	601-436-6243	R	3	0.1
Red Lake Fisheries Association	PO Box 56	Redby	MN	56670	William May	218-679-3813	R	2	<0.1
Roy Stritmatter Seafood	923 Karr Av	Hoquiam	WA	98550	Roy Stritmatter	206-532-0710	R	2	<0.1
Top Catch Inc	87 Sackett St	Brooklyn	NY	11231	Arthur Gentile	718-624-9300	R	2	<0.1
KSM Seafood Corp	PO Box 3057	Baton Rouge	LA	70821	Bo Wallenholm	504-383-1517	R	1•	0.2
St George Packing Company Inc	PO Box 2670	Ft Myers Bch	FL	33932	John L Shafer	813-463-6351	R	1•	<0.1
Todd Seafoods Inc	PO Box 28	Cambridge	MD	21613	Michael W Todd	410-228-1400	R	1	<0.1
Pristine Foods Inc	3126 Hwy 594	Monroe	LA	71203	Dixon Touchstone	318-343-1947	R	1	<0.1
BG Smith and Sons Oyster	PO Box 69	Sharps	VA	22548	Jack Smith	804-394-2721	R	0	<0.1

Source: *Ward's Business Directory of U.S. Private and Public Companies*, Volumes 1 and 2, 1996. The company type code used is as follows: P - Public, R - Private, S - Subsidiary, D - Division, J - Joint Venture, A - Affiliate, G - Group. Sales are in millions of dollars, employees are in thousands. An asterisk (•) indicates an estimated sales volume. The symbol < stands for 'less than'. Company names and addresses are truncated, in some cases, to fit into the available space.

MATERIALS CONSUMED

Material		Quantity	Delivered Cost ($ million)
Materials, ingredients, containers, and supplies		(X)	4,165.0
Alaska pollack	1,000 s tons	79.0	71.7
Tuna	1,000 s tons	3.5*	13.3
Salmon	1,000 s tons	241.2	623.9
Sardines	1,000 s tons	(D)	(D)
Ground fish (cod, cusk, haddock, hake, Atlantic Ocean perch, Atlantic pollock, and whiting)	1,000 s tons	223.5	280.6
Flounder		(X)	28.2
Other fin fish		(X)	377.4
Shrimp		(X)	569.0
Crabs		(X)	280.1
Oysters		(X)	34.7
Clams		(X)	32.1
Other shellfish		(X)	131.5
Surimi	1,000 s tons	35.1	105.8
Frozen fish blocks	1,000 s tons	241.6	570.8
Fats and oils, all types (purchased as such)	mil lb	(D)	(D)
Paperboard containers, boxes, and corrugated paperboard		(X)	91.3
Packaging paper and plastics film, coated and laminated		(X)	31.0
Metal cans, can lids and ends		(X)	26.6
All other materials and components, parts, containers, and supplies		(X)	352.7
Materials, ingredients, containers, and supplies, nsk		(X)	503.1

Source: 1992 *Economic Census*. Explanation of symbols used: (D): Withheld to avoid disclosure of competitive data; na: Not available; (S): Withheld because statistical norms were not met; (X): Not applicable; (Z): Less than half the unit shown; nec: Not elsewhere classified; nsk: Not specified by kind; - : zero; * : 10-19 percent estimated; ** : 20-29 percent estimated.

PRODUCT SHARE DETAILS

Product or Product Class	% Share
Fresh or frozen prepared fish and other seafood	100.00
Prepared fresh fish and other fresh seafood	15.25
Prepared fresh fish	41.62
Prepared fresh blue crab meat	5.36
Prepared fresh rock crab meat	(D)
Prepared fresh snow crab meat	(D)
Other prepared fresh crab meat	1.42
Prepared fresh shrimp	8.86
Prepared fresh oysters	7.61
Prepared fresh clams	2.37
Other prepared fresh shellfish (except surimi and surimi-based products)	5.06
Prepared fresh surimi, except surimi-based products	2.94
Prepared fresh surimi-based products	(D)
Other prepared fresh seafood (roe, squid, etc.)	14.17
Prepared fresh fish and other fresh seafood, nsk	2.62
Prepared frozen fish	42.37
Prepared frozen groundfish (cod, cusk, haddock, hake, perch, pollock, and whiting), fillets and steaks, breaded or battered	16.10
Prepared frozen groundfish (cod, cusk, haddock, hake, perch, pollock, and whiting), plain fillets and steaks	5.37
Prepared frozen groundfish (cod, cusk, haddock, hake, perch, pollock, and whiting), sticks and portions, breaded or battered	21.20
Prepared frozen groundfish (cod, cusk, haddock, hake, perch, pollock, and whiting), plain sticks and portions	0.87
Other prepared frozen groundfish (cod, cusk, haddock, hake, perch, pollock, and whiting)	3.26
Prepared frozen flounder, halibut, and sole, fillets and steaks	1.86
Other prepared frozen flounder, halibut, and sole, fillets and steaks	3.82
All other prepared frozen fish, fillets and steaks, breaded or battered	2.77
All other prepared frozen fish, fillets and steaks, plain	18.84
All other prepared frozen fish, other forms	24.73
Frozen fish, nsk	1.17
Prepared frozen shellfish	24.03
Prepared frozen headless shrimp, raw	9.18
Prepared frozen peeled shrimp, raw	9.36
Prepared frozen peeled shrimp, cooked	9.44
Prepared frozen shrimp, breaded	26.75
Other 100 percent prepared frozen shrimp products	1.18
Prepared frozen blue crab meat	1.43
Prepared frozen snow crab meat	3.96
Prepared frozen dungeness crab meat	0.90
Prepared frozen king crab meat, cooked	1.16
Prepared frozen King crab sections	4.97
Other prepared frozen crabs and parts of crabs	15.76
Other prepared frozen shellfish (including oysters, clams, and parts of lobsters except tails)	13.99
Frozen shellfish, nsk	1.94
Other prepared frozen seafoods	9.26
Prepared frozen surimi, except surimi-based products	29.69
Prepared frozen surimi-based products	20.30
Other prepared frozen seafoods (soups, stews, chowders, pies, fishcakes, crabcakes, shrimpcakes, etc.), except surimi	39.60
Other frozen seafoods, nsk	10.39
Fresh or frozen prepared fish and other seafood, nsk	9.09

Source: 1992 *Economic Census*. The values shown are percent of total shipments in an industry. Values of indented subcategories are summed in the main heading. The symbol (D) appears when data are withheld to prevent disclosure of competitive information. The abbreviation nsk stands for 'not specified by kind' and nec for 'not elsewhere classified'.

INPUTS AND OUTPUTS FOR FRESH OR FROZEN PACKAGED FISH

Economic Sector or Industry Providing Inputs	%	Sector	Economic Sector or Industry Buying Outputs	%	Sector
Commercial fishing	51.1	Agric.	Eating & drinking places	60.4	Trade
Imports	9.8	Foreign	Exports	16.4	Foreign
Wholesale trade	8.4	Trade	Personal consumption expenditures	13.1	
Noncomparable imports	8.1	Foreign	Hospitals	2.0	Services
Miscellaneous livestock	6.8	Agric.	S/L Govt. purch., elem. & secondary education	1.4	S/L Govt
Paperboard containers & boxes	2.5	Manufg.	Change in business inventories	1.3	In House
Motor freight transportation & warehousing	1.4	Util.	Federal Government enterprises nec	1.1	Gov't
Electric services (utilities)	1.3	Util.	S/L Govt. purch., health & hospitals	0.9	S/L Govt
Shortening & cooking oils	1.1	Manufg.	S/L Govt. purch., higher education	0.7	S/L Govt
Fresh or frozen packaged fish	0.7	Manufg.	Fresh or frozen packaged fish	0.6	Manufg.
Miscellaneous plastics products	0.7	Manufg.	S/L Govt. purch., correction	0.5	S/L Govt
Petroleum refining	0.7	Manufg.	Residential care	0.4	Services
Air transportation	0.7	Util.	Amusement & recreation services nec	0.2	Services
Advertising	0.7	Services	Nursing & personal care facilities	0.2	Services
Paper coating & glazing	0.5	Manufg.	Social services, nec	0.2	Services
Water transportation	0.4	Util.	Air transportation	0.1	Util.
Eating & drinking places	0.4	Trade	Railroads & related services	0.1	Util.
Adhesives & sealants	0.3	Manufg.	Water transportation	0.1	Util.
Refrigeration & heating equipment	0.3	Manufg.	Child day care services	0.1	Services
Communications, except radio & TV	0.3	Util.			
Banking	0.3	Fin/R.E.			
Maintenance of nonfarm buildings nec	0.2	Constr.			
Metal barrels, drums, & pails	0.2	Manufg.			
Rubber & plastics hose & belting	0.2	Manufg.			
Gas production & distribution (utilities)	0.2	Util.			
Real estate	0.2	Fin/R.E.			
Equipment rental & leasing services	0.2	Services			
Metal foil & leaf	0.1	Manufg.			
Accounting, auditing & bookkeeping	0.1	Services			
Business/professional associations	0.1	Services			
Detective & protective services	0.1	Services			
Legal services	0.1	Services			
Management & consulting services & labs	0.1	Services			

Source: Benchmark Input-Output Accounts for the U.S. Economy, 1982, U.S. Department of Commerce, Washington, D.C., July 1991. Data, as reported in the source, are organized by the 1977 SIC structure in use in 1982 but have been matched, as closely as is possible, to the 1987 SIC structure used in this book.

OCCUPATIONS EMPLOYED BY SIC 209 - MISCELLANEOUS FOODS AND KINDRED PRODUCTS

Occupation	% of Total 1994	Change to 2005	Occupation	% of Total 1994	Change to 2005
Cannery workers	10.4	26.3	Machine feeders & offbearers	1.9	3.3
Packaging & filling machine operators	8.7	26.3	Industrial truck & tractor operators	1.9	14.8
Hand packers & packagers	8.0	-1.6	Janitors & cleaners, incl maids	1.7	-8.2
Helpers, laborers, & material movers nec	6.7	14.8	Bakers, manufacturing	1.7	35.9
Meat, poultry, & fish cutters & trimmers, hand	5.8	14.8	Maintenance repairers, general utility	1.5	3.3
Cooking, roasting machine operators	3.4	26.3	Inspectors, testers, & graders, precision	1.5	14.8
Truck drivers light & heavy	3.2	18.3	Agricultural workers nec	1.3	14.8
Driver/sales workers	2.8	3.3	Industrial production managers	1.3	14.8
General managers & top executives	2.2	8.9	Bookkeeping, accounting, & auditing clerks	1.2	-13.9
Industrial machinery mechanics	2.2	26.2	Traffic, shipping, & receiving clerks	1.2	10.5
Precision food & tobacco workers nec	2.2	14.8	Secretaries, ex legal & medical	1.2	4.5
Freight, stock, & material movers, hand	2.1	-8.2	Extruding & forming machine workers	1.2	26.3
Crushing & mixing machine operators	2.0	14.8	Butchers & meatcutters	1.2	27.4
Assemblers, fabricators, & hand workers nec	2.0	14.8	General office clerks	1.1	-2.1
Sales & related workers nec	1.9	14.8			

Source: Industry-Occupation Matrix, Bureau of Labor Statistics. These data relate to one or more 3-digit SIC industry groups rather than to a single 4-digit SIC. The change reported for each occupation to the year 2005 is a percent of growth or decline as estimated by the Bureau of Labor Statistics. The abbreviation nec stands for 'not elsewhere classified'.

LOCATION BY STATE AND REGIONAL CONCENTRATION

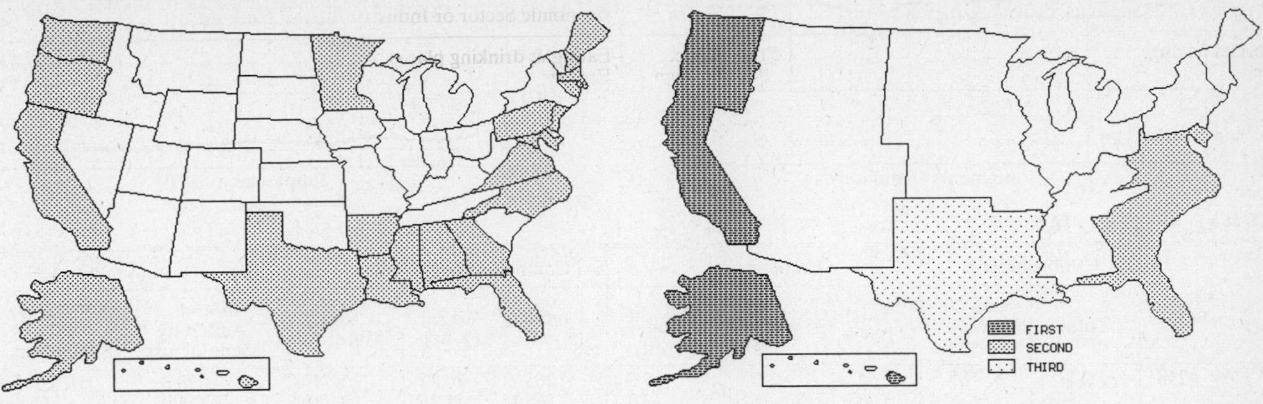

INDUSTRY DATA BY STATE

State	Establish-ments	Shipments Total ($ mil)	Shipments % of U.S.	Shipments Per Establ.	Employment Total Number	Employment % of U.S.	Employment Per Establ.	Wages ($/hour)	Cost as % of Shipments	Investment per Employee ($)
Washington	87	1,447.3	20.7	16.6	7,200	17.4	83	8.73	66.3	3,056
Alaska	84	1,210.4	17.3	14.4	8,000	19.4	95	9.62	62.2	6,675
Massachusetts	42	967.4	13.8	23.0	2,200	5.3	52	10.69	71.9	2,227
Florida	56	511.7	7.3	9.1	3,100	7.5	55	6.00	65.4	1,355
California	52	436.8	6.2	8.4	3,000	7.3	58	7.55	68.8	2,300
Pennsylvania	4	373.2	5.3	93.3	1,000	2.4	250	11.13	64.5	3,500
Mississippi	27	362.3	5.2	13.4	3,700	9.0	137	4.68	69.1	2,000
Maryland	30	177.3	2.5	5.9	1,000	2.4	33	7.33	78.5	4,900
Alabama	17	171.4	2.5	10.1	1,600	3.9	94	5.74	71.8	2,500
Louisiana	57	167.5	2.4	2.9	1,600	3.9	28	5.68	72.3	3,563
Oregon	22	164.9	2.4	7.5	1,300	3.1	59	7.80	64.3	2,385
Texas	25	114.9	1.6	4.6	1,100	2.7	44	6.33	74.2	6,000
Virginia	50	113.2	1.6	2.3	1,300	3.1	26	7.25	58.1	5,000
New Hampshire	10	107.0	1.5	10.7	500	1.2	50	9.22	75.1	6,200
Minnesota	7	97.3	1.4	13.9	600	1.5	86	5.64	51.3	3,833
New Jersey	9	84.5	1.2	9.4	500	1.2	56	7.50	73.1	3,200
North Carolina	31	60.3	0.9	1.9	1,000	2.4	32	6.00	67.3	700
Arkansas	5	46.1	0.7	9.2	300	0.7	60	5.50	51.4	2,000
Rhode Island	5	21.8	0.3	4.4	200	0.5	40	7.00	65.1	-
Maine	14	17.9	0.3	1.3	100	0.2	7	5.50	66.5	-
Georgia	7	(D)	-	-	1,750 *	4.2	250	-	-	-
Hawaii	3	(D)	-	-	175 *	0.4	58	-	-	-
Connecticut	1	(D)	-	-	175 *	0.4	175	-	-	-

Source: 1992 *Economic Census*. The states are in descending order of shipments or establishments (if shipment data are missing for the majority). The symbol (D) appears when data are withheld to prevent disclosure of competitive information. States marked with (D) are sorted by number of establishments. A dash (-) indicates that the data element cannot be calculated; * indicates the midpoint of a range.

2095 - ROASTED COFFEE

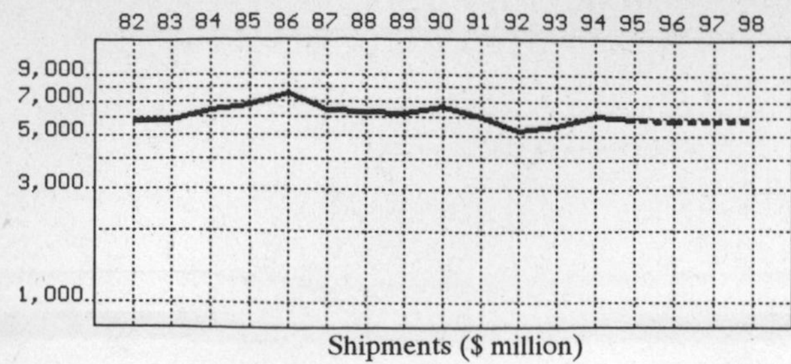

Shipments ($ million)

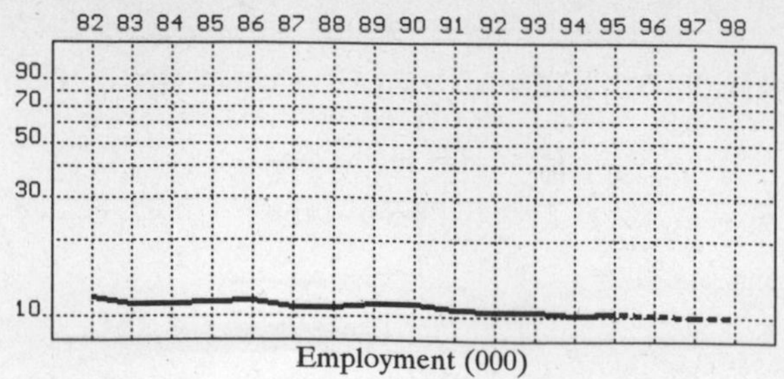

Employment (000)

GENERAL STATISTICS

Year	Com-panies	Establishments: Total	Establishments: with 20 or more employees	Employment: Total (000)	Employment: Production Workers (000)	Employment: Production Hours (Mil)	Compensation: Payroll ($ mil)	Compensation: Wages ($/hr)	Production ($ million): Cost of Materials	Production ($ million): Value Added by Manufacture	Production ($ million): Value of Shipments	Production ($ million): Capital Invest.
1982	118	152	85	11.8	7.4	15.0	265.7	10.47	3,749.0	2,070.3	5,826.9	80.5
1983		150	84	11.1	6.9	13.8	265.1	11.26	3,710.8	2,115.0	5,808.5	96.1
1984		148	83	11.1	7.2	14.5	279.2	11.84	4,178.3	2,220.2	6,378.4	134.1
1985		146	82	11.4	7.5	15.0	294.5	11.87	4,211.2	2,445.8	6,677.1	138.9
1986		141	80	11.5	7.4	15.2	307.1	11.81	5,140.2	2,444.7	7,544.0	147.3
1987	111	141	82	10.7	6.6	13.6	303.0	12.54	3,775.2	2,589.8	6,400.6	155.2
1988		147	89	10.7	6.7	12.7	315.6	13.65	3,526.8	2,795.8	6,332.4	123.2
1989		150	91	11.1	6.5	13.5	303.1	12.76	3,491.6	2,658.1	6,167.2	120.9
1990		147	88	11.0	6.9	14.4	326.7	12.53	3,004.9	3,581.8	6,622.7	114.6
1991		150	85	10.6	6.8	14.2	324.4	13.30	3,035.2	2,868.4	5,919.9	126.6
1992	134	172	90	10.5	6.6	14.0	340.0	13.76	2,530.0	2,752.5	5,292.8	149.1
1993		178	90	10.4	6.5	13.9	339.4	13.59	2,587.8	2,969.6	5,535.7	111.2
1994		164P	90P	10.1	6.1	12.9	333.3	13.93	3,277.5	2,925.1	6,127.1	125.6
1995		166P	91P	10.2P	6.3P	13.4P	351.7P	14.33P	3,148.1P	2,809.6P	5,885.1P	135.2P
1996		168P	91P	10.1P	6.2P	13.3P	358.0P	14.59P	3,123.8P	2,787.9P	5,839.8P	136.7P
1997		170P	92P	10.0P	6.1P	13.2P	364.3P	14.84P	3,099.6P	2,766.3P	5,794.5P	138.2P
1998		172P	93P	9.9P	6.0P	13.1P	370.6P	15.09P	3,075.3P	2,744.6P	5,749.1P	139.7P

Sources: 1982, 1987, 1992 *Economic Census*; *Annual Survey of Manufactures*, 83-86, 88-91, 93-94. Establishment counts for non-Census years are from *County Business Patterns*; establishment values for 83-84 are extrapolations. 'P's show projections by the editors. Industries reclassified in 87 will not have data for prior years.

INDICES OF CHANGE

Year	Com-panies	Establishments: Total	Establishments: with 20 or more employees	Employment: Total (000)	Employment: Production Workers (000)	Employment: Production Hours (Mil)	Compensation: Payroll ($ mil)	Compensation: Wages ($/hr)	Production ($ million): Cost of Materials	Production ($ million): Value Added by Manufacture	Production ($ million): Value of Shipments	Production ($ million): Capital Invest.
1982	88	88	94	112	112	107	78	76	148	75	110	54
1983		87	93	106	105	99	78	82	147	77	110	64
1984		86	92	106	109	104	82	86	165	81	121	90
1985		85	91	109	114	107	87	86	166	89	126	93
1986		82	89	110	112	109	90	86	203	89	143	99
1987	83	82	91	102	100	97	89	91	149	94	121	104
1988		85	99	102	102	91	93	99	139	102	120	83
1989		87	101	106	98	96	89	93	138	97	117	81
1990		85	98	105	105	103	96	91	119	130	125	77
1991		87	94	101	103	101	95	97	120	104	112	85
1992	100	100	100	100	100	100	100	100	100	100	100	100
1993		103	100	99	98	99	100	99	102	108	105	75
1994		95P	100P	96	92	92	98	101	130	106	116	84
1995		96P	101P	97P	95P	95P	103P	104P	124P	102P	111P	91P
1996		98P	102P	96P	94P	95P	105P	106P	123P	101P	110P	92P
1997		99P	102P	95P	92P	94P	107P	108P	123P	101P	109P	93P
1998		100P	103P	94P	91P	93P	109P	110P	122P	100P	109P	94P

Sources: Same as General Statistics. Values reflect change from the base year, 1992. Values above 100 mean greater than 92, values below 100 mean less than 92, and a value of 100 in the 82-91 or 93-98 period means same as 92. 'P's mark projections by the editors.

SELECTED RATIOS

For 1994	Avg. of All Manufact.	Analyzed Industry	Index
Employees per Establishment	49	62	126
Payroll per Establishment	1,500,273	2,032,129	135
Payroll per Employee	30,620	33,000	108
Production Workers per Establishment	34	37	108
Wages per Establishment	853,319	1,095,612	128
Wages per Production Worker	24,861	29,459	118
Hours per Production Worker	2,056	2,115	103
Wages per Hour	12.09	13.93	115
Value Added per Establishment	4,602,255	17,834,328	388
Value Added per Employee	93,930	289,614	308

For 1994	Avg. of All Manufact.	Analyzed Industry	Index
Value Added per Production Worker	134,084	479,525	358
Cost per Establishment	5,045,178	19,982,910	396
Cost per Employee	102,970	324,505	315
Cost per Production Worker	146,988	537,295	366
Shipments per Establishment	9,576,895	37,356,915	390
Shipments per Employee	195,460	606,644	310
Shipments per Production Worker	279,017	1,004,443	360
Investment per Establishment	321,011	765,783	239
Investment per Employee	6,552	12,436	190
Investment per Production Worker	9,352	20,590	220

Sources: Same as General Statistics. The 'Average of All Manufacturing' column represents the average of all manufacturing industries reported for the most recent complete year available. The Index shows the relationship between the Average and the Analyzed Industry. For example, 100 means that they are equal; 500 that the Analyzed Industry is five times the average; 50 means that the Analyzed Industry is half the national average. The abbreviation 'na' is used to show that data are 'not available'.

LEADING COMPANIES

Number shown: **53** Total sales ($ mil): **2,622** Total employment (000): **10.0**

Company Name	Address				CEO Name	Phone	Co. Type	Sales ($ mil)	Empl. (000)
Nestle Beverage Co	PO Box 7449	San Francisco	CA	94120	Paul Miller	415-546-4600	S	840	2.0
Chock Full O'Nuts Corp	370 Lexington Av	New York	NY	10017	Marvin I Haas	212-532-0300	P	266	1.1
Reily Companies Inc	PO Box 60296	New Orleans	LA	70160	William B Reily III	504-524-6131	R	230*	1.1
Superior Coffee and Foods	990 Supreme Dr	Bensenville	IL	60106	Stanley L Greanias	708-860-1400	D	200	0.8
Boyd Coffee Co	PO Box 20547	Portland	OR	97220	Richard Boyd	503-666-4545	R	100*	0.5
Melitta North America Inc	17757 US 19 N	Clearwater	FL	34624	HH Radtke	813-535-2111	S	100	0.2
Brother's Gourmet Coffees Inc	2255 Glades Rd	Boca Raton	FL	33431	Dennis Boyer	407-241-0215	R	83	0.1
Wechsler Coffee Corp	10 Empire Blv	Moonachie	NJ	07074	Michael Slater	201-440-1700	R	79	0.5
Melitta USA Inc	1401 Berlin Rd	Cherry Hill	NJ	08003	H Helmut Radtke	609-428-7202	S	76*	0.2
Royal Cup Inc	PO Box 170971	Birmingham	AL	35217	Hatton Smith	205-849-5836	R	75	0.4
Millstone Coffee Inc	729 100th St SE	Everett	WA	98208	L Jonson	206-347-3995	R	70	0.5
S and D Coffee Inc	PO Box 1628	Concord	NC	28025	JR Davis Jr	704-782-3121	R	52*	0.5
Stanley W Ferguson Inc	365 C St	Boston	MA	02127	CR Ferguson	617-268-6280	R	46	<0.1
Continental Coffee Products Co	321 N Clark St	Chicago	IL	60610	Jim Bankard	312-222-8300	S	40	0.3
Victor Coffee Co	365 C St	South Boston	MA	02127	G Ferguson	617-268-6280	D	40	<0.1
New England Tea and Coffee	100 Charles St	Malden	MA	02148	Stephen Kaloyanides	617-324-8094	R	30	0.1
Caravali Coffees Inc	PO Box 58803	Seattle	WA	98138	Bart Wilson	206-251-9256	R	25*	0.1
Rowland Coffee Roaster Inc	8080 NW 58th St	Miami	FL	33166	JA Souto	305-594-9039	R	22	0.2
Coffee Holding Co	PO Box 208	Brooklyn	NY	11232	Sterling Gordon	718-832-0800	R	20	<0.1
White Coffee Corp	1835 38th St	Long Island Ct	NY	11105	Carole White	718-204-7900	R	19*	<0.1
Greenwich Mills	520 Secaucus Rd	Secaucus	NJ	07094	Marvin Haas	201-865-0200	D	17*	<0.1
Araban Coffee Company Inc	PO Box 235	Boston	MA	02127	HJ Perry	617-439-3900	R	15	<0.1
Autocrat Coffee Inc	PO Box 285	Lincoln	RI	02865	Richard Fields	401-333-3300	R	14*	<0.1
Peerless United Coffee Corp	260 Oak St	Oakland	CA	94607	George Vukasin	510-763-1763	S	12*	<0.1
Richheimer Coffee Co	1127 N Halsted St	Chicago	IL	60622	Michael Slater	312-787-8352	S	12	<0.1
American Tea and Coffee	PO Box 23890	Nashville	TN	37202	Marvin R Bubis	615-329-0079	R	11	<0.1
De Coty Coffee Co	1920 Austin St	San Angelo	TX	76903	Michael J Agan	915-655-5607	R	11	<0.1
Stewarts Private Blend Foods	4110 W Wrightwood	Chicago	IL	60639	WA Stewart	312-489-2500	R	10	<0.1
Coffee Bean International Inc	2181 NW Nicolai St	Portland	OR	97210	Jim Myers	503-227-4490	R	10	<0.1
Woolson Spice Co	894 Queen St	Honolulu	HI	96813	James Delano	808-591-1199	R	8	<0.1
Dallis Brothers Coffee Company	100-30 Atlantic Av	Ozone Park	NY	11416	David Dallis	718-845-3010	R	7	<0.1
Lingle Brothers Coffee Inc	6500 S Garfield Av	Bell Gardens	CA	90201	James B Lingle	310-927-3317	R	7*	<0.1
Fairwinds Gourmet Coffee	17 Tinker Av	Londonderry	NH	03053	Dennis Boyer	603-262-0135	S	6*	<0.1
John Conti Coffee Co	4023 Bardstown Rd	Louisville	KY	40218	John Conti	502-499-8600	R	6*	<0.1
White Cloud	PO Box 1737	Boise	ID	83701	Jerome Eberharter	208-322-1166	R	6	<0.1
American Coffee Company Inc	PO Box 52018	New Orleans	LA	70152		504-581-7234	R	5	<0.1
Damron Corp	4433 W Ohio St	Chicago	IL	60624	Ronald E Damper	312-826-6000	R	5	<0.1
Old Mansion Foods Inc	PO Box 2026	Petersburg	VA	23803	D Patton	804-862-9889	R	5*	<0.1
Piacere International Inc	1101 Airway St	Glendale	CA	91201	Richard Forquer	818-240-7335	R	5	<0.1
SJ McCullagh Inc	245 Swan St	Buffalo	NY	14204	Warren Emblidge Jr	716-856-3473	R	5	0.1
Texas Coffee Co	PO Box 31	Beaumont	TX	77704	Carlo Busceme Jr	409-835-3434	R	5	<0.1
Andresen-Ryan Coffee Co	2206 Winter St	Superior	WI	54880	John C Andresen	715-392-4771	R	4*	<0.1
Cafe de Todd USA Inc	11600 Big John Blv	Houston	TX	77038	Dan Walton	713-445-6744	R	4	<0.1
Cameron Coffee Company Inc	PO Box 627	Hayward	WI	54843	James H Cameron	715-634-3646	R	4	<0.1
Kona Kai Farms	PO Box C	Kealakekua	HI	96750	Bob Rigley	808-323-2911	R	4	<0.1
Berardi's Fresh Roast Coffee Co	12126 York Rd	North Royalton	OH	44133	Michael P Caruso	216-582-4303	R	3	<0.1
Bargreen Coffee	2821 Rucker Av	Everett	WA	98201	Howie Bargreen	206-252-3161	R	2*	<0.1
Scottie MacBean Inc	660 High St	Worthington	OH	43085	Ronald M Kellogg	614-888-3494	R	2	<0.1
Arbuckle Coffee Co	441 Smithfield St	Pittsburgh	PA	15219	John Harvey	412-471-5225	R	1*	<0.1
Nicholas Coffee and Tea Co	23 Market Pl	Pittsburgh	PA	15201	Nicholas Nicholas	412-261-4225	S	1*	<0.1
Ryan Coffee Co	14444 Griffith St	San Leandro	CA	94577	Gregory B Ryan	510-357-1425	R	1*	<0.1
Campbell Coffee Roasting Co	1875 S Bascom Av	Campbell	CA	95008	Fred Naggar	408-559-8040	R	1*	<0.1
Elan Intern Organic Coffees	432 F St	San Diego	CA	92101	Karen Cebreros	619-239-8383	R	1*	<0.1

Source: Ward's Business Directory of U.S. Private and Public Companies, Volumes 1 and 2, 1996. The company type code used is as follows: P - Public, R - Private, S - Subsidiary, D - Division, J - Joint Venture, A - Affiliate, G - Group. Sales are in millions of dollars, employees are in thousands. An asterisk (*) indicates an estimated sales volume. The symbol < stands for 'less than'. Company names and addresses are truncated, in some cases, to fit into the available space.

MATERIALS CONSUMED

Material		Quantity	Delivered Cost ($ million)
Materials, ingredients, containers, and supplies		(X)	2,319.1
Green coffee	1,000 cwt	17,261.7**	1,698.4
Packaging paper and plastics film, coated and laminated		(X)	47.6
Bags; plastics, foil, and coated paper		(X)	56.6
Paperboard containers, boxes, and corrugated paperboard		(X)	60.3
Plastic containers and plastic can and jar lids		(X)	38.5
Glass containers		(X)	29.4
Metal cans, can lids and ends		(X)	166.2
All other materials and components, parts, containers, and supplies		(X)	165.3
Materials, ingredients, containers, and supplies, nsk		(X)	56.9

Source: 1992 *Economic Census*. Explanation of symbols used: (D): Withheld to avoid disclosure of competitive data; na: Not available; (S): Withheld because statistical norms were not met; (X): Not applicable; (Z): Less than half the unit shown; nec: Not elsewhere classified; nsk: Not specified by kind; - : zero; * : 10-19 percent estimated; ** : 20-29 percent estimated.

PRODUCT SHARE DETAILS

Product or Product Class	% Share	Product or Product Class	% Share
Roasted coffee	100.00	Roasted coffee, nsk	0.23
Roasted coffee	80.05	Coffee, concentrated (freeze-dried, spray-dried, frozen, or liquid concentrated or extracts, mixtures, etc.)	17.43
Whole bean roasted coffee	12.50	Roasted coffee, nsk	2.52
Ground roasted coffee (including extended yield)	86.90		
Ground roasted coffee mixtures (with grain, chicory, etc.)	0.37		

Source: 1992 *Economic Census*. The values shown are percent of total shipments in an industry. Values of indented subcategories are summed in the main heading. The symbol (D) appears when data are withheld to prevent disclosure of competitive information. The abbreviation nsk stands for 'not specified by kind' and nec for 'not elsewhere classified'.

INPUTS AND OUTPUTS FOR ROASTED COFFEE

Economic Sector or Industry Providing Inputs	%	Sector	Economic Sector or Industry Buying Outputs	%	Sector
Noncomparable imports	51.1	Foreign	Personal consumption expenditures	64.3	
Motor freight transportation & warehousing	15.4	Util.	Eating & drinking places	25.5	Trade
Wholesale trade	6.7	Trade	Hospitals	3.1	Services
Metal cans	5.7	Manufg.	Exports	2.2	Foreign
Water transportation	3.3	Util.	S/L Govt. purch., health & hospitals	1.4	S/L Govt
Imports	3.3	Foreign	Nursing & personal care facilities	0.6	Services
Miscellaneous plastics products	3.2	Manufg.	Motion pictures	0.5	Services
Advertising	2.0	Services	Residential care	0.4	Services
Commercial printing	1.9	Manufg.	Social services, nec	0.4	Services
Glass containers	1.0	Manufg.	Federal Government enterprises nec	0.4	Gov't
Paperboard containers & boxes	1.0	Manufg.	Change in business inventories	0.3	In House
Crowns & closures	0.6	Manufg.	S/L Govt. purch., correction	0.2	S/L Govt
Electric services (utilities)	0.6	Util.	S/L Govt. purch., higher education	0.2	S/L Govt
Banking	0.6	Fin/R.E.	Amusement & recreation services nec	0.1	Services
Cyclic crudes and organics	0.4	Manufg.			
Gas production & distribution (utilities)	0.4	Util.			
Petroleum refining	0.3	Manufg.			
Rubber & plastics hose & belting	0.3	Manufg.			
Paper coating & glazing	0.2	Manufg.			
Miscellaneous crops	0.1	Agric.			
Industrial gases	0.1	Manufg.			
Communications, except radio & TV	0.1	Util.			
Railroads & related services	0.1	Util.			
Royalties	0.1	Fin/R.E.			
U.S. Postal Service	0.1	Gov't			

Source: Benchmark Input-Output Accounts for the U.S. Economy, 1982, U.S. Department of Commerce, Washington, D.C., July 1991. Data, as reported in the source, are organized by the 1977 SIC structure in use in 1982 but have been matched, as closely as is possible, to the 1987 SIC structure used in this book.

OCCUPATIONS EMPLOYED BY SIC 209 - MISCELLANEOUS FOODS AND KINDRED PRODUCTS

Occupation	% of Total 1994	Change to 2005	Occupation	% of Total 1994	Change to 2005
Cannery workers	10.4	26.3	Machine feeders & offbearers	1.9	3.3
Packaging & filling machine operators	8.7	26.3	Industrial truck & tractor operators	1.9	14.8
Hand packers & packagers	8.0	-1.6	Janitors & cleaners, incl maids	1.7	-8.2
Helpers, laborers, & material movers nec	6.7	14.8	Bakers, manufacturing	1.7	35.9
Meat, poultry, & fish cutters & trimmers, hand	5.8	14.8	Maintenance repairers, general utility	1.5	3.3
Cooking, roasting machine operators	3.4	26.3	Inspectors, testers, & graders, precision	1.5	14.8
Truck drivers light & heavy	3.2	18.3	Agricultural workers nec	1.3	14.8
Driver/sales workers	2.8	3.3	Industrial production managers	1.3	14.8
General managers & top executives	2.2	8.9	Bookkeeping, accounting, & auditing clerks	1.2	-13.9
Industrial machinery mechanics	2.2	26.2	Traffic, shipping, & receiving clerks	1.2	10.5
Precision food & tobacco workers nec	2.2	14.8	Secretaries, ex legal & medical	1.2	4.5
Freight, stock, & material movers, hand	2.1	-8.2	Extruding & forming machine workers	1.2	26.3
Crushing & mixing machine operators	2.0	14.8	Butchers & meatcutters	1.2	27.4
Assemblers, fabricators, & hand workers nec	2.0	14.8	General office clerks	1.1	-2.1
Sales & related workers nec	1.9	14.8			

Source: Industry-Occupation Matrix, Bureau of Labor Statistics. These data relate to one or more 3-digit SIC industry groups rather than to a single 4-digit SIC. The change reported for each occupation to the year 2005 is a percent of growth or decline as estimated by the Bureau of Labor Statistics. The abbreviation nec stands for 'not elsewhere classified'.

LOCATION BY STATE AND REGIONAL CONCENTRATION

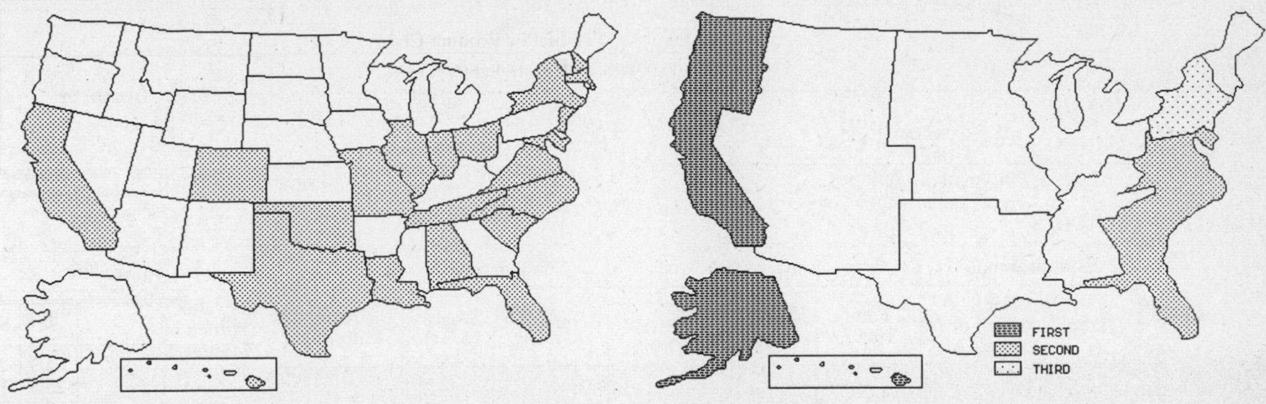

INDUSTRY DATA BY STATE

State	Establish-ments	Shipments			Employment				Cost as % of Shipments	Investment per Employee ($)
		Total ($ mil)	% of U.S.	Per Establ.	Total Number	% of U.S.	Per Establ.	Wages ($/hour)		
Texas	7	971.7	18.4	138.8	1,400	13.3	200	17.64	48.4	-
California	31	956.1	18.1	30.8	1,400	13.3	45	15.50	46.1	11,786
Louisiana	8	727.0	13.7	90.9	800	7.6	100	13.15	39.1	-
Florida	14	522.7	9.9	37.3	700	6.7	50	11.70	46.8	-
New Jersey	9	385.3	7.3	42.8	1,200	11.4	133	15.73	59.0	13,333
Ohio	8	163.8	3.1	20.5	400	3.8	50	14.40	59.5	-
New York	15	162.5	3.1	10.8	600	5.7	40	11.67	49.6	4,833
Illinois	9	154.1	2.9	17.1	500	4.8	56	12.29	70.1	4,000
Massachusetts	3	72.4	1.4	24.1	300	2.9	100	10.00	70.4	-
Maryland	3	55.6	1.1	18.5	100	1.0	33	6.33	51.6	11,000
Missouri	8	(D)	-	-	375 *	3.6	47	-	-	9,867
Colorado	5	(D)	-	-	175 *	1.7	35	-	-	-
Hawaii	5	(D)	-	-	175 *	1.7	35	-	-	-
Virginia	4	(D)	-	-	375 *	3.6	94	-	-	-
Tennessee	3	(D)	-	-	175 *	1.7	58	-	-	-
Indiana	2	(D)	-	-	175 *	1.7	88	-	-	-
North Carolina	2	(D)	-	-	375 *	3.6	188	-	-	-
South Carolina	2	(D)	-	-	175 *	1.7	88	-	-	-
Alabama	1	(D)	-	-	375 *	3.6	375	-	-	-
New Hampshire	1	(D)	-	-	175 *	1.7	175	-	-	-
Oklahoma	1	(D)	-	-	175 *	1.7	175	-	-	-

Source: 1992 *Economic Census*. The states are in descending order of shipments or establishments (if shipment data are missing for the majority). The symbol (D) appears when data are withheld to prevent disclosure of competitive information. States marked with (D) are sorted by number of establishments. A dash (-) indicates that the data element cannot be calculated; * indicates the midpoint of a range.

2096 - POTATO CHIPS, CORN CHIPS & SNACKS

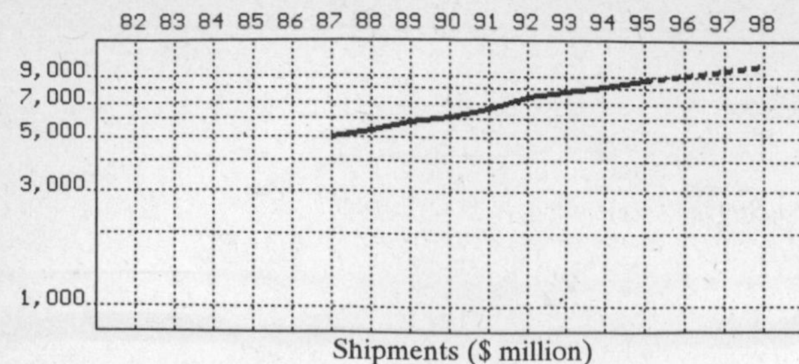

Shipments ($ million)

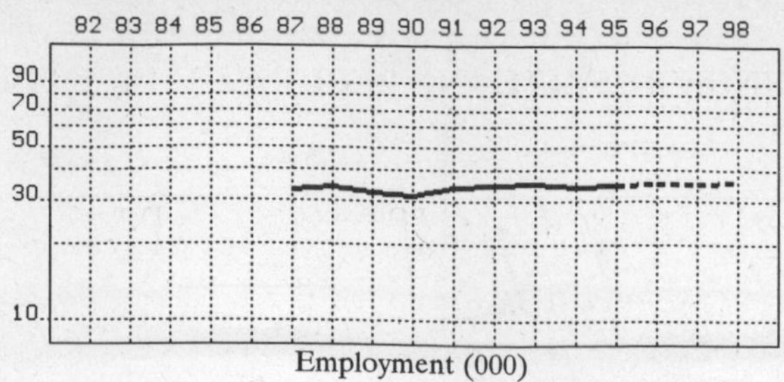

Employment (000)

GENERAL STATISTICS

Year	Companies	Establishments: Total	Establishments: with 20 or more employees	Employment: Total (000)	Employment: Production Workers (000)	Employment: Production Hours (Mil)	Compensation: Payroll ($ mil)	Compensation: Wages ($/hr)	Production ($ million): Cost of Materials	Production ($ million): Value Added by Manufacture	Production ($ million): Value of Shipments	Production ($ million): Capital Invest.
1982												
1983												
1984												
1985												
1986												
1987	273	343	183	33.0	23.2	38.6	622.1	9.72	1,749.3	3,299.6	5,038.6	181.3
1988		359	185	34.1	24.0	39.8	653.0	9.73	1,905.5	3,474.4	5,384.9	102.6
1989		343	186	32.4	23.8	39.4	640.5	9.24	3,187.1	2,608.1	5,788.8	125.9
1990		332	193	31.7	21.4	42.0	696.5	9.08	3,156.2	2,906.3	6,062.1	161.7
1991		351	204	34.0	22.9	42.5	767.0	10.08	3,537.5	3,108.3	6,646.4	189.2
1992	334	409	215	34.9	24.1	45.7	828.8	10.35	3,409.2	3,912.8	7,324.7	259.1
1993		404	216	35.1	24.3	45.9	857.3	10.56	3,406.7	4,335.0	7,734.6	250.1
1994		405P	223P	34.3	23.2	44.4	879.6	11.00	2,770.1	5,405.2	8,167.3	273.0
1995		415P	229P	35.0P	23.6P	47.1P	928.4P	10.90P	2,916.6P	5,691.0P	8,599.2P	289.6P
1996		425P	235P	35.3P	23.6P	48.2P	969.6P	11.11P	3,073.4P	5,997.1P	9,061.6P	311.1P
1997		436P	242P	35.5P	23.7P	49.3P	1,010.8P	11.32P	3,230.3P	6,303.1P	9,524.0P	332.7P
1998		446P	248P	35.8P	23.7P	50.4P	1,052.0P	11.53P	3,387.1P	6,609.1P	9,986.4P	354.2P

Sources: 1982, 1987, 1992 *Economic Census*; *Annual Survey of Manufactures*, 83-86, 88-91, 93-94. Establishment counts for non-Census years are from *County Business Patterns*; establishment values for 83-84 are extrapolations. 'P's show projections by the editors. Industries reclassified in 87 will not have data for prior years.

INDICES OF CHANGE

Year	Companies	Establishments: Total	Establishments: with 20 or more employees	Employment: Total (000)	Employment: Production Workers (000)	Employment: Production Hours (Mil)	Compensation: Payroll ($ mil)	Compensation: Wages ($/hr)	Production ($ million): Cost of Materials	Production ($ million): Value Added by Manufacture	Production ($ million): Value of Shipments	Production ($ million): Capital Invest.
1982												
1983												
1984												
1985												
1986												
1987	82	84	85	95	96	84	75	94	51	84	69	70
1988		88	86	98	100	87	79	94	56	89	74	40
1989		84	87	93	99	86	77	89	93	67	79	49
1990		81	90	91	89	92	84	88	93	74	83	62
1991		86	95	97	95	93	93	97	104	79	91	73
1992	100	100	100	100	100	100	100	100	100	100	100	100
1993		99	100	101	101	100	103	102	100	111	106	97
1994		99P	104P	98	96	97	106	106	81	138	112	105
1995		101P	107P	100P	98P	103P	112P	105P	86P	145P	117P	112P
1996		104P	109P	101P	98P	105P	117P	107P	90P	153P	124P	120P
1997		107P	112P	102P	98P	108P	122P	109P	95P	161P	130P	128P
1998		109P	115P	103P	98P	110P	127P	111P	99P	169P	136P	137P

Sources: Same as General Statistics. Values reflect change from the base year, 1992. Values above 100 mean greater than 92, values below 100 mean less than 92, and a value of 100 in the 82-91 or 93-98 period means same as 92. 'P's mark projections by the editors.

SELECTED RATIOS

For 1994	Avg. of All Manufact.	Analyzed Industry	Index
Employees per Establishment	49	85	173
Payroll per Establishment	1,500,273	2,174,153	145
Payroll per Employee	30,620	25,644	84
Production Workers per Establishment	34	57	167
Wages per Establishment	853,319	1,207,203	141
Wages per Production Worker	24,861	21,052	85
Hours per Production Worker	2,056	1,914	93
Wages per Hour	12.09	11.00	91
Value Added per Establishment	4,602,255	13,360,311	290
Value Added per Employee	93,930	157,586	168

For 1994	Avg. of All Manufact.	Analyzed Industry	Index
Value Added per Production Worker	134,084	232,983	174
Cost per Establishment	5,045,178	6,846,999	136
Cost per Employee	102,970	80,761	78
Cost per Production Worker	146,988	119,401	81
Shipments per Establishment	9,576,895	20,187,535	211
Shipments per Employee	195,460	238,114	122
Shipments per Production Worker	279,017	352,039	126
Investment per Establishment	321,011	674,788	210
Investment per Employee	6,552	7,959	121
Investment per Production Worker	9,352	11,767	126

Sources: Same as General Statistics. The 'Average of All Manufacturing' column represents the average of all manufacturing industries reported for the most recent complete year available. The Index shows the relationship between the Average and the Analyzed Industry. For example, 100 means that they are equal; 500 that the Analyzed Industry is five times the average; 50 means that the Analyzed Industry is half the national average. The abbreviation 'na' is used to show that data are 'not available'.

LEADING COMPANIES

Number shown: **51** Total sales ($ mil): **7,118** Total employment (000): **48.4**

Company Name	Address				CEO Name	Phone	Co. Type	Sales ($ mil)	Empl. (000)
Frito-Lay Inc	PO Box 66034	Dallas	TX	75266	Steven S Reiemund	214-334-7000	S	4,400	30.0
Frito-Lay Inc	105 College Rd E	Princeton	NJ	08540	John Spooner	609-734-6200	D	1,102	4.5
Mission Foods Corp	5445 E Olympic	Los Angeles	CA	90022	Mike Bailey	213-887-6600	R	240	1.3
Golden Flake Snack Foods Inc	PO Box 2447	Birmingham	AL	35201	Wayne Pate	205-323-6161	S	127	1.4
Snyder's of Hanover Inc	PO Box 917	Hanover	PA	17331	John Denton	717-632-4477	R	113	0.8
Herr Foods Inc	PO Box 300	Nottingham	PA	19362	James M Herr	215-932-9330	R	100	1.0
Jays Foods LLC	825 E 99th St	Chicago	IL	60628	Len Japp	312-731-8400	R	95	0.4
Laura Scudder's	PO Box 620	Salt Lake City	UT	84145	Carl Caughran	801-534-4000	R	85	0.8
Guy's Foods Inc	405 S Leonard St	Liberty	MO	64068	Vic Sabatino	816-781-6700	S	68	0.6
Clover Club Foods Co	200 North	Salt Lake City	UT	84110	Carl Caughran	801-531-9848	S	58	0.8
Snyder of Berlin	PO Box 220	Berlin	PA	15530	Michael Gaffney	814-267-4641	D	58	0.4
Wyandot Inc	135 Wyandot Av	Marion	OH	43302	D Warren Brown	614-383-4031	R	58*	0.5
CJ Vitner Company Inc	4202 W 45th St	Chicago	IL	60632	William A Vitner	312-523-7900	R	48	0.4
Seyfert Foods Inc	PO Box 8606	Fort Wayne	IN	46898	Larry L	219-483-9521	R	41	0.5
Troyer Potato Products Inc	PO Box 676	Waterford	PA	16441	Cliff Troyer	814-796-2611	R	41*	0.5
Country Club Foods Inc	1809 S 900 W	Salt Lake City	UT	84104	J Myron Walker	801-972-2555	R	38	0.3
Bon Ton Foods Inc	1120 Zinns Quarry	York	PA	17404	Jim Quellette	717-843-0026	R	36	0.2
Barrel O'Fun Snack Foods Co	PO Box L	Perham	MN	56573	Ken Nelson	218-346-7000	R	35	0.4
Husman Snack Foods Co	1621 Moore St	Cincinnati	OH	45210	David Ray	513-621-5614	S	32	0.2
Moore's Quality Snack Foods	PO Box 1909	Bristol	VA	24203	C Stephen Cregg	703-669-6194	D	30*	0.7
Pacific Snax Corp	1 Civic Plz	Newport Beach	CA	92660	Richard Damion	714-640-4111	P	22	0.1
Romero Foods Inc	15155 Val View Av	Santa Fe Sprgs	CA	90670	Leon Romero	310-802-1858	R	22*	0.2
McCleary Industries Inc	PO Box 187	South Beloit	IL	61080	Pat McCleary	815-389-3053	R	20	0.2
Christie Brown and Co	51 Gibraltar Dr	Morris Plains	NJ	07950		201-984-8086	D	20	<0.1
State Line Snacks Corp	2535 Boston Rd	Wilbraham	MA	01095	William J Salmon	413-596-8331	R	20	0.3
Guiltless Gourmet Inc	3709 Promontory Pt	Austin	TX	78744	John Oudt	512-443-4373	R	19	<0.1
Nally's US Chips and Snacks	PO Box 11046	Tacoma	WA	98411	Helen Whatmough	206-383-1621	D	18	0.2
Nibble with Gibble's Inc	6647 Molly Pitcher	Chambersburg	PA	17201	Robert N Feulner	717-375-2243	R	18	0.2
Husman Snackfoods	1621 Moore St	Cincinnati	OH	45210	David Ray	513-621-5614	D	15	0.2
Boyd Acquisitions Inc	PO Box 550	Lynn	MA	01903	Willis Burbank	617-593-4422	R	12*	0.1
Pate Foods Corp	1455 Gardner St	South Beloit	IL	61080	Larry Polhill	815-389-3426	S	12	0.1
Valley Grain Products/ADM	PO Box 1107	Madera	CA	93639	Jack Rew	209-675-3400	S	12*	0.1
Cross and Peters Co	10148 Gratiot Av	Detroit	MI	48213	Robert Marracino	313-925-4774	R	11*	0.1
Natural Nectar Corp	16010 Phoenix Dr	City of Industry	CA	91748	Robert Tepper	818-913-5880	R	11*	0.1
Kennedy Endeavors Inc	PO Box 2302	Auburn	WA	98071	Helen Whatmough	206-833-0255	D	10*	<0.1
Wachusett Potato Chip Company	759 Water St	Fitchburg	MA	01420	E Krysiak	508-342-6038	R	10	<0.1
Terry's Snack Foods Inc	1400 Newton St	Bristol	VA	24201	John R Terry	703-669-8149	R	9*	0.2
Vincent Potato Chip Co	205 Highland Av	Salem	MA	01970	Thomas G Voyer	508-745-1505	R	9	<0.1
Herr's Potato Chips	476 E 7th St	Chillicothe	OH	45601		614-773-8282	D	8	<0.1
Ira Middleswarth and Son Inc	PO Box 354	Middleburg	PA	17842	B Middleswarth	717-837-1431	R	7	<0.1
Bob's Texas Style Potato Chips	PO Box 66A	Brookshire	TX	77423	Bob Rod	713-391-8903	S	5	<0.1
Great Western Tortilla Co	1761 E 58th Av	Denver	CO	80216	Rally Ralston	303-298-0705	R	5	<0.1
Natural Choices Inc	2101 Com NE	Albuquerque	NM	87102	Hal Newman	505-242-3494	R	3	<0.1
Dennis Inc	Stratford Park	Winston-Salem	NC	27113	Henry B Dennis Jr	919-765-8280	R	3	<0.1
Vegas Chips Inc	2945 N ML King	N Las Vegas	NV	89030	Milton Rudnick	702-647-3800	P	3	<0.1
Tri-Sum Potato Chip Company	68 Cedar St	Leominster	MA	01453	R R Duchesneau	508-537-4088	R	3	<0.1
Happy's Potato Chip Co	3900 Chandler Dr	Minneapolis	MN	55421	Bob Bemmels	612-781-3121	R	2*	<0.1
Pisciotta Inc	860 E 46th St	Tucson	AZ	85713	Ray Pisciotta	602-884-8049	R	2	<0.1
Noahs Potato Chip Company Inc	PO Box 5132	Alexandria	LA	71307	S Bohrer	318-445-0283	R	1*	<0.1
Terra Prima Inc	221 Monroe St N	Hudson	WI	54016	Chuck Walker	715-381-1336	R	1	<0.1
Prince Potato Chip Co	21000 Coolidge Hwy	Oak Park	MI	48237	Susan J Bricker	810-399-9908	R	1*	<0.1

Source: *Ward's Business Directory of U.S. Private and Public Companies*, Volumes 1 and 2, 1996. The company type code used is as follows: P - Public, R - Private, S - Subsidiary, D - Division, J - Joint Venture, A - Affiliate, G - Group. Sales are in millions of dollars, employees are in thousands. An asterisk (*) indicates an estimated sales volume. The symbol < stands for 'less than'. Company names and addresses are truncated, in some cases, to fit into the available space.

MATERIALS CONSUMED

Material		Quantity	Delivered Cost ($ million)
Materials, ingredients, containers, and supplies		(X)	3,144.6
Shelled peanuts	mil lb	29.3	10.0
Sweetcorn, fresh or frozen	1,000 s tons	(D)	(D)
Field corn, whole grain	mil lb	529.6	85.9
White potatoes	1,000 s tons	4,366.0	658.5
Dried vegetables, except potatoes and corn	1,000 s tons	(D)	(D)
Popcorn, whole grain	mil lb	135.1	17.6
Corn grits, meal, and flakes	1,000 cwt	(D)	(D)
Corn flour	1,000 cwt	744.2	128.7
Wheat flour	1,000 cwt	712.8*	10.3
Spices, raw	mil lb	14.3*	12.9
Corn syrup	mil lb	(D)	(D)
Sugar, cane and beet (in terms of sugar solids)	1,000 s tons	3.0	1.7
Fats and oils, all types (purchased as such)	mil lb	958.6	279.0
Paperboard containers, boxes, and corrugated paperboard		(X)	173.8
Packaging paper and plastics film, coated and laminated		(X)	370.3
Bags; plastics, foil, and coated paper		(X)	54.7
Bags; uncoated paper and multiwall		(X)	(D)
Glass containers		(X)	0.2
Metal cans, can lids and ends		(X)	28.4
All other materials and components, parts, containers, and supplies		(X)	840.2
Materials, ingredients, containers, and supplies, nsk		(X)	111.4

Source: 1992 *Economic Census*. Explanation of symbols used: (D): Withheld to avoid disclosure of competitive data; na: Not available; (S): Withheld because statistical norms were not met; (X): Not applicable; (Z): Less than half the unit shown; nec: Not elsewhere classified; nsk: Not specified by kind; - : zero; * : 10-19 percent estimated; ** : 20-29 percent estimated.

PRODUCT SHARE DETAILS

Product or Product Class	% Share	Product or Product Class	% Share
Potato chips and similar products	100.00	Corn chips and related products, nsk	0.05
Potato chips and sticks, plain and flavored	43.26	Other chips, sticks, etc. (bacon rinds, popcorn (except candied), etc.), excluding crackers, pretzels, and nuts	14.20
Corn chips and related products	40.09	Potato chips and similar products, nsk	2.45
Corn chips	75.83		
Corn curls and related products	24.12		

Source: 1992 *Economic Census*. The values shown are percent of total shipments in an industry. Values of indented subcategories are summed in the main heading. The symbol (D) appears when data are withheld to prevent disclosure of competitive information. The abbreviation nsk stands for 'not specified by kind' and nec for 'not elsewhere classified'.

INPUTS AND OUTPUTS FOR FOOD PREPARATIONS, NEC

Economic Sector or Industry Providing Inputs	%	Sector	Economic Sector or Industry Buying Outputs	%	Sector
Miscellaneous plastics products	11.8	Manufg.	Personal consumption expenditures	75.9	
Wholesale trade	11.6	Trade	Eating & drinking places	10.8	Trade
Imports	8.7	Foreign	Exports	1.6	Foreign
Cyclic crudes and organics	5.8	Manufg.	Bread, cake, & related products	1.1	Manufg.
Noncomparable imports	4.0	Foreign	Fluid milk	1.1	Manufg.
Paper coating & glazing	3.9	Manufg.	Sausages & other prepared meats	1.1	Manufg.
Oil bearing crops	3.8	Agric.	Change in business inventories	1.1	In House
Paperboard containers & boxes	3.8	Manufg.	Ice cream & frozen desserts	0.8	Manufg.
Vegetables	3.6	Agric.	Meat packing plants	0.6	Manufg.
Advertising	3.2	Services	Motion pictures	0.6	Services
Motor freight transportation & warehousing	2.9	Util.	Hospitals	0.5	Services
Shortening & cooking oils	2.8	Manufg.	Federal Government purchases, nondefense	0.5	Fed Govt
Glass containers	2.5	Manufg.	Confectionery products	0.4	Manufg.
Sugar	2.2	Manufg.	Residential care	0.4	Services
Commercial printing	2.1	Manufg.	Food preparations, nec	0.3	Manufg.
Bags, except textile	1.9	Manufg.	Pickles, sauces, & salad dressings	0.3	Manufg.
Miscellaneous livestock	1.2	Agric.	Canned fruits & vegetables	0.2	Manufg.
Metal cans	1.2	Manufg.	Frozen specialties	0.2	Manufg.
Electric services (utilities)	1.2	Util.	Prepared feeds, nec	0.2	Manufg.
Miscellaneous crops	1.1	Agric.	Nursing & personal care facilities	0.2	Services
Metal foil & leaf	1.1	Manufg.	Social services, nec	0.2	Services
Gas production & distribution (utilities)	1.1	Util.	S/L Govt. purch., elem. & secondary education	0.2	S/L Govt
Flour & other grain mill products	1.0	Manufg.	S/L Govt. purch., health & hospitals	0.2	S/L Govt
Forestry products	0.9	Agric.	S/L Govt. purch., higher education	0.2	S/L Govt
Feed grains	0.8	Agric.	Cheese, natural & processed	0.1	Manufg.
Eating & drinking places	0.8	Trade	Cookies & crackers	0.1	Manufg.
Chemical preparations, nec	0.7	Manufg.	Federal Government enterprises nec	0.1	Gov't
Cottonseed oil mills	0.7	Manufg.	Federal Government purchases, national defense	0.1	Fed Govt
Industrial inorganic chemicals, nec	0.7	Manufg.			
Railroads & related services	0.7	Util.			
Water transportation	0.7	Util.			

Continued on next page.

INPUTS AND OUTPUTS FOR FOOD PREPARATIONS, NEC - Continued

Economic Sector or Industry Providing Inputs	%	Sector	Economic Sector or Industry Buying Outputs	%	Sector
Business services nec	0.7	Services			
Chocolate & cocoa products	0.5	Manufg.			
Food preparations, nec	0.5	Manufg.			
Wet corn milling	0.5	Manufg.			
Banking	0.5	Fin/R.E.			
Bread, cake, & related products	0.4	Manufg.			
Crowns & closures	0.4	Manufg.			
Dehydrated food products	0.4	Manufg.			
Communications, except radio & TV	0.4	Util.			
Electrical repair shops	0.4	Services			
Maintenance of nonfarm buildings nec	0.3	Constr.			
Cheese, natural & processed	0.3	Manufg.			
Flavoring extracts & syrups, nec	0.3	Manufg.			
Petroleum refining	0.3	Manufg.			
Real estate	0.3	Fin/R.E.			
Equipment rental & leasing services	0.3	Services			
Legal services	0.3	Services			
Management & consulting services & labs	0.3	Services			
U.S. Postal Service	0.3	Gov't			
Sugar crops	0.2	Agric.			
Creamery butter	0.2	Manufg.			
Soybean oil mills	0.2	Manufg.			
Air transportation	0.2	Util.			
Sanitary services, steam supply, irrigation	0.2	Util.			
Royalties	0.2	Fin/R.E.			
Accounting, auditing & bookkeeping	0.2	Services			
Detective & protective services	0.2	Services			
State & local government enterprises, nec	0.2	Gov't			
Alkalies & chlorine	0.1	Manufg.			
Bottled & canned soft drinks	0.1	Manufg.			
Food products machinery	0.1	Manufg.			
Lubricating oils & greases	0.1	Manufg.			
Machinery, except electrical, nec	0.1	Manufg.			
Poultry & egg processing	0.1	Manufg.			
Water supply & sewage systems	0.1	Util.			
Business/professional associations	0.1	Services			
Miscellaneous repair shops	0.1	Services			

Source: Benchmark Input-Output Accounts for the U.S. Economy, 1982, U.S. Department of Commerce, Washington, D.C., July 1991. Data, as reported in the source, are organized by the 1977 SIC structure in use in 1982 but have been matched, as closely as is possible, to the 1987 SIC structure used in this book.

OCCUPATIONS EMPLOYED BY SIC 209 - MISCELLANEOUS FOODS AND KINDRED PRODUCTS

Occupation	% of Total 1994	Change to 2005	Occupation	% of Total 1994	Change to 2005
Cannery workers	10.4	26.3	Machine feeders & offbearers	1.9	3.3
Packaging & filling machine operators	8.7	26.3	Industrial truck & tractor operators	1.9	14.8
Hand packers & packagers	8.0	-1.6	Janitors & cleaners, incl maids	1.7	-8.2
Helpers, laborers, & material movers nec	6.7	14.8	Bakers, manufacturing	1.7	35.9
Meat, poultry, & fish cutters & trimmers, hand	5.8	14.8	Maintenance repairers, general utility	1.5	3.3
Cooking, roasting machine operators	3.4	26.3	Inspectors, testers, & graders, precision	1.5	14.8
Truck drivers light & heavy	3.2	18.3	Agricultural workers nec	1.3	14.8
Driver/sales workers	2.8	3.3	Industrial production managers	1.3	14.8
General managers & top executives	2.2	8.9	Bookkeeping, accounting, & auditing clerks	1.2	-13.9
Industrial machinery mechanics	2.2	26.2	Traffic, shipping, & receiving clerks	1.2	10.5
Precision food & tobacco workers nec	2.2	14.8	Secretaries, ex legal & medical	1.2	4.5
Freight, stock, & material movers, hand	2.1	-8.2	Extruding & forming machine workers	1.2	26.3
Crushing & mixing machine operators	2.0	14.8	Butchers & meatcutters	1.2	27.4
Assemblers, fabricators, & hand workers nec	2.0	14.8	General office clerks	1.1	-2.1
Sales & related workers nec	1.9	14.8			

Source: Industry-Occupation Matrix, Bureau of Labor Statistics. These data relate to one or more 3-digit SIC industry groups rather than to a single 4-digit SIC. The change reported for each occupation to the year 2005 is a percent of growth or decline as estimated by the Bureau of Labor Statistics. The abbreviation nec stands for 'not elsewhere classified'.

LOCATION BY STATE AND REGIONAL CONCENTRATION

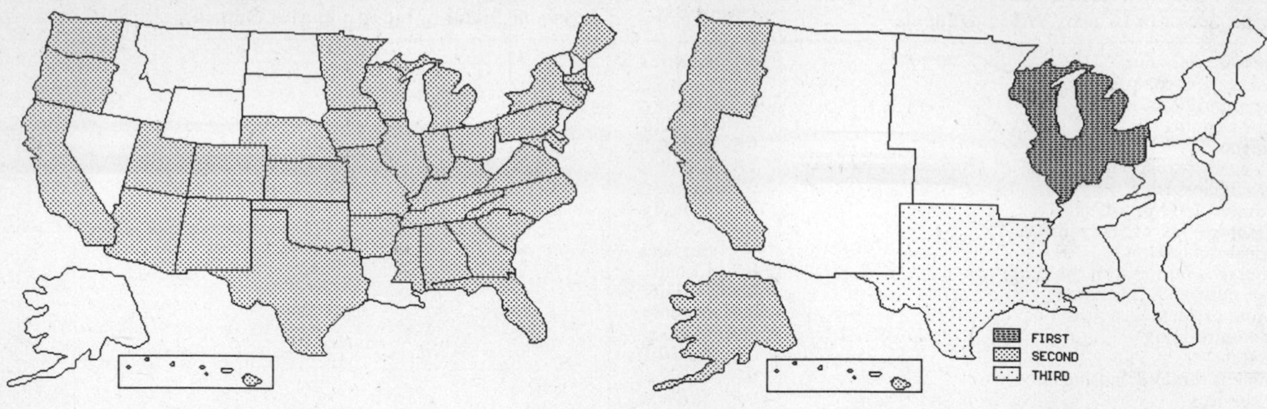

INDUSTRY DATA BY STATE

State	Establish-ments	Shipments			Employment				Cost as % of Shipments	Investment per Employee ($)
		Total ($ mil)	% of U.S.	Per Establ.	Total Number	% of U.S.	Per Establ.	Wages ($/hour)		
Texas	56	890.4	12.2	15.9	3,100	8.9	55	11.18	44.4	-
Pennsylvania	36	814.4	11.1	22.6	5,200	14.9	144	9.71	43.4	4,904
California	54	732.9	10.0	13.6	3,600	10.3	67	11.28	50.1	3,306
Indiana	12	559.4	7.6	46.6	2,000	5.7	167	11.40	43.3	-
Tennessee	9	403.1	5.5	44.8	1,300	3.7	144	11.00	51.6	-
Ohio	27	301.5	4.1	11.2	1,600	4.6	59	10.05	52.1	4,625
Florida	10	181.2	2.5	18.1	800	2.3	80	10.25	52.3	-
Michigan	14	171.9	2.3	12.3	900	2.6	64	13.08	48.9	7,333
Illinois	22	160.5	2.2	7.3	1,100	3.2	50	7.53	50.8	9,636
Kentucky	6	146.4	2.0	24.4	800	2.3	133	8.69	47.3	8,000
Arizona	10	122.8	1.7	12.3	600	1.7	60	10.75	31.7	-
Colorado	11	88.6	1.2	8.1	400	1.1	36	9.50	51.6	-
Oregon	4	72.0	1.0	18.0	500	1.4	125	9.40	51.4	-
Massachusetts	10	67.9	0.9	6.8	600	1.7	60	9.67	45.4	1,833
Iowa	9	62.6	0.9	7.0	400	1.1	44	8.25	26.4	-
Nebraska	4	26.7	0.4	6.7	200	0.6	50	8.00	45.3	-
Hawaii	5	15.7	0.2	3.1	200	0.6	40	10.50	29.3	-
New York	14	(D)	-	-	750 *	2.1	54	-	-	4,800
Wisconsin	12	(D)	-	-	750 *	2.1	63	-	-	-
Missouri	8	(D)	-	-	750 *	2.1	94	-	-	-
North Carolina	8	(D)	-	-	1,750 *	5.0	219	-	-	-
Georgia	6	(D)	-	-	750 *	2.1	125	-	-	-
Kansas	6	(D)	-	-	750 *	2.1	125	-	-	-
Minnesota	5	(D)	-	-	750 *	2.1	150	-	-	-
Washington	5	(D)	-	-	750 *	2.1	150	-	-	-
New Mexico	4	(D)	-	-	175 *	0.5	44	-	-	-
Utah	4	(D)	-	-	375 *	1.1	94	-	-	-
Virginia	4	(D)	-	-	750 *	2.1	188	-	-	-
Arkansas	3	(D)	-	-	375 *	1.1	125	-	-	-
Mississippi	3	(D)	-	-	375 *	1.1	125	-	-	-
Alabama	2	(D)	-	-	1,750 *	5.0	875	-	-	-
Connecticut	2	(D)	-	-	750 *	2.1	375	-	-	-
Maine	2	(D)	-	-	175 *	0.5	88	-	-	-
Maryland	2	(D)	-	-	175 *	0.5	88	-	-	-
Oklahoma	2	(D)	-	-	175 *	0.5	88	-	-	-
South Carolina	1	(D)	-	-	375 *	1.1	375	-	-	-

Source: 1992 *Economic Census*. The states are in descending order of shipments or establishments (if shipment data are missing for the majority). The symbol (D) appears when data are withheld to prevent disclosure of competitive information. States marked with (D) are sorted by number of establishments. A dash (-) indicates that the data element cannot be calculated; * indicates the midpoint of a range.

2097 - MANUFACTURED ICE

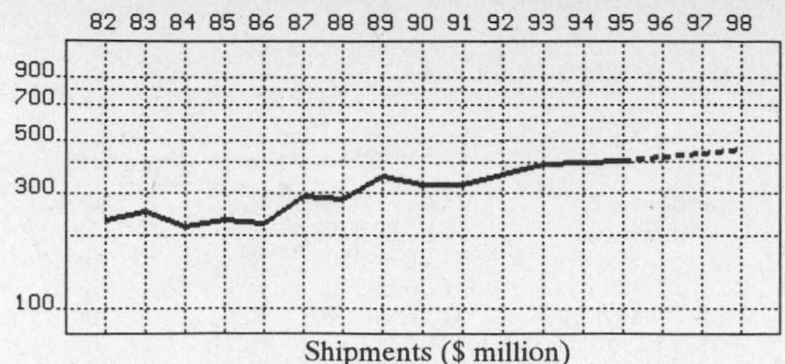

Shipments ($ million)

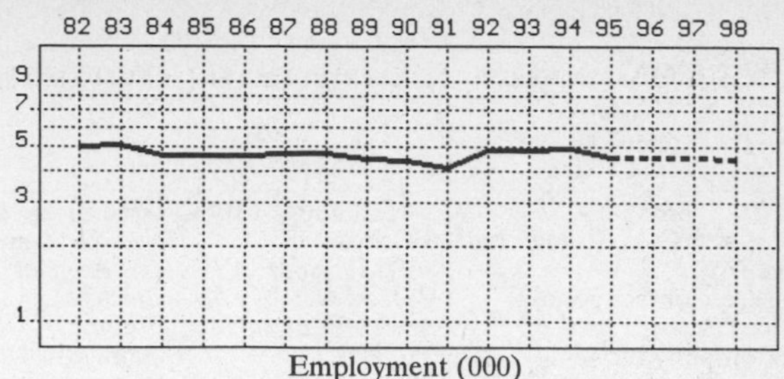

Employment (000)

GENERAL STATISTICS

Year	Companies	Establishments Total	Establishments with 20 or more employees	Employment Total (000)	Production Workers (000)	Production Hours (Mil)	Compensation Payroll ($ mil)	Compensation Wages ($/hr)	Cost of Materials	Value Added by Manufacture	Value of Shipments	Capital Invest.
1982	530	596	64	5.0	3.0	5.5	65.1	6.53	79.0	152.6	229.5	13.4
1983		578	58	5.1	2.7	4.9	66.7	7.67	82.5	172.3	252.0	8.7
1984		560	52	4.6	2.4	3.6	69.1	9.64	71.6	144.2	217.1	26.3
1985		541	47	4.6	2.2	3.8	69.4	9.26	79.7	151.1	230.9	32.1
1986		528	52	4.6	2.6	4.3	65.9	8.51	75.0	148.5	223.6	19.8
1987	502	549	65	4.7	2.8	5.9	77.0	7.08	86.7	202.9	289.6	14.0
1988		517	47	4.7	2.7	5.9	83.1	7.41	71.6	209.0	280.7	9.9
1989		494	47	4.5	3.2	6.1	94.7	9.72	96.4	261.8	355.4	18.0
1990		489	57	4.4	3.0	6.1	78.1	7.74	89.2	238.0	326.7	29.8
1991		508	57	4.1	2.9	6.1	77.2	7.57	81.9	241.1	324.0	21.0
1992	513	562	59	4.8	2.9	6.1	93.3	7.93	103.6	255.1	358.8	13.8
1993		556	61	4.8	3.0	6.1	97.4	8.00	113.8	278.2	394.4	21.4
1994		509P	56P	4.9	2.9	6.1	99.4	8.03	118.2	280.2	398.4	30.3
1995		505P	56P	4.5P	3.0P	6.6P	99.8P	8.08P	121.0P	286.9P	407.9P	23.9P
1996		500P	56P	4.5P	3.1P	6.8P	102.7P	8.08P	125.7P	297.9P	423.5P	24.5P
1997		495P	56P	4.5P	3.1P	6.9P	105.5P	8.08P	130.3P	308.9P	439.2P	25.1P
1998		491P	57P	4.5P	3.1P	7.1P	108.4P	8.08P	134.9P	319.9P	454.8P	25.7P

Sources: 1982, 1987, 1992 *Economic Census*; *Annual Survey of Manufactures*, 83-86, 88-91, 93-94. Establishment counts for non-Census years are from *County Business Patterns*; establishment values for 83-84 are extrapolations. 'P's show projections by the editors. Industries reclassified in 87 will not have data for prior years.

INDICES OF CHANGE

Year	Companies	Establishments Total	Establishments with 20 or more employees	Employment Total (000)	Production Workers (000)	Production Hours (Mil)	Compensation Payroll ($ mil)	Compensation Wages ($/hr)	Cost of Materials	Value Added by Manufacture	Value of Shipments	Capital Invest.
1982	103	106	108	104	103	90	70	82	76	60	64	97
1983		103	98	106	93	80	71	97	80	68	70	63
1984		100	88	96	83	59	74	122	69	57	61	191
1985		96	80	96	76	62	74	117	77	59	64	233
1986		94	88	96	90	70	71	107	72	58	62	143
1987	98	98	110	98	97	97	83	89	84	80	81	101
1988		92	80	98	93	97	89	93	69	82	78	72
1989		88	80	94	110	100	102	123	93	103	99	130
1990		87	97	92	103	100	84	98	86	93	91	216
1991		90	97	85	100	100	83	95	79	95	90	152
1992	100	100	100	100	100	100	100	100	100	100	100	100
1993		99	103	100	103	100	104	101	110	109	110	155
1994		91P	95P	102	100	100	107	101	114	110	111	220
1995		90P	95P	95P	105P	108P	107P	102P	117P	112P	114P	174P
1996		89P	95P	94P	106P	111P	110P	102P	121P	117P	118P	178P
1997		88P	96P	94P	107P	113P	113P	102P	126P	121P	122P	182P
1998		87P	96P	94P	108P	116P	116P	102P	130P	125P	127P	186P

Sources: Same as General Statistics. Values reflect change from the base year, 1992. Values above 100 mean greater than 92, values below 100 mean less than 92, and a value of 100 in the 82-91 or 93-98 period means same as 92. 'P's mark projections by the editors.

SELECTED RATIOS

For 1994	Avg. of All Manufact.	Analyzed Industry	Index	For 1994	Avg. of All Manufact.	Analyzed Industry	Index
Employees per Establishment	49	10	20	Value Added per Production Worker	134,084	96,621	72
Payroll per Establishment	1,500,273	195,157	13	Cost per Establishment	5,045,178	232,068	5
Payroll per Employee	30,620	20,286	66	Cost per Employee	102,970	24,122	23
Production Workers per Establishment	34	6	17	Cost per Production Worker	146,988	40,759	28
Wages per Establishment	853,319	96,171	11	Shipments per Establishment	9,576,895	782,199	8
Wages per Production Worker	24,861	16,891	68	Shipments per Employee	195,460	81,306	42
Hours per Production Worker	2,056	2,103	102	Shipments per Production Worker	279,017	137,379	49
Wages per Hour	12.09	8.03	66	Investment per Establishment	321,011	59,490	19
Value Added per Establishment	4,602,255	550,131	12	Investment per Employee	6,552	6,184	94
Value Added per Employee	93,930	57,184	61	Investment per Production Worker	9,352	10,448	112

Sources: Same as General Statistics. The 'Average of All Manufacturing' column represents the average of all manufacturing industries reported for the most recent complete year available. The Index shows the relationship between the Average and the Analyzed Industry. For example, 100 means that they are equal; 500 that the Analyzed Industry is five times the average; 50 means that the Analyzed Industry is half the national average. The abbreviation 'na' is used to show that data are 'not available'.

LEADING COMPANIES Number shown: 14 Total sales ($ mil): 108 Total employment (000): 0.8

Company Name	Address				CEO Name	Phone	Co. Type	Sales ($ mil)	Empl. (000)
Rice Oil Company Inc	34 Montague City	Greenfield	MA	01301	Timothy Rice	413-772-0227	R	24*	0.2
Pelican Ice and Cold Storage Inc	PO Box 23865	New Orleans	LA	70183	Daniel Behre	504-525-4193	R	16*	0.1
Union Ice Co	6100 E Sheila St	Los Angeles	CA	90040		213-890-3803	R	16*	0.1
Jefferson Ice Company Inc	2248 N Natchez Av	Chicago	IL	60635	RJ Rustman	312-622-9400	R	13*	0.1
Glacier Ice Co	43960 Fremont Blv	Fremont	CA	94538	John Nicholson	510-656-2230	R	10*	<0.1
City Ice Company Inc	PO Box 1333	Gainesville	GA	30503	Carl B Romberg II	404-535-3700	R	6*	<0.1
Reddy Ice Corp	4320 Duncanville	Dallas	TX	75236	Gayle Beshears	214-296-4271	R	6*	<0.1
Happy Refrigerated Services	900 Turk Hill Rd	Fairport	NY	14450	Kerry Chamberlain	716-388-0233	R	5	<0.1
Coachella Valley Ice Co	PO Drawer 10740	Indio	CA	92202	HB Mason	619-347-3529	R	4	<0.1
Riverside Ice Company Inc	4444 Vine St	Riverside	CA	92507	Gary Wittenmyer	909-683-1730	R	3*	<0.1
Diamond Newport Corp	1107 E Walnut St	Santa Ana	CA	92701	Raymond Craft	714-835-8306	R	2*	<0.1
Merchants Ice & Cold Storage	801 Logan St	Louisville	KY	40204	WC Glass	502-584-5321	D	2*	<0.1
Herrin Brothers Coal and Ice Co	PO Box 5291	Charlotte	NC	28225	Marshall L Herrin	704-332-2193	R	1*	<0.1
Chikato Brothers Ice Co	2161 Sacramento St	Los Angeles	CA	90021	Scott Peatross	213-622-4181	R	1	<0.1

Source: *Ward's Business Directory of U.S. Private and Public Companies*, Volumes 1 and 2, 1996. The company type code used is as follows: P - Public, R - Private, S - Subsidiary, D - Division, J - Joint Venture, A - Affiliate, G - Group. Sales are in millions of dollars, employees are in thousands. An asterisk (*) indicates an estimated sales volume. The symbol < stands for 'less than'. Company names and addresses are truncated, in some cases, to fit into the available space.

MATERIALS CONSUMED

Material	Quantity	Delivered Cost ($ million)
No Materials Consumed data available for this industry.		

Source: 1992 *Economic Census*. Explanation of symbols used: (D): Withheld to avoid disclosure of competitive data; na: Not available; (S): Withheld because statistical norms were not met; (X): Not applicable; (Z): Less than half the unit shown; nec: Not elsewhere classified; nsk: Not specified by kind; - : zero; * : 10-19 percent estimated; ** : 20-29 percent estimated.

PRODUCT SHARE DETAILS

Product or Product Class	% Share	Product or Product Class	% Share
Manufactured ice	100.00	Manufactured cubed, crushed, or other processed ice . . .	54.72
Manufactured can or block ice	14.48		

Source: 1992 *Economic Census*. The values shown are percent of total shipments in an industry. Values of indented subcategories are summed in the main heading. The symbol (D) appears when data are withheld to prevent disclosure of competitive information. The abbreviation nsk stands for 'not specified by kind' and nec for 'not elsewhere classified'.

INPUTS AND OUTPUTS FOR MANUFACTURED ICE

Economic Sector or Industry Providing Inputs	%	Sector	Economic Sector or Industry Buying Outputs	%	Sector
Electric services (utilities)	35.3	Util.	Personal consumption expenditures	82.6	
Bags, except textile	31.3	Manufg.	Commercial fishing	15.0	Agric.
Advertising	3.9	Services	Wholesale trade	1.1	Trade
Equipment rental & leasing services	2.7	Services	Change in business inventories	0.6	In House
U.S. Postal Service	2.4	Gov't	Manufactured ice	0.3	Manufg.
Eating & drinking places	2.2	Trade	Motor freight transportation & warehousing	0.2	Util.
Real estate	2.1	Fin/R.E.	Exports	0.1	Foreign
Water supply & sewage systems	1.8	Util.			
Wholesale trade	1.3	Trade			
Gas production & distribution (utilities)	1.1	Util.			
Coal	0.9	Mining			
Communications, except radio & TV	0.8	Util.			
Motor freight transportation & warehousing	0.8	Util.			
Legal services	0.8	Services			
Management & consulting services & labs	0.8	Services			
Manufactured ice	0.7	Manufg.			
Mechanical measuring devices	0.7	Manufg.			
Banking	0.7	Fin/R.E.			
Business/professional associations	0.7	Services			
Laundry, dry cleaning, shoe repair	0.7	Services			
Accounting, auditing & bookkeeping	0.6	Services			
Food products machinery	0.5	Manufg.			
Paperboard containers & boxes	0.5	Manufg.			
Electrical repair shops	0.5	Services			
Machinery, except electrical, nec	0.4	Manufg.			
Manifold business forms	0.4	Manufg.			
Computer & data processing services	0.4	Services			
Maintenance of nonfarm buildings nec	0.3	Constr.			

Continued on next page.

INPUTS AND OUTPUTS FOR MANUFACTURED ICE - Continued

Economic Sector or Industry Providing Inputs	%	Sector	Economic Sector or Industry Buying Outputs	%	Sector
Distilled liquor, except brandy	0.3	Manufg.			
Fabricated rubber products, nec	0.3	Manufg.			
Lubricating oils & greases	0.3	Manufg.			
Railroads & related services	0.3	Util.			
Miscellaneous repair shops	0.3	Services			
Manufacturing industries, nec	0.2	Manufg.			
Petroleum refining	0.2	Manufg.			
Air transportation	0.2	Util.			
Insurance carriers	0.2	Fin/R.E.			
Royalties	0.2	Fin/R.E.			
Automotive repair shops & services	0.2	Services			
Personnel supply services	0.2	Services			
Services to dwellings & other buildings	0.2	Services			
Abrasive products	0.1	Manufg.			
Hand & edge tools, nec	0.1	Manufg.			
Periodicals	0.1	Manufg.			
Photographic equipment & supplies	0.1	Manufg.			
Special dies & tools & machine tool accessories	0.1	Manufg.			
Transit & bus transportation	0.1	Util.			
Detective & protective services	0.1	Services			
Engineering, architectural, & surveying services	0.1	Services			
Imports	0.1	Foreign			

Source: Benchmark Input-Output Accounts for the U.S. Economy, 1982, U.S. Department of Commerce, Washington, D.C., July 1991. Data, as reported in the source, are organized by the 1977 SIC structure in use in 1982 but have been matched, as closely as is possible, to the 1987 SIC structure used in this book.

OCCUPATIONS EMPLOYED BY SIC 209 - MISCELLANEOUS FOODS AND KINDRED PRODUCTS

Occupation	% of Total 1994	Change to 2005	Occupation	% of Total 1994	Change to 2005
Cannery workers	10.4	26.3	Machine feeders & offbearers	1.9	3.3
Packaging & filling machine operators	8.7	26.3	Industrial truck & tractor operators	1.9	14.8
Hand packers & packagers	8.0	-1.6	Janitors & cleaners, incl maids	1.7	-8.2
Helpers, laborers, & material movers nec	6.7	14.8	Bakers, manufacturing	1.7	35.9
Meat, poultry, & fish cutters & trimmers, hand	5.8	14.8	Maintenance repairers, general utility	1.5	3.3
Cooking, roasting machine operators	3.4	26.3	Inspectors, testers, & graders, precision	1.5	14.8
Truck drivers light & heavy	3.2	18.3	Agricultural workers nec	1.3	14.8
Driver/sales workers	2.8	3.3	Industrial production managers	1.3	14.8
General managers & top executives	2.2	8.9	Bookkeeping, accounting, & auditing clerks	1.2	-13.9
Industrial machinery mechanics	2.2	26.2	Traffic, shipping, & receiving clerks	1.2	10.5
Precision food & tobacco workers nec	2.2	14.8	Secretaries, ex legal & medical	1.2	4.5
Freight, stock, & material movers, hand	2.1	-8.2	Extruding & forming machine workers	1.2	26.3
Crushing & mixing machine operators	2.0	14.8	Butchers & meatcutters	1.2	27.4
Assemblers, fabricators, & hand workers nec	2.0	14.8	General office clerks	1.1	-2.1
Sales & related workers nec	1.9	14.8			

Source: Industry-Occupation Matrix, Bureau of Labor Statistics. These data relate to one or more 3-digit SIC industry groups rather than to a single 4-digit SIC. The change reported for each occupation to the year 2005 is a percent of growth or decline as estimated by the Bureau of Labor Statistics. The abbreviation nec stands for 'not elsewhere classified'.

LOCATION BY STATE AND REGIONAL CONCENTRATION

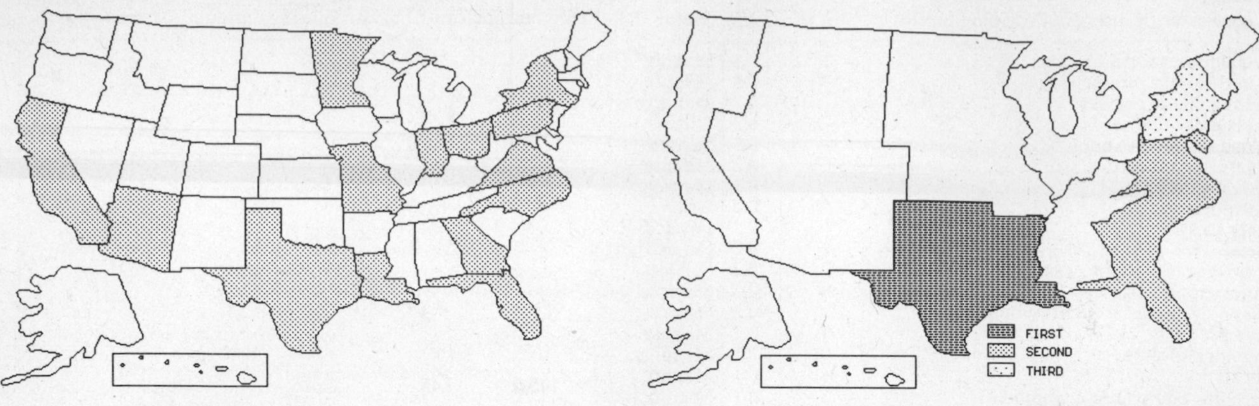

INDUSTRY DATA BY STATE

State	Establish-ments	Shipments			Employment				Cost as % of Shipments	Investment per Employee ($)
		Total ($ mil)	% of U.S.	Per Establ.	Total Number	% of U.S.	Per Establ.	Wages ($/hour)		
California	37	44.0	12.3	1.2	500	10.4	14	9.86	33.9	3,800
Florida	37	27.3	7.6	0.7	300	6.3	8	6.80	30.0	-
New York	22	13.2	3.7	0.6	100	2.1	5	8.00	21.2	5,000
Pennsylvania	26	13.1	3.7	0.5	100	2.1	4	6.00	22.9	2,000
North Carolina	16	13.0	3.6	0.8	200	4.2	13	7.50	42.3	1,000
Georgia	17	11.7	3.3	0.7	100	2.1	6	7.00	28.2	4,000
Missouri	17	10.1	2.8	0.6	200	4.2	12	8.50	24.8	-
Louisiana	24	9.3	2.6	0.4	100	2.1	4	6.00	31.2	2,000
Minnesota	9	7.0	2.0	0.8	200	4.2	22	5.00	18.6	2,000
Virginia	14	5.8	1.6	0.4	100	2.1	7	10.00	27.6	3,000
Texas	65	(D)	-	-	750 *	15.6	12	-	-	2,267
Ohio	19	(D)	-	-	175 *	3.6	9	-	-	-
Indiana	18	(D)	-	-	175 *	3.6	10	-	-	6,286
Arizona	12	(D)	-	-	375 *	7.8	31	-	-	-

Source: 1992 *Economic Census*. The states are in descending order of shipments or establishments (if shipment data are missing for the majority). The symbol (D) appears when data are withheld to prevent disclosure of competitive information. States marked with (D) are sorted by number of establishments. A dash (-) indicates that the data element cannot be calculated; * indicates the midpoint of a range.

2098 - MACARONI AND SPAGHETTI

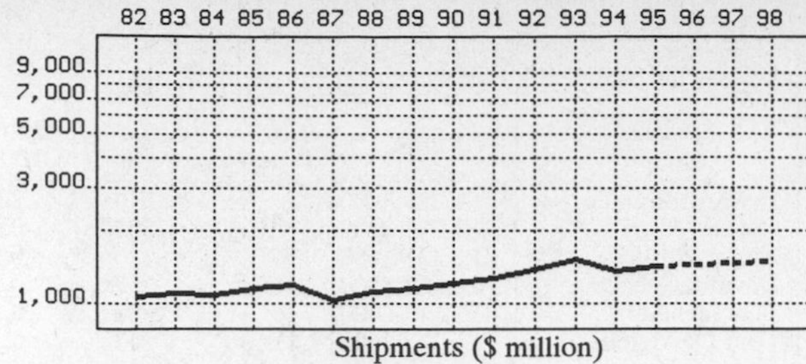

Shipments ($ million)

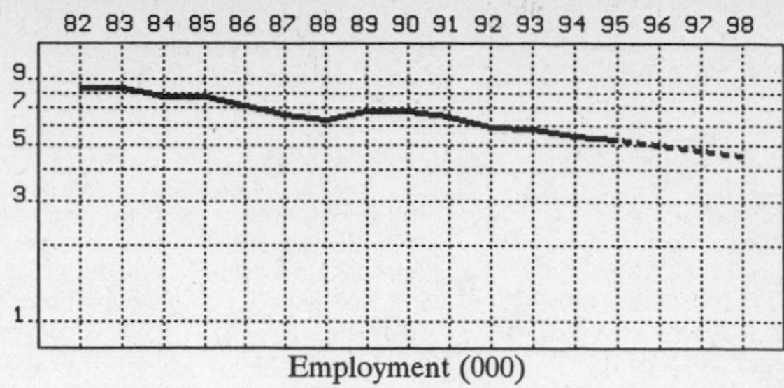

Employment (000)

GENERAL STATISTICS

Year	Companies	Establishments: Total	Establishments: with 20 or more employees	Employment: Total (000)	Production Workers (000)	Production Hours (Mil)	Compensation: Payroll ($ mil)	Compensation: Wages ($/hr)	Production ($ million): Cost of Materials	Value Added by Manufacture	Value of Shipments	Capital Invest.
1982	208	230	81	8.4	6.0	11.9	145.0	7.45	514.6	550.9	1,065.0	48.3
1983		232	79	8.4	5.6	11.3	149.1	8.05	514.4	583.9	1,096.2	44.0
1984		234	77	7.7	5.5	11.1	139.9	7.90	501.4	578.8	1,082.3	26.2
1985		237	75	7.7	5.6	11.7	141.7	7.99	528.1	628.6	1,154.7	31.8
1986		243	75	7.2	5.3	11.2	139.5	8.32	494.1	702.2	1,199.8	32.8
1987	205	218	48	6.6	5.0	9.8	140.0	9.27	435.1	614.0	1,048.1	32.2
1988		229	54	6.3	4.8	9.7	135.1	9.46	480.1	639.0	1,119.5	35.5
1989		213	54	6.8	4.6	9.7	132.0	9.51	512.6	642.3	1,154.0	44.5
1990		199	55	6.8	4.8	10.0	142.4	10.07	507.6	728.7	1,229.6	46.8
1991		206	56	6.4	4.9	10.3	149.2	10.09	527.0	749.3	1,276.8	96.5
1992	182	199	41	5.9	4.6	10.2	146.8	10.25	565.1	830.8	1,389.5	74.7
1993		198	49	5.8	4.6	10.3	150.8	10.49	598.6	915.6	1,518.3	40.7
1994		195P	39P	5.4	4.2	9.3	144.3	11.24	558.1	794.5	1,347.1	19.5
1995		191P	36P	5.2P	4.2P	9.3P	144.8P	11.33P	588.4P	837.6P	1,420.2P	53.3P
1996		187P	32P	5.0P	4.0P	9.1P	145.0P	11.63P	601.1P	855.6P	1,450.8P	54.6P
1997		183P	29P	4.8P	3.9P	9.0P	145.3P	11.93P	613.7P	873.7P	1,481.4P	55.9P
1998		179P	25P	4.5P	3.8P	8.8P	145.6P	12.23P	626.4P	891.7P	1,511.9P	57.3P

Sources: 1982, 1987, 1992 *Economic Census*; *Annual Survey of Manufactures*, 83-86, 88-91, 93-94. Establishment counts for non-Census years are from *County Business Patterns*; establishment values for 83-84 are extrapolations. 'P's show projections by the editors. Industries reclassified in 87 will not have data for prior years.

INDICES OF CHANGE

Year	Companies	Establishments: Total	Establishments: with 20 or more employees	Employment: Total (000)	Production Workers (000)	Production Hours (Mil)	Compensation: Payroll ($ mil)	Compensation: Wages ($/hr)	Production ($ million): Cost of Materials	Value Added by Manufacture	Value of Shipments	Capital Invest.
1982	114	116	198	142	130	117	99	73	91	66	77	65
1983		117	193	142	122	111	102	79	91	70	79	59
1984		118	188	131	120	109	95	77	89	70	78	35
1985		119	183	131	122	115	97	78	93	76	83	43
1986		122	183	122	115	110	95	81	87	85	86	44
1987	113	110	117	112	109	96	95	90	77	74	75	43
1988		115	132	107	104	95	92	92	85	77	81	48
1989		107	132	115	100	95	90	93	91	77	83	60
1990		100	134	115	104	98	97	98	90	88	88	63
1991		104	137	108	107	101	102	98	93	90	92	129
1992	100	100	100	100	100	100	100	100	100	100	100	100
1993		99	120	98	100	101	103	102	106	110	109	54
1994		98P	96P	92	91	91	98	110	99	96	97	26
1995		96P	87P	89P	90P	91P	99P	111P	104P	101P	102P	71P
1996		94P	79P	85P	88P	90P	99P	113P	106P	103P	104P	73P
1997		92P	70P	81P	85P	88P	99P	116P	109P	105P	107P	75P
1998		90P	62P	77P	82P	86P	99P	119P	111P	107P	109P	77P

Sources: Same as General Statistics. Values reflect change from the base year, 1992. Values above 100 mean greater than 92, values below 100 mean less than 92, and a value of 100 in the 82-91 or 93-98 period means same as 92. 'P's mark projections by the editors.

SELECTED RATIOS

For 1994	Avg. of All Manufact.	Analyzed Industry	Index
Employees per Establishment	49	28	57
Payroll per Establishment	1,500,273	741,845	49
Payroll per Employee	30,620	26,722	87
Production Workers per Establishment	34	22	63
Wages per Establishment	853,319	537,398	63
Wages per Production Worker	24,861	24,889	100
Hours per Production Worker	2,056	2,214	108
Wages per Hour	12.09	11.24	93
Value Added per Establishment	4,602,255	4,084,515	89
Value Added per Employee	93,930	147,130	157

For 1994	Avg. of All Manufact.	Analyzed Industry	Index
Value Added per Production Worker	134,084	189,167	141
Cost per Establishment	5,045,178	2,869,185	57
Cost per Employee	102,970	103,352	100
Cost per Production Worker	146,988	132,881	90
Shipments per Establishment	9,576,895	6,925,425	72
Shipments per Employee	195,460	249,463	128
Shipments per Production Worker	279,017	320,738	115
Investment per Establishment	321,011	100,249	31
Investment per Employee	6,552	3,611	55
Investment per Production Worker	9,352	4,643	50

Sources: Same as General Statistics. The 'Average of All Manufacturing' column represents the average of all manufacturing industries reported for the most recent complete year available. The Index shows the relationship between the Average and the Analyzed Industry. For example, 100 means that they are equal; 500 that the Analyzed Industry is five times the average; 50 means that the Analyzed Industry is half the national average. The abbreviation 'na' is used to show that data are 'not available'.

LEADING COMPANIES

Number shown: **25** Total sales ($ mil): **1,360** Total employment (000): **6.0**

Company Name	Address				CEO Name	Phone	Co. Type	Sales ($ mil)	Empl. (000)
Borden Pasta Inc	180 E Broad St	Columbus	OH	43215	Ervin R Shames	614-225-4000	S	510*	2.5
Golden Grain Co	4576 Willow Rd	Pleasanton	CA	94588	Chuck Marcy	510-734-8800	S	305	0.6
Nissin Foods	2001 W Rosecrans	Gardena	CA	90249	Kazuo Hibla	213-321-6453	S	180*	0.9
Noodles By Leonardo Inc	PO Box 860	Devils Lake	ND	58301	David L Speare	701-662-8300	R	57*	0.3
American Italian Pasta Co	1000 Italian Way	Excelsior Sprgs	MO	64024	Tim Webster	816-630-6400	R	50	0.2
San Giorgio Macaroni	749 Gilford St	Lebanon	PA	17006	Tom DeAngelis	717-273-7641	D	47	0.3
Gooch Foods Inc	510 South St	Lincoln	NE	68501	Richard Ross	402-477-4426	S	45	0.2
A Zerega's Sons Inc	PO Box 241	Fair Lawn	NJ	07410	PA Vermylen	201-797-1400	R	30	0.2
Diana's Noodle Corp	PO Box 7555	San Mateo	CA	94403	Diana Cernobori	415-378-5165	R	29*	0.1
Foulds Inc	520 E Church St	Libertyville	IL	60048	Robert J Strom	708-362-3062	R	23	0.1
Philadelphia Macaroni Co	756 S 11th St	Philadelphia	PA	19147	Luke Marano	215-923-3141	R	20	0.2
Original Italian Pasta Products	36 Auburn St	Chelsea	MA	02150	Paul K Stevens	617-884-5211	P	16	<0.1
Consolidated Food	2215 Tradeport Dr	Orlando	FL	32824	Peter Porokscher	407-679-1907	R	14*	<0.1
Gourmet's Fresh Pasta Inc	2220 S Figueroa St	Los Angeles	CA	90007	Michael Yagjian	213-746-1041	R	8	<0.1
Larinascente Macaroni	41 James St	S Hackensack	NJ	07606	JA Natali	201-342-2500	R	5	<0.1
Shade Pasta Inc	PO Box 645	Fremont	NE	68025	Vincent James	402-727-8412	S	5	<0.1
Pasta USA Inc	PO Box 4402	Spokane	WA	99202	Richard Clemson	509-747-2085	R	4	<0.1
OB Macaroni Co	PO Box 53	Fort Worth	TX	76101	JP Laneri	817-335-4629	R	3*	<0.1
Nanka Seimen Company Inc	3030 Leonis Blv	Los Angeles	CA	90058	Shoichi Sayano	213-585-9967	R	2*	<0.1
Maria and Son Italian Products	4201 Hereford St	St Louis	MO	63109	Ralph Cannovo	314-481-9009	R	2	<0.1
Dakota Growers Pasta Co	PO Box 21	Carrington	ND	58421	Tim Dodd	701-652-2855	R	1	0.1
Food City USA Inc	2727 W Barberry Pl	Denver	CO	80204	Dirk Piz	303-629-6937	R	1	<0.1
FunFoods Inc	2 Hudson Pl	Hoboken	NJ	07030	Doug Tintle	201-795-9416	R	1*	<0.1
Serkon Enterprises Inc	11840 Dorsett Rd	Maryland H	MO	63043	Kevin Mendell	314-739-1001	R	1	<0.1
US Durum Products Ltd	PO Box 10126	Lancaster	PA	17605	Jeff Dewey	717-293-8698	R	1	<0.1

Source: *Ward's Business Directory of U.S. Private and Public Companies*, Volumes 1 and 2, 1996. The company type code used is as follows: P - Public, R - Private, S - Subsidiary, D - Division, J - Joint Venture, A - Affiliate, G - Group. Sales are in millions of dollars, employees are in thousands. An asterisk (*) indicates an estimated sales volume. The symbol < stands for 'less than'. Company names and addresses are truncated, in some cases, to fit into the available space.

MATERIALS CONSUMED

Material		Quantity	Delivered Cost ($ million)
Materials, ingredients, containers, and supplies		(X)	506.4
Semolina and durum wheat flour	1,000 cwt	18,205.2	257.9
Other wheat flour (including farina)	1,000 cwt	458.1**	5.2
Packaging paper and plastics film, coated and laminated		(X)	31.4
Bags; plastics, foil, and coated paper		(X)	2.6
Paperboard containers, boxes, and corrugated paperboard		(X)	75.9
All other materials and components, parts, containers, and supplies		(X)	104.7
Materials, ingredients, containers, and supplies, nsk		(X)	28.8

Source: 1992 *Economic Census*. Explanation of symbols used: (D): Withheld to avoid disclosure of competitive data; na: Not available; (S): Withheld because statistical norms were not met; (X): Not applicable; (Z): Less than half the unit shown; nec: Not elsewhere classified; nsk: Not specified by kind; - : zero; * : 10-19 percent estimated; ** : 20-29 percent estimated.

PRODUCT SHARE DETAILS

Product or Product Class	% Share
Macaroni and spaghetti	100.00
Dry macaroni, spaghetti, vermicelli, and other pasta products, except noodles (water content less than 14 percent)	77.85
Refrigerated macaroni, spaghetti, vermicelli, and other pasta products, except noodles	(D)
Dry noodle products of all shapes, sizes, and types, except chinese noodles (water content less than 14 percent)	12.95
Wet noodle products of all shapes, sizes, and types, except chinese noodles (water content 14 percent or more), except refrigerated	(D)
Refrigerated noodle products of all shapes, sizes, and types, except chinese noodles	(D)

Source: 1992 *Economic Census*. The values shown are percent of total shipments in an industry. Values of indented subcategories are summed in the main heading. The symbol (D) appears when data are withheld to prevent disclosure of competitive information. The abbreviation nsk stands for 'not specified by kind' and nec for 'not elsewhere classified'.

INPUTS AND OUTPUTS FOR MACARONI & SPAGHETTI

Economic Sector or Industry Providing Inputs	%	Sector	Economic Sector or Industry Buying Outputs	%	Sector
Flour & other grain mill products	36.3	Manufg.	Personal consumption expenditures	91.1	
Miscellaneous plastics products	12.8	Manufg.	Eating & drinking places	4.9	Trade
Paperboard containers & boxes	12.2	Manufg.	Exports	1.1	Foreign
Wholesale trade	9.6	Trade	S/L Govt. purch., elem. & secondary education	1.0	S/L Govt
Imports	8.5	Foreign	Change in business inventories	0.3	In House
Advertising	3.4	Services	Macaroni & spaghetti	0.2	Manufg.
Railroads & related services	2.4	Util.	Hospitals	0.2	Services
Poultry & egg processing	2.2	Manufg.	Nursing & personal care facilities	0.2	Services
Electric services (utilities)	2.0	Util.	Residential care	0.2	Services
Motor freight transportation & warehousing	1.6	Util.	S/L Govt. purch., health & hospitals	0.2	S/L Govt
Gas production & distribution (utilities)	1.1	Util.	Social services, nec	0.1	Services
Real estate	0.8	Fin/R.E.	S/L Govt. purch., higher education	0.1	S/L Govt
Maintenance of nonfarm buildings nec	0.6	Constr.			
Macaroni & spaghetti	0.5	Manufg.			
Communications, except radio & TV	0.5	Util.			
Eating & drinking places	0.5	Trade			
Banking	0.5	Fin/R.E.			
Drugs	0.4	Manufg.			
Petroleum refining	0.4	Manufg.			
Detective & protective services	0.3	Services			
Equipment rental & leasing services	0.3	Services			
Miscellaneous repair shops	0.3	Services			
Cyclic crudes and organics	0.2	Manufg.			
Royalties	0.2	Fin/R.E.			
Legal services	0.2	Services			
Management & consulting services & labs	0.2	Services			
U.S. Postal Service	0.2	Gov't			
Lubricating oils & greases	0.1	Manufg.			
Mechanical measuring devices	0.1	Manufg.			
Paper coating & glazing	0.1	Manufg.			
Sanitary services, steam supply, irrigation	0.1	Util.			
Accounting, auditing & bookkeeping	0.1	Services			
Computer & data processing services	0.1	Services			
Laundry, dry cleaning, shoe repair	0.1	Services			

Source: Benchmark Input-Output Accounts for the U.S. Economy, 1982, U.S. Department of Commerce, Washington, D.C., July 1991. Data, as reported in the source, are organized by the 1977 SIC structure in use in 1982 but have been matched, as closely as is possible, to the 1987 SIC structure used in this book.

OCCUPATIONS EMPLOYED BY SIC 209 - MISCELLANEOUS FOODS AND KINDRED PRODUCTS

Occupation	% of Total 1994	Change to 2005	Occupation	% of Total 1994	Change to 2005
Cannery workers	10.4	26.3	Machine feeders & offbearers	1.9	3.3
Packaging & filling machine operators	8.7	26.3	Industrial truck & tractor operators	1.9	14.8
Hand packers & packagers	8.0	-1.6	Janitors & cleaners, incl maids	1.7	-8.2
Helpers, laborers, & material movers nec	6.7	14.8	Bakers, manufacturing	1.7	35.9
Meat, poultry, & fish cutters & trimmers, hand	5.8	14.8	Maintenance repairers, general utility	1.5	3.3
Cooking, roasting machine operators	3.4	26.3	Inspectors, testers, & graders, precision	1.5	14.8
Truck drivers light & heavy	3.2	18.3	Agricultural workers nec	1.3	14.8
Driver/sales workers	2.8	3.3	Industrial production managers	1.3	14.8
General managers & top executives	2.2	8.9	Bookkeeping, accounting, & auditing clerks	1.2	-13.9
Industrial machinery mechanics	2.2	26.2	Traffic, shipping, & receiving clerks	1.2	10.5
Precision food & tobacco workers nec	2.2	14.8	Secretaries, ex legal & medical	1.2	4.5
Freight, stock, & material movers, hand	2.1	-8.2	Extruding & forming machine workers	1.2	26.3
Crushing & mixing machine operators	2.0	14.8	Butchers & meatcutters	1.2	27.4
Assemblers, fabricators, & hand workers nec	2.0	14.8	General office clerks	1.1	-2.1
Sales & related workers nec	1.9	14.8			

Source: Industry-Occupation Matrix, Bureau of Labor Statistics. These data relate to one or more 3-digit SIC industry groups rather than to a single 4-digit SIC. The change reported for each occupation to the year 2005 is a percent of growth or decline as estimated by the Bureau of Labor Statistics. The abbreviation nec stands for 'not elsewhere classified'.

LOCATION BY STATE AND REGIONAL CONCENTRATION

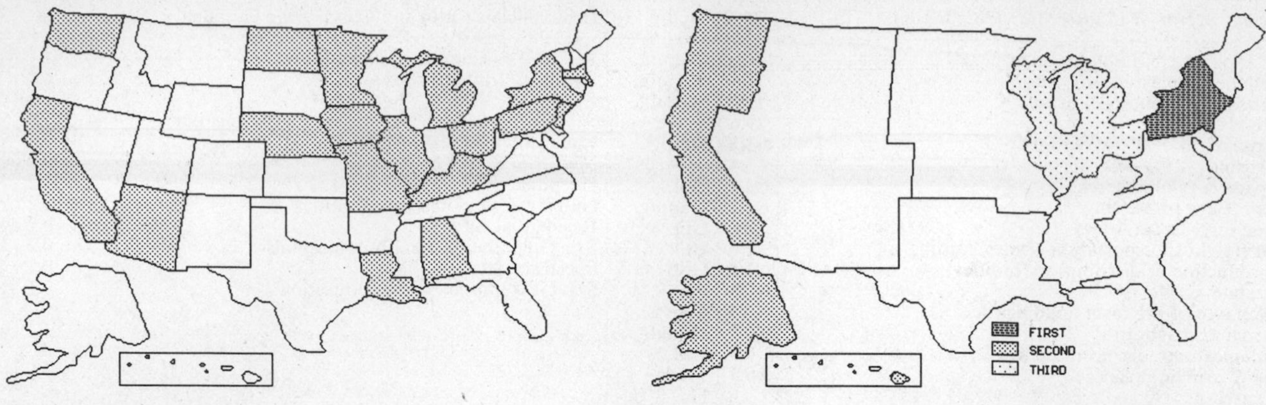

INDUSTRY DATA BY STATE

State	Establish-ments	Shipments			Employment				Cost as % of Shipments	Investment per Employee ($)
		Total ($ mil)	% of U.S.	Per Establ.	Total Number	% of U.S.	Per Establ.	Wages ($/hour)		
New York	37	125.8	9.1	3.4	700	11.9	19	10.08	40.0	1,857
California	38	81.4	5.9	2.1	400	6.8	11	9.38	34.9	17,500
Illinois	9	37.6	2.7	4.2	300	5.1	33	8.20	46.8	3,000
Ohio	6	17.6	1.3	2.9	100	1.7	17	9.50	42.6	6,000
Pennsylvania	13	(D)	-	-	375 *	6.4	29	-	-	-
New Jersey	8	(D)	-	-	750 *	12.7	94	-	-	-
Massachusetts	6	(D)	-	-	375 *	6.4	63	-	-	-
Michigan	5	(D)	-	-	175 *	3.0	35	-	-	-
Iowa	4	(D)	-	-	175 *	3.0	44	-	-	-
Louisiana	4	(D)	-	-	175 *	3.0	44	-	-	-
Minnesota	4	(D)	-	-	375 *	6.4	94	-	-	-
Washington	4	(D)	-	-	175 *	3.0	44	-	-	-
Arizona	3	(D)	-	-	175 *	3.0	58	-	-	-
Missouri	3	(D)	-	-	375 *	6.4	125	-	-	-
Nebraska	3	(D)	-	-	375 *	6.4	125	-	-	4,267
North Dakota	2	(D)	-	-	375 *	6.4	188	-	-	-
Alabama	1	(D)	-	-	175 *	3.0	175	-	-	-
Kentucky	1	(D)	-	-	175 *	3.0	175	-	-	-

Source: 1992 *Economic Census*. The states are in descending order of shipments or establishments (if shipment data are missing for the majority). The symbol (D) appears when data are withheld to prevent disclosure of competitive information. States marked with (D) are sorted by number of establishments. A dash (-) indicates that the data element cannot be calculated; * indicates the midpoint of a range.

2099 - FOOD PREPARATIONS, NEC

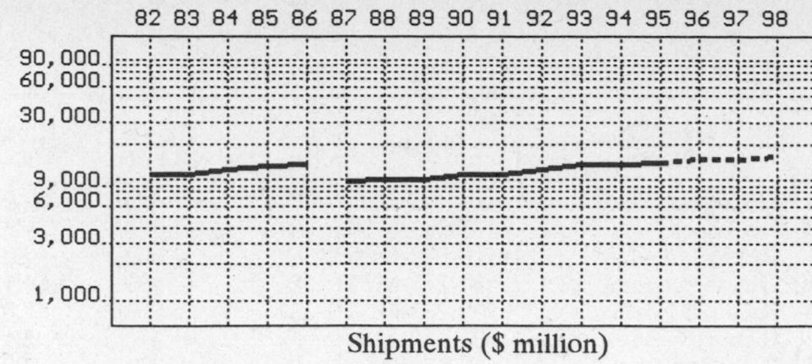

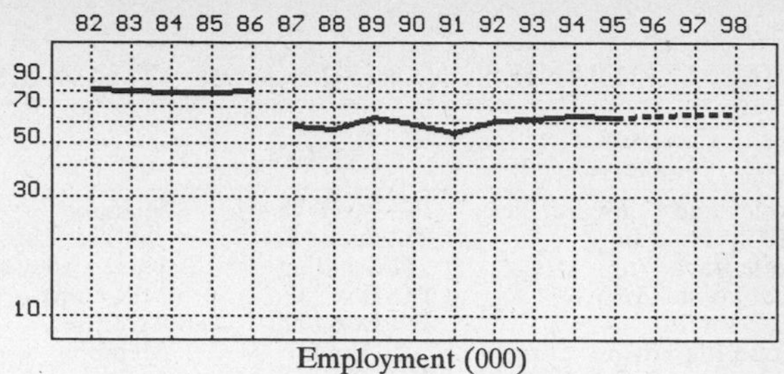

GENERAL STATISTICS

Year	Companies	Establishments: Total	Establishments: with 20 or more employees	Employment: Total (000)	Employment: Production Workers (000)	Employment: Production Hours (Mil)	Compensation: Payroll ($ mil)	Compensation: Wages ($/hr)	Production: Cost of Materials	Production: Value Added by Manufacture	Production: Value of Shipments	Production: Capital Invest.
1982	1,746	1,976	794	81.4	57.9	104.8	1,220.6	7.02	5,344.8	5,663.3	10,979.3	295.4
1983		1,907	788	79.6	56.1	105.9	1,292.0	6.88	5,492.9	5,654.0	11,176.9	254.8
1984		1,838	782	78.7	55.5	106.1	1,344.7	7.48	5,772.5	6,359.1	12,094.5	390.7
1985		1,769	777	78.7	55.7	106.1	1,434.8	8.27	6,193.1	6,713.9	12,906.0	411.7
1986		1,721	768	80.9	56.9	104.8	1,504.6	8.57	6,111.1	7,302.0	13,392.1	408.2
1987*	1,492	1,658	633	57.9	40.8	77.5	1,109.8	8.41	4,702.6	5,126.4	9,787.3	247.5
1988		1,501	628	57.0	40.3	73.9	1,129.6	8.78	4,832.5	5,333.8	10,167.0	204.5
1989		1,425	632	62.5	39.4	75.7	1,085.8	8.33	5,077.4	5,049.2	10,083.6	202.9
1990		1,410	626	58.9	38.1	78.1	1,190.0	8.43	5,590.8	5,458.3	11,047.6	251.7
1991		1,457	627	54.7	37.5	74.9	1,193.2	9.05	5,728.7	5,665.7	11,322.4	296.0
1992	1,644	1,800	637	61.4	43.7	86.4	1,412.4	9.22	6,313.4	5,883.5	12,170.2	332.3
1993		1,709	646	61.9	44.2	87.9	1,469.1	9.45	6,516.3	7,024.2	13,497.2	394.2
1994		1,678P	640P	64.3	45.7	90.5	1,546.5	9.71	6,781.7	6,529.5	13,314.9	356.0
1995		1,706P	642P	63.1P	44.8P	90.8P	1,574.4P	9.77P	7,124.9P	6,859.9P	13,988.7P	400.3P
1996		1,734P	644P	63.9P	45.5P	93.0P	1,642.7P	9.95P	7,415.2P	7,139.4P	14,558.7P	425.8P
1997		1,761P	646P	64.6P	46.3P	95.3P	1,711.0P	10.14P	7,705.5P	7,419.0P	15,128.7P	451.3P
1998		1,789P	648P	65.3P	47.1P	97.6P	1,779.3P	10.33P	7,995.8P	7,698.5P	15,698.7P	476.8P

Sources: 1982, 1987, 1992 *Economic Census*; *Annual Survey of Manufactures*, 83-86, 88-91, 93-94. Establishment counts are from *County Business Patterns* for non-Census years; establishment counts for 83-84 are extrapolations. * indicates that industry content changed in 87; earlier years use 77 SICs. 'P's mark projections.

INDICES OF CHANGE

Year	Companies	Establishments: Total	Establishments: with 20 or more employees	Employment: Total (000)	Employment: Production Workers (000)	Employment: Production Hours (Mil)	Compensation: Payroll ($ mil)	Compensation: Wages ($/hr)	Production: Cost of Materials	Production: Value Added by Manufacture	Production: Value of Shipments	Production: Capital Invest.
1982	106	110	125	133	132	121	86	76	85	96	90	89
1983		106	124	130	128	123	91	75	87	96	92	77
1984		102	123	128	127	123	95	81	91	108	99	118
1985		98	122	128	127	123	102	90	98	114	106	124
1986		96	121	132	130	121	107	93	97	124	110	123
1987*	91	92	99	94	93	90	79	91	74	87	80	74
1988		83	99	93	92	86	80	95	77	91	84	62
1989		79	99	102	90	88	77	90	80	86	83	61
1990		78	98	96	87	90	84	91	89	93	91	76
1991		81	98	89	86	87	84	98	91	96	93	89
1992	100	100	100	100	100	100	100	100	100	100	100	100
1993		95	101	101	101	102	104	102	103	119	111	119
1994		93P	100P	105	105	105	109	105	107	111	109	107
1995		95P	101P	103P	102P	105P	111P	106P	113P	117P	115P	120P
1996		96P	101P	104P	104P	108P	116P	108P	117P	121P	120P	128P
1997		98P	101P	105P	106P	110P	121P	110P	122P	126P	124P	136P
1998		99P	102P	106P	108P	113P	126P	112P	127P	131P	129P	143P

Sources: Same as General Statistics. Values reflect change from the base year, 1992. Values above 100 mean greater than 92, values below 100 mean less than 92, and a value of 100 in the 82-91 or 93-98 period means same as 92. * indicates that industry content changed in 87. Data for earlier years are in 77 SIC format.

SELECTED RATIOS

For 1994	Avg. of All Manufact.	Analyzed Industry	Index	For 1994	Avg. of All Manufact.	Analyzed Industry	Index
Employees per Establishment	49	38	78	Value Added per Production Worker	134,084	142,877	107
Payroll per Establishment	1,500,273	921,868	61	Cost per Establishment	5,045,178	4,042,570	80
Payroll per Employee	30,620	24,051	79	Cost per Employee	102,970	105,470	102
Production Workers per Establishment	34	27	79	Cost per Production Worker	146,988	148,396	101
Wages per Establishment	853,319	523,826	61	Shipments per Establishment	9,576,895	7,937,009	83
Wages per Production Worker	24,861	19,229	77	Shipments per Employee	195,460	207,075	106
Hours per Production Worker	2,056	1,980	96	Shipments per Production Worker	279,017	291,354	104
Wages per Hour	12.09	9.71	80	Investment per Establishment	321,011	212,212	66
Value Added per Establishment	4,602,255	3,892,234	85	Investment per Employee	6,552	5,537	85
Value Added per Employee	93,930	101,547	108	Investment per Production Worker	9,352	7,790	83

Sources: Same as General Statistics. The 'Average of All Manufacturing' column represents the average of all manufacturing industries reported for the most recent complete year available. The Index shows the relationship between the Average and the Analyzed Industry. For example, 100 means that they are equal; 500 that the Analyzed Industry is five times the average; 50 means that the Analyzed Industry is half the national average. The abbreviation 'na' is used to show that data are 'not available'.

LEADING COMPANIES Number shown: **75** Total sales ($ mil): **11,089** Total employment (000): **54.1**

Company Name	Address				CEO Name	Phone	Co. Type	Sales ($ mil)	Empl. (000)
McCormick and Company Inc	PO Box 6000	Sparks	MD	21152	H Eugene Blattman	410-771-7301	P	1,695	9.0
Burns-Philp Food Inc	222 Sutter St	San Francisco	CA	94108	Ian Clack	415-296-5700	S	1,500	1.3
McCormick/Schilling	211 Schilling Cir	Hunt Valley	MD	21031	Robert Lawless	410-527-6000	D	1,000	7.0
Universal Foods Corp	PO Box 737	Milwaukee	WI	53201	Guy A Osborn	414-271-6755	P	930	4.1
Lamb-Weston Inc	PO Box 1900	Tri Cities	WA	99302	Richard Porter	509-735-4651	S	900*	5.0
Kraft Food Ingredients Corp	6410 Poplar Av	Memphis	TN	38119	Robert G McVicker	901-766-2100	D	390	2.4
Griffith Laboratories Inc	1 Griffith Ctr	Alsip	IL	60658	Pete Rhodes	708-371-0900	R	350	2.0
Pfizer Inc	235 E 42nd St	New York	NY	10017	John Venardo	212-573-2548	D	304	1.6
McCormick International	PO Box 6000	Sparks	MD	21031	James Albrecht	410-771-7336	D	300	1.0
Tetley Inc	100 Commerce Dr	Shelton	CT	06484	Henry F McInerney	203-929-9200	S	300	1.3
Land O'Frost Inc	16850 Chicago Av	Lansing	IL	60438	Paul Van Eekeren	708-474-7100	R	230*	1.3
Kelco Division	PO Box 23576	San Diego	CA	92123	Peter Kovacs	619-292-4900	D	200*	1.3
Orval Kent Food Company Inc	120 W Palatine Rd	Wheeling	IL	60090	Richard L Fogg	708-459-9000	J	200	1.4
Fresh Express Inc	PO Box 80599	Salinas	CA	93912	Mark Drever	408-422-5917	S	180*	1.0
Red Star Yeast and Products	1384 5th St	Oakland	CA	94607	Thomas J Degnan	510-272-9033	D	163	0.3
Golden Valley Microwave Foods	7450 Metro Blv	Edina	MN	55439	Jack McKeon	612-835-6900	S	160*	0.9
Specialty Brands	222 Sutter St	San Francisco	CA	94120	J Frank Stephens	415-981-7600	D	130*	0.8
UTZ Quality Foods Inc	PO Box 458	Hanover	PA	17331	RG King	717-637-6644	R	115	1.1
Tone Brothers Inc	PO Box AA	Des Moines	IA	50301	FC Cruger	515-965-2711	S	100*	0.4
Portion Pac Inc	7325 Snider Rd	Mason	OH	45040	Pete Jack	513-398-0400	S	91*	0.5
Fleischmann's Yeast	206 Fabricator Dr	Fenton	MO	63026	Gary Edwards	314-349-1289	D	81	0.5
Blue Ridge Farms Inc	3301 Atlantic Av	Brooklyn	NY	11208	Seymour Siegel	718-827-9000	R	75	0.5
Jacobs Management Corp	100 S 5th St	Minneapolis	MN	55402	Irwin Jacobs	612-339-9500	R	72*	0.4
Celestial Seasonings Inc	4600 Sleepytime Dr	Boulder	CO	80301	Mo Siegel	303-530-5300	P	65	0.2
Algood Food Co	PO Box 17554	Louisville	KY	40217	Cecil C Barnett	502-637-3631	R	60*	0.1
Eastern Foods Inc	1000 Fresh	Atlanta	GA	30349	RH Brooks	404-765-9000	R	60	0.3
La Reina Inc	316 N Ford Blv	Los Angeles	CA	90022	Mauro Robles	213-268-2791	R	60	0.6
Oppenheimer Companies Inc	877 W Main St	Boise	ID	83702	A F Oppenheimer	208-343-2602	R	54*	0.3
Best Brands Inc	1765 Yankee	St Paul	MN	55121	Ken Malecha	612-454-5850	R	50	0.3
Clements Food Company Inc	PO Box 14538	Oklahoma City	OK	73113	Edward B Clements	405-842-3308	R	50	0.2
Heller Seasonings	PO Box 128	Bedford Park	IL	60499	John A Heller	708-581-6800	R	50	0.2
Southern Tea Co	1267 Cobb Indus'l	Marietta	GA	30066	Daniel T Reed	404-428-5555	S	50	0.5
Old Dutch Foods Inc	PO Box 64627	St Paul	MN	55164	Vernon O Anenson	612-633-8810	R	49*	0.4
Baltimore Spice Inc	9740 Reisterstown	Owings Mills	MD	21117	Jack M Irvin Jr	410-363-1700	S	42	0.3
Integrated Ingredients	1420 Harbor Bay	Alameda	CA	94501	David Wilson	510-748-6300	S	42	0.3
Sioux Honey Association	PO Box 388	Sioux City	IA	51102	Gary Evans	712-258-0638	R	42*	<0.1
Cumberland Packing Corp	2 Cumberland St	Brooklyn	NY	11205	M Eisenstadt	718-858-4200	R	41*	0.4
Diamond Crystal Specialty Foods	10 Burlington Av	Wilmington	MA	01887	Ron Tarantino	508-658-3131	R	40	0.3
Griffith Laboratories Inc	6601 Griffith Way	Lithonia	GA	30058	Bruce Blank	404-482-2951	D	40	0.2
General Spice Inc	238 St Nicholas Av	South Plainfield	NJ	07080	Werner F Hiller	908-753-9100	S	36	0.1
Made Rite Foods Inc	2414 Battleground	Greensboro	NC	27408	Jerry A McMasters	919-288-6646	R	36	0.2
Prepared Products Company Inc	6190 E Slauson Av	Los Angeles	CA	90040	Thomas W Lehmer	213-726-2676	R	36*	0.2
Weaver Popcorn Company Inc	PO Box 395	Van Buren	IN	46991	ME Weaver	317-934-2101	R	34	0.3
Mallet and Co	PO Box 474	Carnegie	PA	15106	Robert I Mallet	412-276-9000	R	33	0.1
Reliv' International Inc	PO Box 405	Chesterfield	MO	63006	R L Montgomery	314-537-9715	P	32	<0.1
Hulman and Co	PO Box 150	Terre Haute	IN	47808	Mary H George	812-232-9446	R	32*	0.2
Kalsec Inc	PO Box 50511	Kalamazoo	MI	49005	PH Todd Jr	616-349-9711	R	30*	0.2
Sanofi Bio-Industries Inc	620 Progress Av	Waukesha	WI	53186	Don Combs	414-547-5531	D	29	<0.1
Preferred Products Inc	312 Lake Hazeltine	Chaska	MN	55318	Tom Miller	612-448-5252	S	27*	0.2
Redco Foods Inc	100 Northfield Dr	Windsor	CT	06095	John Rigg	203-688-2121	R	27*	0.2
Custom Food Products Inc	5145 W 123rd St	Alsip	IL	60658	Martin Overton	708-388-8883	S	25	0.1
Dixie Crystal Foodservice Inc	PO Box 9177	Savannah	GA	31412	Oscar Brannon	912-651-5112	S	25	0.2
Zatarain's	PO Box 347	Gretna	LA	70054	Chloe R Anderson	504-367-2950	R	25	<0.1
Regal Food Service Inc	PO Box 21172	Houston	TX	77026	Don Bean	713-222-8231	R	22	0.2
Vestro Natural Foods Inc	PO Box 48006	Gardena	CA	90248	B Allen Lay	310-886-8200	P	22	<0.1
Abco Laboratories Inc	PO Box 5576	Concord	CA	94524	Allen Baron	510-685-1212	R	20	0.1
American Foods Corp	875 Mahler Rd	Burlingame	CA	94010	Hiroyasu Nakano	415-692-1040	S	20*	0.1
Continental Colloids Inc	245 W Roosevelt	West Chicago	IL	60185	Donald Josephson	708-231-8650	R	20	<0.1
Eden Foods Inc	701 Tecumseh Rd	Clinton	MI	49236	Michael Potter	517-456-7424	R	20	<0.1
Maple Grove Farms of Vermont	167 Portland St	St Johnsbury	VT	05819	WF Callahan	802-748-5141	R	20	<0.1
Rogers Foods Inc Chili Products	PO Box H	Greenfield	CA	93927	Allen Sietsema	408-674-5571	D	20*	0.1
Tracy-Luckey Company Inc	PO Box 188	Harlem	GA	30814	FW Tracy	706-556-6216	R	20	0.1
Diamond V Mills Inc	PO Box 74570	Cedar Rapids	IA	52407	William Bloomhall II	319-366-0745	R	19	<0.1
Crest Foods Company Inc	PO Box 371	Ashton	IL	61006	Jeff Meiners	815-453-7411	R	18	0.3
St Clair Foods Inc	3122 Bellbrook Dr	Memphis	TN	38116	Oscar Edmonds III	901-396-8680	R	18*	0.1
Wixon Fontarome Inc	1390 E Bolivar Av	Milwaukee	WI	53207	JH Morgan	414-481-8900	R	18	0.1
Home Orders Inc	PO Box 7555	San Mateo	CA	94403	Kirk Thompson	415-378-5214	R	17*	<0.1
Milani Foods Inc	2525 Armitage	Melrose Park	IL	60160	R Kirshbaum	708-450-3189	D	17	0.3
Butterball Farms Inc	1435 Buchanan Av	Grand Rapids	MI	49507	Leo Peters	616-243-0105	R	16*	0.2
I Rokeach and Sons Inc	80 Av K	Newark	NJ	07105	Howard Freudlich	201-589-4900	R	16*	<0.1
La Canasta of Minnesota Inc	2570 Kasota Av	St Paul	MN	55108	Joel Bachuel	612-646-1888	S	16	0.1
Standard Foods Inc	1101 E Washington	Louisville	KY	40206	Gordon Dabney	502-587-8877	R	16	0.1
Pacific Foods Inc	21612 88th Av S	Kent	WA	98031	Charles Eggert	206-395-9400	R	15*	<0.1
ABI Food Services Inc	PO Box 11128	Chattanooga	TN	37401	Frank Feist	615-624-4681	S	15	0.1
ED Smith Inc	PO Box 489	Byhalia	MS	38611	Llewellyn S Smith	601-838-2121	S	15	0.2

Source: *Ward's Business Directory of U.S. Private and Public Companies*, Volumes 1 and 2, 1996. The company type code used is as follows: P - Public, R - Private, S - Subsidiary, D - Division, J - Joint Venture, A - Affiliate, G - Group. Sales are in millions of dollars, employees are in thousands. An asterisk (*) indicates an estimated sales volume. The symbol < stands for 'less than'. Company names and addresses are truncated, in some cases, to fit into the available space.

MATERIALS CONSUMED

Material		Quantity	Delivered Cost ($ million)
Materials, ingredients, containers, and supplies		(X)	5,809.5
Shelled peanuts	mil lb	635.6	449.4
Sweetcorn, fresh or frozen	1,000 s tons	(D)	(D)
White potatoes	1,000 s tons	180.2**	29.9
Other fresh vegetables	1,000 s tons	427.4**	137.6
Dried vegetables, except potatoes and corn	1,000 s tons	89.9*	84.0
Popcorn, whole grain	mil lb	476.9	76.3
Field corn, whole grain	mil lb	(S)	24.0
Corn grits, meal, and flakes	1,000 cwt	(S)	63.8
Corn flour	1,000 cwt	149.3**	29.0
Wheat flour	1,000 cwt	7,465.8*	159.2
Spices, raw	mil lb	386.5*	414.3
Green coffee	1,000 cwt	(D)	(D)
Raw tea	mil lb	133.2	119.7
Corn syrup	mil lb	201.5	22.6
Sugar, cane and beet (in terms of sugar solids)	1,000 s tons	394.0	204.4
Chocolate (compounds, cocoa, chocolate liquor, coatings, chocolate flavoring, etc.)	mil lb	26.4	18.1
Fats and oils, all types (purchased as such)	mil lb	203.8*	98.9
Paperboard containers, boxes, and corrugated paperboard		(X)	281.3
Packaging paper and plastics film, coated and laminated		(X)	147.3
Bags; plastics, foil, and coated paper		(X)	50.0
Bags; uncoated paper and multiwall		(X)	14.8
Glass containers		(X)	72.9
Metal cans, can lids and ends		(X)	33.1
All other materials and components, parts, containers, and supplies		(X)	2,287.2
Materials, ingredients, containers, and supplies, nsk		(X)	966.2

Source: 1992 *Economic Census*. Explanation of symbols used: (D): Withheld to avoid disclosure of competitive data; na: Not available; (S): Withheld because statistical norms were not met; (X): Not applicable; (Z): Less than half the unit shown; nec: Not elsewhere classified; nsk: Not specified by kind; - : zero; * : 10-19 percent estimated; ** : 20-29 percent estimated.

PRODUCT SHARE DETAILS

Product or Product Class	% Share
Food preparations, nec	100.00
Desserts (ready-to-mix)	4.99
Ready-to-mix desserts with cornstarch base, consumer sizes (less than 1 lb)	28.95
Ready-to-mix desserts with cornstarch base, commercial sizes (1 lb or more)	4.00
Ready-to-mix desserts with gelatin base, consumer sizes (less than 1 lb)	45.78
Ready-to-mix desserts with gelatin base, commercial sizes (1 lb or more)	0.99
Ready-to-mix desserts, other base	6.10
Desserts (ready-to-mix), nsk	14.18
Sweetening syrups and molasses	4.28
Sweetening syrups and molasses containing corn syrup	86.88
Sweetening syrups and molasses not containing corn syrup	9.51
Sweetening syrups and molasses, nsk	3.60
Baking powder and yeast	2.23
Baking powder	19.24
Compressed yeast	52.34
Active dry yeast	(D)
Other yeast products (brewers', primary grown yeast, including torule, extracts, and other yeast products)	9.46
Baking powder and yeast, nsk	(D)
Vinegar and cider	1.61
Cider	21.23
Vinegar, fermented (basis equivalent to 40 grain)	18.16
Vinegar, distilled (basis equivalent to 100 grain)	55.19
Vinegar and cider, nsk	5.43
Perishable prepared foods sold in bulk or packages, not frozen or canned	16.65
Salads sold in bulk or packages, not frozen or canned	21.84
Sandwiches, made from bread, sold in bulk or packages, not frozen or canned	10.90
Vegetables and potatoes, peeled or cut for the trade, sold in bulk or packages, not frozen or canned	5.09
Tortillas sold in bulk or packages, not frozen or canned	27.07
Tamales and other mexican food specialties sold in bulk or packages, not frozen or canned	10.56
Prepared meals, including meat and poultry pies, sold in bulk or packages, not frozen or canned	4.04
Tofu (bean curd) sold in bulk or packages, not frozen or canned	2.99
Pizza sold in bulk or packages, not frozen or canned	4.70
Other perishable prepared foods	9.40
Perishable prepared foods sold in bulk or packages, not frozen or canned, nsk	3.42
Macaroni and noodle products packaged with other ingredients, not canned or frozen	7.91
Dry (less than 14 percent moisture) macaroni, spaghetti, vermicelli, and other macaroni products packaged with other ingredients, not canned or frozen	54.49
Wet (14 percent or more moisture) macaroni, spaghetti, vermicelli, and other macaroni products packaged with other ingredients, not canned, frozen, or refrigerated	(D)
Refrigerated macaroni, spaghetti, vermicelli, and other macaroni products packaged with other ingredients, not canned or frozen	6.16
Dry (less than 14 percent moisture) noodle products of all shapes, sizes, and types (except chinese), packaged with other ingredients, not canned or frozen	14.42
Wet (14 percent or more moisture) noodle products of all shapes, sizes, and types (except chinese), packaged with other ingredients, not canned, frozen, or refrigerated	(D)
Refrigerated noodle products of all shapes, sizes, and types (except chinese), packaged with other ingredients, not canned or frozen	1.12
Macaroni and noodle products packaged with other ingredients, not canned or frozen, nsk	1.44
Dry mix preparations, except macaroni and noodles	15.50
Dry dip mixes	0.75
Dry salad dressing mixes	(D)
Dry gravy and sauce mixes	13.94
Dry seasoning mixes	31.51
Dry frosting mixes	(D)
Dried and dehydrated potatoes, packaged with other ingredients	5.79
Head rice packaged with other ingredients	17.99
Other dry preparations, including bouillon, etc., but excluding imitation dairy mixes	12.27
Tea in consumer packages	7.80
Tea in consumer packages, packed in tea bags	66.19
Instant soluble tea, with or without added flavoring and/or sweetener	31.53
Other tea in consumer packages	1.95
Tea in consumer packages, nsk	0.33
Spices	7.91
Pepper, white and black, in consumer sizes (less than 1 lb)	13.91
Pepper, white and black, in commercial sizes (1 lb or more)	6.38
Other spices in consumer sizes (less than 1 lb)	47.09
Other spices in commercial sizes (1 lb or more)	31.56
Spices, nsk	1.06
Peanut butter	8.95
Peanut butter in consumer sizes	91.40
Peanut butter in commercial sizes and bulk	8.24
Peanut butter, nsk	0.36
Other food preparations, nec	11.71
Coconut, sweetened, creamed, and toasted	2.56
Blended honey, including churned	8.93
Chinese noodles, except canned and frozen	6.14
Pectin (100 grade, dry basis)	1.38
Unpopped popcorn, in consumer packages	40.90
Cracker sandwiches, made from purchased crackers	(D)
Food preparations, not elsewhere classified	38.52
Other food preparations, nec, nsk	(D)
Food preparations, nec, nsk	10.44

Source: 1992 *Economic Census*. The values shown are percent of total shipments in an industry. Values of indented subcategories are summed in the main heading. The symbol (D) appears when data are withheld to prevent disclosure of competitive information. The abbreviation nsk stands for 'not specified by kind' and nec for 'not elsewhere classified'.

INPUTS AND OUTPUTS FOR FOOD PREPARATIONS, NEC

Economic Sector or Industry Providing Inputs	%	Sector	Economic Sector or Industry Buying Outputs	%	Sector
Miscellaneous plastics products	11.8	Manufg.	Personal consumption expenditures	75.9	
Wholesale trade	11.6	Trade	Eating & drinking places	10.8	Trade
Imports	8.7	Foreign	Exports	1.6	Foreign
Cyclic crudes and organics	5.8	Manufg.	Bread, cake, & related products	1.1	Manufg.
Noncomparable imports	4.0	Foreign	Fluid milk	1.1	Manufg.
Paper coating & glazing	3.9	Manufg.	Sausages & other prepared meats	1.1	Manufg.
Oil bearing crops	3.8	Agric.	Change in business inventories	1.1	In House
Paperboard containers & boxes	3.8	Manufg.	Ice cream & frozen desserts	0.8	Manufg.
Vegetables	3.6	Agric.	Meat packing plants	0.6	Manufg.
Advertising	3.2	Services	Motion pictures	0.6	Services
Motor freight transportation & warehousing	2.9	Util.	Hospitals	0.5	Services
Shortening & cooking oils	2.8	Manufg.	Federal Government purchases, nondefense	0.5	Fed Govt
Glass containers	2.5	Manufg.	Confectionery products	0.4	Manufg.
Sugar	2.2	Manufg.	Residential care	0.4	Services
Commercial printing	2.1	Manufg.	Food preparations, nec	0.3	Manufg.
Bags, except textile	1.9	Manufg.	Pickles, sauces, & salad dressings	0.3	Manufg.
Miscellaneous livestock	1.2	Agric.	Canned fruits & vegetables	0.2	Manufg.

Continued on next page.

INPUTS AND OUTPUTS FOR FOOD PREPARATIONS, NEC - Continued

Economic Sector or Industry Providing Inputs	%	Sector	Economic Sector or Industry Buying Outputs	%	Sector
Metal cans	1.2	Manufg.	Frozen specialties	0.2	Manufg.
Electric services (utilities)	1.2	Util.	Prepared feeds, nec	0.2	Manufg.
Miscellaneous crops	1.1	Agric.	Nursing & personal care facilities	0.2	Services
Metal foil & leaf	1.1	Manufg.	Social services, nec	0.2	Services
Gas production & distribution (utilities)	1.1	Util.	S/L Govt. purch., elem. & secondary education	0.2	S/L Govt
Flour & other grain mill products	1.0	Manufg.	S/L Govt. purch., health & hospitals	0.2	S/L Govt
Forestry products	0.9	Agric.	S/L Govt. purch., higher education	0.2	S/L Govt
Feed grains	0.8	Agric.	Cheese, natural & processed	0.1	Manufg.
Eating & drinking places	0.8	Trade	Cookies & crackers	0.1	Manufg.
Chemical preparations, nec	0.7	Manufg.	Federal Government enterprises nec	0.1	Gov't
Cottonseed oil mills	0.7	Manufg.	Federal Government purchases, national defense	0.1	Fed Govt
Industrial inorganic chemicals, nec	0.7	Manufg.			
Railroads & related services	0.7	Util.			
Water transportation	0.7	Util.			
Business services nec	0.7	Services			
Chocolate & cocoa products	0.5	Manufg.			
Food preparations, nec	0.5	Manufg.			
Wet corn milling	0.5	Manufg.			
Banking	0.5	Fin/R.E.			
Bread, cake, & related products	0.4	Manufg.			
Crowns & closures	0.4	Manufg.			
Dehydrated food products	0.4	Manufg.			
Communications, except radio & TV	0.4	Util.			
Electrical repair shops	0.4	Services			
Maintenance of nonfarm buildings nec	0.3	Constr.			
Cheese, natural & processed	0.3	Manufg.			
Flavoring extracts & syrups, nec	0.3	Manufg.			
Petroleum refining	0.3	Manufg.			
Real estate	0.3	Fin/R.E.			
Equipment rental & leasing services	0.3	Services			
Legal services	0.3	Services			
Management & consulting services & labs	0.3	Services			
U.S. Postal Service	0.3	Gov't			
Sugar crops	0.2	Agric.			
Creamery butter	0.2	Manufg.			
Soybean oil mills	0.2	Manufg.			
Air transportation	0.2	Util.			
Sanitary services, steam supply, irrigation	0.2	Util.			
Royalties	0.2	Fin/R.E.			
Accounting, auditing & bookkeeping	0.2	Services			
Detective & protective services	0.2	Services			
State & local government enterprises, nec	0.2	Gov't			
Alkalies & chlorine	0.1	Manufg.			
Bottled & canned soft drinks	0.1	Manufg.			
Food products machinery	0.1	Manufg.			
Lubricating oils & greases	0.1	Manufg.			
Machinery, except electrical, nec	0.1	Manufg.			
Poultry & egg processing	0.1	Manufg.			
Water supply & sewage systems	0.1	Util.			
Business/professional associations	0.1	Services			
Miscellaneous repair shops	0.1	Services			

Source: Benchmark Input-Output Accounts for the U.S. Economy, 1982, U.S. Department of Commerce, Washington, D.C., July 1991. Data, as reported in the source, are organized by the 1977 SIC structure in use in 1982 but have been matched, as closely as is possible, to the 1987 SIC structure used in this book.

OCCUPATIONS EMPLOYED BY SIC 209 - MISCELLANEOUS FOODS AND KINDRED PRODUCTS

Occupation	% of Total 1994	Change to 2005	Occupation	% of Total 1994	Change to 2005
Cannery workers	10.4	26.3	Machine feeders & offbearers	1.9	3.3
Packaging & filling machine operators	8.7	26.3	Industrial truck & tractor operators	1.9	14.8
Hand packers & packagers	8.0	-1.6	Janitors & cleaners, incl maids	1.7	-8.2
Helpers, laborers, & material movers nec	6.7	14.8	Bakers, manufacturing	1.7	35.9
Meat, poultry, & fish cutters & trimmers, hand	5.8	14.8	Maintenance repairers, general utility	1.5	3.3
Cooking, roasting machine operators	3.4	26.3	Inspectors, testers, & graders, precision	1.5	14.8
Truck drivers light & heavy	3.2	18.3	Agricultural workers nec	1.3	14.8
Driver/sales workers	2.8	3.3	Industrial production managers	1.3	14.8
General managers & top executives	2.2	8.9	Bookkeeping, accounting, & auditing clerks	1.2	-13.9
Industrial machinery mechanics	2.2	26.2	Traffic, shipping, & receiving clerks	1.2	10.5
Precision food & tobacco workers nec	2.2	14.8	Secretaries, ex legal & medical	1.2	4.5
Freight, stock, & material movers, hand	2.1	-8.2	Extruding & forming machine workers	1.2	26.3
Crushing & mixing machine operators	2.0	14.8	Butchers & meatcutters	1.2	27.4
Assemblers, fabricators, & hand workers nec	2.0	14.8	General office clerks	1.1	-2.1
Sales & related workers nec	1.9	14.8			

Source: Industry-Occupation Matrix, Bureau of Labor Statistics. These data relate to one or more 3-digit SIC industry groups rather than to a single 4-digit SIC. The change reported for each occupation to the year 2005 is a percent of growth or decline as estimated by the Bureau of Labor Statistics. The abbreviation nec stands for 'not elsewhere classified'.

LOCATION BY STATE AND REGIONAL CONCENTRATION

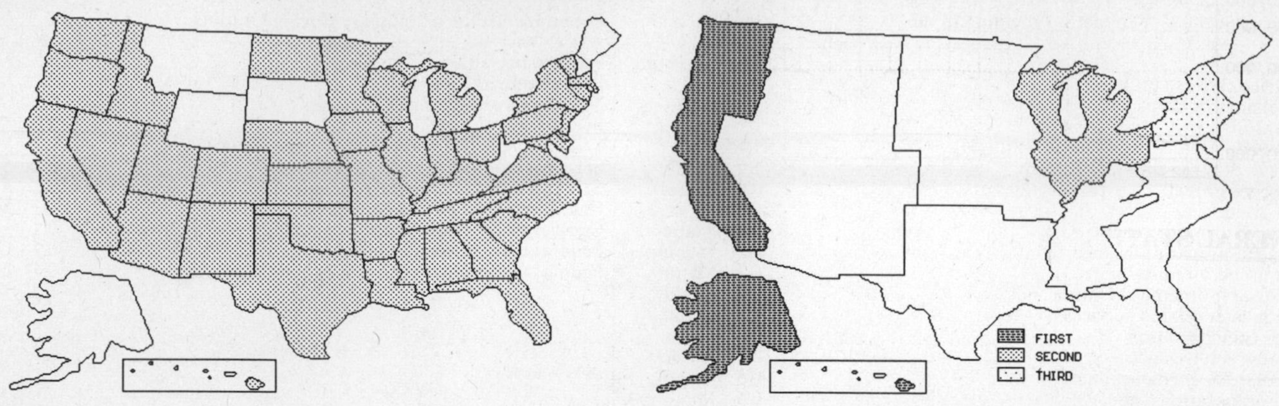

INDUSTRY DATA BY STATE

State	Establish-ments	Shipments			Employment				Cost as % of Shipments	Investment per Employee ($)
		Total ($ mil)	% of U.S.	Per Establ.	Total Number	% of U.S.	Per Establ.	Wages ($/hour)		
California	337	1,932.3	15.9	5.7	12,400	20.2	37	8.26	46.3	3,573
Illinois	97	1,032.1	8.5	10.6	5,200	8.5	54	9.82	48.7	6,173
Maryland	32	746.6	6.1	23.3	2,100	3.4	66	16.83	55.9	10,000
Virginia	20	642.2	5.3	32.1	1,700	2.8	85	11.50	43.2	10,765
Georgia	37	526.2	4.3	14.2	1,600	2.6	43	10.32	68.6	4,563
Texas	174	489.6	4.0	2.8	4,300	7.0	25	6.66	50.9	3,395
Ohio	53	472.4	3.9	8.9	2,100	3.4	40	8.72	42.6	3,333
Kentucky	13	456.4	3.8	35.1	800	1.3	62	10.85	68.1	11,375
Wisconsin	54	421.6	3.5	7.8	1,800	2.9	33	10.92	48.8	-
New York	111	399.1	3.3	3.6	2,700	4.4	24	8.53	50.8	3,148
Indiana	27	368.7	3.0	13.7	1,700	2.8	63	9.04	40.0	4,529
Pennsylvania	66	360.7	3.0	5.5	1,800	2.9	27	9.57	52.6	3,889
New Jersey	54	296.9	2.4	5.5	1,700	2.8	31	10.33	63.3	6,294
Iowa	16	271.2	2.2	17.0	1,000	1.6	63	9.71	68.1	6,000
Minnesota	42	219.5	1.8	5.2	1,200	2.0	29	9.30	42.5	-
Missouri	24	212.3	1.7	8.8	500	0.8	21	9.38	80.9	-
Washington	55	209.6	1.7	3.8	1,400	2.3	25	9.82	51.2	5,429
Michigan	55	186.2	1.5	3.4	1,300	2.1	24	7.33	48.2	2,769
Colorado	37	184.7	1.5	5.0	1,500	2.4	41	7.37	47.0	3,600
Louisiana	28	176.5	1.5	6.3	1,000	1.6	36	8.13	48.0	-
North Carolina	27	147.5	1.2	5.5	1,600	2.6	59	9.36	57.6	7,250
Massachusetts	37	136.8	1.1	3.7	700	1.1	19	10.10	42.0	8,429
Florida	51	121.3	1.0	2.4	700	1.1	14	8.78	45.9	3,143
Oregon	35	118.9	1.0	3.4	700	1.1	20	8.30	45.2	4,143
Alabama	16	108.1	0.9	6.8	700	1.1	44	7.75	66.4	8,857
Arizona	30	78.9	0.6	2.6	900	1.5	30	5.83	52.5	4,000
Hawaii	42	60.7	0.5	1.4	600	1.0	14	7.71	48.3	1,667
Oklahoma	17	58.9	0.5	3.5	400	0.7	24	9.20	75.2	2,500
Nebraska	13	39.4	0.3	3.0	200	0.3	15	11.50	74.9	-
New Mexico	21	39.1	0.3	1.9	400	0.7	19	6.60	49.4	3,000
Connecticut	15	29.2	0.2	1.9	300	0.5	20	9.50	45.2	6,667
Nevada	10	26.4	0.2	2.6	200	0.3	20	12.50	49.6	4,000
Utah	9	20.4	0.2	2.3	200	0.3	22	9.00	54.4	4,000
Tennessee	30	(D)	-	-	750 *	1.2	25	-	-	4,800
Kansas	19	(D)	-	-	1,750 *	2.9	92	-	-	-
Vermont	16	(D)	-	-	175 *	0.3	11	-	-	-
Idaho	10	(D)	-	-	175 *	0.3	18	-	-	-
Arkansas	9	(D)	-	-	1,750 *	2.9	194	-	-	-
Mississippi	8	(D)	-	-	750 *	1.2	94	-	-	-
South Carolina	8	(D)	-	-	750 *	1.2	94	-	-	-
North Dakota	7	(D)	-	-	375 *	0.6	54	-	-	-
Delaware	2	(D)	-	-	1,750 *	2.9	875	-	-	-

Source: 1992 *Economic Census*. The states are in descending order of shipments or establishments (if shipment data are missing for the majority). The symbol (D) appears when data are withheld to prevent disclosure of competitive information. States marked with (D) are sorted by number of establishments. A dash (-) indicates that the data element cannot be calculated; * indicates the midpoint of a range.

2111 - CIGARETTES

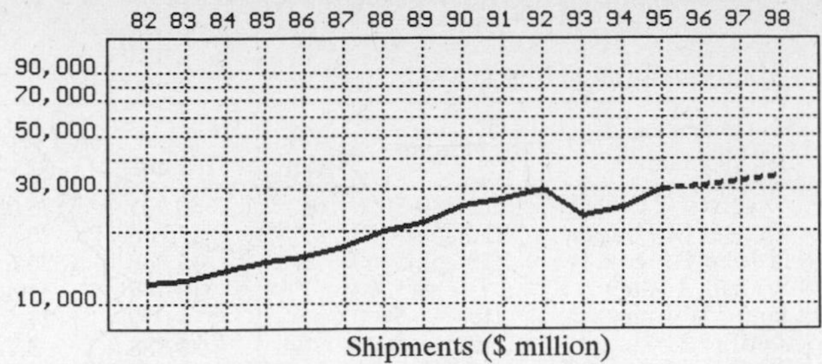

Shipments ($ million)

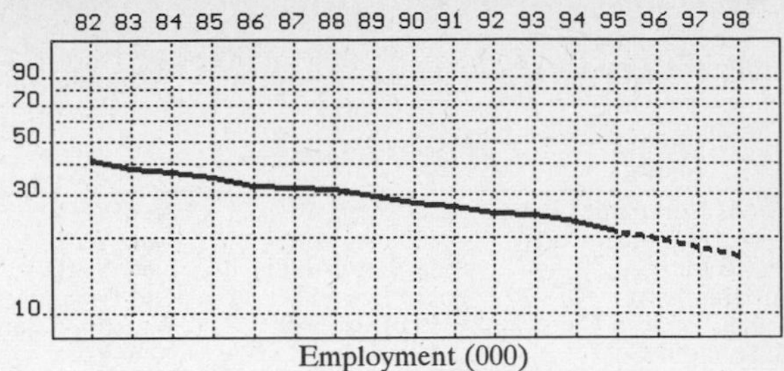

Employment (000)

GENERAL STATISTICS

Year	Companies	Establishments		Employment			Compensation		Production ($ million)			
		Total	with 20 or more employees	Total (000)	Production Workers (000)	Production Hours (Mil)	Payroll ($ mil)	Wages ($/hr)	Cost of Materials	Value Added by Manufacture	Value of Shipments	Capital Invest.
1982	8	14	13	41.5	32.2	58.5	1,093.7	13.69	4,052.3	8,098.3	12,126.8	570.9
1983				38.6	29.2	52.3	1,112.1	15.31	3,986.0	8,624.0	12,610.5	570.0
1984				36.8	27.0	50.2	1,123.0	15.66	4,403.3	9,538.0	13,938.4	624.8
1985				35.5	26.6	47.9	1,130.7	16.70	4,362.1	10,540.7	14,896.8	622.2
1986				32.7	24.0	43.8	1,101.4	17.31	4,205.2	11,501.1	15,699.1	601.6
1987	8	12	12	32.0	23.6	42.9	1,233.7	20.05	4,396.6	12,970.7	17,372.0	410.2
1988				31.9	23.9	41.9	1,238.6	20.42	4,471.1	15,624.0	20,078.3	365.7
1989		13	13	29.6	22.1	39.1	1,212.4	21.28	4,583.6	17,240.1	21,825.1	288.4
1990				27.8	20.2	38.8	1,229.7	21.84	4,874.1	20,628.3	25,522.4	236.7
1991				26.9	19.5	35.1	1,224.0	23.60	4,902.4	22,209.6	27,111.0	341.9
1992	8	11	10	25.4	18.1	33.0	1,205.0	24.58	4,965.6	24,801.9	29,746.1	322.5
1993				24.7	17.8	30.6	1,129.4	24.71	4,634.2	18,652.1	23,266.3	338.6
1994				23.0	16.4	29.9	1,151.7	26.54	5,133.1	19,759.1	24,879.4	347.1
1995				21.1P	14.7P	26.4P	1,217.2P	27.47P	6,125.4P	23,578.8P	29,688.9P	226.1P
1996				19.7P	13.5P	24.2P	1,224.3P	28.52P	6,413.1P	24,686.2P	31,083.3P	196.5P
1997				18.2P	12.4P	22.0P	1,231.3P	29.56P	6,700.8P	25,793.5P	32,477.6P	166.8P
1998				16.8P	11.2P	19.8P	1,238.3P	30.61P	6,988.4P	26,900.9P	33,871.9P	137.1P

Sources: 1982, 1987, 1992 *Economic Census*; *Annual Survey of Manufactures*, 83-86, 88-91, 93-94. Establishment counts for non-Census years are from *County Business Patterns*; establishment values for 83-84 are extrapolations. 'P's show projections by the editors. Industries reclassified in 87 will not have data for prior years.

INDICES OF CHANGE

Year	Companies	Establishments		Employment			Compensation		Production ($ million)			
		Total	with 20 or more employees	Total (000)	Production Workers (000)	Production Hours (Mil)	Payroll ($ mil)	Wages ($/hr)	Cost of Materials	Value Added by Manufacture	Value of Shipments	Capital Invest.
1982	100	127	130	163	178	177	91	56	82	33	41	177
1983				152	161	158	92	62	80	35	42	177
1984				145	149	152	93	64	89	38	47	194
1985				140	147	145	94	68	88	42	50	193
1986				129	133	133	91	70	85	46	53	187
1987	100	109	120	126	130	130	102	82	89	52	58	127
1988				126	132	127	103	83	90	63	67	113
1989		118	130	117	122	118	101	87	92	70	73	89
1990				109	112	118	102	89	98	83	86	73
1991				106	108	106	102	96	99	90	91	106
1992	100	100	100	100	100	100	100	100	100	100	100	100
1993				97	98	93	94	101	93	75	78	105
1994				91	91	91	96	108	103	80	84	108
1995				83P	81P	80P	101P	112P	123P	95P	100P	70P
1996				77P	75P	73P	102P	116P	129P	100P	104P	61P
1997				72P	68P	67P	102P	120P	135P	104P	109P	52P
1998				66P	62P	60P	103P	125P	141P	108P	114P	43P

Sources: Same as General Statistics. Values reflect change from the base year, 1992. Values above 100 mean greater than 92, values below 100 mean less than 92, and a value of 100 in the 82-91 or 93-98 period means same as 92. 'P's mark projections by the editors.

SELECTED RATIOS

For 1992	Avg. of All Manufact.	Analyzed Industry	Index	For 1992	Avg. of All Manufact.	Analyzed Industry	Index
Employees per Establishment	46	2,309	5,057	Value Added per Production Worker	122,353	1,370,271	1,120
Payroll per Establishment	1,332,320	109,545,455	8,222	Cost per Establishment	4,239,462	451,418,182	10,648
Payroll per Employee	29,181	47,441	163	Cost per Employee	92,853	195,496	211
Production Workers per Establishment	31	1,645	5,240	Cost per Production Worker	135,003	274,343	203
Wages per Establishment	734,496	73,740,000	10,040	Shipments per Establishment	8,100,800	2,704,190,909	33,382
Wages per Production Worker	23,390	44,814	192	Shipments per Employee	177,425	1,171,106	660
Hours per Production Worker	2,025	1,823	90	Shipments per Production Worker	257,966	1,643,431	637
Wages per Hour	11.55	24.58	213	Investment per Establishment	278,244	29,318,182	10,537
Value Added per Establishment	3,842,210	2,254,718,182	58,683	Investment per Employee	6,094	12,697	208
Value Added per Employee	84,153	976,453	1,160	Investment per Production Worker	8,861	17,818	201

Sources: Same as General Statistics. The 'Average of All Manufacturing' column represents the average of all manufacturing industries reported for the most recent complete year available. The Index shows the relationship between the Average and the Analyzed Industry. For example, 100 means that they are equal; 500 that the Analyzed Industry is five times the average; 50 means that the Analyzed Industry is half the national average. The abbreviation 'na' is used to show that data are 'not available'.

LEADING COMPANIES

Number shown: 6 Total sales ($ mil): **114,746** Total employment (000): **374.2**

Company Name	Address				CEO Name	Phone	Co. Type	Sales ($ mil)	Empl. (000)
Philip Morris Companies Inc	120 Park Av	New York	NY	10017	Geoffrey C Bible	212-880-5000	P	60,901	173.0
RJR Nabisco Holdings Corp	1301 Av Amer	New York	NY	10019	Charles M Harper	212-258-5600	P	15,366	70.6
RJR Nabisco Inc	1301 Av Amer	New York	NY	10019	H John Greeniaus	212-258-5600	S	15,366	70.6
American Brands Inc	PO Box 811	Old Greenwich	CT	06870	William J Alley	203-698-5000	P	13,146	34.8
RJ Reynolds Tobacco Co	PO Box 2959	Winston-Salem	NC	27102	James W Johnston	919-741-5000	S	8,079	21.5
Lorillard Tobacco Co	1 Park Av	New York	NY	10016	Andrew H Tisch	212-545-3000	S	1,888	3.7

Source: *Ward's Business Directory of U.S. Private and Public Companies*, Volumes 1 and 2, 1996. The company type code used is as follows: P - Public, R - Private, S - Subsidiary, D - Division, J - Joint Venture, A - Affiliate, G - Group. Sales are in millions of dollars, employees are in thousands. An asterisk (*) indicates an estimated sales volume. The symbol < stands for 'less than'. Company names and addresses are truncated, in some cases, to fit into the available space.

MATERIALS CONSUMED

Material		Quantity	Delivered Cost ($ million)
Materials, ingredients, containers, and supplies		(X)	4,589.1
Unstemmed leaf tobacco including green tobacco not packed	mil lb	(D)	(D)
Unstemmed leaf tobacco, redried and packed	mil lb	(D)	(D)
Stemmed leaf tobacco, excluding processed sheet and homogenized tobacco	mil lb	1,013.0	2,157.2
Reconstituted tobacco, processed sheet and homogenized	mil lb	297.9	183.6
Paperboard containers, boxes, and corrugated paperboard		(X)	294.9
Manmade fibers, staple, and tow		(X)	305.3
All other materials and components, parts, containers, and supplies		(X)	1,120.3

Source: 1992 *Economic Census*. Explanation of symbols used: (D): Withheld to avoid disclosure of competitive data; na: Not available; (S): Withheld because statistical norms were not met; (X): Not applicable; (Z): Less than half the unit shown; nec: Not elsewhere classified; nsk: Not specified by kind; - : zero; * : 10-19 percent estimated; ** : 20-29 percent estimated.

PRODUCT SHARE DETAILS

Product or Product Class	% Share
Cigarettes	100.00
Filter tip cigarettes, including nontobacco cigarettes, 80 millimeters long or less	(D)
Filter tip cigarettes, including nontobacco cigarettes, 85 millimeters long	49.91
Filter tip cigarettes, including nontobacco cigarettes, 100 millimeters or more long	(D)
Nonfilter tip cigarettes, including nontobacco cigarettes	2.62

Source: 1992 *Economic Census*. The values shown are percent of total shipments in an industry. Values of indented subcategories are summed in the main heading. The symbol (D) appears when data are withheld to prevent disclosure of competitive information. The abbreviation nsk stands for 'not specified by kind' and nec for 'not elsewhere classified'.

INPUTS AND OUTPUTS FOR CIGARETTES

Economic Sector or Industry Providing Inputs	%	Sector	Economic Sector or Industry Buying Outputs	%	Sector
Tobacco stemming & redrying	51.0	Manufg.	Personal consumption expenditures	92.1	
Paperboard containers & boxes	11.0	Manufg.	Exports	7.9	Foreign
Advertising	8.3	Services			
Wholesale trade	5.8	Trade			
Commercial printing	5.1	Manufg.			
Metal foil & leaf	1.8	Manufg.			
Banking	1.8	Fin/R.E.			
Miscellaneous plastics products	1.6	Manufg.			
Petroleum refining	1.5	Manufg.			
Paper mills, except building paper	1.0	Manufg.			
U.S. Postal Service	1.0	Gov't			
Electric services (utilities)	0.9	Util.			
Paper coating & glazing	0.8	Manufg.			
Motor freight transportation & warehousing	0.5	Util.			
Royalties	0.5	Fin/R.E.			
Business services nec	0.5	Services			
Air transportation	0.4	Util.			
Communications, except radio & TV	0.4	Util.			
Imports	0.4	Foreign			
Cyclic crudes and organics	0.3	Manufg.			
Soap & other detergents	0.3	Manufg.			
Gas production & distribution (utilities)	0.3	Util.			
Eating & drinking places	0.3	Trade			
Automotive rental & leasing, without drivers	0.3	Services			
Equipment rental & leasing services	0.3	Services			
Coal	0.2	Mining			

Continued on next page.

INPUTS AND OUTPUTS FOR CIGARETTES - Continued

Economic Sector or Industry Providing Inputs	%	Sector	Economic Sector or Industry Buying Outputs	%	Sector
Maintenance of nonfarm buildings nec	0.2	Constr.			
Adhesives & sealants	0.2	Manufg.			
Lubricating oils & greases	0.2	Manufg.			
Machinery, except electrical, nec	0.2	Manufg.			
Credit agencies other than banks	0.2	Fin/R.E.			
Insurance carriers	0.2	Fin/R.E.			
Automotive repair shops & services	0.2	Services			
Computer & data processing services	0.2	Services			
Railroads & related services	0.1	Util.			
Real estate	0.1	Fin/R.E.			
Hotels & lodging places	0.1	Services			
Legal services	0.1	Services			
Management & consulting services & labs	0.1	Services			

Source: Benchmark Input-Output Accounts for the U.S. Economy, 1982, U.S. Department of Commerce, Washington, D.C., July 1991. Data, as reported in the source, are organized by the 1977 SIC structure in use in 1982 but have been matched, as closely as is possible, to the 1987 SIC structure used in this book.

OCCUPATIONS EMPLOYED BY SIC 211 - TOBACCO PRODUCTS

Occupation	% of Total 1994	Change to 2005	Occupation	% of Total 1994	Change to 2005
Machine operators nec	12.3	-43.9	Freight, stock, & material movers, hand	2.3	-49.0
Helpers, laborers, & material movers nec	11.3	-36.3	Precision food & tobacco workers nec	2.1	-30.0
Packaging & filling machine operators	7.3	-36.3	Secretaries, ex legal & medical	2.0	-42.0
Industrial machinery mechanics	7.0	-29.9	Science & mathematics technicians	1.4	-36.3
Blue collar worker supervisors	5.5	-39.0	Maintenance repairers, general utility	1.3	-42.7
Sales & related workers nec	4.6	-36.3	General managers & top executives	1.3	-39.5
Industrial truck & tractor operators	3.4	-36.3	Systems analysts	1.3	1.9
Management support workers nec	3.4	-36.3	Industrial production managers	1.1	-36.2
Machine feeders & offbearers	3.3	-42.6	Cooking, roasting machine operators	1.0	-29.9
Inspectors, testers, & graders, precision	2.5	-36.3			

Source: Industry-Occupation Matrix, Bureau of Labor Statistics. These data relate to one or more 3-digit SIC industry groups rather than to a single 4-digit SIC. The change reported for each occupation to the year 2005 is a percent of growth or decline as estimated by the Bureau of Labor Statistics. The abbreviation nec stands for 'not elsewhere classified'.

LOCATION BY STATE AND REGIONAL CONCENTRATION

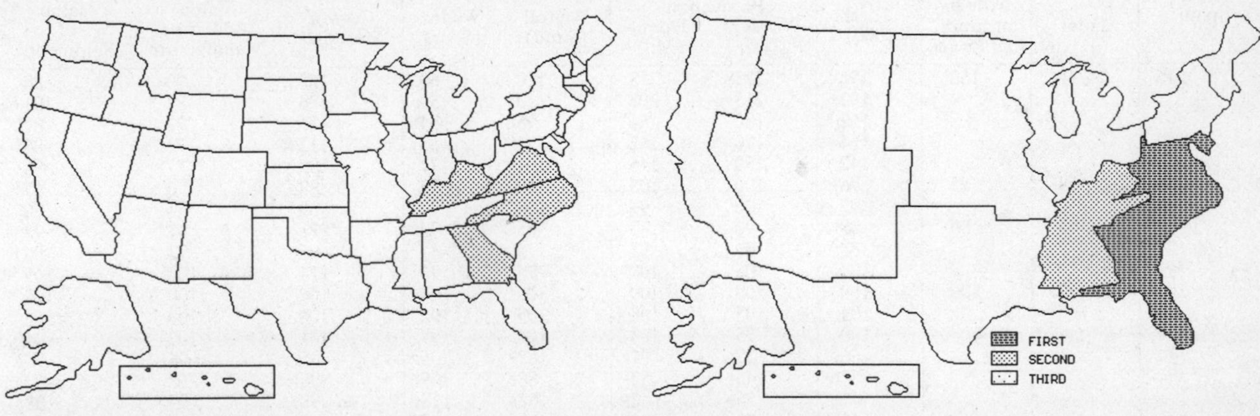

INDUSTRY DATA BY STATE

State	Establish-ments	Shipments: Total ($ mil)	Shipments: % of U.S.	Shipments: Per Establ.	Employment: Total Number	Employment: % of U.S.	Employment: Per Establ.	Employment: Wages ($/hour)	Cost as % of Shipments	Investment per Employee ($)
North Carolina	6	(D)	-	-	17,500 *	68.9	2,917	-	-	-
Kentucky	2	(D)	-	-	3,750 *	14.8	1,875	-	-	-
Georgia	1	(D)	-	-	1,750 *	6.9	1,750	-	-	-
Virginia	1	(D)	-	-	17,500 *	68.9	17,500	-	-	-

Source: 1992 *Economic Census.* The states are in descending order of shipments or establishments (if shipment data are missing for the majority). The symbol (D) appears when data are withheld to prevent disclosure of competitive information. States marked with (D) are sorted by number of establishments. A dash (-) indicates that the data element cannot be calculated; * indicates the midpoint of a range.

2121 - CIGARS

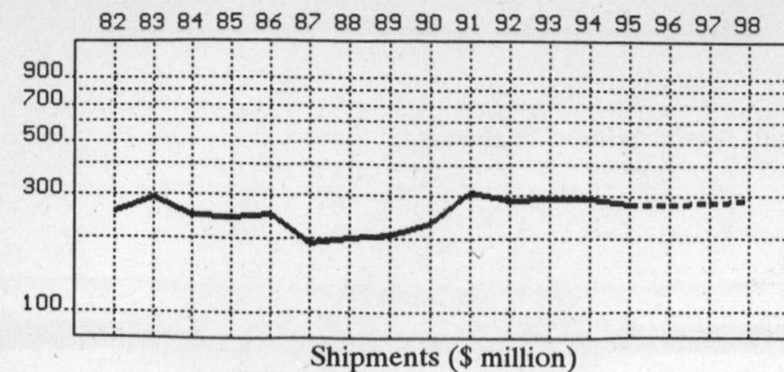

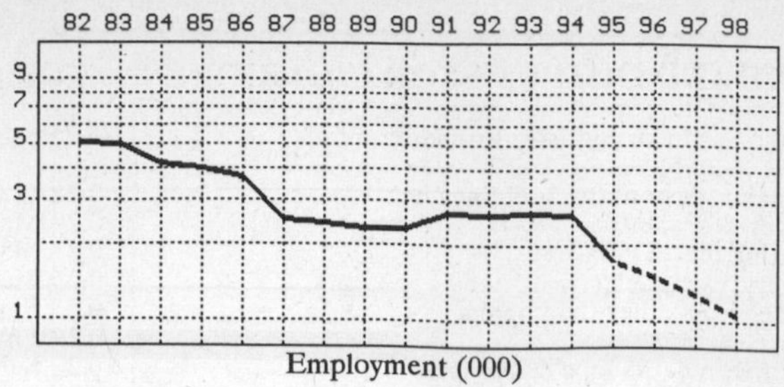

GENERAL STATISTICS

Year	Companies	Establishments: Total	Establishments: with 20 or more employees	Employment: Total (000)	Employment: Production Workers (000)	Employment: Production Hours (Mil)	Compensation: Payroll ($ mil)	Compensation: Wages ($/hr)	Production ($ million): Cost of Materials	Production ($ million): Value Added by Manufacture	Production ($ million): Value of Shipments	Production ($ million): Capital Invest.
1982	54	60	30	5.1	4.5	8.5	58.5	5.34	120.5	133.3	253.7	7.4
1983				5.0	4.3	8.1	58.4	5.28	133.4	156.7	288.9	5.5
1984				4.2	3.6	6.4	50.7	5.78	112.2	135.6	248.3	4.5
1985				4.0	3.4	6.3	50.1	5.62	107.8	136.8	243.8	5.2
1986				3.7	3.0	5.7	55.4	6.68	104.9	147.2	252.1	7.1
1987	16	20	18	2.5	2.0	4.0	35.7	6.55	85.5	106.3	191.5	5.0
1988				2.4	2.0	3.8	33.7	6.32	86.0	115.4	201.7	4.8
1989		20	17	2.3	1.8	3.4	34.5	7.12	87.8	116.8	205.8	3.1
1990				2.3	1.8	3.6	38.6	7.53	92.6	137.0	229.8	3.9
1991				2.7	2.1	3.9	51.3	8.44	110.0	200.8	311.5	3.9
1992	25	27	19	2.6	2.0	3.9	53.3	8.97	96.6	190.1	286.8	3.0
1993				2.7	2.1	4.2	58.1	9.12	104.3	190.2	293.7	2.7
1994				2.6	1.9	3.9	55.2	8.74	97.1	193.2	290.6	0.7
1995				1.7P	1.1P	2.4P	47.1P	9.46P	92.1P	183.3P	275.7P	1.6P
1996				1.5P	0.9P	2.0P	46.9P	9.81P	93.2P	185.4P	278.9P	1.2P
1997				1.3P	0.7P	1.6P	46.6P	10.16P	94.2P	187.5P	282.0P	0.8P
1998				1.1P	0.5P	1.3P	46.4P	10.50P	95.3P	189.6P	285.1P	0.4P

Sources: 1982, 1987, 1992 *Economic Census*; *Annual Survey of Manufactures*, 83-86, 88-91, 93-94. Establishment counts for non-Census years are from *County Business Patterns*; establishment values for 83-84 are extrapolations. 'P's show projections by the editors. Industries reclassified in 87 will not have data for prior years.

INDICES OF CHANGE

Year	Companies	Establishments: Total	Establishments: with 20 or more employees	Employment: Total (000)	Employment: Production Workers (000)	Employment: Production Hours (Mil)	Compensation: Payroll ($ mil)	Compensation: Wages ($/hr)	Production ($ million): Cost of Materials	Production ($ million): Value Added by Manufacture	Production ($ million): Value of Shipments	Production ($ million): Capital Invest.
1982	216	222	158	196	225	218	110	60	125	70	88	247
1983				192	215	208	110	59	138	82	101	183
1984				162	180	164	95	64	116	71	87	150
1985				154	170	162	94	63	112	72	85	173
1986				142	150	146	104	74	109	77	88	237
1987	64	74	95	96	100	103	67	73	89	56	67	167
1988				92	100	97	63	70	89	61	70	160
1989		74	89	88	90	87	65	79	91	61	72	103
1990				88	90	92	72	84	96	72	80	130
1991				104	105	100	96	94	114	106	109	130
1992	100	100	100	100	100	100	100	100	100	100	100	100
1993				104	105	108	109	102	108	100	102	90
1994				100	95	100	104	97	101	102	101	23
1995				66P	57P	61P	88P	106P	95P	96P	96P	53P
1996				57P	46P	52P	88P	109P	96P	98P	97P	40P
1997				49P	35P	42P	88P	113P	98P	99P	98P	26P
1998				40P	24P	32P	87P	117P	99P	100P	99P	13P

Sources: Same as General Statistics. Values reflect change from the base year, 1992. Values above 100 mean greater than 92, values below 100 mean less than 92, and a value of 100 in the 82-91 or 93-98 period means same as 92. 'P's mark projections by the editors.

SELECTED RATIOS

For 1992	Avg. of All Manufact.	Analyzed Industry	Index
Employees per Establishment	46	96	211
Payroll per Establishment	1,332,320	1,974,074	148
Payroll per Employee	29,181	20,500	70
Production Workers per Establishment	31	74	236
Wages per Establishment	734,496	1,295,667	176
Wages per Production Worker	23,390	17,491	75
Hours per Production Worker	2,025	1,950	96
Wages per Hour	11.55	8.97	78
Value Added per Establishment	3,842,210	7,040,741	183
Value Added per Employee	84,153	73,115	87

For 1992	Avg. of All Manufact.	Analyzed Industry	Index
Value Added per Production Worker	122,353	95,050	78
Cost per Establishment	4,239,462	3,577,778	84
Cost per Employee	92,853	37,154	40
Cost per Production Worker	135,003	48,300	36
Shipments per Establishment	8,100,800	10,622,222	131
Shipments per Employee	177,425	110,308	62
Shipments per Production Worker	257,966	143,400	56
Investment per Establishment	278,244	111,111	40
Investment per Employee	6,094	1,154	19
Investment per Production Worker	8,861	1,500	17

Sources: Same as General Statistics. The 'Average of All Manufacturing' column represents the average of all manufacturing industries reported for the most recent complete year available. The Index shows the relationship between the Average and the Analyzed Industry. For example, 100 means that they are equal; 500 that the Analyzed Industry is five times the average; 50 means that the Analyzed Industry is half the national average. The abbreviation 'na' is used to show that data are 'not available'.

LEADING COMPANIES

Number shown: **6** Total sales ($ mil): **443** Total employment (000): **2.1**

Company Name	Address				CEO Name	Phone	Co. Type	Sales ($ mil)	Empl. (000)
General Cigar Co	320 W Newberry Rd	Bloomfield	CT	06002	David Bergh	203-769-3600	S	330*	1.5
Havatampa Inc	PO Box 1261	Tampa	FL	33601	Thomas D Arthur	813-621-3535	R	42*	0.2
Standard Cigar Company Inc	PO Box 2030	Tampa	FL	33601	Eric Newman	813-248-2124	S	29*	0.1
M and N Cigar Manufacturing	PO Box 2030	Tampa	FL	33601	Eric Newman	813-248-2124	R	20	<0.1
Finck Cigar Co	PO Box 831007	San Antonio	TX	78283	Bill Finck	210-226-4191	R	18*	<0.1
National Cigar Corp	PO Box 97	Frankfort	IN	46041	Carl Berger Sr	317-659-3326	R	4	<0.1

Source: *Ward's Business Directory of U.S. Private and Public Companies*, Volumes 1 and 2, 1996. The company type code used is as follows: P - Public, R - Private, S - Subsidiary, D - Division, J - Joint Venture, A - Affiliate, G - Group. Sales are in millions of dollars, employees are in thousands. An asterisk (*) indicates an estimated sales volume. The symbol < stands for 'less than'. Company names and addresses are truncated, in some cases, to fit into the available space.

MATERIALS CONSUMED

Material		Quantity	Delivered Cost ($ million)
Materials, ingredients, containers, and supplies		(X)	78.9
Unstemmed leaf tobacco including green tobacco not packed	mil lb	2.1	6.5
Unstemmed leaf tobacco, redried and packed	mil lb	9.6	10.2
Stemmed leaf tobacco, excluding processed sheet and homogenized tobacco	mil lb	18.0	26.1
Reconstituted tobacco, processed sheet and homogenized	mil lb	4.3	11.1
Paperboard containers, boxes, and corrugated paperboard		(X)	12.3
Manmade fibers, staple, and tow		(X)	0.8
All other materials and components, parts, containers, and supplies		(X)	11.8
Materials, ingredients, containers, and supplies, nsk		(X)	0.1

Source: 1992 *Economic Census*. Explanation of symbols used: (D): Withheld to avoid disclosure of competitive data; na: Not available; (S): Withheld because statistical norms were not met; (X): Not applicable; (Z): Less than half the unit shown; nec: Not elsewhere classified; nsk: Not specified by kind; - : zero; * : 10-19 percent estimated; ** : 20-29 percent estimated.

PRODUCT SHARE DETAILS

Product or Product Class	% Share	Product or Product Class	% Share
Cigars	100.00	Cigarillos weighing 3 to 10 lb per 1,000 cigars	23.28
Little cigars, cigarette-size, weighing less than 3 lb per 1,000 cigars	8.96	Cigars weighing more than 10 lb per 1,000 cigars	67.76

Source: 1992 *Economic Census*. The values shown are percent of total shipments in an industry. Values of indented subcategories are summed in the main heading. The symbol (D) appears when data are withheld to prevent disclosure of competitive information. The abbreviation nsk stands for 'not specified by kind' and nec for 'not elsewhere classified'.

INPUTS AND OUTPUTS FOR CIGARS

Economic Sector or Industry Providing Inputs	%	Sector	Economic Sector or Industry Buying Outputs	%	Sector
Imports	41.8	Foreign	Personal consumption expenditures	97.5	
Tobacco stemming & redrying	28.6	Manufg.	Exports	2.5	Foreign
Paperboard containers & boxes	8.0	Manufg.			
Wholesale trade	4.2	Trade			
Tobacco	1.9	Agric.			
Advertising	1.4	Services			
Metal foil & leaf	1.2	Manufg.			
Electric services (utilities)	1.2	Util.			
Miscellaneous plastics products	1.1	Manufg.			
Banking	1.0	Fin/R.E.			
Eating & drinking places	0.8	Trade			
Paper coating & glazing	0.6	Manufg.			
Machinery, except electrical, nec	0.5	Manufg.			
Periodicals	0.5	Manufg.			
Communications, except radio & TV	0.5	Util.			
Gas production & distribution (utilities)	0.5	Util.			
Lubricating oils & greases	0.4	Manufg.			
Equipment rental & leasing services	0.4	Services			
Maintenance of nonfarm buildings nec	0.3	Constr.			
Motor freight transportation & warehousing	0.3	Util.			
Computer & data processing services	0.3	Services			
Legal services	0.3	Services			
Management & consulting services & labs	0.3	Services			
Noncomparable imports	0.3	Foreign			
Die-cut paper & board	0.2	Manufg.			
Manifold business forms	0.2	Manufg.			

Continued on next page.

INPUTS AND OUTPUTS FOR CIGARS - Continued

Economic Sector or Industry Providing Inputs	%	Sector	Economic Sector or Industry Buying Outputs	%	Sector
Special dies & tools & machine tool accessories	0.2	Manufg.			
Air transportation	0.2	Util.			
Security & commodity brokers	0.2	Fin/R.E.			
Accounting, auditing & bookkeeping	0.2	Services			
Laundry, dry cleaning, shoe repair	0.2	Services			
Distilled liquor, except brandy	0.1	Manufg.			
Gaskets, packing & sealing devices	0.1	Manufg.			
Petroleum refining	0.1	Manufg.			
Soap & other detergents	0.1	Manufg.			
Real estate	0.1	Fin/R.E.			
Automotive repair shops & services	0.1	Services			
Hotels & lodging places	0.1	Services			

Source: Benchmark Input-Output Accounts for the U.S. Economy, 1982, U.S. Department of Commerce, Washington, D.C., July 1991. Data, as reported in the source, are organized by the 1977 SIC structure in use in 1982 but have been matched, as closely as is possible, to the 1987 SIC structure used in this book.

OCCUPATIONS EMPLOYED BY SIC 211 - TOBACCO PRODUCTS

Occupation	% of Total 1994	Change to 2005	Occupation	% of Total 1994	Change to 2005
Machine operators nec	12.3	-43.9	Freight, stock, & material movers, hand	2.3	-49.0
Helpers, laborers, & material movers nec	11.3	-36.3	Precision food & tobacco workers nec	2.1	-30.0
Packaging & filling machine operators	7.3	-36.3	Secretaries, ex legal & medical	2.0	-42.0
Industrial machinery mechanics	7.0	-29.9	Science & mathematics technicians	1.4	-36.3
Blue collar worker supervisors	5.5	-39.0	Maintenance repairers, general utility	1.3	-42.7
Sales & related workers nec	4.6	-36.3	General managers & top executives	1.3	-39.5
Industrial truck & tractor operators	3.4	-36.3	Systems analysts	1.3	1.9
Management support workers nec	3.4	-36.3	Industrial production managers	1.1	-36.2
Machine feeders & offbearers	3.3	-42.6	Cooking, roasting machine operators	1.0	-29.9
Inspectors, testers, & graders, precision	2.5	-36.3			

Source: Industry-Occupation Matrix, Bureau of Labor Statistics. These data relate to one or more 3-digit SIC industry groups rather than to a single 4-digit SIC. The change reported for each occupation to the year 2005 is a percent of growth or decline as estimated by the Bureau of Labor Statistics. The abbreviation nec stands for 'not elsewhere classified'.

LOCATION BY STATE AND REGIONAL CONCENTRATION

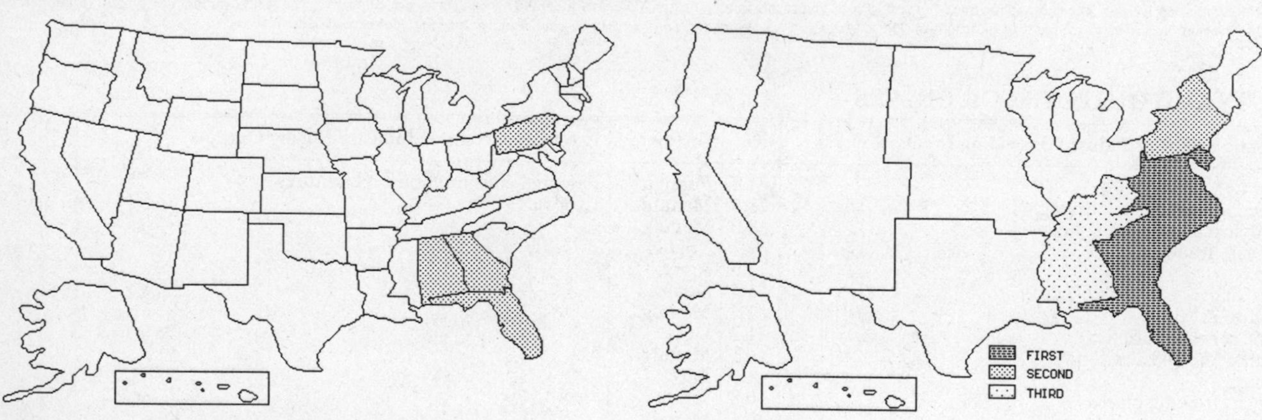

INDUSTRY DATA BY STATE

State	Establish-ments	Shipments Total ($ mil)	Shipments % of U.S.	Shipments Per Establ.	Employment Total Number	Employment % of U.S.	Employment Per Establ.	Wages ($/hour)	Cost as % of Shipments	Investment per Employee ($)
Pennsylvania	6	43.8	15.3	7.3	600	23.1	100	8.67	39.7	-
Florida	12	(D)	-	-	750 *	28.8	63	-	-	-
Alabama	2	(D)	-	-	375 *	14.4	188	-	-	-
Georgia	2	(D)	-	-	375 *	14.4	188	-	-	-

Source: 1992 *Economic Census*. The states are in descending order of shipments or establishments (if shipment data are missing for the majority). The symbol (D) appears when data are withheld to prevent disclosure of competitive information. States marked with (D) are sorted by number of establishments. A dash (-) indicates that the data element cannot be calculated; * indicates the midpoint of a range.

2131 - CHEWING & SMOKING TOBACCO

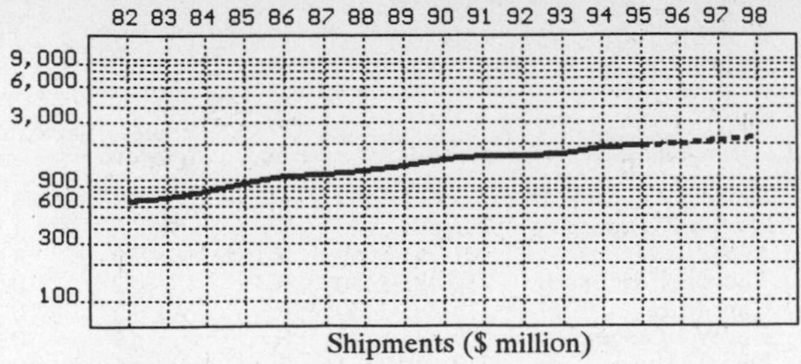

Shipments ($ million)

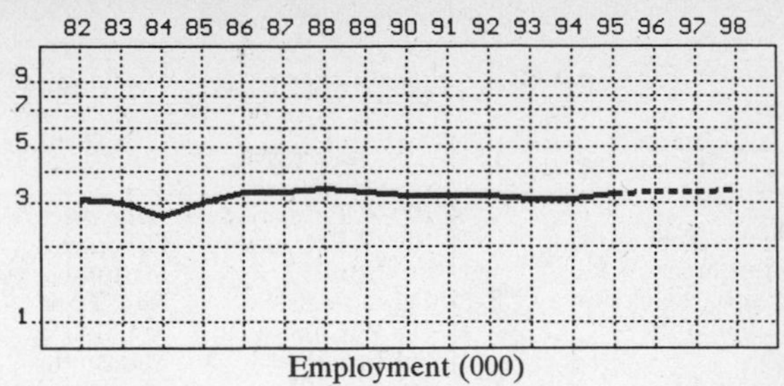

Employment (000)

GENERAL STATISTICS

Year	Com-panies	Establishments		Employment			Compensation		Production ($ million)			
		Total	with 20 or more employees	Total (000)	Production Workers (000)	Production Hours (Mil)	Payroll ($ mil)	Wages ($/hr)	Cost of Materials	Value Added by Manufacture	Value of Shipments	Capital Invest.
1982	21	29	18	3.1	2.4	4.4	51.6	8.50	246.8	420.5	665.4	8.3
1983				3.0	2.4	4.5	53.9	8.42	247.7	449.6	697.9	12.1
1984				2.6	1.9	3.6	52.4	0.97	262.7	544.6	805.0	12.9
1985				3.0	2.1	3.7	61.7	9.86	306.0	641.1	946.6	13.1
1986				3.3	2.2	4.3	78.3	10.91	327.7	730.4	1,062.4	10.1
1987	23	29	19	3.3	2.2	4.3	77.2	10.74	321.5	791.9	1,114.3	8.9
1988				3.4	2.3	4.5	83.8	11.07	312.1	873.0	1,185.0	12.6
1989		29	22	3.3	2.3	4.5	86.3	10.87	359.0	952.2	1,310.1	18.4
1990				3.2	2.1	4.1	84.4	11.32	371.1	1,105.9	1,473.8	16.2
1991				3.2	2.1	4.0	88.0	12.18	394.5	1,202.8	1,601.7	14.3
1992	23	30	19	3.2	2.1	4.1	91.8	12.34	398.0	1,212.5	1,608.4	15.1
1993				3.1	2.0	4.0	94.1	12.63	365.1	1,273.8	1,636.3	15.5
1994				3.1	2.0	4.0	97.6	13.07	370.9	1,500.3	1,871.1	20.3
1995				3.3P	2.0P	4.1P	105.3P	14.14P	381.8P	1,544.4P	1,926.1P	18.4P
1996				3.3P	2.0P	4.1P	109.3P	14.70P	401.6P	1,624.3P	2,025.7P	19.1P
1997				3.3P	2.0P	4.0P	113.3P	15.26P	421.3P	1,704.1P	2,125.3P	19.8P
1998				3.3P	2.0P	4.0P	117.4P	15.82P	441.0P	1,784.0P	2,224.9P	20.4P

Sources: 1982, 1987, 1992 *Economic Census*; *Annual Survey of Manufactures*, 83-86, 88-91, 93-94. Establishment counts for non-Census years are from *County Business Patterns*; establishment values for 83-84 are extrapolations. 'P's show projections by the editors. Industries reclassified in 87 will not have data for prior years.

INDICES OF CHANGE

Year	Com-panies	Establishments		Employment			Compensation		Production ($ million)			
		Total	with 20 or more employees	Total (000)	Production Workers (000)	Production Hours (Mil)	Payroll ($ mil)	Wages ($/hr)	Cost of Materials	Value Added by Manufacture	Value of Shipments	Capital Invest.
1982	91	97	95	97	114	107	56	69	62	35	41	55
1983				94	114	110	59	68	62	37	43	80
1984				81	90	88	57	8	66	45	50	85
1985				94	100	90	67	80	77	53	59	87
1986				103	105	105	85	88	82	60	66	67
1987	100	97	100	103	105	105	84	87	81	65	69	59
1988				106	110	110	91	90	78	72	74	83
1989		97	116	103	110	110	94	88	90	79	81	122
1990				100	100	100	92	92	93	91	92	107
1991				100	100	98	96	99	99	99	100	95
1992	100	100	100	100	100	100	100	100	100	100	100	100
1993				97	95	98	103	102	92	105	102	103
1994				97	95	98	106	106	93	124	116	134
1995				102P	96P	99P	115P	115P	96P	127P	120P	122P
1996				103P	95P	99P	119P	119P	101P	134P	126P	126P
1997				103P	94P	99P	123P	124P	106P	141P	132P	131P
1998				104P	93P	98P	128P	128P	111P	147P	138P	135P

Sources: Same as General Statistics. Values reflect change from the base year, 1992. Values above 100 mean greater than 92, values below 100 mean less than 92, and a value of 100 in the 82-91 or 93-98 period means same as 92. 'P's mark projections by the editors.

SELECTED RATIOS

For 1992	Avg. of All Manufact.	Analyzed Industry	Index	For 1992	Avg. of All Manufact.	Analyzed Industry	Index
Employees per Establishment	46	107	234	Value Added per Production Worker	122,353	577,381	472
Payroll per Establishment	1,332,320	3,060,000	230	Cost per Establishment	4,239,462	13,266,667	313
Payroll per Employee	29,181	28,688	98	Cost per Employee	92,853	124,375	134
Production Workers per Establishment	31	70	223	Cost per Production Worker	135,003	189,524	140
Wages per Establishment	734,496	1,686,467	230	Shipments per Establishment	8,100,800	53,613,333	662
Wages per Production Worker	23,390	24,092	103	Shipments per Employee	177,425	502,625	283
Hours per Production Worker	2,025	1,952	96	Shipments per Production Worker	257,966	765,905	297
Wages per Hour	11.55	12.34	107	Investment per Establishment	278,244	503,333	181
Value Added per Establishment	3,842,210	40,416,667	1,052	Investment per Employee	6,094	4,719	77
Value Added per Employee	84,153	378,906	450	Investment per Production Worker	8,861	7,190	81

Sources: Same as General Statistics. The 'Average of All Manufacturing' column represents the average of all manufacturing industries reported for the most recent complete year available. The Index shows the relationship between the Average and the Analyzed Industry. For example, 100 means that they are equal; 500 that the Analyzed Industry is five times the average; 50 means that the Analyzed Industry is half the national average. The abbreviation 'na' is used to show that data are 'not available'.

LEADING COMPANIES

Number shown: **10** Total sales ($ mil): **2,615** Total employment (000): **7.3**

Company Name	Address				CEO Name	Phone	Co. Type	Sales ($ mil)	Empl. (000)
UST Inc	100 W Putnam Av	Greenwich	CT	06830	Vincent A Gierer Jr	203-661-1100	P	1,223	3.8
United States Tobacco Co	100 W Putnam Av	Greenwich	CT	06830	Joseph R Taddeo	203-661-1100	S	1,058	1.8
Conwood Company LP	PO Box 217	Memphis	TN	38101	JS Wilson Jr	901-761-2050	R	210	1.0
National Tobacco Company LP	444 Park Av S	New York	NY	10016	Thomas F Helms Jr	212-481-1450	R	52	0.3
John Middleton Inc	418 W Church Rd	King of Prussia	PA	19406	Clint Price	215-265-1400	R	30	0.1
JBG Inc	PO Box 1530	Manzanita	OR	97130	Bill WA Geiger	503-636-5529	R	15	0.2
TOP Tobacco LP	PO Box 205	Lk Waccamaw	NC	28450	Donald Levin	919-646-3014	S	15	<0.1
Red Lion International Ltd	PO Box 488	Red Lion	PA	17356	John Woltman	717-244-4501	R	5*	<0.1
Nuway-Microflake Partnership	PO Box 415	E Windsor Hill	CT	06028	Angel Oliva Jr	203-289-6414	J	4	<0.1
Smokey Mountain Chew Inc	4278 Kellwey Cir	Dallas	TX	75244	Philip J Bidwell	214-931-6580	R	3	<0.1

Source: *Ward's Business Directory of U.S. Private and Public Companies*, Volumes 1 and 2, 1996. The company type code used is as follows: P - Public, R - Private, S - Subsidiary, D - Division, J - Joint Venture, A - Affiliate, G - Group. Sales are in millions of dollars, employees are in thousands. An asterisk (*) indicates an estimated sales volume. The symbol < stands for 'less than'. Company names and addresses are truncated, in some cases, to fit into the available space.

MATERIALS CONSUMED

Material		Quantity	Delivered Cost ($ million)
Materials, ingredients, containers, and supplies		(X)	313.2
Unstemmed leaf tobacco including green tobacco not packed	mil lb	22.1	37.8
Unstemmed leaf tobacco, redried and packed	mil lb	15.8	20.7
Stemmed leaf tobacco, excluding processed sheet and homogenized tobacco	mil lb	70.4	110.3
Reconstituted tobacco, processed sheet and homogenized	mil lb	(D)	(D)
Paperboard containers, boxes, and corrugated paperboard		(X)	22.2
Manmade fibers, staple, and tow		(X)	(D)
All other materials and components, parts, containers, and supplies		(X)	86.4
Materials, ingredients, containers, and supplies, nsk		(X)	1.3

Source: 1992 *Economic Census*. Explanation of symbols used: (D): Withheld to avoid disclosure of competitive data; na: Not available; (S): Withheld because statistical norms were not met; (X): Not applicable; (Z): Less than half the unit shown; nec: Not elsewhere classified; nsk: Not specified by kind; - : zero; * : 10-19 percent estimated; ** : 20-29 percent estimated.

PRODUCT SHARE DETAILS

Product or Product Class	% Share	Product or Product Class	% Share
Chewing and smoking tobacco	100.00	Snuff, dry and moist	(D)
Smoking tobacco	10.09	All other chewing tobacco, including fine cut chewing, twist chewing, plug chewing, etc.	12.10
Loose leaf chewing tobacco	(D)		

Source: 1992 *Economic Census*. The values shown are percent of total shipments in an industry. Values of indented subcategories are summed in the main heading. The symbol (D) appears when data are withheld to prevent disclosure of competitive information. The abbreviation nsk stands for 'not specified by kind' and nec for 'not elsewhere classified'.

INPUTS AND OUTPUTS FOR CHEWING & SMOKING TOBACCO

Economic Sector or Industry Providing Inputs	%	Sector	Economic Sector or Industry Buying Outputs	%	Sector
Imports	54.1	Foreign	Personal consumption expenditures	94.1	
Tobacco stemming & redrying	20.6	Manufg.	Exports	5.1	Foreign
Advertising	3.4	Services	Change in business inventories	0.8	In House
Accounting, auditing & bookkeeping	3.2	Services			
Paperboard containers & boxes	2.5	Manufg.			
Wholesale trade	2.0	Trade			
Tobacco	1.9	Agric.			
Cyclic crudes and organics	1.0	Manufg.			
Metal foil & leaf	0.8	Manufg.			
Banking	0.8	Fin/R.E.			
Commercial printing	0.7	Manufg.			
Motor freight transportation & warehousing	0.7	Util.			
Petroleum refining	0.6	Manufg.			
Paper coating & glazing	0.5	Manufg.			
Electric services (utilities)	0.5	Util.			
Business services nec	0.5	Services			
Noncomparable imports	0.5	Foreign			
Industrial gases	0.4	Manufg.			
Gas production & distribution (utilities)	0.4	Util.			
Business/professional associations	0.4	Services			
U.S. Postal Service	0.4	Gov't			
Adhesives & sealants	0.3	Manufg.			

Continued on next page.

INPUTS AND OUTPUTS FOR CHEWING & SMOKING TOBACCO - Continued

Economic Sector or Industry Providing Inputs	%	Sector	Economic Sector or Industry Buying Outputs	%	Sector
Mechanical measuring devices	0.3	Manufg.			
Security & commodity brokers	0.3	Fin/R.E.			
Metal cans	0.2	Manufg.			
Miscellaneous plastics products	0.2	Manufg.			
Soap & other detergents	0.2	Manufg.			
Air transportation	0.2	Util.			
Communications, except radio & TV	0.2	Util.			
Eating & drinking places	0.2	Trade			
Royalties	0.2	Fin/R.E.			
Conveyors & conveying equipment	0.1	Manufg.			
Engineering & scientific instruments	0.1	Manufg.			
Industrial inorganic chemicals, nec	0.1	Manufg.			
Lubricating oils & greases	0.1	Manufg.			
Machinery, except electrical, nec	0.1	Manufg.			
Real estate	0.1	Fin/R.E.			
Automotive rental & leasing, without drivers	0.1	Services			
Equipment rental & leasing services	0.1	Services			

Source: Benchmark Input-Output Accounts for the U.S. Economy, 1982, U.S. Department of Commerce, Washington, D.C., July 1991. Data, as reported in the source, are organized by the 1977 SIC structure in use in 1982 but have been matched, as closely as is possible, to the 1987 SIC structure used in this book.

OCCUPATIONS EMPLOYED BY SIC 211 - TOBACCO PRODUCTS

Occupation	% of Total 1994	Change to 2005	Occupation	% of Total 1994	Change to 2005
Machine operators nec	12.3	-43.9	Freight, stock, & material movers, hand	2.3	-49.0
Helpers, laborers, & material movers nec	11.3	-36.3	Precision food & tobacco workers nec	2.1	-30.0
Packaging & filling machine operators	7.3	-36.3	Secretaries, ex legal & medical	2.0	-42.0
Industrial machinery mechanics	7.0	-29.9	Science & mathematics technicians	1.4	-36.3
Blue collar worker supervisors	5.5	-39.0	Maintenance repairers, general utility	1.3	-42.7
Sales & related workers nec	4.6	-36.3	General managers & top executives	1.3	-39.5
Industrial truck & tractor operators	3.4	-36.3	Systems analysts	1.3	1.9
Management support workers nec	3.4	-36.3	Industrial production managers	1.1	-36.2
Machine feeders & offbearers	3.3	-42.6	Cooking, roasting machine operators	1.0	-29.9
Inspectors, testers, & graders, precision	2.5	-36.3			

Source: Industry-Occupation Matrix, Bureau of Labor Statistics. These data relate to one or more 3-digit SIC industry groups rather than to a single 4-digit SIC. The change reported for each occupation to the year 2005 is a percent of growth or decline as estimated by the Bureau of Labor Statistics. The abbreviation nec stands for 'not elsewhere classified'.

LOCATION BY STATE AND REGIONAL CONCENTRATION

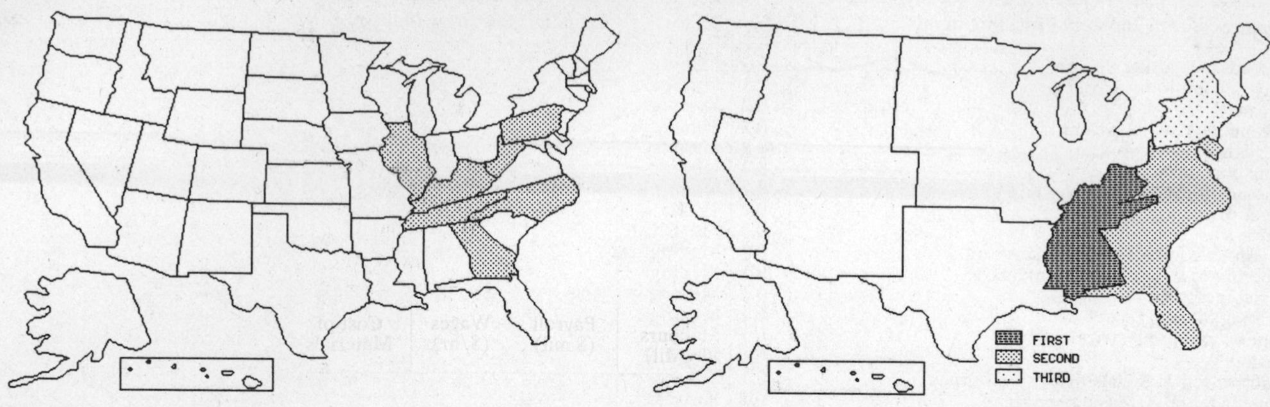

INDUSTRY DATA BY STATE

State	Establish-ments	Shipments			Employment				Cost as % of Shipments	Investment per Employee ($)
		Total ($ mil)	% of U.S.	Per Establ.	Total Number	% of U.S.	Per Establ.	Wages ($/hour)		
Kentucky	6	(D)	-	-	1,750 *	54.7	292	-	-	-
Tennessee	6	(D)	-	-	750 *	23.4	125	-	-	-
North Carolina	4	(D)	-	-	375 *	11.7	94	-	-	-
Pennsylvania	2	(D)	-	-	175 *	5.5	88	-	-	-
Georgia	1	(D)	-	-	175 *	5.5	175	-	-	-
Illinois	1	(D)	-	-	375 *	11.7	375	-	-	-
West Virginia	1	(D)	-	-	175 *	5.5	175	-	-	-

Source: 1992 *Economic Census*. The states are in descending order of shipments or establishments (if shipment data are missing for the majority). The symbol (D) appears when data are withheld to prevent disclosure of competitive information. States marked with (D) are sorted by number of establishments. A dash (-) indicates that the data element cannot be calculated; * indicates the midpoint of a range.

2141 - TOBACCO STEMMING & REDRYING

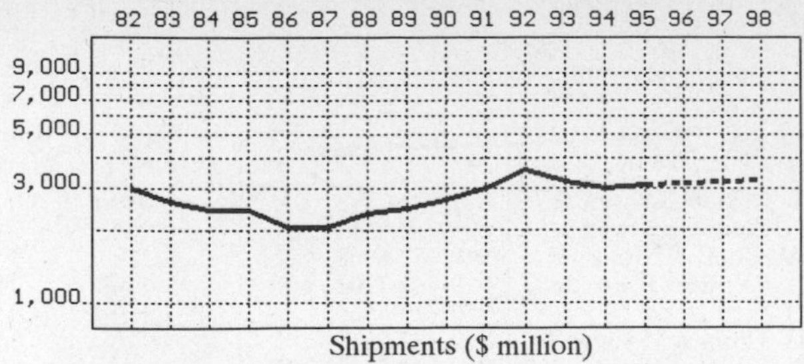

Shipments ($ million)

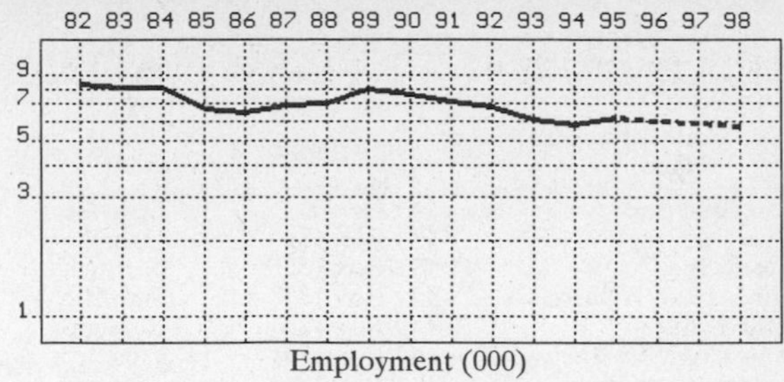

Employment (000)

GENERAL STATISTICS

Year	Com-panies	Establishments		Employment			Compensation		Production ($ million)			
		Total	with 20 or more employees	Total (000)	Production Workers (000)	Production Hours (Mil)	Payroll ($ mil)	Wages ($/hr)	Cost of Materials	Value Added by Manufacture	Value of Shipments	Capital Invest.
1982	34	60	46	8.3	6.2	12.3	119.8	5.96	2,680.2	312.6	3,015.4	110.7
1983				8.2	6.0	12.6	130.6	6.09	2,173.7	461.8	2,654.7	61.0
1984				8.1	6.1	12.5	127.8	6.01	1,904.8	568.4	2,448.0	28.0
1985				6.7	4.8	9.9	126.9	7.00	1,849.8	575.0	2,419.6	28.0
1986				6.4	4.5	9.2	125.3	7.53	1,703.5	345.9	2,059.4	40.3
1987	64	76	34	6.9	4.8	10.2	139.0	7.62	1,687.0	394.9	2,079.2	40.2
1988				7.0	5.0	10.0	145.1	7.91	1,821.4	542.8	2,366.8	26.6
1989		66	29	8.0	5.8	10.8	161.7	8.69	1,845.6	613.3	2,462.0	89.4
1990				7.6	5.4	10.9	163.7	8.59	2,006.3	690.0	2,696.5	21.0
1991				7.1	5.0	10.4	156.6	8.28	2,144.5	871.1	3,007.5	45.2
1992	33	47	32	6.8	4.8	10.3	174.2	9.65	2,555.8	1,002.3	3,557.1	48.6
1993				6.1	4.1	8.7	141.3	8.67	2,476.7	716.2	3,186.9	31.0
1994				5.8	4.0	8.4	136.5	8.89	2,342.5	677.8	2,979.9	18.4
1995				6.2P	4.2P	8.7P	162.5P	9.76P	2,423.9P	701.4P	3,083.5P	23.8P
1996				6.0P	4.0P	8.4P	165.4P	10.05P	2,468.5P	714.2P	3,140.1P	20.7P
1997				5.9P	3.9P	8.2P	168.3P	10.34P	2,513.0P	727.1P	3,196.7P	17.6P
1998				5.7P	3.8P	7.9P	171.2P	10.62P	2,557.5P	740.0P	3,253.4P	14.5P

Sources: 1982, 1987, 1992 *Economic Census*; *Annual Survey of Manufactures*, 83-86, 88-91, 93-94. Establishment counts for non-Census years are from *County Business Patterns*; establishment values for 83-84 are extrapolations. 'P's show projections by the editors. Industries reclassified in 87 will not have data for prior years.

INDICES OF CHANGE

Year	Com-panies	Establishments		Employment			Compensation		Production ($ million)			
		Total	with 20 or more employees	Total (000)	Production Workers (000)	Production Hours (Mil)	Payroll ($ mil)	Wages ($/hr)	Cost of Materials	Value Added by Manufacture	Value of Shipments	Capital Invest.
1982	103	128	144	122	129	119	69	62	105	31	85	228
1983				121	125	122	75	63	85	46	75	126
1984				119	127	121	73	62	75	57	69	58
1985				99	100	96	73	73	72	57	68	58
1986				94	94	89	72	78	67	35	58	83
1987	194	162	106	101	100	99	80	79	66	39	58	83
1988				103	104	97	83	82	71	54	67	55
1989		140	91	118	121	105	93	90	72	61	69	184
1990				112	113	106	94	89	78	69	76	43
1991				104	104	101	90	86	84	87	85	93
1992	100	100	100	100	100	100	100	100	100	100	100	100
1993				90	85	84	81	90	97	71	90	64
1994				85	83	82	78	92	92	68	84	38
1995				90P	87P	84P	93P	101P	95P	70P	87P	49P
1996				88P	84P	82P	95P	104P	97P	71P	88P	43P
1997				86P	81P	80P	97P	107P	98P	73P	90P	36P
1998				84P	79P	77P	98P	110P	100P	74P	91P	30P

Sources: Same as General Statistics. Values reflect change from the base year, 1992. Values above 100 mean greater than 92, values below 100 mean less than 92, and a value of 100 in the 82-91 or 93-98 period means same as 92. 'P's mark projections by the editors.

SELECTED RATIOS

For 1992	Avg. of All Manufact.	Analyzed Industry	Index	For 1992	Avg. of All Manufact.	Analyzed Industry	Index
Employees per Establishment	46	145	317	Value Added per Production Worker	122,353	208,812	171
Payroll per Establishment	1,332,320	3,706,383	278	Cost per Establishment	4,239,462	54,378,723	1,283
Payroll per Employee	29,181	25,618	88	Cost per Employee	92,853	375,853	405
Production Workers per Establishment	31	102	325	Cost per Production Worker	135,003	532,458	394
Wages per Establishment	734,496	2,114,787	288	Shipments per Establishment	8,100,800	75,682,979	934
Wages per Production Worker	23,390	20,707	89	Shipments per Employee	177,425	523,103	295
Hours per Production Worker	2,025	2,146	106	Shipments per Production Worker	257,966	741,063	287
Wages per Hour	11.55	9.65	84	Investment per Establishment	278,244	1,034,043	372
Value Added per Establishment	3,842,210	21,325,532	555	Investment per Employee	6,094	7,147	117
Value Added per Employee	84,153	147,397	175	Investment per Production Worker	8,861	10,125	114

Sources: Same as General Statistics. The 'Average of All Manufacturing' column represents the average of all manufacturing industries reported for the most recent complete year available. The Index shows the relationship between the Average and the Analyzed Industry. For example, 100 means that they are equal; 500 that the Analyzed Industry is five times the average; 50 means that the Analyzed Industry is half the national average. The abbreviation 'na' is used to show that data are 'not available'.

LEADING COMPANIES

Number shown: **9** Total sales ($ mil): **2,727** Total employment (000): **20.2**

Company Name	Address				CEO Name	Phone	Co. Type	Sales ($ mil)	Empl. (000)
Dibrell Brothers Inc	PO Box 681	Danville	VA	24543	Claude B Owen Jr	804-792-7511	S	919	6.3
DiMon Inc	PO Box 681	Danville	VA	24543	Claude B Owen Jr	804-792-7511	P	904	9.4
Monk-Austin Inc	PO Box 166	Farmville	NC	27826	Albert C Monk III	919-753-8000	S	528	3.1
KR Edwards Leaf Tobacco	PO Box 1337	Smithfield	NC	27577	Reginald E Foy Jr	919-934-7101	S	110*	0.6
Flue-Cured Tobacco	PO Box 12300	Raleigh	NC	27605	Fred Bond	919-821-4560	R	100	<0.1
WA Adams Company Inc	PO Box 159	Wilson	NC	27894	Thomas M Evins Jr	919-237-9218	S	70	0.1
Tobacco Processors Inc	PO Box 1989	Wilson	NC	27893	J Wayne Hicks	919-237-5131	S	50	0.3
General Processor Inc	PO Box 246	Oxford	NC	27565	Wayne Pierce	919-693-1116	R	39*	0.4
Parker Tobacco Company Inc	PO Box 428	Maysville	KY	41056	S Alex Parker Jr	606-564-5571	R	7	<0.1

Source: *Ward's Business Directory of U.S. Private and Public Companies*, Volumes 1 and 2, 1996. The company type code used is as follows: P - Public, R - Private, S - Subsidiary, D - Division, J - Joint Venture, A - Affiliate, G - Group. Sales are in millions of dollars, employees are in thousands. An asterisk (*) indicates an estimated sales volume. The symbol < stands for 'less than'. Company names and addresses are truncated, in some cases, to fit into the available space.

MATERIALS CONSUMED

Material		Quantity	Delivered Cost ($ million)
Materials, ingredients, containers, and supplies		(X)	2,256.7
Unstemmed leaf tobacco including green tobacco not packed	mil lb	772.3	1,623.6
Unstemmed leaf tobacco, redried and packed	mil lb	29.7	37.1
Stemmed leaf tobacco, excluding processed sheet and homogenized tobacco	mil lb	457.3	554.0
Reconstituted tobacco, processed sheet and homogenized	mil lb	16.5	6.7
Paperboard containers, boxes, and corrugated paperboard		(X)	6.0
All other materials and components, parts, containers, and supplies		(X)	18.0
Materials, ingredients, containers, and supplies, nsk		(X)	11.3

Source: 1992 *Economic Census*. Explanation of symbols used: (D): Withheld to avoid disclosure of competitive data; na: Not available; (S): Withheld because statistical norms were not met; (X): Not applicable; (Z): Less than half the unit shown; nec: Not elsewhere classified; nsk: Not specified by kind; - : zero; * : 10-19 percent estimated; ** : 20-29 percent estimated.

PRODUCT SHARE DETAILS

Product or Product Class	% Share	Product or Product Class	% Share
Tobacco stemming and redrying	100.00	Stemmed tobacco, packed for use in own manufacturing (interplant transfers), including both aged and not aged leaf	17.33
Unstemmed leaf tobacco redried before packing	(D)	Reconstituted tobacco	(D)
Unstemmed leaf tobacco redried before packing, including interplant transfers	(D)	Reconstituted tobacco (processed sheet and homogenized)	(D)
Tobacco, stemmed	81.83	Tobacco stemming and redrying, nsk	0.34
Stemmed tobacco, packaged for sale as such, aged leaf	12.11		
Stemmed tobacco, packaged for sale as such, not aged leaf	70.56		

Source: 1992 *Economic Census*. The values shown are percent of total shipments in an industry. Values of indented subcategories are summed in the main heading. The symbol (D) appears when data are withheld to prevent disclosure of competitive information. The abbreviation nsk stands for 'not specified by kind' and nec for 'not elsewhere classified'.

INPUTS AND OUTPUTS FOR TOBACCO STEMMING & REDRYING

Economic Sector or Industry Providing Inputs	%	Sector	Economic Sector or Industry Buying Outputs	%	Sector
Tobacco	68.8	Agric.	Cigarettes	48.9	Manufg.
Tobacco stemming & redrying	13.3	Manufg.	Exports	28.6	Foreign
Imports	11.0	Foreign	Tobacco stemming & redrying	11.5	Manufg.
Wholesale trade	2.2	Trade	Change in business inventories	7.0	In House
Motor freight transportation & warehousing	1.1	Util.	Chewing & smoking tobacco	2.5	Manufg.
Petroleum refining	0.6	Manufg.	Cigars	1.4	Manufg.
Banking	0.6	Fin/R.E.			
Electric services (utilities)	0.4	Util.			
Paperboard containers & boxes	0.2	Manufg.			
Gas production & distribution (utilities)	0.2	Util.			
Advertising	0.2	Services			

Source: *Benchmark Input-Output Accounts for the U.S. Economy, 1982*, U.S. Department of Commerce, Washington, D.C., July 1991. Data, as reported in the source, are organized by the 1977 SIC structure in use in 1982 but have been matched, as closely as is possible, to the 1987 SIC structure used in this book.

OCCUPATIONS EMPLOYED BY SIC 211 - TOBACCO PRODUCTS

Occupation	% of Total 1994	Change to 2005	Occupation	% of Total 1994	Change to 2005
Machine operators nec	12.3	-43.9	Freight, stock, & material movers, hand	2.3	-49.0
Helpers, laborers, & material movers nec	11.3	-36.3	Precision food & tobacco workers nec	2.1	-30.0
Packaging & filling machine operators	7.3	-36.3	Secretaries, ex legal & medical	2.0	-42.0
Industrial machinery mechanics	7.0	-29.9	Science & mathematics technicians	1.4	-36.3
Blue collar worker supervisors	5.5	-39.0	Maintenance repairers, general utility	1.3	-42.7
Sales & related workers nec	4.6	-36.3	General managers & top executives	1.3	-39.5
Industrial truck & tractor operators	3.4	-36.3	Systems analysts	1.3	1.9
Management support workers nec	3.4	-36.3	Industrial production managers	1.1	-36.2
Machine feeders & offbearers	3.3	-42.6	Cooking, roasting machine operators	1.0	-29.9
Inspectors, testers, & graders, precision	2.5	-36.3			

Source: Industry-Occupation Matrix, Bureau of Labor Statistics. These data relate to one or more 3-digit SIC industry groups rather than to a single 4-digit SIC. The change reported for each occupation to the year 2005 is a percent of growth or decline as estimated by the Bureau of Labor Statistics. The abbreviation nec stands for 'not elsewhere classified'.

LOCATION BY STATE AND REGIONAL CONCENTRATION

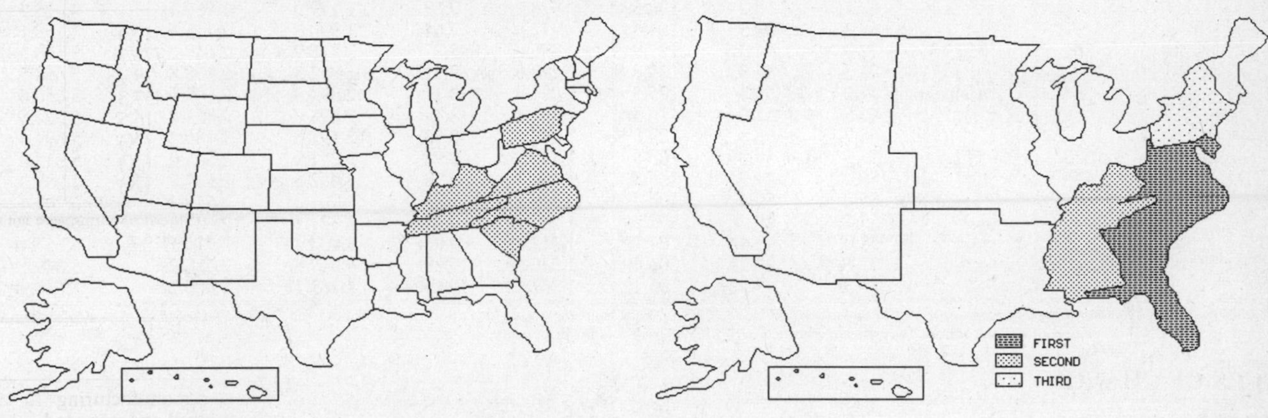

INDUSTRY DATA BY STATE

State	Establish-ments	Shipments Total ($ mil)	Shipments % of U.S.	Shipments Per Establ.	Employment Total Number	Employment % of U.S.	Employment Per Establ.	Wages ($/hour)	Cost as % of Shipments	Investment per Employee ($)
North Carolina	13	(D)	-	-	3,750 *	55.1	288	-	-	-
Virginia	8	(D)	-	-	1,750 *	25.7	219	-	-	-
Kentucky	6	(D)	-	-	750 *	11.0	125	-	-	-
Tennessee	4	(D)	-	-	175 *	2.6	44	-	-	-
Pennsylvania	2	(D)	-	-	175 *	2.6	88	-	-	-
South Carolina	2	(D)	-	-	175 *	2.6	88	-	-	-

Source: 1992 *Economic Census*. The states are in descending order of shipments or establishments (if shipment data are missing for the majority). The symbol (D) appears when data are withheld to prevent disclosure of competitive information. States marked with (D) are sorted by number of establishments. A dash (-) indicates that the data element cannot be calculated; * indicates the midpoint of a range.

2211 - BROADWOVEN FABRIC MILLS, COTTON

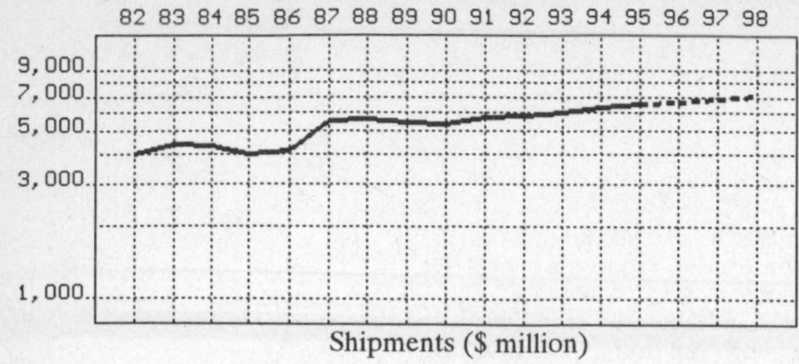

Shipments ($ million)

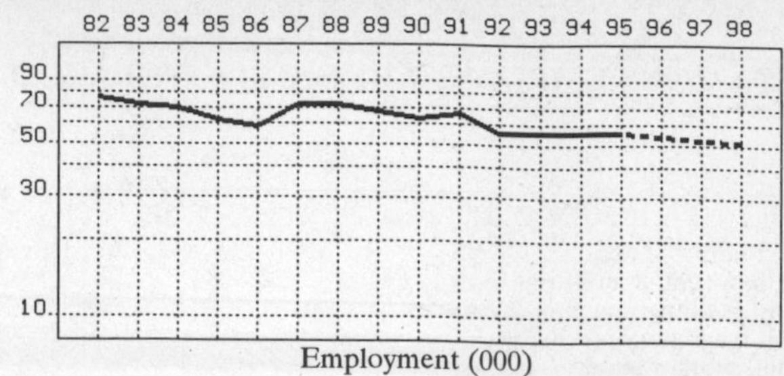

Employment (000)

GENERAL STATISTICS

Year	Com-panies	Establishments		Employment			Compensation		Production ($ million)			
		Total	with 20 or more employees	Total (000)	Production Workers (000)	Production Hours (Mil)	Payroll ($ mil)	Wages ($/hr)	Cost of Materials	Value Added by Manufacture	Value of Shipments	Capital Invest.
1982	212	269	143	76.9	69.2	127.0	964.6	6.44	2,293.7	1,637.5	3,972.0	297.9
1983				71.6	65.2	128.6	1,020.9	6.87	2,540.1	1,870.6	4,391.6	212.8
1984				69.6	63.0	118.3	999.6	7.14	2,433.0	1,928.5	4,347.2	175.7
1985				62.1	56.2	108.5	924.2	7.29	2,177.0	1,767.4	4,025.2	191.6
1986				58.3	52.5	104.4	932.8	7.64	1,980.3	2,115.6	4,155.1	113.9
1987	246	301	151	72.3	64.9	137.9	1,260.0	7.77	2,915.9	2,610.2	5,508.3	198.9
1988				72.3	64.8	129.8	1,228.0	7.91	2,882.5	2,838.8	5,664.5	239.8
1989		284	154	67.2	60.3	125.3	1,221.4	8.17	2,894.3	2,605.7	5,456.6	215.4
1990				62.5	55.6	114.5	1,137.1	8.19	2,891.0	2,457.0	5,324.5	199.1
1991				65.9	58.8	122.8	1,246.4	8.35	3,191.5	2,480.1	5,694.6	160.9
1992	281	323	117	55.9	50.2	105.9	1,146.8	8.92	3,291.9	2,505.0	5,814.0	168.1
1993				55.0	49.9	105.5	1,184.0	9.38	3,462.5	2,539.9	5,989.8	222.6
1994				55.7	50.6	106.7	1,249.5	9.83	3,701.0	2,549.3	6,262.4	262.2
1995				55.4P	49.7P	109.0P	1,287.7P	9.71P	3,821.1P	2,632.0P	6,465.7P	200.7P
1996				54.0P	48.4P	107.7P	1,312.2P	9.96P	3,934.4P	2,710.1P	6,657.4P	200.1P
1997				52.6P	47.2P	106.4P	1,336.6P	10.20P	4,047.8P	2,788.2P	6,849.1P	199.5P
1998				51.3P	45.9P	105.1P	1,361.1P	10.45P	4,161.1P	2,866.2P	7,040.9P	199.0P

Sources: 1982, 1987, 1992 *Economic Census*; *Annual Survey of Manufactures*, 83-86, 88-91, 93-94. Establishment counts for non-Census years are from *County Business Patterns*; establishment values for 83-84 are extrapolations. 'P's show projections by the editors. Industries reclassified in 87 will not have data for prior years.

INDICES OF CHANGE

Year	Com-panies	Establishments		Employment			Compensation		Production ($ million)			
		Total	with 20 or more employees	Total (000)	Production Workers (000)	Production Hours (Mil)	Payroll ($ mil)	Wages ($/hr)	Cost of Materials	Value Added by Manufacture	Value of Shipments	Capital Invest.
1982	75	83	122	138	138	120	84	72	70	65	68	177
1983				128	130	121	89	77	77	75	76	127
1984				125	125	112	87	80	74	77	75	105
1985				111	112	102	81	82	66	71	69	114
1986				104	105	99	81	86	60	84	71	68
1987	88	93	129	129	129	130	110	87	89	104	95	118
1988				129	129	123	107	89	88	113	97	143
1989		88	132	120	120	118	107	92	88	104	94	128
1990				112	111	108	99	92	88	98	92	118
1991				118	117	116	109	94	97	99	98	96
1992	100	100	100	100	100	100	100	100	100	100	100	100
1993				98	99	100	103	105	105	101	103	132
1994				100	101	101	109	110	112	102	108	156
1995				99P	99P	103P	112P	109P	116P	105P	111P	119P
1996				97P	97P	102P	114P	112P	120P	108P	115P	119P
1997				94P	94P	100P	117P	114P	123P	111P	118P	119P
1998				92P	91P	99P	119P	117P	126P	114P	121P	118P

Sources: Same as General Statistics. Values reflect change from the base year, 1992. Values above 100 mean greater than 92, values below 100 mean less than 92, and a value of 100 in the 82-91 or 93-98 period means same as 92. 'P's mark projections by the editors.

SELECTED RATIOS

For 1992	Avg. of All Manufact.	Analyzed Industry	Index
Employees per Establishment	46	173	379
Payroll per Establishment	1,332,320	3,550,464	266
Payroll per Employee	29,181	20,515	70
Production Workers per Establishment	31	155	495
Wages per Establishment	734,496	2,924,545	398
Wages per Production Worker	23,390	18,817	80
Hours per Production Worker	2,025	2,110	104
Wages per Hour	11.55	8.92	77
Value Added per Establishment	3,842,210	7,755,418	202
Value Added per Employee	84,153	44,812	53

For 1992	Avg. of All Manufact.	Analyzed Industry	Index
Value Added per Production Worker	122,353	49,900	41
Cost per Establishment	4,239,462	10,191,641	240
Cost per Employee	92,853	58,889	63
Cost per Production Worker	135,003	65,576	49
Shipments per Establishment	8,100,800	18,000,000	222
Shipments per Employee	177,425	104,007	59
Shipments per Production Worker	257,966	115,817	45
Investment per Establishment	278,244	520,433	187
Investment per Employee	6,094	3,007	49
Investment per Production Worker	8,861	3,349	38

Sources: Same as General Statistics. The 'Average of All Manufacturing' column represents the average of all manufacturing industries reported for the most recent complete year available. The Index shows the relationship between the Average and the Analyzed Industry. For example, 100 means that they are equal; 500 that the Analyzed Industry is five times the average; 50 means that the Analyzed Industry is half the national average. The abbreviation 'na' is used to show that data are 'not available'.

LEADING COMPANIES Number shown: **75** Total sales ($ mil): **15,186** Total employment (000): **154.5**

Company Name	Address				CEO Name	Phone	Co. Type	Sales ($ mil)	Empl. (000)
Springs Industries Inc	205 N White St	Fort Mill	SC	29715	Walter Y Elisha	803-547-1500	P	2,069	20.1
Milliken and Co	PO Box 1926	Spartanburg	SC	29304	Roger Milliken	803-573-2020	R	1,800	14.5
WestPoint Stevens Inc	PO Box 71	West Point	GA	31833	H T Green Jr	706-645-4000	P	1,597	17.4
Triarc Companies Inc	900 3rd Av	New York	NY	10022	Nelson Peltz	212-230-3000	P	1,063	11.3
Delta Woodside Industries Inc	233 N Main St	Greenville	SC	29601	E Erwin Maddrey II	803-232-8301	P	686	8.3
Cone Mills Corp	1201 Maple St	Greensboro	NC	27405	J Patrick Danahy	919-379-6220	P	633	7.8
Dominion Textile	120 W 45th St	New York	NY	10036	Charles Hanto	212-704-7600	S	560*	2.5
RB Pamplin Corp	900 SW 5th Av	Portland	OR	97204	R B Pamplin Jr	503-248-1133	R	550*	5.5
Avondale Mills	900 Avondale Av	Sylacauga	AL	35150	Stephen Felker	205-249-1200	D	500*	4.0
Greenwood Mills Inc	PO Box 1017	Greenwood	SC	29648	W Matt Self	803-229-2571	R	500	7.0
Galey and Lord Inc	PO Box 35528	Greensboro	NC	27425	Arthur C Wiener	910-665-3037	P	451	4.2
Dan River Inc	PO Box 261	Danville	VA	24543	Richard L Williams	804-799-7000	R	430*	5.0
Mount Vernon Mills Inc	PO Box 3478	Greenville	SC	29602	Roger W Chastain	803-233-4151	S	430*	5.0
Graniteville Co	PO Box 128	Graniteville	SC	29829	H D Kingsmore	803-663-7231	S	360	3.5
Texfi Industries Inc	5400 Glenwood Av	Raleigh	NC	27612	William L Remley	919-783-4736	P	283	4.4
Thomaston Mills Inc	115 E Main St	Thomaston	GA	30286	Neil H Hightower	706-647-7131	P	279	2.5
Culp Inc	101 S Main St	High Point	NC	27261	Robert G Culp III	919-889-5161	P	245	1.8
Gray Goods	PO Box 1177	Greenwood	SC	29648	Ted Colcolough	803-227-2121	D	200	2.8
Greenwood Mills Inc	PO Box 1177	Greenwood	SC	29648	Robert E Kaplan	803-227-2121	D	200	4.0
Concord Fabrics Inc	1359 Broadway	New York	NY	10018	Earl Kramer	212-760-0300	P	198	0.6
Lincoln Group Inc	2000 S Beltline Blvd	Columbia	SC	29250	Walton E Burdick	803-799-8800	R	170*	2.0
Johnston Industries Inc	111 W 40th St	New York	NY	10018	David L Chandler	212-768-3750	P	160	1.4
Swift Textiles Inc	PO Box 1400	Columbus	GA	31994	John Boland III	706-324-3623	S	120*	1.4
Inman Mills Inc	PO Box 207	Inman	SC	29349	WM Chapman	803-472-2121	R	110	1.4
Leshner Corp	PO Box 179	Hamilton	OH	45012	Mark Petricoff	513-868-3500	R	98*	1.2
Opp and Micolas Mills Inc	PO Drawer 70	Opp	AL	36467	Roger J Gilmartin	205-493-3531	S	87	1.0
Ramtex Sales Corp	445 5th Av	New York	NY	10016	Thomas Seiler	212-689-7101	R	80	<0.1
RAMTEX Inc	PO Box 307	Ramseur	NC	27316	Donald Yeung	919-824-5600	R	79	0.8
Lindale Manufacturing Inc	PO Box 9	Lindale	GA	30147	W Matt Self	706-234-1621	S	71*	1.0
Collins and Aikman Corp	PO Box 208	Farmville	NC	27828	Millard King	919-753-7400	D	69	0.8
Valdese Weavers Inc	PO Box 70	Valdese	NC	28690	BE McKinnon	704-874-2181	S	60	0.5
Holliston Mills Inc	PO Box 478	Church Hill	TN	37662	Wait Burdick	615-357-6141	S	55	0.5
Hamrick Mills Inc	PO Box 48	Gaffney	SC	29342	Wylie Hamrick	803-489-4731	R	52*	0.6
Copen Associates Inc	350 5th Av	New York	NY	10118	Carin Trundle	212-736-6120	R	50	0.2
Rockland Industries Inc	1601 Edison Hwy	Baltimore	MD	21213	AJ Leaderman	410-522-2505	R	50	0.3
Russell Corp	PO Box 272	Alexander City	AL	35010	JT Taunton Jr	205-329-4000	D	50	0.5
CCP Industries Inc	PO Box 6500	Cleveland	OH	44101	Richard J Sims	216-449-6550	D	45	0.5
Bloomsburg Mills Inc	W & 6th St	Bloomsburg	PA	17815	James P Marion III	717-784-4262	R	42*	0.5
Startex Mills	PO Box 1658	Spartanburg	SC	29304	Dan Brewton	803-439-5258	D	41	0.6
DeRoyal Textiles Inc	PO Box 400	Camden	SC	29020	ES Ward	803-432-2403	R	34	0.4
Hoffman Mills Inc	470 Park Av S	New York	NY	10016	Richard D Hoffman	212-684-3700	R	34*	0.4
Arkwright Mills	PO Box 5628	Spartanburg	SC	29304	ML Cates Jr	803-585-8301	R	30	<0.1
Craftex Mills Inc	450 Sentry Pkwy	Blue Bell	PA	19422	Robert M Blum	610-941-1212	R	30	0.4
Hedaya Brothers	295 5th Av	New York	NY	10016	Joseph Hedaya	212-889-1111	R	30*	0.4
Blumenthal Print Works Inc	905 S Broad St	New Orleans	LA	70125	H J Blumenthal Jr	504-822-4620	R	28*	0.3
Dicey Mills Inc	PO Box 1090	Shelby	NC	28150	HP Neisler	704-487-6324	R	27	0.2
Blair Mills LP	PO Box 97	Belton	SC	29627	Billy Rice Jr	803-338-6611	R	26*	0.3
Marion Fabrics Inc	700 Baldwin Av	Marion	NC	28752	Joseph Tisdale	704-652-3010	S	26*	0.7
Pillowtex Corp	505 Miller St	Monroe	NC	28110	Larry T Mills	704-282-4382	S	25	0.3
Fieldcrest Cannon Inc	1271 Av of America	New York	NY	10020	J M Fitzgibbons	212-536-1200	D	23	0.2
Pittsfield Products Inc	PO Box 1027	Ann Arbor	MI	48106	Ted Fosdick	313-665-3771	R	21*	0.3
Fendrich Industries Inc	PO Box 3645	Evansville	IN	47735	Burkley F McCarthy	812-426-2536	R	20	0.2
Sterile Products Corp	401 Marshall Rd	Valley Park	MO	63088	CC Van Noy	314-225-5151	R	20*	0.2
Stillwater Sales Inc	1040 Av Amer	New York	NY	10018	E Alpert	212-354-7070	R	20	0.3
Fabricut Manufacturing Inc	PO Box 869	Pryor	OK	74361	Harvey Noodleman	918-825-4400	R	17*	0.2
Springs Industries Inc	PO Box 111	Lancaster	SC	29720	WS Hood	803-286-2956	D	17*	0.4
Weave Corp	433 Hackensack Av	Hackensack	NJ	07601	Roger Berkley	201-646-1500	R	17*	0.2
Western Textile Company Inc	421 W Erie St	Chicago	IL	60610	Cary Lichtenstein	312-751-0600	R	16	0.1
Carpostan Industries Inc	PO Box 724	Lake View	SC	29563	JL Smith	803-759-2105	R	15*	0.1
Mt Hope Finishing Co	405 W B St	Butner	NC	27509	John K Milliken	919-575-6501	R	15	0.2
Waverly Fabrics	79 Madison Av	New York	NY	10016	Meri Stevens	212-213-7900	D	15	0.2
Waverly Textile Processing Inc	8401 Fort Darling	Richmond	VA	23237	Michael Robinson	804-275-0400	R	15	0.2
Bell National Corp	4209 Vineland Rd	Orlando	FL	32811	Robert C Shaw	407-849-0290	P	14	<0.1
James Thompson and Company	2 Park Av	New York	NY	10016	RB Judell	212-686-4242	R	13	0.2
Spartan Mills Inc	PO Box 1658	Spartanburg	SC	29304	C Campbell	803-674-5544	D	13	0.2
Advanced Textile Composites	15 Poplar St	Scranton	PA	18509	Paul J Cuccolo	717-346-8421	R	12	0.2
Asheboro Elastics Corp	PO Box 1143	Asheboro	NC	27204	Keith Crisco	919-629-2626	R	12	0.1
KM Fabrics Inc	PO Box 7379	Greenville	SC	29611	Richard K Heusel	803-295-2550	R	11	<0.1
Printed Fabrics Corp	PO Box 220	Carrollton	GA	30117	Bernard Kress	404-832-3561	R	11	0.2
Initial Trends Inc	229 W 36th St	New York	NY	10018	S Schneiderman	212-244-6700	D	10	<0.1
Jaunty Textile	15 Poplar St	Scranton	PA	18509	Paul J Cuccolo	717-346-8421	D	10	0.1
Rose Hill Linen Co	208 Post Rd W	Westport	CT	06880	Jim Pitt	203-454-3700	R	10	<0.1
Santens of America Inc	PO Box 669	Anderson	SC	29622	Wim De Pape	803-226-6422	S	10	<0.1
Bates of Maine	PO Box 591	Lewiston	ME	04243	Alfred Lebel	207-784-7311	R	8*	0.1
Universal Sample Card Company	2016 Pitkin Av	Brooklyn	NY	11207	Mark Moody	718-385-1700	R	8*	0.1

Source: *Ward's Business Directory of U.S. Private and Public Companies*, Volumes 1 and 2, 1996. The company type code used is as follows: P - Public, R - Private, S - Subsidiary, D - Division, J - Joint Venture, A - Affiliate, G - Group. Sales are in millions of dollars, employees are in thousands. An asterisk (*) indicates an estimated sales volume. The symbol < stands for 'less than'. Company names and addresses are truncated, in some cases, to fit into the available space.

MATERIALS CONSUMED

Material		Quantity	Delivered Cost ($ million)
Materials, ingredients, containers, and supplies		(X)	2,982.0
Raw cotton fibers	1,000 bales	3,332.3	1,068.8
Rayon and acetate staple and tow	mil lb	11.3**	12.2
Nylon staple and tow	mil lb	(D)	(D)
Polyester staple and tow	mil lb	131.9	98.3
All other manmade fiber staple and tow (except glass)	mil lb	2.0	1.4
All other fibers (silk, jute, reused wool, waste, etc.)	mil lb	(D)	(D)
Rayon and acetate filament yarns	mil lb	18.6	41.9
Nylon filament yarns	mil lb	(D)	(D)
Polyester filament yarns	mil lb	70.0	62.0
All other filament yarns, except glass	mil lb	3.4	6.3
Glass filament yarn and roving	mil lb	(D)	(D)
Spun yarn, all fibers	mil lb	489.4*	583.2
Broadwoven fabrics	mil sq yd	712.7	461.8
Dyes, lakes, and toners		(X)	112.1
All other materials and components, parts, containers, and supplies		(X)	504.1
Materials, ingredients, containers, and supplies, nsk		(X)	26.2

Source: 1992 *Economic Census*. Explanation of symbols used: (D): Withheld to avoid disclosure of competitive data; na: Not available; (S): Withheld because statistical norms were not met; (X): Not applicable; (Z): Less than half the unit shown; nec: Not elsewhere classified; nsk: Not specified by kind; - : zero; * : 10-19 percent estimated; ** : 20-29 percent estimated.

PRODUCT SHARE DETAILS

Product or Product Class	% Share	Product or Product Class	% Share
Broadwoven fabric mills, cotton	100.00	Plain weave (except pile), other, including lawns, voiles, and batistes	(D)
Cotton broadwoven plain weave fabrics, except pile (gray goods)	16.48	Twill weave (except pile)	60.06
Cotton broadwoven twill weave fabrics, except pile (gray goods)	24.19	Other weaves (except pile), sateens	(D)
Cotton broadwoven fabrics, all other weaves, except pile (gray goods)	9.37	Other weaves (except pile), other, including oxfords, table damask, jacquard, dobby shirting, and birdseye diaper cloth	11.34
Cotton broadwoven pile fabrics (gray goods)	5.27	Pile fabrics (velvets, plushes, corduroy, terry toweling, terry cloth, and others)	(D)
Cotton finished broadwoven fabrics (finished in weaving mills)	21.95	Finished cotton broadwoven fabrics (finished in weaving mills), nsk	0.21
Plain weave (except pile), print cloth	(D)	Cotton towels and washcloths (made in weaving mills)	12.81
Plain weave (except pile), poplin and broadcloth	(D)	Fabricated cotton textile products, except towels and washcloths (made in weaving mills)	8.71
Plain weave (except pile), sheeting, including bedsheeting and osnaburgs	(D)	Broadwoven fabrics mills, cotton, nsk	1.22
Plain weave (except pile), tobacco, cheese, and bandage cloth	(D)		

Source: 1992 *Economic Census*. The values shown are percent of total shipments in an industry. Values of indented subcategories are summed in the main heading. The symbol (D) appears when data are withheld to prevent disclosure of competitive information. The abbreviation nsk stands for 'not specified by kind' and nec for 'not elsewhere classified'.

INPUTS AND OUTPUTS FOR BROADWOVEN FABRIC MILLS

Economic Sector or Industry Providing Inputs	%	Sector	Economic Sector or Industry Buying Outputs	%	Sector
Broadwoven fabric mills	36.6	Manufg.	Apparel made from purchased materials	36.0	Manufg.
Organic fibers, noncellulosic	9.0	Manufg.	Broadwoven fabric mills	30.4	Manufg.
Imports	8.5	Foreign	Housefurnishings, nec	5.0	Manufg.
Cotton	6.1	Agric.	Exports	4.0	Foreign
Yarn mills & finishing of textiles, nec	5.2	Manufg.	Personal consumption expenditures	2.6	
Wholesale trade	5.2	Trade	Upholstered household furniture	2.5	Manufg.
Cyclic crudes and organics	3.2	Manufg.	Curtains & draperies	2.2	Manufg.
Cellulosic manmade fibers	2.9	Manufg.	Automotive & apparel trimmings	1.7	Manufg.
Electric services (utilities)	2.9	Util.	Surgical appliances & supplies	1.3	Manufg.
Business services nec	2.0	Services	Coated fabrics, not rubberized	1.2	Manufg.
Miscellaneous plastics products	1.4	Manufg.	Fabricated textile products, nec	1.1	Manufg.
Gas production & distribution (utilities)	1.1	Util.	Mattresses & bedsprings	0.9	Manufg.
Petroleum refining	1.0	Manufg.	Paper mills, except building paper	0.9	Manufg.
Laundry, dry cleaning, shoe repair	1.0	Services	Rubber & plastics hose & belting	0.7	Manufg.
Banking	0.9	Fin/R.E.	Fabricated rubber products, nec	0.6	Manufg.
Personnel supply services	0.9	Services	Miscellaneous plastics products	0.6	Manufg.
Paperboard containers & boxes	0.8	Manufg.	Sanitary paper products	0.6	Manufg.
Textile machinery	0.8	Manufg.	Textile bags	0.6	Manufg.
Motor freight transportation & warehousing	0.8	Util.	Canvas & related products	0.5	Manufg.
Advertising	0.8	Services	Paperboard mills	0.4	Manufg.
Sanitary services, steam supply, irrigation	0.7	Util.	Rubber & plastics footwear	0.4	Manufg.
Surface active agents	0.6	Manufg.	Bags, except textile	0.3	Manufg.
Textile goods, nec	0.6	Manufg.	Floor coverings	0.3	Manufg.
Maintenance of nonfarm buildings nec	0.5	Constr.	Laundry, dry cleaning, shoe repair	0.3	Services
Glass & glass products, except containers	0.5	Manufg.	Federal Government purchases, national defense	0.3	Fed Govt

Continued on next page.

INPUTS AND OUTPUTS FOR BROADWOVEN FABRIC MILLS - Continued

Economic Sector or Industry Providing Inputs	%	Sector	Economic Sector or Industry Buying Outputs	%	Sector
Lubricating oils & greases	0.5	Manufg.	Tobacco	0.2	Agric.
Eating & drinking places	0.5	Trade	Abrasive products	0.2	Manufg.
Industrial inorganic chemicals, nec	0.4	Manufg.	Aircraft	0.2	Manufg.
U.S. Postal Service	0.3	Gov't	Book printing	0.2	Manufg.
Meat animals	0.2	Agric.	Brooms & brushes	0.2	Manufg.
Coal	0.2	Mining	Burial caskets & vaults	0.2	Manufg.
Conveyors & conveying equipment	0.2	Manufg.	Dolls	0.2	Manufg.
Machinery, except electrical, nec	0.2	Manufg.	Needles, pins, & fasteners	0.2	Manufg.
Communications, except radio & TV	0.2	Util.	Pleating & stitching	0.2	Manufg.
Railroads & related services	0.2	Util.	Sporting & athletic goods, nec	0.2	Manufg.
Business/professional associations	0.2	Services	S/L Govt. purch., elem. & secondary education	0.2	S/L Govt
Computer & data processing services	0.2	Services	S/L Govt. purch., public assistance & relief	0.2	S/L Govt
Equipment rental & leasing services	0.2	Services	Coal	0.1	Mining
Management & consulting services & labs	0.2	Services	Aircraft & missile engines & engine parts	0.1	Manufg.
Scrap	0.2	Scrap	Luggage	0.1	Manufg.
Real estate	0.1	Fin/R.E.	Hotels & lodging places	0.1	Services
Royalties	0.1	Fin/R.E.	Motion pictures	0.1	Services
Automotive rental & leasing, without drivers	0.1	Services	Watch, clock, jewelry, & furniture repair	0.1	Services
Legal services	0.1	Services			

Source: Benchmark Input-Output Accounts for the U.S. Economy, 1982, U.S. Department of Commerce, Washington, D.C., July 1991. Data, as reported in the source, are organized by the 1977 SIC structure in use in 1982 but have been matched, as closely as is possible, to the 1987 SIC structure used in this book.

OCCUPATIONS EMPLOYED BY SIC 221 - WEAVING, FINISHING, YARN AND THREAD MILLS

Occupation	% of Total 1994	Change to 2005	Occupation	% of Total 1994	Change to 2005
Textile draw-out & winding machine operators	32.8	-35.5	Machine feeders & offbearers	2.6	-27.4
Industrial machinery mechanics	6.4	29.1	Machine operators nec	2.2	-28.9
Textile machine setters & set-up operators	4.9	-11.3	Sewing machine operators, non-garment	1.8	21.0
Helpers, laborers, & material movers nec	4.5	-19.3	Industrial truck & tractor operators	1.6	-19.3
Blue collar worker supervisors	4.2	-24.6	Hand packers & packagers	1.3	-30.9
Inspectors, testers, & graders, precision	4.2	-27.4	General managers & top executives	1.3	-23.5
Textile bleaching & dyeing machine operators	4.2	8.9	Maintenance repairers, general utility	1.2	-27.4
Freight, stock, & material movers, hand	2.8	-35.5	Janitors & cleaners, incl maids	1.0	-35.5

Source: Industry-Occupation Matrix, Bureau of Labor Statistics. These data relate to one or more 3-digit SIC industry groups rather than to a single 4-digit SIC. The change reported for each occupation to the year 2005 is a percent of growth or decline as estimated by the Bureau of Labor Statistics. The abbreviation nec stands for 'not elsewhere classified'.

LOCATION BY STATE AND REGIONAL CONCENTRATION

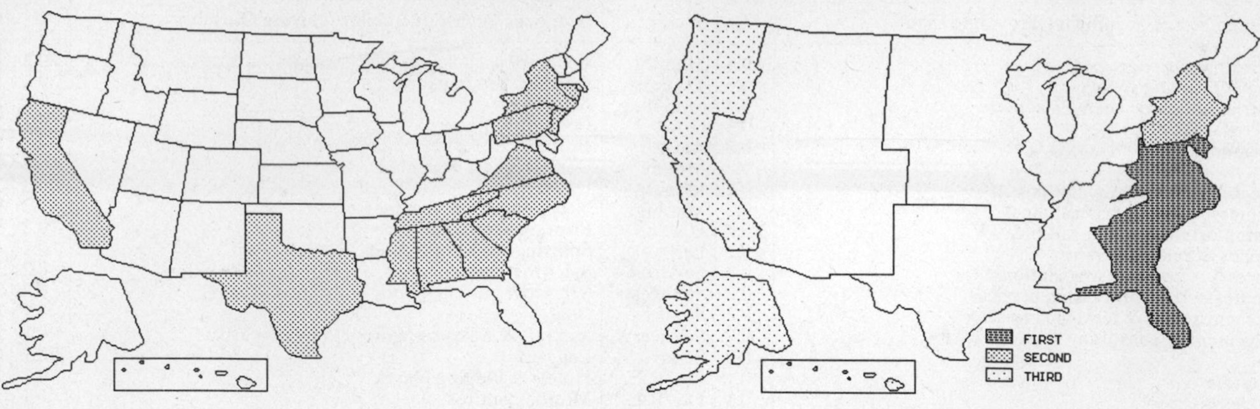

INDUSTRY DATA BY STATE

State	Establish-ments	Shipments			Employment				Cost as % of Shipments	Investment per Employee ($)
		Total ($ mil)	% of U.S.	Per Establ.	Total Number	% of U.S.	Per Establ.	Wages ($/hour)		
North Carolina	39	1,978.4	34.0	50.7	18,600	33.3	477	8.88	64.6	2,661
Georgia	31	1,375.0	23.6	44.4	14,000	25.0	452	8.63	52.1	3,150
South Carolina	41	1,313.0	22.6	32.0	11,900	21.3	290	8.95	57.4	2,496
Alabama	7	434.7	7.5	62.1	4,100	7.3	586	9.43	46.1	5,293
Texas	19	198.5	3.4	10.4	2,100	3.8	111	9.10	46.8	-
Pennsylvania	13	30.1	0.5	2.3	400	0.7	31	9.57	49.8	-
California	35	16.3	0.3	0.5	200	0.4	6	6.50	49.1	1,500
New Jersey	17	15.4	0.3	0.9	200	0.4	12	10.33	52.6	2,000
New York	25	13.4	0.2	0.5	200	0.4	8	7.67	58.2	500
Tennessee	7	(D)	-	-	1,750 *	3.1	250	-	-	-
Connecticut	5	(D)	-	-	375 *	0.7	75	-	-	-
Virginia	2	(D)	-	-	1,750 *	3.1	875	-	-	-
Mississippi	1	(D)	-	-	750 *	1.3	750	-	-	-

Source: 1992 *Economic Census*. The states are in descending order of shipments or establishments (if shipment data are missing for the majority). The symbol (D) appears when data are withheld to prevent disclosure of competitive information. States marked with (D) are sorted by number of establishments. A dash (-) indicates that the data element cannot be calculated; * indicates the midpoint of a range.

2221 - BROADWOVEN FABRIC MILLS, MANMADE

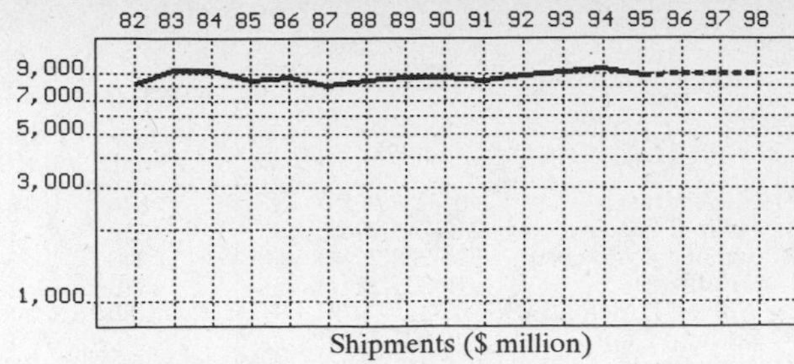

Shipments ($ million)

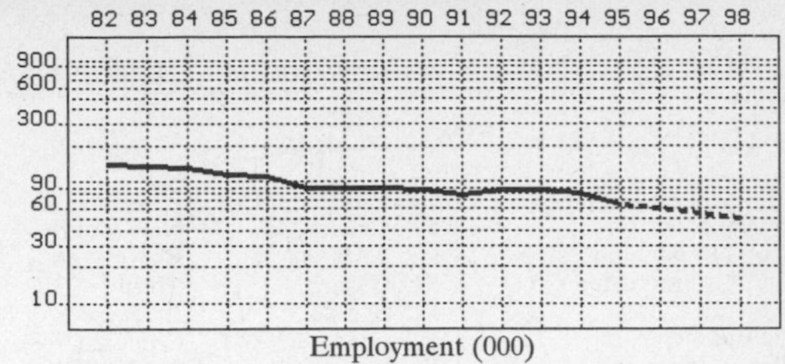

Employment (000)

GENERAL STATISTICS

Year	Com-panies	Establishments		Employment			Compensation		Production ($ million)			
		Total	with 20 or more employees	Total (000)	Production Workers (000)	Production Hours (Mil)	Payroll ($ mil)	Wages ($/hr)	Cost of Materials	Value Added by Manufacture	Value of Shipments	Capital Invest.
1982	340	522	362	140.8	122.9	230.4	1,814.4	6.28	4,644.5	3,486.7	8,186.7	384.8
1983				137.2	120.4	243.0	2,023.6	6.75	5,391.3	3,940.6	9,285.0	380.4
1984				130.6	115.0	229.4	2,005.3	7.04	5,296.2	4,011.5	9,273.9	471.8
1985				115.0	99.9	197.2	1,832.3	7.37	4,791.4	3,542.1	8,401.9	484.4
1986				109.7	95.5	196.1	1,881.7	7.63	4,847.1	3,776.8	8,665.5	350.6
1987	315	436	270	88.3	77.0	163.2	1,595.7	7.80	4,504.0	3,595.9	8,048.9	314.3
1988				90.4	78.8	163.4	1,671.8	8.10	4,775.9	3,753.7	8,462.6	378.8
1989		419	288	88.4	77.6	159.0	1,705.2	8.45	5,025.0	3,706.1	8,690.0	393.2
1990				85.3	74.6	154.0	1,688.4	8.55	4,961.3	3,619.3	8,577.9	440.0
1991				78.3	68.5	141.6	1,600.0	8.68	4,755.9	3,550.5	8,315.2	331.9
1992	321	422	255	87.4	76.9	158.4	1,860.0	9.21	4,824.4	4,031.6	8,793.5	357.3
1993				85.8	75.0	157.0	1,908.3	9.46	5,059.9	4,136.6	9,144.9	433.2
1994				80.7	70.6	148.2	1,869.0	9.88	5,278.3	4,172.2	9,423.8	575.9
1995				64.9P	56.8P	123.8P	1,734.9P	10.02P	4,988.1P	3,942.8P	8,905.6P	436.4P
1996				59.7P	52.2P	115.8P	1,725.0P	10.30P	5,003.5P	3,955.0P	8,933.1P	440.5P
1997				54.4P	47.7P	107.8P	1,715.1P	10.58P	5,018.9P	3,967.1P	8,960.6P	444.7P
1998				49.2P	43.1P	99.7P	1,705.2P	10.85P	5,034.3P	3,979.3P	8,988.1P	448.8P

Sources: 1982, 1987, 1992 *Economic Census*; *Annual Survey of Manufactures*, 83-86, 88-91, 93-94. Establishment counts for non-Census years are from *County Business Patterns*; establishment values for 83-84 are extrapolations. 'P's show projections by the editors. Industries reclassified in 87 will not have data for prior years.

INDICES OF CHANGE

Year	Com-panies	Establishments		Employment			Compensation		Production ($ million)			
		Total	with 20 or more employees	Total (000)	Production Workers (000)	Production Hours (Mil)	Payroll ($ mil)	Wages ($/hr)	Cost of Materials	Value Added by Manufacture	Value of Shipments	Capital Invest.
1982	106	124	142	161	160	145	98	68	96	86	93	108
1983				157	157	153	109	73	112	98	106	106
1984				149	150	145	108	76	110	100	105	132
1985				132	130	124	99	80	99	88	96	136
1986				126	124	124	101	83	100	94	99	98
1987	98	103	106	101	100	103	86	85	93	89	92	88
1988				103	102	103	90	88	99	93	96	106
1989		99	113	101	101	100	92	92	104	92	99	110
1990				98	97	97	91	93	103	90	98	123
1991				90	89	89	86	94	99	88	95	93
1992	100	100	100	100	100	100	100	100	100	100	100	100
1993				98	98	99	103	103	105	103	104	121
1994				92	92	94	100	107	109	103	107	161
1995				74P	74P	78P	93P	109P	103P	98P	101P	122P
1996				68P	68P	73P	93P	112P	104P	98P	102P	123P
1997				62P	62P	68P	92P	115P	104P	98P	102P	124P
1998				56P	56P	63P	92P	118P	104P	99P	102P	126P

Sources: Same as General Statistics. Values reflect change from the base year, 1992. Values above 100 mean greater than 92, values below 100 mean less than 92, and a value of 100 in the 82-91 or 93-98 period means same as 92. 'P's mark projections by the editors.

SELECTED RATIOS

For 1992	Avg. of All Manufact.	Analyzed Industry	Index	For 1992	Avg. of All Manufact.	Analyzed Industry	Index
Employees per Establishment	46	207	454	Value Added per Production Worker	122,353	52,427	43
Payroll per Establishment	1,332,320	4,407,583	331	Cost per Establishment	4,239,462	11,432,227	270
Payroll per Employee	29,181	21,281	73	Cost per Employee	92,853	55,199	59
Production Workers per Establishment	31	182	580	Cost per Production Worker	135,003	62,736	46
Wages per Establishment	734,496	3,457,024	471	Shipments per Establishment	8,100,800	20,837,678	257
Wages per Production Worker	23,390	18,971	81	Shipments per Employee	177,425	100,612	57
Hours per Production Worker	2,025	2,060	102	Shipments per Production Worker	257,966	114,350	44
Wages per Hour	11.55	9.21	80	Investment per Establishment	278,244	846,682	304
Value Added per Establishment	3,842,210	9,553,555	249	Investment per Employee	6,094	4,088	67
Value Added per Employee	84,153	46,128	55	Investment per Production Worker	8,861	4,646	52

Sources: Same as General Statistics. The 'Average of All Manufacturing' column represents the average of all manufacturing industries reported for the most recent complete year available. The Index shows the relationship between the Average and the Analyzed Industry. For example, 100 means that they are equal; 500 that the Analyzed Industry is five times the average; 50 means that the Analyzed Industry is half the national average. The abbreviation 'na' is used to show that data are 'not available'.

LEADING COMPANIES Number shown: **74** Total sales ($ mil): **3,509** Total employment (000): **33.5**

Company Name	Address				CEO Name	Phone	Co. Type	Sales ($ mil)	Empl. (000)
Amoco Fabrics and Fibers Co	900 Circle 75 Pkwy	Atlanta	GA	30339	FG Andrusko	404-956-9025	S	840•	8.0
F Schumacher and Co	79 Madison Av	New York	NY	10016	Philip P Puschel	212-213-7900	R	250	1.5
Burlington House Upholstery	906 Anthony St	Burlington	NC	27217	Stephen C Mischen	919-228-2641	D	240	3.0
Chatham Manufacturing Co	PO Box 620	Elkin	NC	28621	S Raffo	919-835-2211	S	180•	1.7
Clark-Schwebel Inc	PO Box 2627	Anderson	SC	29622	William D Bennison	803-225-7028	S	180	1.6
Synthetic Industries Inc	309 Lafayette Rd	Chickamauga	GA	30707	Leonard Chill	706-375-3121	R	140•	1.9
Texfi-Blends Inc	PO Box 8400	Rocky Mount	NC	27804	Andy Parise	919-443-5001	S	120	1.1
Beacon Manufacturing Co	PO Box 395	Swannanoa	NC	28778	E Randall Chestnut	704-686-3861	S	100	1.2
Highland Industries Inc	629 Green Val Rd	Greensboro	NC	27408	Frank Roe	919-547-1600	S	90	0.5
Cavel	PO Box 643	Roxboro	NC	27573	Andrew Major	919-599-1111	D	80	1.4
AlliedSignal Inc	PO Box 166	Moncure	NC	27559	Butch Forehand	919-542-2200	D	79•	0.8
Frank Ix and Sons Inc	469 7th Av	New York	NY	10018	Douglas Ix	212-239-4480	R	70	0.6
Wangner Systems Corp	525 Piedmont Hwy	Greenville	SC	29605	Horace Cochran	803-295-3000	R	70	0.4
Rossville/Chromatex	PO Box 40	Rossville	GA	30741	Dan Jacobs	706-866-1010	D	60	0.7
Scher Fabrics Inc	119 W 40th St	New York	NY	10018	Robert Scher	212-382-2266	R	60	0.2
Chemfab Corp	PO Box 1137	Merrimack	NH	03054	Duane C Montopoli	603-424-9000	P	52	0.4
Klopman Blended Fabrics	PO Box 21207	Greensboro	NC	27420	Gary Welchman	919-379-2000	D	52•	0.5
Phillips Industries Inc	PO Box 1350	High Point	NC	27261	S Dave Phillips	910-882-3301	R	52•	0.5
Gates Formed-Fibre Products	PO Box 1300	Auburn	ME	04211	David MacMahon	207-784-1118	S	50	0.4
Bloomsburg Mills Inc	111 W 40th St	New York	NY	10018	James P Marion III	212-221-6114	R	49•	0.5
Belding Hausman Inc	1430 Broadway	New York	NY	10018	Nancy Zarin	212-556-4700	S	40	0.3
H Warshow and Sons Inc	PO Box 488	Tappahannock	VA	22560	Pete McBride	804-443-3391	D	36•	0.4
Pontiac Weaving Corp	32 Meeting St	Cumberland	RI	02864	Robert Scher	401-726-4600	S	36•	0.1
JB Martin Company Inc	10 E 53rd St	New York	NY	10022	Loic Dekertanguy	212-421-2020	R	32•	0.4
Galey & Lord	1947 N Fayettebill	Asheboro	NC	27203	Michael Carico	910-672-2111	D	30•	0.3
Biddeford Textile Co	PO Box 624	Biddeford	ME	04005	RW Boisvert	207-282-3376	D	26	0.3
Belding Hausman Weldon Mill	Mill Rd	Emporia	VA	23847	Herbert Nylander Jr	804-634-3101	D	25	0.2
Culp Woven Velvet	PO Box 4088	Anderson	SC	29622	Robert Culp	803-226-2857	D	25•	0.2
Langenthal Corp	PO Box 965	Rural Hall	NC	27045	Dieter H Lantin	910-969-9551	R	22	0.2
Beavertown Mills Inc	441 W Market St	Beavertown	PA	17813	Abraham Bloom	717-658-8041	R	19	0.2
GFF Inc	PO Box 658	Soperton	GA	30457	Ann Graham	912-529-3734	R	19•	0.2
Balson Industries Ltd	PO Box 218	Providence	RI	02901	M Ball	401-724-6000	R	18•	0.2
Dickson Elberton Mills Inc	PO Box 6107	Elberton	GA	30635	Philippe Petot	706-283-3721	R	17	0.2
Patricia Knitting Inc	PO Box 175	Hickory	NC	28603	JR Turner	704-322-5953	R	16	<0.1
Aronsohn Tie Fabrics	14 E 33rd St	New York	NY	10016	Dan Krauss	212-685-9680	R	15•	<0.1
Interglas Inc	PO Box 8233	Ward Hill	MA	01835	Michael Camuso	508-373-2500	S	15•	0.2
McGinley Mills Inc	100 Kuebler Rd	Easton	PA	18042	TJ McGinley	215-559-6400	R	15	0.1
National Filter Media Corp	691 N 400 W	Salt Lake City	UT	84103	Boyd V Rydalch	801-363-6736	R	15•	0.2
Newtex Industries Inc	8050 Victor	Victor	NY	14564	Sudhakar G Dixit	716-924-9135	R	15•	0.1
Noel Joanna Inc	22942 Arroyo Vista	R S Margari	CA	92688	Shirley Pepys	714-858-9717	R	15	<0.1
Biederlack of America	Rte 220	Cumberland	MD	21502	Robert Biederlack	301-759-3633	S	14	0.2
Lebo Peerless Corp	PO Box 540	Armonk	NY	10504	Patrick Mastronardo	914-273-8844	R	14	<0.1
American Velvet Co	22 Bayview Av	Stonington	CT	06378	J Wimpfheimer	203-535-1050	R	13	0.3
Appleton Mills	PO Box 1899	Appleton	WI	54913	TS Scheetz	414-734-9876	S	13	0.3
SynTechnics Inc	700 Terrace Ln	Paducah	KY	42003	John Dane	502-898-7303	S	13•	0.2
Velvet Textile Company Inc	PO Box 86	Blackstone	VA	23824	Frank Carlo	804-292-7211	R	13	0.1
Raxon Fabrics Corp	114 E 32nd St	New York	NY	10016	Jean Baer	212-532-6816	R	12	0.1
Advanced Textiles Inc	2460 Crossroads	Seguin	TX	78155	Peter L DeWalt	210-372-0160	R	11•	<0.1
Bomont Mills Inc	PO Box 1806	Altoona	PA	16603	Leroy McMullen	814-944-9381	S	11	0.1
Miller Industries Inc	PO Box 97	Lisbon Falls	ME	04252	Herbert Miller	207-353-4371	R	10•	0.1
Stern and Stern Industries Inc	PO Box 556	Hornell	NY	14843	Peter Thornton	607-324-4485	R	10•	0.1
Fortune Fabrics Inc	315 Simpson St	Swoyersville	PA	18704	Robert Fortinsky	717-288-3666	R	9•	<0.1
Keystone Weaving Mills Inc	PO Box 208	Lebanon	PA	17042	Eli Caplan	717-272-4665	R	9•	<0.1
WS Libbey Company Inc	PO Box 809	Blythewood	SC	29016	Armand J Favreau	803-482-6688	R	9	<0.1
Donghia Textiles Inc	485 Broadway	New York	NY	10013	Michael Sorrentino	212-925-2777	R	8•	<0.1
Kingstree Manufacturing Co	PO Box 730	Kingstree	SC	29556	RA Rubel	803-354-6164	D	8•	0.2
Berwick Weaving Inc	PO Box 158	Berwick	PA	18603	Elizabeth Hertel	717-752-4516	R	7	0.1
Widder Brothers Inc	570 7th Av	New York	NY	10018	Herman Widder	212-921-5230	R	7	<0.1
Keystone Engineering	6310 Sidney St	Houston	TX	77021	Sandford Ring	713-747-1478	R	6	<0.1
Kings Plush Acquisition Corp	PO Box 398	Kings Mt	NC	28086	Wayne A King	704-739-4503	R	6•	<0.1
Tweave Inc	138 Barrows St	Norton	MA	02766	William Giblin	508-285-6701	R	6	<0.1
Warwick Mills Inc	50 Federal St	Boston	MA	02110	Gordon Osborne	617-357-9125	R	6	0.1
American Nonwovens Inc	PO Box 989	Vernon	AL	35592	Dan Herren	205-695-6067	R	5•	<0.1
American Weavers LP	PO Box 369	Calhoun	GA	30703	Scott Fletcher	706-602-1111	R	5•	<0.1
Supreme Products	406 Scruggs Rd	Chattanooga	TN	37412	Jay Desai	615-855-5252	R	5	0.1
National Select Fabrics Corp	PO Box 485	Berwick	PA	18603	Leonard S Cerullo	717-752-3649	R	3	<0.1
Glasteel Tennessee Inc	1727 Buena Vista	Duarte	CA	91010	Eric Fryer	818-357-8081	R	2•	<0.1
J Robert Scott Textiles Inc	3416 La Cienega	Los Angeles	CA	90016	Sally C Lewis	213-525-1010	D	2•	<0.1
McMillan Fiberglass Stocks Inc	21421 N 14th Av	Phoenix	AZ	85027	Kelly McMillan	602-582-9635	R	2•	<0.1
Pleasure Prod Manufacturing Co	2421 16th Av S	Moorhead	MN	56560	Stewart Ystebo	218-236-1818	R	2	<0.1
Metro Fabrics Inc	1040 6th Av	New York	NY	10018	David Caplan	212-302-8811	R	1•	<0.1
National Hair Technology Ltd	300 Canal St	Lawrence	MA	01840	John Moot	508-686-1497	R	1	<0.1
Spindletop Draperies Inc	1064 Bardstown Rd	Louisville	KY	40204	Patrick M Payne	502-583-5556	R	1•	<0.1
Atron Products and Services Inc	3005 Hadley Rd	South Plainfield	NJ	07080	Greg Prejs	908-668-1624	R	1	<0.1

Source: *Ward's Business Directory of U.S. Private and Public Companies*, Volumes 1 and 2, 1996. The company type code used is as follows: P - Public, R - Private, S - Subsidiary, D - Division, J - Joint Venture, A - Affiliate, G - Group. Sales are in millions of dollars, employees are in thousands. An asterisk (*) indicates an estimated sales volume. The symbol < stands for 'less than'. Company names and addresses are truncated, in some cases, to fit into the available space.

MATERIALS CONSUMED

Material		Quantity	Delivered Cost ($ million)
Materials, ingredients, containers, and supplies		(X)	4,381.5
Raw cotton fibers	1,000 bales	980.0	342.2
Raw wool, mohair, and other animal fibers (scoured weight)	mil lb	(D)	(D)
Wool tops	mil lb	(D)	(D)
Rayon and acetate staple and tow	mil lb	175.1	204.9
Nylon staple and tow	mil lb	19.7**	36.6
Polyester staple and tow	mil lb	504.3	370.4
All other manmade fiber staple and tow (except glass)	mil lb	192.2	90.1
All other fibers (silk, jute, reused wool, waste, etc.)	mil lb	(S)	12.2
Rayon and acetate filament yarns	mil lb	152.6	235.0
Nylon filament yarns	mil lb	173.4	252.2
Polyester filament yarns	mil lb	342.6	504.5
All other filament yarns, except glass	mil lb	157.7	278.4
Glass filament yarn and roving	mil lb	148.2	252.3
Spun yarn, all fibers	mil lb	546.6*	939.5
Broadwoven fabrics	mil sq yd	107.8	103.5
Dyes, lakes, and toners		(X)	41.5
All other materials and components, parts, containers, and supplies		(X)	666.0
Materials, ingredients, containers, and supplies, nsk		(X)	39.1

Source: 1992 *Economic Census*. Explanation of symbols used: (D): Withheld to avoid disclosure of competitive data; na: Not available; (S): Withheld because statistical norms were not met; (X): Not applicable; (Z): Less than half the unit shown; nec: Not elsewhere classified; nsk: Not specified by kind; - : zero; * : 10-19 percent estimated; ** : 20-29 percent estimated.

PRODUCT SHARE DETAILS

Product or Product Class	% Share
Broadwoven fabric mills, manmade fiber and silk	100.00
85 percent or more filament rayon and/or acetate fabrics, including blends chiefly rayon and/or acetate (gray goods)	7.55
85 percent or more filament fabrics, except rayon or acetate (gray goods)	26.24
85 percent or more spun yarn plain weave fabrics, except pile, excluding wool blends (gray goods)	23.05
85 percent or more spun yarn twill weave fabrics, except pile, excluding wool blends (gray goods)	3.56
Other 85 percent or more spun yarn fabrics, except pile, excluding wool blends (gray goods)	4.24
Combinations of spun yarn and filament fabrics, except wool blends, each less than 85 percent of total fiber content (gray goods)	11.61
Other manmade fiber fabrics and silk fabrics (gray goods)	2.80
Pile fabrics (gray goods)	60.05
Other chiefly manmade fiber fabrics, including chiefly manmade fiber blends with wool, and silk fabrics (gray goods)	39.95
Manmade fiber and silk finished broadwoven fabrics (finished in weaving mills)	15.24
85 percent or more spun yarn fabrics, plain weave (except pile), print cloth	2.93
85 percent or more spun yarn fabrics, plain weave (except pile), poplin and broadcloth	(D)
85 percent or more spun yarn fabrics, plain weave (except pile), sheeting, including bedsheeting and osnaburgs	(D)
85 percent or more spun yarn fabrics, plain weave (except pile), other types	3.14
85 percent or more spun yarn fabrics, twill weave (except pile)	25.00
85 percent or more spun yarn fabrics, other weaves (except pile), sateens	(D)
85 percent or more spun yarn fabrics, other weaves (except pile), other (including oxfords, table damask, jacquard, etc)	14.01
85 percent or more spun yarn fabrics, pile (velvets, plushes, corduroy, and others)	3.81
85 percent or more filament yarn fabrics, chiefly rayon and/or acetate	(D)
85 percent or more filament yarn fabrics, chiefly polyester	11.30
85 percent or more filament yarn fabrics, other	15.31
Other, including combinations of spun yarn and filament, blends with wool, silk, and blends with silk	(D)
Finished manmade fiber and silk broadwoven fabrics (finished in weaving mills), nsk	0.33
Sheets and pillowcases, wholly or chiefly manmade fibers and silk (made in weaving mills)	(D)
Fabricated manmade fiber and silk textile products, except sheets and pillowcases (made in weaving mills)	(D)
Fabricated manmade fiber and silk textile products, except sheets and pillowcases (made in weaving mills), quilted	(D)
Fabricated manmade fiber and silk textile products, except sheets and pillowcases (made in weaving mills), nonquilted	(D)
Broadwoven fabrics mills, manmade fiber and silk, nsk	0.84

Source: 1992 *Economic Census*. The values shown are percent of total shipments in an industry. Values of indented subcategories are summed in the main heading. The symbol (D) appears when data are withheld to prevent disclosure of competitive information. The abbreviation nsk stands for 'not specified by kind' and nec for 'not elsewhere classified'.

INPUTS AND OUTPUTS FOR BROADWOVEN FABRIC MILLS

Economic Sector or Industry Providing Inputs	%	Sector	Economic Sector or Industry Buying Outputs	%	Sector
Broadwoven fabric mills	36.6	Manufg.	Apparel made from purchased materials	36.0	Manufg.
Organic fibers, noncellulosic	9.0	Manufg.	Broadwoven fabric mills	30.4	Manufg.
Imports	8.5	Foreign	Housefurnishings, nec	5.0	Manufg.
Cotton	6.1	Agric.	Exports	4.0	Foreign
Yarn mills & finishing of textiles, nec	5.2	Manufg.	Personal consumption expenditures	2.6	
Wholesale trade	5.2	Trade	Upholstered household furniture	2.5	Manufg.
Cyclic crudes and organics	3.2	Manufg.	Curtains & draperies	2.2	Manufg.
Cellulosic manmade fibers	2.9	Manufg.	Automotive & apparel trimmings	1.7	Manufg.
Electric services (utilities)	2.9	Util.	Surgical appliances & supplies	1.3	Manufg.
Business services nec	2.0	Services	Coated fabrics, not rubberized	1.2	Manufg.

Continued on next page.

INPUTS AND OUTPUTS FOR BROADWOVEN FABRIC MILLS - Continued

Economic Sector or Industry Providing Inputs	%	Sector	Economic Sector or Industry Buying Outputs	%	Sector
Miscellaneous plastics products	1.4	Manufg.	Fabricated textile products, nec	1.1	Manufg.
Gas production & distribution (utilities)	1.1	Util.	Mattresses & bedsprings	0.9	Manufg.
Petroleum refining	1.0	Manufg.	Paper mills, except building paper	0.9	Manufg.
Laundry, dry cleaning, shoe repair	1.0	Services	Rubber & plastics hose & belting	0.7	Manufg.
Banking	0.9	Fin/R.E.	Fabricated rubber products, nec	0.6	Manufg.
Personnel supply services	0.9	Services	Miscellaneous plastics products	0.6	Manufg.
Paperboard containers & boxes	0.8	Manufg.	Sanitary paper products	0.6	Manufg.
Textile machinery	0.8	Manufg.	Textile bags	0.6	Manufg.
Motor freight transportation & warehousing	0.8	Util.	Canvas & related products	0.5	Manufg.
Advertising	0.8	Services	Paperboard mills	0.4	Manufg.
Sanitary services, steam supply, irrigation	0.7	Util.	Rubber & plastics footwear	0.4	Manufg.
Surface active agents	0.6	Manufg.	Bags, except textile	0.3	Manufg.
Textile goods, nec	0.6	Manufg.	Floor coverings	0.3	Manufg.
Maintenance of nonfarm buildings nec	0.5	Constr.	Laundry, dry cleaning, shoe repair	0.3	Services
Glass & glass products, except containers	0.5	Manufg.	Federal Government purchases, national defense	0.3	Fed Govt
Lubricating oils & greases	0.5	Manufg.	Tobacco	0.2	Agric.
Eating & drinking places	0.5	Trade	Abrasive products	0.2	Manufg.
Industrial inorganic chemicals, nec	0.4	Manufg.	Aircraft	0.2	Manufg.
U.S. Postal Service	0.3	Gov't	Book printing	0.2	Manufg.
Meat animals	0.2	Agric.	Brooms & brushes	0.2	Manufg.
Coal	0.2	Mining	Burial caskets & vaults	0.2	Manufg.
Conveyors & conveying equipment	0.2	Manufg.	Dolls	0.2	Manufg.
Machinery, except electrical, nec	0.2	Manufg.	Needles, pins, & fasteners	0.2	Manufg.
Communications, except radio & TV	0.2	Util.	Pleating & stitching	0.2	Manufg.
Railroads & related services	0.2	Util.	Sporting & athletic goods, nec	0.2	Manufg.
Business/professional associations	0.2	Services	S/L Govt. purch., elem. & secondary education	0.2	S/L Govt
Computer & data processing services	0.2	Services	S/L Govt. purch., public assistance & relief	0.2	S/L Govt
Equipment rental & leasing services	0.2	Services	Coal	0.1	Mining
Management & consulting services & labs	0.2	Services	Aircraft & missile engines & engine parts	0.1	Manufg.
Scrap	0.2	Scrap	Luggage	0.1	Manufg.
Real estate	0.1	Fin/R.E.	Hotels & lodging places	0.1	Services
Royalties	0.1	Fin/R.E.	Motion pictures	0.1	Services
Automotive rental & leasing, without drivers	0.1	Services	Watch, clock, jewelry, & furniture repair	0.1	Services
Legal services	0.1	Services			

Source: Benchmark Input-Output Accounts for the U.S. Economy, 1982, U.S. Department of Commerce, Washington, D.C., July 1991. Data, as reported in the source, are organized by the 1977 SIC structure in use in 1982 but have been matched, as closely as is possible, to the 1987 SIC structure used in this book.

OCCUPATIONS EMPLOYED BY SIC 222 - WEAVING, FINISHING, YARN AND THREAD MILLS

Occupation	% of Total 1994	Change to 2005	Occupation	% of Total 1994	Change to 2005
Textile draw-out & winding machine operators	32.8	-35.5	Machine feeders & offbearers	2.6	-27.4
Industrial machinery mechanics	6.4	29.1	Machine operators nec	2.2	-28.9
Textile machine setters & set-up operators	4.9	-11.3	Sewing machine operators, non-garment	1.8	21.0
Helpers, laborers, & material movers nec	4.5	-19.3	Industrial truck & tractor operators	1.6	-19.3
Blue collar worker supervisors	4.2	-24.6	Hand packers & packagers	1.3	-30.9
Inspectors, testers, & graders, precision	4.2	-27.4	General managers & top executives	1.3	-23.5
Textile bleaching & dyeing machine operators	4.2	8.9	Maintenance repairers, general utility	1.2	-27.4
Freight, stock, & material movers, hand	2.8	-35.5	Janitors & cleaners, incl maids	1.0	-35.5

Source: Industry-Occupation Matrix, Bureau of Labor Statistics. These data relate to one or more 3-digit SIC industry groups rather than to a single 4-digit SIC. The change reported for each occupation to the year 2005 is a percent of growth or decline as estimated by the Bureau of Labor Statistics. The abbreviation nec stands for 'not elsewhere classified'.

LOCATION BY STATE AND REGIONAL CONCENTRATION

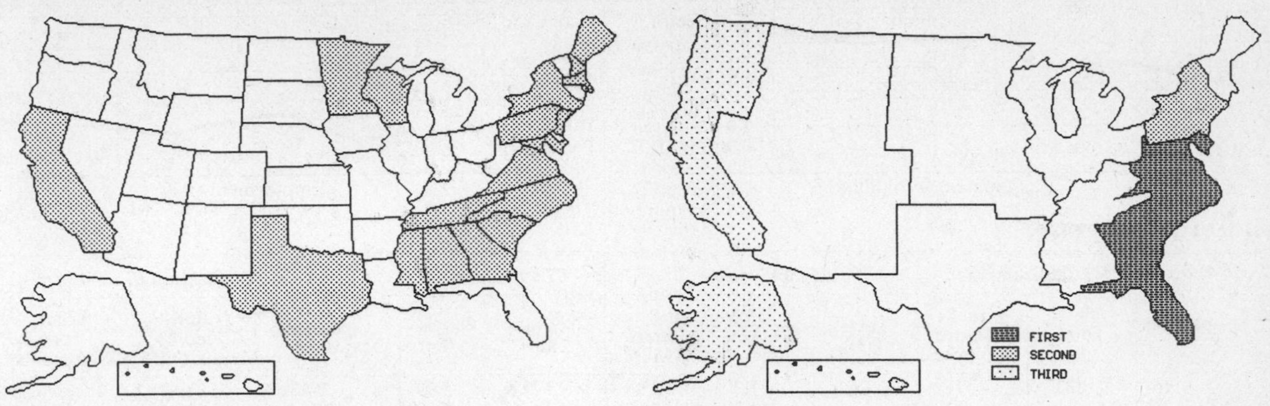

INDUSTRY DATA BY STATE

State	Establish-ments	Shipments			Employment				Cost as % of Shipments	Investment per Employee ($)
		Total ($ mil)	% of U.S.	Per Establ.	Total Number	% of U.S.	Per Establ.	Wages ($/hour)		
South Carolina	88	2,972.5	33.8	33.8	31,000	35.5	352	9.12	54.1	4,652
North Carolina	67	1,858.7	21.1	27.7	19,200	22.0	287	9.15	57.8	4,120
Georgia	31	1,152.5	13.1	37.2	9,800	11.2	316	8.98	57.2	4,602
Virginia	15	973.2	11.1	64.9	9,100	10.4	607	9.29	56.9	3,121
Alabama	19	595.4	6.8	31.3	6,300	7.2	332	9.48	48.4	3,095
Massachusetts	12	381.4	4.3	31.8	3,200	3.7	267	9.37	50.9	3,500
Pennsylvania	30	325.6	3.7	10.9	3,300	3.8	110	9.07	55.4	3,909
Maine	7	106.1	1.2	15.2	1,200	1.4	171	9.52	52.8	-
New Jersey	8	59.0	0.7	7.4	400	0.5	50	10.71	59.3	4,750
New York	20	56.7	0.6	2.8	700	0.8	35	11.64	46.0	2,571
Rhode Island	8	42.7	0.5	5.3	500	0.6	63	8.70	48.5	3,200
Texas	13	38.4	0.4	3.0	300	0.3	23	9.33	43.5	333
California	29	20.8	0.2	0.7	300	0.3	10	7.40	54.3	2,000
Minnesota	4	(D)	-	-	175 *	0.2	44	-	-	-
Maryland	3	(D)	-	-	175 *	0.2	58	-	-	-
Mississippi	3	(D)	-	-	375 *	0.4	125	-	-	-
Tennessee	3	(D)	-	-	750 *	0.9	250	-	-	2,267
New Hampshire	2	(D)	-	-	175 *	0.2	88	-	-	-
Wisconsin	2	(D)	-	-	175 *	0.2	88	-	-	-

Source: 1992 *Economic Census*. The states are in descending order of shipments or establishments (if shipment data are missing for the majority). The symbol (D) appears when data are withheld to prevent disclosure of competitive information. States marked with (D) are sorted by number of establishments. A dash (-) indicates that the data element cannot be calculated; * indicates the midpoint of a range.

2231 - BROADWOVEN FABRIC MILLS, WOOL

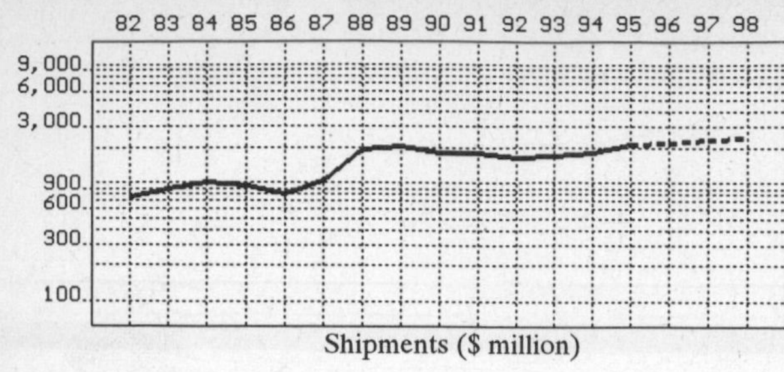

Shipments ($ million)

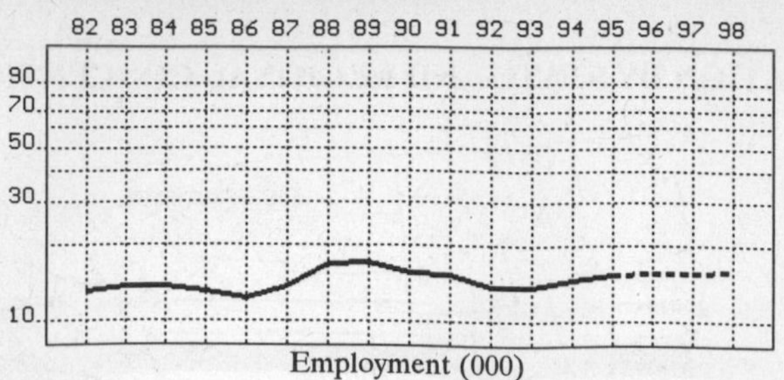

Employment (000)

GENERAL STATISTICS

Year	Com-panies	Establishments Total	Establishments with 20 or more employees	Employment Total (000)	Production Workers (000)	Production Hours (Mil)	Compensation Payroll ($ mil)	Compensation Wages ($/hr)	Cost of Materials	Value Added by Manufacture	Value of Shipments	Capital Invest.
1982	116	131	71	13.1	11.3	22.8	175.8	5.99	394.2	349.4	762.8	27.7
1983				13.6	11.8	24.8	197.8	6.18	477.2	402.7	879.3	20.4
1984				13.7	11.9	25.0	211.2	6.48	564.3	461.5	1,015.7	33.4
1985				13.1	11.2	22.8	203.8	6.79	475.8	461.5	932.5	33.9
1986				12.3	10.6	21.6	194.8	6.91	432.5	371.6	815.0	24.2
1987	105	118	68	13.8	12.1	24.5	232.1	7.39	589.1	498.0	1,050.7	40.1
1988				16.9	14.6	30.0	297.9	7.65	1,274.8	686.2	1,928.4	57.6
1989		115	65	17.2	14.8	30.1	317.6	8.19	1,404.5	657.8	2,068.3	39.6
1990				15.7	13.5	27.6	291.1	8.09	1,116.0	674.6	1,798.3	34.5
1991				15.3	13.2	28.3	295.7	8.03	1,093.3	704.9	1,804.4	30.2
1992	87	99	54	13.7	11.8	25.3	279.4	8.46	947.0	690.5	1,612.4	32.7
1993				13.8	11.9	26.0	302.0	8.87	971.1	707.8	1,681.2	49.6
1994				14.6	12.6	27.1	337.4	9.70	1,091.3	729.0	1,810.2	34.6
1995				15.4P	13.3P	28.4P	345.8P	9.54P	1,266.0P	845.7P	2,100.0P	42.7P
1996				15.5P	13.4P	28.8P	358.5P	9.81P	1,326.5P	886.1P	2,200.4P	43.8P
1997				15.7P	13.5P	29.2P	371.2P	10.09P	1,387.1P	926.6P	2,300.8P	44.8P
1998				15.8P	13.6P	29.5P	384.0P	10.37P	1,447.6P	967.0P	2,401.3P	45.9P

Sources: 1982, 1987, 1992 *Economic Census*; *Annual Survey of Manufactures*, 83-86, 88-91, 93-94. Establishment counts for non-Census years are from *County Business Patterns*; establishment values for 83-84 are extrapolations. 'P's show projections by the editors. Industries reclassified in 87 will not have data for prior years.

INDICES OF CHANGE

Year	Com-panies	Establishments Total	Establishments with 20 or more employees	Employment Total (000)	Production Workers (000)	Production Hours (Mil)	Compensation Payroll ($ mil)	Compensation Wages ($/hr)	Cost of Materials	Value Added by Manufacture	Value of Shipments	Capital Invest.
1982	133	132	131	96	96	90	63	71	42	51	47	85
1983				99	100	98	71	73	50	58	55	62
1984				100	101	99	76	77	60	67	63	102
1985				96	95	90	73	80	50	67	58	104
1986				90	90	85	70	82	46	54	51	74
1987	121	119	126	101	103	97	83	87	62	72	65	123
1988				123	124	119	107	90	135	99	120	176
1989		116	120	126	125	119	114	97	148	95	128	121
1990				115	114	109	104	96	118	98	112	106
1991				112	112	112	106	95	115	102	112	92
1992	100	100	100	100	100	100	100	100	100	100	100	100
1993				101	101	103	108	105	103	103	104	152
1994				107	107	107	121	115	115	106	112	106
1995				112P	112P	112P	124P	113P	134P	122P	130P	131P
1996				113P	113P	114P	128P	116P	140P	128P	136P	134P
1997				115P	115P	115P	133P	119P	146P	134P	143P	137P
1998				116P	116P	117P	137P	123P	153P	140P	149P	140P

Sources: Same as General Statistics. Values reflect change from the base year, 1992. Values above 100 mean greater than 92, values below 100 mean less than 92, and a value of 100 in the 82-91 or 93-98 period means same as 92. 'P's mark projections by the editors.

SELECTED RATIOS

For 1992	Avg. of All Manufact.	Analyzed Industry	Index	For 1992	Avg. of All Manufact.	Analyzed Industry	Index
Employees per Establishment	46	138	303	Value Added per Production Worker	122,353	58,517	48
Payroll per Establishment	1,332,320	2,822,222	212	Cost per Establishment	4,239,462	9,565,657	226
Payroll per Employee	29,181	20,394	70	Cost per Employee	92,853	69,124	74
Production Workers per Establishment	31	119	380	Cost per Production Worker	135,003	80,254	59
Wages per Establishment	734,496	2,162,000	294	Shipments per Establishment	8,100,800	16,286,869	201
Wages per Production Worker	23,390	18,139	78	Shipments per Employee	177,425	117,693	66
Hours per Production Worker	2,025	2,144	106	Shipments per Production Worker	257,966	136,644	53
Wages per Hour	11.55	8.46	73	Investment per Establishment	278,244	330,303	119
Value Added per Establishment	3,842,210	6,974,747	182	Investment per Employee	6,094	2,387	39
Value Added per Employee	84,153	50,401	60	Investment per Production Worker	8,861	2,771	31

Sources: Same as General Statistics. The 'Average of All Manufacturing' column represents the average of all manufacturing industries reported for the most recent complete year available. The Index shows the relationship between the Average and the Analyzed Industry. For example, 100 means that they are equal; 500 that the Analyzed Industry is five times the average; 50 means that the Analyzed Industry is half the national average. The abbreviation 'na' is used to show that data are 'not available'.

LEADING COMPANIES

Number shown: **24** Total sales ($ mil): **2,732** Total employment (000): **33.3**

Company Name	Address				CEO Name	Phone	Co. Type	Sales ($ mil)	Empl. (000)
Burlington Industries Inc	3330 W Friendly	Greensboro	NC	27410	G W Henderson III	919-379-2000	P	2,127	23.8
Forstmann and Company Inc	1185 Avnue of the	New York	NY	10036	C L Schaller	212-642-6900	P	237	3.0
Guilford of Maine Inc	PO Box 179	Guilford	ME	04443	Lyn Sawltor	207-876-3331	S	77*	1.5
American Woolen Co	4000 NW 30th Av	Miami	FL	33142	Richard S Marcus	305-635-4000	R	46	1.2
Worcester Co	1 Greystone Av	Centredale	RI	02911	William Masser	401-231-4500	R	35	0.7
Anglo Fabrics Company Inc	561 7th Av	New York	NY	10018	John Honig	212-736-2230	R	32	0.6
LW Packard and Company Inc	6 Mill St	Ashland	NH	03217	John L Glidden	603-968-3351	R	28	0.3
Dorr Woolen Co	Rte 11	Guild	NH	03754	Merrill Loring	603-863-1196	S	25	0.3
Eastland Woolen Mills Inc	Main St	Corinna	ME	04928	Matthew J Burns	207-278-3101	R	25	0.5
Faribault Woolen Mill Co	PO Box 369	Faribault	MN	55021	Robert K Johnson	507-334-6444	R	18	0.2
Haartz Corp	87 Heyward Rd	Acton	MA	01720	Eric Haartz	508-263-2741	R	15*	0.2
Cascade Woolen Mill Inc	PO Box 157	Oakland	ME	04963	Gerald C Tipper	207-465-2511	R	11*	0.2
Robinson Manufacturing Co	PO Box 195	Oxford	ME	04270	George Robinson	207-539-4481	R	10*	0.2
Kezar Falls Woolen Co	Federal Rd	Kezar Falls	ME	04047	John B Robinson	207-625-3267	D	8*	0.1
Charles W House and Sons Inc	PO Box 158	Unionville	CT	06085	HA Hamlin	203-673-2518	R	7*	<0.1
HAB Industries Inc	15 S Albert St	Allentown	PA	18103	HA Buechele	215-439-1208	R	7*	0.2
Henry Mali Company Inc	257 Park Av S	New York	NY	10010	Fred J Mali	212-475-4960	R	7	<0.1
Anchor Dyeing and Finishing	Adams & Leiper St	Philadelphia	PA	19124	B Shlomm	215-289-5100	S	5	<0.1
Anthra Textile Company Inc	1400 Chestnut St	Kulpmont	PA	17834	Boris Schlomm	717-373-9418	S	3*	<0.1
Navajo Textile Mills Inc	40 W Brown Rd	Mesa	AZ	85201	Albert M Pooley	602-844-9899	R	3	<0.1
Litchfield Woolen Mill Co	PO Box 722	Litchfield	MN	55355	Plymouth D Nelson	612-693-7227	R	2	<0.1
Waterbury Felt Inc	PO Box 549	Oriskany	NY	13424	Peter Earle	315-736-3016	R	2*	<0.1
Ortega's Weaving Shop Inc	PO Box 325	Chimayo	NM	87522	Robert J Ortega	505-351-4215	R	1	<0.1
Jacquard Fabrics Inc	1965 Swathmore	Lakewood	NJ	08701	Len Gliner	908-905-4545	R	1*	<0.1

Source: *Ward's Business Directory of U.S. Private and Public Companies*, Volumes 1 and 2, 1996. The company type code used is as follows: P - Public, R - Private, S - Subsidiary, D - Division, J - Joint Venture, A - Affiliate, G - Group. Sales are in millions of dollars, employees are in thousands. An asterisk (*) indicates an estimated sales volume. The symbol < stands for 'less than'. Company names and addresses are truncated, in some cases, to fit into the available space.

MATERIALS CONSUMED

Material		Quantity	Delivered Cost ($ million)
Materials, ingredients, containers, and supplies		(X)	887.3
Raw cotton fibers	1,000 bales	(D)	(D)
Raw wool, mohair, and other animal fibers (scoured weight)	mil lb	97.0**	196.4
Wool tops	mil lb	26.9**	90.0
Rayon and acetate staple and tow	mil lb	(D)	(D)
Nylon staple and tow	mil lb	(S)	8.0
Polyester staple and tow	mil lb	(D)	(D)
All other manmade fiber staple and tow (except glass)	mil lb	(D)	(D)
All other fibers (silk, jute, reused wool, waste, etc.)	mil lb	(D)	(D)
Rayon and acetate filament yarns	mil lb	(D)	(D)
Nylon filament yarns	mil lb	(D)	(D)
Polyester filament yarns	mil lb	(D)	(D)
All other filament yarns, except glass	mil lb	(D)	(D)
Spun yarn, all fibers	mil lb	50.5	205.8
Broadwoven fabrics	mil sq yd	(D)	(D)
Dyes, lakes, and toners		(X)	33.2
All other materials and components, parts, containers, and supplies		(X)	53.4
Materials, ingredients, containers, and supplies, nsk		(X)	7.3

Source: 1992 *Economic Census*. Explanation of symbols used: (D): Withheld to avoid disclosure of competitive data; na: Not available; (S): Withheld because statistical norms were not met; (X): Not applicable; (Z): Less than half the unit shown; nec: Not elsewhere classified; nsk: Not specified by kind; - : zero; * : 10-19 percent estimated; ** : 20-29 percent estimated.

PRODUCT SHARE DETAILS

Product or Product Class	% Share	Product or Product Class	% Share
Broadwoven fabric mills, wool	100.00	Receipts for commission finishing or sponging of wool fabrics	(D)
Finished wool yarns, tops, or raw stock, not combed or spun at the same establishment	4.57	Fabricated textile products, 36 percent or more wool	(D)
Wool broadwoven fabrics (gray goods)	28.34	Broadwoven fabrics mills, wool, nsk	1.42
Finished broadwoven wool fabrics and felts	63.90		

Source: 1992 *Economic Census*. The values shown are percent of total shipments in an industry. Values of indented subcategories are summed in the main heading. The symbol (D) appears when data are withheld to prevent disclosure of competitive information. The abbreviation nsk stands for 'not specified by kind' and nec for 'not elsewhere classified'.

INPUTS AND OUTPUTS FOR BROADWOVEN FABRIC MILLS

Economic Sector or Industry Providing Inputs	%	Sector	Economic Sector or Industry Buying Outputs	%	Sector
Broadwoven fabric mills	36.6	Manufg.	Apparel made from purchased materials	36.0	Manufg.
Organic fibers, noncellulosic	9.0	Manufg.	Broadwoven fabric mills	30.4	Manufg.
Imports	8.5	Foreign	Housefurnishings, nec	5.0	Manufg.
Cotton	6.1	Agric.	Exports	4.0	Foreign
Yarn mills & finishing of textiles, nec	5.2	Manufg.	Personal consumption expenditures	2.6	
Wholesale trade	5.2	Trade	Upholstered household furniture	2.5	Manufg.
Cyclic crudes and organics	3.2	Manufg.	Curtains & draperies	2.2	Manufg.
Cellulosic manmade fibers	2.9	Manufg.	Automotive & apparel trimmings	1.7	Manufg.
Electric services (utilities)	2.9	Util.	Surgical appliances & supplies	1.3	Manufg.
Business services nec	2.0	Services	Coated fabrics, not rubberized	1.2	Manufg.
Miscellaneous plastics products	1.4	Manufg.	Fabricated textile products, nec	1.1	Manufg.
Gas production & distribution (utilities)	1.1	Util.	Mattresses & bedsprings	0.9	Manufg.
Petroleum refining	1.0	Manufg.	Paper mills, except building paper	0.9	Manufg.
Laundry, dry cleaning, shoe repair	1.0	Services	Rubber & plastics hose & belting	0.7	Manufg.
Banking	0.9	Fin/R.E.	Fabricated rubber products, nec	0.6	Manufg.
Personnel supply services	0.9	Services	Miscellaneous plastics products	0.6	Manufg.
Paperboard containers & boxes	0.8	Manufg.	Sanitary paper products	0.6	Manufg.
Textile machinery	0.8	Manufg.	Textile bags	0.6	Manufg.
Motor freight transportation & warehousing	0.8	Util.	Canvas & related products	0.5	Manufg.
Advertising	0.8	Services	Paperboard mills	0.4	Manufg.
Sanitary services, steam supply, irrigation	0.7	Util.	Rubber & plastics footwear	0.4	Manufg.
Surface active agents	0.6	Manufg.	Bags, except textile	0.3	Manufg.
Textile goods, nec	0.6	Manufg.	Floor coverings	0.3	Manufg.
Maintenance of nonfarm buildings nec	0.5	Constr.	Laundry, dry cleaning, shoe repair	0.3	Services
Glass & glass products, except containers	0.5	Manufg.	Federal Government purchases, national defense	0.3	Fed Govt
Lubricating oils & greases	0.5	Manufg.	Tobacco	0.2	Agric.
Eating & drinking places	0.5	Trade	Abrasive products	0.2	Manufg.
Industrial inorganic chemicals, nec	0.4	Manufg.	Aircraft	0.2	Manufg.
U.S. Postal Service	0.3	Gov't	Book printing	0.2	Manufg.
Meat animals	0.2	Agric.	Brooms & brushes	0.2	Manufg.
Coal	0.2	Mining	Burial caskets & vaults	0.2	Manufg.
Conveyors & conveying equipment	0.2	Manufg.	Dolls	0.2	Manufg.
Machinery, except electrical, nec	0.2	Manufg.	Needles, pins, & fasteners	0.2	Manufg.
Communications, except radio & TV	0.2	Util.	Pleating & stitching	0.2	Manufg.
Railroads & related services	0.2	Util.	Sporting & athletic goods, nec	0.2	Manufg.
Business/professional associations	0.2	Services	S/L Govt. purch., elem. & secondary education	0.2	S/L Govt
Computer & data processing services	0.2	Services	S/L Govt. purch., public assistance & relief	0.2	S/L Govt
Equipment rental & leasing services	0.2	Services	Coal	0.1	Mining
Management & consulting services & labs	0.2	Services	Aircraft & missile engines & engine parts	0.1	Manufg.
Scrap	0.2	Scrap	Luggage	0.1	Manufg.
Real estate	0.1	Fin/R.E.	Hotels & lodging places	0.1	Services
Royalties	0.1	Fin/R.E.	Motion pictures	0.1	Services
Automotive rental & leasing, without drivers	0.1	Services	Watch, clock, jewelry, & furniture repair	0.1	Services
Legal services	0.1	Services			

Source: Benchmark Input-Output Accounts for the U.S. Economy, 1982, U.S. Department of Commerce, Washington, D.C., July 1991. Data, as reported in the source, are organized by the 1977 SIC structure in use in 1982 but have been matched, as closely as is possible, to the 1987 SIC structure used in this book.

OCCUPATIONS EMPLOYED BY SIC 223 - WEAVING, FINISHING, YARN AND THREAD MILLS

Occupation	% of Total 1994	Change to 2005	Occupation	% of Total 1994	Change to 2005
Textile draw-out & winding machine operators	32.8	-35.5	Machine feeders & offbearers	2.6	-27.4
Industrial machinery mechanics	6.4	29.1	Machine operators nec	2.2	-28.9
Textile machine setters & set-up operators	4.9	-11.3	Sewing machine operators, non-garment	1.8	21.0
Helpers, laborers, & material movers nec	4.5	-19.3	Industrial truck & tractor operators	1.6	-19.3
Blue collar worker supervisors	4.2	-24.6	Hand packers & packagers	1.3	-30.9
Inspectors, testers, & graders, precision	4.2	-27.4	General managers & top executives	1.3	-23.5
Textile bleaching & dyeing machine operators	4.2	8.9	Maintenance repairers, general utility	1.2	-27.4
Freight, stock, & material movers, hand	2.8	-35.5	Janitors & cleaners, incl maids	1.0	-35.5

Source: Industry-Occupation Matrix, Bureau of Labor Statistics. These data relate to one or more 3-digit SIC industry groups rather than to a single 4-digit SIC. The change reported for each occupation to the year 2005 is a percent of growth or decline as estimated by the Bureau of Labor Statistics. The abbreviation nec stands for 'not elsewhere classified'.

LOCATION BY STATE AND REGIONAL CONCENTRATION

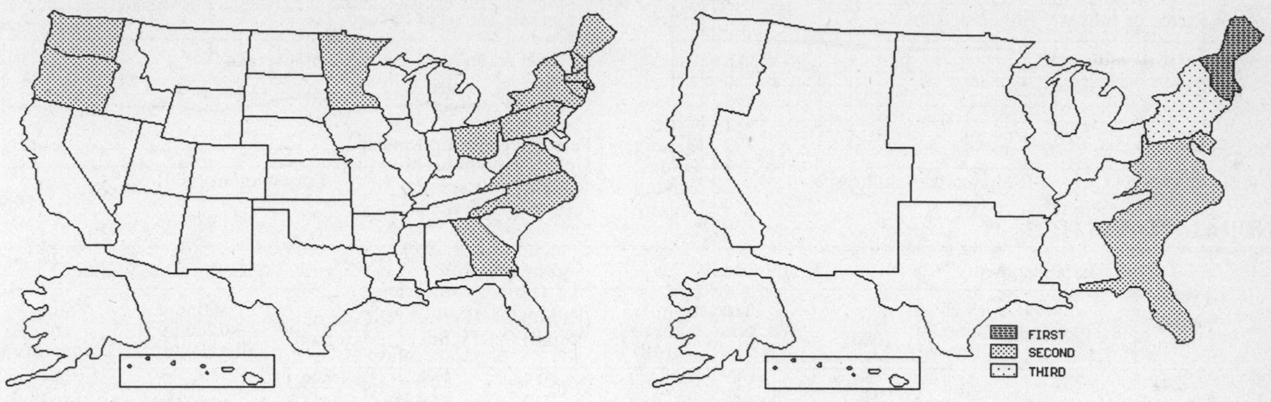

INDUSTRY DATA BY STATE

State	Establish-ments	Shipments			Employment				Cost as % of Shipments	Investment per Employee ($)
		Total ($ mil)	% of U.S.	Per Establ.	Total Number	% of U.S.	Per Establ.	Wages ($/hour)		
Maine	8	122.8	7.6	15.3	1,600	11.7	200	8.36	46.8	3,000
New Hampshire	5	68.4	4.2	13.7	700	5.1	140	9.08	53.4	3,714
Massachusetts	10	38.7	2.4	3.9	500	3.6	50	9.00	30.7	1,200
Pennsylvania	7	25.4	1.6	3.6	800	5.8	114	8.45	22.0	-
New York	8	7.1	0.4	0.9	100	0.7	13	8.50	49.3	1,000
Georgia	11	(D)	-	-	3,750 *	27.4	341	-	-	-
North Carolina	6	(D)	-	-	1,750 *	12.8	292	-	-	-
Rhode Island	6	(D)	-	-	750 *	5.5	125	-	-	-
Virginia	5	(D)	-	-	3,750 *	27.4	750	-	-	-
Connecticut	3	(D)	-	-	375 *	2.7	125	-	-	-
Minnesota	3	(D)	-	-	175 *	1.3	58	-	-	-
Ohio	3	(D)	-	-	175 *	1.3	58	-	-	-
Oregon	2	(D)	-	-	175 *	1.3	88	-	-	-
Washington	1	(D)	-	-	375 *	2.7	375	-	-	-

Source: 1992 *Economic Census*. The states are in descending order of shipments or establishments (if shipment data are missing for the majority). The symbol (D) appears when data are withheld to prevent disclosure of competitive information. States marked with (D) are sorted by number of establishments. A dash (-) indicates that the data element cannot be calculated; * indicates the midpoint of a range.

2241 - NARROW FABRIC MILLS

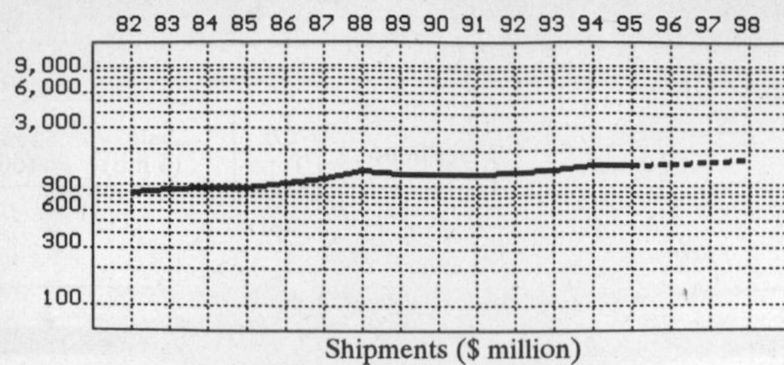

Shipments ($ million)

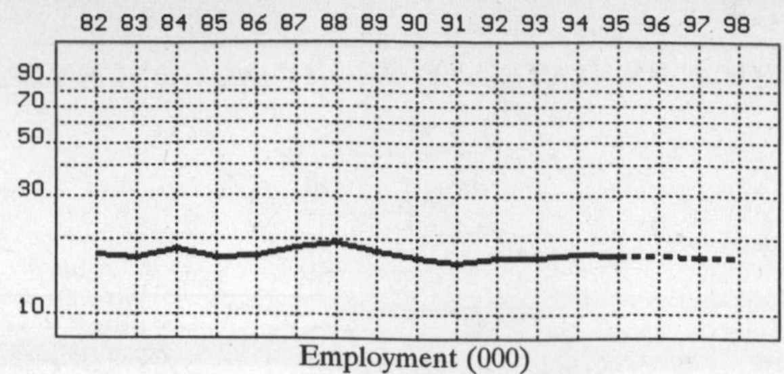

Employment (000)

GENERAL STATISTICS

Year	Companies	Establishments: Total	Establishments: with 20 or more employees	Employment: Total (000)	Employment: Production Workers (000)	Employment: Production Hours (Mil)	Compensation: Payroll ($ mil)	Compensation: Wages ($/hr)	Production ($ million): Cost of Materials	Production ($ million): Value Added by Manufacture	Production ($ million): Value of Shipments	Production ($ million): Capital Invest.
1982	241	281	161	17.5	15.2	28.5	215.5	5.58	388.3	464.7	851.8	22.3
1983				16.9	14.5	28.6	227.3	5.95	414.8	509.0	918.9	18.8
1984				18.1	15.6	29.6	240.1	5.97	409.6	555.2	954.6	55.9
1985				16.9	14.4	27.2	242.3	6.38	415.3	550.0	962.3	28.9
1986				17.2	14.7	27.5	259.7	6.63	452.6	594.5	1,040.0	32.4
1987	248	272	166	18.5	15.7	31.6	295.5	6.67	557.7	580.1	1,135.7	32.5
1988				19.4	16.6	34.3	330.8	6.91	617.5	731.4	1,342.2	35.0
1989		267	157	18.0	15.5	30.5	304.6	7.24	578.9	667.6	1,247.7	28.8
1990				17.0	14.7	30.2	306.7	7.32	588.9	671.4	1,259.7	34.0
1991				16.1	13.9	28.2	290.8	7.53	558.5	697.9	1,247.6	28.3
1992	224	258	131	16.8	14.3	29.0	324.8	8.12	605.2	718.8	1,313.9	50.3
1993				16.9	14.5	28.9	332.4	8.23	614.6	748.5	1,353.0	39.9
1994				17.5	14.2	29.0	358.1	7.69	653.5	834.1	1,470.0	67.3
1995				17.1P	14.4P	29.8P	362.5P	8.40P	665.5P	849.4P	1,496.9P	50.0P
1996				17.1P	14.3P	29.9P	373.3P	8.61P	686.8P	876.6P	1,544.8P	51.9P
1997				17.0P	14.3P	29.9P	384.2P	8.82P	708.1P	903.8P	1,592.8P	53.8P
1998				17.0P	14.2P	30.0P	395.0P	9.03P	729.4P	931.0P	1,640.7P	55.8P

Sources: 1982, 1987, 1992 *Economic Census*; *Annual Survey of Manufactures*, 83-86, 88-91, 93-94. Establishment counts for non-Census years are from *County Business Patterns*; establishment values for 83-84 are extrapolations. 'P's show projections by the editors. Industries reclassified in 87 will not have data for prior years.

INDICES OF CHANGE

Year	Companies	Establishments: Total	Establishments: with 20 or more employees	Employment: Total (000)	Employment: Production Workers (000)	Employment: Production Hours (Mil)	Compensation: Payroll ($ mil)	Compensation: Wages ($/hr)	Production ($ million): Cost of Materials	Production ($ million): Value Added by Manufacture	Production ($ million): Value of Shipments	Production ($ million): Capital Invest.
1982	108	109	123	104	106	98	66	69	64	65	65	44
1983				101	101	99	70	73	69	71	70	37
1984				108	109	102	74	74	68	77	73	111
1985				101	101	94	75	79	69	77	73	57
1986				102	103	95	80	82	75	83	79	64
1987	111	105	127	110	110	109	91	82	92	81	86	65
1988				115	116	118	102	85	102	102	102	70
1989		103	120	107	108	105	94	89	96	93	95	57
1990				101	103	104	94	90	97	93	96	68
1991				96	97	97	90	93	92	97	95	56
1992	100	100	100	100	100	100	100	100	100	100	100	100
1993				101	101	100	102	101	102	104	103	79
1994				104	99	100	110	95	108	116	112	134
1995				102P	101P	103P	112P	103P	110P	118P	114P	99P
1996				102P	100P	103P	115P	106P	113P	122P	118P	103P
1997				101P	100P	103P	118P	109P	117P	126P	121P	107P
1998				101P	99P	103P	122P	111P	121P	130P	125P	111P

Sources: Same as General Statistics. Values reflect change from the base year, 1992. Values above 100 mean greater than 92, values below 100 mean less than 92, and a value of 100 in the 82-91 or 93-98 period means same as 92. 'P's mark projections by the editors.

SELECTED RATIOS

For 1992	Avg. of All Manufact.	Analyzed Industry	Index
Employees per Establishment	46	65	143
Payroll per Establishment	1,332,320	1,258,915	94
Payroll per Employee	29,181	19,333	66
Production Workers per Establishment	31	55	177
Wages per Establishment	734,496	912,713	124
Wages per Production Worker	23,390	16,467	70
Hours per Production Worker	2,025	2,028	100
Wages per Hour	11.55	8.12	70
Value Added per Establishment	3,842,210	2,786,047	73
Value Added per Employee	84,153	42,786	51

For 1992	Avg. of All Manufact.	Analyzed Industry	Index
Value Added per Production Worker	122,353	50,266	41
Cost per Establishment	4,239,462	2,345,736	55
Cost per Employee	92,853	36,024	39
Cost per Production Worker	135,003	42,322	31
Shipments per Establishment	8,100,800	5,092,636	63
Shipments per Employee	177,425	78,208	44
Shipments per Production Worker	257,966	91,881	36
Investment per Establishment	278,244	194,961	70
Investment per Employee	6,094	2,994	49
Investment per Production Worker	8,861	3,517	40

Sources: Same as General Statistics. The 'Average of All Manufacturing' column represents the average of all manufacturing industries reported for the most recent complete year available. The Index shows the relationship between the Average and the Analyzed Industry. For example, 100 means that they are equal; 500 that the Analyzed Industry is five times the average; 50 means that the Analyzed Industry is half the national average. The abbreviation 'na' is used to show that data are 'not available'.

LEADING COMPANIES

Number shown: **71** Total sales ($ mil): **1,619** Total employment (000): **19.5**

Company Name	Address				CEO Name	Phone	Co. Type	Sales ($ mil)	Empl. (000)
Worldtex Inc	PO Box 2363	Hickory	NC	28603	Barry D Setzer	704-328-5381	P	165	1.0
Pendleton Woolen Mills Inc	PO Box 3030	Portland	OR	97208	BH Bishop	503-226-4801	R	160	2.2
BGF Industries Inc	301 N Elm St	Greensboro	NC	27401	Graham Pope	919-333-9570	S	120	1.0
JPS Glass Fabrics	PO Box 260	Slater	SC	29683	Jerry E Hunter	803-836-1362	D	80	0.5
Spanco Industries Inc	PO Box 1288	Sanford	NC	27330	Lamar Beach	919-776-5111	R	75	0.9
Moore Co	36 Beach St	Westerly	RI	02891	Peter Moore	401-596-2816	R	73•	1.0
Regal Manufacturing Company	212 12th Av NE	Hickory	NC	28601	Kenneth W O'Neill	704-328-5381	S	67	0.6
Elastic Corporation of America	455 Hwy 70	Columbiana	AL	35051	Edward Gleadall	205-669-3101	D	65	0.6
NFA Corp	850 Boylston St	Chestnut Hill	MA	02167	David Casty	617-232-6060	R	65•	1.0
Bacova Guild Ltd	1 Main St	Bacova	VA	24412	Benjamin I Johns	703-839-5313	R	48•	0.5
PAXAR Corp	500 E 35th St	Paterson	NJ	07504	Frank Diekmann	201-684-6564	D	48	0.1
United Elastic Corp	PO Box 519	Stuart	VA	24171	Charles Tracy	703-694-7171	D	44	0.6
Conso Products Co	PO Box 326	Union	SC	29379	J Cary Findlay	803-427-9004	P	42	1.2
Artistic Identification Systems	55 Wanaque Av	Pompton Lakes	NJ	07442	Willard G Kluge	201-835-6000	R	32	0.5
Fulflex Inc	PO Box 4549	Middletown	RI	02842	William E Russell	401-849-0600	S	32•	0.5
Monterey Inc	PO Box 271	Janesville	WI	53547	Jay Jensen	608-754-2866	R	29	0.4
Atkins and Pearce Inc	1 Braid Way	Covington	KY	41017	Joseph Head, Jr	606-356-2001	R	25	0.2
Narrow Fabric Industries Inc	7th & Reading Av	West Reading	PA	19611	Stewart R Tait	215-376-2891	R	25	0.4
Lion Ribbon Company Inc	Rte 24, Box 601	Chester	NJ	07930	Claude P Offray Jr	908-879-4700	S	24•	0.3
Industrial Fabrics Corp	7160 Northland Cir	Minneapolis	MN	55428	Rolf Muehlenhaus	612-535-3220	R	20	<0.1
Sher Woven Label Co	62 W 38th St	New York	NY	10018	Eric Sharenow	212-391-8100	R	18	0.3
Tho-Ro Products Inc	335 Paterson Plank	Carlstadt	NJ	07072	Arthur J Simon	201-935-3990	R	17•	0.4
PAXAR Corp	PO Box 735	Lenoir	NC	28645	R Dan Burke	704-758-2338	D	16•	0.4
Sullivan-Carson Inc	1034 Laurel Oak Rd	Voorhees	NJ	08043	Jim Carson	609-784-4222	R	16	0.2
Georgia Narrow Fabrics	2050 Sunset Blv	Jesup	GA	31545	Roland K Knight	912-427-6961	R	15	0.2
Trimtex Company Inc	400 Park Av	Williamsport	PA	17701	W C Henderson	717-326-9135	R	15	0.3
Quality Braid Corp	60-01 31st Av	Woodside	NY	11377	Alan Ferrin	718-204-0002	R	14•	0.2
Southern Webbing Mills Inc	PO Box 13919	Greensboro	NC	27415	Claude I Ruth III	910-375-3103	R	14•	0.2
South Carolina Elastic Co	PO Box 369	Landrum	SC	29356	Jack Elliott	803-457-3388	D	13	0.2
Venus Trimming&Binding Co	41-50 24th St	Long Island Ct	NY	11101	S Sloan	718-729-4300	R	13	0.2
Shelby Elastics Inc	639 N Post Rd	Shelby	NC	28150	Douglas M Shytles	704-487-4301	S	13	0.1
Stanwood Mills Inc	570 7th Av	New York	NY	10018	John Shulman	212-944-4826	R	12	0.1
Wellington Sears Co	3006 Anaconda Rd	Tarboro	NC	27886	Allan Hinkle	919-823-6126	S	12•	0.2
Wayne Mills Company Inc	130 W Berkley St	Philadelphia	PA	19144	Franklin A Milnes	215-842-2134	S	11	0.2
Texfi Elastics	328 W Central Av	Asheboro	NC	27203	David Geer	910-672-3820	S	11	0.4
Bally Ribbon Mills	23 N 7th St	Bally	PA	19503	Ray Harries	610-845-2211	R	10	0.2
Julius Koch USA Inc	PO Box 2900	New Bedford	MA	02741	Lew Coco	508-995-9565	R	10	0.1
National Bias Binding Corp	231 59th St	Brooklyn	NY	11220	S Gagliano	718-439-4800	R	10•	<0.1
Pittsfield Weaving Company Inc	1 Fayette St	Pittsfield	NH	03263	Gilbert Bleckmann	603-435-8301	R	10	0.2
Sheltex Manufacturing Company	14902 SW 74th Pl	Miami	FL	33158	Jon Raphaely	305-670-6639	R	10•	0.2
Gudebrod Inc	PO Box 357	Pottstown	PA	19464	RJ Marquardt	610-327-4050	R	10	<0.1
Chatham Mills Inc	PO Box 616	Pittsboro	NC	27312	P Romeo	919-542-3142	S	9•	0.1
Providence Braid Company Inc	358 Lowden St	Pawtucket	RI	02860	H Huntoon	401-722-2120	R	8	0.1
Carson and Gebel Ribbon Co	PO Box 409	Dover	NJ	07801	Seymour Gebel	201-366-0610	R	7•	0.1
Artistic Woven Labels	W Hwy 6	Holdrege	NE	68949	Lloyd Horner	308-995-8671	S	7•	0.1
CT-Nassau Corp	PO Box 39	Alamance	NC	27201	Alan Thoenen	910-570-0091	R	7	<0.1
Lockwood Industries Inc	21054 Osborne St	Canoga Park	CA	91304	NC Tucker	818-709-1288	R	7•	<0.1
Hickory Brands Inc	PO Box 429	Hickory	NC	28603	Bob Bell	704-322-2600	R	6•	<0.1
Narricot Industries Inc	928 Jaymore Rd	Southampton	PA	18966	Phil Dansky	215-322-3900	R	6	0.4
AH Rice Corp	55 Spring St	Pittsfield	MA	01201	George Unhoch	413-443-6477	S	5	<0.1
AH Weiss Company Inc	2323 S Halsted St	Chicago	IL	60608	LE Robins	312-829-4676	R	5	<0.1
Star Binding and Trimming Corp	1109 Grand Av	North Bergen	NJ	07047	Martin Spatz	201-864-2220	R	5	<0.1
Thomas Taylor and Sons Inc	50 Houghton St	Hudson	MA	01749	Robert Damon	508-562-3401	R	5	<0.1
Suncook Trim Corp	PO Box 234	Suncook	NH	03275	Jonathan A Bresler	603-485-9558	R	5	<0.1
Bo-Buck Mills Inc	PO Box 692	Chesterfield	SC	29709	Andrew F Maner	803-623-2158	R	4	<0.1
Berstone Knitting Mills Inc	418 Lafayette St	New York	NY	10003	Simon Bernstein	212-533-0505	R	3	<0.1
General Shoe Lace Company Inc	642 Starks Bldg	Louisville	KY	40202	Calvin H Raus	502-585-4191	R	3	<0.1
Howard Brothers Mfg	PO Box 1447	Auburn	MA	01501	Walter Jones	508-793-7070	D	3•	<0.1
Leedon Webbing Co	86 Tremont St	Central Falls	RI	02863	William H Janowski	401-722-1044	R	3	<0.1
Alfred Manufacturing Corp	350 Warren St	Jersey City	NJ	07302	Herb Spear	201-332-9100	R	2•	<0.1
Roselin Manufacturing Co	95 Milk St	Willimantic	CT	06226	Stanley Rosenstein	203-423-2568	R	2	<0.1
Henry A Jacobs and Company	PO Box 149	Marlboro	NJ	07746	A Feinman	908-780-9700	R	2	<0.1
AISCO	PO Box 280	Edison	NJ	08818	Susan Gronbeck	908-248-9495	D	1	<0.1
Steelstran Industries	PO Box 280	Edison	NJ	08818	P Gronbeck	908-248-9495	R	1	<0.1
Artray Label Company Inc	107 Grand St	New York	NY	10013	Arthur Rand	212-966-5590	R	1	<0.1
Colonial-Bende Ribbons Inc	182 Autumn St	Passaic	NJ	07055	Andras Bende	201-777-8700	R	1	<0.1
Hooper Industries Inc	2121 Druid Park Dr	Baltimore	MD	21211	Kenneth Mumaw	410-462-4400	R	1	<0.1
York Braid Mills Inc	PO Box 523	York	PA	17405	Ronald Ehrhart	717-846-2837	R	1•	<0.1
Lambeth Band Corp	PO Box 50490	New Bedford	MA	02745	S Braley Gray	508-995-2626	R	1	<0.1
Tennford Weaving Co	PO Box 308	Wartburg	TN	37887	Edwin Collins	615-346-6241	D	1	0.1
Kendrick Company Inc	6139 Germantown	Philadelphia	PA	19144	Lesley DeVine	215-438-1122	R	0	<0.1

Source: Ward's Business Directory of U.S. Private and Public Companies, Volumes 1 and 2, 1996. The company type code used is as follows: P - Public, R - Private, S - Subsidiary, D - Division, J - Joint Venture, A - Affiliate, G - Group. Sales are in millions of dollars, employees are in thousands. An asterisk (•) indicates an estimated sales volume. The symbol < stands for 'less than'. Company names and addresses are truncated, in some cases, to fit into the available space.

MATERIALS CONSUMED

Material	Quantity	Delivered Cost ($ million)
Materials, ingredients, containers, and supplies	(X)	564.5
Cotton yarns	(X)	38.9
Polyester filament yarns	(X)	102.4
Nylon filament yarns	(X)	116.8
Filament rayon and acetate yarns	(X)	6.6
All other yarns	(X)	88.7
Bare rubber thread	(X)	51.5
All other materials and components, parts, containers, and supplies	(X)	103.7
Materials, ingredients, containers, and supplies, nsk	(X)	55.9

Source: 1992 *Economic Census*. Explanation of symbols used: (D): Withheld to avoid disclosure of competitive data; na: Not available; (S): Withheld because statistical norms were not met; (X): Not applicable; (Z): Less than half the unit shown; nec: Not elsewhere classified; nsk: Not specified by kind; - : zero; * : 10-19 percent estimated; ** : 20-29 percent estimated.

PRODUCT SHARE DETAILS

Product or Product Class	% Share
Narrow fabric mills	100.00
Woven narrow fabrics (12 in or less in width)	64.15
Woven elastic narrow fabrics, corset	(D)
Woven elastic narrow fabrics, underwear and other apparel	19.65
Woven elastic narrow fabrics for other uses	3.15
Woven nonelastic labels	17.52
Woven nonelastic ribbons, woven edge	14.53
Woven nonelastic zipper tape	(D)
Woven nonelastic apparel tape, except zipper	1.00
Woven nonelastic tape, except apparel and zipper	(D)
Other woven nonelastic narrow fabrics, including webbing	24.10
Woven narrow fabrics (12 inches or less in width), nsk	9.68
Braided narrow fabrics (12 in or less in width)	15.94
Braided narrow fabrics (12 in or less in width), elastic (flat, round, and tubular)	23.39
Braided nonelastic shoe and corset laces	17.38
Braided narrow fabrics (12 in or less in width), nonelastic, other	54.52
Braided narrow fabrics (12 inches or less in width), nsk	4.72
Covered rubber thread, made in narrow fabric mills	15.65
Narrow fabrics mills, nsk	4.27

Source: 1992 *Economic Census*. The values shown are percent of total shipments in an industry. Values of indented subcategories are summed in the main heading. The symbol (D) appears when data are withheld to prevent disclosure of competitive information. The abbreviation nsk stands for 'not specified by kind' and nec for 'not elsewhere classified'.

INPUTS AND OUTPUTS FOR NARROW FABRIC MILLS

Economic Sector or Industry Providing Inputs	%	Sector	Economic Sector or Industry Buying Outputs	%	Sector
Yarn mills & finishing of textiles, nec	22.4	Manufg.	Apparel made from purchased materials	18.9	Manufg.
Cellulosic manmade fibers	13.5	Manufg.	Exports	10.2	Foreign
Advertising	9.3	Services	Personal consumption expenditures	8.8	
Organic fibers, noncellulosic	8.5	Manufg.	Fabricated textile products, nec	6.5	Manufg.
Wholesale trade	6.1	Trade	Abrasive products	5.9	Manufg.
Imports	5.3	Foreign	Automotive & apparel trimmings	4.4	Manufg.
Nonwoven fabrics	4.0	Manufg.	Carbon paper & inked ribbons	4.3	Manufg.
Fabricated rubber products, nec	3.8	Manufg.	Surgical appliances & supplies	4.0	Manufg.
Miscellaneous plastics products	3.6	Manufg.	Coated fabrics, not rubberized	3.7	Manufg.
Electric services (utilities)	2.4	Util.	Miscellaneous plastics products	3.6	Manufg.
Laundry, dry cleaning, shoe repair	1.9	Services	Motor vehicles & car bodies	2.5	Manufg.
Narrow fabric mills	1.8	Manufg.	Federal Government purchases, national defense	2.5	Fed Govt
Petroleum refining	1.4	Manufg.	Shoes, except rubber	2.1	Manufg.
Synthetic rubber	1.2	Manufg.	Drapery hardware & blinds & shades	1.7	Manufg.
Motor freight transportation & warehousing	1.2	Util.	Canvas & related products	1.4	Manufg.
Glass & glass products, except containers	1.1	Manufg.	Knit underwear mills	1.4	Manufg.
Lubricating oils & greases	1.0	Manufg.	Luggage	1.4	Manufg.
Air transportation	1.0	Util.	Narrow fabric mills	1.4	Manufg.
Eating & drinking places	0.9	Trade	Blankbooks & looseleaf binders	1.3	Manufg.
Maintenance of nonfarm buildings nec	0.6	Constr.	Knit outerwear mills	1.3	Manufg.
Thread mills	0.6	Manufg.	Needles, pins, & fasteners	1.2	Manufg.
Gas production & distribution (utilities)	0.6	Util.	Household refrigerators & freezers	1.1	Manufg.
Banking	0.6	Fin/R.E.	Yarn mills & finishing of textiles, nec	1.1	Manufg.
Textile machinery	0.5	Manufg.	Nonferrous wire drawing & insulating	1.0	Manufg.
Communications, except radio & TV	0.5	Util.	House slippers	0.9	Manufg.
Real estate	0.5	Fin/R.E.	Housefurnishings, nec	0.9	Manufg.
Business/professional associations	0.5	Services	Personal leather goods	0.8	Manufg.
U.S. Postal Service	0.5	Gov't	Rubber & plastics hose & belting	0.8	Manufg.
Royalties	0.4	Fin/R.E.	Upholstered household furniture	0.8	Manufg.
Machinery, except electrical, nec	0.3	Manufg.	Aircraft & missile equipment, nec	0.7	Manufg.
Equipment rental & leasing services	0.3	Services	Rubber & plastics footwear	0.7	Manufg.
Legal services	0.3	Services	Curtains & draperies	0.6	Manufg.
Management & consulting services & labs	0.3	Services	Ship building & repairing	0.6	Manufg.
Accounting, auditing & bookkeeping	0.2	Services	Women's handbags & purses	0.3	Manufg.
Automotive rental & leasing, without drivers	0.2	Services	Floor coverings	0.2	Manufg.
Automotive repair shops & services	0.2	Services	Mattresses & bedsprings	0.2	Manufg.
Computer & data processing services	0.2	Services	Textile bags	0.2	Manufg.
Hotels & lodging places	0.2	Services	Manufacturing industries, nec	0.1	Manufg.
Chemical preparations, nec	0.1	Manufg.			
Manifold business forms	0.1	Manufg.			
Special dies & tools & machine tool accessories	0.1	Manufg.			
Insurance carriers	0.1	Fin/R.E.			
Job training & related services	0.1	Services			
Personnel supply services	0.1	Services			

Source: Benchmark Input-Output Accounts for the U.S. Economy, 1982, U.S. Department of Commerce, Washington, D.C., July 1991. Data, as reported in the source, are organized by the 1977 SIC structure in use in 1982 but have been matched, as closely as is possible, to the 1987 SIC structure used in this book.

OCCUPATIONS EMPLOYED BY SIC 224 - WEAVING, FINISHING, YARN AND THREAD MILLS

Occupation	% of Total 1994	Change to 2005	Occupation	% of Total 1994	Change to 2005
Textile draw-out & winding machine operators	32.8	-35.5	Machine feeders & offbearers	2.6	-27.4
Industrial machinery mechanics	6.4	29.1	Machine operators nec	2.2	-28.9
Textile machine setters & set-up operators	4.9	-11.3	Sewing machine operators, non-garment	1.8	21.0
Helpers, laborers, & material movers nec	4.5	-19.3	Industrial truck & tractor operators	1.6	-19.3
Blue collar worker supervisors	4.2	-24.6	Hand packers & packagers	1.3	-30.9
Inspectors, testers, & graders, precision	4.2	-27.4	General managers & top executives	1.3	-23.5
Textile bleaching & dyeing machine operators	4.2	8.9	Maintenance repairers, general utility	1.2	-27.4
Freight, stock, & material movers, hand	2.8	-35.5	Janitors & cleaners, incl maids	1.0	-35.5

Source: Industry-Occupation Matrix, Bureau of Labor Statistics. These data relate to one or more 3-digit SIC industry groups rather than to a single 4-digit SIC. The change reported for each occupation to the year 2005 is a percent of growth or decline as estimated by the Bureau of Labor Statistics. The abbreviation nec stands for 'not elsewhere classified'.

LOCATION BY STATE AND REGIONAL CONCENTRATION

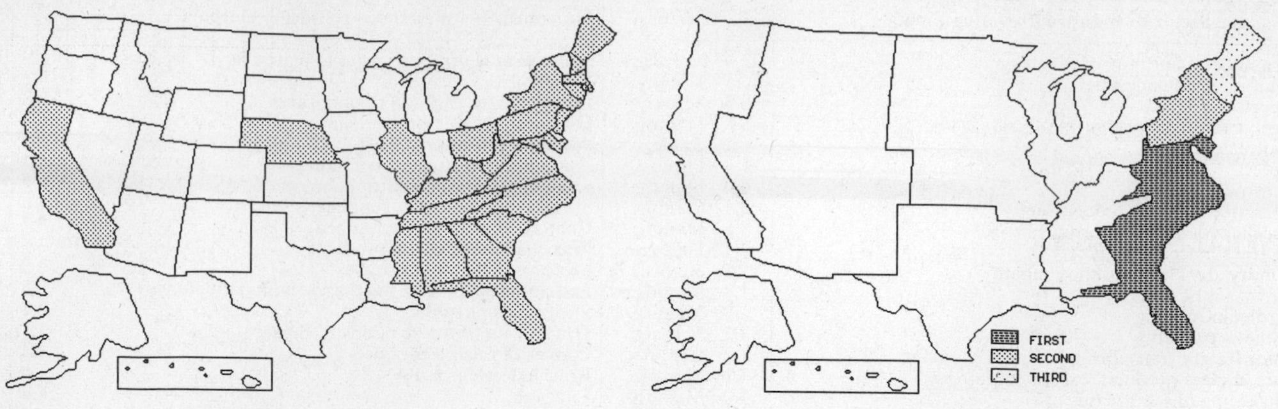

INDUSTRY DATA BY STATE

State	Establish-ments	Shipments			Employment				Cost as % of Shipments	Investment per Employee ($)
		Total ($ mil)	% of U.S.	Per Establ.	Total Number	% of U.S.	Per Establ.	Wages ($/hour)		
Pennsylvania	33	130.9	10.0	4.0	2,100	12.5	64	8.22	39.0	1,619
Rhode Island	18	123.0	9.4	6.8	1,700	10.1	94	7.93	44.8	529
New Jersey	20	57.8	4.4	2.9	800	4.8	40	9.93	45.3	6,375
Virginia	5	56.2	4.3	11.2	1,100	6.5	220	7.05	40.2	1,455
California	14	45.0	3.4	3.2	500	3.0	36	8.11	44.4	8,400
Massachusetts	15	40.4	3.1	2.7	500	3.0	33	9.00	45.8	1,400
Tennessee	6	30.3	2.3	5.1	300	1.8	50	8.17	46.2	2,000
Florida	10	19.9	1.5	2.0	400	2.4	40	7.17	42.2	3,250
New York	20	13.7	1.0	0.7	300	1.8	15	6.80	48.9	1,333
North Carolina	35	(D)	-	-	3,750 *	22.3	107	-	-	4,080
Georgia	13	(D)	-	-	375 *	2.2	29	-	-	-
South Carolina	13	(D)	-	-	1,750 *	10.4	135	-	-	-
Alabama	6	(D)	-	-	750 *	4.5	125	-	-	533
New Hampshire	6	(D)	-	-	750 *	4.5	125	-	-	-
Maryland	5	(D)	-	-	750 *	4.5	150	-	-	-
Connecticut	4	(D)	-	-	175 *	1.0	44	-	-	-
Maine	4	(D)	-	-	175 *	1.0	44	-	-	-
Illinois	3	(D)	-	-	175 *	1.0	58	-	-	-
Ohio	3	(D)	-	-	375 *	2.2	125	-	-	-
Kentucky	2	(D)	-	-	175 *	1.0	88	-	-	-
Mississippi	1	(D)	-	-	175 *	1.0	175	-	-	-
Nebraska	1	(D)	-	-	175 *	1.0	175	-	-	-
West Virginia	1	(D)	-	-	175 *	1.0	175	-	-	-

Source: 1992 *Economic Census*. The states are in descending order of shipments or establishments (if shipment data are missing for the majority). The symbol (D) appears when data are withheld to prevent disclosure of competitive information. States marked with (D) are sorted by number of establishments. A dash (-) indicates that the data element cannot be calculated; * indicates the midpoint of a range.

2251 - WOMEN'S HOSIERY

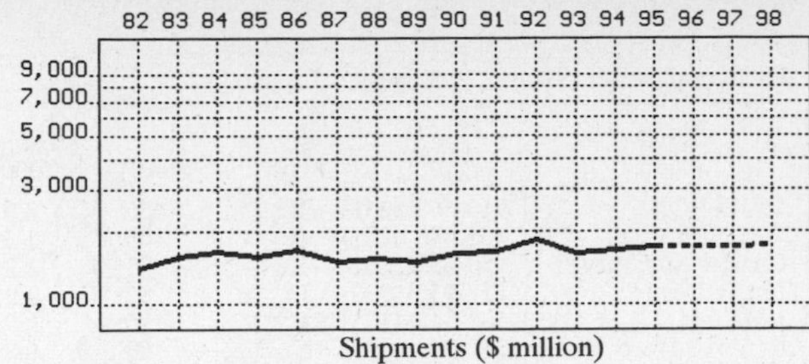

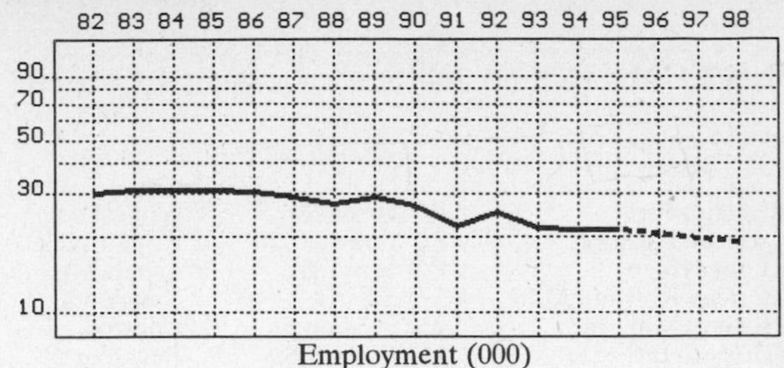

GENERAL STATISTICS

Year	Com-panies	Establishments: Total	Establishments: with 20 or more employees	Employment: Total (000)	Employment: Production Workers (000)	Employment: Production Hours (Mil)	Compensation: Payroll ($ mil)	Compensation: Wages ($/hr)	Production ($ million): Cost of Materials	Production ($ million): Value Added by Manufacture	Production ($ million): Value of Shipments	Production ($ million): Capital Invest.
1982	179	206	118	30.2	26.7	49.6	311.1	4.87	636.8	777.4	1,411.3	26.0
1983		194	119	30.8	27.5	53.2	354.5	5.24	677.3	903.0	1,566.9	26.2
1984		182	120	31.2	27.5	52.6	372.1	5.47	686.7	969.2	1,654.4	27.4
1985		169	120	30.8	27.4	55.5	383.2	5.24	655.2	914.0	1,568.2	36.2
1986		164	116	30.7	27.3	56.5	403.6	5.48	740.1	953.3	1,682.3	28.5
1987	139	161	93	29.3	25.9	53.7	385.9	5.98	715.6	769.5	1,497.5	32.3
1988		155	93	27.5	25.3	51.1	375.8	6.18	682.3	868.2	1,541.2	37.7
1989		145	90	29.2	21.9	40.9	343.4	6.73	649.2	881.5	1,517.0	19.7
1990		144	89	26.8	21.1	42.4	349.5	6.66	713.9	911.2	1,620.7	42.4
1991		151	88	22.3	20.1	40.6	344.7	6.88	749.4	896.0	1,644.6	42.5
1992	127	151	88	25.3	22.8	45.8	398.0	7.02	893.7	977.5	1,843.0	65.0
1993		152	92	21.8	20.0	40.9	353.2	7.11	851.1	789.8	1,624.2	71.8
1994		133P	79P	21.5	19.2	38.7	362.2	7.53	856.7	828.5	1,690.1	47.7
1995		128P	75P	21.6P	18.7P	38.6P	369.7P	7.70P	868.8P	840.2P	1,713.9P	59.6P
1996		123P	72P	20.7P	17.9P	37.3P	370.4P	7.92P	876.7P	847.8P	1,729.5P	62.6P
1997		118P	68P	19.9P	17.2P	35.9P	371.2P	8.14P	884.6P	855.5P	1,745.1P	65.6P
1998		114P	65P	19.0P	16.4P	34.6P	372.0P	8.36P	892.5P	863.1P	1,760.7P	68.5P

Sources: 1982, 1987, 1992 *Economic Census*; *Annual Survey of Manufactures*, 83-86, 88-91, 93-94. Establishment counts for non-Census years are from *County Business Patterns*; establishment values for 83-84 are extrapolations. 'P's show projections by the editors. Industries reclassified in 87 will not have data for prior years.

INDICES OF CHANGE

Year	Com-panies	Establishments: Total	Establishments: with 20 or more employees	Employment: Total (000)	Employment: Production Workers (000)	Employment: Production Hours (Mil)	Compensation: Payroll ($ mil)	Compensation: Wages ($/hr)	Production ($ million): Cost of Materials	Production ($ million): Value Added by Manufacture	Production ($ million): Value of Shipments	Production ($ million): Capital Invest.
1982	141	136	134	119	117	108	78	69	71	80	77	40
1983		128	135	122	121	116	89	75	76	92	85	40
1984		121	136	123	121	115	93	78	77	99	90	42
1985		112	136	122	120	121	96	75	73	94	85	56
1986		109	132	121	120	123	101	78	83	98	91	44
1987	109	107	106	116	114	117	97	85	80	79	81	50
1988		103	106	109	111	112	94	88	76	89	84	58
1989		96	102	115	96	89	86	96	73	90	82	30
1990		95	101	106	93	93	88	95	80	93	88	65
1991		100	100	88	88	89	87	98	84	92	89	65
1992	100	100	100	100	100	100	100	100	100	100	100	100
1993		101	105	86	88	89	89	101	95	81	88	110
1994		88P	90P	85	84	84	91	107	96	85	92	73
1995		85P	86P	85P	82P	84P	93P	110P	97P	86P	93P	92P
1996		82P	82P	82P	79P	81P	93P	113P	98P	87P	94P	96P
1997		78P	78P	79P	75P	78P	93P	116P	99P	88P	95P	101P
1998		75P	73P	75P	72P	76P	93P	119P	100P	88P	96P	105P

Sources: Same as General Statistics. Values reflect change from the base year, 1992. Values above 100 mean greater than 92, values below 100 mean less than 92, and a value of 100 in the 82-91 or 93-98 period means same as 92. 'P's mark projections by the editors.

SELECTED RATIOS

For 1994	Avg. of All Manufact.	Analyzed Industry	Index
Employees per Establishment	49	162	330
Payroll per Establishment	1,500,273	2,723,308	182
Payroll per Employee	30,620	16,847	55
Production Workers per Establishment	34	144	421
Wages per Establishment	853,319	2,191,060	257
Wages per Production Worker	24,861	15,178	61
Hours per Production Worker	2,056	2,016	98
Wages per Hour	12.09	7.53	62
Value Added per Establishment	4,602,255	6,229,323	135
Value Added per Employee	93,930	38,535	41

For 1994	Avg. of All Manufact.	Analyzed Industry	Index
Value Added per Production Worker	134,084	43,151	32
Cost per Establishment	5,045,178	6,441,353	128
Cost per Employee	102,970	39,847	39
Cost per Production Worker	146,988	44,620	30
Shipments per Establishment	9,576,895	12,707,519	133
Shipments per Employee	195,460	78,609	40
Shipments per Production Worker	279,017	88,026	32
Investment per Establishment	321,011	358,647	112
Investment per Employee	6,552	2,219	34
Investment per Production Worker	9,352	2,484	27

Sources: Same as General Statistics. The 'Average of All Manufacturing' column represents the average of all manufacturing industries reported for the most recent complete year available. The Index shows the relationship between the Average and the Analyzed Industry. For example, 100 means that they are equal; 500 that the Analyzed Industry is five times the average; 50 means that the Analyzed Industry is half the national average. The abbreviation 'na' is used to show that data are 'not available'.

LEADING COMPANIES

Number shown: **30** Total sales ($ mil): **1,326** Total employment (000): **20.8**

Company Name	Address				CEO Name	Phone	Co. Type	Sales ($ mil)	Empl. (000)
Ithaca Industries Inc	PO Box 620	Wilkesboro	NC	28697	Jim D Waller	910-667-5231	R	450	8.0
Kentucky Derby Hosiery	PO Drawer 550	Hopkinsville	KY	42240	WH Nichol Jr	502-886-0131	R	100	1.5
Acme-McCrary Corp	PO Box 1287	Asheboro	NC	27204	Charles McCrary Jr	910-625-2161	R	85*	1.2
Great American Knitting Mills	575 5th Av	New York	NY	10017	Jim Williams	212-930-1970	D	82*	1.2
Auburn Hosiery Mills Inc	113 E Main St	Auburn	KY	42206	J Manning	502-542-4175	R	76*	0.7
Pennaco Hosiery Inc	111 W 40th St	New York	NY	10018	Byron A Hero Jr	212-764-4630	S	60	0.8
Shogren Hosiery Mfg Co	304 Winecoff School	Concord	NC	28025	Jack Stanfield	704-792-1870	S	58	0.9
Alba-Waldensian Inc	PO Box 100	Valdese	NC	28690	Thomas F Schuster	704-879-6500	S	57	0.8
US Textile Corp	PO Box 1179	Lancaster	SC	29721	Hans Lengers	803-283-6800	R	42	0.8
Admiration Hosiery Mill Inc	PO Box 33775	Charlotte	NC	28233	Saul Wojnowich	704-525-3162	R	41*	0.6
Hampshire Hosiery Inc	1372 Broadway	New York	NY	10018	Ludwig Kuthner	212-391-2700	S	35	0.2
Trimfit Inc	10450 Drummond	Philadelphia	PA	19154	Arnold Kramer Jr	215-632-3000	R	32	0.6
Holt Hosiery Mills Inc	PO Box 1757	Burlington	NC	27216	Ralph M Holt Jr	910-227-1431	R	25	0.4
Carolina Hosiery Mills Inc	PO Drawer 850	Burlington	NC	27216	Maurice Koury	910-226-5581	R	20*	0.2
Moretz Hosiery Mills Inc	PO Box 580	Newton	NC	28658	John Moretz	704-464-0751	R	20*	0.3
Tower Mills Inc	PO Box 1088	Burlington	NC	27215	JW Maynard	910-227-6221	R	19*	0.5
US Hosiery Corp	PO Box 160	Lincolnton	NC	28092	H Lynn Moretz	704-735-3041	R	17*	0.3
Harriss & Covington	PO Box 1909	High Point	NC	27261	Ned Covington	910-882-6811	R	16	0.3
Willis Hosiery Mills Inc	184 Academy NW	Concord	NC	28025	Claire Cook-Faggart	704-782-4155	R	16*	0.2
Laughlin Hosiery Mills Inc	PO Box 517	Randleman	NC	27317	EW Welborn Jr	910-498-2678	R	15	0.3
Lemco Mills Inc	PO Box 2098	Burlington	NC	27216	Chester Mayer	919-226-5548	S	13*	0.2
International Pantyhose Inc	460 W 34th St	New York	NY	10001	Robert Ross	212-564-7677	R	11	0.2
Pickett Hosiery Mills Inc	PO Box 877	Burlington	NC	27216	James N Harris Jr	910-227-2716	R	8*	0.1
Handcraft Company Inc	Mechanic St	Princeton	WI	54968	PE Hiestand	414-295-6565	R	7	0.1
Cabot Hosiery Mills Inc	35 N Main St	Northfield	VT	05663	Marc Cabot	802-485-6066	R	6*	<0.1
KB Socks Inc	12021 W Jefferson	Culver City	CA	90230	Karen S Bell	310-821-8539	R	5	<0.1
Soft-Wear Hosiery	PO Box 738	Biscoe	NC	27209	Matt Dyer	919-974-4124	D	5	0.1
Linville Hosiery	PO Box 157	Marion	NC	28752	Michael Clevenger	704-652-6311	R	3*	<0.1
Hellam Hosiery Company Inc	198 Beaver St	Hellam	PA	17406	Dennis L Raver	717-755-3831	R	2	<0.1
Giorgio Armani Calze	1450 Broadway	New York	NY	10018	William Bell	212-768-0090	R	1*	<0.1

Source: *Ward's Business Directory of U.S. Private and Public Companies*, Volumes 1 and 2, 1996. The company type code used is as follows: P - Public, R - Private, S - Subsidiary, D - Division, J - Joint Venture, A - Affiliate, G - Group. Sales are in millions of dollars, employees are in thousands. An asterisk (*) indicates an estimated sales volume. The symbol < stands for 'less than'. Company names and addresses are truncated, in some cases, to fit into the available space.

MATERIALS CONSUMED

Material	Quantity	Delivered Cost ($ million)
Materials, ingredients, containers, and supplies	(X)	825.9
Hosiery shipped in the greige, except pantyhose	(X)	23.1
Pantyhose shipped in the greige	(X)	(D)
Cotton yarns	(X)	26.4
Spun nylon yarn	(X)	270.4
Acrylic yarns	(X)	(D)
Nylon filament yarns	(X)	128.9
Spandex filament yarns	(X)	61.8
All other yarns	(X)	37.1
Flexible packaging materials	(X)	41.0
Paperboard containers, boxes, and corrugated paperboard	(X)	48.8
All other materials and components, parts, containers, and supplies	(X)	114.7
Materials, ingredients, containers, and supplies, nsk	(X)	12.3

Source: 1992 *Economic Census*. Explanation of symbols used: (D): Withheld to avoid disclosure of competitive data; na: Not available; (S): Withheld because statistical norms were not met; (X): Not applicable; (Z): Less than half the unit shown; nec: Not elsewhere classified; nsk: Not specified by kind; - : zero; * : 10-19 percent estimated; ** : 20-29 percent estimated.

PRODUCT SHARE DETAILS

Product or Product Class	% Share	Product or Product Class	% Share
Women's hosiery, except socks	100.00	30 denier or heavier, opaque stretch, except socks	18.60
Women's and misses' finished hosiery, full-length and knee-length, except socks	18.24	Elastomer, control top, no leg support, except socks	12.89
Knee-length, stretch and nonstretch, except socks	42.66	Elastomer, leg support, under 35 denier, except socks	9.49
Full-length, stretch, except socks	7.06	Elastomer, leg support, 35 denier or heavier, except socks.	8.61
Full-length, nonstretch, except socks	(D)	Miscellaneous sheers, including fancies, sewed on legs, waist connected legs, replacable legs, nonstretch, etc., except socks	4.16
Full-length, support, except socks	3.72	Women's hosiery, except socks, shipped in the greige	4.56
All other full-length, except socks	(D)	Hosiery shipped in the greige, full-fashioned and seamless, full-length and knee-length (except panty hose and socks).	25.41
Full-length and knee-length, nsk	2.39	Pantyhose, shipped in the greige	74.59
Women's and misses' finished panty hose, including tights, except socks	75.08	Women's hosiery, except socks, nsk	2.12
Less than 30 denier, sheer stretch, except socks	46.26		

Source: 1992 *Economic Census*. The values shown are percent of total shipments in an industry. Values of indented subcategories are summed in the main heading. The symbol (D) appears when data are withheld to prevent disclosure of competitive information. The abbreviation nsk stands for 'not specified by kind' and nec for 'not elsewhere classified'.

INPUTS AND OUTPUTS FOR WOMEN'S HOSIERY, EXCEPT SOCKS

Economic Sector or Industry Providing Inputs	%	Sector	Economic Sector or Industry Buying Outputs	%	Sector
Organic fibers, noncellulosic	28.9	Manufg.	Personal consumption expenditures	89.5	
Women's hosiery, except socks	14.7	Manufg.	Women's hosiery, except socks	8.9	Manufg.
Advertising	9.4	Services	Exports	1.7	Foreign
Yarn mills & finishing of textiles, nec	6.3	Manufg.			
Wholesale trade	4.6	Trade			
Miscellaneous plastics products	4.4	Manufg.			
Paperboard containers & boxes	4.4	Manufg.			
Surface active agents	4.4	Manufg.			
Imports	3.7	Foreign			
Electric services (utilities)	2.5	Util.			
Textile machinery	1.7	Manufg.			
Laundry, dry cleaning, shoe repair	1.3	Services			
Cyclic crudes and organics	1.1	Manufg.			
U.S. Postal Service	1.1	Gov't			
Detective & protective services	1.0	Services			
Gas production & distribution (utilities)	0.8	Util.			
Petroleum refining	0.7	Manufg.			
Motor freight transportation & warehousing	0.7	Util.			
Eating & drinking places	0.6	Trade			
Industrial gases	0.5	Manufg.			
Lubricating oils & greases	0.5	Manufg.			
Communications, except radio & TV	0.4	Util.			
Water transportation	0.4	Util.			
Banking	0.4	Fin/R.E.			
Equipment rental & leasing services	0.4	Services			
Maintenance of nonfarm buildings nec	0.3	Constr.			
Air transportation	0.3	Util.			
Royalties	0.3	Fin/R.E.			
Security & commodity brokers	0.3	Fin/R.E.			
Bags, except textile	0.2	Manufg.			
Paper coating & glazing	0.2	Manufg.			
Real estate	0.2	Fin/R.E.			
Computer & data processing services	0.2	Services			
Engineering, architectural, & surveying services	0.2	Services			
Legal services	0.2	Services			
Management & consulting services & labs	0.2	Services			
Commercial printing	0.1	Manufg.			
Hosiery, nec	0.1	Manufg.			
Industrial inorganic chemicals, nec	0.1	Manufg.			
Machinery, except electrical, nec	0.1	Manufg.			
Manifold business forms	0.1	Manufg.			
Railroads & related services	0.1	Util.			
Credit agencies other than banks	0.1	Fin/R.E.			
Insurance carriers	0.1	Fin/R.E.			
Accounting, auditing & bookkeeping	0.1	Services			
Automotive rental & leasing, without drivers	0.1	Services			
Automotive repair shops & services	0.1	Services			
Theatrical producers, bands, entertainers	0.1	Services			

Source: Benchmark Input-Output Accounts for the U.S. Economy, 1982, U.S. Department of Commerce, Washington, D.C., July 1991. Data, as reported in the source, are organized by the 1977 SIC structure in use in 1982 but have been matched, as closely as is possible, to the 1987 SIC structure used in this book.

OCCUPATIONS EMPLOYED BY SIC 225 - KNITTING MILLS

Occupation	% of Total 1994	Change to 2005	Occupation	% of Total 1994	Change to 2005
Sewing machine operators, garment	22.2	-21.5	Blue collar worker supervisors	3.2	-18.0
Textile draw-out & winding machine operators	14.6	-12.7	Industrial machinery mechanics	3.1	-4.0
Inspectors, testers, & graders, precision	6.1	-4.0	Freight, stock, & material movers, hand	2.6	-30.2
Hand packers & packagers	5.2	-25.2	Machine operators nec	1.5	-23.1
Assemblers, fabricators, & hand workers nec	4.8	-12.7	Traffic, shipping, & receiving clerks	1.2	-16.0
Textile bleaching & dyeing machine operators	4.5	39.6	General managers & top executives	1.2	-17.2
Textile machine setters & set-up operators	3.9	30.9	Pressing machine operators, textiles	1.0	-43.3
Helpers, laborers, & material movers nec	3.7	-12.7			

Source: Industry-Occupation Matrix, Bureau of Labor Statistics. These data relate to one or more 3-digit SIC industry groups rather than to a single 4-digit SIC. The change reported for each occupation to the year 2005 is a percent of growth or decline as estimated by the Bureau of Labor Statistics. The abbreviation nec stands for 'not elsewhere classified'.

LOCATION BY STATE AND REGIONAL CONCENTRATION

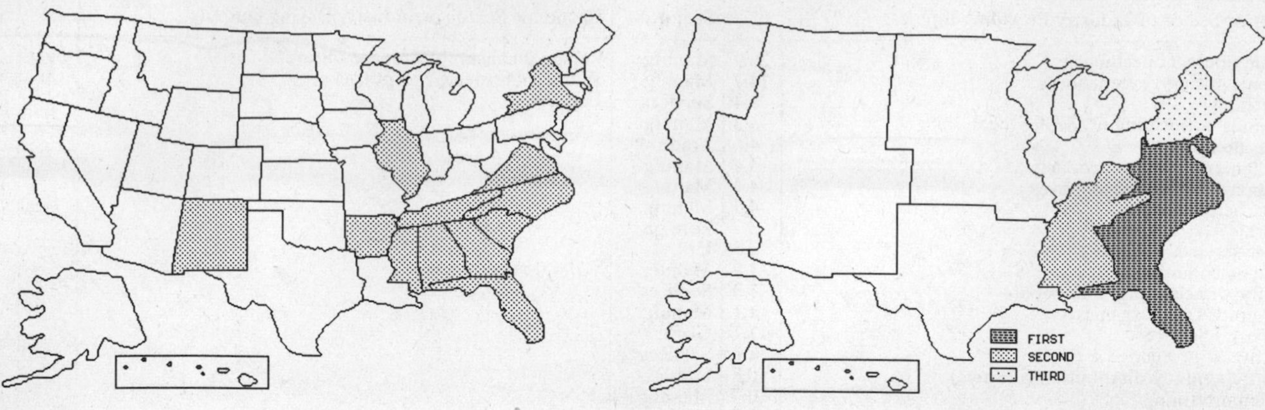

INDUSTRY DATA BY STATE

State	Establish-ments	Shipments			Employment				Cost as % of Shipments	Investment per Employee ($)
		Total ($ mil)	% of U.S.	Per Establ.	Total Number	% of U.S.	Per Establ.	Wages ($/hour)		
North Carolina	98	1,152.6	62.5	11.8	16,700	66.0	170	7.11	47.6	1,725
Tennessee	5	70.7	3.8	14.1	1,400	5.5	280	4.90	57.1	-
New York	10	(D)	-	-	175 *	0.7	18	-	-	-
South Carolina	9	(D)	-	-	3,750 *	14.8	417	-	-	-
Alabama	6	(D)	-	-	175 *	0.7	29	-	-	-
Florida	3	(D)	-	-	1,750 *	6.9	583	-	-	-
Virginia	2	(D)	-	-	175 *	0.7	88	-	-	-
Arkansas	1	(D)	-	-	375 *	1.5	375	-	-	-
Georgia	1	(D)	-	-	175 *	0.7	175	-	-	-
Illinois	1	(D)	-	-	375 *	1.5	375	-	-	-
Mississippi	1	(D)	-	-	750 *	3.0	750	-	-	-
New Mexico	1	(D)	-	-	750 *	3.0	750	-	-	-

Source: 1992 *Economic Census*. The states are in descending order of shipments or establishments (if shipment data are missing for the majority). The symbol (D) appears when data are withheld to prevent disclosure of competitive information. States marked with (D) are sorted by number of establishments. A dash (-) indicates that the data element cannot be calculated; * indicates the midpoint of a range.

2252 - HOSIERY, NEC

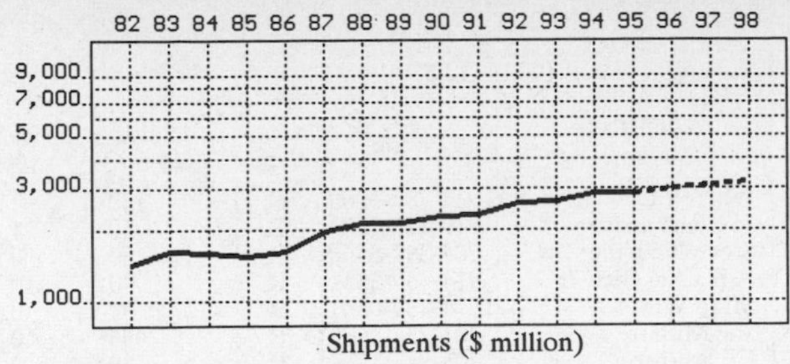

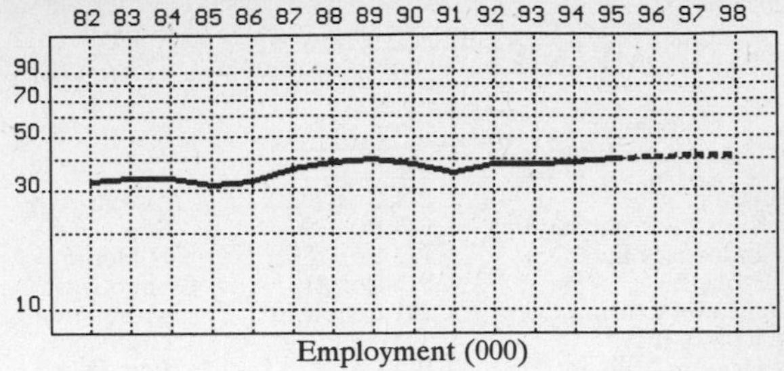

GENERAL STATISTICS

Year	Companies	Establishments Total	Establishments with 20 or more employees	Employment Total (000)	Production Workers (000)	Production Hours (Mil)	Compensation Payroll ($ mil)	Compensation Wages ($/hr)	Production ($ million) Cost of Materials	Value Added by Manufacture	Value of Shipments	Capital Invest.
1982	376	420	263	32.6	28.8	51.2	326.5	5.04	832.2	617.3	1,443.4	31.4
1983		408	258	33.6	30.4	56.0	374.5	5.32	876.8	771.6	1,616.5	26.5
1984		396	253	33.3	28.6	53.7	376.5	5.46	900.1	707.7	1,604.3	35.4
1985		385	248	31.7	27.9	51.1	386.4	5.82	854.5	698.1	1,551.0	31.0
1986		372	246	32.9	28.9	52.9	414.7	6.09	890.4	736.7	1,618.9	29.4
1987	375	426	276	36.5	32.5	59.6	467.8	6.24	1,008.9	960.1	1,952.1	64.6
1988		428	287	39.1	34.9	66.6	511.3	6.20	1,099.1	1,024.3	2,112.5	51.5
1989		416	284	40.0	34.0	65.5	512.3	6.56	1,117.6	1,052.8	2,122.1	47.9
1990		414	276	38.5	35.8	72.1	556.5	6.49	1,255.1	1,062.0	2,277.9	75.3
1991		423	264	35.5	32.7	65.3	533.0	6.85	1,304.0	1,026.2	2,295.9	67.3
1992	403	448	277	38.1	33.1	63.6	596.0	7.32	1,345.3	1,261.5	2,582.5	66.4
1993		451	269	38.1	33.6	65.0	624.6	7.44	1,397.5	1,260.7	2,643.1	81.0
1994		442P	280P	38.8	33.2	66.8	643.0	7.23	1,428.7	1,419.1	2,837.1	107.4
1995		446P	282P	40.1P	35.3P	70.9P	670.8P	7.67P	1,441.9P	1,432.2P	2,863.3P	94.9P
1996		450P	284P	40.7P	35.8P	72.4P	697.2P	7.87P	1,500.4P	1,490.3P	2,979.4P	100.6P
1997		454P	286P	41.2P	36.3P	73.8P	723.5P	8.06P	1,558.8P	1,548.3P	3,095.5P	106.3P
1998		459P	288P	41.8P	36.8P	75.3P	749.9P	8.26P	1,617.3P	1,606.4P	3,211.6P	112.0P

Sources: 1982, 1987, 1992 *Economic Census*; *Annual Survey of Manufactures*, 83-86, 88-91, 93-94. Establishment counts for non-Census years are from *County Business Patterns*; establishment values for 83-84 are extrapolations. 'P's show projections by the editors. Industries reclassified in 87 will not have data for prior years.

INDICES OF CHANGE

Year	Companies	Establishments Total	Establishments with 20 or more employees	Employment Total (000)	Production Workers (000)	Production Hours (Mil)	Compensation Payroll ($ mil)	Compensation Wages ($/hr)	Production ($ million) Cost of Materials	Value Added by Manufacture	Value of Shipments	Capital Invest.
1982	93	94	95	86	87	81	55	69	62	49	56	47
1983		91	93	88	92	88	63	73	65	61	63	40
1984		88	91	87	86	84	63	75	67	56	62	53
1985		86	90	83	84	80	65	80	64	55	60	47
1986		83	89	86	87	83	70	83	66	58	63	44
1987	93	95	100	96	98	94	78	85	75	76	76	97
1988		96	104	103	105	105	86	85	82	81	82	78
1989		93	103	105	103	103	86	90	83	83	82	72
1990		92	100	101	108	113	93	89	93	84	88	113
1991		94	95	93	99	103	89	94	97	81	89	101
1992	100	100	100	100	100	100	100	100	100	100	100	100
1993		101	97	100	102	102	105	102	104	100	102	122
1994		99P	101P	102	100	105	108	99	106	112	110	162
1995		100P	102P	105P	107P	112P	113P	105P	107P	114P	111P	143P
1996		101P	103P	107P	108P	114P	117P	107P	112P	118P	115P	151P
1997		101P	103P	108P	110P	116P	121P	110P	116P	123P	120P	160P
1998		102P	104P	110P	111P	118P	126P	113P	120P	127P	124P	169P

Sources: Same as General Statistics. Values reflect change from the base year, 1992. Values above 100 mean greater than 92, values below 100 mean less than 92, and a value of 100 in the 82-91 or 93-98 period means same as 92. 'P's mark projections by the editors.

SELECTED RATIOS

For 1994	Avg. of All Manufact.	Analyzed Industry	Index	For 1994	Avg. of All Manufact.	Analyzed Industry	Index
Employees per Establishment	49	88	179	Value Added per Production Worker	134,084	42,744	32
Payroll per Establishment	1,500,273	1,454,253	97	Cost per Establishment	5,045,178	3,231,245	64
Payroll per Employee	30,620	16,572	54	Cost per Employee	102,970	36,822	36
Production Workers per Establishment	34	75	219	Cost per Production Worker	146,988	43,033	29
Wages per Establishment	853,319	1,092,304	128	Shipments per Establishment	9,576,895	6,416,579	67
Wages per Production Worker	24,861	14,547	59	Shipments per Employee	195,460	73,121	37
Hours per Production Worker	2,056	2,012	98	Shipments per Production Worker	279,017	85,455	31
Wages per Hour	12.09	7.23	60	Investment per Establishment	321,011	242,903	76
Value Added per Establishment	4,602,255	3,209,533	70	Investment per Employee	6,552	2,768	42
Value Added per Employee	93,930	36,575	39	Investment per Production Worker	9,352	3,235	35

Sources: Same as General Statistics. The 'Average of All Manufacturing' column represents the average of all manufacturing industries reported for the most recent complete year available. The Index shows the relationship between the Average and the Analyzed Industry. For example, 100 means that they are equal; 500 that the Analyzed Industry is five times the average; 50 means that the Analyzed Industry is half the national average. The abbreviation 'na' is used to show that data are 'not available'.

LEADING COMPANIES

Number shown: **50** Total sales ($ mil): **761** Total employment (000): **12.3**

Company Name	Address				CEO Name	Phone	Co. Type	Sales ($ mil)	Empl. (000)
Renfro Corp	PO Box 908	Mount Airy	NC	27030	Warren C Nichols	919-786-3000	R	130*	2.5
Clayson Knitting Company Inc	PO Box 39	Star	NC	27356	Joe Richardson	919-428-2171	R	50	1.0
Neuville Industries Inc	PO Box 286	Hildebran	NC	28637	Steve Neuville	704-397-5566	R	50	0.6
Wigwam Mills Inc	PO Box 818	Sheboygan	WI	53081	R E Chesebro Jr	414-457-5551	R	40	0.4
Premiere Manufacturing Corp	101 Lenoir St	Morganton	NC	28655	Mike Watts	704-437-0661	R	37	0.5
Cricket Hosiery Inc	62 Cherry St	Bridgeport	CT	06605	Vic Mulaire	203-336-3689	R	35*	<0.1
Johnson Hosiery Mills Inc	PO Box 89	Fort Payne	AL	35967	CE Johnson	205-845-1561	R	30	0.4
VI Prewett and Son Inc	PO Box 1069	Fort Payne	AL	35967	Vergil I Prewett Jr	205-845-5234	R	27*	0.5
Ellis Hosiery Mills Inc	PO Box 1088	Hickory	NC	28603	Richard D Stober	704-322-1010	R	25	0.5
Golden City Hosiery Mills Inc	PO Box 939	Villa Rica	GA	30180	Henry G Brown	404-459-4481	S	22	0.3
Fox River Mills Inc	PO Box 298	Osage	IA	50461	John J Lessard	515-732-3798	R	20	0.4
Keepers International Inc	20720 Marilla St	Chatsworth	CA	91311	Sid Levine	818-882-5000	R	18*	<0.1
Nation Hosiery Mills Inc	PO Box 3130	Chattanooga	TN	37404	Steve Kanipe	615-266-3722	S	16*	0.3
Slane Hosiery Mills Inc	PO Box 2486	High Point	NC	27261	John C Slane	919-883-4136	R	16*	0.3
Ben Berger and Son Inc	417 5th Av	New York	NY	10016	Morton Berger	212-684-6664	R	15	<0.1
Peds Products Inc	PO Box 1386	Carrollton	GA	30117	Larry Smith	404-834-4495	S	15	0.2
Twin City Knitting Co	PO Box 1179	Conover	NC	28613	Dewey Houston	704-464-4830	R	15	0.2
Monarch Hosiery Mills Inc	PO Box 1205	Burlington	NC	27216	RC Keziah	910-584-0361	R	14	0.4
Cherokee Hosiery Mill Inc	208 NE 35th St	Fort Payne	AL	35967	VI Prewett	205-845-0004	R	13*	0.3
Lea-Wayne Knitting Mills Inc	5231 Com Blvd	Morristown	TN	37814	DO Ratcliff	615-586-7513	R	11*	0.2
Thor-Lo Inc	PO Box 5399	Statesville	NC	28687	Jim Throneburg	704-872-6522	R	11	0.4
Emby Hosiery Corp	7 W 30th St	New York	NY	10001	E Brody	212-594-5740	R	10	<0.1
Mebane Hosiery Inc	PO Box 427	Mebane	NC	27302	Clyde A Billings	919-563-5943	R	10*	0.2
Meywebb Hosiery Mills Inc	PO Box 266	Meridian	MS	39301	Richard L Meyer	601-485-4129	R	10*	0.2
Paul Lavitt Mills Inc	PO Box 1507	Hickory	NC	28601	Arthur Lavitt	704-328-2463	R	10*	0.2
Johnson Hosiery Mills Inc	PO Box 1389	Hickory	NC	28603	Jill J Patton	704-322-6185	R	8	0.1
Pittsburg Knitting Mills	212 E 1st St	South Pittsburg	TN	37380	William Hawkins	615-837-6794	D	8	0.2
Robinson Hosiery Mill Inc	Rte 1	Valdese	NC	28690	Kenneth Robinson	704-874-2228	R	8*	0.2
Spalding Knitting Mills	PO Drawer K	Griffin	GA	30224	R P Shapard III	404-228-1395	R	8	0.2
Superior Mills Inc	PO Box 732	Chilhowie	VA	24319	Stanley Landis	703-646-8972	R	8*	0.2
Tennessee Machine and Hosiery	PO Drawer 399	Dandridge	TN	37725	F Rimmer	615-397-3155	R	7	0.1
Singer Hosiery Mills Inc	PO Box 758	Thomasville	NC	27360	Gerald Singer	910-475-2161	R	6	<0.1
Hole-in-None Hosiery	PO Drawer 2198	Burlington	NC	27216	BH Bridgers	919-228-1758	R	6	0.1
Bailey Knit Corp	PO Box 1209	Fort Payne	AL	35967	JA Bailey	205-845-0766	R	5*	0.1
Elder Hosiery Mills Inc	PO Box 2377	Burlington	NC	27216	DM Elder Jr	910-226-2229	R	5	0.1
Montgomery Hosiery Mill Inc	PO Box 69	Star	NC	27356	Harold R Russell	919-428-2191	R	4*	0.1
Pilot Hosiery Mills Inc	PO Box 608	Pilot Mountain	NC	27041	WB Thomas Jr	919-368-2291	R	4	0.1
Woodlawn Mills Inc	PO Box 34184	Charlotte	NC	28234	Arch Lineberger	704-825-4252	R	4*	<0.1
Clevenger Industries Inc	PO Box 157	Marion	NC	28752	Jim Clevenger	704-652-6311	R	4	<0.1
Elizabeth-Meade Hosiery Mills	PO Box 1029	Burlington	NC	27216	SE Harper	919-226-7216	R	4	<0.1
Burke Hosiery Mills Inc	PO Box 406	Hildebran	NC	28637	David L Dale Sr	704-328-1725	R	3	<0.1
Country Kids Tights Inc	10 Main St	New Paltz	NY	12561	Josephine Sherratt	212-971-4009	R	3	<0.1
Surratt Hosiery Mills Inc	Rte 1 Box 121 8	Denton	NC	27239	IA Surratt	704-869-4583	R	3	<0.1
Sweetwater Hosiery Mills Inc	818 N Main St	Sweetwater	TN	37874	William Burn	615-337-6161	S	3	0.1
Wrightenberry Mills Inc	PO Box 859	Graham	NC	27253	Jerry Wrightenberry	910-226-5765	R	3*	<0.1
Cormier Corp	144 Lexington Dr	Laconia	NH	03246	Odilon Cormier	603-528-5722	R	3	<0.1
Softspun Knitting Mills Inc	PO Drawer 729	Henderson	NC	27536	John B Baity	919-438-4222	R	2	<0.1
Sunrise Hosiery of Georgia Inc	PO Box 907	La Fayette	GA	30728	Mac Powell	706-638-1242	R	2*	<0.1
Fort Payne Dekalb Hosiery Mills	PO Box 318	Fort Payne	AL	35967	L Cobble	205-845-2731	R	2	<0.1
Troydon Hosiery Mills Inc	PO Box 69	Granite Falls	NC	28630	David Yount	704-396-3138	R	0*	<0.1

Source: *Ward's Business Directory of U.S. Private and Public Companies*, Volumes 1 and 2, 1996. The company type code used is as follows: P - Public, R - Private, S - Subsidiary, D - Division, J - Joint Venture, A - Affiliate, G - Group. Sales are in millions of dollars, employees are in thousands. An asterisk (*) indicates an estimated sales volume. The symbol < stands for 'less than'. Company names and addresses are truncated, in some cases, to fit into the available space.

MATERIALS CONSUMED

Material	Quantity	Delivered Cost ($ million)
Materials, ingredients, containers, and supplies	(X)	1,191.7
Hosiery shipped in the greige, except pantyhose	(X)	355.3
Pantyhose shipped in the greige	(X)	2.7
Cotton yarns	(X)	294.8
Spun nylon yarn	(X)	51.0
Acrylic yarns	(X)	72.2
Nylon filament yarns	(X)	46.0
Spandex filament yarns	(X)	11.3
All other yarns	(X)	100.5
Flexible packaging materials	(X)	55.9
Paperboard containers, boxes, and corrugated paperboard	(X)	25.7
All other materials and components, parts, containers, and supplies	(X)	144.1
Materials, ingredients, containers, and supplies, nsk	(X)	32.3

Source: 1992 *Economic Census*. Explanation of symbols used: (D): Withheld to avoid disclosure of competitive data; na: Not available; (S): Withheld because statistical norms were not met; (X): Not applicable; (Z): Less than half the unit shown; nec: Not elsewhere classified; nsk: Not specified by kind; - : zero; * : 10-19 percent estimated; ** : 20-29 percent estimated.

PRODUCT SHARE DETAILS

Product or Product Class	% Share
Hosiery, nec	100.00
Men's finished seamless hosiery (sizes 10 and up)	45.89
Anklets (including slack socks, crew socks, athletic socks, etc.), natural fibers (cotton and/or wool, etc.)	40.79
Anklets (including slack socks, crew socks, athletic socks, etc.), manmade fibers	19.30
Midcalf (including half hose), natural fibers (cotton and/or wool, etc.)	20.09
Midcalf (including half hose), manmade fibers	8.67
Knee (bermuda, campus, etc.), natural fibers (cotton and/ or wool, etc.)	4.03
Knee (bermuda, campus, etc.), manmade fibers	5.35
All other (including foot socks)	(D)
Not specified by kind	(D)
All other finished hosiery	40.72
Women's and misses' below the knee finished sheer hosiery (foot socks, anklets, and midcalf/crew)	5.70
Women's and misses' finished knee-length socks, all fibers (including bermuda, campus, etc.) (sizes 8-11)	1.64
Women's and misses', girls', and boys' (sizes 8-11), finished anklets, except sheer (including slack, crew, athletic socks, etc.), natural fibers (cotton and/or wool, etc.)	52.66
Women's and misses', girls', and boys' (sizes 8-11), finished anklets, except sheer (including slack, crew, athletic socks, etc.), manmade fibers	6.96
Girls' and boys' (excluding anklets), finished knee-length hosiery (including bermuda, campus, etc.), natural fibers (cotton and/or wool, etc.)	4.61
Girls' and boys' (excluding anklets), finished knee-length hosiery (including bermuda, campus, etc.), manmade fibers	3.50
All other finished hosiery, girls' and boys' (excluding anklets), all others (including foot socks, stockings, and waist-highs)	2.25
Infants' and children's (sizes 3 - 8 1/2), finished anklets (including slack socks, crew socks, athletic socks, etc.), natural fibers (cotton and/or wool, etc.)	16.75
Infants' and children's (sizes 3 - 8 1/2), finished anklets (including slack socks, crew socks, athletic socks, etc.), manmade fibers	2.95
Infants' and children's (sizes 3 - 8 1/2), finished knee-length hosiery (including bermuda, campus, etc.)	0.59
Infants' and children's (sizes 3 - 8 1/2), other finished hosiery (including foot socks, stockings, and waist-highs)	1.29
All other finished hosiery, nsk	1.11
Seamless hosiery shipped in the greige	9.21
Men's, all types (sizes 10 and up)	44.95
Women's and misses' (except full-length and knee-length), girls' and boys'	40.19
Children's and infants'	14.91
Hosiery, nec, nsk	4.18

Source: 1992 *Economic Census*. The values shown are percent of total shipments in an industry. Values of indented subcategories are summed in the main heading. The symbol (D) appears when data are withheld to prevent disclosure of competitive information. The abbreviation nsk stands for 'not specified by kind' and nec for 'not elsewhere classified'.

INPUTS AND OUTPUTS FOR HOSIERY, NEC

Economic Sector or Industry Providing Inputs	%	Sector	Economic Sector or Industry Buying Outputs	%	Sector
Yarn mills & finishing of textiles, nec	31.7	Manufg.	Personal consumption expenditures	82.1	
Hosiery, nec	22.9	Manufg.	Hosiery, nec	15.8	Manufg.
Organic fibers, noncellulosic	8.6	Manufg.	Exports	2.0	Foreign
Wholesale trade	6.5	Trade			
Advertising	4.8	Services			
Surface active agents	3.8	Manufg.			
Commercial printing	2.6	Manufg.			
Paperboard containers & boxes	2.6	Manufg.			
Electric services (utilities)	1.9	Util.			
Textile machinery	1.4	Manufg.			
Imports	1.3	Foreign			
Motor freight transportation & warehousing	1.2	Util.			
Laundry, dry cleaning, shoe repair	1.2	Services			
Gas production & distribution (utilities)	1.1	Util.			
U.S. Postal Service	0.8	Gov't			
Petroleum refining	0.7	Manufg.			
Equipment rental & leasing services	0.7	Services			
Apparel made from purchased materials	0.6	Manufg.			
Eating & drinking places	0.6	Trade			
Lubricating oils & greases	0.5	Manufg.			
Real estate	0.5	Fin/R.E.			
Maintenance of nonfarm buildings nec	0.4	Constr.			
Communications, except radio & TV	0.4	Util.			
Banking	0.3	Fin/R.E.			
Air transportation	0.2	Util.			
Security & commodity brokers	0.2	Fin/R.E.			
Legal services	0.2	Services			
Management & consulting services & labs	0.2	Services			
Machinery, except electrical, nec	0.1	Manufg.			
Royalties	0.1	Fin/R.E.			
Accounting, auditing & bookkeeping	0.1	Services			
Computer & data processing services	0.1	Services			
Engineering, architectural, & surveying services	0.1	Services			
Hotels & lodging places	0.1	Services			
State & local government enterprises, nec	0.1	Gov't			

Source: Benchmark Input-Output Accounts for the U.S. Economy, 1982, U.S. Department of Commerce, Washington, D.C., July 1991. Data, as reported in the source, are organized by the 1977 SIC structure in use in 1982 but have been matched, as closely as is possible, to the 1987 SIC structure used in this book.

OCCUPATIONS EMPLOYED BY SIC 225 - KNITTING MILLS

Occupation	% of Total 1994	Change to 2005	Occupation	% of Total 1994	Change to 2005
Sewing machine operators, garment	22.2	-21.5	Blue collar worker supervisors	3.2	-18.0
Textile draw-out & winding machine operators	14.6	-12.7	Industrial machinery mechanics	3.1	-4.0
Inspectors, testers, & graders, precision	6.1	-4.0	Freight, stock, & material movers, hand	2.6	-30.2
Hand packers & packagers	5.2	-25.2	Machine operators nec	1.5	-23.1
Assemblers, fabricators, & hand workers nec	4.8	-12.7	Traffic, shipping, & receiving clerks	1.2	-16.0
Textile bleaching & dyeing machine operators	4.5	39.6	General managers & top executives	1.2	-17.2
Textile machine setters & set-up operators	3.9	30.9	Pressing machine operators, textiles	1.0	-43.3
Helpers, laborers, & material movers nec	3.7	-12.7			

Source: Industry-Occupation Matrix, Bureau of Labor Statistics. These data relate to one or more 3-digit SIC industry groups rather than to a single 4-digit SIC. The change reported for each occupation to the year 2005 is a percent of growth or decline as estimated by the Bureau of Labor Statistics. The abbreviation nec stands for 'not elsewhere classified'.

LOCATION BY STATE AND REGIONAL CONCENTRATION

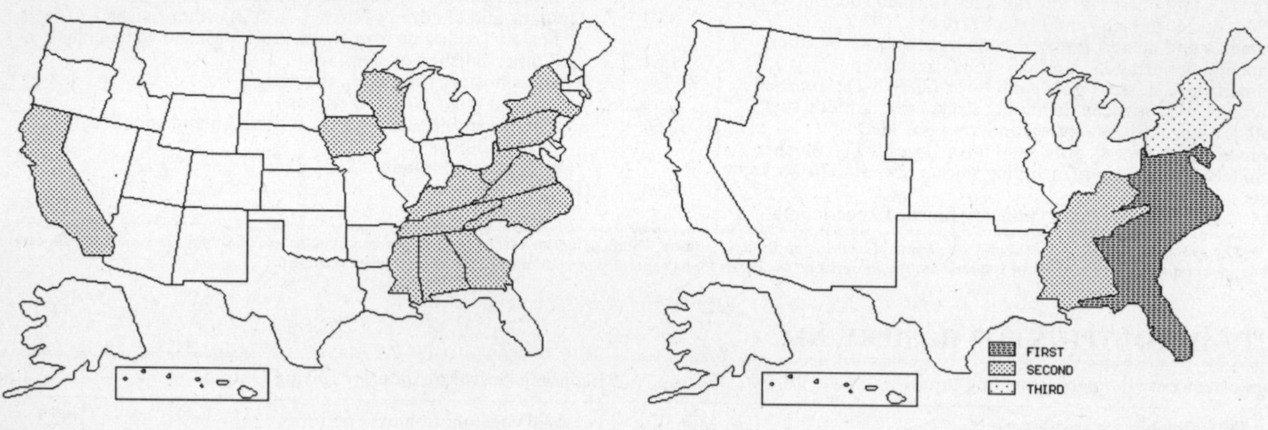

INDUSTRY DATA BY STATE

State	Establish-ments	Shipments Total ($ mil)	Shipments % of U.S.	Shipments Per Establ.	Employment Total Number	Employment % of U.S.	Employment Per Establ.	Wages ($/hour)	Cost as % of Shipments	Investment per Employee ($)
North Carolina	242	1,540.3	59.6	6.4	23,200	60.9	96	7.51	49.6	1,892
Alabama	118	378.5	14.7	3.2	5,400	14.2	46	6.75	60.8	1,519
Tennessee	23	176.3	6.8	7.7	3,100	8.1	135	6.80	52.5	1,710
Georgia	21	161.3	6.2	7.7	2,100	5.5	100	7.06	65.0	1,476
Pennsylvania	6	(D)	-	-	750 *	2.0	125	-	-	-
Virginia	6	(D)	-	-	750 *	2.0	125	-	-	-
New York	5	(D)	-	-	175 *	0.5	35	-	-	-
Kentucky	4	(D)	-	-	750 *	2.0	188	-	-	-
Mississippi	3	(D)	-	-	375 *	1.0	125	-	-	-
California	2	(D)	-	-	375 *	1.0	188	-	-	-
West Virginia	2	(D)	-	-	175 *	0.5	88	-	-	-
Wisconsin	2	(D)	-	-	375 *	1.0	188	-	-	-
Iowa	1	(D)	-	-	375 *	1.0	375	-	-	-

Source: 1992 *Economic Census*. The states are in descending order of shipments or establishments (if shipment data are missing for the majority). The symbol (D) appears when data are withheld to prevent disclosure of competitive information. States marked with (D) are sorted by number of establishments. A dash (-) indicates that the data element cannot be calculated; * indicates the midpoint of a range.

2253 - KNIT OUTERWEAR MILLS

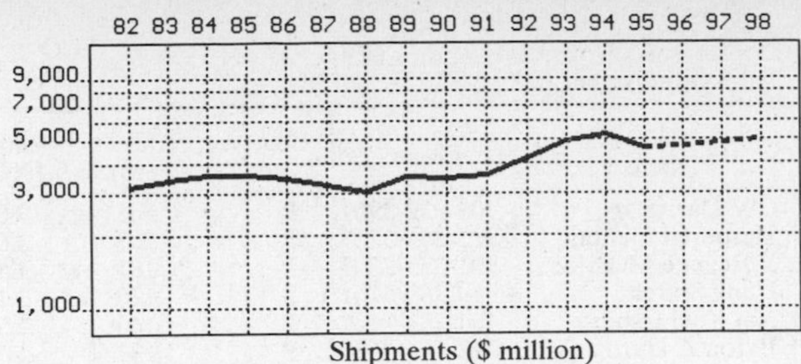

Shipments ($ million)

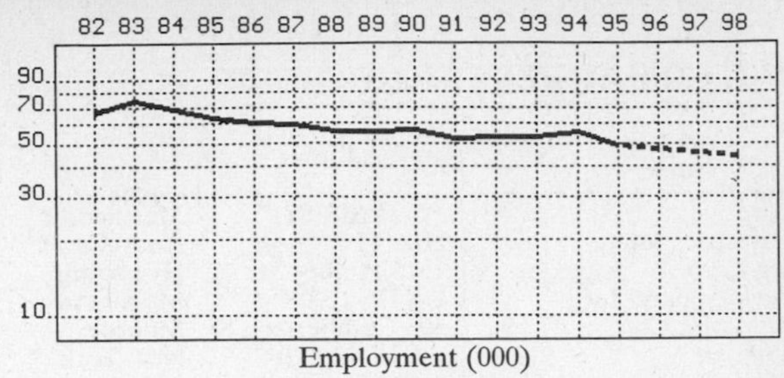

Employment (000)

GENERAL STATISTICS

Year	Companies	Establishments: Total	Establishments: with 20 or more employees	Employment: Total (000)	Employment: Production Workers (000)	Employment: Production Hours (Mil)	Compensation: Payroll ($ mil)	Compensation: Wages ($/hr)	Production ($ million): Cost of Materials	Production ($ million): Value Added by Manufacture	Production ($ million): Value of Shipments	Production ($ million): Capital Invest.
1982	893	923	482	66.8	55.9	102.0	741.4	5.29	1,476.8	1,704.8	3,182.4	53.5
1983		896	479	74.5	63.4	114.5	862.3	5.56	1,609.7	1,842.6	3,410.0	63.8
1984		869	476	67.8	57.2	109.2	835.0	5.58	1,754.5	1,906.4	3,607.1	116.6
1985		843	472	62.7	52.9	97.2	830.2	6.21	1,894.5	1,675.4	3,604.3	86.5
1986		875	480	60.4	51.4	95.2	824.9	6.32	1,741.5	1,695.3	3,447.2	85.6
1987	811	824	440	59.0	50.6	96.9	838.4	6.39	1,614.4	1,677.8	3,255.2	94.0
1988		769	425	55.1	44.5	84.9	786.3	6.86	1,550.8	1,488.0	3,036.8	86.4
1989		712	400	54.9	54.9	102.3	910.1	6.93	1,794.6	1,761.0	3,548.0	96.8
1990		693	361	56.2	56.4	106.4	927.3	6.90	1,715.6	1,783.2	3,456.4	111.4
1991		673	326	52.2	45.7	92.4	798.9	6.64	1,715.9	1,902.3	3,610.6	72.2
1992	646	679	334	53.0	47.2	92.5	875.8	7.60	1,928.9	2,300.0	4,182.3	117.5
1993		658	304	52.8	47.0	89.0	914.1	8.19	2,224.5	2,821.4	4,957.5	117.7
1994		613P	298P	55.9	50.1	92.7	923.8	8.15	2,292.9	2,987.5	5,263.8	124.7
1995		587P	281P	48.7P	45.8P	89.0P	916.8P	8.25P	2,010.1P	2,619.1P	4,614.6P	121.7P
1996		561P	263P	47.2P	44.9P	87.7P	926.1P	8.48P	2,064.8P	2,690.3P	4,740.2P	125.6P
1997		534P	245P	45.6P	44.0P	86.4P	935.4P	8.71P	2,119.5P	2,761.6P	4,865.8P	129.6P
1998		508P	227P	44.1P	43.1P	85.1P	944.8P	8.94P	2,174.2P	2,832.9P	4,991.4P	133.5P

Sources: 1982, 1987, 1992 *Economic Census*; *Annual Survey of Manufactures*, 83-86, 88-91, 93-94. Establishment counts for non-Census years are from *County Business Patterns*; establishment values for 83-84 are extrapolations. 'P's show projections by the editors. Industries reclassified in 87 will not have data for prior years.

INDICES OF CHANGE

Year	Companies	Establishments: Total	Establishments: with 20 or more employees	Employment: Total (000)	Employment: Production Workers (000)	Employment: Production Hours (Mil)	Compensation: Payroll ($ mil)	Compensation: Wages ($/hr)	Production ($ million): Cost of Materials	Production ($ million): Value Added by Manufacture	Production ($ million): Value of Shipments	Production ($ million): Capital Invest.
1982	138	136	144	126	118	110	85	70	77	74	76	46
1983		132	143	141	134	124	98	73	83	80	82	54
1984		128	143	128	121	118	95	73	91	83	86	99
1985		124	141	118	112	105	95	82	98	73	86	74
1986		129	144	114	109	103	94	83	90	74	82	73
1987	126	121	132	111	107	105	96	84	84	73	78	80
1988		113	127	104	94	92	90	90	80	65	73	74
1989		105	120	104	116	111	104	91	93	77	85	82
1990		102	108	106	119	115	106	91	89	78	83	95
1991		99	98	98	97	100	91	87	89	83	86	61
1992	100	100	100	100	100	100	100	100	100	100	100	100
1993		97	91	100	100	96	104	108	115	123	119	100
1994		90P	89P	105	106	100	105	107	119	130	126	106
1995		86P	84P	92P	97P	96P	105P	109P	104P	114P	110P	104P
1996		83P	79P	89P	95P	95P	106P	112P	107P	117P	113P	107P
1997		79P	73P	86P	93P	93P	107P	115P	110P	120P	116P	110P
1998		75P	68P	83P	91P	92P	108P	118P	113P	123P	119P	114P

Sources: Same as General Statistics. Values reflect change from the base year, 1992. Values above 100 mean greater than 92, values below 100 mean less than 92, and a value of 100 in the 82-91 or 93-98 period means same as 92. 'P's mark projections by the editors.

SELECTED RATIOS

For 1994	Avg. of All Manufact.	Analyzed Industry	Index
Employees per Establishment	49	91	186
Payroll per Establishment	1,500,273	1,506,345	100
Payroll per Employee	30,620	16,526	54
Production Workers per Establishment	34	82	238
Wages per Establishment	853,319	1,231,923	144
Wages per Production Worker	24,861	15,080	61
Hours per Production Worker	2,056	1,850	90
Wages per Hour	12.09	8.15	67
Value Added per Establishment	4,602,255	4,871,405	106
Value Added per Employee	93,930	53,444	57

For 1994	Avg. of All Manufact.	Analyzed Industry	Index
Value Added per Production Worker	134,084	59,631	44
Cost per Establishment	5,045,178	3,738,793	74
Cost per Employee	102,970	41,018	40
Cost per Production Worker	146,988	45,766	31
Shipments per Establishment	9,576,895	8,583,131	90
Shipments per Employee	195,460	94,165	48
Shipments per Production Worker	279,017	105,066	38
Investment per Establishment	321,011	203,335	63
Investment per Employee	6,552	2,231	34
Investment per Production Worker	9,352	2,489	27

Sources: Same as General Statistics. The 'Average of All Manufacturing' column represents the average of all manufacturing industries reported for the most recent complete year available. The Index shows the relationship between the Average and the Analyzed Industry. For example, 100 means that they are equal; 500 that the Analyzed Industry is five times the average; 50 means that the Analyzed Industry is half the national average. The abbreviation 'na' is used to show that data are 'not available'.

LEADING COMPANIES Number shown: **71** Total sales ($ mil): **2,249** Total employment (000): **31.7**

Company Name	Address				CEO Name	Phone	Co. Type	Sales ($ mil)	Empl. (000)
Tultex Corp	PO Box 5191	Martinsville	VA	24115	CW Davies Jr	703-632-2961	P	565	7.0
Oneita Industries Inc	Hwy 41	Andrews	SC	29510	Herbert J Fleming	803-264-5225	P	203	3.6
Dyersburg Corp	1315 Phillips St	Dyersburg	TN	38024	T Eugene McBride	901-285-2323	P	181	1.5
Cross Creek Apparel Inc	US Hwy 52 S	Mount Airy	NC	27030	Hank Spires	919-789-6161	S	170*	3.1
Chesterfield Mfg Corp	505 Cuthbertson St	Monroe	NC	28110	Nat Koenigsberg	704-283-7469	R	140*	2.5
Danskin Inc	111 W 40th St	New York	NY	10018	Byron A Hero Jr	212-764-4630	P	132	1.7
St John Knits Inc	17422 Derian Av	Irvine	CA	92713	Robert E Gray	714-863-1171	P	100	1.9
United Merchants	1650 Palisade Av	Teaneck	NJ	07666	Uzi Ruskin	201-837-1700	P	98	1.5
Marisa Christina Inc	415 2nd Av	New Hyde Park	NY	11040	Michael H Lerner	516-352-5050	P	76	0.3
Cullman Industries Inc	215 5th St SE	Cullman	AL	35055	Joe Bachmuth	205-739-1133	R	57	0.7
Kentucky Textiles Inc	1 20th St	Paris	KY	40361	Wayne Shumate	606-987-5228	R	36*	0.6
Brundidge Shirt Corp	555 S Main St	Brundidge	AL	36010	Richard Woodham	205-735-2371	S	35*	0.9
Pine State Knitwear Co	PO Box 631	Mount Airy	NC	27030	Lindsay Holcomb Jr	919-789-9121	S	35	0.5
Neff Athletic Lettering Co	513 E Pine St	Greenville	OH	45331	Lindley Scarlett	513-548-3194	S	29	0.5
Flynt Fabrics and Finishing Inc	PO Box 477	Graham	NC	27253	Charles Flynt	910-226-8476	R	25*	0.5
Winona Knitting Mills Inc	902 E 2nd St	Winona	MN	55987	Pete Woodworth	507-454-4381	R	24	0.4
Acker Knitting Mills Inc	110 W 33rd St	New York	NY	10001	Sanders Acker	212-244-6834	R	20	<0.1
Alpha Mills Corp	122 Margaretta St	Schuylkill H	PA	17972	BR Biever Jr	717-385-0511	R	20	0.3
Berwick Knitwear Inc	232 S Poplar St	Berwick	PA	18603	Charles E Komar	717-752-5985	R	20	0.3
Gotham Apparel Corp	1384 Broadway	New York	NY	10018	Michael Kipperman	212-921-8800	P	20	<0.1
Knitcraft Corp	4020 W 6th St	Winona	MN	55987	Bernhard Brenner	507-454-1163	R	19	0.3
Ridgeview Inc	PO Box 8	Newton	NC	28658	Hugh Gaither	704-464-2972	R	17	0.3
Ocello Inc	PO Box 609	Richland	PA	17087	Charles Haddad	717-866-5778	R	16*	0.3
Castleberry Knits Ltd	530 7th Av	New York	NY	10018	Richard Conrad	212-221-4333	S	15	<0.1
Americana Knitting Mills Inc	12845 NW 45th Av	Opa Locka	FL	33054	A Nickel	305-687-5653	R	12*	0.2
Gilison Knitwear Company Inc	65-89 W John St	Hicksville	NY	11802	Alan Gilison	516-931-0041	R	12	0.1
Granite Knitwear Inc	PO Box 498	Granite Quarry	NC	28072	MR Jones	704-279-5526	R	11	0.2
Alps Sportswear Mfg Co	5 Franklin St	Lawrence	MA	01840	M Axelrod	508-683-2438	R	10	<0.1
Natalie Knitting Mills Inc	PO Box 722	Chilhowie	VA	24319	Mike Ketner	703-646-8941	S	10	0.2
Reliable Knitting Works Inc	PO Box 563	Milwaukee	WI	53201	I Polacheck	414-272-5084	R	10	0.2
Schuessler Knitting Mills Inc	1523 N Fremont St	Chicago	IL	60622	R D Schuessler	312-642-1490	R	8	0.2
Manchester Knitted Fashion Inc	33 S Commercial St	Manchester	NH	03101	Alvin Werner	603-669-5370	R	8	0.1
Aqvila Inc	1901 Winter St	Superior	WI	54880	Gary Gengel	715-392-9779	R	7	0.2
Jacques Moret Inc	1350 Broadway	New York	NY	10018	Joey Harary	212-736-0041	R	7*	<0.1
Minnesota Knitting Mills Inc	1450 Mendota Hght	St Paul	MN	55120	Ted Kuller	612-452-2240	R	7*	<0.1
Oakdale Knitting Mills Inc	1670 Weirfield St	Ridgewood	NY	11385	Edward Yedid	718-417-8880	R	6*	0.1
Drasin Knitting Mills Inc	1721 Trinity St	Los Angeles	CA	90015	Edward Drasin	213-747-5583	R	5	0.1
Fit-All Sportswear Inc	PO Box 1428	Pilot Mountain	NC	27041	Ron Bird	910-368-2227	R	5	<0.1
Mayfair Industries	Old Rte 22	Hamburg	PA	19526	Steve Chernick	215-562-5799	D	5*	0.1
Multiples	1431 Regal Row	Dallas	TX	75247	Ed Vierling	214-637-5300	D	5	0.1
Pressman-Gutman Company Inc	1430 Broadway	New York	NY	10018	James Gutman	212-221-7339	R	5*	0.1
Collegiate-Pacific Co	PO Box 210	Roanoke	VA	24002	Eugene West	703-366-2451	S	4	<0.1
A and G Manufacturing Inc	94 9th St	Brooklyn	NY	11215	Katheryn Balsamo	718-832-0688	R	4*	<0.1
American Research and Knitting	PO Box 1004	Cleveland	TN	37364	Merrill J Woodfin	615-472-7106	R	4	<0.1
Kaufman Knitting Company Inc	123 N 3rd St	Minneapolis	MN	55401	BM Schaak	612-333-0443	R	4*	<0.1
Ohio Knitting Mills Inc	1974 E 61st St	Cleveland	OH	44103	Leonard Rand	216-881-4646	R	4*	<0.1
Happyknit Inc	220 Sunrise Hwy	Rockville Ct	NY	11570	EJ Murphy Jr	516-293-9888	R	4	<0.1
Louis Gallet Inc	120 Delaware Av	Uniontown	PA	15401	Roger Gallet	412-438-8597	R	4	<0.1
Andrews Knitting Mills Inc	3560 Hoffman E	St Paul	MN	55110	Paul G Boening	612-770-4060	R	3	<0.1
Broadway Knitting Mills Inc	2152 Sacramento St	Los Angeles	CA	90021	Thomas A Ainslie	213-680-9694	R	3*	<0.1
Genesis Clothing Consultants	Rte 14	Crossville	TN	38555	Karl Baehr	615-788-6727	R	3	<0.1
Moxvil Manufacturing Company	PO Box 534	Mocksville	NC	27028	Nancy Brooks	704-634-5961	R	3*	<0.1
S and R Knitting Mills Inc	240 Broadway	Brooklyn	NY	11211	Abe Russak	718-387-3472	R	3	0.1
TM Athletics Corp	9622 40th Av SW	Tacoma	WA	98499	M Thevenoux	206-588-3060	R	3	<0.1
Crown Globe Inc	338 Main St	Shoemakersville	PA	19555	DP Wolfe	610-562-2239	R	2	<0.1
Royal Knitting Mills Inc	2007 S California	Chicago	IL	60608	Arnold Newberger	312-247-6300	R	2	<0.1
Tony Lambert Design Group Inc	1450 Broadway	New York	NY	10018	Mark Grebler	212-391-1700	S	2*	<0.1
Wear-A-Knit Corp	1306 18th St	Cloquet	MN	55720	Duane Putikka	218-879-1203	R	2	<0.1
Centralia Knitting Mills Inc	PO Box 269	Centralia	WA	98531	Dorothy Thoreson	206-736-3994	R	2	<0.1
Ultimate Products Inc	4893-D W Waters	Tampa	FL	33634	Jack Hartley	813-881-1575	R	2	<0.1
Bel-Ami Knitwear Company Inc	1350 Broadway	New York	NY	10018	Paul Peterseil	212-736-4985	R	1	<0.1
Binghamton Knitting Co	PO Box 1646	Binghamton	NY	13902	EW Hardler	607-722-6941	R	1	<0.1
Catoosa Knitting Mills Inc	PO Box 526	Crossville	TN	38557	Daniel R Muller	615-484-5191	R	1	<0.1
Cuddle Knit Inc	681 Grand Blv	Deer Park	NY	11729	Jack Lubro	516-586-3200	R	1*	<0.1
Elizabeth Knits Inc	526 7th Av	New York	NY	10018	Mark Weinberg	212-221-6006	R	1*	<0.1
Renaissance Inc	1407 Broadway	New York	NY	10018	Marc Chemtob	212-354-3388	R	1*	<0.1
Penn Keystone Knitting Mills Inc	324 Washington St	Walnutport	PA	18088	Stella J Saas	215-767-2041	R	1	<0.1
Combined Interest Inc	1410 Broadway	New York	NY	10018	Jerry Hammer	212-921-5001	R	1*	<0.1
Norris Knitting Company Inc	1109 N 36th St	Seattle	WA	98103	Simone MJ Studer	206-632-9037	R	0	<0.1
Harlequin Designs Inc	PO Box 147	Valley Forge	PA	19481	Cynthia McKinney	215-935-3391	R	0*	<0.1
Winona Knitting Co	PO Box 5400	Winona	MN	55987	Pete Woodworth	507-454-4381	R	0*	<0.1

Source: *Ward's Business Directory of U.S. Private and Public Companies*, Volumes 1 and 2, 1996. The company type code used is as follows: P - Public, R - Private, S - Subsidiary, D - Division, J - Joint Venture, A - Affiliate, G - Group. Sales are in millions of dollars, employees are in thousands. An asterisk (*) indicates an estimated sales volume. The symbol < stands for 'less than'. Company names and addresses are truncated, in some cases, to fit into the available space.

MATERIALS CONSUMED

Material		Quantity	Delivered Cost ($ million)
Materials, ingredients, containers, and supplies		(X)	1,635.2
Knit fabrics	mil lb	(S)	309.1
Manmade fibers, staple, and tow	mil lb	2.8	8.3
Raw cotton fibers	1,000 bales	(D)	(D)
Raw wool fibers	mil lb	(D)	(D)
Carded cotton yarn	mil lb	239.9**	408.2
Combed cotton yarn	mil lb	(S)	115.0
Spun rayon and acetate yarn	mil lb	(S)	0.8
Spun nylon yarn	mil lb	(D)	(D)
Spun polyester yarns	mil lb	115.7	132.6
Rayon and acetate filament yarns	mil lb	1.0	2.1
Nylon filament yarn	mil lb	(D)	(D)
Polyester filament yarn	mil lb	3.3	6.2
Acrylic yarns	mil lb	101.1	155.4
Wool yarn	mil lb	3.8	15.5
All other yarns	mil lb	9.8*	18.7
All other materials and components, parts, containers, and supplies		(X)	324.1
Materials, ingredients, containers, and supplies, nsk		(X)	120.4

Source: 1992 *Economic Census*. Explanation of symbols used: (D): Withheld to avoid disclosure of competitive data; na: Not available; (S): Withheld because statistical norms were not met; (X): Not applicable; (Z): Less than half the unit shown; nec: Not elsewhere classified; nsk: Not specified by kind; - : zero; * : 10-19 percent estimated; ** : 20-29 percent estimated.

PRODUCT SHARE DETAILS

Product or Product Class	% Share
Knit outerwear mills	100.00
Men's and boys' sweaters (from yarns or from fabrics knit in the same establishment)	4.90
Women's, misses', and juniors' sweaters (from yarns or from fabrics knit in the same establishment)	8.58
Girls', children's, and infants' sweaters (from yarns or from fabrics knit in the same establishment)	0.73
Men's and boys' knit shirts (from yarns or from fabrics knit in the same establishment)	41.14
Women's, misses', and juniors' knit shirts and blouses (from yarns or from fabrics knit in the same establishment)	5.09
Girls', children's, and infants' knit shirts and blouses (from yarns or from fabrics knit in the same establishment)	1.82
All other knit outerwear products	21.13
Women's, misses', and juniors' knit outerwear except sweaters, shirts, and blouses (from yarns or from fabrics knit in the same establishment)	(D)
Men's and boys' knit outerwear except sweaters and shirts (from yarns or from fabrics knit in the same establishment)	61.96
Girls', children's, and infants' knit outerwear except sweaters, shirts, and blouses (from yarns or from fabrics knit in the same establishment)	20.31
All other knit outerwear products, nsk	(D)
Contract and commission receipts for knitting only or knitting and finishing outerwear	11.75
Knit outerwear mills, nsk	4.84

Source: 1992 *Economic Census*. The values shown are percent of total shipments in an industry. Values of indented subcategories are summed in the main heading. The symbol (D) appears when data are withheld to prevent disclosure of competitive information. The abbreviation nsk stands for 'not specified by kind' and nec for 'not elsewhere classified'.

INPUTS AND OUTPUTS FOR KNIT FABRIC MILLS

Economic Sector or Industry Providing Inputs	%	Sector	Economic Sector or Industry Buying Outputs	%	Sector
Yarn mills & finishing of textiles, nec	24.0	Manufg.	Apparel made from purchased materials	79.8	Manufg.
Organic fibers, noncellulosic	22.2	Manufg.	Knit fabric mills	10.6	Manufg.
Knit fabric mills	14.4	Manufg.	Personal consumption expenditures	5.1	
Cellulosic manmade fibers	8.1	Manufg.	Knit outerwear mills	2.0	Manufg.
Wholesale trade	4.8	Trade	Exports	1.7	Foreign
Surface active agents	4.0	Manufg.	Knitting mills, nec	0.2	Manufg.
Miscellaneous plastics products	2.7	Manufg.	Coated fabrics, not rubberized	0.1	Manufg.
Electric services (utilities)	2.5	Util.	Knit underwear mills	0.1	Manufg.
Petroleum refining	2.1	Manufg.	Leather gloves & mittens	0.1	Manufg.
Cyclic crudes and organics	1.7	Manufg.			
Gas production & distribution (utilities)	1.6	Util.			
Textile machinery	1.5	Manufg.			
Motor freight transportation & warehousing	1.2	Util.			
Industrial gases	0.7	Manufg.			
Imports	0.7	Foreign			
Cotton	0.6	Agric.			
Equipment rental & leasing services	0.5	Services			
Laundry, dry cleaning, shoe repair	0.5	Services			
Air transportation	0.4	Util.			
Real estate	0.4	Fin/R.E.			
Paperboard containers & boxes	0.3	Manufg.			
Communications, except radio & TV	0.3	Util.			
Banking	0.3	Fin/R.E.			
U.S. Postal Service	0.3	Gov't			
Maintenance of nonfarm buildings nec	0.2	Constr.			
Ball & roller bearings	0.2	Manufg.			

Continued on next page.

INPUTS AND OUTPUTS FOR KNIT FABRIC MILLS - Continued

Economic Sector or Industry Providing Inputs	%	Sector	Economic Sector or Industry Buying Outputs	%	Sector
Industrial inorganic chemicals, nec	0.2	Manufg.			
Lubricating oils & greases	0.2	Manufg.			
Sanitary services, steam supply, irrigation	0.2	Util.			
Eating & drinking places	0.2	Trade			
Automotive rental & leasing, without drivers	0.2	Services			
Computer & data processing services	0.2	Services			
Detective & protective services	0.2	Services			
State & local government enterprises, nec	0.2	Gov't			
Paper coating & glazing	0.1	Manufg.			
Railroads & related services	0.1	Util.			
Insurance carriers	0.1	Fin/R.E.			
Advertising	0.1	Services			
Automotive repair shops & services	0.1	Services			
Hotels & lodging places	0.1	Services			

Source: Benchmark Input-Output Accounts for the U.S. Economy, 1982, U.S. Department of Commerce, Washington, D.C., July 1991. Data, as reported in the source, are organized by the 1977 SIC structure in use in 1982 but have been matched, as closely as is possible, to the 1987 SIC structure used in this book.

OCCUPATIONS EMPLOYED BY SIC 225 - KNITTING MILLS

Occupation	% of Total 1994	Change to 2005	Occupation	% of Total 1994	Change to 2005
Sewing machine operators, garment	22.2	-21.5	Blue collar worker supervisors	3.2	-18.0
Textile draw-out & winding machine operators	14.6	-12.7	Industrial machinery mechanics	3.1	-4.0
Inspectors, testers, & graders, precision	6.1	-4.0	Freight, stock, & material movers, hand	2.6	-30.2
Hand packers & packagers	5.2	-25.2	Machine operators nec	1.5	-23.1
Assemblers, fabricators, & hand workers nec	4.8	-12.7	Traffic, shipping, & receiving clerks	1.2	-16.0
Textile bleaching & dyeing machine operators	4.5	39.6	General managers & top executives	1.2	-17.2
Textile machine setters & set-up operators	3.9	30.9	Pressing machine operators, textiles	1.0	-43.3
Helpers, laborers, & material movers nec	3.7	-12.7			

Source: Industry-Occupation Matrix, Bureau of Labor Statistics. These data relate to one or more 3-digit SIC industry groups rather than to a single 4-digit SIC. The change reported for each occupation to the year 2005 is a percent of growth or decline as estimated by the Bureau of Labor Statistics. The abbreviation nec stands for 'not elsewhere classified'.

LOCATION BY STATE AND REGIONAL CONCENTRATION

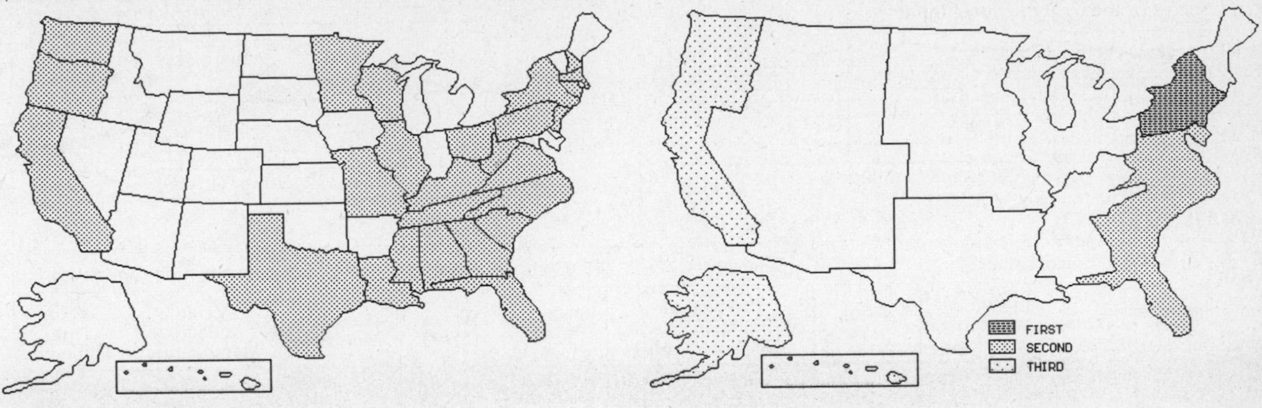

INDUSTRY DATA BY STATE

State	Establish-ments	Shipments			Employment				Cost as % of Shipments	Investment per Employee ($)
		Total ($ mil)	% of U.S.	Per Establ.	Total Number	% of U.S.	Per Establ.	Wages ($/hour)		
North Carolina	53	1,171.3	28.0	22.1	12,500	23.6	236	8.10	53.7	4,528
New York	255	510.8	12.2	2.0	7,600	14.3	30	7.27	48.8	2,724
Tennessee	21	245.7	5.9	11.7	2,900	5.5	138	5.16	55.2	828
Alabama	22	227.4	5.4	10.3	3,600	6.8	164	8.43	48.0	1,111
Pennsylvania	37	195.5	4.7	5.3	2,900	5.5	78	6.80	53.5	1,103
California	70	176.9	4.2	2.5	2,500	4.7	36	6.61	43.6	2,840
Mississippi	4	86.1	2.1	21.5	2,500	4.7	625	8.11	29.4	1,120
New Jersey	55	82.0	2.0	1.5	1,400	2.6	25	7.08	45.0	1,643
Florida	20	41.6	1.0	2.1	900	1.7	45	6.14	37.3	-
South Carolina	11	31.5	0.8	2.9	900	1.7	82	8.09	24.4	1,000
Illinois	11	20.0	0.5	1.8	300	0.6	27	7.60	45.5	1,667
Wisconsin	8	19.7	0.5	2.5	500	0.9	63	5.57	39.1	400
Texas	10	13.0	0.3	1.3	300	0.6	30	5.60	56.2	667
Massachusetts	6	6.3	0.2	1.0	200	0.4	33	10.00	52.4	-
Connecticut	4	5.5	0.1	1.4	100	0.2	25	11.00	47.3	-
Virginia	10	(D)	-	-	1,750 *	3.3	175	-	-	2,057
Washington	9	(D)	-	-	175 *	0.3	19	-	-	-
Georgia	8	(D)	-	-	750 *	1.4	94	-	-	267
Ohio	6	(D)	-	-	375 *	0.7	63	-	-	267
Minnesota	5	(D)	-	-	750 *	1.4	150	-	-	933
Missouri	5	(D)	-	-	175 *	0.3	35	-	-	-
Oregon	5	(D)	-	-	375 *	0.7	75	-	-	-
Kentucky	4	(D)	-	-	3,750 *	7.1	938	-	-	-
Louisiana	4	(D)	-	-	3,750 *	7.1	938	-	-	-
New Hampshire	2	(D)	-	-	175 *	0.3	88	-	-	-
West Virginia	1	(D)	-	-	375 *	0.7	375	-	-	-

Source: 1992 *Economic Census*. The states are in descending order of shipments or establishments (if shipment data are missing for the majority). The symbol (D) appears when data are withheld to prevent disclosure of competitive information. States marked with (D) are sorted by number of establishments. A dash (-) indicates that the data element cannot be calculated; * indicates the midpoint of a range.

2254 - KNIT UNDERWEAR & NIGHTWEAR MILLS

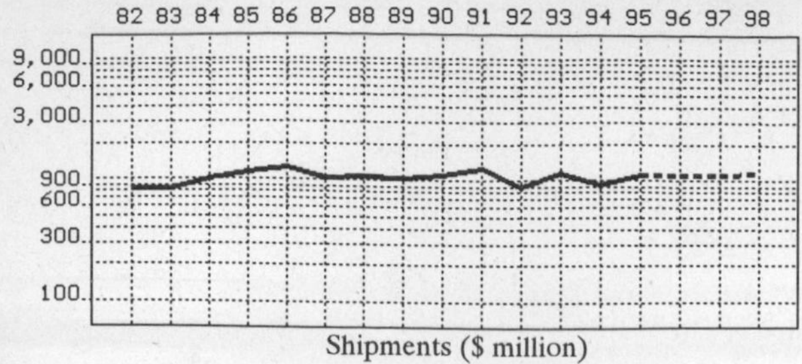

Shipments ($ million)

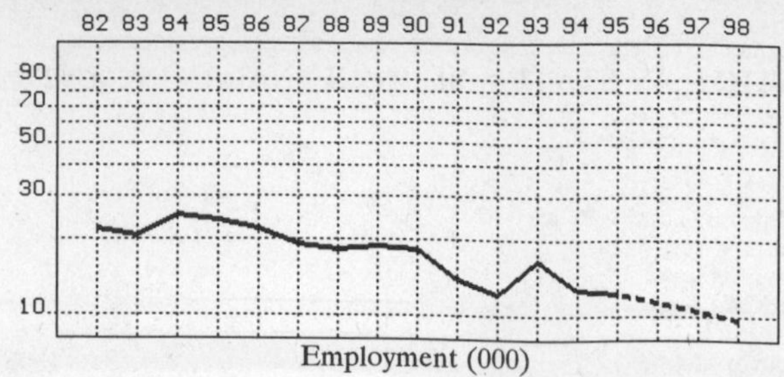

Employment (000)

GENERAL STATISTICS

Year	Companies	Establishments: Total	Establishments: with 20 or more employees	Employment: Total (000)	Employment: Production Workers (000)	Employment: Production Hours (Mil)	Compensation: Payroll ($ mil)	Compensation: Wages ($/hr)	Production ($ million): Cost of Materials	Production ($ million): Value Added by Manufacture	Production ($ million): Value of Shipments	Production ($ million): Capital Invest.
1982	72	84	61	22.3	20.0	35.3	232.3	5.43	369.7	446.2	829.9	9.3
1983		79	59	20.6	18.2	33.4	226.4	5.61	383.1	449.9	824.3	11.6
1984		74	57	25.0	22.1	41.3	302.2	6.00	513.9	492.8	1,010.7	24.1
1985		69	55	24.0	21.6	39.2	301.8	6.38	671.7	491.7	1,136.2	22.7
1986		66	58	22.3	20.5	37.4	301.1	6.73	705.4	559.8	1,277.6	33.5
1987	58	63	44	19.3	17.4	33.1	275.7	6.99	548.3	516.5	1,058.1	27.7
1988		66	46	18.3	16.8	31.5	276.1	7.46	607.1	502.9	1,064.1	41.6
1989		62	42	18.9	15.3	28.4	250.0	7.26	506.0	527.6	1,050.9	30.2
1990		61	47	18.4	14.1	26.3	226.3	7.29	537.1	596.5	1,105.0	50.0
1991		58	46	13.9	12.6	24.1	214.5	7.55	587.2	694.4	1,250.6	39.9
1992	57	69	50	12.0	10.8	20.5	190.2	7.62	403.9	498.8	891.1	35.5
1993		75	56	16.6	15.0	27.4	266.6	8.38	529.2	678.5	1,162.4	33.8
1994		61P	45P	12.7	12.0	22.1	214.6	8.79	395.9	541.9	912.4	38.1
1995		60P	44P	12.3P	10.8P	20.6P	221.7P	8.78P	481.4P	658.9P	1,109.4P	46.6P
1996		58P	43P	11.4P	10.0P	19.1P	217.4P	9.03P	485.4P	664.4P	1,118.7P	48.9P
1997		57P	42P	10.5P	9.2P	17.7P	213.1P	9.28P	489.5P	670.0P	1,128.1P	51.2P
1998		56P	41P	9.6P	8.3P	16.2P	208.7P	9.53P	493.5P	675.5P	1,137.4P	53.5P

Sources: 1982, 1987, 1992 *Economic Census*; *Annual Survey of Manufactures*, 83-86, 88-91, 93-94. Establishment counts for non-Census years are from *County Business Patterns*; establishment values for 83-84 are extrapolations. 'P's show projections by the editors. Industries reclassified in 87 will not have data for prior years.

INDICES OF CHANGE

Year	Companies	Establishments: Total	Establishments: with 20 or more employees	Employment: Total (000)	Employment: Production Workers (000)	Employment: Production Hours (Mil)	Compensation: Payroll ($ mil)	Compensation: Wages ($/hr)	Production ($ million): Cost of Materials	Production ($ million): Value Added by Manufacture	Production ($ million): Value of Shipments	Production ($ million): Capital Invest.
1982	126	122	122	186	185	172	122	71	92	89	93	26
1983		114	118	172	169	163	119	74	95	90	93	33
1984		107	114	208	205	201	159	79	127	99	113	68
1985		100	110	200	200	191	159	84	166	99	128	64
1986		96	116	186	190	182	158	88	175	112	143	94
1987	102	91	88	161	161	161	145	92	136	104	119	78
1988		96	92	152	156	154	145	98	150	101	119	117
1989		90	84	158	142	139	131	95	125	106	118	85
1990		88	94	153	131	128	119	96	133	120	124	141
1991		84	92	116	117	118	113	99	145	139	140	112
1992	100	100	100	100	100	100	100	100	100	100	100	100
1993		109	112	138	139	134	140	110	131	136	130	95
1994		88P	90P	106	111	108	113	115	98	109	102	107
1995		86P	88P	103P	100P	100P	117P	115P	119P	132P	124P	131P
1996		85P	86P	95P	93P	93P	114P	119P	120P	133P	126P	138P
1997		83P	84P	87P	85P	86P	112P	122P	121P	134P	127P	144P
1998		81P	82P	80P	77P	79P	110P	125P	122P	135P	128P	151P

Sources: Same as General Statistics. Values reflect change from the base year, 1992. Values above 100 mean greater than 92, values below 100 mean less than 92, and a value of 100 in the 82-91 or 93-98 period means same as 92. 'P's mark projections by the editors.

SELECTED RATIOS

For 1994	Avg. of All Manufact.	Analyzed Industry	Index
Employees per Establishment	49	209	426
Payroll per Establishment	1,500,273	3,525,037	235
Payroll per Employee	30,620	16,898	55
Production Workers per Establishment	34	197	574
Wages per Establishment	853,319	3,190,914	374
Wages per Production Worker	24,861	16,188	65
Hours per Production Worker	2,056	1,842	90
Wages per Hour	12.09	8.79	73
Value Added per Establishment	4,602,255	8,901,294	193
Value Added per Employee	93,930	42,669	45

For 1994	Avg. of All Manufact.	Analyzed Industry	Index
Value Added per Production Worker	134,084	45,158	34
Cost per Establishment	5,045,178	6,503,086	129
Cost per Employee	102,970	31,173	30
Cost per Production Worker	146,988	32,992	22
Shipments per Establishment	9,576,895	14,987,158	156
Shipments per Employee	195,460	71,843	37
Shipments per Production Worker	279,017	76,033	27
Investment per Establishment	321,011	625,834	195
Investment per Employee	6,552	3,000	46
Investment per Production Worker	9,352	3,175	34

Sources: Same as General Statistics. The 'Average of All Manufacturing' column represents the average of all manufacturing industries reported for the most recent complete year available. The Index shows the relationship between the Average and the Analyzed Industry. For example, 100 means that they are equal; 500 that the Analyzed Industry is five times the average; 50 means that the Analyzed Industry is half the national average. The abbreviation 'na' is used to show that data are 'not available'.

LEADING COMPANIES

Number shown: **10** Total sales ($ mil): **447** Total employment (000): **6.5**

Company Name	Address				CEO Name	Phone	Co. Type	Sales ($ mil)	Empl. (000)
Jockey International Inc	2300 60th St	Kenosha	WI	53140	D Wolf Steigerwaldt	414-658-8111	R	340*	5.0
Medalist Apparel Inc	4201 Pottsville Pike	Reading	PA	19605	Matthew Barrer	610-921-2299	R	48	0.4
Johnstown Knitting Mill Co	PO Box 529	Johnstown	NY	12095	C Easterly	518-762-3156	R	20	0.5
Dundee Mills Inc	PO Box 107	Jackson	GA	30233	Larry Robertson	404-775-7842	D	13*	0.2
Swanknit Inc	PO Box 675	Cohoes	NY	12047	Nancy Leren	518-237-4209	R	6	<0.1
Boltz Knitting Mill Inc	317 N 9th St	Pottsville	PA	17901	Bill Heffner	717-622-4510	D	5	<0.1
Classtex Knitting Mills Inc	E Mifflin St	Orwigsburg	PA	17961	Richard R Rohrer	717-366-0651	R	5	<0.1
Union Knitting Mills Inc	PO Box 60	Schuylkill H	PA	17972	ME Reed	717-385-0730	R	5	0.1
O and H Manufacturing	332 N Front St	Allentown	PA	18102	Gary Jones	215-434-7992	R	3	<0.1
Priamo Designs Ltd	6614 Broadway	West New York	NJ	07093	Priamo Espaillat	201-861-8808	R	2	<0.1

Source: *Ward's Business Directory of U.S. Private and Public Companies*, Volumes 1 and 2, 1996. The company type code used is as follows: P - Public, R - Private, S - Subsidiary, D - Division, J - Joint Venture, A - Affiliate, G - Group. Sales are in millions of dollars, employees are in thousands. An asterisk (*) indicates an estimated sales volume. The symbol < stands for 'less than'. Company names and addresses are truncated, in some cases, to fit into the available space.

MATERIALS CONSUMED

Material		Quantity	Delivered Cost ($ million)
Materials, ingredients, containers, and supplies		(X)	354.4
Knit fabrics	mil lb	(S)	60.0
Manmade fibers, staple, and tow	mil lb	(D)	(D)
Raw cotton fibers	1,000 bales	(D)	(D)
Carded cotton yarn	mil lb	76.2*	100.1
Combed cotton yarn	mil lb	29.6	53.6
Spun nylon yarn	mil lb	(D)	(D)
Spun polyester yarns	mil lb	(S)	11.0
Nylon filament yarn	mil lb	2.7	10.1
Polyester filament yarn	mil lb	3.8	5.1
Acrylic yarns	mil lb	(D)	(D)
Wool yarn	mil lb	(D)	(D)
All other yarns	mil lb	2.3*	6.1
All other materials and components, parts, containers, and supplies		(X)	80.3
Materials, ingredients, containers, and supplies, nsk		(X)	0.8

Source: 1992 *Economic Census*. Explanation of symbols used: (D): Withheld to avoid disclosure of competitive data; na: Not available; (S): Withheld because statistical norms were not met; (X): Not applicable; (Z): Less than half the unit shown; nec: Not elsewhere classified; nsk: Not specified by kind; - : zero; * : 10-19 percent estimated; ** : 20-29 percent estimated.

PRODUCT SHARE DETAILS

Product or Product Class	% Share
Knit underwear mills	100.00
Men's and boys' knit underwear and nightwear	(D)
Women's and children's knit underwear and nightwear	35.54
Women's and children's knit underwear (from yarns or from fabrics knit in the same establishment)	86.72
Women's and children's knit nightwear, except robes (from yarns or from fabrics knit in the same establishment)	13.28

Source: 1992 *Economic Census*. The values shown are percent of total shipments in an industry. Values of indented subcategories are summed in the main heading. The symbol (D) appears when data are withheld to prevent disclosure of competitive information. The abbreviation nsk stands for 'not specified by kind' and nec for 'not elsewhere classified'.

INPUTS AND OUTPUTS FOR KNIT FABRIC MILLS

Economic Sector or Industry Providing Inputs	%	Sector	Economic Sector or Industry Buying Outputs	%	Sector
Yarn mills & finishing of textiles, nec	24.0	Manufg.	Apparel made from purchased materials	79.8	Manufg.
Organic fibers, noncellulosic	22.2	Manufg.	Knit fabric mills	10.6	Manufg.
Knit fabric mills	14.4	Manufg.	Personal consumption expenditures	5.1	
Cellulosic manmade fibers	8.1	Manufg.	Knit outerwear mills	2.0	Manufg.
Wholesale trade	4.8	Trade	Exports	1.7	Foreign
Surface active agents	4.0	Manufg.	Knitting mills, nec	0.2	Manufg.
Miscellaneous plastics products	2.7	Manufg.	Coated fabrics, not rubberized	0.1	Manufg.
Electric services (utilities)	2.5	Util.	Knit underwear mills	0.1	Manufg.
Petroleum refining	2.1	Manufg.	Leather gloves & mittens	0.1	Manufg.
Cyclic crudes and organics	1.7	Manufg.			
Gas production & distribution (utilities)	1.6	Util.			
Textile machinery	1.5	Manufg.			
Motor freight transportation & warehousing	1.2	Util.			
Industrial gases	0.7	Manufg.			
Imports	0.7	Foreign			

Continued on next page.

INPUTS AND OUTPUTS FOR KNIT FABRIC MILLS - Continued

Economic Sector or Industry Providing Inputs	%	Sector	Economic Sector or Industry Buying Outputs	%	Sector
Cotton	0.6	Agric.			
Equipment rental & leasing services	0.5	Services			
Laundry, dry cleaning, shoe repair	0.5	Services			
Air transportation	0.4	Util.			
Real estate	0.4	Fin/R.E.			
Paperboard containers & boxes	0.3	Manufg.			
Communications, except radio & TV	0.3	Util.			
Banking	0.3	Fin/R.E.			
U.S. Postal Service	0.3	Gov't			
Maintenance of nonfarm buildings nec	0.2	Constr.			
Ball & roller bearings	0.2	Manufg.			
Industrial inorganic chemicals, nec	0.2	Manufg.			
Lubricating oils & greases	0.2	Manufg.			
Sanitary services, steam supply, irrigation	0.2	Util.			
Eating & drinking places	0.2	Trade			
Automotive rental & leasing, without drivers	0.2	Services			
Computer & data processing services	0.2	Services			
Detective & protective services	0.2	Services			
State & local government enterprises, nec	0.2	Gov't			
Paper coating & glazing	0.1	Manufg.			
Railroads & related services	0.1	Util.			
Insurance carriers	0.1	Fin/R.E.			
Advertising	0.1	Services			
Automotive repair shops & services	0.1	Services			
Hotels & lodging places	0.1	Services			

Source: Benchmark Input-Output Accounts for the U.S. Economy, 1982, U.S. Department of Commerce, Washington, D.C., July 1991. Data, as reported in the source, are organized by the 1977 SIC structure in use in 1982 but have been matched, as closely as is possible, to the 1987 SIC structure used in this book.

OCCUPATIONS EMPLOYED BY SIC 225 - KNITTING MILLS

Occupation	% of Total 1994	Change to 2005	Occupation	% of Total 1994	Change to 2005
Sewing machine operators, garment	22.2	-21.5	Blue collar worker supervisors	3.2	-18.0
Textile draw-out & winding machine operators	14.6	-12.7	Industrial machinery mechanics	3.1	-4.0
Inspectors, testers, & graders, precision	6.1	-4.0	Freight, stock, & material movers, hand	2.6	-30.2
Hand packers & packagers	5.2	-25.2	Machine operators nec	1.5	-23.1
Assemblers, fabricators, & hand workers nec	4.8	-12.7	Traffic, shipping, & receiving clerks	1.2	-16.0
Textile bleaching & dyeing machine operators	4.5	39.6	General managers & top executives	1.2	-17.2
Textile machine setters & set-up operators	3.9	30.9	Pressing machine operators, textiles	1.0	-43.3
Helpers, laborers, & material movers nec	3.7	-12.7			

Source: Industry-Occupation Matrix, Bureau of Labor Statistics. These data relate to one or more 3-digit SIC industry groups rather than to a single 4-digit SIC. The change reported for each occupation to the year 2005 is a percent of growth or decline as estimated by the Bureau of Labor Statistics. The abbreviation nec stands for 'not elsewhere classified'.

LOCATION BY STATE AND REGIONAL CONCENTRATION

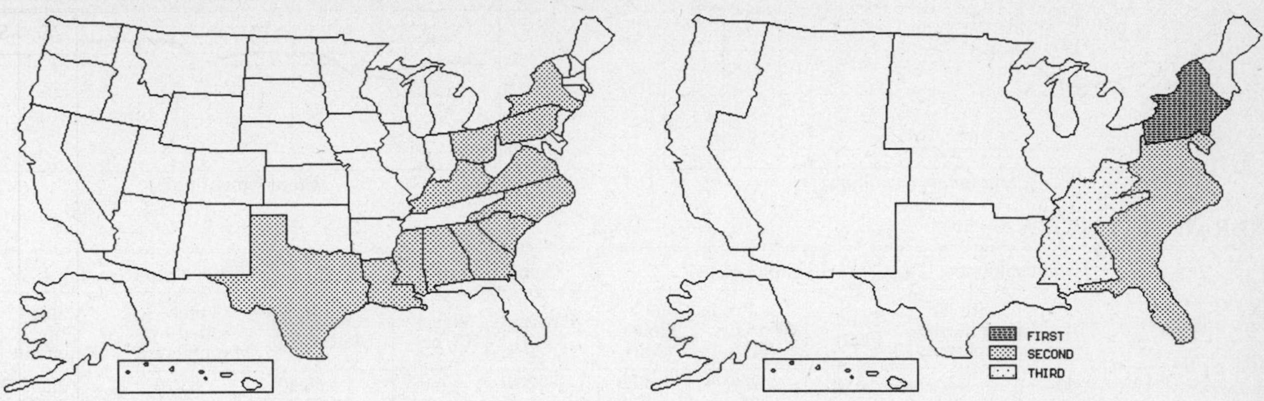

INDUSTRY DATA BY STATE

State	Establish-ments	Shipments			Employment				Cost as % of Shipments	Investment per Employee ($)
		Total ($ mil)	% of U.S.	Per Establ.	Total Number	% of U.S.	Per Establ.	Wages ($/hour)		
North Carolina	13	229.0	25.7	17.6	4,200	35.0	323	8.47	54.1	4,690
Pennsylvania	16	176.7	19.8	11.0	1,600	13.3	100	8.11	35.5	-
New York	6	48.1	5.4	8.0	400	3.3	67	6.83	41.8	1,000
Georgia	4	(D)	-	-	1,750 *	14.6	438	-	-	-
South Carolina	4	(D)	-	-	375 *	3.1	94	-	-	-
Mississippi	3	(D)	-	-	375 *	3.1	125	-	-	-
Alabama	2	(D)	-	-	175 *	1.5	88	-	-	-
Kentucky	1	(D)	-	-	175 *	1.5	175	-	-	-
Louisiana	1	(D)	-	-	375 *	3.1	375	-	-	-
Ohio	1	(D)	-	-	175 *	1.5	175	-	-	-
Texas	1	(D)	-	-	1,750 *	14.6	1,750	-	-	-
Virginia	1	(D)	-	-	750 *	6.3	750	-	-	-

Source: 1992 *Economic Census*. The states are in descending order of shipments or establishments (if shipment data are missing for the majority). The symbol (D) appears when data are withheld to prevent disclosure of competitive information. States marked with (D) are sorted by number of establishments. A dash (-) indicates that the data element cannot be calculated; * indicates the midpoint of a range.

2257 - WEFT KNIT FABRIC MILLS

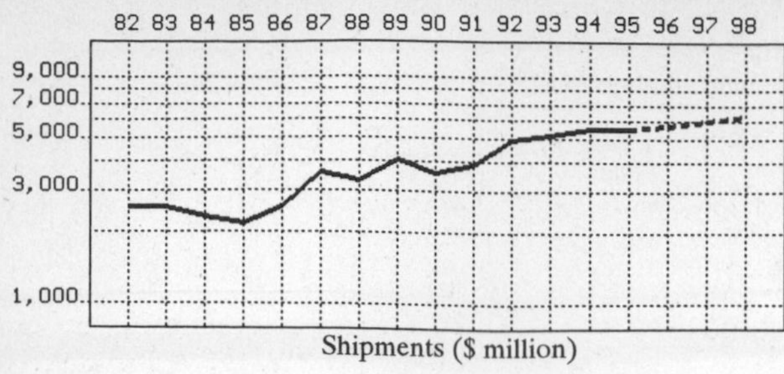

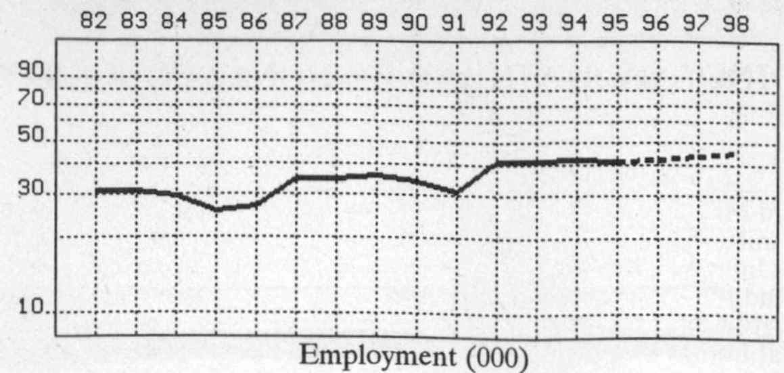

GENERAL STATISTICS

Year	Com-panies	Establishments: Total	Establishments: with 20 or more employees	Employment: Total (000)	Production Workers (000)	Production Hours (Mil)	Compensation: Payroll ($ mil)	Compensation: Wages ($/hr)	Production ($ million): Cost of Materials	Value Added by Manufacture	Value of Shipments	Capital Invest.
1982	384	422	222	31.1	25.7	50.9	420.9	6.07	1,669.0	850.4	2,538.8	68.8
1983		388	208	31.2	25.7	53.0	432.1	5.96	1,715.6	876.7	2,570.6	53.2
1984		354	194	29.7	24.7	46.2	420.3	6.63	1,534.7	772.1	2,319.1	68.8
1985		321	179	25.7	21.1	41.4	418.6	7.24	1,430.2	744.7	2,174.3	66.5
1986		307	190	26.8	22.3	43.9	444.0	7.37	1,642.2	927.4	2,562.2	70.6
1987	305	334	210	34.9	29.2	57.3	577.7	7.41	2,183.0	1,425.6	3,578.5	95.8
1988		332	200	34.7	29.6	59.6	598.3	7.72	2,079.2	1,220.8	3,306.9	107.8
1989		322	202	36.2	29.1	62.5	658.0	8.17	2,414.8	1,677.5	4,057.5	162.9
1990		309	187	34.6	26.0	56.6	596.2	8.10	2,231.6	1,370.0	3,588.7	110.0
1991		323	180	30.8	26.0	58.0	623.5	8.15	2,401.2	1,500.4	3,900.3	120.0
1992	344	387	234	41.7	35.3	72.3	805.6	8.21	3,018.5	1,888.1	4,924.1	159.8
1993		384	228	41.1	34.3	70.3	836.9	8.73	3,236.6	1,975.5	5,205.9	197.1
1994		334P	209P	41.9	35.3	72.2	901.7	9.42	3,370.4	2,187.9	5,560.4	187.4
1995		331P	210P	41.4P	34.4P	72.6P	881.4P	9.37P	3,310.7P	2,149.2P	5,462.0P	193.8P
1996		329P	211P	42.4P	35.3P	74.8P	922.4P	9.62P	3,475.4P	2,256.0P	5,733.6P	205.4P
1997		327P	212P	43.5P	36.2P	77.0P	963.3P	9.87P	3,640.0P	2,362.9P	6,005.2P	216.9P
1998		324P	213P	44.6P	37.1P	79.2P	1,004.2P	10.11P	3,804.7P	2,469.8P	6,276.8P	228.4P

Sources: 1982, 1987, 1992 *Economic Census*; *Annual Survey of Manufactures*, 83-86, 88-91, 93-94. Establishment counts for non-Census years are from *County Business Patterns*; establishment values for 83-84 are extrapolations. 'P's show projections by the editors. Industries reclassified in 87 will not have data for prior years.

INDICES OF CHANGE

Year	Com-panies	Establishments: Total	Establishments: with 20 or more employees	Employment: Total (000)	Production Workers (000)	Production Hours (Mil)	Compensation: Payroll ($ mil)	Compensation: Wages ($/hr)	Production ($ million): Cost of Materials	Value Added by Manufacture	Value of Shipments	Capital Invest.
1982	112	109	95	75	73	70	52	74	55	45	52	43
1983		100	89	75	73	73	54	73	57	46	52	33
1984		91	83	71	70	64	52	81	51	41	47	43
1985		83	76	62	60	57	52	88	47	39	44	42
1986		79	81	64	63	61	55	90	54	49	52	44
1987	89	86	90	84	83	79	72	90	72	76	73	60
1988		86	85	83	84	82	74	94	69	65	67	67
1989		83	86	87	82	86	82	100	80	89	82	102
1990		80	80	83	74	78	74	99	74	73	73	69
1991		83	77	74	74	80	77	99	80	79	79	75
1992	100	100	100	100	100	100	100	100	100	100	100	100
1993		99	97	99	97	97	104	106	107	105	106	123
1994		86P	89P	100	100	100	112	115	112	116	113	117
1995		86P	90P	99P	97P	100P	109P	114P	110P	114P	111P	121P
1996		85P	90P	102P	100P	103P	114P	117P	115P	119P	116P	129P
1997		84P	90P	104P	102P	106P	120P	120P	121P	125P	122P	136P
1998		84P	91P	107P	105P	110P	125P	123P	126P	131P	127P	143P

Sources: Same as General Statistics. Values reflect change from the base year, 1992. Values above 100 mean greater than 92, values below 100 mean less than 92, and a value of 100 in the 82-91 or 93-98 period means same as 92. 'P's mark projections by the editors.

SELECTED RATIOS

For 1994	Avg. of All Manufact.	Analyzed Industry	Index
Employees per Establishment	49	126	256
Payroll per Establishment	1,500,273	2,703,257	180
Payroll per Employee	30,620	21,520	70
Production Workers per Establishment	34	106	308
Wages per Establishment	853,319	2,038,982	239
Wages per Production Worker	24,861	19,267	77
Hours per Production Worker	2,056	2,045	99
Wages per Hour	12.09	9.42	78
Value Added per Establishment	4,602,255	6,559,228	143
Value Added per Employee	93,930	52,217	56

For 1994	Avg. of All Manufact.	Analyzed Industry	Index
Value Added per Production Worker	134,084	61,980	46
Cost per Establishment	5,045,178	10,104,311	200
Cost per Employee	102,970	80,439	78
Cost per Production Worker	146,988	95,479	65
Shipments per Establishment	9,576,895	16,669,834	174
Shipments per Employee	195,460	132,706	68
Shipments per Production Worker	279,017	157,518	56
Investment per Establishment	321,011	561,817	175
Investment per Employee	6,552	4,473	68
Investment per Production Worker	9,352	5,309	57

Sources: Same as General Statistics. The 'Average of All Manufacturing' column represents the average of all manufacturing industries reported for the most recent complete year available. The Index shows the relationship between the Average and the Analyzed Industry. For example, 100 means that they are equal; 500 that the Analyzed Industry is five times the average; 50 means that the Analyzed Industry is half the national average. The abbreviation 'na' is used to show that data are 'not available'.

LEADING COMPANIES

Number shown: **22** Total sales ($ mil): **716** Total employment (000): **6.6**

Company Name	Address				CEO Name	Phone	Co. Type	Sales ($ mil)	Empl. (000)
Guilford Mills	PO Box 1645	Lumberton	NC	28358	Alfred Greenblatt	919-739-8689	D	415	3.0
Stevcoknit Fabrics Co	PO Box 1500	Greer	SC	29652	Robert Humphreys	803-879-6701	S	100	1.5
Andrex Industries Corp	1071 Av Amer	New York	NY	10018	Steven Gottdiener	212-354-8500	R	50	0.2
Cleveland Mills Co	101 W Main St	Lawndale	NC	28090	Watt Jackson	704-538-8511	S	40	0.4
Wilmington Finishing Co	1 Mill Rd	Wilmington	DE	19806	RD Fisher	302-654-5311	R	16*	0.2
National Looms Corp	229 W 36th St	New York	NY	10018	Daniel Honig	212-594-8940	R	15*	<0.1
MoCaro Industries Inc	PO Box 6689	Statesville	NC	28687	TC Spell	704-878-6645	R	13*	0.2
Draper Knitting Company Inc	28 Draper Ln	Canton	MA	02021	Scott Draper	617-828-0029	R	10	<0.1
HH Fessler Knitting Company	Church & Sherman	Orwigsburg	PA	17961	C Beth Heim	717-366-0531	R	8	0.1
Shelby Dyeing and Finishing Inc	1038 S Lattimore	Shelby	NC	28152	Wyett Dellinger	704-487-0641	R	7*	0.1
Kings Mountain Knit Fabrics Inc	PO Box 666	Kings Mt	NC	28086	Claude Suber	704-739-6418	R	6*	<0.1
Clover Knits Inc	PO Box 539	Clover	SC	29710	Harold D McCarter	803-222-3021	R	5	0.1
Knitcraft Inc	PO Box 825	Belmont	NC	28012	George M Howe Jr	704-825-5182	R	5	0.1
Schuylkill H	PO Box 307	Schuylkill H	PA	17972	Edward G Bamford	717-385-2190	R	5	<0.1
Mi-Jan Fabrics Inc	Washington St	Denver	PA	17517	Marie Sharadin	717-336-5595	R	4*	<0.1
Southern Wipers Inc	PO Box 5645	Charlotte	NC	28225	WG MacKinnon	704-377-3448	R	4	0.1
Kenda Knits Inc	PO Box 276	Clover	SC	29710	Stewart Wingate	803-222-3041	R	3*	<0.1
Purl-Knit Fabrics Corp	68 35th St	Brooklyn	NY	11232	K Weissman	718-788-3900	R	3	<0.1
Borg Textile Corp	PO Box 697	Rossville	GA	30741	Patrick J Forde	706-866-1743	R	2*	<0.1
Jasco Fabrics Inc	450 7th Av	New York	NY	10123	George Silver	212-563-2960	R	2*	<0.1
Martin Corp	171 N Pearl St	Bridgeton	NJ	08302	W Martin	609-451-0900	R	2*	<0.1
Edmond Stern Inc	350 5th Av	New York	NY	10118	Alfred Stern	212-695-6480	R	1*	<0.1

Source: *Ward's Business Directory of U.S. Private and Public Companies*, Volumes 1 and 2, 1996. The company type code used is as follows: P - Public, R - Private, S - Subsidiary, D - Division, J - Joint Venture, A - Affiliate, G - Group. Sales are in millions of dollars, employees are in thousands. An asterisk (*) indicates an estimated sales volume. The symbol < stands for 'less than'. Company names and addresses are truncated, in some cases, to fit into the available space.

MATERIALS CONSUMED

Material		Quantity	Delivered Cost ($ million)
Materials, ingredients, containers, and supplies		(X)	2,736.6
Knit fabrics	mil lb	384.9	584.7
Manmade fibers, staple, and tow	mil lb	(S)	37.2
Raw cotton fibers	1,000 bales	144.9**	57.0
Raw wool fibers	mil lb	(D)	(D)
Carded cotton yarn	mil lb	265.8	459.4
Combed cotton yarn	mil lb	133.5	226.7
Spun rayon and acetate yarn	mil lb	(S)	1.2
Spun nylon yarn	mil lb	3.5*	7.6
Spun polyester yarns	mil lb	267.4	395.7
Rayon and acetate filament yarns	mil lb	6.0	10.1
Nylon filament yarn	mil lb	19.9	34.1
Polyester filament yarn	mil lb	27.1*	44.8
Acrylic yarns	mil lb	(D)	(D)
Wool yarn	mil lb	(D)	(D)
All other yarns	mil lb	(S)	190.0
All other materials and components, parts, containers, and supplies		(X)	515.4
Materials, ingredients, containers, and supplies, nsk		(X)	70.4

Source: 1992 *Economic Census*. Explanation of symbols used: (D): Withheld to avoid disclosure of competitive data; na: Not available; (S): Withheld because statistical norms were not met; (X): Not applicable; (Z): Less than half the unit shown; nec: Not elsewhere classified; nsk: Not specified by kind; - : zero; * : 10-19 percent estimated; ** : 20-29 percent estimated.

PRODUCT SHARE DETAILS

Product or Product Class	% Share
Weft knit fabric mills	100.00
Weft (circular) knit fabrics greige goods, except hosiery	25.82
Weft (circular) knit fabrics greige goods, except hosiery, narrow fabrics (12 in wide or less)	1.01
Weft (circular) knit fabrics greige goods, except hosiery, broad fabrics (more than 12 in wide)	98.99
Finished weft (circular) knit fabrics, except hosiery	59.40
Knit and finished in the same establishment, narrow (12 in wide or less)	1.27
Knit and finished in the same establishment, broad (more than 12 in wide)	63.38
Purchased and finished, narrow (12 in wide or less)	0.46
Purchased and finished, broad (more than 12 in wide)	34.90
Contract and commission receipts for knitting only or knitting and finishing weft (circular) knit fabrics	12.57
Weft knit fabrics mills, nsk	2.20

Source: 1992 *Economic Census*. The values shown are percent of total shipments in an industry. Values of indented subcategories are summed in the main heading. The symbol (D) appears when data are withheld to prevent disclosure of competitive information. The abbreviation nsk stands for 'not specified by kind' and nec for 'not elsewhere classified'.

INPUTS AND OUTPUTS FOR KNIT FABRIC MILLS

Economic Sector or Industry Providing Inputs	%	Sector	Economic Sector or Industry Buying Outputs	%	Sector
Yarn mills & finishing of textiles, nec	24.0	Manufg.	Apparel made from purchased materials	79.8	Manufg.
Organic fibers, noncellulosic	22.2	Manufg.	Knit fabric mills	10.6	Manufg.
Knit fabric mills	14.4	Manufg.	Personal consumption expenditures	5.1	
Cellulosic manmade fibers	8.1	Manufg.	Knit outerwear mills	2.0	Manufg.
Wholesale trade	4.8	Trade	Exports	1.7	Foreign
Surface active agents	4.0	Manufg.	Knitting mills, nec	0.2	Manufg.
Miscellaneous plastics products	2.7	Manufg.	Coated fabrics, not rubberized	0.1	Manufg.
Electric services (utilities)	2.5	Util.	Knit underwear mills	0.1	Manufg.
Petroleum refining	2.1	Manufg.	Leather gloves & mittens	0.1	Manufg.
Cyclic crudes and organics	1.7	Manufg.			
Gas production & distribution (utilities)	1.6	Util.			
Textile machinery	1.5	Manufg.			
Motor freight transportation & warehousing	1.2	Util.			
Industrial gases	0.7	Manufg.			
Imports	0.7	Foreign			
Cotton	0.6	Agric.			
Equipment rental & leasing services	0.5	Services			
Laundry, dry cleaning, shoe repair	0.5	Services			
Air transportation	0.4	Util.			
Real estate	0.4	Fin/R.E.			
Paperboard containers & boxes	0.3	Manufg.			
Communications, except radio & TV	0.3	Util.			
Banking	0.3	Fin/R.E.			
U.S. Postal Service	0.3	Gov't			
Maintenance of nonfarm buildings nec	0.2	Constr.			
Ball & roller bearings	0.2	Manufg.			
Industrial inorganic chemicals, nec	0.2	Manufg.			
Lubricating oils & greases	0.2	Manufg.			
Sanitary services, steam supply, irrigation	0.2	Util.			
Eating & drinking places	0.2	Trade			
Automotive rental & leasing, without drivers	0.2	Services			
Computer & data processing services	0.2	Services			
Detective & protective services	0.2	Services			
State & local government enterprises, nec	0.2	Gov't			
Paper coating & glazing	0.1	Manufg.			
Railroads & related services	0.1	Util.			
Insurance carriers	0.1	Fin/R.E.			
Advertising	0.1	Services			
Automotive repair shops & services	0.1	Services			
Hotels & lodging places	0.1	Services			

Source: Benchmark Input-Output Accounts for the U.S. Economy, 1982, U.S. Department of Commerce, Washington, D.C., July 1991. Data, as reported in the source, are organized by the 1977 SIC structure in use in 1982 but have been matched, as closely as is possible, to the 1987 SIC structure used in this book.

OCCUPATIONS EMPLOYED BY SIC 225 - KNITTING MILLS

Occupation	% of Total 1994	Change to 2005	Occupation	% of Total 1994	Change to 2005
Sewing machine operators, garment	22.2	-21.5	Blue collar worker supervisors	3.2	-18.0
Textile draw-out & winding machine operators	14.6	-12.7	Industrial machinery mechanics	3.1	-4.0
Inspectors, testers, & graders, precision	6.1	-4.0	Freight, stock, & material movers, hand	2.6	-30.2
Hand packers & packagers	5.2	-25.2	Machine operators nec	1.5	-23.1
Assemblers, fabricators, & hand workers nec	4.8	-12.7	Traffic, shipping, & receiving clerks	1.2	-16.0
Textile bleaching & dyeing machine operators	4.5	39.6	General managers & top executives	1.2	-17.2
Textile machine setters & set-up operators	3.9	30.9	Pressing machine operators, textiles	1.0	-43.3
Helpers, laborers, & material movers nec	3.7	-12.7			

Source: Industry-Occupation Matrix, Bureau of Labor Statistics. These data relate to one or more 3-digit SIC industry groups rather than to a single 4-digit SIC. The change reported for each occupation to the year 2005 is a percent of growth or decline as estimated by the Bureau of Labor Statistics. The abbreviation nec stands for 'not elsewhere classified'.

LOCATION BY STATE AND REGIONAL CONCENTRATION

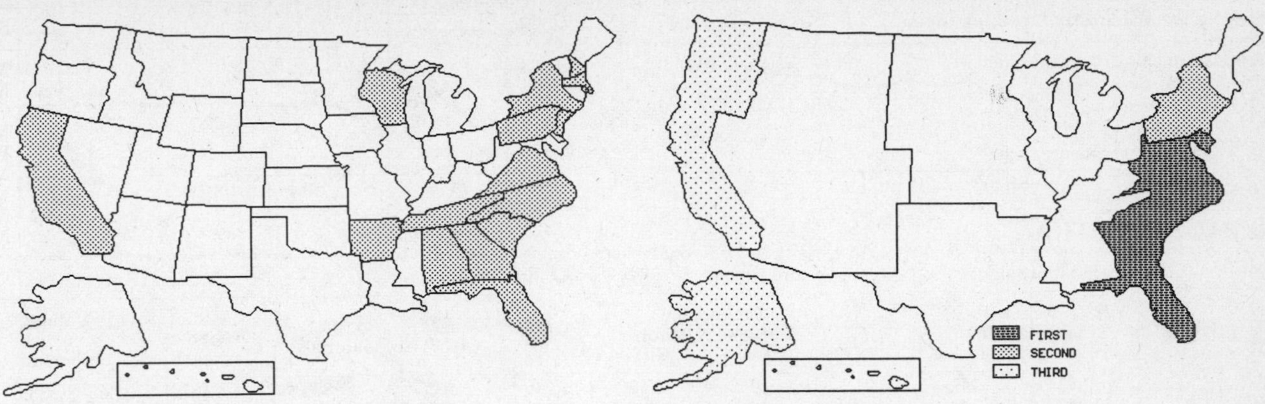

INDUSTRY DATA BY STATE

State	Establish-ments	Shipments Total ($ mil)	Shipments % of U.S.	Shipments Per Establ.	Employment Total Number	Employment % of U.S.	Employment Per Establ.	Employment Wages ($/hour)	Cost as % of Shipments	Investment per Employee ($)
North Carolina	115	2,516.1	51.1	21.9	20,500	49.2	178	8.34	63.1	4,093
California	27	286.7	5.8	10.6	2,000	4.8	74	7.50	67.3	3,500
Alabama	8	284.4	5.8	35.6	2,000	4.8	250	8.08	76.8	-
South Carolina	22	272.5	5.5	12.4	2,700	6.5	123	7.83	55.9	3,296
Tennessee	14	263.0	5.3	18.8	2,200	5.3	157	8.70	48.4	-
Virginia	6	253.4	5.1	42.2	2,200	5.3	367	7.92	60.2	-
New York	83	156.6	3.2	1.9	1,500	3.6	18	8.54	61.9	3,733
Georgia	12	145.0	2.9	12.1	1,800	4.3	150	7.74	55.7	2,833
Pennsylvania	30	126.9	2.6	4.2	1,400	3.4	47	9.08	44.7	3,714
New Jersey	30	70.8	1.4	2.4	800	1.9	27	9.40	55.4	4,000
Wisconsin	5	61.5	1.2	12.3	400	1.0	80	8.63	66.0	-
Florida	12	59.7	1.2	5.0	400	1.0	33	9.57	69.3	3,500
Massachusetts	5	(D)	-	-	3,750 *	9.0	750	-	-	-
Rhode Island	5	(D)	-	-	175 *	0.4	35	-	-	1,143
Arkansas	2	(D)	-	-	750 *	1.8	375	-	-	-
New Hampshire	1	(D)	-	-	175 *	0.4	175	-	-	-

Source: 1992 *Economic Census*. The states are in descending order of shipments or establishments (if shipment data are missing for the majority). The symbol (D) appears when data are withheld to prevent disclosure of competitive information. States marked with (D) are sorted by number of establishments. A dash (-) indicates that the data element cannot be calculated; * indicates the midpoint of a range.

2258 - LACE & WARP KNIT FABRIC MILLS

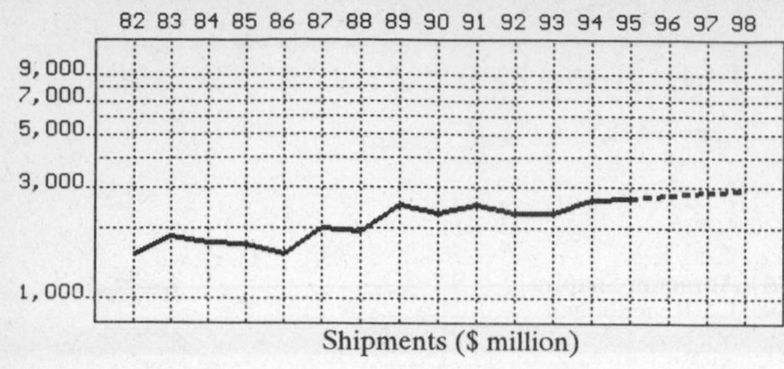

Shipments ($ million)

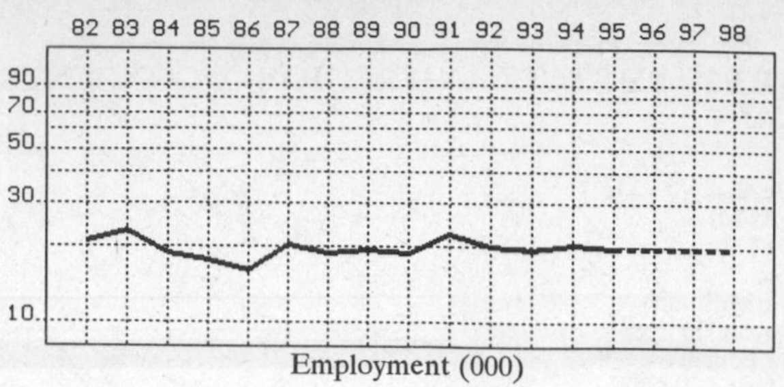

Employment (000)

GENERAL STATISTICS

Year	Com-panies	Establishments		Employment			Compensation		Production ($ million)			
		Total	with 20 or more employees	Total (000)	Production Workers (000)	Production Hours (Mil)	Payroll ($ mil)	Wages ($/hr)	Cost of Materials	Value Added by Manufacture	Value of Shipments	Capital Invest.
1982	124	272	152	21.1	17.0	33.0	286.4	6.28	929.5	580.4	1,538.0	44.9
1983		237	142	23.0	18.5	38.6	350.7	6.65	1,121.6	740.2	1,839.8	40.4
1984		202	132	18.8	15.4	32.9	307.6	6.75	995.0	745.9	1,728.8	74.2
1985		166	123	17.6	14.3	29.1	308.4	7.47	983.5	712.5	1,705.7	74.7
1986		162	119	16.1	13.3	26.8	289.3	7.76	944.1	588.6	1,533.9	55.2
1987	213	241	159	20.5	16.8	35.5	388.2	8.07	1,181.1	812.5	1,992.3	67.3
1988		232	155	18.8	15.3	33.7	380.6	8.04	1,237.5	724.5	1,939.3	65.5
1989		234	155	19.4	18.7	38.8	434.0	8.28	1,520.2	989.8	2,518.0	84.9
1990		220	150	19.0	18.7	39.5	440.0	8.09	1,348.7	931.6	2,298.3	85.7
1991		222	150	22.4	18.8	40.3	442.2	7.97	1,424.9	1,087.3	2,499.0	85.5
1992	252	278	163	20.0	16.5	34.2	417.6	8.86	1,312.4	998.6	2,309.6	75.8
1993		281	164	19.5	16.3	34.0	434.0	9.24	1,350.5	979.8	2,319.7	69.4
1994		254P	163P	20.4	17.0	35.7	469.9	9.53	1,458.8	1,142.7	2,605.2	99.6
1995		257P	165P	19.8P	17.4P	37.1P	484.8P	9.59P	1,490.7P	1,167.7P	2,662.1P	93.7P
1996		261P	167P	19.8P	17.5P	37.4P	499.6P	9.82P	1,538.6P	1,205.2P	2,747.6P	97.0P
1997		265P	170P	19.8P	17.6P	37.8P	514.5P	10.06P	1,586.4P	1,242.7P	2,833.1P	100.2P
1998		269P	172P	19.9P	17.7P	38.1P	529.4P	10.30P	1,634.3P	1,280.2P	2,918.6P	103.5P

Sources: 1982, 1987, 1992 *Economic Census*; *Annual Survey of Manufactures*, 83-86, 88-91, 93-94. Establishment counts for non-Census years are from *County Business Patterns*; establishment values for 83-84 are extrapolations. 'P's show projections by the editors. Industries reclassified in 87 will not have data for prior years.

INDICES OF CHANGE

Year	Com-panies	Establishments		Employment			Compensation		Production ($ million)			
		Total	with 20 or more employees	Total (000)	Production Workers (000)	Production Hours (Mil)	Payroll ($ mil)	Wages ($/hr)	Cost of Materials	Value Added by Manufacture	Value of Shipments	Capital Invest.
1982	49	98	93	106	103	96	69	71	71	58	67	59
1983		85	87	115	112	113	84	75	85	74	80	53
1984		73	81	94	93	96	74	76	76	75	75	98
1985		60	75	88	87	85	74	84	75	71	74	99
1986		58	73	81	81	78	69	88	72	59	66	73
1987	85	87	98	102	102	104	93	91	90	81	86	89
1988		83	95	94	93	99	91	91	94	73	84	86
1989		84	95	97	113	113	104	93	116	99	109	112
1990		79	92	95	113	115	105	91	103	93	100	113
1991		80	92	112	114	118	106	90	109	109	108	113
1992	100	100	100	100	100	100	100	100	100	100	100	100
1993		101	101	98	99	99	104	104	103	98	100	92
1994		91P	100P	102	103	104	113	108	111	114	113	131
1995		93P	101P	99P	106P	109P	116P	108P	114P	117P	115P	124P
1996		94P	103P	99P	106P	109P	120P	111P	117P	121P	119P	128P
1997		95P	104P	99P	107P	110P	123P	114P	121P	124P	123P	132P
1998		97P	106P	99P	108P	111P	127P	116P	125P	128P	126P	136P

Sources: Same as General Statistics. Values reflect change from the base year, 1992. Values above 100 mean greater than 92, values below 100 mean less than 92, and a value of 100 in the 82-91 or 93-98 period means same as 92. 'P's mark projections by the editors.

SELECTED RATIOS

For 1994	Avg. of All Manufact.	Analyzed Industry	Index
Employees per Establishment	49	80	164
Payroll per Establishment	1,500,273	1,853,095	124
Payroll per Employee	30,620	23,034	75
Production Workers per Establishment	34	67	195
Wages per Establishment	853,319	1,341,694	157
Wages per Production Worker	24,861	20,013	80
Hours per Production Worker	2,056	2,100	102
Wages per Hour	12.09	9.53	79
Value Added per Establishment	4,602,255	4,506,346	98
Value Added per Employee	93,930	56,015	60

For 1994	Avg. of All Manufact.	Analyzed Industry	Index
Value Added per Production Worker	134,084	67,218	50
Cost per Establishment	5,045,178	5,752,916	114
Cost per Employee	102,970	71,510	69
Cost per Production Worker	146,988	85,812	58
Shipments per Establishment	9,576,895	10,273,853	107
Shipments per Employee	195,460	127,706	65
Shipments per Production Worker	279,017	153,247	55
Investment per Establishment	321,011	392,782	122
Investment per Employee	6,552	4,882	75
Investment per Production Worker	9,352	5,859	63

Sources: Same as General Statistics. The 'Average of All Manufacturing' column represents the average of all manufacturing industries reported for the most recent complete year available. The Index shows the relationship between the Average and the Analyzed Industry. For example, 100 means that they are equal; 500 that the Analyzed Industry is five times the average; 50 means that the Analyzed Industry is half the national average. The abbreviation 'na' is used to show that data are 'not available'.

LEADING COMPANIES

Number shown: **31** Total sales ($ mil): **1,364** Total employment (000): **11.5**

Company Name	Address				CEO Name	Phone	Co. Type	Sales ($ mil)	Empl. (000)
Guilford Mills Inc	PO Box 26969	Greensboro	NC	27419	Charles A Hayes	919-316-4000	P	704	5.4
Liberty Fabrics Inc	295 5th Av	New York	NY	10016	Matthew Williams	212-684-3100	S	180*	1.4
Lida Inc	2222 South Blv	Charlotte	NC	28203	Isaac Kier	704-376-5609	P	91	0.6
Glenoit Mills Inc	PO Box 1157	Tarboro	NC	27886	Abraham Shapira	919-823-2124	R	50*	0.5
Darlington Fabrics Corp	1359 Broadway	New York	NY	10018	LA Regenbogen	212-279-7733	S	49	0.4
Liberty Penn Corp	PO Box 279	Jamesville	NC	27846	Michael Gottlieb	919-792-8167	S	40*	0.2
Milco Industries Inc	180 Madison Av	New York	NY	10016	Norman Belmonte	212-683-0826	R	40	0.6
Hosposable Products Inc	PO Box 387	Bound Brook	NJ	08805	Leonard Schramm	908-707-1800	P	30	0.2
Apex Mills Corp	168 Doughty Blv	Inwood	NY	11096	Milton Kurz	516-239-4400	R	20	<0.1
Pottsville Bleach and Dye	PO Box 348	Schuylkill H	PA	17972	Richard Hemphill	717-385-4100	D	20	0.3
Charbert Inc	485 7th Av	New York	NY	10018	Nat Weisler	212-564-4866	R	18*	0.2
Bridgton Mills	Portland Rd	Bridgton	ME	04009	Dennis D Ackroyd	207-647-3333	D	15*	0.3
Gehring Textiles Inc	1 W 34th St	New York	NY	10001	G Gregory Gehring	212-689-9700	R	11	0.2
Carolace Embroidery Company	501 Broad Av	Ridgefield	NJ	07657	Bernard Mann	201-945-2151	R	10*	0.1
Continental Fabrics Inc	104 W 40th St	New York	NY	10018	William Conroy	212-354-1373	R	10	<0.1
Nanray Inc	PO Box 1362	Lumberton	NC	28358	Robert E Freeman	910-738-5251	R	10	0.1
Fablok Mills Inc	140 Spring St	Murray Hill	NJ	07974	Alex Fisher	908-464-1950	R	8*	<0.1
Pomona Textile Company Inc	4405 W Riverside	Burbank	CA	91505	Chester J Gelber	213-627-7277	R	8	<0.1
Paris Lace Inc	PO Box 258	Clifton	NJ	07011	I Barr	201-478-9035	R	6	<0.1
Roman Knit Inc	PO Box 889	Norwood	NC	28128	D Foreman	704-474-4123	R	6*	<0.1
Scranton Lace Co	1313 Meylert Av	Scranton	PA	18509	James T Bird	717-344-1121	R	6*	0.2
Aridyne Corp	PO Box 62	Graham	NC	27253	Allan Goldstein	919-578-2550	S	5*	<0.1
Fairlane Inc	PO Box 197	Gibsonville	NC	27249	Harold J Hunnicutt	910-449-4921	R	5*	<0.1
Joseph Titone and Sons Inc	1002 Jacksonville	Burlington	NJ	08016	Alfred Titone	609-386-1147	R	5	<0.1
Helmont Mills Inc	15 Lion Av	St Johnsville	NY	13452	Gregory Gehring	518-568-7913	S	4*	<0.1
Rue de France Inc	28 Jacome Way	Middletown	RI	02842	Pamela Kelley	401-846-2084	R	4	<0.1
Bojud Knitting Mills Inc	66 Willow St	Amsterdam	NY	12010	Matthew Aronoff	518-842-4766	R	3*	<0.1
Mohawk Fabric Company Inc	96 Guy Park Av	Amsterdam	NY	12010	Greg L Needham	518-842-3090	R	3	<0.1
United Veil	28 Bostwick Av	Jersey City	NJ	07305	R Brandell	201-333-1369	R	2*	<0.1
Knit-Wear Fabrics Inc	PO Box 790	Burlington	NC	27215	FD Hornaday III	919-226-4342	R	1	<0.1
Embassy Embroidery Corp	PO Box 543	North Bergen	NJ	07047	Jackie Green	201-863-3915	R	1*	<0.1

Source: *Ward's Business Directory of U.S. Private and Public Companies*, Volumes 1 and 2, 1996. The company type code used is as follows: P - Public, R - Private, S - Subsidiary, D - Division, J - Joint Venture, A - Affiliate, G - Group. Sales are in millions of dollars, employees are in thousands. An asterisk (*) indicates an estimated sales volume. The symbol < stands for 'less than'. Company names and addresses are truncated, in some cases, to fit into the available space.

MATERIALS CONSUMED

Material		Quantity	Delivered Cost ($ million)
Materials, ingredients, containers, and supplies		(X)	1,198.3
Knit fabrics	mil lb	152.7*	297.3
Manmade fibers, staple, and tow	mil lb	7.8	22.4
Raw cotton fibers	1,000 bales	(D)	(D)
Carded cotton yarn	mil lb	21.4	33.1
Combed cotton yarn	mil lb	15.4	26.0
Spun rayon and acetate yarn	mil lb	(D)	(D)
Spun nylon yarn	mil lb	19.1**	55.4
Spun polyester yarns	mil lb	31.8	60.2
Rayon and acetate filament yarns	mil lb	3.2*	6.7
Nylon filament yarn	mil lb	45.5	118.3
Polyester filament yarn	mil lb	66.6*	116.6
Acrylic yarns	mil lb	7.8	15.9
All other yarns	mil lb	26.1	71.3
All other materials and components, parts, containers, and supplies		(X)	341.7
Materials, ingredients, containers, and supplies, nsk		(X)	20.7

Source: 1992 *Economic Census*. Explanation of symbols used: (D): Withheld to avoid disclosure of competitive data; na: Not available; (S): Withheld because statistical norms were not met; (X): Not applicable; (Z): Less than half the unit shown; nec: Not elsewhere classified; nsk: Not specified by kind; - : zero; * : 10-19 percent estimated; ** : 20-29 percent estimated.

PRODUCT SHARE DETAILS

Product or Product Class	% Share	Product or Product Class	% Share
Warp knit fabric mills and lace goods	100.00	Finished warp knit fabrics, purchased and finished, narrow (12 in wide or less)	2.28
Warp knit fabrics greige goods	18.46	Finished warp knit fabrics, purchased and finished, broad (more than 12 in wide)	46.13
Warp knit fabrics greige goods, narrow fabrics (12 in wide or less)	6.69	Lace and net goods, all leavers and Nottingham lace machine products, including bobbinets and barmen laces	2.26
Warp knit fabrics greige goods, broad fabrics (more than 12 in wide)	93.31	Contract and commission receipts for knitting only or knitting and finishing of warp knit fabrics, or finishing lace	10.40
Finished warp knit fabrics	67.11	Warp knit fabrics mills and lace goods, nsk	1.78
Finished warp knit fabrics, knit and finished in the same establishment, narrow (12 in wide or less)	7.59		
Finished warp knit fabrics, knit and finished in the same establishment, broad (more than 12 in wide)	44.00		

Source: 1992 *Economic Census*. The values shown are percent of total shipments in an industry. Values of indented subcategories are summed in the main heading. The symbol (D) appears when data are withheld to prevent disclosure of competitive information. The abbreviation nsk stands for 'not specified by kind' and nec for 'not elsewhere classified'.

INPUTS AND OUTPUTS FOR KNIT FABRIC MILLS

Economic Sector or Industry Providing Inputs	%	Sector	Economic Sector or Industry Buying Outputs	%	Sector
Yarn mills & finishing of textiles, nec	24.0	Manufg.	Apparel made from purchased materials	79.8	Manufg.
Organic fibers, noncellulosic	22.2	Manufg.	Knit fabric mills	10.6	Manufg.
Knit fabric mills	14.4	Manufg.	Personal consumption expenditures	5.1	
Cellulosic manmade fibers	8.1	Manufg.	Knit outerwear mills	2.0	Manufg.
Wholesale trade	4.8	Trade	Exports	1.7	Foreign
Surface active agents	4.0	Manufg.	Knitting mills, nec	0.2	Manufg.
Miscellaneous plastics products	2.7	Manufg.	Coated fabrics, not rubberized	0.1	Manufg.
Electric services (utilities)	2.5	Util.	Knit underwear mills	0.1	Manufg.
Petroleum refining	2.1	Manufg.	Leather gloves & mittens	0.1	Manufg.
Cyclic crudes and organics	1.7	Manufg.			
Gas production & distribution (utilities)	1.6	Util.			
Textile machinery	1.5	Manufg.			
Motor freight transportation & warehousing	1.2	Util.			
Industrial gases	0.7	Manufg.			
Imports	0.7	Foreign			
Cotton	0.6	Agric.			
Equipment rental & leasing services	0.5	Services			
Laundry, dry cleaning, shoe repair	0.5	Services			
Air transportation	0.4	Util.			
Real estate	0.4	Fin/R.E.			
Paperboard containers & boxes	0.3	Manufg.			
Communications, except radio & TV	0.3	Util.			
Banking	0.3	Fin/R.E.			
U.S. Postal Service	0.3	Gov't			
Maintenance of nonfarm buildings nec	0.2	Constr.			
Ball & roller bearings	0.2	Manufg.			
Industrial inorganic chemicals, nec	0.2	Manufg.			
Lubricating oils & greases	0.2	Manufg.			
Sanitary services, steam supply, irrigation	0.2	Util.			
Eating & drinking places	0.2	Trade			
Automotive rental & leasing, without drivers	0.2	Services			
Computer & data processing services	0.2	Services			
Detective & protective services	0.2	Services			
State & local government enterprises, nec	0.2	Gov't			
Paper coating & glazing	0.1	Manufg.			
Railroads & related services	0.1	Util.			
Insurance carriers	0.1	Fin/R.E.			
Advertising	0.1	Services			
Automotive repair shops & services	0.1	Services			
Hotels & lodging places	0.1	Services			

Source: Benchmark Input-Output Accounts for the U.S. Economy, 1982, U.S. Department of Commerce, Washington, D.C., July 1991. Data, as reported in the source, are organized by the 1977 SIC structure in use in 1982 but have been matched, as closely as is possible, to the 1987 SIC structure used in this book.

OCCUPATIONS EMPLOYED BY SIC 225 - KNITTING MILLS

Occupation	% of Total 1994	Change to 2005	Occupation	% of Total 1994	Change to 2005
Sewing machine operators, garment	22.2	-21.5	Blue collar worker supervisors	3.2	-18.0
Textile draw-out & winding machine operators	14.6	-12.7	Industrial machinery mechanics	3.1	-4.0
Inspectors, testers, & graders, precision	6.1	-4.0	Freight, stock, & material movers, hand	2.6	-30.2
Hand packers & packagers	5.2	-25.2	Machine operators nec	1.5	-23.1
Assemblers, fabricators, & hand workers nec	4.8	-12.7	Traffic, shipping, & receiving clerks	1.2	-16.0
Textile bleaching & dyeing machine operators	4.5	39.6	General managers & top executives	1.2	-17.2
Textile machine setters & set-up operators	3.9	30.9	Pressing machine operators, textiles	1.0	-43.3
Helpers, laborers, & material movers nec	3.7	-12.7			

Source: *Industry-Occupation Matrix*, Bureau of Labor Statistics. These data relate to one or more 3-digit SIC industry groups rather than to a single 4-digit SIC. The change reported for each occupation to the year 2005 is a percent of growth or decline as estimated by the Bureau of Labor Statistics. The abbreviation nec stands for 'not elsewhere classified'.

LOCATION BY STATE AND REGIONAL CONCENTRATION

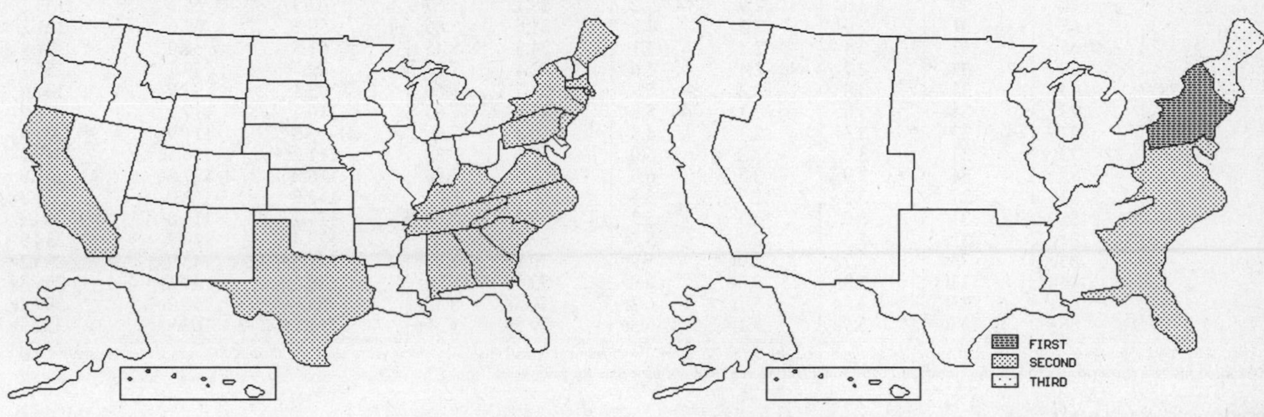

INDUSTRY DATA BY STATE

State	Establish-ments	Shipments			Employment				Cost as % of Shipments	Investment per Employee ($)
		Total ($ mil)	% of U.S.	Per Establ.	Total Number	% of U.S.	Per Establ.	Wages ($/hour)		
North Carolina	55	828.6	35.9	15.1	6,600	33.0	120	8.59	52.7	5,167
New York	58	277.6	12.0	4.8	2,500	12.5	43	9.21	55.1	2,360
Pennsylvania	15	256.5	11.1	17.1	1,900	9.5	127	7.72	57.3	3,526
New Jersey	55	202.9	8.8	3.7	2,400	12.0	44	10.17	45.9	2,042
Rhode Island	12	100.3	4.3	8.4	800	4.0	67	9.57	63.3	3,625
Georgia	7	81.1	3.5	11.6	700	3.5	100	9.23	54.5	-
California	11	23.6	1.0	2.1	300	1.5	27	8.20	46.2	2,333
Alabama	5	22.1	1.0	4.4	300	1.5	60	9.20	55.2	-
Massachusetts	6	20.5	0.9	3.4	200	1.0	33	9.25	41.5	-
South Carolina	9	(D)	-	-	750 *	3.8	83	-	-	-
Tennessee	7	(D)	-	-	175 *	0.9	25	-	-	571
Virginia	6	(D)	-	-	1,750 *	8.8	292	-	-	-
Texas	5	(D)	-	-	175 *	0.9	35	-	-	2,286
Connecticut	4	(D)	-	-	750 *	3.8	188	-	-	-
Maine	4	(D)	-	-	175 *	0.9	44	-	-	-
Kentucky	1	(D)	-	-	375 *	1.9	375	-	-	-

Source: 1992 *Economic Census*. The states are in descending order of shipments or establishments (if shipment data are missing for the majority). The symbol (D) appears when data are withheld to prevent disclosure of competitive information. States marked with (D) are sorted by number of establishments. A dash (-) indicates that the data element cannot be calculated; * indicates the midpoint of a range.

2259 - KNITTING MILLS, NEC

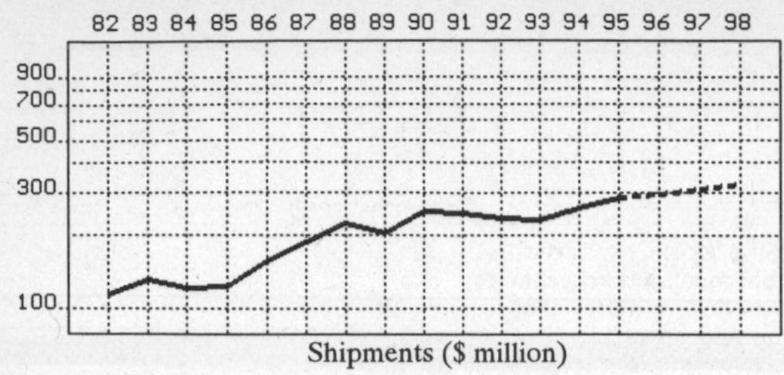

Shipments ($ million)

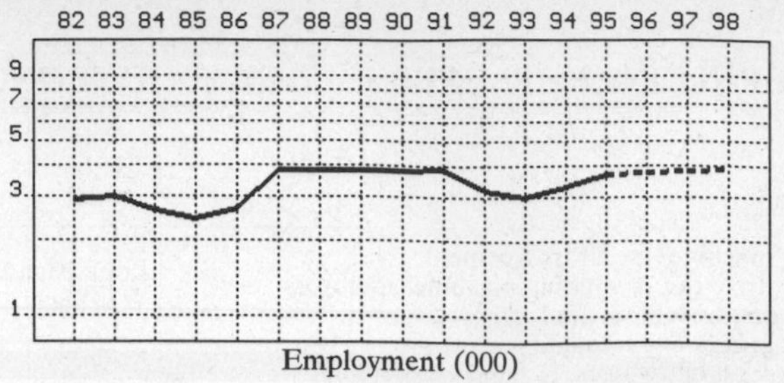

Employment (000)

GENERAL STATISTICS

Year	Companies	Establishments: Total	Establishments: with 20 or more employees	Employment: Total (000)	Employment: Production Workers (000)	Employment: Production Hours (Mil)	Compensation: Payroll ($ mil)	Compensation: Wages ($/hr)	Production ($ million): Cost of Materials	Production ($ million): Value Added by Manufacture	Production ($ million): Value of Shipments	Production ($ million): Capital Invest.
1982	71	72	29	2.9	2.5	4.7	33.8	5.47	57.5	55.4	114.5	1.5
1983		70	30	3.0	2.9	5.2	38.1	5.67	67.5	65.9	133.2	3.0
1984		68	31	2.6	2.3	4.2	31.6	5.86	59.1	62.6	121.2	2.4
1985		65	32	2.4	2.1	3.1	34.3	8.45	61.5	62.0	124.4	1.9
1986		69	33	2.7	2.4	4.6	42.4	7.22	79.7	79.1	157.1	3.5
1987	78	79	35	3.8	3.2	5.8	54.7	6.60	93.1	97.9	187.6	6.6
1988		77	34	3.8	3.1	5.8	57.8	7.05	110.5	117.1	222.9	3.2
1989		71	33	3.8	2.7	4.8	50.8	7.69	93.6	111.9	205.4	3.9
1990		73	34	3.8	3.3	6.0	63.6	7.83	111.2	136.5	249.3	8.4
1991		72	34	3.9	3.3	6.0	65.5	7.88	116.3	137.3	247.8	7.7
1992	82	84	27	3.2	2.7	5.5	60.7	8.05	112.8	123.0	235.8	5.8
1993		85	31	3.0	2.5	5.3	59.5	8.06	114.2	116.8	230.7	5.1
1994		81P	32P	3.3	2.8	5.5	62.7	8.35	129.4	130.7	258.9	3.3
1995		83P	33P	3.7P	3.0P	5.9P	70.8P	8.73P	141.5P	142.9P	283.2P	6.6P
1996		84P	33P	3.8P	3.0P	6.0P	73.7P	8.94P	148.1P	149.6P	296.3P	6.9P
1997		85P	33P	3.8P	3.1P	6.2P	76.6P	9.15P	154.6P	156.2P	309.4P	7.3P
1998		86P	33P	3.9P	3.1P	6.3P	79.5P	9.36P	161.2P	162.8P	322.5P	7.6P

Sources: 1982, 1987, 1992 *Economic Census*; *Annual Survey of Manufactures*, 83-86, 88-91, 93-94. Establishment counts for non-Census years are from *County Business Patterns*; establishment values for 83-84 are extrapolations. 'P's show projections by the editors. Industries reclassified in 87 will not have data for prior years.

INDICES OF CHANGE

Year	Companies	Establishments: Total	Establishments: with 20 or more employees	Employment: Total (000)	Employment: Production Workers (000)	Employment: Production Hours (Mil)	Compensation: Payroll ($ mil)	Compensation: Wages ($/hr)	Production ($ million): Cost of Materials	Production ($ million): Value Added by Manufacture	Production ($ million): Value of Shipments	Production ($ million): Capital Invest.
1982	87	86	107	91	93	85	56	68	51	45	49	26
1983		83	111	94	107	95	63	70	60	54	56	52
1984		81	115	81	85	76	52	73	52	51	51	41
1985		77	119	75	78	56	57	105	55	50	53	33
1986		82	122	84	89	84	70	90	71	64	67	60
1987	95	94	130	119	119	105	90	82	83	80	80	114
1988		92	126	119	115	105	95	88	98	95	95	55
1989		85	122	119	100	87	84	96	83	91	87	67
1990		87	126	119	122	109	105	97	99	111	106	145
1991		86	126	122	122	109	108	98	103	112	105	133
1992	100	100	100	100	100	100	100	100	100	100	100	100
1993		101	115	94	93	96	98	100	101	95	98	88
1994		97P	120P	103	104	100	103	104	115	106	110	57
1995		98P	121P	115P	111P	108P	117P	108P	125P	116P	120P	114P
1996		100P	121P	117P	112P	110P	121P	111P	131P	122P	126P	120P
1997		101P	121P	119P	114P	112P	126P	114P	137P	127P	131P	125P
1998		103P	122P	121P	115P	114P	131P	116P	143P	132P	137P	131P

Sources: Same as General Statistics. Values reflect change from the base year, 1992. Values above 100 mean greater than 92, values below 100 mean less than 92, and a value of 100 in the 82-91 or 93-98 period means same as 92. 'P's mark projections by the editors.

SELECTED RATIOS

For 1994	Avg. of All Manufact.	Analyzed Industry	Index	For 1994	Avg. of All Manufact.	Analyzed Industry	Index
Employees per Establishment	49	40	83	Value Added per Production Worker	134,084	46,679	35
Payroll per Establishment	1,500,273	769,325	51	Cost per Establishment	5,045,178	1,587,730	31
Payroll per Employee	30,620	19,000	62	Cost per Employee	102,970	39,212	38
Production Workers per Establishment	34	34	100	Cost per Production Worker	146,988	46,214	31
Wages per Establishment	853,319	563,497	66	Shipments per Establishment	9,576,895	3,176,687	33
Wages per Production Worker	24,861	16,402	66	Shipments per Employee	195,460	78,455	40
Hours per Production Worker	2,056	1,964	96	Shipments per Production Worker	279,017	92,464	33
Wages per Hour	12.09	8.35	69	Investment per Establishment	321,011	40,491	13
Value Added per Establishment	4,602,255	1,603,681	35	Investment per Employee	6,552	1,000	15
Value Added per Employee	93,930	39,606	42	Investment per Production Worker	9,352	1,179	13

Sources: Same as General Statistics. The 'Average of All Manufacturing' column represents the average of all manufacturing industries reported for the most recent complete year available. The Index shows the relationship between the Average and the Analyzed Industry. For example, 100 means that they are equal; 500 that the Analyzed Industry is five times the average; 50 means that the Analyzed Industry is half the national average. The abbreviation 'na' is used to show that data are 'not available'.

LEADING COMPANIES

Number shown: **8** Total sales ($ mil): **90** Total employment (000): **1.0**

Company Name	Address				CEO Name	Phone	Co. Type	Sales ($ mil)	Empl. (000)
H Warshow and Sons Inc	1375 Broadway	New York	NY	10018	Henry Warshow	212-921-9200	R	50	0.6
Scott Mills Inc	120 W Germ Pk	Plym Meeting	PA	19462	Wesley Edwards	610-828-7261	P	17	0.2
Arlington Hat Company Inc	47-00 34th St	Long Island Ct	NY	11101	LJ Strongin	718-361-3000	R	6*	<0.1
Novelty Textile Mills Inc	PO Box 498	Wauregan	CT	06387	AJ Feinberg	203-774-5000	R	5*	<0.1
Flexlon Fabrics Inc	PO Box 1058	Burlington	NC	27215	WS Foster III	919-578-0111	R	5	<0.1
Cushman and Marden Inc	PO Box 3001	Peabody	MA	01960	Sandra Gray	508-532-1670	R	4	<0.1
Marlee Knitting Mill Inc	51 Beaver St	Gloversville	NY	12078	Martin Krieger	518-725-6767	R	2*	<0.1
Sandler Sanitary Wiping Cloth	2229 S Halsted St	Chicago	IL	60608	Myron Sandler	312-226-1414	R	1	<0.1

Source: Ward's Business Directory of U.S. Private and Public Companies, Volumes 1 and 2, 1996. The company type code used is as follows: P - Public, R - Private, S - Subsidiary, D - Division, J - Joint Venture, A - Affiliate, G - Group. Sales are in millions of dollars, employees are in thousands. An asterisk (*) indicates an estimated sales volume. The symbol < stands for 'less than'. Company names and addresses are truncated, in some cases, to fit into the available space.

MATERIALS CONSUMED

Material		Quantity	Delivered Cost ($ million)
Materials, ingredients, containers, and supplies		(X)	97.0
Knit fabrics	mil lb	(D)	(D)
Raw cotton fibers	1,000 bales	(D)	(D)
Raw wool fibers	mil lb	(D)	(D)
Carded cotton yarn	mil lb	(S)	23.9
Combed cotton yarn	mil lb	(D)	(D)
Spun rayon and acetate yarn	mil lb	(D)	(D)
Spun nylon yarn	mil lb	(D)	(D)
Spun polyester yarns	mil lb	4.4**	7.8
Nylon filament yarn	mil lb	(D)	(D)
Polyester filament yarn	mil lb	(S)	4.6
Acrylic yarns	mil lb	(D)	(D)
Wool yarn	mil lb	(D)	(D)
All other yarns	mil lb	(D)	(D)
All other materials and components, parts, containers, and supplies		(X)	35.3
Materials, ingredients, containers, and supplies, nsk		(X)	5.0

Source: 1992 *Economic Census*. Explanation of symbols used: (D): Withheld to avoid disclosure of competitive data; na: Not available; (S): Withheld because statistical norms were not met; (X): Not applicable; (Z): Less than half the unit shown; nec: Not elsewhere classified; nsk: Not specified by kind; - : zero; * : 10-19 percent estimated; ** : 20-29 percent estimated.

PRODUCT SHARE DETAILS

Product or Product Class	% Share	Product or Product Class	% Share
Knitting mills, nec	100.00	Knit products (made in knitting mills), other knit end products, except fabrics (including towels and washcloths)	48.05
Knit gloves and mittens including fabric-and-leather combination (made in knitting mills)	45.69		

Source: 1992 *Economic Census*. The values shown are percent of total shipments in an industry. Values of indented subcategories are summed in the main heading. The symbol (D) appears when data are withheld to prevent disclosure of competitive information. The abbreviation nsk stands for 'not specified by kind' and nec for 'not elsewhere classified'.

INPUTS AND OUTPUTS FOR KNIT FABRIC MILLS

Economic Sector or Industry Providing Inputs	%	Sector	Economic Sector or Industry Buying Outputs	%	Sector
Yarn mills & finishing of textiles, nec	24.0	Manufg.	Apparel made from purchased materials	79.8	Manufg.
Organic fibers, noncellulosic	22.2	Manufg.	Knit fabric mills	10.6	Manufg.
Knit fabric mills	14.4	Manufg.	Personal consumption expenditures	5.1	
Cellulosic manmade fibers	8.1	Manufg.	Knit outerwear mills	2.0	Manufg.
Wholesale trade	4.8	Trade	Exports	1.7	Foreign
Surface active agents	4.0	Manufg.	Knitting mills, nec	0.2	Manufg.
Miscellaneous plastics products	2.7	Manufg.	Coated fabrics, not rubberized	0.1	Manufg.
Electric services (utilities)	2.5	Util.	Knit underwear mills	0.1	Manufg.
Petroleum refining	2.1	Manufg.	Leather gloves & mittens	0.1	Manufg.
Cyclic crudes and organics	1.7	Manufg.			
Gas production & distribution (utilities)	1.6	Util.			
Textile machinery	1.5	Manufg.			
Motor freight transportation & warehousing	1.2	Util.			
Industrial gases	0.7	Manufg.			
Imports	0.7	Foreign			
Cotton	0.6	Agric.			
Equipment rental & leasing services	0.5	Services			

Continued on next page.

INPUTS AND OUTPUTS FOR KNIT FABRIC MILLS - Continued

Economic Sector or Industry Providing Inputs	%	Sector	Economic Sector or Industry Buying Outputs	%	Sector
Laundry, dry cleaning, shoe repair	0.5	Services			
Air transportation	0.4	Util.			
Real estate	0.4	Fin/R.E.			
Paperboard containers & boxes	0.3	Manufg.			
Communications, except radio & TV	0.3	Util.			
Banking	0.3	Fin/R.E.			
U.S. Postal Service	0.3	Gov't			
Maintenance of nonfarm buildings nec	0.2	Constr.			
Ball & roller bearings	0.2	Manufg.			
Industrial inorganic chemicals, nec	0.2	Manufg.			
Lubricating oils & greases	0.2	Manufg.			
Sanitary services, steam supply, irrigation	0.2	Util.			
Eating & drinking places	0.2	Trade			
Automotive rental & leasing, without drivers	0.2	Services			
Computer & data processing services	0.2	Services			
Detective & protective services	0.2	Services			
State & local government enterprises, nec	0.2	Gov't			
Paper coating & glazing	0.1	Manufg.			
Railroads & related services	0.1	Util.			
Insurance carriers	0.1	Fin/R.E.			
Advertising	0.1	Services			
Automotive repair shops & services	0.1	Services			
Hotels & lodging places	0.1	Services			

Source: Benchmark Input-Output Accounts for the U.S. Economy, 1982, U.S. Department of Commerce, Washington, D.C., July 1991. Data, as reported in the source, are organized by the 1977 SIC structure in use in 1982 but have been matched, as closely as is possible, to the 1987 SIC structure used in this book.

OCCUPATIONS EMPLOYED BY SIC 225 - KNITTING MILLS

Occupation	% of Total 1994	Change to 2005	Occupation	% of Total 1994	Change to 2005
Sewing machine operators, garment	22.2	-21.5	Blue collar worker supervisors	3.2	-18.0
Textile draw-out & winding machine operators	14.6	-12.7	Industrial machinery mechanics	3.1	-4.0
Inspectors, testers, & graders, precision	6.1	-4.0	Freight, stock, & material movers, hand	2.6	-30.2
Hand packers & packagers	5.2	-25.2	Machine operators nec	1.5	-23.1
Assemblers, fabricators, & hand workers nec	4.8	-12.7	Traffic, shipping, & receiving clerks	1.2	-16.0
Textile bleaching & dyeing machine operators	4.5	39.6	General managers & top executives	1.2	-17.2
Textile machine setters & set-up operators	3.9	30.9	Pressing machine operators, textiles	1.0	-43.3
Helpers, laborers, & material movers nec	3.7	-12.7			

Source: Industry-Occupation Matrix, Bureau of Labor Statistics. These data relate to one or more 3-digit SIC industry groups rather than to a single 4-digit SIC. The change reported for each occupation to the year 2005 is a percent of growth or decline as estimated by the Bureau of Labor Statistics. The abbreviation nec stands for 'not elsewhere classified'.

LOCATION BY STATE AND REGIONAL CONCENTRATION

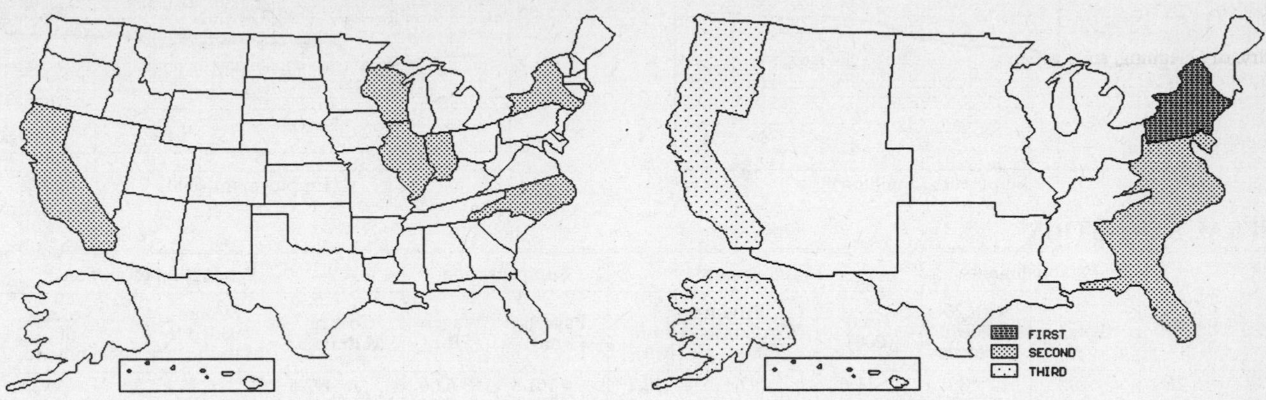

INDUSTRY DATA BY STATE

State	Establish-ments	Shipments			Employment				Cost as % of Shipments	Investment per Employee ($)
		Total ($ mil)	% of U.S.	Per Establ.	Total Number	% of U.S.	Per Establ.	Wages ($/hour)		
North Carolina	16	83.1	35.2	5.2	1,100	34.4	69	8.21	50.5	1,182
New York	18	45.1	19.1	2.5	600	18.8	33	8.73	38.1	3,333
California	5	(D)	-	-	175 *	5.5	35	-	-	-
Illinois	2	(D)	-	-	175 *	5.5	88	-	-	-
Wisconsin	2	(D)	-	-	750 *	23.4	375	-	-	-
Indiana	1	(D)	-	-	175 *	5.5	175	-	-	-

Source: 1992 *Economic Census*. The states are in descending order of shipments or establishments (if shipment data are missing for the majority). The symbol (D) appears when data are withheld to prevent disclosure of competitive information. States marked with (D) are sorted by number of establishments. A dash (-) indicates that the data element cannot be calculated; * indicates the midpoint of a range.

2261 - FINISHING PLANTS, COTTON

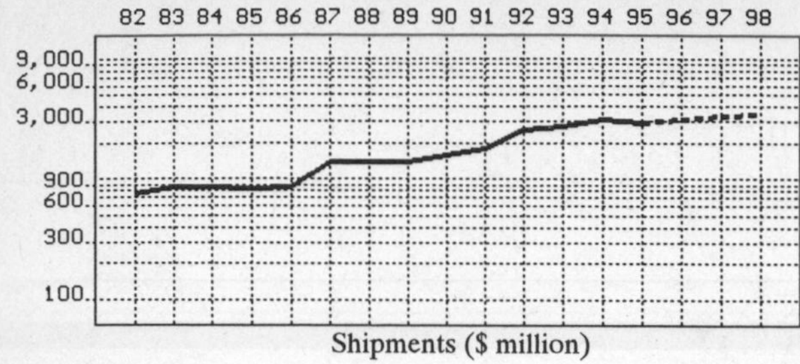

Shipments ($ million)

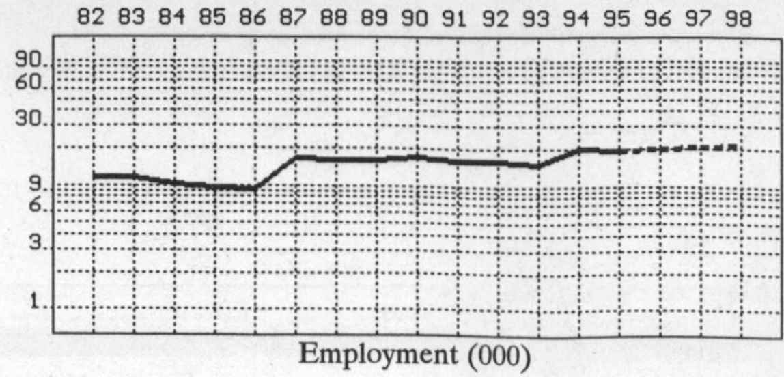

Employment (000)

GENERAL STATISTICS

Year	Companies	Establishments		Employment			Compensation		Production ($ million)			
		Total	with 20 or more employees	Total (000)	Production Workers (000)	Production Hours (Mil)	Payroll ($ mil)	Wages ($/hr)	Cost of Materials	Value Added by Manufacture	Value of Shipments	Capital Invest.
1982	266	275	80	11.6	9.6	18.2	161.8	6.66	492.6	256.1	753.8	24.0
1983		269	78	11.6	9.6	19.3	171.8	6.71	560.7	308.2	867.4	24.2
1984		263	76	10.2	8.5	18.4	153.4	6.43	550.8	307.3	851.1	24.6
1985		256	75	9.4	8.0	15.9	155.6	7.69	586.3	250.6	846.5	27.8
1986		248	76	9.3	7.9	15.3	168.0	8.25	591.1	293.8	873.7	31.3
1987	204	218	105	16.6	13.6	27.5	299.5	7.79	792.3	604.7	1,388.7	48.5
1988		475	109	15.8	12.7	26.0	293.2	8.05	732.3	679.2	1,392.5	34.7
1989		205	114	16.0	12.1	24.4	285.7	8.69	703.5	712.7	1,407.2	50.1
1990		268	113	17.0	12.3	24.5	288.6	8.95	786.9	812.3	1,594.8	40.0
1991		334	118	15.8	13.0	27.5	320.5	8.68	939.2	872.6	1,794.2	43.2
1992	154	168	107	16.0	13.1	28.5	343.8	9.02	1,751.6	824.5	2,570.4	60.2
1993		292	116	15.2	12.6	27.9	339.0	9.16	1,952.6	828.5	2,783.6	44.4
1994		272P	126P	20.0	16.4	34.6	442.8	9.27	2,121.2	981.7	3,100.7	104.7
1995		272P	130P	19.0P	15.2P	32.6P	417.4P	9.78P	1,981.1P	916.8P	2,895.9P	73.4P
1996		271P	135P	19.7P	15.7P	33.9P	439.4P	10.02P	2,112.0P	977.5P	3,087.3P	77.7P
1997		271P	139P	20.4P	16.3P	35.2P	461.4P	10.26P	2,243.0P	1,038.1P	3,278.8P	82.1P
1998		271P	143P	21.1P	16.8P	36.4P	483.5P	10.50P	2,374.0P	1,098.7P	3,470.2P	86.5P

Sources: 1982, 1987, 1992 *Economic Census*; *Annual Survey of Manufactures*, 83-86, 88-91, 93-94. Establishment counts for non-Census years are from *County Business Patterns*; establishment values for 83-84 are extrapolations. 'P's show projections by the editors. Industries reclassified in 87 will not have data for prior years.

INDICES OF CHANGE

Year	Companies	Establishments		Employment			Compensation		Production ($ million)			
		Total	with 20 or more employees	Total (000)	Production Workers (000)	Production Hours (Mil)	Payroll ($ mil)	Wages ($/hr)	Cost of Materials	Value Added by Manufacture	Value of Shipments	Capital Invest.
1982	173	164	75	73	73	64	47	74	28	31	29	40
1983		160	73	73	73	68	50	74	32	37	34	40
1984		157	71	64	65	65	45	71	31	37	33	41
1985		152	70	59	61	56	45	85	33	30	33	46
1986		148	71	58	60	54	49	91	34	36	34	52
1987	132	130	98	104	104	96	87	86	45	73	54	81
1988		283	102	99	97	91	85	89	42	82	54	58
1989		122	107	100	92	86	83	96	40	86	55	83
1990		160	106	106	94	86	84	99	45	99	62	66
1991		199	110	99	99	96	93	96	54	106	70	72
1992	100	100	100	100	100	100	100	100	100	100	100	100
1993		174	108	95	96	98	99	102	111	100	108	74
1994		162P	118P	125	125	121	129	103	121	119	121	174
1995		162P	122P	119P	116P	114P	121P	108P	113P	111P	113P	122P
1996		162P	126P	123P	120P	119P	128P	111P	121P	119P	120P	129P
1997		162P	130P	128P	124P	123P	134P	114P	128P	126P	128P	136P
1998		161P	134P	132P	128P	128P	141P	116P	136P	133P	135P	144P

Sources: Same as General Statistics. Values reflect change from the base year, 1992. Values above 100 mean greater than 92, values below 100 mean less than 92, and a value of 100 in the 82-91 or 93-98 period means same as 92. 'P's mark projections by the editors.

SELECTED RATIOS

For 1994	Avg. of All Manufact.	Analyzed Industry	Index
Employees per Establishment	49	74	150
Payroll per Establishment	1,500,273	1,629,484	109
Payroll per Employee	30,620	22,140	72
Production Workers per Establishment	34	60	176
Wages per Establishment	853,319	1,180,316	138
Wages per Production Worker	24,861	19,557	79
Hours per Production Worker	2,056	2,110	103
Wages per Hour	12.09	9.27	77
Value Added per Establishment	4,602,255	3,612,612	78
Value Added per Employee	93,930	49,085	52

For 1994	Avg. of All Manufact.	Analyzed Industry	Index
Value Added per Production Worker	134,084	59,860	45
Cost per Establishment	5,045,178	7,805,921	155
Cost per Employee	102,970	106,060	103
Cost per Production Worker	146,988	129,341	88
Shipments per Establishment	9,576,895	11,410,438	119
Shipments per Employee	195,460	155,035	79
Shipments per Production Worker	279,017	189,067	68
Investment per Establishment	321,011	385,291	120
Investment per Employee	6,552	5,235	80
Investment per Production Worker	9,352	6,384	68

Sources: Same as General Statistics. The 'Average of All Manufacturing' column represents the average of all manufacturing industries reported for the most recent complete year available. The Index shows the relationship between the Average and the Analyzed Industry. For example, 100 means that they are equal; 500 that the Analyzed Industry is five times the average; 50 means that the Analyzed Industry is half the national average. The abbreviation 'na' is used to show that data are 'not available'.

LEADING COMPANIES
Number shown: **43** Total sales ($ mil): **903** Total employment (000): **9.9**

Company Name	Address				CEO Name	Phone	Co. Type	Sales ($ mil)	Empl. (000)
Cranston Print Works Co	1381 Cranston St	Cranston	RI	02920	George W Shuster	401-943-4800	R	160*	1.8
Santee Print Works	19 Progress St	Sumter	SC	29153	Marty Barocas	803-773-1461	R	50	0.9
Cecil Saydah Co	2935 E 12th St	Los Angeles	CA	90023	Richard Saydah	213-263-9321	R	45*	0.3
Facemate Corp	5 W Main St	Chicopee	MA	01020	Walter Mrozinski	413-594-6661	R	45	0.3
Copland Fabrics Inc	PO Box 1208	Burlington	NC	27216	J R Copland III	919-226-0272	R	43	0.6
American Fast Print	PO Box 5765	Spartanburg	SC	29304	Jaroslav S Fryml	803-578-2020	R	40	0.7
Crazy Shirts Inc	99-969 Iwaena St	Aiea	HI	96701	R Ralston	808-487-9919	R	40	0.6
RA Briggs and Co	650 N Church St	Lake Zurich	IL	60047	Arnie Stevens	708-438-2345	D	40	0.5
Texprint Georgia Inc	2730 Weaver Rd	Macon	GA	31201	Mori Hideki	912-743-0321	R	38*	0.2
Cherokee Finishing Co	PO Box 1658	Spartanburg	SC	29304	Charles Davis	803-487-8200	D	35*	0.4
Cranston Print Works Co	Worster Rd	Webster	MA	01570	Andrew F Sylvia	508-943-0520	D	35	0.5
CS Crable Sportswear Inc	4101 Midland Blv	Batavia	OH	45103	John Hayden	513-753-3400	S	35	0.2
Spectrum Fabrics	267 5th Av	New York	NY	10016	Marjorie Hoyne	212-684-7100	D	32*	<0.1
North Carolina Finishing Co	PO Box 45	Spencer	NC	28159	FH Toney	704-636-3541	D	30	0.4
Perma Color Inc	PO Box 1439	Cleveland	TN	37364	Robert Kaplan	615-479-4102	S	27*	0.3
Bishopville Finishing	PO Box 472	Bishopville	SC	29010	Steve Dawson	803-484-5421	D	25	0.4
Holoubek Inc	W 238 N 1800	Waukesha	WI	53188	Verne R Holoubek	414-547-0500	R	18	0.2
Swan Finishing Company Inc	PO Box 1389	Fall River	MA	02721	P Guerriero	508-674-4611	R	18	0.3
Bradford Dyeing Association Inc	PO Box 539	Westerly	RI	02891	Michael Grills	401-377-2231	R	17*	0.3
Cyrus Clark Company Inc	267 5th Av	New York	NY	10016	Cyrus Clark III	212-684-5312	R	15	<0.1
Perma Glas-Mesh Inc	2201 Progress St	Dover	OH	44622	James Pellikan	216-343-4441	S	15	<0.1
Superba Print Works Inc	PO Box 297	Mooresville	NC	28115	Robert Fotsch	704-664-2711	S	15	0.3
Como Textile Prints Inc	191-195 E Railway	Paterson	NJ	07503	H Blanchfield	201-279-2950	R	13*	<0.1
Republic Converting Company	990 6th Av	New York	NY	10018	Murray Goldberg	212-564-5999	R	9	<0.1
Oxford Textile Inc	PO Box 90	Oxford	NJ	07863	Mario Guarriello Sr	908-453-2121	R	9*	0.2
Facemate PL-GF Inc	200 Main St	Somersworth	NH	03878	AH Jackson	603-692-3622	S	8*	<0.1
Graphic Prints Inc	16540 S Main St	Gardena	CA	90248	Alan Greenberg	310-768-0474	R	7*	<0.1
Tyca Corp	50 Sun St	Waltham	MA	02154	Franklin Hardy	617-891-1811	R	5	0.1
Coral Dyeing and Finishing Corp	555 E 31st St	Paterson	NJ	07513	F Dombrow	201-278-0272	R	4	<0.1
Ideal Textile Company Inc	2425 E 30th St	Vernon	CA	90058	Mark Mosch	213-236-9700	R	4*	<0.1
Nu Quaker Dyeing Inc	320 S 16th St	Easton	PA	18042	William J Guffy	215-258-7264	R	4	<0.1
Crantex Fabrics	469 7th Av	New York	NY	10018	George Shuster	212-967-0770	D	3*	<0.1
JBJ Fabrics Inc	151 W 40th St	New York	NY	10018	Michael Garson	212-382-1500	R	3*	<0.1
Mesa Cutting Corp	601 W 26th St	New York	NY	10001	Clifford Moss	212-366-5318	R	3*	<0.1
Alvarado Dye House Inc	30542 Union City	Union City	CA	94587	Steven Lieberman	510-471-7888	R	2	<0.1
Bank Miller Company Inc	55 W 39th St	New York	NY	10018	Larry Eisendthat	212-869-3916	R	2*	<0.1
Eyecatcher Screen Printing	1301 E El Segundo	El Segundo	CA	90245	Doug Davidge	310-615-0173	R	2*	<0.1
Poughkeepsie Finishing Corp	48 E 5th St	Paterson	NJ	07524	Myron Feldman	201-279-1451	R	2	<0.1
Lawrence Textile Shrinking Co	PO Box 1016	Lawrence	MA	01841	Thomas A Benigno	508-687-7145	R	2*	<0.1
Key West Hand Print	201 Simonton St	Key West	FL	33040	Danio Bazo	305-294-9535	R	2	<0.1
Textile Graphics Inc	1719 Lafayette Av	McMinnville	OR	97128	Jeff Chapman	503-245-6090	R	1	<0.1
Coudray Graphic Technologies	825 Capitolio Way	S L Obispo	CA	93401	Mark Coudray	805-541-1586	R	1*	<0.1
Dek Tillett Ltd	PO Box 760	Sheffield	MA	01257	Dek Tillett	413-229-8764	R	1	<0.1

Source: *Ward's Business Directory of U.S. Private and Public Companies*, Volumes 1 and 2, 1996. The company type code used is as follows: P - Public, R - Private, S - Subsidiary, D - Division, J - Joint Venture, A - Affiliate, G - Group. Sales are in millions of dollars, employees are in thousands. An asterisk (*) indicates an estimated sales volume. The symbol < stands for 'less than'. Company names and addresses are truncated, in some cases, to fit into the available space.

MATERIALS CONSUMED

Material		Quantity	Delivered Cost ($ million)
Materials, ingredients, containers, and supplies		(X)	1,648.3
Spun yarn, all fibers	mil lb	(D)	(D)
Broadwoven fabrics	mil sq yd	1,801.9	1,230.3
Knit fabrics	mil lb	(D)	(D)
Dyes, lakes, and toners		(X)	295.9
All other materials and components, parts, containers, and supplies		(X)	86.3
Materials, ingredients, containers, and supplies, nsk		(X)	20.4

Source: 1992 *Economic Census*. Explanation of symbols used: (D): Withheld to avoid disclosure of competitive data; na: Not available; (S): Withheld because statistical norms were not met; (X): Not applicable; (Z): Less than half the unit shown; nec: Not elsewhere classified; nsk: Not specified by kind; - : zero; * : 10-19 percent estimated; ** : 20-29 percent estimated.

PRODUCT SHARE DETAILS

Product or Product Class	% Share
Finishing plants, cotton	100.00
Finished cotton broadwoven fabrics (not finished in weaving mills)	68.39
Job or commission finishing of cotton broadwoven fabrics	31.40

Source: 1992 *Economic Census*. The values shown are percent of total shipments in an industry. Values of indented subcategories are summed in the main heading. The symbol (D) appears when data are withheld to prevent disclosure of competitive information. The abbreviation nsk stands for 'not specified by kind' and nec for 'not elsewhere classified'.

INPUTS AND OUTPUTS FOR KNIT FABRIC MILLS

Economic Sector or Industry Providing Inputs	%	Sector	Economic Sector or Industry Buying Outputs	%	Sector
Yarn mills & finishing of textiles, nec	24.0	Manufg.	Apparel made from purchased materials	79.8	Manufg.
Organic fibers, noncellulosic	22.2	Manufg.	Knit fabric mills	10.6	Manufg.
Knit fabric mills	14.4	Manufg.	Personal consumption expenditures	5.1	
Cellulosic manmade fibers	8.1	Manufg.	Knit outerwear mills	2.0	Manufg.
Wholesale trade	4.8	Trade	Exports	1.7	Foreign
Surface active agents	4.0	Manufg.	Knitting mills, nec	0.2	Manufg.
Miscellaneous plastics products	2.7	Manufg.	Coated fabrics, not rubberized	0.1	Manufg.
Electric services (utilities)	2.5	Util.	Knit underwear mills	0.1	Manufg.
Petroleum refining	2.1	Manufg.	Leather gloves & mittens	0.1	Manufg.
Cyclic crudes and organics	1.7	Manufg.			
Gas production & distribution (utilities)	1.6	Util.			
Textile machinery	1.5	Manufg.			
Motor freight transportation & warehousing	1.2	Util.			
Industrial gases	0.7	Manufg.			
Imports	0.7	Foreign			
Cotton	0.6	Agric.			
Equipment rental & leasing services	0.5	Services			
Laundry, dry cleaning, shoe repair	0.5	Services			
Air transportation	0.4	Util.			
Real estate	0.4	Fin/R.E.			
Paperboard containers & boxes	0.3	Manufg.			
Communications, except radio & TV	0.3	Util.			
Banking	0.3	Fin/R.E.			
U.S. Postal Service	0.3	Gov't			
Maintenance of nonfarm buildings nec	0.2	Constr.			
Ball & roller bearings	0.2	Manufg.			
Industrial inorganic chemicals, nec	0.2	Manufg.			
Lubricating oils & greases	0.2	Manufg.			
Sanitary services, steam supply, irrigation	0.2	Util.			
Eating & drinking places	0.2	Trade			
Automotive rental & leasing, without drivers	0.2	Services			
Computer & data processing services	0.2	Services			
Detective & protective services	0.2	Services			
State & local government enterprises, nec	0.2	Gov't			
Paper coating & glazing	0.1	Manufg.			
Railroads & related services	0.1	Util.			
Insurance carriers	0.1	Fin/R.E.			
Advertising	0.1	Services			
Automotive repair shops & services	0.1	Services			
Hotels & lodging places	0.1	Services			

Source: Benchmark Input-Output Accounts for the U.S. Economy, 1982, U.S. Department of Commerce, Washington, D.C., July 1991. Data, as reported in the source, are organized by the 1977 SIC structure in use in 1982 but have been matched, as closely as is possible, to the 1987 SIC structure used in this book.

OCCUPATIONS EMPLOYED BY SIC 226 - WEAVING, FINISHING, YARN AND THREAD MILLS

Occupation	% of Total 1994	Change to 2005	Occupation	% of Total 1994	Change to 2005
Textile draw-out & winding machine operators	32.8	-35.5	Machine feeders & offbearers	2.6	-27.4
Industrial machinery mechanics	6.4	29.1	Machine operators nec	2.2	-28.9
Textile machine setters & set-up operators	4.9	-11.3	Sewing machine operators, non-garment	1.8	21.0
Helpers, laborers, & material movers nec	4.5	-19.3	Industrial truck & tractor operators	1.6	-19.3
Blue collar worker supervisors	4.2	-24.6	Hand packers & packagers	1.3	-30.9
Inspectors, testers, & graders, precision	4.2	-27.4	General managers & top executives	1.3	-23.5
Textile bleaching & dyeing machine operators	4.2	8.9	Maintenance repairers, general utility	1.2	-27.4
Freight, stock, & material movers, hand	2.8	-35.5	Janitors & cleaners, incl maids	1.0	-35.5

Source: Industry-Occupation Matrix, Bureau of Labor Statistics. These data relate to one or more 3-digit SIC industry groups rather than to a single 4-digit SIC. The change reported for each occupation to the year 2005 is a percent of growth or decline as estimated by the Bureau of Labor Statistics. The abbreviation nec stands for 'not elsewhere classified'.

LOCATION BY STATE AND REGIONAL CONCENTRATION

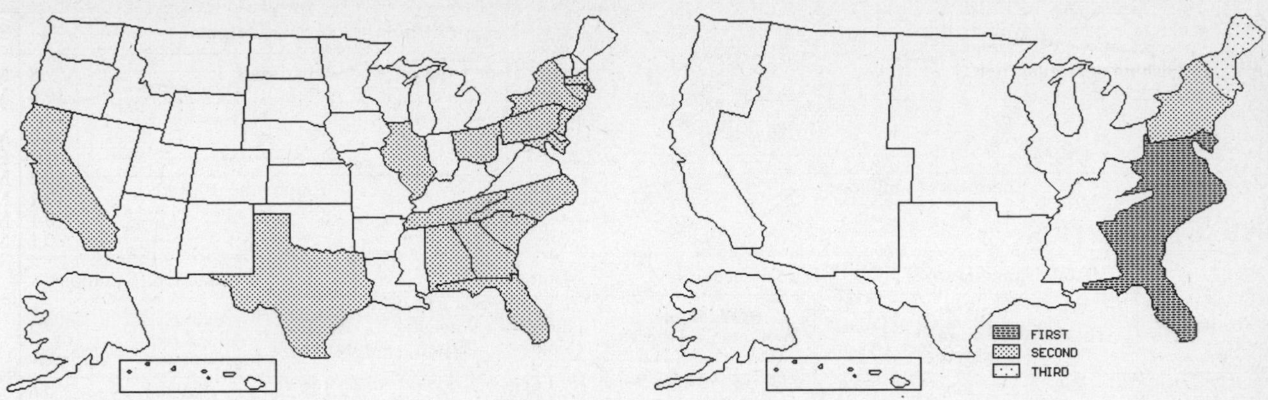

INDUSTRY DATA BY STATE

State	Establish-ments	Shipments			Employment				Cost as % of Shipments	Investment per Employee ($)
		Total ($ mil)	% of U.S.	Per Establ.	Total Number	% of U.S.	Per Establ.	Wages ($/hour)		
South Carolina	24	1,397.3	54.4	58.2	5,500	34.4	229	9.34	75.0	4,582
North Carolina	15	273.4	10.6	18.2	2,400	15.0	160	9.22	56.3	3,083
Georgia	10	206.4	8.0	20.6	1,600	10.0	160	7.43	65.5	-
Massachusetts	7	137.2	5.3	19.6	1,100	6.9	157	10.73	63.1	-
Rhode Island	8	64.8	2.5	8.1	700	4.4	88	11.00	43.1	-
California	10	39.0	1.5	3.9	300	1.9	30	8.33	59.7	1,333
New Jersey	8	31.9	1.2	4.0	400	2.5	50	10.50	44.2	2,250
New York	15	30.6	1.2	2.0	400	2.5	27	8.57	41.5	1,000
Pennsylvania	13	23.2	0.9	1.8	300	1.9	23	10.17	25.9	7,000
Florida	12	(D)	-	-	375 *	2.3	31	-	-	-
Alabama	5	(D)	-	-	375 *	2.3	75	-	-	-
Tennessee	5	(D)	-	-	175 *	1.1	35	-	-	-
Maryland	3	(D)	-	-	375 *	2.3	125	-	-	-
Ohio	3	(D)	-	-	175 *	1.1	58	-	-	-
Connecticut	2	(D)	-	-	175 *	1.1	88	-	-	-
Illinois	2	(D)	-	-	175 *	1.1	88	-	-	-
Texas	2	(D)	-	-	750 *	4.7	375	-	-	-

Source: 1992 *Economic Census*. The states are in descending order of shipments or establishments (if shipment data are missing for the majority). The symbol (D) appears when data are withheld to prevent disclosure of competitive information. States marked with (D) are sorted by number of establishments. A dash (-) indicates that the data element cannot be calculated; * indicates the midpoint of a range.

2262 - FINISHING PLANTS, MANMADE

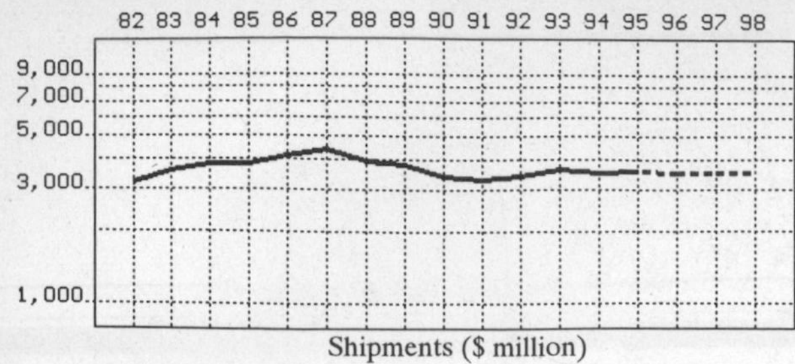

Shipments ($ million)

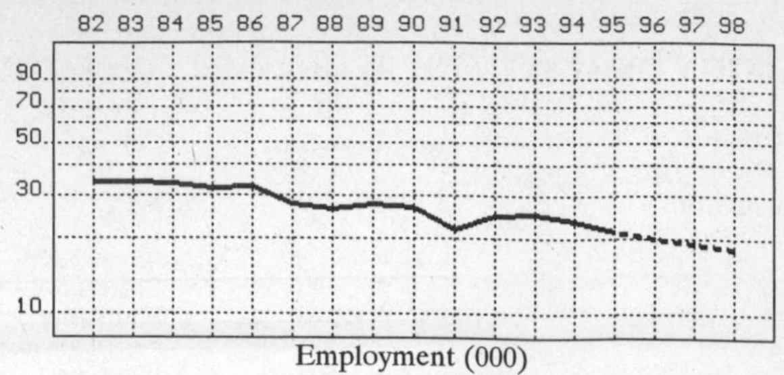

Employment (000)

GENERAL STATISTICS

Year	Companies	Establishments: Total	Establishments: with 20 or more employees	Employment: Total (000)	Employment: Production Workers (000)	Employment: Production Hours (Mil)	Compensation: Payroll ($ mil)	Compensation: Wages ($/hr)	Production ($ million): Cost of Materials	Production ($ million): Value Added by Manufacture	Production ($ million): Value of Shipments	Production ($ million): Capital Invest.
1982	265	296	166	34.4	27.8	55.7	514.8	6.73	2,173.3	999.0	3,186.2	79.0
1983		284	160	34.5	27.9	59.6	578.1	7.12	2,417.2	1,191.2	3,609.9	106.7
1984		272	154	33.9	27.5	56.8	577.2	7.40	2,545.4	1,290.2	3,822.2	105.4
1985		260	147	32.0	25.8	52.9	573.2	7.85	2,600.3	1,129.8	3,787.8	74.5
1986		241	145	32.8	26.6	55.8	605.4	7.80	2,826.6	1,269.6	4,132.1	123.0
1987	245	268	123	27.9	22.3	47.4	545.9	8.17	3,183.3	1,265.2	4,405.8	98.5
1988		261	131	26.6	21.6	45.9	531.8	8.40	2,650.1	1,305.0	3,962.7	96.9
1989		259	129	27.6	19.2	41.1	502.5	8.74	2,584.8	1,239.0	3,822.2	86.7
1990		262	126	26.9	17.9	38.4	486.8	9.00	2,284.2	1,109.7	3,400.9	72.0
1991		277	126	21.7	17.7	39.4	505.8	9.05	1,989.7	1,301.0	3,280.5	80.6
1992	163	180	131	24.9	19.8	43.8	599.9	9.54	1,909.2	1,530.7	3,432.5	104.4
1993		195	124	25.2	20.3	44.4	620.0	9.83	2,003.6	1,625.4	3,628.9	112.2
1994		210P	114P	23.6	18.8	41.6	630.7	10.42	1,835.0	1,659.3	3,484.4	100.7
1995		203P	111P	21.3P	16.1P	36.6P	579.1P	10.42P	1,877.0P	1,697.3P	3,564.2P	97.7P
1996		196P	107P	20.3P	15.2P	35.0P	581.9P	10.70P	1,867.7P	1,688.8P	3,546.4P	98.0P
1997		190P	103P	19.2P	14.3P	33.4P	584.8P	10.98P	1,858.3P	1,680.3P	3,528.6P	98.3P
1998		183P	99P	18.2P	13.3P	31.7P	587.6P	11.26P	1,848.9P	1,671.9P	3,510.8P	98.6P

Sources: 1982, 1987, 1992 *Economic Census*; *Annual Survey of Manufactures*, 83-86, 88-91, 93-94. Establishment counts for non-Census years are from *County Business Patterns*; establishment values for 83-84 are extrapolations. 'P's show projections by the editors. Industries reclassified in 87 will not have data for prior years.

INDICES OF CHANGE

Year	Companies	Establishments: Total	Establishments: with 20 or more employees	Employment: Total (000)	Employment: Production Workers (000)	Employment: Production Hours (Mil)	Compensation: Payroll ($ mil)	Compensation: Wages ($/hr)	Production ($ million): Cost of Materials	Production ($ million): Value Added by Manufacture	Production ($ million): Value of Shipments	Production ($ million): Capital Invest.
1982	163	164	127	138	140	127	86	71	114	65	93	76
1983		158	122	139	141	136	96	75	127	78	105	102
1984		151	118	136	139	130	96	78	133	84	111	101
1985		144	112	129	130	121	96	82	136	74	110	71
1986		134	111	132	134	127	101	82	148	83	120	118
1987	150	149	94	112	113	108	91	86	167	83	128	94
1988		145	100	107	109	105	89	88	139	85	115	93
1989		144	98	111	97	94	84	92	135	81	111	83
1990		146	96	108	90	88	81	94	120	72	99	69
1991		154	96	87	89	90	84	95	104	85	96	77
1992	100	100	100	100	100	100	100	100	100	100	100	100
1993		108	95	101	103	101	103	103	105	106	106	107
1994		117P	87P	95	95	95	105	109	96	108	102	96
1995		113P	84P	86P	81P	84P	97P	109P	98P	111P	104P	94P
1996		109P	82P	81P	77P	80P	97P	112P	98P	110P	103P	94P
1997		105P	79P	77P	72P	76P	97P	115P	97P	110P	103P	94P
1998		102P	76P	73P	67P	72P	98P	118P	97P	109P	102P	94P

Sources: Same as General Statistics. Values reflect change from the base year, 1992. Values above 100 mean greater than 92, values below 100 mean less than 92, and a value of 100 in the 82-91 or 93-98 period means same as 92. 'P's mark projections by the editors.

SELECTED RATIOS

For 1994	Avg. of All Manufact.	Analyzed Industry	Index
Employees per Establishment	49	112	229
Payroll per Establishment	1,500,273	3,001,168	200
Payroll per Employee	30,620	26,725	87
Production Workers per Establishment	34	89	261
Wages per Establishment	853,319	2,062,664	242
Wages per Production Worker	24,861	23,057	93
Hours per Production Worker	2,056	2,213	108
Wages per Hour	12.09	10.42	86
Value Added per Establishment	4,602,255	7,895,732	172
Value Added per Employee	93,930	70,309	75

For 1994	Avg. of All Manufact.	Analyzed Industry	Index
Value Added per Production Worker	134,084	88,261	66
Cost per Establishment	5,045,178	8,731,795	173
Cost per Employee	102,970	77,754	76
Cost per Production Worker	146,988	97,606	66
Shipments per Establishment	9,576,895	16,580,418	173
Shipments per Employee	195,460	147,644	76
Shipments per Production Worker	279,017	185,340	66
Investment per Establishment	321,011	479,178	149
Investment per Employee	6,552	4,267	65
Investment per Production Worker	9,352	5,356	57

Sources: Same as General Statistics. The 'Average of All Manufacturing' column represents the average of all manufacturing industries reported for the most recent complete year available. The Index shows the relationship between the Average and the Analyzed Industry. For example, 100 means that they are equal; 500 that the Analyzed Industry is five times the average; 50 means that the Analyzed Industry is half the national average. The abbreviation 'na' is used to show that data are 'not available'.

LEADING COMPANIES

Number shown: **17** Total sales ($ mil): **148** Total employment (000): **1.8**

Company Name	Address				CEO Name	Phone	Co. Type	Sales ($ mil)	Empl. (000)
Amerbelle Corp	PO Box 150	Vernon	CT	06066	Alan R Schwedel	203-875-3325	R	25	0.3
Kenyon Industries Inc	PO Box 147	Kenyon	RI	02836	Geraldine Kubik	401-364-7761	S	25	0.4
Champagne Dye Works Inc	PO Box 716	Asheboro	NC	27203	EJ Dombrowski	910-672-2164	R	18	0.2
J and J Flock Products Inc	1150 Centre St	Easton	PA	18044	Earl Jaskol	215-252-6181	R	17	0.1
Yates Bleachery Co	PO Box 800	Flintstone	GA	30725	Pierce A Yates	706-820-1531	R	15	0.3
Amatex Corp	1032 Stanbridge St	Norristown	PA	19401	Richard C Howard	610-277-6100	R	10	<0.1
Trio Dyeing and Finishing	440 E 22nd St	Paterson	NJ	07509	Mark Bleender	201-279-5538	R	9*	0.1
Spinnerin Inc	30 Wesley St	S Hackensack	NJ	07606	Jerry W Finney	201-343-5900	S	8	<0.1
Hemmerich Industries Inc	PO Box 286	Denver	PA	17517	Peter Hemmerich	215-267-7594	R	5	0.1
Quip Industries Inc	18th & Jefferson Sts	Carlyle	IL	62231	J Bolk	618-594-2437	R	5	<0.1
Crown Prince Inc	PO Box 37	Brookfield	WI	53008	Richard Yellen	414-783-2200	R	3*	<0.1
Yarnell Group	48 W 38th St	New York	NY	10018	Marvin Yarnell	212-819-1270	R	3*	<0.1
Kent-Bragaline Inc	27-35 Jackson Av	Long Island Ct	NY	11101	Edward Bragaline	718-784-2012	R	2*	<0.1
H and W Shoe Supplies Co	271 Livingston St	Northvale	NJ	07647	Francis Wershing	201-768-7100	R	1	<0.1
PM Design Corp	61 Willett St	Passaic	NJ	07055	Edward Goldfarb	201-471-7706	R	1	<0.1
Paw Prints of California	3166 Bay Rd	Redwood City	CA	94063	GA Eston	415-365-4077	R	1	<0.1
Aerolyn Fabrics Inc	900 Passaic Av	East Newark	NJ	07029	Mark J Macrini	201-483-7288	R	0	<0.1

Source: *Ward's Business Directory of U.S. Private and Public Companies*, Volumes 1 and 2, 1996. The company type code used is as follows: P - Public, R - Private, S - Subsidiary, D - Division, J - Joint Venture, A - Affiliate, G - Group. Sales are in millions of dollars, employees are in thousands. An asterisk (*) indicates an estimated sales volume. The symbol < stands for 'less than'. Company names and addresses are truncated, in some cases, to fit into the available space.

MATERIALS CONSUMED

Material		Quantity	Delivered Cost ($ million)
Materials, ingredients, containers, and supplies		(X)	1,693.5
Spun yarn, all fibers	mil lb	(D)	(D)
Broadwoven fabrics	mil sq yd	1,383.4**	1,006.8
Knit fabrics	mil lb	(D)	(D)
Dyes, lakes, and toners		(X)	380.7
All other materials and components, parts, containers, and supplies		(X)	249.4
Materials, ingredients, containers, and supplies, nsk		(X)	11.1

Source: 1992 *Economic Census*. Explanation of symbols used: (D): Withheld to avoid disclosure of competitive data; na: Not available; (S): Withheld because statistical norms were not met; (X): Not applicable; (Z): Less than half the unit shown; nec: Not elsewhere classified; nsk: Not specified by kind; - : zero; * : 10-19 percent estimated; ** : 20-29 percent estimated.

PRODUCT SHARE DETAILS

Product or Product Class	% Share
Finishing plants, manmade fiber and silk	100.00
Finished manmade fiber and silk broadwoven fabrics (not finished in weaving mills)	60.50
Finished manmade fiber and silk broadwoven fabrics (not finished in weaving mills), 85 percent or more spun yarn fibers, plain weave (except pile), print cloth	9.62
Finished manmade fiber and silk broadwoven fabrics (not finished in weaving mills), 85 percent or more spun yarn fibers, plain weave (except pile), poplin and broadcloth, carded and combed	(D)
Finished manmade fiber and silk broadwoven fabrics (not finished in weaving mills), 85 percent or more spun yarn fibers, plain weave (except pile), sheeting, including bedsheeting and osnaburgs	(D)
Finished manmade fiber and silk broadwoven fabrics (not finished in weaving mills), 85 percent or more spun yarn fibers, plain weave (except pile), lawns, voiles, and batistes	(D)
Finished manmade fiber and silk broadwoven fabrics (not finished in weaving mills), 85 percent or more spun yarn fibers, plain weave (except pile), other types	3.10
Finished manmade fiber and silk broadwoven fabrics (not finished in weaving mills), 85 percent or more spun yarn fibers, twill weave (except pile)	10.15
Finished manmade fiber and silk broadwoven fabrics (not finished in weaving mills), 85 percent or more spun yarn fibers, other weaves (except pile), sateens	1.39
Other finished manmade fiber and silk broadwoven fabrics (not finished in weaving mills), 85 percent or more spun yarn fibers, other weaves (except pile), incl. oxfords, table damask, jacquard, etc.	16.96
Finished manmade fiber and silk broadwoven fabrics (not finished in weaving mills), 85 percent or more spun yarn fibers, pile fabrics (velvets, plushes, corduroy, and others)	3.84
Finished manmade fiber and silk broadwoven fabrics (not finished in weaving mills), 85 percent or more filament yarn fabrics, chiefly rayon and/or acetate	(D)
Finished manmade fiber and silk broadwoven fabrics (not finished in weaving mills), 85 percent or more filament yarn fabrics, chiefly polyester	17.84
Finished manmade fiber and silk broadwoven fabrics (not finished in weaving mills), 85 percent or more filament yarn fabrics, other	7.74
Finished manmade fiber and silk broadwoven fabrics (not finished in weaving mills), other fabrics, including combinations of spun yarn and filament	(D)
Finished manmade fiber and silk broadwoven fabrics (not finished in weaving mills), nsk	1.04
Manmade fiber and silk, job or commission finishing of manmade broadwoven fabrics	39.29
Plain weave (except pile), print cloth	26.73
Plain weave (except pile), poplin and broadcloth	4.07
Plain weave (except pile), sheeting, including bedsheeting and osnaburgs	6.82
Plain weave (except pile), lawns, voiles, and batistes	(D)
Plain weave (except pile), other types	3.19
Twill weave (except pile)	3.35
Other weaves (except pile), sateens	(D)
Other weaves (except pile), including oxfords, table damask, jacquard, etc.	1.47
Pile fabrics (velvets, plushes, corduroy, and others)	(D)
85 percent or more filament yarn fabrics, chiefly rayon or acetate	22.48
85 percent or more filament yarn fabrics, chiefly polyester	14.89
85 percent or more filament yarn fabrics, other	6.38
Other fabrics, including combinations of spun yarn and filament, blends with wool, and blends with silk	1.64
Job or commission finishing of manmade fiber and silk broadwoven fabrics, nsk	3.38
Finishing plants, manmade fiber and silk, nsk	0.21

Source: 1992 *Economic Census*. The values shown are percent of total shipments in an industry. Values of indented subcategories are summed in the main heading. The symbol (D) appears when data are withheld to prevent disclosure of competitive information. The abbreviation nsk stands for 'not specified by kind' and nec for 'not elsewhere classified'.

INPUTS AND OUTPUTS FOR KNIT FABRIC MILLS

Economic Sector or Industry Providing Inputs	%	Sector	Economic Sector or Industry Buying Outputs	%	Sector
Yarn mills & finishing of textiles, nec	24.0	Manufg.	Apparel made from purchased materials	79.8	Manufg.
Organic fibers, noncellulosic	22.2	Manufg.	Knit fabric mills	10.6	Manufg.
Knit fabric mills	14.4	Manufg.	Personal consumption expenditures	5.1	
Cellulosic manmade fibers	8.1	Manufg.	Knit outerwear mills	2.0	Manufg.
Wholesale trade	4.8	Trade	Exports	1.7	Foreign
Surface active agents	4.0	Manufg.	Knitting mills, nec	0.2	Manufg.
Miscellaneous plastics products	2.7	Manufg.	Coated fabrics, not rubberized	0.1	Manufg.
Electric services (utilities)	2.5	Util.	Knit underwear mills	0.1	Manufg.
Petroleum refining	2.1	Manufg.	Leather gloves & mittens	0.1	Manufg.
Cyclic crudes and organics	1.7	Manufg.			
Gas production & distribution (utilities)	1.6	Util.			
Textile machinery	1.5	Manufg.			
Motor freight transportation & warehousing	1.2	Util.			
Industrial gases	0.7	Manufg.			
Imports	0.7	Foreign			
Cotton	0.6	Agric.			
Equipment rental & leasing services	0.5	Services			
Laundry, dry cleaning, shoe repair	0.5	Services			
Air transportation	0.4	Util.			
Real estate	0.4	Fin/R.E.			
Paperboard containers & boxes	0.3	Manufg.			
Communications, except radio & TV	0.3	Util.			
Banking	0.3	Fin/R.E.			
U.S. Postal Service	0.3	Gov't			
Maintenance of nonfarm buildings nec	0.2	Constr.			
Ball & roller bearings	0.2	Manufg.			
Industrial inorganic chemicals, nec	0.2	Manufg.			
Lubricating oils & greases	0.2	Manufg.			
Sanitary services, steam supply, irrigation	0.2	Util.			
Eating & drinking places	0.2	Trade			
Automotive rental & leasing, without drivers	0.2	Services			
Computer & data processing services	0.2	Services			
Detective & protective services	0.2	Services			
State & local government enterprises, nec	0.2	Gov't			
Paper coating & glazing	0.1	Manufg.			
Railroads & related services	0.1	Util.			
Insurance carriers	0.1	Fin/R.E.			
Advertising	0.1	Services			
Automotive repair shops & services	0.1	Services			
Hotels & lodging places	0.1	Services			

Source: Benchmark Input-Output Accounts for the U.S. Economy, 1982, U.S. Department of Commerce, Washington, D.C., July 1991. Data, as reported in the source, are organized by the 1977 SIC structure in use in 1982 but have been matched, as closely as is possible, to the 1987 SIC structure used in this book.

OCCUPATIONS EMPLOYED BY SIC 226 - WEAVING, FINISHING, YARN AND THREAD MILLS

Occupation	% of Total 1994	Change to 2005	Occupation	% of Total 1994	Change to 2005
Textile draw-out & winding machine operators	32.8	-35.5	Machine feeders & offbearers	2.6	-27.4
Industrial machinery mechanics	6.4	29.1	Machine operators nec	2.2	-28.9
Textile machine setters & set-up operators	4.9	-11.3	Sewing machine operators, non-garment	1.8	21.0
Helpers, laborers, & material movers nec	4.5	-19.3	Industrial truck & tractor operators	1.6	-19.3
Blue collar worker supervisors	4.2	-24.6	Hand packers & packagers	1.3	-30.9
Inspectors, testers, & graders, precision	4.2	-27.4	General managers & top executives	1.3	-23.5
Textile bleaching & dyeing machine operators	4.2	8.9	Maintenance repairers, general utility	1.2	-27.4
Freight, stock, & material movers, hand	2.8	-35.5	Janitors & cleaners, incl maids	1.0	-35.5

Source: Industry-Occupation Matrix, Bureau of Labor Statistics. These data relate to one or more 3-digit SIC industry groups rather than to a single 4-digit SIC. The change reported for each occupation to the year 2005 is a percent of growth or decline as estimated by the Bureau of Labor Statistics. The abbreviation nec stands for 'not elsewhere classified'.

LOCATION BY STATE AND REGIONAL CONCENTRATION

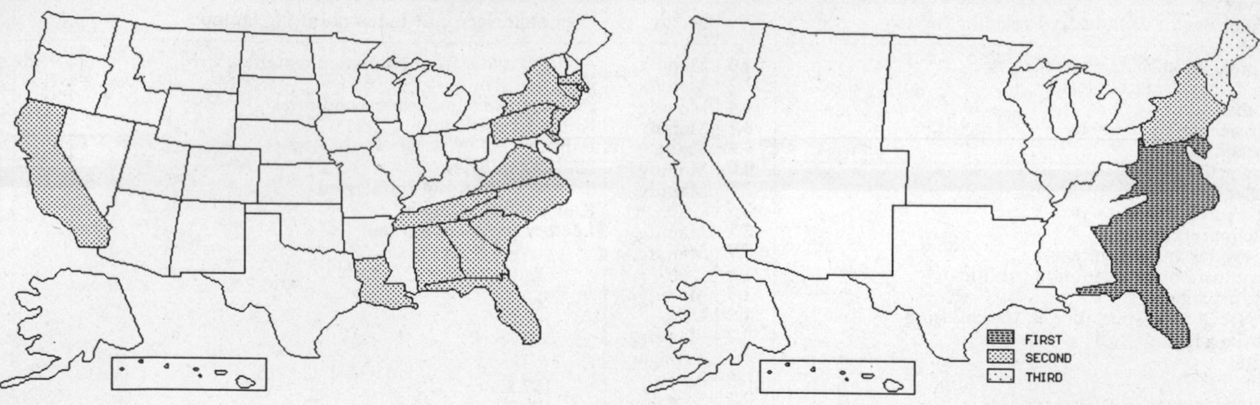

INDUSTRY DATA BY STATE

State	Establish-ments	Shipments			Employment				Cost as % of Shipments	Investment per Employee ($)
		Total ($ mil)	% of U.S.	Per Establ.	Total Number	% of U.S.	Per Establ.	Wages ($/hour)		
South Carolina	20	915.5	26.7	45.8	7,300	29.3	365	9.41	55.6	3,740
North Carolina	25	889.4	25.9	35.6	5,200	20.9	208	8.99	72.2	4,288
New Jersey	29	281.3	8.2	9.7	2,700	10.8	93	12.56	40.5	2,926
Massachusetts	13	256.5	7.5	19.7	2,400	9.6	185	10.27	37.9	6,167
Georgia	7	156.3	4.6	22.3	1,200	4.8	171	8.24	48.1	2,583
California	18	81.9	2.4	4.6	900	3.6	50	9.87	48.5	4,222
Connecticut	4	80.2	2.3	20.0	500	2.0	125	11.56	71.6	5,400
Pennsylvania	9	69.7	2.0	7.7	500	2.0	56	9.89	58.8	3,800
New York	10	67.8	2.0	6.8	700	2.8	70	8.40	60.3	3,571
Rhode Island	3	47.1	1.4	15.7	500	2.0	167	8.50	39.7	-
Florida	4	(D)	-	-	175 *	0.7	44	-	-	-
Alabama	2	(D)	-	-	750 *	3.0	375	-	-	-
Tennessee	2	(D)	-	-	175 *	0.7	88	-	-	-
Virginia	2	(D)	-	-	1,750 *	7.0	875	-	-	-
Delaware	1	(D)	-	-	175 *	0.7	175	-	-	-
Louisiana	1	(D)	-	-	375 *	1.5	375	-	-	-

Source: 1992 *Economic Census*. The states are in descending order of shipments or establishments (if shipment data are missing for the majority). The symbol (D) appears when data are withheld to prevent disclosure of competitive information. States marked with (D) are sorted by number of establishments. A dash (-) indicates that the data element cannot be calculated; * indicates the midpoint of a range.

2269 - FINISHING PLANTS, NEC

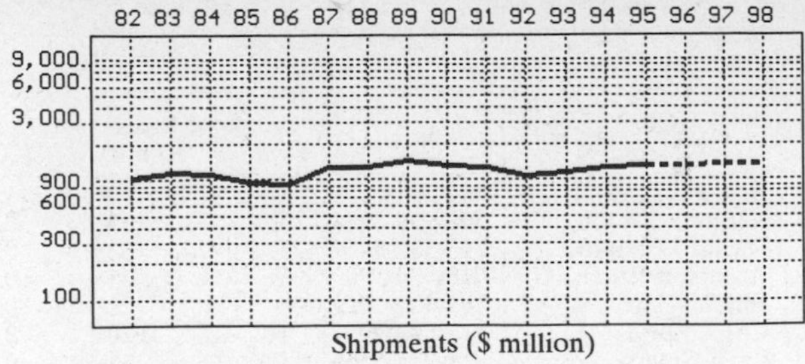

Shipments ($ million)

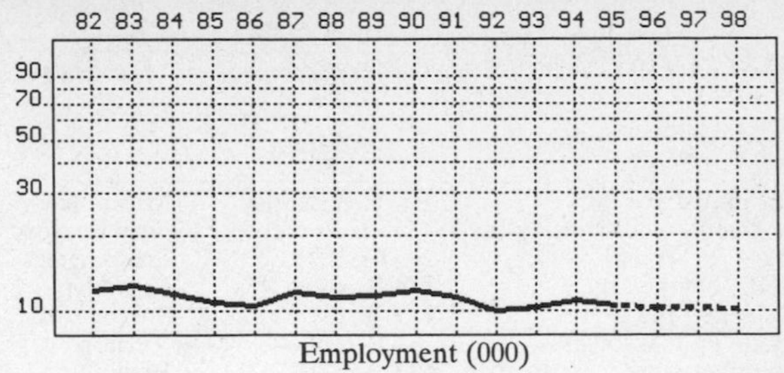

Employment (000)

GENERAL STATISTICS

Year	Com-panies	Establishments		Employment			Compensation		Production ($ million)			
		Total	with 20 or more employees	Total (000)	Production Workers (000)	Production Hours (Mil)	Payroll ($ mil)	Wages ($/hr)	Cost of Materials	Value Added by Manufacture	Value of Shipments	Capital Invest.
1982	177	182	107	12.0	10.0	19.7	157.3	5.64	685.1	335.1	1,031.9	15.1
1983		179	105	12.6	10.3	20.6	178.7	6.29	778.4	399.6	1,164.5	14.8
1984		176	103	11.7	9.8	19.7	163.6	5.96	676.6	422.4	1,098.7	21.2
1985		174	102	10.8	9.1	18.3	158.3	6.18	593.2	377.2	966.7	16.9
1986		168	100	10.5	8.9	17.9	162.2	6.47	585.9	323.3	908.0	20.5
1987	175	183	94	11.8	9.8	20.2	192.7	6.89	816.3	468.5	1,267.5	25.8
1988		180	96	11.4	9.6	19.9	191.5	7.07	844.6	408.4	1,248.0	25.4
1989		174	95	11.5	11.4	23.8	235.7	7.22	943.4	525.1	1,449.9	42.0
1990		172	99	12.0	10.6	22.5	222.5	7.23	864.5	443.6	1,308.1	26.2
1991		175	95	11.3	9.8	21.1	219.6	7.66	815.7	466.9	1,285.7	26.8
1992	123	133	87	9.9	8.4	17.6	196.2	8.15	648.7	426.3	1,074.6	23.6
1993		156	99	10.2	8.7	18.4	209.1	8.35	720.0	448.0	1,169.1	28.4
1994		155P	91P	10.9	9.4	19.3	285.9	9.52	702.3	575.4	1,270.2	43.8
1995		153P	90P	10.4P	9.3P	19.9P	251.9P	9.00P	718.4P	588.6P	1,299.3P	37.2P
1996		150P	89P	10.3P	9.2P	19.9P	259.6P	9.26P	728.4P	596.8P	1,317.4P	38.9P
1997		148P	87P	10.2P	9.2P	19.9P	267.3P	9.53P	738.4P	605.0P	1,335.5P	40.6P
1998		145P	86P	10.1P	9.1P	19.9P	275.0P	9.80P	748.4P	613.2P	1,353.6P	42.3P

Sources: 1982, 1987, 1992 *Economic Census*; *Annual Survey of Manufactures*, 83-86, 88-91, 93-94. Establishment counts for non-Census years are from *County Business Patterns*; establishment values for 83-84 are extrapolations. 'P's show projections by the editors. Industries reclassified in 87 will not have data for prior years.

INDICES OF CHANGE

Year	Com-panies	Establishments		Employment			Compensation		Production ($ million)			
		Total	with 20 or more employees	Total (000)	Production Workers (000)	Production Hours (Mil)	Payroll ($ mil)	Wages ($/hr)	Cost of Materials	Value Added by Manufacture	Value of Shipments	Capital Invest.
1982	144	137	123	121	119	112	80	69	106	79	96	64
1983		135	121	127	123	117	91	77	120	94	108	63
1984		132	118	118	117	112	83	73	104	99	102	90
1985		131	117	109	108	104	81	76	91	88	90	72
1986		126	115	106	106	102	83	79	90	76	84	87
1987	142	138	108	119	117	115	98	85	126	110	118	109
1988		135	110	115	114	113	98	87	130	96	116	108
1989		131	109	116	136	135	120	89	145	123	135	178
1990		129	114	121	126	128	113	89	133	104	122	111
1991		132	109	114	117	120	112	94	126	110	120	114
1992	100	100	100	100	100	100	100	100	100	100	100	100
1993		117	114	103	104	105	107	102	111	105	109	120
1994		117P	104P	110	112	110	146	117	108	135	118	186
1995		115P	103P	106P	111P	113P	128P	110P	111P	138P	121P	158P
1996		113P	102P	104P	110P	113P	132P	114P	112P	140P	123P	165P
1997		111P	100P	103P	109P	113P	136P	117P	114P	142P	124P	172P
1998		109P	99P	102P	109P	113P	140P	120P	115P	144P	126P	179P

Sources: Same as General Statistics. Values reflect change from the base year, 1992. Values above 100 mean greater than 92, values below 100 mean less than 92, and a value of 100 in the 82-91 or 93-98 period means same as 92. 'P's mark projections by the editors.

SELECTED RATIOS

For 1994	Avg. of All Manufact.	Analyzed Industry	Index	For 1994	Avg. of All Manufact.	Analyzed Industry	Index
Employees per Establishment	49	70	143	Value Added per Production Worker	134,084	61,213	46
Payroll per Establishment	1,500,273	1,843,975	123	Cost per Establishment	5,045,178	4,529,639	90
Payroll per Employee	30,620	26,229	86	Cost per Employee	102,970	64,431	63
Production Workers per Establishment	34	61	177	Cost per Production Worker	146,988	74,713	51
Wages per Establishment	853,319	1,185,046	139	Shipments per Establishment	9,576,895	8,192,436	86
Wages per Production Worker	24,861	19,546	79	Shipments per Employee	195,460	116,532	60
Hours per Production Worker	2,056	2,053	100	Shipments per Production Worker	279,017	135,128	48
Wages per Hour	12.09	9.52	79	Investment per Establishment	321,011	282,498	88
Value Added per Establishment	4,602,255	3,711,170	81	Investment per Employee	6,552	4,018	61
Value Added per Employee	93,930	52,789	56	Investment per Production Worker	9,352	4,660	50

Sources: Same as General Statistics. The 'Average of All Manufacturing' column represents the average of all manufacturing industries reported for the most recent complete year available. The Index shows the relationship between the Average and the Analyzed Industry. For example, 100 means that they are equal; 500 that the Analyzed Industry is five times the average; 50 means that the Analyzed Industry is half the national average. The abbreviation 'na' is used to show that data are 'not available'.

LEADING COMPANIES

Number shown: **31** Total sales ($ mil): **452** Total employment (000): **4.3**

Company Name	Address				CEO Name	Phone	Co. Type	Sales ($ mil)	Empl. (000)
Meridian Industries Inc	100 E Wisconsin	Milwaukee	WI	53202	Bruce E Pindyck	414-224-0610	R	190*	1.3
Brittany Dyeing and Printing Inc	1357 E French	New Bedford	MA	02744	Kenneth Joblon	508-999-3281	R	33*	0.3
India Ink	2457 E 27th St	Los Angeles	CA	90058	Richard Benaron	213-589-5471	R	33*	0.3
Cherry Hill Textiles Inc	PO Box 190045	Brooklyn	NY	11219	Abraham Rubashkin	718-439-5800	R	25*	<0.1
J and C Dyeing Inc	PO Box 9000	Shelby	NC	28151	Bill Seagleton	704-487-2322	S	22*	0.2
Chris Stone and Associates	PO Box 58606	Vernon	CA	90058	Chris Stone	213-583-9957	R	20	0.3
Holt Manufacturing Company	PO Box 2017	Burlington	NC	27215	Larry Small	919-227-5561	R	15	0.3
Pisgah Yarn and Dyeing	PO Box 606	Old Fort	NC	28762	Harold J Lonon	704-668-7667	R	14	0.2
Sanford Finishing Co	PO Box 550	Sanford	NC	27330	S Profio	919-776-4321	D	12	0.2
Southampton Textile Co	520 Reese St	Emporia	VA	23847	W Bobby Boswell	804-634-2159	S	12	0.1
Transcolor Corp	Allegheny Cir	Cheverly	MD	20781	M M Lapides Sr	301-341-6100	S	10	0.2
SMS Textile Mills Inc	132 Franklin St	Norwich	CT	06360	Frank A Flynn	203-886-1459	R	9*	<0.1
Wolfe Dye and Bleach Works	25 Ridge Rd	Shoemakersville	PA	19555	Philip D Wolfe	610-562-7639	R	8*	<0.1
Interstate Dyeing and Finishing	35 8th St	Passaic	NJ	07055	John Glasaroski	201-473-8370	R	7	<0.1
Western Piece Dyers	2845 W 48th Pl	Chicago	IL	60632	George Renaldi Jr	312-523-7000	R	7	0.1
Eagle Dyeing and Finish Co	PO Box 180	Mount Holly	NJ	08060	Frank O'Connell	609-267-1040	R	5*	<0.1
Elmore-Pisgah Inc	204 Oak St	Spindale	NC	28160	James E Lonon Jr	704-286-3665	R	5	<0.1
Luithlen Dye Corp	J St & Tioga St	Philadelphia	PA	19134	Douglas Wiegand	215-739-8005	R	4*	<0.1
Dyecraftsmen Inc	437 Whittenton St	Taunton	MA	02780	Neil P Olken	508-823-0741	R	3*	<0.1
Legacy by Friendly Hearts	14140-N Pk Long Ct	Chantilly	VA	22021	Debra Ryan	703-830-6818	R	3	<0.1
GJ Littlewood and Son Inc	4045-61 Main St	Philadelphia	PA	19127	Wallace Littlewood	215-483-3970	R	2	<0.1
Hemco Inc	PO Box 211	Newton Grove	NC	28366	Peter Hemmerich	919-594-1968	R	2	0.1
Just In-Materials Inc	148 W 37th St	New York	NY	10018	Marty Kornfield	212-564-7720	R	2*	<0.1
Rezex Corp	1901 Sacramento St	Los Angeles	CA	90021	Shahrzad Rezai	213-622-2015	R	2*	<0.1
William J Dixon Company Inc	756 Springdale Dr	Exton	PA	19341	John K Dixon	215-524-1131	R	2	<0.1
Dyetex Inc	PO Box 469	Haverhill	MA	01831	Steven Shain	508-374-7401	R	2	<0.1
J and M Dyers Inc	PO Box 550	Sumter	SC	29150	Norman A Halper	803-775-6371	S	1	<0.1
Sibyl Shepard Inc	14526 Garfield Av	Paramount	CA	90723	Christopher Sarris	310-531-8612	R	1*	<0.1
Sterlings Name Tape Co	PO Box 939	Winsted	CT	06098	James Barrett	203-379-5142	R	1	<0.1
Mi Marc Industries Inc	1241 Ford Rd	Bensalem	PA	19020	L B Morgenstern	215-245-6767	R	1*	<0.1
Edmund Erdmann Enterprises	3727 Rose Lake Dr	Charlotte	NC	28217	Daniel Troutman	704-357-6034	S	0	<0.1

Source: *Ward's Business Directory of U.S. Private and Public Companies*, Volumes 1 and 2, 1996. The company type code used is as follows: P - Public, R - Private, S - Subsidiary, D - Division, J - Joint Venture, A - Affiliate, G - Group. Sales are in millions of dollars, employees are in thousands. An asterisk (*) indicates an estimated sales volume. The symbol < stands for 'less than'. Company names and addresses are truncated, in some cases, to fit into the available space.

MATERIALS CONSUMED

Material		Quantity	Delivered Cost ($ million)
Materials, ingredients, containers, and supplies		(X)	592.4
Spun yarn, all fibers	mil lb	274.0	402.3
Broadwoven fabrics	mil sq yd	(D)	(D)
Knit fabrics	mil lb	(D)	(D)
Dyes, lakes, and toners		(X)	80.0
All other materials and components, parts, containers, and supplies		(X)	88.2
Materials, ingredients, containers, and supplies, nsk		(X)	17.9

Source: 1992 *Economic Census*. Explanation of symbols used: (D): Withheld to avoid disclosure of competitive data; na: Not available; (S): Withheld because statistical norms were not met; (X): Not applicable; (Z): Less than half the unit shown; nec: Not elsewhere classified; nsk: Not specified by kind; - : zero; * : 10-19 percent estimated; ** : 20-29 percent estimated.

PRODUCT SHARE DETAILS

Product or Product Class	% Share	Product or Product Class	% Share
Finished yarn, raw stock, and narrow fabrics	100.00	Yarns dyed, all other polyester	10.85
Yarns bleached	(D)	Yarns dyed, other manmade fiber and silk yarns	10.05
Yarns dyed, carded cotton	13.96	Mercerized cotton yarns	6.40
Yarns dyed, combed cotton	11.52	Raw stock, bleached or dyed (except wool)	6.51
Yarns dyed, rayon and/or acetate	4.97	Printed plastics film	(D)
Yarns dyed, acrylic and/or modacrylic	(D)	Finished braided or woven narrow fabrics	4.83
Yarns dyed, polyester blends with cotton	7.67		

Source: 1992 *Economic Census*. The values shown are percent of total shipments in an industry. Values of indented subcategories are summed in the main heading. The symbol (D) appears when data are withheld to prevent disclosure of competitive information. The abbreviation nsk stands for 'not specified by kind' and nec for 'not elsewhere classified'.

INPUTS AND OUTPUTS FOR KNIT FABRIC MILLS

Economic Sector or Industry Providing Inputs	%	Sector	Economic Sector or Industry Buying Outputs	%	Sector
Yarn mills & finishing of textiles, nec	24.0	Manufg.	Apparel made from purchased materials	79.8	Manufg.
Organic fibers, noncellulosic	22.2	Manufg.	Knit fabric mills	10.6	Manufg.
Knit fabric mills	14.4	Manufg.	Personal consumption expenditures	5.1	
Cellulosic manmade fibers	8.1	Manufg.	Knit outerwear mills	2.0	Manufg.
Wholesale trade	4.8	Trade	Exports	1.7	Foreign
Surface active agents	4.0	Manufg.	Knitting mills, nec	0.2	Manufg.
Miscellaneous plastics products	2.7	Manufg.	Coated fabrics, not rubberized	0.1	Manufg.
Electric services (utilities)	2.5	Util.	Knit underwear mills	0.1	Manufg.
Petroleum refining	2.1	Manufg.	Leather gloves & mittens	0.1	Manufg.
Cyclic crudes and organics	1.7	Manufg.			
Gas production & distribution (utilities)	1.6	Util.			
Textile machinery	1.5	Manufg.			
Motor freight transportation & warehousing	1.2	Util.			
Industrial gases	0.7	Manufg.			
Imports	0.7	Foreign			
Cotton	0.6	Agric.			
Equipment rental & leasing services	0.5	Services			
Laundry, dry cleaning, shoe repair	0.5	Services			
Air transportation	0.4	Util.			
Real estate	0.4	Fin/R.E.			
Paperboard containers & boxes	0.3	Manufg.			
Communications, except radio & TV	0.3	Util.			
Banking	0.3	Fin/R.E.			
U.S. Postal Service	0.3	Gov't			
Maintenance of nonfarm buildings nec	0.2	Constr.			
Ball & roller bearings	0.2	Manufg.			
Industrial inorganic chemicals, nec	0.2	Manufg.			
Lubricating oils & greases	0.2	Manufg.			
Sanitary services, steam supply, irrigation	0.2	Util.			
Eating & drinking places	0.2	Trade			
Automotive rental & leasing, without drivers	0.2	Services			
Computer & data processing services	0.2	Services			
Detective & protective services	0.2	Services			
State & local government enterprises, nec	0.2	Gov't			
Paper coating & glazing	0.1	Manufg.			
Railroads & related services	0.1	Util.			
Insurance carriers	0.1	Fin/R.E.			
Advertising	0.1	Services			
Automotive repair shops & services	0.1	Services			
Hotels & lodging places	0.1	Services			

Source: Benchmark Input-Output Accounts for the U.S. Economy, 1982, U.S. Department of Commerce, Washington, D.C., July 1991. Data, as reported in the source, are organized by the 1977 SIC structure in use in 1982 but have been matched, as closely as is possible, to the 1987 SIC structure used in this book.

OCCUPATIONS EMPLOYED BY SIC 226 - WEAVING, FINISHING, YARN AND THREAD MILLS

Occupation	% of Total 1994	Change to 2005	Occupation	% of Total 1994	Change to 2005
Textile draw-out & winding machine operators	32.8	-35.5	Machine feeders & offbearers	2.6	-27.4
Industrial machinery mechanics	6.4	29.1	Machine operators nec	2.2	-28.9
Textile machine setters & set-up operators	4.9	-11.3	Sewing machine operators, non-garment	1.8	21.0
Helpers, laborers, & material movers nec	4.5	-19.3	Industrial truck & tractor operators	1.6	-19.3
Blue collar worker supervisors	4.2	-24.6	Hand packers & packagers	1.3	-30.9
Inspectors, testers, & graders, precision	4.2	-27.4	General managers & top executives	1.3	-23.5
Textile bleaching & dyeing machine operators	4.2	8.9	Maintenance repairers, general utility	1.2	-27.4
Freight, stock, & material movers, hand	2.8	-35.5	Janitors & cleaners, incl maids	1.0	-35.5

Source: Industry-Occupation Matrix, Bureau of Labor Statistics. These data relate to one or more 3-digit SIC industry groups rather than to a single 4-digit SIC. The change reported for each occupation to the year 2005 is a percent of growth or decline as estimated by the Bureau of Labor Statistics. The abbreviation nec stands for 'not elsewhere classified'.

LOCATION BY STATE AND REGIONAL CONCENTRATION

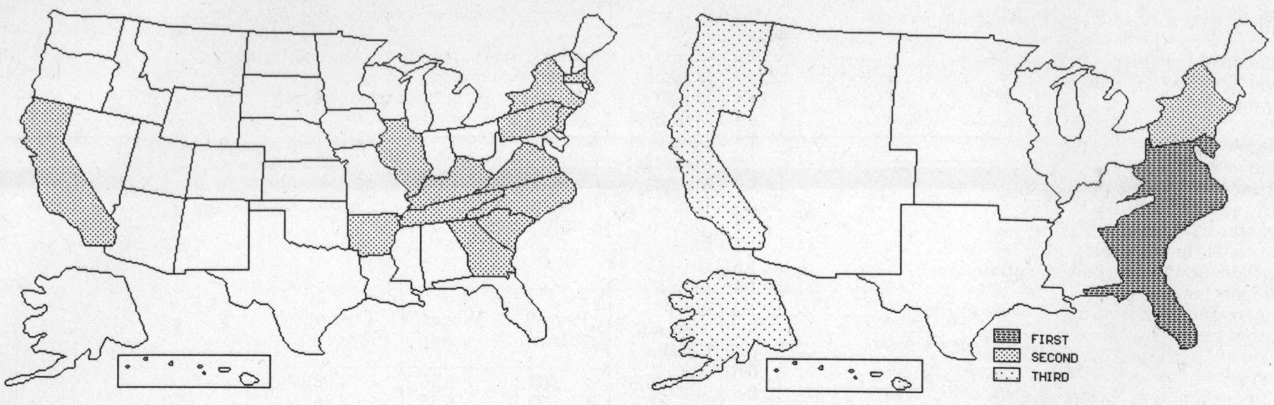

INDUSTRY DATA BY STATE

State	Establish- ments	Shipments			Employment				Cost as % of Shipments	Investment per Employee ($)
		Total ($ mil)	% of U.S.	Per Establ.	Total Number	% of U.S.	Per Establ.	Wages ($/hour)		
North Carolina	27	399.1	37.1	14.8	3,200	32.3	119	8.14	67.3	3,469
Georgia	16	182.5	17.0	11.4	1,500	15.2	94	8.59	51.7	-
Tennessee	8	107.9	10.0	13.5	1,000	10.1	125	7.67	65.8	2,100
California	12	43.2	4.0	3.6	600	6.1	50	7.80	46.3	3,833
New Jersey	10	38.1	3.5	3.8	400	4.0	40	10.00	39.4	750
New York	14	37.9	3.5	2.7	400	4.0	29	7.57	55.9	2,000
South Carolina	6	33.2	3.1	5.5	400	4.0	67	6.14	85.8	2,750
Massachusetts	8	22.6	2.1	2.8	400	4.0	50	8.57	43.8	-
Pennsylvania	8	15.6	1.5	2.0	200	2.0	25	7.25	34.6	-
Illinois	4	(D)	-	-	750 *	7.6	188	-	-	-
Virginia	4	(D)	-	-	750 *	7.6	188	-	-	-
Kentucky	2	(D)	-	-	175 *	1.8	88	-	-	-
Arkansas	1	(D)	-	-	175 *	1.8	175	-	-	-

Source: 1992 *Economic Census*. The states are in descending order of shipments or establishments (if shipment data are missing for the majority). The symbol (D) appears when data are withheld to prevent disclosure of competitive information. States marked with (D) are sorted by number of establishments. A dash (-) indicates that the data element cannot be calculated; * indicates the midpoint of a range.

2273 - CARPETS & RUGS

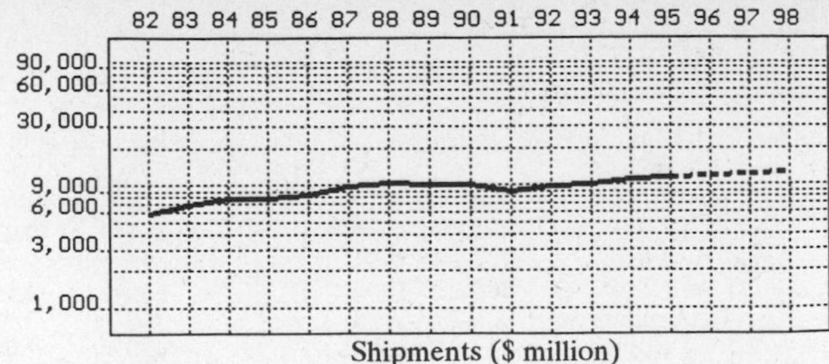

Shipments ($ million)

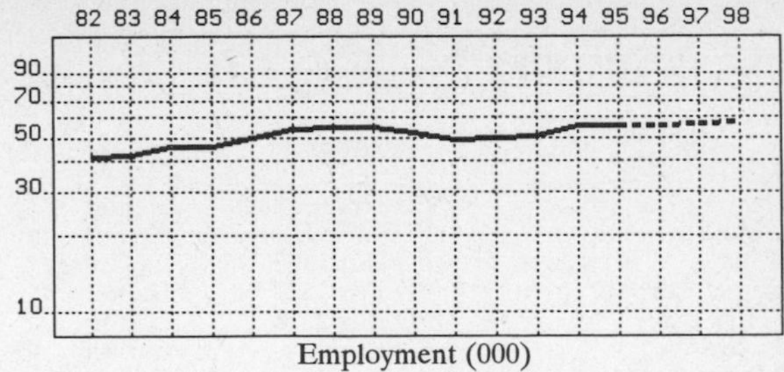

Employment (000)

GENERAL STATISTICS

Year	Companies	Establishments: Total	Establishments: with 20 or more employees	Employment: Total (000)	Employment: Production Workers (000)	Employment: Production Hours (Mil)	Compensation: Payroll ($ mil)	Compensation: Wages ($/hr)	Production ($ million): Cost of Materials	Production ($ million): Value Added by Manufacture	Production ($ million): Value of Shipments	Production ($ million): Capital Invest.
1982		505	243	41.8	32.9	65.0	603.1	6.10	4,089.2	1,711.7	5,807.8	83.9
1983				42.7	33.9	69.6	672.1	6.55	4,862.9	2,144.6	6,879.7	83.8
1984				46.2	36.8	76.6	749.2	6.80	5,624.9	2,257.3	7,804.7	167.0
1985				46.2	36.5	75.3	789.3	7.13	5,640.4	2,195.1	7,868.4	153.4
1986				49.8	37.2	79.6	856.9	7.37	6,064.9	2,382.8	8,432.7	134.8
1987	420	475	245	53.3	40.6	85.2	1,039.2	8.12	6,815.8	3,059.9	9,795.0	222.8
1988				54.6	42.6	92.0	1,078.1	7.83	7,148.7	3,145.7	10,256.0	151.1
1989		434	236	54.5	43.4	94.0	1,104.6	7.97	7,072.5	3,225.7	10,220.0	210.1
1990				51.8	41.0	89.2	1,059.0	7.95	7,026.1	2,917.3	10,038.4	201.7
1991				48.5	37.8	82.4	1,027.9	8.26	6,072.5	2,846.0	8,988.1	179.6
1992	383	447	210	49.4	38.9	81.7	1,088.0	8.83	6,360.2	3,480.5	9,831.0	144.6
1993				50.6	39.6	85.8	1,185.6	9.17	6,662.6	3,689.1	10,234.2	160.1
1994				55.2	43.0	91.1	1,313.6	9.54	7,028.7	3,959.4	10,961.3	249.0
1995				55.2P	43.1P	93.9P	1,327.1P	9.60P	7,325.5P	4,126.6P	11,424.2P	221.8P
1996				55.9P	43.7P	95.6P	1,378.6P	9.85P	7,546.8P	4,251.2P	11,769.2P	229.9P
1997				56.7P	44.3P	97.3P	1,430.1P	10.10P	7,768.0P	4,375.9P	12,114.2P	238.1P
1998				57.5P	44.9P	99.0P	1,481.6P	10.36P	7,989.2P	4,500.5P	12,459.3P	246.2P

Sources: 1982, 1987, 1992 *Economic Census*; *Annual Survey of Manufactures*, 83-86, 88-91, 93-94. Establishment counts for non-Census years are from *County Business Patterns*; establishment values for 83-84 are extrapolations. 'P's show projections by the editors. Industries reclassified in 87 will not have data for prior years.

INDICES OF CHANGE

Year	Companies	Establishments: Total	Establishments: with 20 or more employees	Employment: Total (000)	Employment: Production Workers (000)	Employment: Production Hours (Mil)	Compensation: Payroll ($ mil)	Compensation: Wages ($/hr)	Production ($ million): Cost of Materials	Production ($ million): Value Added by Manufacture	Production ($ million): Value of Shipments	Production ($ million): Capital Invest.
1982		113	116	85	85	80	55	69	64	49	59	58
1983				86	87	85	62	74	76	62	70	58
1984				94	95	94	69	77	88	65	79	115
1985				94	94	92	73	81	89	63	80	106
1986				101	96	97	79	83	95	68	86	93
1987	110	106	117	108	104	104	96	92	107	88	100	154
1988				111	110	113	99	89	112	90	104	104
1989		97	112	110	112	115	102	90	111	93	104	145
1990				105	105	109	97	90	110	84	102	139
1991				98	97	101	94	94	95	82	91	124
1992	100	100	100	100	100	100	100	100	100	100	100	100
1993				102	102	105	109	104	105	106	104	111
1994				112	111	112	121	108	111	114	111	172
1995				112P	111P	115P	122P	109P	115P	119P	116P	153P
1996				113P	112P	117P	127P	112P	119P	122P	120P	159P
1997				115P	114P	119P	131P	114P	122P	126P	123P	165P
1998				116P	115P	121P	136P	117P	126P	129P	127P	170P

Sources: Same as General Statistics. Values reflect change from the base year, 1992. Values above 100 mean greater than 92, values below 100 mean less than 92, and a value of 100 in the 82-91 or 93-98 period means same as 92. 'P's mark projections by the editors.

SELECTED RATIOS

For 1992	Avg. of All Manufact.	Analyzed Industry	Index	For 1992	Avg. of All Manufact.	Analyzed Industry	Index
Employees per Establishment	46	111	242	Value Added per Production Worker	122,353	89,473	73
Payroll per Establishment	1,332,320	2,434,004	183	Cost per Establishment	4,239,462	14,228,635	336
Payroll per Employee	29,181	22,024	75	Cost per Employee	92,853	128,749	139
Production Workers per Establishment	31	87	277	Cost per Production Worker	135,003	163,501	121
Wages per Establishment	734,496	1,613,895	220	Shipments per Establishment	8,100,800	21,993,289	271
Wages per Production Worker	23,390	18,545	79	Shipments per Employee	177,425	199,008	112
Hours per Production Worker	2,025	2,100	104	Shipments per Production Worker	257,966	252,725	98
Wages per Hour	11.55	8.83	76	Investment per Establishment	278,244	323,490	116
Value Added per Establishment	3,842,210	7,786,353	203	Investment per Employee	6,094	2,927	48
Value Added per Employee	84,153	70,455	84	Investment per Production Worker	8,861	3,717	42

Sources: Same as General Statistics. The 'Average of All Manufacturing' column represents the average of all manufacturing industries reported for the most recent complete year available. The Index shows the relationship between the Average and the Analyzed Industry. For example, 100 means that they are equal; 500 that the Analyzed Industry is five times the average; 50 means that the Analyzed Industry is half the national average. The abbreviation 'na' is used to show that data are 'not available'.

LEADING COMPANIES Number shown: **72** Total sales ($ mil): **10,193** Total employment (000): **86.6**

Company Name	Address				CEO Name	Phone	Co. Type	Sales ($ mil)	Empl. (000)
Shaw Industries Inc	PO Drawer 2128	Dalton	GA	30722	Robert E Shaw	706-278-3812	P	2,630	24.0
Mohawk Industries Inc	1775 The Exchange	Atlanta	GA	30339	David L Kolb	404-951-6000	P	1,437	13.3
Interface Inc	PO Box 1503	La Grange	GA	30241	Ray C Anderson	706-882-1891	P	625	3.7
Queen Carpet Corp	PO Box 1527	Dalton	GA	30722	Julian Saul	706-277-1900	R	540•	4.5
Aladdin Mills Inc	PO Box 2208	Dalton	GA	30722	Alan Loberbaum	706-277-1100	S	460	3.5
Masland Corp	PO Box 40	Carlisle	PA	17013	William J Branch	717-249-1866	P	430	3.0
Masland Industries Inc	PO Box 40	Carlisle	PA	17013	William J Branch	717-249-1866	S	430	3.0
World Carpets Inc	PO Box 1448	Dalton	GA	30722	David Polley	706-278-8000	R	360•	3.0
Shelter Components Corp	PO Box 4026	Elkhart	IN	46514	Larry D Renbarger	219-262-4541	P	333	1.2
Diamond Rug and Carpet Mills	PO Box 46	Eton	GA	30724	Linda Weaver	706-695-9446	R	300	2.5
Mohawk Carpet Corp	1755 The Exchange	Atlanta	GA	30339	David L Kolb	404-951-6000	S	274	7.1
Carriage Industries Inc	PO Box 12542	Calhoun	GA	30703	Philip H Barlow	706-629-9234	S	173	0.9
Columbus Mills Inc	4600 River Rd	Columbus	GA	31904	John Dickson	706-324-0111	R	160	1.1
Tuftex Carpet Mills Inc	15305 Valley View	Santa Fe Sprgs	CA	90670	Robert Cook	310-921-0951	R	140•	1.2
Designweave	15305 Valley View	Santa Fe Sprgs	CA	90670	Robert Cook	310-921-0951	D	120•	1.0
Image Industries Inc	PO Box 5555	Armuchee	GA	30105	H Stanley Padgett	706-235-8444	P	104	1.0
Beaulieu of America Inc	PO Box 4539	Dalton	GA	30719	K G Heneyman	706-278-6666	R	100	0.3
Marglen Industries Inc	1748 Ward	Rome	GA	30161	Jerry G Hubbard	706-295-5621	R	100•	0.3
Masland Carpets Inc	PO Box 11467	Mobile	AL	36671	John O Sturdy	205-675-9080	S	86	0.6
Wunda Weve Carpet Co	PO Box 167	Greenville	SC	29602	David S Holt	803-879-8000	R	85	0.5
Conquest Carpet Mills Inc	PO Box 4329	Dalton	GA	30721	Thomas Bouckaert	706-226-8066	R	84•	0.7
Collins & Aikman	PO Box 1447	Dalton	GA	30722	Edgar M Bridger	706-259-9711	S	78•	0.7
Bentley Mills Inc	PO Box 527	City of Industry	CA	91746	Royce Renfore	818-333-4585	R	72•	0.6
J and J Industries Inc	PO Box 1287	Dalton	GA	30722	J Jolly	706-278-4454	R	72	0.6
Multitex Corporation of America	PO Box 628	Dalton	GA	30722	Charles Miller	706-277-2770	R	70	0.4
USAxminster Inc	PO Box 877	Greenville	MS	38702	Barbara Coveny	601-332-1581	R	63•	0.5
Atlas Carpet Mills Inc	2200 Saybrook Av	City of Com	CA	90040	James Horwich	213-724-9000	R	60	0.3
Mannington Carpets Inc	PO Box 12281	Calhoun	GA	30701	Stan Peszat	706-629-7301	S	56	0.5
Regal Inc	819 Buckeye St	North Vernon	IN	47265	Andrew Smithson	812-346-3601	R	54•	0.5
Interface Flooring Systems Inc	PO Box 1503	La Grange	GA	30241	Gordon Whitener	706-882-1891	S	50	0.8
Magee Industrial Enterprises Inc	480 W 5th St	Bloomsburg	PA	17815	Harry M Katerman	717-784-4100	R	50	0.7
Blue Ridge Carpet Mills	PO Box 507	Ellijay	GA	30540	NE Gibbs Jr	706-276-2001	D	45	0.3
Danube Carpet Mills Inc	PO Box 2298	Fort Oglethorpe	GA	30742	M Thomas Johnson	706-866-5327	S	45	0.2
Prince St Technologies Ltd	36 Enterprise Blv	Atlanta	GA	30336	Robert Weiner	404-691-0507	R	43	0.3
Barrett Carpet Mills Inc	PO Box 2045	Dalton	GA	30720	Ray C Barrett	706-277-2114	R	42•	0.2
Princeton Inc	PO Box 100050	Adairsville	GA	30103	Dirk De Vuyst	404-773-3796	S	40	0.2
Vista Corp	201 Princeton Blv	Adairsville	GA	30103	Dirk DeVuyst	404-773-7783	R	40	0.2
Coronet Carpets Inc	PO Box 1736	Gainesville	GA	30503	Don Howard	404-536-0551	S	36•	0.3
DWB Carpet Holdings LP	PO Box 740	Chatsworth	GA	30705	David Turner	706-277-1851	S	36•	0.3
Capel Inc	PO Box 826	Troy	NC	27371	A Leon Capel Jr	919-576-6211	R	30	0.4
Lacey Rug Mills Inc	PO Box 69	Fairmount	GA	30139	Wyatt Bradford	706-337-5331	R	24•	0.2
Specialty Carpets	PO Box 1348	Chatsworth	GA	30705	ME Ralston	706-695-4624	R	23	0.1
Downs Carpet Company Inc	PO Box 475	Willow Grove	PA	19090	GT Downs III	215-672-1100	R	22	0.2
Antigua Mills Inc	PO Box 578	Dalton	GA	30722	LJ Meltz	706-278-9744	R	20	0.3
Georgia Tufters	PO Box 12569	Calhoun	GA	30703	Thomas J Brown Jr	706-629-4516	R	15•	0.1
Lady Madison Inc	PO Box 749	Dalton	GA	30722	Robert Weinstein	706-278-8028	S	13	0.2
Dorsett Carpet Mills Inc	PO Box 805	Dalton	GA	30720	Robert Goodroe	706-278-1961	R	12	<0.1
Patcraft Commercial	PO Box 1527	Dalton	GA	30722	Robert Chandler	706-277-2133	D	11•	0.2
Michaelian and Kohlberg	10 E 21st St	New York	NY	10010	Teddy Sumner	212-505-8525	R	10	<0.1
Peeler Rug and Printing Co	1224 Champion	Gaffney	SC	29341	Bobby J Peeler	803-489-0226	R	10	0.3
Woven Legends Inc	4700 Wissahickon	Philadelphia	PA	19144	George Jevremovich	215-849-8344	R	10	<0.1
Carousel Carpet Mills Inc	1 Carousel Ln	Ukiah	CA	95482	Max Pettlich	707-485-0333	R	7	0.1
Camelot Carpet Mills Inc	1420 S Manhattan	Fullerton	CA	92631	Ken Kazarian	714-774-7330	R	6•	<0.1
Foreign Accents	2825 Broadbent N	Albuquerque	NM	87107	Wolfgang Rempen	505-344-4833	R	5	<0.1
Len Dal Carpets Inc	PO Box 39	Chatsworth	GA	30705	Charles Lents	706-695-4533	R	5	<0.1
Log Cabin Company Inc	PO Box 1083	Dalton	GA	30720	CS Thomas Jr	706-259-4824	R	5	<0.1
Omega Carpet Mills Inc	PO Box 1446	Dalton	GA	30722	Buddy Parker	706-226-2223	R	5	<0.1
Omega Rug Works	PO Box 1446	Dalton	GA	30722	Robert E Garrett	706-226-2223	R	5	<0.1
Pennsylvania Woven Carpet Mills	401 E Allegheny	Philadelphia	PA	19134	Frank J Pisano	215-425-5833	R	5	<0.1
Unituft Inc	PO Box 1676	Dalton	GA	30722	EW Ramsey	706-277-9707	R	5	0.1
Langhorne Carpet Company Inc	PO Box 7175	Penndel	PA	19047	WH Morrow	215-757-5155	R	4	<0.1
Masterlooms Inc	100 Park Plaza Dr	Secaucus	NJ	07094	Nasser Rahmanan	201-319-1696	R	4	<0.1
Merida Meridian Inc	PO Box 1071	Syracuse	NY	13201	Hiram Samel	315-422-4921	R	3	<0.1
Proffitt Manufacturing Co	PO Box 729	Dalton	GA	30722	Jack R Proffitt	706-278-7105	R	3	<0.1
Kendrick Carpets Inc	PO Box 798	Chatsworth	GA	30705	Thomas Kendrick	706-695-4628	R	2•	<0.1
Colonial Carpet Mills Inc	PO Box 347	Union City	CA	94587	Joe Franco	510-471-5700	R	1	<0.1
InnerAsia Trading Company Inc	236 5th Av	New York	NY	10001	Kesang Tashi	212-532-2600	R	1•	<0.1
Jaunty Company Inc	1850 Beverly Blv	Los Angeles	CA	90057	Eddie Mirarooni	213-413-3333	R	1	<0.1
Pilgrim House Rug Co	PO Box 327	Glendale	SC	29346	Peter R Steidle	803-579-9593	R	1	<0.1
Carpeting Concepts	1410 Eisenhower St	Mascoutah	IL	62258	TP Canty	618-566-7847	R	1	<0.1
SET Enterprises Inc	125 8th Av	Cramerton	NC	28032	Hy Spectorman	704-824-5333	R	0•	<0.1
Peter Sachs	1966 San Marco	Jacksonville	FL	32207	Peter Sachs	904-398-4375	R	0•	<0.1

Source: *Ward's Business Directory of U.S. Private and Public Companies*, Volumes 1 and 2, 1996. The company type code used is as follows: P - Public, R - Private, S - Subsidiary, D - Division, J - Joint Venture, A - Affiliate, G - Group. Sales are in millions of dollars, employees are in thousands. An asterisk (*) indicates an estimated sales volume. The symbol < stands for 'less than'. Company names and addresses are truncated, in some cases, to fit into the available space.

MATERIALS CONSUMED

Material		Quantity	Delivered Cost ($ million)
Materials, ingredients, containers, and supplies		(X)	6,043.1
Spun wool and chiefly wool yarns	mil lb	11.1	29.5
Spun nylon yarn	mil lb	802.7*	1,559.9
Spun polyester yarns	mil lb	123.4*	153.7
Spun polypropylene yarns	mil lb	104.2**	121.1
All other spun yarns	mil lb	20.3*	35.8
Nylon filament yarns	mil lb	480.8*	1,006.7
Polyester filament yarns	mil lb	4.6*	6.8
Polypropylene filament yarns	mil lb	188.3	232.0
All other filament yarns	mil lb	26.2*	38.7
Nylon staple and tow	mil lb	(D)	(D)
Polypropylene staple and tow	mil lb	44.7*	36.1
Polyester staple and tow	mil lb	27.0	16.0
All other manmade fiber staple and tow (except glass)	mil lb	2.7*	2.9
All other fibers (silk, jute, reused wool, waste, etc.)	mil lb	(D)	(D)
Polypropylene fiber fabrics primary backing	mil sq yd	659.6**	190.5
All other manmade fiber fabrics primary backing	mil sq yd	106.8*	73.3
All other fabrics (except manmade) primary backing	mil sq yd	4.1	5.1
Jute secondary backing	mil sq yd	(S)	80.0
Foam or high density rubber cushion secondary backing	mil sq yd	30.2	13.7
Other cushion secondary backings (including vinyl, polyurethane, etc.)	mil sq yd	(S)	95.9
Woven and nonwoven manmade fiber fabrics secondary backing	mil sq yd	399.1*	107.3
All other secondary backing (including scrim, solid vinyl, etc.)	mil sq yd	94.1**	47.4
Dyes, lakes, and toners		(X)	185.5
All other materials and components, parts, containers, and supplies		(X)	781.2
Materials, ingredients, containers, and supplies, nsk		(X)	93.8

Source: 1992 *Economic Census*. Explanation of symbols used: (D): Withheld to avoid disclosure of competitive data; na: Not available; (S): Withheld because statistical norms were not met; (X): Not applicable; (Z): Less than half the unit shown; nec: Not elsewhere classified; nsk: Not specified by kind; - : zero; * : 10-19 percent estimated; ** : 20-29 percent estimated.

PRODUCT SHARE DETAILS

Product or Product Class	% Share	Product or Product Class	% Share
Carpets and rugs	100.00	Carpets and rugs, finished only	8.03
Woven carpets and rugs	3.00	Carpets, rugs, and mats, nec	3.48
Carpets and rugs	92.51	Carpets and rugs, nsk	1.01
Carpets and rugs	91.97		

Source: 1992 *Economic Census*. The values shown are percent of total shipments in an industry. Values of indented subcategories are summed in the main heading. The symbol (D) appears when data are withheld to prevent disclosure of competitive information. The abbreviation nsk stands for 'not specified by kind' and nec for 'not elsewhere classified'.

INPUTS AND OUTPUTS FOR FLOOR COVERINGS

Economic Sector or Industry Providing Inputs	%	Sector	Economic Sector or Industry Buying Outputs	%	Sector
Yarn mills & finishing of textiles, nec	30.2	Manufg.	Personal consumption expenditures	39.9	
Organic fibers, noncellulosic	28.6	Manufg.	Gross private fixed investment	23.5	Cap Inv
Wholesale trade	4.2	Trade	Residential 1-unit structures, nonfarm	6.9	Constr.
Synthetic rubber	3.8	Manufg.	Exports	5.0	Foreign
Nonwoven fabrics	3.4	Manufg.	Office buildings	4.8	Constr.
Imports	3.3	Foreign	Maintenance of nonfarm buildings nec	3.7	Constr.
Floor coverings	3.2	Manufg.	Motor vehicles & car bodies	2.8	Manufg.
Cyclic crudes and organics	2.8	Manufg.	Floor coverings	2.5	Manufg.
Fabricated rubber products, nec	2.7	Manufg.	Nonfarm residential structure maintenance	2.3	Constr.
Textile machinery	1.9	Manufg.	Mobile homes	1.5	Manufg.
Motor freight transportation & warehousing	1.6	Util.	Residential additions/alterations, nonfarm	1.3	Constr.
Gas production & distribution (utilities)	1.3	Util.	Construction of stores & restaurants	0.8	Constr.
Broadwoven fabric mills	1.2	Manufg.	Residential garden apartments	0.8	Constr.
Electric services (utilities)	1.1	Util.	Construction of educational buildings	0.6	Constr.
Noncomparable imports	1.1	Foreign	Construction of hospitals	0.6	Constr.
Textile goods, nec	0.9	Manufg.	Industrial buildings	0.6	Constr.
Paperboard containers & boxes	0.6	Manufg.	Residential 2-4 unit structures, nonfarm	0.5	Constr.
Banking	0.6	Fin/R.E.	Residential high-rise apartments	0.3	Constr.
Miscellaneous plastics products	0.5	Manufg.	Amusement & recreation building construction	0.2	Constr.
Advertising	0.5	Services	Construction of nonfarm buildings nec	0.2	Constr.
Petroleum refining	0.4	Manufg.	Resid. & other health facility construction	0.2	Constr.
Surface active agents	0.4	Manufg.	Boat building & repairing	0.2	Manufg.
Communications, except radio & TV	0.4	Util.	Travel trailers & campers	0.2	Manufg.
Water transportation	0.4	Util.	Construction of religious buildings	0.1	Constr.
Eating & drinking places	0.4	Trade	Farm housing units & additions & alterations	0.1	Constr.
Laundry, dry cleaning, shoe repair	0.4	Services	Farm service facilities	0.1	Constr.
Maintenance of nonfarm buildings nec	0.3	Constr.			
Cellulosic manmade fibers	0.3	Manufg.			

Continued on next page.

INPUTS AND OUTPUTS FOR FLOOR COVERINGS - Continued

Economic Sector or Industry Providing Inputs	%	Sector	Economic Sector or Industry Buying Outputs	%	Sector
Industrial inorganic chemicals, nec	0.3	Manufg.			
Real estate	0.3	Fin/R.E.			
Equipment rental & leasing services	0.3	Services			
Plastics materials & resins	0.2	Manufg.			
Railroads & related services	0.2	Util.			
U.S. Postal Service	0.2	Gov't			
Coal	0.1	Mining			
Fabricated textile products, nec	0.1	Manufg.			
Lubricating oils & greases	0.1	Manufg.			
Paper coating & glazing	0.1	Manufg.			
Computer & data processing services	0.1	Services			
Legal services	0.1	Services			
Management & consulting services & labs	0.1	Services			

Source: Benchmark Input-Output Accounts for the U.S. Economy, 1982, U.S. Department of Commerce, Washington, D.C., July 1991. Data, as reported in the source, are organized by the 1977 SIC structure in use in 1982 but have been matched, as closely as is possible, to the 1987 SIC structure used in this book.

OCCUPATIONS EMPLOYED BY SIC 227 - CARPETS AND RUGS

Occupation	% of Total 1994	Change to 2005	Occupation	% of Total 1994	Change to 2005
Textile draw-out & winding machine operators	18.0	-7.3	Mechanics, installers, & repairers nec	2.0	3.0
Helpers, laborers, & material movers nec	7.6	3.0	Hand packers & packagers	1.9	-11.7
Sewing machine operators, non-garment	6.5	23.6	General managers & top executives	1.6	-2.2
Blue collar worker supervisors	4.2	-5.0	General office clerks	1.5	-12.2
Industrial truck & tractor operators	4.1	3.0	Traffic, shipping, & receiving clerks	1.3	-0.9
Machine operators nec	3.9	-9.2	Textile, apparel, & furnishings workers nec	1.2	21.4
Industrial machinery mechanics	3.3	13.3	Coating, painting, & spraying machine workers	1.2	3.1
Inspectors, testers, & graders, precision	3.1	3.0	Assemblers, fabricators, & hand workers nec	1.2	3.0
Textile bleaching & dyeing machine operators	3.1	54.6	Industrial production managers	1.1	3.0
Textile machine setters & set-up operators	2.7	3.1	Adjustment clerks	1.1	23.7
Freight, stock, & material movers, hand	2.5	-17.6	Truck drivers light & heavy	1.1	6.2
Sales & related workers nec	2.4	3.0	Secretaries, ex legal & medical	1.1	-6.2
Machine feeders & offbearers	2.3	-7.3	Cutters & trimmers, hand	1.0	-7.4

Source: *Industry-Occupation Matrix*, Bureau of Labor Statistics. These data relate to one or more 3-digit SIC industry groups rather than to a single 4-digit SIC. The change reported for each occupation to the year 2005 is a percent of growth or decline as estimated by the Bureau of Labor Statistics. The abbreviation nec stands for 'not elsewhere classified'.

LOCATION BY STATE AND REGIONAL CONCENTRATION

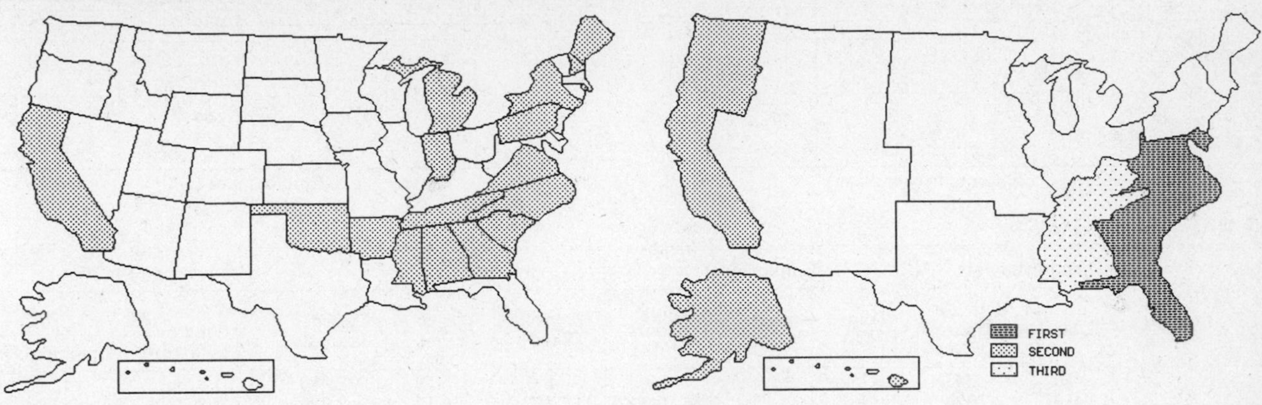

INDUSTRY DATA BY STATE

State	Establish-ments	Shipments			Employment				Cost as % of Shipments	Investment per Employee ($)
		Total ($ mil)	% of U.S.	Per Establ.	Total Number	% of U.S.	Per Establ.	Wages ($/hour)		
Georgia	238	7,165.6	72.9	30.1	31,600	64.0	133	8.76	65.9	3,032
California	38	556.6	5.7	14.6	3,200	6.5	84	9.98	63.6	3,469
North Carolina	29	506.5	5.2	17.5	2,900	5.9	100	7.75	65.4	-
South Carolina	16	417.4	4.2	26.1	2,700	5.5	169	8.16	67.5	3,407
Pennsylvania	10	329.4	3.4	32.9	2,300	4.7	230	10.58	66.5	783
Alabama	6	130.1	1.3	21.7	900	1.8	150	8.56	55.3	3,444
Tennessee	11	120.0	1.2	10.9	700	1.4	64	7.91	61.6	-
Rhode Island	7	22.2	0.2	3.2	400	0.8	57	8.00	56.3	-
New York	8	19.6	0.2	2.5	200	0.4	25	12.00	60.7	500
Michigan	5	(D)	-	-	175 *	0.4	35	-	-	-
Indiana	4	(D)	-	-	375 *	0.8	94	-	-	-
Virginia	3	(D)	-	-	1,750 *	3.5	583	-	-	-
Arkansas	2	(D)	-	-	750 *	1.5	375	-	-	-
Maine	2	(D)	-	-	750 *	1.5	375	-	-	-
New Hampshire	2	(D)	-	-	375 *	0.8	188	-	-	-
Mississippi	1	(D)	-	-	375 *	0.8	375	-	-	-
Oklahoma	1	(D)	-	-	375 *	0.8	375	-	-	-

Source: 1992 *Economic Census*. The states are in descending order of shipments or establishments (if shipment data are missing for the majority). The symbol (D) appears when data are withheld to prevent disclosure of competitive information. States marked with (D) are sorted by number of establishments. A dash (-) indicates that the data element cannot be calculated; * indicates the midpoint of a range.

2281 - YARN SPINNING MILLS

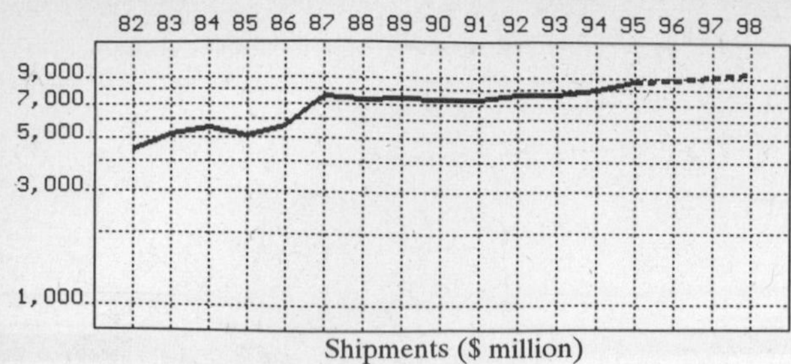

Shipments ($ million)

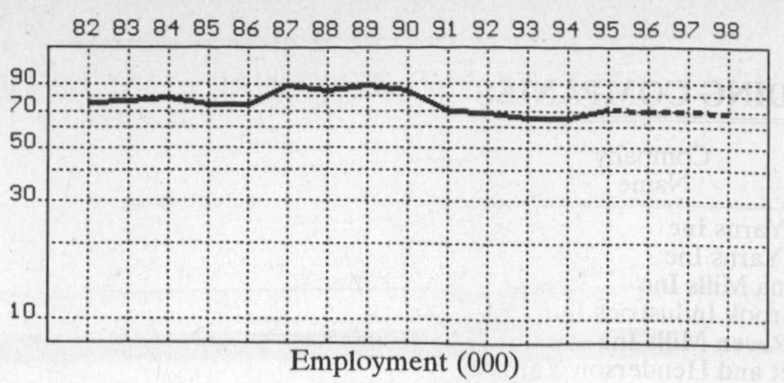

Employment (000)

GENERAL STATISTICS

Year	Companies	Establishments		Employment			Compensation		Production ($ million)			
		Total	with 20 or more employees	Total (000)	Production Workers (000)	Production Hours (Mil)	Payroll ($ mil)	Wages ($/hr)	Cost of Materials	Value Added by Manufacture	Value of Shipments	Capital Invest.
1982		450	347	76.0	69.5	130.5	891.5	5.79	2,913.6	1,575.0	4,512.9	156.6
1983		415	327	76.5	70.0	141.8	1,027.7	6.13	3,386.6	1,874.8	5,240.1	226.0
1984		380	307	79.4	72.5	143.2	1,060.6	6.23	3,612.3	1,890.8	5,503.5	
1985		344	288	73.7	67.3	131.1	1,032.7	6.65	3,167.6	1,874.7	5,087.3	256.5
1986		331	277	73.8	67.7	142.5	1,109.2	6.66	3,500.4	2,139.9	5,664.4	209.5
1987	242	414	351	89.0	81.1	170.8	1,109.2	7.19	4,493.8	3,025.1	7,517.5	340.2
1988		412	339	83.8	76.5	156.0	1,374.0	7.43	4,521.4	2,756.3	7,278.9	
1989		421	350	88.1	71.0	146.6	1,362.2	7.93	4,595.7	2,769.4	7,327.2	348.4
1990		416	345	85.1	68.8	138.2	1,312.6	8.02	4,622.8	2,654.5	7,259.2	342.3
1991		431	354	69.8	63.6	124.4	1,233.1	8.28	4,675.6	2,566.9	7,265.4	363.5
1992	211	396	324	68.7	62.6	126.2	1,288.4	8.48	4,788.4	2,890.6	7,668.6	294.0
1993		401	329	65.6	59.7	127.1	1,316.2	8.62	4,878.5	2,750.6	7,618.1	280.9
1994		407P	342P	65.4	59.6	127.7	1,341.4	8.95	5,222.0	2,796.5	8,005.8	450.0
1995		408P	344P	70.7P	61.9P	130.8P	1,432.0P	9.29P	5,593.0P	2,995.2P	8,574.6P	
1996		409P	346P	69.9P	61.0P	129.6P	1,466.7P	9.56P	5,775.9P	3,093.1P	8,855.0P	
1997		410P	348P	69.1P	60.1P	128.5P	1,501.4P	9.82P	5,958.9P	3,191.1P	9,135.5P	
1998		411P	350P	68.2P	59.1P	127.3P	1,536.1P	10.09P	6,141.8P	3,289.1P	9,415.9P	

Sources: 1982, 1987, 1992 *Economic Census*; *Annual Survey of Manufactures*, 83-86, 88-91, 93-94. Establishment counts for non-Census years are from *County Business Patterns*; establishment values for 83-84 are extrapolations. 'P's show projections by the editors. Industries reclassified in 87 will not have data for prior years.

INDICES OF CHANGE

Year	Companies	Establishments		Employment			Compensation		Production ($ million)			
		Total	with 20 or more employees	Total (000)	Production Workers (000)	Production Hours (Mil)	Payroll ($ mil)	Wages ($/hr)	Cost of Materials	Value Added by Manufacture	Value of Shipments	Capital Invest.
1982		114	107	111	111	103	69	68	61	54	59	53
1983		105	101	111	112	112	80	72	71	65	68	77
1984		96	95	116	116	113	82	73	75	65	72	
1985		87	89	107	108	104	80	78	66	65	66	87
1986		84	85	107	108	113	86	79	73	74	74	71
1987	115	105	108	130	130	135	86	85	94	105	98	116
1988		104	105	122	122	124	107	88	94	95	95	
1989		106	108	128	113	116	106	94	96	96	96	119
1990		105	106	124	110	110	102	95	97	92	95	116
1991		109	109	102	102	99	96	98	98	89	95	124
1992	100	100	100	100	100	100	100	100	100	100	100	100
1993		101	102	95	95	101	102	102	102	95	99	96
1994		103P	105P	95	95	101	104	106	109	97	104	153
1995		103P	106P	103P	99P	104P	111P	110P	117P	104P	112P	
1996		103P	107P	102P	97P	103P	114P	113P	121P	107P	115P	
1997		104P	107P	101P	96P	102P	117P	116P	124P	110P	119P	
1998		104P	108P	99P	94P	101P	119P	119P	128P	114P	123P	

Sources: Same as General Statistics. Values reflect change from the base year, 1992. Values above 100 mean greater than 92, values below 100 mean less than 92, and a value of 100 in the 82-91 or 93-98 period means same as 92. 'P's mark projections by the editors.

SELECTED RATIOS

For 1994	Avg. of All Manufact.	Analyzed Industry	Index
Employees per Establishment	49	161	328
Payroll per Establishment	1,500,273	3,294,474	220
Payroll per Employee	30,620	20,511	67
Production Workers per Establishment	34	146	426
Wages per Establishment	853,319	2,806,995	329
Wages per Production Worker	24,861	19,176	77
Hours per Production Worker	2,056	2,143	104
Wages per Hour	12.09	8.95	74
Value Added per Establishment	4,602,255	6,868,195	149
Value Added per Employee	93,930	42,760	46

For 1994	Avg. of All Manufact.	Analyzed Industry	Index
Value Added per Production Worker	134,084	46,921	35
Cost per Establishment	5,045,178	12,825,215	254
Cost per Employee	102,970	79,847	78
Cost per Production Worker	146,988	87,617	60
Shipments per Establishment	9,576,895	19,662,219	205
Shipments per Employee	195,460	122,413	63
Shipments per Production Worker	279,017	134,326	48
Investment per Establishment	321,011	1,105,199	344
Investment per Employee	6,552	6,881	105
Investment per Production Worker	9,352	7,550	81

Sources: Same as General Statistics. The 'Average of All Manufacturing' column represents the average of all manufacturing industries reported for the most recent complete year available. The Index shows the relationship between the Average and the Analyzed Industry. For example, 100 means that they are equal; 500 that the Analyzed Industry is five times the average; 50 means that the Analyzed Industry is half the national average. The abbreviation 'na' is used to show that data are 'not available'.

LEADING COMPANIES Number shown: **64** Total sales ($ mil): **3,106** Total employment (000): **34.8**

Company Name	Address				CEO Name	Phone	Co. Type	Sales ($ mil)	Empl. (000)
Dixie Yarns Inc	PO Box 751	Chattanooga	TN	37401	Daniel K Frierson	615-698-2501	P	689	6.9
Pharr Yarns Inc	PO Box 1939	Mc Adenville	NC	28101	J M Carstarphen	704-824-3551	R	300	4.0
Carolina Mills Inc	PO Box 157	Maiden	NC	28650	Edward P Schrum	704-428-9911	P	201	2.5
Carisbrook Industries Inc	16 E 34th St	New York	NY	10016	David Krivisky	212-951-5100	S	174	1.5
Glen Raven Mills Inc	1831 N Park Av	Glen Raven	NC	27217	Alan Gant	919-227-6211	R	170	2.1
Harriet and Henderson Yarns	PO Box 789	Henderson	NC	27536	Marshall Cooper Jr	919-430-5000	R	150	2.0
Candlewick	PO Box 1368	Dalton	GA	30720	Paul K Frierson	706-259-4811	D	101	1.3
Burlington Madison Yarn	PO Box 21207	Greensboro	NC	27410	Daniel T Sullivan	910-379-2000	D	100	1.3
Dillon Yarn Inc	PO Box 1247	Dillon	SC	29536	Robert Howell	803-774-7353	S	100	0.2
Dominion Yarn Corp	PO Box 8105	Landis	NC	28088	H Alton Conner	704-857-1121	S	100	0.9
Wiscassett Mills Co	PO Box 40	Albemarle	NC	28001	William T McGhee	704-982-1181	R	66*	0.8
Glen Raven Mills Inc	142 Glenraven Rd	Glen Raven	NC	27217	Charles Grady	919-227-6211	D	56*	0.7
Cheraw Yarn Mills Inc	PO Drawer 807	Cheraw	SC	29520	WM Malloy	803-537-7846	R	50	0.3
First Republic Corporation	302 5th Av	New York	NY	10001	Norman A Halper	212-279-6100	P	48	0.4
Amital Spinning Corp	197 Bosch Blv	New Bern	NC	28562	Milton Gold	919-636-3435	R	40	0.3
Grover Industries Inc	PO Box 79	Grover	NC	28073	Charles F Harry III	704-937-7434	R	40	0.3
Pharr Yarns Inc	PO Box 275	Clover	SC	29710	John Raines	803-631-5212	D	37*	0.5
Artee Industries Inc	PO Box 1509	Shelby	NC	28150	RT Davis	704-482-3826	R	35*	0.3
China Grove Textiles Inc	PO Box 12500	Gastonia	NC	28053	Donald L Warren	704-864-8374	S	35*	0.4
King Mill	PO Box 819	Augusta	GA	30913	Franklin Rachels	706-826-4520	D	35*	0.5
Spray Cotton Mills	PO Box 3207	Eden	NC	27288	Mark Bishopric	910-623-9181	R	35*	0.5
Tuscarora Yarns Inc	PO Box 218	Mount Pleasant	NC	28124	James Fry	704-436-6527	R	35	0.5
Rocky Mount Mills	PO Box 1240	Rocky Mount	NC	27802	John M Mebane Jr	919-442-1145	R	30	0.5
Jones Companies Ltd	PO Box 367	Humboldt	TN	38343	R Jones III	901-784-2832	R	29	0.4
Borden Manufacturing Company	PO.Drawer P	Goldsboro	NC	27533	EB Borden Jr	919-734-4301	R	28*	0.2
Doran Yarn Mill Inc	PO Box 9000	Shelby	NC	28151	Dan Green	704-487-2266	S	25	0.4
Highland Yarn Mills	PO Box 10055	High Point	NC	27261		919-886-4841	D	24	0.4
Kent Manufacturing Co	PO Box 67	Pickens	SC	29671	MB Kent	803-878-6367	R	22	0.2
Pharr Yarns of Georgia	PO Box 2827	Rome	GA	30164	JP Hine	706-235-8215	D	20	0.2
United Spinners Corp	PO Box 6	Lowell	NC	28098	Allen Bates	704-824-3576	S	20	0.2
Waverly Mills Inc	23 3rd St	Laurinburg	NC	28352	Jett L Smith III	919-276-1441	R	20	0.4
Multitex Corporation	PO Box 98	Ulmer	SC	29849	WD Johnson	803-584-3458	D	19	0.1
Fibron	4019 Industry Dr	Chattanooga	TN	37416	Leonard Chill	615-892-8080	D	18*	0.2
Rhyne Mills Inc	PO Box 70	Lincolnton	NC	28092	Joseph M Rhyne	704-732-5560	R	18	0.4
Image Yarn	PO Box 436	Talladega	AL	35160	Charles Pope	205-362-4712	D	16*	0.2
Burlington Menswear	PO Box 523	Bishopville	SC	29010	David York	803-484-5436	D	15*	0.2
OMI Georgia Inc	PO Box 8389	Columbus	GA	31908	T Kawamoto	706-563-6394	J	13	<0.1
Atlantic Spinners Inc	PO Box 1240	Bessemer City	NC	28016	Francis E Beall	704-629-6263	R	12*	0.2
Brodnax Mills Inc	PO Box A	Brodnax	VA	23920	Russell Lawrimore	804-729-2325	R	12*	0.2
Eastern Manufacturing Company	PO Box 98	Selma	NC	27576	Robert W Miller	919-965-3162	R	12*	0.2
Palmetto Spinning Corp	1100 Church St	Laurens	SC	29360	William F Davis Jr	803-984-3556	S	12*	0.2
Wyndmoor Industries Inc	PO Box 818	Lincolnton	NC	28092	W Kaplan	704-732-1171	R	12*	0.2
Crescent Spinning Co	PO Box 231	Belmont	NC	28012	JM Carstarphen	704-825-9611	D	11	0.2
UKI Yarns Inc	541 W 37th St	New York	NY	10018	Morton M Usdan	212-564-2000	R	11	0.2
American Silk Mills Corp	75 Stark St	Plains	PA	18705	John Sullivan	717-822-7147	S	10*	0.1
Chesterfield Yarn Mill	PO Box 427	Pageland	SC	29728	Robert P Neisler	803-672-7211	R	10	0.2
Crescent Woolen Mills Co	1016 School St	Two Rivers	WI	54241	WJ Webster	414-793-3331	R	10	<0.1
Oakdale Cotton Mills	PO Box 787	Jamestown	NC	27282	W G Ragsdale III	919-454-1144	R	10	0.2
Trio Manufacturing Co	PO Drawer 270	Forsyth	GA	31029	Howell W Newton	912-994-2671	R	10	0.1
Coren-Indix Inc	4224 N Front St	Philadelphia	PA	19140	Mark Indix	215-329-9650	R	8*	0.1
Howell Manufacturing Co	PO Box 460	Cherryville	NC	28021	HT White Jr	704-435-3259	R	8*	0.1
Federal Foam	150 Indrial Pk Rd	Cokato	MN	55321	Jim Vanhooser	612-286-2696	D	6	<0.1
Queen Carpet Corp	920 Tinsley St	Dalton	GA	30720	Marrion Smith	706-226-9122	D	6*	<0.1
Paola Yarns Inc	PO Box 5609	Statesville	NC	28687	William A Mills	704-873-1842	R	5	<0.1
Southern Mercerizing Co	PO Drawer H	Tryon	NC	28782	RM Neely	704-859-6671	S	5	<0.1
Robinson Manufacturing Co	PO Box 186	Elizabeth City	NC	27907	C O Robinson III	919-335-5200	R	5	<0.1
J and H Clasgens Company Inc	2383 State Rte 132	New Richmond	OH	45157	JH Clasgens II	513-553-4177	R	4	<0.1
Southwest Textiles Inc	PO Box 710	Abernathy	TX	79311	Joe O Thompson	806-298-2548	R	4	<0.1
Newburgh Yarn Mills Inc	625 Broadway St	Newburgh	NY	12550	Jack T Drennen Jr	914-562-2630	R	4	<0.1
Atlantic Cotton Mill	PO Box 4667	Macon	GA	31208	R L McCommon Jr	912-745-6521	R	3	<0.1
Fibers and Fabrics of Georgia	PO Box 962	Elberton	GA	30635	Abdul Hafeez	404-283-7510	S	2	<0.1
Lowell Worsted Mills Inc	12 Perkins St	Lowell	MA	01854	Patricia Chew	508-454-6041	R	1*	<0.1
Stone Creek Yarn Mill Company	Rte 4	Tallassee	AL	36078	William J Stough	205-283-2170	R	1	<0.1
Quinnehticut Woolen Co	PO Box 522	Norwich	CT	06360	Dale Plummer	203-889-0325	R	1	<0.1

Source: Ward's Business Directory of U.S. Private and Public Companies, Volumes 1 and 2, 1996. The company type code used is as follows: P - Public, R - Private, S - Subsidiary, D - Division, J - Joint Venture, A - Affiliate, G - Group. Sales are in millions of dollars, employees are in thousands. An asterisk (*) indicates an estimated sales volume. The symbol < stands for 'less than'. Company names and addresses are truncated, in some cases, to fit into the available space.

MATERIALS CONSUMED

Material		Quantity	Delivered Cost ($ million)
Materials, ingredients, containers, and supplies		(X)	4,445.4
Raw cotton fibers	1,000 bales	4,975.7	1,649.8
Raw wool, mohair, and other animal fibers (scoured weight)	mil lb	(D)	(D)
Wool tops	mil lb	(D)	(D)
All other fibers (silk, jute, reused wool, waste, etc.)	mil lb	72.3	15.8
Rayon and acetate staple and tow	mil lb	122.5	138.3
Nylon staple and tow	mil lb	926.9	992.1
Polyester staple and tow	mil lb	763.0	598.8
Acrylic staple and tow	mil lb	144.6	159.7
All other manmade fiber staple and tow (except glass)	mil lb	66.7*	108.1
Spun yarn, all fibers	mil lb	32.0*	45.4
Nylon filament yarns	mil lb	95.9	148.5
Polyester filament yarns	mil lb	100.5	97.3
All other manmade filament yarns	mil lb	1.7*	3.4
Dyes, lakes, and toners		(X)	18.9
All other materials and components, parts, containers, and supplies		(X)	330.0
Materials, ingredients, containers, and supplies, nsk		(X)	14.8

Source: 1992 *Economic Census*. Explanation of symbols used: (D): Withheld to avoid disclosure of competitive data; na: Not available; (S): Withheld because statistical norms were not met; (X): Not applicable; (Z): Less than half the unit shown; nec: Not elsewhere classified; nsk: Not specified by kind; - : zero; * : 10-19 percent estimated; ** : 20-29 percent estimated.

PRODUCT SHARE DETAILS

Product or Product Class	% Share	Product or Product Class	% Share
Yarn spinning mills	100.00	Combed cotton yarns, spun gray	8.09
Carded cotton yarns	35.61	Rayon and/or acetate spun yarns, spun gray	3.19
Carded cotton yarns, spun gray	64.13	Spun noncellulosic fiber and silk yarns	49.31
Carded cotton yarns, spun and finished in the same establishment	35.82	Wool yarns	3.32
Carded cotton yarns, nsk	0.05	Yarn spinning mills, nsk	0.48

Source: 1992 *Economic Census*. The values shown are percent of total shipments in an industry. Values of indented subcategories are summed in the main heading. The symbol (D) appears when data are withheld to prevent disclosure of competitive information. The abbreviation nsk stands for 'not specified by kind' and nec for 'not elsewhere classified'.

INPUTS AND OUTPUTS FOR YARN MILLS & FINISHING OF TEXTILES, NEC

Economic Sector or Industry Providing Inputs	%	Sector	Economic Sector or Industry Buying Outputs	%	Sector
Organic fibers, noncellulosic	44.9	Manufg.	Floor coverings	21.8	Manufg.
Yarn mills & finishing of textiles, nec	13.6	Manufg.	Broadwoven fabric mills	14.1	Manufg.
Cotton	8.9	Agric.	Yarn mills & finishing of textiles, nec	11.8	Manufg.
Wholesale trade	5.3	Trade	Knit fabric mills	11.2	Manufg.
Electric services (utilities)	4.9	Util.	Knit outerwear mills	8.6	Manufg.
Imports	2.6	Foreign	Apparel made from purchased materials	8.4	Manufg.
Cellulosic manmade fibers	2.0	Manufg.	Hosiery, nec	4.7	Manufg.
Textile goods, nec	2.0	Manufg.	Narrow fabric mills	2.6	Manufg.
Textile machinery	1.4	Manufg.	Thread mills	2.3	Manufg.
Cyclic crudes and organics	1.3	Manufg.	Personal consumption expenditures	2.2	
Laundry, dry cleaning, shoe repair	1.2	Services	Knit underwear mills	2.2	Manufg.
Petroleum refining	1.1	Manufg.	Exports	1.7	Foreign
Paperboard containers & boxes	1.0	Manufg.	Pleating & stitching	1.5	Manufg.
Gas production & distribution (utilities)	0.9	Util.	Fabricated textile products, nec	1.1	Manufg.
Motor freight transportation & warehousing	0.9	Util.	Women's hosiery, except socks	0.9	Manufg.
Lubricating oils & greases	0.6	Manufg.	Schiffli machine embroideries	0.7	Manufg.
Eating & drinking places	0.6	Trade	Manufacturing industries, nec	0.6	Manufg.
Surface active agents	0.5	Manufg.	Organic fibers, noncellulosic	0.6	Manufg.
Banking	0.5	Fin/R.E.	Canvas & related products	0.5	Manufg.
Maintenance of nonfarm buildings nec	0.4	Constr.	Cellulosic manmade fibers	0.4	Manufg.
Meat animals	0.3	Agric.	Nonwoven fabrics	0.4	Manufg.
Communications, except radio & TV	0.3	Util.	Cordage & twine	0.2	Manufg.
Advertising	0.3	Services	Games, toys, & children's vehicles	0.2	Manufg.
U.S. Postal Service	0.3	Gov't	Knitting mills, nec	0.2	Manufg.
Industrial inorganic chemicals, nec	0.2	Manufg.	Textile goods, nec	0.2	Manufg.
Machinery, except electrical, nec	0.2	Manufg.	Job training & related services	0.2	Services
Narrow fabric mills	0.2	Manufg.	Coated fabrics, not rubberized	0.1	Manufg.
Semiconductors & related devices	0.2	Manufg.	Lace goods	0.1	Manufg.
Railroads & related services	0.2	Util.	Nonferrous wire drawing & insulating	0.1	Manufg.
Real estate	0.2	Fin/R.E.	Padding & upholstery filling	0.1	Manufg.
Computer & data processing services	0.2	Services			
Equipment rental & leasing services	0.2	Services			
Legal services	0.2	Services			
Management & consulting services & labs	0.2	Services			
Paper coating & glazing	0.1	Manufg.			
Processed textile waste	0.1	Manufg.			
Insurance carriers	0.1	Fin/R.E.			
Accounting, auditing & bookkeeping	0.1	Services			
Automotive rental & leasing, without drivers	0.1	Services			
Automotive repair shops & services	0.1	Services			

Source: Benchmark Input-Output Accounts for the U.S. Economy, 1982, U.S. Department of Commerce, Washington, D.C., July 1991. Data, as reported in the source, are organized by the 1977 SIC structure in use in 1982 but have been matched, as closely as is possible, to the 1987 SIC structure used in this book.

OCCUPATIONS EMPLOYED BY SIC 228 - WEAVING, FINISHING, YARN AND THREAD MILLS

Occupation	% of Total 1994	Change to 2005	Occupation	% of Total 1994	Change to 2005
Textile draw-out & winding machine operators	32.8	-35.5	Machine feeders & offbearers	2.6	-27.4
Industrial machinery mechanics	6.4	29.1	Machine operators nec	2.2	-28.9
Textile machine setters & set-up operators	4.9	-11.3	Sewing machine operators, non-garment	1.8	21.0
Helpers, laborers, & material movers nec	4.5	-19.3	Industrial truck & tractor operators	1.6	-19.3
Blue collar worker supervisors	4.2	-24.6	Hand packers & packagers	1.3	-30.9
Inspectors, testers, & graders, precision	4.2	-27.4	General managers & top executives	1.3	-23.5
Textile bleaching & dyeing machine operators	4.2	8.9	Maintenance repairers, general utility	1.2	-27.4
Freight, stock, & material movers, hand	2.8	-35.5	Janitors & cleaners, incl maids	1.0	-35.5

Source: Industry-Occupation Matrix, Bureau of Labor Statistics. These data relate to one or more 3-digit SIC industry groups rather than to a single 4-digit SIC. The change reported for each occupation to the year 2005 is a percent of growth or decline as estimated by the Bureau of Labor Statistics. The abbreviation nec stands for 'not elsewhere classified'.

LOCATION BY STATE AND REGIONAL CONCENTRATION

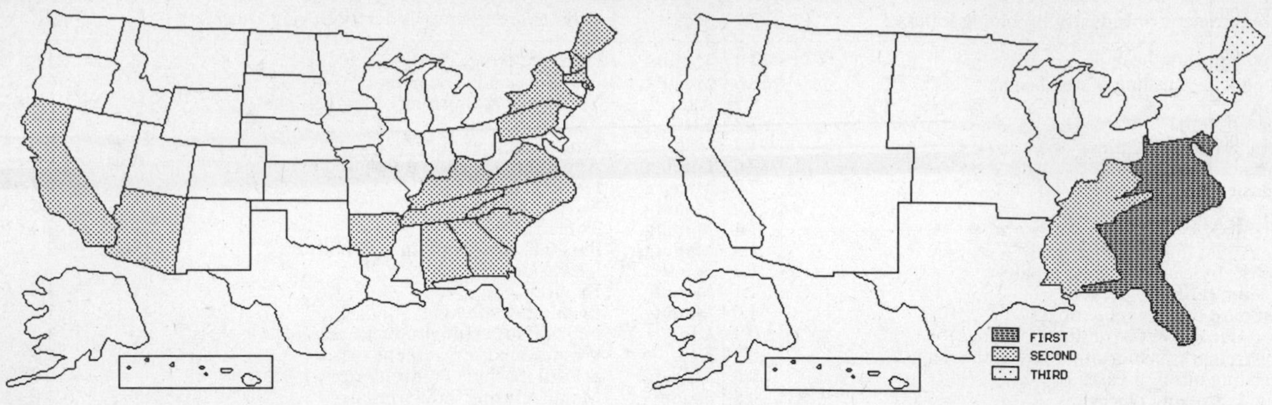

INDUSTRY DATA BY STATE

State	Establish-ments	Shipments			Employment				Cost as % of Shipments	Investment per Employee ($)
		Total ($ mil)	% of U.S.	Per Establ.	Total Number	% of U.S.	Per Establ.	Wages ($/hour)		
North Carolina	168	3,755.0	49.0	22.4	33,400	48.6	199	8.27	59.8	4,305
Georgia	63	1,442.6	18.8	22.9	12,800	18.6	203	8.62	66.4	2,008
South Carolina	42	873.2	11.4	20.8	8,000	11.6	190	8.27	63.1	3,675
Tennessee	11	304.1	4.0	27.6	1,900	2.8	173	9.59	65.2	10,632
Massachusetts	10	20.1	0.3	2.0	200	0.3	20	11.33	60.2	3,500
New York	14	12.5	0.2	0.9	200	0.3	14	6.25	52.8	2,000
Alabama	34	(D)	-	-	7,500 *	10.9	221	-	-	-
Maine	8	(D)	-	-	750 *	1.1	94	-	-	-
California	7	(D)	-	-	750 *	1.1	107	-	-	-
Pennsylvania	7	(D)	-	-	375 *	0.5	54	-	-	-
Rhode Island	3	(D)	-	-	175 *	0.3	58	-	-	-
Virginia	3	(D)	-	-	750 *	1.1	250	-	-	-
Kentucky	2	(D)	-	-	375 *	0.5	188	-	-	-
New Hampshire	2	(D)	-	-	175 *	0.3	88	-	-	-
Arizona	1	(D)	-	-	375 *	0.5	375	-	-	-
Arkansas	1	(D)	-	-	175 *	0.3	175	-	-	-

Source: 1992 *Economic Census*. The states are in descending order of shipments or establishments (if shipment data are missing for the majority). The symbol (D) appears when data are withheld to prevent disclosure of competitive information. States marked with (D) are sorted by number of establishments. A dash (-) indicates that the data element cannot be calculated; * indicates the midpoint of a range.

2282 - THROWING AND WINDING MILLS

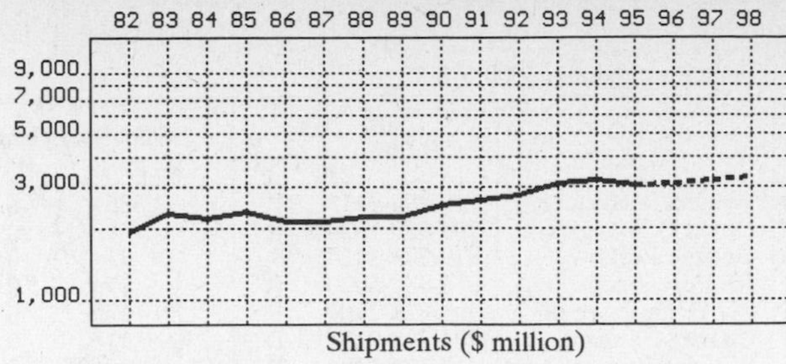

Shipments ($ million)

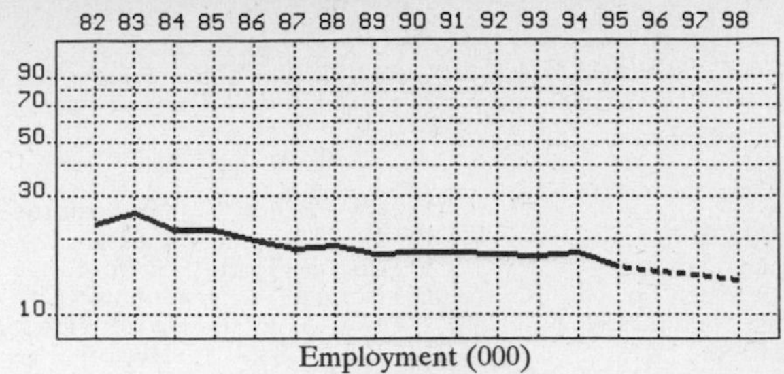

Employment (000)

GENERAL STATISTICS

		Establishments		Employment			Compensation		Production ($ million)			
Year	Companies	Total	with 20 or more employees	Total (000)	Production Workers (000)	Production Hours (Mil)	Payroll ($ mil)	Wages ($/hr)	Cost of Materials	Value Added by Manufacture	Value of Shipments	Capital Invest.
1982	160	189	139	22.8	19.8	37.7	273.0	5.63	1,399.6	527.4	1,944.7	59.0
1983		179	130	25.5	22.5	44.8	326.3	5.74	1,667.3	675.1	2,324.5	52.5
1984		169	121	21.9	19.5	37.1	304.9	6.47	1,628.7	586.9	2,213.7	75.3
1985		158	112	21.9	19.2	37.2	315.0	6.68	1,701.4	628.9	2,340.4	51.5
1986		149	106	19.7	17.5	33.9	291.7	6.87	1,545.1	606.5	2,138.8	39.0
1987	122	138	99	18.3	16.1	31.5	290.5	7.32	1,549.7	588.0	2,123.7	43.1
1988		148	104	19.0	16.8	32.8	305.0	7.41	1,572.2	684.0	2,261.2	61.2
1989		132	94	17.4	16.0	31.4	293.1	7.49	1,603.2	647.8	2,249.0	57.9
1990		138	95	17.8	16.6	33.2	314.1	7.58	1,745.5	769.3	2,521.0	142.8
1991		127	87	17.9	16.1	32.1	312.1	7.67	1,841.6	779.2	2,622.6	125.9
1992	111	137	90	17.3	15.3	31.7	340.1	8.28	1,930.3	842.6	2,771.9	85.5
1993		147	98	17.2	15.2	31.5	351.1	8.68	2,187.5	900.2	3,076.5	128.4
1994		122P	80P	17.7	15.8	32.3	386.3	9.59	2,350.3	852.1	3,197.6	77.3
1995		117P	76P	15.4P	14.0P	29.1P	353.5P	9.27P	2,228.2P	807.8P	3,031.4P	114.4P
1996		113P	72P	14.9P	13.5P	28.4P	358.9P	9.55P	2,289.8P	830.1P	3,115.2P	119.8P
1997		109P	68P	14.3P	13.0P	27.6P	364.3P	9.82P	2,351.3P	852.5P	3,199.0P	125.1P
1998		104P	63P	13.7P	12.6P	26.9P	369.7P	10.10P	2,412.9P	874.8P	3,282.8P	130.5P

Sources: 1982, 1987, 1992 *Economic Census*; *Annual Survey of Manufactures*, 83-86, 88-91, 93-94. Establishment counts for non-Census years are from *County Business Patterns*; establishment values for 83-84 are extrapolations. 'P's show projections by the editors. Industries reclassified in 87 will not have data for prior years.

INDICES OF CHANGE

		Establishments		Employment			Compensation		Production ($ million)			
Year	Companies	Total	with 20 or more employees	Total (000)	Production Workers (000)	Production Hours (Mil)	Payroll ($ mil)	Wages ($/hr)	Cost of Materials	Value Added by Manufacture	Value of Shipments	Capital Invest.
1982	144	138	154	132	129	119	80	68	73	63	70	69
1983		131	144	147	147	141	96	69	86	80	84	61
1984		123	134	127	127	117	90	78	84	70	80	88
1985		115	124	127	125	117	93	81	88	75	84	60
1986		109	118	114	114	107	86	83	80	72	77	46
1987	110	101	110	106	105	99	85	88	80	70	77	50
1988		108	116	110	110	103	90	89	81	81	82	72
1989		96	104	101	105	99	86	90	83	77	81	68
1990		101	106	103	108	105	92	92	90	91	91	167
1991		93	97	103	105	101	92	93	95	92	95	147
1992	100	100	100	100	100	100	100	100	100	100	100	100
1993		107	109	99	99	99	103	105	113	107	111	150
1994		89P	89P	102	103	102	114	116	122	101	115	90
1995		86P	84P	89P	92P	92P	104P	112P	115P	96P	109P	134P
1996		82P	80P	86P	88P	89P	106P	115P	119P	99P	112P	140P
1997		79P	75P	82P	85P	87P	107P	119P	122P	101P	115P	146P
1998		76P	71P	79P	82P	85P	109P	122P	125P	104P	118P	153P

Sources: Same as General Statistics. Values reflect change from the base year, 1992. Values above 100 mean greater than 92, values below 100 mean less than 92, and a value of 100 in the 82-91 or 93-98 period means same as 92. 'P's mark projections by the editors.

SELECTED RATIOS

For 1994	Avg. of All Manufact.	Analyzed Industry	Index	For 1994	Avg. of All Manufact.	Analyzed Industry	Index
Employees per Establishment	49	145	296	Value Added per Production Worker	134,084	53,930	40
Payroll per Establishment	1,500,273	3,167,967	211	Cost per Establishment	5,045,178	19,274,329	382
Payroll per Employee	30,620	21,825	71	Cost per Employee	102,970	132,785	129
Production Workers per Establishment	34	130	378	Cost per Production Worker	146,988	148,753	101
Wages per Establishment	853,319	2,540,254	298	Shipments per Establishment	9,576,895	26,222,863	274
Wages per Production Worker	24,861	19,605	79	Shipments per Employee	195,460	180,655	92
Hours per Production Worker	2,056	2,044	99	Shipments per Production Worker	279,017	202,380	73
Wages per Hour	12.09	9.59	79	Investment per Establishment	321,011	633,921	197
Value Added per Establishment	4,602,255	6,987,898	152	Investment per Employee	6,552	4,367	67
Value Added per Employee	93,930	48,141	51	Investment per Production Worker	9,352	4,892	52

Sources: Same as General Statistics. The 'Average of All Manufacturing' column represents the average of all manufacturing industries reported for the most recent complete year available. The Index shows the relationship between the Average and the Analyzed Industry. For example, 100 means that they are equal; 500 that the Analyzed Industry is five times the average; 50 means that the Analyzed Industry is half the national average. The abbreviation 'na' is used to show that data are 'not available'.

LEADING COMPANIES

Number shown: **16** Total sales ($ mil): **1,574** Total employment (000): **8.5**

Company Name	Address				CEO Name	Phone	Co. Type	Sales ($ mil)	Empl. (000)
Unifi Inc	7201 W Friendly	Greensboro	NC	27410	William T Kretzer	910-294-4410	P	1,385	6.0
Jefferson Mills Inc	PO Box 698	Pulaski	VA	24301	David B Spangler	703-980-1530	R	48	0.4
Unifi Spun Yarn Inc	1921 Boone Trail	Sanford	NC	27330	George Perkins	919-775-1426	S	41*	0.5
Leon-Ferenbach Co	PO Box 450	Johnson City	TN	37605	RS Ferenbach	615-434-5000	R	17	0.3
Concordia Manufacturing	PO Box 151	West Warwick	RI	02893	PO Boghossian III	401-828-1100	R	13	0.2
Hudson Cloth	PO Box 2228	Hickory	NC	28603	Charles Shuford	704-328-2131	D	11*	0.1
Middleburg Yarn Process	909 N Orange St	Selinsgrove	PA	17870	William Brawer	717-374-1284	R	10*	0.1
Roselon Industries Inc	18 S 5th St	Quakertown	PA	18951	Robert Adams	215-536-3275	R	10*	0.1
Sapona Manufacturing Company	PO Box 128	Cedar Falls	NC	27230	S Steele Redding	919-625-2727	R	10	0.2
Liberty Throwing Company Inc	PO Box 1387	Kingston	PA	18704	Larry Sprankle	717-287-1114	R	7*	<0.1
Whitney Yarn	PO Box 1658	Spartanburg	SC	29304	Joe Caton	803-594-5300	D	7*	0.1
Hickory Dyeing and Winding	PO Box 1975	Hickory	NC	28603	Robert F Miller	704-322-1550	R	6	<0.1
Atwater Inc	PO Box 247	Plymouth	PA	18651	Elmo Begliomini	717-779-9568	R	4	0.1
Huntingdon Throwing Mills Inc	117 Walnut St	Mifflinburg	PA	17844	Beulah K Baugher	717-966-3111	R	2	0.1
Westbrook Yarns Inc	PO Box 457	Westbrook	ME	04098	Don Spencer	207-854-8445	R	2	<0.1
North Plains Textiles Inc	PO Box 864	Tulia	TX	79088	Doug Nix	806-995-3190	R	1	<0.1

Source: *Ward's Business Directory of U.S. Private and Public Companies*, Volumes 1 and 2, 1996. The company type code used is as follows: P - Public, R - Private, S - Subsidiary, D - Division, J - Joint Venture, A - Affiliate, G - Group. Sales are in millions of dollars, employees are in thousands. An asterisk (*) indicates an estimated sales volume. The symbol < stands for 'less than'. Company names and addresses are truncated, in some cases, to fit into the available space.

MATERIALS CONSUMED

Material		Quantity	Delivered Cost ($ million)
Materials, ingredients, containers, and supplies		(X)	1,845.6
Spun yarn, all fibers	mil lb	40.6	48.7
Polyester filament yarns	mil lb	693.9	697.1
Nylon filament yarns	mil lb	507.8*	821.5
All other manmade filament yarns	mil lb	49.0	100.6
Dyes, lakes, and toners		(X)	2.7
All other materials and components, parts, containers, and supplies		(X)	167.3
Materials, ingredients, containers, and supplies, nsk		(X)	7.7

Source: 1992 *Economic Census*. Explanation of symbols used: (D): Withheld to avoid disclosure of competitive data; na: Not available; (S): Withheld because statistical norms were not met; (X): Not applicable; (Z): Less than half the unit shown; nec: Not elsewhere classified; nsk: Not specified by kind; - : zero; * : 10-19 percent estimated; ** : 20-29 percent estimated.

PRODUCT SHARE DETAILS

Product or Product Class	% Share
Yarn throwing and winding mills	100.00
Rewound, plied, etc., yarns (not spun or thrown at the same establishment)	5.75
Rewound and novelty yarns, other than wool (not spun or thrown at the same establishment)	34.79
Plied yarns, other than wool (not spun or thrown at the same establishment)	45.83
Winding, warping, etc. of purchased wool yarns	19.38
Thrown filament yarns, except textured	11.00
Nylon yarns	56.60
Polyester yarns	25.01
All other thrown yarns	16.62
Not specified by kind	1.77
Textured, crimped, or bulked filament yarns, including stretch yarn (made from purchased filament yarn)	78.55
Commission throwing, plying, etc., of yarns	4.36
Commission receipts for throwing or texturing of filament yarns	18.59
Commission receipts for winding, warping, etc., of yarn not thrown or spun at the same establishment	76.40
Commission throwing, plying, etc., of yarns, nsk	5.01
Yarn throwing and winding mills, nsk	0.35

Source: 1992 *Economic Census*. The values shown are percent of total shipments in an industry. Values of indented subcategories are summed in the main heading. The symbol (D) appears when data are withheld to prevent disclosure of competitive information. The abbreviation nsk stands for 'not specified by kind' and nec for 'not elsewhere classified'.

INPUTS AND OUTPUTS FOR THREAD MILLS

Economic Sector or Industry Providing Inputs	%	Sector	Economic Sector or Industry Buying Outputs	%	Sector
Yarn mills & finishing of textiles, nec	34.2	Manufg.	Apparel made from purchased materials	41.0	Manufg.
Organic fibers, noncellulosic	15.5	Manufg.	Knit outerwear mills	12.5	Manufg.
Imports	6.7	Foreign	Personal consumption expenditures	11.1	
Cellulosic manmade fibers	6.3	Manufg.	Exports	6.6	Foreign
Wholesale trade	5.5	Trade	Shoes, except rubber	4.5	Manufg.
Electric services (utilities)	4.3	Util.	Automotive & apparel trimmings	4.4	Manufg.
Cotton	4.1	Agric.	Knit underwear mills	2.5	Manufg.
Miscellaneous plastics products	3.0	Manufg.	Rubber & plastics footwear	2.2	Manufg.
Photofinishing labs, commercial photography	2.4	Services	Upholstered household furniture	1.7	Manufg.
Cyclic crudes and organics	1.7	Manufg.	Mattresses & bedsprings	1.4	Manufg.
Textile machinery	1.4	Manufg.	Surgical appliances & supplies	1.4	Manufg.
Air transportation	1.3	Util.	Luggage	1.1	Manufg.
Laundry, dry cleaning, shoe repair	1.3	Services	Women's handbags & purses	1.0	Manufg.
Petroleum refining	1.1	Manufg.	Narrow fabric mills	0.7	Manufg.
Motor freight transportation & warehousing	1.1	Util.	Miscellaneous plastics products	0.6	Manufg.
Paperboard containers & boxes	0.9	Manufg.	House slippers	0.5	Manufg.
Gas production & distribution (utilities)	0.9	Util.	Knitting mills, nec	0.5	Manufg.
Industrial gases	0.8	Manufg.	Leather gloves & mittens	0.5	Manufg.
Thread mills	0.8	Manufg.	Leather goods, nec	0.5	Manufg.
Lubricating oils & greases	0.6	Manufg.	Thread mills	0.5	Manufg.
Eating & drinking places	0.6	Trade	Personal leather goods	0.4	Manufg.
Banking	0.5	Fin/R.E.	Sporting & athletic goods, nec	0.4	Manufg.
U.S. Postal Service	0.4	Gov't	Watch, clock, jewelry, & furniture repair	0.4	Services
Maintenance of nonfarm buildings nec	0.3	Constr.	Canvas & related products	0.3	Manufg.
Communications, except radio & TV	0.3	Util.	Fabricated textile products, nec	0.3	Manufg.
Hotels & lodging places	0.3	Services	Housefurnishings, nec	0.3	Manufg.
Industrial inorganic chemicals, nec	0.2	Manufg.	Schiffli machine embroideries	0.3	Manufg.
Machinery, except electrical, nec	0.2	Manufg.	Yarn mills & finishing of textiles, nec	0.3	Manufg.
Real estate	0.2	Fin/R.E.	Laundry, dry cleaning, shoe repair	0.3	Services
Advertising	0.2	Services	Curtains & draperies	0.2	Manufg.
Computer & data processing services	0.2	Services	Metal household furniture	0.2	Manufg.
Equipment rental & leasing services	0.2	Services	Pleating & stitching	0.2	Manufg.
Legal services	0.2	Services	Public building furniture	0.2	Manufg.
Management & consulting services & labs	0.2	Services	Textile bags	0.2	Manufg.
Coal	0.1	Mining	Blankbooks & looseleaf binders	0.1	Manufg.
Railroads & related services	0.1	Util.	Motion pictures	0.1	Services
Sanitary services, steam supply, irrigation	0.1	Util.	Portrait, photographic studios	0.1	Services
Water supply & sewage systems	0.1	Util.			
Insurance carriers	0.1	Fin/R.E.			
Accounting, auditing & bookkeeping	0.1	Services			

Source: Benchmark Input-Output Accounts for the U.S. Economy, 1982, U.S. Department of Commerce, Washington, D.C., July 1991. Data, as reported in the source, are organized by the 1977 SIC structure in use in 1982 but have been matched, as closely as is possible, to the 1987 SIC structure used in this book.

OCCUPATIONS EMPLOYED BY SIC 228 - WEAVING, FINISHING, YARN AND THREAD MILLS

Occupation	% of Total 1994	Change to 2005	Occupation	% of Total 1994	Change to 2005
Textile draw-out & winding machine operators	32.8	-35.5	Machine feeders & offbearers	2.6	-27.4
Industrial machinery mechanics	6.4	29.1	Machine operators nec	2.2	-28.9
Textile machine setters & set-up operators	4.9	-11.3	Sewing machine operators, non-garment	1.8	21.0
Helpers, laborers, & material movers nec	4.5	-19.3	Industrial truck & tractor operators	1.6	-19.3
Blue collar worker supervisors	4.2	-24.6	Hand packers & packagers	1.3	-30.9
Inspectors, testers, & graders, precision	4.2	-27.4	General managers & top executives	1.3	-23.5
Textile bleaching & dyeing machine operators	4.2	8.9	Maintenance repairers, general utility	1.2	-27.4
Freight, stock, & material movers, hand	2.8	-35.5	Janitors & cleaners, incl maids	1.0	-35.5

Source: Industry-Occupation Matrix, Bureau of Labor Statistics. These data relate to one or more 3-digit SIC industry groups rather than to a single 4-digit SIC. The change reported for each occupation to the year 2005 is a percent of growth or decline as estimated by the Bureau of Labor Statistics. The abbreviation nec stands for 'not elsewhere classified'.

LOCATION BY STATE AND REGIONAL CONCENTRATION

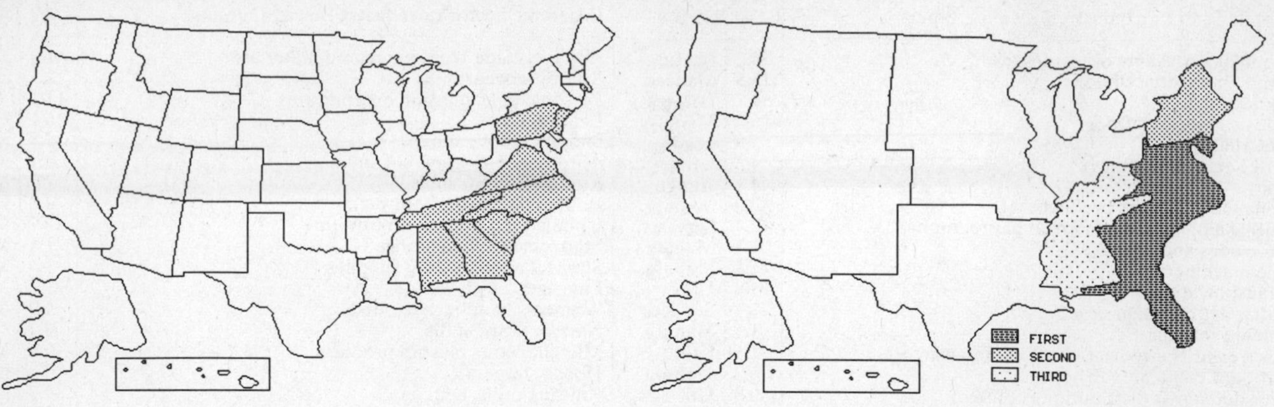

INDUSTRY DATA BY STATE

State	Establish-ments	Shipments			Employment				Cost as % of Shipments	Investment per Employee ($)
		Total ($ mil)	% of U.S.	Per Establ.	Total Number	% of U.S.	Per Establ.	Wages ($/hour)		
North Carolina	36	1,283.9	46.3	35.7	6,200	35.8	172	8.47	67.3	3,274
Pennsylvania	17	64.5	2.3	3.8	900	5.2	53	7.40	50.9	1,111
Rhode Island	5	28.2	1.0	5.6	300	1.7	60	8.00	46.8	667
New Jersey	6	23.4	0.8	3.9	200	1.2	33	8.50	65.8	-
Georgia	32	(D)	-	-	7,500 *	43.4	234	-	-	-
South Carolina	11	(D)	-	-	1,750 *	10.1	159	-	-	-
Virginia	7	(D)	-	-	1,750 *	10.1	250	-	-	-
Tennessee	3	(D)	-	-	750 *	4.3	250	-	-	-
Alabama	2	(D)	-	-	375 *	2.2	188	-	-	-

Source: 1992 *Economic Census*. The states are in descending order of shipments or establishments (if shipment data are missing for the majority). The symbol (D) appears when data are withheld to prevent disclosure of competitive information. States marked with (D) are sorted by number of establishments. A dash (-) indicates that the data element cannot be calculated; * indicates the midpoint of a range.

2284 - THREAD MILLS

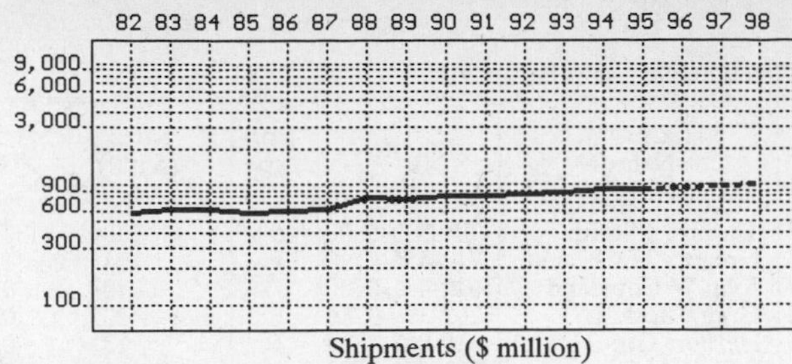

Shipments ($ million)

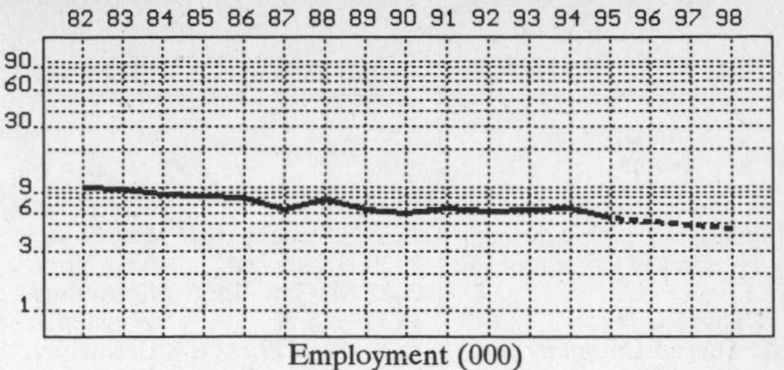

Employment (000)

GENERAL STATISTICS

Year	Companies	Establishments		Employment			Compensation		Production ($ million)			
		Total	with 20 or more employees	Total (000)	Production Workers (000)	Production Hours (Mil)	Payroll ($ mil)	Wages ($/hr)	Cost of Materials	Value Added by Manufacture	Value of Shipments	Capital Invest.
1982	60	75	45	9.8	8.4	15.1	113.2	5.72	360.8	215.5	578.8	15.3
1983		72	44	9.5	8.0	14.8	118.7	6.04	357.6	266.2	615.5	26.5
1984		69	43	8.8	7.5	13.5	117.9	6.39	355.6	253.2	619.9	12.3
1985		66	41	8.5	7.2	13.1	119.7	6.59	343.2	245.3	591.3	12.4
1986		65	42	8.0	6.8	13.1	119.9	6.79	333.4	268.0	600.4	10.4
1987	50	59	38	6.5	5.6	11.0	106.1	7.01	398.9	248.1	635.6	14.1
1988		58	40	7.9	6.9	13.9	123.6	6.88	468.5	318.1	780.1	11.0
1989		59	40	6.5	6.2	12.8	126.2	7.27	434.5	326.1	764.8	29.7
1990		59	39	6.1	6.3	13.4	127.7	7.14	465.9	329.3	794.5	23.8
1991		56	38	6.7	5.9	13.4	124.8	7.06	455.4	338.3	799.3	24.1
1992	50	65	41	6.2	5.6	11.9	115.4	7.34	511.7	328.4	837.0	22.0
1993		75	42	6.5	5.8	12.2	124.3	7.61	530.8	338.0	865.9	24.3
1994		60P	39P	6.7	6.0	12.4	129.1	7.77	541.1	391.8	922.0	35.2
1995		59P	38P	5.5P	5.2P	11.9P	126.8P	7.91P	544.7P	394.4P	928.1P	28.7P
1996		59P	38P	5.2P	5.0P	11.7P	127.7P	8.05P	561.9P	406.8P	957.4P	30.0P
1997		58P	37P	4.9P	4.8P	11.5P	128.6P	8.19P	579.0P	419.2P	986.6P	31.2P
1998		57P	37P	4.6P	4.6P	11.3P	129.5P	8.34P	596.2P	431.7P	1,015.8P	32.4P

Sources: 1982, 1987, 1992 *Economic Census*; *Annual Survey of Manufactures*, 83-86, 88-91, 93-94. Establishment counts for non-Census years are from *County Business Patterns*; establishment values for 83-84 are extrapolations. 'P's show projections by the editors. Industries reclassified in 87 will not have data for prior years.

INDICES OF CHANGE

Year	Companies	Establishments		Employment			Compensation		Production ($ million)			
		Total	with 20 or more employees	Total (000)	Production Workers (000)	Production Hours (Mil)	Payroll ($ mil)	Wages ($/hr)	Cost of Materials	Value Added by Manufacture	Value of Shipments	Capital Invest.
1982	120	115	110	158	150	127	98	78	71	66	69	70
1983		111	107	153	143	124	103	82	70	81	74	120
1984		106	105	142	134	113	102	87	69	77	74	56
1985		102	100	137	129	110	104	90	67	75	71	56
1986		100	102	129	121	110	104	93	65	82	72	47
1987	100	91	93	105	100	92	92	96	78	76	76	64
1988		89	98	127	123	117	107	94	92	97	93	50
1989		91	98	105	111	108	109	99	85	99	91	135
1990		91	95	98	113	113	111	97	91	100	95	108
1991		86	93	108	105	113	108	96	89	103	95	110
1992	100	100	100	100	100	100	100	100	100	100	100	100
1993		115	102	105	104	103	108	104	104	103	103	110
1994		92P	94P	108	107	104	112	106	106	119	110	160
1995		91P	93P	88P	93P	100P	110P	108P	106P	120P	111P	131P
1996		90P	92P	83P	89P	98P	111P	110P	110P	124P	114P	136P
1997		89P	91P	79P	85P	97P	111P	112P	113P	128P	118P	142P
1998		88P	90P	74P	82P	95P	112P	114P	117P	131P	121P	147P

Sources: Same as General Statistics. Values reflect change from the base year, 1992. Values above 100 mean greater than 92, values below 100 mean less than 92, and a value of 100 in the 82-91 or 93-98 period means same as 92. 'P's mark projections by the editors.

SELECTED RATIOS

For 1994	Avg. of All Manufact.	Analyzed Industry	Index
Employees per Establishment	49	111	228
Payroll per Establishment	1,500,273	2,147,870	143
Payroll per Employee	30,620	19,269	63
Production Workers per Establishment	34	100	291
Wages per Establishment	853,319	1,602,966	188
Wages per Production Worker	24,861	16,058	65
Hours per Production Worker	2,056	2,067	101
Wages per Hour	12.09	7.77	64
Value Added per Establishment	4,602,255	6,518,477	142
Value Added per Employee	93,930	58,478	62

For 1994	Avg. of All Manufact.	Analyzed Industry	Index
Value Added per Production Worker	134,084	65,300	49
Cost per Establishment	5,045,178	9,002,420	178
Cost per Employee	102,970	80,761	78
Cost per Production Worker	146,988	90,183	61
Shipments per Establishment	9,576,895	15,339,551	160
Shipments per Employee	195,460	137,612	70
Shipments per Production Worker	279,017	153,667	55
Investment per Establishment	321,011	585,631	182
Investment per Employee	6,552	5,254	80
Investment per Production Worker	9,352	5,867	63

Sources: Same as General Statistics. The 'Average of All Manufacturing' column represents the average of all manufacturing industries reported for the most recent complete year available. The Index shows the relationship between the Average and the Analyzed Industry. For example, 100 means that they are equal; 500 that the Analyzed Industry is five times the average; 50 means that the Analyzed Industry is half the national average. The abbreviation 'na' is used to show that data are 'not available'.

LEADING COMPANIES

Number shown: **12** Total sales ($ mil): **662** Total employment (000): **7.3**

Company Name	Address				CEO Name	Phone	Co. Type	Sales ($ mil)	Empl. (000)
American and Efird Inc	PO Box 507	Mount Holly	NC	28120	John W Copeland	704-827-4311	S	265	2.6
Coats Industrial North America	4135 S Stream Blv	Charlotte	NC	28217	Thomas J Smith	704-329-5800	S	160*	2.0
Belding Heminway Company Inc	1430 Broadway	New York	NY	10018	Gregory H Cheskin	212-556-4700	P	124	1.4
Amer & Efird	2421 McGaw Rd	Columbus	OH	43207	John W Copeland	614-491-0700	D	40*	0.4
Danfield Threads Inc	PO Box 979	Winsted	CT	06098	Greg Cheskin	203-379-0786	S	20	0.2
Synthetic Thread Company Inc	PO Box 1277	Bethlehem	PA	18016	Herbert Greenblatt	610-868-8575	R	12	0.1
Advance Fiber Techn Corp	15 Industrial Rd	Fairfield	NJ	07006	P Phillips	201-882-9500	R	10	0.1
Ludlow Textiles Company Inc	PO Box I	Ludlow	MA	01056	MA Lower	413-583-5051	R	10	0.1
Robison-Anton Textile Co	175 Bergen Blv	Fairview	NJ	07022	Bruce N Anton	201-941-0500	R	10*	0.2
Eddington Thread Mfg Co	PO Box 446	Bensalem	PA	19020	IA Tannenbaum	215-639-8900	R	5	0.1
DMC Corp	10 Port Kearny	South Kearny	NJ	07032	Nicholas Wallaert	201-589-0606	S	4	<0.1
US Thread Inc	PO Box 39	Graysville	TN	37338	Gene Robbins	615-775-0095	S	2	<0.1

Source: *Ward's Business Directory of U.S. Private and Public Companies*, Volumes 1 and 2, 1996. The company type code used is as follows: P - Public, R - Private, S - Subsidiary, D - Division, J - Joint Venture, A - Affiliate, G - Group. Sales are in millions of dollars, employees are in thousands. An asterisk (*) indicates an estimated sales volume. The symbol < stands for 'less than'. Company names and addresses are truncated, in some cases, to fit into the available space.

MATERIALS CONSUMED

Material		Quantity	Delivered Cost ($ million)
Materials, ingredients, containers, and supplies		(X)	480.0
Raw cotton fibers	1,000 bales	(S)	15.9
Nylon staple and tow	mil lb	19.8*	28.5
Rayon and acetate staple and tow	mil lb	(D)	(D)
Polyester staple and tow	mil lb	7.9*	12.7
Spun yarn, all fibers	mil lb	76.8	232.8
Nylon filament yarns	mil lb	11.9	24.9
Polyester filament yarns	mil lb	30.1*	58.9
All other manmade filament yarns	mil lb	22.5*	24.5
Dyes, lakes, and toners		(X)	(D)
All other materials and components, parts, containers, and supplies		(X)	45.3
Materials, ingredients, containers, and supplies, nsk		(X)	11.8

Source: 1992 *Economic Census*. Explanation of symbols used: (D): Withheld to avoid disclosure of competitive data; na: Not available; (S): Withheld because statistical norms were not met; (X): Not applicable; (Z): Less than half the unit shown; nec: Not elsewhere classified; nsk: Not specified by kind; - : zero; * : 10-19 percent estimated; ** : 20-29 percent estimated.

PRODUCT SHARE DETAILS

Product or Product Class	% Share
Thread mills	100.00
Cotton thread, finished, for use in the home	(D)
Cotton thread, finished, for industrial or manufacturers' use (excluding cordage products, such as bag thread, string, or twine)	4.22
Manmade fiber thread and other thread, except silk, filament yarn thread, finished, for use in the home	(D)
Manmade fiber and other thread, except silk, filament yarn thread, finished, for industrial or manufacturers' use (excluding cordage products, such as bag thread, string, twine, rope, etc.)	20.95
Manmade fiber thread and other thread, except silk, spun yarn, finished, for industrial or manufacturers' use (excluding cordage products, such as bag thread, string, or twine)	59.10
Silk thread	(D)
Unfinished thread shipped or transferred to other plants for finishing	(D)

Source: 1992 *Economic Census*. The values shown are percent of total shipments in an industry. Values of indented subcategories are summed in the main heading. The symbol (D) appears when data are withheld to prevent disclosure of competitive information. The abbreviation nsk stands for 'not specified by kind' and nec for 'not elsewhere classified'.

INPUTS AND OUTPUTS FOR THREAD MILLS

Economic Sector or Industry Providing Inputs	%	Sector	Economic Sector or Industry Buying Outputs	%	Sector
Yarn mills & finishing of textiles, nec	34.2	Manufg.	Apparel made from purchased materials	41.0	Manufg.
Organic fibers, noncellulosic	15.5	Manufg.	Knit outerwear mills	12.5	Manufg.
Imports	6.7	Foreign	Personal consumption expenditures	11.1	
Cellulosic manmade fibers	6.3	Manufg.	Exports	6.6	Foreign
Wholesale trade	5.5	Trade	Shoes, except rubber	4.5	Manufg.
Electric services (utilities)	4.3	Util.	Automotive & apparel trimmings	4.4	Manufg.
Cotton	4.1	Agric.	Knit underwear mills	2.5	Manufg.
Miscellaneous plastics products	3.0	Manufg.	Rubber & plastics footwear	2.2	Manufg.
Photofinishing labs, commercial photography	2.4	Services	Upholstered household furniture	1.7	Manufg.
Cyclic crudes and organics	1.7	Manufg.	Mattresses & bedsprings	1.4	Manufg.
Textile machinery	1.4	Manufg.	Surgical appliances & supplies	1.4	Manufg.

Continued on next page.

INPUTS AND OUTPUTS FOR THREAD MILLS - Continued

Economic Sector or Industry Providing Inputs	%	Sector	Economic Sector or Industry Buying Outputs	%	Sector
Air transportation	1.3	Util.	Luggage	1.1	Manufg.
Laundry, dry cleaning, shoe repair	1.3	Services	Women's handbags & purses	1.0	Manufg.
Petroleum refining	1.1	Manufg.	Narrow fabric mills	0.7	Manufg.
Motor freight transportation & warehousing	1.1	Util.	Miscellaneous plastics products	0.6	Manufg.
Paperboard containers & boxes	0.9	Manufg.	House slippers	0.5	Manufg.
Gas production & distribution (utilities)	0.9	Util.	Knitting mills, nec	0.5	Manufg.
Industrial gases	0.8	Manufg.	Leather gloves & mittens	0.5	Manufg.
Thread mills	0.8	Manufg.	Leather goods, nec	0.5	Manufg.
Lubricating oils & greases	0.6	Manufg.	Thread mills	0.5	Manufg.
Eating & drinking places	0.6	Trade	Personal leather goods	0.4	Manufg.
Banking	0.5	Fin/R.E.	Sporting & athletic goods, nec	0.4	Manufg.
U.S. Postal Service	0.4	Gov't	Watch, clock, jewelry, & furniture repair	0.4	Services
Maintenance of nonfarm buildings nec	0.3	Constr.	Canvas & related products	0.3	Manufg.
Communications, except radio & TV	0.3	Util.	Fabricated textile products, nec	0.3	Manufg.
Hotels & lodging places	0.3	Services	Housefurnishings, nec	0.3	Manufg.
Industrial inorganic chemicals, nec	0.2	Manufg.	Schiffli machine embroideries	0.3	Manufg.
Machinery, except electrical, nec	0.2	Manufg.	Yarn mills & finishing of textiles, nec	0.3	Manufg.
Real estate	0.2	Fin/R.E.	Laundry, dry cleaning, shoe repair	0.3	Services
Advertising	0.2	Services	Curtains & draperies	0.2	Manufg.
Computer & data processing services	0.2	Services	Metal household furniture	0.2	Manufg.
Equipment rental & leasing services	0.2	Services	Pleating & stitching	0.2	Manufg.
Legal services	0.2	Services	Public building furniture	0.2	Manufg.
Management & consulting services & labs	0.2	Services	Textile bags	0.2	Manufg.
Coal	0.1	Mining	Blankbooks & looseleaf binders	0.1	Manufg.
Railroads & related services	0.1	Util.	Motion pictures	0.1	Services
Sanitary services, steam supply, irrigation	0.1	Util.	Portrait, photographic studios	0.1	Services
Water supply & sewage systems	0.1	Util.			
Insurance carriers	0.1	Fin/R.E.			
Accounting, auditing & bookkeeping	0.1	Services			

Source: Benchmark Input-Output Accounts for the U.S. Economy, 1982, U.S. Department of Commerce, Washington, D.C., July 1991. Data, as reported in the source, are organized by the 1977 SIC structure in use in 1982 but have been matched, as closely as is possible, to the 1987 SIC structure used in this book.

OCCUPATIONS EMPLOYED BY SIC 228 - WEAVING, FINISHING, YARN AND THREAD MILLS

Occupation	% of Total 1994	Change to 2005	Occupation	% of Total 1994	Change to 2005
Textile draw-out & winding machine operators	32.8	-35.5	Machine feeders & offbearers	2.6	-27.4
Industrial machinery mechanics	6.4	29.1	Machine operators nec	2.2	-28.9
Textile machine setters & set-up operators	4.9	-11.3	Sewing machine operators, non-garment	1.8	21.0
Helpers, laborers, & material movers nec	4.5	-19.3	Industrial truck & tractor operators	1.6	-19.3
Blue collar worker supervisors	4.2	-24.6	Hand packers & packagers	1.3	-30.9
Inspectors, testers, & graders, precision	4.2	-27.4	General managers & top executives	1.3	-23.5
Textile bleaching & dyeing machine operators	4.2	8.9	Maintenance repairers, general utility	1.2	-27.4
Freight, stock, & material movers, hand	2.8	-35.5	Janitors & cleaners, incl maids	1.0	-35.5

Source: Industry-Occupation Matrix, Bureau of Labor Statistics. These data relate to one or more 3-digit SIC industry groups rather than to a single 4-digit SIC. The change reported for each occupation to the year 2005 is a percent of growth or decline as estimated by the Bureau of Labor Statistics. The abbreviation nec stands for 'not elsewhere classified'.

LOCATION BY STATE AND REGIONAL CONCENTRATION

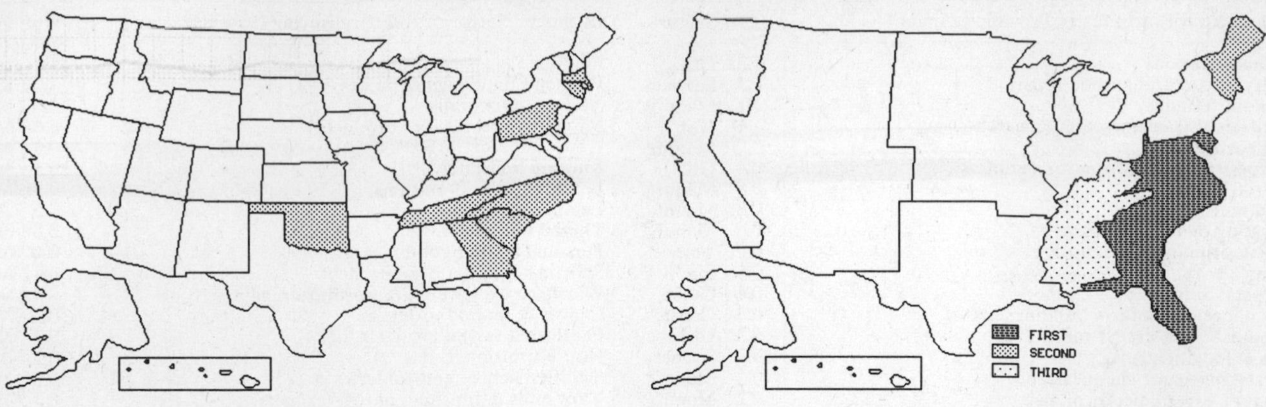

INDUSTRY DATA BY STATE

State	Establish-ments	Shipments			Employment				Cost as % of Shipments	Investment per Employee ($)
		Total ($ mil)	% of U.S.	Per Establ.	Total Number	% of U.S.	Per Establ.	Wages ($/hour)		
North Carolina	19	473.2	56.5	24.9	3,100	50.0	163	7.13	60.8	5,000
Massachusetts	5	25.4	3.0	5.1	200	3.2	40	9.25	54.3	1,500
Georgia	6	(D)	-	-	1,750 *	28.2	292	-	-	-
Connecticut	3	(D)	-	-	750 *	12.1	250	-	-	-
Pennsylvania	3	(D)	-	-	175 *	2.8	58	-	-	-
Tennessee	3	(D)	-	-	175 *	2.8	58	-	-	-
South Carolina	2	(D)	-	-	175 *	2.8	88	-	-	-
Oklahoma	1	(D)	-	-	175 *	2.8	175	-	-	-

Source: 1992 *Economic Census*. The states are in descending order of shipments or establishments (if shipment data are missing for the majority). The symbol (D) appears when data are withheld to prevent disclosure of competitive information. States marked with (D) are sorted by number of establishments. A dash (-) indicates that the data element cannot be calculated; * indicates the midpoint of a range.

2295 - COATED FABRICS, NOT RUBBERIZED

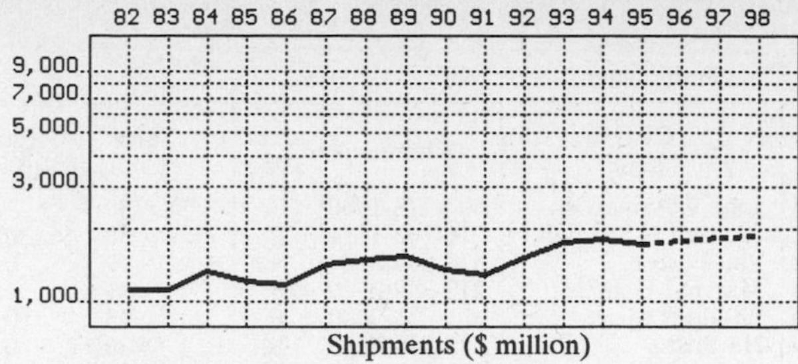

Shipments ($ million)

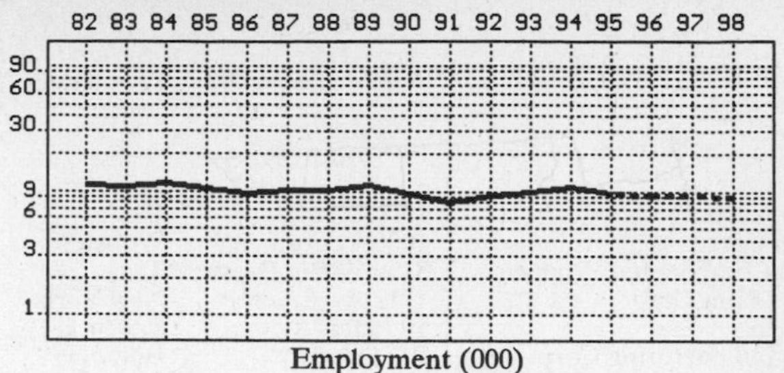

Employment (000)

GENERAL STATISTICS

Year	Com-panies	Establishments		Employment			Compensation		Production ($ million)			
		Total	with 20 or more employees	Total (000)	Production Workers (000)	Production Hours (Mil)	Payroll ($ mil)	Wages ($/hr)	Cost of Materials	Value Added by Manufacture	Value of Shipments	Capital Invest.
1982	188	198	114	11.0	8.0	15.7	198.5	7.69	676.2	435.2	1,115.0	28.4
1983		193	112	10.7	7.7	15.3	205.8	8.28	685.9	435.6	1,129.8	25.9
1984		188	110	11.7	8.6	17.5	235.9	8.47	826.7	514.3	1,336.9	25.0
1985		184	108	10.4	7.7	15.7	221.2	9.03	762.4	464.8	1,228.2	33.9
1986		179	108	9.7	7.2	14.9	218.1	9.36	713.9	457.9	1,172.0	37.4
1987	181	186	92	10.3	7.4	15.8	252.2	10.23	875.0	567.5	1,434.9	63.4
1988		185	93	10.3	7.4	15.7	251.1	10.24	927.7	583.6	1,509.5	38.7
1989		182	90	11.2	6.6	13.4	253.9	11.66	892.4	639.2	1,542.7	59.8
1990		176	90	9.4	6.4	12.8	244.1	11.37	777.4	578.6	1,361.8	52.9
1991		171	84	8.0	5.5	11.6	234.3	12.21	758.5	528.5	1,298.4	54.5
1992	186	193	90	9.2	6.6	13.8	274.1	12.00	912.0	613.7	1,528.1	47.1
1993		199	91	9.9	7.2	15.1	317.3	13.12	1,088.8	696.0	1,773.3	55.8
1994		183P	81P	10.8	7.7	16.3	350.4	13.47	1,005.7	807.6	1,804.3	75.2
1995		182P	78P	9.3P	6.4P	13.7P	316.5P	13.93P	970.8P	779.6P	1,741.8P	69.4P
1996		182P	75P	9.2P	6.3P	13.5P	325.9P	14.42P	997.8P	801.3P	1,790.2P	72.7P
1997		182P	73P	9.1P	6.2P	13.4P	335.3P	14.90P	1,024.8P	823.0P	1,838.6P	76.1P
1998		181P	70P	9.0P	6.1P	13.2P	344.7P	15.38P	1,051.8P	844.7P	1,887.1P	79.4P

Sources: 1982, 1987, 1992 *Economic Census*; *Annual Survey of Manufactures*, 83-86, 88-91, 93-94. Establishment counts for non-Census years are from *County Business Patterns*; establishment values for 83-84 are extrapolations. 'P's show projections by the editors. Industries reclassified in 87 will not have data for prior years.

INDICES OF CHANGE

Year	Com-panies	Establishments		Employment			Compensation		Production ($ million)			
		Total	with 20 or more employees	Total (000)	Production Workers (000)	Production Hours (Mil)	Payroll ($ mil)	Wages ($/hr)	Cost of Materials	Value Added by Manufacture	Value of Shipments	Capital Invest.
1982	101	103	127	120	121	114	72	64	74	71	73	60
1983		100	124	116	117	111	75	69	75	71	74	55
1984		97	122	127	130	127	86	71	91	84	87	53
1985		95	120	113	117	114	81	75	84	76	80	72
1986		93	120	105	109	108	80	78	78	75	77	79
1987	97	96	102	112	112	114	92	85	96	92	94	135
1988		96	103	112	112	114	92	85	102	95	99	82
1989		94	100	122	100	97	93	97	98	104	101	127
1990		91	100	102	97	93	89	95	85	94	89	112
1991		89	93	87	83	84	85	102	83	86	85	116
1992	100	100	100	100	100	100	100	100	100	100	100	100
1993		103	101	108	109	109	116	109	119	113	116	118
1994		95P	90P	117	117	118	128	112	110	132	118	160
1995		95P	87P	102P	97P	99P	115P	116P	106P	127P	114P	147P
1996		94P	84P	100P	95P	98P	119P	120P	109P	131P	117P	154P
1997		94P	81P	99P	94P	97P	122P	124P	112P	134P	120P	161P
1998		94P	78P	98P	92P	96P	126P	128P	115P	138P	123P	169P

Sources: Same as General Statistics. Values reflect change from the base year, 1992. Values above 100 mean greater than 92, values below 100 mean less than 92, and a value of 100 in the 82-91 or 93-98 period means same as 92. 'P's mark projections by the editors.

SELECTED RATIOS

For 1994	Avg. of All Manufact.	Analyzed Industry	Index
Employees per Establishment	49	59	120
Payroll per Establishment	1,500,273	1,914,913	128
Payroll per Employee	30,620	32,444	106
Production Workers per Establishment	34	42	123
Wages per Establishment	853,319	1,199,886	141
Wages per Production Worker	24,861	28,514	115
Hours per Production Worker	2,056	2,117	103
Wages per Hour	12.09	13.47	111
Value Added per Establishment	4,602,255	4,413,480	96
Value Added per Employee	93,930	74,778	80

For 1994	Avg. of All Manufact.	Analyzed Industry	Index
Value Added per Production Worker	134,084	104,883	78
Cost per Establishment	5,045,178	5,496,083	109
Cost per Employee	102,970	93,120	90
Cost per Production Worker	146,988	130,610	89
Shipments per Establishment	9,576,895	9,860,379	103
Shipments per Employee	195,460	167,065	85
Shipments per Production Worker	279,017	234,325	84
Investment per Establishment	321,011	410,963	128
Investment per Employee	6,552	6,963	106
Investment per Production Worker	9,352	9,766	104

Sources: Same as General Statistics. The 'Average of All Manufacturing' column represents the average of all manufacturing industries reported for the most recent complete year available. The Index shows the relationship between the Average and the Analyzed Industry. For example, 100 means that they are equal; 500 that the Analyzed Industry is five times the average; 50 means that the Analyzed Industry is half the national average. The abbreviation 'na' is used to show that data are 'not available'.

LEADING COMPANIES

Number shown: **42** Total sales ($ mil): **680** Total employment (000): **4.7**

Company Name	Address				CEO Name	Phone	Co. Type	Sales ($ mil)	Empl. (000)
Ludlow Corp	2 Tyco Park	Exeter	NH	03833	John C Armacost	603-778-1500	S	130*	1.0
Seaman Corp	1000 Venture Blv	Wooster	OH	44691	Richard N Seaman	216-262-1111	R	50	0.3
Uniroyal Engineered Products	3250 W Big Beaver	Troy	MI	48084	Phil Foster	810-649-8244	S	49	0.3
Health-Chem Corp	1212 Av Amer	New York	NY	10036	Marvin M Speiser	212-398-0700	P	47	0.2
Cooley Inc	50 Esten Av	Pawtucket	RI	02860	Phillip R Siener	401-724-9000	R	35	0.2
Athol Manufacturing Corp	PO Box 105	Butner	NC	27509	HS Post	919-575-6523	R	30	0.2
Great Lakes Paper Co	308 W Erie St	Chicago	IL	60610	Walter Mainieks	312-787-2075	R	30	0.3
JB Group Inc	PO Box 791	Statesville	NC	28677	John Bell Jr	704-872-6303	R	30*	0.2
Uniroyal Engineered Products	PO Box 208	Stoughton	WI	53589	Phil Foster	608-873-6631	D	24	0.2
Alpha Associates Inc	2 Amboy Av	Woodbridge	NJ	07095	AL Avallone	908-634-5700	R	20	<0.1
Starensier Inc	PO Box 408	Newburyport	MA	01950	Louis Rubenfeld	508-462-7311	R	20	<0.1
Herculite Products Inc	PO Box 786	York	PA	17405		717-764-1191	S	19	<0.1
Fairprene Industrial Products	85 Mill Plain Rd	Fairfield	CT	06430	Malcolm Wright	203-259-3351	R	17	0.1
Pajco Products Inc	7740 West St	Lowville	NY	13367	Sam Villanti	315-376-3571	S	16*	0.1
Guardsman Products Inc	PO Box 88010	Grand Rapids	MI	49518	Richard J Marks	616-940-2900	D	15	<0.1
Duracote Corp	PO Box 1209	Ravenna	OH	44266	WR Truog	216-296-9600	R	14*	<0.1
Fabrionics Inc	Rte 130 S	Camargo	IL	61919	Robert E Gray	217-832-2011	R	12*	0.2
Dalton Enterprises Inc	131 Willow St	Cheshire	CT	06410	Peter F Dalton	203-272-3221	R	11	0.1
Emtex Inc	PO Box 505807	Chelsea	MA	02150	Robert I Livinston	617-889-4500	R	10	<0.1
John Boyle and Company Inc	PO Box 791	Statesville	NC	28677	Paul Stelzner	704-872-6303	D	10*	0.2
VyTech Industries Inc	PO Box 5288	Anderson	SC	29623	Thomas J Gilligan	803-224-8771	R	10	0.2
Gem Urethane Corp	PO Box 390	Amsterdam	NY	12010	Klaus Beckman	518-842-0073	S	8	<0.1
Flexfirm Products Inc	2300 N Chico Av	S El Monte	CA	91733	Barry Eichorn	818-448-7627	R	7	<0.1
Best Tape Inc	321 Van Norman	Montebello	CA	90640	Joseph Vidor	310-948-3791	R	7	<0.1
Buckeye Fabric Finishing Co	PO Box 216	Coshocton	OH	43812	Kevin Lee	614-622-3251	R	5	<0.1
O'Dell Williams Inc	60 Acton St	Watertown	MA	02172	Bruce Williams	617-924-4600	R	5*	<0.1
Sauquoit Industries Inc	PO Box 3807	Scranton	PA	18505	Gerald A Scofield	717-348-2751	R	5*	<0.1
Swift Textile Metalizing Corp	PO Box 66	Bloomfield	CT	06002	M Allen Swift	203-243-1122	R	5	<0.1
Deccofelt Corp	PO Box 156	Glendora	CA	91740	Jerry Heinrich	818-963-8511	R	5	<0.1
Engineered Yarns America Inc	939 Currant Rd	Fall River	MA	02720	Gerald Mauretti	508-673-3307	R	4*	<0.1
Fabri Cote Corp	724 E 60th Av	Los Angeles	CA	90001	S Spaulding	213-232-2147	R	4*	<0.1
Marchem Coated Fabrics	2131 Hickory St	St Louis	MO	63100	Marvin Wool	314-621-4200	D	4	<0.1
Manning Fabrics Inc	PO Box 6300	Pinehurst	NC	28374	Edward N Manning	910-295-1970	R	3*	<0.1
McLaughlin International Inc	809 Locust	Scranton	IA	51462	John H McLaughlin	712-652-3911	R	3	<0.1
Regent Manufacturing Co	259 2nd St	Saddle Brook	NJ	07663	Seymour Shimkowitz	201-478-9200	R	3*	<0.1
S and O Corp	PO Box 167	Gallaway	TN	38036	Dolphis Owens	901-867-2223	R	3	<0.1
Tomen-Ein Inc	111 W 40th St	New York	NY	10018	K Toyota	212-930-5600	S	3	<0.1
Process Engineering Corp	PO Box 279	Crystal Lake	IL	60039	George Boyd Sr	815-459-1734	R	3	<0.1
Lakeville Laminating Co	70 Clinton Rd	Fairfield	NJ	07004	AJ Glasser	201-575-1654	R	2	<0.1
New York Cutting and Gumming	150 Wesley St	S Hackensack	NJ	07606	Ralph Mattes	201-487-3093	R	2*	<0.1
Wilcar Products Inc	75 Ontario St	Stratford	CT	06497	David J McClatchie	203-378-5068	R	1	<0.1
Simtec Coatings Inc	16666 Smoke Tree	Hesperia	CA	92345	Simon Devries	619-244-2774	R	1	<0.1

Source: *Ward's Business Directory of U.S. Private and Public Companies*, Volumes 1 and 2, 1996. The company type code used is as follows: P - Public, R - Private, S - Subsidiary, D - Division, J - Joint Venture, A - Affiliate, G - Group. Sales are in millions of dollars, employees are in thousands. An asterisk (*) indicates an estimated sales volume. The symbol < stands for 'less than'. Company names and addresses are truncated, in some cases, to fit into the available space.

MATERIALS CONSUMED

Material		Quantity	Delivered Cost ($ million)
Materials, ingredients, containers, and supplies		(X)	847.4
Manmade fibers, staple, and tow	mil lb	61.3*	27.5
Yarn, all fibers	mil lb	21.0	35.6
Cotton fabrics	mil lin yd	(S)	68.8
Manmade fiber fabrics, including glass	mil lin yd	222.6	201.3
Paper (cellulosic wadding)	mil lb	(S)	11.8
Adhesives and binders (resins)	mil lb	(S)	25.6
Plasticizers	mil lb	66.6**	39.1
Vinyl and vinyl copolymer resins, all forms	mil lb	123.2**	56.5
Plastics resins (except vinyl) consumed in the form of granules, pellets, powders, liquids, etc.	mil lb	50.8*	53.9
Plastics products consumed in the form of sheets, rods, tubes, film, and other shapes		(X)	28.0
Additives (fire retardants, water repellants, softeners, and antistatics, etc.)		(X)	8.1
All other materials and components, parts, containers, and supplies		(X)	177.5
Materials, ingredients, containers, and supplies, nsk		(X)	113.6

Source: 1992 *Economic Census*. Explanation of symbols used: (D): Withheld to avoid disclosure of competitive data; na: Not available; (S): Withheld because statistical norms were not met; (X): Not applicable; (Z): Less than half the unit shown; nec: Not elsewhere classified; nsk: Not specified by kind; - : zero; * : 10-19 percent estimated; ** : 20-29 percent estimated.

PRODUCT SHARE DETAILS

Product or Product Class	% Share	Product or Product Class	% Share
Coated fabrics, not rubberized	100.00	Heavyweight fabrics, more than 16 oz per sq yd finished weight, nonwoven base	4.98
Vinyl coated fabrics, including expanded vinyl coated	42.78	Not speficified by kind	3.31
Lightweight fabrics, 10 oz or less per sq yd finished weight, woven fabrics base	9.72	Other coated or laminated fabrics and coated yarns, not rubberized	50.95
Lightweight fabrics, 10 oz or less per sq yd finished weight, knit fabrics base	8.63	Pyroxylin coated fabrics	7.41
Lightweight fabrics, 10 oz or less per sq yd finished weight, nonwoven base	10.16	Polyurethane coated fabrics	12.00
Mediumweight fabrics, more than 10 oz up to 16 oz per sq yd finished weight, woven fabrics base	14.96	Other coated or laminated fabrics, excluding rubberized and coated yarns, lightweight fabrics, 10 oz or less per sq yd finished weight	24.28
Mediumweight fabrics, more than 10 oz up to 16 oz per sq yd finished weight, knit fabrics base	11.42	Other coated or laminated fabrics, excluding rubberized and coated yarns, mediumweight fabrics, more than 10 oz up to and including 16 oz per sq yd finished weight	23.27
Mediumweight fabrics, more than 10 oz up to 16 oz per sq yd finished weight, nonwoven base	7.21	Other coated or laminated fabrics, excluding rubberized and coated yarns, heavyweight fabrics, more than 16 oz per sq yd finished weight	24.72
Heavyweight fabrics, more than 16 oz per sq yd finished weight, woven fabrics base	22.59	Other coated or laminated yarns, all types except rubberized	7.59
Heavyweight fabrics, more than 16 oz per sq yd finished weight, knit fabrics base	7.00	Other coated or laminated fabrics and coated yarns, nsk	0.71
		Coated fabrics, not rubberized, nsk	6.28

Source: 1992 *Economic Census*. The values shown are percent of total shipments in an industry. Values of indented subcategories are summed in the main heading. The symbol (D) appears when data are withheld to prevent disclosure of competitive information. The abbreviation nsk stands for 'not specified by kind' and nec for 'not elsewhere classified'.

INPUTS AND OUTPUTS FOR COATED FABRICS, NOT RUBBERIZED

Economic Sector or Industry Providing Inputs	%	Sector	Economic Sector or Industry Buying Outputs	%	Sector
Broadwoven fabric mills	27.5	Manufg.	Automotive & apparel trimmings	10.2	Manufg.
Plastics materials & resins	11.2	Manufg.	Games, toys, & children's vehicles	9.1	Manufg.
Nonwoven fabrics	7.8	Manufg.	Shoes, except rubber	6.8	Manufg.
Wholesale trade	6.7	Trade	Metal office furniture	6.7	Manufg.
Advertising	5.9	Services	Exports	6.7	Foreign
Cyclic crudes and organics	4.3	Manufg.	Luggage	4.6	Manufg.
Narrow fabric mills	3.7	Manufg.	Drapery hardware & blinds & shades	4.2	Manufg.
Coated fabrics, not rubberized	3.2	Manufg.	Canvas & related products	3.9	Manufg.
Industrial gases	3.0	Manufg.	House slippers	3.8	Manufg.
Imports	2.7	Foreign	Upholstered household furniture	3.8	Manufg.
Textile goods, nec	1.8	Manufg.	Metal household furniture	3.5	Manufg.
Electric services (utilities)	1.8	Util.	Housefurnishings, nec	2.7	Manufg.
Miscellaneous plastics products	1.7	Manufg.	Coated fabrics, not rubberized	2.6	Manufg.
Fabricated textile products, nec	1.5	Manufg.	Women's handbags & purses	2.4	Manufg.
Gas production & distribution (utilities)	1.5	Util.	Boat building & repairing	2.3	Manufg.
Textile machinery	1.3	Manufg.	Public building furniture	2.2	Manufg.
Chemical preparations, nec	1.0	Manufg.	Motor vehicle parts & accessories	1.7	Manufg.
Motor freight transportation & warehousing	1.0	Util.	Wood office furniture	1.6	Manufg.
Yarn mills & finishing of textiles, nec	0.9	Manufg.	Watch, clock, jewelry, & furniture repair	1.5	Services
Business services nec	0.9	Services	Bookbinding & related work	1.4	Manufg.
Industrial inorganic chemicals, nec	0.8	Manufg.	Fabricated textile products, nec	1.4	Manufg.
Petroleum refining	0.7	Manufg.	Textile bags	1.4	Manufg.
Equipment rental & leasing services	0.7	Services	Blankbooks & looseleaf binders	1.2	Manufg.
Knit fabric mills	0.6	Manufg.	Furniture & fixtures, nec	1.2	Manufg.
Railroads & related services	0.6	Util.	Mattresses & bedsprings	1.2	Manufg.
Banking	0.6	Fin/R.E.	Mobile homes	1.2	Manufg.
U.S. Postal Service	0.6	Gov't	Paperboard mills	1.1	Manufg.
Paints & allied products	0.5	Manufg.	Wood household furniture	1.1	Manufg.
Communications, except radio & TV	0.5	Util.	Personal leather goods	0.9	Manufg.
Laundry, dry cleaning, shoe repair	0.5	Services	Travel trailers & campers	0.9	Manufg.
Real estate	0.4	Fin/R.E.	Motor homes (made on purchased chassis)	0.8	Manufg.
Detective & protective services	0.4	Services	Surgical appliances & supplies	0.7	Manufg.
Sanitary services, steam supply, irrigation	0.3	Util.	Pulp mills	0.6	Manufg.
Eating & drinking places	0.3	Trade	Sporting & athletic goods, nec	0.6	Manufg.
Maintenance of nonfarm buildings nec	0.2	Constr.	Truck trailers	0.6	Manufg.
Paperboard containers & boxes	0.2	Manufg.	Nonferrous wire drawing & insulating	0.5	Manufg.
Royalties	0.2	Fin/R.E.	Truck & bus bodies	0.5	Manufg.
Portrait, photographic studios	0.2	Services	Dental equipment & supplies	0.4	Manufg.
Alkalies & chlorine	0.1	Manufg.	Stationery products	0.4	Manufg.
Lubricating oils & greases	0.1	Manufg.	Wood partitions & fixtures	0.4	Manufg.
Machinery, except electrical, nec	0.1	Manufg.	Commercial fishing	0.3	Agric.
Paper coating & glazing	0.1	Manufg.	Motor vehicles & car bodies	0.3	Manufg.
Pipelines, except natural gas	0.1	Util.	Railroad equipment	0.3	Manufg.
Automotive rental & leasing, without drivers	0.1	Services	Metal partitions & fixtures	0.1	Manufg.
Computer & data processing services	0.1	Services	Surgical & medical instruments	0.1	Manufg.
Legal services	0.1	Services			
Management & consulting services & labs	0.1	Services			

Source: Benchmark Input-Output Accounts for the U.S. Economy, 1982, U.S. Department of Commerce, Washington, D.C., July 1991. Data, as reported in the source, are organized by the 1977 SIC structure in use in 1982 but have been matched, as closely as is possible, to the 1987 SIC structure used in this book.

OCCUPATIONS EMPLOYED BY SIC 229 - MISCELLANEOUS TEXTILE GOODS

Occupation	% of Total 1994	Change to 2005	Occupation	% of Total 1994	Change to 2005
Textile draw-out & winding machine operators	22.1	-3.5	Maintenance repairers, general utility	2.1	-13.1
Blue collar worker supervisors	6.0	-7.8	Industrial truck & tractor operators	2.0	-3.5
Machine operators nec	4.6	-14.9	Traffic, shipping, & receiving clerks	1.9	-7.2
Industrial machinery mechanics	4.2	6.2	Coating, painting, & spraying machine workers	1.9	-3.6
Textile machine setters & set-up operators	3.9	-13.1	Hand packers & packagers	1.8	-17.4
Helpers, laborers, & material movers nec	3.9	-3.5	Freight, stock, & material movers, hand	1.7	-22.8
Inspectors, testers, & graders, precision	3.8	-3.5	Secretaries, ex legal & medical	1.6	-12.1
General managers & top executives	2.5	-8.4	Sewing machine operators, non-garment	1.6	-22.8
Sales & related workers nec	2.3	-3.5	Industrial production managers	1.5	-3.5
Machine feeders & offbearers	2.3	-13.1	Packaging & filling machine operators	1.5	-3.5
Assemblers, fabricators, & hand workers nec	2.3	-3.5	Bookkeeping, accounting, & auditing clerks	1.2	-27.7
Extruding & forming machine workers	2.2	-3.5	Janitors & cleaners, incl maids	1.1	-22.8

Source: Industry-Occupation Matrix, Bureau of Labor Statistics. These data relate to one or more 3-digit SIC industry groups rather than to a single 4-digit SIC. The change reported for each occupation to the year 2005 is a percent of growth or decline as estimated by the Bureau of Labor Statistics. The abbreviation nec stands for 'not elsewhere classified'.

LOCATION BY STATE AND REGIONAL CONCENTRATION

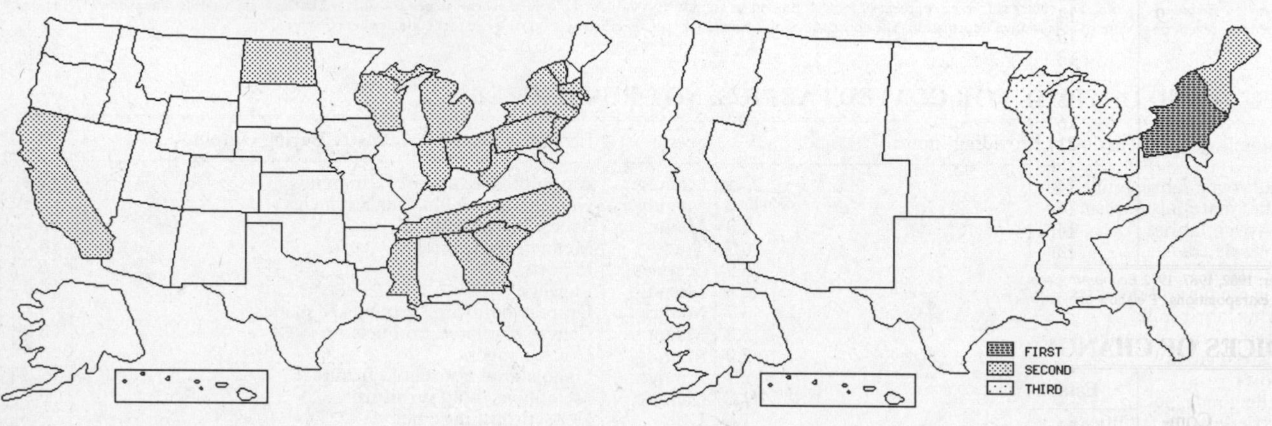

INDUSTRY DATA BY STATE

State	Establish-ments	Shipments: Total ($ mil)	Shipments: % of U.S.	Shipments: Per Establ.	Employment: Total Number	Employment: % of U.S.	Employment: Per Establ.	Wages ($/hour)	Cost as % of Shipments	Investment per Employee ($)
Massachusetts	24	227.6	14.9	9.5	1,100	12.0	46	11.94	64.5	4,182
Ohio	16	191.6	12.5	12.0	1,200	13.0	75	13.35	63.8	3,083
California	22	157.6	10.3	7.2	900	9.8	41	13.67	56.0	5,667
North Carolina	13	118.6	7.8	9.1	700	7.6	54	8.50	62.8	-
New Jersey	17	117.3	7.7	6.9	700	7.6	41	10.70	62.5	5,571
New York	16	106.3	7.0	6.6	600	6.5	38	10.22	55.1	3,000
Tennessee	7	92.3	6.0	13.2	700	7.6	100	12.33	53.0	3,571
Connecticut	7	54.4	3.6	7.8	400	4.3	57	10.40	54.4	-
Pennsylvania	9	37.0	2.4	4.1	200	2.2	22	9.67	55.9	5,000
Georgia	7	9.1	0.6	1.3	100	1.1	14	10.00	64.8	3,000
South Carolina	8	(D)	-	-	175 *	1.9	22	-	-	-
Wisconsin	6	(D)	-	-	375 *	4.1	63	-	-	-
Indiana	5	(D)	-	-	375 *	4.1	75	-	-	-
Michigan	4	(D)	-	-	375 *	4.1	94	-	-	-
Mississippi	1	(D)	-	-	375 *	4.1	375	-	-	-
North Dakota	1	(D)	-	-	175 *	1.9	175	-	-	-
Vermont	1	(D)	-	-	175 *	1.9	175	-	-	-
West Virginia	1	(D)	-	-	175 *	1.9	175	-	-	-

Source: 1992 *Economic Census*. The states are in descending order of shipments or establishments (if shipment data are missing for the majority). The symbol (D) appears when data are withheld to prevent disclosure of competitive information. States marked with (D) are sorted by number of establishments. A dash (-) indicates that the data element cannot be calculated; * indicates the midpoint of a range.

2296 - TIRE CORD AND FABRIC

82 83 84 85 86 87 88 89 90 91 92 93 94 95 96 97 98

9,000
6,000
3,000
900
600
300
100

Shipments ($ million)

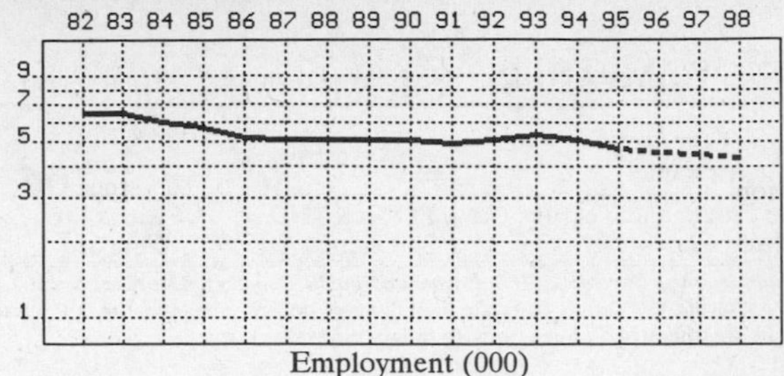

Employment (000)

GENERAL STATISTICS

Year	Com-panies	Establishments		Employment			Compensation		Production ($ million)			
		Total	with 20 or more employees	Total (000)	Production Workers (000)	Production Hours (Mil)	Payroll ($ mil)	Wages ($/hr)	Cost of Materials	Value Added by Manufacture	Value of Shipments	Capital Invest.
1982	12	21	19	6.5	5.6	9.6	90.5	7.26	687.9	289.9	981.5	6.2
1983		20	18	6.4	5.5	10.1	100.5	7.78	737.7	316.9	1,063.7	9.1
1984		19	17	6.0	5.2	10.2	101.4	7.94	801.5	371.6	1,192.1	14.8
1985		19	17	5.7	4.9	9.0	95.4	8.17	718.3	342.6	1,064.4	5.9
1986		20	16	5.2	4.5	8.6	95.1	8.58	653.2	351.6	1,007.8	5.3
1987	9	14	13	5.1	4.4	9.1	100.5	8.80	650.3	395.8	1,040.8	5.5
1988		15	15	5.1	4.5	8.8	96.6	8.60	608.7	337.4	943.3	4.5
1989		13	12	5.1	4.6	8.9	101.0	8.83	702.9	347.9	1,045.9	32.3
1990		14	11	5.1	4.4	8.3	99.3	9.17	654.8	334.3	981.6	10.7
1991		15	14	4.9	4.2	7.9	98.9	9.58	647.2	332.2	982.0	9.8
1992	13	16	15	5.1	4.4	8.7	112.6	9.89	584.6	402.6	981.0	37.2
1993		21	16	5.3	4.5	9.1	118.6	9.95	577.2	263.9	838.0	72.8
1994		15P	13P	5.1	4.3	9.0	127.8	10.81	682.3	252.8	915.9	15.8
1995		14P	12P	4.7P	4.0P	8.3P	117.5P	10.62P	670.9P	248.6P	900.6P	37.5P
1996		14P	12P	4.5P	3.9P	8.2P	119.6P	10.87P	660.0P	244.5P	886.0P	40.3P
1997		14P	11P	4.4P	3.8P	8.1P	121.7P	11.12P	649.1P	240.5P	871.3P	43.2P
1998		13P	11P	4.3P	3.7P	8.0P	123.7P	11.37P	638.2P	236.5P	856.7P	46.0P

Sources: 1982, 1987, 1992 *Economic Census*; *Annual Survey of Manufactures*, 83-86, 88-91, 93-94. Establishment counts for non-Census years are from *County Business Patterns*; establishment values for 83-84 are extrapolations. 'P's show projections by the editors. Industries reclassified in 87 will not have data for prior years.

INDICES OF CHANGE

Year	Com-panies	Establishments		Employment			Compensation		Production ($ million)			
		Total	with 20 or more employees	Total (000)	Production Workers (000)	Production Hours (Mil)	Payroll ($ mil)	Wages ($/hr)	Cost of Materials	Value Added by Manufacture	Value of Shipments	Capital Invest.
1982	92	131	127	127	127	110	80	73	118	72	100	17
1983		125	120	125	125	116	89	79	126	79	108	24
1984		119	113	118	118	117	90	80	137	92	122	40
1985		119	113	112	111	103	85	83	123	85	109	16
1986		125	107	102	102	99	84	87	112	87	103	14
1987	69	88	87	100	100	105	89	89	111	98	106	15
1988		94	100	100	102	101	86	87	104	84	96	12
1989		81	80	100	105	102	90	89	120	86	107	87
1990		88	73	100	100	95	88	93	112	83	100	29
1991		94	93	96	95	91	88	97	111	83	100	26
1992	100	100	100	100	100	100	100	100	100	100	100	100
1993		131	107	104	102	105	105	101	99	66	85	196
1994		92P	83P	100	98	103	113	109	117	63	93	42
1995		90P	81P	91P	91P	95P	104P	107P	115P	62P	92P	101P
1996		88P	78P	89P	89P	94P	106P	110P	113P	61P	90P	108P
1997		85P	75P	87P	86P	93P	108P	112P	111P	60P	89P	116P
1998		83P	72P	85P	84P	92P	110P	115P	109P	59P	87P	124P

Sources: Same as General Statistics. Values reflect change from the base year, 1992. Values above 100 mean greater than 92, values below 100 mean less than 92, and a value of 100 in the 82-91 or 93-98 period means same as 92. 'P's mark projections by the editors.

SELECTED RATIOS

For 1994	Avg. of All Manufact.	Analyzed Industry	Index	For 1994	Avg. of All Manufact.	Analyzed Industry	Index
Employees per Establishment	49	345	705	Value Added per Production Worker	134,084	58,791	44
Payroll per Establishment	1,500,273	8,651,077	577	Cost per Establishment	5,045,178	46,186,462	915
Payroll per Employee	30,620	25,059	82	Cost per Employee	102,970	133,784	130
Production Workers per Establishment	34	291	848	Cost per Production Worker	146,988	158,674	108
Wages per Establishment	853,319	6,585,785	772	Shipments per Establishment	9,576,895	61,999,385	647
Wages per Production Worker	24,861	22,626	91	Shipments per Employee	195,460	179,588	92
Hours per Production Worker	2,056	2,093	102	Shipments per Production Worker	279,017	213,000	76
Wages per Hour	12.09	10.81	89	Investment per Establishment	321,011	1,069,538	333
Value Added per Establishment	4,602,255	17,112,615	372	Investment per Employee	6,552	3,098	47
Value Added per Employee	93,930	49,569	53	Investment per Production Worker	9,352	3,674	39

Sources: Same as General Statistics. The 'Average of All Manufacturing' column represents the average of all manufacturing industries reported for the most recent complete year available. The Index shows the relationship between the Average and the Analyzed Industry. For example, 100 means that they are equal; 500 that the Analyzed Industry is five times the average; 50 means that the Analyzed Industry is half the national average. The abbreviation 'na' is used to show that data are 'not available'.

LEADING COMPANIES Number shown: 2 Total sales ($ mil): 82 Total employment (000): 0.5

Company Name	Address				CEO Name	Phone	Co. Type	Sales ($ mil)	Empl. (000)
Firestone Fibers and Textiles Co	PO Box 1369	Kings Mt	NC	28086	J Anand	704-734-2100	S	80	0.4
Page Belting Co	24 Chenell Dr	Concord	NH	03301	Loyd Rich	603-225-5523	R	2	<0.1

Source: *Ward's Business Directory of U.S. Private and Public Companies*, Volumes 1 and 2, 1996. The company type code used is as follows: P - Public, R - Private, S - Subsidiary, D - Division, J - Joint Venture, A - Affiliate, G - Group. Sales are in millions of dollars, employees are in thousands. An asterisk (*) indicates an estimated sales volume. The symbol < stands for 'less than'. Company names and addresses are truncated, in some cases, to fit into the available space.

MATERIALS CONSUMED

Material		Quantity	Delivered Cost ($ million)
Materials, ingredients, containers, and supplies		(X)	554.3
Raw cotton fibers	1,000 bales	(D)	(D)
Rayon and acetate staple and tow	mil lb	(D)	(D)
Nylon staple and tow	mil lb	(D)	(D)
Polyester staple and tow	mil lb	90.7	100.1
All other manmade fiber staple and tow (except glass)	mil lb	(D)	(D)
Rayon and acetate filament yarns	mil lb	3.5	5.9
Nylon filament yarns	mil lb	49.7	61.5
Polyester filament yarns	mil lb	82.5	110.7
All other filament yarns, except glass	mil lb	(D)	(D)
Glass filament yarn and roving	mil lb	1.5	2.2
Spun yarn, all fibers	mil lb	(D)	(D)
Dyes, lakes, and toners		(X)	(D)
All other materials and components, parts, containers, and supplies		(X)	44.4
Materials, ingredients, containers, and supplies, nsk		(X)	(D)

Source: 1992 *Economic Census*. Explanation of symbols used: (D): Withheld to avoid disclosure of competitive data; na: Not available; (S): Withheld because statistical norms were not met; (X): Not applicable; (Z): Less than half the unit shown; nec: Not elsewhere classified; nsk: Not specified by kind; - : zero; * : 10-19 percent estimated; ** : 20-29 percent estimated.

PRODUCT SHARE DETAILS

Product or Product Class	% Share	Product or Product Class	% Share
Tire cord and tire cord fabrics	100.00		

Source: 1992 *Economic Census*. The values shown are percent of total shipments in an industry. Values of indented subcategories are summed in the main heading. The symbol (D) appears when data are withheld to prevent disclosure of competitive information. The abbreviation nsk stands for 'not specified by kind' and nec for 'not elsewhere classified'.

INPUTS AND OUTPUTS FOR TIRE CORD & FABRIC

Economic Sector or Industry Providing Inputs	%	Sector	Economic Sector or Industry Buying Outputs	%	Sector
Organic fibers, noncellulosic	61.0	Manufg.	Tires & inner tubes	90.9	Manufg.
Glass & glass products, except containers	10.6	Manufg.	Exports	8.8	Foreign
Advertising	7.1	Services	Tire cord & fabric	0.3	Manufg.
Wholesale trade	3.8	Trade			
Electric services (utilities)	3.2	Util.			
Cyclic crudes and organics	1.9	Manufg.			
Textile machinery	1.7	Manufg.			
Synthetic rubber	1.3	Manufg.			
Cellulosic manmade fibers	1.2	Manufg.			
Industrial gases	0.8	Manufg.			
Gas production & distribution (utilities)	0.8	Util.			
Rubber & plastics hose & belting	0.7	Manufg.			
Motor freight transportation & warehousing	0.6	Util.			
Banking	0.5	Fin/R.E.			
Laundry, dry cleaning, shoe repair	0.4	Services			
Chemical preparations, nec	0.3	Manufg.			
Tire cord & fabric	0.3	Manufg.			
Eating & drinking places	0.3	Trade			
Royalties	0.3	Fin/R.E.			
Maintenance of nonfarm buildings nec	0.2	Constr.			
Industrial inorganic chemicals, nec	0.2	Manufg.			
Communications, except radio & TV	0.2	Util.			
Railroads & related services	0.2	Util.			
Detective & protective services	0.2	Services			
Equipment rental & leasing services	0.2	Services			
U.S. Postal Service	0.2	Gov't			
Imports	0.2	Foreign			
Lubricating oils & greases	0.1	Manufg.			

Source: Benchmark Input-Output Accounts for the U.S. Economy, 1982, U.S. Department of Commerce, Washington, D.C., July 1991. Data, as reported in the source, are organized by the 1977 SIC structure in use in 1982 but have been matched, as closely as is possible, to the 1987 SIC structure used in this book.

OCCUPATIONS EMPLOYED BY SIC 229 - MISCELLANEOUS TEXTILE GOODS

Occupation	% of Total 1994	Change to 2005	Occupation	% of Total 1994	Change to 2005
Textile draw-out & winding machine operators	22.1	-3.5	Maintenance repairers, general utility	2.1	-13.1
Blue collar worker supervisors	6.0	-7.8	Industrial truck & tractor operators	2.0	-3.5
Machine operators nec	4.6	-14.9	Traffic, shipping, & receiving clerks	1.9	-7.2
Industrial machinery mechanics	4.2	6.2	Coating, painting, & spraying machine workers	1.9	-3.6
Textile machine setters & set-up operators	3.9	-13.1	Hand packers & packagers	1.8	-17.4
Helpers, laborers, & material movers nec	3.9	-3.5	Freight, stock, & material movers, hand	1.7	-22.8
Inspectors, testers, & graders, precision	3.8	-3.5	Secretaries, ex legal & medical	1.6	-12.1
General managers & top executives	2.5	-8.4	Sewing machine operators, non-garment	1.6	-22.8
Sales & related workers nec	2.3	-3.5	Industrial production managers	1.5	-3.5
Machine feeders & offbearers	2.3	-13.1	Packaging & filling machine operators	1.5	-3.5
Assemblers, fabricators, & hand workers nec	2.3	-3.5	Bookkeeping, accounting, & auditing clerks	1.2	-27.7
Extruding & forming machine workers	2.2	-3.5	Janitors & cleaners, incl maids	1.1	-22.8

Source: Industry-Occupation Matrix, Bureau of Labor Statistics. These data relate to one or more 3-digit SIC industry groups rather than to a single 4-digit SIC. The change reported for each occupation to the year 2005 is a percent of growth or decline as estimated by the Bureau of Labor Statistics. The abbreviation nec stands for 'not elsewhere classified'.

LOCATION BY STATE AND REGIONAL CONCENTRATION

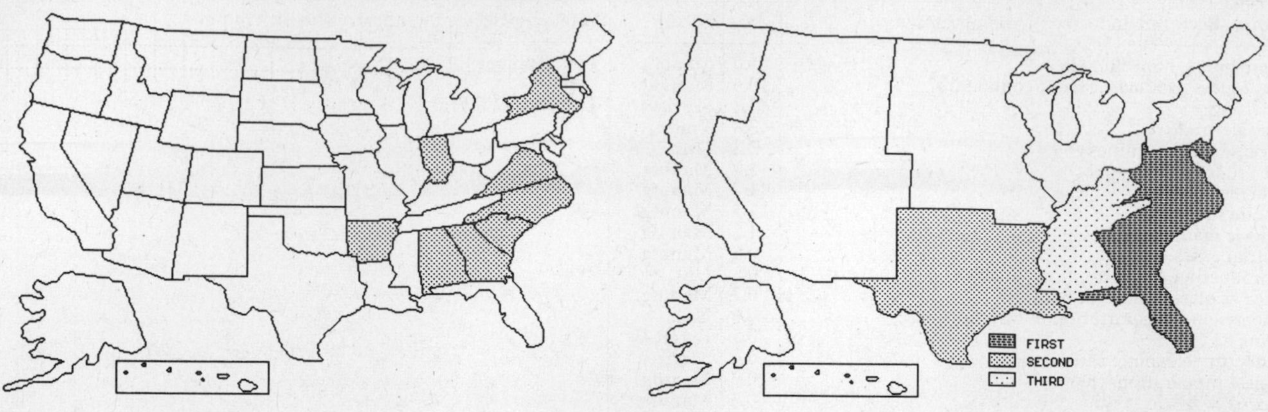

INDUSTRY DATA BY STATE

State	Establish-ments	Shipments			Employment				Cost as % of Shipments	Investment per Employee ($)
		Total ($ mil)	% of U.S.	Per Establ.	Total Number	% of U.S.	Per Establ.	Wages ($/hour)		
Georgia	3	335.6	34.2	111.9	2,000	39.2	667	9.38	56.9	-
North Carolina	3	(D)	-	-	750 *	14.7	250	-	-	-
Alabama	2	(D)	-	-	1,750 *	34.3	875	-	-	-
Arkansas	2	(D)	-	-	175 *	3.4	88	-	-	-
New York	2	(D)	-	-	375 *	7.4	188	-	-	-
Indiana	1	(D)	-	-	175 *	3.4	175	-	-	-
South Carolina	1	(D)	-	-	375 *	7.4	375	-	-	-
Virginia	1	(D)	-	-	175 *	3.4	175	-	-	-

Source: 1992 *Economic Census*. The states are in descending order of shipments or establishments (if shipment data are missing for the majority). The symbol (D) appears when data are withheld to prevent disclosure of competitive information. States marked with (D) are sorted by number of establishments. A dash (-) indicates that the data element cannot be calculated; * indicates the midpoint of a range.

2297 - NONWOVEN FABRICS

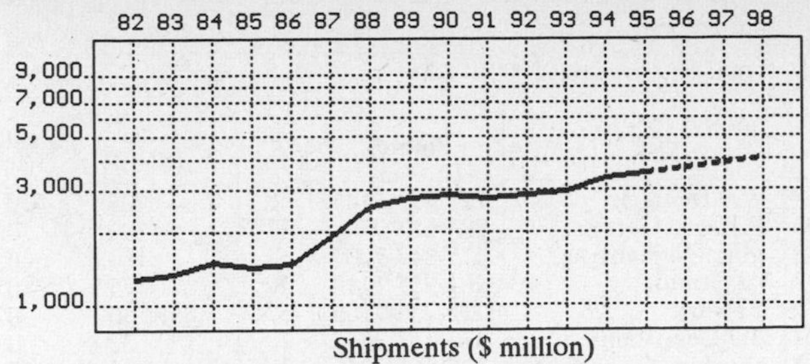

Shipments ($ million)

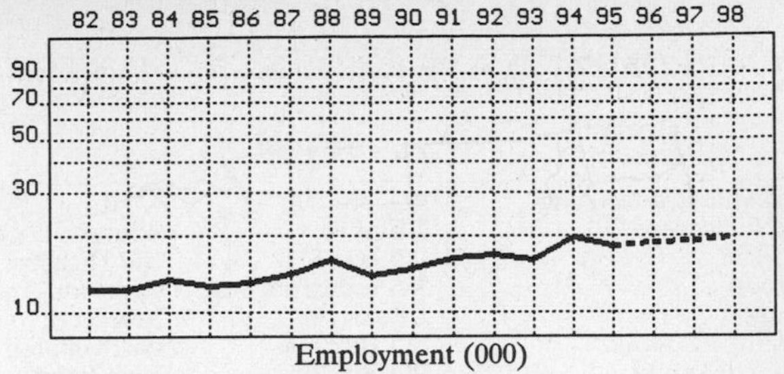

Employment (000)

GENERAL STATISTICS

Year	Com-panies	Establishments		Employment			Compensation		Production ($ million)			
		Total	with 20 or more employees	Total (000)	Production Workers (000)	Production Hours (Mil)	Payroll ($ mil)	Wages ($/hr)	Cost of Materials	Value Added by Manufacture	Value of Shipments	Capital Invest.
1982	144	132	91	12.3	9.5	18.7	198.8	7.28	743.4	544.4	1,278.7	78.7
1983		127	90	12.3	9.4	19.5	211.1	7.56	748.3	591.2	1,338.8	111.4
1984		122	89	13.4	10.4	21.0	236.8	7.93	824.0	668.5	1,489.8	148.2
1985		118	88	12.5	9.8	19.4	237.5	8.36	780.4	640.7	1,426.7	106.7
1986		113	85	13.1	10.2	20.9	260.8	8.29	785.4	702.3	1,478.6	84.4
1987	111	130	93	14.2	10.7	22.0	328.4	9.37	1,073.0	840.5	1,902.9	95.0
1988		126	88	15.9	11.7	24.7	382.1	9.60	1,397.2	1,149.9	2,542.9	122.2
1989		122	87	14.0	12.2	25.8	408.8	10.08	1,556.2	1,232.1	2,756.5	178.6
1990		121	91	14.9	12.9	26.5	416.1	9.92	1,563.9	1,306.9	2,851.0	113.0
1991		129	91	16.2	12.1	25.2	413.5	10.11	1,526.5	1,260.0	2,767.5	124.5
1992	144	168	110	16.8	12.6	26.0	475.6	11.65	1,619.7	1,217.5	2,851.9	166.2
1993		164	104	16.1	12.0	24.9	473.4	12.20	1,641.5	1,329.7	2,954.7	132.6
1994		149P	100P	19.6	14.9	30.8	563.4	11.86	1,805.4	1,557.9	3,355.3	192.1
1995		152P	102P	18.2P	14.0P	29.3P	561.0P	12.43P	1,895.7P	1,635.8P	3,523.0P	167.7P
1996		155P	103P	18.7P	14.4P	30.2P	590.5P	12.84P	1,995.0P	1,721.5P	3,707.7P	173.5P
1997		158P	104P	19.2P	14.8P	31.0P	620.0P	13.25P	2,094.4P	1,807.3P	3,892.4P	179.3P
1998		161P	105P	19.7P	15.2P	31.8P	649.6P	13.66P	2,193.7P	1,893.0P	4,077.0P	185.0P

Sources: 1982, 1987, 1992 *Economic Census*; *Annual Survey of Manufactures*, 83-86, 88-91, 93-94. Establishment counts for non-Census years are from *County Business Patterns*; establishment values for 83-84 are extrapolations. 'P's show projections by the editors. Industries reclassified in 87 will not have data for prior years.

INDICES OF CHANGE

Year	Com-panies	Establishments		Employment			Compensation		Production ($ million)			
		Total	with 20 or more employees	Total (000)	Production Workers (000)	Production Hours (Mil)	Payroll ($ mil)	Wages ($/hr)	Cost of Materials	Value Added by Manufacture	Value of Shipments	Capital Invest.
1982	100	79	83	73	75	72	42	62	46	45	45	47
1983		76	82	73	75	75	44	65	46	49	47	67
1984		73	81	80	83	81	50	68	51	55	52	89
1985		70	80	74	78	75	50	72	48	53	50	64
1986		67	77	78	81	80	55	71	48	58	52	51
1987	77	77	85	85	85	85	69	80	66	69	67	57
1988		75	80	95	93	95	80	82	86	94	89	74
1989		73	79	83	97	99	86	87	96	101	97	107
1990		72	83	89	102	102	87	85	97	107	100	68
1991		77	83	96	96	97	87	87	94	103	97	75
1992	100	100	100	100	100	100	100	100	100	100	100	100
1993		98	95	96	95	96	100	105	101	109	104	80
1994		89P	91P	117	118	118	118	102	111	128	118	116
1995		91P	92P	108P	111P	113P	118P	107P	117P	134P	124P	101P
1996		92P	93P	111P	114P	116P	124P	110P	123P	141P	130P	104P
1997		94P	95P	114P	117P	119P	130P	114P	129P	148P	136P	108P
1998		96P	96P	117P	120P	122P	137P	117P	135P	155P	143P	111P

Sources: Same as General Statistics. Values reflect change from the base year, 1992. Values above 100 mean greater than 92, values below 100 mean less than 92, and a value of 100 in the 82-91 or 93-98 period means same as 92. 'P's mark projections by the editors.

SELECTED RATIOS

For 1994	Avg. of All Manufact.	Analyzed Industry	Index	For 1994	Avg. of All Manufact.	Analyzed Industry	Index
Employees per Establishment	49	131	268	Value Added per Production Worker	134,084	104,557	78
Payroll per Establishment	1,500,273	3,772,002	251	Cost per Establishment	5,045,178	12,087,279	240
Payroll per Employee	30,620	28,745	94	Cost per Employee	102,970	92,112	89
Production Workers per Establishment	34	100	291	Cost per Production Worker	146,988	121,168	82
Wages per Establishment	853,319	2,445,629	287	Shipments per Establishment	9,576,895	22,463,968	235
Wages per Production Worker	24,861	24,516	99	Shipments per Employee	195,460	171,189	88
Hours per Production Worker	2,056	2,067	101	Shipments per Production Worker	279,017	225,188	81
Wages per Hour	12.09	11.86	98	Investment per Establishment	321,011	1,286,123	401
Value Added per Establishment	4,602,255	10,430,250	227	Investment per Employee	6,552	9,801	150
Value Added per Employee	93,930	79,485	85	Investment per Production Worker	9,352	12,893	138

Sources: Same as General Statistics. The 'Average of All Manufacturing' column represents the average of all manufacturing industries reported for the most recent complete year available. The Index shows the relationship between the Average and the Analyzed Industry. For example, 100 means that they are equal; 500 that the Analyzed Industry is five times the average; 50 means that the Analyzed Industry is half the national average. The abbreviation 'na' is used to show that data are 'not available'.

LEADING COMPANIES

Number shown: **15** Total sales ($ mil): **1,431** Total employment (000): **2.3**

Company Name	Address				CEO Name	Phone	Co. Type	Sales ($ mil)	Empl. (000)
Irving Textile Products Inc	PO Box 270	Atglen	PA	19310	WA Irving Jr	215-593-5145	R	705	<0.1
Dexter Nonwovens	2 Elm St	Windsor Locks	CT	06096	R Barry Gettins	203-623-9801	D	300	0.1
Reemay Inc	PO Box 511	Old Hickory	TN	37138	Migo Najbantyan	615-847-7000	S	180	0.6
ATI Group	585 Industrial Rd	Carlstadt	NJ	07072	PJ Gould	201-935-1110	R	75	0.1
Hyosung	1 Penn Plz	New York	NY	10119	YI Park	212-736-7100	S	50	0.4
National Nonwovens	PO Box 150	Easthampton	MA	01027	A J Centofanti	413-527-3445	R	32	0.4
Yarborough and Co	PO Box 308	High Point	NC	27261	Gordon Yarborough	919-861-2345	R	25	<0.1
FiberTech Group Inc	PO Box 360	Landisville	NJ	08326	Jerry Zucker	609-697-1600	R	23*	0.2
Phoenix Manufacturing Company	PO Box 120	London	KY	40743	Rick Schott	606-864-7317	R	14	<0.1
Fiberbond Corp	110 Menke Rd	Michigan City	IN	46360	John Marienau	219-879-4541	R	10	0.1
Delaware Valley Corp	500 Broadway	Lawrence	MA	01841	DP Dimaggio Jr	508-688-6995	R	6	<0.1
Toray Industries	600 3rd Av	New York	NY	10016	Akio Takaya	212-697-8150	S	5*	<0.1
HDK Industries Inc	100 Industrial Pk Dr	Rogersville	TN	37857	Dave Lunceford	615-272-7119	R	4*	<0.1
Tandem Fabrics	52904 County #13	Elkhart	IN	46514	William Hickey	219-262-0121	D	2	<0.1
Engineered Nonwovens Inc	PO Box 1538	Westfield	MA	01086	Marc D Etchells	413-572-7050	R	1	<0.1

Source: *Ward's Business Directory of U.S. Private and Public Companies*, Volumes 1 and 2, 1996. The company type code used is as follows: P - Public, R - Private, S - Subsidiary, D - Division, J - Joint Venture, A - Affiliate, G - Group. Sales are in millions of dollars, employees are in thousands. An asterisk (*) indicates an estimated sales volume. The symbol < stands for 'less than'. Company names and addresses are truncated, in some cases, to fit into the available space.

MATERIALS CONSUMED

Material		Quantity	Delivered Cost ($ million)
Materials, ingredients, containers, and supplies		(X)	1,317.6
Raw cotton fibers	1,000 bales	(D)	(D)
Cotton waste	mil lb	(D)	(D)
Cotton linters (net weight)	mil lb	(D)	(D)
Raw wool, mohair, and other animal fibers (scoured weight)	mil lb	(D)	(D)
Cellulosic (rayon and acetate) manmade textile fibers	mil lb	67.1*	70.8
Noncellulosic (polyester, nylon, etc.) manmade textile fibers	mil lb	352.4**	262.3
Yarn, all fibers	mil lb	40.0**	89.8
Textile fabrics	mil lin yd	(S)	47.9
Paper (cellulosic wadding)	mil lb	59.8*	47.2
Adhesives and binders (resins)	mil lb	83.7*	55.2
Additives (fire retardants, water repellants, softeners, and antistatics, etc.)		(X)	28.8
New and used rags, clips, etc.	mil lb	(D)	(D)
Vinyl and vinyl copolymer resins, all forms	mil lb	(S)	16.7
Plastics resins (except vinyl) consumed in the form of granules, pellets, powders, liquids, etc.	mil lb	516.0**	243.3
Paperboard containers, boxes, and corrugated paperboard		(X)	22.8
All other materials and components, parts, containers, and supplies		(X)	336.3
Materials, ingredients, containers, and supplies, nsk		(X)	59.2

Source: 1992 *Economic Census*. Explanation of symbols used: (D): Withheld to avoid disclosure of competitive data; na: Not available; (S): Withheld because statistical norms were not met; (X): Not applicable; (Z): Less than half the unit shown; nec: Not elsewhere classified; nsk: Not specified by kind; - : zero; * : 10-19 percent estimated; ** : 20-29 percent estimated.

PRODUCT SHARE DETAILS

Product or Product Class	% Share
Nonwoven fabrics	100.00
Nonwoven fabrics	75.22
Laminated and wet laid, less than 1 oz per sq yd	2.50
Laminated and wet laid, 1 oz to 2.5 oz per sq yd.	15.77
Laminated and wet laid, more than 2.5 oz per sq yd	5.80
Spun bonded, dry laid, and other, less than 0.8 oz per sq yd	14.46
Spun bonded, dry laid, and other, 0.8 oz to 1.5 oz per sq yd	32.39
Spun bonded, dry laid, and other, more than 1.5 oz per sq yd	25.08
Not speficified by kind	4.00
Fabricated nonwoven products	22.97
Blankets made from nonwoven fabrics	14.84
Ribbons, for gift tyings, Christmas, made from nonwoven fabrics	6.14
Ribbons, for gift tyings, except Christmas, made from nonwoven fabrics	13.15
Wipers made from nonwoven fabrics (including windshield, industrial, and lithographic)	14.78
Fabricated nonwoven products, all other, excluding diapers and orthopedic, prosthetic, and surgical supplies	50.32
Fabricated nonwoven products, nsk	0.77
Nonwoven fabrics, nsk	1.81

Source: 1992 *Economic Census*. The values shown are percent of total shipments in an industry. Values of indented subcategories are summed in the main heading. The symbol (D) appears when data are withheld to prevent disclosure of competitive information. The abbreviation nsk stands for 'not specified by kind' and nec for 'not elsewhere classified'.

INPUTS AND OUTPUTS FOR NONWOVEN FABRICS

Economic Sector or Industry Providing Inputs	%	Sector	Economic Sector or Industry Buying Outputs	%	Sector
Organic fibers, noncellulosic	18.1	Manufg.	Sanitary paper products	13.7	Manufg.
Cellulosic manmade fibers	9.8	Manufg.	Floor coverings	9.0	Manufg.
Nonwoven fabrics	9.8	Manufg.	Fabricated textile products, nec	8.5	Manufg.
Cyclic crudes and organics	7.8	Manufg.	Automotive & apparel trimmings	8.2	Manufg.
Advertising	7.0	Services	Personal consumption expenditures	7.7	
Imports	6.0	Foreign	Nonwoven fabrics	6.7	Manufg.
Wholesale trade	5.4	Trade	Surgical appliances & supplies	6.5	Manufg.
Adhesives & sealants	5.2	Manufg.	Exports	6.0	Foreign
Industrial gases	3.2	Manufg.	Coated fabrics, not rubberized	4.0	Manufg.
Plastics materials & resins	2.6	Manufg.	Paper coating & glazing	4.0	Manufg.
Electric services (utilities)	2.3	Util.	Housefurnishings, nec	3.5	Manufg.
Textile goods, nec	2.1	Manufg.	General industrial machinery, nec	2.7	Manufg.
Yarn mills & finishing of textiles, nec	2.1	Manufg.	Blowers & fans	2.3	Manufg.
Converted paper products, nec	2.0	Manufg.	Narrow fabric mills	1.7	Manufg.
Motor freight transportation & warehousing	1.5	Util.	Curtains & draperies	1.3	Manufg.
Textile machinery	1.2	Manufg.	Textile bags	1.3	Manufg.
Miscellaneous plastics products	1.1	Manufg.	Miscellaneous plastics products	1.1	Manufg.
Petroleum refining	1.1	Manufg.	Rubber & plastics hose & belting	0.9	Manufg.
Gas production & distribution (utilities)	1.1	Util.	Retail trade, except eating & drinking	0.9	Trade
Processed textile waste	1.0	Manufg.	Luggage	0.8	Manufg.
Industrial inorganic chemicals, nec	0.9	Manufg.	Eating & drinking places	0.8	Trade
Surface active agents	0.8	Manufg.	Polishes & sanitation goods	0.7	Manufg.
Paperboard containers & boxes	0.7	Manufg.	Boot & shoe cutstock & findings	0.6	Manufg.
Railroads & related services	0.6	Util.	Commercial printing	0.6	Manufg.
Chemical preparations, nec	0.5	Manufg.	Shoes, except rubber	0.6	Manufg.
Sanitary services, steam supply, irrigation	0.5	Util.	Residential 1-unit structures, nonfarm	0.5	Constr.
Communications, except radio & TV	0.4	Util.	Automotive repair shops & services	0.5	Services
U.S. Postal Service	0.4	Gov't	Hospitals	0.5	Services
Pulp mills	0.3	Manufg.	Maintenance of nonfarm buildings nec	0.4	Constr.
Banking	0.3	Fin/R.E.	Rubber & plastics footwear	0.4	Manufg.
Real estate	0.3	Fin/R.E.	Converted paper products, nec	0.3	Manufg.
Royalties	0.3	Fin/R.E.	Fabricated rubber products, nec	0.3	Manufg.
Equipment rental & leasing services	0.3	Services	Surgical & medical instruments	0.3	Manufg.
Coal	0.2	Mining	Toilet preparations	0.3	Manufg.
Maintenance of nonfarm buildings nec	0.2	Constr.	Hotels & lodging places	0.3	Services
Paper mills, except building paper	0.2	Manufg.	Nonfarm residential structure maintenance	0.2	Constr.
Water transportation	0.2	Util.	Residential additions/alterations, nonfarm	0.2	Constr.
Business services nec	0.2	Services	Federal Government purchases, nondefense	0.2	Fed Govt
Computer & data processing services	0.2	Services	S/L Govt. purch., health & hospitals	0.2	S/L Govt
Detective & protective services	0.2	Services	Office buildings	0.1	Constr.
Laundry, dry cleaning, shoe repair	0.2	Services	Residential garden apartments	0.1	Constr.
Alkalies & chlorine	0.1	Manufg.			
Pipelines, except natural gas	0.1	Util.			
Eating & drinking places	0.1	Trade			
Hotels & lodging places	0.1	Services			

Source: Benchmark Input-Output Accounts for the U.S. Economy, 1982, U.S. Department of Commerce, Washington, D.C., July 1991. Data, as reported in the source, are organized by the 1977 SIC structure in use in 1982 but have been matched, as closely as is possible, to the 1987 SIC structure used in this book.

OCCUPATIONS EMPLOYED BY SIC 229 - MISCELLANEOUS TEXTILE GOODS

Occupation	% of Total 1994	Change to 2005	Occupation	% of Total 1994	Change to 2005
Textile draw-out & winding machine operators	22.1	-3.5	Maintenance repairers, general utility	2.1	-13.1
Blue collar worker supervisors	6.0	-7.8	Industrial truck & tractor operators	2.0	-3.5
Machine operators nec	4.6	-14.9	Traffic, shipping, & receiving clerks	1.9	-7.2
Industrial machinery mechanics	4.2	6.2	Coating, painting, & spraying machine workers	1.9	-3.6
Textile machine setters & set-up operators	3.9	-13.1	Hand packers & packagers	1.8	-17.4
Helpers, laborers, & material movers nec	3.9	-3.5	Freight, stock, & material movers, hand	1.7	-22.8
Inspectors, testers, & graders, precision	3.8	-3.5	Secretaries, ex legal & medical	1.6	-12.1
General managers & top executives	2.5	-8.4	Sewing machine operators, non-garment	1.6	-22.8
Sales & related workers nec	2.3	-3.5	Industrial production managers	1.5	-3.5
Machine feeders & offbearers	2.3	-13.1	Packaging & filling machine operators	1.5	-3.5
Assemblers, fabricators, & hand workers nec	2.3	-3.5	Bookkeeping, accounting, & auditing clerks	1.2	-27.7
Extruding & forming machine workers	2.2	-3.5	Janitors & cleaners, incl maids	1.1	-22.8

Source: Industry-Occupation Matrix, Bureau of Labor Statistics. These data relate to one or more 3-digit SIC industry groups rather than to a single 4-digit SIC. The change reported for each occupation to the year 2005 is a percent of growth or decline as estimated by the Bureau of Labor Statistics. The abbreviation nec stands for 'not elsewhere classified'.

LOCATION BY STATE AND REGIONAL CONCENTRATION

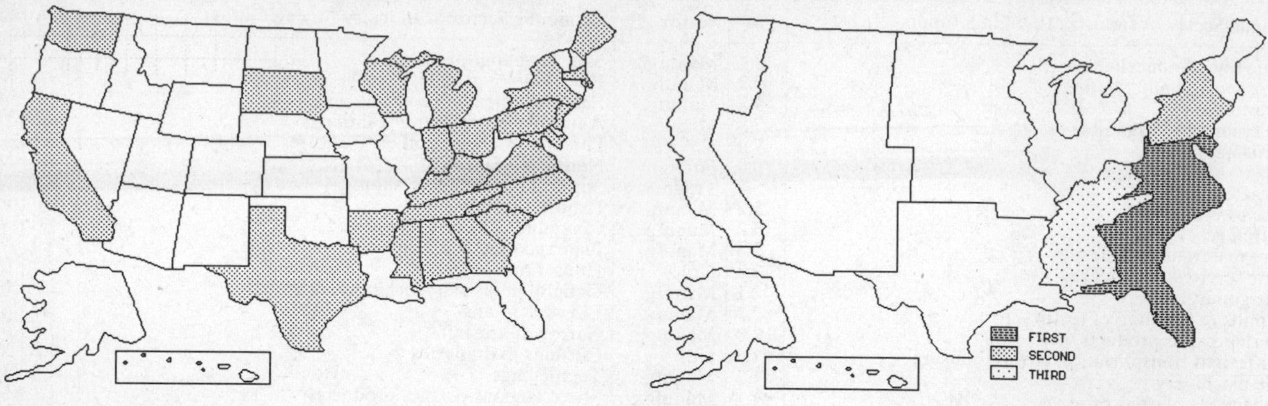

INDUSTRY DATA BY STATE

State	Establish-ments	Shipments			Employment				Cost as % of Shipments	Investment per Employee ($)
		Total ($ mil)	% of U.S.	Per Establ.	Total Number	% of U.S.	Per Establ.	Wages ($/hour)		
North Carolina	22	454.5	15.9	20.7	3,100	18.5	141	10.29	52.2	11,677
South Carolina	12	288.0	10.1	24.0	1,700	10.1	142	11.07	52.6	11,471
Pennsylvania	10	171.5	6.0	17.2	1,200	7.1	120	9.72	49.0	2,333
Georgia	9	166.6	5.8	18.5	1,100	6.5	122	12.87	64.9	-
Massachusetts	10	164.9	5.8	16.5	1,100	6.5	110	16.30	48.9	-
Wisconsin	8	116.7	4.1	14.6	300	1.8	38	14.50	67.2	-
New York	23	114.5	4.0	5.0	1,000	6.0	43	9.87	50.5	3,200
New Jersey	6	74.2	2.6	12.4	400	2.4	67	8.63	62.9	3,250
Alabama	5	17.5	0.6	3.5	200	1.2	40	9.00	56.6	-
California	7	(D)	-	-	175 *	1.0	25	-	-	-
Tennessee	6	(D)	-	-	1,750 *	10.4	292	-	-	2,800
Virginia	6	(D)	-	-	375 *	2.2	63	-	-	-
Mississippi	4	(D)	-	-	750 *	4.5	188	-	-	-
Texas	4	(D)	-	-	375 *	2.2	94	-	-	-
Washington	4	(D)	-	-	375 *	2.2	94	-	-	-
Arkansas	3	(D)	-	-	750 *	4.5	250	-	-	-
Maine	3	(D)	-	-	375 *	2.2	125	-	-	267
Michigan	3	(D)	-	-	375 *	2.2	125	-	-	-
Ohio	3	(D)	-	-	375 *	2.2	125	-	-	-
Rhode Island	3	(D)	-	-	375 *	2.2	125	-	-	-
Indiana	2	(D)	-	-	175 *	1.0	88	-	-	-
Kentucky	2	(D)	-	-	175 *	1.0	88	-	-	-
Maryland	1	(D)	-	-	375 *	2.2	375	-	-	-
South Dakota	1	(D)	-	-	750 *	4.5	750	-	-	-

Source: 1992 *Economic Census*. The states are in descending order of shipments or establishments (if shipment data are missing for the majority). The symbol (D) appears when data are withheld to prevent disclosure of competitive information. States marked with (D) are sorted by number of establishments. A dash (-) indicates that the data element cannot be calculated; * indicates the midpoint of a range.

2298 - CORDAGE AND TWINE

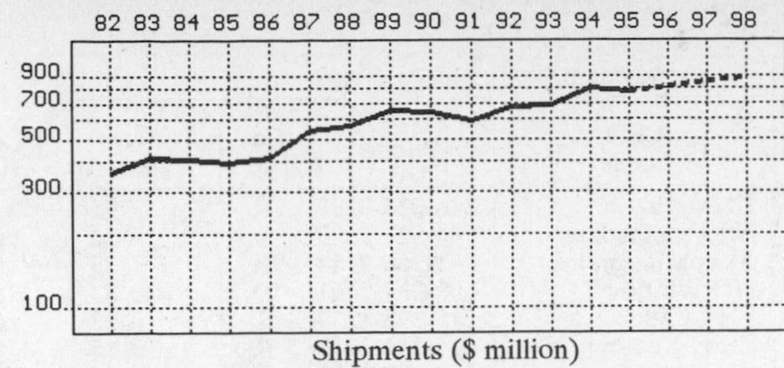

Shipments ($ million)

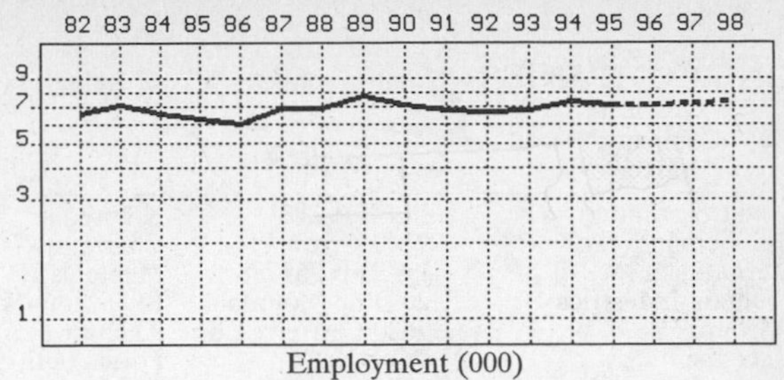

Employment (000)

GENERAL STATISTICS

Year	Com-panies	Establishments: Total	Establishments: with 20 or more employees	Employment: Total (000)	Employment: Production Workers (000)	Employment: Production Hours (Mil)	Compensation: Payroll ($ mil)	Compensation: Wages ($/hr)	Production ($ million): Cost of Materials	Production ($ million): Value Added by Manufacture	Production ($ million): Value of Shipments	Production ($ million): Capital Invest.
1982	164	181	69	6.6	5.2	9.4	77.0	5.50	178.7	181.5	358.7	17.0
1983		175	70	7.2	5.7	10.6	93.6	5.93	206.5	200.4	412.9	15.8
1984		169	71	6.6	5.2	9.6	87.1	6.19	201.9	209.8	408.8	19.0
1985		163	73	6.3	5.0	9.5	92.9	6.49	182.2	211.9	394.5	23.7
1986		164	69	6.0	4.7	9.2	93.8	6.78	182.5	226.2	413.0	9.5
1987	181	197	78	6.9	5.5	10.8	112.3	7.00	261.1	284.0	541.2	12.0
1988		191	87	6.9	5.4	10.7	117.4	7.29	280.4	281.8	560.3	11.0
1989		186	84	7.7	5.6	10.7	124.9	7.38	390.9	258.7	646.3	13.8
1990		187	86	7.2	5.3	11.3	129.7	7.30	387.7	248.8	636.9	23.2
1991		201	83	6.8	5.3	11.4	128.0	7.19	355.0	248.1	588.5	16.6
1992	191	210	78	6.7	5.2	10.8	138.7	7.94	324.8	350.1	672.7	21.5
1993		219	84	6.8	5.2	11.2	147.7	8.02	348.9	333.3	682.4	22.4
1994		213P	88P	7.4	5.8	11.6	158.4	8.21	441.3	354.3	795.0	19.0
1995		217P	89P	7.2P	5.4P	11.7P	159.9P	8.45P	435.1P	349.3P	783.8P	19.7P
1996		221P	91P	7.2P	5.5P	11.9P	166.3P	8.65P	453.8P	364.4P	817.6P	20.0P
1997		225P	92P	7.2P	5.5P	12.0P	172.6P	8.86P	472.6P	379.4P	851.4P	20.4P
1998		229P	94P	7.3P	5.5P	12.2P	179.0P	9.06P	491.4P	394.5P	885.2P	20.7P

Sources: 1982, 1987, 1992 *Economic Census*; *Annual Survey of Manufactures*, 83-86, 88-91, 93-94. Establishment counts for non-Census years are from *County Business Patterns*; establishment values for 83-84 are extrapolations. 'P's show projections by the editors. Industries reclassified in 87 will not have data for prior years.

INDICES OF CHANGE

Year	Com-panies	Establishments: Total	Establishments: with 20 or more employees	Employment: Total (000)	Employment: Production Workers (000)	Employment: Production Hours (Mil)	Compensation: Payroll ($ mil)	Compensation: Wages ($/hr)	Production ($ million): Cost of Materials	Production ($ million): Value Added by Manufacture	Production ($ million): Value of Shipments	Production ($ million): Capital Invest.
1982	86	86	88	99	100	87	56	69	55	52	53	79
1983		83	90	107	110	98	67	75	64	57	61	73
1984		80	91	99	100	89	63	78	62	60	61	88
1985		78	94	94	96	88	67	82	56	61	59	110
1986		78	88	90	90	85	68	85	56	65	61	44
1987	95	94	100	103	106	100	81	88	80	81	80	56
1988		91	112	103	104	99	85	92	86	80	83	51
1989		89	108	115	108	99	90	93	120	74	96	64
1990		89	110	107	102	105	94	92	119	71	95	108
1991		96	106	101	102	106	92	91	109	71	87	77
1992	100	100	100	100	100	100	100	100	100	100	100	100
1993		104	108	101	100	104	106	101	107	95	101	104
1994		101P	112P	110	112	107	114	103	136	101	118	88
1995		103P	114P	107P	105P	108P	115P	106P	134P	100P	117P	92P
1996		105P	116P	107P	105P	110P	120P	109P	140P	104P	122P	93P
1997		107P	118P	108P	105P	112P	124P	112P	146P	108P	127P	95P
1998		109P	120P	109P	106P	113P	129P	114P	151P	113P	132P	96P

Sources: Same as General Statistics. Values reflect change from the base year, 1992. Values above 100 mean greater than 92, values below 100 mean less than 92, and a value of 100 in the 82-91 or 93-98 period means same as 92. 'P's mark projections by the editors.

SELECTED RATIOS

For 1994	Avg. of All Manufact.	Analyzed Industry	Index
Employees per Establishment	49	35	71
Payroll per Establishment	1,500,273	744,509	50
Payroll per Employee	30,620	21,405	70
Production Workers per Establishment	34	27	79
Wages per Establishment	853,319	447,627	52
Wages per Production Worker	24,861	16,420	66
Hours per Production Worker	2,056	2,000	97
Wages per Hour	12.09	8.21	68
Value Added per Establishment	4,602,255	1,665,276	36
Value Added per Employee	93,930	47,878	51

For 1994	Avg. of All Manufact.	Analyzed Industry	Index
Value Added per Production Worker	134,084	61,086	46
Cost per Establishment	5,045,178	2,074,192	41
Cost per Employee	102,970	59,635	58
Cost per Production Worker	146,988	76,086	52
Shipments per Establishment	9,576,895	3,736,647	39
Shipments per Employee	195,460	107,432	55
Shipments per Production Worker	279,017	137,069	49
Investment per Establishment	321,011	89,304	28
Investment per Employee	6,552	2,568	39
Investment per Production Worker	9,352	3,276	35

Sources: Same as General Statistics. The 'Average of All Manufacturing' column represents the average of all manufacturing industries reported for the most recent complete year available. The Index shows the relationship between the Average and the Analyzed Industry. For example, 100 means that they are equal; 500 that the Analyzed Industry is five times the average; 50 means that the Analyzed Industry is half the national average. The abbreviation 'na' is used to show that data are 'not available'.

LEADING COMPANIES

Number shown: **38** Total sales ($ mil): **410** Total employment (000): **4.6**

Company Name	Address				CEO Name	Phone	Co. Type	Sales ($ mil)	Empl. (000)
Wire Rope Corporation	PO Box 288	St Joseph	MO	64501	JP Barclay Jr	816-233-0287	R	95*	1.0
Tolaram Fibers Inc	9140 Arrow Pt	Charlotte	NC	28273	NS Jagannathan	704-521-9607	S	52	0.2
Fitec International Inc	PO Box 751788	Memphis	TN	38175	Joseph R Amore	901-366-9144	R	35	0.5
Blue Mountain Industries	20 Blue Mountain	Blue Mountain	AL	36204	HD Whitlow	205-237-9461	D	32	0.6
Lehigh Group	7620 Cetronia Rd	Allentown	PA	18106	Fred Keller	215-398-1233	S	22	0.1
Mitchellace Inc	PO Box 89	Portsmouth	OH	45662	Kerry Keating	614-354-2813	R	15	0.3
New England Ropes Inc	848 Airport Rd	Fall River	MA	02720	George E Repass	508-999-2351	R	12	0.1
SS White Technologies Inc	151 New Br	Piscataway	NJ	08854	Rahul B Shukla	908-752-8300	R	12	0.1
Wall Industries Inc	PO Box 830	Granite Quarry	NC	28072	Stanley Swider	704-279-7901	R	11	0.2
Bridon Cordage Inc	909 16th St	Albert Lea	MN	56007	William J Adams	507-377-1601	R	10	<0.1
Petco Inc	3050 Walkent NW	Grand Rapids	MI	49504	Dave J Meyers	616-784-5868	R	10*	0.1
Strandflex	6149 Sutliff Rd	Oriskany	NY	13424	Keith Stahl	315-736-5208	D	10	<0.1
Winchester-Auburn Mills Inc	200 Merrimac St	Woburn	MA	01801	Milton Steinberg	617-935-4110	R	10	<0.1
Cortland Line Company Inc	3736 Kellogg	Cortland	NY	13045	SM Zattosky	607-756-2851	R	9	0.1
Rocky Mount Cord Co	PO Box 4304	Rocky Mount	NC	27803	Joseph E Bunn	919-977-9130	R	9	0.2
Gladding Braided Products Inc	PO Box 164	South Otselic	NY	13155	Sparky Christakos	315-653-7211	R	6	<0.1
Brownell and Company Inc	PO Box 362	Moodus	CT	06469	Anthony Ferraz	203-873-8625	S	5	<0.1
Tubbs Rope Works Inc	815 E 18th St	Tucson	AZ	85719	Douglas Coath	602-798-3752	S	5*	<0.1
Ashaway Line & Twine Mfg Co	24 Laurel St	Ashaway	RI	02804	PA Crandall	401-377-2221	R	4*	<0.1
Memphis Net and Twine	PO Box 8331	Memphis	TN	38108	W D McCorkle	901-458-2656	R	4	<0.1
Rome Specialty Company Inc	PO Box 109	Rome	NY	13442	JH Butts	315-337-8200	R	4	<0.1
Samson Ocean Systems Inc	2090 Thornton St	Ferndale	WA	98248	C Swiackey	206-384-4669	R	4*	0.1
January and Wood Company Inc	237 W 2nd St	Maysville	KY	41056	WC Adair	606-564-3301	R	4	0.1
Energy Electric Assembly Inc	272 Rex Blv	Auburn Hills	MI	48321	Curtis Cieszkowski	313-853-6363	R	3	<0.1
First Washington Net Factory	PO Box 310	Blaine	WA	98230	N Smith	206-332-5351	R	3	<0.1
FNT Industries Inc	PO Box 157	Menominee	MI	49858	Werner Haberl	906-863-5531	R	3	<0.1
Star Synthetic Mfg Corp	Rte 145	East Durham	NY	12423	GE Stengel	518-634-2535	R	3	<0.1
Fibre Yarns and Fillers Inc	4309 G St	Philadelphia	PA	19124	Lee A Huff	215-533-8100	R	3	<0.1
Nylon Net Co	PO Box 592	Memphis	TN	38101	George T Slaughter	901-774-1500	R	3	<0.1
US Rigging Supply Corp	4001 Carriage Dr	Santa Ana	CA	92704	Gaylord C Whipple	714-545-7444	R	3	<0.1
Akzo Nobel Geosynthetics Co	PO Box 7249	Asheville	NC	28802	Tom Robrack	704-665-5026	R	2*	<0.1
Research Nets Inc	PO Box 249	Bothell	WA	98041	Jackie Halstead	206-821-7345	R	2*	<0.1
Pelican Rope Works	4001 W Carriage Dr	Santa Ana	CA	92704	Gaylord C Whipple	714-545-0116	R	2	<0.1
Adler Western Inc	6252 Florence Av	Bell Gardens	CA	90201	JM Hezlep Jr	310-927-1321	R	1	<0.1
Badger Cordage Mills Inc	193 N Broadway	Milwaukee	WI	53202	Warren E Buesing	414-225-2880	S	1	<0.1
Coordinated Wire Rope	1707 E Anaheim St	Wilmington	CA	90744	Stanley Fishfader	310-834-8535	S	1	<0.1
Koring Brothers Inc	2020 W 16th St	Long Beach	CA	90813	Berand Koring	310-435-4974	R	1*	<0.1
Sunset Line and Twine Co	PO Box 691	Petaluma	CA	94953	AW Agnew	707-762-2704	R	1	<0.1

Source: *Ward's Business Directory of U.S. Private and Public Companies*, Volumes 1 and 2, 1996. The company type code used is as follows: P - Public, R - Private, S - Subsidiary, D - Division, J - Joint Venture, A - Affiliate, G - Group. Sales are in millions of dollars, employees are in thousands. An asterisk (*) indicates an estimated sales volume. The symbol < stands for 'less than'. Company names and addresses are truncated, in some cases, to fit into the available space.

MATERIALS CONSUMED

Material		Quantity	Delivered Cost ($ million)
Materials, ingredients, containers, and supplies		(X)	263.3
Manmade fibers, staple, and tow	mil lb	25.9	37.7
Yarn, all fibers	mil lb	64.4*	80.4
Cotton fabrics	mil lin yd	(D)	(D)
Manmade fiber fabrics, including glass	mil lin yd	(S)	2.8
Paper (cellulosic wadding)	mil lb	(S)	3.5
Adhesives and binders (resins)	mil lb	(D)	(D)
Plasticizers	mil lb	(D)	(D)
Vinyl and vinyl copolymer resins, all forms	mil lb	(D)	(D)
Plastics resins (except vinyl) consumed in the form of granules, pellets, powders, liquids, etc.	mil lb	122.8	40.9
Plastics products consumed in the form of sheets, rods, tubes, film, and other shapes		(X)	(D)
Additives (fire retardants, water repellants, softeners, and antistatics, etc.)		(X)	2.8
All other materials and components, parts, containers, and supplies		(X)	46.9
Materials, ingredients, containers, and supplies, nsk		(X)	42.4

Source: 1992 *Economic Census*. Explanation of symbols used: (D): Withheld to avoid disclosure of competitive data; na: Not available; (S): Withheld because statistical norms were not met; (X): Not applicable; (Z): Less than half the unit shown; nec: Not elsewhere classified; nsk: Not specified by kind; - : zero; * : 10-19 percent estimated; ** : 20-29 percent estimated.

PRODUCT SHARE DETAILS

Product or Product Class	% Share	Product or Product Class	% Share
Cordage and twine	100.00	Rope 3/16 in. diameter and larger, manmade fiber	33.12
Cordage and twine, hard fiber	19.04	Industrial and agriculture twine, less than 3/16 in. diameter, manmade fiber	24.12
Cordage and twine, hard fiber cordage rope and cable (including products of 3 strands or more) each strand composed of 2 yarns or more	37.06	All other cordage and twine, manmade fiber	19.11
Cordage and twine, hard fiber twine (including products laid or twisted, but not stranded, and twine of hard fiber and paper)	(D)	Cordage and twine, soft fiber (except cotton and manmade, including hemp, jute, and paper)	3.70
Hard fiber cordage and twine, nsk	(D)	Soft fiber cordage and twine (except cotton), nsk	(D)
Cordage and twine, soft fiber (except cotton)	57.11	Cotton cordage and twine	11.84
Fish line, commercial, manmade fiber	1.49	Cotton cordage and twine, braided, regardless of size	24.86
Fish line, recreational, manmade fiber	(D)	Cotton cordage, wrapping, seine, and other twine	30.54
Fish nets and fish netting, commercial, manmade fiber	5.86	All other cotton cordage and twine, including fish nets	24.46
Fish nets and fish netting, recreational, manmade fiber	0.73	Cotton cordage and twine, nsk	20.14
		Cordage and twine, nsk	12.00

Source: 1992 *Economic Census*. The values shown are percent of total shipments in an industry. Values of indented subcategories are summed in the main heading. The symbol (D) appears when data are withheld to prevent disclosure of competitive information. The abbreviation nsk stands for 'not specified by kind' and nec for 'not elsewhere classified'.

INPUTS AND OUTPUTS FOR CORDAGE & TWINE

Economic Sector or Industry Providing Inputs	%	Sector	Economic Sector or Industry Buying Outputs	%	Sector
Noncomparable imports	30.5	Foreign	Personal consumption expenditures	20.7	
Organic fibers, noncellulosic	18.9	Manufg.	Commercial fishing	15.7	Agric.
Wholesale trade	7.8	Trade	Water transportation	13.2	Util.
Advertising	7.6	Services	Wholesale trade	9.8	Trade
Imports	5.7	Foreign	Feed grains	5.4	Agric.
Motor freight transportation & warehousing	4.6	Util.	Exports	4.7	Foreign
Yarn mills & finishing of textiles, nec	4.4	Manufg.	Logging camps & logging contractors	4.1	Manufg.
Textile goods, nec	4.1	Manufg.	S/L Govt. purch., other general government	2.9	S/L Govt
Electric services (utilities)	2.4	Util.	Drapery hardware & blinds & shades	2.3	Manufg.
Miscellaneous plastics products	2.0	Manufg.	S/L Govt. purch., correction	1.8	S/L Govt
Banking	1.0	Fin/R.E.	Boat building & repairing	1.3	Manufg.
Laundry, dry cleaning, shoe repair	1.0	Services	Greenhouse & nursery products	1.2	Agric.
Processed textile waste	0.8	Manufg.	Amusement & recreation services nec	1.2	Services
Eating & drinking places	0.7	Trade	Motor freight transportation & warehousing	1.0	Util.
Maintenance of nonfarm buildings nec	0.6	Constr.	Federal Government purchases, nondefense	0.9	Fed Govt
Paperboard containers & boxes	0.6	Manufg.	Mattresses & bedsprings	0.8	Manufg.
Textile machinery	0.6	Manufg.	Meat animals	0.7	Agric.
Communications, except radio & TV	0.5	Util.	Laundry, dry cleaning, shoe repair	0.6	Services
Gas production & distribution (utilities)	0.5	Util.	Management & consulting services & labs	0.6	Services
Water transportation	0.5	Util.	S/L Govt. purch., elem. & secondary education	0.6	S/L Govt
Security & commodity brokers	0.4	Fin/R.E.	Industrial buildings	0.5	Constr.
Lubricating oils & greases	0.3	Manufg.	Office buildings	0.5	Constr.
Machinery, except electrical, nec	0.3	Manufg.	Miscellaneous fabricated wire products	0.4	Manufg.
Real estate	0.3	Fin/R.E.	Sporting & athletic goods, nec	0.4	Manufg.
Royalties	0.3	Fin/R.E.	U.S. Postal Service	0.4	Gov't
Business services nec	0.3	Services	Federal Government purchases, national defense	0.4	Fed Govt
Equipment rental & leasing services	0.3	Services	S/L Govt. purch., natural resource & recreation.	0.4	S/L Govt
Management & consulting services & labs	0.3	Services	Dairy farm products	0.3	Agric.
U.S. Postal Service	0.3	Gov't	Forestry products	0.3	Agric.
Cordage & twine	0.2	Manufg.	Residential additions/alterations, nonfarm	0.3	Constr.
Petroleum refining	0.2	Manufg.	Food grains	0.2	Agric.
Sanitary services, steam supply, irrigation	0.2	Util.	Oil bearing crops	0.2	Agric.
Accounting, auditing & bookkeeping	0.2	Services	Construction of hospitals	0.2	Constr.
Legal services	0.2	Services	Construction of stores & restaurants	0.2	Constr.
Asbestos products	0.1	Manufg.	Highway & street construction	0.2	Constr.
Manifold business forms	0.1	Manufg.	Hotels & motels	0.2	Constr.
Special dies & tools & machine tool accessories	0.1	Manufg.	Residential garden apartments	0.2	Constr.
Computer & data processing services	0.1	Services	Telephone & telegraph facility construction	0.2	Constr.
			Cordage & twine	0.2	Manufg.
			Shoes, except rubber	0.2	Manufg.
			Hospitals	0.2	Services
			S/L Govt. purch., health & hospitals	0.2	S/L Govt
			S/L Govt. purch., public assistance & relief	0.2	S/L Govt
			Fruits	0.1	Agric.
			Poultry & eggs	0.1	Agric.
			Vegetables	0.1	Agric.
			Construction of educational buildings	0.1	Constr.
			Electric utility facility construction	0.1	Constr.
			Farm service facilities	0.1	Constr.
			Maintenance of farm service facilities	0.1	Constr.
			Maintenance of nonfarm buildings nec	0.1	Constr.
			Nonfarm residential structure maintenance	0.1	Constr.
			Residential high-rise apartments	0.1	Constr.
			Sewer system facility construction	0.1	Constr.
			Periodicals	0.1	Manufg.
			Railroads & related services	0.1	Util.

Source: Benchmark Input-Output Accounts for the U.S. Economy, 1982, U.S. Department of Commerce, Washington, D.C., July 1991. Data, as reported in the source, are organized by the 1977 SIC structure in use in 1982 but have been matched, as closely as is possible, to the 1987 SIC structure used in this book.

OCCUPATIONS EMPLOYED BY SIC 229 - MISCELLANEOUS TEXTILE GOODS

Occupation	% of Total 1994	Change to 2005	Occupation	% of Total 1994	Change to 2005
Textile draw-out & winding machine operators	22.1	-3.5	Maintenance repairers, general utility	2.1	-13.1
Blue collar worker supervisors	6.0	-7.8	Industrial truck & tractor operators	2.0	-3.5
Machine operators nec	4.6	-14.9	Traffic, shipping, & receiving clerks	1.9	-7.2
Industrial machinery mechanics	4.2	6.2	Coating, painting, & spraying machine workers	1.9	-3.6
Textile machine setters & set-up operators	3.9	-13.1	Hand packers & packagers	1.8	-17.4
Helpers, laborers, & material movers nec	3.9	-3.5	Freight, stock, & material movers, hand	1.7	-22.8
Inspectors, testers, & graders, precision	3.8	-3.5	Secretaries, ex legal & medical	1.6	-12.1
General managers & top executives	2.5	-8.4	Sewing machine operators, non-garment	1.6	-22.8
Sales & related workers nec	2.3	-3.5	Industrial production managers	1.5	-3.5
Machine feeders & offbearers	2.3	-13.1	Packaging & filling machine operators	1.5	-3.5
Assemblers, fabricators, & hand workers nec	2.3	-3.5	Bookkeeping, accounting, & auditing clerks	1.2	-27.7
Extruding & forming machine workers	2.2	-3.5	Janitors & cleaners, incl maids	1.1	-22.8

Source: Industry-Occupation Matrix, Bureau of Labor Statistics. These data relate to one or more 3-digit SIC industry groups rather than to a single 4-digit SIC. The change reported for each occupation to the year 2005 is a percent of growth or decline as estimated by the Bureau of Labor Statistics. The abbreviation nec stands for 'not elsewhere classified'.

LOCATION BY STATE AND REGIONAL CONCENTRATION

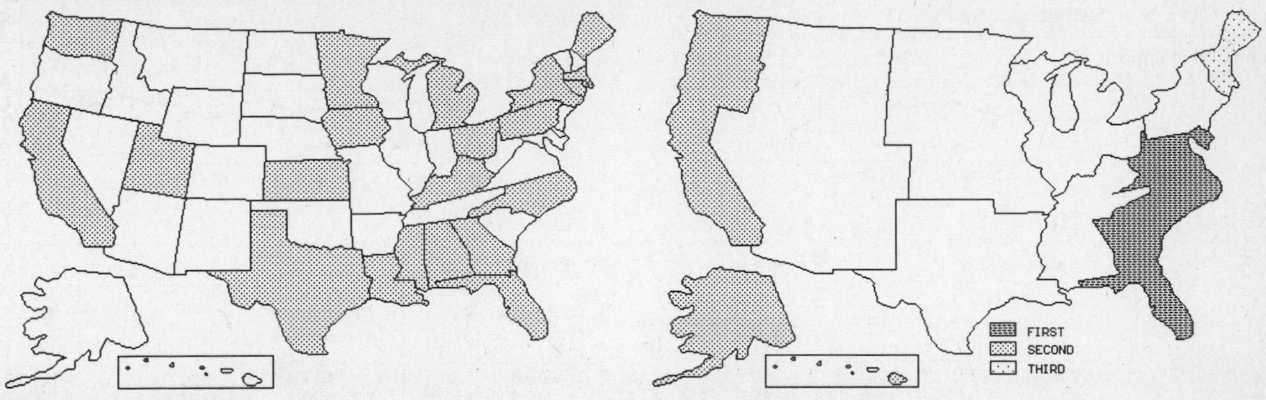

INDUSTRY DATA BY STATE

State	Establish-ments	Shipments			Employment				Cost as % of Shipments	Investment per Employee ($)
		Total ($ mil)	% of U.S.	Per Establ.	Total Number	% of U.S.	Per Establ.	Wages ($/hour)		
Washington	10	52.0	7.7	5.2	400	6.0	40	9.50	55.0	1,500
Pennsylvania	13	51.7	7.7	4.0	400	6.0	31	7.75	63.2	2,750
Alabama	10	50.4	7.5	5.0	800	11.9	80	7.21	38.7	1,375
Georgia	10	30.2	4.5	3.0	400	6.0	40	6.57	47.0	-
California	22	29.9	4.4	1.4	300	4.5	14	7.67	43.8	2,333
Mississippi	5	17.4	2.6	3.5	200	3.0	40	8.67	59.2	-
Florida	15	17.1	2.5	1.1	200	3.0	13	6.50	46.8	-
Massachusetts	7	14.4	2.1	2.1	100	1.5	14	7.50	43.1	-
Rhode Island	6	9.5	1.4	1.6	100	1.5	17	8.50	30.5	1,000
Texas	16	8.9	1.3	0.6	100	1.5	6	7.00	53.9	2,000
Michigan	5	7.1	1.1	1.4	100	1.5	20	5.50	36.6	-
North Carolina	17	(D)	-	-	1,750 *	26.1	103	-	-	1,600
Maine	7	(D)	-	-	375 *	5.6	54	-	-	-
New York	7	(D)	-	-	175 *	2.6	25	-	-	-
Connecticut	5	(D)	-	-	175 *	2.6	35	-	-	-
Kansas	4	(D)	-	-	175 *	2.6	44	-	-	-
Louisiana	3	(D)	-	-	175 *	2.6	58	-	-	-
Ohio	3	(D)	-	-	175 *	2.6	58	-	-	-
Utah	3	(D)	-	-	175 *	2.6	58	-	-	-
Kentucky	2	(D)	-	-	175 *	2.6	88	-	-	-
Minnesota	2	(D)	-	-	175 *	2.6	88	-	-	-
Iowa	1	(D)	-	-	375 *	5.6	375	-	-	-

Source: 1992 *Economic Census*. The states are in descending order of shipments or establishments (if shipment data are missing for the majority). The symbol (D) appears when data are withheld to prevent disclosure of competitive information. States marked with (D) are sorted by number of establishments. A dash (-) indicates that the data element cannot be calculated; * indicates the midpoint of a range.

2299 - TEXTILE GOODS, NEC

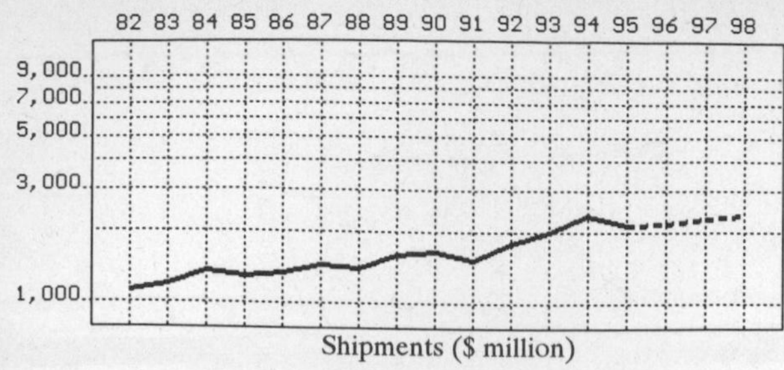

Shipments ($ million)

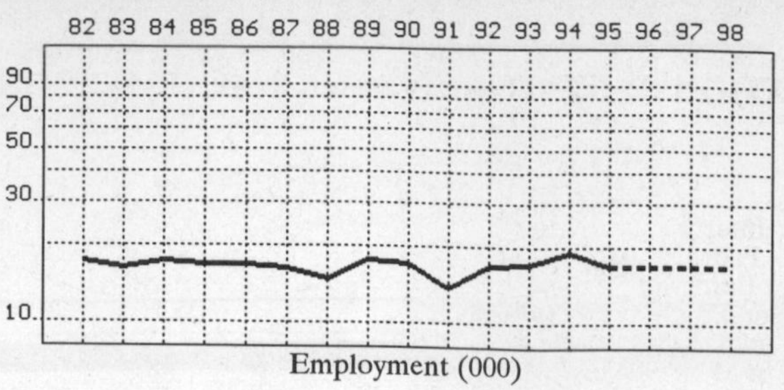

Employment (000)

GENERAL STATISTICS

Year	Com-panies	Establishments Total	Establishments with 20 or more employees	Employment Total (000)	Production Workers (000)	Production Hours (Mil)	Compensation Payroll ($ mil)	Compensation Wages ($/hr)	Cost of Materials	Value Added by Manufacture	Value of Shipments	Capital Invest.
1982	506	523	179	17.3	14.0	27.8	242.8	5.97	617.8	507.0	1,129.2	47.0
1983		419	143	16.3	13.3	27.2	248.9	6.25	679.3	524.4	1,186.8	26.0
1984		315	107	17.5	14.5	29.1	272.5	6.74	693.5	660.9	1,352.5	33.9
1985		211	71	17.0	14.2	28.4	273.6	6.82	660.2	632.0	1,296.1	33.0
1986		189	65	17.0	14.0	28.0	285.2	7.34	636.3	708.7	1,333.1	57.3
1987	522	551	173	16.4	13.0	26.4	314.5	7.95	742.3	718.6	1,452.4	85.1
1988		488	181	14.8	11.5	22.5	295.0	8.51	739.6	676.8	1,411.0	68.2
1989		446	186	17.8	12.8	26.6	330.6	8.33	831.5	804.9	1,608.0	44.1
1990		434	172	17.2	11.3	23.9	302.8	8.36	847.3	823.4	1,646.5	77.1
1991		433	171	13.7	10.6	22.8	301.0	8.66	777.4	708.2	1,523.2	74.1
1992	537	573	188	16.7	12.6	27.1	400.4	9.12	875.5	947.2	1,795.7	83.3
1993		507	174	17.1	12.8	27.7	418.3	9.20	1,009.5	1,024.5	2,017.9	66.5
1994		512P	189P	19.1	14.4	30.4	464.3	9.53	1,158.5	1,193.5	2,360.6	83.9
1995		525P	195P	16.9P	12.1P	26.2P	427.7P	9.97P	1,038.3P	1,069.6P	2,115.6P	88.6P
1996		539P	201P	16.9P	11.9P	26.1P	443.2P	10.26P	1,078.1P	1,110.7P	2,196.8P	92.6P
1997		552P	206P	16.9P	11.8P	26.0P	458.7P	10.56P	1,118.0P	1,151.8P	2,278.1P	96.7P
1998		566P	212P	17.0P	11.7P	26.0P	474.2P	10.85P	1,157.8P	1,192.8P	2,359.3P	100.8P

Sources: 1982, 1987, 1992 *Economic Census*; *Annual Survey of Manufactures*, 83-86, 88-91, 93-94. Establishment counts for non-Census years are from *County Business Patterns*; establishment values for 83-84 are extrapolations. 'P's show projections by the editors. Industries reclassified in 87 will not have data for prior years.

INDICES OF CHANGE

Year	Com-panies	Establishments Total	Establishments with 20 or more employees	Employment Total (000)	Production Workers (000)	Production Hours (Mil)	Compensation Payroll ($ mil)	Compensation Wages ($/hr)	Cost of Materials	Value Added by Manufacture	Value of Shipments	Capital Invest.
1982	94	91	95	104	111	103	61	65	71	54	63	56
1983		73	76	98	106	100	62	69	78	55	66	31
1984		55	57	105	115	107	68	74	79	70	75	41
1985		37	38	102	113	105	68	75	75	67	72	40
1986		33	35	102	111	103	71	80	73	75	74	69
1987	97	96	92	98	103	97	79	87	85	76	81	102
1988		85	96	89	91	83	74	93	84	71	79	82
1989		78	99	107	102	98	83	91	95	85	90	53
1990		76	91	103	90	88	76	92	97	87	92	93
1991		76	91	82	84	84	75	95	89	75	85	89
1992	100	100	100	100	100	100	100	100	100	100	100	100
1993		88	93	102	102	102	104	101	115	108	112	80
1994		89P	100P	114	114	112	116	104	132	126	131	101
1995		92P	104P	101P	96P	97P	107P	109P	119P	113P	118P	106P
1996		94P	107P	101P	95P	96P	111P	113P	123P	117P	122P	111P
1997		96P	110P	101P	94P	96P	115P	116P	128P	122P	127P	116P
1998		99P	113P	102P	93P	96P	118P	119P	132P	126P	131P	121P

Sources: Same as General Statistics. Values reflect change from the base year, 1992. Values above 100 mean greater than 92, values below 100 mean less than 92, and a value of 100 in the 82-91 or 93-98 period means same as 92. 'P's mark projections by the editors.

SELECTED RATIOS

For 1994	Avg. of All Manufact.	Analyzed Industry	Index	For 1994	Avg. of All Manufact.	Analyzed Industry	Index
Employees per Establishment	49	37	76	Value Added per Production Worker	134,084	82,882	62
Payroll per Establishment	1,500,273	907,212	60	Cost per Establishment	5,045,178	2,263,633	45
Payroll per Employee	30,620	24,309	79	Cost per Employee	102,970	60,654	59
Production Workers per Establishment	34	28	82	Cost per Production Worker	146,988	80,451	55
Wages per Establishment	853,319	566,078	66	Shipments per Establishment	9,576,895	4,612,458	48
Wages per Production Worker	24,861	20,119	81	Shipments per Employee	195,460	123,592	63
Hours per Production Worker	2,056	2,111	103	Shipments per Production Worker	279,017	163,931	59
Wages per Hour	12.09	9.53	79	Investment per Establishment	321,011	163,935	51
Value Added per Establishment	4,602,255	2,332,021	51	Investment per Employee	6,552	4,393	67
Value Added per Employee	93,930	62,487	67	Investment per Production Worker	9,352	5,826	62

Sources: Same as General Statistics. The 'Average of All Manufacturing' column represents the average of all manufacturing industries reported for the most recent complete year available. The Index shows the relationship between the Average and the Analyzed Industry. For example, 100 means that they are equal; 500 that the Analyzed Industry is five times the average; 50 means that the Analyzed Industry is half the national average. The abbreviation 'na' is used to show that data are 'not available'.

LEADING COMPANIES Number shown: **67** Total sales ($ mil): **1,906** Total employment (000): **17.6**

Company Name	Address				CEO Name	Phone	Co. Type	Sales ($ mil)	Empl. (000)
Albany International Corp	PO Box 1907	Albany	NY	12201	Francis L McKone	518-445-2200	P	568	5.4
Quaker Fabric Corp	941 Grinnell St	Fall River	MA	02721	Larry A Liebenow	508-678-1951	P	165	1.6
William Barnet and Son Inc	PO Box 131	Arcadia	SC	29320	William Barnet III	803-576-7154	R	100	0.6
Barth and Dreyfuss of California	PO Box 21811	Los Angeles	CA	90021	Julian Galperson	213-627-6000	S	95	0.6
BDK Holdings Inc	2260 E 15th St	Los Angeles	CA	90021	Julian Galsperson	213-627-6000	R	95	0.6
Southern Mills Inc	PO Box 289	Union City	GA	30291	W Douglas Ellis	404-969-1000	R	80	0.5
Tex-Tech Industries Inc	PO Box 8	N Monmouth	ME	04265	CF Lynch	207-933-4404	R	70	0.5
Albany International Corp	PO Box 1907	Albany	NY	12201	Francis McKone	518-447-6400	D	50*	0.5
Troy Mills Inc	30 Monadnock St	Troy	NH	03465	BF Ripley	603-242-7711	P	46	0.4
Ace-Tex Corp	7601 Central	Detroit	MI	48210	Irving Laker	313-834-4000	R	41*	0.6
Franco Manufacturing Company	555 Prospect St	Metuchen	NJ	08840	Louis Franco	908-494-0500	R	39	0.5
Arden Corp	26899 Northwestern	Southfield	MI	48034	RS Sachs	313-355-1101	R	35	0.4
Kasbar National Industries Inc	370 Reed Rd	Broomall	PA	19008	Jeffrey D Shapiro	215-544-9799	R	29	0.2
Prouvost USA Inc	PO Box 98	Jamestown	SC	29453	JC Mazingue	803-257-2212	S	27	0.3
Amicale Industries Inc	1375 Broadway	New York	NY	10018	Borris Shlomm	212-398-0300	R	25	0.4
Orcon Corp	1570 Atlantic St	Union City	CA	94587	Hollis H Bascom	510-489-8100	R	25*	0.2
Clark-Cutler-McDermott Corp	PO Box 269	Franklin	MA	02038	T R McDermott	508-528-1200	R	18	0.2
Fairfield Processing Corp	PO Drawer 1157	Danbury	CT	06813	R Young	203-744-2090	R	18*	0.2
Orr Felt Co	PO Box 908	Piqua	OH	45356	C M Nicholas	513-773-0551	R	18	0.2
Norman W Paschall Company	PO Box 2100	Peachtree City	GA	30269	NW Paschall	404-487-7945	R	16	<0.1
DashMat Co	1502 W Hatcher Rd	Phoenix	AZ	85021	Brad Poston	602-870-3022	R	15*	0.2
John R Lyman Co	PO Box 157	Chicopee	MA	01014	William S Wright	413-598-8344	R	15	0.2
Lortex Inc	PO Box 1936	Des Moines	IA	50306	Patric J Curry	515-243-8155	R	15	<0.1
Carpet Cushion Company Inc	PO Box 128	Hickory	NC	28603	Neil Underdown	704-328-2201	S	14*	0.1
GS Fibers	PO Box 190	Claremont	NC	28610	M B Hamilton Jr	704-459-7645	D	14*	0.2
Lightron Corp	100 Jericho	Jericho	NY	11753	Robert Balemian	516-938-5544	S	14	0.1
Mount Vernon Press Fabrics	PO Box 16119	Greenville	SC	29606	Cliff Smith	803-963-4400	D	14*	0.1
Porritts and Spencer Inc	PO Box 1411	Wilson	NC	27893	Carlyle Smith	919-291-3800	S	14*	0.2
Buffalo Industries Inc	99 S Spokane St	Seattle	WA	98134	Lawrence J Benezra	206-682-9900	R	13*	0.1
Dunsirn Industries Inc	2415 Industrial Dr	Neenah	WI	54956	Brian Dunsirn	414-725-3814	R	13*	0.2
Osterneck Industries	PO Box 859	Lumberton	NC	28359	Guy Osterneck	919-738-2416	R	13*	0.2
Albany Mount Vernon	PO Box 5837	Greenville	SC	29606	RL King Jr	803-967-7641	D	12*	0.2
Hendrix Batting Company Inc	PO Box 7408	High Point	NC	27264	KL Hendrix	910-431-1181	R	12*	0.1
Dazians Inc	423 W 55th St	New York	NY	10016	Louis Fienberg	212-307-7800	R	11	<0.1
Hobbs Bonded Fibers	PO Box 2521	Waco	TX	76702	Carey Hobbs	817-741-0040	R	11*	0.1
O'Neill	PO Box 758	Villa Rica	GA	30180	Robert K Pease	404-459-1800	D	10*	0.1
Slosman Corp	PO Box 3019	Asheville	NC	28802	Fred N Slosman	704-274-2100	R	10	<0.1
United Textile Company Inc	2225 Grant Av	San Lorenzo	CA	94580	Steve Gradin	510-276-2288	R	10	0.2
Consolidated Textiles Inc	PO Box 240416	Charlotte	NC	28224	Robert P Kunik	704-554-8621	R	9*	<0.1
Lindsay Wire	220 Price St	Florence	MS	39073	Kai Chiu	601-845-2202	R	8*	0.1
Safegard Corp	315 E 15th St	Covington	KY	41011	RE Sammis	606-431-7651	R	8	0.2
All Felt Products Inc	538 S Sycamore St	Genoa	IL	60135	Gerald Leinberg	815-784-5800	R	7*	<0.1
Baxter Corp	PO Box 645	Franklin Lakes	NJ	07417	George A Bowen	201-337-1212	R	7*	0.1
Atlas Mill Supply	PO Box 01530	Los Angeles	CA	90001	Erwin A Raffle	213-589-8992	R	6*	0.2
Fairmont Corp	2245 W Pershing Rd	Chicago	IL	60609	Leonard Herman	312-376-1300	R	5*	<0.1
M Chasen and Son Inc	20 Esther St	Newark	NJ	07105	P Chasen	201-589-8700	R	5	<0.1
Sorbent Products Company Inc	645 Howard Av	Somerset	NJ	08873	Michael P Mobin	908-302-0080	R	5*	<0.1
Windle Industries Inc	PO Box 232	Millbury	MA	01527	Terrence B Windle	508-865-4461	R	5	<0.1
Houston Wiper	PO Box 24962	Houston	TX	77229	Michael J Brown	713-672-0571	R	5	0.1
Aetna Felt Corp	2401 W Emaus Av	Allentown	PA	18103	Wilfred W Weppler	215-791-0900	R	5	<0.1
Aetna Felt Corp	2401 W Emaus Av	Allentown	PA	18103	WW Weppler	215-791-5791	D	4	<0.1
Earl of Arkansas Corp	PO Box 238	Earle	AR	72331	B Posner	501-792-8671	R	4*	<0.1
Fiber Conversion Inc	15 E Elm St	Broadalbin	NY	12025	DB Kissinger	518-883-3431	R	4*	<0.1
Huntingdon Yarn Mill Inc	3114 E Thompson	Philadelphia	PA	19134	RN Birkenbach	215-425-5656	R	4*	<0.1
Novelty Cord and Tassel	107-20 Av D	Brooklyn	NY	11236	CJ Imershein	718-272-8800	R	4	<0.1
Oklahoma Waste&Wiping Rag	2013 SE 18th St	Oklahoma City	OK	73129	V Williamson	405-670-3100	R	4	<0.1
Acme Felt Works	PO Box 01227	Los Angeles	CA	90001	Steven A Stone	213-752-3778	S	3	<0.1
New Haven Moving Equip Corp	1518 Paloma St	Los Angeles	CA	90021	J Paul Levine	213-749-8181	R	3	<0.1
Columbia Wool Scouring Mills	PO Box 17097	Portland	OR	97217	David Taft	503-289-3642	D	2	<0.1
Metlon Corp	133 Frances Av	Cranston	RI	02910		401-467-3435	R	2	<0.1
Textile Products Inc	2512 Woodland Dr	Anaheim	CA	92801	Kevin C Gearin	714-761-0401	R	2	<0.1
Simtex Yarns Inc	PO Box 56	Armonk	NY	10504	Stephen Simon	914-273-5300	R	2	<0.1
TLK Industries Inc	902 Ogden Av	Superior	WI	54880	Thomas Karon	715-392-6253	R	1	<0.1
Acme Wiping Materials Co	1327 Palmetto St	Los Angeles	CA	90013	M Fischer	213-624-8756	R	1	<0.1
D'Kei Inc	PO Box 450	Lisle	IL	60532	Keith Axtell	708-963-2093	R	1	<0.1
Vincent Manufacturing Company	560 E Mill St	Little Falls	NY	13365	AN Vincent	315-823-0280	R	1	<0.1
Lumured Corp	292 E Smith St	Woodbridge	NJ	07095	Adolf Baumgarten	908-634-1313	R	0	<0.1

Source: Ward's Business Directory of U.S. Private and Public Companies, Volumes 1 and 2, 1996. The company type code is used as follows: P - Public, R - Private, S - Subsidiary, D - Division, J - Joint Venture, A - Affiliate, G - Group. Sales are in millions of dollars, employees are in thousands. An asterisk (*) indicates an estimated sales volume. The symbol < stands for 'less than'. Company names and addresses are truncated, in some cases, to fit into the available space.

MATERIALS CONSUMED

Material		Quantity	Delivered Cost ($ million)
Materials, ingredients, containers, and supplies		(X)	740.5
Raw cotton fibers	1,000 bales	39.7	7.0
Cotton waste	mil lb	170.6*	20.1
Cotton linters (net weight)	mil lb	22.2**	4.3
Raw wool, mohair, and other animal fibers (scoured weight)	mil lb	8.8	23.8
Wool noils and waste	mil lb	19.4	8.5
Cellulosic (rayon and acetate) manmade textile fibers	mil lb	6.9*	15.2
Noncellulosic (polyester, nylon, etc.) manmade textile fibers	mil lb	490.6	213.0
Yarn, all fibers	mil lb	45.7*	40.2
Textile fabrics	mil lin yd	(S)	11.4
Paper (cellulosic wadding)	mil lb	(D)	(D)
Adhesives and binders (resins)	mil lb	69.3**	22.3
Additives (fire retardants, water repellants, softeners, and antistatics, etc.)		(X)	6.7
New and used rags, clips, etc.	mil lb	138.5	24.1
Vinyl and vinyl copolymer resins, all forms	mil lb	(S)	4.9
Plastics resins (except vinyl) consumed in the form of granules, pellets, powders, liquids, etc.	mil lb	(D)	(D)
Paperboard containers, boxes, and corrugated paperboard		(X)	8.0
All other materials and components, parts, containers, and supplies		(X)	151.0
Materials, ingredients, containers, and supplies, nsk		(X)	168.8

Source: 1992 *Economic Census*. Explanation of symbols used: (D): Withheld to avoid disclosure of competitive data; na: Not available; (S): Withheld because statistical norms were not met; (X): Not applicable; (Z): Less than half the unit shown; nec: Not elsewhere classified; nsk: Not specified by kind; - : zero; * : 10-19 percent estimated; ** : 20-29 percent estimated.

PRODUCT SHARE DETAILS

Product or Product Class	% Share
Textile goods, nec	100.00
Pressed, punched, or needled felts, except hats	34.53
Pressed felts, except hats	21.45
Punched or needled, felts (including stitch bonded), hair and/or jute felts, including carpet and rug linings and cushions, except hats	15.25
Punched or needled, wool and manmade fiber, (including stitch bonded), excluding carpet and rug suitable for outdoor use (indoor/outdoor), except hats	62.93
Pressed, punched, or needled felts, except hats, nsk	0.38
Recovered fibers, processed mill waste and related products	15.89
Fibers recovered from mill waste, manmade fibers	46.07
Fibers recovered from mill waste, all other fibers, including oakum	17.12
Flock, all fibers (new stock, waste, or reclaimed fiber) processed mill waste and related products	31.20
Recovered fibers, processed mill waste and related products, nsk	5.60
Paddings and upholstery filling, batting, and wadding (excluding foam rubber and plastics)	29.02
Paddings, batting, and wadding (excluding foam rubber and plastics), automotive pads	15.23
Paddings, batting, and wadding (excluding foam rubber and plastics), all other paddings	15.19
Paddings, batting, wadding, and mattress felts (excluding foam rubber and plastics), made from cotton linters, cotton waste, and raw cotton	(D)
Paddings, batting, wadding, and mattress felts (excluding foam rubber and plastics), made from manmade fibers	26.53
Paddings, batting, wadding, and mattress felts (excluding foam rubber and plastics), made from all other fibers	(D)
Upholstery filling (excluding foam rubber and plastics)	14.41
Paddings and upholstery filling, batting, and wadding (excluding foam rubber and plastics), nsk	7.26
Jute goods and scouring and combing mill products	9.49
Jute yarn, bagging, and all other jute woven goods (except felt, cordage, or twine)	(D)
Linen thread, fabrics, and other linen goods, except cordage or twine	60.90
Scouring and combing mill products, tops and noils, including top or sliver converted from tow without combing	17.97
Scouring and combing mill products, scoured wool and other scouring and combing mill products, including nubs and slubs, etc.	16.83
Jute goods and scouring and combing mill products, nsk	(D)
Textile goods, nec, nsk	11.08

Source: 1992 *Economic Census*. The values shown are percent of total shipments in an industry. Values of indented subcategories are summed in the main heading. The symbol (D) appears when data are withheld to prevent disclosure of competitive information. The abbreviation nsk stands for 'not specified by kind' and nec for 'not elsewhere classified'.

INPUTS AND OUTPUTS FOR TEXTILE GOODS, NEC

Economic Sector or Industry Providing Inputs	%	Sector	Economic Sector or Industry Buying Outputs	%	Sector
Imports	37.3	Foreign	Yarn mills & finishing of textiles, nec	17.8	Manufg.
Meat animals	23.8	Agric.	Broadwoven fabric mills	15.8	Manufg.
Textile goods, nec	6.5	Manufg.	Exports	8.8	Foreign
Noncomparable imports	6.1	Foreign	Agricultural, forestry, & fishery services	8.6	Agric.
Advertising	3.0	Services	Floor coverings	6.8	Manufg.
Wholesale trade	2.6	Trade	Housefurnishings, nec	5.3	Manufg.
Yarn mills & finishing of textiles, nec	2.5	Manufg.	Textile goods, nec	4.1	Manufg.
Electric services (utilities)	2.1	Util.	Nonwoven fabrics	4.0	Manufg.
Cyclic crudes and organics	1.6	Manufg.	Prepared feeds, nec	3.7	Manufg.
Chemical preparations, nec	1.1	Manufg.	Knit outerwear mills	2.9	Manufg.
Paperboard containers & boxes	1.1	Manufg.	Coated fabrics, not rubberized	2.6	Manufg.
Motor freight transportation & warehousing	1.1	Util.	Felt goods, nec	2.3	Manufg.
Petroleum refining	1.0	Manufg.	Cordage & twine	2.2	Manufg.
U.S. Postal Service	1.0	Gov't	Dairy farm products	1.9	Agric.
Gas production & distribution (utilities)	0.9	Util.	Automotive & apparel trimmings	1.9	Manufg.

Continued on next page.

INPUTS AND OUTPUTS FOR TEXTILE GOODS, NEC - Continued

Economic Sector or Industry Providing Inputs	%	Sector	Economic Sector or Industry Buying Outputs	%	Sector
Laundry, dry cleaning, shoe repair	0.9	Services	Shoes, except rubber	1.9	Manufg.
Textile machinery	0.7	Manufg.	House slippers	1.4	Manufg.
Industrial gases	0.6	Manufg.	Padding & upholstery filling	1.4	Manufg.
Eating & drinking places	0.6	Trade	Greenhouse & nursery products	0.9	Agric.
Wood products, nec	0.4	Manufg.	Boot & shoe cutstock & findings	0.9	Manufg.
Banking	0.4	Fin/R.E.	Machinery, except electrical, nec	0.8	Manufg.
Equipment rental & leasing services	0.4	Services	Paper coating & glazing	0.7	Manufg.
Lubricating oils & greases	0.3	Manufg.	Processed textile waste	0.7	Manufg.
Real estate	0.3	Fin/R.E.	Commercial fishing	0.3	Agric.
Maintenance of nonfarm buildings nec	0.2	Constr.	Boat building & repairing	0.3	Manufg.
Industrial inorganic chemicals, nec	0.2	Manufg.	Pleating & stitching	0.3	Manufg.
Machinery, except electrical, nec	0.2	Manufg.	Soap & other detergents	0.3	Manufg.
Communications, except radio & TV	0.2	Util.	Cereal breakfast foods	0.2	Manufg.
Water supply & sewage systems	0.2	Util.	Dog, cat, & other pet food	0.2	Manufg.
Accounting, auditing & bookkeeping	0.2	Services	Motion pictures	0.2	Services
Legal services	0.2	Services	Forestry products	0.1	Agric.
Management & consulting services & labs	0.2	Services	Abrasive products	0.1	Manufg.
Railroads & related services	0.1	Util.	Lace goods	0.1	Manufg.
Royalties	0.1	Fin/R.E.			
Business/professional associations	0.1	Services			
State & local government enterprises, nec	0.1	Gov't			

Source: Benchmark Input-Output Accounts for the U.S. Economy, 1982, U.S. Department of Commerce, Washington, D.C., July 1991. Data, as reported in the source, are organized by the 1977 SIC structure in use in 1982 but have been matched, as closely as is possible, to the 1987 SIC structure used in this book.

OCCUPATIONS EMPLOYED BY SIC 229 - MISCELLANEOUS TEXTILE GOODS

Occupation	% of Total 1994	Change to 2005	Occupation	% of Total 1994	Change to 2005
Textile draw-out & winding machine operators	22.1	-3.5	Maintenance repairers, general utility	2.1	-13.1
Blue collar worker supervisors	6.0	-7.8	Industrial truck & tractor operators	2.0	-3.5
Machine operators nec	4.6	-14.9	Traffic, shipping, & receiving clerks	1.9	-7.2
Industrial machinery mechanics	4.2	6.2	Coating, painting, & spraying machine workers	1.9	-3.6
Textile machine setters & set-up operators	3.9	-13.1	Hand packers & packagers	1.8	-17.4
Helpers, laborers, & material movers nec	3.9	-3.5	Freight, stock, & material movers, hand	1.7	-22.8
Inspectors, testers, & graders, precision	3.8	-3.5	Secretaries, ex legal & medical	1.6	-12.1
General managers & top executives	2.5	-8.4	Sewing machine operators, non-garment	1.6	-22.8
Sales & related workers nec	2.3	-3.5	Industrial production managers	1.5	-3.5
Machine feeders & offbearers	2.3	-13.1	Packaging & filling machine operators	1.5	-3.5
Assemblers, fabricators, & hand workers nec	2.3	-3.5	Bookkeeping, accounting, & auditing clerks	1.2	-27.7
Extruding & forming machine workers	2.2	-3.5	Janitors & cleaners, incl maids	1.1	-22.8

Source: Industry-Occupation Matrix, Bureau of Labor Statistics. These data relate to one or more 3-digit SIC industry groups rather than to a single 4-digit SIC. The change reported for each occupation to the year 2005 is a percent of growth or decline as estimated by the Bureau of Labor Statistics. The abbreviation nec stands for 'not elsewhere classified'.

LOCATION BY STATE AND REGIONAL CONCENTRATION

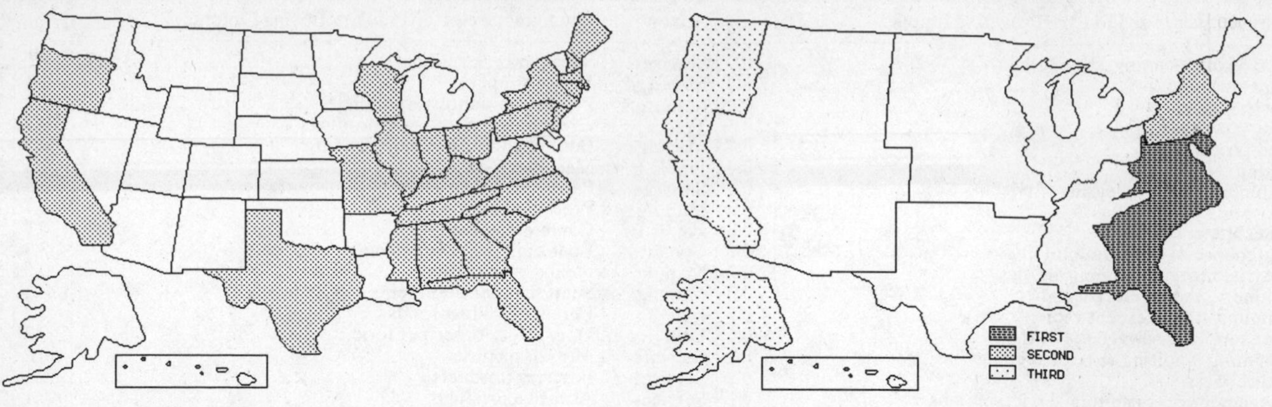

INDUSTRY DATA BY STATE

State	Establish-ments	Shipments			Employment				Cost as % of Shipments	Investment per Employee ($)
		Total ($ mil)	% of U.S.	Per Establ.	Total Number	% of U.S.	Per Establ.	Wages ($/hour)		
South Carolina	29	334.0	18.6	11.5	2,600	15.6	90	11.21	47.4	9,231
Massachusetts	30	183.1	10.2	6.1	1,300	7.8	43	10.22	61.8	2,846
New York	79	162.4	9.0	2.1	1,800	10.8	23	7.06	42.2	2,500
North Carolina	52	151.8	8.5	2.9	2,000	12.0	38	7.87	52.6	2,600
Georgia	40	130.2	7.3	3.3	1,000	6.0	25	9.50	48.2	8,800
California	64	106.0	5.9	1.7	1,200	7.2	19	7.05	52.1	5,333
Virginia	7	59.1	3.3	8.4	700	4.2	100	8.89	23.7	-
New Jersey	37	53.7	3.0	1.5	700	4.2	19	9.30	52.1	4,000
Pennsylvania	25	49.6	2.8	2.0	400	2.4	16	10.00	37.1	2,250
New Hampshire	5	48.8	2.7	9.8	500	3.0	100	14.87	46.7	-
Connecticut	12	41.1	2.3	3.4	300	1.8	25	8.60	52.1	2,333
Mississippi	5	34.5	1.9	6.9	300	1.8	60	8.40	57.1	1,333
Kentucky	6	28.6	1.6	4.8	200	1.2	33	9.50	38.8	-
Rhode Island	4	28.5	1.6	7.1	200	1.2	50	7.00	62.8	-
Texas	22	23.7	1.3	1.1	300	1.8	14	7.50	42.2	3,333
Illinois	12	23.3	1.3	1.9	200	1.2	17	10.00	52.8	1,000
Indiana	6	17.2	1.0	2.9	200	1.2	33	8.00	44.2	-
Florida	18	(D)	-	-	175 *	1.0	10	-	-	4,000
Missouri	14	(D)	-	-	375 *	2.2	27	-	-	-
Tennessee	10	(D)	-	-	375 *	2.2	38	-	-	-
Alabama	9	(D)	-	-	375 *	2.2	42	-	-	800
Ohio	9	(D)	-	-	375 *	2.2	42	-	-	-
Wisconsin	6	(D)	-	-	375 *	2.2	63	-	-	-
Maine	5	(D)	-	-	375 *	2.2	75	-	-	-
Oregon	4	(D)	-	-	175 *	1.0	44	-	-	-

Source: 1992 *Economic Census*. The states are in descending order of shipments or establishments (if shipment data are missing for the majority). The symbol (D) appears when data are withheld to prevent disclosure of competitive information. States marked with (D) are sorted by number of establishments. A dash (-) indicates that the data element cannot be calculated; * indicates the midpoint of a range.

2311 - MEN'S & BOYS' SUITS AND COATS

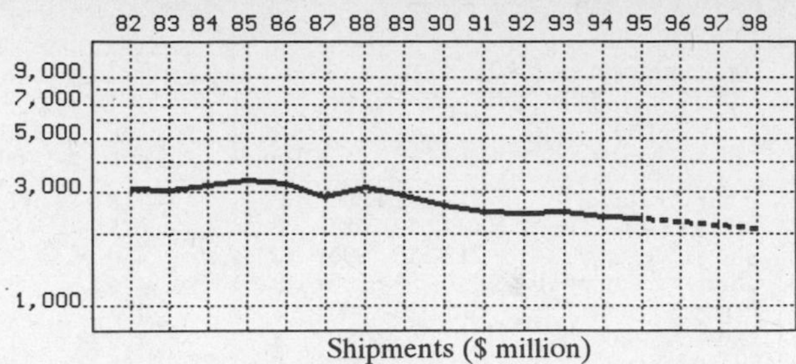

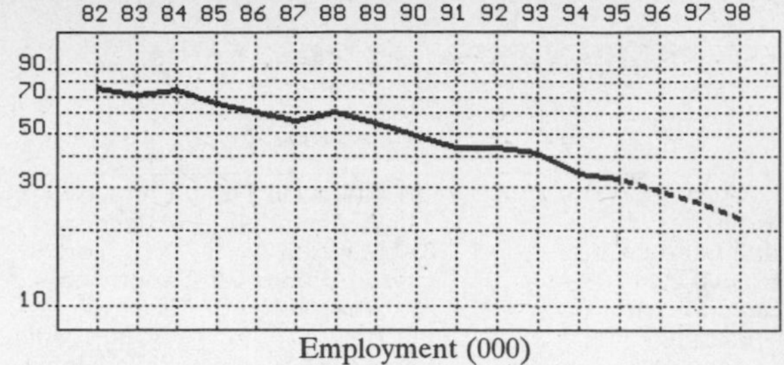

GENERAL STATISTICS

Year	Companies	Establishments		Employment			Compensation		Production ($ million)			
		Total	with 20 or more employees	Total (000)	Production Workers (000)	Production Hours (Mil)	Payroll ($ mil)	Wages ($/hr)	Cost of Materials	Value Added by Manufacture	Value of Shipments	Capital Invest.
1982	443	528	343	75.0	64.8	116.5	876.7	5.65	1,397.4	1,681.2	3,059.7	24.6
1983				70.8	60.4	108.9	849.6	5.94	1,376.0	1,674.1	3,045.7	28.4
1984				73.9	63.9	115.4	916.5	5.82	1,462.6	1,788.9	3,208.8	38.0
1985				64.9	57.4	102.8	862.5	6.49	1,456.2	1,879.8	3,321.0	23.8
1986				59.5	52.8	94.9	808.3	6.60	1,362.1	1,871.9	3,242.0	29.0
1987	291	337	236	55.2	48.1	85.8	779.0	6.95	1,110.8	1,761.2	2,863.3	29.1
1988				60.0	51.7	93.5	877.5	7.09	1,328.9	1,864.6	3,169.4	
1989		309	222	54.5	47.0	83.9	832.7	7.58	1,258.3	1,658.5	2,918.2	30.4
1990				48.4	41.3	73.6	768.1	7.84	1,107.7	1,500.8	2,622.4	21.6
1991				43.6	36.5	66.0	743.0	8.14	1,070.5	1,399.7	2,466.8	24.3
1992	249	302	199	43.8	37.2	66.9	720.3	7.97	1,024.2	1,372.5	2,426.0	22.2
1993				41.2	34.7	62.9	688.2	8.32	955.6	1,524.6	2,463.3	23.2
1994				34.0	28.7	52.6	604.1	8.35	937.3	1,430.9	2,361.5	25.4
1995				32.6P	27.3P	49.4P	655.4P	8.86P	921.4P	1,406.6P	2,321.4P	
1996				29.3P	24.4P	44.1P	635.6P	9.10P	890.9P	1,360.1P	2,244.6P	
1997				26.0P	21.4P	38.9P	615.7P	9.35P	860.4P	1,313.5P	2,167.8P	
1998				22.7P	18.4P	33.6P	595.9P	9.59P	829.9P	1,267.0P	2,091.0P	

Sources: 1982, 1987, 1992 *Economic Census*; *Annual Survey of Manufactures*, 83-86, 88-91, 93-94. Establishment counts for non-Census years are from *County Business Patterns*; establishment values for 83-84 are extrapolations. 'P's show projections by the editors. Industries reclassified in 87 will not have data for prior years.

INDICES OF CHANGE

Year	Companies	Establishments		Employment			Compensation		Production ($ million)			
		Total	with 20 or more employees	Total (000)	Production Workers (000)	Production Hours (Mil)	Payroll ($ mil)	Wages ($/hr)	Cost of Materials	Value Added by Manufacture	Value of Shipments	Capital Invest.
1982	178	175	172	171	174	174	122	71	136	122	126	111
1983				162	162	163	118	75	134	122	126	128
1984				169	172	172	127	73	143	130	132	171
1985				148	154	154	120	81	142	137	137	107
1986				136	142	142	112	83	133	136	134	131
1987	117	112	119	126	129	128	108	87	108	128	118	131
1988				137	139	140	122	89	130	136	131	
1989		102	112	124	126	125	116	95	123	121	120	137
1990				111	111	110	107	98	108	109	108	97
1991				100	98	99	103	102	105	102	102	109
1992	100	100	100	100	100	100	100	100	100	100	100	100
1993				94	93	94	96	104	93	111	102	105
1994				78	77	79	84	105	92	104	97	114
1995				74P	73P	74P	91P	111P	90P	102P	96P	
1996				67P	65P	66P	88P	114P	87P	99P	93P	
1997				59P	58P	58P	85P	117P	84P	96P	89P	
1998				52P	50P	50P	83P	120P	81P	92P	86P	

Sources: Same as General Statistics. Values reflect change from the base year, 1992. Values above 100 mean greater than 92, values below 100 mean less than 92, and a value of 100 in the 82-91 or 93-98 period means same as 92. 'P's mark projections by the editors.

SELECTED RATIOS

For 1992	Avg. of All Manufact.	Analyzed Industry	Index
Employees per Establishment	46	145	318
Payroll per Establishment	1,332,320	2,385,099	179
Payroll per Employee	29,181	16,445	56
Production Workers per Establishment	31	123	392
Wages per Establishment	734,496	1,765,540	240
Wages per Production Worker	23,390	14,333	61
Hours per Production Worker	2,025	1,798	89
Wages per Hour	11.55	7.97	69
Value Added per Establishment	3,842,210	4,544,702	118
Value Added per Employee	84,153	31,336	37

For 1992	Avg. of All Manufact.	Analyzed Industry	Index
Value Added per Production Worker	122,353	36,895	30
Cost per Establishment	4,239,462	3,391,391	80
Cost per Employee	92,853	23,384	25
Cost per Production Worker	135,003	27,532	20
Shipments per Establishment	8,100,800	8,033,113	99
Shipments per Employee	177,425	55,388	31
Shipments per Production Worker	257,966	65,215	25
Investment per Establishment	278,244	73,510	26
Investment per Employee	6,094	507	8
Investment per Production Worker	8,861	597	7

Sources: Same as General Statistics. The 'Average of All Manufacturing' column represents the average of all manufacturing industries reported for the most recent complete year available. The Index shows the relationship between the Average and the Analyzed Industry. For example, 100 means that they are equal; 500 that the Analyzed Industry is five times the average; 50 means that the Analyzed Industry is half the national average. The abbreviation 'na' is used to show that data are 'not available'.

LEADING COMPANIES Number shown: **60** Total sales ($ mil): **3,310** Total employment (000): **42.0**

Company Name	Address				CEO Name	Phone	Co. Type	Sales ($ mil)	Empl. (000)
Hartmarx Corp	101 N Wacker Dr	Chicago	IL	60606	Elbert O Hand	312-372-6300	P	718	11.0
Oxford Industries Inc	222 Piedmont NE	Atlanta	GA	30308	J Hicks Lanier	404-659-2424	P	625	9.8
Polo/Ralph Lauren Corp	650 Madison Av	New York	NY	10022	Cheryl Sterling	212-318-7000	R	450	2.7
Crystal Brands Inc	Crystal Brands Rd	Southport	CT	06490	Charles J Campbell	203-254-6200	P	444	3.3
Horace Small Apparel Co	350 28th Av N	Nashville	TN	37209	Douglas Small	615-320-1000	S	105	1.2
J Schoeneman Inc	PO Box 17	Owings Mills	MD	21117	James J Stankovic	410-363-0100	S	100	1.7
Pincus Brothers Inc	Indep Mall E	Philadelphia	PA	19106	David Pincus	215-922-4900	R	80	1.2
Hickey-Freeman Company Inc	PO Box 200	Rochester	NY	14601	Steven Weiner	716-467-7240	S	76	0.8
Shepard Clothing Company Inc	800 Acushnet Av	New Bedford	MA	02740	Paul Kussell	508-993-2662	R	67•	1.0
Polo Clothing Company Inc	4100 Beechwood Dr	Greensboro	NC	27410	Ralph Lauren	910-632-5000	S	56•	0.3
Stafford (USA) Ltd	1290 Av Amer	New York	NY	10010	Jerry Klanfer	212-765-2780	R	45•	<0.1
Raffinati Men's Apparel Inc	3 University Plz	Hackensack	NJ	07601	Robert Bennett	201-343-8180	S	40	0.6
Whiteville Apparel Co	Rte 2	Whiteville	NC	28472	David A Dabb	919-642-7701	D	37•	0.6
Bauman Carter Patterson Corp	PO Box 13643	Greensboro	NC	27415	David Carter	919-375-0060	R	33•	0.5
Hardwick Clothes Inc	PO Box 2310	Cleveland	TN	37311	Joe V Williams III	615-476-6534	R	30	0.7
Sidran Inc	2875 Merrill Rd	Dallas	TX	75229	Roland S Mizrahi	214-352-7979	R	30•	0.5
Dunbrooke Sportswear Co	PO Box 1900	Independence	MO	64055	Steve McMullen	816-795-7722	S	26•	0.4
Lanier Clothes Co	1600 S Green St	Tupelo	MS	38801	Wayne Branley	601-842-5252	D	25•	0.4
Oxxford Clothes Inc	1220 W Van Buren	Chicago	IL	60607	G Chrysler Fisher	312-829-3600	R	25•	0.5
American Fashions Inc	642 Arizona St	Chula Vista	CA	91911	Steve Kurtzman	619-426-1212	R	20•	0.4
Fashion World Career Apparel	38-09 43rd Av	Long Island Ct	NY	11101	Howard Weschsler	718-706-1414	D	20•	<0.1
Nu-Look Fashions Inc	5080 Sinclair Rd	Columbus	OH	43229	L Fannin	614-885-4936	R	18	0.1
Hubbard Company Inc	202 N Georgia Av	Bremen	GA	30110	John S Hubbard	404-537-2341	S	16	0.2
Stanley Blacker Inc	Syms Way	Secaucus	NJ	07094	Stanley Blacker	201-902-9824	R	15	0.1
Weintraub Brothers Co	2695 Philmont Av	Huntingdon Vl	PA	19006	TE Weintraub	215-938-7540	R	14	<0.1
Harve Benard Ltd	205 W 39th St	New York	NY	10018	Bernard Holtzman	212-354-8420	R	13•	0.2
Taylor Clothing Inc	200 E High St	Taylor	PA	18517	Fritz Johannesen	717-562-2140	R	12•	0.2
Bradley-Scott Clothes Inc	PO Box 326	Fall River	MA	02724	BS Silver	508-676-1078	R	11•	0.2
Ippoliti Inc	7300 Lindbergh	Philadelphia	PA	19153	Nicholas Ippoliti Jr	215-365-1600	R	10	0.2
Warren Sewell Clothing	PO Box 625	Bremen	GA	30110	Robin S Worley	404-537-2391	R	10	<0.1
Haas Tailoring Co	3425 Sinclair Ln	Baltimore	MD	21213	John M Haas	410-732-3800	R	9	0.3
Trooper Inc	PO Box 3386	Augusta	GA	30904	Warren Gary	706-738-2543	R	9	0.2
Estill Manufacturing Co	PO Box 38	Estill	SC	29918	Larry Kea	803-625-2631	D	8	0.1
Kane Industries Inc	413 N Ward Av	Morgantown	KY	42261	Warren Naylor	502-526-3301	S	8	0.2
Protexall Inc	77 S Henderson St	Galesburg	IL	61401	LW Williams	309-342-3106	R	8	0.2
Westmoor Manufacturing	PO Box 162749	Fort Worth	TX	76161	Jeffery S Hochster	817-625-2841	R	8	0.1
Bowdon Manufacturing Co	127 N Carroll St	Bowdon	GA	30108	E P Buttimer	404-258-7242	R	7	0.1
Oakloom Clothes Inc	1800 Johnson St	Baltimore	MD	21230	Malcolm P Katzen	410-837-6763	R	7•	0.1
Stanwood Corp	PO Box 538	Pelahatchie	MS	39145	Bob Kelley	601-854-8133	S	7	0.2
Davis Clothing Co	115 Westgate Dr	Brockton	MA	02401	Charles J First	508-583-8900	R	6•	0.1
Freedom Industries Inc	PO Box 457	Liberty	MS	39645	Marvin Pollock	601-657-4309	S	6	0.1
Globe Corp	490 E McMillan St	Cincinnati	OH	45206	EA Heimann	513-961-0200	R	6•	0.2
Hartz and Co	1341 Hughes Ford	Frederick	MD	21705	Al Cohen	301-662-7500	S	6•	0.1
Sandess Manufacturing Company	19th & Lehigh Av	Philadelphia	PA	19132	Ned Santerian	215-226-2900	S	6•	0.1
Phar-Shar Manufacturing	115 Sequoia Dr	Leitchfield	KY	42754	Osco Pharris	502-259-3845	R	5	0.3
Flight Suits Ltd	1675 Pioneer Way	El Cajon	CA	92020	James Wegge	619-440-2700	R	4	<0.1
Parker School Uniforms	2315 Karbach	Houston	TX	77092	Mac Shuford	713-681-4045	R	4•	<0.1
Henry Segal Co	511 Coney Island	Brooklyn	NY	11218	Robert Segal	718-282-4100	R	4	<0.1
Leon of Paris Company Inc	1290 Av Amer	New York	NY	10104	Paul Wattenberg	212-765-8100	R	3	<0.1
Racewear Designs Inc	340 Coogan Way	El Cajon	CA	92020	T Alden	619-442-9651	R	3	<0.1
Badger Shirt Co	PO Box 608	Racine	WI	53401	DO Lange	414-634-6612	R	3	<0.1
Jacob Siegel Company Inc	1843 W Allegheny	Philadelphia	PA	19132	Stephen R Saft	215-229-9900	R	2•	<0.1
Lee McClain Co	1857 Midland Trail	Shelbyville	KY	40065	Morton M Webb Jr	502-633-3823	R	2	<0.1
Miller Manufacturing Co	4755 State Hwy 30	Amsterdam	NY	12010	Dorothy B Miller	518-842-6460	R	2	<0.1
Toluca Garment Co	604 E Sante Fe Av	Toluca	IL	61369	L M Magliano Jr	815-452-2325	R	2	0.1
Alan Flusser Enterprises Inc	50 Trinity Pl	New York	NY	10006	Martin Flusser	212-363-1704	R	1•	<0.1
Axis Clothing Corp	1769 E 41st Pl	Los Angeles	CA	90058	Rick Solomon	213-745-7722	R	1•	<0.1
Mancillas International Ltd	1000 Skokie Blv	Wilmette	IL	60091	Marcial Mancillas	708-256-0050	R	1•	<0.1
Saint Laurie Ltd	897 Broadway	New York	NY	10003	Carey Graeber	212-473-0100	R	1•	<0.1
Mister Coats Inc	15 Union St	Lawrence	MA	01840	David H Cohen	508-688-0375	R	1	<0.1

Source: *Ward's Business Directory of U.S. Private and Public Companies*, Volumes 1 and 2, 1996. The company type code used is as follows: P - Public, R - Private, S - Subsidiary, D - Division, J - Joint Venture, A - Affiliate, G - Group. Sales are in millions of dollars, employees are in thousands. An asterisk (•) indicates an estimated sales volume. The symbol < stands for 'less than'. Company names and addresses are truncated, in some cases, to fit into the available space.

MATERIALS CONSUMED

Material	Quantity	Delivered Cost ($ million)
Materials, ingredients, containers, and supplies	(X)	803.5
Broadwoven fabrics (piece goods)	(X)	602.7
Narrow fabrics (12 inches or less in width)	(X)	30.4
Knit fabrics	(X)	8.7
Yarn, all fibers	(X)	6.6
Buttons, zippers, and slide fasteners	(X)	21.7
All other materials and components, parts, containers, and supplies	(X)	115.8
Materials, ingredients, containers, and supplies, nsk	(X)	17.6

Source: 1992 *Economic Census*. Explanation of symbols used: (D): Withheld to avoid disclosure of competitive data; na: Not available; (S): Withheld because statistical norms were not met; (X): Not applicable; (Z): Less than half the unit shown; nec: Not elsewhere classified; nsk: Not specified by kind; - : zero; * : 10-19 percent estimated; ** : 20-29 percent estimated.

PRODUCT SHARE DETAILS

Product or Product Class	% Share	Product or Product Class	% Share
Men's and boys' suits and coats	100.00	Receipts for contract and commission work on men's and boys' suits and tailored coats and jackets	11.82
Men's and boys' suits, including uniform	48.96	Receipts for contract and commission work on men's and boys' suits and tailored coats and jackets	99.08
Men's and boys' overcoats, topcoats, and tailored car and suburban coats (including uniform and wool water-repellent), excluding raincoats	2.31	Receipts for contract and commission work on men's and boys' suits and tailored coats and jackets, nsk	0.96
Men's and boys' tailored dress and sport coats (including uniform and separate leisure-type) and tailored vests	35.99	Men's and boys' suits and coats, nsk	0.93

Source: 1992 *Economic Census*. The values shown are percent of total shipments in an industry. Values of indented subcategories are summed in the main heading. The symbol (D) appears when data are withheld to prevent disclosure of competitive information. The abbreviation nsk stands for 'not specified by kind' and nec for 'not elsewhere classified'.

INPUTS AND OUTPUTS FOR APPAREL MADE FROM PURCHASED MATERIALS

Economic Sector or Industry Providing Inputs	%	Sector	Economic Sector or Industry Buying Outputs	%	Sector
Imports	29.1	Foreign	Personal consumption expenditures	82.7	
Broadwoven fabric mills	20.2	Manufg.	Apparel made from purchased materials	12.0	Manufg.
Apparel made from purchased materials	18.3	Manufg.	Exports	1.5	Foreign
Knit fabric mills	8.6	Manufg.	Federal Government purchases, national defense	0.9	Fed Govt
Wholesale trade	3.8	Trade	S/L Govt. purch., correction	0.5	S/L Govt
Advertising	2.4	Services	Pleating & stitching	0.3	Manufg.
Yarn mills & finishing of textiles, nec	1.4	Manufg.	Knit outerwear mills	0.2	Manufg.
Pleating & stitching	1.1	Manufg.	Hospitals	0.2	Services
Banking	1.1	Fin/R.E.	Laundry, dry cleaning, shoe repair	0.2	Services
Petroleum refining	1.0	Manufg.	S/L Govt. purch., health & hospitals	0.2	S/L Govt
Electric services (utilities)	1.0	Util.	Portrait, photographic studios	0.1	Services
Automotive & apparel trimmings	0.9	Manufg.	S/L Govt. purch., public assistance & relief	0.1	S/L Govt
Needles, pins, & fasteners	0.8	Manufg.			
Thread mills	0.7	Manufg.			
Communications, except radio & TV	0.7	Util.			
Eating & drinking places	0.7	Trade			
U.S. Postal Service	0.7	Gov't			
Leather tanning & finishing	0.5	Manufg.			
Narrow fabric mills	0.5	Manufg.			
Schiffli machine embroideries	0.4	Manufg.			
Motor freight transportation & warehousing	0.4	Util.			
Real estate	0.4	Fin/R.E.			
Royalties	0.4	Fin/R.E.			
Forestry products	0.3	Agric.			
Buttons	0.3	Manufg.			
Paperboard containers & boxes	0.3	Manufg.			
Air transportation	0.3	Util.			
Maintenance of nonfarm buildings nec	0.2	Constr.			
Lace goods	0.2	Manufg.			
Gas production & distribution (utilities)	0.2	Util.			
Automotive rental & leasing, without drivers	0.2	Services			
Electrical repair shops	0.2	Services			
Equipment rental & leasing services	0.2	Services			
Legal services	0.2	Services			
Management & consulting services & labs	0.2	Services			
Artificial trees & flowers	0.1	Manufg.			
Insurance carriers	0.1	Fin/R.E.			
Accounting, auditing & bookkeeping	0.1	Services			
Automotive repair shops & services	0.1	Services			

Source: Benchmark Input-Output Accounts for the U.S. Economy, 1982, U.S. Department of Commerce, Washington, D.C., July 1991. Data, as reported in the source, are organized by the 1977 SIC structure in use in 1982 but have been matched, as closely as is possible, to the 1987 SIC structure used in this book.

OCCUPATIONS EMPLOYED BY SIC 231 - APPAREL

Occupation	% of Total 1994	Change to 2005	Occupation	% of Total 1994	Change to 2005
Sewing machine operators, garment	56.1	-33.1	Cutters & trimmers, hand	1.7	-24.8
Inspectors, testers, & graders, precision	3.5	-16.4	Patternmakers, layout workers, fabric & apparel	1.5	25.4
Blue collar worker supervisors	3.0	-24.0	General managers & top executives	1.4	-20.7
Assemblers, fabricators, & hand workers nec	2.5	-16.4	Sewing machine operators, non-garment	1.3	-37.3
Pressing machine operators, textiles	2.4	-45.7	Helpers, laborers, & material movers nec	1.1	-16.4
Hand packers & packagers	2.0	-21.2	Industrial machinery mechanics	1.1	0.3
Freight, stock, & material movers, hand	1.8	-33.1	Pressers, hand	1.1	-58.2
Traffic, shipping, & receiving clerks	1.8	-19.6	Sewers, hand	1.0	-10.7

Source: Industry-Occupation Matrix, Bureau of Labor Statistics. These data relate to one or more 3-digit SIC industry groups rather than to a single 4-digit SIC. The change reported for each occupation to the year 2005 is a percent of growth or decline as estimated by the Bureau of Labor Statistics. The abbreviation nec stands for 'not elsewhere classified'.

LOCATION BY STATE AND REGIONAL CONCENTRATION

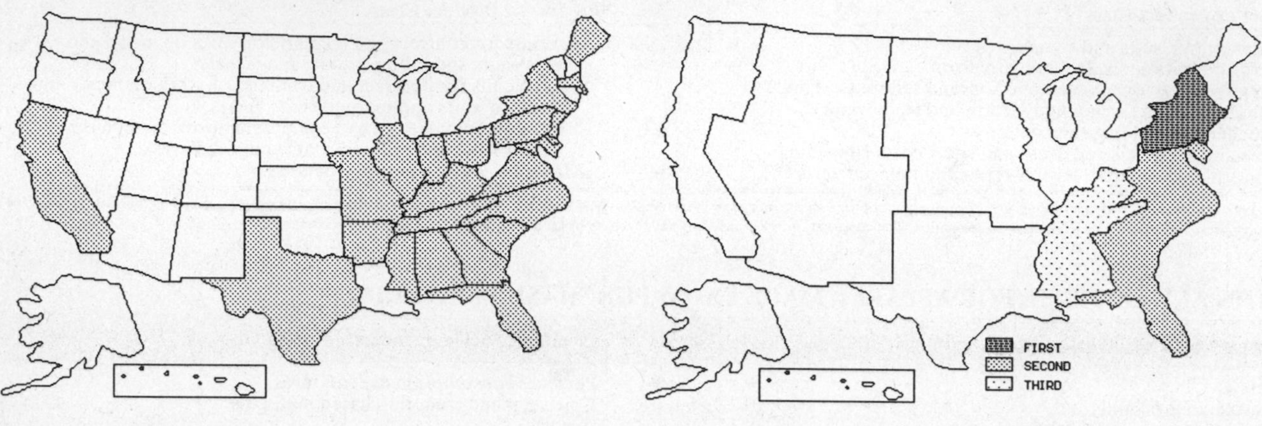

INDUSTRY DATA BY STATE

State	Establish-ments	Shipments Total ($ mil)	Shipments % of U.S.	Shipments Per Establ.	Employment Total Number	Employment % of U.S.	Employment Per Establ.	Wages ($/hour)	Cost as % of Shipments	Investment per Employee ($)
New York	66	468.3	19.3	7.1	5,300	12.1	80	8.96	52.1	623
Pennsylvania	46	445.5	18.4	9.7	8,500	19.4	185	8.69	38.0	447
Massachusetts	13	295.8	12.2	22.8	3,200	7.3	246	9.25	46.3	531
Georgia	20	231.7	9.6	11.6	5,200	11.9	260	6.35	45.7	500
Tennessee	11	129.6	5.3	11.8	2,100	4.8	191	7.71	53.3	-
Maryland	10	118.9	4.9	11.9	1,700	3.9	170	8.28	35.7	294
Illinois	10	116.1	4.8	11.6	2,600	5.9	260	9.61	31.9	192
Kentucky	10	82.7	3.4	8.3	2,400	5.5	240	7.97	23.0	-
New Jersey	17	58.6	2.4	3.4	1,000	2.3	59	8.92	54.4	-
Florida	5	41.7	1.7	8.3	600	1.4	120	7.43	67.9	-
Texas	10	34.4	1.4	3.4	1,600	3.7	160	5.71	22.1	125
North Carolina	7	33.9	1.4	4.8	1,500	3.4	214	6.77	27.7	933
South Carolina	4	22.8	0.9	5.7	900	2.1	225	8.29	28.9	-
Arkansas	3	5.2	0.2	1.7	300	0.7	100	5.50	15.4	-
California	28	(D)	-	-	750 *	1.7	27	-	-	400
Ohio	8	(D)	-	-	1,750 *	4.0	219	-	-	-
Alabama	6	(D)	-	-	1,750 *	4.0	292	-	-	-
Missouri	4	(D)	-	-	1,750 *	4.0	438	-	-	-
Mississippi	3	(D)	-	-	750 *	1.7	250	-	-	-
Delaware	2	(D)	-	-	175 *	0.4	88	-	-	-
Indiana	2	(D)	-	-	375 *	0.9	188	-	-	-
Maine	1	(D)	-	-	175 *	0.4	175	-	-	-
Virginia	1	(D)	-	-	750 *	1.7	750	-	-	-

Source: 1992 *Economic Census*. The states are in descending order of shipments or establishments (if shipment data are missing for the majority). The symbol (D) appears when data are withheld to prevent disclosure of competitive information. States marked with (D) are sorted by number of establishments. A dash (-) indicates that the data element cannot be calculated; * indicates the midpoint of a range.

2321 - MEN'S & BOYS' SHIRTS

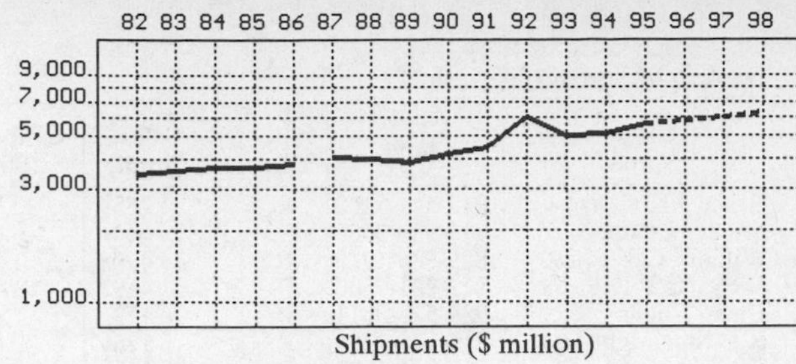

Shipments ($ million)

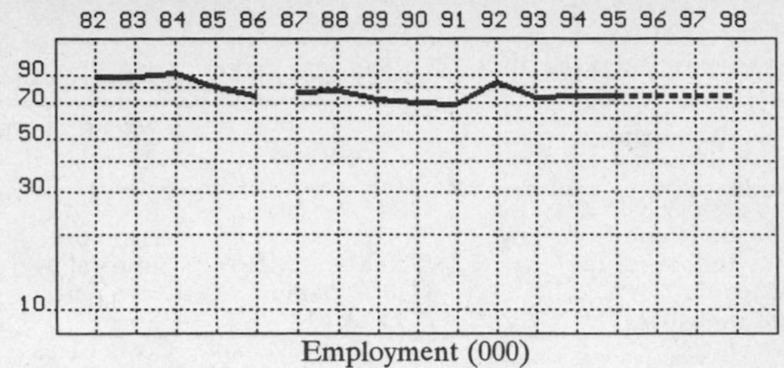

Employment (000)

GENERAL STATISTICS

Year	Com-panies	Establishments		Employment			Compensation		Production ($ million)			
		Total	with 20 or more employees	Total (000)	Production Workers (000)	Production Hours (Mil)	Payroll ($ mil)	Wages ($/hr)	Cost of Materials	Value Added by Manufacture	Value of Shipments	Capital Invest.
1982	535	741	560	88.7	76.0	132.9	819.0	4.62	1,676.0	1,785.5	3,477.7	37.2
1983		703	535	88.3	74.7	134.3	854.3	4.78	1,725.0	1,851.0	3,573.4	38.7
1984		665	510	90.9	78.5	136.7	905.4	5.00	1,753.5	2,071.6	3,688.8	59.6
1985		628	484	80.1	69.1	120.7	823.5	5.08	1,802.2	1,824.6	3,673.8	45.5
1986		603	462	74.8	65.8	118.4	811.9	5.33	1,857.4	1,909.7	3,795.4	59.7
1987*	460	601	470	76.7	66.6	121.8	868.9	5.45	1,897.7	2,185.4	4,075.0	51.7
1988		575	447	77.4	68.0	122.8	915.8	5.77	2,013.6	2,023.6	4,031.3	
1989		550	426	72.6	65.1	118.6	942.6	6.29	1,848.3	2,026.1	3,872.6	52.5
1990		514	402	69.1	61.7	111.2	922.8	6.46	2,047.3	2,197.7	4,242.6	45.2
1991		512	375	68.8	60.9	112.8	987.8	6.87	2,071.5	2,371.6	4,494.0	46.3
1992	528	658	479	84.4	74.3	136.0	1,205.9	6.84	2,853.3	3,181.2	5,915.5	84.5
1993		654	460	72.7	64.1	114.5	1,041.4	6.90	2,580.4	2,411.8	5,011.7	69.8
1994		622P	435P	73.6	66.8	124.7	1,078.9	6.95	2,526.3	2,513.3	5,088.0	84.9
1995		632P	434P	73.9P	66.4P	122.0P	1,153.7P	7.42P	2,768.4P	2,754.2P	5,575.6P	
1996		642P	433P	73.8P	66.5P	122.4P	1,188.9P	7.63P	2,877.0P	2,862.2P	5,794.3P	
1997		652P	433P	73.6P	66.6P	122.8P	1,224.0P	7.85P	2,985.6P	2,970.3P	6,013.1P	
1998		663P	432P	73.5P	66.7P	123.2P	1,259.2P	8.07P	3,094.2P	3,078.3P	6,231.8P	

Sources: 1982, 1987, 1992 *Economic Census*; *Annual Survey of Manufactures*, 83-86, 88-91, 93-94. Establishment counts are from *County Business Patterns* for non-Census years; establishment counts for 83-84 are extrapolations. * indicates that industry content changed in 87; earlier years use 77 SICs. 'P's mark projections.

INDICES OF CHANGE

Year	Com-panies	Establishments		Employment			Compensation		Production ($ million)			
		Total	with 20 or more employees	Total (000)	Production Workers (000)	Production Hours (Mil)	Payroll ($ mil)	Wages ($/hr)	Cost of Materials	Value Added by Manufacture	Value of Shipments	Capital Invest.
1982	101	113	117	105	102	98	68	68	59	56	59	44
1983		107	112	105	101	99	71	70	60	58	60	46
1984		101	106	108	106	101	75	73	61	65	62	71
1985		95	101	95	93	89	68	74	63	57	62	54
1986		92	96	89	89	87	67	78	65	60	64	71
1987*	87	91	98	91	90	90	72	80	67	69	69	61
1988		87	93	92	92	90	76	84	71	64	68	
1989		84	89	86	88	87	78	92	65	64	65	62
1990		78	84	82	83	82	77	94	72	69	72	53
1991		78	78	82	82	83	82	100	73	75	76	55
1992	100	100	100	100	100	100	100	100	100	100	100	100
1993		99	96	86	86	84	86	101	90	76	85	83
1994		94P	91P	87	90	92	89	102	89	79	86	100
1995		96P	91P	88P	89P	90P	96P	108P	97P	87P	94P	
1996		98P	90P	87P	90P	90P	99P	112P	101P	90P	98P	
1997		99P	90P	87P	90P	90P	102P	115P	105P	93P	102P	
1998		101P	90P	87P	90P	91P	104P	118P	108P	97P	105P	

Sources: Same as General Statistics. Values reflect change from the base year, 1992. Values above 100 mean greater than 92, values below 100 mean less than 92, and a value of 100 in the 82-91 or 93-98 period means same as 92. * indicates that industry content changed in 87. Data for earlier years are in 77 SIC format.

SELECTED RATIOS

For 1994	Avg. of All Manufact.	Analyzed Industry	Index	For 1994	Avg. of All Manufact.	Analyzed Industry	Index
Employees per Establishment	49	118	242	Value Added per Production Worker	134,084	37,624	28
Payroll per Establishment	1,500,273	1,735,762	116	Cost per Establishment	5,045,178	4,064,376	81
Payroll per Employee	30,620	14,659	48	Cost per Employee	102,970	34,325	33
Production Workers per Establishment	34	107	313	Cost per Production Worker	146,988	37,819	26
Wages per Establishment	853,319	1,394,313	163	Shipments per Establishment	9,576,895	8,185,704	85
Wages per Production Worker	24,861	12,974	52	Shipments per Employee	195,460	69,130	35
Hours per Production Worker	2,056	1,867	91	Shipments per Production Worker	279,017	76,168	27
Wages per Hour	12.09	6.95	57	Investment per Establishment	321,011	136,589	43
Value Added per Establishment	4,602,255	4,043,461	88	Investment per Employee	6,552	1,154	18
Value Added per Employee	93,930	34,148	36	Investment per Production Worker	9,352	1,271	14

Sources: Same as General Statistics. The 'Average of All Manufacturing' column represents the average of all manufacturing industries reported for the most recent complete year available. The Index shows the relationship between the Average and the Analyzed Industry. For example, 100 means that they are equal; 500 that the Analyzed Industry is five times the average; 50 means that the Analyzed Industry is half the national average. The abbreviation 'na' is used to show that data are 'not available'.

LEADING COMPANIES Number shown: **75** Total sales ($ mil): **4,748** Total employment (000): **46.1**

Company Name	Address				CEO Name	Phone	Co. Type	Sales ($ mil)	Empl. (000)
Phillips-Van Heusen Corp	1290 Av Amer	New York	NY	10104	Bruce J Klatsky	212-541-5200	P	1,255	13.8
Cluett, Peabody and Company	575 5th Av	New York	NY	10017	Michel Zelnik	212-930-3000	S	640*	8.0
Bugle Boy Industries Inc	2900 Madera Rd	Simi Valley	CA	93065	William CW Mow	805-582-1010	R	490*	1.5
Salant Corp	1114 Av Amer	New York	NY	10036	Nicholas P DiPaolo	212-221-7500	P	419	4.0
Hampton Industries Inc	PO Box 614	Kinston	NC	28502	David Fuchs	919-527-8011	P	172	1.6
Quiksilver Inc	1740 Monrovia Av	Costa Mesa	CA	92627	R B McKnight Jr	714-645-1395	P	126	0.4
Cherokee Inc	9545 Wentworth St	Sunland	CA	91040	Bryan Marsal	818-951-1002	P	114	0.3
Santana Ltd	21 E Union Av	E Rutherford	NJ	07073	Norman Spiro	201-804-0600	R	100	0.2
Supreme International Corp	7495 NW 48th St	Miami	FL	33166	George Feldenkreis	305-592-2760	P	90	0.1
USA Classic Inc	350 5th Av	New York	NY	10118	Milton M Adams	212-629-0320	P	79	0.5
TJFC Holding Co	184 Riverview W	Cleveland	OH	44101	John Dejeagher	216-961-6000	R	72*	0.9
Apparel Group	1370 Av Amer	New York	NY	10019	Norman Goldberg	212-399-3500	R	69	1.2
Stage II Apparel Corp	350 5th Av	New York	NY	10118	Robert Plotkin	212-564-5865	P	65	<0.1
Fun-Tees Inc	PO Box 187	Concord	NC	28026	LG Reid Jr	704-788-3003	R	65	0.6
Val-Dor Inc	350 5th Av	New York	NY	10118	Martin Granoff	212-594-7050	R	48*	0.6
Whisper Knits Inc	PO Box 777	Vass	NC	28394	JH Morgan	919-245-7716	R	48	0.7
Oxford Industries Inc	PO Box 510	Lyons	GA	30436	Earl Norton	912-526-1100	D	43	0.6
Oxford of Vidalia	PO Box 408	Vidalia	GA	30474	Tom Meredith	912-537-8821	D	43*	0.8
Bonhomme Shirtmakers Ltd	350 5th Av	New York	NY	10118	Al Goodman	212-947-8600	R	42	0.4
Harper Industries Inc	350 5th Av	New York	NY	10118	Thomas S Friedland	212-971-9200	R	42*	0.4
Kenneth Gordon New Orleans	1209 Dist Row	New Orleans	LA	70123	Kenneth S Gordon	504-734-1433	R	32	0.5
B Lippman Inc	505 Morris Av	Springfield	NJ	07081	Patrick Esposito	201-564-8600	R	30	0.5
La Mode Sportswear Group	13301 S Main St	Los Angeles	CA	90061	Eddie Kahn	310-327-5188	R	30	0.3
Sherry Manufacturing Company	3287 NW 65th St	Miami	FL	33147	Gary Sandler	305-693-7000	R	30	0.3
Indiana Knitwear Corp	PO Box 309	Greenfield	IN	46140	Leonard Berkowitz	317-462-4413	R	28*	0.4
Lucedale Sportswear Co	110 Virginia St	Lucedale	MS	39452	Randy Kogon	601-947-2747	S	26	0.3
Samsons Manufacturing Corp	418 Brown St	Washington	NC	27889	Mayford Sells	919-946-5191	S	25*	0.2
Snake Creek Manufacturing Co	350 5th Av	New York	NY	10118	Jack Troy	212-239-8640	R	22	0.3
Jem Sportswear Inc	459 Park Av	San Fernando	CA	91340	EE Marine	818-365-9361	R	20*	0.3
Marathon Corp	621 N 31st St	Birmingham	AL	35203	Thomas E Jernigan	205-251-4735	R	20	0.2
Oxford of Lyons	State Farm Rd	Lyons	GA	30436	Tommy Burk	912-526-1318	D	20*	0.3
Toll-Gate Garment Co	Rte 3	Hamilton	AL	35570	Robert Moore	205-921-3163	R	20	0.3
Flushing Shirt Manufacturing Co	505 Morris Av	Springfield	NJ	07081	Patrick Esposito	201-564-8600	S	19	0.3
Duffel Sportswear	1870 NW 173rd Av	Beaverton	OR	97006	John Herman	503-629-8777	D	17*	<0.1
Ebert Sportswear Inc	PO Box 21747	Columbia	SC	29221	John Dyer	803-772-2752	R	17*	0.4
Block Industries Inc	525 N Collige Rd	Wilmington	NC	28405	Richard Thrush	910-392-2100	R	16*	0.3
Ely and Walker Co	PO Box 1326	Lebanon	TN	37087	Ivar Aavatsark	615-443-1878	R	16*	<0.1
Fast Clothing Inc	549 S Dawson St	Seattle	WA	98108	Richard Lentz	206-869-4886	R	16	<0.1
Surrey's of Florida Inc	5125 NW 77th Av	Miami	FL	33166	P Shiekman	305-592-8300	R	16	0.2
Blanchard Shirt Corp	PO Box 369	Mountain View	AR	72560	Donald Cooper	501-269-3801	S	15*	0.2
M Rubin and Sons Inc	34-01 38th Av	Long Island Ct	NY	11101	Don Rubin	718-361-2800	R	15	<0.1
Paul Davril Inc	5401 S Soto St	Los Angeles	CA	90058	Charles Perez	213-588-5338	R	15	0.3
After Six Ltd	9108-Yellow Br	Baltimore	MD	21237	Saul Offit	410-682-4400	R	12*	0.2
D'Avila Inc	576 NW 28th St	Miami	FL	33127	James Bakas	305-576-2700	R	12*	0.2
Marathon Apparel Corp	621 N 31st St	Birmingham	AL	35203	Thomas E Jernign	205-251-4735	S	12	0.2
Milfam Inc	PO Box 698	Roseboro	NC	28382	Bruce Miller	919-525-5118	R	12*	0.2
Spot International Inc	17032 Murphy Av	Irvine	CA	92714	John Bernard	714-955-1016	R	12*	<0.1
Star Knitwear Inc	8700 Dayton Pike	Soddy Daisy	TN	37379	Arthur Levy	615-332-9467	R	12*	0.2
Fleetwood Shirt Corp	26 E Locust St	Fleetwood	PA	19522	Leonard Abrams	610-944-7636	R	11*	0.1
In Private Inc	350 5th Av	New York	NY	10118	Michael Castle	212-279-0786	R	11	<0.1
Edgewood Apparel Inc	PO Box 585	Lexington	NC	27292	J Dillon	704-249-9981	R	10*	0.1
Merrill-Sharpe Ltd	47-00 33rd St	Long Island Ct	NY	11101	Larry Schwartz	718-706-8686	R	10*	<0.1
Oxford of Alamo	PO Box 406	Alamo	GA	30411	J Webster	912-568-7121	D	10	0.2
Rivera Manufacturing Inc	PO Box 207	Pontotoc	MS	38863	Melvin Lev	601-489-1561	R	10*	0.1
Roseboro Manufacturing Co	PO Box 698	Roseboro	NC	28382	Rebecca Hall	919-525-5118	D	10*	0.1
Abbeville Shirtmaker Inc	206 Barnett St	Abbeville	SC	29620	Frank A Annese	803-459-5437	R	9*	0.2
BD Baggies	1370 Avnue of the	New York	NY	10019	Tom Witthuhn	212-399-3500	D	8*	0.1
Nantucket Inc	PO Drawer 429	Kinston	NC	28501	Fred A Rouse	919-523-7001	R	7	<0.1
Daren LA Kid Inc	524 S Mateo St	Los Angeles	CA	90013	Mona L Ghaleb	213-620-8774	R	7	<0.1
Action Apparel Inc	PO Box 846	Starkville	MS	39759	RA Smith	601-323-0008	R	6	0.4
California Ranchwear Inc	14600 S Main St	Gardena	CA	90248	S Christenfeld	310-532-8980	R	6*	<0.1
Jetricks	PO Box 428	Selmer	TN	38375	Ray Surratt	901-645-3455	D	6	0.2
Morgan Shirt Corp	PO Box 867	Morgantown	WV	26507	Robert Thomas	304-292-8451	R	6	0.3
Mule Skins	2900 W Main St	Galesburg	IL	61401	Richard Lindville	309-343-1191	D	6	0.2
Sweet-Orr and Company Inc	1290 Av Amer	New York	NY	10104	Arnold Ginsburg	212-757-7733	R	6*	<0.1
Triumph of California Inc	2900 S Main St	Los Angeles	CA	90007	Alex Birnbaum	213-747-6172	R	6	<0.1
Berkley Shirt Company Inc	358 5th Av	New York	NY	10001	Carl Stapf	212-594-1225	R	5*	<0.1
Cinnabar Traders Ltd	1460 Broadway	New York	NY	10036	Arnold Blair	212-302-0960	R	5*	<0.1
Clifton Shirt Co	529 Main St	Loveland	OH	45140	Ed Levy	513-683-2130	R	5*	0.1
International News Inc	19226 70th Av S	Kent	WA	98032	Michael Alesco	206-872-3542	R	5*	<0.1
Itawamba Manufacturing	PO Box 909	Fulton	MS	38843	Andy Holiman	601-862-3134	R	5*	0.4
Seattle Pacific Industries	1848 Westlake N	Seattle	WA	98109	Brian Leung	206-282-8889	D	5	<0.1
Organik Technologies Inc	4020 S 56th St	Tacoma	WA	98409	John C Lindsey	206-471-9900	P	4	0.2
Carlyle Golf Inc	10550 E 54th Av	Denver	CO	80239	David J Bullock	303-371-2889	P	4	<0.1
Chadco Inc	PO Box 911	Corinth	MS	38834	Lawrence Flax	601-287-1417	R	4*	<0.1

Source: *Ward's Business Directory of U.S. Private and Public Companies*, Volumes 1 and 2, 1996. The company type code used is as follows: P - Public, R - Private, S - Subsidiary, D - Division, J - Joint Venture, A - Affiliate, G - Group. Sales are in millions of dollars, employees are in thousands. An asterisk (*) indicates an estimated sales volume. The symbol < stands for 'less than'. Company names and addresses are truncated, in some cases, to fit into the available space.

MATERIALS CONSUMED

Material	Quantity	Delivered Cost ($ million)
Materials, ingredients, containers, and supplies	(X)	2,240.7
Broadwoven fabrics (piece goods)	(X)	464.0
Narrow fabrics (12 inches or less in width)	(X)	30.2
Knit fabrics	(X)	1,372.2
Yarn, all fibers	(X)	88.6
Buttons, zippers, and slide fasteners	(X)	39.5
All other materials and components, parts, containers, and supplies	(X)	201.4
Materials, ingredients, containers, and supplies, nsk	(X)	44.8

Source: 1992 *Economic Census*. Explanation of symbols used: (D): Withheld to avoid disclosure of competitive data; na: Not available; (S): Withheld because statistical norms were not met; (X): Not applicable; (Z): Less than half the unit shown; nec: Not elsewhere classified; nsk: Not specified by kind; - : zero; * : 10-19 percent estimated; ** : 20-29 percent estimated.

PRODUCT SHARE DETAILS

Product or Product Class	% Share
Men's and boys' shirts	100.00
Men's and boys' knit shirts, dress and sport (including polo, tennis, sweat, tank-tops, T-shirts for outerwear, etc.), made from purchased fabrics	66.76
Men's and boys' woven dress and sport shirts (including military-type uniform shirts)	20.89
Receipts for contract and commission work on men's and boys' shirts, except work shirts	11.37
Receipts for contract and commission work on men's and boys' shirts, except work shirts	98.94
Receipts for contract and commission work on men's and boys' shirts, except work shirts, nsk	1.06
Men's and boys' shirts, nsk	0.98

Source: 1992 *Economic Census*. The values shown are percent of total shipments in an industry. Values of indented subcategories are summed in the main heading. The symbol (D) appears when data are withheld to prevent disclosure of competitive information. The abbreviation nsk stands for 'not specified by kind' and nec for 'not elsewhere classified'.

INPUTS AND OUTPUTS FOR APPAREL MADE FROM PURCHASED MATERIALS

Economic Sector or Industry Providing Inputs	%	Sector	Economic Sector or Industry Buying Outputs	%	Sector
Imports	29.1	Foreign	Personal consumption expenditures	82.7	
Broadwoven fabric mills	20.2	Manufg.	Apparel made from purchased materials	12.0	Manufg.
Apparel made from purchased materials	18.3	Manufg.	Exports	1.5	Foreign
Knit fabric mills	8.6	Manufg.	Federal Government purchases, national defense	0.9	Fed Govt
Wholesale trade	3.8	Trade	S/L Govt. purch., correction	0.5	S/L Govt
Advertising	2.4	Services	Pleating & stitching	0.3	Manufg.
Yarn mills & finishing of textiles, nec	1.4	Manufg.	Knit outerwear mills	0.2	Manufg.
Pleating & stitching	1.1	Manufg.	Hospitals	0.2	Services
Banking	1.1	Fin/R.E.	Laundry, dry cleaning, shoe repair	0.2	Services
Petroleum refining	1.0	Manufg.	S/L Govt. purch., health & hospitals	0.2	S/L Govt
Electric services (utilities)	1.0	Util.	Portrait, photographic studios	0.1	Services
Automotive & apparel trimmings	0.9	Manufg.	S/L Govt. purch., public assistance & relief	0.1	S/L Govt
Needles, pins, & fasteners	0.8	Manufg.			
Thread mills	0.7	Manufg.			
Communications, except radio & TV	0.7	Util.			
Eating & drinking places	0.7	Trade			
U.S. Postal Service	0.7	Gov't			
Leather tanning & finishing	0.5	Manufg.			
Narrow fabric mills	0.5	Manufg.			
Schiffli machine embroideries	0.4	Manufg.			
Motor freight transportation & warehousing	0.4	Util.			
Real estate	0.4	Fin/R.E.			
Royalties	0.4	Fin/R.E.			
Forestry products	0.3	Agric.			
Buttons	0.3	Manufg.			
Paperboard containers & boxes	0.3	Manufg.			
Air transportation	0.3	Util.			
Maintenance of nonfarm buildings nec	0.2	Constr.			
Lace goods	0.2	Manufg.			
Gas production & distribution (utilities)	0.2	Util.			
Automotive rental & leasing, without drivers	0.2	Services			
Electrical repair shops	0.2	Services			
Equipment rental & leasing services	0.2	Services			
Legal services	0.2	Services			
Management & consulting services & labs	0.2	Services			
Artificial trees & flowers	0.1	Manufg.			
Insurance carriers	0.1	Fin/R.E.			
Accounting, auditing & bookkeeping	0.1	Services			
Automotive repair shops & services	0.1	Services			

Source: Benchmark Input-Output Accounts for the U.S. Economy, 1982, U.S. Department of Commerce, Washington, D.C., July 1991. Data, as reported in the source, are organized by the 1977 SIC structure in use in 1982 but have been matched, as closely as is possible, to the 1987 SIC structure used in this book.

OCCUPATIONS EMPLOYED BY SIC 232 - APPAREL

Occupation	% of Total 1994	Change to 2005	Occupation	% of Total 1994	Change to 2005
Sewing machine operators, garment	56.1	-33.1	Cutters & trimmers, hand	1.7	-24.8
Inspectors, testers, & graders, precision	3.5	-16.4	Patternmakers, layout workers, fabric & apparel	1.5	25.4
Blue collar worker supervisors	3.0	-24.0	General managers & top executives	1.4	-20.7
Assemblers, fabricators, & hand workers nec	2.5	-16.4	Sewing machine operators, non-garment	1.3	-37.3
Pressing machine operators, textiles	2.4	-45.7	Helpers, laborers, & material movers nec	1.1	-16.4
Hand packers & packagers	2.0	-21.2	Industrial machinery mechanics	1.1	0.3
Freight, stock, & material movers, hand	1.8	-33.1	Pressers, hand	1.1	-58.2
Traffic, shipping, & receiving clerks	1.8	-19.6	Sewers, hand	1.0	-10.7

Source: Industry-Occupation Matrix, Bureau of Labor Statistics. These data relate to one or more 3-digit SIC industry groups rather than to a single 4-digit SIC. The change reported for each occupation to the year 2005 is a percent of growth or decline as estimated by the Bureau of Labor Statistics. The abbreviation nec stands for 'not elsewhere classified'.

LOCATION BY STATE AND REGIONAL CONCENTRATION

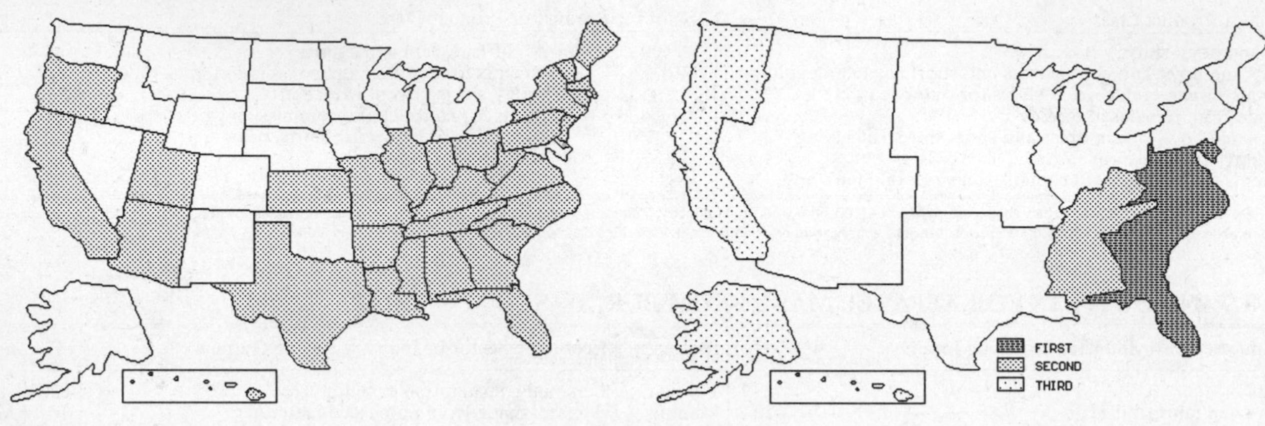

INDUSTRY DATA BY STATE

State	Establish-ments	Shipments Total ($ mil)	Shipments % of U.S.	Shipments Per Establ.	Employment Total Number	Employment % of U.S.	Employment Per Establ.	Wages ($/hour)	Cost as % of Shipments	Investment per Employee ($)
North Carolina	89	975.7	16.5	11.0	13,000	15.4	146	6.73	55.9	1,108
Alabama	52	614.4	10.4	11.8	10,900	12.9	210	7.49	43.8	890
Kentucky	9	612.9	10.4	68.1	5,400	6.4	600	7.67	30.2	981
South Carolina	35	549.8	9.3	15.7	7,400	8.8	211	6.71	45.4	1,216
Georgia	35	462.6	7.8	13.2	6,800	8.1	194	6.24	52.3	544
New York	53	403.5	6.8	7.6	1,400	1.7	26	8.06	59.9	857
California	86	339.9	5.7	4.0	3,700	4.4	43	6.96	56.9	1,784
Florida	39	334.7	5.7	8.6	4,300	5.1	110	6.58	49.3	-
Virginia	15	277.8	4.7	18.5	3,700	4.4	247	7.91	68.3	1,135
Pennsylvania	41	236.9	4.0	5.8	4,700	5.6	115	7.00	48.1	596
Tennessee	47	207.7	3.5	4.4	5,500	6.5	117	6.27	38.6	491
Mississippi	23	165.5	2.8	7.2	4,000	4.7	174	5.48	23.5	525
Arkansas	17	90.4	1.5	5.3	3,300	3.9	194	5.96	21.7	394
New Jersey	10	84.1	1.4	8.4	1,100	1.3	110	6.81	46.4	818
Kansas	6	72.3	1.2	12.0	900	1.1	150	8.75	58.0	-
Texas	15	52.8	0.9	3.5	600	0.7	40	6.00	68.2	-
Hawaii	19	22.5	0.4	1.2	600	0.7	32	6.33	39.1	667
Arizona	5	5.5	0.1	1.1	200	0.2	40	5.67	27.3	-
Missouri	11	(D)	-	-	1,750 *	2.1	159	-	-	-
Ohio	7	(D)	-	-	375 *	0.4	54	-	-	267
Indiana	4	(D)	-	-	375 *	0.4	94	-	-	-
Louisiana	4	(D)	-	-	1,750 *	2.1	438	-	-	457
Massachusetts	3	(D)	-	-	375 *	0.4	125	-	-	-
Oregon	3	(D)	-	-	375 *	0.4	125	-	-	-
Utah	3	(D)	-	-	375 *	0.4	125	-	-	-
Vermont	3	(D)	-	-	175 *	0.2	58	-	-	-
Connecticut	2	(D)	-	-	175 *	0.2	88	-	-	-
Illinois	2	(D)	-	-	375 *	0.4	188	-	-	-
West Virginia	2	(D)	-	-	375 *	0.4	188	-	-	-
Maine	1	(D)	-	-	750 *	0.9	750	-	-	-

Source: 1992 *Economic Census.* The states are in descending order of shipments or establishments (if shipment data are missing for the majority). The symbol (D) appears when data are withheld to prevent disclosure of competitive information. States marked with (D) are sorted by number of establishments. A dash (-) indicates that the data element cannot be calculated; * indicates the midpoint of a range.

2322 - MEN'S & BOYS' UNDERWEAR & NIGHTWEAR

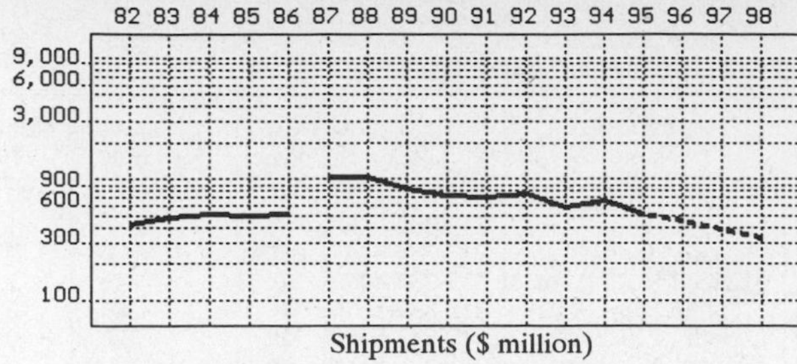

Shipments ($ million)

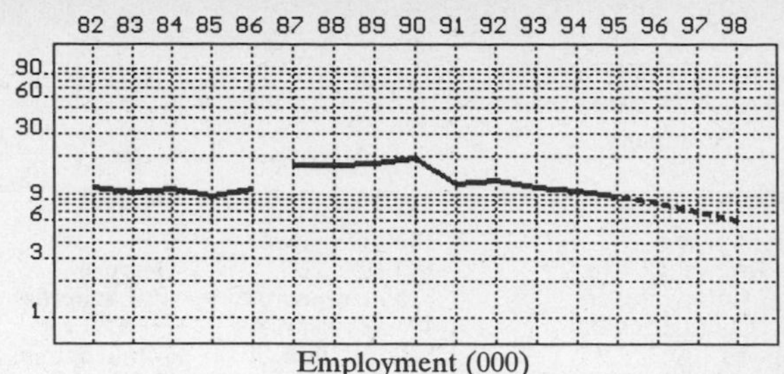

Employment (000)

GENERAL STATISTICS

Year	Companies	Establishments: Total	Establishments: with 20 or more employees	Employment: Total (000)	Employment: Production Workers (000)	Employment: Production Hours (Mil)	Compensation: Payroll ($ mil)	Compensation: Wages ($/hr)	Production ($ million): Cost of Materials	Production ($ million): Value Added by Manufacture	Production ($ million): Value of Shipments	Production ($ million): Capital Invest.
1982	61	77	51	11.0	10.0	16.8	99.1	4.88	206.7	210.2	429.4	3.3
1983		73	52	10.3	9.2	16.1	97.4	5.11	228.7	242.8	484.9	1.4
1984		69	53	10.7	10.2	18.7	115.5	5.64	234.5	276.4	514.1	
1985		66	53	9.6	9.3	16.4	107.4	5.99	220.1	285.5	505.0	2.3
1986		65	47	10.7	10.4	18.8	129.5	6.24	229.9	288.1	514.2	4.4
1987*	74	96	76	17.2	16.2	29.5	200.1	5.98	465.2	577.8	1,045.4	7.6
1988		99	77	17.1	16.1	29.5	207.2	6.20	488.7	556.6	1,044.5	
1989		89	71	17.6	15.3	27.0	190.8	6.21	395.9	432.1	827.9	27.2
1990		90	73	19.2	14.4	26.5	183.8	6.07	333.7	381.7	724.9	11.8
1991		94	71	11.8	10.9	19.1	165.0	7.42	333.0	371.7	709.9	6.2
1992	66	85	62	12.8	11.8	22.2	172.0	6.72	360.6	398.7	749.2	6.9
1993		98	68	11.3	10.5	18.7	143.2	6.48	313.5	263.4	581.1	8.0
1994		91P	63P	10.5	10.1	19.4	152.2	7.03	350.1	314.6	664.4	7.1
1995		90P	61P	9.5P	8.6P	16.1P	137.7P	7.14P	270.3P	242.9P	513.0P	
1996		89P	60P	8.3P	7.6P	14.4P	129.0P	7.28P	237.5P	213.4P	450.6P	
1997		89P	58P	7.1P	6.6P	12.7P	120.3P	7.41P	204.6P	183.9P	388.3P	
1998		88P	56P	6.0P	5.6P	10.9P	111.6P	7.55P	171.8P	154.4P	326.0P	

Sources: 1982, 1987, 1992 *Economic Census*; *Annual Survey of Manufactures*, 83-86, 88-91, 93-94. Establishment counts are from *County Business Patterns* for non-Census years; establishment counts for 83-84 are extrapolations. * indicates that industry content changed in 87; earlier years use 77 SICs. 'P's mark projections.

INDICES OF CHANGE

Year	Companies	Establishments: Total	Establishments: with 20 or more employees	Employment: Total (000)	Employment: Production Workers (000)	Employment: Production Hours (Mil)	Compensation: Payroll ($ mil)	Compensation: Wages ($/hr)	Production ($ million): Cost of Materials	Production ($ million): Value Added by Manufacture	Production ($ million): Value of Shipments	Production ($ million): Capital Invest.
1982	92	91	82	86	85	76	58	73	57	53	57	48
1983		86	84	80	78	73	57	76	63	61	65	20
1984		81	85	84	86	84	67	84	65	69	69	
1985		78	85	75	79	74	62	89	61	72	67	33
1986		76	76	84	88	85	75	93	64	72	69	64
1987*	112	113	123	134	137	133	116	89	129	145	140	110
1988		116	124	134	136	133	120	92	136	140	139	
1989		105	115	138	130	122	111	92	110	108	111	394
1990		106	118	150	122	119	107	90	93	96	97	171
1991		111	115	92	92	86	96	110	92	93	95	90
1992	100	100	100	100	100	100	100	100	100	100	100	100
1993		115	110	88	89	84	83	96	87	66	78	116
1994		107P	102P	82	86	87	88	105	97	79	89	103
1995		106P	99P	74P	73P	73P	80P	106P	75P	61P	68P	
1996		105P	96P	65P	65P	65P	75P	108P	66P	54P	60P	
1997		104P	93P	56P	56P	57P	70P	110P	57P	46P	52P	
1998		104P	90P	47P	47P	49P	65P	112P	48P	39P	44P	

Sources: Same as General Statistics. Values reflect change from the base year, 1992. Values above 100 mean greater than 92, values below 100 mean less than 92, and a value of 100 in the 82-91 or 93-98 period means same as 92. * indicates that industry content changed in 87. Data for earlier years are in 77 SIC format.

SELECTED RATIOS

For 1994	Avg. of All Manufact.	Analyzed Industry	Index	For 1994	Avg. of All Manufact.	Analyzed Industry	Index
Employees per Establishment	49	116	237	Value Added per Production Worker	134,084	31,149	23
Payroll per Establishment	1,500,273	1,680,442	112	Cost per Establishment	5,045,178	3,865,457	77
Payroll per Employee	30,620	14,495	47	Cost per Employee	102,970	33,343	32
Production Workers per Establishment	34	112	325	Cost per Production Worker	146,988	34,663	24
Wages per Establishment	853,319	1,505,795	176	Shipments per Establishment	9,576,895	7,335,647	77
Wages per Production Worker	24,861	13,503	54	Shipments per Employee	195,460	63,276	32
Hours per Production Worker	2,056	1,921	93	Shipments per Production Worker	279,017	65,782	24
Wages per Hour	12.09	7.03	58	Investment per Establishment	321,011	78,391	24
Value Added per Establishment	4,602,255	3,473,502	75	Investment per Employee	6,552	676	10
Value Added per Employee	93,930	29,962	32	Investment per Production Worker	9,352	703	8

Sources: Same as General Statistics. The 'Average of All Manufacturing' column represents the average of all manufacturing industries reported for the most recent complete year available. The Index shows the relationship between the Average and the Analyzed Industry. For example, 100 means that they are equal; 500 that the Analyzed Industry is five times the average; 50 means that the Analyzed Industry is half the national average. The abbreviation 'na' is used to show that data are 'not available'.

LEADING COMPANIES

Number shown: **10** Total sales ($ mil): **2,638** Total employment (000): **42.5**

Company Name	Address				CEO Name	Phone	Co. Type	Sales ($ mil)	Empl. (000)
Fruit of the Loom Inc	233 S Wacker Dr	Chicago	IL	60606	William Farley	312-876-1724	P	2,298	37.4
Host Apparel Inc	1430 Broadway	New York	NY	10018	Irving Cohen	212-302-0800	R	109	1.0
Wrights Knitwear Corp	PO Box 518	Auburn	PA	17922	Donald Handal	717-754-3261	R	51*	0.9
Harwood Companies Inc	3355 Enterprise Av	Ft Lauderdale	FL	33331	Michael Rothbaum	305-384-4400	R	45*	1.5
Nantucket Industries Inc	105 Madison Av	New York	NY	10016	Stephen Samberg	212-889-5656	P	42	0.5
Munsingwear Inc	8000 W 78th St	Minneapolis	MN	55439	Lowell M Fisher	612-943-5000	P	37	0.3
Wex-Tex of Ashford Inc	PO Box X	Ashford	AL	36312	William Nomberg	205-899-5116	R	31*	0.4
Union Underwear	1 Fruit of the Loom	Bowling Green	KY	42103	Jeff Caplenor	502-781-6400	D	13*	0.3
Stone Mfg Co Menswear	Wrenn St	Johnston	SC	29832	Fred Allen	803-275-4992	D	9	0.2
Green Apparel Inc	PO Box 88	Greenfield	TN	38230	Robert L Green	901-235-2247	R	4	<0.1

Source: *Ward's Business Directory of U.S. Private and Public Companies*, Volumes 1 and 2, 1996. The company type code used is as follows: P - Public, R - Private, S - Subsidiary, D - Division, J - Joint Venture, A - Affiliate, G - Group. Sales are in millions of dollars, employees are in thousands. An asterisk (*) indicates an estimated sales volume. The symbol < stands for 'less than'. Company names and addresses are truncated, in some cases, to fit into the available space.

MATERIALS CONSUMED

Material	Quantity	Delivered Cost ($ million)
Materials, ingredients, containers, and supplies	(X)	332.8
Broadwoven fabrics (piece goods)	(X)	50.7
Narrow fabrics (12 inches or less in width)	(X)	4.1
Knit fabrics	(X)	222.6
Yarn, all fibers	(X)	(D)
Buttons, zippers, and slide fasteners	(X)	(D)
All other materials and components, parts, containers, and supplies	(X)	24.9
Materials, ingredients, containers, and supplies, nsk	(X)	4.0

Source: 1992 *Economic Census*. Explanation of symbols used: (D): Withheld to avoid disclosure of competitive data; na: Not available; (S): Withheld because statistical norms were not met; (X): Not applicable; (Z): Less than half the unit shown; nec: Not elsewhere classified; nsk: Not specified by kind; - : zero; * : 10-19 percent estimated; ** : 20-29 percent estimated.

PRODUCT SHARE DETAILS

Product or Product Class	% Share	Product or Product Class	% Share
Men's and boys' underwear and nightwear	100.00	Receipts for contract and commission work on men's and boys' underwear and nightwear	7.22
Men's and boys' underwear, made from purchased fabrics	77.41	Men's and boys' underwear and nightwear, nsk	0.80
Men's and boys' nightwear (including pajamas, night shirts, etc.), excluding robes	14.57		

Source: 1992 *Economic Census*. The values shown are percent of total shipments in an industry. Values of indented subcategories are summed in the main heading. The symbol (D) appears when data are withheld to prevent disclosure of competitive information. The abbreviation nsk stands for 'not specified by kind' and nec for 'not elsewhere classified'.

INPUTS AND OUTPUTS FOR APPAREL MADE FROM PURCHASED MATERIALS

Economic Sector or Industry Providing Inputs	%	Sector	Economic Sector or Industry Buying Outputs	%	Sector
Imports	29.1	Foreign	Personal consumption expenditures	82.7	
Broadwoven fabric mills	20.2	Manufg.	Apparel made from purchased materials	12.0	Manufg.
Apparel made from purchased materials	18.3	Manufg.	Exports	1.5	Foreign
Knit fabric mills	8.6	Manufg.	Federal Government purchases, national defense	0.9	Fed Govt
Wholesale trade	3.8	Trade	S/L Govt. purch., correction	0.5	S/L Govt
Advertising	2.4	Services	Pleating & stitching	0.3	Manufg.
Yarn mills & finishing of textiles, nec	1.4	Manufg.	Knit outerwear mills	0.2	Manufg.
Pleating & stitching	1.1	Manufg.	Hospitals	0.2	Services
Banking	1.1	Fin/R.E.	Laundry, dry cleaning, shoe repair	0.2	Services
Petroleum refining	1.0	Manufg.	S/L Govt. purch., health & hospitals	0.2	S/L Govt
Electric services (utilities)	1.0	Util.	Portrait, photographic studios	0.1	Services
Automotive & apparel trimmings	0.9	Manufg.	S/L Govt. purch., public assistance & relief	0.1	S/L Govt
Needles, pins, & fasteners	0.8	Manufg.			
Thread mills	0.7	Manufg.			
Communications, except radio & TV	0.7	Util.			
Eating & drinking places	0.7	Trade			
U.S. Postal Service	0.7	Gov't			
Leather tanning & finishing	0.5	Manufg.			
Narrow fabric mills	0.5	Manufg.			
Schiffli machine embroideries	0.4	Manufg.			
Motor freight transportation & warehousing	0.4	Util.			
Real estate	0.4	Fin/R.E.			

Continued on next page.

INPUTS AND OUTPUTS FOR APPAREL MADE FROM PURCHASED MATERIALS - Continued

Economic Sector or Industry Providing Inputs	%	Sector	Economic Sector or Industry Buying Outputs	%	Sector
Royalties	0.4	Fin/R.E.			
Forestry products	0.3	Agric.			
Buttons	0.3	Manufg.			
Paperboard containers & boxes	0.3	Manufg.			
Air transportation	0.3	Util.			
Maintenance of nonfarm buildings nec	0.2	Constr.			
Lace goods	0.2	Manufg.			
Gas production & distribution (utilities)	0.2	Util.			
Automotive rental & leasing, without drivers	0.2	Services			
Electrical repair shops	0.2	Services			
Equipment rental & leasing services	0.2	Services			
Legal services	0.2	Services			
Management & consulting services & labs	0.2	Services			
Artificial trees & flowers	0.1	Manufg.			
Insurance carriers	0.1	Fin/R.E.			
Accounting, auditing & bookkeeping	0.1	Services			
Automotive repair shops & services	0.1	Services			

Source: Benchmark Input-Output Accounts for the U.S. Economy, 1982, U.S. Department of Commerce, Washington, D.C., July 1991. Data, as reported in the source, are organized by the 1977 SIC structure in use in 1982 but have been matched, as closely as is possible, to the 1987 SIC structure used in this book.

OCCUPATIONS EMPLOYED BY SIC 232 - APPAREL

Occupation	% of Total 1994	Change to 2005	Occupation	% of Total 1994	Change to 2005
Sewing machine operators, garment	56.1	-33.1	Cutters & trimmers, hand	1.7	-24.8
Inspectors, testers, & graders, precision	3.5	-16.4	Patternmakers, layout workers, fabric & apparel	1.5	25.4
Blue collar worker supervisors	3.0	-24.0	General managers & top executives	1.4	-20.7
Assemblers, fabricators, & hand workers nec	2.5	-16.4	Sewing machine operators, non-garment	1.3	-37.3
Pressing machine operators, textiles	2.4	-45.7	Helpers, laborers, & material movers nec	1.1	-16.4
Hand packers & packagers	2.0	-21.2	Industrial machinery mechanics	1.1	0.3
Freight, stock, & material movers, hand	1.8	-33.1	Pressers, hand	1.1	-58.2
Traffic, shipping, & receiving clerks	1.8	-19.6	Sewers, hand	1.0	-10.7

Source: Industry-Occupation Matrix, Bureau of Labor Statistics. These data relate to one or more 3-digit SIC industry groups rather than to a single 4-digit SIC. The change reported for each occupation to the year 2005 is a percent of growth or decline as estimated by the Bureau of Labor Statistics. The abbreviation nec stands for 'not elsewhere classified'.

LOCATION BY STATE AND REGIONAL CONCENTRATION

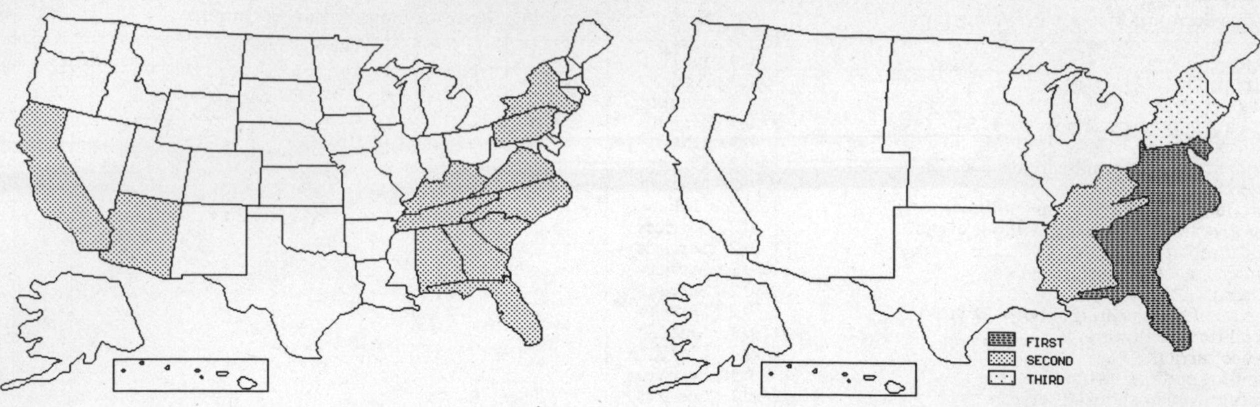

INDUSTRY DATA BY STATE

State	Establish-ments	Shipments Total ($ mil)	Shipments % of U.S.	Shipments Per Establ.	Employment Total Number	Employment % of U.S.	Employment Per Establ.	Wages ($/hour)	Cost as % of Shipments	Investment per Employee ($)
Georgia	11	154.1	20.6	14.0	2,600	20.3	236	6.13	56.2	423
Tennessee	8	83.0	11.1	10.4	1,400	10.9	175	6.33	53.5	429
Pennsylvania	6	63.8	8.5	10.6	800	6.3	133	7.46	48.1	-
North Carolina	8	60.5	8.1	7.6	1,100	8.6	138	7.39	51.9	-
Alabama	4	32.7	4.4	8.2	600	4.7	150	6.00	54.7	-
Virginia	7	29.2	3.9	4.2	900	7.0	129	6.38	41.1	-
New York	8	(D)	-	-	375 *	2.9	47	-	-	-
South Carolina	7	(D)	-	-	1,750 *	13.7	250	-	-	-
California	5	(D)	-	-	175 *	1.4	35	-	-	-
Florida	5	(D)	-	-	375 *	2.9	75	-	-	-
Kentucky	4	(D)	-	-	3,750 *	29.3	938	-	-	-
Arizona	3	(D)	-	-	750 *	5.9	250	-	-	-

Source: 1992 *Economic Census*. The states are in descending order of shipments or establishments (if shipment data are missing for the majority). The symbol (D) appears when data are withheld to prevent disclosure of competitive information. States marked with (D) are sorted by number of establishments. A dash (-) indicates that the data element cannot be calculated; * indicates the midpoint of a range.

2323 - MEN'S & BOYS' NECKWEAR

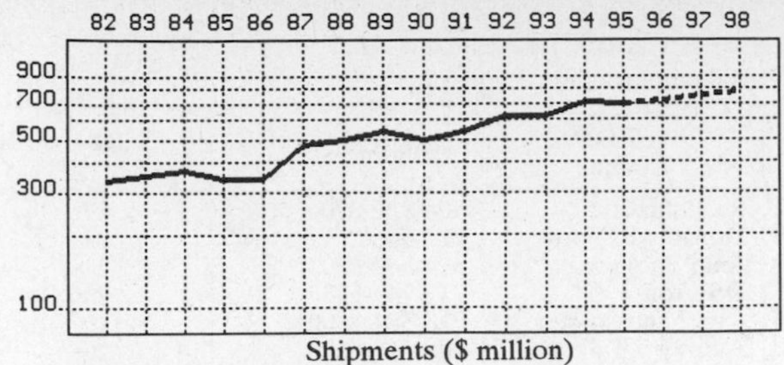

Shipments ($ million)

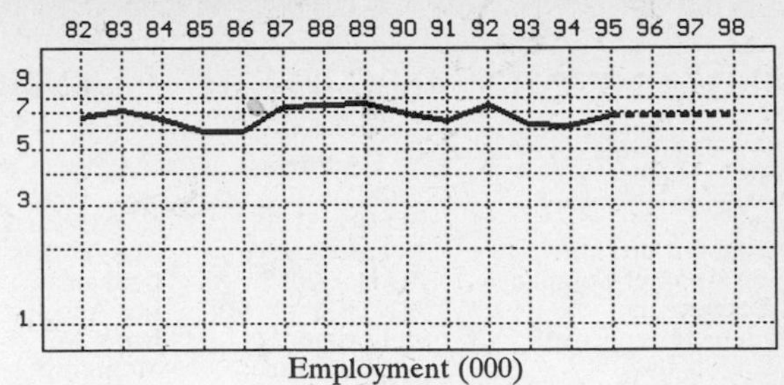

Employment (000)

GENERAL STATISTICS

Year	Com-panies	Establishments		Employment			Compensation		Production ($ million)			
		Total	with 20 or more employees	Total (000)	Production Workers (000)	Production Hours (Mil)	Payroll ($ mil)	Wages ($/hr)	Cost of Materials	Value Added by Manufacture	Value of Shipments	Capital Invest.
1982	165	170	91	6.7	5.3	9.0	83.0	5.58	148.3	184.5	335.0	4.9
1983		165	89	7.1	5.7	9.4	110.4	7.74	134.5	217.1	355.5	7.3
1984		160	87	6.6	5.2	9.0	86.9	5.74	174.2	187.1	367.1	
1985		154	85	5.9	4.8	8.2	80.4	5.84	161.3	174.8	341.9	1.5
1986		154	84	5.9	4.8	8.2	79.9	6.09	162.4	179.6	341.5	1.4
1987	139	142	84	7.4	6.2	11.0	117.0	6.98	223.6	251.4	475.6	6.2
1988		131	84	7.5	6.2	11.0	123.0	7.15	241.6	258.0	499.9	
1989		127	85	7.6	6.6	10.6	124.6	7.04	249.3	285.2	533.9	4.8
1990		121	77	6.9	6.0	9.5	120.1	7.28	231.2	268.5	499.9	5.3
1991		129	74	6.4	5.1	9.0	124.7	8.02	251.8	287.5	532.0	3.8
1992	132	136	80	7.5	5.8	10.4	130.2	7.39	301.1	319.1	618.2	6.0
1993		138	76	6.3	4.8	8.4	126.0	8.43	304.0	311.5	619.3	5.0
1994		119P	74P	6.2	4.6	8.1	119.4	9.21	342.6	366.1	704.5	2.4
1995		115P	73P	6.8P	5.4P	9.4P	136.2P	8.68P	335.4P	358.5P	689.8P	
1996		112P	72P	6.8P	5.4P	9.4P	140.0P	8.91P	350.1P	374.1P	719.9P	
1997		108P	71P	6.8P	5.3P	9.4P	143.8P	9.13P	364.8P	389.8P	750.1P	
1998		104P	69P	6.8P	5.3P	9.4P	147.6P	9.36P	379.4P	405.4P	780.2P	

Sources: 1982, 1987, 1992 *Economic Census*; *Annual Survey of Manufactures*, 83-86, 88-91, 93-94. Establishment counts for non-Census years are from *County Business Patterns*; establishment values for 83-84 are extrapolations. 'P's show projections by the editors. Industries reclassified in 87 will not have data for prior years.

INDICES OF CHANGE

Year	Com-panies	Establishments		Employment			Compensation		Production ($ million)			
		Total	with 20 or more employees	Total (000)	Production Workers (000)	Production Hours (Mil)	Payroll ($ mil)	Wages ($/hr)	Cost of Materials	Value Added by Manufacture	Value of Shipments	Capital Invest.
1982	125	125	114	89	91	87	64	76	49	58	54	82
1983		121	111	95	98	90	85	105	45	68	58	122
1984		118	109	88	90	87	67	78	58	59	59	
1985		113	106	79	83	79	62	79	54	55	55	25
1986		113	105	79	83	79	61	82	54	56	55	23
1987	105	104	105	99	107	106	90	94	74	79	77	103
1988		96	105	100	107	106	94	97	80	81	81	
1989		93	106	101	114	102	96	95	83	89	86	80
1990		89	96	92	103	91	92	99	77	84	81	88
1991		95	93	85	88	87	96	109	84	90	86	63
1992	100	100	100	100	100	100	100	100	100	100	100	100
1993		101	95	84	83	81	97	114	101	98	100	83
1994		88P	93P	83	79	78	92	125	114	115	114	40
1995		85P	91P	90P	93P	90P	105P	118P	111P	112P	112P	
1996		82P	90P	90P	92P	90P	108P	121P	116P	117P	116P	
1997		79P	88P	90P	92P	90P	110P	124P	121P	122P	121P	
1998		76P	87P	90P	92P	90P	113P	127P	126P	127P	126P	

Sources: Same as General Statistics. Values reflect change from the base year, 1992. Values above 100 mean greater than 92, values below 100 mean less than 92, and a value of 100 in the 82-91 or 93-98 period means same as 92. 'P's mark projections by the editors.

SELECTED RATIOS

For 1994	Avg. of All Manufact.	Analyzed Industry	Index	For 1994	Avg. of All Manufact.	Analyzed Industry	Index
Employees per Establishment	49	52	106	Value Added per Production Worker	134,084	79,587	59
Payroll per Establishment	1,500,273	1,001,576	67	Cost per Establishment	5,045,178	2,873,869	57
Payroll per Employee	30,620	19,258	63	Cost per Employee	102,970	55,258	54
Production Workers per Establishment	34	39	112	Cost per Production Worker	146,988	74,478	51
Wages per Establishment	853,319	625,784	73	Shipments per Establishment	9,576,895	5,909,634	62
Wages per Production Worker	24,861	16,218	65	Shipments per Employee	195,460	113,629	58
Hours per Production Worker	2,056	1,761	86	Shipments per Production Worker	279,017	153,152	55
Wages per Hour	12.09	9.21	76	Investment per Establishment	321,011	20,132	6
Value Added per Establishment	4,602,255	3,070,996	67	Investment per Employee	6,552	387	6
Value Added per Employee	93,930	59,048	63	Investment per Production Worker	9,352	522	6

Sources: Same as General Statistics. The 'Average of All Manufacturing' column represents the average of all manufacturing industries reported for the most recent complete year available. The Index shows the relationship between the Average and the Analyzed Industry. For example, 100 means that they are equal; 500 that the Analyzed Industry is five times the average; 50 means that the Analyzed Industry is half the national average. The abbreviation 'na' is used to show that data are 'not available'.

LEADING COMPANIES

Number shown: 27 Total sales ($ mil): 273 Total employment (000): 3.2

Company Name	Address				CEO Name	Phone	Co. Type	Sales ($ mil)	Empl. (000)
Wemco Inc	PO Box 51119	New Orleans	LA	70151	SC Pulitzer	504-822-3700	R	69*	0.9
Echo Design Group Inc	10 E 40th St	New York	NY	10016	Dorothy Roberts	212-686-8771	R	35	0.1
Remington Apparel Company	PO Box 2015	Graham	TX	76450	John Babiarz	817-549-8304	S	25*	0.4
Castle Neckwear Inc	1415 S Maple St	Los Angeles	CA	90015	D Baron	213-749-5487	R	20*	0.2
Fabil Manufacturing Corp	95 Lorimer St	Brooklyn	NY	11206	Sam Landau	718-384-8300	R	20	0.1
Robert Talbott Inc	2901 M-Salinas	Monterey	CA	93940	Audrey S Talbott	408-649-6000	R	20*	0.3
Barry Wells	690 E Lamar	Arlington	TX	76011	Anthony Briggle	214-905-1331	R	15*	0.2
Kantor Brothers Neckwear	575 E 10th Av	Hialeah	FL	33010	T Kantor	305-885-4056	R	11	0.1
Hollyvogue Ties Corp	3671 S Broadway	Los Angeles	CA	90007	Bluma Samuels	213-233-4286	R	7*	0.1
Isaco International Corp	3651 NW 79th Av	Miami	FL	33166	Isaac Zelcer	305-594-4455	R	7*	0.1
MMG Corp	1717 Olive St	St Louis	MO	63103	Donald L Eisenberg	314-421-2182	R	7	0.2
Bost Neckwear Company Inc	PO Box 1065	Asheboro	NC	27204	Don Cox	919-625-6650	R	6	0.1
Zanzara International Ltd	1330 W North Av	Chicago	IL	60622	Joseph Farinella	312-486-5700	R	5	<0.1
Spiegel Neckwear Company Inc	350 5th Av	New York	NY	10118	F Spiegel	212-563-3360	R	5	0.1
A Schreter and Sons Inc	600 S Pulaski St	Baltimore	MD	21223	William Kerch	410-945-3600	S	4*	0.1
Ralph Marlin and Company Inc	PO Box 999	Hartland	WI	53029	Mark Abramoff	414-369-8800	R	4*	<0.1
Brown and Church Co	PO Drawer AJ	Pilot Mountain	NC	27041	Larry Marshall	919-368-5502	S	3	<0.1
Hudson Neckware Company Inc	36 E 31st St	New York	NY	10016	William Berger	212-689-3244	R	3	<0.1
Charles W Kamil and Son Inc	4310 23rd St	Long Island Ct	NY	11101	Gerald Horowitz	718-729-0074	R	1*	<0.1
Fashion Point Accessories Inc	42 W 39th St 8th Fl	New York	NY	10018	Charles Junger	212-921-5934	R	1*	<0.1
MBP Neckwear Inc	240 Madison Av	New York	NY	10016	Mel Cohen	212-808-9777	R	1*	<0.1
Salem Neckwear Corp	PO Box 38	Randleman	NC	27317	Jim Trogdon	910-498-2022	R	1*	<0.1
Nasett International Corp	693 5th Av	New York	NY	10022	Toshiya Takahashi	212-758-0024	R	1*	<0.1
Park Lane Neckwear Inc	109 E 38th St	New York	NY	10016	Ted Lazarus	212-679-6040	S	1*	<0.1
Ack-Ti-Linings Inc	210 Madison 6th Fl	New York	NY	10016	Allan Lerner	212-684-6990	S	1*	<0.1
Philip Klein Neckwear Inc	19 W 26th St	New York	NY	10010	Joseph Klein	212-684-7632	R	1	<0.1
Steven Krauss Menswear Cies	5645 Park Oak Pl	Los Angeles	CA	90068	Steven J Krauss	213-464-5316	R	0*	<0.1

Source: *Ward's Business Directory of U.S. Private and Public Companies*, Volumes 1 and 2, 1996. The company type code used is as follows: P - Public, R - Private, S - Subsidiary, D - Division, J - Joint Venture, A - Affiliate, G - Group. Sales are in millions of dollars, employees are in thousands. An asterisk (*) indicates an estimated sales volume. The symbol < stands for 'less than'. Company names and addresses are truncated, in some cases, to fit into the available space.

MATERIALS CONSUMED

Material	Quantity	Delivered Cost ($ million)
Materials, ingredients, containers, and supplies	(X)	242.0
Broadwoven fabrics (piece goods)	(X)	150.0
Narrow fabrics (12 inches or less in width)	(X)	36.1
Knit fabrics	(X)	2.8
Yarn, all fibers	(X)	(D)
Finished leather	(X)	(D)
Buttons, zippers, and slide fasteners	(X)	(D)
All other materials and components, parts, containers, and supplies	(X)	18.9
Materials, ingredients, containers, and supplies, nsk	(X)	31.6

Source: 1992 *Economic Census*. Explanation of symbols used: (D): Withheld to avoid disclosure of competitive data; na: Not available; (S): Withheld because statistical norms were not met; (X): Not applicable; (Z): Less than half the unit shown; nec: Not elsewhere classified; nsk: Not specified by kind; - : zero; * : 10-19 percent estimated; ** : 20-29 percent estimated.

PRODUCT SHARE DETAILS

Product or Product Class	% Share
Men's and boys' neckwear	100.00
Neckties made from woven fabrics (including prints), all silk	62.18
Neckties made from woven fabrics (including prints), all polyester	13.54
Neckties made from woven fabrics (including prints), all other fabrics (including blends)	8.93
All other men's and boys' neckwear (including leather neckties and knit or woven mufflers and scarves)	1.59

Source: 1992 *Economic Census*. The values shown are percent of total shipments in an industry. Values of indented subcategories are summed in the main heading. The symbol (D) appears when data are withheld to prevent disclosure of competitive information. The abbreviation nsk stands for 'not specified by kind' and nec for 'not elsewhere classified'.

INPUTS AND OUTPUTS FOR APPAREL MADE FROM PURCHASED MATERIALS

Economic Sector or Industry Providing Inputs	%	Sector	Economic Sector or Industry Buying Outputs	%	Sector
Imports	29.1	Foreign	Personal consumption expenditures	82.7	
Broadwoven fabric mills	20.2	Manufg.	Apparel made from purchased materials	12.0	Manufg.
Apparel made from purchased materials	18.3	Manufg.	Exports	1.5	Foreign
Knit fabric mills	8.6	Manufg.	Federal Government purchases, national defense	0.9	Fed Govt
Wholesale trade	3.8	Trade	S/L Govt. purch., correction	0.5	S/L Govt
Advertising	2.4	Services	Pleating & stitching	0.3	Manufg.
Yarn mills & finishing of textiles, nec	1.4	Manufg.	Knit outerwear mills	0.2	Manufg.
Pleating & stitching	1.1	Manufg.	Hospitals	0.2	Services
Banking	1.1	Fin/R.E.	Laundry, dry cleaning, shoe repair	0.2	Services
Petroleum refining	1.0	Manufg.	S/L Govt. purch., health & hospitals	0.2	S/L Govt
Electric services (utilities)	1.0	Util.	Portrait, photographic studios	0.1	Services
Automotive & apparel trimmings	0.9	Manufg.	S/L Govt. purch., public assistance & relief	0.1	S/L Govt
Needles, pins, & fasteners	0.8	Manufg.			
Thread mills	0.7	Manufg.			
Communications, except radio & TV	0.7	Util.			
Eating & drinking places	0.7	Trade			
U.S. Postal Service	0.7	Gov't			
Leather tanning & finishing	0.5	Manufg.			
Narrow fabric mills	0.5	Manufg.			
Schiffli machine embroideries	0.4	Manufg.			
Motor freight transportation & warehousing	0.4	Util.			
Real estate	0.4	Fin/R.E.			
Royalties	0.4	Fin/R.E.			
Forestry products	0.3	Agric.			
Buttons	0.3	Manufg.			
Paperboard containers & boxes	0.3	Manufg.			
Air transportation	0.3	Util.			
Maintenance of nonfarm buildings nec	0.2	Constr.			
Lace goods	0.2	Manufg.			
Gas production & distribution (utilities)	0.2	Util.			
Automotive rental & leasing, without drivers	0.2	Services			
Electrical repair shops	0.2	Services			
Equipment rental & leasing services	0.2	Services			
Legal services	0.2	Services			
Management & consulting services & labs	0.2	Services			
Artificial trees & flowers	0.1	Manufg.			
Insurance carriers	0.1	Fin/R.E.			
Accounting, auditing & bookkeeping	0.1	Services			
Automotive repair shops & services	0.1	Services			

Source: Benchmark Input-Output Accounts for the U.S. Economy, 1982, U.S. Department of Commerce, Washington, D.C., July 1991. Data, as reported in the source, are organized by the 1977 SIC structure in use in 1982 but have been matched, as closely as is possible, to the 1987 SIC structure used in this book.

OCCUPATIONS EMPLOYED BY SIC 232 - APPAREL

Occupation	% of Total 1994	Change to 2005	Occupation	% of Total 1994	Change to 2005
Sewing machine operators, garment	56.1	-33.1	Cutters & trimmers, hand	1.7	-24.8
Inspectors, testers, & graders, precision	3.5	-16.4	Patternmakers, layout workers, fabric & apparel	1.5	25.4
Blue collar worker supervisors	3.0	-24.0	General managers & top executives	1.4	-20.7
Assemblers, fabricators, & hand workers nec	2.5	-16.4	Sewing machine operators, non-garment	1.3	-37.3
Pressing machine operators, textiles	2.4	-45.7	Helpers, laborers, & material movers nec	1.1	-16.4
Hand packers & packagers	2.0	-21.2	Industrial machinery mechanics	1.1	0.3
Freight, stock, & material movers, hand	1.8	-33.1	Pressers, hand	1.1	-58.2
Traffic, shipping, & receiving clerks	1.8	-19.6	Sewers, hand	1.0	-10.7

Source: *Industry-Occupation Matrix*, Bureau of Labor Statistics. These data relate to one or more 3-digit SIC industry groups rather than to a single 4-digit SIC. The change reported for each occupation to the year 2005 is a percent of growth or decline as estimated by the Bureau of Labor Statistics. The abbreviation nec stands for 'not elsewhere classified'.

LOCATION BY STATE AND REGIONAL CONCENTRATION

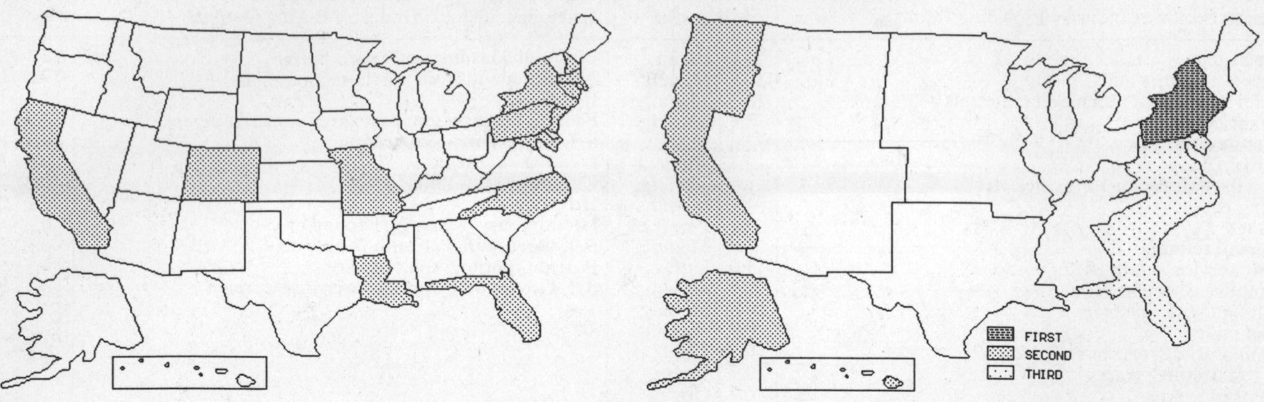

INDUSTRY DATA BY STATE

State	Establish-ments	Shipments			Employment				Cost as % of Shipments	Investment per Employee ($)
		Total ($ mil)	% of U.S.	Per Establ.	Total Number	% of U.S.	Per Establ.	Wages ($/hour)		
New York	57	225.8	36.5	4.0	2,400	32.0	42	8.38	55.5	542
California	19	177.6	28.7	9.3	1,500	20.0	79	8.06	48.9	1,400
North Carolina	8	41.2	6.7	5.2	800	10.7	100	5.38	46.4	1,125
Pennsylvania	8	12.5	2.0	1.6	200	2.7	25	7.00	36.0	-
New Jersey	6	6.5	1.1	1.1	200	2.7	33	6.75	30.8	-
Massachusetts	6	(D)	-	-	175 *	2.3	29	-	-	-
Connecticut	5	(D)	-	-	175 *	2.3	35	-	-	-
Florida	4	(D)	-	-	175 *	2.3	44	-	-	-
Louisiana	4	(D)	-	-	750 *	10.0	188	-	-	-
Colorado	3	(D)	-	-	175 *	2.3	58	-	-	-
Maryland	3	(D)	-	-	175 *	2.3	58	-	-	-
Missouri	2	(D)	-	-	375 *	5.0	188	-	-	-
New Hampshire	1	(D)	-	-	175 *	2.3	175	-	-	-

Source: 1992 *Economic Census*. The states are in descending order of shipments or establishments (if shipment data are missing for the majority). The symbol (D) appears when data are withheld to prevent disclosure of competitive information. States marked with (D) are sorted by number of establishments. A dash (-) indicates that the data element cannot be calculated; * indicates the midpoint of a range.

2325 - MEN'S & BOYS' TROUSERS AND SLACKS

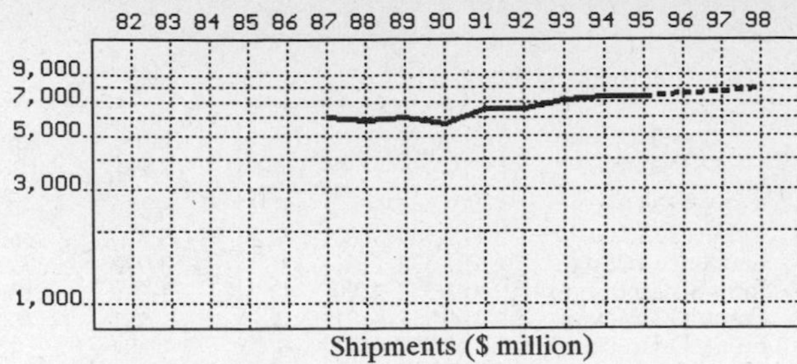

Shipments ($ million)

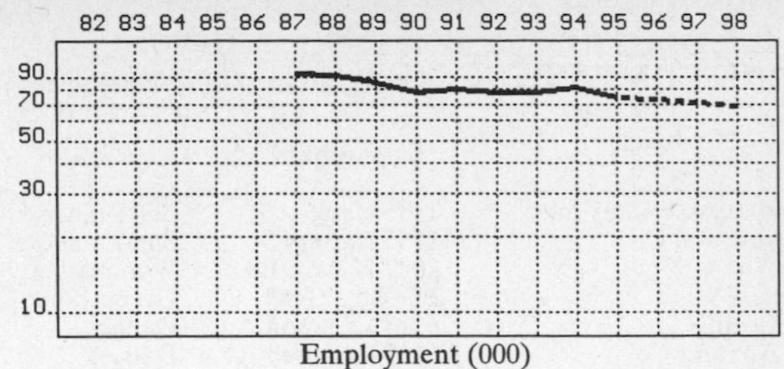

Employment (000)

GENERAL STATISTICS

Year	Com-panies	Establishments		Employment			Compensation		Production ($ million)			
		Total	with 20 or more employees	Total (000)	Production Workers (000)	Production Hours (Mil)	Payroll ($ mil)	Wages ($/hr)	Cost of Materials	Value Added by Manufacture	Value of Shipments	Capital Invest.
1982												
1983												
1984												
1985												
1986												
1987	312	484	413	93.3	82.3	145.6	1,102.5	5.88	2,742.8	3,273.2	6,013.6	74.5
1988		475	403	91.9	80.8	139.3	1,129.6	6.26	2,659.6	3,108.1	5,767.3	
1989		449	379	86.0	76.7	136.9	1,106.9	6.17	2,596.8	3,440.5	5,983.0	50.1
1990		428	356	78.0	71.6	122.7	1,024.4	6.43	2,546.4	3,016.7	5,657.3	60.9
1991		410	336	80.5	70.8	127.6	1,038.8	6.36	2,970.6	3,495.4	6,466.8	60.9
1992	278	424	360	78.3	69.2	128.4	1,098.5	6.86	2,843.7	3,644.0	6,489.7	92.0
1993		434	343	78.5	68.4	128.3	1,188.2	7.15	3,229.3	3,905.2	7,054.8	92.9
1994		402P	322P	82.2	71.9	132.0	1,223.3	7.03	3,191.7	4,068.0	7,225.7	82.4
1995		391P	309P	74.7P	65.5P	123.4P	1,174.4P	7.29P	3,205.3P	4,085.3P	7,256.5P	
1996		381P	297P	72.8P	63.6P	121.4P	1,187.9P	7.47P	3,296.0P	4,201.0P	7,461.9P	
1997		371P	285P	70.8P	61.7P	119.4P	1,201.3P	7.64P	3,386.7P	4,316.6P	7,667.2P	
1998		360P	273P	68.8P	59.8P	117.3P	1,214.7P	7.81P	3,477.5P	4,432.2P	7,872.6P	

Sources: 1982, 1987, 1992 *Economic Census*; *Annual Survey of Manufactures*, 83-86, 88-91, 93-94. Establishment counts for non-Census years are from *County Business Patterns*; establishment values for 83-84 are extrapolations. 'P's show projections by the editors. Industries reclassified in 87 will not have data for prior years.

INDICES OF CHANGE

Year	Com-panies	Establishments		Employment			Compensation		Production ($ million)			
		Total	with 20 or more employees	Total (000)	Production Workers (000)	Production Hours (Mil)	Payroll ($ mil)	Wages ($/hr)	Cost of Materials	Value Added by Manufacture	Value of Shipments	Capital Invest.
1982												
1983												
1984												
1985												
1986												
1987	112	114	115	119	119	113	100	86	96	90	93	81
1988		112	112	117	117	108	103	91	94	85	89	
1989		106	105	110	111	107	101	90	91	94	92	54
1990		101	99	100	103	96	93	94	90	83	87	66
1991		97	93	103	102	99	95	93	104	96	100	66
1992	100	100	100	100	100	100	100	100	100	100	100	100
1993		102	95	100	99	100	108	104	114	107	109	101
1994		95P	89P	105	104	103	111	102	112	112	111	90
1995		92P	86P	95P	95P	96P	107P	106P	113P	112P	112P	
1996		90P	83P	93P	92P	95P	108P	109P	116P	115P	115P	
1997		87P	79P	90P	89P	93P	109P	111P	119P	118P	118P	
1998		85P	76P	88P	86P	91P	111P	114P	122P	122P	121P	

Sources: Same as General Statistics. Values reflect change from the base year, 1992. Values above 100 mean greater than 92, values below 100 mean less than 92, and a value of 100 in the 82-91 or 93-98 period means same as 92. 'P's mark projections by the editors.

SELECTED RATIOS

For 1994	Avg. of All Manufact.	Analyzed Industry	Index	For 1994	Avg. of All Manufact.	Analyzed Industry	Index
Employees per Establishment	49	205	417	Value Added per Production Worker	134,084	56,579	42
Payroll per Establishment	1,500,273	3,044,117	203	Cost per Establishment	5,045,178	7,942,375	157
Payroll per Employee	30,620	14,882	49	Cost per Employee	102,970	38,828	38
Production Workers per Establishment	34	179	521	Cost per Production Worker	146,988	44,391	30
Wages per Establishment	853,319	2,309,179	271	Shipments per Establishment	9,576,895	17,980,768	188
Wages per Production Worker	24,861	12,906	52	Shipments per Employee	195,460	87,904	45
Hours per Production Worker	2,056	1,836	89	Shipments per Production Worker	279,017	100,497	36
Wages per Hour	12.09	7.03	58	Investment per Establishment	321,011	205,048	64
Value Added per Establishment	4,602,255	10,123,000	220	Investment per Employee	6,552	1,002	15
Value Added per Employee	93,930	49,489	53	Investment per Production Worker	9,352	1,146	12

Sources: Same as General Statistics. The 'Average of All Manufacturing' column represents the average of all manufacturing industries reported for the most recent complete year available. The Index shows the relationship between the Average and the Analyzed Industry. For example, 100 means that they are equal; 500 that the Analyzed Industry is five times the average; 50 means that the Analyzed Industry is half the national average. The abbreviation 'na' is used to show that data are 'not available'.

LEADING COMPANIES Number shown: **68** Total sales ($ mil): **21,193** Total employment (000): **211.5**

Company Name	Address				CEO Name	Phone	Co. Type	Sales ($ mil)	Empl. (000)
Levi Strauss Associates Inc	1155 Battery St	San Francisco	CA	94111	Robert D Haas	415-544-6000	R	6,100	36.0
Levi Strauss and Co	1155 Battery St	San Francisco	CA	94111	Robert D Haas	415-544-6000	S	5,890	36.0
VF Corp	1047 N Park Rd	Wyomissing	PA	19610	Lawrence R Pugh	610-378-1151	P	4,972	72.2
Wrangler	PO Box 21488	Greensboro	NC	27420	John Schamberger	919-373-3400	D	1,000	13.0
Haggar Corp	6113 Lemmon Av	Dallas	TX	75209	Frank D Bracken	214-352-8481	P	491	6.4
Haggar Apparel Co	6113 Lemmon Av	Dallas	TX	75209	Frank D Bracken	214-352-8481	S	394	4.5
Williamson-Dickie Mfg Co	PO Box 1779	Fort Worth	TX	76101	Steven Lefler	817-336-7201	R	370	4.0
Jordache Enterprises Inc	226 W 37th St	New York	NY	10018	Joseph Nakash	212-643-8400	R	280*	3.0
Farah Inc	8889 Gateway W	El Paso	TX	79925	Richard C Allender	915-593-4444	P	243	6.0
Glen Oaks Industries Inc	16 E 34th St	New York	NY	10016	Milton Askinas	212-679-9020	R	140*	1.5
Flynn Enterprises Inc	PO Box 1047	Hopkinsville	KY	42241	Bill Flynn	502-886-0223	R	100*	1.8
HealthTex Inc	PO Box 21488	Greensboro	NC	27420	Gary Simmons	910-316-1000	S	100	1.5
Chic By HIS Inc	1372 Broadway	New York	NY	10018	Roland F Luehers	212-302-6400	R	86	5.0
Thomson Co	1114 Av of Amer	New York	NY	10036	Steven Leslie	212-221-7500	S	84	1.0
Europe Craft Imports Inc	475 5th Av	New York	NY	10016	Ed Wachtel	212-686-5050	R	70	0.2
Glenn Enterprises Inc	PO Box 188	Sulligent	AL	35586	Coy F Glenn	205-698-9125	R	70	2.4
Trans-Apparel Group	PO Box 700	Michigan City	IN	46360	R Royden Ricks	219-879-7341	S	64	1.9
American Trouser Inc	PO Box 391	Columbus	MS	39703	Daniel Berry	601-328-1556	R	60	1.0
Hagale Industries Inc	PO Box 190	Ozark	MO	65721	JA Hagale	417-581-2351	R	47	1.3
Elder Manufacturing Co	PO Box 273	St Louis	MO	63166	Ron Sher	314-469-1120	R	42	0.4
Reed Manufacturing Company	PO Box 650	Tupelo	MS	38801	Edward Nelson	601-842-4472	R	40*	1.0
Oxford of Luverne Inc	PO Box 312	Luverne	AL	36049	Henry G Edwards	205-335-6561	D	33*	0.4
Glenn's All-American Sportswear	PO Box 188	Sulligent	AL	35586	Coy Glenn	205-698-9125	S	31*	1.1
Mannor Corp	PO Box 669	Bay Minette	AL	36507	Norman Feinberg	205-937-6767	R	30	0.7
Barrow Manufacturing Company	PO Box 460	Winder	GA	30680	WH Jennings Jr	404-867-2121	R	28*	0.3
Jonbil Inc	1350 Broadway	New York	NY	10018	Herbert M Winkler	212-594-2051	R	28	0.7
Marietta Sportswear Co	300 NE 6th St	Marietta	OK	73448	Milton Askinas	405-276-3376	D	28*	0.3
Shorebreak	4000 Ruffin Rd	San Diego	CA	92123	Douglas Tudor	619-565-7158	R	23	0.3
E-Town Sportswear Corp	Drawer E	Elizabethtown	KY	42701	Don Osborne	502-769-3361	S	21	0.4
Jay Garment Co	PO Box 907	Portland	IN	47371	John G Young	219-726-7151	R	18*	0.4
Master Casualwear	Hwy 51 S	Ripley	TN	38063	CR Hargett	901-635-9415	D	18	0.2
Albert Given Manufacturing Co	1301 W Chicago	East Chicago	IN	46312	J R Wickemeyer	219-397-3200	D	16	0.3
Stephenson Enterprises Inc	PO Box 98	Folkston	GA	31537	NH Stephenson	912-496-7355	R	16*	0.2
Dozier Manufacturing Company	PO Box 97	Dozier	AL	36028	Nathaniel Wright	205-496-3852	R	15*	0.2
Sierra Pacific Apparel Company	1120 N Santa Fe	Visalia	CA	93292	Jeffrey Paul	209-732-8707	R	15	0.3
Gips Manufacturing Company	PO Box 100	Hartwell	GA	30643	Scott Hardigree	706-376-8001	R	14*	0.2
HPH Apparel Manufacturing Co	136 Indrial Pk Rd	Piney Flats	TN	37686	HP Hendrickson	615-538-7159	R	14*	0.2
Paris Manufacturing Co	Maple & Elm Sts	Paris	AR	72855	Mark A Fogley	501-963-2182	R	14*	0.2
Berle Manufacturing Company	PO Box 71445	Charleston	SC	29415	H Berlinsky	803-744-4213	R	13	0.3
Taylor Togs Inc	PO Box 180	Micaville	NC	28755	Grier A Lackey	704-675-4153	R	12	0.5
Big J Apparel Inc	PO Box 3368	Waco	TX	76707	C Jack Tucker	817-754-5487	R	11*	0.1
McCoy Manufacturing Inc	PO Box 188	Sulligent	AL	35586	CF Glenn	205-698-9125	S	11*	0.4
HR Kaminsky and Sons Inc	136 Bowen's Mill	Fitzgerald	GA	31750	Larry E Kaminsky	912-423-4396	R	10	0.3
Reidbord Brothers Company Inc	5000 Baum Blv	Pittsburgh	PA	15213	MS Reidbord	412-687-3000	R	10*	0.5
W and J Rives Inc	PO Box 1761	High Point	NC	27261	Jeff Rives	919-434-4181	R	10	0.2
Apparel Brands Inc	602 S Marcus St	Wrightsville	GA	31096	W Jack Brinson	912-864-3342	R	9	0.3
Continental Apparel Mfg	PO Box 1426	De Funiak Sp	FL	32433	Janusz R Janczewski	904-892-2161	R	9*	0.2
Franklin Sportswear Inc	PO Box 99	Canon	GA	30520	Walter Brown	706-245-7366	R	9	0.1
M and W Sportswear Co	PO Box 8	Sycamore	GA	31790	Ben E Walker	912-567-3433	R	9*	<0.1
Reed Manufacturing Company	Rte 5	Fulton	MS	38843	Jerry Brady	601-862-9717	D	9*	0.1
Vernon Manufacturing Co	PO Box 339	Vernon	AL	35592	Excene Cantrell	205-695-7126	S	9*	0.2
Glenn Slacks	PO Box 517	Bruce	MS	38915	Robert Smith	601-983-4335	D	8	0.4
DeWitt Apparel Inc	PO Box 538	Uniontown	AL	36786	JD Shivers	205-628-2141	R	8	0.2
IC Isaacs and Co Newton Co	300 N Newton Av	Newton	MS	39345	Gary Brashers	601-683-2011	D	6*	0.2
Summer Manufacturing Co	447 Hwy 51 N	Winona	MS	38967	Herbert Summers	601-283-1372	R	6*	<0.1
Hagale Manufacturing Co	179 George St	Marshfield	MO	65706	Robert Heins	417-859-4432	D	4*	0.1
South Monroe Sportswear Inc	PO Box 117	Hamilton	MS	39746	Billy Ogden	601-343-8369	R	4	<0.1
R and R Manufacturing	PO Box 49	Auburn	GA	30203	John E Withers	404-963-4846	R	3	0.2
Solomon Company Inc	PO Box 6	Leeds	AL	35094	A Solomon	205-699-2221	R	3*	0.2
Superior Garment Company Inc	24 Windlawn Av	Winder	GA	30680	RD Maxwell	404-867-2178	R	3*	<0.1
WPM Manufacturing Company	PO Box 667	Monticello	KY	42633	Michael D Blevins	606-348-9215	R	3	0.2
Fine Vines Inc	PO Box 873	Greenville	MS	38701	Hal Hall	601-378-9224	S	3	0.2
Kalikow Brothers Inc	34 W 33rd St	New York	NY	10001	Norman Kalikow	212-643-0315	R	2*	<0.1
Magliano Pants Co	PO Box 6846	Cincinnati	OH	45206	Luis Magliano Jr	513-961-5164	R	2*	<0.1
Castlewood Apparel Corp	350 5th Av	New York	NY	10118	Henry Sutton	212-564-3600	R	1*	<0.1
Sergio Valente	1450 Broadway	New York	NY	10018	Leo Zelkin	212-398-2222	D	1*	<0.1
Southland Manufacturing	PO Box 457	Ashland	AL	36251	Don Adams	205-354-2172	R	1	0.1
Pawnee Pants Manufacturing	101-105 Lackawanna	Olyphant	PA	18447	Louis A Bisignani	717-489-7544	R	1*	0.1

Source: *Ward's Business Directory of U.S. Private and Public Companies*, Volumes 1 and 2, 1996. The company type code used is as follows: P - Public, R - Private, S - Subsidiary, D - Division, J - Joint Venture, A - Affiliate, G - Group. Sales are in millions of dollars, employees are in thousands. An asterisk (*) indicates an estimated sales volume. The symbol < stands for 'less than'. Company names and addresses are truncated, in some cases, to fit into the available space.

MATERIALS CONSUMED

Material	Quantity	Delivered Cost ($ million)
Materials, ingredients, containers, and supplies	(X)	1,969.9
Broadwoven fabrics (piece goods)	(X)	1,539.3
Narrow fabrics (12 inches or less in width)	(X)	61.6
Knit fabrics	(X)	55.9
Yarn, all fibers	(X)	43.7
Buttons, zippers, and slide fasteners	(X)	45.6
All other materials and components, parts, containers, and supplies	(X)	187.7
Materials, ingredients, containers, and supplies, nsk	(X)	36.3

Source: 1992 *Economic Census*. Explanation of symbols used: (D): Withheld to avoid disclosure of competitive data; na: Not available; (S): Withheld because statistical norms were not met; (X): Not applicable; (Z): Less than half the unit shown; nec: Not elsewhere classified; nsk: Not specified by kind; - : zero; * : 10-19 percent estimated; ** : 20-29 percent estimated.

PRODUCT SHARE DETAILS

Product or Product Class	% Share
Men's and boys' trousers and slacks	100.00
Men's and boys' separate dress and sport trousers, pants, and slacks (including military-type uniform pants), excluding jeans	25.52
Men's and boys' jeans (including dungarees and jean-cut casual slacks)	63.76
Receipts for contract and commission work on men's and boys' trousers and slacks	10.37
Receipts for contract and commission work on men's and boys' trousers and slacks	99.82
Receipts for contract and commission work on men's and boys' trousers and slacks, nsk	0.19
Men's and boys' trousers and slacks, nsk	0.35

Source: 1992 *Economic Census*. The values shown are percent of total shipments in an industry. Values of indented subcategories are summed in the main heading. The symbol (D) appears when data are withheld to prevent disclosure of competitive information. The abbreviation nsk stands for 'not specified by kind' and nec for 'not elsewhere classified'.

INPUTS AND OUTPUTS FOR APPAREL MADE FROM PURCHASED MATERIALS

Economic Sector or Industry Providing Inputs	%	Sector	Economic Sector or Industry Buying Outputs	%	Sector
Imports	29.1	Foreign	Personal consumption expenditures	82.7	
Broadwoven fabric mills	20.2	Manufg.	Apparel made from purchased materials	12.0	Manufg.
Apparel made from purchased materials	18.3	Manufg.	Exports	1.5	Foreign
Knit fabric mills	8.6	Manufg.	Federal Government purchases, national defense	0.9	Fed Govt
Wholesale trade	3.8	Trade	S/L Govt. purch., correction	0.5	S/L Govt
Advertising	2.4	Services	Pleating & stitching	0.3	Manufg.
Yarn mills & finishing of textiles, nec	1.4	Manufg.	Knit outerwear mills	0.2	Manufg.
Pleating & stitching	1.1	Manufg.	Hospitals	0.2	Services
Banking	1.1	Fin/R.E.	Laundry, dry cleaning, shoe repair	0.2	Services
Petroleum refining	1.0	Manufg.	S/L Govt. purch., health & hospitals	0.2	S/L Govt
Electric services (utilities)	1.0	Util.	Portrait, photographic studios	0.1	Services
Automotive & apparel trimmings	0.9	Manufg.	S/L Govt. purch., public assistance & relief	0.1	S/L Govt
Needles, pins, & fasteners	0.8	Manufg.			
Thread mills	0.7	Manufg.			
Communications, except radio & TV	0.7	Util.			
Eating & drinking places	0.7	Trade			
U.S. Postal Service	0.7	Gov't			
Leather tanning & finishing	0.5	Manufg.			
Narrow fabric mills	0.5	Manufg.			
Schiffli machine embroideries	0.4	Manufg.			
Motor freight transportation & warehousing	0.4	Util.			
Real estate	0.4	Fin/R.E.			
Royalties	0.4	Fin/R.E.			
Forestry products	0.3	Agric.			
Buttons	0.3	Manufg.			
Paperboard containers & boxes	0.3	Manufg.			
Air transportation	0.3	Util.			
Maintenance of nonfarm buildings nec	0.2	Constr.			
Lace goods	0.2	Manufg.			
Gas production & distribution (utilities)	0.2	Util.			
Automotive rental & leasing, without drivers	0.2	Services			
Electrical repair shops	0.2	Services			
Equipment rental & leasing services	0.2	Services			
Legal services	0.2	Services			
Management & consulting services & labs	0.2	Services			
Artificial trees & flowers	0.1	Manufg.			
Insurance carriers	0.1	Fin/R.E.			
Accounting, auditing & bookkeeping	0.1	Services			
Automotive repair shops & services	0.1	Services			

Source: *Benchmark Input-Output Accounts for the U.S. Economy, 1982*, U.S. Department of Commerce, Washington, D.C., July 1991. Data, as reported in the source, are organized by the 1977 SIC structure in use in 1982 but have been matched, as closely as is possible, to the 1987 SIC structure used in this book.

OCCUPATIONS EMPLOYED BY SIC 232 - APPAREL

Occupation	% of Total 1994	Change to 2005	Occupation	% of Total 1994	Change to 2005
Sewing machine operators, garment	56.1	-33.1	Cutters & trimmers, hand	1.7	-24.8
Inspectors, testers, & graders, precision	3.5	-16.4	Patternmakers, layout workers, fabric & apparel	1.5	25.4
Blue collar worker supervisors	3.0	-24.0	General managers & top executives	1.4	-20.7
Assemblers, fabricators, & hand workers nec	2.5	-16.4	Sewing machine operators, non-garment	1.3	-37.3
Pressing machine operators, textiles	2.4	-45.7	Helpers, laborers, & material movers nec	1.1	-16.4
Hand packers & packagers	2.0	-21.2	Industrial machinery mechanics	1.1	0.3
Freight, stock, & material movers, hand	1.8	-33.1	Pressers, hand	1.1	-58.2
Traffic, shipping, & receiving clerks	1.8	-19.6	Sewers, hand	1.0	-10.7

Source: *Industry-Occupation Matrix*, Bureau of Labor Statistics. These data relate to one or more 3-digit SIC industry groups rather than to a single 4-digit SIC. The change reported for each occupation to the year 2005 is a percent of growth or decline as estimated by the Bureau of Labor Statistics. The abbreviation nec stands for 'not elsewhere classified'.

LOCATION BY STATE AND REGIONAL CONCENTRATION

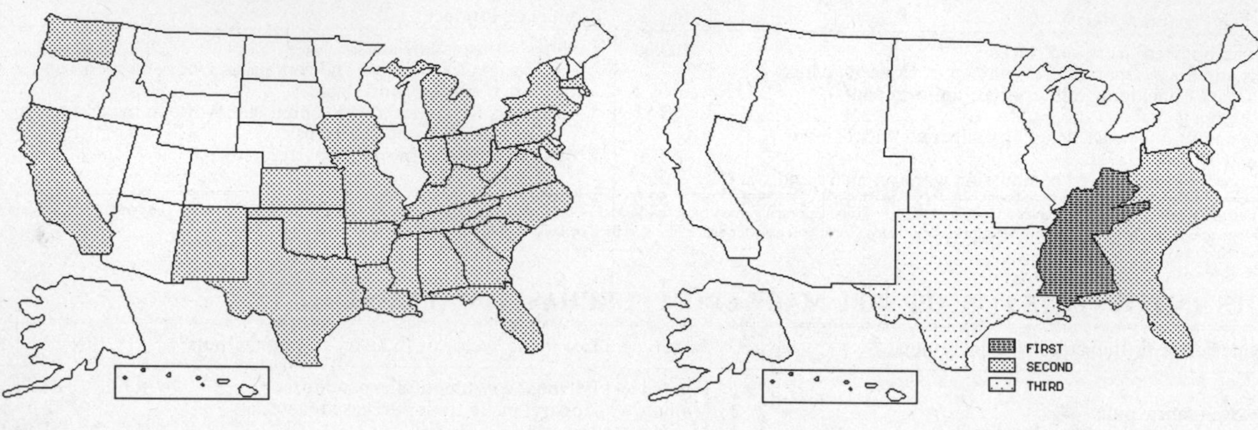

INDUSTRY DATA BY STATE

State	Establish-ments	Shipments: Total ($ mil)	Shipments: % of U.S.	Shipments: Per Establ.	Employment: Total Number	Employment: % of U.S.	Employment: Per Establ.	Employment: Wages ($/hour)	Cost as % of Shipments	Investment per Employee ($)
Texas	40	1,709.3	26.3	42.7	15,400	19.7	385	7.47	39.6	1,123
Tennessee	31	612.8	9.4	19.8	8,300	10.6	268	6.94	29.8	964
Georgia	52	388.8	6.0	7.5	8,200	10.5	158	6.39	34.7	756
Alabama	33	365.6	5.6	11.1	8,400	10.7	255	6.39	36.9	917
North Carolina	13	270.4	4.2	20.8	2,300	2.9	177	7.25	40.0	1,217
Virginia	9	214.0	3.3	23.8	2,700	3.4	300	6.81	52.1	-
Mississippi	27	186.4	2.9	6.9	5,600	7.2	207	6.03	38.3	554
Kentucky	25	160.4	2.5	6.4	4,600	5.9	184	6.71	40.2	478
Arkansas	11	150.5	2.3	13.7	3,000	3.8	273	6.84	33.0	-
New York	23	127.5	2.0	5.5	800	1.0	35	8.00	56.5	1,375
Pennsylvania	21	105.2	1.6	5.0	1,600	2.0	76	8.91	36.8	313
Florida	14	103.3	1.6	7.4	1,500	1.9	107	5.78	52.6	667
Missouri	17	87.9	1.4	5.2	3,400	4.3	200	6.72	28.9	618
Massachusetts	3	31.1	0.5	10.4	500	0.6	167	7.44	32.2	400
Louisiana	5	23.8	0.4	4.8	1,000	1.3	200	5.94	33.2	-
California	50	(D)	-	-	3,750 *	4.8	75	-	-	453
Oklahoma	8	(D)	-	-	1,750 *	2.2	219	-	-	-
Indiana	5	(D)	-	-	1,750 *	2.2	350	-	-	-
Iowa	4	(D)	-	-	750 *	1.0	188	-	-	-
South Carolina	4	(D)	-	-	375 *	0.5	94	-	-	-
Washington	4	(D)	-	-	375 *	0.5	94	-	-	-
West Virginia	4	(D)	-	-	750 *	1.0	188	-	-	-
Maryland	3	(D)	-	-	175 *	0.2	58	-	-	-
Ohio	3	(D)	-	-	375 *	0.5	125	-	-	-
Michigan	2	(D)	-	-	175 *	0.2	88	-	-	-
New Mexico	2	(D)	-	-	1,750 *	2.2	875	-	-	-
Kansas	1	(D)	-	-	175 *	0.2	175	-	-	-

Source: 1992 *Economic Census*. The states are in descending order of shipments or establishments (if shipment data are missing for the majority). The symbol (D) appears when data are withheld to prevent disclosure of competitive information. States marked with (D) are sorted by number of establishments. A dash (-) indicates that the data element cannot be calculated; * indicates the midpoint of a range.

2326 - MEN'S & BOYS' WORK CLOTHING

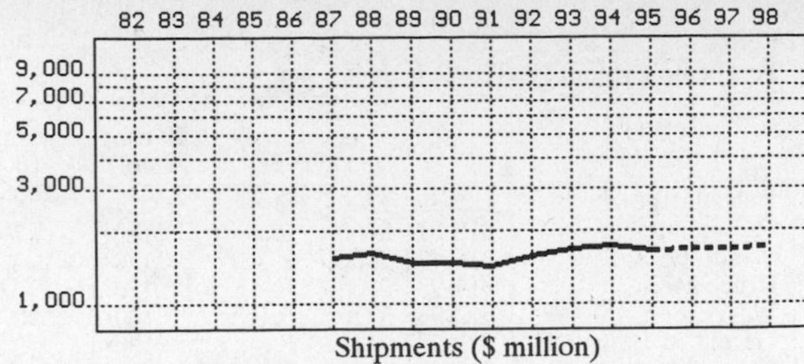

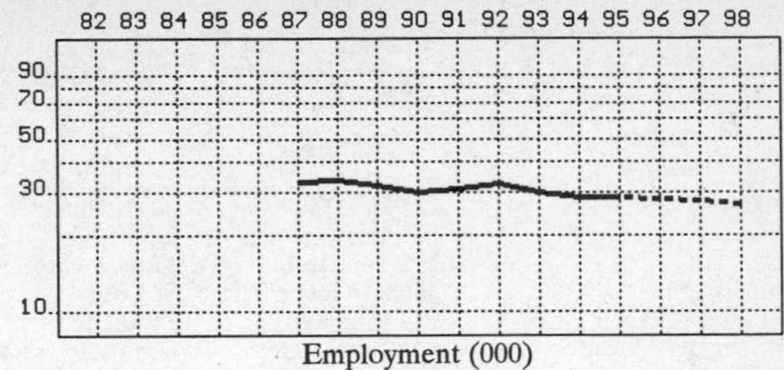

GENERAL STATISTICS

Year	Companies	Establishments		Employment			Compensation		Production ($ million)			
		Total	with 20 or more employees	Total (000)	Production Workers (000)	Production Hours (Mil)	Payroll ($ mil)	Wages ($/hr)	Cost of Materials	Value Added by Manufacture	Value of Shipments	Capital Invest.
1982												
1983												
1984												
1985												
1986												
1987	177	255	191	33.1	29.0	50.9	335.6	5.17	665.1	870.1	1,541.6	14.3
1988		257	198	33.3	29.5	54.5	353.2	5.17	713.9	913.8	1,632.9	
1989		237	192	32.2	30.0	52.3	360.7	5.41	616.5	856.2	1,464.2	17.5
1990		228	189	30.0	27.8	50.6	350.6	5.46	618.9	846.3	1,461.7	19.3
1991		229	185	30.8	27.2	50.0	359.8	5.68	627.2	825.7	1,426.1	18.2
1992	188	284	190	32.6	28.4	52.9	409.6	5.97	708.4	860.3	1,572.5	24.9
1993		275	185	30.0	26.5	47.9	399.1	6.47	762.8	919.9	1,670.1	22.6
1994		267P	184P	28.5	24.4	45.4	378.3	6.49	811.2	933.5	1,714.4	22.6
1995		271P	183P	28.8P	25.0P	46.8P	405.0P	6.67P	781.1P	898.8P	1,650.7P	
1996		275P	181P	28.3P	24.4P	46.0P	413.2P	6.88P	790.6P	909.7P	1,670.8P	
1997		279P	180P	27.7P	23.8P	45.1P	421.3P	7.09P	800.0P	920.7P	1,690.8P	
1998		282P	178P	27.1P	23.2P	44.3P	429.5P	7.30P	809.5P	931.6P	1,710.9P	

Sources: 1982, 1987, 1992 *Economic Census*; *Annual Survey of Manufactures*, 83-86, 88-91, 93-94. Establishment counts for non-Census years are from *County Business Patterns*; establishment values for 83-84 are extrapolations. 'P's show projections by the editors. Industries reclassified in 87 will not have data for prior years.

INDICES OF CHANGE

Year	Companies	Establishments		Employment			Compensation		Production ($ million)			
		Total	with 20 or more employees	Total (000)	Production Workers (000)	Production Hours (Mil)	Payroll ($ mil)	Wages ($/hr)	Cost of Materials	Value Added by Manufacture	Value of Shipments	Capital Invest.
1982												
1983												
1984												
1985												
1986												
1987	94	90	101	102	102	96	82	87	94	101	98	57
1988		90	104	102	104	103	86	87	101	106	104	
1989		83	101	99	106	99	88	91	87	100	93	70
1990		80	99	92	98	96	86	91	87	98	93	78
1991		81	97	94	96	95	88	95	89	96	91	73
1992	100	100	100	100	100	100	100	100	100	100	100	100
1993		97	97	92	93	91	97	108	108	107	106	91
1994		94P	97P	87	86	86	92	109	115	109	109	91
1995		95P	96P	88P	88P	88P	99P	112P	110P	104P	105P	
1996		97P	95P	87P	86P	87P	101P	115P	112P	106P	106P	
1997		98P	95P	85P	84P	85P	103P	119P	113P	107P	108P	
1998		99P	94P	83P	82P	84P	105P	122P	114P	108P	109P	

Sources: Same as General Statistics. Values reflect change from the base year, 1992. Values above 100 mean greater than 92, values below 100 mean less than 92, and a value of 100 in the 82-91 or 93-98 period means same as 92. 'P's mark projections by the editors.

SELECTED RATIOS

For 1994	Avg. of All Manufact.	Analyzed Industry	Index	For 1994	Avg. of All Manufact.	Analyzed Industry	Index
Employees per Establishment	49	107	218	Value Added per Production Worker	134,084	38,258	29
Payroll per Establishment	1,500,273	1,415,339	94	Cost per Establishment	5,045,178	3,034,955	60
Payroll per Employee	30,620	13,274	43	Cost per Employee	102,970	28,463	28
Production Workers per Establishment	34	91	266	Cost per Production Worker	146,988	33,246	23
Wages per Establishment	853,319	1,102,363	129	Shipments per Establishment	9,576,895	6,414,110	67
Wages per Production Worker	24,861	12,076	49	Shipments per Employee	195,460	60,154	31
Hours per Production Worker	2,056	1,861	90	Shipments per Production Worker	279,017	70,262	25
Wages per Hour	12.09	6.49	54	Investment per Establishment	321,011	84,554	26
Value Added per Establishment	4,602,255	3,492,517	76	Investment per Employee	6,552	793	12
Value Added per Employee	93,930	32,754	35	Investment per Production Worker	9,352	926	10

Sources: Same as General Statistics. The 'Average of All Manufacturing' column represents the average of all manufacturing industries reported for the most recent complete year available. The Index shows the relationship between the Average and the Analyzed Industry. For example, 100 means that they are equal; 500 that the Analyzed Industry is five times the average; 50 means that the Analyzed Industry is half the national average. The abbreviation 'na' is used to show that data are 'not available'.

LEADING COMPANIES

Number shown: **51** Total sales ($ mil): **2,002** Total employment (000): **32.1**

Company Name	Address				CEO Name	Phone	Co. Type	Sales ($ mil)	Empl. (000)
Red Kap Industries	PO Box 140995	Nashville	TN	37214	Bob Matthews	615-391-1200	D	424	6.0
Carhartt Inc	PO Box 600	Dearborn	MI	48121	RC Valade	313-271-8460	R	180	2.4
Unitog Co	101 W 11th St	Kansas City	MO	64105	Randolph K Rolf	816-474-7000	P	170	3.2
Todd Uniform Inc	3668 S Geyer Rd	St Louis	MO	63127	Bruce Main	314-984-0365	R	170	3.0
Riverside Manufacturing Co	PO Box 460	Moultrie	GA	31776	WJ Vereen	912-985-5210	R	140*	2.4
Superior Surgical Manufacturing	PO Box 4002	Seminole	FL	34642	Gerald M Benstock	813-397-9611	P	130	2.2
Best Manufacturing Inc	1633 Broadway	New York	NY	10019	Lester Maslow	212-974-1100	R	100*	1.0
Fechheimer Brothers Co	4545 Malsbary Rd	Cincinnati	OH	45242	Richard E Benchley	513-793-5400	S	100*	1.1
Walls Industries Inc	PO Box 98	Cleburne	TX	76031	Albert Archer	817-645-4366	S	70	1.4
American Uniform Co	PO Box 2130	Cleveland	TN	37320	Gary K Smith	615-476-6561	S	60	1.0
Lion Apparel Inc	6450 Poe Av	Dayton	OH	45413	Richard Lapedes	513-898-1949	R	47*	0.8
Ottenheimer and Company Inc	2275 Halfday Rd	Bannockburn	IL	60015	Kenneth A Merlau	708-940-8000	R	35	0.8
Elbeco Inc	PO Box 13099	Reading	PA	19612	Lee H Lurio	215-921-0651	R	33	0.6
JH Rutter-Rex Manufacturing	PO Box 24010	New Orleans	LA	70184	Eugene J Rutter Jr	504-283-7373	R	32*	0.6
United Pioneer Corp	10 W 33rd St	New York	NY	10001	B Braverman	212-279-3931	R	32*	0.6
Rivco	PO Box 460	Moultrie	GA	31768	W Jerry Vereen	912-985-5210	D	31	0.2
Barco of California	350 W Rosecrantz	Gardena	CA	90248	Michael Donner	310-323-7315	R	28	0.3
Garment Corporation	801 W 41st St	Miami	FL	33140	J Shulevitz	305-531-4040	R	27	0.5
Topps Manufacturing Co	PO Box 750	Rochester	IN	46975	LR Elin	219-223-4311	R	15	0.4
Jomac Products Inc	863 Easton Rd	Warrington	PA	18976	WS Colehower	215-343-0800	S	13	0.3
Medline Industries Inc	3927 Miles Pkwy	Pell City	AL	35125	JoAnn Fambrough	205-884-1560	R	13	0.3
Safeguard America Inc	PO Box 1649	Clanton	AL	35045	James Moore	205-755-7710	R	13	0.3
Starke Uniform Mfg Co	PO Box 1150	Starke	FL	32091	Steve Zalman	904-964-5090	D	13*	0.2
Mar-Mac Manufacturing	PO Box 278	McBee	SC	29101	John S McLeod Jr	803-335-8211	R	12	0.3
Melton Shirt Company Inc	56 Harvester Av	Batavia	NY	14020	Monroe A Davidson	716-343-8750	R	11	0.1
Crest Uniform Company Inc	9 W 24th St	New York	NY	10010	Ed Kaye	212-691-4600	R	11*	0.2
Euclid Garment Mfg Co	333 Martinel Dr	Kent	OH	44240	CB Rosenblatt	216-673-7413	R	9	0.1
Polkton Manufacturing Company	PO Box 220	Marshville	NC	28103	HM Efird	704-624-3200	R	8*	0.1
Anson Shirt Co	PO Box 311	Wadesboro	NC	28170	Alice Pegram	704-694-5148	D	7*	<0.1
Amplaco Group Inc	810 E 152nd St	Bronx	NY	10455	Joseph Biff	718-585-4111	R	7	0.1
LC King Manufacturing Co	PO Box 367	Bristol	TN	37621	Jack R King	615-764-5188	R	6	0.1
Ihling Bros Everard Co	2022 Fulford St	Kalamazoo	MI	49001	EL Ihling	616-381-1340	R	6	<0.1
Dickson Industries Inc	2425 Dean Av	Des Moines	IA	50317	Arthur W Dickson	515-262-8061	R	5	<0.1
McGehee Industries Inc	Hwy 65	McGehee	AR	71654	Michael Benstock	501-222-3085	S	5*	0.1
Panhandle Slim	PO Box 162749	Fort Worth	TX	76161	Jeff Hochster	817-625-2841	S	5*	0.1
Werner Works Inc	PO Box 974	Roseburg	OR	97470	Carolyn Werner	503-672-3213	R	5	0.1
Cadet Uniform Supply Co	11113 Penrose St	Sun Valley	CA	91352	William Troy	818-767-8030	R	4	0.1
Doyle Shirt Manufacturing Corp	3965 R Viking	Las Vegas	NV	89121	Robert Roggen	702-737-3383	R	4	0.3
Edmonton Manufacturing Co	210 Industrial Rd	Greensburg	KY	42743	Louis Elin	502-932-4247	S	3*	0.1
Pella Manufacturing Corp	707 E 3rd St	Pella	IA	50219	Sanford Eckerling	515-628-3923	S	3	<0.1
JB Battle Uniform Co	PO Box 24028	Oklahoma City	OK	73124	D Randy Battle	405-232-6431	R	2*	<0.1
Locknane Inc	720 132nd St SW	Everett	WA	98204	Duane R Locknane	206-742-5187	R	2	<0.1
Meyers and Son Manufacturing	202 Jefferson St	Madison	IN	47250	D Meyers	812-265-5421	R	2	<0.1
Mr T's Apparel Inc	PO Box 799	Crystal Springs	MS	39059	Edwin E Tinsley	601-892-2571	R	2	0.1
Atlas Uniform Co	5943 W Lawrence	Chicago	IL	60630	Steven Grys	312-725-1220	R	1*	<0.1
Avon Enterprises Inc	PO Box 216	Avon	SD	57315	Bob Behan	605-286-3232	S	1*	<0.1
Bearden Enterprises Inc	PO Box 419	Bearden	AR	71720	V Epting	501-687-2242	R	1	0.1
Commercial Textiles Inc	510 E 8th Av	Homestead	PA	15120	David Frischman	412-461-4600	R	1	<0.1
Dirt Shirts Co	PO Box 458	Titusville	FL	32781	C Adams	407-267-2919	R	1*	<0.1
Flagstaff Industries Inc	PO Box 1330	Bensalem	PA	19020	Marvin L Pollack	215-638-9662	R	1*	0.1
Peerless Uniform Mfg Co	21600 Lassen St	Chatsworth	CA	91311	Jan Rome	818-341-0700	D	1	<0.1

Source: *Ward's Business Directory of U.S. Private and Public Companies*, Volumes 1 and 2, 1996. The company type code used is as follows: P - Public, R - Private, S - Subsidiary, D - Division, J - Joint Venture, A - Affiliate, G - Group. Sales are in millions of dollars, employees are in thousands. An asterisk (*) indicates an estimated sales volume. The symbol < stands for 'less than'. Company names and addresses are truncated, in some cases, to fit into the available space.

MATERIALS CONSUMED

Material	Quantity	Delivered Cost ($ million)
Materials, ingredients, containers, and supplies	(X)	642.5
Broadwoven fabrics (piece goods)	(X)	465.2
Narrow fabrics (12 inches or less in width)	(X)	13.2
Knit fabrics	(X)	36.8
Yarn, all fibers	(X)	3.6
Buttons, zippers, and slide fasteners	(X)	23.8
All other materials and components, parts, containers, and supplies	(X)	51.7
Materials, ingredients, containers, and supplies, nsk	(X)	48.3

Source: 1992 *Economic Census*. Explanation of symbols used: (D): Withheld to avoid disclosure of competitive data; na: Not available; (S): Withheld because statistical norms were not met; (X): Not applicable; (Z): Less than half the unit shown; nec: Not elsewhere classified; nsk: Not specified by kind; - : zero; * : 10-19 percent estimated; ** : 20-29 percent estimated.

PRODUCT SHARE DETAILS

Product or Product Class	% Share	Product or Product Class	% Share
Men's and boys' work clothing	100.00	slacks	8.06
Men's and boys' work shirts	25.83	Receipts for contract and commission work on men's and boys' work clothing, except jeans and jean-cut casual slacks	99.18
Men's and boys' work clothing, except shirts and jeans, and washable service apparel (work pants, overalls, work jackets, etc.)	64.71	Receipts for contract and commission work on men's and boys' work clothing, nsk	0.82
Receipts for contract and commission work on men's and boys' work clothing, except jeans and jean-cut casual		Men's and boys' work clothing, nsk	1.40

Source: 1992 *Economic Census*. The values shown are percent of total shipments in an industry. Values of indented subcategories are summed in the main heading. The symbol (D) appears when data are withheld to prevent disclosure of competitive information. The abbreviation nsk stands for 'not specified by kind' and nec for 'not elsewhere classified'.

INPUTS AND OUTPUTS FOR APPAREL MADE FROM PURCHASED MATERIALS

Economic Sector or Industry Providing Inputs	%	Sector	Economic Sector or Industry Buying Outputs	%	Sector
Imports	29.1	Foreign	Personal consumption expenditures	82.7	
Broadwoven fabric mills	20.2	Manufg.	Apparel made from purchased materials	12.0	Manufg.
Apparel made from purchased materials	18.3	Manufg.	Exports	1.5	Foreign
Knit fabric mills	8.6	Manufg.	Federal Government purchases, national defense	0.9	Fed Govt
Wholesale trade	3.8	Trade	S/L Govt. purch., correction	0.5	S/L Govt
Advertising	2.4	Services	Pleating & stitching	0.3	Manufg.
Yarn mills & finishing of textiles, nec	1.4	Manufg.	Knit outerwear mills	0.2	Manufg.
Pleating & stitching	1.1	Manufg.	Hospitals	0.2	Services
Banking	1.1	Fin/R.E.	Laundry, dry cleaning, shoe repair	0.2	Services
Petroleum refining	1.0	Manufg.	S/L Govt. purch., health & hospitals	0.2	S/L Govt
Electric services (utilities)	1.0	Util.	Portrait, photographic studios	0.1	Services
Automotive & apparel trimmings	0.9	Manufg.	S/L Govt. purch., public assistance & relief	0.1	S/L Govt
Needles, pins, & fasteners	0.8	Manufg.			
Thread mills	0.7	Manufg.			
Communications, except radio & TV	0.7	Util.			
Eating & drinking places	0.7	Trade			
U.S. Postal Service	0.7	Gov't			
Leather tanning & finishing	0.5	Manufg.			
Narrow fabric mills	0.5	Manufg.			
Schiffli machine embroideries	0.4	Manufg.			
Motor freight transportation & warehousing	0.4	Util.			
Real estate	0.4	Fin/R.E.			
Royalties	0.4	Fin/R.E.			
Forestry products	0.3	Agric.			
Buttons	0.3	Manufg.			
Paperboard containers & boxes	0.3	Manufg.			
Air transportation	0.3	Util.			
Maintenance of nonfarm buildings nec	0.2	Constr.			
Lace goods	0.2	Manufg.			
Gas production & distribution (utilities)	0.2	Util.			
Automotive rental & leasing, without drivers	0.2	Services			
Electrical repair shops	0.2	Services			
Equipment rental & leasing services	0.2	Services			
Legal services	0.2	Services			
Management & consulting services & labs	0.2	Services			
Artificial trees & flowers	0.1	Manufg.			
Insurance carriers	0.1	Fin/R.E.			
Accounting, auditing & bookkeeping	0.1	Services			
Automotive repair shops & services	0.1	Services			

Source: Benchmark Input-Output Accounts for the U.S. Economy, 1982, U.S. Department of Commerce, Washington, D.C., July 1991. Data, as reported in the source, are organized by the 1977 SIC structure in use in 1982 but have been matched, as closely as is possible, to the 1987 SIC structure used in this book.

OCCUPATIONS EMPLOYED BY SIC 232 - APPAREL

Occupation	% of Total 1994	Change to 2005	Occupation	% of Total 1994	Change to 2005
Sewing machine operators, garment	56.1	-33.1	Cutters & trimmers, hand	1.7	-24.8
Inspectors, testers, & graders, precision	3.5	-16.4	Patternmakers, layout workers, fabric & apparel	1.5	25.4
Blue collar worker supervisors	3.0	-24.0	General managers & top executives	1.4	-20.7
Assemblers, fabricators, & hand workers nec	2.5	-16.4	Sewing machine operators, non-garment	1.3	-37.3
Pressing machine operators, textiles	2.4	-45.7	Helpers, laborers, & material movers nec	1.1	-16.4
Hand packers & packagers	2.0	-21.2	Industrial machinery mechanics	1.1	0.3
Freight, stock, & material movers, hand	1.8	-33.1	Pressers, hand	1.1	-58.2
Traffic, shipping, & receiving clerks	1.8	-19.6	Sewers, hand	1.0	-10.7

Source: Industry-Occupation Matrix, Bureau of Labor Statistics. These data relate to one or more 3-digit SIC industry groups rather than to a single 4-digit SIC. The change reported for each occupation to the year 2005 is a percent of growth or decline as estimated by the Bureau of Labor Statistics. The abbreviation nec stands for 'not elsewhere classified'.

LOCATION BY STATE AND REGIONAL CONCENTRATION

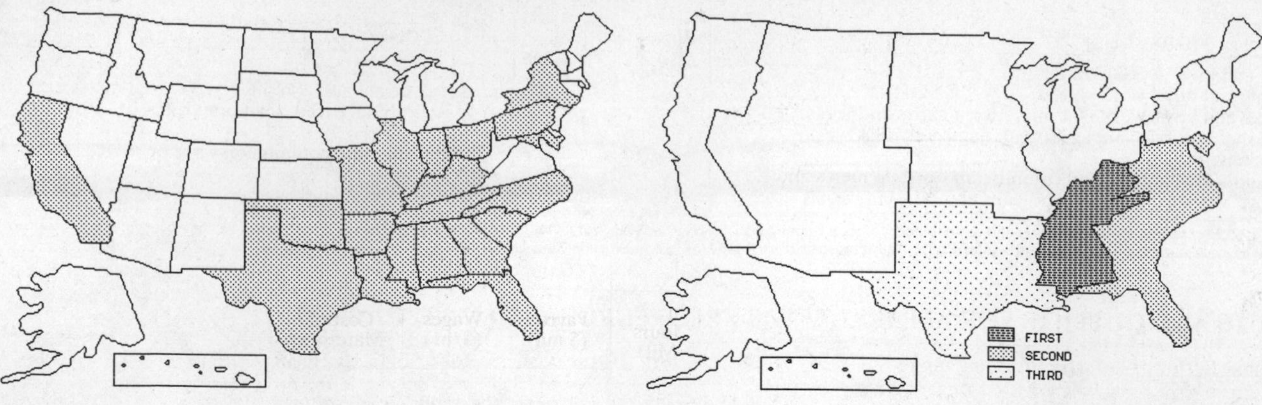

INDUSTRY DATA BY STATE

State	Establish-ments	Shipments			Employment				Cost as % of Shipments	Investment per Employee ($)
		Total ($ mil)	% of U.S.	Per Establ.	Total Number	% of U.S.	Per Establ.	Wages ($/hour)		
Mississippi	36	327.2	20.8	9.1	6,700	20.6	186	5.47	46.1	806
Tennessee	31	260.1	16.5	8.4	6,200	19.0	200	5.75	50.2	565
Texas	20	187.7	11.9	9.4	3,000	9.2	150	5.80	41.0	-
Kentucky	13	184.5	11.7	14.2	2,900	8.9	223	7.32	38.7	2,034
Georgia	16	125.6	8.0	7.8	2,700	8.3	169	5.28	38.6	593
Alabama	24	124.2	7.9	5.2	2,700	8.3	113	6.57	53.5	481
Missouri	12	57.1	3.6	4.8	1,600	4.9	133	6.04	49.4	688
Illinois	8	35.0	2.2	4.4	500	1.5	63	8.38	52.3	1,400
Pennsylvania	8	32.6	2.1	4.1	400	1.2	50	7.67	59.8	250
Arkansas	9	29.2	1.9	3.2	1,100	3.4	122	4.14	40.8	-
California	29	23.9	1.5	0.8	800	2.5	28	6.08	36.4	-
North Carolina	6	22.7	1.4	3.8	400	1.2	67	7.00	55.9	-
Maryland	4	13.6	0.9	3.4	400	1.2	100	9.20	30.9	-
Florida	12	12.3	0.8	1.0	500	1.5	42	5.50	17.9	400
Ohio	5	11.9	0.8	2.4	200	0.6	40	8.33	53.8	-
Oklahoma	4	2.2	0.1	0.6	100	0.3	25	11.00	18.2	-
New York	12	(D)	-	-	750 *	2.3	63	-	-	-
Indiana	4	(D)	-	-	750 *	2.3	188	-	-	-
Louisiana	4	(D)	-	-	375 *	1.2	94	-	-	-
South Carolina	1	(D)	-	-	375 *	1.2	375	-	-	-

Source: 1992 *Economic Census*. The states are in descending order of shipments or establishments (if shipment data are missing for the majority). The symbol (D) appears when data are withheld to prevent disclosure of competitive information. States marked with (D) are sorted by number of establishments. A dash (-) indicates that the data element cannot be calculated; * indicates the midpoint of a range.

2329 - MEN'S & BOYS' CLOTHING, NEC

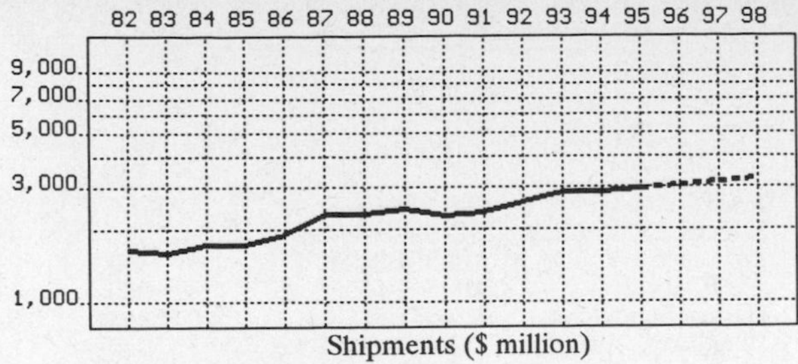

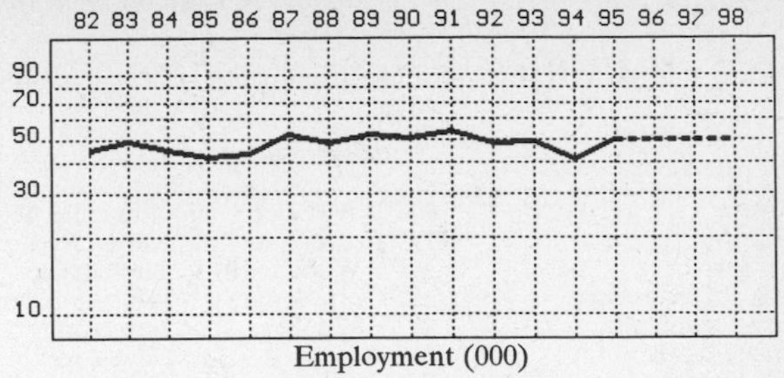

GENERAL STATISTICS

Year	Companies	Establishments: Total	Establishments: with 20 or more employees	Employment: Total (000)	Employment: Production Workers (000)	Employment: Production Hours (Mil)	Compensation: Payroll ($ mil)	Compensation: Wages ($/hr)	Production ($ million): Cost of Materials	Production ($ million): Value Added by Manufacture	Production ($ million): Value of Shipments	Production ($ million): Capital Invest.
1982	575	646	386	44.6	38.6	68.5	432.8	4.72	745.3	931.3	1,658.3	18.3
1983		615	377	48.2	39.5	71.0	473.6	4.45	641.8	954.3	1,595.4	28.0
1984		584	368	44.9	38.9	69.9	474.1	5.03	727.2	1,003.5	1,730.1	22.2
1985		553	359	42.2	36.2	65.3	455.7	5.12	718.4	1,021.1	1,727.9	24.5
1986		524	332	43.5	37.5	68.5	497.2	5.44	785.5	1,136.3	1,910.0	27.5
1987	540	616	393	52.2	45.6	83.1	621.4	5.65	1,010.0	1,315.8	2,289.6	34.4
1988		579	371	48.1	41.7	75.1	592.8	5.83	968.9	1,370.3	2,317.8	33.1
1989		575	395	51.9	45.3	82.0	639.8	5.85	994.0	1,425.6	2,406.8	23.5
1990		591	384	50.2	46.6	84.1	673.2	5.99	987.1	1,340.6	2,286.6	26.0
1991		615	376	53.9	47.2	85.7	694.8	6.23	985.8	1,328.5	2,359.1	32.0
1992	624	701	403	47.9	40.7	74.9	658.3	6.47	1,113.6	1,514.8	2,588.8	36.4
1993		739	414	49.1	42.5	76.4	687.8	6.67	1,212.5	1,638.3	2,834.5	37.1
1994		664P	400P	41.6	35.4	66.7	608.4	6.76	1,269.2	1,568.9	2,826.7	48.4
1995		672P	403P	49.4P	43.3P	79.6P	729.6P	7.01P	1,320.6P	1,632.4P	2,941.1P	41.3P
1996		680P	406P	49.6P	43.6P	80.3P	751.3P	7.19P	1,368.4P	1,691.6P	3,047.7P	42.9P
1997		689P	409P	49.9P	43.9P	81.0P	773.0P	7.38P	1,416.3P	1,750.7P	3,154.3P	44.5P
1998		697P	413P	50.1P	44.2P	81.7P	794.7P	7.56P	1,464.2P	1,809.9P	3,260.9P	46.1P

Sources: 1982, 1987, 1992 *Economic Census*; *Annual Survey of Manufactures*, 83-86, 88-91, 93-94. Establishment counts for non-Census years are from *County Business Patterns*; establishment values for 83-84 are extrapolations. 'P's show projections by the editors. Industries reclassified in 87 will not have data for prior years.

INDICES OF CHANGE

Year	Companies	Establishments: Total	Establishments: with 20 or more employees	Employment: Total (000)	Employment: Production Workers (000)	Employment: Production Hours (Mil)	Compensation: Payroll ($ mil)	Compensation: Wages ($/hr)	Production ($ million): Cost of Materials	Production ($ million): Value Added by Manufacture	Production ($ million): Value of Shipments	Production ($ million): Capital Invest.
1982	92	92	96	93	95	91	66	73	67	61	64	50
1983		88	94	101	97	95	72	69	58	63	62	77
1984		83	91	94	96	93	72	78	65	66	67	61
1985		79	89	88	89	87	69	79	65	67	67	67
1986		75	82	91	92	91	76	84	71	75	74	76
1987	87	88	98	109	112	111	94	87	91	87	88	95
1988		83	92	100	102	100	90	90	87	90	90	91
1989		82	98	108	111	109	97	90	89	94	93	65
1990		84	95	105	114	112	102	93	89	89	88	71
1991		88	93	113	116	114	106	96	89	88	91	88
1992	100	100	100	100	100	100	100	100	100	100	100	100
1993		105	103	103	104	102	104	103	109	108	109	102
1994		95P	99P	87	87	89	92	104	114	104	109	133
1995		96P	100P	103P	106P	106P	111P	108P	119P	108P	114P	114P
1996		97P	101P	104P	107P	107P	114P	111P	123P	112P	118P	118P
1997		98P	102P	104P	108P	108P	117P	114P	127P	116P	122P	122P
1998		99P	102P	105P	109P	109P	121P	117P	131P	119P	126P	127P

Sources: Same as General Statistics. Values reflect change from the base year, 1992. Values above 100 mean greater than 92, values below 100 mean less than 92, and a value of 100 in the 82-91 or 93-98 period means same as 92. 'P's mark projections by the editors.

SELECTED RATIOS

For 1994	Avg. of All Manufact.	Analyzed Industry	Index
Employees per Establishment	49	63	128
Payroll per Establishment	1,500,273	915,952	61
Payroll per Employee	30,620	14,625	48
Production Workers per Establishment	34	53	155
Wages per Establishment	853,319	678,822	80
Wages per Production Worker	24,861	12,737	51
Hours per Production Worker	2,056	1,884	92
Wages per Hour	12.09	6.76	56
Value Added per Establishment	4,602,255	2,361,993	51
Value Added per Employee	93,930	37,714	40

For 1994	Avg. of All Manufact.	Analyzed Industry	Index
Value Added per Production Worker	134,084	44,319	33
Cost per Establishment	5,045,178	1,910,792	38
Cost per Employee	102,970	30,510	30
Cost per Production Worker	146,988	35,853	24
Shipments per Establishment	9,576,895	4,255,622	44
Shipments per Employee	195,460	67,950	35
Shipments per Production Worker	279,017	79,850	29
Investment per Establishment	321,011	72,867	23
Investment per Employee	6,552	1,163	18
Investment per Production Worker	9,352	1,367	15

Sources: Same as General Statistics. The 'Average of All Manufacturing' column represents the average of all manufacturing industries reported for the most recent complete year available. The Index shows the relationship between the Average and the Analyzed Industry. For example, 100 means that they are equal; 500 that the Analyzed Industry is five times the average; 50 means that the Analyzed Industry is half the national average. The abbreviation 'na' is used to show that data are 'not available'.

LEADING COMPANIES

Number shown: **75** Total sales ($ mil): **5,158** Total employment (000): **75.6**

Company Name	Address				CEO Name	Phone	Co. Type	Sales ($ mil)	Empl. (000)
Russell Corp	PO Box 272	Alexander City	AL	35010	John C Adams	205-329-4000	P	1,098	16.8
Russell Corp	PO Box 272	Alexander City	AL	35010	Eugene C Gwaltney	205-329-4000	D	490*	9.0
Angelica Corp	424 S Woods Mill	Chesterfield	MO	63017	Lawrence J Young	314-854-3800	P	473	9.8
Champion Products Inc	475 Corp Square	Winston-Salem	NC	27105	Joe Fontino	910-519-6500	S	200	4.5
Nautica Enterprises Inc	40 W 57th St	New York	NY	10019	Harvey Sanders	212-541-5757	P	193	0.1
Coordinated Apparel Inc	350 5th Av	New York	NY	10118	Ellen Constantinides	212-613-9200	R	180*	2.8
Authentic Fitness Corp	7911 Haskell Av	Van Nuys	CA	91410	Linda J Wachner	818-376-0300	P	179	1.4
Garan Inc	350 5th Av	New York	NY	10118	S Lichtenstein	212-563-2000	P	173	3.0
Fishman and Tobin Inc	625 Ridge Pike	Conshohocken	PA	19428	Mark Fishman	215-828-8400	R	160*	2.5
Winning Ways Inc	9700 Com Pkwy	Lenexa	KS	66219	John Menghini	913-888-0445	R	120*	0.6
Sun Sportswear Inc	6520 S 190th St	Kent	WA	98032	Larry Mounger	206-251-3565	P	113	0.5
Sports Apparel Corp	9700 Com Pkwy	Lenexa	KS	66219	John Menghini	913-888-0640	S	108*	0.5
Signal Apparel Company Inc	PO Box 4296	Chattanooga	TN	37405	Marvin Winkler	615-752-2032	P	96	1.8
Robinson Manufacturing	520 S Market St	Dayton	TN	37321	TJ Robinson	615-775-2212	R	93	1.4
Jansport Inc	PO Box 1817	Appleton	WI	54913	Paul Delorey	414-734-5708	S	85*	0.6
Swingster Marketing	10450 Holmes Rd	Kansas City	MO	64131	James O'Brien	816-943-5000	D	85	1.7
K-Products Inc	PO Box 147	Orange City	IA	51041	Thomas Kohout	712-737-4925	R	80	1.6
Orbit International Corp	80 Cabot Ct	Hauppauge	NY	11788	Max Reissman	516-435-8300	P	73	0.6
Nazareth/Century Mills Inc	350 5th Av	New York	NY	10118	Harvey Roisman	212-613-0500	R	68	1.4
Artex Manufacturing Company	7600 Wedd Rd	Overland Park	KS	66204	Bruce Pratt	913-631-4040	S	65*	1.0
DeLong Sportswear Inc	PO Box 189	Grinnell	IA	50112	S Lannom	515-236-3106	R	56	0.8
Pacific Trail Inc	1310 Mercer St	Seattle	WA	98109	James Milligan	206-622-8730	S	52*	0.2
Thaw Corp	PO Box 3978	Seattle	WA	98124	Jim Cross	206-624-4277	S	43	0.4
King Louie International Inc	13500 15th St	Grandview	MO	64030	Robert V Palan	816-765-5212	R	41*	1.0
Rugged Sportswear Inc	1914 S Elm St	High Point	NC	27261	Edwin Monroe	910-889-2992	R	41	0.6
National Garment Co	514 Earth City	St Louis	MO	63045	R D Rothbarth	314-291-8540	R	40	0.8
L and L Manufacturing Co	2250 S Maple Av	Los Angeles	CA	90011	Leonard Feldman	213-747-6164	R	39*	0.6
Goodman Knitting Company Inc	300 Manley St	Brockton	MA	02403	Peter Goodman	508-588-7200	S	36	0.1
Apparel America Inc	1175 State St	New Haven	CT	06511	Burton I Koffman	203-777-5531	P	34	0.6
Hind Inc	PO Box 12609	S L Obispo	CA	93406	Greg W Hind	805-544-8555	R	30*	0.5
Pomare Ltd	700 N Nimitz Hwy	Honolulu	HI	96817	Jim S Romig	808-524-3966	R	26*	0.4
Globe Manufacturing Co	PO Box 128	Pittsfield	NH	03263	George E Freese	603-435-8323	R	25	0.2
Darwood Manufacturing Co	PO Box 625	Pelham	GA	31779	HA Burford	912-294-4932	R	23*	0.4
Kent Sportswear Inc	PO Box 216	Curwensville	PA	16833	Robert Bayer	814-236-2110	R	22*	0.5
Game Inc	7100 Jamesson Rd	Midland	GA	31820	Greg Yates	706-563-2773	S	21*	0.4
DVB Enterprises	9237 Ward Pkwy	Kansas City	MO	64114	Patrick Bachofer	816-363-4000	R	20	0.4
Majestic Athletic Wear Ltd	636 Pen Argyl St	Pen Argyl	PA	18072	FE Capobianco	610-863-6161	R	20	0.4
Russell Athletic	PO Box 272	Alexander City	AL	35010	Frank Hall	205-329-4000	D	19*	0.3
Fab-Knit Manufacturing	1415 N 4th St	Waco	TX	76707	Bob Landon	817-752-2511	S	18	0.3
Great Pacific Iron Works	259 W Santa Clara	Ventura	CA	93001	Peter Noone	805-643-8616	S	18	0.1
Sportif USA Inc	445 E Glendale Av	Sparks	NV	89431	John Kirsch	702-359-6400	R	18	<0.1
David Peyser Sportswear Inc	90 Spence St	Bay Shore	NY	11706	Paul Peyser	516-231-7788	R	16*	0.3
Four Seasons Garment Co	1111 Western Row	Mason	OH	45040	Jim T Stevens	513-398-3695	S	16	0.2
Lexington Fabrics Inc	Old Mill Rd	Lexington	AL	35648	Bill McCreary	205-229-6611	R	16*	0.3
Roffe Inc	808 Howell St	Seattle	WA	98101	GR Jones	206-622-0456	R	16*	0.3
Brookhurst Inc	107 W Carob St	Compton	CA	90220	Bill Ott	310-631-3500	R	15	<0.1
Famous-Fraternity	2060 Hardy Pkwy	Grove City	OH	43123	GW McClure	614-875-8180	R	15	0.1
Holloway Sportswear Inc	PO Box AB	Jackson Center	OH	45334	Roy E Leasure Jr	513-596-6193	R	15	0.3
JM Associates Inc	1870 NW 173rd Av	Beaverton	OR	97006	Barry Garlick	503-629-8777	R	15	<0.1
Swell-Wear Inc	1407 Broadway	New York	NY	10018	Shirley Bren	212-997-2300	R	15	<0.1
Big Sky USA Inc	4020 S 56th St	Tacoma	WA	98409	Finn E Walstad	206-471-9900	P	14	0.2
Bogner of America Inc	PO Box 644	Newport	VT	05855	William Bogner	802-334-6507	R	13*	0.2
Fox Point Sportswear Inc	PO Box 507	Merrill	WI	54452	JJ Bocke	715-536-9461	R	13	0.3
Golden Manufacturing Co	PO Drawer 390	Golden	MS	38847	James Fennell	601-454-3428	R	13*	0.2
Quiltex Company Inc	168 39th St	Brooklyn	NY	11232	Alan Scelenfreund	718-788-3158	R	13	0.2
Rockmount Ranch Wear Mfg Co	1626 Wazee St	Denver	CO	80202	Jack A Weil	303-629-7777	R	13	0.2
Katzenberg Brothers Inc	3500 Parkdale Av	Baltimore	MD	21211	J Katzenberg	410-669-4400	R	12*	0.2
Virginia Apparel Corp	PO Box 589	Rocky Mount	VA	24151	Thomas W Mason	703-483-0231	R	12	0.3
Sports Belle Inc	6723 Pleasant Ridge	Knoxville	TN	37921	JC Lee	615-938-2063	R	11*	0.2
RefrigiWear Inc	PO Box 39	Dahlonega	GA	30533	M Breakstone	706-864-5757	R	10	0.1
Comstock-Tivolie	1776 Broadway	New York	NY	10019	Edward Coll III	212-586-2736	R	10	<0.1
Dakota Industries Inc	PO Box 932	Sioux Falls	SD	57101	D P Mackintosh	605-368-2773	R	10	0.2
Butwin Sportswear Co	3401 Spring St NE	Minneapolis	MN	55413	Irving D Butwin	612-331-3300	R	9*	0.2
Fitigues Inc	700 N Sangamon	Chicago	IL	60611	Steven Rosenstein	312-455-8866	R	9	<0.1
Roytex Inc	16 E 34th St	New York	NY	10016	Dennis Mourry	212-686-3500	R	9*	0.2
Gotcha International LP	9600 Toledo Way	Irvine	CA	92718	Michael Thompson	714-457-9999	R	8*	0.1
Hummer Sportswear Inc	PO Box 65116	Fayetteville	NC	28306	Bruce Miller	919-423-4866	R	8	0.3
Piccolino USA Inc	100 W 33rd St	New York	NY	10001	Sam Honig	212-279-3004	S	8	<0.1
Winning Moves Inc	Apparel Ctr	Chicago	IL	60654	Avers Wexler	312-828-9400	R	8*	0.1
Andrews Apparel Co	PO Box 487	Andrews	SC	29510	Larry F Urtz	803-264-3431	R	7*	0.1
Bacon and Company Inc	200 Summit Hill Dr	Knoxville	TN	37902	Jack E Dance	615-523-9181	R	7*	<0.1
College House Inc	601 Cantiague Rock	Westbury	NY	11590	Peter S Blumberg	516-334-7600	R	7*	0.1
Cornish Knit Goods Mfg Corp	121 Ingraham St	Brooklyn	NY	11237	Michael Alper	718-366-9853	R	7*	<0.1
Head Sportswear International	9189 Red Branch	Columbia	MD	21045	Clayton P Fisher III	410-730-8300	S	7*	0.1
Owenby Co	5775 Murphy Hwy	Blairsville	GA	30512	Paul Owenby	706-745-5531	R	7	0.3

Source: *Ward's Business Directory of U.S. Private and Public Companies*, Volumes 1 and 2, 1996. The company type code used is as follows: P - Public, R - Private, S - Subsidiary, D - Division, J - Joint Venture, A - Affiliate, G - Group. Sales are in millions of dollars, employees are in thousands. An asterisk (*) indicates an estimated sales volume. The symbol < stands for 'less than'. Company names and addresses are truncated, in some cases, to fit into the available space.

MATERIALS CONSUMED

Material	Quantity	Delivered Cost ($ million)
Materials, ingredients, containers, and supplies	(X)	894.2
Broadwoven fabrics (piece goods)	(X)	395.3
Narrow fabrics (12 inches or less in width)	(X)	62.7
Knit fabrics	(X)	186.8
Yarn, all fibers	(X)	42.2
Buttons, zippers, and slide fasteners	(X)	30.6
All other materials and components, parts, containers, and supplies	(X)	117.9
Materials, ingredients, containers, and supplies, nsk	(X)	58.6

Source: 1992 *Economic Census*. Explanation of symbols used: (D): Withheld to avoid disclosure of competitive data; na: Not available; (S): Withheld because statistical norms were not met; (X): Not applicable; (Z): Less than half the unit shown; nec: Not elsewhere classified; nsk: Not specified by kind; - : zero; * : 10-19 percent estimated; ** : 20-29 percent estimated.

PRODUCT SHARE DETAILS

Product or Product Class	% Share
Men's and boys' clothing, nec	100.00
Men's and boys' heavy nontailored outerwear coats, jackets, and vests, except ski wear (mackinaws, meltons, lumber jackets, etc.)	22.71
Men's and boys' other outerwear	56.09
Men's and boys' swimwear and shorts	42.43
Men's and boys' athletic uniforms sold as such	13.66
Men's and boys' sweaters (including sweater vests), made from purchased fabrics	5.16
Men's and boys' other outerwear, nec (ski and snow pants, leggings, light outerwear jackets, etc.)	38.00
Men's and boys' other outerwear made from purchased fabrics, nsk	0.75
Receipts for contract and commission work on men's and boys' outerwear, nec	18.21
Receipts for contract and commission work on men's and boys' outerwear, nec	99.37
Receipts for contract and commission work on men's and boys' outerwear, nec, nsk	0.63
Men's and boys' clothing, nec, nsk	3.00

Source: 1992 *Economic Census*. The values shown are percent of total shipments in an industry. Values of indented subcategories are summed in the main heading. The symbol (D) appears when data are withheld to prevent disclosure of competitive information. The abbreviation nsk stands for 'not specified by kind' and nec for 'not elsewhere classified'.

INPUTS AND OUTPUTS FOR APPAREL MADE FROM PURCHASED MATERIALS

Economic Sector or Industry Providing Inputs	%	Sector	Economic Sector or Industry Buying Outputs	%	Sector
Imports	29.1	Foreign	Personal consumption expenditures	82.7	
Broadwoven fabric mills	20.2	Manufg.	Apparel made from purchased materials	12.0	Manufg.
Apparel made from purchased materials	18.3	Manufg.	Exports	1.5	Foreign
Knit fabric mills	8.6	Manufg.	Federal Government purchases, national defense	0.9	Fed Govt
Wholesale trade	3.8	Trade	S/L Govt. purch., correction	0.5	S/L Govt
Advertising	2.4	Services	Pleating & stitching	0.3	Manufg.
Yarn mills & finishing of textiles, nec	1.4	Manufg.	Knit outerwear mills	0.2	Manufg.
Pleating & stitching	1.1	Manufg.	Hospitals	0.2	Services
Banking	1.1	Fin/R.E.	Laundry, dry cleaning, shoe repair	0.2	Services
Petroleum refining	1.0	Manufg.	S/L Govt. purch., health & hospitals	0.2	S/L Govt
Electric services (utilities)	1.0	Util.	Portrait, photographic studios	0.1	Services
Automotive & apparel trimmings	0.9	Manufg.	S/L Govt. purch., public assistance & relief	0.1	S/L Govt
Needles, pins, & fasteners	0.8	Manufg.			
Thread mills	0.7	Manufg.			
Communications, except radio & TV	0.7	Util.			
Eating & drinking places	0.7	Trade			
U.S. Postal Service	0.7	Gov't			
Leather tanning & finishing	0.5	Manufg.			
Narrow fabric mills	0.5	Manufg.			
Schiffli machine embroideries	0.4	Manufg.			
Motor freight transportation & warehousing	0.4	Util.			
Real estate	0.4	Fin/R.E.			
Royalties	0.4	Fin/R.E.			
Forestry products	0.3	Agric.			
Buttons	0.3	Manufg.			
Paperboard containers & boxes	0.3	Manufg.			
Air transportation	0.3	Util.			
Maintenance of nonfarm buildings nec	0.2	Constr.			
Lace goods	0.2	Manufg.			
Gas production & distribution (utilities)	0.2	Util.			
Automotive rental & leasing, without drivers	0.2	Services			
Electrical repair shops	0.2	Services			
Equipment rental & leasing services	0.2	Services			
Legal services	0.2	Services			
Management & consulting services & labs	0.2	Services			
Artificial trees & flowers	0.1	Manufg.			
Insurance carriers	0.1	Fin/R.E.			
Accounting, auditing & bookkeeping	0.1	Services			
Automotive repair shops & services	0.1	Services			

Source: Benchmark Input-Output Accounts for the U.S. Economy, 1982, U.S. Department of Commerce, Washington, D.C., July 1991. Data, as reported in the source, are organized by the 1977 SIC structure in use in 1982 but have been matched, as closely as is possible, to the 1987 SIC structure used in this book.

OCCUPATIONS EMPLOYED BY SIC 232 - APPAREL

Occupation	% of Total 1994	Change to 2005	Occupation	% of Total 1994	Change to 2005
Sewing machine operators, garment	56.1	-33.1	Cutters & trimmers, hand	1.7	-24.8
Inspectors, testers, & graders, precision	3.5	-16.4	Patternmakers, layout workers, fabric & apparel	1.5	25.4
Blue collar worker supervisors	3.0	-24.0	General managers & top executives	1.4	-20.7
Assemblers, fabricators, & hand workers nec	2.5	-16.4	Sewing machine operators, non-garment	1.3	-37.3
Pressing machine operators, textiles	2.4	-45.7	Helpers, laborers, & material movers nec	1.1	-16.4
Hand packers & packagers	2.0	-21.2	Industrial machinery mechanics	1.1	0.3
Freight, stock, & material movers, hand	1.8	-33.1	Pressers, hand	1.1	-58.2
Traffic, shipping, & receiving clerks	1.8	-19.6	Sewers, hand	1.0	-10.7

Source: *Industry-Occupation Matrix*, Bureau of Labor Statistics. These data relate to one or more 3-digit SIC industry groups rather than to a single 4-digit SIC. The change reported for each occupation to the year 2005 is a percent of growth or decline as estimated by the Bureau of Labor Statistics. The abbreviation nec stands for 'not elsewhere classified'.

LOCATION BY STATE AND REGIONAL CONCENTRATION

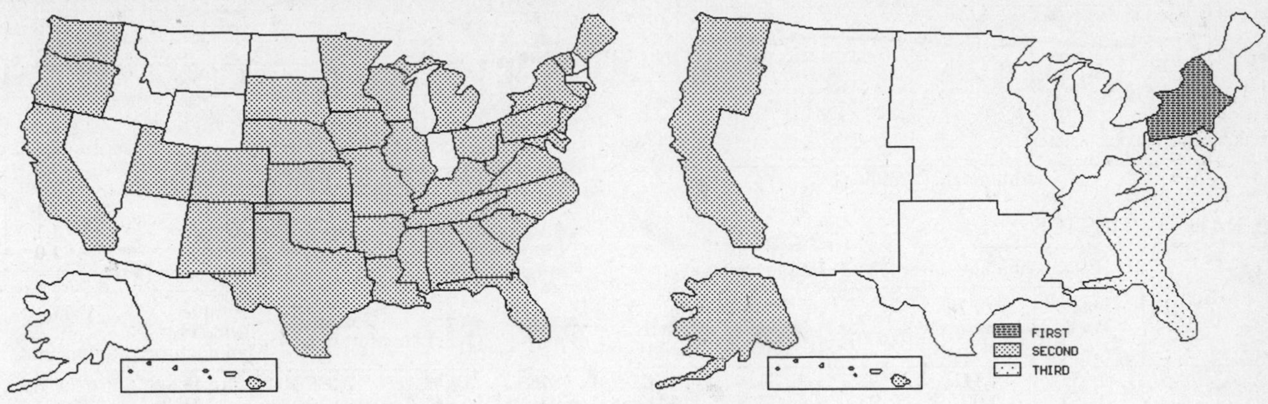

INDUSTRY DATA BY STATE

State	Establish-ments	Shipments			Employment				Cost as % of Shipments	Investment per Employee ($)
		Total ($ mil)	% of U.S.	Per Establ.	Total Number	% of U.S.	Per Establ.	Wages ($/hour)		
Tennessee	43	336.2	13.0	7.8	6,100	12.7	142	6.27	46.0	590
California	111	243.4	9.4	2.2	4,400	9.2	40	6.93	35.5	523
New York	93	227.1	8.8	2.4	4,100	8.6	44	6.20	51.9	707
North Carolina	36	180.5	7.0	5.0	3,200	6.7	89	7.18	29.8	1,844
Alabama	14	138.3	5.3	9.9	2,400	5.0	171	7.94	52.1	-
Virginia	9	135.1	5.2	15.0	3,100	6.5	344	7.00	21.1	-
Ohio	9	96.5	3.7	10.7	900	1.9	100	6.43	65.2	2,222
Missouri	17	90.1	3.5	5.3	1,300	2.7	76	6.53	52.2	538
Georgia	19	87.9	3.4	4.6	1,400	2.9	74	5.09	68.0	429
Pennsylvania	37	57.8	2.2	1.6	2,100	4.4	57	6.24	29.6	286
Texas	25	47.4	1.8	1.9	1,700	3.5	68	5.37	39.9	353
Arkansas	8	45.2	1.7	5.7	900	1.9	113	6.38	25.2	-
Florida	27	43.0	1.7	1.6	900	1.9	33	5.47	27.0	444
Illinois	7	22.8	0.9	3.3	400	0.8	57	6.14	44.7	-
Wisconsin	11	20.8	0.8	1.9	600	1.3	55	5.89	40.4	-
New Jersey	20	15.8	0.6	0.8	400	0.8	20	9.00	42.4	250
Colorado	13	12.5	0.5	1.0	300	0.6	23	7.00	36.8	667
Washington	25	(D)	-	-	1,750 *	3.7	70	-	-	-
Minnesota	16	(D)	-	-	375 *	0.8	23	-	-	-
Iowa	13	(D)	-	-	750 *	1.6	58	-	-	-
Michigan	12	(D)	-	-	175 *	0.4	15	-	-	571
South Carolina	12	(D)	-	-	1,750 *	3.7	146	-	-	-
Mississippi	11	(D)	-	-	1,750 *	3.7	159	-	-	-
Kentucky	10	(D)	-	-	1,750 *	3.7	175	-	-	-
Louisiana	8	(D)	-	-	750 *	1.6	94	-	-	-
Kansas	7	(D)	-	-	375 *	0.8	54	-	-	-
Oregon	7	(D)	-	-	175 *	0.4	25	-	-	-
South Dakota	7	(D)	-	-	375 *	0.8	54	-	-	-
Utah	7	(D)	-	-	375 *	0.8	54	-	-	-
Maryland	6	(D)	-	-	375 *	0.8	63	-	-	267
Connecticut	5	(D)	-	-	375 *	0.8	75	-	-	-
Nebraska	4	(D)	-	-	375 *	0.8	94	-	-	-
Oklahoma	4	(D)	-	-	750 *	1.6	188	-	-	-
Hawaii	3	(D)	-	-	750 *	1.6	250	-	-	-
West Virginia	3	(D)	-	-	750 *	1.6	250	-	-	-
Maine	2	(D)	-	-	175 *	0.4	88	-	-	-
New Mexico	2	(D)	-	-	175 *	0.4	88	-	-	-
Vermont	1	(D)	-	-	175 *	0.4	175	-	-	-

Source: 1992 *Economic Census*. The states are in descending order of shipments or establishments (if shipment data are missing for the majority). The symbol (D) appears when data are withheld to prevent disclosure of competitive information. States marked with (D) are sorted by number of establishments. A dash (-) indicates that the data element cannot be calculated; * indicates the midpoint of a range.

2331 - WOMEN'S AND MISSES' BLOUSES & SHIRTS

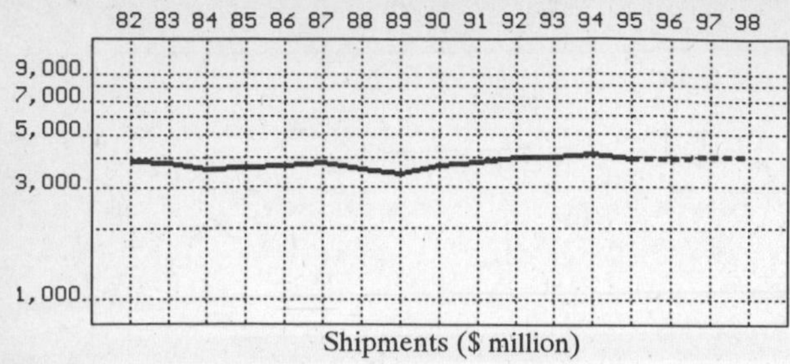

Shipments ($ million)

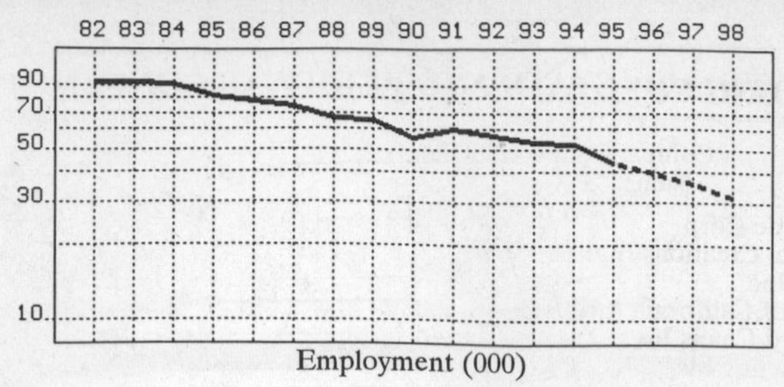

Employment (000)

GENERAL STATISTICS

Year	Com-panies	Establishments: Total	Establishments: with 20 or more employees	Employment: Total (000)	Employment: Production Workers (000)	Employment: Production Hours (Mil)	Compensation: Payroll ($ mil)	Compensation: Wages ($/hr)	Production ($ million): Cost of Materials	Production ($ million): Value Added by Manufacture	Production ($ million): Value of Shipments	Production ($ million): Capital Invest.
1982	1,825	1,955	1,111	92.3	79.4	141.1	876.1	4.42	2,038.3	1,843.6	3,896.2	29.4
1983		1,764	1,007	93.1	79.3	141.8	921.2	4.62	2,030.9	1,774.2	3,804.1	40.2
1984		1,573	903	91.5	76.5	137.3	897.4	4.65	1,875.3	1,738.3	3,579.3	72.5
1985		1,380	800	82.1	70.0	126.3	845.6	4.62	1,876.3	1,729.0	3,642.9	33.8
1986		1,211	734	78.2	66.2	119.3	835.6	4.66	1,907.5	1,808.0	3,694.4	35.0
1987	1,408	1,496	860	73.4	63.2	109.0	856.6	5.38	1,943.3	1,918.1	3,831.2	40.1
1988		1,357	814	67.0	56.7	100.7	832.1	5.65	1,827.9	1,741.0	3,573.5	
1989		1,177	726	64.7	55.2	98.6	817.4	5.70	1,700.5	1,713.2	3,402.2	22.2
1990		1,057	622	55.9	54.3	97.9	865.8	5.85	1,801.7	1,954.9	3,733.0	35.6
1991		1,044	606	59.5	49.4	88.5	814.0	5.93	1,855.1	1,943.2	3,800.9	25.2
1992	1,411	1,473	674	56.2	47.2	85.3	832.4	6.44	2,002.3	1,967.9	3,978.2	38.2
1993		1,423	602	52.9	44.7	81.8	827.9	6.96	2,031.9	1,969.1	4,011.7	26.0
1994		1,090P	524P	51.8	42.2	79.7	794.1	6.61	2,214.9	1,948.3	4,146.5	32.6
1995		1,041P	483P	43.5P	37.0P	68.1P	797.7P	6.98P	2,104.7P	1,851.4P	3,940.2P	
1996		992P	442P	39.6P	33.6P	62.4P	790.6P	7.20P	2,117.2P	1,862.4P	3,963.6P	
1997		943P	402P	35.7P	30.3P	56.7P	783.5P	7.41P	2,129.7P	1,873.4P	3,987.0P	
1998		894P	361P	31.9P	27.0P	50.9P	776.4P	7.62P	2,142.2P	1,884.4P	4,010.4P	

Sources: 1982, 1987, 1992 *Economic Census*; *Annual Survey of Manufactures*, 83-86, 88-91, 93-94. Establishment counts for non-Census years are from *County Business Patterns*; establishment values for 83-84 are extrapolations. 'P's show projections by the editors. Industries reclassified in 87 will not have data for prior years.

INDICES OF CHANGE

Year	Com-panies	Establishments: Total	Establishments: with 20 or more employees	Employment: Total (000)	Employment: Production Workers (000)	Employment: Production Hours (Mil)	Compensation: Payroll ($ mil)	Compensation: Wages ($/hr)	Production ($ million): Cost of Materials	Production ($ million): Value Added by Manufacture	Production ($ million): Value of Shipments	Production ($ million): Capital Invest.
1982	129	133	165	164	168	165	105	69	102	94	98	77
1983		120	149	166	168	166	111	72	101	90	96	105
1984		107	134	163	162	161	108	72	94	88	90	190
1985		94	119	146	148	148	102	72	94	88	92	88
1986		82	109	139	140	140	100	72	95	92	93	92
1987	100	102	128	131	134	128	103	84	97	97	96	105
1988		92	121	119	120	118	100	88	91	88	90	
1989		80	108	115	117	116	98	89	85	87	86	58
1990		72	92	99	115	115	104	91	90	99	94	93
1991		71	90	106	105	104	98	92	93	99	96	66
1992	100	100	100	100	100	100	100	100	100	100	100	100
1993		97	89	94	95	96	99	108	101	100	101	68
1994		74P	78P	92	89	93	95	103	111	99	104	85
1995		71P	72P	77P	78P	80P	96P	108P	105P	94P	99P	
1996		67P	66P	70P	71P	73P	95P	112P	106P	95P	100P	
1997		64P	60P	64P	64P	66P	94P	115P	106P	95P	100P	
1998		61P	54P	57P	57P	60P	93P	118P	107P	96P	101P	

Sources: Same as General Statistics. Values reflect change from the base year, 1992. Values above 100 mean greater than 92, values below 100 mean less than 92, and a value of 100 in the 82-91 or 93-98 period means same as 92. 'P's mark projections by the editors.

SELECTED RATIOS

For 1994	Avg. of All Manufact.	Analyzed Industry	Index
Employees per Establishment	49	48	97
Payroll per Establishment	1,500,273	728,330	49
Payroll per Employee	30,620	15,330	50
Production Workers per Establishment	34	39	113
Wages per Establishment	853,319	483,184	57
Wages per Production Worker	24,861	12,484	50
Hours per Production Worker	2,056	1,889	92
Wages per Hour	12.09	6.61	55
Value Added per Establishment	4,602,255	1,786,934	39
Value Added per Employee	93,930	37,612	40

For 1994	Avg. of All Manufact.	Analyzed Industry	Index
Value Added per Production Worker	134,084	46,168	34
Cost per Establishment	5,045,178	2,031,454	40
Cost per Employee	102,970	42,759	42
Cost per Production Worker	146,988	52,486	36
Shipments per Establishment	9,576,895	3,803,071	40
Shipments per Employee	195,460	80,048	41
Shipments per Production Worker	279,017	98,258	35
Investment per Establishment	321,011	29,900	9
Investment per Employee	6,552	629	10
Investment per Production Worker	9,352	773	8

Sources: Same as General Statistics. The 'Average of All Manufacturing' column represents the average of all manufacturing industries reported for the most recent complete year available. The Index shows the relationship between the Average and the Analyzed Industry. For example, 100 means that they are equal; 500 that the Analyzed Industry is five times the average; 50 means that the Analyzed Industry is half the national average. The abbreviation 'na' is used to show that data are 'not available'.

LEADING COMPANIES Number shown: **66** Total sales ($ mil): **3,297** Total employment (000): **18.1**

Company Name	Address				CEO Name	Phone	Co. Type	Sales ($ mil)	Empl. (000)
Esprit de Corp	900 Minnesota St	San Francisco	CA	94107	David Folkman	415-648-6900	R	900	4.0
Capucci Creations Internationale	9565 Santa Monica	Beverly Hills	CA	90210	Albert Fenster	310-275-0700	R	474	0.5
Koret Inc	611 Mission St	San Francisco	CA	94105	Steve Rudin	415-957-2000	R	300	1.4
Koret of California Inc	611 Mission St	San Francisco	CA	94105	Steve Rudin	415-957-2000	S	300	1.4
Bernard Chaus Inc	1410 Broadway	New York	NY	10018	Josephine Chaus	212-354-1280	P	236	0.9
Donnkenny Inc	1411 Broadway	New York	NY	10018	Richard Rubin	212-730-7770	P	159	1.5
Rampage Clothing Co	1731 S Santa Fe Av	Los Angeles	CA	90021	Larry Hansel	213-584-1300	R	110*	1.0
Tennessee River Inc	4050 Helton Dr	Florence	AL	35630	Jeannette Hennessee	205-767-5220	R	90*	0.8
Oak Hill Sportswear Corp	1411 Broadway	New York	NY	10018	Arthur L Asch	212-789-8900	P	84	0.4
Land and Sea Inc	1375 Broadway #2	New York	NY	10018	Seymor Sobel	212-244-1010	R	72	1.0
Judy Bond Inc	330 W 34th St	New York	NY	10001	Andrew Postal	212-868-4800	R	55	0.8
Tess Inc	1410 Broadway	New York	NY	10018	Gary Dahan	212-719-5762	R	55	0.2
Biscayne Holdings Inc	1373 Broad St	Clifton	NJ	07013	Earl W Powell	201-473-3240	P	53	0.5
Adrianna Papell Ltd	498 7th Av	New York	NY	10018	Harvey Berkman	212-695-5244	R	50	<0.1
Monarch Knit and Sportswear	122 E Washington	Los Angeles	CA	90015	Sheldon N Goldman	213-746-5800	R	28	<0.1
YES Clothing Co	1380 W Washington	Los Angeles	CA	90007	George W Randall	213-765-7800	P	28	0.1
Hilton Active Apparel	6850 N Central Park	Lincolnwood	IL	60645	Frank Leibow	708-675-1010	D	27*	<0.1
Sharilove Fashions Inc	175 Broadway	Paterson	NJ	07505	Jack Brem	201-278-4400	R	24*	<0.1
Segrets Inc	66 Cherry Hill Dr	Beverly	MA	01915	Edward Jones	508-927-6601	R	22	<0.1
Lucky Winner Inc	525 7th Av	New York	NY	10018	Marco Yeshoua	212-354-9464	R	18*	0.2
Tara-Lee Sportswear Company	601 Water St	New Berlin	PA	17855	Larry Pfirman	717-966-3817	R	17*	0.2
Albain Shirt Co	PO Box 429	Kinston	NC	28501	Michael R Bain	919-523-2151	R	14	0.4
Elberton Manufacturing Co	PO Box 878	Elberton	GA	30635	Anri Konfino	706-283-2751	S	13*	0.2
Bleyle Inc	14 St John Cir	Shenandoah	GA	30265	Micheal Young	404-253-2792	R	11	0.1
DARUE of California Inc	PO Box 59918	Los Angeles	CA	90059	Richard P McElrath	310-323-1350	R	11	<0.1
Holiday Togs Inc	141 W 36th St	New York	NY	10018	Gilbert Davret	212-971-9500	R	10	0.1
Smart Novelty Blouse Company	1370 Broadway	New York	NY	10018	AS Feinerman	212-736-7314	R	10	<0.1
Red Level Fashions Inc	PO Box 186	Red Level	AL	36474	David Chapman	205-469-5317	S	9	0.2
G and J Sportswear Inc	231 Morristown Dr	Bath	PA	18014	Tony Diodoardo	215-837-1846	R	8	0.1
Marin Apparel Co	7049 Redwood Blv	Novato	CA	94945	Clark A Hodges	415-892-6674	R	8	<0.1
Shane Hunter Inc	1400 6th St	San Francisco	CA	94107	Wayne Mallin	415-255-6044	R	8*	<0.1
Merry Maid Inc	25 Messenger St	Bangor	PA	18013	Faust Ruggiero	610-588-0927	R	7*	0.2
Vantage Point Fashions Inc	462 7th Av	New York	NY	10018	Harold G Feltman	212-695-3671	R	7	<0.1
Park Manufacturing Company	PO Box 634	Jamestown	TN	38556	Joe Williams	615-879-5894	R	6	0.1
Street Life Inc	72 Spring St	New York	NY	10012	John Frisch	212-219-3880	R	6	<0.1
Susan Bristol Inc	529 Main St	Boston	MA	02129	Robert Lurie	617-241-5300	R	6	<0.1
Mariall Apparel Inc	101 Townsend St	San Francisco	CA	94107	G Robert Allen	415-495-7300	R	5	<0.1
Utah Tailoring Mills	3088 Washington	Ogden	UT	84401	Boyd Bingham	801-394-4517	R	5*	<0.1
Mary Fashion Manufacturing	380 W Main St	Bath	PA	18014	Umberto Fantozzi	610-837-6763	R	4	0.2
Oxford of Belton	PO Box 126	Belton	SC	29627	Norman Sellars	803-338-5221	D	4	0.1
WHK Inc	501 7th Av	New York	NY	10018	Ingrid Fagen	212-354-2255	S	4	<0.1
Amy Lynn of California	555 4th St	San Fernando	CA	91340	Lewis D Joella	818-365-0674	R	3	<0.1
FL Malik Inc	7138 Envoy Ct	Dallas	TX	75247	David A Neumann	214-638-0550	R	3	<0.1
Perry Ellis International Inc	575 7th Av	New York	NY	10018	Claudia Thomas	212-921-8500	R	3*	<0.1
We Be Bop Inc	1380 10th St	Berkeley	CA	94710	Neil Zussman	510-528-0761	R	3	<0.1
William Pearson Inc	719 S Los Angeles	Los Angeles	CA	90014	Randy Randazzo	213-629-4307	R	3	<0.1
Gamco Manufacturing Co	422 Industrial Dr	Jamestown	TN	38556	Hollis D Gammon	615-879-9712	R	3	0.1
Angelique Imports Inc	4800 W Side Av	North Bergen	NJ	07047	Naresh Mahtni	201-864-5714	R	2*	<0.1
Pine Place Sportswear	14th and Laurel St	Pottsville	PA	17901	Jay Mitchell	717-622-1126	D	2	0.1
Prive Inc	470 7th Av	New York	NY	10018	Ivan Strougo	212-244-4082	R	2*	<0.1
K and M Manufacturing Co	PO Box 403	Barnwell	SC	29812	Kenneth McElveen	803-259-1742	R	2	<0.1
New Fashion Inc	PO Box 148	Iva	SC	29655	William Epstein	803-348-6151	R	2	<0.1
Sock Hop Inc	929 S Broadway	Los Angeles	CA	90015	Jackie Schwartz	213-488-9710	R	2	<0.1
Sportswear Unlimited Inc	PO Box 148	Iva	SC	29655	W Epstein	803-348-6151	R	2	0.1
Weston Wear Inc	900 Alabama St	San Francisco	CA	94110	Julienne Weston	415-550-8869	R	1	<0.1
Maklihon Group Corp	241 W 37th St	New York	NY	10018	David Pearson	212-819-1123	R	1	<0.1
Marsina Inc	525 7th Av	New York	NY	10018	Antoine Doummar	212-768-1923	R	1*	<0.1
Pageland Manufacturing Inc	600 N Pearl St	Pageland	SC	29728	Worcester Morrell	803-672-6357	R	1*	<0.1
Rita's Sportswear Inc	101 Lincoln St	Moscow	PA	18444	Nicholas Cortazzo	717-842-7661	R	1	<0.1
Rob-Ran Corp	PO Box 117	Geneva	AL	36340	Lois Riley	205-684-3711	R	1	<0.1
Utah Sportswear Inc	250 W 500 S	Spanish Fork	UT	84660	W Wallace Osborn	801-798-9511	R	1	<0.1
Robespierre Inc	225 W 35th St	New York	NY	10001	Robert Savage	212-594-0012	R	1*	<0.1
Fuller Sportswear Company Inc	215 Quarry St	Fullerton	PA	18052	Aaron Feinerman	610-264-4554	R	0*	<0.1
Caberra Inc	512 7th Av	New York	NY	10028	Cynthia Fitzgerald	212-869-1064	R	0*	<0.1
Hino and Malee Boutique	50 E Oak St	Chicago	IL	60611	Kayuyoshi Hino	312-664-7475	R	0*	<0.1
Lena Fiore Inc	1949 Coltman St	Cleveland	OH	44106	Celeste Massullo	216-795-1020	R	0	<0.1

Source: Ward's Business Directory of U.S. Private and Public Companies, Volumes 1 and 2, 1996. The company type code used is as follows: P - Public, R - Private, S - Subsidiary, D - Division, J - Joint Venture, A - Affiliate, G - Group. Sales are in millions of dollars, employees are in thousands. An asterisk (*) indicates an estimated sales volume. The symbol < stands for 'less than'. Company names and addresses are truncated, in some cases, to fit into the available space.

MATERIALS CONSUMED

Material	Quantity	Delivered Cost ($ million)
Materials, ingredients, containers, and supplies	(X)	1,336.6
Broadwoven fabrics (piece goods)	(X)	552.3
Narrow fabrics (12 inches or less in width)	(X)	39.9
Knit fabrics	(X)	462.5
Yarn, all fibers	(X)	17.9
Buttons, zippers, and slide fasteners	(X)	31.9
All other materials and components, parts, containers, and supplies	(X)	72.5
Materials, ingredients, containers, and supplies, nsk	(X)	159.7

Source: 1992 *Economic Census*. Explanation of symbols used: (D): Withheld to avoid disclosure of competitive data; na: Not available; (S): Withheld because statistical norms were not met; (X): Not applicable; (Z): Less than half the unit shown; nec: Not elsewhere classified; nsk: Not specified by kind; - : zero; * : 10-19 percent estimated; ** : 20-29 percent estimated.

PRODUCT SHARE DETAILS

Product or Product Class	% Share
Women's, misses', and juniors' shirts and blouses	100.00
Women's, misses', and juniors' knit shirts and blouses (polo, tennis, cowal, tank, T-shirts, sweat, etc.), made from purchased fabrics	35.46
Women's, misses', and juniors' woven shirts and blouses	44.38
Receipts for contract and commission work on women's, misses', and juniors' shirts and blouses	17.42
Receipts for contract and commission work on women's, misses', and juniors' shirts and blouses	98.77
Receipts for contract and commission work on women's, misses', and juniors' shirts and blouses, nsk	1.23
Women's, misses', and juniors' shirts and blouses, nsk	2.74

Source: 1992 *Economic Census*. The values shown are percent of total shipments in an industry. Values of indented subcategories are summed in the main heading. The symbol (D) appears when data are withheld to prevent disclosure of competitive information. The abbreviation nsk stands for 'not specified by kind' and nec for 'not elsewhere classified'.

INPUTS AND OUTPUTS FOR APPAREL MADE FROM PURCHASED MATERIALS

Economic Sector or Industry Providing Inputs	%	Sector	Economic Sector or Industry Buying Outputs	%	Sector
Imports	29.1	Foreign	Personal consumption expenditures	82.7	
Broadwoven fabric mills	20.2	Manufg.	Apparel made from purchased materials	12.0	Manufg.
Apparel made from purchased materials	18.3	Manufg.	Exports	1.5	Foreign
Knit fabric mills	8.6	Manufg.	Federal Government purchases, national defense	0.9	Fed Govt
Wholesale trade	3.8	Trade	S/L Govt. purch., correction	0.5	S/L Govt
Advertising	2.4	Services	Pleating & stitching	0.3	Manufg.
Yarn mills & finishing of textiles, nec	1.4	Manufg.	Knit outerwear mills	0.2	Manufg.
Pleating & stitching	1.1	Manufg.	Hospitals	0.2	Services
Banking	1.1	Fin/R.E.	Laundry, dry cleaning, shoe repair	0.2	Services
Petroleum refining	1.0	Manufg.	S/L Govt. purch., health & hospitals	0.2	S/L Govt
Electric services (utilities)	1.0	Util.	Portrait, photographic studios	0.1	Services
Automotive & apparel trimmings	0.9	Manufg.	S/L Govt. purch., public assistance & relief	0.1	S/L Govt
Needles, pins, & fasteners	0.8	Manufg.			
Thread mills	0.7	Manufg.			
Communications, except radio & TV	0.7	Util.			
Eating & drinking places	0.7	Trade			
U.S. Postal Service	0.7	Gov't			
Leather tanning & finishing	0.5	Manufg.			
Narrow fabric mills	0.5	Manufg.			
Schiffli machine embroideries	0.4	Manufg.			
Motor freight transportation & warehousing	0.4	Util.			
Real estate	0.4	Fin/R.E.			
Royalties	0.4	Fin/R.E.			
Forestry products	0.3	Agric.			
Buttons	0.3	Manufg.			
Paperboard containers & boxes	0.3	Manufg.			
Air transportation	0.3	Util.			
Maintenance of nonfarm buildings nec	0.2	Constr.			
Lace goods	0.2	Manufg.			
Gas production & distribution (utilities)	0.2	Util.			
Automotive rental & leasing, without drivers	0.2	Services			
Electrical repair shops	0.2	Services			
Equipment rental & leasing services	0.2	Services			
Legal services	0.2	Services			
Management & consulting services & labs	0.2	Services			
Artificial trees & flowers	0.1	Manufg.			
Insurance carriers	0.1	Fin/R.E.			
Accounting, auditing & bookkeeping	0.1	Services			
Automotive repair shops & services	0.1	Services			

Source: Benchmark Input-Output Accounts for the U.S. Economy, 1982, U.S. Department of Commerce, Washington, D.C., July 1991. Data, as reported in the source, are organized by the 1977 SIC structure in use in 1982 but have been matched, as closely as is possible, to the 1987 SIC structure used in this book.

OCCUPATIONS EMPLOYED BY SIC 233 - APPAREL

Occupation	% of Total 1994	Change to 2005	Occupation	% of Total 1994	Change to 2005
Sewing machine operators, garment	56.1	-33.1	Cutters & trimmers, hand	1.7	-24.8
Inspectors, testers, & graders, precision	3.5	-16.4	Patternmakers, layout workers, fabric & apparel	1.5	25.4
Blue collar worker supervisors	3.0	-24.0	General managers & top executives	1.4	-20.7
Assemblers, fabricators, & hand workers nec	2.5	-16.4	Sewing machine operators, non-garment	1.3	-37.3
Pressing machine operators, textiles	2.4	-45.7	Helpers, laborers, & material movers nec	1.1	-16.4
Hand packers & packagers	2.0	-21.2	Industrial machinery mechanics	1.1	0.3
Freight, stock, & material movers, hand	1.8	-33.1	Pressers, hand	1.1	-58.2
Traffic, shipping, & receiving clerks	1.8	-19.6	Sewers, hand	1.0	-10.7

Source: *Industry-Occupation Matrix*, Bureau of Labor Statistics. These data relate to one or more 3-digit SIC industry groups rather than to a single 4-digit SIC. The change reported for each occupation to the year 2005 is a percent of growth or decline as estimated by the Bureau of Labor Statistics. The abbreviation nec stands for 'not elsewhere classified'.

LOCATION BY STATE AND REGIONAL CONCENTRATION

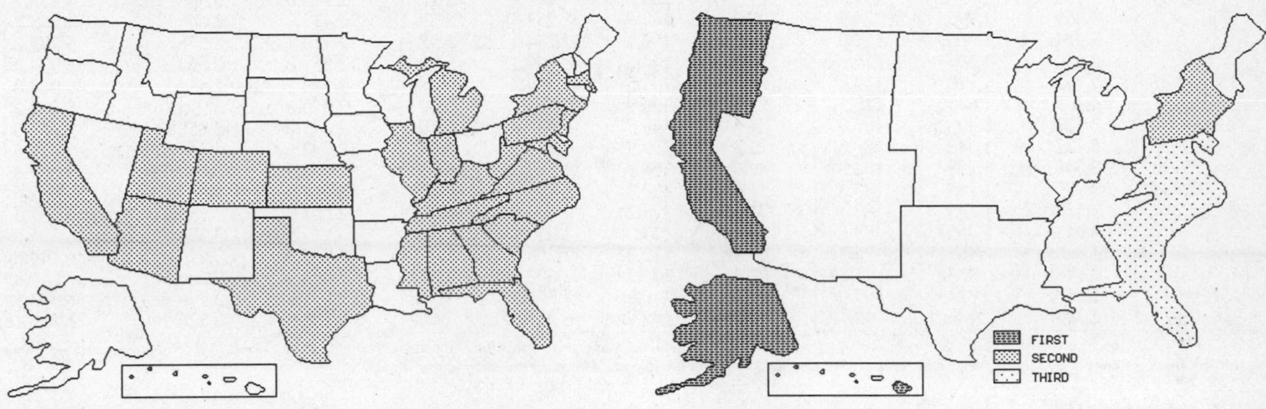

INDUSTRY DATA BY STATE

State	Establish-ments	Shipments Total ($ mil)	Shipments % of U.S.	Shipments Per Establ.	Employment Total Number	Employment % of U.S.	Employment Per Establ.	Wages ($/hour)	Cost as % of Shipments	Investment per Employee ($)
California	566	1,750.5	44.0	3.1	16,000	28.5	28	6.96	56.5	1,044
New York	289	537.4	13.5	1.9	6,900	12.3	24	6.34	48.6	420
New Jersey	67	302.0	7.6	4.5	3,000	5.3	45	7.15	56.3	533
Pennsylvania	117	260.4	6.5	2.2	5,300	9.4	45	5.92	38.5	-
Virginia	20	185.6	4.7	9.3	2,800	5.0	140	7.34	56.8	321
North Carolina	43	159.5	4.0	3.7	3,600	6.4	84	7.27	43.8	861
South Carolina	34	141.0	3.5	4.1	4,200	7.5	124	5.50	44.8	524
Florida	87	136.0	3.4	1.6	2,600	4.6	30	6.36	43.2	1,308
Alabama	23	104.3	2.6	4.5	2,100	3.7	91	5.06	17.4	333
Texas	43	69.9	1.8	1.6	1,100	2.0	26	7.69	47.5	1,000
Tennessee	40	57.7	1.5	1.4	2,400	4.3	60	5.27	38.1	250
Georgia	18	36.1	0.9	2.0	1,300	2.3	72	5.68	31.6	-
Massachusetts	21	36.0	0.9	1.7	700	1.2	33	9.00	31.4	286
Kentucky	8	24.6	0.6	3.1	800	1.4	100	4.60	43.9	625
Illinois	10	18.9	0.5	1.9	200	0.4	20	6.25	38.6	500
Indiana	5	9.2	0.2	1.8	400	0.7	80	6.50	9.8	-
Michigan	4	6.5	0.2	1.6	100	0.2	25	10.00	40.0	-
Maryland	6	2.8	0.1	0.5	100	0.2	17	5.50	7.1	-
Arizona	6	(D)	-	-	375 *	0.7	63	-	-	-
Mississippi	6	(D)	-	-	375 *	0.7	63	-	-	-
Utah	5	(D)	-	-	750 *	1.3	150	-	-	-
Colorado	4	(D)	-	-	175 *	0.3	44	-	-	-
Kansas	4	(D)	-	-	175 *	0.3	44	-	-	-
West Virginia	4	(D)	-	-	375 *	0.7	94	-	-	-

Source: 1992 *Economic Census*. The states are in descending order of shipments or establishments (if shipment data are missing for the majority). The symbol (D) appears when data are withheld to prevent disclosure of competitive information. States marked with (D) are sorted by number of establishments. A dash (-) indicates that the data element cannot be calculated; * indicates the midpoint of a range.

2335 - WOMEN'S, JUNIORS', & MISSES' DRESSES

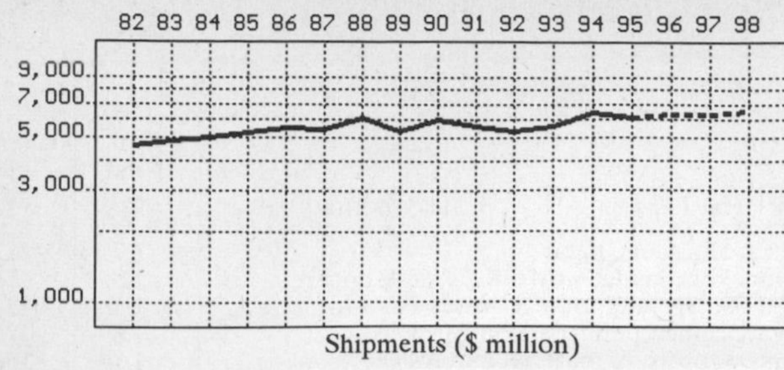

Shipments ($ million)

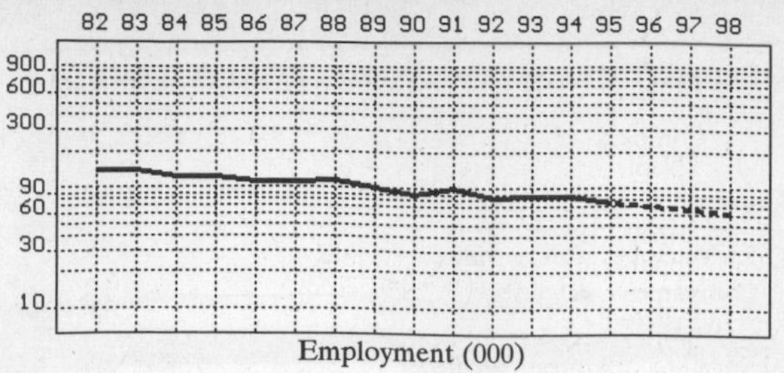

Employment (000)

GENERAL STATISTICS

Year	Com-panies	Establishments		Employment			Compensation		Production ($ million)			
		Total	with 20 or more employees	Total (000)	Production Workers (000)	Production Hours (Mil)	Payroll ($ mil)	Wages ($/hr)	Cost of Materials	Value Added by Manufacture	Value of Shipments	Capital Invest.
1982	5,489	5,627	2,055	137.9	120.0	210.7	1,268.3	4.56	2,210.7	2,413.2	4,623.3	68.1
1983		4,993	1,925	139.5	121.7	225.0	1,543.0	5.18	2,328.0	2,548.3	4,858.9	34.8
1984		4,359	1,795	124.3	107.0	169.0	1,253.3	5.39	2,415.0	2,640.8	4,995.9	52.8
1985		3,724	1,666	121.0	105.2	152.3	1,254.9	5.92	2,716.1	2,576.6	5,277.2	58.4
1986		3,650	1,591	111.8	94.5	144.2	1,240.1	5.98	2,851.2	2,664.3	5,504.2	36.6
1987	5,425	5,471	1,720	112.7	91.5	141.5	1,359.5	6.08	2,582.7	2,580.2	5,447.8	31.4
1988		4,235	1,641	115.1	91.8	136.9	1,454.9	6.40	2,920.3	3,093.1	6,037.2	
1989		3,521	1,493	100.9	89.2	148.7	1,335.9	6.10	2,485.0	2,860.0	5,365.8	48.2
1990		3,122	1,343	88.8	93.3	159.9	1,359.8	5.93	2,593.6	3,346.8	5,914.5	59.0
1991		2,948	1,258	102.3	89.6	148.8	1,342.3	6.30	2,673.9	3,019.3	5,664.8	30.8
1992	3,938	3,996	1,187	83.3	71.0	120.0	1,204.3	6.81	2,608.6	2,813.5	5,352.0	42.3
1993		3,538	1,145	87.1	74.5	128.2	1,277.9	6.71	2,661.0	2,959.0	5,602.3	40.0
1994		3,043P	1,059P	87.5	74.8	133.3	1,353.1	7.10	3,119.5	3,306.3	6,396.2	53.8
1995		2,880P	981P	76.2P	67.1P	112.3P	1,306.2P	7.17P	2,996.8P	3,176.3P	6,144.6P	
1996		2,718P	903P	71.6P	63.3P	106.2P	1,303.2P	7.34P	3,044.2P	3,226.5P	6,241.8P	
1997		2,555P	824P	67.0P	59.4P	100.1P	1,300.3P	7.50P	3,091.6P	3,276.7P	6,338.9P	
1998		2,393P	746P	62.4P	55.6P	93.9P	1,297.3P	7.66P	3,138.9P	3,326.9P	6,436.1P	

Sources: 1982, 1987, 1992 *Economic Census*; *Annual Survey of Manufactures*, 83-86, 88-91, 93-94. Establishment counts for non-Census years are from *County Business Patterns*; establishment values for 83-84 are extrapolations. 'P's show projections by the editors. Industries reclassified in 87 will not have data for prior years.

INDICES OF CHANGE

Year	Com-panies	Establishments		Employment			Compensation		Production ($ million)			
		Total	with 20 or more employees	Total (000)	Production Workers (000)	Production Hours (Mil)	Payroll ($ mil)	Wages ($/hr)	Cost of Materials	Value Added by Manufacture	Value of Shipments	Capital Invest.
1982	139	141	173	166	169	176	105	67	85	86	86	161
1983		125	162	167	171	188	128	76	89	91	91	82
1984		109	151	149	151	141	104	79	93	94	93	125
1985		93	140	145	148	127	104	87	104	92	99	138
1986		91	134	134	133	120	103	88	109	95	103	87
1987	138	137	145	135	129	118	113	89	99	92	102	74
1988		106	138	138	129	114	121	94	112	110	113	
1989		88	126	121	126	124	111	90	95	102	100	114
1990		78	113	107	131	133	113	87	99	119	111	139
1991		74	106	123	126	124	111	93	103	107	106	73
1992	100	100	100	100	100	100	100	100	100	100	100	100
1993		89	96	105	105	107	106	99	102	105	105	95
1994		76P	89P	105	105	111	112	104	120	118	120	127
1995		72P	83P	92P	95P	94P	108P	105P	115P	113P	115P	
1996		68P	76P	86P	89P	89P	108P	108P	117P	115P	117P	
1997		64P	69P	80P	84P	83P	108P	110P	119P	116P	118P	
1998		60P	63P	75P	78P	78P	108P	113P	120P	118P	120P	

Sources: Same as General Statistics. Values reflect change from the base year, 1992. Values above 100 mean greater than 92, values below 100 mean less than 92, and a value of 100 in the 82-91 or 93-98 period means same as 92. 'P's mark projections by the editors.

SELECTED RATIOS

For 1994	Avg. of All Manufact.	Analyzed Industry	Index
Employees per Establishment	49	29	59
Payroll per Establishment	1,500,273	444,702	30
Payroll per Employee	30,620	15,464	51
Production Workers per Establishment	34	25	72
Wages per Establishment	853,319	311,048	36
Wages per Production Worker	24,861	12,653	51
Hours per Production Worker	2,056	1,782	87
Wages per Hour	12.09	7.10	59
Value Added per Establishment	4,602,255	1,086,629	24
Value Added per Employee	93,930	37,786	40

For 1994	Avg. of All Manufact.	Analyzed Industry	Index
Value Added per Production Worker	134,084	44,202	33
Cost per Establishment	5,045,178	1,025,237	20
Cost per Employee	102,970	35,651	35
Cost per Production Worker	146,988	41,705	28
Shipments per Establishment	9,576,895	2,102,138	22
Shipments per Employee	195,460	73,099	37
Shipments per Production Worker	279,017	85,511	31
Investment per Establishment	321,011	17,682	6
Investment per Employee	6,552	615	9
Investment per Production Worker	9,352	719	8

Sources: Same as General Statistics. The 'Average of All Manufacturing' column represents the average of all manufacturing industries reported for the most recent complete year available. The Index shows the relationship between the Average and the Analyzed Industry. For example, 100 means that they are equal; 500 that the Analyzed Industry is five times the average; 50 means that the Analyzed Industry is half the national average. The abbreviation 'na' is used to show that data are 'not available'.

LEADING COMPANIES

Number shown: **70** Total sales ($ mil): **2,252** Total employment (000): **25.0**

Company Name	Address				CEO Name	Phone	Co. Type	Sales ($ mil)	Empl. (000)
Kellwood Co	PO Box 14374	St Louis	MO	63178	Hal J Upbin	314-576-3100	P	1,203	15.5
Jessica McClintock Inc	1400 16th St	San Francisco	CA	94103	J G McClintock	415-495-3030	R	140	0.4
Donnkenny Apparel Inc	1411 Broadway	New York	NY	10018	Richard Rubin	212-730-7770	S	110*	1.6
Tanner Companies Inc	PO Box 1139	Rutherfordton	NC	28139	Dave DeFeo	704-287-4205	R	72*	0.8
Harkham Industries Inc	1157 S Crocker St	Los Angeles	CA	90021	Uri Harkham	213-624-6696	R	50	0.4
Jerell Inc	1431 Regal Row	Dallas	TX	75247	Ed Vierling	214-637-5300	R	50	0.4
SPN Inc	PO Box 749	Collinsville	IL	62234	Daniel P Shea	618-345-2345	R	50	0.6
Expo Inc	1400 Broadway	New York	NY	10018	Beau Baker	212-382-3777	R	41*	<0.1
Depeche Mode Inc	498 7th Av	New York	NY	10018	Marvin Singer	212-563-9700	R	38	0.1
Little Laura of California Inc	1655 Mateo St	Los Angeles	CA	90021	Neil Miller	213-688-0170	R	36	0.2
Kingley Manufacturing Corp	70 W 36th St	New York	NY	10018	Arthur Mintz	212-279-3240	R	34*	0.4
Lanz Inc	8680 Hayden Pl	Culver City	CA	90232	Alexis Scharff	310-558-0200	R	30	0.2
Cape Cod-Cricket Lane	PO Box 542	W Bridgewater	MA	02379	Jack Finkelman	508-586-4343	D	29*	0.4
Breli Originals Inc	520 8th Av	New York	NY	10018	Alvin Bressler	212-695-5111	R	25	<0.1
David Stevens Manufacturing	109 N Black Horse	Blackwood	NJ	08012	Herbert Kane	609-227-0655	R	21*	0.2
House of Bianchi Inc	1 Brainard Av	Medford	MA	02155	Joseph V Massa	617-391-6111	R	20	0.3
Oxford of Alma Inc	Rte 2	Alma	GA	31510	FF Lockaby	912-632-7236	S	19*	0.2
Surf and Turf of California Inc	3833 S Hill St	Los Angeles	CA	90037	Seymour Rothman	213-749-5251	R	16*	<0.1
Ursula of Switzerland Inc	PO Box 418	Waterford	NY	12188	U G-Rickenbacher	518-237-2580	R	16	<0.1
Wilroy Inc	1111 Secaucus Rd	Secaucus	NJ	07094	Kenneth Grossman	201-348-1111	R	15	<0.1
Caron Inc	350 W Kinzie St	Chicago	IL	60610	Phil Sudakoff	312-670-3700	R	15	0.1
Keyser Garment Company Inc	PO Box 819	Keyser	WV	26726	P Grogan	304-788-3481	R	15*	0.2
Howard B Wolf Inc	3809 Parry Av	Dallas	TX	75226	Robert D Wolf	214-823-9941	P	14	<0.1
Scarlett Nite	501 7th Av	New York	NY	10018	Richard Sims	212-382-1414	R	13*	0.2
Milady Bridals Inc	1375 Broadway	New York	NY	10018	Eve Muscio	212-302-0050	R	12*	<0.1
HL Miller and Son Inc	25 W Miller Rd	Iola	KS	66749	EJ Miller	316-365-2174	R	11	0.1
Russell Apparel Corp	219 Norwood St	Radford	VA	24141	GR Quesenberry	703-639-5761	R	11*	0.1
Victor Costa Inc	7600 Ambass	Dallas	TX	75247	Victor Costa	214-634-1133	R	10	<0.1
Lady Carol Dresses Inc	1400 Broadway	New York	NY	10018	Sheldon Ratner	212-391-7880	R	10*	0.1
Miss Elliette Inc	4701 S Santa Fe Av	Los Angeles	CA	90058	Robert Ellis	213-585-2222	R	10	<0.1
Dan Howard Industries Inc	4245 N Knox Av	Chicago	IL	60641	Daniel S Kirsch	312-263-6700	R	9	0.1
Mike Benet Formals Mfg	PO Drawer 43	Pittsburg	TX	75686	Michael Crowell	903-856-3648	R	7	0.2
Oscar de la Renta Ltd	550 7th Av	New York	NY	10018	Gerald Shaw	212-354-6777	R	7*	<0.1
Danny and Nicole Inc	49 W 37th St 10th Fl	New York	NY	10018	Danial Zar	212-704-9603	R	6	0.1
Elias Sayour Company Inc	183 Madison Av	New York	NY	10016	Paul Sayour	212-686-7560	R	6	<0.1
Lady Hope Dress Company Inc	1400 Chestnut St	Kulpmont	PA	17834	Stephen Kent	717-373-9416	R	6*	<0.1
Prattville Apparel	Hwy 82 Bypass	Prattville	AL	36067	J Smoler	205-365-5921	D	6*	0.1
Priscilla of Boston Inc	40 Cambridge St	Charlestown	MA	02129	Patricia C Kaneb	617-242-2677	R	6	0.1
Sol Walter Enterprises Inc	PO Box 808	Nyack	NY	10960	Samuel Walter	914-358-0979	R	5	<0.1
JLT Inc	2818 Virgo Ln	Dallas	TX	75229	Jason Lucks	214-243-0700	R	4*	<0.1
Jones of Dallas Manufacturing	8505 Chancell	Dallas	TX	75247	Gerald R Lofland	214-638-0321	R	4*	<0.1
Mori Lee Associates	498 7th Av	New York	NY	10018	Marvin Leibowitz	212-947-3490	R	4*	<0.1
Helga Inc	722 S Los Angeles	Los Angeles	CA	90014	Michael S Shore	213-627-0806	R	3	<0.1
Krist Gudnason Inc	PO Box 8427	Emeryville	CA	94608	Krist Gudnason	510-655-9212	R	3	<0.1
Vijack Fashions Inc	213 W 35th St	New York	NY	10001	Henry Lippolt	212-695-6677	R	3	<0.1
Carolina Dress Corp	PO Box 328	Hayesville	NC	28904	W Fuller	704-389-8888	R	3	0.1
Irene Kasmer Inc	910 S Los Angeles	Los Angeles	CA	90015	Irene Kasmer	213-622-1046	R	3	<0.1
Royes Fashion Inc	756 S Spring St	Los Angeles	CA	90014	Gene Roye	213-629-9031	R	3	<0.1
Ruffolo Brothers Inc	530 7th Av	New York	NY	10018	Aurora Ruffolo	212-354-9250	R	2*	<0.1
Achievers Unlimited Corp	46 Pondfield Rd	Bronxville	NY	10708	Marcella Luiso	914-337-2234	R	2*	<0.1
Carolina Maid Products Inc	PO Box 308	Granite Quarry	NC	28072	David W Swaim	704-279-7221	R	2	<0.1
Cattiva Inc	498 7th Av	New York	NY	10018	Charles Schwartz	212-239-8808	R	2*	<0.1
Fink Brothers Inc	1385 Broadway	New York	NY	10018	Morris Fink	212-921-5683	R	2	<0.1
Glad Rags Inc	PO Box 189	Buchanan	VA	24066	Peter J Ragone	703-254-1361	R	2	0.1
Summit Station Manufacturing	194 S Tulpehocken	Pine Grove	PA	17963	S Katzman	717-345-4191	R	2	<0.1
Treage Ltd	2529 Royal Ln	Dallas	TX	75229	Gary Warner	214-620-7640	S	2	<0.1
IH Marshall Ltd	530 7th Av	New York	NY	10018	Ildi Marshall	212-730-2823	R	1	<0.1
San Carlin Manufacturing	738 S Range Av	Denham Sp	LA	70726	Carla Jumonville	504-667-0462	R	1	<0.1
Alexander Brown	846 S Broadway	Los Angeles	CA	90014	D Alexander	213-614-0418	R	1*	<0.1
Len-Jef Inc	110 Maple St	Kulpmont	PA	17834	Daniel S Shimko	717-373-5841	R	1	0.1
San Martin Bridals	3353 Verdugo Rd	Los Angeles	CA	90065	T Martin	213-257-5333	R	1*	<0.1
Sancor Inc	1417 Santee St	Los Angeles	CA	90015	Mark Naim	213-622-5176	R	1	<0.1
Victoria Royal Inc	530 7th Av	New York	NY	10018	Alan Sealove	212-944-6844	R	1*	<0.1
E Nola Inc	10762 Weaver Av	S El Monte	CA	91733	E Nola	818-452-9247	R	1*	<0.1
Style-Rite Manufacturing	1220 Moores Grove	Winterville	GA	30683	Ruby K Smith	706-742-7200	R	1	<0.1
Tiff and Griff Designs Ltd	1801 Larchmont St	Chicago	IL	60613	Tiffani Kim	312-281-7555	R	1*	<0.1
By Susan Inc	1633 Spruce St	Philadelphia	PA	19103	Susan Lunenfeld	215-546-5115	R	1*	<0.1
Ballinger Gold Inc	1450 Broadway	New York	NY	10018	Babette Ballinger	212-730-7880	R	1*	<0.1
Argentum USA Inc	566 7th Av	New York	NY	10018	Anna Blumenfeld	212-840-0987	R	1	<0.1
AKIRA Corp	200 W 57th St	New York	NY	10019	Akira Maki	212-397-0720	R	0	<0.1

Source: *Ward's Business Directory of U.S. Private and Public Companies*, Volumes 1 and 2, 1996. The company type code used is as follows: P - Public, R - Private, S - Subsidiary, D - Division, J - Joint Venture, A - Affiliate, G - Group. Sales are in millions of dollars, employees are in thousands. An asterisk (*) indicates an estimated sales volume. The symbol < stands for 'less than'. Company names and addresses are truncated, in some cases, to fit into the available space.

MATERIALS CONSUMED

Material	Quantity	Delivered Cost ($ million)
Materials, ingredients, containers, and supplies	(X)	1,667.4
Broadwoven fabrics (piece goods)	(X)	758.4
Narrow fabrics (12 inches or less in width)	(X)	57.4
Knit fabrics	(X)	114.1
Yarn, all fibers	(X)	28.7
Buttons, zippers, and slide fasteners	(X)	77.3
All other materials and components, parts, containers, and supplies	(X)	78.7
Materials, ingredients, containers, and supplies, nsk	(X)	552.9

Source: 1992 *Economic Census*. Explanation of symbols used: (D): Withheld to avoid disclosure of competitive data; na: Not available; (S): Withheld because statistical norms were not met; (X): Not applicable; (Z): Less than half the unit shown; nec: Not elsewhere classified; nsk: Not specified by kind; - : zero; * : 10-19 percent estimated; ** : 20-29 percent estimated.

PRODUCT SHARE DETAILS

Product or Product Class	% Share
Women's, misses', and juniors' dresses	100.00
Women's, misses', and juniors' dresses	75.46
Receipts for contract and commission work on women's, misses', and juniors' dresses	19.32
Receipts for contract and commission work on women's, misses', and juniors' dresses	98.20
Receipts for contract and commission work on women's, misses', and juniors' dresses, nsk	1.79
Women's, misses', and juniors' dresses, nsk	5.22

Source: 1992 *Economic Census*. The values shown are percent of total shipments in an industry. Values of indented subcategories are summed in the main heading. The symbol (D) appears when data are withheld to prevent disclosure of competitive information. The abbreviation nsk stands for 'not specified by kind' and nec for 'not elsewhere classified'.

INPUTS AND OUTPUTS FOR APPAREL MADE FROM PURCHASED MATERIALS

Economic Sector or Industry Providing Inputs	%	Sector	Economic Sector or Industry Buying Outputs	%	Sector
Imports	29.1	Foreign	Personal consumption expenditures	82.7	
Broadwoven fabric mills	20.2	Manufg.	Apparel made from purchased materials	12.0	Manufg.
Apparel made from purchased materials	18.3	Manufg.	Exports	1.5	Foreign
Knit fabric mills	8.6	Manufg.	Federal Government purchases, national defense	0.9	Fed Govt
Wholesale trade	3.8	Trade	S/L Govt. purch., correction	0.5	S/L Govt
Advertising	2.4	Services	Pleating & stitching	0.3	Manufg.
Yarn mills & finishing of textiles, nec	1.4	Manufg.	Knit outerwear mills	0.2	Manufg.
Pleating & stitching	1.1	Manufg.	Hospitals	0.2	Services
Banking	1.1	Fin/R.E.	Laundry, dry cleaning, shoe repair	0.2	Services
Petroleum refining	1.0	Manufg.	S/L Govt. purch., health & hospitals	0.2	S/L Govt
Electric services (utilities)	1.0	Util.	Portrait, photographic studios	0.1	Services
Automotive & apparel trimmings	0.9	Manufg.	S/L Govt. purch., public assistance & relief	0.1	S/L Govt
Needles, pins, & fasteners	0.8	Manufg.			
Thread mills	0.7	Manufg.			
Communications, except radio & TV	0.7	Util.			
Eating & drinking places	0.7	Trade			
U.S. Postal Service	0.7	Gov't			
Leather tanning & finishing	0.5	Manufg.			
Narrow fabric mills	0.5	Manufg.			
Schiffli machine embroideries	0.4	Manufg.			
Motor freight transportation & warehousing	0.4	Util.			
Real estate	0.4	Fin/R.E.			
Royalties	0.4	Fin/R.E.			
Forestry products	0.3	Agric.			
Buttons	0.3	Manufg.			
Paperboard containers & boxes	0.3	Manufg.			
Air transportation	0.3	Util.			
Maintenance of nonfarm buildings nec	0.2	Constr.			
Lace goods	0.2	Manufg.			
Gas production & distribution (utilities)	0.2	Util.			
Automotive rental & leasing, without drivers	0.2	Services			
Electrical repair shops	0.2	Services			
Equipment rental & leasing services	0.2	Services			
Legal services	0.2	Services			
Management & consulting services & labs	0.2	Services			
Artificial trees & flowers	0.1	Manufg.			
Insurance carriers	0.1	Fin/R.E.			
Accounting, auditing & bookkeeping	0.1	Services			
Automotive repair shops & services	0.1	Services			

Source: Benchmark Input-Output Accounts for the U.S. Economy, 1982, U.S. Department of Commerce, Washington, D.C., July 1991. Data, as reported in the source, are organized by the 1977 SIC structure in use in 1982 but have been matched, as closely as is possible, to the 1987 SIC structure used in this book.

OCCUPATIONS EMPLOYED BY SIC 233 - APPAREL

Occupation	% of Total 1994	Change to 2005	Occupation	% of Total 1994	Change to 2005
Sewing machine operators, garment	56.1	-33.1	Cutters & trimmers, hand	1.7	-24.8
Inspectors, testers, & graders, precision	3.5	-16.4	Patternmakers, layout workers, fabric & apparel	1.5	25.4
Blue collar worker supervisors	3.0	-24.0	General managers & top executives	1.4	-20.7
Assemblers, fabricators, & hand workers nec	2.5	-16.4	Sewing machine operators, non-garment	1.3	-37.3
Pressing machine operators, textiles	2.4	-45.7	Helpers, laborers, & material movers nec	1.1	-16.4
Hand packers & packagers	2.0	-21.2	Industrial machinery mechanics	1.1	0.3
Freight, stock, & material movers, hand	1.8	-33.1	Pressers, hand	1.1	-58.2
Traffic, shipping, & receiving clerks	1.8	-19.6	Sewers, hand	1.0	-10.7

Source: Industry-Occupation Matrix, Bureau of Labor Statistics. These data relate to one or more 3-digit SIC industry groups rather than to a single 4-digit SIC. The change reported for each occupation to the year 2005 is a percent of growth or decline as estimated by the Bureau of Labor Statistics. The abbreviation nec stands for 'not elsewhere classified'.

LOCATION BY STATE AND REGIONAL CONCENTRATION

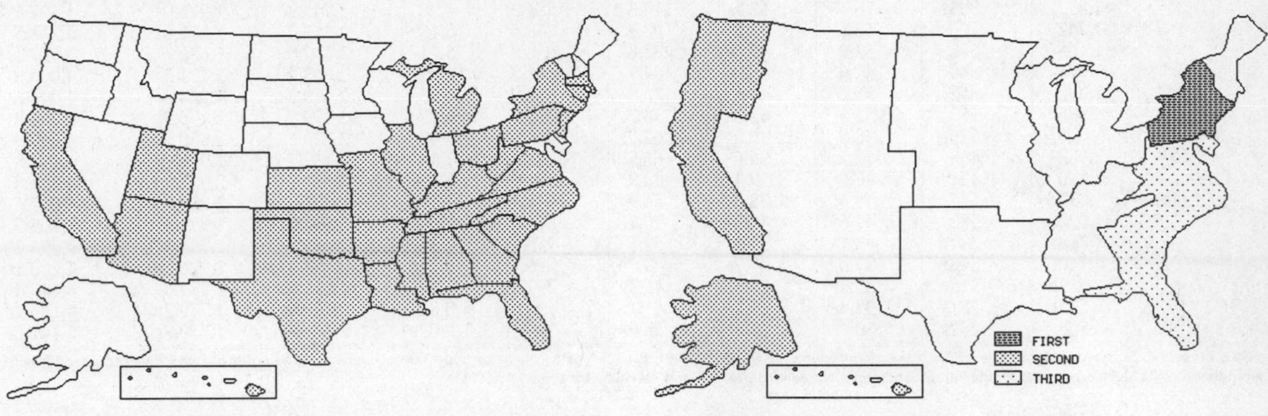

INDUSTRY DATA BY STATE

State	Establish-ments	Shipments Total ($ mil)	Shipments % of U.S.	Shipments Per Establ.	Employment Total Number	Employment % of U.S.	Employment Per Establ.	Wages ($/hour)	Cost as % of Shipments	Investment per Employee ($)
New York	1,310	2,409.1	45.0	1.8	27,100	32.5	21	7.65	52.7	491
California	1,339	1,680.0	31.4	1.3	23,800	28.6	18	6.83	49.7	655
Pennsylvania	215	403.5	7.5	1.9	8,000	9.6	37	6.15	44.2	388
Texas	141	188.2	3.5	1.3	2,700	3.2	19	7.55	48.4	852
Illinois	59	101.1	1.9	1.7	1,500	1.8	25	7.10	41.4	333
New Jersey	155	90.2	1.7	0.6	2,200	2.6	14	6.76	41.1	364
Florida	236	88.6	1.7	0.4	2,800	3.4	12	6.38	33.4	929
North Carolina	52	46.5	0.9	0.9	2,200	2.6	42	5.39	31.0	273
Massachusetts	37	35.7	0.7	1.0	900	1.1	24	6.73	36.7	222
Georgia	28	27.3	0.5	1.0	1,600	1.9	57	5.43	37.4	188
Tennessee	34	26.3	0.5	0.8	1,500	1.8	44	5.96	14.1	200
Hawaii	42	19.5	0.4	0.5	600	0.7	14	5.78	37.4	500
Alabama	32	18.8	0.4	0.6	1,400	1.7	44	5.26	23.9	357
South Carolina	27	16.5	0.3	0.6	1,000	1.2	37	6.00	23.0	200
Missouri	11	14.6	0.3	1.3	300	0.4	27	6.25	34.2	-
West Virginia	10	9.4	0.2	0.9	500	0.6	50	6.00	31.9	200
Kentucky	8	7.8	0.1	1.0	300	0.4	38	5.75	39.7	-
Ohio	18	6.2	0.1	0.3	300	0.4	17	5.50	29.0	333
Connecticut	15	5.7	0.1	0.4	300	0.4	20	5.75	24.6	333
Louisiana	9	5.1	0.1	0.6	200	0.2	22	6.00	23.5	-
Michigan	19	5.0	0.1	0.3	200	0.2	11	6.67	14.0	500
Arizona	13	4.7	0.1	0.4	300	0.4	23	5.50	29.8	333
Utah	10	3.0	0.1	0.3	200	0.2	20	6.50	20.0	-
Oklahoma	13	2.3	0.0	0.2	100	0.1	8	5.00	17.4	-
Virginia	30	(D)	-	-	1,750 *	2.1	58	-	-	-
Mississippi	14	(D)	-	-	375 *	0.5	27	-	-	267
Arkansas	8	(D)	-	-	175 *	0.2	22	-	-	-
Kansas	3	(D)	-	-	175 *	0.2	58	-	-	-

Source: 1992 *Economic Census*. The states are in descending order of shipments or establishments (if shipment data are missing for the majority). The symbol (D) appears when data are withheld to prevent disclosure of competitive information. States marked with (D) are sorted by number of establishments. A dash (-) indicates that the data element cannot be calculated; * indicates the midpoint of a range.

2337 - WOMEN'S AND MISSES' SUITS AND COATS

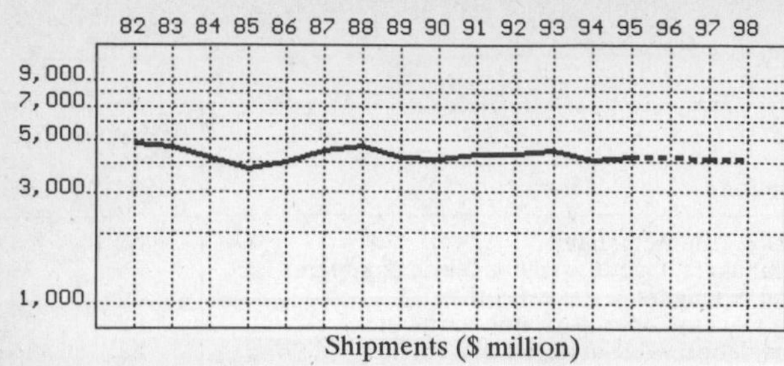

Shipments ($ million)

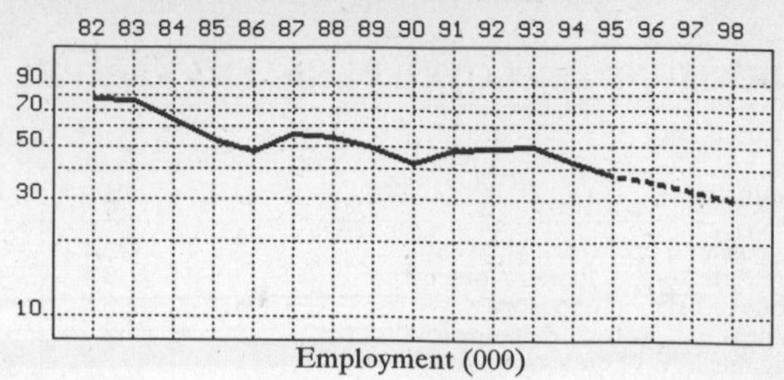

Employment (000)

GENERAL STATISTICS

Year	Com-panies	Establishments		Employment			Compensation		Production ($ million)			
		Total	with 20 or more employees	Total (000)	Production Workers (000)	Production Hours (Mil)	Payroll ($ mil)	Wages ($/hr)	Cost of Materials	Value Added by Manufacture	Value of Shipments	Capital Invest.
1982	1,431	1,512	900	78.2	63.2	125.8	871.1	4.60	2,772.6	2,067.1	4,886.7	30.5
1983		1,377	803	76.4	62.1	117.8	881.3	4.98	2,745.2	1,976.9	4,697.5	28.0
1984		1,242	706	63.8	52.5	93.9	758.4	5.15	2,362.2	1,872.6	4,238.5	35.4
1985		1,106	608	52.9	43.6	73.8	658.8	5.51	2,107.8	1,630.6	3,752.1	23.2
1986		975	540	47.6	38.3	64.7	641.7	6.01	2,303.0	1,731.3	4,005.3	27.3
1987	1,044	1,092	652	55.2	44.6	78.0	818.9	6.53	2,459.3	1,964.0	4,446.6	24.5
1988		986	553	53.3	42.2	73.7	817.7	6.57	2,499.7	2,196.9	4,704.8	
1989		874	526	48.5	36.0	63.9	758.0	7.02	2,220.6	2,030.7	4,240.8	16.0
1990		788	448	42.5	36.6	66.5	769.5	7.00	2,187.7	1,979.0	4,162.8	27.6
1991		778	421	47.9	39.3	70.7	802.4	7.09	2,322.7	2,033.2	4,324.0	24.1
1992	1,008	1,037	547	48.6	38.0	66.9	848.4	7.53	2,371.3	2,019.9	4,369.6	31.5
1993		1,032	502	49.6	40.0	70.1	871.5	7.64	2,534.9	1,993.1	4,508.7	27.5
1994		758P	382P	43.1	34.1	59.6	750.0	7.68	2,339.7	1,734.1	4,055.2	24.7
1995		710P	348P	37.6P	29.7P	49.5P	796.4P	8.27P	2,423.3P	1,796.0P	4,200.1P	
1996		663P	315P	35.2P	27.7P	45.3P	797.5P	8.54P	2,411.9P	1,787.6P	4,180.4P	
1997		615P	281P	32.8P	25.7P	41.1P	798.7P	8.81P	2,400.6P	1,779.2P	4,160.7P	
1998		568P	247P	30.4P	23.7P	36.9P	799.8P	9.07P	2,389.2P	1,770.8P	4,141.0P	

Sources: 1982, 1987, 1992 *Economic Census*; *Annual Survey of Manufactures*, 83-86, 88-91, 93-94. Establishment counts for non-Census years are from *County Business Patterns*; establishment values for 83-84 are extrapolations. 'P's show projections by the editors. Industries reclassified in 87 will not have data for prior years.

INDICES OF CHANGE

Year	Com-panies	Establishments		Employment			Compensation		Production ($ million)			
		Total	with 20 or more employees	Total (000)	Production Workers (000)	Production Hours (Mil)	Payroll ($ mil)	Wages ($/hr)	Cost of Materials	Value Added by Manufacture	Value of Shipments	Capital Invest.
1982	142	146	165	161	166	188	103	61	117	102	112	97
1983		133	147	157	163	176	104	66	116	98	108	89
1984		120	129	131	138	140	89	68	100	93	97	112
1985		107	111	109	115	110	78	73	89	81	86	74
1986		94	99	98	101	97	76	80	97	86	92	87
1987	104	105	119	114	117	117	97	87	104	97	102	78
1988		95	101	110	111	110	96	87	105	109	108	
1989		84	96	100	95	96	89	93	94	101	97	51
1990		76	82	87	96	99	91	93	92	98	95	88
1991		75	77	99	103	106	95	94	98	101	99	77
1992	100	100	100	100	100	100	100	100	100	100	100	100
1993		100	92	102	105	105	103	101	107	99	103	87
1994		73P	70P	89	90	89	88	102	99	86	93	78
1995		68P	64P	77P	78P	74P	94P	110P	102P	89P	96P	
1996		64P	58P	72P	73P	68P	94P	113P	102P	89P	96P	
1997		59P	51P	68P	68P	61P	94P	117P	101P	88P	95P	
1998		55P	45P	63P	62P	55P	94P	121P	101P	88P	95P	

Sources: Same as General Statistics. Values reflect change from the base year, 1992. Values above 100 mean greater than 92, values below 100 mean less than 92, and a value of 100 in the 82-91 or 93-98 period means same as 92. 'P's mark projections by the editors.

SELECTED RATIOS

For 1994	Avg. of All Manufact.	Analyzed Industry	Index
Employees per Establishment	49	57	116
Payroll per Establishment	1,500,273	989,723	66
Payroll per Employee	30,620	17,401	57
Production Workers per Establishment	34	45	131
Wages per Establishment	853,319	604,032	71
Wages per Production Worker	24,861	13,423	54
Hours per Production Worker	2,056	1,748	85
Wages per Hour	12.09	7.68	64
Value Added per Establishment	4,602,255	2,288,371	50
Value Added per Employee	93,930	40,234	43

For 1994	Avg. of All Manufact.	Analyzed Industry	Index
Value Added per Production Worker	134,084	50,853	38
Cost per Establishment	5,045,178	3,087,539	61
Cost per Employee	102,970	54,285	53
Cost per Production Worker	146,988	68,613	47
Shipments per Establishment	9,576,895	5,351,366	56
Shipments per Employee	195,460	94,088	48
Shipments per Production Worker	279,017	118,921	43
Investment per Establishment	321,011	32,595	10
Investment per Employee	6,552	573	9
Investment per Production Worker	9,352	724	8

Sources: Same as General Statistics. The 'Average of All Manufacturing' column represents the average of all manufacturing industries reported for the most recent complete year available. The Index shows the relationship between the Average and the Analyzed Industry. For example, 100 means that they are equal; 500 that the Analyzed Industry is five times the average; 50 means that the Analyzed Industry is half the national average. The abbreviation 'na' is used to show that data are 'not available'.

LEADING COMPANIES

Number shown: **44** Total sales ($ mil): **786** Total employment (000): **5.0**

Company Name	Address				CEO Name	Phone	Co. Type	Sales ($ mil)	Empl. (000)
Norton McNaughton of Squire	463 7th Av	New York	NY	10018	Sanford Greenberg	212-947-2960	S	169	0.2
Norton McNaughton Inc	463 7th Av	New York	NY	10018	Sanford Greenberg	212-947-2960	P	169	0.2
JH Collectibles Inc	200 W Vogel Av	Milwaukee	WI	53207	Bruce Ross	414-744-5080	R	130	0.7
School Apparel Inc	4610 Mission St	San Francisco	CA	94112	KW Knoss	415-239-1900	R	42	0.6
CMT Industries Inc	208 Octavia St	El Paso	TX	79901	Juergen Kuehnel	915-532-2619	R	33*	0.5
Joyce Sportswear Co	350 N Orleans St	Chicago	IL	60654	Jack Goodman	312-828-0800	R	22	0.4
Apparel Group Inc	13800 S Figueroa St	Los Angeles	CA	90061	Stewart Weiser	310-516-0531	R	20*	<0.1
Leon Max Inc	127 E 9th St	Los Angeles	CA	90015	Leon Max	213-629-5030	R	20*	<0.1
Sunny Lady	7777 Hines Pl	Dallas	TX	75235	Sol Munles	214-637-4333	D	20	<0.1
Sunny South Fashions	7777 Hines Pl	Dallas	TX	75235	Murray Munves	214-637-4333	R	20	0.1
M Shapiro and Company Inc	10151 National Blv	Los Angeles	CA	90034	Ronald Shapiro	310-815-9471	R	13*	<0.1
Gloria Gay Coats Inc	500 7th Av	New York	NY	10018	William Hartman	212-736-1810	R	11	<0.1
Oxford of Burgaw Co	1090 Wilmington St	Burgaw	NC	28425	George Arrington	910-259-5794	D	10	0.1
Pants Plus Inc	225 W 35th St	New York	NY	10001	Cary Goldberg	212-695-7973	R	10*	<0.1
Kay Lynn Sportswear Inc	1820 W Spring St	Palestine	TX	75801	W L Morgan Jr	903-729-3103	R	9	0.1
Marlin Manufacturing Company	PO Box 1100	Marlin	TX	76661	Amnon DeNur	817-883-3581	R	9	0.3
Deanna Dee Inc	860 S Los Angeles	Los Angeles	CA	90014	Mari Achwarz	213-622-9103	R	6	<0.1
Loring Coat Inc	8-18 S Lander St	Newburgh	NY	12550	Abraham Fuhr	914-562-1124	R	6	0.1
Annette Fashions Corp	162 P-Adamsbrg	Jeannette	PA	15644	Berardo Maragni	412-523-5476	R	5*	<0.1
Cuddlecoat Inc	512 7th Av	New York	NY	10018	JR Lipman	212-944-7500	R	5*	<0.1
Lamesa Apparel Inc	1010 N 4th St	Lamesa	TX	79331	Larry Whitman	806-872-8817	R	5*	<0.1
La-Del Manufacturing Company	PO Box 128	Lawrenceburg	TN	38464	Henry Blankenship	615-762-7412	R	5	0.1
Mayes Manufacturing Co	1950 Dawn Dr SE	Cleveland	TN	37311	Susan Ferreri	615-479-5179	R	5	0.1
Truly Yours Inc	33 Dover St	Brockton	MA	02401	Fred Bennett	508-583-3320	R	5*	<0.1
Vicki Clothing Company Inc	327 Liberty St	Newburgh	NY	12550	AF Giordano	914-561-2024	R	5*	<0.1
Herzman and Company Inc	661-63 N 8th St	Lebanon	PA	17042	Seymour Kaplan	717-272-4481	R	4	<0.1
Malco Modes Inc	1596 Howard St	San Francisco	CA	94103	Albert C Malouf	415-621-0840	R	4	<0.1
Mackintosh of New England	331 Page St	Stoughton	MA	02072	Bernard Moller	617-344-4404	S	3	<0.1
Mar-Cal Inc	1628 N Indiana St	Los Angeles	CA	90063	Sal Capitano	909-626-9737	R	3	<0.1
Paula Fashions Inc	50 Dwight St	New Britain	CT	06051	Sal Gozzo	203-229-6760	R	3	<0.1
Second Shot Inc	820 Exposition #5	Dallas	TX	75226	Julie Esping	214-823-2727	R	3	<0.1
ShaLor Designs Inc	200 Park Av S	New York	NY	10003	Mark Carson	212-736-1137	R	2*	<0.1
Kneeland Skirt Company Inc	119 Braintree St	Boston	MA	02134	Rocco Freni	617-783-8955	R	2	0.1
Babette	28 S Park St	San Francisco	CA	94107	Babette Pinsky	415-267-0280	R	1	<0.1
Ilie Wacs Inc	530 7th Av	New York	NY	10018	Ilie Wacs	212-354-9080	R	1*	<0.1
L-7 Inc	8918 Governors	Dallas	TX	75247	Todd Oldham	214-638-2937	R	1*	<0.1
Mamo Howell Inc	1020 Auahi	Honolulu	HI	96814	Mamo Howell	808-592-0611	R	1*	<0.1
Pola-Marie Fashions Inc	270 Arch St	New Britain	CT	06051	Carmen Pavano	203-223-5056	R	1	<0.1
Pretty Made Coat Company Inc	60 Railroad Av	Copiague	NY	11726	Tony Pisciotta	516-264-4452	R	1*	<0.1
Steel Sportswear Inc	5675 Boyle Av	Vernon	CA	90058	Vivian Baisley	213-582-2030	R	1	<0.1
Suz-ette Fashions Inc	14 Burma Rd	Jersey City	NJ	07305	Robert Mincow	201-333-7500	R	1	<0.1
Yeohlee Inc	530 7th Av	New York	NY	10018	Yeohlee Teng	212-704-9600	R	1*	<0.1
RCM Design Inc	512 7th Av	New York	NY	10018	Michael Kaufman	212-827-0310	S	1*	<0.1
Fashion Enterprises Inc	11355 Rojas Dr	El Paso	TX	79936	Peter Cowal	915-591-1233	R	1*	<0.1

Source: *Ward's Business Directory of U.S. Private and Public Companies*, Volumes 1 and 2, 1996. The company type code used is as follows; P - Public, R - Private, S - Subsidiary, D - Division, J - Joint Venture, A - Affiliate, G - Group. Sales are in millions of dollars, employees are in thousands. An asterisk (*) indicates an estimated sales volume. The symbol < stands for 'less than'. Company names and addresses are truncated, in some cases, to fit into the available space.

MATERIALS CONSUMED

Material	Quantity	Delivered Cost ($ million)
Materials, ingredients, containers, and supplies	(X)	1,454.1
Broadwoven fabrics (piece goods)	(X)	1,037.8
Narrow fabrics (12 inches or less in width)	(X)	85.2
Knit fabrics	(X)	80.8
Yarn, all fibers	(X)	23.7
Buttons, zippers, and slide fasteners	(X)	75.7
All other materials and components, parts, containers, and supplies	(X)	60.4
Materials, ingredients, containers, and supplies, nsk	(X)	90.5

Source: 1992 *Economic Census*. Explanation of symbols used: (D): Withheld to avoid disclosure of competitive data; na: Not available; (S): Withheld because statistical norms were not met; (X): Not applicable; (Z): Less than half the unit shown; nec: Not elsewhere classified; nsk: Not specified by kind; - : zero; * : 10-19 percent estimated; ** : 20-29 percent estimated.

PRODUCT SHARE DETAILS

Product or Product Class	% Share	Product or Product Class	% Share
Women's, misses', and juniors' suits, skirts, and coats	100.00	jackets), excluding fur and leather	41.67
Women's, misses', and juniors' coats and capes, except fur, leather, down-and feather-filled, and ski	13.33	Skirts, tailored jackets, and vests, nsk	0.67
Women's, misses', and juniors' suits, pantsuits, and military-type uniform jackets, except ski and snow suits	8.30	Receipts for contract and commission work on women's, misses', and juniors' coats, suits, skirts, and jackets	14.19
Women's, misses', and juniors' skirts, tailored jackets, and vests	63.49	Receipts for contract and commission work on women's, misses', and juniors' coats, suits, skirts, and jackets	98.87
Separate skirts (including military-type uniform skirts)	57.66	Receipts for contract and commission work on women's, misses', and juniors' coats, suits, skirts, and jackets, nsk	1.13
Jackets and vests, tailored (including military-type uniform		Women's, misses', and juniors' suits, skirts, and coats, nsk	0.69

Source: 1992 *Economic Census*. The values shown are percent of total shipments in an industry. Values of indented subcategories are summed in the main heading. The symbol (D) appears when data are withheld to prevent disclosure of competitive information. The abbreviation nsk stands for 'not specified by kind' and nec for 'not elsewhere classified'.

INPUTS AND OUTPUTS FOR APPAREL MADE FROM PURCHASED MATERIALS

Economic Sector or Industry Providing Inputs	%	Sector	Economic Sector or Industry Buying Outputs	%	Sector
Imports	29.1	Foreign	Personal consumption expenditures	82.7	
Broadwoven fabric mills	20.2	Manufg.	Apparel made from purchased materials	12.0	Manufg.
Apparel made from purchased materials	18.3	Manufg.	Exports	1.5	Foreign
Knit fabric mills	8.6	Manufg.	Federal Government purchases, national defense	0.9	Fed Govt
Wholesale trade	3.8	Trade	S/L Govt. purch., correction	0.5	S/L Govt
Advertising	2.4	Services	Pleating & stitching	0.3	Manufg.
Yarn mills & finishing of textiles, nec	1.4	Manufg.	Knit outerwear mills	0.2	Manufg.
Pleating & stitching	1.1	Manufg.	Hospitals	0.2	Services
Banking	1.1	Fin/R.E.	Laundry, dry cleaning, shoe repair	0.2	Services
Petroleum refining	1.0	Manufg.	S/L Govt. purch., health & hospitals	0.2	S/L Govt
Electric services (utilities)	1.0	Util.	Portrait, photographic studios	0.1	Services
Automotive & apparel trimmings	0.9	Manufg.	S/L Govt. purch., public assistance & relief	0.1	S/L Govt
Needles, pins, & fasteners	0.8	Manufg.			
Thread mills	0.7	Manufg.			
Communications, except radio & TV	0.7	Util.			
Eating & drinking places	0.7	Trade			
U.S. Postal Service	0.7	Gov't			
Leather tanning & finishing	0.5	Manufg.			
Narrow fabric mills	0.5	Manufg.			
Schiffli machine embroideries	0.4	Manufg.			
Motor freight transportation & warehousing	0.4	Util.			
Real estate	0.4	Fin/R.E.			
Royalties	0.4	Fin/R.E.			
Forestry products	0.3	Agric.			
Buttons	0.3	Manufg.			
Paperboard containers & boxes	0.3	Manufg.			
Air transportation	0.3	Util.			
Maintenance of nonfarm buildings nec	0.2	Constr.			
Lace goods	0.2	Manufg.			
Gas production & distribution (utilities)	0.2	Util.			
Automotive rental & leasing, without drivers	0.2	Services			
Electrical repair shops	0.2	Services			
Equipment rental & leasing services	0.2	Services			
Legal services	0.2	Services			
Management & consulting services & labs	0.2	Services			
Artificial trees & flowers	0.1	Manufg.			
Insurance carriers	0.1	Fin/R.E.			
Accounting, auditing & bookkeeping	0.1	Services			
Automotive repair shops & services	0.1	Services			

Source: Benchmark Input-Output Accounts for the U.S. Economy, 1982, U.S. Department of Commerce, Washington, D.C., July 1991. Data, as reported in the source, are organized by the 1977 SIC structure in use in 1982 but have been matched, as closely as is possible, to the 1987 SIC structure used in this book.

OCCUPATIONS EMPLOYED BY SIC 233 - APPAREL

Occupation	% of Total 1994	Change to 2005	Occupation	% of Total 1994	Change to 2005
Sewing machine operators, garment	56.1	-33.1	Cutters & trimmers, hand	1.7	-24.8
Inspectors, testers, & graders, precision	3.5	-16.4	Patternmakers, layout workers, fabric & apparel	1.5	25.4
Blue collar worker supervisors	3.0	-24.0	General managers & top executives	1.4	-20.7
Assemblers, fabricators, & hand workers nec	2.5	-16.4	Sewing machine operators, non-garment	1.3	-37.3
Pressing machine operators, textiles	2.4	-45.7	Helpers, laborers, & material movers nec	1.1	-16.4
Hand packers & packagers	2.0	-21.2	Industrial machinery mechanics	1.1	0.3
Freight, stock, & material movers, hand	1.8	-33.1	Pressers, hand	1.1	-58.2
Traffic, shipping, & receiving clerks	1.8	-19.6	Sewers, hand	1.0	-10.7

Source: *Industry-Occupation Matrix*, Bureau of Labor Statistics. These data relate to one or more 3-digit SIC industry groups rather than to a single 4-digit SIC. The change reported for each occupation to the year 2005 is a percent of growth or decline as estimated by the Bureau of Labor Statistics. The abbreviation nec stands for 'not elsewhere classified'.

LOCATION BY STATE AND REGIONAL CONCENTRATION

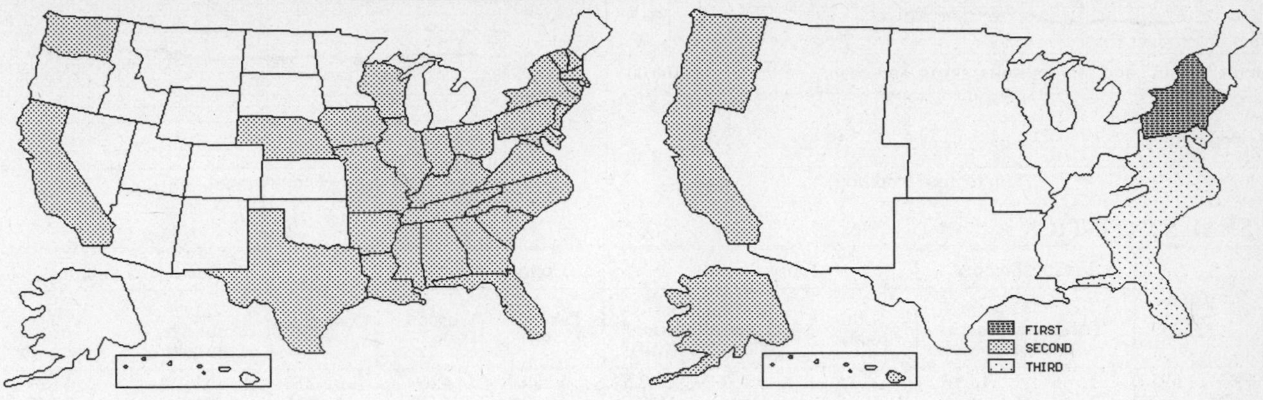

INDUSTRY DATA BY STATE

State	Establish-ments	Shipments			Employment				Cost as % of Shipments	Investment per Employee ($)
		Total ($ mil)	% of U.S.	Per Establ.	Total Number	% of U.S.	Per Establ.	Wages ($/hour)		
New York	339	1,435.5	32.9	4.2	12,700	26.1	37	7.94	56.9	465
California	203	587.4	13.4	2.9	5,600	11.5	28	8.26	51.1	589
Pennsylvania	50	463.5	10.6	9.3	3,000	6.2	60	7.09	67.4	-
Massachusetts	50	440.6	10.1	8.8	4,000	8.2	80	7.78	58.9	425
New Jersey	140	418.2	9.6	3.0	6,300	13.0	45	7.57	41.8	397
Georgia	13	157.3	3.6	12.1	1,200	2.5	92	8.73	73.6	-
Tennessee	16	115.0	2.6	7.2	2,500	5.1	156	5.90	39.3	640
North Carolina	17	114.9	2.6	6.8	2,000	4.1	118	7.21	49.1	650
Florida	32	72.8	1.7	2.3	1,600	3.3	50	8.47	40.2	375
Texas	38	65.1	1.5	1.7	1,000	2.1	26	7.85	51.8	400
Alabama	19	46.3	1.1	2.4	1,700	3.5	89	6.65	24.0	294
Kentucky	7	37.1	0.8	5.3	1,000	2.1	143	5.75	65.8	-
Missouri	10	27.0	0.6	2.7	600	1.2	60	5.30	32.2	-
Vermont	5	15.6	0.4	3.1	200	0.4	40	6.67	42.3	-
Illinois	13	12.6	0.3	1.0	300	0.6	23	8.50	31.7	-
Mississippi	3	10.7	0.2	3.6	400	0.8	133	7.57	6.5	-
South Carolina	7	8.7	0.2	1.2	500	1.0	71	6.00	8.0	-
Connecticut	8	5.7	0.1	0.7	400	0.8	50	5.57	7.0	-
New Hampshire	4	3.7	0.1	0.9	200	0.4	50	6.33	8.1	-
Ohio	5	2.7	0.1	0.5	100	0.2	20	7.00	22.2	-
Maryland	6	(D)	-	-	175 *	0.4	29	-	-	-
Washington	6	(D)	-	-	375 *	0.8	63	-	-	-
Wisconsin	5	(D)	-	-	750 *	1.5	150	-	-	-
Indiana	4	(D)	-	-	375 *	0.8	94	-	-	-
Nebraska	4	(D)	-	-	750 *	1.5	188	-	-	-
Iowa	3	(D)	-	-	175 *	0.4	58	-	-	-
Virginia	3	(D)	-	-	375 *	0.8	125	-	-	-
Arkansas	1	(D)	-	-	375 *	0.8	375	-	-	-
Louisiana	1	(D)	-	-	175 *	0.4	175	-	-	-

Source: 1992 *Economic Census*. The states are in descending order of shipments or establishments (if shipment data are missing for the majority). The symbol (D) appears when data are withheld to prevent disclosure of competitive information. States marked with (D) are sorted by number of establishments. A dash (-) indicates that the data element cannot be calculated; * indicates the midpoint of a range.

2339 - WOMEN'S AND MISSES' OUTERWEAR, NEC

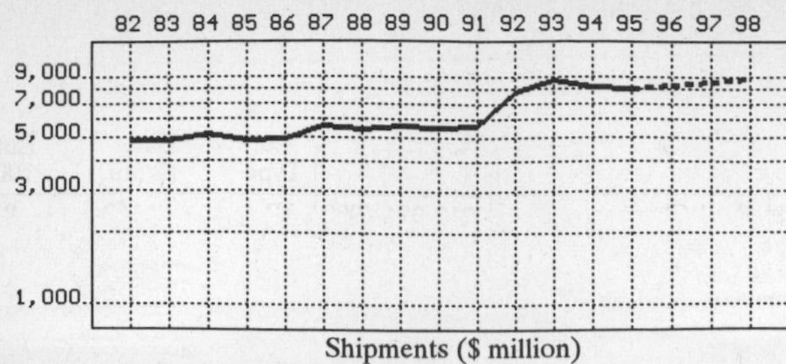

Shipments ($ million)

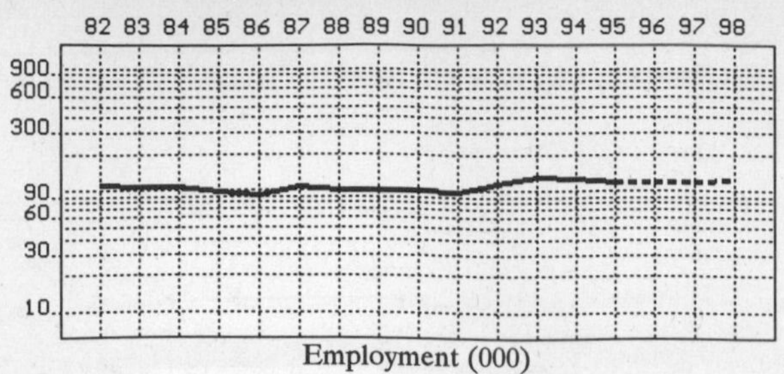

Employment (000)

GENERAL STATISTICS

Year	Com-panies	Establishments		Employment			Compensation		Production ($ million)			
		Total	with 20 or more employees	Total (000)	Production Workers (000)	Production Hours (Mil)	Payroll ($ mil)	Wages ($/hr)	Cost of Materials	Value Added by Manufacture	Value of Shipments	Capital Invest.
1982	1,595	1,746	1,039	110.9	93.5	163.5	1,099.0	4.69	2,560.0	2,261.2	4,833.9	85.4
1983		1,649	986	108.2	90.8	162.2	1,109.9	4.58	2,493.0	2,365.7	4,847.5	51.9
1984		1,552	933	108.3	92.1	161.3	1,151.1	4.85	2,689.3	2,597.6	5,239.0	50.2
1985		1,454	880	98.7	84.0	140.5	1,106.0	5.48	2,460.2	2,348.9	4,816.2	47.3
1986		1,411	828	92.3	77.7	135.7	1,081.8	5.44	2,424.3	2,503.9	4,911.2	49.3
1987	2,088	2,198	985	107.3	90.9	156.3	1,261.7	5.68	2,790.7	2,914.3	5,663.4	65.0
1988		1,997	1,019	102.3	87.0	148.5	1,224.9	5.80	2,696.1	2,745.4	5,435.7	52.5
1989		1,736	951	102.7	87.3	156.3	1,285.9	5.91	2,821.3	2,892.3	5,671.2	141.1
1990		2,632	954	101.2	87.4	163.3	1,320.6	5.92	2,562.7	2,911.7	5,528.4	56.6
1991		3,457	1,234	97.7	83.6	155.4	1,284.9	5.95	2,667.4	2,957.1	5,643.2	46.0
1992	2,917	3,015	1,164	115.8	97.7	177.7	1,666.8	6.57	3,851.7	3,929.3	7,766.6	88.8
1993		3,785	1,189	133.5	115.5	207.1	1,940.6	6.77	4,257.2	4,420.6	8,583.6	62.5
1994		3,463P	1,153P	126.2	107.7	189.5	1,842.6	6.96	4,065.3	4,152.1	8,135.9	87.5
1995		3,654P	1,174P	118.0P	101.4P	183.9P	1,787.2P	7.05P	3,968.1P	4,052.9P	7,941.4P	79.8P
1996		3,846P	1,196P	119.4P	102.7P	186.9P	1,851.6P	7.24P	4,111.8P	4,199.6P	8,229.0P	81.5P
1997		4,037P	1,217P	120.9P	104.1P	189.9P	1,916.0P	7.42P	4,255.5P	4,346.3P	8,516.5P	83.2P
1998		4,228P	1,239P	122.3P	105.4P	192.9P	1,980.4P	7.61P	4,399.1P	4,493.0P	8,804.0P	84.9P

Sources: 1982, 1987, 1992 *Economic Census*; *Annual Survey of Manufactures*, 83-86, 88-91, 93-94. Establishment counts for non-Census years are from *County Business Patterns*; establishment values for 83-84 are extrapolations. 'P's show projections by the editors. Industries reclassified in 87 will not have data for prior years.

INDICES OF CHANGE

Year	Com-panies	Establishments		Employment			Compensation		Production ($ million)			
		Total	with 20 or more employees	Total (000)	Production Workers (000)	Production Hours (Mil)	Payroll ($ mil)	Wages ($/hr)	Cost of Materials	Value Added by Manufacture	Value of Shipments	Capital Invest.
1982	55	58	89	96	96	92	66	71	66	58	62	96
1983		55	85	93	93	91	67	70	65	60	62	58
1984		51	80	94	94	91	69	74	70	66	67	57
1985		48	76	85	86	79	66	83	64	60	62	53
1986		47	71	80	80	76	65	83	63	64	63	56
1987	72	73	85	93	93	88	76	86	72	74	73	73
1988		66	88	88	89	84	73	88	70	70	70	59
1989		58	82	89	89	88	77	90	73	74	73	159
1990		87	82	87	89	92	79	90	67	74	71	64
1991		115	106	84	86	87	77	91	69	75	73	52
1992	100	100	100	100	100	100	100	100	100	100	100	100
1993		126	102	115	118	117	116	103	111	113	111	70
1994		115P	99P	109	110	107	111	106	106	106	105	99
1995		121P	101P	102P	104P	103P	107P	107P	103P	103P	102P	90P
1996		128P	103P	103P	105P	105P	111P	110P	107P	107P	106P	92P
1997		134P	105P	104P	107P	107P	115P	113P	110P	111P	110P	94P
1998		140P	106P	106P	108P	109P	119P	116P	114P	114P	113P	96P

Sources: Same as General Statistics. Values reflect change from the base year, 1992. Values above 100 mean greater than 92, values below 100 mean less than 92, and a value of 100 in the 82-91 or 93-98 period means same as 92. 'P's mark projections by the editors.

SELECTED RATIOS

For 1994	Avg. of All Manufact.	Analyzed Industry	Index	For 1994	Avg. of All Manufact.	Analyzed Industry	Index
Employees per Establishment	49	36	74	Value Added per Production Worker	134,084	38,552	29
Payroll per Establishment	1,500,273	532,080	35	Cost per Establishment	5,045,178	1,173,919	23
Payroll per Employee	30,620	14,601	48	Cost per Employee	102,970	32,213	31
Production Workers per Establishment	34	31	91	Cost per Production Worker	146,988	37,747	26
Wages per Establishment	853,319	380,859	45	Shipments per Establishment	9,576,895	2,349,369	25
Wages per Production Worker	24,861	12,246	49	Shipments per Employee	195,460	64,468	33
Hours per Production Worker	2,056	1,760	86	Shipments per Production Worker	279,017	75,542	27
Wages per Hour	12.09	6.96	58	Investment per Establishment	321,011	25,267	8
Value Added per Establishment	4,602,255	1,198,984	26	Investment per Employee	6,552	693	11
Value Added per Employee	93,930	32,901	35	Investment per Production Worker	9,352	812	9

Sources: Same as General Statistics. The 'Average of All Manufacturing' column represents the average of all manufacturing industries reported for the most recent complete year available. The Index shows the relationship between the Average and the Analyzed Industry. For example, 100 means that they are equal; 500 that the Analyzed Industry is five times the average; 50 means that the Analyzed Industry is half the national average. The abbreviation 'na' is used to show that data are 'not available'.

LEADING COMPANIES Number shown: **75** Total sales ($ mil): **3,866** Total employment (000): **22.5**

Company Name	Address				CEO Name	Phone	Co. Type	Sales ($ mil)	Empl. (000)
Liz Claiborne Inc	1441 Broadway	New York	NY	10018	Paul Charron	212-354-4900	P	2,163	8.0
Baron-Abramson Inc	4000 Mystic Valley	Medford	MA	02155	Donald F Baron	617-396-2000	R	130	<0.1
Liz Claiborne Inc	1450 Broadway	New York	NY	10018	Harvey Rosencweig	212-626-5800	S	120•	0.5
Eudora Garment Corp	PO Drawer B	Eudora	AR	71640	Ray Anderson	501-355-8381	S	110	0.7
A and H Sportswear Company	500 Williams St	Pen Argyl	PA	18072	Herman Waldman	610-863-4176	R	100•	0.9
Orbit Industries Inc	PO Box 275	Helen	GA	30545	Robert Fowler	706-878-2283	R	90	1.2
Weekend Exercise Company Inc	8960 Carroll Way	San Diego	CA	92121	Norm Zwail	619-295-4124	R	65•	0.2
Don Shapiro Industries Inc	1931 Myrtle Av	El Paso	TX	79901	Don Shapiro	915-532-4481	R	62	0.5
Cambridge Dry Goods Company	PO Box 500	Newton	MA	02166	Robert Matura	617-965-7080	S	50	0.2
CDG Holdings Inc	269 Grove St	Newton	MA	02166	Donald M Horning	617-965-7080	R	50	0.2
National Spirit Group Ltd	PO Box 660359	Dallas	TX	75266	Lance Wagers	214-840-1344	R	50	0.5
Issac Hazan and Company Inc	470 Vanderbilt Av	Brooklyn	NY	11238	Murray Hazan	718-636-0200	R	45	0.2
Lucia Inc	PO Box 12129	Winston-Salem	NC	27117	H Pfohe	910-788-4901	R	43	0.6
Spectravest Inc	320 Shaw Rd	S San Francisco	CA	94080	Todd Magaline	415-871-4500	R	42•	0.4
Donegal Industries Inc	PO Box 507	Mount Joy	PA	17552	L S Bernstein	717-653-1486	R	40•	0.3
Dennis Uniform Mfg Co	135 SE Hawthorne	Portland	OR	97214	Douglas W Donaca	503-238-7123	R	37•	0.3
Wilkins Industries Inc	PO Box 1512	Athens	GA	30603	John J Wilkins III	706-546-7960	R	33	0.7
Saul Brothers and Company Inc	6500 Peachtree	Norcross	GA	30071	Robert C Thomas	404-881-1833	R	31	<0.1
Sirena Apparel Group Inc	PO Box 3307	S El Monte	CA	91733	Douglas Arbetman	818-442-6680	P	29	0.3
Mr Remo of California Inc	PO Box 990	Duarte	CA	91010	Robert Birkle	818-357-3867	R	27•	<0.1
Carthage Co	PO Box 438	Carthage	MS	39051	Charles Boutwell	601-267-9672	D	26•	0.5
Pyke Manufacturing Co	PO Box 30326	Salt Lake City	UT	84130	Ernest D Mariani	801-973-2200	R	26•	0.4
Baldanza Inc	209 W 38th St	New York	NY	10018	Sandy Baldanza	212-921-7650	R	25	<0.1
Denise Lingerie Corp	129 Roland St	Johnson City	TN	37601	Curtis Marshall	615-928-8261	S	22•	0.3
House of Perfection Inc	131 W 33rd St	New York	NY	10001	Gene J Goldfarb	212-239-9780	R	21	0.4
Gabar Inc	590 Smith St	Farmingdale	NY	11735	Gabriel Colasante	516-420-1400	R	19	0.1
Artistic Creations Inc	PO Box 520	Monticello	FL	32344	Rodney Ganis	904-997-2466	R	18•	0.2
Tom Togs Inc	PO Box 26	Farmville	NC	27828	Thomas Glennon	919-753-7161	R	17	0.8
Ronnie Manufacturing Inc	70 Kilburn St	New Bedford	MA	02740	N Glassman	508-999-4584	R	16	0.3
TechKnits Inc	10 Grand Av	Brooklyn	NY	11205	S Taub	718-875-3299	P	15	0.2
Leon Levin Sons Inc	1411 Broadway	New York	NY	10018	Neil Weiss	212-575-1900	R	15	0.1
Malbon Co	PO Box 100	Hiram	GA	30141	Donald Ray	404-943-3586	R	15•	0.1
Mevisto Inc	1466 Broadway	New York	NY	10036	Ivan Strougo	212-730-5137	R	15	<0.1
Oxford of Hickory Grove	PO Box 38	Hickory Grove	SC	29717	Janet Barton	803-925-2106	D	13•	0.1
Neosport Inc	1760 Evergreen St	Duarte	CA	91010	Armen Gregorian	818-303-0099	P	12	<0.1
Carole Wren Inc	75 9th Av	New York	NY	10011	Martin Leff	212-675-7023	R	12•	0.1
Cleveland Sportswear Co	Rte 2	Cleveland	GA	30528	Larry Hood	706-865-4415	R	12•	0.1
North State Garment Company	PO Box 215	Farmville	NC	27828	William E Jones	919-753-3266	R	12•	0.1
David H Smith Inc	48 Main St	North Reading	MA	01864	RJ Smith	508-664-3600	R	10•	<0.1
Durlacher and Company Inc	47-11 Van Dam St	Long Island Ct	NY	11101	Jules C Ventura	718-706-1700	R	10•	0.1
Holly Bra of California	1112 N Seward St	Hollywood	CA	90038	Dave Young	213-469-1623	R	10•	0.2
Jennifer Dawn Inc	5300 Barksdale Blv	Bossier City	LA	71112	Robert Aufrichtig	318-747-9100	R	10•	<0.1
K and R Sportswear Inc	602 W Branch St	Spring Hope	NC	27882	Peter Kessner	919-478-3173	D	10	0.2
Kayo of California Inc	161 W 39th St	Los Angeles	CA	90037	Jeff Michaels	213-233-6107	R	10•	<0.1
Metter Manufacturing Co	800 E Broad St	Metter	GA	30439	CH Peterson	912-685-2156	R	9•	<0.1
Excelsior Inc	2151 N Soto St	Los Angeles	CA	90032	Daniel Kwok	213-221-8383	R	9	<0.1
Kass and Co	3829 S Broadway	Los Angeles	CA	90037	Irving Kass	213-232-4411	R	9•	0.2
Canvasbacks Inc	224 W Washington	Milwaukee	WI	53204	Janice Lutton	414-384-4484	R	8	<0.1
Clifton Heights Sportswear Inc	Bridgeport Ind'l Pk	Bridgeport	PA	19405	Valentine De Noia	215-272-6810	R	8•	<0.1
McBee Manufacturing Co	PO Box 158	McBee	SC	29101	J B Campolong Jr	803-335-8234	R	8•	<0.1
Riverview Sportswear Inc	1 Ironside Ct	Willingboro	NJ	08046	M Macaluso	609-871-8888	R	8	0.3
Kirby Manufacturing Company	PO Box 8	McClure	PA	17841	S Kirby Bubb	717-658-8425	R	7	0.1
RCM Enterprises Inc	PO Box 279	Baconton	GA	31716	Bonnie Rackley	912-787-5021	R	7	0.1
Univogue Inc	3633 W Miller Rd	Garland	TX	75041	Curtis Hoguland	214-341-7300	R	7	<0.1
CranBarry Inc	PO Box 488	East Boston	MA	02128	Tom Cronin	617-567-9737	R	6•	<0.1
Crane Manufacturing Company	30 Washington St	Marionville	MO	65705	Nicholas L Weinsaft	417-463-2534	R	6	0.2
Dance France	2503 Main St	Santa Monica	CA	90405	Jennifer Falconer	310-392-9786	D	6	<0.1
Elkin Valley Apparel Co	Hwy 268 W	Elkin	NC	28621	Robert H Ball	919-835-6406	R	6	0.1
Paddy-Lee Fashions Co	33/02 Skillman Av	Long Island Ct	NY	11101	R Covelli	718-786-6020	R	6	<0.1
Niver Western Wear Inc	1221 Hemphill St	Fort Worth	TX	76104	Bert G Niver	817-336-2389	R	5	<0.1
Double D Ranchwear Inc	318 E Morris St	Yoakum	TX	77995	Margie L McMullen	512-293-2394	R	5	<0.1
Leadtec California Inc	836 Arroyo St	San Fernando	CA	91340	FG Lucas	818-365-9601	R	5	0.1
Stafford Higgins Industries Inc	PO Box 446	Norwalk	CT	06856	Walter Baum	203-846-1666	R	5	0.3
Ujena Inc	1400 N Shoreline	Mountain View	CA	94043	Robert Anderson	408-524-9900	R	5	<0.1
Little King Manufacturing	PO Box 287	Alamo	TN	38001	Jimmy Nolen	901-696-5517	R	4	0.1
Alorna Coat Corp	463 7th Av	New York	NY	10018	Elliot Satnick	212-290-4000	R	4	<0.1
Banner Industries	469 7th Av	New York	NY	10018	Robert Kaplan	212-564-3400	R	4•	<0.1
Bendigo International Inc	75 W Hayden Av	Hayden Lake	ID	83835	Herman Roup	208-772-7394	R	4•	<0.1
Darbo Manufacturing Company	182 N Cypress St	Pomona	CA	91768	Fred W Freehling	909-622-0321	R	4	<0.1
Grady Garment	Rte 1	Homer	GA	30547	Brenda Heffner	706-677-2213	D	4	<0.1
Just Bikinis Inc	PO Box 6170	Newport Beach	CA	92658	Joyce Holder-Stone	714-644-5634	R	4•	<0.1
Raisin Company Inc	33171 Paseo	S J Capistrano	CA	92675	Tom Lingo	714-493-0640	S	4•	<0.1
Sideffects of California Inc	1763 Flower St	Glendale	CA	91201	Gean LaMar	818-241-8882	R	4•	<0.1
Cotton Stuff Inc	2221 S Main St	Los Angeles	CA	90007	Stewart Briar	213-748-9724	R	4	<0.1
Her Majesty Industries Inc	100 W 33rd St	New York	NY	10001	Nicholas La Rosa	212-695-2770	R	4	<0.1

Source: *Ward's Business Directory of U.S. Private and Public Companies*, Volumes 1 and 2, 1996. The company type code used is as follows: P - Public, R - Private, S - Subsidiary, D - Division, J - Joint Venture, A - Affiliate, G - Group. Sales are in millions of dollars, employees are in thousands. An asterisk (*) indicates an estimated sales volume. The symbol < stands for 'less than'. Company names and addresses are truncated, in some cases, to fit into the available space.

MATERIALS CONSUMED

Material	Quantity	Delivered Cost ($ million)
Materials, ingredients, containers, and supplies	(X)	2,441.6
Broadwoven fabrics (piece goods)	(X)	1,275.0
Narrow fabrics (12 inches or less in width)	(X)	146.7
Knit fabrics	(X)	444.7
Yarn, all fibers	(X)	35.5
Buttons, zippers, and slide fasteners	(X)	114.0
All other materials and components, parts, containers, and supplies	(X)	154.4
Materials, ingredients, containers, and supplies, nsk	(X)	271.9

Source: 1992 *Economic Census*. Explanation of symbols used: (D): Withheld to avoid disclosure of competitive data; na: Not available; (S): Withheld because statistical norms were not met; (X): Not applicable; (Z): Less than half the unit shown; nec: Not elsewhere classified; nsk: Not specified by kind; - : zero; * : 10-19 percent estimated; ** : 20-29 percent estimated.

PRODUCT SHARE DETAILS

Product or Product Class	% Share
Women's, misses', and juniors' outerwear, nec	100.00
Women's, misses', and juniors' washable service apparel (aprons, smocks, hoovers, uniforms for maids, nurses, etc., and hospital patient wear)	3.70
Women's, misses', and juniors' bathing suits	8.17
Women's, misses', and juniors' slacks (including jeans and jean-cut casual slacks)	47.78
Women's, misses', and juniors' outerwear, nec	19.42
Athletic uniforms, sold as such	2.07
Sweaters (including sweater vests), made from purchased fabrics	13.59
Play garments (including shorts, pedal pushers, bermudas, and jamaicas)	43.16
Scarfs, dickies, and other neckwear	2.10
Other outerwear (including jogging pants and suits, ski suits and jackets, leotards, nontailored jackets, etc.)	35.16
Outerwear, nec, nsk	3.91
Receipts for contract and commission work on women's, misses', and juniors' outerwear, nec	16.59
Receipts for contract and commission work on women's, misses', and juniors' outerwear, nec	98.80
Receipts for contract and commission work on women's, misses', and juniors' outerwear, nec, nsk	1.21
Women's, misses', and juniors' outerwear, nec, nsk	4.35

Source: 1992 *Economic Census*. The values shown are percent of total shipments in an industry. Values of indented subcategories are summed in the main heading. The symbol (D) appears when data are withheld to prevent disclosure of competitive information. The abbreviation nsk stands for 'not specified by kind' and nec for 'not elsewhere classified'.

INPUTS AND OUTPUTS FOR APPAREL MADE FROM PURCHASED MATERIALS

Economic Sector or Industry Providing Inputs	%	Sector	Economic Sector or Industry Buying Outputs	%	Sector
Imports	29.1	Foreign	Personal consumption expenditures	82.7	
Broadwoven fabric mills	20.2	Manufg.	Apparel made from purchased materials	12.0	Manufg.
Apparel made from purchased materials	18.3	Manufg.	Exports	1.5	Foreign
Knit fabric mills	8.6	Manufg.	Federal Government purchases, national defense	0.9	Fed Govt
Wholesale trade	3.8	Trade	S/L Govt. purch., correction	0.5	S/L Govt
Advertising	2.4	Services	Pleating & stitching	0.3	Manufg.
Yarn mills & finishing of textiles, nec	1.4	Manufg.	Knit outerwear mills	0.2	Manufg.
Pleating & stitching	1.1	Manufg.	Hospitals	0.2	Services
Banking	1.1	Fin/R.E.	Laundry, dry cleaning, shoe repair	0.2	Services
Petroleum refining	1.0	Manufg.	S/L Govt. purch., health & hospitals	0.2	S/L Govt
Electric services (utilities)	1.0	Util.	Portrait, photographic studios	0.1	Services
Automotive & apparel trimmings	0.9	Manufg.	S/L Govt. purch., public assistance & relief	0.1	S/L Govt
Needles, pins, & fasteners	0.8	Manufg.			
Thread mills	0.7	Manufg.			
Communications, except radio & TV	0.7	Util.			
Eating & drinking places	0.7	Trade			
U.S. Postal Service	0.7	Gov't			
Leather tanning & finishing	0.5	Manufg.			
Narrow fabric mills	0.5	Manufg.			
Schiffli machine embroideries	0.4	Manufg.			
Motor freight transportation & warehousing	0.4	Util.			
Real estate	0.4	Fin/R.E.			
Royalties	0.4	Fin/R.E.			
Forestry products	0.3	Agric.			
Buttons	0.3	Manufg.			
Paperboard containers & boxes	0.3	Manufg.			
Air transportation	0.3	Util.			
Maintenance of nonfarm buildings nec	0.2	Constr.			
Lace goods	0.2	Manufg.			
Gas production & distribution (utilities)	0.2	Util.			
Automotive rental & leasing, without drivers	0.2	Services			
Electrical repair shops	0.2	Services			
Equipment rental & leasing services	0.2	Services			
Legal services	0.2	Services			
Management & consulting services & labs	0.2	Services			
Artificial trees & flowers	0.1	Manufg.			
Insurance carriers	0.1	Fin/R.E.			
Accounting, auditing & bookkeeping	0.1	Services			
Automotive repair shops & services	0.1	Services			

Source: Benchmark Input-Output Accounts for the U.S. Economy, 1982, U.S. Department of Commerce, Washington, D.C., July 1991. Data, as reported in the source, are organized by the 1977 SIC structure in use in 1982 but have been matched, as closely as is possible, to the 1987 SIC structure used in this book.

OCCUPATIONS EMPLOYED BY SIC 233 - APPAREL

Occupation	% of Total 1994	Change to 2005	Occupation	% of Total 1994	Change to 2005
Sewing machine operators, garment	56.1	-33.1	Cutters & trimmers, hand	1.7	-24.8
Inspectors, testers, & graders, precision	3.5	-16.4	Patternmakers, layout workers, fabric & apparel	1.5	25.4
Blue collar worker supervisors	3.0	-24.0	General managers & top executives	1.4	-20.7
Assemblers, fabricators, & hand workers nec	2.5	-16.4	Sewing machine operators, non-garment	1.3	-37.3
Pressing machine operators, textiles	2.4	-45.7	Helpers, laborers, & material movers nec	1.1	-16.4
Hand packers & packagers	2.0	-21.2	Industrial machinery mechanics	1.1	0.3
Freight, stock, & material movers, hand	1.8	-33.1	Pressers, hand	1.1	-58.2
Traffic, shipping, & receiving clerks	1.8	-19.6	Sewers, hand	1.0	-10.7

Source: Industry-Occupation Matrix, Bureau of Labor Statistics. These data relate to one or more 3-digit SIC industry groups rather than to a single 4-digit SIC. The change reported for each occupation to the year 2005 is a percent of growth or decline as estimated by the Bureau of Labor Statistics. The abbreviation nec stands for 'not elsewhere classified'.

LOCATION BY STATE AND REGIONAL CONCENTRATION

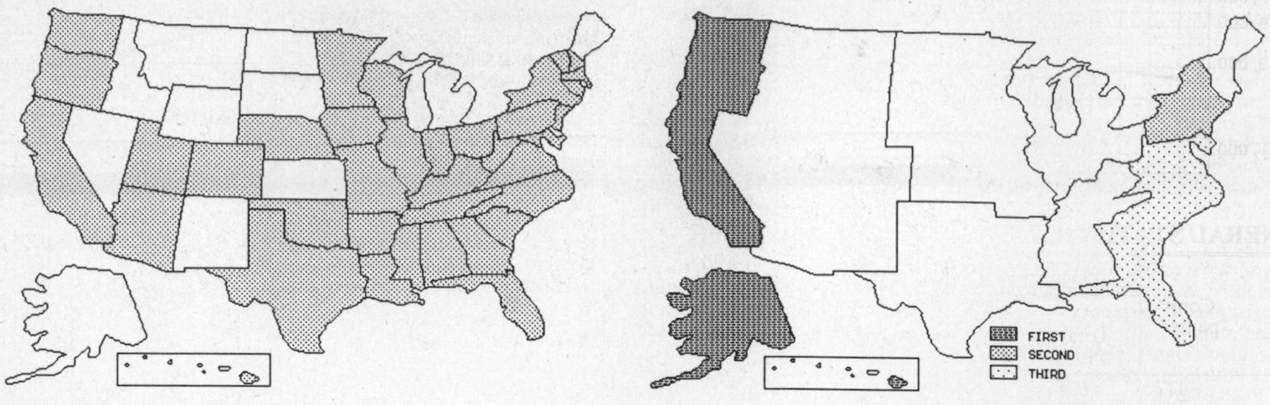

INDUSTRY DATA BY STATE

State	Establish-ments	Shipments			Employment				Cost as % of Shipments	Investment per Employee ($)
		Total ($ mil)	% of U.S.	Per Establ.	Total Number	% of U.S.	Per Establ.	Wages ($/hour)		
California	1,289	2,245.2	28.9	1.7	33,400	28.8	26	6.58	49.9	1,078
New York	617	1,221.8	15.7	2.0	13,400	11.6	22	7.40	54.1	679
New Jersey	101	626.8	8.1	6.2	3,500	3.0	35	8.07	57.3	686
Georgia	69	541.5	7.0	7.8	6,600	5.7	96	5.63	59.0	470
Texas	130	472.3	6.1	3.6	7,300	6.3	56	6.06	43.6	795
Tennessee	59	457.9	5.9	7.8	7,500	6.5	127	6.45	38.9	547
Pennsylvania	118	335.0	4.3	2.8	6,700	5.8	57	6.65	41.9	597
Mississippi	30	287.1	3.7	9.6	4,600	4.0	153	5.81	46.3	500
Virginia	27	245.9	3.2	9.1	3,500	3.0	130	6.98	51.6	1,486
Florida	156	230.8	3.0	1.5	4,000	3.5	26	6.21	50.7	550
South Carolina	42	169.9	2.2	4.0	3,900	3.4	93	5.98	42.5	385
Kentucky	21	136.3	1.8	6.5	3,300	2.8	157	6.47	39.7	1,333
Alabama	22	121.5	1.6	5.5	2,500	2.2	114	7.31	60.3	480
North Carolina	53	110.1	1.4	2.1	4,100	3.5	77	5.64	34.4	610
Massachusetts	32	76.0	1.0	2.4	1,100	0.9	34	7.78	45.3	364
Washington	22	53.1	0.7	2.4	900	0.8	41	6.87	44.6	-
Connecticut	9	49.9	0.6	5.5	500	0.4	56	11.50	52.3	-
Maryland	10	30.2	0.4	3.0	400	0.3	40	6.80	71.2	500
Illinois	20	25.8	0.3	1.3	700	0.6	35	7.50	25.2	429
Indiana	7	20.4	0.3	2.9	200	0.2	29	5.67	47.1	-
Oregon	14	20.1	0.3	1.4	600	0.5	43	7.33	27.4	333
Utah	6	19.6	0.3	3.3	300	0.3	50	6.33	29.1	667
Ohio	11	14.9	0.2	1.4	400	0.3	36	6.00	40.9	-
New Hampshire	10	12.6	0.2	1.3	500	0.4	50	7.38	8.7	-
Arkansas	6	9.7	0.1	1.6	400	0.3	67	7.33	33.0	500
Oklahoma	9	9.2	0.1	1.0	300	0.3	33	5.40	52.2	-
Minnesota	15	7.8	0.1	0.5	300	0.3	20	5.40	35.9	333
Colorado	10	7.3	0.1	0.7	200	0.2	20	6.33	35.6	500
Arizona	7	7.1	0.1	1.0	100	0.1	14	4.00	52.1	-
Wisconsin	9	5.5	0.1	0.6	200	0.2	22	5.33	36.4	-
Hawaii	16	3.6	0.0	0.2	100	0.1	6	5.50	33.3	1,000
Missouri	14	(D)	-	-	1,750 *	1.5	125	-	-	-
Louisiana	8	(D)	-	-	1,750 *	1.5	219	-	-	-
Nebraska	5	(D)	-	-	175 *	0.2	35	-	-	-
Iowa	4	(D)	-	-	175 *	0.2	44	-	-	-
West Virginia	4	(D)	-	-	175 *	0.2	44	-	-	-
Vermont	3	(D)	-	-	375 *	0.3	125	-	-	-

Source: 1992 *Economic Census*. The states are in descending order of shipments or establishments (if shipment data are missing for the majority). The symbol (D) appears when data are withheld to prevent disclosure of competitive information. States marked with (D) are sorted by number of establishments. A dash (-) indicates that the data element cannot be calculated; * indicates the midpoint of a range.

2341 - WOMEN'S AND CHILDREN'S UNDERWEAR

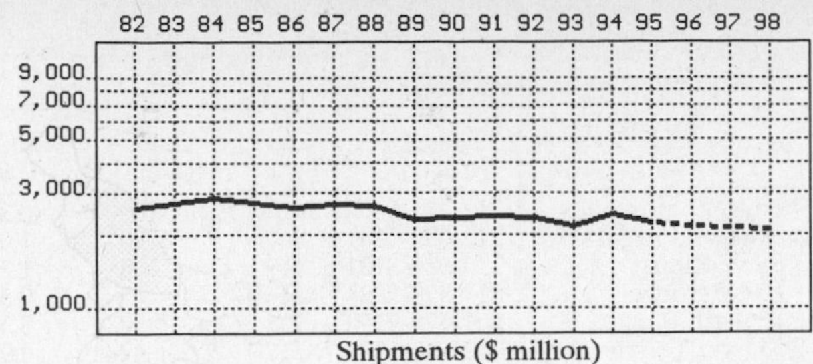

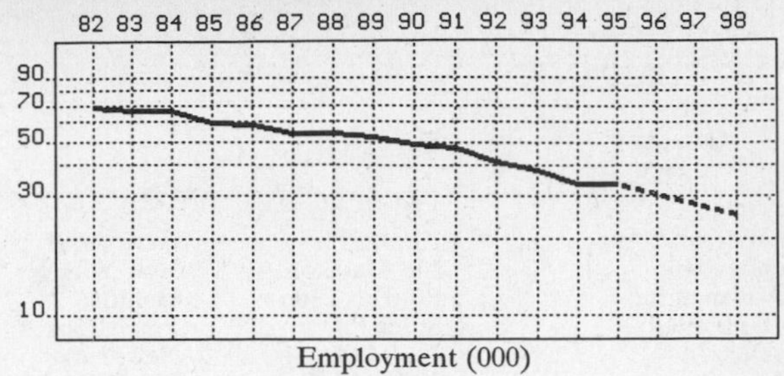

GENERAL STATISTICS

Year	Companies	Establishments		Employment			Compensation		Production ($ million)			
		Total	with 20 or more employees	Total (000)	Production Workers (000)	Production Hours (Mil)	Payroll ($ mil)	Wages ($/hr)	Cost of Materials	Value Added by Manufacture	Value of Shipments	Capital Invest.
1982	477	604	422	67.8	57.4	104.0	640.8	4.60	1,247.5	1,350.8	2,602.4	30.4
1983		579	412	66.7	57.2	105.1	677.4	4.82	1,373.0	1,359.7	2,734.9	34.2
1984		554	402	66.2	56.9	102.0	700.2	5.10	1,418.2	1,427.5	2,827.1	34.7
1985		530	391	59.4	51.7	92.1	658.7	5.35	1,344.2	1,357.0	2,715.2	34.8
1986		501	387	58.6	51.1	91.2	662.3	5.50	1,254.4	1,335.9	2,588.1	29.9
1987	325	434	334	53.7	46.5	85.4	644.9	5.72	1,229.6	1,429.6	2,658.3	44.9
1988		409	307	53.9	46.7	86.0	664.9	5.83	1,215.6	1,426.4	2,621.4	
1989		383	300	52.0	43.2	80.0	614.3	5.68	1,048.4	1,256.9	2,301.1	18.3
1990		369	275	48.6	42.3	76.9	610.4	5.96	1,035.0	1,298.4	2,337.4	25.6
1991		383	268	46.9	40.7	77.3	619.2	6.10	1,033.0	1,362.5	2,386.1	20.2
1992	264	354	266	41.5	35.8	65.5	578.3	6.46	1,054.6	1,306.7	2,364.6	29.1
1993		337	229	38.0	33.0	59.3	521.2	6.54	965.5	1,205.4	2,154.5	21.0
1994		286P	214P	33.5	29.0	55.2	483.1	6.51	1,215.8	1,242.2	2,437.5	12.7
1995		261P	195P	33.3P	29.0P	54.4P	526.3P	6.81P	1,110.2P	1,134.3P	2,225.8P	
1996		235P	177P	30.5P	26.6P	50.3P	512.7P	6.96P	1,089.4P	1,113.1P	2,184.1P	
1997		209P	159P	27.7P	24.3P	46.2P	499.2P	7.12P	1,068.6P	1,091.8P	2,142.4P	
1998		183P	140P	25.0P	21.9P	42.1P	485.6P	7.28P	1,047.8P	1,070.6P	2,100.7P	

Sources: 1982, 1987, 1992 *Economic Census*; *Annual Survey of Manufactures*, 83-86, 88-91, 93-94. Establishment counts for non-Census years are from *County Business Patterns*; establishment values for 83-84 are extrapolations. 'P's show projections by the editors. Industries reclassified in 87 will not have data for prior years.

INDICES OF CHANGE

Year	Companies	Establishments		Employment			Compensation		Production ($ million)			
		Total	with 20 or more employees	Total (000)	Production Workers (000)	Production Hours (Mil)	Payroll ($ mil)	Wages ($/hr)	Cost of Materials	Value Added by Manufacture	Value of Shipments	Capital Invest.
1982	181	171	159	163	160	159	111	71	118	103	110	104
1983		164	155	161	160	160	117	75	130	104	116	118
1984		156	151	160	159	156	121	79	134	109	120	119
1985		150	147	143	144	141	114	83	127	104	115	120
1986		142	145	141	143	139	115	85	119	102	109	103
1987	123	123	126	129	130	130	112	89	117	109	112	154
1988		116	115	130	130	131	115	90	115	109	111	
1989		108	113	125	121	122	106	88	99	96	97	63
1990		104	103	117	118	117	106	92	98	99	99	88
1991		108	101	113	114	118	107	94	98	104	101	69
1992	100	100	100	100	100	100	100	100	100	100	100	100
1993		95	86	92	92	91	90	101	92	92	91	72
1994		81P	80P	81	81	84	84	101	115	95	103	44
1995		74P	73P	80P	81P	83P	91P	105P	105P	87P	94P	
1996		66P	67P	74P	74P	77P	89P	108P	103P	85P	92P	
1997		59P	60P	67P	68P	70P	86P	110P	101P	84P	91P	
1998		52P	53P	60P	61P	64P	84P	113P	99P	82P	89P	

Sources: Same as General Statistics. Values reflect change from the base year, 1992. Values above 100 mean greater than 92, values below 100 mean less than 92, and a value of 100 in the 82-91 or 93-98 period means same as 92. 'P's mark projections by the editors.

SELECTED RATIOS

For 1994	Avg. of All Manufact.	Analyzed Industry	Index
Employees per Establishment	49	117	239
Payroll per Establishment	1,500,273	1,687,998	113
Payroll per Employee	30,620	14,421	47
Production Workers per Establishment	34	101	295
Wages per Establishment	853,319	1,255,611	147
Wages per Production Worker	24,861	12,391	50
Hours per Production Worker	2,056	1,903	93
Wages per Hour	12.09	6.51	54
Value Added per Establishment	4,602,255	4,340,367	94
Value Added per Employee	93,930	37,081	39

For 1994	Avg. of All Manufact.	Analyzed Industry	Index
Value Added per Production Worker	134,084	42,834	32
Cost per Establishment	5,045,178	4,248,123	84
Cost per Employee	102,970	36,293	35
Cost per Production Worker	146,988	41,924	29
Shipments per Establishment	9,576,895	8,516,862	89
Shipments per Employee	195,460	72,761	37
Shipments per Production Worker	279,017	84,052	30
Investment per Establishment	321,011	44,375	14
Investment per Employee	6,552	379	6
Investment per Production Worker	9,352	438	5

Sources: Same as General Statistics. The 'Average of All Manufacturing' column represents the average of all manufacturing industries reported for the most recent complete year available. The Index shows the relationship between the Average and the Analyzed Industry. For example, 100 means that they are equal; 500 that the Analyzed Industry is five times the average; 50 means that the Analyzed Industry is half the national average. The abbreviation 'na' is used to show that data are 'not available'.

LEADING COMPANIES Number shown: **70** Total sales ($ mil): **1,164** Total employment (000): **21.1**

Company Name	Address				CEO Name	Phone	Co. Type	Sales ($ mil)	Empl. (000)
NAP Inc	171 Madison Av	New York	NY	10016	Pano Zomopoulos	212-481-5000	R	100	0.3
Wundies Industries Inc	1 Penn Plz	New York	NY	10119	Michael Fitzgerald	212-695-8181	R	90	1.0
Sid Greenberg Inc	148 Madison Av	New York	NY	10016	Steve Klein	212-689-3131	R	68*	1.2
Russell-Newman Inc	PO Box 2306	Denton	TX	76202	FN Martino	817-898-8888	R	65	0.3
Vanities Unlimited	Stiles Ln	Pine Brook	NJ	07058	Prakash Bahatt	201-575-7290	D	50	3.5
Jennifer Dale Inc	180 Madison #1900	New York	NY	10016	Marvin Tolkin	212-532-5522	R	47	0.9
Natori Co	40 E 34th St	New York	NY	10016	Josefina Natori	212-532-7796	R	45	0.1
LV Myles Inc	135 Madison Av	New York	NY	10016	Paul Miller	212-725-0900	R	43	0.7
Burlen Corp	PO Box 168	Tifton	GA	31794	B Klein	912-382-4100	R	42*	1.2
S Schwab Company Inc	PO Box 1742	Cumberland	MD	21501	Sam Schwab	301-729-4488	R	35	0.5
Lee's Manufacturing Company	500 W Washington	Cannon Falls	MN	55009	John R McCarthy	507-263-3941	R	30	0.7
Nashville Textile Corp	202 Industrial Dr	Nashville	GA	31639	Irving Paparo	912-686-5581	S	30	0.5
Waterbury Garment Corp	1669 Thomaston	Waterbury	CT	06704	Jack Brownstein	203-574-3811	R	25	<0.1
Unity Knitting Mill Inc	PO Box 827	Wadesboro	NC	28170	VR Hughes	704-694-6544	R	23	0.5
Lewis Frimel Company Inc	1411 Broadway	New York	NY	10018	Stanley Goldick	212-730-7770	S	22*	0.5
Beam Corp	301 Centre Av	Buckeye	AZ	85326	Mark Horwitch	602-386-4493	S	21*	0.5
Deena Inc	3040 N 44th St	Phoenix	AZ	85018	BS Horwitch	602-912-4200	R	21*	0.5
Lady Ester Lingerie Corp	404 E 10th St	Berwick	PA	18603	Robert T Sadock	717-752-4521	R	21*	0.4
O'Bryan Brothers Inc	4220 W Belmont	Chicago	IL	60641	Mike L O'Bryan	312-283-3000	R	21*	0.5
Heckler Mfg	400 Bon Air St	Mauldin	SC	29662	John J Heckler	803-288-5450	R	20	0.5
Russell Group Ltd	PO Box 1927	Rockingham	NC	28379	Charles J Russell	919-997-6622	R	18	0.3
Leading Lady Companies Inc	24050 Com Pk Rd	Beachwood	OH	44122	Alfred G Corrado	216-464-5490	R	17	0.4
Cassie Cotillion Inc	112 W 34th St	New York	NY	10120	Leo Garter	212-564-0111	R	15	0.3
Chic Lingerie Co	3435 S Broadway	Los Angeles	CA	90007	J Balton	213-233-7121	R	15	0.5
I-C Manufacturing Co	PO Box 1060	El Campo	TX	77437	GL Collier	409-543-2724	R	15	0.3
Spotlight Company Inc	38 E 32nd St	New York	NY	10016	Jules Seiff	212-532-7533	R	15*	0.3
Glencraft Lingerie Inc	38 E 32nd St	New York	NY	10016	Harvey Jacobson	212-689-5990	R	14	0.3
East Tennessee	PO Box 100	Elizabethton	TN	37643	Leo Greenberg	615-542-4146	R	13*	0.2
Intimate Fashions Inc	15 E 32nd St	New York	NY	10016	B Segan	212-686-1530	R	13	0.2
Tam Industries Inc	PO Box 423	Glennville	GA	30427	Gary Thigpen	912-654-3075	R	13	0.2
Gerber Childrenswear Ballinger	PO Box 535	Ballinger	TX	76821	Ron Boone	915-365-2513	D	12*	0.3
Diplomat Corp	25 Kay Fries Dr	Stony Point	NY	10980	Sheldon R Rose	914-786-5552	P	10	<0.1
Wondermaid Inc	801 Terry Ln	Washington	MO	63090	Ronald Cross	314-239-3696	R	10	0.2
Dutchess Lingerie Inc	180 Madison Av	New York	NY	10016	Rene T Selver	212-684-3020	R	9	0.2
Sand Mountain Industries Inc	PO Box 150	Rainsville	AL	35986	Jimmy G Lloyd	205-638-4476	S	9*	0.2
Zelig Strauss Company Inc	234 16th St	Jersey City	NJ	07302	Zelig Strauss	201-963-6700	R	9*	0.1
Bareville Garment Corp	Grist Mill Rd	Martindale	PA	17549	Ronald Boltz	215-445-4343	R	8	0.2
Sylray Inc	216 Independence	Orwigsburg	PA	17961	RF Koehler Sr	717-366-0537	R	8*	0.2
Faris Brothers of California Inc	12801 Arroyo St	Sylmar	CA	91342	P Faris	818-898-2377	R	8	0.2
Bliss Manufacturing Inc	1049 Park St	Peekskill	NY	10566	Lawerence Teich	914-737-7300	R	7*	0.1
Industrial Seaming Co	PO Box 481	Granite Falls	NC	28630	Carl Wilson	704-396-2171	R	7*	0.2
National Corset Supply House	3240 E 26th St	Vernon	CA	90023	Roy Schlobohm	213-261-0265	R	7*	0.2
Body Slimmers Inc	500 5th Av	New York	NY	10110	Nancy Ganz	212-575-5800	R	6	<0.1
Elsie Undergarment Corp	PO Box 4788	Hialeah	FL	33014	Isaac Silberberg	305-822-6981	R	6	0.2
Milaca Mills Inc	10401 Bren Rd E	Minnetonka	MN	55343	Ralph Green	612-935-8440	R	6*	0.1
VB Caribe Inc	PO Box 11	New York	NY	10021	Richard Gimble	212-889-9054	R	6	0.2
Boutique Industries Inc	40 E 34th St	New York	NY	10016	Edwin Polsky	212-679-2270	R	5*	0.1
Boyertown Apparel Inc	320 S Franklin St	Boyertown	PA	19512	A W Albrecht	215-367-2161	R	5	<0.1
Intime of California	1865 Cordova St	Los Angeles	CA	90007	B Bernstein	213-735-1131	R	5	0.1
King Nancy Textiles Inc	PO Box 848	N Wilkesboro	NC	28659	WM Day	910-667-1194	R	5	0.1
Lawrence Corp	900 Pickens St	Moulton	AL	35650	Keith Spry	205-974-0656	S	5*	0.1
Triangle Lingerie Corp	183 Madison Av	New York	NY	10016	Richard Schneierson	212-725-2585	R	5	<0.1
AFR Apparel International Inc	16542 Arminta St	Van Nuys	CA	91406	Amir Z Moghadam	818-782-6000	R	4	<0.1
Ladyfair Mills Inc	PO Box 159	Ratcliff	AR	72951	David Suarez	501-635-4571	S	4*	0.1
Paris Blues Inc	343 E Jefferson	Los Angeles	CA	90011	Jose Quant	213-235-8235	R	4*	0.1
Shady Character Ltd	35 W 35th St 12th Fl	New York	NY	10001	Linda Rae Tepper	212-629-9500	R	4	<0.1
Dixie Belle Textiles Inc	PO Box 316	Gibsonville	NC	27249	V F Westmoreland	910-449-6262	R	3	<0.1
L and D Manufacturing Inc	20 S Elder St	Easton	PA	18042	LL Rosenfelt	215-258-6366	R	3	<0.1
Magnolia Hosiery Mill Inc	PO Box 472	Corinth	MS	38834	Troy Bumpas	601-286-2221	R	3	0.2
Mr Carmen Inc	PO Box 119E	Selinsgrove	PA	17870	Carmen L Folio	717-374-4444	R	3	<0.1
Rohr Lingerie Inc	209 Dunn Av	Old Forge	PA	18518	N W Witiak Jr	717-562-1902	R	3*	<0.1
Beco Helman Inc	801 Washington N	Minneapolis	MN	55401	Frank Thomas	612-338-5634	R	3	<0.1
Berklee Manufacturing Co	735 Pittston St	Allentown	PA	18103	Edward Nissenbaum	215-434-0431	R	2*	<0.1
Kiki International Corp	180 Madison Av	New York	NY	10016	Steve Silverstein	212-685-7920	R	1	<0.1
Mallory and Kraft Ltd	180 Madison Av	New York	NY	10016	John Yen Sr	212-532-0888	R	1	<0.1
Lou Lingerie Inc	185 Madison Av	New York	NY	10016	Carola Bernota	212-686-1012	S	0	<0.1
Phases Inc	40 E 34th St	New York	NY	10016	Norman Gottlieb	212-213-5252	R	0	<0.1
Heidi's Joy Ltd	10 Carlisle Dr	Old Brookville	NY	11545	Heidi Weinstein	516-626-6806	R	0	<0.1
Laracris Corp	2300 W 95th St	Chicago	IL	60643	Carol Green	312-445-8891	R	0*	<0.1
Sunrise Undergarment Co	53 Bridge St	Brooklyn	NY	11201	Charles Russo	718-855-2421	R	0*	<0.1

Source: *Ward's Business Directory of U.S. Private and Public Companies*, Volumes 1 and 2, 1996. The company type code used is as follows: P - Public, R - Private, S - Subsidiary, D - Division, J - Joint Venture, A - Affiliate, G - Group. Sales are in millions of dollars, employees are in thousands. An asterisk (*) indicates an estimated sales volume. The symbol < stands for 'less than'. Company names and addresses are truncated, in some cases, to fit into the available space.

MATERIALS CONSUMED

Material	Quantity	Delivered Cost ($ million)
Materials, ingredients, containers, and supplies	(X)	830.1
Broadwoven fabrics (piece goods)	(X)	177.3
Narrow fabrics (12 inches or less in width)	(X)	37.1
Knit fabrics	(X)	419.5
Yarn, all fibers	(X)	38.3
Buttons, zippers, and slide fasteners	(X)	35.9
All other materials and components, parts, containers, and supplies	(X)	97.4
Materials, ingredients, containers, and supplies, nsk	(X)	24.6

Source: 1992 *Economic Census*. Explanation of symbols used: (D): Withheld to avoid disclosure of competitive data; na: Not available; (S): Withheld because statistical norms were not met; (X): Not applicable; (Z): Less than half the unit shown; nec: Not elsewhere classified; nsk: Not specified by kind; - : zero; * : 10-19 percent estimated; ** : 20-29 percent estimated.

PRODUCT SHARE DETAILS

Product or Product Class	% Share
Women's, children's, and infants' underwear and nightwear	100.00
Women's, children's, and infants' underwear, except brassieres, corsets, and girdles (including slips, teddies, etc.), made from purchased fabrics	44.67
Women's, children's, and infants' nightwear (including pajamas, gowns, etc.), except robes, etc., intended for separate sale	42.82
Receipts for contract and commission work on women's and children's underwear and nightwear	10.77
Receipts for contract and commission work on women's and children's underwear and nightwear	98.38
Receipts for contract and commission work on women's and children's underwear and nightwear, nsk	1.62
Women's, children's, and infants' underwear and nightwear, nsk	1.75

Source: 1992 *Economic Census*. The values shown are percent of total shipments in an industry. Values of indented subcategories are summed in the main heading. The symbol (D) appears when data are withheld to prevent disclosure of competitive information. The abbreviation nsk stands for 'not specified by kind' and nec for 'not elsewhere classified'.

INPUTS AND OUTPUTS FOR APPAREL MADE FROM PURCHASED MATERIALS

Economic Sector or Industry Providing Inputs	%	Sector	Economic Sector or Industry Buying Outputs	%	Sector
Imports	29.1	Foreign	Personal consumption expenditures	82.7	
Broadwoven fabric mills	20.2	Manufg.	Apparel made from purchased materials	12.0	Manufg.
Apparel made from purchased materials	18.3	Manufg.	Exports	1.5	Foreign
Knit fabric mills	8.6	Manufg.	Federal Government purchases, national defense	0.9	Fed Govt
Wholesale trade	3.8	Trade	S/L Govt. purch., correction	0.5	S/L Govt
Advertising	2.4	Services	Pleating & stitching	0.3	Manufg.
Yarn mills & finishing of textiles, nec	1.4	Manufg.	Knit outerwear mills	0.2	Manufg.
Pleating & stitching	1.1	Manufg.	Hospitals	0.2	Services
Banking	1.1	Fin/R.E.	Laundry, dry cleaning, shoe repair	0.2	Services
Petroleum refining	1.0	Manufg.	S/L Govt. purch., health & hospitals	0.2	S/L Govt
Electric services (utilities)	1.0	Util.	Portrait, photographic studios	0.1	Services
Automotive & apparel trimmings	0.9	Manufg.	S/L Govt. purch., public assistance & relief	0.1	S/L Govt
Needles, pins, & fasteners	0.8	Manufg.			
Thread mills	0.7	Manufg.			
Communications, except radio & TV	0.7	Util.			
Eating & drinking places	0.7	Trade			
U.S. Postal Service	0.7	Gov't			
Leather tanning & finishing	0.5	Manufg.			
Narrow fabric mills	0.5	Manufg.			
Schiffli machine embroideries	0.4	Manufg.			
Motor freight transportation & warehousing	0.4	Util.			
Real estate	0.4	Fin/R.E.			
Royalties	0.4	Fin/R.E.			
Forestry products	0.3	Agric.			
Buttons	0.3	Manufg.			
Paperboard containers & boxes	0.3	Manufg.			
Air transportation	0.3	Util.			
Maintenance of nonfarm buildings nec	0.2	Constr.			
Lace goods	0.2	Manufg.			
Gas production & distribution (utilities)	0.2	Util.			
Automotive rental & leasing, without drivers	0.2	Services			
Electrical repair shops	0.2	Services			
Equipment rental & leasing services	0.2	Services			
Legal services	0.2	Services			
Management & consulting services & labs	0.2	Services			
Artificial trees & flowers	0.1	Manufg.			
Insurance carriers	0.1	Fin/R.E.			
Accounting, auditing & bookkeeping	0.1	Services			
Automotive repair shops & services	0.1	Services			

Source: Benchmark Input-Output Accounts for the U.S. Economy, 1982, U.S. Department of Commerce, Washington, D.C., July 1991. Data, as reported in the source, are organized by the 1977 SIC structure in use in 1982 but have been matched, as closely as is possible, to the 1987 SIC structure used in this book.

OCCUPATIONS EMPLOYED BY SIC 234 - APPAREL

Occupation	% of Total 1994	Change to 2005	Occupation	% of Total 1994	Change to 2005
Sewing machine operators, garment	56.1	-33.1	Cutters & trimmers, hand	1.7	-24.8
Inspectors, testers, & graders, precision	3.5	-16.4	Patternmakers, layout workers, fabric & apparel	1.5	25.4
Blue collar worker supervisors	3.0	-24.0	General managers & top executives	1.4	-20.7
Assemblers, fabricators, & hand workers nec	2.5	-16.4	Sewing machine operators, non-garment	1.3	-37.3
Pressing machine operators, textiles	2.4	-45.7	Helpers, laborers, & material movers nec	1.1	-16.4
Hand packers & packagers	2.0	-21.2	Industrial machinery mechanics	1.1	0.3
Freight, stock, & material movers, hand	1.8	-33.1	Pressers, hand	1.1	-58.2
Traffic, shipping, & receiving clerks	1.8	-19.6	Sewers, hand	1.0	-10.7

Source: *Industry-Occupation Matrix*, Bureau of Labor Statistics. These data relate to one or more 3-digit SIC industry groups rather than to a single 4-digit SIC. The change reported for each occupation to the year 2005 is a percent of growth or decline as estimated by the Bureau of Labor Statistics. The abbreviation nec stands for 'not elsewhere classified'.

LOCATION BY STATE AND REGIONAL CONCENTRATION

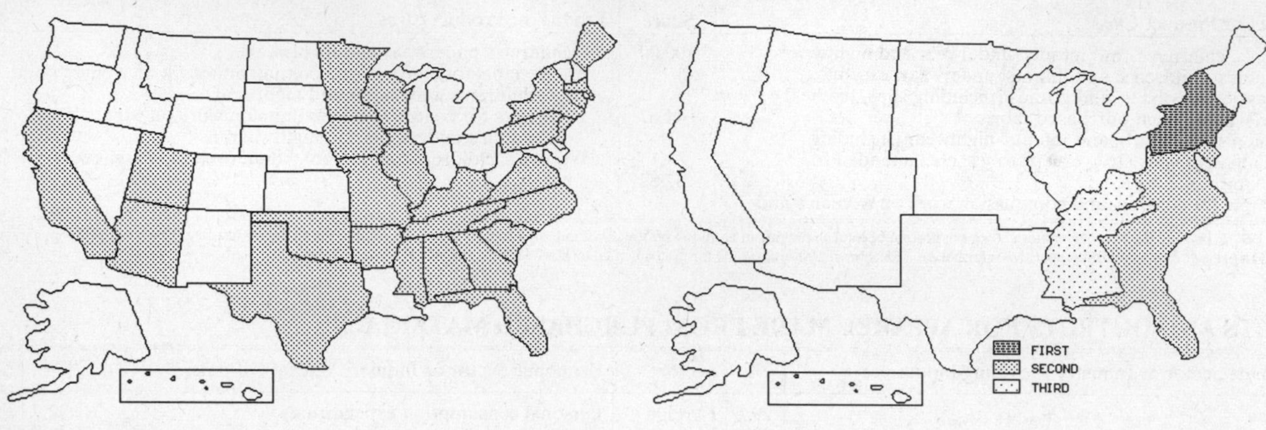

INDUSTRY DATA BY STATE

State	Establish-ments	Shipments Total ($ mil)	Shipments % of U.S.	Shipments Per Establ.	Employment Total Number	Employment % of U.S.	Employment Per Establ.	Wages ($/hour)	Cost as % of Shipments	Investment per Employee ($)
New York	55	268.8	11.4	4.9	2,800	6.7	51	6.78	49.9	679
Pennsylvania	56	265.9	11.2	4.7	5,300	12.8	95	6.28	49.0	302
California	40	177.4	7.5	4.4	2,000	4.8	50	6.52	48.9	-
Mississippi	15	116.0	4.9	7.7	2,300	5.5	153	6.46	27.4	696
Florida	12	66.0	2.8	5.5	1,500	3.6	125	6.30	37.0	267
South Carolina	8	47.6	2.0	5.9	1,400	3.4	175	6.23	41.2	-
New Jersey	20	29.3	1.2	1.5	900	2.2	45	7.20	38.9	-
Massachusetts	7	29.2	1.2	4.2	800	1.9	114	6.77	25.7	250
North Carolina	31	(D)	-	-	3,750 *	9.0	121	-	-	-
Georgia	29	(D)	-	-	7,500 *	18.1	259	-	-	-
Alabama	13	(D)	-	-	7,500 *	18.1	577	-	-	-
Tennessee	10	(D)	-	-	750 *	1.8	75	-	-	-
Texas	9	(D)	-	-	1,750 *	4.2	194	-	-	-
Virginia	6	(D)	-	-	750 *	1.8	125	-	-	400
Iowa	5	(D)	-	-	375 *	0.9	75	-	-	-
Kentucky	5	(D)	-	-	1,750 *	4.2	350	-	-	-
Connecticut	4	(D)	-	-	175 *	0.4	44	-	-	-
Missouri	4	(D)	-	-	375 *	0.9	94	-	-	-
Arkansas	3	(D)	-	-	375 *	0.9	125	-	-	-
Wisconsin	3	(D)	-	-	375 *	0.9	125	-	-	-
Arizona	2	(D)	-	-	375 *	0.9	188	-	-	-
Minnesota	2	(D)	-	-	175 *	0.4	88	-	-	-
Oklahoma	2	(D)	-	-	175 *	0.4	88	-	-	-
Illinois	1	(D)	-	-	175 *	0.4	175	-	-	-
Maine	1	(D)	-	-	375 *	0.9	375	-	-	-
Utah	1	(D)	-	-	375 *	0.9	375	-	-	-

Source: 1992 *Economic Census*. The states are in descending order of shipments or establishments (if shipment data are missing for the majority). The symbol (D) appears when data are withheld to prevent disclosure of competitive information. States marked with (D) are sorted by number of establishments. A dash (-) indicates that the data element cannot be calculated; * indicates the midpoint of a range.

2342 - BRAS, GIRDLES, AND ALLIED GARMENTS

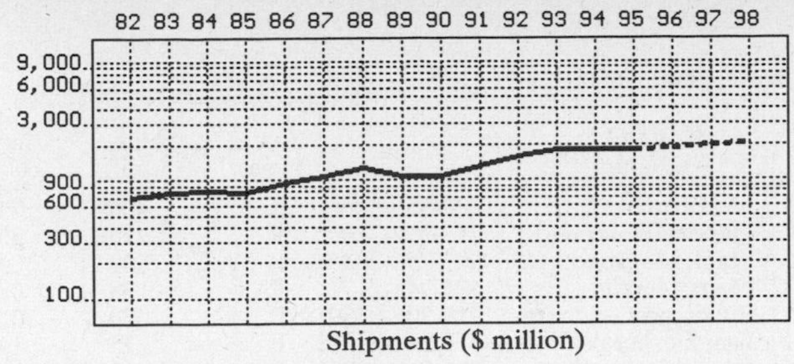

Shipments ($ million)

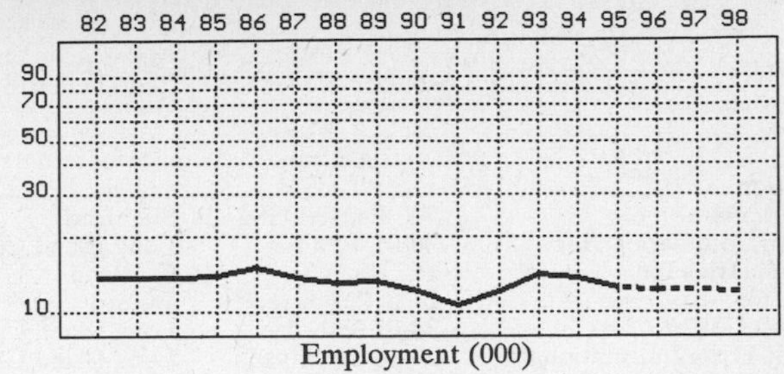

Employment (000)

GENERAL STATISTICS

Year	Companies	Establishments: Total	Establishments: with 20 or more employees	Employment: Total (000)	Production Workers (000)	Production Hours (Mil)	Compensation: Payroll ($ mil)	Compensation: Wages ($/hr)	Production ($ million): Cost of Materials	Value Added by Manufacture	Value of Shipments	Capital Invest.
1982	134	151	97	13.8	11.3	19.5	142.3	4.58	334.5	370.8	720.3	7.5
1983		146	93	13.7	11.1	19.3	151.5	4.88	355.7	434.4	770.2	4.8
1984		141	89	13.8	11.3	20.4	163.6	5.28	380.1	459.7	811.1	8.1
1985		137	86	13.9	10.9	20.1	169.5	5.26	378.0	402.1	775.2	12.3
1986		124	87	15.2	11.7	21.7	193.4	5.24	458.0	476.4	944.7	8.9
1987	109	128	88	13.8	9.7	18.2	198.8	5.63	514.4	576.3	1,079.9	6.7
1988		125	88	12.9	9.3	17.2	192.2	6.03	596.6	663.4	1,262.7	
1989		118	83	13.2	8.4	14.7	181.9	6.16	529.5	541.1	1,064.4	11.1
1990		113	78	12.0	8.5	15.6	187.5	6.34	517.1	560.6	1,086.9	7.6
1991		118	84	10.6	7.8	14.0	191.2	7.01	552.3	809.9	1,297.0	7.7
1992	106	125	78	12.1	9.7	17.3	219.8	7.79	701.1	887.5	1,579.3	12.9
1993		119	78	14.1	10.7	19.9	262.7	7.93	882.6	900.0	1,788.6	19.9
1994		110P	76P	13.6	10.4	21.0	263.5	7.22	923.1	879.5	1,807.3	13.5
1995		107P	74P	12.4P	8.9P	17.1P	253.1P	7.99P	913.4P	870.3P	1,788.3P	
1996		104P	73P	12.3P	8.7P	16.9P	261.6P	8.26P	959.8P	914.4P	1,879.1P	
1997		101P	71P	12.2P	8.5P	16.7P	270.1P	8.53P	1,006.1P	958.6P	1,969.9P	
1998		98P	70P	12.0P	8.4P	16.5P	278.5P	8.80P	1,052.5P	1,002.8P	2,060.6P	

Sources: 1982, 1987, 1992 *Economic Census*; *Annual Survey of Manufactures*, 83-86, 88-91, 93-94. Establishment counts for non-Census years are from *County Business Patterns*; establishment values for 83-84 are extrapolations. 'P's show projections by the editors. Industries reclassified in 87 will not have data for prior years.

INDICES OF CHANGE

Year	Companies	Establishments: Total	Establishments: with 20 or more employees	Employment: Total (000)	Production Workers (000)	Production Hours (Mil)	Compensation: Payroll ($ mil)	Compensation: Wages ($/hr)	Production ($ million): Cost of Materials	Value Added by Manufacture	Value of Shipments	Capital Invest.
1982	126	121	124	114	116	113	65	59	48	42	46	58
1983		117	119	113	114	112	69	63	51	49	49	37
1984		113	114	114	116	118	74	68	54	52	51	63
1985		110	110	115	112	116	77	68	54	45	49	95
1986		99	112	126	121	125	88	67	65	54	60	69
1987	103	102	113	114	100	105	90	72	73	65	68	52
1988		100	113	107	96	99	87	77	85	75	80	
1989		94	106	109	87	85	83	79	76	61	67	86
1990		90	100	99	88	90	85	81	74	63	69	59
1991		94	108	88	80	81	87	90	79	91	82	60
1992	100	100	100	100	100	100	100	100	100	100	100	100
1993		95	100	117	110	115	120	102	126	101	113	154
1994		88P	97P	112	107	121	120	93	132	99	114	105
1995		85P	95P	103P	92P	99P	115P	103P	130P	98P	113P	
1996		83P	94P	101P	90P	97P	119P	106P	137P	103P	119P	
1997		81P	92P	100P	88P	96P	123P	110P	144P	108P	125P	
1998		78P	90P	99P	86P	95P	127P	113P	150P	113P	130P	

Sources: Same as General Statistics. Values reflect change from the base year, 1992. Values above 100 mean greater than 92, values below 100 mean less than 92, and a value of 100 in the 82-91 or 93-98 period means same as 92. 'P's mark projections by the editors.

SELECTED RATIOS

For 1994	Avg. of All Manufact.	Analyzed Industry	Index	For 1994	Avg. of All Manufact.	Analyzed Industry	Index
Employees per Establishment	49	124	253	Value Added per Production Worker	134,084	84,567	63
Payroll per Establishment	1,500,273	2,404,397	160	Cost per Establishment	5,045,178	8,423,144	167
Payroll per Employee	30,620	19,375	63	Cost per Employee	102,970	67,875	66
Production Workers per Establishment	34	95	276	Cost per Production Worker	146,988	88,760	60
Wages per Establishment	853,319	1,383,509	162	Shipments per Establishment	9,576,895	16,491,331	172
Wages per Production Worker	24,861	14,579	59	Shipments per Employee	195,460	132,890	68
Hours per Production Worker	2,056	2,019	98	Shipments per Production Worker	279,017	173,779	62
Wages per Hour	12.09	7.22	60	Investment per Establishment	321,011	123,185	38
Value Added per Establishment	4,602,255	8,025,301	174	Investment per Employee	6,552	993	15
Value Added per Employee	93,930	64,669	69	Investment per Production Worker	9,352	1,298	14

Sources: Same as General Statistics. The 'Average of All Manufacturing' column represents the average of all manufacturing industries reported for the most recent complete year available. The Index shows the relationship between the Average and the Analyzed Industry. For example, 100 means that they are equal; 500 that the Analyzed Industry is five times the average; 50 means that the Analyzed Industry is half the national average. The abbreviation 'na' is used to show that data are 'not available'.

LEADING COMPANIES

Number shown: **23** Total sales ($ mil): **849** Total employment (000): **15.5**

Company Name	Address				CEO Name	Phone	Co. Type	Sales ($ mil)	Empl. (000)
Playtex Apparel Inc	700 Fairfield Av	Stamford	CT	06904	Joe Chaden	203-356-8000	S	400*	7.8
Bestform Foundations Inc	38-01 47th Av	Long Island Ct	NY	11101	Marvin Bienenfeld	718-392-2200	R	110*	2.2
NCC Industries Inc	165 Main St	Cortland	NY	13045	Frank Magrone	607-756-2841	P	100	0.9
Lovable Co	2121 Peachtree	Buford	GA	30518	Frank Garson	404-945-2171	R	38	0.6
Gold Seal Garter Corp	34-01 38th Av	Long Island Ct	NY	11101	Raymond Goldberg	718-706-0350	R	30	0.1
Splendor Form International Inc	29-10 Thompson	Long Island Ct	NY	11101	Jack Desperak	718-392-6600	R	25	1.4
Aristotle Corp	129 Church St	New Haven	CT	06510	John J Crawford	203-867-4090	P	18	0.2
Strouse, Adler Co	PO Box 1770	New Haven	CT	06507	David S Howell	203-777-3484	S	18	0.2
Kern Manufacturing Company	100 Trowbridge Rd	Neoga	IL	62447	Al Corrado	217-895-3602	R	16	0.4
Revelation Brassiere Company	156 Porter St	East Boston	MA	02128	Arnold Jaccobson	617-569-3000	R	13*	0.3
Glamorise Foundations Inc	135 Madison Av	New York	NY	10016	Richard Rosner	212-684-5025	R	13	0.2
Metric Products Inc	4671 Leahy St	Culver City	CA	90230	Shirley Magidson	213-870-9121	R	12	0.3
Lily of France Inc	136 Madison Av	New York	NY	10016	M Bienenfeld	212-696-1110	S	10*	0.2
Reach Road Mfg Corp	2729 Reach Rd	Williamsport	PA	17701	R Rosner	717-322-7806	S	10	0.2
Carnival Creations	1050 Edward St	Linden	NJ	07036	F Klein	908-862-8400	R	9*	0.2
Preferred Foundations	216 N Main St	Freeport	NY	11520	Myron Bienenfeld	516-623-7777	R	8	<0.1
Q-T Foundations Company Inc	1 McDermott Pl	Bergenfield	NJ	07621	M Kutzin	201-384-7000	R	5	0.1
Trim-Line Foundations	PO Box 37066	Charlotte	NC	28237	Joseph Farel	704-375-5665	D	5	<0.1
Jo La Foundations Inc	6101 16th Av	Brooklyn	NY	11204	Joel Radbell	718-259-6800	R	3*	<0.1
Basic Comfort Inc	445 Lincoln St	Denver	CO	80203	Ron Ives	303-778-7535	R	2*	<0.1
Carmen Foundations Inc	843 W Adams St	Chicago	IL	60607	HM Lehman	312-829-1801	R	2	<0.1
Cortland Corset Company Inc	PO Box 546	Cortland	NY	13045	Charles K Wanish	607-756-7566	R	2	<0.1
Merit Foundations Inc	PO Box 3365	Bridgeport	CT	06605	Harvey Gaberman	203-334-9148	R	1	<0.1

Source: *Ward's Business Directory of U.S. Private and Public Companies*, Volumes 1 and 2, 1996. The company type code used is as follows: P - Public, R - Private, S - Subsidiary, D - Division, J - Joint Venture, A - Affiliate, G - Group. Sales are in millions of dollars, employees are in thousands. An asterisk (*) indicates an estimated sales volume. The symbol < stands for 'less than'. Company names and addresses are truncated, in some cases, to fit into the available space.

MATERIALS CONSUMED

Material	Quantity	Delivered Cost ($ million)
Materials, ingredients, containers, and supplies	(X)	552.1
Broadwoven fabrics (piece goods)	(X)	45.8
Narrow fabrics (12 inches or less in width)	(X)	41.3
Knit fabrics	(X)	354.3
Yarn, all fibers	(X)	1.2
Buttons, zippers, and slide fasteners	(X)	4.2
All other materials and components, parts, containers, and supplies	(X)	73.4
Materials, ingredients, containers, and supplies, nsk	(X)	31.9

Source: 1992 *Economic Census*. Explanation of symbols used: (D): Withheld to avoid disclosure of competitive data; na: Not available; (S): Withheld because statistical norms were not met; (X): Not applicable; (Z): Less than half the unit shown; nec: Not elsewhere classified; nsk: Not specified by kind; - : zero; * : 10-19 percent estimated; ** : 20-29 percent estimated.

PRODUCT SHARE DETAILS

Product or Product Class	% Share	Product or Product Class	% Share
Brassieres, girdles, and allied garments	100.00	Receipts for contract and commission work on brassieres, corsets, and allied garments	1.40
Brassieres (including maternity), bra-lettes, and bandeaux	74.66	Brassieres, girdles, and allied garments, nsk	2.82
Corsets, girdles, combinations, and accessories	21.11		

Source: 1992 *Economic Census*. The values shown are percent of total shipments in an industry. Values of indented subcategories are summed in the main heading. The symbol (D) appears when data are withheld to prevent disclosure of competitive information. The abbreviation nsk stands for 'not specified by kind' and nec for 'not elsewhere classified'.

INPUTS AND OUTPUTS FOR APPAREL MADE FROM PURCHASED MATERIALS

Economic Sector or Industry Providing Inputs	%	Sector	Economic Sector or Industry Buying Outputs	%	Sector
Imports	29.1	Foreign	Personal consumption expenditures	82.7	
Broadwoven fabric mills	20.2	Manufg.	Apparel made from purchased materials	12.0	Manufg.
Apparel made from purchased materials	18.3	Manufg.	Exports	1.5	Foreign
Knit fabric mills	8.6	Manufg.	Federal Government purchases, national defense	0.9	Fed Govt
Wholesale trade	3.8	Trade	S/L Govt. purch., correction	0.5	S/L Govt
Advertising	2.4	Services	Pleating & stitching	0.3	Manufg.
Yarn mills & finishing of textiles, nec	1.4	Manufg.	Knit outerwear mills	0.2	Manufg.
Pleating & stitching	1.1	Manufg.	Hospitals	0.2	Services
Banking	1.1	Fin/R.E.	Laundry, dry cleaning, shoe repair	0.2	Services
Petroleum refining	1.0	Manufg.	S/L Govt. purch., health & hospitals	0.2	S/L Govt

Continued on next page.

INPUTS AND OUTPUTS FOR APPAREL MADE FROM PURCHASED MATERIALS - Continued

Economic Sector or Industry Providing Inputs	%	Sector	Economic Sector or Industry Buying Outputs	%	Sector
Electric services (utilities)	1.0	Util.	Portrait, photographic studios	0.1	Services
Automotive & apparel trimmings	0.9	Manufg.	S/L Govt. purch., public assistance & relief	0.1	S/L Govt
Needles, pins, & fasteners	0.8	Manufg.			
Thread mills	0.7	Manufg.			
Communications, except radio & TV	0.7	Util.			
Eating & drinking places	0.7	Trade			
U.S. Postal Service	0.7	Gov't			
Leather tanning & finishing	0.5	Manufg.			
Narrow fabric mills	0.5	Manufg.			
Schiffli machine embroideries	0.4	Manufg.			
Motor freight transportation & warehousing	0.4	Util.			
Real estate	0.4	Fin/R.E.			
Royalties	0.4	Fin/R.E.			
Forestry products	0.3	Agric.			
Buttons	0.3	Manufg.			
Paperboard containers & boxes	0.3	Manufg.			
Air transportation	0.3	Util.			
Maintenance of nonfarm buildings nec	0.2	Constr.			
Lace goods	0.2	Manufg.			
Gas production & distribution (utilities)	0.2	Util.			
Automotive rental & leasing, without drivers	0.2	Services			
Electrical repair shops	0.2	Services			
Equipment rental & leasing services	0.2	Services			
Legal services	0.2	Services			
Management & consulting services & labs	0.2	Services			
Artificial trees & flowers	0.1	Manufg.			
Insurance carriers	0.1	Fin/R.E.			
Accounting, auditing & bookkeeping	0.1	Services			
Automotive repair shops & services	0.1	Services			

Source: Benchmark Input-Output Accounts for the U.S. Economy, 1982, U.S. Department of Commerce, Washington, D.C., July 1991. Data, as reported in the source, are organized by the 1977 SIC structure in use in 1982 but have been matched, as closely as is possible, to the 1987 SIC structure used in this book.

OCCUPATIONS EMPLOYED BY SIC 234 - APPAREL

Occupation	% of Total 1994	Change to 2005	Occupation	% of Total 1994	Change to 2005
Sewing machine operators, garment	56.1	-33.1	Cutters & trimmers, hand	1.7	-24.8
Inspectors, testers, & graders, precision	3.5	-16.4	Patternmakers, layout workers, fabric & apparel	1.5	25.4
Blue collar worker supervisors	3.0	-24.0	General managers & top executives	1.4	-20.7
Assemblers, fabricators, & hand workers nec	2.5	-16.4	Sewing machine operators, non-garment	1.3	-37.3
Pressing machine operators, textiles	2.4	-45.7	Helpers, laborers, & material movers nec	1.1	-16.4
Hand packers & packagers	2.0	-21.2	Industrial machinery mechanics	1.1	0.3
Freight, stock, & material movers, hand	1.8	-33.1	Pressers, hand	1.1	-58.2
Traffic, shipping, & receiving clerks	1.8	-19.6	Sewers, hand	1.0	-10.7

Source: Industry-Occupation Matrix, Bureau of Labor Statistics. These data relate to one or more 3-digit SIC industry groups rather than to a single 4-digit SIC. The change reported for each occupation to the year 2005 is a percent of growth or decline as estimated by the Bureau of Labor Statistics. The abbreviation nec stands for 'not elsewhere classified'.

LOCATION BY STATE AND REGIONAL CONCENTRATION

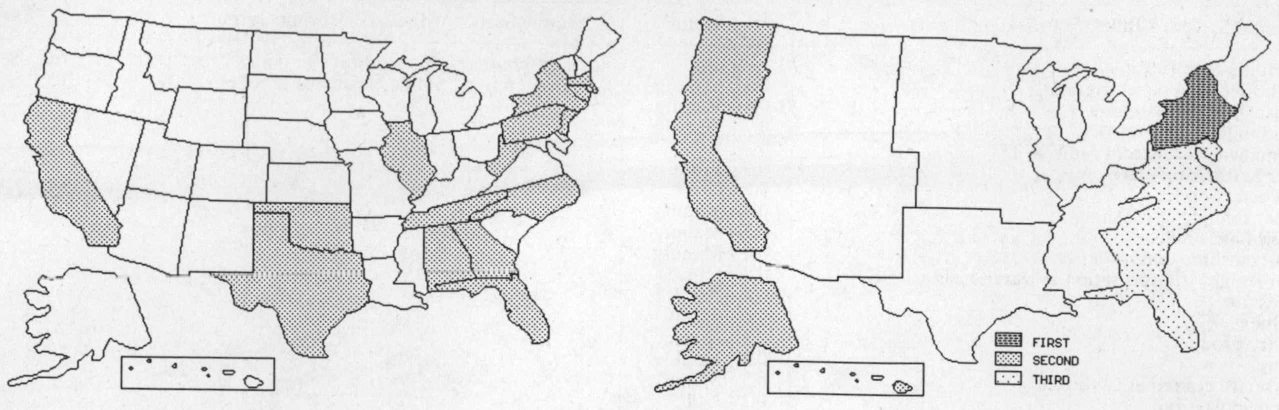

INDUSTRY DATA BY STATE

State	Establish-ments	Shipments Total ($ mil)	Shipments % of U.S.	Shipments Per Establ.	Employment Total Number	Employment % of U.S.	Employment Per Establ.	Wages ($/hour)	Cost as % of Shipments	Investment per Employee ($)
New York	41	422.5	26.8	10.3	2,900	24.0	71	8.89	38.2	862
New Jersey	12	237.5	15.0	19.8	1,500	12.4	125	7.14	48.7	-
California	22	158.1	10.0	7.2	1,500	12.4	68	8.00	45.4	-
Pennsylvania	7	50.5	3.2	7.2	1,100	9.1	157	9.00	29.9	273
Massachusetts	5	22.5	1.4	4.5	300	2.5	60	7.40	47.1	667
Florida	3	13.7	0.9	4.6	300	2.5	100	6.00	39.4	667
Connecticut	5	(D)	-	-	375 *	3.1	75	-	-	-
Illinois	5	(D)	-	-	375 *	3.1	75	-	-	-
North Carolina	5	(D)	-	-	375 *	3.1	75	-	-	-
Georgia	3	(D)	-	-	1,750 *	14.5	583	-	-	-
Tennessee	3	(D)	-	-	375 *	3.1	125	-	-	-
Alabama	2	(D)	-	-	750 *	6.2	375	-	-	-
Texas	2	(D)	-	-	375 *	3.1	188	-	-	-
West Virginia	2	(D)	-	-	175 *	1.4	88	-	-	-
Oklahoma	1	(D)	-	-	750 *	6.2	750	-	-	-

Source: 1992 *Economic Census*. The states are in descending order of shipments or establishments (if shipment data are missing for the majority). The symbol (D) appears when data are withheld to prevent disclosure of competitive information. States marked with (D) are sorted by number of establishments. A dash (-) indicates that the data element cannot be calculated; * indicates the midpoint of a range.

2353 - HATS, CAPS & MILLINERY

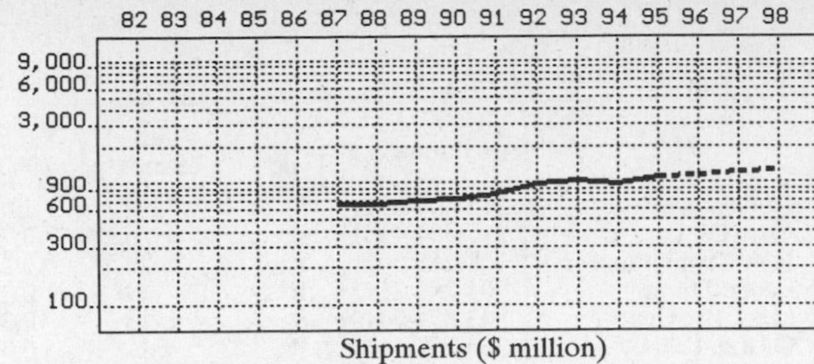

Shipments ($ million)

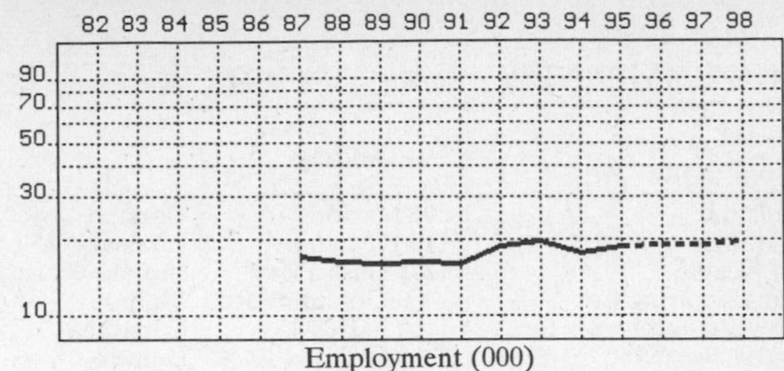

Employment (000)

GENERAL STATISTICS

Year	Companies	Establishments		Employment			Compensation		Production ($ million)			
		Total	with 20 or more employees	Total (000)	Production Workers (000)	Production Hours (Mil)	Payroll ($ mil)	Wages ($/hr)	Cost of Materials	Value Added by Manufacture	Value of Shipments	Capital Invest.
1982												
1983												
1984												
1985												
1986												
1987	440	462	170	17.2	14.6	26.5	204.4	5.60	294.6	368.0	662.7	7.2
1988				16.4	14.0	24.3	208.8	6.11	297.7	377.5	671.4	7.2
1989		380	167	16.0	13.8	24.3	210.4	6.12	310.0	418.9	722.4	6.5
1990				16.5	14.4	25.4	227.3	6.33	316.8	424.3	736.6	7.3
1991				15.9	13.6	26.0	228.2	6.05	347.0	455.3	800.5	10.3
1992	346	370	170	18.8	15.6	29.6	281.4	7.08	436.3	573.5	978.4	21.5
1993				19.7	16.6	32.2	312.0	7.39	465.2	597.4	1,054.6	21.9
1994				17.6	14.2	27.2	295.6	7.82	417.8	572.8	990.3	14.8
1995				18.7P	15.4P	30.2P	319.3P	7.88P	462.9P	634.6P	1,097.2P	21.4P
1996				19.0P	15.6P	30.9P	335.6P	8.17P	488.2P	669.3P	1,157.2P	23.5P
1997				19.4P	15.7P	31.7P	351.9P	8.46P	513.5P	704.0P	1,217.2P	25.6P
1998				19.7P	15.9P	32.4P	368.2P	8.75P	538.8P	738.8P	1,277.2P	27.7P

Sources: 1982, 1987, 1992 *Economic Census*; *Annual Survey of Manufactures*, 83-86, 88-91, 93-94. Establishment counts for non-Census years are from *County Business Patterns*; establishment values for 83-84 are extrapolations. 'P's show projections by the editors. Industries reclassified in 87 will not have data for prior years.

INDICES OF CHANGE

Year	Companies	Establishments		Employment			Compensation		Production ($ million)			
		Total	with 20 or more employees	Total (000)	Production Workers (000)	Production Hours (Mil)	Payroll ($ mil)	Wages ($/hr)	Cost of Materials	Value Added by Manufacture	Value of Shipments	Capital Invest.
1982												
1983												
1984												
1985												
1986												
1987	127	125	100	91	94	90	73	79	68	64	68	33
1988				87	90	82	74	86	68	66	69	33
1989		103	98	85	88	82	75	86	71	73	74	30
1990				88	92	86	81	89	73	74	75	34
1991				85	87	88	81	85	80	79	82	48
1992	100	100	100	100	100	100	100	100	100	100	100	100
1993				105	106	109	111	104	107	104	108	102
1994				94	91	92	105	110	96	100	101	69
1995				100P	99P	102P	113P	111P	106P	111P	112P	100P
1996				101P	100P	104P	119P	115P	112P	117P	118P	109P
1997				103P	101P	107P	125P	120P	118P	123P	124P	119P
1998				105P	102P	109P	131P	124P	124P	129P	131P	129P

Sources: Same as General Statistics. Values reflect change from the base year, 1992. Values above 100 mean greater than 92, values below 100 mean less than 92, and a value of 100 in the 82-91 or 93-98 period means same as 92. 'P's mark projections by the editors.

SELECTED RATIOS

For 1992	Avg. of All Manufact.	Analyzed Industry	Index	For 1992	Avg. of All Manufact.	Analyzed Industry	Index
Employees per Establishment	46	51	111	Value Added per Production Worker	122,353	36,763	30
Payroll per Establishment	1,332,320	760,541	57	Cost per Establishment	4,239,462	1,179,189	28
Payroll per Employee	29,181	14,968	51	Cost per Employee	92,853	23,207	25
Production Workers per Establishment	31	42	134	Cost per Production Worker	135,003	27,968	21
Wages per Establishment	734,496	566,400	77	Shipments per Establishment	8,100,800	2,644,324	33
Wages per Production Worker	23,390	13,434	57	Shipments per Employee	177,425	52,043	29
Hours per Production Worker	2,025	1,897	94	Shipments per Production Worker	257,966	62,718	24
Wages per Hour	11.55	7.08	61	Investment per Establishment	278,244	58,108	21
Value Added per Establishment	3,842,210	1,550,000	40	Investment per Employee	6,094	1,144	19
Value Added per Employee	84,153	30,505	36	Investment per Production Worker	8,861	1,378	16

Sources: Same as General Statistics. The 'Average of All Manufacturing' column represents the average of all manufacturing industries reported for the most recent complete year available. The Index shows the relationship between the Average and the Analyzed Industry. For example, 100 means that they are equal; 500 that the Analyzed Industry is five times the average; 50 means that the Analyzed Industry is half the national average. The abbreviation 'na' is used to show that data are 'not available'.

LEADING COMPANIES

Number shown: **44** Total sales ($ mil): **482** Total employment (000): **6.6**

Company Name	Address				CEO Name	Phone	Co. Type	Sales ($ mil)	Empl. (000)
Hat Brands Inc	601 Marion Dr	Garland	TX	75042	Robert Stec	214-494-0511	S	200	1.0
Bollman Hat Co	110 E Main St	Adamstown	PA	19501	Curt Glass	215-484-4361	R	35	0.7
American Needle	1275 Bush Pkwy	Buffalo Grove	IL	60089	R A Kronenberger	708-215-0011	R	23	0.2
Dunn Manufacturing Co	1400 Goldmine Rd	Monroe	NC	28110	Lance Dunn	704-283-2147	R	19*	0.4
Miller Brothers Industries Inc	1101 N Bus 45	Corsicana	TX	75110	Mike Broyles	903-874-7446	S	18	0.3
Imperial Headwear Inc	5200 E Evans Av	Denver	CO	80222	Gloria Teague	303-757-1166	R	16*	0.3
Louisville Manufacturing Co	PO Box 1436	Louisville	KY	40201	Michael Heideman	502-774-8711	R	16	0.3
F and M Hat Company Inc	103 Walnut St	Denver	PA	17517	F B Fichthorn	717-336-5505	R	15*	0.3
Texace Corp	PO Box 7429	San Antonio	TX	78285	Bob W Coleman	210-227-7551	R	14	0.4
Virginia Garment Company Inc	501 N 17th St	Richmond	VA	23219	Joseph Fekete	804-648-3422	R	11	0.3
M Grossman and Sons Inc	245 4th St	Passaic	NJ	07055	M Grossman	201-779-4651	R	10*	0.2
DeLong Sportswear Inc	PO Box 299	Crowell	TX	79227	Tim Christopher	817-684-1561	D	9*	0.2
M and B Headwear Company	2323 E Main St	Richmond	VA	23223	Sheldon Bigler	804-648-1603	R	8	0.2
Strohm Manufacturing Inc	PO Box 1516	Clarksdale	MS	38614	Fred Strohm	601-627-2670	R	8*	0.2
Crown Clothing Company Inc	609 Paul St	Vineland	NJ	08360	Howard Levin	609-691-0343	R	7*	0.1
Eleja Casuals Corp	42 W 38th St	New York	NY	10018	H Smith	212-921-8166	R	7	0.1
Town Talk Cap Mfg Co	PO Box 58157	Louisville	KY	40268	Wayne O Joplin	502-584-2163	R	7	0.1
Stratton Hats Inc	3200 Randolph St	Bellwood	IL	60104	Leon Stratton	708-544-5220	R	6	<0.1
Julie Hat Company Inc	PO Drawer 518	Patterson	GA	31557	L Dunaway	912-647-2031	R	5	0.2
Northern Cap Manufacturing Co	510 N 1st Av	Minneapolis	MN	55403	Samuel Rafowitz	612-332-8979	R	5	<0.1
Hypnotic Hats Ltd	95 Horatio St	New York	NY	10014	Michael Pascal	212-645-7147	R	4*	<0.1
Milano Hat Co	10203 Corkwood Rd	Dallas	TX	75238	John Milano	214-342-0071	R	4	<0.1
Mad Bomber Co	139 Windy Hill Ln	Winchester	VA	22602	Brent Reynolds	703-662-8840	R	4	<0.1
David Banash and Son Inc	100 Chauncy St	Boston	MA	02111	Angel Algeri	617-482-5478	R	3	<0.1
Derby Cap Manufacturing	PO Box 34220	Louisville	KY	40232	FG Cogswell	502-587-8495	R	3	<0.1
Manhattan-Miami Corp	5019 NW 165 St	Hialeah	FL	33014	A Edelstein	305-628-3630	R	3	<0.1
Adver-Togs Inc	555 Mount Tabor	New Albany	IN	47150	William L Allen III	812-948-2351	R	3	<0.1
Dorel Hat Company Inc	1 Main St	Beacon	NY	12508	Salvador Cumella	914-831-5231	R	3	<0.1
Benay Hat Co	4710 Roanoke Av	Newport News	VA	23607	Stanley Molin	804-244-0807	R	2*	<0.1
Fit Rite Headwear Inc	92 S Empire St	Wilkes-Barre	PA	18702	SS Schonwetter	717-825-3459	R	2	0.1
Outdoor Research Inc	1000 1st Av S	Seattle	WA	98134	Ron Gregg	206-467-8197	R	2*	0.2
New Jersey Headwear Corp	150 Bay St	Jersey City	NJ	07302	Mitchell Cahn	201-420-5900	R	2	<0.1
Lancaster Uniform Cap	PO Box 21489	Los Angeles	CA	90021	Ernest Aguilar	213-626-4661	R	2	<0.1
Keystone Uniform Cap Corp	428 N 13th St	Philadelphia	PA	19123	Harold Selvin	215-922-5493	R	2	<0.1
Camp Cap Company Inc	PO Box 726	Villa Rica	GA	30180	WR Camp	404-459-3647	R	1	<0.1
Do Rags Inc	205 S 26th St	Waco	TX	76710	Richard Dix	817-754-3537	R	1	<0.1
Eric Javits Hats	406 W 31st St	New York	NY	10001	Eric Javits	212-967-8410	R	1	<0.1
Korber Hats Inc	PO Box 336	Fall River	MA	02724	Michael Korber	508-672-7033	R	1*	<0.1
Barbara Creations Inc	225 W 37th St	New York	NY	10018	MH Weiss	212-827-0480	R	1	<0.1
Makins Hats Ltd	212 W 35th St	New York	NY	10001	Marsha Akins	212-594-6666	R	1	<0.1
MU Industries Inc	110 N 5th St	Minneapolis	MN	55403	William Lipkin	612-338-8245	R	1	<0.1
Alexander and Baum Corp	707 S Broadway	Los Angeles	CA	90014	Leon Berlin	213-622-7064	R	1	<0.1
Moriarty Hat and Sweater Co	PO Box 1117	Stowe	VT	05672	E W Morrison	802-253-4052	R	0	<0.1
Jesterwear Inc	10121 Evergreen	Everett	WA	98204	Mark McKenzie	206-334-9757	R	0*	<0.1

Source: *Ward's Business Directory of U.S. Private and Public Companies*, Volumes 1 and 2, 1996. The company type code used is as follows: P - Public, R - Private, S - Subsidiary, D - Division, J - Joint Venture, A - Affiliate, G - Group. Sales are in millions of dollars, employees are in thousands. An asterisk (*) indicates an estimated sales volume. The symbol < stands for 'less than'. Company names and addresses are truncated, in some cases, to fit into the available space.

MATERIALS CONSUMED

Material	Quantity	Delivered Cost ($ million)
Materials, ingredients, containers, and supplies	(X)	353.4
Broadwoven fabrics (piece goods)	(X)	95.1
Narrow fabrics (12 inches or less in width)	(X)	40.8
Wool felt	(X)	6.7
Hat bodies	(X)	71.7
All other materials and components, parts, containers, and supplies	(X)	72.8
Materials, ingredients, containers, and supplies, nsk	(X)	66.5

Source: 1992 *Economic Census*. Explanation of symbols used: (D): Withheld to avoid disclosure of competitive data; na: Not available; (S): Withheld because statistical norms were not met; (X): Not applicable; (Z): Less than half the unit shown; nec: Not elsewhere classified; nsk: Not specified by kind; - : zero; * : 10-19 percent estimated; ** : 20-29 percent estimated.

PRODUCT SHARE DETAILS

Product or Product Class	% Share	Product or Product Class	% Share
Hats, caps, and millinery	100.00	Cloth hats and caps, nsk	1.98
Hats and hat bodies, except cloth and millinery	20.60	Millinery (women's, children's, and infants' trimmed hats made from hat bodies or other millinery materials)	10.91
Finished straw hats, except harvest hats, men's and boys'	31.30	Women's, children's, and infants' fur-felt and wool-felt millinery	33.62
Wool-felt finished hats, excluding millinery	19.43	Women's, children's, and infants' fabrics millinery, made from all types of fabrics (including ribbon and pile fabrics)	30.02
Fur-felt finished hats, excluding millinery	24.92	Women's, children's, and infants' all other millinery, including flowered millinery, straw (natural or synthetic), whimseys, miniatures, and hat frames	32.98
Hat bodies, except hat bodies finished into hats or millinery in the same plant	24.36	Millinery (women's, children's and infants' trimmed hats made from hat bodies or other millinery materials), nsk	3.49
Cloth hats and caps	56.50	Hats, caps, and millinery, nsk	11.98
Men's and boys' cloth hats, except uniform	14.92		
Men's and boys' caps, except uniform	68.87		
Men's and boys' uniform hats and caps	8.98		
All other hats and caps (harvest hats, women's uniform hats and caps, headwear made from purchased knit fabrics, etc.)	5.25		

Source: 1992 *Economic Census*. The values shown are percent of total shipments in an industry. Values of indented subcategories are summed in the main heading. The symbol (D) appears when data are withheld to prevent disclosure of competitive information. The abbreviation nsk stands for 'not specified by kind' and nec for 'not elsewhere classified'.

INPUTS AND OUTPUTS FOR FELT GOODS, NEC

Economic Sector or Industry Providing Inputs	%	Sector	Economic Sector or Industry Buying Outputs	%	Sector
Processed textile waste	17.2	Manufg.	Asphalt felts & coatings	12.2	Manufg.
Advertising	11.7	Services	Machinery, except electrical, nec	11.4	Manufg.
Textile goods, nec	8.6	Manufg.	General industrial machinery, nec	7.9	Manufg.
Wholesale trade	7.3	Trade	Exports	6.8	Foreign
Motor freight transportation & warehousing	5.7	Util.	Blowers & fans	6.7	Manufg.
Cyclic crudes and organics	5.0	Manufg.	Surgical appliances & supplies	6.7	Manufg.
Petroleum refining	4.8	Manufg.	Photographic equipment & supplies	6.1	Manufg.
Fabricated rubber products, nec	3.7	Manufg.	Padding & upholstery filling	5.2	Manufg.
Plastics materials & resins	3.0	Manufg.	Pens & mechanical pencils	5.2	Manufg.
Electric services (utilities)	2.8	Util.	Personal consumption expenditures	4.4	
Noncomparable imports	2.7	Foreign	Mattresses & bedsprings	2.2	Manufg.
Industrial gases	2.0	Manufg.	Gross private fixed investment	2.1	Cap Inv
Gas production & distribution (utilities)	1.7	Util.	Lead pencils & art goods	2.0	Manufg.
Textile machinery	1.5	Manufg.	Sporting & athletic goods, nec	2.0	Manufg.
Sanitary services, steam supply, irrigation	1.5	Util.	State & local electric utilities	2.0	Gov't
Soap & other detergents	1.4	Manufg.	Apparel made from purchased materials	1.9	Manufg.
Meat animals	1.3	Agric.	Housefurnishings, nec	1.9	Manufg.
Automotive repair shops & services	1.2	Services	Motors & generators	1.7	Manufg.
Water transportation	1.0	Util.	Pleating & stitching	1.7	Manufg.
Laundry, dry cleaning, shoe repair	1.0	Services	Boot & shoe cutstock & findings	1.4	Manufg.
Felt goods, nec	0.9	Manufg.	Luggage	1.3	Manufg.
Banking	0.9	Fin/R.E.	Engine electrical equipment	1.1	Manufg.
Automotive rental & leasing, without drivers	0.9	Services	Office buildings	0.7	Constr.
Detective & protective services	0.9	Services	Musical instruments	0.7	Manufg.
Imports	0.9	Foreign	Felt goods, nec	0.6	Manufg.
Communications, except radio & TV	0.7	Util.	Nonfarm residential structure maintenance	0.4	Constr.
Eating & drinking places	0.7	Trade	Construction of educational buildings	0.2	Constr.
Industrial inorganic chemicals, nec	0.6	Manufg.	Construction of hospitals	0.2	Constr.
Yarn mills & finishing of textiles, nec	0.6	Manufg.	Construction of stores & restaurants	0.2	Constr.
Lubricating oils & greases	0.5	Manufg.	Maintenance of nonfarm buildings nec	0.2	Constr.
Royalties	0.5	Fin/R.E.	Residential 1-unit structures, nonfarm	0.2	Constr.
Equipment rental & leasing services	0.5	Services	Residential garden apartments	0.2	Constr.
U.S. Postal Service	0.5	Gov't	Mobile homes	0.2	Manufg.
Maintenance of nonfarm buildings nec	0.4	Constr.	Motor homes (made on purchased chassis)	0.2	Manufg.
Miscellaneous plastics products	0.4	Manufg.	Retail trade, except eating & drinking	0.2	Trade
Paperboard containers & boxes	0.4	Manufg.	Wholesale trade	0.2	Trade
Organic fibers, noncellulosic	0.3	Manufg.	Local government passenger transit	0.2	Gov't
Railroads & related services	0.3	Util.	Amusement & recreation building construction	0.1	Constr.
Insurance carriers	0.3	Fin/R.E.	Construction of nonfarm buildings nec	0.1	Constr.
Real estate	0.3	Fin/R.E.	Prefabricated wood buildings	0.1	Manufg.
Scrap	0.3	Scrap	Travel trailers & campers	0.1	Manufg.
Machinery, except electrical, nec	0.2	Manufg.	Real estate	0.1	Fin/R.E.
Tires & inner tubes	0.2	Manufg.	Doctors & dentists	0.1	Services
Pipelines, except natural gas	0.2	Util.	Legal services	0.1	Services
Retail trade, except eating & drinking	0.2	Trade			
Accounting, auditing & bookkeeping	0.2	Services			
Computer & data processing services	0.2	Services			
Legal services	0.2	Services			
Management & consulting services & labs	0.2	Services			
Alkalies & chlorine	0.1	Manufg.			
Manifold business forms	0.1	Manufg.			
Motor vehicle parts & accessories	0.1	Manufg.			
Special dies & tools & machine tool accessories	0.1	Manufg.			
Air transportation	0.1	Util.			

Source: Benchmark Input-Output Accounts for the U.S. Economy, 1982, U.S. Department of Commerce, Washington, D.C., July 1991. Data, as reported in the source, are organized by the 1977 SIC structure in use in 1982 but have been matched, as closely as is possible, to the 1987 SIC structure used in this book.

OCCUPATIONS EMPLOYED BY SIC 235 - APPAREL

Occupation	% of Total 1994	Change to 2005	Occupation	% of Total 1994	Change to 2005
Sewing machine operators, garment	56.1	-33.1	Cutters & trimmers, hand	1.7	-24.8
Inspectors, testers, & graders, precision	3.5	-16.4	Patternmakers, layout workers, fabric & apparel	1.5	25.4
Blue collar worker supervisors	3.0	-24.0	General managers & top executives	1.4	-20.7
Assemblers, fabricators, & hand workers nec	2.5	-16.4	Sewing machine operators, non-garment	1.3	-37.3
Pressing machine operators, textiles	2.4	-45.7	Helpers, laborers, & material movers nec	1.1	-16.4
Hand packers & packagers	2.0	-21.2	Industrial machinery mechanics	1.1	0.3
Freight, stock, & material movers, hand	1.8	-33.1	Pressers, hand	1.1	-58.2
Traffic, shipping, & receiving clerks	1.8	-19.6	Sewers, hand	1.0	-10.7

Source: Industry-Occupation Matrix, Bureau of Labor Statistics. These data relate to one or more 3-digit SIC industry groups rather than to a single 4-digit SIC. The change reported for each occupation to the year 2005 is a percent of growth or decline as estimated by the Bureau of Labor Statistics. The abbreviation nec stands for 'not elsewhere classified'.

LOCATION BY STATE AND REGIONAL CONCENTRATION

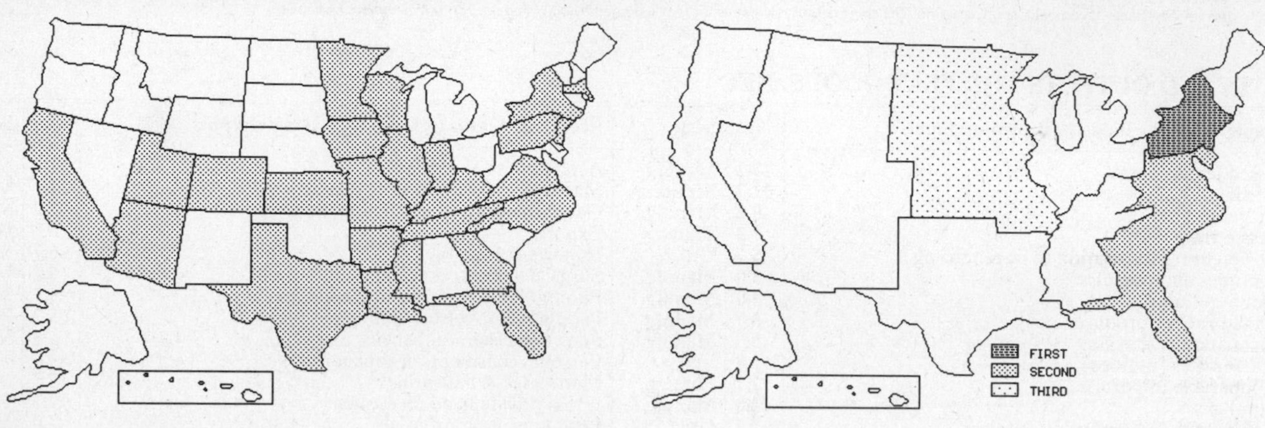

INDUSTRY DATA BY STATE

State	Establish-ments	Shipments: Total ($ mil)	Shipments: % of U.S.	Shipments: Per Establ.	Employment: Total Number	Employment: % of U.S.	Employment: Per Establ.	Employment: Wages ($/hour)	Cost as % of Shipments	Investment per Employee ($)
Missouri	36	178.0	18.2	4.9	3,400	18.1	94	5.88	33.1	912
New York	95	173.2	17.7	1.8	2,700	14.4	28	7.79	51.7	1,407
Pennsylvania	15	102.9	10.5	6.9	1,600	8.5	107	9.61	36.2	1,625
Texas	22	98.3	10.0	4.5	1,600	8.5	73	5.97	49.8	1,250
Virginia	10	59.8	6.1	6.0	900	4.8	90	7.19	69.9	-
California	36	39.9	4.1	1.1	1,100	5.9	31	6.07	42.4	-
Georgia	13	28.8	2.9	2.2	1,000	5.3	77	6.15	36.1	1,000
Colorado	12	24.1	2.5	2.0	600	3.2	50	7.00	24.5	-
Kentucky	7	24.0	2.5	3.4	500	2.7	71	7.25	57.1	1,600
Tennessee	10	15.0	1.5	1.5	400	2.1	40	8.00	41.3	1,500
North Carolina	7	12.1	1.2	1.7	300	1.6	43	5.33	35.5	667
Minnesota	4	11.5	1.2	2.9	200	1.1	50	7.00	40.0	-
Massachusetts	9	7.7	0.8	0.9	100	0.5	11	6.50	37.7	-
Florida	19	(D)	-	-	375 *	2.0	20	-	-	533
New Jersey	17	(D)	-	-	750 *	4.0	44	-	-	400
Illinois	6	(D)	-	-	175 *	0.9	29	-	-	571
Wisconsin	5	(D)	-	-	175 *	0.9	35	-	-	-
Arizona	4	(D)	-	-	175 *	0.9	44	-	-	-
Utah	4	(D)	-	-	175 *	0.9	44	-	-	-
Arkansas	2	(D)	-	-	175 *	0.9	88	-	-	-
Indiana	2	(D)	-	-	175 *	0.9	88	-	-	-
Kansas	2	(D)	-	-	175 *	0.9	88	-	-	-
Mississippi	2	(D)	-	-	175 *	0.9	88	-	-	-
Iowa	1	(D)	-	-	1,750 *	9.3	1,750	-	-	-
Louisiana	1	(D)	-	-	175 *	0.9	175	-	-	-

Source: 1992 *Economic Census*. The states are in descending order of shipments or establishments (if shipment data are missing for the majority). The symbol (D) appears when data are withheld to prevent disclosure of competitive information. States marked with (D) are sorted by number of establishments. A dash (-) indicates that the data element cannot be calculated; * indicates the midpoint of a range.

2361 - GIRLS' & CHILDREN'S DRESSES, BLOUSES

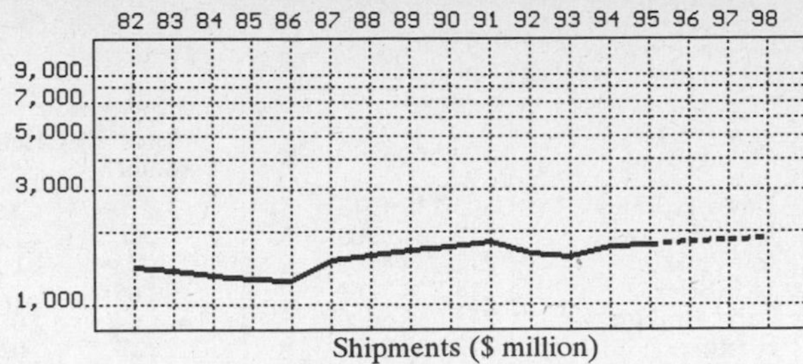

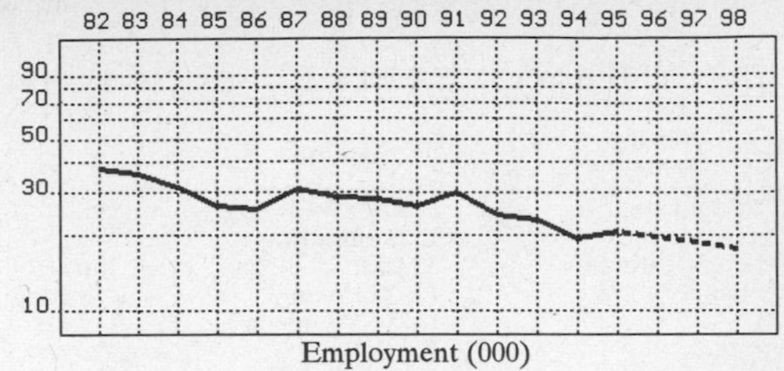

GENERAL STATISTICS

Year	Com-panies	Establishments: Total	Establishments: with 20 or more employees	Employment: Total (000)	Employment: Production Workers (000)	Employment: Production Hours (Mil)	Compensation: Payroll ($ mil)	Compensation: Wages ($/hr)	Production ($ million): Cost of Materials	Production ($ million): Value Added by Manufacture	Production ($ million): Value of Shipments	Capital Invest.
1982	490	556	391	37.7	32.4	57.5	357.3	4.52	667.6	745.9	1,417.7	11.6
1983		524	362	36.0	30.9	54.9	342.1	4.25	673.1	762.9	1,400.9	7.6
1984		492	333	31.4	26.4	45.5	327.4	5.07	655.8	682.7	1,332.0	11.3
1985		460	304	26.7	22.3	37.1	291.9	5.52	579.6	678.6	1,268.7	13.2
1986		442	298	25.6	21.3	37.4	287.2	5.41	564.1	685.2	1,247.3	6.8
1987	401	454	307	30.9	26.2	45.0	350.4	5.71	735.9	790.4	1,518.6	12.6
1988		413	287	28.9	23.7	43.2	360.0	5.70	778.5	831.1	1,603.6	
1989		378	266	28.2	25.6	45.1	372.7	5.64	809.9	866.6	1,670.6	9.8
1990		367	247	26.5	24.2	43.7	370.7	5.80	821.0	903.8	1,724.5	15.3
1991		373	240	30.2	25.6	46.4	394.6	5.94	851.6	943.4	1,799.8	20.9
1992	364	397	249	24.2	19.4	36.9	367.3	6.49	803.6	826.7	1,625.9	13.2
1993		419	245	23.1	18.6	35.8	344.4	6.24	810.3	710.0	1,566.5	11.4
1994		345P	211P	19.5	15.2	31.6	325.4	6.53	864.0	864.9	1,716.2	13.2
1995		330P	198P	21.0P	17.2P	33.7P	363.8P	6.74P	896.1P	897.0P	1,780.0P	
1996		315P	185P	19.9P	16.2P	32.3P	366.5P	6.91P	914.1P	915.0P	1,815.6P	
1997		301P	172P	18.8P	15.2P	31.0P	369.1P	7.07P	932.0P	933.0P	1,851.3P	
1998		286P	159P	17.8P	14.2P	29.6P	371.7P	7.23P	950.0P	951.0P	1,887.0P	

Sources: 1982, 1987, 1992 *Economic Census*; *Annual Survey of Manufactures*, 83-86, 88-91, 93-94. Establishment counts for non-Census years are from *County Business Patterns*; establishment values for 83-84 are extrapolations. 'P's show projections by the editors. Industries reclassified in 87 will not have data for prior years.

INDICES OF CHANGE

Year	Com-panies	Establishments: Total	Establishments: with 20 or more employees	Employment: Total (000)	Employment: Production Workers (000)	Employment: Production Hours (Mil)	Compensation: Payroll ($ mil)	Compensation: Wages ($/hr)	Production ($ million): Cost of Materials	Production ($ million): Value Added by Manufacture	Production ($ million): Value of Shipments	Capital Invest.
1982	135	140	157	156	167	156	97	70	83	90	87	88
1983		132	145	149	159	149	93	65	84	92	86	58
1984		124	134	130	136	123	89	78	82	83	82	86
1985		116	122	110	115	101	79	85	72	82	78	100
1986		111	120	106	110	101	78	83	70	83	77	52
1987	110	114	123	128	135	122	95	88	92	96	93	95
1988		104	115	119	122	117	98	88	97	101	99	
1989		95	107	117	132	122	101	87	101	105	103	74
1990		92	99	110	125	118	101	89	102	109	106	116
1991		94	96	125	132	126	107	92	106	114	111	158
1992	100	100	100	100	100	100	100	100	100	100	100	100
1993		106	98	95	96	97	94	96	101	86	96	86
1994		87P	85P	81	78	86	89	101	108	105	106	100
1995		83P	79P	87P	88P	91P	99P	104P	112P	109P	109P	
1996		79P	74P	82P	83P	88P	100P	106P	114P	111P	112P	
1997		76P	69P	78P	78P	84P	100P	109P	116P	113P	114P	
1998		72P	64P	73P	73P	80P	101P	111P	118P	115P	116P	

Sources: Same as General Statistics. Values reflect change from the base year, 1992. Values above 100 mean greater than 92, values below 100 mean less than 92, and a value of 100 in the 82-91 or 93-98 period means same as 92. 'P's mark projections by the editors.

SELECTED RATIOS

For 1994	Avg. of All Manufact.	Analyzed Industry	Index
Employees per Establishment	49	57	116
Payroll per Establishment	1,500,273	944,391	63
Payroll per Employee	30,620	16,687	54
Production Workers per Establishment	34	44	129
Wages per Establishment	853,319	598,873	70
Wages per Production Worker	24,861	13,576	55
Hours per Production Worker	2,056	2,079	101
Wages per Hour	12.09	6.53	54
Value Added per Establishment	4,602,255	2,510,153	55
Value Added per Employee	93,930	44,354	47

For 1994	Avg. of All Manufact.	Analyzed Industry	Index
Value Added per Production Worker	134,084	56,901	42
Cost per Establishment	5,045,178	2,507,541	50
Cost per Employee	102,970	44,308	43
Cost per Production Worker	146,988	56,842	39
Shipments per Establishment	9,576,895	4,980,836	52
Shipments per Employee	195,460	88,010	45
Shipments per Production Worker	279,017	112,908	40
Investment per Establishment	321,011	38,310	12
Investment per Employee	6,552	677	10
Investment per Production Worker	9,352	868	9

Sources: Same as General Statistics. The 'Average of All Manufacturing' column represents the average of all manufacturing industries reported for the most recent complete year available. The Index shows the relationship between the Average and the Analyzed Industry. For example, 100 means that they are equal; 500 that the Analyzed Industry is five times the average; 50 means that the Analyzed Industry is half the national average. The abbreviation 'na' is used to show that data are 'not available'.

LEADING COMPANIES

Number shown: **40** Total sales ($ mil): **885** Total employment (000): **12.5**

Company Name	Address				CEO Name	Phone	Co. Type	Sales ($ mil)	Empl. (000)
Gerber Childrenswear Inc	PO Box 3010	Greenville	SC	29602	David H Jones	803-235-1615	S	220	3.9
House of Ronnie Inc	1333 Broadway	New York	NY	10018	Irving Paparo	212-564-0900	R	90	1.6
Allison Manufacturing Co	350 5th Av	New York	NY	10118	Jeff Pinkow	212-239-4500	S	72•	1.2
Kleinert's Inc	120 Germant	Plym Meeting	PA	19462	Jack Brier	215-828-7261	P	69	1.0
Jalate Ltd	1675 S Alameda St	Los Angeles	CA	90021	Larry Brahim	213-765-5000	P	64	0.1
Baby Togs Inc	460 W 34 St	New York	NY	10001	E Sitt	212-868-2100	R	50	0.3
Dobie Industries Inc	1333 Broadway	New York	NY	10018	Howard Rosenfeld	212-239-8950	R	48•	0.8
Bryan Industries Inc	9120 Br Arrow	Tulsa	OK	74145	Stan Kinnamon	918-663-2230	R	34•	0.5
Gemini Shirtmakers Inc	1701 E 41st Pl	Los Angeles	CA	90058	Stuart North	213-235-2190	S	28	<0.1
Baylis Brothers Co	224 E 8th St	Cincinnati	OH	45202	Shirley Hoffman	513-721-7020	D	27	0.2
Star Childrens Dress Co	100 W 33rd St	New York	NY	10001	E Rosen	212-244-1390	R	25	0.5
United Brands International	498 7th Av	New York	NY	10018	Lance Walsky	212-594-4925	R	25	<0.1
Gerson and Gerson Inc	112 W 34ht St	New York	NY	10120	Matthew Gerson	212-279-1130	R	22	0.4
Carolina Industries Inc	PO Box 726	St George	SC	29477	J Capitano	803-563-3555	R	13	0.2
May Apparel Group Inc	PO Box 190	Mebane	NC	27302	Neal Anderson	919-563-5521	R	12	0.3
Isabella Inc	112 W 34th St	New York	NY	10120	Peter Kessner	212-564-8680	S	9	0.2
Mini World Inc	1460 N Riversidez	Provo	UT	84604		801-375-1700	R	9•	0.2
Camptown Togs Inc	PO Box 1950	Clanton	AL	35045	M C Rosenfield	205-755-0540	R	9	0.2
Sweet Potatoes Inc	1716 4th St	Berkeley	CA	94710	Anna Tokunaga	510-527-7633	R	8	<0.1
Florence Eiseman Inc	PO Box 0704	Milwaukee	WI	53201	Frank Botto	414-272-3222	R	6•	0.1
Patsy Aiken Designs Inc	PO Box 97457	Raleigh	NC	27624	Patsy Aiken	919-872-8789	R	6•	0.1
Simi Inc	10580 Newkirk St	Dallas	TX	75220	Frances A Johnston	214-401-2870	R	5	<0.1
Officially for Kids Inc	1701 N Miami Av	Miami	FL	33136	Ruben Moreno	305-577-0052	R	4	<0.1
Don's Manufacturing Company	PO Box 467	Rich Square	NC	27869	Sue Beal	919-539-2873	R	4•	<0.1
Quality Textiles Inc	PO Box 580	Bailey	NC	27807	Steve Johnson	919-235-3665	R	4	<0.1
Amelia Dress Company Inc	PO Box 385	Farmville	VA	23901	Robert G Stewart	804-352-7145	R	3	0.2
Cradle Togs Inc	77 S 1st St	Elizabeth	NJ	07206	Irving Maleh	908-351-4477	R	3•	<0.1
Trans World Textile Corp	313 5th Av	New York	NY	10016	Abe Kassin	212-889-7601	R	3•	<0.1
Frog Pond Kids Inc	747 Miami Cir	Atlanta	GA	30324	Joyce Prince	404-237-2263	R	3	<0.1
Nannette Manufacturing	3800 Frankford Av	Philadelphia	PA	19124	Jeremy Rosenau	215-289-1000	R	2•	<0.1
Dee's Manufacturing Co	PO Box 157	Tishomingo	OK	73460	Doug Blackwell	405-371-3319	R	2	<0.1
Little Miss Tennis TV Sports	PO Box 17442	Memphis	TN	38187	Marilyn Kosten	901-371-0291	R	2	<0.1
Baby Bag of Maine	PO Box 566	Cumberld Ctr	ME	04021	Elizabeth Andrews	207-829-5037	R	1	<0.1
Chicken Noodle Inc	605 Addison St	Berkeley	CA	94710	April Ward	510-848-8882	R	1•	<0.1
Hollywood Needlecraft Inc	3777 S Main St	Los Angeles	CA	90007	William C Roen	213-233-4105	R	1	<0.1
Mousefeathers Inc	1003 Camelia St	Berkeley	CA	94710	Stephanie Upham	510-526-4900	R	1	<0.1
Rococo	1003 Camelia St	Berkeley	CA	94710	Stephanie Upham	510-526-4900	D	1	<0.1
Bentex Kiddie Corp	100 W 33rd St	New York	NY	10001	Ronald Benun	212-594-4250	R	1	<0.1
New World Kids Co	4950 Keller Spgs Rd	Dallas	TX	75248	Emmanuel Charhon	214-661-2262	R	0•	<0.1
Chloe's Closet	2234 N Gower St	Hollywood	CA	90068	Judy Stimmel	213-463-4323	R	0•	<0.1

Source: *Ward's Business Directory of U.S. Private and Public Companies*, Volumes 1 and 2, 1996. The company type code used is as follows: P - Public, R - Private, S - Subsidiary, D - Division, J - Joint Venture, A - Affiliate, G - Group. Sales are in millions of dollars, employees are in thousands. An asterisk (•) indicates an estimated sales volume. The symbol < stands for 'less than'. Company names and addresses are truncated, in some cases, to fit into the available space.

MATERIALS CONSUMED

Material	Quantity	Delivered Cost ($ million)
Materials, ingredients, containers, and supplies	(X)	484.3
Broadwoven fabrics (piece goods)	(X)	196.2
Narrow fabrics (12 inches or less in width)	(X)	(D)
Knit fabrics	(X)	138.4
Yarn, all fibers	(X)	(D)
Buttons, zippers, and slide fasteners	(X)	30.2
All other materials and components, parts, containers, and supplies	(X)	31.4
Materials, ingredients, containers, and supplies, nsk	(X)	68.9

Source: 1992 *Economic Census*. Explanation of symbols used: (D): Withheld to avoid disclosure of competitive data; na: Not available; (S): Withheld because statistical norms were not met; (X): Not applicable; (Z): Less than half the unit shown; nec: Not elsewhere classified; nsk: Not specified by kind; - : zero; * : 10-19 percent estimated; ** : 20-29 percent estimated.

PRODUCT SHARE DETAILS

Product or Product Class	% Share	Product or Product Class	% Share
Girls', children's, and infants' dresses, blouses, and shirts	100.00	Receipts for contract and commission work on girls', children's, and infants' dresses, blouses, and shirts	99.65
Girls', children's, and infants' knit blouses and shirts (polo, tennis, tank, sweat, T-shirts for outerwear, etc.), made from purchased fabrics	36.79	Receipts for contract and commission work on girls', children's, and infants' dresses, blouses, and shirts, nsk.	0.35
Girls', children's, and infants' woven blouses and shirts	12.66	Girls', children's, and infants' dresses, blouses, and shirts, nsk	1.64
Girls', children's, and infants' dresses	35.63		
Receipts for contract and commission work on girls', children's, and infants' dresses, blouses, and shirts	13.29		

Source: 1992 *Economic Census*. The values shown are percent of total shipments in an industry. Values of indented subcategories are summed in the main heading. The symbol (D) appears when data are withheld to prevent disclosure of competitive information. The abbreviation nsk stands for 'not specified by kind' and nec for 'not elsewhere classified'.

INPUTS AND OUTPUTS FOR APPAREL MADE FROM PURCHASED MATERIALS

Economic Sector or Industry Providing Inputs	%	Sector	Economic Sector or Industry Buying Outputs	%	Sector
Imports	29.1	Foreign	Personal consumption expenditures	82.7	
Broadwoven fabric mills	20.2	Manufg.	Apparel made from purchased materials	12.0	Manufg.
Apparel made from purchased materials	18.3	Manufg.	Exports	1.5	Foreign
Knit fabric mills	8.6	Manufg.	Federal Government purchases, national defense	0.9	Fed Govt
Wholesale trade	3.8	Trade	S/L Govt. purch., correction	0.5	S/L Govt
Advertising	2.4	Services	Pleating & stitching	0.3	Manufg.
Yarn mills & finishing of textiles, nec	1.4	Manufg.	Knit outerwear mills	0.2	Manufg.
Pleating & stitching	1.1	Manufg.	Hospitals	0.2	Services
Banking	1.1	Fin/R.E.	Laundry, dry cleaning, shoe repair	0.2	Services
Petroleum refining	1.0	Manufg.	S/L Govt. purch., health & hospitals	0.2	S/L Govt
Electric services (utilities)	1.0	Util.	Portrait, photographic studios	0.1	Services
Automotive & apparel trimmings	0.9	Manufg.	S/L Govt. purch., public assistance & relief	0.1	S/L Govt
Needles, pins, & fasteners	0.8	Manufg.			
Thread mills	0.7	Manufg.			
Communications, except radio & TV	0.7	Util.			
Eating & drinking places	0.7	Trade			
U.S. Postal Service	0.7	Gov't			
Leather tanning & finishing	0.5	Manufg.			
Narrow fabric mills	0.5	Manufg.			
Schiffli machine embroideries	0.4	Manufg.			
Motor freight transportation & warehousing	0.4	Util.			
Real estate	0.4	Fin/R.E.			
Royalties	0.4	Fin/R.E.			
Forestry products	0.3	Agric.			
Buttons	0.3	Manufg.			
Paperboard containers & boxes	0.3	Manufg.			
Air transportation	0.3	Util.			
Maintenance of nonfarm buildings nec	0.2	Constr.			
Lace goods	0.2	Manufg.			
Gas production & distribution (utilities)	0.2	Util.			
Automotive rental & leasing, without drivers	0.2	Services			
Electrical repair shops	0.2	Services			
Equipment rental & leasing services	0.2	Services			
Legal services	0.2	Services			
Management & consulting services & labs	0.2	Services			
Artificial trees & flowers	0.1	Manufg.			
Insurance carriers	0.1	Fin/R.E.			
Accounting, auditing & bookkeeping	0.1	Services			
Automotive repair shops & services	0.1	Services			

Source: Benchmark Input-Output Accounts for the U.S. Economy, 1982, U.S. Department of Commerce, Washington, D.C., July 1991. Data, as reported in the source, are organized by the 1977 SIC structure in use in 1982 but have been matched, as closely as is possible, to the 1987 SIC structure used in this book.

OCCUPATIONS EMPLOYED BY SIC 236 - APPAREL

Occupation	% of Total 1994	Change to 2005	Occupation	% of Total 1994	Change to 2005
Sewing machine operators, garment	56.1	-33.1	Cutters & trimmers, hand	1.7	-24.8
Inspectors, testers, & graders, precision	3.5	-16.4	Patternmakers, layout workers, fabric & apparel	1.5	25.4
Blue collar worker supervisors	3.0	-24.0	General managers & top executives	1.4	-20.7
Assemblers, fabricators, & hand workers nec	2.5	-16.4	Sewing machine operators, non-garment	1.3	-37.3
Pressing machine operators, textiles	2.4	-45.7	Helpers, laborers, & material movers nec	1.1	-16.4
Hand packers & packagers	2.0	-21.2	Industrial machinery mechanics	1.1	0.3
Freight, stock, & material movers, hand	1.8	-33.1	Pressers, hand	1.1	-58.2
Traffic, shipping, & receiving clerks	1.8	-19.6	Sewers, hand	1.0	-10.7

Source: Industry-Occupation Matrix, Bureau of Labor Statistics. These data relate to one or more 3-digit SIC industry groups rather than to a single 4-digit SIC. The change reported for each occupation to the year 2005 is a percent of growth or decline as estimated by the Bureau of Labor Statistics. The abbreviation nec stands for 'not elsewhere classified'.

LOCATION BY STATE AND REGIONAL CONCENTRATION

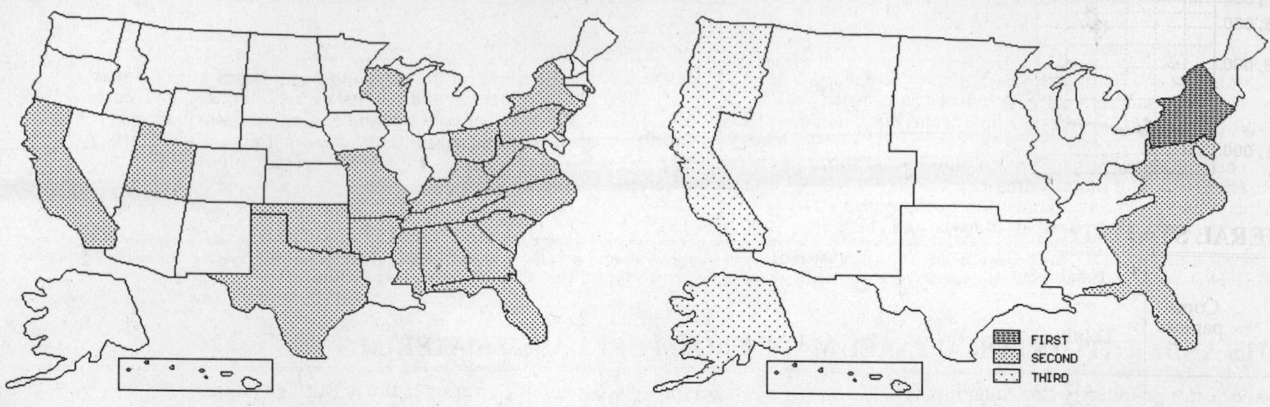

INDUSTRY DATA BY STATE

State	Establish-ments	Shipments			Employment				Cost as % of Shipments	Investment per Employee ($)
		Total ($ mil)	% of U.S.	Per Establ.	Total Number	% of U.S.	Per Establ.	Wages ($/hour)		
New York	78	428.9	26.4	5.5	2,700	11.2	35	7.91	60.8	704
California	77	321.8	19.8	4.2	3,500	14.5	45	7.81	60.9	514
North Carolina	27	143.0	8.8	5.3	2,900	12.0	107	6.02	35.2	
Pennsylvania	47	124.4	7.7	2.6	2,900	12.0	62	6.50	44.3	586
New Jersey	18	106.9	6.6	5.9	500	2.1	28	6.83	66.0	1,600
Florida	19	50.9	3.1	2.7	1,000	4.1	53	5.81	54.8	200
South Carolina	9	43.8	2.7	4.9	1,200	5.0	133	5.59	45.7	250
Virginia	24	40.4	2.5	1.7	2,200	9.1	92	5.68	13.1	182
Utah	8	32.8	2.0	4.1	800	3.3	100	5.90	48.5	-
Texas	9	29.0	1.8	3.2	700	2.9	78	5.50	43.8	-
Arkansas	3	14.1	0.9	4.7	300	1.2	100	5.50	41.1	-
Oklahoma	9	10.8	0.7	1.2	600	2.5	67	5.18	15.7	-
Tennessee	9	(D)	-	-	1,750 *	7.2	194	-	-	-
Georgia	8	(D)	-	-	750 *	3.1	94	-	-	-
Ohio	7	(D)	-	-	750 *	3.1	107	-	-	-
Wisconsin	5	(D)	-	-	750 *	3.1	150	-	-	-
Alabama	4	(D)	-	-	375 *	1.5	94	-	-	-
Mississippi	4	(D)	-	-	375 *	1.5	94	-	-	-
Missouri	2	(D)	-	-	175 *	0.7	88	-	-	-
Rhode Island	2	(D)	-	-	175 *	0.7	88	-	-	-
West Virginia	2	(D)	-	-	175 *	0.7	88	-	-	-
Kentucky	1	(D)	-	-	175 *	0.7	175	-	-	-

Source: 1992 *Economic Census*. The states are in descending order of shipments or establishments (if shipment data are missing for the majority). The symbol (D) appears when data are withheld to prevent disclosure of competitive information. States marked with (D) are sorted by number of establishments. A dash (-) indicates that the data element cannot be calculated; * indicates the midpoint of a range.

2369 - GIRLS' AND CHILDREN'S OUTERWEAR, NEC

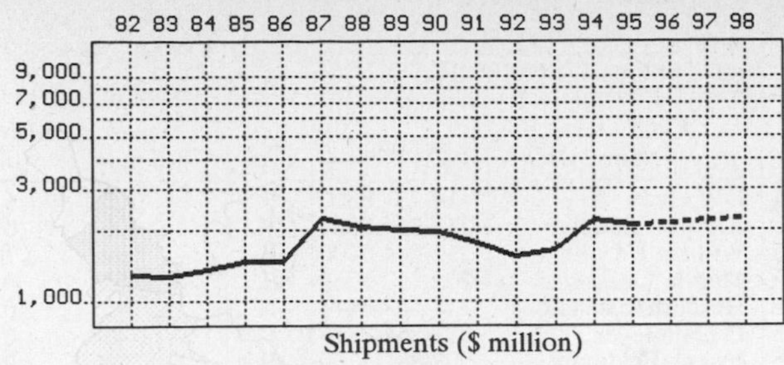

Shipments ($ million)

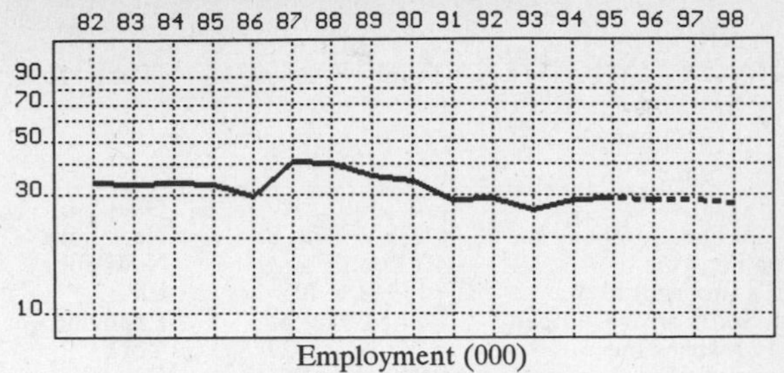

Employment (000)

GENERAL STATISTICS

Year	Com-panies	Establishments		Employment			Compensation		Production ($ million)			
		Total	with 20 or more employees	Total (000)	Production Workers (000)	Production Hours (Mil)	Payroll ($ mil)	Wages ($/hr)	Cost of Materials	Value Added by Manufacture	Value of Shipments	Capital Invest.
1982		412	266	33.7	28.6	51.5	313.9	4.52	589.8	699.9	1,293.7	18.5
1983		380	248	33.2	27.3	49.3	313.6	4.53	563.5	706.9	1,279.4	14.6
1984		348	230	33.5	29.0	51.7	340.6	4.86	601.4	771.5	1,362.7	10.8
1985		316	213	33.2	28.5	50.5	356.3	5.13	659.0	791.7	1,472.2	13.4
1986		321	212	29.7	25.1	44.2	327.6	5.27	686.4	805.3	1,477.1	11.9
1987	311	381	265	40.8	34.7	62.0	475.4	5.69	1,052.6	1,193.3	2,234.5	22.1
1988		357	236	40.0	33.9	62.5	467.2	5.44	972.1	1,070.5	2,069.8	
1989		319	231	36.2	30.9	59.1	455.6	5.65	878.2	1,181.6	2,020.2	22.9
1990		305	222	34.6	26.5	56.6	440.8	5.31	835.8	1,141.9	1,973.2	24.6
1991		309	211	28.6	24.1	48.5	396.5	5.51	792.9	963.7	1,779.3	15.2
1992	323	362	230	29.5	24.6	45.2	413.4	6.26	678.9	849.9	1,533.5	10.7
1993		360	220	26.1	21.2	41.9	430.4	6.97	681.9	974.5	1,654.7	14.0
1994		323P	215P	28.5	23.2	45.1	465.1	6.96	915.9	1,325.3	2,210.1	15.5
1995		319P	213P	29.4P	23.9P	48.1P	480.9P	6.84P	868.3P	1,256.5P	2,095.3P	
1996		315P	210P	28.9P	23.3P	47.6P	492.5P	7.02P	890.5P	1,288.6P	2,148.9P	
1997		311P	208P	28.4P	22.8P	47.2P	504.0P	7.21P	912.8P	1,320.8P	2,202.5P	
1998		307P	205P	27.9P	22.3P	46.7P	515.6P	7.39P	935.0P	1,352.9P	2,256.1P	

Sources: 1982, 1987, 1992 *Economic Census*; *Annual Survey of Manufactures*, 83-86, 88-91, 93-94. Establishment counts for non-Census years are from *County Business Patterns*; establishment values for 83-84 are extrapolations. 'P's show projections by the editors. Industries reclassified in 87 will not have data for prior years.

INDICES OF CHANGE

Year	Com-panies	Establishments		Employment			Compensation		Production ($ million)			
		Total	with 20 or more employees	Total (000)	Production Workers (000)	Production Hours (Mil)	Payroll ($ mil)	Wages ($/hr)	Cost of Materials	Value Added by Manufacture	Value of Shipments	Capital Invest.
1982		114	116	114	116	114	76	72	87	82	84	173
1983		105	108	113	111	109	76	72	83	83	83	136
1984		96	100	114	118	114	82	78	89	91	89	101
1985		87	93	113	116	112	86	82	97	93	96	125
1986		89	92	101	102	98	79	84	101	95	96	111
1987	96	105	115	138	141	137	115	91	155	140	146	207
1988		99	103	136	138	138	113	87	143	126	135	
1989		88	100	123	126	131	110	90	129	139	132	214
1990		84	97	117	108	125	107	85	123	134	129	230
1991		85	92	97	98	107	96	88	117	113	116	142
1992	100	100	100	100	100	100	100	100	100	100	100	100
1993		99	96	88	86	93	104	111	100	115	108	131
1994		89P	94P	97	94	100	113	111	135	156	144	145
1995		88P	93P	100P	97P	106P	116P	109P	128P	148P	137P	
1996		87P	91P	98P	95P	105P	119P	112P	131P	152P	140P	
1997		86P	90P	96P	93P	104P	122P	115P	134P	155P	144P	
1998		85P	89P	94P	91P	103P	125P	118P	138P	159P	147P	

Sources: Same as General Statistics. Values reflect change from the base year, 1992. Values above 100 mean greater than 92, values below 100 mean less than 92, and a value of 100 in the 82-91 or 93-98 period means same as 92. 'P's mark projections by the editors.

SELECTED RATIOS

For 1994	Avg. of All Manufact.	Analyzed Industry	Index	For 1994	Avg. of All Manufact.	Analyzed Industry	Index
Employees per Establishment	49	88	180	Value Added per Production Worker	134,084	57,125	43
Payroll per Establishment	1,500,273	1,441,358	96	Cost per Establishment	5,045,178	2,838,400	56
Payroll per Employee	30,620	16,319	53	Cost per Employee	102,970	32,137	31
Production Workers per Establishment	34	72	209	Cost per Production Worker	146,988	39,478	27
Wages per Establishment	853,319	972,773	114	Shipments per Establishment	9,576,895	6,849,162	72
Wages per Production Worker	24,861	13,530	54	Shipments per Employee	195,460	77,547	40
Hours per Production Worker	2,056	1,944	95	Shipments per Production Worker	279,017	95,263	34
Wages per Hour	12.09	6.96	58	Investment per Establishment	321,011	48,035	15
Value Added per Establishment	4,602,255	4,107,142	89	Investment per Employee	6,552	544	8
Value Added per Employee	93,930	46,502	50	Investment per Production Worker	9,352	668	7

Sources: Same as General Statistics. The 'Average of All Manufacturing' column represents the average of all manufacturing industries reported for the most recent complete year available. The Index shows the relationship between the Average and the Analyzed Industry. For example, 100 means that they are equal; 500 that the Analyzed Industry is five times the average; 50 means that the Analyzed Industry is half the national average. The abbreviation 'na' is used to show that data are 'not available'.

LEADING COMPANIES

Number shown: **31** Total sales ($ mil): **968** Total employment (000): **14.4**

Company Name	Address				CEO Name	Phone	Co. Type	Sales ($ mil)	Empl. (000)
Oshkosh B'Gosh Inc	112 Otter Av	Oshkosh	WI	54901	DW Hyde	414-231-8800	P	363	6.6
Rothschild and Company Inc	225 W 37th St	New York	NY	10018	Isidore Friedman	212-354-8550	R	100	0.4
Andover Togs Inc	1 Penn Plz	New York	NY	10119	William L Cohen	212-244-0700	P	89	1.3
Kleinert's Incorporated	PO Box 705	Elba	AL	36323	Marvin Grossman	205-897-5764	S	55*	0.8
General Sportswear Company	23 Market St	Ellenville	NY	12428	Herbert Rosenstock	914-647-4411	R	45	0.8
Dallco Industries Inc	PO Box 2727	York	PA	17405	D Dallmeyer	717-854-7875	R	43*	0.8
Isfel Company Inc	900 Hart St	Rahway	NJ	07065	Joseph Feldman	908-382-3100	R	30	<0.1
Maurice Silvera Inc	131 W 33rd St	New York	NY	10001	Ralph Silvera	212-594-6620	R	27*	0.5
Hilb and Company Inc	4600 E 48th Av	Denver	CO	80216	Tom Hilb	303-399-2100	R	25	<0.1
Good Lad Co	431 E Tioga St	Philadelphia	PA	19134	P Scheintoch	215-739-0200	R	25*	0.5
Robin International	100 W 33rd St	New York	NY	10001	Howard Davidson	212-967-6800	S	25	0.1
Kessner and Rabinowitz Inc	350 5th Av	New York	NY	10118	Peter Kessner	212-564-7030	R	21*	0.4
Collection Bebe	PO Box 383	Gainesville	GA	30503	Gus Whalen	404-535-3000	D	20*	0.5
Devil Dog Manufacturing	PO Box 69	Zebulon	NC	27597	Macky Howard	919-269-7485	D	16*	0.3
D Glasgow and Sons Inc	382 Fayette Dr	Perth Amboy	NJ	08861	Andrew Glasgow	908-826-3900	R	16*	0.3
California Infanteen Togs	2345 E 37th St	Vernon	CA	90058	S Fell	213-747-6178	R	12	0.2
Wellmade Industries Inc	131 W 33rd St	New York	NY	10001	Dennis Spitalnick	212-564-3526	R	11	<0.1
Rosbro Sportswear Company Inc	55 Washington St	Brooklyn	NY	11201	D Rosenberg	718-875-6329	R	9	0.1
Marksville Industries Inc	PO Box 312	Marksville	LA	71351	Maureen Benson	318-253-6523	S	7	0.2
Pikeville Manufacturing Co	Rte 1	Pikeville	NC	27863	Robert Gamballa	919-736-0945	R	7*	0.1
Wayne Manufacturing Company	200 N 117 By-Pass	Goldsboro	NC	27530	Nicolas Gambella	919-736-7724	R	6	0.2
Franklin Apparel Inc	PO Box 306	Louisburg	NC	27549	Reece Duncan	919-496-2954	R	5	<0.1
Streat Garment Co	PO Box 245	Nicholls	GA	31554	Wilbur Streat	912-345-2965	R	5	<0.1
Baby Rooth Inc	16 Bassett St	Providence	RI	02903	Melissa Oman	401-831-3080	R	1	<0.1
Millicents of San Francisco Inc	275 9th St	San Francisco	CA	94103	David Kulka	415-863-2232	R	1	<0.1
Biscotti Inc	144 Linden St	Oakland	CA	94607	Bernadette Reiss	510-272-9122	R	1*	<0.1
Genuine Kids	350 5th Av	New York	NY	10118	BR Widder-Lowry	212-244-3550	S	1*	<0.1
Malley and Co	2805 National Dr	Garland	TX	75041	Malley Gaulding	214-840-6433	R	1*	<0.1
Boo-Boo-Baby Inc	450 7th Av	New York	NY	10023	Belinda Hughes	212-465-8407	R	0	<0.1
Malina Inc	3314 W Pico Blv	Santa Monica	CA	90405	Malina Gerber	310-395-5965	R	0*	<0.1
Software by Malina	3314 W Pico Blv	Santa Monica	CA	90405	Malina Gerber	310-395-5965	D	0*	<0.1

Source: *Ward's Business Directory of U.S. Private and Public Companies*, Volumes 1 and 2, 1996. The company type code used is as follows: P - Public, R - Private, S - Subsidiary, D - Division, J - Joint Venture, A - Affiliate, G - Group. Sales are in millions of dollars, employees are in thousands. An asterisk (*) indicates an estimated sales volume. The symbol < stands for 'less than'. Company names and addresses are truncated, in some cases, to fit into the available space.

MATERIALS CONSUMED

Material	Quantity	Delivered Cost ($ million)
Materials, ingredients, containers, and supplies	(X)	511.8
Broadwoven fabrics (piece goods)	(X)	151.3
Narrow fabrics (12 inches or less in width)	(X)	37.0
Knit fabrics	(X)	191.8
Yarn, all fibers	(X)	6.1
Buttons, zippers, and slide fasteners	(X)	22.6
All other materials and components, parts, containers, and supplies	(X)	39.8
Materials, ingredients, containers, and supplies, nsk	(X)	63.3

Source: 1992 *Economic Census*. Explanation of symbols used: (D): Withheld to avoid disclosure of competitive data; na: Not available; (S): Withheld because statistical norms were not met; (X): Not applicable; (Z): Less than half the unit shown; nec: Not elsewhere classified; nsk: Not specified by kind; - : zero; * : 10-19 percent estimated; ** : 20-29 percent estimated.

PRODUCT SHARE DETAILS

Product or Product Class	% Share
Girls', children's, and infants' other outerwear, nec	100.00
Girls', children's, and infants' coats, jackets, suits, snowsuits, and coat-and-legging sets, excluding raincoats and wash suits	5.87
Girls', children's, and infants' play garments and sweaters	81.59
Play garments (including playsuits, playshorts, dungarees, jeans, slacks, halter tops, creepers, rompers and overalls)	81.50
Sweaters (including sweater vests), made from purchased fabrics	2.04
Robes and dressing gowns	0.62
Other outerwear (neckwear, headwear, swimwear, skirts, leotards, sweatpants, etc.)	14.38
Play garments and sweaters, nsk	1.46
Receipts for contract and commission work on girls', children's, and infants' outerwear, nec	10.57
Receipts for contract and commission work on girls', children's, and infants' outerwear, nec	98.89
Receipts for contract and commission work on girls', children's, and infants' outerwear, nec, nsk	1.11
Girls', children's, and infants' other outerwear, nec, nsk	1.97

Source: 1992 *Economic Census*. The values shown are percent of total shipments in an industry. Values of indented subcategories are summed in the main heading. The symbol (D) appears when data are withheld to prevent disclosure of competitive information. The abbreviation nsk stands for 'not specified by kind' and nec for 'not elsewhere classified'.

INPUTS AND OUTPUTS FOR APPAREL MADE FROM PURCHASED MATERIALS

Economic Sector or Industry Providing Inputs	%	Sector	Economic Sector or Industry Buying Outputs	%	Sector
Imports	29.1	Foreign	Personal consumption expenditures	82.7	
Broadwoven fabric mills	20.2	Manufg.	Apparel made from purchased materials	12.0	Manufg.
Apparel made from purchased materials	18.3	Manufg.	Exports	1.5	Foreign
Knit fabric mills	8.6	Manufg.	Federal Government purchases, national defense	0.9	Fed Govt
Wholesale trade	3.8	Trade	S/L Govt. purch., correction	0.5	S/L Govt
Advertising	2.4	Services	Pleating & stitching	0.3	Manufg.
Yarn mills & finishing of textiles, nec	1.4	Manufg.	Knit outerwear mills	0.2	Manufg.
Pleating & stitching	1.1	Manufg.	Hospitals	0.2	Services
Banking	1.1	Fin/R.E.	Laundry, dry cleaning, shoe repair	0.2	Services
Petroleum refining	1.0	Manufg.	S/L Govt. purch., health & hospitals	0.2	S/L Govt
Electric services (utilities)	1.0	Util.	Portrait, photographic studios	0.1	Services
Automotive & apparel trimmings	0.9	Manufg.	S/L Govt. purch., public assistance & relief	0.1	S/L Govt
Needles, pins, & fasteners	0.8	Manufg.			
Thread mills	0.7	Manufg.			
Communications, except radio & TV	0.7	Util.			
Eating & drinking places	0.7	Trade			
U.S. Postal Service	0.7	Gov't			
Leather tanning & finishing	0.5	Manufg.			
Narrow fabric mills	0.5	Manufg.			
Schiffli machine embroideries	0.4	Manufg.			
Motor freight transportation & warehousing	0.4	Util.			
Real estate	0.4	Fin/R.E.			
Royalties	0.4	Fin/R.E.			
Forestry products	0.3	Agric.			
Buttons	0.3	Manufg.			
Paperboard containers & boxes	0.3	Manufg.			
Air transportation	0.3	Util.			
Maintenance of nonfarm buildings nec	0.2	Constr.			
Lace goods	0.2	Manufg.			
Gas production & distribution (utilities)	0.2	Util.			
Automotive rental & leasing, without drivers	0.2	Services			
Electrical repair shops	0.2	Services			
Equipment rental & leasing services	0.2	Services			
Legal services	0.2	Services			
Management & consulting services & labs	0.2	Services			
Artificial trees & flowers	0.1	Manufg.			
Insurance carriers	0.1	Fin/R.E.			
Accounting, auditing & bookkeeping	0.1	Services			
Automotive repair shops & services	0.1	Services			

Source: Benchmark Input-Output Accounts for the U.S. Economy, 1982, U.S. Department of Commerce, Washington, D.C., July 1991. Data, as reported in the source, are organized by the 1977 SIC structure in use in 1982 but have been matched, as closely as is possible, to the 1987 SIC structure used in this book.

OCCUPATIONS EMPLOYED BY SIC 236 - APPAREL

Occupation	% of Total 1994	Change to 2005	Occupation	% of Total 1994	Change to 2005
Sewing machine operators, garment	56.1	-33.1	Cutters & trimmers, hand	1.7	-24.8
Inspectors, testers, & graders, precision	3.5	-16.4	Patternmakers, layout workers, fabric & apparel	1.5	25.4
Blue collar worker supervisors	3.0	-24.0	General managers & top executives	1.4	-20.7
Assemblers, fabricators, & hand workers nec	2.5	-16.4	Sewing machine operators, non-garment	1.3	-37.3
Pressing machine operators, textiles	2.4	-45.7	Helpers, laborers, & material movers nec	1.1	-16.4
Hand packers & packagers	2.0	-21.2	Industrial machinery mechanics	1.1	0.3
Freight, stock, & material movers, hand	1.8	-33.1	Pressers, hand	1.1	-58.2
Traffic, shipping, & receiving clerks	1.8	-19.6	Sewers, hand	1.0	-10.7

Source: Industry-Occupation Matrix, Bureau of Labor Statistics. These data relate to one or more 3-digit SIC industry groups rather than to a single 4-digit SIC. The change reported for each occupation to the year 2005 is a percent of growth or decline as estimated by the Bureau of Labor Statistics. The abbreviation nec stands for 'not elsewhere classified'.

LOCATION BY STATE AND REGIONAL CONCENTRATION

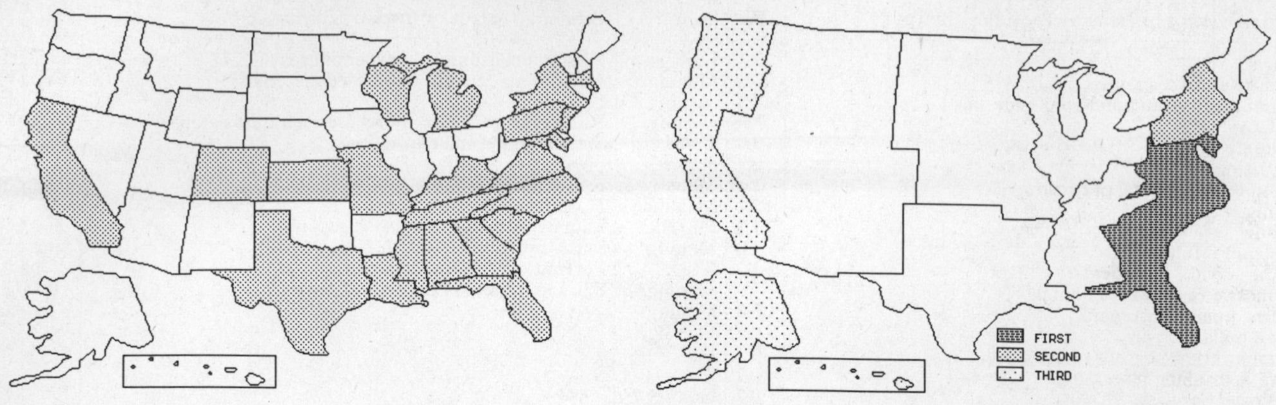

INDUSTRY DATA BY STATE

State	Establish-ments	Shipments			Employment				Cost as % of Shipments	Investment per Employee ($)
		Total ($ mil)	% of U.S.	Per Establ.	Total Number	% of U.S.	Per Establ.	Wages ($/hour)		
New York	50	159.6	10.4	3.2	1,500	5.1	30	8.76	59.0	600
Virginia	16	144.0	9.4	9.0	2,900	9.8	181	6.40	66.1	276
California	57	130.7	8.5	2.3	2,500	8.5	44	4.43	50.3	280
New Jersey	17	108.7	7.1	6.4	700	2.4	41	11.22	61.5	571
North Carolina	38	102.9	6.7	2.7	3,600	12.2	95	5.63	37.8	-
Pennsylvania	32	92.5	6.0	2.9	1,900	6.4	59	6.57	36.3	53
Florida	26	57.4	3.7	2.2	1,100	3.7	42	6.20	44.1	455
South Carolina	9	26.8	1.7	3.0	700	2.4	78	5.17	36.6	-
Massachusetts	6	22.7	1.5	3.8	400	1.4	67	8.71	38.8	-
Texas	13	6.3	0.4	0.5	300	1.0	23	5.50	34.9	-
Georgia	16	(D)	-	-	1,750 *	5.9	109	-	-	-
Alabama	14	(D)	-	-	3,750 *	12.7	268	-	-	-
Tennessee	9	(D)	-	-	1,750 *	5.9	194	-	-	-
Missouri	7	(D)	-	-	750 *	2.5	107	-	-	-
Louisiana	6	(D)	-	-	1,750 *	5.9	292	-	-	-
Mississippi	5	(D)	-	-	1,750 *	5.9	350	-	-	-
Colorado	4	(D)	-	-	375 *	1.3	94	-	-	-
Kentucky	3	(D)	-	-	375 *	1.3	125	-	-	-
Maryland	3	(D)	-	-	750 *	2.5	250	-	-	-
Kansas	2	(D)	-	-	375 *	1.3	188	-	-	-
Michigan	2	(D)	-	-	750 *	2.5	375	-	-	-
Wisconsin	1	(D)	-	-	375 *	1.3	375	-	-	-

Source: 1992 *Economic Census*. The states are in descending order of shipments or establishments (if shipment data are missing for the majority). The symbol (D) appears when data are withheld to prevent disclosure of competitive information. States marked with (D) are sorted by number of establishments. A dash (-) indicates that the data element cannot be calculated; * indicates the midpoint of a range.

2371 - FUR GOODS

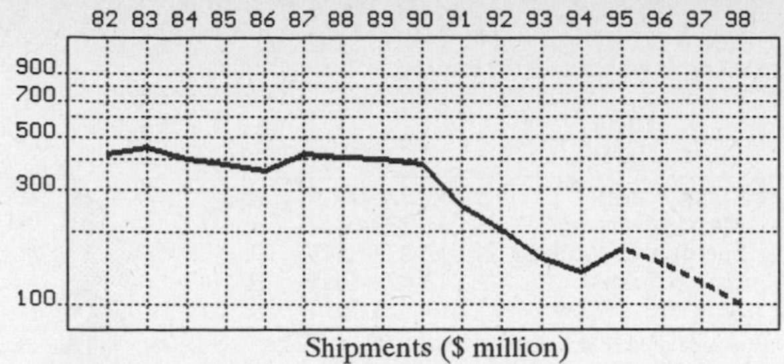

Shipments ($ million)

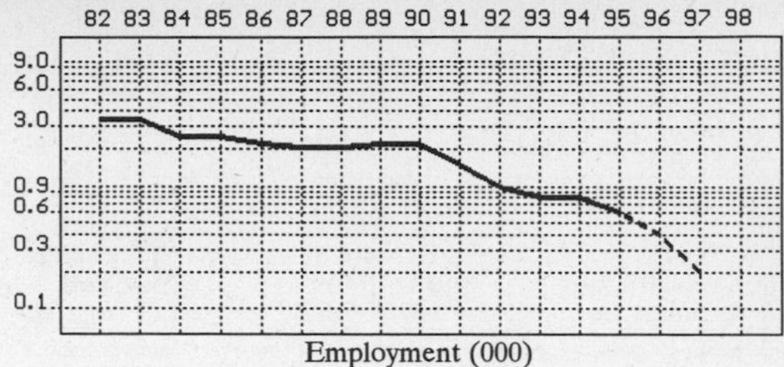

Employment (000)

GENERAL STATISTICS

Year	Com-panies	Establishments		Employment			Compensation		Production ($ million)			
		Total	with 20 or more employees	Total (000)	Production Workers (000)	Production Hours (Mil)	Payroll ($ mil)	Wages ($/hr)	Cost of Materials	Value Added by Manufacture	Value of Shipments	Capital Invest.
1982	503	504	43	3.4	2.5	4.5	59.6	9.16	287.2	131.6	419.3	0.3
1983				3.4	2.6	5.7	63.5	7.42	283.4	156.4	444.5	1.1
1984				2.5	1.7	3.6	50.5	8.83	274.5	124.6	398.1	1.0
1985				2.5	1.7	3.4	46.4	9.03	273.9	108.0	383.7	0.5
1986				2.2	1.6	3.2	44.4	9.31	251.2	104.7	360.4	0.5
1987	380	380	17	2.1	1.5	2.7	48.2	10.41	292.6	131.2	422.6	1.2
1988				2.1	1.4	2.6	44.1	10.12	277.4	129.4	407.2	0.2
1989		324	14	2.2	1.5	2.6	47.7	10.73	277.8	127.7	402.4	0.6
1990				2.2	1.5	2.5	46.2	10.64	263.3	103.6	378.7	1.9
1991				1.5	1.0	1.6	29.2	9.25	189.5	69.9	257.4	
1992	211	211	9	1.0	0.7	1.3	23.5	11.46	123.7	81.4	205.4	1.9
1993				0.8	0.6	1.1	17.1	11.55	94.1	58.9	153.8	1.0
1994				0.8	0.5	0.9	16.0	10.44	85.6	54.9	136.7	1.2
1995				0.6P	0.4P	0.4P	16.3P	11.51P	107.4P	68.9P	171.5P	
1996				0.4P	0.2P	0.1P	12.7P	11.74P	92.6P	59.4P	147.9P	
1997				0.2P	0.0P		9.1P	11.97P	77.9P	50.0P	124.4P	
1998							5.5P	12.21P	63.2P	40.5P	100.9P	

Sources: 1982, 1987, 1992 *Economic Census; Annual Survey of Manufactures*, 83-86, 88-91, 93-94. Establishment counts for non-Census years are from *County Business Patterns*; establishment values for 83-84 are extrapolations. 'P's show projections by the editors. Industries reclassified in 87 will not have data for prior years.

INDICES OF CHANGE

Year	Com-panies	Establishments		Employment			Compensation		Production ($ million)			
		Total	with 20 or more employees	Total (000)	Production Workers (000)	Production Hours (Mil)	Payroll ($ mil)	Wages ($/hr)	Cost of Materials	Value Added by Manufacture	Value of Shipments	Capital Invest.
1982	238	239	478	340	357	346	254	80	232	162	204	16
1983				340	371	438	270	65	229	192	216	58
1984				250	243	277	215	77	222	153	194	53
1985				250	243	262	197	79	221	133	187	26
1986				220	229	246	189	81	203	129	175	26
1987	180	180	189	210	214	208	205	91	237	161	206	63
1988				210	200	200	188	88	224	159	198	11
1989		154	156	220	214	200	203	94	225	157	196	32
1990				220	214	192	197	93	213	127	184	100
1991				150	143	123	124	81	153	86	125	
1992	100	100	100	100	100	100	100	100	100	100	100	100
1993				80	86	85	73	101	76	72	75	53
1994				80	71	69	68	91	69	67	67	63
1995				61P	51P	32P	69P	100P	87P	85P	83P	
1996				41P	29P	6P	54P	102P	75P	73P	72P	
1997				20P	7P		39P	104P	63P	61P	61P	
1998							24P	107P	51P	50P	49P	

Sources: Same as General Statistics. Values reflect change from the base year, 1992. Values above 100 mean greater than 92, values below 100 mean less than 92, and a value of 100 in the 82-91 or 93-98 period means same as 92. 'P's mark projections by the editors.

SELECTED RATIOS

For 1992	Avg. of All Manufact.	Analyzed Industry	Index
Employees per Establishment	46	5	10
Payroll per Establishment	1,332,320	111,374	8
Payroll per Employee	29,181	23,500	81
Production Workers per Establishment	31	3	11
Wages per Establishment	734,496	70,607	10
Wages per Production Worker	23,390	21,283	91
Hours per Production Worker	2,025	1,857	92
Wages per Hour	11.55	11.46	99
Value Added per Establishment	3,842,210	385,782	10
Value Added per Employee	84,153	81,400	97

For 1992	Avg. of All Manufact.	Analyzed Industry	Index
Value Added per Production Worker	122,353	116,286	95
Cost per Establishment	4,239,462	586,256	14
Cost per Employee	92,853	123,700	133
Cost per Production Worker	135,003	176,714	131
Shipments per Establishment	8,100,800	973,460	12
Shipments per Employee	177,425	205,400	116
Shipments per Production Worker	257,966	293,429	114
Investment per Establishment	278,244	9,005	3
Investment per Employee	6,094	1,900	31
Investment per Production Worker	8,861	2,714	31

Sources: Same as General Statistics. The 'Average of All Manufacturing' column represents the average of all manufacturing industries reported for the most recent complete year available. The Index shows the relationship between the Average and the Analyzed Industry. For example, 100 means that they are equal; 500 that the Analyzed Industry is five times the average; 50 means that the Analyzed Industry is half the national average. The abbreviation 'na' is used to show that data are 'not available'.

LEADING COMPANIES

Number shown: **5** Total sales ($ mil): **23** Total employment (000): **0.0**

Company Name	Address				CEO Name	Phone	Co. Type	Sales ($ mil)	Empl. (000)
Mohl Fur Company Inc	345 7th Av	New York	NY	10001	Manny Mohl	212-736-7676	R	14*	<0.1
Elika Ltd	345 7th Av	New York	NY	10001	Marvin Berger	212-279-6417	R	4	<0.1
LA Rockler Fur Co	16 N 4th St	Minneapolis	MN	55401	Sheldon G Rockler	612-332-8643	R	3	<0.1
Sekas International Ltd	330 7th Av	New York	NY	10001	Gus N Sekas	212-629-6095	R	2	<0.1
Meshekow Brothers Corp	527 W 7th St	Los Angeles	CA	90014	Alex Meshekow	213-623-7177	R	1*	<0.1

Source: *Ward's Business Directory of U.S. Private and Public Companies*, Volumes 1 and 2, 1996. The company type code used is as follows: P - Public, R - Private, S - Subsidiary, D - Division, J - Joint Venture, A - Affiliate, G - Group. Sales are in millions of dollars, employees are in thousands. An asterisk (*) indicates an estimated sales volume. The symbol < stands for 'less than'. Company names and addresses are truncated, in some cases, to fit into the available space.

MATERIALS CONSUMED

Material	Quantity	Delivered Cost ($ million)
No Materials Consumed data available for this industry.		

Source: 1992 *Economic Census*. Explanation of symbols used: (D): Withheld to avoid disclosure of competitive data; na: Not available; (S): Withheld because statistical norms were not met; (X): Not applicable; (Z): Less than half the unit shown; nec: Not elsewhere classified; nsk: Not specified by kind; - : zero; * : 10-19 percent estimated; ** : 20-29 percent estimated.

PRODUCT SHARE DETAILS

Product or Product Class	% Share	Product or Product Class	% Share
Fur goods	100.00		

Source: 1992 *Economic Census*. The values shown are percent of total shipments in an industry. Values of indented subcategories are summed in the main heading. The symbol (D) appears when data are withheld to prevent disclosure of competitive information. The abbreviation nsk stands for 'not specified by kind' and nec for 'not elsewhere classified'.

INPUTS AND OUTPUTS FOR TEXTILE GOODS, NEC

Economic Sector or Industry Providing Inputs	%	Sector	Economic Sector or Industry Buying Outputs	%	Sector
Imports	37.3	Foreign	Yarn mills & finishing of textiles, nec	17.8	Manufg.
Meat animals	23.8	Agric.	Broadwoven fabric mills	15.8	Manufg.
Textile goods, nec	6.5	Manufg.	Exports	8.8	Foreign
Noncomparable imports	6.1	Foreign	Agricultural, forestry, & fishery services	8.6	Agric.
Advertising	3.0	Services	Floor coverings	6.8	Manufg.
Wholesale trade	2.6	Trade	Housefurnishings, nec	5.3	Manufg.
Yarn mills & finishing of textiles, nec	2.5	Manufg.	Textile goods, nec	4.1	Manufg.
Electric services (utilities)	2.1	Util.	Nonwoven fabrics	4.0	Manufg.
Cyclic crudes and organics	1.6	Manufg.	Prepared feeds, nec	3.7	Manufg.
Chemical preparations, nec	1.1	Manufg.	Knit outerwear mills	2.9	Manufg.
Paperboard containers & boxes	1.1	Manufg.	Coated fabrics, not rubberized	2.6	Manufg.
Motor freight transportation & warehousing	1.1	Util.	Felt goods, nec	2.3	Manufg.
Petroleum refining	1.0	Manufg.	Cordage & twine	2.2	Manufg.
U.S. Postal Service	1.0	Gov't	Dairy farm products	1.9	Agric.
Gas production & distribution (utilities)	0.9	Util.	Automotive & apparel trimmings	1.9	Manufg.
Laundry, dry cleaning, shoe repair	0.9	Services	Shoes, except rubber	1.9	Manufg.
Textile machinery	0.7	Manufg.	House slippers	1.4	Manufg.
Industrial gases	0.6	Manufg.	Padding & upholstery filling	1.4	Manufg.
Eating & drinking places	0.6	Trade	Greenhouse & nursery products	0.9	Agric.
Wood products, nec	0.4	Manufg.	Boot & shoe cutstock & findings	0.9	Manufg.
Banking	0.4	Fin/R.E.	Machinery, except electrical, nec	0.8	Manufg.
Equipment rental & leasing services	0.4	Services	Paper coating & glazing	0.7	Manufg.
Lubricating oils & greases	0.3	Manufg.	Processed textile waste	0.7	Manufg.
Real estate	0.3	Fin/R.E.	Commercial fishing	0.3	Agric.
Maintenance of nonfarm buildings nec	0.2	Constr.	Boat building & repairing	0.3	Manufg.
Industrial inorganic chemicals, nec	0.2	Manufg.	Pleating & stitching	0.3	Manufg.
Machinery, except electrical, nec	0.2	Manufg.	Soap & other detergents	0.3	Manufg.
Communications, except radio & TV	0.2	Util.	Cereal breakfast foods	0.2	Manufg.
Water supply & sewage systems	0.2	Util.	Dog, cat, & other pet food	0.2	Manufg.
Accounting, auditing & bookkeeping	0.2	Services	Motion pictures	0.2	Services
Legal services	0.2	Services	Forestry products	0.1	Agric.
Management & consulting services & labs	0.2	Services	Abrasive products	0.1	Manufg.
Railroads & related services	0.1	Util.	Lace goods	0.1	Manufg.
Royalties	0.1	Fin/R.E.			
Business/professional associations	0.1	Services			
State & local government enterprises, nec	0.1	Gov't			

Source: Benchmark Input-Output Accounts for the U.S. Economy, 1982, U.S. Department of Commerce, Washington, D.C., July 1991. Data, as reported in the source, are organized by the 1977 SIC structure in use in 1982 but have been matched, as closely as is possible, to the 1987 SIC structure used in this book.

OCCUPATIONS EMPLOYED BY SIC 237 - APPAREL

Occupation	% of Total 1994	Change to 2005	Occupation	% of Total 1994	Change to 2005
Sewing machine operators, garment	56.1	-33.1	Cutters & trimmers, hand	1.7	-24.8
Inspectors, testers, & graders, precision	3.5	-16.4	Patternmakers, layout workers, fabric & apparel	1.5	25.4
Blue collar worker supervisors	3.0	-24.0	General managers & top executives	1.4	-20.7
Assemblers, fabricators, & hand workers nec	2.5	-16.4	Sewing machine operators, non-garment	1.3	-37.3
Pressing machine operators, textiles	2.4	-45.7	Helpers, laborers, & material movers nec	1.1	-16.4
Hand packers & packagers	2.0	-21.2	Industrial machinery mechanics	1.1	0.3
Freight, stock, & material movers, hand	1.8	-33.1	Pressers, hand	1.1	-58.2
Traffic, shipping, & receiving clerks	1.8	-19.6	Sewers, hand	1.0	-10.7

Source: *Industry-Occupation Matrix*, Bureau of Labor Statistics. These data relate to one or more 3-digit SIC industry groups rather than to a single 4-digit SIC. The change reported for each occupation to the year 2005 is a percent of growth or decline as estimated by the Bureau of Labor Statistics. The abbreviation nec stands for 'not elsewhere classified'.

LOCATION BY STATE AND REGIONAL CONCENTRATION

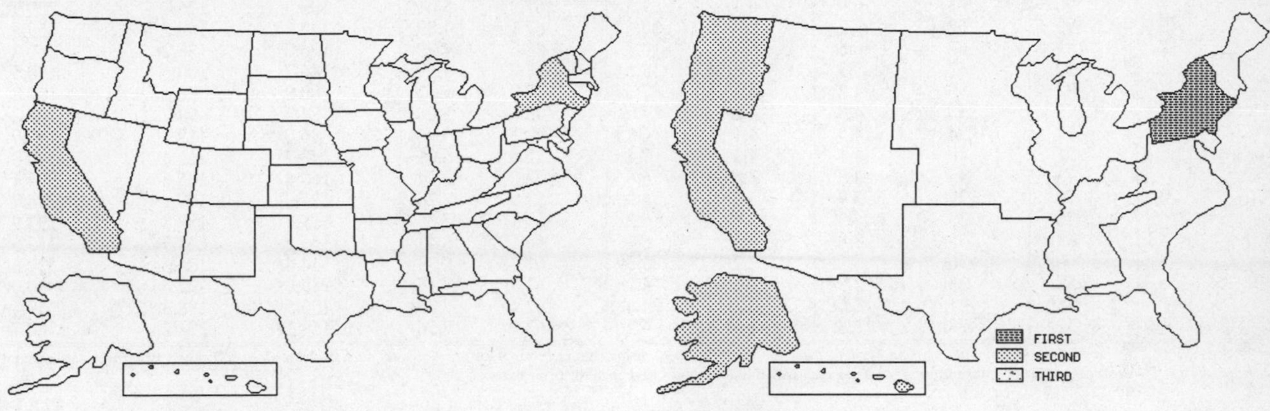

INDUSTRY DATA BY STATE

State	Establish-ments	Shipments: Total ($ mil)	Shipments: % of U.S.	Shipments: Per Establ.	Employment: Total Number	Employment: % of U.S.	Employment: Per Establ.	Employment: Wages ($/hour)	Cost as % of Shipments	Investment per Employee ($)
New York	166	136.8	66.6	0.8	600	60.0	4	12.12	60.5	2,333
California	13	(D)	-	-	175 *	17.5	13	-	-	-

Source: 1992 *Economic Census*. The states are in descending order of shipments or establishments (if shipment data are missing for the majority). The symbol (D) appears when data are withheld to prevent disclosure of competitive information. States marked with (D) are sorted by number of establishments. A dash (-) indicates that the data element cannot be calculated; * indicates the midpoint of a range.

2381 - FABRIC DRESS AND WORK GLOVES

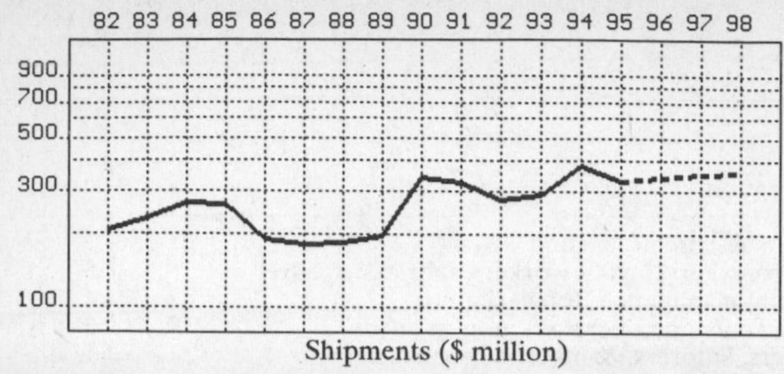

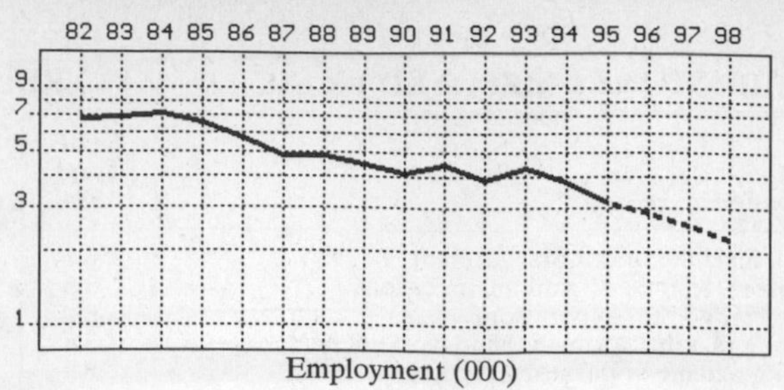

GENERAL STATISTICS

Year	Companies	Establishments Total	Establishments with 20 or more employees	Employment Total (000)	Production Workers (000)	Production Hours (Mil)	Compensation Payroll ($ mil)	Compensation Wages ($/hr)	Cost of Materials	Value Added by Manufacture	Value of Shipments	Capital Invest.
1982	78	102	64	6.8	6.1	9.2	51.2	4.52	98.9	104.7	208.4	3.4
1983		96	63	6.9	6.1	9.5	61.3	5.01	103.3	126.7	229.9	3.1
1984		90	62	7.2	6.3	10.6	67.1	4.89	130.3	143.2	269.8	2.7
1985		83	62	6.6	6.0	10.1	58.5	4.72	126.0	138.2	261.3	1.5
1986		80	62	5.7	5.2	8.2	48.3	4.79	86.2	100.6	190.5	1.0
1987	62	82	58	4.8	4.3	7.3	47.9	5.12	80.8	98.2	180.8	1.5
1988		75	53	4.8	4.2	7.0	46.6	5.06	84.2	99.7	185.2	1.1
1989		77	54	4.5	4.1	6.9	48.8	4.96	86.0	119.5	197.9	1.3
1990		71	49	4.1	4.3	7.7	72.8	6.01	143.2	212.4	340.8	4.7
1991		73	45	4.5	3.6	6.6	72.0	6.74	160.4	165.6	324.4	2.0
1992	58	70	39	3.9	3.2	6.0	57.9	6.28	127.0	148.1	278.7	2.8
1993		70	39	4.3	3.8	6.2	63.1	7.35	155.4	153.8	293.9	6.0
1994		63P	38P	3.8	3.2	6.1	56.1	6.41	166.2	214.7	379.3	5.6
1995		60P	36P	3.1P	2.7P	5.3P	61.4P	6.95P	144.4P	186.6P	329.6P	4.2P
1996		58P	33P	2.8P	2.4P	4.9P	61.9P	7.15P	149.0P	192.4P	340.0P	4.4P
1997		55P	31P	2.6P	2.1P	4.6P	62.4P	7.35P	153.5P	198.3P	350.4P	4.6P
1998		52P	28P	2.3P	1.9P	4.2P	62.9P	7.56P	158.1P	204.2P	360.7P	4.8P

Sources: 1982, 1987, 1992 *Economic Census*; *Annual Survey of Manufactures*, 83-86, 88-91, 93-94. Establishment counts for non-Census years are from *County Business Patterns*; establishment values for 83-84 are extrapolations. 'P's show projections by the editors. Industries reclassified in 87 will not have data for prior years.

INDICES OF CHANGE

Year	Companies	Establishments Total	Establishments with 20 or more employees	Employment Total (000)	Production Workers (000)	Production Hours (Mil)	Compensation Payroll ($ mil)	Compensation Wages ($/hr)	Cost of Materials	Value Added by Manufacture	Value of Shipments	Capital Invest.
1982	134	146	164	174	191	153	88	72	78	71	75	121
1983		137	162	177	191	158	106	80	81	86	82	111
1984		129	159	185	197	177	116	78	103	97	97	96
1985		119	159	169	188	168	101	75	99	93	94	54
1986		114	159	146	162	137	83	76	68	68	68	36
1987	107	117	149	123	134	122	83	82	64	66	65	54
1988		107	136	123	131	117	80	81	66	67	66	39
1989		110	138	115	128	115	84	79	68	81	71	46
1990		101	126	105	134	128	126	96	113	143	122	168
1991		104	115	115	113	110	124	107	126	112	116	71
1992	100	100	100	100	100	100	100	100	100	100	100	100
1993		100	100	110	119	103	109	117	122	104	105	214
1994		90P	98P	97	100	102	97	102	131	145	136	200
1995		86P	92P	81P	84P	88P	106P	111P	114P	126P	118P	151P
1996		82P	85P	73P	76P	82P	107P	114P	117P	130P	122P	159P
1997		78P	79P	65P	67P	76P	108P	117P	121P	134P	126P	166P
1998		74P	73P	58P	58P	70P	109P	120P	124P	138P	129P	173P

Sources: Same as General Statistics. Values reflect change from the base year, 1992. Values above 100 mean greater than 92, values below 100 mean less than 92, and a value of 100 in the 82-91 or 93-98 period means same as 92. 'P's mark projections by the editors.

SELECTED RATIOS

For 1994	Avg. of All Manufact.	Analyzed Industry	Index
Employees per Establishment	49	60	123
Payroll per Establishment	1,500,273	890,476	59
Payroll per Employee	30,620	14,763	48
Production Workers per Establishment	34	51	148
Wages per Establishment	853,319	620,651	73
Wages per Production Worker	24,861	12,219	49
Hours per Production Worker	2,056	1,906	93
Wages per Hour	12.09	6.41	53
Value Added per Establishment	4,602,255	3,407,937	74
Value Added per Employee	93,930	56,500	60

For 1994	Avg. of All Manufact.	Analyzed Industry	Index
Value Added per Production Worker	134,084	67,094	50
Cost per Establishment	5,045,178	2,638,095	52
Cost per Employee	102,970	43,737	42
Cost per Production Worker	146,988	51,937	35
Shipments per Establishment	9,576,895	6,020,635	63
Shipments per Employee	195,460	99,816	51
Shipments per Production Worker	279,017	118,531	42
Investment per Establishment	321,011	88,889	28
Investment per Employee	6,552	1,474	22
Investment per Production Worker	9,352	1,750	19

Sources: Same as General Statistics. The 'Average of All Manufacturing' column represents the average of all manufacturing industries reported for the most recent complete year available. The Index shows the relationship between the Average and the Analyzed Industry. For example, 100 means that they are equal; 500 that the Analyzed Industry is five times the average; 50 means that the Analyzed Industry is half the national average. The abbreviation 'na' is used to show that data are 'not available'.

LEADING COMPANIES

Number shown: **19** Total sales ($ mil): **263** Total employment (000): **4.6**

Company Name	Address				CEO Name	Phone	Co. Type	Sales ($ mil)	Empl. (000)
Wells Lamont Corp	6640 W Touhy Av	Niles	IL	60714	Lloyd F Rogers	708-647-8200	S	110	2.0
Golden Needles	PO Box 803	Wilkesboro	NC	28697	Harold Plemmons	919-667-5102	R	27*	0.5
Southern Glove Manufacturing	PO Box 579	Conover	NC	28613	Thomas E Moser	704-464-4884	R	16	0.5
Tom Thumb Glove Co	PO Box 640	Wilkesboro	NC	28697	Harold Plemmons	919-667-1281	R	15	0.2
Avon Glove Corp	1966 Broad Hollow	New York	NY	11735	Jeffrey Schwartz	516-752-1212	R	15*	<0.1
Sand and Siman Inc	10 W 33rd St	New York	NY	10001	Jeffrey Schwartz	212-564-4484	D	15	<0.1
Magid Glove	2060 N Kolmar	Chicago	IL	60639	Abe Cohen	312-384-2072	R	11*	0.3
Midwest Quality Gloves Inc	PO Box 260	Chillicothe	MO	64601	Stephen J Franke	816-646-2165	R	10	0.1
Lambert Manufacturing Co	PO Box 740	Chillicothe	MO	64601	James Lambert	816-646-2150	R	8	0.3
Perfect Fit Glove Company Inc	85 Innsbruck Dr	Buffalo	NY	14227	Joseph Hoerner	716-668-2000	R	6*	0.1
Star Glove Company Inc	25159 Dequindre	Madison H	MI	48071	GA Brydell	810-548-6100	R	6	0.1
Brookville Glove Mfg Co	PO Box 188	Brookville	PA	15825	Ned Stanley	814-849-7324	R	4	<0.1
Maine Brand Manufacturing Inc	PO Box 860	Houlton	ME	04730	Glenn Clarke	207-538-9577	R	4	<0.1
Seal Glove Manufacturing Inc	E North St	Millersburg	PA	17061	WA Specht Jr	717-692-4747	R	4	<0.1
American Made Products Inc	1155 E Morgan St	Carlinville	IL	62626	L Burns	217-854-4496	R	3	<0.1
Glove Corp	PO Box 117	Alexandria	IN	46001	Frank C Sturm	317-724-4481	R	3	0.1
Knoxville Glove Co	PO Box 138	Knoxville	TN	37901	R Townsend Jr	615-573-4555	R	3	0.1
Jasper Glove Co	PO Box 189	Jasper	IN	47546	Charles F Habig	812-482-4473	R	1	<0.1
Edina Manufacturing Company	PO Box 130	Edina	MO	63537	Jerry R Novak	816-397-2291	R	1	<0.1

Source: *Ward's Business Directory of U.S. Private and Public Companies*, Volumes 1 and 2, 1996. The company type code used is as follows: P - Public, R - Private, S - Subsidiary, D - Division, J - Joint Venture, A - Affiliate, G - Group. Sales are in millions of dollars, employees are in thousands. An asterisk (*) indicates an estimated sales volume. The symbol < stands for 'less than'. Company names and addresses are truncated, in some cases, to fit into the available space.

MATERIALS CONSUMED

Material		Quantity	Delivered Cost ($ million)
Materials, ingredients, containers, and supplies		(X)	81.5
Broadwoven fabrics (piece goods)	mil lin yd	491.8	17.1
Knit fabrics	mil lb	4.3**	10.1
Yarn, all fibers	mil lb	9.1	13.3
Plastics resins consumed in the form of granules, pellets, powders, liquids, etc.	mil lb	2.4	2.5
Finished leather	mil sq ft	(S)	5.5
All other materials and components, parts, containers, and supplies		(X)	22.2
Materials, ingredients, containers, and supplies, nsk		(X)	10.9

Source: 1992 *Economic Census*. Explanation of symbols used: (D): Withheld to avoid disclosure of competitive data; na: Not available; (S): Withheld because statistical norms were not met; (X): Not applicable; (Z): Less than half the unit shown; nec: Not elsewhere classified; nsk: Not specified by kind; - : zero; * : 10-19 percent estimated; ** : 20-29 percent estimated.

PRODUCT SHARE DETAILS

Product or Product Class	% Share	Product or Product Class	% Share
Dress and work gloves and mittens	100.00	Dress and work gloves and mittens made from leather-and-fabrics combinations	10.54
Dress and work gloves and mittens made from woven or purchased knit fabrics	87.47	Dress and work gloves and mittens, nsk	1.99

Source: 1992 *Economic Census*. The values shown are percent of total shipments in an industry. Values of indented subcategories are summed in the main heading. The symbol (D) appears when data are withheld to prevent disclosure of competitive information. The abbreviation nsk stands for 'not specified by kind' and nec for 'not elsewhere classified'.

INPUTS AND OUTPUTS FOR APPAREL MADE FROM PURCHASED MATERIALS

Economic Sector or Industry Providing Inputs	%	Sector	Economic Sector or Industry Buying Outputs	%	Sector
Imports	29.1	Foreign	Personal consumption expenditures	82.7	
Broadwoven fabric mills	20.2	Manufg.	Apparel made from purchased materials	12.0	Manufg.
Apparel made from purchased materials	18.3	Manufg.	Exports	1.5	Foreign
Knit fabric mills	8.6	Manufg.	Federal Government purchases, national defense	0.9	Fed Govt
Wholesale trade	3.8	Trade	S/L Govt. purch., correction	0.5	S/L Govt
Advertising	2.4	Services	Pleating & stitching	0.3	Manufg.
Yarn mills & finishing of textiles, nec	1.4	Manufg.	Knit outerwear mills	0.2	Manufg.
Pleating & stitching	1.1	Manufg.	Hospitals	0.2	Services
Banking	1.1	Fin/R.E.	Laundry, dry cleaning, shoe repair	0.2	Services
Petroleum refining	1.0	Manufg.	S/L Govt. purch., health & hospitals	0.2	S/L Govt
Electric services (utilities)	1.0	Util.	Portrait, photographic studios	0.1	Services
Automotive & apparel trimmings	0.9	Manufg.	S/L Govt. purch., public assistance & relief	0.1	S/L Govt
Needles, pins, & fasteners	0.8	Manufg.			
Thread mills	0.7	Manufg.			

Continued on next page.

INPUTS AND OUTPUTS FOR APPAREL MADE FROM PURCHASED MATERIALS - Continued

Economic Sector or Industry Providing Inputs	%	Sector	Economic Sector or Industry Buying Outputs	%	Sector
Communications, except radio & TV	0.7	Util.			
Eating & drinking places	0.7	Trade			
U.S. Postal Service	0.7	Gov't			
Leather tanning & finishing	0.5	Manufg.			
Narrow fabric mills	0.5	Manufg.			
Schiffli machine embroideries	0.4	Manufg.			
Motor freight transportation & warehousing	0.4	Util.			
Real estate	0.4	Fin/R.E.			
Royalties	0.4	Fin/R.E.			
Forestry products	0.3	Agric.			
Buttons	0.3	Manufg.			
Paperboard containers & boxes	0.3	Manufg.			
Air transportation	0.3	Util.			
Maintenance of nonfarm buildings nec	0.2	Constr.			
Lace goods	0.2	Manufg.			
Gas production & distribution (utilities)	0.2	Util.			
Automotive rental & leasing, without drivers	0.2	Services			
Electrical repair shops	0.2	Services			
Equipment rental & leasing services	0.2	Services			
Legal services	0.2	Services			
Management & consulting services & labs	0.2	Services			
Artificial trees & flowers	0.1	Manufg.			
Insurance carriers	0.1	Fin/R.E.			
Accounting, auditing & bookkeeping	0.1	Services			
Automotive repair shops & services	0.1	Services			

Source: Benchmark Input-Output Accounts for the U.S. Economy, 1982, U.S. Department of Commerce, Washington, D.C., July 1991. Data, as reported in the source, are organized by the 1977 SIC structure in use in 1982 but have been matched, as closely as is possible, to the 1987 SIC structure used in this book.

OCCUPATIONS EMPLOYED BY SIC 238 - APPAREL

Occupation	% of Total 1994	Change to 2005	Occupation	% of Total 1994	Change to 2005
Sewing machine operators, garment	56.1	-33.1	Cutters & trimmers, hand	1.7	-24.8
Inspectors, testers, & graders, precision	3.5	-16.4	Patternmakers, layout workers, fabric & apparel	1.5	25.4
Blue collar worker supervisors	3.0	-24.0	General managers & top executives	1.4	-20.7
Assemblers, fabricators, & hand workers nec	2.5	-16.4	Sewing machine operators, non-garment	1.3	-37.3
Pressing machine operators, textiles	2.4	-45.7	Helpers, laborers, & material movers nec	1.1	-16.4
Hand packers & packagers	2.0	-21.2	Industrial machinery mechanics	1.1	0.3
Freight, stock, & material movers, hand	1.8	-33.1	Pressers, hand	1.1	-58.2
Traffic, shipping, & receiving clerks	1.8	-19.6	Sewers, hand	1.0	-10.7

Source: Industry-Occupation Matrix, Bureau of Labor Statistics. These data relate to one or more 3-digit SIC industry groups rather than to a single 4-digit SIC. The change reported for each occupation to the year 2005 is a percent of growth or decline as estimated by the Bureau of Labor Statistics. The abbreviation nec stands for 'not elsewhere classified'.

LOCATION BY STATE AND REGIONAL CONCENTRATION

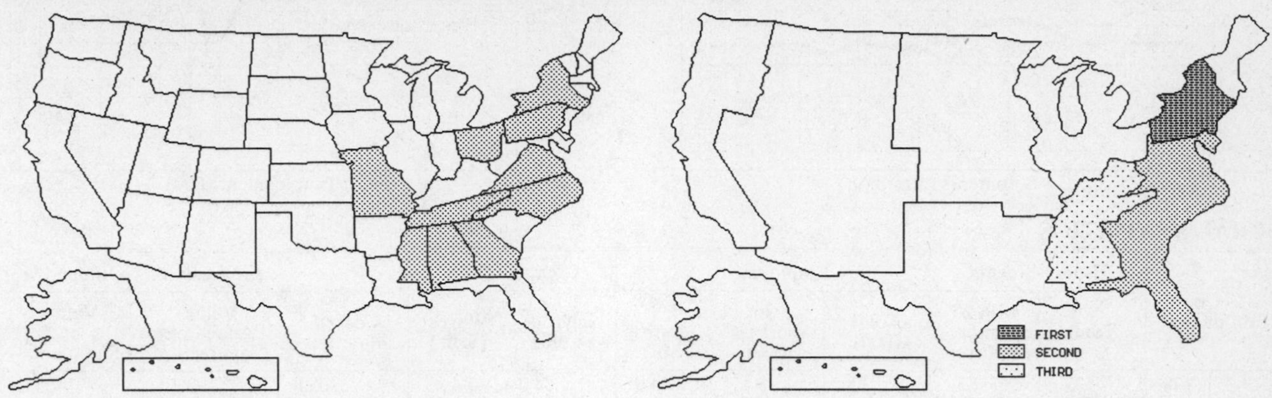

INDUSTRY DATA BY STATE

State	Establish-ments	Shipments			Employment				Cost as % of Shipments	Investment per Employee ($)
		Total ($ mil)	% of U.S.	Per Establ.	Total Number	% of U.S.	Per Establ.	Wages ($/hour)		
North Carolina	11	52.3	18.8	4.8	900	23.1	82	7.00	51.1	556
Mississippi	7	44.4	15.9	6.3	900	23.1	129	5.82	47.1	-
New York	12	10.8	3.9	0.9	300	7.7	25	6.25	63.9	1,000
Pennsylvania	5	9.0	3.2	1.8	200	5.1	40	6.00	43.3	-
Georgia	4	5.8	2.1	1.5	200	5.1	50	6.00	48.3	-
Missouri	3	(D)	-	-	175 *	4.5	58	-	-	-
Ohio	3	(D)	-	-	750 *	19.2	250	-	-	-
Alabama	2	(D)	-	-	175 *	4.5	88	-	-	-
Virginia	2	(D)	-	-	175 *	4.5	88	-	-	-
Tennessee	1	(D)	-	-	175 *	4.5	175	-	-	-

Source: 1992 *Economic Census*. The states are in descending order of shipments or establishments (if shipment data are missing for the majority). The symbol (D) appears when data are withheld to prevent disclosure of competitive information. States marked with (D) are sorted by number of establishments. A dash (-) indicates that the data element cannot be calculated; * indicates the midpoint of a range.

2384 - ROBES AND DRESSING GOWNS

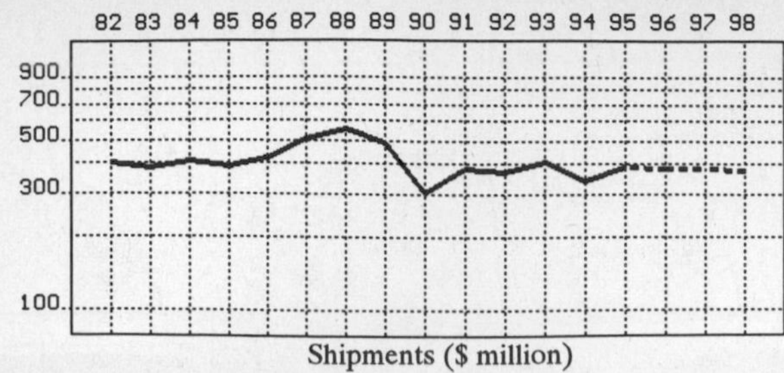

Shipments ($ million)

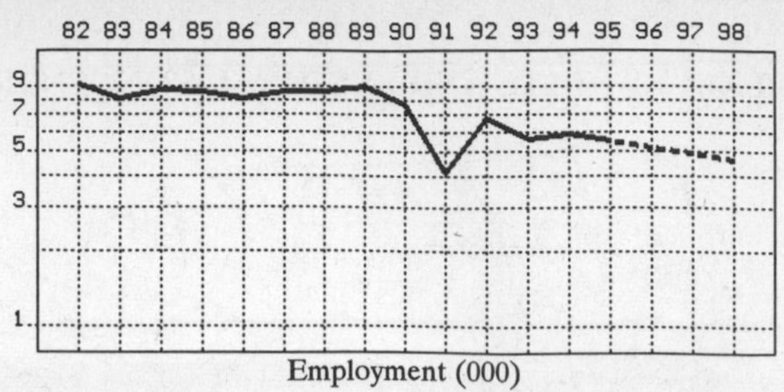

Employment (000)

GENERAL STATISTICS

Year	Companies	Establishments Total	Establishments with 20 or more employees	Employment Total (000)	Production Workers (000)	Production Hours (Mil)	Compensation Payroll ($ mil)	Compensation Wages ($/hr)	Cost of Materials	Value Added by Manufacture	Value of Shipments	Capital Invest.
1982	128	135	83	9.3	8.1	14.8	88.0	4.35	205.6	193.1	403.6	3.9
1983		122	77	8.1	6.7	12.3	85.1	4.72	216.0	163.4	381.4	2.8
1984		109	71	8.8	7.3	13.6	91.1	4.49	201.4	199.9	407.0	2.1
1985		96	64	8.6	6.9	12.4	83.5	4.50	198.2	185.8	386.8	2.4
1986		92	57	8.1	6.6	12.0	85.3	4.61	225.8	198.7	422.6	2.2
1987	85	96	74	8.7	7.3	13.1	101.4	5.36	278.3	228.0	502.6	3.3
1988		97	78	8.7	7.0	12.7	110.5	5.54	319.7	240.5	552.6	5.0
1989		97	72	9.0	5.7	10.9	87.3	5.62	239.7	236.9	484.2	4.4
1990		82	61	7.7	3.8	7.5	58.0	5.23	173.3	119.7	306.3	3.2
1991		73	52	4.1	4.1	8.0	62.9	5.30	197.5	176.0	383.3	2.9
1992	70	81	54	6.8	5.7	10.2	85.9	5.88	192.8	182.8	373.5	2.2
1993		75	49	5.6	4.7	8.9	72.9	5.81	216.8	194.9	406.3	1.7
1994		66P	51P	5.9	4.7	8.5	74.0	5.80	199.2	139.8	339.0	1.0
1995		61P	48P	5.5P	4.0P	7.6P	72.1P	6.08P	226.9P	159.2P	386.1P	2.2P
1996		57P	46P	5.2P	3.7P	7.1P	70.5P	6.21P	224.8P	157.8P	382.5P	2.1P
1997		52P	43P	4.9P	3.5P	6.6P	68.9P	6.34P	222.7P	156.3P	378.9P	2.0P
1998		47P	41P	4.6P	3.2P	6.0P	67.3P	6.47P	220.5P	154.8P	375.3P	1.9P

Sources: 1982, 1987, 1992 *Economic Census*; *Annual Survey of Manufactures*, 83-86, 88-91, 93-94. Establishment counts for non-Census years are from *County Business Patterns*; establishment values for 83-84 are extrapolations. 'P's show projections by the editors. Industries reclassified in 87 will not have data for prior years.

INDICES OF CHANGE

Year	Companies	Establishments Total	Establishments with 20 or more employees	Employment Total (000)	Production Workers (000)	Production Hours (Mil)	Compensation Payroll ($ mil)	Compensation Wages ($/hr)	Cost of Materials	Value Added by Manufacture	Value of Shipments	Capital Invest.
1982	183	167	154	137	142	145	102	74	107	106	108	177
1983		151	143	119	118	121	99	80	112	89	102	127
1984		135	131	129	128	133	106	76	104	109	109	95
1985		119	119	126	121	122	97	77	103	102	104	109
1986		114	106	119	116	118	99	78	117	109	113	100
1987	121	119	137	128	128	128	118	91	144	125	135	150
1988		120	144	128	123	125	129	94	166	132	148	227
1989		120	133	132	100	107	102	96	124	130	130	200
1990		101	113	113	67	74	68	89	90	65	82	145
1991		90	96	60	72	78	73	90	102	96	103	132
1992	100	100	100	100	100	100	100	100	100	100	100	100
1993		93	91	82	82	87	85	99	112	107	109	77
1994		81P	94P	87	82	83	86	99	103	76	91	45
1995		76P	89P	81P	71P	74P	84P	103P	118P	87P	103P	98P
1996		70P	85P	77P	66P	69P	82P	106P	117P	86P	102P	94P
1997		64P	80P	73P	61P	64P	80P	108P	115P	85P	101P	89P
1998		58P	76P	68P	56P	59P	78P	110P	114P	85P	100P	85P

Sources: Same as General Statistics. Values reflect change from the base year, 1992. Values above 100 mean greater than 92, values below 100 mean less than 92, and a value of 100 in the 82-91 or 93-98 period means same as 92. 'P's mark projections by the editors.

SELECTED RATIOS

For 1994	Avg. of All Manufact.	Analyzed Industry	Index
Employees per Establishment	49	90	183
Payroll per Establishment	1,500,273	1,122,759	75
Payroll per Employee	30,620	12,542	41
Production Workers per Establishment	34	71	208
Wages per Establishment	853,319	748,000	88
Wages per Production Worker	24,861	10,489	42
Hours per Production Worker	2,056	1,809	88
Wages per Hour	12.09	5.80	48
Value Added per Establishment	4,602,255	2,121,103	46
Value Added per Employee	93,930	23,695	25

For 1994	Avg. of All Manufact.	Analyzed Industry	Index
Value Added per Production Worker	134,084	29,745	22
Cost per Establishment	5,045,178	3,022,345	60
Cost per Employee	102,970	33,763	33
Cost per Production Worker	146,988	42,383	29
Shipments per Establishment	9,576,895	5,143,448	54
Shipments per Employee	195,460	57,458	29
Shipments per Production Worker	279,017	72,128	26
Investment per Establishment	321,011	15,172	5
Investment per Employee	6,552	169	3
Investment per Production Worker	9,352	213	2

Sources: Same as General Statistics. The 'Average of All Manufacturing' column represents the average of all manufacturing industries reported for the most recent complete year available. The Index shows the relationship between the Average and the Analyzed Industry. For example, 100 means that they are equal; 500 that the Analyzed Industry is five times the average; 50 means that the Analyzed Industry is half the national average. The abbreviation 'na' is used to show that data are 'not available'.

LEADING COMPANIES

Number shown: **11** Total sales ($ mil): **346** Total employment (000): **6.0**

Company Name	Address				CEO Name	Phone	Co. Type	Sales ($ mil)	Empl. (000)
I Appel Corp	136 Madison Av	New York	NY	10016	N Katz	212-592-8600	R	110*	1.9
Movie Star Inc	136 Madison Av	New York	NY	10016	Mark M David	212-679-7260	P	103	1.9
Marengo Mills	PO Box 80	Demopolis	AL	36732	Thomas A Williams	205-289-0680	D	30*	0.5
Foster Industries Inc	358 5th Av	New York	NY	10001	Robert Yaspan	212-563-2054	R	23*	0.4
Wagener Manufacturing Co	PO Box 145	Wagener	SC	29164	Ed Carver	803-564-3144	D	23	0.4
Crowntuft Manufacturing Corp	180 Madison Av	New York	NY	10016	G N Hakim Sr	212-684-4866	D	20	0.4
Damy Industries Inc	PO Box 969	Athens	TN	37303	Les Farnum	615-745-7620	R	17	0.3
Hampco Apparel Inc	PO Box 71	Chatham	VA	24531	Ken Miles	804-432-2861	S	10	0.1
Carolyn of Virginia Inc	21 Washington St	Bristol	VA	24201	Morris Lipson	703-466-3231	R	7*	0.1
Irving Marks Nite Wear Corp	350 5th Av	New York	NY	10118	Malvin Marks	212-695-1698	R	3	0.1
Miami Robes International	14652 Biscayne Blv	Miami	FL	33181	Richard Rosenblum	305-940-3377	R	1	<0.1

Source: *Ward's Business Directory of U.S. Private and Public Companies*, Volumes 1 and 2, 1996. The company type code used is as follows: P - Public, R - Private, S - Subsidiary, D - Division, J - Joint Venture, A - Affiliate, G - Group. Sales are in millions of dollars, employees are in thousands. An asterisk (*) indicates an estimated sales volume. The symbol < stands for 'less than'. Company names and addresses are truncated, in some cases, to fit into the available space.

MATERIALS CONSUMED

Material	Quantity	Delivered Cost ($ million)
Materials, ingredients, containers, and supplies	(X)	135.9
Broadwoven fabrics (piece goods)	(X)	52.9
Knit fabrics	(X)	58.2
Yarn, all fibers	(X)	7.7
All other materials and components, parts, containers, and supplies	(X)	12.4
Materials, ingredients, containers, and supplies, nsk	(X)	4.8

Source: 1992 *Economic Census*. Explanation of symbols used: (D): Withheld to avoid disclosure of competitive data; na: Not available; (S): Withheld because statistical norms were not met; (X): Not applicable; (Z): Less than half the unit shown; nec: Not elsewhere classified; nsk: Not specified by kind; - : zero; * : 10-19 percent estimated; ** : 20-29 percent estimated.

PRODUCT SHARE DETAILS

Product or Product Class	% Share	Product or Product Class	% Share
Robes and dressing gowns	100.00	smoking jackets)	20.21
Men's and boys' robes and dressing gowns (including		Women's, misses', and juniors' robes and dressing gowns	78.37

Source: 1992 *Economic Census*. The values shown are percent of total shipments in an industry. Values of indented subcategories are summed in the main heading. The symbol (D) appears when data are withheld to prevent disclosure of competitive information. The abbreviation nsk stands for 'not specified by kind' and nec for 'not elsewhere classified'.

INPUTS AND OUTPUTS FOR APPAREL MADE FROM PURCHASED MATERIALS

Economic Sector or Industry Providing Inputs	%	Sector	Economic Sector or Industry Buying Outputs	%	Sector
Imports	29.1	Foreign	Personal consumption expenditures	82.7	
Broadwoven fabric mills	20.2	Manufg.	Apparel made from purchased materials	12.0	Manufg.
Apparel made from purchased materials	18.3	Manufg.	Exports	1.5	Foreign
Knit fabric mills	8.6	Manufg.	Federal Government purchases, national defense	0.9	Fed Govt
Wholesale trade	3.8	Trade	S/L Govt. purch., correction	0.5	S/L Govt
Advertising	2.4	Services	Pleating & stitching	0.3	Manufg.
Yarn mills & finishing of textiles, nec	1.4	Manufg.	Knit outerwear mills	0.2	Manufg.
Pleating & stitching	1.1	Manufg.	Hospitals	0.2	Services
Banking	1.1	Fin/R.E.	Laundry, dry cleaning, shoe repair	0.2	Services
Petroleum refining	1.0	Manufg.	S/L Govt. purch., health & hospitals	0.2	S/L Govt
Electric services (utilities)	1.0	Util.	Portrait, photographic studios	0.1	Services
Automotive & apparel trimmings	0.9	Manufg.	S/L Govt. purch., public assistance & relief	0.1	S/L Govt
Needles, pins, & fasteners	0.8	Manufg.			
Thread mills	0.7	Manufg.			
Communications, except radio & TV	0.7	Util.			
Eating & drinking places	0.7	Trade			
U.S. Postal Service	0.7	Gov't			
Leather tanning & finishing	0.5	Manufg.			
Narrow fabric mills	0.5	Manufg.			
Schiffli machine embroideries	0.4	Manufg.			
Motor freight transportation & warehousing	0.4	Util.			
Real estate	0.4	Fin/R.E.			
Royalties	0.4	Fin/R.E.			
Forestry products	0.3	Agric.			
Buttons	0.3	Manufg.			

Continued on next page.

INPUTS AND OUTPUTS FOR APPAREL MADE FROM PURCHASED MATERIALS - Continued

Economic Sector or Industry Providing Inputs	%	Sector	Economic Sector or Industry Buying Outputs	%	Sector
Paperboard containers & boxes	0.3	Manufg.			
Air transportation	0.3	Util.			
Maintenance of nonfarm buildings nec	0.2	Constr.			
Lace goods	0.2	Manufg.			
Gas production & distribution (utilities)	0.2	Util.			
Automotive rental & leasing, without drivers	0.2	Services			
Electrical repair shops	0.2	Services			
Equipment rental & leasing services	0.2	Services			
Legal services	0.2	Services			
Management & consulting services & labs	0.2	Services			
Artificial trees & flowers	0.1	Manufg.			
Insurance carriers	0.1	Fin/R.E.			
Accounting, auditing & bookkeeping	0.1	Services			
Automotive repair shops & services	0.1	Services			

Source: Benchmark Input-Output Accounts for the U.S. Economy, 1982, U.S. Department of Commerce, Washington, D.C., July 1991. Data, as reported in the source, are organized by the 1977 SIC structure in use in 1982 but have been matched, as closely as is possible, to the 1987 SIC structure used in this book.

OCCUPATIONS EMPLOYED BY SIC 238 - APPAREL

Occupation	% of Total 1994	Change to 2005	Occupation	% of Total 1994	Change to 2005
Sewing machine operators, garment	56.1	-33.1	Cutters & trimmers, hand	1.7	-24.8
Inspectors, testers, & graders, precision	3.5	-16.4	Patternmakers, layout workers, fabric & apparel	1.5	25.4
Blue collar worker supervisors	3.0	-24.0	General managers & top executives	1.4	-20.7
Assemblers, fabricators, & hand workers nec	2.5	-16.4	Sewing machine operators, non-garment	1.3	-37.3
Pressing machine operators, textiles	2.4	-45.7	Helpers, laborers, & material movers nec	1.1	-16.4
Hand packers & packagers	2.0	-21.2	Industrial machinery mechanics	1.1	0.3
Freight, stock, & material movers, hand	1.8	-33.1	Pressers, hand	1.1	-58.2
Traffic, shipping, & receiving clerks	1.8	-19.6	Sewers, hand	1.0	-10.7

Source: Industry-Occupation Matrix, Bureau of Labor Statistics. These data relate to one or more 3-digit SIC industry groups rather than to a single 4-digit SIC. The change reported for each occupation to the year 2005 is a percent of growth or decline as estimated by the Bureau of Labor Statistics. The abbreviation nec stands for 'not elsewhere classified'.

LOCATION BY STATE AND REGIONAL CONCENTRATION

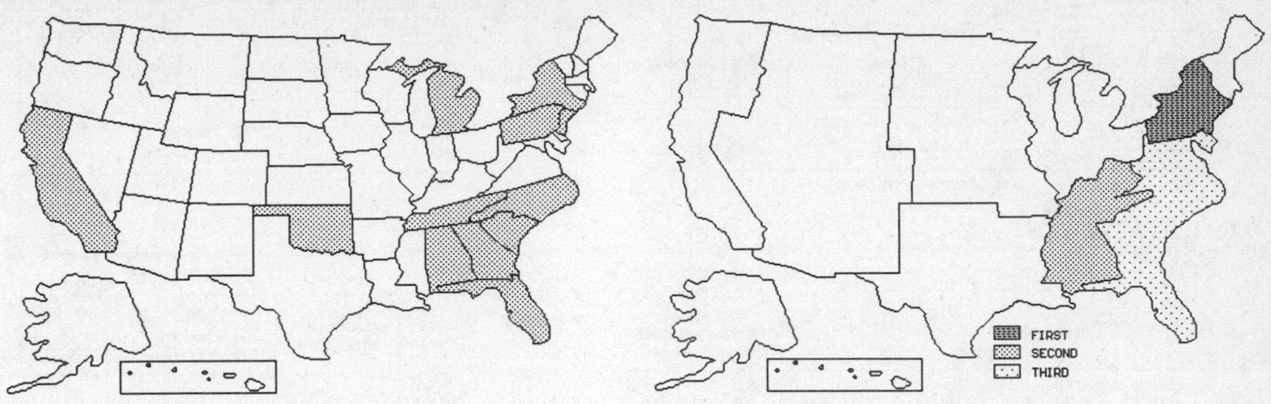

INDUSTRY DATA BY STATE

State	Establish-ments	Shipments			Employment				Cost as % of Shipments	Investment per Employee ($)
		Total ($ mil)	% of U.S.	Per Establ.	Total Number	% of U.S.	Per Establ.	Wages ($/hour)		
New York	20	83.2	22.3	4.2	800	11.8	40	6.08	60.6	750
Tennessee	9	54.2	14.5	6.0	1,400	20.6	156	5.25	44.5	71
California	13	31.9	8.5	2.5	700	10.3	54	4.50	52.7	-
Georgia	3	7.9	2.1	2.6	300	4.4	100	7.00	63.3	-
Pennsylvania	5	2.8	0.7	0.6	200	2.9	40	6.00	10.7	-
Alabama	6	(D)	-	-	750 *	11.0	125	-	-	-
South Carolina	5	(D)	-	-	750 *	11.0	150	-	-	-
North Carolina	4	(D)	-	-	750 *	11.0	188	-	-	-
Florida	3	(D)	-	-	750 *	11.0	250	-	-	-
New Jersey	3	(D)	-	-	175 *	2.6	58	-	-	-
Oklahoma	3	(D)	-	-	750 *	11.0	250	-	-	-
Michigan	2	(D)	-	-	175 *	2.6	88	-	-	-

Source: 1992 *Economic Census*. The states are in descending order of shipments or establishments (if shipment data are missing for the majority). The symbol (D) appears when data are withheld to prevent disclosure of competitive information. States marked with (D) are sorted by number of establishments. A dash (-) indicates that the data element cannot be calculated; * indicates the midpoint of a range.

2385 - WATERPROOF OUTERWEAR

Shipments ($ million)

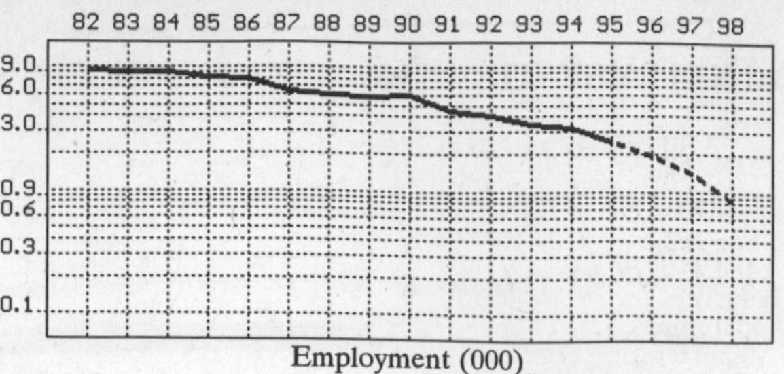

Employment (000)

GENERAL STATISTICS

Year	Companies	Establishments: Total	Establishments: with 20 or more employees	Employment: Total (000)	Production Workers (000)	Production Hours (Mil)	Compensation: Payroll ($ mil)	Compensation: Wages ($/hr)	Cost of Materials	Value Added by Manufacture	Value of Shipments	Capital Invest.
1982	98	112	76	9.3	8.0	13.9	101.1	5.36	205.8	246.0	449.2	4.6
1983		108	71	9.0	7.7	13.6	95.1	5.25	213.7	247.2	449.5	3.7
1984		104	66	9.1	7.9	14.4	107.6	5.68	208.3	241.7	439.3	4.0
1985		99	62	8.3	7.3	12.6	95.6	5.99	193.7	182.9	386.1	5.0
1986		99	63	8.1	7.1	12.5	93.4	5.73	188.3	159.2	360.5	2.7
1987	60	67	39	6.4	5.3	9.5	85.5	6.41	162.5	172.5	333.0	3.2
1988		65	35	6.0	4.8	9.1	96.5	7.65	161.7	157.5	317.8	3.0
1989		58	38	5.8	3.8	7.1	65.3	6.85	108.5	99.1	208.8	2.7
1990		59	34	5.9	3.7	6.7	63.9	7.42	108.5	113.0	219.3	0.7
1991		63	38	4.5	3.7	6.9	64.5	7.32	124.8	100.5	231.8	1.2
1992	61	71	37	4.1	3.2	5.6	64.5	7.23	110.5	146.0	268.4	2.5
1993		66	34	3.4	2.7	4.8	56.9	7.56	66.7	131.8	196.6	1.0
1994		48P	23P	3.2	2.7	4.5	51.8	7.98	65.5	118.7	189.2	0.3
1995		43P	18P	2.5P	1.6P	2.9P	48.1P	8.24P	49.6P	89.8P	143.1P	0.3P
1996		38P	14P	2.0P	1.1P	2.0P	43.6P	8.46P	41.2P	74.7P	119.1P	
1997		33P	10P	1.4P	0.5P	1.1P	39.0P	8.69P	32.9P	59.6P	95.0P	
1998		28P	6P	0.8P	0.0P	0.2P	34.4P	8.92P	24.6P	44.5P	71.0P	

Sources: 1982, 1987, 1992 *Economic Census; Annual Survey of Manufactures*, 83-86, 88-91, 93-94. Establishment counts for non-Census years are from *County Business Patterns*; establishment values for 83-84 are extrapolations. 'P's show projections by the editors. Industries reclassified in 87 will not have data for prior years.

INDICES OF CHANGE

Year	Companies	Establishments: Total	Establishments: with 20 or more employees	Employment: Total (000)	Production Workers (000)	Production Hours (Mil)	Compensation: Payroll ($ mil)	Compensation: Wages ($/hr)	Cost of Materials	Value Added by Manufacture	Value of Shipments	Capital Invest.
1982	161	158	205	227	250	248	157	74	186	168	167	184
1983		152	192	220	241	243	147	73	193	169	167	148
1984		146	178	222	247	257	167	79	189	166	164	160
1985		139	168	202	228	225	148	83	175	125	144	200
1986		139	170	198	222	223	145	79	170	109	134	108
1987	98	94	105	156	166	170	133	89	147	118	124	128
1988		92	95	146	150	163	150	106	146	108	118	120
1989		82	103	141	119	127	101	95	98	68	78	108
1990		83	92	144	116	120	99	103	98	77	82	28
1991		89	103	110	116	123	100	101	113	69	86	48
1992	100	100	100	100	100	100	100	100	100	100	100	100
1993		93	92	83	84	86	88	105	60	90	73	40
1994		68P	61P	78	84	80	80	110	59	81	70	12
1995		60P	50P	61P	49P	52P	75P	114P	45P	62P	53P	12P
1996		53P	39P	48P	33P	36P	68P	117P	37P	51P	44P	
1997		46P	27P	34P	17P	19P	60P	120P	30P	41P	35P	
1998		39P	16P	21P	1P	3P	53P	123P	22P	30P	26P	

Sources: Same as General Statistics. Values reflect change from the base year, 1992. Values above 100 mean greater than 92, values below 100 mean less than 92, and a value of 100 in the 82-91 or 93-98 period means same as 92. 'P's mark projections by the editors.

SELECTED RATIOS

For 1994	Avg. of All Manufact.	Analyzed Industry	Index
Employees per Establishment	49	67	136
Payroll per Establishment	1,500,273	1,080,531	72
Payroll per Employee	30,620	16,187	53
Production Workers per Establishment	34	56	164
Wages per Establishment	853,319	749,071	88
Wages per Production Worker	24,861	13,300	53
Hours per Production Worker	2,056	1,667	81
Wages per Hour	12.09	7.98	66
Value Added per Establishment	4,602,255	2,476,043	54
Value Added per Employee	93,930	37,094	39

For 1994	Avg. of All Manufact.	Analyzed Industry	Index
Value Added per Production Worker	134,084	43,963	33
Cost per Establishment	5,045,178	1,366,308	27
Cost per Employee	102,970	20,469	20
Cost per Production Worker	146,988	24,259	17
Shipments per Establishment	9,576,895	3,946,650	41
Shipments per Employee	195,460	59,125	30
Shipments per Production Worker	279,017	70,074	25
Investment per Establishment	321,011	6,258	2
Investment per Employee	6,552	94	1
Investment per Production Worker	9,352	111	1

Sources: Same as General Statistics. The 'Average of All Manufacturing' column represents the average of all manufacturing industries reported for the most recent complete year available. The Index shows the relationship between the Average and the Analyzed Industry. For example, 100 means that they are equal; 500 that the Analyzed Industry is five times the average; 50 means that the Analyzed Industry is half the national average. The abbreviation 'na' is used to show that data are 'not available'.

LEADING COMPANIES

Number shown: **17** Total sales ($ mil): **586** Total employment (000): **4.4**

Company Name	Address				CEO Name	Phone	Co. Type	Sales ($ mil)	Empl. (000)
Londontown Corp	1332 Londontown	Eldersburg	MD	21784	Arnold P Cohen	410-795-5900	S	350	1.9
London Fog Industries Inc	1332 London Town	Eldersburg	MD	21784	James Milligan	410-795-5900	R	100*	0.5
Rainfair Inc	PO Box 1647	Racine	WI	53401	Craig L Leipold	414-554-7000	R	20	0.2
Neese Industries Inc	PO Box 1059	Gonzales	LA	70707	Sam Speligene	504-647-6553	R	17*	0.3
Chief Apparel Inc	1350 Av Amer	New York	NY	10001	Peter Cannold	212-974-1070	R	16	0.1
Blauer Manufacturing Co	20 Aberdeen St	Boston	MA	02215	Charles L Blauer	617-536-6606	R	12	0.4
Chemprene Inc	PO Box 471	Beacon	NY	12508	EB Kerin	914-831-2800	R	12	0.2
Forecaster of Boston Inc	192 Friend St	Boston	MA	02114	A Forman	617-742-6230	R	11*	0.2
Cerf Brothers Bag Company Inc	2827 S Brentwood	St Louis	MO	63144	Jerome Michelson	314-961-7939	R	9	0.2
Fleet Street Ltd	512 7th Av	New York	NY	10018	Manny Haber	212-354-8990	R	8*	0.1
Wippette International Inc	500 7th Av	New York	NY	10018	Lewis Bernstein	212-852-4900	R	8	<0.1
Wippette Rainthings Inc	500 7th Av	New York	NY	10018	Lewis M Bernstein	212-852-4900	S	8	<0.1
Falcon Industries Inc	PO Box 97	Estill	SC	29918	Gerald E Morris	803-625-3165	R	5*	0.1
Diving Unlimited International	1148 Delevan Dr	San Diego	CA	92102	Richard Long	619-236-1203	R	4	<0.1
Marathon Rubber Products Co	510 Sherman St	Wausau	WI	54401	HL Cohan	715-845-6255	R	3	<0.1
Loveline Industries Inc	385 Gerard Av	Bronx	NY	10451	Morton Goldstein	212-402-3500	R	2	<0.1
Wippette Kids	112 W 34th St	New York	NY	10120	Lisa O'Toole	212-695-6735	D	1	<0.1

Source: *Ward's Business Directory of U.S. Private and Public Companies*, Volumes 1 and 2, 1996. The company type code used is as follows: P - Public, R - Private, S - Subsidiary, D - Division, J - Joint Venture, A - Affiliate, G - Group. Sales are in millions of dollars, employees are in thousands. An asterisk (*) indicates an estimated sales volume. The symbol < stands for 'less than'. Company names and addresses are truncated, in some cases, to fit into the available space.

MATERIALS CONSUMED

Material	Quantity	Delivered Cost ($ million)
Materials, ingredients, containers, and supplies	(X)	88.1
Broadwoven fabrics (piece goods)	(X)	(D)
Narrow fabrics (12 inches or less in width)	(X)	0.6
Buttons, zippers, and slide fasteners	(X)	7.6
All other materials and components, parts, containers, and supplies	(X)	16.7
Materials, ingredients, containers, and supplies, nsk	(X)	1.5

Source: 1992 *Economic Census*. Explanation of symbols used: (D): Withheld to avoid disclosure of competitive data; na: Not available; (S): Withheld because statistical norms were not met; (X): Not applicable; (Z): Less than half the unit shown; nec: Not elsewhere classified; nsk: Not specified by kind; - : zero; * : 10-19 percent estimated; ** : 20-29 percent estimated.

PRODUCT SHARE DETAILS

Product or Product Class	% Share	Product or Product Class	% Share
Waterproof outerwear	100.00	Receipts for contract and commission work on raincoats and other waterproof outergarments	8.28
Raincoats and other waterproof outergarments	90.67	Receipts for contract and commission work on raincoats and other waterproof outergarments	98.53
Raincoats and raincapes	78.48	Waterproof outerwear, nsk	1.10
Baby pants and diaper covers, plastics and rubberized	5.95		
All other plastics or rubberized waterproof outergarments (including aprons, smocks, bibs, dress shields, etc.)	15.57		

Source: 1992 *Economic Census*. The values shown are percent of total shipments in an industry. Values of indented subcategories are summed in the main heading. The symbol (D) appears when data are withheld to prevent disclosure of competitive information. The abbreviation nsk stands for 'not specified by kind' and nec for 'not elsewhere classified'.

INPUTS AND OUTPUTS FOR APPAREL MADE FROM PURCHASED MATERIALS

Economic Sector or Industry Providing Inputs	%	Sector	Economic Sector or Industry Buying Outputs	%	Sector
Imports	29.1	Foreign	Personal consumption expenditures	82.7	
Broadwoven fabric mills	20.2	Manufg.	Apparel made from purchased materials	12.0	Manufg.
Apparel made from purchased materials	18.3	Manufg.	Exports	1.5	Foreign
Knit fabric mills	8.6	Manufg.	Federal Government purchases, national defense	0.9	Fed Govt
Wholesale trade	3.8	Trade	S/L Govt. purch., correction	0.5	S/L Govt
Advertising	2.4	Services	Pleating & stitching	0.3	Manufg.
Yarn mills & finishing of textiles, nec	1.4	Manufg.	Knit outerwear mills	0.2	Manufg.
Pleating & stitching	1.1	Manufg.	Hospitals	0.2	Services
Banking	1.1	Fin/R.E.	Laundry, dry cleaning, shoe repair	0.2	Services
Petroleum refining	1.0	Manufg.	S/L Govt. purch., health & hospitals	0.2	S/L Govt
Electric services (utilities)	1.0	Util.	Portrait, photographic studios	0.1	Services
Automotive & apparel trimmings	0.9	Manufg.	S/L Govt. purch., public assistance & relief	0.1	S/L Govt
Needles, pins, & fasteners	0.8	Manufg.			
Thread mills	0.7	Manufg.			
Communications, except radio & TV	0.7	Util.			

Continued on next page.

INPUTS AND OUTPUTS FOR APPAREL MADE FROM PURCHASED MATERIALS - Continued

Economic Sector or Industry Providing Inputs	%	Sector	Economic Sector or Industry Buying Outputs	%	Sector
Eating & drinking places	0.7	Trade			
U.S. Postal Service	0.7	Gov't			
Leather tanning & finishing	0.5	Manufg.			
Narrow fabric mills	0.5	Manufg.			
Schiffli machine embroideries	0.4	Manufg.			
Motor freight transportation & warehousing	0.4	Util.			
Real estate	0.4	Fin/R.E.			
Royalties	0.4	Fin/R.E.			
Forestry products	0.3	Agric.			
Buttons	0.3	Manufg.			
Paperboard containers & boxes	0.3	Manufg.			
Air transportation	0.3	Util.			
Maintenance of nonfarm buildings nec	0.2	Constr.			
Lace goods	0.2	Manufg.			
Gas production & distribution (utilities)	0.2	Util.			
Automotive rental & leasing, without drivers	0.2	Services			
Electrical repair shops	0.2	Services			
Equipment rental & leasing services	0.2	Services			
Legal services	0.2	Services			
Management & consulting services & labs	0.2	Services			
Artificial trees & flowers	0.1	Manufg.			
Insurance carriers	0.1	Fin/R.E.			
Accounting, auditing & bookkeeping	0.1	Services			
Automotive repair shops & services	0.1	Services			

Source: Benchmark Input-Output Accounts for the U.S. Economy, 1982, U.S. Department of Commerce, Washington, D.C., July 1991. Data, as reported in the source, are organized by the 1977 SIC structure in use in 1982 but have been matched, as closely as is possible, to the 1987 SIC structure used in this book.

OCCUPATIONS EMPLOYED BY SIC 238 - APPAREL

Occupation	% of Total 1994	Change to 2005	Occupation	% of Total 1994	Change to 2005
Sewing machine operators, garment	56.1	-33.1	Cutters & trimmers, hand	1.7	-24.8
Inspectors, testers, & graders, precision	3.5	-16.4	Patternmakers, layout workers, fabric & apparel	1.5	25.4
Blue collar worker supervisors	3.0	-24.0	General managers & top executives	1.4	-20.7
Assemblers, fabricators, & hand workers nec	2.5	-16.4	Sewing machine operators, non-garment	1.3	-37.3
Pressing machine operators, textiles	2.4	-45.7	Helpers, laborers, & material movers nec	1.1	-16.4
Hand packers & packagers	2.0	-21.2	Industrial machinery mechanics	1.1	0.3
Freight, stock, & material movers, hand	1.8	-33.1	Pressers, hand	1.1	-58.2
Traffic, shipping, & receiving clerks	1.8	-19.6	Sewers, hand	1.0	-10.7

Source: Industry-Occupation Matrix, Bureau of Labor Statistics. These data relate to one or more 3-digit SIC industry groups rather than to a single 4-digit SIC. The change reported for each occupation to the year 2005 is a percent of growth or decline as estimated by the Bureau of Labor Statistics. The abbreviation nec stands for 'not elsewhere classified'.

LOCATION BY STATE AND REGIONAL CONCENTRATION

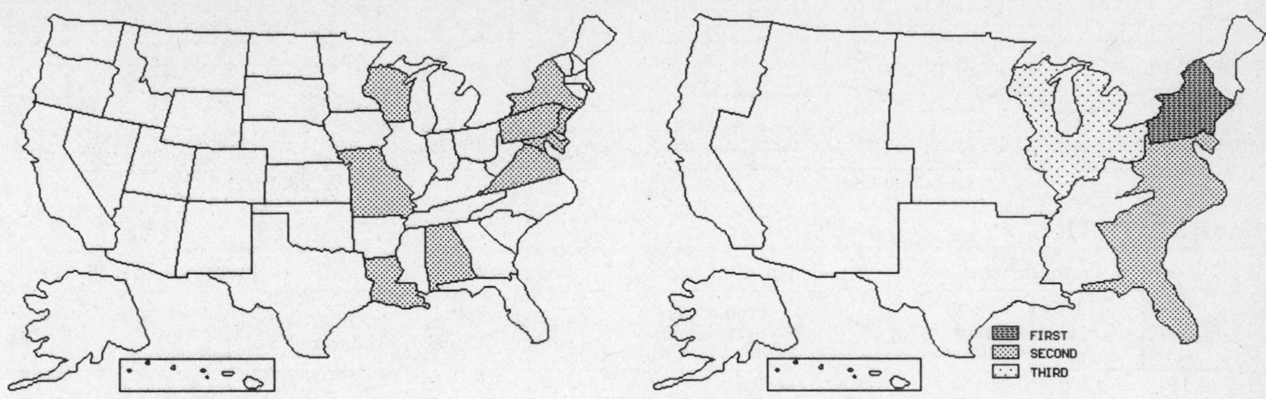

INDUSTRY DATA BY STATE

State	Establish-ments	Shipments			Employment				Cost as % of Shipments	Investment per Employee ($)
		Total ($ mil)	% of U.S.	Per Establ.	Total Number	% of U.S.	Per Establ.	Wages ($/hour)		
New York	9	16.2	6.0	1.8	300	7.3	33	8.25	48.1	-
Maryland	9	(D)	-	-	1,750 *	42.7	194	-	-	-
New Jersey	8	(D)	-	-	375 *	9.1	47	-	-	-
Pennsylvania	3	(D)	-	-	175 *	4.3	58	-	-	-
Virginia	3	(D)	-	-	375 *	9.1	125	-	-	-
Wisconsin	3	(D)	-	-	175 *	4.3	58	-	-	-
Alabama	1	(D)	-	-	750 *	18.3	750	-	-	-
Louisiana	1	(D)	-	-	175 *	4.3	175	-	-	-
Missouri	1	(D)	-	-	175 *	4.3	175	-	-	-

Source: 1992 *Economic Census*. The states are in descending order of shipments or establishments (if shipment data are missing for the majority). The symbol (D) appears when data are withheld to prevent disclosure of competitive information. States marked with (D) are sorted by number of establishments. A dash (-) indicates that the data element cannot be calculated; * indicates the midpoint of a range.

2386 - LEATHER AND SHEEP LINED CLOTHING

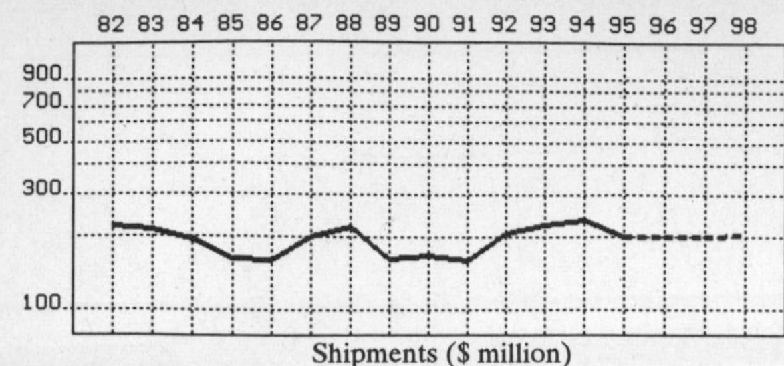

Shipments ($ million)

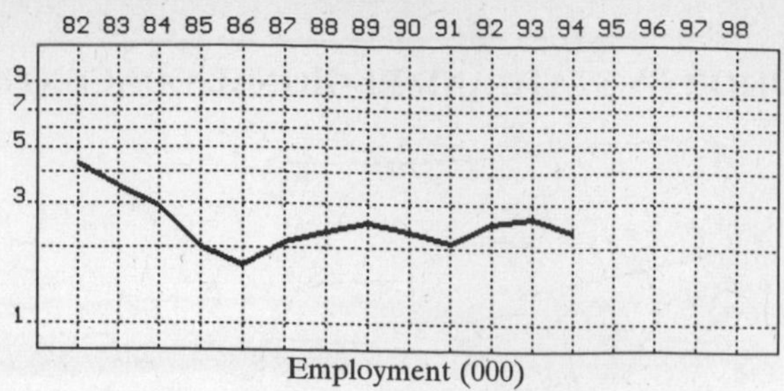

Employment (000)

GENERAL STATISTICS

Year	Com-panies	Establishments: Total	Establishments: with 20 or more employees	Employment: Total (000)	Employment: Production Workers (000)	Employment: Production Hours (Mil)	Compensation: Payroll ($ mil)	Compensation: Wages ($/hr)	Production ($ million): Cost of Materials	Production ($ million): Value Added by Manufacture	Production ($ million): Value of Shipments	Production ($ million): Capital Invest.
1982	186	186	52	4.3	3.6	6.4	48.9	5.69	122.9	95.7	221.3	0.9
1983		175	48	3.5	3.0	5.4	47.4	6.50	118.3	91.8	212.8	0.4
1984		164	44	2.9	2.4	4.2	39.0	6.69	113.6	84.9	194.4	1.1
1985		152	41	2.0	1.5	2.8	31.0	7.89	107.5	58.3	164.3	0.8
1986		142	37	1.7	1.3	2.3	29.8	8.52	102.6	56.0	161.4	0.4
1987	130	131	32	2.1	1.7	2.9	33.8	7.72	110.3	92.1	201.8	0.9
1988		134	30			3.2	35.9		123.1	97.1	220.5	0.5
1989		129	34	2.5	1.6	2.9	30.4	6.93	90.9	72.8	163.0	0.8
1990		134	34	2.3	1.8	3.2	32.8	6.81	91.4	73.0	166.6	0.4
1991		132	32	2.1	1.8	3.2	31.2	6.47	87.5	70.7	158.6	0.3
1992	116	117	32	2.5	2.0	3.7	45.9	7.73	123.8	92.2	209.2	1.3
1993		114	29	2.6	2.1	4.0	48.7	7.55	138.2	86.7	224.1	1.6
1994		105P	25P	2.3	2.0	3.5	41.3	7.83	119.8	115.6	237.6	0.1
1995		99P	23P			2.8P	37.8P		101.6P	98.0P	201.5P	0.7P
1996		93P	21P			2.6P	37.8P		102.1P	98.5P	202.4P	0.7P
1997		87P	20P			2.5P	37.8P		102.5P	98.9P	203.4P	0.8P
1998		81P	18P			2.4P	37.7P		103.0P	99.4P	204.3P	0.8P

Sources: 1982, 1987, 1992 *Economic Census*; *Annual Survey of Manufactures*, 83-86, 88-91, 93-94. Establishment counts for non-Census years are from *County Business Patterns*; establishment values for 83-84 are extrapolations. 'P's show projections by the editors. Industries reclassified in 87 will not have data for prior years.

INDICES OF CHANGE

Year	Com-panies	Establishments: Total	Establishments: with 20 or more employees	Employment: Total (000)	Employment: Production Workers (000)	Employment: Production Hours (Mil)	Compensation: Payroll ($ mil)	Compensation: Wages ($/hr)	Production ($ million): Cost of Materials	Production ($ million): Value Added by Manufacture	Production ($ million): Value of Shipments	Production ($ million): Capital Invest.
1982	160	159	163	172	180	173	107	74	99	104	106	69
1983		150	150	140	150	146	103	84	96	100	102	31
1984		140	138	116	120	114	85	87	92	92	93	85
1985		130	128	80	75	76	68	102	87	63	79	62
1986		121	116	68	65	62	65	110	83	61	77	31
1987	112	112	100	84	85	78	74	100	89	100	96	69
1988		115	94			86	78		99	105	105	38
1989		110	106	100	80	78	66	90	73	79	78	62
1990		115	106	92	90	86	71	88	74	79	80	31
1991		113	100	84	90	86	68	84	71	77	76	23
1992	100	100	100	100	100	100	100	100	100	100	100	100
1993		97	91	104	105	108	106	98	112	94	107	123
1994		89P	78P	92	100	95	90	101	97	125	114	8
1995		84P	73P			75P	82P		82P	106P	96P	57P
1996		80P	67P			71P	82P		82P	107P	97P	58P
1997		75P	61P			68P	82P		83P	107P	97P	58P
1998		70P	55P			64P	82P		83P	108P	98P	58P

Sources: Same as General Statistics. Values reflect change from the base year, 1992. Values above 100 mean greater than 92, values below 100 mean less than 92, and a value of 100 in the 82-91 or 93-98 period means same as 92. 'P's mark projections by the editors.

SELECTED RATIOS

For 1994	Avg. of All Manufact.	Analyzed Industry	Index	For 1994	Avg. of All Manufact.	Analyzed Industry	Index
Employees per Establishment	49	22	45	Value Added per Production Worker	134,084	57,800	43
Payroll per Establishment	1,500,273	394,529	26	Cost per Establishment	5,045,178	1,144,420	23
Payroll per Employee	30,620	17,957	59	Cost per Employee	102,970	52,087	51
Production Workers per Establishment	34	19	56	Cost per Production Worker	146,988	59,900	41
Wages per Establishment	853,319	261,793	31	Shipments per Establishment	9,576,895	2,269,735	24
Wages per Production Worker	24,861	13,702	55	Shipments per Employee	195,460	103,304	53
Hours per Production Worker	2,056	1,750	85	Shipments per Production Worker	279,017	118,800	43
Wages per Hour	12.09	7.83	65	Investment per Establishment	321,011	955	0
Value Added per Establishment	4,602,255	1,104,299	24	Investment per Employee	6,552	43	1
Value Added per Employee	93,930	50,261	54	Investment per Production Worker	9,352	50	1

Sources: Same as General Statistics. The 'Average of All Manufacturing' column represents the average of all manufacturing industries reported for the most recent complete year available. The Index shows the relationship between the Average and the Analyzed Industry. For example, 100 means that they are equal; 500 that the Analyzed Industry is five times the average; 50 means that the Analyzed Industry is half the national average. The abbreviation 'na' is used to show that data are 'not available'.

LEADING COMPANIES

Number shown: **9** Total sales ($ mil): **76** Total employment (000): **0.7**

Company Name	Address				CEO Name	Phone	Co. Type	Sales ($ mil)	Empl. (000)
Tivolie Fashions Inc	1350 Broadway	New York	NY	10018	Edward Coll III	212-564-3656	R	45	<0.1
Schott Brothers Inc	PO Box 506	Perth Amboy	NJ	08861	M Schott	908-442-2486	R	10	0.5
Avanti Outerwear Inc	512 7th Av	New York	NY	10018	Stephen Bass	212-391-2230	D	9	<0.1
Berlin Glove Company Inc	275 June St	Berlin	WI	54923	Ray Katt	414-361-5050	R	5*	0.1
Brooks Leather Sportswear Inc	14511 W 11 Mile Rd	Oak Park	MI	48237	Steven Weiss	313-548-8633	R	3	<0.1
Ardney Ltd	200 S Water St	Milwaukee	WI	53204	John G Abler	414-271-6260	R	1*	<0.1
Winfield Cover Company Inc	763 Brannan St	San Francisco	CA	94103	Gerald M Buhrz	415-431-1323	R	1	<0.1
T and B Leather Fashions Inc	230 W 38th St	New York	NY	10018	Roberto Larin	212-221-6622	R	1	<0.1
Leathers and Inc	10 E 33rd St	New York	NY	10016	CJ Leffeld	212-683-7460	R	1*	<0.1

Source: *Ward's Business Directory of U.S. Private and Public Companies*, Volumes 1 and 2, 1996. The company type code used is as follows: P - Public, R - Private, S - Subsidiary, D - Division, J - Joint Venture, A - Affiliate, G - Group. Sales are in millions of dollars, employees are in thousands. An asterisk (*) indicates an estimated sales volume. The symbol < stands for 'less than'. Company names and addresses are truncated, in some cases, to fit into the available space.

MATERIALS CONSUMED

Material	Quantity	Delivered Cost ($ million)
Materials, ingredients, containers, and supplies	(X)	107.5
Broadwoven fabrics (piece goods)	(X)	(D)
Narrow fabrics (12 inches or less in width)	(X)	1.5
Finished leather	(X)	80.1
Buttons, zippers, and slide fasteners	(X)	4.6
All other materials and components, parts, containers, and supplies	(X)	6.6
Materials, ingredients, containers, and supplies, nsk	(X)	7.2

Source: 1992 *Economic Census*. Explanation of symbols used: (D): Withheld to avoid disclosure of competitive data; na: Not available; (S): Withheld because statistical norms were not met; (X): Not applicable; (Z): Less than half the unit shown; nec: Not elsewhere classified; nsk: Not specified by kind; - : zero; * : 10-19 percent estimated; ** : 20-29 percent estimated.

PRODUCT SHARE DETAILS

Product or Product Class	% Share	Product or Product Class	% Share
Leather and sheep-lined clothing	100.00	All other leather clothing and sheep-lined clothing, including children's	14.02
Men's and boys' leather coats and jackets	49.40		
Women's, misses', and juniors' leather coats and jackets	30.35		

Source: 1992 *Economic Census*. The values shown are percent of total shipments in an industry. Values of indented subcategories are summed in the main heading. The symbol (D) appears when data are withheld to prevent disclosure of competitive information. The abbreviation nsk stands for 'not specified by kind' and nec for 'not elsewhere classified'.

INPUTS AND OUTPUTS FOR TEXTILE GOODS, NEC

Economic Sector or Industry Providing Inputs	%	Sector	Economic Sector or Industry Buying Outputs	%	Sector
Imports	37.3	Foreign	Yarn mills & finishing of textiles, nec	17.8	Manufg.
Meat animals	23.8	Agric.	Broadwoven fabric mills	15.8	Manufg.
Textile goods, nec	6.5	Manufg.	Exports	8.8	Foreign
Noncomparable imports	6.1	Foreign	Agricultural, forestry, & fishery services	8.6	Agric.
Advertising	3.0	Services	Floor coverings	6.8	Manufg.
Wholesale trade	2.6	Trade	Housefurnishings, nec	5.3	Manufg.
Yarn mills & finishing of textiles, nec	2.5	Manufg.	Textile goods, nec	4.1	Manufg.
Electric services (utilities)	2.1	Util.	Nonwoven fabrics	4.0	Manufg.
Cyclic crudes and organics	1.6	Manufg.	Prepared feeds, nec	3.7	Manufg.
Chemical preparations, nec	1.1	Manufg.	Knit outerwear mills	2.9	Manufg.
Paperboard containers & boxes	1.1	Manufg.	Coated fabrics, not rubberized	2.6	Manufg.
Motor freight transportation & warehousing	1.1	Util.	Felt goods, nec	2.3	Manufg.
Petroleum refining	1.0	Manufg.	Cordage & twine	2.2	Manufg.
U.S. Postal Service	1.0	Gov't	Dairy farm products	1.9	Agric.
Gas production & distribution (utilities)	0.9	Util.	Automotive & apparel trimmings	1.9	Manufg.
Laundry, dry cleaning, shoe repair	0.9	Services	Shoes, except rubber	1.9	Manufg.
Textile machinery	0.7	Manufg.	House slippers	1.4	Manufg.
Industrial gases	0.6	Manufg.	Padding & upholstery filling	1.4	Manufg.
Eating & drinking places	0.6	Trade	Greenhouse & nursery products	0.9	Agric.
Wood products, nec	0.4	Manufg.	Boot & shoe cutstock & findings	0.9	Manufg.
Banking	0.4	Fin/R.E.	Machinery, except electrical, nec	0.8	Manufg.
Equipment rental & leasing services	0.4	Services	Paper coating & glazing	0.7	Manufg.
Lubricating oils & greases	0.3	Manufg.	Processed textile waste	0.7	Manufg.
Real estate	0.3	Fin/R.E.	Commercial fishing	0.3	Agric.
Maintenance of nonfarm buildings nec	0.2	Constr.	Boat building & repairing	0.3	Manufg.

Continued on next page.

INPUTS AND OUTPUTS FOR TEXTILE GOODS, NEC - Continued

Economic Sector or Industry Providing Inputs	%	Sector	Economic Sector or Industry Buying Outputs	%	Sector
Industrial inorganic chemicals, nec	0.2	Manufg.	Pleating & stitching	0.3	Manufg.
Machinery, except electrical, nec	0.2	Manufg.	Soap & other detergents	0.3	Manufg.
Communications, except radio & TV	0.2	Util.	Cereal breakfast foods	0.2	Manufg.
Water supply & sewage systems	0.2	Util.	Dog, cat, & other pet food	0.2	Manufg.
Accounting, auditing & bookkeeping	0.2	Services	Motion pictures	0.2	Services
Legal services	0.2	Services	Forestry products	0.1	Agric.
Management & consulting services & labs	0.2	Services	Abrasive products	0.1	Manufg.
Railroads & related services	0.1	Util.	Lace goods	0.1	Manufg.
Royalties	0.1	Fin/R.E.			
Business/professional associations	0.1	Services			
State & local government enterprises, nec	0.1	Gov't			

Source: *Benchmark Input-Output Accounts for the U.S. Economy, 1982*, U.S. Department of Commerce, Washington, D.C., July 1991. Data, as reported in the source, are organized by the 1977 SIC structure in use in 1982 but have been matched, as closely as is possible, to the 1987 SIC structure used in this book.

OCCUPATIONS EMPLOYED BY SIC 238 - APPAREL

Occupation	% of Total 1994	Change to 2005	Occupation	% of Total 1994	Change to 2005
Sewing machine operators, garment	56.1	-33.1	Cutters & trimmers, hand	1.7	-24.8
Inspectors, testers, & graders, precision	3.5	-16.4	Patternmakers, layout workers, fabric & apparel	1.5	25.4
Blue collar worker supervisors	3.0	-24.0	General managers & top executives	1.4	-20.7
Assemblers, fabricators, & hand workers nec	2.5	-16.4	Sewing machine operators, non-garment	1.3	-37.3
Pressing machine operators, textiles	2.4	-45.7	Helpers, laborers, & material movers nec	1.1	-16.4
Hand packers & packagers	2.0	-21.2	Industrial machinery mechanics	1.1	0.3
Freight, stock, & material movers, hand	1.8	-33.1	Pressers, hand	1.1	-58.2
Traffic, shipping, & receiving clerks	1.8	-19.6	Sewers, hand	1.0	-10.7

Source: *Industry-Occupation Matrix*, Bureau of Labor Statistics. These data relate to one or more 3-digit SIC industry groups rather than to a single 4-digit SIC. The change reported for each occupation to the year 2005 is a percent of growth or decline as estimated by the Bureau of Labor Statistics. The abbreviation nec stands for 'not elsewhere classified'.

LOCATION BY STATE AND REGIONAL CONCENTRATION

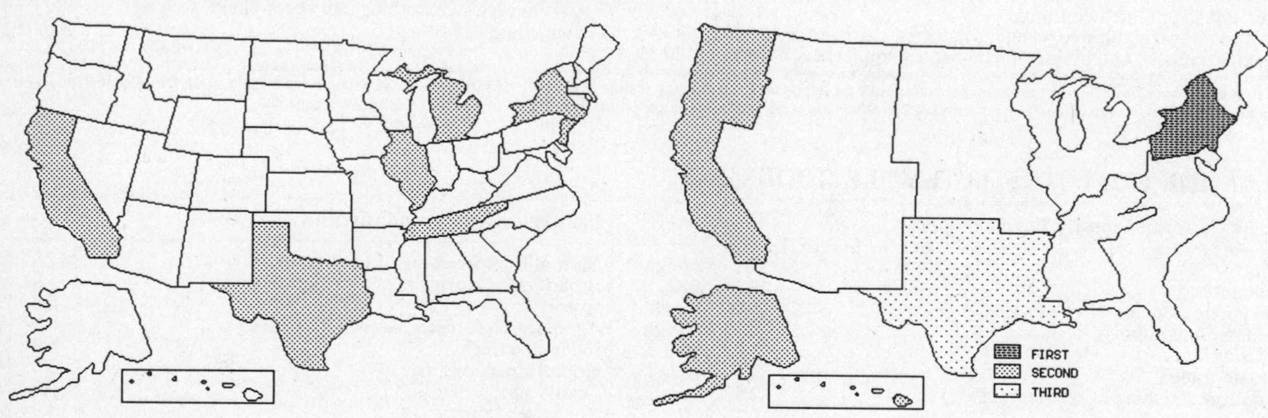

INDUSTRY DATA BY STATE

State	Establish-ments	Shipments			Employment				Cost as % of Shipments	Investment per Employee ($)
		Total ($ mil)	% of U.S.	Per Establ.	Total Number	% of U.S.	Per Establ.	Wages ($/hour)		
California	24	62.1	29.7	2.6	900	36.0	38	8.07	61.5	556
New York	50	33.4	16.0	0.7	400	16.0	8	7.33	55.7	-
Texas	6	(D)	-	-	175 *	7.0	29	-	-	-
New Jersey	5	(D)	-	-	375 *	15.0	75	-	-	-
Illinois	3	(D)	-	-	175 *	7.0	58	-	-	-
Michigan	2	(D)	-	-	175 *	7.0	88	-	-	-
Tennessee	2	(D)	-	-	175 *	7.0	88	-	-	-

Source: 1992 *Economic Census*. The states are in descending order of shipments or establishments (if shipment data are missing for the majority). The symbol (D) appears when data are withheld to prevent disclosure of competitive information. States marked with (D) are sorted by number of establishments. A dash (-) indicates that the data element cannot be calculated; * indicates the midpoint of a range.

2387 - APPAREL BELTS

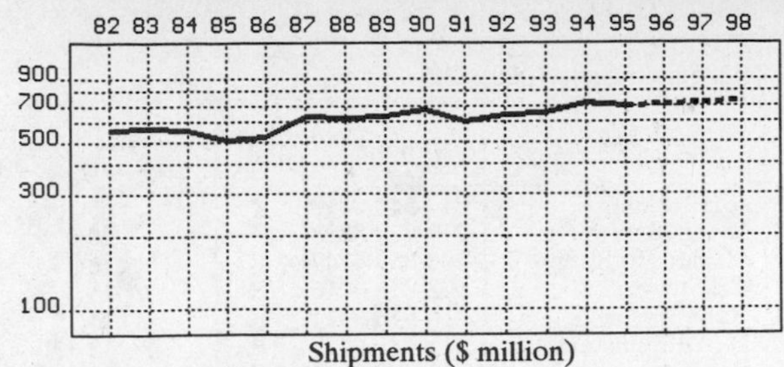

Shipments ($ million)

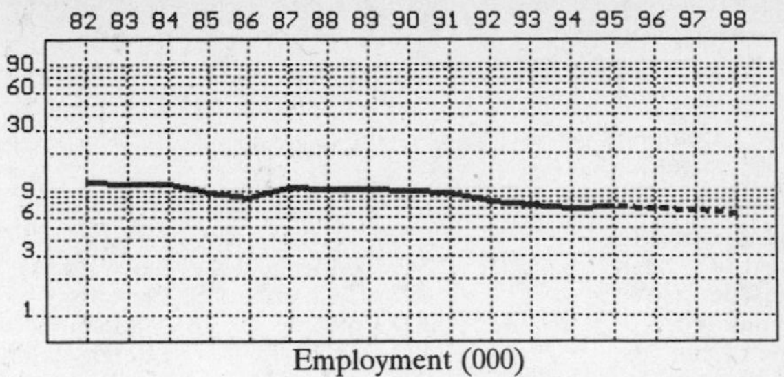

Employment (000)

GENERAL STATISTICS

Year	Companies	Establishments: Total	Establishments: with 20 or more employees	Employment: Total (000)	Employment: Production Workers (000)	Employment: Production Hours (Mil)	Compensation: Payroll ($ mil)	Compensation: Wages ($/hr)	Production: Cost of Materials	Production: Value Added by Manufacture	Production: Value of Shipments	Production: Capital Invest.
1982	317	319	143	11.7	9.2	17.2	137.1	4.74	250.6	305.4	556.5	8.3
1983		306	137	11.1	8.7	17.1	138.2	4.76	245.3	318.2	568.8	6.9
1984		293	131	11.1	8.9	17.3	136.6	4.64	252.5	299.8	551.7	5.6
1985		281	124	9.5	7.5	13.8	120.5	5.12	223.4	278.3	504.9	2.2
1986		260	109	8.8	6.9	12.9	116.5	5.46	229.2	293.7	521.0	2.5
1987	264	265	126	10.5	7.8	14.8	151.0	5.78	294.5	339.5	627.8	3.1
1988		255	121	10.1	7.7	15.1	153.6	5.84	285.7	337.3	618.6	2.8
1989		234	123	10.2	8.6	16.5	165.0	6.07	268.0	371.3	634.5	4.5
1990		240	110	9.8	8.4	15.4	175.4	6.31	296.7	386.1	673.4	3.5
1991		239	95	9.6	7.2	13.5	160.4	6.54	269.0	344.8	603.2	3.0
1992	245	245	85	8.0	6.1	11.3	150.6	7.19	305.3	343.8	639.6	5.2
1993		232	84	7.6	5.7	10.7	142.8	6.51	317.1	323.5	642.3	3.1
1994		215P	84P	7.1	5.4	11.2	152.7	7.13	331.1	394.6	718.7	4.9
1995		207P	79P	7.5P	5.8P	11.1P	162.5P	7.37P	319.3P	380.5P	693.1P	2.9P
1996		199P	74P	7.2P	5.5P	10.6P	164.8P	7.59P	325.1P	387.5P	705.7P	2.7P
1997		192P	69P	6.9P	5.3P	10.1P	167.2P	7.81P	330.9P	394.4P	718.4P	2.5P
1998		184P	64P	6.6P	5.0P	9.6P	169.5P	8.03P	336.8P	401.4P	731.0P	2.3P

Sources: 1982, 1987, 1992 *Economic Census*; *Annual Survey of Manufactures*, 83-86, 88-91, 93-94. Establishment counts for non-Census years are from *County Business Patterns*; establishment values for 83-84 are extrapolations. 'P's show projections by the editors. Industries reclassified in 87 will not have data for prior years.

INDICES OF CHANGE

Year	Companies	Establishments: Total	Establishments: with 20 or more employees	Employment: Total (000)	Employment: Production Workers (000)	Employment: Production Hours (Mil)	Compensation: Payroll ($ mil)	Compensation: Wages ($/hr)	Production: Cost of Materials	Production: Value Added by Manufacture	Production: Value of Shipments	Production: Capital Invest.
1982	129	130	168	146	151	152	91	66	82	89	87	160
1983		125	161	139	143	151	92	66	80	93	89	133
1984		120	154	139	146	153	91	65	83	87	86	108
1985		115	146	119	123	122	80	71	73	81	79	42
1986		106	128	110	113	114	77	76	75	85	81	48
1987	108	108	148	131	128	131	100	80	96	99	98	60
1988		104	142	126	126	134	102	81	94	98	97	54
1989		96	145	127	141	146	110	84	88	108	99	87
1990		98	129	123	138	136	116	88	97	112	105	67
1991		98	112	120	118	119	107	91	88	100	94	58
1992	100	100	100	100	100	100	100	100	100	100	100	100
1993		95	99	95	93	95	95	91	104	94	100	60
1994		88P	99P	89	89	99	101	99	108	115	112	94
1995		84P	93P	94P	95P	98P	108P	103P	105P	111P	108P	56P
1996		81P	87P	90P	90P	94P	109P	106P	106P	113P	110P	52P
1997		78P	81P	86P	86P	89P	111P	109P	108P	115P	112P	49P
1998		75P	76P	82P	82P	85P	113P	112P	110P	117P	114P	45P

Sources: Same as General Statistics. Values reflect change from the base year, 1992. Values above 100 mean greater than 92, values below 100 mean less than 92, and a value of 100 in the 82-91 or 93-98 period means same as 92. 'P's mark projections by the editors.

SELECTED RATIOS

For 1994	Avg. of All Manufact.	Analyzed Industry	Index	For 1994	Avg. of All Manufact.	Analyzed Industry	Index
Employees per Establishment	49	33	68	Value Added per Production Worker	134,084	73,074	54
Payroll per Establishment	1,500,273	711,536	47	Cost per Establishment	5,045,178	1,542,827	31
Payroll per Employee	30,620	21,507	70	Cost per Employee	102,970	46,634	45
Production Workers per Establishment	34	25	73	Cost per Production Worker	146,988	61,315	42
Wages per Establishment	853,319	372,105	44	Shipments per Establishment	9,576,895	3,348,927	35
Wages per Production Worker	24,861	14,788	59	Shipments per Employee	195,460	101,225	52
Hours per Production Worker	2,056	2,074	101	Shipments per Production Worker	279,017	133,093	48
Wages per Hour	12.09	7.13	59	Investment per Establishment	321,011	22,833	7
Value Added per Establishment	4,602,255	1,838,718	40	Investment per Employee	6,552	690	11
Value Added per Employee	93,930	55,577	59	Investment per Production Worker	9,352	907	10

Sources: Same as General Statistics. The 'Average of All Manufacturing' column represents the average of all manufacturing industries reported for the most recent complete year available. The Index shows the relationship between the Average and the Analyzed Industry. For example, 100 means that they are equal; 500 that the Analyzed Industry is five times the average; 50 means that the Analyzed Industry is half the national average. The abbreviation 'na' is used to show that data are 'not available'.

LEADING COMPANIES

Number shown: **20** Total sales ($ mil): **192** Total employment (000): **2.5**

Company Name	Address				CEO Name	Phone	Co. Type	Sales ($ mil)	Empl. (000)
Tandy Brands Accessories Inc	690 E Lamar Blv	Arlington	TX	76011	JSB Jenkins	817-548-0090	P	68	0.7
Harmal Industries Inc	3300 Northern Blv	Long Island Ct	NY	11101	Irving Malawer	718-729-8833	S	20	0.1
Trafalgar Ltd	349 Connecticut Av	Norwalk	CT	06854	Marley Hodgson	203-853-4747	R	16*	0.2
Chambers Belt Co	2920 E Chambers St	Phoenix	AZ	85034	CE Stewart	602-276-0016	R	15	0.2
Gem Dandy Inc	PO Box 657	Madison	NC	27025	Rahn Boyer	910-548-9624	R	14	0.2
Bethlehem Lynn	PO Box 20070	Lehigh Valley	PA	18002	N M Braunstein	215-433-6477	R	12	0.2
Tex Tan Western Leather Co	808 S Hwy 77A	Yoakum	TX	77995	Pat Hybner	512-293-2314	R	12	0.3
Lejon Inc	1229 Railroad St	Corona	CA	91720	Jack Shirinian	909-736-1229	R	7	0.1
Max Leather Group Inc	1415 Redfern Av	Far Rockaway	NY	11691	Steven Kahn	718-471-3300	R	5*	<0.1
New England Accessories	PO Box 630	Old Saybrook	CT	06475	Richard Whitney	203-388-3522	D	5	<0.1
Debi Belt Inc	53 Bridge St	Brooklyn	NY	11201	Alan Hangad	718-492-8295	R	3	<0.1
Jameco Metal Products Co	94-34 158th St	Jamaica	NY	11433	Michael Silverman	718-297-2056	R	3	<0.1
Princess Belt and Novelty Inc	9008 Chancellor	Dallas	TX	75247	David Marks	214-638-7770	R	3	<0.1
Dan Dee Belt and Bag Company	PO Box M-461	Hoboken	NJ	07030	Charles Rotondi	201-659-5951	R	2*	<0.1
United Belt of California	585 Howard St	San Francisco	CA	94105	H Schwartz	415-982-8904	R	2	<0.1
Benjamin Worth Inc	929 S Broadway	Los Angeles	CA	90015	Cheryl Trammell	213-623-5748	R	1	<0.1
Crown Pacific USA Inc	16 W 32nd St	New York	NY	10001	Daniel Friedman	212-947-6040	R	1*	<0.1
Austin Trading Company Inc	PO Box 4275	Austin	TX	78765	Peter Eacott	512-452-4828	R	1	<0.1
Berkeley Belt Inc	20 W 36th St	New York	NY	10018	Larry Cohen	212-244-5577	R	1*	<0.1
Kleinberg Sherrill Inc	56 E Andrews NW	Atlanta	GA	30305	William Kleinberg	404-355-2778	R	1	<0.1

Source: *Ward's Business Directory of U.S. Private and Public Companies*, Volumes 1 and 2, 1996. The company type code used is as follows: P - Public, R - Private, S - Subsidiary, D - Division, J - Joint Venture, A - Affiliate, G - Group. Sales are in millions of dollars, employees are in thousands. An asterisk (*) indicates an estimated sales volume. The symbol < stands for 'less than'. Company names and addresses are truncated, in some cases, to fit into the available space.

MATERIALS CONSUMED

Material	Quantity	Delivered Cost ($ million)
Materials, ingredients, containers, and supplies	(X)	229.7
Broadwoven fabrics (piece goods)	(X)	14.6
Narrow fabrics (12 inches or less in width)	(X)	5.4
Knit fabrics	(X)	7.2
Finished leather	(X)	100.4
Buttons, zippers, and slide fasteners	(X)	6.9
All other materials and components, parts, containers, and supplies	(X)	74.9
Materials, ingredients, containers, and supplies, nsk	(X)	20.4

Source: 1992 *Economic Census*. Explanation of symbols used: (D): Withheld to avoid disclosure of competitive data; na: Not available; (S): Withheld because statistical norms were not met; (X): Not applicable; (Z): Less than half the unit shown; nec: Not elsewhere classified; nsk: Not specified by kind; - : zero; * : 10-19 percent estimated; ** : 20-29 percent estimated.

PRODUCT SHARE DETAILS

Product or Product Class	% Share	Product or Product Class	% Share
Apparel belts	100.00	Women's and children's belts other than leather, made for sale to apparel firms	33.76
Leather belts	63.55	Women's and children's belts other than leather, made for sale separately	25.14
Women's and children's leather belts, made for sale to apparel firms	21.40	Men's and boys' belts other than leather, made for sale to apparel firms	20.46
Women's and children's leather belts, made for sale separately	12.49	Men's and boys' belts other than leather, made for sale separately	17.00
Men's and boys' leather belts, made for sale to apparel firms	24.84	Belts other than leather, nsk	3.64
Men's and boys' leather belts, made for sale separately	40.70	Apparel belts, nsk	6.41
Leather belts, nsk.	0.57		
Belts other than leather	30.06		

Source: 1992 *Economic Census*. The values shown are percent of total shipments in an industry. Values of indented subcategories are summed in the main heading. The symbol (D) appears when data are withheld to prevent disclosure of competitive information. The abbreviation nsk stands for 'not specified by kind' and nec for 'not elsewhere classified'.

INPUTS AND OUTPUTS FOR APPAREL MADE FROM PURCHASED MATERIALS

Economic Sector or Industry Providing Inputs	%	Sector	Economic Sector or Industry Buying Outputs	%	Sector
Imports	29.1	Foreign	Personal consumption expenditures	82.7	
Broadwoven fabric mills	20.2	Manufg.	Apparel made from purchased materials	12.0	Manufg.
Apparel made from purchased materials	18.3	Manufg.	Exports	1.5	Foreign
Knit fabric mills	8.6	Manufg.	Federal Government purchases, national defense	0.9	Fed Govt
Wholesale trade	3.8	Trade	S/L Govt. purch., correction	0.5	S/L Govt
Advertising	2.4	Services	Pleating & stitching	0.3	Manufg.
Yarn mills & finishing of textiles, nec	1.4	Manufg.	Knit outerwear mills	0.2	Manufg.
Pleating & stitching	1.1	Manufg.	Hospitals	0.2	Services
Banking	1.1	Fin/R.E.	Laundry, dry cleaning, shoe repair	0.2	Services
Petroleum refining	1.0	Manufg.	S/L Govt. purch., health & hospitals	0.2	S/L Govt
Electric services (utilities)	1.0	Util.	Portrait, photographic studios	0.1	Services
Automotive & apparel trimmings	0.9	Manufg.	S/L Govt. purch., public assistance & relief	0.1	S/L Govt
Needles, pins, & fasteners	0.8	Manufg.			
Thread mills	0.7	Manufg.			
Communications, except radio & TV	0.7	Util.			
Eating & drinking places	0.7	Trade			
U.S. Postal Service	0.7	Gov't			
Leather tanning & finishing	0.5	Manufg.			
Narrow fabric mills	0.5	Manufg.			
Schiffli machine embroideries	0.4	Manufg.			
Motor freight transportation & warehousing	0.4	Util.			
Real estate	0.4	Fin/R.E.			
Royalties	0.4	Fin/R.E.			
Forestry products	0.3	Agric.			
Buttons	0.3	Manufg.			
Paperboard containers & boxes	0.3	Manufg.			
Air transportation	0.3	Util.			
Maintenance of nonfarm buildings nec	0.2	Constr.			
Lace goods	0.2	Manufg.			
Gas production & distribution (utilities)	0.2	Util.			
Automotive rental & leasing, without drivers	0.2	Services			
Electrical repair shops	0.2	Services			
Equipment rental & leasing services	0.2	Services			
Legal services	0.2	Services			
Management & consulting services & labs	0.2	Services			
Artificial trees & flowers	0.1	Manufg.			
Insurance carriers	0.1	Fin/R.E.			
Accounting, auditing & bookkeeping	0.1	Services			
Automotive repair shops & services	0.1	Services			

Source: Benchmark Input-Output Accounts for the U.S. Economy, 1982, U.S. Department of Commerce, Washington, D.C., July 1991. Data, as reported in the source, are organized by the 1977 SIC structure in use in 1982 but have been matched, as closely as is possible, to the 1987 SIC structure used in this book.

OCCUPATIONS EMPLOYED BY SIC 238 - APPAREL

Occupation	% of Total 1994	Change to 2005	Occupation	% of Total 1994	Change to 2005
Sewing machine operators, garment	56.1	-33.1	Cutters & trimmers, hand	1.7	-24.8
Inspectors, testers, & graders, precision	3.5	-16.4	Patternmakers, layout workers, fabric & apparel	1.5	25.4
Blue collar worker supervisors	3.0	-24.0	General managers & top executives	1.4	-20.7
Assemblers, fabricators, & hand workers nec	2.5	-16.4	Sewing machine operators, non-garment	1.3	-37.3
Pressing machine operators, textiles	2.4	-45.7	Helpers, laborers, & material movers nec	1.1	-16.4
Hand packers & packagers	2.0	-21.2	Industrial machinery mechanics	1.1	0.3
Freight, stock, & material movers, hand	1.8	-33.1	Pressers, hand	1.1	-58.2
Traffic, shipping, & receiving clerks	1.8	-19.6	Sewers, hand	1.0	-10.7

Source: Industry-Occupation Matrix, Bureau of Labor Statistics. These data relate to one or more 3-digit SIC industry groups rather than to a single 4-digit SIC. The change reported for each occupation to the year 2005 is a percent of growth or decline as estimated by the Bureau of Labor Statistics. The abbreviation nec stands for 'not elsewhere classified'.

LOCATION BY STATE AND REGIONAL CONCENTRATION

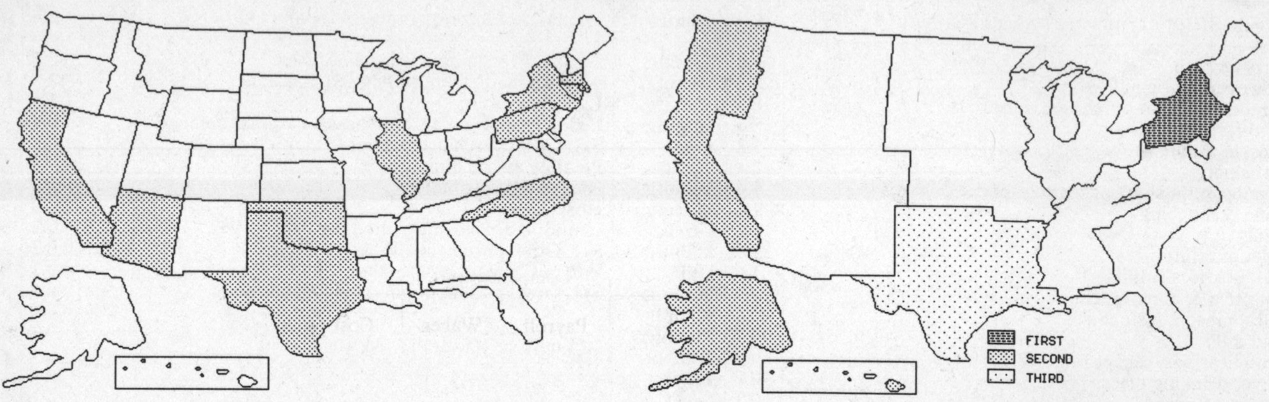

INDUSTRY DATA BY STATE

State	Establish-ments	Shipments			Employment				Cost as % of Shipments	Investment per Employee ($)
		Total ($ mil)	% of U.S.	Per Establ.	Total Number	% of U.S.	Per Establ.	Wages ($/hour)		
New York	116	160.1	25.0	1.4	2,200	27.5	19	7.26	51.7	318
California	44	149.5	23.4	3.4	2,000	25.0	45	7.38	39.3	1,200
Texas	18	56.0	8.8	3.1	1,000	12.5	56	5.50	46.4	100
Pennsylvania	9	25.6	4.0	2.8	300	3.8	33	8.00	53.9	333
Connecticut	6	(D)	-	-	750 *	9.4	125	-	-	-
Massachusetts	4	(D)	-	-	375 *	4.7	94	-	-	-
Rhode Island	4	(D)	-	-	175 *	2.2	44	-	-	-
Illinois	3	(D)	-	-	750 *	9.4	250	-	-	-
North Carolina	3	(D)	-	-	175 *	2.2	58	-	-	-
Arizona	2	(D)	-	-	175 *	2.2	88	-	-	-
Oklahoma	1	(D)	-	-	175 *	2.2	175	-	-	-

Source: 1992 *Economic Census*. The states are in descending order of shipments or establishments (if shipment data are missing for the majority). The symbol (D) appears when data are withheld to prevent disclosure of competitive information. States marked with (D) are sorted by number of establishments. A dash (-) indicates that the data element cannot be calculated; * indicates the midpoint of a range.

2389 - APPAREL AND ACCESSORIES, NEC

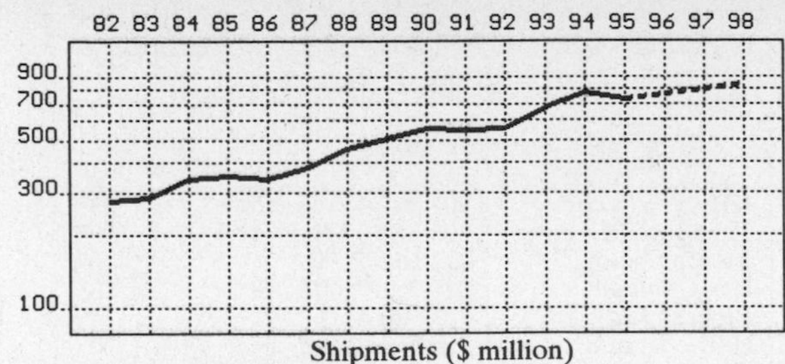

Shipments ($ million)

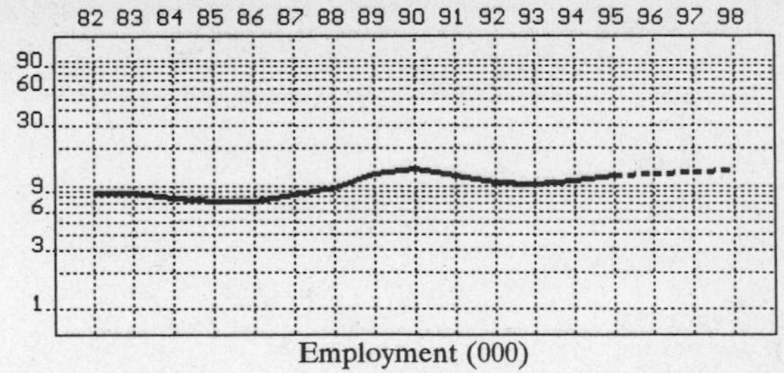

Employment (000)

GENERAL STATISTICS

Year	Com-panies	Establishments		Employment			Compensation		Production ($ million)			
		Total	with 20 or more employees	Total (000)	Production Workers (000)	Production Hours (Mil)	Payroll ($ mil)	Wages ($/hr)	Cost of Materials	Value Added by Manufacture	Value of Shipments	Capital Invest.
1982	362	369	109	8.7	7.1	12.6	86.2	4.72	125.6	152.7	279.2	3.6
1983		348	112	8.8	7.0	12.8	89.1	4.85	130.2	153.9	283.5	1.2
1984		327	115	7.9	6.5	12.2	83.2	4.93	162.7	200.0	340.3	5.8
1985		306	117	7.5	6.4	11.9	81.7	5.30	161.3	193.6	350.0	1.7
1986		293	106	7.4	6.4	12.1	85.2	5.36	153.4	190.5	344.0	2.5
1987	332	340	105	8.3	6.5	11.5	98.1	5.61	166.9	220.8	383.4	2.9
1988		420	122	9.4	7.5	13.2	117.9	5.70	191.8	262.4	454.0	3.0
1989		388	151	12.3	8.9	15.6	141.0	6.10	221.8	293.2	503.3	2.7
1990		403	157	13.4	9.6	16.4	143.4	5.74	227.1	333.8	550.1	4.1
1991		404	153	11.8	9.9	17.7	154.7	5.82	230.9	309.8	542.3	4.5
1992	403	407	123	10.4	8.5	14.7	149.2	6.93	240.6	316.5	552.9	5.4
1993		439	118	10.3	8.1	13.4	148.7	7.69	315.8	360.8	668.5	9.3
1994		431P	143P	10.9	8.9	16.2	168.9	6.96	346.7	442.7	772.9	8.2
1995		441P	145P	12.1P	9.5P	16.4P	174.3P	7.30P	326.0P	416.3P	726.7P	7.2P
1996		450P	148P	12.4P	9.7P	16.7P	182.2P	7.51P	342.9P	437.8P	764.4P	7.6P
1997		460P	151P	12.7P	9.9P	17.1P	190.1P	7.73P	359.7P	459.4P	802.0P	8.1P
1998		469P	154P	13.1P	10.2P	17.4P	198.0P	7.94P	376.6P	480.9P	839.6P	8.5P

Sources: 1982, 1987, 1992 *Economic Census*; *Annual Survey of Manufactures*, 83-86, 88-91, 93-94. Establishment counts for non-Census years are from *County Business Patterns*; establishment values for 83-84 are extrapolations. 'P's show projections by the editors. Industries reclassified in 87 will not have data for prior years.

INDICES OF CHANGE

Year	Com-panies	Establishments		Employment			Compensation		Production ($ million)			
		Total	with 20 or more employees	Total (000)	Production Workers (000)	Production Hours (Mil)	Payroll ($ mil)	Wages ($/hr)	Cost of Materials	Value Added by Manufacture	Value of Shipments	Capital Invest.
1982	90	91	89	84	84	86	58	68	52	48	50	67
1983		86	91	85	82	87	60	70	54	49	51	22
1984		80	93	76	76	83	56	71	68	63	62	107
1985		75	95	72	75	81	55	76	67	61	63	31
1986		72	86	71	75	82	57	77	64	60	62	46
1987	82	84	85	80	76	78	66	81	69	70	69	54
1988		103	99	90	88	90	79	82	80	83	82	56
1989		95	123	118	105	106	95	88	92	93	91	50
1990		99	128	129	113	112	96	83	94	105	99	76
1991		99	124	113	116	120	104	84	96	98	98	83
1992	100	100	100	100	100	100	100	100	100	100	100	100
1993		108	96	99	95	91	100	111	131	114	121	172
1994		106P	116P	105	105	110	113	100	144	140	140	152
1995		108P	118P	116P	111P	111P	117P	105P	135P	132P	131P	134P
1996		111P	121P	119P	114P	114P	122P	108P	143P	138P	138P	142P
1997		113P	123P	122P	117P	116P	127P	111P	150P	145P	145P	150P
1998		115P	125P	125P	120P	119P	133P	115P	157P	152P	152P	157P

Sources: Same as General Statistics. Values reflect change from the base year, 1992. Values above 100 mean greater than 92, values below 100 mean less than 92, and a value of 100 in the 82-91 or 93-98 period means same as 92. 'P's mark projections by the editors.

SELECTED RATIOS

For 1994	Avg. of All Manufact.	Analyzed Industry	Index	For 1994	Avg. of All Manufact.	Analyzed Industry	Index
Employees per Establishment	49	25	52	Value Added per Production Worker	134,084	49,742	37
Payroll per Establishment	1,500,273	391,453	26	Cost per Establishment	5,045,178	803,533	16
Payroll per Employee	30,620	15,495	51	Cost per Employee	102,970	31,807	31
Production Workers per Establishment	34	21	60	Cost per Production Worker	146,988	38,955	27
Wages per Establishment	853,319	261,321	31	Shipments per Establishment	9,576,895	1,791,319	19
Wages per Production Worker	24,861	12,669	51	Shipments per Employee	195,460	70,908	36
Hours per Production Worker	2,056	1,820	89	Shipments per Production Worker	279,017	86,843	31
Wages per Hour	12.09	6.96	58	Investment per Establishment	321,011	19,005	6
Value Added per Establishment	4,602,255	1,026,028	22	Investment per Employee	6,552	752	11
Value Added per Employee	93,930	40,615	43	Investment per Production Worker	9,352	921	10

Sources: Same as General Statistics. The 'Average of All Manufacturing' column represents the average of all manufacturing industries reported for the most recent complete year available. The Index shows the relationship between the Average and the Analyzed Industry. For example, 100 means that they are equal; 500 that the Analyzed Industry is five times the average; 50 means that the Analyzed Industry is half the national average. The abbreviation 'na' is used to show that data are 'not available'.

LEADING COMPANIES

Number shown: **42** Total sales ($ mil): **372** Total employment (000): **6.1**

Company Name	Address				CEO Name	Phone	Co. Type	Sales ($ mil)	Empl. (000)
Varsity Spirit Corp	PO Box 341609	Memphis	TN	38184	Jeffrey G Webb	901-387-4300	P	63	1.8
Paris Accessories Inc	350 5th Av	New York	NY	10118	Theodore Markson	212-868-0500	R	50	0.8
I Shalom and Company Inc	411 5th Av	New York	NY	10016	Joseph Shalom	212-532-7911	R	40	0.2
Herff Jones	1000 N Market St	Champaign	IL	61820	Rex Crandall	217-351-9500	D	29*	0.5
Sterile Recoveries Inc	28100 US Hwy 19 N	Clearwater	FL	34621	Richard Isel	813-726-4421	R	26	0.4
Damin Industries Inc	117 S Front St	Burbank	CA	91502	Harry Sagheb	818-563-9749	R	20	<0.1
AJ Siris Products Corp	PO Box AV	Paterson	NJ	07501	Donald F Ryan	201-684-7700	R	15	0.2
Kufner Textile Corp	PO Box 428	Simpsonville	SC	29681	Josef Kufner	803-963-5463	S	12	<0.1
De Moulin Brothers and Co	1000 S 4th St	Greenville	IL	62246	W R De Moulin	618-664-2000	R	11	0.2
Tighe Industries Inc	PO Box 709	York	PA	17405	L King Jr	717-252-1578	R	10*	0.3
Washington Garter Corp	195 Front St	Brooklyn	NY	11201	Sam Susswein	718-852-1255	R	9	0.1
Carolina Manufacturing Inc	PO Box 9138	Greenville	SC	29604	David M Moore	803-299-0600	D	9	<0.1
Lewis Industries	1681 Walton Rd	St Louis	MO	63114	Tom Bearman	314-427-1421	S	7	<0.1
Lockwoven Co	1681 Walton Rd	St Louis	MO	63114	Bernard L Bearman	314-427-2013	R	7*	0.1
Eaves and Brooks Costume Co	21-07 41st Av	Long Island Ct	NY	11101	Daniel Eoly	718-729-1010	R	6	0.1
Graduate Supply House Inc	PO Box 1034	Jackson	MS	39205	Charles L Scott	601-354-5323	R	6	<0.1
Stanbury Uniforms Inc	PO Box 100	Brookfield	MO	64628	Gary F Roberts	816-258-2246	R	6	0.2
Berkshire Handkerchief Inc	1 W 37th St	New York	NY	10018	Ike B Dweck	212-221-1542	R	5	0.1
Melco Inc	PO Box 1754	Wilmington	DE	19899	LS Epstein	302-429-3999	R	5	0.1
Party Professionals Inc	8610 Milliken Av	R Cucamonga	CA	91730	Bill Atcheson	909-944-3559	R	5	<0.1
Cal Themes Inc	5277 Cameron St	Las Vegas	NV	89118	Gary Spiegler	702-251-4461	R	3*	<0.1
Great Cover Up	8610 Milliken Av	R Cucamonga	CA	91730	Bill Atcheson	909-944-3559	D	3	<0.1
Thomas Creative Apparel Inc	1 Harmony Pl	New London	OH	44851	Vicky Hall	419-929-1506	R	3*	<0.1
North River Apparel Inc	PO Box 419	Berry	AL	35546	Larry Johnson	205-689-5259	R	3	0.2
Accessory Street Inc	411 5th Av	New York	NY	10016	Robert Friedlander	212-725-1300	R	2	<0.1
Art Needlecraft Inc	400 1st Av N	Minneapolis	MN	55401	Frederick Gaspard	612-333-7949	R	2	<0.1
Don Post Studios Inc	8610 Milliken Av	R Cucamonga	CA	91730	Bill Atcheson	909-944-3559	D	2	<0.1
Ethel Maid	PO Box 211	Schuylkill Haven	PA	17972	Richard L Gardinier	717-385-2721	D	2	<0.1
Gardinier Associates Inc	202 E Liberty St	Schuylkill Haven	PA	17972	Richard L Gardinier	717-385-2721	R	2	<0.1
J Press Inc	262 York St	New Haven	CT	06511	Takashi Sudo	203-772-1310	R	2*	<0.1
San Brushardi Inc	489 5th Av	New York	NY	10017	Sheldon Sontog	212-986-6611	R	2*	<0.1
Bentley and Simon Inc	PO Box 1078	Salem	VA	24153	Malcolm Rosenberg	703-387-0000	S	1	<0.1
Jan Michaels Inc	590 York St	San Francisco	CA	94110	Jan Michaels	415-621-0101	R	1	<0.1
Joe Benbasset Inc	253 W 35th St	New York	NY	10001	Joe Benbasset	212-594-8440	R	1*	<0.1
Theatrical Accessories Inc	5277 Cameron St	Las Vegas	NV	89118	Gary Spiegler	702-251-4461	R	1*	<0.1
ProtectAide Inc	605 White Hills Dr	Rockwall	TX	75087	Mitchell Davis	214-722-0018	R	1*	<0.1
Oxy-Therm Products Inc	8491 Sunset Blv	Los Angeles	CA	90069	Mark Davis	619-661-7290	R	1*	<0.1
House of Hansen	4223 W Irving Pk	Chicago	IL	60641	Clem P Arens	312-372-8750	R	0*	<0.1
Diaperaps Ltd	PO Box 3050	Granada Hills	CA	91344	Rachel Flug	818-886-7471	R	0*	<0.1
Debra Moises Group	244 W 74th St	New York	NY	10023	Debra Moises	212-496-6811	R	0*	<0.1
CatHouse Fashions Inc	889 Edwards Rd	Parsippany	NJ	07054	Jenny Distler	201-882-5652	R	0*	<0.1
No Moon Co	8681-39 Mallorca	La Jolla	CA	92037	Tim Russell	619-457-4339	R	0	<0.1

Source: *Ward's Business Directory of U.S. Private and Public Companies*, Volumes 1 and 2, 1996. The company type code used is as follows: P - Public, R - Private, S - Subsidiary, D - Division, J - Joint Venture, A - Affiliate, G - Group. Sales are in millions of dollars, employees are in thousands. An asterisk (*) indicates an estimated sales volume. The symbol < stands for 'less than'. Company names and addresses are truncated, in some cases, to fit into the available space.

MATERIALS CONSUMED

Material	Quantity	Delivered Cost ($ million)
Materials, ingredients, containers, and supplies	(X)	184.8
Broadwoven fabrics (piece goods)	(X)	41.9
Narrow fabrics (12 inches or less in width)	(X)	9.3
Knit fabrics	(X)	13.7
Finished leather	(X)	1.3
Buttons, zippers, and slide fasteners	(X)	2.3
All other materials and components, parts, containers, and supplies	(X)	40.9
Materials, ingredients, containers, and supplies, nsk	(X)	75.3

Source: 1992 *Economic Census*. Explanation of symbols used: (D): Withheld to avoid disclosure of competitive data; na: Not available; (S): Withheld because statistical norms were not met; (X): Not applicable; (Z): Less than half the unit shown; nec: Not elsewhere classified; nsk: Not specified by kind; - : zero; * : 10-19 percent estimated; ** : 20-29 percent estimated.

PRODUCT SHARE DETAILS

Product or Product Class	% Share	Product or Product Class	% Share
Apparel and accessories, nec	100.00	Academic caps and gowns, and costumes (including theatrical)	41.50
Garters, hose supporters, arm bands, and suspenders	7.03	Ecclesiastical vestments, special garments for fraternal orders, except tailored clothing and military-type uniforms	12.51
Men's and boys' handkerchiefs	(D)		
Garter belts	3.13		
Burial garments	(D)		

Source: 1992 *Economic Census*. The values shown are percent of total shipments in an industry. Values of indented subcategories are summed in the main heading. The symbol (D) appears when data are withheld to prevent disclosure of competitive information. The abbreviation nsk stands for 'not specified by kind' and nec for 'not elsewhere classified'.

INPUTS AND OUTPUTS FOR APPAREL MADE FROM PURCHASED MATERIALS

Economic Sector or Industry Providing Inputs	%	Sector	Economic Sector or Industry Buying Outputs	%	Sector
Imports	29.1	Foreign	Personal consumption expenditures	82.7	
Broadwoven fabric mills	20.2	Manufg.	Apparel made from purchased materials	12.0	Manufg.
Apparel made from purchased materials	18.3	Manufg.	Exports	1.5	Foreign
Knit fabric mills	8.6	Manufg.	Federal Government purchases, national defense	0.9	Fed Govt
Wholesale trade	3.8	Trade	S/L Govt. purch., correction	0.5	S/L Govt
Advertising	2.4	Services	Pleating & stitching	0.3	Manufg.
Yarn mills & finishing of textiles, nec	1.4	Manufg.	Knit outerwear mills	0.2	Manufg.
Pleating & stitching	1.1	Manufg.	Hospitals	0.2	Services
Banking	1.1	Fin/R.E.	Laundry, dry cleaning, shoe repair	0.2	Services
Petroleum refining	1.0	Manufg.	S/L Govt. purch., health & hospitals	0.2	S/L Govt
Electric services (utilities)	1.0	Util.	Portrait, photographic studios	0.1	Services
Automotive & apparel trimmings	0.9	Manufg.	S/L Govt. purch., public assistance & relief	0.1	S/L Govt
Needles, pins, & fasteners	0.8	Manufg.			
Thread mills	0.7	Manufg.			
Communications, except radio & TV	0.7	Util.			
Eating & drinking places	0.7	Trade			
U.S. Postal Service	0.7	Gov't			
Leather tanning & finishing	0.5	Manufg.			
Narrow fabric mills	0.5	Manufg.			
Schiffli machine embroideries	0.4	Manufg.			
Motor freight transportation & warehousing	0.4	Util.			
Real estate	0.4	Fin/R.E.			
Royalties	0.4	Fin/R.E.			
Forestry products	0.3	Agric.			
Buttons	0.3	Manufg.			
Paperboard containers & boxes	0.3	Manufg.			
Air transportation	0.3	Util.			
Maintenance of nonfarm buildings nec	0.2	Constr.			
Lace goods	0.2	Manufg.			
Gas production & distribution (utilities)	0.2	Util.			
Automotive rental & leasing, without drivers	0.2	Services			
Electrical repair shops	0.2	Services			
Equipment rental & leasing services	0.2	Services			
Legal services	0.2	Services			
Management & consulting services & labs	0.2	Services			
Artificial trees & flowers	0.1	Manufg.			
Insurance carriers	0.1	Fin/R.E.			
Accounting, auditing & bookkeeping	0.1	Services			
Automotive repair shops & services	0.1	Services			

Source: Benchmark Input-Output Accounts for the U.S. Economy, 1982, U.S. Department of Commerce, Washington, D.C., July 1991. Data, as reported in the source, are organized by the 1977 SIC structure in use in 1982 but have been matched, as closely as is possible, to the 1987 SIC structure used in this book.

OCCUPATIONS EMPLOYED BY SIC 238 - APPAREL

Occupation	% of Total 1994	Change to 2005	Occupation	% of Total 1994	Change to 2005
Sewing machine operators, garment	56.1	-33.1	Cutters & trimmers, hand	1.7	-24.8
Inspectors, testers, & graders, precision	3.5	-16.4	Patternmakers, layout workers, fabric & apparel	1.5	25.4
Blue collar worker supervisors	3.0	-24.0	General managers & top executives	1.4	-20.7
Assemblers, fabricators, & hand workers nec	2.5	-16.4	Sewing machine operators, non-garment	1.3	-37.3
Pressing machine operators, textiles	2.4	-45.7	Helpers, laborers, & material movers nec	1.1	-16.4
Hand packers & packagers	2.0	-21.2	Industrial machinery mechanics	1.1	0.3
Freight, stock, & material movers, hand	1.8	-33.1	Pressers, hand	1.1	-58.2
Traffic, shipping, & receiving clerks	1.8	-19.6	Sewers, hand	1.0	-10.7

Source: Industry-Occupation Matrix, Bureau of Labor Statistics. These data relate to one or more 3-digit SIC industry groups rather than to a single 4-digit SIC. The change reported for each occupation to the year 2005 is a percent of growth or decline as estimated by the Bureau of Labor Statistics. The abbreviation nec stands for 'not elsewhere classified'.

LOCATION BY STATE AND REGIONAL CONCENTRATION

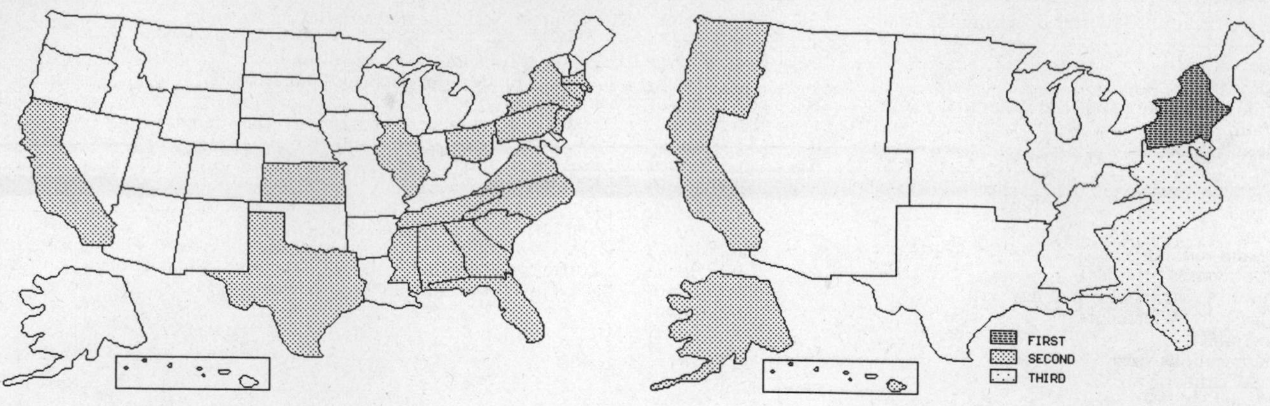

INDUSTRY DATA BY STATE

State	Establish-ments	Shipments Total ($ mil)	Shipments % of U.S.	Shipments Per Establ.	Employment Total Number	Employment % of U.S.	Employment Per Establ.	Wages ($/hour)	Cost as % of Shipments	Investment per Employee ($)
Pennsylvania	32	94.1	17.0	2.9	1,300	12.5	41	8.65	47.3	231
California	71	92.2	16.7	1.3	1,800	17.3	25	6.00	46.1	278
New York	66	61.4	11.1	0.9	1,100	10.6	17	8.31	47.4	182
South Carolina	11	47.4	8.6	4.3	800	7.7	73	6.08	41.6	625
Florida	18	36.6	6.6	2.0	600	5.8	33	6.30	48.9	-
North Carolina	16	17.2	3.1	1.1	200	1.9	13	6.75	60.5	-
Virginia	7	15.5	2.8	2.2	300	2.9	43	7.50	35.5	-
New Jersey	17	15.5	2.8	0.9	400	3.8	24	6.75	52.3	-
Tennessee	9	13.4	2.4	1.5	600	5.8	67	6.45	19.4	-
Georgia	9	13.2	2.4	1.5	400	3.8	44	5.83	51.5	-
Massachusetts	12	11.0	2.0	0.9	200	1.9	17	6.00	48.2	500
Texas	23	10.4	1.9	0.5	300	2.9	13	6.67	46.2	667
Ohio	13	8.0	1.4	0.6	300	2.9	23	6.00	38.8	-
Illinois	20	(D)	-	-	750 *	7.2	38	-	-	-
Alabama	5	(D)	-	-	175 *	1.7	35	-	-	-
Mississippi	4	(D)	-	-	175 *	1.7	44	-	-	-
Connecticut	3	(D)	-	-	175 *	1.7	58	-	-	-
Kansas	1	(D)	-	-	175 *	1.7	175	-	-	-

Source: 1992 *Economic Census*. The states are in descending order of shipments or establishments (if shipment data are missing for the majority). The symbol (D) appears when data are withheld to prevent disclosure of competitive information. States marked with (D) are sorted by number of establishments. A dash (-) indicates that the data element cannot be calculated; * indicates the midpoint of a range.

2391 - CURTAINS AND DRAPERIES

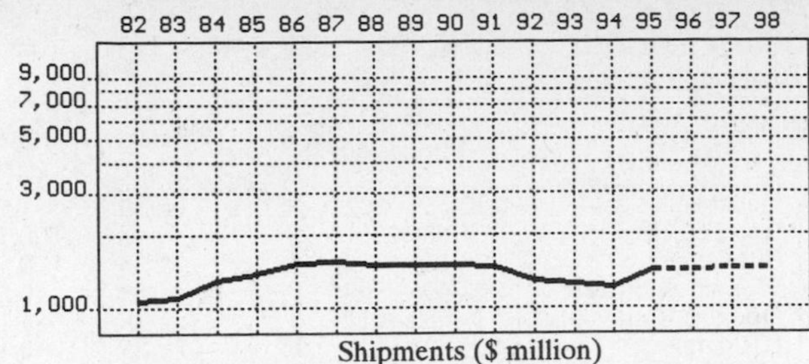

Shipments ($ million)

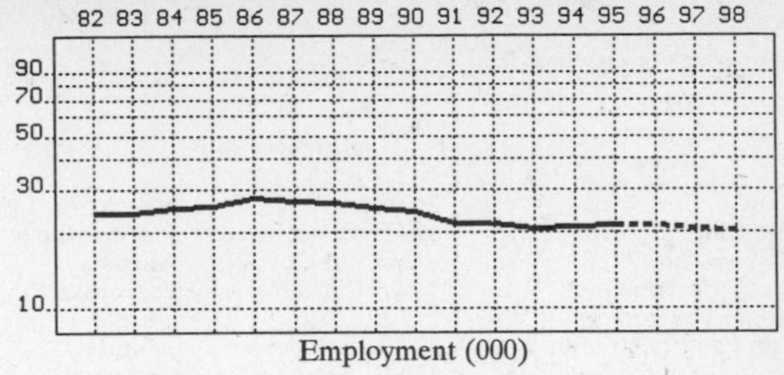

Employment (000)

GENERAL STATISTICS

Year	Com-panies	Establishments		Employment			Compensation		Production ($ million)			
		Total	with 20 or more employees	Total (000)	Production Workers (000)	Production Hours (Mil)	Payroll ($ mil)	Wages ($/hr)	Cost of Materials	Value Added by Manufacture	Value of Shipments	Capital Invest.
1982	1,327	1,371	254	24.1	19.7	33.8	233.7	5.04	614.9	442.1	1,062.0	6.3
1983		1,342	253	24.0	19.8	34.4	232.5	4.89	644.8	462.0	1,098.0	4.0
1984		1,313	252	25.2	21.0	35.6	272.4	5.43	727.4	562.0	1,282.7	7.5
1985		1,284	252	25.6	20.5	38.4	300.3	5.25	785.4	589.1	1,379.0	6.8
1986		1,254	254	27.8	22.6	43.6	323.5	5.19	852.9	685.6	1,530.7	10.4
1987	1,221	1,250	239	27.1	21.4	39.3	342.7	5.85	823.6	720.1	1,539.6	14.9
1988		1,175	247	26.3	21.0	37.5	338.1	5.93	809.1	700.3	1,496.1	10.4
1989		1,132	229	25.2	19.4	35.9	331.7	6.21	867.4	653.8	1,502.7	12.0
1990		1,115	220	24.5	18.5	34.4	329.5	6.28	824.8	685.4	1,499.2	10.5
1991		1,073	192	21.7	17.0	31.4	320.7	6.68	789.6	677.3	1,461.9	14.7
1992	1,004	1,040	177	21.8	16.7	31.2	337.3	7.02	690.2	593.3	1,284.1	16.1
1993		987	161	20.7	15.6	29.5	311.9	7.28	662.1	581.4	1,248.9	16.8
1994		969P	174P	21.1	16.1	30.0	325.8	7.05	639.5	582.5	1,218.8	17.4
1995		935P	166P	21.6P	16.1P	30.9P	356.6P	7.44P	747.8P	681.2P	1,425.3P	18.5P
1996		900P	158P	21.2P	15.6P	30.3P	363.6P	7.64P	753.2P	686.0P	1,435.4P	19.5P
1997		866P	149P	20.9P	15.2P	29.7P	370.6P	7.85P	758.5P	690.9P	1,445.6P	20.6P
1998		831P	141P	20.5P	14.8P	29.1P	377.6P	8.05P	763.8P	695.8P	1,455.8P	21.6P

Sources: 1982, 1987, 1992 *Economic Census*; *Annual Survey of Manufactures*, 83-86, 88-91, 93-94. Establishment counts for non-Census years are from *County Business Patterns*; establishment values for 83-84 are extrapolations. 'P's show projections by the editors. Industries reclassified in 87 will not have data for prior years.

INDICES OF CHANGE

Year	Com-panies	Establishments		Employment			Compensation		Production ($ million)			
		Total	with 20 or more employees	Total (000)	Production Workers (000)	Production Hours (Mil)	Payroll ($ mil)	Wages ($/hr)	Cost of Materials	Value Added by Manufacture	Value of Shipments	Capital Invest.
1982	132	132	144	111	118	108	69	72	89	75	83	39
1983		129	143	110	119	110	69	70	93	78	86	25
1984		126	142	116	126	114	81	77	105	95	100	47
1985		123	142	117	123	123	89	75	114	99	107	42
1986		121	144	128	135	140	96	74	124	116	119	65
1987	122	120	135	124	128	126	102	83	119	121	120	93
1988		113	140	121	126	120	100	84	117	118	117	65
1989		109	129	116	116	115	98	88	126	110	117	75
1990		107	124	112	111	110	98	89	120	116	117	65
1991		103	108	100	102	101	95	95	114	114	114	91
1992	100	100	100	100	100	100	100	100	100	100	100	100
1993		95	91	95	93	95	92	104	96	98	97	104
1994		93P	98P	97	96	96	97	100	93	98	95	108
1995		90P	94P	99P	96P	99P	106P	106P	108P	115P	111P	115P
1996		87P	89P	97P	94P	97P	108P	109P	109P	116P	112P	121P
1997		83P	84P	96P	91P	95P	110P	112P	110P	116P	113P	128P
1998		80P	80P	94P	88P	93P	112P	115P	111P	117P	113P	134P

Sources: Same as General Statistics. Values reflect change from the base year, 1992. Values above 100 mean greater than 92, values below 100 mean less than 92, and a value of 100 in the 82-91 or 93-98 period means same as 92. 'P's mark projections by the editors.

SELECTED RATIOS

For 1994	Avg. of All Manufact.	Analyzed Industry	Index	For 1994	Avg. of All Manufact.	Analyzed Industry	Index
Employees per Establishment	49	22	44	Value Added per Production Worker	134,084	36,180	27
Payroll per Establishment	1,500,273	336,055	22	Cost per Establishment	5,045,178	659,629	13
Payroll per Employee	30,620	15,441	50	Cost per Employee	102,970	30,308	29
Production Workers per Establishment	34	17	48	Cost per Production Worker	146,988	39,720	27
Wages per Establishment	853,319	218,157	26	Shipments per Establishment	9,576,895	1,257,163	13
Wages per Production Worker	24,861	13,137	53	Shipments per Employee	195,460	57,763	30
Hours per Production Worker	2,056	1,863	91	Shipments per Production Worker	279,017	75,702	27
Wages per Hour	12.09	7.05	58	Investment per Establishment	321,011	17,948	6
Value Added per Establishment	4,602,255	600,835	13	Investment per Employee	6,552	825	13
Value Added per Employee	93,930	27,607	29	Investment per Production Worker	9,352	1,081	12

Sources: Same as General Statistics. The 'Average of All Manufacturing' column represents the average of all manufacturing industries reported for the most recent complete year available. The Index shows the relationship between the Average and the Analyzed Industry. For example, 100 means that they are equal; 500 that the Analyzed Industry is five times the average; 50 means that the Analyzed Industry is half the national average. The abbreviation 'na' is used to show that data are 'not available'.

LEADING COMPANIES

Number shown: **41** Total sales ($ mil): **575** Total employment (000): **8.4**

Company Name	Address				CEO Name	Phone	Co. Type	Sales ($ mil)	Empl. (000)
Croscill Inc	261 5th Av	New York	NY	10016	David Kahn	212-689-7222	R	150	1.5
Draymore Manufacturing Corp	150 By-Pass Rd	Mooresville	NC	28115	Bob Fotsch	704-664-2711	S	46	0.7
Carole Fabrics Inc	PO Box 1436-13	Augusta	GA	30913	Bill Geiger	706-863-4742	R	35•	0.5
Decorator Industries Inc	10011 Pines Blv	Pembroke Pines	FL	33024	William A Bassett	305-436-8909	P	33	0.5
Royal Home Fashions Inc	PO Box 930	Durham	NC	27702	Douglas Kahn	919-683-8011	S	26	1.1
Robertson Factories Inc	33 Chandler Av	Taunton	MA	02780	RR Anglin	508-823-5141	R	25	0.3
Curtain and Drapery Fashions	420 W Franklin	Gastonia	NC	28052	Johnnie E Nichols	704-861-8416	R	22•	0.3
Cadillac Curtain Corp	261 5th Av	New York	NY	10016	Seymour Brown	212-679-3684	R	20	0.4
Marietta Drapery	PO Box 569	Marietta	GA	30061	Jack Bentley	404-428-3335	R	20	0.3
Corona Curtain Manufacturing	23 Drydock Av	Boston	MA	02210	Paul Sheiber	617-350-6970	S	18	0.2
Curtron Curtains Inc	PO Box 248	Travelers Rest	SC	29690	Gerald Greenberg	803-834-7217	R	16	0.3
Max Kahn Curtain Corp	PO Box 470	Evergreen	AL	36401	Steven Markowitz	334-578-1720	R	16	0.2
Weeks Textile Co	PO Box 112	Quitman	GA	31643	RC Weeks	912-263-4123	R	15•	0.2
Wesco Fabrics Inc	4001 Forest St	Denver	CO	80216	Richard Gentry	303-388-4101	R	14	0.2
Steven Fabrics Co	1400 Van Buren NE	Minneapolis	MN	55413	R M Schommer	612-781-6671	R	12	0.1
Custom Drapery and Blinds Inc	1312 Live Oak St	Houston	TX	77003	AR Klein	713-225-9211	R	10	0.1
Dirigo Inc	11 Steward Av	Skowhegan	ME	04976	Peter Schultz	207-474-8421	R	10•	0.1
Mitchel Manufacturing Company	PO Box F	Honea Path	SC	29654	Mitchel Butchwalter	803-369-2831	R	10•	0.1
Bay State Curtain Manufacturing	PO Box 2267	Fitchburg	MA	01420	T Zonderman	508-343-6984	R	9	<0.1
Charm House Fabrics	PO Box 1376	Sumter	SC	29150	Melanie Brown	803-775-2388	D	9•	0.1
Stanwood Drapery Company Inc	27 Drydock Av	Boston	MA	02210	MS Burack	617-737-1566	R	7	0.1
Imperial Fabrics	PO Box 1886	Elkhart	IN	46515	Clark Peters	219-293-2575	D	6	0.1
Richmark International Inc	PO Box 426	Boston	MA	02128	John Levanchy	617-569-6353	R	5	0.2
Anthony House Inc	1819 Kahai St	Honolulu	HI	96819	Theodore K Taketa	808-841-4521	R	4•	<0.1
Arlee Home Fashions Inc	261 5th Av	New York	NY	10016	Bud Frankel	212-689-0020	R	4•	<0.1
Kenney Drapery Associates Inc	135 E 144th St	Bronx	NY	10451	Dean Belmont	718-665-9200	R	4	<0.1
Charles Curtain Company Inc	1352 Crampton St	Dallas	TX	75207	Charles M Ross	214-630-7967	R	3	<0.1
Janson Industries	1200 Garfield SW	Canton	OH	44706	R Janson	216-455-2241	R	3•	<0.1
Seattle Curtains Mfg Co	104 12th Av	Seattle	WA	98122	Morrie Capeluto	206-324-0692	R	3	<0.1
GLK Inc	PO Box 353	Milford	DE	19963	Herbert Konowitz	302-422-8021	R	3	<0.1
Lady Linda Covers Inc	PO Box 353	Milford	DE	19963	H H Konowitz	302-422-8021	S	3	<0.1
Lachina Draperies Co	6401 Penn Av	Pittsburgh	PA	15206	Patsy Lachina	412-665-4900	R	2•	<0.1
Leonard's Draperies Inc	10441 Rhode Island	Beltsville	MD	20705	Jay Marks	301-441-2600	R	2	<0.1
Merrill Y Landis Ltd	PO Box 249	Telford	PA	18969	Richard Landis	215-723-8177	R	2	0.1
National Curtain Corp	261 5th Av	New York	NY	10016	Aaron Jacoby	212-685-7575	R	2	<0.1
Penn Needle Art Co	6945 Lynn Way	Pittsburgh	PA	15208	L Berger	412-441-7551	R	2	<0.1
Trends of Hawaii	1804 Hart St	Honolulu	HI	96819	A Shintani	808-841-8731	R	2•	<0.1
Bautex Window Automation	10827 Alder Cir	Dallas	TX	75238	Jon Virlenk	214-343-1610	S	1	<0.1
Custom Fabricating Industries	1703 E End Av	Chicago Hts	IL	60411	Carol Hemmer	708-756-1350	R	1	<0.1
M and S Drapery Workroom	3933 W Irving Pk	Chicago	IL	60618	Hyman Mann	312-583-7906	R	1	<0.1
Aero Drapery Corp	PO Box 419	Westfield	IN	46074	Ed Mullins	317-896-2521	R	1	<0.1

Source: *Ward's Business Directory of U.S. Private and Public Companies*, Volumes 1 and 2, 1996. The company type code used is as follows: P - Public, R - Private, S - Subsidiary, D - Division, J - Joint Venture, A - Affiliate, G - Group. Sales are in millions of dollars, employees are in thousands. An asterisk (•) indicates an estimated sales volume. The symbol < stands for 'less than'. Company names and addresses are truncated, in some cases, to fit into the available space.

MATERIALS CONSUMED

Material		Quantity	Delivered Cost ($ million)
Materials, ingredients, containers, and supplies		(X)	624.1
Cotton broadwoven fabrics (piece goods)	mil sq yd	(S)	48.8
Rayon and acetate broadwoven fabrics (piece goods)	mil sq yd	50.7	74.5
Polyester broadwoven fabrics (piece goods)	mil sq yd	(S)	79.1
Nylon broadwoven fabrics (piece goods)	mil sq yd	(S)	3.9
Other broadwoven fabrics (piece goods)	mil sq yd	89.6	119.8
Yarn, all fibers	mil lb	(S)	36.3
Plastics coated, impregnated, or laminated fabrics	mil sq yd	(S)	6.1
Manmade fibers, staple, and tow	mil lb	(S)	0.6
Plastics products consumed in the form of sheets, rods, tubes, film, and other shapes		(X)	3.4
All other materials and components, parts, containers, and supplies		(X)	77.7
Materials, ingredients, containers, and supplies, nsk		(X)	173.8

Source: 1992 *Economic Census*. Explanation of symbols used: (D): Withheld to avoid disclosure of competitive data; na: Not available; (S): Withheld because statistical norms were not met; (X): Not applicable; (Z): Less than half the unit shown; nec: Not elsewhere classified; nsk: Not specified by kind; - : zero; * : 10-19 percent estimated; ** : 20-29 percent estimated.

PRODUCT SHARE DETAILS

Product or Product Class	% Share	Product or Product Class	% Share
Curtains and draperies	100.00	Woven window curtains, other materials	4.39
Curtains and draperies, knit, except lace	7.40	Woven draperies, wholly or chiefly cotton	8.90
Woven window curtains, wholly or chiefly cotton	9.48	Woven draperies, rayon and/or acetate fabrics	7.87
Woven window curtains, rayon and/or acetate fabrics	5.22	Woven draperies, all other manmade fiber fabrics, including glass	14.84
Woven window curtains, all other manmade fiber fabrics, including glass	13.97	Woven draperies, other materials	5.25

Source: 1992 *Economic Census*. The values shown are percent of total shipments in an industry. Values of indented subcategories are summed in the main heading. The symbol (D) appears when data are withheld to prevent disclosure of competitive information. The abbreviation nsk stands for 'not specified by kind' and nec for 'not elsewhere classified'.

INPUTS AND OUTPUTS FOR CURTAINS & DRAPERIES

Economic Sector or Industry Providing Inputs	%	Sector	Economic Sector or Industry Buying Outputs	%	Sector
Broadwoven fabric mills	62.2	Manufg.	Personal consumption expenditures	83.5	
Curtains & draperies	9.4	Manufg.	Curtains & draperies	5.9	Manufg.
Wholesale trade	6.1	Trade	S/L Govt. purch., other general government	1.4	S/L Govt
Nonwoven fabrics	3.2	Manufg.	Travel trailers & campers	1.1	Manufg.
Imports	2.7	Foreign	Retail trade, except eating & drinking	1.0	Trade
Banking	2.2	Fin/R.E.	Exports	1.0	Foreign
Noncomparable imports	1.5	Foreign	Insurance carriers	0.7	Fin/R.E.
Advertising	1.1	Services	Federal Government purchases, national defense	0.5	Fed Govt
Electric services (utilities)	1.0	Util.	Wholesale trade	0.4	Trade
Eating & drinking places	0.9	Trade	Real estate	0.4	Fin/R.E.
Real estate	0.9	Fin/R.E.	S/L Govt. purch., highways	0.4	S/L Govt
Narrow fabric mills	0.8	Manufg.	Eating & drinking places	0.3	Trade
Motor freight transportation & warehousing	0.8	Util.	Banking	0.2	Fin/R.E.
U.S. Postal Service	0.8	Gov't	S/L Govt. purch., public assistance & relief	0.2	S/L Govt
Paperboard containers & boxes	0.7	Manufg.	Mobile homes	0.1	Manufg.
Lace goods	0.6	Manufg.	Credit agencies other than banks	0.1	Fin/R.E.
Communications, except radio & TV	0.4	Util.	Insurance agents, brokers, & services	0.1	Fin/R.E.
Maintenance of nonfarm buildings nec	0.3	Constr.	S/L Govt. purch., correction	0.1	S/L Govt
Detective & protective services	0.3	Services	S/L Govt. purch., health & hospitals	0.1	S/L Govt
Equipment rental & leasing services	0.3	Services			
Management & consulting services & labs	0.3	Services			
Thread mills	0.2	Manufg.			
Gas production & distribution (utilities)	0.2	Util.			
Security & commodity brokers	0.2	Fin/R.E.			
Accounting, auditing & bookkeeping	0.2	Services			
Business/professional associations	0.2	Services			
Hotels & lodging places	0.2	Services			
Legal services	0.2	Services			
Lubricating oils & greases	0.1	Manufg.			
Machinery, except electrical, nec	0.1	Manufg.			
Manifold business forms	0.1	Manufg.			
Miscellaneous plastics products	0.1	Manufg.			
Royalties	0.1	Fin/R.E.			

Source: Benchmark Input-Output Accounts for the U.S. Economy, 1982, U.S. Department of Commerce, Washington, D.C., July 1991. Data, as reported in the source, are organized by the 1977 SIC structure in use in 1982 but have been matched, as closely as is possible, to the 1987 SIC structure used in this book.

OCCUPATIONS EMPLOYED BY SIC 239 - MISCELLANEOUS FABRICATED TEXTILE PRODUCTS

Occupation	% of Total 1994	Change to 2005	Occupation	% of Total 1994	Change to 2005
Sewing machine operators, non-garment	21.5	-26.0	Cutters & trimmers, hand	1.9	-25.9
Sewing machine operators, garment	11.0	36.7	Sales & related workers nec	1.8	13.9
Assemblers, fabricators, & hand workers nec	8.6	13.9	Textile draw-out & winding machine operators	1.8	2.5
Hand packers & packagers	3.9	-2.4	Machine feeders & offbearers	1.5	2.5
Blue collar worker supervisors	3.6	4.6	Machine operators nec	1.4	0.4
General managers & top executives	3.1	8.1	Bookkeeping, accounting, & auditing clerks	1.4	-14.6
Helpers, laborers, & material movers nec	2.7	13.9	Industrial machinery mechanics	1.3	25.3
Inspectors, testers, & graders, precision	2.6	13.9	General office clerks	1.2	-2.9
Screen printing machine setters & set-up operators	2.3	36.7	Industrial production managers	1.2	13.9
Freight, stock, & material movers, hand	2.3	-8.9	Secretaries, ex legal & medical	1.1	3.7
Traffic, shipping, & receiving clerks	2.1	9.6	Cutting & slicing machine setters, operators	1.0	25.3

Source: *Industry-Occupation Matrix*, Bureau of Labor Statistics. These data relate to one or more 3-digit SIC industry groups rather than to a single 4-digit SIC. The change reported for each occupation to the year 2005 is a percent of growth or decline as estimated by the Bureau of Labor Statistics. The abbreviation nec stands for 'not elsewhere classified'.

LOCATION BY STATE AND REGIONAL CONCENTRATION

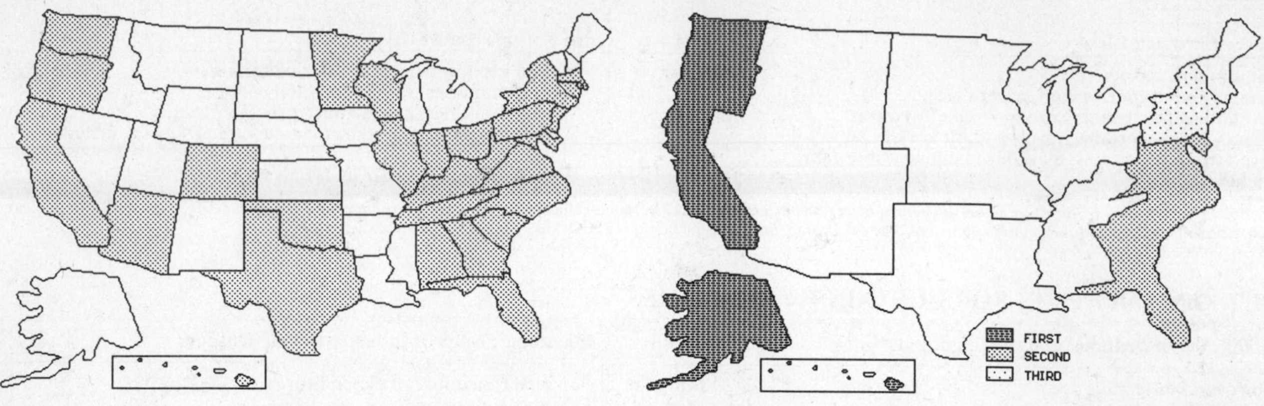

INDUSTRY DATA BY STATE

State	Establish-ments	Shipments			Employment				Cost as % of Shipments	Investment per Employee ($)
		Total ($ mil)	% of U.S.	Per Establ.	Total Number	% of U.S.	Per Establ.	Wages ($/hour)		
North Carolina	40	247.1	19.2	6.2	4,500	20.6	113	7.48	45.3	1,689
Massachusetts	40	178.6	13.9	4.5	2,500	11.5	63	7.56	67.4	400
Texas	78	137.5	10.7	1.8	2,100	9.6	27	6.58	62.7	-
New York	66	92.8	7.2	1.4	1,200	5.5	18	8.29	52.2	667
California	187	84.5	6.6	0.5	1,500	6.9	8	6.96	56.1	267
Georgia	45	71.3	5.6	1.6	1,700	7.8	38	6.10	50.4	824
Indiana	22	41.1	3.2	1.9	800	3.7	36	6.58	60.1	250
South Carolina	24	41.1	3.2	1.7	900	4.1	38	5.71	53.5	222
Maryland	21	34.9	2.7	1.7	500	2.3	24	7.40	38.7	-
Florida	59	31.4	2.4	0.5	500	2.3	8	5.88	50.0	200
New Jersey	25	31.0	2.4	1.2	500	2.3	20	9.88	40.3	200
Alabama	13	30.6	2.4	2.4	500	2.3	38	6.38	51.3	200
Ohio	27	26.8	2.1	1.0	400	1.8	15	8.00	51.1	-
Oklahoma	7	21.9	1.7	3.1	300	1.4	43	5.67	58.4	-
Pennsylvania	39	20.7	1.6	0.5	400	1.8	10	6.00	46.4	250
Virginia	24	20.2	1.6	0.8	300	1.4	13	7.67	54.5	-
Illinois	50	17.5	1.4	0.4	300	1.4	6	7.00	52.6	-
Connecticut	8	14.0	1.1	1.8	300	1.4	38	5.40	49.3	-
Arizona	23	13.5	1.1	0.6	300	1.4	13	7.25	51.1	333
Oregon	20	13.5	1.1	0.7	200	0.9	10	8.00	51.9	500
Rhode Island	8	12.1	0.9	1.5	200	0.9	25	9.00	55.4	-
Wisconsin	14	9.7	0.8	0.7	100	0.5	7	13.00	55.7	-
Colorado	24	8.8	0.7	0.4	200	0.9	8	8.00	51.1	500
Washington	16	8.7	0.7	0.5	200	0.9	13	8.50	50.6	-
Kentucky	10	8.5	0.7	0.9	200	0.9	20	5.67	61.2	-
Hawaii	5	5.8	0.5	1.2	100	0.5	20	12.00	53.4	-
Minnesota	23	5.1	0.4	0.2	200	0.9	9	7.00	43.1	-
Tennessee	19	(D)	-	-	175 *	0.8	9	-	-	-
West Virginia	2	(D)	-	-	175 *	0.8	88	-	-	-

Source: 1992 *Economic Census*. The states are in descending order of shipments or establishments (if shipment data are missing for the majority). The symbol (D) appears when data are withheld to prevent disclosure of competitive information. States marked with (D) are sorted by number of establishments. A dash (-) indicates that the data element cannot be calculated; * indicates the midpoint of a range.

2392 - HOUSEFURNISHINGS, NEC

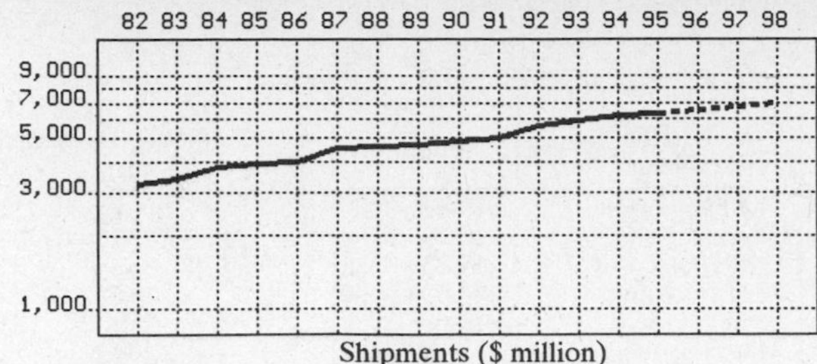

Shipments ($ million)

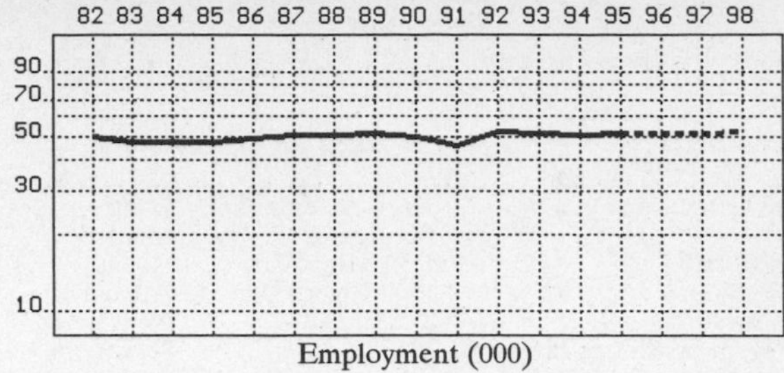

Employment (000)

GENERAL STATISTICS

Year	Companies	Establishments		Employment			Compensation		Production ($ million)			
		Total	with 20 or more employees	Total (000)	Production Workers (000)	Production Hours (Mil)	Payroll ($ mil)	Wages ($/hr)	Cost of Materials	Value Added by Manufacture	Value of Shipments	Capital Invest.
1982	882	958	399	49.3	39.8	77.6	518.2	4.76	1,994.3	1,249.0	3,262.2	38.8
1983		936	390	46.8	37.8	76.9	503.8	4.63	2,223.5	1,307.4	3,440.6	25.0
1984		914	381	46.8	38.7	74.3	588.4	5.62	2,383.7	1,371.5	3,800.0	57.7
1985		892	373	47.5	39.3	74.5	612.2	5.74	2,537.4	1,405.2	3,951.4	38.7
1986		843	371	48.5	39.8	78.6	649.6	5.75	2,622.5	1,412.0	4,035.7	43.5
1987	867	944	402	50.5	42.8	83.8	713.7	6.19	2,816.4	1,759.3	4,530.0	44.2
1988		906	384	50.5	42.6	82.1	723.3	6.27	2,766.2	1,839.7	4,625.9	46.3
1989		867	386	50.9	38.2	75.2	673.1	6.43	2,780.9	1,934.0	4,665.2	63.6
1990		830	369	49.4	37.7	73.9	672.4	6.50	2,904.3	1,967.3	4,871.9	66.7
1991		837	356	45.4	38.3	77.8	714.6	6.63	3,028.7	2,007.2	5,021.0	63.7
1992	791	868	353	52.0	44.3	87.8	870.3	7.33	3,269.6	2,374.2	5,614.3	83.6
1993		860	356	51.4	43.9	86.4	904.0	7.96	3,269.8	2,668.7	5,904.9	110.9
1994		831P	355P	50.4	43.1	81.9	892.6	8.22	3,473.1	2,743.4	6,206.6	90.6
1995		822P	351P	51.0P	42.8P	83.9P	913.8P	8.18P	3,489.2P	2,756.1P	6,235.4P	97.4P
1996		813P	348P	51.2P	43.2P	84.5P	945.1P	8.45P	3,619.2P	2,858.8P	6,467.6P	102.8P
1997		805P	344P	51.5P	43.5P	85.2P	976.3P	8.72P	3,749.1P	2,961.4P	6,699.8P	108.2P
1998		796P	341P	51.7P	43.8P	85.8P	1,007.6P	8.98P	3,879.0P	3,064.1P	6,932.0P	113.6P

Sources: 1982, 1987, 1992 *Economic Census*; *Annual Survey of Manufactures*, 83-86, 88-91, 93-94. Establishment counts for non-Census years are from *County Business Patterns*; establishment values for 83-84 are extrapolations. 'P's show projections by the editors. Industries reclassified in 87 will not have data for prior years.

INDICES OF CHANGE

Year	Companies	Establishments		Employment			Compensation		Production ($ million)			
		Total	with 20 or more employees	Total (000)	Production Workers (000)	Production Hours (Mil)	Payroll ($ mil)	Wages ($/hr)	Cost of Materials	Value Added by Manufacture	Value of Shipments	Capital Invest.
1982	112	110	113	95	90	88	60	65	61	53	58	46
1983		108	110	90	85	88	58	63	68	55	61	30
1984		105	108	90	87	85	68	77	73	58	68	69
1985		103	106	91	89	85	70	78	78	59	70	46
1986		97	105	93	90	90	75	78	80	59	72	52
1987	110	109	114	97	97	95	82	84	86	74	81	53
1988		104	109	97	96	94	83	86	85	77	82	55
1989		100	109	98	86	86	77	88	85	81	83	76
1990		96	105	95	85	84	77	89	89	83	87	80
1991		96	101	87	86	89	82	90	93	85	89	76
1992	100	100	100	100	100	100	100	100	100	100	100	100
1993		99	101	99	99	98	104	109	100	112	105	133
1994		96P	100P	97	97	93	103	112	106	116	111	108
1995		95P	99P	98P	97P	96P	105P	112P	107P	116P	111P	116P
1996		94P	99P	98P	97P	96P	109P	115P	111P	120P	115P	123P
1997		93P	98P	99P	98P	97P	112P	119P	115P	125P	119P	129P
1998		92P	97P	99P	99P	98P	116P	123P	119P	129P	123P	136P

Sources: Same as General Statistics. Values reflect change from the base year, 1992. Values above 100 mean greater than 92, values below 100 mean less than 92, and a value of 100 in the 82-91 or 93-98 period means same as 92. 'P's mark projections by the editors.

SELECTED RATIOS

For 1994	Avg. of All Manufact.	Analyzed Industry	Index	For 1994	Avg. of All Manufact.	Analyzed Industry	Index
Employees per Establishment	49	61	124	Value Added per Production Worker	134,084	63,652	47
Payroll per Establishment	1,500,273	1,074,147	72	Cost per Establishment	5,045,178	4,179,499	83
Payroll per Employee	30,620	17,710	58	Cost per Employee	102,970	68,911	67
Production Workers per Establishment	34	52	151	Cost per Production Worker	146,988	80,582	55
Wages per Establishment	853,319	810,145	95	Shipments per Establishment	9,576,895	7,468,969	78
Wages per Production Worker	24,861	15,620	63	Shipments per Employee	195,460	123,147	63
Hours per Production Worker	2,056	1,900	92	Shipments per Production Worker	279,017	144,005	52
Wages per Hour	12.09	8.22	68	Investment per Establishment	321,011	109,027	34
Value Added per Establishment	4,602,255	3,301,384	72	Investment per Employee	6,552	1,798	27
Value Added per Employee	93,930	54,433	58	Investment per Production Worker	9,352	2,102	22

Sources: Same as General Statistics. The 'Average of All Manufacturing' column represents the average of all manufacturing industries reported for the most recent complete year available. The Index shows the relationship between the Average and the Analyzed Industry. For example, 100 means that they are equal; 500 that the Analyzed Industry is five times the average; 50 means that the Analyzed Industry is half the national average. The abbreviation 'na' is used to show that data are 'not available'.

LEADING COMPANIES Number shown: 75 Total sales ($ mil): 3,470 Total employment (000): 41.0

Company Name	Address				CEO Name	Phone	Co. Type	Sales ($ mil)	Empl. (000)
Fieldcrest Cannon Inc	326 E Stadium Dr	Eden	NC	27288	J M Fitzgibbons	910-627-3000	P	1,064	13.9
Bibb Co	PO Box 4207	Macon	GA	31208	Thomas Foley	912-752-6700	R	450	6.4
Pillowtex Corp	4111 Mint Way	Dallas	TX	75237	C M Hansen Jr	214-333-3225	P	352	3.8
Crown Crafts Inc	1600 River Edge	Atlanta	GA	30328	M H Bernstein	404-644-6400	P	187	1.9
Home Innovations	295 5th Av	New York	NY	10016	Robert Fotsch	212-686-2080	R	170	2.0
Dawson Home Fashions Inc	295 5th Av	New York	NY	10016	Tim Hogan	212-689-6300	S	100	1.0
Fieldcrest Cannon Surefit	E Broad & Wood St	Bethlehem	PA	18016	Bert Shlensky	215-867-7581	R	55	0.5
Brentwood Originals Inc	PO Box 6272	Carson	CA	90749	H Alden	310-637-6804	S	53*	0.6
Jayark Corp	6116 Skyline Dr	Houston	TX	77057	David L Koffman	713-783-7822	P	50	0.1
Rosalco Inc	257 America Pl	Jeffersonville	IN	47130	Robert Glick	812-284-0022	S	49	<0.1
Beacon Manufacturing Co	110 Parkview St	Westminster	SC	29693	Jeff Blair	803-647-5461	D	43	0.6
Company Store Inc	500 Company Store	La Crosse	WI	54601	C Pellenberg	608-785-1400	R	40	0.7
Gold Medal Inc	PO Box 2028	Richmond	VA	23216	Michael Luczkovich	804-233-4337	R	40	0.3
Sunweave Linen Corp	530 5th Av	New York	NY	10036	Joseph A Cohen	212-997-1050	R	40	0.2
Charles D Owen Manufacturing	PO Box 457	Swannanoa	NC	28778	Charles D Owen	704-298-6802	R	35	0.5
Madison Industries Inc	279 5th Av	New York	NY	10016	Robert Weinstein	212-679-5110	R	35*	0.4
Messina and Zucker Inc	295 5th Av	New York	NY	10016	Clyde S Zucker	212-889-3750	R	35	<0.1
Minette-Bates Inc	PO Box 49	Grover	NC	28073	Bull Little	704-937-7611	R	35*	0.4
Whiting Manufacturing Company	9999 Carver Rd	Cincinnati	OH	45242	Dick Whiting	513-791-9100	R	32*	0.4
California Feather	11842 S Alameda St	Lynwood	CA	90262	Jeff Goldman	310-898-1900	R	30	0.2
Liebhardt Mills Inc	PO Box 249	Middletown	IN	47356	James Liebhardt	317-378-4010	R	30	0.4
Piedmont Home Textile Corp	PO Box 267	Walhalla	SC	29691	Alfred Mizhir	803-638-3636	S	30	0.3
Select Comfort Corp	6105 Trenton Ln	Plymouth	MN	55442	Mark de Naray	612-551-7000	R	30	0.3
Designer Collection Inc	8181 Ambassador	Dallas	TX	75247	Jeffrey B Zisk	214-634-8040	R	26	0.3
Earle Industries Inc	PO Box 28	Earle	AR	72331	D Felsenthal	501-792-8694	R	25	0.3
Dakotah Inc	PO Box 120	Webster	SD	57274	George C Whyte	605-345-4646	P	23	0.4
Tennessee Woolen Mills	218 N Maple St	Lebanon	TN	37087	Steve Davidson	615-444-6060	D	21	0.3
Jay Franco and Sons Inc	295 5th Av	New York	NY	10016	Nathan Franco	212-679-3022	R	20	<0.1
Phoenix Down Corp	85 Rte 46 W	Totowa	NJ	07012	John Facateselis	201-812-8100	R	20	<0.1
Superior Shade and Blind	1541 N Powerline	Pompano Bch	FL	33069	David Fryburg	305-975-8122	R	20	0.2
Eastern Home Products Inc	1536 Grant St	Elkhart	IN	46514	William Reading	219-264-0662	R	17	<0.1
Bardwil Industries Inc	1071 of the Amer	New York	NY	10018	Elias G Bardwil	212-944-1870	R	15*	0.2
Manny Industries	6000 Sheila St	Los Angeles	CA	90040	Harriette Rinkov	213-722-3181	R	15	0.2
Southern Quilters	PO Drawer 1638	Henderson	NC	27536	Richard Aldrich	919-492-0051	R	15	0.7
Lincoln Textile Product	PO Box 331	Nazareth	PA	18064	Harry Sugarman	215-759-6211	R	14*	0.2
Crystal Lake Manufacturing Inc	PO Box 159	Autaugaville	AL	36003	James A Pearson	205-365-3342	R	13	0.2
Yonah Realty Co	105 Chattahoochee	Cornelia	GA	30531	JL Bruce Sr	706-778-2126	R	13*	0.2
Decor Home Fashions Inc	140 58th St	Brooklyn	NY	11220	Gene Baranof	718-921-1030	R	12*	0.1
American Home Fashions Inc	PO Box 309	Calhoun	GA	30703	Reid Ruttenberg	706-629-8231	R	10*	0.1
American Textile Co	Harrison & 49th Sts	Pittsburgh	PA	15201	Reid W Ruttenberg	412-681-9404	R	10	0.1
Bechik Products Inc	1140 Homer St	St Paul	MN	55116	Anthony Bechik	612-698-0364	R	10	<0.1
Bess Manufacturing Co	1807-27 Hunt	Philadelphia	PA	19125	David Ashe	215-425-9450	R	10	0.1
Showeray Corp	225 25th St	Brooklyn	NY	11232	A Grazi	718-965-3633	R	10	0.1
Alagold Corp	PO Drawer 4959	Montgomery	AL	36103	A Goldman	205-834-6900	R	9	0.2
Kennebunk Weavers Inc	PO Box 153	Suncook	NH	03275	Arthur J Feinberg	603-485-7511	R	9	<0.1
Acme Laundry Products Inc	21600 Lassen St	Chatsworth	CA	91311	Jan Rome	818-341-0700	R	8*	0.1
Bloch/New England Inc	PO Box 296	Worcester	MA	01603	AL Bloch	508-754-3204	R	8	<0.1
Bright of America Inc	300 Greenbrier Rd	Summersville	WV	26651	Stephen Pridemore	304-872-3000	S	8	0.2
J Lamb Inc	PO Box 312	Englewood	NJ	07631	Bruce Strongwater	201-569-0001	R	8	<0.1
Royal Mills Associates	275 5th Av	New York	NY	10016	Sam Gindi	212-683-5970	R	8	0.1
K-C Products Company Inc	1600 E 6th St	Los Angeles	CA	90023	K Cahn	213-267-1600	R	7	0.2
MIT International Inc	8000 Market St	Houston	TX	77029	Doug Knight	713-675-0075	S	7*	<0.1
Originals Bi Judi Inc	PO Box 12307	Scottsdale	AZ	85267	Jack Rist	602-991-5885	R	7*	<0.1
Quiltcraft Industries Inc	1233 Lavee St	Dallas	TX	75207	Larry Pearson	214-741-1662	R	7*	<0.1
Riverdale Decorative Products	PO Box 4959	Montgomery	AL	36103	Allan Goldman	205-834-6900	D	7	0.1
Tailored Baby Inc	17042 Devonshire St	Northridge	CA	91324		818-368-4703	R	7*	0.1
Greenwood Mop and Broom Inc	PO Drawer 1426	Greenwood	SC	29648	Henry Bonds	803-227-8411	R	7	<0.1
Echota Fabrics Inc	PO Box 625	Calhoun	GA	30703	Joel Ostuw	706-629-9750	R	5*	<0.1
Penthouse Industries Inc	84 N 9th St	Brooklyn	NY	11211	Irving Wilensky	718-384-5800	R	5	<0.1
Active Quilting	20 S River St	Plains	PA	18705	Walter Levy	717-823-3127	D	4*	<0.1
Catalina Products Corp	2455 McDonald Av	Brooklyn	NY	11223	Norman R Harris	718-336-8288	R	4	<0.1
Devin Lane Collections	510 1st Av N	Minneapolis	MN	55403	Lois Sonstegard	612-338-0622	R	4	<0.1
Page Foam Cushion Products	850 Eisenhower	Johnstown	PA	15904	Walter F Page	814-266-6969	R	4	<0.1
Porterco Inc	PO Box 1560	Magnolia	AR	71753	Calvin M Porter	501-234-6600	R	4	<0.1
Vantage Industries Inc	PO Box 43944	Atlanta	GA	30336	Robert F Weber	404-691-9500	D	4*	<0.1
J Marie Martin Co	1880 Como Av	St Paul	MN	55108	Lyndsay Franck	612-646-4463	D	3	<0.1
Lydon-Bricher Manufacturing	1880 Como Av	St Paul	MN	55102	Steven McKay	612-646-4463	R	3	<0.1
Mayfield Manufacturing	PO Box 272	Thomson	GA	30824	Neil Colvin	706-595-6551	R	3*	<0.1
Phoenixware Ltd	4022 S 20th St	Phoenix	AZ	85040	David Wagner	602-233-1000	R	3*	<0.1
Royal Bedding of Buffalo	PO Box 538	Buffalo	NY	14212	Daniel Kantor	716-895-1414	R	3	<0.1
Domestex USA Ltd	PO Box 50098	Fort Worth	TX	76105	Vickie Ennis	817-536-7355	R	2	<0.1
Hutton Industries Inc	PO Box 1092	St Helens	OR	97051	Deanice Hutton	503-397-3769	R	2*	<0.1
Malden Novelty Company Inc	PO Box 207	Malden	MA	02148	B Sugarman	617-322-6131	R	2	<0.1
Pacific Cotton Goods Company	2525 Mandela Pkwy	Oakland	CA	94607	William M Hart	510-835-8177	R	2*	<0.1
Three Weavers Inc	150 Bennington St	Houston	TX	77022	Pete Johnson	713-697-3995	S	2*	<0.1

Source: *Ward's Business Directory of U.S. Private and Public Companies*, Volumes 1 and 2, 1996. The company type code used is as follows: P - Public, R - Private, S - Subsidiary, D - Division, J - Joint Venture, A - Affiliate, G - Group. Sales are in millions of dollars, employees are in thousands. An asterisk (*) indicates an estimated sales volume. The symbol < stands for 'less than'. Company names and addresses are truncated, in some cases, to fit into the available space.

MATERIALS CONSUMED

Material		Quantity	Delivered Cost ($ million)
Materials, ingredients, containers, and supplies		(X)	3,095.8
Cotton broadwoven fabrics (piece goods)	mil sq yd	578.3**	761.5
Rayon and acetate broadwoven fabrics (piece goods)	mil sq yd	(S)	12.9
Polyester broadwoven fabrics (piece goods)	mil sq yd	(S)	396.3
Nylon broadwoven fabrics (piece goods)	mil sq yd	(S)	26.5
Other broadwoven fabrics (piece goods)	mil sq yd	263.3*	298.4
Narrow fabrics (12 inches or less in width)	mil sq yd	43.8**	33.6
Yarn, all fibers	mil lb	(S)	179.4
Plastics coated, impregnated, or laminated fabrics	mil sq yd	27.1*	35.2
Manmade fibers, staple, and tow	mil lb	(S)	119.5
Plastics products consumed in the form of sheets, rods, tubes, film, and other shapes		(X)	60.0
All other materials and components, parts, containers, and supplies		(X)	857.2
Materials, ingredients, containers, and supplies, nsk		(X)	315.2

Source: 1992 *Economic Census*. Explanation of symbols used: (D): Withheld to avoid disclosure of competitive data; na: Not available; (S): Withheld because statistical norms were not met; (X): Not applicable; (Z): Less than half the unit shown; nec: Not elsewhere classified; nsk: Not specified by kind; - : zero; * : 10-19 percent estimated; ** : 20-29 percent estimated.

PRODUCT SHARE DETAILS

Product or Product Class	% Share	Product or Product Class	% Share
Housefurnishings, nec	100.00	Table linen, knitted or crocheted (tablecloths, napkins, place mats, etc.)	0.50
Bedspreads and bedsets (not made in a weaving mill)	8.27	Tablecloths and napkins, cotton	4.28
Knit and/or crocheted bedspreads, not made in a weaving mill	1.63	Other table linen, cotton, (including place mats and place mat sets)	0.49
Tailored bedspreads (except knit), wholly or chiefly cotton fabrics, quilted, not made in a weaving mill	16.40	Tablecloths and napkins, linen	(D)
Tailored bedspreads (except knit), wholly or chiefly manmade fiber fabrics, quilted, not made in a weaving mill	30.55	Other (including place mats and place mat sets), linen	(D)
Tailored bedspreads (except knit), wholly or chiefly cotton fabrics, nonquilted, not made in a weaving mill	0.68	Tablecloths and napkins, manmade fibers	1.34
Tailored bedspreads (except knit), wholly or chiefly manmade fiber fabrics, nonquilted, not made in a weaving mill	9.58	Other (including place mats and place mat sets), manmade fibers	(D)
Nontailored bedspreads, wholly or chiefly cotton fabrics, not made in a weaving mill	30.75	Tablecloths and napkins, other materials, including plastics	1.74
Nontailored bedspreads, wholly or chiefly manmade fiber fabrics, not made in a weaving mill	5.90	Other (including place mats and place mat sets), other materials, including plastics	0.37
Bedspreads and bedsets (made from purchased fabrics), nsk	4.52	Other related articles, except lace (dresser covers and scarves, doilies, tray cloths, etc., including plastics)	0.79
Sheets and pillowcases (made from purchased fabrics)	18.71	Bed pillows, manmade fiber-filled	8.39
Towels and washcloths (made from purchased fabrics)	11.42	Bed pillows, other materials (including foam)	3.37
Other housefurnishings	58.07	Fancy pillows and cushions, foam rubber	2.39
Shower bath curtains, including plastics (unsupported film), coated fabrics, and all others	5.03	Fancy pillows and cushions, other materials	8.24
Quilted comforters and quilts, wholly or chiefly cotton (except down-filled)	9.18	Furniture slipcovers made from fabrics, plastics, and other material (except paper products)	3.56
Quilted comforters and quilts, wholly or chiefly manmade fiber (except down-filled)	15.49	Mattress slipcovers, nonquilted	(D)
Quilted comforters and quilts, down-filled	3.36	Other slipcovers	1.68
Quilted mattress protectors (including mattress covers), wholly or chiefly cotton	2.10	Dry mops and dusters (excluding dusting cloths, including refills)	1.45
Quilted mattress protectors (including mattress covers), all other fabrics	3.46	Wet mops (except sponge mops, including refills)	3.43
Other quilted products	0.55	Sponge mops (including refills)	2.93
		Laundry, wardrobe, and shoe bags (including storage bags of textiles with or without external supporting frames)	1.22
		Blankets	3.70
		All other housefurnishings	6.86
		Other housefurnishings (made from purchased fabrics), nsk	2.91
		Housefurnishings, nec, nsk	3.54

Source: 1992 *Economic Census*. The values shown are percent of total shipments in an industry. Values of indented subcategories are summed in the main heading. The symbol (D) appears when data are withheld to prevent disclosure of competitive information. The abbreviation nsk stands for 'not specified by kind' and nec for 'not elsewhere classified'.

INPUTS AND OUTPUTS FOR HOUSEFURNISHINGS, NEC

Economic Sector or Industry Providing Inputs	%	Sector	Economic Sector or Industry Buying Outputs	%	Sector
Broadwoven fabric mills	45.5	Manufg.	Personal consumption expenditures	73.5	
Imports	13.2	Foreign	Hospitals	6.7	Services
Wholesale trade	9.1	Trade	Hotels & lodging places	5.1	Services
Housefurnishings, nec	3.5	Manufg.	Laundry, dry cleaning, shoe repair	4.5	Services
Nonwoven fabrics	2.6	Manufg.	Exports	3.4	Foreign
Schiffli machine embroideries	2.4	Manufg.	Housefurnishings, nec	1.6	Manufg.
Organic fibers, noncellulosic	2.2	Manufg.	Nursing & personal care facilities	1.3	Services
Paperboard containers & boxes	2.2	Manufg.	S/L Govt. purch., health & hospitals	1.0	S/L Govt
Padding & upholstery filling	2.1	Manufg.	S/L Govt. purch., elem. & secondary education	0.5	S/L Govt
Textile goods, nec	1.4	Manufg.	S/L Govt. purch., other general government	0.3	S/L Govt
Coated fabrics, not rubberized	1.3	Manufg.	S/L Govt. purch., police	0.3	S/L Govt

Continued on next page.

INPUTS AND OUTPUTS FOR HOUSEFURNISHINGS, NEC - Continued

Economic Sector or Industry Providing Inputs	%	Sector	Economic Sector or Industry Buying Outputs	%	Sector
Advertising	1.3	Services	Residential care	0.2	Services
Electric services (utilities)	1.1	Util.	S/L Govt. purch., correction	0.2	S/L Govt
Miscellaneous plastics products	1.0	Manufg.	S/L Govt. purch., natural resource & recreation.	0.2	S/L Govt
Sanitary services, steam supply, irrigation	1.0	Util.	S/L Govt. purch., other education & libraries	0.2	S/L Govt
Communications, except radio & TV	0.7	Util.	S/L Govt. purch., public assistance & relief	0.2	S/L Govt
Banking	0.7	Fin/R.E.	Miscellaneous plastics products	0.1	Manufg.
Wood products, nec	0.6	Manufg.			
Motor freight transportation & warehousing	0.6	Util.			
Gas production & distribution (utilities)	0.5	Util.			
Eating & drinking places	0.5	Trade			
Real estate	0.5	Fin/R.E.			
U.S. Postal Service	0.5	Gov't			
Cellulosic manmade fibers	0.4	Manufg.			
Narrow fabric mills	0.4	Manufg.			
Noncomparable imports	0.4	Foreign			
Job training & related services	0.3	Services			
Maintenance of nonfarm buildings nec	0.2	Constr.			
Felt goods, nec	0.2	Manufg.			
Lace goods	0.2	Manufg.			
Petroleum refining	0.2	Manufg.			
Royalties	0.2	Fin/R.E.			
Business/professional associations	0.2	Services			
Detective & protective services	0.2	Services			
Equipment rental & leasing services	0.2	Services			
Management & consulting services & labs	0.2	Services			
Air transportation	0.1	Util.			
Accounting, auditing & bookkeeping	0.1	Services			
Electrical repair shops	0.1	Services			
Hotels & lodging places	0.1	Services			
Legal services	0.1	Services			

Source: Benchmark Input-Output Accounts for the U.S. Economy, 1982, U.S. Department of Commerce, Washington, D.C., July 1991. Data, as reported in the source, are organized by the 1977 SIC structure in use in 1982 but have been matched, as closely as is possible, to the 1987 SIC structure used in this book.

OCCUPATIONS EMPLOYED BY SIC 239 - MISCELLANEOUS FABRICATED TEXTILE PRODUCTS

Occupation	% of Total 1994	Change to 2005	Occupation	% of Total 1994	Change to 2005
Sewing machine operators, non-garment	21.5	-26.0	Cutters & trimmers, hand	1.9	-25.9
Sewing machine operators, garment	11.0	36.7	Sales & related workers nec	1.8	13.9
Assemblers, fabricators, & hand workers nec	8.6	13.9	Textile draw-out & winding machine operators	1.8	2.5
Hand packers & packagers	3.9	-2.4	Machine feeders & offbearers	1.5	2.5
Blue collar worker supervisors	3.6	4.6	Machine operators nec	1.4	0.4
General managers & top executives	3.1	8.1	Bookkeeping, accounting, & auditing clerks	1.4	-14.6
Helpers, laborers, & material movers nec	2.7	13.9	Industrial machinery mechanics	1.3	25.3
Inspectors, testers, & graders, precision	2.6	13.9	General office clerks	1.2	-2.9
Screen printing machine setters & set-up operators	2.3	36.7	Industrial production managers	1.2	13.9
Freight, stock, & material movers, hand	2.3	-8.9	Secretaries, ex legal & medical	1.1	3.7
Traffic, shipping, & receiving clerks	2.1	9.6	Cutting & slicing machine setters, operators	1.0	25.3

Source: Industry-Occupation Matrix, Bureau of Labor Statistics. These data relate to one or more 3-digit SIC industry groups rather than to a single 4-digit SIC. The change reported for each occupation to the year 2005 is a percent of growth or decline as estimated by the Bureau of Labor Statistics. The abbreviation nec stands for 'not elsewhere classified'.

LOCATION BY STATE AND REGIONAL CONCENTRATION

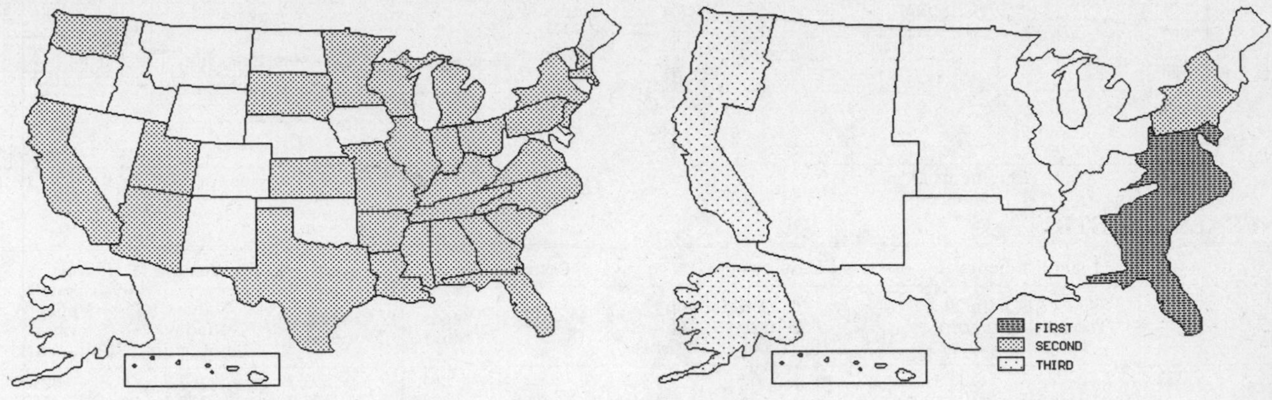

INDUSTRY DATA BY STATE

State	Establish-ments	Shipments			Employment				Cost as % of Shipments	Investment per Employee ($)
		Total ($ mil)	% of U.S.	Per Establ.	Total Number	% of U.S.	Per Establ.	Wages ($/hour)		
North Carolina	64	1,177.9	21.0	18.4	10,200	19.6	159	7.49	52.6	1,167
South Carolina	40	861.8	15.4	21.5	6,300	12.1	158	8.10	64.8	2,762
Alabama	20	538.1	9.6	26.9	3,800	7.3	190	8.27	65.2	-
Georgia	47	455.3	8.1	9.7	4,700	9.0	100	6.62	50.2	2,319
California	125	408.8	7.3	3.3	4,300	8.3	34	7.25	52.6	698
New York	109	222.4	4.0	2.0	2,400	4.6	22	5.87	64.3	708
Texas	39	204.1	3.6	5.2	1,100	2.1	28	8.00	71.7	2,364
Pennsylvania	37	186.7	3.3	5.0	2,100	4.0	57	7.56	49.7	619
New Jersey	38	171.5	3.1	4.5	2,000	3.8	53	7.00	56.9	750
Ohio	20	171.0	3.0	8.6	1,900	3.7	95	6.00	60.5	842
Virginia	12	165.6	2.9	13.8	1,000	1.9	83	7.40	82.5	-
Mississippi	10	155.0	2.8	15.5	1,800	3.5	180	7.07	52.9	3,611
Illinois	35	143.9	2.6	4.1	1,400	2.7	40	7.23	49.0	643
Kentucky	11	117.5	2.1	10.7	1,000	1.9	91	8.59	57.5	-
Florida	47	116.1	2.1	2.5	1,500	2.9	32	7.29	58.1	-
Indiana	14	80.1	1.4	5.7	1,000	1.9	71	6.72	62.4	400
Wisconsin	9	66.1	1.2	7.3	500	1.0	56	11.50	35.1	-
Massachusetts	19	56.2	1.0	3.0	800	1.5	42	7.18	55.7	500
Tennessee	17	48.4	0.9	2.8	600	1.2	35	6.50	77.3	-
Arkansas	10	45.7	0.8	4.6	700	1.3	70	5.91	49.7	-
Washington	12	41.6	0.7	3.5	400	0.8	33	9.00	59.4	-
Minnesota	10	21.7	0.4	2.2	500	1.0	50	6.57	59.4	-
Louisiana	8	14.0	0.2	1.8	200	0.4	25	6.00	61.4	-
Missouri	14	13.4	0.2	1.0	200	0.4	14	5.67	59.0	-
Michigan	7	10.8	0.2	1.5	100	0.2	14	7.50	57.4	-
Utah	5	9.6	0.2	1.9	100	0.2	20	4.50	64.6	-
Arizona	10	(D)	-	-	175 *	0.3	18	-	-	-
Kansas	6	(D)	-	-	375 *	0.7	63	-	-	-
New Hampshire	5	(D)	-	-	175 *	0.3	35	-	-	-
South Dakota	5	(D)	-	-	375 *	0.7	75	-	-	-

Source: 1992 *Economic Census*. The states are in descending order of shipments or establishments (if shipment data are missing for the majority). The symbol (D) appears when data are withheld to prevent disclosure of competitive information. States marked with (D) are sorted by number of establishments. A dash (-) indicates that the data element cannot be calculated; * indicates the midpoint of a range.

2393 - TEXTILE BAGS

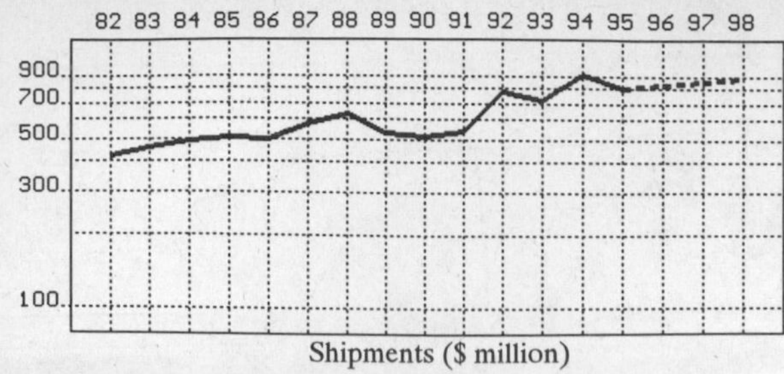

Shipments ($ million)

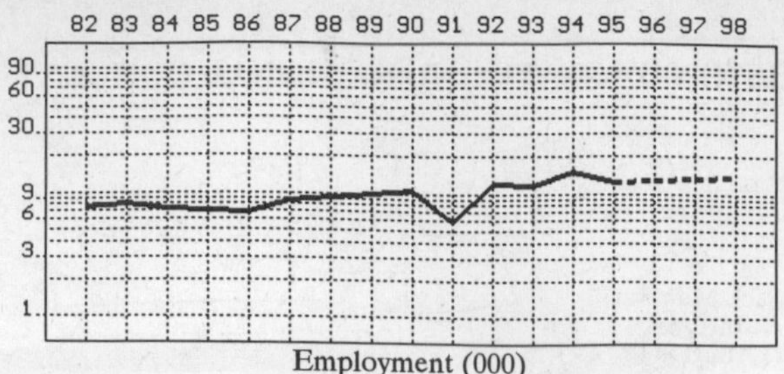

Employment (000)

GENERAL STATISTICS

Year	Com-panies	Establishments		Employment			Compensation		Production ($ million)			
		Total	with 20 or more employees	Total (000)	Production Workers (000)	Production Hours (Mil)	Payroll ($ mil)	Wages ($/hr)	Cost of Materials	Value Added by Manufacture	Value of Shipments	Capital Invest.
1982	233	249	108	7.7	6.5	12.2	89.5	5.31	252.7	167.8	421.8	5.9
1983		244	106	8.2	7.0	13.0	94.6	5.18	276.3	175.4	455.7	5.3
1984		239	104	7.4	6.3	11.9	92.6	5.38	279.0	209.4	487.9	5.4
1985		233	102	7.1	6.0	10.5	87.9	5.60	291.6	219.0	502.0	4.6
1986		227	90	6.9	5.8	10.6	86.4	5.35	296.3	207.3	499.8	4.2
1987	255	262	116	8.8	7.3	13.5	118.0	5.65	336.4	239.9	571.5	5.8
1988		262	117	9.2	7.4	14.9	133.7	5.68	361.3	266.8	626.1	6.2
1989		253	114	10.0	5.2	9.3	108.4	7.25	291.2	238.5	528.6	5.0
1990		265	119	10.4	4.6	8.7	98.6	7.38	288.3	230.0	513.0	5.6
1991		282	117	5.8	4.7	8.9	104.8	7.83	299.3	239.4	537.6	6.1
1992	298	311	131	11.9	9.6	19.0	185.9	6.48	443.4	336.2	778.5	12.0
1993		312	133	11.5	9.2	18.8	190.4	6.71	400.9	317.6	723.2	19.4
1994		303P	130P	14.7	11.9	22.8	226.3	6.58	515.4	403.0	914.7	12.2
1995		310P	133P	12.3P	8.9P	17.6P	191.3P	7.41P	447.9P	350.2P	794.9P	12.9P
1996		316P	135P	12.8P	9.2P	18.1P	200.8P	7.59P	465.1P	363.7P	825.4P	13.7P
1997		323P	138P	13.2P	9.4P	18.7P	210.4P	7.77P	482.3P	377.1P	855.9P	14.5P
1998		329P	141P	13.6P	9.7P	19.3P	219.9P	7.94P	499.4P	390.5P	886.4P	15.3P

Sources: 1982, 1987, 1992 *Economic Census*; *Annual Survey of Manufactures*, 83-86, 88-91, 93-94. Establishment counts for non-Census years are from *County Business Patterns*; establishment values for 83-84 are extrapolations. 'P's show projections by the editors. Industries reclassified in 87 will not have data for prior years.

INDICES OF CHANGE

Year	Com-panies	Establishments		Employment			Compensation		Production ($ million)			
		Total	with 20 or more employees	Total (000)	Production Workers (000)	Production Hours (Mil)	Payroll ($ mil)	Wages ($/hr)	Cost of Materials	Value Added by Manufacture	Value of Shipments	Capital Invest.
1982	78	80	82	65	68	64	48	82	57	50	54	49
1983		78	81	69	73	68	51	80	62	52	59	44
1984		77	79	62	66	63	50	83	63	62	63	45
1985		75	78	60	63	55	47	86	66	65	64	38
1986		73	69	58	60	56	46	83	67	62	64	35
1987	86	84	89	74	76	71	63	87	76	71	73	48
1988		84	89	77	77	78	72	88	81	79	80	52
1989		81	87	84	54	49	58	112	66	71	68	42
1990		85	91	87	48	46	53	114	65	68	66	47
1991		91	89	49	49	47	56	121	68	71	69	51
1992	100	100	100	100	100	100	100	100	100	100	100	100
1993		100	102	97	96	99	102	104	90	94	93	162
1994		98P	99P	124	124	120	122	102	116	120	117	102
1995		100P	101P	103P	93P	92P	103P	114P	101P	104P	102P	108P
1996		102P	103P	107P	95P	96P	108P	117P	105P	108P	106P	114P
1997		104P	105P	111P	98P	99P	113P	120P	109P	112P	110P	121P
1998		106P	107P	115P	101P	102P	118P	123P	113P	116P	114P	127P

Sources: Same as General Statistics. Values reflect change from the base year, 1992. Values above 100 mean greater than 92, values below 100 mean less than 92, and a value of 100 in the 82-91 or 93-98 period means same as 92. 'P's mark projections by the editors.

SELECTED RATIOS

For 1994	Avg. of All Manufact.	Analyzed Industry	Index
Employees per Establishment	49	48	99
Payroll per Establishment	1,500,273	746,156	50
Payroll per Employee	30,620	15,395	50
Production Workers per Establishment	34	39	114
Wages per Establishment	853,319	494,659	58
Wages per Production Worker	24,861	12,607	51
Hours per Production Worker	2,056	1,916	93
Wages per Hour	12.09	6.58	54
Value Added per Establishment	4,602,255	1,328,771	29
Value Added per Employee	93,930	27,415	29

For 1994	Avg. of All Manufact.	Analyzed Industry	Index
Value Added per Production Worker	134,084	33,866	25
Cost per Establishment	5,045,178	1,699,376	34
Cost per Employee	102,970	35,061	34
Cost per Production Worker	146,988	43,311	29
Shipments per Establishment	9,576,895	3,015,946	31
Shipments per Employee	195,460	62,224	32
Shipments per Production Worker	279,017	76,866	28
Investment per Establishment	321,011	40,226	13
Investment per Employee	6,552	830	13
Investment per Production Worker	9,352	1,025	11

Sources: Same as General Statistics. The 'Average of All Manufacturing' column represents the average of all manufacturing industries reported for the most recent complete year available. The Index shows the relationship between the Average and the Analyzed Industry. For example, 100 means that they are equal; 500 that the Analyzed Industry is five times the average; 50 means that the Analyzed Industry is half the national average. The abbreviation 'na' is used to show that data are 'not available'.

LEADING COMPANIES

Number shown: **36** Total sales ($ mil): **403** Total employment (000): **4.9**

Company Name	Address				CEO Name	Phone	Co. Type	Sales ($ mil)	Empl. (000)
BHA Group Inc	8800 E 63rd St	Kansas City	MO	64133	James E Lund	816-356-8400	P	89	0.6
Menardi-Criswell	PO Box 160	Trenton	SC	29847	Len Boesger	803-663-6551	S	30	0.3
MFRI Inc	PO Box 2075	Winchester	VA	22601	David Unger	703-667-8500	P	30	0.2
Super Sack Manufacturing Corp	PO Box 245	Savoy	TX	75479	David Kellenberger	903-340-7060	R	25	0.3
Bulk Lift International Inc	202 Springhill Dr	Carpentersville	IL	60110	Peter Nattrass	708-428-6059	R	22*	0.4
Innovo Group Inc	PO Box 576	Springfield	TN	37172	Pat Anderson	615-384-0100	P	18	0.2
Cady Bag Company Inc	PO Box 68	Pearson	GA	31642	Wanda C Walker	912-422-3298	R	16	0.3
Kenneth Fox Supply Co	2200 Fox Rd	McAllen	TX	78501	Kenneth Fox	210-682-6176	R	13*	0.2
J and M Industries Inc	PO Box 3188	New Orleans	LA	70177	Maurice Gaudet	504-947-1002	R	13	0.2
Central Bag Co	1323 W 13th St	Kansas City	MO	64102	Tom Simone	816-471-0388	R	12*	<0.1
Custom Packaging Systems Inc	PO Box 183	Manistee	MI	49660	Lee LaFleur	616-723-5211	R	10	0.4
US Lawn Products Inc	3110 Ranchview Ln	Minneapolis	MN	55447	Steve Sullivan	612-559-1092	R	10	<0.1
Innovo Inc	27 N Main St	Springfield	TN	37172	Pat D Anderson	615-384-0100	S	9*	0.2
Allied Duralux Inc	PO Box 1017	Beulaville	NC	28518	Arthur Lux	910-298-5154	R	8*	<0.1
Athletic Bag Co	PO Box 27273	Salt Lake City	UT	84127	David L Whiting	801-972-4866	R	7	0.1
A Rifkin Co	PO Box 878	Wilkes-Barre	PA	18703	AS Rifkin	717-825-9551	R	7*	0.2
Designer Line	1045 W 500 N	Logan	UT	84321	Peter Erenfeld	801-753-7560	R	7	0.2
American Bag and Burlap Co	32 Arlington St	Chelsea	MA	02150	Elliot Corman	617-884-7600	R	6	<0.1
Halsted Corp	78 Halladay St	Jersey City	NJ	07304	HL Jaszewski	201-433-3323	R	6*	<0.1
Morgan Brothers Bag Company	PO Box 25577	Richmond	VA	23260	GD Morgan Jr	804-355-9107	R	6	<0.1
RM Crow Co	PO Box 20908	Waco	TX	76702	Edna Kunze	817-772-5280	R	6*	<0.1
Augusta Bag Company Inc	PO Box 335	Evans	GA	30809	HL Hamilton Jr	706-860-3499	R	5*	<0.1
Bearse Manufacturing Co	3815 W Cortland	Chicago	IL	60647	JA Erickson	312-235-8710	R	5	0.2
Birt Inc	PO Box 15352	Houston	TX	77020	AB Dowling II	713-675-5323	R	5	<0.1
Dyersburg Fabrics Inc	PO Drawer 107	Trenton	TN	38382	KD Holder	901-855-1323	D	5	0.2
Fisher Bag Company Inc	1560 1st Av S	Seattle	WA	98134	L J Fisher	206-623-1966	R	5	<0.1
Mountain Equipment Inc	4776 E Jensen Av	Fresno	CA	93725	Paul M Honkavaara	209-486-8211	R	5	<0.1
United Bags Inc	PO Box 297	St Louis	MO	63166	Herbert Greenberg	314-421-3700	R	5	<0.1
Ace Bag and Burlap Company	166 Frelinghuysen	Newark	NJ	07114	R Jay Sherman	201-242-2200	R	5	<0.1
Billboard Concepts Inc	861 E Hennepin	Minneapolis	MN	55414	Michar Miller	612-378-3200	R	4	<0.1
Tough Traveler Inc	1012 State St	Schenectady	NY	12307	Nancy Gold	518-377-8526	R	4	<0.1
Fulton-Denver Co	3500 Winekoop St	Denver	CO	80216	D Pope	303-294-9292	R	3*	<0.1
Chase Line	PO Box 398	Reidsville	NC	27323	Phil Brooks	910-342-1313	R	2*	<0.1
BJ Seaman and Co	1801 S Lumber St	Chicago	IL	60616	Bert J Seaman	312-666-6580	R	1	<0.1
Berg Bag Co	410 3rd Av N	Minneapolis	MN	55401	A Berg	612-332-8845	R	1*	<0.1
Tree Saver Inc	PO Box 22745	Denver	CO	80222	Trisha Hood	303-695-6163	R	0	<0.1

Source: *Ward's Business Directory of U.S. Private and Public Companies*, Volumes 1 and 2, 1996. The company type code used is as follows: P - Public, R - Private, S - Subsidiary, D - Division, J - Joint Venture, A - Affiliate, G - Group. Sales are in millions of dollars, employees are in thousands. An asterisk (*) indicates an estimated sales volume. The symbol < stands for 'less than'. Company names and addresses are truncated, in some cases, to fit into the available space.

MATERIALS CONSUMED

Material		Quantity	Delivered Cost ($ million)
Materials, ingredients, containers, and supplies		(X)	389.2
Cotton broadwoven fabrics (piece goods)	mil sq yd	44.8*	47.2
Rayon and acetate broadwoven fabrics (piece goods)	mil sq yd	3.0*	2.2
Polyester broadwoven fabrics (piece goods)	mil sq yd	11.0*	16.9
Nylon broadwoven fabrics (piece goods)	mil sq yd	12.9*	31.9
Other broadwoven fabrics (piece goods)	mil sq yd	(S)	48.5
Narrow fabrics (12 inches or less in width)	mil sq yd	(S)	11.9
Yarn, all fibers	mil lb	9.2**	11.5
Plastics coated, impregnated, or laminated fabrics	mil sq yd	42.1**	34.0
Manmade fibers, staple, and tow	mil lb	29.2	12.3
Plastics products consumed in the form of sheets, rods, tubes, film, and other shapes		(X)	16.3
All other materials and components, parts, containers, and supplies		(X)	107.3
Materials, ingredients, containers, and supplies, nsk		(X)	49.2

Source: 1992 *Economic Census*. Explanation of symbols used: (D): Withheld to avoid disclosure of competitive data; na: Not available; (S): Withheld because statistical norms were not met; (X): Not applicable; (Z): Less than half the unit shown; nec: Not elsewhere classified; nsk: Not specified by kind; - : zero; * : 10-19 percent estimated; ** : 20-29 percent estimated.

PRODUCT SHARE DETAILS

Product or Product Class	% Share	Product or Product Class	% Share
Textile bags	100.00	Duffle bags and knapsacks, wholly or chiefly manmade fiber fabrics	10.94
Duffle bags and knapsacks, wholly or chiefly cotton (including cotton canvas and open-mesh cotton)	4.06	Split polyethylene or polypropylene strip (except duffle), wholly or chiefly manmade fiber fabrics	9.31
Other bags, wholly or chiefly cotton (including cotton canvas and open-mesh cotton)	23.65	Other manmade fiber fabrics, except duffle	10.52
Textile bags (except laundry, wardrobe, and shoe), spun paper	(D)	Textile bags (except laundry, wardrobe, and shoe), other fabrics	(D)
Textile bags (except laundry, wardrobe, and shoe), burlap	9.24		

Source: 1992 *Economic Census*. The values shown are percent of total shipments in an industry. Values of indented subcategories are summed in the main heading. The symbol (D) appears when data are withheld to prevent disclosure of competitive information. The abbreviation nsk stands for 'not specified by kind' and nec for 'not elsewhere classified'.

INPUTS AND OUTPUTS FOR TEXTILE BAGS

Economic Sector or Industry Providing Inputs	%	Sector	Economic Sector or Industry Buying Outputs	%	Sector
Broadwoven fabric mills	42.7	Manufg.	Personal consumption expenditures	22.5	
Noncomparable imports	15.6	Foreign	Banking	19.9	Fin/R.E.
Nonwoven fabrics	7.8	Manufg.	Agricultural, forestry, & fishery services	13.1	Agric.
Wholesale trade	7.4	Trade	Wholesale trade	12.1	Trade
Coated fabrics, not rubberized	5.3	Manufg.	Prepared feeds, nec	4.0	Manufg.
Miscellaneous plastics products	3.0	Manufg.	Flour & other grain mill products	3.9	Manufg.
Imports	2.9	Foreign	Vegetables	3.8	Agric.
Motor freight transportation & warehousing	2.5	Util.	Exports	3.4	Foreign
Water transportation	1.8	Util.	Fruits	2.8	Agric.
Advertising	1.0	Services	Pleating & stitching	2.6	Manufg.
Electric services (utilities)	0.9	Util.	Fertilizers, mixing only	2.0	Manufg.
Narrow fabric mills	0.8	Manufg.	Federal Government purchases, national defense	1.8	Fed Govt
Eating & drinking places	0.8	Trade	Automotive & apparel trimmings	1.1	Manufg.
Real estate	0.8	Fin/R.E.	Dog, cat, & other pet food	1.1	Manufg.
Paperboard containers & boxes	0.6	Manufg.	Knit outerwear mills	0.9	Manufg.
Thread mills	0.6	Manufg.	U.S. Postal Service	0.9	Gov't
Gas production & distribution (utilities)	0.6	Util.	Knit underwear mills	0.7	Manufg.
Textile bags	0.4	Manufg.	Laundry, dry cleaning, shoe repair	0.6	Services
Banking	0.3	Fin/R.E.	S/L Govt. purch., sanitation	0.5	S/L Govt
Detective & protective services	0.3	Services	Tree nuts	0.4	Agric.
Equipment rental & leasing services	0.3	Services	Hospitals	0.4	Services
Management & consulting services & labs	0.3	Services	Textile bags	0.3	Manufg.
U.S. Postal Service	0.3	Gov't	Local government passenger transit	0.3	Gov't
Maintenance of nonfarm buildings nec	0.2	Constr.	State & local government enterprises, nec	0.3	Gov't
Fabricated textile products, nec	0.2	Manufg.	Grass seeds	0.2	Agric.
Communications, except radio & TV	0.2	Util.	Cereal breakfast foods	0.1	Manufg.
Accounting, auditing & bookkeeping	0.2	Services			
Electrical repair shops	0.2	Services			
Laundry, dry cleaning, shoe repair	0.2	Services			
Legal services	0.2	Services			
Machinery, except electrical, nec	0.1	Manufg.			
Yarn mills & finishing of textiles, nec	0.1	Manufg.			
Insurance carriers	0.1	Fin/R.E.			
Royalties	0.1	Fin/R.E.			
Computer & data processing services	0.1	Services			

Source: Benchmark Input-Output Accounts for the U.S. Economy, 1982, U.S. Department of Commerce, Washington, D.C., July 1991. Data, as reported in the source, are organized by the 1977 SIC structure in use in 1982 but have been matched, as closely as is possible, to the 1987 SIC structure used in this book.

OCCUPATIONS EMPLOYED BY SIC 239 - MISCELLANEOUS FABRICATED TEXTILE PRODUCTS

Occupation	% of Total 1994	Change to 2005	Occupation	% of Total 1994	Change to 2005
Sewing machine operators, non-garment	21.5	-26.0	Cutters & trimmers, hand	1.9	-25.9
Sewing machine operators, garment	11.0	36.7	Sales & related workers nec	1.8	13.9
Assemblers, fabricators, & hand workers nec	8.6	13.9	Textile draw-out & winding machine operators	1.8	2.5
Hand packers & packagers	3.9	-2.4	Machine feeders & offbearers	1.5	2.5
Blue collar worker supervisors	3.6	4.6	Machine operators nec	1.4	0.4
General managers & top executives	3.1	8.1	Bookkeeping, accounting, & auditing clerks	1.4	-14.6
Helpers, laborers, & material movers nec	2.7	13.9	Industrial machinery mechanics	1.3	25.3
Inspectors, testers, & graders, precision	2.6	13.9	General office clerks	1.2	-2.9
Screen printing machine setters & set-up operators	2.3	36.7	Industrial production managers	1.2	13.9
Freight, stock, & material movers, hand	2.3	-8.9	Secretaries, ex legal & medical	1.1	3.7
Traffic, shipping, & receiving clerks	2.1	9.6	Cutting & slicing machine setters, operators	1.0	25.3

Source: Industry-Occupation Matrix, Bureau of Labor Statistics. These data relate to one or more 3-digit SIC industry groups rather than to a single 4-digit SIC. The change reported for each occupation to the year 2005 is a percent of growth or decline as estimated by the Bureau of Labor Statistics. The abbreviation nec stands for 'not elsewhere classified'.

LOCATION BY STATE AND REGIONAL CONCENTRATION

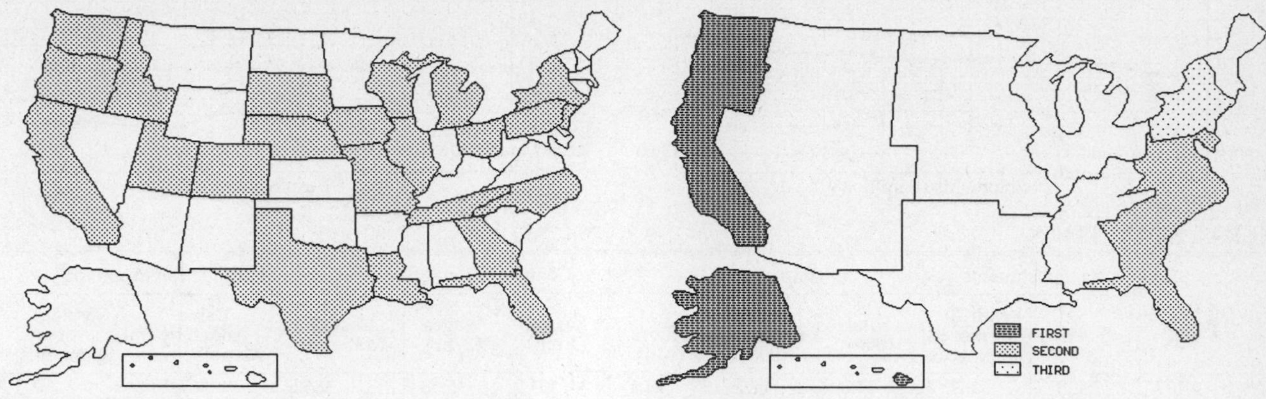

INDUSTRY DATA BY STATE

State	Establish-ments	Shipments			Employment				Cost as % of Shipments	Investment per Employee ($)
		Total ($ mil)	% of U.S.	Per Establ.	Total Number	% of U.S.	Per Establ.	Wages ($/hour)		
California	38	101.1	13.0	2.7	1,300	10.9	34	6.36	62.5	1,000
Missouri	8	85.0	10.9	10.6	600	5.0	75	5.36	70.8	-
Georgia	18	82.2	10.6	4.6	1,300	10.9	72	6.24	52.8	923
Texas	26	45.3	5.8	1.7	900	7.6	35	6.21	52.8	333
North Carolina	13	43.7	5.6	3.4	700	5.9	54	6.33	56.5	1,000
New Jersey	9	31.4	4.0	3.5	500	4.2	56	7.00	66.2	400
Pennsylvania	11	29.0	3.7	2.6	400	3.4	36	7.00	52.4	1,250
New York	18	25.5	3.3	1.4	400	3.4	22	8.40	45.5	-
Wisconsin	6	25.2	3.2	4.2	400	3.4	67	8.13	52.8	1,250
Tennessee	9	24.2	3.1	2.7	300	2.5	33	7.25	56.2	1,000
Louisiana	7	23.9	3.1	3.4	300	2.5	43	5.33	59.8	-
Florida	11	22.8	2.9	2.1	600	5.0	55	5.70	44.3	-
Washington	10	22.2	2.9	2.2	400	3.4	40	6.29	54.5	500
Illinois	12	21.8	2.8	1.8	400	3.4	33	5.71	54.1	1,750
Iowa	7	18.3	2.4	2.6	300	2.5	43	5.00	53.6	-
Ohio	9	17.8	2.3	2.0	300	2.5	33	7.75	51.7	1,000
Colorado	8	17.5	2.2	2.2	300	2.5	38	6.20	53.1	1,000
Utah	11	15.3	2.0	1.4	400	3.4	36	6.00	40.5	-
Michigan	6	14.0	1.8	2.3	200	1.7	33	9.00	57.9	1,500
Oregon	6	(D)	-	-	375 *	3.2	63	-	-	-
Idaho	5	(D)	-	-	175 *	1.5	35	-	-	-
South Dakota	5	(D)	-	-	375 *	3.2	75	-	-	-
Nebraska	2	(D)	-	-	175 *	1.5	88	-	-	-

Source: 1992 *Economic Census*. The states are in descending order of shipments or establishments (if shipment data are missing for the majority). The symbol (D) appears when data are withheld to prevent disclosure of competitive information. States marked with (D) are sorted by number of establishments. A dash (-) indicates that the data element cannot be calculated; * indicates the midpoint of a range.

2394 - CANVAS AND RELATED PRODUCTS

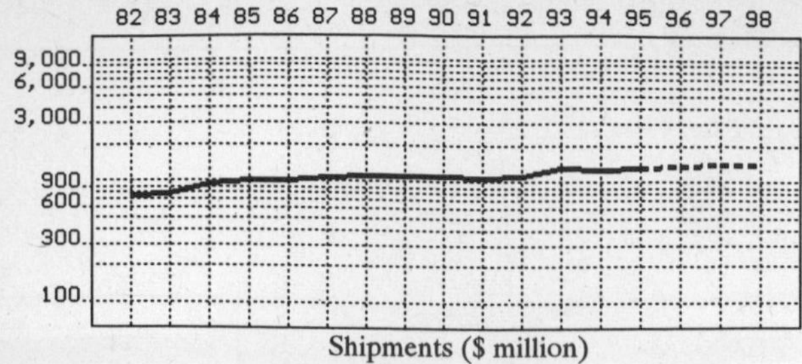

Shipments ($ million)

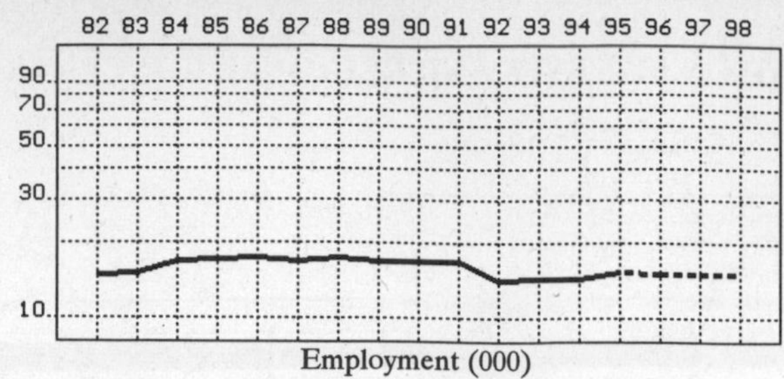

Employment (000)

GENERAL STATISTICS

Year	Com-panies	Establishments		Employment			Compensation		Production ($ million)			
		Total	with 20 or more employees	Total (000)	Production Workers (000)	Production Hours (Mil)	Payroll ($ mil)	Wages ($/hr)	Cost of Materials	Value Added by Manufacture	Value of Shipments	Capital Invest.
1982	1,107	1,128	162	14.8	11.3	21.1	181.2	5.58	384.5	367.7	752.3	17.8
1983		1,128	165	15.2	11.8	22.5	197.1	5.62	409.7	391.8	791.9	12.6
1984		1,128	168	16.9	12.9	28.2	230.3	5.63	468.3	507.1	953.0	20.8
1985		1,127	170	17.2	13.6	29.4	247.7	5.91	546.6	462.2	1,013.8	19.8
1986		1,135	184	17.5	13.8	27.9	263.0	6.48	536.4	474.3	1,019.9	23.7
1987	1,261	1,273	196	16.7	12.6	23.8	270.6	7.20	525.0	550.0	1,064.7	20.1
1988		1,207	190	17.3	12.9	24.6	296.8	7.61	549.7	564.7	1,118.7	9.5
1989		1,207	195	16.7	13.9	24.3	291.6	7.42	562.3	524.2	1,094.8	22.5
1990		1,220	191	16.8	13.8	24.8	306.0	7.54	605.3	531.1	1,134.9	21.5
1991		1,233	179	16.7	13.3	23.2	304.2	8.03	548.4	517.6	1,063.8	19.2
1992	1,291	1,307	179	14.2	10.4	19.7	275.3	8.46	538.6	578.8	1,107.8	19.2
1993		1,336	183	14.5	11.4	20.8	293.1	8.85	732.5	567.2	1,302.4	26.2
1994		1,322P	193P	14.4	11.4	21.9	267.3	8.73	639.2	625.7	1,250.1	28.2
1995		1,340P	195P	15.3P	12.1P	21.6P	319.3P	9.28P	666.8P	652.7P	1,304.0P	24.7P
1996		1,358P	197P	15.2P	12.1P	21.3P	327.3P	9.58P	685.2P	670.8P	1,340.1P	25.4P
1997		1,377P	199P	15.1P	12.0P	20.9P	335.3P	9.88P	703.7P	688.8P	1,376.2P	26.0P
1998		1,395P	201P	15.0P	11.9P	20.6P	343.2P	10.18P	722.1P	706.9P	1,412.3P	26.7P

Sources: 1982, 1987, 1992 *Economic Census*; *Annual Survey of Manufactures*, 83-86, 88-91, 93-94. Establishment counts for non-Census years are from *County Business Patterns*; establishment values for 83-84 are extrapolations. 'P's show projections by the editors. Industries reclassified in 87 will not have data for prior years.

INDICES OF CHANGE

Year	Com-panies	Establishments		Employment			Compensation		Production ($ million)			
		Total	with 20 or more employees	Total (000)	Production Workers (000)	Production Hours (Mil)	Payroll ($ mil)	Wages ($/hr)	Cost of Materials	Value Added by Manufacture	Value of Shipments	Capital Invest.
1982	86	86	91	104	109	107	66	66	71	64	68	93
1983		86	92	107	113	114	72	66	76	68	71	66
1984		86	94	119	124	143	84	67	87	88	86	108
1985		86	95	121	131	149	90	70	101	80	92	103
1986		87	103	123	133	142	96	77	100	82	92	123
1987	98	97	109	118	121	121	98	85	97	95	96	105
1988		92	106	122	124	125	108	90	102	98	101	49
1989		92	109	118	134	123	106	88	104	91	99	117
1990		93	107	118	133	126	111	89	112	92	102	112
1991		94	100	118	128	118	110	95	102	89	96	100
1992	100	100	100	100	100	100	100	100	100	100	100	100
1993		102	102	102	110	106	106	105	136	98	118	136
1994		101P	108P	101	110	111	97	103	119	108	113	147
1995		103P	109P	108P	117P	110P	116P	110P	124P	113P	118P	129P
1996		104P	110P	107P	116P	108P	119P	113P	127P	116P	121P	132P
1997		105P	111P	106P	115P	106P	122P	117P	131P	119P	124P	136P
1998		107P	112P	106P	115P	105P	125P	120P	134P	122P	127P	139P

Sources: Same as General Statistics. Values reflect change from the base year, 1992. Values above 100 mean greater than 92, values below 100 mean less than 92, and a value of 100 in the 82-91 or 93-98 period means same as 92. 'P's mark projections by the editors.

SELECTED RATIOS

For 1994	Avg. of All Manufact.	Analyzed Industry	Index	For 1994	Avg. of All Manufact.	Analyzed Industry	Index
Employees per Establishment	49	11	22	Value Added per Production Worker	134,084	54,886	41
Payroll per Establishment	1,500,273	202,238	13	Cost per Establishment	5,045,178	483,615	10
Payroll per Employee	30,620	18,562	61	Cost per Employee	102,970	44,389	43
Production Workers per Establishment	34	9	25	Cost per Production Worker	146,988	56,070	38
Wages per Establishment	853,319	144,651	17	Shipments per Establishment	9,576,895	945,819	10
Wages per Production Worker	24,861	16,771	67	Shipments per Employee	195,460	86,812	44
Hours per Production Worker	2,056	1,921	93	Shipments per Production Worker	279,017	109,658	39
Wages per Hour	12.09	8.73	72	Investment per Establishment	321,011	21,336	7
Value Added per Establishment	4,602,255	473,401	10	Investment per Employee	6,552	1,958	30
Value Added per Employee	93,930	43,451	46	Investment per Production Worker	9,352	2,474	26

Sources: Same as General Statistics. The 'Average of All Manufacturing' column represents the average of all manufacturing industries reported for the most recent complete year available. The Index shows the relationship between the Average and the Analyzed Industry. For example, 100 means that they are equal; 500 that the Analyzed Industry is five times the average; 50 means that the Analyzed Industry is half the national average. The abbreviation 'na' is used to show that data are 'not available'.

LEADING COMPANIES

Number shown: **59** Total sales ($ mil): **403** Total employment (000): **4.3**

Company Name	Address				CEO Name	Phone	Co. Type	Sales ($ mil)	Empl. (000)
American Recreation Products	1224 Fern Ridge Pk	St Louis	MO	63141	G J Grabner Jr	314-576-8000	S	70	0.6
North Sails Group Inc	66 Quirk Rd	Milford	CT	06460	Tom Whidden	203-877-8234	S	35	0.3
Outdoor Venture Corp	PO Box 337	Stearns	KY	42647	James C Egnew	606-376-5021	R	35	0.2
CR Daniels Inc	3451 Ellicott Ctr	Ellicott City	MD	21043	GV Abel	410-461-2100	R	20	0.5
Hoover Industries Inc	PO Box 522337	Miami	FL	33152	Ron Nobles	305-888-9791	S	20*	0.3
Birdair Inc	65 Lawrence Bell	Amherst	NY	14221	L James Newman	716-633-9500	R	14	0.1
NSC Corp	1601 Mountain St	Aurora	IL	60505	Louis Levin	312-379-9190	R	13	0.2
Clamshell Building Inc	1990 Knoll Dr	Ventura	CA	93003	Sandford Waddell	805-650-1700	R	12	<0.1
Midwest Canvas Corp	4635 W Lake St	Chicago	IL	60644	Gary R Handwerker	312-287-4400	R	12	0.2
Attwoot Corp	1526 E Forrest Av	East Point	GA	30344	Dirk Hyde	404-766-0259	R	10	<0.1
Canvas Specialty	7344 E Bandini Blvd	Los Angeles	CA	90040	P Friedman	213-722-1156	R	10	0.1
Harry Miller Company Inc	120 Southampton St	Boston	MA	02118	SL Miller	617-427-2300	R	10	<0.1
John Johnson Co	1481 14th St	Detroit	MI	48216	C A Keersmaeker	313-496-0600	R	10	0.1
Loop-Loc Ltd	100 Engineers Rd	Hauppauge	NY	11788	William Donaton	516-582-2626	R	10*	0.1
Wahpeton Canvas Co	PO Box 713	Yankton	SD	57078	William Shorma	605-665-6000	R	10	0.1
Diamond Brand Canvas	Hwy 25 N	Naples	NC	28760	Arnold Kemp	704-684-6261	R	7*	0.1
DC Humphreys Company Inc	5744 Woodland Av	Philadelphia	PA	19143	Ronald Nissenbaum	215-724-8181	R	7	<0.1
Carpenter Rigging	222 Napoleon St	San Francisco	CA	94124	Bernard Martin	415-285-1954	R	6*	<0.1
M Putterman and Company Inc	4834 S Oakley	Chicago	IL	60609	Edward E Reicin	312-927-4120	R	6*	<0.1
Rainier Industries Ltd	620 S Indrial Way	Seattle	WA	98108	Scott C Campbell	206-622-8219	R	6	<0.1
DC May Ma-Crepe Corp	PO Box 1926	Durham	NC	27702	Mike D May	919-682-6511	R	5	<0.1
Tensar Industries Inc	13550 Bloomingdale	Akron	NY	14001	James Cornell	716-542-5888	R	5	<0.1
Canvas Products Co	10411 Capital Av	Oak Park	MI	48237	C Keersmaekers	810-398-3500	R	4	<0.1
Campbell Manufacturing	4301 S Fitzhugh Av	Dallas	TX	75210	H P Campbell Jr	214-428-7454	R	4*	<0.1
Eide Industries Inc	16215 Piuma Av	Cerritos	CA	90703	DJ Araiza	310-402-8335	R	4	<0.1
Phoenix Industries of Huntsville	2939 Johnson SW	Huntsville	AL	35805	HB Dodson	205-880-0671	R	4	0.1
Bailey and Staub Inc	PO Box 67	New London	CT	06320	Nicholas Staub II	203-442-5621	R	3	<0.1
Budge Industries Inc	821 Tech Dr	Telford	PA	18969	Bruce Baron	215-721-6700	R	3*	<0.1
Cabo Rico Yachts Inc	2258 SE 17th St	Ft Lauderdale	FL	33316	Fraser W Smith	305-462-6699	R	3	<0.1
Canamer International Inc	PO Box 82	Winona	MN	55987	PB Double	507-452-1700	R	3	<0.1
Detroit Cover Co	4892 Grand River	Detroit	MI	48208	RH Dancy	313-898-9202	R	3	<0.1
Webb Manufacturing Corp	1241 Carpenter St	Philadelphia	PA	19147	Steve Krupnick	215-336-5570	R	3*	<0.1
KD Kanopy Inc	3755 W 69th Pl	Westminster	CO	80030	James P Lynch	303-650-1310	R	3	<0.1
JC Goss Co	6330 E Jefferson	Detroit	MI	48207	Richard A Dancy Jr	313-259-3520	R	3	<0.1
Steele Canvas Basket Corp	PO Box 6267	Chelsea	MA	02150	John J Lordan	617-889-0202	R	3	<0.1
Baltimore Canvas Products	2861 W Franklin St	Baltimore	MD	21223	Rick Hansen	410-947-7890	R	2	<0.1
Ecotat Systems Company Inc	2200 Com Pkwy	Virginia Beach	VA	23454	Monroe Ozment	804-340-0866	R	2	<0.1
Moss Inc	146 Northport Av	Belfast	ME	04915	Maryln Moss	207-236-8368	R	2*	<0.1
Service Canvas Company Inc	149 Swan St	Buffalo	NY	14203	Jerry H Eron	716-853-0558	R	2	<0.1
Sommer Awning Co	5060 E 62nd St	Indianapolis	IN	46220	Stephen Sommer	317-257-4300	R	2	<0.1
CBF Industries Inc	PO Box 540204	Dallas	TX	75354	Jeannine Franklin	214-358-3281	R	2	<0.1
Josephson Bag and Canvas Inc	PO Box 398	Bridgeport	CT	06601	Adam Y Scheps	203-335-2109	R	2	<0.1
Mankato Tent and Awning Co	1021 Range St	North Mankato	MN	56001	Charles Gasswint	507-625-5115	R	2	<0.1
Thurston Sails Inc	112 Tupelo St	Bristol	RI	02809	Steve Thurston	401-254-0970	R	1	<0.1
Austin Canvas Specialty Inc	1014 N Graham St	Charlotte	NC	28206	R Hall	704-375-7321	R	1*	<0.1
AL Robertson Inc	331 S Kresson St	Baltimore	MD	21224	David R Bullock	410-327-6320	R	1	<0.1
Cotton Goods Manufacturing	216 N Clinton St	Chicago	IL	60661	Edward M Lewis	312-346-2097	R	1	<0.1
Federal Sales Corp	511 30th Av SE	Minneapolis	MN	55414	Sigmund M Harris	612-331-1829	R	1	<0.1
Hood Sailmakers Inc	200 High Point Av	Portsmouth	RI	02871	J T Woodhouse III	401-683-4660	R	1*	<0.1
Philip A Stitt Agencies	3900 Stockton Blv	Sacramento	CA	95820	Philip L Stitt	916-451-2801	R	1	<0.1
Rose City Awning Co	1638 NW Overton	Portland	OR	97209	Jack Neustadter	503-226-2761	R	1	<0.1
Teral Inc	PO Box 238	Cheshire	OR	97419	Terri May Kwake	503-998-8504	R	1*	<0.1
T Williams and Son Inc	211 N Northwest	Barrington	IL	60010	Lee J Ford Jr	708-381-1992	R	1	<0.1
McGregor Agri Corporation Inc	PO Box 189	McGregor	MN	55760	Paul McCarron	218-768-4811	R	1	<0.1
TD Industrial Coverings Inc	7330 Nineteen Mile	Sterling Hts	MI	48314	Thomas D'Andreta	810-731-2080	R	1	<0.1
Smith Rents Tents of Florida Inc	1079 Cephas Rd	Clearwater	FL	34625	Bruce Smith	813-448-0987	R	1*	<0.1
C and C Canvas Co	10900 E Faucett	S El Monte	CA	91733	Terry Bleick	818-442-4493	R	1*	<0.1
Crosley Canvas	2370 S Blue Island	Chicago	IL	60608	Joel Levit	312-247-1631	R	1	<0.1
Nomadics Tipi Makers	17671 Snow Creek	Bend	OR	97701	Jeb Barton	503-389-3980	R	0	<0.1

Source: Ward's Business Directory of U.S. Private and Public Companies, Volumes 1 and 2, 1996. The company type code used is as follows: P - Public, R - Private, S - Subsidiary, D - Division, J - Joint Venture, A - Affiliate, G - Group. Sales are in millions of dollars, employees are in thousands. An asterisk (*) indicates an estimated sales volume. The symbol < stands for 'less than'. Company names and addresses are truncated, in some cases, to fit into the available space.

MATERIALS CONSUMED

Material		Quantity	Delivered Cost ($ million)
Materials, ingredients, containers, and supplies		(X)	469.3
Cotton broadwoven fabrics (piece goods)	mil sq yd	19.9*	27.2
Rayon and acetate broadwoven fabrics (piece goods)	mil sq yd	0.5*	1.1
Polyester broadwoven fabrics (piece goods)	mil sq yd	5.6*	16.6
Nylon broadwoven fabrics (piece goods)	mil sq yd	(S)	23.3
Other broadwoven fabrics (piece goods)	mil sq yd	(S)	21.1
Narrow fabrics (12 inches or less in width)	mil sq yd	(S)	5.7
Yarn, all fibers	mil lb	(S)	1.0
Plastics coated, impregnated, or laminated fabrics	mil sq yd	20.3**	54.3
Manmade fibers, staple, and tow	mil lb	(S)	1.1
Plastics products consumed in the form of sheets, rods, tubes, film, and other shapes		(X)	3.0
All other materials and components, parts, containers, and supplies		(X)	108.6
Materials, ingredients, containers, and supplies, nsk		(X)	206.3

Source: 1992 *Economic Census*. Explanation of symbols used: (D): Withheld to avoid disclosure of competitive data; na: Not available; (S): Withheld because statistical norms were not met; (X): Not applicable; (Z): Less than half the unit shown; nec: Not elsewhere classified; nsk: Not specified by kind; - : zero; * : 10-19 percent estimated; ** : 20-29 percent estimated.

PRODUCT SHARE DETAILS

Product or Product Class	% Share	Product or Product Class	% Share
Canvas and related products	100.00	Tarpaulins and other covers, flat, made from cotton, nylon, polyester, and other industrial fabrics	12.56
Canvas and related products (made from cotton, nylon, polyester, and other industrial fabrics), awnings	20.53	Tarpaulins and other covers, fitted, made from cotton, nylon, polyester, and other industrial fabrics	11.53
Camping tents made from cotton, nylon, polyester, and other industrial fabrics	6.58	Canvas sails, made from cotton, nylon, polyester, and other industrial fabrics	4.41
Other tents, including air supported structures and tension structures, made from cotton, nylon, polyester, and other industrial fabrics	7.86	All other canvas products, except bags, made from cotton, nylon, polyester, and other industrial fabrics	15.39

Source: 1992 *Economic Census*. The values shown are percent of total shipments in an industry. Values of indented subcategories are summed in the main heading. The symbol (D) appears when data are withheld to prevent disclosure of competitive information. The abbreviation nsk stands for 'not specified by kind' and nec for 'not elsewhere classified'.

INPUTS AND OUTPUTS FOR CANVAS & RELATED PRODUCTS

Economic Sector or Industry Providing Inputs	%	Sector	Economic Sector or Industry Buying Outputs	%	Sector
Broadwoven fabric mills	31.6	Manufg.	Personal consumption expenditures	27.2	
Coated fabrics, not rubberized	13.2	Manufg.	Pipelines, except natural gas	9.2	Util.
Yarn mills & finishing of textiles, nec	9.7	Manufg.	Water transportation	6.5	Util.
Wholesale trade	9.3	Trade	Vegetables	5.3	Agric.
Fabricated textile products, nec	6.9	Manufg.	Retail trade, except eating & drinking	4.0	Trade
Narrow fabric mills	3.8	Manufg.	Fruits	3.8	Agric.
Needles, pins, & fasteners	3.3	Manufg.	Theatrical producers, bands, entertainers	3.8	Services
Chemical preparations, nec	2.5	Manufg.	U.S. Postal Service	3.7	Gov't
Textile machinery	2.3	Manufg.	Games, toys, & children's vehicles	3.0	Manufg.
Advertising	2.3	Services	Metal household furniture	2.8	Manufg.
Canvas & related products	1.5	Manufg.	Advertising	2.5	Services
Electric services (utilities)	1.4	Util.	Federal Government purchases, national defense	2.2	Fed Govt
Eating & drinking places	1.3	Trade	Boat building & repairing	2.0	Manufg.
Real estate	1.2	Fin/R.E.	Ship building & repairing	2.0	Manufg.
Motor freight transportation & warehousing	0.9	Util.	Eating & drinking places	2.0	Trade
Communications, except radio & TV	0.7	Util.	Commercial fishing	1.8	Agric.
Banking	0.6	Fin/R.E.	Membership sports & recreation clubs	1.7	Services
Equipment rental & leasing services	0.6	Services	Motor freight transportation & warehousing	1.6	Util.
U.S. Postal Service	0.6	Gov't	S/L Govt. purch., public assistance & relief	1.5	S/L Govt
Thread mills	0.5	Manufg.	Exports	1.3	Foreign
Management & consulting services & labs	0.5	Services	Change in business inventories	1.1	In House
Maintenance of nonfarm buildings nec	0.4	Constr.	Forestry products	1.0	Agric.
Gas production & distribution (utilities)	0.4	Util.	Industrial buildings	0.7	Constr.
Imports	0.4	Foreign	Canvas & related products	0.7	Manufg.
Royalties	0.3	Fin/R.E.	Tree nuts	0.5	Agric.
Accounting, auditing & bookkeeping	0.3	Services	Office buildings	0.5	Constr.
Business/professional associations	0.3	Services	Residential garden apartments	0.5	Constr.
Legal services	0.3	Services	Air transportation	0.5	Util.
Lubricating oils & greases	0.2	Manufg.	Residential high-rise apartments	0.4	Constr.
Manifold business forms	0.2	Manufg.	Travel trailers & campers	0.4	Manufg.
Paperboard containers & boxes	0.2	Manufg.	Construction of hospitals	0.3	Constr.
Machinery, except electrical, nec	0.1	Manufg.	Construction of stores & restaurants	0.3	Constr.
Special dies & tools & machine tool accessories	0.1	Manufg.	Residential 1-unit structures, nonfarm	0.3	Constr.
Air transportation	0.1	Util.	Residential additions/alterations, nonfarm	0.3	Constr.
Railroads & related services	0.1	Util.	Colleges, universities, & professional schools	0.3	Services
Insurance carriers	0.1	Fin/R.E.	Motion pictures	0.3	Services
Laundry, dry cleaning, shoe repair	0.1	Services	S/L Govt. purch., health & hospitals	0.3	S/L Govt

Continued on next page.

INPUTS AND OUTPUTS FOR CANVAS & RELATED PRODUCTS - Continued

Economic Sector or Industry Providing Inputs	%	Sector	Economic Sector or Industry Buying Outputs	%	Sector
Personnel supply services	0.1	Services	Grass seeds	0.2	Agric.
			Construction of educational buildings	0.2	Constr.
			Electric utility facility construction	0.2	Constr.
			Highway & street construction	0.2	Constr.
			Hotels & motels	0.2	Constr.
			Maintenance of nonfarm buildings nec	0.2	Constr.
			Residential 2-4 unit structures, nonfarm	0.2	Constr.
			Bowling alleys, billiard & pool establishments	0.2	Services
			S/L Govt. purch., correction	0.2	S/L Govt
			S/L Govt. purch., other general government	0.2	S/L Govt
			Farm service facilities	0.1	Constr.
			Blast furnaces & steel mills	0.1	Manufg.
			Amusement & recreation services nec	0.1	Services

Source: Benchmark Input-Output Accounts for the U.S. Economy, 1982, U.S. Department of Commerce, Washington, D.C., July 1991. Data, as reported in the source, are organized by the 1977 SIC structure in use in 1982 but have been matched, as closely as is possible, to the 1987 SIC structure used in this book.

OCCUPATIONS EMPLOYED BY SIC 239 - MISCELLANEOUS FABRICATED TEXTILE PRODUCTS

Occupation	% of Total 1994	Change to 2005	Occupation	% of Total 1994	Change to 2005
Sewing machine operators, non-garment	21.5	-26.0	Cutters & trimmers, hand	1.9	-25.9
Sewing machine operators, garment	11.0	36.7	Sales & related workers nec	1.8	13.9
Assemblers, fabricators, & hand workers nec	8.6	13.9	Textile draw-out & winding machine operators	1.8	2.5
Hand packers & packagers	3.9	-2.4	Machine feeders & offbearers	1.5	2.5
Blue collar worker supervisors	3.6	4.6	Machine operators nec	1.4	0.4
General managers & top executives	3.1	8.1	Bookkeeping, accounting, & auditing clerks	1.4	-14.6
Helpers, laborers, & material movers nec	2.7	13.9	Industrial machinery mechanics	1.3	25.3
Inspectors, testers, & graders, precision	2.6	13.9	General office clerks	1.2	-2.9
Screen printing machine setters & set-up operators	2.3	36.7	Industrial production managers	1.2	13.9
Freight, stock, & material movers, hand	2.3	-8.9	Secretaries, ex legal & medical	1.1	3.7
Traffic, shipping, & receiving clerks	2.1	9.6	Cutting & slicing machine setters, operators	1.0	25.3

Source: Industry-Occupation Matrix, Bureau of Labor Statistics. These data relate to one or more 3-digit SIC industry groups rather than to a single 4-digit SIC. The change reported for each occupation to the year 2005 is a percent of growth or decline as estimated by the Bureau of Labor Statistics. The abbreviation nec stands for 'not elsewhere classified'.

LOCATION BY STATE AND REGIONAL CONCENTRATION

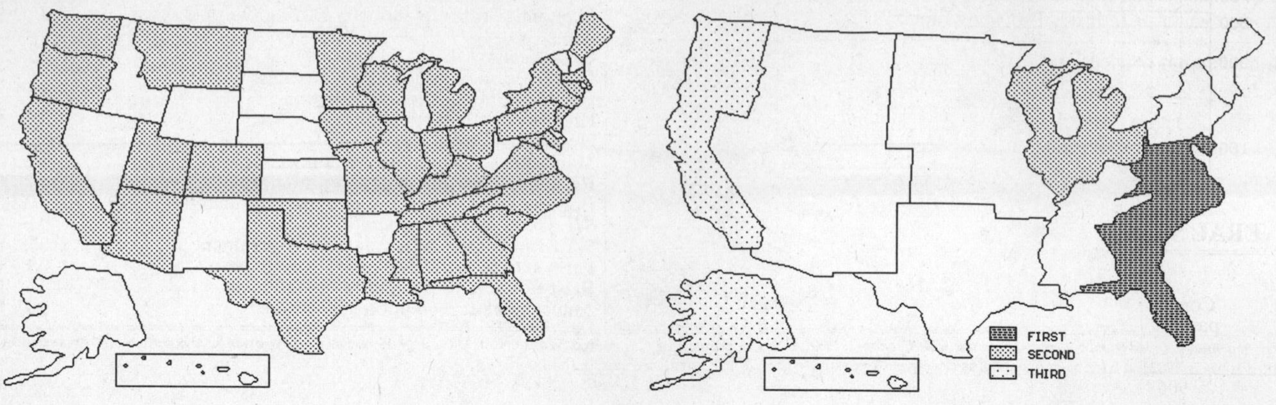

INDUSTRY DATA BY STATE

State	Establish-ments	Shipments			Employment				Cost as % of Shipments	Investment per Employee ($)
		Total ($ mil)	% of U.S.	Per Establ.	Total Number	% of U.S.	Per Establ.	Wages ($/hour)		
New York	90	113.3	10.2	1.3	1,100	7.7	12	9.07	53.5	1,273
California	127	85.9	7.8	0.7	1,200	8.5	9	9.56	46.9	917
Texas	55	75.4	6.8	1.4	800	5.6	15	7.91	43.8	1,000
Illinois	45	67.7	6.1	1.5	800	5.6	18	9.80	47.4	1,125
Indiana	29	59.3	5.4	2.0	900	6.3	31	8.54	48.2	778
Florida	143	51.0	4.6	0.4	900	6.3	6	8.00	45.5	778
Ohio	64	50.1	4.5	0.8	600	4.2	9	7.78	54.3	1,500
Tennessee	19	48.8	4.4	2.6	600	4.2	32	7.11	45.5	333
Wisconsin	34	46.9	4.2	1.4	400	2.8	12	8.40	63.1	2,250
Georgia	25	44.2	4.0	1.8	600	4.2	24	8.00	50.5	-
Michigan	51	40.3	3.6	0.8	600	4.2	12	8.25	46.2	1,000
Connecticut	27	32.4	2.9	1.2	300	2.1	11	9.75	43.8	1,667
Missouri	24	30.6	2.8	1.3	500	3.5	21	8.14	50.3	1,000
Colorado	21	30.5	2.8	1.5	300	2.1	14	8.75	48.5	1,333
Washington	50	29.5	2.7	0.6	400	2.8	8	9.20	40.0	750
Pennsylvania	54	28.0	2.5	0.5	400	2.8	7	9.00	44.3	750
Massachusetts	33	25.6	2.3	0.8	300	2.1	9	9.67	49.6	1,000
Maryland	43	25.0	2.3	0.6	300	2.1	7	9.00	45.6	667
Kentucky	10	21.7	2.0	2.2	300	2.1	30	7.50	57.6	-
Utah	12	20.0	1.8	1.7	200	1.4	17	9.50	44.0	-
South Carolina	16	17.3	1.6	1.1	200	1.4	13	6.50	51.4	-
Arizona	15	15.7	1.4	1.0	200	1.4	13	7.25	48.4	500
North Carolina	28	14.1	1.3	0.5	200	1.4	7	7.67	50.4	1,000
New Jersey	46	13.7	1.2	0.3	200	1.4	4	9.00	46.7	1,000
Oregon	19	11.1	1.0	0.6	200	1.4	11	10.00	51.4	500
Maine	19	10.4	0.9	0.5	100	0.7	5	9.00	39.4	1,000
Virginia	22	9.6	0.9	0.4	200	1.4	9	8.00	50.0	500
Mississippi	10	8.5	0.8	0.9	100	0.7	10	5.50	62.4	1,000
Alabama	16	7.7	0.7	0.5	200	1.4	13	7.50	44.2	500
Louisiana	10	7.0	0.6	0.7	100	0.7	10	6.00	41.4	1,000
Minnesota	21	6.9	0.6	0.3	100	0.7	5	14.00	47.8	1,000
Iowa	14	6.8	0.6	0.5	100	0.7	7	6.00	45.6	1,000
Montana	6	6.5	0.6	1.1	200	1.4	33	6.50	27.7	-
Oklahoma	16	6.1	0.6	0.4	100	0.7	6	4.50	45.9	1,000

Source: 1992 *Economic Census*. The states are in descending order of shipments or establishments (if shipment data are missing for the majority). The symbol (D) appears when data are withheld to prevent disclosure of competitive information. States marked with (D) are sorted by number of establishments. A dash (-) indicates that the data element cannot be calculated; * indicates the midpoint of a range.

2395 - PLEATING AND STITCHING

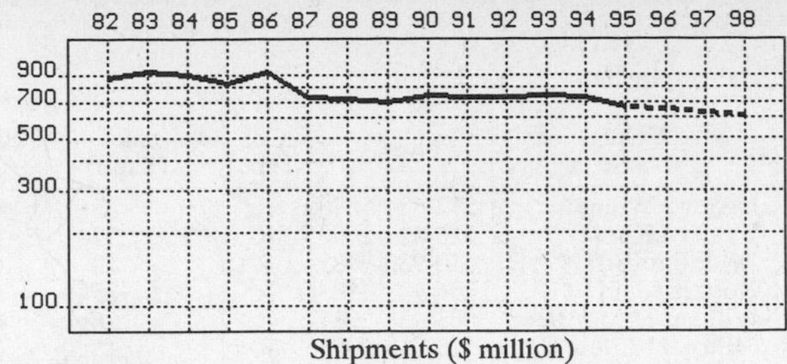

Shipments ($ million)

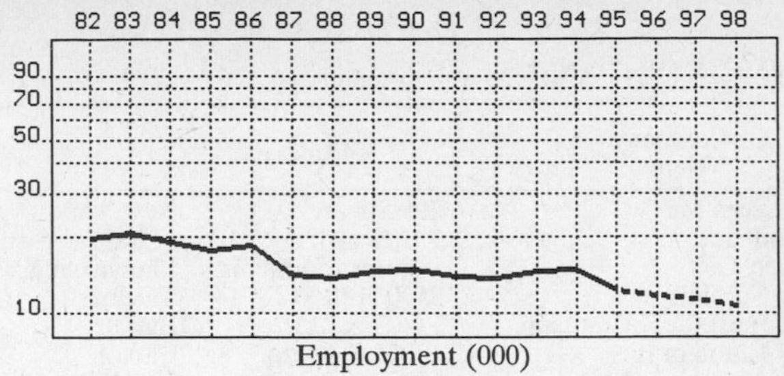

Employment (000)

GENERAL STATISTICS

Year	Companies	Establishments: Total	Establishments: with 20 or more employees	Employment: Total (000)	Production Workers (000)	Production Hours (Mil)	Compensation: Payroll ($ mil)	Compensation: Wages ($/hr)	Production ($ million): Cost of Materials	Value Added by Manufacture	Value of Shipments	Capital Invest.
1982	906	912	269	19.8	16.4	29.0	204.5	5.18	420.5	452.6	873.1	17.0
1983		875	260	20.8	17.3	29.2	207.4	5.21	462.0	474.8	933.4	7.9
1984		838	251	19.2	15.9	27.2	219.4	5.46	453.9	451.2	896.1	13.3
1985		801	243	17.8	14.5	25.3	204.9	5.19	421.3	403.9	829.3	13.1
1986		775	247	18.6	15.2	25.9	229.5	5.70	488.9	432.8	922.1	22.6
1987	679	685	169	14.1	11.8	20.9	174.4	5.75	346.1	396.8	728.0	12.1
1988		661	181	13.7	11.3	20.0	173.6	6.15	338.8	383.0	723.6	7.4
1989		631	185	14.6	11.7	21.4	181.8	5.99	333.1	359.4	691.2	15.6
1990		645	176	14.7	12.1	22.0	186.0	5.96	360.9	388.1	742.7	17.3
1991		654	166	14.0	12.0	22.0	189.0	6.00	307.2	426.0	725.9	16.4
1992	747	756	148	13.7	11.0	20.7	205.0	6.71	355.4	383.3	726.6	22.8
1993		762	141	14.6	11.8	21.9	221.0	6.79	355.1	362.4	732.6	17.0
1994		630P	123P	14.9	12.1	23.8	245.5	6.90	319.9	415.1	729.4	23.5
1995		612P	111P	12.3P	10.0P	19.5P	208.2P	6.94P	291.1P	377.7P	663.8P	20.7P
1996		594P	98P	11.7P	9.5P	18.9P	208.9P	7.08P	283.3P	367.6P	645.9P	21.4P
1997		575P	86P	11.2P	9.0P	18.3P	209.6P	7.23P	275.5P	357.4P	628.1P	22.0P
1998		557P	74P	10.6P	8.6P	17.7P	210.3P	7.37P	267.6P	347.3P	610.2P	22.7P

Sources: 1982, 1987, 1992 *Economic Census*; *Annual Survey of Manufactures*, 83-86, 88-91, 93-94. Establishment counts for non-Census years are from *County Business Patterns*; establishment values for 83-84 are extrapolations. 'P's show projections by the editors. Industries reclassified in 87 will not have data for prior years.

INDICES OF CHANGE

Year	Companies	Establishments: Total	Establishments: with 20 or more employees	Employment: Total (000)	Production Workers (000)	Production Hours (Mil)	Compensation: Payroll ($ mil)	Compensation: Wages ($/hr)	Production ($ million): Cost of Materials	Value Added by Manufacture	Value of Shipments	Capital Invest.
1982	121	121	182	145	149	140	100	77	118	118	120	75
1983		116	176	152	157	141	101	78	130	124	128	35
1984		111	170	140	145	131	107	81	128	118	123	58
1985		106	164	130	132	122	100	77	119	105	114	57
1986		103	167	136	138	125	112	85	138	113	127	99
1987	91	91	114	103	107	101	85	86	97	104	100	53
1988		87	122	100	103	97	85	92	95	100	100	32
1989		83	125	107	106	103	89	89	94	94	95	68
1990		85	119	107	110	106	91	89	102	101	102	76
1991		87	112	102	109	106	92	89	86	111	100	72
1992	100	100	100	100	100	100	100	100	100	100	100	100
1993		101	95	107	107	106	108	101	100	95	101	75
1994		83P	83P	109	110	115	120	103	90	108	100	103
1995		81P	75P	90P	91P	94P	102P	103P	82P	99P	91P	91P
1996		79P	66P	86P	86P	91P	102P	106P	80P	96P	89P	94P
1997		76P	58P	82P	82P	88P	102P	108P	78P	93P	86P	97P
1998		74P	50P	78P	78P	86P	103P	110P	75P	91P	84P	100P

Sources: Same as General Statistics. Values reflect change from the base year, 1992. Values above 100 mean greater than 92, values below 100 mean less than 92, and a value of 100 in the 82-91 or 93-98 period means same as 92. 'P's mark projections by the editors.

SELECTED RATIOS

For 1994	Avg. of All Manufact.	Analyzed Industry	Index
Employees per Establishment	49	24	48
Payroll per Establishment	1,500,273	389,448	26
Payroll per Employee	30,620	16,477	54
Production Workers per Establishment	34	19	56
Wages per Establishment	853,319	260,510	31
Wages per Production Worker	24,861	13,572	55
Hours per Production Worker	2,056	1,967	96
Wages per Hour	12.09	6.90	57
Value Added per Establishment	4,602,255	658,493	14
Value Added per Employee	93,930	27,859	30

For 1994	Avg. of All Manufact.	Analyzed Industry	Index
Value Added per Production Worker	134,084	34,306	26
Cost per Establishment	5,045,178	507,473	10
Cost per Employee	102,970	21,470	21
Cost per Production Worker	146,988	26,438	18
Shipments per Establishment	9,576,895	1,157,082	12
Shipments per Employee	195,460	48,953	25
Shipments per Production Worker	279,017	60,281	22
Investment per Establishment	321,011	37,279	12
Investment per Employee	6,552	1,577	24
Investment per Production Worker	9,352	1,942	21

Sources: Same as General Statistics. The 'Average of All Manufacturing' column represents the average of all manufacturing industries reported for the most recent complete year available. The Index shows the relationship between the Average and the Analyzed Industry. For example, 100 means that they are equal; 500 that the Analyzed Industry is five times the average; 50 means that the Analyzed Industry is half the national average. The abbreviation 'na' is used to show that data are 'not available'.

LEADING COMPANIES Number shown: 26 Total sales ($ mil): 230 Total employment (000): 2.5

Company Name	Address				CEO Name	Phone	Co. Type	Sales ($ mil)	Empl. (000)
Wiener Laces Inc	295 5th Av	New York	NY	10016	Lester J Wiener	212-684-5870	R	35	0.3
Fabri Quilt Inc	901 E 14th Av	N Kansas City	MO	64116	Lionel J Kunst	816-421-2000	R	32	0.2
Kimberton Co	Walnut & Lincoln	Phoenixville	PA	19460	Jay F Smith Jr	610-933-8985	R	28	0.1
Morning Sun Inc	3500 20th St E	Tacoma	WA	98424	Robert Klein	206-922-6589	R	25	0.2
Jubilee Embroidery Company	PO Box 215	Lugoff	SC	29078	William H McAbee	803-438-2934	R	16*	0.2
National Emblem Inc	17036 S Avalon	Carson	CA	90749	Milton H Lubin Sr	310-515-5055	R	15	0.3
United Embroidery Inc	1122 53rd St	North Bergen	NJ	07047	Larry Severini	201-863-0070	R	11*	0.1
Vogue Originals Inc	5101 NW 36th Av	Miami	FL	33142	Yehuda Bilu	305-634-6677	R	10	0.3
St Louis Embroidery	1759 Scherer Pkwy	St Charles	MO	63303	David Schniepp	314-724-2200	D	9*	0.1
DME Industries Inc	37-11 35th Av	Astoria	NY	11101	Jack Greenberg	718-392-7171	R	8	0.1
3 Strikes Custom Design USA	45 Church St	Stamford	CT	06906	Mark Kaufman	203-359-4559	R	5	<0.1
Swiss Maid Inc	RR 1	Greentown	PA	18426	Robert Koch	717-676-3336	R	5	<0.1
Modern Quilters Inc	62038 Hwy 24	Litchfield	MN	55355	John Merrill	612-693-7987	R	5	<0.1
All Kind Quilting Corp	128 Wythe Av	Brooklyn	NY	11211	Israel Fredman	718-388-3013	R	4	<0.1
Needleworks Inc	PO Box 245	Millersburg	PA	17061	Frederick Trimmer	717-692-2144	R	4	<0.1
Action Embroidery Corp	1325 W Brooks St	Ontario	CA	91762	Ozzie Silna	909-983-1359	R	4	0.1
Peerless Embroidery Co	2817 N Western	Chicago	IL	60618	John Lenzinger	312-276-0000	R	4	<0.1
Branded Emblem Company Inc	7920 Foster St	Overland Park	KS	66204	David Willson	913-648-7920	R	3	<0.1
All American Emblem Corp	PO Box 54-9013	Opa Locka	FL	33054	J Lewis Brody	305-688-8800	R	2*	<0.1
DJC Design Studio	227 Sheep Davis Rd	Concord	NH	03301	Diane Jackson-Cole	603-228-0488	R	2	<0.1
I Johns Company Inc	PO Box 550-A	North Bergen	NJ	07047	Alcibiades Cabrera	201-869-3574	R	2	<0.1
Kenmar Comfort Company Inc	1517 S Mateo St	Los Angeles	CA	90021	Abe Popowitz	213-747-2532	R	1*	<0.1
Marilyn Embroidery Corp	PO Box 35106	Dallas	TX	75235	James Santangelo	214-630-6591	R	1*	<0.1
Deborah Mallow	276 5th Av	New York	NY	10001	Brian Chenensky	212-779-0540	R	1	<0.1
UniCargo Group International	7000 W 111th St	Worth	IL	60482	Bob Haberkorn	708-448-1660	R	0	<0.1
Brookfield Enterprises	84 Union Av	Laconia	NH	03246	K H Wakefield	603-524-5973	R	0	<0.1

Source: *Ward's Business Directory of U.S. Private and Public Companies*, Volumes 1 and 2, 1996. The company type code used is as follows: P - Public, R - Private, S - Subsidiary, D - Division, J - Joint Venture, A - Affiliate, G - Group. Sales are in millions of dollars, employees are in thousands. An asterisk (*) indicates an estimated sales volume. The symbol < stands for 'less than'. Company names and addresses are truncated, in some cases, to fit into the available space.

MATERIALS CONSUMED

Material	Quantity	Delivered Cost ($ million)
No Materials Consumed data available for this industry.		

Source: 1992 *Economic Census*. Explanation of symbols used: (D): Withheld to avoid disclosure of competitive data; na: Not available; (S): Withheld because statistical norms were not met; (X): Not applicable; (Z): Less than half the unit shown; nec: Not elsewhere classified; nsk: Not specified by kind; - : zero; * : 10-19 percent estimated; ** : 20-29 percent estimated.

PRODUCT SHARE DETAILS

Product or Product Class	% Share
Pleating and stitching	100.00
Embroideries (except Schiffli machine products)	52.44
Receipts for commission work on materials owned by others	24.31
Receipts for commission embroidering (other than Schiffli machine) on materials owned by others	45.53
Receipts for commission tucking, pleating, hemstitching, and buttonholing for the trade	47.62
Receipts for commission work on materials owned by others, nsk	6.86
Pleating and stitching, nsk	23.25

Source: 1992 *Economic Census*. The values shown are percent of total shipments in an industry. Values of indented subcategories are summed in the main heading. The symbol (D) appears when data are withheld to prevent disclosure of competitive information. The abbreviation nsk stands for 'not specified by kind' and nec for 'not elsewhere classified'.

INPUTS AND OUTPUTS FOR PLEATING & STITCHING

Economic Sector or Industry Providing Inputs	%	Sector	Economic Sector or Industry Buying Outputs	%	Sector
Apparel made from purchased materials	24.6	Manufg.	Personal consumption expenditures	50.7	
Yarn mills & finishing of textiles, nec	16.3	Manufg.	Apparel made from purchased materials	44.4	Manufg.
Printing ink	7.7	Manufg.	Pleating & stitching	3.7	Manufg.
Banking	7.1	Fin/R.E.	Exports	1.1	Foreign
Wholesale trade	6.9	Trade			
Broadwoven fabric mills	6.1	Manufg.			
Pleating & stitching	5.7	Manufg.			
Electrical repair shops	4.7	Services			
Miscellaneous plastics products	4.1	Manufg.			
Textile bags	1.8	Manufg.			
Advertising	1.8	Services			
Motor freight transportation & warehousing	1.5	Util.			

Continued on next page.

INPUTS AND OUTPUTS FOR PLEATING & STITCHING - Continued

Economic Sector or Industry Providing Inputs	%	Sector	Economic Sector or Industry Buying Outputs	%	Sector
Needles, pins, & fasteners	1.4	Manufg.			
Electric services (utilities)	1.2	Util.			
Real estate	1.0	Fin/R.E.			
Communications, except radio & TV	0.9	Util.			
Hotels & lodging places	0.8	Services			
Felt goods, nec	0.7	Manufg.			
Eating & drinking places	0.7	Trade			
Paperboard containers & boxes	0.6	Manufg.			
Gas production & distribution (utilities)	0.5	Util.			
Maintenance of nonfarm buildings nec	0.3	Constr.			
Textile goods, nec	0.3	Manufg.			
Thread mills	0.3	Manufg.			
Equipment rental & leasing services	0.3	Services			
Management & consulting services & labs	0.3	Services			
Royalties	0.2	Fin/R.E.			
Legal services	0.2	Services			
U.S. Postal Service	0.2	Gov't			
Lubricating oils & greases	0.1	Manufg.			
Petroleum refining	0.1	Manufg.			
Railroads & related services	0.1	Util.			
Accounting, auditing & bookkeeping	0.1	Services			
Business/professional associations	0.1	Services			

Source: Benchmark Input-Output Accounts for the U.S. Economy, 1982, U.S. Department of Commerce, Washington, D.C., July 1991. Data, as reported in the source, are organized by the 1977 SIC structure in use in 1982 but have been matched, as closely as is possible, to the 1987 SIC structure used in this book.

OCCUPATIONS EMPLOYED BY SIC 239 - MISCELLANEOUS FABRICATED TEXTILE PRODUCTS

Occupation	% of Total 1994	Change to 2005	Occupation	% of Total 1994	Change to 2005
Sewing machine operators, non-garment	21.5	-26.0	Cutters & trimmers, hand	1.9	-25.9
Sewing machine operators, garment	11.0	36.7	Sales & related workers nec	1.8	13.9
Assemblers, fabricators, & hand workers nec	8.6	13.9	Textile draw-out & winding machine operators	1.8	2.5
Hand packers & packagers	3.9	-2.4	Machine feeders & offbearers	1.5	2.5
Blue collar worker supervisors	3.6	4.6	Machine operators nec	1.4	0.4
General managers & top executives	3.1	8.1	Bookkeeping, accounting, & auditing clerks	1.4	-14.6
Helpers, laborers, & material movers nec	2.7	13.9	Industrial machinery mechanics	1.3	25.3
Inspectors, testers, & graders, precision	2.6	13.9	General office clerks	1.2	-2.9
Screen printing machine setters & set-up operators	2.3	36.7	Industrial production managers	1.2	13.9
Freight, stock, & material movers, hand	2.3	-8.9	Secretaries, ex legal & medical	1.1	3.7
Traffic, shipping, & receiving clerks	2.1	9.6	Cutting & slicing machine setters, operators	1.0	25.3

Source: Industry-Occupation Matrix, Bureau of Labor Statistics. These data relate to one or more 3-digit SIC industry groups rather than to a single 4-digit SIC. The change reported for each occupation to the year 2005 is a percent of growth or decline as estimated by the Bureau of Labor Statistics. The abbreviation nec stands for 'not elsewhere classified'.

LOCATION BY STATE AND REGIONAL CONCENTRATION

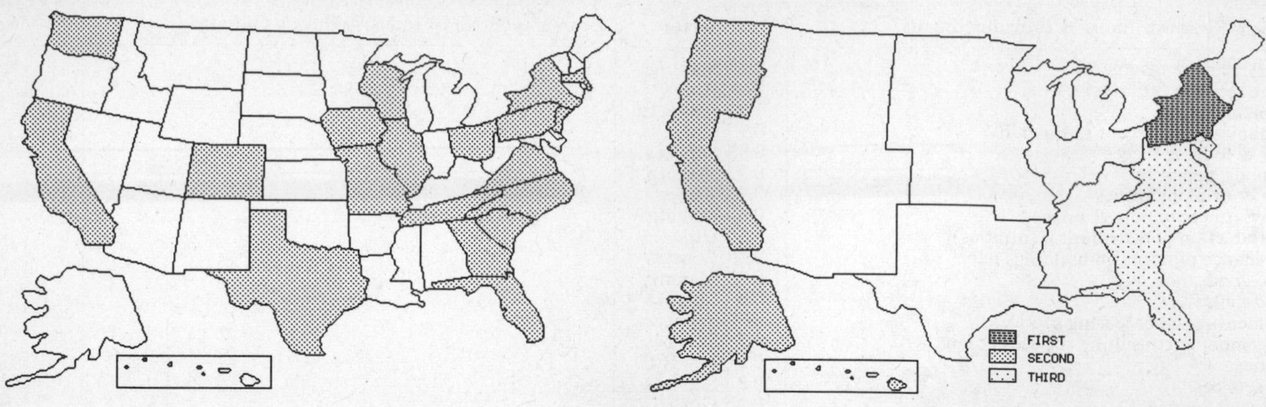

INDUSTRY DATA BY STATE

State	Establish-ments	Shipments			Employment				Cost as % of Shipments	Investment per Employee ($)
		Total ($ mil)	% of U.S.	Per Establ.	Total Number	% of U.S.	Per Establ.	Wages ($/hour)		
California	116	121.9	16.8	1.1	2,400	17.5	21	6.61	53.2	1,417
New York	126	91.0	12.5	0.7	1,500	10.9	12	7.00	46.4	1,533
New Jersey	116	80.6	11.1	0.7	1,500	10.9	13	7.89	51.7	1,467
North Carolina	38	67.0	9.2	1.8	1,900	13.9	50	6.13	36.3	1,684
Illinois	22	45.6	6.3	2.1	700	5.1	32	8.30	52.2	1,143
Florida	43	44.6	6.1	1.0	1,000	7.3	23	5.54	48.2	1,400
Missouri	15	37.7	5.2	2.5	400	2.9	27	7.33	46.9	2,250
South Carolina	16	25.1	3.5	1.6	800	5.8	50	5.15	38.6	1,625
Massachusetts	14	9.1	1.3	0.7	200	1.5	14	10.50	45.1	1,500
Colorado	10	8.3	1.1	0.8	100	0.7	10	7.00	47.0	4,000
Washington	14	7.1	1.0	0.5	200	1.5	14	7.00	47.9	1,000
Texas	36	(D)	-	-	750 *	5.5	21	-	-	533
Pennsylvania	18	(D)	-	-	175 *	1.3	10	-	-	5,143
Ohio	17	(D)	-	-	750 *	5.5	44	-	-	-
Georgia	16	(D)	-	-	175 *	1.3	11	-	-	2,857
Wisconsin	11	(D)	-	-	175 *	1.3	16	-	-	1,714
Tennessee	9	(D)	-	-	175 *	1.3	19	-	-	1,714
Virginia	5	(D)	-	-	175 *	1.3	35	-	-	571
Iowa	4	(D)	-	-	175 *	1.3	44	-	-	-

Source: 1992 *Economic Census*. The states are in descending order of shipments or establishments (if shipment data are missing for the majority). The symbol (D) appears when data are withheld to prevent disclosure of competitive information. States marked with (D) are sorted by number of establishments. A dash (-) indicates that the data element cannot be calculated; * indicates the midpoint of a range.

2396 - AUTOMOTIVE AND APPAREL TRIMMINGS

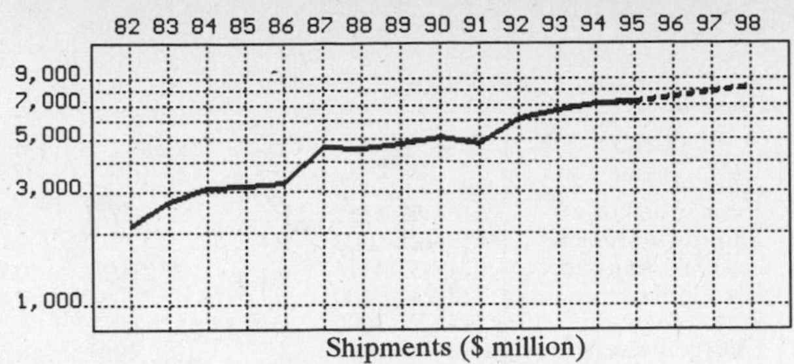

Shipments ($ million)

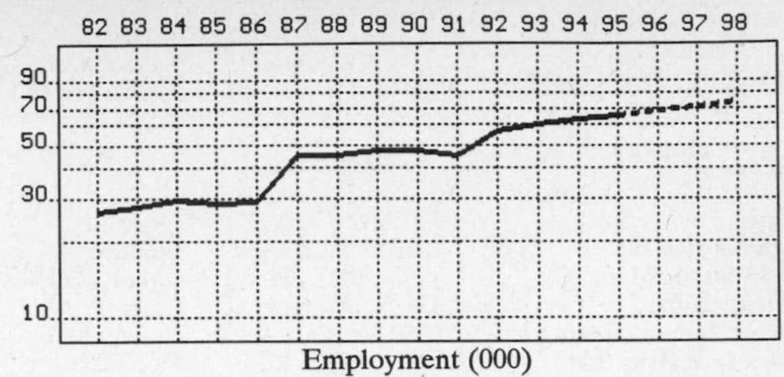

Employment (000)

GENERAL STATISTICS

Year	Companies	Establishments: Total	Establishments: with 20 or more employees	Employment: Total (000)	Production Workers (000)	Production Hours (Mil)	Compensation: Payroll ($ mil)	Compensation: Wages ($/hr)	Production ($ million): Cost of Materials	Value Added by Manufacture	Value of Shipments	Capital Invest.
1982	801	826	201	26.2	21.8	38.8	505.2	9.99	1,120.3	1,000.4	2,130.2	41.1
1983		808	201	27.8	23.3	44.2	600.1	10.69	1,397.3	1,335.3	2,723.0	42.9
1984		790	201	29.7	25.3	49.5	686.9	10.86	1,620.7	1,521.6	3,109.3	54.8
1985		773	201	28.7	23.4	47.9	725.4	11.80	1,666.1	1,467.5	3,156.5	91.8
1986		748	203	29.0	23.6	47.8	765.9	12.54	1,768.7	1,471.4	3,227.3	114.7
1987	1,534	1,560	339	44.8	35.8	67.5	1,007.9	11.01	2,609.8	2,053.4	4,633.7	115.8
1988		1,172	365	45.1	36.9	69.5	1,053.2	11.43	2,673.4	1,906.2	4,564.6	79.1
1989		1,375	375	47.2	35.6	64.8	1,056.7	12.25	2,685.2	2,110.1	4,762.5	134.5
1990		1,583	377	47.7	37.7	68.8	1,119.9	12.17	2,862.8	2,267.4	5,104.8	141.6
1991		1,717	367	45.0	35.7	66.8	1,083.1	12.03	2,555.7	2,179.0	4,753.2	131.4
1992	2,419	2,469	484	57.1	44.5	84.5	1,334.3	11.15	3,399.2	2,721.2	6,093.1	139.7
1993		2,453	521	60.1	47.6	90.6	1,367.5	10.74	3,677.9	2,974.1	6,627.2	165.1
1994		2,376P	516P	62.6	48.5	94.1	1,528.3	11.21	3,816.3	3,221.0	7,010.9	266.2
1995		2,533P	546P	64.6P	50.1P	95.0P	1,540.9P	11.76P	3,877.5P	3,272.7P	7,123.3P	212.7P
1996		2,690P	577P	67.8P	52.4P	99.4P	1,620.0P	11.81P	4,085.1P	3,447.9P	7,504.7P	226.4P
1997		2,847P	607P	71.0P	54.8P	103.8P	1,699.1P	11.87P	4,292.7P	3,623.1P	7,886.1P	240.1P
1998		3,004P	637P	74.2P	57.1P	108.2P	1,778.2P	11.92P	4,500.3P	3,798.3P	8,267.5P	253.8P

Sources: 1982, 1987, 1992 *Economic Census*; *Annual Survey of Manufactures*, 83-86, 88-91, 93-94. Establishment counts for non-Census years are from *County Business Patterns*; establishment values for 83-84 are extrapolations. 'P's show projections by the editors. Industries reclassified in 87 will not have data for prior years.

INDICES OF CHANGE

Year	Companies	Establishments: Total	Establishments: with 20 or more employees	Employment: Total (000)	Production Workers (000)	Production Hours (Mil)	Compensation: Payroll ($ mil)	Compensation: Wages ($/hr)	Production ($ million): Cost of Materials	Value Added by Manufacture	Value of Shipments	Capital Invest.
1982	33	33	42	46	49	46	38	90	33	37	35	29
1983		33	42	49	52	52	45	96	41	49	45	31
1984		32	42	52	57	59	51	97	48	56	51	39
1985		31	42	50	53	57	54	106	49	54	52	66
1986		30	42	51	53	57	57	112	52	54	53	82
1987	63	63	70	78	80	80	76	99	77	75	76	83
1988		47	75	79	83	82	79	103	79	70	75	57
1989		56	77	83	80	77	79	110	79	78	78	96
1990		64	78	84	85	81	84	109	84	83	84	101
1991		70	76	79	80	79	81	108	75	80	78	94
1992	100	100	100	100	100	100	100	100	100	100	100	100
1993		99	108	105	107	107	102	96	108	109	109	118
1994		96P	107P	110	109	111	115	101	112	118	115	191
1995		103P	113P	113P	113P	112P	115P	105P	114P	120P	117P	152P
1996		109P	119P	119P	118P	118P	121P	106P	120P	127P	123P	162P
1997		115P	125P	124P	123P	123P	127P	106P	126P	133P	129P	172P
1998		122P	132P	130P	128P	128P	133P	107P	132P	140P	136P	182P

Sources: Same as General Statistics. Values reflect change from the base year, 1992. Values above 100 mean greater than 92, values below 100 mean less than 92, and a value of 100 in the 82-91 or 93-98 period means same as 92. 'P's mark projections by the editors.

SELECTED RATIOS

For 1994	Avg. of All Manufact.	Analyzed Industry	Index	For 1994	Avg. of All Manufact.	Analyzed Industry	Index
Employees per Establishment	49	26	54	Value Added per Production Worker	134,084	66,412	50
Payroll per Establishment	1,500,273	643,191	43	Cost per Establishment	5,045,178	1,606,105	32
Payroll per Employee	30,620	24,414	80	Cost per Employee	102,970	60,963	59
Production Workers per Establishment	34	20	59	Cost per Production Worker	146,988	78,687	54
Wages per Establishment	853,319	443,942	52	Shipments per Establishment	9,576,895	2,950,565	31
Wages per Production Worker	24,861	21,750	87	Shipments per Employee	195,460	111,995	57
Hours per Production Worker	2,056	1,940	94	Shipments per Production Worker	279,017	144,555	52
Wages per Hour	12.09	11.21	93	Investment per Establishment	321,011	112,031	35
Value Added per Establishment	4,602,255	1,355,571	29	Investment per Employee	6,552	4,252	65
Value Added per Employee	93,930	51,454	55	Investment per Production Worker	9,352	5,489	59

Sources: Same as General Statistics. The 'Average of All Manufacturing' column represents the average of all manufacturing industries reported for the most recent complete year available. The Index shows the relationship between the Average and the Analyzed Industry. For example, 100 means that they are equal; 500 that the Analyzed Industry is five times the average; 50 means that the Analyzed Industry is half the national average. The abbreviation 'na' is used to show that data are 'not available'.

LEADING COMPANIES

Number shown: **52** Total sales ($ mil): **1,971** Total employment (000): **12.0**

Company Name	Address				CEO Name	Phone	Co. Type	Sales ($ mil)	Empl. (000)
Prince Corp	1 Prince Ctr	Holland	MI	49423	John Spoelhof	616-392-5151	R	700	4.0
Findlay Industries Inc	4000 Fostoria Rd	Findlay	OH	45840	Phillip Gardner Sr	419-422-1302	R	425	3.0
TS Trim Industries Inc	59 Gender Rd	Canal Winches	OH	43110	Toshiaki Fujiwara	614-837-4114	S	220	0.8
QST Industries Inc	231 S Jefferson St	Chicago	IL	60661	Ely Lionheart	312-930-9400	R	200	0.4
Velva-Sheen Manufacturing Co	3860 Virginia Av	Cincinnati	OH	45227	Peter Singleton	513-272-3600	D	60	0.3
Fair Haven Industries Inc	7445 Mayer Rd	Fair Haven	MI	48023	George Powers	313-725-2411	S	40*	0.5
Mid-South Textile Co	338 Commerce St	Jackson	TN	38301	Robert Jones	901-424-2525	D	38	0.1
MALCO Inc	PO Box 436	Union	IL	60180	Wayne Ombry Sr	815-923-2127	R	34	0.2
Mutual Industries Inc	707 W Grange St	Philadelphia	PA	19120	EM Dun	215-927-6000	R	25	0.1
HFI Inc	2421 McGaw Rd	Columbus	OH	43207	Walter E Dennis Jr	614-491-0700	R	20	0.2
John Solomon Inc	PO Box 217	Somerville	MA	02143	Salvatore A Paterna	617-666-4411	R	14	<0.1
Screen Prints Inc	PO Drawer A	Smyrna	SC	29743	Jimmy Moss	803-925-2197	R	11*	0.1
Acme Pad Corp	330 N Warwick Av	Baltimore	MD	21223	P Gary Cohen Sr	410-947-2700	R	10	0.2
Ad South Inc	4600 E Shelby Dr	Memphis	TN	38118	William Fay	901-366-5842	S	10	<0.1
Classic Company Inc	PO Box 5606	Fort Wayne	IN	46895	Gary Bennett	219-484-9061	R	10	0.1
Insta Graphics Systems	13925 E 166th St	Cerritos	CA	90702	Herbert A Wells	310-404-3000	R	10	0.1
Transcolor West Inc	6687 Flotilla St	Commerce	CA	90040	Saul Grossman	213-887-9995	S	10	0.1
Carolina Binding	2826 Tophill Rd	Monroe	NC	28110	Robert Blumenthal	704-283-5002	S	9*	<0.1
Penn Pad Co	300 E Clearfield St	Philadelphia	PA	19134	Edwin Michie	215-426-2000	R	8	0.1
Amster Novelty Co	75-13 71st Av	Middle Village	NY	11379	Harold Tepper	718-894-8660	R	7	0.1
Dallas Bias Fabrics Inc	1401 N Carroll Av	Dallas	TX	75204	Stuart Kipness	214-824-2036	R	7	<0.1
H and L Products Inc	PO Box 1445	National City	CA	91951	Lorneva Johnson	619-477-2738	R	7	<0.1
Alco Manufacturing Company	PO Box 724	Logan	UT	84323	J Kenneth Dobbins	801-753-5805	S	7	<0.1
Hy-Ko Products Co	7370 Northfield Rd	Walton Hills	OH	44146	Bert A Ross	216-232-8223	R	6	<0.1
State Coat Front Co	90 Wareham St	Boston	MA	02118	L Fraidin	617-482-6591	R	6	<0.1
American Coat Pad Co	1220 Curtain Av	Baltimore	MD	21218	Martin Grand	410-889-7777	R	5*	<0.1
Foreign Embroidery Inc	1033 Jefferson St	Hoboken	NJ	07030	Leonard Gross	201-798-6333	R	5	<0.1
International Molders Inc	3578 Hayden Av	Culver City	CA	90230	J Howard	213-870-1200	S	5	<0.1
Japenamelac Corp	25 Katrina Rd	Chelmsford	MA	01824	Jack Schulz	508-256-2212	S	5*	<0.1
Sportsprint Inc	252 S Florissant Rd	St Louis	MO	63135	R F Rockamann Jr	314-521-9000	R	5	<0.1
Superior Trim Inc	PO Box 118	Findlay	OH	45839	MP Whalen III	419-422-5335	R	4	<0.1
Flow-Eze Co	3209 Auburn St	Rockford	IL	61101	Alice M McCarren	815-965-1062	R	4	<0.1
Brizel Leather Corp	180 Varick St	New York	NY	10014	Victor Brizel	212-620-3800	R	4	<0.1
Continental Screen Printing	151 Kent Av	Brooklyn	NY	11211	Alan Paler	718-782-7706	R	4*	<0.1
Mar-Kal Products Corp	105 Walnut St	Montclair	NJ	07042	Hans F Schmid	201-783-7155	R	4	<0.1
Artwork Reproduction Inc	43-45 Ball St	Port Jervis	NY	12771		914-858-8630	R	3*	<0.1
Fashion Ribbon Company Inc	34-01 38th Av	Long Island Ct	NY	11101	J Rosenzweig	718-482-0100	R	3*	<0.1
Louis Krieger Co	2000 S Main St	Los Angeles	CA	90007	Saul Tanzman	213-746-1000	R	3	<0.1
Nevlen Co	96 Audubon Rd	Wakefield	MA	01880	MC Nickerson	617-245-2433	R	3	<0.1
Rico Sportswear Inc	71 W 35th St	New York	NY	10001	Leon Barocas	212-279-0168	S	3	<0.1
Silk Screen Technology Inc	141 Lanza Av	Garfield	NJ	07026	Laurence Scheer	201-546-1606	R	3	<0.1
Collegiate Pacific West Inc	1460 E 29th St	Long Beach	CA	90806	Dennis Parker	310-427-9798	R	2	<0.1
M and M Designs Inc	3000 Old Houston	Huntsville	TX	77340	Rob Myers	409-295-2682	R	2	<0.1
Marionat Bridal Veils Inc	1375 Broadway	New York	NY	10018	Philip Levitt	212-921-5046	R	2*	<0.1
National/Beatty Page Inc	Br Navy Yrd	Brooklyn	NY	11205	Harvard G Gordon	718-330-1280	R	2	<0.1
Universal Screen Printing Co	PO Box 12657	Gastonia	NC	28052	Ray Gaeto	704-864-7841	R	2	<0.1
Screen Wear Corp	345 Lively Blv	Elk Grove Vill	IL	60007	Gary Kurz	708-228-1737	R	1	<0.1
Ad Graphic Inc	1414 Spring Garden	Pittsburgh	PA	15212	David Baney	412-321-9118	R	1	<0.1
Extreme Sportswear	PO Box 159	Charlotte	NC	28126	Richard Mitchell	704-596-0200	R	1	<0.1
Ground Control	525 S Loop 288	Denton	TX	76205	Bill Cates	817-898-8864	S	1	<0.1
Spectator Sports Services Inc	5029 WT Harris #A	Charlotte	NC	28269	Dannie R Smith	704-596-2223	R	1	<0.1
Chance Bridal Veils Inc	124 Spear St	San Francisco	CA	94105	Stacy K Turner	415-777-9531	R	0	<0.1

Source: *Ward's Business Directory of U.S. Private and Public Companies*, Volumes 1 and 2, 1996. The company type code used is as follows: P - Public, R - Private, S - Subsidiary, D - Division, J - Joint Venture, A - Affiliate, G - Group. Sales are in millions of dollars, employees are in thousands. An asterisk (*) indicates an estimated sales volume. The symbol < stands for 'less than'. Company names and addresses are truncated, in some cases, to fit into the available space.

MATERIALS CONSUMED

Material	Quantity	Delivered Cost ($ million)
No Materials Consumed data available for this industry.		

Source: 1992 *Economic Census*. Explanation of symbols used: (D): Withheld to avoid disclosure of competitive data; na: Not available; (S): Withheld because statistical norms were not met; (X): Not applicable; (Z): Less than half the unit shown; nec: Not elsewhere classified; nsk: Not specified by kind; - : zero; * : 10-19 percent estimated; ** : 20-29 percent estimated.

PRODUCT SHARE DETAILS

Product or Product Class	% Share
Automotive trimmings, apparel findings, and related products	100.00
Mens' and boys' suit and coat findings, hatters' fur, and other hat and cap materials	3.94
Mens' and boys' coat, suit, and trouser findings	74.67
Hat bands, hat linings, tip printing and stamping, sweats, cap fronts, and hatters' fur, cut or blown, for sale as such	(D)
Mens' and boys' suit and coat findings, hatters' fur, and other hat and cap materials, nsk	(D)
Automobile trimmings	43.84
Other trimmings and findings	11.18
Women's and children's apparel findings and trimmings	44.57
All other (including furniture trimmings) (except automobile)	11.61
Bias binding for the apparel trade and notion trade (except fused or sealed edge)	9.59
Ribbons, fused or sealed edge (not woven with fast edges)	31.37
Other trimmings and findings, nsk	2.85
Printing on garments and apparel accessories (including silk screen printing), stamped art goods for embroidering, punching, and needlework	37.47
Printing on garments and apparel accessories (including silk screen printing)	96.15
Stamped art goods for embroidering, punching, and needlework	1.68
Printing on garments and apparel accessories (including silk screen printing) and stamped art goods, nsk	2.17
Automotive trimmings, apparel findings, and related products, nsk	3.57

Source: 1992 *Economic Census*. The values shown are percent of total shipments in an industry. Values of indented subcategories are summed in the main heading. The symbol (D) appears when data are withheld to prevent disclosure of competitive information. The abbreviation nsk stands for 'not specified by kind' and nec for 'not elsewhere classified'.

INPUTS AND OUTPUTS FOR AUTOMOTIVE & APPAREL TRIMMINGS

Economic Sector or Industry Providing Inputs	%	Sector	Economic Sector or Industry Buying Outputs	%	Sector
Broadwoven fabric mills	25.3	Manufg.	Motor vehicles & car bodies	65.2	Manufg.
Miscellaneous plastics products	15.0	Manufg.	Apparel made from purchased materials	16.8	Manufg.
Leather tanning & finishing	10.3	Manufg.	Automotive stampings	3.8	Manufg.
Nonwoven fabrics	9.9	Manufg.	Personal consumption expenditures	2.1	
Wholesale trade	8.1	Trade	Aircraft	2.1	Manufg.
Coated fabrics, not rubberized	8.0	Manufg.	Motorcycles, bicycles, & parts	1.5	Manufg.
Narrow fabric mills	2.8	Manufg.	Automotive & apparel trimmings	1.3	Manufg.
Thread mills	2.0	Manufg.	Ship building & repairing	1.2	Manufg.
Automotive & apparel trimmings	1.9	Manufg.	Travel trailers & campers	1.2	Manufg.
Plastics materials & resins	1.8	Manufg.	Railroad equipment	1.0	Manufg.
Job training & related services	1.4	Services	Boat building & repairing	0.9	Manufg.
Advertising	1.0	Services	Mobile homes	0.9	Manufg.
Business services nec	1.0	Services	Motor homes (made on purchased chassis)	0.6	Manufg.
Commercial printing	0.9	Manufg.	Upholstered household furniture	0.5	Manufg.
Textile goods, nec	0.9	Manufg.	Exports	0.4	Foreign
Electric services (utilities)	0.9	Util.	Public building furniture	0.1	Manufg.
Die-cut paper & board	0.8	Manufg.	Truck & bus bodies	0.1	Manufg.
Motor freight transportation & warehousing	0.7	Util.			
Paperboard containers & boxes	0.6	Manufg.			
Eating & drinking places	0.5	Trade			
Banking	0.5	Fin/R.E.			
U.S. Postal Service	0.5	Gov't			
Communications, except radio & TV	0.4	Util.			
Real estate	0.4	Fin/R.E.			
Needles, pins, & fasteners	0.3	Manufg.			
Petroleum refining	0.3	Manufg.			
Textile bags	0.3	Manufg.			
Gas production & distribution (utilities)	0.3	Util.			
Colleges, universities, & professional schools	0.3	Services			
Equipment rental & leasing services	0.3	Services			
Maintenance of nonfarm buildings nec	0.2	Constr.			
Lace goods	0.2	Manufg.			
Royalties	0.2	Fin/R.E.			
Business/professional associations	0.2	Services			
Hotels & lodging places	0.2	Services			
Legal services	0.2	Services			
Management & consulting services & labs	0.2	Services			
Railroads & related services	0.1	Util.			
Accounting, auditing & bookkeeping	0.1	Services			
Detective & protective services	0.1	Services			
Electrical repair shops	0.1	Services			

Source: Benchmark Input-Output Accounts for the U.S. Economy, 1982, U.S. Department of Commerce, Washington, D.C., July 1991. Data, as reported in the source, are organized by the 1977 SIC structure in use in 1982 but have been matched, as closely as is possible, to the 1987 SIC structure used in this book.

OCCUPATIONS EMPLOYED BY SIC 239 - MISCELLANEOUS FABRICATED TEXTILE PRODUCTS

Occupation	% of Total 1994	Change to 2005	Occupation	% of Total 1994	Change to 2005
Sewing machine operators, non-garment	21.5	-26.0	Cutters & trimmers, hand	1.9	-25.9
Sewing machine operators, garment	11.0	36.7	Sales & related workers nec	1.8	13.9
Assemblers, fabricators, & hand workers nec	8.6	13.9	Textile draw-out & winding machine operators	1.8	2.5
Hand packers & packagers	3.9	-2.4	Machine feeders & offbearers	1.5	2.5
Blue collar worker supervisors	3.6	4.6	Machine operators nec	1.4	0.4
General managers & top executives	3.1	8.1	Bookkeeping, accounting, & auditing clerks	1.4	-14.6
Helpers, laborers, & material movers nec	2.7	13.9	Industrial machinery mechanics	1.3	25.3
Inspectors, testers, & graders, precision	2.6	13.9	General office clerks	1.2	-2.9
Screen printing machine setters & set-up operators	2.3	36.7	Industrial production managers	1.2	13.9
Freight, stock, & material movers, hand	2.3	-8.9	Secretaries, ex legal & medical	1.1	3.7
Traffic, shipping, & receiving clerks	2.1	9.6	Cutting & slicing machine setters, operators	1.0	25.3

Source: Industry-Occupation Matrix, Bureau of Labor Statistics. These data relate to one or more 3-digit SIC industry groups rather than to a single 4-digit SIC. The change reported for each occupation to the year 2005 is a percent of growth or decline as estimated by the Bureau of Labor Statistics. The abbreviation nec stands for 'not elsewhere classified'.

LOCATION BY STATE AND REGIONAL CONCENTRATION

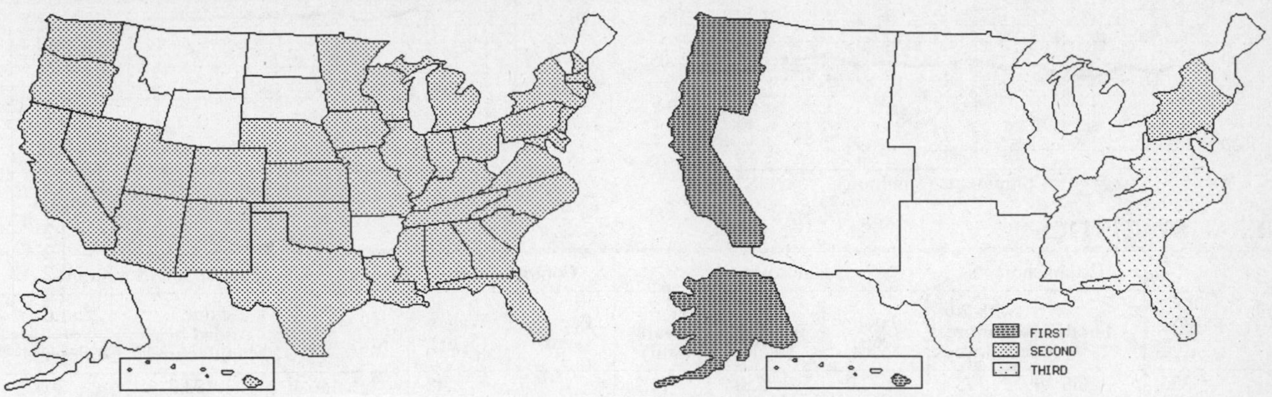

INDUSTRY DATA BY STATE

State	Establish-ments	Shipments			Employment				Cost as % of Shipments	Investment per Employee ($)
		Total ($ mil)	% of U.S.	Per Establ.	Total Number	% of U.S.	Per Establ.	Wages ($/hour)		
Michigan	87	1,836.4	30.1	21.1	11,900	20.8	137	18.54	61.2	3,025
California	380	653.0	10.7	1.7	8,100	14.2	21	8.48	51.9	2,370
Ohio	88	539.9	8.9	6.1	4,000	7.0	45	10.91	54.9	2,050
New York	240	454.3	7.5	1.9	5,300	9.3	22	8.82	41.3	1,038
Tennessee	59	273.2	4.5	4.6	1,900	3.3	32	8.27	68.0	8,947
North Carolina	89	217.9	3.6	2.4	1,900	3.3	21	7.89	46.2	1,789
New Jersey	105	214.9	3.5	2.0	2,200	3.9	21	10.06	51.9	1,455
Florida	133	191.1	3.1	1.4	2,400	4.2	18	8.26	53.9	1,792
Indiana	37	175.1	2.9	4.7	1,700	3.0	46	8.92	65.6	2,941
Pennsylvania	99	137.7	2.3	1.4	1,700	3.0	17	9.46	41.4	2,824
Massachusetts	51	132.0	2.2	2.6	1,500	2.6	29	9.32	50.5	1,400
Washington	53	103.6	1.7	2.0	900	1.6	17	9.46	63.6	444
South Carolina	49	100.5	1.6	2.1	1,100	1.9	22	6.87	62.2	1,636
Missouri	62	93.1	1.5	1.5	900	1.6	15	7.46	57.5	1,333
Illinois	64	87.4	1.4	1.4	900	1.6	14	11.92	54.8	2,667
Virginia	52	83.9	1.4	1.6	1,000	1.8	19	8.33	61.0	1,600
Texas	139	82.3	1.4	0.6	1,100	1.9	8	7.94	54.2	1,273
Georgia	66	76.7	1.3	1.2	1,100	1.9	17	8.64	58.3	2,273
Wisconsin	54	70.5	1.2	1.3	800	1.4	15	8.08	63.0	3,750
Maryland	32	70.1	1.2	2.2	700	1.2	22	10.33	54.6	1,286
Minnesota	48	52.6	0.9	1.1	500	0.9	10	11.14	57.6	2,400
Iowa	19	40.9	0.7	2.2	500	0.9	26	11.33	44.0	1,400
Rhode Island	13	39.9	0.7	3.1	400	0.7	31	16.33	57.1	-
Utah	23	37.6	0.6	1.6	400	0.7	17	9.17	55.3	2,750
Hawaii	22	28.1	0.5	1.3	200	0.4	9	9.00	65.8	-
Louisiana	17	25.6	0.4	1.5	300	0.5	18	7.50	67.6	1,000
Colorado	40	22.0	0.4	0.6	300	0.5	8	7.00	52.7	2,000
Nebraska	21	20.4	0.3	1.0	300	0.5	14	7.50	59.8	1,333
Arizona	39	19.0	0.3	0.5	300	0.5	8	6.75	47.9	1,667
Alabama	31	18.0	0.3	0.6	400	0.7	13	7.17	50.0	2,000
Nevada	13	14.4	0.2	1.1	200	0.4	15	6.67	70.8	-
Oklahoma	27	14.1	0.2	0.5	100	0.2	4	11.00	61.7	2,000
Connecticut	21	13.8	0.2	0.7	200	0.4	10	8.33	47.8	-
Mississippi	18	12.8	0.2	0.7	200	0.4	11	6.67	74.2	500
Oregon	34	12.1	0.2	0.4	200	0.4	6	10.00	58.7	2,000
Kentucky	24	11.9	0.2	0.5	200	0.4	8	10.00	44.5	1,000
Kansas	19	7.8	0.1	0.4	100	0.2	5	5.50	61.5	1,000
New Mexico	13	6.8	0.1	0.5	100	0.2	8	11.00	60.3	-
New Hampshire	7	(D)	-	-	375 *	0.7	54	-	-	-

Source: 1992 *Economic Census*. The states are in descending order of shipments or establishments (if shipment data are missing for the majority). The symbol (D) appears when data are withheld to prevent disclosure of competitive information. States marked with (D) are sorted by number of establishments. A dash (-) indicates that the data element cannot be calculated; * indicates the midpoint of a range.

2397 - SCHIFFLI MACHINE EMBROIDERIES

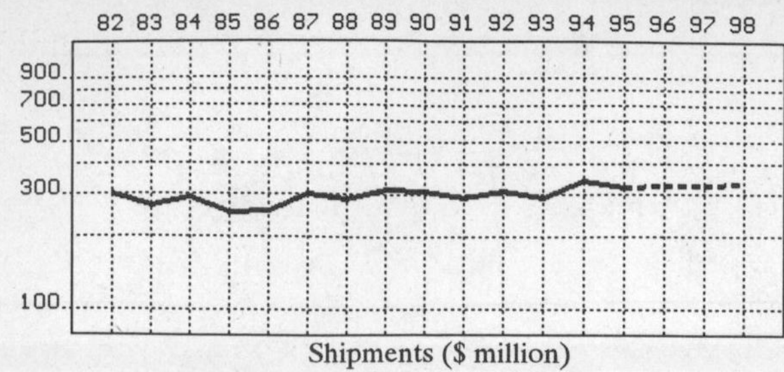

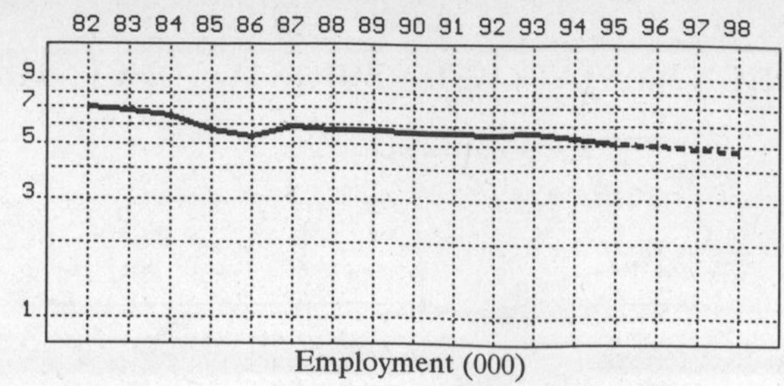

GENERAL STATISTICS

Year	Companies	Establishments		Employment			Compensation		Production ($ million)			
		Total	with 20 or more employees	Total (000)	Production Workers (000)	Production Hours (Mil)	Payroll ($ mil)	Wages ($/hr)	Cost of Materials	Value Added by Manufacture	Value of Shipments	Capital Invest.
1982	356	366	75	7.0	5.8	11.2	96.7	6.48	116.4	188.9	303.3	7.4
1983		349	70	6.8	5.6	10.8	90.4	6.20	98.6	170.9	268.5	3.0
1984		332	65	6.5	5.5	10.5	95.0	6.75	116.0	181.7	291.7	7.6
1985		314	60	5.7	4.8	9.4	90.4	7.17	95.7	159.2	252.8	6.0
1986		282	57	5.3	4.5	8.8	81.2	6.92	105.8	149.8	254.8	5.4
1987	264	271	53	5.9	5.0	9.6	98.2	7.43	137.6	167.0	302.0	5.9
1988		247	51	5.7	4.9	9.1	95.1	7.78	122.2	166.5	284.0	3.3
1989		233	52	5.7	5.2	9.5	95.3	7.48	139.3	175.7	314.4	4.6
1990		215	50	5.6	5.1	9.3	97.0	7.74	135.8	172.9	309.2	6.4
1991		211	51	5.6	4.8	9.0	93.0	7.58	125.7	168.4	293.1	8.0
1992	220	221	44	5.5	4.6	8.6	100.2	8.49	124.6	186.0	311.3	6.7
1993		216	55	5.6	4.7	8.7	102.6	8.84	114.4	179.4	293.2	4.9
1994		173P	43P	5.3	4.3	8.2	102.5	8.66	155.1	188.5	344.1	3.1
1995		158P	41P	5.1P	4.4P	8.0P	101.1P	8.89P	144.5P	175.6P	320.5P	5.1P
1996		143P	39P	5.0P	4.3P	7.8P	101.9P	9.09P	146.2P	177.7P	324.3P	5.0P
1997		128P	36P	4.9P	4.2P	7.6P	102.8P	9.29P	147.9P	179.7P	328.1P	4.9P
1998		113P	34P	4.8P	4.1P	7.4P	103.6P	9.49P	149.6P	181.8P	331.9P	4.8P

Sources: 1982, 1987, 1992 *Economic Census*; *Annual Survey of Manufactures*, 83-86, 88-91, 93-94. Establishment counts for non-Census years are from *County Business Patterns*; establishment values for 83-84 are extrapolations. 'P's show projections by the editors. Industries reclassified in 87 will not have data for prior years.

INDICES OF CHANGE

Year	Companies	Establishments		Employment			Compensation		Production ($ million)			
		Total	with 20 or more employees	Total (000)	Production Workers (000)	Production Hours (Mil)	Payroll ($ mil)	Wages ($/hr)	Cost of Materials	Value Added by Manufacture	Value of Shipments	Capital Invest.
1982	162	166	170	127	126	130	97	76	93	102	97	110
1983		158	159	124	122	126	90	73	79	92	86	45
1984		150	148	118	120	122	95	80	93	98	94	113
1985		142	136	104	104	109	90	84	77	86	81	90
1986		128	130	96	98	102	81	82	85	81	82	81
1987	120	123	120	107	109	112	98	88	110	90	97	88
1988		112	116	104	107	106	95	92	98	90	91	49
1989		105	118	104	113	110	95	88	112	94	101	69
1990		97	114	102	111	108	97	91	109	93	99	96
1991		95	116	102	104	105	93	89	101	91	94	119
1992	100	100	100	100	100	100	100	100	100	100	100	100
1993		98	125	102	102	101	102	104	92	96	94	73
1994		78P	97P	96	93	95	102	102	124	101	111	46
1995		72P	92P	93P	95P	93P	101P	105P	116P	94P	103P	75P
1996		65P	88P	91P	93P	91P	102P	107P	117P	96P	104P	74P
1997		58P	83P	89P	91P	89P	103P	109P	119P	97P	105P	73P
1998		51P	78P	86P	90P	86P	103P	112P	120P	98P	107P	72P

Sources: Same as General Statistics. Values reflect change from the base year, 1992. Values above 100 mean greater than 92, values below 100 mean less than 92, and a value of 100 in the 82-91 or 93-98 period means same as 92. 'P's mark projections by the editors.

SELECTED RATIOS

For 1994	Avg. of All Manufact.	Analyzed Industry	Index	For 1994	Avg. of All Manufact.	Analyzed Industry	Index
Employees per Establishment	49	31	62	Value Added per Production Worker	134,084	43,837	33
Payroll per Establishment	1,500,273	591,294	39	Cost per Establishment	5,045,178	894,729	18
Payroll per Employee	30,620	19,340	63	Cost per Employee	102,970	29,264	28
Production Workers per Establishment	34	25	72	Cost per Production Worker	146,988	36,070	25
Wages per Establishment	853,319	409,649	48	Shipments per Establishment	9,576,895	1,985,019	21
Wages per Production Worker	24,861	16,514	66	Shipments per Employee	195,460	64,925	33
Hours per Production Worker	2,056	1,907	93	Shipments per Production Worker	279,017	80,023	29
Wages per Hour	12.09	8.66	72	Investment per Establishment	321,011	17,883	6
Value Added per Establishment	4,602,255	1,087,405	24	Investment per Employee	6,552	585	9
Value Added per Employee	93,930	35,566	38	Investment per Production Worker	9,352	721	8

Sources: Same as General Statistics. The 'Average of All Manufacturing' column represents the average of all manufacturing industries reported for the most recent complete year available. The Index shows the relationship between the Average and the Analyzed Industry. For example, 100 means that they are equal; 500 that the Analyzed Industry is five times the average; 50 means that the Analyzed Industry is half the national average. The abbreviation 'na' is used to show that data are 'not available'.

LEADING COMPANIES

Number shown: **4** Total sales ($ mil): **19** Total employment (000): **0.2**

Company Name	Address				CEO Name	Phone	Co. Type	Sales ($ mil)	Empl. (000)
Moritz Embroidery Works Inc	PO Box 187	Mount Pocono	PA	18344	Carl J Moritz Jr	717-839-9600	R	8	0.1
Schweizer Emblem Company Inc	3345 N Wolcott Av	Chicago	IL	60657	Joe Binder	312-525-6465	R	8	<0.1
Joseph C Gilardone and Son Inc	PO Box 186	Virginville	PA	19564	JC Gilardone Jr	610-562-2229	R	2	<0.1
Samuel Ehrman Company Inc	561 7th Av	New York	NY	10018	Samuel K Ehrman	212-354-6750	R	1*	<0.1

Source: *Ward's Business Directory of U.S. Private and Public Companies*, Volumes 1 and 2, 1996. The company type code used is as follows: P - Public, R - Private, S - Subsidiary, D - Division, J - Joint Venture, A - Affiliate, G - Group. Sales are in millions of dollars, employees are in thousands. An asterisk (*) indicates an estimated sales volume. The symbol < stands for 'less than'. Company names and addresses are truncated, in some cases, to fit into the available space.

MATERIALS CONSUMED

Material		Quantity	Delivered Cost ($ million)
Materials, ingredients, containers, and supplies		(X)	3,118.8
Polyester broadwoven fabrics (piece goods)	mil sq yd	144.2	185.9
Cotton broadwoven fabrics (piece goods)	mil sq yd	73.2**	76.0
Rayon and acetate broadwoven fabrics (piece goods)	mil sq yd	(S)	35.8
Other broadwoven fabrics (piece goods)	mil sq yd	156.2	259.5
Narrow fabrics (12 inches or less in width)	mil sq yd	(S)	29.7
Yarn, all fibers	mil lb	(S)	29.2
Plastics coated, impregnated, or laminated fabrics	mil sq yd	(S)	99.5
Garments purchased to be printed and resold		(X)	347.7
Printing ink, for printing on garments		(X)	53.6
Plastics resins consumed in the form of granules, pellets, powders, liquids, etc.	mil lb	(S)	133.6
Plastics products consumed in the form of sheets, rods, tubes, film, and other shapes		(X)	17.1
All other materials and components, parts, containers, and supplies		(X)	1,208.0
Materials, ingredients, containers, and supplies, nsk		(X)	643.3

Source: 1992 *Economic Census*. Explanation of symbols used: (D): Withheld to avoid disclosure of competitive data; na: Not available; (S): Withheld because statistical norms were not met; (X): Not applicable; (Z): Less than half the unit shown; nec: Not elsewhere classified; nsk: Not specified by kind; - : zero; * : 10-19 percent estimated; ** : 20-29 percent estimated.

PRODUCT SHARE DETAILS

Product or Product Class	% Share	Product or Product Class	% Share
Schiffli machine embroideries	100.00		

Source: 1992 *Economic Census*. The values shown are percent of total shipments in an industry. Values of indented subcategories are summed in the main heading. The symbol (D) appears when data are withheld to prevent disclosure of competitive information. The abbreviation nsk stands for 'not specified by kind' and nec for 'not elsewhere classified'.

INPUTS AND OUTPUTS FOR SCHIFFLI MACHINE EMBROIDERIES

Economic Sector or Industry Providing Inputs	%	Sector	Economic Sector or Industry Buying Outputs	%	Sector
Yarn mills & finishing of textiles, nec	31.3	Manufg.	Apparel made from purchased materials	53.2	Manufg.
Schiffli machine embroideries	22.2	Manufg.	Personal consumption expenditures	17.7	
Broadwoven fabric mills	11.6	Manufg.	Housefurnishings, nec	17.7	Manufg.
Imports	10.7	Foreign	Schiffli machine embroideries	10.9	Manufg.
Wholesale trade	3.5	Trade	Change in business inventories	0.5	In House
Electric services (utilities)	2.3	Util.			
Advertising	2.3	Services			
Motor freight transportation & warehousing	1.7	Util.			
Thread mills	1.4	Manufg.			
Real estate	1.3	Fin/R.E.			
Paperboard containers & boxes	1.2	Manufg.			
Textile machinery	1.2	Manufg.			
Gas production & distribution (utilities)	1.0	Util.			
Communications, except radio & TV	0.8	Util.			
Personnel supply services	0.8	Services			
Eating & drinking places	0.7	Trade			
Banking	0.6	Fin/R.E.			
Detective & protective services	0.6	Services			
U.S. Postal Service	0.6	Gov't			
Knit fabric mills	0.5	Manufg.			
Equipment rental & leasing services	0.5	Services			
Business/professional associations	0.4	Services			
Maintenance of nonfarm buildings nec	0.3	Constr.			
Royalties	0.3	Fin/R.E.			
Laundry, dry cleaning, shoe repair	0.3	Services			

Continued on next page.

INPUTS AND OUTPUTS FOR SCHIFFLI MACHINE EMBROIDERIES - Continued

Economic Sector or Industry Providing Inputs	%	Sector	Economic Sector or Industry Buying Outputs	%	Sector
Management & consulting services & labs	0.3	Services			
Computer & data processing services	0.2	Services			
Hotels & lodging places	0.2	Services			
Legal services	0.2	Services			
Manifold business forms	0.1	Manufg.			
Insurance carriers	0.1	Fin/R.E.			
Accounting, auditing & bookkeeping	0.1	Services			
Electrical repair shops	0.1	Services			
Engineering, architectural, & surveying services	0.1	Services			

Source: Benchmark Input-Output Accounts for the U.S. Economy, 1982, U.S. Department of Commerce, Washington, D.C., July 1991. Data, as reported in the source, are organized by the 1977 SIC structure in use in 1982 but have been matched, as closely as is possible, to the 1987 SIC structure used in this book.

OCCUPATIONS EMPLOYED BY SIC 239 - MISCELLANEOUS FABRICATED TEXTILE PRODUCTS

Occupation	% of Total 1994	Change to 2005	Occupation	% of Total 1994	Change to 2005
Sewing machine operators, non-garment	21.5	-26.0	Cutters & trimmers, hand	1.9	-25.9
Sewing machine operators, garment	11.0	36.7	Sales & related workers nec	1.8	13.9
Assemblers, fabricators, & hand workers nec	8.6	13.9	Textile draw-out & winding machine operators	1.8	2.5
Hand packers & packagers	3.9	-2.4	Machine feeders & offbearers	1.5	2.5
Blue collar worker supervisors	3.6	4.6	Machine operators nec	1.4	0.4
General managers & top executives	3.1	8.1	Bookkeeping, accounting, & auditing clerks	1.4	-14.6
Helpers, laborers, & material movers nec	2.7	13.9	Industrial machinery mechanics	1.3	25.3
Inspectors, testers, & graders, precision	2.6	13.9	General office clerks	1.2	-2.9
Screen printing machine setters & set-up operators	2.3	36.7	Industrial production managers	1.2	13.9
Freight, stock, & material movers, hand	2.3	-8.9	Secretaries, ex legal & medical	1.1	3.7
Traffic, shipping, & receiving clerks	2.1	9.6	Cutting & slicing machine setters, operators	1.0	25.3

Source: Industry-Occupation Matrix, Bureau of Labor Statistics. These data relate to one or more 3-digit SIC industry groups rather than to a single 4-digit SIC. The change reported for each occupation to the year 2005 is a percent of growth or decline as estimated by the Bureau of Labor Statistics. The abbreviation nec stands for 'not elsewhere classified'.

LOCATION BY STATE AND REGIONAL CONCENTRATION

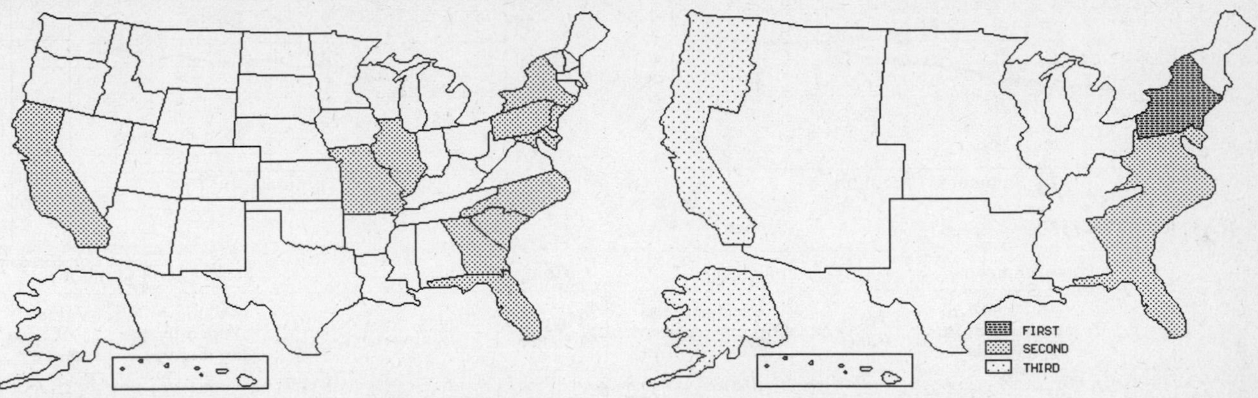

INDUSTRY DATA BY STATE

State	Establish-ments	Shipments			Employment				Cost as % of Shipments	Investment per Employee ($)
		Total ($ mil)	% of U.S.	Per Establ.	Total Number	% of U.S.	Per Establ.	Wages ($/hour)		
New Jersey	142	143.7	46.2	1.0	1,800	32.7	13	10.96	47.3	1,222
New York	10	27.4	8.8	2.7	400	7.3	40	8.17	36.5	-
North Carolina	3	19.3	6.2	6.4	600	10.9	200	6.33	29.5	333
California	14	17.2	5.5	1.2	400	7.3	29	6.25	33.1	1,750
Illinois	6	6.1	2.0	1.0	100	1.8	17	14.00	47.5	-
Florida	6	3.7	1.2	0.6	100	1.8	17	10.00	45.9	1,000
Pennsylvania	4	(D)	-	-	375 *	6.8	94	-	-	800
South Carolina	4	(D)	-	-	750 *	13.6	188	-	-	-
Missouri	3	(D)	-	-	175 *	3.2	58	-	-	-
Georgia	2	(D)	-	-	175 *	3.2	88	-	-	-
Maryland	1	(D)	-	-	375 *	6.8	375	-	-	-

Source: 1992 *Economic Census*. The states are in descending order of shipments or establishments (if shipment data are missing for the majority). The symbol (D) appears when data are withheld to prevent disclosure of competitive information. States marked with (D) are sorted by number of establishments. A dash (-) indicates that the data element cannot be calculated; * indicates the midpoint of a range.

2399 - FABRICATED TEXTILE PRODUCTS, NEC

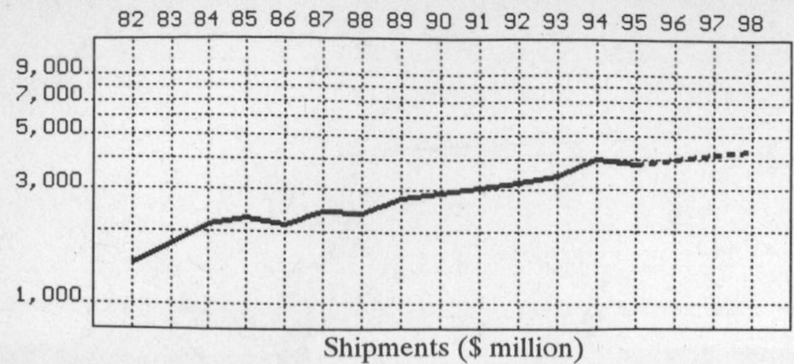

Shipments ($ million)

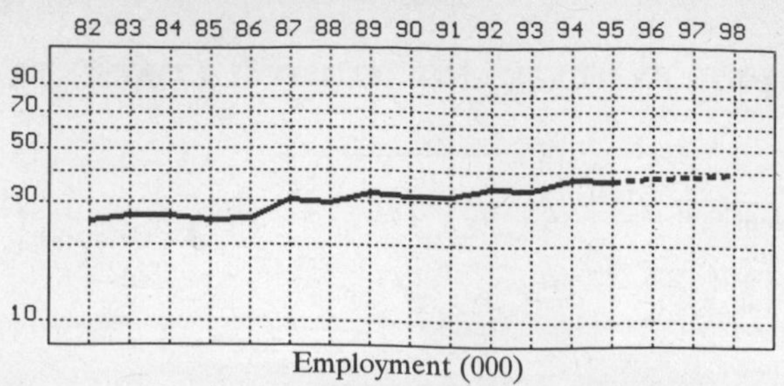

Employment (000)

GENERAL STATISTICS

Year	Companies	Establishments: Total	Establishments: with 20 or more employees	Employment: Total (000)	Employment: Production Workers (000)	Employment: Production Hours (Mil)	Compensation: Payroll ($ mil)	Compensation: Wages ($/hr)	Production ($ million): Cost of Materials	Production ($ million): Value Added by Manufacture	Production ($ million): Value of Shipments	Production ($ million): Capital Invest.
1982	770	801	259	25.1	20.5	36.8	290.7	5.37	841.7	629.9	1,475.9	23.5
1983		766	266	26.3	21.7	39.7	327.3	5.53	986.7	763.2	1,747.5	80.8
1984		731	273	26.6	22.3	41.0	353.2	6.00	1,288.2	876.8	2,147.9	55.0
1985		697	280	25.4	21.1	40.6	370.5	6.40	1,331.1	934.7	2,265.7	62.5
1986		649	268	25.7	21.3	40.3	379.8	6.46	1,242.0	921.2	2,152.0	39.4
1987	887	916	311	30.5	25.0	46.7	430.2	6.21	1,346.8	1,097.2	2,442.1	33.1
1988		899	309	29.6	23.9	43.7	437.4	6.86	1,325.4	1,062.3	2,393.8	28.4
1989		823	315	32.3	25.5	47.4	493.1	7.02	1,468.3	1,300.0	2,779.7	51.8
1990		834	310	31.8	25.4	48.5	513.9	7.29	1,548.3	1,376.6	2,910.3	61.1
1991		827	296	31.9	25.9	50.1	564.1	7.63	1,629.7	1,412.2	3,037.4	57.8
1992	1,140	1,182	337	34.3	27.2	52.6	606.7	7.57	1,786.3	1,408.4	3,195.0	59.4
1993		1,089	313	33.5	26.9	51.0	618.5	8.06	1,963.5	1,498.3	3,431.8	74.7
1994		1,051P	333P	37.4	30.0	57.1	706.8	8.27	2,172.3	1,819.2	3,969.8	84.9
1995		1,081P	339P	36.7P	29.2P	56.2P	694.7P	8.46P	2,097.1P	1,756.2P	3,832.3P	70.3P
1996		1,112P	345P	37.7P	29.9P	57.7P	727.0P	8.69P	2,192.5P	1,836.1P	4,006.7P	72.5P
1997		1,143P	351P	38.6P	30.6P	59.2P	759.3P	8.92P	2,287.9P	1,916.0P	4,181.1P	74.8P
1998		1,173P	357P	39.6P	31.3P	60.7P	791.6P	9.16P	2,383.4P	1,996.0P	4,355.6P	77.0P

Sources: 1982, 1987, 1992 *Economic Census*; *Annual Survey of Manufactures*, 83-86, 88-91, 93-94. Establishment counts for non-Census years are from *County Business Patterns*; establishment values for 83-84 are extrapolations. 'P's show projections by the editors. Industries reclassified in 87 will not have data for prior years.

INDICES OF CHANGE

Year	Companies	Establishments: Total	Establishments: with 20 or more employees	Employment: Total (000)	Employment: Production Workers (000)	Employment: Production Hours (Mil)	Compensation: Payroll ($ mil)	Compensation: Wages ($/hr)	Production ($ million): Cost of Materials	Production ($ million): Value Added by Manufacture	Production ($ million): Value of Shipments	Production ($ million): Capital Invest.
1982	68	68	77	73	75	70	48	71	47	45	46	40
1983		65	79	77	80	75	54	73	55	54	55	136
1984		62	81	78	82	78	58	79	72	62	67	93
1985		59	83	74	78	77	61	85	75	66	71	105
1986		55	80	75	78	77	63	85	70	65	67	66
1987	78	77	92	89	92	89	71	82	75	78	76	56
1988		76	92	86	88	83	72	91	74	75	75	48
1989		70	93	94	94	90	81	93	82	92	87	87
1990		71	92	93	93	92	85	96	87	98	91	103
1991		70	88	93	95	95	93	101	91	100	95	97
1992	100	100	100	100	100	100	100	100	100	100	100	100
1993		92	93	98	99	97	102	106	110	106	107	126
1994		89P	99P	109	110	109	116	109	122	129	124	143
1995		91P	101P	107P	107P	107P	115P	112P	117P	125P	120P	118P
1996		94P	102P	110P	110P	110P	120P	115P	123P	130P	125P	122P
1997		97P	104P	113P	112P	112P	125P	118P	128P	136P	131P	126P
1998		99P	106P	115P	115P	115P	130P	121P	133P	142P	136P	130P

Sources: Same as General Statistics. Values reflect change from the base year, 1992. Values above 100 mean greater than 92, values below 100 mean less than 92, and a value of 100 in the 82-91 or 93-98 period means same as 92. 'P's mark projections by the editors.

SELECTED RATIOS

For 1994	Avg. of All Manufact.	Analyzed Industry	Index	For 1994	Avg. of All Manufact.	Analyzed Industry	Index
Employees per Establishment	49	36	73	Value Added per Production Worker	134,084	60,640	45
Payroll per Establishment	1,500,273	672,774	45	Cost per Establishment	5,045,178	2,067,723	41
Payroll per Employee	30,620	18,898	62	Cost per Employee	102,970	58,083	56
Production Workers per Establishment	34	29	83	Cost per Production Worker	146,988	72,410	49
Wages per Establishment	853,319	449,484	53	Shipments per Establishment	9,576,895	3,778,690	39
Wages per Production Worker	24,861	15,741	63	Shipments per Employee	195,460	106,144	54
Hours per Production Worker	2,056	1,903	93	Shipments per Production Worker	279,017	132,327	47
Wages per Hour	12.09	8.27	68	Investment per Establishment	321,011	80,813	25
Value Added per Establishment	4,602,255	1,731,622	38	Investment per Employee	6,552	2,270	35
Value Added per Employee	93,930	48,642	52	Investment per Production Worker	9,352	2,830	30

Sources: Same as General Statistics. The 'Average of All Manufacturing' column represents the average of all manufacturing industries reported for the most recent complete year available. The Index shows the relationship between the Average and the Analyzed Industry. For example, 100 means that they are equal; 500 that the Analyzed Industry is five times the average; 50 means that the Analyzed Industry is half the national average. The abbreviation 'na' is used to show that data are 'not available'.

LEADING COMPANIES Number shown: **66** Total sales ($ mil): **2,284** Total employment (000): **27.1**

Company Name	Address				CEO Name	Phone	Co. Type	Sales ($ mil)	Empl. (000)
TRW Vehicle Safety Systems Inc	4505 W 26 Mile Rd	Washington	MI	48094	John Janitz	810-781-5511	S	1,002	11.0
Takata Inc	2500 Takata Dr	Auburn Hills	MI	48326	Stanley Groner	810-377-6130	S	375	6.0
Guilford Mills Inc Automotive	1754 NC Hwy 903	Kenansville	NC	28349	John Emrich	910-296-5200	D	267	2.1
TechnoTrim Inc	31478 Industrial Rd	Livonia	MI	48150	M Enami	313-421-7660	S	72*	1.0
Acme Group	5151 Loraine Av	Detroit	MI	48208	James Colman	313-894-7110	R	70	0.2
Saddleman Inc	PO Box 3656	Logan	UT	84321	Kenneth J Dobbins	801-753-6340	R	55	0.8
Sagaz Industries Inc	16241 NW 48th Av	Hialeah	FL	33014	Stewart Wallach	305-620-1851	R	48	0.3
Western Textile Products Co	PO Box 7139	St Louis	MO	63177	Charles Van Dyke	314-225-9400	R	30	0.4
Collegeville Flag	PO Box 98	Collegeville	PA	19426	David Cornish	215-489-4131	R	24	0.3
Annin and Co	1 Annin Dr	Roseland	NJ	07068	CR Beard Jr	201-228-9400	R	22	0.4
Snow Filtration Co	6386 Gano Rd	West Chester	OH	45069	Stephen G Vollmer	513-777-6200	R	22*	0.1
Mills Manufacturing Corp	PO Box 8100	Asheville	NC	28814	JW Turner	704-645-3061	R	20	0.4
Dettra Flag Company Inc	PO Box 408	Oaks	PA	19456	WC Spangler	610-666-5050	R	18	0.2
Pioneer Aerospace Corp	PO Box 207	South Windsor	CT	06074	Jilles Debray	203-528-0092	S	17	0.3
Arden/Benhar Mills	26899 Northwestern	Southfield	MI	48034	Robert Sachs	313-355-1101	D	16*	0.2
Action Co	PO Box 8008	McKinney	TX	75069	F D Motsenbocker	214-542-8700	R	15*	0.3
Am-Safe Inc	240 N 48th Av	Phoenix	AZ	85043	Tony Pritzker	602-233-2802	S	15*	0.1
NET Systems Inc	7910 NE Day Rd W	Bainbridge Isl	WA	98110	Gary Loverich	206-842-5623	R	15	0.1
Fabriko Inc	745 South St	Green Lake	WI	54941	CL Chelstrom	414-294-3387	R	13	0.2
Switlik Parachute Co	1325 E State St	Trenton	NJ	08607	Richard Switlik Sr	609-587-3300	R	11*	0.2
Flexcon and Systems Inc	204-A Easy St	Lafayette	LA	70506	Daniel R Schnaars	318-234-3211	R	10	0.2
Henderson Camp Products Inc	PO Box 867	Henderson	NC	27536	Melvin L Hughes	919-492-6061	R	10	0.2
National Banner Co	11938 Harry Hines	Dallas	TX	75234	Abraham Goldfarb	214-241-2131	R	10*	0.2
Acme Sample Books Inc	PO Box 1588	High Point	NC	27261	Keith F Lambeth	910-883-4187	R	8	0.1
Para-Flite Inc	5800 Magnolia Av	Pennsauken	NJ	08109	Elek Puskas	609-663-1275	R	8*	0.1
Olympus Flag and Banner Inc	8939 N 55th St	Milwaukee	WI	53223	Helmet Adam	414-355-2010	R	7	0.1
Caribou Mountaineering Inc	PO Box 3696	Chico	CA	95927	Robert Irvine	916-891-6415	R	6*	0.1
Jen Cel Lite Corp	954 E Union St	Seattle	WA	98122	Robert Reinking	206-322-3030	R	6	<0.1
Kelty Pack Inc	1224 Fern Ridge	St Louis	MO	63141	Dennis Brune	314-576-8005	D	6	0.2
Meca Sportswear Inc	1752 Terrace Dr	St Paul	MN	55113	Tom A Bramwell	612-638-3800	R	6	0.2
Morning Glory Products	302 Highland Dr	Taylor	TX	76574	William Easterling	512-352-6311	D	6	<0.1
Aerial Machine and Tool Corp	PO Box 222	Vesta	VA	24177	Peter Coe	703-952-2006	R	5	<0.1
Dow Cover Company Inc	373 Lexington Av	New Haven	CT	06513	Mark Steinhardt	203-469-5394	R	5	<0.1
Liftex Inc	204 Railroad Dr	Ivyland	PA	18974	JD Heppner	215-322-9095	R	5	<0.1
Standard Safety Equipment Co	PO Box 188	Palatine	IL	60078	George G Dickson	708-359-1400	R	5	<0.1
Bumkins International Inc	1945 E Watkins St	Phoenix	AZ	85034	David R Liberman	602-254-2626	R	4	<0.1
International Electrical	131 Franklin St	Bloomfield	NJ	07003	Thomas Potenzone	201-429-3111	R	4	<0.1
Seamcraft Inc	932 W Dakin St	Chicago	IL	60613	Stephen S Stack	312-281-5150	R	4	<0.1
Denmark Military Equip Co	37-11 35th Av	Long Island Ct	NY	11101	Jack Greenberg	718-392-7171	D	3	0.1
Dixie Flag Manufacturing Co	PO Box 8618	San Antonio	TX	78208	HP Van de Putte	210-227-5039	R	3	<0.1
Drulane Co	PO Box 570	Farmington	WV	26571	Edwin B Pound	304-825-6697	R	3*	<0.1
Fabri-Tech Inc	13333 Britton Pk Rd	Fishers	IN	46038	D L Menchhofer	317-849-7755	R	3	<0.1
Aero Products Co	815 E Rosecrans	Los Angeles	CA	90059	William Ballard	310-639-6900	R	3	<0.1
Gates Flag and Banner Co	25 Rte 46	Clifton	NJ	07011	William Gates	201-478-7600	R	3	<0.1
Adco Products Inc	PO Box 626	Mishawaka	IN	46546	Allen Ein	219-259-5281	R	2*	<0.1
National Capital Flag Company	100 S Quaker Ln	Alexandria	VA	22314	Claude L Haynes Jr	703-751-2411	R	2	<0.1
Regalia Manufacturing Co	2018 4th Av	Rock Island	IL	61204	PR Jahn	309-788-7471	R	2	<0.1
Safe-Strap Company Inc	180 Old Tappan Rd	Old Tappan	NJ	07675	Paul Giampavolo	201-767-7450	R	2	<0.1
CTA Manufacturing Inc	6430 Dale St	Buena Park	CA	90621	GH Whittier	714-523-8670	R	2	<0.1
BH Awning/Tent	2275 M-139	Benton Harbor	MI	49022	CR Dill	616-925-2187	R	2	<0.1
Finney Co	3943 Meadowbrook	Minneapolis	MN	55426	Janet A Zahn	612-938-9330	R	2	<0.1
Gemsco Inc	PO Box 532	Milford	CT	06460	Leonard Elkies	203-877-0305	R	2	<0.1
FW Haxel Company Inc	200-202 N Pearl St	Baltimore	MD	21201	Philip F Haxel Jr	410-539-7025	R	1	<0.1
Ballistic Recovery Systems Inc	1845 Henry Av	South St Paul	MN	55075	Darrel D Brandt	612-457-7491	P	1	<0.1
Achievement Badge	1518 W 7th St	Los Angeles	CA	90017	George C Armes	213-483-7981	R	1	<0.1
Airborne Industries Inc	290 Dodge Av	East Haven	CT	06512	Anthony Gentile	203-466-1400	R	1*	<0.1
Flag Place	2595 Mountain	Tucker	GA	30084	Sherman Ledford	404-493-1973	R	1*	<0.1
Flagman of America	PO Box 440	Avon	CT	06001	David A Dimesky	203-678-0275	R	1	<0.1
Oates Flag Company Inc	10951 Electron Dr	Louisville	KY	40299	Randy R Oates	502-267-8200	R	1*	<0.1
World Division USA	11929 Denton Dr	Dallas	TX	75234	Francois Louis	214-241-2612	R	1*	<0.1
Koryn Rolstad/Bannerworks Inc	558 1st Av S	Seattle	WA	98104	Koryn Rolstab	206-622-8734	R	1	<0.1
Slumberjack Inc	PO Box 7048-A	St Louis	MO	63177	George Grabner	314-576-8000	D	1	<0.1
ByCobra Inc	1843 Floradale Av	S El Monte	CA	91733	Dennis L Carpenter	818-443-4197	R	0*	<0.1
Acme Emblem Corp	150 Coolidge Av	Englewood	NJ	07631	S Marks	201-569-1000	R	0*	<0.1
California Flag and Sign Co	441 S 4th Av	Oakdale	CA	95361	Michael Richardson	209-848-4735	R	0	<0.1
Hortie-Van Innovation	1940 E Walnut St	Pasadena	CA	91107	H H Vanderwyck	818-577-1776	R	0*	<0.1

Source: *Ward's Business Directory of U.S. Private and Public Companies*, Volumes 1 and 2, 1996. The company type code used is as follows: P - Public, R - Private, S - Subsidiary, D - Division, J - Joint Venture, A - Affiliate, G - Group. Sales are in millions of dollars, employees are in thousands. An asterisk (*) indicates an estimated sales volume. The symbol < stands for 'less than'. Company names and addresses are truncated, in some cases, to fit into the available space.

MATERIALS CONSUMED

Material		Quantity	Delivered Cost ($ million)
Materials, ingredients, containers, and supplies		(X)	1,613.4
Cotton broadwoven fabrics (piece goods)	mil sq yd	(S)	54.4
Rayon and acetate broadwoven fabrics (piece goods)	mil sq yd	(S)	7.8
Polyester broadwoven fabrics (piece goods)	mil sq yd	67.3	90.1
Nylon broadwoven fabrics (piece goods)	mil sq yd	52.2*	142.5
Other broadwoven fabrics (piece goods)	mil sq yd	(S)	157.4
Narrow fabrics (12 inches or less in width)	mil sq yd	71.4*	25.5
Yarn, all fibers	mil lb	(S)	126.1
Plastics coated, impregnated, or laminated fabrics	mil sq yd	(S)	78.3
Manmade fibers, staple, and tow	mil lb	24.2	22.9
Plastics products consumed in the form of sheets, rods, tubes, film, and other shapes		(X)	35.0
All other materials and components, parts, containers, and supplies		(X)	694.0
Materials, ingredients, containers, and supplies, nsk		(X)	179.3

Source: 1992 *Economic Census*. Explanation of symbols used: (D): Withheld to avoid disclosure of competitive data; na: Not available; (S): Withheld because statistical norms were not met; (X): Not applicable; (Z): Less than half the unit shown; nec: Not elsewhere classified; nsk: Not specified by kind; - : zero; * : 10-19 percent estimated; ** : 20-29 percent estimated.

PRODUCT SHARE DETAILS

Product or Product Class	% Share	Product or Product Class	% Share
Fabricated textile products, nec	100.00	Fabricated industrial shop towels	1.24
Fabricated automobile seat covers	12.65	Fabricated carpet tiles (tufted and needlepunched) cut from broadloom	7.28
Fabricated seat or safety belts (including shoulder harnesses; except leather)	15.83	Fabricated carpet and rugs made from carpeting not made in this plant (cutting, sewing, and binding only)	8.32
Fabricated sleeping bags	6.34	All other fabricated textile products, including diapers	27.63
Fabricated, flags, banners, and similar emblems	9.52		
Fabricated parachutes	2.73		

Source: 1992 *Economic Census*. The values shown are percent of total shipments in an industry. Values of indented subcategories are summed in the main heading. The symbol (D) appears when data are withheld to prevent disclosure of competitive information. The abbreviation nsk stands for 'not specified by kind' and nec for 'not elsewhere classified'.

INPUTS AND OUTPUTS FOR FABRICATED TEXTILE PRODUCTS, NEC

Economic Sector or Industry Providing Inputs	%	Sector	Economic Sector or Industry Buying Outputs	%	Sector
Broadwoven fabric mills	24.5	Manufg.	Personal consumption expenditures	30.0	
Nonwoven fabrics	15.2	Manufg.	Motor vehicles & car bodies	16.3	Manufg.
Imports	10.0	Foreign	Exports	13.4	Foreign
Wholesale trade	8.3	Trade	Aircraft	5.9	Manufg.
Yarn mills & finishing of textiles, nec	7.4	Manufg.	Fabricated textile products, nec	3.7	Manufg.
Fabricated textile products, nec	6.1	Manufg.	Nonfarm residential structure maintenance	3.3	Constr.
Narrow fabric mills	6.1	Manufg.	Federal Government purchases, national defense	3.0	Fed Govt
Padding & upholstery filling	2.5	Manufg.	Sporting & athletic goods, nec	2.4	Manufg.
Miscellaneous plastics products	1.8	Manufg.	S/L Govt. purch., public assistance & relief	2.3	S/L Govt
Chemical preparations, nec	1.6	Manufg.	Wholesale trade	2.2	Trade
Coated fabrics, not rubberized	1.6	Manufg.	Games, toys, & children's vehicles	2.0	Manufg.
Electric services (utilities)	1.4	Util.	Mattresses & bedsprings	1.8	Manufg.
Advertising	1.4	Services	Manufacturing industries, nec	1.6	Manufg.
Organic fibers, noncellulosic	1.2	Manufg.	Canvas & related products	1.5	Manufg.
Paperboard containers & boxes	1.0	Manufg.	S/L Govt. purch., other general government	1.4	S/L Govt
Needles, pins, & fasteners	0.9	Manufg.	S/L Govt. purch., elem. & secondary education	1.2	S/L Govt
Motor freight transportation & warehousing	0.7	Util.	Federal Government purchases, nondefense	1.1	Fed Govt
Eating & drinking places	0.6	Trade	Coated fabrics, not rubberized	0.9	Manufg.
Communications, except radio & TV	0.5	Util.	Labor, civic, social, & fraternal associations	0.9	Services
Real estate	0.5	Fin/R.E.	Cyclic crudes and organics	0.7	Manufg.
Cellulosic manmade fibers	0.4	Manufg.	Truck & bus bodies	0.7	Manufg.
Gas production & distribution (utilities)	0.4	Util.	Chemical preparations, nec	0.5	Manufg.
Banking	0.4	Fin/R.E.	Laundry, dry cleaning, shoe repair	0.5	Services
Business/professional associations	0.4	Services	S/L Govt. purch., natural resource & recreation.	0.5	S/L Govt
Maintenance of nonfarm buildings nec	0.3	Constr.	Floor coverings	0.4	Manufg.
Credit agencies other than banks	0.3	Fin/R.E.	Hospitals	0.4	Services
Detective & protective services	0.3	Services	Watch, clock, jewelry, & furniture repair	0.3	Services
Equipment rental & leasing services	0.3	Services	U.S. Postal Service	0.3	Gov't
U.S. Postal Service	0.3	Gov't	S/L Govt. purch., higher education	0.2	S/L Govt
Knit fabric mills	0.2	Manufg.	Colleges, universities, & professional schools	0.1	Services
Petroleum refining	0.2	Manufg.	Motion pictures	0.1	Services
Thread mills	0.2	Manufg.	S/L Govt. purch., health & hospitals	0.1	S/L Govt
Royalties	0.2	Fin/R.E.			
Security & commodity brokers	0.2	Fin/R.E.			
Electrical repair shops	0.2	Services			
Job training & related services	0.2	Services			
Legal services	0.2	Services			
Management & consulting services & labs	0.2	Services			
Noncomparable imports	0.2	Foreign			
Air transportation	0.1	Util.			
Railroads & related services	0.1	Util.			
Accounting, auditing & bookkeeping	0.1	Services			

Source: Benchmark Input-Output Accounts for the U.S. Economy, 1982, U.S. Department of Commerce, Washington, D.C., July 1991. Data, as reported in the source, are organized by the 1977 SIC structure in use in 1982 but have been matched, as closely as is possible, to the 1987 SIC structure used in this book.

OCCUPATIONS EMPLOYED BY SIC 239 - MISCELLANEOUS FABRICATED TEXTILE PRODUCTS

Occupation	% of Total 1994	Change to 2005	Occupation	% of Total 1994	Change to 2005
Sewing machine operators, non-garment	21.5	-26.0	Cutters & trimmers, hand	1.9	-25.9
Sewing machine operators, garment	11.0	36.7	Sales & related workers nec	1.8	13.9
Assemblers, fabricators, & hand workers nec	8.6	13.9	Textile draw-out & winding machine operators	1.8	2.5
Hand packers & packagers	3.9	-2.4	Machine feeders & offbearers	1.5	2.5
Blue collar worker supervisors	3.6	4.6	Machine operators nec	1.4	0.4
General managers & top executives	3.1	8.1	Bookkeeping, accounting, & auditing clerks	1.4	-14.6
Helpers, laborers, & material movers nec	2.7	13.9	Industrial machinery mechanics	1.3	25.3
Inspectors, testers, & graders, precision	2.6	13.9	General office clerks	1.2	-2.9
Screen printing machine setters & set-up operators	2.3	36.7	Industrial production managers	1.2	13.9
Freight, stock, & material movers, hand	2.3	-8.9	Secretaries, ex legal & medical	1.1	3.7
Traffic, shipping, & receiving clerks	2.1	9.6	Cutting & slicing machine setters, operators	1.0	25.3

Source: Industry-Occupation Matrix, Bureau of Labor Statistics. These data relate to one or more 3-digit SIC industry groups rather than to a single 4-digit SIC. The change reported for each occupation to the year 2005 is a percent of growth or decline as estimated by the Bureau of Labor Statistics. The abbreviation nec stands for 'not elsewhere classified'.

LOCATION BY STATE AND REGIONAL CONCENTRATION

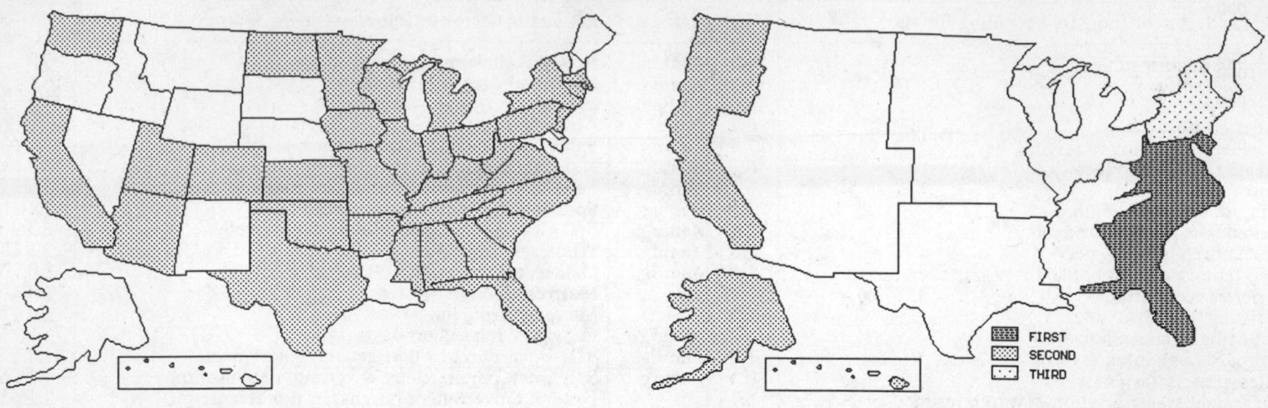

INDUSTRY DATA BY STATE

State	Establish-ments	Shipments			Employment				Cost as % of Shipments	Investment per Employee ($)
		Total ($ mil)	% of U.S.	Per Establ.	Total Number	% of U.S.	Per Establ.	Wages ($/hour)		
Georgia	57	381.9	12.0	6.7	3,500	10.2	61	8.09	54.8	3,829
California	182	311.8	9.8	1.7	3,800	11.1	21	7.07	52.6	947
Texas	74	211.6	6.6	2.9	1,400	4.1	19	6.48	58.1	1,000
New York	105	196.6	6.2	1.9	2,000	5.8	19	7.39	60.3	800
South Carolina	20	182.9	5.7	9.1	2,100	6.1	105	7.81	60.3	857
Tennessee	30	180.7	5.7	6.0	1,900	5.5	63	6.65	60.5	1,526
Indiana	24	163.2	5.1	6.8	1,500	4.4	63	8.09	55.7	2,867
Alabama	23	133.4	4.2	5.8	1,300	3.8	57	7.85	59.1	462
Florida	80	125.2	3.9	1.6	1,500	4.4	19	7.57	53.8	800
Pennsylvania	45	124.9	3.9	2.8	1,400	4.1	31	8.43	50.9	714
Michigan	31	112.5	3.5	3.6	1,000	2.9	32	11.12	59.2	-
Illinois	40	92.0	2.9	2.3	1,000	2.9	25	6.74	53.2	900
New Jersey	60	76.1	2.4	1.3	1,100	3.2	18	8.28	57.3	1,091
North Carolina	42	73.6	2.3	1.8	1,400	4.1	33	5.95	52.2	429
Ohio	32	60.2	1.9	1.9	900	2.6	28	6.93	53.0	556
Mississippi	13	59.5	1.9	4.6	700	2.0	54	7.75	77.6	-
Missouri	21	53.8	1.7	2.6	800	2.3	38	7.07	72.7	875
Utah	18	51.7	1.6	2.9	600	1.7	33	8.78	55.7	1,667
Oklahoma	12	41.6	1.3	3.5	300	0.9	25	9.50	68.0	1,667
Connecticut	10	39.2	1.2	3.9	700	2.0	70	6.00	54.3	286
Massachusetts	33	36.2	1.1	1.1	500	1.5	15	8.67	50.0	1,000
Washington	35	34.5	1.1	1.0	500	1.5	14	10.29	53.9	2,400
Arizona	10	29.1	0.9	2.9	400	1.2	40	6.50	33.7	500
Kansas	6	16.9	0.5	2.8	300	0.9	50	5.75	50.9	-
Minnesota	18	13.6	0.4	0.8	200	0.6	11	6.67	50.0	1,000
Virginia	22	13.4	0.4	0.6	300	0.9	14	8.33	43.3	667
Wisconsin	11	12.6	0.4	1.1	200	0.6	18	7.50	37.3	500
Rhode Island	10	9.3	0.3	0.9	100	0.3	10	9.50	37.6	-
Iowa	7	7.2	0.2	1.0	100	0.3	14	5.50	51.4	-
Colorado	21	(D)	-	-	750 *	2.2	36	-	-	-
Kentucky	13	(D)	-	-	1,750 *	5.1	135	-	-	-
Arkansas	8	(D)	-	-	175 *	0.5	22	-	-	-
North Dakota	4	(D)	-	-	175 *	0.5	44	-	-	-
West Virginia	2	(D)	-	-	175 *	0.5	88	-	-	-

Source: 1992 *Economic Census*. The states are in descending order of shipments or establishments (if shipment data are missing for the majority). The symbol (D) appears when data are withheld to prevent disclosure of competitive information. States marked with (D) are sorted by number of establishments. A dash (-) indicates that the data element cannot be calculated; * indicates the midpoint of a range.

2411 - LOGGING

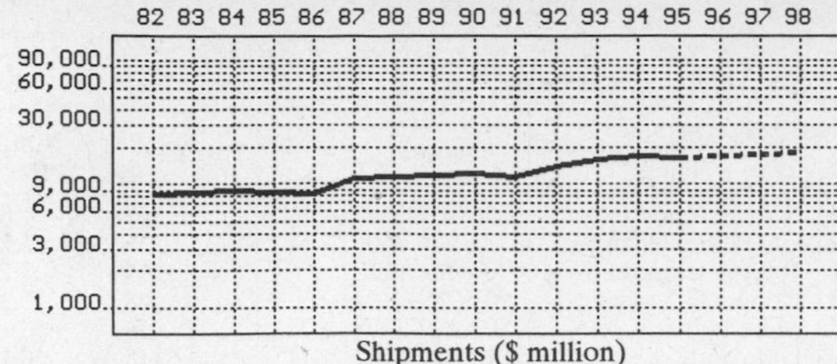

Shipments ($ million)

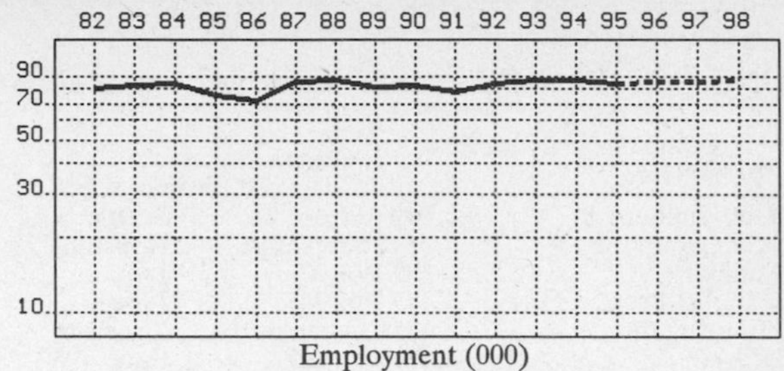

Employment (000)

GENERAL STATISTICS

Year	Com-panies	Establishments		Employment			Compensation		Production ($ million)			
		Total	with 20 or more employees	Total (000)	Production Workers (000)	Production Hours (Mil)	Payroll ($ mil)	Wages ($/hr)	Cost of Materials	Value Added by Manufacture	Value of Shipments	Capital Invest.
1982	11,541	11,658	657	80.8	69.1	121.3	1,207.9	8.27	5,630.2	2,501.9	8,274.0	249.0
1983				83.5	73.0	129.2	1,310.8	8.54	5,916.6	2,780.9	8,731.0	237.0
1984				84.7	72.1	131.5	1,362.5	8.47	5,993.2	2,939.3	8,987.9	328.2
1985				76.3	65.2	116.1	1,259.5	8.90	5,524.9	2,944.0	8,518.0	356.0
1986				72.3	60.6	112.2	1,250.0	9.11	5,306.5	2,892.3	8,235.7	341.3
1987	11,852	11,936	803	85.8	72.2	131.3	1,515.5	9.14	6,801.5	4,075.2	10,938.2	349.3
1988				86.9	73.0	136.5	1,591.4	9.09	7,350.6	4,324.0	11,663.8	221.5
1989		11,915	814	81.7	68.0	132.4	1,595.6	9.50	7,576.3	4,512.6	12,017.4	353.9
1990				83.4	68.9	134.4	1,647.3	9.55	7,930.4	4,313.2	12,229.0	405.9
1991				78.1	65.4	126.0	1,560.6	9.80	7,280.2	4,097.4	11,434.3	292.9
1992	12,916	13,010	727	83.6	69.4	131.2	1,693.1	9.96	8,763.3	5,119.3	13,844.5	375.5
1993				86.2	71.6	138.9	1,774.9	9.86	10,121.3	5,904.4	15,976.4	366.0
1994				87.2	71.7	142.4	1,820.2	9.96	10,856.7	5,947.6	16,817.7	469.0
1995				85.1P	69.7P	139.1P	1,856.7P	10.27P	10,429.8P	5,713.7P	16,156.4P	415.0P
1996				85.5P	69.7P	140.4P	1,906.6P	10.41P	10,872.2P	5,956.1P	16,841.7P	426.5P
1997				85.9P	69.8P	141.8P	1,956.6P	10.56P	11,314.6P	6,198.5P	17,527.1P	438.1P
1998				86.2P	69.8P	143.2P	2,006.6P	10.71P	11,757.0P	6,440.8P	18,212.4P	449.6P

Sources: 1982, 1987, 1992 *Economic Census*; *Annual Survey of Manufactures*, 83-86, 88-91, 93-94. Establishment counts for non-Census years are from *County Business Patterns*; establishment values for 83-84 are extrapolations. 'P's show projections by the editors. Industries reclassified in 87 will not have data for prior years.

INDICES OF CHANGE

Year	Com-panies	Establishments		Employment			Compensation		Production ($ million)			
		Total	with 20 or more employees	Total (000)	Production Workers (000)	Production Hours (Mil)	Payroll ($ mil)	Wages ($/hr)	Cost of Materials	Value Added by Manufacture	Value of Shipments	Capital Invest.
1982	89	90	90	97	100	92	71	83	64	49	60	66
1983				100	105	98	77	86	68	54	63	63
1984				101	104	100	80	85	68	57	65	87
1985				91	94	88	74	89	63	58	62	95
1986				86	87	86	74	91	61	56	59	91
1987	92	92	110	103	104	100	90	92	78	80	79	93
1988				104	105	104	94	91	84	84	84	59
1989		92	112	98	98	101	94	95	86	88	87	94
1990				100	99	102	97	96	90	84	88	108
1991				93	94	96	92	98	83	80	83	78
1992	100	100	100	100	100	100	100	100	100	100	100	100
1993				103	103	106	105	99	115	115	115	97
1994				104	103	109	108	100	124	116	121	125
1995				102P	100P	106P	110P	103P	119P	112P	117P	111P
1996				102P	100P	107P	113P	105P	124P	116P	122P	114P
1997				103P	101P	108P	116P	106P	129P	121P	127P	117P
1998				103P	101P	109P	119P	107P	134P	126P	132P	120P

Sources: Same as General Statistics. Values reflect change from the base year, 1992. Values above 100 mean greater than 92, values below 100 mean less than 92, and a value of 100 in the 82-91 or 93-98 period means same as 92. 'P's mark projections by the editors.

SELECTED RATIOS

For 1992	Avg. of All Manufact.	Analyzed Industry	Index	For 1992	Avg. of All Manufact.	Analyzed Industry	Index
Employees per Establishment	46	6	14	Value Added per Production Worker	122,353	73,765	60
Payroll per Establishment	1,332,320	130,138	10	Cost per Establishment	4,239,462	673,582	16
Payroll per Employee	29,181	20,252	69	Cost per Employee	92,853	104,824	113
Production Workers per Establishment	31	5	17	Cost per Production Worker	135,003	126,272	94
Wages per Establishment	734,496	100,442	14	Shipments per Establishment	8,100,800	1,064,143	13
Wages per Production Worker	23,390	18,829	81	Shipments per Employee	177,425	165,604	93
Hours per Production Worker	2,025	1,890	93	Shipments per Production Worker	257,966	199,488	77
Wages per Hour	11.55	9.96	86	Investment per Establishment	278,244	28,862	10
Value Added per Establishment	3,842,210	393,490	10	Investment per Employee	6,094	4,492	74
Value Added per Employee	84,153	61,236	73	Investment per Production Worker	8,861	5,411	61

Sources: Same as General Statistics. The 'Average of All Manufacturing' column represents the average of all manufacturing industries reported for the most recent complete year available. The Index shows the relationship between the Average and the Analyzed Industry. For example, 100 means that they are equal; 500 that the Analyzed Industry is five times the average; 50 means that the Analyzed Industry is half the national average. The abbreviation 'na' is used to show that data are 'not available'.

LEADING COMPANIES

Number shown: **29** Total sales ($ mil): **1,232** Total employment (000): **5.6**

Company Name	Address				CEO Name	Phone	Co. Type	Sales ($ mil)	Empl. (000)
Plum Creek Timber LP	999 3rd Av	Seattle	WA	98104	Rick R Holley	206-467-3600	P	579	1.8
MAXXAM Group Inc	5847 San Felipe St	Houston	TX	77057	Charles E Hurwitz	713-975-7600	S	233	1.2
Pacific Lumber Co	PO Box 37	Scotia	CA	95565	John A Campbell	707-764-2222	S	204	1.2
Klukwan Forest Products Inc	PO Box 34659	Juneau	AK	99803	Robert G Loiselle	907-789-7104	S	48	0.3
B and S Logging Inc	1110 Laughlin Rd	Prineville	OR	97754	Mike Brown	503-447-3175	R	16	<0.1
Kane Hardware	PO Box 807	Kane	PA	16735	Dale Slate	814-837-6941	D	15	<0.1
Wimer Logging Company Inc	600 Goldfish Farm	Albany	OR	97321	Donald L Wimer	503-928-8585	S	15	<0.1
Midwest Walnut Co	PO Box 97	Council Bluffs	IA	51502	James Plowman	712-325-9191	R	14	0.1
Starfire Lumber Co	PO Box 547	Cottage Grove	OR	97424	Foster Robinson	503-942-0168	R	11*	<0.1
Allen and Gibbons Logging Inc	PO Box 754	Canyonville	OR	97417	Lawrence Gibbons	503-839-4590	R	10*	<0.1
Acrowood Corp	PO Box 1028	Everett	WA	98206	Farhang Javid	206-258-3555	R	10	0.1
Nygaard Logging Company Inc	PO Box 157	Warrenton	OR	97146	John Nygaard	503-861-3305	R	10*	<0.1
Papac Logging Inc	PO Box 149	Montesano	WA	98563	Peter Papac	206-249-4175	R	8	<0.1
Talmo Inc	PO Box 492	Gig Harbor	WA	98335	James O Tallman	206-858-8444	R	8	<0.1
Cascade Timber Company Inc	PO Box 940	Klamath Falls	OR	97601	Leonard Putnam	503-882-3143	R	7*	<0.1
JI Morgan Inc	PO Box D	New Meadows	ID	83654	William E Kerby	208-347-2222	R	7	0.1
SURCO Log Inc	PO Box 1057	Springfield	OR	97478	Rod Surcamp	503-746-3213	R	6*	<0.1
Barclay Contractors	PO Box 40	Sisters	OR	97759	Eldon J Howard	503-549-3666	R	5	<0.1
Hopkes Logging Company Inc	PO Box 279	Tillamook	OR	97141	Marvin G Hopkes	503-842-2491	R	5	<0.1
Warrenton Fiber Co	PO Box 100	Warrenton	OR	97146	Martin Nygaard	503-861-3305	R	5*	<0.1
Zee Brothers Inc	PO Box M	Bellingham	WA	98227	Pete Zender	206-734-1920	R	4*	<0.1
Emerson Logging Company Inc	PO Box 817	Jackson	CA	95642	John Emerson	209-223-2814	R	4	<0.1
Future Logging Co	3112 Industrial Av	Springfield	OR	97478	Rick Christian	503-747-2311	R	2*	<0.1
Harmon Wood Company Inc	PO Box 518	Homer	LA	71040	Eddie R Harmon	318-927-3567	R	2	<0.1
Banco Lumber Company Inc	PO Box 235	Burnsville	NC	28714	William A Banks	704-682-2187	R	1	<0.1
Lee Smith Logging Inc	HC 30 Box 130	Chemult	OR	97731	Lee Smith	503-365-2272	R	1	<0.1
Washington Loggers Corp	3949 Iron Gate Rd	Bellingham	WA	98226	H Hammer	206-734-3660	R	1	<0.1
Al Peirce Co	PO Box 300	Coos Bay	OR	97420	Hilda V Peirce	503-267-4113	R	1	<0.1
Williams Forest Products Corp	PO Box 1713	Cleveland	TX	77327	Harry N Williams	713-592-6406	R	0*	<0.1

Source: *Ward's Business Directory of U.S. Private and Public Companies*, Volumes 1 and 2, 1996. The company type code used is as follows: P - Public, R - Private, S - Subsidiary, D - Division, J - Joint Venture, A - Affiliate, G - Group. Sales are in millions of dollars, employees are in thousands. An asterisk (*) indicates an estimated sales volume. The symbol < stands for 'less than'. Company names and addresses are truncated, in some cases, to fit into the available space.

MATERIALS CONSUMED

Material	Quantity	Delivered Cost ($ million)
Materials, ingredients, containers, and supplies	(X)	6,408.8
Stumpage cost (cost of timber, excluding land, cut and consumed at same establishment)	(X)	1,934.3
All other materials and components, parts, containers, and supplies	(X)	556.2
Materials, ingredients, containers, and supplies, nsk	(X)	3,918.3

Source: 1992 *Economic Census*. Explanation of symbols used: (D): Withheld to avoid disclosure of competitive data; na: Not available; (S): Withheld because statistical norms were not met; (X): Not applicable; (Z): Less than half the unit shown; nec: Not elsewhere classified; nsk: Not specified by kind; - : zero; * : 10-19 percent estimated; ** : 20-29 percent estimated.

PRODUCT SHARE DETAILS

Product or Product Class	% Share	Product or Product Class	% Share
Logging	100.00	Other roundwood products	3.56
Softwood logs, bolts, and timber	34.21	Wood poles, piles, and posts, untreated, not more than 15 feet in length	6.14
Redwood logs, bolts, and timber	2.07	Softwood poles, piles, and posts, untreated, more than 15 feet in length	22.09
Southern yellow pine logs, bolts, and timber	22.26	Hardwood poles, piles, and posts, untreated, more than 15 feet in length	2.00
Ponderosa pine logs, bolts, and timber	6.06	Softwood chips produced in the field, measured in short tons	26.64
Spruce logs, bolts, and timber	5.71	Softwood chips produced in the field, measured in standard units (one standard unit, 200 cu ft of gravity packed chips, one standard cord)	10.60
Douglas fir logs, bolts, and timber	34.22	Hardwood chips produced in the field, measured in short tons	10.41
Hemlock logs, bolts, and timber	13.37	Hardwood chips produced in the field, measured in standard units (one standard unit, 200 cu ft of gravity packed chips, one standard cord)	4.72
Western red cedar logs, bolts, and timber	2.66	Other logging roundwood products and wood in the rough, nec, including brierwood, stumps, sticks, burls, fuelwood, etc.	7.10
Other softwood species logs, bolts, and timber	5.92	Other roundwood products, nsk	10.33
Softwood logs, bolts, and timber, nsk	7.74	Receipts for contract logging of timber owned by others	18.37
Hardwood logs, bolts, and timber	4.01	Logging, nsk	32.30
Maple logs, bolts, and timber	7.67		
Red oak logs, bolts, and timber	18.97		
White oak logs, bolts, and timber	13.52		
Ash logs, bolts, and timber	4.03		
Yellow poplar logs, bolts, and timber	4.34		
Other hardwood species logs, bolts, and timber, including beech	40.03		
Hardwood logs, bolts, and timber, nsk	11.44		
Pulpwood logs, bolts, and timber	7.56		
Softwood pulpwood logs, bolts, and timber	67.75		
Hardwood pulpwood logs, bolts, and timber	27.60		
Pulpwood, nsk	4.65		

Source: 1992 *Economic Census*. The values shown are percent of total shipments in an industry. Values of indented subcategories are summed in the main heading. The symbol (D) appears when data are withheld to prevent disclosure of competitive information. The abbreviation nsk stands for 'not specified by kind' and nec for 'not elsewhere classified'.

INPUTS AND OUTPUTS FOR LOGGING CAMPS & LOGGING CONTRACTORS

Economic Sector or Industry Providing Inputs	%	Sector	Economic Sector or Industry Buying Outputs	%	Sector
Forestry products	57.8	Agric.	Sawmills & planning mills, general	42.2	Manufg.
Logging camps & logging contractors	11.0	Manufg.	Veneer & plywood	14.4	Manufg.
Petroleum refining	3.9	Manufg.	Exports	10.0	Foreign
Miscellaneous fabricated wire products	3.5	Manufg.	Paper mills, except building paper	9.2	Manufg.
Wholesale trade	3.1	Trade	Paperboard mills	8.1	Manufg.
Machinery, except electrical, nec	2.1	Manufg.	Logging camps & logging contractors	7.2	Manufg.
Miscellaneous plastics products	1.5	Manufg.	Pulp mills	3.2	Manufg.
Automotive repair shops & services	1.2	Services	Wood preserving	1.9	Manufg.
Metal stampings, nec	1.0	Manufg.	Coal	0.7	Mining
Power transmission equipment	0.9	Manufg.	Wood products, nec	0.7	Manufg.
Power driven hand tools	0.8	Manufg.	Special product sawmills, nec	0.6	Manufg.
Screw machine and related products	0.8	Manufg.	Wood pallets & skids	0.6	Manufg.
Libraries, vocation education	0.8	Services	Hardwood dimension & flooring mills	0.4	Manufg.
Fabricated metal products, nec	0.6	Manufg.	Gum & wood chemicals	0.2	Manufg.
Imports	0.6	Foreign	Particleboard	0.2	Manufg.
Explosives	0.5	Manufg.	Wood containers	0.2	Manufg.
Hand saws & saw blades	0.5	Manufg.	Millwork	0.1	Manufg.
Motor freight transportation & warehousing	0.5	Util.			
Banking	0.5	Fin/R.E.			
Automotive rental & leasing, without drivers	0.5	Services			
Equipment rental & leasing services	0.5	Services			
Nitrogenous & phosphatic fertilizers	0.4	Manufg.			
Maintenance of nonbuilding facilities nec	0.3	Constr.			
Industrial trucks & tractors	0.3	Manufg.			
Rubber & plastics hose & belting	0.3	Manufg.			
Sawmills & planning mills, general	0.3	Manufg.			
Special dies & tools & machine tool accessories	0.3	Manufg.			
Business/professional associations	0.3	Services			
Maintenance of nonfarm buildings nec	0.2	Constr.			
Cordage & twine	0.2	Manufg.			
Cyclic crudes and organics	0.2	Manufg.			
Fabricated rubber products, nec	0.2	Manufg.			
Hand & edge tools, nec	0.2	Manufg.			
Lighting fixtures & equipment	0.2	Manufg.			
Motors & generators	0.2	Manufg.			
Nonferrous wire drawing & insulating	0.2	Manufg.			
Paints & allied products	0.2	Manufg.			
Tires & inner tubes	0.2	Manufg.			
Communications, except radio & TV	0.2	Util.			
Electric services (utilities)	0.2	Util.			
Sanitary services, steam supply, irrigation	0.2	Util.			
Water transportation	0.2	Util.			
Eating & drinking places	0.2	Trade			
Retail trade, except eating & drinking	0.2	Trade			
Insurance carriers	0.2	Fin/R.E.			
Asbestos products	0.1	Manufg.			
Motor vehicle parts & accessories	0.1	Manufg.			

Source: Benchmark Input-Output Accounts for the U.S. Economy, 1982, U.S. Department of Commerce, Washington, D.C., July 1991. Data, as reported in the source, are organized by the 1977 SIC structure in use in 1982 but have been matched, as closely as is possible, to the 1987 SIC structure used in this book.

OCCUPATIONS EMPLOYED BY SIC 241 - LOGGING

Occupation	% of Total 1994	Change to 2005	Occupation	% of Total 1994	Change to 2005
Logging tractor operators	22.9	0.1	Bookkeeping, accounting, & auditing clerks	2.4	-31.8
Fallers & buckers	16.5	-18.1	General office clerks	1.7	-22.5
Truck drivers light & heavy	15.4	-6.2	Secretaries, ex legal & medical	1.6	-17.2
Timber workers nec	7.5	-18.1	Mobile heavy equipment mechanics	1.4	-10.9
Log handling equipment operators	7.5	-9.0	Hoist & winch operators	1.4	-27.2
General managers & top executives	4.4	-13.7	Grader, dozer, & scraper operators	1.2	-9.1
Supervisors, farming, forestry	4.1	0.1	Freight, stock, & material movers, hand	1.0	-27.2
Head sawyers & sawing machine workers	2.5	36.4			

Source: Industry-Occupation Matrix, Bureau of Labor Statistics. These data relate to one or more 3-digit SIC industry groups rather than to a single 4-digit SIC. The change reported for each occupation to the year 2005 is a percent of growth or decline as estimated by the Bureau of Labor Statistics. The abbreviation nec stands for 'not elsewhere classified'.

LOCATION BY STATE AND REGIONAL CONCENTRATION

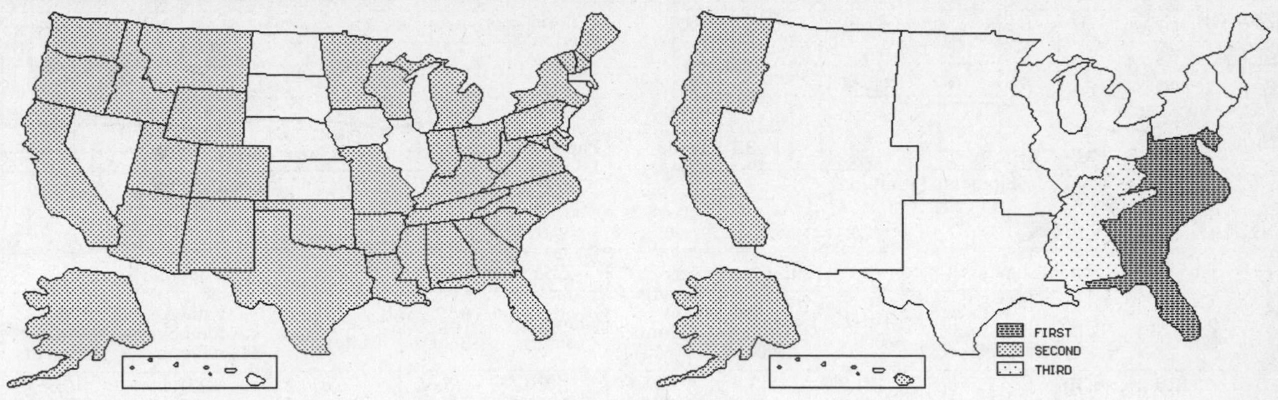

INDUSTRY DATA BY STATE

State	Establish-ments	Shipments			Employment				Cost as % of Shipments	Investment per Employee ($)
		Total ($ mil)	% of U.S.	Per Establ.	Total Number	% of U.S.	Per Establ.	Wages ($/hour)		
Washington	1,033	2,367.3	17.1	2.3	9,100	10.9	9	13.38	69.2	5,253
Oregon	1,308	2,132.9	15.4	1.6	9,900	11.8	8	12.38	59.4	4,242
Alabama	998	844.5	6.1	0.8	6,700	8.0	7	7.88	64.0	4,970
Maine	475	774.6	5.6	1.6	3,300	3.9	7	9.17	70.3	3,424
Mississippi	680	670.5	4.8	1.0	4,300	5.1	6	8.05	71.1	5,395
North Carolina	714	658.0	4.8	0.9	4,200	5.0	6	8.21	69.9	4,595
Georgia	776	628.7	4.5	0.8	5,600	6.7	7	8.29	61.6	4,464
California	519	611.8	4.4	1.2	4,200	5.0	8	12.78	51.4	4,452
Florida	344	572.7	4.1	1.7	2,700	3.2	8	10.59	61.9	4,778
Arkansas	544	528.8	3.8	1.0	3,200	3.8	6	7.87	63.3	5,031
Texas	355	503.0	3.6	1.4	2,000	2.4	6	10.27	67.0	5,700
Idaho	412	475.3	3.4	1.2	3,100	3.7	8	11.82	59.7	3,000
Louisiana	487	439.6	3.2	0.9	3,200	3.8	7	8.37	66.0	4,719
South Carolina	531	424.3	3.1	0.8	3,700	4.4	7	7.87	64.5	3,973
Alaska	52	382.1	2.8	7.3	1,700	2.0	33	16.87	42.9	5,176
Montana	323	238.0	1.7	0.7	1,600	1.9	5	10.20	67.4	3,688
Virginia	448	230.6	1.7	0.5	2,200	2.6	5	8.22	55.7	4,136
Wisconsin	435	166.0	1.2	0.4	1,600	1.9	4	7.42	57.5	3,750
Michigan	356	159.0	1.1	0.4	1,600	1.9	4	7.92	60.3	4,750
Pennsylvania	267	109.3	0.8	0.4	1,000	1.2	4	8.07	60.2	3,400
Oklahoma	26	108.9	0.8	4.2	300	0.4	12	13.60	69.7	4,667
New York	244	86.3	0.6	0.4	800	1.0	3	8.77	55.4	3,875
West Virginia	241	82.9	0.6	0.3	1,000	1.2	4	7.60	55.7	5,100
Tennessee	178	74.4	0.5	0.4	800	1.0	4	7.08	61.3	3,500
Minnesota	189	72.1	0.5	0.4	700	0.8	4	9.18	57.0	4,714
Ohio	120	72.0	0.5	0.6	500	0.6	4	8.25	61.8	5,000
New Hampshire	134	59.6	0.4	0.4	500	0.6	4	8.00	53.2	3,600
Kentucky	153	57.4	0.4	0.4	700	0.8	5	6.10	64.5	2,143
Arizona	52	50.6	0.4	1.0	500	0.6	10	10.38	53.0	3,000
Vermont	98	42.4	0.3	0.4	300	0.4	3	8.40	56.6	-
Indiana	83	35.9	0.3	0.4	400	0.5	5	8.14	56.0	9,750
Maryland	58	31.7	0.2	0.5	300	0.4	5	7.40	61.8	6,333
Wyoming	73	26.9	0.2	0.4	300	0.4	4	7.40	55.0	3,667
Colorado	49	23.8	0.2	0.5	200	0.2	4	7.75	64.3	2,500
Missouri	76	18.5	0.1	0.2	200	0.2	3	6.33	63.2	3,500
Utah	16	17.8	0.1	1.1	200	0.2	13	9.75	66.3	2,500
New Mexico	28	15.7	0.1	0.6	200	0.2	7	6.33	54.1	1,500

Source: 1992 *Economic Census*. The states are in descending order of shipments or establishments (if shipment data are missing for the majority). The symbol (D) appears when data are withheld to prevent disclosure of competitive information. States marked with (D) are sorted by number of establishments. A dash (-) indicates that the data element cannot be calculated; * indicates the midpoint of a range.

2421 - SAWMILLS AND PLANING MILLS, GENERAL

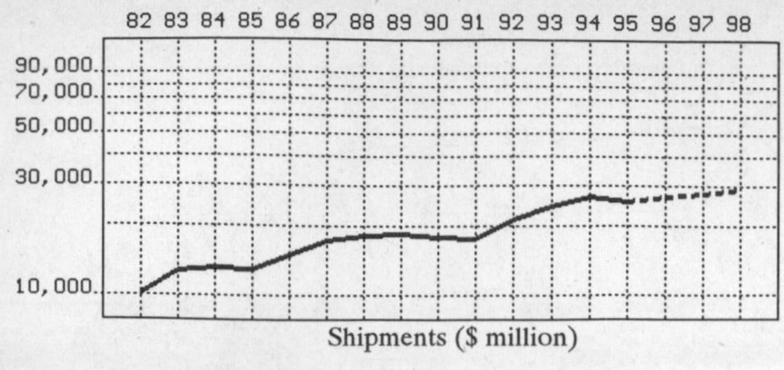

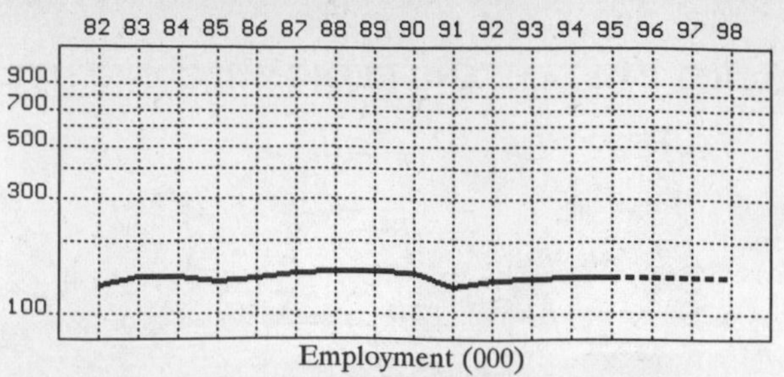

GENERAL STATISTICS

Year	Companies	Establishments: Total	Establishments: with 20 or more employees	Employment: Total (000)	Employment: Production Workers (000)	Employment: Production Hours (Mil)	Compensation: Payroll ($ mil)	Compensation: Wages ($/hr)	Production ($ million): Cost of Materials	Production ($ million): Value Added by Manufacture	Production ($ million): Value of Shipments	Production ($ million): Capital Invest.
1982	5,810	6,316	1,556	131.9	113.9	215.5	2,020.2	7.66	6,674.2	3,237.5	10,065.2	408.4
1983		6,183	1,575	142.8	125.0	244.9	2,333.6	7.86	8,184.3	4,619.5	12,663.9	370.2
1984		6,050	1,594	142.7	125.3	245.2	2,419.9	8.08	8,369.0	4,765.8	13,118.2	558.4
1985		5,917	1,613	136.3	119.9	238.3	2,411.6	8.22	8,334.4	4,665.0	12,973.9	443.8
1986		5,626	1,592	141.1	123.8	247.7	2,547.3	8.43	9,247.0	5,774.8	14,953.3	440.6
1987	5,244	5,742	1,697	148.3	129.1	272.1	2,816.5	8.45	10,636.0	6,757.5	17,357.1	512.2
1988		5,569	1,757	152.0	131.7	278.5	3,007.9	8.75	11,361.4	7,031.5	18,260.4	581.3
1989		5,423	1,724	150.1	125.5	265.3	2,936.9	8.94	11,701.8	6,918.8	18,479.1	573.3
1990		5,336	1,675	148.5	124.5	258.9	2,913.1	9.23	11,877.3	6,184.3	17,923.0	522.1
1991		5,286	1,549	129.5	116.1	241.0	2,746.6	9.33	11,603.7	5,865.9	17,485.0	464.3
1992	5,500	6,004	1,604	138.1	118.0	249.1	3,045.5	9.63	13,311.1	7,783.6	21,065.9	457.1
1993		5,864	1,679	141.6	122.4	265.0	3,288.6	9.83	15,937.7	8,878.5	24,459.8	548.3
1994		5,421P	1,682P	142.2	121.8	267.4	3,413.0	9.99	17,347.7	9,476.2	26,760.8	694.9
1995		5,367P	1,689P	143.2P	122.5P	270.3P	3,434.3P	10.16P	16,522.2P	9,025.2P	25,487.3P	601.5P
1996		5,312P	1,696P	143.4P	122.5P	272.8P	3,530.4P	10.36P	17,275.6P	9,436.8P	26,649.6P	615.2P
1997		5,258P	1,703P	143.6P	122.4P	275.3P	3,626.5P	10.55P	18,029.1P	9,848.4P	27,811.9P	628.9P
1998		5,203P	1,710P	143.8P	122.4P	277.8P	3,722.6P	10.75P	18,782.5P	10,260.0P	28,974.2P	642.6P

Sources: 1982, 1987, 1992 *Economic Census*; *Annual Survey of Manufactures*, 83-86, 88-91, 93-94. Establishment counts for non-Census years are from *County Business Patterns*; establishment values for 83-84 are extrapolations. 'P's show projections by the editors. Industries reclassified in 87 will not have data for prior years.

INDICES OF CHANGE

Year	Companies	Establishments: Total	Establishments: with 20 or more employees	Employment: Total (000)	Employment: Production Workers (000)	Employment: Production Hours (Mil)	Compensation: Payroll ($ mil)	Compensation: Wages ($/hr)	Production ($ million): Cost of Materials	Production ($ million): Value Added by Manufacture	Production ($ million): Value of Shipments	Production ($ million): Capital Invest.
1982	106	105	97	96	97	87	66	80	50	42	48	89
1983		103	98	103	106	98	77	82	61	59	60	81
1984		101	99	103	106	98	79	84	63	61	62	122
1985		99	101	99	102	96	79	85	63	60	62	97
1986		94	99	102	105	99	84	88	69	74	71	96
1987	95	96	106	107	109	109	92	88	80	87	82	112
1988		93	110	110	112	112	99	91	85	90	87	127
1989		90	107	109	106	107	96	93	88	89	88	125
1990		89	104	108	106	104	96	96	89	79	85	114
1991		88	97	94	98	97	90	97	87	75	83	102
1992	100	100	100	100	100	100	100	100	100	100	100	100
1993		98	105	103	104	106	108	102	120	114	116	120
1994		90P	105P	103	103	107	112	104	130	122	127	152
1995		89P	105P	104P	104P	109P	113P	106P	124P	116P	121P	132P
1996		88P	106P	104P	104P	110P	116P	108P	130P	121P	127P	135P
1997		88P	106P	104P	104P	111P	119P	110P	135P	127P	132P	138P
1998		87P	107P	104P	104P	112P	122P	112P	141P	132P	138P	141P

Sources: Same as General Statistics. Values reflect change from the base year, 1992. Values above 100 mean greater than 92, values below 100 mean less than 92, and a value of 100 in the 82-91 or 93-98 period means same as 92. 'P's mark projections by the editors.

SELECTED RATIOS

For 1994	Avg. of All Manufact.	Analyzed Industry	Index
Employees per Establishment	49	26	54
Payroll per Establishment	1,500,273	629,545	42
Payroll per Employee	30,620	24,001	78
Production Workers per Establishment	34	22	65
Wages per Establishment	853,319	492,739	58
Wages per Production Worker	24,861	21,932	88
Hours per Production Worker	2,056	2,195	107
Wages per Hour	12.09	9.99	83
Value Added per Establishment	4,602,255	1,747,932	38
Value Added per Employee	93,930	66,640	71

For 1994	Avg. of All Manufact.	Analyzed Industry	Index
Value Added per Production Worker	134,084	77,801	58
Cost per Establishment	5,045,178	3,199,869	63
Cost per Employee	102,970	121,995	118
Cost per Production Worker	146,988	142,428	97
Shipments per Establishment	9,576,895	4,936,161	52
Shipments per Employee	195,460	188,191	96
Shipments per Production Worker	279,017	219,711	79
Investment per Establishment	321,011	128,178	40
Investment per Employee	6,552	4,887	75
Investment per Production Worker	9,352	5,705	61

Sources: Same as General Statistics. The 'Average of All Manufacturing' column represents the average of all manufacturing industries reported for the most recent complete year available. The Index shows the relationship between the Average and the Analyzed Industry. For example, 100 means that they are equal; 500 that the Analyzed Industry is five times the average; 50 means that the Analyzed Industry is half the national average. The abbreviation 'na' is used to show that data are 'not available'.

LEADING COMPANIES Number shown: 75 Total sales ($ mil): 21,543 Total employment (000): 88.8

Company Name	Address				CEO Name	Phone	Co. Type	Sales ($ mil)	Empl. (000)
Georgia-Pacific Corp	PO Box 105605	Atlanta	GA	30348	AD Correll	404-521-4000	P	12,738	47.0
Louisiana-Pacific Corp	111 SW 5th Av	Portland	OR	97204	Harry A Merlo	503-221-0800	P	3,039	13.0
Universal Forest Products Inc	2801 E Beltline NE	Grand Rapids	MI	49505	William G Currie	616-364-6161	P	866	2.2
Sierra Pacific Industries	PO Box 496028	Redding	CA	96049	AA Emmerson	916-365-3721	R	750	2.5
Louisiana-Pacific Corp	PO Box 3107	Conroe	TX	77305	Ronnie Paul	409-756-0511	D	280*	1.3
Potlatch Corp	PO Box 1016	Lewiston	ID	83501	Richard K Kelly	208-799-1850	D	263	2.5
Idaho Timber Corp	PO Box 67	Boise	ID	83707	Larry Williams	208-377-3000	R	250	0.6
Kaibab Industries Inc	PO Box 52111	Phoenix	AZ	85072	R Bruce Whiting	602-840-5555	R	140*	0.9
New South Inc	PO Box 29	Conway	SC	29526	JM Singleton	803-347-4284	R	140	0.5
Stimson Lumber Co	308 Pacific Bldg	Portland	OR	97204	D Dutton	503-222-1676	R	130	1.4
Coe Manufacturing Co	PO Box 520	Painesville	OH	44077	FW Fields	216-352-9381	R	120*	0.7
Vanport Manufacturing Inc	PO Box 97	Boring	OR	97009	G Adolph Hertrich	503-663-4466	R	110	0.3
Potlatch Corp	PO Box 390	Warren	AR	71671	Richard Bullard	501-226-2611	D	100	0.7
Michigan-California Lumber Co	PO Box 486	Camino	CA	95709	Pete Himmel	916-644-2311	R	95	0.3
RSG Forest Products	985 NW 2nd	Kalama	WA	98625	Robert C Sanders	206-673-2825	R	93*	0.6
Contact Lumber Co	1881 SW Front Av	Portland	OR	97201	Robert L Donnelly	503-228-7361	R	90	0.5
Omak Wood Products Inc	Rte 2	Omak	WA	98841	Bob Harris	509-826-1460	R	90	0.5
Deltic Farm and Timber	200 Peach St	El Dorado	AR	71730	Ron L Pearce	501-862-6411	S	88	0.3
Northwest Hardwoods	10220 Greenburg	Portland	OR	97223	A Curtis	503-246-5700	D	84*	0.6
Simpson Timber Co	PO Box 1169	Arcata	CA	95521	Dave Kaney	707-822-0371	D	75	0.5
Eel River Sawmills Inc	1053 Northwestern	Fortuna	CA	95540	Dennis Scott	707-725-6911	R	70	0.5
Buchanan Hardwood Inc	PO Box 960	Selma	AL	36702	Wallace Buchanan	205-872-0491	R	66	0.5
Hankins Lumber Co	PO Box 1397	Grenada	MS	38901	Albert B Hankins	601-226-2961	R	65*	0.5
Jemison Investment Company	320 Park Place Twr	Birmingham	AL	35203	James Davis	205-324-7681	R	64*	0.4
Hanel Lumber Company Inc	4865 Hwy 35	Hood River	OR	97031	Robert L Hanel	503-354-1484	R	60	0.3
Taylor-Ramsey Corp	PO Box 11888	Lynchburg	VA	24506	G P Ramsey Jr	804-929-7443	R	60	0.7
Allied Forest Products Inc	1130 SW Morrison	Portland	OR	97205	John B Souther	503-224-4051	R	59*	0.4
Langdale Forest Products Co	PO Box 1088	Valdosta	GA	31603	John W Langdale Jr	912-333-2500	R	54	0.5
DR Johnson Lumber Co	PO Box 66	Riddle	OR	97469	Don R Johnson	503-874-2231	R	53	0.4
Manke Lumber Company Inc	1717 Marine View	Tacoma	WA	98422	Charles Manke	206-572-6252	R	53	0.5
Webster Lumber Co	PO Box 297	Bangor	WI	54614	PD Webster	608-486-2341	R	45	0.4
Bibler Brothers Inc	PO Box 490	Russellville	AR	72811	James A Bibler	501-968-4986	R	42	0.3
Nagel Lumber Company Inc	PO Box 209	Land O Lakes	WI	54540	E Nagel	715-547-3361	R	41*	0.2
Algoma Lumber Company Inc	1400 Perry St	Algoma	WI	54201	R Krause	414-487-3511	R	40	<0.1
Merritt Brothers Lumber	PO Box 190	Athol	ID	83801	Wilbur Merritt	208-683-3321	R	40	<0.1
Shuqualak Lumber Company Inc	PO Box 87	Shuqualak	MS	39361	William A Thomas	601-793-4528	R	40	0.2
TR Miller Mill Company Inc	PO Box 708	Brewton	AL	36427	Gordon W Ahrens	205-867-4331	R	40*	0.4
Warm Springs	PO Box 810	Warm Springs	OR	97761	Eric Saunders	503-553-1131	R	40*	0.2
Frank Lumber Company Inc	PO Drawer 79	Mill City	OR	97360	DD Frank	503-897-2371	R	38	0.1
Rex Lumber Co	Hwy 2 E	Graceville	FL	32440	C Finley McRae	904-263-4457	R	38*	0.2
Taylor Lumber and Treating Inc	PO Box 567	Beaverton	OR	97075	Walter H Parks	503-291-2550	R	38*	0.1
Welco Lumber Co	PO Box 125	Marysville	WA	98270	EP Garrett	360-435-6630	R	38	0.2
Enterprise Lumber Co	3210 Smokey Pt Dr	Arlington	WA	98223	HE York	206-435-1111	D	36	0.1
Arcata Redwood	PO Box 1089	Arcata	CA	95521	Tom Ingham	707-443-5031	D	35*	0.3
Wetsel-Oviatt Lumber Co	PO Box 910	Folsom	CA	95763	CL Wetsel	916-939-8700	R	35	0.1
Bennett Lumber Products Inc	PO Box 49	Princeton	ID	83857	Frank Bennett	208-875-1121	R	34	0.2
Tillamook Lumber Co	PO Box 314	Tillamook	OR	97141	Harvey Chandler	503-842-6641	S	34	0.2
Cersosimo Lumber Company Inc	1103 Vernon St	Brattleboro	VT	05301	Dominic Cersosimo	802-254-4508	R	33*	0.3
American Timber Co	PO Box 128	Olney	MT	59927	L Peter Larson	406-881-2311	R	30	0.1
Balfour Lumber Company Inc	PO Box 1337	Thomasville	GA	31799	RC Balfour III	912-226-0611	R	30*	0.2
CM Tucker Lumber Corp	PO Box 7	Pageland	SC	29728	CM Tucker III	803-672-6135	R	30	0.2
Ochoco Lumber Co	PO Box 668	Prineville	OR	97754	SJ Shelk Jr	503-447-6296	R	30	0.3
Rosboro Lumber Co	PO Box 20	Springfield	OR	97477	P Cole	503-746-8411	R	30*	0.3
Hoge Lumber Co	S Main St	New Knoxville	OH	45871	JH Hoge	419-753-2263	R	29	0.2
Lafayette Manufacturing Co	915 Red Boiling	Lafayette	TN	37083	Douglas A Habic	615-666-2165	S	29	0.2
Hammond Lumber Co	PO Box 500	Belgrade	ME	04917	Clifton Hammond	207-495-3303	R	28*	0.2
Hughes Resources Inc	FM 2626 N	Bon Wier	TX	75928	James E Hughes Sr	409-397-4221	P	28	0.1
Riley Creek Lumber Co	PO Box 220	Laclede	ID	83841	Mark Brinkmeyer	208-263-7574	R	28	0.2
Superior Lumber Co	PO Box 250	Glendale	OR	97442	RG Swanson	503-832-1121	R	27*	0.2
Modoc Lumber Co	PO Box 257	Klamath Falls	OR	97601	TJ Shaw	503-884-3177	R	27	0.2
Federal Paper Board Company	PO Box 697	Newberry	SC	29108	Greg Hart	803-276-4311	D	26	0.2
Avison Lumber Company Inc	PO Box 419	Molalla	OR	97038	WJ Avison	503-829-9131	R	25	0.1
Ellingson Lumber Co	PO Box 549	Baker City	OR	97814	RP Ellingson III	503-523-4404	R	25*	0.2
Fremont Sawmill	PO Box 1340	Lakeview	OR	97630	Paul Harlan	503-947-2018	D	25	0.1
Jordan Lumber and Supply Inc	PO Box 98	Mount Gilead	NC	27306	Robert B Jordan III	919-439-6121	R	25	0.2
Mongold Lumber Enterprises	Rte 1	Elkins	WV	26241	Max Armentrout	304-636-2081	S	25	0.2
Oregon Cedar Products Co	PO Box 280	Springfield	OR	97477	J Laduke	503-746-2502	R	25	0.1
Ostrander Resources Co	1618 SW 1st Av	Portland	OR	97201	James E Quinn	503-227-1219	R	25	0.1
Delson Lumber Co	PO Box 858	Olympia	WA	98507	DW Smyth	206-352-7633	R	24	0.1
Pinkham Lumber	PO Box O	Ashland	ME	04732	Randy Caron	207-435-3281	D	24	0.1
Suwannee Lumber Mfg Co	PO Box 5090	Cross City	FL	32628	George Dickert	904-498-3363	R	24*	0.1
WM Sheppard Lumber	PO Box 38	Brooklet	GA	30415	W M Sheppard	912-842-2197	R	24*	0.1
Bowater Lumber	660 Industrial Blv	Albertville	AL	35950	Ben M Rooke Jr	205-878-7987	D	23*	0.1
Pyramid Mountain Lumber Inc	PO Box 549	Seeley Lake	MT	59868	Roger Johnson	406-677-2201	R	22	0.1
Brazier Forest Industries Inc	701 5th Av	Seattle	WA	98104	JM Brazier	206-386-5800	R	22	<0.1

Source: *Ward's Business Directory of U.S. Private and Public Companies*, Volumes 1 and 2, 1996. The company type code used is as follows: P - Public, R - Private, S - Subsidiary, D - Division, J - Joint Venture, A - Affiliate, G - Group. Sales are in millions of dollars, employees are in thousands. An asterisk (*) indicates an estimated sales volume. The symbol < stands for 'less than'. Company names and addresses are truncated, in some cases, to fit into the available space.

MATERIALS CONSUMED

Material		Quantity	Delivered Cost ($ million)
Materials, ingredients, containers, and supplies		(X)	11,870.6
Stumpage cost (cost of timber, excluding land, cut and consumed at same establishment)		(X)	1,060.9
Hardwood logs, bolts, and unsliced flitches	mil ft log scale	4,018.4*	935.7
Softwood logs, bolts, and unsliced flitches	mil ft log scale	20,810.9	5,438.5
Hardwood rough lumber	mil bd ft	797.9**	367.1
Softwood rough lumber	mil bd ft	2,541.0*	788.6
Hardwood dressed lumber	mil bd ft	45.4**	31.3
Softwood dressed lumber	mil bd ft	702.1**	243.8
Glues and adhesives	mil lb	(S)	8.9
All other materials and components, parts, containers, and supplies		(X)	655.6
Materials, ingredients, containers, and supplies, nsk		(X)	2,340.3

Source: 1992 *Economic Census*. Explanation of symbols used: (D): Withheld to avoid disclosure of competitive data; na: Not available; (S): Withheld because statistical norms were not met; (X): Not applicable; (Z): Less than half the unit shown; nec: Not elsewhere classified; nsk: Not specified by kind; - : zero; * : 10-19 percent estimated; ** : 20-29 percent estimated.

PRODUCT SHARE DETAILS

Product or Product Class	% Share
Sawmills and planing mills, general	100.00
Hardwood lumber, rough and dressed, except siding	15.00
Beech rough lumber, except siding	1.79
Oak rough lumber, except siding	36.18
Other hardwood rough lumber, except siding	33.08
Hardwood dressed lumber, edged worked (tongued, grooved, rabbeted, etc.), including ceiling, framing, and shiplapped lumber (except siding)	1.77
Hardwood dressed lumber, not edge worked, including ceiling, framing, and shiplapped lumber (except siding)	9.90
Hardwood lumber, rough and dressed, except siding, nsk	17.28
Softwood lumber, rough and dressed, except siding	56.41
Softwood rough boards, less than 2 inches in nominal thickness, except siding	9.02
Softwood rough 2-inch lumber, 2 inches in nominal thickness only	12.26
Softwood rough lumber and timbers, more than 2 inches in nominal thickness	5.45
Softwood dressed lumber, edge worked (tongued, grooved, rabbeted, etc.), including ceiling, framing, matched, and shiplapped (except siding)	1.57
Softwood dressed boards, not edged worked, less than 2 inches in nominal thickness (except siding)	15.95
Softwood dressed 2-inch lumber, not edge worked, 2 inches in nominal thickness only (except siding)	40.73
Softwood dressed lumber and timbers more than 2 inches in nominal thickness, not edge worked (except siding)	7.37
Softwood lumber, rough and dressed, except siding, nsk	7.64
Wood chips, except field chips	12.60
Softwood chips, except field chips, measured in short tons	40.48
Softwood chips, except field chips, measured in standard units (one standard unit, 200 cu ft of gravity packed chips, one standard cord)	32.26
Hardwood chips, except field chips, measured in short tons	12.40
Hardwood chips, except field chips, measured in standard units (one standard unit, 200 cu ft of gravity packed chips, one standard cord)	9.26
Wood chips, except field chips, nsk	5.59
Softwood cut stock	3.28
Softwood furniture cut stock	8.94
Softwood industrial cut stock	78.80
Softwood cut stock, nsk	12.26
Softwood flooring, siding, and other general sawmill and planing mill products	1.38
Softwood flooring	4.32
Softwood siding (weatherboards or clapboards), including drilled or treated, except treated with permanent wood preservatives	16.44
Softwood railway crossties and mine ties (untreated)	18.11
Softwood wood lath	3.86
Softwood fence pickets, palings, and rails not assembled into fence sections	11.34
Other softwood planing mill and sawmill products	35.65
Softwood flooring, siding, and other general sawmill and planing mill products, nsk	10.31
Receipts from contract or custom sawing, kiln drying, planing, etc.	0.79
Receipts for contract or custom sawing of logs owned by others	23.39
Receipts for contract kiln drying, planing, resawing, or other manufacturing of lumber owned by others	72.89
Receipts from contract or custom sawing, kiln drying, planing, etc., nsk	3.72
Sawmills and planing mills, general, nsk	10.54

Source: 1992 *Economic Census*. The values shown are percent of total shipments in an industry. Values of indented subcategories are summed in the main heading. The symbol (D) appears when data are withheld to prevent disclosure of competitive information. The abbreviation nsk stands for 'not specified by kind' and nec for 'not elsewhere classified'.

INPUTS AND OUTPUTS FOR SAWMILLS & PLANNING MILLS, GENERAL

Economic Sector or Industry Providing Inputs	%	Sector	Economic Sector or Industry Buying Outputs	%	Sector
Logging camps & logging contractors	54.9	Manufg.	Residential 1-unit structures, nonfarm	16.1	Constr.
Imports	21.4	Foreign	Paperboard mills	7.6	Manufg.
Sawmills & planning mills, general	5.3	Manufg.	Millwork	7.1	Manufg.
Electric services (utilities)	2.8	Util.	Exports	6.8	Foreign
Wholesale trade	2.7	Trade	Paper mills, except building paper	6.6	Manufg.
Railroads & related services	2.1	Util.	Residential additions/alterations, nonfarm	5.1	Constr.
Petroleum refining	1.6	Manufg.	Sawmills & planning mills, general	3.8	Manufg.
Motor freight transportation & warehousing	1.4	Util.	Maintenance of nonfarm buildings nec	3.6	Constr.
Banking	0.6	Fin/R.E.	Wood household furniture	3.2	Manufg.
Maintenance of nonfarm buildings nec	0.5	Constr.	Wood pallets & skids	2.3	Manufg.
Gas production & distribution (utilities)	0.4	Util.	Wood preserving	2.3	Manufg.
Eating & drinking places	0.4	Trade	Wood products, nec	2.3	Manufg.
Maintenance of nonbuilding facilities nec	0.3	Constr.	Pulp mills	2.2	Manufg.
Communications, except radio & TV	0.3	Util.	Structural wood members, nec	2.2	Manufg.
Water transportation	0.3	Util.	Nonfarm residential structure maintenance	2.0	Constr.

Continued on next page.

INPUTS AND OUTPUTS FOR SAWMILLS & PLANNING MILLS, GENERAL - Continued

Economic Sector or Industry Providing Inputs	%	Sector	Economic Sector or Industry Buying Outputs	%	Sector
Cyclic crudes and organics	0.2	Manufg.	Mobile homes	1.7	Manufg.
Metal stampings, nec	0.2	Manufg.	Residential garden apartments	1.6	Constr.
Veneer & plywood	0.2	Manufg.	Hardwood dimension & flooring mills	1.6	Manufg.
Sanitary services, steam supply, irrigation	0.2	Util.	Prefabricated wood buildings	1.5	Manufg.
Advertising	0.2	Services	Wood containers	1.3	Manufg.
Automotive rental & leasing, without drivers	0.2	Services	Maintenance of railroads	1.2	Constr.
Automotive repair shops & services	0.2	Services	Wood kitchen cabinets	1.2	Manufg.
Equipment rental & leasing services	0.2	Services	Residential 2-4 unit structures, nonfarm	0.9	Constr.
Management & consulting services & labs	0.2	Services	Sanitary services, steam supply, irrigation	0.8	Util.
U.S. Postal Service	0.2	Gov't	Upholstered household furniture	0.7	Manufg.
Abrasive products	0.1	Manufg.	Particleboard	0.6	Manufg.
Adhesives & sealants	0.1	Manufg.	Office buildings	0.5	Constr.
Woodworking machinery	0.1	Manufg.	Manufacturing industries, nec	0.5	Manufg.
Insurance carriers	0.1	Fin/R.E.	Farm service facilities	0.4	Constr.
Real estate	0.1	Fin/R.E.	Industrial buildings	0.4	Constr.
Accounting, auditing & bookkeeping	0.1	Services	Wood office furniture	0.4	Manufg.
Legal services	0.1	Services	Wood partitions & fixtures	0.4	Manufg.
			Electric utility facility construction	0.3	Constr.
			Farm housing units & additions & alterations	0.3	Constr.
			Mattresses & bedsprings	0.3	Manufg.
			Sheet metal work	0.3	Manufg.
			Construction of educational buildings	0.2	Constr.
			Construction of stores & restaurants	0.2	Constr.
			Maintenance of farm service facilities	0.2	Constr.
			Residential high-rise apartments	0.2	Constr.
			Boat building & repairing	0.2	Manufg.
			Burial caskets & vaults	0.2	Manufg.
			Furniture & fixtures, nec	0.2	Manufg.
			Games, toys, & children's vehicles	0.2	Manufg.
			Iron & steel foundries	0.2	Manufg.
			Logging camps & logging contractors	0.2	Manufg.
			Musical instruments	0.2	Manufg.
			Public building furniture	0.2	Manufg.
			Pumps & compressors	0.2	Manufg.
			Sporting & athletic goods, nec	0.2	Manufg.
			Travel trailers & campers	0.2	Manufg.
			Veneer & plywood	0.2	Manufg.
			Motion pictures	0.2	Services
			S/L Govt. purch., elem. & secondary education	0.2	S/L Govt
			Nonferrous metal ores, except copper	0.1	Mining
			Maintenance of highways & streets	0.1	Constr.
			Maintenance of nonbuilding facilities nec	0.1	Constr.
			Nonbuilding facilities nec	0.1	Constr.
			Telephone & telegraph facility construction	0.1	Constr.
			Aluminum rolling & drawing	0.1	Manufg.
			Ammunition, except for small arms, nec	0.1	Manufg.
			Building paper & board mills	0.1	Manufg.
			Glass & glass products, except containers	0.1	Manufg.
			Gum & wood chemicals	0.1	Manufg.
			Miscellaneous fabricated wire products	0.1	Manufg.
			Radio & TV communication equipment	0.1	Manufg.
			Ready-mixed concrete	0.1	Manufg.
			Refrigeration & heating equipment	0.1	Manufg.
			Ship building & repairing	0.1	Manufg.
			Signs & advertising displays	0.1	Manufg.
			Telephone & telegraph apparatus	0.1	Manufg.
			Truck trailers	0.1	Manufg.
			Wood TV & radio cabinets	0.1	Manufg.

Source: Benchmark Input-Output Accounts for the U.S. Economy, 1982, U.S. Department of Commerce, Washington, D.C., July 1991. Data, as reported in the source, are organized by the 1977 SIC structure in use in 1982 but have been matched, as closely as is possible, to the 1987 SIC structure used in this book.

OCCUPATIONS EMPLOYED BY SIC 242 - SAWMILLS AND PLANING MILLS

Occupation	% of Total 1994	Change to 2005	Occupation	% of Total 1994	Change to 2005
Head sawyers & sawing machine workers	12.9	-18.3	Wood machinists	2.3	63.5
Machine feeders & offbearers	11.0	-26.4	Maintenance repairers, general utility	1.7	-26.5
Freight, stock, & material movers, hand	7.8	-34.6	Timber workers nec	1.6	-26.4
Helpers, laborers, & material movers nec	6.8	-18.3	Assemblers, fabricators, & hand workers nec	1.3	-18.3
Woodworking machine workers	4.6	-26.4	General office clerks	1.3	-30.3
Industrial truck & tractor operators	4.6	-18.3	Hand packers & packagers	1.3	-29.9
Blue collar worker supervisors	3.8	-23.8	Secretaries, ex legal & medical	1.2	-25.6
Inspectors, testers, & graders, precision	3.4	-18.3	Bookkeeping, accounting, & auditing clerks	1.2	-38.7
Truck drivers light & heavy	3.0	-15.7	Furnace, kiln, or kettle operators	1.1	-10.1
Industrial machinery mechanics	2.9	-10.1	Millwrights	1.1	-18.3
General managers & top executives	2.4	-22.5	Precision metal workers nec	1.1	-18.3
Log handling equipment operators	2.4	-18.3	Material moving equipment operators nec	1.1	-34.6

Source: *Industry-Occupation Matrix*, Bureau of Labor Statistics. These data relate to one or more 3-digit SIC industry groups rather than to a single 4-digit SIC. The change reported for each occupation to the year 2005 is a percent of growth or decline as estimated by the Bureau of Labor Statistics. The abbreviation nec stands for 'not elsewhere classified'.

LOCATION BY STATE AND REGIONAL CONCENTRATION

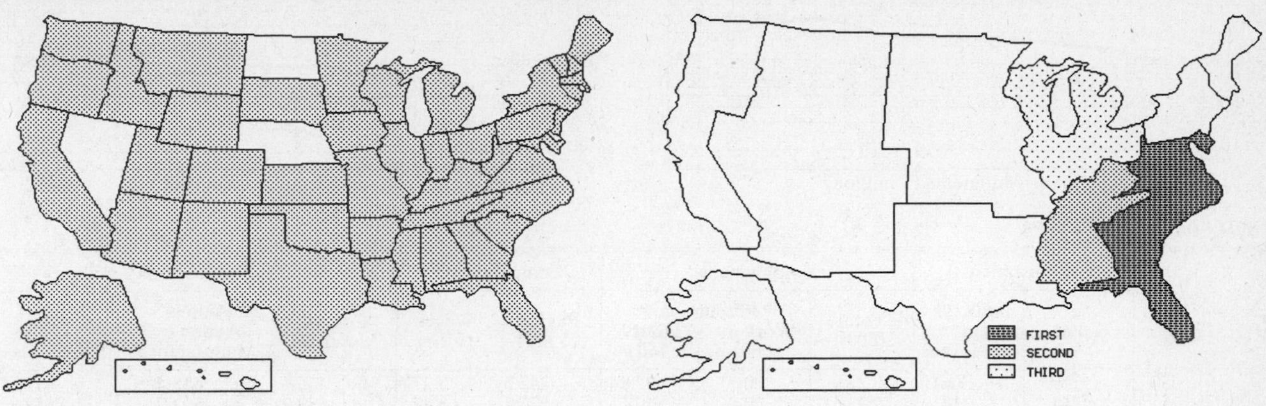

INDUSTRY DATA BY STATE

State	Establish-ments	Shipments			Employment				Cost as % of Shipments	Investment per Employee ($)
		Total ($ mil)	% of U.S.	Per Establ.	Total Number	% of U.S.	Per Establ.	Wages ($/hour)		
Oregon	269	3,205.3	15.2	11.9	14,700	10.6	55	12.07	70.9	3,660
California	236	2,370.1	11.3	10.0	11,600	8.4	49	12.08	58.7	3,310
Washington	241	2,176.2	10.3	9.0	11,200	8.1	46	12.63	65.4	4,973
Mississippi	173	1,097.9	5.2	6.3	7,000	5.1	40	8.27	61.4	3,371
Georgia	187	1,064.9	5.1	5.7	6,500	4.7	35	8.39	64.9	3,723
Alabama	194	946.5	4.5	4.9	6,800	4.9	35	8.28	63.1	2,574
Idaho	94	945.1	4.5	10.1	4,600	3.3	49	11.86	65.3	3,652
North Carolina	346	801.9	3.8	2.3	6,600	4.8	19	8.14	61.8	2,864
Arkansas	195	800.5	3.8	4.1	5,700	4.1	29	8.97	63.2	5,105
South Carolina	108	613.2	2.9	5.7	3,500	2.5	32	8.95	65.5	-
Pennsylvania	412	596.1	2.8	1.4	5,500	4.0	13	7.76	59.5	2,891
Virginia	312	517.9	2.5	1.7	4,900	3.5	16	7.64	57.5	2,102
Texas	155	455.3	2.2	2.9	3,100	2.2	20	8.61	66.0	3,935
Louisiana	107	433.7	2.1	4.1	3,000	2.2	28	8.98	66.0	2,267
Wisconsin	223	390.8	1.9	1.8	3,500	2.5	16	8.50	59.0	2,429
West Virginia	184	337.0	1.6	1.8	3,100	2.2	17	7.31	55.6	3,323
Maine	100	292.2	1.4	2.9	2,200	1.6	22	9.66	55.2	3,591
Kentucky	218	292.1	1.4	1.3	3,300	2.4	15	6.62	58.6	2,333
New York	185	270.8	1.3	1.5	2,000	1.4	11	8.91	58.9	4,250
Florida	100	269.6	1.3	2.7	2,000	1.4	20	8.16	61.0	1,850
Michigan	219	261.2	1.2	1.2	2,300	1.7	11	8.36	57.2	3,696
Indiana	147	257.4	1.2	1.8	2,000	1.4	14	8.00	59.1	2,700
Ohio	163	255.8	1.2	1.6	2,300	1.7	14	7.79	60.9	4,217
Missouri	278	180.9	0.9	0.7	2,200	1.6	8	6.54	55.7	1,818
Minnesota	94	97.4	0.5	1.0	900	0.7	10	8.31	58.1	-
Wyoming	27	86.0	0.4	3.2	800	0.6	30	9.29	56.4	1,250
Vermont	54	82.0	0.4	1.5	700	0.5	13	8.85	52.7	3,857
South Dakota	17	80.6	0.4	4.7	700	0.5	41	11.60	63.5	-
Colorado	47	70.9	0.3	1.5	600	0.4	13	8.40	56.1	2,167
Illinois	85	56.4	0.3	0.7	700	0.5	8	7.80	58.0	-
Massachusetts	59	42.9	0.2	0.7	400	0.3	7	9.00	50.3	2,500
Connecticut	23	31.3	0.1	1.4	300	0.2	13	12.75	61.7	3,333
Kansas	12	14.0	0.1	1.2	100	0.1	8	9.50	54.3	1,000
Tennessee	310	(D)	-	-	3,750 *	2.7	12	-	-	2,347
New Hampshire	70	(D)	-	-	1,750 *	1.3	25	-	-	-
Montana	67	(D)	-	-	3,750 *	2.7	56	-	-	-
Maryland	59	(D)	-	-	750 *	0.5	13	-	-	-
Iowa	39	(D)	-	-	375 *	0.3	10	-	-	-
New Mexico	33	(D)	-	-	750 *	0.5	23	-	-	-
Utah	30	(D)	-	-	375 *	0.3	13	-	-	-
Arizona	28	(D)	-	-	1,750 *	1.3	63	-	-	-
Oklahoma	24	(D)	-	-	375 *	0.3	16	-	-	-
New Jersey	22	(D)	-	-	175 *	0.1	8	-	-	-
Alaska	20	(D)	-	-	750 *	0.5	38	-	-	-

Source: 1992 *Economic Census*. The states are in descending order of shipments or establishments (if shipment data are missing for the majority). The symbol (D) appears when data are withheld to prevent disclosure of competitive information. States marked with (D) are sorted by number of establishments. A dash (-) indicates that the data element cannot be calculated; * indicates the midpoint of a range.

2426 - HARDWOOD DIMENSION & FLOORING MILLS

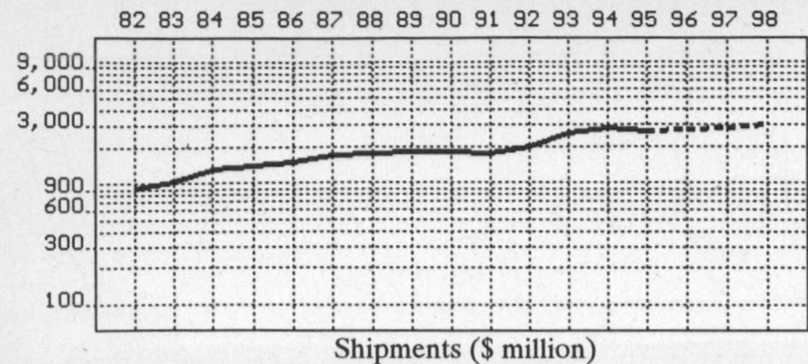

Shipments ($ million)

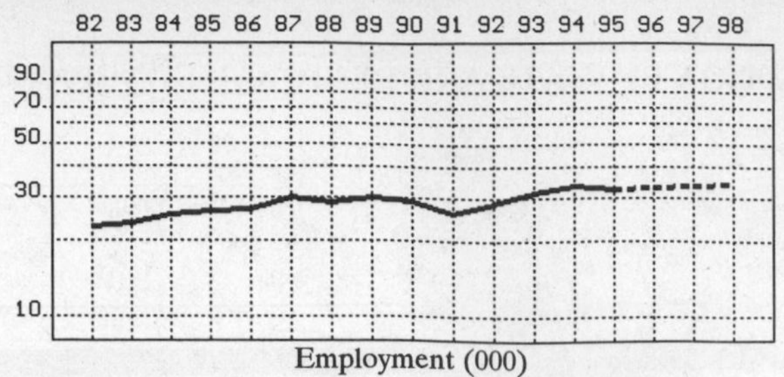

Employment (000)

GENERAL STATISTICS

Year	Companies	Establishments: Total	Establishments: with 20 or more employees	Employment: Total (000)	Employment: Production Workers (000)	Employment: Production Hours (Mil)	Compensation: Payroll ($ mil)	Compensation: Wages ($/hr)	Production ($ million): Cost of Materials	Production ($ million): Value Added by Manufacture	Production ($ million): Value of Shipments	Production ($ million): Capital Invest.
1982	750	789	306	22.9	20.1	37.8	252.6	5.27	465.6	445.4	912.6	24.3
1983		761	314	23.6	20.9	40.4	275.2	5.47	553.2	522.7	1,053.8	25.0
1984		733	322	25.7	22.5	45.0	334.7	5.84	679.1	649.7	1,315.2	37.2
1985		704	331	26.2	23.2	45.4	347.7	6.08	705.7	688.3	1,392.4	36.5
1986		688	316	27.2	23.8	48.2	386.1	6.34	793.2	718.1	1,503.0	52.7
1987	696	737	343	29.9	26.2	53.2	440.8	6.49	866.7	853.9	1,714.0	66.3
1988		719	339	28.9	25.2	51.2	454.9	6.90	916.2	840.5	1,730.0	49.8
1989		694	334	30.0	26.0	52.9	471.7	7.01	909.0	882.1	1,787.1	44.5
1990		729	331	29.4	26.0	53.3	475.0	6.93	893.9	908.8	1,800.5	88.0
1991		718	308	26.1	22.9	48.3	462.0	7.26	866.8	863.8	1,738.8	66.6
1992	781	831	339	28.5	24.8	49.9	501.9	7.76	1,037.3	993.9	2,027.2	47.8
1993		812	338	31.4	27.4	55.1	582.4	8.21	1,374.8	1,172.1	2,529.4	48.2
1994		763P	339P	33.4	29.9	60.8	618.6	8.16	1,443.2	1,379.7	2,799.5	63.1
1995		767P	341P	32.5P	28.5P	59.0P	621.5P	8.44P	1,345.5P	1,286.3P	2,610.1P	70.4P
1996		770P	342P	33.1P	29.1P	60.3P	648.7P	8.68P	1,411.4P	1,349.3P	2,737.8P	73.3P
1997		773P	344P	33.7P	29.7P	61.7P	675.9P	8.92P	1,477.3P	1,412.3P	2,865.6P	76.2P
1998		776P	346P	34.4P	30.2P	63.1P	703.2P	9.16P	1,543.2P	1,475.3P	2,993.4P	79.1P

Sources: 1982, 1987, 1992 *Economic Census*; *Annual Survey of Manufactures*, 83-86, 88-91, 93-94. Establishment counts for non-Census years are from *County Business Patterns*; establishment values for 83-84 are extrapolations. 'P's show projections by the editors. Industries reclassified in 87 will not have data for prior years.

INDICES OF CHANGE

Year	Companies	Establishments: Total	Establishments: with 20 or more employees	Employment: Total (000)	Employment: Production Workers (000)	Employment: Production Hours (Mil)	Compensation: Payroll ($ mil)	Compensation: Wages ($/hr)	Production ($ million): Cost of Materials	Production ($ million): Value Added by Manufacture	Production ($ million): Value of Shipments	Production ($ million): Capital Invest.
1982	96	95	90	80	81	76	50	68	45	45	45	51
1983		92	93	83	84	81	55	70	53	53	52	52
1984		88	95	90	91	90	67	75	65	65	65	78
1985		85	98	92	94	91	69	78	68	69	69	76
1986		83	93	95	96	97	77	82	76	72	74	110
1987	89	89	101	105	106	107	88	84	84	86	85	139
1988		87	100	101	102	103	91	89	88	85	85	104
1989		84	99	105	105	106	94	90	88	89	88	93
1990		88	98	103	105	107	95	89	86	91	89	184
1991		86	91	92	92	97	92	94	84	87	86	139
1992	100	100	100	100	100	100	100	100	100	100	100	100
1993		98	100	110	110	110	116	106	133	118	125	101
1994		92P	100P	117	121	122	123	105	139	139	138	132
1995		92P	100P	114P	115P	118P	124P	109P	130P	129P	129P	147P
1996		93P	101P	116P	117P	121P	129P	112P	136P	136P	135P	153P
1997		93P	102P	118P	120P	124P	135P	115P	142P	142P	141P	159P
1998		93P	102P	121P	122P	126P	140P	118P	149P	148P	148P	166P

Sources: Same as General Statistics. Values reflect change from the base year, 1992. Values above 100 mean greater than 92, values below 100 mean less than 92, and a value of 100 in the 82-91 or 93-98 period means same as 92. 'P's mark projections by the editors.

SELECTED RATIOS

For 1994	Avg. of All Manufact.	Analyzed Industry	Index	For 1994	Avg. of All Manufact.	Analyzed Industry	Index
Employees per Establishment	49	44	89	Value Added per Production Worker	134,084	46,144	34
Payroll per Establishment	1,500,273	810,280	54	Cost per Establishment	5,045,178	1,890,392	37
Payroll per Employee	30,620	18,521	60	Cost per Employee	102,970	43,210	42
Production Workers per Establishment	34	39	114	Cost per Production Worker	146,988	48,268	33
Wages per Establishment	853,319	649,859	76	Shipments per Establishment	9,576,895	3,666,958	38
Wages per Production Worker	24,861	16,593	67	Shipments per Employee	195,460	83,817	43
Hours per Production Worker	2,056	2,033	99	Shipments per Production Worker	279,017	93,629	34
Wages per Hour	12.09	8.16	67	Investment per Establishment	321,011	82,652	26
Value Added per Establishment	4,602,255	1,807,216	39	Investment per Employee	6,552	1,889	29
Value Added per Employee	93,930	41,308	44	Investment per Production Worker	9,352	2,110	23

Sources: Same as General Statistics. The 'Average of All Manufacturing' column represents the average of all manufacturing industries reported for the most recent complete year available. The Index shows the relationship between the Average and the Analyzed Industry. For example, 100 means that they are equal; 500 that the Analyzed Industry is five times the average; 50 means that the Analyzed Industry is half the national average. The abbreviation 'na' is used to show that data are 'not available'.

LEADING COMPANIES

Number shown: **75** Total sales ($ mil): **2,140** Total employment (000): **20.5**

Company Name	Address				CEO Name	Phone	Co. Type	Sales ($ mil)	Empl. (000)
Triangle Pacific Corp	PO Box 660100	Dallas	TX	75266	Floyd F Sherman	214-931-3000	P	346	3.5
Triangle Pacific Corp	16803 Dallas Pkwy	Dallas	TX	75248	James E Price	214-931-3000	D	244	2.4
Crown Pacific Partners LP	121 SW Morrison St	Portland	OR	97204	Peter W Stott	503-274-2300	P	221	1.6
Crown Pacific LP	121 SW Morrison St	Portland	OR	97204	Peter W Stott	503-274-2300	S	221	1.6
Coastal Lumber Co	PO Box 829	Weldon	NC	27890	Paul B Barringer	919-536-4211	R	200	1.6
Anthony Timberlands Inc	PO Box 137	Bearden	AR	71720	John Anthony	501-687-3611	R	66	0.4
Woodcraft Industries Inc	525 Lincoln SE	St Cloud	MN	56304	TR Ritsche	612-252-1503	R	58	0.7
Robbins Inc	4777 Eastern Av	Cincinnati	OH	45226	James Stoehr	513-871-8988	R	50	0.6
Walter H Weaber Sons Inc	RD 4	Lebanon	PA	17042	G Weaber	717-867-2212	R	50*	0.4
Memphis Hardwood	1551 Thomas St	Memphis	TN	38107	Thomas Cathey	901-526-7306	R	40	0.6
Catawissa Lumber and Specialty	PO Box 176	Catawissa	PA	17820	William Gittler Sr	717-356-2349	R	37	0.3
Ross-Simmons	PO Box 366	Longview	WA	98632	Warren Morris	360-423-8210	R	28	0.2
Endeavor Lumber Co	PO Box 67	Endeavor	PA	16322	Barry Lettie	814-463-7701	D	26*	<0.1
Fitzpatrick and Weller Inc	PO Box 490	Ellicottville	NY	14731	Gerard Fitzpatrick	716-699-2393	R	25	0.2
Harris-Tarkett Inc	PO Box 300	Johnson City	TN	37605	David Wootton	615-928-3122	S	25*	0.4
PermaGrain Products Inc	4789 W Chester Pk	Newtown Sq	PA	19073	AR Witt	610-353-8801	R	22	0.2
Cascade Hardwood Inc	PO Box 269	Chehalis	WA	98532	D F Princehouse	206-748-0178	S	20*	<0.1
Northern Hardwoods	PO Box 189	South Range	MI	49963	Emmerentia Guthrie	906-487-6400	D	20	0.2
Dixon Lumber Company Inc	PO Box 907	Galax	VA	24333	Latham Wlliams	703-236-9963	R	17	0.3
Fred Netterville Lumber	PO Box 857	Woodville	MS	39669	Fred Netterville	601-888-4343	R	16	0.2
Hassell and Hughes Lumber	PO Box 68	Collinwood	TN	38450	William H Hughes	615-724-9191	R	16	0.2
Lebanon Oak Flooring Co	215 Taylor Av	Lebanon	KY	40033	Robert L Goodin	502-692-2128	R	15	0.1
Van Keulen	245 54th St SW	Grand Rapids	MI	49548	John D Bouwer	616-532-3678	R	15	<0.1
Cumberland Lumber	202 Red Rd	McMinnville	TN	37110	Ray Spivey	615-473-9542	R	14	0.1
AMF Bowling Inc	Utica Blv	Lowville	NY	13367	Rodney Mallette	315-376-6541	D	13*	0.2
Blalock Manufacturing	125 Sweeten Creek	Asheville	NC	28803	Mike Latta	704-274-0335	D	12	0.1
JP Price Lumber Co	PO Box 536	Monticello	AR	71655	JP Price	501-367-9751	S	12*	0.1
Searcy Flooring Inc	PO Box 906	Searcy	AR	72145	LV Witt	501-268-8694	S	12	0.1
Smith Flooring Inc	1501 W Hwy 60	Mountain View	MO	65548	Van K Smith	417-934-2291	R	12	0.1
Calion Lumber Company Inc	PO Box 348	Calion	AR	71724	Edwin Thomas Jr	501-748-2411	R	11*	<0.1
Carolina Hardwoods LLC	PO Box 5456	Lenoir	NC	28645	Robert H Green	704-728-8402	R	11*	0.1
Woodcraft Inc	PO Box 1819	Morristown	TN	37816	JC Elliot	615-581-5413	R	11*	0.1
Cranford Woodcarving Inc	PO Box 2426	Hickory	NC	28603	Jessie Cranford	704-328-4538	R	10	0.2
Ideal Frame Company Inc	PO Box 935	Taylorsville	NC	28681	Phil C Lackey	704-632-3771	R	10	0.1
Sherman Lumber Co	PO Box 70	Sherman St	ME	04777	M A Robinson	207-365-4211	R	10	<0.1
Carving Craft Inc	PO Box 2388	Hickory	NC	28603	Catharine Fuller	704-322-5625	R	9*	0.1
Connor AGA	PO Box 246	Amasa	MI	49903	Brad Karnstedt	906-822-7311	S	9*	0.1
Fayette Enterprises Inc	PO Box 188	Fayette	MS	39069	Connie Kanoy	601-786-3473	S	9	<0.1
Giffin Interior and Fixture Inc	500 Scotti Dr	Bridgeville	PA	15017	Gordon D Giffin	412-221-1166	R	9	0.1
Hardwood Dimensions Inc	Hwy 301 S	Dunn	NC	28334	Albert Murray Jr	910-892-8118	R	9*	0.1
McMinnville Manufacturing Co	PO Box 151	McMinnville	TN	37110	James B Mullican	615-473-2131	R	9	0.1
Bear Paw Lumber Corp	PO Box 20	Fryeburg	ME	04037	DE Keaten	207-935-2951	R	8	<0.1
Horner Flooring Company Inc	250 S Maple Av	Dollar Bay	MI	49922	Doug Hamar	906-482-1180	R	8	<0.1
S and K Industries Inc	PO Box G	Lexington	MO	64067	Thomas R Stout	816-259-4691	R	8	0.3
Ste Genevieve Manufacturing	805 Moreau St	Ste Genevieve	MO	63670	Gerald Trautman	314-883-7451	R	8	<0.1
Walter Dimension Co	PO Box 843	Jamestown	TN	38556	P Harden	615-879-8151	R	8	0.1
Smith Inc	PO Box 87	S Londonderry	VT	05155	NW Smith	802-824-5515	R	7	<0.1
Wagner Woodcraft Inc	10417 S Main St	Archdale	NC	27263	JD Edwards	919-431-1197	R	7	<0.1
Wood Products Co	PO Box 689	Newport	TN	37821	CT Rhyne Jr	615-623-3003	R	7	0.1
Custom Dimensions Inc	PO Box 555	Calhoun City	MS	38916	Tom Therrell	601-628-6641	R	7*	<0.1
Pacific Hardwoods	PO Box 185	South Bend	WA	98586	Tom McGogh	206-942-5525	S	7	<0.1
Cortrim Hardwood Parts Co	1320 Georgia Av	Bristol	TN	37620	Robert Spiegle	615-764-6127	R	7	0.2
Holmes and Company Inc	PO Box 370	Columbia City	IN	46725	L E Almendinger	219-244-6149	R	6*	<0.1
Roman Empire	4466 Worth St	Los Angeles	CA	90063	Roman Amezquita	213-264-8857	R	6	<0.1
Thomson Oak Flooring Co	946 Mesena Rd NW	Thomson	GA	30824	Monroe Kimbrel	706-595-2577	R	6	0.1
Newport Furniture Parts Corp	PO Box 788	Newport	VT	05855	Jean M Laforce	802-334-2875	R	5	<0.1
Bagley Hardwood Products	PO Box C	Bagley	MN	56621	Wes Renneberg	218-694-6141	R	5	<0.1
National Wood Products	216 Industrial Dr	Glasgow	KY	42141	James D Manning	502-651-8804	D	5*	<0.1
Rhyne Lumber Company Inc	PO Box 709	Newport	TN	37821	BG Williams	615-623-2324	R	5	<0.1
Superior Moulding Company Inc	PO Box 409	Troy	AL	36081	HK Brown Jr	205-566-0164	R	5	0.1
Adams Wood Turning Inc	216 Woodbine St	High Point	NC	27260	Walter S Blackburn	910-884-7344	R	4*	<0.1
American Walnut Company Inc	1021 S 18th St	Kansas City	KS	66105	John R Worrell	913-371-1820	R	4*	<0.1
Angelina Hardwood Sales	PO Box 3659	Lufkin	TX	75903	GH Henderson Jr	409-634-4415	R	4	<0.1
MJ Wood Products Inc	RR 1	Morrisville	VT	05661	Geoffrey Jackson	802-888-7974	R	4	<0.1
Penn Wood Products Inc	102 Locust St	East Berlin	PA	17316	Newell E Coxon Jr	717-259-9551	R	4	<0.1
Rich Lumber Co	PO Box 317	Beardstown	IL	62618	Danny Rich	217-323-1718	R	4*	<0.1
Champion Wood Products Inc	PO Box 178	Jeffersonville	IN	47131	EC Rucker Jr	812-282-9460	R	4	<0.1
Sparta Spoke Factory	PO Box 240	Sparta	TN	38583	RL Tubb	615-738-2231	R	3	<0.1
C and C Smith Lumber Company	RR #1	Summerhill	PA	15958	CB Smith	814-495-4712	R	3	0.1
Hotz Manufacturing Company	PO Box 120	Shawano	WI	54166	John Swanke	715-526-3154	S	3*	<0.1
Carrick Turning Works Inc	PO Box 1868	High Point	NC	27261	FR Carrick	910-475-2111	R	3	0.1
Jefferson Wood Working	PO Box 3505	Louisville	KY	40201	Allen Mercke	502-635-5227	R	3	<0.1
Mountain Lumber Co	PO Box 289	Ruckersville	VA	22968	William Drake	804-985-3646	R	2	<0.1
Peace Flooring Company Inc	PO Box 87	Magnolia	AR	71753	John S Duke	501-234-2310	R	2	<0.1
Wood-Crafts Company Inc	PO Box 88	N Manchester	IN	46962	Richard E Miller	219-982-2186	R	1	<0.1

Source: *Ward's Business Directory of U.S. Private and Public Companies*, Volumes 1 and 2, 1996. The company type code used is as follows: P - Public, R - Private, S - Subsidiary, D - Division, J - Joint Venture, A - Affiliate, G - Group. Sales are in millions of dollars, employees are in thousands. An asterisk (*) indicates an estimated sales volume. The symbol < stands for 'less than'. Company names and addresses are truncated, in some cases, to fit into the available space.

MATERIALS CONSUMED

Material		Quantity	Delivered Cost ($ million)
Materials, ingredients, containers, and supplies		(X)	938.1
Stumpage cost (cost of timber, excluding land, cut and consumed at same establishment)		(X)	4.9
Hardwood logs, bolts, and unsliced flitches	mil ft log scale	165.5*	46.5
Hardwood rough lumber	mil bd ft	908.2*	407.1
Softwood rough lumber	mil bd ft	37.1*	12.9
Hardwood dressed lumber	mil bd ft	124.6**	65.4
Softwood dressed lumber	mil bd ft	16.0*	6.5
Glues and adhesives	mil lb	19.3**	10.3
All other materials and components, parts, containers, and supplies		(X)	163.5
Materials, ingredients, containers, and supplies, nsk		(X)	221.0

Source: 1992 *Economic Census*. Explanation of symbols used: (D): Withheld to avoid disclosure of competitive data; na: Not available; (S): Withheld because statistical norms were not met; (X): Not applicable; (Z): Less than half the unit shown; nec: Not elsewhere classified; nsk: Not specified by kind; - : zero; * : 10-19 percent estimated; ** : 20-29 percent estimated.

PRODUCT SHARE DETAILS

Product or Product Class	% Share	Product or Product Class	% Share
Hardwood dimension and flooring mills	100.00	laminates, completely fabricated and ready for assembly, including furniture parts, except frames	29.60
Hardwood flooring	33.42	Rough industrial hardwood dimension stock (for handles, golf clubs, etc.)	5.64
Oak flooring (3/4 inch, 1/2 inch, 3/8 inch T and G and EM, and 5/16 inch square edge strip)	57.99	Semifabricated industrial hardwood dimension stock (for handles, golf clubs, etc.)	1.46
Oak parquetry	6.46	Completely fabricated industrial hardwood dimension stock (for handles, golf clubs, etc.)	16.27
Other oak flooring, including plank, block, and specialty	12.25	Compression-modified or densified hardwood dimension stock, furniture parts, and vehicle stock (whether or not impregnated with synthetic resin)	0.17
Maple flooring, including strip, block, parquetry	3.99	Hardwood dimension stock, furniture parts, and vehicle stock, nsk	4.29
Glued laminated hardwood truck trailer flooring and railroad car decking	12.31	Hardwood furniture frames for household furniture	13.89
Other hardwood flooring	3.66	Hardwood furniture frames for household seating	82.95
Hardwood flooring, nsk	3.37	Hardwood furniture frames for other household furniture	13.16
Hardwood dimension stock, furniture parts, and vehicle stock	38.82	Wood furniture frames for household furniture, nsk	3.89
Hardwood furniture dimension stock, including glued laminates, rough or surfaced, cut to size	27.37	Hardwood dimension and flooring mills, nsk	13.86
Hardwood furniture dimension stock, including glued laminates, semifabricated	15.21		
Hardwood furniture dimension stock, including glued			

Source: 1992 *Economic Census*. The values shown are percent of total shipments in an industry. Values of indented subcategories are summed in the main heading. The symbol (D) appears when data are withheld to prevent disclosure of competitive information. The abbreviation nsk stands for 'not specified by kind' and nec for 'not elsewhere classified'.

INPUTS AND OUTPUTS FOR HARDWOOD DIMENSION & FLOORING MILLS

Economic Sector or Industry Providing Inputs	%	Sector	Economic Sector or Industry Buying Outputs	%	Sector
Sawmills & planning mills, general	30.9	Manufg.	Wood household furniture	22.1	Manufg.
Imports	12.0	Foreign	Upholstered household furniture	15.8	Manufg.
Wholesale trade	11.0	Trade	Wood kitchen cabinets	7.0	Manufg.
Petroleum refining	8.1	Manufg.	Residential additions/alterations, nonfarm	6.2	Constr.
Logging camps & logging contractors	8.0	Manufg.	Mattresses & bedsprings	4.6	Manufg.
Electric services (utilities)	4.0	Util.	Residential 1-unit structures, nonfarm	3.9	Constr.
Motor freight transportation & warehousing	2.2	Util.	Truck trailers	3.9	Manufg.
Advertising	1.9	Services	Wood products, nec	3.7	Manufg.
Railroads & related services	1.7	Util.	Exports	3.5	Foreign
Automotive rental & leasing, without drivers	1.7	Services	Wood office furniture	2.7	Manufg.
Automotive repair shops & services	1.7	Services	Nonfarm residential structure maintenance	2.4	Constr.
Paperboard containers & boxes	1.3	Manufg.	Maintenance of nonfarm buildings nec	2.0	Constr.
Maintenance of nonfarm buildings nec	1.1	Constr.	Prefabricated wood buildings	2.0	Manufg.
Eating & drinking places	1.0	Trade	Residential garden apartments	1.7	Constr.
Royalties	0.9	Fin/R.E.	Small arms	1.6	Manufg.
Gas production & distribution (utilities)	0.8	Util.	Drapery hardware & blinds & shades	1.5	Manufg.
Hardwood dimension & flooring mills	0.7	Manufg.	Millwork	1.3	Manufg.
Adhesives & sealants	0.6	Manufg.	Wood partitions & fixtures	0.9	Manufg.
Hand saws & saw blades	0.6	Manufg.	Wood TV & radio cabinets	0.9	Manufg.
Communications, except radio & TV	0.6	Util.	Games, toys, & children's vehicles	0.8	Manufg.
Banking	0.6	Fin/R.E.	Leather goods, nec	0.7	Manufg.
Paints & allied products	0.5	Manufg.	Lighting fixtures & equipment	0.7	Manufg.
Tires & inner tubes	0.5	Manufg.	Watch, clock, jewelry, & furniture repair	0.7	Services
Water transportation	0.5	Util.	Office buildings	0.6	Constr.
Retail trade, except eating & drinking	0.5	Trade	Residential 2-4 unit structures, nonfarm	0.6	Constr.
Insurance carriers	0.5	Fin/R.E.	Mobile homes	0.6	Manufg.
Real estate	0.5	Fin/R.E.	Sporting & athletic goods, nec	0.6	Manufg.
Motor vehicle parts & accessories	0.4	Manufg.	Residential high-rise apartments	0.5	Constr.
Management & consulting services & labs	0.4	Services	Boot & shoe cutstock & findings	0.5	Manufg.
U.S. Postal Service	0.4	Gov't	Hardwood dimension & flooring mills	0.5	Manufg.

Continued on next page.

INPUTS AND OUTPUTS FOR HARDWOOD DIMENSION & FLOORING MILLS - Continued

Economic Sector or Industry Providing Inputs	%	Sector	Economic Sector or Industry Buying Outputs	%	Sector
Woodworking machinery	0.3	Manufg.	Miscellaneous plastics products	0.5	Manufg.
Accounting, auditing & bookkeeping	0.3	Services	Railroad equipment	0.5	Manufg.
Equipment rental & leasing services	0.3	Services	Ship building & repairing	0.5	Manufg.
Legal services	0.3	Services	Shoes, except rubber	0.5	Manufg.
Abrasive products	0.2	Manufg.	Special product sawmills, nec	0.5	Manufg.
Lubricating oils & greases	0.2	Manufg.	Motion pictures	0.5	Services
Machinery, except electrical, nec	0.2	Manufg.	Household furniture, nec	0.4	Manufg.
Business/professional associations	0.2	Services	Brooms & brushes	0.3	Manufg.
Engineering, architectural, & surveying services	0.2	Services	Concrete products, nec	0.3	Manufg.
Laundry, dry cleaning, shoe repair	0.2	Services	Household appliances, nec	0.3	Manufg.
Manifold business forms	0.1	Manufg.	Metal partitions & fixtures	0.3	Manufg.
Sanitary services, steam supply, irrigation	0.1	Util.	Textile machinery	0.3	Manufg.
Security & commodity brokers	0.1	Fin/R.E.	Luggage	0.2	Manufg.
Detective & protective services	0.1	Services	Farm housing units & additions & alterations	0.1	Constr.
State & local government enterprises, nec	0.1	Gov't			

Source: Benchmark Input-Output Accounts for the U.S. Economy, 1982, U.S. Department of Commerce, Washington, D.C., July 1991. Data, as reported in the source, are organized by the 1977 SIC structure in use in 1982 but have been matched, as closely as is possible, to the 1987 SIC structure used in this book.

OCCUPATIONS EMPLOYED BY SIC 242 - SAWMILLS AND PLANING MILLS

Occupation	% of Total 1994	Change to 2005	Occupation	% of Total 1994	Change to 2005
Head sawyers & sawing machine workers	12.9	-18.3	Wood machinists	2.3	63.5
Machine feeders & offbearers	11.0	-26.4	Maintenance repairers, general utility	1.7	-26.5
Freight, stock, & material movers, hand	7.8	-34.6	Timber workers nec	1.6	-26.4
Helpers, laborers, & material movers nec	6.8	-18.3	Assemblers, fabricators, & hand workers nec	1.3	-18.3
Woodworking machine workers	4.6	-26.4	General office clerks	1.3	-30.3
Industrial truck & tractor operators	4.6	-18.3	Hand packers & packagers	1.3	-29.9
Blue collar worker supervisors	3.8	-23.8	Secretaries, ex legal & medical	1.2	-25.6
Inspectors, testers, & graders, precision	3.4	-18.3	Bookkeeping, accounting, & auditing clerks	1.2	-38.7
Truck drivers light & heavy	3.0	-15.7	Furnace, kiln, or kettle operators	1.1	-10.1
Industrial machinery mechanics	2.9	-10.1	Millwrights	1.1	-18.3
General managers & top executives	2.4	-22.5	Precision metal workers nec	1.1	-18.3
Log handling equipment operators	2.4	-18.3	Material moving equipment operators nec	1.1	-34.6

Source: Industry-Occupation Matrix, Bureau of Labor Statistics. These data relate to one or more 3-digit SIC industry groups rather than to a single 4-digit SIC. The change reported for each occupation to the year 2005 is a percent of growth or decline as estimated by the Bureau of Labor Statistics. The abbreviation nec stands for 'not elsewhere classified'.

LOCATION BY STATE AND REGIONAL CONCENTRATION

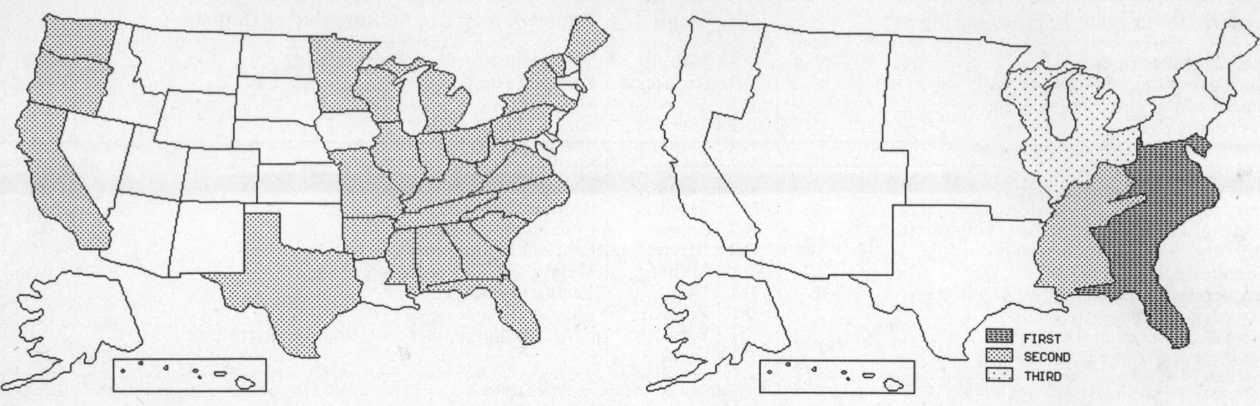

INDUSTRY DATA BY STATE

State	Establish-ments	Shipments Total ($ mil)	Shipments % of U.S.	Shipments Per Establ.	Employment Total Number	Employment % of U.S.	Employment Per Establ.	Employment Wages ($/hour)	Cost as % of Shipments	Investment per Employee ($)
Tennessee	63	360.5	17.8	5.7	4,500	15.8	71	7.29	52.8	-
Missouri	23	128.4	6.3	5.6	1,500	5.3	65	8.42	47.1	-
Arkansas	25	111.9	5.5	4.5	1,500	5.3	60	6.81	43.8	933
Kentucky	22	104.5	5.2	4.8	1,400	4.9	64	7.88	56.4	-
Michigan	21	52.8	2.6	2.5	600	2.1	29	9.40	50.8	2,500
Ohio	16	51.3	2.5	3.2	600	2.1	38	9.10	58.9	-
California	56	49.5	2.4	0.9	900	3.2	16	6.75	51.3	-
Texas	15	38.1	1.9	2.5	500	1.8	33	8.67	60.4	1,200
Maine	10	33.0	1.6	3.3	600	2.1	60	7.00	46.7	1,833
South Carolina	9	20.5	1.0	2.3	400	1.4	44	7.71	46.3	-
Washington	6	19.9	1.0	3.3	200	0.7	33	7.50	52.8	-
Illinois	13	16.7	0.8	1.3	300	1.1	23	7.60	54.5	-
Alabama	11	15.5	0.8	1.4	400	1.4	36	5.43	60.0	750
Oregon	9	14.3	0.7	1.6	200	0.7	22	8.25	48.3	500
Vermont	9	12.3	0.6	1.4	200	0.7	22	7.00	33.3	1,000
North Carolina	180	(D)	-	-	3,750 *	13.2	21	-	-	-
Mississippi	70	(D)	-	-	1,750 *	6.1	25	-	-	-
Pennsylvania	58	(D)	-	-	1,750 *	6.1	30	-	-	-
Indiana	40	(D)	-	-	1,750 *	6.1	44	-	-	1,486
New York	40	(D)	-	-	750 *	2.6	19	-	-	-
Virginia	24	(D)	-	-	1,750 *	6.1	73	-	-	-
Wisconsin	23	(D)	-	-	750 *	2.6	33	-	-	-
Florida	11	(D)	-	-	175 *	0.6	16	-	-	1,143
Minnesota	11	(D)	-	-	750 *	2.6	68	-	-	-
West Virginia	10	(D)	-	-	375 *	1.3	38	-	-	-
Georgia	4	(D)	-	-	375 *	1.3	94	-	-	-

Source: 1992 *Economic Census*. The states are in descending order of shipments or establishments (if shipment data are missing for the majority). The symbol (D) appears when data are withheld to prevent disclosure of competitive information. States marked with (D) are sorted by number of establishments. A dash (-) indicates that the data element cannot be calculated; * indicates the midpoint of a range.

2429 - SPECIAL PRODUCT SAWMILLS, NEC

Shipments ($ million)

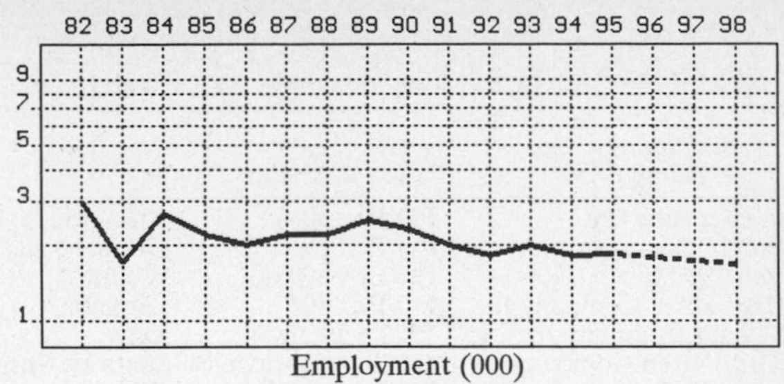

Employment (000)

GENERAL STATISTICS

Year	Companies	Establishments Total	Establishments with 20 or more employees	Employment Total (000)	Production Workers (000)	Production Hours (Mil)	Compensation Payroll ($ mil)	Compensation Wages ($/hr)	Cost of Materials	Value Added by Manufacture	Value of Shipments	Capital Invest.
1982	266	298	47	3.0	2.7	4.0	33.1	6.52	91.5	65.0	154.6	2.9
1983		275	43	1.7	1.5	3.1	27.2	8.00	70.8	64.9	138.9	3.6
1984		252	39	2.7	2.5	3.6	31.4	6.69	85.9	48.4	138.0	1.6
1985		230	36	2.2	2.0	2.7	28.8	8.19	70.5	43.9	110.4	1.5
1986		212	36	2.0	1.7	2.4	26.5	8.75	56.2	40.8	97.0	1.3
1987	220	234	32	2.2	1.9	3.2	32.6	8.03	86.0	60.1	149.2	3.2
1988		215	28	2.2	2.0	3.2	34.0	8.84	90.6	56.9	143.2	4.4
1989		206	32	2.5	1.9	3.1	36.1	9.06	105.1	67.5	175.2	1.8
1990		222	24	2.3	2.1	3.6	40.6	8.83	128.2	81.5	211.3	1.7
1991		197	29	2.0	1.7	2.9	35.7	9.38	113.5	73.8	185.5	1.8
1992	175	192	23	1.8	1.5	2.8	31.3	8.43	83.5	62.0	144.0	4.8
1993		191	23	2.0	1.6	3.1	35.0	7.90	108.5	73.3	181.7	6.1
1994		173P	19P	1.8	1.5	2.8	31.6	7.86	85.2	67.9	154.1	3.0
1995		164P	17P	1.8P	1.5P	2.8P	35.8P	8.93P	99.5P	79.3P	180.0P	3.9P
1996		156P	15P	1.8P	1.4P	2.8P	36.2P	9.04P	101.7P	81.1P	184.0P	4.1P
1997		148P	13P	1.7P	1.4P	2.7P	36.7P	9.14P	103.9P	82.8P	187.9P	4.2P
1998		139P	11P	1.7P	1.3P	2.7P	37.1P	9.25P	106.1P	84.5P	191.8P	4.3P

Sources: 1982, 1987, 1992 *Economic Census*; *Annual Survey of Manufactures*, 83-86, 88-91, 93-94. Establishment counts for non-Census years are from *County Business Patterns*; establishment values for 83-84 are extrapolations. 'P's show projections by the editors. Industries reclassified in 87 will not have data for prior years.

INDICES OF CHANGE

Year	Companies	Establishments Total	Establishments with 20 or more employees	Employment Total (000)	Production Workers (000)	Production Hours (Mil)	Compensation Payroll ($ mil)	Compensation Wages ($/hr)	Cost of Materials	Value Added by Manufacture	Value of Shipments	Capital Invest.
1982	152	155	204	167	180	143	106	77	110	105	107	60
1983		143	187	94	100	111	87	95	85	105	96	75
1984		131	170	150	167	129	100	79	103	78	96	33
1985		120	157	122	133	96	92	97	84	71	77	31
1986		110	157	111	113	86	85	104	67	66	67	27
1987	126	122	139	122	127	114	104	95	103	97	104	67
1988		112	122	122	133	114	109	105	109	92	99	92
1989		107	139	139	127	111	115	107	126	109	122	37
1990		116	104	128	140	129	130	105	154	131	147	35
1991		103	126	111	113	104	114	111	136	119	129	37
1992	100	100	100	100	100	100	100	100	100	100	100	100
1993		99	100	111	107	111	112	94	130	118	126	127
1994		90P	84P	100	100	100	101	93	102	110	107	63
1995		86P	75P	102P	98P	101P	114P	106P	119P	128P	125P	81P
1996		81P	66P	99P	95P	99P	116P	107P	122P	131P	128P	84P
1997		77P	57P	97P	91P	98P	117P	108P	124P	134P	130P	87P
1998		73P	48P	94P	87P	97P	119P	110P	127P	136P	133P	90P

Sources: Same as General Statistics. Values reflect change from the base year, 1992. Values above 100 mean greater than 92, values below 100 mean less than 92, and a value of 100 in the 82-91 or 93-98 period means same as 92. 'P's mark projections by the editors.

SELECTED RATIOS

For 1994	Avg. of All Manufact.	Analyzed Industry	Index	For 1994	Avg. of All Manufact.	Analyzed Industry	Index
Employees per Establishment	49	10	21	Value Added per Production Worker	134,084	45,267	34
Payroll per Establishment	1,500,273	182,899	12	Cost per Establishment	5,045,178	493,133	10
Payroll per Employee	30,620	17,556	57	Cost per Employee	102,970	47,333	46
Production Workers per Establishment	34	9	25	Cost per Production Worker	146,988	56,800	39
Wages per Establishment	853,319	127,381	15	Shipments per Establishment	9,576,895	891,923	9
Wages per Production Worker	24,861	14,672	59	Shipments per Employee	195,460	85,611	44
Hours per Production Worker	2,056	1,867	91	Shipments per Production Worker	279,017	102,733	37
Wages per Hour	12.09	7.86	65	Investment per Establishment	321,011	17,364	5
Value Added per Establishment	4,602,255	393,002	9	Investment per Employee	6,552	1,667	25
Value Added per Employee	93,930	37,722	40	Investment per Production Worker	9,352	2,000	21

Sources: Same as General Statistics. The 'Average of All Manufacturing' column represents the average of all manufacturing industries reported for the most recent complete year available. The Index shows the relationship between the Average and the Analyzed Industry. For example, 100 means that they are equal; 500 that the Analyzed Industry is five times the average; 50 means that the Analyzed Industry is half the national average. The abbreviation 'na' is used to show that data are 'not available'.

LEADING COMPANIES

Number shown: **11** Total sales ($ mil): **201** Total employment (000): **1.5**

Company Name	Address				CEO Name	Phone	Co. Type	Sales ($ mil)	Empl. (000)
American Excelsior Co	PO Box 5067	Arlington	TX	76005	RL Gregenson	817-640-1555	R	90	0.7
Miller Shingle Company Inc	PO Box 29	Granite Falls	WA	98252	Bruce L Miller II	206-691-7727	R	36*	0.2
Shakertown 1992 Inc	PO Box 400	Winlock	WA	98596	Edward Stanton	206-785-3501	R	24*	0.2
Independent Stave Company Inc	PO Box 104	Lebanon	MO	65536	John J Boswell	417-588-4151	R	23	0.4
Colonial Cedar Company Inc	7800 S 206th St	Kent	WA	98032	JG Prendergast	206-364-1936	R	14	<0.1
John H Van Patten Company	13320 Cambridge St	Santa Fe Sprgs	CA	90670	TE Hagerman	310-921-4491	R	5*	<0.1
Kennedy Wood Products Inc	701 By-Pass Rd	Clinton	NC	28328	Monte B Bristow	919-592-6131	R	4	<0.1
Hurn Shingle Company Inc	PO Box 799	Concrete	WA	98237	Larry W Hurn	206-853-8151	R	3	<0.1
Robertson Shake Mill Inc	365 Chehalis Av	Chehalis	WA	98532	Dencil Robertson	206-748-9411	R	1*	<0.1
Pugsley Cedar Products Inc	4713 123rd Av	Lake Stevens	WA	98258	Ferris Pugsley	206-334-2868	R	1*	<0.1
Hinchen Brothers Shingle	PO Box 2116	Forks	WA	98331	Terry Hinchen	206-374-9821	R	1	<0.1

Source: *Ward's Business Directory of U.S. Private and Public Companies*, Volumes 1 and 2, 1996. The company type code used is as follows: P - Public, R - Private, S - Subsidiary, D - Division, J - Joint Venture, A - Affiliate, G - Group. Sales are in millions of dollars, employees are in thousands. An asterisk (*) indicates an estimated sales volume. The symbol < stands for 'less than'. Company names and addresses are truncated, in some cases, to fit into the available space.

MATERIALS CONSUMED

Material		Quantity	Delivered Cost ($ million)
Materials, ingredients, containers, and supplies		(X)	76.5
Stumpage cost (cost of timber, excluding land, cut and consumed at same establishment)		(X)	2.3
Hardwood logs, bolts, and unsliced flitches	mil ft log scale	67.8**	21.2
Softwood logs, bolts, and unsliced flitches	mil ft log scale	(S)	13.3
All other materials and components, parts, containers, and supplies		(X)	13.1
Materials, ingredients, containers, and supplies, nsk		(X)	26.7

Source: 1992 *Economic Census*. Explanation of symbols used: (D): Withheld to avoid disclosure of competitive data; na: Not available; (S): Withheld because statistical norms were not met; (X): Not applicable; (Z): Less than half the unit shown; nec: Not elsewhere classified; nsk: Not specified by kind; - : zero; * : 10-19 percent estimated; ** : 20-29 percent estimated.

PRODUCT SHARE DETAILS

Product or Product Class	% Share	Product or Product Class	% Share
Special product sawmills, nec	100.00	Shingles and shakes, except red cedar	9.65
Red cedar shingles, including remanufactured shingles	10.51	Tight and slack cooperage stock (staves and heading) and excelsior products (including wood wool, pads and wrappers)	39.60
Red cedar handsplit shakes (handsplit and resawn, tapersawn, straight split, and tapersplit)	15.12		

Source: 1992 *Economic Census*. The values shown are percent of total shipments in an industry. Values of indented subcategories are summed in the main heading. The symbol (D) appears when data are withheld to prevent disclosure of competitive information. The abbreviation nsk stands for 'not specified by kind' and nec for 'not elsewhere classified'.

INPUTS AND OUTPUTS FOR SPECIAL PRODUCT SAWMILLS, NEC

Economic Sector or Industry Providing Inputs	%	Sector	Economic Sector or Industry Buying Outputs	%	Sector
Imports	40.8	Foreign	Office buildings	28.1	Constr.
Logging camps & logging contractors	25.2	Manufg.	Residential 1-unit structures, nonfarm	19.2	Constr.
Wholesale trade	9.0	Trade	Wood containers	10.2	Manufg.
Sawmills & planning mills, general	4.1	Manufg.	Residential additions/alterations, nonfarm	9.0	Constr.
Petroleum refining	3.6	Manufg.	Nonfarm residential structure maintenance	7.7	Constr.
Miscellaneous plastics products	2.3	Manufg.	Maintenance of nonfarm buildings nec	5.2	Constr.
Maintenance of nonbuilding facilities nec	2.1	Constr.	Industrial buildings	4.6	Constr.
Hardwood dimension & flooring mills	1.8	Manufg.	Exports	2.0	Foreign
Motor freight transportation & warehousing	1.8	Util.	Wood products, nec	1.6	Manufg.
Railroads & related services	1.0	Util.	Residential 2-4 unit structures, nonfarm	1.3	Constr.
Advertising	0.7	Services	Residential garden apartments	1.3	Constr.
Electric services (utilities)	0.6	Util.	Prefabricated wood buildings	1.1	Manufg.
Automotive rental & leasing, without drivers	0.6	Services	Wood TV & radio cabinets	1.0	Manufg.
Automotive repair shops & services	0.6	Services	Games, toys, & children's vehicles	0.9	Manufg.
Detective & protective services	0.6	Services	Glass containers	0.9	Manufg.
Security & commodity brokers	0.5	Fin/R.E.	Wholesale trade	0.9	Trade
Eating & drinking places	0.4	Trade	Maintenance of farm residential buildings	0.7	Constr.
Maintenance of nonfarm buildings nec	0.3	Constr.	Construction of stores & restaurants	0.5	Constr.
Hand saws & saw blades	0.3	Manufg.	Glass & glass products, except containers	0.5	Manufg.
Banking	0.3	Fin/R.E.	Construction of religious buildings	0.4	Constr.
Royalties	0.3	Fin/R.E.	Farm housing units & additions & alterations	0.4	Constr.
Tires & inner tubes	0.2	Manufg.	Construction of educational buildings	0.3	Constr.
Communications, except radio & TV	0.2	Util.	Upholstered household furniture	0.3	Manufg.

Continued on next page.

INPUTS AND OUTPUTS FOR SPECIAL PRODUCT SAWMILLS, NEC - Continued

Economic Sector or Industry Providing Inputs	%	Sector	Economic Sector or Industry Buying Outputs	%	Sector
Sanitary services, steam supply, irrigation	0.2	Util.	Amusement & recreation building construction	0.2	Constr.
Retail trade, except eating & drinking	0.2	Trade	Construction of nonfarm buildings nec	0.2	Constr.
Insurance carriers	0.2	Fin/R.E.	Maintenance of railroads	0.2	Constr.
U.S. Postal Service	0.2	Gov't	Federal Government purchases, national defense	0.2	Fed Govt
Woodworking machinery	0.1	Manufg.	Construction of hospitals	0.1	Constr.
Water transportation	0.1	Util.	Maintenance of farm service facilities	0.1	Constr.
Real estate	0.1	Fin/R.E.	Resid. & other health facility construction	0.1	Constr.
Accounting, auditing & bookkeeping	0.1	Services	Telephone & telegraph facility construction	0.1	Constr.
Business/professional associations	0.1	Services	Warehouses	0.1	Constr.
Electrical repair shops	0.1	Services	Particleboard	0.1	Manufg.
Equipment rental & leasing services	0.1	Services	Wood household furniture	0.1	Manufg.
Management & consulting services & labs	0.1	Services	Federal Government purchases, nondefense	0.1	Fed Govt

Source: Benchmark Input-Output Accounts for the U.S. Economy, 1982, U.S. Department of Commerce, Washington, D.C., July 1991. Data, as reported in the source, are organized by the 1977 SIC structure in use in 1982 but have been matched, as closely as is possible, to the 1987 SIC structure used in this book.

OCCUPATIONS EMPLOYED BY SIC 242 - SAWMILLS AND PLANING MILLS

Occupation	% of Total 1994	Change to 2005	Occupation	% of Total 1994	Change to 2005
Head sawyers & sawing machine workers	12.9	-18.3	Wood machinists	2.3	63.5
Machine feeders & offbearers	11.0	-26.4	Maintenance repairers, general utility	1.7	-26.5
Freight, stock, & material movers, hand	7.8	-34.6	Timber workers nec	1.6	-26.4
Helpers, laborers, & material movers nec	6.8	-18.3	Assemblers, fabricators, & hand workers nec	1.3	-18.3
Woodworking machine workers	4.6	-26.4	General office clerks	1.3	-30.3
Industrial truck & tractor operators	4.6	-18.3	Hand packers & packagers	1.3	-29.9
Blue collar worker supervisors	3.8	-23.8	Secretaries, ex legal & medical	1.2	-25.6
Inspectors, testers, & graders, precision	3.4	-18.3	Bookkeeping, accounting, & auditing clerks	1.2	-38.7
Truck drivers light & heavy	3.0	-15.7	Furnace, kiln, or kettle operators	1.1	-10.1
Industrial machinery mechanics	2.9	-10.1	Millwrights	1.1	-18.3
General managers & top executives	2.4	-22.5	Precision metal workers nec	1.1	-18.3
Log handling equipment operators	2.4	-18.3	Material moving equipment operators nec	1.1	-34.6

Source: Industry-Occupation Matrix, Bureau of Labor Statistics. These data relate to one or more 3-digit SIC industry groups rather than to a single 4-digit SIC. The change reported for each occupation to the year 2005 is a percent of growth or decline as estimated by the Bureau of Labor Statistics. The abbreviation nec stands for 'not elsewhere classified'.

LOCATION BY STATE AND REGIONAL CONCENTRATION

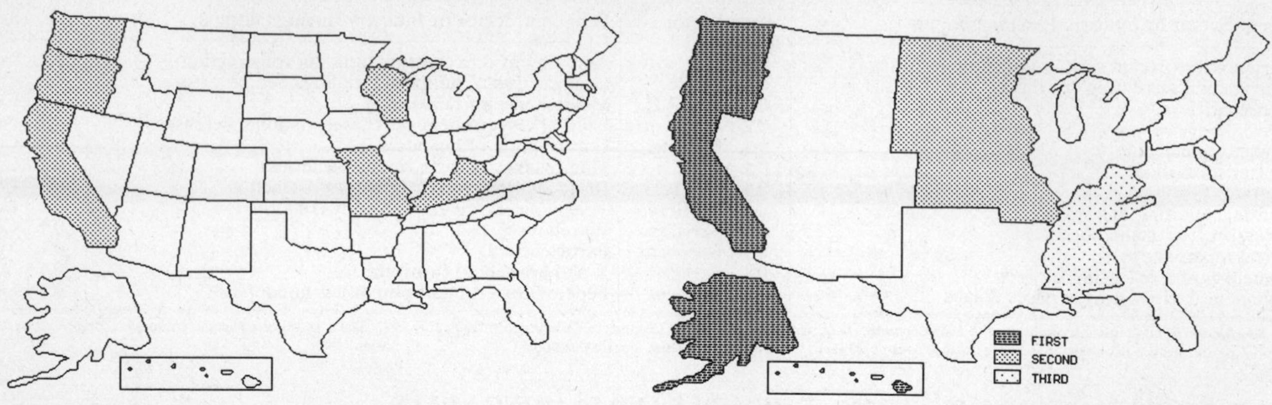

INDUSTRY DATA BY STATE

State	Establish-ments	Shipments			Employment				Cost as % of Shipments	Investment per Employee ($)
		Total ($ mil)	% of U.S.	Per Establ.	Total Number	% of U.S.	Per Establ.	Wages ($/hour)		
Washington	84	46.0	31.9	0.5	500	27.8	6	11.00	60.0	-
Missouri	18	17.7	12.3	1.0	300	16.7	17	6.00	57.6	-
Oregon	16	11.8	8.2	0.7	100	5.6	6	7.50	55.1	1,000
California	5	10.5	7.3	2.1	100	5.6	20	10.00	55.2	-
Kentucky	7	6.4	4.4	0.9	100	5.6	14	5.50	62.5	-
Wisconsin	3	(D)	-	-	175 *	9.7	58	-	-	-

Source: 1992 *Economic Census*. The states are in descending order of shipments or establishments (if shipment data are missing for the majority). The symbol (D) appears when data are withheld to prevent disclosure of competitive information. States marked with (D) are sorted by number of establishments. A dash (-) indicates that the data element cannot be calculated; * indicates the midpoint of a range.

2431 - MILLWORK

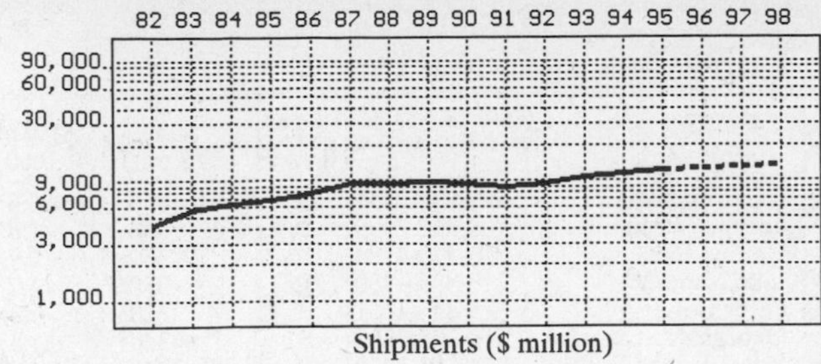

Shipments ($ million)

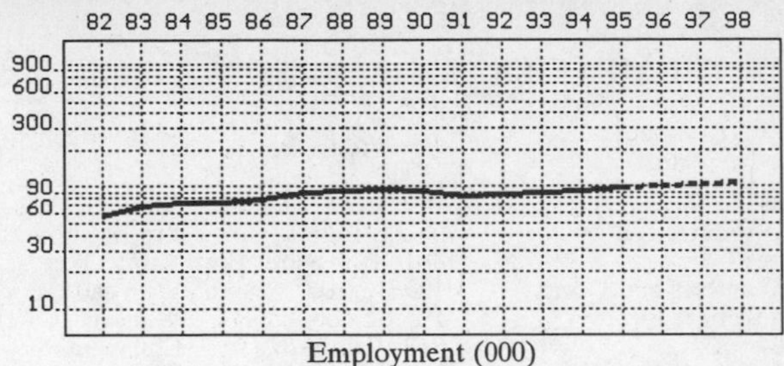

Employment (000)

GENERAL STATISTICS

Year	Com-panies	Establishments		Employment			Compensation		Production ($ million)			
		Total	with 20 or more employees	Total (000)	Production Workers (000)	Production Hours (Mil)	Payroll ($ mil)	Wages ($/hr)	Cost of Materials	Value Added by Manufacture	Value of Shipments	Capital Invest.
1982	2,192	2,321	642	56.8	44.7	83.5	895.4	7.73	2,502.0	1,712.6	4,248.3	79.9
1983		2,336	687	67.9	54.7	106.5	1,125.6	7.69	3,437.6	2,268.7	5,627.3	103.1
1984		2,351	732	74.1	60.3	115.4	1,277.0	7.85	3,860.8	2,641.5	6,489.3	139.1
1985		2,365	777	73.1	59.2	115.5	1,359.5	8.32	4,186.7	2,637.6	6,812.8	137.4
1986		2,378	813	77.2	61.1	119.8	1,493.4	8.81	4,692.9	3,091.0	7,748.9	164.9
1987	2,639	2,782	855	89.0	71.6	140.6	1,809.8	9.27	5,467.2	3,932.1	9,326.9	184.4
1988		2,709	896	90.7	73.0	141.3	2,013.7	10.36	5,553.1	3,899.6	9,385.2	155.9
1989		2,635	906	93.7	73.5	140.2	1,976.7	10.22	5,755.1	3,864.7	9,654.3	205.4
1990		2,723	894	92.7	72.1	140.1	1,960.9	9.83	5,655.3	3,851.6	9,524.7	197.5
1991		2,980	816	84.9	66.7	130.9	1,835.9	9.96	5,235.4	3,732.9	8,969.4	140.6
1992	3,009	3,155	799	86.3	68.8	136.9	1,983.9	10.20	5,627.6	4,048.4	9,639.8	190.7
1993		3,230	774	89.1	71.9	141.9	2,096.6	10.40	6,433.5	4,467.5	10,861.8	184.7
1994		3,215P	889P	92.3	73.8	148.5	2,205.3	10.39	6,856.8	4,802.7	11,592.5	177.3
1995		3,300P	903P	99.0P	78.6P	156.2P	2,390.0P	11.11P	7,119.5P	4,986.7P	12,036.6P	208.3P
1996		3,385P	917P	101.4P	80.5P	160.3P	2,489.3P	11.37P	7,422.3P	5,198.8P	12,548.6P	215.4P
1997		3,470P	931P	103.8P	82.4P	164.3P	2,588.6P	11.63P	7,725.2P	5,410.9P	13,060.6P	222.5P
1998		3,554P	944P	106.3P	84.2P	168.4P	2,687.9P	11.88P	8,028.0P	5,623.1P	13,572.6P	229.7P

Sources: 1982, 1987, 1992 *Economic Census*; *Annual Survey of Manufactures*, 83-86, 88-91, 93-94. Establishment counts for non-Census years are from *County Business Patterns*; establishment values for 83-84 are extrapolations. 'P's show projections by the editors. Industries reclassified in 87 will not have data for prior years.

INDICES OF CHANGE

Year	Com-panies	Establishments		Employment			Compensation		Production ($ million)			
		Total	with 20 or more employees	Total (000)	Production Workers (000)	Production Hours (Mil)	Payroll ($ mil)	Wages ($/hr)	Cost of Materials	Value Added by Manufacture	Value of Shipments	Capital Invest.
1982	73	74	80	66	65	61	45	76	44	42	44	42
1983		74	86	79	80	78	57	75	61	56	58	54
1984		75	92	86	88	84	64	77	69	65	67	73
1985		75	97	85	86	84	69	82	74	65	71	72
1986		75	102	89	89	88	75	86	83	76	80	86
1987	88	88	107	103	104	103	91	91	97	97	97	97
1988		86	112	105	106	103	102	102	99	96	97	82
1989		84	113	109	107	102	100	100	102	95	100	108
1990		86	112	107	105	102	99	96	100	95	99	104
1991		94	102	98	97	96	93	98	93	92	93	74
1992	100	100	100	100	100	100	100	100	100	100	100	100
1993		102	97	103	105	104	106	102	114	110	113	97
1994		102P	111P	107	107	108	111	102	122	119	120	93
1995		105P	113P	115P	114P	114P	120P	109P	127P	123P	125P	109P
1996		107P	115P	118P	117P	117P	125P	111P	132P	128P	130P	113P
1997		110P	116P	120P	120P	120P	130P	114P	137P	134P	135P	117P
1998		113P	118P	123P	122P	123P	135P	116P	143P	139P	141P	120P

Sources: Same as General Statistics. Values reflect change from the base year, 1992. Values above 100 mean greater than 92, values below 100 mean less than 92, and a value of 100 in the 82-91 or 93-98 period means same as 92. 'P's mark projections by the editors.

SELECTED RATIOS

For 1994	Avg. of All Manufact.	Analyzed Industry	Index
Employees per Establishment	49	29	59
Payroll per Establishment	1,500,273	685,912	46
Payroll per Employee	30,620	23,893	78
Production Workers per Establishment	34	23	67
Wages per Establishment	853,319	479,891	56
Wages per Production Worker	24,861	20,907	84
Hours per Production Worker	2,056	2,012	98
Wages per Hour	12.09	10.39	86
Value Added per Establishment	4,602,255	1,493,778	32
Value Added per Employee	93,930	52,034	55

For 1994	Avg. of All Manufact.	Analyzed Industry	Index
Value Added per Production Worker	134,084	65,077	49
Cost per Establishment	5,045,178	2,132,662	42
Cost per Employee	102,970	74,288	72
Cost per Production Worker	146,988	92,911	63
Shipments per Establishment	9,576,895	3,605,601	38
Shipments per Employee	195,460	125,596	64
Shipments per Production Worker	279,017	157,080	56
Investment per Establishment	321,011	55,145	17
Investment per Employee	6,552	1,921	29
Investment per Production Worker	9,352	2,402	26

Sources: Same as General Statistics. The 'Average of All Manufacturing' column represents the average of all manufacturing industries reported for the most recent complete year available. The Index shows the relationship between the Average and the Analyzed Industry. For example, 100 means that they are equal; 500 that the Analyzed Industry is five times the average; 50 means that the Analyzed Industry is half the national average. The abbreviation 'na' is used to show that data are 'not available'.

LEADING COMPANIES Number shown: **75** Total sales ($ mil): **5,261** Total employment (000): **39.3**

Company Name	Address				CEO Name	Phone	Co. Type	Sales ($ mil)	Empl. (000)
Jeld-Wen Inc	PO Box 1329	Klamath Falls	OR	97601	RC Wendt	503-882-3451	R	850*	6.6
Morgan Products Ltd	75 Tri-State	Lincolnshire	IL	60069	Larry R Robinette	708-317-2400	P	358	1.6
Jim Walter Corp	4010 Boy Scout Blv	Tampa	FL	33607	Dennis Ross	813-873-4194	R	350*	2.7
Marvin Windows and Doors	PO Box 100	Warroad	MN	56763	Jake Marvin	218-386-1430	R	350*	2.7
SNE Enterprises Inc	PO Box 8007	Wausau	WI	54402	Peter Balint	715-845-1161	S	320*	1.8
Clopay Corp	312 Walnut St	Cincinnati	OH	45202	George A Strutz Jr	513-381-4800	S	310*	1.5
Huttig Sash and Door Co	PO Box 1041	Chesterfield	MO	63006	Jim B Edens	314-878-2222	S	240*	1.9
Blackstone Company Inc	PO Box 1069	East Brunswick	NJ	08816	William A Schwartz	908-254-5550	R	140	1.0
Babcock Lumber Company Inc	PO Box 8348	Pittsburgh	PA	15218	Carl P Stillitano	412-351-3515	R	100*	0.4
Marley Mouldings Inc	PO Box 610	Marion	VA	24354	Larry L Davis	703-783-8161	D	90	0.8
Kolbe and Kolbe Millwork	1323 S 11th Av	Wausau	WI	54401	Herb Kolbe	715-842-5666	R	86	1.3
Norco Windows Inc	380 E Park Ctr Blvd	Boise	ID	83706	Nick Dye	208-364-1400	S	86	0.9
Louisiana-Pacific Corp	324 Wooster Rd N	Barberton	OH	44203	Melf U Lorenzen	216-745-1661	D	85*	0.8
Conestoga Wood Specialties Inc	PO Box 158	East Earl	PA	17519	N Hahn	717-445-6701	R	70	1.1
Gunton Corp	26150 Richmond Rd	Bedford Hts	OH	44146	Mark Mead	216-831-2420	R	70	0.4
Cascade Wood Products Inc	PO Box 2429	White City	OR	97503	TD Collins	503-826-2911	R	65*	0.5
Jessup Door Co	PO Box 240	Dowagiac	MI	49047	Guy R Harper	616-782-2183	D	65	0.5
Lyman Lumber Co	PO Box 40	Excelsior	MN	55331	Thomas P Lowe	612-474-5991	R	65	0.5
Semling-Menke Company Inc	PO Box 378	Merrill	WI	54452	John P Semling	715-536-9411	R	65	0.5
Setzer Forest Products Co	2555 3rd St	Sacramento	CA	95818	D Mark Kable	916-442-2555	R	60	0.3
Vega Industries Inc	1125 Ford St	Maumee	OH	43537	Paul Jaquith	419-893-3311	R	52*	0.4
Tomkins Industries Inc	PO Box 397	Malta	OH	43758	Roy Speaks	614-962-3131	D	50	0.7
Riverside Millwork Company Inc	77 Merrimack St	Penacook	NH	03303	W Healey	603-753-6318	R	46	0.3
Haley Brothers Inc	6291 Orangethorpe	Buena Park	CA	90620	Tom J Cobb	714-670-2112	R	45*	0.4
Fiberboard Box	PO Box 430	Red Bluff	CA	96080	John Roach	916-527-9113	S	44*	0.5
Ferche Millwork Inc	PO Box 39	Rice	MN	56367	RJ Ferche	612-393-2288	S	41	0.2
Shaw Lumber Co	217 Como Av	St Paul	MN	55103	M Lindgren	612-488-2525	R	41	0.2
Buffelen Woodworking Co	PO Box 1383	Tacoma	WA	98421	J Guizzetti	206-627-1191	R	40	0.5
Steves and Sons Inc	PO Drawer S	San Antonio	TX	78211	Edward G Steves	210-924-5111	R	40	0.3
Atrium Door and Window Co	PO Box 226957	Dallas	TX	75222	Randall Fojtasek	214-634-9663	D	39	0.3
Jeld-Wen Inc Young Door Co	2526 N Western	Plymouth	IN	46563	Bill O'Dell	219-936-2183	D	39*	0.3
Sunset Moulding Co	PO Box 326	Yuba City	CA	95992	Kenneth Olson	916-695-1801	R	39*	0.3
Sealrite Windows Inc	PO Box 4468	Lincoln	NE	68504	J Grigsby	402-464-0202	R	36	0.1
Automated Building Components	PO Box 40	Excelsior	MN	55331	Thomas P Lowe	612-474-4374	R	35	0.4
M W Windows	175 10th St	Ste Genevieve	MO	63670	C Alexander Swan	314-883-3571	D	32*	0.3
Northcutt Woodworks LP	PO Box 820	Crockett	TX	75835	Larry Christopher	409-544-2028	R	32	0.3
Algoma Hardwoods Inc	1001 Perry St	Algoma	WI	54201	WE Ellsworth	414-487-5221	R	30	0.4
Dorris Lumber and Molding Co	2601 Redding Av	Sacramento	CA	95820	E Chase Israelson	916-452-7531	R	30*	0.2
Ideal Door Co	PO Box 106	Baldwin	WI	54002	OM Hinrichs	715-684-3223	R	30	0.3
McPhillips Manufacturing	PO Box 169	Mobile	AL	36601	JM McPhillips	205-438-1681	R	30*	0.2
Wenco/Pennsylvania	PO Box 259	Ringtown	PA	17967	JD Tomtishen	717-889-3173	D	30	0.3
Premdor Corp	PO Box 1	Walkerton	IN	46574	Philip Orsino	219-586-3192	S	29*	0.2
Taney Corp	5130 Allendale Ln	Taneytown	MD	21787	Jeffrey S Glass	410-756-6671	R	29	0.2
Commercial & Architectural	PO Box 250	Dover	OH	44622	RS Campbell	216-343-6621	R	28*	0.2
Woodwork Corporation	1432 W 21st St	Chicago	IL	60608	Robert F Kay	312-226-4800	R	27	0.4
Maywood Inc	PO Box 30550	Amarillo	TX	79120	JC Maynard	806-374-2835	R	26	0.4
Eggers Industries Inc	164 N Lake St	Neenah	WI	54957	Harry Reichwald	414-722-6444	D	25	0.2
Wahlfeld's	1100 SW Wash	Peoria	IL	61602	Ted Wahlfeld	309-673-4421	R	25	<0.1
Panelfold Inc	10700 NW 36th Av	Miami	FL	33167	Guy E Dixon Jr	305-688-3501	R	22	0.2
Jay-K Independent Lumber	PO Box 378	New Hartford	NY	13413	Kevin M Kelly	315-735-4475	R	21	0.1
Stow Davis	850 Elkton Dr	Co Springs	CO	80907	E Wigand Jr	719-599-8887	S	21	0.1
Temple Products Inc	PO Box 1008	Temple	TX	76503	John M Chupik	817-778-5537	R	20	0.2
Alexander Moulding Mill	PO Box 312	Hamilton	TX	76531	John Alexander	817-386-3187	R	19*	<0.1
Dayton Showcase Co	2601 W Dorothy Ln	Dayton	OH	45439	J Mothersole	513-294-0321	R	18	0.2
Holmes Garage Door Company	PO Box 1976	Auburn	WA	98071	James A Stiles	206-931-8900	S	18	0.1
Southern Cross	PO Box 907	O'Fallon	MO	63366	John A Kelly	314-240-6226	R	18	<0.1
Pella Window and Door Co	PO Box 9004	Valley Forge	PA	19485	RJ Gunton	215-631-9500	D	17	0.1
Rockdale Sash and Trim	PO Box 2099	Joliet	IL	60434	James R Beirnes	815-725-5491	R	17*	0.1
Cole Sewell Corp	2288 University Av	St Paul	MN	55114	Fred E Sewell	612-646-7873	R	16*	0.1
Gerber Industries Inc	1 Gerber Indrial Dr	St Peters	MO	63376	Frances Gerber	314-278-5710	R	16*	0.1
Missoula White Pine Sash	PO Box 7009	Missoula	MT	59807	DR Duff	406-728-4010	D	16	0.2
Parenti and Raffaelli Ltd	215 E Prospect Av	Mt Prospect	IL	60056	Robert F Parenti	708-253-5550	R	16	0.1
Foreign and Domestic Woods	PO Box 449	Bowling Green	VA	22427	Harvey Ross	804-633-5001	R	16*	0.1
Andover Wood Products Inc	PO Box 38	Andover	ME	04216	Donald Stecher	207-392-2101	S	15	<0.1
Annona Manufacturing Co	PO Box 287	Annona	TX	75550	Jimmy Peak	903-697-3591	R	15*	0.1
CW Ohio Inc	1209 Maple Av	Conneaut	OH	44030	Dale P Webb	216-593-5800	R	15	0.2
King Sash and Door Inc	PO Box 787	Clemmons	NC	27012	T Bumgarner	910-768-4650	R	15	<0.1
Mims and Thomas Inc	3535 NW 50th St	Miami	FL	33142	Jerry Alexander	305-633-9575	S	15	0.1
Moss Supply Co	PO Box 26338	Charlotte	NC	28221	Harry C Moss	704-596-8717	R	15	0.1
Sierra Lumber Manufacturers	PO Box 6216	Stockton	CA	95206	Joseph Eger	209-943-7777	R	15*	0.1
West Coast Door Inc	PO Box 110936	Tacoma	WA	98411	WB Swensen	206-272-4269	R	15	0.2
NT Jenkins Manufacturing	PO Box 249	Anniston	AL	36202	Robert Sage	205-831-7000	S	14	0.1
Tewa Moulding Corp	PO Box 10291	Albuquerque	NM	87184	Carl Bonner	505-898-0420	R	14	<0.1
Young Manufacturing Company	PO Box 167	Beaver Dam	KY	42320	CT Young	502-274-3306	R	14	0.1
Black Millwork Company Inc	PO Box 27	Allendale	NJ	07401	Ted Councilor	201-934-0100	R	13*	0.1

Source: *Ward's Business Directory of U.S. Private and Public Companies*, Volumes 1 and 2, 1996. The company type code used is as follows: P - Public, R - Private, S - Subsidiary, D - Division, J - Joint Venture, A - Affiliate, G - Group. Sales are in millions of dollars, employees are in thousands. An asterisk (*) indicates an estimated sales volume. The symbol < stands for 'less than'. Company names and addresses are truncated, in some cases, to fit into the available space.

MATERIALS CONSUMED

Material	Quantity	Delivered Cost ($ million)
Materials, ingredients, containers, and supplies	(X)	5,164.2
Hardwood rough lumber	(X)	249.8
Softwood rough lumber	(X)	679.1
Hardwood dressed lumber	(X)	125.2
Softwood dressed lumber	(X)	503.4
Softwood cut stock, including window and cabinet parts	(X)	533.7
Hardwood dimension and parts, excluding furniture frames	(X)	48.4
Hardwood veneer	(X)	101.3
Hardwood plywood	(X)	77.8
Softwood plywood	(X)	20.8
Particleboard (wood)	(X)	52.9
Hardboard (wood fiberboard)	(X)	61.7
Medium density fiberboard (MDF)	(X)	26.1
Glass (float, sheet and plate)	(X)	257.0
Plastics products consumed in the form of sheets, rods, tubes, film, and other shapes	(X)	47.1
Builders' hardware (including door locks, locksets, lock trim, screen hardware, etc.)	(X)	241.0
Paperboard containers, boxes, and corrugated paperboard	(X)	49.6
All other materials and components, parts, containers, and supplies	(X)	742.6
Materials, ingredients, containers, and supplies, nsk	(X)	1,346.7

Source: 1992 *Economic Census*. Explanation of symbols used: (D): Withheld to avoid disclosure of competitive data; na: Not available; (S): Withheld because statistical norms were not met; (X): Not applicable; (Z): Less than half the unit shown; nec: Not elsewhere classified; nsk: Not specified by kind; - : zero; * : 10-19 percent estimated; ** : 20-29 percent estimated.

PRODUCT SHARE DETAILS

Product or Product Class	% Share
Millwork	100.00
Wood window units	25.89
Double hung wood window units, cladded	29.40
Other double hung wood window units	9.39
Wood awning window units	1.22
Casement wood window units, cladded	31.99
Other casement wood window units	7.94
Horizontal sliding wood window units	3.81
All other wood window units, including single hung	14.32
Wood window units, nsk	1.94
Wood sash, excluding window units	1.43
Knockdown and open wood sash, excluding window units	54.21
Glazed wood sash, excluding window units	43.43
Wood sash, excluding window units, nsk	2.35
Wood window and door frames, and door frames shipped in door units	4.88
Wood window frames	31.53
Wood door frames, including door frames shipped as door units	66.00
Wood window and door frames, and door frames shipped in door units, nsk	2.48
Wood doors, interior and exterior, including those with glazed sections	16.39
Panel-type douglas fir doors, interior and exterior, including those with glazed sections	10.99
Panel-type western pine doors, interior and exterior, including those with glazed sections	15.52
Other panel-type wood doors, interior and exterior, including those with glazed sections	7.41
Flush-type, hollow core, softwood faced doors, interior and exterior, including those with glazed sections	3.74
Flush-type, hollow core, hardwood faced doors (including lauan, birch, oak, etc.), interior and exterior, including those with glazed sections	16.73
Flush-type, hollow core, hardboard faced doors, interior and exterior, including those with glazed sections	11.17
Flush-type, hollow core, other wood faced doors, interior and exterior, including those with glazed sections	1.57
Flush-type, solid wood core, hardwood faced doors (including lauan, birch, oak, etc.), interior and exterior, including those with glazed sections	7.01
Flush-type, solid composition core, hardwood faced doors (including lauan, birch, oak, etc.), interior and exterior, including those with glazed sections	13.70
Flush-type, solid core, hardboard faced doors, interior and exterior, including those with glazed sections	1.07
Flush-type, solid core, softwood and other faced doors, interior and exterior, including those with glazed sections	3.67
Wood doors, interior and exterior, including those with glazed sections, nsk	7.41
Other wood doors, including garage, screen, storm, etc.	10.57
Wood garage doors	12.32
Wood screen doors and combination screen and storm doors	2.14
Wood louver doors	4.02
Wood bifold doors	10.76
Wood patio doors, sliding	24.48
Wood patio doors, swinging	20.46
Other wood doors, including storm, cabinet, toilet, grain, etc.	22.26
Other wood doors, including garage, screen, storm, etc., nsk	3.56
Wood moldings, except prefinished moldings made from purchased moldings, including moldings covered with metal, plastics, etc.	12.27
Pine wood moldings, except prefinished moldings made from purchased moldings, including moldings covered with metal, plastics, etc.	58.72
Other softwood moldings, except prefinished moldings made from purchased moldings, including moldings covered with metal, plastics, etc.	10.07
Hardwood moldings (including lauan, and hardwood covered with metal, plastics, etc.), except prefinished moldings made from purchased moldings	24.80
Wood moldings except prefinished moldings made from purchased moldings, nsk	6.41
Prefinished wood moldings made from purchased moldings, including moldings covered with metal, plastics, etc.	1.65
Prefinished softwood moldings made from purchased moldings, including softwood covered with metal, plastics, etc.	67.66
Prefinished hardwood moldings made from purchased moldings, including lauan and hardwood covered with metal, plastics, etc.	10.12
Prefinished wood moldings made from purchased moldings, nsk	22.29
Other millwork products, including stairwork and exterior millwork	10.66
Softwood stairwork, including treads, risers, balusters, brackets, crooks, newels, etc.	11.72
Hardwood stairwork, including treads, risers, balusters, brackets, crooks, newels, etc.	17.57
Exterior wood blinds and shutters, with or without their hardware (excluding fibrous vegetable materials)	2.49
Exterior millwork, including porch columns, porch rails, newels, trellises, and entrances	6.41
Nonstandard or specialty softwood moldings, carvings, and ornaments	5.16
Nonstandard or specialty hardwood moldings, carvings, and ornaments	7.69
Other millwork products, nec, including interior millwork	44.31
Other millwork products, including stairwork and exterior millwork, nsk	4.64
Millwork, nsk	16.25

Source: 1992 *Economic Census*. The values shown are percent of total shipments in an industry. Values of indented subcategories are summed in the main heading. The symbol (D) appears when data are withheld to prevent disclosure of competitive information. The abbreviation nsk stands for 'not specified by kind' and nec for 'not elsewhere classified'.

INPUTS AND OUTPUTS FOR MILLWORK

Economic Sector or Industry Providing Inputs	%	Sector	Economic Sector or Industry Buying Outputs	%	Sector
Sawmills & planning mills, general	34.0	Manufg.	Residential 1-unit structures, nonfarm	28.7	Constr.
Wholesale trade	13.1	Trade	Residential additions/alterations, nonfarm	26.5	Constr.
Veneer & plywood	5.3	Manufg.	Maintenance of nonfarm buildings nec	10.4	Constr.
Hardware, nec	4.4	Manufg.	Nonfarm residential structure maintenance	6.5	Constr.
Screw machine and related products	4.2	Manufg.	Industrial buildings	6.0	Constr.
Wood products, nec	3.7	Manufg.	Office buildings	3.8	Constr.
Advertising	2.8	Services	Residential garden apartments	3.4	Constr.
Imports	2.8	Foreign	Residential 2-4 unit structures, nonfarm	1.8	Constr.
Motor freight transportation & warehousing	2.7	Util.	Mobile homes	1.4	Manufg.
Glass & glass products, except containers	2.4	Manufg.	Exports	1.4	Foreign
Metal stampings, nec	2.4	Manufg.	Construction of educational buildings	1.0	Constr.
Railroads & related services	1.8	Util.	Construction of stores & restaurants	1.0	Constr.
Electric services (utilities)	1.7	Util.	Farm housing units & additions & alterations	1.0	Constr.
Paints & allied products	1.6	Manufg.	Warehouses	0.9	Constr.
Fabricated metal products, nec	1.5	Manufg.	Prefabricated wood buildings	0.8	Manufg.
Millwork	0.9	Manufg.	Nonbuilding facilities nec	0.7	Constr.
Adhesives & sealants	0.8	Manufg.	Millwork	0.6	Manufg.
Particleboard	0.8	Manufg.	Maintenance of farm residential buildings	0.5	Constr.

Continued on next page.

INPUTS AND OUTPUTS FOR MILLWORK - Continued

Economic Sector or Industry Providing Inputs	%	Sector	Economic Sector or Industry Buying Outputs	%	Sector
Banking	0.8	Fin/R.E.	Maintenance of farm service facilities	0.5	Constr.
Maintenance of nonfarm buildings nec	0.7	Constr.	Residential high-rise apartments	0.4	Constr.
Miscellaneous plastics products	0.7	Manufg.	Travel trailers & campers	0.4	Manufg.
Petroleum refining	0.7	Manufg.	Construction of hospitals	0.2	Constr.
Real estate	0.7	Fin/R.E.	Construction of nonfarm buildings nec	0.2	Constr.
Hand & edge tools, nec	0.6	Manufg.	Hotels & motels	0.2	Constr.
Logging camps & logging contractors	0.6	Manufg.	Maintenance of highways & streets	0.2	Constr.
Paperboard containers & boxes	0.6	Manufg.	Maintenance of nonbuilding facilities nec	0.2	Constr.
Communications, except radio & TV	0.6	Util.	Resid. & other health facility construction	0.2	Constr.
Eating & drinking places	0.6	Trade	Telephone & telegraph facility construction	0.2	Constr.
Royalties	0.6	Fin/R.E.	Amusement & recreation building construction	0.1	Constr.
Hardwood dimension & flooring mills	0.5	Manufg.	Construction of conservation facilities	0.1	Constr.
Water transportation	0.5	Util.	Dormitories & other group housing	0.1	Constr.
Equipment rental & leasing services	0.5	Services	Garage & service station construction	0.1	Constr.
Power driven hand tools	0.4	Manufg.	Highway & street construction	0.1	Constr.
Gas production & distribution (utilities)	0.4	Util.			
U.S. Postal Service	0.3	Gov't			
Abrasive products	0.2	Manufg.			
Miscellaneous fabricated wire products	0.2	Manufg.			
Woodworking machinery	0.2	Manufg.			
Accounting, auditing & bookkeeping	0.2	Services			
Legal services	0.2	Services			
Management & consulting services & labs	0.2	Services			
Lubricating oils & greases	0.1	Manufg.			
Machinery, except electrical, nec	0.1	Manufg.			
Air transportation	0.1	Util.			
Sanitary services, steam supply, irrigation	0.1	Util.			
Water supply & sewage systems	0.1	Util.			
Insurance carriers	0.1	Fin/R.E.			
Automotive rental & leasing, without drivers	0.1	Services			
Automotive repair shops & services	0.1	Services			
Engineering, architectural, & surveying services	0.1	Services			

Source: Benchmark Input-Output Accounts for the U.S. Economy, 1982, U.S. Department of Commerce, Washington, D.C., July 1991. Data, as reported in the source, are organized by the 1977 SIC structure in use in 1982 but have been matched, as closely as is possible, to the 1987 SIC structure used in this book.

OCCUPATIONS EMPLOYED BY SIC 243 - MILLWORK, PLYWOOD, AND STRUCTURAL MEMBERS

Occupation	% of Total 1994	Change to 2005	Occupation	% of Total 1994	Change to 2005
Assemblers, fabricators, & hand workers nec	13.6	-2.8	Truck drivers light & heavy	2.0	0.2
Cabinetmakers & bench carpenters	10.9	-2.8	Inspectors, testers, & graders, precision	1.7	-2.8
Woodworking machine workers	6.1	-22.2	Coating, painting, & spraying machine workers	1.7	-22.2
Machine feeders & offbearers	5.1	-12.5	Carpenters	1.7	-22.2
Head sawyers & sawing machine workers	4.6	-22.2	Cement & gluing machine operators	1.7	6.9
Helpers, laborers, & material movers nec	4.4	-2.8	Precision woodworkers nec	1.4	94.4
Wood machinists	4.3	-12.5	Secretaries, ex legal & medical	1.4	-11.5
Blue collar worker supervisors	3.9	-8.3	Industrial machinery mechanics	1.3	6.9
General managers & top executives	2.8	-7.8	Bookkeeping, accounting, & auditing clerks	1.2	-27.1
Freight, stock, & material movers, hand	2.7	-22.2	General office clerks	1.2	-17.1
Sales & related workers nec	2.3	-2.8	Industrial production managers	1.2	-2.8
Industrial truck & tractor operators	2.3	-2.8	Drafters	1.0	-24.3

Source: Industry-Occupation Matrix, Bureau of Labor Statistics. These data relate to one or more 3-digit SIC industry groups rather than to a single 4-digit SIC. The change reported for each occupation to the year 2005 is a percent of growth or decline as estimated by the Bureau of Labor Statistics. The abbreviation nec stands for 'not elsewhere classified'.

LOCATION BY STATE AND REGIONAL CONCENTRATION

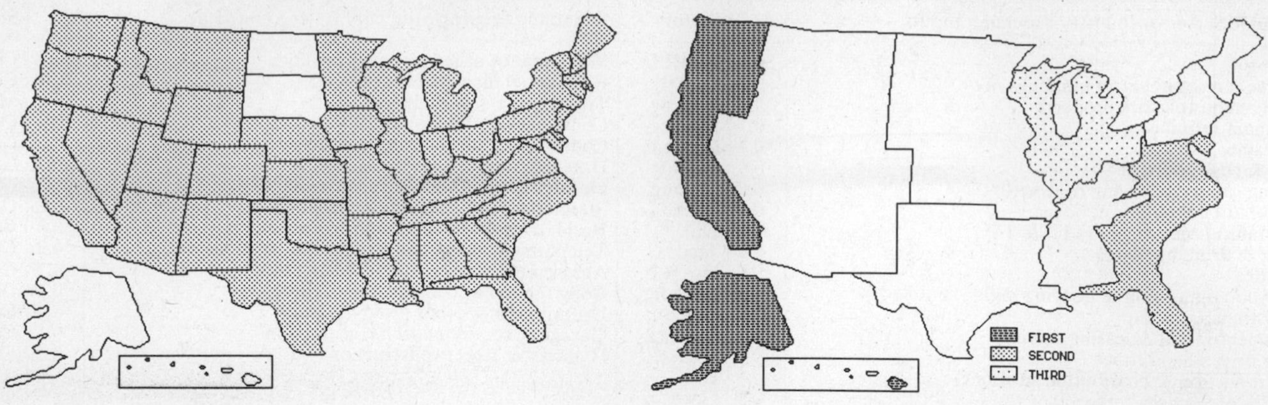

INDUSTRY DATA BY STATE

State	Establish-ments	Shipments			Employment				Cost as % of Shipments	Investment per Employee ($)
		Total ($ mil)	% of U.S.	Per Establ.	Total Number	% of U.S.	Per Establ.	Wages ($/hour)		
California	418	1,018.8	10.6	2.4	8,300	9.6	20	9.63	63.7	1,470
Wisconsin	110	1,016.5	10.5	9.2	8,900	10.3	81	10.86	60.7	2,180
Oregon	88	644.9	6.7	7.3	5,700	6.6	65	9.76	66.4	1,860
Texas	165	449.2	4.7	2.7	4,900	5.7	30	7.20	59.0	1,469
Washington	118	381.0	4.0	3.2	3,200	3.7	27	10.85	59.4	1,844
Ohio	109	365.9	3.8	3.4	4,000	4.6	37	9.32	57.7	1,825
Iowa	20	355.9	3.7	17.8	3,900	4.5	195	12.69	53.3	6,333
Pennsylvania	146	332.9	3.5	2.3	3,300	3.8	23	10.32	56.4	1,364
Illinois	125	282.0	2.9	2.3	2,800	3.2	22	11.43	52.3	2,429
Georgia	107	255.4	2.6	2.4	2,200	2.5	21	9.59	57.7	2,409
Virginia	76	252.3	2.6	3.3	2,700	3.1	36	9.09	51.8	1,963
Indiana	85	250.4	2.6	2.9	2,400	2.8	28	8.87	55.2	1,667
Michigan	106	242.9	2.5	2.3	2,200	2.5	21	9.70	59.0	1,545
North Carolina	105	237.9	2.5	2.3	2,300	2.7	22	7.86	63.1	3,174
New York	158	218.2	2.3	1.4	2,100	2.4	13	11.00	56.8	1,571
Alabama	61	203.4	2.1	3.3	1,900	2.2	31	7.66	63.6	2,263
Idaho	25	168.2	1.7	6.7	1,300	1.5	52	9.00	66.9	-
Florida	156	141.3	1.5	0.9	1,700	2.0	11	8.38	53.9	1,353
Arizona	78	123.3	1.3	1.6	1,500	1.7	19	8.04	54.0	1,333
South Carolina	38	116.4	1.2	3.1	1,000	1.2	26	8.00	65.8	2,100
Tennessee	56	112.9	1.2	2.0	1,400	1.6	25	7.48	56.9	3,857
Maryland	41	108.1	1.1	2.6	1,000	1.2	24	9.85	63.5	1,100
Massachusetts	73	104.9	1.1	1.4	900	1.0	12	10.92	56.7	1,444
New Jersey	60	78.8	0.8	1.3	700	0.8	12	13.11	58.6	2,286
Colorado	61	75.1	0.8	1.2	800	0.9	13	8.54	52.9	1,125
New Mexico	26	69.9	0.7	2.7	500	0.6	19	9.00	73.7	2,000
Kentucky	37	68.6	0.7	1.9	700	0.8	19	8.73	51.2	2,000
Missouri	53	68.5	0.7	1.3	700	0.8	13	8.50	55.5	1,571
Kansas	31	63.2	0.7	2.0	600	0.7	19	7.89	51.1	-
New Hampshire	25	50.8	0.5	2.0	600	0.7	24	8.50	66.7	1,167
Arkansas	31	48.2	0.5	1.6	500	0.6	16	8.13	61.2	1,400
Nebraska	18	47.4	0.5	2.6	300	0.3	17	7.60	63.7	-
Connecticut	54	44.2	0.5	0.8	400	0.5	7	11.25	46.8	1,750
West Virginia	18	42.7	0.4	2.4	700	0.8	39	9.58	47.1	-
Mississippi	27	36.7	0.4	1.4	400	0.5	15	7.50	65.9	2,250
Utah	34	36.5	0.4	1.1	600	0.7	18	8.67	71.8	833
Oklahoma	21	35.3	0.4	1.7	400	0.5	19	10.17	55.5	2,750
Montana	11	26.5	0.3	2.4	300	0.3	27	11.50	54.0	-
Maine	22	25.3	0.3	1.1	300	0.3	14	8.80	57.3	1,667
Louisiana	28	21.3	0.2	0.8	300	0.3	11	7.60	48.8	1,333
Vermont	15	17.8	0.2	1.2	200	0.2	13	8.33	62.9	1,000
Nevada	14	15.5	0.2	1.1	200	0.2	14	9.67	53.5	2,500
Delaware	8	12.9	0.1	1.6	100	0.1	13	10.50	64.3	1,000
Rhode Island	17	10.1	0.1	0.6	100	0.1	6	9.50	48.5	-
Minnesota	51	(D)	-	-	7,500 *	8.7	147	-	-	3,000
Wyoming	4	(D)	-	-	175 *	0.2	44	-	-	-

Source: 1992 *Economic Census*. The states are in descending order of shipments or establishments (if shipment data are missing for the majority). The symbol (D) appears when data are withheld to prevent disclosure of competitive information. States marked with (D) are sorted by number of establishments. A dash (-) indicates that the data element cannot be calculated; * indicates the midpoint of a range.

2434 - WOOD KITCHEN CABINETS

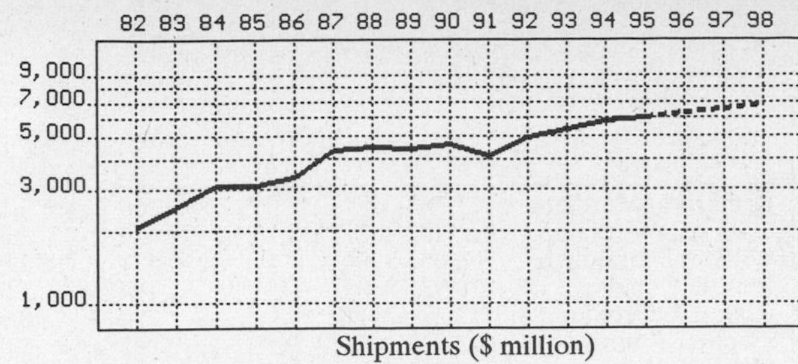

Shipments ($ million)

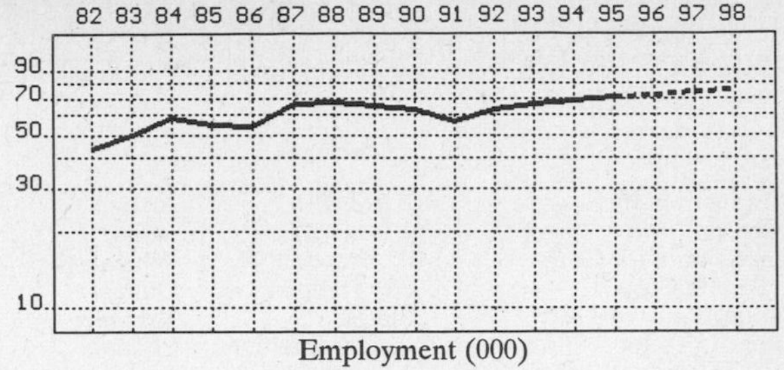

Employment (000)

GENERAL STATISTICS

Year	Companies	Establishments: Total	Establishments: with 20 or more employees	Employment: Total (000)	Production Workers (000)	Production Hours (Mil)	Compensation: Payroll ($ mil)	Compensation: Wages ($/hr)	Production ($ million): Cost of Materials	Value Added by Manufacture	Value of Shipments	Capital Invest.
1982	2,902	2,964	489	43.6	34.6	67.1	606.9	6.59	906.8	1,144.3	2,060.7	43.8
1983		2,879	522	49.5	40.7	79.0	678.4	6.42	1,067.8	1,421.9	2,482.7	52.5
1984		2,794	555	58.4	48.1	98.1	841.1	6.13	1,434.2	1,645.9	3,061.4	74.5
1985		2,710	588	54.5	44.6	89.1	863.5	6.86	1,425.9	1,659.4	3,083.6	67.3
1986		2,618	587	53.4	42.3	85.8	901.7	7.26	1,501.9	1,842.9	3,342.2	81.9
1987	3,642	3,713	668	67.0	53.7	107.9	1,184.8	7.72	1,908.6	2,495.1	4,376.6	101.0
1988		3,446	681	67.3	54.1	105.6	1,214.0	8.16	1,914.9	2,581.9	4,484.0	86.2
1989		3,166	670	65.5	49.6	98.3	1,196.7	8.61	1,962.7	2,437.5	4,393.2	108.6
1990		3,547	637	63.6	51.0	101.4	1,217.4	8.55	2,066.7	2,540.1	4,610.0	92.0
1991		3,737	577	57.1	46.2	91.3	1,139.0	8.84	1,877.9	2,277.5	4,164.9	60.5
1992	4,273	4,323	627	62.8	49.8	99.7	1,307.5	9.29	2,214.7	2,728.3	4,933.5	89.1
1993		4,473	616	66.1	51.6	104.0	1,380.0	9.28	2,573.1	2,846.9	5,397.1	89.3
1994		4,313P	670P	68.9	55.0	110.7	1,477.5	9.45	2,694.5	3,136.0	5,804.2	119.2
1995		4,459P	680P	70.6P	55.6P	111.4P	1,541.7P	9.99P	2,762.3P	3,214.9P	5,950.2P	109.0P
1996		4,605P	691P	72.1P	56.7P	113.7P	1,608.0P	10.29P	2,890.6P	3,364.3P	6,226.7P	112.9P
1997		4,751P	701P	73.6P	57.8P	116.1P	1,674.3P	10.58P	3,019.0P	3,513.6P	6,503.2P	116.7P
1998		4,897P	712P	75.2P	58.9P	118.4P	1,740.6P	10.88P	3,147.3P	3,663.0P	6,779.6P	120.6P

Sources: 1982, 1987, 1992 *Economic Census*; *Annual Survey of Manufactures*, 83-86, 88-91, 93-94. Establishment counts for non-Census years are from *County Business Patterns*; establishment values for 83-84 are extrapolations. 'P's show projections by the editors. Industries reclassified in 87 will not have data for prior years.

INDICES OF CHANGE

Year	Companies	Establishments: Total	Establishments: with 20 or more employees	Employment: Total (000)	Production Workers (000)	Production Hours (Mil)	Compensation: Payroll ($ mil)	Compensation: Wages ($/hr)	Production ($ million): Cost of Materials	Value Added by Manufacture	Value of Shipments	Capital Invest.
1982	68	69	78	69	69	67	46	71	41	42	42	49
1983		67	83	79	82	79	52	69	48	52	50	59
1984		65	89	93	97	98	64	66	65	60	62	84
1985		63	94	87	90	89	66	74	64	61	63	76
1986		61	94	85	85	86	69	78	68	68	68	92
1987	85	86	107	107	108	108	91	83	86	91	89	113
1988		80	109	107	109	106	93	88	86	95	91	97
1989		73	107	104	100	99	92	93	89	89	89	122
1990		82	102	101	102	102	93	92	93	93	93	103
1991		86	92	91	93	92	87	95	85	83	84	68
1992	100	100	100	100	100	100	100	100	100	100	100	100
1993		103	98	105	104	104	106	100	116	104	109	100
1994		100P	107P	110	110	111	113	102	122	115	118	134
1995		103P	108P	112P	112P	112P	118P	108P	125P	118P	121P	122P
1996		107P	110P	115P	114P	114P	123P	111P	131P	123P	126P	127P
1997		110P	112P	117P	116P	116P	128P	114P	136P	129P	132P	131P
1998		113P	114P	120P	118P	119P	133P	117P	142P	134P	137P	135P

Sources: Same as General Statistics. Values reflect change from the base year, 1992. Values above 100 mean greater than 92, values below 100 mean less than 92, and a value of 100 in the 82-91 or 93-98 period means same as 92. 'P's mark projections by the editors.

SELECTED RATIOS

For 1994	Avg. of All Manufact.	Analyzed Industry	Index	For 1994	Avg. of All Manufact.	Analyzed Industry	Index
Employees per Establishment	49	16	33	Value Added per Production Worker	134,084	57,018	43
Payroll per Establishment	1,500,273	342,552	23	Cost per Establishment	5,045,178	624,708	12
Payroll per Employee	30,620	21,444	70	Cost per Employee	102,970	39,107	38
Production Workers per Establishment	34	13	37	Cost per Production Worker	146,988	48,991	33
Wages per Establishment	853,319	242,537	28	Shipments per Establishment	9,576,895	1,345,679	14
Wages per Production Worker	24,861	19,020	77	Shipments per Employee	195,460	84,241	43
Hours per Production Worker	2,056	2,013	98	Shipments per Production Worker	279,017	105,531	38
Wages per Hour	12.09	9.45	78	Investment per Establishment	321,011	27,636	9
Value Added per Establishment	4,602,255	727,068	16	Investment per Employee	6,552	1,730	26
Value Added per Employee	93,930	45,515	48	Investment per Production Worker	9,352	2,167	23

Sources: Same as General Statistics. The 'Average of All Manufacturing' column represents the average of all manufacturing industries reported for the most recent complete year available. The Index shows the relationship between the Average and the Analyzed Industry. For example, 100 means that they are equal; 500 that the Analyzed Industry is five times the average; 50 means that the Analyzed Industry is half the national average. The abbreviation 'na' is used to show that data are 'not available'.

LEADING COMPANIES

Number shown: **75** Total sales ($ mil): **2,032** Total employment (000): **24.3**

Company Name	Address				CEO Name	Phone	Co. Type	Sales ($ mil)	Empl. (000)
Merillat Industries Inc	PO Box 1946	Adrian	MI	49221	Richard D Merillat	517-263-0771	S	250*	3.1
Aristokraft Inc	PO Box 420	Jasper	IN	47547	Gilbert D Verkamp	812-482-2527	S	220	2.3
American Woodmark Corp	3102 Shawnee Dr	Winchester	VA	22601	William F Brandt Jr	703-665-9100	P	171	2.0
Triangle Pacific Corp	16803 Dallas Pkwy	Dallas	TX	75248	John G Conklin	214-931-3000	D	147	1.5
Wood-Mode Industries Inc	1 2nd St	Kreamer	PA	17833	Robert L Gronlund	717-374-2711	R	90	0.9
Distributors USA Inc	2425 E Camelback	Phoenix	AZ	85016	Stephen T White	602-946-8008	R	82*	1.0
Schrock-WCI Cabinet Group	217 S Oak St	Arthur	IL	61911	Merv Plank	217-543-3311	D	72	0.7
HomeCrest Corp	PO Box 595	Goshen	IN	46526	Russell S Warner	219-533-9571	R	65	0.9
Kitchen Kompact Inc	PO Box 868	Jeffersonville	IN	47130	D Gahm	812-282-6681	R	60	0.3
Wellborn Cabinet Inc	PO Box 1210	Ashland	AL	36251	Paul Wellborn	205-354-7151	R	60	1.0
Yorktowne Inc	PO Box 231	Red Lion	PA	17356	John P Edl	717-244-4011	R	55	0.8
Norcraft Companies Inc	30 E Plato Blv	St Paul	MN	55107	Harold Dokmo	612-297-0661	R	52	0.7
Crystal Cabinet Works Inc	1100 Crystal Dr	Princeton	MN	55371	Jeffery R Hammer	612-389-4187	R	50	0.8
Weskar Inc	2425 E Camelback	Phoenix	AZ	85016	James M Mantle	602-946-8008	S	40*	0.4
Cardell Cabinets Inc	PO Box 200850	San Antonio	TX	78220	BJ Tidwell	210-225-0290	R	36	0.5
Starmark Inc	700 E 48th St	Sioux Falls	SD	57104	Tony Bour	605-335-8600	D	35	0.5
Diamond Cabinets	PO Box 547	Hillsboro	OR	97123	Michael Dulac	503-648-3104	D	32	0.5
McConnell Cabinets Inc	3017 N Rumford	El Monte	CA	91732	W R McConnell	818-444-2653	R	28	0.2
Facelifters Home Systems Inc	800 Snediker Av	Brooklyn	NY	11207	Mark Honigsfeld	718-257-9700	P	26	0.4
LesCare Kitchens Inc	1 LesCare Dr	Waterbury	CT	06705	James Lestorti	203-755-1100	R	26	0.2
Medallion Kitchens of Minnesota	180 Industrial Blv	Waconia	MN	55387	Jack Edl	612-442-5171	R	26*	0.3
Dura Supreme Inc	300 Dura Dr	Howard Lake	MN	55349	Keith Stotts	612-543-3872	R	23	0.3
Mobilcraft Wood Products	2018 Fieldhouse	Elkhart	IN	46517	David Lung	219-293-0521	D	22	0.2
Rutt Custom Cabinetry	1564 Main St	Goodville	PA	17528	Jerry Price	215-445-6751	D	17	0.2
Grandview Products Co	PO Box 874	Parsons	KS	67357	Emil F Zetmeir	316-421-6950	R	16	0.2
Brandom Manufacturing Inc	211 Campus Dr	Keene	TX	76059	Hannu T Halminen	817-645-8841	R	15	0.2
Karman Kitchens Inc	PO Box 57086	Salt Lake City	UT	84157	Matt Pettibone	801-268-3581	S	15	0.2
Leedo Manufacturing Co	PO Box AA	East Bernard	TX	77435	JV Samuels	713-342-4989	R	15*	0.2
McCarthy Cabinet Co	3255 W Osborn Rd	Phoenix	AZ	85017	Kevin McCarthy	602-269-9731	R	15	0.3
Regal Kitchens Inc	8600 S River NW	Miami	FL	33166	RE Sweeney	305-885-0111	R	15*	0.2
Brakur Custom Cabinetry Inc	Rte 59	Shorewood	IL	60435	KT Kurtz	815-436-4970	R	13	0.2
Fashion Cabinet Manufacturing	5440 W 9620 S	West Jordan	UT	84084	G Kelsch	801-566-0646	R	13	0.1
Ampco Products Inc	PO Box 4190	Hialeah	FL	33014	Stanley L Krieger	305-821-5700	R	12	0.1
Plain 'N Fancy Kitchens Inc	PO Box 519	Schaefferstown	PA	17088	John Achey	717-949-6571	R	12	0.2
Mastercraft Industries Inc	120 W Allen St	Rice Lake	WI	54868	HH Johnston	715-234-8111	R	11	0.2
Cabinet Supply Inc	1700 NW 5th St	Richmond	IN	47374	D Karn	317-966-6893	R	10	<0.1
Custom Wood Products Inc	PO Box 4500	Roanoke	VA	24015	RA Ungerer	703-345-8821	R	10	0.1
Plato Woodwork Inc	PO Box 98	Plato	MN	55370	Timothy Pinske	612-238-2193	R	10	<0.1
Rosebud Manufacturing Co	PO Box 409	Madison	SD	57042	Don Grayson	605-256-4561	R	10	<0.1
Shamrock Cabinet & Fixture	10201 E 65th St	Raytown	MO	64133	William J Price	816-737-2300	R	10*	0.1
Kinzee Industries Inc	1 Paul Kohner Pl	Elmwood Park	NJ	07407	J Solomon	201-797-4700	R	9	<0.1
Trendlines Inc	9912 Governor	Williamsport	MD	21795	J Terry Thompson	301-223-8900	R	8	<0.1
Columbia Woodworking Inc	945 Brentwood NE	Washington	DC	20018	D Seagraves	202-526-2387	S	7	0.1
Calmar Manufacturing Co	402 E Main St	Calmar	IA	52132	Bruce Anderson	319-562-3261	R	7	<0.1
California Kitchen	385 Woodview Av	Morgan Hill	CA	95037	Chris Fajardo	408-779-9229	R	6*	0.1
Coppes Napanee Co	401 E Market St	Nappanee	IN	46550	Paul R Herrold	219-773-4141	R	6	<0.1
Martin Cabinet Inc	336 S Washington	Plainville	CT	06062	Jean Martin	203-747-5769	R	6	<0.1
Rich Maid Kabinetry Inc	633 W Lincoln Av	Myerstown	PA	17067	Ray Martin	717-866-2112	R	6*	<0.1
Saco Industries Inc	PO Box 518	Frankfort	IL	60423	Ron Bergstrom	815-469-4663	R	6*	<0.1
Chemcraft	PO Box 1086	Elkhart	IN	46515	W F Henningfeld	219-264-3121	R	5	<0.1
Mid-America Cabinets Inc	PO Box 219	Gentry	AR	72734	Robert J Hosteter	501-736-2671	R	5	0.1
Millbrook Kitchens Inc	Rte 20	Nassau	NY	12123	Joesph E Hochberg	518-766-3033	R	5	<0.1
Belmont Corp	60 Crystal Pond Pl	Bristol	CT	06010	David T Clark	203-589-5700	R	5	<0.1
Prime Wood Inc	2217 N 9th St	Wahpeton	ND	58075	Edward Shourma	701-642-2727	R	5	0.6
Schmidt Cabinet Co	PO Box 68	New Salisbury	IN	47161	OC Schmidt	812-347-2434	R	4	<0.1
Carrollton Manufacturing	PO Box 9	North Carrolton	MS	38947	Mark R Warren	601-237-6806	R	4	<0.1
Dura-Craft Industries Inc	110 W Oak St	Gillespie	IL	62033	Clifford Crispens	217-839-2151	R	4	<0.1
Hart Tie and Lumber Co	PO Box 10	Black Riv Fls	WI	54615	Olita Hart	715-284-5616	R	4	<0.1
Murray Cabinet and Fixtures	6360 Federal Blv	San Diego	CA	92114	Lillian Paul	619-582-3162	R	4	<0.1
Superior Woodwork Inc	9230 Billy The Kid	El Paso	TX	79907	William Russell	915-860-1493	R	4	<0.1
Pennville Custom Cabinet	PO Box 1266	Portland	IN	47371	Mark Goldman	219-726-9357	D	3	<0.1
Custom Craft Cabinets Inc	458 Bell Rd	Nashville	TN	37217	C Anderson	615-361-4020	R	3	<0.1
AYR Cabinet Co	1074 Hwy 6	Nappanee	IN	46550	D Miller Jr	219-773-7973	R	3	<0.1
Birchcraft Kitchens Inc	1612 Thorn St	Reading	PA	19601	RR Whitmoyer	610-375-4392	R	3	<0.1
Del-Wood Kitchens Inc	RR 10	Hanover	PA	17331	C W Grubb Jr	717-637-9320	R	3*	<0.1
Dun-Rite Kitchen Cabinet Corp	571 Hempstead Tpk	Elmont	NY	11003	V Perciballi	516-437-3040	R	3*	<0.1
DW Industries Inc	9175 N Bradford St	Portland	OR	97203	Tracy Wilson	503-285-0058	S	3	<0.1
Cabinet Maker Inc	534 Sowers Rd	Statesville	NC	28677	Virgil L Elliott	704-876-2808	R	2	<0.1
JT Parsons Cabinet Company	PO Box 445	Osceola	AR	72370	Joe Parsons	501-563-2696	R	2	<0.1
Elish and Company Inc	PO Box 4546	Eighty Four	PA	15330	Laura Elish	412-228-3737	R	2	<0.1
Terry Manufacturing Co	PO Box 1398	Palestine	TX	75802	Richard Terry	903-729-6804	R	2	<0.1
Fred K Anderson and Sons Inc	725 S Kohler St	Los Angeles	CA	90021	Earl Anderson	213-627-3667	R	2	<0.1
Artistic Cabinets	1863 Commercial St	Escondido	CA	92025	Larry Niggli	619-746-8631	R	1*	<0.1
Barnhill Trading Company Inc	PO Box 311775	New Braunfels	TX	78131	Gilford Barnhill	210-629-5887	R	1*	<0.1
Eurotech Cabinets/Salientte	8204 Sovereign Row	Dallas	TX	75247	Neal Seidner	214-630-7766	R	1	<0.1

Source: *Ward's Business Directory of U.S. Private and Public Companies*, Volumes 1 and 2, 1996. The company type code used is as follows: P - Public, R - Private, S - Subsidiary, D - Division, J - Joint Venture, A - Affiliate, G - Group. Sales are in millions of dollars, employees are in thousands. An asterisk (*) indicates an estimated sales volume. The symbol < stands for 'less than'. Company names and addresses are truncated, in some cases, to fit into the available space.

MATERIALS CONSUMED

Material	Quantity	Delivered Cost ($ million)
Materials, ingredients, containers, and supplies	(X)	2,049.6
Hardwood rough lumber	(X)	98.4
Softwood rough lumber	(X)	9.0
Hardwood dressed lumber	(X)	107.4
Softwood dressed lumber	(X)	14.2
Softwood cut stock, including window and cabinet parts	(X)	8.8
Hardwood dimension and parts, excluding furniture frames	(X)	272.1
Hardwood veneer	(X)	20.1
Hardwood plywood	(X)	90.2
Softwood plywood	(X)	16.7
Particleboard (wood)	(X)	160.2
Hardboard (wood fiberboard)	(X)	11.6
Medium density fiberboard (MDF)	(X)	29.5
Glass (float, sheet and plate)	(X)	4.0
Plastics products consumed in the form of sheets, rods, tubes, film, and other shapes	(X)	36.8
Builders' hardware (including door locks, locksets, lock trim, screen hardware, etc.)	(X)	151.4
Paperboard containers, boxes, and corrugated paperboard	(X)	45.5
All other materials and components, parts, containers, and supplies	(X)	333.6
Materials, ingredients, containers, and supplies, nsk	(X)	640.2

Source: 1992 *Economic Census*. Explanation of symbols used: (D): Withheld to avoid disclosure of competitive data; na: Not available; (S): Withheld because statistical norms were not met; (X): Not applicable; (Z): Less than half the unit shown; nec: Not elsewhere classified; nsk: Not specified by kind; - : zero; * : 10-19 percent estimated; ** : 20-29 percent estimated.

PRODUCT SHARE DETAILS

Product or Product Class	% Share	Product or Product Class	% Share
Wood kitchen cabinets	100.00	laminated	68.88
Cabinets and cabinetwork, stock line	40.42	Cabinets and cabinetwork, custom, plastics laminated	22.84
Cabinets and cabinetwork, stock line, except plastics laminated	86.87	Cabinets and cabinetwork, custom, nsk	8.28
Cabinets and cabinetwork, stock line, plastics laminated	9.17	Wood vanities and other cabinetwork	10.61
Cabinets and cabinetwork, stock line, nsk	3.96	Vanities and other cabinetwork, stock line	53.40
Cabinets and cabinetwork, custom	28.59	Vanities and other cabinetwork, custom	41.00
Cabinets and cabinetwork, custom, except plastics		Vanities and other cabinetwork, nsk	5.62
		Wood kitchen cabinets, nsk	20.39

Source: 1992 *Economic Census*. The values shown are percent of total shipments in an industry. Values of indented subcategories are summed in the main heading. The symbol (D) appears when data are withheld to prevent disclosure of competitive information. The abbreviation nsk stands for 'not specified by kind' and nec for 'not elsewhere classified'.

INPUTS AND OUTPUTS FOR WOOD KITCHEN CABINETS

Economic Sector or Industry Providing Inputs	%	Sector	Economic Sector or Industry Buying Outputs	%	Sector
Sawmills & planning mills, general	13.9	Manufg.	Residential additions/alterations, nonfarm	32.0	Constr.
Wholesale trade	10.6	Trade	Residential 1-unit structures, nonfarm	30.2	Constr.
Veneer & plywood	8.2	Manufg.	Residential garden apartments	16.8	Constr.
Particleboard	7.2	Manufg.	Nonfarm residential structure maintenance	5.8	Constr.
Hardwood dimension & flooring mills	6.3	Manufg.	Residential 2-4 unit structures, nonfarm	3.7	Constr.
Hardware, nec	5.0	Manufg.	Office buildings	2.8	Constr.
Advertising	4.8	Services	Farm housing units & additions & alterations	1.7	Constr.
Wood products, nec	4.3	Manufg.	Construction of educational buildings	1.4	Constr.
Paints & allied products	4.0	Manufg.	Residential high-rise apartments	1.3	Constr.
Adhesives & sealants	3.9	Manufg.	Mobile homes	1.3	Manufg.
Motor freight transportation & warehousing	2.8	Util.	Industrial buildings	0.9	Constr.
Metal stampings, nec	2.6	Manufg.	Exports	0.5	Foreign
Paperboard containers & boxes	2.6	Manufg.	Maintenance of farm residential buildings	0.4	Constr.
Miscellaneous plastics products	2.5	Manufg.	Prefabricated wood buildings	0.3	Manufg.
Electric services (utilities)	2.2	Util.	Wood kitchen cabinets	0.3	Manufg.
Petroleum refining	1.8	Manufg.	Construction of stores & restaurants	0.2	Constr.
Railroads & related services	1.5	Util.	Travel trailers & campers	0.2	Manufg.
Real estate	1.2	Fin/R.E.			
Maintenance of nonfarm buildings nec	1.0	Constr.			
Communications, except radio & TV	1.0	Util.			
Eating & drinking places	1.0	Trade			
Banking	0.9	Fin/R.E.			
Royalties	0.9	Fin/R.E.			
Fabricated metal products, nec	0.8	Manufg.			
Hand & edge tools, nec	0.8	Manufg.			
Equipment rental & leasing services	0.8	Services			
Gas production & distribution (utilities)	0.6	Util.			
Wood kitchen cabinets	0.5	Manufg.			
Paper coating & glazing	0.4	Manufg.			
Screw machine and related products	0.4	Manufg.			
Management & consulting services & labs	0.4	Services			

Continued on next page.

INPUTS AND OUTPUTS FOR WOOD KITCHEN CABINETS - Continued

Economic Sector or Industry Providing Inputs	%	Sector	Economic Sector or Industry Buying Outputs	%	Sector
Woodworking machinery	0.3	Manufg.			
Water transportation	0.3	Util.			
Accounting, auditing & bookkeeping	0.3	Services			
Automotive rental & leasing, without drivers	0.3	Services			
Automotive repair shops & services	0.3	Services			
Legal services	0.3	Services			
U.S. Postal Service	0.3	Gov't			
Abrasive products	0.2	Manufg.			
Lubricating oils & greases	0.2	Manufg.			
Machinery, except electrical, nec	0.2	Manufg.			
Sanitary services, steam supply, irrigation	0.2	Util.			
Insurance carriers	0.2	Fin/R.E.			
Business/professional associations	0.2	Services			
Engineering, architectural, & surveying services	0.2	Services			
Manifold business forms	0.1	Manufg.			
Computer & data processing services	0.1	Services			
Detective & protective services	0.1	Services			

Source: Benchmark Input-Output Accounts for the U.S. Economy, 1982, U.S. Department of Commerce, Washington, D.C., July 1991. Data, as reported in the source, are organized by the 1977 SIC structure in use in 1982 but have been matched, as closely as is possible, to the 1987 SIC structure used in this book.

OCCUPATIONS EMPLOYED BY SIC 243 - MILLWORK, PLYWOOD, AND STRUCTURAL MEMBERS

Occupation	% of Total 1994	Change to 2005	Occupation	% of Total 1994	Change to 2005
Assemblers, fabricators, & hand workers nec	13.6	-2.8	Truck drivers light & heavy	2.0	0.2
Cabinetmakers & bench carpenters	10.9	-2.8	Inspectors, testers, & graders, precision	1.7	-2.8
Woodworking machine workers	6.1	-22.2	Coating, painting, & spraying machine workers	1.7	-22.2
Machine feeders & offbearers	5.1	-12.5	Carpenters	1.7	-22.2
Head sawyers & sawing machine workers	4.6	-22.2	Cement & gluing machine operators	1.7	6.9
Helpers, laborers, & material movers nec	4.4	-2.8	Precision woodworkers nec	1.4	94.4
Wood machinists	4.3	-12.5	Secretaries, ex legal & medical	1.4	-11.5
Blue collar worker supervisors	3.9	-8.3	Industrial machinery mechanics	1.3	6.9
General managers & top executives	2.8	-7.8	Bookkeeping, accounting, & auditing clerks	1.2	-27.1
Freight, stock, & material movers, hand	2.7	-22.2	General office clerks	1.2	-17.1
Sales & related workers nec	2.3	-2.8	Industrial production managers	1.2	-2.8
Industrial truck & tractor operators	2.3	-2.8	Drafters	1.0	-24.3

Source: Industry-Occupation Matrix, Bureau of Labor Statistics. These data relate to one or more 3-digit SIC industry groups rather than to a single 4-digit SIC. The change reported for each occupation to the year 2005 is a percent of growth or decline as estimated by the Bureau of Labor Statistics. The abbreviation nec stands for 'not elsewhere classified'.

LOCATION BY STATE AND REGIONAL CONCENTRATION

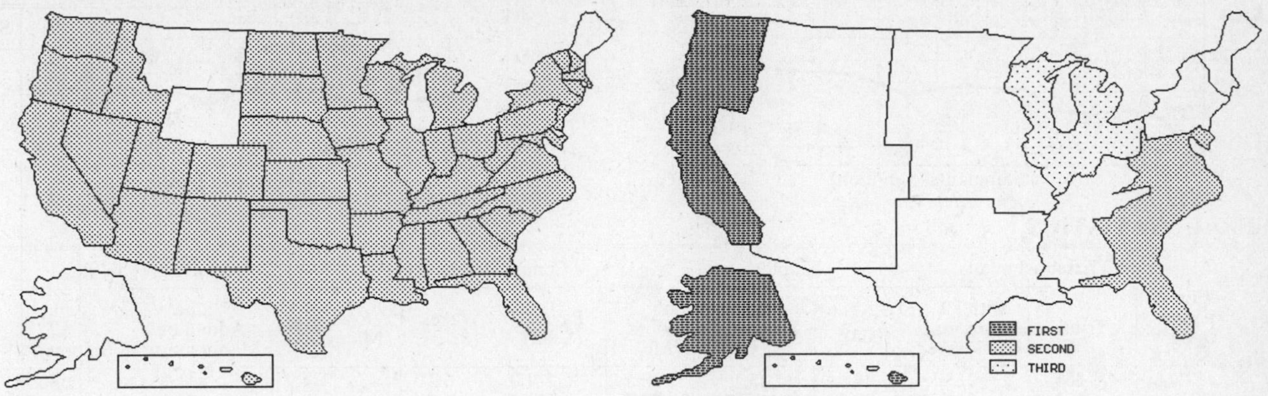

INDUSTRY DATA BY STATE

State	Establish-ments	Shipments			Employment				Cost as % of Shipments	Investment per Employee ($)
		Total ($ mil)	% of U.S.	Per Establ.	Total Number	% of U.S.	Per Establ.	Wages ($/hour)		
California	791	475.5	9.6	0.6	7,300	11.6	9	10.15	40.4	753
Pennsylvania	202	360.4	7.3	1.8	4,900	7.8	24	10.54	41.8	898
Indiana	84	360.2	7.3	4.3	3,300	5.3	39	9.44	55.9	1,576
Ohio	135	322.8	6.5	2.4	2,900	4.6	21	9.08	45.0	3,862
Minnesota	115	302.7	6.1	2.6	2,900	4.6	25	8.94	47.7	1,103
Texas	226	273.1	5.5	1.2	4,100	6.5	18	7.62	47.5	1,366
Virginia	128	234.7	4.8	1.8	2,200	3.5	17	9.91	42.4	955
Illinois	128	178.6	3.6	1.4	2,200	3.5	17	9.42	44.0	1,182
Florida	337	171.1	3.5	0.5	3,100	4.9	9	7.66	45.2	677
Georgia	175	143.5	2.9	0.8	1,700	2.7	10	9.19	35.5	882
Washington	118	139.5	2.8	1.2	1,900	3.0	16	10.31	41.7	1,211
Oregon	91	136.3	2.8	1.5	1,600	2.5	18	10.36	44.2	938
New York	176	131.2	2.7	0.7	1,800	2.9	10	9.83	43.0	1,111
North Carolina	105	131.0	2.7	1.2	1,700	2.7	16	8.55	48.1	2,941
Iowa	30	122.8	2.5	4.1	1,400	2.2	47	10.26	42.9	5,071
Alabama	121	106.8	2.2	0.9	1,600	2.5	13	7.96	50.3	3,750
Wisconsin	106	102.5	2.1	1.0	1,600	2.5	15	8.85	42.6	1,313
Tennessee	111	98.4	2.0	0.9	1,300	2.1	12	8.71	51.5	615
Massachusetts	70	97.9	2.0	1.4	800	1.3	11	10.85	45.1	1,000
Michigan	67	92.6	1.9	1.4	900	1.4	13	10.46	52.2	-
Missouri	93	88.7	1.8	1.0	1,500	2.4	16	9.05	43.5	933
Kansas	38	88.4	1.8	2.3	1,200	1.9	32	8.21	49.3	2,583
Arizona	73	88.0	1.8	1.2	1,100	1.8	15	9.00	34.0	455
Utah	63	84.0	1.7	1.3	1,100	1.8	17	9.24	43.7	909
New Jersey	108	70.5	1.4	0.7	900	1.4	8	10.71	41.1	889
Connecticut	53	55.6	1.1	1.0	700	1.1	13	12.80	40.3	-
Colorado	61	44.6	0.9	0.7	600	1.0	10	8.89	42.8	1,500
South Dakota	11	42.9	0.9	3.9	600	1.0	55	7.11	42.7	1,333
Nevada	18	40.3	0.8	2.2	400	0.6	22	9.71	61.8	-
Arkansas	36	39.6	0.8	1.1	600	1.0	17	7.22	38.9	667
Kentucky	43	31.5	0.6	0.7	500	0.8	12	9.25	45.7	1,000
Oklahoma	27	28.1	0.6	1.0	500	0.8	19	7.75	43.8	-
North Dakota	17	25.5	0.5	1.5	400	0.6	24	10.60	46.3	3,750
Mississippi	33	22.3	0.5	0.7	500	0.8	15	6.25	47.5	800
Hawaii	20	15.7	0.3	0.8	200	0.3	10	14.00	45.9	1,000
New Mexico	35	14.4	0.3	0.4	300	0.5	9	6.60	35.4	333
Idaho	32	12.3	0.2	0.4	200	0.3	6	7.25	38.2	-
Vermont	12	10.7	0.2	0.9	200	0.3	17	7.50	31.8	-
West Virginia	14	9.3	0.2	0.7	200	0.3	14	8.00	48.4	500
Maryland	48	(D)	-	-	375 *	0.6	8	-	-	2,400
South Carolina	42	(D)	-	-	375 *	0.6	9	-	-	-
Louisiana	35	(D)	-	-	375 *	0.6	11	-	-	800
Nebraska	27	(D)	-	-	375 *	0.6	14	-	-	2,400
New Hampshire	16	(D)	-	-	375 *	0.6	23	-	-	-

Source: 1992 *Economic Census*. The states are in descending order of shipments or establishments (if shipment data are missing for the majority). The symbol (D) appears when data are withheld to prevent disclosure of competitive information. States marked with (D) are sorted by number of establishments. A dash (-) indicates that the data element cannot be calculated; * indicates the midpoint of a range.

2435 - HARDWOOD VENEER AND PLYWOOD

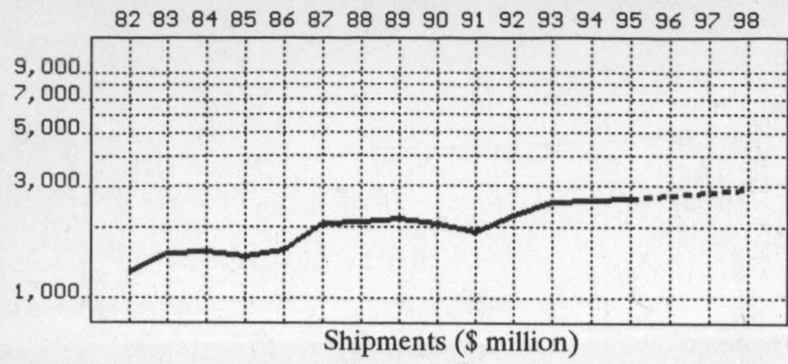

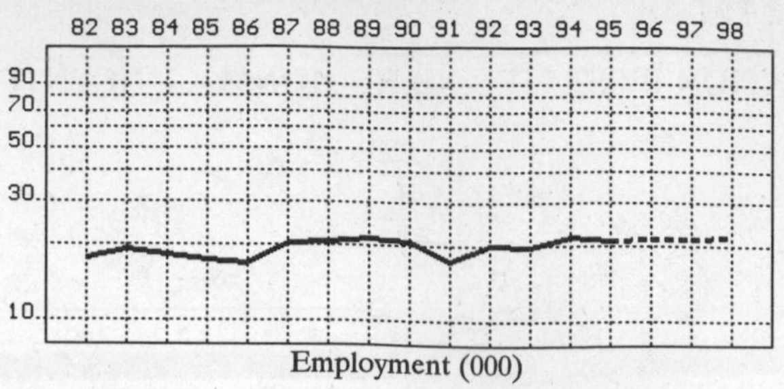

GENERAL STATISTICS

Year	Companies	Establishments		Employment			Compensation		Production ($ million)			
		Total	with 20 or more employees	Total (000)	Production Workers (000)	Production Hours (Mil)	Payroll ($ mil)	Wages ($/hr)	Cost of Materials	Value Added by Manufacture	Value of Shipments	Capital Invest.
1982	268	306	213	17.8	15.1	28.5	241.0	6.21	844.9	441.3	1,304.4	22.2
1983		304	213	19.3	16.5	32.7	271.2	6.20	978.6	553.8	1,537.1	17.3
1984		302	213	18.3	15.6	31.2	272.8	6.36	1,010.7	571.0	1,578.8	40.3
1985		299	213	17.3	14.8	29.2	273.8	6.67	939.3	552.0	1,510.0	34.9
1986		303	209	17.0	14.3	29.7	268.7	6.65	946.9	632.0	1,585.2	38.0
1987	274	310	213	20.5	17.4	35.2	339.6	6.99	1,320.9	750.6	2,060.5	31.3
1988		307	215	20.6	17.3	35.1	347.5	7.20	1,415.4	702.9	2,100.3	37.2
1989		301	212	21.5	17.0	34.3	356.2	7.58	1,445.1	741.0	2,184.6	47.2
1990		297	211	21.0	15.7	31.6	334.5	7.83	1,350.4	706.6	2,051.7	40.8
1991		298	208	17.3	14.8	29.4	320.1	8.03	1,203.3	683.4	1,896.5	45.5
1992	283	318	213	20.1	17.0	35.1	394.7	8.12	1,401.9	856.4	2,247.5	47.0
1993		316	202	19.8	16.8	35.0	417.3	8.55	1,646.5	930.4	2,537.2	46.6
1994		309P	208P	21.9	18.7	39.3	436.0	8.21	1,728.2	846.8	2,599.1	52.3
1995		310P	207P	21.1P	17.4P	36.5P	431.6P	8.73P	1,740.2P	852.7P	2,617.1P	54.2P
1996		311P	207P	21.3P	17.6P	37.0P	446.3P	8.94P	1,804.7P	884.3P	2,714.2P	56.4P
1997		311P	206P	21.6P	17.8P	37.5P	461.0P	9.15P	1,869.2P	915.9P	2,811.2P	58.6P
1998		312P	206P	21.8P	17.9P	38.0P	475.7P	9.35P	1,933.8P	947.5P	2,908.3P	60.9P

Sources: 1982, 1987, 1992 *Economic Census*; *Annual Survey of Manufactures*, 83-86, 88-91, 93-94. Establishment counts for non-Census years are from *County Business Patterns*; establishment values for 83-84 are extrapolations. 'P's show projections by the editors. Industries reclassified in 87 will not have data for prior years.

INDICES OF CHANGE

Year	Companies	Establishments		Employment			Compensation		Production ($ million)			
		Total	with 20 or more employees	Total (000)	Production Workers (000)	Production Hours (Mil)	Payroll ($ mil)	Wages ($/hr)	Cost of Materials	Value Added by Manufacture	Value of Shipments	Capital Invest.
1982	95	96	100	89	89	81	61	76	60	52	58	47
1983		96	100	96	97	93	69	76	70	65	68	37
1984		95	100	91	92	89	69	78	72	67	70	86
1985		94	100	86	87	83	69	82	67	64	67	74
1986		95	98	85	84	85	68	82	68	74	71	81
1987	97	97	100	102	102	100	86	86	94	88	92	67
1988		97	101	102	102	100	88	89	101	82	93	79
1989		95	100	107	100	98	90	93	103	87	97	100
1990		93	99	104	92	90	85	96	96	83	91	87
1991		94	98	86	87	84	81	99	86	80	84	97
1992	100	100	100	100	100	100	100	100	100	100	100	100
1993		99	95	99	99	100	106	105	117	109	113	99
1994		97P	98P	109	110	112	110	101	123	99	116	111
1995		97P	97P	105P	103P	104P	109P	108P	124P	100P	116P	115P
1996		98P	97P	106P	104P	105P	113P	110P	129P	103P	121P	120P
1997		98P	97P	107P	105P	107P	117P	113P	133P	107P	125P	125P
1998		98P	97P	108P	106P	108P	121P	115P	138P	111P	129P	130P

Sources: Same as General Statistics. Values reflect change from the base year, 1992. Values above 100 mean greater than 92, values below 100 mean less than 92, and a value of 100 in the 82-91 or 93-98 period means same as 92. 'P's mark projections by the editors.

SELECTED RATIOS

For 1994	Avg. of All Manufact.	Analyzed Industry	Index
Employees per Establishment	49	71	144
Payroll per Establishment	1,500,273	1,409,276	94
Payroll per Employee	30,620	19,909	65
Production Workers per Establishment	34	60	176
Wages per Establishment	853,319	1,042,906	122
Wages per Production Worker	24,861	17,254	69
Hours per Production Worker	2,056	2,102	102
Wages per Hour	12.09	8.21	68
Value Added per Establishment	4,602,255	2,737,098	59
Value Added per Employee	93,930	38,667	41

For 1994	Avg. of All Manufact.	Analyzed Industry	Index
Value Added per Production Worker	134,084	45,283	34
Cost per Establishment	5,045,178	5,586,033	111
Cost per Employee	102,970	78,913	77
Cost per Production Worker	146,988	92,417	63
Shipments per Establishment	9,576,895	8,401,028	88
Shipments per Employee	195,460	118,680	61
Shipments per Production Worker	279,017	138,989	50
Investment per Establishment	321,011	169,048	53
Investment per Employee	6,552	2,388	36
Investment per Production Worker	9,352	2,797	30

Sources: Same as General Statistics. The 'Average of All Manufacturing' column represents the average of all manufacturing industries reported for the most recent complete year available. The Index shows the relationship between the Average and the Analyzed Industry. For example, 100 means that they are equal; 500 that the Analyzed Industry is five times the average; 50 means that the Analyzed Industry is half the national average. The abbreviation 'na' is used to show that data are 'not available'.

LEADING COMPANIES Number shown: **71** Total sales ($ mil): **2,307** Total employment (000): **18.0**

Company Name	Address				CEO Name	Phone	Co. Type	Sales ($ mil)	Empl. (000)
Ply Gem Industries Inc	777 3rd Av	New York	NY	10017	Jeffrey S Silverman	212-832-1550	P	796	4.0
Columbia Forest Products Inc	2020 SW 4th Av	Portland	OR	97201	Andrew J Honzel	503-224-5300	R	200*	3.0
Fibreboard Corp	PO Box 218	Standard	CA	95373	Jim Costello	209-532-7141	D	180	0.6
Timber Products Co Medford	PO Box 1669	Medford	OR	97501	J H Gonyea III	503-773-6681	D	130	0.6
Chesapeake Hardwood Products	201 W Dexter	Chesapeake	VA	23324	James N Haynie	804-543-1601	R	60	0.2
David R Webb Inc	PO Box 8	Edinburgh	IN	46124	JA Grunwald	812-526-2601	R	60	0.6
States Industries Inc	PO Box 7037	Eugene	OR	97401	D Montoya	503-688-7871	R	60	0.4
Atlantic Veneer Corp	PO Box 660	Beaufort	NC	28516	K Heinz Moehring	919-728-3169	S	50	0.6
Day Companies Inc	PO Box 240188	Memphis	TN	38111	Clarence Day	901-685-9500	R	50	0.2
Besse Forest Products Group	PO Box 352	Gladstone	MI	49837	John Besse	906-428-3113	R	42	0.5
Birds Eye Veneer Co	PO Box 352	Gladstone	MI	49837	John O Beese	906-428-3113	S	42	0.5
Northern Michigan Veneers Inc	PO Box 352	Gladstone	MI	49837	John Besse	906-428-3113	S	42	0.5
Eggers Industries Inc	PO Box 88	Two Rivers	WI	54241	Jim Lester	414-793-1351	R	40	0.4
Indian Head	PO Box 605	Newport	VT	05855	TN Jewett	802-334-6711	D	40	0.4
Marion Plywood Corp	PO Box 497	Marion	WI	54950	Peter T Rogers	715-754-5231	R	35	0.5
Brand S Corp	PO Box 1087	Corvallis	OR	97339	John S Brandis Jr	503-757-7777	R	30*	0.4
International Veneer Company	1551 Montgomery	South Hill	VA	23970	Olvid C Edwards	804-447-7100	R	25	0.2
MacBeath Hardwood Company	2150 Oakdale Av	San Francisco	CA	94124	J Cortese	415-647-0782	R	24	0.1
Pavco Industries Inc	PO Box 612	Pascagoula	MS	39567	Roy L Ausserer	601-762-3172	R	16*	0.1
Day Plywood Inc	PO Drawer 429	Cuthbert	GA	31740	Ron Tews	912-732-3701	S	15	0.2
G-L Veneer Company Inc	2224 E Slauson Av	Huntington Pk	CA	90255	JB Levin	213-582-5203	R	15	<0.1
Wisconsin Veneer and Plywood	PO Box 140	Mattoon	WI	54450	John Besse	715-489-3611	S	15	0.2
McKnight Plywood Inc	PO Box 3349	West Helena	AR	72390	J Brooks	501-572-2501	R	13	0.1
Danville Plywood Corp	PO Box 2249	Danville	VA	24541	G B Buchanan Jr	804-793-4626	R	12*	0.1
Davis Wood Products Inc	PO Box 604	Hudson	NC	28638	Marc Davis	704-728-8444	R	12	0.2
Dillon Veneer and Plywood	PO Box 310	Dillon	SC	29536	EC Carr Jr	803-774-4124	R	12*	0.1
Flexible Materials Inc	11209 Electron Dr	Jeffersontown	KY	40337	Ron Humin	502-267-7717	R	12*	0.2
RS Bacon Veneer Co	100 S Mannheim Rd	Hillside	IL	60162	James A McCracken	708-547-6673	R	12*	0.1
Standard Plywood Inc	PO Box 1155	Clinton	SC	29325	Robert Anderson	803-833-6250	R	12*	0.1
Superior Hardwoods	PO Box 7	Philomath	OR	97370	Jack Brandis Jr	503-757-7777	D	12	<0.1
Freeman Corp	PO Box 96	Winchester	KY	40391	George T Freeman	606-744-4311	R	11	0.2
North American Wood Products	PO Box 306	Seymour	IN	47274	Walter Seremek	812-522-1121	R	11	0.2
Amos-Hill Associates Inc	PO Box 7	Edinburgh	IN	46124	RL Wertz	812-526-2671	R	10	0.1
Birchwood Lumber and Veneer	PO Box 68	Birchwood	WI	54817	BG Kennen	715-354-3441	R	10	0.2
Dean Co	PO Box 1239	Princeton	WV	24740	AH McClaugherty	304-425-8701	R	10	0.2
East Perry Lumber Co	PO Box 105	Frohna	MO	63748	MP Petzoldt	314-824-5272	R	10	<0.1
Erath Veneer Corporation	PO Box 507	Rocky Mount	VA	24151	GS Erath	703-483-5223	R	10	<0.1
Forestex Co	PO Box 68	Forest Grove	OR	97116	Dan Dutton	503-357-2131	S	10	<0.1
Paramount Plywood Products	PO Box 469	New Albany	IN	47150	W Cobb	812-944-2294	R	9*	<0.1
Evansville Veneer and Lumber	100 S Kentucky St	Evansville	IN	47714	Douglas Richardson	812-423-6491	D	9	<0.1
Arkansas Face Veneer Company	PO Box 706	Benton	AR	72018	Bill Hartzell	501-778-7412	S	8*	<0.1
Henry County Plywood Corp	PO Box 406	Ridgeway	VA	24148	E Gravely	703-956-3121	R	8	0.1
StemWood Corp	PO Box 1316	New Albany	IN	47151	David E Wunderlin	812-945-6646	R	8	<0.1
Thiesing Veneer Company Inc	300 Park Dr	Mooresville	IN	46158	David Mathers	317-831-4040	R	8*	<0.1
Grays Harbor Veneer	PO Box 239	Hoquiam	WA	98550	Gary L Earl	206-532-3540	D	7	<0.1
Hasty Plywood Co	PO Box 417	Maxton	NC	28364	Stephen Floyd	910-844-5267	R	7	<0.1
Keller Products Inc	PO Box 4105	Manchester	NH	03108	Richard Steinberg	603-627-7887	S	7*	<0.1
Birchwood Manufacturing Co	PO Box 540	Rice Lake	WI	54868	RB Lillyblad	715-234-8181	R	6	0.1
Lenderink Inc	PO Box 98	Belmont	MI	49306	Tom A Lenderink	616-887-8257	R	6	<0.1
Benton Veneer Co	PO Box 202	Benton	AR	72018	MP Lawrence	501-776-0681	R	5*	<0.1
Bradford Veneer and Panel Co	PO Box 379	Bradford	VT	05033	Gary W Best	802-222-5241	R	5	<0.1
Columbia Panel Manufacturing	PO Box 7447	High Point	NC	27264	Gaylord R Rush	910-861-4100	R	5	<0.1
Ellstrom Manufacturing	1540 NW Ballard	Seattle	WA	98107	Sven Ellstrom	206-789-3000	R	5*	<0.1
Rankin Brothers Co	PO Box 876	Fayetteville	NC	28302	James H Wilson III	919-483-1478	R	5	<0.1
Swords Veneer and Lumber Co	PO Box 6157	Rock Island	IL	61204	M Elefant	309-788-4515	S	5*	0.1
Weber Veneer	PO Box 89	Shawano	WI	54166	RK Weber	715-526-3165	R	5	0.1
Capital Veneer Works Inc	PO Box 240785	Montgomery	AL	36124	Ella C Adams	205-264-1401	R	4*	<0.1
EM Cummings Veneers Inc	PO Box 49	New Albany	IN	47151	Edward Zoeller	812-944-2269	R	4	<0.1
Winnsboro Plywood Company	PO Box 449	Winnsboro	SC	29180	Quay McMaster	803-635-4696	R	4	0.1
Kearse Manufacturing Company	PO Box 138	Olar	SC	29843	WH Kearse	803-368-8130	R	4	<0.1
AR Taylor Veneer Co	PO Box 985	Demopolis	AL	36732	AR Taylor Jr	205-289-3671	R	4	<0.1
Mill City Plywood Co	7301 Walker St	St Louis Park	MN	55426	Paul Erickson	612-938-2729	R	4	<0.1
BL Curry and Sons Inc	PO Box 439	New Albany	IN	47151	Jerry Curry	812-945-6623	R	3	<0.1
Calypso Panel Company Inc	PO Box 407	Calypso	NC	28325	Gary Tyler	919-658-2542	R	3	<0.1
Chowan Veneer Company Inc	PO Box 297	Edenton	NC	27932	James E Darnell	919-482-4411	R	3	<0.1
Jasper Veneers Inc	PO Box 226	Jasper	IN	47546	Herb Manthei	812-482-5022	R	3	<0.1
Burkeville Veneer Co	PO Box 128	Burkeville	VA	23922	James L Minter	804-767-5559	D	3	0.1
Memphis Plywood Corp	337 E Mallory Av	Memphis	TN	38109	WS Decker	901-948-5531	R	2	<0.1
Plywood Manufacturing	2201 Dominguez St	Torrance	CA	90501	Alec E Gilad	310-328-7986	R	2	<0.1
Panel Techn Building Systems	14853 Martin Dr	Fort Myers	FL	33908	Scott Bartels	813-433-4110	R	1*	<0.1
Sanders Manufacturing Company	1000 Moran St	Gainesville	TX	76240	Dave Sanders, Jr	817-668-7228	R	1	<0.1

Source: *Ward's Business Directory of U.S. Private and Public Companies*, Volumes 1 and 2, 1996. The company type code used is as follows: P - Public, R - Private, S - Subsidiary, D - Division, J - Joint Venture, A - Affiliate, G - Group. Sales are in millions of dollars, employees are in thousands. An asterisk (*) indicates an estimated sales volume. The symbol < stands for 'less than'. Company names and addresses are truncated, in some cases, to fit into the available space.

MATERIALS CONSUMED

Material		Quantity	Delivered Cost ($ million)
Materials, ingredients, containers, and supplies		(X)	1,228.5
Stumpage cost (cost of timber, excluding land, cut and consumed at same establishment)		(X)	43.1
Hardwood logs, bolts, and unsliced flitches	mil ft log scale	430.0**	183.2
Softwood logs, bolts, and unsliced flitches	mil ft log scale	155.5	54.8
Rough and dressed lumber	mil bd ft	12.8*	9.3
Hardwood veneer	mil sq ft sm	2,583.3	351.2
Softwood veneer	mil.sq ft (1 in. bas	867.9	61.5
Hardwood plywood	mil sq ft sm	(S)	134.3
Softwood plywood	mil sq ft (3/8 in. b	(D)	(D)
Particleboard (wood)	mil sq ft (3/4 in. b	183.9**	43.8
Medium density fiberboard (MDF)	mil sq ft (3/4 in. b	109.5*	34.9
Hardboard (wood fiberboard)	mil sq ft (1/8 in. b	(D)	(D)
Glues and adhesives		(X)	29.1
All other materials and components, parts, containers, and supplies		(X)	115.5
Materials, ingredients, containers, and supplies, nsk		(X)	152.5

Source: 1992 *Economic Census*. Explanation of symbols used: (D): Withheld to avoid disclosure of competitive data; na: Not available; (S): Withheld because statistical norms were not met; (X): Not applicable; (Z): Less than half the unit shown; nec: Not elsewhere classified; nsk: Not specified by kind; - : zero; * : 10-19 percent estimated; ** : 20-29 percent estimated.

PRODUCT SHARE DETAILS

Product or Product Class	% Share	Product or Product Class	% Share
Hardwood veneer and plywood	100.00	Other hardwood plywood type products, including cellular panels and curved and molded plywood	28.58
Hardwood plywood	33.39	Hardwood plywood type products, nsk	9.20
Hardwood plywood, veneer core	67.10	Hardwood veneer, not reinforced or backed	29.06
Hardwood plywood, particleboard core	12.88	Birch veneer, not reinforced or backed	5.09
Hardwood plywood, medium density fiberboard (MDF) core	10.49	Maple veneer, not reinforced or backed	6.70
Hardwood plywood, other core, including lumber, hardboard, oriented strand board or waferboard	4.43	Oak veneer, not reinforced or backed	37.47
Hardwood plywood, nsk	5.10	Walnut veneer, not reinforced or backed	6.87
Prefinished hardwood plywood made from purchased plywood	9.35	Other domestic hardwood veneers, not reinforced or backed	26.05
Hardwood plywood type products	23.54	Imported hardwood veneers, not reinforced or backed	1.02
Hardwood veneered panels	62.23	Hardwood veneer, not reinforced or backed, nsk	16.79
		Hardwood veneer and plywood, nsk	4.67

Source: 1992 *Economic Census*. The values shown are percent of total shipments in an industry. Values of indented subcategories are summed in the main heading. The symbol (D) appears when data are withheld to prevent disclosure of competitive information. The abbreviation nsk stands for 'not specified by kind' and nec for 'not elsewhere classified'.

INPUTS AND OUTPUTS FOR VENEER & PLYWOOD

Economic Sector or Industry Providing Inputs	%	Sector	Economic Sector or Industry Buying Outputs	%	Sector
Logging camps & logging contractors	43.0	Manufg.	Residential 1-unit structures, nonfarm	14.6	Constr.
Veneer & plywood	16.5	Manufg.	Veneer & plywood	14.0	Manufg.
Imports	12.9	Foreign	Residential additions/alterations, nonfarm	10.5	Constr.
Wholesale trade	4.8	Trade	Exports	4.2	Foreign
Adhesives & sealants	3.4	Manufg.	Wood household furniture	3.4	Manufg.
Electric services (utilities)	3.1	Util.	Millwork	3.1	Manufg.
Railroads & related services	2.4	Util.	Mobile homes	2.9	Manufg.
Motor freight transportation & warehousing	1.8	Util.	Nonfarm residential structure maintenance	2.4	Constr.
Particleboard	1.3	Manufg.	Residential garden apartments	2.2	Constr.
Petroleum refining	1.1	Manufg.	Maintenance of nonfarm buildings nec	2.0	Constr.
Wood products, nec	1.0	Manufg.	Prefabricated metal buildings	2.0	Manufg.
Gas production & distribution (utilities)	1.0	Util.	Wood kitchen cabinets	2.0	Manufg.
Banking	0.8	Fin/R.E.	Office buildings	1.9	Constr.
Paints & allied products	0.6	Manufg.	Signs & advertising displays	1.9	Manufg.
Advertising	0.6	Services	Engineering & scientific instruments	1.5	Manufg.
Maintenance of nonfarm buildings nec	0.5	Constr.	Theatrical producers, bands, entertainers	1.5	Services
Hand & edge tools, nec	0.5	Manufg.	Metal household furniture	1.3	Manufg.
Sawmills & planning mills, general	0.5	Manufg.	Wood office furniture	1.2	Manufg.
Communications, except radio & TV	0.4	Util.	Maintenance of highways & streets	1.0	Constr.
Eating & drinking places	0.4	Trade	Prefabricated wood buildings	1.0	Manufg.
Plastics materials & resins	0.3	Manufg.	Travel trailers & campers	0.9	Manufg.
Water transportation	0.3	Util.	Wood containers	0.9	Manufg.
Miscellaneous plastics products	0.2	Manufg.	Wood partitions & fixtures	0.9	Manufg.
Sanitary services, steam supply, irrigation	0.2	Util.	Farm service facilities	0.8	Constr.
Woodworking machinery	0.1	Manufg.	Maintenance of petroleum & natural gas wells	0.8	Constr.
Insurance carriers	0.1	Fin/R.E.	Residential 2-4 unit structures, nonfarm	0.8	Constr.
Equipment rental & leasing services	0.1	Services	Luggage	0.8	Manufg.
Legal services	0.1	Services	Highway & street construction	0.7	Constr.
Management & consulting services & labs	0.1	Services	Boat building & repairing	0.7	Manufg.
			Farm machinery & equipment	0.7	Manufg.

Continued on next page.

INPUTS AND OUTPUTS FOR VENEER & PLYWOOD - Continued

Economic Sector or Industry Providing Inputs	%	Sector	Economic Sector or Industry Buying Outputs	%	Sector
			Sporting & athletic goods, nec	0.7	Manufg.
			Wood products, nec	0.7	Manufg.
			Construction of stores & restaurants	0.6	Constr.
			Warehouses	0.6	Constr.
			Games, toys, & children's vehicles	0.6	Manufg.
			Household refrigerators & freezers	0.6	Manufg.
			Musical instruments	0.6	Manufg.
			Upholstered household furniture	0.6	Manufg.
			Industrial buildings	0.5	Constr.
			Maintenance of farm service facilities	0.5	Constr.
			Furniture & fixtures, nec	0.5	Manufg.
			Manufacturing industries, nec	0.5	Manufg.
			Mattresses & bedsprings	0.5	Manufg.
			Radio & TV receiving sets	0.5	Manufg.
			Metal office furniture	0.4	Manufg.
			Motor homes (made on purchased chassis)	0.4	Manufg.
			Public building furniture	0.4	Manufg.
			Sawmills & planning mills, general	0.4	Manufg.
			Wood pallets & skids	0.4	Manufg.
			Construction of hospitals	0.3	Constr.
			Hotels & motels	0.3	Constr.
			Aircraft & missile engines & engine parts	0.3	Manufg.
			Drapery hardware & blinds & shades	0.3	Manufg.
			Industrial patterns	0.3	Manufg.
			Motor vehicle parts & accessories	0.3	Manufg.
			Surgical & medical instruments	0.3	Manufg.
			Truck trailers	0.3	Manufg.
			Motion pictures	0.3	Services
			Construction of educational buildings	0.2	Constr.
			Construction of nonfarm buildings nec	0.2	Constr.
			Farm housing units & additions & alterations	0.2	Constr.
			Maintenance of farm residential buildings	0.2	Constr.
			Maintenance of telephone & telegraph facilities	0.2	Constr.
			Resid. & other health facility construction	0.2	Constr.
			Residential high-rise apartments	0.2	Constr.
			Telephone & telegraph facility construction	0.2	Constr.
			Brooms & brushes	0.2	Manufg.
			Concrete products, nec	0.2	Manufg.
			Household furniture, nec	0.2	Manufg.
			Industrial trucks & tractors	0.2	Manufg.
			Particleboard	0.2	Manufg.
			Refrigeration & heating equipment	0.2	Manufg.
			Switchgear & switchboard apparatus	0.2	Manufg.
			Wood TV & radio cabinets	0.2	Manufg.
			Amusement & recreation building construction	0.1	Constr.
			Brick & structural clay tile	0.1	Manufg.
			Ship building & repairing	0.1	Manufg.
			Structural wood members, nec	0.1	Manufg.
			Transportation equipment, nec	0.1	Manufg.
			Truck & bus bodies	0.1	Manufg.

Source: Benchmark Input-Output Accounts for the U.S. Economy, 1982, U.S. Department of Commerce, Washington, D.C., July 1991. Data, as reported in the source, are organized by the 1977 SIC structure in use in 1982 but have been matched, as closely as is possible, to the 1987 SIC structure used in this book.

OCCUPATIONS EMPLOYED BY SIC 243 - MILLWORK, PLYWOOD, AND STRUCTURAL MEMBERS

Occupation	% of Total 1994	Change to 2005	Occupation	% of Total 1994	Change to 2005
Assemblers, fabricators, & hand workers nec	13.6	-2.8	Truck drivers light & heavy	2.0	0.2
Cabinetmakers & bench carpenters	10.9	-2.8	Inspectors, testers, & graders, precision	1.7	-2.8
Woodworking machine workers	6.1	-22.2	Coating, painting, & spraying machine workers	1.7	-22.2
Machine feeders & offbearers	5.1	-12.5	Carpenters	1.7	-22.2
Head sawyers & sawing machine workers	4.6	-22.2	Cement & gluing machine operators	1.7	6.9
Helpers, laborers, & material movers nec	4.4	-2.8	Precision woodworkers nec	1.4	94.4
Wood machinists	4.3	-12.5	Secretaries, ex legal & medical	1.4	-11.5
Blue collar worker supervisors	3.9	-8.3	Industrial machinery mechanics	1.3	6.9
General managers & top executives	2.8	-7.8	Bookkeeping, accounting, & auditing clerks	1.2	-27.1
Freight, stock, & material movers, hand	2.7	-22.2	General office clerks	1.2	-17.1
Sales & related workers nec	2.3	-2.8	Industrial production managers	1.2	-2.8
Industrial truck & tractor operators	2.3	-2.8	Drafters	1.0	-24.3

Source: Industry-Occupation Matrix, Bureau of Labor Statistics. These data relate to one or more 3-digit SIC industry groups rather than to a single 4-digit SIC. The change reported for each occupation to the year 2005 is a percent of growth or decline as estimated by the Bureau of Labor Statistics. The abbreviation nec stands for 'not elsewhere classified'.

LOCATION BY STATE AND REGIONAL CONCENTRATION

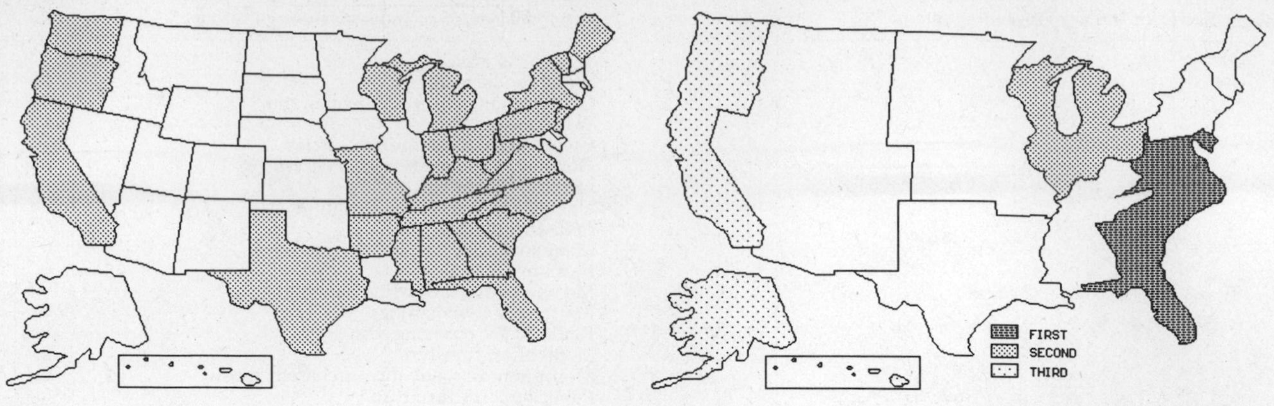

INDUSTRY DATA BY STATE

State	Establish-ments	Shipments			Employment				Cost as % of Shipments	Investment per Employee ($)
		Total ($ mil)	% of U.S.	Per Establ.	Total Number	% of U.S.	Per Establ.	Wages ($/hour)		
Oregon	11	313.1	13.9	28.5	1,600	8.0	145	10.60	71.4	1,813
North Carolina	67	300.6	13.4	4.5	3,900	19.4	58	7.55	53.6	1,615
California	24	234.4	10.4	9.8	1,300	6.5	54	10.35	73.1	-
Indiana	34	233.7	10.4	6.9	2,400	11.9	71	8.36	51.3	3,167
Virginia	19	214.9	9.6	11.3	1,400	7.0	74	7.75	70.1	3,571
Wisconsin	21	141.7	6.3	6.7	2,000	10.0	95	7.41	49.1	2,800
Georgia	8	123.7	5.5	15.5	800	4.0	100	6.75	73.4	-
Arkansas	10	73.7	3.3	7.4	500	2.5	50	6.78	71.8	1,600
Alabama	12	50.9	2.3	4.2	500	2.5	42	7.10	70.9	2,400
Vermont	4	50.5	2.2	12.6	600	3.0	150	8.55	53.7	-
South Carolina	14	45.4	2.0	3.2	800	4.0	57	5.67	61.0	1,500
Washington	6	26.3	1.2	4.4	300	1.5	50	8.00	61.2	2,000
Kentucky	5	25.4	1.1	5.1	400	2.0	80	7.33	63.8	750
Mississippi	6	24.1	1.1	4.0	200	1.0	33	6.33	58.1	3,000
New York	7	17.9	0.8	2.6	200	1.0	29	8.67	54.2	-
Texas	4	13.2	0.6	3.3	100	0.5	25	4.33	65.9	-
Michigan	10	(D)	-	-	750 *	3.7	75	-	-	2,800
Florida	8	(D)	-	-	375 *	1.9	47	-	-	-
Ohio	7	(D)	-	-	375 *	1.9	54	-	-	-
Pennsylvania	6	(D)	-	-	750 *	3.7	125	-	-	3,067
New Jersey	5	(D)	-	-	175 *	0.9	35	-	-	-
Tennessee	5	(D)	-	-	175 *	0.9	35	-	-	-
Maine	2	(D)	-	-	175 *	0.9	88	-	-	-
Missouri	2	(D)	-	-	175 *	0.9	88	-	-	-
West Virginia	1	(D)	-	-	175 *	0.9	175	-	-	-

Source: 1992 *Economic Census*. The states are in descending order of shipments or establishments (if shipment data are missing for the majority). The symbol (D) appears when data are withheld to prevent disclosure of competitive information. States marked with (D) are sorted by number of establishments. A dash (-) indicates that the data element cannot be calculated; * indicates the midpoint of a range.

2436 - SOFTWOOD VENEER AND PLYWOOD

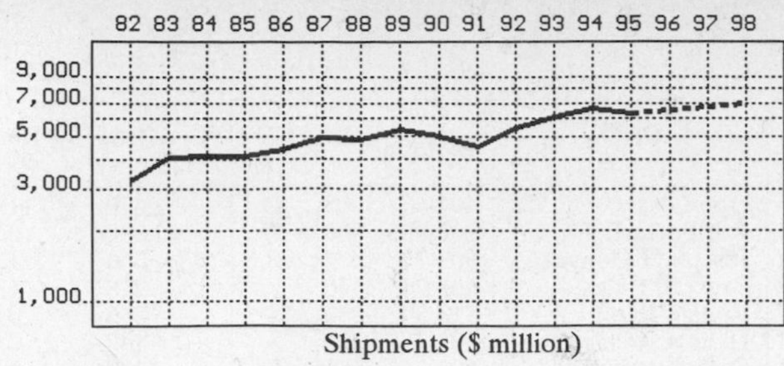

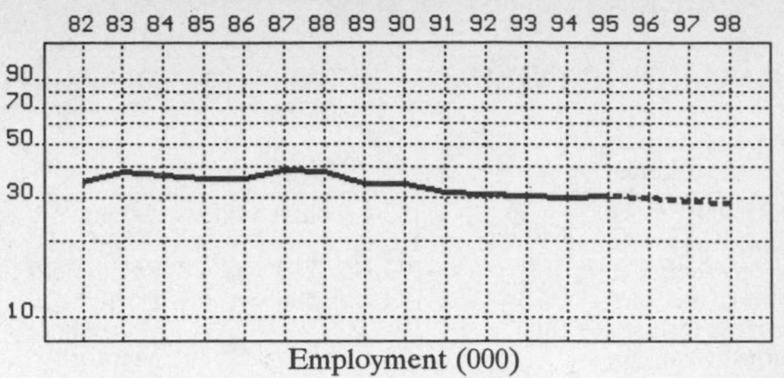

GENERAL STATISTICS

Year	Companies	Establishments Total	Establishments with 20 or more employees	Employment Total (000)	Production Workers (000)	Production Hours (Mil)	Payroll ($ mil)	Wages ($/hr)	Cost of Materials	Value Added by Manufacture	Value of Shipments	Capital Invest.
1982	135	250	199	34.9	31.1	63.7	667.3	8.93	2,363.9	831.5	3,221.5	99.7
1983		243	193	38.1	34.4	72.4	785.9	9.41	2,747.7	1,333.9	4,062.7	86.5
1984		236	187	37.5	33.7	72.2	823.4	9.87	2,773.5	1,332.6	4,108.4	101.8
1985		228	181	35.7	32.1	70.0	798.7	9.88	2,578.4	1,495.4	4,091.2	130.9
1986		221	179	35.9	32.3	71.9	826.1	9.89	2,727.6	1,678.4	4,401.1	95.8
1987	130	231	190	38.9	35.2	76.9	888.0	9.97	2,962.2	1,956.0	4,919.6	110.2
1988		227	191	38.4	34.7	76.6	900.4	10.09	3,083.5	1,766.9	4,848.4	126.1
1989		216	176	34.6	32.9	73.3	887.5	10.34	3,282.5	2,017.3	5,310.0	139.8
1990		206	169	34.6	32.2	71.5	880.6	10.44	3,379.0	1,669.2	5,030.4	103.0
1991		202	158	31.7	28.6	63.6	810.4	10.78	3,114.7	1,473.9	4,592.4	86.7
1992	123	201	159	31.3	28.0	63.5	827.4	11.10	3,265.3	2,185.9	5,447.0	98.7
1993		191	154	30.7	27.7	63.5	846.6	11.42	3,630.5	2,442.1	6,035.4	118.2
1994		189P	154P	30.3	27.2	62.5	856.1	11.83	4,150.4	2,401.5	6,552.7	150.4
1995		184P	150P	30.7P	28.0P	65.1P	892.0P	11.71P	3,985.5P	2,306.1P	6,292.3P	125.3P
1996		180P	146P	30.1P	27.5P	64.5P	900.8P	11.91P	4,118.9P	2,383.3P	6,503.0P	127.3P
1997		175P	142P	29.5P	27.0P	63.9P	909.6P	12.11P	4,252.4P	2,460.5P	6,713.8P	129.3P
1998		170P	139P	28.9P	26.5P	63.3P	918.3P	12.31P	4,385.9P	2,537.8P	6,924.6P	131.2P

Sources: 1982, 1987, 1992 *Economic Census*; *Annual Survey of Manufactures*, 83-86, 88-91, 93-94. Establishment counts for non-Census years are from *County Business Patterns*; establishment values for 83-84 are extrapolations. 'P's show projections by the editors. Industries reclassified in 87 will not have data for prior years.

INDICES OF CHANGE

Year	Companies	Establishments Total	Establishments with 20 or more employees	Employment Total (000)	Production Workers (000)	Production Hours (Mil)	Payroll ($ mil)	Wages ($/hr)	Cost of Materials	Value Added by Manufacture	Value of Shipments	Capital Invest.
1982	110	124	125	112	111	100	81	80	72	38	59	101
1983		121	121	122	123	114	95	85	84	61	75	88
1984		117	118	120	120	114	100	89	85	61	75	103
1985		113	114	114	115	110	97	89	79	68	75	133
1986		110	113	115	115	113	100	89	84	77	81	97
1987	106	115	119	124	126	121	107	90	91	89	90	112
1988		113	120	123	124	121	109	91	94	81	89	128
1989		107	111	111	118	115	107	93	101	92	97	142
1990		102	106	111	115	113	106	94	103	76	92	104
1991		100	99	101	102	100	98	97	95	67	84	88
1992	100	100	100	100	100	100	100	100	100	100	100	100
1993		95	97	98	99	100	102	103	111	112	111	120
1994		94P	97P	97	97	98	103	107	127	110	120	152
1995		92P	94P	98P	100P	103P	108P	105P	122P	105P	116P	127P
1996		89P	92P	96P	98P	102P	109P	107P	126P	109P	119P	129P
1997		87P	90P	94P	96P	101P	110P	109P	130P	113P	123P	131P
1998		84P	87P	92P	94P	100P	111P	111P	134P	116P	127P	133P

Sources: Same as General Statistics. Values reflect change from the base year, 1992. Values above 100 mean greater than 92, values below 100 mean less than 92, and a value of 100 in the 82-91 or 93-98 period means same as 92. 'P's mark projections by the editors.

SELECTED RATIOS

For 1994	Avg. of All Manufact.	Analyzed Industry	Index	For 1994	Avg. of All Manufact.	Analyzed Industry	Index
Employees per Establishment	49	160	327	Value Added per Production Worker	134,084	88,290	66
Payroll per Establishment	1,500,273	4,522,017	301	Cost per Establishment	5,045,178	21,922,881	435
Payroll per Employee	30,620	28,254	92	Cost per Employee	102,970	136,977	133
Production Workers per Establishment	34	144	419	Cost per Production Worker	146,988	152,588	104
Wages per Establishment	853,319	3,905,462	458	Shipments per Establishment	9,576,895	34,612,101	361
Wages per Production Worker	24,861	27,183	109	Shipments per Employee	195,460	216,261	111
Hours per Production Worker	2,056	2,298	112	Shipments per Production Worker	279,017	240,908	86
Wages per Hour	12.09	11.83	98	Investment per Establishment	321,011	794,430	247
Value Added per Establishment	4,602,255	12,684,994	276	Investment per Employee	6,552	4,964	76
Value Added per Employee	93,930	79,257	84	Investment per Production Worker	9,352	5,529	59

Sources: Same as General Statistics. The 'Average of All Manufacturing' column represents the average of all manufacturing industries reported for the most recent complete year available. The Index shows the relationship between the Average and the Analyzed Industry. For example, 100 means that they are equal; 500 that the Analyzed Industry is five times the average; 50 means that the Analyzed Industry is half the national average. The abbreviation 'na' is used to show that data are 'not available'.

LEADING COMPANIES

Number shown: **33** Total sales ($ mil): **4,519** Total employment (000): **25.2**

Company Name	Address				CEO Name	Phone	Co. Type	Sales ($ mil)	Empl. (000)
Georgia-Pacific Corp	133 Peachtree NE	Atlanta	GA	30303	Don Glass	404-652-5005	D	1,470	11.0
Champion International	1 Champion Plz	Stamford	CT	06921	R L Porterfield	203-358-7000	D	1,310*	6.3
Timber Products Co	PO Box 269	Springfield	OR	97477	Joseph H Gonyea	503-747-4577	R	360	1.0
WTD Industries Inc	PO Box 5805	Portland	OR	97228	Bruce L Engel	503-246-3440	P	278	1.1
Kirby Forest Industries Inc	Rte 1	Cleveland	TX	77327	Ronald Paul	713-592-0563	S	260*	0.8
Stone Southwest	PO Box 820	Medford	OR	97501	Dennis Spencer	503-776-5750	S	140	0.9
Springfield Forest Products LP	72B Cen Loop	Eugene	OR	97401	Dick Baldwin	503-344-4886	R	100	0.7
Borden Inc	1154 Reco Av	St Louis	MO	63126	Tom Gilson	314-822-3880	D	90	0.5
Freres Lumber Co	PO Box 276	Lyons	OR	97358	Robert T Freres	503-859-2121	R	75	0.3
Decor Gravure Corp	PO Box 111	Fairfield	AL	35064	Dale Glasscock	205-785-8000	R	50	0.2
Philomath Forest Products Co	PO Box 218	Philomath	OR	97370	Bob Nix	503-929-3205	S	41*	0.3
K-Ply Inc	PO Box 2318	Port Angeles	WA	98362	Ernie Van Ogle	206-457-4421	S	40	0.2
Murphy Co	PO Box 2810	Eugene	OR	97402	Peter C Murphy Jr	503-344-4747	R	36*	0.3
Tecton Laminates Corp	PO Box 587	Hines	OR	97738	AJ Trimble	503-573-2312	R	31	0.2
North Santiam Plywood Inc	PO Box 377	Mill City	OR	97360	James D Morgan	503-897-2391	S	29	0.2
Lane Plywood Inc	65 N Bertelsen Rd	Eugene	OR	97402	Carl Wiley	503-342-5561	R	27	0.2
Westbrook Wood Products Inc	PO Box 248	Coquille	OR	97423	H Westbrook	503-396-2196	R	25	0.2
Bald Knob Land and Timber Co	9414 SW Barber	Portland	OR	97219	George Walker	503-293-1221	R	16*	<0.1
Langboard Inc	PO Box 837	Quitman	GA	31643	John Robinson	912-263-8943	S	16	0.1
Hayworth Roll and Panel Co	PO Box 2244	High Point	NC	27261	Mark A Trexler	910-883-0131	R	15	0.2
Hazama	PO Box 1029	Creswell	OR	97426	Jerry Solomon	503-895-2151	D	14*	<0.1
Medply Corp	PO Box 2488	White City	OR	97503	Clyde Lang	503-826-3142	R	14	0.1
Sedro-Woolley Lumber Co	PO Box 639	Sedro Woolley	WA	98284	Bill McKinley	206-855-2125	S	14*	0.1
Tumwater Lumber Co	PO Box 4158	Tumwater	WA	98501	Larry Nelson	206-352-1548	S	14	0.2
Ply-Gem Manufacturing Co	PO Box 189	Gloucester City	NJ	08030	Howard Steinberg	609-456-9100	D	13	<0.1
Ero/Goodrich Forest Products	Tualatin-Sherwood	Sherwood	OR	97140	Jere Goodrich	503-625-2555	R	12*	<0.1
Pacific Softwoods Co	PO Box 370	Philomath	OR	97370	Richard Bragg	503-929-2902	S	12	<0.1
Plytrim West Inc	1524 Center St	Tacoma	WA	98409	Harry Hoffman	206-572-7300	R	9*	<0.1
Trinity Furniture Inc	PO Box 30	Jacksonville	TX	75766	David Johnson	903-586-2511	D	3	<0.1
Trask River Lumber Co	5900 Moffett Rd	Tillamook	OR	97141	Mitch Cramer	503-842-4007	S	2*	<0.1
Textured Forest Products	PO Box 125	Washougal	WA	98671	GA Weber	360-835-2164	R	2	<0.1
Blue Ridge Veneer	Rte 1	Aston	VA	22920	Yi-Chun Tseng	703-456-6842	R	1	<0.1
Young and Morgan Timber Inc	PO Box 377	Mill City	OR	97360	James D Morgan	503-897-2391	S	1	<0.1

Source: *Ward's Business Directory of U.S. Private and Public Companies*, Volumes 1 and 2, 1996. The company type code used is as follows: P - Public, R - Private, S - Subsidiary, D - Division, J - Joint Venture, A - Affiliate, G - Group. Sales are in millions of dollars, employees are in thousands. An asterisk (*) indicates an estimated sales volume. The symbol < stands for 'less than'. Company names and addresses are truncated, in some cases, to fit into the available space.

MATERIALS CONSUMED

Material		Quantity	Delivered Cost ($ million)
Materials, ingredients, containers, and supplies		(X)	3,056.7
Stumpage cost (cost of timber, excluding land, cut and consumed at same establishment)		(X)	471.7
Hardwood logs, bolts, and unsliced flitches	mil ft log scale	100.2	26.6
Softwood logs, bolts, and unsliced flitches	mil ft log scale	4,535.3	1,498.2
Rough and dressed lumber	mil bd ft	9.5	2.9
Hardwood veneer	mil sq ft sm	224.1*	28.5
Softwood veneer	mil.sq ft (1 in. bas	(S)	402.3
Hardwood plywood	mil sq ft sm	(D)	(D)
Softwood plywood	mil sq ft (3/8 in. b	53.9**	11.4
Particleboard (wood)	mil sq ft (3/4 in. b	(D)	(D)
Medium density fiberboard (MDF)	mil sq ft (3/4 in. b	(D)	(D)
Hardboard (wood fiberboard)	mil sq ft (1/8 in. b	2.3	0.4
Glues and adhesives		(X)	198.4
All other materials and components, parts, containers, and supplies		(X)	316.4
Materials, ingredients, containers, and supplies, nsk		(X)	95.6

Source: 1992 *Economic Census*. Explanation of symbols used: (D): Withheld to avoid disclosure of competitive data; na: Not available; (S): Withheld because statistical norms were not met; (X): Not applicable; (Z): Less than half the unit shown; nec: Not elsewhere classified; nsk: Not specified by kind; - : zero; * : 10-19 percent estimated; ** : 20-29 percent estimated.

PRODUCT SHARE DETAILS

Product or Product Class	% Share	Product or Product Class	% Share
Softwood veneer and plywood	100.00	C -C (plugged)	3.55
Softwood plywood type products	2.78	Softwood plywood, rough, including touch sanded, interior and exterior, nsk	4.29
Softwood veneered panels	80.00	Softwood plywood, sanded	16.55
Other softwood plywood type products, including cellular panels, and curved and molded plywood	19.92	Interior softwood plywood, sanded	5.21
Softwood veneer, not reinforced or backed	12.57	Exterior softwood plywood, sanded, A - C	42.27
Softwood plywood, rough, including touch sanded, interior and exterior	57.01	Exterior softwood plywood, sanded, B - B plyform	9.24
Interior softwood plywood, rough, including touch sanded, C -D exterior glue	61.39	Exterior softwood plywood, sanded, B - C	29.69
Interior softwood plywood, rough, including touch sanded, underlayment exterior glue	19.93	Other exterior softwood plywood, sanded	4.36
Other interior softwood plywood, rough, including touch sanded	8.31	Softwood plywood, sanded, nsk	9.22
Exterior softwood plywood, rough, including touch sanded, C -C (not plugged)	2.53	Softwood plywood specialties	9.87
Exterior softwood plywood, rough, including touch sanded,		Softwood plywood siding	52.44
		Softwood plywood overlays	15.23
		Softwood plywood interior decoratives	(D)
		Other softwood plywood specialties	19.85
		Softwood plywood specialties, nsk	(D)
		Softwood veneer and plywood, nsk	1.23

Source: 1992 *Economic Census*. The values shown are percent of total shipments in an industry. Values of indented subcategories are summed in the main heading. The symbol (D) appears when data are withheld to prevent disclosure of competitive information. The abbreviation nsk stands for 'not specified by kind' and nec for 'not elsewhere classified'.

INPUTS AND OUTPUTS FOR VENEER & PLYWOOD

Economic Sector or Industry Providing Inputs	%	Sector	Economic Sector or Industry Buying Outputs	%	Sector
Logging camps & logging contractors	43.0	Manufg.	Residential 1-unit structures, nonfarm	14.6	Constr.
Veneer & plywood	16.5	Manufg.	Veneer & plywood	14.0	Manufg.
Imports	12.9	Foreign	Residential additions/alterations, nonfarm	10.5	Constr.
Wholesale trade	4.8	Trade	Exports	4.2	Foreign
Adhesives & sealants	3.4	Manufg.	Wood household furniture	3.4	Manufg.
Electric services (utilities)	3.1	Util.	Millwork	3.1	Manufg.
Railroads & related services	2.4	Util.	Mobile homes	2.9	Manufg.
Motor freight transportation & warehousing	1.8	Util.	Nonfarm residential structure maintenance	2.4	Constr.
Particleboard	1.3	Manufg.	Residential garden apartments	2.2	Constr.
Petroleum refining	1.1	Manufg.	Maintenance of nonfarm buildings nec	2.0	Constr.
Wood products, nec	1.0	Manufg.	Prefabricated metal buildings	2.0	Manufg.
Gas production & distribution (utilities)	1.0	Util.	Wood kitchen cabinets	2.0	Manufg.
Banking	0.8	Fin/R.E.	Office buildings	1.9	Constr.
Paints & allied products	0.6	Manufg.	Signs & advertising displays	1.9	Manufg.
Advertising	0.6	Services	Engineering & scientific instruments	1.5	Manufg.
Maintenance of nonfarm buildings nec	0.5	Constr.	Theatrical producers, bands, entertainers	1.5	Services
Hand & edge tools, nec	0.5	Manufg.	Metal household furniture	1.3	Manufg.
Sawmills & planning mills, general	0.5	Manufg.	Wood office furniture	1.2	Manufg.
Communications, except radio & TV	0.4	Util.	Maintenance of highways & streets	1.0	Constr.
Eating & drinking places	0.4	Trade	Prefabricated wood buildings	1.0	Manufg.
Plastics materials & resins	0.3	Manufg.	Travel trailers & campers	0.9	Manufg.
Water transportation	0.3	Util.	Wood containers	0.9	Manufg.
Miscellaneous plastics products	0.2	Manufg.	Wood partitions & fixtures	0.9	Manufg.
Sanitary services, steam supply, irrigation	0.2	Util.	Farm service facilities	0.8	Constr.
Woodworking machinery	0.1	Manufg.	Maintenance of petroleum & natural gas wells	0.8	Constr.
Insurance carriers	0.1	Fin/R.E.	Residential 2-4 unit structures, nonfarm	0.8	Constr.
Equipment rental & leasing services	0.1	Services	Luggage	0.8	Manufg.
Legal services	0.1	Services	Highway & street construction	0.7	Constr.
Management & consulting services & labs	0.1	Services	Boat building & repairing	0.7	Manufg.
			Farm machinery & equipment	0.7	Manufg.
			Sporting & athletic goods, nec	0.7	Manufg.
			Wood products, nec	0.7	Manufg.
			Construction of stores & restaurants	0.6	Constr.
			Warehouses	0.6	Constr.
			Games, toys, & children's vehicles	0.6	Manufg.
			Household refrigerators & freezers	0.6	Manufg.
			Musical instruments	0.6	Manufg.
			Upholstered household furniture	0.6	Manufg.
			Industrial buildings	0.5	Constr.
			Maintenance of farm service facilities	0.5	Constr.
			Furniture & fixtures, nec	0.5	Manufg.
			Manufacturing industries, nec	0.5	Manufg.
			Mattresses & bedsprings	0.5	Manufg.
			Radio & TV receiving sets	0.5	Manufg.
			Metal office furniture	0.4	Manufg.
			Motor homes (made on purchased chassis)	0.4	Manufg.
			Public building furniture	0.4	Manufg.
			Sawmills & planning mills, general	0.4	Manufg.
			Wood pallets & skids	0.4	Manufg.
			Construction of hospitals	0.3	Constr.
			Hotels & motels	0.3	Constr.
			Aircraft & missile engines & engine parts	0.3	Manufg.
			Drapery hardware & blinds & shades	0.3	Manufg.

Continued on next page.

INPUTS AND OUTPUTS FOR VENEER & PLYWOOD - Continued

Economic Sector or Industry Providing Inputs	%	Sector	Economic Sector or Industry Buying Outputs	%	Sector
			Industrial patterns	0.3	Manufg.
			Motor vehicle parts & accessories	0.3	Manufg.
			Surgical & medical instruments	0.3	Manufg.
			Truck trailers	0.3	Manufg.
			Motion pictures	0.3	Services
			Construction of educational buildings	0.2	Constr.
			Construction of nonfarm buildings nec	0.2	Constr.
			Farm housing units & additions & alterations	0.2	Constr.
			Maintenance of farm residential buildings	0.2	Constr.
			Maintenance of telephone & telegraph facilities	0.2	Constr.
			Resid. & other health facility construction	0.2	Constr.
			Residential high-rise apartments	0.2	Constr.
			Telephone & telegraph facility construction	0.2	Constr.
			Brooms & brushes	0.2	Manufg.
			Concrete products, nec	0.2	Manufg.
			Household furniture, nec	0.2	Manufg.
			Industrial trucks & tractors	0.2	Manufg.
			Particleboard	0.2	Manufg.
			Refrigeration & heating equipment	0.2	Manufg.
			Switchgear & switchboard apparatus	0.2	Manufg.
			Wood TV & radio cabinets	0.2	Manufg.
			Amusement & recreation building construction	0.1	Constr.
			Brick & structural clay tile	0.1	Manufg.
			Ship building & repairing	0.1	Manufg.
			Structural wood members, nec	0.1	Manufg.
			Transportation equipment, nec	0.1	Manufg.
			Truck & bus bodies	0.1	Manufg.

Source: Benchmark Input-Output Accounts for the U.S. Economy, 1982, U.S. Department of Commerce, Washington, D.C., July 1991. Data, as reported in the source, are organized by the 1977 SIC structure in use in 1982 but have been matched, as closely as is possible, to the 1987 SIC structure used in this book.

OCCUPATIONS EMPLOYED BY SIC 243 - MILLWORK, PLYWOOD, AND STRUCTURAL MEMBERS

Occupation	% of Total 1994	Change to 2005	Occupation	% of Total 1994	Change to 2005
Assemblers, fabricators, & hand workers nec	13.6	-2.8	Truck drivers light & heavy	2.0	0.2
Cabinetmakers & bench carpenters	10.9	-2.8	Inspectors, testers, & graders, precision	1.7	-2.8
Woodworking machine workers	6.1	-22.2	Coating, painting, & spraying machine workers	1.7	-22.2
Machine feeders & offbearers	5.1	-12.5	Carpenters	1.7	-22.2
Head sawyers & sawing machine workers	4.6	-22.2	Cement & gluing machine operators	1.7	6.9
Helpers, laborers, & material movers nec	4.4	-2.8	Precision woodworkers nec	1.4	94.4
Wood machinists	4.3	-12.5	Secretaries, ex legal & medical	1.4	-11.5
Blue collar worker supervisors	3.9	-8.3	Industrial machinery mechanics	1.3	6.9
General managers & top executives	2.8	-7.8	Bookkeeping, accounting, & auditing clerks	1.2	-27.1
Freight, stock, & material movers, hand	2.7	-22.2	General office clerks	1.2	-17.1
Sales & related workers nec	2.3	-2.8	Industrial production managers	1.2	-2.8
Industrial truck & tractor operators	2.3	-2.8	Drafters	1.0	-24.3

Source: *Industry-Occupation Matrix*, Bureau of Labor Statistics. These data relate to one or more 3-digit SIC industry groups rather than to a single 4-digit SIC. The change reported for each occupation to the year 2005 is a percent of growth or decline as estimated by the Bureau of Labor Statistics. The abbreviation nec stands for 'not elsewhere classified'.

LOCATION BY STATE AND REGIONAL CONCENTRATION

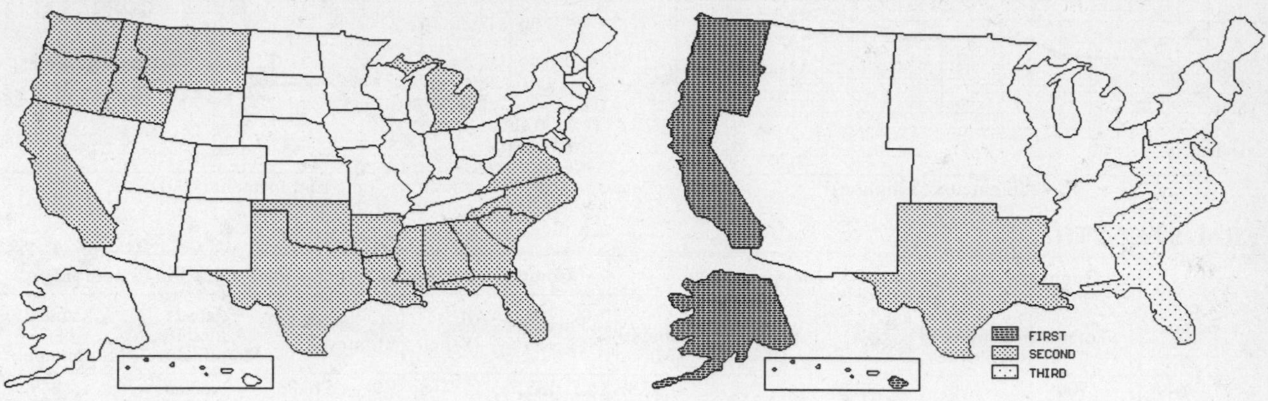

INDUSTRY DATA BY STATE

State	Establish-ments	Shipments			Employment				Cost as % of Shipments	Investment per Employee ($)
		Total ($ mil)	% of U.S.	Per Establ.	Total Number	% of U.S.	Per Establ.	Wages ($/hour)		
Oregon	70	1,832.6	33.6	26.2	9,300	29.7	133	12.01	67.4	2,484
Louisiana	13	597.0	11.0	45.9	3,600	11.5	277	10.14	55.0	3,306
Texas	10	433.3	8.0	43.3	2,700	8.6	270	10.02	55.2	741
Arkansas	8	420.4	7.7	52.5	2,400	7.7	300	10.92	52.8	4,583
Washington	22	331.8	6.1	15.1	2,300	7.3	105	11.57	66.3	4,348
Mississippi	10	309.8	5.7	31.0	1,800	5.8	180	10.23	56.7	2,222
Alabama	8	302.9	5.6	37.9	1,600	5.1	200	10.97	57.0	1,438
Idaho	5	168.6	3.1	33.7	900	2.9	180	13.28	62.6	4,000
California	9	48.2	0.9	5.4	300	1.0	33	10.33	70.5	-
Georgia	8	(D)	-	-	1,750 *	5.6	219	-	-	-
North Carolina	7	(D)	-	-	1,750 *	5.6	250	-	-	-
Florida	4	(D)	-	-	750 *	2.4	188	-	-	-
Michigan	4	(D)	-	-	175 *	0.6	44	-	-	-
Montana	3	(D)	-	-	1,750 *	5.6	583	-	-	-
South Carolina	3	(D)	-	-	750 *	2.4	250	-	-	-
Virginia	3	(D)	-	-	375 *	1.2	125	-	-	-
Oklahoma	1	(D)	-	-	175 *	0.6	175	-	-	-

Source: 1992 *Economic Census*. The states are in descending order of shipments or establishments (if shipment data are missing for the majority). The symbol (D) appears when data are withheld to prevent disclosure of competitive information. States marked with (D) are sorted by number of establishments. A dash (-) indicates that the data element cannot be calculated; * indicates the midpoint of a range.

2439 - STRUCTURAL WOOD MEMBERS, NEC

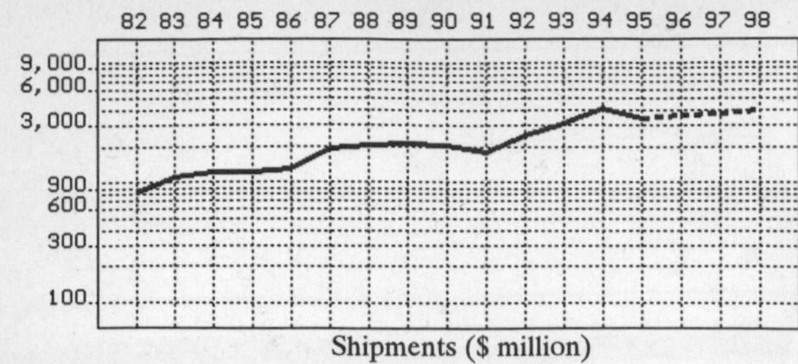

Shipments ($ million)

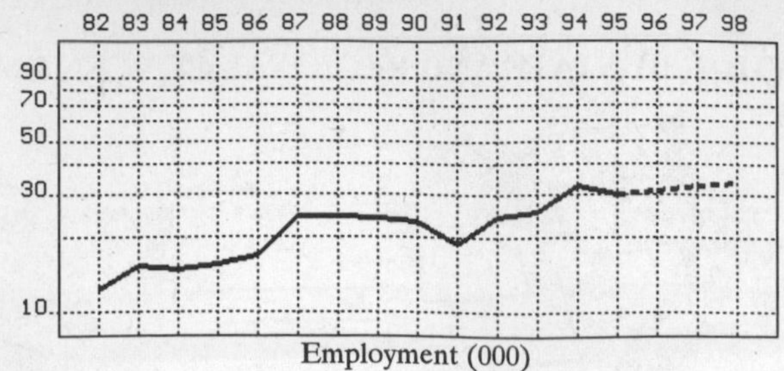

Employment (000)

GENERAL STATISTICS

Year	Com-panies	Establishments		Employment			Compensation		Production ($ million)			
		Total	with 20 or more employees	Total (000)	Production Workers (000)	Production Hours (Mil)	Payroll ($ mil)	Wages ($/hr)	Cost of Materials	Value Added by Manufacture	Value of Shipments	Capital Invest.
1982	649	704	190	12.2	9.3	17.8	185.5	7.08	516.8	330.5	847.9	16.1
1983		707	224	15.4	12.3	23.7	236.6	6.94	714.4	430.0	1,134.4	37.8
1984		710	258	14.7	11.0	21.8	228.2	6.36	738.0	500.9	1,233.8	25.3
1985		714	291	15.5	11.2	20.5	267.1	7.80	739.9	467.7	1,209.6	37.9
1986		725	325	16.7	11.9	22.4	292.3	8.21	850.3	473.3	1,327.2	33.5
1987	831	893	396	24.6	18.5	35.1	434.7	7.76	1,159.9	770.8	1,928.8	46.5
1988		841	393	24.2	18.0	35.5	446.1	7.98	1,259.6	769.1	2,040.7	45.7
1989		800	391	24.1	18.9	36.5	449.3	8.11	1,294.4	849.8	2,134.9	82.0
1990		801	377	23.2	17.0	33.2	429.4	8.31	1,219.9	810.1	2,028.4	37.8
1991		833	328	18.9	14.5	28.4	381.7	8.52	1,104.7	717.6	1,825.0	25.1
1992	829	895	408	24.3	18.1	35.7	515.1	8.85	1,483.5	1,034.2	2,505.3	42.5
1993		910	400	25.6	18.9	38.1	569.7	9.02	1,885.9	1,237.3	3,094.3	65.0
1994		918P	447P	32.7	24.9	51.2	715.7	8.84	2,528.7	1,625.5	4,140.0	106.3
1995		937P	465P	30.0P	22.5P	45.2P	651.1P	9.28P	2,090.7P	1,343.9P	3,422.8P	75.2P
1996		956P	483P	31.3P	23.4P	47.2P	687.6P	9.46P	2,218.5P	1,426.1P	3,632.1P	79.3P
1997		975P	501P	32.6P	24.4P	49.3P	724.0P	9.65P	2,346.3P	1,508.3P	3,841.4P	83.4P
1998		994P	518P	33.8P	25.4P	51.3P	760.4P	9.83P	2,474.2P	1,590.4P	4,050.7P	87.6P

Sources: 1982, 1987, 1992 *Economic Census*; *Annual Survey of Manufactures*, 83-86, 88-91, 93-94. Establishment counts for non-Census years are from *County Business Patterns*; establishment values for 83-84 are extrapolations. 'P's show projections by the editors. Industries reclassified in 87 will not have data for prior years.

INDICES OF CHANGE

Year	Com-panies	Establishments		Employment			Compensation		Production ($ million)			
		Total	with 20 or more employees	Total (000)	Production Workers (000)	Production Hours (Mil)	Payroll ($ mil)	Wages ($/hr)	Cost of Materials	Value Added by Manufacture	Value of Shipments	Capital Invest.
1982	78	79	47	50	51	50	36	80	35	32	34	38
1983		79	55	63	68	66	46	78	48	42	45	89
1984		79	63	60	61	61	44	72	50	48	49	60
1985		80	71	64	62	57	52	88	50	45	48	89
1986		81	80	69	66	63	57	93	57	46	53	79
1987	100	100	97	101	102	98	84	88	78	75	77	109
1988		94	96	100	99	99	87	90	85	74	81	108
1989		89	96	99	104	102	87	92	87	82	85	193
1990		89	92	95	94	93	83	94	82	78	81	89
1991		93	80	78	80	80	74	96	74	69	73	59
1992	100	100	100	100	100	100	100	100	100	100	100	100
1993		102	98	105	104	107	111	102	127	120	124	153
1994		103P	110P	135	138	143	139	100	170	157	165	250
1995		105P	114P	123P	124P	127P	126P	105P	141P	130P	137P	177P
1996		107P	118P	129P	130P	132P	133P	107P	150P	138P	145P	187P
1997		109P	123P	134P	135P	138P	141P	109P	158P	146P	153P	196P
1998		111P	127P	139P	140P	144P	148P	111P	167P	154P	162P	206P

Sources: Same as General Statistics. Values reflect change from the base year, 1992. Values above 100 mean greater than 92, values below 100 mean less than 92, and a value of 100 in the 82-91 or 93-98 period means same as 92. 'P's mark projections by the editors.

SELECTED RATIOS

For 1994	Avg. of All Manufact.	Analyzed Industry	Index	For 1994	Avg. of All Manufact.	Analyzed Industry	Index
Employees per Establishment	49	36	73	Value Added per Production Worker	134,084	65,281	49
Payroll per Establishment	1,500,273	779,836	52	Cost per Establishment	5,045,178	2,755,303	55
Payroll per Employee	30,620	21,887	71	Cost per Employee	102,970	77,330	75
Production Workers per Establishment	34	27	79	Cost per Production Worker	146,988	101,554	69
Wages per Establishment	853,319	493,167	58	Shipments per Establishment	9,576,895	4,510,995	47
Wages per Production Worker	24,861	18,177	73	Shipments per Employee	195,460	126,606	65
Hours per Production Worker	2,056	2,056	100	Shipments per Production Worker	279,017	166,265	60
Wages per Hour	12.09	8.84	73	Investment per Establishment	321,011	115,826	36
Value Added per Establishment	4,602,255	1,771,165	38	Investment per Employee	6,552	3,251	50
Value Added per Employee	93,930	49,709	53	Investment per Production Worker	9,352	4,269	46

Sources: Same as General Statistics. The 'Average of All Manufacturing' column represents the average of all manufacturing industries reported for the most recent complete year available. The Index shows the relationship between the Average and the Analyzed Industry. For example, 100 means that they are equal; 500 that the Analyzed Industry is five times the average; 50 means that the Analyzed Industry is half the national average. The abbreviation 'na' is used to show that data are 'not available'.

LEADING COMPANIES Number shown: **52** Total sales ($ mil): **1,342** Total employment (000): **10.0**

Company Name	Address				CEO Name	Phone	Co. Type	Sales ($ mil)	Empl. (000)
TJ International Inc	PO Box 65	Boise	ID	83702	Walter C Minnick	208-364-3300	P	551	3.6
TJ International	3210 E Amity Rd	Boise	ID	83707	Robert Dingman	208-343-7771	D	200	1.3
Frank Calandra Inc	PO Box 187	Cresson	PA	16630	John M Calandra	814-886-4121	R	100*	0.5
Richardson Industries Inc	904 Monroe St	Sheboygan Fls	WI	53085	J Richardson III	414-467-2671	R	85	1.0
Trussway Inc	9411 Alcorn St	Houston	TX	77093	Richard L Rotto	713-691-6900	R	56*	0.5
Shelter Systems of NJ Inc	Hainesport Ind Pk	Hainesport	NJ	08036	Edward Maul	609-261-2000	R	20	0.2
Truss-Com Co	PO Box 37	Taneytown	MD	21787	Karen C Wilson	410-848-6300	D	20*	0.2
CBS Builders Supply Inc	PO Box 120158	Clermont	FL	34712	Denise Anastasia	904-394-2118	R	18*	0.1
Aviston Lumber Co	101 S Clement Av	Aviston	IL	62216	Maurice Netemeyer	618-228-7247	R	17	<0.1
Blue Ox Industries Inc	PO Box 1547	Kernersville	NC	27285	TO Moore Jr	919-993-4541	R	15	0.3
Columbia Cascade Co	1975 SW 5th Av	Portland	OR	97201	SK Kirn	503-223-1157	R	15*	0.1
Automated Products Inc	PO Box 808	Marshfield	WI	54449	Gary Kopela	715-387-3426	R	14	0.1
Wood Structures Inc	PO Box 347	Biddeford	ME	04005	Dave Gould	207-282-7556	R	14	<0.1
Automated Building Components	129 N Main St	N Baltimore	OH	45872	HL McCarty	419-257-2152	R	12	0.2
Blue Ridge Truss and Supply Inc	1099 Orkney Grade	Basye	VA	22810	Willard Fansler	703-856-2191	R	12	0.1
Gang Nail Truss Company Inc	PO Box 3163	Visalia	CA	93278	Timothy M Rouch	209-651-2121	R	11	0.1
SS Steele and Company Inc	4951 Government	Mobile	AL	36693	SS Steele	334-661-9600	R	11	<0.1
Villaume Industries Inc	2926 Lone Oak Cir	St Paul	MN	55121	JN Linsmayer	612-454-3610	R	11	0.1
Florida Forest Products Ltd	PO Box 1345	Largo	FL	34649	J I Heidenreich	813-585-2067	R	10	<0.1
Shook Builder Supply Co	PO Box 1790	Hickory	NC	28603	Dent F Allison	704-328-2051	R	9	<0.1
Armstrong Lumber Company	2709 Auburn Way N	Auburn	WA	98002	James R Armstrong	206-833-6666	R	8*	0.1
Norwood Sash	4953 Section Av	Norwood	OH	45212	Mike P Klekamp	513-531-5700	R	8*	<0.1
Truss Manufacturing Company	Park St & Elm St	Westfield	IN	46074	CD Krothe	317-896-2571	R	8	0.1
Buettner Brothers Lumber Co	PO Box 1087	Cullman	AL	35056	Charles Buettner	205-734-4221	R	7*	<0.1
Structural Wood Systems	321 Dohrmier St	Greenville	AL	36037	Carlton Whittle	205-382-6534	D	7	<0.1
Tilton Truss Manufacturers Inc	PO Box 267	Woodinville	WA	98072	Ed Tilton	206-483-8585	R	7	<0.1
Truss-Span Corp	19340 NE 80th St	Redmond	WA	98053	Frank Novak	206-868-3100	R	7*	<0.1
Fabricated Wood Products Inc	PO Box 154	Owatonna	MN	55060	Charles Spitzack	507-451-1019	R	7	<0.1
B and R Lumber and Truss Co	119 Didion Rd	St Peters	MO	63376	Wallace Randall	314-278-2246	R	7	<0.1
Citation Homes Inc	PO Box A-F	Spirit Lake	IA	51360	Mike Stineman	712-336-2156	R	6	<0.1
KS Enterprises Inc	PO Box 27427	Albuquerque	NM	87125	James Stafford	505-877-0770	R	6	<0.1
Best Homes Inc	1230 W 171st St	Hazel Crest	IL	60429	Robert Arquilla	708-335-2000	R	5	<0.1
Burns Construction Inc	6676 S Old US Hwy	Macy	IN	46951	Dan B Burns	219-382-2315	R	5*	<0.1
Columbus Roof Trusses Inc	2525 Fisher Rd	Columbus	OH	43204	E Iacovetta	614-272-6464	R	5*	<0.1
Fullerton Building Systems Inc	PO Box 308	Worthington	MN	56187	RJ Clough	507-376-3128	S	5	<0.1
Phillips Manufacturing Company	PO Box 1708	Anniston	AL	36202	Roger Hutcheson	205-831-4881	R	5*	<0.1
Ottawa Truss LLC	6640 96th Av	Zeeland	MI	49464	Jack Weaver	616-875-8157	R	4	<0.1
Enwood Structures Inc	PO Box A	Morrisville	NC	27560	Mark A Schwartz	919-467-6151	R	4	<0.1
Construction Components Inc	PO Box 755	Greenville	AL	36037	EB Shirley	205-382-2657	R	3	<0.1
LOC Inc	PO Box 8068	Erie	PA	16505	LH Lazenby	814-833-7734	R	3	<0.1
Montgomery Truss and Panel	803 W Main St	Grove City	PA	16127	C B Montgomery	412-458-7500	R	3	<0.1
Tacoma Truss Systems Inc	20617 Mountain	Spanaway	WA	98387	Michael L Hart	206-847-2204	R	3	<0.1
UBC Inc	320 W Main St	Branford	CT	06405	Marshall D'Onofrio	203-488-7207	R	3	<0.1
Building Components Unlimited	6260 Arnold Rd	Williamsburg	MI	49690	Charles B Walter	616-267-5322	R	2	<0.1
Calvert Company Inc	218 V St	Vancouver	WA	98661	Douglas A Calvert	206-693-0971	R	2	<0.1
Maugansville Elevator & Lumber	PO Box 278	Maugansville	MD	21767	James S Martin	301-739-4220	R	2	<0.1
Mills and Nebraska Truss Co	PO Box 536548	Orlando	FL	32853	Tom Pulsifer	407-295-1891	S	2	<0.1
Olympic Structures Inc	1850 93rd Av	Olympia	WA	98512	M Manning	206-943-5433	R	2*	<0.1
Sentry Building Components Inc	PO Box 1162	Jennings	LA	70546	Frances E Boisture	318-824-4865	R	2	<0.1
Precision Truss Systems Inc	PO Box 38	Kirklin	IN	46050	JP Fettig	317-279-8848	R	2	<0.1
American Building Components	PO Box 2098	Dublin	CA	94568	Ed P Omernik	510-828-0400	R	1	<0.1
Dakota Craft Co	PO Box 2488	Rapid City	SD	57709	Alan Thornburg	605-341-6100	R	1	<0.1

Source: *Ward's Business Directory of U.S. Private and Public Companies*, Volumes 1 and 2, 1996. The company type code used is as follows: P - Public, R - Private, S - Subsidiary, D - Division, J - Joint Venture, A - Affiliate, G - Group. Sales are in millions of dollars, employees are in thousands. An asterisk (*) indicates an estimated sales volume. The symbol < stands for 'less than'. Company names and addresses are truncated, in some cases, to fit into the available space.

MATERIALS CONSUMED

Material		Quantity	Delivered Cost ($ million)
Materials, ingredients, containers, and supplies		(X)	1,342.4
Hardwood rough lumber	mil bd ft	(S)	59.1
Softwood rough lumber	mil bd ft	498.5**	169.3
Hardwood dressed lumber	mil bd ft	(S)	39.2
Softwood dressed lumber	mil bd ft	1,272.5**	400.2
Softwood plywood	mil sq ft (3/8 in. b	164.1*	40.8
Gypsum building board		(X)	0.2
Builders' hardware (including door locks, locksets, lock trim, screen hardware, etc.)		(X)	15.6
Mineral wool insulation (fibrous glass, rock wool, etc.)		(X)	(D)
Windows and window units, including wood, metal, and vinyl	thousands	96.2*	6.3
Wood doors and door units		(X)	2.3
Metal doors and door units	thousands	26.6*	2.2
Kitchen cabinets, wood		(X)	0.4
Reconstituted wood products		(X)	43.8
Metal siding, including aluminum, steel		(X)	1.1
Fabricated structural iron, steel, and aluminum including truss plates		(X)	42.1
Current-carrying wiring devices, including switches, connectors, lampholders, etc.		(X)	(D)
Household appliances, including refrigerators, cooking equipment, and other household appliances		(X)	(D)
Floor coverings, textile		(X)	3.7
All other materials and components, parts, containers, and supplies		(X)	201.5
Materials, ingredients, containers, and supplies, nsk		(X)	313.6

Source: 1992 *Economic Census*. Explanation of symbols used: (D): Withheld to avoid disclosure of competitive data; na: Not available; (S): Withheld because statistical norms were not met; (X): Not applicable; (Z): Less than half the unit shown; nec: Not elsewhere classified; nsk: Not specified by kind; - : zero; * : 10-19 percent estimated; ** : 20-29 percent estimated.

PRODUCT SHARE DETAILS

Product or Product Class	% Share	Product or Product Class	% Share
Structural wood members, nec	100.00	Combination of glued, laminated, and sawn structural lumber for heavy timber construction	1.04
Glued laminated structural lumber for heavy timber construction, except combinations of glued, laminated, and sawn	11.61	Roof trusses made of sawn lumber, light construction, sold separately	52.74
Sawn structural lumber for heavy timber construction, except combinations of glued, laminated, and sawn	2.65	Other fabricated structural wood products, including floor trusses, nec	21.91

Source: 1992 *Economic Census*. The values shown are percent of total shipments in an industry. Values of indented subcategories are summed in the main heading. The symbol (D) appears when data are withheld to prevent disclosure of competitive information. The abbreviation nsk stands for 'not specified by kind' and nec for 'not elsewhere classified'.

INPUTS AND OUTPUTS FOR STRUCTURAL WOOD MEMBERS, NEC

Economic Sector or Industry Providing Inputs	%	Sector	Economic Sector or Industry Buying Outputs	%	Sector
Sawmills & planning mills, general	48.5	Manufg.	Residential additions/alterations, nonfarm	24.7	Constr.
Wholesale trade	13.0	Trade	Office buildings	11.1	Constr.
Paints & allied products	4.0	Manufg.	Industrial buildings	11.0	Constr.
Fabricated structural metal	3.9	Manufg.	Residential garden apartments	8.3	Constr.
Motor freight transportation & warehousing	3.5	Util.	Hotels & motels	6.9	Constr.
Screw machine and related products	2.1	Manufg.	Construction of hospitals	4.4	Constr.
Railroads & related services	2.1	Util.	Construction of educational buildings	4.1	Constr.
Advertising	2.0	Services	Construction of stores & restaurants	3.7	Constr.
Petroleum refining	1.9	Manufg.	Electric utility facility construction	3.2	Constr.
Fabricated metal products, nec	1.6	Manufg.	Nonfarm residential structure maintenance	2.6	Constr.
Electric services (utilities)	1.5	Util.	Residential 1-unit structures, nonfarm	2.2	Constr.
Hardware, nec	1.1	Manufg.	Construction of religious buildings	1.8	Constr.
Adhesives & sealants	0.9	Manufg.	Residential 2-4 unit structures, nonfarm	1.5	Constr.
Particleboard	0.9	Manufg.	Amusement & recreation building construction	1.3	Constr.
Veneer & plywood	0.9	Manufg.	Maintenance of nonfarm buildings nec	1.3	Constr.
Paperboard containers & boxes	0.8	Manufg.	Dormitories & other group housing	1.2	Constr.
Banking	0.8	Fin/R.E.	Resid. & other health facility construction	1.2	Constr.
Equipment rental & leasing services	0.8	Services	Residential high-rise apartments	1.1	Constr.
Real estate	0.7	Fin/R.E.	Construction of nonfarm buildings nec	1.0	Constr.
Maintenance of nonfarm buildings nec	0.6	Constr.	Highway & street construction	1.0	Constr.
Hand & edge tools, nec	0.6	Manufg.	Warehouses	0.9	Constr.
Communications, except radio & TV	0.6	Util.	Sewer system facility construction	0.8	Constr.
Eating & drinking places	0.6	Trade	Local transit facility construction	0.5	Constr.
Water transportation	0.5	Util.	Maintenance of electric utility facilities	0.5	Constr.
Royalties	0.4	Fin/R.E.	Telephone & telegraph facility construction	0.5	Constr.
Hand saws & saw blades	0.3	Manufg.	Exports	0.5	Foreign
Wood products, nec	0.3	Manufg.	Federal Government purchases, national defense	0.4	Fed Govt
Gas production & distribution (utilities)	0.3	Util.	Farm service facilities	0.3	Constr.
Security & commodity brokers	0.3	Fin/R.E.	Maintenance of highways & streets	0.3	Constr.
Automotive rental & leasing, without drivers	0.3	Services	Maintenance of local transit facilities	0.2	Constr.
Automotive repair shops & services	0.3	Services	Garage & service station construction	0.1	Constr.

Continued on next page.

INPUTS AND OUTPUTS FOR STRUCTURAL WOOD MEMBERS, NEC - Continued

Economic Sector or Industry Providing Inputs	%	Sector	Economic Sector or Industry Buying Outputs	%	Sector
Business services nec	0.3	Services	Maintenance of military facilities	0.1	Constr.
Woodworking machinery	0.2	Manufg.	Maintenance of sewer facilities	0.1	Constr.
Sanitary services, steam supply, irrigation	0.2	Util.	Water supply facility construction	0.1	Constr.
Accounting, auditing & bookkeeping	0.2	Services			
Legal services	0.2	Services			
Management & consulting services & labs	0.2	Services			
Imports	0.2	Foreign			
Abrasive products	0.1	Manufg.			
Lighting fixtures & equipment	0.1	Manufg.			
Lubricating oils & greases	0.1	Manufg.			
Machinery, except electrical, nec	0.1	Manufg.			
Plastics materials & resins	0.1	Manufg.			
Structural wood members, nec	0.1	Manufg.			
Insurance carriers	0.1	Fin/R.E.			
Business/professional associations	0.1	Services			
U.S. Postal Service	0.1	Gov't			

Source: Benchmark Input-Output Accounts for the U.S. Economy, 1982, U.S. Department of Commerce, Washington, D.C., July 1991. Data, as reported in the source, are organized by the 1977 SIC structure in use in 1982 but have been matched, as closely as is possible, to the 1987 SIC structure used in this book.

OCCUPATIONS EMPLOYED BY SIC 243 - MILLWORK, PLYWOOD, AND STRUCTURAL MEMBERS

Occupation	% of Total 1994	Change to 2005	Occupation	% of Total 1994	Change to 2005
Assemblers, fabricators, & hand workers nec	13.6	-2.8	Truck drivers light & heavy	2.0	0.2
Cabinetmakers & bench carpenters	10.9	-2.8	Inspectors, testers, & graders, precision	1.7	-2.8
Woodworking machine workers	6.1	-22.2	Coating, painting, & spraying machine workers	1.7	-22.2
Machine feeders & offbearers	5.1	-12.5	Carpenters	1.7	-22.2
Head sawyers & sawing machine workers	4.6	-22.2	Cement & gluing machine operators	1.7	6.9
Helpers, laborers, & material movers nec	4.4	-2.8	Precision woodworkers nec	1.4	94.4
Wood machinists	4.3	-12.5	Secretaries, ex legal & medical	1.4	-11.5
Blue collar worker supervisors	3.9	-8.3	Industrial machinery mechanics	1.3	6.9
General managers & top executives	2.8	-7.8	Bookkeeping, accounting, & auditing clerks	1.2	-27.1
Freight, stock, & material movers, hand	2.7	-22.2	General office clerks	1.2	-17.1
Sales & related workers nec	2.3	-2.8	Industrial production managers	1.2	-2.8
Industrial truck & tractor operators	2.3	-2.8	Drafters	1.0	-24.3

Source: Industry-Occupation Matrix, Bureau of Labor Statistics. These data relate to one or more 3-digit SIC industry groups rather than to a single 4-digit SIC. The change reported for each occupation to the year 2005 is a percent of growth or decline as estimated by the Bureau of Labor Statistics. The abbreviation nec stands for 'not elsewhere classified'.

LOCATION BY STATE AND REGIONAL CONCENTRATION

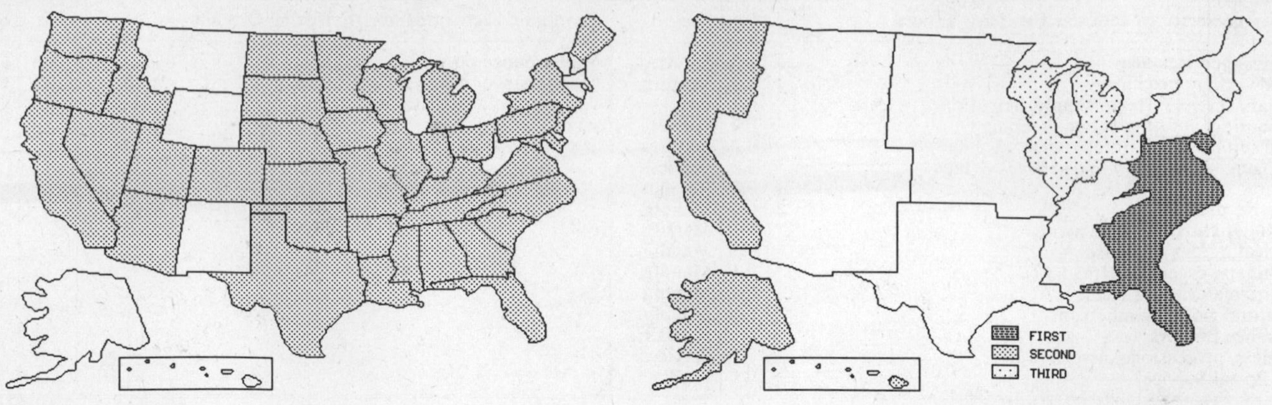

INDUSTRY DATA BY STATE

State	Establish-ments	Shipments			Employment				Cost as % of Shipments	Investment per Employee ($)
		Total ($ mil)	% of U.S.	Per Establ.	Total Number	% of U.S.	Per Establ.	Wages ($/hour)		
Oregon	40	344.0	13.7	8.6	1,500	6.2	38	12.54	71.1	2,467
Florida	102	204.3	8.2	2.0	3,200	13.2	31	7.20	56.5	969
California	92	197.5	7.9	2.1	2,200	9.1	24	9.39	56.9	864
Ohio	30	120.6	4.8	4.0	1,000	4.1	33	7.81	56.6	-
Minnesota	18	109.6	4.4	6.1	900	3.7	50	10.50	48.4	6,444
Michigan	24	95.6	3.8	4.0	1,000	4.1	42	10.36	56.1	2,000
Washington	42	90.3	3.6	2.2	1,000	4.1	24	9.50	50.7	2,000
Texas	29	78.4	3.1	2.7	600	2.5	21	7.11	71.0	-
Maryland	11	66.2	2.6	6.0	400	1.6	36	9.17	79.9	-
Arizona	25	62.1	2.5	2.5	700	2.9	28	8.00	58.3	1,286
Illinois	18	61.0	2.4	3.4	600	2.5	33	10.90	48.9	2,333
Wisconsin	19	59.4	2.4	3.1	600	2.5	32	8.56	52.0	1,833
Pennsylvania	24	58.8	2.3	2.5	600	2.5	25	9.75	56.3	-
Idaho	14	52.0	2.1	3.7	400	1.6	29	9.83	65.2	2,000
New York	19	48.2	1.9	2.5	400	1.6	21	8.14	49.4	1,000
Colorado	22	38.0	1.5	1.7	500	2.1	23	9.50	52.4	-
Arkansas	24	32.6	1.3	1.4	400	1.6	17	8.20	53.1	1,500
Nevada	12	32.0	1.3	2.7	400	1.6	33	7.14	50.6	1,000
Alabama	19	31.0	1.2	1.6	500	2.1	26	9.40	62.9	400
Iowa	10	27.7	1.1	2.8	200	0.8	20	7.00	63.5	2,000
Kentucky	18	27.4	1.1	1.5	400	1.6	22	7.60	50.7	1,250
Tennessee	18	24.7	1.0	1.4	300	1.2	17	6.60	59.5	-
South Carolina	11	21.0	0.8	1.9	300	1.2	27	7.25	56.2	667
Kansas	7	17.3	0.7	2.5	200	0.8	29	6.33	31.8	-
South Dakota	8	12.1	0.5	1.5	100	0.4	13	8.50	61.2	-
North Dakota	7	12.1	0.5	1.7	100	0.4	14	7.50	57.9	-
Mississippi	6	10.3	0.4	1.7	100	0.4	17	7.00	55.3	1,000
Georgia	35	(D)	-	-	750 *	3.1	21	-	-	2,933
North Carolina	34	(D)	-	-	1,750 *	7.2	51	-	-	-
Missouri	25	(D)	-	-	375 *	1.5	15	-	-	-
Virginia	22	(D)	-	-	750 *	3.1	34	-	-	-
Indiana	18	(D)	-	-	750 *	3.1	42	-	-	-
Oklahoma	13	(D)	-	-	175 *	0.7	13	-	-	-
Utah	12	(D)	-	-	375 *	1.5	31	-	-	533
New Jersey	9	(D)	-	-	375 *	1.5	42	-	-	-
Nebraska	5	(D)	-	-	375 *	1.5	75	-	-	-
Louisiana	3	(D)	-	-	175 *	0.7	58	-	-	-
Maine	2	(D)	-	-	175 *	0.7	88	-	-	-

Source: 1992 *Economic Census*. The states are in descending order of shipments or establishments (if shipment data are missing for the majority). The symbol (D) appears when data are withheld to prevent disclosure of competitive information. States marked with (D) are sorted by number of establishments. A dash (-) indicates that the data element cannot be calculated; * indicates the midpoint of a range.

2441 - NAILED WOOD BOXES AND SHOOK

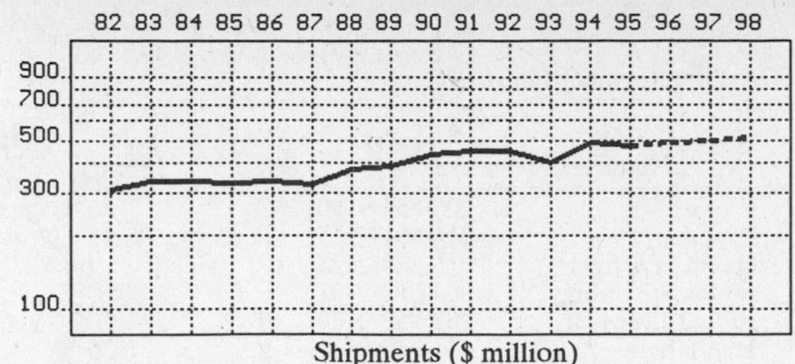

Shipments ($ million)

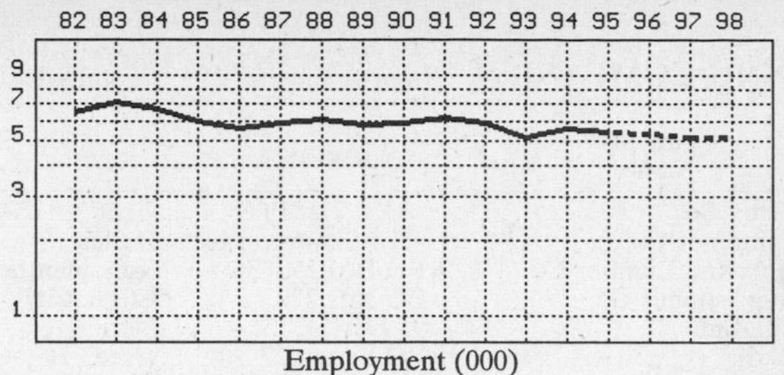

Employment (000)

GENERAL STATISTICS

Year	Companies	Establishments: Total	Establishments: with 20 or more employees	Employment: Total (000)	Production Workers (000)	Production Hours (Mil)	Compensation: Payroll ($ mil)	Compensation: Wages ($/hr)	Production: Cost of Materials	Production: Value Added by Manufacture	Production: Value of Shipments	Capital Invest.
1982	332	338	90	6.4	5.3	9.4	76.5	5.96	166.7	137.9	306.8	6.9
1983		322	90	7.1	6.0	10.6	84.6	5.48	184.8	153.9	334.8	12.5
1984		306	90	6.7	5.8	10.0	80.9	5.93	187.4	147.6	336.8	14.0
1985		289	89	6.0	4.8	8.9	79.1	6.29	179.6	146.8	329.7	4.8
1986		282	93	5.6	4.5	8.2	77.3	6.67	181.8	157.1	338.5	6.5
1987	304	308	95	5.9	4.9	9.0	84.7	6.38	182.0	146.5	325.0	5.5
1988		287	91	6.1	4.9	9.9	88.4	5.98	193.6	183.0	378.0	8.4
1989		283	91	5.8	4.9	10.0	94.5	6.45	229.0	168.5	392.9	9.0
1990		273	86	5.9	4.8	9.4	97.5	7.20	240.6	191.6	431.3	4.6
1991		276	81	6.2	5.0	10.2	100.0	7.18	245.9	199.3	443.7	4.7
1992	291	304	87	5.9	4.7	9.1	101.2	7.37	255.8	189.3	444.0	7.8
1993		299	80	5.2	4.1	8.1	98.0	7.81	240.4	155.6	399.4	4.9
1994		277P	83P	5.6	4.5	8.9	106.8	8.15	274.5	209.0	481.6	3.9
1995		274P	83P	5.4P	4.3P	8.9P	107.0P	8.00P	269.2P	205.0P	472.3P	4.1P
1996		271P	82P	5.3P	4.2P	8.8P	109.4P	8.19P	276.7P	210.7P	485.5P	3.6P
1997		267P	81P	5.2P	4.1P	8.8P	111.9P	8.38P	284.2P	216.4P	498.7P	3.2P
1998		264P	80P	5.1P	4.0P	8.7P	114.3P	8.57P	291.7P	222.1P	511.8P	2.7P

Sources: 1982, 1987, 1992 *Economic Census*; *Annual Survey of Manufactures*, 83-86, 88-91, 93-94. Establishment counts for non-Census years are from *County Business Patterns*; establishment values for 83-84 are extrapolations. 'P's show projections by the editors. Industries reclassified in 87 will not have data for prior years.

INDICES OF CHANGE

Year	Companies	Establishments: Total	Establishments: with 20 or more employees	Employment: Total (000)	Production Workers (000)	Production Hours (Mil)	Compensation: Payroll ($ mil)	Compensation: Wages ($/hr)	Production: Cost of Materials	Production: Value Added by Manufacture	Production: Value of Shipments	Capital Invest.
1982	114	111	103	108	113	103	76	81	65	73	69	88
1983		106	103	120	128	116	84	74	72	81	75	160
1984		101	103	114	123	110	80	80	73	78	76	179
1985		95	102	102	102	98	78	85	70	78	74	62
1986		93	107	95	96	90	76	91	71	83	76	83
1987	104	101	109	100	104	99	84	87	71	77	73	71
1988		94	105	103	104	109	87	81	76	97	85	108
1989		93	105	98	104	110	93	88	90	89	88	115
1990		90	99	100	102	103	96	98	94	101	97	59
1991		91	93	105	106	112	99	97	96	105	100	60
1992	100	100	100	100	100	100	100	100	100	100	100	100
1993		98	92	88	87	89	97	106	94	82	90	63
1994		91P	96P	95	96	98	106	111	107	110	108	50
1995		90P	95P	92P	91P	98P	106P	109P	105P	108P	106P	52P
1996		89P	94P	90P	89P	97P	108P	111P	108P	111P	109P	46P
1997		88P	93P	88P	87P	96P	111P	114P	111P	114P	112P	41P
1998		87P	92P	87P	85P	96P	113P	116P	114P	117P	115P	35P

Sources: Same as General Statistics. Values reflect change from the base year, 1992. Values above 100 mean greater than 92, values below 100 mean less than 92, and a value of 100 in the 82-91 or 93-98 period means same as 92. 'P's mark projections by the editors.

SELECTED RATIOS

For 1994	Avg. of All Manufact.	Analyzed Industry	Index
Employees per Establishment	49	20	41
Payroll per Establishment	1,500,273	385,813	26
Payroll per Employee	30,620	19,071	62
Production Workers per Establishment	34	16	47
Wages per Establishment	853,319	262,031	31
Wages per Production Worker	24,861	16,119	65
Hours per Production Worker	2,056	1,978	96
Wages per Hour	12.09	8.15	67
Value Added per Establishment	4,602,255	755,008	16
Value Added per Employee	93,930	37,321	40

For 1994	Avg. of All Manufact.	Analyzed Industry	Index
Value Added per Production Worker	134,084	46,444	35
Cost per Establishment	5,045,178	991,626	20
Cost per Employee	102,970	49,018	48
Cost per Production Worker	146,988	61,000	41
Shipments per Establishment	9,576,895	1,739,770	18
Shipments per Employee	195,460	86,000	44
Shipments per Production Worker	279,017	107,022	38
Investment per Establishment	321,011	14,089	4
Investment per Employee	6,552	696	11
Investment per Production Worker	9,352	867	9

Sources: Same as General Statistics. The 'Average of All Manufacturing' column represents the average of all manufacturing industries reported for the most recent complete year available. The Index shows the relationship between the Average and the Analyzed Industry. For example, 100 means that they are equal; 500 that the Analyzed Industry is five times the average; 50 means that the Analyzed Industry is half the national average. The abbreviation 'na' is used to show that data are 'not available'.

LEADING COMPANIES

Number shown: **21** Total sales ($ mil): **101** Total employment (000): **0.9**

Company Name	Address				CEO Name	Phone	Co. Type	Sales ($ mil)	Empl. (000)
Seattle Box Co	23400 71st Pl S	Kent	WA	98032	FJ Nist	206-854-9700	R	20	0.1
Lane Container Co	4301 Simonton Rd	Dallas	TX	75244	RJ Lane	214-991-5263	R	10	<0.1
Florin Box and Lumber Co	PO Box 292338	Sacramento	CA	95829	David W Engel	916-383-2675	R	9*	0.1
Spaulding Lumber Co	PO Box 220	Chase City	VA	23924	James Spaulding	804-372-2101	R	8	<0.1
Pack-Rite Inc	95 Day St	Newington	CT	06111	Richard Mercer	203-953-0120	R	6	<0.1
Tosca Ltd	PO Box 8127	Green Bay	WI	54308	Jere Dhein	414-465-8534	R	6	<0.1
Allied Container Corp	435 E Hedding St	San Jose	CA	95112	Evelynn Johnson	408-293-3628	R	5	<0.1
Ward-Davis Inc	PO Box 1894	Texarkana	TX	75504	Joe Knight	903-793-5559	R	5	<0.1
Abbot and Abbot Box Corp	37-11 10th St	Long Island Ct	NY	11101	Stuart A Gleiber	718-392-2600	R	4	<0.1
Ruszel Woodworks Inc	2980 Bayshore Rd	Benicia	CA	94510	Jack Ruszel	707-745-6979	R	4	<0.1
Burch Manufacturing Company	Box 17	Summit Point	WV	25446	Tom Burch	304-725-9215	R	3	<0.1
Day Lumber Corp	PO Box 9	Westfield	MA	01086	Deborah S Simpson	413-568-3511	R	3	<0.1
Delaware Valley	2651 E State St	Trenton	NJ	08619	CC Gould	609-890-8202	R	3	<0.1
Ockerlund Industries Inc	PO Box 97	Forest Park	IL	60130	Wayne Troyer	708-771-7707	R	3	<0.1
Pomona Box Co	301 W Imperial	La Habra	CA	90631	DE Votaw	714-871-0932	R	3	<0.1
Stearnswood Inc	PO Box 50	Hutchinson	MN	55350	Roger R Stearns	612-587-2137	R	3	<0.1
Bea Maurer Inc	14522 Lee Rd	Chantilly	VA	22021	Bea Maurer	703-631-6363	R	2	<0.1
Cedar Box Company Inc	2012 Cedar Av	Minneapolis	MN	55404	Charles Skjeveland	612-332-4287	R	1	<0.1
Ockerlund Wood Products	PO Box 97	Forest Park	IL	60130	W Troyer	708-771-7707	D	1	<0.1
Pine Point Wood Products Inc	PO Box 1900	Dayton	MN	55327	James R Talbot	612-428-4301	R	1*	<0.1
A and M Wood Products Inc	9900 S Madison St	Hinsdale	IL	60521	M Marwitz	708-323-2555	R	1	<0.1

Source: *Ward's Business Directory of U.S. Private and Public Companies*, Volumes 1 and 2, 1996. The company type code used is as follows: P - Public, R - Private, S - Subsidiary, D - Division, J - Joint Venture, A - Affiliate, G - Group. Sales are in millions of dollars, employees are in thousands. An asterisk (*) indicates an estimated sales volume. The symbol < stands for 'less than'. Company names and addresses are truncated, in some cases, to fit into the available space.

MATERIALS CONSUMED

Material		Quantity	Delivered Cost ($ million)
Materials, ingredients, containers, and supplies		(X)	220.2
Logs, bolts, and unsliced flitches	mil ft log scale	18.4**	3.9
Hardwood rough lumber		(X)	7.3
Softwood rough lumber	mil bd ft	(S)	11.8
Hardwood dressed lumber	mil bd ft	(S)	9.0
Softwood dressed lumber	mil bd ft	205.4*	64.7
Veneer and plywood		(X)	28.6
All other materials and components, parts, containers, and supplies		(X)	42.7
Materials, ingredients, containers, and supplies, nsk		(X)	52.3

Source: 1992 *Economic Census*. Explanation of symbols used: (D): Withheld to avoid disclosure of competitive data; na: Not available; (S): Withheld because statistical norms were not met; (X): Not applicable; (Z): Less than half the unit shown; nec: Not elsewhere classified; nsk: Not specified by kind; - : zero; * : 10-19 percent estimated; ** : 20-29 percent estimated.

PRODUCT SHARE DETAILS

Product or Product Class	% Share
Nailed wood boxes and shook	100.00
Nailed or lock-corner wooden boxes	30.06
Nailed or lock-corner wood boxes made from lumber	51.97
Nailed or lock-corner wood boxes made from veneer and plywood, and combination wood and fiber boxes, including wood and part wooden cigar boxes	44.15
Nailed or lock-corner wooden boxes, nsk	3.87
Wooden box and crate shook	54.50
Wood box and crate shook made from lumber, for fruits and vegetables	26.54
Wood box and crate shook made from lumber, for industrial and other uses	49.72
Wood box and crate shook made from veneer and plywood for fruits, vegetables, meat, industrial, and other uses	17.73
Wooden box and crate shook, nsk	6.01
Nailed wood boxes and shook, nsk	15.44

Source: 1992 *Economic Census*. The values shown are percent of total shipments in an industry. Values of indented subcategories are summed in the main heading. The symbol (D) appears when data are withheld to prevent disclosure of competitive information. The abbreviation nsk stands for 'not specified by kind' and nec for 'not elsewhere classified'.

INPUTS AND OUTPUTS FOR WOOD CONTAINERS

Economic Sector or Industry Providing Inputs	%	Sector	Economic Sector or Industry Buying Outputs	%	Sector
Sawmills & planning mills, general	31.5	Manufg.	Fruits	55.0	Agric.
Wholesale trade	12.8	Trade	Wholesale trade	12.8	Trade
Veneer & plywood	8.0	Manufg.	Distilled liquor, except brandy	11.8	Manufg.
Paperboard containers & boxes	6.7	Manufg.	Glass & glass products, except containers	9.7	Manufg.
Logging camps & logging contractors	5.2	Manufg.	Refrigeration & heating equipment	2.3	Manufg.
Special product sawmills, nec	5.2	Manufg.	Vegetables	1.9	Agric.
Motor freight transportation & warehousing	2.7	Util.	Wood containers	1.9	Manufg.
Railroads & related services	2.5	Util.	Exports	1.1	Foreign
Wood containers	2.3	Manufg.	Service industry machines, nec	1.0	Manufg.
Imports	2.1	Foreign	Federal Government purchases, national defense	0.7	Fed Govt
Electric services (utilities)	1.7	Util.	Musical instruments	0.4	Manufg.
Advertising	1.7	Services	Poultry & eggs	0.3	Agric.
Security & commodity brokers	1.4	Fin/R.E.	Commercial laundry equipment	0.3	Manufg.
Petroleum refining	1.2	Manufg.	Household refrigerators & freezers	0.3	Manufg.
Eating & drinking places	1.1	Trade	Federal Government purchases, nondefense	0.3	Fed Govt
Detective & protective services	1.1	Services	Tree nuts	0.2	Agric.
Maintenance of nonfarm buildings nec	0.9	Constr.	Automatic merchandising machines	0.2	Manufg.
Banking	0.9	Fin/R.E.			
Plastics materials & resins	0.8	Manufg.			
Wood pallets & skids	0.7	Manufg.			
Gas production & distribution (utilities)	0.6	Util.			
Hand saws & saw blades	0.5	Manufg.			
Communications, except radio & TV	0.5	Util.			
Job training & related services	0.5	Services			
Management & consulting services & labs	0.5	Services			
Sanitary services, steam supply, irrigation	0.4	Util.			
Water transportation	0.4	Util.			
Real estate	0.4	Fin/R.E.			
Equipment rental & leasing services	0.4	Services			
U.S. Postal Service	0.4	Gov't			
Abrasive products	0.3	Manufg.			
Machinery, except electrical, nec	0.3	Manufg.			
Woodworking machinery	0.3	Manufg.			
Automotive repair shops & services	0.3	Services			
Engineering, architectural, & surveying services	0.3	Services			
Legal services	0.3	Services			
Steel wire & related products	0.2	Manufg.			
Air transportation	0.2	Util.			
Accounting, auditing & bookkeeping	0.2	Services			
Automotive rental & leasing, without drivers	0.2	Services			
Electrical repair shops	0.2	Services			
Laundry, dry cleaning, shoe repair	0.2	Services			
Lubricating oils & greases	0.1	Manufg.			
Manifold business forms	0.1	Manufg.			
Special dies & tools & machine tool accessories	0.1	Manufg.			
Credit agencies other than banks	0.1	Fin/R.E.			
Insurance carriers	0.1	Fin/R.E.			
Royalties	0.1	Fin/R.E.			
Business/professional associations	0.1	Services			

Source: Benchmark Input-Output Accounts for the U.S. Economy, 1982, U.S. Department of Commerce, Washington, D.C., July 1991. Data, as reported in the source, are organized by the 1977 SIC structure in use in 1982 but have been matched, as closely as is possible, to the 1987 SIC structure used in this book.

OCCUPATIONS EMPLOYED BY SIC 244 - WOOD CONTAINERS AND MISCELLANEOUS WOOD PRODUCTS

Occupation	% of Total 1994	Change to 2005	Occupation	% of Total 1994	Change to 2005
Assemblers, fabricators, & hand workers nec	15.4	10.0	Industrial machinery mechanics	2.3	21.0
Woodworking machine workers	9.3	-12.0	Sales & related workers nec	1.8	10.0
Head sawyers & sawing machine workers	7.6	-45.0	Inspectors, testers, & graders, precision	1.7	10.0
Machine feeders & offbearers	5.1	-1.0	Industrial production managers	1.6	10.0
Blue collar worker supervisors	4.5	0.7	Secretaries, ex legal & medical	1.5	0.2
Helpers, laborers, & material movers nec	4.2	10.0	Bookkeeping, accounting, & auditing clerks	1.5	-17.5
Wood machinists	4.1	10.0	General office clerks	1.5	-6.2
Industrial truck & tractor operators	4.0	10.0	Traffic, shipping, & receiving clerks	1.3	5.9
Freight, stock, & material movers, hand	3.8	-12.0	Carpenters	1.1	-12.0
General managers & top executives	3.7	4.4	Cabinetmakers & bench carpenters	1.1	-1.0
Truck drivers light & heavy	3.0	13.4	Extruding & forming machine workers	1.0	21.0
Coating, painting, & spraying machine workers	2.5	10.0			

Source: *Industry-Occupation Matrix*, Bureau of Labor Statistics. These data relate to one or more 3-digit SIC industry groups rather than to a single 4-digit SIC. The change reported for each occupation to the year 2005 is a percent of growth or decline as estimated by the Bureau of Labor Statistics. The abbreviation nec stands for 'not elsewhere classified'.

LOCATION BY STATE AND REGIONAL CONCENTRATION

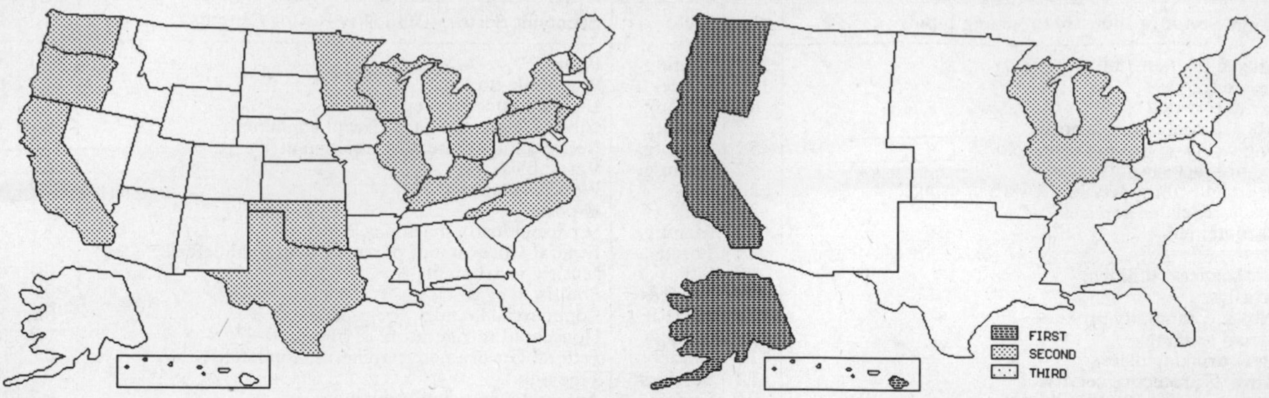

INDUSTRY DATA BY STATE

State	Establish-ments	Shipments			Employment				Cost as % of Shipments	Investment per Employee ($)
		Total ($ mil)	% of U.S.	Per Establ.	Total Number	% of U.S.	Per Establ.	Wages ($/hour)		
California	73	163.0	36.7	2.2	1,800	30.5	25	7.27	64.8	1,833
Washington	10	41.8	9.4	4.2	300	5.1	30	8.60	72.7	3,333
Ohio	18	23.7	5.3	1.3	300	5.1	17	6.80	54.0	-
Michigan	13	20.9	4.7	1.6	400	6.8	31	6.17	45.5	1,000
Texas	16	18.8	4.2	1.2	400	6.8	25	6.50	54.8	500
North Carolina	13	16.9	3.8	1.3	200	3.4	15	5.80	56.2	1,000
Oregon	5	13.6	3.1	2.7	300	5.1	60	8.00	64.7	-
Oklahoma	6	10.3	2.3	1.7	100	1.7	17	8.00	48.5	2,000
Pennsylvania	9	8.6	1.9	1.0	100	1.7	11	7.00	51.2	2,000
New Hampshire	4	6.2	1.4	1.5	100	1.7	25	6.50	67.7	-
New York	22	(D)	-	-	375 *	6.4	17	-	-	-
New Jersey	12	(D)	-	-	175 *	3.0	15	-	-	-
Wisconsin	9	(D)	-	-	175 *	3.0	19	-	-	571
Illinois	8	(D)	-	-	175 *	3.0	22	-	-	-
Kentucky	4	(D)	-	-	175 *	3.0	44	-	-	-
Minnesota	3	(D)	-	-	175 *	3.0	58	-	-	-

Source: 1992 *Economic Census*. The states are in descending order of shipments or establishments (if shipment data are missing for the majority). The symbol (D) appears when data are withheld to prevent disclosure of competitive information. States marked with (D) are sorted by number of establishments. A dash (-) indicates that the data element cannot be calculated; * indicates the midpoint of a range.

2448 - WOOD PALLETS AND SKIDS

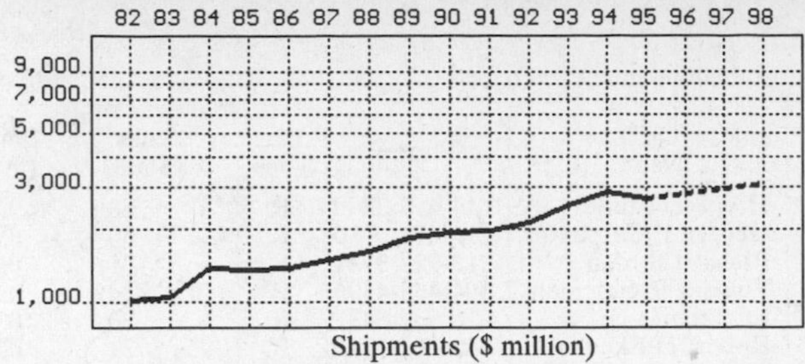

Shipments ($ million)

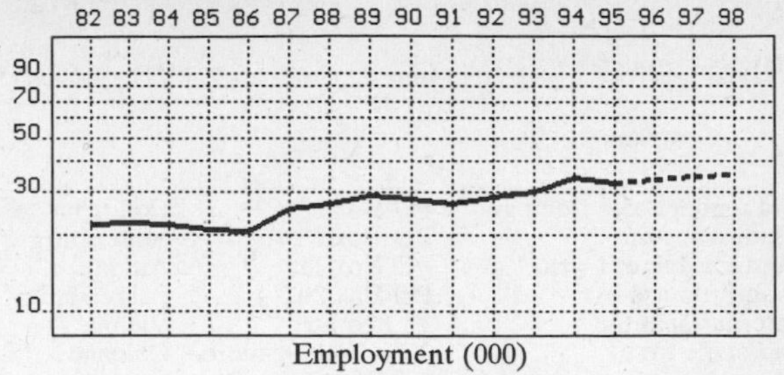

Employment (000)

GENERAL STATISTICS

Year	Companies	Establishments		Employment			Compensation		Production ($ million)			
		Total	with 20 or more employees	Total (000)	Production Workers (000)	Production Hours (Mil)	Payroll ($ mil)	Wages ($/hr)	Cost of Materials	Value Added by Manufacture	Value of Shipments	Capital Invest.
1982	1,642	1,677	362	22.1	18.4	32.7	230.4	5.05	589.1	420.5	1,012.3	29.4
1983		1,642	381	22.5	19.3	34.4	237.0	4.95	627.1	412.4	1,051.8	34.3
1984		1,607	400	22.3	18.8	34.3	268.2	5.85	804.2	602.7	1,400.9	34.5
1985		1,571	418	21.2	17.4	33.2	301.8	6.30	771.9	598.3	1,363.9	39.7
1986		1,542	412	20.7	16.3	27.9	284.6	6.86	803.5	588.8	1,394.1	28.3
1987	1,678	1,701	415	25.7	21.7	38.0	328.0	6.26	880.2	616.8	1,496.1	43.8
1988		1,669	470	26.9	22.8	42.0	362.7	6.00	1,026.7	625.5	1,644.1	38.1
1989		1,634	471	29.0	24.5	44.1	394.6	6.37	1,080.8	767.5	1,843.7	49.2
1990		1,699	454	28.3	24.0	45.5	416.6	6.53	1,155.1	802.0	1,948.6	62.3
1991		1,756	445	27.1	22.8	43.1	413.4	6.86	1,173.2	813.0	1,987.3	48.8
1992	1,883	1,912	457	28.7	23.4	44.8	449.4	6.94	1,183.8	961.4	2,143.3	52.8
1993		1,920	486	30.1	25.1	49.0	492.0	6.99	1,373.7	1,115.7	2,480.9	50.7
1994		1,854P	494P	34.4	28.7	55.9	569.4	7.18	1,536.9	1,341.4	2,865.9	72.5
1995		1,879P	504P	32.8P	27.3P	52.9P	546.0P	7.41P	1,440.3P	1,257.1P	2,685.7P	64.7P
1996		1,903P	513P	33.7P	28.1P	54.7P	571.8P	7.57P	1,512.7P	1,320.2P	2,820.7P	67.6P
1997		1,928P	523P	34.7P	28.9P	56.5P	597.6P	7.73P	1,585.0P	1,383.4P	2,955.7P	70.4P
1998		1,952P	533P	35.6P	29.7P	58.2P	623.4P	7.88P	1,657.4P	1,446.6P	3,090.6P	73.2P

Sources: 1982, 1987, 1992 *Economic Census*; *Annual Survey of Manufactures*, 83-86, 88-91, 93-94. Establishment counts for non-Census years are from *County Business Patterns*; establishment values for 83-84 are extrapolations. 'P's show projections by the editors. Industries reclassified in 87 will not have data for prior years.

INDICES OF CHANGE

Year	Companies	Establishments		Employment			Compensation		Production ($ million)			
		Total	with 20 or more employees	Total (000)	Production Workers (000)	Production Hours (Mil)	Payroll ($ mil)	Wages ($/hr)	Cost of Materials	Value Added by Manufacture	Value of Shipments	Capital Invest.
1982	87	88	79	77	79	73	51	73	50	44	47	56
1983		86	83	78	82	77	53	71	53	43	49	65
1984		84	88	78	80	77	60	84	68	63	65	65
1985		82	91	74	74	74	67	91	65	62	64	75
1986		81	90	72	70	62	63	99	68	61	65	54
1987	89	89	91	90	93	85	73	90	74	64	70	83
1988		87	103	94	97	94	81	86	87	65	77	72
1989		85	103	101	105	98	88	92	91	80	86	93
1990		89	99	99	103	102	93	94	98	83	91	118
1991		92	97	94	97	96	92	99	99	85	93	92
1992	100	100	100	100	100	100	100	100	100	100	100	100
1993		100	106	105	107	109	109	101	116	116	116	96
1994		97P	108P	120	123	125	127	103	130	140	134	137
1995		98P	110P	114P	117P	118P	121P	107P	122P	131P	125P	123P
1996		100P	112P	117P	120P	122P	127P	109P	128P	137P	132P	128P
1997		101P	114P	121P	123P	126P	133P	111P	134P	144P	138P	133P
1998		102P	117P	124P	127P	130P	139P	114P	140P	150P	144P	139P

Sources: Same as General Statistics. Values reflect change from the base year, 1992. Values above 100 mean greater than 92, values below 100 mean less than 92, and a value of 100 in the 82-91 or 93-98 period means same as 92. 'P's mark projections by the editors.

SELECTED RATIOS

For 1994	Avg. of All Manufact.	Analyzed Industry	Index
Employees per Establishment	49	19	38
Payroll per Establishment	1,500,273	307,130	20
Payroll per Employee	30,620	16,552	54
Production Workers per Establishment	34	15	45
Wages per Establishment	853,319	216,491	25
Wages per Production Worker	24,861	13,985	56
Hours per Production Worker	2,056	1,948	95
Wages per Hour	12.09	7.18	59
Value Added per Establishment	4,602,255	723,540	16
Value Added per Employee	93,930	38,994	42

For 1994	Avg. of All Manufact.	Analyzed Industry	Index
Value Added per Production Worker	134,084	46,739	35
Cost per Establishment	5,045,178	828,992	16
Cost per Employee	102,970	44,677	43
Cost per Production Worker	146,988	53,551	36
Shipments per Establishment	9,576,895	1,545,843	16
Shipments per Employee	195,460	83,311	43
Shipments per Production Worker	279,017	99,857	36
Investment per Establishment	321,011	39,106	12
Investment per Employee	6,552	2,108	32
Investment per Production Worker	9,352	2,526	27

Sources: Same as General Statistics. The 'Average of All Manufacturing' column represents the average of all manufacturing industries reported for the most recent complete year available. The Index shows the relationship between the Average and the Analyzed Industry. For example, 100 means that they are equal; 500 that the Analyzed Industry is five times the average; 50 means that the Analyzed Industry is half the national average. The abbreviation 'na' is used to show that data are 'not available'.

LEADING COMPANIES Number shown: **69** Total sales ($ mil): **519** Total employment (000): **4.8**

Company Name	Address				CEO Name	Phone	Co. Type	Sales ($ mil)	Empl. (000)
Morgan Lumber Sales Company	PO Box 20369	Columbus	OH	43220	H W Reinstetle	614-457-3390	R	50	<0.1
Semac Industries Inc	PO Box 289	Millersburg	OH	44654	George E Carpenter	216-674-6080	R	50	0.2
Woodland Container Corp	PO Box 110	Aitkin	MN	56431	Richard Jordan	218-927-3721	R	31	0.3
Gatewood Products Inc	PO Box 207	Parkersburg	WV	26102	Edward R Gateman	304-485-4406	R	30•	0.2
Litco International Inc	1 Litco Dr	Vienna	OH	44473	LF Trebilcock	216-539-5433	R	30	<0.1
Sonoma Pacific Co	2100 Embarcadero	Oakland	CA	94606	Robert D Ekedahl	510-261-1843	R	21	<0.1
Fraser Industries Inc	208 W 3rd St	Big Spring	TX	79720	Troy Fraser	915-263-1307	R	20	0.3
Yoder Lumber Company Inc	3799 Rte 70	Sugarcreek	OH	44681	E Yoder	216-893-3131	R	15	0.1
Edwards Wood Products Inc	PO Box 219	Marshville	NC	28103	Carroll Edwards	704-624-5098	R	12	0.3
Nelson Co	2116 Sparrows Pt	Baltimore	MD	21219	AP Caltrider	410-477-3000	R	12	<0.1
United Wholesale Lumber	8009 W Doe Av	Visalia	CA	93291	Tom Thayer	209-651-2037	R	12•	<0.1
Girard Wood Products Inc	PO Box 830	Puyallup	WA	98371	J Vipond	206-845-0505	R	11	<0.1
George Bassi Distributing Co	PO Box 1169	Watsonville	CA	95077	George Bassi Sr	408-724-1028	R	10	<0.1
Abell Industries	PO Box 339	Lawrenceville	VA	23868	JC Lucy III	804-848-2164	R	9	0.2
Hunter Woodworks Inc	PO Box 4937	Carson	CA	90749	William M Hunter	310-835-5671	R	9	0.1
Keene	10100 East Rd	Potter Valley	CA	95469	Stuart Lerner	707-743-1154	D	9•	<0.1
Treen Box and Pallet Corp	PO Box 368	Bensalem	PA	19020	George Geiges	215-639-5100	R	9	<0.1
Anderson Forest Products Inc	PO Box 520	Tompkinsville	KY	42167	Bill J Anderson	502-487-6778	R	8•	<0.1
Precision Wood Products Inc	PO Box 529	Vancouver	WA	98666	Marley B Peterson	360-694-8322	R	8	<0.1
Edwards Wood Products Inc	3130 Alpine Rd	Portola Valley	CA	94028	Thomas F Turner	408-971-6571	R	7	<0.1
Nepa Pallet and Container	PO Box 399	Snohomish	WA	98291	Denton Sherry	206-568-3185	R	7	0.1
Packing Material Co	27280 Haggerty	Farmington Hls	MI	48331	JB Foster	810-489-7000	R	7	<0.1
Williamsburg Millwork	PO Box 427	Bowling Green	VA	22427	MR Piland III	804-994-2151	R	7	<0.1
Brunswick Box Company Inc	PO Box 7	Lawrenceville	VA	23868	John D Clary	804-848-2222	R	6	<0.1
Mallery Lumber Corp	Star Rte	Emporium	PA	15834	G Mee	814-486-3764	R	6	<0.1
Sheffield Lumber and Pallet Inc	165 Turkey Foot Rd	Mocksville	NC	27028	AG Reavis	704-492-5565	R	6•	<0.1
Bennett Box and Pallet Company	PO Box 249	Ahoskie	NC	27910	BB Perry	919-332-5026	R	6	0.1
Hinchcliff Lumber Co	PO Box 386	Parsons	WV	26287	Ned H Phillips	304-478-2500	R	6	<0.1
Mt Valley Farms & Lumber	1240 Nawakwa Rd	Biglerville	PA	17307	Henry L Taylor	717-677-6166	R	6	<0.1
Cutter Lumber Products Inc	10 Rickerbacker Cir	Livermore	CA	94550	Tony Palma	510-444-5959	R	5	<0.1
Konz Wood Products Inc	PO Box 1717	Appleton	WI	54913	LA Konz	414-734-7770	R	5	<0.1
Sterling Lumber and Supply	PO Box 88	Goodwater	AL	35072	Charles F Thomas	205-839-6371	R	5	<0.1
WNC Pallet	PO Box 38	Candler	NC	28715	Thomas L Thrash	704-667-5426	R	5	0.1
NE Michigan Rehab	PO Box 645	Alpena	MI	49707	Howard P French	517-356-6141	R	5	0.2
Ball Brothers Forest Products	PO Box 548	Koshkonong	MO	65692	Fred Ball Jr	417-867-5664	R	5	<0.1
Daniel Lumber Co	PO Box 340	La Grange	GA	30240	Joesph E Daniel Jr	706-884-5686	R	4	<0.1
Savanna Pallet Inc	PO Box 308	McGregor	MN	55760	Lawrence S Raushel	218-768-2077	R	4	<0.1
Smalley Package Company Inc	PO Box 231	Berryville	VA	22611	R W Smalley Jr	703-955-2550	R	4	0.1
Spring Wood Products Inc	4267 Austin Rd	Geneva	OH	44041	Jacob A Castrilla	216-466-1135	R	4	<0.1
Thunder Pallet Inc	W 137 N 9418 Hwy	Menomonee Fls	WI	53051	Clarence F Pelkey	414-251-0300	R	4	<0.1
Delisa Pallet Corp	91-97 Blanchard St	Newark	NJ	07105	JF Delisa	201-344-8600	R	4	<0.1
Champlin Co	236 Hamilton St	Hartford	CT	06106	Rolland S Champlin	203-951-9217	R	3	<0.1
Howatt Company Inc	12540 Admiralty	Everett	WA	98204	M L Makemson	206-743-4682	R	3	<0.1
L & H Wood Manufacturing Co	PO Box 441	Farmington	MI	48332	Robert T Lindbert	313-474-9000	R	3	<0.1
Pallet Masters Inc	655 E Florence Av	Los Angeles	CA	90001	Steve H Anderson	213-758-6559	R	3•	<0.1
Viking Pallet Corp	PO Box 167	Osseo	MN	55369	DW Colson	612-425-6707	R	3•	<0.1
Mid-Valley Rehabilitation Inc	16700 Hwy 99 W	Amity	OR	97101	David Wiegan	503-835-2971	R	3	0.1
Patterson Industries Inc	216 W Broad St	Bethlehem	PA	18018	Dushane Patterson	610-865-0288	R	3	<0.1
New River Valley Workshop	103 Duncan Ln	Radford	VA	24141	BJ Huff	703-639-9027	R	2	0.1
Booth Inc	671 E Kittle Rd	Mio	MI	48647	C Booth	517-848-5973	R	2	<0.1
J and J Enterprise of Louisiana	1229 Hwy 190 W	Port Allen	LA	70767	Jeff Simpson	504-344-1507	R	2	<0.1
N Central Sheltered	127 Av M	Fort Dodge	IA	50501	Q Weidner	515-576-2126	R	2	0.1
Precision Pallets Co	721 Parkwood Av	Romeoville	IL	60441	Robert S Wojcik	815-886-1061	R	2	<0.1
Troy Wood Products Inc	PO Box 865	Monroe	MI	48161	A M Hubbard	313-242-1848	R	2	<0.1
Findley Industries Inc	7841 N US Hwy 31	Seymour	IN	47274	N Findley-Russell	812-522-1501	R	2	<0.1
Millersville Box Co	931 Millersville Av	Howards Grove	WI	53083	Lester Sprenger	414-565-3331	R	2	<0.1
Southern Pallet and Crate	PO Box 4123	Macon	GA	31208	WP Simmons Jr	912-742-1431	R	2	<0.1
Tranter Industries Inc	PO Box 220	Franklin	IN	46131	Robert R Tranter	317-736-5134	R	2	<0.1
J and J Pallet	PO Box 583	New Albany	IN	47151	Chris Jones	812-944-8670	R	1	<0.1
B and S Pallet Corp	550 W Root	Chicago	IL	60609	Brad Kendall	312-373-2700	R	1	<0.1
Cardinal Wood Products Inc	Rte 2	Marble Hill	MO	63764	Bill Ward	314-238-2145	R	1•	<0.1
Daniel Boone Lumber Industries	1375 Clearfork N	Morehead	KY	40351	GS Lincoln	606-784-7586	R	1	<0.1
Harbor Pallet Co	PO Box 4443	Anaheim	CA	92803	RW Gilroy	714-533-4940	R	1•	<0.1
Klinger's Skid and Pallet	1845 Millcreek Rd	York	PA	17404	RA Klinger	717-292-2342	R	1	<0.1
Manufacturers Assistance Group	PO Box 632	Poplar Bluff	MO	63901	David Peters	314-785-1624	R	1•	<0.1
Acme Pallet Company Inc	45-10 Court Sq	Long Island Ct	NY	11101	Nick Vassiliou	718-784-8020	R	0	<0.1
Coxco Inc	PO Box 793	Bessemer	AL	35023	Renee Cox	205-428-6223	R	0•	<0.1
Comprehensive Industries	PO Box 98	Elma	IA	50628	Donna Fangman	515-393-2126	D	0	<0.1
Wilson Pallet Co	504 Albert Av	Wilson	NC	27893	Ray Baker	919-237-4992	R	0	<0.1

Source: *Ward's Business Directory of U.S. Private and Public Companies*, Volumes 1 and 2, 1996. The company type code used is as follows: P - Public, R - Private, S - Subsidiary, D - Division, J - Joint Venture, A - Affiliate, G - Group. Sales are in millions of dollars, employees are in thousands. An asterisk (•) indicates an estimated sales volume. The symbol < stands for 'less than'. Company names and addresses are truncated, in some cases, to fit into the available space.

MATERIALS CONSUMED

Material		Quantity	Delivered Cost ($ million)
Materials, ingredients, containers, and supplies		(X)	1,080.6
Logs, bolts, and unsliced flitches	mil ft log scale	(S)	71.8
Hardwood rough lumber		(X)	277.5
Softwood rough lumber	mil bd ft	(S)	66.4
Hardwood dressed lumber	mil bd ft	275.1**	60.2
Softwood dressed lumber	mil bd ft	531.1*	103.6
Veneer and plywood		(X)	13.0
All other materials and components, parts, containers, and supplies		(X)	90.3
Materials, ingredients, containers, and supplies, nsk		(X)	397.8

Source: 1992 *Economic Census*. Explanation of symbols used: (D): Withheld to avoid disclosure of competitive data; na: Not available; (S): Withheld because statistical norms were not met; (X): Not applicable; (Z): Less than half the unit shown; nec: Not elsewhere classified; nsk: Not specified by kind; - : zero; * : 10-19 percent estimated; ** : 20-29 percent estimated.

PRODUCT SHARE DETAILS

Product or Product Class	% Share	Product or Product Class	% Share
Wood pallets and skids	100.00	Wood skids	5.24
Wood pallets, flat	71.74	Pallets and skids, wood and metal combination	4.58
Wood pallet containers	3.64		

Source: 1992 *Economic Census*. The values shown are percent of total shipments in an industry. Values of indented subcategories are summed in the main heading. The symbol (D) appears when data are withheld to prevent disclosure of competitive information. The abbreviation nsk stands for 'not specified by kind' and nec for 'not elsewhere classified'.

INPUTS AND OUTPUTS FOR WOOD PALLETS & SKIDS

Economic Sector or Industry Providing Inputs	%	Sector	Economic Sector or Industry Buying Outputs	%	Sector
Sawmills & planning mills, general	43.3	Manufg.	Wholesale trade	71.0	Trade
Wholesale trade	11.2	Trade	Refrigeration & heating equipment	2.2	Manufg.
Logging camps & logging contractors	10.2	Manufg.	Aircraft & missile equipment, nec	1.7	Manufg.
Motor freight transportation & warehousing	3.4	Util.	Motor vehicle parts & accessories	1.6	Manufg.
Electric services (utilities)	3.0	Util.	Freight forwarders	1.6	Util.
Veneer & plywood	2.9	Manufg.	Canned fruits & vegetables	1.3	Manufg.
Railroads & related services	2.5	Util.	Motor freight transportation & warehousing	1.2	Util.
Screw machine and related products	2.3	Manufg.	Metal cans	1.1	Manufg.
Advertising	2.0	Services	Paperboard mills	1.1	Manufg.
Adhesives & sealants	1.9	Manufg.	Paper mills, except building paper	0.8	Manufg.
Petroleum refining	1.9	Manufg.	Exports	0.8	Foreign
Eating & drinking places	1.3	Trade	Fabricated metal products, nec	0.7	Manufg.
Banking	1.2	Fin/R.E.	Glass containers	0.7	Manufg.
Maintenance of nonfarm buildings nec	1.1	Constr.	Hardware, nec	0.7	Manufg.
Equipment rental & leasing services	0.8	Services	Iron & steel foundries	0.7	Manufg.
Fabricated metal products, nec	0.7	Manufg.	Retail trade, except eating & drinking	0.7	Trade
Real estate	0.7	Fin/R.E.	Motors & generators	0.6	Manufg.
Steel wire & related products	0.6	Manufg.	Nonferrous wire drawing & insulating	0.6	Manufg.
Communications, except radio & TV	0.6	Util.	Paper coating & glazing	0.6	Manufg.
Management & consulting services & labs	0.6	Services	Agricultural chemicals, nec	0.5	Manufg.
Wood pallets & skids	0.5	Manufg.	Automotive stampings	0.5	Manufg.
Water transportation	0.5	Util.	Clay refractories	0.5	Manufg.
Job training & related services	0.5	Services	Cement, hydraulic	0.4	Manufg.
Abrasive products	0.4	Manufg.	Metal partitions & fixtures	0.4	Manufg.
Paperboard containers & boxes	0.4	Manufg.	Wood containers	0.4	Manufg.
Gas production & distribution (utilities)	0.4	Util.	Aluminum rolling & drawing	0.3	Manufg.
Machinery, except electrical, nec	0.3	Manufg.	Blast furnaces & steel mills	0.3	Manufg.
Woodworking machinery	0.3	Manufg.	Electrical industrial apparatus, nec	0.3	Manufg.
Air transportation	0.3	Util.	Metal stampings, nec	0.3	Manufg.
Accounting, auditing & bookkeeping	0.3	Services	Miscellaneous plastics products	0.3	Manufg.
Business/professional associations	0.3	Services	Nonclay refractories	0.3	Manufg.
Legal services	0.3	Services	Switchgear & switchboard apparatus	0.3	Manufg.
Lubricating oils & greases	0.2	Manufg.	Wood pallets & skids	0.3	Manufg.
Wood products, nec	0.2	Manufg.	Cold finishing of steel shapes	0.2	Manufg.
Automotive rental & leasing, without drivers	0.2	Services	Electrometallurgical products	0.2	Manufg.
Automotive repair shops & services	0.2	Services	Farm machinery & equipment	0.2	Manufg.
Engineering, architectural, & surveying services	0.2	Services	Food products machinery	0.2	Manufg.
U.S. Postal Service	0.2	Gov't	Heating equipment, except electric	0.2	Manufg.
Manifold business forms	0.1	Manufg.	Household laundry equipment	0.2	Manufg.
Miscellaneous fabricated wire products	0.1	Manufg.	Miscellaneous metal work	0.2	Manufg.
Plastics materials & resins	0.1	Manufg.	Periodicals	0.2	Manufg.
Special dies & tools & machine tool accessories	0.1	Manufg.	Power transmission equipment	0.2	Manufg.
Sanitary services, steam supply, irrigation	0.1	Util.	Radio & TV receiving sets	0.2	Manufg.
Credit agencies other than banks	0.1	Fin/R.E.	Special dies & tools & machine tool accessories	0.2	Manufg.
Insurance carriers	0.1	Fin/R.E.	Wood products, nec	0.2	Manufg.
Royalties	0.1	Fin/R.E.	Federal Government purchases, national defense	0.2	Fed Govt
Computer & data processing services	0.1	Services	S/L Govt. purch., elem. & secondary education	0.2	S/L Govt
Laundry, dry cleaning, shoe repair	0.1	Services	Building paper & board mills	0.1	Manufg.
			Construction machinery & equipment	0.1	Manufg.
			Miscellaneous fabricated wire products	0.1	Manufg.
			Radio & TV communication equipment	0.1	Manufg.
			Steel wire & related products	0.1	Manufg.
			Telephone & telegraph apparatus	0.1	Manufg.
			Welding apparatus, electric	0.1	Manufg.

Source: Benchmark Input-Output Accounts for the U.S. Economy, 1982, U.S. Department of Commerce, Washington, D.C., July 1991. Data, as reported in the source, are organized by the 1977 SIC structure in use in 1982 but have been matched, as closely as is possible, to the 1987 SIC structure used in this book.

OCCUPATIONS EMPLOYED BY SIC 244 - WOOD CONTAINERS AND MISCELLANEOUS WOOD PRODUCTS

Occupation	% of Total 1994	Change to 2005	Occupation	% of Total 1994	Change to 2005
Assemblers, fabricators, & hand workers nec	15.4	10.0	Industrial machinery mechanics	2.3	21.0
Woodworking machine workers	9.3	-12.0	Sales & related workers nec	1.8	10.0
Head sawyers & sawing machine workers	7.6	-45.0	Inspectors, testers, & graders, precision	1.7	10.0
Machine feeders & offbearers	5.1	-1.0	Industrial production managers	1.6	10.0
Blue collar worker supervisors	4.5	0.7	Secretaries, ex legal & medical	1.5	0.2
Helpers, laborers, & material movers nec	4.2	10.0	Bookkeeping, accounting, & auditing clerks	1.5	-17.5
Wood machinists	4.1	10.0	General office clerks	1.5	-6.2
Industrial truck & tractor operators	4.0	10.0	Traffic, shipping, & receiving clerks	1.3	5.9
Freight, stock, & material movers, hand	3.8	-12.0	Carpenters	1.1	-12.0
General managers & top executives	3.7	4.4	Cabinetmakers & bench carpenters	1.1	-1.0
Truck drivers light & heavy	3.0	13.4	Extruding & forming machine workers	1.0	21.0
Coating, painting, & spraying machine workers	2.5	10.0			

Source: Industry-Occupation Matrix, Bureau of Labor Statistics. These data relate to one or more 3-digit SIC industry groups rather than to a single 4-digit SIC. The change reported for each occupation to the year 2005 is a percent of growth or decline as estimated by the Bureau of Labor Statistics. The abbreviation nec stands for 'not elsewhere classified'.

LOCATION BY STATE AND REGIONAL CONCENTRATION

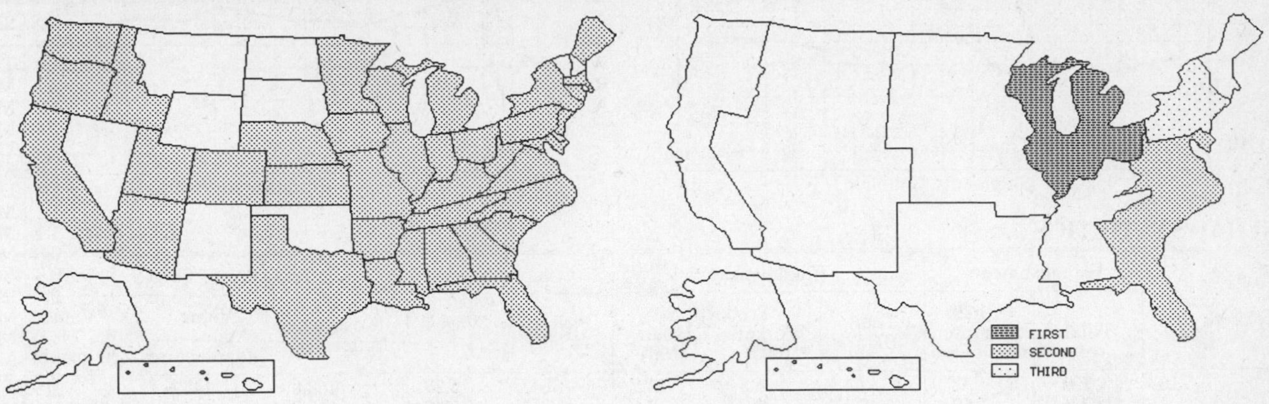

INDUSTRY DATA BY STATE

State	Establish-ments	Shipments			Employment				Cost as % of Shipments	Investment per Employee ($)
		Total ($ mil)	% of U.S.	Per Establ.	Total Number	% of U.S.	Per Establ.	Wages ($/hour)		
California	103	204.4	9.5	2.0	2,200	7.7	21	7.54	57.6	1,636
Pennsylvania	154	156.3	7.3	1.0	1,800	6.3	12	7.57	52.7	2,111
Michigan	113	149.7	7.0	1.3	1,500	5.2	13	7.39	56.5	1,667
Ohio	142	133.9	6.2	0.9	1,900	6.6	13	6.40	53.4	1,684
Texas	79	125.4	5.9	1.6	1,800	6.3	23	6.20	58.3	1,944
Wisconsin	96	117.8	5.5	1.2	1,700	5.9	18	7.33	54.8	1,235
North Carolina	70	101.9	4.8	1.5	1,500	5.2	21	6.48	54.3	2,067
Indiana	105	89.8	4.2	0.9	1,500	5.2	14	6.86	52.2	1,400
Missouri	78	82.3	3.8	1.1	1,100	3.8	14	6.50	54.7	2,182
Georgia	63	80.7	3.8	1.3	1,100	3.8	17	7.12	52.5	1,727
Illinois	75	77.9	3.6	1.0	1,100	3.8	15	7.29	53.5	1,818
Arkansas	44	71.2	3.3	1.6	900	3.1	20	6.47	60.8	-
Virginia	47	65.8	3.1	1.4	900	3.1	19	7.47	55.0	3,333
Kentucky	63	64.0	3.0	1.0	900	3.1	14	5.80	56.3	1,778
New York	57	60.6	2.8	1.1	700	2.4	12	8.08	51.2	3,429
Tennessee	90	60.3	2.8	0.7	900	3.1	10	6.21	56.4	1,778
Iowa	37	47.8	2.2	1.3	600	2.1	16	7.22	57.1	2,333
Alabama	44	41.4	1.9	0.9	600	2.1	14	6.09	51.7	2,000
Florida	31	38.4	1.8	1.2	500	1.7	16	7.57	60.4	1,800
Washington	23	37.2	1.7	1.6	600	2.1	26	7.88	65.3	1,333
South Carolina	33	26.8	1.3	0.8	500	1.7	15	6.00	54.5	600
Minnesota	38	23.6	1.1	0.6	300	1.0	8	6.80	58.9	1,667
New Jersey	32	23.0	1.1	0.7	300	1.0	9	8.00	51.3	667
Oregon	15	21.0	1.0	1.4	200	0.7	13	6.50	61.9	6,000
Connecticut	14	14.8	0.7	1.1	200	0.7	14	8.67	52.0	-
Massachusetts	28	14.5	0.7	0.5	200	0.7	7	7.67	53.1	1,500
Arizona	17	14.1	0.7	0.8	200	0.7	12	5.67	58.9	1,500
Colorado	13	8.2	0.4	0.6	100	0.3	8	6.00	46.3	2,000
Mississippi	38	(D)	-	-	750 *	2.6	20	-	-	2,000
Louisiana	26	(D)	-	-	375 *	1.3	14	-	-	-
Nebraska	15	(D)	-	-	175 *	0.6	12	-	-	-
Kansas	14	(D)	-	-	175 *	0.6	13	-	-	-
West Virginia	14	(D)	-	-	375 *	1.3	27	-	-	533
Maryland	12	(D)	-	-	175 *	0.6	15	-	-	-
Utah	12	(D)	-	-	175 *	0.6	15	-	-	2,286
Idaho	10	(D)	-	-	175 *	0.6	18	-	-	-
Maine	10	(D)	-	-	175 *	0.6	18	-	-	-

Source: 1992 *Economic Census*. The states are in descending order of shipments or establishments (if shipment data are missing for the majority). The symbol (D) appears when data are withheld to prevent disclosure of competitive information. States marked with (D) are sorted by number of establishments. A dash (-) indicates that the data element cannot be calculated; * indicates the midpoint of a range.

2449 - WOOD CONTAINERS, NEC

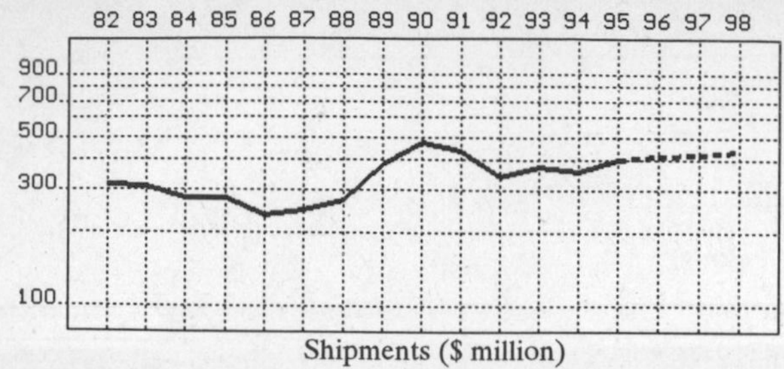

Shipments ($ million)

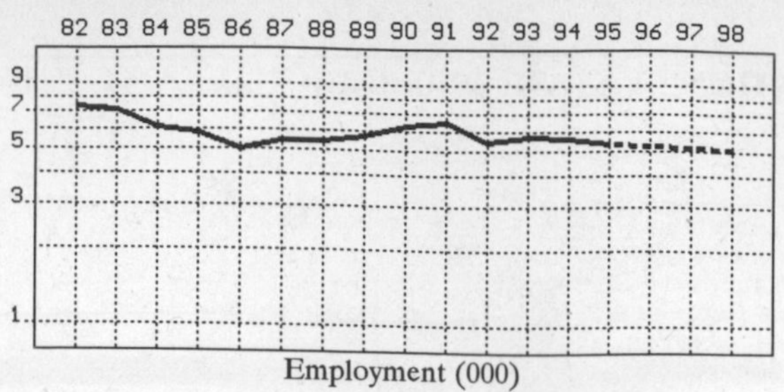

Employment (000)

GENERAL STATISTICS

Year	Com-panies	Establishments		Employment			Compensation		Production ($ million)			
		Total	with 20 or more employees	Total (000)	Production Workers (000)	Production Hours (Mil)	Payroll ($ mil)	Wages ($/hr)	Cost of Materials	Value Added by Manufacture	Value of Shipments	Capital Invest.
1982	216	235	72	7.4	6.5	12.5	84.0	5.27	168.8	144.6	315.8	3.7
1983		226	69	7.1	6.2	12.6	85.7	5.40	169.8	131.4	309.2	4.0
1984		217	66	6.1	5.3	10.0	68.6	5.29	147.6	121.3	275.1	2.8
1985		209	64	5.8	5.1	9.6	69.4	5.63	183.6	96.0	279.3	2.1
1986		207	63	5.0	4.4	8.2	58.3	5.63	151.0	84.0	235.8	3.0
1987	198	208	51	5.4	4.7	8.6	70.4	5.86	136.2	111.6	248.3	2.8
1988		200	60	5.4	4.7	8.9	73.6	5.94	148.8	130.1	272.3	1.3
1989		194	54	5.7	5.7	10.6	110.5	7.42	225.3	158.2	380.5	4.8
1990		225	65	6.3	5.9	10.7	121.5	7.79	277.6	195.6	470.2	5.2
1991		258	62	6.5	5.4	9.9	120.3	8.43	251.0	190.9	433.1	5.3
1992	217	225	50	5.4	4.4	8.6	89.4	6.81	178.0	164.2	343.3	6.1
1993		236	57	5.7	4.7	9.2	95.8	7.20	200.7	173.7	375.2	4.9
1994		227P	53P	5.6	4.6	9.2	91.5	7.12	201.4	158.0	360.1	3.3
1995		228P	51P	5.4P	4.5P	8.6P	106.8P	8.00P	226.5P	177.7P	404.9P	5.0P
1996		230P	50P	5.3P	4.4P	8.4P	109.5P	8.22P	232.4P	182.3P	415.5P	5.2P
1997		231P	49P	5.2P	4.3P	8.2P	112.2P	8.45P	238.3P	187.0P	426.1P	5.3P
1998		232P	47P	5.1P	4.2P	8.0P	115.0P	8.67P	244.3P	191.6P	436.7P	5.5P

Sources: 1982, 1987, 1992 *Economic Census*; *Annual Survey of Manufactures*, 83-86, 88-91, 93-94. Establishment counts for non-Census years are from *County Business Patterns*; establishment values for 83-84 are extrapolations. 'P's show projections by the editors. Industries reclassified in 87 will not have data for prior years.

INDICES OF CHANGE

Year	Com-panies	Establishments		Employment			Compensation		Production ($ million)			
		Total	with 20 or more employees	Total (000)	Production Workers (000)	Production Hours (Mil)	Payroll ($ mil)	Wages ($/hr)	Cost of Materials	Value Added by Manufacture	Value of Shipments	Capital Invest.
1982	100	104	144	137	148	145	94	77	95	88	92	61
1983		100	138	131	141	147	96	79	95	80	90	66
1984		96	132	113	120	116	77	78	83	74	80	46
1985		93	128	107	116	112	78	83	103	58	81	34
1986		92	126	93	100	95	65	83	85	51	69	49
1987	91	92	102	100	107	100	79	86	77	68	72	46
1988		89	120	100	107	103	82	87	84	79	79	21
1989		86	108	106	130	123	124	109	127	96	111	79
1990		100	130	117	134	124	136	114	156	119	137	85
1991		115	124	120	123	115	135	124	141	116	126	87
1992	100	100	100	100	100	100	100	100	100	100	100	100
1993		105	114	106	107	107	107	106	113	106	109	80
1994		101P	105P	104	105	107	102	105	113	96	105	54
1995		102P	102P	99P	103P	100P	119P	117P	127P	108P	118P	82P
1996		102P	100P	98P	101P	97P	122P	121P	131P	111P	121P	85P
1997		103P	97P	96P	98P	95P	126P	124P	134P	114P	124P	88P
1998		103P	94P	94P	96P	93P	129P	127P	137P	117P	127P	90P

Sources: Same as General Statistics. Values reflect change from the base year, 1992. Values above 100 mean greater than 92, values below 100 mean less than 92, and a value of 100 in the 82-91 or 93-98 period means same as 92. 'P's mark projections by the editors.

SELECTED RATIOS

For 1994	Avg. of All Manufact.	Analyzed Industry	Index	For 1994	Avg. of All Manufact.	Analyzed Industry	Index
Employees per Establishment	49	25	50	Value Added per Production Worker	134,084	34,348	26
Payroll per Establishment	1,500,273	402,519	27	Cost per Establishment	5,045,178	885,983	18
Payroll per Employee	30,620	16,339	53	Cost per Employee	102,970	35,964	35
Production Workers per Establishment	34	20	59	Cost per Production Worker	146,988	43,783	30
Wages per Establishment	853,319	288,160	34	Shipments per Establishment	9,576,895	1,584,123	17
Wages per Production Worker	24,861	14,240	57	Shipments per Employee	195,460	64,304	33
Hours per Production Worker	2,056	2,000	97	Shipments per Production Worker	279,017	78,283	28
Wages per Hour	12.09	7.12	59	Investment per Establishment	321,011	14,517	5
Value Added per Establishment	4,602,255	695,061	15	Investment per Employee	6,552	589	9
Value Added per Employee	93,930	28,214	30	Investment per Production Worker	9,352	717	8

Sources: Same as General Statistics. The 'Average of All Manufacturing' column represents the average of all manufacturing industries reported for the most recent complete year available. The Index shows the relationship between the Average and the Analyzed Industry. For example, 100 means that they are equal; 500 that the Analyzed Industry is five times the average; 50 means that the Analyzed Industry is half the national average. The abbreviation 'na' is used to show that data are 'not available'.

LEADING COMPANIES

Number shown: **41** Total sales ($ mil): **368** Total employment (000): **4.1**

Company Name	Address				CEO Name	Phone	Co. Type	Sales ($ mil)	Empl. (000)
Calpine Containers Inc	PO Box 5050	Walnut Creek	CA	94596	Ted Rathbun	510-798-3010	R	95	0.3
Elberta Crate and Box Co	PO Box 795	Bainbridge	GA	31717	DR Simmons	912-246-2266	R	35	0.4
Napa Valley Box Company Inc	11995 El Cam Real	San Diego	CA	92130	Jeff White	619-259-3000	R	25	0.2
Growers Container Cooperative	PO Box 491355	Leesburg	FL	34749	William Talley Jr	904-787-3579	R	24*	0.3
Mid-States Container Corp	PO Box 339	De Graff	OH	43318	DR Lamb	513-585-5361	R	19*	0.2
Kay Home Products	2077 Parkwood Av	Columbus	OH	43219	Felix Tarorick	614-267-1296	R	15*	0.1
Marvil Package Co	PO Box 210	Wilmington	NC	28402	W Albert Corbett	919-763-9991	R	15	0.3
Georgia Crate and Basket	PO Box 46	Thomasville	GA	31799	B Jones IV	912-226-2541	R	13*	0.3
Great Amer Wirebound Box Co	PO Box 179	Fernwood	MS	39635	A Boyd Carter	601-684-7311	R	11*	0.3
Peacock Crate Factory Inc	1511 S Jackson St	Jacksonville	TX	75766	J Hoke Peacock	903-586-5321	R	8*	<0.1
Wisconsin Box Co	PO Box 718	Wausau	WI	54402	William J Davis	715-842-2248	R	8	0.1
McIntosh Box and Pallet Co	PO Box 127	East Syracuse	NY	13057	Thomas J Ryan	315-446-9350	R	8	0.1
Lionel Industries	2623 Monaco Ter	P Bch Gardens	FL	33410	Jani B Whitney	407-624-9093	R	6	<0.1
Martin Brothers	PO Box 87	Martin	TN	38237	D Bebione	901-587-3171	R	6*	<0.1
Yakima Pallet and Bin Inc	51 N Mitchell Dr	Yakima	WA	98908	Clif Cope	509-966-4610	R	6	<0.1
Carter Manufacturing Company	PO Box 250	Lake City	SC	29560	James W Carter	803-394-8123	R	5*	<0.1
Corbett Package Co	PO Box 210	Wilmington	NC	28402	Wilbur A Corbett	910-763-9991	R	5	0.2
Franklin Crates Inc	PO Box 279	Micanopy	FL	32667	Ben Franklin III	904-466-3141	R	5	<0.1
Industrial and Wholesale Lumber	4401 N 25th Av	Schiller Park	IL	60176	Russel W Kathrein	708-678-0480	R	5	<0.1
Little Rock Crate and Basket Co	1623 E 14th St	Little Rock	AR	72202	Dudley Swann	501-376-6961	R	5	0.1
MBX Packaging Specialists	PO Box 929	Wausau	WI	54401	Frank Pederson	715-845-1171	R	5	0.1
St Vincent DePaul	4867 NE Union	Portland	OR	97211	C Graham	503-281-1289	R	5*	0.2
Nashville Crate Co	PO Box 29	Nashville	AR	71852	D Swann	501-845-2885	S	4*	<0.1
O'Malley Wood Products Inc	PO Box 207	Gardners	PA	17324	Patrick P O'Malley	717-432-2961	R	4	<0.1
Texas Basket Co	PO Box 1110	Jacksonville	TX	75766	Martin Swanson	903-586-8014	R	4	0.1
Rownd and Son Inc	PO Box 1126	Dillon	SC	29536	HL Rownd	803-774-8264	R	3	<0.1
TE Brown Inc	14361 Chapman Rd	San Leandro	CA	94578	William B Brown	510-357-4840	R	3	<0.1
Stewart's Forest Products	803 Transfer Rd	St Paul	MN	55114	George Stewart	612-645-8266	R	3	<0.1
American Pallet Inc	PO Box 1413	Oakdale	CA	95361	Ray Fauria	209-847-6122	R	2	<0.1
Cases Inc	PO Box 3248	Arlington	WA	98223	D Lorang	206-435-6688	R	2	<0.1
HA Davidson Box Co	PO Box 27066	Detroit	MI	48227	JH Davidson	313-834-6770	D	2	<0.1
Texas Crating Inc	5021 Statesman Dr	Irving	TX	75063	Sam Kurgkendall	214-929-2255	S	2*	<0.1
Tipton Box Company Inc	PO Box 49	Caruthersville	MO	63830	Ronald E Stutzman	314-757-6588	R	2	<0.1
Walling Crate Co	PO Box 329	Leesburg	FL	32749	Robert Walling	904-787-5211	R	2	<0.1
Custom Industries Inc	2 S Grove St	Bradford	MA	01835	L Frank Sirois	508-374-6331	R	2	<0.1
Ash-Lin Inc	4197 US Hwy 52	New Palestine	IN	46163	James R Lyddan	317-861-1540	R	1	<0.1
DGGR Packaging	1450 S Manhattan	Fullerton	CA	92631	Joseph Di Benedetto	714-635-0055	R	1	<0.1
Erickson Wood Products	PO Box 61	Belmont	CA	94002	Arthur W Erickson	415-591-5785	R	1	<0.1
Smith Kramer Inc	1622 Westport Rd	Kansas City	MO	64111	David Smith	816-756-3777	R	1	<0.1
Wood Space Industries Inc	1399 N Miller St	Anaheim	CA	92806	David E Reed	714-996-4552	R	1*	<0.1
Bridgeport Crating Co	PO Box 479	Bridgeport	NY	13030	WO Winans	315-463-4747	R	0	<0.1

Source: *Ward's Business Directory of U.S. Private and Public Companies*, Volumes 1 and 2, 1996. The company type code used is as follows: P - Public, R - Private, S - Subsidiary, D - Division, J - Joint Venture, A - Affiliate, G - Group. Sales are in millions of dollars, employees are in thousands. An asterisk (*) indicates an estimated sales volume. The symbol < stands for 'less than'. Company names and addresses are truncated, in some cases, to fit into the available space.

MATERIALS CONSUMED

Material		Quantity	Delivered Cost ($ million)
Materials, ingredients, containers, and supplies		(X)	160.7
Logs, bolts, and unsliced flitches	mil ft log scale	(S)	14.6
Hardwood rough lumber		(X)	39.1
Softwood rough lumber	mil bd ft	(S)	1.7
Hardwood dressed lumber	mil bd ft	(S)	3.1
Softwood dressed lumber	mil bd ft	(S)	4.7
Veneer and plywood		(X)	24.3
All other materials and components, parts, containers, and supplies		(X)	33.4
Materials, ingredients, containers, and supplies, nsk		(X)	39.7

Source: 1992 *Economic Census*. Explanation of symbols used: (D): Withheld to avoid disclosure of competitive data; na: Not available; (S): Withheld because statistical norms were not met; (X): Not applicable; (Z): Less than half the unit shown; nec: Not elsewhere classified; nsk: Not specified by kind; - : zero; * : 10-19 percent estimated; ** : 20-29 percent estimated.

PRODUCT SHARE DETAILS

Product or Product Class	% Share
Wood containers, nec.	100.00
Wirebound boxes made from lumber	7.82
Wirebound boxes made from wood veneer and plywood, for fruits and vegetables	24.01
Wirebound boxes made from wood veneer and plywood, for industrial and other uses, including meat and poultry	6.53
Veneer and plywood containers, including pails, drums, tubs, fruit and vegetable baskets, hampers, etc.	9.58
Wood slack and tight cooperage (hogsheads, barrels, kegs, tubs, etc.) new and recoopered used	29.99

Source: 1992 *Economic Census*. The values shown are percent of total shipments in an industry. Values of indented subcategories are summed in the main heading. The symbol (D) appears when data are withheld to prevent disclosure of competitive information. The abbreviation nsk stands for 'not specified by kind' and nec for 'not elsewhere classified'.

INPUTS AND OUTPUTS FOR WOOD CONTAINERS

Economic Sector or Industry Providing Inputs	%	Sector	Economic Sector or Industry Buying Outputs	%	Sector
Sawmills & planning mills, general	31.5	Manufg.	Fruits	55.0	Agric.
Wholesale trade	12.8	Trade	Wholesale trade	12.8	Trade
Veneer & plywood	8.0	Manufg.	Distilled liquor, except brandy	11.8	Manufg.
Paperboard containers & boxes	6.7	Manufg.	Glass & glass products, except containers	9.7	Manufg.
Logging camps & logging contractors	5.2	Manufg.	Refrigeration & heating equipment	2.3	Manufg.
Special product sawmills, nec	5.2	Manufg.	Vegetables	1.9	Agric.
Motor freight transportation & warehousing	2.7	Util.	Wood containers	1.9	Manufg.
Railroads & related services	2.5	Util.	Exports	1.1	Foreign
Wood containers	2.3	Manufg.	Service industry machines, nec	1.0	Manufg.
Imports	2.1	Foreign	Federal Government purchases, national defense	0.7	Fed Govt
Electric services (utilities)	1.7	Util.	Musical instruments	0.4	Manufg.
Advertising	1.7	Services	Poultry & eggs	0.3	Agric.
Security & commodity brokers	1.4	Fin/R.E.	Commercial laundry equipment	0.3	Manufg.
Petroleum refining	1.2	Manufg.	Household refrigerators & freezers	0.3	Manufg.
Eating & drinking places	1.1	Trade	Federal Government purchases, nondefense	0.3	Fed Govt
Detective & protective services	1.1	Services	Tree nuts	0.2	Agric.
Maintenance of nonfarm buildings nec	0.9	Constr.	Automatic merchandising machines	0.2	Manufg.
Banking	0.9	Fin/R.E.			
Plastics materials & resins	0.8	Manufg.			
Wood pallets & skids	0.7	Manufg.			
Gas production & distribution (utilities)	0.6	Util.			
Hand saws & saw blades	0.5	Manufg.			
Communications, except radio & TV	0.5	Util.			
Job training & related services	0.5	Services			
Management & consulting services & labs	0.5	Services			
Sanitary services, steam supply, irrigation	0.4	Util.			
Water transportation	0.4	Util.			
Real estate	0.4	Fin/R.E.			
Equipment rental & leasing services	0.4	Services			
U.S. Postal Service	0.4	Gov't			
Abrasive products	0.3	Manufg.			
Machinery, except electrical, nec	0.3	Manufg.			
Woodworking machinery	0.3	Manufg.			
Automotive repair shops & services	0.3	Services			
Engineering, architectural, & surveying services	0.3	Services			
Legal services	0.3	Services			
Steel wire & related products	0.2	Manufg.			
Air transportation	0.2	Util.			
Accounting, auditing & bookkeeping	0.2	Services			
Automotive rental & leasing, without drivers	0.2	Services			
Electrical repair shops	0.2	Services			
Laundry, dry cleaning, shoe repair	0.2	Services			
Lubricating oils & greases	0.1	Manufg.			
Manifold business forms	0.1	Manufg.			
Special dies & tools & machine tool accessories	0.1	Manufg.			
Credit agencies other than banks	0.1	Fin/R.E.			
Insurance carriers	0.1	Fin/R.E.			
Royalties	0.1	Fin/R.E.			
Business/professional associations	0.1	Services			

Source: Benchmark Input-Output Accounts for the U.S. Economy, 1982, U.S. Department of Commerce, Washington, D.C., July 1991. Data, as reported in the source, are organized by the 1977 SIC structure in use in 1982 but have been matched, as closely as is possible, to the 1987 SIC structure used in this book.

OCCUPATIONS EMPLOYED BY SIC 244 - WOOD CONTAINERS AND MISCELLANEOUS WOOD PRODUCTS

Occupation	% of Total 1994	Change to 2005	Occupation	% of Total 1994	Change to 2005
Assemblers, fabricators, & hand workers nec	15.4	10.0	Industrial machinery mechanics	2.3	21.0
Woodworking machine workers	9.3	-12.0	Sales & related workers nec	1.8	10.0
Head sawyers & sawing machine workers	7.6	-45.0	Inspectors, testers, & graders, precision	1.7	10.0
Machine feeders & offbearers	5.1	-1.0	Industrial production managers	1.6	10.0
Blue collar worker supervisors	4.5	0.7	Secretaries, ex legal & medical	1.5	0.2
Helpers, laborers, & material movers nec	4.2	10.0	Bookkeeping, accounting, & auditing clerks	1.5	-17.5
Wood machinists	4.1	10.0	General office clerks	1.5	-6.2
Industrial truck & tractor operators	4.0	10.0	Traffic, shipping, & receiving clerks	1.3	5.9
Freight, stock, & material movers, hand	3.8	-12.0	Carpenters	1.1	-12.0
General managers & top executives	3.7	4.4	Cabinetmakers & bench carpenters	1.1	-1.0
Truck drivers light & heavy	3.0	13.4	Extruding & forming machine workers	1.0	21.0
Coating, painting, & spraying machine workers	2.5	10.0			

Source: Industry-Occupation Matrix, Bureau of Labor Statistics. These data relate to one or more 3-digit SIC industry groups rather than to a single 4-digit SIC. The change reported for each occupation to the year 2005 is a percent of growth or decline as estimated by the Bureau of Labor Statistics. The abbreviation nec stands for 'not elsewhere classified'.

LOCATION BY STATE AND REGIONAL CONCENTRATION

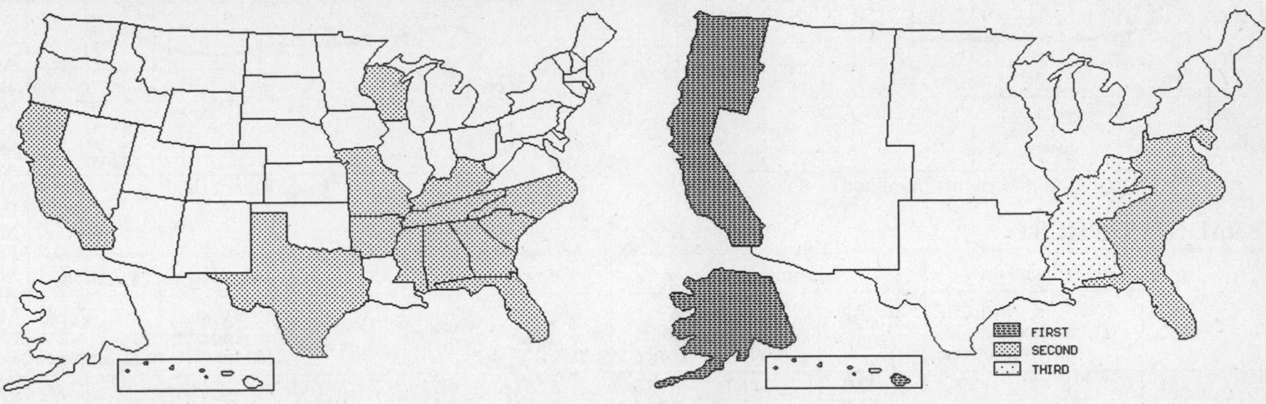

INDUSTRY DATA BY STATE

State	Establish-ments	Shipments			Employment				Cost as % of Shipments	Investment per Employee ($)
		Total ($ mil)	% of U.S.	Per Establ.	Total Number	% of U.S.	Per Establ.	Wages ($/hour)		
Georgia	6	39.1	11.4	6.5	700	13.0	117	5.75	45.8	-
California	38	38.6	11.2	1.0	500	9.3	13	7.17	60.9	1,400
North Carolina	13	24.9	7.3	1.9	600	11.1	46	5.80	56.6	833
Florida	9	18.1	5.3	2.0	300	5.6	33	6.80	68.0	-
Tennessee	5	14.5	4.2	2.9	300	5.6	60	5.67	55.2	333
Texas	14	11.9	3.5	0.9	300	5.6	21	6.00	45.4	333
Kentucky	7	(D)	-	-	375 *	6.9	54	-	-	-
Alabama	6	(D)	-	-	175 *	3.2	29	-	-	-
Missouri	6	(D)	-	-	375 *	6.9	63	-	-	-
South Carolina	6	(D)	-	-	375 *	6.9	63	-	-	-
Wisconsin	6	(D)	-	-	175 *	3.2	29	-	-	-
Arkansas	4	(D)	-	-	175 *	3.2	44	-	-	-
Mississippi	4	(D)	-	-	175 *	3.2	44	-	-	-

Source: 1992 *Economic Census*. The states are in descending order of shipments or establishments (if shipment data are missing for the majority). The symbol (D) appears when data are withheld to prevent disclosure of competitive information. States marked with (D) are sorted by number of establishments. A dash (-) indicates that the data element cannot be calculated; * indicates the midpoint of a range.

2451 - MOBILE HOMES

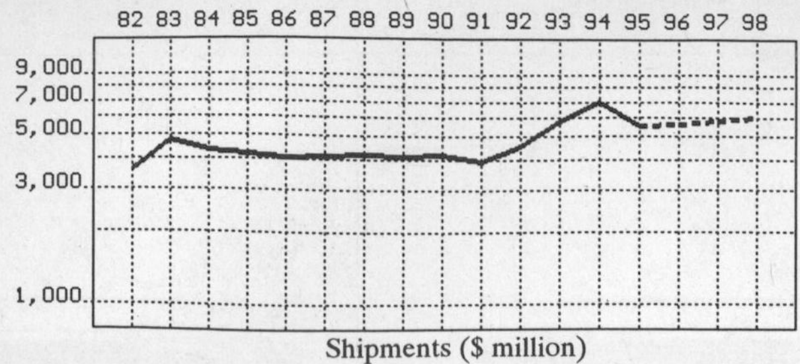

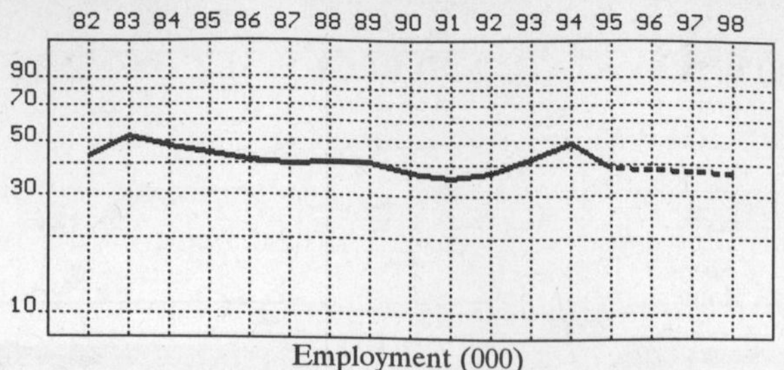

GENERAL STATISTICS

Year	Companies	Establishments		Employment			Compensation		Production ($ million)			
		Total	with 20 or more employees	Total (000)	Production Workers (000)	Production Hours (Mil)	Payroll ($ mil)	Wages ($/hr)	Cost of Materials	Value Added by Manufacture	Value of Shipments	Capital Invest.
1982	261	516	406	42.8	34.6	63.9	622.4	6.73	2,410.1	1,187.4	3,606.4	47.7
1983		491	393	51.9	42.7	82.1	820.8	7.26	3,219.1	1,582.7	4,785.2	67.6
1984		466	380	46.8	38.6	71.9	759.4	7.39	2,875.2	1,440.3	4,311.8	66.9
1985		442	366	44.3	36.2	68.7	764.0	7.68	2,783.8	1,465.5	4,236.5	68.5
1986		417	340	41.8	34.1	64.3	735.4	7.72	2,636.1	1,400.1	4,053.4	67.9
1987	207	395	315	39.9	32.4	62.0	734.2	8.19	2,639.9	1,466.0	4,102.4	42.8
1988		374	308	40.8	33.4	63.3	772.5	8.42	2,734.7	1,493.3	4,222.4	51.0
1989		341	290	40.9	32.7	62.4	768.7	8.61	2,683.4	1,437.3	4,127.8	25.4
1990		327	269	36.8	31.7	59.7	769.1	8.88	2,697.5	1,501.6	4,202.5	26.6
1991		311	250	35.1	28.7	55.0	713.7	8.91	2,555.0	1,381.8	3,930.2	16.9
1992	155	286	239	37.0	30.9	61.5	813.2	9.40	2,891.2	1,644.5	4,531.8	51.1
1993		290	235	42.4	35.7	71.4	999.4	10.07	3,715.0	2,081.9	5,786.4	78.4
1994		246P	206P	48.5	40.6	82.4	1,161.2	10.16	4,479.2	2,501.4	6,965.5	118.2
1995		224P	190P	38.8P	32.6P	65.5P	967.7P	10.31P	3,541.0P	1,977.5P	5,506.5P	62.2P
1996		203P	173P	38.3P	32.3P	65.3P	991.3P	10.58P	3,630.9P	2,027.7P	5,646.3P	63.1P
1997		181P	156P	37.8P	32.0P	65.1P	1,014.9P	10.84P	3,720.8P	2,077.9P	5,786.2P	63.9P
1998		159P	139P	37.3P	31.7P	64.9P	1,038.4P	11.11P	3,810.7P	2,128.1P	5,926.0P	64.8P

Sources: 1982, 1987, 1992 *Economic Census*; *Annual Survey of Manufactures*, 83-86, 88-91, 93-94. Establishment counts for non-Census years are from *County Business Patterns*; establishment values for 83-84 are extrapolations. 'P's show projections by the editors. Industries reclassified in 87 will not have data for prior years.

INDICES OF CHANGE

Year	Companies	Establishments		Employment			Compensation		Production ($ million)			
		Total	with 20 or more employees	Total (000)	Production Workers (000)	Production Hours (Mil)	Payroll ($ mil)	Wages ($/hr)	Cost of Materials	Value Added by Manufacture	Value of Shipments	Capital Invest.
1982	168	180	170	116	112	104	77	72	83	72	80	93
1983		172	164	140	138	133	101	77	111	96	106	132
1984		163	159	126	125	117	93	79	99	88	95	131
1985		155	153	120	117	112	94	82	96	89	93	134
1986		146	142	113	110	105	90	82	91	85	89	133
1987	134	138	132	108	105	101	90	87	91	89	91	84
1988		131	129	110	108	103	95	90	95	91	93	100
1989		119	121	111	106	101	95	92	93	87	91	50
1990		114	113	99	103	97	95	94	93	91	93	52
1991		109	105	95	93	89	88	95	88	84	87	33
1992	100	100	100	100	100	100	100	100	100	100	100	100
1993		101	98	115	116	116	123	107	128	127	128	153
1994		86P	86P	131	131	134	143	108	155	152	154	231
1995		78P	79P	105P	106P	107P	119P	110P	122P	120P	122P	122P
1996		71P	72P	104P	105P	106P	122P	113P	126P	123P	125P	123P
1997		63P	65P	102P	104P	106P	125P	115P	129P	126P	128P	125P
1998		56P	58P	101P	102P	106P	128P	118P	132P	129P	131P	127P

Sources: Same as General Statistics. Values reflect change from the base year, 1992. Values above 100 mean greater than 92, values below 100 mean less than 92, and a value of 100 in the 82-91 or 93-98 period means same as 92. 'P's mark projections by the editors.

SELECTED RATIOS

For 1994	Avg. of All Manufact.	Analyzed Industry	Index
Employees per Establishment	49	197	402
Payroll per Establishment	1,500,273	4,716,839	314
Payroll per Employee	30,620	23,942	78
Production Workers per Establishment	34	165	480
Wages per Establishment	853,319	3,400,674	399
Wages per Production Worker	24,861	20,620	83
Hours per Production Worker	2,056	2,030	99
Wages per Hour	12.09	10.16	84
Value Added per Establishment	4,602,255	10,160,783	221
Value Added per Employee	93,930	51,575	55

For 1994	Avg. of All Manufact.	Analyzed Industry	Index
Value Added per Production Worker	134,084	61,611	46
Cost per Establishment	5,045,178	18,194,682	361
Cost per Employee	102,970	92,355	90
Cost per Production Worker	146,988	110,325	75
Shipments per Establishment	9,576,895	28,294,129	295
Shipments per Employee	195,460	143,619	73
Shipments per Production Worker	279,017	171,564	61
Investment per Establishment	321,011	480,133	150
Investment per Employee	6,552	2,437	37
Investment per Production Worker	9,352	2,911	31

Sources: Same as General Statistics. The 'Average of All Manufacturing' column represents the average of all manufacturing industries reported for the most recent complete year available. The Index shows the relationship between the Average and the Analyzed Industry. For example, 100 means that they are equal; 500 that the Analyzed Industry is five times the average; 50 means that the Analyzed Industry is half the national average. The abbreviation 'na' is used to show that data are 'not available'.

LEADING COMPANIES

Number shown: **39** Total sales ($ mil): **4,557** Total employment (000): **35.6**

Company Name	Address				CEO Name	Phone	Co. Type	Sales ($ mil)	Empl. (000)
Clayton Homes Inc	PO Box 15169	Knoxville	TN	37901	James L Clayton	615-970-7200	P	628	4.0
Champion Enterprises Inc	2701 University Dr	Auburn Hills	MI	48326	Walter R Young Jr	810-340-9090	P	616	4.5
Oakwood Homes Corp	PO Box 7386	Greensboro	NC	27417	N J St George	919-855-2400	P	506	3.6
Redman Homes Inc	2550 Walnut Hill Ln	Dallas	TX	75229	Robert Linton	214-353-3600	S	443	3.6
Redman Industries Inc	2550 Walnut Hill Ln	Dallas	TX	75229	Thomas W Sturgess	214-353-3600	P	443	3.7
Schult Homes Corp	PO Box 151	Middlebury	IN	46540	Walter E Wells	219-825-5881	P	260	2.1
Fairmont Homes Inc	PO Box 27	Nappanee	IN	46550	Edward Ludwick	219-773-7941	R	200	1.8
Cavalier Homes Inc	PO Box 300	Addison	AL	35540	Jerry F Wilson	205-747-1575	P	156	1.6
Horton Homes Inc	PO Drawer 4410	Eatonton	GA	31024	Nevils D Horton Jr	706-485-8506	R	144	0.7
Southern Energy Homes Inc	PO Box 269	Addison	AL	35540	W L Batchelor	205-747-1544	P	144	1.3
Commodore Corp	PO Box 577	Goshen	IN	46526	Barry Shein	219-533-7100	R	130*	0.9
Liberty Homes Inc	PO Box 35	Goshen	IN	46526	Edward J Hussey	219-533-0431	P	125	1.0
American Homestar Corp	812 NASA	Webster	TX	77598	Finis F Teeter	713-333-5601	P	119	0.9
Belmont Homes Inc	PO Box 280	Belmont	MS	38827	Jerold Kennedy	601-454-9217	P	107	0.7
Homes of Merit Inc	PO Box 1606	Bartow	FL	33830	William Harriss	813-533-0593	R	80	0.7
Wick Building Systems Inc	PO Box 490	Mazomanie	WI	53560	JF Wick	608-795-4281	R	80	0.7
Fuqua Homes Inc	7100 S Cooper St	Arlington	TX	76017	Phillip R Daniels	817-465-3211	R	50	0.4
Jacobsen Manufacturing Inc	901 4th St N	Safety Harbor	FL	34695	WR Jacobsen	813-726-1138	R	33	0.2
Skyline Mobile Homes	1650 Swan Lake Rd	Bossier City	LA	71111	Tom K Duncan	318-746-5001	D	30	0.2
Sunshine Homes Inc	PO Box 507	Red Bay	AL	35582	John Bostick	205-356-4428	R	24	0.4
Mascot Homes Inc	PO Box 127	Gramling	SC	29348	WE Mitchell	803-472-2041	R	23	0.2
Giles Industries	PO Box 750	New Tazewell	TN	37825	James Giles	615-626-7243	R	23	0.1
R-Anell Custom Homes Inc	PO Box 428	Denver	NC	28037	DL Jones	704-483-5511	R	21	0.2
Oak Creek Homes Inc	4805 E Loop 820 S	Fort Worth	TX	76119	Laurence A Dawson	817-478-5551	R	20*	0.2
Skyline Homes Inc	PO Box 670	San Jacinto	CA	92581	William Metzger	909-654-9321	S	18*	0.1
Chariot Eagle Inc	931 NW 37th Av	Ocala	FL	32675	Robert Holliday	904-629-7007	R	17*	0.1
Crimson Industries Inc	PO Box 1086	Haleyville	AL	35565	Troy B Oliver	205-486-9222	R	16*	0.3
Contempri Homes Inc	PO Box 84	Taylor	PA	18504	Stephen Bassett	717-562-0110	P	13	0.2
Glen River Industries Inc	PO Box 810	Centralia	WA	98531	Robert McCullough	206-736-1341	R	13	0.1
Fleetwood Homes of Florida Inc	PO Box 37	Haines City	FL	33845	Phil Tanner	813-422-7591	S	12*	0.2
Mansion Homes Inc	PO Box 39	Robbins	NC	27325	Tony Castle	910-948-2141	R	11*	0.2
HOMARK Company Inc	PO Box 309	Red Lake Falls	MN	56750	Dave Johnson	218-253-2777	R	10	0.1
Oxford Homes Inc	PO Box 167	Oxford	ME	04270	Peter N Connell	207-539-4412	R	10	0.2
Elliott Manufactured Homes Inc	PO Box 209	Waurika	OK	73573	Jerry J Elliott	405-228-2339	R	9*	0.1
Custom Villa	POBox 100	Howe	IN	46746	CA Wilkinson	219-562-2341	D	8*	<0.1
Richards & Malloy Mfg	PO Box 1889	Carrollton	GA	30117	Tom Richards	404-832-6376	R	8	0.1
Homette	PO Box 2648	Ocala	FL	34478	Vaughn Houseworth	904-629-7571	D	4	0.1
McCarthy's Portable Structures	PO Box 610	Lynnfield	MA	01940	James McCarthy	617-595-7300	R	3	<0.1
Diversified Mobile Prod Corp	4240 Pine Creek Rd	Elkhart	IN	46516	Lawrence Graf	219-293-9555	R	1	<0.1

Source: *Ward's Business Directory of U.S. Private and Public Companies*, Volumes 1 and 2, 1996. The company type code used is as follows: P - Public, R - Private, S - Subsidiary, D - Division, J - Joint Venture, A - Affiliate, G - Group. Sales are in millions of dollars, employees are in thousands. An asterisk (*) indicates an estimated sales volume. The symbol < stands for 'less than'. Company names and addresses are truncated, in some cases, to fit into the available space.

MATERIALS CONSUMED

Material	Quantity	Delivered Cost ($ million)
Materials, ingredients, containers, and supplies	(X)	2,828.9
Metal mill shapes and forms, including castings (steel, aluminum, etc.)	(X)	40.9
Metal siding, including aluminum, steel	(X)	104.9
Metal plumbing fixtures, fittings, and trim (including enameled) (except forgings)	(X)	40.1
Metal doors and door units, windows and window units	(X)	112.3
Metal bolts, nuts, screws, washers, rivets, and other screw machine products	(X)	42.4
Plastics fabricated pipe and pipe fittings	(X)	50.1
Plywood	(X)	50.4
Particleboard (wood)	(X)	68.9
Oriented strand board (OSB) and waferboard	(X)	64.3
Gypsum building board	(X)	133.7
Dressed lumber	(X)	273.1
Wood millwork, including molding, doors, and windows	(X)	67.5
Kitchen cabinets, wood	(X)	50.4
Floor coverings, textile	(X)	83.3
Linoleum and other hard-surfaced floor covering	(X)	29.3
Heating equipment and air conditioners, including heat pumps	(X)	58.4
Current-carrying wiring devices, including switches, connectors, lampholders, etc.	(X)	74.1
Mineral fiber blankets, batts, and boards	(X)	64.8
Loose fill insulating materials (mineral fiber, cellulose fiber, and other)	(X)	28.6
Builders' hardware (including door locks, locksets, lock trim, screen hardware, etc.)	(X)	30.3
Household-type furniture, including tables, sofas, beds, mattresses, etc.	(X)	33.0
Household appliances, including refrigerators, cooking equipment, and other household appliances	(X)	132.7
Trailer axles, wheels, brakes, undercarriages, and other metal vehicular parts	(X)	157.2
Pneumatic tires and inner tubes	(X)	42.6
All other materials and components, parts, containers, and supplies	(X)	348.2
Materials, ingredients, containers, and supplies, nsk	(X)	647.5

Source: 1992 *Economic Census*. Explanation of symbols used: (D): Withheld to avoid disclosure of competitive data; na: Not available; (S): Withheld because statistical norms were not met; (X): Not applicable; (Z): Less than half the unit shown; nec: Not elsewhere classified; nsk: Not specified by kind; - : zero; * : 10-19 percent estimated; ** : 20-29 percent estimated.

PRODUCT SHARE DETAILS

Product or Product Class	% Share	Product or Product Class	% Share
Mobile homes	100.00	Mobile homes, nsk	6.70
Mobile homes (35 feet or more in length)	88.92	Mobile buildings, nonresidential	2.91
Mobile homes, 8 feet to 11 feet 11 inches in width	0.68	Mobile office and other commercial buildings	49.50
Mobile homes, 12 feet in width	1.35	Other manufactured (mobile) nonresidential buildings, including classroom and industrial buildings	47.89
Mobile homes, 12 feet 1 inch to 13 feet 11 inches in width	3.46	Manufactured (mobile) buildings, nonresidential, nsk	2.61
Mobile homes, 14 feet or more in width	32.17	Mobile homes, nsk	8.18
Mobile homes, double wides	55.64		

Source: 1992 *Economic Census*. The values shown are percent of total shipments in an industry. Values of indented subcategories are summed in the main heading. The symbol (D) appears when data are withheld to prevent disclosure of competitive information. The abbreviation nsk stands for 'not specified by kind' and nec for 'not elsewhere classified'.

INPUTS AND OUTPUTS FOR PREFABRICATED WOOD BUILDINGS

Economic Sector or Industry Providing Inputs	%	Sector	Economic Sector or Industry Buying Outputs	%	Sector
Sawmills & planning mills, general	23.5	Manufg.	Residential 1-unit structures, nonfarm	36.8	Constr.
Wholesale trade	10.9	Trade	Office buildings	19.4	Constr.
Veneer & plywood	5.9	Manufg.	Residential additions/alterations, nonfarm	12.6	Constr.
Metal doors, sash, & trim	5.0	Manufg.	Residential garden apartments	5.8	Constr.
Fabricated structural metal	4.9	Manufg.	Construction of stores & restaurants	3.4	Constr.
Millwork	4.3	Manufg.	Warehouses	3.3	Constr.
Advertising	4.3	Services	Exports	3.2	Foreign
Motor freight transportation & warehousing	2.6	Util.	Resid. & other health facility construction	2.5	Constr.
Hardwood dimension & flooring mills	2.5	Manufg.	Farm housing units & additions & alterations	2.1	Constr.
Mineral wool	2.3	Manufg.	Residential 2-4 unit structures, nonfarm	1.9	Constr.
Maintenance of nonfarm buildings nec	2.2	Constr.	Residential high-rise apartments	1.6	Constr.
Gypsum products	1.9	Manufg.	Construction of educational buildings	1.5	Constr.
Sheet metal work	1.8	Manufg.	Amusement & recreation building construction	1.3	Constr.
Refrigeration & heating equipment	1.7	Manufg.	Federal Government purchases, national defense	1.1	Fed Govt
Asphalt felts & coatings	1.6	Manufg.	Construction of nonfarm buildings nec	1.0	Constr.
Hardware, nec	1.6	Manufg.	Prefabricated wood buildings	0.7	Manufg.
Railroads & related services	1.6	Util.	Change in business inventories	0.6	In House
Machinery, except electrical, nec	1.2	Manufg.	Dormitories & other group housing	0.4	Constr.
Prefabricated wood buildings	1.2	Manufg.	Garage & service station construction	0.4	Constr.
Wood products, nec	1.1	Manufg.	Construction of conservation facilities	0.3	Constr.
Electric services (utilities)	1.1	Util.	Nonbuilding facilities nec	0.1	Constr.
Banking	1.1	Fin/R.E.			
Screw machine and related products	0.9	Manufg.			
Petroleum refining	0.8	Manufg.			
Communications, except radio & TV	0.8	Util.			
Imports	0.8	Foreign			
Particleboard	0.7	Manufg.			
Wood kitchen cabinets	0.7	Manufg.			
Eating & drinking places	0.7	Trade			
Business services nec	0.7	Services			
Air transportation	0.6	Util.			
Equipment rental & leasing services	0.6	Services			
Nonferrous wire drawing & insulating	0.5	Manufg.			
Paints & allied products	0.5	Manufg.			
Gas production & distribution (utilities)	0.5	Util.			
Real estate	0.5	Fin/R.E.			
Miscellaneous plastics products	0.4	Manufg.			
Pipe, valves, & pipe fittings	0.4	Manufg.			
Special product sawmills, nec	0.4	Manufg.			
Fabricated rubber products, nec	0.3	Manufg.			
Hard surface floor coverings	0.3	Manufg.			
Lighting fixtures & equipment	0.3	Manufg.			
Water transportation	0.3	Util.			
Credit agencies other than banks	0.3	Fin/R.E.			
Management & consulting services & labs	0.3	Services			
U.S. Postal Service	0.3	Gov't			
Paperboard containers & boxes	0.2	Manufg.			
Insurance carriers	0.2	Fin/R.E.			
Royalties	0.2	Fin/R.E.			
Accounting, auditing & bookkeeping	0.2	Services			
Automotive rental & leasing, without drivers	0.2	Services			
Automotive repair shops & services	0.2	Services			
Hotels & lodging places	0.2	Services			
Legal services	0.2	Services			
Heating equipment, except electric	0.1	Manufg.			
Steel wire & related products	0.1	Manufg.			
Wiring devices	0.1	Manufg.			
Woodworking machinery	0.1	Manufg.			
Sanitary services, steam supply, irrigation	0.1	Util.			
Engineering, architectural, & surveying services	0.1	Services			

Source: Benchmark Input-Output Accounts for the U.S. Economy, 1982, U.S. Department of Commerce, Washington, D.C., July 1991. Data, as reported in the source, are organized by the 1977 SIC structure in use in 1982 but have been matched, as closely as is possible, to the 1987 SIC structure used in this book.

OCCUPATIONS EMPLOYED BY SIC 245 - WOOD BUILDINGS AND MOBILE HOMES

Occupation	% of Total 1994	Change to 2005	Occupation	% of Total 1994	Change to 2005
Assemblers, fabricators, & hand workers nec	29.5	5.0	Plumbers, pipefitters, & steamfitters	1.7	5.0
Carpenters	20.2	-16.0	Truck drivers light & heavy	1.6	8.2
Blue collar worker supervisors	4.2	3.3	Head sawyers & sawing machine workers	1.4	-16.1
Sales & related workers nec	3.6	4.9	Secretaries, ex legal & medical	1.3	-4.4
Extraction & related workers nec	3.1	5.0	Helpers, laborers, & material movers nec	1.3	5.0
Helpers, construction trades	2.8	5.0	Industrial production managers	1.3	4.9
Electricians	2.7	-1.5	Wood machinists	1.3	4.9
Drafters	2.3	-18.2	Painters & paperhangers	1.2	5.0
General managers & top executives	2.1	-0.4	Freight, stock, & material movers, hand	1.2	-16.0
Cabinetmakers & bench carpenters	1.9	-5.5	Bookkeeping, accounting, & auditing clerks	1.0	-21.3

Source: Industry-Occupation Matrix, Bureau of Labor Statistics. These data relate to one or more 3-digit SIC industry groups rather than to a single 4-digit SIC. The change reported for each occupation to the year 2005 is a percent of growth or decline as estimated by the Bureau of Labor Statistics. The abbreviation nec stands for 'not elsewhere classified'.

LOCATION BY STATE AND REGIONAL CONCENTRATION

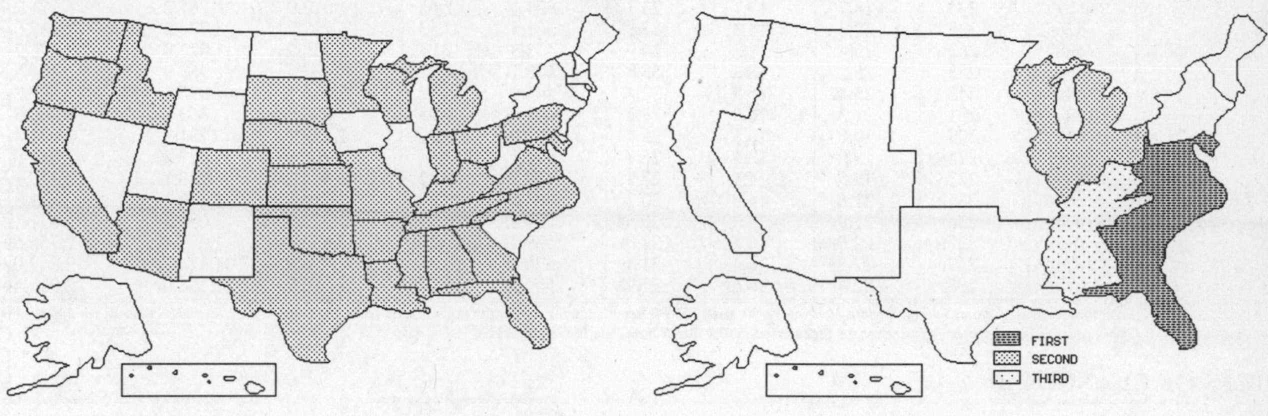

INDUSTRY DATA BY STATE

State	Establish-ments	Shipments			Employment				Cost as % of Shipments	Investment per Employee ($)
		Total ($ mil)	% of U.S.	Per Establ.	Total Number	% of U.S.	Per Establ.	Wages ($/hour)		
Indiana	34	643.2	14.2	18.9	4,900	13.2	144	10.78	66.3	1,122
Georgia	22	445.2	9.8	20.2	3,600	9.7	164	8.82	69.9	722
Alabama	25	443.3	9.8	17.7	4,000	10.8	160	7.84	66.8	800
North Carolina	25	425.3	9.4	17.0	3,400	9.2	136	8.91	65.0	971
Florida	25	301.3	6.6	12.1	2,400	6.5	96	10.29	61.2	667
Oregon	10	260.7	5.8	26.1	2,100	5.7	210	9.78	61.3	762
Tennessee	14	253.7	5.6	18.1	1,900	5.1	136	9.06	62.4	-
Pennsylvania	18	250.6	5.5	13.9	1,900	5.1	106	11.36	61.6	-
California	23	217.2	4.8	9.4	2,300	6.2	100	8.65	55.7	609
Texas	9	177.4	3.9	19.7	1,300	3.5	144	9.44	61.5	4,308
Mississippi	8	128.5	2.8	16.1	1,100	3.0	138	7.55	68.4	1,455
Arizona	8	116.4	2.6	14.5	1,000	2.7	125	8.45	61.3	-
Wisconsin	5	107.4	2.4	21.5	900	2.4	180	9.64	61.2	-
Idaho	6	101.1	2.2	16.9	800	2.2	133	9.62	61.8	875
Minnesota	6	89.6	2.0	14.9	700	1.9	117	11.00	63.7	1,857
Washington	5	84.2	1.9	16.8	800	2.2	160	10.15	56.7	-
Ohio	5	71.2	1.6	14.2	500	1.4	100	9.00	66.6	-
Virginia	3	70.6	1.6	23.5	600	1.6	200	9.78	60.9	-
Kansas	4	(D)	-	-	375 *	1.0	94	-	-	-
Michigan	4	(D)	-	-	175 *	0.5	44	-	-	-
Nebraska	4	(D)	-	-	750 *	2.0	188	-	-	-
Arkansas	2	(D)	-	-	175 *	0.5	88	-	-	-
Colorado	2	(D)	-	-	175 *	0.5	88	-	-	-
Missouri	2	(D)	-	-	175 *	0.5	88	-	-	-
Oklahoma	2	(D)	-	-	375 *	1.0	188	-	-	-
Kentucky	1	(D)	-	-	175 *	0.5	175	-	-	-
Louisiana	1	(D)	-	-	175 *	0.5	175	-	-	-
Maryland	1	(D)	-	-	175 *	0.5	175	-	-	-
South Dakota	1	(D)	-	-	175 *	0.5	175	-	-	-

Source: 1992 *Economic Census*. The states are in descending order of shipments or establishments (if shipment data are missing for the majority). The symbol (D) appears when data are withheld to prevent disclosure of competitive information. States marked with (D) are sorted by number of establishments. A dash (-) indicates that the data element cannot be calculated; * indicates the midpoint of a range.

2452 - PREFABRICATED WOOD BUILDINGS

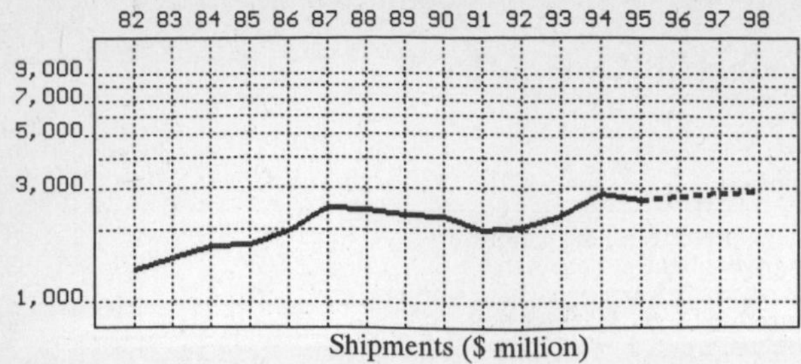

Shipments ($ million)

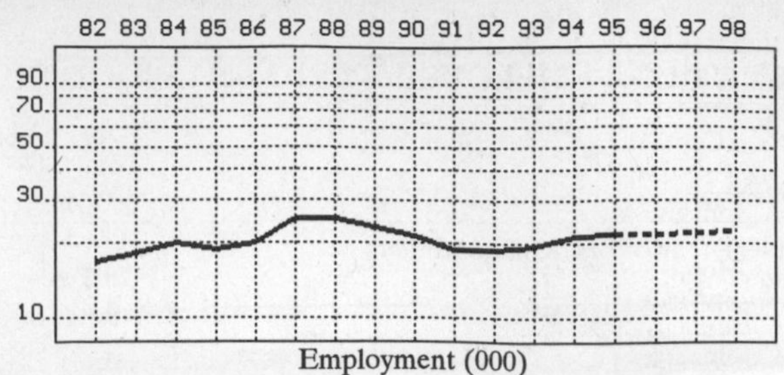

Employment (000)

GENERAL STATISTICS

Year	Com-panies	Establishments		Employment			Compensation		Production ($ million)			
		Total	with 20 or more employees	Total (000)	Production Workers (000)	Production Hours (Mil)	Payroll ($ mil)	Wages ($/hr)	Cost of Materials	Value Added by Manufacture	Value of Shipments	Capital Invest.
1982	598	647	206	16.8	11.4	20.8	257.8	6.88	794.0	553.4	1,349.0	17.4
1983		651	215	18.2	12.6	23.6	290.9	6.73	915.6	624.1	1,532.2	20.2
1984		655	224	20.2	14.3	26.7	325.1	6.81	1,031.1	670.1	1,698.2	33.3
1985		659	233	18.7	13.1	23.7	324.1	7.62	1,013.0	701.2	1,714.2	35.6
1986		626	228	20.3	14.3	27.8	361.5	7.53	1,207.7	777.2	1,987.0	34.6
1987	603	688	262	25.4	18.5	34.9	473.3	7.97	1,456.9	1,022.8	2,471.7	57.4
1988		660	253	25.2	18.2	35.8	478.7	7.91	1,433.5	969.9	2,404.8	21.9
1989		645	243	23.4	16.5	30.4	441.9	8.82	1,410.1	897.3	2,297.2	41.9
1990		637	231	21.3	16.0	29.2	448.0	9.05	1,393.9	863.2	2,268.5	32.7
1991		659	209	19.0	13.6	25.1	392.0	9.37	1,229.1	791.2	2,021.4	23.5
1992	561	655	224	19.0	13.4	25.1	414.1	9.64	1,206.8	847.4	2,055.6	24.2
1993		699	227	19.5	14.1	27.9	437.9	9.32	1,414.2	913.1	2,327.1	39.9
1994		669P	235P	21.6	15.8	30.2	493.0	9.88	1,714.5	1,116.2	2,821.8	48.8
1995		671P	236P	21.9P	16.0P	30.6P	504.8P	10.25P	1,622.9P	1,056.6P	2,671.1P	40.7P
1996		673P	237P	22.0P	16.2P	31.0P	520.4P	10.53P	1,674.8P	1,090.4P	2,756.5P	41.8P
1997		675P	237P	22.2P	16.4P	31.4P	536.1P	10.81P	1,726.8P	1,124.2P	2,842.0P	42.8P
1998		677P	238P	22.4P	16.6P	31.9P	551.7P	11.10P	1,778.7P	1,158.0P	2,927.4P	43.9P

Sources: 1982, 1987, 1992 *Economic Census*; *Annual Survey of Manufactures*, 83-86, 88-91, 93-94. Establishment counts for non-Census years are from *County Business Patterns*; establishment values for 83-84 are extrapolations. 'P's show projections by the editors. Industries reclassified in 87 will not have data for prior years.

INDICES OF CHANGE

Year	Com-panies	Establishments		Employment			Compensation		Production ($ million)			
		Total	with 20 or more employees	Total (000)	Production Workers (000)	Production Hours (Mil)	Payroll ($ mil)	Wages ($/hr)	Cost of Materials	Value Added by Manufacture	Value of Shipments	Capital Invest.
1982	107	99	92	88	85	83	62	71	66	65	66	72
1983		99	96	96	94	94	70	70	76	74	75	83
1984		100	100	106	107	106	79	71	85	79	83	138
1985		101	104	98	98	94	78	79	84	83	83	147
1986		96	102	107	107	111	87	78	100	92	97	143
1987	107	105	117	134	138	139	114	83	121	121	120	237
1988		101	113	133	136	143	116	82	119	114	117	90
1989		98	108	123	123	121	107	91	117	106	112	173
1990		97	103	112	119	116	108	94	116	102	110	135
1991		101	93	100	101	100	95	97	102	93	98	97
1992	100	100	100	100	100	100	100	100	100	100	100	100
1993		107	101	103	105	111	106	97	117	108	113	165
1994		102P	105P	114	118	120	119	102	142	132	137	202
1995		102P	105P	115P	120P	122P	122P	106P	134P	125P	130P	168P
1996		103P	106P	116P	121P	124P	126P	109P	139P	129P	134P	173P
1997		103P	106P	117P	122P	125P	129P	112P	143P	133P	138P	177P
1998		103P	106P	118P	124P	127P	133P	115P	147P	137P	142P	181P

Sources: Same as General Statistics. Values reflect change from the base year, 1992. Values above 100 mean greater than 92, values below 100 mean less than 92, and a value of 100 in the 82-91 or 93-98 period means same as 92. 'P's mark projections by the editors.

SELECTED RATIOS

For 1994	Avg. of All Manufact.	Analyzed Industry	Index	For 1994	Avg. of All Manufact.	Analyzed Industry	Index
Employees per Establishment	49	32	66	Value Added per Production Worker	134,084	70,646	53
Payroll per Establishment	1,500,273	736,520	49	Cost per Establishment	5,045,178	2,561,388	51
Payroll per Employee	30,620	22,824	75	Cost per Employee	102,970	79,375	77
Production Workers per Establishment	34	24	69	Cost per Production Worker	146,988	108,513	74
Wages per Establishment	853,319	445,761	52	Shipments per Establishment	9,576,895	4,215,646	44
Wages per Production Worker	24,861	18,885	76	Shipments per Employee	195,460	130,639	67
Hours per Production Worker	2,056	1,911	93	Shipments per Production Worker	279,017	178,595	64
Wages per Hour	12.09	9.88	82	Investment per Establishment	321,011	72,905	23
Value Added per Establishment	4,602,255	1,667,554	36	Investment per Employee	6,552	2,259	34
Value Added per Employee	93,930	51,676	55	Investment per Production Worker	9,352	3,089	33

Sources: Same as General Statistics. The 'Average of All Manufacturing' column represents the average of all manufacturing industries reported for the most recent complete year available. The Index shows the relationship between the Average and the Analyzed Industry. For example, 100 means that they are equal; 500 that the Analyzed Industry is five times the average; 50 means that the Analyzed Industry is half the national average. The abbreviation 'na' is used to show that data are 'not available'.

LEADING COMPANIES Number shown: **69** Total sales ($ mil): **2,975** Total employment (000): **15.3**

Company Name	Address				CEO Name	Phone	Co. Type	Sales ($ mil)	Empl. (000)
Guerdon Homes Inc	5285 SW Meadows	Lake Oswego	OR	97035	Al Preusch	503-624-6400	R	1,200	0.8
Skyline Corp	PO Box 743	Elkhart	IN	46515	Arthur J Decio	219-294-6521	P	580	3.6
Champion Home Builders Co	2701 University Dr	Auburn Hills	MI	48326	James Gurch	313-340-9090	S	250	2.0
Wausau Homes Inc	PO Box 8005	Wausau	WI	54402	Marvin Schuette	715-359-7272	R	90	0.4
Cavco Industries Inc	301 E Bethany	Phoenix	AZ	85012	Alfred R Ghelfi	602-265-0580	P	64	0.9
Western Home Center Inc	7600 Colerain Av	Cincinnati	OH	45239	Edward A Friesz	513-931-6300	R	59	0.3
Morgan Buildings and Spas	PO Box 660280	Dallas	TX	75222	G Morgan	214-840-1200	R	40*	0.5
Lindal Cedar Homes Inc	PO Box 24426	Seattle	WA	98124	Douglas F Lindal	206-725-0900	P	40	0.3
Miller Structures Inc	PO Box 1283	Elkhart	IN	46515	JM Davis	219-295-1214	S	38*	0.3
Bonnavilla Homes	PO Box 127	Aurora	NE	68818	Melvin R Auch	402-694-5250	D	36	0.3
Muncy Building Enterprises LP	PO Box 246	Muncy	PA	17756	Phillip A Schaivoni	717-546-5444	S	33	0.3
Nationwide Homes Inc	PO Box 5511	Martinsville	VA	24115	Frederick J Betz	703-632-7100	R	31	0.3
North American Housing Corp	PO Box 145	Point Of Rocks	MD	21777	RC Benna	301-694-9100	R	25*	0.4
Curt Bullock Builders Inc	720 S Gilbert St	Danville	IL	61834	RC Bullock	217-431-6400	R	25*	0.5
Design Homes Inc	PO Box 239	Prairie du Chien	WI	53821	F Weeks	608-326-6041	R	25*	0.3
Wisconsin Homes Inc	PO Box 250	Marshfield	WI	54449	Lamont Nienast	715-384-2161	R	25	0.3
Haven Homes Inc	PO Box 178	Beech Creek	PA	16822	C Mogish	717-962-2111	R	20	0.2
Simplex Industries Inc	1 Simplex Dr	Scranton	PA	18504	Henry P Fricchione	717-346-5113	R	20	0.3
Aurora Modular Industries	16833 Krameria Av	Riverside	CA	92504	Michael D Henning	909-789-7196	R	19	<0.1
Stratford Homes LP	PO Box 37	Stratford	WI	54484	Robert White	715-687-3133	R	18	0.2
Evergreen Mobile Co	PO Box 687	Redmond	WA	98073	Roland O Undi	206-861-7400	R	17	0.2
Active Homes Group	PO Box 127	Marlette	MI	48453	HA Drettmann	517-635-3532	S	15	0.2
Kan Build Inc	PO Box 259	Osage City	KS	66523	John Samples	913-528-4163	R	15	0.3
Northeastern Log Homes	PO Box 46	Kenduskeag	ME	04450	Jonathan French	207-884-7000	R	15	0.1
Timberland Homes Inc	1201 37th St NW	Auburn	WA	98001	GW Wood	206-735-3435	R	14	<0.1
West Coast Mills Inc	PO Box 480	Chehalis	WA	98532	Ben L Jones	360-748-3351	R	14	<0.1
Lena Builders Inc	209 N Bridge St	Eleroy	IL	61027	Stuart Duth	815-235-7176	R	13	0.2
Dynamic Homes Inc	525 Roosevelt Av	Detroit Lakes	MN	56501	Vern Muzik	218-847-2611	P	12	0.1
Magnolia	PO Box 657	Gering	NE	69341	J Fillingham	308-436-3131	D	12	0.2
Rycenga Homes Inc	PO Box 534	Spring Lake	MI	49456	Ronald Retsema	616-842-8040	R	12	0.1
Northern Products Log Homes	Bomarc Rd	Bangor	ME	04401	David Caliendo	207-945-6413	R	11*	0.1
Ramtech Building Systems Inc	1400 US Hwy 287 S	Mansfield	TX	76063	Michael T Slataper	817-473-9376	S	11*	0.1
Atlantic Meeco Inc	1501 E Gene Stipe	McAlester	OK	74501	Chris Clark	918-423-6833	R	10	<0.1
Deck House Inc	930 Main St	Acton	MA	01720	Michael S Harris	617-259-9450	R	10	0.1
Homes by Keystone Inc	PO Box 69	Waynesboro	PA	17268	Guy W Miller Jr	717-762-1104	R	10	0.1
Town and Country Cedar Homes	4772 US Hwy 131 S	Petoskey	MI	49770	Steven Biggs	616-347-4360	R	10	<0.1
New England Homes Inc	270 Ocean Rd	Greenland	NH	03840	Daniel J Donahue	603-436-8830	R	10	<0.1
Western Wood Structures Inc	PO Box 130	Tualatin	OR	97062	Marshall R Turner	503-692-6900	R	10	<0.1
Mod-U-Kraf Homes Inc	PO Box 573	Rocky Mount	VA	24151	Dale H Powell	703-483-0291	P	9	0.1
Rocky Mountain Log Homes	1883 Hwy 93 S	Hamilton	MT	59840	Jim Schueler	406-363-5680	R	9	<0.1
AmerLink Ltd	PO Box 669	Battleboro	NC	27809	Richard Spoor	919-977-2545	R	9	<0.1
Modern Home and Equipment	2467 N Dog River	Mobile	AL	36605	James D McPhillip	334-476-8343	R	8	0.1
Acorn Structures Inc	PO Box 1445	Concord	MA	01742	Stephen Stuntz	508-369-4111	R	7*	<0.1
Clearspan Components Inc	PO Box 4195	Meridian	MS	39304	JA Herrington	601-483-3941	R	7	<0.1
ASI of New York Inc	5911 Loomis Rd	Farmington	NY	14425	JR Malta	716-924-7151	R	6	<0.1
Pacific Modern Homes Inc	PO Box 670	Elk Grove	CA	95759	Mac Dyer	916-423-3150	R	6	<0.1
Pan Abode Cedar Homes Inc	4350 Lk Wash	Renton	WA	98056	John L Hubbard	206-255-8261	R	6	<0.1
Ward Log Homes	PO Box 72	Houlton	ME	04730	MA McLaughlin	207-532-6531	R	6	<0.1
Adrian Home Builders Inc	PO Box 430	Adrian	GA	31002	William E Simmons	912-668-3232	R	5	0.1
Mobile Structures Inc	PO Box 368	Pinckneyville	IL	62274	Joseph M Holder	618-357-2138	R	5	<0.1
Pittsville Homes Inc	PO Box C	Pittsville	WI	54466	Jim Hoogesteger	715-884-2511	R	5*	<0.1
Best Panel Homes Inc	11301 Paddy Run	Hamilton	OH	45013	Anthony J Otte	513-738-1212	R	4	<0.1
New England Corp	PO Box 5427	Hamden	CT	06518	Leonard F Suzio	203-562-9981	R	4*	<0.1
Design Homes of Minnesota	PO Box 462	Waseca	MN	56093	Frank Weeks	507-835-4451	S	3	<0.1
Woodmaster Inc	PO Box 16295	Hooksett	NH	03106	D R Lagerquist	603-669-1650	R	3	<0.1
Bay Wood Homes Inc	PO Box 368	Bay City	MI	48707	RG Haight	517-895-8001	R	2	<0.1
American Timber Homes Inc	PO Box 496	Escanaba	MI	49829	J Walbridge Jr	906-786-4550	R	2	<0.1
Homera Homes of Minnesota	Tracy Industrial Pk	Tracy	MN	56175	Bradley Johnson	507-629-3493	R	2	<0.1
Permabilt Manufactured Homes	330 S Kalamazoo	Marshall	MI	49068	Jimmie L Young	616-781-2887	R	2	<0.1
Cedarmark Home Corp	PO Box 4109	Bellevue	WA	98009	Michael O Hook	206-454-3966	R	2	<0.1
Stimpert Enterprises Inc	501 Burnside St SE	Sleepy Eye	MN	56085	Merton A Stimpert	507-794-3491	R	2	<0.1
World Wide Homes Inc	9536 Grand Av	Duluth	MN	55808	August Stoffel	218-626-2739	R	2	<0.1
Northwoods Log Homes Inc	HCR 70	Laporte	MN	56461	Ray Kerby	218-224-2251	R	1	<0.1
HWH Corp	755 York Rd	Warminster	PA	18974	John Norton	215-661-2000	S	1*	<0.1
LC Andrew	35 Main St	Windham	ME	04062	Laurence Clark	207-892-8561	R	1	<0.1
Frankton Port-A Buildings Inc	PO Box 177	Frankton	IN	46044	L Young	317-754-7012	R	1	<0.1
Napoleon Lumber Company Inc	PO Box 88	Napoleon	IN	47034	Neal Dean	812-852-4545	R	1	<0.1
Shelter-Kit Inc	22 Mill St	Tilton	NH	03276	Andy Prokosch	603-286-7611	R	0	<0.1
Composting Toilet Systems	PO Box 1928	Newport	WA	99156	MJ Jacobsen	509-447-3708	R	0	<0.1

Source: *Ward's Business Directory of U.S. Private and Public Companies*, Volumes 1 and 2, 1996. The company type code used is as follows: P - Public, R - Private, S - Subsidiary, D - Division, J - Joint Venture, A - Affiliate, G - Group. Sales are in millions of dollars, employees are in thousands. An asterisk (*) indicates an estimated sales volume. The symbol < stands for 'less than'. Company names and addresses are truncated, in some cases, to fit into the available space.

MATERIALS CONSUMED

Material		Quantity	Delivered Cost ($ million)
Materials, ingredients, containers, and supplies		(X)	1,113.7
Hardwood rough lumber	mil bd ft	(S)	24.6
Softwood rough lumber	mil bd ft	190.5	61.0
Hardwood dressed lumber	mil bd ft	(S)	12.5
Softwood dressed lumber	mil bd ft	325.0**	128.0
Softwood plywood	mil sq ft (3/8 in. b	113.9**	37.7
Gypsum building board		(X)	16.7
Builders' hardware (including door locks, locksets, lock trim, screen hardware, etc.)		(X)	15.5
Mineral wool insulation (fibrous glass, rock wool, etc.)		(X)	13.5
Windows and window units, including wood, metal, and vinyl	thousands	405.8*	54.9
Wood doors and door units		(X)	15.0
Metal doors and door units	thousands	83.2**	13.7
Kitchen cabinets, wood		(X)	30.3
Reconstituted wood products		(X)	22.4
Metal siding, including aluminum, steel		(X)	39.0
Fabricated structural iron, steel, and aluminum including truss plates		(X)	15.5
Current-carrying wiring devices, including switches, connectors, lampholders, etc.		(X)	17.5
Household appliances, including refrigerators, cooking equipment, and other household appliances		(X)	7.9
Floor coverings, textile		(X)	18.6
All other materials and components, parts, containers, and supplies		(X)	184.1
Materials, ingredients, containers, and supplies, nsk		(X)	385.4

Source: 1992 *Economic Census*. Explanation of symbols used: (D): Withheld to avoid disclosure of competitive data; na: Not available; (S): Withheld because statistical norms were not met; (X): Not applicable; (Z): Less than half the unit shown; nec: Not elsewhere classified; nsk: Not specified by kind; - : zero; * : 10-19 percent estimated; ** : 20-29 percent estimated.

PRODUCT SHARE DETAILS

Product or Product Class	% Share
Prefabricated wood buildings	100.00
Components for prefabricated stationary wood buildings (not sold as complete units)	10.28
Components for prefabricated stationary wood residential buildings (homes, townhouses, and apartments) (not sold as complete units)	80.88
Components for prefabricated stationary wood nonresidential buildings (including motels and hotels) (not sold as complete units)	16.86
Components for stationary buildings (not sold as complete units), nsk	2.26
Precut packages for prefabricated stationary wood buildings (complete units)	19.68
Precut packages for prefabricated residential log homes, sold as complete units	29.85
Precut packages for other prefabricated stationary residential wood buildings, including homes, townhouses, and apartments	21.34
Precut packages for prefabricated stationary nonresidential wood buildings (including motels and hotels)	47.99
Precut packages for stationary buildings (complete units), nsk	0.79
Prefabricated stationary wood buildings sold as complete units and shipped in panel form	17.22
Prefabricated stationary residential single family wood buildings, including townhouses, sold as complete units and shipped in panel form	71.67
Prefabricated stationary residential multifamily wood buildings sold as complete units and shipped in panel form	1.63
Prefabricated stationary nonresidential wood buildings (including motels and hotels) sold as complete units and shipped in panel form	11.05
Stationary buildings sold as complete units and shipped in panel form, nsk	15.64
Prefabricated stationary wood buildings shipped in three-dimensional assemblies	35.74
Prefabricated stationary residential wood buildings (including homes, townhouses, and apartments) shipped in three-dimensional assemblies	76.02
Prefabricated stationary nonresidential wood buildings (including motels and hotels) shipped in three-dimensional assemblies	17.93
Stationary buildings shipped in three-dimensional assemblies, nsk	6.04
Prefabricated wood buildings, nsk	17.07

Source: 1992 *Economic Census*. The values shown are percent of total shipments in an industry. Values of indented subcategories are summed in the main heading. The symbol (D) appears when data are withheld to prevent disclosure of competitive information. The abbreviation nsk stands for 'not specified by kind' and nec for 'not elsewhere classified'.

INPUTS AND OUTPUTS FOR PREFABRICATED WOOD BUILDINGS

Economic Sector or Industry Providing Inputs	%	Sector	Economic Sector or Industry Buying Outputs	%	Sector
Sawmills & planning mills, general	23.5	Manufg.	Residential 1-unit structures, nonfarm	36.8	Constr.
Wholesale trade	10.9	Trade	Office buildings	19.4	Constr.
Veneer & plywood	5.9	Manufg.	Residential additions/alterations, nonfarm	12.6	Constr.
Metal doors, sash, & trim	5.0	Manufg.	Residential garden apartments	5.8	Constr.
Fabricated structural metal	4.9	Manufg.	Construction of stores & restaurants	3.4	Constr.
Millwork	4.3	Manufg.	Warehouses	3.3	Constr.
Advertising	4.3	Services	Exports	3.2	Foreign
Motor freight transportation & warehousing	2.6	Util.	Resid. & other health facility construction	2.5	Constr.
Hardwood dimension & flooring mills	2.5	Manufg.	Farm housing units & additions & alterations	2.1	Constr.
Mineral wool	2.3	Manufg.	Residential 2-4 unit structures, nonfarm	1.9	Constr.
Maintenance of nonfarm buildings nec	2.2	Constr.	Residential high-rise apartments	1.6	Constr.
Gypsum products	1.9	Manufg.	Construction of educational buildings	1.5	Constr.
Sheet metal work	1.8	Manufg.	Amusement & recreation building construction	1.3	Constr.
Refrigeration & heating equipment	1.7	Manufg.	Federal Government purchases, national defense	1.1	Fed Govt

Continued on next page.

INPUTS AND OUTPUTS FOR PREFABRICATED WOOD BUILDINGS - Continued

Economic Sector or Industry Providing Inputs	%	Sector	Economic Sector or Industry Buying Outputs	%	Sector
Asphalt felts & coatings	1.6	Manufg.	Construction of nonfarm buildings nec	1.0	Constr.
Hardware, nec	1.6	Manufg.	Prefabricated wood buildings	0.7	Manufg.
Railroads & related services	1.6	Util.	Change in business inventories	0.6	In House
Machinery, except electrical, nec	1.2	Manufg.	Dormitories & other group housing	0.4	Constr.
Prefabricated wood buildings	1.2	Manufg.	Garage & service station construction	0.4	Constr.
Wood products, nec	1.1	Manufg.	Construction of conservation facilities	0.3	Constr.
Electric services (utilities)	1.1	Util.	Nonbuilding facilities nec	0.1	Constr.
Banking	1.1	Fin/R.E.			
Screw machine and related products	0.9	Manufg.			
Petroleum refining	0.8	Manufg.			
Communications, except radio & TV	0.8	Util.			
Imports	0.8	Foreign			
Particleboard	0.7	Manufg.			
Wood kitchen cabinets	0.7	Manufg.			
Eating & drinking places	0.7	Trade			
Business services nec	0.7	Services			
Air transportation	0.6	Util.			
Equipment rental & leasing services	0.6	Services			
Nonferrous wire drawing & insulating	0.5	Manufg.			
Paints & allied products	0.5	Manufg.			
Gas production & distribution (utilities)	0.5	Util.			
Real estate	0.5	Fin/R.E.			
Miscellaneous plastics products	0.4	Manufg.			
Pipe, valves, & pipe fittings	0.4	Manufg.			
Special product sawmills, nec	0.4	Manufg.			
Fabricated rubber products, nec	0.3	Manufg.			
Hard surface floor coverings	0.3	Manufg.			
Lighting fixtures & equipment	0.3	Manufg.			
Water transportation	0.3	Util.			
Credit agencies other than banks	0.3	Fin/R.E.			
Management & consulting services & labs	0.3	Services			
U.S. Postal Service	0.3	Gov't			
Paperboard containers & boxes	0.2	Manufg.			
Insurance carriers	0.2	Fin/R.E.			
Royalties	0.2	Fin/R.E.			
Accounting, auditing & bookkeeping	0.2	Services			
Automotive rental & leasing, without drivers	0.2	Services			
Automotive repair shops & services	0.2	Services			
Hotels & lodging places	0.2	Services			
Legal services	0.2	Services			
Heating equipment, except electric	0.1	Manufg.			
Steel wire & related products	0.1	Manufg.			
Wiring devices	0.1	Manufg.			
Woodworking machinery	0.1	Manufg.			
Sanitary services, steam supply, irrigation	0.1	Util.			
Engineering, architectural, & surveying services	0.1	Services			

Source: Benchmark Input-Output Accounts for the U.S. Economy, 1982, U.S. Department of Commerce, Washington, D.C., July 1991. Data, as reported in the source, are organized by the 1977 SIC structure in use in 1982 but have been matched, as closely as is possible, to the 1987 SIC structure used in this book.

OCCUPATIONS EMPLOYED BY SIC 245 - WOOD BUILDINGS AND MOBILE HOMES

Occupation	% of Total 1994	Change to 2005	Occupation	% of Total 1994	Change to 2005
Assemblers, fabricators, & hand workers nec	29.5	5.0	Plumbers, pipefitters, & steamfitters	1.7	5.0
Carpenters	20.2	-16.0	Truck drivers light & heavy	1.6	8.2
Blue collar worker supervisors	4.2	3.3	Head sawyers & sawing machine workers	1.4	-16.1
Sales & related workers nec	3.6	4.9	Secretaries, ex legal & medical	1.3	-4.4
Extraction & related workers nec	3.1	5.0	Helpers, laborers, & material movers nec	1.3	5.0
Helpers, construction trades	2.8	5.0	Industrial production managers	1.3	4.9
Electricians	2.7	-1.5	Wood machinists	1.3	4.9
Drafters	2.3	-18.2	Painters & paperhangers	1.2	5.0
General managers & top executives	2.1	-0.4	Freight, stock, & material movers, hand	1.2	-16.0
Cabinetmakers & bench carpenters	1.9	-5.5	Bookkeeping, accounting, & auditing clerks	1.0	-21.3

Source: Industry-Occupation Matrix, Bureau of Labor Statistics. These data relate to one or more 3-digit SIC industry groups rather than to a single 4-digit SIC. The change reported for each occupation to the year 2005 is a percent of growth or decline as estimated by the Bureau of Labor Statistics. The abbreviation nec stands for 'not elsewhere classified'.

LOCATION BY STATE AND REGIONAL CONCENTRATION

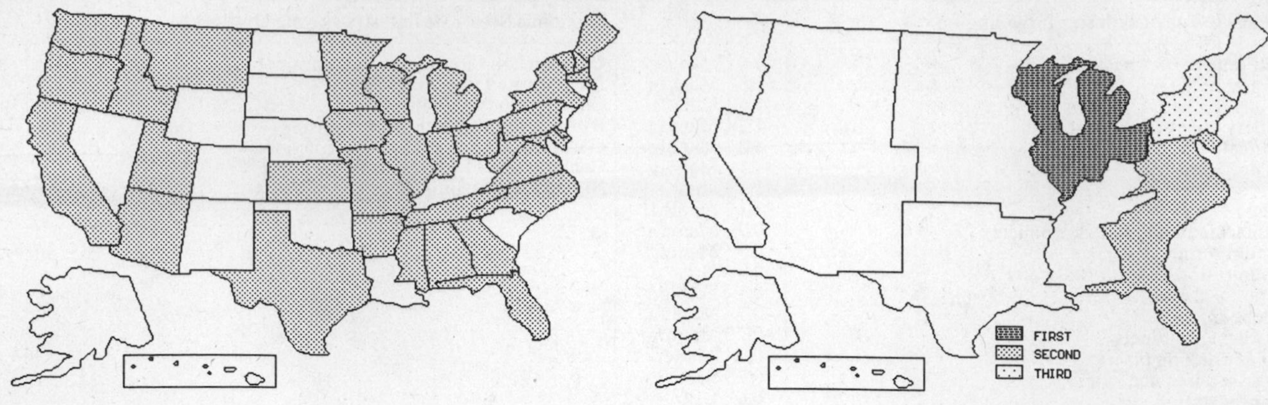

INDUSTRY DATA BY STATE

State	Establish-ments	Shipments			Employment				Cost as % of Shipments	Investment per Employee ($)
		Total ($ mil)	% of U.S.	Per Establ.	Total Number	% of U.S.	Per Establ.	Wages ($/hour)		
Pennsylvania	55	361.5	17.6	6.6	3,700	19.5	67	10.11	57.5	-
Wisconsin	26	181.6	8.8	7.0	1,400	7.4	54	9.30	63.7	-
Indiana	25	104.0	5.1	4.2	900	4.7	36	10.38	55.3	1,000
Virginia	24	80.9	3.9	3.4	1,000	5.3	42	8.62	59.7	-
Minnesota	20	79.6	3.9	4.0	500	2.6	25	9.00	60.7	1,200
Texas	25	71.7	3.5	2.9	700	3.7	28	9.22	61.4	1,143
Ohio	18	65.8	3.2	3.7	400	2.1	22	9.67	52.6	-
Arizona	8	60.3	2.9	7.5	300	1.6	38	8.80	66.3	-
California	41	58.6	2.9	1.4	600	3.2	15	9.00	60.8	1,167
Tennessee	20	42.6	2.1	2.1	700	3.7	35	6.86	52.6	-
North Carolina	21	37.0	1.8	1.8	300	1.6	14	9.00	58.6	1,333
Washington	22	35.3	1.7	1.6	300	1.6	14	12.25	56.4	-
Alabama	14	34.7	1.7	2.5	300	1.6	21	9.00	62.0	2,333
New Hampshire	17	33.0	1.6	1.9	300	1.6	18	11.00	53.6	667
Florida	15	27.2	1.3	1.8	400	2.1	27	7.20	51.8	750
Georgia	17	26.5	1.3	1.6	300	1.6	18	7.75	61.5	1,667
Massachusetts	7	24.9	1.2	3.6	200	1.1	29	14.50	63.1	-
Oregon	19	24.6	1.2	1.3	200	1.1	11	11.33	65.9	500
West Virginia	10	16.4	0.8	1.6	300	1.6	30	9.67	57.9	667
Idaho	9	12.1	0.6	1.3	200	1.1	22	10.00	60.3	1,000
Mississippi	6	6.7	0.3	1.1	100	0.5	17	9.00	55.2	1,000
New York	32	(D)	-	-	750 *	3.9	23	-	-	-
Michigan	29	(D)	-	-	750 *	3.9	26	-	-	-
Illinois	25	(D)	-	-	750 *	3.9	30	-	-	-
Montana	18	(D)	-	-	375 *	2.0	21	-	-	-
Maryland	12	(D)	-	-	750 *	3.9	63	-	-	-
Missouri	12	(D)	-	-	175 *	0.9	15	-	-	-
Maine	11	(D)	-	-	375 *	2.0	34	-	-	-
Vermont	10	(D)	-	-	175 *	0.9	18	-	-	-
Arkansas	9	(D)	-	-	175 *	0.9	19	-	-	-
Utah	8	(D)	-	-	175 *	0.9	22	-	-	-
Iowa	4	(D)	-	-	175 *	0.9	44	-	-	-
Kansas	3	(D)	-	-	175 *	0.9	58	-	-	-
Delaware	1	(D)	-	-	750 *	3.9	750	-	-	-

Source: 1992 *Economic Census*. The states are in descending order of shipments or establishments (if shipment data are missing for the majority). The symbol (D) appears when data are withheld to prevent disclosure of competitive information. States marked with (D) are sorted by number of establishments. A dash (-) indicates that the data element cannot be calculated; * indicates the midpoint of a range.

2491 - WOOD PRESERVING

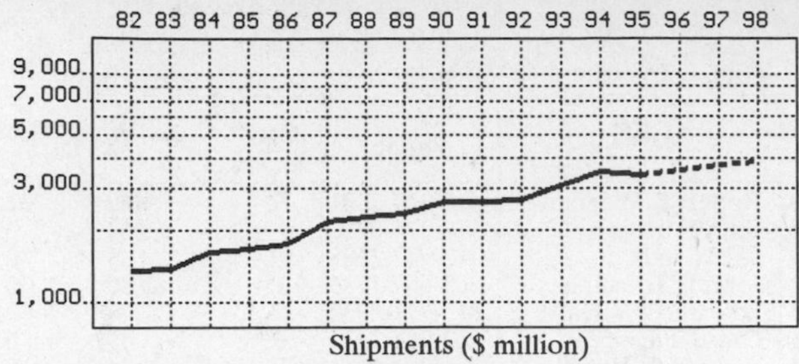

Shipments ($ million)

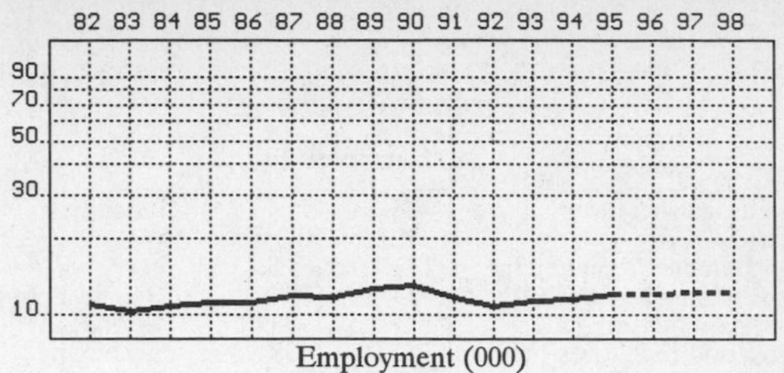

Employment (000)

GENERAL STATISTICS

Year	Companies	Establishments: Total	Establishments: with 20 or more employees	Employment: Total (000)	Employment: Production Workers (000)	Employment: Production Hours (Mil)	Compensation: Payroll ($ mil)	Compensation: Wages ($/hr)	Production: Cost of Materials	Production: Value Added by Manufacture	Production: Value of Shipments	Production: Capital Invest.
1982	428	524	184	10.9	8.6	16.5	159.4	6.56	978.5	383.7	1,360.2	35.9
1983		508	189	10.2	8.1	15.7	155.7	6.90	1,031.7	334.3	1,378.4	23.8
1984		492	194	10.7	8.8	18.3	171.7	6.94	1,177.4	495.2	1,625.5	43.5
1985		475	200	11.1	9.0	18.2	184.0	7.33	1,206.4	525.9	1,683.5	47.7
1986		489	207	11.1	8.6	17.1	181.1	7.48	1,269.3	504.1	1,774.0	35.3
1987	456	540	202	11.8	9.1	18.2	207.7	7.73	1,620.1	552.6	2,169.6	44.1
1988		522	202	11.7	8.8	18.0	214.3	8.06	1,670.3	605.0	2,265.0	46.2
1989		505	207	12.6	9.4	17.4	223.4	8.45	1,768.3	579.9	2,366.2	45.4
1990		494	207	12.9	10.2	18.8	245.8	8.61	1,977.5	696.5	2,642.7	57.2
1991		505	193	11.7	9.1	17.3	232.8	8.86	1,932.8	657.6	2,605.0	42.0
1992	407	486	179	10.8	8.3	17.2	232.8	8.74	2,046.7	678.5	2,694.8	56.2
1993		481	183	11.3	8.7	17.5	252.1	8.87	2,483.9	697.0	3,095.2	52.8
1994		491P	194P	11.5	9.1	19.5	259.4	8.84	2,803.0	701.8	3,495.9	58.6
1995		490P	194P	12.0P	9.2P	18.5P	271.5P	9.42P	2,734.9P	684.8P	3,411.0P	59.1P
1996		488P	193P	12.1P	9.3P	18.7P	280.4P	9.64P	2,868.7P	718.3P	3,577.9P	61.1P
1997		487P	193P	12.2P	9.3P	18.8P	289.3P	9.85P	3,002.5P	751.8P	3,744.8P	63.1P
1998		485P	193P	12.3P	9.3P	18.9P	298.1P	10.06P	3,136.4P	785.3P	3,911.7P	65.1P

Sources: 1982, 1987, 1992 *Economic Census*; *Annual Survey of Manufactures*, 83-86, 88-91, 93-94. Establishment counts for non-Census years are from *County Business Patterns*; establishment values for 83-84 are extrapolations. 'P's show projections by the editors. Industries reclassified in 87 will not have data for prior years.

INDICES OF CHANGE

Year	Companies	Establishments: Total	Establishments: with 20 or more employees	Employment: Total (000)	Employment: Production Workers (000)	Employment: Production Hours (Mil)	Compensation: Payroll ($ mil)	Compensation: Wages ($/hr)	Production: Cost of Materials	Production: Value Added by Manufacture	Production: Value of Shipments	Production: Capital Invest.
1982	105	108	103	101	104	96	68	75	48	57	50	64
1983		105	106	94	98	91	67	79	50	49	51	42
1984		101	108	99	106	106	74	79	58	73	60	77
1985		98	112	103	108	106	79	84	59	78	62	85
1986		101	116	103	104	99	78	86	62	74	66	63
1987	112	111	113	109	110	106	89	88	79	81	81	78
1988		107	113	108	106	105	92	92	82	89	84	82
1989		104	116	117	113	101	96	97	86	85	88	81
1990		102	116	119	123	109	106	99	97	103	98	102
1991		104	108	108	110	101	100	101	94	97	97	75
1992	100	100	100	100	100	100	100	100	100	100	100	100
1993		99	102	105	105	102	108	101	121	103	115	94
1994		101P	108P	106	110	113	111	101	137	103	130	104
1995		101P	108P	111P	111P	108P	117P	108P	134P	101P	127P	105P
1996		100P	108P	112P	111P	108P	120P	110P	140P	106P	133P	109P
1997		100P	108P	113P	112P	109P	124P	113P	147P	111P	139P	112P
1998		100P	108P	114P	112P	110P	128P	115P	153P	116P	145P	116P

Sources: Same as General Statistics. Values reflect change from the base year, 1992. Values above 100 mean greater than 92, values below 100 mean less than 92, and a value of 100 in the 82-91 or 93-98 period means same as 92. 'P's mark projections by the editors.

SELECTED RATIOS

For 1994	Avg. of All Manufact.	Analyzed Industry	Index	For 1994	Avg. of All Manufact.	Analyzed Industry	Index
Employees per Establishment	49	23	48	Value Added per Production Worker	134,084	77,121	58
Payroll per Establishment	1,500,273	527,870	35	Cost per Establishment	5,045,178	5,704,005	113
Payroll per Employee	30,620	22,557	74	Cost per Employee	102,970	243,739	237
Production Workers per Establishment	34	19	54	Cost per Production Worker	146,988	308,022	210
Wages per Establishment	853,319	350,787	41	Shipments per Establishment	9,576,895	7,114,032	74
Wages per Production Worker	24,861	18,943	76	Shipments per Employee	195,460	303,991	156
Hours per Production Worker	2,056	2,143	104	Shipments per Production Worker	279,017	384,165	138
Wages per Hour	12.09	8.84	73	Investment per Establishment	321,011	119,249	37
Value Added per Establishment	4,602,255	1,428,138	31	Investment per Employee	6,552	5,096	78
Value Added per Employee	93,930	61,026	65	Investment per Production Worker	9,352	6,440	69

Sources: Same as General Statistics. The 'Average of All Manufacturing' column represents the average of all manufacturing industries reported for the most recent complete year available. The Index shows the relationship between the Average and the Analyzed Industry. For example, 100 means that they are equal; 500 that the Analyzed Industry is five times the average; 50 means that the Analyzed Industry is half the national average. The abbreviation 'na' is used to show that data are 'not available'.

LEADING COMPANIES

Number shown: 35 Total sales ($ mil): **1,454** Total employment (000): **8.4**

Company Name	Address				CEO Name	Phone	Co. Type	Sales ($ mil)	Empl. (000)
Koppers Industries Inc	436 7th Av	Pittsburgh	PA	15219	Robert K Wagner	412-227-2001	R	465	1.8
Fibreboard Corp	2121 N California	Walnut Creek	CA	94596	John D Roach	510-274-0700	P	364	3.5
Tolleson Lumber Company Inc	PO Drawer E	Perry	GA	31069	WJ Wood	912-987-2105	R	85	0.4
Walker-Williams Lumber Co	PO Box 170	Hatchechubbee	AL	36858	John D Hite Jr	205-667-7736	R	80	0.3
Robbins Manufacturing Co	PO Box 17939	Tampa	FL	33682	Lawrence W Hall	813-971-3030	R	70*	0.3
Atlantic Wood Industries Inc	PO Box 1608	Savannah	GA	31498	David T Bryce	912-964-1234	R	45	0.2
Burke-Parsons-Bowlby Corp	PO Box 231	Ripley	WV	25271	Richard E Bowlby	304-372-2211	P	44	0.3
LD McFarland Company Ltd	PO Box 1496	Tacoma	WA	98401	BC McFarland	206-572-3033	R	40*	0.2
McFarland Cascade	PO Box 1496	Tacoma	WA	98401	BC McFarland	206-572-3033	R	40	0.2
JH Baxter and Co	PO Box 5902	San Mateo	CA	94402	Richard H Baxter	415-349-0201	R	38	0.2
Perry Builders Inc	PO Box 589	Henderson	NC	27536	LW Perry	919-492-9171	R	35	<0.1
Great Southern Wood Preserving	PO Box 610	Abbeville	AL	36310	James W Rane	205-585-2291	R	16*	0.1
Texas Electric Cooperatives Inc	PO Box 9589	Austin	TX	78766	James Morris	512-454-0311	R	16*	0.2
Brown Wood Preserving	6201 Camp Ground	Louisville	KY	40216	Lowell Stanley	502-448-2337	R	13	0.1
Western Wood Preserving Co	PO Box 1250	Sumner	WA	98390	Robert D Reimer	206-863-8191	R	13	<0.1
Conroe Creosoting Inc	PO Box 9	Conroe	TX	77305	HM Hawthorne	409-539-2245	R	10	<0.1
Atlantic Wood	PO Box 1608	Savannah	GA	31498	David T Bryce	912-964-1234	S	8	<0.1
Oeser Co	PO Box 156	Bellingham	WA	98227	C M Secrist	206-734-1480	R	8*	<0.1
Sumter Wood Preserving	PO Box 637	Sumter	SC	29151	Michael V Mecionis	803-775-5301	R	8*	<0.1
Artistic Finishes Inc	2224 Terminal Rd	Roseville	MN	55113	Thomas R Leach	612-631-2807	R	7*	<0.1
Wood Preservers Inc	PO Box 158	Warsaw	VA	22572	WM Wright	804-333-4022	R	7	<0.1
Appalachian Timber Service Inc	PO Box 7518	Charleston	WV	25356	William E Gadd	304-776-3109	R	6*	<0.1
Bell Lumber and Pole Co	778 1st St NW	New Brighton	MN	55112	MJ Bell III	612-633-4334	R	6	<0.1
Carolina Wood Preserving	PO Box 310	Scotland Neck	NC	27874	F Fathful	919-826-4151	D	5*	<0.1
Camirn Company Inc	13467 64th Pl NE	Kirkland	WA	98034	Kirin DePriest	206-932-0445	R	5	<0.1
Ellijay Lumber	Hwy 5 S	Ellijay	GA	30540	Garland Thomas	706-635-4751	R	4	<0.1
Girard Custom Coaters Inc	2148 Port Tacoma	Tacoma	WA	98421	Nick Iverson	206-627-1141	R	4	<0.1
Land O Lakes	PO Box 87	Tenstrike	MN	56683	RL Fellows	218-586-2203	R	4	<0.1
Kennedy Sawmills Inc	PO Box 54	Shreveport	LA	71161	John E Kennedy	318-222-8491	R	3	<0.1
Dura-Wood Treating Co	PO Box 1926	Alexandria	LA	71309	Clyde M Norton	318-442-5733	S	2	<0.1
MacGillis and Gibbs Co	PO Box 120576	New Brighton	MN	55112	AJ Bumby	612-636-6191	R	2*	<0.1
Bow House Inc	92 Randall Rd	Bolton	MA	01740	Gwendolen Rogers	508-779-6464	R	2	<0.1
Page and Hill Forest Products	PO Box 7	Big Falls	MN	56627	VR Hufnagle	218-276-2251	R	1*	<0.1
San Diego Wood Preserving Co	2010 Haffley Av	National City	CA	91950	Gerald Baker	619-474-6441	R	1	<0.1
Environmental Manufacturing	PO Box 269	Plymouth	NH	03264	Charlie Brosseau	603-536-7400	R	0*	<0.1

Source: *Ward's Business Directory of U.S. Private and Public Companies*, Volumes 1 and 2, 1996. The company type code used is as follows: P - Public, R - Private, S - Subsidiary, D - Division, J - Joint Venture, A - Affiliate, G - Group. Sales are in millions of dollars, employees are in thousands. An asterisk (*) indicates an estimated sales volume. The symbol < stands for 'less than'. Company names and addresses are truncated, in some cases, to fit into the available space.

MATERIALS CONSUMED

Material		Quantity	Delivered Cost ($ million)
Materials, ingredients, containers, and supplies		(X)	1,913.0
Poles, piling, and other round or hewn wood products treated in the same establishment		(X)	216.3
Hardwood rough lumber	mil bd ft	(S)	132.3
Softwood rough lumber	mil bd ft	(S)	360.8
Dressed lumber	mil bd ft	1,704.1*	540.9
Creosote oil consumed in the same establishment	mil gal	46.7**	38.3
Pentachlorophenol consumed in the same establishment	mil lb	(S)	24.0
Water-born salts consumed in the same establishment	mil lb	(S)	78.0
Flame retardants consumed in the same establishment		(X)	6.8
All other materials and components, parts, containers, and supplies		(X)	196.3
Materials, ingredients, containers, and supplies, nsk		(X)	319.4

Source: 1992 *Economic Census*. Explanation of symbols used: (D): Withheld to avoid disclosure of competitive data; na: Not available; (S): Withheld because statistical norms were not met; (X): Not applicable; (Z): Less than half the unit shown; nec: Not elsewhere classified; nsk: Not specified by kind; - : zero; * : 10-19 percent estimated; ** : 20-29 percent estimated.

PRODUCT SHARE DETAILS

Product or Product Class	% Share
Wood preserving	100.00
Wood poles, piles, and posts owned and treated by same establishment	20.72
Treated with pentachlorophenol, up to 15 feet in length	5.79
Treated with arsenical chemicals, up to 15 feet in length	15.71
Treated with creosote, up to 15 feet in length	1.20
Treated with other chemicals, up to 15 feet in length	0.30
Treated with pentachlorophenol, more than 15 feet in length	31.31
Treated with arsenical chemicals, more than 15 feet in length	13.10
Treated with creosote, more than 15 feet in length	17.30
Treated with other chemicals, more than 15 feet in length	6.03
Treated by same establishment, nsk	9.25
Other wood products owned and treated by same establishment	66.07
Railway crossties and mine ties (except switch or bridge) owned and treated by the same establishment	9.77
Rough and dressed lumber (interior and exterior), not edged, owned and treated with fire-retardant by the same establishment	2.70

Continued on next page.

PRODUCT SHARE DETAILS - Continued

Product or Product Class	% Share	Product or Product Class	% Share
with pentachlorophenol by the same establishment	3.67	paling, and rails	5.90
Rough and dressed lumber, not edged, owned and treated with arsenical chemicals by the same establishment	59.94	Other wood products owned and treated by same establishment, nsk	9.71
Rough and dressed lumber, not edged, owned and treated with other chemicals by the same establishment	5.19	Contract wood preserving	4.70
Wood siding, flooring, and other edged lumber owned and treated by the same establishment	1.43	Receipts for treating wood owned by others with arsenical chemicals	37.11
Switch and bridge ties owned and treated by the same establishment	1.69	Receipts for treating wood owned by others with creosote	34.34
Other wood products owned and treated by the same establishment, including plywood, wood fence pickets,		Receipts for treating wood owned by others with other chemicals, including fire-retardant and pentachlorophenol	22.27
		Contract wood preserving, nsk	6.28
		Wood preserving, nsk	8.51

Source: 1992 *Economic Census*. The values shown are percent of total shipments in an industry. Values of indented subcategories are summed in the main heading. The symbol (D) appears when data are withheld to prevent disclosure of competitive information. The abbreviation nsk stands for 'not specified by kind' and nec for 'not elsewhere classified'.

INPUTS AND OUTPUTS FOR WOOD PRESERVING

Economic Sector or Industry Providing Inputs	%	Sector	Economic Sector or Industry Buying Outputs	%	Sector
Sawmills & planning mills, general	26.9	Manufg.	Electric utility facility construction	26.5	Constr.
Logging camps & logging contractors	20.7	Manufg.	Industrial buildings	12.3	Constr.
Cyclic crudes and organics	12.7	Manufg.	Nonfarm residential structure maintenance	9.0	Constr.
Wholesale trade	7.5	Trade	Maintenance of electric utility facilities	8.7	Constr.
Petroleum refining	4.7	Manufg.	Warehouses	7.0	Constr.
Paints & allied products	3.4	Manufg.	Telephone & telegraph facility construction	5.9	Constr.
Industrial inorganic chemicals, nec	3.0	Manufg.	Maintenance of railroads	3.0	Constr.
Railroads & related services	2.7	Util.	Office buildings	2.7	Constr.
Motor freight transportation & warehousing	2.5	Util.	Exports	2.7	Foreign
Advertising	1.8	Services	Construction of conservation facilities	2.4	Constr.
Gas production & distribution (utilities)	1.4	Util.	Maintenance of farm service facilities	1.9	Constr.
Electric services (utilities)	1.3	Util.	Change in business inventories	1.8	In House
Wood preserving	1.0	Manufg.	Farm service facilities	1.5	Constr.
Banking	1.0	Fin/R.E.	Maintenance of telephone & telegraph facilities	1.4	Constr.
Business services nec	1.0	Services	Maintenance of nonfarm buildings nec	1.3	Constr.
Coal	0.8	Mining	Residential 1-unit structures, nonfarm	1.1	Constr.
Imports	0.8	Foreign	Highway & street construction	1.0	Constr.
Water transportation	0.7	Util.	Railroad construction	0.9	Constr.
Maintenance of nonfarm buildings nec	0.5	Constr.	Wood preserving	0.8	Manufg.
Fabricated metal products, nec	0.5	Manufg.	Local transit facility construction	0.7	Constr.
Alkalies & chlorine	0.4	Manufg.	Residential additions/alterations, nonfarm	0.7	Constr.
Eating & drinking places	0.4	Trade	Sewer system facility construction	0.7	Constr.
Communications, except radio & TV	0.3	Util.	Copper ore	0.6	Mining
Detective & protective services	0.3	Services	Coal	0.5	Mining
Equipment rental & leasing services	0.3	Services	Maintenance of highways & streets	0.5	Constr.
Abrasive products	0.2	Manufg.	Construction of educational buildings	0.4	Constr.
Paperboard containers & boxes	0.2	Manufg.	Maintenance of farm residential buildings	0.4	Constr.
Air transportation	0.2	Util.	Maintenance of military facilities	0.4	Constr.
Engineering, architectural, & surveying services	0.2	Services	Maintenance, conservation & development facilities	0.4	Constr.
Management & consulting services & labs	0.2	Services	Nonbuilding facilities nec	0.4	Constr.
Hand saws & saw blades	0.1	Manufg.	Nonferrous metal ores, except copper	0.3	Mining
Machinery, except electrical, nec	0.1	Manufg.	Maintenance of local transit facilities	0.3	Constr.
Insurance carriers	0.1	Fin/R.E.	Maintenance of nonbuilding facilities nec	0.3	Constr.
Royalties	0.1	Fin/R.E.	Construction of hospitals	0.2	Constr.
Legal services	0.1	Services	Residential garden apartments	0.2	Constr.
U.S. Postal Service	0.1	Gov't	Residential high-rise apartments	0.2	Constr.
			Federal Government purchases, national defense	0.2	Fed Govt
			Garage & service station construction	0.1	Constr.
			Maintenance of sewer facilities	0.1	Constr.
			Water supply facility construction	0.1	Constr.
			Federal Government purchases, nondefense	0.1	Fed Govt

Source: Benchmark Input-Output Accounts for the U.S. Economy, 1982, U.S. Department of Commerce, Washington, D.C., July 1991. Data, as reported in the source, are organized by the 1977 SIC structure in use in 1982 but have been matched, as closely as is possible, to the 1987 SIC structure used in this book.

OCCUPATIONS EMPLOYED BY SIC 249 - WOOD CONTAINERS AND MISCELLANEOUS WOOD PRODUCTS

Occupation	% of Total 1994	Change to 2005	Occupation	% of Total 1994	Change to 2005
Assemblers, fabricators, & hand workers nec	15.4	10.0	Industrial machinery mechanics	2.3	21.0
Woodworking machine workers	9.3	-12.0	Sales & related workers nec	1.8	10.0
Head sawyers & sawing machine workers	7.6	-45.0	Inspectors, testers, & graders, precision	1.7	10.0
Machine feeders & offbearers	5.1	-1.0	Industrial production managers	1.6	10.0
Blue collar worker supervisors	4.5	0.7	Secretaries, ex legal & medical	1.5	0.2
Helpers, laborers, & material movers nec	4.2	10.0	Bookkeeping, accounting, & auditing clerks	1.5	-17.5
Wood machinists	4.1	10.0	General office clerks	1.5	-6.2
Industrial truck & tractor operators	4.0	10.0	Traffic, shipping, & receiving clerks	1.3	5.9
Freight, stock, & material movers, hand	3.8	-12.0	Carpenters	1.1	-12.0
General managers & top executives	3.7	4.4	Cabinetmakers & bench carpenters	1.1	-1.0
Truck drivers light & heavy	3.0	13.4	Extruding & forming machine workers	1.0	21.0
Coating, painting, & spraying machine workers	2.5	10.0			

Source: Industry-Occupation Matrix, Bureau of Labor Statistics. These data relate to one or more 3-digit SIC industry groups rather than to a single 4-digit SIC. The change reported for each occupation to the year 2005 is a percent of growth or decline as estimated by the Bureau of Labor Statistics. The abbreviation nec stands for 'not elsewhere classified'.

LOCATION BY STATE AND REGIONAL CONCENTRATION

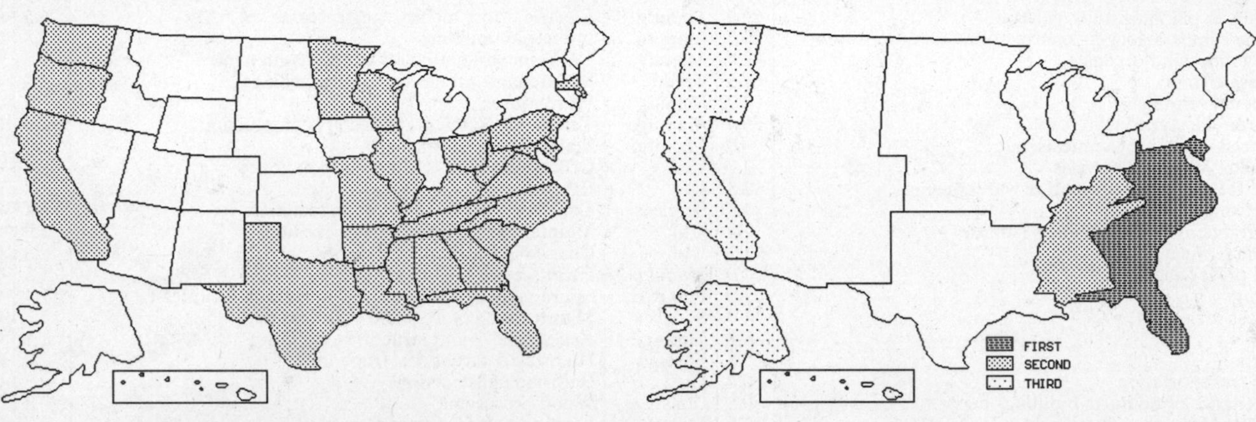

INDUSTRY DATA BY STATE

State	Establish-ments	Shipments Total ($ mil)	Shipments % of U.S.	Shipments Per Establ.	Employment Total Number	Employment % of U.S.	Employment Per Establ.	Employment Wages ($/hour)	Cost as % of Shipments	Investment per Employee ($)
Alabama	29	298.4	11.1	10.3	1,300	12.0	45	8.24	76.2	6,615
Virginia	20	237.6	8.8	11.9	800	7.4	40	9.08	76.9	8,750
Washington	16	191.9	7.1	12.0	700	6.5	44	11.64	66.2	3,714
South Carolina	16	180.7	6.7	11.3	700	6.5	44	8.50	77.7	5,286
North Carolina	31	166.8	6.2	5.4	500	4.6	16	7.75	84.1	4,400
Georgia	24	134.4	5.0	5.6	500	4.6	21	8.86	76.3	5,800
Arkansas	12	122.7	4.6	10.2	500	4.6	42	8.88	76.9	3,400
Texas	26	115.1	4.3	4.4	800	7.4	31	8.46	65.9	2,625
Florida	18	113.4	4.2	6.3	300	2.8	17	7.40	82.8	3,667
Pennsylvania	21	107.9	4.0	5.1	400	3.7	19	9.17	79.3	3,750
Wisconsin	12	74.6	2.8	6.2	200	1.9	17	9.00	86.7	3,000
Oregon	13	71.0	2.6	5.5	300	2.8	23	10.17	68.6	6,000
Maryland	8	66.0	2.4	8.3	100	0.9	13	9.00	77.4	-
Illinois	16	59.8	2.2	3.7	200	1.9	13	11.67	73.9	15,000
California	25	57.7	2.1	2.3	300	2.8	12	8.20	69.8	6,333
West Virginia	9	57.5	2.1	6.4	200	1.9	22	7.25	81.7	5,500
Massachusetts	7	52.4	1.9	7.5	100	0.9	14	8.00	87.6	9,000
Ohio	16	49.9	1.9	3.1	200	1.9	13	9.00	81.6	-
Louisiana	12	43.2	1.6	3.6	200	1.9	17	8.00	72.5	-
Minnesota	11	43.1	1.6	3.9	200	1.9	18	5.75	72.4	-
Kentucky	11	43.0	1.6	3.9	200	1.9	18	6.67	80.5	-
Tennessee	9	42.1	1.6	4.7	200	1.9	22	6.25	83.4	4,000
Mississippi	18	(D)	-	-	375 *	3.5	21	-	-	-
Missouri	14	(D)	-	-	175 *	1.6	13	-	-	-
New Jersey	5	(D)	-	-	175 *	1.6	35	-	-	-

Source: 1992 *Economic Census*. The states are in descending order of shipments or establishments (if shipment data are missing for the majority). The symbol (D) appears when data are withheld to prevent disclosure of competitive information. States marked with (D) are sorted by number of establishments. A dash (-) indicates that the data element cannot be calculated; * indicates the midpoint of a range.

2493 - RECONSTITUTED WOOD PRODUCTS

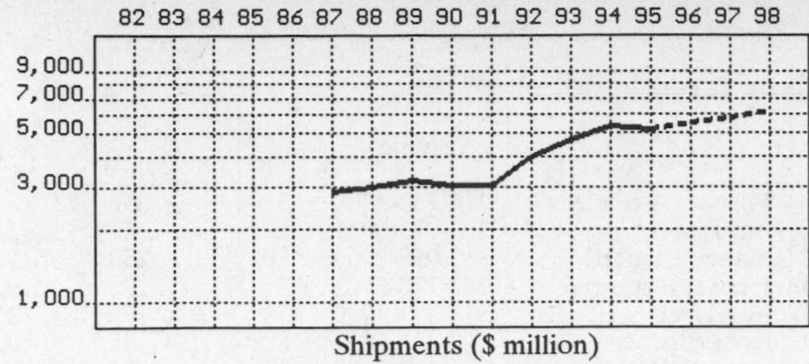

Shipments ($ million)

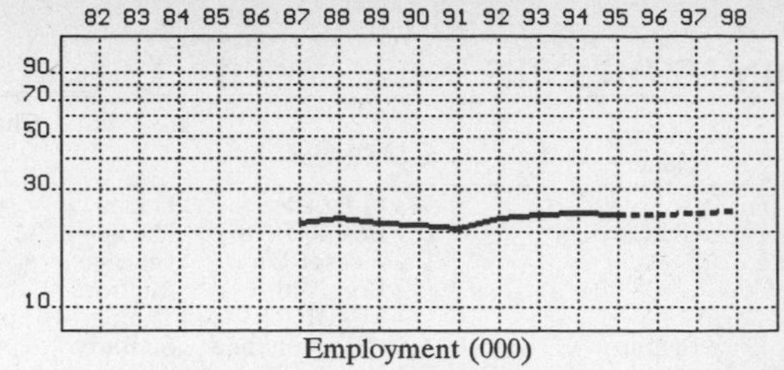

Employment (000)

GENERAL STATISTICS

Year	Com-panies	Establishments		Employment			Compensation		Production ($ million)			
		Total	with 20 or more employees	Total (000)	Production Workers (000)	Production Hours (Mil)	Payroll ($ mil)	Wages ($/hr)	Cost of Materials	Value Added by Manufacture	Value of Shipments	Capital Invest.
1982												
1983												
1984												
1985												
1986												
1987	158	240	154	22.0	17.7	37.1	504.5	9.98	1,488.9	1,371.1	2,864.9	149.9
1988		254	166	22.8	18.3	38.7	532.0	10.16	1,584.0	1,390.8	2,971.3	215.6
1989		268	163	21.8	18.2	39.5	546.6	10.15	1,706.8	1,476.5	3,198.8	132.9
1990		261	164	21.5	18.2	39.1	554.3	10.41	1,778.8	1,285.0	3,042.6	130.2
1991		269	162	21.0	17.1	36.9	537.0	10.73	1,756.1	1,284.6	3,040.6	187.3
1992	195	288	180	22.8	18.5	39.9	614.3	11.50	2,029.8	1,930.7	3,980.6	142.8
1993		300	190	23.5	19.2	41.9	659.7	11.72	2,258.2	2,414.1	4,669.3	170.6
1994		304P	188P	24.1	19.5	42.8	684.1	11.84	2,528.9	2,840.8	5,358.4	333.1
1995		313P	193P	23.5P	19.2P	42.4P	690.6P	12.16P	2,433.5P	2,733.6P	5,156.2P	244.1P
1996		322P	197P	23.8P	19.4P	43.1P	715.4P	12.46P	2,592.4P	2,912.2P	5,493.0P	257.7P
1997		331P	202P	24.0P	19.6P	43.7P	740.1P	12.76P	2,751.4P	3,090.7P	5,829.8P	271.3P
1998		340P	207P	24.3P	19.8P	44.4P	764.9P	13.06P	2,910.3P	3,269.2P	6,166.5P	285.0P

Sources: 1982, 1987, 1992 *Economic Census*; *Annual Survey of Manufactures*, 83-86, 88-91, 93-94. Establishment counts for non-Census years are from *County Business Patterns*; establishment values for 83-84 are extrapolations. 'P's show projections by the editors. Industries reclassified in 87 will not have data for prior years.

INDICES OF CHANGE

Year	Com-panies	Establishments		Employment			Compensation		Production ($ million)			
		Total	with 20 or more employees	Total (000)	Production Workers (000)	Production Hours (Mil)	Payroll ($ mil)	Wages ($/hr)	Cost of Materials	Value Added by Manufacture	Value of Shipments	Capital Invest.
1982												
1983												
1984												
1985												
1986												
1987	81	83	86	96	96	93	82	87	73	71	72	105
1988		88	92	100	99	97	87	88	78	72	75	151
1989		93	91	96	98	99	89	88	84	76	80	93
1990		91	91	94	98	98	90	91	88	67	76	91
1991		93	90	92	92	92	87	93	87	67	76	131
1992	100	100	100	100	100	100	100	100	100	100	100	100
1993		104	106	103	104	105	107	102	111	125	117	119
1994		106P	104P	106	105	107	111	103	125	147	135	233
1995		109P	107P	103P	104P	106P	112P	106P	120P	142P	130P	171P
1996		112P	110P	104P	105P	108P	116P	108P	128P	151P	138P	180P
1997		115P	112P	105P	106P	110P	120P	111P	136P	160P	146P	190P
1998		118P	115P	107P	107P	111P	125P	114P	143P	169P	155P	200P

Sources: Same as General Statistics. Values reflect change from the base year, 1992. Values above 100 mean greater than 92, values below 100 mean less than 92, and a value of 100 in the 82-91 or 93-98 period means same as 92. 'P's mark projections by the editors.

SELECTED RATIOS

For 1994	Avg. of All Manufact.	Analyzed Industry	Index	For 1994	Avg. of All Manufact.	Analyzed Industry	Index
Employees per Establishment	49	79	162	Value Added per Production Worker	134,084	145,682	109
Payroll per Establishment	1,500,273	2,249,272	150	Cost per Establishment	5,045,178	8,314,843	165
Payroll per Employee	30,620	28,386	93	Cost per Employee	102,970	104,934	102
Production Workers per Establishment	34	64	187	Cost per Production Worker	146,988	129,687	88
Wages per Establishment	853,319	1,666,164	195	Shipments per Establishment	9,576,895	17,618,037	184
Wages per Production Worker	24,861	25,987	105	Shipments per Employee	195,460	222,340	114
Hours per Production Worker	2,056	2,195	107	Shipments per Production Worker	279,017	274,790	98
Wages per Hour	12.09	11.84	98	Investment per Establishment	321,011	1,095,209	341
Value Added per Establishment	4,602,255	9,340,348	203	Investment per Employee	6,552	13,822	211
Value Added per Employee	93,930	117,876	125	Investment per Production Worker	9,352	17,082	183

Sources: Same as General Statistics. The 'Average of All Manufacturing' column represents the average of all manufacturing industries reported for the most recent complete year available. The Index shows the relationship between the Average and the Analyzed Industry. For example, 100 means that they are equal; 500 that the Analyzed Industry is five times the average; 50 means that the Analyzed Industry is half the national average. The abbreviation 'na' is used to show that data are 'not available'.

LEADING COMPANIES

Number shown: 22 Total sales ($ mil): **1,566** Total employment (000): **14.2**

Company Name	Address				CEO Name	Phone	Co. Type	Sales ($ mil)	Empl. (000)
Valcor Inc	5430 LBJ Fwy	Dallas	TX	75240	Michael A Snetzer	214-233-1700	S	350	5.3
Louisiana-Pacific Corp	PO Box 4000-98	Hayden Lake	ID	83835	Jim Eisses	208-772-6011	D	350*	2.8
Masonite Corp	1 S Wacker Dr	Chicago	IL	60606	Manco L Snapp	312-750-0900	D	250	1.3
Medite Corp	PO Box 4040	Medford	OR	97501	Jerry L Bramwell	503-773-2522	S	200	0.7
Celotex Corp	PO Box 31602	Tampa	FL	33631	Ken Hyatt	813-873-4000	S	190*	2.7
Celotex Corp Sunbury	1400 Susquehanna	Sunbury	PA	17801	Robert Frost	717-286-5831	D	45	0.1
Ponderosa Products Inc	PO Box 25506	Albuquerque	NM	87125	James D Harrison	505-843-7400	S	28	0.2
Woods Group Inc	PO Box 25506	Albuquerque	NM	87125	E Steward	505-843-7400	R	28	0.2
Tectum Inc	PO Box 3002	Newark	OH	43058	S Mihaly	614-345-9691	R	20*	0.1
GVK America Inc	157 GVK Dr	Biscoe	NC	27209	GVK Reddy	910-428-3080	S	16	<0.1
Rodman Industries	PO Box 76	Marinette	WI	54143	Larry Starkweather	715-735-9500	D	14	<0.1
Lydall Inc	PO Box 599	Covington	TN	38019	J Cook	901-476-7174	D	13	0.1
Lionite Hardboard Co	PO Box 138	Phillips	WI	54555	Don Olson	715-339-2111	S	11	<0.1
Indian Country Inc	HC 86	Deposit	NY	13754	Gerard Kamp	607-467-3801	R	10	0.1
Panel Processing of Texas Inc	PO Box 871	Jacksonville	TX	75766	RW Murdock	903-586-2424	S	8	<0.1
Groovfold Inc	PO Box 317	Newcomerstown	OH	43832	Chris Cornell	614-498-8363	R	6	<0.1
Sylvan Sales Inc	PO Box 310	Lake City	PA	16423	C Senzel	814-774-3186	R	6	<0.1
Bally Block Co	PO Box 188	Bally	PA	19503	J Dau	610-845-7511	R	5	0.1
Nuwoods Inc	PO Box 706	Lenoir	NC	28645	Fred H Fulmer	704-758-4463	S	5	<0.1
New York Hardboard	129 30th St	Brooklyn	NY	11232	S Sigman	718-768-4830	R	4	<0.1
Service Products Inc	5900 W 51st St	Chicago	IL	60638	Randy Horst	312-767-2360	R	4	<0.1
Fiberwood Inc	5854 88th St	Sacramento	CA	95828	Stu Douglass	916-387-9754	R	3	<0.1

Source: *Ward's Business Directory of U.S. Private and Public Companies*, Volumes 1 and 2, 1996. The company type code used is as follows: P - Public, R - Private, S - Subsidiary, D - Division, J - Joint Venture, A - Affiliate, G - Group. Sales are in millions of dollars, employees are in thousands. An asterisk (*) indicates an estimated sales volume. The symbol < stands for 'less than'. Company names and addresses are truncated, in some cases, to fit into the available space.

MATERIALS CONSUMED

Material		Quantity	Delivered Cost ($ million)
Materials, ingredients, containers, and supplies		(X)	1,727.8
Logs, bolts, and unsliced flitches	mil ft log scale	(D)	(D)
Pulpwood	1,000 standard cords	(D)	(D)
Chips, slabs, edgings, sawdust, and other wood waste, except planer shavings	1,000 s tons	5,767.8	174.5
Planer shavings	1,000 s tons	4,376.2	139.7
Hardboard (wood fiberboard)	mil sq ft (1/8 in. b	(S)	37.8
Medium density fiberboard (MDF)	mil sq ft (3/4 in. b	93.3*	30.1
Particleboard (wood)	mil sq ft (3/4 in. b	477.1*	106.1
Paints, varnishes, lacquers, stains, shellacs, japans, enamels, and allied products	1,000 gallons	7,496.9**	62.2
Urea and melamine resins	mil lb (dry basis)	1,617.2*	184.5
Phenolic and other tar acid resins	mil lb (dry basis)	462.2**	114.2
Petroleum wax	mil lb (dry basis)	266.1*	44.7
Vinyl and paper overlays	mil sq ft sm	1,688.8*	86.8
Plastic laminates		(X)	6.2
All other plastics resins consumed in the form of granules, pellets, powders, liquids, etc.		(X)	27.7
All other materials and components, parts, containers, and supplies		(X)	377.6
Materials, ingredients, containers, and supplies, nsk		(X)	93.3

Source: 1992 *Economic Census*. Explanation of symbols used: (D): Withheld to avoid disclosure of competitive data; na: Not available; (S): Withheld because statistical norms were not met; (X): Not applicable; (Z): Less than half the unit shown; nec: Not elsewhere classified; nsk: Not specified by kind; - : zero; * : 10-19 percent estimated; ** : 20-29 percent estimated.

PRODUCT SHARE DETAILS

Product or Product Class	% Share
Reconstituted wood products	100.00
Particleboard, produced at this location	23.87
Particleboard floor underlayment, produced at this location	6.36
Particleboard industrial board (furniture, fixtures, cabinets, toys, games, electronic cabinets, etc.), produced at this location	69.94
Other particleboard, including stepping, siding, shelving, and door core, etc., produced at this location	18.23
Particleboard, produced at this location, nsk	5.48
Waferboard and oriented strand board	28.44
Waferboard and oriented strand board sheathing panels	61.93
Waferboard and oriented strand board underlayment panels	9.71
Waferboard and oriented strand board panels with surface treatment (overlays, filled, and sanded)	(D)
Other waferboard and oriented strand board panels, nec	(D)
Medium density fiberboard (MDF) produced at this location	9.63
Standard panel medium density fiberboard, not coated or prefinished, produced at this location	61.09
All other medium density fiberboard, including cut to size, prefinished, produced at this location	37.01
Medium density fiberboard (mdf) produced at this location, nsk	1.93
Hardboard products made from hardboard produced at this location	17.14
Standard hardboard (not machined or coated) made from hardboard produced at this location	17.14
Service, tempered, and other basic hardboard (not machined or coated) made from hardboard produced at this location	(D)
Machined and cut hardboard (including molded, cut to size, perforated, panel stock, etc.), not coated, made from hardboard produced at this location	(D)
Coated or laminated hardboard interior paneling, made from hardboard produced at this location	3.75

Continued on next page.

PRODUCT SHARE DETAILS - Continued

Product or Product Class	% Share	Product or Product Class	% Share
Coated or laminated hardboard exterior siding, made from hardboard produced at this location	44.23	Other coated or laminated hardboard products, including doorskins, garage door panels, furniture stock, and siding, made from purchased hardboard	35.38
Other coated or laminated hardboard products, including doorskins, garage door panels, and furniture stock, made from hardboard produced at this location	(D)	Hardboard products made from purchased hardboard, nsk	24.93
Hardboard products made from hardboard produced at this location, nsk	1.99	Prefinished particleboard and medium density fiberboard (MDF) made from purchased particleboard and MDF	10.92
Cellulosic fiberboard (insulating board)	2.62	Prefinished particleboard made from purchased particleboard	72.18
Hardboard products made from purchased hardboard	4.37	Prefinished or coated medium density fiberboard (MDF) made from purchased MDF	16.54
Machined and cut hardboard, including molded, cut to size, perforated, panel stock, etc., not coated, made from purchased hardboard	13.04	Prefinished particleboard and medium density fiberboard (mdf) made from purchased particleboard and mdf, nsk	11.27
Coated or laminated hardboard interior paneling, made from purchased hardboard	26.65	Reconstituted wood products, nsk	3.00

Source: 1992 *Economic Census*. The values shown are percent of total shipments in an industry. Values of indented subcategories are summed in the main heading. The symbol (D) appears when data are withheld to prevent disclosure of competitive information. The abbreviation nsk stands for 'not specified by kind' and nec for 'not elsewhere classified'.

INPUTS AND OUTPUTS FOR PARTICLEBOARD

Economic Sector or Industry Providing Inputs	%	Sector	Economic Sector or Industry Buying Outputs	%	Sector
Adhesives & sealants	20.0	Manufg.	Wood household furniture	13.2	Manufg.
Sawmills & planning mills, general	17.9	Manufg.	Mobile homes	10.9	Manufg.
Imports	14.6	Foreign	Wood kitchen cabinets	10.7	Manufg.
Electric services (utilities)	9.2	Util.	Wood partitions & fixtures	10.2	Manufg.
Wholesale trade	7.2	Trade	Veneer & plywood	6.6	Manufg.
Logging camps & logging contractors	4.4	Manufg.	Wood products, nec	4.9	Manufg.
Motor freight transportation & warehousing	4.1	Util.	Ship building & repairing	3.5	Manufg.
Gas production & distribution (utilities)	2.9	Util.	Exports	3.0	Foreign
Petroleum refining	2.8	Manufg.	Wood office furniture	2.9	Manufg.
Veneer & plywood	2.0	Manufg.	Residential 1-unit structures, nonfarm	2.8	Constr.
Miscellaneous plastics products	1.9	Manufg.	Millwork	2.8	Manufg.
Railroads & related services	1.5	Util.	Metal household furniture	2.7	Manufg.
Metal stampings, nec	1.3	Manufg.	Residential garden apartments	2.5	Constr.
Paints & allied products	1.2	Manufg.	Boat building & repairing	2.4	Manufg.
Fabricated metal products, nec	0.8	Manufg.	Metal office furniture	2.3	Manufg.
Banking	0.8	Fin/R.E.	Residential additions/alterations, nonfarm	2.2	Constr.
Advertising	0.6	Services	Public building furniture	2.0	Manufg.
Eating & drinking places	0.5	Trade	Wood TV & radio cabinets	2.0	Manufg.
Automotive rental & leasing, without drivers	0.5	Services	Metal partitions & fixtures	1.4	Manufg.
Maintenance of nonfarm buildings nec	0.4	Constr.	Office buildings	0.8	Constr.
Automotive repair shops & services	0.4	Services	Residential high-rise apartments	0.8	Constr.
Detective & protective services	0.4	Services	Prefabricated wood buildings	0.8	Manufg.
Communications, except radio & TV	0.3	Util.	Furniture & fixtures, nec	0.7	Manufg.
Sanitary services, steam supply, irrigation	0.3	Util.	Miscellaneous plastics products	0.7	Manufg.
Water transportation	0.3	Util.	Structural wood members, nec	0.7	Manufg.
Business services nec	0.3	Services	Nonfarm residential structure maintenance	0.6	Constr.
Air transportation	0.2	Util.	Residential 2-4 unit structures, nonfarm	0.5	Constr.
Water supply & sewage systems	0.2	Util.	Sporting & athletic goods, nec	0.5	Manufg.
Insurance carriers	0.2	Fin/R.E.	Construction of educational buildings	0.4	Constr.
Management & consulting services & labs	0.2	Services	Construction of hospitals	0.4	Constr.
U.S. Postal Service	0.2	Gov't	Hotels & motels	0.4	Constr.
Coal	0.1	Mining	Industrial buildings	0.4	Constr.
Abrasive products	0.1	Manufg.	Construction of stores & restaurants	0.3	Constr.
Machinery, except electrical, nec	0.1	Manufg.	Fabricated plate work (boiler shops)	0.2	Manufg.
Legal services	0.1	Services	Paper mills, except building paper	0.2	Manufg.
			Signs & advertising displays	0.2	Manufg.
			Upholstered household furniture	0.2	Manufg.
			Warehouses	0.1	Constr.
			Fabricated structural metal	0.1	Manufg.
			Surgical & medical instruments	0.1	Manufg.
			S/L Govt. purch., higher education	0.1	S/L Govt

Source: Benchmark Input-Output Accounts for the U.S. Economy, 1982, U.S. Department of Commerce, Washington, D.C., July 1991. Data, as reported in the source, are organized by the 1977 SIC structure in use in 1982 but have been matched, as closely as is possible, to the 1987 SIC structure used in this book.

OCCUPATIONS EMPLOYED BY SIC 249 - WOOD CONTAINERS AND MISCELLANEOUS WOOD PRODUCTS

Occupation	% of Total 1994	Change to 2005	Occupation	% of Total 1994	Change to 2005
Assemblers, fabricators, & hand workers nec	15.4	10.0	Industrial machinery mechanics	2.3	21.0
Woodworking machine workers	9.3	-12.0	Sales & related workers nec	1.8	10.0
Head sawyers & sawing machine workers	7.6	-45.0	Inspectors, testers, & graders, precision	1.7	10.0
Machine feeders & offbearers	5.1	-1.0	Industrial production managers	1.6	10.0
Blue collar worker supervisors	4.5	0.7	Secretaries, ex legal & medical	1.5	0.2
Helpers, laborers, & material movers nec	4.2	10.0	Bookkeeping, accounting, & auditing clerks	1.5	-17.5
Wood machinists	4.1	10.0	General office clerks	1.5	-6.2
Industrial truck & tractor operators	4.0	10.0	Traffic, shipping, & receiving clerks	1.3	5.9
Freight, stock, & material movers, hand	3.8	-12.0	Carpenters	1.1	-12.0
General managers & top executives	3.7	4.4	Cabinetmakers & bench carpenters	1.1	-1.0
Truck drivers light & heavy	3.0	13.4	Extruding & forming machine workers	1.0	21.0
Coating, painting, & spraying machine workers	2.5	10.0			

Source: Industry-Occupation Matrix, Bureau of Labor Statistics. These data relate to one or more 3-digit SIC industry groups rather than to a single 4-digit SIC. The change reported for each occupation to the year 2005 is a percent of growth or decline as estimated by the Bureau of Labor Statistics. The abbreviation nec stands for 'not elsewhere classified'.

LOCATION BY STATE AND REGIONAL CONCENTRATION

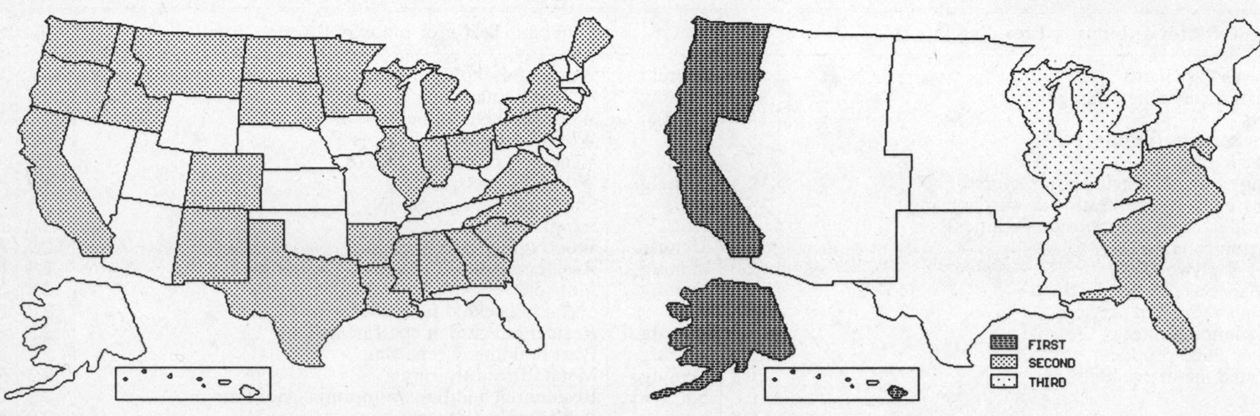

INDUSTRY DATA BY STATE

State	Establish-ments	Shipments Total ($ mil)	Shipments % of U.S.	Shipments Per Establ.	Employment Total Number	Employment % of U.S.	Employment Per Establ.	Wages ($/hour)	Cost as % of Shipments	Investment per Employee ($)
Oregon	24	461.9	11.6	19.2	2,400	10.5	100	13.45	60.4	4,667
Minnesota	11	325.8	8.2	29.6	1,300	5.7	118	15.23	36.5	6,462
Michigan	16	300.1	7.5	18.8	1,400	6.1	88	13.78	44.9	6,000
North Carolina	20	286.9	7.2	14.3	2,100	9.2	105	10.30	63.5	6,667
Georgia	14	260.4	6.5	18.6	1,200	5.3	86	10.95	48.9	11,250
Texas	16	251.0	6.3	15.7	1,100	4.8	69	11.10	48.9	9,545
California	27	229.0	5.8	8.5	1,500	6.6	56	11.48	59.8	4,200
Wisconsin	8	211.6	5.3	26.5	900	3.9	113	11.25	48.1	3,000
Pennsylvania	11	203.2	5.1	18.5	1,000	4.4	91	13.10	41.3	8,300
Virginia	11	197.0	4.9	17.9	1,300	5.7	118	10.00	49.0	3,769
South Carolina	9	143.5	3.6	15.9	1,000	4.4	111	11.71	61.6	7,000
Louisiana	6	134.0	3.4	22.3	900	3.9	150	11.94	57.2	-
Ohio	8	84.6	2.1	10.6	400	1.8	50	11.20	45.4	-
Illinois	9	59.9	1.5	6.7	800	3.5	89	6.54	55.3	2,125
Arkansas	3	59.1	1.5	19.7	400	1.8	133	10.50	52.8	500
Washington	10	38.8	1.0	3.9	300	1.3	30	8.00	47.9	7,000
Indiana	12	36.6	0.9	3.0	400	1.8	33	8.17	33.6	8,750
Mississippi	8	(D)	-	-	1,750 *	7.7	219	-	-	-
Alabama	7	(D)	-	-	375 *	1.6	54	-	-	2,400
Colorado	4	(D)	-	-	175 *	0.8	44	-	-	-
Maine	4	(D)	-	-	375 *	1.6	94	-	-	-
Idaho	3	(D)	-	-	175 *	0.8	58	-	-	-
Montana	3	(D)	-	-	375 *	1.6	125	-	-	-
New Mexico	3	(D)	-	-	375 *	1.6	125	-	-	-
New York	3	(D)	-	-	175 *	0.8	58	-	-	-
North Dakota	1	(D)	-	-	375 *	1.6	375	-	-	-
South Dakota	1	(D)	-	-	375 *	1.6	375	-	-	-

Source: 1992 *Economic Census*. The states are in descending order of shipments or establishments (if shipment data are missing for the majority). The symbol (D) appears when data are withheld to prevent disclosure of competitive information. States marked with (D) are sorted by number of establishments. A dash (-) indicates that the data element cannot be calculated; * indicates the midpoint of a range.

2499 - WOOD PRODUCTS, NEC

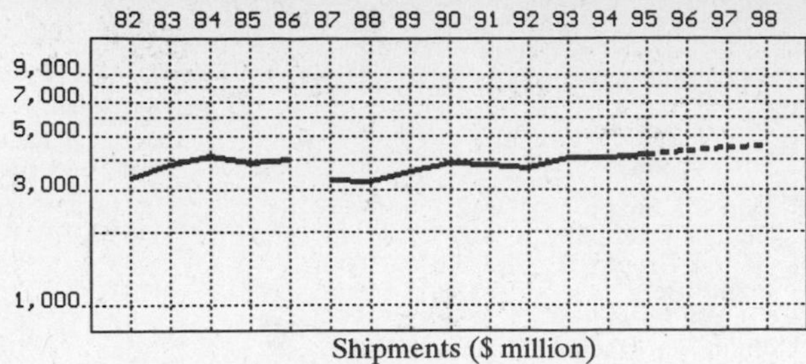

Shipments ($ million)

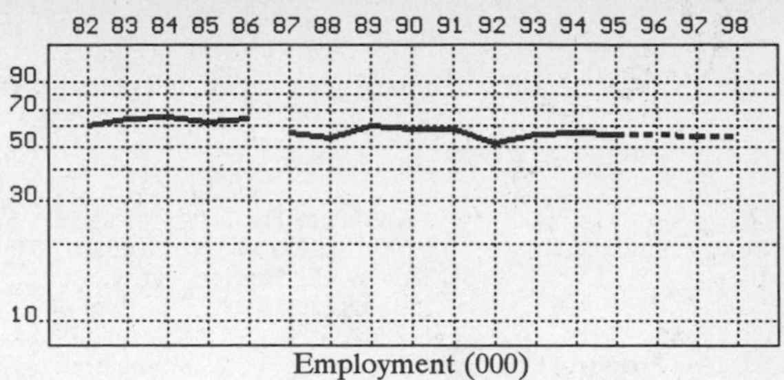

Employment (000)

GENERAL STATISTICS

		Establishments		Employment			Compensation		Production ($ million)			
Year	Com-panies	Total	with 20 or more employees	Total (000)	Production Workers (000)	Production Hours (Mil)	Payroll ($ mil)	Wages ($/hr)	Cost of Materials	Value Added by Manufacture	Value of Shipments	Capital Invest.
1982	3,226	3,387	644	60.6	49.4	90.0	799.6	6.21	1,677.8	1,645.6	3,347.8	142.3
1983		3,179	656	64.1	52.7	97.7	875.1	6.21	1,798.4	2,019.1	3,786.0	84.9
1984		2,971	668	65.2	53.6	100.4	947.7	6.57	2,053.9	2,087.6	4,118.2	116.4
1985		2,762	681	61.9	50.9	95.1	919.4	6.79	1,981.5	1,935.7	3,895.5	146.7
1986		2,608	677	64.3	52.0	96.2	941.7	6.85	1,989.1	2,003.0	3,986.1	115.0
1987*	3,223	3,324	671	56.1	46.4	86.5	824.2	6.67	1,587.0	1,726.0	3,295.5	74.3
1988		2,932	701	54.0	45.0	84.0	817.4	6.75	1,572.5	1,667.3	3,241.5	41.2
1989		2,653	688	59.7	45.7	90.0	872.6	6.85	1,760.0	1,850.9	3,585.5	88.9
1990		2,732	666	58.0	50.3	93.3	944.8	7.16	1,894.8	1,996.3	3,871.8	67.2
1991		2,752	617	58.1	47.7	93.1	936.1	7.25	1,922.7	1,890.2	3,816.0	60.9
1992	2,644	2,754	589	51.1	42.3	81.0	889.4	7.50	1,726.6	2,007.0	3,716.8	67.7
1993		2,772	604	55.0	47.5	91.6	928.6	7.45	2,017.9	2,078.2	4,065.8	74.7
1994		2,572P	577P	56.5	47.4	88.9	961.3	7.77	1,963.7	2,136.3	4,072.4	73.8
1995		2,504P	559P	55.1P	46.9P	90.0P	980.2P	7.88P	2,043.7P	2,223.4P	4,238.4P	73.6P
1996		2,436P	542P	54.9P	47.0P	90.4P	998.8P	8.04P	2,100.6P	2,285.2P	4,356.2P	74.7P
1997		2,367P	524P	54.7P	47.1P	90.7P	1,017.3P	8.20P	2,157.4P	2,347.0P	4,474.1P	75.9P
1998		2,299P	506P	54.5P	47.1P	91.0P	1,035.9P	8.36P	2,214.2P	2,408.8P	4,591.9P	77.0P

Sources: 1982, 1987, 1992 *Economic Census*; *Annual Survey of Manufactures*, 83-86, 88-91, 93-94. Establishment counts are from *County Business Patterns* for non-Census years; establishment counts for 83-84 are extrapolations. * indicates that industry content changed in 87; earlier years use 77 SICs. 'P's mark projections.

INDICES OF CHANGE

		Establishments		Employment			Compensation		Production ($ million)			
Year	Com-panies	Total	with 20 or more employees	Total (000)	Production Workers (000)	Production Hours (Mil)	Payroll ($ mil)	Wages ($/hr)	Cost of Materials	Value Added by Manufacture	Value of Shipments	Capital Invest.
1982	122	123	109	119	117	111	90	83	97	82	90	210
1983		115	111	125	125	121	98	83	104	101	102	125
1984		108	113	128	127	124	107	88	119	104	111	172
1985		100	116	121	120	117	103	91	115	96	105	217
1986		95	115	126	123	119	106	91	115	100	107	170
1987*	122	121	114	110	110	107	93	89	92	86	89	110
1988		106	119	106	106	104	92	90	91	83	87	61
1989		96	117	117	108	111	98	91	102	92	96	131
1990		99	113	114	119	115	106	95	110	99	104	99
1991		100	105	114	113	115	105	97	111	94	103	90
1992	100	100	100	100	100	100	100	100	100	100	100	100
1993		101	103	108	112	113	104	99	117	104	109	110
1994		93P	98P	111	112	110	108	104	114	106	110	109
1995		91P	95P	108P	111P	111P	110P	105P	118P	111P	114P	109P
1996		88P	92P	107P	111P	112P	112P	107P	122P	114P	117P	110P
1997		86P	89P	107P	111P	112P	114P	109P	125P	117P	120P	112P
1998		83P	86P	107P	111P	112P	116P	111P	128P	120P	124P	114P

Sources: Same as General Statistics. Values reflect change from the base year, 1992. Values above 100 mean greater than 92, values below 100 mean less than 92, and a value of 100 in the 82-91 or 93-98 period means same as 92. * indicates that industry content changed in 87. Data for earlier years are in 77 SIC format.

SELECTED RATIOS

For 1994	Avg. of All Manufact.	Analyzed Industry	Index	For 1994	Avg. of All Manufact.	Analyzed Industry	Index
Employees per Establishment	49	22	45	Value Added per Production Worker	134,084	45,070	34
Payroll per Establishment	1,500,273	373,714	25	Cost per Establishment	5,045,178	763,407	15
Payroll per Employee	30,620	17,014	56	Cost per Employee	102,970	34,756	34
Production Workers per Establishment	34	18	54	Cost per Production Worker	146,988	41,428	28
Wages per Establishment	853,319	268,537	31	Shipments per Establishment	9,576,895	1,583,183	17
Wages per Production Worker	24,861	14,573	59	Shipments per Employee	195,460	72,078	37
Hours per Production Worker	2,056	1,876	91	Shipments per Production Worker	279,017	85,916	31
Wages per Hour	12.09	7.77	64	Investment per Establishment	321,011	28,690	9
Value Added per Establishment	4,602,255	830,506	18	Investment per Employee	6,552	1,306	20
Value Added per Employee	93,930	37,811	40	Investment per Production Worker	9,352	1,557	17

Sources: Same as General Statistics. The 'Average of All Manufacturing' column represents the average of all manufacturing industries reported for the most recent complete year available. The Index shows the relationship between the Average and the Analyzed Industry. For example, 100 means that they are equal; 500 that the Analyzed Industry is five times the average; 50 means that the Analyzed Industry is half the national average. The abbreviation 'na' is used to show that data are 'not available'.

LEADING COMPANIES

Number shown: 75 Total sales ($ mil): 2,025 Total employment (000): 21.2

Company Name	Address				CEO Name	Phone	Co. Type	Sales ($ mil)	Empl. (000)
Masonite Corp	1 S Wacker Dr	Chicago	IL	60606	Manco L Snapp	312-750-0900	S	264*	3.0
ABT Building Products Corp	1 Neenah Ctr	Neenah	WI	54956	George T Brophy	414-751-8611	P	203	1.4
ABTCO Inc	3250 W Big Beaver	Troy	MI	48084	George Brophy	313-649-3300	S	203	1.4
Norco	1821 University Av	St Paul	MN	55104	John P Berg	612-645-5557	D	130*	1.5
Larson-Juhl Inc	422 3rd St W	Ashland	WI	54806	Craig A Ponzio	715-682-5257	R	87*	1.0
California Cedar Products Co	PO Box 528	Stockton	CA	95201	Philip Berolzheimer	209-944-5800	R	56*	0.6
Magee Co	PO Box 507	Pocahontas	AR	72455	B Frank Bigger	501-892-5227	S	46*	0.7
Olsonite Corp	8801 Conant Av	Detroit	MI	48211	TA Caponi	313-875-5831	R	45	0.5
National Picture and Frame Co	PO Box 1910	Greenwood	MS	38930	Jesse C Luxton	601-453-6686	P	44	1.1
MCS Industries Inc	2280 Newlins Mill	Easton	PA	18045	Richard Master	215-253-6268	R	42	0.4
Acme Frame Products Inc	1 American Rd	Cleveland	OH	44144	Gary E Johnston	216-476-2263	S	40	0.5
Badger Cork	PO Box 25	Trevor	WI	53179	Henry W Fleck	414-862-2311	D	40	0.2
Pine Mountain Corp	1375 Grand Av	Piedmont	CA	94610	N L Brockbank	510-654-7880	R	40	<0.1
Interaction Marketing	4960 Singleton Blv	Dallas	TX	75212	Keith Wolfe	214-638-1518	R	30*	0.4
Panel Processing Inc	PO Box 457	Alpena	MI	49707	RM Granum	517-356-9007	R	30	0.2
Solon Manufacturing Company	PO Box 285	Solon	ME	04979	HV Tewksbury	207-643-2210	R	30	0.4
Lynn Ladder and Scaffolding	PO Box 346	West Lynn	MA	01905	Bernard M Kline	617-598-6010	R	29*	0.3
Kottler Industries Inc	2650 W Fulton St	Chicago	IL	60612	Edward M Kottler	312-826-3900	R	26*	0.3
Saunders Brothers Inc	PO Box 1016	Westbrook	ME	04098	Bruce J Saunders	207-854-2551	R	26	0.4
Malden International Designs	20 Kendrick Rd	Wareham	MA	02571	John Aucello	508-291-1104	R	25	<0.1
Nagel Manufacturing	PO Box 9386	Austin	TX	78766	WG Nagel	512-837-4800	R	25	0.4
Acme Frame Products	1301 S Illinois St	Harrisburg	AR	72432	Steve Johnson	501-578-2486	D	24*	0.3
Cooper Wood Products Inc	PO Box 489	Rocky Mount	VA	24151	William L Cooper	703-483-9201	R	22	0.3
Hudson ICS	PO Box 2338	San Leandro	CA	94577	Larry Hood	510-351-5872	R	21*	0.3
Dellen Wood Products Inc	N 3014 Flora Rd	Spokane	WA	99216	WE Lentes	509-928-1397	R	20	0.2
IXL Manufacturing Company	PO Box 149	Bernie	MO	63822	BN Keathley	314-293-5341	R	20	0.2
OP Link Handle Company Inc	PO Box 350	Salem	IN	47167	Norman Link	812-883-2981	R	20	0.4
Pioneer Southern Inc	275 Kenyon Rd	Suffolk	VA	23434	JC Adams II	804-539-7489	R	19*	0.2
Master Woodcraft Inc	1 Hanson Pl	Brooklyn	NY	11243	LB Moss	718-636-9100	R	16	0.2
Walpole Woodworkers Inc	767 East St	Walpole	MA	02081	Louis Maglio	508-668-2800	R	16*	0.2
Capitol Interior Inc	493 S Ellis Av	Peshtigo	WI	54157	Don Lingkan	715-582-4212	R	15	0.2
Cascade Wood Components Inc	PO Box 100	Cascade Locks	OR	97014	Gary Hegeweld	503-374-8413	R	15*	<0.1
HB Williamson Co	206 N Summit	Wayne City	IL	62895	Terry Schaubert	618-895-2158	R	15	0.3
Tygart Moulding Corp	PO Box 7747	Charlottesville	VA	22906	W David Abbott	804-979-0715	R	15	0.2
Rochester Shoe Tree Company	PO Box 746	Ashland	NH	03217	Jay Conley	603-968-3301	R	13	0.2
Brooks Manufacturing Co	PO Box 7	Bellingham	WA	98227	John Ferlin	360-733-1700	R	12	<0.1
Strauser Manufacturing Inc	PO Box 991	Walla Walla	WA	99362	JW Strauser	509-529-6284	R	12	0.2
North American Enclosures Inc	85 Jetson Ln	Central Islip	NY	11722	Richard Schwartz	516-234-9500	R	11	0.1
Dadant and Sons Inc	51 S 2nd St	Hamilton	IL	62341	Charles C Dadant	217-847-3324	R	10	<0.1
Industrial Ladder Co	1212 Powell St	Oakland	CA	94608	David E Forristall	510-653-0969	R	10	<0.1
Manchester Wood Inc	PO Box 180	Granville	NY	12832	Clifford F Pierce	518-642-9518	S	10	0.2
Northwest Design Products Inc	7717 New Market St	Olympia	WA	98501	Woody Hill	206-943-6374	R	10*	<0.1
Basketville Inc	PO Box 710	Putney	VT	05346	Greg Wilson	802-387-5509	R	10	0.2
Commercial Carving Company	PO Box 878	Thomasville	NC	27361	BC Murphy	910-475-2301	R	9	0.2
Fordick Corp	PO Box 3186	Shawnee Msn	KS	66203	C Wagoner	913-599-0009	R	9	0.1
Lambert of Arkansas Inc	PO Box 826	Hughes	AR	72348	Stephen L Kroul	501-339-2365	R	9	0.1
Pride Manufacturing Co	RFD 3	Guilford	ME	04443	SG Pride	207-876-3315	R	9	0.2
Idaho Cedar Sales Inc	PO Box 399	Troy	ID	83871	Wendle G Minkler	208-835-2161	S	9	<0.1
Best Molding Corp	PO Box 10259	Albuquerque	NM	87184	Frank Demott	505-898-6770	R	8	<0.1
Duraflame Inc	PO Box 1230	Stockton	CA	95201	Philip Berolzheimer	209-461-6600	R	8	<0.1
Edco Products Inc	845 Excelsior Av E	Hopkins	MN	55343	Gerald Gustafson	612-938-6313	R	8*	0.1
Eureka Manufacturing Co	47 Elm St	Norton	MA	02766	David McLoughlin	508-285-9881	S	8	0.1
Janco Designs Inc	1240 Dielman	St Louis	MO	63132	Lee M Rogers	314-993-1332	R	8*	0.1
Lasercraft Inc	PO Box 696	Santa Rosa	CA	95402	Ralph Skidmore	707-528-1060	R	8	0.1
Arrow Pattern and Foundry Co	9725 S Industrial Dr	Bridgeview	IL	60455	SJ Kuchay	708-598-0300	R	7	<0.1
Brown Wood Products Co	PO Box 8246-W	Northfield	IL	60093	Terry Gross	708-446-5200	R	7	<0.1
Caviness Woodworking Co	PO Drawer 710	Calhoun City	MS	38916	Donald Caviness	601-628-5195	R	7*	<0.1
Dicksons Inc	PO Box 368	Seymour	IN	47274	David Vandivier	812-522-1308	R	7*	0.1
Heath Manufacturing Co	PO Box 105	Coopersville	MI	49404	DE Heath	616-837-8181	R	7	<0.1
National Home Products	535 Schoolhouse Rd	Telford	PA	18969	R Plechner	215-723-8959	R	7	<0.1
New Kearsarge Corp	PO Box 775	Bradford	NH	03221	Peter Moyer	603-938-2266	R	7*	<0.1
Sexton Metalcraft Inc	PO Box 9518	Raytown	MO	64133	Leland Sexton	816-353-4350	R	7	<0.1
Turner, Day	205 N Webb Av	Crossville	TN	38555	Terry Milam	615-484-8491	S	7	0.1
Vermillion Inc	1207 S Scenic Dr	Springfield	MO	65802	P Driscoll	417-862-3785	R	7	0.2
Hill Wood Products Inc	PO Box 398	Cook	MN	55723	S Hill	218-666-5933	R	6	0.1
Chicago Dowel Company Inc	4700 W Grand Av	Chicago	IL	60639	Ralph Iacono	312-622-2000	R	6*	0.1
Creative Designs International	34 State St	Ossining	NY	10562	T Izukawa	914-762-1134	R	6	<0.1
CB Cummings and Sons Co	PO Box 346	Norway	ME	04268	SB Cummings	207-743-6326	R	6	0.2
International Bath Accessories	14260 SW 136th St	Miami	FL	33186	Tony Mears	305-253-8533	R	6	<0.1
Thompson Maple Products Inc	PO Box 99	Corry	PA	16407	CP Henness	814-664-7717	R	6	<0.1
Universal Woods Inc	2600 Grassland Dr	Louisville	KY	40299	Paul T Neumann	502-491-1461	R	6	<0.1
West Coast Forest Products Inc	19406 68th Dr NE	Arlington	WA	98223	Yukiya Wada	206-435-2175	S	6*	0.1
HY-JO Mfg Imports Corp	1830 J Towers Av	El Cajon	CA	92020	Joseph Hayko	619-449-7700	R	6	<0.1
Mid-States Container Corp	PO Box 148	Brookville	OH	45309	Walter Lamb	513-833-4041	D	6	<0.1
August Lotz Company Inc	PO Box 39	Boyd	WI	54726	Mark Schlichter	715-667-5121	R	5	0.1

Source: Ward's Business Directory of U.S. Private and Public Companies, Volumes 1 and 2, 1996. The company type code used is as follows: P - Public, R - Private, S - Subsidiary, D - Division, J - Joint Venture, A - Affiliate, G - Group. Sales are in millions of dollars, employees are in thousands. An asterisk (*) indicates an estimated sales volume. The symbol < stands for 'less than'. Company names and addresses are truncated, in some cases, to fit into the available space.

MATERIALS CONSUMED

Material		Quantity	Delivered Cost ($ million)
Materials, ingredients, containers, and supplies		(X)	1,533.1
Hardwood logs, bolts, and unsliced flitches	mil ft log scale	(S)	54.8
Softwood logs, bolts, and unsliced flitches	mil ft log scale	(S)	10.5
Hardwood rough lumber	mil bd ft	(S)	101.9
Softwood rough lumber	mil bd ft	120.4*	58.4
Hardwood dressed lumber	mil bd ft	(S)	45.3
Softwood dressed lumber	mil bd ft	(S)	91.1
Chips, slabs, edgings, shavings, sawdust, and other wood waste	1,000 s tons	(S)	22.9
Hardwood dimension and parts, excluding furniture frames	mil bd ft	(S)	21.1
Hardwood plywood	mil sq ft sm	45.7**	19.4
Softwood plywood	mil sq ft (3/8 in. b	(S)	27.4
Reconstituted wood products		(X)	21.9
Paints, varnishes, lacquers, stains, shellacs, japans, enamels, and allied products	1,000 gallons	(S)	20.6
Glass (float, sheet and plate)		(X)	21.2
Fabricated metal products, including forgings		(X)	29.7
Paperboard containers, boxes, and corrugated paperboard		(X)	37.6
All other materials and components, parts, containers, and supplies		(X)	397.3
Materials, ingredients, containers, and supplies, nsk		(X)	551.8

Source: 1992 *Economic Census*. Explanation of symbols used: (D): Withheld to avoid disclosure of competitive data; na: Not available; (S): Withheld because statistical norms were not met; (X): Not applicable; (Z): Less than half the unit shown; nec: Not elsewhere classified; nsk: Not specified by kind; - : zero; * : 10-19 percent estimated; ** : 20-29 percent estimated.

PRODUCT SHARE DETAILS

Product or Product Class	% Share	Product or Product Class	% Share
Wood products, nec	100.00	Bamboo, rattan, willow, and chip basketwork, wickerwork, and related products of fibrous vegetable substances	2.16
Mirror and picture frames	23.17	Lasts for boots and shoes (wood and other materials), remodeled last sole patterns and forms, shoe trees, and stretchers	0.59
Wood frames for mirrors and pictures	36.00	Wood striking tool handles (axe, pick, hammer, etc.)	1.25
Metal frames for mirrors and pictures	14.68	Other wood handtool handles, including spade, shovel, rake, scythe, and other mechanics, farm, garden, household, etc.	1.53
Finished wood moldings for mirrors and pictures	6.63	Wood broom, mop, and paintbrush handles	1.21
Finished metal moldings for mirrors and pictures	2.66	Other wood handles: wooden tools, tool bodies, and backs for brooms, mops, and brushes	0.89
Wood framed pictures	24.67	Wood dowels and dowel pins (plain or sanded, grooved, or otherwise advanced in condition)	2.57
Framed pictures other than wood (metal, plastics, fiber)	7.26	Wood stepladders	2.75
Mirror and picture frames, nsk	8.12	Wood rung ladders (nonextension, extension, and scaffolding ladders)	0.69
Cork and cork products, including natural and waste and articles made of natural, granulated, and composition cork	1.95	Wooden reels for wire and cable	8.15
Miscellaneous wood products	56.93	Wood flour	1.28
Wood jewelry boxes, silverware chests, instrument cases, cigar and cigarette boxes, microscope, tool, or utensil cases, etc.	2.14	Other wood fabricated industrial parts, except hardwood furniture parts	2.53
Wood statuettes and other ornaments, including ashtrays, bookends, etc.	2.79	Wood toilet seats, including molded wood	5.05
Wood tableware and kitchenware	2.50	Miscellaneous wooden products, nec, including articles of wood, nec, and wood turnings (except handles)	50.51
Wood fences, palings, and rails assembled into fence sections	2.53	Miscellaneous wood products, nsk	2.30
Wood toothpicks, skewers, candy sticks, ice cream sticks, tongue depressors, drink mixers, and similar small wood wares	2.96	Wood products, nec, nsk	17.96
Firewood and fuel wood containing an added binder, including compressed logs	3.62		

Source: 1992 *Economic Census*. The values shown are percent of total shipments in an industry. Values of indented subcategories are summed in the main heading. The symbol (D) appears when data are withheld to prevent disclosure of competitive information. The abbreviation nsk stands for 'not specified by kind' and nec for 'not elsewhere classified'.

INPUTS AND OUTPUTS FOR WOOD PRODUCTS, NEC

Economic Sector or Industry Providing Inputs	%	Sector	Economic Sector or Industry Buying Outputs	%	Sector
Imports	18.0	Foreign	Personal consumption expenditures	21.9	
Sawmills & planning mills, general	13.0	Manufg.	Wood products, nec	4.5	Manufg.
Wholesale trade	8.5	Trade	Office buildings	4.0	Constr.
Wood products, nec	7.7	Manufg.	Exports	3.5	Foreign
Electric services (utilities)	5.5	Util.	Wood household furniture	3.2	Manufg.
Adhesives & sealants	4.4	Manufg.	Glass & glass products, except containers	2.8	Manufg.
Logging camps & logging contractors	3.8	Manufg.	Miscellaneous plastics products	2.7	Manufg.
Advertising	3.2	Services	Millwork	2.5	Manufg.
Metal stampings, nec	3.1	Manufg.	Paperboard mills	2.3	Manufg.
Gas production & distribution (utilities)	2.3	Util.	Manufacturing industries, nec	2.0	Manufg.
Paints & allied products	2.2	Manufg.	Residential 1-unit structures, nonfarm	1.9	Constr.
Motor freight transportation & warehousing	2.2	Util.	Electric housewares & fans	1.9	Manufg.
Miscellaneous plastics products	2.0	Manufg.	Job training & related services	1.9	Services
Hardwood dimension & flooring mills	1.7	Manufg.	Nonfarm residential structure maintenance	1.8	Constr.

Continued on next page.

INPUTS AND OUTPUTS FOR WOOD PRODUCTS, NEC - Continued

Economic Sector or Industry Providing Inputs	%	Sector	Economic Sector or Industry Buying Outputs	%	Sector
Petroleum refining	1.7	Manufg.	Games, toys, & children's vehicles	1.7	Manufg.
Particleboard	1.6	Manufg.	Mobile homes	1.7	Manufg.
Veneer & plywood	1.4	Manufg.	Residential additions/alterations, nonfarm	1.6	Constr.
Railroads & related services	1.2	Util.	Signs & advertising displays	1.6	Manufg.
Paperboard containers & boxes	1.1	Manufg.	Drapery hardware & blinds & shades	1.5	Manufg.
Screw machine and related products	1.1	Manufg.	Lead pencils & art goods	1.4	Manufg.
Eating & drinking places	1.0	Trade	Construction of educational buildings	1.3	Constr.
Maintenance of nonfarm buildings nec	0.9	Constr.	Wood kitchen cabinets	1.3	Manufg.
Real estate	0.9	Fin/R.E.	Veneer & plywood	1.0	Manufg.
Fabricated metal products, nec	0.8	Manufg.	Blast furnaces & steel mills	0.9	Manufg.
Communications, except radio & TV	0.8	Util.	Primary metal products, nec	0.9	Manufg.
Banking	0.8	Fin/R.E.	Retail trade, except eating & drinking	0.9	Trade
Plastics materials & resins	0.7	Manufg.	Maintenance of nonfarm buildings nec	0.8	Constr.
Glass & glass products, except containers	0.5	Manufg.	Brooms & brushes	0.8	Manufg.
Hardware, nec	0.5	Manufg.	Hardware, nec	0.8	Manufg.
Miscellaneous fabricated wire products	0.4	Manufg.	Paving mixtures & blocks	0.8	Manufg.
Equipment rental & leasing services	0.4	Services	Fabricated metal products, nec	0.7	Manufg.
Management & consulting services & labs	0.4	Services	Hand & edge tools, nec	0.7	Manufg.
Abrasive products	0.3	Manufg.	Ship building & repairing	0.7	Manufg.
Paper coating & glazing	0.3	Manufg.	Upholstered household furniture	0.7	Manufg.
Air transportation	0.3	Util.	Wood partitions & fixtures	0.7	Manufg.
Sanitary services, steam supply, irrigation	0.3	Util.	Wholesale trade	0.7	Trade
Water transportation	0.3	Util.	S/L Govt. purch., other general government	0.7	S/L Govt
Legal services	0.3	Services	Ice cream & frozen desserts	0.6	Manufg.
U.S. Postal Service	0.3	Gov't	Miscellaneous fabricated wire products	0.6	Manufg.
Coal	0.2	Mining	Steel wire & related products	0.6	Manufg.
Machinery, except electrical, nec	0.2	Manufg.	Eating & drinking places	0.6	Trade
Special product sawmills, nec	0.2	Manufg.	Boat building & repairing	0.5	Manufg.
Steel wire & related products	0.2	Manufg.	Costume jewelry	0.5	Manufg.
Woodworking machinery	0.2	Manufg.	Hard surface floor coverings	0.5	Manufg.
Insurance carriers	0.2	Fin/R.E.	Petroleum refining	0.5	Manufg.
Royalties	0.2	Fin/R.E.	Industrial buildings	0.4	Constr.
Accounting, auditing & bookkeeping	0.2	Services	Residential garden apartments	0.4	Constr.
Automotive rental & leasing, without drivers	0.2	Services	Gaskets, packing & sealing devices	0.4	Manufg.
Automotive repair shops & services	0.2	Services	Housefurnishings, nec	0.4	Manufg.
Engineering, architectural, & surveying services	0.2	Services	Lighting fixtures & equipment	0.4	Manufg.
Lubricating oils & greases	0.1	Manufg.	Musical instruments	0.4	Manufg.
Manifold business forms	0.1	Manufg.	Wood TV & radio cabinets	0.4	Manufg.
Special dies & tools & machine tool accessories	0.1	Manufg.	Meat animals	0.3	Agric.
Credit agencies other than banks	0.1	Fin/R.E.	Construction of hospitals	0.3	Constr.
Business/professional associations	0.1	Services	Aluminum rolling & drawing	0.3	Manufg.
State & local government enterprises, nec	0.1	Gov't	Chemical preparations, nec	0.3	Manufg.
			Marking devices	0.3	Manufg.
			Metal office furniture	0.3	Manufg.
			Metal partitions & fixtures	0.3	Manufg.
			Public building furniture	0.3	Manufg.
			Wood office furniture	0.3	Manufg.
			Real estate	0.3	Fin/R.E.
			Doctors & dentists	0.3	Services
			S/L Govt. purch., public assistance & relief	0.3	S/L Govt
			Feed grains	0.2	Agric.
			Construction of stores & restaurants	0.2	Constr.
			Highway & street construction	0.2	Constr.
			Maintenance of petroleum & natural gas wells	0.2	Constr.
			Maintenance of sewer facilities	0.2	Constr.
			Residential 2-4 unit structures, nonfarm	0.2	Constr.
			Copper rolling & drawing	0.2	Manufg.
			Crowns & closures	0.2	Manufg.
			Cutlery	0.2	Manufg.
			Explosives	0.2	Manufg.
			Metal stampings, nec	0.2	Manufg.
			Motor vehicle parts & accessories	0.2	Manufg.
			Pipe, valves, & pipe fittings	0.2	Manufg.
			Prefabricated wood buildings	0.2	Manufg.
			Shoes, except rubber	0.2	Manufg.
			Sporting & athletic goods, nec	0.2	Manufg.
			Travel trailers & campers	0.2	Manufg.
			Labor, civic, social, & fraternal associations	0.2	Services
			Legal services	0.2	Services
			Dairy farm products	0.1	Agric.
			Maintenance of highways & streets	0.1	Constr.
			Maintenance of nonbuilding facilities nec	0.1	Constr.
			Telephone & telegraph facility construction	0.1	Constr.
			Electrical equipment & supplies, nec	0.1	Manufg.
			Metal household furniture	0.1	Manufg.

Continued on next page.

INPUTS AND OUTPUTS FOR WOOD PRODUCTS, NEC - Continued

Economic Sector or Industry Providing Inputs	%	Sector	Economic Sector or Industry Buying Outputs	%	Sector
			Truck trailers	0.1	Manufg.
			Computer & data processing services	0.1	Services
			Management & consulting services & labs	0.1	Services
			S/L Govt. purch., elem. & secondary education	0.1	S/L Govt
			S/L Govt. purch., higher education	0.1	S/L Govt

Source: Benchmark Input-Output Accounts for the U.S. Economy, 1982, U.S. Department of Commerce, Washington, D.C., July 1991. Data, as reported in the source, are organized by the 1977 SIC structure in use in 1982 but have been matched, as closely as is possible, to the 1987 SIC structure used in this book.

OCCUPATIONS EMPLOYED BY SIC 249 - WOOD CONTAINERS AND MISCELLANEOUS WOOD PRODUCTS

Occupation	% of Total 1994	Change to 2005	Occupation	% of Total 1994	Change to 2005
Assemblers, fabricators, & hand workers nec	15.4	10.0	Industrial machinery mechanics	2.3	21.0
Woodworking machine workers	9.3	-12.0	Sales & related workers nec	1.8	10.0
Head sawyers & sawing machine workers	7.6	-45.0	Inspectors, testers, & graders, precision	1.7	10.0
Machine feeders & offbearers	5.1	-1.0	Industrial production managers	1.6	10.0
Blue collar worker supervisors	4.5	0.7	Secretaries, ex legal & medical	1.5	0.2
Helpers, laborers, & material movers nec	4.2	10.0	Bookkeeping, accounting, & auditing clerks	1.5	-17.5
Wood machinists	4.1	10.0	General office clerks	1.5	-6.2
Industrial truck & tractor operators	4.0	10.0	Traffic, shipping, & receiving clerks	1.3	5.9
Freight, stock, & material movers, hand	3.8	-12.0	Carpenters	1.1	-12.0
General managers & top executives	3.7	4.4	Cabinetmakers & bench carpenters	1.1	-1.0
Truck drivers light & heavy	3.0	13.4	Extruding & forming machine workers	1.0	21.0
Coating, painting, & spraying machine workers	2.5	10.0			

Source: Industry-Occupation Matrix, Bureau of Labor Statistics. These data relate to one or more 3-digit SIC industry groups rather than to a single 4-digit SIC. The change reported for each occupation to the year 2005 is a percent of growth or decline as estimated by the Bureau of Labor Statistics. The abbreviation nec stands for 'not elsewhere classified'.

LOCATION BY STATE AND REGIONAL CONCENTRATION

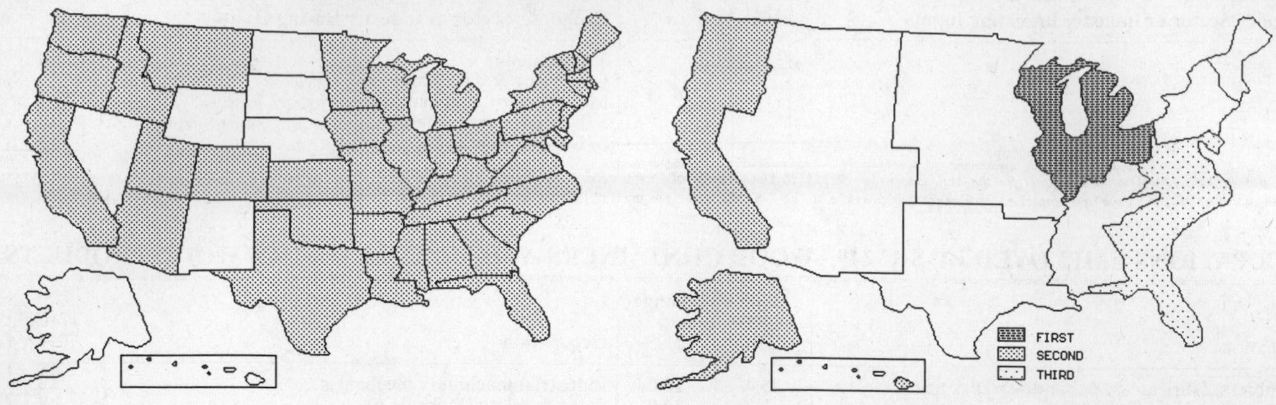

INDUSTRY DATA BY STATE

State	Establish-ments	Shipments			Employment				Cost as % of Shipments	Investment per Employee ($)
		Total ($ mil)	% of U.S.	Per Establ.	Total Number	% of U.S.	Per Establ.	Wages ($/hour)		
California	309	561.2	15.1	1.8	6,600	12.9	21	7.44	53.2	1,136
Ohio	142	397.7	10.7	2.8	4,100	8.0	29	8.64	31.3	2,000
North Carolina	111	203.1	5.5	1.8	2,500	4.9	23	8.05	42.9	1,320
New York	168	202.4	5.4	1.2	3,100	6.1	18	8.00	47.3	-
Texas	129	189.0	5.1	1.5	2,600	5.1	20	6.91	46.6	1,346
Illinois	106	170.2	4.6	1.6	2,600	5.1	25	7.70	43.2	846
Mississippi	50	164.6	4.4	3.3	2,400	4.7	48	6.29	48.0	2,250
Maine	63	155.8	4.2	2.5	2,800	5.5	44	7.60	35.8	1,071
Indiana	85	104.5	2.8	1.2	1,700	3.3	20	6.92	52.5	-
Arkansas	47	103.5	2.8	2.2	1,400	2.7	30	6.33	47.2	1,143
Florida	92	102.1	2.7	1.1	1,400	2.7	15	6.35	55.9	929
Missouri	89	98.3	2.6	1.1	1,600	3.1	18	6.50	46.8	1,063
Michigan	87	96.0	2.6	1.1	1,000	2.0	11	8.50	51.0	1,300
Wisconsin	94	93.0	2.5	1.0	1,600	3.1	17	8.28	45.4	1,375
Massachusetts	65	92.1	2.5	1.4	1,100	2.2	17	8.94	49.1	727
Tennessee	71	86.4	2.3	1.2	1,500	2.9	21	6.48	47.8	733
Virginia	56	71.9	1.9	1.3	1,400	2.7	25	6.81	49.9	1,214
Washington	76	68.0	1.8	0.9	900	1.8	12	9.42	46.0	1,778
Pennsylvania	108	67.2	1.8	0.6	900	1.8	8	8.00	52.5	1,222
Vermont	35	59.8	1.6	1.7	700	1.4	20	9.55	50.5	-
Minnesota	62	59.6	1.6	1.0	900	1.8	15	7.21	48.5	-
Oregon	96	52.3	1.4	0.5	900	1.8	9	6.58	49.5	1,111
Georgia	51	48.7	1.3	1.0	700	1.4	14	7.30	55.9	1,571
New Hampshire	41	44.4	1.2	1.1	700	1.4	17	8.08	37.4	1,429
New Jersey	43	40.0	1.1	0.9	500	1.0	12	7.57	54.7	600
South Carolina	32	32.8	0.9	1.0	600	1.2	19	6.30	48.2	1,167
Connecticut	21	24.1	0.6	1.1	300	0.6	14	10.00	58.9	-
Kansas	23	19.5	0.5	0.8	300	0.6	13	7.50	30.3	667
Arizona	30	19.0	0.5	0.6	400	0.8	13	6.60	47.9	500
Oklahoma	21	18.8	0.5	0.9	200	0.4	10	9.33	47.3	1,000
Louisiana	21	14.4	0.4	0.7	200	0.4	10	5.75	52.1	2,000
West Virginia	19	12.0	0.3	0.6	200	0.4	11	7.50	46.7	2,500
Colorado	35	11.3	0.3	0.3	200	0.4	6	6.33	38.9	-
Montana	22	10.1	0.3	0.5	200	0.4	9	6.67	46.5	500
Idaho	16	7.7	0.2	0.5	100	0.2	6	6.00	57.1	-
Alabama	54	(D)	-	-	750 *	1.5	14	-	-	4,667
Iowa	32	(D)	-	-	750 *	1.5	23	-	-	533
Kentucky	30	(D)	-	-	750 *	1.5	25	-	-	1,600
Maryland	24	(D)	-	-	375 *	0.7	16	-	-	4,000
Utah	18	(D)	-	-	175 *	0.3	10	-	-	-

Source: 1992 *Economic Census*. The states are in descending order of shipments or establishments (if shipment data are missing for the majority). The symbol (D) appears when data are withheld to prevent disclosure of competitive information. States marked with (D) are sorted by number of establishments. A dash (-) indicates that the data element cannot be calculated; * indicates the midpoint of a range.

2511 - WOOD HOUSEHOLD FURNITURE

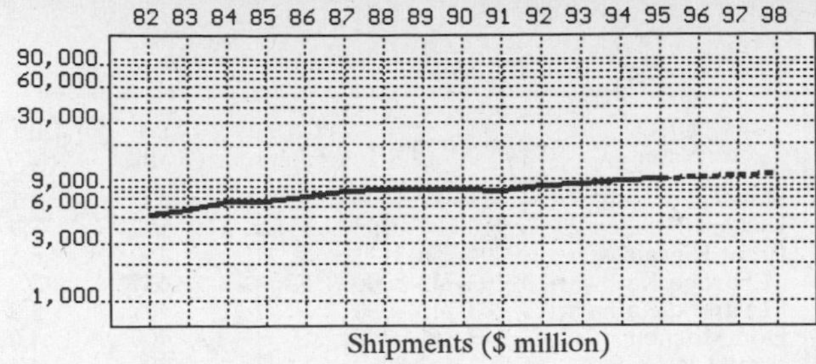

Shipments ($ million)

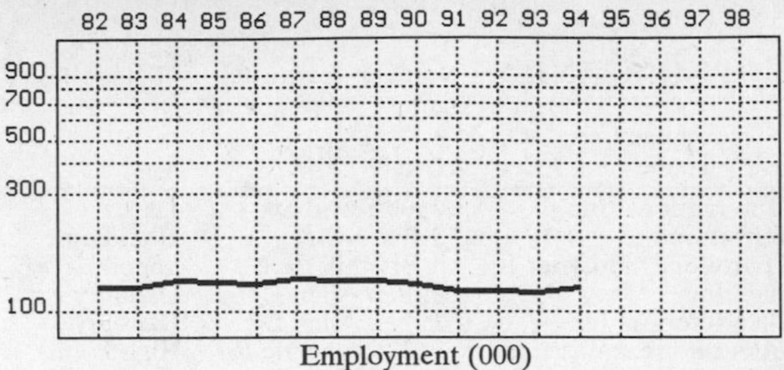

Employment (000)

GENERAL STATISTICS

Year	Com-panies	Establishments: Total	Establishments: with 20 or more employees	Employment: Total (000)	Production Workers (000)	Production Hours (Mil)	Compensation: Payroll ($ mil)	Compensation: Wages ($/hr)	Cost of Materials	Value Added by Manufacture	Value of Shipments	Capital Invest.
1982	2,430	2,607	833	125.6	109.2	197.2	1,402.7	5.43	2,317.8	2,715.0	5,056.6	119.1
1983		2,556	837	125.7	109.7	208.0	1,532.0	5.70	2,640.2	3,088.5	5,702.4	111.5
1984		2,505	841	134.9	118.1	227.0	1,717.9	5.86	3,223.5	3,459.0	6,613.2	138.7
1985		2,453	845	133.2	115.9	221.1	1,748.8	6.12	3,194.6	3,526.7	6,727.6	151.6
1986		2,502	851	128.6	114.1	223.1	1,799.5	6.34	3,468.6	3,802.8	7,237.5	138.5
1987	2,770	2,948	864	135.8	118.8	235.2	2,017.1	6.67	3,784.2	4,265.5	7,982.0	196.9
1988		2,754	866			232.1	2,111.8		3,915.6	4,463.4	8,275.4	212.4
1989		2,583	829	134.0	116.4	226.6	2,114.1	7.07	4,153.3	4,339.7	8,460.7	263.7
1990		2,627	771	129.6	112.6	219.2	2,097.1	7.16	3,991.8	4,399.0	8,302.9	184.6
1991		2,588	735	121.4	103.8	199.0	2,004.9	7.49	3,834.6	4,169.3	7,979.8	166.1
1992	2,634	2,786	720	121.1	105.3	205.7	2,173.5	8.00	4,055.4	4,726.2	8,737.0	197.4
1993		2,827	724	119.0	105.4	201.9	2,182.7	8.39	4,529.1	4,847.8	9,267.2	237.5
1994		2,781P	732P	125.4	110.6	215.5	2,362.6	8.44	4,765.1	5,247.7	9,918.5	257.3
1995		2,802P	720P			212.9P	2,416.4P		4,848.2P	5,339.2P	10,091.5P	255.7P
1996		2,823P	708P			212.4P	2,483.9P		5,011.5P	5,519.0P	10,431.3P	266.1P
1997		2,844P	696P			211.9P	2,551.5P		5,174.8P	5,698.9P	10,771.2P	276.5P
1998		2,865P	684P			211.4P	2,619.0P		5,338.1P	5,878.7P	11,111.1P	286.9P

Sources: 1982, 1987, 1992 *Economic Census*; *Annual Survey of Manufactures*, 83-86, 88-91, 93-94. Establishment counts for non-Census years are from *County Business Patterns*; establishment values for 83-84 are extrapolations. 'P's show projections by the editors. Industries reclassified in 87 will not have data for prior years.

INDICES OF CHANGE

Year	Com-panies	Establishments: Total	Establishments: with 20 or more employees	Employment: Total (000)	Production Workers (000)	Production Hours (Mil)	Compensation: Payroll ($ mil)	Compensation: Wages ($/hr)	Cost of Materials	Value Added by Manufacture	Value of Shipments	Capital Invest.
1982	92	94	116	104	104	96	65	68	57	57	58	60
1983		92	116	104	104	101	70	71	65	65	65	56
1984		90	117	111	112	110	79	73	79	73	76	70
1985		88	117	110	110	107	80	77	79	75	77	77
1986		90	118	106	108	108	83	79	86	80	83	70
1987	105	106	120	112	113	114	93	83	93	90	91	100
1988		99	120			113	97		97	94	95	108
1989		93	115	111	111	110	97	88	102	92	97	134
1990		94	107	107	107	107	96	90	98	93	95	94
1991		93	102	100	99	97	92	94	95	88	91	84
1992	100	100	100	100	100	100	100	100	100	100	100	100
1993		101	101	98	100	98	100	105	112	103	106	120
1994		100P	102P	104	105	105	109	106	118	111	114	130
1995		101P	100P			103P	111P		120P	113P	116P	130P
1996		101P	98P			103P	114P		124P	117P	119P	135P
1997		102P	97P			103P	117P		128P	121P	123P	140P
1998		103P	95P			103P	120P		132P	124P	127P	145P

Sources: Same as General Statistics. Values reflect change from the base year, 1992. Values above 100 mean greater than 92, values below 100 mean less than 92, and a value of 100 in the 82-91 or 93-98 period means same as 92. 'P's mark projections by the editors.

SELECTED RATIOS

For 1994	Avg. of All Manufact.	Analyzed Industry	Index	For 1994	Avg. of All Manufact.	Analyzed Industry	Index
Employees per Establishment	49	45	92	Value Added per Production Worker	134,084	47,448	35
Payroll per Establishment	1,500,273	849,611	57	Cost per Establishment	5,045,178	1,713,570	34
Payroll per Employee	30,620	18,841	62	Cost per Employee	102,970	37,999	37
Production Workers per Establishment	34	40	116	Cost per Production Worker	146,988	43,084	29
Wages per Establishment	853,319	654,063	77	Shipments per Establishment	9,576,895	3,566,775	37
Wages per Production Worker	24,861	16,445	66	Shipments per Employee	195,460	79,095	40
Hours per Production Worker	2,056	1,948	95	Shipments per Production Worker	279,017	89,679	32
Wages per Hour	12.09	8.44	70	Investment per Establishment	321,011	92,527	29
Value Added per Establishment	4,602,255	1,887,117	41	Investment per Employee	6,552	2,052	31
Value Added per Employee	93,930	41,848	45	Investment per Production Worker	9,352	2,326	25

Sources: Same as General Statistics. The 'Average of All Manufacturing' column represents the average of all manufacturing industries reported for the most recent complete year available. The Index shows the relationship between the Average and the Analyzed Industry. For example, 100 means that they are equal; 500 that the Analyzed Industry is five times the average; 50 means that the Analyzed Industry is half the national average. The abbreviation 'na' is used to show that data are 'not available'.

LEADING COMPANIES Number shown: **75** Total sales ($ mil): **7,157** Total employment (000): **89.8**

Company Name	Address				CEO Name	Phone	Co. Type	Sales ($ mil)	Empl. (000)
Kimball International Inc	1600 Royal St	Jasper	IN	47549	Douglas A Habig	812-482-1600	P	823	8.1
LADD Furniture Inc	1 Plaza Ctr	High Point	NC	27261	Richard R Allen	910-889-0333	P	592	7.9
Broyhill Furniture Industries Inc	1 Broyhill Park	Lenoir	NC	28633	Brent Kincaid	704-758-3111	S	450	6.5
Ethan Allen Inc	Ethan Allen Dr	Danbury	CT	06801	M Farooq Kathwari	203-743-8000	S	437	5.9
Ethan Allen Interiors Inc	Ethan Allen Dr	Danbury	CT	06801	M Farooq Kathwari	203-743-8000	P	437	5.9
Universal Furniture Industries	2622 Uwharrie Rd	High Point	NC	27263	Don Mitchell	919-861-7200	S	400	4.0
Drexel Heritage Furnishings Inc	101 N Main St	Drexel	NC	28619	Daniel M Grow	704-433-3000	S	300	4.4
Bush Industries Inc	PO Box 460	Jamestown	NY	14702	Paul S Bush	716-665-2000	P	213	1.7
Stanley Furniture	PO Box 30	Stanleytown	VA	24168	Albert Prillaman	703-629-7561	D	184	2.9
Stanley Furniture Company Inc	PO Box 30	Stanleytown	VA	24168	Albert L Prillaman	703-627-2000	P	184	2.9
Bernhardt Furniture Company	PO Box 740	Lenoir	NC	28645	G Alex Bernhardt	704-758-9811	R	150	2.2
Ditri Associates Inc	15 Valley Dr	Greenwich	CT	06831	Arnold Ditri	203-869-1100	R	150	1.2
Pulaski Furniture Corp	PO Box 1371	Pulaski	VA	24301	Bernard C Wampler	703-980-7330	P	148	2.3
Singer Furniture Co	PO Box 5337	Roanoke	VA	24012	Dennis Ammons	703-366-0361	R	140	2.4
WinsLoew Furniture Inc	201 Cahaba Val	Pelham	AL	35124	Bobby Tesney	205-870-0897	P	138	1.5
Century Furniture Industries	PO Box 608	Hickory	NC	28603	Harley F Shuford Jr	704-328-1851	R	135	1.6
Ashley Furniture Industries Inc	1 Ashley Way	Arcadia	WI	54612	Ron Wanek	608-323-3377	R	130	1.9
Ameriwood Indust Intern Corp	171 Monroe NW	Grand Rapids	MI	49503	Joseph J Miglore	616-336-9400	P	105	0.8
Riverside Furniture Corp	PO Box 1427	Fort Smith	AR	72902	Howard J Spradlin	501-785-8100	R	98	1.5
Amer Moulding & Millwork Co	2801 W Lane	Stockton	CA	95208	GB Sloop	209-946-5800	R	88	0.8
General Marble Co	350 N 321 Bypass	Lincolnton	NC	28092	Hans Wade	704-732-5000	S	87	0.5
JDI Group Inc	PO Box 7240	St Louis	MO	63177	Ronald Pass	314-291-0400	R	75*	3.0
Ameriwood Furniture	PO Box 270	Dowagiac	MI	49047	Joseph J Milgore	616-782-8661	D	68	0.4
L and JG Stickley Inc	PO Box 480	Manlius	NY	13104	Alfred J Audi	315-682-5500	R	66	0.6
DMI Furniture Inc	101 Bullitt Ln	Louisville	KY	40222	Donald D Dreher	502-426-4351	P	61	0.6
Charleswood Corp	PO Box 346	Wright City	MO	63390	Richard Jackson	314-745-3351	S	60	0.4
Royal Creations Inc	PO Box 698	Villa Rica	GA	30180	M Riegsecker	404-459-5767	R	60	0.1
Standard Furniture Mfg Co	PO Box 1089	Bay Minette	AL	36507	William Hodgson Jr	205-937-6741	R	60	0.6
Korn Industries Inc	PO Box 100	Sumter	SC	29151	RH Hudson	803-778-5444	R	53	0.8
Hickory Chair Co	PO Box 2147	Hickory	NC	28603	C Michael Younts	704-328-1801	D	52	0.8
Hammary Furniture Company	PO Box 760	Lenoir	NC	28645	Fred Preddy	704-728-3231	D	50	0.5
Henredon Furniture Industries	Altapass Rd	Spruce Pine	NC	28777	Richard Crisp	704-765-9641	D	50*	0.9
Howard Miller Clock Co	860 E Main St	Zeeland	MI	49464	JH Miller	616-772-9131	R	50	0.5
SK Products Corp	125 Entin Rd	Clifton	NJ	07015	Joze Obersnel	201-473-0700	R	50	0.1
Florida Furniture Industries Inc	PO Box 610	Palatka	FL	32178	Howard Gardner Jr	904-328-3444	R	48	0.6
Good Tables Inc	1118 E 223rd St	Carson	CA	90745	Dave Finegood	213-775-8541	R	48*	0.7
US Furniture Industries Inc	PO Box 2127	High Point	NC	27261	G Davis Beaston	919-884-7375	R	48	0.6
Vaughan-Bassett Furniture Co	PO Box 1549	Galax	VA	24333	John D Bassett III	703-236-6161	R	46*	0.9
Young-Hinkle Corp	PO Box 1537	Lexington	NC	27293	Julius S Young	704-249-5100	S	43	0.7
Virginia House Furniture Corp	PO Box 138	Atkins	VA	24311	GW Greer III	703-783-7217	R	41*	0.6
Harden Furniture Company Inc	Mill Pond Way	McConnellsv	NY	13401	David Harden	315-245-1000	R	38*	0.6
Keller Manufacturing Co	PO Box 8	Corydon	IN	47112	Robert W Byrd	812-738-2222	R	35*	0.6
Crawford Furniture Mfg Corp	1021 Allen St Ext	Jamestown	NY	14701	Carl Cappa	716-661-9100	R	34*	0.5
Whittier Wood Products Inc	3787 W 1st Av	Eugene	OR	97402	Scott Whittier	503-687-0213	R	32	0.4
Webb Furniture Enterprises Inc	PO Box 1277	Galax	VA	24333	DE Ward Jr	703-236-2984	R	32	0.6
Boyd Furniture Company Inc	6355 E Washington	Los Angeles	CA	90040	Robert M Clark	213-726-6767	R	30	0.2
Hekman Furniture Co	1400 Buchanan SW	Grand Rapids	MI	49507	Dan Henslee	616-452-1411	S	30	0.2
Lehigh Portland Cement Co	PO Box 640	Marianna	FL	32447	W H Boyenton	904-526-2811	D	30*	0.5
Telescope Casual Furniture Inc	85 Church St	Granville	NY	12832	H Vanderminden	518-642-1100	R	30	0.3
Okla Homer Smith	PO Box 1148	Fort Smith	AR	72902	OB Smith	501-783-6191	D	26*	0.2
Hood Furniture Mfg Co	PO Box 55568	Jackson	MS	39296	Ken Fonville	601-981-1551	R	25	0.5
Khoury Inc	PO Box 729	Iron Mountain	MI	49801	Daniel Khoury	906-774-6333	R	25	0.3
Rose Hill Company Inc	105 S Childs St	Okolona	MS	38860	WE Hughes	601-447-5425	R	25	0.3
Chatham County	PO Box 2127	High Point	NC	27260	G Davis Beaston	919-431-2156	S	20	<0.1
Dawson Heritage Inc	209 W Broadway	Webb City	MO	64870	James S Dawson	417-673-5012	R	20	0.2
Harper Furniture Co	1 Broyhill Park	Lenoir	NC	28633	D Powell	704-754-6473	D	19*	0.3
Orleans Furniture Inc	PO Drawer 867	Columbia	MS	39429	PE Simmons	601-736-9002	R	19	0.3
Oak Canyon Inc	3711 W Clarendon	Phoenix	AZ	85019	R D MacMillan	602-233-0224	R	18	0.2
Blacksmith Shop Co	PO Box 2127	High Point	NC	27261	Davis Beaston	919-431-1151	S	18	0.2
Carolina Furniture Works Inc	PO Box 1120	Sumter	SC	29151	Ernest M Weeks Jr	803-775-6381	R	16	0.2
Crescent Enterprises Inc	PO Box 1438	Gallatin	TN	37066	Charles Tomkins III	615-452-1671	R	16*	0.2
Kindel Furniture Co	PO Box 2047	Grand Rapids	MI	49501	R Fogarty	616-243-3676	S	16	0.3
Borkholder Corp	PO Box 5	Nappanee	IN	46550	F D Borkholder	219-773-3144	R	15*	0.1
Cherry Hill	77 S Main St	Union City	PA	16438	Tom Brockman	814-438-3868	D	15*	0.2
Robinson Furniture Mfg	N 14225 Robinson	Wilson	MI	49896	Roger Robinson	906-639-2151	R	15	0.3
Sandberg Furniture Mfg	3251 Slauson Av	Los Angeles	CA	90058	A Sandberg	213-582-0711	R	15	0.4
Silver Furniture Co	PO Box 3820	Knoxville	TN	37927	Robert Ivins	615-637-4541	R	15	0.2
Weiman Co	PO Box 670	Bassett	VA	24055	RH Spilman	703-629-7592	D	15	0.3
Councill Craftsmen Inc	PO Box 398	Denton	NC	27239	FM Councill	704-869-2155	R	14	0.4
Doxey Furniture Corp	Hwy 211-E	Aberdeen	NC	28315	Richard Henkel	910-944-7101	R	14	0.1
La Barge Inc	PO Box 1769	Holland	MI	49422	James La Barge	616-392-1473	S	14	<0.1
Dinaire Corp	145 Gruner Rd	Buffalo	NY	14227	Carmelo Gugino Jr	716-894-1201	R	13	0.2
Fort Smith Table & Furniture	PO Box 6115	Fort Smith	AR	72906	Bob Taylor	501-646-4741	S	13	0.1
Great	13477 Benson Av	Chino	CA	91710	Earl Payton	909-613-1732	S	13*	0.2
Hekman Furniture Co	1400 Buchanan SW	Grand Rapids	MI	49507	Dan Henslee	616-452-1411	D	13	<0.1

Source: *Ward's Business Directory of U.S. Private and Public Companies*, Volumes 1 and 2, 1996. The company type code used is as follows: P - Public, R - Private, S - Subsidiary, D - Division, J - Joint Venture, A - Affiliate, G - Group. Sales are in millions of dollars, employees are in thousands. An asterisk (*) indicates an estimated sales volume. The symbol < stands for 'less than'. Company names and addresses are truncated, in some cases, to fit into the available space.

MATERIALS CONSUMED

Material		Quantity	Delivered Cost ($ million)
Materials, ingredients, containers, and supplies		(X)	3,525.4
Hardwood lumber, rough and dressed	mil bd ft	(S)	445.5
Softwood lumber, rough and dressed	mil bd ft	853.9*	115.7
Hardwood dimension and parts, excluding furniture frames		(X)	238.3
Softwood plywood	mil sq ft (3/8 in. b	(S)	21.2
Hardwood plywood	mil sq ft sm	(S)	92.7
Hardwood veneer		(X)	126.1
Particleboard (wood)	mil sq ft (3/4 in. b	(S)	240.8
Medium density fiberboard (MDF)	mil sq ft (3/4 in. b	451.1	65.9
Hardboard (wood fiberboard)		(X)	34.3
Furniture frames, wood		(X)	156.8
Paints, varnishes, lacquers, stains, shellacs, japans, enamels, and allied products		(X)	142.0
Adhesives and sealants		(X)	15.9
Plastics resins consumed in the form of granules, pellets, powders, liquids, etc.	mil lb	(S)	11.2
Plastics parts, components, sheets, and other shapes (excluding plastics resins)		(X)	50.3
Flat glass (plate, float, and sheet)		(X)	46.8
Mirrors, framed and unframed		(X)	47.6
Fabrics, all types		(X)	35.2
Furniture and builders' hardware		(X)	254.6
Paperboard containers, boxes, and corrugated paperboard		(X)	199.4
All other materials and components, parts, containers, and supplies		(X)	501.7
Materials, ingredients, containers, and supplies, nsk		(X)	683.4

Source: 1992 *Economic Census*. Explanation of symbols used: (D): Withheld to avoid disclosure of competitive data; na: Not available; (S): Withheld because statistical norms were not met; (X): Not applicable; (Z): Less than half the unit shown; nec: Not elsewhere classified; nsk: Not specified by kind; - : zero; * : 10-19 percent estimated; ** : 20-29 percent estimated.

PRODUCT SHARE DETAILS

Product or Product Class	% Share
Wood household furniture	100.00
Wood living room, library, family room, and den furniture	20.32
Cabinets, including record, music, sewing, smoking, etc., except sewing machine, radio, phono, and television cabinets	11.24
Chairs, except dining room	4.18
Rockers	4.34
Tables (all types), except card and telephone tables	30.80
Wood household desks	8.20
Credenzas, bookcases, and bookshelves, except wall units	5.35
Wall units (desk, bookcase, and storage type)	16.45
Other nonupholstered wood living room, library, family room, and den seating, including settees, loveseats, benches, stools, etc.	3.17
Other wood living room, library, family room, and den nonupholstered furniture (secretaries, breakfronts, bars, magazine racks, smoking stands, etc.)	9.08
Wood living room, library, family room, and den furniture, nsk	7.21
Wood dining room and kitchen furniture, except kitchen cabinets	19.90
Tables, 30 x 40 inches or greater	23.92
Chairs	36.63
Buffets and servers	9.00
China and corner cabinets	19.49
Other wood dining room and kitchen seating	1.25
Other wood dining room and kitchen furniture, including junior dining furniture sets	5.28
Wood dining room and kitchen furniture, except kitchen cabinets, nsk	4.43
Wood bedroom furniture	31.07
Wood beds, excluding headboards, headboard beds, bunk beds, cribs, cradles, Hollywood beds, and youth beds	8.78
Wood headboards and headboard beds, including padded	12.07
Wood bunk beds, excluding mattresses and detachable springs	2.04
Wood conventional water beds	3.93
Dressers, vanities, and dressing tables	19.66
Wardrobes, chifforobes, armoires, and wardrobe-type cabinets	5.54
Chests of drawers	15.79
Cedar chests	1.18
Night tables and stands	10.10
Other wood bedroom nonupholstered furniture, including commodes, bed rails, chairs, valet stands, etc.	11.58
Wood bedroom furniture, nsk	9.33
Infants' and children's wood furniture	3.96
Infants' and children's wood cribs, including springs sold as part of the crib	35.36
Infants' and children's wood seating (chairs, nursery seats, high chairs, etc.)	3.70
Other infants' and children's wood bedroom furniture, including youth beds	39.18
Other infants' and children's wood furniture	18.75
Infants' and children's wood furniture, nsk	3.04
Wood outdoor furniture, unpainted wood furniture, and ready-to-assemble wood furniture	13.57
Porch, lawn, beach, and similar wood outdoor furniture	5.28
Unpainted wood furniture, assembled (furniture-in-the-white), including bookcases, chairs, tables, desks, vanities, etc.	6.91
Ready-to-assemble wood household seating, unpainted or finished, sold in kits	2.06
Ready-to-assemble wood kitchen furniture, unpainted or finished, sold in kits	11.50
Ready-to-assemble wood bedroom furniture, unpainted or finished, sold in kits	5.99
Ready-to-assemble wood home entertainment centers, unpainted or finished, sold in kits	9.84
Other ready-to-assemble wood furniture, unpainted or finished, sold in kits	55.86
Wood outdoor furniture, unpainted wood furniture, and ready-to-assemble wood furniture, nsk	2.57
Wood household furniture, nsk	11.17

Source: 1992 *Economic Census*. The values shown are percent of total shipments in an industry. Values of indented subcategories are summed in the main heading. The symbol (D) appears when data are withheld to prevent disclosure of competitive information. The abbreviation nsk stands for 'not specified by kind' and nec for 'not elsewhere classified'.

INPUTS AND OUTPUTS FOR WOOD HOUSEHOLD FURNITURE

Economic Sector or Industry Providing Inputs	%	Sector	Economic Sector or Industry Buying Outputs	%	Sector
Imports	20.0	Foreign	Personal consumption expenditures	88.2	
Sawmills & planning mills, general	11.6	Manufg.	Gross private fixed investment	7.2	Cap Inv
Wholesale trade	10.2	Trade	Exports	2.4	Foreign
Hardwood dimension & flooring mills	6.2	Manufg.	Mobile homes	0.7	Manufg.
Veneer & plywood	4.4	Manufg.	Federal Government purchases, nondefense	0.4	Fed Govt
Advertising	3.6	Services	Travel trailers & campers	0.3	Manufg.
Wood products, nec	3.5	Manufg.	Federal Government purchases, national defense	0.2	Fed Govt
Paints & allied products	3.4	Manufg.	S/L Govt. purch., elem. & secondary education	0.2	S/L Govt
Hardware, nec	3.2	Manufg.	S/L Govt. purch., higher education	0.2	S/L Govt
Particleboard	2.8	Manufg.	Wood household furniture	0.1	Manufg.
Business services nec	2.6	Services			
Electric services (utilities)	2.4	Util.			
Motor freight transportation & warehousing	1.8	Util.			
Paperboard containers & boxes	1.7	Manufg.			
Maintenance of nonfarm buildings nec	1.5	Constr.			
Glass & glass products, except containers	1.5	Manufg.			
Petroleum refining	1.5	Manufg.			
Screw machine and related products	1.5	Manufg.			
Eating & drinking places	1.4	Trade			
Miscellaneous plastics products	1.2	Manufg.			
Railroads & related services	1.1	Util.			
Abrasive products	0.8	Manufg.			
Banking	0.8	Fin/R.E.			
Hand & edge tools, nec	0.6	Manufg.			
Real estate	0.6	Fin/R.E.			
Adhesives & sealants	0.5	Manufg.			
Broadwoven fabric mills	0.5	Manufg.			
Communications, except radio & TV	0.5	Util.			
Management & consulting services & labs	0.5	Services			
Coated fabrics, not rubberized	0.4	Manufg.			
Air transportation	0.4	Util.			
Legal services	0.4	Services			
U.S. Postal Service	0.4	Gov't			
Fabricated metal products, nec	0.3	Manufg.			
Machinery, except electrical, nec	0.3	Manufg.			
Woodworking machinery	0.3	Manufg.			
Gas production & distribution (utilities)	0.3	Util.			
Sanitary services, steam supply, irrigation	0.3	Util.			
Accounting, auditing & bookkeeping	0.3	Services			
Equipment rental & leasing services	0.3	Services			
Lubricating oils & greases	0.2	Manufg.			
Manifold business forms	0.2	Manufg.			
Paper coating & glazing	0.2	Manufg.			
Special dies & tools & machine tool accessories	0.2	Manufg.			
Steel wire & related products	0.2	Manufg.			
Wood household furniture	0.2	Manufg.			
Water transportation	0.2	Util.			
Insurance carriers	0.2	Fin/R.E.			
Royalties	0.2	Fin/R.E.			
Automotive rental & leasing, without drivers	0.2	Services			
Automotive repair shops & services	0.2	Services			
Business/professional associations	0.2	Services			
Computer & data processing services	0.2	Services			
Commercial printing	0.1	Manufg.			
Mechanical measuring devices	0.1	Manufg.			
Engineering, architectural, & surveying services	0.1	Services			
Hotels & lodging places	0.1	Services			
Personnel supply services	0.1	Services			

Source: Benchmark Input-Output Accounts for the U.S. Economy, 1982, U.S. Department of Commerce, Washington, D.C., July 1991. Data, as reported in the source, are organized by the 1977 SIC structure in use in 1982 but have been matched, as closely as is possible, to the 1987 SIC structure used in this book.

OCCUPATIONS EMPLOYED BY SIC 251 - HOUSEHOLD FURNITURE

Occupation	% of Total 1994	Change to 2005	Occupation	% of Total 1994	Change to 2005
Assemblers, fabricators, & hand workers nec	13.5	-6.7	Hand packers & packagers	1.9	-20.0
Upholsterers	7.7	12.4	Truck drivers light & heavy	1.9	-3.8
Sewing machine operators, non-garment	7.1	26.0	General managers & top executives	1.7	-11.5
Woodworking machine workers	5.6	-25.3	Machine feeders & offbearers	1.7	-16.0
Cabinetmakers & bench carpenters	4.8	58.6	Traffic, shipping, & receiving clerks	1.7	-10.2
Wood machinists	4.5	30.6	Cutters & trimmers, hand	1.6	-6.7
Blue collar worker supervisors	3.9	-13.5	Sales & related workers nec	1.5	-6.7
Furniture finishers	3.7	21.8	Inspectors, testers, & graders, precision	1.5	-6.7
Head sawyers & sawing machine workers	3.0	-39.3	Grinders & polishers, hand	1.2	-25.4
Helpers, laborers, & material movers nec	2.9	-6.7	General office clerks	1.1	-20.4
Freight, stock, & material movers, hand	2.5	-25.3	Precision woodworkers nec	1.0	2.7
Coating, painting, & spraying machine workers	2.0	16.6			

Source: *Industry-Occupation Matrix*, Bureau of Labor Statistics. These data relate to one or more 3-digit SIC industry groups rather than to a single 4-digit SIC. The change reported for each occupation to the year 2005 is a percent of growth or decline as estimated by the Bureau of Labor Statistics. The abbreviation nec stands for 'not elsewhere classified'.

LOCATION BY STATE AND REGIONAL CONCENTRATION

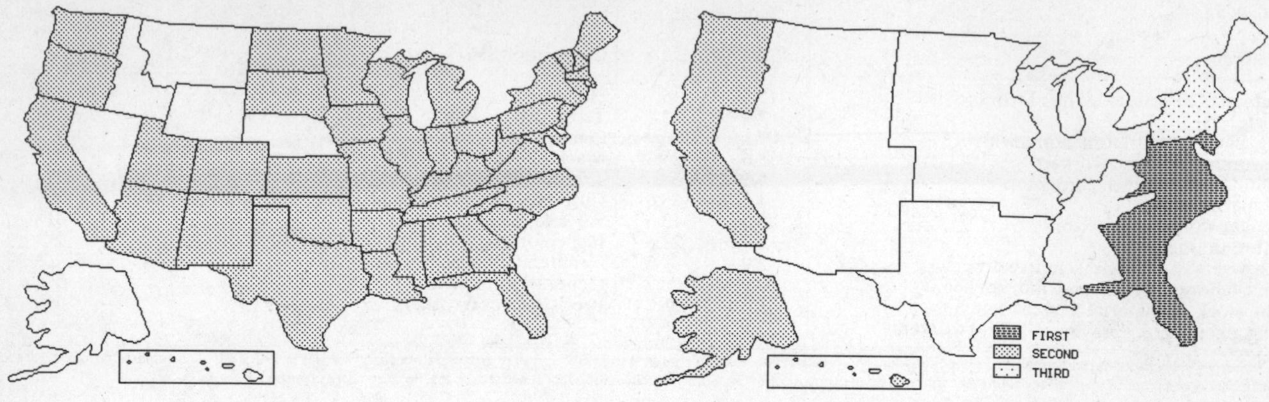

INDUSTRY DATA BY STATE

State	Establish-ments	Shipments			Employment				Cost as % of Shipments	Investment per Employee ($)
		Total ($ mil)	% of U.S.	Per Establ.	Total Number	% of U.S.	Per Establ.	Wages ($/hour)		
North Carolina	218	2,162.5	24.8	9.9	34,500	28.5	158	8.71	43.5	1,093
Virginia	76	976.1	11.2	12.8	15,200	12.6	200	7.63	45.9	1,053
California	414	720.4	8.2	1.7	10,400	8.6	25	6.79	49.3	846
Ohio	87	424.2	4.9	4.9	3,400	2.8	39	10.04	50.9	-
New York	184	409.5	4.7	2.2	5,000	4.1	27	9.43	40.2	1,060
Wisconsin	77	386.6	4.4	5.0	4,100	3.4	53	6.68	48.5	1,683
Tennessee	99	380.8	4.4	3.8	5,900	4.9	60	6.85	49.6	1,864
Missouri	49	339.3	3.9	6.9	3,000	2.5	61	9.49	49.5	2,433
Indiana	56	321.3	3.7	5.7	4,000	3.3	71	8.73	42.5	2,850
Pennsylvania	133	314.9	3.6	2.4	3,600	3.0	27	8.43	40.9	2,111
Alabama	98	289.7	3.3	3.0	4,100	3.4	42	6.52	51.8	1,561
Florida	196	202.9	2.3	1.0	2,900	2.4	15	7.04	40.3	897
Michigan	62	182.1	2.1	2.9	2,300	1.9	37	8.95	43.6	1,261
Illinois	73	166.9	1.9	2.3	1,700	1.4	23	8.32	56.6	941
Georgia	70	164.7	1.9	2.4	2,100	1.7	30	6.39	58.2	952
Arkansas	38	142.4	1.6	3.7	2,100	1.7	55	7.31	55.1	1,000
South Carolina	28	129.6	1.5	4.5	2,000	1.7	71	7.57	46.1	1,600
Mississippi	33	114.1	1.3	3.5	2,200	1.8	67	5.33	48.1	364
Massachusetts	58	98.7	1.1	1.7	1,100	0.9	19	9.72	46.7	1,364
Arizona	46	81.3	0.9	1.8	1,200	1.0	26	6.59	50.3	2,833
Texas	82	69.9	0.8	0.9	1,000	0.8	12	6.22	45.6	700
Oregon	38	62.5	0.7	1.6	700	0.6	18	9.67	43.2	1,857
New Jersey	60	52.4	0.6	0.9	500	0.4	8	10.25	48.7	1,200
New Hampshire	23	50.5	0.6	2.2	500	0.4	22	8.00	45.5	1,400
Kentucky	35	43.0	0.5	1.2	600	0.5	17	6.80	54.4	-
Minnesota	42	37.5	0.4	0.9	600	0.5	14	7.22	48.0	1,833
Colorado	48	36.3	0.4	0.8	500	0.4	10	8.13	59.8	-
Maryland	26	32.6	0.4	1.3	400	0.3	15	10.00	39.3	1,500
Washington	50	29.3	0.3	0.6	500	0.4	10	9.14	44.7	-
Connecticut	23	23.1	0.3	1.0	300	0.2	13	11.00	38.5	667
Utah	30	22.1	0.3	0.7	300	0.2	10	7.25	48.4	4,333
Maine	24	18.8	0.2	0.8	400	0.3	17	7.83	33.0	750
Louisiana	16	16.7	0.2	1.0	200	0.2	13	5.50	67.7	-
Kansas	18	11.1	0.1	0.6	100	0.1	6	5.33	55.0	2,000
New Mexico	26	9.4	0.1	0.4	200	0.2	8	6.67	52.1	1,000
Iowa	15	9.1	0.1	0.6	200	0.2	13	5.75	49.5	-
Oklahoma	19	7.6	0.1	0.4	200	0.2	11	7.33	47.4	500
Vermont	32	(D)	-	-	1,750 *	1.4	55	-	-	-
West Virginia	9	(D)	-	-	175 *	0.1	19	-	-	-
North Dakota	5	(D)	-	-	750 *	0.6	150	-	-	-
South Dakota	4	(D)	-	-	175 *	0.1	44	-	-	-

Source: 1992 *Economic Census*. The states are in descending order of shipments or establishments (if shipment data are missing for the majority). The symbol (D) appears when data are withheld to prevent disclosure of competitive information. States marked with (D) are sorted by number of establishments. A dash (-) indicates that the data element cannot be calculated; * indicates the midpoint of a range.

2512 - UPHOLSTERED HOUSEHOLD FURNITURE

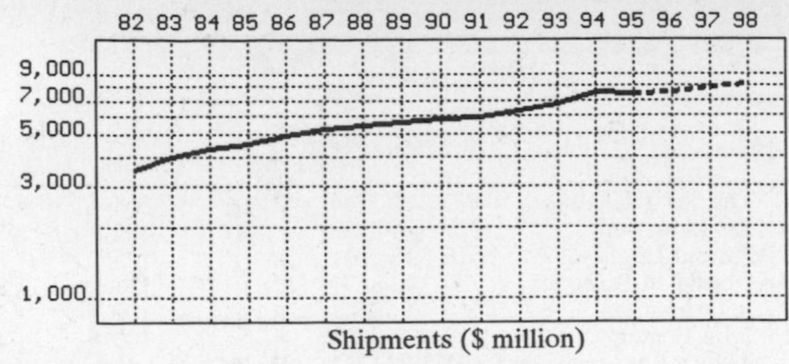

Shipments ($ million)

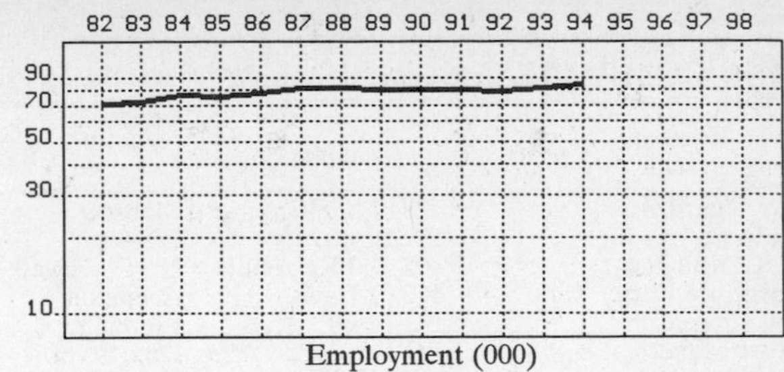

Employment (000)

GENERAL STATISTICS

Year	Companies	Establishments		Employment			Compensation		Production ($ million)			
		Total	with 20 or more employees	Total (000)	Production Workers (000)	Production Hours (Mil)	Payroll ($ mil)	Wages ($/hr)	Cost of Materials	Value Added by Manufacture	Value of Shipments	Capital Invest.
1982	1,129	1,227	602	70.6	59.8	105.6	849.9	6.03	1,761.5	1,745.3	3,505.3	57.2
1983		1,197	604	72.5	62.6	115.1	944.9	6.34	2,006.6	1,990.8	3,989.7	61.5
1984		1,167	606	76.5	64.8	120.7	1,076.7	6.67	2,282.5	2,108.7	4,362.7	64.1
1985		1,136	607	76.0	64.3	118.2	1,116.9	7.03	2,352.2	2,193.0	4,550.7	60.1
1986		1,113	579	77.9	65.6	125.0	1,206.2	7.17	2,463.8	2,489.2	4,945.0	79.1
1987	1,030	1,150	576	82.1	69.6	132.4	1,295.2	7.42	2,630.9	2,661.2	5,263.1	77.4
1988		1,095	572			131.3	1,338.3		2,770.2	2,644.8	5,408.5	84.8
1989		1,041	558	81.0	68.9	131.5	1,397.7	7.94	2,883.2	2,751.5	5,618.1	56.3
1990		1,047	517	79.5	71.5	137.6	1,486.7	8.05	3,042.4	2,809.1	5,815.3	73.0
1991		1,078	506	80.3	68.5	128.5	1,460.7	8.49	3,058.5	2,827.2	5,859.4	49.9
1992	1,077	1,184	524	79.2	67.1	128.9	1,535.2	8.68	3,236.6	3,009.9	6,223.3	73.6
1993		1,157	500	81.5	69.4	130.1	1,618.3	9.37	3,515.5	3,195.2	6,689.9	70.2
1994		1,082P	493P	84.9	73.9	145.3	1,758.2	9.25	3,952.4	3,509.5	7,445.0	79.6
1995		1,074P	482P			142.4P	1,789.1P		3,878.6P	3,444.0P	7,306.0P	74.1P
1996		1,067P	472P			144.6P	1,856.9P		4,026.2P	3,575.0P	7,584.0P	74.9P
1997		1,059P	461P			146.8P	1,924.7P		4,173.8P	3,706.1P	7,862.1P	75.7P
1998		1,051P	450P			149.0P	1,992.6P		4,321.4P	3,837.2P	8,140.1P	76.6P

Sources: 1982, 1987, 1992 *Economic Census*; *Annual Survey of Manufactures*, 83-86, 88-91, 93-94. Establishment counts for non-Census years are from *County Business Patterns*; establishment values for 83-84 are extrapolations. 'P's show projections by the editors. Industries reclassified in 87 will not have data for prior years.

INDICES OF CHANGE

Year	Companies	Establishments		Employment			Compensation		Production ($ million)			
		Total	with 20 or more employees	Total (000)	Production Workers (000)	Production Hours (Mil)	Payroll ($ mil)	Wages ($/hr)	Cost of Materials	Value Added by Manufacture	Value of Shipments	Capital Invest.
1982	105	104	115	89	89	82	55	69	54	58	56	78
1983		101	115	92	93	89	62	73	62	66	64	84
1984		99	116	97	97	94	70	77	71	70	70	87
1985		96	116	96	96	92	73	81	73	73	73	82
1986		94	110	98	98	97	79	83	76	83	79	107
1987	96	97	110	104	104	103	84	85	81	88	85	105
1988		92	109			102	87		86	88	87	115
1989		88	106	102	103	102	91	91	89	91	90	76
1990		88	99	100	107	107	97	93	94	93	93	99
1991		91	97	101	102	100	95	98	94	94	94	68
1992	100	100	100	100	100	100	100	100	100	100	100	100
1993		98	95	103	103	101	105	108	109	106	107	95
1994		91P	94P	107	110	113	115	107	122	117	120	108
1995		91P	92P			110P	117P		120P	114P	117P	101P
1996		90P	90P			112P	121P		124P	119P	122P	102P
1997		89P	88P			114P	125P		129P	123P	126P	103P
1998		89P	86P			116P	130P		134P	127P	131P	104P

Sources: Same as General Statistics. Values reflect change from the base year, 1992. Values above 100 mean greater than 92, values below 100 mean less than 92, and a value of 100 in the 82-91 or 93-98 period means same as 92. 'P's mark projections by the editors.

SELECTED RATIOS

For 1994	Avg. of All Manufact.	Analyzed Industry	Index	For 1994	Avg. of All Manufact.	Analyzed Industry	Index
Employees per Establishment	49	78	160	Value Added per Production Worker	134,084	47,490	35
Payroll per Establishment	1,500,273	1,624,840	108	Cost per Establishment	5,045,178	3,652,609	72
Payroll per Employee	30,620	20,709	68	Cost per Employee	102,970	46,554	45
Production Workers per Establishment	34	68	199	Cost per Production Worker	146,988	53,483	36
Wages per Establishment	853,319	1,242,080	146	Shipments per Establishment	9,576,895	6,880,295	72
Wages per Production Worker	24,861	18,187	73	Shipments per Employee	195,460	87,691	45
Hours per Production Worker	2,056	1,966	96	Shipments per Production Worker	279,017	100,744	36
Wages per Hour	12.09	9.25	76	Investment per Establishment	321,011	73,562	23
Value Added per Establishment	4,602,255	3,243,303	70	Investment per Employee	6,552	938	14
Value Added per Employee	93,930	41,337	44	Investment per Production Worker	9,352	1,077	12

Sources: Same as General Statistics. The 'Average of All Manufacturing' column represents the average of all manufacturing industries reported for the most recent complete year available. The Index shows the relationship between the Average and the Analyzed Industry. For example, 100 means that they are equal; 500 that the Analyzed Industry is five times the average; 50 means that the Analyzed Industry is half the national average. The abbreviation 'na' is used to show that data are 'not available'.

LEADING COMPANIES

Number shown: **75** Total sales ($ mil): **2,942** Total employment (000): **36.8**

Company Name	Address				CEO Name	Phone	Co. Type	Sales ($ mil)	Empl. (000)
La-Z-Boy Chair Co	1284 N Telegraph	Monroe	MI	48161	Charles T Knabusch	313-242-1444	P	805	8.7
Flexsteel Industries Inc	PO Box 877	Dubuque	IA	52004	KB Lauritsen	319-556-7730	P	195	2.3
England/Corsair Inc	402 Old Knoxville	New Tazewell	TN	37825	Arnold England	615-626-5211	R	125	1.6
Rowe Furniture Corp	1725 J Davis	Arlington	VA	22202	Gerald M Birnbach	703-389-8671	P	111	1.3
Cleveland Chair Co	PO Box 1359	Cleveland	TN	37364	R Jackson	615-476-8544	R	100	1.3
Lea Industries Inc	PO Box HP3	High Point	NC	27261	John Foster	910-889-0333	S	100	1.4
Mohasco Corp	Hwy 178 W	New Albany	MS	38652	Robert Shaughnessy	601-534-4762	D	85*	1.0
Sherrill Furniture Co	PO Box 189	Hickory	NC	28603	Harold Sherrill	704-322-2640	R	81*	1.0
Franklin Corp	PO Box 569	Houston	MS	38851	HH Franklin	601-456-4286	R	80	1.0
Schnadig Corp	4820 W Belmont	Chicago	IL	60641	Donald A Belgrad	312-545-2300	R	80	1.0
River Oaks Furniture Inc	PO Box 277	Fulton	MS	38843	Stephen L Simons	601-862-7774	P	70	0.8
Alexvale Furniture Inc	PO Box 817	Taylorsville	NC	28681	Charles Bolick	704-632-9774	R	60	0.6
Hickory White Co	PO Box 1600	High Point	NC	27261	Randolph L Austin	919-885-1200	S	51*	0.8
Gaines Furniture Mfg Co	PO Box 550	McKenzie	TN	38201	Ben Gaines Jr	901-352-3376	S	45	0.6
Jackson Manufacturing Co	PO Box 1359	Cleveland	TN	37311	Wayne Johnson	615-476-8544	D	43*	0.7
Schweiger Industries Inc	116 W Washington	Jefferson	WI	53549	Gary Maykew	414-674-2440	R	43	0.4
Brookwood Furniture Company	PO Box 540	Pontotoc	MS	38863	J Diffee	601-489-1100	R	40	0.7
Classic Leather Inc	PO Box 2404	Hickory	NC	28603	E Gerald Tuttle	704-328-2046	R	40	0.5
Fairfield Chair Company Inc	PO Box 1710	Lenoir	NC	28645	J Beall III	704-758-5571	R	40*	0.5
Pem-Kay Furniture Company	PO Box 547	Conover	NC	28613	Dennis Soboti	704-464-2408	R	40*	0.5
Hickory Hill Furniture Corp	501 Hoyle St	Valdese	NC	28690	William E Adkins	704-874-2124	S	36	0.5
Les Brown Chair Co	PO Box 218	Hermansville	MI	49847	Robert Brown	906-498-7721	R	30	0.4
Carlton Manufacturing Inc	317 W Franklin St	Elkhart	IN	46516	Doug Mercier	219-293-4507	R	25	0.3
Sam Moore Furniture Industries	1556 Dawn Dr	Bedford	VA	24523	J K Boardman Jr	703-586-8253	R	25	0.3
Highland House Inc	PO 2467	Hickory	NC	28603	William Hayes	704-323-8600	S	24	0.3
Alan White Co	PO Box 249	Stamps	AR	71860	David White	501-533-4471	R	21*	0.3
CM Furniture Inc	PO Box 617	Maiden	NC	28650	John Wells	704-428-9978	S	21	0.4
Cooke Manufacturing Company	PO Box 4230	Cleveland	TN	37320	Jimmy Cooke Sr	615-476-5536	R	20	0.2
Hickory Craft Furniture Inc	PO Box 1733	Hickory	NC	28603	Birger Rasmussen	704-322-5995	D	20*	0.2
Marge Carson Inc	9056 E Garvey Av	Rosemead	CA	91770	Jim LaBarge	818-571-1111	S	20*	0.3
RM Wieland Company Inc	PO Box 1000	Grabill	IN	46741	Roy Wieland	219-627-3686	R	19	0.2
Charles Schneider and Co	518 N 10th St	Council Bluffs	IA	51503	Al Stevens	712-328-1587	D	16*	0.2
Precedent Inc	PO Box 730	Newton	NC	28658	Bill Councill	704-465-0844	S	16*	0.2
Randolph and Hein Inc	1 Arkansas St	San Francisco	CA	94107	Howard Hein	415-864-3371	R	16*	<0.1
Shaw Manufacturing Company	PO Box 267	Okolona	MS	38860	William Doughty	601-447-3358	R	16*	0.2
Southwood Furniture Corp	PO Box 2245	Hickory	NC	28601	Rocky Holscher	704-465-1776	R	16	0.2
Brooks Furniture Manufacturing	PO Box 199	Tazewell	TN	37879	JH Brooks Jr	615-626-1111	R	15	0.2
Ficks Reed Company Inc	4900 Charlemar Dr	Cincinnati	OH	45227	Lee B Ficks	513-561-2100	R	15	0.1
Mastercraft Furniture	1111 N 13th St	Omaha	NE	68102	Mike Katzman	402-345-8550	R	14	0.2
Broyhill Investments Corp	PO Box 500	Lenoir	NC	28645	Paul Broyhill	704-758-6100	R	12*	0.2
CR Laine Furniture Company	PO Box 2128	Hickory	NC	28603	CE Roseman Jr	704-328-1831	R	12	0.2
Interior Crafts Inc	2513 W Cullerton St	Chicago	IL	60608	JL Seiff	312-376-8160	R	12*	0.2
Key City Furniture Co	PO Box 1049	N Wilkesboro	NC	28659	FD Forester III	919-838-4191	R	12	0.2
Oak Land Furniture Mfg	PO Box 151	Okolona	MS	38860	Gene Welch	601-447-3371	R	12*	0.2
Comfort Designs Inc	PO Box 3000	Kingston	PA	18704	John H Graham	717-288-6657	R	11	0.1
Conover Chair Company Inc	PO Box 759	Conover	NC	28613	FL Sherrill Jr	704-464-0251	R	11	0.2
Ethan Allen Inc	Rd 1	Eldred	PA	16731	John Werlan	814-225-4744	D	11*	0.2
Kingsley Furniture Company Inc	102 Park St	La Porte	IN	46350	NH Wenig	219-326-0550	R	11*	0.1
Sheffield Furniture Corp	2100 E 38th St	Los Angeles	CA	90058	Charles Koch	213-232-4161	R	11*	0.1
Bryant Manufacturing Company	2320 G Wallace	Albertville	AL	35950	James A Jackson	205-878-3561	R	10	0.1
Frankline Inc	PO Box 446	Hernando	MS	38632	David High	601-429-5201	R	10	0.1
Hayes Manufacturing Company	PO Box 7229	Oakland	CA	94601	Ed Abadie	510-534-4511	R	10*	<0.1
Home-Style Industries Inc	PO Box 396	Nampa	ID	83653	Randy D Raptosh	208-466-8481	R	10*	0.2
North Hickory Furniture Co	PO Drawer 759	Hickory	NC	28601	James W Floyd	704-328-1841	R	10*	0.1
Oak Brook Equities Inc	1010 Jorie Blv	Oak Brook	IL	60521	Henry A Porterfield	708-990-7100	R	10	0.1
Bright Chair Co	51 Railroad Av	Middletown	NY	10940	Stan Gottlieb	914-343-2196	S	9*	0.2
David Edward Inc	1407 Parker Rd	Baltimore	MD	21227	Edward Pitts	410-242-2222	R	9*	0.3
HH Hiatt Furniture Mfg	12520 S Chadron	Hawthorne	CA	90250	Homer Hiatt	213-772-5574	R	9*	0.1
Modern of Marshfield Inc	137 W 9th St	Marshfield	WI	54449	WJ Mork	715-387-1181	R	9	<0.1
Covington Furniture Mfg Corp	11481 Gulf Stream	Arlington	TN	38002	JK Patten	901-867-2986	R	8*	0.1
Custom Sofa Gallery Mfg	PO Box 500	Lenoir	NC	28645	Hunt Broyhill	704-758-6100	D	8*	0.1
Hallagan Manufacturing	PO Box 268	Newark	NY	14513	Charles Hallagan	315-331-4640	R	8*	0.1
La-Z-Boy South	33 Scanlan St	Newton	MS	39345	Earl Bryan	601-683-3356	D	8*	1.1
Panache	840 England Indrial	New Tazewell	TN	37825	Rodney England	615-626-4008	D	8	<0.1
Shaver-Howard Co	PO Box 698	N Wilkesboro	NC	28659	Joseph A Johnston	919-838-5178	R	8	0.1
Cavalier Manufacturing Inc	12765 E 166th St	Cerritos	CA	90703	S Button	310-926-1353	R	7	0.1
Fairchild of California	8146 S Byron Rd	Whittier	CA	90606	Walter Haigh	310-698-7988	R	7*	<0.1
Hickory Fry Furniture Company	PO Box 817	Taylorsville	NC	28681	Charles Bolick	704-632-0084	S	7*	0.1
International Furniture Corp	PO Box 1269	Corona	CA	91718	Collia D'Cruz	909-737-5722	S	7	0.1
Jackson Furniture of Danville	PO Box 169	Danville	KY	40422	Tom Yow	606-236-2604	R	7*	0.1
Howard Furniture Inc	PO Box 554	Fulton	MS	38843	Howard Gaskin	601-862-2949	R	6	<0.1
Imperial of Morristown Inc	2052 S Economy Rd	Morristown	TN	37814	M Wayne Crider	615-586-2821	R	6	0.1
Kinder Manufacturing Corp	PO Box 1207	Elkhart	IN	46515	Hank Porterfield	219-293-3531	R	6	<0.1
Lancer Inc	PO Box 848	Star	NC	27356	Randy B Deese	919-428-2181	R	6	0.1
Berne Furniture Co	PO Box 329	Berne	IN	46711	Jay J Yager	219-589-2173	R	5*	0.1

Source: *Ward's Business Directory of U.S. Private and Public Companies*, Volumes 1 and 2, 1996. The company type code used is as follows: P - Public, R - Private, S - Subsidiary, D - Division, J - Joint Venture, A - Affiliate, G - Group. Sales are in millions of dollars, employees are in thousands. An asterisk (*) indicates an estimated sales volume. The symbol < stands for 'less than'. Company names and addresses are truncated, in some cases, to fit into the available space.

MATERIALS CONSUMED

Material	Quantity	Delivered Cost ($ million)
Materials, ingredients, containers, and supplies	(X)	3,118.6
Hardwood lumber, rough and dressed	(X)	142.9
Softwood lumber, rough and dressed	(X)	25.0
Hardwood dimension and parts, excluding furniture frames	(X)	39.1
Furniture frames, wood	(X)	307.7
Woven cotton upholstery fabrics, excluding ticking	(X)	253.4
Other woven upholstery fabrics (rayon, nylon, polyester, etc.), excluding ticking	(X)	560.8
Paddings, battings, and fillings, except rubber and plastics foam	(X)	137.8
Coated or laminated fabrics, including vinyl coated	(X)	128.2
Springs, innerspring units, and box spring constructions	(X)	71.9
Furniture and builders' hardware	(X)	151.0
Constructions (sleeper mechanisms) for dual purpose sleep furniture	(X)	76.1
Foam cores for mattresses, including latex, excluding topper pads	(X)	40.7
Formed and slab stock for pillows, cushions, seating, etc. (urethane)	(X)	327.5
All other materials and components, parts, containers, and supplies	(X)	424.6
Materials, ingredients, containers, and supplies, nsk	(X)	432.2

Source: 1992 *Economic Census*. Explanation of symbols used: (D): Withheld to avoid disclosure of competitive data; na: Not available; (S): Withheld because statistical norms were not met; (X): Not applicable; (Z): Less than half the unit shown; nec: Not elsewhere classified; nsk: Not specified by kind; - : zero; * : 10-19 percent estimated; ** : 20-29 percent estimated.

PRODUCT SHARE DETAILS

Product or Product Class	% Share	Product or Product Class	% Share
Upholstered household furniture	100.00	Upholstered household sectional sofa pieces, including pieces seating one person, except dual-purpose sleep furniture	6.89
Upholstered household sofas, davenports, settees, and loveseats, excluding chairs sold as part of suites and sectional sofa pieces, except dual-purpose sleep furniture	44.97	Upholstered household rockers, including swivel rockers	5.90
Upholstered household swivel chairs with variable height adjustment	0.86	Upholstered household reclining chairs, all types	13.31
Other upholstered household chairs, except reclining and dual-purpose sleep furniture	12.02	Other upholstered household furniture (ottomans, hassocks, benches, chaise lounges, etc.), except dual-purpose sleep furniture	1.66

Source: 1992 *Economic Census*. The values shown are percent of total shipments in an industry. Values of indented subcategories are summed in the main heading. The symbol (D) appears when data are withheld to prevent disclosure of competitive information. The abbreviation nsk stands for 'not specified by kind' and nec for 'not elsewhere classified'.

INPUTS AND OUTPUTS FOR UPHOLSTERED HOUSEHOLD FURNITURE

Economic Sector or Industry Providing Inputs	%	Sector	Economic Sector or Industry Buying Outputs	%	Sector
Broadwoven fabric mills	25.3	Manufg.	Personal consumption expenditures	89.7	
Wholesale trade	8.4	Trade	Gross private fixed investment	7.7	Cap Inv
Miscellaneous plastics products	7.5	Manufg.	Exports	1.2	Foreign
Hardwood dimension & flooring mills	7.3	Manufg.	Mobile homes	1.0	Manufg.
Miscellaneous fabricated wire products	4.5	Manufg.	Federal Government purchases, nondefense	0.1	Fed Govt
Sawmills & planning mills, general	4.3	Manufg.			
Padding & upholstery filling	3.6	Manufg.			
Banking	3.4	Fin/R.E.			
Leather tanning & finishing	3.2	Manufg.			
Coated fabrics, not rubberized	2.0	Manufg.			
Fabricated rubber products, nec	1.6	Manufg.			
Petroleum refining	1.5	Manufg.			
Eating & drinking places	1.5	Trade			
Advertising	1.5	Services			
Maintenance of nonfarm buildings nec	1.4	Constr.			
Electric services (utilities)	1.3	Util.			
Veneer & plywood	1.2	Manufg.			
Wood products, nec	1.2	Manufg.			
Motor freight transportation & warehousing	1.2	Util.			
Needles, pins, & fasteners	1.1	Manufg.			
Hardware, nec	1.0	Manufg.			
Abrasive products	0.8	Manufg.			
Credit agencies other than banks	0.8	Fin/R.E.			
Adhesives & sealants	0.7	Manufg.			
Hand & edge tools, nec	0.7	Manufg.			
Railroads & related services	0.7	Util.			
Paints & allied products	0.6	Manufg.			
Real estate	0.6	Fin/R.E.			
Security & commodity brokers	0.6	Fin/R.E.			
Automotive & apparel trimmings	0.5	Manufg.			
Paperboard containers & boxes	0.5	Manufg.			
Thread mills	0.5	Manufg.			
Air transportation	0.5	Util.			
Communications, except radio & TV	0.5	Util.			

Continued on next page.

INPUTS AND OUTPUTS FOR UPHOLSTERED HOUSEHOLD FURNITURE - Continued

Economic Sector or Industry Providing Inputs	%	Sector	Economic Sector or Industry Buying Outputs	%	Sector
Management & consulting services & labs	0.5	Services			
U.S. Postal Service	0.5	Gov't			
Cottonseed oil mills	0.4	Manufg.			
Gas production & distribution (utilities)	0.4	Util.			
Equipment rental & leasing services	0.4	Services			
Legal services	0.4	Services			
Noncomparable imports	0.4	Foreign			
Machinery, except electrical, nec	0.3	Manufg.			
Narrow fabric mills	0.3	Manufg.			
Paper coating & glazing	0.3	Manufg.			
Steel wire & related products	0.3	Manufg.			
Accounting, auditing & bookkeeping	0.3	Services			
Automotive rental & leasing, without drivers	0.3	Services			
Lubricating oils & greases	0.2	Manufg.			
Manifold business forms	0.2	Manufg.			
Special dies & tools & machine tool accessories	0.2	Manufg.			
Insurance carriers	0.2	Fin/R.E.			
Automotive repair shops & services	0.2	Services			
Mechanical measuring devices	0.1	Manufg.			
Upholstered household furniture	0.1	Manufg.			
Sanitary services, steam supply, irrigation	0.1	Util.			
Water transportation	0.1	Util.			
Royalties	0.1	Fin/R.E.			
Computer & data processing services	0.1	Services			
Engineering, architectural, & surveying services	0.1	Services			
Hotels & lodging places	0.1	Services			
Personnel supply services	0.1	Services			

Source: Benchmark Input-Output Accounts for the U.S. Economy, 1982, U.S. Department of Commerce, Washington, D.C., July 1991. Data, as reported in the source, are organized by the 1977 SIC structure in use in 1982 but have been matched, as closely as is possible, to the 1987 SIC structure used in this book.

OCCUPATIONS EMPLOYED BY SIC 251 - HOUSEHOLD FURNITURE

Occupation	% of Total 1994	Change to 2005	Occupation	% of Total 1994	Change to 2005
Assemblers, fabricators, & hand workers nec	13.5	-6.7	Hand packers & packagers	1.9	-20.0
Upholsterers	7.7	12.4	Truck drivers light & heavy	1.9	-3.8
Sewing machine operators, non-garment	7.1	26.0	General managers & top executives	1.7	-11.5
Woodworking machine workers	5.6	-25.3	Machine feeders & offbearers	1.7	-16.0
Cabinetmakers & bench carpenters	4.8	58.6	Traffic, shipping, & receiving clerks	1.7	-10.2
Wood machinists	4.5	30.6	Cutters & trimmers, hand	1.6	-6.7
Blue collar worker supervisors	3.9	-13.5	Sales & related workers nec	1.5	-6.7
Furniture finishers	3.7	21.8	Inspectors, testers, & graders, precision	1.5	-6.7
Head sawyers & sawing machine workers	3.0	-39.3	Grinders & polishers, hand	1.2	-25.4
Helpers, laborers, & material movers nec	2.9	-6.7	General office clerks	1.1	-20.4
Freight, stock, & material movers, hand	2.5	-25.3	Precision woodworkers nec	1.0	2.7
Coating, painting, & spraying machine workers	2.0	16.6			

Source: Industry-Occupation Matrix, Bureau of Labor Statistics. These data relate to one or more 3-digit SIC industry groups rather than to a single 4-digit SIC. The change reported for each occupation to the year 2005 is a percent of growth or decline as estimated by the Bureau of Labor Statistics. The abbreviation nec stands for 'not elsewhere classified'.

LOCATION BY STATE AND REGIONAL CONCENTRATION

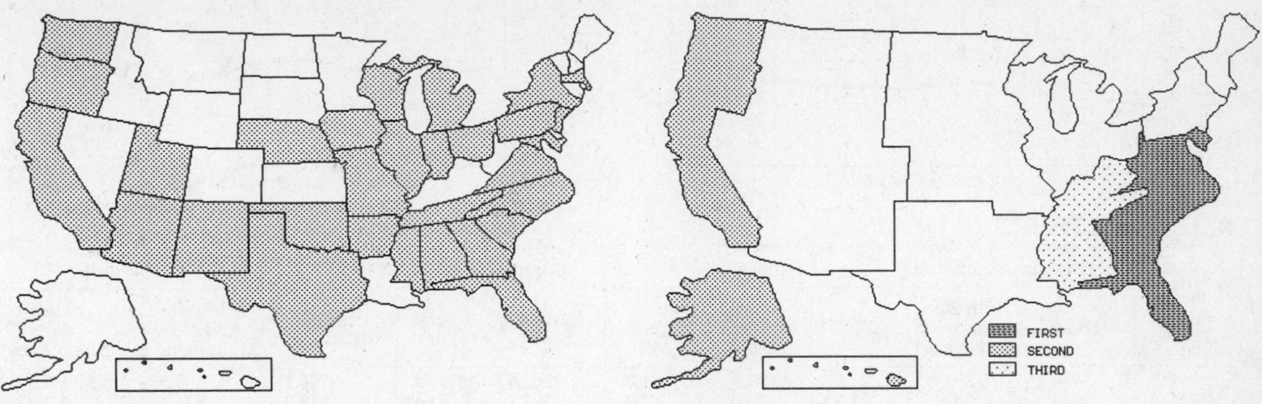

INDUSTRY DATA BY STATE

State	Establish-ments	Shipments			Employment				Cost as % of Shipments	Investment per Employee ($)
		Total ($ mil)	% of U.S.	Per Establ.	Total Number	% of U.S.	Per Establ.	Wages ($/hour)		
North Carolina	288	1,929.9	31.0	6.7	24,200	30.6	84	9.39	52.9	851
Mississippi	135	1,537.1	24.7	11.4	18,200	23.0	135	8.63	56.2	1,132
California	195	626.5	10.1	3.2	7,700	9.7	39	8.73	50.6	506
Tennessee	58	584.6	9.4	10.1	8,700	11.0	150	7.84	45.8	1,034
Indiana	22	148.5	2.4	6.8	1,600	2.0	73	9.20	58.6	-
Iowa	6	145.1	2.3	24.2	1,700	2.1	283	9.89	53.2	-
Missouri	8	137.8	2.2	17.2	1,600	2.0	200	9.42	43.7	-
Pennsylvania	36	125.4	2.0	3.5	1,400	1.8	39	7.63	50.4	643
Texas	44	115.9	1.9	2.6	1,600	2.0	36	6.93	44.4	688
Virginia	15	94.3	1.5	6.3	1,300	1.6	87	7.81	59.7	-
Arkansas	14	70.4	1.1	5.0	1,000	1.3	71	7.18	51.1	300
Wisconsin	16	66.5	1.1	4.2	800	1.0	50	6.38	34.6	375
Georgia	19	62.4	1.0	3.3	1,000	1.3	53	5.81	59.9	1,200
Oregon	19	49.6	0.8	2.6	700	0.9	37	8.30	49.2	286
Alabama	12	38.3	0.6	3.2	600	0.8	50	6.44	48.3	1,000
Florida	48	38.1	0.6	0.8	700	0.9	15	6.73	49.3	571
New Jersey	17	36.6	0.6	2.2	300	0.4	18	10.00	57.4	1,000
Michigan	15	35.2	0.6	2.3	400	0.5	27	9.14	65.9	250
New York	47	34.0	0.5	0.7	600	0.8	13	8.67	49.1	333
Arizona	19	32.7	0.5	1.7	600	0.8	32	5.64	52.9	333
Illinois	18	21.9	0.4	1.2	400	0.5	22	8.33	47.5	500
Washington	14	21.2	0.3	1.5	400	0.5	29	9.20	49.5	-
Massachusetts	20	18.6	0.3	0.9	300	0.4	15	8.80	47.3	333
Utah	17	(D)	-	-	750 *	0.9	44	-	-	-
Ohio	14	(D)	-	-	1,750 *	2.2	125	-	-	171
Oklahoma	8	(D)	-	-	175 *	0.2	22	-	-	571
New Mexico	5	(D)	-	-	175 *	0.2	35	-	-	-
Nebraska	4	(D)	-	-	175 *	0.2	44	-	-	-
South Carolina	4	(D)	-	-	375 *	0.5	94	-	-	-
Maryland	3	(D)	-	-	175 *	0.2	58	-	-	-

Source: 1992 *Economic Census*. The states are in descending order of shipments or establishments (if shipment data are missing for the majority). The symbol (D) appears when data are withheld to prevent disclosure of competitive information. States marked with (D) are sorted by number of establishments. A dash (-) indicates that the data element cannot be calculated; * indicates the midpoint of a range.

2514 - METAL HOUSEHOLD FURNITURE

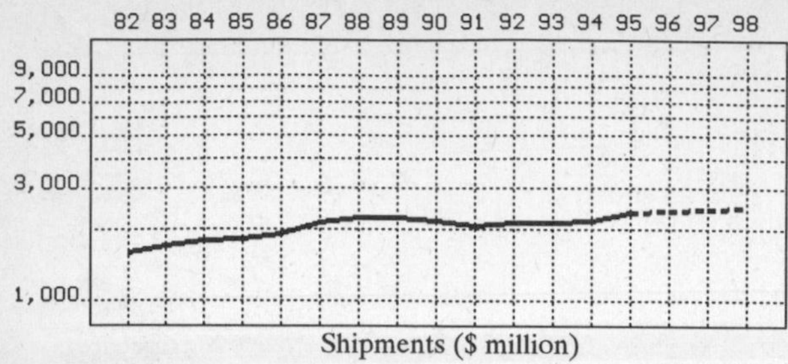

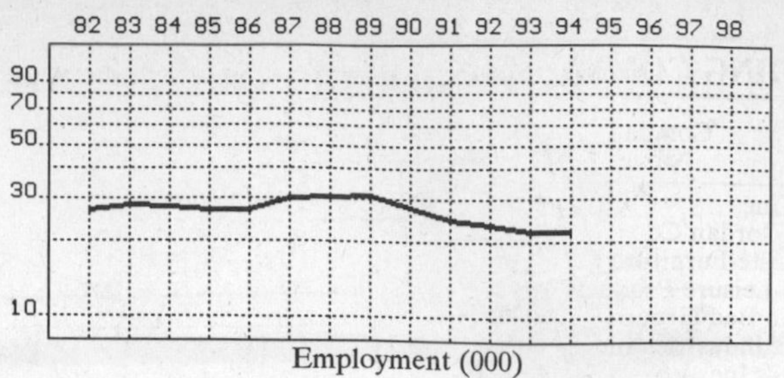

GENERAL STATISTICS

Year	Com-panies	Establishments: Total	Establishments: with 20 or more employees	Employment: Total (000)	Employment: Production Workers (000)	Employment: Production Hours (Mil)	Compensation: Payroll ($ mil)	Compensation: Wages ($/hr)	Production ($ million): Cost of Materials	Production ($ million): Value Added by Manufacture	Production ($ million): Value of Shipments	Production ($ million): Capital Invest.
1982	413	454	205	27.0	21.5	41.8	362.4	5.75	774.1	807.0	1,590.7	25.4
1983		443	209	28.3	23.0	45.2	391.2	5.64	854.9	836.4	1,701.0	23.1
1984		432	213	27.6	22.8	43.9	406.8	6.17	916.0	893.2	1,796.2	38.5
1985		421	218	27.2	22.4	42.9	420.5	6.52	939.3	885.3	1,828.9	36.9
1986		402	208	26.9	21.7	43.0	438.2	6.73	980.0	941.7	1,901.5	29.7
1987	374	418	211	30.1	24.3	47.7	498.0	6.93	1,103.0	1,047.6	2,141.2	37.7
1988		383	196			48.2	510.3		1,139.1	1,105.6	2,224.7	27.9
1989		365	190	31.3	23.3	47.0	483.6	7.12	1,147.9	1,058.6	2,228.5	33.6
1990		344	174	27.7	22.2	43.7	471.2	7.20	1,136.3	1,032.4	2,184.1	35.7
1991		341	161	24.9	20.7	39.8	441.5	7.36	1,048.8	1,054.4	2,089.8	34.1
1992	323	353	166	23.8	18.9	36.6	468.8	8.42	1,044.1	1,084.7	2,111.7	36.8
1993		349	161	22.1	17.6	34.5	442.6	8.61	1,078.0	1,080.6	2,141.1	27.1
1994		321P	158P	22.2	17.6	33.9	462.3	9.02	1,165.6	1,011.5	2,190.7	50.7
1995		310P	153P			36.8P	492.8P		1,243.4P	1,079.0P	2,336.8P	40.0P
1996		299P	147P			36.1P	499.5P		1,268.2P	1,100.5P	2,383.5P	40.9P
1997		288P	142P			35.3P	506.2P		1,293.0P	1,122.1P	2,430.2P	41.8P
1998		277P	137P			34.5P	512.9P		1,317.9P	1,143.7P	2,476.9P	42.7P

Sources: 1982, 1987, 1992 *Economic Census*; *Annual Survey of Manufactures*, 83-86, 88-91, 93-94. Establishment counts for non-Census years are from *County Business Patterns*; establishment values for 83-84 are extrapolations. 'P's show projections by the editors. Industries reclassified in 87 will not have data for prior years.

INDICES OF CHANGE

Year	Com-panies	Establishments: Total	Establishments: with 20 or more employees	Employment: Total (000)	Employment: Production Workers (000)	Employment: Production Hours (Mil)	Compensation: Payroll ($ mil)	Compensation: Wages ($/hr)	Production ($ million): Cost of Materials	Production ($ million): Value Added by Manufacture	Production ($ million): Value of Shipments	Production ($ million): Capital Invest.
1982	128	129	123	113	114	114	77	68	74	74	75	69
1983		125	126	119	122	123	83	67	82	77	81	63
1984		122	128	116	121	120	87	73	88	82	85	105
1985		119	131	114	119	117	90	77	90	82	87	100
1986		114	125	113	115	117	93	80	94	87	90	81
1987	116	118	127	126	129	130	106	82	106	97	101	102
1988		108	118			132	109		109	102	105	76
1989		103	114	132	123	128	103	85	110	98	106	91
1990		97	105	116	117	119	101	86	109	95	103	97
1991		97	97	105	110	109	94	87	100	97	99	93
1992	100	100	100	100	100	100	100	100	100	100	100	100
1993		99	97	93	93	94	94	102	103	100	101	74
1994		91P	95P	93	93	93	99	107	112	93	104	138
1995		88P	92P			101P	105P		119P	99P	111P	109P
1996		85P	89P			99P	107P		121P	101P	113P	111P
1997		82P	86P			96P	108P		124P	103P	115P	113P
1998		78P	82P			94P	109P		126P	105P	117P	116P

Sources: Same as General Statistics. Values reflect change from the base year, 1992. Values above 100 mean greater than 92, values below 100 mean less than 92, and a value of 100 in the 82-91 or 93-98 period means same as 92. 'P's mark projections by the editors.

SELECTED RATIOS

For 1994	Avg. of All Manufact.	Analyzed Industry	Index
Employees per Establishment	49	69	141
Payroll per Establishment	1,500,273	1,440,731	96
Payroll per Employee	30,620	20,824	68
Production Workers per Establishment	34	55	160
Wages per Establishment	853,319	952,939	112
Wages per Production Worker	24,861	17,374	70
Hours per Production Worker	2,056	1,926	94
Wages per Hour	12.09	9.02	75
Value Added per Establishment	4,602,255	3,152,281	68
Value Added per Employee	93,930	45,563	49

For 1994	Avg. of All Manufact.	Analyzed Industry	Index
Value Added per Production Worker	134,084	57,472	43
Cost per Establishment	5,045,178	3,632,524	72
Cost per Employee	102,970	52,505	51
Cost per Production Worker	146,988	66,227	45
Shipments per Establishment	9,576,895	6,827,189	71
Shipments per Employee	195,460	98,680	50
Shipments per Production Worker	279,017	124,472	45
Investment per Establishment	321,011	158,004	49
Investment per Employee	6,552	2,284	35
Investment per Production Worker	9,352	2,881	31

Sources: Same as General Statistics. The 'Average of All Manufacturing' column represents the average of all manufacturing industries reported for the most recent complete year available. The Index shows the relationship between the Average and the Analyzed Industry. For example, 100 means that they are equal; 500 that the Analyzed Industry is five times the average; 50 means that the Analyzed Industry is half the national average. The abbreviation 'na' is used to show that data are 'not available'.

LEADING COMPANIES

Number shown: 31 Total sales ($ mil): 815 Total employment (000): 7.3

Company Name	Address				CEO Name	Phone	Co. Type	Sales ($ mil)	Empl. (000)
Cosco Inc	2525 State St	Columbus	IN	47201	Nick Costides	812-372-0141	S	110	1.2
Brown Jordan Co	PO Box 5688	El Monte	CA	91734	James Mueller	818-443-8971	S	71	0.6
Samsonite Furniture Co	PO Box 189	Murfreesboro	TN	37133	Bill Echols	615-893-0300	R	70	0.5
Crown Leisure Products Inc	PO Box 280	Owosso	MI	48867	Ben Rhenda	517-723-7881	S	60*	0.3
Fashion Bed Group	5950 W 51st St	Chicago	IL	60638	John Elting	708-458-1800	S	59	0.6
Kessler Industries Inc	8600 Gateway E	El Paso	TX	79907	CK Kessler	915-591-8161	R	54	0.6
Stainless Inc	1 Stainless Plz	Deerfield Bch	FL	33441	Gregory Kassab	305-421-4290	R	36*	0.2
All-Luminum Products Inc	10981 Decatur Rd	Philadelphia	PA	19154	Warren Cohen	215-632-2800	R	35	0.3
Homecrest Industries Inc	PO Box 350	Wadena	MN	56482	D L Bottemiller	218-631-1000	R	35	0.3
Flanders Industries Inc	PO Box 1788	Fort Smith	AR	72902	DH Flanders	501-785-2351	R	33	0.1
Sico Inc	PO Box 1169	Minneapolis	MN	55440	Harold K Wilson	612-941-1700	R	30	0.3
Chautauqua Hardware Corp	31 Water St	Jamestown	NY	14701	JC Crighton	716-488-1161	S	29*	0.3
Jack-Post Corp	800 E 3rd St	Buchanan	MI	49107	JT Bycraft	616-695-7000	R	29	0.3
Duro Metal Manufacturing	410 Hillburn Dr	Dallas	TX	75217	WD Rosenberg	214-391-3181	D	25	0.2
Mantua Manufacturing Co	7900 Northfield Rd	Walton Hills	OH	44146	Edward Weintraub	216-232-8865	R	22	0.1
Kay Home Products Inc	90 McMillen Rd	Antioch	IL	60002	Felix tarorick	708-395-3300	D	20	0.2
Douglas Furniture of California	4000 Freeman Blv	Redondo Beach	CA	90278	Morton R Cohen	310-643-7200	R	19*	0.2
Kolcraft Enterprises Inc	3455 W 31st Pl	Chicago	IL	60623	Sanfred Koltun	312-247-4494	R	13*	0.2
Duray/JF Duncan Industries	9301ewart & Gray	Downey	CA	90241	John Wong	310-862-4269	R	12*	0.1
Burnett Manufacturing Corp	240 Roberts Av	Philadelphia	PA	19144	F Schluckebier	215-842-9010	R	10	<0.1
Hatteras Hammocks	PO Box 1602	Greenville	NC	27834	Walter Perkins Jr	919-758-0641	R	9*	0.1
Tradewinds Outdoor	16301 NW 15th Av	Miami	FL	33169	Arnie Ditri	305-624-4411	D	9*	0.1
Western Bed Products Company	444 Tiffany St	Bronx	NY	10474	D Imber	718-328-7428	R	6	<0.1
Algoma Net Co	1525 Mueller St	Algoma	WI	54201	James L Westrich	414-487-5578	D	5	0.1
Medallion Leisure	800 NW 166th St	Miami	FL	33169	Robert L Gass Jr	305-626-0000	R	4	<0.1
Buffalo Metal Fabricating Corp	50 Wacker St	Buffalo	NY	14215	Nicholas Moroczko	716-892-7800	R	3*	<0.1
Parent Metal Products	6800 State Rd	Philadelphia	PA	19135	Edward Pickell	215-332-6800	R	3*	<0.1
SAK Industries	PO Box 725	Monrovia	CA	91016	Stanley L Kreizel	818-359-5351	R	2	<0.1
Dutro Co Steel Core Plastics	PO Box 88447	Emeryville	CA	94662	William A Dutro	510-652-9130	D	1	<0.1
M and L Products Inc	Rte 80	Killingworth	CT	06419	W Loveland	203-526-5387	R	1*	<0.1
Buffalo Maid Cabinets Inc	71 Roberts Av	Buffalo	NY	14206	Steven D Krasinski	716-828-0304	R	1	<0.1

Source: *Ward's Business Directory of U.S. Private and Public Companies*, Volumes 1 and 2, 1996. The company type code used is as follows: P - Public, R - Private, S - Subsidiary, D - Division, J - Joint Venture, A - Affiliate, G - Group. Sales are in millions of dollars, employees are in thousands. An asterisk (*) indicates an estimated sales volume. The symbol < stands for 'less than'. Company names and addresses are truncated, in some cases, to fit into the available space.

MATERIALS CONSUMED

Material	Quantity	Delivered Cost ($ million)
Materials, ingredients, containers, and supplies	(X)	942.2
Metal stampings	(X)	11.5
Other fabricated metal products, except forgings	(X)	52.9
Forgings	(X)	(D)
Castings (rough and semifinished)	(X)	(D)
Steel sheet and strip, including tin plate	(X)	88.8
All other steel shapes and forms (except castings, forgings, and fabricated metal products)	(X)	83.6
Aluminum and aluminum-base alloy sheet, plate, foil, and welded tubing	(X)	39.3
All other aluminum and aluminum-base alloy shapes and forms	(X)	21.3
Other nonferrous shapes and forms (except castings, forgings, and fabricated metal products)	(X)	1.2
Plastics parts, components, sheets, and other shapes (excluding plastics resins)	(X)	47.9
Hardwood dimension and parts, including wood furniture frames	(X)	40.1
Particleboard (wood)	(X)	14.9
Flat glass (plate, float, and sheet)	(X)	18.1
Coated or laminated fabrics, including vinyl coated	(X)	59.0
Paints, varnishes, lacquers, stains, shellacs, japans, enamels, and allied products	(X)	20.9
Furniture and builders' hardware	(X)	39.1
Paperboard containers, boxes, and corrugated paperboard	(X)	46.5
All other materials and components, parts, containers, and supplies	(X)	226.1
Materials, ingredients, containers, and supplies, nsk	(X)	115.9

Source: 1992 *Economic Census*. Explanation of symbols used: (D): Withheld to avoid disclosure of competitive data; na: Not available; (S): Withheld because statistical norms were not met; (X): Not applicable; (Z): Less than half the unit shown; nec: Not elsewhere classified; nsk: Not specified by kind; - : zero; * : 10-19 percent estimated; ** : 20-29 percent estimated.

PRODUCT SHARE DETAILS

Product or Product Class	% Share	Product or Product Class	% Share
Metal household furniture	100.00	Other cast and wrought iron porch, lawn, outdoor, and casual furniture, including gliders, hammocks, and tables	8.00
Metal household dining room and kitchen furniture	19.82	Other metal porch, lawn, outdoor, and casual furniture, including picnic tables	11.89
Tubular metal dining, dinette, and breakfast set tables	21.92	Metal porch, lawn, outdoor, and casual furniture, nsk	3.57
Tubular metal dining, dinette, and breakfast set chairs	26.87	Other metal household furniture	36.92
Tubular metal dining, dinette, and breakfast tables (not sold with a set)	9.58	Metal household folding cots, rollable cots, army cots, and other beds	8.39
Tubular metal dining, dinette, and breakfast chairs (not sold with a set)	22.26	Metal household bed frames (complete metal bed frames, sold separately, with or without a headboard)	26.92
Metal kitchen cabinets, such as base, top and base, wall, utility, etc.	3.37	Metal household card tables and chairs	(D)
Metal kitchen stools, padded and plain	6.37	Metal household medicine cabinets, including "wall type" and "insert type"	12.30
Other metal dining room and kitchen furniture, including hostess carts	5.92	Metal and plastics infants' high chairs	5.18
Metal household dining room and kitchen furniture, nsk	3.71	Metal and plastics infants' car seats	16.81
Metal porch, lawn, outdoor, and casual furniture	32.60	Other metal infants' and children's furniture, including chairs, tables, playpens, play yards, and portable cribs	13.25
Tubular aluminum porch, lawn, outdoor, and casual chairs, rockers, benches, chaise lounges, and settees	51.73	Other metal household furniture, including upholstered furniture, metal folding trays, etc.	12.69
Other tubular aluminum porch, lawn, outdoor, and casual furniture, including gliders, swings, hammocks, and tables	11.42	Other metal household furniture, nsk	(D)
Cast and wrought iron porch, lawn, outdoor, and casual chairs, rockers, benches, chaise lounges, and settees	13.41	Metal household furniture, nsk	10.66

Source: 1992 *Economic Census*. The values shown are percent of total shipments in an industry. Values of indented subcategories are summed in the main heading. The symbol (D) appears when data are withheld to prevent disclosure of competitive information. The abbreviation nsk stands for 'not specified by kind' and nec for 'not elsewhere classified'.

INPUTS AND OUTPUTS FOR METAL HOUSEHOLD FURNITURE

Economic Sector or Industry Providing Inputs	%	Sector	Economic Sector or Industry Buying Outputs	%	Sector
Blast furnaces & steel mills	14.3	Manufg.	Personal consumption expenditures	82.2	
Wholesale trade	10.0	Trade	Gross private fixed investment	6.3	Cap Inv
Aluminum rolling & drawing	8.0	Manufg.	Exports	2.7	Foreign
Veneer & plywood	5.7	Manufg.	Nonfarm residential structure maintenance	1.3	Constr.
Miscellaneous plastics products	5.0	Manufg.	Construction of hospitals	1.0	Constr.
Advertising	4.9	Services	Radio & TV receiving sets	0.9	Manufg.
Paperboard containers & boxes	4.6	Manufg.	Residential 1-unit structures, nonfarm	0.8	Constr.
Coated fabrics, not rubberized	4.0	Manufg.	Office buildings	0.7	Constr.
Hardware, nec	2.7	Manufg.	Residential additions/alterations, nonfarm	0.6	Constr.
Metal stampings, nec	2.3	Manufg.	Construction of stores & restaurants	0.4	Constr.
Glass & glass products, except containers	2.1	Manufg.	Resid. & other health facility construction	0.4	Constr.
Canvas & related products	2.0	Manufg.	Mobile homes	0.3	Manufg.
Business services nec	2.0	Services	S/L Govt. purch., elem. & secondary education	0.3	S/L Govt
Paints & allied products	1.9	Manufg.	S/L Govt. purch., higher education	0.3	S/L Govt
Particleboard	1.9	Manufg.	Hotels & motels	0.2	Constr.
Fabricated metal products, nec	1.8	Manufg.	Maintenance of nonfarm buildings nec	0.2	Constr.
Motor freight transportation & warehousing	1.7	Util.	Residential garden apartments	0.2	Constr.
Fabricated rubber products, nec	1.5	Manufg.	S/L Govt. purch., correction	0.2	S/L Govt
Electric services (utilities)	1.4	Util.	Amusement & recreation building construction	0.1	Constr.
Sawmills & planning mills, general	1.2	Manufg.	Federal Government purchases, national defense	0.1	Fed Govt
Petroleum refining	1.0	Manufg.			
Eating & drinking places	1.0	Trade			
Real estate	1.0	Fin/R.E.			
Maintenance of nonfarm buildings nec	0.9	Constr.			
Equipment rental & leasing services	0.9	Services			
Credit agencies other than banks	0.8	Fin/R.E.			
Business/professional associations	0.8	Services			
Padding & upholstery filling	0.7	Manufg.			
Railroads & related services	0.7	Util.			
Security & commodity brokers	0.7	Fin/R.E.			
Colleges, universities, & professional schools	0.7	Services			
Theatrical producers, bands, entertainers	0.7	Services			
Abrasive products	0.6	Manufg.			
Adhesives & sealants	0.6	Manufg.			
Communications, except radio & TV	0.6	Util.			
Gas production & distribution (utilities)	0.6	Util.			
Banking	0.6	Fin/R.E.			
Screw machine and related products	0.5	Manufg.			
Wood products, nec	0.5	Manufg.			
Royalties	0.5	Fin/R.E.			
Detective & protective services	0.5	Services			
U.S. Postal Service	0.5	Gov't			
Air transportation	0.4	Util.			
Water supply & sewage systems	0.4	Util.			
Miscellaneous fabricated wire products	0.3	Manufg.			
Legal services	0.3	Services			
Management & consulting services & labs	0.3	Services			
Machinery, except electrical, nec	0.2	Manufg.			
Paper coating & glazing	0.2	Manufg.			

Continued on next page.

INPUTS AND OUTPUTS FOR METAL HOUSEHOLD FURNITURE - Continued

Economic Sector or Industry Providing Inputs	%	Sector	Economic Sector or Industry Buying Outputs	%	Sector
Accounting, auditing & bookkeeping	0.2	Services			
Automotive repair shops & services	0.2	Services			
Computer & data processing services	0.2	Services			
Coal	0.1	Mining			
Apparel made from purchased materials	0.1	Manufg.			
Lubricating oils & greases	0.1	Manufg.			
Manifold business forms	0.1	Manufg.			
Metal household furniture	0.1	Manufg.			
Special dies & tools & machine tool accessories	0.1	Manufg.			
Sanitary services, steam supply, irrigation	0.1	Util.			
Insurance carriers	0.1	Fin/R.E.			
Automotive rental & leasing, without drivers	0.1	Services			
Engineering, architectural, & surveying services	0.1	Services			
Hotels & lodging places	0.1	Services			
Laundry, dry cleaning, shoe repair	0.1	Services			

Source: Benchmark Input-Output Accounts for the U.S. Economy, 1982, U.S. Department of Commerce, Washington, D.C., July 1991. Data, as reported in the source, are organized by the 1977 SIC structure in use in 1982 but have been matched, as closely as is possible, to the 1987 SIC structure used in this book.

OCCUPATIONS EMPLOYED BY SIC 251 - HOUSEHOLD FURNITURE

Occupation	% of Total 1994	Change to 2005	Occupation	% of Total 1994	Change to 2005
Assemblers, fabricators, & hand workers nec	13.5	-6.7	Hand packers & packagers	1.9	-20.0
Upholsterers	7.7	12.4	Truck drivers light & heavy	1.9	-3.8
Sewing machine operators, non-garment	7.1	26.0	General managers & top executives	1.7	-11.5
Woodworking machine workers	5.6	-25.3	Machine feeders & offbearers	1.7	-16.0
Cabinetmakers & bench carpenters	4.8	58.6	Traffic, shipping, & receiving clerks	1.7	-10.2
Wood machinists	4.5	30.6	Cutters & trimmers, hand	1.6	-6.7
Blue collar worker supervisors	3.9	-13.5	Sales & related workers nec	1.5	-6.7
Furniture finishers	3.7	21.8	Inspectors, testers, & graders, precision	1.5	-6.7
Head sawyers & sawing machine workers	3.0	-39.3	Grinders & polishers, hand	1.2	-25.4
Helpers, laborers, & material movers nec	2.9	-6.7	General office clerks	1.1	-20.4
Freight, stock, & material movers, hand	2.5	-25.3	Precision woodworkers nec	1.0	2.7
Coating, painting, & spraying machine workers	2.0	16.6			

Source: Industry-Occupation Matrix, Bureau of Labor Statistics. These data relate to one or more 3-digit SIC industry groups rather than to a single 4-digit SIC. The change reported for each occupation to the year 2005 is a percent of growth or decline as estimated by the Bureau of Labor Statistics. The abbreviation nec stands for 'not elsewhere classified'.

LOCATION BY STATE AND REGIONAL CONCENTRATION

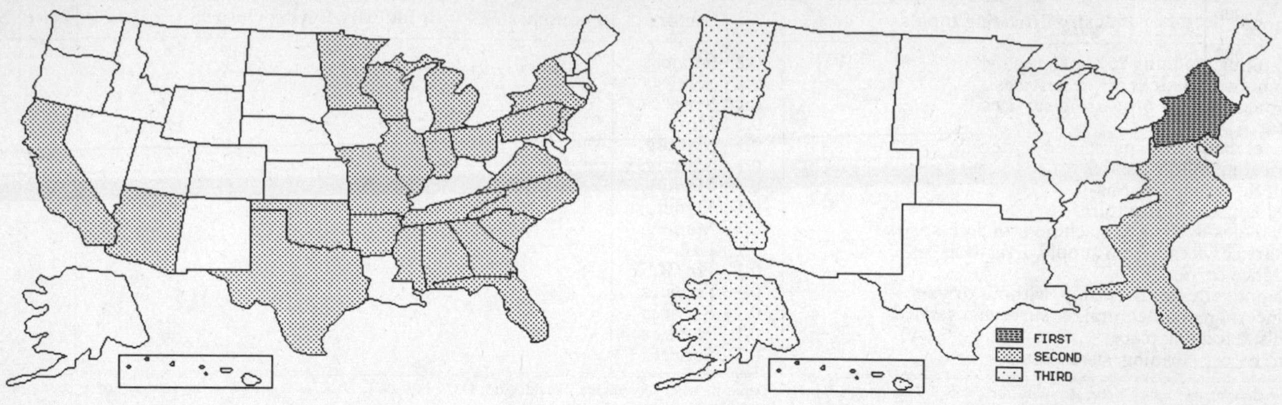

INDUSTRY DATA BY STATE

State	Establish-ments	Shipments			Employment				Cost as % of Shipments	Investment per Employee ($)
		Total ($ mil)	% of U.S.	Per Establ.	Total Number	% of U.S.	Per Establ.	Wages ($/hour)		
California	68	345.6	16.4	5.1	3,800	16.0	56	8.02	51.6	1,342
Tennessee	8	279.0	13.2	34.9	3,900	16.4	488	7.21	47.3	1,641
Pennsylvania	22	196.3	9.3	8.9	1,800	7.6	82	9.18	52.9	1,722
Indiana	16	160.0	7.6	10.0	2,000	8.4	125	9.42	45.1	-
Illinois	17	134.7	6.4	7.9	1,200	5.0	71	7.88	54.1	750
Alabama	8	116.8	5.5	14.6	1,000	4.2	125	8.63	39.5	-
Mississippi	7	101.4	4.8	14.5	1,200	5.0	171	10.82	45.5	583
Ohio	8	97.5	4.6	12.2	800	3.4	100	8.80	65.9	-
Texas	17	91.8	4.3	5.4	900	3.8	53	6.88	49.1	778
New York	40	90.8	4.3	2.3	1,100	4.6	28	10.50	44.3	909
Michigan	10	77.0	3.6	7.7	700	2.9	70	8.36	42.9	2,143
Florida	34	53.0	2.5	1.6	700	2.9	21	7.45	42.3	1,429
New Jersey	8	19.3	0.9	2.4	100	0.4	13	9.00	48.7	1,000
Arizona	5	12.1	0.6	2.4	200	0.8	40	9.00	51.2	-
North Carolina	22	(D)	-	-	1,750 *	7.4	80	-	-	-
Georgia	6	(D)	-	-	175 *	0.7	29	-	-	-
Virginia	6	(D)	-	-	750 *	3.2	125	-	-	-
Arkansas	5	(D)	-	-	375 *	1.6	75	-	-	-
Minnesota	5	(D)	-	-	375 *	1.6	75	-	-	-
Oklahoma	4	(D)	-	-	175 *	0.7	44	-	-	1,143
Missouri	3	(D)	-	-	175 *	0.7	58	-	-	-
Wisconsin	3	(D)	-	-	175 *	0.7	58	-	-	-
South Carolina	2	(D)	-	-	175 *	0.7	88	-	-	-

Source: 1992 *Economic Census*. The states are in descending order of shipments or establishments (if shipment data are missing for the majority). The symbol (D) appears when data are withheld to prevent disclosure of competitive information. States marked with (D) are sorted by number of establishments. A dash (-) indicates that the data element cannot be calculated; * indicates the midpoint of a range.

2515 - MATTRESSES AND BEDSPRINGS

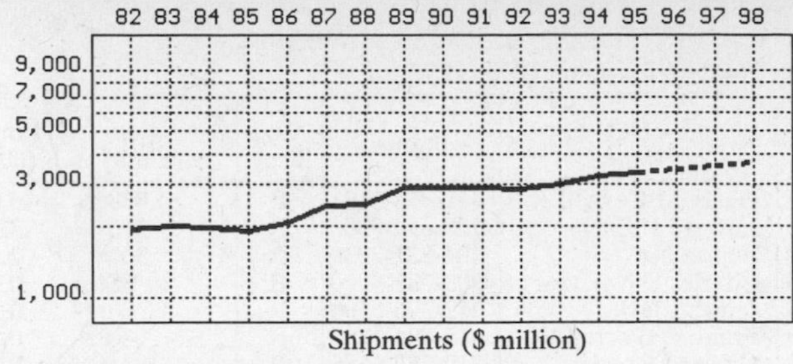

Shipments ($ million)

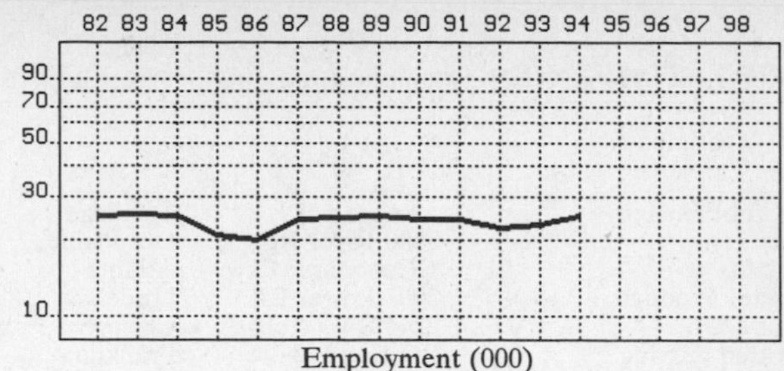

Employment (000)

GENERAL STATISTICS

Year	Companies	Establishments Total	Establishments with 20 or more employees	Employment Total (000)	Production Workers (000)	Production Hours (Mil)	Compensation Payroll ($ mil)	Compensation Wages ($/hr)	Cost of Materials	Value Added by Manufacture	Value of Shipments	Capital Invest.
1982	786	902	336	25.4	19.0	35.6	357.4	6.15	1,047.4	882.4	1,935.4	25.0
1983		889	340	25.6	19.2	37.3	387.2	6.23	1,127.4	907.3	2,026.1	34.7
1984		876	344	25.0	18.6	35.6	358.9	5.90	1,095.5	860.8	1,956.3	29.2
1985		863	349	21.1	15.3	28.8	369.7	7.38	1,057.4	856.3	1,920.9	27.6
1986		853	344	20.3	14.5	28.7	376.7	7.56	1,112.3	961.5	2,074.6	23.7
1987	721	839	335	24.4	17.9	34.8	448.2	7.44	1,259.5	1,164.5	2,417.3	34.2
1988		820	340			35.7	451.9		1,311.2	1,149.4	2,457.4	20.2
1989		793	338	25.1	18.8	36.9	507.3	8.14	1,539.6	1,347.3	2,892.9	30.6
1990		787	324	24.4	17.7	35.1	490.9	8.07	1,572.0	1,331.4	2,904.9	28.2
1991		793	323	24.3	17.7	33.8	508.9	8.54	1,528.9	1,393.3	2,922.9	35.5
1992	700	790	322	22.6	16.4	33.2	488.0	8.55	1,436.0	1,404.5	2,842.6	31.2
1993		790	327	23.3	16.9	34.4	518.1	8.70	1,513.7	1,481.2	3,000.5	38.6
1994		758P	323P	25.3	19.0	37.5	563.8	9.08	1,691.3	1,584.4	3,267.1	29.6
1995		747P	321P			35.1P	568.0P		1,728.0P	1,618.8P	3,338.0P	33.1P
1996		735P	319P			35.2P	585.1P		1,789.3P	1,676.2P	3,456.4P	33.6P
1997		724P	317P			35.3P	602.2P		1,850.6P	1,733.6P	3,574.8P	34.0P
1998		712P	315P			35.4P	619.4P		1,911.9P	1,791.0P	3,693.2P	34.5P

Sources: 1982, 1987, 1992 *Economic Census*; *Annual Survey of Manufactures*, 83-86, 88-91, 93-94. Establishment counts for non-Census years are from *County Business Patterns*; establishment values for 83-84 are extrapolations. 'P's show projections by the editors. Industries reclassified in 87 will not have data for prior years.

INDICES OF CHANGE

Year	Companies	Establishments Total	Establishments with 20 or more employees	Employment Total (000)	Production Workers (000)	Production Hours (Mil)	Compensation Payroll ($ mil)	Compensation Wages ($/hr)	Cost of Materials	Value Added by Manufacture	Value of Shipments	Capital Invest.
1982	112	114	104	112	116	107	73	72	73	63	68	80
1983		113	106	113	117	112	79	73	79	65	71	111
1984		111	107	111	113	107	74	69	76	61	69	94
1985		109	108	93	93	87	76	86	74	61	68	88
1986		108	107	90	88	86	77	88	77	68	73	76
1987	103	106	104	108	109	105	92	87	88	83	85	110
1988		104	106			108	93		91	82	86	65
1989		100	105	111	115	111	104	95	107	96	102	98
1990		100	101	108	108	106	101	94	109	95	102	90
1991		100	100	108	108	102	104	100	106	99	103	114
1992	100	100	100	100	100	100	100	100	100	100	100	100
1993		100	102	103	103	104	106	102	105	105	106	124
1994		96P	100P	112	116	113	116	106	118	113	115	95
1995		95P	100P			106P	116P		120P	115P	117P	106P
1996		93P	99P			106P	120P		125P	119P	122P	108P
1997		92P	98P			106P	123P		129P	123P	126P	109P
1998		90P	98P			107P	127P		133P	128P	130P	111P

Sources: Same as General Statistics. Values reflect change from the base year, 1992. Values above 100 mean greater than 92, values below 100 mean less than 92, and a value of 100 in the 82-91 or 93-98 period means same as 92. 'P's mark projections by the editors.

SELECTED RATIOS

For 1994	Avg. of All Manufact.	Analyzed Industry	Index	For 1994	Avg. of All Manufact.	Analyzed Industry	Index
Employees per Establishment	49	33	68	Value Added per Production Worker	134,084	83,389	62
Payroll per Establishment	1,500,273	743,502	50	Cost per Establishment	5,045,178	2,230,375	44
Payroll per Employee	30,620	22,285	73	Cost per Employee	102,970	66,850	65
Production Workers per Establishment	34	25	73	Cost per Production Worker	146,988	89,016	61
Wages per Establishment	853,319	449,029	53	Shipments per Establishment	9,576,895	4,308,436	45
Wages per Production Worker	24,861	17,921	72	Shipments per Employee	195,460	129,134	66
Hours per Production Worker	2,056	1,974	96	Shipments per Production Worker	279,017	171,953	62
Wages per Hour	12.09	9.08	75	Investment per Establishment	321,011	39,035	12
Value Added per Establishment	4,602,255	2,089,402	45	Investment per Employee	6,552	1,170	18
Value Added per Employee	93,930	62,625	67	Investment per Production Worker	9,352	1,558	17

Sources: Same as General Statistics. The 'Average of All Manufacturing' column represents the average of all manufacturing industries reported for the most recent complete year available. The Index shows the relationship between the Average and the Analyzed Industry. For example, 100 means that they are equal; 500 that the Analyzed Industry is five times the average; 50 means that the Analyzed Industry is half the national average. The abbreviation 'na' is used to show that data are 'not available'.

LEADING COMPANIES

Number shown: **65** Total sales ($ mil): **2,985** Total employment (000): **25.3**

Company Name	Address				CEO Name	Phone	Co. Type	Sales ($ mil)	Empl. (000)
Leggett and Platt Inc	1 Leggett Rd	Carthage	MO	64836	Harry M Cornell Jr	417-358-8131	P	1,858	16.0
Serta Inc	2800 River Rd	Des Plaines	IL	60018	Edward F Lilly	708-699-9300	R	300*	2.1
Simmons Co	1 Concourse Pkwy	Atlanta	GA	30338	Zenon Nie	404-321-3030	R	300*	2.5
Sleepmaster Products LP	2001 Lower Rd	Linden	NJ	07036	Charles Schweitzer	908-381-5000	R	35*	0.3
Flexi-Mat Corp	2244 S Western Av	Chicago	IL	60608	James Elesh	312-376-5500	R	30	0.3
Jamison Bedding Inc	PO Box 518	Franklin	TN	37065	Frank C Gorrell III	615-794-1883	R	30	0.3
Ortho Mattress Inc	1515 W 178th St	Gardena	CA	90248	Howard Roeder	310-527-6555	R	24*	0.2
Atlas Spring Mfg Corp	150 E 157th St	Gardena	CA	90248	Mel Bayer	213-321-4600	R	18*	0.2
Serta of Southern California	4774 Airport Dr	Ontario	CA	91761	Bob Sherman	909-390-0145	D	18	<0.1
Serta Mattress Co	3777 Vacaville Val	Vacaville	CA	95688	Donald S Simon	707-446-7999	R	17*	0.1
Park Place Corp	PO Box 3827	Greenville	SC	29608	JB Orders III	803-242-4900	R	16	0.2
Schubert Industries Inc	1510 Bauer Blv	Akron	OH	44305	JR Schubert	216-733-8302	R	16	0.1
Latex Foam Products Inc	20 W Main St	Ansonia	CT	06401	William Coffey	203-735-8641	R	15	0.1
Paramount Industrial Companies	1112 Kingwood Av	Norfolk	VA	23502	J Diamonstein	804-855-3321	R	15	0.1
Sealy Stearns and Foster Inc	279 Industrial Dr	Pontotoc	MS	38863	John Beeby	601-489-7650	S	14	0.1
Namaco Industries Inc	PO Box 1450	Huntington	WV	25716	Joan C Edwards	304-522-7334	R	13	0.2
Spring Air Mattress of California	PO Box 890	Union City	CA	94587	DC Vesey	510-471-7110	R	13	<0.1
Spring Air Co	PO Box 7240	Des Plaines	IL	60018	Jeff Holmes	708-297-5577	R	12	<0.1
Lions Club Industries Inc	PO Box 11305	Durham	NC	27703	Bill Hudson	919-596-8277	R	11*	0.1
Peerless Mattress & Furniture	816 S Saginaw St	Flint	MI	48502	J A Pemberton	810-232-7121	R	11	<0.1
Imperial Bedding Co	PO Box 5347	Huntington	WV	25703	James R Rowe	304-529-3321	R	10	<0.1
Serta Mattress Co	PO Box 11363	Tacoma	WA	98411	David E Puterbaugh	206-474-8447	D	10	<0.1
Clearwater Mattress Inc	8325 Ulmerton Rd	Largo	FL	34641	Mel Jones	813-539-1600	R	9	0.1
Comfortex Inc	PO Box 850	Winona	MN	55987	Edmund Kelley	507-454-6579	R	8	<0.1
Herr Manufacturing Co	PO Box 4623	Lancaster	PA	17604	John K Herr	717-392-4168	R	8	<0.1
Spring Air Mattress of Colorado	1055 S Jason	Denver	CO	80223	Dallas G Yeargain	303-777-6683	R	8	<0.1
Leonetti Furniture Mfg Co	5150 SW Western	Beaverton	OR	97005	Douglas Leonetti	503-646-1145	R	8*	<0.1
Tiffany Furniture Industries Inc	7150 NW 37th Av	Miami	FL	33147	EM Salomon Jr	305-696-8400	R	8	<0.1
Spring Air Bedding Inc	6200 Melrose Ln	Oklahoma City	OK	73127	Ike Tennyson	405-495-3521	R	7	<0.1
Angel Echevarria Company Inc	1000 Apex St	Nashville	TN	37206	Angel Echevarria	615-228-9000	R	7*	<0.1
Blue Bell Mattress Co	770 Bloomfield Av	Windsor	CT	06095	Frank Stavis	203-688-6496	R	7*	<0.1
Premier Sleep Products Inc	PO Box 080384	Brooklyn	NY	11208	Steve Simon	718-272-1010	R	7	<0.1
Serta Mattress	PO Box 4623	Lancaster	PA	17604	John K Herr III	717-392-4168	D	7	<0.1
Spiller Spring Co	PO Box 1023	Sheboygan	WI	53082	Stuart Spiller	414-457-3649	S	7*	0.1
Standard Mattress Co	PO Box 89	Hartford	CT	06141	R J Naboicheck	203-549-2000	R	7	<0.1
World Sleep Products Inc	12 Esquire Rd	North Billerica	MA	01862	Charles Warshaver	508-667-6648	R	7	<0.1
Coyne Mattress Company Ltd	94-134 Leowwena St	Waipahu	HI	96797	Donald E Lee	808-671-4071	R	6	<0.1
Diamond Mattress Company Inc	3112 Hermanas	Compton	CA	90221	R D Pennington	310-638-0363	R	6*	<0.1
Meridian Mattress Factory Inc	PO Box 5127	Meridian	MS	39302	GT Crudup	601-693-3875	R	6	<0.1
Southern Mattress Co	PO Box 6026	New Orleans	LA	70174	Betsy Birdsong	504-561-1106	R	6	<0.1
Springwall Mattress	1510 Bauer Blv	Akron	OH	44305	James Schubert	216-733-8302	D	6*	<0.1
Penfield Manufacturing Co	1710 N Salina St	Syracuse	NY	13208	Charles L Gordon	315-471-7145	R	6	<0.1
Bowles Mattress Company Inc	1220 Watt St	Jeffersonville	IN	47130	George E Bowles	812-288-8614	R	5	<0.1
Automatic Bedding Corp	735 Lorimer St	Brooklyn	NY	11211	Alvin Gursky	718-388-1560	R	4	<0.1
Northwest Futon Co	PO Box 14952	Portland	OR	97214	Valko Sichel	503-224-3199	R	4*	<0.1
Restwell Mattress Co	3540 Belt Line Blv	St Louis Park	MN	55416	Chuck Carlson	612-920-3348	R	4*	<0.1
Scott Bedding Co	PO Box 687	Americus	GA	31709	George A Scott	912-924-6911	R	4*	<0.1
US Mattress Corp	84 Coit St	Irvington	NJ	07111	Steve Ardussi	201-374-8800	R	4	<0.1
Aireloom Bedding Co	PO Box 4638	El Monte	CA	91734	Don Rob	818-442-4440	R	3	<0.1
Doppelt Industries Inc	649 39th St	Brooklyn	NY	11232	JK Doppelt	718-853-7000	R	3	<0.1
Los Angeles Spring Co	945 S Birch St	Los Angeles	CA	90021	Larry Harrow	213-622-2219	R	3*	<0.1
Sleep-Aire Mattress Company	19022 N Aurora	Seattle	WA	98133	Mike Peason	206-546-4195	R	3	<0.1
Troy Mattress Company Inc	PO Box 4367	Albany	NY	12204	Stanley Falk	518-449-7733	R	3*	<0.1
Elkhart Bedding Co	2124 Sterling Av	Elkhart	IN	46516	J Darr	219-293-6200	R	3	<0.1
Sleeper Lounge Mfg Corp	701 E Kings Hill Pl	Carson	CA	90746	Jay W Watai	310-329-6421	R	3	<0.1
Charles H Beckley Inc	749 E 137th St	Bronx	NY	10454	Theodore Marschke	718-665-2218	R	2*	<0.1
Kinder Manufacturing Corp	PO Box 5038	Riverside	CA	92507	William Gunn	909-653-2125	D	2	<0.1
Salt Lake Mattress & Mfg	PO Box 783	Salt Lake City	UT	84110	Curt P Crowther	801-363-3878	R	2	<0.1
Universal Bedding Inc	1337 Farmville Rd	Memphis	TN	38122	Gene Kennedy	901-324-6779	R	2	<0.1
McRoskey Airflex Mattress	1687 Market St	San Francisco	CA	94103	Robin Azevedo	415-861-4532	R	2	<0.1
Acme Mattress Factory Inc	18429 Pacific St	Fountain Val	CA	92708	Charles C Wyatt	714-965-8868	R	1	<0.1
Melrose Mattress Inc	8241 Lankershim	N Hollywood	CA	91605	Harry Myers	818-982-2234	R	1	<0.1
Valley Mattress Co	4160 14th Av	Sacramento	CA	95820	Paul W Cronick	916-455-3019	R	1	<0.1
Riviera Convertibles Inc	3876 S Santa Fe Av	Los Angeles	CA	90058	Michael H Seigel	213-587-4165	R	1*	<0.1
Cotton Cloud Futon	3125 E Burnside St	Portland	OR	97214	Terri Treat	503-234-6567	R	1	<0.1

Source: Ward's Business Directory of U.S. Private and Public Companies, Volumes 1 and 2, 1996. The company type code used is as follows: P - Public, R - Private, S - Subsidiary, D - Division, J - Joint Venture, A - Affiliate, G - Group. Sales are in millions of dollars, employees are in thousands. An asterisk (*) indicates an estimated sales volume. The symbol < stands for 'less than'. Company names and addresses are truncated, in some cases, to fit into the available space.

MATERIALS CONSUMED

Material	Quantity	Delivered Cost ($ million)
Materials, ingredients, containers, and supplies	(X)	1,371.9
Hardwood dimension and parts, including furniture frames	(X)	55.6
Plastics products consumed in the form of sheets, rods, tubes, film, and other shapes	(X)	21.9
Metal mill shapes and forms, including castings (steel, aluminum, etc.)	(X)	9.9
Springs, innerspring units, and box spring constructions	(X)	302.4
Constructions (sleeper mechanisms) for dual purpose sleep furniture	(X)	16.6
Foam cores for mattresses, including latex, excluding topper pads	(X)	37.6
Woven upholstery fabrics (cotton, nylon, polyester, rayon, etc.), excluding ticking	(X)	42.6
Ticking (mattress)	(X)	186.4
Cotton linters and cotton waste	(X)	12.1
Padding, foam (except mattress cores)	(X)	115.1
Cotton felt filling materials, purchased premade	(X)	18.1
Insulators, all types, except cotton felt, purchased premade	(X)	50.5
Other cushioning materials, purchased premade	(X)	18.4
Paper and paperboard containers, including shipping sacks and other paper packaging supplies	(X)	8.4
All other materials and components, parts, containers, and supplies	(X)	158.4
Materials, ingredients, containers, and supplies, nsk	(X)	317.9

Source: 1992 *Economic Census*. Explanation of symbols used: (D): Withheld to avoid disclosure of competitive data; na: Not available; (S): Withheld because statistical norms were not met; (X): Not applicable; (Z): Less than half the unit shown; nec: Not elsewhere classified; nsk: Not specified by kind; - : zero; * : 10-19 percent estimated; ** : 20-29 percent estimated.

PRODUCT SHARE DETAILS

Product or Product Class	% Share
Mattresses, foundations, and convertible beds	100.00
Innerspring mattresses, excluding crib size, including those with topper pads and those sold as part of Hollywood beds	37.92
Other mattresses, including crib mattresses and mattress inserts	6.59
Crib mattresses, all types, including crib size mattresses made with innersprings, foam, hair, cotton felt, etc.	26.16
Foam core mattresses, other than crib size	16.81
Other mattresses, including inflatable air chambered, cotton felt, hair, etc. (excludes sleep system ensembles)	33.22
Mattress inserts for dual-purpose sleep furniture (innerspring and foam), and futons shipped without frames	18.62
Other mattresses, including crib mattresses and mattress inserts, nsk	5.19
Foundations, excluding innerspring units and those incorporated into hybrid-type flotation and adjustable ensembles	22.08
Spring foundations, excluding innerspring units and those incorporated into hybrid-type flotation and adjustable ensembles	85.21
Foam foundations, excluding those incorporated into hybrid-type flotation and adjustable ensembles	6.94
Other foundations, including platform, excluding those incorporated into hybrid-type flotation and adjustable ensembles	5.66
Foundations, excl. innerspring units and those incorporated into hybrid-type flotation and adjustable ensembles, nsk	2.19
Dual-purpose sleep furniture, including convertible sofas, futons shipped with frames, studio couches, etc..	16.16
Sleep system ensembles, excluding conventional water beds	4.25
Hybrid-type sleep system flotation ensembles, excluding conventional water beds	25.30
Electric adjustable sleep system ensemble, excluding hospital and conventional water beds	68.09
Sleep system ensembles, excluding conventional water beds, nsk	6.53
Mattresses, foundations, and convertible beds, nsk	13.00

Source: 1992 *Economic Census*. The values shown are percent of total shipments in an industry. Values of indented subcategories are summed in the main heading. The symbol (D) appears when data are withheld to prevent disclosure of competitive information. The abbreviation nsk stands for 'not specified by kind' and nec for 'not elsewhere classified'.

INPUTS AND OUTPUTS FOR MATTRESSES & BEDSPRINGS

Economic Sector or Industry Providing Inputs	%	Sector	Economic Sector or Industry Buying Outputs	%	Sector
Miscellaneous fabricated wire products	22.0	Manufg.	Personal consumption expenditures	89.0	
Broadwoven fabric mills	14.4	Manufg.	Gross private fixed investment	7.5	Cap Inv
Miscellaneous plastics products	7.7	Manufg.	S/L Govt. purch., higher education	1.0	S/L Govt
Wholesale trade	7.4	Trade	Mobile homes	0.9	Manufg.
Advertising	4.5	Services	Exports	0.8	Foreign
Accounting, auditing & bookkeeping	4.4	Services	S/L Govt. purch., health & hospitals	0.2	S/L Govt
Fabricated rubber products, nec	3.7	Manufg.	S/L Govt. purch., elem. & secondary education	0.1	S/L Govt
Hardwood dimension & flooring mills	3.3	Manufg.	S/L Govt. purch., other education & libraries	0.1	S/L Govt
Sawmills & planning mills, general	2.7	Manufg.			
Fabricated textile products, nec	2.1	Manufg.			
Padding & upholstery filling	1.7	Manufg.			
Veneer & plywood	1.7	Manufg.			
Banking	1.7	Fin/R.E.			
Business services nec	1.5	Services			
Cyclic crudes and organics	1.1	Manufg.			
Metal stampings, nec	1.1	Manufg.			
Real estate	1.1	Fin/R.E.			
Coated fabrics, not rubberized	1.0	Manufg.			
Cottonseed oil mills	1.0	Manufg.			
Maintenance of nonfarm buildings nec	0.8	Constr.			
Paperboard containers & boxes	0.8	Manufg.			

Continued on next page.

INPUTS AND OUTPUTS FOR MATTRESSES & BEDSPRINGS - Continued

Economic Sector or Industry Providing Inputs	%	Sector	Economic Sector or Industry Buying Outputs	%	Sector
Electric services (utilities)	0.8	Util.			
Motor freight transportation & warehousing	0.8	Util.			
Eating & drinking places	0.8	Trade			
Petroleum refining	0.7	Manufg.			
Thread mills	0.7	Manufg.			
Blast furnaces & steel mills	0.6	Manufg.			
Job training & related services	0.6	Services			
Railroads & related services	0.5	Util.			
Water transportation	0.5	Util.			
Royalties	0.5	Fin/R.E.			
Imports	0.5	Foreign			
Abrasive products	0.4	Manufg.			
Felt goods, nec	0.4	Manufg.			
Air transportation	0.4	Util.			
Communications, except radio & TV	0.4	Util.			
Equipment rental & leasing services	0.4	Services			
U.S. Postal Service	0.4	Gov't			
Apparel made from purchased materials	0.3	Manufg.			
Business/professional associations	0.3	Services			
Management & consulting services & labs	0.3	Services			
Cordage & twine	0.2	Manufg.			
Machinery, except electrical, nec	0.2	Manufg.			
Narrow fabric mills	0.2	Manufg.			
Paper coating & glazing	0.2	Manufg.			
Processed textile waste	0.2	Manufg.			
Gas production & distribution (utilities)	0.2	Util.			
Credit agencies other than banks	0.2	Fin/R.E.			
Legal services	0.2	Services			
Industrial inorganic chemicals, nec	0.1	Manufg.			
Manifold business forms	0.1	Manufg.			
Mattresses & bedsprings	0.1	Manufg.			
Special dies & tools & machine tool accessories	0.1	Manufg.			
Sanitary services, steam supply, irrigation	0.1	Util.			
Insurance carriers	0.1	Fin/R.E.			
Automotive rental & leasing, without drivers	0.1	Services			
Automotive repair shops & services	0.1	Services			

Source: Benchmark Input-Output Accounts for the U.S. Economy, 1982, U.S. Department of Commerce, Washington, D.C., July 1991. Data, as reported in the source, are organized by the 1977 SIC structure in use in 1982 but have been matched, as closely as is possible, to the 1987 SIC structure used in this book.

OCCUPATIONS EMPLOYED BY SIC 251 - HOUSEHOLD FURNITURE

Occupation	% of Total 1994	Change to 2005	Occupation	% of Total 1994	Change to 2005
Assemblers, fabricators, & hand workers nec	13.5	-6.7	Hand packers & packagers	1.9	-20.0
Upholsterers	7.7	12.4	Truck drivers light & heavy	1.9	-3.8
Sewing machine operators, non-garment	7.1	26.0	General managers & top executives	1.7	-11.5
Woodworking machine workers	5.6	-25.3	Machine feeders & offbearers	1.7	-16.0
Cabinetmakers & bench carpenters	4.8	58.6	Traffic, shipping, & receiving clerks	1.7	-10.2
Wood machinists	4.5	30.6	Cutters & trimmers, hand	1.6	-6.7
Blue collar worker supervisors	3.9	-13.5	Sales & related workers nec	1.5	-6.7
Furniture finishers	3.7	21.8	Inspectors, testers, & graders, precision	1.5	-6.7
Head sawyers & sawing machine workers	3.0	-39.3	Grinders & polishers, hand	1.2	-25.4
Helpers, laborers, & material movers nec	2.9	-6.7	General office clerks	1.1	-20.4
Freight, stock, & material movers, hand	2.5	-25.3	Precision woodworkers nec	1.0	2.7
Coating, painting, & spraying machine workers	2.0	16.6			

Source: Industry-Occupation Matrix, Bureau of Labor Statistics. These data relate to one or more 3-digit SIC industry groups rather than to a single 4-digit SIC. The change reported for each occupation to the year 2005 is a percent of growth or decline as estimated by the Bureau of Labor Statistics. The abbreviation nec stands for 'not elsewhere classified'.

LOCATION BY STATE AND REGIONAL CONCENTRATION

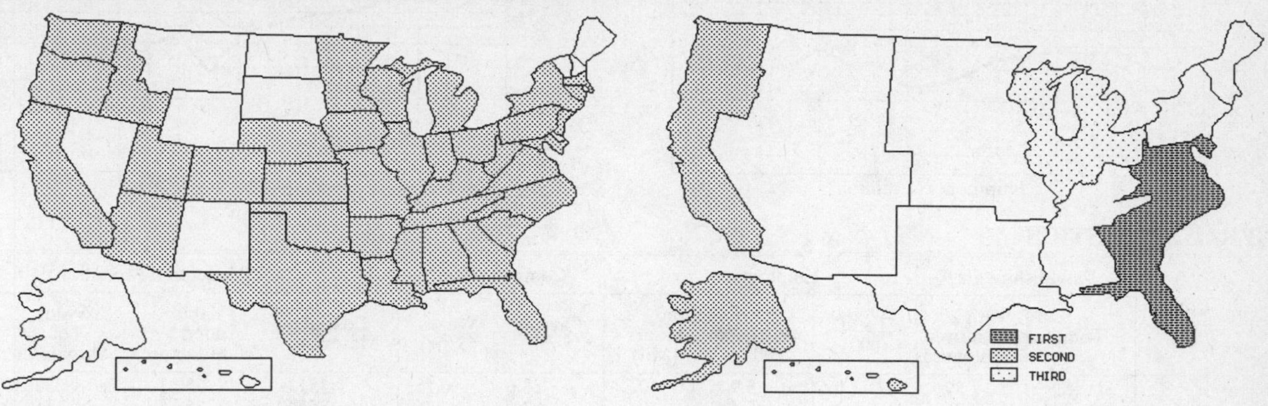

INDUSTRY DATA BY STATE

State	Establish-ments	Shipments			Employment				Cost as % of Shipments	Investment per Employee ($)
		Total ($ mil)	% of U.S.	Per Establ.	Total Number	% of U.S.	Per Establ.	Wages ($/hour)		
California	105	408.9	14.4	3.9	2,900	12.8	28	8.98	46.4	1,241
Florida	47	225.6	7.9	4.8	1,800	8.0	38	7.63	53.7	2,000
Texas	52	191.6	6.7	3.7	1,700	7.5	33	7.42	50.1	1,412
North Carolina	42	164.2	5.8	3.9	1,600	7.1	38	8.30	54.5	1,125
New Jersey	23	147.7	5.2	6.4	1,000	4.4	43	9.75	51.7	1,100
Ohio	24	126.2	4.4	5.3	800	3.5	33	10.25	47.7	1,125
Georgia	27	100.9	3.5	3.7	700	3.1	26	8.45	50.0	3,000
Wisconsin	21	100.2	3.5	4.8	600	2.7	29	9.40	50.2	2,000
Pennsylvania	32	99.0	3.5	3.1	800	3.5	25	8.50	49.8	875
Massachusetts	24	90.5	3.2	3.8	700	3.1	29	9.22	50.9	1,429
Mississippi	18	81.4	2.9	4.5	800	3.5	44	7.83	58.1	750
Illinois	23	76.5	2.7	3.3	600	2.7	26	9.75	45.6	2,167
Maryland	11	74.0	2.6	6.7	600	2.7	55	9.50	51.4	667
New York	38	72.4	2.5	1.9	800	3.5	21	8.00	49.0	750
Washington	22	54.9	1.9	2.5	500	2.2	23	9.00	49.7	1,600
Minnesota	13	52.6	1.9	4.0	300	1.3	23	9.25	42.0	-
Indiana	20	49.8	1.8	2.5	500	2.2	25	8.83	57.4	1,000
Michigan	16	49.7	1.7	3.1	400	1.8	25	8.60	45.9	1,250
Colorado	8	46.2	1.6	5.8	300	1.3	38	8.60	49.8	1,667
Connecticut	12	44.4	1.6	3.7	300	1.3	25	9.75	42.3	1,000
Nebraska	5	42.8	1.5	8.6	300	1.3	60	10.50	63.6	2,000
Arizona	26	39.2	1.4	1.5	300	1.3	12	8.75	49.2	1,333
Oregon	14	38.6	1.4	2.8	200	0.9	14	9.67	46.9	1,500
Kansas	9	33.9	1.2	3.8	300	1.3	33	8.00	53.1	333
Alabama	17	29.6	1.0	1.7	300	1.3	18	7.00	58.4	-
Oklahoma	10	19.3	0.7	1.9	200	0.9	20	9.00	57.5	1,000
South Carolina	5	19.1	0.7	3.8	200	0.9	40	7.00	50.3	-
Arkansas	13	18.7	0.7	1.4	300	1.3	23	6.50	51.3	1,000
Utah	7	17.5	0.6	2.5	100	0.4	14	7.00	52.0	3,000
Iowa	6	17.3	0.6	2.9	100	0.4	17	14.00	49.1	-
Kentucky	6	17.0	0.6	2.8	100	0.4	17	8.00	49.4	-
West Virginia	5	14.4	0.5	2.9	100	0.4	20	7.50	56.9	-
Louisiana	6	14.1	0.5	2.3	100	0.4	17	6.00	54.6	-
Tennessee	21	(D)	-	-	750 *	3.3	36	-	-	-
Missouri	20	(D)	-	-	375 *	1.7	19	-	-	1,600
Virginia	14	(D)	-	-	375 *	1.7	27	-	-	2,667
Idaho	4	(D)	-	-	175 *	0.8	44	-	-	-

Source: 1992 *Economic Census*. The states are in descending order of shipments or establishments (if shipment data are missing for the majority). The symbol (D) appears when data are withheld to prevent disclosure of competitive information. States marked with (D) are sorted by number of establishments. A dash (-) indicates that the data element cannot be calculated; * indicates the midpoint of a range.

2517 - WOOD TV AND RADIO CABINETS

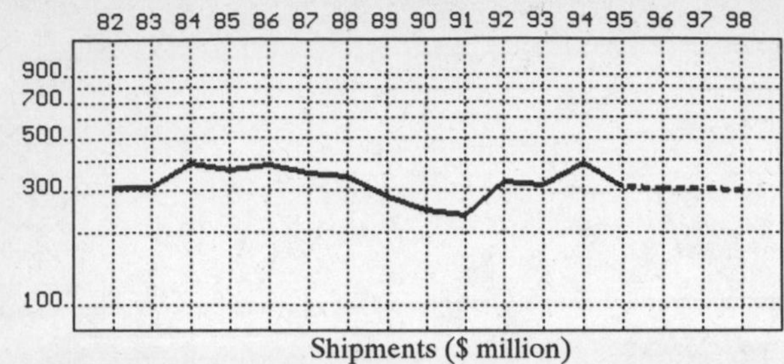

Shipments ($ million)

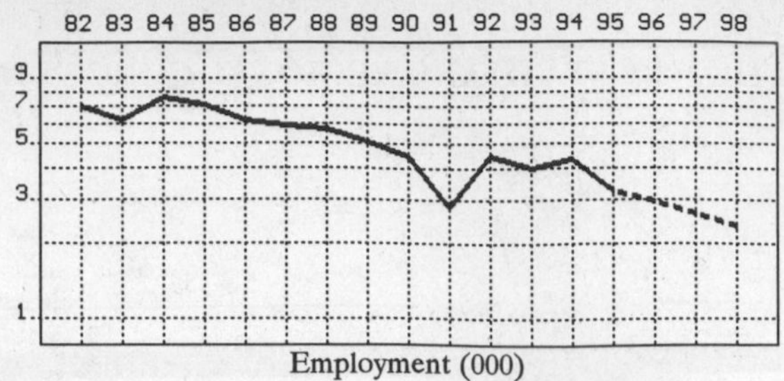

Employment (000)

GENERAL STATISTICS

Year	Companies	Establishments: Total	Establishments: with 20 or more employees	Employment: Total (000)	Production Workers (000)	Production Hours (Mil)	Compensation: Payroll ($ mil)	Compensation: Wages ($/hr)	Production ($ million): Cost of Materials	Value Added by Manufacture	Value of Shipments	Capital Invest.
1982	82	83	37	7.0	5.9	10.8	88.6	6.15	151.8	152.1	306.6	7.3
1983		79	36	6.2	5.4	10.0	83.1	6.26	155.8	155.5	310.3	6.3
1984		75	35	7.6	6.6	12.1	103.7	6.69	206.4	191.3	393.2	16.5
1985		72	35	7.2	6.2	11.2	98.9	6.79	186.0	177.2	364.4	9.4
1986		72	35	6.2	5.4	10.2	95.1	7.43	196.0	189.6	382.1	8.0
1987	79	80	36	5.9	5.1	10.3	91.5	6.85	182.0	167.5	351.1	7.0
1988		72	33	5.7	4.8	9.4	87.5	7.00	170.8	171.4	340.9	6.7
1989		74	31	5.1	3.5	6.4	72.5	8.58	133.1	151.3	281.2	10.3
1990		78	32	4.5	2.7	5.0	64.7	9.48	116.4	132.6	246.9	6.2
1991		75	23	2.8	2.4	4.7	59.7	9.83	114.6	118.1	235.3	3.8
1992	104	105	36	4.5	3.9	7.6	83.5	8.33	153.1	171.6	327.7	3.9
1993		103	29	4.0	3.5	6.8	77.8	8.93	163.1	151.9	314.6	5.8
1994		92P	29P	4.3	3.7	7.7	89.8	9.32	207.0	185.3	390.7	6.4
1995		93P	28P	3.3P	2.5P	5.3P	72.9P	9.89P	163.6P	146.4P	308.7P	4.6P
1996		95P	27P	3.0P	2.3P	4.8P	71.3P	10.19P	162.2P	145.2P	306.2P	4.2P
1997		97P	26P	2.6P	2.0P	4.4P	69.6P	10.48P	160.9P	144.0P	303.6P	3.8P
1998		98P	26P	2.3P	1.7P	3.9P	68.0P	10.78P	159.5P	142.8P	301.1P	3.4P

Sources: 1982, 1987, 1992 *Economic Census*; *Annual Survey of Manufactures*, 83-86, 88-91, 93-94. Establishment counts for non-Census years are from *County Business Patterns*; establishment values for 83-84 are extrapolations. 'P's show projections by the editors. Industries reclassified in 87 will not have data for prior years.

INDICES OF CHANGE

Year	Companies	Establishments: Total	Establishments: with 20 or more employees	Employment: Total (000)	Production Workers (000)	Production Hours (Mil)	Compensation: Payroll ($ mil)	Compensation: Wages ($/hr)	Production ($ million): Cost of Materials	Value Added by Manufacture	Value of Shipments	Capital Invest.
1982	79	79	103	156	151	142	106	74	99	89	94	187
1983		75	100	138	138	132	100	75	102	91	95	162
1984		71	97	169	169	159	124	80	135	111	120	423
1985		69	97	160	159	147	118	82	121	103	111	241
1986		69	97	138	138	134	114	89	128	110	117	205
1987	76	76	100	131	131	136	110	82	119	98	107	179
1988		69	92	127	123	124	105	84	112	100	104	172
1989		70	86	113	90	84	87	103	87	88	86	264
1990		74	89	100	69	66	77	114	76	77	75	159
1991		71	64	62	62	62	71	118	75	69	72	97
1992	100	100	100	100	100	100	100	100	100	100	100	100
1993		98	81	89	90	89	93	107	107	89	96	149
1994		87P	79P	96	95	101	108	112	135	108	119	164
1995		89P	77P	73P	65P	70P	87P	119P	107P	85P	94P	118P
1996		90P	75P	66P	58P	64P	85P	122P	106P	85P	93P	108P
1997		92P	73P	59P	51P	57P	83P	126P	105P	84P	93P	97P
1998		94P	72P	52P	43P	51P	81P	129P	104P	83P	92P	86P

Sources: Same as General Statistics. Values reflect change from the base year, 1992. Values above 100 mean greater than 92, values below 100 mean less than 92, and a value of 100 in the 82-91 or 93-98 period means same as 92. 'P's mark projections by the editors.

SELECTED RATIOS

For 1994	Avg. of All Manufact.	Analyzed Industry	Index	For 1994	Avg. of All Manufact.	Analyzed Industry	Index
Employees per Establishment	49	47	96	Value Added per Production Worker	134,084	50,081	37
Payroll per Establishment	1,500,273	980,122	65	Cost per Establishment	5,045,178	2,259,302	45
Payroll per Employee	30,620	20,884	68	Cost per Employee	102,970	48,140	47
Production Workers per Establishment	34	40	118	Cost per Production Worker	146,988	55,946	38
Wages per Establishment	853,319	783,268	92	Shipments per Establishment	9,576,895	4,264,296	45
Wages per Production Worker	24,861	19,396	78	Shipments per Employee	195,460	90,860	46
Hours per Production Worker	2,056	2,081	101	Shipments per Production Worker	279,017	105,595	38
Wages per Hour	12.09	9.32	77	Investment per Establishment	321,011	69,853	22
Value Added per Establishment	4,602,255	2,022,457	44	Investment per Employee	6,552	1,488	23
Value Added per Employee	93,930	43,093	46	Investment per Production Worker	9,352	1,730	18

Sources: Same as General Statistics. The 'Average of All Manufacturing' column represents the average of all manufacturing industries reported for the most recent complete year available. The Index shows the relationship between the Average and the Analyzed Industry. For example, 100 means that they are equal; 500 that the Analyzed Industry is five times the average; 50 means that the Analyzed Industry is half the national average. The abbreviation 'na' is used to show that data are 'not available'.

LEADING COMPANIES

Number shown: 2 Total sales ($ mil): **13** Total employment (000): **0.5**

Company Name	Address				CEO Name	Phone	Co. Type	Sales ($ mil)	Empl. (000)
American Quality Mfg Corp	PO Drawer 640	Conway	AR	72038	DeWayne Davis	501-327-6085	S	10	0.4
Panex Corp	400 E Burnett St	Beaver Dam	WI	53916	Robert E Panthofer	414-885-3338	R	4	<0.1

Source: *Ward's Business Directory of U.S. Private and Public Companies*, Volumes 1 and 2, 1996. The company type code used is as follows: P - Public, R - Private, S - Subsidiary, D - Division, J - Joint Venture, A - Affiliate, G - Group. Sales are in millions of dollars, employees are in thousands. An asterisk (*) indicates an estimated sales volume. The symbol < stands for 'less than'. Company names and addresses are truncated, in some cases, to fit into the available space.

MATERIALS CONSUMED

Material		Quantity	Delivered Cost ($ million)
Materials, ingredients, containers, and supplies		(X)	146.0
Hardwood lumber, rough and dressed	mil bd ft	254.7	12.3
Softwood lumber, rough and dressed	mil bd ft	(D)	(D)
Hardwood dimension and parts, excluding furniture frames		(X)	(D)
Softwood plywood	mil sq ft (3/8 in. b	(S)	0.5
Hardwood plywood	mil sq ft sm	284.7	6.0
Hardwood veneer		(X)	1.2
Particleboard (wood)	mil sq ft (3/4 in. b	(S)	16.5
Medium density fiberboard (MDF)	mil sq ft (3/4 in. b	16.4*	7.9
Hardboard (wood fiberboard)		(X)	(D)
Furniture frames, wood		(X)	(D)
Paints, varnishes, lacquers, stains, shellacs, japans, enamels, and allied products		(X)	4.9
Adhesives and sealants		(X)	1.3
Plastics resins consumed in the form of granules, pellets, powders, liquids, etc.	mil lb	(D)	(D)
Plastics parts, components, sheets, and other shapes (excluding plastics resins)		(X)	4.2
Flat glass (plate, float, and sheet)		(X)	1.7
Mirrors, framed and unframed		(X)	(D)
Fabrics, all types		(X)	1.5
Furniture and builders' hardware		(X)	13.4
Paperboard containers, boxes, and corrugated paperboard		(X)	13.7
All other materials and components, parts, containers, and supplies		(X)	7.5
Materials, ingredients, containers, and supplies, nsk		(X)	29.8

Source: 1992 *Economic Census*. Explanation of symbols used: (D): Withheld to avoid disclosure of competitive data; na: Not available; (S): Withheld because statistical norms were not met; (X): Not applicable; (Z): Less than half the unit shown; nec: Not elsewhere classified; nsk: Not specified by kind; - : zero; * : 10-19 percent estimated; ** : 20-29 percent estimated.

PRODUCT SHARE DETAILS

Product or Product Class	% Share	Product or Product Class	% Share
Wood television and radio cabinets	100.00	Wood audio cabinets, including radio, stereo, phonograph, and speaker cabinets.	19.13
Wood television cabinets and combinations (television, stereo, and radio).	64.90	Wood sewing machine cabinets	4.44

Source: 1992 *Economic Census*. The values shown are percent of total shipments in an industry. Values of indented subcategories are summed in the main heading. The symbol (D) appears when data are withheld to prevent disclosure of competitive information. The abbreviation nsk stands for 'not specified by kind' and nec for 'not elsewhere classified'.

INPUTS AND OUTPUTS FOR WOOD TV & RADIO CABINETS

Economic Sector or Industry Providing Inputs	%	Sector	Economic Sector or Industry Buying Outputs	%	Sector
Wholesale trade	10.8	Trade	Radio & TV receiving sets	66.9	Manufg.
Wood products, nec	7.7	Manufg.	Radio & TV communication equipment	17.3	Manufg.
Particleboard	7.5	Manufg.	Personal consumption expenditures	7.9	
Miscellaneous plastics products	7.1	Manufg.	Electronic components nec	3.7	Manufg.
Sawmills & planning mills, general	6.6	Manufg.	Semiconductors & related devices	2.4	Manufg.
Veneer & plywood	5.5	Manufg.	Wood TV & radio cabinets	1.1	Manufg.
Imports	5.1	Foreign	Electrical repair shops	0.4	Services
Hardware, nec	4.4	Manufg.	Federal Government purchases, national defense	0.2	Fed Govt
Hardwood dimension & flooring mills	4.3	Manufg.			
Paints & allied products	3.7	Manufg.			
Petroleum refining	3.6	Manufg.			
Advertising	2.3	Services			
Motor freight transportation & warehousing	2.1	Util.			
Electric services (utilities)	2.0	Util.			
Wood TV & radio cabinets	1.9	Manufg.			
Maintenance of nonfarm buildings nec	1.7	Constr.			
Special product sawmills, nec	1.5	Manufg.			

Continued on next page.

INPUTS AND OUTPUTS FOR WOOD TV & RADIO CABINETS - Continued

Economic Sector or Industry Providing Inputs	%	Sector	Economic Sector or Industry Buying Outputs	%	Sector
Eating & drinking places	1.5	Trade			
Fabricated metal products, nec	1.1	Manufg.			
Detective & protective services	1.1	Services			
Miscellaneous fabricated wire products	1.0	Manufg.			
Railroads & related services	1.0	Util.			
Real estate	1.0	Fin/R.E.			
U.S. Postal Service	1.0	Gov't			
Sanitary services, steam supply, irrigation	0.9	Util.			
Abrasive products	0.8	Manufg.			
Hand saws & saw blades	0.8	Manufg.			
Gas production & distribution (utilities)	0.8	Util.			
Automotive rental & leasing, without drivers	0.8	Services			
Hand & edge tools, nec	0.7	Manufg.			
Paperboard containers & boxes	0.7	Manufg.			
Automotive repair shops & services	0.7	Services			
Adhesives & sealants	0.5	Manufg.			
Air transportation	0.5	Util.			
Communications, except radio & TV	0.5	Util.			
Banking	0.5	Fin/R.E.			
Management & consulting services & labs	0.5	Services			
Laundry, dry cleaning, shoe repair	0.4	Services			
Legal services	0.4	Services			
Machinery, except electrical, nec	0.3	Manufg.			
Screw machine and related products	0.3	Manufg.			
Insurance carriers	0.3	Fin/R.E.			
Accounting, auditing & bookkeeping	0.3	Services			
Equipment rental & leasing services	0.3	Services			
Lubricating oils & greases	0.2	Manufg.			
Manifold business forms	0.2	Manufg.			
Miscellaneous publishing	0.2	Manufg.			
Plastics materials & resins	0.2	Manufg.			
Special dies & tools & machine tool accessories	0.2	Manufg.			
Tires & inner tubes	0.2	Manufg.			
Retail trade, except eating & drinking	0.2	Trade			
Computer & data processing services	0.2	Services			
Engineering, architectural, & surveying services	0.2	Services			
Hotels & lodging places	0.2	Services			
Coal	0.1	Mining			
Distilled liquor, except brandy	0.1	Manufg.			
Gaskets, packing & sealing devices	0.1	Manufg.			
Manufacturing industries, nec	0.1	Manufg.			
Mechanical measuring devices	0.1	Manufg.			
Motor vehicle parts & accessories	0.1	Manufg.			
Royalties	0.1	Fin/R.E.			
Business/professional associations	0.1	Services			
Personnel supply services	0.1	Services			
Services to dwellings & other buildings	0.1	Services			

Source: Benchmark Input-Output Accounts for the U.S. Economy, 1982, U.S. Department of Commerce, Washington, D.C., July 1991. Data, as reported in the source, are organized by the 1977 SIC structure in use in 1982 but have been matched, as closely as is possible, to the 1987 SIC structure used in this book.

OCCUPATIONS EMPLOYED BY SIC 251 - HOUSEHOLD FURNITURE

Occupation	% of Total 1994	Change to 2005	Occupation	% of Total 1994	Change to 2005
Assemblers, fabricators, & hand workers nec	13.5	-6.7	Hand packers & packagers	1.9	-20.0
Upholsterers	7.7	12.4	Truck drivers light & heavy	1.9	-3.8
Sewing machine operators, non-garment	7.1	26.0	General managers & top executives	1.7	-11.5
Woodworking machine workers	5.6	-25.3	Machine feeders & offbearers	1.7	-16.0
Cabinetmakers & bench carpenters	4.8	58.6	Traffic, shipping, & receiving clerks	1.7	-10.2
Wood machinists	4.5	30.6	Cutters & trimmers, hand	1.6	-6.7
Blue collar worker supervisors	3.9	-13.5	Sales & related workers nec	1.5	-6.7
Furniture finishers	3.7	21.8	Inspectors, testers, & graders, precision	1.5	-6.7
Head sawyers & sawing machine workers	3.0	-39.3	Grinders & polishers, hand	1.2	-25.4
Helpers, laborers, & material movers nec	2.9	-6.7	General office clerks	1.1	-20.4
Freight, stock, & material movers, hand	2.5	-25.3	Precision woodworkers nec	1.0	2.7
Coating, painting, & spraying machine workers	2.0	16.6			

Source: Industry-Occupation Matrix, Bureau of Labor Statistics. These data relate to one or more 3-digit SIC industry groups rather than to a single 4-digit SIC. The change reported for each occupation to the year 2005 is a percent of growth or decline as estimated by the Bureau of Labor Statistics. The abbreviation nec stands for 'not elsewhere classified'.

LOCATION BY STATE AND REGIONAL CONCENTRATION

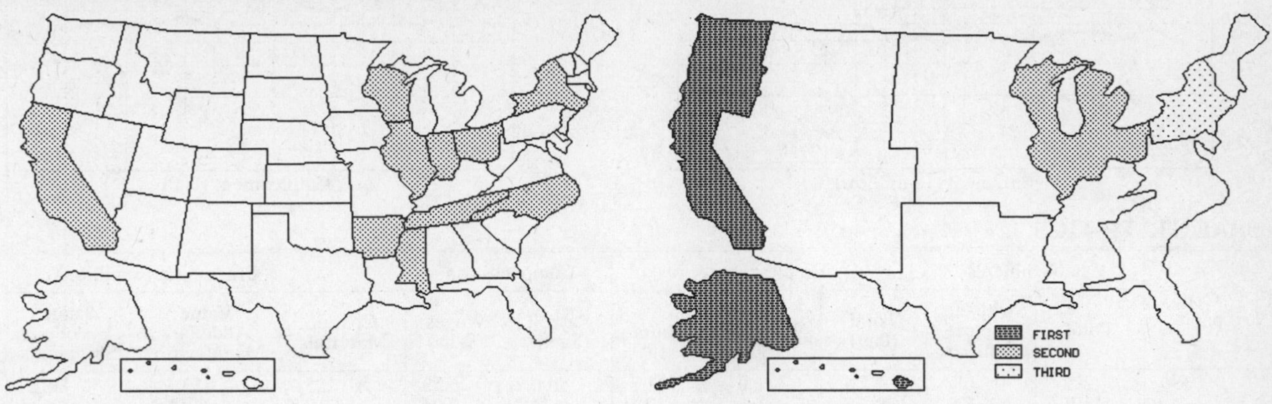

INDUSTRY DATA BY STATE

State	Establish-ments	Shipments			Employment				Cost as % of Shipments	Investment per Employee ($)
		Total ($ mil)	% of U.S.	Per Establ.	Total Number	% of U.S.	Per Establ.	Wages ($/hour)		
California	23	46.8	14.3	2.0	500	11.1	22	7.11	41.7	-
Illinois	4	15.1	4.6	3.8	200	4.4	50	11.67	50.3	-
New York	10	7.8	2.4	0.8	200	4.4	20	9.50	43.6	500
Indiana	7	(D)	-	-	750 *	16.7	107	-	-	-
Wisconsin	6	(D)	-	-	175 *	3.9	29	-	-	-
Tennessee	4	(D)	-	-	750 *	16.7	188	-	-	-
North Carolina	3	(D)	-	-	750 *	16.7	250	-	-	-
Ohio	3	(D)	-	-	375 *	8.3	125	-	-	-
Arkansas	2	(D)	-	-	175 *	3.9	88	-	-	-
Mississippi	1	(D)	-	-	375 *	8.3	375	-	-	-

Source: 1992 *Economic Census*. The states are in descending order of shipments or establishments (if shipment data are missing for the majority). The symbol (D) appears when data are withheld to prevent disclosure of competitive information. States marked with (D) are sorted by number of establishments. A dash (-) indicates that the data element cannot be calculated; * indicates the midpoint of a range.

2519 - HOUSEHOLD FURNITURE, NEC

Shipments ($ million)

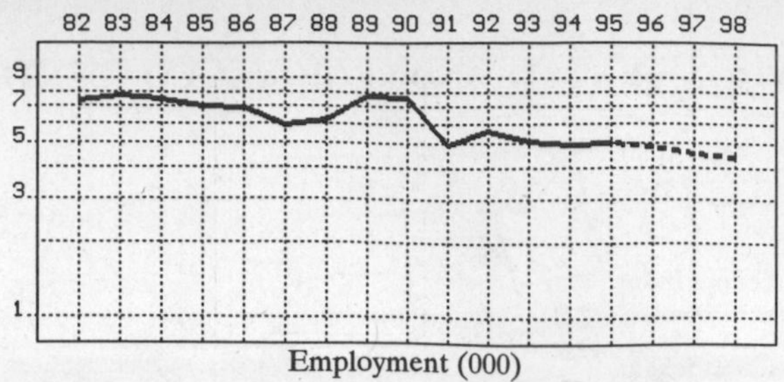

Employment (000)

GENERAL STATISTICS

Year	Companies	Establishments Total	Establishments with 20 or more employees	Employment Total (000)	Production Workers (000)	Production Hours (Mil)	Compensation Payroll ($ mil)	Compensation Wages ($/hr)	Cost of Materials	Value Added by Manufacture	Value of Shipments	Capital Invest.
1982	196	202	63	7.4	6.0	11.7	100.7	6.53	225.6	153.3	381.1	11.9
1983		196	62	7.7	6.5	12.2	114.7	7.04	258.8	219.1	462.0	12.4
1984		190	61	7.5	6.3	12.3	114.1	7.02	239.9	185.7	423.4	13.4
1985		185	59	7.0	5.9	11.3	105.4	6.96	257.7	188.6	445.7	12.2
1986		175	67	6.9	5.8	11.5	108.9	7.00	253.5	192.9	450.3	21.9
1987	175	177	51	5.9	5.0	10.1	101.4	7.25	227.3	178.2	403.9	24.1
1988		181	59	6.2	5.3	10.1	107.9	7.72	225.6	199.1	424.0	20.9
1989		166	57	7.8	5.3	10.0	111.4	8.31	267.6	209.7	473.4	19.7
1990		156	56	7.6	4.7	8.2	107.8	9.56	270.7	173.7	458.7	18.8
1991		172	62	4.9	3.9	6.5	99.9	10.98	254.9	160.8	411.8	7.6
1992	197	200	51	5.6	4.7	8.0	113.0	10.35	256.0	193.0	451.2	10.8
1993		187	48	5.1	3.9	8.1	106.5	9.60	256.4	237.4	492.6	13.9
1994		173P	51P	4.9	4.0	7.7	90.4	8.96	256.3	196.3	451.2	13.7
1995		171P	50P	5.0P	3.7P	6.6P	101.9P	10.52P	265.0P	202.9P	466.5P	14.9P
1996		170P	49P	4.8P	3.4P	6.2P	101.2P	10.84P	267.1P	204.5P	470.1P	14.8P
1997		168P	48P	4.6P	3.2P	5.7P	100.6P	11.17P	269.1P	206.1P	473.8P	14.7P
1998		167P	47P	4.4P	3.0P	5.3P	99.9P	11.49P	271.2P	207.7P	477.5P	14.6P

Sources: 1982, 1987, 1992 *Economic Census*; *Annual Survey of Manufactures*, 83-86, 88-91, 93-94. Establishment counts for non-Census years are from *County Business Patterns*; establishment values for 83-84 are extrapolations. 'P's show projections by the editors. Industries reclassified in 87 will not have data for prior years.

INDICES OF CHANGE

Year	Companies	Establishments Total	Establishments with 20 or more employees	Employment Total (000)	Production Workers (000)	Production Hours (Mil)	Compensation Payroll ($ mil)	Compensation Wages ($/hr)	Cost of Materials	Value Added by Manufacture	Value of Shipments	Capital Invest.
1982	99	101	124	132	128	146	89	63	88	79	84	110
1983		98	122	138	138	152	102	68	101	114	102	115
1984		95	120	134	134	154	101	68	94	96	94	124
1985		93	116	125	126	141	93	67	101	98	99	113
1986		88	131	123	123	144	96	68	99	100	100	203
1987	89	89	100	105	106	126	90	70	89	92	90	223
1988		91	116	111	113	126	95	75	88	103	94	194
1989		83	112	139	113	125	99	80	105	109	105	182
1990		78	110	136	100	102	95	92	106	90	102	174
1991		86	122	88	83	81	88	106	100	83	91	70
1992	100	100	100	100	100	100	100	100	100	100	100	100
1993		94	94	91	83	101	94	93	100	123	109	129
1994		86P	101P	88	85	96	80	87	100	102	100	127
1995		86P	99P	90P	78P	83P	90P	102P	104P	105P	103P	138P
1996		85P	97P	86P	73P	77P	90P	105P	104P	106P	104P	137P
1997		84P	95P	82P	69P	72P	89P	108P	105P	107P	105P	136P
1998		83P	93P	78P	64P	66P	88P	111P	106P	108P	106P	135P

Sources: Same as General Statistics. Values reflect change from the base year, 1992. Values above 100 mean greater than 92, values below 100 mean less than 92, and a value of 100 in the 82-91 or 93-98 period means same as 92. 'P's mark projections by the editors.

SELECTED RATIOS

For 1994	Avg. of All Manufact.	Analyzed Industry	Index
Employees per Establishment	49	28	58
Payroll per Establishment	1,500,273	523,644	35
Payroll per Employee	30,620	18,449	60
Production Workers per Establishment	34	23	68
Wages per Establishment	853,319	399,638	47
Wages per Production Worker	24,861	17,248	69
Hours per Production Worker	2,056	1,925	94
Wages per Hour	12.09	8.96	74
Value Added per Establishment	4,602,255	1,137,072	25
Value Added per Employee	93,930	40,061	43

For 1994	Avg. of All Manufact.	Analyzed Industry	Index
Value Added per Production Worker	134,084	49,075	37
Cost per Establishment	5,045,178	1,484,623	29
Cost per Employee	102,970	52,306	51
Cost per Production Worker	146,988	64,075	44
Shipments per Establishment	9,576,895	2,613,586	27
Shipments per Employee	195,460	92,082	47
Shipments per Production Worker	279,017	112,800	40
Investment per Establishment	321,011	79,358	25
Investment per Employee	6,552	2,796	43
Investment per Production Worker	9,352	3,425	37

Sources: Same as General Statistics. The 'Average of All Manufacturing' column represents the average of all manufacturing industries reported for the most recent complete year available. The Index shows the relationship between the Average and the Analyzed Industry. For example, 100 means that they are equal; 500 that the Analyzed Industry is five times the average; 50 means that the Analyzed Industry is half the national average. The abbreviation 'na' is used to show that data are 'not available'.

LEADING COMPANIES

Number shown: **25** Total sales ($ mil): **326** Total employment (000): **3.1**

Company Name	Address				CEO Name	Phone	Co. Type	Sales ($ mil)	Empl. (000)
Syroco Inc	175 McClellan Hwy	East Boston	MA	02128	Leonard Florenec	617-561-1473	S	87	0.4
Grosfillex Inc	Old West Penn Av	Robesonia	PA	19551	Carel Harmsen	610-693-5835	S	40*	0.2
Lloyd Flanders Industries Inc	PO Box 550	Menominee	MI	49858	Gene Davenport	906-863-4491	R	35	0.4
Tropitone Furniture Company	5 Marconi	Irvine	CA	92718	Michael Echolds	714-951-2010	R	31*	0.4
AB Plastics Corp	15730 S Figueroa St	Gardena	CA	90248	James S Adams	213-770-8771	R	24*	0.3
Emerson Leather Inc	816 13th St NE	Hickory	NC	28601	Leslie W Flippo	704-328-1701	R	24	0.2
Burlington Basket Company Inc	PO Box 808	Burlington	IA	52601	CH Thompson Jr	319-754-6508	R	12	0.2
Now Products Inc	4800 W Roosevelt	Cicero	IL	60650	Max Aronoff	312-379-4000	D	12	0.3
Acacia Furniture Inc	PO Box 426	Conover	NC	28613	Alex Te	704-465-1700	R	10	<0.1
Gem Southeast Inc	PO Box 610	Toccoa	GA	30577	E E Berriman III	706-886-8431	S	10*	0.1
McGuire Furniture Co	1201 Bryant St	San Francisco	CA	94131	Frank Doodha	415-626-1414	S	7*	0.1
Standard Container of Edgar	PO Box 227	Edgar	WI	54426	Jon Rasmussen	715-352-2311	R	7	0.2
SoundTech Inc	4430 Eastland Dr	Elkhart	IN	46516	Rudy Schlacher	219-522-1692	S	5	<0.1
Herbert Ritts Inc	8441 Santa Monica	W Hollywood	CA	90069	Shirley Ritts	213-656-2947	R	4	<0.1
Stanco Corp	2001 Windsor Av	Baltimore	MD	21217	A McIver	410-462-6400	R	3*	<0.1
Whitecraft Rattan Inc	PO Box 380309	Miami	FL	33238	Perry Solomon	305-757-3407	R	3*	<0.1
Clark Casual Furniture Inc	214 Industrial Rd	Greensburg	KY	42743	William E Clark	502-932-4273	R	3	<0.1
Custom Mattress Co	PO Box 1988	Louisville	KY	40201	John R Bloodworth	502-585-5959	R	2*	<0.1
L&R Furniture Manufacturing	700 W 16th St	Long Beach	CA	90813	Larry Griffin	310-432-0404	R	2*	<0.1
Seating Components Mfg	4520 E La Palma	Anaheim	CA	92807	Daryl Fossier	714-693-3376	R	1	<0.1
Creative Point Inc	4121 Clipper Ct	Fremont	CA	94538	Jerry Long	510-659-8222	S	1*	<0.1
Calder Industries Inc	1322 Loop Rd	Lancaster	PA	17601	James Calder	717-394-5641	R	1*	<0.1
Goldman Arts Inc	107 South St	Boston	MA	02111	Nicole Goldman	617-423-6606	R	1	<0.1
Poly-Wood Inc	207 N Huntington	Syracuse	IN	46567	Mark Phillabaum	219-457-3284	R	1	<0.1
Hartman USA Inc	9801 W Kincey Av	Huntersville	NC	28078	Erwin R Gremmer	704-875-9190	S	0*	<0.1

Source: *Ward's Business Directory of U.S. Private and Public Companies*, Volumes 1 and 2, 1996. The company type code used is as follows: P - Public, R - Private, S - Subsidiary, D - Division, J - Joint Venture, A - Affiliate, G - Group. Sales are in millions of dollars, employees are in thousands. An asterisk (*) indicates an estimated sales volume. The symbol < stands for 'less than'. Company names and addresses are truncated, in some cases, to fit into the available space.

MATERIALS CONSUMED

Material		Quantity	Delivered Cost ($ million)
Materials, ingredients, containers, and supplies		(X)	241.6
Hardwood lumber, rough and dressed	mil bd ft	(S)	0.4
Softwood lumber, rough and dressed	mil bd ft	(D)	(D)
Hardwood dimension and parts, excluding furniture frames		(X)	(D)
Softwood plywood	mil sq ft (3/8 in. b	(S)	0.2
Hardwood plywood	mil sq ft sm	(S)	0.2
Hardwood veneer		(X)	(D)
Particleboard (wood)	mil sq ft (3/4 in. b	(S)	0.1
Medium density fiberboard (MDF)	mil sq ft (3/4 in. b	1.0*	0.4
Hardboard (wood fiberboard)		(X)	0.1
Furniture frames, wood		(X)	(D)
Paints, varnishes, lacquers, stains, shellacs, japans, enamels, and allied products		(X)	5.5
Adhesives and sealants		(X)	0.3
Plastics resins consumed in the form of granules, pellets, powders, liquids, etc.	mil lb	(S)	103.0
Plastics parts, components, sheets, and other shapes (excluding plastics resins)		(X)	5.2
Flat glass (plate, float, and sheet)		(X)	0.9
Mirrors, framed and unframed		(X)	0.1
Fabrics, all types		(X)	2.3
Furniture and builders' hardware		(X)	0.6
Paperboard containers, boxes, and corrugated paperboard		(X)	15.2
All other materials and components, parts, containers, and supplies		(X)	51.9
Materials, ingredients, containers, and supplies, nsk		(X)	53.2

Source: 1992 *Economic Census*. Explanation of symbols used: (D): Withheld to avoid disclosure of competitive data; na: Not available; (S): Withheld because statistical norms were not met; (X): Not applicable; (Z): Less than half the unit shown; nec: Not elsewhere classified; nsk: Not specified by kind; - : zero; * : 10-19 percent estimated; ** : 20-29 percent estimated.

PRODUCT SHARE DETAILS

Product or Product Class	% Share	Product or Product Class	% Share
Household furniture, nec	100.00	Other plastics and fibrous glass household furniture	6.66
Plastics and fibrous glass household cabinets, including radio, phonograph, television, stereo, and combinations thereof	52.31	Reed and rattan household seating, including willow, wicker, and cane	10.95
Plastics and fibrous glass household seating	1.78	Other reed and rattan household furniture	8.63
		Other household furniture, nec, except wood or metal	4.30

Source: 1992 *Economic Census*. The values shown are percent of total shipments in an industry. Values of indented subcategories are summed in the main heading. The symbol (D) appears when data are withheld to prevent disclosure of competitive information. The abbreviation nsk stands for 'not specified by kind' and nec for 'not elsewhere classified'.

INPUTS AND OUTPUTS FOR HOUSEHOLD FURNITURE, NEC

Economic Sector or Industry Providing Inputs	%	Sector	Economic Sector or Industry Buying Outputs	%	Sector
Imports	41.6	Foreign	Personal consumption expenditures	62.1	
Plastics materials & resins	12.3	Manufg.	Radio & TV receiving sets	14.1	Manufg.
Wholesale trade	7.2	Trade	Exports	12.5	Foreign
Miscellaneous plastics products	6.3	Manufg.	Gross private fixed investment	4.6	Cap Inv
Real estate	3.3	Fin/R.E.	Radio & TV communication equipment	1.7	Manufg.
Adhesives & sealants	3.0	Manufg.	Electron tubes	1.3	Manufg.
Veneer & plywood	3.0	Manufg.	Household furniture, nec	1.1	Manufg.
Noncomparable imports	3.0	Foreign	Surgical & medical instruments	0.6	Manufg.
Electric services (utilities)	2.2	Util.	Aircraft	0.5	Manufg.
Petroleum refining	1.7	Manufg.	Aircraft & missile engines & engine parts	0.5	Manufg.
Household furniture, nec	1.6	Manufg.	Aircraft & missile equipment, nec	0.5	Manufg.
Motor freight transportation & warehousing	1.6	Util.	Federal Government purchases, nondefense	0.5	Fed Govt
Glass & glass products, except containers	1.3	Manufg.			
Hardwood dimension & flooring mills	1.3	Manufg.			
Paperboard containers & boxes	1.2	Manufg.			
Screw machine and related products	1.2	Manufg.			
Railroads & related services	0.6	Util.			
Eating & drinking places	0.6	Trade			
Equipment rental & leasing services	0.6	Services			
Maintenance of nonfarm buildings nec	0.5	Constr.			
Communications, except radio & TV	0.5	Util.			
Gas production & distribution (utilities)	0.5	Util.			
Banking	0.5	Fin/R.E.			
Abrasive products	0.3	Manufg.			
Hand saws & saw blades	0.3	Manufg.			
Automotive rental & leasing, without drivers	0.3	Services			
Business services nec	0.3	Services			
Coal	0.2	Mining			
Coated fabrics, not rubberized	0.2	Manufg.			
Hardware, nec	0.2	Manufg.			
Steel wire & related products	0.2	Manufg.			
Air transportation	0.2	Util.			
Water transportation	0.2	Util.			
Automotive repair shops & services	0.2	Services			
Laundry, dry cleaning, shoe repair	0.2	Services			
Management & consulting services & labs	0.2	Services			
Advertising	0.1	Services			
Computer & data processing services	0.1	Services			
Legal services	0.1	Services			

Source: Benchmark Input-Output Accounts for the U.S. Economy, 1982, U.S. Department of Commerce, Washington, D.C., July 1991. Data, as reported in the source, are organized by the 1977 SIC structure in use in 1982 but have been matched, as closely as is possible, to the 1987 SIC structure used in this book.

OCCUPATIONS EMPLOYED BY SIC 251 - HOUSEHOLD FURNITURE

Occupation	% of Total 1994	Change to 2005	Occupation	% of Total 1994	Change to 2005
Assemblers, fabricators, & hand workers nec	13.5	-6.7	Hand packers & packagers	1.9	-20.0
Upholsterers	7.7	12.4	Truck drivers light & heavy	1.9	-3.8
Sewing machine operators, non-garment	7.1	26.0	General managers & top executives	1.7	-11.5
Woodworking machine workers	5.6	-25.3	Machine feeders & offbearers	1.7	-16.0
Cabinetmakers & bench carpenters	4.8	58.6	Traffic, shipping, & receiving clerks	1.7	-10.2
Wood machinists	4.5	30.6	Cutters & trimmers, hand	1.6	-6.7
Blue collar worker supervisors	3.9	-13.5	Sales & related workers nec	1.5	-6.7
Furniture finishers	3.7	21.8	Inspectors, testers, & graders, precision	1.5	-6.7
Head sawyers & sawing machine workers	3.0	-39.3	Grinders & polishers, hand	1.2	-25.4
Helpers, laborers, & material movers nec	2.9	-6.7	General office clerks	1.1	-20.4
Freight, stock, & material movers, hand	2.5	-25.3	Precision woodworkers nec	1.0	2.7
Coating, painting, & spraying machine workers	2.0	16.6			

Source: Industry-Occupation Matrix, Bureau of Labor Statistics. These data relate to one or more 3-digit SIC industry groups rather than to a single 4-digit SIC. The change reported for each occupation to the year 2005 is a percent of growth or decline as estimated by the Bureau of Labor Statistics. The abbreviation nec stands for 'not elsewhere classified'.

LOCATION BY STATE AND REGIONAL CONCENTRATION

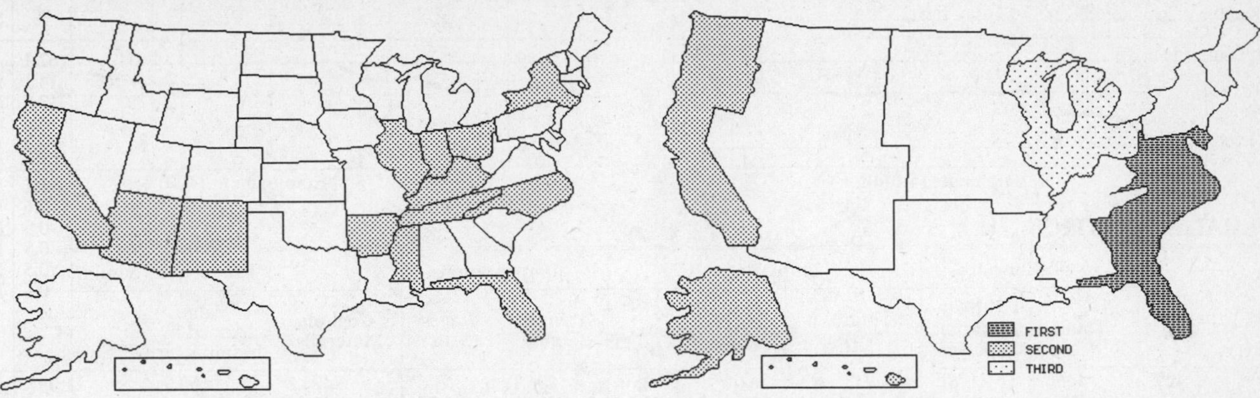

INDUSTRY DATA BY STATE

State	Establish-ments	Shipments			Employment				Cost as % of Shipments	Investment per Employee ($)
		Total ($ mil)	% of U.S.	Per Establ.	Total Number	% of U.S.	Per Establ.	Wages ($/hour)		
California	29	72.9	16.2	2.5	900	16.1	31	8.27	46.6	-
Florida	50	49.6	11.0	1.0	600	10.7	12	8.20	51.8	1,333
Illinois	8	26.5	5.9	3.3	400	7.1	50	10.60	51.3	-
New York	9	6.0	1.3	0.7	100	1.8	11	10.00	40.0	1,000
Kentucky	5	5.2	1.2	1.0	100	1.8	20	6.00	38.5	-
North Carolina	7	(D)	-	-	375 *	6.7	54	-	-	-
Arizona	6	(D)	-	-	375 *	6.7	63	-	-	-
Indiana	5	(D)	-	-	1,750 *	31.3	350	-	-	-
Arkansas	3	(D)	-	-	375 *	6.7	125	-	-	-
Mississippi	3	(D)	-	-	375 *	6.7	125	-	-	-
New Mexico	3	(D)	-	-	175 *	3.1	58	-	-	-
Ohio	3	(D)	-	-	175 *	3.1	58	-	-	-
Tennessee	3	(D)	-	-	175 *	3.1	58	-	-	-

Source: 1992 *Economic Census*. The states are in descending order of shipments or establishments (if shipment data are missing for the majority). The symbol (D) appears when data are withheld to prevent disclosure of competitive information. States marked with (D) are sorted by number of establishments. A dash (-) indicates that the data element cannot be calculated; * indicates the midpoint of a range.

2521 - WOOD OFFICE FURNITURE

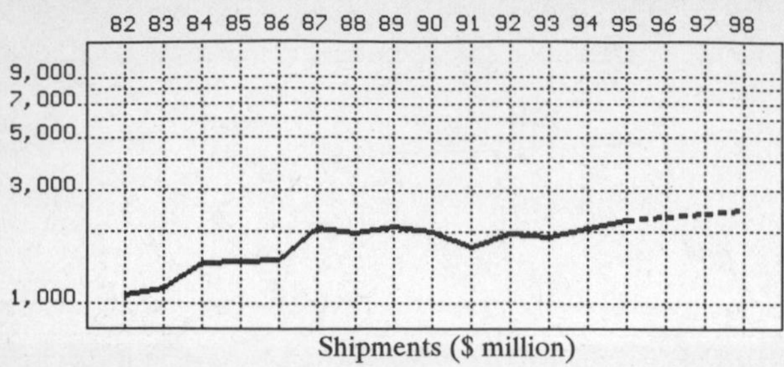

Shipments ($ million)

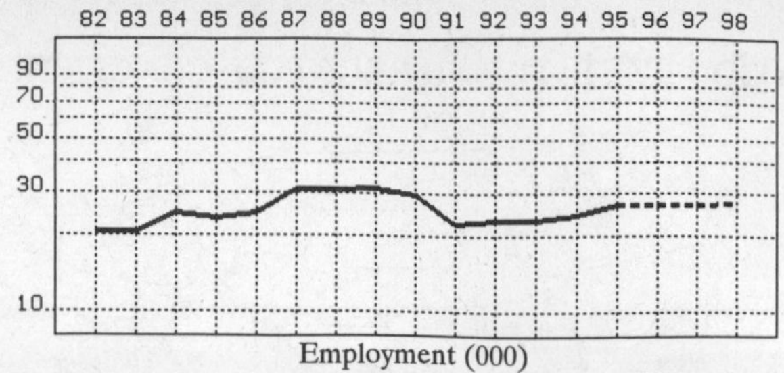

Employment (000)

GENERAL STATISTICS

Year	Companies	Establishments: Total	Establishments: with 20 or more employees	Employment: Total (000)	Production Workers (000)	Production Hours (Mil)	Compensation: Payroll ($ mil)	Compensation: Wages ($/hr)	Production ($ million): Cost of Materials	Value Added by Manufacture	Value of Shipments	Capital Invest.
1982	429	446	176	21.0	16.6	32.0	296.1	6.06	424.2	659.0	1,087.4	32.6
1983		465	186	20.8	16.6	32.6	324.0	6.51	473.4	712.6	1,166.6	47.0
1984		484	196	24.8	19.6	39.1	406.6	6.97	586.7	909.4	1,477.9	45.2
1985		503	207	23.7	18.5	37.0	410.5	7.30	557.4	942.8	1,505.4	54.8
1986		513	212	24.8	19.8	37.9	426.2	7.62	608.9	913.8	1,530.2	42.1
1987	625	649	233	31.0	24.4	48.4	562.2	7.83	829.0	1,261.8	2,084.1	48.3
1988		636	240	30.8	24.6	47.2	557.7	7.85	822.0	1,163.4	1,984.8	36.4
1989		636	236	31.4	24.3	49.0	601.7	8.14	916.2	1,186.9	2,101.3	40.5
1990		621	239	29.8	22.1	44.1	572.4	8.67	878.3	1,100.8	1,998.8	34.7
1991		587	206	22.5	17.0	34.1	493.4	9.24	708.5	986.4	1,720.7	22.4
1992	611	635	192	23.4	18.5	38.4	529.1	9.11	853.8	1,101.0	1,964.6	37.4
1993		623	196	23.0	18.4	38.6	548.4	9.60	844.0	1,079.0	1,929.1	46.1
1994		683P	223P	24.6	19.7	41.2	572.5	9.28	884.0	1,211.0	2,079.8	51.5
1995		701P	225P	26.8P	20.9P	43.3P	632.8P	10.00P	957.6P	1,311.8P	2,252.9P	39.8P
1996		719P	227P	27.0P	21.0P	43.8P	654.0P	10.28P	988.7P	1,354.4P	2,326.1P	39.6P
1997		737P	229P	27.2P	21.2P	44.3P	675.1P	10.56P	1,019.8P	1,397.0P	2,399.2P	39.4P
1998		755P	231P	27.4P	21.3P	44.7P	696.3P	10.85P	1,050.9P	1,439.6P	2,472.4P	39.1P

Sources: 1982, 1987, 1992 *Economic Census*; *Annual Survey of Manufactures*, 83-86, 88-91, 93-94. Establishment counts for non-Census years are from *County Business Patterns*; establishment values for 83-84 are extrapolations. 'P's show projections by the editors. Industries reclassified in 87 will not have data for prior years.

INDICES OF CHANGE

Year	Companies	Establishments: Total	Establishments: with 20 or more employees	Employment: Total (000)	Production Workers (000)	Production Hours (Mil)	Compensation: Payroll ($ mil)	Compensation: Wages ($/hr)	Production ($ million): Cost of Materials	Value Added by Manufacture	Value of Shipments	Capital Invest.
1982	70	70	92	90	90	83	56	67	50	60	55	87
1983		73	97	89	90	85	61	71	55	65	59	126
1984		76	102	106	106	102	77	77	69	83	75	121
1985		79	108	101	100	96	78	80	65	86	77	147
1986		81	110	106	107	99	81	84	71	83	78	113
1987	102	102	121	132	132	126	106	86	97	115	106	129
1988		100	125	132	133	123	105	86	96	106	101	97
1989		100	123	134	131	128	114	89	107	108	107	108
1990		98	124	127	119	115	108	95	103	100	102	93
1991		92	107	96	92	89	93	101	83	90	88	60
1992	100	100	100	100	100	100	100	100	100	100	100	100
1993		98	102	98	99	101	104	105	99	98	98	123
1994		108P	116P	105	106	107	108	102	104	110	106	138
1995		110P	117P	115P	113P	113P	120P	110P	112P	119P	115P	107P
1996		113P	118P	115P	114P	114P	124P	113P	116P	123P	118P	106P
1997		116P	119P	116P	114P	115P	128P	116P	119P	127P	122P	105P
1998		119P	120P	117P	115P	116P	132P	119P	123P	131P	126P	105P

Sources: Same as General Statistics. Values reflect change from the base year, 1992. Values above 100 mean greater than 92, values below 100 mean less than 92, and a value of 100 in the 82-91 or 93-98 period means same as 92. 'P's mark projections by the editors.

SELECTED RATIOS

For 1994	Avg. of All Manufact.	Analyzed Industry	Index	For 1994	Avg. of All Manufact.	Analyzed Industry	Index
Employees per Establishment	49	36	73	Value Added per Production Worker	134,084	61,472	46
Payroll per Establishment	1,500,273	837,712	56	Cost per Establishment	5,045,178	1,293,515	26
Payroll per Employee	30,620	23,272	76	Cost per Employee	102,970	35,935	35
Production Workers per Establishment	34	29	84	Cost per Production Worker	146,988	44,873	31
Wages per Establishment	853,319	559,454	66	Shipments per Establishment	9,576,895	3,043,272	32
Wages per Production Worker	24,861	19,408	78	Shipments per Employee	195,460	84,545	43
Hours per Production Worker	2,056	2,091	102	Shipments per Production Worker	279,017	105,574	38
Wages per Hour	12.09	9.28	77	Investment per Establishment	321,011	75,357	23
Value Added per Establishment	4,602,255	1,771,999	39	Investment per Employee	6,552	2,093	32
Value Added per Employee	93,930	49,228	52	Investment per Production Worker	9,352	2,614	28

Sources: Same as General Statistics. The 'Average of All Manufacturing' column represents the average of all manufacturing industries reported for the most recent complete year available. The Index shows the relationship between the Average and the Analyzed Industry. For example, 100 means that they are equal; 500 that the Analyzed Industry is five times the average; 50 means that the Analyzed Industry is half the national average. The abbreviation 'na' is used to show that data are 'not available'.

LEADING COMPANIES Number shown: **75** Total sales ($ mil): **4,440** Total employment (000): **36.0**

Company Name	Address				CEO Name	Phone	Co. Type	Sales ($ mil)	Empl. (000)
Haworth Inc	1 Haworth Ctr	Holland	MI	49423	G B Johanneson	616-393-3000	R	1,005	7.0
Herman Miller Inc	PO Box 302	Zeeland	MI	49464	J Kermit Campbell	616-654-3000	P	953	5.4
HON Industries Inc	PO Box 1109	Muscatine	IA	52761	Jack D Michaels	319-264-7400	P	780	6.3
O'Sullivan Industries Inc	1900 Gulf St	Lamar	MO	64759	Daniel F O'Sullivan	417-682-3322	S	246	1.9
O'Sullivan Industries Holdings	1900 Gulf St	Lamar	MO	64759	Daniel F O'Sullivan	417-682-3322	P	246	1.9
Shelby Williams Industries Inc	1348 Merch	Chicago	IL	60654	Paul N Steinfield	312-527-3593	P	159	1.4
Phoenix Designs Inc	10875 Chicago Dr	Zeeland	MI	49464	Bix Norman	616-772-1630	S	70*	0.4
Gunlocke Co	1 Gunlocke Dr	Wayland	NY	14572	Joseph Wisniewski	716-728-5111	S	60*	0.8
Murphy-Miller Co	931 Wing Av	Owensboro	KY	42301	Bill Glover	502-684-4221	D	40*	0.3
Trendway Corp	PO Box 9016	Holland	MI	49422	Donald G Heeringa	616-399-3900	R	39*	0.4
Styline Industries Inc	PO Box 100	Huntingburg	IN	47542	RH Menke Jr	812-683-4848	R	38	0.6
Executive Furniture Inc	PO Box 167	Huntingburg	IN	47542	CL Brosmer	812-683-3334	R	35	0.3
Brayton International	PO Box 7288	High Point	NC	27264	Scott Hartkopf	910-434-4151	S	32	0.3
Howe Furniture Corp	12 Cambridge Dr	Trumbull	CT	06611	H Howe Jr	203-374-7833	R	30	0.2
Jofco Inc	PO Box 71	Jasper	IN	47547	Joseph Steurer	812-482-5154	R	30	0.4
Sligh Furniture Co	1201 Industrial Av	Holland	MI	49423	Robert L Sligh Jr	616-392-7101	R	30	0.3
High Point Furniture Industries	PO Box 2063	High Point	NC	27261	Harry Samet	910-431-7101	R	30	0.5
Indiana Desk Company Inc	PO Box 270	Jasper	IN	47547	Jim Webb	812-482-5727	S	28	0.4
Indiana Furniture Industries Inc	PO Box 270	Jasper	IN	47547	Jim Webb	812-482-5727	R	28	0.4
Superior Chair	PO Box 725	Belton	TX	76513	Mike Webster	817-939-3517	D	28	0.2
Tiffany Industries Inc	1015 Corp Sq Dr	St Louis	MO	63132	Dave Ridgeway	314-991-1700	R	25	0.3
Paoli Inc	PO Box 30	Paoli	IN	47454	Thomas A Tolone	812-723-2791	S	24	0.6
Hickory Business Furniture	PO Box 8	Hickory	NC	28603	William E Hamlin	704-328-2064	D	20	0.2
Taylor Chair Co	75 Taylor St	Bedford	OH	44146	Taylor Meals	216-232-0700	R	20	0.2
Goebel Fixture Co	528 S Dale St	Hutchinson	MN	55350	Bill Aschinger	612-587-2112	R	19	0.1
Loewenstein Inc	1801 N Andrews Ext	Pompano Bch	FL	33061	Craig Watts	305-960-1100	S	19*	0.2
Lunstead Inc	8655 S 208th St	Kent	WA	98031	Pete Goldman	206-872-8835	S	18	0.2
Miller Desk Inc	PO Drawer HP-11	High Point	NC	27261	Felix F Miller Jr	919-886-7061	R	18	0.5
JG Furniture Systems Inc	PO Box 9002	Quakertown	PA	18951	CD Isaac	215-538-5800	R	16	0.2
La-Z-Boy Chair Co	1111 Godfrey SW	Grand Rapids	MI	49503	Thomas Grealish	616-246-0246	D	15	0.1
Nucraft Furniture Co	5151 W River Dr	Comstock Park	MI	49321	TO Schad	616-784-6016	R	15	0.1
Thonet Industries Inc	PO Box 5909	Statesville	NC	28687	Martha Wadsworth	704-878-2222	S	15	0.3
Gasser Chair Co	4136 Loganway Av	Youngstown	OH	44505	Gary Gasser	216-759-2234	R	13	0.2
GO Furniture Inc	4451 Eucalyptus	Chino	CA	91710	John Meruelo	909-393-4431	R	13*	0.1
Jasper Seating Inc	PO Box 231	Jasper	IN	47547	M Elliott	812-482-3204	R	13	0.2
John Boos and Company Inc	PO Box 609	Effingham	IL	62401	TS Gravenhorst Sr	217-347-7701	R	12	0.1
Omni International Inc	PO Box 1409	Vernon	AL	35592	JL Riley	205-695-9173	R	12	0.1
Novikoff Inc	2100 E Richmond St	Fort Worth	TX	76104	Leon Novikoff	817-535-0826	R	11	0.1
Jansko Inc	4101 Ravenswood	Ft Lauderdale	FL	33312	Benjamin Friedman	305-359-0159	P	11	0.1
Councill Co	PO Box 398	Denton	NC	27239	FM Councill	704-869-2155	R	10	0.1
Patrician Furniture Co	PO Box 2353	High Point	NC	27261	Darrell Stout	910-889-6186	D	10	0.1
Rough Rider Industries	PO Box 5521	Bismarck	ND	58502	Dennis Fracassi	701-221-6161	R	10	0.1
Westin Nielsen Corp	4301 White Bear	St Paul	MN	55110	WJ Nielsen	612-426-4625	R	10*	<0.1
Whitehall Furniture Inc	PO Box 745	Owensboro	KY	42302	Edward C Wathen	502-683-3585	R	10	0.1
Inwood Office Furniture	PO Box 646	Jasper	IN	47547	Glen M Sturm	812-482-6121	R	9*	0.1
LUI Corp	5500 E Lombard St	Baltimore	MD	21224	James Crystal	410-522-4135	R	9	<0.1
Magna Design Inc	5804 204th St SW	Lynnwood	WA	98036	Tom A Sehrer	206-776-2181	R	9*	<0.1
Princeton Upholstery Co	51 Railroad Av	Middletown	NY	10940	Stan Gottlieb	914-343-2196	R	9*	0.2
Nova Office Furniture Inc	421 W Indrial Av	Effingham	IL	62401	John Lechman	217-342-7070	R	8	<0.1
Quaker Furniture Inc	PO Box 1973	Hickory	NC	28603	Gary N Lail	704-322-1794	R	8*	0.1
Taylor Desk Co	11020 Santa Fe Av	Lynwood	CA	90262	Alan Paull	310-631-6727	S	8	0.1
Jasper Desk Co	PO Box 111	Jasper	IN	47547	W Price	812-482-4132	R	8	0.1
Gregson Furniture Industries	PO Box 1269	Liberty	NC	27298	Chester Wooten	919-622-2201	S	7*	0.1
Mode Corp	14700 Doolittle	San Leandro	CA	94577	M Nachuk	510-895-6600	R	7	<0.1
CCN International Inc	200 Lehigh St	Geneva	NY	14456	Richard Conoyer	315-789-4400	R	7	<0.1
Aspects Inc	PO Box 1799	Redlands	CA	92373	RG Zacky	909-794-7722	R	6	<0.1
Conwed Designscape	275 Market St	Minneapolis	MN	55405	Larry Scott	612-333-9166	D	6	0.1
FE Hale Manufacturing	650 W German St	Herkimer	NY	13350	James D Benson	315-866-4250	R	6	<0.1
Berco Industries Inc	1120 Montrose	St Louis	MO	63104	R Berkowitz	314-772-4700	R	5	0.1
Charlotte Company Inc	815 Front St	Belding	MI	48809	Mary Klein	616-794-1700	D	5	<0.1
Cleator Corp	8725 Production	San Diego	CA	92121	RK Cleator	619-566-6850	R	5	0.1
John Savoy and Son Inc	PO Box 248	Montoursville	PA	17754	John A Savoy	717-368-2424	R	5	0.1
Kittinger Co	1893 Elmwood Av	Buffalo	NY	14207	Nicholas J Defino	716-876-1000	S	5*	<0.1
Stuart-Clark Manufacturing Inc	PO Box 707	Lexington	NC	27292	Donald Clark	704-249-1428	S	5*	<0.1
Stuart-Clark Inc	PO Box 707	Lexington	NC	27292	OK Hogan	704-249-1428	R	5*	<0.1
Dependable Furniture Mfg Co	111 San Leandro	San Leandro	CA	94577	Kevin Sarkisian	510-635-1111	R	4*	<0.1
Intrex Corp	93 Triangle St	Danbury	CT	06810	Paul LePage	203-792-7400	R	4	<0.1
Moser Corp	PO Box 1984	Rogers	AR	72757	Harley Moser Jr	501-636-3481	R	4*	0.1
Tesco Industries Inc	PO Box 736	Bellville	TX	77418	A Jackson	409-865-3176	R	4	<0.1
AT Foote Woodworking Co	726 Windsor St	Hartford	CT	06120	Arthur T Foote	203-249-6821	R	4	<0.1
Arnold Furniture Manufacturers	400 Coit St	Irvington	NJ	07111	Julius Arnold	201-399-0505	R	3	<0.1
B and W Corp	110 Gateway Rd	Bensenville	IL	60106	Ronald Wood Sr	708-766-5100	R	3*	<0.1
Premier Furniture Inc	2057 S Broadway	Denver	CO	80210	Dave Raeder	303-722-2270	R	3	<0.1
Wood Design Inc	PO Box 31	French Lick	IN	47432	Robert Elsby	812-936-9977	R	3	<0.1
Balt Inc	201 N Crockett	Cameron	TX	76520	Lorraine Moore	817-697-4953	R	3	<0.1

Source: Ward's Business Directory of U.S. Private and Public Companies, Volumes 1 and 2, 1996. The company type code used is as follows: P - Public, R - Private, S - Subsidiary, D - Division, J - Joint Venture, A - Affiliate, G - Group. Sales are in millions of dollars, employees are in thousands. An asterisk (*) indicates an estimated sales volume. The symbol < stands for 'less than'. Company names and addresses are truncated, in some cases, to fit into the available space.

MATERIALS CONSUMED

Material	Quantity	Delivered Cost ($ million)
Materials, ingredients, containers, and supplies	(X)	753.2
Metal stampings	(X)	4.1
All other fabricated metal products (except castings and forgings)	(X)	9.9
Forgings	(X)	0.2
Castings (rough and semifinished)	(X)	0.3
Steel sheet and strip, including tin plate	(X)	4.0
All other steel shapes and forms (except castings, forgings, and fabricated metal products)	(X)	5.0
Aluminum and aluminum-base alloy sheet, plate, foil, and welded tubing	(X)	(Z)
All other aluminum and aluminum-base alloy shapes and forms	(X)	0.8
Other nonferrous shapes and forms (except castings, forgings, and fabricated metal products)	(X)	(D)
Hardwood lumber, rough and dressed	(X)	53.3
Softwood lumber, rough and dressed	(X)	5.3
Hardwood dimension and parts, including wood furniture frames	(X)	51.3
Hardwood veneer	(X)	33.5
Hardwood plywood	(X)	57.0
Softwood plywood	(X)	(D)
Particleboard (wood)	(X)	45.7
Medium density fiberboard (MDF)	(X)	5.7
Hardboard (wood fiberboard)	(X)	8.5
Plastics laminated sheets	(X)	26.6
Plastics furniture parts and components	(X)	8.9
Formed and slab stock for pillows, cushions, seating, etc. (urethane)	(X)	8.7
Coated or laminated fabrics, including vinyl coated	(X)	13.4
Uncoated broadwoven fabrics for upholstery	(X)	23.0
Flat glass (plate, float, and sheet)	(X)	2.6
Adhesives and sealants	(X)	3.1
Paints, varnishes, lacquers, stains, shellacs, japans, enamels, and allied products	(X)	17.2
Furniture and builders' hardware	(X)	62.3
Paperboard containers, boxes, and corrugated paperboard	(X)	28.3
All other materials and components, parts, containers, and supplies	(X)	71.4
Materials, ingredients, containers, and supplies, nsk	(X)	177.2

Source: 1992 *Economic Census*. Explanation of symbols used: (D): Withheld to avoid disclosure of competitive data; na: Not available; (S): Withheld because statistical norms were not met; (X): Not applicable; (Z): Less than half the unit shown; nec: Not elsewhere classified; nsk: Not specified by kind; - : zero; * : 10-19 percent estimated; ** : 20-29 percent estimated.

PRODUCT SHARE DETAILS

Product or Product Class	% Share	Product or Product Class	% Share
Wood office furniture	100.00		

Source: 1992 *Economic Census*. The values shown are percent of total shipments in an industry. Values of indented subcategories are summed in the main heading. The symbol (D) appears when data are withheld to prevent disclosure of competitive information. The abbreviation nsk stands for 'not specified by kind' and nec for 'not elsewhere classified'.

INPUTS AND OUTPUTS FOR WOOD OFFICE FURNITURE

Economic Sector or Industry Providing Inputs	%	Sector	Economic Sector or Industry Buying Outputs	%	Sector
Wholesale trade	10.5	Trade	Gross private fixed investment	86.9	Cap Inv
Veneer & plywood	8.9	Manufg.	S/L Govt. purch., other general government	3.4	S/L Govt
Sawmills & planning mills, general	8.3	Manufg.	Exports	2.1	Foreign
Business services nec	7.7	Services	S/L Govt. purch., elem. & secondary education	2.1	S/L Govt
Hardware, nec	6.1	Manufg.	S/L Govt. purch., higher education	1.1	S/L Govt
Accounting, auditing & bookkeeping	6.1	Services	S/L Govt. purch., other education & libraries	1.1	S/L Govt
Hardwood dimension & flooring mills	4.4	Manufg.	S/L Govt. purch., police	1.1	S/L Govt
Particleboard	3.6	Manufg.	S/L Govt. purch., highways	0.4	S/L Govt
Advertising	3.4	Services	Wood office furniture	0.3	Manufg.
Coated fabrics, not rubberized	3.1	Manufg.	S/L Govt. purch., water	0.3	S/L Govt
Banking	2.8	Fin/R.E.	S/L Govt. purch., gas & electric utilities	0.2	S/L Govt
Petroleum refining	2.5	Manufg.	S/L Govt. purch., urban renewal & commun. facilities	0.2	S/L Govt
Paperboard containers & boxes	2.2	Manufg.	Federal Government purchases, nondefense	0.1	Fed Govt
Wood products, nec	2.1	Manufg.	S/L Govt. purch., fire	0.1	S/L Govt
Miscellaneous plastics products	2.0	Manufg.			
Real estate	1.8	Fin/R.E.			
Maintenance of nonfarm buildings nec	1.7	Constr.			
Paints & allied products	1.7	Manufg.			
Electric services (utilities)	1.6	Util.			
Eating & drinking places	1.6	Trade			
Motor freight transportation & warehousing	1.5	Util.			
Blast furnaces & steel mills	1.4	Manufg.			
Railroads & related services	1.1	Util.			
Abrasive products	0.9	Manufg.			
Leather tanning & finishing	0.9	Manufg.			
Communications, except radio & TV	0.8	Util.			

Continued on next page.

INPUTS AND OUTPUTS FOR WOOD OFFICE FURNITURE - Continued

Economic Sector or Industry Providing Inputs	%	Sector	Economic Sector or Industry Buying Outputs	%	Sector
Electrical repair shops	0.8	Services			
Adhesives & sealants	0.6	Manufg.			
Fabricated rubber products, nec	0.6	Manufg.			
Padding & upholstery filling	0.6	Manufg.			
Wood office furniture	0.5	Manufg.			
Automotive rental & leasing, without drivers	0.5	Services			
Management & consulting services & labs	0.5	Services			
Gas production & distribution (utilities)	0.4	Util.			
Security & commodity brokers	0.4	Fin/R.E.			
Equipment rental & leasing services	0.4	Services			
Legal services	0.4	Services			
Machinery, except electrical, nec	0.3	Manufg.			
Air transportation	0.3	Util.			
Automotive repair shops & services	0.3	Services			
Aluminum rolling & drawing	0.2	Manufg.			
Lubricating oils & greases	0.2	Manufg.			
Manifold business forms	0.2	Manufg.			
Paper coating & glazing	0.2	Manufg.			
Special dies & tools & machine tool accessories	0.2	Manufg.			
Steel wire & related products	0.2	Manufg.			
Insurance carriers	0.2	Fin/R.E.			
Royalties	0.2	Fin/R.E.			
Computer & data processing services	0.2	Services			
Broadwoven fabric mills	0.1	Manufg.			
Mechanical measuring devices	0.1	Manufg.			
Tires & inner tubes	0.1	Manufg.			
Sanitary services, steam supply, irrigation	0.1	Util.			
Water transportation	0.1	Util.			
Laundry, dry cleaning, shoe repair	0.1	Services			
Personnel supply services	0.1	Services			
U.S. Postal Service	0.1	Gov't			

Source: Benchmark Input-Output Accounts for the U.S. Economy, 1982, U.S. Department of Commerce, Washington, D.C., July 1991. Data, as reported in the source, are organized by the 1977 SIC structure in use in 1982 but have been matched, as closely as is possible, to the 1987 SIC structure used in this book.

OCCUPATIONS EMPLOYED BY SIC 252 - OFFICE AND MISCELLANEOUS FURNITURE AND FIXTURES

Occupation	% of Total 1994	Change to 2005	Occupation	% of Total 1994	Change to 2005
Assemblers, fabricators, & hand workers nec	21.5	6.5	Hand packers & packagers	1.6	-8.7
Blue collar worker supervisors	4.2	1.0	Welders & cutters	1.6	6.5
Cabinetmakers & bench carpenters	3.9	59.7	Inspectors, testers, & graders, precision	1.6	6.5
Upholsterers	2.8	10.1	Machine forming operators, metal & plastic	1.4	6.5
Welding machine setters, operators	2.8	-4.2	Head sawyers & sawing machine workers	1.3	-14.8
Sales & related workers nec	2.6	6.5	Secretaries, ex legal & medical	1.3	-3.1
Wood machinists	2.5	43.7	General office clerks	1.3	-9.2
General managers & top executives	2.2	1.0	Industrial truck & tractor operators	1.2	6.5
Furniture finishers	2.2	30.3	Industrial production managers	1.2	6.5
Coating, painting, & spraying machine workers	2.1	6.5	Drafters	1.2	-17.1
Machine tool cutting & forming etc. nec	2.0	6.5	Grinders & polishers, hand	1.1	6.5
Freight, stock, & material movers, hand	2.0	-14.8	Bookkeeping, accounting, & auditing clerks	1.1	-20.1
Woodworking machine workers	2.0	-57.4	Truck drivers light & heavy	1.1	9.8
Traffic, shipping, & receiving clerks	1.9	2.4			

Source: Industry-Occupation Matrix, Bureau of Labor Statistics. These data relate to one or more 3-digit SIC industry groups rather than to a single 4-digit SIC. The change reported for each occupation to the year 2005 is a percent of growth or decline as estimated by the Bureau of Labor Statistics. The abbreviation nec stands for 'not elsewhere classified'.

LOCATION BY STATE AND REGIONAL CONCENTRATION

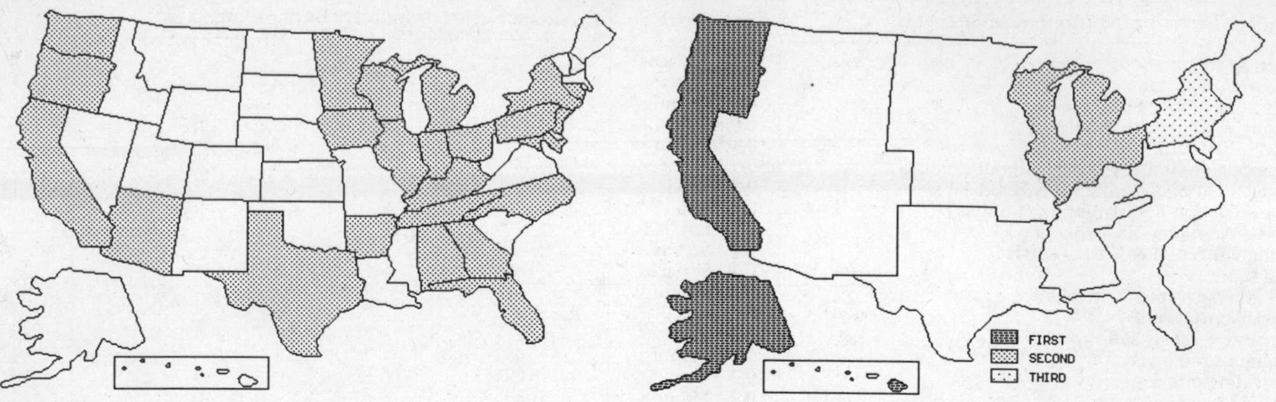

INDUSTRY DATA BY STATE

State	Establish-ments	Shipments			Employment				Cost as % of Shipments	Investment per Employee ($)
		Total ($ mil)	% of U.S.	Per Establ.	Total Number	% of U.S.	Per Establ.	Wages ($/hour)		
Indiana	31	367.7	18.7	11.9	4,200	17.9	135	9.38	45.7	1,952
North Carolina	32	283.7	14.4	8.9	4,200	17.9	131	7.75	45.4	1,333
California	115	250.2	12.7	2.2	2,700	11.5	23	7.68	46.2	1,407
Michigan	26	145.2	7.4	5.6	1,500	6.4	58	11.71	38.8	2,200
New York	60	142.2	7.2	2.4	1,800	7.7	30	9.21	39.7	1,056
Illinois	28	103.2	5.3	3.7	1,000	4.3	36	13.33	39.8	200
Pennsylvania	18	62.9	3.2	3.5	800	3.4	44	9.42	48.6	625
Washington	25	60.9	3.1	2.4	700	3.0	28	9.67	40.9	-
New Jersey	19	60.2	3.1	3.2	500	2.1	26	12.14	26.2	-
Wisconsin	15	39.9	2.0	2.7	400	1.7	27	10.00	43.1	1,750
Georgia	13	36.0	1.8	2.8	500	2.1	38	9.57	30.0	-
Minnesota	17	26.9	1.4	1.6	300	1.3	18	8.80	40.9	-
Connecticut	6	26.4	1.3	4.4	300	1.3	50	8.50	36.0	1,000
Texas	31	26.2	1.3	0.8	400	1.7	13	8.17	43.1	500
Ohio	9	20.4	1.0	2.3	200	0.9	22	7.00	43.6	1,500
Tennessee	9	19.6	1.0	2.2	300	1.3	33	9.00	49.5	1,000
Arizona	14	19.5	1.0	1.4	300	1.3	21	7.00	70.3	-
Florida	31	14.9	0.8	0.5	300	1.3	10	8.50	45.6	333
Maryland	12	(D)	-	-	175 *	0.7	15	-	-	-
Oregon	12	(D)	-	-	175 *	0.7	15	-	-	-
Alabama	10	(D)	-	-	750 *	3.2	75	-	-	-
Arkansas	10	(D)	-	-	175 *	0.7	18	-	-	571
Kentucky	5	(D)	-	-	1,750 *	7.5	350	-	-	-
Iowa	4	(D)	-	-	175 *	0.7	44	-	-	-

Source: 1992 *Economic Census*. The states are in descending order of shipments or establishments (if shipment data are missing for the majority). The symbol (D) appears when data are withheld to prevent disclosure of competitive information. States marked with (D) are sorted by number of establishments. A dash (-) indicates that the data element cannot be calculated; * indicates the midpoint of a range.

2522 - OFFICE FURNITURE, EXCEPT WOOD

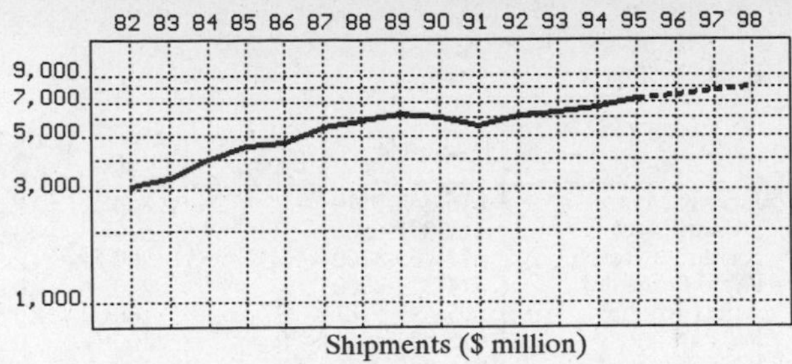

Shipments ($ million)

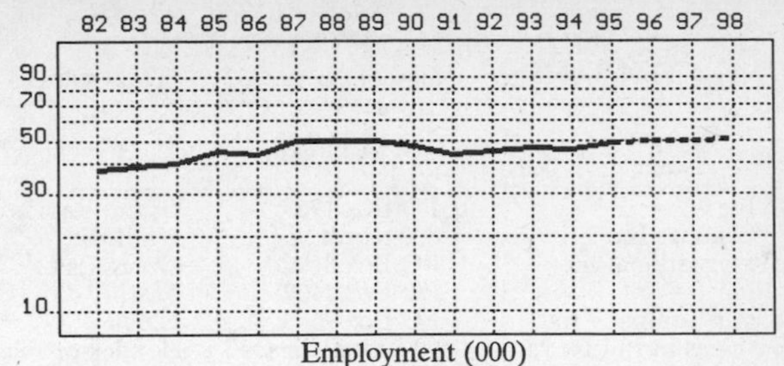

Employment (000)

GENERAL STATISTICS

Year	Companies	Establishments		Employment			Compensation		Production ($ million)			
		Total	with 20 or more employees	Total (000)	Production Workers (000)	Production Hours (Mil)	Payroll ($ mil)	Wages ($/hr)	Cost of Materials	Value Added by Manufacture	Value of Shipments	Capital Invest.
1982	224	254	162	37.8	27.3	53.2	754.8	9.10	1,230.9	1,817.9	3,062.7	114.2
1983		256	165	39.1	28.4	53.8	816.5	9.65	1,313.9	2,073.4	3,350.5	185.0
1984		258	168	40.4	29.4	59.4	931.1	10.02	1,567.7	2,487.4	4,027.2	159.5
1985		259	171	44.6	31.8	62.9	1,036.1	10.66	1,847.6	2,687.9	4,530.2	171.9
1986		261	173	43.7	30.8	61.0	1,072.5	11.14	1,861.7	2,874.1	4,728.9	218.3
1987	291	337	206	49.7	35.8	69.6	1,227.4	11.16	1,987.9	3,479.4	5,453.6	234.1
1988		324	211	49.8	36.3	72.1	1,327.5	11.81	2,251.2	3,534.2	5,794.1	270.0
1989		321	215	49.7	35.1	70.9	1,365.2	12.11	2,478.9	3,654.8	6,155.7	261.4
1990		307	213	47.0	33.4	68.6	1,324.8	11.99	2,401.2	3,618.7	6,031.4	257.4
1991		306	202	43.6	30.8	62.8	1,267.9	11.82	2,374.8	3,141.9	5,542.2	150.2
1992	327	386	222	44.5	31.9	70.0	1,337.7	11.78	2,505.6	3,533.0	6,043.1	164.1
1993		388	225	46.5	33.8	72.7	1,402.2	12.04	2,664.2	3,672.6	6,336.0	188.7
1994		382P	235P	45.6	33.6	73.3	1,449.1	12.22	2,768.8	3,829.5	6,583.3	191.9
1995		394P	241P	48.8P	35.1P	75.9P	1,564.8P	12.88P	3,004.5P	4,155.5P	7,143.7P	218.3P
1996		405P	247P	49.3P	35.5P	77.4P	1,620.0P	13.12P	3,121.1P	4,316.7P	7,420.9P	221.3P
1997		417P	254P	49.9P	36.0P	78.9P	1,675.3P	13.36P	3,237.7P	4,478.0P	7,698.2P	224.3P
1998		429P	260P	50.5P	36.4P	80.4P	1,730.6P	13.60P	3,354.3P	4,639.3P	7,975.4P	227.3P

Sources: 1982, 1987, 1992 *Economic Census*; *Annual Survey of Manufactures*, 83-86, 88-91, 93-94. Establishment counts for non-Census years are from *County Business Patterns*; establishment values for 83-84 are extrapolations. 'P's show projections by the editors. Industries reclassified in 87 will not have data for prior years.

INDICES OF CHANGE

Year	Companies	Establishments		Employment			Compensation		Production ($ million)			
		Total	with 20 or more employees	Total (000)	Production Workers (000)	Production Hours (Mil)	Payroll ($ mil)	Wages ($/hr)	Cost of Materials	Value Added by Manufacture	Value of Shipments	Capital Invest.
1982	69	66	73	85	86	76	56	77	49	51	51	70
1983		66	74	88	89	77	61	82	52	59	55	113
1984		67	76	91	92	85	70	85	63	70	67	97
1985		67	77	100	100	90	77	90	74	76	75	105
1986		68	78	98	97	87	80	95	74	81	78	133
1987	89	87	93	112	112	99	92	95	79	98	90	143
1988		84	95	112	114	103	99	100	90	100	96	165
1989		83	97	112	110	101	102	103	99	103	102	159
1990		80	96	106	105	98	99	102	96	102	100	157
1991		79	91	98	97	90	95	100	95	89	92	92
1992	100	100	100	100	100	100	100	100	100	100	100	100
1993		101	101	104	106	104	105	102	106	104	105	115
1994		99P	106P	102	105	105	108	104	111	108	109	117
1995		102P	109P	110P	110P	108P	117P	109P	120P	118P	118P	133P
1996		105P	111P	111P	111P	111P	121P	111P	125P	122P	123P	135P
1997		108P	114P	112P	113P	113P	125P	113P	129P	127P	127P	137P
1998		111P	117P	113P	114P	115P	129P	115P	134P	131P	132P	139P

Sources: Same as General Statistics. Values reflect change from the base year, 1992. Values above 100 mean greater than 92, values below 100 mean less than 92, and a value of 100 in the 82-91 or 93-98 period means same as 92. 'P's mark projections by the editors.

SELECTED RATIOS

For 1994	Avg. of All Manufact.	Analyzed Industry	Index
Employees per Establishment	49	119	244
Payroll per Establishment	1,500,273	3,796,166	253
Payroll per Employee	30,620	31,779	104
Production Workers per Establishment	34	88	256
Wages per Establishment	853,319	2,346,508	275
Wages per Production Worker	24,861	26,659	107
Hours per Production Worker	2,056	2,182	106
Wages per Hour	12.09	12.22	101
Value Added per Establishment	4,602,255	10,032,031	218
Value Added per Employee	93,930	83,980	89

For 1994	Avg. of All Manufact.	Analyzed Industry	Index
Value Added per Production Worker	134,084	113,973	85
Cost per Establishment	5,045,178	7,253,346	144
Cost per Employee	102,970	60,719	59
Cost per Production Worker	146,988	82,405	56
Shipments per Establishment	9,576,895	17,246,082	180
Shipments per Employee	195,460	144,371	74
Shipments per Production Worker	279,017	195,932	70
Investment per Establishment	321,011	502,715	157
Investment per Employee	6,552	4,208	64
Investment per Production Worker	9,352	5,711	61

Sources: Same as General Statistics. The 'Average of All Manufacturing' column represents the average of all manufacturing industries reported for the most recent complete year available. The Index shows the relationship between the Average and the Analyzed Industry. For example, 100 means that they are equal; 500 that the Analyzed Industry is five times the average; 50 means that the Analyzed Industry is half the national average. The abbreviation 'na' is used to show that data are 'not available'.

LEADING COMPANIES

Number shown: **62** Total sales ($ mil): **5,190** Total employment (000): **34.2**

Company Name	Address				CEO Name	Phone	Co. Type	Sales ($ mil)	Empl. (000)
Steelcase Inc	PO Box 1967	Grand Rapids	MI	49501	Jerry K Myers	616-247-2710	R	2,800	17.0
HMK Enterprises Inc	800 South St	Waltham	MA	02154	Steven Karol	617-891-6660	R	600*	3.0
Krueger International Inc	PO Box 8100	Green Bay	WI	54308	Richard J Resch	414-468-8100	R	289	2.3
Steelcase Inc	PO Box 2409	Tustin	CA	92681	Pablo Gonzalez	714-259-8000	D	250	0.9
United Chair Company Inc	PO Box 96	Leeds	AL	35094	James Ritchey	205-699-5181	S	160*	0.5
Globe Business Furniture Inc	90 Volunteer Dr	Hendersonville	TN	37075	JW Park	615-822-4968	R	100*	0.7
Meridian Inc	PO Box 768	Spring Lake	MI	49456	Rick Smith	616-846-0280	S	100	0.7
Tennsco Corp	PO Box 1888	Dickson	TN	37056	Lester Speyer	615-446-8000	R	70	0.6
Fixtures Manufacturing Corp	1642 Crystal	Kansas City	MO	64126	Norman Polsky	816-241-4500	R	55	0.4
Centercore Inc	110 Summit Dr	Exton	PA	19341	George E Mitchell	215-524-1905	P	53	0.3
Steelworks Inc	1st & New York	Des Moines	IA	50313	G Wayne Stewart	515-288-7414	R	50	0.5
Vecta	PO Box 534013	Grand Prairie	TX	75053	Michael Love	214-641-2860	S	43	0.3
Harter Corp	PO Box 400	Sturgis	MI	49091	Gary Gottschalk	616-651-3201	R	35	0.4
Wright Line Inc	160 Gold Star Blv	Worcester	MA	01606	Phil Burkart	508-852-4300	S	33*	0.4
Haskell of Pittsburgh Inc	231 Haskell Ln	Verona	PA	15147	Joseph Wojdak	412-828-6000	R	31*	0.3
General Metalcraft Inc	PO Box 557	Dover	DE	19903	Mike Amsterdam	302-678-3454	R	30*	0.3
Harvard Interiors Manufacturing	4321 Semple Av	St Louis	MO	63120	Thomas Jenkins	314-382-5590	D	30	0.3
Marvel Group Inc	3843 W 43rd St	Chicago	IL	60632	John J Dellamore	312-523-4804	S	30	0.4
Metalworks Inc	PO Box 689	Ludington	MI	49431	Tom Paine	616-845-5136	R	27*	0.3
Panel Concepts Inc	PO Box C-25100	Santa Ana	CA	92799	Van Jacobsen	714-433-3300	R	24	0.3
EAC Corp	347 N Lindbergh	St Louis	MO	63141	MW Rogers III	314-993-8100	R	20	0.2
Mayline Company Inc	PO Box 728	Sheboygan	WI	53082	Paul Simons	414-457-5537	R	20	0.3
Plan Hold Corp	17421 Von Karman	Irvine	CA	92714	PJ Massa	714-660-0400	S	20	0.2
Luxor	2245 Delany Rd	Waukegan	IL	60085	Donald Nichoalds	708-244-1800	D	18*	0.2
McDowell & Craig Mfg Co	13146 E Firestone	Norwalk	CA	90650	JC McDowell	213-773-3451	R	17*	0.2
Hamilton Sorter Company Inc	PO Box 18008	Fairfield	OH	45018	Thadius Jarozewicz	513-870-4400	R	16	0.1
Jebco Inc	PO Box 112	Warrenton	GA	30828	James E Barrow	706-465-3378	R	16	0.2
Anderson-Hickey Co	PO Box 80	Henderson	TX	75652	Jimmy Ritchey	903-657-9531	S	15*	0.3
Teichman Enterprises Inc	PO Box 58263	Los Angeles	CA	90058	S Teichman	213-234-9053	R	15	0.1
Alabama Metal Products Inc	PO Box 608	Rosedale	MS	38769	RL Kanary	601-759-3521	R	13	0.2
Spectrum Industries Inc	1600 Johnson St	Chippewa Falls	WI	54729	D Hancock	715-723-6750	R	13	0.3
Sandusky Cabinets Inc	PO Box 1040	Sandusky	OH	44870	John Stoever	419-626-5465	R	13	0.1
Toledo Metals Furniture	W Main St	Stroudsburg	PA	18360	Michael J Stirr	717-421-4110	D	12	0.2
Transwall Corp	PO Box 1930	West Chester	PA	19380	HH Aikens	215-647-3040	R	12	<0.1
Anthro Corp	3221 NW Yeon St	Portland	OR	97210	Shoaib Tareen	503-241-7113	R	10	<0.1
Brewer Co	13901 Main St	Menomonee Fls	WI	53051	Jeffrey Beischel	414-251-9530	R	10	0.1
Kemper Industries Inc	PO Box 6	Littlestown	PA	17340	ML Kemper	717-359-4111	R	10	0.1
Mills Co	6690 Beta Dr	Cleveland	OH	44143	John M Plumpton	216-442-2900	R	10	<0.1
Russ Bassett Co	8189 Byron Rd	Whittier	CA	90606	Mike Dressendorfer	310-945-2445	R	10	<0.1
Virginia Manufacturing Inc	PO Box 340	Pennington Gap	VA	24277	Robert J Parkey	703-546-3328	R	10	0.2
Mity-Lite Inc	1301 W 400 N	Orem	UT	84057	Gregory L Wilson	801-224-0589	P	10	<0.1
C-2 Office Gear Inc	2762 N Clybourn	Chicago	IL	60614	Mark Swislow	312-327-9200	R	9*	0.1
October Company Inc	PO Box 71	Easthampton	MA	01027	H Michael Schaefer	413-527-9380	R	9	0.1
ACME Design Technology Co	1000 Allview Dr	Crozet	VA	22932	Thomas D Hall	804-823-4351	R	8*	<0.1
Kwik-File Inc	500 73rd Av NE	Minneapolis	MN	55432	James Gray	612-572-1980	R	8*	<0.1
MicroComputer Accessories Inc	9920 La Cienega	Inglewood	CA	90301	Gerry Cleinjan	310-301-9400	S	6*	<0.1
MLP Seating Corp	2125 Lively Blv	Elk Grove Vill	IL	60007	RD Samuel	708-956-1700	R	6	<0.1
Neutral Posture Ergonomics Inc	2301 Fountain Av	Bryan	TX	77801	Rebecca Boenigk	409-822-5080	R	6*	<0.1
Emeco Industries Inc	805 Elm Av	Hanover	PA	17331	Jay Buchbinder	717-637-5951	R	5	0.1
Glen Upton Inc	6300 Saint John Av	Kansas City	MO	64123	Glen A Upton	816-921-1195	R	5	<0.1
RJ Taylor Corp	9410 S Meridan Rd	Clarklake	MI	49234	Robert J Taylor	517-529-4007	R	5	<0.1
Biltrite Metal Products Inc	100 E North St	Leland	IL	60531	Linda Thomas	815-495-2211	R	5	<0.1
Brandrud Furniture Inc	PO Box C	Auburn	WA	98071	Larry C Green	206-838-6500	R	4*	<0.1
Datum Filing Systems Inc	915 Borom Rd	York	PA	17404	Thomas Potter	717-764-6350	R	4	<0.1
Bevco Precision Mfg Co	W 227 N 752	Waukesha	WI	53186	John Bevington	414-547-6990	R	2	<0.1
Fortress Inc	4880 Murietta St	Chino	CA	91710	Donald I Wolper	909-627-4270	R	2*	<0.1
Maury Office Systems Inc	1330 Sycamore	Memphis	TN	38134	ER Bean	901-388-8080	R	2	<0.1
Monarch Systems	PO Box 110	Frenchtown	NJ	08825	Ron Rienecker	908-996-3113	D	2*	<0.1
Data-MATE Inc	PO Box 408	Nashua	NH	03061	Alfred M Norton	603-882-5142	R	1	<0.1
Watson Industries Inc	PO Box 1028	Jamestown	NY	14702	BN Okwumabua	716-487-1901	R	1*	<0.1
Currier Manufacturing	1211 P Butler	St Paul	MN	55104	Mark Olson	612-647-5410	D	1	<0.1
Input-Ez Corp	1440 W 3rd Av	Denver	CO	80223	Margery Johnson	303-571-5571	R	0	<0.1

Source: *Ward's Business Directory of U.S. Private and Public Companies*, Volumes 1 and 2, 1996. The company type code used is as follows: P - Public, R - Private, S - Subsidiary, D - Division, J - Joint Venture, A - Affiliate, G - Group. Sales are in millions of dollars, employees are in thousands. An asterisk (*) indicates an estimated sales volume. The symbol < stands for 'less than'. Company names and addresses are truncated, in some cases, to fit into the available space.

MATERIALS CONSUMED

Material	Quantity	Delivered Cost ($ million)
Materials, ingredients, containers, and supplies	(X)	2,267.4
Metal stampings	(X)	(D)
All other fabricated metal products (except castings and forgings)	(X)	41.2
Forgings	(X)	(D)
Castings (rough and semifinished)	(X)	17.4
Steel sheet and strip, including tin plate	(X)	323.4
All other steel shapes and forms (except castings, forgings, and fabricated metal products)	(X)	63.0
Aluminum and aluminum-base alloy sheet, plate, foil, and welded tubing	(X)	10.2
All other aluminum and aluminum-base alloy shapes and forms	(X)	31.5
Other nonferrous shapes and forms (except castings, forgings, and fabricated metal products)	(X)	(D)
Hardwood lumber, rough and dressed	(X)	26.0
Softwood lumber, rough and dressed	(X)	3.1
Hardwood dimension and parts, including wood furniture frames	(X)	121.2
Hardwood veneer	(X)	7.3
Hardwood plywood	(X)	8.9
Softwood plywood	(X)	4.4
Particleboard (wood)	(X)	23.6
Medium density fiberboard (MDF)	(X)	(D)
Hardboard (wood fiberboard)	(X)	10.7
Plastics laminated sheets	(X)	28.2
Plastics furniture parts and components	(X)	100.2
Formed and slab stock for pillows, cushions, seating, etc. (urethane)	(X)	48.4
Coated or laminated fabrics, including vinyl coated	(X)	189.8
Uncoated broadwoven fabrics for upholstery	(X)	209.5
Flat glass (plate, float, and sheet)	(X)	1.5
Adhesives and sealants	(X)	8.3
Paints, varnishes, lacquers, stains, shellacs, japans, enamels, and allied products	(X)	63.0
Furniture and builders' hardware	(X)	147.7
Paperboard containers, boxes, and corrugated paperboard	(X)	85.0
All other materials and components, parts, containers, and supplies	(X)	241.0
Materials, ingredients, containers, and supplies, nsk	(X)	277.5

Source: 1992 *Economic Census*. Explanation of symbols used: (D): Withheld to avoid disclosure of competitive data; na: Not available; (S): Withheld because statistical norms were not met; (X): Not applicable; (Z): Less than half the unit shown; nec: Not elsewhere classified; nsk: Not specified by kind; - : zero; * : 10-19 percent estimated; ** : 20-29 percent estimated.

PRODUCT SHARE DETAILS

Product or Product Class	% Share	Product or Product Class	% Share
Office furniture, except wood	100.00	Office panel and modular systems furniture and all other nonwood office furniture, nec	40.18
Office seating, including upholstered, except wood	24.74	Office furniture, except wood, nsk	2.44
Office desks and extensions, except wood	6.49		
Office storage units, files, and tables, except wood	26.15		

Source: 1992 *Economic Census*. The values shown are percent of total shipments in an industry. Values of indented subcategories are summed in the main heading. The symbol (D) appears when data are withheld to prevent disclosure of competitive information. The abbreviation nsk stands for 'not specified by kind' and nec for 'not elsewhere classified'.

INPUTS AND OUTPUTS FOR METAL OFFICE FURNITURE

Economic Sector or Industry Providing Inputs	%	Sector	Economic Sector or Industry Buying Outputs	%	Sector
Blast furnaces & steel mills	18.8	Manufg.	Gross private fixed investment	84.3	Cap Inv
Wholesale trade	11.2	Trade	S/L Govt. purch., other general government	5.1	S/L Govt
Accounting, auditing & bookkeeping	8.8	Services	S/L Govt. purch., higher education	2.5	S/L Govt
Banking	5.9	Fin/R.E.	S/L Govt. purch., elem. & secondary education	2.4	S/L Govt
Coated fabrics, not rubberized	4.8	Manufg.	Exports	1.9	Foreign
Business services nec	3.9	Services	Federal Government purchases, nondefense	0.8	Fed Govt
Advertising	3.8	Services	Federal Government purchases, national defense	0.5	Fed Govt
Hardware, nec	3.3	Manufg.	S/L Govt. purch., police	0.4	S/L Govt
Miscellaneous plastics products	3.1	Manufg.	S/L Govt. purch., urban renewal & commun. facilities	0.4	S/L Govt
Paperboard containers & boxes	2.8	Manufg.	Metal office furniture	0.2	Manufg.
Fabricated metal products, nec	2.7	Manufg.	S/L Govt. purch., health & hospitals	0.2	S/L Govt
Metal stampings, nec	2.7	Manufg.	S/L Govt. purch., highways	0.2	S/L Govt
Paints & allied products	2.5	Manufg.	S/L Govt. purch., other education & libraries	0.2	S/L Govt
Electric services (utilities)	1.7	Util.	S/L Govt. purch., sewerage	0.1	S/L Govt
Aluminum rolling & drawing	1.5	Manufg.	S/L Govt. purch., water	0.1	S/L Govt
Motor freight transportation & warehousing	1.5	Util.	S/L Govt. purch., water & air facilities	0.1	S/L Govt
Veneer & plywood	1.3	Manufg.			
Screw machine and related products	1.2	Manufg.			
Particleboard	1.1	Manufg.			
Petroleum refining	1.0	Manufg.			
Gas production & distribution (utilities)	1.0	Util.			
Maintenance of nonfarm buildings nec	0.9	Constr.			
Communications, except radio & TV	0.9	Util.			

Continued on next page.

INPUTS AND OUTPUTS FOR METAL OFFICE FURNITURE - Continued

Economic Sector or Industry Providing Inputs	%	Sector	Economic Sector or Industry Buying Outputs	%	Sector
Real estate	0.9	Fin/R.E.			
Ball & roller bearings	0.8	Manufg.			
Fabricated rubber products, nec	0.8	Manufg.			
Sawmills & planning mills, general	0.8	Manufg.			
Equipment rental & leasing services	0.8	Services			
Eating & drinking places	0.7	Trade			
Cyclic crudes and organics	0.6	Manufg.			
Wood products, nec	0.6	Manufg.			
Adhesives & sealants	0.5	Manufg.			
Railroads & related services	0.5	Util.			
Abrasive products	0.4	Manufg.			
Metal office furniture	0.4	Manufg.			
Detective & protective services	0.4	Services			
General industrial machinery, nec	0.3	Manufg.			
Miscellaneous fabricated wire products	0.3	Manufg.			
Plastics materials & resins	0.3	Manufg.			
Air transportation	0.3	Util.			
Credit agencies other than banks	0.3	Fin/R.E.			
Paper coating & glazing	0.2	Manufg.			
Insurance carriers	0.2	Fin/R.E.			
Royalties	0.2	Fin/R.E.			
Security & commodity brokers	0.2	Fin/R.E.			
Automotive rental & leasing, without drivers	0.2	Services			
Automotive repair shops & services	0.2	Services			
Computer & data processing services	0.2	Services			
Legal services	0.2	Services			
Management & consulting services & labs	0.2	Services			
U.S. Postal Service	0.2	Gov't			
Machinery, except electrical, nec	0.1	Manufg.			
Laundry, dry cleaning, shoe repair	0.1	Services			

Source: Benchmark Input-Output Accounts for the U.S. Economy, 1982, U.S. Department of Commerce, Washington, D.C., July 1991. Data, as reported in the source, are organized by the 1977 SIC structure in use in 1982 but have been matched, as closely as is possible, to the 1987 SIC structure used in this book.

OCCUPATIONS EMPLOYED BY SIC 252 - OFFICE AND MISCELLANEOUS FURNITURE AND FIXTURES

Occupation	% of Total 1994	Change to 2005	Occupation	% of Total 1994	Change to 2005
Assemblers, fabricators, & hand workers nec	21.5	6.5	Hand packers & packagers	1.6	-8.7
Blue collar worker supervisors	4.2	1.0	Welders & cutters	1.6	6.5
Cabinetmakers & bench carpenters	3.9	59.7	Inspectors, testers, & graders, precision	1.6	6.5
Upholsterers	2.8	10.1	Machine forming operators, metal & plastic	1.4	6.5
Welding machine setters, operators	2.8	-4.2	Head sawyers & sawing machine workers	1.3	-14.8
Sales & related workers nec	2.6	6.5	Secretaries, ex legal & medical	1.3	-3.1
Wood machinists	2.5	43.7	General office clerks	1.3	-9.2
General managers & top executives	2.2	1.0	Industrial truck & tractor operators	1.2	6.5
Furniture finishers	2.2	30.3	Industrial production managers	1.2	6.5
Coating, painting, & spraying machine workers	2.1	6.5	Drafters	1.2	-17.1
Machine tool cutting & forming etc. nec	2.0	6.5	Grinders & polishers, hand	1.1	6.5
Freight, stock, & material movers, hand	2.0	-14.8	Bookkeeping, accounting, & auditing clerks	1.1	-20.1
Woodworking machine workers	2.0	-57.4	Truck drivers light & heavy	1.1	9.8
Traffic, shipping, & receiving clerks	1.9	2.4			

Source: Industry-Occupation Matrix, Bureau of Labor Statistics. These data relate to one or more 3-digit SIC industry groups rather than to a single 4-digit SIC. The change reported for each occupation to the year 2005 is a percent of growth or decline as estimated by the Bureau of Labor Statistics. The abbreviation nec stands for 'not elsewhere classified'.

LOCATION BY STATE AND REGIONAL CONCENTRATION

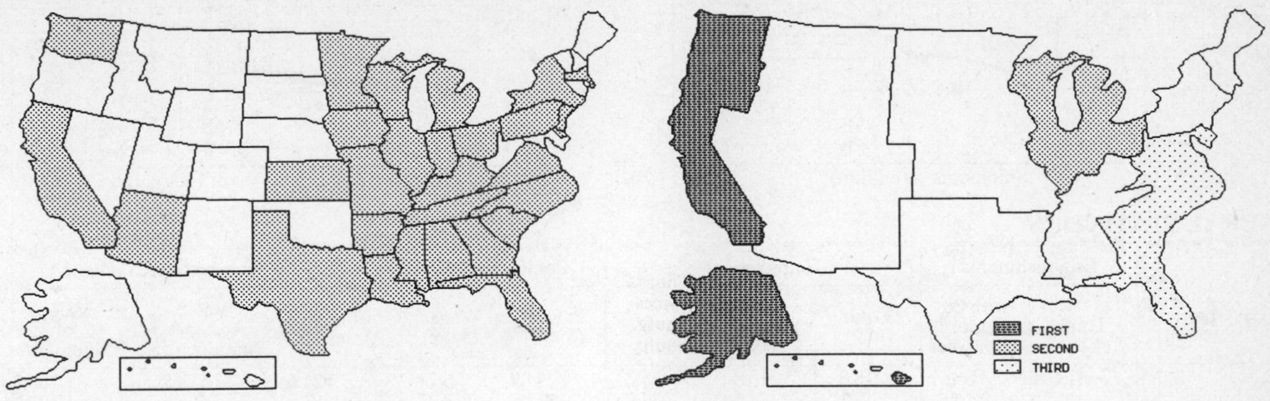

INDUSTRY DATA BY STATE

State	Establish-ments	Shipments Total ($ mil)	Shipments % of U.S.	Shipments Per Establ.	Employment Total Number	Employment % of U.S.	Employment Per Establ.	Employment Wages ($/hour)	Cost as % of Shipments	Investment per Employee ($)
Michigan	31	2,693.2	44.6	86.9	16,100	36.2	519	14.51	39.0	6,404
California	77	531.1	8.8	6.9	4,900	11.0	64	11.40	37.8	1,714
Pennsylvania	17	349.4	5.8	20.6	2,900	6.5	171	12.76	50.8	1,759
Tennessee	12	266.8	4.4	22.2	2,100	4.7	175	8.21	54.6	1,286
Georgia	9	220.4	3.6	24.5	1,200	2.7	133	10.29	51.5	-
North Carolina	22	181.4	3.0	8.2	2,100	4.7	95	7.62	46.8	2,571
Texas	17	165.4	2.7	9.7	1,600	3.6	94	7.90	47.5	1,625
Wisconsin	11	162.5	2.7	14.8	1,100	2.5	100	9.56	43.4	3,727
Ohio	12	150.8	2.5	12.6	1,300	2.9	108	11.88	37.0	2,077
Illinois	9	150.5	2.5	16.7	1,500	3.4	167	12.65	39.9	3,067
Mississippi	5	93.5	1.5	18.7	700	1.6	140	8.08	40.6	-
New York	33	87.9	1.5	2.7	1,100	2.5	33	8.29	38.5	1,182
Indiana	9	58.7	1.0	6.5	800	1.8	89	9.15	38.3	625
Florida	25	49.3	0.8	2.0	700	1.6	28	7.50	44.6	2,143
Minnesota	7	49.1	0.8	7.0	500	1.1	71	13.83	35.0	-
New Jersey	11	29.9	0.5	2.7	400	0.9	36	9.00	47.2	-
Washington	8	21.3	0.4	2.7	300	0.7	38	8.50	39.4	-
Kansas	5	12.5	0.2	2.5	100	0.2	20	10.00	37.6	-
Arizona	4	8.6	0.1	2.2	100	0.2	25	8.50	36.0	-
Iowa	7	(D)	-	-	1,750 *	3.9	250	-	-	-
Missouri	7	(D)	-	-	750 *	1.7	107	-	-	-
Alabama	6	(D)	-	-	1,750 *	3.9	292	-	-	-
Massachusetts	6	(D)	-	-	375 *	0.8	63	-	-	-
Arkansas	4	(D)	-	-	375 *	0.8	94	-	-	1,333
South Carolina	4	(D)	-	-	175 *	0.4	44	-	-	-
Kentucky	3	(D)	-	-	175 *	0.4	58	-	-	-
Virginia	3	(D)	-	-	375 *	0.8	125	-	-	-
Delaware	1	(D)	-	-	375 *	0.8	375	-	-	-
Louisiana	1	(D)	-	-	175 *	0.4	175	-	-	-

Source: 1992 *Economic Census*. The states are in descending order of shipments or establishments (if shipment data are missing for the majority). The symbol (D) appears when data are withheld to prevent disclosure of competitive information. States marked with (D) are sorted by number of establishments. A dash (-) indicates that the data element cannot be calculated; * indicates the midpoint of a range.

2531 - PUBLIC BUILDING & RELATED FURNITURE

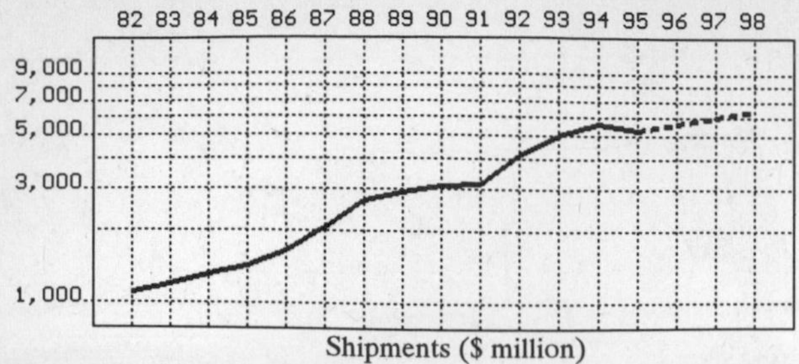

Shipments ($ million)

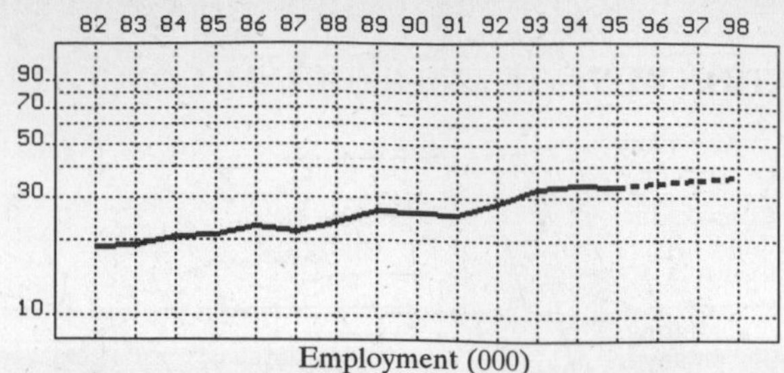

Employment (000)

GENERAL STATISTICS

Year	Com-panies	Establishments		Employment			Compensation		Production ($ million)			
		Total	with 20 or more employees	Total (000)	Production Workers (000)	Production Hours (Mil)	Payroll ($ mil)	Wages ($/hr)	Cost of Materials	Value Added by Manufacture	Value of Shipments	Capital Invest.
1982	393	413	181	18.8	13.8	26.2	294.9	6.71	521.6	578.8	1,102.8	24.8
1983				19.1	14.0	26.9	318.8	7.07	586.8	609.4	1,197.8	25.4
1984				20.7	15.4	30.5	350.1	7.16	640.5	683.9	1,317.0	42.3
1985				21.2	15.8	31.0	369.9	7.50	687.5	728.2	1,415.8	46.0
1986				22.9	17.4	33.0	399.7	7.80	831.6	827.7	1,654.8	42.1
1987	465	491	209	21.8	16.6	33.0	396.8	7.85	1,191.3	901.1	2,088.3	45.0
1988				23.5	17.9	34.8	457.4	8.20	1,622.2	1,037.4	2,660.8	40.7
1989		472	215	26.2	19.8	39.6	519.0	8.17	1,795.9	1,108.2	2,883.7	59.7
1990				26.0	20.1	42.6	543.9	8.31	1,979.0	1,147.1	3,112.4	46.6
1991				25.9	19.8	40.5	558.8	8.73	1,909.8	1,259.1	3,136.4	47.9
1992	473	516	223	28.9	21.4	44.5	677.9	9.32	2,529.4	1,607.1	4,135.2	69.0
1993				32.4	24.5	51.1	776.8	9.51	3,222.4	1,797.3	5,017.8	105.4
1994				33.9	25.7	52.8	839.6	10.03	3,766.5	1,905.0	5,640.6	108.6
1995				33.0P	25.1P	52.5P	802.1P	9.94P	3,523.6P	1,782.2P	5,276.9P	94.1P
1996				34.1P	26.0P	54.6P	845.2P	10.19P	3,767.5P	1,905.5P	5,642.1P	99.8P
1997				35.3P	27.0P	56.8P	888.3P	10.45P	4,011.4P	2,028.9P	6,007.3P	105.5P
1998				36.5P	27.9P	58.9P	931.4P	10.70P	4,255.3P	2,152.2P	6,372.6P	111.2P

Sources: 1982, 1987, 1992 *Economic Census*; *Annual Survey of Manufactures*, 83-86, 88-91, 93-94. Establishment counts for non-Census years are from *County Business Patterns*; establishment values for 83-84 are extrapolations. 'P's show projections by the editors. Industries reclassified in 87 will not have data for prior years.

INDICES OF CHANGE

Year	Com-panies	Establishments		Employment			Compensation		Production ($ million)			
		Total	with 20 or more employees	Total (000)	Production Workers (000)	Production Hours (Mil)	Payroll ($ mil)	Wages ($/hr)	Cost of Materials	Value Added by Manufacture	Value of Shipments	Capital Invest.
1982	83	80	81	65	64	59	44	72	21	36	27	36
1983				66	65	60	47	76	23	38	29	37
1984				72	72	69	52	77	25	43	32	61
1985				73	74	70	55	80	27	45	34	67
1986				79	81	74	59	84	33	52	40	61
1987	98	95	94	75	78	74	59	84	47	56	51	65
1988				81	84	78	67	88	64	65	64	59
1989		91	96	91	93	89	77	88	71	69	70	87
1990				90	94	96	80	89	78	71	75	68
1991				90	93	91	82	94	76	78	76	69
1992	100	100	100	100	100	100	100	100	100	100	100	100
1993				112	114	115	115	102	127	112	121	153
1994				117	120	119	124	108	149	119	136	157
1995				114P	117P	118P	118P	107P	139P	111P	128P	136P
1996				118P	122P	123P	125P	109P	149P	119P	136P	145P
1997				122P	126P	128P	131P	112P	159P	126P	145P	153P
1998				126P	130P	132P	137P	115P	168P	134P	154P	161P

Sources: Same as General Statistics. Values reflect change from the base year, 1992. Values above 100 mean greater than 92, values below 100 mean less than 92, and a value of 100 in the 82-91 or 93-98 period means same as 92. 'P's mark projections by the editors.

SELECTED RATIOS

For 1992	Avg. of All Manufact.	Analyzed Industry	Index
Employees per Establishment	46	56	123
Payroll per Establishment	1,332,320	1,313,760	99
Payroll per Employee	29,181	23,457	80
Production Workers per Establishment	31	41	132
Wages per Establishment	734,496	803,760	109
Wages per Production Worker	23,390	19,380	83
Hours per Production Worker	2,025	2,079	103
Wages per Hour	11.55	9.32	81
Value Added per Establishment	3,842,210	3,114,535	81
Value Added per Employee	84,153	55,609	66

For 1992	Avg. of All Manufact.	Analyzed Industry	Index
Value Added per Production Worker	122,353	75,098	61
Cost per Establishment	4,239,462	4,901,938	116
Cost per Employee	92,853	87,522	94
Cost per Production Worker	135,003	118,196	88
Shipments per Establishment	8,100,800	8,013,953	99
Shipments per Employee	177,425	143,087	81
Shipments per Production Worker	257,966	193,234	75
Investment per Establishment	278,244	133,721	48
Investment per Employee	6,094	2,388	39
Investment per Production Worker	8,861	3,224	36

Sources: Same as General Statistics. The 'Average of All Manufacturing' column represents the average of all manufacturing industries reported for the most recent complete year available. The Index shows the relationship between the Average and the Analyzed Industry. For example, 100 means that they are equal; 500 that the Analyzed Industry is five times the average; 50 means that the Analyzed Industry is half the national average. The abbreviation 'na' is used to show that data are 'not available'.

LEADING COMPANIES Number shown: **67** Total sales ($ mil): **14,386** Total employment (000): **115.9**

Company Name	Address				CEO Name	Phone	Co. Type	Sales ($ mil)	Empl. (000)
Johnson Controls Inc	PO Box 591	Milwaukee	WI	53201	James H Keyes	414-228-1200	P	6,870	54.8
Lear Seating Corp	21557 Telegraph Rd	Southfield	MI	48034	Kenneth L Way	810-746-1500	P	3,147	25.0
Johnson Controls	PO Box 8010	Plymouth	MI	48170	John Barth	313-454-5000	D	2,874	21.0
Vintec Co	PO Box 1258	Murfreesboro	TN	37133	Thomas W Bobo	615-890-5559	J	260	0.3
Virco Manufacturing Corp	15134 S Vermont	Los Angeles	CA	90247	Robert A Virtue	310-533-0474	P	206	3.0
Hill Rom Company Inc	1069 State Rte 46	Batesville	IN	47006	William M Kelley	812-934-7777	S	180	2.0
Weber Aircraft Inc	1300 E Valencia Dr	Fullerton	CA	92631	Michel LaBarre	714-449-3000	S	80*	0.8
Hussey Seating Company Inc	Dyer St	North Berwick	ME	03906	Philip W Hussey Jr	207-676-2271	R	65	0.4
Gerry Baby Products Co	1500 E 128th Av	Denver	CO	80241	Darlye Lovett	303-457-0926	S	47*	0.5
Simula Inc	401 W Baseline	Phoenix	AZ	85283	Donald Townsend	602-752-8919	P	41	0.5
Artco-Bell Corp	PO Box 608	Temple	TX	76503	Thomas W Oliver	817-778-1811	R	38	0.5
Greensteel	29 Laing Av	Dixonville	PA	15734	N Roy Anderson	412-254-4321	D	38	0.2
Bostrom Seating Inc	PO Box 566	Piedmont	AL	36272	Harrison R Horan	205-447-9051	R	35	0.3
Information Display Technology	29 Laing Av	Dixonville	PA	15734	N Roy Anderson	412-254-4321	P	32	0.5
Keiper Recaro Seating Inc	905 W Maple	Clawson	MI	48017	Hans Milobinski	313-288-6800	S	30	0.3
Smith System Manufacturing Co	PO Box 860415	Plano	TX	75086	Charles Risdall	713-328-1061	R	30	0.3
Seats Inc	PO Box 60	Reedsburg	WI	53959	EW Sauey	608-524-4316	R	28	0.3
Claridge Products&Equipment	PO Box 910	Harrison	AR	72602	Paul Clavey	501-743-2200	R	26	0.4
Baker Manufacturing Co	PO Box 4120	Pineville	LA	71361	William M Agee	318-640-8077	R	23	0.3
Sauder Manufacturing Company	600 Middle St	Archbold	OH	43502	V Miller	419-445-7670	D	22	0.3
Foldcraft Co	615 Centennial Dr	Kenyon	MN	55946	Chuck Mayhew	507-789-5111	R	20	0.3
Michigan Tube Swagers	1244 W Dean Rd	Temperance	MI	48182	PH Swy	313-847-3875	R	20	0.2
Counterpoint South	PO Box 128	Hudson	IN	46747	Tom James Sr	219-587-3231	S	16	<0.1
Library Bureau Inc	801 Park Av	Herkimer	NY	13350	Rudolph F Scialdo	315-866-1330	P	15	0.2
Carolina Business Furniture	PO Box 2127	High Point	NC	27261	G Davis Beaston	910-884-7375	D	15	0.2
Ghent Manufacturing Inc	PO Box 410	Lebanon	OH	45036	GL Leasure	513-932-3445	R	15	0.1
Buckstaff Company Inc	1127 S Main St	Oshkosh	WI	54901	JD Buckstaff	414-235-5890	R	13	0.2
American Desk Mfg Co	PO Box 1069	Taylor	TX	76574	Paul Kerr	512-352-6371	D	12	0.3
Coach and Car Equipment Corp	1951 Arthur Av	Elk Grove Vill	IL	60007	Chuck Covington	708-437-5760	R	12*	0.2
KR Industries Inc	1200 S 54th Av	Cicero	IL	60650	S Wolkoff	708-863-1200	R	12	0.2
Royal Seating Corp	PO Box 753	Cameron	TX	76520	David Petty	817-697-6421	R	12	0.3
Hi-Tech Seating Products Inc	8990 S Atlantic	South Gate	CA	90280	Ron D Belk	213-564-4481	R	10	0.2
French Baby Style Inc	1 Freedom Ct	Greer	SC	29650	Yves Nania	803-848-0569	R	9	<0.1
Worcester Manufacturing Inc	35 New St	Worcester	MA	01605	Charles Flanagan	508-753-2654	R	9	0.1
LL Sams Inc	PO Box 1430	Waco	TX	76703	David Petty	817-752-9751	S	9*	0.2
Knoedler Manufacturers Inc	904 E Kent St	Streator	IL	61364	Wilhelm Sturhan	815-673-2341	R	8	<0.1
Modern Contract Furniture Co	424 Main St	Gardner	MA	01440	Norman R Caouette	508-632-4700	R	8*	0.1
Allied Plastics Company Inc	PO Box 3125	Jacksonville	FL	32206	Gregory Berger	904-359-0386	R	7	0.1
Sturdisteel	PO Box 2655	Waco	TX	76702	Fred Schultz	817-857-3744	D	7*	<0.1
Taylor-Ramsey Dimensions	507 Northwest Av	Blackstone	VA	23824	Marty Cogar	804-292-7266	D	7*	<0.1
Tuohy Furniture Corp	42 St Albans Pl	Chatfield	MN	55923	Daniel Tuohy	507-867-4280	R	7	0.2
Caseworks Furniture Mfg	8350 E Old Vail Rd	Tucson	AZ	85747	Lester Weinman	602-884-8500	R	5	<0.1
Imperial Woodworks Inc	PO Box 7835	Waco	TX	76714	Jim Hilliard	817-756-5431	R	5	<0.1
Norse Furniture Co	1202-A Black Lake	Olympia	WA	98502	Lyle Morse	360-943-5090	R	5	<0.1
Othmar Klem Furniture Co	PO Box 125	St Anthony	IN	47575	Othmar Klem	812-326-2361	R	5	<0.1
Sams Manufacturing Company	PO Box 1430	Waco	TX	76703	Conrad Robison	817-752-9751	S	5	0.2
Simon Corp	PO Box 620188	Middleton	WI	53562	James S Billian	608-836-1911	R	5	0.1
Texwood Furniture	PO Box 6280	Austin	TX	78762	Carolyn Gallagher	512-385-3323	R	5	<0.1
Southside Manufacturing Corp	PO Box 207	Danville	VA	24541	S B Houghton III	804-836-6347	R	4	<0.1
Bangor Cork Company Inc	William St & D St	Pen Argyl	PA	18072	Frank S Brumbaugh	610-863-9041	R	4	<0.1
Monroe Co	316 N Walnut St	Colfax	IA	50054	Barbara A Monroe	515-674-3511	R	4	<0.1
Am Fab	2525 Miller Rd	Kalamazoo	MI	49001	Michael Sinkgraven	616-385-2938	D	3	<0.1
Helikon Furniture Company Inc	607 Norwich Av	Taftville	CT	06380	Jack Bernhardt	203-886-2301	R	3*	<0.1
Richardson Seating Corp	2545 W Arthington	Chicago	IL	60612	E Lichtenstein	312-829-4040	R	3	<0.1
Flight Equip & Eng Corp	PO Box 522173	Miami	FL	33152	LC Ke	305-871-3590	R	2	<0.1
Lindsey Manufacturing Company	PO Box 429	Lawrenceburg	TN	38464	Edward M Lindsey	615-762-2249	R	2	<0.1
Med Service Inc	PO Box 1296	Batesville	MS	38606	Gary W Cox	601-563-8130	R	2	<0.1
Worcester Manufacturing Inc	508 Boston Tpk	Shrewsbury	MA	01545	Ed Swider	508-842-4190	D	2	<0.1
Alden Supply & Mfg Co	3030 Main St	Hartford	CT	06120	Barry Goldenthal	203-522-1189	R	1	<0.1
Best-Rite	201 N Crockett	Cameron	TX	76520	Lorraine Moore	817-697-4953	D	1	<0.1
Lor-Rog Industries Inc	PO Box 388	Garnett	KS	66032	Roger Cranford	913-448-3141	R	1	<0.1
A-1 Visual Systems	2856 Vail Av	City of Com	CA	90040	Albert Berookhim	213-728-2680	R	1	<0.1
National Church Furnishings Inc	2600 Commercial	Centralia	WA	98531	W Widholm	206-736-9323	R	1*	<0.1
Custom Aircraft Interiors Inc	3701 Industry Av	Lakewood	CA	90712	Patricia Erwin	310-426-5098	R	1	<0.1
Walter Jacobi and Sons Inc	PO Box 471	Belmont	CA	94002	Leo Jacoby	415-593-6815	R	1	<0.1
Millard Heath Enterprises Inc	PO Box 1983	Denton	TX	76202	Millard Heath	817-383-1688	R	1	<0.1
Concept Seating Inc	W 227N6193 Sussex	Sussex	WI	53089	John Vento	414-246-0900	R	0	<0.1

Source: *Ward's Business Directory of U.S. Private and Public Companies*, Volumes 1 and 2, 1996. The company type code used is as follows: P - Public, R - Private, S - Subsidiary, D - Division, J - Joint Venture, A - Affiliate, G - Group. Sales are in millions of dollars, employees are in thousands. An asterisk (*) indicates an estimated sales volume. The symbol < stands for 'less than'. Company names and addresses are truncated, in some cases, to fit into the available space.

MATERIALS CONSUMED

Material	Quantity	Delivered Cost ($ million)
Materials, ingredients, containers, and supplies	(X)	2,393.7
Metal stampings	(X)	178.9
All other fabricated metal products (except castings and forgings)	(X)	199.3
Forgings	(X)	2.6
Castings (rough and semifinished)	(X)	3.9
Steel sheet and strip, including tin plate	(X)	71.1
All other steel shapes and forms (except castings, forgings, and fabricated metal products)	(X)	131.4
Aluminum and aluminum-base alloy sheet, plate, foil, and welded tubing	(X)	35.0
All other aluminum and aluminum-base alloy shapes and forms	(X)	21.0
Other nonferrous shapes and forms (except castings, forgings, and fabricated metal products)	(X)	0.1
Hardwood lumber, rough and dressed	(X)	30.9
Softwood lumber, rough and dressed	(X)	3.8
Hardwood dimension and parts, including wood furniture frames	(X)	129.1
Hardwood veneer	(X)	7.0
Hardwood plywood	(X)	16.7
Softwood plywood	(X)	5.2
Particleboard (wood)	(X)	16.3
Medium density fiberboard (MDF)	(X)	6.3
Hardboard (wood fiberboard)	(X)	4.3
Plastics laminated sheets	(X)	24.1
Plastics furniture parts and components	(X)	122.2
Formed and slab stock for pillows, cushions, seating, etc. (urethane)	(X)	147.2
Coated or laminated fabrics, including vinyl coated	(X)	498.8
Uncoated broadwoven fabrics for upholstery	(X)	148.5
Flat glass (plate, float, and sheet)	(X)	1.2
Adhesives and sealants	(X)	4.7
Paints, varnishes, lacquers, stains, shellacs, japans, enamels, and allied products	(X)	11.4
Furniture and builders' hardware	(X)	89.8
Paperboard containers, boxes, and corrugated paperboard	(X)	23.0
All other materials and components, parts, containers, and supplies	(X)	267.7
Materials, ingredients, containers, and supplies, nsk	(X)	192.0

Source: 1992 *Economic Census*. Explanation of symbols used: (D): Withheld to avoid disclosure of competitive data; na: Not available; (S): Withheld because statistical norms were not met; (X): Not applicable; (Z): Less than half the unit shown; nec: Not elsewhere classified; nsk: Not specified by kind; - : zero; * : 10-19 percent estimated; ** : 20-29 percent estimated.

PRODUCT SHARE DETAILS

Product or Product Class	% Share
Public building and related furniture	100.00
School furniture, except stone and concrete (excluding library furniture)	11.77
School single-pupil units, excluding library	24.09
School chairs, all-purpose (nonfolding), excluding library	20.61
School storage cabinets, excluding library	15.70
Other school furniture, designed specifically for use in schools (including teachers' desks, study carrels, etc.), except stone and concrete, excluding library furniture	36.28
School furniture, except stone and concrete (excluding library furniture), nsk	3.29
Public building and related furniture, except school and restaurant furniture	83.63
Seats for public conveyances (except aircraft), including automobiles, trucks, buses, and van conversion seats	69.12
Seats for aircraft	7.83
Church pews	1.01
Church furniture other than pews (pulpits, altars, lecterns, etc.)	0.55
Folding tables, including folding banquet tables, except school, restaurant, household, office, or library	2.04
Fixed chairs and seats, including theater, auditorium, and institutional (except school, restaurant, household, office, or library)	1.57
Portable folding chairs, single or ganged, including theater, auditorium, and institutional (except school, restaurant, household, office, or library)	1.11
Stacking chairs and seats, including theater, auditorium, and institutional (except school, restaurant, household, office, or library)	2.31
Other chairs and seats, including freestanding, theater, auditorium, and institutional (except school, restaurant, household, office, or library)	1.53
Stadium and bleacher seating, including grandstands	3.81
Library furniture, all types (including chairs, charging desks, study carrels, reading tables, etc.)	0.83
Other public building furniture, nec	2.40
Public building and related furniture, except school and restaurant furniture, nsk	5.90
Public building and related furniture, nsk	4.60

Source: 1992 *Economic Census*. The values shown are percent of total shipments in an industry. Values of indented subcategories are summed in the main heading. The symbol (D) appears when data are withheld to prevent disclosure of competitive information. The abbreviation nsk stands for 'not specified by kind' and nec for 'not elsewhere classified'.

INPUTS AND OUTPUTS FOR PUBLIC BUILDING FURNITURE

Economic Sector or Industry Providing Inputs	%	Sector	Economic Sector or Industry Buying Outputs	%	Sector
Imports	27.3	Foreign	Gross private fixed investment	40.1	Cap Inv
Public building furniture	8.3	Manufg.	S/L Govt. purch., elem. & secondary education	11.5	S/L Govt
Blast furnaces & steel mills	7.4	Manufg.	Aircraft	11.1	Manufg.
Wholesale trade	6.6	Trade	Motor vehicles & car bodies	7.9	Manufg.
Miscellaneous plastics products	3.7	Manufg.	Public building furniture	5.9	Manufg.
Accounting, auditing & bookkeeping	3.1	Services	Aircraft & missile equipment, nec	5.4	Manufg.
Aluminum rolling & drawing	2.8	Manufg.	S/L Govt. purch., higher education	3.6	S/L Govt
Coated fabrics, not rubberized	2.6	Manufg.	S/L Govt. purch., natural resource & recreation.	2.8	S/L Govt
Sawmills & planning mills, general	2.5	Manufg.	Industrial trucks & tractors	2.3	Manufg.
Business services nec	2.2	Services	Construction of educational buildings	1.8	Constr.
U.S. Postal Service	2.2	Gov't	Motor homes (made on purchased chassis)	1.4	Manufg.
Hardware, nec	2.0	Manufg.	S/L Govt. purch., other education & libraries	1.3	S/L Govt
Veneer & plywood	1.7	Manufg.	Nonbuilding facilities nec	1.1	Constr.
Metal stampings, nec	1.6	Manufg.	Amusement & recreation building construction	0.7	Constr.
Banking	1.6	Fin/R.E.	Construction of nonfarm buildings nec	0.6	Constr.
Advertising	1.6	Services	Maintenance of nonbuilding facilities nec	0.5	Constr.
Particleboard	1.5	Manufg.	Truck trailers	0.4	Manufg.
Padding & upholstery filling	1.4	Manufg.	Truck & bus bodies	0.3	Manufg.
Screw machine and related products	1.3	Manufg.	Federal Government purchases, national defense	0.3	Fed Govt
Electric services (utilities)	1.3	Util.	S/L Govt. purch., other general government	0.3	S/L Govt
Paperboard containers & boxes	1.2	Manufg.	Federal Government purchases, nondefense	0.2	Fed Govt
Petroleum refining	1.1	Manufg.	S/L Govt. purch., correction	0.2	S/L Govt
Wood products, nec	1.1	Manufg.	Maintenance of farm service facilities	0.1	Constr.
Motor freight transportation & warehousing	1.1	Util.	S/L Govt. purch., police	0.1	S/L Govt
Maintenance of nonfarm buildings nec	1.0	Constr.			
Eating & drinking places	0.9	Trade			
Paints & allied products	0.8	Manufg.			
Communications, except radio & TV	0.6	Util.			
Real estate	0.6	Fin/R.E.			
Abrasive products	0.5	Manufg.			
Air transportation	0.5	Util.			
Gas production & distribution (utilities)	0.5	Util.			
State & local government enterprises, nec	0.5	Gov't			
Adhesives & sealants	0.4	Manufg.			
Copper rolling & drawing	0.4	Manufg.			
Fabricated metal products, nec	0.4	Manufg.			
Miscellaneous fabricated wire products	0.4	Manufg.			
Railroads & related services	0.4	Util.			
Business/professional associations	0.4	Services			
Automotive & apparel trimmings	0.3	Manufg.			
Equipment rental & leasing services	0.3	Services			
Management & consulting services & labs	0.3	Services			
Machinery, except electrical, nec	0.2	Manufg.			
Steel wire & related products	0.2	Manufg.			
Security & commodity brokers	0.2	Fin/R.E.			
Automotive rental & leasing, without drivers	0.2	Services			
Automotive repair shops & services	0.2	Services			
Legal services	0.2	Services			
Cutstone & stone products	0.1	Manufg.			
Lubricating oils & greases	0.1	Manufg.			
Manifold business forms	0.1	Manufg.			
Paper coating & glazing	0.1	Manufg.			
Special dies & tools & machine tool accessories	0.1	Manufg.			
Thread mills	0.1	Manufg.			
Insurance carriers	0.1	Fin/R.E.			
Computer & data processing services	0.1	Services			
Laundry, dry cleaning, shoe repair	0.1	Services			

Source: Benchmark Input-Output Accounts for the U.S. Economy, 1982, U.S. Department of Commerce, Washington, D.C., July 1991. Data, as reported in the source, are organized by the 1977 SIC structure in use in 1982 but have been matched, as closely as is possible, to the 1987 SIC structure used in this book.

OCCUPATIONS EMPLOYED BY SIC 253 - OFFICE AND MISCELLANEOUS FURNITURE AND FIXTURES

Occupation	% of Total 1994	Change to 2005	Occupation	% of Total 1994	Change to 2005
Assemblers, fabricators, & hand workers nec	21.5	6.5	Hand packers & packagers	1.6	-8.7
Blue collar worker supervisors	4.2	1.0	Welders & cutters	1.6	6.5
Cabinetmakers & bench carpenters	3.9	59.7	Inspectors, testers, & graders, precision	1.6	6.5
Upholsterers	2.8	10.1	Machine forming operators, metal & plastic	1.4	6.5
Welding machine setters, operators	2.8	-4.2	Head sawyers & sawing machine workers	1.3	-14.8
Sales & related workers nec	2.6	6.5	Secretaries, ex legal & medical	1.3	-3.1
Wood machinists	2.5	43.7	General office clerks	1.3	-9.2
General managers & top executives	2.2	1.0	Industrial truck & tractor operators	1.2	6.5
Furniture finishers	2.2	30.3	Industrial production managers	1.2	6.5
Coating, painting, & spraying machine workers	2.1	6.5	Drafters	1.2	-17.1
Machine tool cutting & forming etc. nec	2.0	6.5	Grinders & polishers, hand	1.1	6.5
Freight, stock, & material movers, hand	2.0	-14.8	Bookkeeping, accounting, & auditing clerks	1.1	-20.1
Woodworking machine workers	2.0	-57.4	Truck drivers light & heavy	1.1	9.8
Traffic, shipping, & receiving clerks	1.9	2.4			

Source: *Industry-Occupation Matrix*, Bureau of Labor Statistics. These data relate to one or more 3-digit SIC industry groups rather than to a single 4-digit SIC. The change reported for each occupation to the year 2005 is a percent of growth or decline as estimated by the Bureau of Labor Statistics. The abbreviation nec stands for 'not elsewhere classified'.

LOCATION BY STATE AND REGIONAL CONCENTRATION

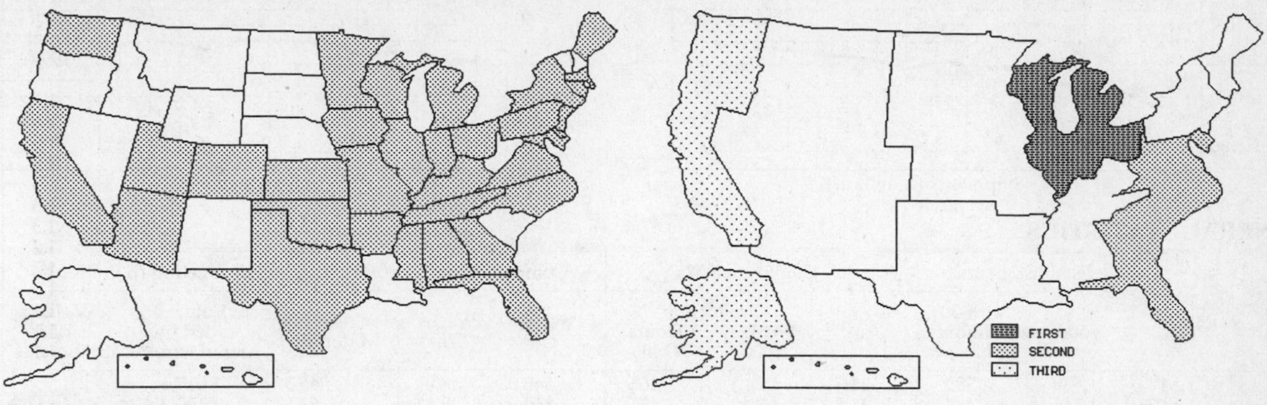

INDUSTRY DATA BY STATE

State	Establish-ments	Shipments			Employment				Cost as % of Shipments	Investment per Employee ($)
		Total ($ mil)	% of U.S.	Per Establ.	Total Number	% of U.S.	Per Establ.	Wages ($/hour)		
Michigan	35	785.4	19.0	22.4	3,300	11.4	94	11.73	67.7	1,727
Tennessee	20	297.3	7.2	14.9	1,800	6.2	90	7.70	72.4	-
Wisconsin	20	285.4	6.9	14.3	2,200	7.6	110	10.09	56.4	2,273
Indiana	41	270.4	6.5	6.6	2,700	9.3	66	8.57	58.4	-
Texas	43	269.1	6.5	6.3	3,000	10.4	70	8.04	50.5	1,600
California	53	256.5	6.2	4.8	2,200	7.6	42	8.56	54.7	773
Arkansas	16	223.9	5.4	14.0	2,200	7.6	138	12.91	48.1	-
Ohio	24	212.6	5.1	8.9	1,000	3.5	42	7.63	56.1	-
Illinois	21	174.5	4.2	8.3	900	3.1	43	10.08	77.6	1,444
North Carolina	22	108.3	2.6	4.9	1,200	4.2	55	8.25	49.0	2,333
Alabama	15	73.1	1.8	4.9	700	2.4	47	7.67	52.4	1,000
Pennsylvania	17	53.3	1.3	3.1	800	2.8	47	7.83	64.5	1,375
New York	14	45.6	1.1	3.3	200	0.7	14	11.67	66.9	-
Massachusetts	12	37.3	0.9	3.1	400	1.4	33	8.17	48.3	1,250
Iowa	7	34.7	0.8	5.0	300	1.0	43	12.25	54.2	-
Florida	23	20.5	0.5	0.9	200	0.7	9	7.67	45.4	500
Georgia	10	19.7	0.5	2.0	200	0.7	20	7.00	57.4	-
Arizona	7	19.2	0.5	2.7	300	1.0	43	9.00	45.3	-
New Jersey	8	14.6	0.4	1.8	100	0.3	13	10.50	52.7	3,000
Virginia	8	12.7	0.3	1.6	300	1.0	38	7.40	43.3	1,000
Utah	5	11.9	0.3	2.4	100	0.3	20	7.00	45.4	-
Kansas	6	8.1	0.2	1.4	100	0.3	17	10.00	43.2	-
Washington	13	(D)	-	-	375 *	1.3	29	-	-	-
Mississippi	9	(D)	-	-	750 *	2.6	83	-	-	-
Kentucky	7	(D)	-	-	750 *	2.6	107	-	-	-
Minnesota	7	(D)	-	-	375 *	1.3	54	-	-	-
Missouri	7	(D)	-	-	175 *	0.6	25	-	-	-
Colorado	5	(D)	-	-	375 *	1.3	75	-	-	-
Connecticut	5	(D)	-	-	750 *	2.6	150	-	-	-
Maine	3	(D)	-	-	375 *	1.3	125	-	-	-
Maryland	3	(D)	-	-	375 *	1.3	125	-	-	-
Oklahoma	2	(D)	-	-	175 *	0.6	88	-	-	-
Delaware	1	(D)	-	-	175 *	0.6	175	-	-	-

Source: 1992 *Economic Census*. The states are in descending order of shipments or establishments (if shipment data are missing for the majority). The symbol (D) appears when data are withheld to prevent disclosure of competitive information. States marked with (D) are sorted by number of establishments. A dash (-) indicates that the data element cannot be calculated; * indicates the midpoint of a range.

2541 - WOOD PARTITIONS AND FIXTURES

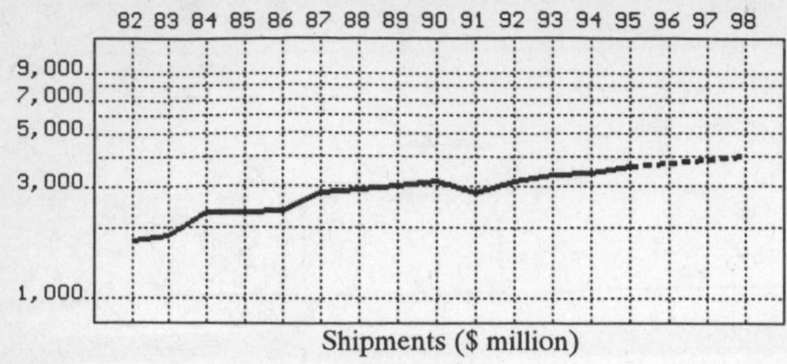

Shipments ($ million)

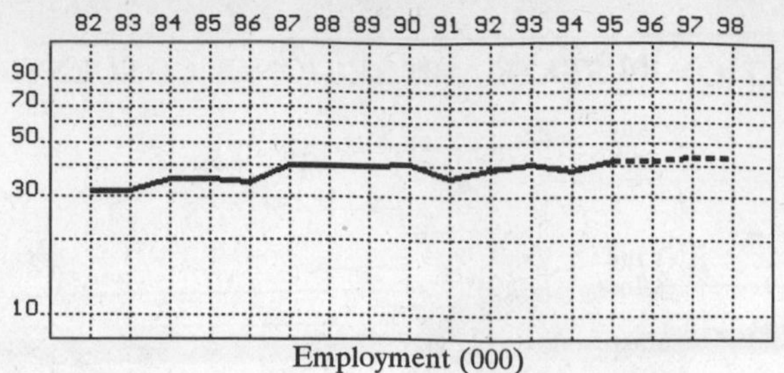

Employment (000)

GENERAL STATISTICS

Year	Companies	Establishments		Employment			Compensation		Production ($ million)			
		Total	with 20 or more employees	Total (000)	Production Workers (000)	Production Hours (Mil)	Payroll ($ mil)	Wages ($/hr)	Cost of Materials	Value Added by Manufacture	Value of Shipments	Capital Invest.
1982	1,547	1,580	389	31.7	24.3	46.9	543.0	8.09	746.3	1,017.1	1,766.7	39.2
1983		1,545	414	31.5	24.2	43.7	560.9	8.81	753.5	1,100.3	1,851.2	24.7
1984		1,510	439	35.0	26.7	51.1	687.9	9.22	998.2	1,304.0	2,288.4	42.4
1985		1,476	465	35.6	27.3	52.8	703.0	9.15	988.6	1,325.8	2,315.3	62.9
1986		1,491	474	34.0	26.3	51.9	721.0	9.40	993.1	1,349.3	2,337.9	75.7
1987	1,832	1,866	557	40.5	30.3	60.9	861.0	9.30	1,211.6	1,608.9	2,814.9	65.7
1988		1,779	557	40.3	30.0	62.6	918.3	9.70	1,272.2	1,623.8	2,891.5	109.5
1989		1,671	545	40.6	30.2	58.8	916.5	9.97	1,339.7	1,668.6	2,978.3	75.5
1990		1,673	549	41.0	29.6	58.7	952.5	10.14	1,360.2	1,788.5	3,147.2	81.5
1991		1,686	507	35.9	26.8	52.1	841.8	10.06	1,241.1	1,527.0	2,804.3	61.8
1992	1,905	1,936	523	39.4	28.5	58.5	950.3	9.97	1,369.6	1,747.4	3,132.7	48.5
1993		1,877	531	40.8	29.5	60.7	1,005.7	10.26	1,481.6	1,904.9	3,375.4	71.6
1994		1,889P	579P	38.6	28.3	59.3	999.9	10.47	1,557.8	1,895.7	3,432.7	70.8
1995		1,922P	592P	41.9P	30.3P	62.9P	1,087.4P	10.71P	1,649.7P	2,007.6P	3,635.2P	81.8P
1996		1,955P	604P	42.6P	30.6P	64.0P	1,125.6P	10.87P	1,710.2P	2,081.1P	3,768.4P	84.3P
1997		1,988P	617P	43.3P	30.9P	65.0P	1,163.8P	11.03P	1,770.6P	2,154.7P	3,901.6P	86.9P
1998		2,021P	630P	43.9P	31.3P	66.1P	1,202.0P	11.20P	1,831.1P	2,228.2P	4,034.9P	89.5P

Sources: 1982, 1987, 1992 *Economic Census*; *Annual Survey of Manufactures*, 83-86, 88-91, 93-94. Establishment counts for non-Census years are from *County Business Patterns*; establishment values for 83-84 are extrapolations. 'P's show projections by the editors. Industries reclassified in 87 will not have data for prior years.

INDICES OF CHANGE

Year	Companies	Establishments		Employment			Compensation		Production ($ million)			
		Total	with 20 or more employees	Total (000)	Production Workers (000)	Production Hours (Mil)	Payroll ($ mil)	Wages ($/hr)	Cost of Materials	Value Added by Manufacture	Value of Shipments	Capital Invest.
1982	81	82	74	80	85	80	57	81	54	58	56	81
1983		80	79	80	85	75	59	88	55	63	59	51
1984		78	84	89	94	87	72	92	73	75	73	87
1985		76	89	90	96	90	74	92	72	76	74	130
1986		77	91	86	92	89	76	94	73	77	75	156
1987	96	96	107	103	106	104	91	93	88	92	90	135
1988		92	107	102	105	107	97	97	93	93	92	226
1989		86	104	103	106	101	96	100	98	95	95	156
1990		86	105	104	104	100	100	102	99	102	100	168
1991		87	97	91	94	89	89	101	91	87	90	127
1992	100	100	100	100	100	100	100	100	100	100	100	100
1993		97	102	104	104	104	106	103	108	109	108	148
1994		98P	111P	98	99	101	105	105	114	108	110	146
1995		99P	113P	106P	106P	107P	114P	107P	120P	115P	116P	169P
1996		101P	116P	108P	107P	109P	118P	109P	125P	119P	120P	174P
1997		103P	118P	110P	109P	111P	122P	111P	129P	123P	125P	179P
1998		104P	120P	111P	110P	113P	126P	112P	134P	128P	129P	184P

Sources: Same as General Statistics. Values reflect change from the base year, 1992. Values above 100 mean greater than 92, values below 100 mean less than 92, and a value of 100 in the 82-91 or 93-98 period means same as 92. 'P's mark projections by the editors.

SELECTED RATIOS

For 1994	Avg. of All Manufact.	Analyzed Industry	Index	For 1994	Avg. of All Manufact.	Analyzed Industry	Index
Employees per Establishment	49	20	42	Value Added per Production Worker	134,084	66,986	50
Payroll per Establishment	1,500,273	529,306	35	Cost per Establishment	5,045,178	824,636	16
Payroll per Employee	30,620	25,904	85	Cost per Employee	102,970	40,358	39
Production Workers per Establishment	34	15	44	Cost per Production Worker	146,988	55,046	37
Wages per Establishment	853,319	328,664	39	Shipments per Establishment	9,576,895	1,817,132	19
Wages per Production Worker	24,861	21,939	88	Shipments per Employee	195,460	88,930	45
Hours per Production Worker	2,056	2,095	102	Shipments per Production Worker	279,017	121,297	43
Wages per Hour	12.09	10.47	87	Investment per Establishment	321,011	37,479	12
Value Added per Establishment	4,602,255	1,003,507	22	Investment per Employee	6,552	1,834	28
Value Added per Employee	93,930	49,111	52	Investment per Production Worker	9,352	2,502	27

Sources: Same as General Statistics. The 'Average of All Manufacturing' column represents the average of all manufacturing industries reported for the most recent complete year available. The Index shows the relationship between the Average and the Analyzed Industry. For example, 100 means that they are equal; 500 that the Analyzed Industry is five times the average; 50 means that the Analyzed Industry is half the national average. The abbreviation 'na' is used to show that data are 'not available'.

LEADING COMPANIES Number shown: **72** Total sales ($ mil): **904** Total employment (000): **9.7**

Company Name	Address				CEO Name	Phone	Co. Type	Sales ($ mil)	Empl. (000)
Lozier Corp	6336 Pershing Dr	Omaha	NE	68110	Allan Lozier	402-457-8000	R	190•	1.9
MII Inc	2100 W 5th St	Lincoln	IL	62656	William J Hunt	217-735-1241	R	60	0.5
Harbor Industries Inc	14130 172nd St	Grand Haven	MI	49417	T Parker	616-842-5330	R	48	0.4
Stevens Industries Inc	704 W Main St	Teutopolis	IL	62467	CA Stevens	217-857-6411	R	42	0.4
Dorfile Storage	4533 Old Lamar	Memphis	TN	38118	Don Bergman	901-365-0479	S	35•	0.6
Store Kraft Manufacturing Co	PO Box 807	Beatrice	NE	68310	Jim Evans	402-223-2348	R	33	0.6
Hufcor Inc	2101 Kennedy Rd	Janesville	WI	53545	J Michael Borden	608-756-1241	R	27•	0.3
Huck Fixture Co	1100 N 28th St	Quincy	IL	62301	Helmut H Weid	217-222-0713	S	23	0.3
R Reynolds Corp	PO Box 1174	Lynnwood	WA	98046	Paul Abodeely	206-775-2551	R	22	0.1
Lundia	600 Capitol Way	Jacksonville	IL	62650	Gary Frye	217-243-8585	D	20	0.1
Abrams Fixture Corp	PO Box 1969	Atlanta	GA	30301	Steven Curvino	404-681-1820	S	18	0.3
Amertec-Granada Inc	7007 N Waterway	Miami	FL	33155	C Frank	305-266-6200	R	15•	0.2
Modar Inc	1394 E Empire Av	Benton Harbor	MI	49022	Gary Cichon	616-925-0671	S	14	<0.1
Standard Cabinet Works Inc	1800 E Washington	Los Angeles	CA	90021	Don Esters	213-749-2111	R	14	0.2
Carts of Colorado Inc	PO Box 16249	Denver	CO	80216	Stanley Gallery	303-288-1000	R	13	0.1
Contempo Design Inc	1800 Industrial Dr	Libertyville	IL	60048	Rob Shaw	708-549-6600	S	12	0.1
Modern Woodcrafts Inc	PO Box 464	Farmington	CT	06034	Donald C Ramsey	203-677-7371	R	12	0.2
Multiplex Display Fixtures	1555 Williams	Fenton	MO	63026	Frank G Grelle	314-343-5700	R	12	<0.1
Camden Industries Company Inc	108 Franklin St	Manchester	NH	03101	Ralph E Still	603-623-8833	R	11	0.1
CDS Mestel Construction Corp	124 Forrest St	Brooklyn	NY	11206	Leonard Hoffman	718-497-2380	R	11	<0.1
Greenwood Fixture	PO Box 360	Greenwood	AR	72936	Jim Evans	501-996-4166	D	11	0.2
Bruewer Woodwork Mfg Co	10000 Cilley Rd	Cleves	OH	45002	August B Bruewer	513-353-3505	R	10	<0.1
Emco Industries Inc	10850 Lakeview Av	Lenexa	KS	66219	Don Alexander	913-492-7414	R	10•	0.1
Miller Manufacturing Company	PO Box 1356	Richmond	VA	23211	David Reynolds	804-232-4551	R	10•	0.1
National Partitions and Interiors	PO Box 4368	Hialeah	FL	33014	Frank D'Andrea	305-822-3721	R	10	0.1
Stanly Fixtures Company Inc	PO Box 616	Norwood	NC	28128	J Almond	704-474-3184	R	10	0.2
West Coast Industries Inc	3150 18th St	San Francisco	CA	94110	Harry Liss	415-621-6656	R	10•	0.1
Environments Inc	5700 Baker Rd	Minnetonka	MN	55345	Roger Wothe	612-933-9981	R	9	<0.1
Dublin Management	7 Campus Dr	Burlington	NJ	08016	John J McDonald	609-387-1600	R	9	0.1
Johnston's Trading Post Inc	11 N County Rd 101	Woodland	CA	95776	Jim Johnston	916-661-6152	R	9	0.1
Modular Casework Systems Inc	377 Kansas St	Redlands	CA	92373	Glenn H Engstrom	909-793-2706	R	9	<0.1
Zell Brothers Inc	PO Box 327	Red Lion	PA	17356	Martin Zell	717-244-7661	R	9	0.2
Bankcrafters Inc	12 E Oregon Av	Philadelphia	PA	19148	D S Bernheim Jr	215-467-3700	R	9	<0.1
Savoy Manufacturing	200 Holdworth Dr	Kerrville	TX	78028	Richard Kibel	210-896-6464	D	8	<0.1
Wind Mill Woodworking Inc	200 Balsom Rd	Sheboygan Fls	WI	53085	JB Hogfeldt	414-467-2402	R	8	<0.1
Woodworkers of Denver Inc	1475 S Acoma St	Denver	CO	80223	John Rilko	303-777-7656	R	8	<0.1
Hallmark Marketing Inc	PO Box 511	Center	TX	75935	Dave Millen	409-598-5645	S	8	0.1
American Woodcraft Inc	PO Box 38	Union City	MI	49094	Charles Cady	517-741-3723	R	7	0.1
Millrock Inc	PO Box 974	Sanford	ME	04073	Martin Liebmann	207-324-0041	R	6	0.1
Woodland Products Company	1480 E Grand Av	Pomona	CA	91766	FD Robertson	909-622-3456	R	6	<0.1
Art-Phyl Creations	16250 NW 48th Av	Miami	FL	33014	A Hochman	305-624-2333	R	5	0.1
Ferrante Manufacturing Co	6626 Gratiot Av	Detroit	MI	48207	Sante Ferrante	313-571-1111	R	5	<0.1
I Ginsberg and Sons Inc	98 Condor St	East Boston	MA	02128	Steven Ginsberg	617-567-9525	R	5•	<0.1
Fixtures International Inc	PO Box 7774	Houston	TX	77270	David Danburg	713-869-3228	R	5	<0.1
Suba Manufacturing Inc	921 Bayshore Rd	Benicia	CA	94510	J Bell	707-745-0358	R	5	<0.1
Display Fixtures Inc	PO Box 7245	Charlotte	NC	28241	JC Blakeney	704-588-0880	R	4	0.1
Jamestown Laminating Co	PO Box 1336	Jamestown	NY	14702	WH Lindquist	716-665-3224	D	4	<0.1
Jensen Cabinet Inc	PO Box 10599	Fort Wayne	IN	46803	Dennis Jensen	219-456-2131	R	4•	<0.1
Kwik Wall Co	PO Box 3267	Springfield	IL	62708	Ray Neisewander	217-522-5553	R	4	<0.1
Michigan Maple Block Company	PO Box 245	Petoskey	MI	49770	John J Dau	616-347-4170	S	4•	<0.1
Modular Systems Inc	PO Box 399	Fruitport	MI	49415	Pat Chilton	616-865-3167	R	4	<0.1
Newood Display Fixture Mfg Co	PO Box 21808	Eugene	OR	97402	Gerry Moshofsky	503-688-0907	R	4	<0.1
Showbest Fixture Corp	PO Box 25336	Richmond	VA	23260	James A Schubert	804-643-3600	R	4	<0.1
Lloyd Gordon Manufacturing	5225 Central Av	Richmond	CA	94804	John Lancaster Sr	510-526-4414	R	4	<0.1
Exhibit Systems Inc	1367 S 700 W	Salt Lake City	UT	84104	Randy Pridgen	801-978-9000	R	3	<0.1
Leo Prager Inc	138 W 25th St	New York	NY	10001	Leo Prager	212-243-4113	R	3•	<0.1
RC Smith Co	801 E 79th St	Minneapolis	MN	55420	Richard C Smith	612-854-0711	R	3	<0.1
Santa Cruz Industries Inc	411 Swift St	Santa Cruz	CA	95060	Thomas E Eklof	408-423-9211	R	3•	<0.1
WMC Corp	12300 Montague St	Pacoima	CA	91331	James D Olsen	818-899-0217	R	3•	<0.1
Zephyr Systems Inc	PO Box 5290	Riverside	CA	92517	JC Moore	909-274-0707	R	3	<0.1
Brewster Corp	PO Box B	Old Saybrook	CT	06475	Leslie C Weinstein	203-388-4441	R	2	<0.1
Decimet Sales Inc	PO Box 173	Rogers	MN	55374	Jack W Hines	612-428-4321	R	2	<0.1
Farmington Displays Inc	PO Box 6868	Hartford	CT	06106	Paul DiTommaso Sr	203-676-2222	R	2•	<0.1
Guilford Corp	901 9th St S	Rockford	IL	61104	J Swanson	815-962-5362	R	2	<0.1
HC Osvold Co	2828 University S	Minneapolis	MN	55414	Beuce Osvold	612-331-1581	R	2	<0.1
Kosakura and Associates Inc	1321 N Blue Gum	Anaheim	CA	92806	Tak Kosakura	714-630-4553	R	2	<0.1
Pacific Fixture Company Inc	21115 Oxnard St	Woodland Hills	CA	91367	Keith Stark	818-340-0070	R	2	<0.1
Sinicrope and Sons Inc	1124 Westminster	Alhambra	CA	91803	G Sinicrope	213-283-5131	R	2	<0.1
Strata Design Inc	PO Box 6250	Traverse City	MI	49685	CT Cady	616-929-2140	R	2	<0.1
Family Movie Centers	111 E Voris St	Akron	OH	44311	T Greathouse	216-643-0750	R	1•	<0.1
General Office Manufacturing	2088 Burroughs Av	San Leandro	CA	94577	Jacek Pasternak	510-352-9221	R	1	<0.1
Mikes Fixture Company Inc	409 Johnson NE	Minneapolis	MN	55413	Michael Iwaskewycz	612-379-2200	R	1	<0.1

Source: *Ward's Business Directory of U.S. Private and Public Companies*, Volumes 1 and 2, 1996. The company type code used is as follows: P - Public, R - Private, S - Subsidiary, D - Division, J - Joint Venture, A - Affiliate, G - Group. Sales are in millions of dollars, employees are in thousands. An asterisk (*) indicates an estimated sales volume. The symbol < stands for 'less than'. Company names and addresses are truncated, in some cases, to fit into the available space.

MATERIALS CONSUMED

Material	Quantity	Delivered Cost ($ million)
Materials, ingredients, containers, and supplies	(X)	1,141.0
Metal stampings	(X)	(D)
All other fabricated metal products (except castings and forgings)	(X)	25.1
Forgings	(X)	(D)
Castings (rough and semifinished)	(X)	0.6
Steel sheet and strip, including tin plate	(X)	10.2
All other steel shapes and forms (except castings, forgings, and fabricated metal products)	(X)	8.0
Aluminum and aluminum-base alloy sheet, plate, foil, and welded tubing	(X)	0.4
All other aluminum and aluminum-base alloy shapes and forms	(X)	5.6
Other nonferrous shapes and forms (except castings, forgings, and fabricated metal products)	(X)	2.2
Hardwood lumber, rough and dressed	(X)	36.9
Softwood lumber, rough and dressed	(X)	9.5
Hardwood dimension and parts, including wood furniture frames	(X)	9.0
Hardwood veneer	(X)	11.3
Hardwood plywood	(X)	25.9
Softwood plywood	(X)	14.3
Particleboard (wood)	(X)	102.0
Medium density fiberboard (MDF)	(X)	33.3
Hardboard (wood fiberboard)	(X)	11.8
Plastics laminated sheets	(X)	113.2
Plastics furniture parts and components	(X)	25.2
Formed and slab stock for pillows, cushions, seating, etc. (urethane)	(X)	0.6
Coated or laminated fabrics, including vinyl coated	(X)	0.9
Uncoated broadwoven fabrics for upholstery	(X)	0.9
Flat glass (plate, float, and sheet)	(X)	11.9
Adhesives and sealants	(X)	10.0
Paints, varnishes, lacquers, stains, shellacs, japans, enamels, and allied products	(X)	15.9
Furniture and builders' hardware	(X)	35.8
Paperboard containers, boxes, and corrugated paperboard	(X)	15.7
All other materials and components, parts, containers, and supplies	(X)	175.1
Materials, ingredients, containers, and supplies, nsk	(X)	411.9

Source: 1992 *Economic Census.* Explanation of symbols used: (D): Withheld to avoid disclosure of competitive data; na: Not available; (S): Withheld because statistical norms were not met; (X): Not applicable; (Z): Less than half the unit shown; nec: Not elsewhere classified; nsk: Not specified by kind; - : zero; * : 10-19 percent estimated; ** : 20-29 percent estimated.

PRODUCT SHARE DETAILS

Product or Product Class	% Share
Wood partitions and fixtures	100.00
Wood partitions, shelving, and lockers	7.71
Prefabricated wood partitions (assembled or knocked-down)	23.95
Wood shelving	61.33
Wood lockers	5.42
Wood partitions, shelving, and lockers, nsk	9.26
Plastics laminated fixture tops (including tops for drainboards, sinks, cabinets, tables, counters, and fixtures)	17.91
Wood fixtures for stores, banks, and offices, and other miscellaneous fixtures	53.27
Wood walls and wall fixtures, custom, for retail stores, except food stores	12.10
Wood center floor tables and gondolas, custom, for retail stores, except food stores	8.66
Other wood fixtures and displays, custom, for retail stores, except food stores	19.05
Wood walls and wall fixtures, manufacturers' standard, for retail stores, except food stores	3.32
Wood center floor tables and gondolas, manufacturers' standard, for retail stores, except food stores	2.08
Other wood fixtures and displays, manufacturers' standard, for retail stores, except food stores	7.00
Wood store fixtures for retail food stores	8.89
Other wood show and display cases, including wall types, and tables, nec	6.03
Wood cabinets, floor or wall types, for stores, banks, and offices	8.13
Wood counters, except bank counters	3.40
Wood bank fixtures, including bank counters	1.84
Other wood partitions and fixtures, including window backs, telephone booths, miscellaneous display fixtures, cashier stands, etc., nec	6.32
Wood fixtures for stores, banks, and offices, and other miscellaneous fixtures, nsk	13.18
Wood partitions and fixtures, nsk	21.11

Source: 1992 *Economic Census.* The values shown are percent of total shipments in an industry. Values of indented subcategories are summed in the main heading. The symbol (D) appears when data are withheld to prevent disclosure of competitive information. The abbreviation nsk stands for 'not specified by kind' and nec for 'not elsewhere classified'.

INPUTS AND OUTPUTS FOR WOOD PARTITIONS & FIXTURES

Economic Sector or Industry Providing Inputs	%	Sector	Economic Sector or Industry Buying Outputs	%	Sector
Wholesale trade	10.3	Trade	Gross private fixed investment	73.1	Cap Inv
Particleboard	8.9	Manufg.	Office buildings	6.3	Constr.
Miscellaneous plastics products	7.9	Manufg.	Nonfarm residential structure maintenance	3.8	Constr.
Blast furnaces & steel mills	5.9	Manufg.	Construction of educational buildings	2.3	Constr.
Sawmills & planning mills, general	5.2	Manufg.	Construction of hospitals	1.5	Constr.
Veneer & plywood	5.1	Manufg.	Industrial buildings	1.2	Constr.
Cyclic crudes and organics	4.4	Manufg.	Residential additions/alterations, nonfarm	1.2	Constr.
Hardware, nec	4.4	Manufg.	Residential 1-unit structures, nonfarm	1.1	Constr.
Wood products, nec	3.1	Manufg.	Exports	1.1	Foreign
Business services nec	3.1	Services	Construction of stores & restaurants	1.0	Constr.
Advertising	3.0	Services	Amusement & recreation building construction	0.8	Constr.
Metal stampings, nec	2.3	Manufg.	Federal Government purchases, nondefense	0.8	Fed Govt
Motor freight transportation & warehousing	2.3	Util.	Maintenance of nonfarm buildings nec	0.6	Constr.
Electric services (utilities)	1.9	Util.	Residential garden apartments	0.6	Constr.
Paints & allied products	1.8	Manufg.	S/L Govt. purch., other education & libraries	0.6	S/L Govt
Real estate	1.8	Fin/R.E.	Residential high-rise apartments	0.5	Constr.
Banking	1.7	Fin/R.E.	Wood partitions & fixtures	0.5	Manufg.
Paperboard containers & boxes	1.5	Manufg.	Construction of nonfarm buildings nec	0.4	Constr.
Maintenance of nonfarm buildings nec	1.4	Constr.	S/L Govt. purch., elem. & secondary education	0.4	S/L Govt
Fabricated metal products, nec	1.4	Manufg.	Resid. & other health facility construction	0.3	Constr.
Petroleum refining	1.4	Manufg.	Farm housing units & additions & alterations	0.2	Constr.
Eating & drinking places	1.4	Trade	Maintenance of military facilities	0.2	Constr.
Glass & glass products, except containers	1.1	Manufg.	Residential 2-4 unit structures, nonfarm	0.2	Constr.
Hardwood dimension & flooring mills	1.1	Manufg.	Federal Government purchases, national defense	0.2	Fed Govt
Wood partitions & fixtures	1.0	Manufg.	S/L Govt. purch., higher education	0.2	S/L Govt
Communications, except radio & TV	0.9	Util.	Household appliances, nec	0.1	Manufg.
Gas production & distribution (utilities)	0.9	Util.	S/L Govt. purch., police	0.1	S/L Govt
Railroads & related services	0.9	Util.			
Abrasive products	0.8	Manufg.			
Aluminum rolling & drawing	0.8	Manufg.			
Hand & edge tools, nec	0.8	Manufg.			
Screw machine and related products	0.7	Manufg.			
Business/professional associations	0.7	Services			
Adhesives & sealants	0.6	Manufg.			
Coated fabrics, not rubberized	0.6	Manufg.			
Detective & protective services	0.6	Services			
Industrial inorganic chemicals, nec	0.5	Manufg.			
Management & consulting services & labs	0.5	Services			
U.S. Postal Service	0.5	Gov't			
Air transportation	0.4	Util.			
Colleges, universities, & professional schools	0.4	Services			
Equipment rental & leasing services	0.4	Services			
Legal services	0.4	Services			
Machinery, except electrical, nec	0.3	Manufg.			
Accounting, auditing & bookkeeping	0.3	Services			
Automotive rental & leasing, without drivers	0.3	Services			
Lighting fixtures & equipment	0.2	Manufg.			
Manifold business forms	0.2	Manufg.			
Paper coating & glazing	0.2	Manufg.			
Special dies & tools & machine tool accessories	0.2	Manufg.			
Sanitary services, steam supply, irrigation	0.2	Util.			
Water transportation	0.2	Util.			
Insurance carriers	0.2	Fin/R.E.			
Royalties	0.2	Fin/R.E.			
Security & commodity brokers	0.2	Fin/R.E.			
Automotive repair shops & services	0.2	Services			
Computer & data processing services	0.2	Services			
Engineering, architectural, & surveying services	0.2	Services			
Job training & related services	0.2	Services			
Laundry, dry cleaning, shoe repair	0.2	Services			
Lubricating oils & greases	0.1	Manufg.			
Mechanical measuring devices	0.1	Manufg.			
Hotels & lodging places	0.1	Services			
Personnel supply services	0.1	Services			

Source: Benchmark Input-Output Accounts for the U.S. Economy, 1982, U.S. Department of Commerce, Washington, D.C., July 1991. Data, as reported in the source, are organized by the 1977 SIC structure in use in 1982 but have been matched, as closely as is possible, to the 1987 SIC structure used in this book.

OCCUPATIONS EMPLOYED BY SIC 254 - PARTITIONS AND FIXTURES

Occupation	% of Total 1994	Change to 2005	Occupation	% of Total 1994	Change to 2005
Cabinetmakers & bench carpenters	13.8	4.3	Woodworking machine workers	1.8	-42.1
Assemblers, fabricators, & hand workers nec	9.5	15.9	Helpers, laborers, & material movers nec	1.7	15.9
Blue collar worker supervisors	4.3	6.1	Sheet metal workers & duct installers	1.6	15.9
General managers & top executives	3.4	9.9	Hand packers & packagers	1.6	-0.7
Wood machinists	3.0	97.0	Traffic, shipping, & receiving clerks	1.6	11.5
Welding machine setters, operators	2.9	4.3	General office clerks	1.5	-1.2
Machine forming operators, metal & plastic	2.7	15.9	Bookkeeping, accounting, & auditing clerks	1.4	-13.0
Coating, painting, & spraying machine workers	2.6	15.9	Secretaries, ex legal & medical	1.4	5.4
Freight, stock, & material movers, hand	2.5	-7.3	Industrial production managers	1.4	15.9
Carpenters	2.5	-7.3	Head sawyers & sawing machine workers	1.3	-7.4
Machine tool cutting & forming etc. nec	2.4	15.9	Truck drivers light & heavy	1.3	19.5
Sales & related workers nec	2.3	15.8	Grinders & polishers, hand	1.2	15.9
Welders & cutters	2.3	15.9	Combination machine tool operators	1.0	27.5
Drafters	1.8	-9.7	Furniture finishers	1.0	3.9
Industrial truck & tractor operators	1.8	15.9			

Source: *Industry-Occupation Matrix*, Bureau of Labor Statistics. These data relate to one or more 3-digit SIC industry groups rather than to a single 4-digit SIC. The change reported for each occupation to the year 2005 is a percent of growth or decline as estimated by the Bureau of Labor Statistics. The abbreviation nec stands for 'not elsewhere classified'.

LOCATION BY STATE AND REGIONAL CONCENTRATION

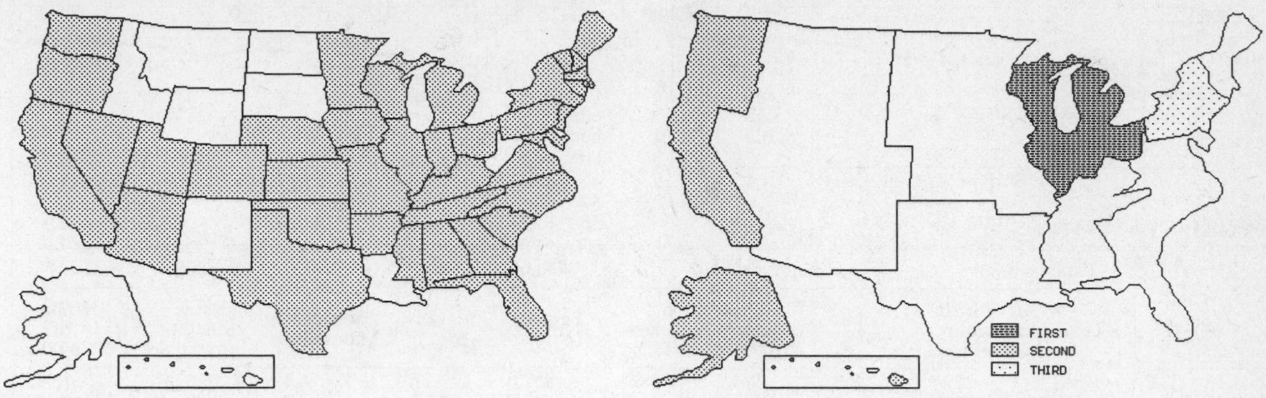

INDUSTRY DATA BY STATE

State	Establish-ments	Shipments Total ($ mil)	Shipments % of U.S.	Shipments Per Establ.	Employment Total Number	Employment % of U.S.	Employment Per Establ.	Wages ($/hour)	Cost as % of Shipments	Investment per Employee ($)
California	271	400.8	12.8	1.5	4,500	11.4	17	10.23	44.6	1,178
New York	147	240.3	7.7	1.6	3,100	7.9	21	10.95	37.4	1,065
Illinois	114	215.7	6.9	1.9	2,200	5.6	19	12.39	51.0	1,227
Ohio	106	205.8	6.6	1.9	2,200	5.6	21	10.57	50.3	1,227
Texas	86	154.9	4.9	1.8	2,200	5.6	26	9.03	42.2	1,136
Pennsylvania	90	146.5	4.7	1.6	2,000	5.1	22	10.15	42.1	1,150
Wisconsin	60	134.0	4.3	2.2	1,700	4.3	28	10.16	42.5	2,118
North Carolina	46	131.6	4.2	2.9	1,600	4.1	35	9.43	49.8	1,063
Michigan	73	129.9	4.1	1.8	2,000	5.1	27	9.63	41.4	1,100
Minnesota	52	110.4	3.5	2.1	1,100	2.8	21	11.94	37.0	1,909
New Jersey	76	104.0	3.3	1.4	1,200	3.0	16	11.50	38.8	1,250
Indiana	48	94.8	3.0	2.0	1,100	2.8	23	8.80	55.7	1,455
Georgia	53	94.7	3.0	1.8	1,000	2.5	19	9.19	46.1	1,000
Florida	99	76.5	2.4	0.8	1,100	2.8	11	8.78	42.1	909
Oklahoma	20	58.8	1.9	2.9	1,000	2.5	50	7.43	49.5	400
Massachusetts	42	57.8	1.8	1.4	700	1.8	17	11.60	36.2	1,000
Oregon	33	52.6	1.7	1.6	700	1.8	21	8.60	40.9	714
Washington	49	50.5	1.6	1.0	700	1.8	14	10.30	39.6	-
Maryland	45	50.1	1.6	1.1	600	1.5	13	13.40	30.1	-
Missouri	42	44.3	1.4	1.1	700	1.8	17	9.70	44.2	857
Virginia	30	42.0	1.3	1.4	600	1.5	20	9.10	40.2	833
Colorado	36	38.7	1.2	1.1	600	1.5	17	10.00	37.0	1,333
Rhode Island	15	32.6	1.0	2.2	400	1.0	27	10.00	38.0	1,250
Nebraska	12	29.1	0.9	2.4	500	1.3	42	9.75	35.7	-
Connecticut	24	28.9	0.9	1.2	300	0.8	13	13.00	29.4	333
Arizona	35	26.9	0.9	0.8	300	0.8	9	10.00	28.3	-
Kentucky	15	25.6	0.8	1.7	400	1.0	27	9.17	41.0	1,750
Alabama	19	20.1	0.6	1.1	300	0.8	16	8.00	51.2	667
New Hampshire	12	18.0	0.6	1.5	200	0.5	17	10.33	41.1	1,000
Mississippi	8	15.7	0.5	2.0	200	0.5	25	7.33	70.7	-
Kansas	11	15.6	0.5	1.4	200	0.5	18	9.67	51.3	1,500
Vermont	7	15.2	0.5	2.2	200	0.5	29	14.00	32.2	500
Iowa	16	15.0	0.5	0.9	200	0.5	13	10.67	39.3	500
Nevada	16	9.3	0.3	0.6	100	0.3	6	11.50	34.4	-
Tennessee	32	(D)	-	-	750 *	1.9	23	-	-	533
Utah	26	(D)	-	-	750 *	1.9	29	-	-	-
Arkansas	13	(D)	-	-	750 *	1.9	58	-	-	-
South Carolina	11	(D)	-	-	750 *	1.9	68	-	-	-
Maine	9	(D)	-	-	175 *	0.4	19	-	-	-

Source: 1992 *Economic Census*. The states are in descending order of shipments or establishments (if shipment data are missing for the majority). The symbol (D) appears when data are withheld to prevent disclosure of competitive information. States marked with (D) are sorted by number of establishments. A dash (-) indicates that the data element cannot be calculated; * indicates the midpoint of a range.

2542 - PARTITIONS AND FIXTURES, EXCEPT WOOD

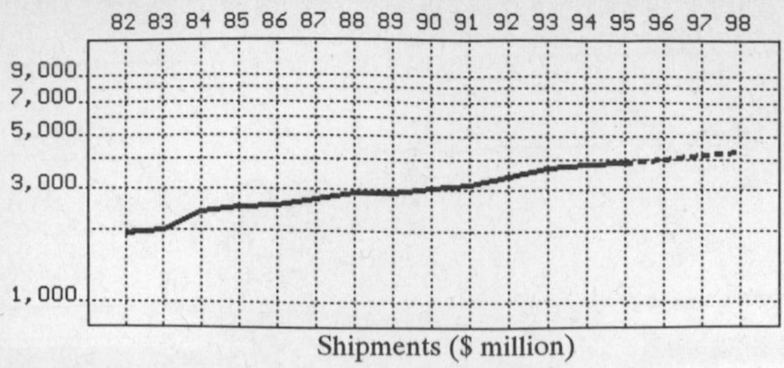

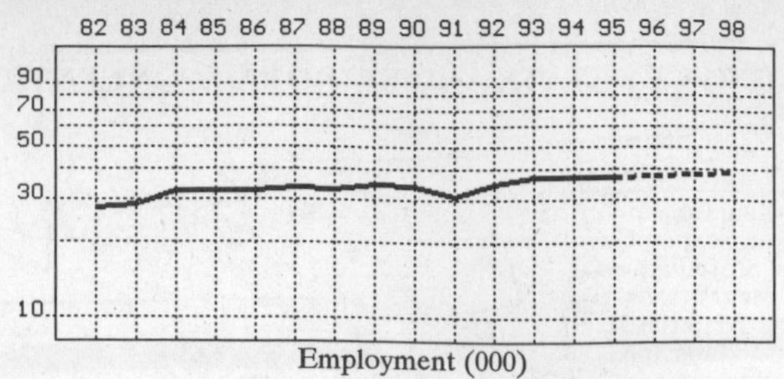

GENERAL STATISTICS

Year	Com-panies	Establishments: Total	Establishments: with 20 or more employees	Employment: Total (000)	Employment: Production Workers (000)	Employment: Production Hours (Mil)	Compensation: Payroll ($ mil)	Compensation: Wages ($/hr)	Production ($ million): Cost of Materials	Production ($ million): Value Added by Manufacture	Production ($ million): Value of Shipments	Production ($ million): Capital Invest.
1982	533	568	299	28.0	20.5	38.9	482.0	7.57	874.4	1,062.5	1,943.2	48.1
1983		560	303	28.7	21.3	41.0	510.0	7.61	915.7	1,090.4	2,000.9	32.5
1984		552	307	32.8	25.1	46.8	601.1	8.18	1,126.2	1,295.1	2,390.9	50.2
1985		545	311	32.3	24.2	45.9	615.0	8.46	1,166.8	1,308.4	2,490.5	61.8
1986		534	297	32.4	23.9	47.5	641.1	8.56	1,178.2	1,374.3	2,554.2	50.2
1987	567	592	299	33.5	24.6	49.2	691.0	8.76	1,237.9	1,502.6	2,721.3	59.2
1988		581	304	33.2	24.4	49.4	716.2	9.08	1,306.9	1,593.8	2,879.2	47.0
1989		564	308	34.7	23.8	47.0	712.9	9.36	1,367.6	1,544.3	2,909.4	58.1
1990		572	305	34.0	23.5	48.0	748.4	9.46	1,427.0	1,620.8	3,045.8	68.0
1991		614	303	31.0	21.9	47.7	779.7	9.89	1,436.5	1,683.3	3,125.0	70.1
1992	743	786	332	34.8	26.0	54.6	863.8	9.82	1,562.4	1,889.6	3,445.9	66.3
1993		779	332	37.5	28.2	56.7	932.9	10.25	1,699.1	2,019.2	3,701.2	82.9
1994		718P	322P	37.0	28.0	59.3	930.5	9.73	1,792.3	2,016.3	3,804.9	82.2
1995		735P	324P	37.2P	27.1P	57.7P	962.9P	10.50P	1,829.7P	2,058.4P	3,884.3P	82.1P
1996		753P	326P	37.8P	27.5P	59.0P	999.1P	10.71P	1,899.5P	2,136.9P	4,032.4P	85.3P
1997		770P	328P	38.3P	28.0P	60.3P	1,035.3P	10.93P	1,969.3P	2,215.4P	4,180.6P	88.4P
1998		788P	331P	38.9P	28.4P	61.6P	1,071.5P	11.14P	2,039.1P	2,293.9P	4,328.8P	91.6P

Sources: 1982, 1987, 1992 *Economic Census*; *Annual Survey of Manufactures*, 83-86, 88-91, 93-94. Establishment counts for non-Census years are from *County Business Patterns*; establishment values for 83-84 are extrapolations. 'P's show projections by the editors. Industries reclassified in 87 will not have data for prior years.

INDICES OF CHANGE

Year	Com-panies	Establishments: Total	Establishments: with 20 or more employees	Employment: Total (000)	Employment: Production Workers (000)	Employment: Production Hours (Mil)	Compensation: Payroll ($ mil)	Compensation: Wages ($/hr)	Production ($ million): Cost of Materials	Production ($ million): Value Added by Manufacture	Production ($ million): Value of Shipments	Production ($ million): Capital Invest.
1982	72	72	90	80	79	71	56	77	56	56	56	73
1983		71	91	82	82	75	59	77	59	58	58	49
1984		70	92	94	97	86	70	83	72	69	69	76
1985		69	94	93	93	84	71	86	75	69	72	93
1986		68	89	93	92	87	74	87	75	73	74	76
1987	76	75	90	96	95	90	80	89	79	80	79	89
1988		74	92	95	94	90	83	92	84	84	84	71
1989		72	93	100	92	86	83	95	88	82	84	88
1990		73	92	98	90	88	87	96	91	86	88	103
1991		78	91	89	84	87	90	101	92	89	91	106
1992	100	100	100	100	100	100	100	100	100	100	100	100
1993		99	100	108	108	104	108	104	109	107	107	125
1994		91P	97P	106	108	109	108	99	115	107	110	124
1995		94P	98P	107P	104P	106P	111P	107P	117P	109P	113P	124P
1996		96P	98P	108P	106P	108P	116P	109P	122P	113P	117P	129P
1997		98P	99P	110P	108P	110P	120P	111P	126P	117P	121P	133P
1998		100P	100P	112P	109P	113P	124P	113P	131P	121P	126P	138P

Sources: Same as General Statistics. Values reflect change from the base year, 1992. Values above 100 mean greater than 92, values below 100 mean less than 92, and a value of 100 in the 82-91 or 93-98 period means same as 92. 'P's mark projections by the editors.

SELECTED RATIOS

For 1994	Avg. of All Manufact.	Analyzed Industry	Index
Employees per Establishment	49	52	105
Payroll per Establishment	1,500,273	1,296,645	86
Payroll per Employee	30,620	25,149	82
Production Workers per Establishment	34	39	114
Wages per Establishment	853,319	804,030	94
Wages per Production Worker	24,861	20,607	83
Hours per Production Worker	2,056	2,118	103
Wages per Hour	12.09	9.73	80
Value Added per Establishment	4,602,255	2,809,700	61
Value Added per Employee	93,930	54,495	58

For 1994	Avg. of All Manufact.	Analyzed Industry	Index
Value Added per Production Worker	134,084	72,011	54
Cost per Establishment	5,045,178	2,497,557	50
Cost per Employee	102,970	48,441	47
Cost per Production Worker	146,988	64,011	44
Shipments per Establishment	9,576,895	5,302,101	55
Shipments per Employee	195,460	102,835	53
Shipments per Production Worker	279,017	135,889	49
Investment per Establishment	321,011	114,545	36
Investment per Employee	6,552	2,222	34
Investment per Production Worker	9,352	2,936	31

Sources: Same as General Statistics. The 'Average of All Manufacturing' column represents the average of all manufacturing industries reported for the most recent complete year available. The Index shows the relationship between the Average and the Analyzed Industry. For example, 100 means that they are equal; 500 that the Analyzed Industry is five times the average; 50 means that the Analyzed Industry is half the national average. The abbreviation 'na' is used to show that data are 'not available'.

LEADING COMPANIES Number shown: 75 Total sales ($ mil): **2,092** Total employment (000): **20.5**

Company Name	Address				CEO Name	Phone	Co. Type	Sales ($ mil)	Empl. (000)
LA Darling Co	PO Box 970	Paragould	AR	72451	Kent E Toomey	501-239-9564	S	165	2.7
American Seating Co	401 Am Seating	Grand Rapids	MI	49504	Edward Clark	616-732-6600	R	130*	1.0
Darling Store Fixtures	PO Box 970	Paragould	AR	72451	Kent E Toomey	501-239-9564	D	125	2.0
Madix Inc	PO Box 729	Terrell	TX	75160	Alley Sharaway	214-563-5744	R	120	1.0
Interlake Material Handling	550 Warrenville Rd	Lisle	IL	60532	Daniel P Wilson	708-852-8800	D	100	0.5
Stanley-Vidmar Inc	PO Box 1151	Allentown	PA	18105	James C Lorence	215-797-6600	S	100	0.5
RHC/Spacemaster Corp	1400 N 25th Av	Melrose Park	IL	60160	AR Umans	708-345-2500	R	90	1.0
V-T Industries Inc	1000 Industrial Park	Holstein	IA	51025	Douglas Clausen	712-368-4381	R	90	0.6
Syndicate Store Fixtures Inc	PO Box 70	Middlebury	IN	46540	Jerry Burris	219-825-9561	S	84	0.9
Frazier Industrial Co	Fairview Av	Long Valley	NJ	07853	WL Mascharka	908-876-3001	R	60	0.1
Lyon Metal Products Inc	PO Box 671	Aurora	IL	60507	RP Washington	708-892-8941	R	56	0.7
Republic Storage Systems	1038 Belden Av NE	Canton	OH	44705	J O'Leary	216-438-5800	R	53	0.6
Kardex Systems Inc	PO Box 171	Marietta	OH	45750	Jack E Smith	614-374-9300	S	50	0.5
Penco Products	Brower Av	Oaks	PA	19456	Arthur M Muti	610-666-0500	S	48	0.4
Borroughs Corp	3002 N Burdick St	Kalamazoo	MI	49007	MW Barrett	616-342-0161	R	45	0.4
Aurora Equipment Co	225 S Highland Av	Aurora	IL	60506	Tom Matyas	708-859-1000	R	35	0.3
Dann Dee Display Fixtures Inc	7555 N Caldwell	Niles	IL	60714	Earl Dann	708-588-1600	R	35	0.1
Ridg-U-Rak Inc	120 S Lake St	North East	PA	16428	John Pellegrino Sr	814-725-8751	R	34	0.3
Equipto	4814 Cass St	Dallas	TX	75235	Jim Rollins	214-634-9550	D	30*	<0.1
Packard Industries Inc	1515 US 31 N	Niles	MI	49120	EH Mark	616-684-2550	R	30*	<0.1
Clestra Hauserman Inc	29525 Fountain	Cleveland	OH	44139	William Hogan	216-498-5000	S	25	0.1
Gower Corp	PO Box 6767	Greenville	SC	29606	H Park	803-271-7630	R	25	0.4
Rapid Rack Industries Inc	14421 Bonelli St	City of Industry	CA	91746	K Blankenhorn	818-333-7225	R	24	<0.1
Boston Metal Products Corp	400 Riverside Av	Medford	MA	02155	Richard J Rubin	617-395-7417	R	20*	0.1
Frick-Gallagher Mfg Co	PO Box 788	Lancaster	OH	43130	PH Frick Jr	614-653-5700	R	20*	0.1
Royal Engineering Co	330 Pennington Av	Trenton	NJ	08618	Larry H Bowen	609-396-4506	R	20	0.5
Seiz Corp	PO Box 217	Perkasie	PA	18944	Frederick G Seiz	215-257-3600	R	20	0.2
Piper Products Inc	530 McClellan St	Wausau	WI	54403	Roger Sweeney	715-842-2724	R	18*	0.2
Kent Corp	PO Box 170399	Birmingham	AL	35217	MA Oztekin	205-853-3420	R	17	0.2
Lodi Metal Tech Inc	213 S Kelly St	Lodi	CA	95241	D Allen Gross	209-334-2500	R	15	0.1
Feeny Manufacturing Co	PO Box 191	Muncie	IN	47308	Tim L Kuzma	317-288-8730	S	15*	0.2
Kiechler	PO Box 550	Harrison	OH	45030	Frank Shipkowski	513-367-2700	D	15	0.2
Lista International Corp	106 Lowland St	Holliston	MA	01746	Donald Brown	508-429-1350	R	15	0.2
Metpar Corp	95 State St	Westbury	NY	11590	John Fallarino	516-333-2600	R	15	0.1
Western Pacific Storage Systems	1532 S California	Monrovia	CA	91016	Jan Newsam	818-359-4522	R	15*	<0.1
Medart Equipment Inc	PO Box 658	Greenwood	MS	38935		601-453-2506	R	14	0.3
Acoustics Development Corp	3800 S 48th Ter	St Joseph	MO	64503	Larry R Pointelin	816-233-8061	R	13	0.1
Brand Manufacturing Corp	744 Berriman St	Brooklyn	NY	11208	Marvin Weiner	718-272-9393	R	13*	0.3
List Industries Inc	401 NW 12th Av	Deerfield Bch	FL	33442	Herbert A List	305-429-9155	R	12	0.3
Benner-Nawman Inc	3070 Bay Vista Ct	Benicia	CA	94510	Edward R Kientz	707-746-0500	R	12	0.1
Hallmark Industries Inc	E Ohio St	McClure	PA	17841	Allan Lozier	717-658-8111	S	12*	0.2
Knickerbocker Partition Corp	PO Box 3035	Freeport	NY	11520	David Markbreiter	516-546-0550	R	12	0.1
Paltier	1701 Kentucky St	Michigan City	IN	46360	JP Washington	219-872-7238	D	12	<0.1
Reeve Store Equipment Co	PO Box 276	Pico Rivera	CA	90660	Edgar H Reeve	310-949-2535	R	12	0.1
Steiner Company Inc	1 E Superior St	Chicago	IL	60611	Guy Marchesi	312-642-1242	S	12	0.1
Cannon Equipment West	12822 Monarch St	Garden Grove	CA	92641	Darren J Coyle	714-373-5800	D	10	0.1
LMT Steel Products Inc	550 9th St	Hoboken	NJ	07030	David Teitelbaum	201-659-1680	R	10*	0.1
Perma-Steel Corp	1065 Shepherd Av	Brooklyn	NY	11208	Robert Grgas	718-649-6800	R	10	0.1
Glen O'Brien Movable Partition	PO Box 300200	Kansas City	MO	64130	Stephen R Nichols	816-523-7416	R	10	0.1
Virginia Metal Industries Inc	PO Box 709	Orange	VA	22960	David P Hoyt	703-672-2800	S	9	0.1
Sama Plastics Corp	800 Eastern Way	Carlstadt	NJ	07072	Martin Wolfberg	201-896-8080	R	9	0.2
Southern Metal Industries Inc	PO Box 219	Ringgold	GA	30736	W Smith	706-935-4486	R	9	<0.1
Artco Corp	PO Box 430	Hatfield	PA	19440	Ruth Moore	215-723-6041	R	8*	0.1
Butler Group Inc	1901 S 7th St	Louisville	KY	40208	Brian O'Hagan	502-636-3461	R	8	<0.1
Erickson Displays Inc	1917 Dean Av	Des Moines	IA	50316	Ron Waddell	515-265-6151	D	8	0.1
L and S Products Inc	340 Jay St	Coldwater	MI	49036	W Neesley	517-279-9526	R	8	0.1
Clark Specialty Company Inc	8440 Rte 54	Hammondsport	NY	14840	Stanley M Clark	607-569-2191	R	8	0.1
Remstar International Inc	41 Eisenhower Dr	Westbrook	ME	04092	Gary Gould	207-854-1861	D	8	<0.1
Adapto Storage Products	PO Box 111660	Hialeah	FL	33011	Paul N Taylor	305-887-9563	R	7	<0.1
National Products Displays Inc	PO Box 187	Grand Haven	MI	49417	Valerie Eggert	616-842-6830	R	7	<0.1
Beagle Manufacturing Company	4377 N Baldwin Av	El Monte	CA	91731	R S McCracken	818-442-1168	R	7	0.2
Acoustic Systems Inc	PO Box 3610	Austin	TX	78764	David Michalek	512-444-1961	R	6*	<0.1
Athena Industries Inc	51 Shore Dr	Burr Ridge	IL	60521	Dale Razee	708-325-9670	R	6*	<0.1
Clymer Enterprises Inc	PO Box 266	Pandora	OH	45877	Gary Clymer	419-384-3211	R	6	<0.1
Decter International Inc	1118 E 8th St	Los Angeles	CA	90021	Thomas L Decter	213-627-9842	R	6*	0.1
Gorilla Rack	14421 E Bonelli Av	City of Industry	CA	91746	K A Blankenhorn	818-333-7225	D	6*	<0.1
Lingo Manufacturing Company	PO Box 426	Florence	KY	41022	Charles R Lingo	606-371-2662	R	6	<0.1
Lockwood Manufacturing Co	31251 Industrial Rd	Livonia	MI	48150	FW Lamson	313-425-5330	R	6*	<0.1
RB White Inc	1204 N Linden St	Bloomington	IL	61701	Robert White	309-828-6295	R	6	<0.1
General Partitions Mfg Corp	PO Box 8370	Erie	PA	16505	GM Zehner	814-833-1154	R	6	<0.1
Advanced Equipment Corp	2401 Commonw	Fullerton	CA	92633	Wesley B Dickson	714-635-5350	R	5*	<0.1
Advance Products Company Inc	PO Box 2178	Wichita	KS	67201	WD Devore	316-263-4231	R	5	0.1
Redyref-Pressed and Welded Inc	38-61 11th St	Long Island Ct	NY	11101	Lawrence J Torn	718-784-3690	R	5	<0.1
General Plastics Corp	1300 N Washington	Marion	IN	46952	WF Morrison	317-664-6221	R	4	<0.1
Major Partitions Inc	PO Box 2167	Irwindale	CA	91706	Dorothy Gallonio	818-969-4385	R	4	<0.1

Source: *Ward's Business Directory of U.S. Private and Public Companies*, Volumes 1 and 2, 1996. The company type code used is as follows: P - Public, R - Private, S - Subsidiary, D - Division, J - Joint Venture, A - Affiliate, G - Group. Sales are in millions of dollars, employees are in thousands. An asterisk (*) indicates an estimated sales volume. The symbol < stands for 'less than'. Company names and addresses are truncated, in some cases, to fit into the available space.

MATERIALS CONSUMED

Material	Quantity	Delivered Cost ($ million)
Materials, ingredients, containers, and supplies	(X)	1,334.7
Metal stampings	(X)	19.1
All other fabricated metal products (except castings and forgings)	(X)	56.2
Forgings	(X)	0.1
Castings (rough and semifinished)	(X)	3.6
Steel sheet and strip, including tin plate	(X)	438.3
All other steel shapes and forms (except castings, forgings, and fabricated metal products)	(X)	119.0
Aluminum and aluminum-base alloy sheet, plate, foil, and welded tubing	(X)	6.0
All other aluminum and aluminum-base alloy shapes and forms	(X)	15.5
Other nonferrous shapes and forms (except castings, forgings, and fabricated metal products)	(X)	5.3
Hardwood lumber, rough and dressed	(X)	9.9
Softwood lumber, rough and dressed	(X)	3.1
Hardwood dimension and parts, including wood furniture frames	(X)	31.8
Hardwood veneer	(X)	2.5
Hardwood plywood	(X)	4.3
Softwood plywood	(X)	1.9
Particleboard (wood)	(X)	31.9
Medium density fiberboard (MDF)	(X)	4.1
Hardboard (wood fiberboard)	(X)	14.0
Plastics laminated sheets	(X)	27.9
Plastics furniture parts and components	(X)	5.6
Formed and slab stock for pillows, cushions, seating, etc. (urethane)	(X)	0.3
Coated or laminated fabrics, including vinyl coated	(X)	2.7
Uncoated broadwoven fabrics for upholstery	(X)	1.3
Flat glass (plate, float, and sheet)	(X)	4.0
Adhesives and sealants	(X)	2.3
Paints, varnishes, lacquers, stains, shellacs, japans, enamels, and allied products	(X)	71.8
Furniture and builders' hardware	(X)	38.1
Paperboard containers, boxes, and corrugated paperboard	(X)	41.8
All other materials and components, parts, containers, and supplies	(X)	195.3
Materials, ingredients, containers, and supplies, nsk	(X)	177.2

Source: 1992 *Economic Census*. Explanation of symbols used: (D): Withheld to avoid disclosure of competitive data; na: Not available; (S): Withheld because statistical norms were not met; (X): Not applicable; (Z): Less than half the unit shown; nec: Not elsewhere classified; nsk: Not specified by kind; - : zero; * : 10-19 percent estimated; ** : 20-29 percent estimated.

PRODUCT SHARE DETAILS

Product or Product Class	% Share
Partitions and fixtures, except wood	100.00
Prefabricated partitions, assembled or knocked-down, except wood	6.84
Toilet partitions, except wood	35.29
Movable partitions, except freestanding and wood	56.62
Other partitions (excluding accordion and folding-type doors), except wood	5.18
Partitions, prefabricated (assembled or knocked-down), except wood, nsk	2.86
Shelving and lockers, except wood	23.00
Commercial shelving (factory, store, etc.), except wood	56.78
Bookstacks (library, office, and school), except wood	5.13
Other shelving, including office shelving for correspondence, computer tapes, microfilm, etc., except wood	16.87
Lockers, except wood	19.06
Shelving and lockers, except wood, nsk	2.15
Storage racks and accessories, except wood	20.16
Drive-in/drive-thru and gravity conveyor pallet storage racks, except wood	10.99
Cantilever storage racks, except wood	7.36
Portable stacking racks and frames, except wood	11.04
Stacker-racks (pallet support, beams perpendicular to the storage aisle), except wood	11.14
Other racks, including conventional pallet racks and accessories, except wood	50.47
Storage racks and accessories, except wood, nsk	9.01
Fixtures for stores, banks, and offices, and miscellaneous fixtures, except wood	39.80
Custom store fixtures, retail (except food stores), except wood	33.31
Manufacturers' standard store fixtures, retail (except food stores), except wood	18.10
Store fixtures for retail food stores, except wood	14.85
Other show and display cases (including wall types) and tables, nec, except wood	7.05
Cabinets (floor or wall types), nec, except wood, for stores, banks, and offices	12.14
Other fixtures (counters, window backs, telephone booths, miscellaneous display fixtures, cashier stands, etc.), nec, except wood	10.28
Fixtures for stores, banks, and offices, and miscellaneous fixtures, except wood, nsk	4.28
Partitions and fixtures, except wood, nsk	10.20

Source: 1992 *Economic Census*. The values shown are percent of total shipments in an industry. Values of indented subcategories are summed in the main heading. The symbol (D) appears when data are withheld to prevent disclosure of competitive information. The abbreviation nsk stands for 'not specified by kind' and nec for 'not elsewhere classified'.

INPUTS AND OUTPUTS FOR METAL PARTITIONS & FIXTURES

Economic Sector or Industry Providing Inputs	%	Sector	Economic Sector or Industry Buying Outputs	%	Sector
Blast furnaces & steel mills	36.0	Manufg.	Gross private fixed investment	83.9	Cap Inv
Wholesale trade	9.6	Trade	Office buildings	2.3	Constr.
Business services nec	4.1	Services	Exports	2.2	Foreign
Advertising	3.0	Services	S/L Govt. purch., other education & libraries	1.3	S/L Govt
Metal stampings, nec	2.6	Manufg.	Construction of stores & restaurants	1.0	Constr.
Paints & allied products	2.5	Manufg.	S/L Govt. purch., elem. & secondary education	1.0	S/L Govt
Screw machine and related products	2.5	Manufg.	Industrial buildings	0.7	Constr.
Paperboard containers & boxes	2.4	Manufg.	Metal partitions & fixtures	0.7	Manufg.
Metalworking machinery, nec	2.2	Manufg.	Construction of hospitals	0.6	Constr.
Electric services (utilities)	2.2	Util.	Construction of nonfarm buildings nec	0.6	Constr.
Banking	1.9	Fin/R.E.	Maintenance of nonfarm buildings nec	0.6	Constr.
Hardware, nec	1.8	Manufg.	S/L Govt. purch., higher education	0.6	S/L Govt
Aluminum rolling & drawing	1.6	Manufg.	Residential 1-unit structures, nonfarm	0.5	Constr.
Motor freight transportation & warehousing	1.6	Util.	Federal Government purchases, national defense	0.5	Fed Govt
Petroleum refining	1.5	Manufg.	Amusement & recreation building construction	0.4	Constr.
Gas production & distribution (utilities)	1.5	Util.	Construction of educational buildings	0.4	Constr.
Metal partitions & fixtures	1.3	Manufg.	Hotels & motels	0.3	Constr.
Sanitary services, steam supply, irrigation	1.3	Util.	Blast furnaces & steel mills	0.3	Manufg.
Real estate	1.3	Fin/R.E.	Residential garden apartments	0.2	Constr.
Wood products, nec	1.2	Manufg.	Retail trade, except eating & drinking	0.2	Trade
Maintenance of nonfarm buildings nec	1.1	Constr.	Wholesale trade	0.2	Trade
Communications, except radio & TV	1.1	Util.	Federal Government purchases, nondefense	0.2	Fed Govt
Eating & drinking places	1.1	Trade	Dormitories & other group housing	0.1	Constr.
Particleboard	1.0	Manufg.	S/L Govt. purch., police	0.1	S/L Govt
Fabricated metal products, nec	0.7	Manufg.			
Miscellaneous plastics products	0.7	Manufg.			
Railroads & related services	0.7	Util.			
Equipment rental & leasing services	0.7	Services			
Abrasive products	0.6	Manufg.			
Adhesives & sealants	0.6	Manufg.			
Cyclic crudes and organics	0.6	Manufg.			
Sawmills & planning mills, general	0.6	Manufg.			
Metal coating & allied services	0.5	Manufg.			
U.S. Postal Service	0.5	Gov't			
Chemical preparations, nec	0.4	Manufg.			
Veneer & plywood	0.4	Manufg.			
Wood pallets & skids	0.4	Manufg.			
Air transportation	0.4	Util.			
Management & consulting services & labs	0.4	Services			
Fabricated rubber products, nec	0.3	Manufg.			
Hardwood dimension & flooring mills	0.3	Manufg.			
Automotive rental & leasing, without drivers	0.3	Services			
Legal services	0.3	Services			
Copper rolling & drawing	0.2	Manufg.			
Machinery, except electrical, nec	0.2	Manufg.			
Paper coating & glazing	0.2	Manufg.			
Insurance carriers	0.2	Fin/R.E.			
Royalties	0.2	Fin/R.E.			
Security & commodity brokers	0.2	Fin/R.E.			
Accounting, auditing & bookkeeping	0.2	Services			
Automotive repair shops & services	0.2	Services			
Computer & data processing services	0.2	Services			
Coated fabrics, not rubberized	0.1	Manufg.			
Glass & glass products, except containers	0.1	Manufg.			
Lighting fixtures & equipment	0.1	Manufg.			
Lubricating oils & greases	0.1	Manufg.			
Manifold business forms	0.1	Manufg.			
Special dies & tools & machine tool accessories	0.1	Manufg.			
Credit agencies other than banks	0.1	Fin/R.E.			
Business/professional associations	0.1	Services			
Hotels & lodging places	0.1	Services			
Laundry, dry cleaning, shoe repair	0.1	Services			

Source: Benchmark Input-Output Accounts for the U.S. Economy, 1982, U.S. Department of Commerce, Washington, D.C., July 1991. Data, as reported in the source, are organized by the 1977 SIC structure in use in 1982 but have been matched, as closely as is possible, to the 1987 SIC structure used in this book.

OCCUPATIONS EMPLOYED BY SIC 254 - PARTITIONS AND FIXTURES

Occupation	% of Total 1994	Change to 2005	Occupation	% of Total 1994	Change to 2005
Cabinetmakers & bench carpenters	13.8	4.3	Woodworking machine workers	1.8	-42.1
Assemblers, fabricators, & hand workers nec	9.5	15.9	Helpers, laborers, & material movers nec	1.7	15.9
Blue collar worker supervisors	4.3	6.1	Sheet metal workers & duct installers	1.6	15.9
General managers & top executives	3.4	9.9	Hand packers & packagers	1.6	-0.7
Wood machinists	3.0	97.0	Traffic, shipping, & receiving clerks	1.6	11.5
Welding machine setters, operators	2.9	4.3	General office clerks	1.5	-1.2
Machine forming operators, metal & plastic	2.7	15.9	Bookkeeping, accounting, & auditing clerks	1.4	-13.0
Coating, painting, & spraying machine workers	2.6	15.9	Secretaries, ex legal & medical	1.4	5.4
Freight, stock, & material movers, hand	2.5	-7.3	Industrial production managers	1.4	15.9
Carpenters	2.5	-7.3	Head sawyers & sawing machine workers	1.3	-7.4
Machine tool cutting & forming etc. nec	2.4	15.9	Truck drivers light & heavy	1.3	19.5
Sales & related workers nec	2.3	15.8	Grinders & polishers, hand	1.2	15.9
Welders & cutters	2.3	15.9	Combination machine tool operators	1.0	27.5
Drafters	1.8	-9.7	Furniture finishers	1.0	3.9
Industrial truck & tractor operators	1.8	15.9			

Source: *Industry-Occupation Matrix*, Bureau of Labor Statistics. These data relate to one or more 3-digit SIC industry groups rather than to a single 4-digit SIC. The change reported for each occupation to the year 2005 is a percent of growth or decline as estimated by the Bureau of Labor Statistics. The abbreviation nec stands for 'not elsewhere classified'.

LOCATION BY STATE AND REGIONAL CONCENTRATION

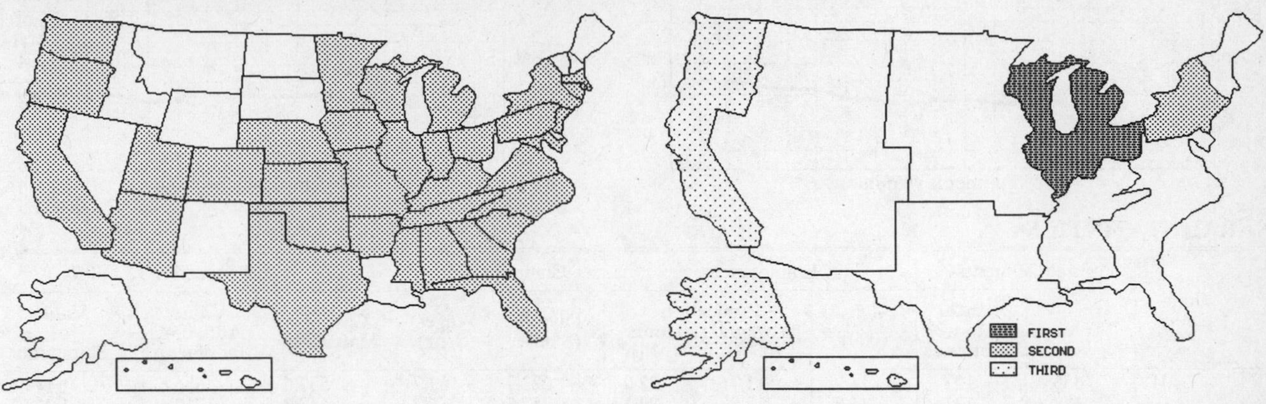

INDUSTRY DATA BY STATE

State	Establish-ments	Shipments			Employment				Cost as % of Shipments	Investment per Employee ($)
		Total ($ mil)	% of U.S.	Per Establ.	Total Number	% of U.S.	Per Establ.	Wages ($/hour)		
Illinois	60	472.1	13.7	7.9	3,700	10.6	62	10.73	45.0	1,622
California	118	260.6	7.6	2.2	2,700	7.8	23	10.31	46.7	1,815
New York	82	215.6	6.3	2.6	2,700	7.8	33	9.17	44.8	1,519
Indiana	21	209.1	6.1	10.0	2,100	6.0	100	10.49	44.8	3,667
Pennsylvania	40	190.9	5.5	4.8	1,800	5.2	45	12.73	46.8	2,278
Ohio	50	184.0	5.3	3.7	2,300	6.6	46	10.06	49.5	1,087
Michigan	43	175.9	5.1	4.1	1,800	5.2	42	9.50	53.4	1,444
New Jersey	34	174.3	5.1	5.1	1,600	4.6	47	10.04	50.0	2,188
Alabama	9	163.7	4.8	18.2	1,200	3.4	133	7.52	46.4	3,000
Minnesota	18	156.2	4.5	8.7	1,600	4.6	89	14.59	39.2	1,375
Texas	31	117.3	3.4	3.8	1,400	4.0	45	8.65	41.9	2,571
Missouri	27	108.2	3.1	4.0	1,200	3.4	44	8.42	39.1	1,333
Georgia	29	101.4	2.9	3.5	1,100	3.2	38	7.90	47.1	2,000
Florida	32	77.4	2.2	2.4	1,000	2.9	31	8.00	45.0	800
Wisconsin	19	70.9	2.1	3.7	800	2.3	42	10.00	39.2	2,250
Mississippi	4	63.7	1.8	15.9	500	1.4	125	7.63	47.6	-
Massachusetts	12	42.8	1.2	3.6	500	1.4	42	11.71	48.1	2,800
Kansas	9	40.8	1.2	4.5	600	1.7	67	8.00	37.5	833
Kentucky	11	38.1	1.1	3.5	500	1.4	45	7.22	50.7	3,800
Colorado	10	31.9	0.9	3.2	300	0.9	30	9.00	39.2	4,000
North Carolina	15	22.8	0.7	1.5	400	1.1	27	8.00	37.3	1,000
Washington	14	18.0	0.5	1.3	200	0.6	14	13.50	39.4	-
Virginia	9	17.1	0.5	1.9	300	0.9	33	7.75	49.1	667
Connecticut	9	16.3	0.5	1.8	200	0.6	22	9.00	44.2	1,000
Maryland	5	12.8	0.4	2.6	100	0.3	20	11.50	40.6	-
Oregon	9	10.6	0.3	1.2	100	0.3	11	8.00	43.4	2,000
Arizona	8	10.5	0.3	1.3	100	0.3	13	9.50	49.5	-
Rhode Island	7	8.3	0.2	1.2	100	0.3	14	6.00	39.8	-
Oklahoma	6	8.2	0.2	1.4	100	0.3	17	13.00	36.6	-
Tennessee	10	(D)	-	-	375 *	1.1	38	-	-	-
Arkansas	7	(D)	-	-	1,750 *	5.0	250	-	-	-
Nebraska	7	(D)	-	-	750 *	2.2	107	-	-	-
South Carolina	4	(D)	-	-	175 *	0.5	44	-	-	-
Iowa	3	(D)	-	-	175 *	0.5	58	-	-	-
Utah	3	(D)	-	-	175 *	0.5	58	-	-	-

Source: 1992 *Economic Census*. The states are in descending order of shipments or establishments (if shipment data are missing for the majority). The symbol (D) appears when data are withheld to prevent disclosure of competitive information. States marked with (D) are sorted by number of establishments. A dash (-) indicates that the data element cannot be calculated; * indicates the midpoint of a range.

2591 - DRAPERY HARDWARE & BLINDS & SHADES

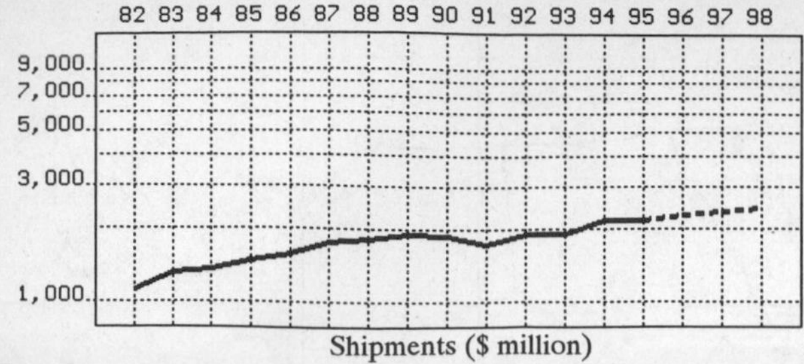

Shipments ($ million)

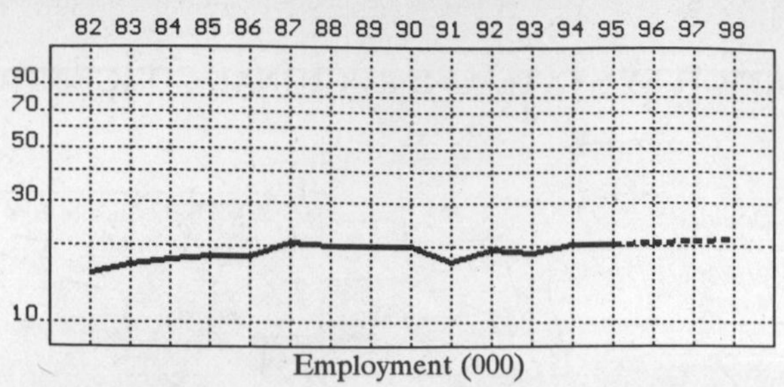

Employment (000)

GENERAL STATISTICS

Year	Companies	Establishments		Employment			Compensation		Production ($ million)			
		Total	with 20 or more employees	Total (000)	Production Workers (000)	Production Hours (Mil)	Payroll ($ mil)	Wages ($/hr)	Cost of Materials	Value Added by Manufacture	Value of Shipments	Capital Invest.
1982	404	435	127	15.7	11.7	22.0	223.7	6.67	557.6	556.6	1,114.4	31.3
1983		428	131	16.8	12.5	24.1	257.5	6.77	649.2	712.4	1,332.1	18.7
1984		421	135	17.7	13.5	26.2	274.8	6.65	706.0	660.8	1,354.2	35.1
1985		414	140	18.4	14.2	27.3	294.9	6.95	768.3	692.3	1,473.6	26.1
1986		434	135	18.2	13.7	26.8	296.2	7.04	822.6	748.5	1,570.6	15.9
1987	443	489	142	20.6	15.9	31.2	342.2	7.16	887.0	898.8	1,780.4	27.3
1988		504	153	20.0	15.6	30.8	341.3	7.42	900.5	929.1	1,830.0	24.8
1989		490	157	20.1	15.4	30.7	359.6	7.78	948.2	984.2	1,927.0	25.6
1990		494	160	20.2	13.7	26.6	360.6	8.42	890.2	1,005.1	1,886.3	27.8
1991		505	137	17.3	12.2	24.7	341.6	8.27	778.0	928.0	1,712.5	24.9
1992	502	556	157	19.4	13.0	26.3	395.5	8.38	941.2	959.9	1,915.6	27.6
1993		536	137	18.8	12.6	26.0	390.9	8.40	959.5	957.9	1,914.7	21.9
1994		554P	155P	20.5	14.0	27.8	436.7	9.03	1,085.3	1,114.5	2,191.1	24.6
1995		566P	157P	20.5P	13.9P	28.3P	436.4P	9.02P	1,088.2P	1,117.4P	2,196.9P	24.1P
1996		578P	158P	20.8P	13.9P	28.5P	451.3P	9.22P	1,123.8P	1,154.1P	2,268.9P	23.9P
1997		590P	160P	21.0P	14.0P	28.7P	466.2P	9.42P	1,159.5P	1,190.7P	2,341.0P	23.7P
1998		602P	162P	21.3P	14.0P	28.9P	481.1P	9.62P	1,195.2P	1,227.4P	2,413.0P	23.5P

Sources: 1982, 1987, 1992 *Economic Census*; *Annual Survey of Manufactures*, 83-86, 88-91, 93-94. Establishment counts for non-Census years are from *County Business Patterns*; establishment values for 83-84 are extrapolations. 'P's show projections by the editors. Industries reclassified in 87 will not have data for prior years.

INDICES OF CHANGE

Year	Companies	Establishments		Employment			Compensation		Production ($ million)			
		Total	with 20 or more employees	Total (000)	Production Workers (000)	Production Hours (Mil)	Payroll ($ mil)	Wages ($/hr)	Cost of Materials	Value Added by Manufacture	Value of Shipments	Capital Invest.
1982	80	78	81	81	90	84	57	80	59	58	58	113
1983		77	83	87	96	92	65	81	69	74	70	68
1984		76	86	91	104	100	69	79	75	69	71	127
1985		74	89	95	109	104	75	83	82	72	77	95
1986		78	86	94	105	102	75	84	87	78	82	58
1987	88	88	90	106	122	119	87	85	94	94	93	99
1988		91	97	103	120	117	86	89	96	97	96	90
1989		88	100	104	118	117	91	93	101	103	101	93
1990		89	102	104	105	101	91	100	95	105	98	101
1991		91	87	89	94	94	86	99	83	97	89	90
1992	100	100	100	100	100	100	100	100	100	100	100	100
1993		96	87	97	97	99	99	100	102	100	100	79
1994		100P	99P	106	108	106	110	108	115	116	114	89
1995		102P	100P	106P	107P	108P	110P	108P	116P	116P	115P	87P
1996		104P	101P	107P	107P	109P	114P	110P	119P	120P	118P	87P
1997		106P	102P	108P	108P	109P	118P	112P	123P	124P	122P	86P
1998		108P	103P	110P	108P	110P	122P	115P	127P	128P	126P	85P

Sources: Same as General Statistics. Values reflect change from the base year, 1992. Values above 100 mean greater than 92, values below 100 mean less than 92, and a value of 100 in the 82-91 or 93-98 period means same as 92. 'P's mark projections by the editors.

SELECTED RATIOS

For 1994	Avg. of All Manufact.	Analyzed Industry	Index	For 1994	Avg. of All Manufact.	Analyzed Industry	Index
Employees per Establishment	49	37	76	Value Added per Production Worker	134,084	79,607	59
Payroll per Establishment	1,500,273	788,914	53	Cost per Establishment	5,045,178	1,960,634	39
Payroll per Employee	30,620	21,302	70	Cost per Employee	102,970	52,941	51
Production Workers per Establishment	34	25	74	Cost per Production Worker	146,988	77,521	53
Wages per Establishment	853,319	453,502	53	Shipments per Establishment	9,576,895	3,958,302	41
Wages per Production Worker	24,861	17,931	72	Shipments per Employee	195,460	106,883	55
Hours per Production Worker	2,056	1,986	97	Shipments per Production Worker	279,017	156,507	56
Wages per Hour	12.09	9.03	75	Investment per Establishment	321,011	44,441	14
Value Added per Establishment	4,602,255	2,013,385	44	Investment per Employee	6,552	1,200	18
Value Added per Employee	93,930	54,366	58	Investment per Production Worker	9,352	1,757	19

Sources: Same as General Statistics. The 'Average of All Manufacturing' column represents the average of all manufacturing industries reported for the most recent complete year available. The Index shows the relationship between the Average and the Analyzed Industry. For example, 100 means that they are equal; 500 that the Analyzed Industry is five times the average; 50 means that the Analyzed Industry is half the national average. The abbreviation 'na' is used to show that data are 'not available'.

LEADING COMPANIES

Number shown: **33** Total sales ($ mil): **1,782** Total employment (000): **16.2**

Company Name	Address				CEO Name	Phone	Co. Type	Sales ($ mil)	Empl. (000)
Hunter Douglas Inc	2 Pkway & Rte 17 S	U Saddle Rvr	NJ	07458	Marvin Hopkins	201-327-8200	R	600	5.0
Kirsch	PO Box 0370	Sturgis	MI	49091	Geoffery Spark	616-659-5100	D	250	3.0
Springs Window Fashions	7549 Graber Rd	Middleton	WI	53562	Lance W Devereaux	608-836-1011	D	250	2.4
Levolor Corp	7614 Business Pk	Greensboro	NC	27409	Don McIlnay	910-668-9862	D	180	1.4
Home Fashions Inc	PO Box 70	Westminster	CA	92683	Joe Berghold	714-891-4311	R	110*	1.0
Kenney Manufacturing Co	1000 Jefferson Blv	Warwick	RI	02886	GD Kenney	401-739-2200	R	100	0.6
Newell Window Furnishing Co	916 S Arcade Av	Freeport	IL	61032	Stephen Thomas	815-235-4171	S	71	0.7
Home Fashions Del Mar	PO Box 70	Westminster	CA	92683	Joseph Cole	714-891-4311	D	44*	0.3
Hunter Douglas Fabrication	2390 Zanker Rd	San Jose	CA	95131	George Snell	408-435-8844	S	32	0.1
Blind Maker Inc	2013 Centimeter Cir	Austin	TX	78758	Ray Hicks	512-835-5333	R	20	0.2
Nanik	PO Box 1766	Wausau	WI	54402	Susan Lang	715-843-4653	D	19	0.2
Beauti-Vue Products Corp	Bristol Industrial	Bristol	WI	53104	J Grumbeck	414-857-2329	R	13	0.1
Mark Window Products	2900 S Fairview St	Santa Ana	CA	92704	B Jackowski	714-641-1411	R	13*	0.1
C-Mor Co	7 Jewell St	Garfield	NJ	07026	S P Gershuny	201-478-3900	R	11	0.1
Andrew Dutton Company Inc	284 Bodwell St	Avon	MA	02322	William Colby	508-586-4100	R	10	<0.1
Acme Window Coverings Ltd	3000 Madison St	Bellwood	IL	60104	Josh Krengel	708-544-5000	R	9	0.1
Empire Carpet Mills Inc	20735 Superior St	Chatsworth	CA	91311	Ruben Sarkissian	818-882-2700	R	7	<0.1
Source North West Inc	PO Box 1458	Woodinville	WA	98072	Laren Olsen	206-483-3535	R	6	<0.1
Warren Shade Company Inc	275 Market St	Minneapolis	MN	55413	Mike Mann	612-331-5939	R	6*	<0.1
Aeroshade Inc	PO Box 559	Waukesha	WI	53187	David M Duval	414-547-2101	R	5*	<0.1
Bailey and Weston Inc	80 Sharp St	Hingham	MA	02043	CR Thurston	617-337-6786	R	4	<0.1
Kenfair Manufacturing Co	840 S Pickett St	Alexandria	VA	22304	N Fairbanks	703-751-5900	R	4	0.5
Ambassador Industries	2754 W Temple St	Los Angeles	CA	90026	Mike Lahav	213-383-1171	R	3	<0.1
Dynamic Dimensions Inc	20 W 201 101st St	Lemont	IL	60439	Mark Teller	708-910-6200	R	3	<0.1
Northern Cross Industries Inc	PO Box 975	Brattleboro	VT	05301	William Hoag	802-257-4501	D	3	<0.1
Ralph Friedland and Brothers	17 Industrial Dr	Keyport	NJ	07735	Ely Tawil	908-290-9800	R	3*	<0.1
Gould-Mersereau Company Inc	PO Box 1231	Long Island Ct	NY	11101	Tony Lentino	718-361-8120	R	3	<0.1
Berkshire Industries Inc	230 J Downey Dr	New Britain	CT	06051	Irving Spivack	203-225-9477	R	1*	<0.1
Kingman Industries	1500 E Chestnut	Santa Ana	CA	92701	Luis Contreras	714-542-0790	S	1	<0.1
Spring Crest Company Inc	190 Arrow Vista Cir	Brea	CA	92621	Jack W Long	714-529-9993	R	1	<0.1
Modern Window Shade Co	3400 Cedar Av S	Minneapolis	MN	55407	AL Quimby Jr	612-729-8256	R	1	<0.1
Plastic-View Transparent Shades	4585 Runway	Simi Valley	CA	93063	Sonny C Voges	805-520-9390	R	1	<0.1
Quaker Blind and Drape Co	303 N Fredericks	Ventnor	NJ	08406	Frances Cohen	609-641-3162	R	0*	<0.1

Source: *Ward's Business Directory of U.S. Private and Public Companies*, Volumes 1 and 2, 1996. The company type code used is as follows: P - Public, R - Private, S - Subsidiary, D - Division, J - Joint Venture, A - Affiliate, G - Group. Sales are in millions of dollars, employees are in thousands. An asterisk (*) indicates an estimated sales volume. The symbol < stands for 'less than'. Company names and addresses are truncated, in some cases, to fit into the available space.

MATERIALS CONSUMED

Material	Quantity	Delivered Cost ($ million)
Materials, ingredients, containers, and supplies	(X)	818.2
Fabricated metal products, including forgings	(X)	43.8
Castings (rough and semifinished)	(X)	0.4
Steel shapes and forms (except castings, forgings, and fabricated metal products)	(X)	44.6
Aluminum and aluminum-base alloy sheet, plate, foil, and welded tubing	(X)	(D)
All other aluminum and aluminum-base alloy shapes and forms	(X)	57.3
Other nonferrous shapes and forms (except castings, forgings, and fabricated metal products)	(X)	(D)
Plastics coated fabrics and shade cloth	(X)	92.7
Cordage	(X)	(D)
Woven narrow tape and webbing	(X)	2.1
Plastics products consumed in the form of sheets, rods, tubes, film, and other shapes	(X)	43.2
Paperboard containers, boxes, and corrugated paperboard	(X)	23.4
All other materials and components, parts, containers, and supplies	(X)	118.7
Materials, ingredients, containers, and supplies, nsk	(X)	302.8

Source: 1992 *Economic Census*. Explanation of symbols used: (D): Withheld to avoid disclosure of competitive data; na: Not available; (S): Withheld because statistical norms were not met; (X): Not applicable; (Z): Less than half the unit shown; nec: Not elsewhere classified; nsk: Not specified by kind; - : zero; * : 10-19 percent estimated; ** : 20-29 percent estimated.

PRODUCT SHARE DETAILS

Product or Product Class	% Share	Product or Product Class	% Share
Drapery hardware and blinds and shades	100.00	vertical and horizontal	13.57
Window shades and accessories	15.91	Venetian blinds, nsk	1.88
Plastics window shades	18.28	Other shades and blinds, nec, and curtain and drapery rods, poles, and fixtures	21.87
Window shades other than plastics, including cloth, paper, etc.	57.25	Other shades and blinds, nec, except canvas and other textile fabrics, including wood, metal, plastics, chip, bamboo, etc.	12.80
Window shade accessories and rollers, sold separately	23.01	Curtain and drapery rods, poles, and fixtures, excluding window shade accessories	83.79
Window shades and accessories, nsk	1.49	Other shades and blinds, nec, and curtain and drapery rods, poles, and fixtures, nsk	3.44
Venetian blinds	49.32	Drapery hardware and blinds and shades, nsk	12.91
Aluminum-slat venetian blinds, complete, vertical and horizontal	52.44		
Venetian blinds other than aluminum-slat, complete, vertical and horizontal, including wood, plastics, steel, etc.	32.09		
Unassembled venetian blinds, parts, and components,			

Source: 1992 *Economic Census*. The values shown are percent of total shipments in an industry. Values of indented subcategories are summed in the main heading. The symbol (D) appears when data are withheld to prevent disclosure of competitive information. The abbreviation nsk stands for 'not specified by kind' and nec for 'not elsewhere classified'.

INPUTS AND OUTPUTS FOR DRAPERY HARDWARE & BLINDS & SHADES

Economic Sector or Industry Providing Inputs	%	Sector	Economic Sector or Industry Buying Outputs	%	Sector
Blast furnaces & steel mills	16.2	Manufg.	Personal consumption expenditures	82.2	
Aluminum rolling & drawing	13.6	Manufg.	Gross private fixed investment	12.4	Cap Inv
Wholesale trade	8.5	Trade	Exports	1.7	Foreign
Wood products, nec	8.4	Manufg.	S/L Govt. purch., higher education	1.5	S/L Govt
Coated fabrics, not rubberized	7.1	Manufg.	Drapery hardware & blinds & shades	0.7	Manufg.
Imports	6.6	Foreign	Change in business inventories	0.6	In House
Miscellaneous plastics products	5.9	Manufg.	Mobile homes	0.3	Manufg.
Advertising	2.8	Services	S/L Govt. purch., health & hospitals	0.2	S/L Govt
Narrow fabric mills	2.3	Manufg.	Paper coating & glazing	0.1	Manufg.
Screw machine and related products	2.3	Manufg.	Paper mills, except building paper	0.1	Manufg.
Hardwood dimension & flooring mills	2.1	Manufg.			
Maintenance of nonfarm buildings nec	1.8	Constr.			
Veneer & plywood	1.8	Manufg.			
Nonferrous wire drawing & insulating	1.6	Manufg.			
Cordage & twine	1.2	Manufg.			
Metal stampings, nec	1.2	Manufg.			
Motor freight transportation & warehousing	1.2	Util.			
Cyclic crudes and organics	1.1	Manufg.			
Drapery hardware & blinds & shades	1.1	Manufg.			
Petroleum refining	1.0	Manufg.			
Electric services (utilities)	1.0	Util.			
Eating & drinking places	1.0	Trade			
Real estate	0.8	Fin/R.E.			
Communications, except radio & TV	0.7	Util.			
Railroads & related services	0.7	Util.			
Gas production & distribution (utilities)	0.6	Util.			
Banking	0.6	Fin/R.E.			
Abrasive products	0.5	Manufg.			
Equipment rental & leasing services	0.5	Services			
Paints & allied products	0.4	Manufg.			
Paperboard containers & boxes	0.4	Manufg.			
Metal coating & allied services	0.3	Manufg.			
Air transportation	0.3	Util.			
Legal services	0.3	Services			
Management & consulting services & labs	0.3	Services			
U.S. Postal Service	0.3	Gov't			
Machinery, except electrical, nec	0.2	Manufg.			
Accounting, auditing & bookkeeping	0.2	Services			
Automotive rental & leasing, without drivers	0.2	Services			
Automotive repair shops & services	0.2	Services			
Industrial inorganic chemicals, nec	0.1	Manufg.			
Lubricating oils & greases	0.1	Manufg.			
Manifold business forms	0.1	Manufg.			
Special dies & tools & machine tool accessories	0.1	Manufg.			
Insurance carriers	0.1	Fin/R.E.			
Royalties	0.1	Fin/R.E.			
Computer & data processing services	0.1	Services			
Hotels & lodging places	0.1	Services			
Job training & related services	0.1	Services			
Laundry, dry cleaning, shoe repair	0.1	Services			

Source: Benchmark Input-Output Accounts for the U.S. Economy, 1982, U.S. Department of Commerce, Washington, D.C., July 1991. Data, as reported in the source, are organized by the 1977 SIC structure in use in 1982 but have been matched, as closely as is possible, to the 1987 SIC structure used in this book.

OCCUPATIONS EMPLOYED BY SIC 259 - OFFICE AND MISCELLANEOUS FURNITURE AND FIXTURES

Occupation	% of Total 1994	Change to 2005	Occupation	% of Total 1994	Change to 2005
Assemblers, fabricators, & hand workers nec	21.5	6.5	Hand packers & packagers	1.6	-8.7
Blue collar worker supervisors	4.2	1.0	Welders & cutters	1.6	6.5
Cabinetmakers & bench carpenters	3.9	59.7	Inspectors, testers, & graders, precision	1.6	6.5
Upholsterers	2.8	10.1	Machine forming operators, metal & plastic	1.4	6.5
Welding machine setters, operators	2.8	-4.2	Head sawyers & sawing machine workers	1.3	-14.8
Sales & related workers nec	2.6	6.5	Secretaries, ex legal & medical	1.3	-3.1
Wood machinists	2.5	43.7	General office clerks	1.3	-9.2
General managers & top executives	2.2	1.0	Industrial truck & tractor operators	1.2	6.5
Furniture finishers	2.2	30.3	Industrial production managers	1.2	6.5
Coating, painting, & spraying machine workers	2.1	6.5	Drafters	1.2	-17.1
Machine tool cutting & forming etc. nec	2.0	6.5	Grinders & polishers, hand	1.1	6.5
Freight, stock, & material movers, hand	2.0	-14.8	Bookkeeping, accounting, & auditing clerks	1.1	-20.1
Woodworking machine workers	2.0	-57.4	Truck drivers light & heavy	1.1	9.8
Traffic, shipping, & receiving clerks	1.9	2.4			

Source: Industry-Occupation Matrix, Bureau of Labor Statistics. These data relate to one or more 3-digit SIC industry groups rather than to a single 4-digit SIC. The change reported for each occupation to the year 2005 is a percent of growth or decline as estimated by the Bureau of Labor Statistics. The abbreviation nec stands for 'not elsewhere classified'.

LOCATION BY STATE AND REGIONAL CONCENTRATION

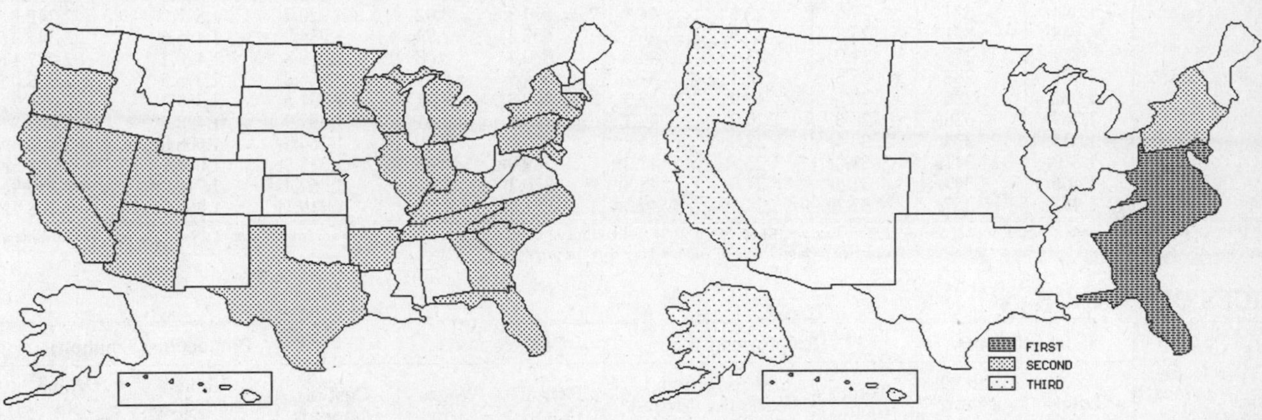

INDUSTRY DATA BY STATE

State	Establish-ments	Shipments Total ($ mil)	Shipments % of U.S.	Shipments Per Establ.	Employment Total Number	Employment % of U.S.	Employment Per Establ.	Employment Wages ($/hour)	Cost as % of Shipments	Investment per Employee ($)
California	88	418.1	21.8	4.8	4,400	22.7	50	8.43	41.7	773
Illinois	28	165.5	8.6	5.9	1,300	6.7	46	9.16	36.9	1,000
Texas	34	162.5	8.5	4.8	1,500	7.7	44	6.57	41.1	1,067
Michigan	15	147.0	7.7	9.8	1,100	5.7	73	11.31	46.9	-
Pennsylvania	35	117.8	6.1	3.4	1,500	7.7	43	7.75	63.7	733
Florida	98	105.6	5.5	1.1	1,500	7.7	15	6.56	56.0	1,200
Georgia	11	74.0	3.9	6.7	600	3.1	55	7.90	44.3	1,167
New Jersey	26	63.8	3.3	2.5	700	3.6	27	7.20	44.2	714
New York	51	62.5	3.3	1.2	800	4.1	16	7.73	54.9	1,250
Connecticut	8	27.4	1.4	3.4	200	1.0	25	10.00	41.2	-
Maryland	10	19.0	1.0	1.9	300	1.5	30	7.00	49.5	-
North Carolina	9	13.8	0.7	1.5	200	1.0	22	8.50	50.7	-
Indiana	14	(D)	-	-	750 *	3.9	54	-	-	-
Arizona	8	(D)	-	-	175 *	0.9	22	-	-	571
Wisconsin	7	(D)	-	-	1,750 *	9.0	250	-	-	-
Tennessee	6	(D)	-	-	375 *	1.9	63	-	-	533
Minnesota	5	(D)	-	-	175 *	0.9	35	-	-	-
Nevada	4	(D)	-	-	175 *	0.9	44	-	-	-
Oregon	4	(D)	-	-	175 *	0.9	44	-	-	-
Utah	4	(D)	-	-	375 *	1.9	94	-	-	-
Arkansas	2	(D)	-	-	175 *	0.9	88	-	-	-
Kentucky	2	(D)	-	-	175 *	0.9	88	-	-	-
Rhode Island	2	(D)	-	-	750 *	3.9	375	-	-	-
South Carolina	2	(D)	-	-	175 *	0.9	88	-	-	-

Source: 1992 *Economic Census*. The states are in descending order of shipments or establishments (if shipment data are missing for the majority). The symbol (D) appears when data are withheld to prevent disclosure of competitive information. States marked with (D) are sorted by number of establishments. A dash (-) indicates that the data element cannot be calculated; * indicates the midpoint of a range.

2599 - FURNITURE & FIXTURES, NEC

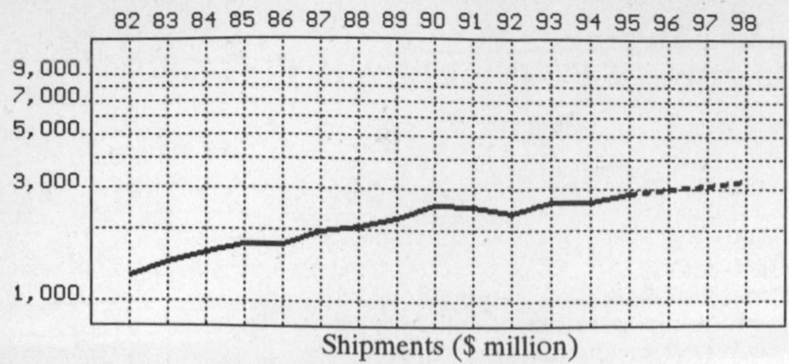

Shipments ($ million)

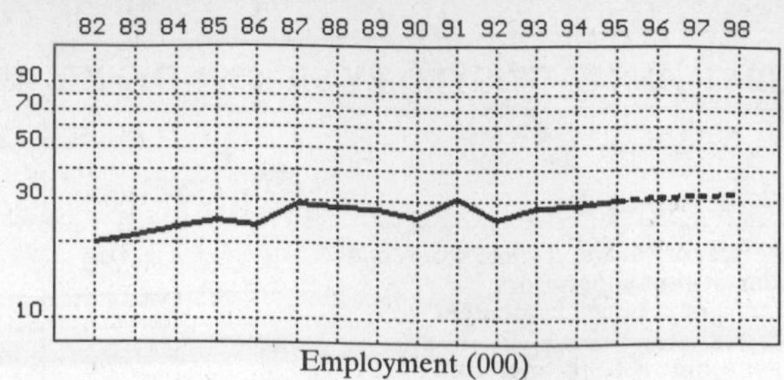

Employment (000)

GENERAL STATISTICS

Year	Companies	Establishments: Total	Establishments: with 20 or more employees	Employment: Total (000)	Employment: Production Workers (000)	Employment: Production Hours (Mil)	Compensation: Payroll ($ mil)	Compensation: Wages ($/hr)	Production ($ million): Cost of Materials	Production ($ million): Value Added by Manufacture	Production ($ million): Value of Shipments	Production ($ million): Capital Invest.
1982	819	832	221	20.1	14.9	29.4	327.4	6.97	595.8	682.0	1,275.7	30.0
1983		754	226	21.6	15.9	32.5	374.4	7.10	691.6	785.9	1,457.9	17.8
1984		676	231	23.1	17.0	34.8	415.9	7.21	737.0	866.4	1,599.8	49.6
1985		598	235	24.8	18.2	36.4	465.0	7.73	760.9	966.2	1,724.7	42.0
1986		563	234	23.9	17.1	34.0	449.1	8.04	719.8	994.0	1,713.7	32.8
1987	1,569	1,597	352	29.3	21.6	41.9	549.7	7.93	791.1	1,171.4	1,959.7	38.3
1988		1,248	355	28.3	21.0	41.0	561.4	8.22	815.3	1,238.8	2,054.7	34.7
1989		1,084	324	27.6	22.8	44.1	576.2	8.02	920.7	1,327.0	2,242.3	51.1
1990		948	301	25.8	23.9	46.8	630.2	7.94	1,084.7	1,485.6	2,547.3	54.0
1991		881	273	31.0	23.1	44.6	630.4	8.08	1,059.8	1,420.1	2,487.1	54.5
1992	1,386	1,409	288	25.3	18.1	37.2	604.5	8.87	966.8	1,396.3	2,359.0	47.6
1993		1,082	286	28.3	19.9	42.3	700.3	8.91	1,081.6	1,569.4	2,636.7	64.1
1994		1,269P	326P	28.6	20.9	42.1	728.8	9.61	1,161.9	1,478.6	2,643.3	48.2
1995		1,315P	334P	30.4P	23.0P	46.2P	757.8P	9.30P	1,264.2P	1,608.8P	2,876.0P	59.8P
1996		1,360P	342P	31.0P	23.5P	47.2P	789.0P	9.48P	1,315.8P	1,674.5P	2,993.5P	62.1P
1997		1,406P	349P	31.6P	24.0P	48.3P	820.2P	9.65P	1,367.4P	1,740.2P	3,110.9P	64.5P
1998		1,452P	357P	32.2P	24.5P	49.3P	851.4P	9.83P	1,419.1P	1,805.9P	3,228.4P	66.8P

Sources: 1982, 1987, 1992 *Economic Census*; *Annual Survey of Manufactures*, 83-86, 88-91, 93-94. Establishment counts for non-Census years are from *County Business Patterns*; establishment values for 83-84 are extrapolations. 'P's show projections by the editors. Industries reclassified in 87 will not have data for prior years.

INDICES OF CHANGE

Year	Companies	Establishments: Total	Establishments: with 20 or more employees	Employment: Total (000)	Employment: Production Workers (000)	Employment: Production Hours (Mil)	Compensation: Payroll ($ mil)	Compensation: Wages ($/hr)	Production ($ million): Cost of Materials	Production ($ million): Value Added by Manufacture	Production ($ million): Value of Shipments	Production ($ million): Capital Invest.
1982	59	59	77	79	82	79	54	79	62	49	54	63
1983		54	78	85	88	87	62	80	72	56	62	37
1984		48	80	91	94	94	69	81	76	62	68	104
1985		42	82	98	101	98	77	87	79	69	73	88
1986		40	81	94	94	91	74	91	74	71	73	69
1987	113	113	122	116	119	113	91	89	82	84	83	80
1988		89	123	112	116	110	93	93	84	89	87	73
1989		77	113	109	126	119	95	90	95	95	95	107
1990		67	105	102	132	126	104	90	112	106	108	113
1991		63	95	123	128	120	104	91	110	102	105	114
1992	100	100	100	100	100	100	100	100	100	100	100	100
1993		77	99	112	110	114	116	100	112	112	112	135
1994		90P	113P	113	115	113	121	108	120	106	112	101
1995		93P	116P	120P	127P	124P	125P	105P	131P	115P	122P	126P
1996		97P	119P	122P	130P	127P	131P	107P	136P	120P	127P	131P
1997		100P	121P	125P	133P	130P	136P	109P	141P	125P	132P	135P
1998		103P	124P	127P	135P	133P	141P	111P	147P	129P	137P	140P

Sources: Same as General Statistics. Values reflect change from the base year, 1992. Values above 100 mean greater than 92, values below 100 mean less than 92, and a value of 100 in the 82-91 or 93-98 period means same as 92. 'P's mark projections by the editors.

SELECTED RATIOS

For 1994	Avg. of All Manufact.	Analyzed Industry	Index
Employees per Establishment	49	23	46
Payroll per Establishment	1,500,273	574,256	38
Payroll per Employee	30,620	25,483	83
Production Workers per Establishment	34	16	48
Wages per Establishment	853,319	318,788	37
Wages per Production Worker	24,861	19,358	78
Hours per Production Worker	2,056	2,014	98
Wages per Hour	12.09	9.61	79
Value Added per Establishment	4,602,255	1,165,058	25
Value Added per Employee	93,930	51,699	55

For 1994	Avg. of All Manufact.	Analyzed Industry	Index
Value Added per Production Worker	134,084	70,746	53
Cost per Establishment	5,045,178	915,515	18
Cost per Employee	102,970	40,626	39
Cost per Production Worker	146,988	55,593	38
Shipments per Establishment	9,576,895	2,082,780	22
Shipments per Employee	195,460	92,423	47
Shipments per Production Worker	279,017	126,474	45
Investment per Establishment	321,011	37,979	12
Investment per Employee	6,552	1,685	26
Investment per Production Worker	9,352	2,306	25

Sources: Same as General Statistics. The 'Average of All Manufacturing' column represents the average of all manufacturing industries reported for the most recent complete year available. The Index shows the relationship between the Average and the Analyzed Industry. For example, 100 means that they are equal; 500 that the Analyzed Industry is five times the average; 50 means that the Analyzed Industry is half the national average. The abbreviation 'na' is used to show that data are 'not available'.

LEADING COMPANIES

Number shown: **49** Total sales ($ mil): **882** Total employment (000): **7.4**

Company Name	Address				CEO Name	Phone	Co. Type	Sales ($ mil)	Empl. (000)
Kinetic Concepts Inc	8023 Vantage Dr	San Antonio	TX	78230	James R Leininger	210-524-9000	P	270	2.2
Robertson Furniture Company	PO Box 847	Toccoa	GA	30577	Forester L Hodges	706-886-1494	R	87	0.1
Kewaunee Scientific Corp	PO Box 1842	Statesville	NC	28687	Eli Manchester Jr	704-873-7202	P	66	0.6
Smith & Davis Mfg Co	1100 Corp Square	St Louis	MO	63132	Richard C Piaza	314-569-3515	S	47	0.3
Joerns Healthcare Inc	5001 Joerns Dr	Stevens Point	WI	54481	Dennis McCarthy	715-341-3600	D	40	0.4
Masterack	PO Box 100055	Atlanta	GA	30348	L Crabbe	404-659-9316	D	39*	0.4
Metal Masters Foodservice	655 Glenwood Av	Smyrna	DE	19977	Larry McAllister	302-653-3000	R	28	0.5
HARD Manufacturing Company	230 Grider St	Buffalo	NY	14215	W Godin	716-893-1800	R	25	<0.1
Hausted Inc	PO Box 710	Medina	OH	44258	Jerry G Silvertooth	216-723-3271	R	23	0.2
UMBRA USA Inc	1705 Broadway	Buffalo	NY	14212	Les Mandelbaum	716-892-8852	R	20	0.1
Amedco Health Care Inc	PO Box 544	Wright City	MO	63390	Bevil Hogg	314-745-3173	S	19*	0.2
Shafer Commercial Seating Inc	4101 E 48th Av	Denver	CO	80216	Byron A Shafer	303-322-7792	R	17	0.2
Vanguard Studios Inc	PO Box C-4521	Pacoima	CA	91333	Michael H Greeley	818-896-7551	R	17	0.2
Doninger Metal Products Corp	Jeffery Way	Youngsville	NC	27596	Michael Doninger	919-554-1500	R	14	0.2
Stutz-Horowitz Company Inc	42 W 39th St	New York	NY	10018	P Horowitz	212-719-5555	R	14	<0.1
King Arthur Inc	PO Box 6040	Statesville	NC	28677	John McCalla	704-872-0300	S	12	0.1
Lamsteel Corporation	PO Box 90	Hartsville	TN	37074	JJ Weitzman	615-374-2261	R	12	0.1
Carlin Manufacturing Inc	3714 N Valentine	Fresno	CA	93722	Ralph H Goldbeck	209-276-0123	S	10	<0.1
L and B Products West Corp	PO Box 405	Perris	CA	92572	Leonard Einhorn	909-943-6220	S	10	<0.1
Custom Seating Inc	341 S 41st St E	Muskogee	OK	74403	Charles Gresham	918-682-4400	R	9*	0.1
Mitchell Manufacturing Co	PO Box 1156	Milwaukee	WI	53201	DE Read	414-342-3111	R	8	<0.1
Progressive International Corp	8300 Military Rd S	Seattle	WA	98108	Kevin Wold	206-762-8300	R	8*	<0.1
Shure Manufacturing Corp	1601 S Hanley Rd	St Louis	MO	63144	D E Richardson	314-781-2500	R	8*	0.1
Chairmasters Inc	200 E 146th St	Bronx	NY	10451	J Jahier	718-292-0600	R	7	0.2
Batesville American Mfg Co	PO Box 838	Batesville	MS	38606	Jim Hartfield	601-563-4646	S	6	0.1
Sci-O-Tech Inc	PO Box 4428	Lancaster	PA	17604	Tyler Schueler	717-397-0308	R	6*	<0.1
Vitro Seating Products Inc	PO Box 5440	St Louis	MO	63147	Steven Scott	314-241-2265	R	6	0.1
Waymatic Inc	PO Box 5320	South Fulton	TN	38257	RM Easterwood	901-479-1741	R	6	0.1
E-J Industries Inc	1275 S Campbell	Chicago	IL	60608	Leonard Weitzman	312-226-5023	R	5	<0.1
Willoughby Industries Inc	2210 W Morris St	Indianapolis	IN	46221	Tim Willoughby	317-638-2381	R	5	<0.1
Yorkraft Inc	PO Box 2386	York	PA	17405	William C Imhoff	717-845-3666	R	5	<0.1
Trouvailles Inc	64 Grove St	Watertown	MA	02172	David Israel	617-926-2520	R	4*	<0.1
Production Industries Inc	240 N Teller St	Corona	CA	91719	Thomas J Scavone	909-272-0555	R	3	<0.1
Spec-Built Systems Inc	PO Box 2577	National City	CA	91951	George Woodward	619-474-0403	R	3*	<0.1
SFS Corp	5055 W River NE	Comstock Park	MI	49321	William F Fisher	616-784-7199	R	3	<0.1
JH Carr and Sons Furniture Inc	37 S Hudson St	Seattle	WA	98134	James Carr	206-763-1937	R	3	<0.1
Stronglite Inc	255 Davidson Av	Cottage Grove	OR	97424	John Lloyd	503-942-0130	R	2	<0.1
BioFit Engineered Seating	PO Box 109	Waterville	OH	43566	Dale E Barnard	419-823-1861	R	2*	0.1
CB Technical Sources Inc	6130 Springer Way	San Jose	CA	95123	Cindy Blanton	408-727-2203	R	2*	<0.1
Metal-Fab	2641 Walnut Av	Tustin	CA	92680	Peter J Anello	714-669-9940	D	2	<0.1
Gentry's Cabinet Inc	PO Box 168	Anderson	IN	46015	W Clay	317-643-6611	R	2	<0.1
Sutton Products Inc	PO Box 160	Bergman	AR	72615	BL Sutton	501-741-6181	R	2	<0.1
Hans C Egloff Inc	120 N Abington Rd	Clarks Summit	PA	18411	Hans C Egloff	717-586-1323	R	1	<0.1
Lectus Inc	150 W 20th Av	San Mateo	CA	94403	Art Bruno	415-358-0588	R	1*	<0.1
North Star Distributors Inc	2210 Hewitt Av	Everett	WA	98201	Craig Bunney	206-252-9600	R	1*	<0.1
Sunbrite Casual Furniture Inc	3019 J Young Pkwy	Orlando	FL	32804	Luigi Brandi	407-294-9041	R	1*	<0.1
IBR Corp Harbortown	900 Lunt Av	Elk Grove Vill	IL	60007	CJ Rhee	708-427-1900	D	1*	<0.1
TDG Aerospace Inc	7031 Koll Ctr Pkwy	Pleasanton	CA	94566	David Wensley	510-417-0910	R	1*	<0.1
NK Medical Products Inc	210 John Glenn Dr	Amherst	NY	14228	Norman Kurlander	716-691-1111	R	0	<0.1

Source: Ward's Business Directory of U.S. Private and Public Companies, Volumes 1 and 2, 1996. The company type code used is as follows: P - Public, R - Private, S - Subsidiary, D - Division, J - Joint Venture, A - Affiliate, G - Group. Sales are in millions of dollars, employees are in thousands. An asterisk (*) indicates an estimated sales volume. The symbol < stands for 'less than'. Company names and addresses are truncated, in some cases, to fit into the available space.

MATERIALS CONSUMED

Material	Quantity	Delivered Cost ($ million)
Materials, ingredients, containers, and supplies	(X)	785.9
Metal stampings	(X)	3.1
All other fabricated metal products (except castings and forgings)	(X)	22.8
Forgings	(X)	(Z)
Castings (rough and semifinished)	(X)	3.7
Steel sheet and strip, including tin plate	(X)	58.4
All other steel shapes and forms (except castings, forgings, and fabricated metal products)	(X)	29.1
Aluminum and aluminum-base alloy sheet, plate, foil, and welded tubing	(X)	5.1
All other aluminum and aluminum-base alloy shapes and forms	(X)	3.3
Other nonferrous shapes and forms (except castings, forgings, and fabricated metal products)	(X)	3.9
Hardwood lumber, rough and dressed	(X)	43.0
Softwood lumber, rough and dressed	(X)	2.7
Hardwood dimension and parts, including wood furniture frames	(X)	29.2
Hardwood veneer	(X)	1.0
Hardwood plywood	(X)	9.5
Softwood plywood	(X)	3.3
Particleboard (wood)	(X)	5.4
Medium density fiberboard (MDF)	(X)	1.9
Hardboard (wood fiberboard)	(X)	1.3

Continued on next page.

MATERIALS CONSUMED - Continued

Material	Quantity	Delivered Cost ($ million)
Plastics laminated sheets	(X)	11.3
Plastics furniture parts and components	(X)	14.1
Formed and slab stock for pillows, cushions, seating, etc. (urethane)	(X)	6.3
Coated or laminated fabrics, including vinyl coated	(X)	12.2
Uncoated broadwoven fabrics for upholstery	(X)	4.6
Flat glass (plate, float, and sheet)	(X)	2.6
Adhesives and sealants	(X)	2.1
Paints, varnishes, lacquers, stains, shellacs, japans, enamels, and allied products	(X)	8.4
Furniture and builders' hardware	(X)	46.1
Paperboard containers, boxes, and corrugated paperboard	(X)	12.4
All other materials and components, parts, containers, and supplies	(X)	159.1
Materials, ingredients, containers, and supplies, nsk	(X)	280.2

Source: 1992 *Economic Census*. Explanation of symbols used: (D): Withheld to avoid disclosure of competitive data; na: Not available; (S): Withheld because statistical norms were not met; (X): Not applicable; (Z): Less than half the unit shown; nec: Not elsewhere classified; nsk: Not specified by kind; - : zero; * : 10-19 percent estimated; ** : 20-29 percent estimated.

PRODUCT SHARE DETAILS

Product or Product Class	% Share	Product or Product Class	% Share
Furniture and fixtures, nec	100.00	Other restaurant, cafeteria, bar, and bowling center furniture and fixtures, nec, except warming, cooking, and refrigeration	48.94
Hospital beds	17.77	Restaurant, cafeteria, and bar furniture and fixtures, nsk	11.17
Restaurant, cafeteria, and bar furniture and fixtures	43.53	All other furniture and fixtures, nec	18.15
Upholstered wood chairs and stools for restaurants, cafeterias, and bars	16.03	Industrial work benches and stools	16.46
Nonupholstered wood chairs and stools for restaurants, cafeterias, and bars	3.15	Other furniture and fixtures, nec (including ship furniture, amusement game cabinets, etc.)	74.34
Metal chairs and stools for restaurants, cafeterias, and bars	8.52	All other furniture and fixtures, nec, nsk	9.17
Booths, bars, and back bars for retaurants, cafeterias, and bars	12.20	Furniture and fixtures, nec, nsk	20.56

Source: 1992 *Economic Census*. The values shown are percent of total shipments in an industry. Values of indented subcategories are summed in the main heading. The symbol (D) appears when data are withheld to prevent disclosure of competitive information. The abbreviation nsk stands for 'not specified by kind' and nec for 'not elsewhere classified'.

INPUTS AND OUTPUTS FOR FURNITURE & FIXTURES, NEC

Economic Sector or Industry Providing Inputs	%	Sector	Economic Sector or Industry Buying Outputs	%	Sector
Imports	40.8	Foreign	Gross private fixed investment	82.0	Cap Inv
Blast furnaces & steel mills	12.5	Manufg.	Exports	8.8	Foreign
Wholesale trade	8.9	Trade	Ship building & repairing	2.3	Manufg.
Power transmission equipment	2.4	Manufg.	Personal consumption expenditures	2.0	
Sawmills & planning mills, general	2.4	Manufg.	S/L Govt. purch., health & hospitals	2.0	S/L Govt
Aluminum rolling & drawing	2.2	Manufg.	Musical instruments	1.2	Manufg.
Advertising	2.2	Services	Furniture & fixtures, nec	0.6	Manufg.
Veneer & plywood	2.1	Manufg.	S/L Govt. purch., higher education	0.6	S/L Govt
Hardware, nec	2.0	Manufg.	Federal Government purchases, nondefense	0.2	Fed Govt
Motors & generators	2.0	Manufg.	Federal Government purchases, national defense	0.1	Fed Govt
Screw machine and related products	2.0	Manufg.	Change in business inventories	0.1	In House
Metal stampings, nec	1.7	Manufg.			
Coated fabrics, not rubberized	1.4	Manufg.			
Miscellaneous plastics products	1.4	Manufg.			
Real estate	1.1	Fin/R.E.			
Furniture & fixtures, nec	1.0	Manufg.			
Paints & allied products	1.0	Manufg.			
Motor freight transportation & warehousing	1.0	Util.			
Paperboard containers & boxes	0.9	Manufg.			
Electric services (utilities)	0.9	Util.			
Petroleum refining	0.7	Manufg.			
Maintenance of nonfarm buildings nec	0.6	Constr.			
Fabricated metal products, nec	0.6	Manufg.			
Particleboard	0.5	Manufg.			
Eating & drinking places	0.5	Trade			
Banking	0.5	Fin/R.E.			
Primary copper	0.4	Manufg.			
Wood products, nec	0.4	Manufg.			
Communications, except radio & TV	0.4	Util.			
Gas production & distribution (utilities)	0.4	Util.			
Railroads & related services	0.4	Util.			
Abrasive products	0.3	Manufg.			
Padding & upholstery filling	0.3	Manufg.			
Detective & protective services	0.3	Services			
Equipment rental & leasing services	0.3	Services			
Fabricated rubber products, nec	0.2	Manufg.			

Continued on next page.

INPUTS AND OUTPUTS FOR FURNITURE & FIXTURES, NEC - Continued

Economic Sector or Industry Providing Inputs	%	Sector	Economic Sector or Industry Buying Outputs	%	Sector
Steel wire & related products	0.2	Manufg.			
Air transportation	0.2	Util.			
Legal services	0.2	Services			
Management & consulting services & labs	0.2	Services			
Glass & glass products, except containers	0.1	Manufg.			
Machinery, except electrical, nec	0.1	Manufg.			
Insurance carriers	0.1	Fin/R.E.			
Royalties	0.1	Fin/R.E.			
Accounting, auditing & bookkeeping	0.1	Services			
Automotive rental & leasing, without drivers	0.1	Services			
Automotive repair shops & services	0.1	Services			
U.S. Postal Service	0.1	Gov't			
Noncomparable imports	0.1	Foreign			

Source: Benchmark Input-Output Accounts for the U.S. Economy, 1982, U.S. Department of Commerce, Washington, D.C., July 1991. Data, as reported in the source, are organized by the 1977 SIC structure in use in 1982 but have been matched, as closely as is possible, to the 1987 SIC structure used in this book.

OCCUPATIONS EMPLOYED BY SIC 259 - OFFICE AND MISCELLANEOUS FURNITURE AND FIXTURES

Occupation	% of Total 1994	Change to 2005	Occupation	% of Total 1994	Change to 2005
Assemblers, fabricators, & hand workers nec	21.5	6.5	Hand packers & packagers	1.6	-8.7
Blue collar worker supervisors	4.2	1.0	Welders & cutters	1.6	6.5
Cabinetmakers & bench carpenters	3.9	59.7	Inspectors, testers, & graders, precision	1.6	6.5
Upholsterers	2.8	10.1	Machine forming operators, metal & plastic	1.4	6.5
Welding machine setters, operators	2.8	-4.2	Head sawyers & sawing machine workers	1.3	-14.8
Sales & related workers nec	2.6	6.5	Secretaries, ex legal & medical	1.3	-3.1
Wood machinists	2.5	43.7	General office clerks	1.3	-9.2
General managers & top executives	2.2	1.0	Industrial truck & tractor operators	1.2	6.5
Furniture finishers	2.2	30.3	Industrial production managers	1.2	6.5
Coating, painting, & spraying machine workers	2.1	6.5	Drafters	1.2	-17.1
Machine tool cutting & forming etc. nec	2.0	6.5	Grinders & polishers, hand	1.1	6.5
Freight, stock, & material movers, hand	2.0	-14.8	Bookkeeping, accounting, & auditing clerks	1.1	-20.1
Woodworking machine workers	2.0	-57.4	Truck drivers light & heavy	1.1	9.8
Traffic, shipping, & receiving clerks	1.9	2.4			

Source: Industry-Occupation Matrix, Bureau of Labor Statistics. These data relate to one or more 3-digit SIC industry groups rather than to a single 4-digit SIC. The change reported for each occupation to the year 2005 is a percent of growth or decline as estimated by the Bureau of Labor Statistics. The abbreviation nec stands for 'not elsewhere classified'.

LOCATION BY STATE AND REGIONAL CONCENTRATION

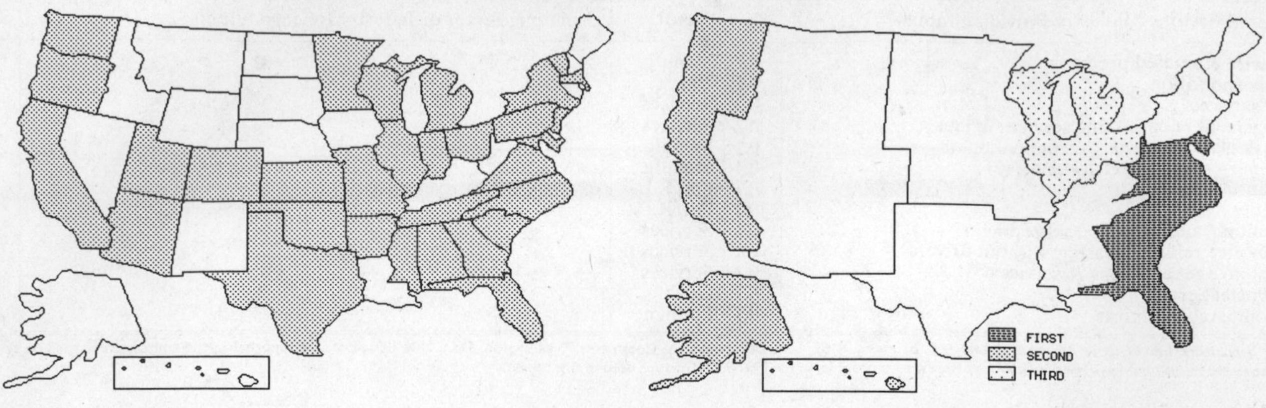

INDUSTRY DATA BY STATE

State	Establish-ments	Shipments			Employment				Cost as % of Shipments	Investment per Employee ($)
		Total ($ mil)	% of U.S.	Per Establ.	Total Number	% of U.S.	Per Establ.	Wages ($/hour)		
California	204	276.1	11.7	1.4	3,300	13.0	16	8.29	42.6	1,364
Missouri	34	182.3	7.7	5.4	1,700	6.7	50	9.88	42.6	-
Florida	124	114.9	4.9	0.9	1,500	5.9	12	7.05	51.0	1,200
Michigan	59	95.8	4.1	1.6	1,100	4.3	19	9.71	45.6	-
Illinois	58	87.8	3.7	1.5	1,100	4.3	19	8.53	45.9	909
North Carolina	67	77.7	3.3	1.2	1,000	4.0	15	7.50	52.5	-
Texas	73	66.6	2.8	0.9	800	3.2	11	8.21	45.2	2,250
New York	103	62.7	2.7	0.6	1,000	4.0	10	9.20	34.9	-
Pennsylvania	51	61.4	2.6	1.2	600	2.4	12	9.44	47.1	2,667
New Jersey	36	46.2	2.0	1.3	500	2.0	14	12.14	39.0	3,600
Georgia	41	43.2	1.8	1.1	600	2.4	15	8.67	39.1	-
Ohio	35	41.9	1.8	1.2	500	2.0	14	10.14	40.3	1,600
Colorado	24	38.0	1.6	1.6	400	1.6	17	8.71	41.1	-
Massachusetts	23	33.8	1.4	1.5	400	1.6	17	8.57	44.1	2,250
Virginia	18	28.3	1.2	1.6	400	1.6	22	9.83	40.6	1,750
Maryland	12	25.6	1.1	2.1	200	0.8	17	8.67	39.8	-
Alabama	26	20.1	0.9	0.8	400	1.6	15	6.83	39.3	-
Mississippi	46	(D)	-	-	1,750 *	6.9	38	-	-	-
Washington	43	(D)	-	-	375 *	1.5	9	-	-	-
Indiana	29	(D)	-	-	1,750 *	6.9	60	-	-	-
Minnesota	28	(D)	-	-	750 *	3.0	27	-	-	-
Oregon	27	(D)	-	-	375 *	1.5	14	-	-	-
Tennessee	25	(D)	-	-	1,750 *	6.9	70	-	-	1,086
Wisconsin	24	(D)	-	-	750 *	3.0	31	-	-	-
Arizona	20	(D)	-	-	175 *	0.7	9	-	-	-
Kansas	18	(D)	-	-	375 *	1.5	21	-	-	-
Arkansas	16	(D)	-	-	375 *	1.5	23	-	-	-
South Carolina	16	(D)	-	-	750 *	3.0	47	-	-	-
Utah	12	(D)	-	-	175 *	0.7	15	-	-	-
Oklahoma	11	(D)	-	-	175 *	0.7	16	-	-	-
Vermont	7	(D)	-	-	175 *	0.7	25	-	-	-

Source: 1992 *Economic Census*. The states are in descending order of shipments or establishments (if shipment data are missing for the majority). The symbol (D) appears when data are withheld to prevent disclosure of competitive information. States marked with (D) are sorted by number of establishments. A dash (-) indicates that the data element cannot be calculated; * indicates the midpoint of a range.

2611 - PULP MILLS

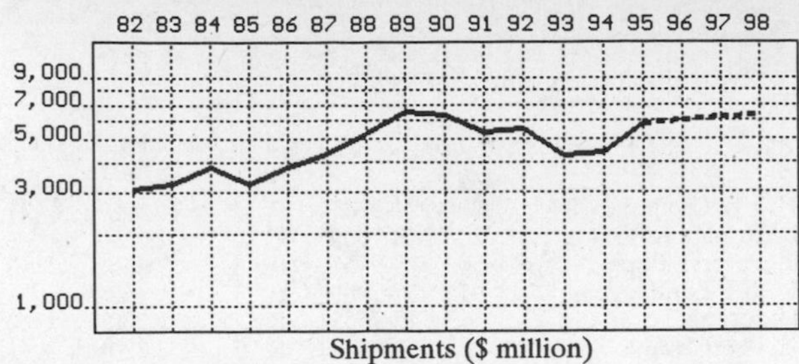

Shipments ($ million)

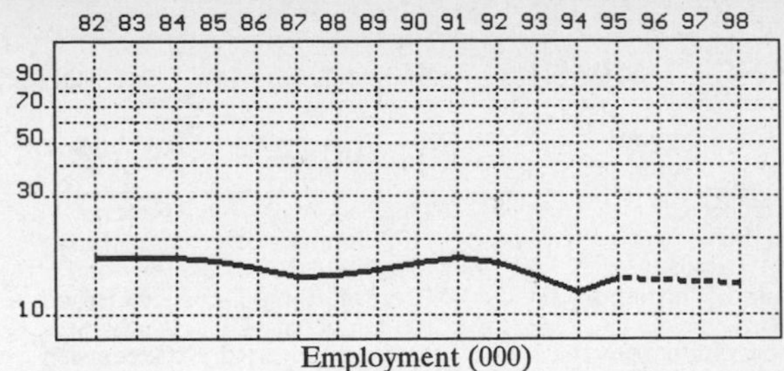

Employment (000)

GENERAL STATISTICS

Year	Com-panies	Establishments		Employment			Compensation		Production ($ million)			
		Total	with 20 or more employees	Total (000)	Production Workers (000)	Production Hours (Mil)	Payroll ($ mil)	Wages ($/hr)	Cost of Materials	Value Added by Manufacture	Value of Shipments	Capital Invest.
1982	29	43	41	16.7	12.8	24.8	467.5	13.88	1,986.5	1,113.8	3,110.4	658.6
1983				16.9	12.9	25.9	508.7	14.55	2,003.8	1,239.4	3,261.4	915.7
1984				16.8	12.9	26.5	549.0	15.54	2,267.3	1,599.4	3,841.1	600.4
1985				16.3	12.4	25.5	555.4	16.20	2,095.0	1,133.1	3,228.0	745.0
1986				15.3	11.8	25.6	593.7	17.53	2,212.7	1,590.8	3,837.3	874.6
1987	26	39	38	14.2	11.0	23.9	535.1	16.60	2,019.4	2,281.4	4,313.7	231.2
1988				14.4	11.2	23.9	559.5	17.28	2,159.5	3,116.5	5,260.1	309.2
1989		46	38	15.2	11.7	25.4	602.6	17.43	2,547.5	3,938.6	6,416.1	696.8
1990				16.1	12.3	27.7	668.0	17.48	2,885.3	3,416.4	6,239.1	1,053.6
1991				16.8	12.8	27.6	697.3	18.36	2,889.6	2,446.2	5,329.4	990.9
1992	29	45	44	15.9	12.1	26.3	689.1	19.07	2,957.7	2,554.7	5,465.6	772.3
1993				14.2	10.8	23.1	627.1	19.49	2,487.8	1,711.1	4,282.1	426.0
1994				12.3	9.4	20.3	569.8	19.98	2,445.5	1,926.4	4,423.9	258.9
1995				14.0P	10.7P	24.0P	679.0P	20.36P	3,204.3P	2,524.1P	5,796.5P	556.5P
1996				13.7P	10.5P	23.8P	692.2P	20.82P	3,303.6P	2,602.3P	5,976.1P	542.2P
1997				13.5P	10.3P	23.6P	705.4P	21.27P	3,402.9P	2,680.5P	6,155.8P	527.9P
1998				13.3P	10.1P	23.5P	718.7P	21.72P	3,502.2P	2,758.8P	6,335.4P	513.7P

Sources: 1982, 1987, 1992 *Economic Census*; *Annual Survey of Manufactures*, 83-86, 88-91, 93-94. Establishment counts for non-Census years are from *County Business Patterns*; establishment values for 83-84 are extrapolations. 'P's show projections by the editors. Industries reclassified in 87 will not have data for prior years.

INDICES OF CHANGE

Year	Com-panies	Establishments		Employment			Compensation		Production ($ million)			
		Total	with 20 or more employees	Total (000)	Production Workers (000)	Production Hours (Mil)	Payroll ($ mil)	Wages ($/hr)	Cost of Materials	Value Added by Manufacture	Value of Shipments	Capital Invest.
1982	100	96	93	105	106	94	68	73	67	44	57	85
1983				106	107	98	74	76	68	49	60	119
1984				106	107	101	80	81	77	63	70	78
1985				103	102	97	81	85	71	44	59	96
1986				96	98	97	86	92	75	62	70	113
1987	90	87	86	89	91	91	78	87	68	89	79	30
1988				91	93	91	81	91	73	122	96	40
1989		102	86	96	97	97	87	91	86	154	117	90
1990				101	102	105	97	92	98	134	114	136
1991				106	106	105	101	96	98	96	98	128
1992	100	100	100	100	100	100	100	100	100	100	100	100
1993				89	89	88	91	102	84	67	78	55
1994				77	78	77	83	105	83	75	81	34
1995				88P	88P	91P	99P	107P	108P	99P	106P	72P
1996				86P	87P	91P	100P	109P	112P	102P	109P	70P
1997				85P	85P	90P	102P	112P	115P	105P	113P	68P
1998				84P	84P	89P	104P	114P	118P	108P	116P	67P

Sources: Same as General Statistics. Values reflect change from the base year, 1992. Values above 100 mean greater than 92, values below 100 mean less than 92, and a value of 100 in the 82-91 or 93-98 period means same as 92. 'P's mark projections by the editors.

SELECTED RATIOS

For 1992	Avg. of All Manufact.	Analyzed Industry	Index	For 1992	Avg. of All Manufact.	Analyzed Industry	Index
Employees per Establishment	46	353	774	Value Added per Production Worker	122,353	211,132	173
Payroll per Establishment	1,332,320	15,313,333	1,149	Cost per Establishment	4,239,462	65,726,667	1,550
Payroll per Employee	29,181	43,340	149	Cost per Employee	92,853	186,019	200
Production Workers per Establishment	31	269	856	Cost per Production Worker	135,003	244,438	181
Wages per Establishment	734,496	11,145,356	1,517	Shipments per Establishment	8,100,800	121,457,778	1,499
Wages per Production Worker	23,390	41,450	177	Shipments per Employee	177,425	343,748	194
Hours per Production Worker	2,025	2,174	107	Shipments per Production Worker	257,966	451,702	175
Wages per Hour	11.55	19.07	165	Investment per Establishment	278,244	17,162,222	6,168
Value Added per Establishment	3,842,210	56,771,111	1,478	Investment per Employee	6,094	48,572	797
Value Added per Employee	84,153	160,673	191	Investment per Production Worker	8,861	63,826	720

Sources: Same as General Statistics. The 'Average of All Manufacturing' column represents the average of all manufacturing industries reported for the most recent complete year available. The Index shows the relationship between the Average and the Analyzed Industry. For example, 100 means that they are equal; 500 that the Analyzed Industry is five times the average; 50 means that the Analyzed Industry is half the national average. The abbreviation 'na' is used to show that data are 'not available'.

LEADING COMPANIES

Number shown: **16** Total sales ($ mil): **13,875** Total employment (000): **49.9**

Company Name	Address				CEO Name	Phone	Co. Type	Sales ($ mil)	Empl. (000)
Weyerhaeuser Co	33663 W Way	Federal Way	WA	98003	J W Creighton Jr	206-924-2345	P	10,398	37.0
Rayonier Inc	1177 Summer St	Stamford	CT	06904	Ronald M Gross	203-348-7000	P	1,069	2.6
Pope and Talbot Inc	1500 SW 1st Av	Portland	OR	97201	Peter T Pope	503-228-9161	P	660	3.0
Parsons and Whittemore Inc	4 International Dr	Rye Brook	NY	10573	G F Landegger	914-937-9009	R	440	1.5
Preco Corp	100 University Dr	Amherst	MA	01004	Joseph Toras	413-549-7635	R	230	0.6
Brant Allen Industries Inc	80 Field Point Rd	Greenwich	CT	06830	Peter Brant	203-661-3344	R	220*	1.0
Georgia-Pacific Corp	PO Box 1438	Brunswick	GA	31521	WW Jones	912-265-5780	D	200	0.8
Simpson Tacoma Kraft Co	1501 Market St	Tacoma	WA	98402	Bryce Seidl	206-596-0174	D	200	0.6
Interstate Resources Inc	1800 N Kent St	Rosslyn	VA	22209	Terry L Brubaker	703-243-3355	R	190	0.9
Port Townsend Paper Corp	750 Ericksen NE	Bainbridge Isl	WA	98110	Ted Swain Jr	206-842-0611	S	100	0.5
Kraft	PO Box 8050	Wis Rapids	WI	54495	Steven Enz	715-422-3111	D	98*	0.4
Southern Cellulose Products Inc	PO Box 2278	Chattanooga	TN	37409	S Pala Jr	615-821-1561	R	30*	0.1
Idaho Pulp and Paperboard	PO Box 1016	Lewiston	ID	83501	C Bill Morton	208-799-1666	D	22	0.8
International Filler Corp	PO Box 50	N Tonawanda	NY	14120	R W Bowen II	716-693-4040	R	11	<0.1
Cheney Pulp and Paper Co	PO Box 215	Franklin	OH	45005	James H Snyder	513-746-9991	R	6*	<0.1
Trans-Rim Enterprises	1100 SW 27th St	Renton	WA	98055	Hans Koch	206-227-0300	R	1*	<0.1

Source: *Ward's Business Directory of U.S. Private and Public Companies*, Volumes 1 and 2, 1996. The company type code used is as follows: P - Public, R - Private, S - Subsidiary, D - Division, J - Joint Venture, A - Affiliate, G - Group. Sales are in millions of dollars, employees are in thousands. An asterisk (*) indicates an estimated sales volume. The symbol < stands for 'less than'. Company names and addresses are truncated, in some cases, to fit into the available space.

MATERIALS CONSUMED

Material		Quantity	Delivered Cost ($ million)
Materials, ingredients, containers, and supplies		(X)	2,532.6
Spruce and true fir pulpwood bolts and logs	1,000 standard cords	(D)	(D)
Hemlock pulpwood bolts and logs	1,000 standard cords	1,183.8	94.9
Southern pine pulpwood bolts and logs	1,000 standard cords	4,669.2	301.5
Other softwood pulpwood bolts and logs, including Douglas fir and Jack pine	1,000 standard cords	(D)	(D)
Softwood pulpwood wood chips, slabs, cores, sawdust, bark, and other mill residues	1,000 standard cords	4,940.6	459.8
Southern mixed hardwood pulpwood bolts and logs	1,000 standard cords	2,866.6	175.3
Other hardwood pulpwood bolts and logs	1,000 standard cords	1,270.6	80.6
Hardwood pulpwood wood chips, slabs, cores, sawdust, bark, and other mill residues	1,000 standard cords	1,939.1	131.9
Chlorine (100 percent Cl basis)	1,000 s tons	268.6	24.2
Sodium hydroxide (caustic soda)(100 percent NaOH)	1,000 s tons	688.8	178.9
Sodium chlorate (100 percent NaClO3)	1,000 s tons	281.6	96.3
Other sodium compounds		(X)	10.9
Aluminum sulfate (17 percent Al2O3)	1,000 s tons	20.6	2.3
Rosin sizing	mil lb (dry basis)	9.1	3.8
Lime	1,000 s tons	314.1	21.1
Kaolin and ball clay	1,000 s tons	114.8	17.3
Starch	mil lb	67.2	12.2
Synthetic resins	mil lb	(D)	(D)
Titanium dioxide, composite and pure (100 percent TiO2)	mil lb	16.7	14.4
Calcium carbonate, precipitated (100 percent CaCO2)	1,000 s tons	(D)	(D)
All other chemicals, including organic		(X)	155.7
Woodpulp produced at affiliated or associated mills at other locations	1,000 s tons	(D)	(D)
Woodpulp purchased market wood pulp	1,000 s tons	42.6	21.3
Mixed wastepaper, except plant's own broke paper	1,000 s tons	(D)	(D)
Corrugated wastepaper, including kraft, except plant's own broke paper	1,000 s tons	14.2	0.9
High grade pulp substitutes wastepaper, except plant's own broke paper	1,000 s tons	(D)	(D)
High grade deinking wastepaper, except plant's own broke paper	1,000 s tons	(D)	(D)
Cotton linters (net weight)	mil lb	429.7	44.9
Other fibrous materials, including rags, straw, and bagasse	1,000 s tons	(D)	(D)
Paperboard containers, boxes, and corrugated paperboard		(X)	3.3
All other materials and components, parts, containers, and supplies		(X)	527.4
Materials, ingredients, containers, and supplies, nsk		(X)	8.7

Source: 1992 *Economic Census*. Explanation of symbols used: (D): Withheld to avoid disclosure of competitive data; na: Not available; (S): Withheld because statistical norms were not met; (X): Not applicable; (Z): Less than half the unit shown; nec: Not elsewhere classified; nsk: Not specified by kind; - : zero; * : 10-19 percent estimated; ** : 20-29 percent estimated.

PRODUCT SHARE DETAILS

Product or Product Class	% Share	Product or Product Class	% Share
Pulp mills	100.00	Pulp, other than wood, and pulp mill byproducts, nec	8.03
Special alpha and dissolving woodpulp (sulfite and sulfate for chemical conversion, papermaking, and other uses)	15.10	Cotton linter pulp	38.34
Sulfate woodpulp, including soda	72.28	Other pulp, including pulp made from straw, rag, flax, deinked paper, bagasse, etc..	42.06
Sulfate woodpulp, bleached and semibleached, including soda	98.22	Turpentine, sulfate	5.49
Sulfate woodpulp, unbleached	1.78	Other cooking liquor pulp mill byproducts (skimmings, binders, fuel, etc.)	14.11
Sulfite and other woodpulp	4.59		

Source: 1992 *Economic Census*. The values shown are percent of total shipments in an industry. Values of indented subcategories are summed in the main heading. The symbol (D) appears when data are withheld to prevent disclosure of competitive information. The abbreviation nsk stands for 'not specified by kind' and nec for 'not elsewhere classified'.

INPUTS AND OUTPUTS FOR PULP MILLS

Economic Sector or Industry Providing Inputs	%	Sector	Economic Sector or Industry Buying Outputs	%	Sector
Imports	40.2	Foreign	Paper mills, except building paper	50.6	Manufg.
Logging camps & logging contractors	9.5	Manufg.	Exports	25.9	Foreign
Sawmills & planning mills, general	7.1	Manufg.	Sanitary paper products	11.2	Manufg.
Cyclic crudes and organics	5.3	Manufg.	Cellulosic manmade fibers	5.4	Manufg.
Petroleum refining	5.2	Manufg.	Cyclic crudes and organics	3.5	Manufg.
Sanitary services, steam supply, irrigation	4.7	Util.	Pulp mills	1.8	Manufg.
Wholesale trade	3.6	Trade	Paperboard mills	0.6	Manufg.
Alkalies & chlorine	3.4	Manufg.	Organic fibers, noncellulosic	0.4	Manufg.
Electric services (utilities)	2.6	Util.	Plastics materials & resins	0.2	Manufg.
Pulp mills	2.5	Manufg.	Pressed & molded pulp goods	0.2	Manufg.
Gas production & distribution (utilities)	2.4	Util.			
Railroads & related services	1.5	Util.			
Motor freight transportation & warehousing	1.3	Util.			
Industrial inorganic chemicals, nec	1.2	Manufg.			
Cottonseed oil mills	0.7	Manufg.			
Water supply & sewage systems	0.7	Util.			
Pipe, valves, & pipe fittings	0.5	Manufg.			
Scrap	0.5	Scrap			
Fabricated rubber products, nec	0.4	Manufg.			
Water transportation	0.4	Util.			
Maintenance of nonfarm buildings nec	0.3	Constr.			
Lime	0.3	Manufg.			
Banking	0.3	Fin/R.E.			
Advertising	0.3	Services			
Computer & data processing services	0.3	Services			
Equipment rental & leasing services	0.3	Services			
Chemical & fertilizer mineral	0.2	Mining			
Coal	0.2	Mining			
Coated fabrics, not rubberized	0.2	Manufg.			
Surface active agents	0.2	Manufg.			
Wet corn milling	0.2	Manufg.			
Air transportation	0.2	Util.			
Automotive rental & leasing, without drivers	0.2	Services			
Detective & protective services	0.2	Services			
Paper industries machinery	0.1	Manufg.			
Communications, except radio & TV	0.1	Util.			
Eating & drinking places	0.1	Trade			
Insurance carriers	0.1	Fin/R.E.			
Security & commodity brokers	0.1	Fin/R.E.			
Automotive repair shops & services	0.1	Services			
State & local government enterprises, nec	0.1	Gov't			

Source: Benchmark Input-Output Accounts for the U.S. Economy, 1982, U.S. Department of Commerce, Washington, D.C., July 1991. Data, as reported in the source, are organized by the 1977 SIC structure in use in 1982 but have been matched, as closely as is possible, to the 1987 SIC structure used in this book.

OCCUPATIONS EMPLOYED BY SIC 261 - PULP, PAPER, AND PAPERBOARD MILLS

Occupation	% of Total 1994	Change to 2005	Occupation	% of Total 1994	Change to 2005
Machine operators nec	11.9	13.8	Extruding & forming machine workers	1.8	19.8
Helpers, laborers, & material movers nec	7.6	-7.8	Machine feeders & offbearers	1.7	-17.0
Blue collar worker supervisors	6.0	0.1	Coating, painting, & spraying machine workers	1.4	-26.2
Paper goods machine setters & set-up operators	4.4	-26.2	Secretaries, ex legal & medical	1.4	-16.1
Industrial machinery mechanics	3.8	1.4	Packaging & filling machine operators	1.4	-7.8
Industrial truck & tractor operators	3.5	-7.8	Plumbers, pipefitters, & steamfitters	1.3	-7.8
Maintenance repairers, general utility	3.0	-7.8	Freight, stock, & material movers, hand	1.2	-26.2
Millwrights	2.9	-26.2	Chemical equipment controllers, operators	1.2	-26.2
Crushing & mixing machine operators	2.7	-17.0	Precision instrument repairers	1.1	19.9
Cutting & slicing machine setters, operators	2.6	10.6	Industrial production managers	1.1	-7.8
Inspectors, testers, & graders, precision	2.5	1.4	Boiler operators, low pressure	1.1	-7.8
Electricians	2.2	-13.5			

Source: Industry-Occupation Matrix, Bureau of Labor Statistics. These data relate to one or more 3-digit SIC industry groups rather than to a single 4-digit SIC. The change reported for each occupation to the year 2005 is a percent of growth or decline as estimated by the Bureau of Labor Statistics. The abbreviation nec stands for 'not elsewhere classified'.

LOCATION BY STATE AND REGIONAL CONCENTRATION

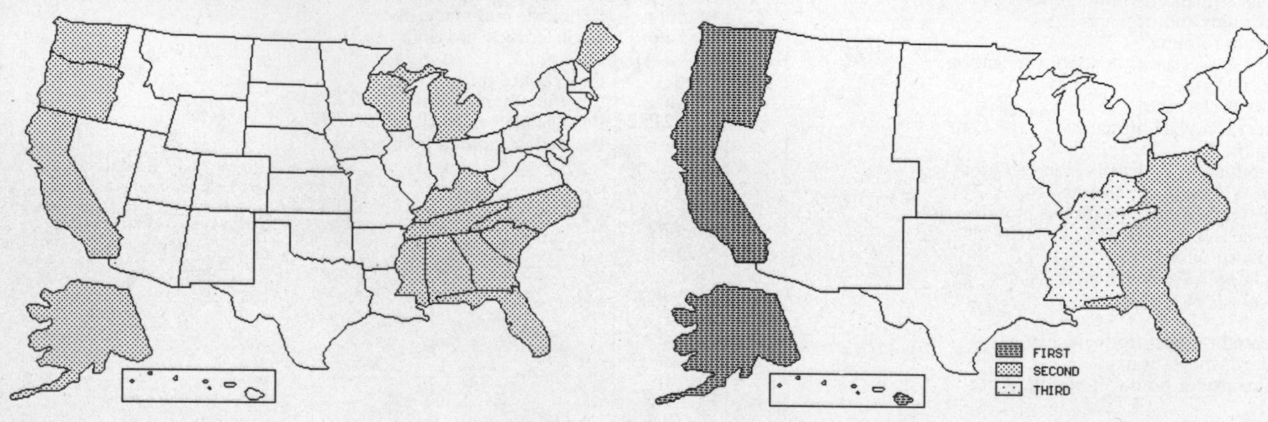

INDUSTRY DATA BY STATE

State	Establish-ments	Shipments Total ($ mil)	Shipments % of U.S.	Shipments Per Establ.	Employment Total Number	Employment % of U.S.	Employment Per Establ.	Employment Wages ($/hour)	Cost as % of Shipments	Investment per Employee ($)
Georgia	4	886.9	16.2	221.7	2,600	16.4	650	16.21	45.7	-
Florida	3	673.9	12.3	224.6	2,000	12.6	667	16.22	58.3	-
Washington	5	388.0	7.1	77.6	1,700	10.7	340	20.76	63.2	13,118
Wisconsin	6	227.3	4.2	37.9	600	3.8	100	18.20	54.0	98,167
California	4	(D)	-	-	750 *	4.7	188	-	-	-
Alabama	3	(D)	-	-	1,750 *	11.0	583	-	-	-
Mississippi	3	(D)	-	-	1,750 *	11.0	583	-	-	-
North Carolina	3	(D)	-	-	1,750 *	11.0	583	-	-	-
Tennessee	3	(D)	-	-	375 *	2.4	125	-	-	14,400
Alaska	2	(D)	-	-	750 *	4.7	375	-	-	-
Oregon	2	(D)	-	-	375 *	2.4	188	-	-	-
Kentucky	1	(D)	-	-	175 *	1.1	175	-	-	-
Maine	1	(D)	-	-	750 *	4.7	750	-	-	-
Michigan	1	(D)	-	-	750 *	4.7	750	-	-	-
South Carolina	1	(D)	-	-	750 *	4.7	750	-	-	-

Source: 1992 *Economic Census*. The states are in descending order of shipments or establishments (if shipment data are missing for the majority). The symbol (D) appears when data are withheld to prevent disclosure of competitive information. States marked with (D) are sorted by number of establishments. A dash (-) indicates that the data element cannot be calculated; * indicates the midpoint of a range.

2621 - PAPER MILLS

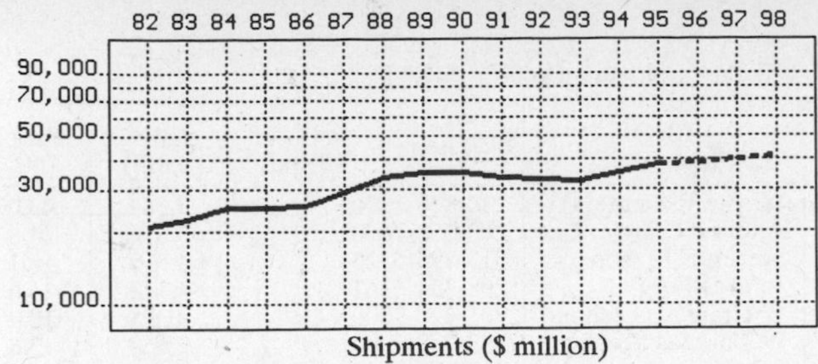

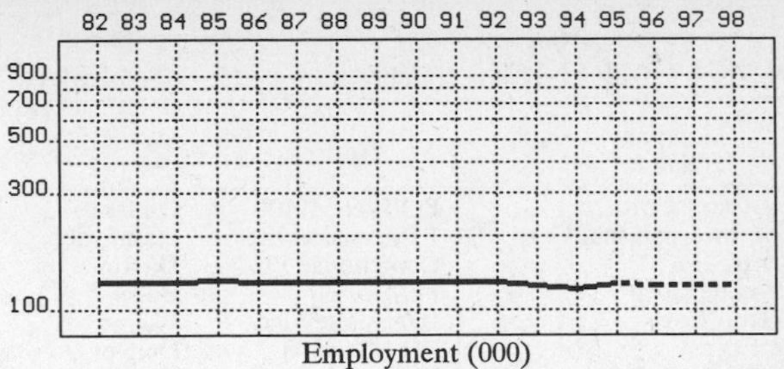

GENERAL STATISTICS

Year	Com-panies	Establishments: Total	Establishments: with 20 or more employees	Employment: Total (000)	Production Workers (000)	Production Hours (Mil)	Compensation: Payroll ($ mil)	Compensation: Wages ($/hr)	Production ($ million): Cost of Materials	Value Added by Manufacture	Value of Shipments	Capital Invest.
1982	135	299	281	129.0	100.1	208.4	3,430.6	12.30	12,136.7	8,954.1	20,994.6	1,856.1
1983				128.6	100.0	210.5	3,703.5	13.25	12,552.1	9,701.6	22,284.0	2,239.3
1984				129.5	100.6	214.7	4,021.6	14.13	14,162.5	11,165.7	25,195.0	2,412.4
1985				131.8	101.5	212.0	4,259.4	15.01	13,929.7	11,074.4	24,980.1	2,484.3
1986				128.8	99.4	210.1	4,405.0	15.63	13,640.9	12,032.9	25,705.9	2,153.3
1987	122	282	276	129.1	99.2	210.4	4,597.0	16.17	14,856.0	14,021.9	28,915.5	2,759.9
1988				130.4	101.1	215.1	4,773.0	16.43	16,782.1	16,866.2	33,545.8	3,299.5
1989		316	284	130.1	100.6	214.0	4,927.1	16.96	18,481.0	17,100.6	35,387.1	5,236.6
1990				130.1	98.6	210.6	5,061.5	17.43	18,861.1	16,599.8	35,321.8	4,277.5
1991				130.3	99.4	212.1	5,223.5	17.82	17,983.1	15,510.3	33,344.0	3,637.7
1992	127	280	276	130.6	100.4	215.2	5,420.5	18.20	17,971.4	14,847.7	32,786.4	2,911.5
1993				126.2	97.2	212.3	5,365.3	18.45	17,717.1	14,511.7	32,102.6	2,863.5
1994				122.8	94.9	210.0	5,519.1	19.29	19,815.4	15,012.3	35,071.3	3,137.5
1995				127.3P	97.4P	212.9P	5,861.0P	19.97P	21,426.3P	16,232.7P	37,922.4P	3,905.0P
1996				127.0P	97.2P	213.1P	6,031.1P	20.50P	22,092.8P	16,737.7P	39,102.1P	4,031.3P
1997				126.8P	96.9P	213.2P	6,201.3P	21.03P	22,759.4P	17,242.7P	40,281.9P	4,157.6P
1998				126.5P	96.6P	213.4P	6,371.5P	21.57P	23,426.0P	17,747.7P	41,461.6P	4,283.9P

Sources: 1982, 1987, 1992 *Economic Census*; *Annual Survey of Manufactures*, 83-86, 88-91, 93-94. Establishment counts for non-Census years are from *County Business Patterns*; establishment values for 83-84 are extrapolations. 'P's show projections by the editors. Industries reclassified in 87 will not have data for prior years.

INDICES OF CHANGE

Year	Com-panies	Establishments: Total	Establishments: with 20 or more employees	Employment: Total (000)	Production Workers (000)	Production Hours (Mil)	Compensation: Payroll ($ mil)	Compensation: Wages ($/hr)	Production ($ million): Cost of Materials	Value Added by Manufacture	Value of Shipments	Capital Invest.
1982	106	107	102	99	100	97	63	68	68	60	64	64
1983				98	100	98	68	73	70	65	68	77
1984				99	100	100	74	78	79	75	77	83
1985				101	101	99	79	82	78	75	76	85
1986				99	99	98	81	86	76	81	78	74
1987	96	101	100	99	99	98	85	89	83	94	88	95
1988				100	101	100	88	90	93	114	102	113
1989		113	103	100	100	99	91	93	103	115	108	180
1990				100	98	98	93	96	105	112	108	147
1991				100	99	99	96	98	100	104	102	125
1992	100	100	100	100	100	100	100	100	100	100	100	100
1993				97	97	99	99	101	99	98	98	98
1994				94	95	98	102	106	110	101	107	108
1995				97P	97P	99P	108P	110P	119P	109P	116P	134P
1996				97P	97P	99P	111P	113P	123P	113P	119P	138P
1997				97P	96P	99P	114P	116P	127P	116P	123P	143P
1998				97P	96P	99P	118P	119P	130P	120P	126P	147P

Sources: Same as General Statistics. Values reflect change from the base year, 1992. Values above 100 mean greater than 92, values below 100 mean less than 92, and a value of 100 in the 82-91 or 93-98 period means same as 92. 'P's mark projections by the editors.

SELECTED RATIOS

For 1992	Avg. of All Manufact.	Analyzed Industry	Index	For 1992	Avg. of All Manufact.	Analyzed Industry	Index
Employees per Establishment	46	466	1,022	Value Added per Production Worker	122,353	147,885	121
Payroll per Establishment	1,332,320	19,358,929	1,453	Cost per Establishment	4,239,462	64,183,571	1,514
Payroll per Employee	29,181	41,505	142	Cost per Employee	92,853	137,606	148
Production Workers per Establishment	31	359	1,142	Cost per Production Worker	135,003	178,998	133
Wages per Establishment	734,496	13,988,000	1,904	Shipments per Establishment	8,100,800	117,094,286	1,445
Wages per Production Worker	23,390	39,010	167	Shipments per Employee	177,425	251,044	141
Hours per Production Worker	2,025	2,143	106	Shipments per Production Worker	257,966	326,558	127
Wages per Hour	11.55	18.20	158	Investment per Establishment	278,244	10,398,214	3,737
Value Added per Establishment	3,842,210	53,027,500	1,380	Investment per Employee	6,094	22,293	366
Value Added per Employee	84,153	113,688	135	Investment per Production Worker	8,861	28,999	327

Sources: Same as General Statistics. The 'Average of All Manufacturing' column represents the average of all manufacturing industries reported for the most recent complete year available. The Index shows the relationship between the Average and the Analyzed Industry. For example, 100 means that they are equal; 500 that the Analyzed Industry is five times the average; 50 means that the Analyzed Industry is half the national average. The abbreviation 'na' is used to show that data are 'not available'.

LEADING COMPANIES Number shown: **75** Total sales ($ mil): **48,914** Total employment (000): **242.9**

Company Name	Address				CEO Name	Phone	Co. Type	Sales ($ mil)	Empl. (000)
Kimberly-Clark Corp	PO Box 619100	Dallas	TX	75261	Wayne R Sanders	214-830-1200	P	7,364	43.0
Champion International Corp	1 Champion Plz	Stamford	CT	06921	Andrew C Sigler	203-358-7000	P	5,319	24.6
Mead Corp	Courthouse Plz NE	Dayton	OH	45463	Steven C Mason	513-495-6323	P	4,558	16.1
Boise Cascade Corp	PO Box 50	Boise	ID	83728	John B Fery	208-384-6161	P	4,140	16.6
Union Camp Corp	1600 Valley Rd	Wayne	NJ	07470	W Craig McClelland	201-628-2000	P	3,395	18.9
Manville Corp	PO Box 5108	Denver	CO	80217	W Thomas Stephens	303-978-2000	P	2,560	13.6
Westvaco Corp	299 Park Av	New York	NY	10171	John Luke	212-688-5000	P	2,345	14.4
Champion International Corp	1 Champion Plz	Stamford	CT	06921	W H Burchfield	203-358-7000	D	1,700	9.3
Pentair Inc	1500 County, B2 W	St Paul	MN	55113	Winslow H Buxton	612-636-7920	P	1,649	10.3
Potlatch Corp	PO Box 193591	San Francisco	CA	94119	John M Richards	415-576-8800	P	1,471	7.5
Bowater Inc	PO Box 1028	Greenville	SC	29602	Anthony P Gammie	803-271-7733	P	1,359	6.0
SD Warren Co	225 Franklin St	Boston	MA	02110	Richard Leaman	617-423-7300	S	1,030	4.0
Mead Fine Paper	PO Box 2500	Chillicothe	OH	45601	Steven C Mason	614-772-3111	D	1,000	3.8
James River Paper Company Inc	300 Lakeside Dr	Oakland	CA	94612	Ernest S Leopold	510-874-3400	D	897	5.8
Simpson Paper Co	1301 5th Av	Seattle	WA	98101	Raymond Tennison	206-224-5700	S	870*	5.3
Newsprint and Kraft	1 Champion Plz	Stamford	CT	06921	B G MacArthur Jr	203-358-7000	D	810*	2.5
Union Camp Corp	PO Box 178	Franklin	VA	23851	CH Greiner Jr	804-569-4321	D	775	3.1
Great Northern Paper Inc	1 Katahdin Av	Millinocket	ME	04462	WP Gregory	207-723-5131	S	430	2.0
Wausau Paper Mills Co	PO Box 1408	Wausau	WI	54402	Sam W Orr Jr	715-845-5266	P	426	1.7
Gilman Paper Co	111 W 50th St	New York	NY	10020	Howard Gilman	212-246-3300	R	400	2.4
Thilmany	PO Box 600	Kaukauna	WI	54130	Bruno Carre	414-766-4611	D	400	1.0
Northwest Paper	PO Box 510	Cloquet	MN	55720	Robert V Hershey	218-879-2300	D	365	1.8
Waldorf Corp	2250 Wabash Av	St Paul	MN	55114	Eugene Frey	612-641-4938	R	360	2.0
North Pacific Paper Corp	33663 W Way	Federal Way	WA	98003	James Keller	206-924-2462	J	350	0.5
Blandin Paper Co	115 1st St SW	Grand Rapids	MN	55744	Alfred Wallace	218-327-6200	S	300	1.1
Smurfit Newsprint Corp	427 Main St	Oregon City	OR	97045	T L Sturdevant	503-650-4211	S	271	0.8
Wausau Papers	PO Box 305	Brokaw	WI	54417	Daniel D King	715-675-3361	D	240	1.0
Kimberly-Clark Corp	Hwy 235	Coosa Pines	AL	35044	BH Knight	205-378-5541	D	220	1.7
Boise Cascade Corp	2nd St	Intern Fls	MN	56649	Jeff Lowe	218-285-5011	D	200	1.0
Simpson Pasadena Paper Co	PO Box 872	Pasadena	TX	77501	Charles S Rose	713-475-6200	S	200	1.1
Potlatch Corp	PO Box 8162	Walnut Creek	CA	94596	Rich Paulson	510-947-4721	D	195	0.8
Bowater Inc	US Hwy 11	Calhoun	TN	37309	James A Breaux	615-336-2211	D	175	1.6
Wausau Paper Mills Co	515 W Davenport St	Rhinelander	WI	54501	Mel Davidson	715-369-4100	S	168	0.7
Consolidated Papers Inc	PO Box 8050	Wis Rapids	WI	54495	Ronald Swanson	715-422-3111	D	160*	1.0
Marcal Paper Mills Inc	1 Market St	Elmwood Park	NJ	07407	R L Marcalus Sr	201-796-4000	R	160	1.0
Niagara	1101 Mill St	Niagara	WI	54151	G Robert Gey	715-251-3151	S	160	0.6
Strathmore Paper Co	39 S Broad St	Westfield	MA	01085	C David Trader	413-568-9111	D	160	1.0
Bowater Communication Papers	PO Box 8801	Moline	IL	61265	Sheldon B Saidman	309-797-1389	S	130*	0.6
Cross Pointe Paper Corp	1295 Bandana N	St Paul	MN	55108	Wilson Blackburn	612-644-3644	S	130	1.0
Burrows Paper Corp	501 W Main St	Little Falls	NY	13365	RW Burrows Jr	315-823-2300	R	120	0.7
Southeast Paper Mfg Co	PO Box 1169	Dublin	GA	31040	James L Burke	912-272-1600	R	110	0.7
Daishowa America Ltd	701 5th Av	Seattle	WA	98104	Steve Taniguchi	206-623-1772	S	105	0.4
Fletcher Paper Co	318 W Fletcher St	Alpena	MI	49707	Paul Hoelderle	517-354-2131	R	100*	0.4
Lincoln Pulp and Paper Co	Katahdin Av	Lincoln	ME	04457	JH Torras	207-794-6721	S	95	0.6
Nicolet Paper Co	200 Main Av	De Pere	WI	54115	Thomas G Kadien	414-336-4211	D	90	0.4
Penntech Papers	181 Harbor Dr	Stamford	CT	06902		203-356-1850	D	89*	0.5
Ahlstrom Filtration Inc	1 Union Sq	Chattanooga	TN	37401	Edward A Leinss	615-821-4090	S	82	0.3
Erving Industries Inc	120 E Main St	Erving	MA	01344	Charles Housen	508-544-3215	R	82	0.5
Mohawk Paper Mills Inc	465 Saratoga St	Cohoes	NY	12047	T O'Connor	518-237-1740	R	80	0.3
Mead Corp	Rte 102	South Lee	MA	01260	T R McLevish	413-243-1231	D	79	0.4
Kimberly-Clark Corp	501 E Munising Av	Munising	MI	49862	Mark E Kerstetter	906-387-2700	D	76*	0.5
Garden State Paper Company	950 River Rd	Elmwood Park	NJ	07407	Thomas M Hahn	201-796-0600	S	73	0.3
Beckett Paper Co	400 Dayton St	Hamilton	OH	45011	David E Herlt	513-863-5641	D	70	0.5
TST/Impreso Inc	PO Box 506	Coppell	TX	75019	M D Sorokwasz	214-462-0100	R	62	0.3
Fox River Paper	PO Box 2215	Appleton	WI	54913	Robert L Esten	414-733-7341	D	60*	0.6
EB Eddy Paper Inc	1700 Washington	Port Huron	MI	48060	A Richard Wagner	313-982-0191	S	56	0.3
Lake Superior Paper Industries	100 N Central Av	Duluth	MN	55807	Wilson Blackburn	218-628-5100	J	56	0.4
Monadnock Paper Mills Inc	117 Antrim Rd	Bennington	NH	03442	Richard G Verney	603-588-3311	R	55	0.3
Sorg Paper Co	901 Manchester Av	Middletown	OH	45042	Richard Early	513-420-5300	S	50	0.2
Tagsons Papers Inc	PO Box 1999	Albany	NY	12201		518-462-0200	R	49	0.3
Cross Pointe Paper Corp	PO Box 66	West Carrollton	OH	45449	Jobe B Morrison	513-859-5101	D	48	0.3
Merrimac Paper Company Inc	9 S Canal St	Lawrence	MA	01843	Gerard J Griffin	508-683-2754	R	40	0.1
Bemiss-Jason Corp	37600 Central Ct	Newark	CA	94560	Gordon Case	510-713-6400	R	36	0.6
Southeast Paper	1800 Parkway Pl	Marietta	GA	30067	Ronald F Willson	404-919-7502	S	34*	0.2
Ponderay Newsprint Co	422767 Hwy 20	Usk	WA	99180	William Meany	509-445-1511	R	32*	0.2
Manistique Papers Inc	453 S Mackinac	Manistique	MI	49854	L Christensen	906-341-2175	S	28	0.2
Tufco Technologies Inc	PO Box 23500	Green Bay	WI	54305	Samuel J Bero	414-336-0054	P	27	0.2
Manning Non Woven	PO Box 328	Troy	NY	12181	JP Carolan	518-273-6320	D	26	0.1
Ahlstrom Filtration	PO Box A	Mt Holly Sprgs	PA	17065	Edward Leines	717-486-3438	D	25	0.1
CPM Inc	PO Box 1280	Claremont	NH	03743	HD Hill	603-542-2592	R	25	0.1
Seaman Paper of Massachusetts	PO Box 21	Baldwinville	MA	01436	George Jones Sr	508-939-5356	R	25	0.1
Mundet Inc	PO Box 70	Colonial Hts	VA	23834	Woody Brown	804-748-3319	R	23	0.1
Rising Paper	Park St	Housatonic	MA	01236	Robert Esten	413-274-3345	D	22	0.2
Byron Weston	30 South St	Dalton	MA	01226	Thomas A White	413-684-2600	D	21*	0.2
Chiyoda America Inc	PO Box 470	Morgantown	PA	19543	John Sato	215-286-3100	S	20	0.2

Source: Ward's Business Directory of U.S. Private and Public Companies, Volumes 1 and 2, 1996. The company type code used is as follows: P - Public, R - Private, S - Subsidiary, D - Division, J - Joint Venture, A - Affiliate, G - Group. Sales are in millions of dollars, employees are in thousands. An asterisk (*) indicates an estimated sales volume. The symbol < stands for 'less than'. Company names and addresses are truncated, in some cases, to fit into the available space.

MATERIALS CONSUMED

Material		Quantity	Delivered Cost ($ million)
Materials, ingredients, containers, and supplies		(X)	14,644.2
Spruce and true fir pulpwood bolts and logs	1,000 standard cords	2,476.5	202.2
Hemlock pulpwood bolts and logs	1,000 standard cords	1,154.2	94.2
Southern pine pulpwood bolts and logs	1,000 standard cords	9,278.9	628.5
Other softwood pulpwood bolts and logs, including Douglas fir and Jack pine	1,000 standard cords	2,060.8	152.7
Softwood pulpwood wood chips, slabs, cores, sawdust, bark, and other mill residues	1,000 standard cords	13,109.1	969.9
Southern mixed hardwood pulpwood bolts and logs	1,000 standard cords	5,447.5	338.0
Other hardwood pulpwood bolts and logs	1,000 standard cords	3,647.2	203.5
Hardwood pulpwood wood chips, slabs, cores, sawdust, bark, and other mill residues	1,000 standard cords	6,943.7	462.9
Chlorine (100 percent Cl basis)	1,000 s tons	671.9	74.4
Sodium hydroxide (caustic soda)(100 percent NaOH)	1,000 s tons	1,383.1	314.7
Sodium chlorate (100 percent NaClO3)	1,000 s tons	436.1	158.8
Other sodium compounds		(X)	65.4
Aluminum sulfate (17 percent Al2O3)	1,000 s tons	262.2	35.2
Rosin sizing	mil lb (dry basis)	183.2*	77.9
Lime	1,000 s tons	768.8	49.8
Kaolin and ball clay	1,000 s tons	2,643.3	402.1
Starch	mil lb	2,189.2	408.9
Synthetic resins	mil lb	479.3	260.2
Titanium dioxide, composite and pure (100 percent TiO2)	mil lb	445.4	384.1
Calcium carbonate, precipitated (100 percent CaCO2)	1,000 s tons	1,168.5	170.5
All other chemicals, including organic		(X)	1,275.1
Woodpulp produced at affiliated or associated mills at other locations	1,000 s tons	2,268.1	975.2
Woodpulp purchased market wood pulp	1,000 s tons	5,308.9	2,480.6
Mixed wastepaper, except plant's own broke paper	1,000 s tons	1,239.2	185.6
Mechanical news wastepaper, except plant's own broke paper	1,000 s tons	2,548.7	147.5
Other mechanical wastepaper, except plant's own broke paper	1,000 s tons	280.6	28.5
Corrugated wastepaper, including kraft, except plant's own broke paper	1,000 s tons	766.1	111.6
High grade pulp substitutes wastepaper, except plant's own broke paper	1,000 s tons	524.5	159.2
High grade deinking wastepaper, except plant's own broke paper	1,000 s tons	1,536.5	210.5
Cotton linters (net weight)	mil lb	42.4	22.9
Linter pulp	1,000 s tons	29.5	33.3
Other fibrous materials, including rags, straw, and bagasse	1,000 s tons	133.4	65.6
Paperboard containers, boxes, and corrugated paperboard		(X)	121.9
All other materials and components, parts, containers, and supplies		(X)	3,157.0
Materials, ingredients, containers, and supplies, nsk		(X)	215.8

Source: 1992 *Economic Census*. Explanation of symbols used: (D): Withheld to avoid disclosure of competitive data; na: Not available; (S): Withheld because statistical norms were not met; (X): Not applicable; (Z): Less than half the unit shown; nec: Not elsewhere classified; nsk: Not specified by kind; - : zero; * : 10-19 percent estimated; ** : 20-29 percent estimated.

PRODUCT SHARE DETAILS

Product or Product Class	% Share
Paper mills	100.00
Newsprint	9.48
Uncoated groundwood paper	2.67
Supercalendered uncoated groundwood publication and printing paper	88.00
Other converting and miscellaneous uncoated groundwood paper, including form bond, wallpaper base, and body stock for coating	9.49
Uncoated groundwood paper (containing more than 10 percent mechanical fiber), nsk	2.52
Clay coated printing and converting paper	24.34
Clay coated groundwood printing and coverting paper	43.11
Clay coated freesheet printing and coverting paper, coated one side	12.31
Clay coated freesheet printing and coverting paper, coated two sides	44.38
Clay coated printing and converting paper, nsk	0.20
Uncoated freesheet paper	28.17
Bond and writing paper, including protective check, uncoated freesheet	21.51
Form bond paper in rolls, uncoated freesheet	12.58
Body stock for communication, copying, and related papers, uncoated freesheet	3.05
Other uncoated freesheet technical and reproduction papers, including mimeograph and gelatin and spirit process duplicating	12.66
Writing tablet paper, uncoated freesheet	2.23
Other writing paper, including ledger, onion skin, papeterie and wedding, etc., uncoated freesheet	0.82
Plain publication and printing paper, uncoated freesheet, including machine finish, English finish, antique, bulking, eggshell, and supercalendered	4.01
Offset publication and printing paper, uncoated freesheet	17.25
Other uncoated publication and printing freesheet paper	7.24
Cover and text papers, uncoated freesheet	6.93
Envelope (white wove) paper, uncoated freesheet	6.25
Kraft envelope (bleached kraft and brown kraft) paper, uncoated freesheet	2.42
Other uncoated freesheet body stock paper for coating (base or raw stock for conversion of off-machine coating) and miscellaneous uncoated freesheet	2.84
Uncoated freesheet (containing not more than 10 percent mechanical fiber), nsk	0.21
Bleached bristols (weight more than 150 g/m2), excluding cotton fiber index and bogus	3.74
Uncoated bristol tag stock, bleached (weight more than 150 g/m2)	13.01
Uncoated bristol file folder stock, bleached (weight more than 150 g/m2)	15.68
Other uncoated bristols, including tabulating card, index, printing, and postcard stock, bleached (weight more than 150 g/m2), excluding cotton fiber index and bogus	24.30
Coated bleached bristols (weight more than 150 g/m2), excludng cotton fiber index and bogus	47.01
Cotton fiber paper and thin paper	2.61
Bond and writing cotton fiber paper	49.09
Other cotton fiber paper	2.06
Thin paper (including carbonizing), Bible paper, dermatype, mimeotype, and duplicating stencil paper, india paper, cigarette paper, etc.	48.10
Cotton fiber paper and thin paper, nsk	0.73
Unbleached kraft packaging and industrial converting paper	4.21
Unbleached kraft shipping sack paper (which meets minimum Federal specifications UU-S-48) and other unbleached kraft shipping sack paper	25.54
Unbleached kraft bag and sack paper (except shipping), including grocers and other unbleached kraft bag and sack for notion, millinery, etc., packaging and industrial converting paper	52.02
Unbleached kraft wrapping and specialty packaging paper	

Continued on next page.

PRODUCT SHARE DETAILS - Continued

Product or Product Class	% Share	Product or Product Class	% Share
(92 lb or less), including flour, sugar, dog food, fast foods, dairy products, etc.	8.31	unbleached kraft, nsk	1.01
Other unbleached kraft converting paper, including creping (92 lb or less) (asphalting paper, coating and laminating, gumming, etc.).	13.63	Special industrial paper, except specialty packaging, including absorbent, battery separator, electrical papers, etc.	4.73
Unbleached kraft (not less than 80 percent) packaging and industrial converting paper, nsk	0.49	Tissue paper and other machine-creped paper	16.28
Packaging and industrial converting paper, except unbleached kraft	3.08	Toilet tissue stock	39.28
Shipping sack paper (except unbleached kraft), including combination kraft and rope, bleached and semibleached	14.11	Facial tissue stock, except toweling, napkin, and toilet	9.83
Other bag and sack paper, except unbleached kraft and shipping, including grocers', liquor, millinery, notion, variety, etc.	7.96	Napkin paper stock, except sanitary napkin stock wadding	10.65
Specialty packaging (92 lb or less) and wrapping paper, except unbleached kraft (butcher, flour, sugar, fast foods, confectionery, etc.)	54.80	Toweling paper stock, except wiper stock	28.26
Waxing paper stock, except unbleached kraft, 19 lb or more.	4.07	Wiper tissue stock, regular, facial, and wadding stock	2.14
Other converting paper stock, except unbleached kraft, including asphalting and creping stocks (92 lb or less), coating and laminating, etc.	7.62	Other sanitary paper stock, including sanitary napkin stock wadding, aseptic paper stock, reinforced paper stock, etc.	5.18
Glassine, greaseproof, and vegetable parchment, all grades regardless of end use (92 lb or less)	10.43	Wrapping tissue, including florist tissue stock, hosiery paper, interleaving, antitarnish, etc.	2.68
Packaging and industrial converting papers, except		Other tissue paper stock, including waxing tissue stock, creped wadding for interior packaging (excluding sanitary and thin)	1.06
		Tissue paper and other machine-creped paper, nsk	0.91
		Construction paper	0.52
		Roofing felts, saturating and dry	44.15
		Other construction paper (including sheathing paper, floor covering felts, automotive, insulating paper blankets, etc.)	44.84
		Construction paper, nsk	11.01
		Paper mills, nsk	0.18

Source: 1992 *Economic Census*. The values shown are percent of total shipments in an industry. Values of indented subcategories are summed in the main heading. The symbol (D) appears when data are withheld to prevent disclosure of competitive information. The abbreviation nsk stands for 'not specified by kind' and nec for 'not elsewhere classified'.

INPUTS AND OUTPUTS FOR PAPER MILLS, EXCEPT BUILDING PAPER

Economic Sector or Industry Providing Inputs	%	Sector	Economic Sector or Industry Buying Outputs	%	Sector
Imports	19.4	Foreign	Commercial printing	20.8	Manufg.
Pulp mills	14.9	Manufg.	Newspapers	16.6	Manufg.
Electric services (utilities)	6.2	Util.	Sanitary paper products	8.2	Manufg.
Logging camps & logging contractors	6.0	Manufg.	Manifold business forms	6.6	Manufg.
Wholesale trade	5.6	Trade	Periodicals	5.0	Manufg.
Petroleum refining	4.7	Manufg.	Bags, except textile	4.9	Manufg.
Sawmills & planning mills, general	4.6	Manufg.	Paper coating & glazing	4.3	Manufg.
Gas production & distribution (utilities)	4.3	Util.	Exports	2.8	Foreign
Cyclic crudes and organics	4.0	Manufg.	Envelopes	2.3	Manufg.
Miscellaneous plastics products	2.8	Manufg.	Book publishing	1.8	Manufg.
Motor freight transportation & warehousing	2.3	Util.	Converted paper products, nec	1.8	Manufg.
Railroads & related services	2.0	Util.	Book printing	1.6	Manufg.
Scrap	1.7	Scrap	Retail trade, except eating & drinking	1.5	Trade
Alkalies & chlorine	1.4	Manufg.	Personal consumption expenditures	1.4	
Broadwoven fabric mills	1.2	Manufg.	Wholesale trade	1.4	Trade
Coal	1.1	Mining	Elementary & secondary schools	1.4	Services
Synthetic rubber	1.1	Manufg.	Stationery products	1.3	Manufg.
Clay, ceramic, & refractory minerals	1.0	Mining	Change in business inventories	1.0	In House
Wet corn milling	1.0	Manufg.	S/L Govt. purch., elem. & secondary education	1.0	S/L Govt
Inorganic pigments	0.9	Manufg.	Blankbooks & looseleaf binders	0.8	Manufg.
Advertising	0.8	Services	Die-cut paper & board	0.8	Manufg.
Paperboard containers & boxes	0.7	Manufg.	Paperboard containers & boxes	0.8	Manufg.
Sanitary services, steam supply, irrigation	0.7	Util.	Greeting card publishing	0.6	Manufg.
Maintenance of nonfarm buildings nec	0.6	Constr.	Miscellaneous publishing	0.6	Manufg.
Industrial inorganic chemicals, nec	0.6	Manufg.	Doctors & dentists	0.6	Services
Water supply & sewage systems	0.6	Util.	Membership organizations nec	0.6	Services
Fabricated rubber products, nec	0.5	Manufg.	Real estate	0.5	Fin/R.E.
Miscellaneous fabricated wire products	0.5	Manufg.	Computer & data processing services	0.5	Services
Surface active agents	0.5	Manufg.	Carbon paper & inked ribbons	0.4	Manufg.
Water transportation	0.4	Util.	Cyclic crudes and organics	0.4	Manufg.
Banking	0.4	Fin/R.E.	Photographic equipment & supplies	0.4	Manufg.
Forestry products	0.3	Agric.	Banking	0.4	Fin/R.E.
Fabricated metal products, nec	0.3	Manufg.	Colleges, universities, & professional schools	0.4	Services
Nitrogenous & phosphatic fertilizers	0.3	Manufg.	Legal services	0.4	Services
Pipe, valves, & pipe fittings	0.3	Manufg.	Religious organizations	0.4	Services
Plastics materials & resins	0.3	Manufg.	S/L Govt. purch., other education & libraries	0.4	S/L Govt
Air transportation	0.3	Util.	Abrasive products	0.3	Manufg.
Communications, except radio & TV	0.3	Util.	Labor, civic, social, & fraternal associations	0.3	Services
Eating & drinking places	0.3	Trade	S/L Govt. purch., public assistance & relief	0.3	S/L Govt
Computer & data processing services	0.3	Services	Cigarettes	0.2	Manufg.
Equipment rental & leasing services	0.3	Services	Engraving & plate printing	0.2	Manufg.
State & local government enterprises, nec	0.3	Gov't	Mineral wool	0.2	Manufg.
Chemical preparations, nec	0.2	Manufg.	Surgical & medical instruments	0.2	Manufg.
Lime	0.2	Manufg.	Eating & drinking places	0.2	Trade
Machinery, except electrical, nec	0.2	Manufg.	Engineering, architectural, & surveying services	0.2	Services
Paper industries machinery	0.2	Manufg.	Management & consulting services & labs	0.2	Services

Continued on next page.

INPUTS AND OUTPUTS FOR PAPER MILLS, EXCEPT BUILDING PAPER - Continued

Economic Sector or Industry Providing Inputs	%	Sector	Economic Sector or Industry Buying Outputs	%	Sector
Automotive rental & leasing, without drivers	0.2	Services	Social services, nec	0.2	Services
U.S. Postal Service	0.2	Gov't	S/L Govt. purch., other general government	0.2	S/L Govt
Nonferrous metal ores, except copper	0.1	Mining	Surgical appliances & supplies	0.1	Manufg.
Lubricating oils & greases	0.1	Manufg.	Transformers	0.1	Manufg.
Paper mills, except building paper	0.1	Manufg.	Business services nec	0.1	Services
Insurance carriers	0.1	Fin/R.E.	Child day care services	0.1	Services
Security & commodity brokers	0.1	Fin/R.E.	Hotels & lodging places	0.1	Services
Automotive repair shops & services	0.1	Services	Libraries, vocation education	0.1	Services
Hotels & lodging places	0.1	Services	Medical & health services, nec	0.1	Services
Legal services	0.1	Services	S/L Govt. purch., higher education	0.1	S/L Govt
Management & consulting services & labs	0.1	Services			
Noncomparable imports	0.1	Foreign			

Source: Benchmark Input-Output Accounts for the U.S. Economy, 1982, U.S. Department of Commerce, Washington, D.C., July 1991. Data, as reported in the source, are organized by the 1977 SIC structure in use in 1982 but have been matched, as closely as is possible, to the 1987 SIC structure used in this book.

OCCUPATIONS EMPLOYED BY SIC 262 - PULP, PAPER, AND PAPERBOARD MILLS

Occupation	% of Total 1994	Change to 2005	Occupation	% of Total 1994	Change to 2005
Machine operators nec	11.9	13.8	Extruding & forming machine workers	1.8	19.8
Helpers, laborers, & material movers nec	7.6	-7.8	Machine feeders & offbearers	1.7	-17.0
Blue collar worker supervisors	6.0	0.1	Coating, painting, & spraying machine workers	1.4	-26.2
Paper goods machine setters & set-up operators	4.4	-26.2	Secretaries, ex legal & medical	1.4	-16.1
Industrial machinery mechanics	3.8	1.4	Packaging & filling machine operators	1.4	-7.8
Industrial truck & tractor operators	3.5	-7.8	Plumbers, pipefitters, & steamfitters	1.3	-7.8
Maintenance repairers, general utility	3.0	-7.8	Freight, stock, & material movers, hand	1.2	-26.2
Millwrights	2.9	-26.2	Chemical equipment controllers, operators	1.2	-26.2
Crushing & mixing machine operators	2.7	-17.0	Precision instrument repairers	1.1	19.9
Cutting & slicing machine setters, operators	2.6	10.6	Industrial production managers	1.1	-7.8
Inspectors, testers, & graders, precision	2.5	1.4	Boiler operators, low pressure	1.1	-7.8
Electricians	2.2	-13.5			

Source: Industry-Occupation Matrix, Bureau of Labor Statistics. These data relate to one or more 3-digit SIC industry groups rather than to a single 4-digit SIC. The change reported for each occupation to the year 2005 is a percent of growth or decline as estimated by the Bureau of Labor Statistics. The abbreviation nec stands for 'not elsewhere classified'.

LOCATION BY STATE AND REGIONAL CONCENTRATION

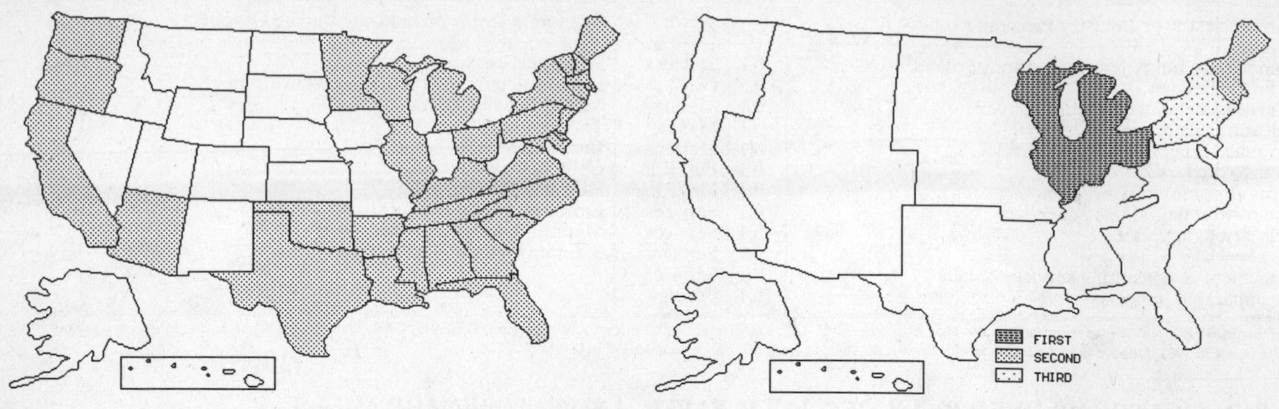

INDUSTRY DATA BY STATE

State	Establish-ments	Shipments: Total ($ mil)	Shipments: % of U.S.	Shipments: Per Establ.	Employment: Total Number	Employment: % of U.S.	Employment: Per Establ.	Employment: Wages ($/hour)	Cost as % of Shipments	Investment per Employee ($)
Wisconsin	35	4,446.7	13.6	127.0	19,200	14.7	549	17.30	54.9	21,755
Maine	13	2,934.5	9.0	225.7	12,500	9.6	962	18.03	60.9	19,864
Alabama	7	2,314.3	7.1	330.6	8,800	6.7	1,257	19.09	48.7	38,852
Washington	13	2,098.8	6.4	161.4	7,100	5.4	546	20.63	62.3	29,254
Louisiana	7	1,629.6	5.0	232.8	4,500	3.4	643	19.93	49.1	41,800
New York	32	1,567.1	4.8	49.0	7,400	5.7	231	15.69	56.9	13,162
Michigan	18	1,563.4	4.8	86.9	6,200	4.7	344	17.13	52.5	11,000
Pennsylvania	16	1,453.9	4.4	90.9	6,300	4.8	394	16.95	55.9	40,730
Ohio	11	1,364.4	4.2	124.0	6,000	4.6	545	17.54	49.9	16,850
Minnesota	7	1,340.4	4.1	191.5	5,400	4.1	771	19.98	56.6	21,741
Georgia	7	1,224.2	3.7	174.9	3,300	2.5	471	17.50	51.3	23,818
South Carolina	4	975.1	3.0	243.8	2,500	1.9	625	19.56	50.1	10,720
North Carolina	3	963.9	2.9	321.3	5,000	3.8	1,667	19.64	50.0	-
Massachusetts	26	879.9	2.7	33.8	4,700	3.6	181	14.57	57.7	13,787
Oregon	6	830.7	2.5	138.5	2,600	2.0	433	24.15	72.1	28,538
Tennessee	6	802.5	2.4	133.7	3,600	2.8	600	19.84	46.9	10,583
Mississippi	6	709.9	2.2	118.3	2,100	1.6	350	17.00	50.4	-
New Hampshire	10	369.4	1.1	36.9	2,400	1.8	240	13.29	53.5	-
New Jersey	6	362.7	1.1	60.4	1,500	1.1	250	17.79	53.2	-
Vermont	4	138.3	0.4	34.6	700	0.5	175	12.45	52.5	13,286
California	9	(D)	-	-	1,750 *	1.3	194	-	-	-
Arkansas	5	(D)	-	-	3,750 *	2.9	750	-	-	-
Connecticut	4	(D)	-	-	750 *	0.6	188	-	-	-
Texas	4	(D)	-	-	3,750 *	2.9	938	-	-	-
Illinois	3	(D)	-	-	375 *	0.3	125	-	-	-
Maryland	3	(D)	-	-	1,750 *	1.3	583	-	-	-
Oklahoma	3	(D)	-	-	750 *	0.6	250	-	-	-
Virginia	3	(D)	-	-	1,750 *	1.3	583	-	-	-
Arizona	2	(D)	-	-	750 *	0.6	375	-	-	-
Delaware	2	(D)	-	-	175 *	0.1	88	-	-	-
Florida	2	(D)	-	-	1,750 *	1.3	875	-	-	-
Kentucky	2	(D)	-	-	750 *	0.6	375	-	-	-

Source: 1992 *Economic Census*. The states are in descending order of shipments or establishments (if shipment data are missing for the majority). The symbol (D) appears when data are withheld to prevent disclosure of competitive information. States marked with (D) are sorted by number of establishments. A dash (-) indicates that the data element cannot be calculated; * indicates the midpoint of a range.

2631 - PAPERBOARD MILLS

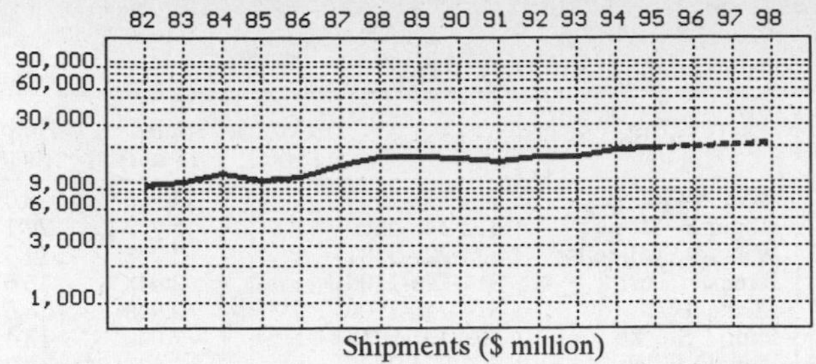

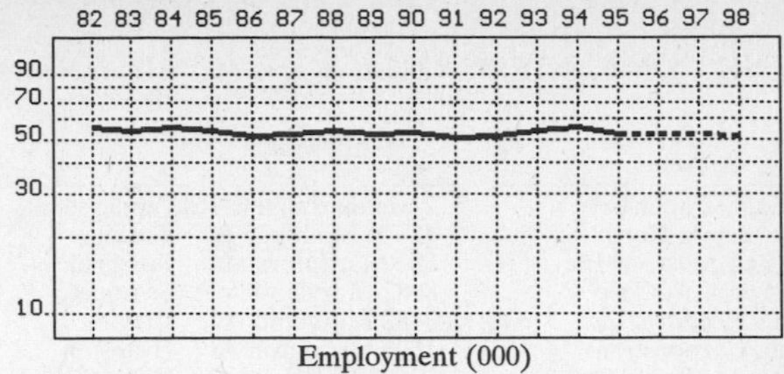

GENERAL STATISTICS

Year	Companies	Establishments: Total	Establishments: with 20 or more employees	Employment: Total (000)	Production Workers (000)	Production Hours (Mil)	Compensation: Payroll ($ mil)	Compensation: Wages ($/hr)	Cost of Materials	Value Added by Manufacture	Value of Shipments	Capital Invest.
1982	106	222	212	55.6	43.0	88.5	1,501.5	12.63	5,842.3	3,739.8	9,531.1	1,286.7
1983				53.6	41.4	87.0	1,558.7	13.50	6,098.4	3,985.7	10,099.9	527.3
1984				55.7	42.5	90.0	1,677.6	14.14	6,708.7	5,238.5	11,880.6	680.2
1985				53.9	41.1	86.5	1,668.4	14.35	6,171.7	4,299.6	10,494.0	1,043.4
1986				51.0	39.2	85.3	1,713.9	15.02	6,133.3	4,947.2	11,160.3	999.6
1987	91	205	200	52.3	40.1	88.5	1,858.8	15.56	6,839.7	6,914.3	13,729.7	772.6
1988				53.6	41.1	90.8	1,964.4	15.97	7,340.6	8,778.5	16,094.2	1,517.5
1989		221	202	52.1	40.3	89.2	1,958.3	16.26	7,563.6	8,798.6	16,319.3	1,653.3
1990				53.1	40.7	90.5	2,048.7	16.44	7,804.8	8,123.0	15,919.3	2,976.6
1991				50.6	39.0	86.5	2,027.4	16.90	7,781.1	7,257.2	15,013.1	2,152.3
1992	89	204	200	51.5	39.4	88.4	2,136.4	17.36	8,013.4	8,195.3	16,140.0	2,040.7
1993				53.3	40.5	90.0	2,244.2	17.69	8,657.0	7,525.7	16,164.8	1,643.3
1994				54.9	41.4	94.5	2,392.3	17.99	9,771.9	8,893.5	18,749.0	1,432.1
1995				52.1P	39.6P	91.0P	2,382.9P	18.65P	9,841.1P	8,956.5P	18,881.7P	2,211.8P
1996				51.9P	39.4P	91.3P	2,451.3P	19.07P	10,208.6P	9,290.9P	19,586.9P	2,322.0P
1997				51.8P	39.3P	91.7P	2,519.7P	19.49P	10,576.1P	9,625.4P	20,292.0P	2,432.2P
1998				51.6P	39.1P	92.0P	2,588.2P	19.92P	10,943.6P	9,959.9P	20,997.1P	2,542.4P

Sources: 1982, 1987, 1992 *Economic Census*; *Annual Survey of Manufactures*, 83-86, 88-91, 93-94. Establishment counts for non-Census years are from *County Business Patterns*; establishment values for 83-84 are extrapolations. 'P's show projections by the editors. Industries reclassified in 87 will not have data for prior years.

INDICES OF CHANGE

Year	Companies	Establishments: Total	Establishments: with 20 or more employees	Employment: Total (000)	Production Workers (000)	Production Hours (Mil)	Compensation: Payroll ($ mil)	Compensation: Wages ($/hr)	Cost of Materials	Value Added by Manufacture	Value of Shipments	Capital Invest.
1982	119	109	106	108	109	100	70	73	73	46	59	63
1983				104	105	98	73	78	76	49	63	26
1984				108	108	102	79	81	84	64	74	33
1985				105	104	98	78	83	77	52	65	51
1986				99	99	96	80	87	77	60	69	49
1987	102	100	100	102	102	100	87	90	85	84	85	38
1988				104	104	103	92	92	92	107	100	74
1989		108	101	101	102	101	92	94	94	107	101	81
1990				103	103	102	96	95	97	99	99	146
1991				98	99	98	95	97	97	89	93	105
1992	100	100	100	100	100	100	100	100	100	100	100	100
1993				103	103	102	105	102	108	92	100	81
1994				107	105	107	112	104	122	109	116	70
1995				101P	101P	103P	112P	107P	123P	109P	117P	108P
1996				101P	100P	103P	115P	110P	127P	113P	121P	114P
1997				101P	100P	104P	118P	112P	132P	117P	126P	119P
1998				100P	99P	104P	121P	115P	137P	122P	130P	125P

Sources: Same as General Statistics. Values reflect change from the base year, 1992. Values above 100 mean greater than 92, values below 100 mean less than 92, and a value of 100 in the 82-91 or 93-98 period means same as 92. 'P's mark projections by the editors.

SELECTED RATIOS

For 1992	Avg. of All Manufact.	Analyzed Industry	Index	For 1992	Avg. of All Manufact.	Analyzed Industry	Index
Employees per Establishment	46	252	553	Value Added per Production Worker	122,353	208,003	170
Payroll per Establishment	1,332,320	10,472,549	786	Cost per Establishment	4,239,462	39,281,373	927
Payroll per Employee	29,181	41,483	142	Cost per Employee	92,853	155,600	168
Production Workers per Establishment	31	193	615	Cost per Production Worker	135,003	203,386	151
Wages per Establishment	734,496	7,522,667	1,024	Shipments per Establishment	8,100,800	79,117,647	977
Wages per Production Worker	23,390	38,950	167	Shipments per Employee	177,425	313,398	177
Hours per Production Worker	2,025	2,244	111	Shipments per Production Worker	257,966	409,645	159
Wages per Hour	11.55	17.36	150	Investment per Establishment	278,244	10,003,431	3,595
Value Added per Establishment	3,842,210	40,173,039	1,046	Investment per Employee	6,094	39,625	650
Value Added per Employee	84,153	159,132	189	Investment per Production Worker	8,861	51,794	585

Sources: Same as General Statistics. The 'Average of All Manufacturing' column represents the average of all manufacturing industries reported for the most recent complete year available. The Index shows the relationship between the Average and the Analyzed Industry. For example, 100 means that they are equal; 500 that the Analyzed Industry is five times the average; 50 means that the Analyzed Industry is half the national average. The abbreviation 'na' is used to show that data are 'not available'.

LEADING COMPANIES

Number shown: **51** Total sales ($ mil): **40,518** Total employment (000): **209.9**

Company Name	Address				CEO Name	Phone	Co. Type	Sales ($ mil)	Empl. (000)
International Paper Co	2 Manhattanville Rd	Purchase	NY	10577	John A Georges	914-397-1500	P	14,966	70.0
Stone Container Corp	150 N Michigan Av	Chicago	IL	60601	Roger W Stone	312-346-6600	P	5,749	29.1
Willamette Industries Inc	3800 1st Interstate	Portland	OR	97201	William Swindells	503-227-5581	P	3,008	12.3
Jefferson Smurfit Corp	8182 Maryland Av	St Louis	MO	63105	James E Terrill	314-746-1100	P	2,948	16.6
SIBV/MS Holdings Inc	8182 Maryland Av	Clayton	MO	63105	Michael Smurfit	314-746-1100	J	2,948	16.6
Packaging Corporation	1603 Orrington Av	Evanston	IL	60201	Paul T Stecko	708-492-5713	S	2,000	13.4
Weyerhaeuser Paper Co	33663 W Way	Federal Way	WA	98003	Ronald Glick	206-924-2345	D	1,640*	7.0
Federal Paper Board Company	75 Chestnut Ridge	Montvale	NJ	07645	John R Kennedy	201-391-1776	P	1,387	6.8
Riverwood Intern Corp	3350 Cumbrlnd	Atlanta	GA	30339	Thomas H Johnson	404-664-3000	P	1,283	8.5
Chesapeake Corp	PO Box 2350	Richmond	VA	23218	J Carter Fox	804-697-1000	P	885	4.8
St Joe Paper Co	1650 Prudential Dr	Jacksonville	FL	32207	Winfred L Thornton	904-396-6600	P	592	5.0
Westvaco Corp	PO Box 118005	Charleston	SC	29423	BD Thomas	803-745-3000	D	520*	1.4
Newark Group Inc	20 Jackson Dr	Cranford	NJ	07016	Fred G von Zuben	908-276-4000	R	481	2.6
Gulf States Paper Corp	PO Box 48999	Tuscaloosa	AL	35404	J Edward Woods	205-553-6200	R	340	2.0
MacMillan Bloedel Inc	PO Box 235016	Montgomery	AL	36123	Fred V Ernst	205-213-6100	S	320	2.5
Simkins Industries Inc	260 East St	New Haven	CT	06511	Leon J Simkins	203-787-7171	R	210	2.0
Menominee Paper Company Inc	PO Box 310	Menominee	MI	49858	Marshall Schneider	906-863-5595	S	200	0.4
Mead Coated Board Inc	PO Box 940	Phenix City	AL	36868	Boyd Giles	205-855-4711	S	120*	0.7
St Joe Forest Products Co	PO Box 190	Port St Joe	FL	32456	Robert Nedley	904-227-1171	S	110	0.9
Specialty Paperboard Inc	PO Box 498	Brattleboro	VT	05301	Alex Kwader	802-257-0365	P	105	0.5
Sonoco Products Co	PO Box 160	Hartsville	SC	29550	CW Claypool	803-383-7000	D	85	1.6
EHV Weidmann Industries Inc	PO Box 903	St Johnsbury	VT	05819	RC Fuehrer	802-748-8106	S	62*	0.4
Riverwood International Georgia	PO Box 3215	Macon	GA	31298	Thomas Johnson	912-788-6160	S	61*	0.5
Shippers Paper Products Co	3610 W Lake Av	Glenview	IL	60025	Michael Loeschen	708-657-5222	S	51	0.4
US Paper Mills Corp	PO Box 3309	De Pere	WI	54115	Thomas Olson	414-336-4229	R	43	0.2
Green Bay Packaging Inc	PO Box 711	Morrilton	AR	72110	Jim Kress	501-354-4521	D	33*	0.4
Cascade-Niagara Falls Inc	4001 Packard Rd	Niagara Falls	NY	14303	Yves LaFontaine	716-285-3681	S	28	0.1
Davey Co	164 Laidlaw Av	Jersey City	NJ	07306	Alfred C Brooks	201-653-0606	R	25	0.3
Ivex Packaging Corp	292 Logan Av	Joliet	IL	60433	Lew Brown	815-740-3838	D	25	0.2
Yorktowne Paper Mills Inc	PO Box 2426	York	PA	17405	D Jack Sparler	717-843-8061	R	25*	0.4
Halifax Paper Board Company	1213 Mall Dr	Richmond	VA	23235	James Walls	804-794-8539	R	24	0.1
Haverhill Paperboard Corp	PO Box 31	Haverhill	MA	01831	Michael Cummings	508-373-4111	S	23*	0.2
Jet Corr Inc	1781 Conyersation	Conyers	GA	30207	Richard A Brown	404-483-7458	S	20	0.3
Salwen Paper Company Inc	PO Box 4008	Edison	NJ	08818	Harry Salwen	908-225-4000	R	20	0.1
Newman and Company Inc	6101 Tacony St	Philadelphia	PA	19135	Bernard Newman	215-333-8700	R	19	0.1
Halltown Paperboard Co	PO Box 10	Halltown	WV	25423	C C Hammann	304-725-2076	S	17	0.2
Cincinnati Paperboard Corp	5500 Wooster Rd	Cincinnati	OH	45226	Paul W Nelson	513-871-7112	D	15*	0.1
Sweetwater Paperboard Co	PO Box 665	Austell	GA	30001	Tom C Dawson Jr	404-944-9350	S	15*	<0.1
US Paper Mills Corp	69 Washington St	Menasha	WI	54952	Keith Mutchler	414-725-7115	D	15	0.1
McCowat-Mercer Press Inc	202 Riverside Dr	Jackson	TN	38301	T H Butler III	901-427-3376	R	14	0.2
American Corrugated Products	PO Box 28575	Columbus	OH	43228	Donald R Youell	614-870-2000	R	13	0.1
Gleason Industries	1347 Shore St	W Sacramento	CA	95691	Mike Richards	916-373-6770	R	12	<0.1
Aurora Paperboard	705 N Farnsworth	Aurora	IL	60505	Stephen C Dodd	708-898-4231	D	10	0.1
Banner Fibreboard Co	22nd and Com Sts	Wellsburg	WV	26070	DL Laughlin	304-737-3711	R	10	<0.1
Converters Paperboard Co	PO Box 560	Rockford	MI	49341	J Isabell	616-866-3421	D	10*	<0.1
Tenax Corp	1850 W Oliver Av	Indianapolis	IN	46221	John A Bratt	317-631-8708	R	8	0.1
Yorktowne Paper Mills of Maine	721 Water St	Gardiner	ME	04345	Joseph W Emerson	207-582-3230	S	7	<0.1
Beloit Box Board Company Inc	PO Box 386	Beloit	WI	53512	J H Chamberlain	608-365-6671	R	6	<0.1
Custom Sheeting Corp	PO Box EG	Livingston	AL	35470	Tom Neuhauser	205-652-7692	R	5	<0.1
C-Case Corp	822 Hillgrove Av	Western Springs	IL	60558	William Dobias	708-887-7000	R	4*	<0.1
Shryock Brothers Inc	PO Box 157	Downingtown	PA	19335	Charlie Barber	215-269-0115	R	4	<0.1

Source: *Ward's Business Directory of U.S. Private and Public Companies*, Volumes 1 and 2, 1996. The company type code used is as follows: P - Public, R - Private, S - Subsidiary, D - Division, J - Joint Venture, A - Affiliate, G - Group. Sales are in millions of dollars, employees are in thousands. An asterisk (*) indicates an estimated sales volume. The symbol < stands for 'less than'. Company names and addresses are truncated, in some cases, to fit into the available space.

MATERIALS CONSUMED

Material		Quantity	Delivered Cost ($ million)
Materials, ingredients, containers, and supplies		(X)	6,319.9
Spruce and true fir pulpwood bolts and logs	1,000 standard cords	480.6	39.6
Hemlock pulpwood bolts and logs	1,000 standard cords	(D)	(D)
Southern pine pulpwood bolts and logs	1,000 standard cords	15,610.9	1,138.0
Other softwood pulpwood bolts and logs, including Douglas fir and Jack pine	1,000 standard cords	769.4	100.9
Softwood pulpwood wood chips, slabs, cores, sawdust, bark, and other mill residues	1,000 standard cords	10,715.9	794.7
Southern mixed hardwood pulpwood bolts and logs	1,000 standard cords	3,980.5	232.2
Other hardwood pulpwood bolts and logs	1,000 standard cords	1,214.1	84.2
Hardwood pulpwood wood chips, slabs, cores, sawdust, bark, and other mill residues	1,000 standard cords	4,158.2	266.2
Chlorine (100 percent Cl basis)	1,000 s tons	172.8	20.9
Sodium hydroxide (caustic soda)(100 percent NaOH)	1,000 s tons	717.6	174.1
Sodium chlorate (100 percent NaClO3)	1,000 s tons	142.5	50.5
Other sodium compounds		(X)	52.8
Aluminum sulfate (17 percent Al2O3)	1,000 s tons	246.9	26.5
Rosin sizing	mil lb (dry basis)	142.7*	51.4
Lime	1,000 s tons	361.3	23.5
Kaolin and ball clay	1,000 s tons	405.8	56.3

Continued on next page.

MATERIALS CONSUMED - Continued

Material		Quantity	Delivered Cost ($ million)
Starch	mil lb	496.4	103.8
Synthetic resins	mil lb	214.9	90.3
Titanium dioxide, composite and pure (100 percent TiO2)	mil lb	95.1	85.3
Calcium carbonate, precipitated (100 percent CaCO2)	1,000 s tons	92.7	9.8
All other chemicals, including organic		(X)	410.4
Woodpulp produced at affiliated or associated mills at other locations	1,000 s tons	(D)	(D)
Woodpulp purchased market wood pulp	1,000 s tons	86.0	37.2
Mixed wastepaper, except plant's own broke paper	1,000 s tons	1,215.2**	44.4
Mechanical news wastepaper, except plant's own broke paper	1,000 s tons	1,267.6	47.3
Other mechanical wastepaper, except plant's own broke paper	1,000 s tons	548.4	31.5
Corrugated wastepaper, including kraft, except plant's own broke paper	1,000 s tons	10,020.5	599.3
High grade pulp substitutes wastepaper, except plant's own broke paper	1,000 s tons	546.4	117.1
High grade deinking wastepaper, except plant's own broke paper	1,000 s tons	189.5	35.2
Cotton linters (net weight)	mil lb	(D)	(D)
Other fibrous materials, including rags, straw, and bagasse	1,000 s tons	(D)	(D)
Paperboard containers, boxes, and corrugated paperboard		(X)	57.5
All other materials and components, parts, containers, and supplies		(X)	1,371.0
Materials, ingredients, containers, and supplies, nsk		(X)	102.8

Source: 1992 *Economic Census*. Explanation of symbols used: (D): Withheld to avoid disclosure of competitive data; na: Not available; (S): Withheld because statistical norms were not met; (X): Not applicable; (Z): Less than half the unit shown; nec: Not elsewhere classified; nsk: Not specified by kind; - : zero; * : 10-19 percent estimated; ** : 20-29 percent estimated.

PRODUCT SHARE DETAILS

Product or Product Class	% Share	Product or Product Class	% Share
Paperboard mills	100.00	Recycled paperboard	26.03
Unbleached kraft packaging and industrial converting paperboard	45.43	Recycled linerboard	14.17
Unbleached kraft linerboard	83.92	Recycled corrugating medium	23.09
Other unbleached kraft packaging and industrial converting paperboard, including tube, can, and drum paperboard, corrugating paperboard medium, folding carton-type board, etc.	16.08	Recycled container chip and filler board	4.28
Bleached packaging and industrial converting paperboard (80 percent or more virgin pulp)	20.41	Recycled folding carton unlined chipboard	3.45
Bleached linerboard	6.23	Recycled kraft-lined folding carton board	0.49
Bleached folding carton-type paperboard	46.61	Recycled white-lined folding carton board	1.64
Bleached milk carton board	24.06	Recycled clay-coated folding carton board	21.88
Bleached heavyweight cup and round nested food container paperboard	11.92	Recycled setup board	1.05
Bleached plate, dish, and tray paperboard stock	5.96	Recycled tube, can, and drum paperboard stock	9.89
Other solid bleached paperboard, including paperboard for moist, liquid, and oily foods	5.22	Recycled gypsum linerboard	3.78
Semichemical paperboard, including corrugating medium	7.43	Other recycled paperboard, including panelboard and wallboard stock and other special combination packaging and industrial converting paperboard	10.74
		Recycled paperboard, nsk	5.54
		Wet machine board, including binders' board and shoe board	0.50
		Paperboard mills, nsk	0.20

Source: 1992 *Economic Census*. The values shown are percent of total shipments in an industry. Values of indented subcategories are summed in the main heading. The symbol (D) appears when data are withheld to prevent disclosure of competitive information. The abbreviation nsk stands for 'not specified by kind' and nec for 'not elsewhere classified'.

INPUTS AND OUTPUTS FOR PAPERBOARD MILLS

Economic Sector or Industry Providing Inputs	%	Sector	Economic Sector or Industry Buying Outputs	%	Sector
Sawmills & planning mills, general	13.5	Manufg.	Paperboard containers & boxes	75.2	Manufg.
Logging camps & logging contractors	13.4	Manufg.	Exports	10.6	Foreign
Gas production & distribution (utilities)	9.4	Util.	Die-cut paper & board	5.1	Manufg.
Petroleum refining	8.1	Manufg.	Miscellaneous plastics products	3.4	Manufg.
Electric services (utilities)	6.6	Util.	Converted paper products, nec	1.0	Manufg.
Wholesale trade	6.3	Trade	Gypsum products	1.0	Manufg.
Cyclic crudes and organics	5.1	Manufg.	Commercial printing	0.9	Manufg.
Scrap	4.6	Scrap	Games, toys, & children's vehicles	0.5	Manufg.
Motor freight transportation & warehousing	3.0	Util.	Blankbooks & looseleaf binders	0.4	Manufg.
Railroads & related services	2.3	Util.	Book printing	0.4	Manufg.
Alkalies & chlorine	2.1	Manufg.	Bookbinding & related work	0.3	Manufg.
Coal	1.4	Mining	Stationery products	0.3	Manufg.
Broadwoven fabric mills	1.4	Manufg.	Surgical & medical instruments	0.2	Manufg.
Industrial inorganic chemicals, nec	1.4	Manufg.	Sanitary paper products	0.1	Manufg.
Wood products, nec	1.3	Manufg.			
Surface active agents	1.2	Manufg.			
Maintenance of nonfarm buildings nec	0.8	Constr.			
Communications, except radio & TV	0.8	Util.			
Water supply & sewage systems	0.8	Util.			
Computer & data processing services	0.8	Services			
Miscellaneous fabricated wire products	0.7	Manufg.			

Continued on next page.

INPUTS AND OUTPUTS FOR PAPERBOARD MILLS - Continued

Economic Sector or Industry Providing Inputs	%	Sector	Economic Sector or Industry Buying Outputs	%	Sector
Synthetic rubber	0.7	Manufg.			
Fabricated metal products, nec	0.6	Manufg.			
Paperboard containers & boxes	0.6	Manufg.			
Pipe, valves, & pipe fittings	0.6	Manufg.			
Wet corn milling	0.6	Manufg.			
Sanitary services, steam supply, irrigation	0.6	Util.			
Advertising	0.6	Services			
Chemical preparations, nec	0.5	Manufg.			
Fabricated rubber products, nec	0.5	Manufg.			
Air transportation	0.5	Util.			
Water transportation	0.5	Util.			
Banking	0.5	Fin/R.E.			
Automotive rental & leasing, without drivers	0.5	Services			
Imports	0.5	Foreign			
Inorganic pigments	0.4	Manufg.			
Plastics materials & resins	0.4	Manufg.			
Pulp mills	0.4	Manufg.			
Paper industries machinery	0.3	Manufg.			
Pumps & compressors	0.3	Manufg.			
Insurance carriers	0.3	Fin/R.E.			
Automotive repair shops & services	0.3	Services			
Equipment rental & leasing services	0.3	Services			
State & local government enterprises, nec	0.3	Gov't			
Clay, ceramic, & refractory minerals	0.2	Mining			
Coated fabrics, not rubberized	0.2	Manufg.			
Lime	0.2	Manufg.			
Paper coating & glazing	0.2	Manufg.			
Wood pallets & skids	0.2	Manufg.			
Eating & drinking places	0.2	Trade			
Security & commodity brokers	0.2	Fin/R.E.			
Electrical repair shops	0.2	Services			
Hotels & lodging places	0.2	Services			
U.S. Postal Service	0.2	Gov't			
Adhesives & sealants	0.1	Manufg.			
Lubricating oils & greases	0.1	Manufg.			
Machinery, except electrical, nec	0.1	Manufg.			
Tires & inner tubes	0.1	Manufg.			
Retail trade, except eating & drinking	0.1	Trade			
Legal services	0.1	Services			

Source: Benchmark Input-Output Accounts for the U.S. Economy, 1982, U.S. Department of Commerce, Washington, D.C., July 1991. Data, as reported in the source, are organized by the 1977 SIC structure in use in 1982 but have been matched, as closely as is possible, to the 1987 SIC structure used in this book.

OCCUPATIONS EMPLOYED BY SIC 263 - PULP, PAPER, AND PAPERBOARD MILLS

Occupation	% of Total 1994	Change to 2005	Occupation	% of Total 1994	Change to 2005
Machine operators nec	11.9	13.8	Extruding & forming machine workers	1.8	19.8
Helpers, laborers, & material movers nec	7.6	-7.8	Machine feeders & offbearers	1.7	-17.0
Blue collar worker supervisors	6.0	0.1	Coating, painting, & spraying machine workers	1.4	-26.2
Paper goods machine setters & set-up operators	4.4	-26.2	Secretaries, ex legal & medical	1.4	-16.1
Industrial machinery mechanics	3.8	1.4	Packaging & filling machine operators	1.4	-7.8
Industrial truck & tractor operators	3.5	-7.8	Plumbers, pipefitters, & steamfitters	1.3	-7.8
Maintenance repairers, general utility	3.0	-7.8	Freight, stock, & material movers, hand	1.2	-26.2
Millwrights	2.9	-26.2	Chemical equipment controllers, operators	1.2	-26.2
Crushing & mixing machine operators	2.7	-17.0	Precision instrument repairers	1.1	19.9
Cutting & slicing machine setters, operators	2.6	10.6	Industrial production managers	1.1	-7.8
Inspectors, testers, & graders, precision	2.5	1.4	Boiler operators, low pressure	1.1	-7.8
Electricians	2.2	-13.5			

Source: Industry-Occupation Matrix, Bureau of Labor Statistics. These data relate to one or more 3-digit SIC industry groups rather than to a single 4-digit SIC. The change reported for each occupation to the year 2005 is a percent of growth or decline as estimated by the Bureau of Labor Statistics. The abbreviation nec stands for 'not elsewhere classified'.

LOCATION BY STATE AND REGIONAL CONCENTRATION

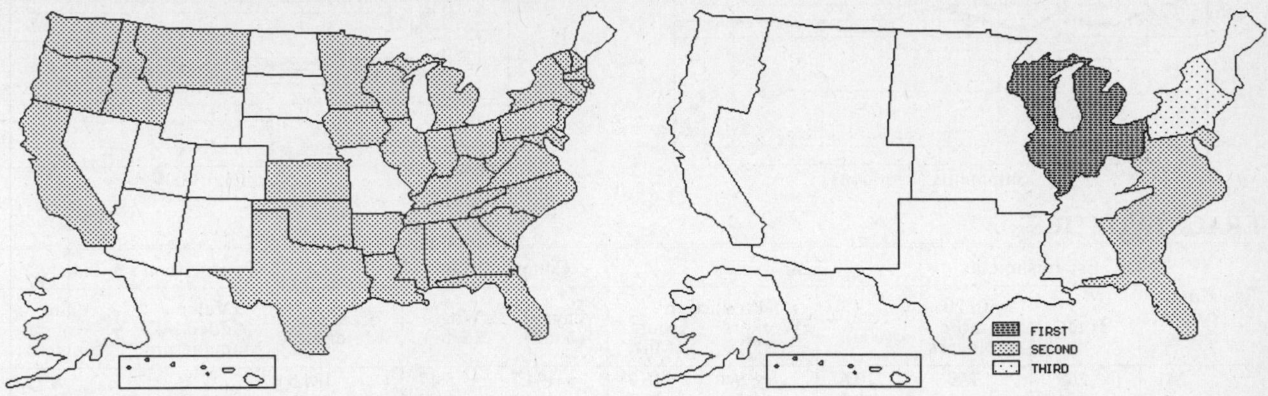

INDUSTRY DATA BY STATE

State	Establish-ments	Shipments Total ($ mil)	Shipments % of U.S.	Shipments Per Establ.	Employment Total Number	Employment % of U.S.	Employment Per Establ.	Wages ($/hour)	Cost as % of Shipments	Investment per Employee ($)
Georgia	12	1,947.5	12.1	162.3	5,800	11.3	483	17.80	48.7	44,103
Alabama	8	1,618.4	10.0	202.3	4,200	8.2	525	16.59	51.2	-
Virginia	9	1,290.7	8.0	143.4	4,500	8.7	500	16.50	44.3	54,467
Louisiana	5	1,262.4	7.8	252.5	2,600	5.0	520	19.65	45.8	40,115
Oregon	5	779.4	4.8	155.9	2,000	3.9	400	22.23	64.9	21,600
Florida	4	760.9	4.7	190.2	2,100	4.1	525	15.53	58.8	-
Arkansas	3	737.3	4.6	245.8	2,200	4.3	733	18.78	54.0	20,273
South Carolina	5	718.1	4.4	143.6	2,300	4.5	460	18.41	44.2	45,087
Michigan	13	607.7	3.8	46.7	2,600	5.0	200	15.90	40.3	34,538
California	15	598.7	3.7	39.9	1,700	3.3	113	17.48	46.1	16,941
Ohio	15	458.8	2.8	30.6	2,000	3.9	133	14.92	42.4	-
Wisconsin	6	351.2	2.2	58.5	1,100	2.1	183	15.26	31.9	21,091
Pennsylvania	12	288.7	1.8	24.1	1,300	2.5	108	14.88	42.2	8,385
New York	13	138.3	0.9	10.6	900	1.7	69	13.31	44.3	12,667
Indiana	9	(D)	-	-	1,750 *	3.4	194	-	-	-
New Jersey	8	(D)	-	-	750 *	1.5	94	-	-	8,400
Illinois	7	(D)	-	-	750 *	1.5	107	-	-	-
Tennessee	6	(D)	-	-	1,750 *	3.4	292	-	-	13,257
Texas	6	(D)	-	-	3,750 *	7.3	625	-	-	-
Connecticut	5	(D)	-	-	750 *	1.5	150	-	-	11,467
Massachusetts	4	(D)	-	-	750 *	1.5	188	-	-	-
North Carolina	4	(D)	-	-	750 *	1.5	188	-	-	-
Oklahoma	4	(D)	-	-	750 *	1.5	188	-	-	-
Washington	4	(D)	-	-	1,750 *	3.4	438	-	-	-
New Hampshire	3	(D)	-	-	175 *	0.3	58	-	-	-
Iowa	2	(D)	-	-	175 *	0.3	88	-	-	-
Kentucky	2	(D)	-	-	175 *	0.3	88	-	-	-
Maryland	2	(D)	-	-	375 *	0.7	188	-	-	-
Mississippi	2	(D)	-	-	750 *	1.5	375	-	-	-
Vermont	2	(D)	-	-	375 *	0.7	188	-	-	-
West Virginia	2	(D)	-	-	175 *	0.3	88	-	-	-
Idaho	1	(D)	-	-	750 *	1.5	750	-	-	-
Kansas	1	(D)	-	-	175 *	0.3	175	-	-	-
Minnesota	1	(D)	-	-	750 *	1.5	750	-	-	-
Montana	1	(D)	-	-	750 *	1.5	750	-	-	-

Source: 1992 *Economic Census*. The states are in descending order of shipments or establishments (if shipment data are missing for the majority). The symbol (D) appears when data are withheld to prevent disclosure of competitive information. States marked with (D) are sorted by number of establishments. A dash (-) indicates that the data element cannot be calculated; * indicates the midpoint of a range.

2652 - SETUP PAPERBOARD BOXES

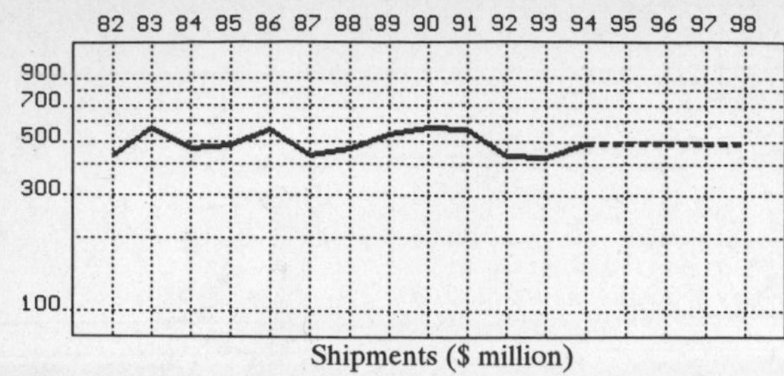

Shipments ($ million)

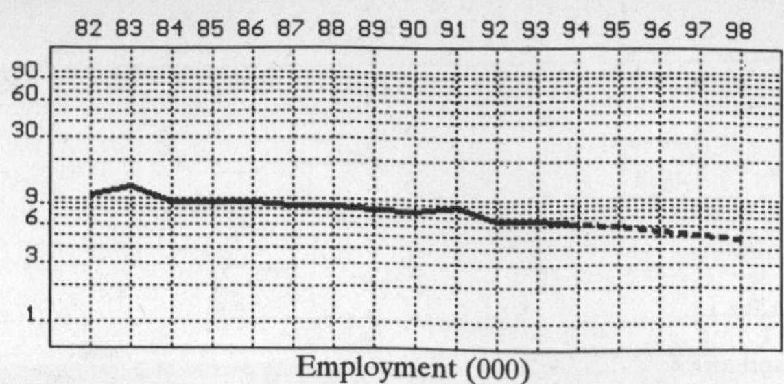

Employment (000)

GENERAL STATISTICS

Year	Companies	Establishments: Total	Establishments: with 20 or more employees	Employment: Total (000)	Employment: Production Workers (000)	Employment: Production Hours (Mil)	Compensation: Payroll ($ mil)	Compensation: Wages ($/hr)	Production ($ million): Cost of Materials	Production ($ million): Value Added by Manufacture	Production ($ million): Value of Shipments	Production ($ million): Capital Invest.
1982	241	265	165	10.6	8.9	16.7	134.7	5.47	184.5	250.2	433.2	10.0
1983		254	158	12.3	10.5	20.1	162.6	5.69	244.9	323.1	568.6	14.1
1984		243	151	9.3	7.7	15.7	131.6	5.65	199.5	268.3	466.1	18.0
1985		232	143	9.2	7.7	15.1	126.8	5.72	230.4	244.0	479.0	16.8
1986		226	136	9.1	7.4	15.4	127.5	5.90	280.0	267.8	552.0	13.2
1987	180	200	120	8.7	7.2	13.9	131.0	6.36	202.7	236.0	436.5	10.3
1988		190	119	8.8	7.5	14.6	135.2	6.29	218.0	249.0	464.4	5.9
1989		183	118	8.0	7.3	14.1	141.2	6.82	243.0	293.6	531.1	12.2
1990		177	117	7.8	7.5	14.5	145.9	7.02	259.0	312.9	565.1	14.4
1991		173	112	8.7	7.3	14.0	149.8	7.30	249.8	305.1	554.9	11.0
1992	146	155	102	6.6	5.1	10.7	129.2	7.92	197.5	240.3	435.7	10.0
1993		159	97	6.7	5.3	11.6	134.5	7.95	207.1	218.2	430.3	6.6
1994		137P	89P	6.3P	5.4P	11.1P	136.7P	8.05P			488.3P	8.6P
1995		127P	83P	6.0P	5.0P	10.5P	136.6P	8.29P			487.5P	8.1P
1996		117P	77P	5.6P	4.7P	10.0P	136.5P	8.53P			486.8P	7.6P
1997		106P	71P	5.2P	4.4P	9.4P	136.4P	8.77P			486.1P	7.1P
1998		96P	65P	4.8P	4.1P	8.9P	136.2P	9.01P			485.3P	6.6P

Sources: 1982, 1987, 1992 *Economic Census*; *Annual Survey of Manufactures*, 83-86, 88-91, 93-94. Establishment counts for non-Census years are from *County Business Patterns*; establishment values for 83-84 are extrapolations. 'P's show projections by the editors. Industries reclassified in 87 will not have data for prior years.

INDICES OF CHANGE

Year	Companies	Establishments: Total	Establishments: with 20 or more employees	Employment: Total (000)	Employment: Production Workers (000)	Employment: Production Hours (Mil)	Compensation: Payroll ($ mil)	Compensation: Wages ($/hr)	Production ($ million): Cost of Materials	Production ($ million): Value Added by Manufacture	Production ($ million): Value of Shipments	Production ($ million): Capital Invest.
1982	165	171	162	161	175	156	104	69	93	104	99	100
1983		164	155	186	206	188	126	72	124	134	131	141
1984		157	148	141	151	147	102	71	101	112	107	180
1985		150	140	139	151	141	98	72	117	102	110	168
1986		146	133	138	145	144	99	74	142	111	127	132
1987	123	129	118	132	141	130	101	80	103	98	100	103
1988		123	117	133	147	136	105	79	110	104	107	59
1989		118	116	121	143	132	109	86	123	122	122	122
1990		114	115	118	147	136	113	89	131	130	130	144
1991		112	110	132	143	131	116	92	126	127	127	110
1992	100	100	100	100	100	100	100	100	100	100	100	100
1993		103	95	102	104	108	104	100	105	91	99	66
1994		89P	88P	96P	105P	104P	106P	102P			112P	86P
1995		82P	82P	90P	99P	98P	106P	105P			112P	81P
1996		75P	76P	85P	92P	93P	106P	108P			112P	76P
1997		69P	70P	79P	86P	88P	106P	111P			112P	71P
1998		62P	64P	73P	80P	83P	105P	114P			111P	66P

Sources: Same as General Statistics. Values reflect change from the base year, 1992. Values above 100 mean greater than 92, values below 100 mean less than 92, and a value of 100 in the 82-91 or 93-98 period means same as 92. 'P's mark projections by the editors.

SELECTED RATIOS

For 1994	Avg. of All Manufact.	Analyzed Industry	Index
Employees per Establishment	49	46	94
Payroll per Establishment	1,500,273	994,610	66
Payroll per Employee	30,620	21,535	70
Production Workers per Establishment	34	39	114
Wages per Establishment	853,319	649,940	76
Wages per Production Worker	24,861	16,670	67
Hours per Production Worker	2,056	2,070	101
Wages per Hour	12.09	8.05	67
Value Added per Establishment	4,602,255	na	na
Value Added per Employee	93,930	na	na

For 1994	Avg. of All Manufact.	Analyzed Industry	Index
Value Added per Production Worker	134,084	na	na
Cost per Establishment	5,045,178	na	na
Cost per Employee	102,970	na	na
Cost per Production Worker	146,988	na	na
Shipments per Establishment	9,576,895	3,552,348	37
Shipments per Employee	195,460	76,914	39
Shipments per Production Worker	279,017	91,114	33
Investment per Establishment	321,011	62,798	20
Investment per Employee	6,552	1,360	21
Investment per Production Worker	9,352	1,611	17

Sources: Same as General Statistics. The 'Average of All Manufacturing' column represents the average of all manufacturing industries reported for the most recent complete year available. The Index shows the relationship between the Average and the Analyzed Industry. For example, 100 means that they are equal; 500 that the Analyzed Industry is five times the average; 50 means that the Analyzed Industry is half the national average. The abbreviation 'na' is used to show that data are 'not available'.

LEADING COMPANIES

Number shown: **37** Total sales ($ mil): **879** Total employment (000): **9.1**

Company Name	Address				CEO Name	Phone	Co. Type	Sales ($ mil)	Empl. (000)
Caraustar Industries Inc	PO Box 115	Austell	GA	30001	Thomas V Brown	404-948-3101	P	456	3.4
Old Dominion Box Company Inc	PO Box 680	Lynchburg	VA	24505	FH Buhler	804-929-6701	R	70	1.1
Ward Paper Box Co	1000 Walnut St	Kansas City	MO	64106	Donald L Robbins	816-842-9240	D	63	0.5
Schiffenhaus Industries Inc	2013 McCarter Hwy	Newark	NJ	07104	Jay A Schiffenhaus	201-484-5000	R	35*	0.2
FN Burt Company Inc	2345 Walden Av	Buffalo	NY	14225	W Russell Hurd	716-684-2345	R	32	0.3
FM Howell and Company Inc	PO Box 286	Elmira	NY	14902	George L Howell	607-734-6291	R	21*	0.3
Apex Paper Box Corp	5601 Walworth Av	Cleveland	OH	44102	Donald Zaas	216-631-4000	R	20	0.4
Fuller Box Co	150 Chestnut St	N Attleboro	MA	02760	Peter Fuller	508-695-2525	R	19*	0.2
Simkins Corp	2824 N 2nd St	Philadelphia	PA	19133	Morton Simkins	215-739-4033	R	14	0.4
Continental Paper Box Company	1147 N 4th St	Philadelphia	PA	19123	Benzion Berman	215-627-5060	R	10*	0.1
Mid State Paper Box Co	PO Box 627	Randleman	NC	27317	MA Bryant	910-498-2631	R	10	0.1
Modern Packaging Corp	504 Huber St	Monroe	MI	48161	DE Heindel	313-242-4014	D	10	<0.1
Rice Packaging Inc	356 Somers Rd	Ellington	CT	06029	Clifford Rice	203-872-8341	R	10	0.1
Superior Packaging Inc	PO Box 2034	Melville	NY	11747	Robert Lovett	516-249-5500	R	8*	0.1
Utah Paper Box Company Inc	340 W 200 S	Salt Lake City	UT	84101	Paul B Keyser	801-363-0093	R	8*	0.1
Brick and Ballerstein Inc	1085 Irving Av	Ridgewood	NY	11385	R Levinson	718-497-1400	R	7	0.1
L Gordon Packaging Inc	1050 S Paca St	Baltimore	MD	21230	FJ Brush Jr	410-539-6537	R	7*	0.2
Carolina Paper Box Company	Drawer 240	Burlington	NC	27215	Joseph L Linens	910-226-1616	S	6*	<0.1
Finn Industries Inc	1921 S Business	Ontario	CA	91761	William L Finn	909-930-1500	R	6	<0.1
Mason Box Company Inc	PO Box 129	N Attleboro	MA	02761	Hugh D Mason	508-695-9381	R	6*	0.1
Paul T Freund Corp	PO Box 187	Palmyra	NY	14522	Dennis C Baron	315-986-9040	R	6*	<0.1
Centralia Container Inc	PO Box 828	Centralia	IL	62801	C Connor	618-532-6784	R	5	<0.1
Jesse Jones Box Corp	499 E Erie Av	Philadelphia	PA	19134	William R Fenkel	215-425-6600	R	5	0.1
Mautner Company Inc	498 Nepperhan Av	Yonkers	NY	10701	J Jay Mautner	914-969-1700	R	5	0.3
OE Clark Paper Box Co	2716 Leonis Blv	Vernon	CA	90058	OE Clark Jr	213-589-3255	R	5	<0.1
Paragon Packaging Inc	49 Sherwood Ter	Lake Bluff	IL	60044	Ron F Cohn	708-615-0065	R	5*	<0.1
Aaron Fink Group	281 Astor St	Newark	NJ	07114	A Fink	201-824-1414	R	4	0.1
Atlantic Paper Box Co	270 Albany St	Cambridge	MA	02139	I Polansky	617-354-3132	R	4	0.2
Old Colony Box Company Inc	1st & Robertson St	Radford	VA	24141	RB Nolan	703-639-2431	R	4	<0.1
Palmetto Box Company Inc	PO Box 8069	Greenville	SC	29604	Frank Buhler	803-235-1681	R	4	<0.1
Salmon Paper Box Co	PO Box 421	Matawan	NJ	07747	WL Salmon	908-566-6300	R	4	0.1
Texas Packaging Company Inc	PO Box 250	Mineral Wells	TX	76068	DL Wyss	817-325-1354	R	3	<0.1
Master Paper Box Co	3641 S Iron St	Chicago	IL	60609	William Farago	312-927-0252	R	2	<0.1
Pharmacy Ellegant Paperbox	5253 W Roosevelt	Chicago	IL	60650	Aaron Hershinow	708-652-3400	R	2*	<0.1
Universal Paper Box Co	644 NW 44th St	Seattle	WA	98107	James Finch	206-782-7105	R	2	<0.1
Avalon Paper Box Company Inc	8723 Avalon Blv	Los Angeles	CA	90003	OH Rieth	213-752-3185	R	1*	<0.1
Jordan Box Co	PO Box 1054	Syracuse	NY	13201	Richard M Casper	315-422-3419	R	1	<0.1

Source: *Ward's Business Directory of U.S. Private and Public Companies*, Volumes 1 and 2, 1996. The company type code used is as follows: P - Public, R - Private, S - Subsidiary, D - Division, J - Joint Venture, A - Affiliate, G - Group. Sales are in millions of dollars, employees are in thousands. An asterisk (*) indicates an estimated sales volume. The symbol < stands for 'less than'. Company names and addresses are truncated, in some cases, to fit into the available space.

MATERIALS CONSUMED

Material		Quantity	Delivered Cost ($ million)
Materials, ingredients, containers, and supplies		(X)	179.2
Paper and paperboard, except boxes and containers	1,000 s tons	(S)	85.9
Fabricated plastics products, including closures, ends, film, and strapping, etc.		(X)	2.3
Steel sheet and strip, including tin plate		(X)	0.6
Glues and adhesives		(X)	3.7
Printing inks (complete formulations)	mil lb	(S)	2.3
All other materials and components, parts, containers, and supplies		(X)	24.7
Materials, ingredients, containers, and supplies, nsk		(X)	59.6

Source: 1992 Economic Census. Explanation of symbols used: (D): Withheld to avoid disclosure of competitive data; na: Not available; (S): Withheld because statistical norms were not met; (X): Not applicable; (Z): Less than half the unit shown; nec: Not elsewhere classified; nsk: Not specified by kind; - : zero; * : 10-19 percent estimated; ** : 20-29 percent estimated.

PRODUCT SHARE DETAILS

Product or Product Class	% Share	Product or Product Class	% Share
Setup paperboard boxes	100.00	For cosmetics, including soap	6.56
For textiles, wearing apparel, and hosiery	12.57	For stationery and office supplies	6.31
For department stores and other retail stores	13.94	For hardware and household supplies	2.24
For confections	10.11	For all other end uses not specified	30.63

Source: 1992 *Economic Census*. The values shown are percent of total shipments in an industry. Values of indented subcategories are summed in the main heading. The symbol (D) appears when data are withheld to prevent disclosure of competitive information. The abbreviation nsk stands for 'not specified by kind' and nec for 'not elsewhere classified'.

INPUTS AND OUTPUTS FOR PAPERBOARD CONTAINERS & BOXES

Economic Sector or Industry Providing Inputs	%	Sector	Economic Sector or Industry Buying Outputs	%	Sector
Paperboard mills	58.2	Manufg.	Wholesale trade	7.2	Trade
Paperboard containers & boxes	6.0	Manufg.	Eating & drinking places	4.7	Trade
Railroads & related services	4.0	Util.	Paperboard containers & boxes	3.9	Manufg.
Motor freight transportation & warehousing	3.6	Util.	Glass containers	3.3	Manufg.
Petroleum refining	3.1	Manufg.	Fluid milk	3.1	Manufg.
Wholesale trade	2.2	Trade	Miscellaneous plastics products	3.1	Manufg.
Electric services (utilities)	1.8	Util.	Cigarettes	2.9	Manufg.
Paper mills, except building paper	1.6	Manufg.	Sanitary paper products	2.3	Manufg.
Die-cut paper & board	1.4	Manufg.	Meat packing plants	1.8	Manufg.
Plastics materials & resins	1.4	Manufg.	Toilet preparations	1.7	Manufg.
Printing ink	1.4	Manufg.	Retail trade, except eating & drinking	1.7	Trade
Sheet metal work	1.4	Manufg.	Food preparations, nec	1.6	Manufg.
Adhesives & sealants	1.2	Manufg.	Personal consumption expenditures	1.5	
Gas production & distribution (utilities)	1.1	Util.	Frozen specialties	1.5	Manufg.
Equipment rental & leasing services	0.7	Services	Malt beverages	1.5	Manufg.
Converted paper products, nec	0.6	Manufg.	Soap & other detergents	1.5	Manufg.
Cyclic crudes and organics	0.6	Manufg.	Fruits	1.4	Agric.
Communications, except radio & TV	0.6	Util.	Exports	1.4	Foreign
Eating & drinking places	0.6	Trade	Cereal breakfast foods	1.3	Manufg.
Metal foil & leaf	0.5	Manufg.	Drugs	1.3	Manufg.
Real estate	0.5	Fin/R.E.	Confectionery products	1.2	Manufg.
Maintenance of nonfarm buildings nec	0.4	Constr.	Cookies & crackers	1.2	Manufg.
Miscellaneous plastics products	0.4	Manufg.	Bottled & canned soft drinks	1.1	Manufg.
Imports	0.4	Foreign	Bread, cake, & related products	1.1	Manufg.
Aluminum rolling & drawing	0.3	Manufg.	Electronic computing equipment	1.1	Manufg.
Paints & allied products	0.3	Manufg.	Ice cream & frozen desserts	1.1	Manufg.
Paper industries machinery	0.3	Manufg.	Frozen fruits, fruit juices & vegetables	1.0	Manufg.
Air transportation	0.3	Util.	Polishes & sanitation goods	1.0	Manufg.
Banking	0.3	Fin/R.E.	Poultry dressing plants	1.0	Manufg.
Automotive rental & leasing, without drivers	0.3	Services	Broadwoven fabric mills	0.8	Manufg.
Automotive repair shops & services	0.3	Services	Canned fruits & vegetables	0.8	Manufg.
Computer & data processing services	0.3	Services	Apparel made from purchased materials	0.7	Manufg.
Fabricated metal products, nec	0.2	Manufg.	Cheese, natural & processed	0.7	Manufg.
Lubricating oils & greases	0.2	Manufg.	Dog, cat, & other pet food	0.7	Manufg.
Machinery, except electrical, nec	0.2	Manufg.	Games, toys, & children's vehicles	0.7	Manufg.
Paper coating & glazing	0.2	Manufg.	Metal foil & leaf	0.7	Manufg.
Sanitary services, steam supply, irrigation	0.2	Util.	Sausages & other prepared meats	0.7	Manufg.
Water transportation	0.2	Util.	Chemical preparations, nec	0.6	Manufg.
Insurance carriers	0.2	Fin/R.E.	Cyclic crudes and organics	0.6	Manufg.
Advertising	0.2	Services	Organic fibers, noncellulosic	0.6	Manufg.
Detective & protective services	0.2	Services	Paper mills, except building paper	0.6	Manufg.
Legal services	0.2	Services	Petroleum refining	0.6	Manufg.
Management & consulting services & labs	0.2	Services	Bags, except textile	0.5	Manufg.
U.S. Postal Service	0.2	Gov't	Blended & prepared flour	0.5	Manufg.
Special dies & tools & machine tool accessories	0.1	Manufg.	Fresh or frozen packaged fish	0.5	Manufg.
Accounting, auditing & bookkeeping	0.1	Services	Glass & glass products, except containers	0.5	Manufg.
Engineering, architectural, & surveying services	0.1	Services	Manufacturing industries, nec	0.5	Manufg.
			Plastics materials & resins	0.5	Manufg.
			Shortening & cooking oils	0.5	Manufg.
			Sugar	0.5	Manufg.
			Agricultural, forestry, & fishery services	0.4	Agric.
			Canned specialties	0.4	Manufg.
			Electric housewares & fans	0.4	Manufg.
			Electronic components nec	0.4	Manufg.
			Lighting fixtures & equipment	0.4	Manufg.
			Lubricating oils & greases	0.4	Manufg.
			Macaroni & spaghetti	0.4	Manufg.
			Photographic equipment & supplies	0.4	Manufg.
			Shoes, except rubber	0.4	Manufg.
			Book publishing	0.3	Manufg.
			Condensed & evaporated milk	0.3	Manufg.
			Dehydrated food products	0.3	Manufg.
			Electric lamps	0.3	Manufg.
			Hardware, nec	0.3	Manufg.
			Housefurnishings, nec	0.3	Manufg.
			Household cooking equipment	0.3	Manufg.
			Machinery, except electrical, nec	0.3	Manufg.
			Metal household furniture	0.3	Manufg.
			Metal stampings, nec	0.3	Manufg.
			Motor vehicle parts & accessories	0.3	Manufg.
			Paper coating & glazing	0.3	Manufg.
			Pickles, sauces, & salad dressings	0.3	Manufg.
			Refrigeration & heating equipment	0.3	Manufg.
			Roasted coffee	0.3	Manufg.
			Sporting & athletic goods, nec	0.3	Manufg.
			Surgical & medical instruments	0.3	Manufg.
			Surgical appliances & supplies	0.3	Manufg.
			Wet corn milling	0.3	Manufg.

Continued on next page.

INPUTS AND OUTPUTS FOR PAPERBOARD CONTAINERS & BOXES - Continued

Economic Sector or Industry Providing Inputs	%	Sector	Economic Sector or Industry Buying Outputs	%	Sector
			Wood household furniture	0.3	Manufg.
			Yarn mills & finishing of textiles, nec	0.3	Manufg.
			Adhesives & sealants	0.2	Manufg.
			Agricultural chemicals, nec	0.2	Manufg.
			Chocolate & cocoa products	0.2	Manufg.
			Commercial printing	0.2	Manufg.
			Converted paper products, nec	0.2	Manufg.
			Envelopes	0.2	Manufg.
			Fabricated rubber products, nec	0.2	Manufg.
			Flavoring extracts & syrups, nec	0.2	Manufg.
			Floor coverings	0.2	Manufg.
			Gum & wood chemicals	0.2	Manufg.
			Hand & edge tools, nec	0.2	Manufg.
			Household laundry equipment	0.2	Manufg.
			Household refrigerators & freezers	0.2	Manufg.
			Industrial inorganic chemicals, nec	0.2	Manufg.
			Manifold business forms	0.2	Manufg.
			Mechanical measuring devices	0.2	Manufg.
			Metal cans	0.2	Manufg.
			Metal office furniture	0.2	Manufg.
			Miscellaneous fabricated wire products	0.2	Manufg.
			Motors & generators	0.2	Manufg.
			Paints & allied products	0.2	Manufg.
			Paperboard mills	0.2	Manufg.
			Paving mixtures & blocks	0.2	Manufg.
			Poultry & egg processing	0.2	Manufg.
			Pumps & compressors	0.2	Manufg.
			Radio & TV communication equipment	0.2	Manufg.
			Radio & TV receiving sets	0.2	Manufg.
			Sheet metal work	0.2	Manufg.
			Signs & advertising displays	0.2	Manufg.
			Special dies & tools & machine tool accessories	0.2	Manufg.
			Wiring devices	0.2	Manufg.
			Women's hosiery, except socks	0.2	Manufg.
			Wood containers	0.2	Manufg.
			Wood kitchen cabinets	0.2	Manufg.
			Motor freight transportation & warehousing	0.2	Util.
			Hospitals	0.2	Services
			Federal Government purchases, national defense	0.2	Fed Govt
			S/L Govt. purch., health & hospitals	0.2	S/L Govt
			Abrasive products	0.1	Manufg.
			Architectural metal work	0.1	Manufg.
			Asphalt felts & coatings	0.1	Manufg.
			Automotive stampings	0.1	Manufg.
			Blast furnaces & steel mills	0.1	Manufg.
			Canned & cured seafoods	0.1	Manufg.
			Chewing gum	0.1	Manufg.
			Cigars	0.1	Manufg.
			Cutlery	0.1	Manufg.
			Die-cut paper & board	0.1	Manufg.
			Engine electrical equipment	0.1	Manufg.
			Flour & other grain mill products	0.1	Manufg.
			Hosiery, nec	0.1	Manufg.
			Household appliances, nec	0.1	Manufg.
			Lawn & garden equipment	0.1	Manufg.
			Metal partitions & fixtures	0.1	Manufg.
			Pens & mechanical pencils	0.1	Manufg.
			Pipe, valves, & pipe fittings	0.1	Manufg.
			Service industry machines, nec	0.1	Manufg.
			Stationery products	0.1	Manufg.
			Storage batteries	0.1	Manufg.
			Telephone & telegraph apparatus	0.1	Manufg.
			Typewriters & office machines, nec	0.1	Manufg.
			Wines, brandy, & brandy spirits	0.1	Manufg.
			Wood products, nec	0.1	Manufg.
			S/L Govt. purch., correction	0.1	S/L Govt
			S/L Govt. purch., higher education	0.1	S/L Govt

Source: Benchmark Input-Output Accounts for the U.S. Economy, 1982, U.S. Department of Commerce, Washington, D.C., July 1991. Data, as reported in the source, are organized by the 1977 SIC structure in use in 1982 but have been matched, as closely as is possible, to the 1987 SIC structure used in this book.

OCCUPATIONS EMPLOYED BY SIC 265 - PAPERBOARD CONTAINERS AND BOXES

Occupation	% of Total 1994	Change to 2005	Occupation	% of Total 1994	Change to 2005
Paper goods machine setters & set-up operators	8.4	-12.0	Cement & gluing machine operators	3.0	-28.5
Machine feeders & offbearers	8.3	-1.0	Truck drivers light & heavy	2.6	13.4
Printing press machine setters, operators	6.2	10.0	Maintenance repairers, general utility	2.2	9.9
Cutting & slicing machine setters, operators	5.9	32.0	General managers & top executives	2.0	4.3
Blue collar worker supervisors	5.3	12.4	Industrial machinery mechanics	2.0	20.9
Helpers, laborers, & material movers nec	5.2	10.0	Freight, stock, & material movers, hand	1.6	-12.0
Machine operators nec	4.9	35.7	Inspectors, testers, & graders, precision	1.5	20.9
Sales & related workers nec	4.4	10.0	Traffic, shipping, & receiving clerks	1.3	5.8
Industrial truck & tractor operators	4.2	10.0	Industrial production managers	1.2	9.9
Assemblers, fabricators, & hand workers nec	4.0	10.0	Packaging & filling machine operators	1.2	10.0
Hand packers & packagers	3.6	-5.7	Bookkeeping, accounting, & auditing clerks	1.0	-17.5

Source: Industry-Occupation Matrix, Bureau of Labor Statistics. These data relate to one or more 3-digit SIC industry groups rather than to a single 4-digit SIC. The change reported for each occupation to the year 2005 is a percent of growth or decline as estimated by the Bureau of Labor Statistics. The abbreviation nec stands for 'not elsewhere classified'.

LOCATION BY STATE AND REGIONAL CONCENTRATION

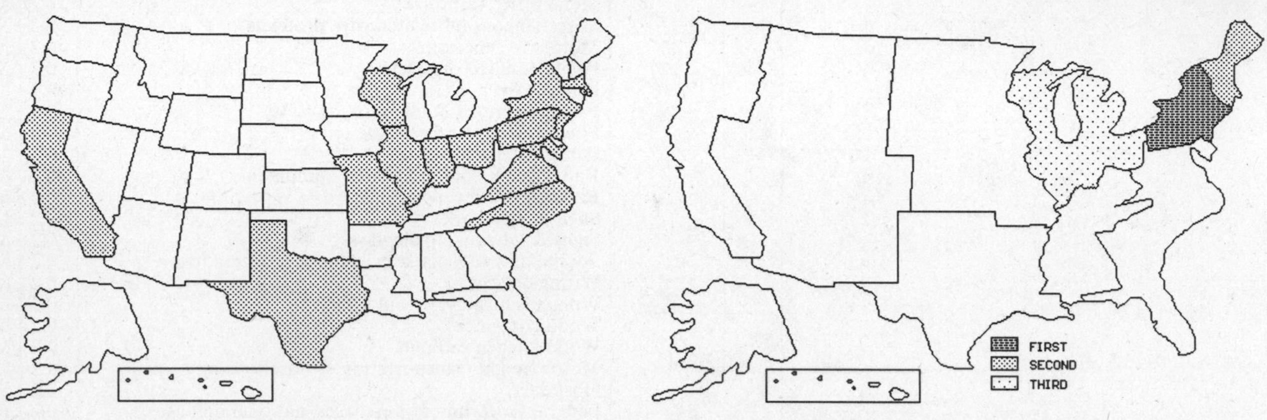

INDUSTRY DATA BY STATE

State	Establish-ments	Shipments: Total ($ mil)	Shipments: % of U.S.	Shipments: Per Establ.	Employment: Total Number	Employment: % of U.S.	Employment: Per Establ.	Employment: Wages ($/hour)	Cost as % of Shipments	Investment per Employee ($)
New York	25	77.6	17.8	3.1	1,300	19.7	52	8.36	42.4	-
Massachusetts	17	60.0	13.8	3.5	700	10.6	41	8.82	49.2	1,429
Pennsylvania	14	43.7	10.0	3.1	700	10.6	50	7.67	39.4	1,286
Rhode Island	12	27.9	6.4	2.3	400	6.1	33	7.83	50.9	1,250
Ohio	7	23.4	5.4	3.3	300	4.5	43	7.17	57.3	-
California	8	20.3	4.7	2.5	300	4.5	38	8.00	47.3	2,333
Illinois	7	14.3	3.3	2.0	200	3.0	29	7.25	43.4	-
Indiana	5	12.0	2.8	2.4	200	3.0	40	9.00	52.5	-
Virginia	3	8.0	1.8	2.7	100	1.5	33	6.50	32.5	-
North Carolina	8	(D)	-	-	375 *	5.7	47	-	-	-
New Jersey	7	(D)	-	-	175 *	2.7	25	-	-	-
Missouri	4	(D)	-	-	375 *	5.7	94	-	-	-
Texas	4	(D)	-	-	175 *	2.7	44	-	-	-
Maryland	3	(D)	-	-	175 *	2.7	58	-	-	571
Wisconsin	2	(D)	-	-	175 *	2.7	88	-	-	-

Source: 1992 *Economic Census*. The states are in descending order of shipments or establishments (if shipment data are missing for the majority). The symbol (D) appears when data are withheld to prevent disclosure of competitive information. States marked with (D) are sorted by number of establishments. A dash (-) indicates that the data element cannot be calculated; * indicates the midpoint of a range.

2653 - CORRUGATED AND SOLID FIBER BOXES

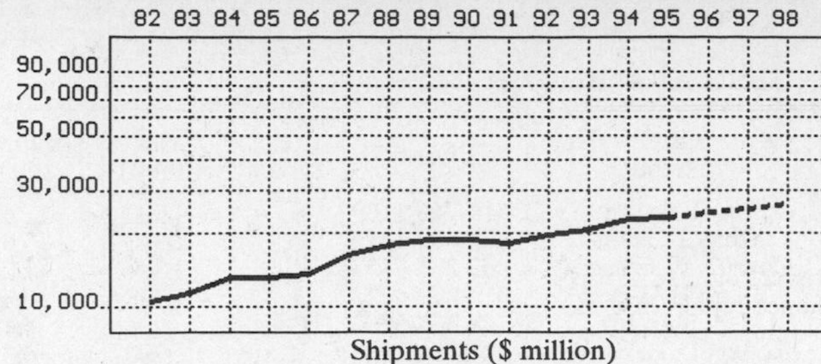

Shipments ($ million)

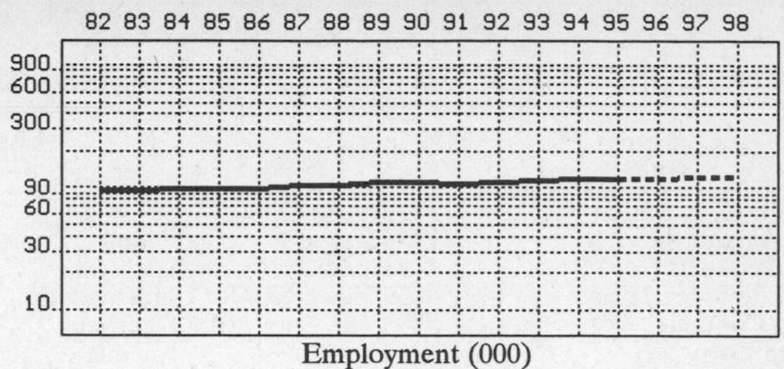

Employment (000)

GENERAL STATISTICS

Year	Companies	Establishments: Total	Establishments: with 20 or more employees	Employment: Total (000)	Employment: Production Workers (000)	Employment: Production Hours (Mil)	Compensation: Payroll ($ mil)	Compensation: Wages ($/hr)	Production ($ million): Cost of Materials	Production ($ million): Value Added by Manufacture	Production ($ million): Value of Shipments	Capital Invest.
1982	907	1,491	1,066	94.3	67.2	131.7	1,857.7	8.69	6,870.7	3,656.6	10,543.9	283.4
1983		1,477	1,080	96.9	68.9	139.7	2,038.1	9.05	7,450.5	3,974.8	11,410.7	248.1
1984		1,463	1,094	98.9	71.5	145.2	2,185.3	9.45	8,696.6	4,461.3	13,110.6	426.2
1985		1,448	1,108	97.9	71.1	142.3	2,231.8	9.77	8,501.0	4,565.1	13,092.9	420.3
1986		1,486	1,122	99.2	71.9	146.4	2,366.9	10.11	8,754.1	4,737.8	13,465.6	433.5
1987	953	1,601	1,165	105.7	77.2	160.4	2,610.1	10.22	10,686.7	5,477.6	16,104.0	468.8
1988		1,593	1,205	106.1	78.1	162.7	2,725.7	10.43	12,232.2	5,630.3	17,806.6	502.8
1989		1,594	1,224	110.2	81.3	170.4	2,927.6	10.47	13,056.9	5,813.9	18,862.3	606.1
1990		1,584	1,206	109.9	80.0	168.0	2,983.7	10.70	12,655.7	5,901.9	18,572.2	606.5
1991		1,584	1,171	108.7	79.4	166.1	3,047.4	11.10	11,959.9	6,063.9	18,025.9	468.1
1992	966	1,646	1,233	111.7	80.9	173.1	3,263.9	11.38	13,079.2	6,738.4	19,789.9	461.0
1993		1,619	1,229	114.2	82.6	177.5	3,461.1	11.85	13,510.3	7,143.0	20,623.3	530.0
1994		1,657P	1,262P	119.1	89.1	190.7	3,712.8	11.89	15,086.7	7,766.3	22,801.5	562.0
1995		1,674P	1,278P	118.9P	87.7P	189.5P	3,745.5P	12.18P	15,332.9P	7,893.1P	23,173.7P	610.8P
1996		1,691P	1,294P	120.8P	89.3P	193.8P	3,891.4P	12.43P	15,965.9P	8,218.9P	24,130.2P	631.9P
1997		1,707P	1,310P	122.7P	90.8P	198.1P	4,037.3P	12.68P	16,598.8P	8,544.7P	25,086.8P	653.1P
1998		1,724P	1,325P	124.5P	92.4P	202.4P	4,183.2P	12.94P	17,231.7P	8,870.5P	26,043.4P	674.2P

Sources: 1982, 1987, 1992 *Economic Census*; *Annual Survey of Manufactures*, 83-86, 88-91, 93-94. Establishment counts for non-Census years are from *County Business Patterns*; establishment values for 83-84 are extrapolations. 'P's show projections by the editors. Industries reclassified in 87 will not have data for prior years.

INDICES OF CHANGE

Year	Companies	Establishments: Total	Establishments: with 20 or more employees	Employment: Total (000)	Employment: Production Workers (000)	Employment: Production Hours (Mil)	Compensation: Payroll ($ mil)	Compensation: Wages ($/hr)	Production ($ million): Cost of Materials	Production ($ million): Value Added by Manufacture	Production ($ million): Value of Shipments	Capital Invest.
1982	94	91	86	84	83	76	57	76	53	54	53	61
1983		90	88	87	85	81	62	80	57	59	58	54
1984		89	89	89	88	84	67	83	66	66	66	92
1985		88	90	88	88	82	68	86	65	68	66	91
1986		90	91	89	89	85	73	89	67	70	68	94
1987	99	97	94	95	95	93	80	90	82	81	81	102
1988		97	98	95	97	94	84	92	94	84	90	109
1989		97	99	99	100	98	90	92	100	86	95	131
1990		96	98	98	99	97	91	94	97	88	94	132
1991		96	95	97	98	96	93	98	91	90	91	102
1992	100	100	100	100	100	100	100	100	100	100	100	100
1993		98	100	102	102	103	106	104	103	106	104	115
1994		101P	102P	107	110	110	114	104	115	115	115	122
1995		102P	104P	106P	108P	109P	115P	107P	117P	117P	117P	132P
1996		103P	105P	108P	110P	112P	119P	109P	122P	122P	122P	137P
1997		104P	106P	110P	112P	114P	124P	111P	127P	127P	127P	142P
1998		105P	107P	111P	114P	117P	128P	114P	132P	132P	132P	146P

Sources: Same as General Statistics. Values reflect change from the base year, 1992. Values above 100 mean greater than 92, values below 100 mean less than 92, and a value of 100 in the 82-91 or 93-98 period means same as 92. 'P's mark projections by the editors.

SELECTED RATIOS

For 1994	Avg. of All Manufact.	Analyzed Industry	Index
Employees per Establishment	49	72	147
Payroll per Establishment	1,500,273	2,240,287	149
Payroll per Employee	30,620	31,174	102
Production Workers per Establishment	34	54	157
Wages per Establishment	853,319	1,368,153	160
Wages per Production Worker	24,861	25,448	102
Hours per Production Worker	2,056	2,140	104
Wages per Hour	12.09	11.89	98
Value Added per Establishment	4,602,255	4,686,150	102
Value Added per Employee	93,930	65,208	69

For 1994	Avg. of All Manufact.	Analyzed Industry	Index
Value Added per Production Worker	134,084	87,164	65
Cost per Establishment	5,045,178	9,103,246	180
Cost per Employee	102,970	126,673	123
Cost per Production Worker	146,988	169,323	115
Shipments per Establishment	9,576,895	13,758,322	144
Shipments per Employee	195,460	191,448	98
Shipments per Production Worker	279,017	255,909	92
Investment per Establishment	321,011	339,108	106
Investment per Employee	6,552	4,719	72
Investment per Production Worker	9,352	6,308	67

Sources: Same as General Statistics. The 'Average of All Manufacturing' column represents the average of all manufacturing industries reported for the most recent complete year available. The Index shows the relationship between the Average and the Analyzed Industry. For example, 100 means that they are equal; 500 that the Analyzed Industry is five times the average; 50 means that the Analyzed Industry is half the national average. The abbreviation 'na' is used to show that data are 'not available'.

LEADING COMPANIES Number shown: 75 Total sales ($ mil): **15,843** Total employment (000): **84.1**

Company Name	Address				CEO Name	Phone	Co. Type	Sales ($ mil)	Empl. (000)
Container Corporation	PO Box 66820	St Louis	MO	63166	James B Malloy	314-746-1100	S	4,500	17.0
Temple-Inland Inc	PO Drawer N	Diboll	TX	75941	Clifford J Grum	409-829-1313	P	2,938	15.0
Sonoco Products Co	PO Box 160	Hartsville	SC	29551	Charles W Coker	803-383-7437	P	2,300	17.2
Inland Container Corp	4030 Vincennes Rd	Indianapolis	IN	46268	William B Howes	317-879-4222	S	1,438	7.5
Gaylord Container Corp	500 Lake Cook Rd	Deerfield	IL	60015	M A Pomerantz	708-405-5500	P	784	4.1
Menasha Corp	PO Box 367	Neenah	WI	54957	Robert D Bero	414-751-1000	R	700	4.3
St Joe Container Co	PO Box 1380	Jacksonville	FL	32201	Howard L Brainin	904-396-6600	S	350*	2.0
Chesapeake Packaging Co	2104 W Laburnum	Richmond	VA	23227	Samuel Taylor	804-353-6400	D	280	1.8
Bell Packaging Corp	1415 S Vernon St	Dallas	TX	75224	John L Bell	214-944-2929	R	200	1.0
Stephen Gould Paper Company	35 S Jefferson Rd	Whippany	NJ	07981	M Golden	201-428-1510	R	152	0.5
Tharco	2222 Grant Av	San Lorenzo	CA	94580	JF Aitchison	510-276-8600	R	102	0.7
Crockett Container Corp	9211 Norwalk Blv	Santa Fe Sprgs	CA	90670	Randy Crockett	310-692-9465	S	85*	0.3
Greater New York Box Co	149 Entin Rd	Clifton	NJ	07014	L Edelman	201-472-3600	S	75	0.5
Packaging Un-Limited Inc	1121 W Kentucky St	Louisville	KY	40210	Bob Faller	502-584-4331	R	59*	0.4
Lawless Container Corp	51 Robinson St	N Tonawanda	NY	14120	David Chapin	716-692-6510	R	52*	0.4
Liberty Carton Co	5600 N Hwy 169	New Hope	MN	55428	Michael Fiterman	612-536-6600	D	52*	0.4
Tecumseh Corrugated Box Co	PO Box 427	Tecumseh	MI	49286	Jeffrey T Robideau	517-423-2126	R	52*	0.4
Buckeye Corrugated Inc	PO Box 954	Wooster	OH	44691	Roy K Allen	216-264-6336	R	50	0.3
Santa Clara Folding	2500 De La Cruz	Santa Clara	CA	95050	D Dawsen	408-496-5000	D	50	0.2
J and J South Central	PO Box 3387	Huntsville	AL	35810	Bud Handell	205-859-5770	D	48	0.2
MacMillan Bloedel	PO Box 1308	Little Rock	AR	72203	James O Murray	501-376-4461	D	48	0.3
Weyerhaeuser Co	2000 S 18th St	Manitowoc	WI	54220	John M Kaestle	414-684-4454	D	45	0.3
Bates Container Inc	PO Box 822028	N Richland Hls	TX	76182	Allen H Sanders	817-498-3200	R	40	0.2
Connecticut Container Corp	455 Sackett Pt Rd	North Haven	CT	06473	Lawrence Perkins	203-248-2161	R	40	0.3
Lawrence Paper Company Inc	PO Box 887	Lawrence	KS	66044	Alan M Hill	913-843-8111	R	40*	0.3
MannKraft Corp	1000 US Hwy 1	Newark	NJ	07114	Richard Pachillo	201-589-7400	R	40	0.2
North American Container Corp	5851 Riverview Rd	Mableton	GA	30059	John M Grigsby	404-691-0611	R	40	0.6
Weyerhaeuser Paper Co	PO Box 3658	Modesto	CA	95352	Ray Raffo	209-529-9950	D	40	0.2
David Weber Company Inc	3500 Richmond St	Philadelphia	PA	19134	Jim Doherty	215-426-3500	R	38	0.1
Weyerhaeuser Paper Co	1699 W 9th St	Wh Bear Lk	MN	55110		612-426-0345	D	38	0.1
Wabash Pioneer Container Corp	PO Box 45	Cedarburg	WI	53012	James Woodard	414-377-2442	S	36	0.3
Advance Packaging Corp	PO Box 888311	Grand Rapids	MI	49588	Richard Strauss	616-949-6610	R	35	0.3
Kalamazoo Container	PO Box 50071	Kalamazoo	MI	49005	James Devlin	616-382-0050	D	35	0.2
Schiffenhaus Packaging Corp	2013 McCarter Hwy	Newark	NJ	07104	L C Schiffenhaus	201-484-5000	S	35	0.2
Seattle Packaging Corp	3701 S Norfolk St	Seattle	WA	98118	Gordon M Younger	206-725-3000	R	35	0.2
Star Corrugated Box Company	PO Box 9	Maspeth	NY	11378	Robert L Karlin	718-386-3200	R	34	0.3
Weyerhaeuser Co	3001 Otto St	Belleville	IL	62223	David Neal	618-233-5460	D	31*	0.1
Castle Rock Container Co	PO Box 530	Adams	WI	53910	R J Schweitzer	608-339-3371	D	30*	0.2
Ideal Box Co	4800 S Austin Av	Chicago	IL	60638	Stephen Eisen	708-594-3100	R	30	0.2
Lewisburg Container Co	PO Box 39	Lewisburg	OH	45338	J McKinney	513-962-2681	S	30	0.2
Longview Fibre Co	PO Box 2008	Milwaukee	WI	53201	RP Wollenberg	414-264-8100	D	30	0.1
Oak Paper Products Company	3686 E Olympic	Los Angeles	CA	90023	Max Weissberg	213-268-0507	R	30	0.2
Weyerhaeuser Co	PO Box 9	Butler	IN	46721	Ian Mercer	219-868-2151	D	30	0.1
York Container Co	PO Box 3008	York	PA	17402	Charles S Wolf	717-757-7611	R	30	0.2
Columbus Container Inc	3460 Commerce Dr	Columbus	IN	47201	Bob Haddad	812-376-9301	R	29*	0.2
Orange County Container Inc	14500 Valley Blv	City of Industry	CA	91744	Michael Feterick	818-333-6363	R	29*	0.2
Delta Corrugated	W Ruby & Railroad	Palisades Park	NJ	07650	Maurice Helsel	201-941-1910	R	28*	0.2
Tri-Pack	2828 S Lock St	Chicago	IL	60608	Byron Pollock	312-247-5500	D	28*	0.2
Weyerhaeuser Paper Co	PO Box 657	Closter	NJ	07624	Joe Andrews	201-768-6161	D	27	0.1
Atlas Container Corp	8140 Telegraph Rd	Odenton	MD	21113	Don Fleegle	410-551-6300	R	26*	0.2
Chesapeake Corp	PO Box 1240	Binghamton	NY	13902	Edward Badyna	607-775-1550	D	26	0.2
Cameo Container Corp	1415 W 44th St	Chicago	IL	60609	Darrell Holman	312-254-1030	S	25	0.2
Color-Box Inc	623 S G St	Richmond	IN	47374	Jack L Creech	317-966-7588	S	25*	0.2
Midland Container Corp	827 Koeln Av	St Louis	MO	63111	EE Elzemeyer Jr	314-638-0028	R	25	0.2
Quality Packaging Materials	PO Box 2200	Flemington	NJ	08822	Larry Trittipl	908-782-0505	D	25*	0.3
Royal Continental Box Co	1301 S 47th Av	Cicero	IL	60650	J Nerenberg	708-656-2020	R	25*	0.2
Arvco Container Corp	351 Rochester Av	Kalamazoo	MI	49007	Gregory Arvanigian	616-381-0900	R	24	0.2
Bicknell and Fuller Co	Peabody Industrial	Peabody	MA	01960	H Seigel	508-532-0200	R	24	0.1
Independent Container Inc	7831 National Tpk	Louisville	KY	40214	Neil MacDonald	502-367-6105	R	24	0.2
Union Camp Corp Kansas City	4343 Clary Blv	Kansas City	MO	64130	Andrew Fox	816-861-4343	D	24	0.2
Commander Packaging Corp	5555 W 73rd Pl	Bedford Park	IL	60638	Randy Mohler	708-563-6400	R	22*	0.1
Container Corporation	122 Quentin Av	New Brunswick	NJ	08901	Bob Degoria	908-247-5200	D	22	0.1
Mack-Chicago Corp	2445 S Rockwell St	Chicago	IL	60608	William Swisshelm	312-376-8100	R	22	0.2
Miller Container Corp	PO Box 1130	Milan	IL	61264	G J Van Severen	309-787-6161	R	22	0.2
Union Camp Corp Lakeland	PO Box 1608	Lakeland	FL	33802	P Brown	813-682-0123	D	22	0.1
A Klein and Co	PO Box 610	Claremont	NC	28610	Jesse L Salwen	704-459-9261	R	20	0.3
Beacon Container	700 W 1st St	Birdsboro	PA	19508	I Grossman	215-582-2222	R	20	0.2
Express Container Corp	105 Av L	Newark	NJ	07105	Stephen Weil	201-589-2155	R	20	0.2
Traub Container Corp	22475 Aurora Rd	Bedford Hts	OH	44146	DL Simon	216-475-5100	R	20	0.1
Enterprise Corrugated	575 N Midland Av	Saddle Brook	NJ	07662	Dominic Palamenti	201-797-7200	R	19*	0.2
Massachusetts Container Corp	PO Box H	Marlborough	MA	01752	Harry Perkins	508-481-1100	S	19*	0.1
Page Packaging Corp	1950 Marina Blv	San Leandro	CA	94577	Peter Mehiel	510-614-1600	S	19	<0.1
Consolidated Converting Co	PO Box 4960	Whittier	CA	90607	George Richter	310-692-9421	D	18	0.1
Key Container Company Inc	4224 Santa Ana St	South Gate	CA	90280	William Watts	213-564-4211	R	18	0.1
New England Wooden	75 Logan St	Gardner	MA	01440	AW Urquhart Jr	508-632-3600	R	18	0.1

Source: *Ward's Business Directory of U.S. Private and Public Companies*, Volumes 1 and 2, 1996. The company type code used is as follows: P - Public, R - Private, S - Subsidiary, D - Division, J - Joint Venture, A - Affiliate, G - Group. Sales are in millions of dollars, employees are in thousands. An asterisk (*) indicates an estimated sales volume. The symbol < stands for 'less than'. Company names and addresses are truncated, in some cases, to fit into the available space.

MATERIALS CONSUMED

Material		Quantity	Delivered Cost ($ million)
Materials, ingredients, containers, and supplies		(X)	12,267.4
Paper and paperboard, except boxes and containers	1,000 s tons	27,070.2*	10,014.5
Fabricated plastics products, including closures, ends, film, and strapping, etc.		(X)	47.5
Steel sheet and strip, including tin plate		(X)	5.5
Petroleum wax	mil lb	286.4**	95.0
Glues and adhesives		(X)	214.4
Printing inks (complete formulations)	mil lb	(S)	132.2
All other materials and components, parts, containers, and supplies		(X)	609.5
Materials, ingredients, containers, and supplies, nsk		(X)	1,148.8

Source: 1992 *Economic Census*. Explanation of symbols used: (D): Withheld to avoid disclosure of competitive data; na: Not available; (S): Withheld because statistical norms were not met; (X): Not applicable; (Z): Less than half the unit shown; nec: Not elsewhere classified; nsk: Not specified by kind; - : zero; * : 10-19 percent estimated; ** : 20-29 percent estimated.

PRODUCT SHARE DETAILS

Product or Product Class	% Share
Corrugated and solid fiber boxes	100.00
Corrugated shipping containers for food and beverages	22.09
Corrugated carryout boxes for retail food	0.90
Corrugated shipping containers for paper and allied products	9.15
Corrugated shipping containers for glass, clay, and stone products	3.07
Corrugated shipping containers for metal products, machinery, equipment, and supplies, except electrical	4.37
Corrugated shipping containers for electrical machinery, equipment, supplies, and appliances	3.56
Corrugated shipping containers for chemicals and drugs, including paints, varnishes, cosmetics, and soaps	4.06
Corrugated shipping containers for lumber and wood products, including furniture	2.73
Corrugated shipping containers for all other end uses not specified (leather, rubber, plastics, petroleum, etc.)	21.11
Corrugated solid fiber containers	2.28
Corrugated paperboard in sheets and rolls, lined and unlined	7.76
Corrugated and solid fiber pallets, pads, and partitions	2.56
Other corrugated and solid fiber products, including point-of-purchase displays, etc.	7.18

Source: 1992 *Economic Census*. The values shown are percent of total shipments in an industry. Values of indented subcategories are summed in the main heading. The symbol (D) appears when data are withheld to prevent disclosure of competitive information. The abbreviation nsk stands for 'not specified by kind' and nec for 'not elsewhere classified'.

INPUTS AND OUTPUTS FOR PAPERBOARD CONTAINERS & BOXES

Economic Sector or Industry Providing Inputs	%	Sector	Economic Sector or Industry Buying Outputs	%	Sector
Paperboard mills	58.2	Manufg.	Wholesale trade	7.2	Trade
Paperboard containers & boxes	6.0	Manufg.	Eating & drinking places	4.7	Trade
Railroads & related services	4.0	Util.	Paperboard containers & boxes	3.9	Manufg.
Motor freight transportation & warehousing	3.6	Util.	Glass containers	3.3	Manufg.
Petroleum refining	3.1	Manufg.	Fluid milk	3.1	Manufg.
Wholesale trade	2.2	Trade	Miscellaneous plastics products	3.1	Manufg.
Electric services (utilities)	1.8	Util.	Cigarettes	2.9	Manufg.
Paper mills, except building paper	1.6	Manufg.	Sanitary paper products	2.3	Manufg.
Die-cut paper & board	1.4	Manufg.	Meat packing plants	1.8	Manufg.
Plastics materials & resins	1.4	Manufg.	Toilet preparations	1.7	Manufg.
Printing ink	1.4	Manufg.	Retail trade, except eating & drinking	1.7	Trade
Sheet metal work	1.4	Manufg.	Food preparations, nec	1.6	Manufg.
Adhesives & sealants	1.2	Manufg.	Personal consumption expenditures	1.5	
Gas production & distribution (utilities)	1.1	Util.	Frozen specialties	1.5	Manufg.
Equipment rental & leasing services	0.7	Services	Malt beverages	1.5	Manufg.
Converted paper products, nec	0.6	Manufg.	Soap & other detergents	1.5	Manufg.
Cyclic crudes and organics	0.6	Manufg.	Fruits	1.4	Agric.
Communications, except radio & TV	0.6	Util.	Exports	1.4	Foreign
Eating & drinking places	0.6	Trade	Cereal breakfast foods	1.3	Manufg.
Metal foil & leaf	0.5	Manufg.	Drugs	1.3	Manufg.
Real estate	0.5	Fin/R.E.	Confectionery products	1.2	Manufg.
Maintenance of nonfarm buildings nec	0.4	Constr.	Cookies & crackers	1.2	Manufg.
Miscellaneous plastics products	0.4	Manufg.	Bottled & canned soft drinks	1.1	Manufg.
Imports	0.4	Foreign	Bread, cake, & related products	1.1	Manufg.
Aluminum rolling & drawing	0.3	Manufg.	Electronic computing equipment	1.1	Manufg.
Paints & allied products	0.3	Manufg.	Ice cream & frozen desserts	1.1	Manufg.
Paper industries machinery	0.3	Manufg.	Frozen fruits, fruit juices & vegetables	1.0	Manufg.
Air transportation	0.3	Util.	Polishes & sanitation goods	1.0	Manufg.
Banking	0.3	Fin/R.E.	Poultry dressing plants	1.0	Manufg.
Automotive rental & leasing, without drivers	0.3	Services	Broadwoven fabric mills	0.8	Manufg.
Automotive repair shops & services	0.3	Services	Canned fruits & vegetables	0.8	Manufg.
Computer & data processing services	0.3	Services	Apparel made from purchased materials	0.7	Manufg.
Fabricated metal products, nec	0.2	Manufg.	Cheese, natural & processed	0.7	Manufg.
Lubricating oils & greases	0.2	Manufg.	Dog, cat, & other pet food	0.7	Manufg.
Machinery, except electrical, nec	0.2	Manufg.	Games, toys, & children's vehicles	0.7	Manufg.
Paper coating & glazing	0.2	Manufg.	Metal foil & leaf	0.7	Manufg.
Sanitary services, steam supply, irrigation	0.2	Util.	Sausages & other prepared meats	0.7	Manufg.

Continued on next page.

INPUTS AND OUTPUTS FOR PAPERBOARD CONTAINERS & BOXES - Continued

Economic Sector or Industry Providing Inputs	%	Sector	Economic Sector or Industry Buying Outputs	%	Sector
Water transportation	0.2	Util.	Chemical preparations, nec	0.6	Manufg.
Insurance carriers	0.2	Fin/R.E.	Cyclic crudes and organics	0.6	Manufg.
Advertising	0.2	Services	Organic fibers, noncellulosic	0.6	Manufg.
Detective & protective services	0.2	Services	Paper mills, except building paper	0.6	Manufg.
Legal services	0.2	Services	Petroleum refining	0.6	Manufg.
Management & consulting services & labs	0.2	Services	Bags, except textile	0.5	Manufg.
U.S. Postal Service	0.2	Gov't	Blended & prepared flour	0.5	Manufg.
Special dies & tools & machine tool accessories	0.1	Manufg.	Fresh or frozen packaged fish	0.5	Manufg.
Accounting, auditing & bookkeeping	0.1	Services	Glass & glass products, except containers	0.5	Manufg.
Engineering, architectural, & surveying services	0.1	Services	Manufacturing industries, nec	0.5	Manufg.
			Plastics materials & resins	0.5	Manufg.
			Shortening & cooking oils	0.5	Manufg.
			Sugar	0.5	Manufg.
			Agricultural, forestry, & fishery services	0.4	Agric.
			Canned specialties	0.4	Manufg.
			Electric housewares & fans	0.4	Manufg.
			Electronic components nec	0.4	Manufg.
			Lighting fixtures & equipment	0.4	Manufg.
			Lubricating oils & greases	0.4	Manufg.
			Macaroni & spaghetti	0.4	Manufg.
			Photographic equipment & supplies	0.4	Manufg.
			Shoes, except rubber	0.4	Manufg.
			Book publishing	0.3	Manufg.
			Condensed & evaporated milk	0.3	Manufg.
			Dehydrated food products	0.3	Manufg.
			Electric lamps	0.3	Manufg.
			Hardware, nec	0.3	Manufg.
			Housefurnishings, nec	0.3	Manufg.
			Household cooking equipment	0.3	Manufg.
			Machinery, except electrical, nec	0.3	Manufg.
			Metal household furniture	0.3	Manufg.
			Metal stampings, nec	0.3	Manufg.
			Motor vehicle parts & accessories	0.3	Manufg.
			Paper coating & glazing	0.3	Manufg.
			Pickles, sauces, & salad dressings	0.3	Manufg.
			Refrigeration & heating equipment	0.3	Manufg.
			Roasted coffee	0.3	Manufg.
			Sporting & athletic goods, nec	0.3	Manufg.
			Surgical & medical instruments	0.3	Manufg.
			Surgical appliances & supplies	0.3	Manufg.
			Wet corn milling	0.3	Manufg.
			Wood household furniture	0.3	Manufg.
			Yarn mills & finishing of textiles, nec	0.3	Manufg.
			Adhesives & sealants	0.2	Manufg.
			Agricultural chemicals, nec	0.2	Manufg.
			Chocolate & cocoa products	0.2	Manufg.
			Commercial printing	0.2	Manufg.
			Converted paper products, nec	0.2	Manufg.
			Envelopes	0.2	Manufg.
			Fabricated rubber products, nec	0.2	Manufg.
			Flavoring extracts & syrups, nec	0.2	Manufg.
			Floor coverings	0.2	Manufg.
			Gum & wood chemicals	0.2	Manufg.
			Hand & edge tools, nec	0.2	Manufg.
			Household laundry equipment	0.2	Manufg.
			Household refrigerators & freezers	0.2	Manufg.
			Industrial inorganic chemicals, nec	0.2	Manufg.
			Manifold business forms	0.2	Manufg.
			Mechanical measuring devices	0.2	Manufg.
			Metal cans	0.2	Manufg.
			Metal office furniture	0.2	Manufg.
			Miscellaneous fabricated wire products	0.2	Manufg.
			Motors & generators	0.2	Manufg.
			Paints & allied products	0.2	Manufg.
			Paperboard mills	0.2	Manufg.
			Paving mixtures & blocks	0.2	Manufg.
			Poultry & egg processing	0.2	Manufg.
			Pumps & compressors	0.2	Manufg.
			Radio & TV communication equipment	0.2	Manufg.
			Radio & TV receiving sets	0.2	Manufg.
			Sheet metal work	0.2	Manufg.
			Signs & advertising displays	0.2	Manufg.
			Special dies & tools & machine tool accessories	0.2	Manufg.
			Wiring devices	0.2	Manufg.
			Women's hosiery, except socks	0.2	Manufg.

Continued on next page.

INPUTS AND OUTPUTS FOR PAPERBOARD CONTAINERS & BOXES - Continued

Economic Sector or Industry Providing Inputs	%	Sector	Economic Sector or Industry Buying Outputs	%	Sector
			Wood containers	0.2	Manufg.
			Wood kitchen cabinets	0.2	Manufg.
			Motor freight transportation & warehousing	0.2	Util.
			Hospitals	0.2	Services
			Federal Government purchases, national defense	0.2	Fed Govt
			S/L Govt. purch., health & hospitals	0.2	S/L Govt
			Abrasive products	0.1	Manufg.
			Architectural metal work	0.1	Manufg.
			Asphalt felts & coatings	0.1	Manufg.
			Automotive stampings	0.1	Manufg.
			Blast furnaces & steel mills	0.1	Manufg.
			Canned & cured seafoods	0.1	Manufg.
			Chewing gum	0.1	Manufg.
			Cigars	0.1	Manufg.
			Cutlery	0.1	Manufg.
			Die-cut paper & board	0.1	Manufg.
			Engine electrical equipment	0.1	Manufg.
			Flour & other grain mill products	0.1	Manufg.
			Hosiery, nec	0.1	Manufg.
			Household appliances, nec	0.1	Manufg.
			Lawn & garden equipment	0.1	Manufg.
			Metal partitions & fixtures	0.1	Manufg.
			Pens & mechanical pencils	0.1	Manufg.
			Pipe, valves, & pipe fittings	0.1	Manufg.
			Service industry machines, nec	0.1	Manufg.
			Stationery products	0.1	Manufg.
			Storage batteries	0.1	Manufg.
			Telephone & telegraph apparatus	0.1	Manufg.
			Typewriters & office machines, nec	0.1	Manufg.
			Wines, brandy, & brandy spirits	0.1	Manufg.
			Wood products, nec	0.1	Manufg.
			S/L Govt. purch., correction	0.1	S/L Govt
			S/L Govt. purch., higher education	0.1	S/L Govt

Source: Benchmark Input-Output Accounts for the U.S. Economy, 1982, U.S. Department of Commerce, Washington, D.C., July 1991. Data, as reported in the source, are organized by the 1977 SIC structure in use in 1982 but have been matched, as closely as is possible, to the 1987 SIC structure used in this book.

OCCUPATIONS EMPLOYED BY SIC 265 - PAPERBOARD CONTAINERS AND BOXES

Occupation	% of Total 1994	Change to 2005	Occupation	% of Total 1994	Change to 2005
Paper goods machine setters & set-up operators	8.4	-12.0	Cement & gluing machine operators	3.0	-28.5
Machine feeders & offbearers	8.3	-1.0	Truck drivers light & heavy	2.6	13.4
Printing press machine setters, operators	6.2	10.0	Maintenance repairers, general utility	2.2	9.9
Cutting & slicing machine setters, operators	5.9	32.0	General managers & top executives	2.0	4.3
Blue collar worker supervisors	5.3	12.4	Industrial machinery mechanics	2.0	20.9
Helpers, laborers, & material movers nec	5.2	10.0	Freight, stock, & material movers, hand	1.6	-12.0
Machine operators nec	4.9	35.7	Inspectors, testers, & graders, precision	1.5	20.9
Sales & related workers nec	4.4	10.0	Traffic, shipping, & receiving clerks	1.3	5.8
Industrial truck & tractor operators	4.2	10.0	Industrial production managers	1.2	9.9
Assemblers, fabricators, & hand workers nec	4.0	10.0	Packaging & filling machine operators	1.2	10.0
Hand packers & packagers	3.6	-5.7	Bookkeeping, accounting, & auditing clerks	1.0	-17.5

Source: Industry-Occupation Matrix, Bureau of Labor Statistics. These data relate to one or more 3-digit SIC industry groups rather than to a single 4-digit SIC. The change reported for each occupation to the year 2005 is a percent of growth or decline as estimated by the Bureau of Labor Statistics. The abbreviation nec stands for 'not elsewhere classified'.

LOCATION BY STATE AND REGIONAL CONCENTRATION

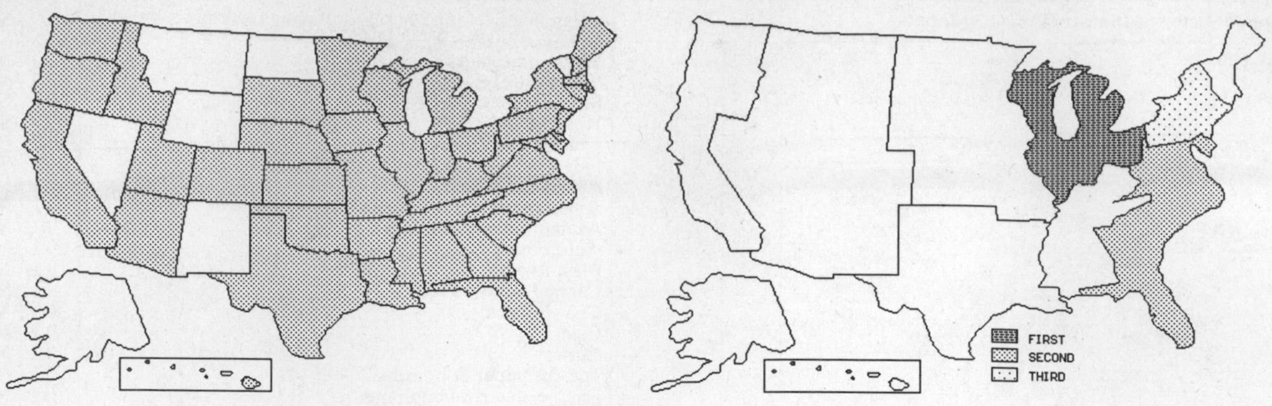

INDUSTRY DATA BY STATE

State	Establish-ments	Shipments			Employment				Cost as % of Shipments	Investment per Employee ($)
		Total ($ mil)	% of U.S.	Per Establ.	Total Number	% of U.S.	Per Establ.	Wages ($/hour)		
California	157	2,528.7	12.8	16.1	11,400	10.2	73	13.01	69.9	3,860
Illinois	112	1,372.7	6.9	12.3	8,100	7.3	72	11.20	61.7	5,407
Ohio	125	1,182.8	6.0	9.5	6,600	5.9	53	11.28	66.7	3,727
Texas	95	1,107.9	5.6	11.7	6,300	5.6	66	10.53	67.2	2,635
Pennsylvania	93	1,103.2	5.6	11.9	6,300	5.6	68	11.80	65.6	3,683
Georgia	67	862.2	4.4	12.9	4,800	4.3	72	11.04	68.3	6,083
Wisconsin	54	768.6	3.9	14.2	4,300	3.8	80	12.52	62.2	3,535
New Jersey	71	759.7	3.8	10.7	5,100	4.6	72	11.53	60.7	5,569
New York	87	724.9	3.7	8.3	4,700	4.2	54	11.08	60.9	2,191
Indiana	63	693.5	3.5	11.0	4,200	3.8	67	10.80	68.8	5,905
North Carolina	59	688.1	3.5	11.7	4,400	3.9	75	10.33	66.0	4,432
Michigan	76	685.3	3.5	9.0	4,200	3.8	55	11.37	64.2	3,833
Tennessee	58	581.4	2.9	10.0	3,500	3.1	60	10.18	68.4	3,657
Florida	44	547.8	2.8	12.4	2,900	2.6	66	10.52	67.4	4,655
Minnesota	28	516.5	2.6	18.4	2,800	2.5	100	11.98	63.5	5,000
Missouri	46	510.3	2.6	11.1	2,800	2.5	61	10.40	67.6	4,179
Virginia	32	454.0	2.3	14.2	2,600	2.3	81	11.49	64.0	6,346
Massachusetts	35	414.0	2.1	11.8	2,600	2.3	74	11.50	64.3	2,385
Washington	25	398.5	2.0	15.9	1,700	1.5	68	15.58	73.8	4,647
South Carolina	29	364.3	1.8	12.6	2,300	2.1	79	9.53	67.7	3,739
Arkansas	31	357.3	1.8	11.5	2,200	2.0	71	10.72	65.6	3,318
Kentucky	26	323.0	1.6	12.4	1,800	1.6	69	11.85	66.9	-
Mississippi	23	302.2	1.5	13.1	1,900	1.7	83	11.03	65.3	2,842
Iowa	17	301.8	1.5	17.8	1,500	1.3	88	11.65	68.9	3,600
Alabama	28	269.8	1.4	9.6	1,600	1.4	57	9.65	68.2	3,813
Louisiana	11	239.7	1.2	21.8	1,200	1.1	109	11.38	65.9	4,000
Connecticut	24	226.8	1.1	9.4	1,500	1.3	63	10.87	62.1	3,400
Maryland	21	212.7	1.1	10.1	1,300	1.2	62	10.38	62.5	2,231
Colorado	17	210.0	1.1	12.4	1,100	1.0	65	11.53	65.5	5,364
Kansas	9	166.3	0.8	18.5	1,100	1.0	122	12.24	68.1	3,273
Arizona	12	141.7	0.7	11.8	600	0.5	50	10.09	64.3	3,167
Oregon	8	140.1	0.7	17.5	700	0.6	88	13.27	62.7	-
Nebraska	5	80.9	0.4	16.2	400	0.4	80	10.00	65.3	-
Utah	6	77.6	0.4	12.9	400	0.4	67	11.67	74.9	-
Maine	4	67.6	0.3	16.9	400	0.4	100	10.67	63.3	-
Rhode Island	7	32.3	0.2	4.6	300	0.3	43	11.25	57.0	1,667
West Virginia	5	22.2	0.1	4.4	200	0.2	40	10.33	60.8	-
Oklahoma	14	(D)	-	-	750 *	0.7	54	-	-	-
New Hampshire	5	(D)	-	-	175 *	0.2	35	-	-	-
Idaho	4	(D)	-	-	375 *	0.3	94	-	-	-
South Dakota	4	(D)	-	-	175 *	0.2	44	-	-	-
Delaware	2	(D)	-	-	175 *	0.2	88	-	-	-
Hawaii	2	(D)	-	-	175 *	0.2	88	-	-	-

Source: 1992 *Economic Census*. The states are in descending order of shipments or establishments (if shipment data are missing for the majority). The symbol (D) appears when data are withheld to prevent disclosure of competitive information. States marked with (D) are sorted by number of establishments. A dash (-) indicates that the data element cannot be calculated; * indicates the midpoint of a range.

2655 - FIBER CANS, DRUMS & SIMILAR PRODUCTS

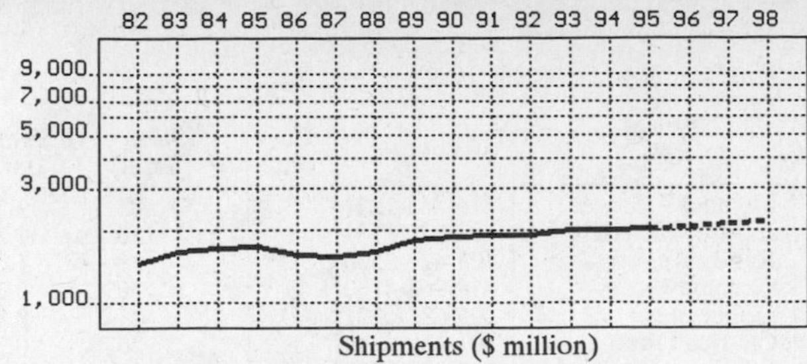

Shipments ($ million)

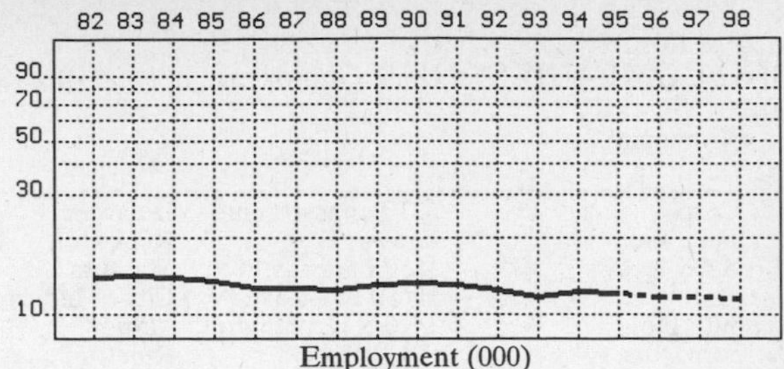

Employment (000)

GENERAL STATISTICS

Year	Com-panies	Establishments		Employment			Compensation		Production ($ million)			
		Total	with 20 or more employees	Total (000)	Production Workers (000)	Production Hours (Mil)	Payroll ($ mil)	Wages ($/hr)	Cost of Materials	Value Added by Manufacture	Value of Shipments	Capital Invest.
1982	151	305	189	13.9	11.3	21.8	247.8	8.30	887.7	566.6	1,456.4	31.0
1983		300	191	14.1	11.4	22.5	275.8	9.05	995.8	628.2	1,627.5	35.0
1984		295	193	13.9	11.4	22.7	280.1	9.14	1,065.1	631.3	1,692.2	41.1
1985		290	196	13.5	11.0	21.8	284.8	9.58	1,060.2	633.5	1,696.7	60.5
1986		283	192	12.6	10.2	20.8	275.1	9.74	977.5	594.2	1,571.3	63.1
1987	137	282	188	12.6	10.2	20.8	281.4	9.87	905.8	629.8	1,536.6	34.0
1988		288	195	12.4	10.2	21.0	289.7	10.14	984.9	650.9	1,630.9	28.2
1989		284	187	13.1	11.1	23.6	328.9	10.13	1,101.0	730.9	1,829.0	38.3
1990		287	185	13.2	11.1	22.9	341.3	10.82	1,134.9	750.6	1,884.9	45.8
1991		292	184	12.9	10.7	22.5	340.5	10.98	1,138.7	770.7	1,912.2	41.6
1992	153	300	185	12.4	10.1	21.6	337.1	11.31	1,138.3	783.1	1,922.1	46.7
1993		299	191	11.7	9.4	19.5	335.1	12.60	1,187.7	815.3	2,004.1	37.7
1994		290P	186P	12.3	10.1	22.0	350.2	11.70	1,173.4	830.2	2,002.0	38.3
1995		290P	186P	11.9P	9.8P	21.5P	362.4P	12.31P	1,198.7P	848.1P	2,045.2P	41.4P
1996		289P	185P	11.8P	9.7P	21.4P	370.5P	12.61P	1,223.3P	865.5P	2,087.1P	41.3P
1997		289P	184P	11.6P	9.6P	21.4P	378.7P	12.90P	1,247.9P	882.9P	2,129.1P	41.3P
1998		289P	184P	11.4P	9.5P	21.3P	386.9P	13.20P	1,272.5P	900.3P	2,171.1P	41.2P

Sources: 1982, 1987, 1992 *Economic Census*; *Annual Survey of Manufactures*, 83-86, 88-91, 93-94. Establishment counts for non-Census years are from *County Business Patterns*; establishment values for 83-84 are extrapolations. 'P's show projections by the editors. Industries reclassified in 87 will not have data for prior years.

INDICES OF CHANGE

Year	Com-panies	Establishments		Employment			Compensation		Production ($ million)			
		Total	with 20 or more employees	Total (000)	Production Workers (000)	Production Hours (Mil)	Payroll ($ mil)	Wages ($/hr)	Cost of Materials	Value Added by Manufacture	Value of Shipments	Capital Invest.
1982	99	102	102	112	112	101	74	73	78	72	76	66
1983		100	103	114	113	104	82	80	87	80	85	75
1984		98	104	112	113	105	83	81	94	81	88	88
1985		97	106	109	109	101	84	85	93	81	88	130
1986		94	104	102	101	96	82	86	86	76	82	135
1987	90	94	102	102	101	96	83	87	80	80	80	73
1988		96	105	100	101	97	86	90	87	83	85	60
1989		95	101	106	110	109	98	90	97	93	95	82
1990		96	100	106	110	106	101	96	100	96	98	98
1991		97	99	104	106	104	101	97	100	98	99	89
1992	100	100	100	100	100	100	100	100	100	100	100	100
1993		100	103	94	93	90	99	111	104	104	104	81
1994		97P	101P	99	100	102	104	103	103	106	104	82
1995		97P	100P	96P	97P	99P	107P	109P	105P	108P	106P	89P
1996		96P	100P	95P	96P	99P	110P	111P	107P	111P	109P	88P
1997		96P	100P	94P	95P	99P	112P	114P	110P	113P	111P	88P
1998		96P	99P	92P	94P	99P	115P	117P	112P	115P	113P	88P

Sources: Same as General Statistics. Values reflect change from the base year, 1992. Values above 100 mean greater than 92, values below 100 mean less than 92, and a value of 100 in the 82-91 or 93-98 period means same as 92. 'P's mark projections by the editors.

SELECTED RATIOS

For 1994	Avg. of All Manufact.	Analyzed Industry	Index	For 1994	Avg. of All Manufact.	Analyzed Industry	Index
Employees per Establishment	49	42	87	Value Added per Production Worker	134,084	82,198	61
Payroll per Establishment	1,500,273	1,207,712	80	Cost per Establishment	5,045,178	4,046,630	80
Payroll per Employee	30,620	28,472	93	Cost per Employee	102,970	95,398	93
Production Workers per Establishment	34	35	101	Cost per Production Worker	146,988	116,178	79
Wages per Establishment	853,319	887,679	104	Shipments per Establishment	9,576,895	6,904,170	72
Wages per Production Worker	24,861	25,485	103	Shipments per Employee	195,460	162,764	83
Hours per Production Worker	2,056	2,178	106	Shipments per Production Worker	279,017	198,218	71
Wages per Hour	12.09	11.70	97	Investment per Establishment	321,011	132,083	41
Value Added per Establishment	4,602,255	2,863,058	62	Investment per Employee	6,552	3,114	48
Value Added per Employee	93,930	67,496	72	Investment per Production Worker	9,352	3,792	41

Sources: Same as General Statistics. The 'Average of All Manufacturing' column represents the average of all manufacturing industries reported for the most recent complete year available. The Index shows the relationship between the Average and the Analyzed Industry. For example, 100 means that they are equal; 500 that the Analyzed Industry is five times the average; 50 means that the Analyzed Industry is half the national average. The abbreviation 'na' is used to show that data are 'not available'.

LEADING COMPANIES

Number shown: **31** Total sales ($ mil): **1,069** Total employment (000): **9.5**

Company Name	Address				CEO Name	Phone	Co. Type	Sales ($ mil)	Empl. (000)
Greif Bros Corp	621 Pennsylvania	Delaware	OH	43015	Michael J Gasser	614-363-1271	P	583	4.5
Star Paper Tube Inc	Drawer B	Rock Hill	SC	29732	Jimmy A Russell	803-329-2131	S	150	1.2
Sonoco Prod Co	1850 Parkway Pl	Marietta	GA	30067	Randy Kelley	404-423-2500	D	98	1.2
Anvil Cases Inc	15650 Salt Lake Av	City of Industry	CA	91745	Gerome Gross	818-968-4100	S	30	0.2
Niemand South Inc	1410 S Washington	Marion	AL	36756	D Geerdes	205-683-6121	D	25	0.3
Real-Reel Corp	PO Box 4798	Rumford	RI	02916	Charles Dunn	401-438-4240	R	20	0.3
Berenfield Containers Inc	PO Box 350	Mason	OH	45040	L H Berenfield	513-398-1300	R	19*	0.2
Nelson-Ball Paper Products Inc	PO Box 3016	Longview	WA	98632	Andy Stewart	206-423-3420	R	15	0.1
NYSCO Products Inc	2350 Lafayette Av	Bronx	NY	10473	Barry Kramer	718-792-9000	R	13*	0.1
Sonoco Products Co	166 N Baldwin Park	City of Industry	CA	91749	Charles Coker	818-369-6611	D	13*	<0.1
Multi-Line Cans Inc	PO Box 1194	Dade City	FL	34297	Cecil Perrette	904-521-2391	S	11*	0.1
American Paper Products Co	2113 E Rush St	Philadelphia	PA	19134	LJ Perelman	215-739-5718	R	10*	0.2
Baxter Tube Co	25221 Miles Rd	Warrensville H	OH	44128	Dennis H Kelly	216-831-8828	D	10	0.1
Lewis Steel Works Inc	PO Box 338	Wrens	GA	30833	RA Lewis	706-547-6561	R	10	0.1
Michael's Cooperage Inc	363 W Pershing Rd	Chicago	IL	60609	Michael Pogwizd	312-268-6281	R	7*	<0.1
Precision Paper Tube Co	1033 S Noel Av	Wheeling	IL	60090	RL Hatton	708-537-4250	R	7	0.2
New England Paper Tube Co	173 Weeden St	Pawtucket	RI	02860	K W Douglas Jr	401-725-2610	R	6*	0.2
Cin-Made Corp	1780 Dreman Av	Cincinnati	OH	45223	Bob Frey	513-681-3600	R	5	<0.1
Marshall Paper Tube Company	52 Marshall St	Randolph	MA	02368	S Grodberg	617-963-5555	R	5*	<0.1
Nu Container Corp	PO Box 970	Atlanta	TX	75551	Randy E Barnes	903-796-2877	D	5	<0.1
Stonington Corp	61 Tpk Industrial Pk	Westfield	MA	01085	Andrew G Niss	413-562-8300	R	5	<0.1
Chicago Mailing Tube Co	400 N Leavitt St	Chicago	IL	60612	Kenneth Barmore	312-243-6050	R	4	<0.1
Arrow Paper Products Co	1301 Wheeler	Saginaw	MI	48602	MH Stark	517-793-4820	R	3	<0.1
Centracor Inc	PO Box 159	Winnebago	WI	54985	Michael Curler	414-235-4299	R	3	<0.1
Greif Bros Corp	170 N Field Av	Edison	NJ	08818	Robert G Straley	908-417-0100	D	3*	<0.1
Acme Spirally Wound Paper	4810 W 139th St	Cleveland	OH	44135	C M Kobak-Moore	216-267-2950	R	3	<0.1
Newark Paperboard Products	10 State St	Nashua	NH	03063	Michael Teske	603-883-8005	D	2	<0.1
LCH Packaging Corp	249 E Lothenbach	West St Paul	MN	55118	MF Hoaglund	612-455-1218	R	1*	<0.1
Master Package Corp	PO Box 338	Owen	WI	54460	N Pabich	715-229-2156	R	1*	<0.1
Middlesex Paper Tube Company	PO Box 588	Lowell	MA	01853	Harry Kaplan	508-458-4686	R	1	<0.1
Midwest Paper Tube & Can	PO Box 6	New Berlin	WI	53151	Gerald J Mahoney	414-782-7300	R	1	<0.1

Source: *Ward's Business Directory of U.S. Private and Public Companies*, Volumes 1 and 2, 1996. The company type code used is as follows: P - Public, R - Private, S - Subsidiary, D - Division, J - Joint Venture, A - Affiliate, G - Group. Sales are in millions of dollars, employees are in thousands. An asterisk (*) indicates an estimated sales volume. The symbol < stands for 'less than'. Company names and addresses are truncated, in some cases, to fit into the available space.

MATERIALS CONSUMED

Material		Quantity	Delivered Cost ($ million)
Materials, ingredients, containers, and supplies		(X)	1,061.9
Paper and paperboard, except boxes and containers	1,000 s tons	1,112.1	424.0
Fabricated plastics products, including closures, ends, film, and strapping, etc.		(X)	13.8
Steel sheet and strip, including tin plate		(X)	182.7
Petroleum wax	mil lb	(S)	1.1
Glues and adhesives		(X)	31.1
Printing inks (complete formulations)	mil lb	1.0**	5.2
All other materials and components, parts, containers, and supplies		(X)	265.6
Materials, ingredients, containers, and supplies, nsk		(X)	138.3

Source: 1992 *Economic Census*. Explanation of symbols used: (D): Withheld to avoid disclosure of competitive data; na: Not available; (S): Withheld because statistical norms were not met; (X): Not applicable; (Z): Less than half the unit shown; nec: Not elsewhere classified; nsk: Not specified by kind; - : zero; * : 10-19 percent estimated; ** : 20-29 percent estimated.

PRODUCT SHARE DETAILS

Product or Product Class	% Share	Product or Product Class	% Share
Fiber cans, drums, and similar products	100.00	Paperboard cones, reels, spools, bobbins, and blocks	5.06
Paperboard fiber drums with ends of any material	20.53	All vulcanized fiber products (boxes, cans, tubes, drums, etc.)	5.34
Fiber cans, tubes, and similar fiber products	70.86	Fiber cans, tubes, and similar fiber products, nsk	5.98
Fiber cans, all fiber and composite	38.93	Fiber cans, drums, and similar products, nsk	8.61
Fiber cores and tubes	44.69		

Source: 1992 *Economic Census*. The values shown are percent of total shipments in an industry. Values of indented subcategories are summed in the main heading. The symbol (D) appears when data are withheld to prevent disclosure of competitive information. The abbreviation nsk stands for 'not specified by kind' and nec for 'not elsewhere classified'.

INPUTS AND OUTPUTS FOR PAPERBOARD CONTAINERS & BOXES

Economic Sector or Industry Providing Inputs	%	Sector	Economic Sector or Industry Buying Outputs	%	Sector
Paperboard mills	58.2	Manufg.	Wholesale trade	7.2	Trade
Paperboard containers & boxes	6.0	Manufg.	Eating & drinking places	4.7	Trade
Railroads & related services	4.0	Util.	Paperboard containers & boxes	3.9	Manufg.
Motor freight transportation & warehousing	3.6	Util.	Glass containers	3.3	Manufg.
Petroleum refining	3.1	Manufg.	Fluid milk	3.1	Manufg.
Wholesale trade	2.2	Trade	Miscellaneous plastics products	3.1	Manufg.
Electric services (utilities)	1.8	Util.	Cigarettes	2.9	Manufg.
Paper mills, except building paper	1.6	Manufg.	Sanitary paper products	2.3	Manufg.
Die-cut paper & board	1.4	Manufg.	Meat packing plants	1.8	Manufg.
Plastics materials & resins	1.4	Manufg.	Toilet preparations	1.7	Manufg.
Printing ink	1.4	Manufg.	Retail trade, except eating & drinking	1.7	Trade
Sheet metal work	1.4	Manufg.	Food preparations, nec	1.6	Manufg.
Adhesives & sealants	1.2	Manufg.	Personal consumption expenditures	1.5	
Gas production & distribution (utilities)	1.1	Util.	Frozen specialties	1.5	Manufg.
Equipment rental & leasing services	0.7	Services	Malt beverages	1.5	Manufg.
Converted paper products, nec	0.6	Manufg.	Soap & other detergents	1.5	Manufg.
Cyclic crudes and organics	0.6	Manufg.	Fruits	1.4	Agric.
Communications, except radio & TV	0.6	Util.	Exports	1.4	Foreign
Eating & drinking places	0.6	Trade	Cereal breakfast foods	1.3	Manufg.
Metal foil & leaf	0.5	Manufg.	Drugs	1.3	Manufg.
Real estate	0.5	Fin/R.E.	Confectionery products	1.2	Manufg.
Maintenance of nonfarm buildings nec	0.4	Constr.	Cookies & crackers	1.2	Manufg.
Miscellaneous plastics products	0.4	Manufg.	Bottled & canned soft drinks	1.1	Manufg.
Imports	0.4	Foreign	Bread, cake, & related products	1.1	Manufg.
Aluminum rolling & drawing	0.3	Manufg.	Electronic computing equipment	1.1	Manufg.
Paints & allied products	0.3	Manufg.	Ice cream & frozen desserts	1.1	Manufg.
Paper industries machinery	0.3	Manufg.	Frozen fruits, fruit juices & vegetables	1.0	Manufg.
Air transportation	0.3	Util.	Polishes & sanitation goods	1.0	Manufg.
Banking	0.3	Fin/R.E.	Poultry dressing plants	1.0	Manufg.
Automotive rental & leasing, without drivers	0.3	Services	Broadwoven fabric mills	0.8	Manufg.
Automotive repair shops & services	0.3	Services	Canned fruits & vegetables	0.8	Manufg.
Computer & data processing services	0.3	Services	Apparel made from purchased materials	0.7	Manufg.
Fabricated metal products, nec	0.2	Manufg.	Cheese, natural & processed	0.7	Manufg.
Lubricating oils & greases	0.2	Manufg.	Dog, cat, & other pet food	0.7	Manufg.
Machinery, except electrical, nec	0.2	Manufg.	Games, toys, & children's vehicles	0.7	Manufg.
Paper coating & glazing	0.2	Manufg.	Metal foil & leaf	0.7	Manufg.
Sanitary services, steam supply, irrigation	0.2	Util.	Sausages & other prepared meats	0.7	Manufg.
Water transportation	0.2	Util.	Chemical preparations, nec	0.6	Manufg.
Insurance carriers	0.2	Fin/R.E.	Cyclic crudes and organics	0.6	Manufg.
Advertising	0.2	Services	Organic fibers, noncellulosic	0.6	Manufg.
Detective & protective services	0.2	Services	Paper mills, except building paper	0.6	Manufg.
Legal services	0.2	Services	Petroleum refining	0.6	Manufg.
Management & consulting services & labs	0.2	Services	Bags, except textile	0.5	Manufg.
U.S. Postal Service	0.2	Gov't	Blended & prepared flour	0.5	Manufg.
Special dies & tools & machine tool accessories	0.1	Manufg.	Fresh or frozen packaged fish	0.5	Manufg.
Accounting, auditing & bookkeeping	0.1	Services	Glass & glass products, except containers	0.5	Manufg.
Engineering, architectural, & surveying services	0.1	Services	Manufacturing industries, nec	0.5	Manufg.
			Plastics materials & resins	0.5	Manufg.
			Shortening & cooking oils	0.5	Manufg.
			Sugar	0.5	Manufg.
			Agricultural, forestry, & fishery services	0.4	Agric.
			Canned specialties	0.4	Manufg.
			Electric housewares & fans	0.4	Manufg.
			Electronic components nec	0.4	Manufg.
			Lighting fixtures & equipment	0.4	Manufg.
			Lubricating oils & greases	0.4	Manufg.
			Macaroni & spaghetti	0.4	Manufg.
			Photographic equipment & supplies	0.4	Manufg.
			Shoes, except rubber	0.4	Manufg.
			Book publishing	0.3	Manufg.
			Condensed & evaporated milk	0.3	Manufg.
			Dehydrated food products	0.3	Manufg.
			Electric lamps	0.3	Manufg.
			Hardware, nec	0.3	Manufg.
			Housefurnishings, nec	0.3	Manufg.
			Household cooking equipment	0.3	Manufg.
			Machinery, except electrical, nec	0.3	Manufg.
			Metal household furniture	0.3	Manufg.
			Metal stampings, nec	0.3	Manufg.
			Motor vehicle parts & accessories	0.3	Manufg.
			Paper coating & glazing	0.3	Manufg.
			Pickles, sauces, & salad dressings	0.3	Manufg.
			Refrigeration & heating equipment	0.3	Manufg.
			Roasted coffee	0.3	Manufg.
			Sporting & athletic goods, nec	0.3	Manufg.
			Surgical & medical instruments	0.3	Manufg.
			Surgical appliances & supplies	0.3	Manufg.
			Wet corn milling	0.3	Manufg.

Continued on next page.

INPUTS AND OUTPUTS FOR PAPERBOARD CONTAINERS & BOXES - Continued

Economic Sector or Industry Providing Inputs	%	Sector	Economic Sector or Industry Buying Outputs	%	Sector
			Wood household furniture	0.3	Manufg.
			Yarn mills & finishing of textiles, nec	0.3	Manufg.
			Adhesives & sealants	0.2	Manufg.
			Agricultural chemicals, nec	0.2	Manufg.
			Chocolate & cocoa products	0.2	Manufg.
			Commercial printing	0.2	Manufg.
			Converted paper products, nec	0.2	Manufg.
			Envelopes	0.2	Manufg.
			Fabricated rubber products, nec	0.2	Manufg.
			Flavoring extracts & syrups, nec	0.2	Manufg.
			Floor coverings	0.2	Manufg.
			Gum & wood chemicals	0.2	Manufg.
			Hand & edge tools, nec	0.2	Manufg.
			Household laundry equipment	0.2	Manufg.
			Household refrigerators & freezers	0.2	Manufg.
			Industrial inorganic chemicals, nec	0.2	Manufg.
			Manifold business forms	0.2	Manufg.
			Mechanical measuring devices	0.2	Manufg.
			Metal cans	0.2	Manufg.
			Metal office furniture	0.2	Manufg.
			Miscellaneous fabricated wire products	0.2	Manufg.
			Motors & generators	0.2	Manufg.
			Paints & allied products	0.2	Manufg.
			Paperboard mills	0.2	Manufg.
			Paving mixtures & blocks	0.2	Manufg.
			Poultry & egg processing	0.2	Manufg.
			Pumps & compressors	0.2	Manufg.
			Radio & TV communication equipment	0.2	Manufg.
			Radio & TV receiving sets	0.2	Manufg.
			Sheet metal work	0.2	Manufg.
			Signs & advertising displays	0.2	Manufg.
			Special dies & tools & machine tool accessories	0.2	Manufg.
			Wiring devices	0.2	Manufg.
			Women's hosiery, except socks	0.2	Manufg.
			Wood containers	0.2	Manufg.
			Wood kitchen cabinets	0.2	Manufg.
			Motor freight transportation & warehousing	0.2	Util.
			Hospitals	0.2	Services
			Federal Government purchases, national defense	0.2	Fed Govt
			S/L Govt. purch., health & hospitals	0.2	S/L Govt
			Abrasive products	0.1	Manufg.
			Architectural metal work	0.1	Manufg.
			Asphalt felts & coatings	0.1	Manufg.
			Automotive stampings	0.1	Manufg.
			Blast furnaces & steel mills	0.1	Manufg.
			Canned & cured seafoods	0.1	Manufg.
			Chewing gum	0.1	Manufg.
			Cigars	0.1	Manufg.
			Cutlery	0.1	Manufg.
			Die-cut paper & board	0.1	Manufg.
			Engine electrical equipment	0.1	Manufg.
			Flour & other grain mill products	0.1	Manufg.
			Hosiery, nec	0.1	Manufg.
			Household appliances, nec	0.1	Manufg.
			Lawn & garden equipment	0.1	Manufg.
			Metal partitions & fixtures	0.1	Manufg.
			Pens & mechanical pencils	0.1	Manufg.
			Pipe, valves, & pipe fittings	0.1	Manufg.
			Service industry machines, nec	0.1	Manufg.
			Stationery products	0.1	Manufg.
			Storage batteries	0.1	Manufg.
			Telephone & telegraph apparatus	0.1	Manufg.
			Typewriters & office machines, nec	0.1	Manufg.
			Wines, brandy, & brandy spirits	0.1	Manufg.
			Wood products, nec	0.1	Manufg.
			S/L Govt. purch., correction	0.1	S/L Govt
			S/L Govt. purch., higher education	0.1	S/L Govt

Source: Benchmark Input-Output Accounts for the U.S. Economy, 1982, U.S. Department of Commerce, Washington, D.C., July 1991. Data, as reported in the source, are organized by the 1977 SIC structure in use in 1982 but have been matched, as closely as is possible, to the 1987 SIC structure used in this book.

OCCUPATIONS EMPLOYED BY SIC 265 - PAPERBOARD CONTAINERS AND BOXES

Occupation	% of Total 1994	Change to 2005	Occupation	% of Total 1994	Change to 2005
Paper goods machine setters & set-up operators	8.4	-12.0	Cement & gluing machine operators	3.0	-28.5
Machine feeders & offbearers	8.3	-1.0	Truck drivers light & heavy	2.6	13.4
Printing press machine setters, operators	6.2	10.0	Maintenance repairers, general utility	2.2	9.9
Cutting & slicing machine setters, operators	5.9	32.0	General managers & top executives	2.0	4.3
Blue collar worker supervisors	5.3	12.4	Industrial machinery mechanics	2.0	20.9
Helpers, laborers, & material movers nec	5.2	10.0	Freight, stock, & material movers, hand	1.6	-12.0
Machine operators nec	4.9	35.7	Inspectors, testers, & graders, precision	1.5	20.9
Sales & related workers nec	4.4	10.0	Traffic, shipping, & receiving clerks	1.3	5.8
Industrial truck & tractor operators	4.2	10.0	Industrial production managers	1.2	9.9
Assemblers, fabricators, & hand workers nec	4.0	10.0	Packaging & filling machine operators	1.2	10.0
Hand packers & packagers	3.6	-5.7	Bookkeeping, accounting, & auditing clerks	1.0	-17.5

Source: *Industry-Occupation Matrix*, Bureau of Labor Statistics. These data relate to one or more 3-digit SIC industry groups rather than to a single 4-digit SIC. The change reported for each occupation to the year 2005 is a percent of growth or decline as estimated by the Bureau of Labor Statistics. The abbreviation nec stands for 'not elsewhere classified'.

LOCATION BY STATE AND REGIONAL CONCENTRATION

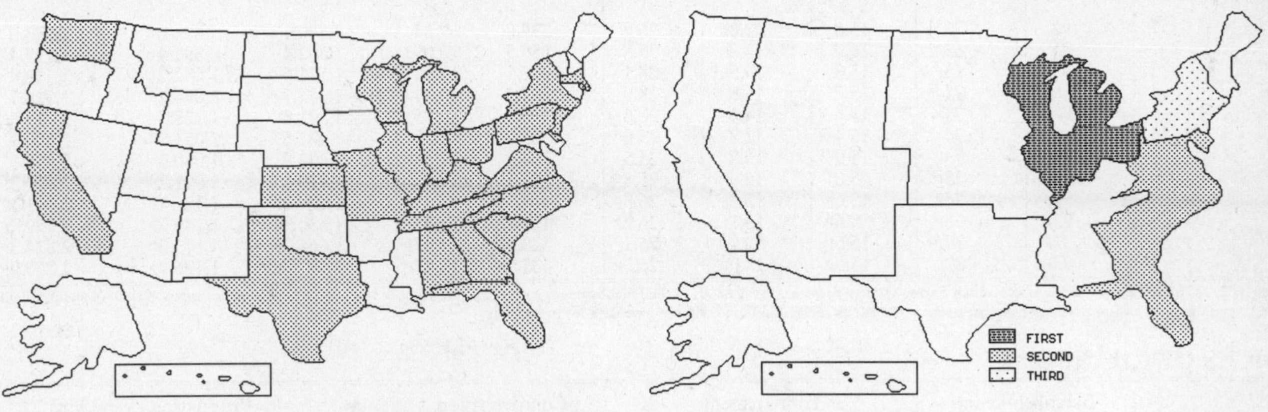

INDUSTRY DATA BY STATE

State	Establish-ments	Shipments Total ($ mil)	Shipments % of U.S.	Shipments Per Establ.	Employment Total Number	Employment % of U.S.	Employment Per Establ.	Wages ($/hour)	Cost as % of Shipments	Investment per Employee ($)
Ohio	25	186.2	9.7	7.4	1,200	9.7	48	11.40	64.9	2,833
Wisconsin	15	131.9	6.9	8.8	800	6.5	53	12.31	62.6	-
New York	15	124.8	6.5	8.3	900	7.3	60	10.06	52.6	3,667
Illinois	19	116.4	6.1	6.1	800	6.5	42	10.75	56.7	7,000
North Carolina	13	108.0	5.6	8.3	900	7.3	69	10.38	52.2	4,111
New Jersey	16	106.5	5.5	6.7	700	5.6	44	11.31	56.8	-
Texas	18	90.4	4.7	5.0	600	4.8	33	10.60	58.5	-
California	18	88.0	4.6	4.9	600	4.8	33	11.70	56.0	2,167
Florida	12	73.0	3.8	6.1	400	3.2	33	13.40	76.4	-
Massachusetts	13	62.5	3.3	4.8	500	4.0	38	12.63	51.4	3,000
Pennsylvania	11	59.5	3.1	5.4	500	4.0	45	11.25	58.5	2,000
Michigan	9	28.7	1.5	3.2	200	1.6	22	11.00	55.7	-
Missouri	6	13.7	0.7	2.3	100	0.8	17	8.00	48.2	-
Georgia	16	(D)	-	-	750 *	6.0	47	-	-	2,667
Alabama	11	(D)	-	-	375 *	3.0	34	-	-	1,067
South Carolina	10	(D)	-	-	750 *	6.0	75	-	-	-
Indiana	8	(D)	-	-	375 *	3.0	47	-	-	-
Tennessee	7	(D)	-	-	375 *	3.0	54	-	-	-
Virginia	6	(D)	-	-	175 *	1.4	29	-	-	-
Kentucky	4	(D)	-	-	175 *	1.4	44	-	-	-
Washington	4	(D)	-	-	175 *	1.4	44	-	-	-
Kansas	3	(D)	-	-	175 *	1.4	58	-	-	-
Rhode Island	3	(D)	-	-	175 *	1.4	58	-	-	-
Delaware	1	(D)	-	-	175 *	1.4	175	-	-	-

Source: 1992 *Economic Census*. The states are in descending order of shipments or establishments (if shipment data are missing for the majority). The symbol (D) appears when data are withheld to prevent disclosure of competitive information. States marked with (D) are sorted by number of establishments. A dash (-) indicates that the data element cannot be calculated; * indicates the midpoint of a range.

2656 - SANITARY FOOD CONTAINERS

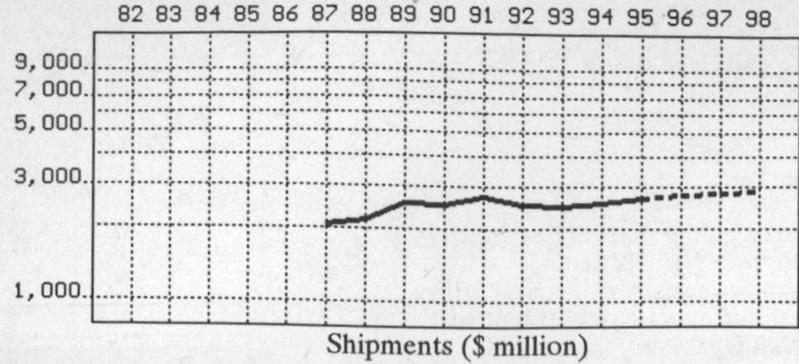

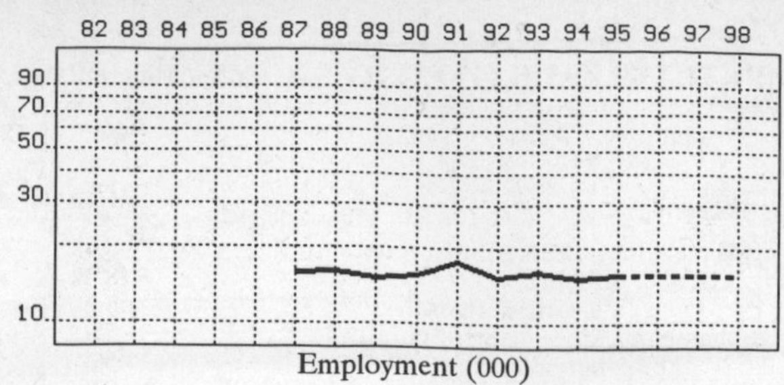

GENERAL STATISTICS

Year	Companies	Establishments: Total	Establishments: with 20 or more employees	Employment: Total (000)	Production Workers (000)	Production Hours (Mil)	Compensation: Payroll ($ mil)	Compensation: Wages ($/hr)	Production ($ million): Cost of Materials	Value Added by Manufacture	Value of Shipments	Capital Invest.
1982												
1983												
1984												
1985												
1986												
1987	57	92	72	15.8	12.8	25.7	339.8	9.83	1,200.1	893.8	2,083.0	95.5
1988		84	63	16.0	12.8	25.8	356.5	10.09	1,302.4	891.4	2,193.4	79.9
1989		85	65	15.2	14.5	28.1	382.5	10.50	1,511.6	1,052.2	2,543.8	64.4
1990		86	71	15.7	14.3	28.0	392.3	10.33	1,454.7	1,074.4	2,518.7	51.4
1991		93	74	17.6	14.4	28.6	410.9	10.35	1,571.8	1,138.5	2,715.6	55.5
1992	46	89	74	15.4	12.8	25.8	385.9	11.42	1,431.6	1,051.8	2,490.8	69.3
1993		91	73	15.9	13.2	25.5	394.4	11.88	1,432.9	1,030.3	2,456.0	68.4
1994		91P	75P	15.0	12.6	25.8	394.1	11.98	1,519.4	1,071.2	2,569.3	89.2
1995		91P	76P	15.6P	13.2P	26.3P	414.1P	12.23P	1,597.3P	1,126.1P	2,701.1P	67.3P
1996		92P	78P	15.6P	13.1P	26.2P	421.2P	12.55P	1,630.8P	1,149.7P	2,757.7P	66.3P
1997		92P	79P	15.5P	13.1P	26.1P	428.4P	12.87P	1,664.3P	1,173.3P	2,814.3P	65.3P
1998		93P	80P	15.5P	13.0P	26.0P	435.5P	13.19P	1,697.7P	1,196.9P	2,870.9P	64.3P

Sources: 1982, 1987, 1992 *Economic Census*; *Annual Survey of Manufactures*, 83-86, 88-91, 93-94. Establishment counts for non-Census years are from *County Business Patterns*; establishment values for 83-84 are extrapolations. 'P's show projections by the editors. Industries reclassified in 87 will not have data for prior years.

INDICES OF CHANGE

Year	Companies	Establishments: Total	Establishments: with 20 or more employees	Employment: Total (000)	Production Workers (000)	Production Hours (Mil)	Compensation: Payroll ($ mil)	Compensation: Wages ($/hr)	Production ($ million): Cost of Materials	Value Added by Manufacture	Value of Shipments	Capital Invest.
1982												
1983												
1984												
1985												
1986												
1987	124	103	97	103	100	100	88	86	84	85	84	138
1988		94	85	104	100	100	92	88	91	85	88	115
1989		96	88	99	113	109	99	92	106	100	102	93
1990		97	96	102	112	109	102	90	102	102	101	74
1991		104	100	114	113	111	106	91	110	108	109	80
1992	100	100	100	100	100	100	100	100	100	100	100	100
1993		102	99	103	103	99	102	104	100	98	99	99
1994		102P	102P	97	98	100	102	105	106	102	103	129
1995		103P	103P	102P	103P	102P	107P	107P	112P	107P	108P	97P
1996		103P	105P	101P	103P	102P	109P	110P	114P	109P	111P	96P
1997		104P	106P	101P	102P	101P	111P	113P	116P	112P	113P	94P
1998		104P	108P	101P	102P	101P	113P	115P	119P	114P	115P	93P

Sources: Same as General Statistics. Values reflect change from the base year, 1992. Values above 100 mean greater than 92, values below 100 mean less than 92, and a value of 100 in the 82-91 or 93-98 period means same as 92. 'P's mark projections by the editors.

SELECTED RATIOS

For 1994	Avg. of All Manufact.	Analyzed Industry	Index	For 1994	Avg. of All Manufact.	Analyzed Industry	Index
Employees per Establishment	49	165	337	Value Added per Production Worker	134,084	85,016	63
Payroll per Establishment	1,500,273	4,344,409	290	Cost per Establishment	5,045,178	16,749,291	332
Payroll per Employee	30,620	26,273	86	Cost per Employee	102,970	101,293	98
Production Workers per Establishment	34	139	405	Cost per Production Worker	146,988	120,587	82
Wages per Establishment	853,319	3,407,225	399	Shipments per Establishment	9,576,895	28,322,992	296
Wages per Production Worker	24,861	24,530	99	Shipments per Employee	195,460	171,287	88
Hours per Production Worker	2,056	2,048	100	Shipments per Production Worker	279,017	203,913	73
Wages per Hour	12.09	11.98	99	Investment per Establishment	321,011	983,307	306
Value Added per Establishment	4,602,255	11,808,504	257	Investment per Employee	6,552	5,947	91
Value Added per Employee	93,930	71,413	76	Investment per Production Worker	9,352	7,079	76

Sources: Same as General Statistics. The 'Average of All Manufacturing' column represents the average of all manufacturing industries reported for the most recent complete year available. The Index shows the relationship between the Average and the Analyzed Industry. For example, 100 means that they are equal; 500 that the Analyzed Industry is five times the average; 50 means that the Analyzed Industry is half the national average. The abbreviation 'na' is used to show that data are 'not available'.

LEADING COMPANIES

Number shown: **13** Total sales ($ mil): **1,407** Total employment (000): **8.5**

Company Name	Address				CEO Name	Phone	Co. Type	Sales ($ mil)	Empl. (000)
Imperial Bondware Inc	75 Chestnut Ridge	Montvale	NJ	07645	Mike Balduino	201-391-1776	S	350	0.8
Champion International Corp	1 Champion Plz	Stamford	CT	06921	Howard J Gidez	203-358-7000	D	320*	1.3
Sealright Company Inc	7101 College Blv	Overland Park	KS	66210	Marvin W Ozley	913-344-9000	P	276	1.9
Solo Cup Co	1505 E Main St	Urbana	IL	61801	RL Hulseman	217-384-1800	S	230	2.4
Sealright Company Inc	9201 Packaging Dr	DeSoto	KS	66018	Don Wooton	913-321-5002	D	56*	0.4
Hayes Manufacturing Group Inc	PO Box 595	Neenah	WI	54957	James R Hayes	414-725-7056	R	50	0.2
Sherwood Industries Inc	PO Box 7118	Kensington	CT	06037	Paul Corazzo	203-828-4161	R	37*	0.3
Fonda Group Inc	PO Box 329	St Albans	VT	05478	Kenneth Freer	802-524-5966	D	30	0.3
Sherri Cup Inc	PO Box 7118	Kensington	CT	06037	Paul Corazzo	203-828-6338	S	27*	0.2
Ryt-Way Packaging Co	1407 Armstrong Rd	Northfield	MN	55057	GW Hasse Jr	507-663-1281	R	20	0.7
EPCO Packaging Products Inc	PO Box 3560	Framingham	MA	01701	Arthur Bash	508-877-7079	R	5	<0.1
Pride-Made Products Inc	PO Box 530	Matawan	NJ	07747	Roy A Olsen	908-583-3030	R	4*	<0.1
Cascade Continental Foods Inc	1089 Essex Av	Richmond	CA	94801	Gary Spakosky	510-232-3103	R	2	<0.1

Source: *Ward's Business Directory of U.S. Private and Public Companies*, Volumes 1 and 2, 1996. The company type code used is as follows: P - Public, R - Private, S - Subsidiary, D - Division, J - Joint Venture, A - Affiliate, G - Group. Sales are in millions of dollars, employees are in thousands. An asterisk (*) indicates an estimated sales volume. The symbol < stands for 'less than'. Company names and addresses are truncated, in some cases, to fit into the available space.

MATERIALS CONSUMED

Material		Quantity	Delivered Cost ($ million)
Materials, ingredients, containers, and supplies		(X)	1,336.8
Paper and paperboard, except boxes and containers	1,000 s tons	1,236.0	975.8
Fabricated plastics products, including closures, ends, film, and strapping, etc.		(X)	37.6
Petroleum wax	mil lb	115.6	36.2
Glues and adhesives		(X)	5.8
Printing inks (complete formulations)	mil lb	12.9*	34.2
All other materials and components, parts, containers, and supplies		(X)	159.6
Materials, ingredients, containers, and supplies, nsk		(X)	87.5

Source: 1992 *Economic Census*. Explanation of symbols used: (D): Withheld to avoid disclosure of competitive data; na: Not available; (S): Withheld because statistical norms were not met; (X): Not applicable; (Z): Less than half the unit shown; nec: Not elsewhere classified; nsk: Not specified by kind; - : zero; * : 10-19 percent estimated; ** : 20-29 percent estimated.

PRODUCT SHARE DETAILS

Product or Product Class	% Share
Sanitary food containers, except folding	100.00
Milk and milk-type paperboard cartons, including juices, beverages, and other products	28.16
Cups and liquid-tight paper and paperboard containers	46.25
Liquid-tight and round-nested paperboard food containers, including lids and tops	15.72
Paperboard drinking cups and portion serving cups	83.51
Cups and liquid-tight paper and paperboard containers, nsk	0.77
Other sanitary paper and paperboard food containers, boards, and trays, except folding	23.30
Pressed paperboard plates, dishes, spoons, and similar products	75.29
Ovenable paperboard food trays	23.87
Other sanitary paper and paperboard food containers, boards, and trays, except folding, nsk	0.84
Sanitary food containers, except folding, nsk	2.30

Source: 1992 *Economic Census*. The values shown are percent of total shipments in an industry. Values of indented subcategories are summed in the main heading. The symbol (D) appears when data are withheld to prevent disclosure of competitive information. The abbreviation nsk stands for 'not specified by kind' and nec for 'not elsewhere classified'.

INPUTS AND OUTPUTS FOR SANITARY PAPER PRODUCTS

Economic Sector or Industry Providing Inputs	%	Sector	Economic Sector or Industry Buying Outputs	%	Sector
Paper mills, except building paper	41.5	Manufg.	Personal consumption expenditures	79.1	
Pulp mills	12.5	Manufg.	Eating & drinking places	6.1	Trade
Paperboard containers & boxes	9.2	Manufg.	Exports	2.9	Foreign
Wholesale trade	7.6	Trade	S/L Govt. purch., elem. & secondary education	1.3	S/L Govt
Nonwoven fabrics	5.1	Manufg.	Hotels & lodging places	1.1	Services
Broadwoven fabric mills	2.7	Manufg.	Services to dwellings & other buildings	0.9	Services
Miscellaneous plastics products	2.7	Manufg.	Hospitals	0.8	Services
Advertising	2.5	Services	S/L Govt. purch., health & hospitals	0.8	S/L Govt
Motor freight transportation & warehousing	2.0	Util.	Change in business inventories	0.7	In House
Petroleum refining	1.8	Manufg.	Retail trade, except eating & drinking	0.5	Trade
Railroads & related services	1.7	Util.	Real estate	0.4	Fin/R.E.
Electric services (utilities)	1.4	Util.	Religious organizations	0.4	Services
Adhesives & sealants	1.3	Manufg.	Elementary & secondary schools	0.3	Services
Air transportation	0.9	Util.	Nursing & personal care facilities	0.3	Services
Hotels & lodging places	0.5	Services	S/L Govt. purch., higher education	0.3	S/L Govt

Continued on next page.

INPUTS AND OUTPUTS FOR SANITARY PAPER PRODUCTS - Continued

Economic Sector or Industry Providing Inputs	%	Sector	Economic Sector or Industry Buying Outputs	%	Sector
Gas production & distribution (utilities)	0.4	Util.	S/L Govt. purch., other general government	0.3	S/L Govt
Sanitary services, steam supply, irrigation	0.4	Util.	Wholesale trade	0.2	Trade
Banking	0.4	Fin/R.E.	Colleges, universities, & professional schools	0.2	Services
Paper coating & glazing	0.3	Manufg.	Federal Government purchases, nondefense	0.2	Fed Govt
Paper industries machinery	0.3	Manufg.	Banking	0.1	Fin/R.E.
Plastics materials & resins	0.3	Manufg.	Federal Government purchases, national defense	0.1	Fed Govt
Communications, except radio & TV	0.3	Util.			
Automotive rental & leasing, without drivers	0.3	Services			
Maintenance of nonfarm buildings nec	0.2	Constr.			
Paperboard mills	0.2	Manufg.			
Printing ink	0.2	Manufg.			
Eating & drinking places	0.2	Trade			
Insurance carriers	0.2	Fin/R.E.			
Real estate	0.2	Fin/R.E.			
Royalties	0.2	Fin/R.E.			
Automotive repair shops & services	0.2	Services			
Equipment rental & leasing services	0.2	Services			
Water transportation	0.1	Util.			
Business/professional associations	0.1	Services			
Computer & data processing services	0.1	Services			

Source: Benchmark Input-Output Accounts for the U.S. Economy, 1982, U.S. Department of Commerce, Washington, D.C., July 1991. Data, as reported in the source, are organized by the 1977 SIC structure in use in 1982 but have been matched, as closely as is possible, to the 1987 SIC structure used in this book.

OCCUPATIONS EMPLOYED BY SIC 265 - PAPERBOARD CONTAINERS AND BOXES

Occupation	% of Total 1994	Change to 2005	Occupation	% of Total 1994	Change to 2005
Paper goods machine setters & set-up operators	8.4	-12.0	Cement & gluing machine operators	3.0	-28.5
Machine feeders & offbearers	8.3	-1.0	Truck drivers light & heavy	2.6	13.4
Printing press machine setters, operators	6.2	10.0	Maintenance repairers, general utility	2.2	9.9
Cutting & slicing machine setters, operators	5.9	32.0	General managers & top executives	2.0	4.3
Blue collar worker supervisors	5.3	12.4	Industrial machinery mechanics	2.0	20.9
Helpers, laborers, & material movers nec	5.2	10.0	Freight, stock, & material movers, hand	1.6	-12.0
Machine operators nec	4.9	35.7	Inspectors, testers, & graders, precision	1.5	20.9
Sales & related workers nec	4.4	10.0	Traffic, shipping, & receiving clerks	1.3	5.8
Industrial truck & tractor operators	4.2	10.0	Industrial production managers	1.2	9.9
Assemblers, fabricators, & hand workers nec	4.0	10.0	Packaging & filling machine operators	1.2	10.0
Hand packers & packagers	3.6	-5.7	Bookkeeping, accounting, & auditing clerks	1.0	-17.5

Source: Industry-Occupation Matrix, Bureau of Labor Statistics. These data relate to one or more 3-digit SIC industry groups rather than to a single 4-digit SIC. The change reported for each occupation to the year 2005 is a percent of growth or decline as estimated by the Bureau of Labor Statistics. The abbreviation nec stands for 'not elsewhere classified'.

LOCATION BY STATE AND REGIONAL CONCENTRATION

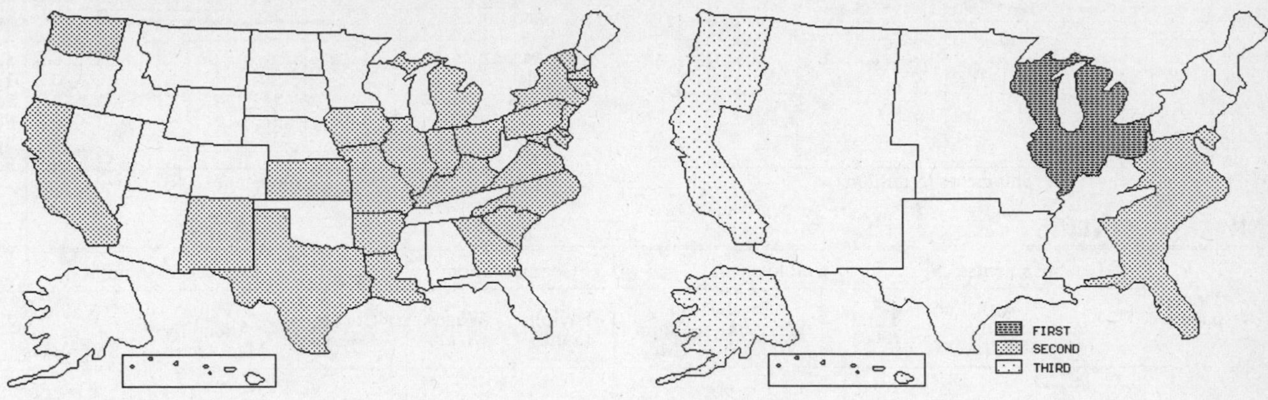

INDUSTRY DATA BY STATE

State	Establish-ments	Shipments			Employment				Cost as % of Shipments	Investment per Employee ($)
		Total ($ mil)	% of U.S.	Per Establ.	Total Number	% of U.S.	Per Establ.	Wages ($/hour)		
Georgia	7	228.6	9.2	32.7	1,100	7.1	157	10.10	70.4	-
California	11	193.4	7.8	17.6	1,000	6.5	91	12.40	60.0	10,200
Ohio	6	149.3	6.0	24.9	900	5.8	150	11.93	58.5	-
Illinois	5	125.2	5.0	25.0	1,100	7.1	220	12.27	57.9	-
Pennsylvania	6	107.6	4.3	17.9	700	4.5	117	9.50	54.3	4,000
Kansas	3	105.4	4.2	35.1	300	1.9	100	10.40	42.5	-
Michigan	4	80.4	3.2	20.1	400	2.6	100	10.00	73.4	-
New York	4	33.8	1.4	8.4	200	1.3	50	8.20	62.7	-
Maryland	4	(D)	-	-	3,750 *	24.4	938	-	-	-
Massachusetts	4	(D)	-	-	175 *	1.1	44	-	-	-
Iowa	3	(D)	-	-	175 *	1.1	58	-	-	-
Kentucky	3	(D)	-	-	750 *	4.9	250	-	-	-
Missouri	3	(D)	-	-	1,750 *	11.4	583	-	-	-
Connecticut	2	(D)	-	-	175 *	1.1	88	-	-	-
Indiana	2	(D)	-	-	175 *	1.1	88	-	-	-
New Jersey	2	(D)	-	-	175 *	1.1	88	-	-	-
South Carolina	2	(D)	-	-	750 *	4.9	375	-	-	-
Texas	2	(D)	-	-	750 *	4.9	375	-	-	-
Arkansas	1	(D)	-	-	750 *	4.9	750	-	-	-
Delaware	1	(D)	-	-	375 *	2.4	375	-	-	-
Louisiana	1	(D)	-	-	175 *	1.1	175	-	-	-
New Mexico	1	(D)	-	-	175 *	1.1	175	-	-	-
North Carolina	1	(D)	-	-	175 *	1.1	175	-	-	-
Rhode Island	1	(D)	-	-	375 *	2.4	375	-	-	-
Vermont	1	(D)	-	-	175 *	1.1	175	-	-	-
Virginia	1	(D)	-	-	175 *	1.1	175	-	-	-
Washington	1	(D)	-	-	175 *	1.1	175	-	-	-

Source: 1992 *Economic Census*. The states are in descending order of shipments or establishments (if shipment data are missing for the majority). The symbol (D) appears when data are withheld to prevent disclosure of competitive information. States marked with (D) are sorted by number of establishments. A dash (-) indicates that the data element cannot be calculated; * indicates the midpoint of a range.

2657 - FOLDING PAPERBOARD BOXES

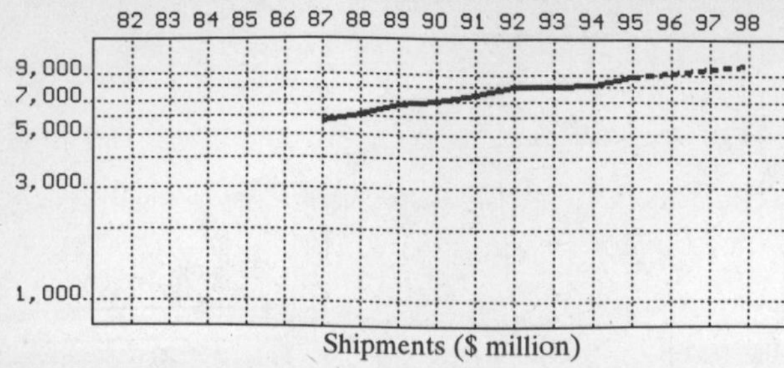

Shipments ($ million)

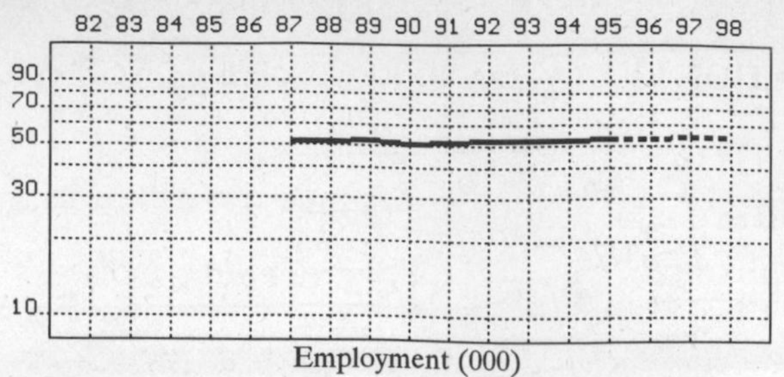

Employment (000)

GENERAL STATISTICS

Year	Companies	Establishments		Employment			Compensation		Production ($ million)			
		Total	with 20 or more employees	Total (000)	Production Workers (000)	Production Hours (Mil)	Payroll ($ mil)	Wages ($/hr)	Cost of Materials	Value Added by Manufacture	Value of Shipments	Capital Invest.
1982												
1983												
1984												
1985												
1986												
1987	461	606	448	50.7	39.9	83.7	1,255.8	10.40	3,144.6	2,586.8	5,705.3	180.5
1988		594	449	51.1	40.5	85.3	1,330.6	10.60	3,398.9	2,772.3	6,098.1	216.6
1989		577	445	52.0	41.2	86.2	1,363.8	11.01	3,753.7	3,080.3	6,715.2	244.2
1990		568	427	50.4	40.6	85.9	1,381.5	11.12	3,910.0	3,042.4	6,969.4	279.8
1991		561	421	50.7	40.9	86.1	1,443.0	11.59	4,127.5	3,252.3	7,368.7	253.8
1992	446	588	436	52.7	41.7	90.0	1,590.1	12.15	4,358.0	3,565.0	7,932.7	295.7
1993		585	436	52.5	41.5	89.1	1,609.6	12.63	4,372.2	3,600.4	8,009.4	332.9
1994		570P	425P	52.5	42.3	92.6	1,659.9	12.38	4,542.4	3,723.7	8,221.6	280.6
1995		566P	422P	52.8P	42.3P	92.3P	1,720.2P	12.98P	4,862.1P	3,985.7P	8,800.2P	336.1P
1996		563P	419P	53.0P	42.6P	93.4P	1,779.3P	13.31P	5,067.4P	4,154.1P	9,171.9P	352.9P
1997		560P	416P	53.3P	42.9P	94.6P	1,838.4P	13.64P	5,272.8P	4,322.4P	9,543.6P	369.7P
1998		557P	413P	53.5P	43.2P	95.7P	1,897.5P	13.98P	5,478.1P	4,490.8P	9,915.3P	386.5P

Sources: 1982, 1987, 1992 *Economic Census*; *Annual Survey of Manufactures*, 83-86, 88-91, 93-94. Establishment counts for non-Census years are from *County Business Patterns*; establishment values for 83-84 are extrapolations. 'P's show projections by the editors. Industries reclassified in 87 will not have data for prior years.

INDICES OF CHANGE

Year	Companies	Establishments		Employment			Compensation		Production ($ million)			
		Total	with 20 or more employees	Total (000)	Production Workers (000)	Production Hours (Mil)	Payroll ($ mil)	Wages ($/hr)	Cost of Materials	Value Added by Manufacture	Value of Shipments	Capital Invest.
1982												
1983												
1984												
1985												
1986												
1987	103	103	103	96	96	93	79	86	72	73	72	61
1988		101	103	97	97	95	84	87	78	78	77	73
1989		98	102	99	99	96	86	91	86	86	85	83
1990		97	98	96	97	95	87	92	90	85	88	95
1991		95	97	96	98	96	91	95	95	91	93	86
1992	100	100	100	100	100	100	100	100	100	100	100	100
1993		99	100	100	100	99	101	104	100	101	101	113
1994		97P	98P	100	101	103	104	102	104	104	104	95
1995		96P	97P	100P	102P	103P	108P	107P	112P	112P	111P	114P
1996		96P	96P	101P	102P	104P	112P	110P	116P	117P	116P	119P
1997		95P	95P	101P	103P	105P	116P	112P	121P	121P	120P	125P
1998		95P	95P	102P	104P	106P	119P	115P	126P	126P	125P	131P

Sources: Same as General Statistics. Values reflect change from the base year, 1992. Values above 100 mean greater than 92, values below 100 mean less than 92, and a value of 100 in the 82-91 or 93-98 period means same as 92. 'P's mark projections by the editors.

SELECTED RATIOS

For 1994	Avg. of All Manufact.	Analyzed Industry	Index
Employees per Establishment	49	92	188
Payroll per Establishment	1,500,273	2,913,566	194
Payroll per Employee	30,620	31,617	103
Production Workers per Establishment	34	74	216
Wages per Establishment	853,319	2,012,216	236
Wages per Production Worker	24,861	27,101	109
Hours per Production Worker	2,056	2,189	106
Wages per Hour	12.09	12.38	102
Value Added per Establishment	4,602,255	6,536,083	142
Value Added per Employee	93,930	70,928	76

For 1994	Avg. of All Manufact.	Analyzed Industry	Index
Value Added per Production Worker	134,084	88,031	66
Cost per Establishment	5,045,178	7,973,119	158
Cost per Employee	102,970	86,522	84
Cost per Production Worker	146,988	107,385	73
Shipments per Establishment	9,576,895	14,431,093	151
Shipments per Employee	195,460	156,602	80
Shipments per Production Worker	279,017	194,364	70
Investment per Establishment	321,011	492,528	153
Investment per Employee	6,552	5,345	82
Investment per Production Worker	9,352	6,634	71

Sources: Same as General Statistics. The 'Average of All Manufacturing' column represents the average of all manufacturing industries reported for the most recent complete year available. The Index shows the relationship between the Average and the Analyzed Industry. For example, 100 means that they are equal; 500 that the Analyzed Industry is five times the average; 50 means that the Analyzed Industry is half the national average. The abbreviation 'na' is used to show that data are 'not available'.

LEADING COMPANIES Number shown: 75 Total sales ($ mil): 3,286 Total employment (000): 22.4

Company Name	Address				CEO Name	Phone	Co. Type	Sales ($ mil)	Empl. (000)
Rock-Tenn Co	PO Box 4098	Norcross	GA	30091	Bradley Currey Jr	404-448-2193	P	706	5.5
Field Container Corp	1500 Nicholas Blv	Elk Grove Vill	IL	60007	Laurence Field	708-437-1700	R	383	0.7
Westvaco Corp	320 Hull St	Richmond	VA	23224	Harry K Williams	804-233-9205	D	250	0.9
Universal Packaging Corp	PO Box 918	Concord	NH	03302	Jack R Hutton	603-224-2333	R	180	1.0
Adage Inc	625 Willowbrook Ln	West Chester	PA	19382	D FU Goebert	215-430-3900	P	127	0.9
Gibraltar Packaging Group Inc	2115 Rexford Rd	Charlotte	NC	28211	Deke C Abbott Jr	704-366-2929	P	76	1.0
Mebane Packaging Group	PO Box 408	Mebane	NC	27302	George Krall	919-563-3516	R	72	0.8
Union Camp Corp	PO Box 555-C	Clifton	NJ	07012	Anthony W Ruvo	201-779-1700	D	65	0.4
Malnove Inc	13434 F St	Omaha	NE	68137	Ron Martin	402-330-1100	R	60	0.3
Climax Manufacturing Company	Climax St	Castorland	NY	13620	LT Hirschey	315-493-3390	R	45	0.4
International Paper Co	100 Progress Pl	Cincinnati	OH	45246	Roger Lague	513-782-6100	D	42*	0.4
Corson Manufacturing Company	20-24 Michigan Av	Lockport	NY	14094	Chad E Hoyme	716-434-8871	R	40	0.2
Shorewood Packaging Co	815 Chapman Way	Newport News	VA	23602	Lance Repert	804-877-1234	S	39*	0.3
Artistic Carton Co	1975 Big Timber Rd	Elgin	IL	60123	PA Traeger	708-741-0247	R	38	0.2
Queens Group Indiana Inc	PO Box 21069	Indianapolis	IN	46221	Eric Kaltman	317-635-7777	S	37*	0.4
Fold-Pak Corp	Van Buren St	Newark	NY	14513	Karl Demay	315-331-3200	R	36	0.3
Malnove Incorporated of Florida	4115 University	Jacksonville	FL	32217	Glen Miller	904-733-4770	S	36	0.2
Hub Folding Box Company Inc	774 Norfolk St	Mansfield	MA	02048	JF Dirico	508-339-0005	R	35	0.2
Renton Folding	PO Box 479	Renton	WA	98057	LA Ramirez	206-235-3331	D	32	0.2
Arkay Packaging Corp	PO Box 6000	Hauppauge	NY	11788	Howard Kaneff	516-273-2000	R	30	0.3
Etta Packaging Inc	PO Box 580	Marion	NC	28752	CB Shaw	704-652-5511	S	30*	0.2
Rex Packaging Inc	PO Box 18247	Jacksonville	FL	32229	Young E Hall Jr	904-757-5210	S	30	0.2
YE Hall Inc	PO Box 18247	Jacksonville	FL	32229	Young E Hall Jr	904-757-5210	R	30	0.2
Crane Carton Co	555 N Tripp St	Chicago	IL	60624	A Crane	312-722-0555	R	28	0.2
Dot Group	6223 Constitution	Fort Wayne	IN	46804	K Moudy	219-432-3822	R	28	0.2
Fort Orange Paper Co	1900 River Rd	Castltn/Hdsn	NY	12033	John Hay Jr	518-732-7722	S	28*	0.2
Americraft Carton Inc	164 Meadowcroft St	Lowell	MA	01853	John F McLaughlin	508-459-9328	R	26*	0.2
San Joaquin Packaging Corp	PO Box 720	Stockton	CA	95201	Dennis Herrick	209-464-7000	R	25	0.2
Astronics Corp	1801 Elmwood Av	Buffalo	NY	14207	Kevin T Keane	716-662-6640	P	25	0.3
Michigan Carton	79 E Fountain St	Battle Creek	MI	49016	Bryan King	616-963-4004	R	24	0.2
Colbert Packaging Corp	28355 Bradley Rd	Lake Forest	IL	60045	John A Neuman	708-367-5990	R	23	0.2
Diamond Packaging	111 Commerce Dr	Rochester	NY	14623	HF Voss	716-334-8030	R	22*	0.2
Carton-Craft Corp	115-121 Ash St	Buffalo	NY	14204	TS Ortolani	716-852-7910	R	20	0.2
Curtis Packaging Corp	Rte 34	Sandy Hook	CT	06482	Donald R Droppo	203-426-5861	R	20	0.2
Richmond Gravure	3400 Deepwater	Richmond	VA	23234	John Georges	804-232-1201	S	20	0.3
Royal-Pioneer Inc	2345 Castor Av	Philadelphia	PA	19134	Mitchell Marks	215-289-8050	R	20	0.2
Rexham Packaging	PO Box 240007	Charlotte	NC	28224	James B Buchanan	704-889-7262	D	19	0.3
AB Cowles and Company Inc	49 N Main St	Manchester	NY	14504	R A Cowles Jr	716-924-3016	R	18*	0.2
Columbia Corrugated Box Co	12777 SW	Tualatin	OR	97062	Marvin Lince	503-692-3344	R	18*	0.2
Glenmark Industries Inc	1000 Pidco Dr	Plymouth	IN	46563	Don T Kindt	219-936-2118	R	18	0.1
Innovative Folding Carton Co	901 Durham Av	South Plainfield	NJ	07080	Sal Cannizzaro	908-757-6000	R	18*	0.2
Los Angeles Paper	PO Box 60830	Los Angeles	CA	90060	W H Kewell III	213-685-8900	R	18	0.2
Tropical Paper Box Co	7000 NW 25th St	Miami	FL	33122	H Quartin	305-592-5520	R	18*	0.2
Wilkata Packaging Corp	300 Hoyt St	Kearny	NJ	07032	James Trimm	201-991-4800	D	18	0.2
Boutwell Owens and Company	549 Westminster St	Fitchburg	MA	01420	WW McLaughlin	508-343-3067	R	17	0.2
Flashfold Carton	PO Box 11467	Fort Wayne	IN	46858	Clyde Potts	219-423-9431	D	17	0.2
Economy Folding Box Corp	2601 S La Salle St	Chicago	IL	60616	JC Moos	312-225-2000	R	16	0.2
Harvard Folding Box Company	71 Linden St	Lynn	MA	01905	Leon Simkins	617-598-1600	S	16	0.1
Pacific Coast Packaging Corp	1401 S Madera Av	Kerman	CA	93630	Brent H Hutchings	209-846-6644	R	16	0.1
Rand Whitney	Rte 2	Harrington	DE	19952	Robert Crafton	302-398-4211	S	16*	0.1
Atlantic Coast Carton	PO Box 668607	Charlotte	NC	28266	C D Haithcock	704-333-6645	D	15	<0.1
Amco Folding Cartons Inc	PO Box 98	Towaco	NJ	07082	John Como	201-334-3030	R	15	0.1
Chapco Carton Co	1810 5th Av	River Grove	IL	60171	CG Kiolbasa Jr	708-452-6942	R	15	0.1
Eastfield Carton Co	1501 Russell St	Baltimore	MD	21230	Timothy Eunice	410-727-3838	S	15	0.1
Lengsfield Brothers Inc	PO Box 50020	New Orleans	LA	70150	Jack T Lengsfield	504-529-2235	R	15*	0.1
Neff Folding Box Co	PO Box 235	Dayton	OH	45404	RS Neff	513-233-3333	R	15	0.1
Razorback	PO Box 4190	Fort Smith	AR	72914	B Mack	501-782-6014	D	15	0.2
Americraft Carton Inc	403 Fillmore Av E	St Paul	MN	55107	Paul Hile	612-227-6655	S	15	0.1
Victory Specialty Packaging Inc	42 Gates Av	Victory Mills	NY	12884	Eugene Holcombe	518-695-3211	R	14*	0.2
Mid-Cities Paper Box Company	PO Box 2096	Bell Gardens	CA	90201	Ken W Sipple	213-773-0233	R	13*	0.1
MOD-PAC Corp	1801 Elmwood Av	Buffalo	NY	14207	Kevin T Keane	716-873-0640	S	13	0.1
Nordic Packaging Inc	5017 Boone Av N	New Hope	MN	55428	OA Bjorkedal	612-535-6440	R	13	<0.1
Seaboard Folding Box Corp	35 Daniels St	Fitchburg	MA	01420	Alan Rabinow	508-342-8921	R	13*	0.1
Boelter Industries Inc	PO Box 916	Winona	MN	55987	LB Boelter	507-452-2315	R	12*	0.1
BF Nelson Folding Carton Inc	752 30th Av SE	Minneapolis	MN	55414	Larry Ross	612-331-1193	R	12*	0.1
Franklyn Folding Box Co	3511 Prince St	Flushing	NY	11354	WF Kornfield Jr	718-539-0900	R	12*	0.1
San Diego Paper Box Co	PO Drawer 1219	Spring Valley	CA	91979	Sidney B Chapman	619-660-9566	R	12*	0.1
Scott and Daniells Inc	264 Freestone Av	Portland	CT	06480	David Preston	203-342-1932	R	11	0.1
Thoro-Packaging	1467 Davril Cir	Corona	CA	91720	Janet Steiner	909-278-2100	R	10	<0.1
Admiral Folding Box Inc	102 Pleasant Valley	Methuen	MA	01844	James Goldman	508-685-0033	R	10	0.2
Arko Paper Products Company	4100 N Brunswick	Piscataway	NJ	08854	A R Kolenski Jr	908-424-2100	R	10	<0.1
Dot Packaging Printpak Inc	PO Box 5972	Spartanburg	SC	29304	Richard Rosenbach	803-579-2280	D	10	<0.1
Eagle Paper Box Company Inc	106 S 28th St	Tacoma	WA	98402	Richard A Barakat	206-627-3125	R	10*	<0.1
F and S Carton Co	PO Box 8606	Grand Rapids	MI	49508	Robert J Scranton	616-538-9400	R	10	0.1
Rose City Paper Box Inc	3100 NW Industrial	Portland	OR	97210	Dick Safranski	503-241-6486	R	10	<0.1

Source: *Ward's Business Directory of U.S. Private and Public Companies*, Volumes 1 and 2, 1996. The company type code used is as follows: P - Public, R - Private, S - Subsidiary, D - Division, J - Joint Venture, A - Affiliate, G - Group. Sales are in millions of dollars, employees are in thousands. An asterisk (*) indicates an estimated sales volume. The symbol < stands for 'less than'. Company names and addresses are truncated, in some cases, to fit into the available space.

MATERIALS CONSUMED

Material		Quantity	Delivered Cost ($ million)
Materials, ingredients, containers, and supplies		(X)	4,072.4
Paper and paperboard, except boxes and containers	1,000 s tons	4,717.2**	2,945.5
Fabricated plastics products, including closures, ends, film, and strapping, etc.		(X)	30.0
Steel sheet and strip, including tin plate		(X)	26.7
Petroleum wax	mil lb	(S)	5.7
Glues and adhesives		(X)	29.6
Printing inks (complete formulations)	mil lb	85.1**	219.3
All other materials and components, parts, containers, and supplies		(X)	432.4
Materials, ingredients, containers, and supplies, nsk		(X)	383.2

Source: 1992 *Economic Census*. Explanation of symbols used: (D): Withheld to avoid disclosure of competitive data; na: Not available; (S): Withheld because statistical norms were not met; (X): Not applicable; (Z): Less than half the unit shown; nec: Not elsewhere classified; nsk: Not specified by kind; - : zero; * : 10-19 percent estimated; ** : 20-29 percent estimated.

PRODUCT SHARE DETAILS

Product or Product Class	% Share	Product or Product Class	% Share
Folding paperboard boxes	100.00	For paper goods or products, including book mailers	6.32
For dry food and produce, including pet and animal food	10.56	For fresh bakery products	2.66
For biscuits and crackers	2.23	For butter and ice cream packages and food pails	3.87
For bottled and canned beverages, including carriers for alcoholic and nonalcoholic beverages	10.22	For processed meats, margarine, lard, and shortening	1.69
For soaps and detergents	4.39	For frozen foods	4.87
For tobacco	4.73	Folding paperboard carryout boxes and trays for retail food	4.60
For hardware and household supplies	5.52	Paperboard backs for blister and skin packaging	1.00
For candy	2.65	Folding paperboard boxes, packaging, and packaging components for all other end uses, not elsewhere classified	15.68
For cosmetics and medicinal products	8.23		

Source: 1992 *Economic Census*. The values shown are percent of total shipments in an industry. Values of indented subcategories are summed in the main heading. The symbol (D) appears when data are withheld to prevent disclosure of competitive information. The abbreviation nsk stands for 'not specified by kind' and nec for 'not elsewhere classified'.

INPUTS AND OUTPUTS FOR PAPERBOARD CONTAINERS & BOXES

Economic Sector or Industry Providing Inputs	%	Sector	Economic Sector or Industry Buying Outputs	%	Sector
Paperboard mills	58.2	Manufg.	Wholesale trade	7.2	Trade
Paperboard containers & boxes	6.0	Manufg.	Eating & drinking places	4.7	Trade
Railroads & related services	4.0	Util.	Paperboard containers & boxes	3.9	Manufg.
Motor freight transportation & warehousing	3.6	Util.	Glass containers	3.3	Manufg.
Petroleum refining	3.1	Manufg.	Fluid milk	3.1	Manufg.
Wholesale trade	2.2	Trade	Miscellaneous plastics products	3.1	Manufg.
Electric services (utilities)	1.8	Util.	Cigarettes	2.9	Manufg.
Paper mills, except building paper	1.6	Manufg.	Sanitary paper products	2.3	Manufg.
Die-cut paper & board	1.4	Manufg.	Meat packing plants	1.8	Manufg.
Plastics materials & resins	1.4	Manufg.	Toilet preparations	1.7	Manufg.
Printing ink	1.4	Manufg.	Retail trade, except eating & drinking	1.7	Trade
Sheet metal work	1.4	Manufg.	Food preparations, nec	1.6	Manufg.
Adhesives & sealants	1.2	Manufg.	Personal consumption expenditures	1.5	
Gas production & distribution (utilities)	1.1	Util.	Frozen specialties	1.5	Manufg.
Equipment rental & leasing services	0.7	Services	Malt beverages	1.5	Manufg.
Converted paper products, nec	0.6	Manufg.	Soap & other detergents	1.5	Manufg.
Cyclic crudes and organics	0.6	Manufg.	Fruits	1.4	Agric.
Communications, except radio & TV	0.6	Util.	Exports	1.4	Foreign
Eating & drinking places	0.6	Trade	Cereal breakfast foods	1.3	Manufg.
Metal foil & leaf	0.5	Manufg.	Drugs	1.3	Manufg.
Real estate	0.5	Fin/R.E.	Confectionery products	1.2	Manufg.
Maintenance of nonfarm buildings nec	0.4	Constr.	Cookies & crackers	1.2	Manufg.
Miscellaneous plastics products	0.4	Manufg.	Bottled & canned soft drinks	1.1	Manufg.
Imports	0.4	Foreign	Bread, cake, & related products	1.1	Manufg.
Aluminum rolling & drawing	0.3	Manufg.	Electronic computing equipment	1.1	Manufg.
Paints & allied products	0.3	Manufg.	Ice cream & frozen desserts	1.1	Manufg.
Paper industries machinery	0.3	Manufg.	Frozen fruits, fruit juices & vegetables	1.0	Manufg.
Air transportation	0.3	Util.	Polishes & sanitation goods	1.0	Manufg.
Banking	0.3	Fin/R.E.	Poultry dressing plants	1.0	Manufg.
Automotive rental & leasing, without drivers	0.3	Services	Broadwoven fabric mills	0.8	Manufg.
Automotive repair shops & services	0.3	Services	Canned fruits & vegetables	0.8	Manufg.
Computer & data processing services	0.3	Services	Apparel made from purchased materials	0.7	Manufg.
Fabricated metal products, nec	0.2	Manufg.	Cheese, natural & processed	0.7	Manufg.
Lubricating oils & greases	0.2	Manufg.	Dog, cat, & other pet food	0.7	Manufg.
Machinery, except electrical, nec	0.2	Manufg.	Games, toys, & children's vehicles	0.7	Manufg.
Paper coating & glazing	0.2	Manufg.	Metal foil & leaf	0.7	Manufg.
Sanitary services, steam supply, irrigation	0.2	Util.	Sausages & other prepared meats	0.7	Manufg.
Water transportation	0.2	Util.	Chemical preparations, nec	0.6	Manufg.
Insurance carriers	0.2	Fin/R.E.	Cyclic crudes and organics	0.6	Manufg.

Continued on next page.

INPUTS AND OUTPUTS FOR PAPERBOARD CONTAINERS & BOXES - Continued

Economic Sector or Industry Providing Inputs	%	Sector	Economic Sector or Industry Buying Outputs	%	Sector
Advertising	0.2	Services	Organic fibers, noncellulosic	0.6	Manufg.
Detective & protective services	0.2	Services	Paper mills, except building paper	0.6	Manufg.
Legal services	0.2	Services	Petroleum refining	0.6	Manufg.
Management & consulting services & labs	0.2	Services	Bags, except textile	0.5	Manufg.
U.S. Postal Service	0.2	Gov't	Blended & prepared flour	0.5	Manufg.
Special dies & tools & machine tool accessories	0.1	Manufg.	Fresh or frozen packaged fish	0.5	Manufg.
Accounting, auditing & bookkeeping	0.1	Services	Glass & glass products, except containers	0.5	Manufg.
Engineering, architectural, & surveying services	0.1	Services	Manufacturing industries, nec	0.5	Manufg.
			Plastics materials & resins	0.5	Manufg.
			Shortening & cooking oils	0.5	Manufg.
			Sugar	0.5	Manufg.
			Agricultural, forestry, & fishery services	0.4	Agric.
			Canned specialties	0.4	Manufg.
			Electric housewares & fans	0.4	Manufg.
			Electronic components nec	0.4	Manufg.
			Lighting fixtures & equipment	0.4	Manufg.
			Lubricating oils & greases	0.4	Manufg.
			Macaroni & spaghetti	0.4	Manufg.
			Photographic equipment & supplies	0.4	Manufg.
			Shoes, except rubber	0.4	Manufg.
			Book publishing	0.3	Manufg.
			Condensed & evaporated milk	0.3	Manufg.
			Dehydrated food products	0.3	Manufg.
			Electric lamps	0.3	Manufg.
			Hardware, nec	0.3	Manufg.
			Housefurnishings, nec	0.3	Manufg.
			Household cooking equipment	0.3	Manufg.
			Machinery, except electrical, nec	0.3	Manufg.
			Metal household furniture	0.3	Manufg.
			Metal stampings, nec	0.3	Manufg.
			Motor vehicle parts & accessories	0.3	Manufg.
			Paper coating & glazing	0.3	Manufg.
			Pickles, sauces, & salad dressings	0.3	Manufg.
			Refrigeration & heating equipment	0.3	Manufg.
			Roasted coffee	0.3	Manufg.
			Sporting & athletic goods, nec	0.3	Manufg.
			Surgical & medical instruments	0.3	Manufg.
			Surgical appliances & supplies	0.3	Manufg.
			Wet corn milling	0.3	Manufg.
			Wood household furniture	0.3	Manufg.
			Yarn mills & finishing of textiles, nec	0.3	Manufg.
			Adhesives & sealants	0.2	Manufg.
			Agricultural chemicals, nec	0.2	Manufg.
			Chocolate & cocoa products	0.2	Manufg.
			Commercial printing	0.2	Manufg.
			Converted paper products, nec	0.2	Manufg.
			Envelopes	0.2	Manufg.
			Fabricated rubber products, nec	0.2	Manufg.
			Flavoring extracts & syrups, nec	0.2	Manufg.
			Floor coverings	0.2	Manufg.
			Gum & wood chemicals	0.2	Manufg.
			Hand & edge tools, nec	0.2	Manufg.
			Household laundry equipment	0.2	Manufg.
			Household refrigerators & freezers	0.2	Manufg.
			Industrial inorganic chemicals, nec	0.2	Manufg.
			Manifold business forms	0.2	Manufg.
			Mechanical measuring devices	0.2	Manufg.
			Metal cans	0.2	Manufg.
			Metal office furniture	0.2	Manufg.
			Miscellaneous fabricated wire products	0.2	Manufg.
			Motors & generators	0.2	Manufg.
			Paints & allied products	0.2	Manufg.
			Paperboard mills	0.2	Manufg.
			Paving mixtures & blocks	0.2	Manufg.
			Poultry & egg processing	0.2	Manufg.
			Pumps & compressors	0.2	Manufg.
			Radio & TV communication equipment	0.2	Manufg.
			Radio & TV receiving sets	0.2	Manufg.
			Sheet metal work	0.2	Manufg.
			Signs & advertising displays	0.2	Manufg.
			Special dies & tools & machine tool accessories	0.2	Manufg.
			Wiring devices	0.2	Manufg.
			Women's hosiery, except socks	0.2	Manufg.
			Wood containers	0.2	Manufg.
			Wood kitchen cabinets	0.2	Manufg.

Continued on next page.

INPUTS AND OUTPUTS FOR PAPERBOARD CONTAINERS & BOXES - Continued

Economic Sector or Industry Providing Inputs	%	Sector	Economic Sector or Industry Buying Outputs	%	Sector
			Motor freight transportation & warehousing	0.2	Util.
			Hospitals	0.2	Services
			Federal Government purchases, national defense	0.2	Fed Govt
			S/L Govt. purch., health & hospitals	0.2	S/L Govt
			Abrasive products	0.1	Manufg.
			Architectural metal work	0.1	Manufg.
			Asphalt felts & coatings	0.1	Manufg.
			Automotive stampings	0.1	Manufg.
			Blast furnaces & steel mills	0.1	Manufg.
			Canned & cured seafoods	0.1	Manufg.
			Chewing gum	0.1	Manufg.
			Cigars	0.1	Manufg.
			Cutlery	0.1	Manufg.
			Die-cut paper & board	0.1	Manufg.
			Engine electrical equipment	0.1	Manufg.
			Flour & other grain mill products	0.1	Manufg.
			Hosiery, nec	0.1	Manufg.
			Household appliances, nec	0.1	Manufg.
			Lawn & garden equipment	0.1	Manufg.
			Metal partitions & fixtures	0.1	Manufg.
			Pens & mechanical pencils	0.1	Manufg.
			Pipe, valves, & pipe fittings	0.1	Manufg.
			Service industry machines, nec	0.1	Manufg.
			Stationery products	0.1	Manufg.
			Storage batteries	0.1	Manufg.
			Telephone & telegraph apparatus	0.1	Manufg.
			Typewriters & office machines, nec	0.1	Manufg.
			Wines, brandy, & brandy spirits	0.1	Manufg.
			Wood products, nec	0.1	Manufg.
			S/L Govt. purch., correction	0.1	S/L Govt
			S/L Govt. purch., higher education	0.1	S/L Govt

Source: Benchmark Input-Output Accounts for the U.S. Economy, 1982, U.S. Department of Commerce, Washington, D.C., July 1991. Data, as reported in the source, are organized by the 1977 SIC structure in use in 1982 but have been matched, as closely as is possible, to the 1987 SIC structure used in this book.

OCCUPATIONS EMPLOYED BY SIC 265 - PAPERBOARD CONTAINERS AND BOXES

Occupation	% of Total 1994	Change to 2005	Occupation	% of Total 1994	Change to 2005
Paper goods machine setters & set-up operators	8.4	-12.0	Cement & gluing machine operators	3.0	-28.5
Machine feeders & offbearers	8.3	-1.0	Truck drivers light & heavy	2.6	13.4
Printing press machine setters, operators	6.2	10.0	Maintenance repairers, general utility	2.2	9.9
Cutting & slicing machine setters, operators	5.9	32.0	General managers & top executives	2.0	4.3
Blue collar worker supervisors	5.3	12.4	Industrial machinery mechanics	2.0	20.9
Helpers, laborers, & material movers nec	5.2	10.0	Freight, stock, & material movers, hand	1.6	-12.0
Machine operators nec	4.9	35.7	Inspectors, testers, & graders, precision	1.5	20.9
Sales & related workers nec	4.4	10.0	Traffic, shipping, & receiving clerks	1.3	5.8
Industrial truck & tractor operators	4.2	10.0	Industrial production managers	1.2	9.9
Assemblers, fabricators, & hand workers nec	4.0	10.0	Packaging & filling machine operators	1.2	10.0
Hand packers & packagers	3.6	-5.7	Bookkeeping, accounting, & auditing clerks	1.0	-17.5

Source: Industry-Occupation Matrix, Bureau of Labor Statistics. These data relate to one or more 3-digit SIC industry groups rather than to a single 4-digit SIC. The change reported for each occupation to the year 2005 is a percent of growth or decline as estimated by the Bureau of Labor Statistics. The abbreviation nec stands for 'not elsewhere classified'.

LOCATION BY STATE AND REGIONAL CONCENTRATION

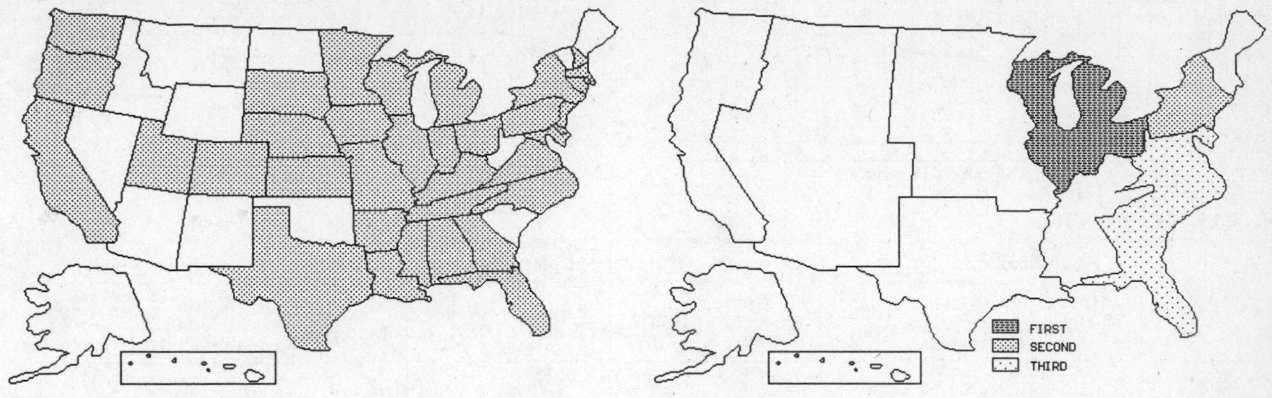

INDUSTRY DATA BY STATE

State	Establish-ments	Shipments			Employment				Cost as % of Shipments	Investment per Employee ($)
		Total ($ mil)	% of U.S.	Per Establ.	Total Number	% of U.S.	Per Establ.	Wages ($/hour)		
Illinois	55	919.4	11.6	16.7	5,700	10.8	104	13.15	56.4	5,491
Ohio	50	628.4	7.9	12.6	4,300	8.2	86	11.53	54.4	4,884
California	49	615.1	7.8	12.6	3,800	7.2	78	13.63	53.4	5,763
New York	53	460.9	5.8	8.7	3,800	7.2	72	12.21	52.1	2,447
North Carolina	25	435.7	5.5	17.4	2,900	5.5	116	11.74	50.8	4,414
Pennsylvania	48	411.5	5.2	8.6	2,900	5.5	60	11.24	55.3	2,483
Tennessee	26	344.6	4.3	13.3	2,300	4.4	88	10.62	56.1	6,478
Georgia	12	337.2	4.3	28.1	1,800	3.4	150	11.87	61.5	6,778
Virginia	10	325.7	4.1	32.6	1,800	3.4	180	13.34	59.1	7,611
Indiana	18	298.1	3.8	16.6	2,100	4.0	117	12.26	54.7	6,238
New Jersey	26	292.6	3.7	11.3	2,300	4.4	88	13.33	40.2	5,130
Wisconsin	13	282.2	3.6	21.7	1,700	3.2	131	13.83	54.0	3,294
Michigan	16	239.2	3.0	14.9	1,500	2.8	94	14.54	62.9	6,667
Massachusetts	23	205.7	2.6	8.9	1,800	3.4	78	11.31	47.1	3,556
Missouri	16	190.0	2.4	11.9	1,300	2.5	81	12.45	57.9	13,077
Texas	23	177.5	2.2	7.7	1,400	2.7	61	9.58	56.9	3,429
Connecticut	17	132.4	1.7	7.8	1,200	2.3	71	11.52	49.4	-
Colorado	5	113.9	1.4	22.8	500	0.9	100	13.37	59.0	4,800
Maryland	6	108.7	1.4	18.1	800	1.5	133	10.38	46.7	-
Kentucky	6	104.1	1.3	17.4	600	1.1	100	11.00	61.4	-
Arkansas	6	100.5	1.3	16.7	700	1.3	117	9.67	54.4	-
Alabama	10	96.7	1.2	9.7	600	1.1	60	9.23	59.6	1,500
Nebraska	5	77.8	1.0	15.6	600	1.1	120	12.25	50.9	-
Washington	6	63.1	0.8	10.5	400	0.8	67	13.71	53.2	-
Florida	7	61.7	0.8	8.8	500	0.9	71	12.12	50.7	14,200
Rhode Island	6	49.3	0.6	8.2	500	0.9	83	11.63	36.7	-
Oregon	4	30.1	0.4	7.5	200	0.4	50	11.50	55.5	-
Minnesota	17	(D)	-	-	1,750 *	3.3	103	-	-	-
Louisiana	6	(D)	-	-	750 *	1.4	125	-	-	-
Iowa	3	(D)	-	-	750 *	1.4	250	-	-	-
Kansas	3	(D)	-	-	375 *	0.7	125	-	-	-
Mississippi	3	(D)	-	-	375 *	0.7	125	-	-	-
New Hampshire	3	(D)	-	-	375 *	0.7	125	-	-	-
Utah	3	(D)	-	-	375 *	0.7	125	-	-	-
Delaware	1	(D)	-	-	175 *	0.3	175	-	-	-
South Dakota	1	(D)	-	-	175 *	0.3	175	-	-	-

Source: 1992 *Economic Census*. The states are in descending order of shipments or establishments (if shipment data are missing for the majority). The symbol (D) appears when data are withheld to prevent disclosure of competitive information. States marked with (D) are sorted by number of establishments. A dash (-) indicates that the data element cannot be calculated; * indicates the midpoint of a range.

2671 - PAPER COATED & LAMINATED, PACKAGING

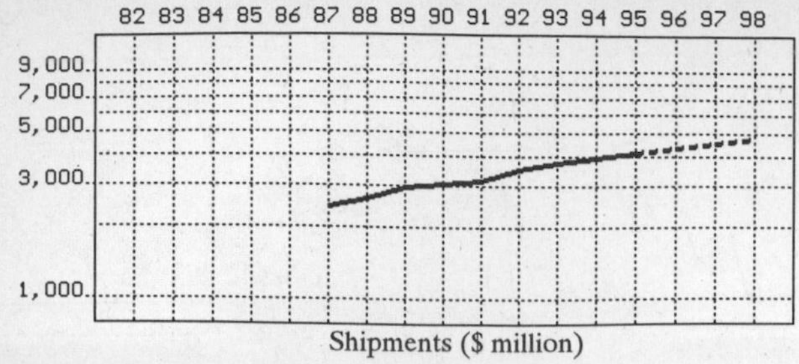

Shipments ($ million)

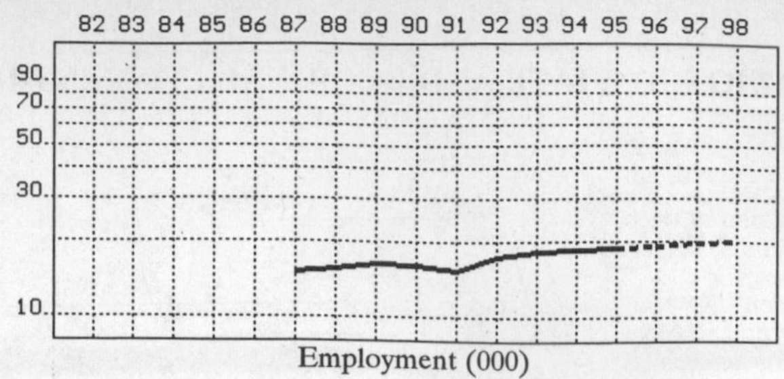

Employment (000)

GENERAL STATISTICS

Year	Companies	Establishments		Employment			Compensation		Production ($ million)			
		Total	with 20 or more employees	Total (000)	Production Workers (000)	Production Hours (Mil)	Payroll ($ mil)	Wages ($/hr)	Cost of Materials	Value Added by Manufacture	Value of Shipments	Capital Invest.
1982												
1983												
1984												
1985												
1986												
1987	89	120	111	15.0	10.4	22.0	406.2	11.53	1,442.0	997.0	2,416.0	128.3
1988		128	117	15.5	10.9	23.5	434.5	11.76	1,648.4	1,018.9	2,640.1	85.2
1989		140	117	16.3	11.3	23.7	458.3	12.05	1,845.9	1,094.6	2,938.8	113.9
1990		143	121	16.0	11.4	23.8	488.5	12.59	1,899.1	1,133.4	3,026.7	101.4
1991		164	120	15.4	11.0	24.0	492.1	12.96	1,907.0	1,261.1	3,145.8	122.7
1992	156	204	136	17.3	12.9	27.8	533.9	12.52	2,068.8	1,427.4	3,508.0	129.4
1993		234	161	18.1	13.5	29.4	574.7	12.85	2,228.5	1,505.7	3,739.1	126.0
1994		236P	153P	18.5	13.8	30.5	614.3	13.16	2,422.1	1,593.9	3,944.0	140.9
1995		254P	160P	18.7P	14.1P	31.0P	628.2P	13.43P	2,539.4P	1,671.1P	4,135.0P	137.8P
1996		273P	167P	19.1P	14.6P	32.2P	656.7P	13.65P	2,671.2P	1,757.8P	4,349.5P	142.0P
1997		291P	174P	19.6P	15.1P	33.4P	685.1P	13.87P	2,802.9P	1,844.5P	4,564.0P	146.3P
1998		310P	181P	20.1P	15.6P	34.6P	713.5P	14.09P	2,934.6P	1,931.2P	4,778.5P	150.6P

Sources: 1982, 1987, 1992 *Economic Census*; *Annual Survey of Manufactures*, 83-86, 88-91, 93-94. Establishment counts for non-Census years are from *County Business Patterns*; establishment values for 83-84 are extrapolations. 'P's show projections by the editors. Industries reclassified in 87 will not have data for prior years.

INDICES OF CHANGE

Year	Companies	Establishments		Employment			Compensation		Production ($ million)			
		Total	with 20 or more employees	Total (000)	Production Workers (000)	Production Hours (Mil)	Payroll ($ mil)	Wages ($/hr)	Cost of Materials	Value Added by Manufacture	Value of Shipments	Capital Invest.
1982												
1983												
1984												
1985												
1986												
1987	57	59	82	87	81	79	76	92	70	70	69	99
1988		63	86	90	84	85	81	94	80	71	75	66
1989		69	86	94	88	85	86	96	89	77	84	88
1990		70	89	92	88	86	91	101	92	79	86	78
1991		80	88	89	85	86	92	104	92	88	90	95
1992	100	100	100	100	100	100	100	100	100	100	100	100
1993		115	118	105	105	106	108	103	108	105	107	97
1994		116P	113P	107	107	110	115	105	117	112	112	109
1995		125P	118P	108P	109P	112P	118P	107P	123P	117P	118P	106P
1996		134P	123P	111P	113P	116P	123P	109P	129P	123P	124P	110P
1997		143P	128P	113P	117P	120P	128P	111P	135P	129P	130P	113P
1998		152P	133P	116P	121P	125P	134P	113P	142P	135P	136P	116P

Sources: Same as General Statistics. Values reflect change from the base year, 1992. Values above 100 mean greater than 92, values below 100 mean less than 92, and a value of 100 in the 82-91 or 93-98 period means same as 92. 'P's mark projections by the editors.

SELECTED RATIOS

For 1994	Avg. of All Manufact.	Analyzed Industry	Index
Employees per Establishment	49	78	160
Payroll per Establishment	1,500,273	2,604,543	174
Payroll per Employee	30,620	33,205	108
Production Workers per Establishment	34	59	170
Wages per Establishment	853,319	1,701,793	199
Wages per Production Worker	24,861	29,086	117
Hours per Production Worker	2,056	2,210	107
Wages per Hour	12.09	13.16	109
Value Added per Establishment	4,602,255	6,757,904	147
Value Added per Employee	93,930	86,157	92

For 1994	Avg. of All Manufact.	Analyzed Industry	Index
Value Added per Production Worker	134,084	115,500	86
Cost per Establishment	5,045,178	10,269,352	204
Cost per Employee	102,970	130,924	127
Cost per Production Worker	146,988	175,514	119
Shipments per Establishment	9,576,895	16,721,987	175
Shipments per Employee	195,460	213,189	109
Shipments per Production Worker	279,017	285,797	102
Investment per Establishment	321,011	597,396	186
Investment per Employee	6,552	7,616	116
Investment per Production Worker	9,352	10,210	109

Sources: Same as General Statistics. The 'Average of All Manufacturing' column represents the average of all manufacturing industries reported for the most recent complete year available. The Index shows the relationship between the Average and the Analyzed Industry. For example, 100 means that they are equal; 500 that the Analyzed Industry is five times the average; 50 means that the Analyzed Industry is half the national average. The abbreviation 'na' is used to show that data are 'not available'.

LEADING COMPANIES

Number shown: **41** Total sales ($ mil): **4,711** Total employment (000): **29.2**

Company Name	Address				CEO Name	Phone	Co. Type	Sales ($ mil)	Empl. (000)
Bemis Company Inc	222 S 9th St	Minneapolis	MN	55402	John H Roe	612-376-3000	P	1,230	7.6
Consolidated Papers Inc	PO Box 8050	Wis Rapids	WI	54495	Patrick F Brennan	715-422-3111	P	1,028	4.9
Printpack Inc	PO Box 43687	Atlanta	GA	30378	Dennis M Love	404-691-5830	R	500	2.7
Instrument Systems Corp	100 Jericho	Jericho	NY	11753	Robert Balemian	516-938-5544	P	489	4.5
Minnesota Mining & Mfg	3M Ctr	St Paul	MN	55125	Paul Ackerman	612-733-1110	D	190*	1.2
Arrow Industries Inc	PO Box 810489	Dallas	TX	75381	Steven Rosenberg	214-416-6500	S	180*	1.4
Daubert Industries Inc	1 Westbrook Corp	Westchester	IL	60154	ML Garman	708-409-5000	R	110	0.5
Hargro Packaging Corp	415 Eagleview Blv	Exton	PA	19341	John Woolford Jr	610-458-7422	S	100	0.8
Curwood Inc	PO Box 2968	Oshkosh	WI	54903	JH Curler	414-236-7300	S	75	1.2
Milprint Inc	PO Box 2968	Oshkosh	WI	54903	Tom Sall	414-236-8600	S	65	0.3
Tekra Corp	16700 W Lincoln	New Berlin	WI	53151	WG Godfrey	414-784-5533	R	62	0.2
Consolidated Papers Inc	PO Box 227	Stevens Point	WI	54481	John B Steele	715-345-8000	D	58*	0.3
Star Tex Corp	8235 220th St W	Lakeville	MN	55044	Dave Timmons	612-469-5461	S	42*	0.2
Papercon Inc	2700 Apple Val NE	Atlanta	GA	30319	Gaby Ajram	404-261-7205	R	39*	0.2
Ideal Tape Company Inc	1400 Middlesex St	Lowell	MA	01851	J Dennis Burns	508-458-6833	S	38	0.2
Central Products Co	531 N Stiles St	Linden	NJ	07036	John Powers	908-925-0900	S	36	0.2
Packaging Industries Inc	2450 Alvarado St	San Leandro	CA	94577	William Kelly	510-352-2262	S	36*	0.2
Plastic Packaging Co	PO Box 5003	Muncie	IN	47307	Robert W Armen	317-281-5000	D	33	<0.1
Minnesota Mining & Mfg	8124 Pacific Av	White City	OR	97503	Don Cady	503-826-4511	D	32*	0.2
Bonar Packaging Inc	PO Box 818	Tyler	TX	75710	Mac Eltin	903-593-1793	S	30*	0.3
Burrows Paper Corp	1722 53rd St	Fort Madison	IA	52627	John C Schuldt	319-372-4241	D	30*	0.1
Placon Corp	PO Box 8246	Madison	WI	53708	David C Boyer	608-271-5634	R	30	0.2
Superpac Inc	PO Box 189	Southampton	PA	18966	Lee Marchetti	215-322-1010	R	26*	0.1
Adchem Corp	625 Main St	Westbury	NY	11590	JJ Pufahl	516-333-3843	R	25	0.1
C and H Packaging Inc	1401 W Taylor St	Merrill	WI	54452	John Clark	715-536-5400	R	25	0.1
Cello-Pack Corp	PO Box 159	Buffalo	NY	14224	William Yardley	716-668-3111	R	24*	0.2
Worthen Industries Inc	3 E Spit Brook Rd	Nashua	NH	03060	Robert F Worthen	603-888-5443	R	24	0.2
Flex Products Inc	2793 Northpoint	Santa Rosa	CA	95407	Michael Sullivan	707-525-9200	R	23	0.1
Western Summit Mfg Corp	9120 Juniper St	Los Angeles	CA	90002	Donald Clark	213-567-1411	R	18	0.1
Zenith Specialty Bag Company	PO Box 8445	City of Industry	CA	91748	S Anderson	818-912-2481	R	16	0.1
Betham Corp	87 Lincoln Blv	Middlesex	NJ	08846	G Laurence Liedel	908-356-2870	R	15	0.1
Norpak Corp	70 Blanchard St	Newark	NJ	07105	Anthony A Coraci	201-589-4200	R	14*	0.1
Kleartone Inc	695 Summa Av	Westbury	NY	11590	Alfred W Levy	516-334-1400	R	11	<0.1
Kalex Chemical Products Inc	235 Gardner Av	Brooklyn	NY	11211	Alex Kaufman	718-417-8282	R	10*	<0.1
US Packaging Company Inc	PO Box 77057	Greensboro	NC	27417	Mark Speckman	910-852-4311	R	10*	0.1
Pioneer Paper Corp	50 Triangle Blv	Carlstadt	NJ	07072	M Gross	201-935-0123	R	9	0.2
Flexo Transparent Inc	PO Box 128	Buffalo	NY	14240	Ronald D Mabry	716-825-7710	R	8*	<0.1
Tolas Health Care	905 Pennsylvania	Feasterville	PA	19053	CD Marotta	215-322-7900	R	8	0.1
Zorn Packaging Inc	1315 Hwy 34	Farmingdale	NJ	07727	Daniel CM Crabbe	908-938-5031	R	7	<0.1
Ehrlich Manufacturing Company	102 Cabot St	Holyoke	MA	01040	Wendy Ehrlich	413-533-7141	R	4	<0.1
Arcon Coating Mills Inc	PO Box 486	Oceanside	NY	11572	David Kruft	516-766-8800	R	3	<0.1

Source: *Ward's Business Directory of U.S. Private and Public Companies*, Volumes 1 and 2, 1996. The company type code used is as follows: P - Public, R - Private, S - Subsidiary, D - Division, J - Joint Venture, A - Affiliate, G - Group. Sales are in millions of dollars, employees are in thousands. An asterisk (*) indicates an estimated sales volume. The symbol < stands for 'less than'. Company names and addresses are truncated, in some cases, to fit into the available space.

MATERIALS CONSUMED

Material		Quantity	Delivered Cost ($ million)
Materials, ingredients, containers, and supplies		(X)	1,975.5
Paper	1,000 s tons	515.9*	506.0
Plastics resins consumed in the form of granules, pellets, powders, liquids, etc.	mil lb	525.3*	330.6
Plastics products consumed in the form of sheets, rods, tubes, film, and other shapes		(X)	513.0
Aluminum foil, plain	mil lb	30.8	47.8
Glues and adhesives		(X)	47.4
Printing inks (complete formulations)	mil lb	(S)	99.3
Paperboard containers, boxes, and corrugated paperboard		(X)	29.2
All other materials and components, parts, containers, and supplies		(X)	273.0
Materials, ingredients, containers, and supplies, nsk		(X)	129.2

Source: 1992 *Economic Census*. Explanation of symbols used: (D): Withheld to avoid disclosure of competitive data; na: Not available; (S): Withheld because statistical norms were not met; (X): Not applicable; (Z): Less than half the unit shown; nec: Not elsewhere classified; nsk: Not specified by kind; - : zero; * : 10-19 percent estimated; ** : 20-29 percent estimated.

PRODUCT SHARE DETAILS

Product or Product Class	% Share
Paper coating and laminating, packaging	100.00
Single-web paper, coated rolls and sheets, including waxed, for packaging uses	23.31
Plastics-coated single-web paper, rolls and sheets, for packaging uses	40.84
Coated single-web paper (other than plastics-coated), rolls and sheets, including waxed, for packaging uses	56.30
Single-web paper, coated rolls and sheets, including waxed, for packaging uses, nsk	2.86
Coated single-web film, rolls and sheets, including coextruded, for packaging uses	28.14
Coated single-web film, rolls and sheets, for packaging uses	51.01
Coextruded single-web film, for packaging uses	45.63
Single-web film, coated rolls and sheets, including coextruded, for packaging uses, nsk	3.35
Paper/paper multiweb laminated rolls and sheets, for packaging uses	5.36
Polyethylene laminated rolls and sheets, coated, for packaging uses	35.02
Polyethylene laminated rolls and sheets, uncoated, for packaging uses	47.97
Laminated rolls and sheets for packaging uses, nsk	16.96
Multiweb laminated rolls and sheets, except paper/paper and foil, for packaging uses	38.24
Film/paper multiweb laminated rolls and sheets, for packaging uses	10.45
Polypropylene/polypropylene multiweb laminated rolls and sheets, for packaging uses	34.52
Metalized film/film laminates multiweb laminated rolls and sheets, for packaging uses	11.19
Celophane/other film multiweb laminated rolls and sheets, for packaging uses	3.33
Other film/film multiweb laminated rolls and sheets, for packaging uses	29.25
Multiweb laminated rolls and sheets, except paper/paper and foil, for packaging uses, nsk	11.27
Paper coating and laminating, packaging, nsk	4.95

Source: 1992 *Economic Census*. The values shown are percent of total shipments in an industry. Values of indented subcategories are summed in the main heading. The symbol (D) appears when data are withheld to prevent disclosure of competitive information. The abbreviation nsk stands for 'not specified by kind' and nec for 'not elsewhere classified'.

INPUTS AND OUTPUTS FOR PAPER COATING & GLAZING

Economic Sector or Industry Providing Inputs	%	Sector	Economic Sector or Industry Buying Outputs	%	Sector
Paper mills, except building paper	31.0	Manufg.	Commercial printing	7.1	Manufg.
Wholesale trade	9.8	Trade	Food preparations, nec	6.3	Manufg.
Miscellaneous plastics products	8.5	Manufg.	Exports	5.6	Foreign
Plastics materials & resins	6.8	Manufg.	Retail trade, except eating & drinking	4.7	Trade
Cyclic crudes and organics	5.2	Manufg.	Personal consumption expenditures	4.6	
Imports	4.3	Foreign	Bread, cake, & related products	4.6	Manufg.
Adhesives & sealants	3.9	Manufg.	Wholesale trade	4.6	Trade
Motor freight transportation & warehousing	2.9	Util.	Cheese, natural & processed	3.2	Manufg.
Nonwoven fabrics	2.1	Manufg.	Change in business inventories	3.0	In House
Petroleum refining	2.1	Manufg.	Condensed & evaporated milk	2.3	Manufg.
Electric services (utilities)	2.0	Util.	Cookies & crackers	2.2	Manufg.
Paperboard containers & boxes	1.9	Manufg.	Plastics materials & resins	2.2	Manufg.
Printing ink	1.4	Manufg.	Confectionery products	2.1	Manufg.
Paper coating & glazing	1.2	Manufg.	Photographic equipment & supplies	2.1	Manufg.
Gas production & distribution (utilities)	1.2	Util.	Membership organizations nec	2.0	Services
Railroads & related services	1.2	Util.	S/L Govt. purch., other general government	2.0	S/L Govt
Advertising	1.2	Services	Fruits	1.8	Agric.
Air transportation	0.9	Util.	Doctors & dentists	1.8	Services
Aluminum rolling & drawing	0.8	Manufg.	Drugs	1.7	Manufg.
Communications, except radio & TV	0.7	Util.	Real estate	1.5	Fin/R.E.
Fabricated rubber products, nec	0.6	Manufg.	S/L Govt. purch., higher education	1.4	S/L Govt
Industrial inorganic chemicals, nec	0.6	Manufg.	S/L Govt. purch., elem. & secondary education	1.3	S/L Govt
Clay, ceramic, & refractory minerals	0.5	Mining	Legal services	1.1	Services
Eating & drinking places	0.5	Trade	Ice cream & frozen desserts	1.0	Manufg.
Hotels & lodging places	0.5	Services	Labor, civic, social, & fraternal associations	1.0	Services
Paper industries machinery	0.4	Manufg.	Frozen specialties	0.9	Manufg.
Wet corn milling	0.4	Manufg.	Cigarettes	0.8	Manufg.
Banking	0.4	Fin/R.E.	Paper coating & glazing	0.8	Manufg.
Real estate	0.4	Fin/R.E.	Canned fruits & vegetables	0.7	Manufg.
Equipment rental & leasing services	0.4	Services	Cereal breakfast foods	0.7	Manufg.
Maintenance of nonfarm buildings nec	0.3	Constr.	Chewing gum	0.7	Manufg.
Broadwoven fabric mills	0.3	Manufg.	Frozen fruits, fruit juices & vegetables	0.7	Manufg.
Sanitary services, steam supply, irrigation	0.3	Util.	Meat packing plants	0.7	Manufg.
Water transportation	0.3	Util.	Eating & drinking places	0.6	Trade
Lubricating oils & greases	0.2	Manufg.	Computer & data processing services	0.6	Services
Machinery, except electrical, nec	0.2	Manufg.	Management & consulting services & labs	0.6	Services
Paints & allied products	0.2	Manufg.	Chocolate & cocoa products	0.5	Manufg.
Primary nonferrous metals, nec	0.2	Manufg.	Paperboard containers & boxes	0.5	Manufg.
Wood pallets & skids	0.2	Manufg.	S/L Govt. purch., health & hospitals	0.5	S/L Govt
Insurance carriers	0.2	Fin/R.E.	Apparel made from purchased materials	0.4	Manufg.
Automotive rental & leasing, without drivers	0.2	Services	Broadwoven fabric mills	0.4	Manufg.
Computer & data processing services	0.2	Services	Miscellaneous plastics products	0.4	Manufg.
Legal services	0.2	Services	Sausages & other prepared meats	0.4	Manufg.
Management & consulting services & labs	0.2	Services	Business services nec	0.4	Services
U.S. Postal Service	0.2	Gov't	Hotels & lodging places	0.4	Services
Noncomparable imports	0.2	Foreign	Job training & related services	0.4	Services
General industrial machinery, nec	0.1	Manufg.	Federal Government purchases, national defense	0.4	Fed Govt
Mechanical measuring devices	0.1	Manufg.	Industrial buildings	0.3	Constr.
Metal foil & leaf	0.1	Manufg.	Office buildings	0.3	Constr.
Sawmills & planning mills, general	0.1	Manufg.	Residential 1-unit structures, nonfarm	0.3	Constr.
Special dies & tools & machine tool accessories	0.1	Manufg.	Residential additions/alterations, nonfarm	0.3	Constr.

Continued on next page.

INPUTS AND OUTPUTS FOR PAPER COATING & GLAZING - Continued

Economic Sector or Industry Providing Inputs	%	Sector	Economic Sector or Industry Buying Outputs	%	Sector
Textile goods, nec	0.1	Manufg.	Canned specialties	0.3	Manufg.
Credit agencies other than banks	0.1	Fin/R.E.	Electronic components nec	0.3	Manufg.
Royalties	0.1	Fin/R.E.	Fluid milk	0.3	Manufg.
Accounting, auditing & bookkeeping	0.1	Services	Fresh or frozen packaged fish	0.3	Manufg.
Automotive repair shops & services	0.1	Services	Motor vehicles & car bodies	0.3	Manufg.
			Paper mills, except building paper	0.3	Manufg.
			Sanitary paper products	0.3	Manufg.
			Transformers	0.3	Manufg.
			Medical & health services, nec	0.3	Services
			S/L Govt. purch., other education & libraries	0.3	S/L Govt
			S/L Govt. purch., public assistance & relief	0.3	S/L Govt
			Highway & street construction	0.2	Constr.
			Blended & prepared flour	0.2	Manufg.
			Creamery butter	0.2	Manufg.
			Dehydrated food products	0.2	Manufg.
			Distilled liquor, except brandy	0.2	Manufg.
			Fabricated rubber products, nec	0.2	Manufg.
			Games, toys, & children's vehicles	0.2	Manufg.
			Industrial controls	0.2	Manufg.
			Manifold business forms	0.2	Manufg.
			Paperboard mills	0.2	Manufg.
			Polishes & sanitation goods	0.2	Manufg.
			Poultry dressing plants	0.2	Manufg.
			Roasted coffee	0.2	Manufg.
			Surgical appliances & supplies	0.2	Manufg.
			Yarn mills & finishing of textiles, nec	0.2	Manufg.
			Motor freight transportation & warehousing	0.2	Util.
			Advertising	0.2	Services
			Hospitals	0.2	Services
			Personnel supply services	0.2	Services
			Construction of hospitals	0.1	Constr.
			Construction of stores & restaurants	0.1	Constr.
			Carbon paper & inked ribbons	0.1	Manufg.
			Electronic computing equipment	0.1	Manufg.
			Floor coverings	0.1	Manufg.
			Glass & glass products, except containers	0.1	Manufg.
			Motors & generators	0.1	Manufg.
			Toilet preparations	0.1	Manufg.
			Upholstered household furniture	0.1	Manufg.
			Wood household furniture	0.1	Manufg.
			Wood products, nec	0.1	Manufg.
			Communications, except radio & TV	0.1	Util.
			Amusement & recreation services nec	0.1	Services
			Automotive rental & leasing, without drivers	0.1	Services
			Automotive repair shops & services	0.1	Services
			Motion pictures	0.1	Services
			Nursing & personal care facilities	0.1	Services
			Photofinishing labs, commercial photography	0.1	Services
			Portrait, photographic studios	0.1	Services
			Religious organizations	0.1	Services
			S/L Govt. purch., natural resource & recreation.	0.1	S/L Govt

Source: Benchmark Input-Output Accounts for the U.S. Economy, 1982, U.S. Department of Commerce, Washington, D.C., July 1991. Data, as reported in the source, are organized by the 1977 SIC structure in use in 1982 but have been matched, as closely as is possible, to the 1987 SIC structure used in this book.

OCCUPATIONS EMPLOYED BY SIC 267 - MISCELLANEOUS CONVERTED PAPER PRODUCTS

Occupation	% of Total 1994	Change to 2005	Occupation	% of Total 1994	Change to 2005
Paper goods machine setters & set-up operators	9.0	-15.9	Machine feeders & offbearers	2.5	-5.4
Machine operators nec	6.8	29.7	Industrial machinery mechanics	2.1	15.6
Hand packers & packagers	5.7	-9.9	Inspectors, testers, & graders, precision	2.1	15.6
Blue collar worker supervisors	4.5	6.8	Packaging & filling machine operators	2.1	5.1
Assemblers, fabricators, & hand workers nec	4.4	5.1	Freight, stock, & material movers, hand	2.0	-15.9
Printing press machine setters, operators	4.3	5.1	Maintenance repairers, general utility	2.0	5.1
Cutting & slicing machine setters, operators	4.0	26.1	Traffic, shipping, & receiving clerks	1.9	1.1
Sales & related workers nec	3.0	5.1	General managers & top executives	1.8	-0.3
Helpers, laborers, & material movers nec	2.9	5.1	Machine forming operators, metal & plastic	1.7	57.6
Extruding & forming machine workers	2.8	36.6	Coating, painting, & spraying machine workers	1.7	-15.9
Printing, binding, & related workers nec	2.6	5.1	Secretaries, ex legal & medical	1.6	-4.3
Industrial truck & tractor operators	2.6	5.1	Industrial production managers	1.2	5.1

Source: Industry-Occupation Matrix, Bureau of Labor Statistics. These data relate to one or more 3-digit SIC industry groups rather than to a single 4-digit SIC. The change reported for each occupation to the year 2005 is a percent of growth or decline as estimated by the Bureau of Labor Statistics. The abbreviation nec stands for 'not elsewhere classified'.

LOCATION BY STATE AND REGIONAL CONCENTRATION

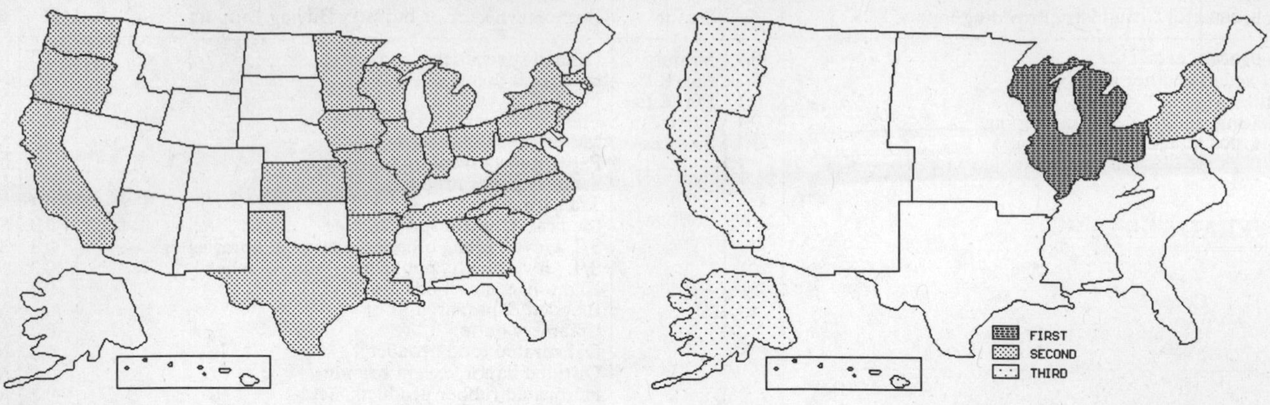

INDUSTRY DATA BY STATE

State	Establish-ments	Shipments			Employment				Cost as % of Shipments	Investment per Employee ($)
		Total ($ mil)	% of U.S.	Per Establ.	Total Number	% of U.S.	Per Establ.	Wages ($/hour)		
Wisconsin	24	859.3	24.5	35.8	3,700	21.4	154	12.42	57.5	10,000
Illinois	17	244.9	7.0	14.4	1,300	7.5	76	11.71	53.9	2,923
Georgia	9	227.9	6.5	25.3	900	5.2	100	13.47	58.6	-
Tennessee	8	204.6	5.8	25.6	1,100	6.4	138	13.08	65.4	7,727
Pennsylvania	10	175.0	5.0	17.5	1,100	6.4	110	14.92	52.6	1,818
Ohio	14	162.0	4.6	11.6	800	4.6	57	11.92	59.9	11,625
Missouri	7	150.7	4.3	21.5	800	4.6	114	12.07	61.4	8,375
California	18	146.9	4.2	8.2	1,000	5.8	56	12.43	58.4	3,600
Massachusetts	7	137.5	3.9	19.6	400	2.3	57	16.20	64.7	18,500
Indiana	9	115.6	3.3	12.8	700	4.0	78	13.92	54.1	3,857
New Jersey	7	107.6	3.1	15.4	600	3.5	86	12.36	53.4	2,667
Michigan	6	102.6	2.9	17.1	500	2.9	83	11.56	70.5	-
Texas	8	80.4	2.3	10.1	600	3.5	75	11.22	64.6	1,833
Minnesota	5	79.5	2.3	15.9	400	2.3	80	11.83	64.5	11,750
Virginia	3	67.7	1.9	22.6	300	1.7	100	12.67	67.9	2,333
North Carolina	5	55.5	1.6	11.1	300	1.7	60	14.50	53.7	16,667
New York	9	39.4	1.1	4.4	300	1.7	33	13.00	54.8	-
Arkansas	5	(D)	-	-	375 *	2.2	75	-	-	-
Iowa	3	(D)	-	-	375 *	2.2	125	-	-	-
Louisiana	3	(D)	-	-	375 *	2.2	125	-	-	-
South Carolina	3	(D)	-	-	175 *	1.0	58	-	-	-
Kansas	2	(D)	-	-	375 *	2.2	188	-	-	-
Oregon	2	(D)	-	-	375 *	2.2	188	-	-	-
Washington	2	(D)	-	-	175 *	1.0	88	-	-	-

Source: 1992 *Economic Census*. The states are in descending order of shipments or establishments (if shipment data are missing for the majority). The symbol (D) appears when data are withheld to prevent disclosure of competitive information. States marked with (D) are sorted by number of establishments. A dash (-) indicates that the data element cannot be calculated; * indicates the midpoint of a range.

2672 - PAPER COATED & LAMINATED, NEC

Shipments ($ million)

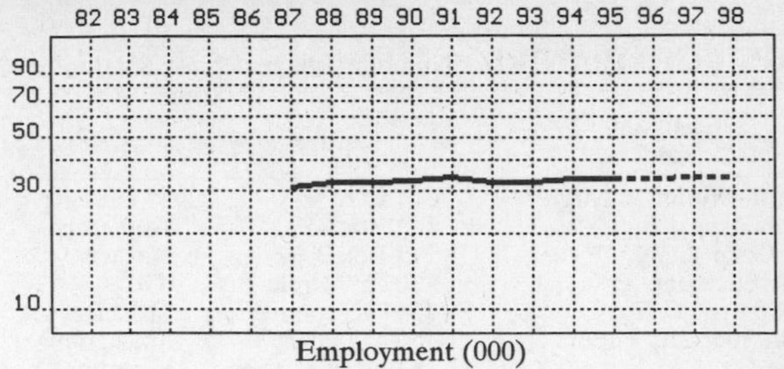

Employment (000)

GENERAL STATISTICS

Year	Companies	Establishments		Employment			Compensation		Production ($ million)			
		Total	with 20 or more employees	Total (000)	Production Workers (000)	Production Hours (Mil)	Payroll ($ mil)	Wages ($/hr)	Cost of Materials	Value Added by Manufacture	Value of Shipments	Capital Invest.
1982												
1983												
1984												
1985												
1986												
1987	362	412	226	30.9	21.1	43.5	838.7	11.55	3,034.5	2,861.4	5,891.7	201.3
1988		411	229	32.5	22.5	48.0	908.4	11.60	3,490.9	3,361.7	6,821.2	203.8
1989		412	237	32.4	24.5	51.4	973.0	11.62	3,731.1	3,419.3	7,145.1	217.1
1990		414	236	33.2	23.5	48.2	985.4	11.98	3,736.4	3,321.0	7,077.8	290.8
1991		422	237	34.2	23.1	46.8	991.5	12.29	3,951.5	3,401.1	7,381.1	243.3
1992	385	453	242	32.4	22.1	47.9	1,041.6	13.01	4,144.1	3,551.2	7,688.3	270.1
1993		451	235	32.6	22.5	48.9	1,085.8	13.61	4,275.9	3,801.2	8,071.0	209.5
1994		455P	242P	33.4	23.0	51.3	1,168.7	13.67	4,616.5	4,288.2	8,872.3	317.1
1995		463P	244P	33.7P	23.1P	50.8P	1,181.8P	13.99P	4,643.7P	4,313.5P	8,924.6P	295.1P
1996		470P	246P	33.9P	23.2P	51.3P	1,222.3P	14.34P	4,823.6P	4,480.6P	9,270.4P	306.4P
1997		478P	248P	34.2P	23.2P	51.9P	1,262.9P	14.69P	5,003.6P	4,647.7P	9,616.2P	317.7P
1998		485P	250P	34.4P	23.3P	52.5P	1,303.5P	15.04P	5,183.5P	4,814.9P	9,962.0P	329.0P

Sources: 1982, 1987, 1992 *Economic Census*; *Annual Survey of Manufactures*, 83-86, 88-91, 93-94. Establishment counts for non-Census years are from *County Business Patterns*; establishment values for 83-84 are extrapolations. 'P's show projections by the editors. Industries reclassified in 87 will not have data for prior years.

INDICES OF CHANGE

Year	Companies	Establishments		Employment			Compensation		Production ($ million)			
		Total	with 20 or more employees	Total (000)	Production Workers (000)	Production Hours (Mil)	Payroll ($ mil)	Wages ($/hr)	Cost of Materials	Value Added by Manufacture	Value of Shipments	Capital Invest.
1982												
1983												
1984												
1985												
1986												
1987	94	91	93	95	95	91	81	89	73	81	77	75
1988		91	95	100	102	100	87	89	84	95	89	75
1989		91	98	100	111	107	93	89	90	96	93	80
1990		91	98	102	106	101	95	92	90	94	92	108
1991		93	98	106	105	98	95	94	95	96	96	90
1992	100	100	100	100	100	100	100	100	100	100	100	100
1993		100	97	101	102	102	104	105	103	107	105	78
1994		100P	100P	103	104	107	112	105	111	121	115	117
1995		102P	101P	104P	104P	106P	113P	108P	112P	121P	116P	109P
1996		104P	102P	105P	105P	107P	117P	110P	116P	126P	121P	113P
1997		105P	102P	105P	105P	108P	121P	113P	121P	131P	125P	118P
1998		107P	103P	106P	105P	110P	125P	116P	125P	136P	130P	122P

Sources: Same as General Statistics. Values reflect change from the base year, 1992. Values above 100 mean greater than 92, values below 100 mean less than 92, and a value of 100 in the 82-91 or 93-98 period means same as 92. 'P's mark projections by the editors.

SELECTED RATIOS

For 1994	Avg. of All Manufact.	Analyzed Industry	Index	For 1994	Avg. of All Manufact.	Analyzed Industry	Index
Employees per Establishment	49	73	150	Value Added per Production Worker	134,084	186,443	139
Payroll per Establishment	1,500,273	2,567,765	171	Cost per Establishment	5,045,178	10,142,969	201
Payroll per Employee	30,620	34,991	114	Cost per Employee	102,970	138,219	134
Production Workers per Establishment	34	51	147	Cost per Production Worker	146,988	200,717	137
Wages per Establishment	853,319	1,540,771	181	Shipments per Establishment	9,576,895	19,493,440	204
Wages per Production Worker	24,861	30,490	123	Shipments per Employee	195,460	265,638	136
Hours per Production Worker	2,056	2,230	108	Shipments per Production Worker	279,017	385,752	138
Wages per Hour	12.09	13.67	113	Investment per Establishment	321,011	696,704	217
Value Added per Establishment	4,602,255	9,421,657	205	Investment per Employee	6,552	9,494	145
Value Added per Employee	93,930	128,389	137	Investment per Production Worker	9,352	13,787	147

Sources: Same as General Statistics. The 'Average of All Manufacturing' column represents the average of all manufacturing industries reported for the most recent complete year available. The Index shows the relationship between the Average and the Analyzed Industry. For example, 100 means that they are equal; 500 that the Analyzed Industry is five times the average; 50 means that the Analyzed Industry is half the national average. The abbreviation 'na' is used to show that data are 'not available'.

LEADING COMPANIES

Number shown: 72 Total sales ($ mil): **19,793** Total employment (000): **106.2**

Company Name	Address				CEO Name	Phone	Co. Type	Sales ($ mil)	Empl. (000)
Minnesota Mining & Mfg	3M Ctr	St Paul	MN	55144	LD DeSimone	612-733-1110	P	15,079	85.2
Appleton Papers Inc	PO Box 359	Appleton	WI	54912	Dale Schumaker	414-734-9841	S	1,200	4.0
Nashua Corp	PO Box 2002	Nashua	NH	03061	William E Mitchell	603-880-2323	P	479	3.1
TIDI Products Inc	1304 E Maple Rd	Troy	MI	48083	John Naglick Jr	313-588-2989	S	430*	0.4
Mosinee Paper Corp	1244 Kronenwetter	Mosinee	WI	54455	Daniel R Olvey	715-693-4470	P	267	1.3
Kenzacki Specialty Papers	1500 Main St	Springfield	MA	01115	R W Champigny	413-736-3216	S	140	0.3
Shurtape	PO Drawer 1530	Hickory	NC	28603	Glenn C Hilton Jr	704-322-2700	D	130	0.7
American Tape Co	317 Kendall Av	Marysville	MI	48040	JJ Choi	313-364-9000	R	120	0.5
Anchor Continental Inc	PO Drawer G	Columbia	SC	29250	Stephen J Britt	803-799-8800	S	120*	0.8
Tesa Tuck Inc	5825 Carnegie Blv	Charlotte	NC	28209	Ebbe Knudsen	704-554-0707	S	120*	0.9
Decorative Specialties Intern	1 Canal St	South Hadley	MA	01075	Anthony MacLaurin	413-533-0699	S	100	0.6
Kanzaki Specialty Papers Inc	PO Box 2002	Ware	MA	01082	Robert Champigvy	413-967-6204	S	100	0.3
Stora Newton Falls Inc	PO Box 253	Newton Falls	NY	13666	Dennis Bunnell	315-848-3321	S	100	0.5
Manco Inc	830 Canterbury Rd	Westlake	OH	44145	Jack Kahl Jr	216-892-4505	R	85	0.2
Otis Specialty Papers Inc	PO Box 10	Jay	ME	04239	Charles F Miller	207-897-7200	S	83	0.3
MPI Label Systems	PO Box 70	Sebring	OH	44672	Donald McDaniel	216-938-2134	R	80	0.5
DRG Medical Packaging Inc	1919 S Butterfield	Mundelein	IL	60060	Rob Gluskin	708-362-9000	S	75*	0.4
Fortifiber Corp	4489 Bandini Blv	Los Angeles	CA	90023	GS Yount	213-268-6783	R	70	0.3
Riverside Paper Corp	PO Box 175	Appleton	WI	54912	Harold J Bergman	414-789-2222	R	70	0.5
Epsen Hillmer Graphics Co	511 N 20th St	Omaha	NE	68102	Gary Thrasher	402-342-7000	R	54	0.4
Fasson Specialty	9292 9th St	R Cucamonga	CA	91730	Ronald F Kishen	909-987-4631	D	50	0.1
Hazen Paper Co	PO Box 189	Holyoke	MA	01041	RB Hazen	413-538-8204	R	46	0.2
Fitchburg Coated Products Inc	PO Box 1106	Scranton	PA	18510	Curtis Clarke	717-347-2035	S	40	0.3
Sekisui TA Industries Inc	7089 Belgrave Av	Garden Grove	CA	92641	Marty Tanaka	714-898-0344	D	40	0.2
Holland Manufacturing	15 Main St	Succasunna	NJ	07876	John A Holland	201-584-8141	R	39	0.3
Duralam Inc	PO Box 862	Appleton	WI	54912	Marv Schneider	414-734-6698	S	35*	0.2
Label Art Inc	1 Riverside Way	Wilton	NH	03086	Thomas Cobery	603-654-6131	S	35	0.3
Bomarko Inc	PO Box K	Plymouth	IN	46563	J D Azzar	219-936-9901	R	34*	0.2
Venture Tape Corp	30 Commerce Rd	Rockland	MA	02370	Lewis S Cohen	617-331-5900	R	32	0.1
Data Documents Inc	3403 Dan Morton	Dallas	TX	75236	A Plejdrup	214-296-0567	D	32*	0.1
Fiberesin Industries Inc	PO Box 88	Oconomowoc	WI	53066	LD Starkweather	414-567-4427	R	31	0.3
Tape Inc	PO Box 11067	Green Bay	WI	54307	Ken Glowacki	414-499-0601	R	31	0.1
TimeMed Labeling Systems Inc	144 Tower Dr	Burr Ridge	IL	60521	J Nerad	708-986-1800	R	31	0.2
Custom Tapes Inc	7125 W Gunnison	Harwood H	IL	60656	Joesph J Palmer	708-867-6060	R	27*	0.1
Crowell Corp	PO Box 3227	Newport	DE	19804	HB Adelman	302-998-0557	R	25	0.2
Media Design Corp	29350ephenson Hwy	Madison H	MI	48071	B Campbell	810-691-9100	D	25	<0.1
Rexford Paper Company	PO Box 411	Milwaukee	WI	53201	William J Filo	414-352-1221	D	25	<0.1
ADM Corp	100 Lincoln Blv	Middlesex	NJ	08846	William N Burnett	908-469-0900	R	24	0.1
CFC International	500 State St	Chicago Hts	IL	60411	RF Hruby	708-891-3456	R	24	0.2
Salem Label Company Inc	PO Box 39	Salem	OH	44460	B Anderson II	216-332-1591	R	24	0.2
Drug Package Inc	901ug Package Ln	O'Fallon	MO	63366	Mike Greco	314-272-6261	R	22*	0.1
Excello Specialty Co	4495 Cranwood	Cleveland	OH	44128	WR Jones	216-581-2600	R	20	0.2
Best Label Company Inc	13260 Moore St	Cerritos	CA	90703	Don Ingle	310-926-1432	R	19	0.1
RJM Manufacturing Inc	1626 Bridgewater	Bensalem	PA	19020	TJ Dodd	215-245-1800	R	17	<0.1
Celia Corp	320 Union St	Sparta	MI	49345	J Clay	616-887-7387	R	15	0.1
General Formulations	320 S Union St	Sparta	MI	49345	J Clay	616-887-7387	D	15	0.1
Highland Supply Corp	1111 6th St	Highland	IL	62249	Donald E Weder	618-654-2161	R	12*	0.2
Paper Coating Co	3536 E Medford St	Los Angeles	CA	90063	A Levine	213-264-2222	R	12*	<0.1
Adhesive Products Inc	520 Cleveland Av	Albany	CA	94710	Paul C Shattuck	510-526-7616	R	10	<0.1
Computype Inc	2285 W County C	St Paul	MN	55113	William E Roach	612-633-0633	R	10	0.1
Deluxe Packages	800 N Walton Av	Yuba City	CA	95993	Mark Williams	916-671-9000	D	10*	<0.1
Permalite Repromedia Corp	230 E Alondra Blv	Gardena	CA	90248	David J Morrison	310-327-0244	R	8	<0.1
Fibre Leather Mfg Corp	686 Belleville Av	New Bedford	MA	02745	Louis D Finger	508-997-4557	R	7	<0.1
Handy Wacks Corp	PO Box 26	Sparta	MI	49345	H Fairchild	616-887-8268	R	7*	<0.1
Laminated Papers Inc	54 Winter St	Holyoke	MA	01040	Bernard L Adams	413-533-3906	R	6	<0.1
Avon Tape Inc	PO Box 1423	Brockton	MA	02403	H Shuman	508-584-8273	R	5	<0.1
Universal Label Printers Inc	12521 McCann Dr	Santa Fe Sprgs	CA	90670	Francis T Mulcahey	310-944-0234	R	5*	<0.1
Blue Ribbon Label Corp	241 Hudson St	Hackensack	NJ	07601	Frances Reichman	201-489-6003	R	4	<0.1
Finite Industries Inc	746 Gotham Pkwy	Carlstadt	NJ	07072	Robert Freidenrich	201-939-0565	R	4*	<0.1
Markal Finishing Corp	400 Bostwick Av	Bridgeport	CT	06605	Craig Sanden	203-384-8219	R	4*	<0.1
Alcop Adhesive Label Co	826 Perkins Ln	Beverly	NJ	08010	W P Webster Jr	609-871-4400	R	3	<0.1
Alfax Paper and Engineering Co	35 Washington St	Westborough	MA	01581	Arnold Kraft	508-366-8227	S	3	<0.1
Dielectric Polymers Inc	218 Race St	Holyoke	MA	01040	Lawrence G Kuntz	413-532-3288	S	3	<0.1
Hurst Labeling Systems Inc	PO Box 6903	Burbank	CA	91510	Sam Allenburg	818-842-9370	R	3	<0.1
JL Darling Corp	2212 Port Tacoma	Tacoma	WA	98421	Scott E Silver	206-383-1714	R	3	<0.1
Mask-Off Company Inc	PO Box 1148	Monrovia	CA	91017	Steve B Sites	818-359-3261	R	3	<0.1
Penmar Industries Inc	1 Bates Ct	Norwalk	CT	06854	Tony Soegaard	203-853-4868	R	3	<0.1
Thomas Tape Co	PO Box 207	Springfield	OH	45501	Robert E Schwartz	513-325-6414	S	3	<0.1
Scioto Sign Company Inc	PO Box 110	Kenton	OH	43326	BA Lange	419-673-1261	R	3	<0.1
Evergreen Solutions Inc	550 39th Av NE	Minneapolis	MN	55421	Daniel L Hanlon	612-944-9080	R	1*	<0.1
Keller Ticket Co	89 Dell Glen Av	Lodi	NJ	07644	Robert Mazzella	201-472-8950	R	1*	<0.1
Keystone Packaging Service	555 Warren St	Phillipsburg	NJ	08865	John Schoeneck	908-454-8567	R	1	<0.1

Source: *Ward's Business Directory of U.S. Private and Public Companies*, Volumes 1 and 2, 1996. The company type code used is as follows: P - Public, R - Private, S - Subsidiary, D - Division, J - Joint Venture, A - Affiliate, G - Group. Sales are in millions of dollars, employees are in thousands. An asterisk (*) indicates an estimated sales volume. The symbol < stands for 'less than'. Company names and addresses are truncated, in some cases, to fit into the available space.

MATERIALS CONSUMED

Material		Quantity	Delivered Cost ($ million)
Materials, ingredients, containers, and supplies		(X)	3,866.7
Paper	1,000 s tons	1,421.9**	1,526.0
Plastics resins consumed in the form of granules, pellets, powders, liquids, etc.	mil lb	(S)	192.4
Plastics products consumed in the form of sheets, rods, tubes, film, and other shapes		(X)	178.3
Aluminum foil, plain	mil lb	(S)	22.4
Glues and adhesives		(X)	329.0
Printing inks (complete formulations)	mil lb	(S)	33.2
Paperboard containers, boxes, and corrugated paperboard		(X)	90.5
All other materials and components, parts, containers, and supplies		(X)	1,015.5
Materials, ingredients, containers, and supplies, nsk		(X)	479.3

Source: 1992 *Economic Census*. Explanation of symbols used: (D): Withheld to avoid disclosure of competitive data; na: Not available; (S): Withheld because statistical norms were not met; (X): Not applicable; (Z): Less than half the unit shown; nec: Not elsewhere classified; nsk: Not specified by kind; - : zero; * : 10-19 percent estimated; ** : 20-29 percent estimated.

PRODUCT SHARE DETAILS

Product or Product Class	% Share
Paper coating and laminating, nec	100.00
Printing paper, coated at establishments other than where paper was produced	3.22
Printing paper, coated one side (for labels and similar uses), coated at establishments other than where paper was produced	41.74
Printing paper, coated two sides (for printing of magazines, directories, catalogs, and similar uses), coated at establishments other than where paper was produced	55.87
Printing paper coated at establishments other than where paper was produced, nsk	2.43
Gummed paper products	3.19
Gummed sealing tape, paper base and reinforced base, used for sealing and securing	66.08
Other gummed paper products, including flat gummed papers, unprinted stock labels, corrugators' kraft tapes, etc.	26.11
Gummed products, nsk	7.82
Pressure-sensitive products	64.09
Single-faced tape, paper backing, excluding electrical	11.44
Single-faced tape, cloth backing, excluding surgical and electrical	2.69
Single-faced tape, film backing, electrical	25.07
Single-faced tape, electrical, all backings (except rubber)	4.26
Single-faced tape, reinforced and laminated, all backings, except surgical and rubber-backed	2.52
Single-faced tape, other, excluding surgical and rubber-backed	2.26
Double-faced tape, excluding surgical and rubber-backed	4.80
Labels, unprinted	5.33
Base stock for labels	25.65
Base stock for other than labels	2.06
Other pressure-sensitive products, not elsewhere classified, unprinted	6.79
Pressure-sensitive products, nsk	7.14
Other coated and processed papers, except for packaging uses	20.43
Processed papers (embossed, leatherette, etc.), except for packaging uses	3.45
Waxed and wax-laminated paper for nonpackaging uses, including household	8.10
Plastics-coated paper, except for packaging uses	4.65
Carbonless paper, coated at establishments other than where paper was produced	76.04
Other coated and processed papers, except for packaging uses, nsk	7.76
Paper coating and laminating, nec, nsk	9.07

Source: 1992 *Economic Census*. The values shown are percent of total shipments in an industry. Values of indented subcategories are summed in the main heading. The symbol (D) appears when data are withheld to prevent disclosure of competitive information. The abbreviation nsk stands for 'not specified by kind' and nec for 'not elsewhere classified'.

INPUTS AND OUTPUTS FOR PAPER COATING & GLAZING

Economic Sector or Industry Providing Inputs	%	Sector	Economic Sector or Industry Buying Outputs	%	Sector
Paper mills, except building paper	31.0	Manufg.	Commercial printing	7.1	Manufg.
Wholesale trade	9.8	Trade	Food preparations, nec	6.3	Manufg.
Miscellaneous plastics products	8.5	Manufg.	Exports	5.6	Foreign
Plastics materials & resins	6.8	Manufg.	Retail trade, except eating & drinking	4.7	Trade
Cyclic crudes and organics	5.2	Manufg.	Personal consumption expenditures	4.6	
Imports	4.3	Foreign	Bread, cake, & related products	4.6	Manufg.
Adhesives & sealants	3.9	Manufg.	Wholesale trade	4.6	Trade
Motor freight transportation & warehousing	2.9	Util.	Cheese, natural & processed	3.2	Manufg.
Nonwoven fabrics	2.1	Manufg.	Change in business inventories	3.0	In House
Petroleum refining	2.1	Manufg.	Condensed & evaporated milk	2.3	Manufg.
Electric services (utilities)	2.0	Util.	Cookies & crackers	2.2	Manufg.
Paperboard containers & boxes	1.9	Manufg.	Plastics materials & resins	2.2	Manufg.
Printing ink	1.4	Manufg.	Confectionery products	2.1	Manufg.
Paper coating & glazing	1.2	Manufg.	Photographic equipment & supplies	2.1	Manufg.
Gas production & distribution (utilities)	1.2	Util.	Membership organizations nec	2.0	Services
Railroads & related services	1.2	Util.	S/L Govt. purch., other general government	2.0	S/L Govt
Advertising	1.2	Services	Fruits	1.8	Agric.
Air transportation	0.9	Util.	Doctors & dentists	1.8	Services
Aluminum rolling & drawing	0.8	Manufg.	Drugs	1.7	Manufg.
Communications, except radio & TV	0.7	Util.	Real estate	1.5	Fin/R.E.
Fabricated rubber products, nec	0.6	Manufg.	S/L Govt. purch., higher education	1.4	S/L Govt
Industrial inorganic chemicals, nec	0.6	Manufg.	S/L Govt. purch., elem. & secondary education	1.3	S/L Govt
Clay, ceramic, & refractory minerals	0.5	Mining	Legal services	1.1	Services
Eating & drinking places	0.5	Trade	Ice cream & frozen desserts	1.0	Manufg.

Continued on next page.

INPUTS AND OUTPUTS FOR PAPER COATING & GLAZING - Continued

Economic Sector or Industry Providing Inputs	%	Sector
Hotels & lodging places	0.5	Services
Paper industries machinery	0.4	Manufg.
Wet corn milling	0.4	Manufg.
Banking	0.4	Fin/R.E.
Real estate	0.4	Fin/R.E.
Equipment rental & leasing services	0.4	Services
Maintenance of nonfarm buildings nec	0.3	Constr.
Broadwoven fabric mills	0.3	Manufg.
Sanitary services, steam supply, irrigation	0.3	Util.
Water transportation	0.3	Util.
Lubricating oils & greases	0.2	Manufg.
Machinery, except electrical, nec	0.2	Manufg.
Paints & allied products	0.2	Manufg.
Primary nonferrous metals, nec	0.2	Manufg.
Wood pallets & skids	0.2	Manufg.
Insurance carriers	0.2	Fin/R.E.
Automotive rental & leasing, without drivers	0.2	Services
Computer & data processing services	0.2	Services
Legal services	0.2	Services
Management & consulting services & labs	0.2	Services
U.S. Postal Service	0.2	Gov't
Noncomparable imports	0.2	Foreign
General industrial machinery, nec	0.1	Manufg.
Mechanical measuring devices	0.1	Manufg.
Metal foil & leaf	0.1	Manufg.
Sawmills & planning mills, general	0.1	Manufg.
Special dies & tools & machine tool accessories	0.1	Manufg.
Textile goods, nec	0.1	Manufg.
Credit agencies other than banks	0.1	Fin/R.E.
Royalties	0.1	Fin/R.E.
Accounting, auditing & bookkeeping	0.1	Services
Automotive repair shops & services	0.1	Services

Economic Sector or Industry Buying Outputs	%	Sector
Labor, civic, social, & fraternal associations	1.0	Services
Frozen specialties	0.9	Manufg.
Cigarettes	0.8	Manufg.
Paper coating & glazing	0.8	Manufg.
Canned fruits & vegetables	0.7	Manufg.
Cereal breakfast foods	0.7	Manufg.
Chewing gum	0.7	Manufg.
Frozen fruits, fruit juices & vegetables	0.7	Manufg.
Meat packing plants	0.7	Manufg.
Eating & drinking places	0.6	Trade
Computer & data processing services	0.6	Services
Management & consulting services & labs	0.6	Services
Chocolate & cocoa products	0.5	Manufg.
Paperboard containers & boxes	0.5	Manufg.
S/L Govt. purch., health & hospitals	0.5	S/L Govt
Apparel made from purchased materials	0.4	Manufg.
Broadwoven fabric mills	0.4	Manufg.
Miscellaneous plastics products	0.4	Manufg.
Sausages & other prepared meats	0.4	Manufg.
Business services nec	0.4	Services
Hotels & lodging places	0.4	Services
Job training & related services	0.4	Services
Federal Government purchases, national defense	0.4	Fed Govt
Industrial buildings	0.3	Constr.
Office buildings	0.3	Constr.
Residential 1-unit structures, nonfarm	0.3	Constr.
Residential additions/alterations, nonfarm	0.3	Constr.
Canned specialties	0.3	Manufg.
Electronic components nec	0.3	Manufg.
Fluid milk	0.3	Manufg.
Fresh or frozen packaged fish	0.3	Manufg.
Motor vehicles & car bodies	0.3	Manufg.
Paper mills, except building paper	0.3	Manufg.
Sanitary paper products	0.3	Manufg.
Transformers	0.3	Manufg.
Medical & health services, nec	0.3	Services
S/L Govt. purch., other education & libraries	0.3	S/L Govt
S/L Govt. purch., public assistance & relief	0.3	S/L Govt
Highway & street construction	0.2	Constr.
Blended & prepared flour	0.2	Manufg.
Creamery butter	0.2	Manufg.
Dehydrated food products	0.2	Manufg.
Distilled liquor, except brandy	0.2	Manufg.
Fabricated rubber products, nec	0.2	Manufg.
Games, toys, & children's vehicles	0.2	Manufg.
Industrial controls	0.2	Manufg.
Manifold business forms	0.2	Manufg.
Paperboard mills	0.2	Manufg.
Polishes & sanitation goods	0.2	Manufg.
Poultry dressing plants	0.2	Manufg.
Roasted coffee	0.2	Manufg.
Surgical appliances & supplies	0.2	Manufg.
Yarn mills & finishing of textiles, nec	0.2	Manufg.
Motor freight transportation & warehousing	0.2	Util.
Advertising	0.2	Services
Hospitals	0.2	Services
Personnel supply services	0.2	Services
Construction of hospitals	0.1	Constr.
Construction of stores & restaurants	0.1	Constr.
Carbon paper & inked ribbons	0.1	Manufg.
Electronic computing equipment	0.1	Manufg.
Floor coverings	0.1	Manufg.
Glass & glass products, except containers	0.1	Manufg.
Motors & generators	0.1	Manufg.
Toilet preparations	0.1	Manufg.
Upholstered household furniture	0.1	Manufg.
Wood household furniture	0.1	Manufg.
Wood products, nec	0.1	Manufg.
Communications, except radio & TV	0.1	Util.
Amusement & recreation services nec	0.1	Services
Automotive rental & leasing, without drivers	0.1	Services
Automotive repair shops & services	0.1	Services
Motion pictures	0.1	Services
Nursing & personal care facilities	0.1	Services
Photofinishing labs, commercial photography	0.1	Services

Continued on next page.

INPUTS AND OUTPUTS FOR PAPER COATING & GLAZING - Continued

Economic Sector or Industry Providing Inputs	%	Sector	Economic Sector or Industry Buying Outputs	%	Sector
			Portrait, photographic studios	0.1	Services
			Religious organizations	0.1	Services
			S/L Govt. purch., natural resource & recreation.	0.1	S/L Govt

Source: Benchmark Input-Output Accounts for the U.S. Economy, 1982, U.S. Department of Commerce, Washington, D.C., July 1991. Data, as reported in the source, are organized by the 1977 SIC structure in use in 1982 but have been matched, as closely as is possible, to the 1987 SIC structure used in this book.

OCCUPATIONS EMPLOYED BY SIC 267 - MISCELLANEOUS CONVERTED PAPER PRODUCTS

Occupation	% of Total 1994	Change to 2005	Occupation	% of Total 1994	Change to 2005
Paper goods machine setters & set-up operators	9.0	-15.9	Machine feeders & offbearers	2.5	-5.4
Machine operators nec	6.8	29.7	Industrial machinery mechanics	2.1	15.6
Hand packers & packagers	5.7	-9.9	Inspectors, testers, & graders, precision	2.1	15.6
Blue collar worker supervisors	4.5	6.8	Packaging & filling machine operators	2.1	5.1
Assemblers, fabricators, & hand workers nec	4.4	5.1	Freight, stock, & material movers, hand	2.0	-15.9
Printing press machine setters, operators	4.3	5.1	Maintenance repairers, general utility	2.0	5.1
Cutting & slicing machine setters, operators	4.0	26.1	Traffic, shipping, & receiving clerks	1.9	1.1
Sales & related workers nec	3.0	5.1	General managers & top executives	1.8	-0.3
Helpers, laborers, & material movers nec	2.9	5.1	Machine forming operators, metal & plastic	1.7	57.6
Extruding & forming machine workers	2.8	36.6	Coating, painting, & spraying machine workers	1.7	-15.9
Printing, binding, & related workers nec	2.6	5.1	Secretaries, ex legal & medical	1.6	-4.3
Industrial truck & tractor operators	2.6	5.1	Industrial production managers	1.2	5.1

Source: *Industry-Occupation Matrix*, Bureau of Labor Statistics. These data relate to one or more 3-digit SIC industry groups rather than to a single 4-digit SIC. The change reported for each occupation to the year 2005 is a percent of growth or decline as estimated by the Bureau of Labor Statistics. The abbreviation nec stands for 'not elsewhere classified'.

LOCATION BY STATE AND REGIONAL CONCENTRATION

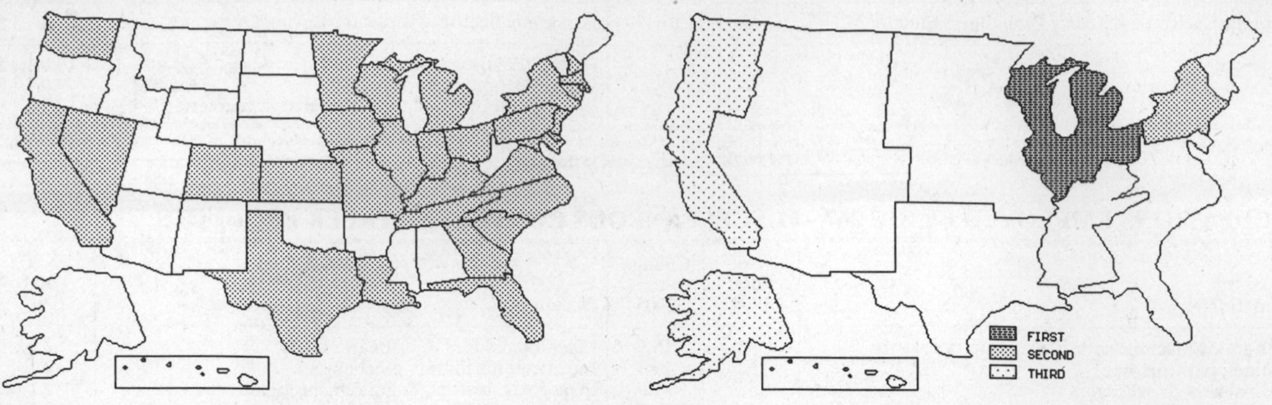

INDUSTRY DATA BY STATE

State	Establish-ments	Shipments			Employment				Cost as % of Shipments	Investment per Employee ($)
		Total ($ mil)	% of U.S.	Per Establ.	Total Number	% of U.S.	Per Establ.	Wages ($/hour)		
Pennsylvania	30	821.3	10.7	27.4	2,700	8.3	90	14.48	57.5	15,741
Wisconsin	24	804.4	10.5	33.5	2,800	8.6	117	13.76	59.4	12,286
Ohio	37	779.0	10.1	21.1	3,000	9.3	81	12.31	57.6	4,067
Illinois	33	689.8	9.0	20.9	3,200	9.9	97	14.15	44.3	3,406
New Jersey	29	367.8	4.8	12.7	2,100	6.5	72	12.33	60.0	6,000
Massachusetts	32	340.2	4.4	10.6	2,200	6.8	69	14.46	48.3	4,364
California	48	291.7	3.8	6.1	2,200	6.8	46	12.78	51.7	4,182
Indiana	10	283.0	3.7	28.3	800	2.5	80	12.71	66.1	7,125
New York	31	271.0	3.5	8.7	1,300	4.0	42	12.74	56.8	6,769
Georgia	10	207.0	2.7	20.7	500	1.5	50	14.33	59.2	7,200
North Carolina	10	179.5	2.3	18.0	1,000	3.1	100	8.79	64.0	2,200
Michigan	9	135.5	1.8	15.1	800	2.5	89	12.09	50.2	8,375
Virginia	7	110.2	1.4	15.7	300	0.9	43	11.25	61.2	-
Texas	20	81.5	1.1	4.1	400	1.2	20	12.40	54.0	3,000
Missouri	9	55.0	0.7	6.1	400	1.2	44	9.00	64.2	3,000
Rhode Island	6	52.0	0.7	8.7	300	0.9	50	11.25	54.8	5,000
Connecticut	10	50.7	0.7	5.1	300	0.9	30	9.67	50.3	3,000
Colorado	3	39.1	0.5	13.0	200	0.6	67	12.00	70.6	-
Nevada	4	29.7	0.4	7.4	200	0.6	50	9.67	78.5	8,000
Washington	9	28.2	0.4	3.1	100	0.3	11	11.50	58.5	5,000
Maryland	6	18.1	0.2	3.0	200	0.6	33	8.33	47.0	4,000
Minnesota	13	(D)	-	-	3,750 *	11.6	288	-	-	-
Florida	8	(D)	-	-	175 *	0.5	22	-	-	3,429
Tennessee	8	(D)	-	-	175 *	0.5	22	-	-	-
Kentucky	6	(D)	-	-	1,750 *	5.4	292	-	-	-
Iowa	5	(D)	-	-	750 *	2.3	150	-	-	-
New Hampshire	5	(D)	-	-	750 *	2.3	150	-	-	-
South Carolina	4	(D)	-	-	1,750 *	5.4	438	-	-	-
Kansas	3	(D)	-	-	175 *	0.5	58	-	-	-
Louisiana	3	(D)	-	-	175 *	0.5	58	-	-	-
Delaware	1	(D)	-	-	175 *	0.5	175	-	-	-

Source: 1992 *Economic Census*. The states are in descending order of shipments or establishments (if shipment data are missing for the majority). The symbol (D) appears when data are withheld to prevent disclosure of competitive information. States marked with (D) are sorted by number of establishments. A dash (-) indicates that the data element cannot be calculated; * indicates the midpoint of a range.

2673 - BAGS: PLASTIC, LAMINATED, & COATED

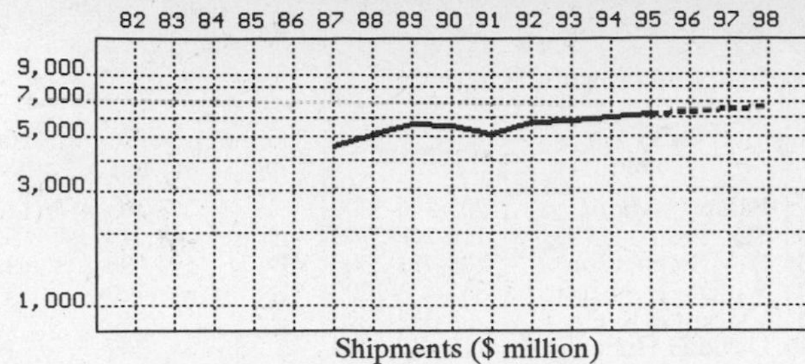

Shipments ($ million)

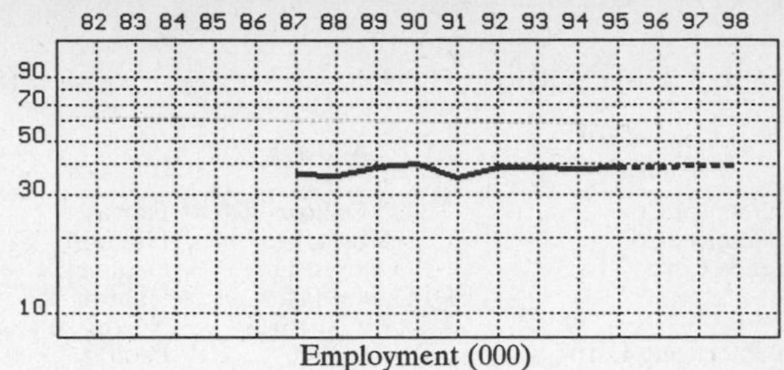

Employment (000)

GENERAL STATISTICS

Year	Companies	Establishments Total	Establishments with 20 or more employees	Employment Total (000)	Production Workers (000)	Production Hours (Mil)	Compensation Payroll ($ mil)	Compensation Wages ($/hr)	Cost of Materials	Value Added by Manufacture	Value of Shipments	Capital Invest.
1982												
1983												
1984												
1985												
1986												
1987	414	483	301	36.6	29.0	59.8	783.7	9.07	2,367.6	2,215.0	4,576.9	199.1
1988		463	300	36.2	29.3	61.1	790.1	9.07	2,746.7	2,349.0	5,058.0	201.6
1989		467	311	38.8	31.4	65.6	882.1	9.47	3,024.3	2,682.7	5,646.3	219.2
1990		460	309	39.9	30.0	63.7	869.9	9.60	2,870.3	2,625.1	5,494.6	213.1
1991		462	295	35.4	28.5	61.0	875.1	10.18	2,685.8	2,364.3	5,083.6	178.3
1992	458	521	306	38.7	30.5	64.7	988.7	10.41	2,871.4	2,853.7	5,708.2	185.6
1993		515	321	39.4	31.0	66.6	1,016.6	10.40	3,004.4	2,786.8	5,813.3	226.6
1994		511P	314P	38.1	30.0	64.6	1,046.4	10.68	3,173.9	2,870.8	6,019.9	215.1
1995		519P	316P	39.0P	30.6P	66.4P	1,083.2P	11.00P	3,245.9P	2,935.9P	6,156.5P	210.3P
1996		526P	318P	39.3P	30.7P	67.0P	1,122.4P	11.26P	3,331.6P	3,013.4P	6,319.0P	211.5P
1997		533P	320P	39.6P	30.8P	67.7P	1,161.7P	11.51P	3,417.3P	3,090.9P	6,481.5P	212.7P
1998		541P	322P	39.8P	31.0P	68.4P	1,200.9P	11.76P	3,503.0P	3,168.4P	6,644.0P	213.9P

Sources: 1982, 1987, 1992 *Economic Census*; *Annual Survey of Manufactures*, 83-86, 88-91, 93-94. Establishment counts for non-Census years are from *County Business Patterns*; establishment values for 83-84 are extrapolations. 'P's show projections by the editors. Industries reclassified in 87 will not have data for prior years.

INDICES OF CHANGE

Year	Companies	Establishments Total	Establishments with 20 or more employees	Employment Total (000)	Production Workers (000)	Production Hours (Mil)	Compensation Payroll ($ mil)	Compensation Wages ($/hr)	Cost of Materials	Value Added by Manufacture	Value of Shipments	Capital Invest.
1982												
1983												
1984												
1985												
1986												
1987	90	93	98	95	95	92	79	87	82	78	80	107
1988		89	98	94	96	94	80	87	96	82	89	109
1989		90	102	100	103	101	89	91	105	94	99	118
1990		88	101	103	98	98	88	92	100	92	96	115
1991		89	96	91	93	94	89	98	94	83	89	96
1992	100	100	100	100	100	100	100	100	100	100	100	100
1993		99	105	102	102	103	103	100	105	98	102	122
1994		98P	103P	98	98	100	106	103	111	101	105	116
1995		100P	103P	101P	100P	103P	110P	106P	113P	103P	108P	113P
1996		101P	104P	102P	101P	104P	114P	108P	116P	106P	111P	114P
1997		102P	105P	102P	101P	105P	117P	111P	119P	108P	114P	115P
1998		104P	105P	103P	102P	106P	121P	113P	122P	111P	116P	115P

Sources: Same as General Statistics. Values reflect change from the base year, 1992. Values above 100 mean greater than 92, values below 100 mean less than 92, and a value of 100 in the 82-91 or 93-98 period means same as 92. 'P's mark projections by the editors.

SELECTED RATIOS

For 1994	Avg. of All Manufact.	Analyzed Industry	Index	For 1994	Avg. of All Manufact.	Analyzed Industry	Index
Employees per Establishment	49	75	152	Value Added per Production Worker	134,084	95,693	71
Payroll per Establishment	1,500,273	2,047,177	136	Cost per Establishment	5,045,178	6,209,419	123
Payroll per Employee	30,620	27,465	90	Cost per Employee	102,970	83,304	81
Production Workers per Establishment	34	59	171	Cost per Production Worker	146,988	105,797	72
Wages per Establishment	853,319	1,349,775	158	Shipments per Establishment	9,576,895	11,777,334	123
Wages per Production Worker	24,861	22,998	93	Shipments per Employee	195,460	158,003	81
Hours per Production Worker	2,056	2,153	105	Shipments per Production Worker	279,017	200,663	72
Wages per Hour	12.09	10.68	88	Investment per Establishment	321,011	420,822	131
Value Added per Establishment	4,602,255	5,616,434	122	Investment per Employee	6,552	5,646	86
Value Added per Employee	93,930	75,349	80	Investment per Production Worker	9,352	7,170	77

Sources: Same as General Statistics. The 'Average of All Manufacturing' column represents the average of all manufacturing industries reported for the most recent complete year available. The Index shows the relationship between the Average and the Analyzed Industry. For example, 100 means that they are equal; 500 that the Analyzed Industry is five times the average; 50 means that the Analyzed Industry is half the national average. The abbreviation 'na' is used to show that data are 'not available'.

LEADING COMPANIES

Number shown: 55 Total sales ($ mil): **8,407** Total employment (000): **34.3**

Company Name	Address				CEO Name	Phone	Co. Type	Sales ($ mil)	Empl. (000)
Mobil Chemical Co	3225 Gallows Rd	Fairfax	VA	22037	Philip W Matos	703-846-3000	S	3,408	11.8
Mobil Chemical Co	1159 Pittsford	Pittsford	NY	14534	SD Pryor	716-248-5700	D	1,719	5.5
First Brands Corp	PO Box 1911	Danbury	CT	06813	W V Stephenson	203-731-2300	P	1,086	3.7
Cryovac	PO Box 464	Duncan	SC	29334	William B Sturgis	803-433-2000	D	720*	3.5
Scholle Corp	200 W North Av	Northlake	IL	60164	Vincent E Keefe	708-562-7290	R	250*	1.2
Graphic Packaging Corp	PO Box 500	Paoli	PA	19301	David H Hofmann	215-647-0500	S	209	1.0
North American Plastics Corp	921 Industrial Dr	Aurora	IL	60506	Gary Kerlagon	708-896-6200	R	115	0.8
Heritage Bag Co	4434 McEwen Rd	Dallas	TX	75244	Carl Allen	214-233-6130	R	90	0.4
Webster Industries Inc	58 Pulaski St	Peabody	MA	01960	Ron Casty	508-532-2000	S	80	0.6
Himolene Inc	PO Box 1911	Danbury	CT	06813	Paul T Hart	203-731-3600	S	50	0.2
Zeta Consumer Products Corp	777 Terrace Av	Hasbrouck H	NJ	07604	Raj Bal	201-288-3370	S	50	0.4
Rex-Rosenlew International Inc	PO Box 1167	Thomasville	NC	27361	C Warr	910-476-3131	R	44	0.2
CP Converters Inc	15 Grumbacher Rd	York	PA	17402	E England	717-764-1193	R	35	0.1
Uniflex Inc	383 W John St	Hicksville	NY	11802	Herbert Barry	516-932-2000	P	30	0.3
KCL Corp	Hodell and Prospect	Shelbyville	IN	46176	Robert C Stolmeier	317-392-2521	R	30	0.5
Pitt Plastic Inc	PO Box 356	Pittsburg	KS	66762	Kurt A DeRuy	316-231-4030	R	30	0.3
Chicago Transparent Products	2700 N Paulina St	Chicago	IL	60614	Stan Manne	312-281-3040	R	24	0.2
Star Packaging Corp	453 85 Circle	College Park	GA	30349	Ollie B Wilson Jr	404-763-2800	R	23	0.2
Poly Pak America Inc	2939 E Washington	Los Angeles	CA	90023	Richard Gerwitz	213-264-2400	R	22	0.1
Stewart Sutherland Inc	PO Box 162	Vicksburg	MI	49097	John C Stewart	616-649-0530	R	21	0.1
Aluf Plastics	3 Glenshaw St	Orangeburg	NY	10962	Rubin Rosenberg	914-365-2200	D	20*	0.1
API Industries Inc	Glenshaw St	Orangeburg	NY	10962	Reuvan Rosenberg	914-365-2200	R	20	0.2
Fortune Plastics Inc	310 Hartmann Dr	Lebanon	TN	37087	Henry A Schumpf	615-444-4004	D	20	0.1
Home Care Industries Inc	1 Libson St	Clifton	NJ	07013	MJ Bosses	201-365-1600	R	20*	0.3
Mid-America Bag Co	2332 Commonw	North Chicago	IL	60064	RW Byrne	708-689-8610	R	20	0.2
Charleston Packaging Company	4229 Domino Av	N Charleston	SC	29405	MP Allred	803-744-1646	S	19*	<0.1
Noteworthy Co	100 Church St	Amsterdam	NY	12010	Carol Constantino	518-842-2660	R	19	0.2
Aargus Plastics Inc	1415 Redeker Rd	Des Plaines	IL	60016	Jerome Starr	708-298-2131	R	18	0.1
Cajun Bag and Supply Co	PO Box 330	Crowley	LA	70527	Jules Maraist	318-783-8105	D	18*	0.3
Pacquet Oneida Inc	PO Box 449	Clifton	NJ	07015	Peter L Adams	201-777-5600	S	17*	0.3
Brown Paper Goods Co	804 E Church St	Libertyville	IL	60048	Allen B Mons	708-362-1450	R	15	0.1
Reef Industries Inc	PO Box 750250	Houston	TX	77275	P Cameron	713-943-0070	R	14	0.3
Capital Poly Bag Inc	3980 Groves Rd	Columbus	OH	43232	Wallace H O'Dowd	614-868-8660	R	12*	<0.1
Continental Extrusion Corp	11 Cliffside Dr	Cedar Grove	NJ	07009	Michael Cooke	201-239-4030	S	12	0.1
Ace Cellophane	75 Underdunk Av	Ridgewood	NY	11385	Jacob Dutch	718-628-8244	R	11*	<0.1
Specialty Container Corp	1608 Plantation Rd	Dallas	TX	75235	John R Dale	214-637-0160	R	11	<0.1
Ace Cellophane Inc	75 Onderdonk Av	Ridgewood	NY	11385	Jacob Deutsch	718-628-8244	R	10*	<0.1
Action Packaging Corp	667 Atkins Av	Brooklyn	NY	11208	Robert Kugler	718-649-2800	R	10	0.1
PPC Industries Inc	PO Box 400	Pleasant Prairie	WI	53158	Thomas Cowan	414-947-0900	R	8	<0.1
Rollpak Corp	1413 Eisenhower S	Goshen	IN	46526	Dale Weaver	219-533-0541	R	8*	<0.1
Coastal Plastic Corp	627 N Lane Av	Jacksonville	FL	32205	Richard Britebart	904-786-2031	R	7*	<0.1
CMC Printed Bag Company	2630 Pacific Park Dr	Whittier	CA	90601	Dick Carlson	310-692-9144	R	7	<0.1
Great American Packaging Inc	2025 E 48th St	Los Angeles	CA	90058	G Gurewitz	213-582-2247	R	7	<0.1
Great Eastern Industries Inc	28-20 Borden Av	Long Island Ct	NY	11101	Gerald Levine	718-784-1364	R	7	<0.1
Western Summit	13051 Saticoy St	N Hollywood	CA	91605	Don Clark	818-759-2500	R	6*	<0.1
Riley and Geehr Inc	2205 Lee St	Evanston	IL	60202	TE Riley Jr	708-869-8100	R	6	<0.1
Poly Shapes Inc	46 E End Dr	Gilberts	IL	60136	Jim Hendershot	708-428-5311	R	5*	<0.1
Woodstock Plastic Company Inc	22521 W Grant Hwy	Marengo	IL	60152	Brian D Jenkner	815-568-5281	R	5	0.1
JAD Corporation of America Inc	PO Box 560241	College Point	NY	11356	Joseph A Dee Jr	718-762-8900	R	4	<0.1
Mohawk Plastics Inc	PO Box 574	South Deerfield	MA	01337	Terry Anderson	413-648-9211	R	4*	<0.1
Lamcor Inc	PO Box 70	Le Sueur	MN	56058	Toby Jensen	612-332-1997	P	4	<0.1
Manhattan Portage Ltd	242 W 30th St	New York	NY	10001	John Peters	212-594-7068	R	3	<0.1
Seaboard Bag Corp	PO Box 25577	Richmond	VA	23260	G D Morgan Jr	804-358-0928	S	3	<0.1
Chalmur Bag Company Inc	PO Box 3692	Philadelphia	PA	19125	M Levin	215-425-2400	R	2	<0.1
Sunland Manufacturing Co	6800 Shingle Creek	Brooklyn Ct	MN	55430	Janet Lanning	612-560-7711	R	1	<0.1

Source: *Ward's Business Directory of U.S. Private and Public Companies*, Volumes 1 and 2, 1996. The company type code used is as follows: P - Public, R - Private, S - Subsidiary, D - Division, J - Joint Venture, A - Affiliate, G - Group. Sales are in millions of dollars, employees are in thousands. An asterisk (*) indicates an estimated sales volume. The symbol < stands for 'less than'. Company names and addresses are truncated, in some cases, to fit into the available space.

MATERIALS CONSUMED

Material		Quantity	Delivered Cost ($ million)
Materials, ingredients, containers, and supplies		(X)	2,574.6
Paper	1,000 s tons	(S)	107.8
Plastics resins consumed in the form of granules, pellets, powders, liquids, etc.	mil lb	3,453.5*	1,200.6
Plastics products consumed in the form of sheets, rods, tubes, film, and other shapes		(X)	325.3
Aluminum foil, plain	mil lb	10.0**	20.5
Glues and adhesives		(X)	39.0
Printing inks (complete formulations)	mil lb	(S)	69.8
Paperboard containers, boxes, and corrugated paperboard		(X)	182.6
All other materials and components, parts, containers, and supplies		(X)	239.2
Materials, ingredients, containers, and supplies, nsk		(X)	389.9

Source: 1992 *Economic Census*. Explanation of symbols used: (D): Withheld to avoid disclosure of competitive data; na: Not available; (S): Withheld because statistical norms were not met; (X): Not applicable; (Z): Less than half the unit shown; nec: Not elsewhere classified; nsk: Not specified by kind; - : zero; * : 10-19 percent estimated; ** : 20-29 percent estimated.

PRODUCT SHARE DETAILS

Product or Product Class	% Share	Product or Product Class	% Share
Bags: plastics, laminated, and coated	100.00	Other single-web film specialty bags and liners	3.50
Coated single-web paper specialty bags and liners	4.81	Specialty bags and liners, single-web film, nsk	9.26
Single-web film specialty bags and liners	77.37	Bags: plastics, laminated, and coated, specialty bags and liners, multiweb laminations and foil	9.03
Polyethylene grocery and variety bags	17.38	Multiweb specialty bags and liners, paper combinations, except paper/foil	13.86
Polyethylene refuse bags	27.52	Multiweb specialty bags and liners, foil and foil combinations	10.98
Polyethylene produce bags	3.00	Multiweb specialty bags and liners, other multiweb combinations	72.21
Polyethylene textile and clothing bags	5.19	Specialty bags and liners, multiweb laminations and foil, nsk	2.92
Polyethylene drum and box liners	3.11	Bags: plastics, laminated, and coated, nsk	8.79
Polyethylene shipping sacks	1.68		
Polyethylene household food storage bags (sandwich and freezer)	9.22		
Other polyethylene specialty bags and liners	11.40		
Coextruded film specialty bags and liners	8.74		

Source: 1992 *Economic Census*. The values shown are percent of total shipments in an industry. Values of indented subcategories are summed in the main heading. The symbol (D) appears when data are withheld to prevent disclosure of competitive information. The abbreviation nsk stands for 'not specified by kind' and nec for 'not elsewhere classified'.

INPUTS AND OUTPUTS FOR BAGS, EXCEPT TEXTILE

Economic Sector or Industry Providing Inputs	%	Sector	Economic Sector or Industry Buying Outputs	%	Sector
Paper mills, except building paper	36.6	Manufg.	Retail trade, except eating & drinking	59.4	Trade
Plastics materials & resins	20.6	Manufg.	Personal consumption expenditures	8.5	
Wholesale trade	7.2	Trade	Wholesale trade	6.7	Trade
Miscellaneous plastics products	6.3	Manufg.	Food preparations, nec	3.0	Manufg.
Paperboard containers & boxes	2.8	Manufg.	Bread, cake, & related products	2.2	Manufg.
Electric services (utilities)	2.7	Util.	Dog, cat, & other pet food	2.0	Manufg.
Motor freight transportation & warehousing	2.3	Util.	Prepared feeds, nec	1.7	Manufg.
Printing ink	2.0	Manufg.	Vegetables	1.4	Agric.
Broadwoven fabric mills	1.8	Manufg.	Exports	1.2	Foreign
Petroleum refining	1.4	Manufg.	Cookies & crackers	1.1	Manufg.
Railroads & related services	1.4	Util.	Fruits	1.0	Agric.
Imports	1.3	Foreign	Confectionery products	1.0	Manufg.
Advertising	1.0	Services	Flour & other grain mill products	0.8	Manufg.
Air transportation	0.9	Util.	Manufactured ice	0.6	Manufg.
Adhesives & sealants	0.8	Manufg.	S/L Govt. purch., public assistance & relief	0.6	S/L Govt
Electrical repair shops	0.8	Services	Cement, hydraulic	0.5	Manufg.
Cyclic crudes and organics	0.6	Manufg.	Fertilizers, mixing only	0.5	Manufg.
Communications, except radio & TV	0.6	Util.	Cyclic crudes and organics	0.4	Manufg.
Sanitary services, steam supply, irrigation	0.6	Util.	Frozen specialties	0.4	Manufg.
Real estate	0.6	Fin/R.E.	Minerals, ground or treated	0.4	Manufg.
Engraving & plate printing	0.5	Manufg.	S/L Govt. purch., health & hospitals	0.4	S/L Govt
Eating & drinking places	0.5	Trade	Agricultural chemicals, nec	0.3	Manufg.
Hotels & lodging places	0.5	Services	Canned fruits & vegetables	0.3	Manufg.
Paper industries machinery	0.4	Manufg.	Cereal breakfast foods	0.3	Manufg.
Gas production & distribution (utilities)	0.4	Util.	Chewing gum	0.3	Manufg.
Maintenance of nonfarm buildings nec	0.3	Constr.	Frozen fruits, fruit juices & vegetables	0.3	Manufg.
Banking	0.3	Fin/R.E.	Gypsum products	0.3	Manufg.
Equipment rental & leasing services	0.3	Services	Federal Government purchases, nondefense	0.3	Fed Govt
Lubricating oils & greases	0.2	Manufg.	Chemical preparations, nec	0.2	Manufg.
Machinery, except electrical, nec	0.2	Manufg.	Chocolate & cocoa products	0.2	Manufg.
Insurance carriers	0.2	Fin/R.E.	Drugs	0.2	Manufg.
Automotive rental & leasing, without drivers	0.2	Services	Mineral wool	0.2	Manufg.
Automotive repair shops & services	0.2	Services	Nitrogenous & phosphatic fertilizers	0.2	Manufg.
Computer & data processing services	0.2	Services	Sausages & other prepared meats	0.2	Manufg.
Legal services	0.2	Services	S/L Govt. purch., higher education	0.2	S/L Govt
Management & consulting services & labs	0.2	Services	S/L Govt. purch., other general government	0.2	S/L Govt
U.S. Postal Service	0.2	Gov't	Tree nuts	0.1	Agric.
Aluminum rolling & drawing	0.1	Manufg.	Apparel made from purchased materials	0.1	Manufg.
Bags, except textile	0.1	Manufg.	Blended & prepared flour	0.1	Manufg.
Fabricated rubber products, nec	0.1	Manufg.	Canned specialties	0.1	Manufg.
General industrial machinery, nec	0.1	Manufg.	Cheese, natural & processed	0.1	Manufg.
Mechanical measuring devices	0.1	Manufg.	Electronic components nec	0.1	Manufg.
Metal foil & leaf	0.1	Manufg.	Lime	0.1	Manufg.
Credit agencies other than banks	0.1	Fin/R.E.	Poultry dressing plants	0.1	Manufg.
Accounting, auditing & bookkeeping	0.1	Services			
Business/professional associations	0.1	Services			

Source: Benchmark Input-Output Accounts for the U.S. Economy, 1982, U.S. Department of Commerce, Washington, D.C., July 1991. Data, as reported in the source, are organized by the 1977 SIC structure in use in 1982 but have been matched, as closely as is possible, to the 1987 SIC structure used in this book.

OCCUPATIONS EMPLOYED BY SIC 267 - MISCELLANEOUS CONVERTED PAPER PRODUCTS

Occupation	% of Total 1994	Change to 2005	Occupation	% of Total 1994	Change to 2005
Paper goods machine setters & set-up operators	9.0	-15.9	Machine feeders & offbearers	2.5	-5.4
Machine operators nec	6.8	29.7	Industrial machinery mechanics	2.1	15.6
Hand packers & packagers	5.7	-9.9	Inspectors, testers, & graders, precision	2.1	15.6
Blue collar worker supervisors	4.5	6.8	Packaging & filling machine operators	2.1	5.1
Assemblers, fabricators, & hand workers nec	4.4	5.1	Freight, stock, & material movers, hand	2.0	-15.9
Printing press machine setters, operators	4.3	5.1	Maintenance repairers, general utility	2.0	5.1
Cutting & slicing machine setters, operators	4.0	26.1	Traffic, shipping, & receiving clerks	1.9	1.1
Sales & related workers nec	3.0	5.1	General managers & top executives	1.8	-0.3
Helpers, laborers, & material movers nec	2.9	5.1	Machine forming operators, metal & plastic	1.7	57.6
Extruding & forming machine workers	2.8	36.6	Coating, painting, & spraying machine workers	1.7	-15.9
Printing, binding, & related workers nec	2.6	5.1	Secretaries, ex legal & medical	1.6	-4.3
Industrial truck & tractor operators	2.6	5.1	Industrial production managers	1.2	5.1

Source: *Industry-Occupation Matrix*, Bureau of Labor Statistics. These data relate to one or more 3-digit SIC industry groups rather than to a single 4-digit SIC. The change reported for each occupation to the year 2005 is a percent of growth or decline as estimated by the Bureau of Labor Statistics. The abbreviation nec stands for 'not elsewhere classified'.

LOCATION BY STATE AND REGIONAL CONCENTRATION

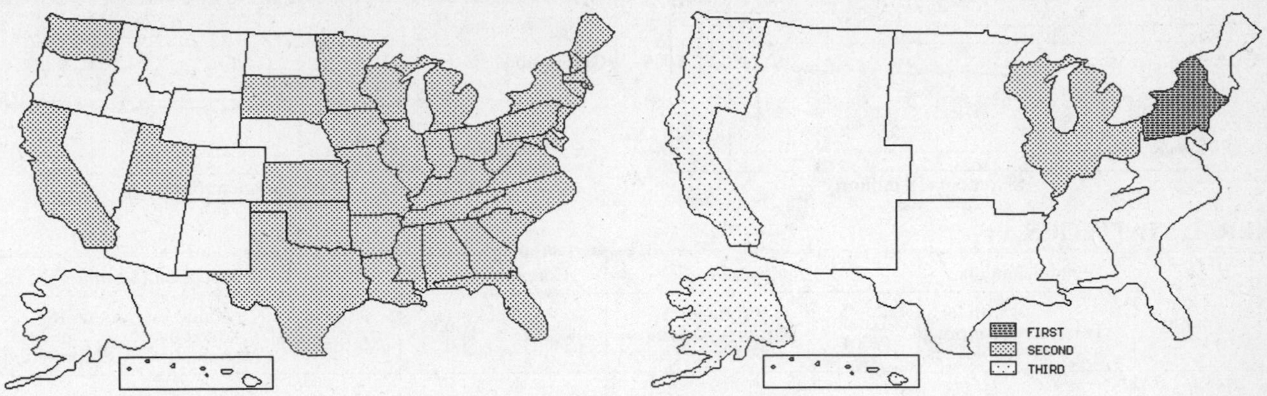

INDUSTRY DATA BY STATE

State	Establish-ments	Shipments			Employment				Cost as % of Shipments	Investment per Employee ($)
		Total ($ mil)	% of U.S.	Per Establ.	Total Number	% of U.S.	Per Establ.	Wages ($/hour)		
Illinois	37	629.9	11.0	17.0	4,100	10.6	111	10.03	44.1	4,317
Texas	36	545.1	9.5	15.1	3,300	8.5	92	9.69	58.8	5,273
California	75	495.1	8.7	6.6	2,900	7.5	39	9.36	46.9	4,207
New York	65	379.9	6.7	5.8	3,300	8.5	51	10.38	47.6	3,061
Indiana	12	353.5	6.2	29.5	2,300	5.9	192	11.23	53.2	8,000
Georgia	13	306.4	5.4	23.6	1,900	4.9	146	9.83	51.1	5,105
New Jersey	36	297.2	5.2	8.3	1,800	4.7	50	10.74	47.9	5,056
Wisconsin	17	265.6	4.7	15.6	1,900	4.9	112	12.23	46.1	4,211
Pennsylvania	19	212.9	3.7	11.2	1,600	4.1	84	11.03	54.3	3,000
North Carolina	14	199.5	3.5	14.2	1,400	3.6	100	10.75	49.1	9,643
Michigan	15	163.1	2.9	10.9	800	2.1	53	16.33	53.5	-
Missouri	11	140.4	2.5	12.8	1,000	2.6	91	9.88	46.3	6,300
Ohio	16	137.0	2.4	8.6	1,000	2.6	63	12.06	50.3	5,400
Florida	23	121.7	2.1	5.3	1,100	2.8	48	8.10	53.7	3,273
Tennessee	14	112.7	2.0	8.1	900	2.3	64	9.35	69.6	4,000
Massachusetts	17	99.4	1.7	5.8	700	1.8	41	10.55	52.5	2,857
Washington	6	93.8	1.6	15.6	800	2.1	133	12.85	56.7	-
Minnesota	13	84.8	1.5	6.5	600	1.6	46	10.11	52.9	3,000
Louisiana	7	71.8	1.3	10.3	600	1.6	86	7.60	52.8	4,167
Kansas	5	55.5	1.0	11.1	400	1.0	80	8.38	60.0	2,750
South Carolina	6	36.3	0.6	6.1	300	0.8	50	10.00	52.9	-
Oklahoma	6	34.9	0.6	5.8	300	0.8	50	15.33	29.8	-
Mississippi	4	28.5	0.5	7.1	300	0.8	75	6.83	42.8	-
New Hampshire	4	26.5	0.5	6.6	400	1.0	100	8.67	49.4	-
Maryland	5	17.8	0.3	3.6	100	0.3	20	8.50	42.1	-
Iowa	5	(D)	-	-	750 *	1.9	150	-	-	-
Alabama	4	(D)	-	-	375 *	1.0	94	-	-	-
Rhode Island	4	(D)	-	-	175 *	0.5	44	-	-	-
Virginia	4	(D)	-	-	750 *	1.9	188	-	-	-
Arkansas	3	(D)	-	-	1,750 *	4.5	583	-	-	-
Connecticut	3	(D)	-	-	375 *	1.0	125	-	-	-
Kentucky	3	(D)	-	-	375 *	1.0	125	-	-	-
South Dakota	2	(D)	-	-	375 *	1.0	188	-	-	-
West Virginia	2	(D)	-	-	175 *	0.5	88	-	-	-
Maine	1	(D)	-	-	175 *	0.5	175	-	-	-
Utah	1	(D)	-	-	375 *	1.0	375	-	-	-

Source: 1992 *Economic Census*. The states are in descending order of shipments or establishments (if shipment data are missing for the majority). The symbol (D) appears when data are withheld to prevent disclosure of competitive information. States marked with (D) are sorted by number of establishments. A dash (-) indicates that the data element cannot be calculated; * indicates the midpoint of a range.

2674 - BAGS: UNCOATED PAPER & MULTIWALL

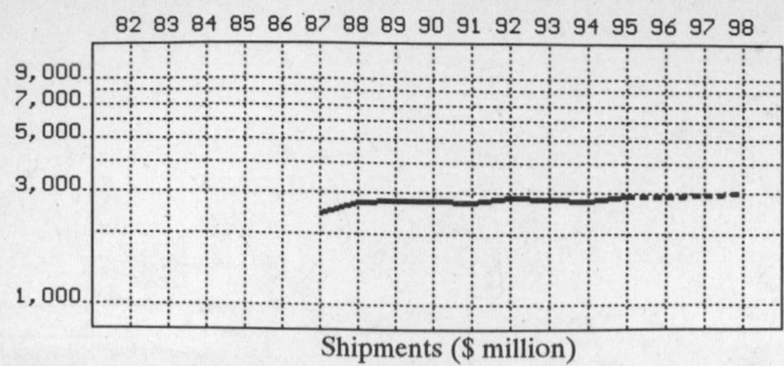

Shipments ($ million)

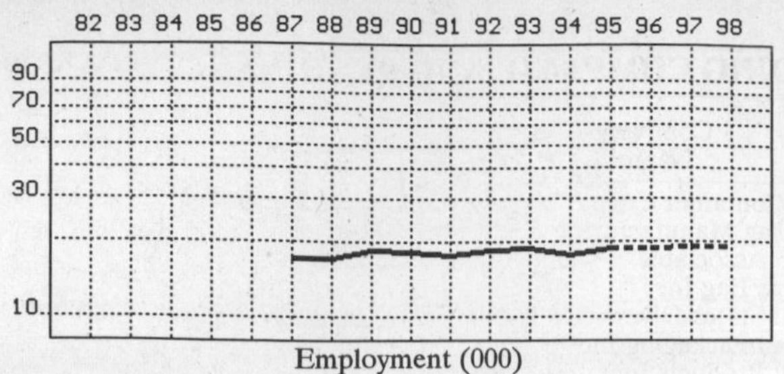

Employment (000)

GENERAL STATISTICS

Year	Com- panies	Establishments		Employment			Compensation		Production ($ million)			
		Total	with 20 or more employees	Total (000)	Production Workers (000)	Production Hours (Mil)	Payroll ($ mil)	Wages ($/hr)	Cost of Materials	Value Added by Manufacture	Value of Shipments	Capital Invest.
1982												
1983												
1984												
1985												
1986												
1987	77	132	112	17.1	14.3	29.0	347.8	9.14	1,588.9	874.8	2,448.0	46.2
1988		135	119	17.2	14.5	29.6	364.7	9.52	1,808.8	934.5	2,731.8	87.4
1989		136	120	18.5	14.4	28.7	357.7	9.43	1,899.8	910.1	2,787.2	53.5
1990		138	121	18.3	14.3	29.0	374.3	9.73	1,881.8	877.1	2,750.1	63.8
1991		136	119	17.9	15.0	29.7	398.4	10.06	1,837.4	895.5	2,735.8	50.6
1992	79	143	123	18.6	15.5	32.0	438.3	10.16	1,824.0	1,024.3	2,846.0	55.1
1993		151	125	18.7	15.5	33.1	453.6	10.10	1,799.3	1,002.6	2,802.6	32.4
1994		149P	126P	17.9	15.0	31.7	430.7	10.17	1,731.0	1,044.4	2,770.3	32.5
1995		152P	128P	18.7P	15.6P	32.9P	464.8P	10.47P	1,801.1P	1,086.7P	2,882.5P	32.4P
1996		154P	130P	18.9P	15.7P	33.4P	480.2P	10.62P	1,821.7P	1,099.1P	2,915.5P	27.9P
1997		157P	131P	19.0P	15.9P	34.0P	495.6P	10.77P	1,842.3P	1,111.6P	2,948.5P	23.3P
1998		160P	133P	19.2P	16.1P	34.5P	510.9P	10.92P	1,863.0P	1,124.0P	2,981.5P	18.8P

Sources: 1982, 1987, 1992 *Economic Census*; *Annual Survey of Manufactures*, 83-86, 88-91, 93-94. Establishment counts for non-Census years are from *County Business Patterns*; establishment values for 83-84 are extrapolations. 'P's show projections by the editors. Industries reclassified in 87 will not have data for prior years.

INDICES OF CHANGE

Year	Com- panies	Establishments		Employment			Compensation		Production ($ million)			
		Total	with 20 or more employees	Total (000)	Production Workers (000)	Production Hours (Mil)	Payroll ($ mil)	Wages ($/hr)	Cost of Materials	Value Added by Manufacture	Value of Shipments	Capital Invest.
1982												
1983												
1984												
1985												
1986												
1987	97	92	91	92	92	91	79	90	87	85	86	84
1988		94	97	92	94	93	83	94	99	91	96	159
1989		95	98	99	93	90	82	93	104	89	98	97
1990		97	98	98	92	91	85	96	103	86	97	116
1991		95	97	96	97	93	91	99	101	87	96	92
1992	100	100	100	100	100	100	100	100	100	100	100	100
1993		106	102	101	100	103	103	99	99	98	98	59
1994		104P	103P	96	97	99	98	100	95	102	97	59
1995		106P	104P	101P	100P	103P	106P	103P	99P	106P	101P	59P
1996		108P	105P	101P	101P	104P	110P	104P	100P	107P	102P	51P
1997		110P	107P	102P	103P	106P	113P	106P	101P	109P	104P	42P
1998		112P	108P	103P	104P	108P	117P	107P	102P	110P	105P	34P

Sources: Same as General Statistics. Values reflect change from the base year, 1992. Values above 100 mean greater than 92, values below 100 mean less than 92, and a value of 100 in the 82-91 or 93-98 period means same as 92. 'P's mark projections by the editors.

SELECTED RATIOS

For 1994	Avg. of All Manufact.	Analyzed Industry	Index
Employees per Establishment	49	120	245
Payroll per Establishment	1,500,273	2,887,835	192
Payroll per Employee	30,620	24,061	79
Production Workers per Establishment	34	101	293
Wages per Establishment	853,319	2,161,612	253
Wages per Production Worker	24,861	21,493	86
Hours per Production Worker	2,056	2,113	103
Wages per Hour	12.09	10.17	84
Value Added per Establishment	4,602,255	7,002,682	152
Value Added per Employee	93,930	58,346	62

For 1994	Avg. of All Manufact.	Analyzed Industry	Index
Value Added per Production Worker	134,084	69,627	52
Cost per Establishment	5,045,178	11,606,322	230
Cost per Employee	102,970	96,704	94
Cost per Production Worker	146,988	115,400	79
Shipments per Establishment	9,576,895	18,574,808	194
Shipments per Employee	195,460	154,765	79
Shipments per Production Worker	279,017	184,687	66
Investment per Establishment	321,011	217,912	68
Investment per Employee	6,552	1,816	28
Investment per Production Worker	9,352	2,167	23

Sources: Same as General Statistics. The 'Average of All Manufacturing' column represents the average of all manufacturing industries reported for the most recent complete year available. The Index shows the relationship between the Average and the Analyzed Industry. For example, 100 means that they are equal; 500 that the Analyzed Industry is five times the average; 50 means that the Analyzed Industry is half the national average. The abbreviation 'na' is used to show that data are 'not available'.

LEADING COMPANIES

Number shown: **19** Total sales ($ mil): **1,014** Total employment (000): **8.6**

Company Name	Address				CEO Name	Phone	Co. Type	Sales ($ mil)	Empl. (000)
Stone Container Corp	150 N Michigan Av	Chicago	IL	60601	Tom Cadden	312-580-4749	D	262	2.6
Duro Bag Manufacturing Co	Davies & Oak Sts	Ludlow	KY	41016	Charles L Shor	606-581-8200	R	190*	1.5
Hargro Associates	1 Landmark Sq	Stamford	CT	06901	FC Oatway	203-324-9707	R	120*	1.0
Bancroft Bag Inc	PO Box 35807	West Monroe	LA	71294	TO Bancroft Jr	318-387-2550	R	110	0.7
Central States Diversified Inc	9322 Manchester	St Louis	MO	63119	JR Flowers	314-961-4300	R	75	0.5
Werthan Packaging Inc	PO Box 1310	Nashville	TN	37202	Bernard Werthan Jr	615-259-9331	R	58	0.5
Studley Products Inc	95 Inip Dr	Inwood	NY	11696	Garson Studley	516-239-4000	S	50	0.5
Langston Companies Inc	PO Box 60	Memphis	TN	38101	Robert E Langston	901-774-4440	R	48	0.4
Gaylord Bag Partnership	500 Lake Cook Rd	Deerfield	IL	60015	Marvin Pomerantz	708-405-5500	R	26*	0.2
RonPak Inc	4301 N Brunswick	South Plainfield	NJ	07080	Ronald Sedley	908-968-8000	R	20	0.2
El Dorado Paper Bag Mfg	PO Box 1585	El Dorado	AR	71730	LT Hall	501-862-4977	R	18	0.2
BAG Corp	11510 Data Dr	Dallas	TX	75218	RR Williamson	214-340-7060	R	10*	0.2
First Midwest Corp	6127 Willowmere	Des Moines	IA	50321	R M Pomerantz	515-243-0768	R	7	<0.1
Capitol City Container Corp	5005 W 81st St	Indianapolis	IN	46268	John R Purcell	317-875-0290	R	6	<0.1
Westland Packaging Inc	PO Box 330730	Pacoima	CA	91333	Morton Nagler	818-899-2566	R	6	<0.1
Pioneer Container Corp	1000 Ellerbrook Rd	N Kansas City	MO	64116	Louis Brown	816-471-0556	R	4	<0.1
A-Guild Paper and Plastic	42 Bayview Av	Manhasset	NY	11030	David Gilson	516-365-2255	R	3	<0.1
Modern Arts Package Inc	38 W 39th St	New York	NY	10018	Alex Lindsay	212-221-6300	R	1	<0.1
Pacific Bag Inc	300 120th Av NE	Bellevue	WA	98005	Edward Urquhart	206-455-1128	R	1*	<0.1

Source: *Ward's Business Directory of U.S. Private and Public Companies*, Volumes 1 and 2, 1996. The company type code used is as follows: P - Public, R - Private, S - Subsidiary, D - Division, J - Joint Venture, A - Affiliate, G - Group. Sales are in millions of dollars, employees are in thousands. An asterisk (*) indicates an estimated sales volume. The symbol < stands for 'less than'. Company names and addresses are truncated, in some cases, to fit into the available space.

MATERIALS CONSUMED

Material		Quantity	Delivered Cost ($ million)
Materials, ingredients, containers, and supplies		(X)	1,716.2
Paper	1,000 s tons	2,384.0*	1,316.4
Plastics resins consumed in the form of granules, pellets, powders, liquids, etc.	mil lb	227.0*	91.5
Plastics products consumed in the form of sheets, rods, tubes, film, and other shapes		(X)	43.7
Glues and adhesives		(X)	43.9
Printing inks (complete formulations)	mil lb	39.7*	63.8
Paperboard containers, boxes, and corrugated paperboard		(X)	25.5
All other materials and components, parts, containers, and supplies		(X)	95.7
Materials, ingredients, containers, and supplies, nsk		(X)	35.6

Source: 1992 *Economic Census*. Explanation of symbols used: (D): Withheld to avoid disclosure of competitive data; na: Not available; (S): Withheld because statistical norms were not met; (X): Not applicable; (Z): Less than half the unit shown; nec: Not elsewhere classified; nsk: Not specified by kind; - : zero; * : 10-19 percent estimated; ** : 20-29 percent estimated.

PRODUCT SHARE DETAILS

Product or Product Class	% Share
Bags: uncoated paper and multiwall	100.00
Uncoated paper grocers' bags and sacks and variety and shopping bags	43.08
Uncoated paper grocers' bags and sacks	67.93
Uncoated paper variety bags (merchandise)	7.95
Uncoated paper shopping bags	9.77
Other uncoated paper bags, nec, including specialty bags, mothproof bags, etc.	12.41
Grocers' bags and sacks and variety and shopping bags, uncoated paper, nsk	1.94
Shipping sacks and multiwall bags, all materials except textiles	55.57
Single and double wall shipping sacks and bags, all materials except textiles	16.72
Multiwall (three-ply or more) shipping sacks and bags, all materials except textiles	80.93
Shipping sacks and multiwall bags, all materials except textiles, nsk	2.35
Bags: uncoated paper and multiwall, nsk	1.35

Source: 1992 *Economic Census*. The values shown are percent of total shipments in an industry. Values of indented subcategories are summed in the main heading. The symbol (D) appears when data are withheld to prevent disclosure of competitive information. The abbreviation nsk stands for 'not specified by kind' and nec for 'not elsewhere classified'.

INPUTS AND OUTPUTS FOR BAGS, EXCEPT TEXTILE

Economic Sector or Industry Providing Inputs	%	Sector	Economic Sector or Industry Buying Outputs	%	Sector
Paper mills, except building paper	36.6	Manufg.	Retail trade, except eating & drinking	59.4	Trade
Plastics materials & resins	20.6	Manufg.	Personal consumption expenditures	8.5	
Wholesale trade	7.2	Trade	Wholesale trade	6.7	Trade
Miscellaneous plastics products	6.3	Manufg.	Food preparations, nec	3.0	Manufg.
Paperboard containers & boxes	2.8	Manufg.	Bread, cake, & related products	2.2	Manufg.
Electric services (utilities)	2.7	Util.	Dog, cat, & other pet food	2.0	Manufg.
Motor freight transportation & warehousing	2.3	Util.	Prepared feeds, nec	1.7	Manufg.
Printing ink	2.0	Manufg.	Vegetables	1.4	Agric.
Broadwoven fabric mills	1.8	Manufg.	Exports	1.2	Foreign
Petroleum refining	1.4	Manufg.	Cookies & crackers	1.1	Manufg.
Railroads & related services	1.4	Util.	Fruits	1.0	Agric.
Imports	1.3	Foreign	Confectionery products	1.0	Manufg.
Advertising	1.0	Services	Flour & other grain mill products	0.8	Manufg.
Air transportation	0.9	Util.	Manufactured ice	0.6	Manufg.
Adhesives & sealants	0.8	Manufg.	S/L Govt. purch., public assistance & relief	0.6	S/L Govt
Electrical repair shops	0.8	Services	Cement, hydraulic	0.5	Manufg.
Cyclic crudes and organics	0.6	Manufg.	Fertilizers, mixing only	0.5	Manufg.
Communications, except radio & TV	0.6	Util.	Cyclic crudes and organics	0.4	Manufg.
Sanitary services, steam supply, irrigation	0.6	Util.	Frozen specialties	0.4	Manufg.
Real estate	0.6	Fin/R.E.	Minerals, ground or treated	0.4	Manufg.
Engraving & plate printing	0.5	Manufg.	S/L Govt. purch., health & hospitals	0.4	S/L Govt
Eating & drinking places	0.5	Trade	Agricultural chemicals, nec	0.3	Manufg.
Hotels & lodging places	0.5	Services	Canned fruits & vegetables	0.3	Manufg.
Paper industries machinery	0.4	Manufg.	Cereal breakfast foods	0.3	Manufg.
Gas production & distribution (utilities)	0.4	Util.	Chewing gum	0.3	Manufg.
Maintenance of nonfarm buildings nec	0.3	Constr.	Frozen fruits, fruit juices & vegetables	0.3	Manufg.
Banking	0.3	Fin/R.E.	Gypsum products	0.3	Manufg.
Equipment rental & leasing services	0.3	Services	Federal Government purchases, nondefense	0.3	Fed Govt
Lubricating oils & greases	0.2	Manufg.	Chemical preparations, nec	0.2	Manufg.
Machinery, except electrical, nec	0.2	Manufg.	Chocolate & cocoa products	0.2	Manufg.
Insurance carriers	0.2	Fin/R.E.	Drugs	0.2	Manufg.
Automotive rental & leasing, without drivers	0.2	Services	Mineral wool	0.2	Manufg.
Automotive repair shops & services	0.2	Services	Nitrogenous & phosphatic fertilizers	0.2	Manufg.
Computer & data processing services	0.2	Services	Sausages & other prepared meats	0.2	Manufg.
Legal services	0.2	Services	S/L Govt. purch., higher education	0.2	S/L Govt
Management & consulting services & labs	0.2	Services	S/L Govt. purch., other general government	0.2	S/L Govt
U.S. Postal Service	0.2	Gov't	Tree nuts	0.1	Agric.
Aluminum rolling & drawing	0.1	Manufg.	Apparel made from purchased materials	0.1	Manufg.
Bags, except textile	0.1	Manufg.	Blended & prepared flour	0.1	Manufg.
Fabricated rubber products, nec	0.1	Manufg.	Canned specialties	0.1	Manufg.
General industrial machinery, nec	0.1	Manufg.	Cheese, natural & processed	0.1	Manufg.
Mechanical measuring devices	0.1	Manufg.	Electronic components nec	0.1	Manufg.
Metal foil & leaf	0.1	Manufg.	Lime	0.1	Manufg.
Credit agencies other than banks	0.1	Fin/R.E.	Poultry dressing plants	0.1	Manufg.
Accounting, auditing & bookkeeping	0.1	Services			
Business/professional associations	0.1	Services			

Source: Benchmark Input-Output Accounts for the U.S. Economy, 1982, U.S. Department of Commerce, Washington, D.C., July 1991. Data, as reported in the source, are organized by the 1977 SIC structure in use in 1982 but have been matched, as closely as is possible, to the 1987 SIC structure used in this book.

OCCUPATIONS EMPLOYED BY SIC 267 - MISCELLANEOUS CONVERTED PAPER PRODUCTS

Occupation	% of Total 1994	Change to 2005	Occupation	% of Total 1994	Change to 2005
Paper goods machine setters & set-up operators	9.0	-15.9	Machine feeders & offbearers	2.5	-5.4
Machine operators nec	6.8	29.7	Industrial machinery mechanics	2.1	15.6
Hand packers & packagers	5.7	-9.9	Inspectors, testers, & graders, precision	2.1	15.6
Blue collar worker supervisors	4.5	6.8	Packaging & filling machine operators	2.1	5.1
Assemblers, fabricators, & hand workers nec	4.4	5.1	Freight, stock, & material movers, hand	2.0	-15.9
Printing press machine setters, operators	4.3	5.1	Maintenance repairers, general utility	2.0	5.1
Cutting & slicing machine setters, operators	4.0	26.1	Traffic, shipping, & receiving clerks	1.9	1.1
Sales & related workers nec	3.0	5.1	General managers & top executives	1.8	-0.3
Helpers, laborers, & material movers nec	2.9	5.1	Machine forming operators, metal & plastic	1.7	57.6
Extruding & forming machine workers	2.8	36.6	Coating, painting, & spraying machine workers	1.7	-15.9
Printing, binding, & related workers nec	2.6	5.1	Secretaries, ex legal & medical	1.6	-4.3
Industrial truck & tractor operators	2.6	5.1	Industrial production managers	1.2	5.1

Source: Industry-Occupation Matrix, Bureau of Labor Statistics. These data relate to one or more 3-digit SIC industry groups rather than to a single 4-digit SIC. The change reported for each occupation to the year 2005 is a percent of growth or decline as estimated by the Bureau of Labor Statistics. The abbreviation nec stands for 'not elsewhere classified'.

LOCATION BY STATE AND REGIONAL CONCENTRATION

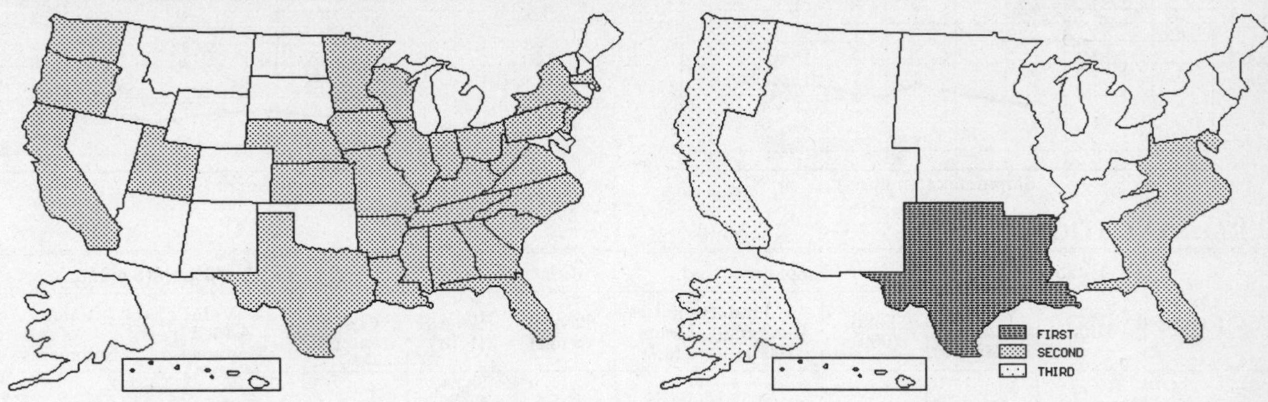

INDUSTRY DATA BY STATE

State	Establish-ments	Shipments			Employment				Cost as % of Shipments	Investment per Employee ($)
		Total ($ mil)	% of U.S.	Per Establ.	Total Number	% of U.S.	Per Establ.	Wages ($/hour)		
Arkansas	14	314.1	11.0	22.4	2,300	12.4	164	9.61	61.8	2,826
Kentucky	5	202.2	7.1	40.4	1,400	7.5	280	10.96	57.6	-
Illinois	9	202.1	7.1	22.5	1,500	8.1	167	9.44	58.5	3,000
Florida	6	167.9	5.9	28.0	700	3.8	117	10.25	73.7	-
Georgia	4	157.7	5.5	39.4	1,300	7.0	325	9.82	67.2	2,385
Louisiana	4	155.9	5.5	39.0	1,100	5.9	275	10.22	70.2	-
Tennessee	7	143.4	5.0	20.5	900	4.8	129	10.87	61.5	1,778
Texas	8	124.5	4.4	15.6	700	3.8	88	10.36	60.8	-
Missouri	5	116.5	4.1	23.3	700	3.8	140	9.83	58.3	1,000
New Jersey	5	109.1	3.8	21.8	600	3.2	120	12.60	79.0	1,833
California	8	106.1	3.7	13.3	600	3.2	75	10.50	60.6	-
New York	6	86.3	3.0	14.4	700	3.8	117	10.08	62.3	-
Washington	5	72.5	2.5	14.5	400	2.2	80	14.00	61.5	1,250
North Carolina	5	66.8	2.3	13.4	500	2.7	100	9.86	52.5	400
Oregon	5	66.0	2.3	13.2	400	2.2	80	10.67	73.5	1,250
Pennsylvania	4	58.5	2.1	14.6	400	2.2	100	9.67	58.6	500
Wisconsin	4	37.1	1.3	9.3	200	1.1	50	10.67	62.0	-
Kansas	3	25.6	0.9	8.5	200	1.1	67	9.67	57.8	1,500
Iowa	4	(D)	-	-	750 *	4.0	188	-	-	-
Massachusetts	4	(D)	-	-	175 *	0.9	44	-	-	-
Virginia	4	(D)	-	-	750 *	4.0	188	-	-	-
Indiana	3	(D)	-	-	175 *	0.9	58	-	-	-
Mississippi	2	(D)	-	-	175 *	0.9	88	-	-	-
Ohio	2	(D)	-	-	375 *	2.0	188	-	-	-
South Carolina	2	(D)	-	-	750 *	4.0	375	-	-	-
West Virginia	2	(D)	-	-	175 *	0.9	88	-	-	-
Alabama	1	(D)	-	-	375 *	2.0	375	-	-	-
Minnesota	1	(D)	-	-	175 *	0.9	175	-	-	-
Nebraska	1	(D)	-	-	175 *	0.9	175	-	-	-
Utah	1	(D)	-	-	375 *	2.0	375	-	-	-

Source: 1992 *Economic Census*. The states are in descending order of shipments or establishments (if shipment data are missing for the majority). The symbol (D) appears when data are withheld to prevent disclosure of competitive information. States marked with (D) are sorted by number of establishments. A dash (-) indicates that the data element cannot be calculated; * indicates the midpoint of a range.

2675 - DIE-CUT PAPER AND BOARD

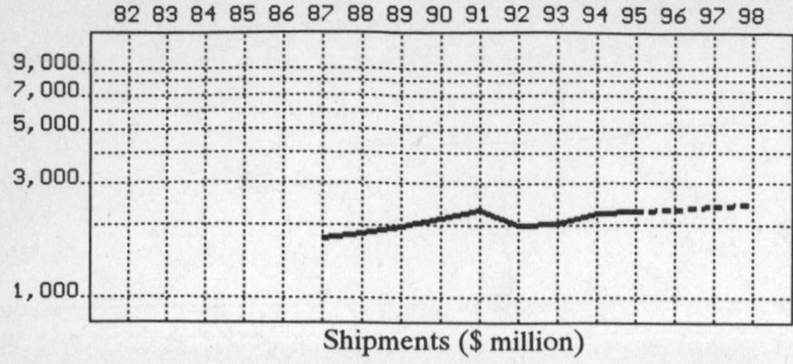

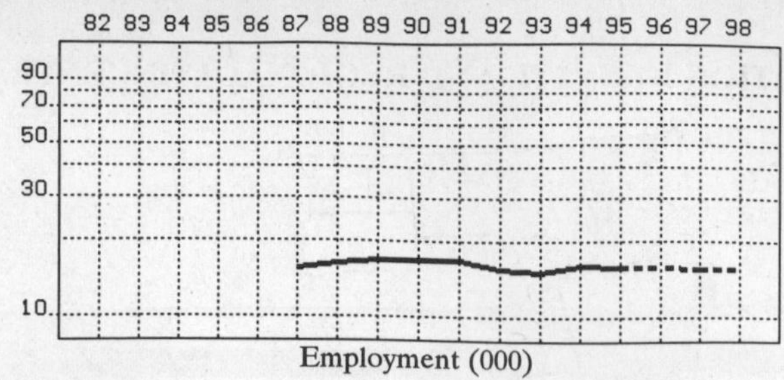

GENERAL STATISTICS

Year	Companies	Establishments Total	Establishments with 20 or more employees	Employment Total (000)	Production Workers (000)	Production Hours (Mil)	Compensation Payroll ($ mil)	Compensation Wages ($/hr)	Cost of Materials	Value Added by Manufacture	Value of Shipments	Capital Invest.
1982												
1983												
1984												
1985												
1986												
1987	371	399	172	15.7	12.5	24.9	307.8	8.24	1,086.1	680.8	1,749.3	33.4
1988		385	172	16.2	13.1	25.9	329.4	8.59	1,140.4	712.7	1,850.8	31.9
1989		372	173	16.8	12.8	26.5	384.0	9.52	1,019.9	989.6	1,984.2	68.8
1990		360	166	16.9	13.5	27.0	395.4	9.40	1,068.8	1,045.7	2,119.0	44.1
1991		378	170	17.0	14.0	28.2	407.5	9.90	1,240.5	1,053.1	2,290.6	91.3
1992	355	381	163	15.6	12.4	25.0	375.2	9.92	1,168.1	845.4	2,011.1	52.6
1993		399	167	15.2	12.0	23.5	392.6	10.83	1,177.7	849.0	2,029.7	35.7
1994		382P	164P	16.0	12.8	25.6	402.7	10.40	1,317.9	913.1	2,236.4	77.5
1995		382P	163P	15.8P	12.7P	25.3P	426.1P	11.10P	1,342.4P	930.1P	2,278.0P	71.9P
1996		382P	161P	15.8P	12.6P	25.1P	437.6P	11.43P	1,374.4P	952.2P	2,332.2P	75.8P
1997		381P	160P	15.7P	12.6P	25.0P	449.1P	11.77P	1,406.3P	974.4P	2,386.5P	79.7P
1998		381P	159P	15.6P	12.5P	24.9P	460.6P	12.10P	1,438.3P	996.5P	2,440.7P	83.5P

Sources: 1982, 1987, 1992 *Economic Census*; *Annual Survey of Manufactures*, 83-86, 88-91, 93-94. Establishment counts for non-Census years are from *County Business Patterns*; establishment values for 83-84 are extrapolations. 'P's show projections by the editors. Industries reclassified in 87 will not have data for prior years.

INDICES OF CHANGE

Year	Companies	Establishments Total	Establishments with 20 or more employees	Employment Total (000)	Production Workers (000)	Production Hours (Mil)	Compensation Payroll ($ mil)	Compensation Wages ($/hr)	Cost of Materials	Value Added by Manufacture	Value of Shipments	Capital Invest.
1982												
1983												
1984												
1985												
1986												
1987	105	105	106	101	101	100	82	83	93	81	87	63
1988		101	106	104	106	104	88	87	98	84	92	61
1989		98	106	108	103	106	102	96	87	117	99	131
1990		94	102	108	109	108	105	95	91	124	105	84
1991		99	104	109	113	113	109	100	106	125	114	174
1992	100	100	100	100	100	100	100	100	100	100	100	100
1993		105	102	97	97	94	105	109	101	100	101	68
1994		100P	101P	103	103	102	107	105	113	108	111	147
1995		100P	100P	101P	102P	101P	114P	112P	115P	110P	113P	137P
1996		100P	99P	101P	102P	101P	117P	115P	118P	113P	116P	144P
1997		100P	98P	101P	101P	100P	120P	119P	120P	115P	119P	151P
1998		100P	97P	100P	101P	100P	123P	122P	123P	118P	121P	159P

Sources: Same as General Statistics. Values reflect change from the base year, 1992. Values above 100 mean greater than 92, values below 100 mean less than 92, and a value of 100 in the 82-91 or 93-98 period means same as 92. 'P's mark projections by the editors.

SELECTED RATIOS

For 1994	Avg. of All Manufact.	Analyzed Industry	Index
Employees per Establishment	49	42	86
Payroll per Establishment	1,500,273	1,054,978	70
Payroll per Employee	30,620	25,169	82
Production Workers per Establishment	34	34	98
Wages per Establishment	853,319	697,485	82
Wages per Production Worker	24,861	20,800	84
Hours per Production Worker	2,056	2,000	97
Wages per Hour	12.09	10.40	86
Value Added per Establishment	4,602,255	2,392,103	52
Value Added per Employee	93,930	57,069	61

For 1994	Avg. of All Manufact.	Analyzed Industry	Index
Value Added per Production Worker	134,084	71,336	53
Cost per Establishment	5,045,178	3,452,582	68
Cost per Employee	102,970	82,369	80
Cost per Production Worker	146,988	102,961	70
Shipments per Establishment	9,576,895	5,858,832	61
Shipments per Employee	195,460	139,775	72
Shipments per Production Worker	279,017	174,719	63
Investment per Establishment	321,011	203,031	63
Investment per Employee	6,552	4,844	74
Investment per Production Worker	9,352	6,055	65

Sources: Same as General Statistics. The 'Average of All Manufacturing' column represents the average of all manufacturing industries reported for the most recent complete year available. The Index shows the relationship between the Average and the Analyzed Industry. For example, 100 means that they are equal; 500 that the Analyzed Industry is five times the average; 50 means that the Analyzed Industry is half the national average. The abbreviation 'na' is used to show that data are 'not available'.

LEADING COMPANIES

Number shown: **43** Total sales ($ mil): **1,220** Total employment (000): **6.8**

Company Name	Address				CEO Name	Phone	Co. Type	Sales ($ mil)	Empl. (000)
Esselte Pendaflex Corp	71 Clinton Rd	Garden City	NY	11530	Robert K Scribner	516-741-3200	S	300	1.0
Fleer Corp	1120 Rte 73	Mount Laurel	NJ	08054	Paul H Mullan	609-231-6200	S	185	0.5
Chesapeake Display	PO Box 12669	Winston-Salem	NC	27117	George Barnes	919-784-0445	S	125	0.7
Book Covers Inc	84 Lockwood St	Newark	NJ	07105	Robert Mullen	201-817-9000	D	100	0.4
Advertising Display Company	570 Sylvan Av	Englewood Clfs	NJ	07632	Steven L Marks	201-569-9100	R	70	0.4
Simplex Products	PO Box 10	Adrian	MI	49221	RE Doyle	517-263-8881	D	70	0.4
RMA/KOLKO Corp	20 Jetview Dr	Rochester	NY	14623	Michael I Zimet	716-328-9500	R	62*	0.2
Austell Box Board Corp	PO Box 157	Austell	GA	30001	Gary Cran	404-948-3100	S	40*	0.4
Niemand Industries Inc	2500 W Front St	Statesville	NC	28677	D Geerdes	704-873-6364	S	25	0.3
Colwell General Inc	PO Box 329	Fort Wayne	IN	46801	Alexander Pursley	219-424-5000	S	19	0.1
E and E Specialties Inc	910 E 29th St	Lawrence	KS	66046	Edward C White	913-843-9240	R	19	0.3
Graphic Converting Inc	6701 W Oakton St	Niles	IL	60714	John Tinnon	708-967-3300	R	17*	0.2
Morrisette Paper Co	PO Box 20768	Greensboro	NC	27420	Bill Morrisette	910-375-1515	R	17*	0.2
Gussco Manufacturing Inc	5112 2nd Av	Brooklyn	NY	11232	J Kremsdorf	718-492-7900	R	15	0.2
Metro Litho Inc	101 Moonachie Av	Moonachie	NJ	07074	Manny De Torres	201-935-1450	R	15	<0.1
University Products Inc	PO Box 101	Holyoke	MA	01041	David L Magoon	413-532-3372	R	13	0.1
Nielsen and Bainbridge	40 Eisenhower Dr	Paramus	NJ	07652	Jack Forbes	201-368-9191	D	12	<0.1
Vertiflex Co	630 W 41st St	Chicago	IL	60609	Stephen Barth	312-927-9800	R	11*	0.1
Westark Specialites Inc	PO Box 6365	Fort Smith	AR	72906	William R Henson	501-646-6225	R	9*	<0.1
General Bag Corp	PO Box 110028	Cleveland	OH	44111	RL Sprosty	216-941-1191	R	9	<0.1
Freedman Die Cutters Inc	85 10th Av	New York	NY	10011	David Halpern	212-929-7000	R	8*	0.2
Gross-Medick-Barrows Inc	PO Box 12727	El Paso	TX	79913	MJ Williams	915-584-8133	R	8	0.2
Acme Die Cutting Services Inc	581 Mateo St	Los Angeles	CA	90013	Donald Risner	213-622-5182	R	7	<0.1
Loroco Industries Inc	5000 Creek Rd	Cincinnati	OH	45242	Lee H Rozin	513-891-9544	R	7	<0.1
Arrow Ace Die Cutting Company	780 E 133rd St	Bronx	NY	10454	N Feuerstein	718-665-7400	R	6	0.1
Victor Cornelius Inc	PO Box 71	Eastland	TX	76448	Cary Meeks	817-629-2626	R	6*	<0.1
Westcott Paper Products	450 Amsterdam Rd	Detroit	MI	48202	AG Campbell Jr	313-872-1200	R	6	<0.1
Alvah Bushnell Co	519 E Chelten Av	Philadelphia	PA	19144	Arthur Bushnell	215-842-9520	R	5*	<0.1
AV Emmett	5700 Mitchelldale	Houston	TX	77092	A V Emmett Jr	713-956-0211	R	4	<0.1
Chicago Steel Rule	6630 W Wrightwood	Chicago	IL	60635	Jerry Guanci	312-237-2235	R	4	<0.1
File-Ez Folder Inc	E 4111 Mission Av	Spokane	WA	99201	Gary F Lawton	509-534-1044	R	4	<0.1
American Coaster Co	3685 Lockpart Rd	Sanborn	NY	14132	Thomas Muraca	716-731-9193	R	3	<0.1
Bryson Capital Corp	24 Shawmut Av	Holyoke	MA	01040	David Bryson	413-536-4250	R	3*	<0.1
Pacific Forest Industries Inc	4803 Everett Av	Vernon	CA	90058	Merl Seastrom	213-581-7223	R	3*	<0.1
Penn Photomounts Inc	POBox 2191	Aston	PA	19014	Dave Matthias	610-459-8303	R	3	<0.1
Alfred Envelope Company Inc	3536 N Mascher St	Philadelphia	PA	19140	OA Comer	215-739-1500	R	2*	<0.1
New Cooler Corp	PO Box 44027	Atlanta	GA	30336	Mike Olvey	404-631-1663	R	2*	<0.1
SFI Inc	475 Bailey Rd	El Dorado	AR	71730	D Byrd	501-863-5184	R	2*	<0.1
Animated Advertising Inc	710 W Jackson Blv	Chicago	IL	60606	Anthony J March	312-372-4692	R	2	<0.1
Blackhawk Manufacturing Inc	69 Ottawa Av	Dixon	IL	61021	David Becker	815-284-4466	R	1	<0.1
Don Paper Co	175 2nd St	Oakland	CA	94607	James E Croft	510-763-3642	R	1	<0.1
Valentine Foil	1796 Indian Val	Novato	CA	94947	Gary Valentine	415-883-9606	R	0*	<0.1
Index Print Inc	PO Box 4208	Santa Fe Sprgs	CA	90670	Gary Grossman	310-949-5800	R	0*	<0.1

Source: *Ward's Business Directory of U.S. Private and Public Companies*, Volumes 1 and 2, 1996. The company type code used is as follows: P - Public, R - Private, S - Subsidiary, D - Division, J - Joint Venture, A - Affiliate, G - Group. Sales are in millions of dollars, employees are in thousands. An asterisk (*) indicates an estimated sales volume. The symbol < stands for 'less than'. Company names and addresses are truncated, in some cases, to fit into the available space.

MATERIALS CONSUMED

Material		Quantity	Delivered Cost ($ million)
Materials, ingredients, containers, and supplies		(X)	1,060.4
Paper and paperboard, except boxes and containers	1,000 s tons	1,249.7*	727.2
Plastics film and sheet, unsupported		(X)	47.6
Glassine film		(X)	2.2
Glues and adhesives	mil lb	(S)	13.8
Paperboard containers, boxes, and corrugated paperboard		(X)	29.7
All other materials and components, parts, containers, and supplies		(X)	112.5
Materials, ingredients, containers, and supplies, nsk		(X)	127.4

Source: 1992 *Economic Census*. Explanation of symbols used: (D): Withheld to avoid disclosure of competitive data; na: Not available; (S): Withheld because statistical norms were not met; (X): Not applicable; (Z): Less than half the unit shown; nec: Not elsewhere classified; nsk: Not specified by kind; - : zero; * : 10-19 percent estimated; ** : 20-29 percent estimated.

PRODUCT SHARE DETAILS

Product or Product Class	% Share	Product or Product Class	% Share
Die-cut paper and board	100.00	etc.	24.46
Die-cut paper and board office supplies	46.96	Die-cut paper and paperboard office supplies, nsk	4.64
Hanging file folders, all types and materials	18.74	Die-cut paper and paperboard products, except office supplies	6.37
Expanding file folders (including wallets), all types and materials	10.42	Cards, die-cut and designed, not printed	29.64
Other file folders (including file jackets and file pockets), all types and materials	38.11	Automotive paperboard products (for panel, trim, etc.)	65.75
Tabulating cards, single-cut	3.62	Die-cut paper and paperboard products, except office supplies, nsk	4.60
Other die-cut paper and board office supplies, including index cards, guide cards, presentation and report covers,		Pasted, lined, laminated, or surface-coated paperboard	37.62
		Die-cut paper and paperboard, nsk	9.05

Source: 1992 *Economic Census*. The values shown are percent of total shipments in an industry. Values of indented subcategories are summed in the main heading. The symbol (D) appears when data are withheld to prevent disclosure of competitive information. The abbreviation nsk stands for 'not specified by kind' and nec for 'not elsewhere classified'.

INPUTS AND OUTPUTS FOR DIE-CUT PAPER & BOARD

Economic Sector or Industry Providing Inputs	%	Sector	Economic Sector or Industry Buying Outputs	%	Sector
Paperboard mills	49.8	Manufg.	Paperboard containers & boxes	10.6	Manufg.
Paper mills, except building paper	18.6	Manufg.	Surgical appliances & supplies	4.5	Manufg.
Railroads & related services	3.7	Util.	Portrait, photographic studios	3.7	Services
Wholesale trade	3.7	Trade	Blankbooks & looseleaf binders	3.3	Manufg.
Motor freight transportation & warehousing	3.4	Util.	Typewriters & office machines, nec	2.6	Manufg.
Paperboard containers & boxes	2.5	Manufg.	Membership organizations nec	2.6	Services
Die-cut paper & board	2.3	Manufg.	Electrical industrial apparatus, nec	2.5	Manufg.
Miscellaneous plastics products	2.1	Manufg.	Signs & advertising displays	2.4	Manufg.
Noncomparable imports	1.7	Foreign	Motor vehicles & car bodies	2.3	Manufg.
Advertising	1.4	Services	Insurance carriers	2.3	Fin/R.E.
Electric services (utilities)	1.2	Util.	Real estate	2.3	Fin/R.E.
Air transportation	1.1	Util.	Doctors & dentists	2.3	Services
Adhesives & sealants	0.8	Manufg.	Manufacturing industries, nec	2.1	Manufg.
Gas production & distribution (utilities)	0.6	Util.	Electronic computing equipment	2.0	Manufg.
Petroleum refining	0.5	Manufg.	S/L Govt. purch., other general government	2.0	S/L Govt
Communications, except radio & TV	0.5	Util.	S/L Govt. purch., elem. & secondary education	1.9	S/L Govt
Eating & drinking places	0.5	Trade	Retail trade, except eating & drinking	1.7	Trade
Hotels & lodging places	0.5	Services	Wholesale trade	1.7	Trade
Maintenance of nonfarm buildings nec	0.4	Constr.	Telephone & telegraph apparatus	1.6	Manufg.
Real estate	0.4	Fin/R.E.	Hospitals	1.6	Services
Equipment rental & leasing services	0.4	Services	Radio & TV receiving sets	1.5	Manufg.
Paper industries machinery	0.3	Manufg.	Die-cut paper & board	1.4	Manufg.
Banking	0.3	Fin/R.E.	Legal services	1.4	Services
Lubricating oils & greases	0.2	Manufg.	Communications, except radio & TV	1.3	Util.
Machinery, except electrical, nec	0.2	Manufg.	Banking	1.3	Fin/R.E.
Computer & data processing services	0.2	Services	Labor, civic, social, & fraternal associations	1.3	Services
Detective & protective services	0.2	Services	Federal Government purchases, national defense	1.3	Fed Govt
Legal services	0.2	Services	S/L Govt. purch., higher education	1.3	S/L Govt
Management & consulting services & labs	0.2	Services	Miscellaneous plastics products	1.2	Manufg.
U.S. Postal Service	0.2	Gov't	Business/professional associations	1.2	Services
Sanitary services, steam supply, irrigation	0.1	Util.	Federal Government purchases, nondefense	1.2	Fed Govt
Insurance carriers	0.1	Fin/R.E.	Jewelry, precious metal	1.0	Manufg.
Royalties	0.1	Fin/R.E.	Water supply & sewage systems	1.0	Util.
Accounting, auditing & bookkeeping	0.1	Services	Colleges, universities, & professional schools	1.0	Services
Automotive rental & leasing, without drivers	0.1	Services	Fluid milk	0.9	Manufg.
			Computer & data processing services	0.8	Services
			Management & consulting services & labs	0.8	Services
			Automotive & apparel trimmings	0.7	Manufg.
			Manifold business forms	0.7	Manufg.
			Libraries, vocation education	0.7	Services
			S/L Govt. purch., health & hospitals	0.7	S/L Govt
			S/L Govt. purch., natural resource & recreation.	0.7	S/L Govt
			Canned fruits & vegetables	0.6	Manufg.
			Insurance agents, brokers, & services	0.6	Fin/R.E.
			Business services nec	0.6	Services
			Calculating & accounting machines	0.5	Manufg.
			Motors & generators	0.5	Manufg.
			Motor freight transportation & warehousing	0.5	Util.
			Credit agencies other than banks	0.5	Fin/R.E.
			Hotels & lodging places	0.5	Services
			S/L Govt. purch., police	0.5	S/L Govt
			S/L Govt. purch., public assistance & relief	0.5	S/L Govt
			Accounting, auditing & bookkeeping	0.4	Services
			Elementary & secondary schools	0.4	Services
			Medical & health services, nec	0.4	Services
			Social services, nec	0.4	Services
			Poultry & eggs	0.3	Agric.
			Commercial printing	0.3	Manufg.
			Motor vehicle parts & accessories	0.3	Manufg.
			Radio & TV communication equipment	0.3	Manufg.

Continued on next page.

INPUTS AND OUTPUTS FOR DIE-CUT PAPER & BOARD - Continued

Economic Sector or Industry Providing Inputs	%	Sector	Economic Sector or Industry Buying Outputs	%	Sector
			Truck & bus bodies	0.3	Manufg.
			Advertising	0.3	Services
			Child day care services	0.3	Services
			Engineering, architectural, & surveying services	0.3	Services
			Job training & related services	0.3	Services
			Exports	0.3	Foreign
			S/L Govt. purch., correction	0.3	S/L Govt
			Chemical preparations, nec	0.2	Manufg.
			Fabricated rubber products, nec	0.2	Manufg.
			Gaskets, packing & sealing devices	0.2	Manufg.
			Industrial furnaces & ovens	0.2	Manufg.
			Newspapers	0.2	Manufg.
			Electric services (utilities)	0.2	Util.
			Radio & TV broadcasting	0.2	Util.
			Security & commodity brokers	0.2	Fin/R.E.
			Amusement & recreation services nec	0.2	Services
			Motion pictures	0.2	Services
			Personnel supply services	0.2	Services
			Photofinishing labs, commercial photography	0.2	Services
			Religious organizations	0.2	Services
			S/L Govt. purch., other education & libraries	0.2	S/L Govt
			Agricultural, forestry, & fishery services	0.1	Agric.
			Aircraft	0.1	Manufg.
			Commercial laundry equipment	0.1	Manufg.
			Drugs	0.1	Manufg.
			Electronic components nec	0.1	Manufg.
			Semiconductors & related devices	0.1	Manufg.
			Air transportation	0.1	Util.
			Railroads & related services	0.1	Util.
			Eating & drinking places	0.1	Trade
			Automotive rental & leasing, without drivers	0.1	Services
			Automotive repair shops & services	0.1	Services
			Equipment rental & leasing services	0.1	Services
			Laundry, dry cleaning, shoe repair	0.1	Services
			Membership sports & recreation clubs	0.1	Services
			Miscellaneous repair shops	0.1	Services
			Nursing & personal care facilities	0.1	Services
			Services to dwellings & other buildings	0.1	Services
			Theatrical producers, bands, entertainers	0.1	Services

Source: Benchmark Input-Output Accounts for the U.S. Economy, 1982, U.S. Department of Commerce, Washington, D.C., July 1991. Data, as reported in the source, are organized by the 1977 SIC structure in use in 1982 but have been matched, as closely as is possible, to the 1987 SIC structure used in this book.

OCCUPATIONS EMPLOYED BY SIC 267 - MISCELLANEOUS CONVERTED PAPER PRODUCTS

Occupation	% of Total 1994	Change to 2005	Occupation	% of Total 1994	Change to 2005
Paper goods machine setters & set-up operators	9.0	-15.9	Machine feeders & offbearers	2.5	-5.4
Machine operators nec	6.8	29.7	Industrial machinery mechanics	2.1	15.6
Hand packers & packagers	5.7	-9.9	Inspectors, testers, & graders, precision	2.1	15.6
Blue collar worker supervisors	4.5	6.8	Packaging & filling machine operators	2.1	5.1
Assemblers, fabricators, & hand workers nec	4.4	5.1	Freight, stock, & material movers, hand	2.0	-15.9
Printing press machine setters, operators	4.3	5.1	Maintenance repairers, general utility	2.0	5.1
Cutting & slicing machine setters, operators	4.0	26.1	Traffic, shipping, & receiving clerks	1.9	1.1
Sales & related workers nec	3.0	5.1	General managers & top executives	1.8	-0.3
Helpers, laborers, & material movers nec	2.9	5.1	Machine forming operators, metal & plastic	1.7	57.6
Extruding & forming machine workers	2.8	36.6	Coating, painting, & spraying machine workers	1.7	-15.9
Printing, binding, & related workers nec	2.6	5.1	Secretaries, ex legal & medical	1.6	-4.3
Industrial truck & tractor operators	2.6	5.1	Industrial production managers	1.2	5.1

Source: Industry-Occupation Matrix, Bureau of Labor Statistics. These data relate to one or more 3-digit SIC industry groups rather than to a single 4-digit SIC. The change reported for each occupation to the year 2005 is a percent of growth or decline as estimated by the Bureau of Labor Statistics. The abbreviation nec stands for 'not elsewhere classified'.

LOCATION BY STATE AND REGIONAL CONCENTRATION

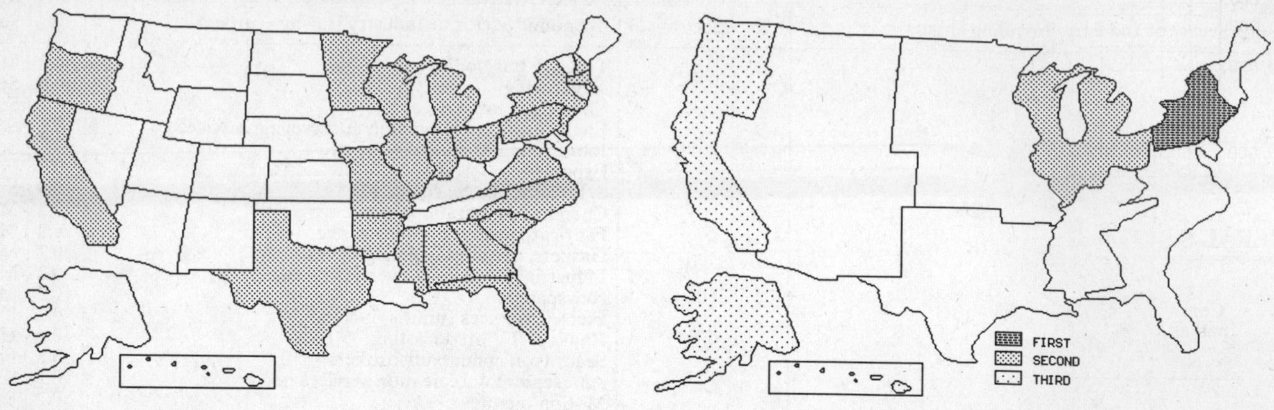

INDUSTRY DATA BY STATE

State	Establish-ments	Shipments			Employment				Cost as % of Shipments	Investment per Employee ($)
		Total ($ mil)	% of U.S.	Per Establ.	Total Number	% of U.S.	Per Establ.	Wages ($/hour)		
Illinois	33	217.2	10.8	6.6	1,600	10.3	48	9.84	51.8	3,188
California	48	185.7	9.2	3.9	1,400	9.0	29	10.52	57.6	2,857
New York	55	150.3	7.5	2.7	2,200	14.1	40	8.14	44.3	1,091
Georgia	11	109.5	5.4	10.0	500	3.2	45	10.63	71.3	-
New Jersey	29	98.5	4.9	3.4	900	5.8	31	10.60	49.4	1,222
Indiana	5	95.0	4.7	19.0	600	3.8	120	9.90	70.6	-
Ohio	19	88.8	4.4	4.7	800	5.1	42	10.08	46.4	-
Massachusetts	9	77.0	3.8	8.6	700	4.5	78	10.91	42.9	3,143
Wisconsin	12	75.3	3.7	6.3	500	3.2	42	11.50	52.9	-
Mississippi	10	73.3	3.6	7.3	600	3.8	60	7.60	67.9	1,333
Texas	15	68.1	3.4	4.5	700	4.5	47	10.36	51.5	571
Pennsylvania	19	53.6	2.7	2.8	700	4.5	37	9.30	56.0	1,857
Florida	15	40.1	2.0	2.7	400	2.6	27	12.40	64.3	1,250
Michigan	18	34.8	1.7	1.9	300	1.9	17	8.17	60.1	-
Alabama	8	24.0	1.2	3.0	200	1.3	25	6.33	37.1	29,000
South Carolina	3	15.6	0.8	5.2	200	1.3	67	7.33	55.1	1,000
Arkansas	3	4.3	0.2	1.4	100	0.6	33	5.00	44.2	-
Missouri	9	(D)	-	-	375 *	2.4	42	-	-	-
North Carolina	9	(D)	-	-	750 *	4.8	83	-	-	2,800
New Hampshire	5	(D)	-	-	175 *	1.1	35	-	-	-
Oregon	5	(D)	-	-	175 *	1.1	35	-	-	-
Minnesota	3	(D)	-	-	1,750 *	11.2	583	-	-	-
Virginia	3	(D)	-	-	175 *	1.1	58	-	-	-

Source: 1992 *Economic Census*. The states are in descending order of shipments or establishments (if shipment data are missing for the majority). The symbol (D) appears when data are withheld to prevent disclosure of competitive information. States marked with (D) are sorted by number of establishments. A dash (-) indicates that the data element cannot be calculated; * indicates the midpoint of a range.

2676 - SANITARY PAPER PRODUCTS

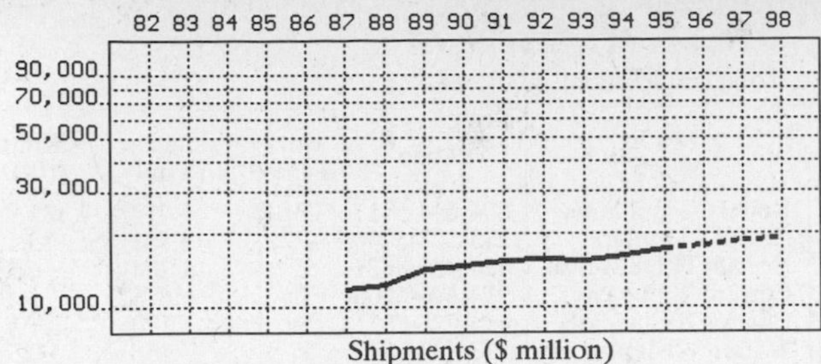

Shipments ($ million)

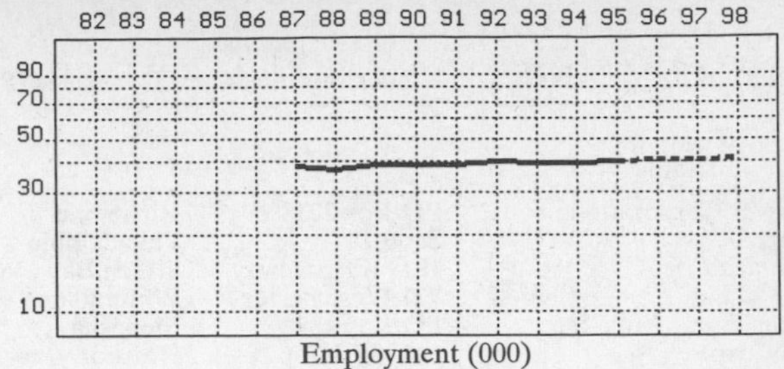

Employment (000)

GENERAL STATISTICS

Year	Companies	Establishments: Total	Establishments: with 20 or more employees	Employment: Total (000)	Employment: Production Workers (000)	Employment: Production Hours (Mil)	Compensation: Payroll ($ mil)	Compensation: Wages ($/hr)	Production ($ million): Cost of Materials	Production ($ million): Value Added by Manufacture	Production ($ million): Value of Shipments	Production ($ million): Capital Invest.
1982												
1983												
1984												
1985												
1986												
1987	76	133	111	38.4	29.9	62.5	1,155.0	13.77	5,500.9	6,309.3	11,698.4	430.4
1988		136	113	37.5	29.4	62.1	1,197.7	14.23	6,078.7	6,294.3	12,312.3	478.7
1989		134	118	38.9	29.6	61.9	1,234.8	14.95	6,627.1	7,741.0	14,332.2	630.2
1990		137	122	39.3	31.0	65.3	1,299.2	15.11	6,887.4	7,896.2	14,709.2	526.2
1991		146	126	38.8	31.1	65.5	1,342.9	15.45	6,818.0	8,747.0	15,593.5	460.6
1992	80	150	125	40.5	32.7	68.1	1,451.1	16.08	7,369.9	8,220.4	15,622.7	418.5
1993		152	124	39.6	32.4	68.9	1,443.9	16.26	7,177.9	8,400.9	15,525.1	634.7
1994		155P	130P	39.7	32.6	69.7	1,470.1	16.54	7,381.0	8,858.9	16,199.6	469.3
1995		158P	133P	40.4P	33.4P	71.0P	1,545.5P	17.08P	7,883.5P	9,462.0P	17,302.4P	524.9P
1996		162P	135P	40.7P	33.9P	72.3P	1,594.7P	17.48P	8,167.3P	9,802.7P	17,925.4P	529.1P
1997		165P	138P	40.9P	34.4P	73.5P	1,643.9P	17.87P	8,451.1P	10,143.3P	18,548.3P	533.3P
1998		169P	140P	41.2P	35.0P	74.7P	1,693.0P	18.27P	8,735.0P	10,484.0P	19,171.3P	537.5P

Sources: 1982, 1987, 1992 *Economic Census*; *Annual Survey of Manufactures*, 83-86, 88-91, 93-94. Establishment counts for non-Census years are from *County Business Patterns*; establishment values for 83-84 are extrapolations. 'P's show projections by the editors. Industries reclassified in 87 will not have data for prior years.

INDICES OF CHANGE

Year	Companies	Establishments: Total	Establishments: with 20 or more employees	Employment: Total (000)	Employment: Production Workers (000)	Employment: Production Hours (Mil)	Compensation: Payroll ($ mil)	Compensation: Wages ($/hr)	Production ($ million): Cost of Materials	Production ($ million): Value Added by Manufacture	Production ($ million): Value of Shipments	Production ($ million): Capital Invest.
1982												
1983												
1984												
1985												
1986												
1987	95	89	89	95	91	92	80	86	75	77	75	103
1988		91	90	93	90	91	83	88	82	77	79	114
1989		89	94	96	91	91	85	93	90	94	92	151
1990		91	98	97	95	96	90	94	93	96	94	126
1991		97	101	96	95	96	93	96	93	106	100	110
1992	100	100	100	100	100	100	100	100	100	100	100	100
1993		101	99	98	99	101	100	101	97	102	99	152
1994		103P	104P	98	100	102	101	103	100	108	104	112
1995		106P	106P	100P	102P	104P	107P	106P	107P	115P	111P	125P
1996		108P	108P	100P	104P	106P	110P	109P	111P	119P	115P	126P
1997		110P	110P	101P	105P	108P	113P	111P	115P	123P	119P	127P
1998		113P	112P	102P	107P	110P	117P	114P	119P	128P	123P	128P

Sources: Same as General Statistics. Values reflect change from the base year, 1992. Values above 100 mean greater than 92, values below 100 mean less than 92, and a value of 100 in the 82-91 or 93-98 period means same as 92. 'P's mark projections by the editors.

SELECTED RATIOS

For 1994	Avg. of All Manufact.	Analyzed Industry	Index
Employees per Establishment	49	256	523
Payroll per Establishment	1,500,273	9,484,516	632
Payroll per Employee	30,620	37,030	121
Production Workers per Establishment	34	210	613
Wages per Establishment	853,319	7,437,665	872
Wages per Production Worker	24,861	35,363	142
Hours per Production Worker	2,056	2,138	104
Wages per Hour	12.09	16.54	137
Value Added per Establishment	4,602,255	57,154,194	1,242
Value Added per Employee	93,930	223,146	238

For 1994	Avg. of All Manufact.	Analyzed Industry	Index
Value Added per Production Worker	134,084	271,745	203
Cost per Establishment	5,045,178	47,619,355	944
Cost per Employee	102,970	185,919	181
Cost per Production Worker	146,988	226,411	154
Shipments per Establishment	9,576,895	104,513,548	1,091
Shipments per Employee	195,460	408,050	209
Shipments per Production Worker	279,017	496,920	178
Investment per Establishment	321,011	3,027,742	943
Investment per Employee	6,552	11,821	180
Investment per Production Worker	9,352	14,396	154

Sources: Same as General Statistics. The 'Average of All Manufacturing' column represents the average of all manufacturing industries reported for the most recent complete year available. The Index shows the relationship between the Average and the Analyzed Industry. For example, 100 means that they are equal; 500 that the Analyzed Industry is five times the average; 50 means that the Analyzed Industry is half the national average. The abbreviation 'na' is used to show that data are 'not available'.

LEADING COMPANIES

Number shown: **34** Total sales ($ mil): **12,179** Total employment (000): **68.7**

Company Name	Address				CEO Name	Phone	Co. Type	Sales ($ mil)	Empl. (000)
James River Corporation	PO Box 2218	Richmond	VA	23217	Robert C Williams	804-644-5411	P	5,417	33.8
Scott Paper Co	Scott Plz	Philadelphia	PA	19113	Albert J Dunlap	215-522-5000	P	3,581	15.1
Fort Howard Corp	1919 S Broadway	Green Bay	WI	54304	Donald H DeMeuse	414-435-8821	P	1,274	6.8
Tambrands Inc	777 Westchester	White Plains	NY	10604	Edward T Fogarty	914-696-6000	P	645	3.4
Wisconsin Tissue Mills Inc	PO Box 489	Menasha	WI	54952	Charles S Cianciola	414-725-7031	S	170	1.5
Drypers Corp	1415 W Loop N	Houston	TX	77055	Walter V Klemp	713-682-6848	P	156	0.5
Tranzonic Cos	30195 Chagrin Blv	Pepper Pike	OH	44124	Robert S Reitman	216-831-5757	P	149	1.6
Nice-Pak Products Inc	2 Nice-Pak Park	Orangeburg	NY	10962	Robert Julius	914-365-1700	R	94	0.9
Whitestone Products Inc	40 Turner Pl	Piscataway	NJ	08854	John Brennan	908-752-2700	R	85	0.5
Statler Industries Inc	300 Middlesex Av	Medford	MA	02155	Leonard Sugarman	617-395-7770	R	70	0.7
INBRAND Corp	PO Box 1181	Marietta	GA	30061	Garnett A Smith	404-422-3036	P	70	0.3
Statler Tissue Corp	300 Middlesex Av	Medford	MA	02155	Leonard Sugarman	617-395-7770	S	65	0.7
Hospital Specialty Co	7501 Carnegie Av	Cleveland	OH	44103	ML Reitman	216-361-1230	D	60	0.4
Encore Paper Company Inc	1 River St	S Glens Falls	NY	12803	William New	518-793-5684	R	50	0.3
Paper-Pak Products Inc	PO Box 1060	La Verne	CA	91750	WG Hopkins	909-396-4300	R	50	0.3
APL Corp	3005 Greene St	Hollywood	FL	33020		305-929-8400	S	35	0.5
Cellu Tissue Corp	2 Forbes St	East Hartford	CT	06108	Edward P Foote Jr	203-289-7496	R	25	0.1
R Sabee Co	1718 W 8th St	Appleton	WI	54914	Michael Sabee	414-734-9551	R	22	0.2
Amjems Inc	3725 E 10th Ct	Hialeah	FL	33013	Roberto Baspanzuri	305-835-8046	R	21*	0.2
Busse Hospital Disposables	75 Arkay Dr	Hauppauge	NY	11788	E Cardinale	516-435-4711	D	18	0.1
Paterson Pacific Parchment Co	625 Greg St	Sparks	NV	89431	Thomas Buckley	702-353-3000	R	18	<0.1
Standard Cos	3110 S Shields Av	Chicago	IL	60616	G Bonomo	312-225-2777	R	14	<0.1
Principle Business Enterprises	PO Box 129	Dunbridge	OH	43414	Charles A Stocking	419-352-1551	R	13	0.1
Veragon	1415 W Loop N	Houston	TX	77055	Walter V Klemp	713-682-6848	D	13*	0.1
Great Lakes Tissue Co	437 S Main St	Cheboygan	MI	49721	Clarence Roznowski	616-627-0200	R	12*	<0.1
Riverside Group	226 Jay St	Rochester	NY	14608	Peter Pape	716-263-2800	R	11	0.2
SQP Inc	PO Box 2023	Scotia	NY	12302	John Gargiulo	518-374-0770	S	10*	<0.1
IFC Disposable Inc	PO Box 1561	Jackson	TN	38302	James S Dykes	901-423-4350	R	9*	<0.1
WR Rayson Co	PO Box 1459	Burgaw	NC	28425	Michael DiMartino	919-259-8100	R	9	<0.1
Clark Paper Converting Corp	1625 Potrero Av	S El Monte	CA	91733	Ted Pasternack	213-686-1917	R	5	<0.1
National Empire Manufacturing	4782-B Bs Ferry	Atlanta	GA	30336	Harold Itkin	404-699-7511	S	5*	<0.1
Sandler Brothers Inc	3621 Medford St	Los Angeles	CA	90063	Barry Sandler	213-269-0494	R	1	<0.1
Gelok International	Pine Lake Industrial	Dunbridge	OH	43414	Jim Mitchell	419-352-1482	R	1	<0.1
Paperades Inc	27 W Broad St	Pawcatuck	CT	06379	Frank Deciantis	203-599-1480	R	1	<0.1

Source: Ward's Business Directory of U.S. Private and Public Companies, Volumes 1 and 2, 1996. The company type code used is as follows: P - Public, R - Private, S - Subsidiary, D - Division, J - Joint Venture, A - Affiliate, G - Group. Sales are in millions of dollars, employees are in thousands. An asterisk (*) indicates an estimated sales volume. The symbol < stands for 'less than'. Company names and addresses are truncated, in some cases, to fit into the available space.

MATERIALS CONSUMED

Material		Quantity	Delivered Cost ($ million)
Materials, ingredients, containers, and supplies		(X)	7,087.0
Paper	1,000 s tons	4,357.7	3,340.8
Woodpulp (air dry basis)	1,000 s tons	1,274.9	654.7
Wastepaper, all types	1,000 s tons	446.7	64.7
Glues and adhesives	mil lb	176.7	149.8
Plastics resins consumed in the form of granules, pellets, powders, liquids, etc.	mil lb	149.6	176.0
Plastics products consumed in the form of sheets, rods, tubes, film, and other shapes		(X)	333.0
Nonwoven fabrics	mil sq yd	11,196.8*	483.6
Packaging paper and plastics film, coated, laminated, printed, etc.		(X)	371.1
Paperboard containers, boxes, and corrugated paperboard		(X)	437.7
All other materials and components, parts, containers, and supplies		(X)	925.2
Materials, ingredients, containers, and supplies, nsk		(X)	150.4

Source: 1992 *Economic Census*. Explanation of symbols used: (D): Withheld to avoid disclosure of competitive data; na: Not available; (S): Withheld because statistical norms were not met; (X): Not applicable; (Z): Less than half the unit shown; nec: Not elsewhere classified; nsk: Not specified by kind; - : zero; * : 10-19 percent estimated; ** : 20-29 percent estimated.

PRODUCT SHARE DETAILS

Product or Product Class	% Share
Sanitary paper products	100.00
Sanitary napkins and tampons	11.20
Disposable diapers, except adult (usually containing pulp or cellulose fibers), including disposable training pants	27.75
Sanitary tissue paper products	59.49
Facial tissues and handkerchiefs, including sputum wipes	8.70
Paper table napkins, industrial (bulk and dispenser type), regular type, single-ply, bulk	2.53
Paper table napkins, industrial (bulk and dispenser type), regular type, single-ply, dispenser	3.46
Paper table napkins, industrial (bulk or dispenser type), facial tissue type, two-ply or more	1.90
Paper table napkins, retail packages (resale), regular type, single-ply	2.62
Paper table napkins, retail packages (resale), facial tissue type, two-ply or more	4.09
Toilet tissue, rolls and ovals, industrial, facial tissue type, two-ply or more	6.38
Toilet tissue, rolls and ovals, industrial, regular type, single-ply	5.15
Toilet tissue, rolls and ovals, retail packages (resale), facial tissue type, two-ply or more	12.96
Toilet tissue, rolls and ovals, retail packages (resale), regular type, single-ply	16.30
Paper towels (rolled, folded, or interfolded), industrial	10.03
Paper towels (rolled, folded, or interfolded), retail packages (resale), single-ply	7.06
Paper towels (rolled, folded, or interfolded), retail packages (resale), two-ply or more	14.96
Paper wipers (windshield, industrial, and lithographic plate), except nonwoven	1.22
Other sanitary paper products, including absorbent pads, toilet seat covers, bibs, headrests, tray covers, etc., except surgical and medical	2.04
Sanitary tissue paper products, nsk	0.61
Sanitary paper products, nsk	1.56

Source: 1992 *Economic Census*. The values shown are percent of total shipments in an industry. Values of indented subcategories are summed in the main heading. The symbol (D) appears when data are withheld to prevent disclosure of competitive information. The abbreviation nsk stands for 'not specified by kind' and nec for 'not elsewhere classified'.

INPUTS AND OUTPUTS FOR SANITARY PAPER PRODUCTS

Economic Sector or Industry Providing Inputs	%	Sector	Economic Sector or Industry Buying Outputs	%	Sector
Paper mills, except building paper	41.5	Manufg.	Personal consumption expenditures	79.1	
Pulp mills	12.5	Manufg.	Eating & drinking places	6.1	Trade
Paperboard containers & boxes	9.2	Manufg.	Exports	2.9	Foreign
Wholesale trade	7.6	Trade	S/L Govt. purch., elem. & secondary education	1.3	S/L Govt
Nonwoven fabrics	5.1	Manufg.	Hotels & lodging places	1.1	Services
Broadwoven fabric mills	2.7	Manufg.	Services to dwellings & other buildings	0.9	Services
Miscellaneous plastics products	2.7	Manufg.	Hospitals	0.8	Services
Advertising	2.5	Services	S/L Govt. purch., health & hospitals	0.8	S/L Govt
Motor freight transportation & warehousing	2.0	Util.	Change in business inventories	0.7	In House
Petroleum refining	1.8	Manufg.	Retail trade, except eating & drinking	0.5	Trade
Railroads & related services	1.7	Util.	Real estate	0.4	Fin/R.E.
Electric services (utilities)	1.4	Util.	Religious organizations	0.4	Services
Adhesives & sealants	1.3	Manufg.	Elementary & secondary schools	0.3	Services
Air transportation	0.9	Util.	Nursing & personal care facilities	0.3	Services
Hotels & lodging places	0.5	Services	S/L Govt. purch., higher education	0.3	S/L Govt
Gas production & distribution (utilities)	0.4	Util.	S/L Govt. purch., other general government	0.3	S/L Govt
Sanitary services, steam supply, irrigation	0.4	Util.	Wholesale trade	0.2	Trade
Banking	0.4	Fin/R.E.	Colleges, universities, & professional schools	0.2	Services
Paper coating & glazing	0.3	Manufg.	Federal Government purchases, nondefense	0.2	Fed Govt
Paper industries machinery	0.3	Manufg.	Banking	0.1	Fin/R.E.
Plastics materials & resins	0.3	Manufg.	Federal Government purchases, national defense	0.1	Fed Govt
Communications, except radio & TV	0.3	Util.			
Automotive rental & leasing, without drivers	0.3	Services			
Maintenance of nonfarm buildings nec	0.2	Constr.			
Paperboard mills	0.2	Manufg.			
Printing ink	0.2	Manufg.			
Eating & drinking places	0.2	Trade			
Insurance carriers	0.2	Fin/R.E.			
Real estate	0.2	Fin/R.E.			
Royalties	0.2	Fin/R.E.			
Automotive repair shops & services	0.2	Services			
Equipment rental & leasing services	0.2	Services			
Water transportation	0.1	Util.			
Business/professional associations	0.1	Services			
Computer & data processing services	0.1	Services			

Source: Benchmark Input-Output Accounts for the U.S. Economy, 1982, U.S. Department of Commerce, Washington, D.C., July 1991. Data, as reported in the source, are organized by the 1977 SIC structure in use in 1982 but have been matched, as closely as is possible, to the 1987 SIC structure used in this book.

OCCUPATIONS EMPLOYED BY SIC 267 - MISCELLANEOUS CONVERTED PAPER PRODUCTS

Occupation	% of Total 1994	Change to 2005	Occupation	% of Total 1994	Change to 2005
Paper goods machine setters & set-up operators	9.0	-15.9	Machine feeders & offbearers	2.5	-5.4
Machine operators nec	6.8	29.7	Industrial machinery mechanics	2.1	15.6
Hand packers & packagers	5.7	-9.9	Inspectors, testers, & graders, precision	2.1	15.6
Blue collar worker supervisors	4.5	6.8	Packaging & filling machine operators	2.1	5.1
Assemblers, fabricators, & hand workers nec	4.4	5.1	Freight, stock, & material movers, hand	2.0	-15.9
Printing press machine setters, operators	4.3	5.1	Maintenance repairers, general utility	2.0	5.1
Cutting & slicing machine setters, operators	4.0	26.1	Traffic, shipping, & receiving clerks	1.9	1.1
Sales & related workers nec	3.0	5.1	General managers & top executives	1.8	-0.3
Helpers, laborers, & material movers nec	2.9	5.1	Machine forming operators, metal & plastic	1.7	57.6
Extruding & forming machine workers	2.8	36.6	Coating, painting, & spraying machine workers	1.7	-15.9
Printing, binding, & related workers nec	2.6	5.1	Secretaries, ex legal & medical	1.6	-4.3
Industrial truck & tractor operators	2.6	5.1	Industrial production managers	1.2	5.1

Source: *Industry-Occupation Matrix*, Bureau of Labor Statistics. These data relate to one or more 3-digit SIC industry groups rather than to a single 4-digit SIC. The change reported for each occupation to the year 2005 is a percent of growth or decline as estimated by the Bureau of Labor Statistics. The abbreviation nec stands for 'not elsewhere classified'.

LOCATION BY STATE AND REGIONAL CONCENTRATION

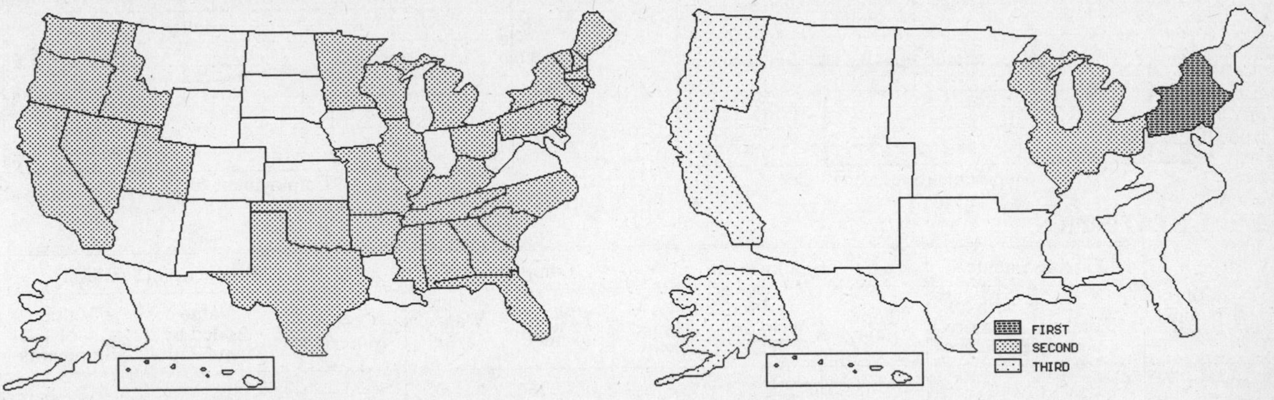

INDUSTRY DATA BY STATE

State	Establish-ments	Shipments			Employment				Cost as % of Shipments	Investment per Employee ($)
		Total ($ mil)	% of U.S.	Per Establ.	Total Number	% of U.S.	Per Establ.	Wages ($/hour)		
Wisconsin	15	2,815.7	18.0	187.7	7,600	18.8	507	17.19	52.4	6,553
Pennsylvania	12	2,067.1	13.2	172.3	4,600	11.4	383	19.42	42.5	12,348
Georgia	7	1,411.2	9.0	201.6	2,900	7.2	414	17.66	50.3	9,759
California	14	1,044.4	6.7	74.6	2,400	5.9	171	15.50	50.6	-
Washington	4	661.5	4.2	165.4	1,300	3.2	325	18.04	68.3	8,769
Texas	4	403.1	2.6	100.8	1,100	2.7	275	13.92	71.8	-
New York	16	322.1	2.1	20.1	1,500	3.7	94	11.07	53.6	8,133
New Jersey	10	319.3	2.0	31.9	1,700	4.2	170	14.47	36.2	-
Maine	3	217.5	1.4	72.5	1,200	3.0	400	13.35	49.4	-
Vermont	4	181.4	1.2	45.3	700	1.7	175	9.45	32.8	2,714
Kentucky	4	117.5	0.8	29.4	500	1.2	125	10.13	67.8	13,200
Ohio	4	96.8	0.6	24.2	400	1.0	100	10.29	53.7	20,750
Mississippi	3	75.8	0.5	25.3	300	0.7	100	12.80	62.7	-
Michigan	5	(D)	-	-	750 *	1.9	150	-	-	-
Florida	4	(D)	-	-	750 *	1.9	188	-	-	-
Illinois	4	(D)	-	-	750 *	1.9	188	-	-	-
Massachusetts	4	(D)	-	-	375 *	0.9	94	-	-	-
Oklahoma	4	(D)	-	-	1,750 *	4.3	438	-	-	-
Missouri	3	(D)	-	-	1,750 *	4.3	583	-	-	-
Tennessee	3	(D)	-	-	750 *	1.9	250	-	-	-
Alabama	2	(D)	-	-	1,750 *	4.3	875	-	-	-
Arkansas	2	(D)	-	-	750 *	1.9	375	-	-	-
Connecticut	2	(D)	-	-	1,750 *	4.3	875	-	-	-
Minnesota	2	(D)	-	-	175 *	0.4	88	-	-	-
Nevada	2	(D)	-	-	175 *	0.4	88	-	-	-
New Hampshire	2	(D)	-	-	750 *	1.9	375	-	-	-
North Carolina	2	(D)	-	-	175 *	0.4	88	-	-	-
Oregon	2	(D)	-	-	750 *	1.9	375	-	-	-
South Carolina	2	(D)	-	-	750 *	1.9	375	-	-	-
Delaware	1	(D)	-	-	1,750 *	4.3	1,750	-	-	-
Idaho	1	(D)	-	-	750 *	1.9	750	-	-	-
Utah	1	(D)	-	-	750 *	1.9	750	-	-	-

Source: 1992 *Economic Census*. The states are in descending order of shipments or establishments (if shipment data are missing for the majority). The symbol (D) appears when data are withheld to prevent disclosure of competitive information. States marked with (D) are sorted by number of establishments. A dash (-) indicates that the data element cannot be calculated; * indicates the midpoint of a range.

2677 - ENVELOPES

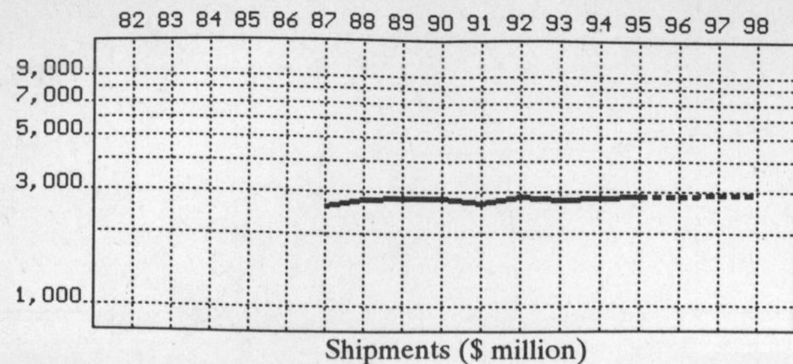

Shipments ($ million)

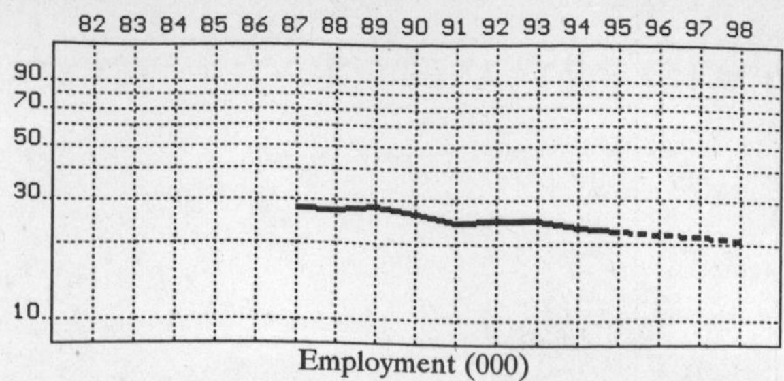

Employment (000)

GENERAL STATISTICS

Year	Com-panies	Establishments		Employment			Compensation		Production ($ million)			
		Total	with 20 or more employees	Total (000)	Production Workers (000)	Production Hours (Mil)	Payroll ($ mil)	Wages ($/hr)	Cost of Materials	Value Added by Manufacture	Value of Shipments	Capital Invest.
1982												
1983												
1984												
1985												
1986												
1987	202	298	215	27.6	20.8	43.4	612.8	9.39	1,403.8	1,192.9	2,598.1	61.3
1988		301	220	27.5	20.8	42.9	628.4	9.82	1,537.5	1,253.1	2,769.4	66.9
1989		279	212	28.2	21.1	43.3	644.8	9.97	1,578.3	1,246.9	2,816.0	75.5
1990		277	213	26.6	20.3	42.4	648.4	10.20	1,620.6	1,194.9	2,816.6	66.8
1991		276	206	24.5	19.0	38.8	615.5	10.57	1,458.1	1,195.1	2,668.9	43.9
1992	192	283	207	24.9	19.0	39.0	672.3	11.41	1,488.4	1,361.7	2,854.1	55.3
1993		272	201	24.7	19.1	39.2	673.1	11.48	1,496.3	1,284.6	2,772.8	46.6
1994		267P	200P	23.0	18.1	37.6	632.7	11.12	1,551.1	1,262.6	2,816.5	29.4
1995		263P	197P	22.8P	17.9P	36.8P	663.1P	11.84P	1,566.8P	1,275.4P	2,845.1P	33.8P
1996		259P	195P	22.1P	17.5P	35.9P	668.0P	12.14P	1,576.8P	1,283.5P	2,863.1P	29.0P
1997		254P	192P	21.4P	17.1P	35.0P	672.9P	12.44P	1,586.7P	1,291.6P	2,881.1P	24.1P
1998		250P	189P	20.7P	16.7P	34.1P	677.8P	12.74P	1,596.6P	1,299.6P	2,899.1P	19.3P

Sources: 1982, 1987, 1992 *Economic Census*; *Annual Survey of Manufactures*, 83-86, 88-91, 93-94. Establishment counts for non-Census years are from *County Business Patterns*; establishment values for 83-84 are extrapolations. 'P's show projections by the editors. Industries reclassified in 87 will not have data for prior years.

INDICES OF CHANGE

Year	Com-panies	Establishments		Employment			Compensation		Production ($ million)			
		Total	with 20 or more employees	Total (000)	Production Workers (000)	Production Hours (Mil)	Payroll ($ mil)	Wages ($/hr)	Cost of Materials	Value Added by Manufacture	Value of Shipments	Capital Invest.
1982												
1983												
1984												
1985												
1986												
1987	105	105	104	111	109	111	91	82	94	88	91	111
1988		106	106	110	109	110	93	86	103	92	97	121
1989		99	102	113	111	111	96	87	106	92	99	137
1990		98	103	107	107	109	96	89	109	88	99	121
1991		98	100	98	100	99	92	93	98	88	94	79
1992	100	100	100	100	100	100	100	100	100	100	100	100
1993		96	97	99	101	101	100	101	101	94	97	84
1994		94P	97P	92	95	96	94	97	104	93	99	53
1995		93P	95P	91P	94P	94P	99P	104P	105P	94P	100P	61P
1996		91P	94P	89P	92P	92P	99P	106P	106P	94P	100P	52P
1997		90P	93P	86P	90P	90P	100P	109P	107P	95P	101P	44P
1998		88P	92P	83P	88P	87P	101P	112P	107P	95P	102P	35P

Sources: Same as General Statistics. Values reflect change from the base year, 1992. Values above 100 mean greater than 92, values below 100 mean less than 92, and a value of 100 in the 82-91 or 93-98 period means same as 92. 'P's mark projections by the editors.

SELECTED RATIOS

For 1994	Avg. of All Manufact.	Analyzed Industry	Index
Employees per Establishment	49	86	176
Payroll per Establishment	1,500,273	2,369,663	158
Payroll per Employee	30,620	27,509	90
Production Workers per Establishment	34	68	198
Wages per Establishment	853,319	1,565,963	184
Wages per Production Worker	24,861	23,100	93
Hours per Production Worker	2,056	2,077	101
Wages per Hour	12.09	11.12	92
Value Added per Establishment	4,602,255	4,728,839	103
Value Added per Employee	93,930	54,896	58

For 1994	Avg. of All Manufact.	Analyzed Industry	Index
Value Added per Production Worker	134,084	69,757	52
Cost per Establishment	5,045,178	5,809,363	115
Cost per Employee	102,970	67,439	65
Cost per Production Worker	146,988	85,696	58
Shipments per Establishment	9,576,895	10,548,689	110
Shipments per Employee	195,460	122,457	63
Shipments per Production Worker	279,017	155,608	56
Investment per Establishment	321,011	110,112	34
Investment per Employee	6,552	1,278	20
Investment per Production Worker	9,352	1,624	17

Sources: Same as General Statistics. The 'Average of All Manufacturing' column represents the average of all manufacturing industries reported for the most recent complete year available. The Index shows the relationship between the Average and the Analyzed Industry. For example, 100 means that they are equal; 500 that the Analyzed Industry is five times the average; 50 means that the Analyzed Industry is half the national average. The abbreviation 'na' is used to show that data are 'not available'.

LEADING COMPANIES Number shown: **60** Total sales ($ mil): **2,267** Total employment (000): **20.6**

Company Name	Address				CEO Name	Phone	Co. Type	Sales ($ mil)	Empl. (000)
American Business Products Inc	PO Box 105684	Atlanta	GA	30348	Thomas R Carmody	404-953-8300	P	563	4.2
Mail-Well Envelope Co	23 Inverness Way E	Englewood	CO	80112	Gerald Mahoney	303-397-7440	R	280	2.6
New York Envelope Corp	29-10 Hunters Point	Long Island Ct	NY	11101	William Ungar	718-786-0300	R	160*	1.5
Tension Envelope Corp	819 E 19th St	Kansas City	MO	64108	William S Berkley	816-471-3800	R	145	1.5
Baltimore Envelope Co	PO Box 741267	Atlanta	GA	30374	Randy Zook	404-351-5011	D	94	0.9
Quality Park Products Co	2520 Como Av	St Paul	MN	55108	Kenneth E Templin	612-645-0251	S	86*	0.5
Old Colony Envelope Co	94 N Elm St	Westfield	MA	01086	W W Stinger Jr	413-568-2431	D	76	0.6
Ames Safety Envelope Co	21 Properzi Way	Somerville	MA	02143	William E Shea	617-776-3360	R	50	0.5
International Envelope Co	2 Tabas Ln	Exton	PA	19341	Tom Isola	215-363-0900	R	50*	0.3
Western States Envelope Co	4480 N 132nd St	Butler	WI	53007	GF Moss	414-781-5540	R	45	0.4
Gilmore Envelope Corp	4540 Worth St	Los Angeles	CA	90063	HN Gilmore Jr	213-268-3401	R	44*	0.4
Gilmore Envelope Corp	4540 Worth St	Los Angeles	CA	90063	HN Gilmore Jr	213-268-3401	D	41	0.3
Mackay Envelope Corp	2100 Elm St SE	Minneapolis	MN	55414	Harvey B Mackay	612-331-9311	R	40	0.4
American Envelope Co	3001 N Rockwell St	Chicago	IL	60618	Stan Dvorak	312-267-3600	D	36*	0.3
Williamshouse	PO Box 3009	Miamisburg	OH	45342	Steven Oglesbee	513-859-9300	S	34*	0.2
Oles Envelope Corp	532 E 25th St	Baltimore	MD	21218	JR Young	410-243-1520	R	32	0.3
Williamhouse Sales Corp	28 W 23rd St	New York	NY	10010	Jerry Salafrio	212-691-2000	S	31*	0.4
Worcester Envelope Co	PO Box 406	Auburn	MA	01501	Eldon D Pond Jr	508-832-5394	R	31	0.2
American Paper Group Ltd	8401 Southern Blv	Youngstown	OH	44512	C Preston Miller	216-758-4545	R	30	0.5
Double Envelope Co	PO Box 7000	Roanoke	VA	24019	Rob Miklas	703-362-3311	S	26	0.5
National Fiberstok Corp	2051 Potshop Ln	Norristown	PA	19403	Robert M Miklas	610-631-6454	R	26	0.5
American Paper Products Co	8401 Southern Blv	Youngstown	OH	44512	CP Miller	216-758-4545	D	25	0.3
Berlin and Jones Co	2 E Union Av	E Rutherford	NJ	07073	Duncan Whyte Jr	201-933-5900	R	24	0.2
National Envelope Central	13871 Pks Steed Dr	Earth City	MO	63045	D Schroeder	314-291-2722	D	22	0.2
American Envelope Co	100 Center Dr	Orchard Park	NY	14127	RA Fitzgerald	716-662-2800	D	21*	0.2
Victor Envelope Mfg Corp	301 Arthur Ct	Bensenville	IL	60106	H Burgess	708-616-2750	R	21*	0.2
Frank G Love Envelope Co	1130 Quaker St	Dallas	TX	75207	Mike Love	214-637-5900	R	20*	0.2
Pavey Envelope and Tag Inc	25 Linden Av E	Jersey City	NJ	07305	G Napiorkowski	201-434-2100	S	15	0.2
Brenner Paper Products	66-31 Otto Rd	Glendale	NY	11385	RB Levenson	718-456-7817	R	15	0.1
Huxley Envelope Corp	145 West St	Brooklyn	NY	11222	Roy Grover	718-389-7800	R	14	0.1
New England Envelope Mfg Co	237 Chandler St	Worcester	MA	01609	EF Bickley Jr	508-798-3736	R	13*	0.2
Bowers Envelope Company Inc	PO Box 20271	Indianapolis	IN	46220	James E Bowers	317-253-4321	R	12	0.1
Darling Envelope Corp	PO Box 657	Shawnee Msn	KS	66201	Bert Darling	913-831-2525	R	12	0.1
Wolf Detroit Envelope Co	725 S Adams Rd	Birmingham	MI	48009	Hugh F Mahler	313-258-5700	R	11	0.1
General Business Envelope	10 Midland	Hartford	CT	06120	L Martyn	203-727-9100	D	8	<0.1
Publishers Envelope	PO Box 27226	Richmond	VA	23261	Bob N Posey	804-355-8039	D	8	0.1
Wolf Envelope Company Inc	248 Artino St	Oberlin	OH	44074	Jeff L Anspach	216-774-8470	R	8	<0.1
Northeastern Envelope Co	PO Box T	Clarks Summit	PA	18411	James F Ferrario	717-586-1061	R	8	<0.1
Roodhouse Envelope Co	414 S State St	Roodhouse	IL	62082	Gary Randall	217-589-4321	R	7	0.1
Griffin Envelope Inc	PO Box 24267	Seattle	WA	98124	Donald Wilson	206-682-4400	R	7	<0.1
Milwaukee Envelope Inc	PO Box 1001	Oconomowoc	WI	53006	Deborah C Quirk	414-782-5550	R	7	0.1
National Church Supply	PO Box 269	Chester	WV	26034	Charles D Taylor	304-387-5200	R	7	0.1
Northeastern Envelope	1515 Washington St	Braintree	MA	02184	Gerald P Mitchell	617-843-4900	R	7*	<0.1
Design Distributors Inc	45 E Industry Ct	Deer Park	NY	11729	SJ Avrick	516-242-2000	R	6	<0.1
Springfield Tablet Mfg Co	PO Box 2145	Springfield	MO	65801	KG Wells	417-862-6638	R	6	<0.1
ABC Die Cutting Corp	601 W 26th St	New York	NY	10001	Irvin Fox	212-675-4110	R	5*	<0.1
Federal Envelope Co	850 Arthur Av	Elk Grove Vill	IL	60007	Howard Shaw Sr	708-593-2000	R	5*	<0.1
Rays Envelope Corp	7521 Pulaski Hwy	Baltimore	MD	21237	RH Hettchen	410-866-3550	R	5	<0.1
Information Packaging Corp	1670 N Wayne Port	Macedon	NY	14502	Jim Sellar	315-986-5793	R	4	<0.1
Pacific Envelope Co	2164 N Glassell St	Orange	CA	92665	Robert L Cashman	714-637-0773	R	4	<0.1
Envelope Co	PO Box 23853	Oakland	CA	94623	Don Hansen	510-251-6100	R	3	<0.1
Gaw-O'Hara Envelope Co	500 N Sacramento	Chicago	IL	60612	JG Warble	312-638-1200	R	3*	<0.1
Gray Envelope Co	225 N Bruns	Piscataway	NJ	08854	Kevin T Robinson	908-981-0933	R	3	<0.1
Seaboard Envelope Co	15601 Cypress St	Irwindale	CA	91706	Bill Niedringhaus	818-960-4559	R	3*	<0.1
Custom Envelope Corp	4990 Iris St	Wheat Ridge	CO	80033	Robert Tucker	303-456-8000	R	3	<0.1
Envelope Man Plus	2536 W Penn Way	Kansas City	MO	64108	Paul Guignon	816-474-5555	R	2*	<0.1
Reed Envelope Company Inc	6310 Gravel Av	Alexandria	VA	22310	Christopher Reed	703-922-4200	R	2	<0.1
Associated Enterprises Inc	498 Nepperhan Av	Yonkers	NY	10701		914-423-6500	R	2	<0.1
Heinrich Envelope Corp	925 Zane Av N	Golden Valley	MN	55422	Anthony A Popp	612-544-3571	R	1*	<0.1
SeedPrint Inc	16820 SW Allen Rd	Lake Oswego	OR	97035	Doug Oliphant	503-635-2880	R	1*	<0.1

Source: *Ward's Business Directory of U.S. Private and Public Companies*, Volumes 1 and 2, 1996. The company type code used is as follows: P - Public, R - Private, S - Subsidiary, D - Division, J - Joint Venture, A - Affiliate, G - Group. Sales are in millions of dollars, employees are in thousands. An asterisk (*) indicates an estimated sales volume. The symbol < stands for 'less than'. Company names and addresses are truncated, in some cases, to fit into the available space.

MATERIALS CONSUMED

Material		Quantity	Delivered Cost ($ million)
Materials, ingredients, containers, and supplies		(X)	1,273.8
Paper and paperboard, except boxes and containers	1,000 s tons	1,111.2**	788.3
Plastics film and sheet, unsupported		(X)	34.6
Glassine film		(X)	17.1
Glues and adhesives	mil lb	(S)	36.5
Paperboard containers, boxes, and corrugated paperboard		(X)	72.0
All other materials and components, parts, containers, and supplies		(X)	102.6
Materials, ingredients, containers, and supplies, nsk		(X)	222.6

Source: 1992 *Economic Census*. Explanation of symbols used: (D): Withheld to avoid disclosure of competitive data; na: Not available; (S): Withheld because statistical norms were not met; (X): Not applicable; (Z): Less than half the unit shown; nec: Not elsewhere classified; nsk: Not specified by kind; - : zero; * : 10-19 percent estimated; ** : 20-29 percent estimated.

PRODUCT SHARE DETAILS

Product or Product Class	% Share	Product or Product Class	% Share
Envelopes	100.00	Commercial, kraft mailing, except clasp and string-and-button types	8.73
Commercial, clasp and string-and-button types, including mailing	3.79	Commercial, all other types including padded shipping envelopes	10.90
Commercial, white or colored mailing, except clasp and string-and-button types	61.23		

Source: 1992 *Economic Census*. The values shown are percent of total shipments in an industry. Values of indented subcategories are summed in the main heading. The symbol (D) appears when data are withheld to prevent disclosure of competitive information. The abbreviation nsk stands for 'not specified by kind' and nec for 'not elsewhere classified'.

INPUTS AND OUTPUTS FOR ENVELOPES

Economic Sector or Industry Providing Inputs	%	Sector	Economic Sector or Industry Buying Outputs	%	Sector
Paper mills, except building paper	59.0	Manufg.	Banking	9.8	Fin/R.E.
Wholesale trade	10.1	Trade	Business services nec	6.5	Services
Paperboard containers & boxes	4.7	Manufg.	Computer & data processing services	4.2	Services
Adhesives & sealants	2.9	Manufg.	Commercial printing	4.0	Manufg.
Electric services (utilities)	2.6	Util.	Personal consumption expenditures	3.9	
Motor freight transportation & warehousing	2.2	Util.	Retail trade, except eating & drinking	3.7	Trade
Real estate	1.9	Fin/R.E.	S/L Govt. purch., elem. & secondary education	3.5	S/L Govt
Railroads & related services	1.4	Util.	Insurance carriers	3.4	Fin/R.E.
Miscellaneous plastics products	1.1	Manufg.	S/L Govt. purch., other general government	3.3	S/L Govt
Communications, except radio & TV	1.1	Util.	Credit agencies other than banks	3.1	Fin/R.E.
Advertising	1.1	Services	Hospitals	3.1	Services
Petroleum refining	1.0	Manufg.	Wholesale trade	2.9	Trade
Air transportation	0.9	Util.	Federal Government purchases, nondefense	2.4	Fed Govt
Envelopes	0.8	Manufg.	Religious organizations	2.3	Services
Eating & drinking places	0.8	Trade	S/L Govt. purch., higher education	2.3	S/L Govt
Equipment rental & leasing services	0.7	Services	Labor, civic, social, & fraternal associations	2.1	Services
Maintenance of nonfarm buildings nec	0.5	Constr.	Real estate	2.0	Fin/R.E.
Hotels & lodging places	0.5	Services	Insurance agents, brokers, & services	1.4	Fin/R.E.
Machinery, except electrical, nec	0.4	Manufg.	Doctors & dentists	1.4	Services
Gas production & distribution (utilities)	0.4	Util.	Federal Government purchases, national defense	1.4	Fed Govt
Banking	0.4	Fin/R.E.	S/L Govt. purch., health & hospitals	1.3	S/L Govt
Detective & protective services	0.4	Services	Exports	1.2	Foreign
Lubricating oils & greases	0.3	Manufg.	Air transportation	1.0	Util.
Paper coating & glazing	0.3	Manufg.	S/L Govt. purch., public assistance & relief	1.0	S/L Govt
Paper industries machinery	0.3	Manufg.	Communications, except radio & TV	0.9	Util.
Paperboard mills	0.3	Manufg.	Accounting, auditing & bookkeeping	0.9	Services
Computer & data processing services	0.3	Services	Legal services	0.9	Services
Legal services	0.3	Services	Colleges, universities, & professional schools	0.7	Services
Management & consulting services & labs	0.3	Services	Engineering, architectural, & surveying services	0.7	Services
U.S. Postal Service	0.3	Gov't	Crude petroleum & natural gas	0.6	Mining
Special dies & tools & machine tool accessories	0.2	Manufg.	Greeting card publishing	0.6	Manufg.
Insurance carriers	0.2	Fin/R.E.	Miscellaneous publishing	0.6	Manufg.
Accounting, auditing & bookkeeping	0.2	Services	Motor freight transportation & warehousing	0.6	Util.
Automotive rental & leasing, without drivers	0.2	Services	Business/professional associations	0.6	Services
Automotive repair shops & services	0.2	Services	Electric services (utilities)	0.5	Util.
Manifold business forms	0.1	Manufg.	Eating & drinking places	0.5	Trade
Royalties	0.1	Fin/R.E.	Security & commodity brokers	0.5	Fin/R.E.
Laundry, dry cleaning, shoe repair	0.1	Services	Management & consulting services & labs	0.5	Services
Imports	0.1	Foreign	S/L Govt. purch., police	0.5	S/L Govt
			Electronic computing equipment	0.4	Manufg.
			Envelopes	0.4	Manufg.
			Freight forwarders	0.4	Util.
			Newspapers	0.3	Manufg.
			Radio & TV communication equipment	0.3	Manufg.
			Elementary & secondary schools	0.3	Services

Continued on next page.

INPUTS AND OUTPUTS FOR ENVELOPES - Continued

Economic Sector or Industry Providing Inputs	%	Sector	Economic Sector or Industry Buying Outputs	%	Sector
			Hotels & lodging places	0.3	Services
			Membership organizations nec	0.3	Services
			Social services, nec	0.3	Services
			S/L Govt. purch., correction	0.3	S/L Govt
			Industrial buildings	0.2	Constr.
			Office buildings	0.2	Constr.
			Residential 1-unit structures, nonfarm	0.2	Constr.
			Aircraft	0.2	Manufg.
			Apparel made from purchased materials	0.2	Manufg.
			Chemical preparations, nec	0.2	Manufg.
			Cyclic crudes and organics	0.2	Manufg.
			Drugs	0.2	Manufg.
			Guided missiles & space vehicles	0.2	Manufg.
			Machinery, except electrical, nec	0.2	Manufg.
			Manufacturing industries, nec	0.2	Manufg.
			Miscellaneous plastics products	0.2	Manufg.
			Motor vehicle parts & accessories	0.2	Manufg.
			Motor vehicles & car bodies	0.2	Manufg.
			Gas production & distribution (utilities)	0.2	Util.
			Radio & TV broadcasting	0.2	Util.
			Advertising	0.2	Services
			Job training & related services	0.2	Services
			Medical & health services, nec	0.2	Services
			Federal Government enterprises nec	0.2	Gov't
			State & local government enterprises, nec	0.2	Gov't
			S/L Govt. purch., fire	0.2	S/L Govt
			S/L Govt. purch., natural resource & recreation.	0.2	S/L Govt
			S/L Govt. purch., other education & libraries	0.2	S/L Govt
			Feed grains	0.1	Agric.
			Meat animals	0.1	Agric.
			Maintenance of nonfarm buildings nec	0.1	Constr.
			Nonfarm residential structure maintenance	0.1	Constr.
			Aircraft & missile engines & engine parts	0.1	Manufg.
			Blast furnaces & steel mills	0.1	Manufg.
			Broadwoven fabric mills	0.1	Manufg.
			Electronic components nec	0.1	Manufg.
			Industrial inorganic chemicals, nec	0.1	Manufg.
			Petroleum refining	0.1	Manufg.
			Photographic equipment & supplies	0.1	Manufg.
			Semiconductors & related devices	0.1	Manufg.
			Arrangement of passenger transportation	0.1	Util.
			Railroads & related services	0.1	Util.
			Amusement & recreation services nec	0.1	Services
			Child day care services	0.1	Services
			Libraries, vocation education	0.1	Services
			Personnel supply services	0.1	Services
			S/L Govt. purch., highways	0.1	S/L Govt

Source: Benchmark Input-Output Accounts for the U.S. Economy, 1982, U.S. Department of Commerce, Washington, D.C., July 1991. Data, as reported in the source, are organized by the 1977 SIC structure in use in 1982 but have been matched, as closely as is possible, to the 1987 SIC structure used in this book.

OCCUPATIONS EMPLOYED BY SIC 267 - MISCELLANEOUS CONVERTED PAPER PRODUCTS

Occupation	% of Total 1994	Change to 2005	Occupation	% of Total 1994	Change to 2005
Paper goods machine setters & set-up operators	9.0	-15.9	Machine feeders & offbearers	2.5	-5.4
Machine operators nec	6.8	29.7	Industrial machinery mechanics	2.1	15.6
Hand packers & packagers	5.7	-9.9	Inspectors, testers, & graders, precision	2.1	15.6
Blue collar worker supervisors	4.5	6.8	Packaging & filling machine operators	2.1	5.1
Assemblers, fabricators, & hand workers nec	4.4	5.1	Freight, stock, & material movers, hand	2.0	-15.9
Printing press machine setters, operators	4.3	5.1	Maintenance repairers, general utility	2.0	5.1
Cutting & slicing machine setters, operators	4.0	26.1	Traffic, shipping, & receiving clerks	1.9	1.1
Sales & related workers nec	3.0	5.1	General managers & top executives	1.8	-0.3
Helpers, laborers, & material movers nec	2.9	5.1	Machine forming operators, metal & plastic	1.7	57.6
Extruding & forming machine workers	2.8	36.6	Coating, painting, & spraying machine workers	1.7	-15.9
Printing, binding, & related workers nec	2.6	5.1	Secretaries, ex legal & medical	1.6	-4.3
Industrial truck & tractor operators	2.6	5.1	Industrial production managers	1.2	5.1

Source: Industry-Occupation Matrix, Bureau of Labor Statistics. These data relate to one or more 3-digit SIC industry groups rather than to a single 4-digit SIC. The change reported for each occupation to the year 2005 is a percent of growth or decline as estimated by the Bureau of Labor Statistics. The abbreviation nec stands for 'not elsewhere classified'.

LOCATION BY STATE AND REGIONAL CONCENTRATION

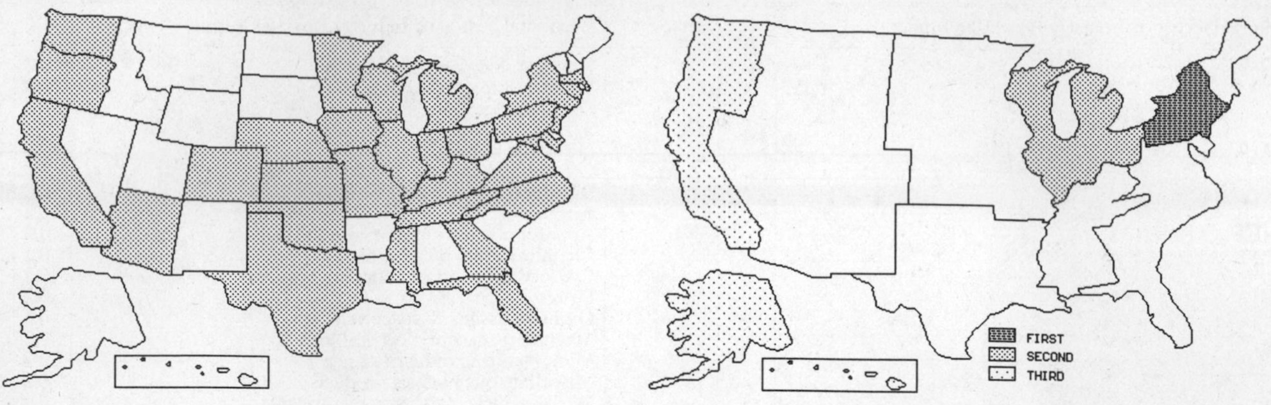

INDUSTRY DATA BY STATE

State	Establish-ments	Shipments			Employment				Cost as % of Shipments	Investment per Employee ($)
		Total ($ mil)	% of U.S.	Per Establ.	Total Number	% of U.S.	Per Establ.	Wages ($/hour)		
California	35	306.2	10.7	8.7	2,100	8.4	60	12.79	53.3	2,143
New York	29	246.7	8.6	8.5	2,400	9.6	83	11.69	51.0	1,667
Illinois	21	223.7	7.8	10.7	2,000	8.0	95	11.21	50.7	1,400
Pennsylvania	13	196.3	6.9	15.1	1,600	6.4	123	10.52	55.0	2,563
Massachusetts	15	182.2	6.4	12.1	1,600	6.4	107	12.08	55.2	3,125
Missouri	12	166.7	5.8	13.9	1,600	6.4	133	11.79	52.2	1,250
Ohio	14	144.9	5.1	10.3	1,200	4.8	86	10.40	58.8	1,000
New Jersey	12	136.9	4.8	11.4	1,300	5.2	108	11.70	56.5	923
Texas	15	125.5	4.4	8.4	1,100	4.4	73	10.41	53.4	2,636
Tennessee	5	99.7	3.5	19.9	900	3.6	180	10.42	42.4	4,333
Minnesota	10	98.7	3.5	9.9	800	3.2	80	12.00	55.2	1,750
Florida	12	85.2	3.0	7.1	800	3.2	67	11.00	57.5	875
Wisconsin	4	81.6	2.9	20.4	700	2.8	175	14.22	55.3	2,857
Virginia	6	75.0	2.6	12.5	800	3.2	133	11.17	49.5	-
Kansas	4	54.6	1.9	13.6	500	2.0	125	12.57	51.1	-
Iowa	4	53.9	1.9	13.5	400	1.6	100	10.86	54.2	1,000
Kentucky	6	52.4	1.8	8.7	400	1.6	67	11.50	50.8	2,750
Colorado	6	40.7	1.4	6.8	400	1.6	67	11.00	44.5	1,750
Washington	6	39.4	1.4	6.6	300	1.2	50	16.50	52.0	2,333
Michigan	10	38.1	1.3	3.8	400	1.6	40	10.80	48.3	-
Oklahoma	7	25.4	0.9	3.6	200	0.8	29	13.00	52.4	-
Georgia	8	(D)	-	-	750 *	3.0	94	-	-	3,467
Arizona	3	(D)	-	-	375 *	1.5	125	-	-	-
Indiana	3	(D)	-	-	375 *	1.5	125	-	-	-
Maryland	3	(D)	-	-	375 *	1.5	125	-	-	-
Nebraska	3	(D)	-	-	175 *	0.7	58	-	-	-
Oregon	3	(D)	-	-	375 *	1.5	125	-	-	-
Mississippi	2	(D)	-	-	750 *	3.0	375	-	-	-
North Carolina	2	(D)	-	-	175 *	0.7	88	-	-	-
Connecticut	1	(D)	-	-	175 *	0.7	175	-	-	-

Source: 1992 *Economic Census*. The states are in descending order of shipments or establishments (if shipment data are missing for the majority). The symbol (D) appears when data are withheld to prevent disclosure of competitive information. States marked with (D) are sorted by number of establishments. A dash (-) indicates that the data element cannot be calculated; * indicates the midpoint of a range.

2678 - STATIONERY PRODUCTS

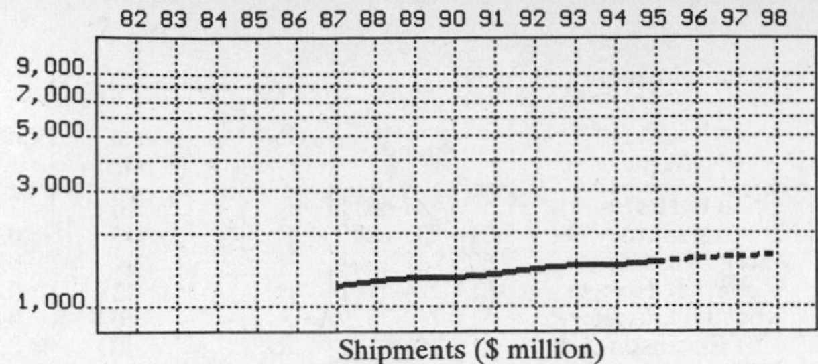

Shipments ($ million)

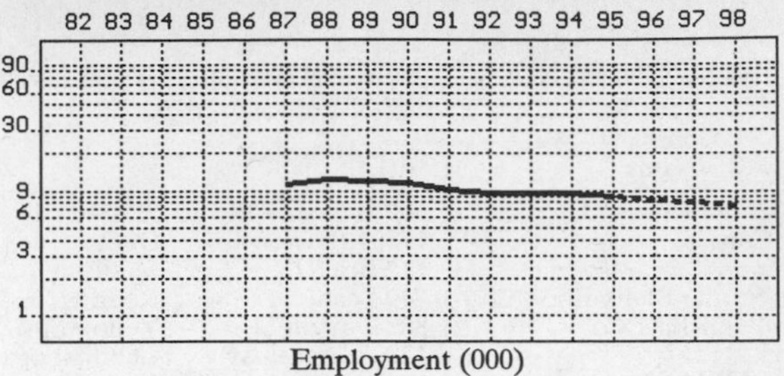

Employment (000)

GENERAL STATISTICS

Year	Com-panies	Establishments: Total	Establishments: with 20 or more employees	Employment: Total (000)	Employment: Production Workers (000)	Employment: Production Hours (Mil)	Compensation: Payroll ($ mil)	Compensation: Wages ($/hr)	Production ($ million): Cost of Materials	Production ($ million): Value Added by Manufacture	Production ($ million): Value of Shipments	Production ($ million): Capital Invest.
1982												
1983												
1984												
1985												
1986												
1987	170	189	92	11.2	8.5	16.4	205.9	8.25	690.8	520.7	1,216.4	25.1
1988		185	94	12.4	9.5	18.2	215.9	7.96	724.9	598.1	1,280.4	19.3
1989		177	94	11.8	8.0	15.5	202.9	8.43	749.8	568.9	1,316.1	38.4
1990		168	92	11.5	7.6	14.6	202.6	9.05	751.2	577.9	1,332.1	42.1
1991		163	84	10.1	7.6	15.1	209.3	9.12	746.1	602.2	1,359.1	25.0
1992	160	177	79	9.5	7.0	13.6	220.9	10.15	730.7	694.7	1,423.7	28.0
1993		175	74	9.4	7.2	13.7	223.3	10.32	790.2	705.6	1,482.5	26.2
1994		166P	74P	9.7	7.1	13.4	225.5	10.54	759.2	695.6	1,475.0	20.7
1995		163P	70P	8.9P	6.5P	12.5P	225.9P	11.00P	787.8P	721.8P	1,530.5P	25.7P
1996		161P	67P	8.5P	6.2P	11.9P	228.7P	11.39P	807.2P	739.6P	1,568.3P	25.2P
1997		158P	63P	8.1P	5.9P	11.3P	231.5P	11.79P	826.6P	757.4P	1,606.0P	24.6P
1998		156P	60P	7.7P	5.6P	10.7P	234.3P	12.18P	846.1P	775.2P	1,643.7P	24.1P

Sources: 1982, 1987, 1992 *Economic Census*; *Annual Survey of Manufactures*, 83-86, 88-91, 93-94. Establishment counts for non-Census years are from *County Business Patterns*; establishment values for 83-84 are extrapolations. 'P's show projections by the editors. Industries reclassified in 87 will not have data for prior years.

INDICES OF CHANGE

Year	Com-panies	Establishments: Total	Establishments: with 20 or more employees	Employment: Total (000)	Employment: Production Workers (000)	Employment: Production Hours (Mil)	Compensation: Payroll ($ mil)	Compensation: Wages ($/hr)	Production ($ million): Cost of Materials	Production ($ million): Value Added by Manufacture	Production ($ million): Value of Shipments	Production ($ million): Capital Invest.
1982												
1983												
1984												
1985												
1986												
1987	106	107	116	118	121	121	93	81	95	75	85	90
1988		105	119	131	136	134	98	78	99	86	90	69
1989		100	119	124	114	114	92	83	103	82	92	137
1990		95	116	121	109	107	92	89	103	83	94	150
1991		92	106	106	109	111	95	90	102	87	95	89
1992	100	100	100	100	100	100	100	100	100	100	100	100
1993		99	94	99	103	101	101	102	108	102	104	94
1994		94P	93P	102	101	99	102	104	104	100	104	74
1995		92P	89P	94P	93P	92P	102P	108P	108P	104P	108P	92P
1996		91P	85P	89P	89P	87P	104P	112P	110P	106P	110P	90P
1997		89P	80P	85P	85P	83P	105P	116P	113P	109P	113P	88P
1998		88P	76P	81P	81P	79P	106P	120P	116P	112P	115P	86P

Sources: Same as General Statistics. Values reflect change from the base year, 1992. Values above 100 mean greater than 92, values below 100 mean less than 92, and a value of 100 in the 82-91 or 93-98 period means same as 92. 'P's mark projections by the editors.

SELECTED RATIOS

For 1994	Avg. of All Manufact.	Analyzed Industry	Index	For 1994	Avg. of All Manufact.	Analyzed Industry	Index
Employees per Establishment	49	58	119	Value Added per Production Worker	134,084	97,972	73
Payroll per Establishment	1,500,273	1,358,434	91	Cost per Establishment	5,045,178	4,573,494	91
Payroll per Employee	30,620	23,247	76	Cost per Employee	102,970	78,268	76
Production Workers per Establishment	34	43	125	Cost per Production Worker	146,988	106,930	73
Wages per Establishment	853,319	850,819	100	Shipments per Establishment	9,576,895	8,885,542	93
Wages per Production Worker	24,861	19,892	80	Shipments per Employee	195,460	152,062	78
Hours per Production Worker	2,056	1,887	92	Shipments per Production Worker	279,017	207,746	74
Wages per Hour	12.09	10.54	87	Investment per Establishment	321,011	124,699	39
Value Added per Establishment	4,602,255	4,190,361	91	Investment per Employee	6,552	2,134	33
Value Added per Employee	93,930	71,711	76	Investment per Production Worker	9,352	2,915	31

Sources: Same as General Statistics. The 'Average of All Manufacturing' column represents the average of all manufacturing industries reported for the most recent complete year available. The Index shows the relationship between the Average and the Analyzed Industry. For example, 100 means that they are equal; 500 that the Analyzed Industry is five times the average; 50 means that the Analyzed Industry is half the national average. The abbreviation 'na' is used to show that data are 'not available'.

LEADING COMPANIES

Number shown: **30** Total sales ($ mil): **710** Total employment (000): **6.7**

Company Name	Address				CEO Name	Phone	Co. Type	Sales ($ mil)	Empl. (000)
Smead Manufacturing Co	600 E Smead Blv	Hastings	MN	55033	Ebba C Hoffman	612-437-4111	R	210	2.4
Ampad Corp	17304 Preston Rd	Dallas	TX	75252	Russell Gard	214-733-6200	R	47	0.4
Demco Inc	PO Box 7488	Madison	WI	53707	Greg M Larson	608-241-1201	R	44	0.4
Roaring Spring Blank Book Co	740 Spang St	Roaring Spring	PA	16673	Robert R Hoover	814-224-5141	R	43*	0.3
Antioch Publishing Co	888 Dayton St	Yellow Springs	OH	45387	Michael Gardner	513-767-7379	R	40	0.4
Top Flight Inc	1300 Central Av	Chattanooga	TN	37408	EM Robinson	615-266-8171	R	40	0.3
Top Flight Paper Products	1300 Central Av	Chattanooga	TN	37408	H T Robinson Jr	615-266-8171	S	40	0.3
Southworth Co	Front St	W Springfield	MA	01089	Kent Tarrant	413-732-5141	R	31*	0.3
Julius Blumberg Inc	62 White St	New York	NY	10013	RH Blumberg	212-431-5000	R	24	0.2
Kurtz Bros Inc	PO Box 392	Clearfield	PA	16830	Robert M Kurtz	814-765-6561	R	23	0.3
B and W Press Inc	401 East Main St	Georgetown	MA	01833	Paul J Beegan	508-352-6100	R	18	0.1
Gordon Paper Company Inc	PO Box 1806	Norfolk	VA	23501	Tavia F Gordon	804-464-3581	R	17	0.1
PCI Paper Conversions Inc	6761 Thompson N	Syracuse	NY	13211	Bruce K Lane	315-437-1641	R	17	0.2
B and J Supply Inc	PO Box 1792	Appleton	WI	54913	Robert J Bridell	414-739-9491	S	16	0.1
EMB Giftware Inc	590 Franklin Av	Mount Vernon	NY	10550	Paul Ross	516-694-9494	R	16*	0.1
JM Co	777 Terrace Av	Hasbrock H	NJ	07604	Alfred Magid	201-869-8200	R	15*	0.2
Pratt and Austin Co	642 S Summer St	Holyoke	MA	01040	Bruce Pratt	413-532-1491	R	12*	0.1
Everett Pad and Paper Company	PO Box 1268	Everett	WA	98206	Richard F Kenna	206-259-2133	R	11*	0.1
Silvanus Products Inc	40 Merchants St	Ste Genevieve	MO	63670	Walter Timm	314-883-3521	R	10	0.2
Cascade School Supplies	1 Brown St	North Adams	MA	01247	Paul O Cote	413-663-3716	R	8	<0.1
Artistic Office Products	721 E 133rd St	Bronx	NY	10454	Steve Mayo	718-665-5510	R	6	<0.1
Lehman Brothers Inc	PO Box 1888	New Haven	CT	06508	Albert P Lehman	203-624-9911	R	5	<0.1
Sainberg and Company Inc	63-20 Austin St	Rego Park	NY	11374	RB Sainberg	718-897-7000	R	5*	<0.1
United Bindery Service Inc	1845 W Carroll Av	Chicago	IL	60612	Bruce Kosaka	312-243-0240	R	3	<0.1
Admiral Envelope and Printing	1300 N Fulton Av	Baltimore	MD	21217	Gary Zorn	410-523-1500	R	3	<0.1
Banning Enterprises Ltd	590 Franklin Av	Mount Vernon	NY	10550		914-699-1400	S	3*	<0.1
School Stationers Corp	1641 S Main St	Oshkosh	WI	54901	Robert Stauffer Jr	414-426-1300	R	1	<0.1
Arkansas Lighthouse	PO Box 192666	Little Rock	AR	72219	J Avants	501-562-2222	R	1	<0.1
Global Goods Corp	160 Kneeland St	Boston	MA	02111	Donald Levy	617-482-8824	R	0*	<0.1
Catherine's Rare Paper Inc	455 N 3rd St	Phoenix	AZ	85004	Cass Rankin	602-252-6960	R	0*	<0.1

Source: *Ward's Business Directory of U.S. Private and Public Companies*, Volumes 1 and 2, 1996. The company type code used is as follows: P - Public, R - Private, S - Subsidiary, D - Division, J - Joint Venture, A - Affiliate, G - Group. Sales are in millions of dollars, employees are in thousands. An asterisk (*) indicates an estimated sales volume. The symbol < stands for 'less than'. Company names and addresses are truncated, in some cases, to fit into the available space.

MATERIALS CONSUMED

Material		Quantity	Delivered Cost ($ million)
Materials, ingredients, containers, and supplies		(X)	646.1
Paper and paperboard, except boxes and containers	1,000 s tons	594.2**	396.4
Glues and adhesives		(X)	4.7
Printing inks (complete formulations)		(X)	4.0
Coated or laminated fabrics, including vinyl coated		(X)	4.6
Paperboard containers, boxes, and corrugated paperboard		(X)	21.7
All other materials and components, parts, containers, and supplies		(X)	46.1
Materials, ingredients, containers, and supplies, nsk		(X)	168.7

Source: 1992 *Economic Census*. Explanation of symbols used: (D): Withheld to avoid disclosure of competitive data; na: Not available; (S): Withheld because statistical norms were not met; (X): Not applicable; (Z): Less than half the unit shown; nec: Not elsewhere classified; nsk: Not specified by kind; - : zero; * : 10-19 percent estimated; ** : 20-29 percent estimated.

PRODUCT SHARE DETAILS

Product or Product Class	% Share	Product or Product Class	% Share
Stationery, tablets, and related products	100.00	Tablets and pads, all other	16.85
Stationery	26.08	Notebooks, bound with wire (except columnar), staples, plastics, etc. (including composition, memo, and stenographic)	27.17
Boxed stationery and portfolios	32.07	Looseleaf paper fillers, school and commercial types (quantity is on 100-sheet basis)	12.35
Wedding and social announcements, paper, cards, and envelopes	25.35	Wrapped ream paper (exclude looseleaf fillers, sensitized photographic and photocopy paper, and paper for fax machines)	10.68
All other stationary products, including packaged paper and envelopes	31.80	All other tablets, pads, and related products, not listed elsewhere	3.14
Stationery, nsk	10.80	Tablets, pads, and related products, nsk	19.38
Tablets, pads, and related products	64.05	Stationery, tablets, and related products, nsk	9.87
Tablets and pads, 8 1/2 in. x 11 in. and 8 1/2 in. x 14 in., except columnar	8.08		
Tablets and pads, columnar, including bound and wire bound	2.35		

Source: 1992 *Economic Census*. The values shown are percent of total shipments in an industry. Values of indented subcategories are summed in the main heading. The symbol (D) appears when data are withheld to prevent disclosure of competitive information. The abbreviation nsk stands for 'not specified by kind' and nec for 'not elsewhere classified'.

INPUTS AND OUTPUTS FOR STATIONERY PRODUCTS

Economic Sector or Industry Providing Inputs	%	Sector	Economic Sector or Industry Buying Outputs	%	Sector
Paper mills, except building paper	56.8	Manufg.	Personal consumption expenditures	51.4	
Wholesale trade	9.1	Trade	Retail trade, except eating & drinking	5.4	Trade
Paperboard mills	5.8	Manufg.	Water supply & sewage systems	5.1	Util.
Paperboard containers & boxes	4.3	Manufg.	Wholesale trade	3.9	Trade
Motor freight transportation & warehousing	2.1	Util.	Change in business inventories	3.6	In House
Railroads & related services	1.7	Util.	S/L Govt. purch., higher education	2.3	S/L Govt
Petroleum refining	1.5	Manufg.	Doctors & dentists	2.0	Services
Miscellaneous plastics products	1.4	Manufg.	Real estate	1.7	Fin/R.E.
Electric services (utilities)	1.4	Util.	Hospitals	1.5	Services
Real estate	1.4	Fin/R.E.	Legal services	1.2	Services
Stationery products	1.2	Manufg.	Exports	1.2	Foreign
Advertising	1.2	Services	State & local government enterprises, nec	1.1	Gov't
Coated fabrics, not rubberized	1.0	Manufg.	Air transportation	1.0	Util.
Air transportation	1.0	Util.	Engineering, architectural, & surveying services	1.0	Services
Communications, except radio & TV	0.8	Util.	Labor, civic, social, & fraternal associations	1.0	Services
Sanitary services, steam supply, irrigation	0.8	Util.	Banking	0.9	Fin/R.E.
Equipment rental & leasing services	0.6	Services	Stationery products	0.7	Manufg.
Hotels & lodging places	0.6	Services	Eating & drinking places	0.7	Trade
Adhesives & sealants	0.5	Manufg.	Computer & data processing services	0.7	Services
Eating & drinking places	0.5	Trade	Management & consulting services & labs	0.7	Services
Maintenance of nonfarm buildings nec	0.4	Constr.	Electric services (utilities)	0.6	Util.
Paper coating & glazing	0.4	Manufg.	Credit agencies other than banks	0.6	Fin/R.E.
Banking	0.4	Fin/R.E.	Child day care services	0.6	Services
U.S. Postal Service	0.4	Gov't	S/L Govt. purch., other education & libraries	0.6	S/L Govt
Paper industries machinery	0.3	Manufg.	S/L Govt. purch., public assistance & relief	0.6	S/L Govt
Printing ink	0.3	Manufg.	Business services nec	0.5	Services
Gas production & distribution (utilities)	0.3	Util.	Freight forwarders	0.4	Util.
Automotive rental & leasing, without drivers	0.3	Services	Hotels & lodging places	0.4	Services
Automotive repair shops & services	0.3	Services	Medical & health services, nec	0.4	Services
Detective & protective services	0.3	Services	S/L Govt. purch., natural resource & recreation.	0.4	S/L Govt
Lubricating oils & greases	0.2	Manufg.	S/L Govt. purch., other general government	0.4	S/L Govt
Machinery, except electrical, nec	0.2	Manufg.	Sanitary services, steam supply, irrigation	0.3	Util.
Insurance carriers	0.2	Fin/R.E.	Advertising	0.3	Services
Computer & data processing services	0.2	Services	Federal Government purchases, nondefense	0.3	Fed Govt
Legal services	0.2	Services	Chemical preparations, nec	0.2	Manufg.
Management & consulting services & labs	0.2	Services	Communications, except radio & TV	0.2	Util.
Imports	0.2	Foreign	Motor freight transportation & warehousing	0.2	Util.
Royalties	0.1	Fin/R.E.	Water transportation	0.2	Util.
Accounting, auditing & bookkeeping	0.1	Services	Amusement & recreation services nec	0.2	Services
			Personnel supply services	0.2	Services
			Social services, nec	0.2	Services
			Federal Government purchases, national defense	0.2	Fed Govt
			S/L Govt. purch., correction	0.2	S/L Govt
			S/L Govt. purch., elem. & secondary education	0.2	S/L Govt
			S/L Govt. purch., highways	0.2	S/L Govt
			Crude petroleum & natural gas	0.1	Mining
			Commercial printing	0.1	Manufg.
			Fluid milk	0.1	Manufg.
			Machinery, except electrical, nec	0.1	Manufg.
			Periodicals	0.1	Manufg.
			Photographic equipment & supplies	0.1	Manufg.
			Radio & TV communication equipment	0.1	Manufg.
			Arrangement of passenger transportation	0.1	Util.
			Insurance agents, brokers, & services	0.1	Fin/R.E.
			Security & commodity brokers	0.1	Fin/R.E.
			Automotive rental & leasing, without drivers	0.1	Services
			Automotive repair shops & services	0.1	Services
			Colleges, universities, & professional schools	0.1	Services
			Elementary & secondary schools	0.1	Services
			Equipment rental & leasing services	0.1	Services
			Laundry, dry cleaning, shoe repair	0.1	Services
			Miscellaneous repair shops	0.1	Services
			Motion pictures	0.1	Services
			Nursing & personal care facilities	0.1	Services
			Photofinishing labs, commercial photography	0.1	Services
			Portrait, photographic studios	0.1	Services
			Services to dwellings & other buildings	0.1	Services
			State & local electric utilities	0.1	Gov't
			U.S. Postal Service	0.1	Gov't
			S/L Govt. purch., police	0.1	S/L Govt

Source: Benchmark Input-Output Accounts for the U.S. Economy, 1982, U.S. Department of Commerce, Washington, D.C., July 1991. Data, as reported in the source, are organized by the 1977 SIC structure in use in 1982 but have been matched, as closely as is possible, to the 1987 SIC structure used in this book.

OCCUPATIONS EMPLOYED BY SIC 267 - MISCELLANEOUS CONVERTED PAPER PRODUCTS

Occupation	% of Total 1994	Change to 2005	Occupation	% of Total 1994	Change to 2005
Paper goods machine setters & set-up operators	9.0	-15.9	Machine feeders & offbearers	2.5	-5.4
Machine operators nec	6.8	29.7	Industrial machinery mechanics	2.1	15.6
Hand packers & packagers	5.7	-9.9	Inspectors, testers, & graders, precision	2.1	15.6
Blue collar worker supervisors	4.5	6.8	Packaging & filling machine operators	2.1	5.1
Assemblers, fabricators, & hand workers nec	4.4	5.1	Freight, stock, & material movers, hand	2.0	-15.9
Printing press machine setters, operators	4.3	5.1	Maintenance repairers, general utility	2.0	5.1
Cutting & slicing machine setters, operators	4.0	26.1	Traffic, shipping, & receiving clerks	1.9	1.1
Sales & related workers nec	3.0	5.1	General managers & top executives	1.8	-0.3
Helpers, laborers, & material movers nec	2.9	5.1	Machine forming operators, metal & plastic	1.7	57.6
Extruding & forming machine workers	2.8	36.6	Coating, painting, & spraying machine workers	1.7	-15.9
Printing, binding, & related workers nec	2.6	5.1	Secretaries, ex legal & medical	1.6	-4.3
Industrial truck & tractor operators	2.6	5.1	Industrial production managers	1.2	5.1

Source: *Industry-Occupation Matrix*, Bureau of Labor Statistics. These data relate to one or more 3-digit SIC industry groups rather than to a single 4-digit SIC. The change reported for each occupation to the year 2005 is a percent of growth or decline as estimated by the Bureau of Labor Statistics. The abbreviation nec stands for 'not elsewhere classified'.

LOCATION BY STATE AND REGIONAL CONCENTRATION

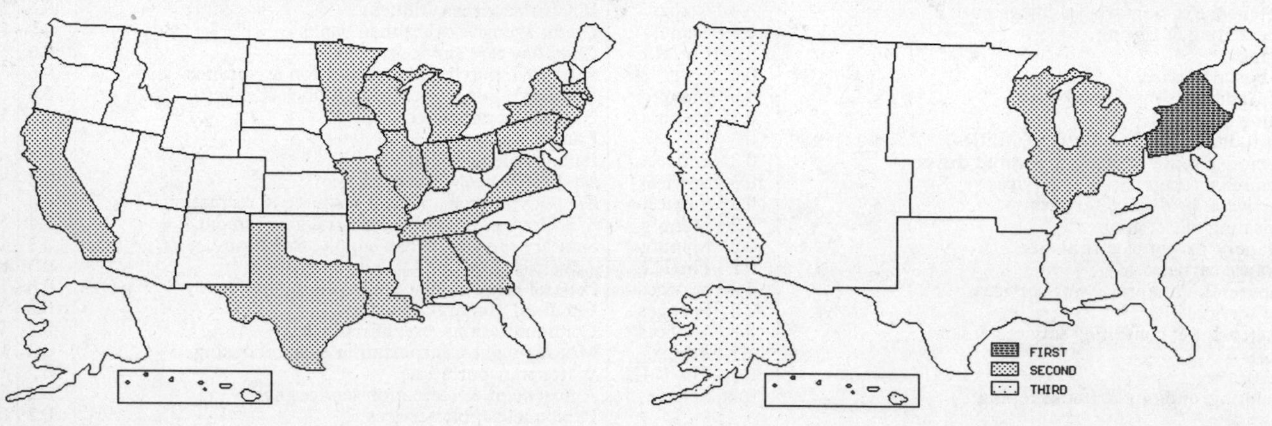

INDUSTRY DATA BY STATE

State	Establish-ments	Shipments			Employment				Cost as % of Shipments	Investment per Employee ($)
		Total ($ mil)	% of U.S.	Per Establ.	Total Number	% of U.S.	Per Establ.	Wages ($/hour)		
Pennsylvania	11	212.3	14.9	19.3	1,700	17.9	155	10.90	56.8	2,294
California	24	130.0	9.1	5.4	900	9.5	38	9.53	41.0	2,889
Massachusetts	16	93.0	6.5	5.8	800	8.4	50	10.73	57.2	1,000
Texas	12	64.0	4.5	5.3	400	4.2	33	9.60	39.2	-
New York	22	59.5	4.2	2.7	600	6.3	27	8.44	49.4	1,833
Wisconsin	6	43.9	3.1	7.3	300	3.2	50	10.50	59.0	3,333
Minnesota	6	27.0	1.9	4.5	200	2.1	33	10.00	48.1	9,000
Indiana	5	25.2	1.8	5.0	400	4.2	80	9.60	50.4	-
New Jersey	7	23.2	1.6	3.3	300	3.2	43	8.00	54.7	-
Illinois	5	(D)	-	-	375 *	3.9	75	-	-	-
Missouri	5	(D)	-	-	1,750 *	18.4	350	-	-	-
Ohio	5	(D)	-	-	175 *	1.8	35	-	-	2,286
Connecticut	4	(D)	-	-	175 *	1.8	44	-	-	-
Georgia	4	(D)	-	-	375 *	3.9	94	-	-	-
Michigan	4	(D)	-	-	375 *	3.9	94	-	-	-
Alabama	3	(D)	-	-	375 *	3.9	125	-	-	-
Virginia	3	(D)	-	-	175 *	1.8	58	-	-	-
Louisiana	2	(D)	-	-	175 *	1.8	88	-	-	-
Tennessee	1	(D)	-	-	175 *	1.8	175	-	-	-

Source: 1992 *Economic Census*. The states are in descending order of shipments or establishments (if shipment data are missing for the majority). The symbol (D) appears when data are withheld to prevent disclosure of competitive information. States marked with (D) are sorted by number of establishments. A dash (-) indicates that the data element cannot be calculated; * indicates the midpoint of a range.

2679 - CONVERTED PAPER PRODUCTS, NEC

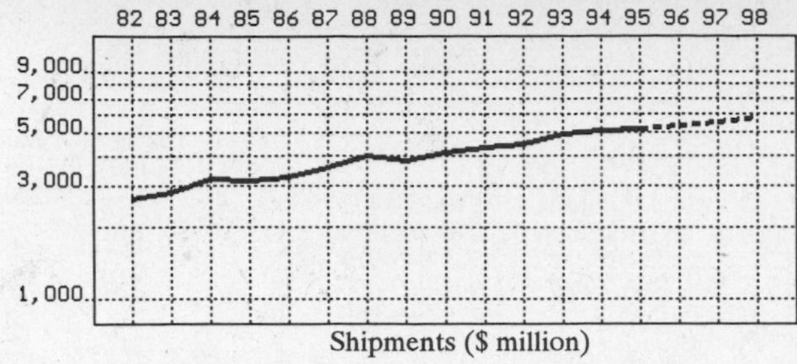

Shipments ($ million)

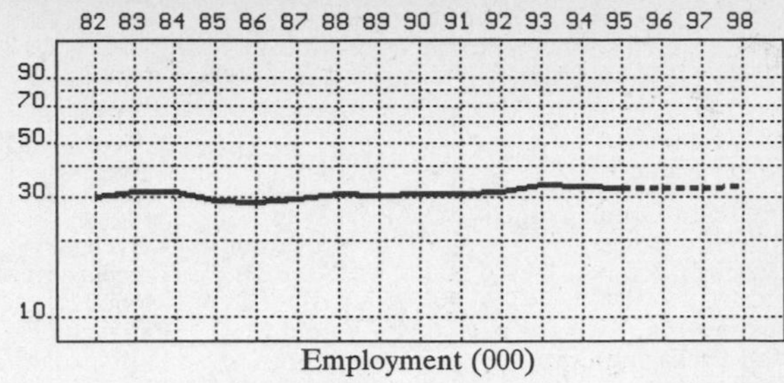

Employment (000)

GENERAL STATISTICS

Year	Companies	Establishments: Total	Establishments: with 20 or more employees	Employment: Total (000)	Employment: Production Workers (000)	Employment: Production Hours (Mil)	Compensation: Payroll ($ mil)	Compensation: Wages ($/hr)	Production ($ million): Cost of Materials	Production ($ million): Value Added by Manufacture	Production ($ million): Value of Shipments	Production ($ million): Capital Invest.
1982	742	809	317	30.4	22.3	43.7	496.3	7.19	1,336.0	1,291.3	2,637.7	74.3
1983				31.7	23.5	44.6	523.5	7.66	1,400.9	1,431.9	2,816.8	36.2
1984				31.6	23.5	45.2	568.7	8.09	1,596.4	1,651.5	3,195.7	70.1
1985				29.3	21.6	42.0	556.4	8.40	1,575.2	1,595.7	3,136.2	70.4
1986				28.4	20.7	41.2	571.1	8.77	1,665.0	1,588.6	3,222.5	73.0
1987	728	821	299	29.6	21.5	43.5	593.1	8.55	1,785.3	1,796.3	3,570.1	74.5
1988		754	323	31.0	23.0	46.8	621.8	8.49	2,154.3	1,878.0	3,998.5	76.2
1989		693	327	30.7	22.8	45.6	627.4	9.06	2,046.5	1,746.3	3,796.4	98.7
1990		675	315	30.8	23.2	47.0	659.2	9.25	2,197.9	1,930.7	4,127.9	155.2
1991		674	310	30.9	23.4	48.7	710.6	9.75	2,259.2	2,017.1	4,301.9	182.1
1992	725	790	311	31.6	23.6	48.7	802.9	10.57	2,294.1	2,167.7	4,437.2	148.5
1993		752	319	33.9	25.4	52.1	865.5	10.79	2,597.0	2,365.5	4,953.4	124.0
1994				33.0	25.0	51.3	862.2	10.67	2,759.5	2,281.8	5,059.0	160.1
1995				32.4P	24.5P	51.2P	862.8P	11.02P	2,815.8P	2,328.4P	5,162.2P	172.2P
1996				32.6P	24.7P	51.9P	893.1P	11.30P	2,922.8P	2,416.9P	5,358.4P	182.1P
1997				32.8P	24.9P	52.7P	923.4P	11.59P	3,029.9P	2,505.4P	5,554.6P	191.9P
1998				33.0P	25.1P	53.4P	953.7P	11.87P	3,136.9P	2,593.9P	5,750.9P	201.7P

Sources: 1982, 1987, 1992 *Economic Census*; *Annual Survey of Manufactures*, 83-86, 88-91, 93-94. Establishment counts for non-Census years are from *County Business Patterns*; establishment values for 83-84 are extrapolations. 'P's show projections by the editors. Industries reclassified in 87 will not have data for prior years.

INDICES OF CHANGE

Year	Companies	Establishments: Total	Establishments: with 20 or more employees	Employment: Total (000)	Employment: Production Workers (000)	Employment: Production Hours (Mil)	Compensation: Payroll ($ mil)	Compensation: Wages ($/hr)	Production ($ million): Cost of Materials	Production ($ million): Value Added by Manufacture	Production ($ million): Value of Shipments	Production ($ million): Capital Invest.
1982	102	102	102	96	94	90	62	68	58	60	59	50
1983				100	100	92	65	72	61	66	63	24
1984				100	100	93	71	77	70	76	72	47
1985				93	92	86	69	79	69	74	71	47
1986				90	88	85	71	83	73	73	73	49
1987	100	104	96	94	91	89	74	81	78	83	80	50
1988		95	104	98	97	96	77	80	94	87	90	51
1989		88	105	97	97	94	78	86	89	81	86	66
1990		85	101	97	98	97	82	88	96	89	93	105
1991		85	100	98	99	100	89	92	98	93	97	123
1992	100	100	100	100	100	100	100	100	100	100	100	100
1993		95	103	107	108	107	108	102	113	109	112	84
1994				104	106	105	107	101	120	105	114	108
1995				103P	104P	105P	107P	104P	123P	107P	116P	116P
1996				103P	105P	107P	111P	107P	127P	111P	121P	123P
1997				104P	106P	108P	115P	110P	132P	116P	125P	129P
1998				105P	106P	110P	119P	112P	137P	120P	130P	136P

Sources: Same as General Statistics. Values reflect change from the base year, 1992. Values above 100 mean greater than 92, values below 100 mean less than 92, and a value of 100 in the 82-91 or 93-98 period means same as 92. 'P's mark projections by the editors.

SELECTED RATIOS

For 1992	Avg. of All Manufact.	Analyzed Industry	Index	For 1992	Avg. of All Manufact.	Analyzed Industry	Index
Employees per Establishment	46	40	88	Value Added per Production Worker	122,353	91,852	75
Payroll per Establishment	1,332,320	1,016,329	76	Cost per Establishment	4,239,462	2,903,924	68
Payroll per Employee	29,181	25,408	87	Cost per Employee	92,853	72,598	78
Production Workers per Establishment	31	30	95	Cost per Production Worker	135,003	97,208	72
Wages per Establishment	734,496	651,594	89	Shipments per Establishment	8,100,800	5,616,709	69
Wages per Production Worker	23,390	21,812	93	Shipments per Employee	177,425	140,418	79
Hours per Production Worker	2,025	2,064	102	Shipments per Production Worker	257,966	188,017	73
Wages per Hour	11.55	10.57	91	Investment per Establishment	278,244	187,975	68
Value Added per Establishment	3,842,210	2,743,924	71	Investment per Employee	6,094	4,699	77
Value Added per Employee	84,153	68,598	82	Investment per Production Worker	8,861	6,292	71

Sources: Same as General Statistics. The 'Average of All Manufacturing' column represents the average of all manufacturing industries reported for the most recent complete year available. The Index shows the relationship between the Average and the Analyzed Industry. For example, 100 means that they are equal; 500 that the Analyzed Industry is five times the average; 50 means that the Analyzed Industry is half the national average. The abbreviation 'na' is used to show that data are 'not available'.

LEADING COMPANIES

Number shown: 75 Total sales ($ mil): **4,497** Total employment (000): **29.5**

Company Name	Address				CEO Name	Phone	Co. Type	Sales ($ mil)	Empl. (000)
Continental Can Company Inc	1 Aerial Way	Syosset	NY	11791	Donald J Bainton	516-822-4940	P	537	3.7
Imperial Wallcoverings	23645 Mercantile	Cleveland	OH	44122	William Brucchieri	216-464-3700	D	410	2.8
Ivex Packaging Corp	100 Tri State Dr	Lincolnshire	IL	60069	George Bayly	708-945-9100	R	400	2.2
Cleo Inc	4025 Viscount St	Memphis	TN	38118	N Jack Rohrbach	901-369-6300	S	220*	1.7
CSS Industries Inc	1845 Walnut St	Philadelphia	PA	19103	Jack Farber	215-569-9900	P	218	2.8
Shorewood Packaging Corp	55 Engineers Ln	Farmingdale	NY	11735	Paul B Shore	516-694-2900	P	217	2.2
American Packaging Corp	Grant & Ashton Rd	Philadelphia	PA	19114	Steven B Schottland	215-698-4800	R	200	0.9
CST Office Products Inc	540 W Allendale Dr	Wheeling	IL	60090	Keith Koski	708-459-7600	R	195	0.3
PM Co	9800 Bustleton Av	Philadelphia	PA	19115	Donald O'Neill	215-673-4500	R	150	0.5
Hollingsworth and Vose Co	112 Washington St	East Walpole	MA	02032	Gordon W Moran	508-668-0295	R	130	0.9
Creative Expressions Group	7240 Shadelan	Indianapolis	IN	46256	Jeff Narkin	317-841-9999	D	110	0.2
Stuart Hall Company Inc	PO Box 200915	Kansas City	MO	64120	James Tiffany	816-221-8480	S	110	0.5
PM Co	24 Triangle Park Dr	cincinnati	OH	45246	William J Fecht	513-772-5057	D	100*	0.3
Beistle Co	PO Box 10	Shippensburg	PA	17257	Stephen F Luhrs	717-532-2131	R	85	0.7
Ludlow Corp	PO Box 749	Homer	LA	71040	Steve Mc Donough	318-927-2531	D	80	0.3
Berwick Industries Inc	PO Box 428	Berwick	PA	18603	John Pinti	717-752-5934	S	76*	0.9
Soabar Systems	7722 Dungan Rd	Philadelphia	PA	19111	Don McKee	215-725-4700	D	58	0.4
TAPEMARK Company Inc	150 E Marie Av	West St Paul	MN	55118	RC Klas Sr	612-455-1611	R	44*	0.3
Chesapeake Consumer Prod Co	PO Box 1039	Appleton	WI	54912	William Raaths	414-739-8233	S	43	0.2
Hexacomb Corp	75 Tri-State	Lincolnshire	IL	60069	Douglas Walmsley	708-317-1991	R	42	0.4
Bleyer Industries Inc	260 W Sunrise Hwy	Valley Stream	NY	11581	Gus Poulis	516-374-3800	R	40*	0.3
Richter Manufacturing Corp	159 N San Antonio	Pomona	CA	91767	Alfred Richter	909-622-1151	R	40	0.2
West Carrollton Parchment Co	PO Box 98	West Carrollton	OH	45449	Hobart Lake	513-859-3621	R	39	0.2
Pressware International Inc	2120 Westbelt Dr	Columbus	OH	43228	Harry Gardner	614-771-5400	S	38	0.2
J Josephson Inc	20 Horizon Blv	S Hackensack	NJ	07606	Mark Goodman	201-440-7000	R	37	0.2
Rockline Industries Inc	PO Box 1007	Sheboygan	WI	53082	Randy H Rudolph	414-452-3004	R	36*	0.3
Cascades Diamond Inc	PO Box 627	Thorndike	MA	01079	Richard Rylko	413-283-8301	S	30	0.3
Ecological Fibers Inc	40 Pioneer Dr	Lunenburg	MA	01462	Stephen F Quill	508-537-0003	R	30	0.1
L and E Packaging Inc	PO Box 14429	Greensboro	NC	27415	Phillip C Wray	910-621-2570	R	30	0.2
Stephen Lawrence Co	35 State St	Moonachie	NJ	07074	Shirley Lawrence	201-807-0500	R	30	0.1
York Wall Coverings Inc	PO Box 5166	York	PA	17405	Carl J Vizzi	717-846-4456	R	30*	0.2
Labelon Corp	10 Chapin St	Canandaigua	NY	14424	W Irwin	716-394-6220	R	29*	0.2
George Schmitt and Company	PO Box 812	Branford	CT	06405	JR Gunther	203-481-2371	R	28	0.3
Eisenhart Wallcoverings Co	PO Box 464	Hanover	PA	17331	SF Eisenhart Jr	717-632-5918	S	27*	0.3
Mellon Corp	351 W 35th St	New York	NY	10001	J Weston	212-563-5278	R	26	0.2
Paper Systems Inc	PO Box 150	Springboro	OH	45066	Lawrence L Curk	513-746-6841	R	26	0.1
Zimmer Paper Products Inc	1450 E 20th St	Indianapolis	IN	46218	Karl R Zimmer	317-636-3333	R	26	0.1
Laminations Corp	PO Box 469	Neenah	WI	54957	R Detienne	414-725-8368	R	25	0.1
Pacon Corp	2525 N Casoloma	Appleton	WI	54911	Gerard H Van Hoof	414-749-5050	R	25	0.2
Permafiber Corp	109 W 26th St	New York	NY	10001	Ronald Shapiro	212-627-7750	R	25	<0.1
St Clair Pakwell	120 25th Av	Bellwood	IL	60104	Joe Kaplan	708-547-7500	D	22	0.1
Butler Printing and Laminating	PO Box 836	Butler	NJ	07405	James Berezny	201-838-8550	R	19	0.1
Rytex Co	PO Box 68187	Indianapolis	IN	46268	Stephen R Lett	317-872-8553	R	19*	0.2
Robert Busse and Company Inc	75 Arkay Dr	Hauppauge	NY	11788	E Cardinale	516-435-4711	R	18	0.1
THT Inc	33 Riverside Av	Westport	CT	06880	F A Rossetti	203-226-6408	P	17	0.1
Beveridge Paper Co	717 W Washington	Indianapolis	IN	46204	Richard Munson	317-635-4391	D	16	0.1
Ennis Tag and Label Co	PO Bin D	Wolfe City	TX	75496	Burl Linebarger	903-496-2244	S	16	0.2
Fibre Converters Inc	1 Industrial Dr	Constantine	MI	49042	JD Stuck	616-435-8681	R	15	<0.1
GreenStone Industries Inc	6500 Rock Spring	Bethesda	MD	20817	Joel Tranmer	301-564-5900	P	15	0.3
Putney Paper Company Inc	PO Box 226	Putney	VT	05346	Ian Smith	802-387-5571	R	15	0.1
Peacock Papers Inc	273 Summer St	Boston	MA	02210	Sharon P Whiteley	617-423-2868	R	14*	0.1
Holyoke Card and Paper Co	PO Box 3450	Springfield	MA	01101	F W Fuller III	413-732-2107	R	14	<0.1
Garlock Printing	164 Fredette St	Gardner	MA	01440	Peter Garlock	508-630-1028	R	13*	<0.1
Brown Products Inc	PO Box 43805	Atlanta	GA	30336	E Alan Erb	404-691-7696	S	13	0.2
Clearprint Paper Co	1482 67th St	Emeryville	CA	94608	Ira Weinberg	510-652-4762	R	13	<0.1
H and L Enterprises	1844 Friendship Dr	El Cajon	CA	92020	Howard Lorsch	619-448-0883	R	13	0.1
Lydall Inc	PO Box 9550	Richmond	VA	23228	RJ Lanzi	804-266-9611	D	13*	<0.1
Party Time Manufacturing Co	421 Parsonage St	Hughestown	PA	18640	James Rosentel	717-655-1689	R	13*	0.1
Pac-Paper Inc	6416 NW Whitney	Vancouver	WA	98665	John T Fike	360-695-7771	R	13	<0.1
Bradford Co	PO Box 1199	Holland	MI	49422	JT Bradford	616-399-3000	R	12	0.1
Cedartown Paper Board Co	PO Box 227	Cedartown	GA	30125	Fred Von Zubern	404-748-3715	D	12*	0.1
Crocker Technical Papers	431 Westminster St	Fitchburg	MA	01420	Andrew F Zephir	508-345-7771	R	12	<0.1
O'Grady Containers Inc	PO Box 9737	Fort Worth	TX	76147	WD O'Grady	817-338-4000	R	12	<0.1
Deltapaper Corp	400 Mack Dr	Croydon	PA	19021	Bill Bregman	215-788-1800	R	11	<0.1
Fidelity Paper Supply Inc	5 Lawrence St	Bloomfield	NJ	07003	Pierre Guariglia	201-748-3475	R	11	<0.1
Flexseal Intern Packaging Corp	24 Seneca Av	Rochester	NY	14621	Donna M Steele	716-544-2500	S	11	<0.1
Compac Corp	Old Flanders Rd	Netcong	NJ	07857	JF Dickinson	201-347-3900	S	10	0.1
Enviro Pac Inc	46 Brooklyn St	Portville	NY	14770	JG Collins	716-933-8703	R	10	0.2
Indian Ribbon Inc	PO Box 355	Wolcott	IN	47995	Joseph G Hickman	219-279-2113	R	10	0.2
Plymkraft	PO Box 1577	Newport News	VA	23601	Norman Bergeron	804-595-0364	D	10	0.1
Wise Tag and Label Company	7035 Central Hwy	Pennsauken	NJ	08109	WS Wise	609-663-2400	R	10	<0.1
Autron Inc	4205 McEwen Rd	Farmers Branch	TX	75244	Steve Richards	214-386-6700	D	9	<0.1
Fidelity Industries Inc	559 Rte 23	Wayne	NJ	07470	M Rivkin	201-696-9120	R	9	<0.1
Central Fiber Corp	4814 Fiber Ln	Wellsville	KS	66092	Donald Meeker	913-883-4600	R	8	<0.1
Premier Industries Inc	PO Box 628	Covington	KY	41012	Viea Taylor	606-581-1390	R	8	<0.1

Source: *Ward's Business Directory of U.S. Private and Public Companies*, Volumes 1 and 2, 1996. The company type code used is as follows: P - Public, R - Private, S - Subsidiary, D - Division, J - Joint Venture, A - Affiliate, G - Group. Sales are in millions of dollars, employees are in thousands. An asterisk (*) indicates an estimated sales volume. The symbol < stands for 'less than'. Company names and addresses are truncated, in some cases, to fit into the available space.

MATERIALS CONSUMED

Material		Quantity	Delivered Cost ($ million)
Materials, ingredients, containers, and supplies		(X)	1,978.3
Paper and paperboard, except boxes and containers	1,000 s tons	(S)	863.5
Wastepaper, all types	1,000 s tons	(S)	57.2
Glues and adhesives		(X)	11.1
Printing inks (complete formulations)		(X)	46.3
Coated or laminated fabrics, including vinyl coated		(X)	24.3
Paperboard containers, boxes, and corrugated paperboard		(X)	49.1
All other materials and components, parts, containers, and supplies		(X)	423.5
Materials, ingredients, containers, and supplies, nsk		(X)	503.4

Source: 1992 *Economic Census*. Explanation of symbols used: (D): Withheld to avoid disclosure of competitive data; na: Not available; (S): Withheld because statistical norms were not met; (X): Not applicable; (Z): Less than half the unit shown; nec: Not elsewhere classified; nsk: Not specified by kind; - : zero; * : 10-19 percent estimated; ** : 20-29 percent estimated.

PRODUCT SHARE DETAILS

Product or Product Class	% Share
Converted paper products, nec	100.00
Wallcoverings	11.08
Paper with less than 2 mils of coating	31.25
Paper-backed, coated or laminated with 2 mils or more of plastics, prepasted	10.43
Paper-backed, coated or laminated with 2 mils or more of plastics, nonpasted	4.76
Fabrics-backed, coated or laminated, woven	28.62
Fabrics-backed, coated or laminated, nonwoven	20.08
Other wallcoverings, including scenic and panel decorations, but excluding those that contain no paper and/or fabrics	0.83
Wallcoverings, nsk	4.02
Gift wrap paper	14.50
Retail counter items, all types and weights, in rolls	41.96
Retail counter items, all types and weights, in folds	30.47
Other paper gift wrapping, including counter rolls and flat sheets for stores' own use	25.49
Gift wrap paper, nsk	2.09
Paper supplies for business machines and other miscellaneous unprinted paper office supplies, nec	9.95
Paper rolls for adding and other business machines, except rolls for facsimile and photocopy machines	44.14
Other unprinted paper office supplies, nec, including safety paper, facsimile paper, manifold carbon paper sets, teletype paper, etc.	39.28
Paper supplies for business machines and other miscellaneous unprinted paper office supplies, nec, nsk	16.58
Molded pulp goods, including egg cartons, florist pots, food trays, etc.	8.53
Other converted paper and paperboard products	40.27
Paper party and holiday goods and accessories (novelties, decorations (except crepe paper), party hats, displays, etc.)	8.91
Cellulose insulation	3.40
Paper doilies, place mats, and tray doilies (or tray covers)	3.25
Paper folders and mounts, all types, except file folders	4.02
Paper coffee filters	5.85
Paper filters other than coffee	1.11
Paper wrapping products, not elsewhere classified, including creped wadding and crepe paper (except fine crepe paper)	4.91
Other miscellaneous converted paper and paperboard products, not elsewhere classified, including fine crepe paper, laminated and tiled wallboard, unprinted tags, etc.	60.23
Other converted paper and paperboard products, nsk	8.32
Converted paper products, nec, nsk	15.67

Source: 1992 *Economic Census*. The values shown are percent of total shipments in an industry. Values of indented subcategories are summed in the main heading. The symbol (D) appears when data are withheld to prevent disclosure of competitive information. The abbreviation nsk stands for 'not specified by kind' and nec for 'not elsewhere classified'.

INPUTS AND OUTPUTS FOR CONVERTED PAPER PRODUCTS, NEC

Economic Sector or Industry Providing Inputs	%	Sector	Economic Sector or Industry Buying Outputs	%	Sector
Paper mills, except building paper	28.3	Manufg.	Personal consumption expenditures	28.5	
Imports	21.0	Foreign	Wholesale trade	11.0	Trade
Wholesale trade	9.2	Trade	Maintenance of nonfarm buildings nec	8.1	Constr.
Paperboard mills	6.6	Manufg.	Exports	6.4	Foreign
Plastics materials & resins	2.5	Manufg.	Doctors & dentists	5.4	Services
Paperboard containers & boxes	2.2	Manufg.	Hospitals	4.9	Services
Cyclic crudes and organics	2.1	Manufg.	Office buildings	3.1	Constr.
Printing ink	2.0	Manufg.	Paperboard containers & boxes	2.8	Manufg.
Electric services (utilities)	2.0	Util.	Retail trade, except eating & drinking	2.5	Trade
Motor freight transportation & warehousing	1.9	Util.	Industrial buildings	2.0	Constr.
Petroleum refining	1.7	Manufg.	Eating & drinking places	1.9	Trade
Railroads & related services	1.4	Util.	Engineering, architectural, & surveying services	1.9	Services
Advertising	1.4	Services	Residential additions/alterations, nonfarm	1.7	Constr.
Real estate	1.1	Fin/R.E.	Construction of educational buildings	1.1	Constr.
Miscellaneous plastics products	1.0	Manufg.	Jewelry, precious metal	0.9	Manufg.
Air transportation	1.0	Util.	Nonwoven fabrics	0.9	Manufg.
Gas production & distribution (utilities)	0.9	Util.	S/L Govt. purch., higher education	0.9	S/L Govt
Scrap	0.8	Scrap	Farm service facilities	0.8	Constr.
Converted paper products, nec	0.7	Manufg.	Nonfarm residential structure maintenance	0.7	Constr.
Communications, except radio & TV	0.7	Util.	Residential 1-unit structures, nonfarm	0.6	Constr.
Eating & drinking places	0.7	Trade	Laundry, dry cleaning, shoe repair	0.6	Services
Adhesives & sealants	0.6	Manufg.	Change in business inventories	0.6	In House
Business services nec	0.6	Services	S/L Govt. purch., other general government	0.5	S/L Govt
Hotels & lodging places	0.6	Services	Converted paper products, nec	0.4	Manufg.
Carbon black	0.5	Manufg.	Real estate	0.4	Fin/R.E.
Detective & protective services	0.5	Services	S/L Govt. purch., elem. & secondary education	0.4	S/L Govt

Continued on next page.

INPUTS AND OUTPUTS FOR CONVERTED PAPER PRODUCTS, NEC - Continued

Economic Sector or Industry Providing Inputs	%	Sector	Economic Sector or Industry Buying Outputs	%	Sector
Equipment rental & leasing services	0.5	Services	S/L Govt. purch., public assistance & relief	0.4	S/L Govt
Noncomparable imports	0.5	Foreign	Construction of hospitals	0.3	Constr.
Aluminum rolling & drawing	0.4	Manufg.	Construction of stores & restaurants	0.3	Constr.
Typesetting	0.4	Manufg.	Residential high-rise apartments	0.3	Constr.
Banking	0.4	Fin/R.E.	Warehouses	0.3	Constr.
Maintenance of nonfarm buildings nec	0.3	Constr.	Adhesives & sealants	0.3	Manufg.
Lubricating oils & greases	0.3	Manufg.	Miscellaneous plastics products	0.3	Manufg.
Machinery, except electrical, nec	0.3	Manufg.	Insurance carriers	0.3	Fin/R.E.
Metal foil & leaf	0.3	Manufg.	Advertising	0.3	Services
Nonwoven fabrics	0.3	Manufg.	Federal Government purchases, national defense	0.3	Fed Govt
Paper industries machinery	0.3	Manufg.	Hotels & motels	0.2	Constr.
Photofinishing labs, commercial photography	0.3	Services	Maintenance of farm residential buildings	0.2	Constr.
U.S. Postal Service	0.3	Gov't	Engineering & scientific instruments	0.2	Manufg.
Industrial inorganic chemicals, nec	0.2	Manufg.	General industrial machinery, nec	0.2	Manufg.
Sanitary services, steam supply, irrigation	0.2	Util.	Instruments to measure electricity	0.2	Manufg.
Water transportation	0.2	Util.	Mechanical measuring devices	0.2	Manufg.
Insurance carriers	0.2	Fin/R.E.	Transit & bus transportation	0.2	Util.
Accounting, auditing & bookkeeping	0.2	Services	Banking	0.2	Fin/R.E.
Automotive rental & leasing, without drivers	0.2	Services	Labor, civic, social, & fraternal associations	0.2	Services
Automotive repair shops & services	0.2	Services	Legal services	0.2	Services
Computer & data processing services	0.2	Services	Religious organizations	0.2	Services
Legal services	0.2	Services	Federal Government purchases, nondefense	0.2	Fed Govt
Management & consulting services & labs	0.2	Services	S/L Govt. purch., health & hospitals	0.2	S/L Govt
Manifold business forms	0.1	Manufg.	S/L Govt. purch., natural resource & recreation.	0.2	S/L Govt
Special dies & tools & machine tool accessories	0.1	Manufg.	Farm housing units & additions & alterations	0.1	Constr.
Royalties	0.1	Fin/R.E.	Residential garden apartments	0.1	Constr.
Services to dwellings & other buildings	0.1	Services	Chemical preparations, nec	0.1	Manufg.
			Gaskets, packing & sealing devices	0.1	Manufg.
			Insurance agents, brokers, & services	0.1	Fin/R.E.
			Business/professional associations	0.1	Services
			Colleges, universities, & professional schools	0.1	Services
			Computer & data processing services	0.1	Services
			Management & consulting services & labs	0.1	Services
			S/L Govt. purch., other education & libraries	0.1	S/L Govt
			S/L Govt. purch., police	0.1	S/L Govt

Source: Benchmark Input-Output Accounts for the U.S. Economy, 1982, U.S. Department of Commerce, Washington, D.C., July 1991. Data, as reported in the source, are organized by the 1977 SIC structure in use in 1982 but have been matched, as closely as is possible, to the 1987 SIC structure used in this book.

OCCUPATIONS EMPLOYED BY SIC 267 - MISCELLANEOUS CONVERTED PAPER PRODUCTS

Occupation	% of Total 1994	Change to 2005	Occupation	% of Total 1994	Change to 2005
Paper goods machine setters & set-up operators	9.0	-15.9	Machine feeders & offbearers	2.5	-5.4
Machine operators nec	6.8	29.7	Industrial machinery mechanics	2.1	15.6
Hand packers & packagers	5.7	-9.9	Inspectors, testers, & graders, precision	2.1	15.6
Blue collar worker supervisors	4.5	6.8	Packaging & filling machine operators	2.1	5.1
Assemblers, fabricators, & hand workers nec	4.4	5.1	Freight, stock, & material movers, hand	2.0	-15.9
Printing press machine setters, operators	4.3	5.1	Maintenance repairers, general utility	2.0	5.1
Cutting & slicing machine setters, operators	4.0	26.1	Traffic, shipping, & receiving clerks	1.9	1.1
Sales & related workers nec	3.0	5.1	General managers & top executives	1.8	-0.3
Helpers, laborers, & material movers nec	2.9	5.1	Machine forming operators, metal & plastic	1.7	57.6
Extruding & forming machine workers	2.8	36.6	Coating, painting, & spraying machine workers	1.7	-15.9
Printing, binding, & related workers nec	2.6	5.1	Secretaries, ex legal & medical	1.6	-4.3
Industrial truck & tractor operators	2.6	5.1	Industrial production managers	1.2	5.1

Source: Industry-Occupation Matrix, Bureau of Labor Statistics. These data relate to one or more 3-digit SIC industry groups rather than to a single 4-digit SIC. The change reported for each occupation to the year 2005 is a percent of growth or decline as estimated by the Bureau of Labor Statistics. The abbreviation nec stands for 'not elsewhere classified'.

LOCATION BY STATE AND REGIONAL CONCENTRATION

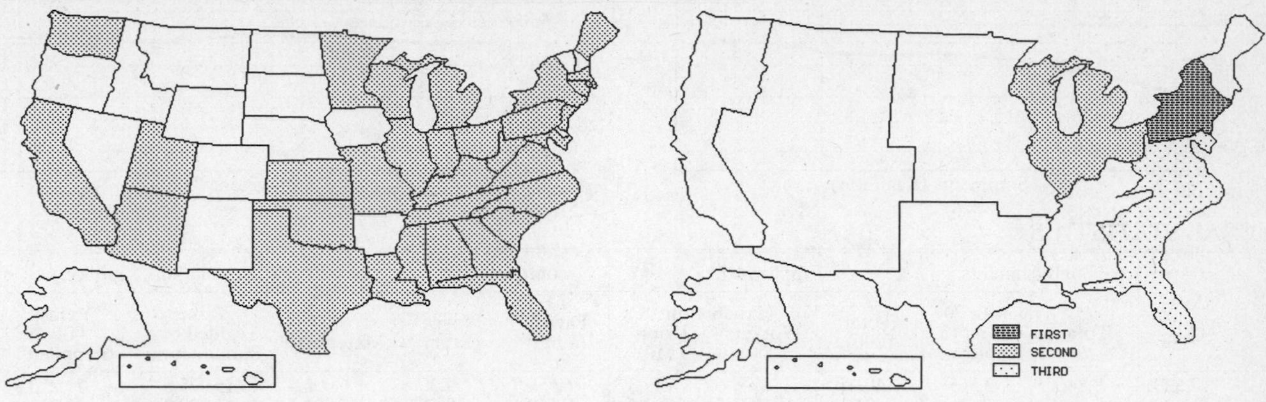

INDUSTRY DATA BY STATE

State	Establish-ments	Shipments			Employment				Cost as % of Shipments	Investment per Employee ($)
		Total ($ mil)	% of U.S.	Per Establ.	Total Number	% of U.S.	Per Establ.	Wages ($/hour)		
Tennessee	14	528.2	11.9	37.7	4,300	13.6	307	9.11	55.3	3,535
Pennsylvania	46	325.5	7.3	7.1	2,500	7.9	54	9.05	51.4	3,800
New York	80	312.2	7.0	3.9	2,300	7.3	29	10.69	53.4	4,000
California	92	304.5	6.9	3.3	2,100	6.6	23	11.31	50.4	5,905
Ohio	41	271.5	6.1	6.6	2,000	6.3	49	11.75	53.7	4,550
Indiana	19	234.9	5.3	12.4	1,800	5.7	95	10.08	51.5	6,778
Illinois	38	205.8	4.6	5.4	1,200	3.8	32	11.60	58.5	2,167
New Jersey	35	172.1	3.9	4.9	1,300	4.1	37	12.06	58.3	2,769
Massachusetts	27	144.6	3.3	5.4	1,600	5.1	59	10.60	48.7	2,500
Georgia	24	138.9	3.1	5.8	1,200	3.8	50	11.11	51.3	9,333
Wisconsin	30	133.1	3.0	4.4	800	2.5	27	10.27	59.0	10,125
North Carolina	36	131.6	3.0	3.7	1,000	3.2	28	10.57	50.7	5,400
Texas	38	117.2	2.6	3.1	800	2.5	21	10.09	57.5	4,125
South Carolina	14	104.4	2.4	7.5	400	1.3	29	9.67	72.8	2,500
Michigan	31	99.3	2.2	3.2	900	2.8	29	9.50	47.2	4,222
Virginia	13	98.0	2.2	7.5	700	2.2	54	9.08	61.6	3,429
Alabama	21	96.0	2.2	4.6	500	1.6	24	9.50	37.8	4,000
Kentucky	8	85.1	1.9	10.6	400	1.3	50	8.14	70.2	-
Arizona	12	70.1	1.6	5.8	500	1.6	42	13.00	60.1	2,400
Washington	15	69.5	1.6	4.6	500	1.6	33	8.88	52.8	-
Connecticut	13	54.0	1.2	4.2	300	0.9	23	10.17	53.9	4,667
Florida	31	37.3	0.8	1.2	400	1.3	13	8.17	52.5	3,500
Louisiana	6	30.6	0.7	5.1	200	0.6	33	9.33	55.6	7,500
Maryland	7	15.8	0.4	2.3	100	0.3	14	8.00	57.0	4,000
Missouri	7	14.3	0.3	2.0	100	0.3	14	8.50	52.4	-
Minnesota	11	13.2	0.3	1.2	100	0.3	9	7.50	53.8	3,000
Oklahoma	8	11.6	0.3	1.5	100	0.3	13	5.50	55.2	3,000
Utah	10	(D)	-	-	175 *	0.6	18	-	-	2,857
Kansas	6	(D)	-	-	750 *	2.4	125	-	-	-
Mississippi	5	(D)	-	-	750 *	2.4	150	-	-	-
Rhode Island	5	(D)	-	-	375 *	1.2	75	-	-	-
Maine	3	(D)	-	-	750 *	2.4	250	-	-	-
West Virginia	2	(D)	-	-	375 *	1.2	188	-	-	-

Source: 1992 *Economic Census*. The states are in descending order of shipments or establishments (if shipment data are missing for the majority). The symbol (D) appears when data are withheld to prevent disclosure of competitive information. States marked with (D) are sorted by number of establishments. A dash (-) indicates that the data element cannot be calculated; * indicates the midpoint of a range.

2711 - NEWSPAPERS

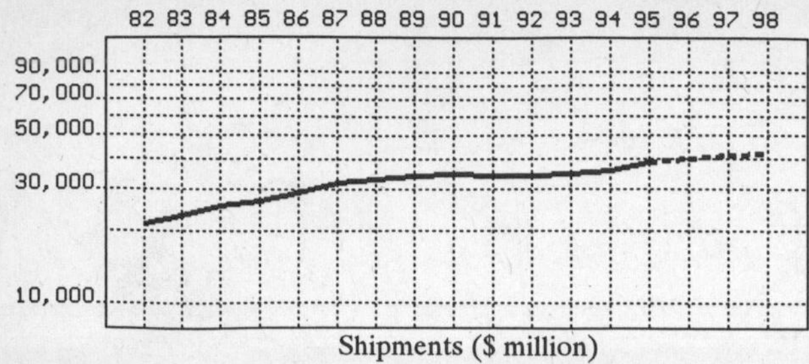

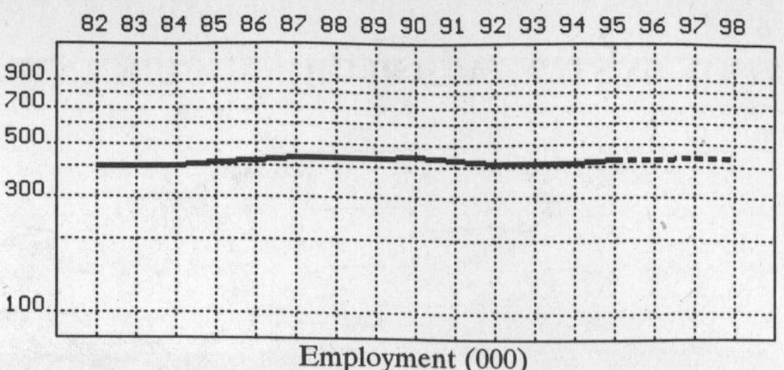

GENERAL STATISTICS

Year	Companies	Establishments		Employment			Compensation		Production ($ million)			
		Total	with 20 or more employees	Total (000)	Production Workers (000)	Production Hours (Mil)	Payroll ($ mil)	Wages ($/hr)	Cost of Materials	Value Added by Manufacture	Value of Shipments	Capital Invest.
1982	7,520	8,846	2,555	401.5	147.2	259.3	6,554.7	9.20	6,006.4	15,275.3	21,276.3	1,029.2
1983				404.1	150.0	263.6	7,059.1	9.86	5,991.5	17,298.2	23,259.4	991.3
1984				398.6	148.5	264.9	7,366.7	10.24	6,429.3	18,871.7	25,302.2	1,086.6
1985				411.0	151.3	265.9	7,904.7	10.64	6,584.6	20,426.3	27,014.7	1,429.7
1986				420.0	151.9	270.0	8,380.5	10.79	7,024.5	22,168.6	29,205.9	1,296.0
1987	7,465	9,091	2,617	434.4	148.4	262.6	9,025.0	11.38	7,533.4	24,310.7	31,850.1	1,522.7
1988				432.4	146.4	262.5	9,348.9	11.42	8,038.3	24,891.9	32,926.8	1,631.3
1989		8,605	2,832	430.9	147.4	253.8	9,842.3	11.82	8,218.4	25,929.7	34,145.8	1,984.5
1990				443.4	149.2	253.2	10,407.1	12.37	8,087.2	26,559.6	34,641.7	1,885.9
1991				428.4	145.1	251.6	10,308.7	12.27	7,606.2	26,092.7	33,702.1	1,537.8
1992	6,762	8,679	2,629	417.0	135.3	235.8	10,506.4	12.89	6,874.0	27,247.0	34,124.3	1,667.4
1993				410.3	131.9	223.8	10,395.5	12.90	6,906.6	27,744.7	34,651.0	1,262.4
1994				410.1	133.7	219.7	10,584.8	13.40	7,018.4	28,817.7	35,837.0	1,329.7
1995				428.3P	135.5P	228.3P	11,572.0P	13.76P	7,598.0P	31,197.7P	38,796.7P	1,721.4P
1996				429.7P	134.1P	224.8P	11,931.9P	14.09P	7,827.1P	32,138.1P	39,966.2P	1,762.3P
1997				431.1P	132.8P	221.3P	12,291.8P	14.42P	8,056.1P	33,078.5P	41,135.6P	1,803.2P
1998				432.5P	131.4P	217.8P	12,651.8P	14.74P	8,285.1P	34,018.9P	42,305.1P	1,844.2P

Sources: 1982, 1987, 1992 *Economic Census*; *Annual Survey of Manufactures*, 83-86, 88-91, 93-94. Establishment counts for non-Census years are from *County Business Patterns*; establishment values for 83-84 are extrapolations. 'P's show projections by the editors. Industries reclassified in 87 will not have data for prior years.

INDICES OF CHANGE

Year	Companies	Establishments		Employment			Compensation		Production ($ million)			
		Total	with 20 or more employees	Total (000)	Production Workers (000)	Production Hours (Mil)	Payroll ($ mil)	Wages ($/hr)	Cost of Materials	Value Added by Manufacture	Value of Shipments	Capital Invest.
1982	111	102	97	96	109	110	62	71	87	56	62	62
1983				97	111	112	67	76	87	63	68	59
1984				96	110	112	70	79	94	69	74	65
1985				99	112	113	75	83	96	75	79	86
1986				101	112	115	80	84	102	81	86	78
1987	110	105	100	104	110	111	86	88	110	89	93	91
1988				104	108	111	89	89	117	91	96	98
1989		99	108	103	109	108	94	92	120	95	100	119
1990				106	110	107	99	96	118	97	102	113
1991				103	107	107	98	95	111	96	99	92
1992	100	100	100	100	100	100	100	100	100	100	100	100
1993				98	97	95	99	100	100	102	102	76
1994				98	99	93	101	104	102	106	105	80
1995				103P	100P	97P	110P	107P	111P	114P	114P	103P
1996				103P	99P	95P	114P	109P	114P	118P	117P	106P
1997				103P	98P	94P	117P	112P	117P	121P	121P	108P
1998				104P	97P	92P	120P	114P	121P	125P	124P	111P

Sources: Same as General Statistics. Values reflect change from the base year, 1992. Values above 100 mean greater than 92, values below 100 mean less than 92, and a value of 100 in the 82-91 or 93-98 period means same as 92. 'P's mark projections by the editors.

SELECTED RATIOS

For 1992	Avg. of All Manufact.	Analyzed Industry	Index	For 1992	Avg. of All Manufact.	Analyzed Industry	Index
Employees per Establishment	46	48	105	Value Added per Production Worker	122,353	201,382	165
Payroll per Establishment	1,332,320	1,210,554	91	Cost per Establishment	4,239,462	792,027	19
Payroll per Employee	29,181	25,195	86	Cost per Employee	92,853	16,484	18
Production Workers per Establishment	31	16	50	Cost per Production Worker	135,003	50,806	38
Wages per Establishment	734,496	350,209	48	Shipments per Establishment	8,100,800	3,931,824	49
Wages per Production Worker	23,390	22,465	96	Shipments per Employee	177,425	81,833	46
Hours per Production Worker	2,025	1,743	86	Shipments per Production Worker	257,966	252,212	98
Wages per Hour	11.55	12.89	112	Investment per Establishment	278,244	192,119	69
Value Added per Establishment	3,842,210	3,139,417	82	Investment per Employee	6,094	3,999	66
Value Added per Employee	84,153	65,341	78	Investment per Production Worker	8,861	12,324	139

Sources: Same as General Statistics. The 'Average of All Manufacturing' column represents the average of all manufacturing industries reported for the most recent complete year available. The Index shows the relationship between the Average and the Analyzed Industry. For example, 100 means that they are equal; 500 that the Analyzed Industry is five times the average; 50 means that the Analyzed Industry is half the national average. The abbreviation 'na' is used to show that data are 'not available'.

LEADING COMPANIES

Number shown: **75** Total sales ($ mil): **41,704** Total employment (000): **351.5**

Company Name	Address				CEO Name	Phone	Co. Type	Sales ($ mil)	Empl. (000)
Gannett Company Inc	1100 Wilson Blv	Arlington	VA	22234	John J Curley	703-284-6000	P	3,824	36.0
Times Mirror Co	Times Mirror Sq	Los Angeles	CA	90053	Robert F Erburu	213-237-3700	P	3,357	18.0
Gannett Company Inc	1100 Wilson Blv	Arlington	VA	22234	Gary Watson	703-284-6000	D	2,980	31.9
Knight-Ridder Inc	1 Herald Plz	Miami	FL	33132	James K Batten	305-376-3800	P	2,649	21.0
Tribune Co	435 N Michigan Av	Chicago	IL	60611	C T Brumback	312-222-9100	P	2,155	10.5
Dow Jones and Company Inc	200 Liberty St	New York	NY	10281	Peter R Kann	212-416-2000	P	2,091	10.3
New York Times Co	229 W 43rd St	New York	NY	10036	A O Sulzberger	212-556-1234	P	2,020	13.0
Advance Publications Inc	950 Fingerboard Rd	Staten Island	NY	10305	Donald Newhouse	718-981-1234	R	1,830•	19.0
Washington Post Co	1150 15th St NW	Washington	DC	20071	Donald E Graham	202-334-6000	P	1,614	6.8
Hearst Corp	959 8th Av	New York	NY	10019	F A Bennack Jr	212-649-2000	R	1,300•	13.5
Tribune Publishing Co	435 N Michigan Av	Chicago	IL	60611	John W Madigan	312-222-3232	S	1,292	7.7
EW Scripps Co	1105 N Market St	Wilmington	DE	19801	Lawrence A Leser	302-478-4141	P	1,220	7.7
Journal Communications Inc	PO Box 661	Milwaukee	WI	53201	Robert Kahlor	414-224-2000	R	635	6.4
Multimedia Inc	PO Box 1688	Greenville	SC	29602	Donald D Sbarra	803-298-4373	P	631	3.5
AH Belo Corp	400 S Record St	Dallas	TX	75202	Robert W Decherd	214-977-6606	P	628	3.1
Media General Inc	PO Box 85333	Richmond	VA	23293	J Stewart Bryan III	804-649-6000	P	601	7.3
Freedom Communications Inc	17666 Fitch	Irvine	CA	92714	James N Rosse	714-553-9292	R	530•	5.5
Central Newspapers Inc	135 N Pennsylvania	Indianapolis	IN	46204	Frank E Russell	317-231-9200	P	520	5.0
Oklahoma Publishing Co	PO Box 25125	Oklahoma City	OK	73125	Edward L Gaylord	405-475-3311	R	480•	6.0
McClatchy Newspapers Inc	2100 Q St	Sacramento	CA	95816	Erwin Potts	916-321-1846	P	471	6.2
Pulitzer Publishing Co	900 N Tucker Blv	St Louis	MO	63101	Michael E Pulitzer	314-622-7000	P	427	3.0
Harte-Hanks Communications	PO Box 269	San Antonio	TX	78291	Larry Franklin	210-829-9000	P	423	6.1
Philadelphia Newspapers Inc	PO Box 8263	Philadelphia	PA	19101	Bob Hall	215-854-2000	S	423	3.4
American Publishing Co	PO Box 1000	West Frankfort	IL	62896	Larry J Perrotto	618-937-6411	P	423	7.2
Lee Enterprises Inc	215 N Main St	Davenport	IA	52801	Richard D Gottlieb	319-383-2202	P	403	4.7
Morris Communications Corp	PO Box 936	Augusta	GA	30913	William S Morris III	706-724-0851	R	360	3.8
Copley Press Inc	7776 Ivanhoe Av	La Jolla	CA	92037	David C Copley	619-454-0411	R	330•	3.5
Miami Herald Publishing	1 Herald Plz	Miami	FL	33132	Roberto Suarez	305-350-2111	S	308	2.4
Phoenix Newspapers Inc	120 E Van Buren St	Phoenix	AZ	85004	Lewis A Weil III	602-271-8000	S	292	2.7
Sun-Times Co	401 N Wabash Av	Chicago	IL	60611	Sam McKeel	312-321-3000	S	282	3.0
Morris Communications Inc	PO Box 936	Augusta	GA	30903	WS Morris III	706-724-0851	R	280•	3.0
Seattle Times Co	PO Box 70	Seattle	WA	98111	H Mason Sizemore	206-464-2111	R	280	2.4
Tribune Co	PO Box 191	Tampa	FL	33601	Jack Butcher	813-272-7711	S	270	3.5
Booth Newspapers Inc	PO Box 2168	Grand Rapids	MI	49501	Werner Veit	616-459-3824	R	260	2.7
Houston Chronicle Pub Co	PO Box 4260	Houston	TX	77210	Richard J Johnson	713-220-7171	S	250	2.0
San Francisco Newspaper Agency	925 Mission St	San Francisco	CA	94103	James Hale	415-777-5700	R	250	2.8
Ottaway Newspapers Inc	PO Box 401	Campbell Hall	NY	10916	Richard A Myers	914-294-8181	S	245	3.5
Chronicle Publishing Co	901 Mission St	San Francisco	CA	94103	Richard Thieriot	415-777-1111	R	240•	2.5
Times Publishing Co	PO Box 1121	St Petersburg	FL	33731	Andrew Barnes	813-893-8111	R	230	3.3
Detroit Free Press Inc	321 W Lafayette	Detroit	MI	48231	Neal Shine	313-222-6400	S	204	0.3
Sentinel Communications Co	PO Box 2833	Orlando	FL	32802	John P Puerner	407-420-5000	S	202	1.4
Howard Publications Inc	PO Box 570	Oceanside	CA	92049	Robert S Howard	619-433-5771	R	200	2.5
Lesher Communications Inc	2640 Shadelands Dr	Walnut Creek	CA	94598	George Riggs	510-935-2525	R	200	2.5
Tower Media Inc	PO Box 4200	Woodland Hills	CA	91365	Jack K Cooke	818-713-3800	R	190•	2.0
Macromedia Inc	150 River St	Hackensack	NJ	07601	Malcolm Borg	201-646-4000	R	180	1.9
Calkins Newspapers Inc	8400 Rte 13	Levittown	PA	19057	Grover J Friend	215-949-4011	R	180•	1.9
Journal/Sentinel Inc	PO Box 661	Milwaukee	WI	53201	James Currow	414-224-2000	S	180	1.5
Kansas City Star Co	1729 Grand Blv	Kansas City	MO	64108	R C Woodworth	816-234-4141	S	170	1.8
Cincinnati Enquirer	312 Elm St	Cincinnati	OH	45202	Harry M Whipple	513-721-2700	D	160	1.0
Indianapolis Newspapers Inc	PO Box 145	Indianapolis	IN	46206	M W Applegate	317-633-1240	S	153	1.9
Denver Post Corp	1560 Broadway	Denver	CO	80202	Ryan McKibben	303-820-1010	S	150•	1.5
San Jose Mercury News Inc	750 Ridder Park Dr	San Jose	CA	95190	Jay T Harris	408-920-5000	S	150•	1.5
Small Newspaper Group Inc	1720 5th Av	Moline	IL	61265	Rob Small	309-764-4344	R	150	1.6
Guy Gannett Publishing Co	PO Box 15277	Portland	ME	04101	James B Shaffer	207-828-8100	R	147	1.7
Asbury Park Press Inc	3601 Hwy 66	Neptune	NJ	07754	E Donald Lass	908-922-6000	R	140•	1.5
Blade Communications Inc	541 N Superior St	Toledo	OH	43660	William Block Jr	419-245-6000	R	140•	1.5
Buffalo News	PO Box 100	Buffalo	NY	14240	Stanford Lipsey	716-849-3434	S	130	1.1
Dispatch Printing Co	34 S 3rd St	Columbus	OH	43216	John F Wolfe	614-461-5000	R	130	1.3
Fort Worth Star-Telegram Inc	PO Box 1870	Fort Worth	TX	76101	Richard Connor	817-390-7400	S	130•	1.4
Morris Newspaper Corp	27 Abercorn St	Savannah	GA	31412	Charles H Morris	912-233-1281	R	120•	1.3
Star-Telegram Inc	PO Box 1870	Fort Worth	TX	76101	Richard L Connor	817-390-7400	S	120•	1.2
PG Publishing Co	34 Blv of the Allies	Pittsburgh	PA	15222	William Block	412-263-1100	D	110•	1.2
Richmond Newspapers Inc	333 E Grace St	Richmond	VA	23219	J Stewart Bryan III	804-649-6000	S	110	0.9
Union-Tribune Publishing Co	PO Box 191	San Diego	CA	92112	Gene Bell	619-299-3131	D	110•	1.2
Woodward Communications Inc	PO Box 688	Dubuque	IA	52004	William Skemp	319-588-5687	R	110	0.7
Gannett Rochester Newspapers	55 Exchange Blv	Rochester	NY	14614	David J Mack	716-232-7100	D	100	1.4
Houston Post Co	PO Box 4747	Houston	TX	77210	Ike Massey	713-840-5600	S	100	1.1
Northwest Publications Inc	345 Cedar St	St Paul	MN	55101	Peter Ridder	612-222-5011	S	99	0.9
Saint Paul Pioneer Press	345 Cedar St	St Paul	MN	55101	Peter Ridder	612-222-5011	S	99	0.9
Scripps League Newspaper Inc	HCR 1	Charlottesville	VA	22901	Edward W Scripps	804-973-3345	R	96	1.0
Albuquerque Publishing Co	7777 Jefferson NE	Albuquerque	NM	87109	Thomas H Lang	505-823-7777	R	95	1.0
News & Observer Publishing Co	215 S McDowell St	Raleigh	NC	27602	Frank A Daniels Jr	919-829-4500	R	90	0.9
American City Business Journals	128 S Tryon St	Charlotte	NC	28202	Ray Shaw	704-375-7404	P	87	0.9
Century Graphics Corp	1013 McDermott	Metairie	LA	70001	Carl J Eberts	504-836-6000	R	85	0.4
Memphis Publishing Co	495 Union Av	Memphis	TN	38101	Angus McEachran	901-529-2211	D	85	1.0

Source: *Ward's Business Directory of U.S. Private and Public Companies*, Volumes 1 and 2, 1996. The company type code is used as follows: P - Public, R - Private, S - Subsidiary, D - Division, J - Joint Venture, A - Affiliate, G - Group. Sales are in millions of dollars, employees are in thousands. An asterisk (*) indicates an estimated sales volume. The symbol < stands for 'less than'. Company names and addresses are truncated, in some cases, to fit into the available space.

MATERIALS CONSUMED

Material		Quantity	Delivered Cost ($ million)
Materials, ingredients, containers, and supplies		(X)	5,850.3
Newsprint, basis wt. 30 lb.	1,000 metric tons	6,914.4	3,202.2
Newspaper, other basis wt.	1,000 metric tons	1,384.9	629.5
Coated paper		(X)	37.9
All other paper, except light sensitive		(X)	43.9
Letterpress printing inks, including news		(X)	33.7
Lithographic (offset) printing inks		(X)	114.9
Other printing inks, including gravure, flexographic, and screen process		(X)	24.3
Lithographic (offset) printing plates, exposed, prepared for printing		(X)	23.7
Letterpress printing plates, exposed, prepared for printing		(X)	17.1
Other printing plates, exposed, prepared for printing		(X)	11.0
Lithographic (offset) printing plates, unexposed photosensitive		(X)	33.1
Letterpress printing plates, unexposed photosensitive		(X)	18.7
Other printing plates, unexposed photosensitive		(X)	3.5
Light sensitive films		(X)	52.5
Light sensitive papers (including photographic paper and diffusion transfer paper)		(X)	18.9
All other materials and components, parts, containers, and supplies		(X)	472.5
Materials, ingredients, containers, and supplies, nsk		(X)	1,112.8

Source: 1992 *Economic Census*. Explanation of symbols used: (D): Withheld to avoid disclosure of competitive data; na: Not available; (S): Withheld because statistical norms were not met; (X): Not applicable; (Z): Less than half the unit shown; nec: Not elsewhere classified; nsk: Not specified by kind; - : zero; * : 10-19 percent estimated; ** : 20-29 percent estimated.

PRODUCT SHARE DETAILS

Product or Product Class	% Share	Product or Product Class	% Share
Newspapers	100.00	Weekly and other newspapers (receipts from subscriptions and sales)	2.00
Daily and Sunday newspapers (receipts from subscriptions and sales)	20.28	Weekly and other newspapers (receipts from advertising)	6.54
Daily and Sunday newspapers (receipts from advertising)	62.38	Newspapers, nsk	8.81

Source: 1992 *Economic Census*. The values shown are percent of total shipments in an industry. Values of indented subcategories are summed in the main heading. The symbol (D) appears when data are withheld to prevent disclosure of competitive information. The abbreviation nsk stands for 'not specified by kind' and nec for 'not elsewhere classified'.

INPUTS AND OUTPUTS FOR NEWSPAPERS

Economic Sector or Industry Providing Inputs	%	Sector	Economic Sector or Industry Buying Outputs	%	Sector
Paper mills, except building paper	35.9	Manufg.	Personal consumption expenditures	91.5	
Communications, except radio & TV	7.0	Util.	Newspapers	2.5	Manufg.
U.S. Postal Service	5.0	Gov't	Change in business inventories	1.4	In House
Wholesale trade	4.7	Trade	Membership organizations nec	1.1	Services
Air transportation	4.5	Util.	S/L Govt. purch., public assistance & relief	0.7	S/L Govt
Petroleum refining	3.7	Manufg.	Banking	0.6	Fin/R.E.
Business services nec	3.3	Services	Social services, nec	0.6	Services
Commercial printing	3.2	Manufg.	S/L Govt. purch., other education & libraries	0.6	S/L Govt
Advertising	3.2	Services	Exports	0.4	Foreign
Royalties	2.5	Fin/R.E.	Credit agencies other than banks	0.1	Fin/R.E.
Eating & drinking places	2.3	Trade			
Legal services	2.0	Services			
Banking	1.9	Fin/R.E.			
Electric services (utilities)	1.6	Util.			
Newspapers	1.5	Manufg.			
Motor freight transportation & warehousing	1.5	Util.			
Photographic equipment & supplies	1.1	Manufg.			
Printing ink	1.1	Manufg.			
Railroads & related services	0.9	Util.			
Computer & data processing services	0.9	Services			
Maintenance of nonfarm buildings nec	0.8	Constr.			
Management & consulting services & labs	0.8	Services			
Real estate	0.7	Fin/R.E.			
Automotive rental & leasing, without drivers	0.7	Services			
Equipment rental & leasing services	0.7	Services			
Imports	0.6	Foreign			
Lithographic platemaking & services	0.5	Manufg.			
Mechanical measuring devices	0.5	Manufg.			
Printing trades machinery	0.5	Manufg.			
Accounting, auditing & bookkeeping	0.5	Services			
Automotive repair shops & services	0.5	Services			
Business/professional associations	0.5	Services			
Engraving & plate printing	0.4	Manufg.			
Manifold business forms	0.4	Manufg.			
Gas production & distribution (utilities)	0.3	Util.			
Insurance carriers	0.3	Fin/R.E.			

Continued on next page.

INPUTS AND OUTPUTS FOR NEWSPAPERS - Continued

Economic Sector or Industry Providing Inputs	%	Sector	Economic Sector or Industry Buying Outputs	%	Sector
Personnel supply services	0.3	Services			
Motor vehicle parts & accessories	0.2	Manufg.			
Periodicals	0.2	Manufg.			
Tires & inner tubes	0.2	Manufg.			
Sanitary services, steam supply, irrigation	0.2	Util.			
Transit & bus transportation	0.2	Util.			
Retail trade, except eating & drinking	0.2	Trade			
Electrical repair shops	0.2	Services			
Hotels & lodging places	0.2	Services			
Lubricating oils & greases	0.1	Manufg.			
Machinery, except electrical, nec	0.1	Manufg.			
Credit agencies other than banks	0.1	Fin/R.E.			
Security & commodity brokers	0.1	Fin/R.E.			

Source: Benchmark Input-Output Accounts for the U.S. Economy, 1982, U.S. Department of Commerce, Washington, D.C., July 1991. Data, as reported in the source, are organized by the 1977 SIC structure in use in 1982 but have been matched, as closely as is possible, to the 1987 SIC structure used in this book.

OCCUPATIONS EMPLOYED BY SIC 271 - NEWSPAPERS

Occupation	% of Total 1994	Change to 2005	Occupation	% of Total 1994	Change to 2005
Sales & related workers nec	13.5	-1.0	Marketing, advertising, & PR managers	1.7	-0.9
Reporters & correspondents	8.2	-10.9	Marketing & sales worker supervisors	1.7	-1.0
Writers & editors, incl technical writers	8.0	-1.0	Adjustment clerks	1.7	18.9
Hand packers & packagers	3.9	-6.6	Duplicating, mail, & office machine operators	1.6	-42.2
Driver/sales workers	3.8	18.9	Photographers	1.6	-1.9
Truck drivers light & heavy	2.6	2.1	Artists & commercial artists	1.5	9.8
Advertising clerks	2.6	-10.9	Secretaries, ex legal & medical	1.5	-9.8
Paste-up workers	2.4	-35.6	Helpers, laborers, & material movers nec	1.4	-1.0
General office clerks	2.2	-15.5	Managers & administrators nec	1.3	-1.0
General managers & top executives	2.2	-6.0	Clerical supervisors & managers	1.3	1.3
Offset lithographic press operators	2.1	-1.0	Letterpress operators	1.3	-75.2
Printing press machine setters, operators	2.1	-20.8	Typesetting & composing machine operators	1.1	-75.2
Blue collar worker supervisors	2.0	-8.3	Janitors & cleaners, incl maids	1.1	-20.8
Machine feeders & offbearers	1.9	-10.9	Electronic pagination systems workers	1.1	58.5
Bookkeeping, accounting, & auditing clerks	1.8	-25.7			

Source: *Industry-Occupation Matrix*, Bureau of Labor Statistics. These data relate to one or more 3-digit SIC industry groups rather than to a single 4-digit SIC. The change reported for each occupation to the year 2005 is a percent of growth or decline as estimated by the Bureau of Labor Statistics. The abbreviation nec stands for 'not elsewhere classified'.

LOCATION BY STATE AND REGIONAL CONCENTRATION

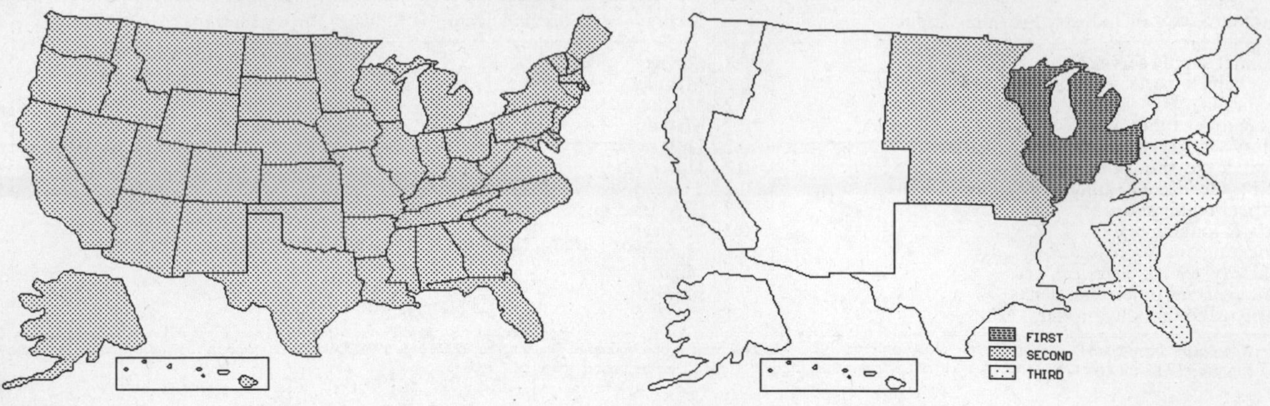

INDUSTRY DATA BY STATE

State	Establish-ments	Shipments			Employment				Cost as % of Shipments	Investment per Employee ($)
		Total ($ mil)	% of U.S.	Per Establ.	Total Number	% of U.S.	Per Establ.	Wages ($/hour)		
California	692	4,443.4	13.0	6.4	52,300	12.5	76	12.93	20.0	2,843
New York	504	3,341.4	9.8	6.6	31,600	7.6	63	18.34	21.0	5,927
Florida	329	2,189.3	6.4	6.7	22,800	5.5	69	12.51	19.7	2,162
Texas	634	1,938.4	5.7	3.1	20,800	5.0	33	10.33	24.8	1,572
Illinois	430	1,788.3	5.2	4.2	19,700	4.7	46	13.25	19.3	3,386
Pennsylvania	306	1,677.1	4.9	5.5	21,900	5.3	72	14.85	20.4	12,484
Ohio	286	1,364.0	4.0	4.8	16,600	4.0	58	12.63	20.0	7,446
Massachusetts	188	1,191.2	3.5	6.3	14,800	3.5	79	14.82	17.7	2,203
New Jersey	186	1,134.6	3.3	6.1	11,900	2.9	64	17.18	23.1	5,689
Virginia	174	1,065.6	3.1	6.1	11,300	2.7	65	10.24	22.2	1,699
Michigan	230	1,025.4	3.0	4.5	14,100	3.4	61	14.27	22.9	3,745
Washington	186	720.1	2.1	3.9	10,400	2.5	56	15.35	18.1	3,538
Georgia	233	695.6	2.0	3.0	10,200	2.4	44	10.28	20.8	4,833
North Carolina	215	671.9	2.0	3.1	9,900	2.4	46	11.27	19.7	1,737
Missouri	292	665.3	1.9	2.3	8,200	2.0	28	12.40	21.7	2,512
Wisconsin	235	624.8	1.8	2.7	10,900	2.6	46	10.80	20.5	1,541
Indiana	208	621.1	1.8	3.0	10,300	2.5	50	11.81	19.1	2,981
Minnesota	287	596.6	1.7	2.1	8,500	2.0	30	13.87	18.9	1,776
Arizona	110	592.3	1.7	5.4	6,300	1.5	57	12.10	19.0	-
Connecticut	91	525.7	1.5	5.8	7,200	1.7	79	14.33	16.8	1,861
Tennessee	167	489.0	1.4	2.9	7,400	1.8	44	9.92	17.3	1,500
Maryland	86	486.6	1.4	5.7	4,900	1.2	57	15.92	16.7	2,673
Colorado	150	482.0	1.4	3.2	6,800	1.6	45	13.25	24.2	10,353
Iowa	241	375.9	1.1	1.6	6,100	1.5	25	10.06	20.3	1,738
Oregon	121	370.8	1.1	3.1	4,800	1.2	40	13.67	22.3	5,000
Louisiana	107	342.5	1.0	3.2	4,300	1.0	40	11.74	23.8	2,977
Oklahoma	175	337.1	1.0	1.9	4,700	1.1	27	11.46	18.7	3,128
Kentucky	156	320.9	0.9	2.1	4,400	1.1	28	10.50	19.5	2,250
South Carolina	105	309.7	0.9	2.9	4,500	1.1	43	9.63	19.4	2,511
Alabama	132	302.5	0.9	2.3	4,100	1.0	31	8.94	18.0	1,610
Hawaii	23	261.4	0.8	11.4	1,500	0.4	65	17.25	11.6	3,333
Kansas	184	220.7	0.6	1.2	4,100	1.0	22	10.17	17.1	1,171
Nevada	37	199.3	0.6	5.4	1,600	0.4	43	12.40	17.9	1,438
Nebraska	139	194.2	0.6	1.4	3,200	0.8	23	8.67	20.2	1,594
Arkansas	117	188.7	0.6	1.6	3,500	0.8	30	8.08	22.5	2,000
Mississippi	105	165.7	0.5	1.6	2,600	0.6	25	8.89	22.6	1,923
Utah	58	163.6	0.5	2.8	2,800	0.7	48	8.63	19.6	1,143
Rhode Island	22	162.4	0.5	7.4	2,300	0.6	105	17.75	23.2	-
West Virginia	80	151.6	0.4	1.9	2,900	0.7	36	9.88	19.7	1,379
Maine	68	140.9	0.4	2.1	2,400	0.6	35	12.36	18.2	1,417
New Mexico	57	140.3	0.4	2.5	2,100	0.5	37	9.00	18.5	2,524
New Hampshire	55	118.4	0.3	2.2	2,100	0.5	38	12.50	17.3	1,238
Idaho	60	97.3	0.3	1.6	1,700	0.4	28	10.10	17.6	1,294
Montana	76	94.9	0.3	1.2	1,500	0.4	20	8.33	17.1	1,533
Delaware	18	94.8	0.3	5.3	900	0.2	50	11.40	20.0	-
North Dakota	68	85.2	0.2	1.3	1,500	0.4	22	9.18	17.0	1,067
South Dakota	91	81.5	0.2	0.9	1,600	0.4	18	8.11	19.6	1,500
Vermont	53	67.9	0.2	1.3	1,100	0.3	21	10.00	18.6	-
Alaska	37	55.4	0.2	1.5	1,200	0.3	32	11.40	22.4	1,833
Wyoming	42	(D)	-	-	750 *	0.2	18	-	-	-
D.C.	33	(D)	-	-	3,750 *	0.9	114	-	-	2,667

Source: 1992 *Economic Census*. The states are in descending order of shipments or establishments (if shipment data are missing for the majority). The symbol (D) appears when data are withheld to prevent disclosure of competitive information. States marked with (D) are sorted by number of establishments. A dash (-) indicates that the data element cannot be calculated; * indicates the midpoint of a range.

2721 - PERIODICALS

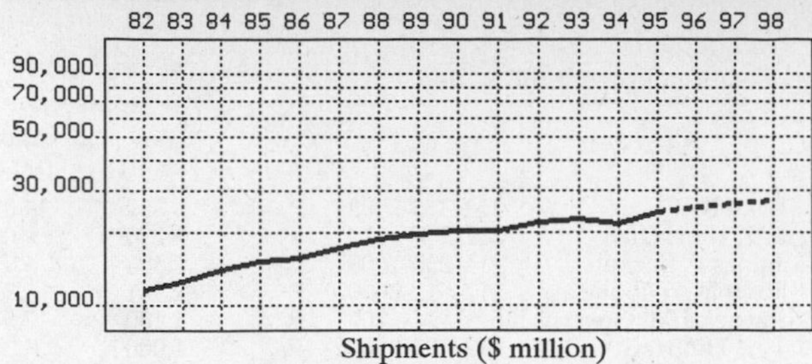

Shipments ($ million)

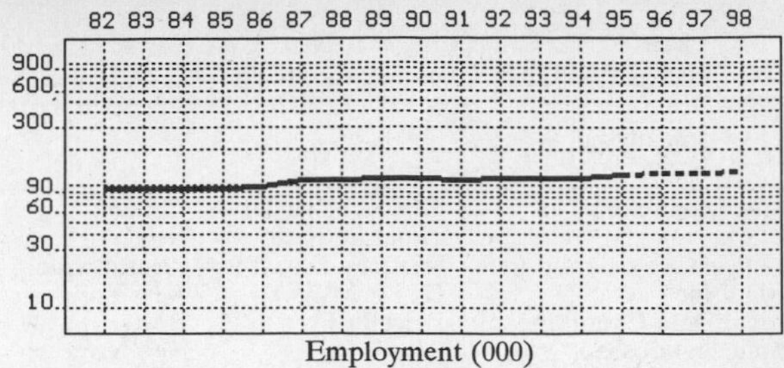

Employment (000)

GENERAL STATISTICS

Year	Companies	Establishments		Employment			Compensation		Production ($ million)			
		Total	with 20 or more employees	Total (000)	Production Workers (000)	Production Hours (Mil)	Payroll ($ mil)	Wages ($/hr)	Cost of Materials	Value Added by Manufacture	Value of Shipments	Capital Invest.
1982	3,144	3,328	690	94.0	17.4	31.9	1,986.1	7.62	4,568.1	6,910.9	11,478.0	194.8
1983				93.4	17.3	31.9	2,073.7	8.03	4,603.6	7,868.9	12,436.7	251.7
1984				93.5	16.2	28.8	2,231.7	8.71	5,117.6	8,943.9	14,052.6	267.4
1985				95.8	16.2	28.4	2,554.5	9.59	5,579.8	9,678.1	15,246.4	339.7
1986				98.1	14.2	24.9	2,710.9	11.60	5,558.1	10,196.0	15,719.4	274.1
1987	3,757	4,020	876	110.0	18.3	32.4	2,982.7	11.06	5,872.7	11,452.1	17,329.2	246.4
1988				111.4	19.1	33.8	3,152.1	11.99	6,201.9	12,439.6	18,611.8	246.1
1989		4,101	872	115.9	20.7	32.6	3,422.8	12.45	6,581.0	13,248.4	19,787.2	272.2
1990				115.2	21.6	35.4	3,658.5	13.09	6,579.6	13,847.7	20,396.7	274.8
1991				110.6	20.7	35.4	3,661.0	13.21	6,459.0	13,794.4	20,345.1	223.0
1992	4,390	4,699	991	116.2	20.1	39.0	4,074.5	13.40	6,200.9	15,833.0	22,033.9	234.4
1993				117.1	19.7	37.4	4,305.3	12.51	6,391.2	16,271.9	22,652.5	289.5
1994				116.4	18.3	34.5	4,273.9	12.97	5,903.1	15,821.4	21,723.3	306.6
1995				123.2P	20.9P	37.7P	4,618.7P	14.65P	6,638.9P	17,793.6P	24,431.2P	278.7P
1996				125.6P	21.2P	38.3P	4,827.0P	15.14P	6,895.1P	18,480.2P	25,373.9P	280.9P
1997				127.9P	21.6P	39.0P	5,035.3P	15.62P	7,151.3P	19,166.8P	26,316.7P	283.2P
1998				130.3P	21.9P	39.7P	5,243.6P	16.11P	7,407.5P	19,853.5P	27,259.5P	285.4P

Sources: 1982, 1987, 1992 *Economic Census; Annual Survey of Manufactures,* 83-86, 88-91, 93-94. Establishment counts for non-Census years are from *County Business Patterns*; establishment values for 83-84 are extrapolations. 'P's show projections by the editors. Industries reclassified in 87 will not have data for prior years.

INDICES OF CHANGE

Year	Companies	Establishments		Employment			Compensation		Production ($ million)			
		Total	with 20 or more employees	Total (000)	Production Workers (000)	Production Hours (Mil)	Payroll ($ mil)	Wages ($/hr)	Cost of Materials	Value Added by Manufacture	Value of Shipments	Capital Invest.
1982	72	71	70	81	87	82	49	57	74	44	52	83
1983				80	86	82	51	60	74	50	56	107
1984				80	81	74	55	65	83	56	64	114
1985				82	81	73	63	72	90	61	69	145
1986				84	71	64	67	87	90	64	71	117
1987	86	86	88	95	91	83	73	83	95	72	79	105
1988				96	95	87	77	89	100	79	84	105
1989		87	88	100	103	84	84	93	106	84	90	116
1990				99	107	91	90	98	106	87	93	117
1991				95	103	91	90	99	104	87	92	95
1992	100	100	100	100	100	100	100	100	100	100	100	100
1993				101	98	96	106	93	103	103	103	124
1994				100	91	88	105	97	95	100	99	131
1995				106P	104P	97P	113P	109P	107P	112P	111P	119P
1996				108P	106P	98P	118P	113P	111P	117P	115P	120P
1997				110P	107P	100P	124P	117P	115P	121P	119P	121P
1998				112P	109P	102P	129P	120P	119P	125P	124P	122P

Sources: Same as General Statistics. Values reflect change from the base year, 1992. Values above 100 mean greater than 92, values below 100 mean less than 92, and a value of 100 in the 82-91 or 93-98 period means same as 92. 'P's mark projections by the editors.

SELECTED RATIOS

For 1992	Avg. of All Manufact.	Analyzed Industry	Index	For 1992	Avg. of All Manufact.	Analyzed Industry	Index
Employees per Establishment	46	25	54	Value Added per Production Worker	122,353	787,711	644
Payroll per Establishment	1,332,320	867,099	65	Cost per Establishment	4,239,462	1,319,621	31
Payroll per Employee	29,181	35,065	120	Cost per Employee	92,853	53,364	57
Production Workers per Establishment	31	4	14	Cost per Production Worker	135,003	308,502	229
Wages per Establishment	734,496	111,215	15	Shipments per Establishment	8,100,800	4,689,062	58
Wages per Production Worker	23,390	26,000	111	Shipments per Employee	177,425	189,620	107
Hours per Production Worker	2,025	1,940	96	Shipments per Production Worker	257,966	1,096,214	425
Wages per Hour	11.55	13.40	116	Investment per Establishment	278,244	49,883	18
Value Added per Establishment	3,842,210	3,369,440	88	Investment per Employee	6,094	2,017	33
Value Added per Employee	84,153	136,256	162	Investment per Production Worker	8,861	11,662	132

Sources: Same as General Statistics. The 'Average of All Manufacturing' column represents the average of all manufacturing industries reported for the most recent complete year available. The Index shows the relationship between the Average and the Analyzed Industry. For example, 100 means that they are equal; 500 that the Analyzed Industry is five times the average; 50 means that the Analyzed Industry is half the national average. The abbreviation 'na' is used to show that data are 'not available'.

LEADING COMPANIES

Number shown: 75 Total sales ($ mil): 27,289 Total employment (000): 148.0

Company Name	Address				CEO Name	Phone	Co. Type	Sales ($ mil)	Empl. (000)
RR Donnelley and Sons Co	77 W Wacker Dr	Chicago	IL	60601	John R Walter	312-326-8000	P	4,889	39.0
Time Inc	TimeLife Bldg	New York	NY	10020	R K Brack Jr	212-586-1212	S	3,270	9.0
Reader's Digest Association Inc	Reader's Digest Rd	Pleasantville	NY	10570	James P, Schadt	914-238-1000	P	2,806	6.7
McGraw-Hill Inc	1221 Av Amer	New York	NY	10020	Joseph L Dionne	212-512-2000	P	2,761	15.3
International Data Group Inc	1 Exeter Plz	Boston	MA	02116	Patrick J McGovern	617-534-1200	R	1,100	7.5
Ziff Communications Co	1 Park Av	New York	NY	10016	Eric Hippeau	212-503-3500	R	1,000	4.3
Printing Holdings LP	101 Park Av	New York	NY	10178	Robert G Burton	212-986-2440	R	950*	6.2
World Color Press Inc	101 Park Av	New York	NY	10178	Robert G Burton	212-986-2440	S	950	6.2
Meredith Corp	1716 Locust St	Des Moines	IA	50309	Jack D Rehm	515-284-3000	P	800	2.2
Scholastic Corp	555 Broadway	New York	NY	10012	Richard Robinson	212-343-6100	P	632	3.1
Scholastic Inc	730 Broadway	New York	NY	10003	Richard Robinson	212-505-3000	S	552	2.6
Marvel Entertainment Group	387 Park Av S	New York	NY	10016	William C Bevins Jr	212-696-0808	P	515	1.6
Cahners Publishing Co	275 Washington St	Newton	MA	02158	Robert Krakoff	617-964-3030	D	430	2.8
Sullivan Graphics Inc	100 Winners Cir	Brentwood	TN	37027	James Sullivan	615-377-0377	R	415	2.3
Moody's Investors Service	99 Church St	New York	NY	10007	John Bohn	212-553-0300	S	364	1.3
Brown Printing Co	PO Box 1549	Waseca	MN	56093	Dan Nitz	507-835-2410	S	350	3.0
Newsweek Inc	251 W 57th St	New York	NY	10019	Richard M Smith	212-445-4000	S	333	1.0
Enquirer/Star Group Inc	600 S East Coast	Lantana	FL	33462	Peter J Callahan	407-586-1111	P	300	1.6
Enquirer/Star Inc	600 S East Coast	Lantana	FL	33462	Peter J Callahan	407-586-1111	S	300	1.6
Standard and Poor's Corp	25 Broadway	New York	NY	10004	H W McGraw III	212-208-8000	S	290	1.9
Trader Publishing Co	100 W Plume St	Norfolk	VA	23510	Conrad Hall	804-640-4000	J	250	3.6
CMP Publications Inc	600 Community Dr	Manhasset	NY	11030	Michael Leeds	516-562-5000	R	240*	1.5
Playboy Enterprises Inc	680 N Lake Shore	Chicago	IL	60611	Christie Hefner	312-751-8000	P	219	0.6
Congressional Quarterly Inc	1414 22nd St NW	Washington	DC	20037	Neil Skene	202-887-8500	D	200*	0.3
Harmon Publishing Co	15400 Knoll Trail	Dallas	TX	75248	Nigel A Donaldson	214-701-0244	D	200	2.0
Penton Publishing Inc	1100 Superior Av	Cleveland	OH	44114	Sal F Marino	216-696-7000	S	165	1.3
Penthouse International Ltd	1965 Broadway	New York	NY	10023	Richard Cohen	212-496-6100	R	160	0.4
Chilton Co	201 King of Prussia	Radnor	PA	19089	Leon C Hufnagel Jr	610-964-4000	S	140	0.9
Southern Progress Corp	2100 Lakeshore Dr	Birmingham	AL	35209	James G Nelson	205-877-6000	S	140*	0.9
Fry Communications Inc	800 W Church Rd	Mechanicsburg	PA	17055	Henry Fry	717-766-0211	R	130	1.2
Publishers Printing Co	PO Box 37500	Louisville	KY	40233	Nicholas X Simon	502-543-2251	R	120*	1.7
Advanstar Communications Inc	7500 Old Oak Blv	Cleveland	OH	44130	Gary R Ingersoll	216-243-8100	S	110	1.0
Advanstar Holdings Trust	7500 Old Oak Blv	Cleveland	OH	44130	Gary R Ingersoll	216-243-8100	R	110	1.0
Bureau of Business Practice	24 Rope Ferry Rd	Waterford	CT	06386	Martin E Kenney Jr	203-442-4365	D	100	0.6
LFP Inc	9171 Wilshire Blv	Beverly Hills	CA	90210	J Kohls	310-858-7100	R	88	0.3
Highlights for Children Inc	PO Box 269	Columbus	OH	43216	GC Myers III	614-486-0631	R	75	0.7
Lebhar-Friedman Inc	425 Park Av	New York	NY	10022	J Roger Friedman	212-756-5000	R	75	0.3
National Information Corp	1101 King St	Alexandria	VA	22314	Allie Ash	703-548-2400	R	75	0.1
PennWell Publishing Co	PO Box 1260	Tulsa	OK	74101	Joseph Wolking	918-835-3161	R	75	0.5
Curtis Publishing Co	1000 Waterway Blv	Indianapolis	IN	46202	Beurt Servaas	317-636-1000	S	71*	0.6
Bill Communications Inc	355 Park Av S	New York	NY	10010	John Wickersham	212-592-6200	R	70	0.3
Standard Publishing Co	8121 Hamilton Av	Cincinnati	OH	45231	Robert Dittrich	513-931-4050	D	69	0.4
General Media International Ltd	1965 Broadway	New York	NY	10023	Bob Guccione	212-496-6100	R	66*	0.4
Imperial Printing Co	PO Box 26	St Joseph	MI	49085	Greg Forbes	616-983-7105	S	60	0.5
Sunset Publishing Corp	80 Willow Rd	Menlo Park	CA	94025	Robin Wolaner	415-321-3600	S	58*	0.3
WD Hoard and Sons Co	PO Box 801	Fort Atkinson	WI	53538	William D Knox	414-563-5551	R	55	0.3
Gordon Publications Inc	301 Gibraltar Dr	Morris Plains	NJ	07950	William R Rakay	201-292-5100	D	50*	0.3
Institutional Investor Inc	488 Madison Av	New York	NY	10022	Peter Derou	212-303-3300	S	50	0.3
Our Sunday Visitor Inc	200 Noll Plz	Huntington	IN	46750	Robert P Lockwood	219-356-8400	R	50	0.5
Springhouse Corp	1111 Bethlehem Pk	Spring House	PA	19477	Kevin M Hurley	215-646-8700	S	50	0.2
A-S-M Communications Inc	1515 Broadway	New York	NY	10010	John Babeack	212-529-5500	S	49*	0.3
Reed Travel	2000 Clearwater Dr	Oak Brook	IL	60521	Martin Nathan	708-574-6000	S	49*	0.3
RFD Publications Inc	9600 SW Boeckman	Wilsonville	OR	97070	Larry Miller	503-682-1881	S	49*	0.3
F and W Publications Inc	1507 Dana Av	Cincinnati	OH	45207	RH Rosenthal	513-531-2222	R	47	0.2
Farm Progress Co	191 S Gary Av	Carol Stream	IL	60188	Allan Johnson	708-690-5600	S	42	0.3
New Yorker Magazine Inc	20 W 43rd St	New York	NY	10036	Thomas A Florio	212-840-3800	S	42*	0.3
Cowles Magazines Inc	PO Box 8200	Harrisburg	PA	17105	Ruth Barnet	717-657-9555	R	41*	0.3
Adis International Inc	940 Town Ctr Dr	Langhorne	PA	19047	Philip Smith	215-741-5200	R	40	0.3
AB Hirschfeld Press Inc	5200 Smith Rd	Denver	CO	80216	A Berry Hirschfeld	303-320-8500	R	40	0.2
Elsevier Science Inc	655 Av Amer	New York	NY	10010	R Schlosser	212-989-5800	S	40	0.2
Kalmbach Publishing Co	PO Box 1612	Waukesha	WI	53187	W J Mundschau	414-796-8776	R	40	0.2
Weider Publications Inc	21100 Erwin St	Woodland Hills	CA	91367	Michael Carr	818-884-6800	R	40	0.2
Dark Horse Publications Inc	10956 SE Main St	Milwaukie	OR	97222	Mike Richardson	503-652-8815	R	38*	<0.1
American Lawyer Media LP	600 3rd Av	New York	NY	10016	Steven Brill	212-973-2800	S	37*	0.5
Clement Communications Inc	Concord Industrial	Concordville	PA	19331	George Clement	215-459-4200	R	37	0.2
Entrepreneur Media Inc	2392 Morse Av	Irvine	CA	92714	Peter Shea	714-261-2325	R	35	<0.1
Farm Journal Inc	230 W Wash Sq	Philadelphia	PA	19106	Dale E Smith	215-829-4700	R	35*	0.3
Morningstar Inc	225 W Wacker Dr	Chicago	IL	60604	Joseph Mansueto	312-696-6000	R	35	0.4
PJB Publications Ltd	1775 Broadway	New York	NY	10019	Philip J Brown	212-262-8230	S	35	0.2
Taunton Press Inc	PO Box 5506	Newtown	CT	06470	Paul Roman	203-426-8171	R	35	0.2
InfoWorld Publishing Corp	155 Bovet Rd	San Mateo	CA	94402	Jim Martin	415-572-7341	S	33*	0.2
American Mathematical Society	PO Box 6248	Providence	RI	02940	W Jaco	401-455-4000	R	31*	0.3
Press of Ohio	3765 Sunnybrook	Brimfield	OH	44240	David H Bracken	216-678-5868	R	31	0.2
BASS Inc	PO Box 17900	Montgomery	AL	36141	Helen Sevier	205-272-9530	R	30	0.2
Grass Roots Publishing Co	950 Third Av	New York	NY	10022	Suzanne Hochman	212-888-1855	R	30	<0.1

Source: *Ward's Business Directory of U.S. Private and Public Companies*, Volumes 1 and 2, 1996. The company type code used is as follows: P - Public, R - Private, S - Subsidiary, D - Division, J - Joint Venture, A - Affiliate, G - Group. Sales are in millions of dollars, employees are in thousands. An asterisk (*) indicates an estimated sales volume. The symbol < stands for 'less than'. Company names and addresses are truncated, in some cases, to fit into the available space.

MATERIALS CONSUMED

Material	Quantity	Delivered Cost ($ million)
Materials, ingredients, containers, and supplies	(X)	2,417.1
Newsprint	(X)	66.3
Coated paper	(X)	986.1
Uncoated paper	(X)	185.2
Printing inks (complete formulations)	(X)	220.8
All other materials and components, parts, containers, and supplies	(X)	165.9
Materials, ingredients, containers, and supplies, nsk	(X)	792.8

Source: 1992 *Economic Census*. Explanation of symbols used: (D): Withheld to avoid disclosure of competitive data; na: Not available; (S): Withheld because statistical norms were not met; (X): Not applicable; (Z): Less than half the unit shown; nec: Not elsewhere classified; nsk: Not specified by kind; - : zero; * : 10-19 percent estimated; ** : 20-29 percent estimated.

PRODUCT SHARE DETAILS

Product or Product Class	% Share
Periodical publishing	100.00
Farm periodicals (receipts from subscriptions, sales, and advertising)	0.96
Specialized business and professional periodicals (receipts from subscriptions and single copy sales)	12.10
Specialized business and professional periodicals (receipts from advertising)	17.79
General and consumer periodicals (receipts from subscriptions)	17.33
General and consumer periodicals (receipts from single copy sales)	8.91
General and consumer periodicals (receipts from advertising)	24.57
Other periodicals, except shopping news, catalogs, or directories, nec	3.30
Periodical publishing, nsk	15.04

Source: 1992 *Economic Census*. The values shown are percent of total shipments in an industry. Values of indented subcategories are summed in the main heading. The symbol (D) appears when data are withheld to prevent disclosure of competitive information. The abbreviation nsk stands for 'not specified by kind' and nec for 'not elsewhere classified'.

INPUTS AND OUTPUTS FOR PERIODICALS

Economic Sector or Industry Providing Inputs	%	Sector	Economic Sector or Industry Buying Outputs	%	Sector
Commercial printing	21.4	Manufg.	Personal consumption expenditures	66.7	
Paper mills, except building paper	18.4	Manufg.	Exports	5.8	Foreign
Book printing	7.2	Manufg.	Lithographic platemaking & services	2.1	Manufg.
Photofinishing labs, commercial photography	4.9	Services	S/L Govt. purch., higher education	2.1	S/L Govt
Eating & drinking places	4.6	Trade	Retail trade, except eating & drinking	1.9	Trade
Advertising	4.4	Services	Libraries, vocation education	1.7	Services
U.S. Postal Service	4.3	Gov't	Banking	1.4	Fin/R.E.
Computer & data processing services	3.8	Services	Wholesale trade	1.2	Trade
Wholesale trade	3.7	Trade	Colleges, universities, & professional schools	1.1	Services
Accounting, auditing & bookkeeping	3.4	Services	S/L Govt. purch., elem. & secondary education	0.8	S/L Govt
Air transportation	3.1	Util.	Social services, nec	0.7	Services
Royalties	2.0	Fin/R.E.	Hospitals	0.6	Services
Real estate	1.8	Fin/R.E.	Periodicals	0.5	Manufg.
Typesetting	1.7	Manufg.	S/L Govt. purch., health & hospitals	0.5	S/L Govt
Banking	1.4	Fin/R.E.	Credit agencies other than banks	0.4	Fin/R.E.
Petroleum refining	1.1	Manufg.	Hotels & lodging places	0.4	Services
Communications, except radio & TV	0.9	Util.	S/L Govt. purch., other education & libraries	0.4	S/L Govt
Motor freight transportation & warehousing	0.8	Util.	Newspapers	0.3	Manufg.
Imports	0.8	Foreign	Communications, except radio & TV	0.3	Util.
Business services nec	0.7	Services	Motor freight transportation & warehousing	0.3	Util.
Equipment rental & leasing services	0.7	Services	Insurance carriers	0.3	Fin/R.E.
Hotels & lodging places	0.7	Services	Engineering, architectural, & surveying services	0.3	Services
Printing ink	0.6	Manufg.	Job training & related services	0.3	Services
Electric services (utilities)	0.6	Util.	Labor, civic, social, & fraternal associations	0.3	Services
Periodicals	0.5	Manufg.	Federal Government purchases, nondefense	0.3	Fed Govt
Railroads & related services	0.5	Util.	S/L Govt. purch., other general government	0.3	S/L Govt
Business/professional associations	0.5	Services	Eating & drinking places	0.2	Trade
Bookbinding & related work	0.4	Manufg.	Real estate	0.2	Fin/R.E.
Cyclic crudes and organics	0.4	Manufg.	Business services nec	0.2	Services
Mechanical measuring devices	0.4	Manufg.	Computer & data processing services	0.2	Services
Printing trades machinery	0.4	Manufg.	Management & consulting services & labs	0.2	Services
Legal services	0.4	Services	S/L Govt. purch., public assistance & relief	0.2	S/L Govt
Management & consulting services & labs	0.4	Services	Meat animals	0.1	Agric.
Chemical preparations, nec	0.3	Manufg.	Crude petroleum & natural gas	0.1	Mining
Electrical repair shops	0.3	Services	Office buildings	0.1	Constr.
Maintenance of nonfarm buildings nec	0.2	Constr.	Residential 1-unit structures, nonfarm	0.1	Constr.
Manifold business forms	0.2	Manufg.	Commercial printing	0.1	Manufg.
Credit agencies other than banks	0.2	Fin/R.E.	Electronic computing equipment	0.1	Manufg.
Insurance carriers	0.2	Fin/R.E.	Insurance agents, brokers, & services	0.1	Fin/R.E.
Automotive rental & leasing, without drivers	0.2	Services	Amusement & recreation services nec	0.1	Services
Automotive repair shops & services	0.2	Services	Automotive repair shops & services	0.1	Services
Lithographic platemaking & services	0.1	Manufg.	Doctors & dentists	0.1	Services
Photographic equipment & supplies	0.1	Manufg.	Elementary & secondary schools	0.1	Services
Gas production & distribution (utilities)	0.1	Util.	Laundry, dry cleaning, shoe repair	0.1	Services
			Membership organizations nec	0.1	Services
			Religious organizations	0.1	Services
			Federal Government purchases, national defense	0.1	Fed Govt

Source: Benchmark Input-Output Accounts for the U.S. Economy, 1982, U.S. Department of Commerce, Washington, D.C., July 1991. Data, as reported in the source, are organized by the 1977 SIC structure in use in 1982 but have been matched, as closely as is possible, to the 1987 SIC structure used in this book.

OCCUPATIONS EMPLOYED BY SIC 272 - PERIODICALS

Occupation	% of Total 1994	Change to 2005	Occupation	% of Total 1994	Change to 2005
Writers & editors, incl technical writers	15.0	28.7	Marketing & sales worker supervisors	1.7	28.7
Sales & related workers nec	10.8	28.7	Typists & word processors	1.6	-35.7
Secretaries, ex legal & medical	5.1	17.2	Management support workers nec	1.5	28.6
General managers & top executives	5.0	22.1	Professional workers nec	1.4	54.4
Artists & commercial artists	3.7	60.4	Order clerks, materials, merchandise, & service	1.3	26.0
Marketing, advertising, & PR managers	3.3	28.7	Advertising clerks	1.3	41.6
General office clerks	3.3	9.7	Computer programmers	1.2	4.2
Bookkeeping, accounting, & auditing clerks	2.9	-3.5	Data entry keyers, ex composing	1.2	-5.0
Clerical supervisors & managers	2.4	31.6	Clerical support workers nec	1.2	2.9
Proofreaders & copy markers	2.3	-16.3	Production, planning, & expediting clerks	1.1	28.6
Managers & administrators nec	2.2	28.6	Offset lithographic press operators	1.1	3.0
Machine feeders & offbearers	1.8	15.8	Adjustment clerks	1.1	54.4
Reporters & correspondents	1.7	3.0	Mail clerks, ex machine operators, postal service	1.1	-7.3

Source: Industry-Occupation Matrix, Bureau of Labor Statistics. These data relate to one or more 3-digit SIC industry groups rather than to a single 4-digit SIC. The change reported for each occupation to the year 2005 is a percent of growth or decline as estimated by the Bureau of Labor Statistics. The abbreviation nec stands for 'not elsewhere classified'.

LOCATION BY STATE AND REGIONAL CONCENTRATION

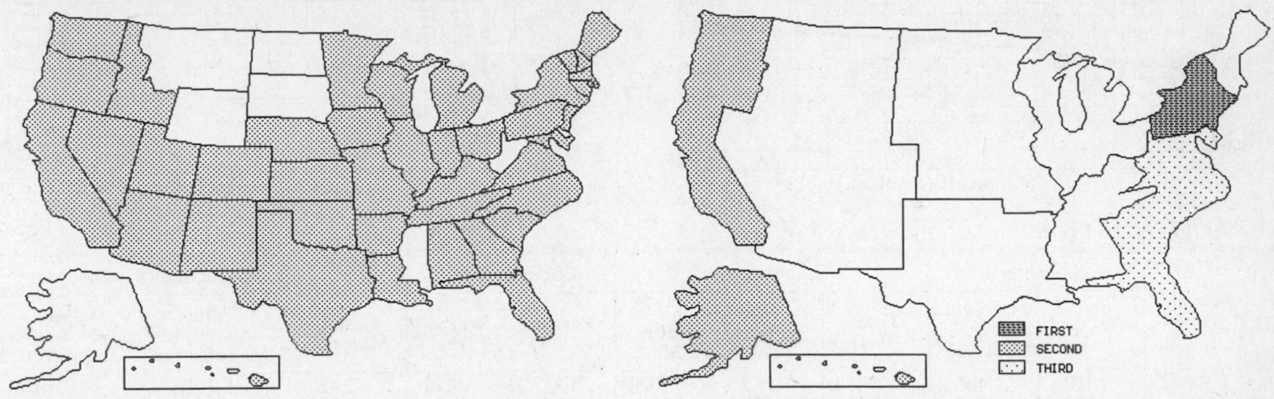

INDUSTRY DATA BY STATE

State	Establish-ments	Shipments			Employment				Cost as % of Shipments	Investment per Employee ($)
		Total ($ mil)	% of U.S.	Per Establ.	Total Number	% of U.S.	Per Establ.	Wages ($/hour)		
New York	622	9,618.1	43.7	15.5	34,000	29.3	55	21.74	28.1	2,876
California	646	1,923.9	8.7	3.0	11,100	9.6	17	10.72	26.6	1,559
Illinois	249	1,451.1	6.6	5.8	11,900	10.2	48	13.33	28.6	1,370
Pennsylvania	159	1,192.4	5.4	7.5	4,700	4.0	30	12.56	35.9	1,340
D.C.	84	956.0	4.3	11.4	4,600	4.0	55	14.75	25.8	3,391
New Jersey	195	683.4	3.1	3.5	4,000	3.4	21	11.76	26.7	2,300
Massachusetts	183	634.4	2.9	3.5	3,600	3.1	20	12.10	28.2	1,750
Ohio	120	476.2	2.2	4.0	3,500	3.0	29	10.64	23.7	1,771
Connecticut	108	463.5	2.1	4.3	2,600	2.2	24	12.91	27.4	1,769
Florida	281	368.7	1.7	1.3	3,400	2.9	12	9.77	31.8	1,235
Georgia	108	319.5	1.5	3.0	2,400	2.1	22	12.31	28.6	1,708
Texas	204	301.2	1.4	1.5	3,100	2.7	15	8.65	28.5	-
Wisconsin	97	296.3	1.3	3.1	2,000	1.7	21	8.70	25.4	3,150
Minnesota	109	294.2	1.3	2.7	1,600	1.4	15	10.60	20.8	-
Maryland	103	222.1	1.0	2.2	1,600	1.4	16	14.57	26.5	2,750
Alabama	42	212.0	1.0	5.0	1,000	0.9	24	8.33	23.4	1,200
Tennessee	68	196.4	0.9	2.9	2,400	2.1	35	11.12	14.9	-
Virginia	133	194.7	0.9	1.5	1,800	1.5	14	10.14	23.7	1,000
Michigan	106	181.6	0.8	1.7	1,900	1.6	18	11.71	26.0	1,263
Missouri	77	176.6	0.8	2.3	2,400	2.1	31	10.25	26.2	1,167
Colorado	99	140.9	0.6	1.4	1,100	0.9	11	12.50	26.3	1,818
North Carolina	77	133.1	0.6	1.7	1,100	0.9	14	11.00	33.6	1,727
New Hampshire	33	131.9	0.6	4.0	600	0.5	18	12.00	21.1	1,000
Indiana	65	131.3	0.6	2.0	1,100	0.9	17	10.00	31.0	1,000
Kansas	35	111.2	0.5	3.2	500	0.4	14	6.00	26.5	3,600
Oklahoma	33	93.8	0.4	2.8	400	0.3	12	7.00	17.9	-
Washington	102	76.4	0.3	0.7	900	0.8	9	15.50	27.4	1,222
Oregon	46	69.0	0.3	1.5	500	0.4	11	11.67	31.3	1,800
Arizona	72	59.4	0.3	0.8	600	0.5	8	7.33	34.5	-
Nebraska	26	49.4	0.2	1.9	400	0.3	15	12.00	29.8	-
Vermont	20	44.3	0.2	2.2	300	0.3	15	13.00	32.1	1,000
Utah	23	36.8	0.2	1.6	300	0.3	13	10.00	28.5	2,333
Idaho	21	29.8	0.1	1.4	300	0.3	14	13.50	27.5	1,000
Hawaii	28	28.1	0.1	1.0	200	0.2	7	9.00	28.1	-
Maine	23	24.3	0.1	1.1	200	0.2	9	6.00	32.5	1,500
Rhode Island	13	21.3	0.1	1.6	200	0.2	15	8.00	20.7	-
Louisiana	36	15.3	0.1	0.4	200	0.2	6	6.00	32.7	500
South Carolina	35	14.6	0.1	0.4	200	0.2	6	5.00	34.2	-
Nevada	18	13.5	0.1	0.8	100	0.1	6	12.00	25.2	-
New Mexico	28	11.9	0.1	0.4	100 *	0.1	4	-	33.6	1,000
Kentucky	45	(D)	-	-	375 *	0.3	8	-	-	1,867
Iowa	40	(D)	-	-	1,750 *	1.5	44	-	-	-
Arkansas	18	(D)	-	-	175 *	0.2	10	-	-	-

Source: 1992 *Economic Census*. The states are in descending order of shipments or establishments (if shipment data are missing for the majority). The symbol (D) appears when data are withheld to prevent disclosure of competitive information. States marked with (D) are sorted by number of establishments. A dash (-) indicates that the data element cannot be calculated; * indicates the midpoint of a range.

2731 - BOOK PUBLISHING

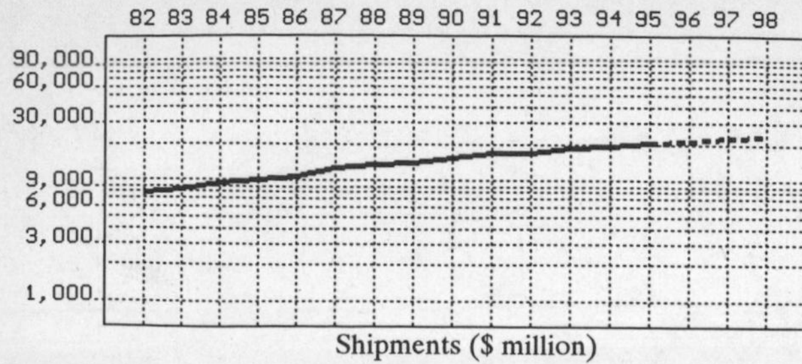

Shipments ($ million)

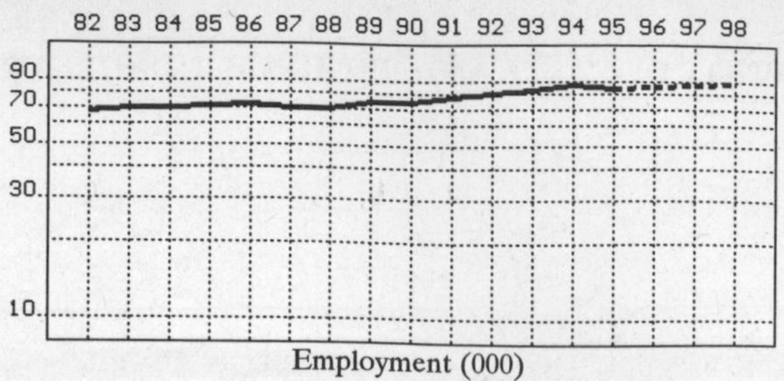

Employment (000)

GENERAL STATISTICS

Year	Com-panies	Establishments: Total	Establishments: with 20 or more employees	Employment: Total (000)	Employment: Production Workers (000)	Employment: Production Hours (Mil)	Compensation: Payroll ($ mil)	Compensation: Wages ($/hr)	Production ($ million): Cost of Materials	Production ($ million): Value Added by Manufacture	Production ($ million): Value of Shipments	Production ($ million): Capital Invest.
1982	2,007	2,130	420	67.1	15.2	30.8	1,327.3	7.70	2,420.0	5,291.5	7,740.0	174.1
1983		2,094	427	69.3	17.1	33.0	1,474.9	8.42	2,683.2	5,823.8	8,427.4	163.6
1984		2,058	434	69.4	14.9	27.2	1,600.3	9.86	2,890.1	6,722.9	9,459.2	199.4
1985		2,023	440	70.9	15.6	28.6	1,672.1	9.78	3,021.1	7,395.8	10,196.2	232.1
1986		2,013	449	71.6	14.4	25.6	1,775.6	10.13	3,099.8	7,755.9	10,731.5	202.8
1987	2,180	2,298	424	70.1	15.9	28.7	1,859.8	10.67	3,663.2	9,110.7	12,619.5	239.7
1988		2,180	428	70.2	16.5	30.4	2,009.8	10.76	3,988.1	9,851.9	13,570.7	302.4
1989		2,164	463	73.6	17.1	30.2	2,132.3	11.56	4,365.5	9,915.5	14,074.2	319.1
1990		2,144	448	74.4	17.3	31.2	2,299.9	11.68	4,465.5	10,919.5	15,317.9	329.1
1991		2,284	451	77.3	17.1	30.0	2,514.1	12.72	5,001.4	11,683.3	16,596.1	330.5
1992	2,504	2,644	500	79.6	18.6	35.5	2,675.7	12.49	5,337.7	11,494.4	16,731.1	326.7
1993		2,699	473	83.2	18.2	34.5	2,799.2	12.90	5,806.8	12,742.9	18,615.9	282.0
1994		2,540P	479P	87.1	18.7	34.8	2,935.6	13.27	5,826.7	13,681.0	19,418.9	283.0
1995		2,588P	484P	84.1P	18.7P	33.9P	3,022.0P	13.96P	6,081.0P	14,278.1P	20,266.5P	352.0P
1996		2,636P	489P	85.5P	19.0P	34.4P	3,156.2P	14.40P	6,377.7P	14,974.6P	21,255.1P	365.0P
1997		2,684P	494P	86.9P	19.3P	34.8P	3,290.4P	14.83P	6,674.3P	15,671.1P	22,243.7P	378.1P
1998		2,732P	499P	88.3P	19.6P	35.3P	3,424.6P	15.27P	6,970.9P	16,367.6P	23,232.3P	391.2P

Sources: 1982, 1987, 1992 *Economic Census*; *Annual Survey of Manufactures*, 83-86, 88-91, 93-94. Establishment counts for non-Census years are from *County Business Patterns*; establishment values for 83-84 are extrapolations. 'P's show projections by the editors. Industries reclassified in 87 will not have data for prior years.

INDICES OF CHANGE

Year	Com-panies	Establishments: Total	Establishments: with 20 or more employees	Employment: Total (000)	Employment: Production Workers (000)	Employment: Production Hours (Mil)	Compensation: Payroll ($ mil)	Compensation: Wages ($/hr)	Production ($ million): Cost of Materials	Production ($ million): Value Added by Manufacture	Production ($ million): Value of Shipments	Production ($ million): Capital Invest.
1982	80	81	84	84	82	87	50	62	45	46	46	53
1983		79	85	87	92	93	55	67	50	51	50	50
1984		78	87	87	80	77	60	79	54	58	57	61
1985		77	88	89	84	81	62	78	57	64	61	71
1986		76	90	90	77	72	66	81	58	67	64	62
1987	87	87	85	88	85	81	70	85	69	79	75	73
1988		82	86	88	89	86	75	86	75	86	81	93
1989		82	93	92	92	85	80	93	82	86	84	98
1990		81	90	93	93	88	86	94	84	95	92	101
1991		86	90	97	92	85	94	102	94	102	99	101
1992	100	100	100	100	100	100	100	100	100	100	100	100
1993		102	95	105	98	97	105	103	109	111	111	86
1994		96P	96P	109	101	98	110	106	109	119	116	87
1995		98P	97P	106P	100P	96P	113P	112P	114P	124P	121P	108P
1996		100P	98P	107P	102P	97P	118P	115P	119P	130P	127P	112P
1997		102P	99P	109P	104P	98P	123P	119P	125P	136P	133P	116P
1998		103P	100P	111P	105P	99P	128P	122P	131P	142P	139P	120P

Sources: Same as General Statistics. Values reflect change from the base year, 1992. Values above 100 mean greater than 92, values below 100 mean less than 92, and a value of 100 in the 82-91 or 93-98 period means same as 92. 'P's mark projections by the editors.

SELECTED RATIOS

For 1994	Avg. of All Manufact.	Analyzed Industry	Index
Employees per Establishment	49	34	70
Payroll per Establishment	1,500,273	1,155,907	77
Payroll per Employee	30,620	33,704	110
Production Workers per Establishment	34	7	21
Wages per Establishment	853,319	181,834	21
Wages per Production Worker	24,861	24,695	99
Hours per Production Worker	2,056	1,861	91
Wages per Hour	12.09	13.27	110
Value Added per Establishment	4,602,255	5,386,960	117
Value Added per Employee	93,930	157,072	167

For 1994	Avg. of All Manufact.	Analyzed Industry	Index
Value Added per Production Worker	134,084	731,604	546
Cost per Establishment	5,045,178	2,294,291	45
Cost per Employee	102,970	66,897	65
Cost per Production Worker	146,988	311,588	212
Shipments per Establishment	9,576,895	7,646,285	80
Shipments per Employee	195,460	222,949	114
Shipments per Production Worker	279,017	1,038,444	372
Investment per Establishment	321,011	111,433	35
Investment per Employee	6,552	3,249	50
Investment per Production Worker	9,352	15,134	162

Sources: Same as General Statistics. The 'Average of All Manufacturing' column represents the average of all manufacturing industries reported for the most recent complete year available. The Index shows the relationship between the Average and the Analyzed Industry. For example, 100 means that they are equal; 500 that the Analyzed Industry is five times the average; 50 means that the Analyzed Industry is half the national average. The abbreviation 'na' is used to show that data are 'not available'.

LEADING COMPANIES

Number shown: **75** Total sales ($ mil): **13,758** Total employment (000): **67.8**

Company Name	Address				CEO Name	Phone	Co. Type	Sales ($ mil)	Empl. (000)
McGraw-Hill Inc	1221 Av Amer	New York	NY	10020	Robert S Christie	212-512-2000	D	1,300	0.5
West Publishing Co	PO Box 64526	St Paul	MN	55164	D D Opperman	612-687-7000	R	1,170	6.0
Harcourt Brace and Co	6277 Sea Harbor Dr	Orlando	FL	32887	Robert J Tarr Jr	407-345-2000	S	920	4.5
Reed Publishing	275 Washington St	Newton	MA	02158	Robert Krakoff	617-964-3030	S	840	4.3
K-III Communications Corp	745 5th Av	New York	NY	10151	William F Reilly	212-745-0100	R	800	3.5
Western Publishing Group Inc	444 Madison Av	New York	NY	10022	R A Bernstein	212-688-4500	P	614	3.3
Western Publishing Company	1220 Mound Av	Racine	WI	53404	George Oess	414-633-2431	S	560*	3.0
Insilco Corp	425 Metro Pl N	Dublin	OH	43017	Robert Smialek	614-792-0468	P	544	5.0
HarperCollins Publishers	10 E 53rd St	New York	NY	10022	George Craig	212-207-7000	S	500	2.8
Houghton Mifflin Co	222 Berkeley St	Boston	MA	02116	Nader F Darehshori	617-351-5000	P	483	2.0
Encyclopaedia Britannica Inc	310 S Michigan Av	Chicago	IL	60604	Peter Norton	312-347-7000	R	453	2.3
McGraw-Hill Inc	1221 Av of the	New York	NY	10020	Stephen B Bonner	212-512-2000	D	410*	2.1
John Wiley and Sons Inc	605 3rd Av	New York	NY	10158	Charles R Ellis	212-850-6000	P	294	1.7
Putnam Berkley Group Inc	200 Madison Av	New York	NY	10016	Phyllis Grann	212-951-8400	S	275	0.9
Thomas Nelson Inc	PO Box 141000	Nashville	TN	37214	Sam Moore	615-889-9000	P	265	1.1
Addison-Wesley Publishing Co	1 Jacob Way	Reading	MA	01867	Warren Stone	617-944-3700	S	210*	1.1
David C Cook Publishing Co	850 N Grove Av	Elgin	IL	60120	David Mehlis	708-741-2400	R	200*	1.0
Wolters Kluwer US Corp	1185 Av of the	New York	NY	10036	Frans van Eysinga	212-930-9640	S	200	0.9
Deseret Management Corp	36 S State St	Salt Lake City	UT	84111	Robert D Hales	801-538-0651	R	190	1.4
Warner-Chappell Music Inc	15800 NW 48th Av	Miami	FL	33014	Jay Morgenstern	305-620-1500	S	190*	1.0
RR Bowker	121 Chanlon Rd	New Providence	NJ	07974	Andrew W Meyer	908-464-6800	D	189	1.5
Shepard's/McGraw-Hill Inc	PO Box 35300	Co Springs	CO	80935	B Hall	719-488-3000	S	170*	0.9
Warner Books Inc	1271 Av Amer	New York	NY	10020	Larry Kirschbaum	212-522-5040	S	170	0.2
Little, Brown and Company Inc	34 Beacon St	Boston	MA	02108	Charles Hayward	617-227-0730	S	136	0.6
South-Western Publishing Co	5101 Madison Rd	Cincinnati	OH	45227	C C Lucido Jr	513-271-8811	S	130	0.6
Waverly Inc	428 E Preston St	Baltimore	MD	21202	E B Hutton Jr	410-528-4000	P	122	0.4
Encyclopaedia Britannica	310 S Michigan Av	Chicago	IL	60604	Joseph Esposito	312-347-7000	S	120*	0.5
Southwestern/Great American	PO Box 305140	Nashville	TN	37230	Ralph W Mosley	615-391-2500	R	120	0.6
Academic Press Inc	525 B St	San Diego	CA	92101	Peter Bolman	619-699-6719	S	100*	0.3
Michie Co	PO Box 7587	Charlottesville	VA	22906	D Harriman	804-295-6171	S	100*	0.6
Hart Graphics Inc	PO Box 968	Austin	TX	78767	WL Hart	512-454-4761	R	95	0.8
Tab McGraw-Hill Inc	13311 Monterey Av	Blue Ridge Sum	PA	17294	Joseph Dionne	717-794-2191	S	88	0.5
PAGES Inc	801 94th Av N	St Petersburg	FL	33702	Richard A Stimmel	813-578-3300	P	79	0.4
JJ Keller and Associates	PO Box 368	Neenah	WI	54957	Robert L Keller	414-722-2848	R	73*	0.6
Richard D Irwin Inc	1333 Burr Ridge	Burr Ridge	IL	60521	Jeff Sund	708-789-4000	S	70	0.5
GP Putnam's Sons	200 Madison Av	New York	NY	10016	Phyllis Grann	212-951-8400	S	68*	0.4
McDougal Littell Inc	PO Box 1667	Evanston	IL	60204	Julie McGee	708-869-2300	D	60	0.3
Riverside Book and Bible House	Hwy 65 S	Iowa Falls	IA	50126	Skip Knapp	515-648-4271	R	60	0.3
Lorenz Corp	PO Box 802	Dayton	OH	45401	Geoffrey Lorenz	513-228-6118	R	58	0.5
Oxford University Press Inc	198 Madison Av	New York	NY	10016	E Barry	212-679-7300	R	58	0.3
Glencoe	936 Eastwind Dr	Westerville	OH	43081	Jack Witmer	614-890-1111	D	56	0.5
Raintree Publishers LP	PO Box 26015	Austin	TX	78755	Sam Yau	512-343-8227	S	54	0.4
Steck-Vaughn Co	PO Box 26015	Austin	TX	78755	Roy E Mayers	512-343-8227	S	54	0.4
Steck-Vaughn Publishing Corp	PO Box 26015	Austin	TX	78755	Roy E Mayers	512-343-8227	P	54	0.4
Prentice Hall Computer Pub	201 W 103rd St	Indianapolis	IN	46290	Scott Flanders	317-581-3500	D	53*	0.3
Plenum Publishing Corp	233 Spring St	New York	NY	10013	Martin E Tash	212-620-8000	P	53	0.3
Delmar Publishers Inc	3 Columbia Cir	Albany	NY	12203	Joseph P Reynolds	518-464-3500	D	51	0.3
Deseret Book Co	PO Box 30178	Salt Lake City	UT	84130	R Millett	801-534-1515	S	50	0.8
Harry N Abrams Inc	100 5th Av	New York	NY	10011	Paul Gottlieb	212-206-7715	S	45	0.1
AM Best Company Inc	Ambest Rd	Oldwick	NJ	08858	Arthur Snyder	908-439-2200	R	41	0.4
Brooks/Cole Publishing Co	511 Forest Lodge	Pacific Grove	CA	93950	William Roberts	408-373-0728	D	40	<0.1
Newbridge Communications Inc	333 E 38th St	New York	NY	10016	Peter Quandt	212-455-5000	R	39*	0.2
St Anthony Publishing	500 Montgomery St	Alexandria	VA	22314	Jim Miller	703-549-0100	R	38*	0.2
Concordia Publishing House	3558 S Jefferson	St Louis	MO	63118	JW Gerber	314-664-7000	R	35	0.4
EMC Publishing Corp	300 York Av	St Paul	MN	55101	David E Feinberg	612-771-1555	R	35*	0.2
William Morrow and Company	1350 of Americas	New York	NY	10019	Allen Marchioni	212-261-6500	S	35	0.2
Abbey Press	Hill Dr	St Meinrad	IN	47577	C Deitchman	812-357-8011	R	34*	0.3
Walt Disney Publications Inc	500 S Buena Vista	Burbank	CA	91521	John Skipper	818-567-5739	D	33	<0.1
American Press Inc	1 American Pl	Gordonsville	VA	22942	M J Pettygrove	703-832-2253	R	30	0.2
Axon Communications Inc	747 Dresher Rd	Horsham	PA	19044	Kenneth Kahn	215-784-0860	R	30	0.3
Marcel Dekker Inc	270 Madison Av	New York	NY	10016	Marcel Dekker	212-696-9000	R	30	0.2
Modern Curriculum Press	PO Box 2649	Columbus	OH	43216		216-238-2222	D	30	<0.1
Peterson's Guides Inc	PO Box 2123	Princeton	NJ	08543	Peter W Hegener	609-243-9111	R	30	0.3
Trade Service Corp	10996 Torreyana Rd	San Diego	CA	92121	A Simpson	619-457-5920	R	30	0.5
Collins Publishers	1160 Battery St	San Francisco	CA	94111	Clayton Carlson	415-616-4700	D	28	<0.1
Dover Publications Inc	31 E 2nd St	Mineola	NY	11501	H Cirker	516-294-7000	R	28	0.1
Hazelden Educational Materials	PO Box 176	Center City	MN	55012	Alan Borne	612-257-4010	R	28	0.1
University Press of America Inc	4720 Boston Way	Lanham	MD	20706	James Lyons	301-459-3366	R	28	0.1
B and H Publishing Inc	127 9th Av N	Nashville	TN	37234	Charles A Wilson	615-251-2520	R	27	0.1
Krames Communications Inc	1100 Grundy Ln	San Bruno	CA	94066	Peter Bergen	415-742-0400	S	27	0.1
Randall Publishing Company Inc	PO Box 2029	Tuscaloosa	AL	35403	HP Randall	205-349-2990	R	27	0.3
Allyn and Bacon	160 Gould St	Needham H	MA	02194	Bill Barke	617-455-1200	D	26*	0.2
Aspen Publishers Inc	200 Orchard Ridge	Gaithersburg	MD	20878	John Marozan	301-417-7500	S	26*	0.1
Dorling Kindersley Publishing	95 Madison Av	New York	NY	10016	John Sargent	212-213-4800	S	26	<0.1
Matthew Bender and Company	11 Penn Plz	New York	NY	10001	LW Peterson	212-967-7707	S	26*	1.0

Source: *Ward's Business Directory of U.S. Private and Public Companies*, Volumes 1 and 2, 1996. The company type code used is as follows: P - Public, R - Private, S - Subsidiary, D - Division, J - Joint Venture, A - Affiliate, G - Group. Sales are in millions of dollars, employees are in thousands. An asterisk (*) indicates an estimated sales volume. The symbol < stands for 'less than'. Company names and addresses are truncated, in some cases, to fit into the available space.

MATERIALS CONSUMED

Material	Quantity	Delivered Cost ($ million)
Materials, ingredients, containers, and supplies	(X)	1,613.7
Newsprint	(X)	76.9
Coated paper	(X)	192.2
Uncoated paper	(X)	305.6
Printing inks (complete formulations)	(X)	45.9
All other materials and components, parts, containers, and supplies	(X)	549.1
Materials, ingredients, containers, and supplies, nsk	(X)	444.1

Source: 1992 *Economic Census*. Explanation of symbols used: (D): Withheld to avoid disclosure of competitive data; na: Not available; (S): Withheld because statistical norms were not met; (X): Not applicable; (Z): Less than half the unit shown; nec: Not elsewhere classified; nsk: Not specified by kind; - : zero; * : 10-19 percent estimated; ** : 20-29 percent estimated.

PRODUCT SHARE DETAILS

Product or Product Class	% Share
Book publishing	100.00
Textbook publishing, including teachers' editions	26.20
Hardbound elementary school (grades K through 8) textbook publishing, including teachers' editions	16.96
Paperbound elementary school (grades K through 8) textbook publishing, including teachers' editions	5.33
Hardbound high school (grades 9 through 12) textbook publishing, including teachers' editions	11.07
Paperbound high school (grades 9 through 12) textbook publishing, including teachers' editions	4.60
Hardbound college (grades 13 and up, for post high school level courses) textbook publishing	28.85
Paperbound college (grades 13 and up, for post high school level courses) textbook publishing	9.89
Paperbound elementary school (grades K through 8) workbook, textbook-related objective test, manual, etc. publishing	7.22
Paperbound high school (grades 9 through 12) workbook, textbook-related objective test, manual, etc. publishing	2.17
Paperbound college (grades 13 and up, for post high school level courses) workbook, textbook-related objective test, manual, etc. publishing	3.66
Standardized test publishing, including both tests and answer sheets, paperbound	5.45
Textbooks, including teachers' editions, nsk	4.83
Technical, scientific, and professional book publishing	16.83
Hardbound law book publishing, including supplements (designed for the profession)	33.66
Paperbound law book publishing, including supplements (designed for the profession)	10.85
Hardbound medical book publishing, including dental subjects (designed for the profession)	15.00
Paperbound medical book publishing, including dental subjects (designed for the profession)	3.59
Hardbound business book publishing (nonfiction for readers in the profession)	4.00
Paperbound business book publishing (nonfiction for readers in the profession)	7.20
Other hardbound technical, scientific, and professional book publishing	13.14
Other paperbound technical, scientific, and professional book publishing	7.46
Technical, scientific, and professional books, nsk	5.10
Religious book publishing	4.94
Hardbound (including flexible cover) Bible and testament publishing	11.24
Paperbound Bible and testament publishing	2.56
Hymnal and devotional publishing, including prayer books and missals, hardbound and paperbound	3.10
Other hardbound religious book publishing, including subscription reference books	19.41
Other paperbound religious book publishing, including subscription reference books	16.76
Religious books, nsk	46.93
Mass market rack-size paperbound book publishing	6.20
Book club book publishing	5.04
Mail order book publishing	4.81
Hardbound mail order book publishing	90.31
Paperbound mail order book publishing	8.39
Mail order books, nsk	1.29
Adult trade and juvenile book publishing	17.90
Hardbound adult trade book publishing, whether by trade or mass market publishers	45.43
Paperbound (excluding mass market rack-size) adult trade book publishing, whether by trade or mass market publishers	20.09
Hardbound juvenile book publishing (fiction and nonfiction, excluding toy and coloring books)	13.97
Paperbound juvenile book publishing (fiction and nonfiction, excluding toy and coloring books)	4.10
Adult trade and juvenile books, nsk	16.41
General reference book publishing	3.32
Encyclopedia publishing	33.06
Dictionary and thesaurus publishing	11.59
Other general reference book publishing	48.73
General reference books, nsk	6.62
Other book publishing, excluding pamphlets	2.64
Hardbound university press book publishing	28.05
Paperbound university press book publishing, excluding pamphlets	20.41
Music book publishing (hardbound and paperbound), excluding pamphlets	24.26
Other hardbound book publishing, nec	15.06
Other paperbound book publishing, nec, excluding pamphlets	9.07
Other books, excluding pamphlets, nsk	3.15
Pamphlet publishing (5 through 48 pages)	0.91
Music pamphlet publishing (5 through 48 pages)	23.22
Other pamphlet publishing (5 through 48 pages), including religious and text	76.11
Pamphlets (5 through 48 pages), nsk	0.74
Audio book publishing (books recorded on audio cassettes)	0.24
Book publishing, nsk	10.96

Source: 1992 *Economic Census*. The values shown are percent of total shipments in an industry. Values of indented subcategories are summed in the main heading. The symbol (D) appears when data are withheld to prevent disclosure of competitive information. The abbreviation nsk stands for 'not specified by kind' and nec for 'not elsewhere classified'.

INPUTS AND OUTPUTS FOR BOOK PUBLISHING

Economic Sector or Industry Providing Inputs	%	Sector	Economic Sector or Industry Buying Outputs	%	Sector
Book printing	27.8	Manufg.	Personal consumption expenditures	60.6	
Paper mills, except building paper	10.3	Manufg.	S/L Govt. purch., elem. & secondary education	11.1	S/L Govt
Wholesale trade	8.9	Trade	Exports	7.4	Foreign
Imports	7.4	Foreign	Legal services	3.4	Services
Bookbinding & related work	7.2	Manufg.	S/L Govt. purch., other education & libraries	2.8	S/L Govt
U.S. Postal Service	5.9	Gov't	Doctors & dentists	2.3	Services
Royalties	4.4	Fin/R.E.	Colleges, universities, & professional schools	1.8	Services
Advertising	4.1	Services	Elementary & secondary schools	1.6	Services
Banking	2.0	Fin/R.E.	Engineering, architectural, & surveying services	1.1	Services
Commercial printing	1.7	Manufg.	Membership organizations nec	1.1	Services
Typesetting	1.7	Manufg.	S/L Govt. purch., other general government	1.1	S/L Govt
Book publishing	1.3	Manufg.	Libraries, vocation education	0.9	Services
Petroleum refining	1.3	Manufg.	Religious organizations	0.7	Services
Paperboard containers & boxes	1.2	Manufg.	Book publishing	0.6	Manufg.
Communications, except radio & TV	1.2	Util.	Business/professional associations	0.4	Services
Eating & drinking places	1.2	Trade	Eating & drinking places	0.3	Trade
Real estate	1.1	Fin/R.E.	Retail trade, except eating & drinking	0.3	Trade
Equipment rental & leasing services	1.0	Services	Banking	0.3	Fin/R.E.
Hotels & lodging places	0.9	Services	Wholesale trade	0.2	Trade
Air transportation	0.6	Util.	Residential care	0.2	Services
Motor freight transportation & warehousing	0.6	Util.			
Noncomparable imports	0.6	Foreign			
Mechanical measuring devices	0.5	Manufg.			
Chemical preparations, nec	0.4	Manufg.			
Lithographic platemaking & services	0.4	Manufg.			
Electric services (utilities)	0.4	Util.			
Legal services	0.4	Services			
Management & consulting services & labs	0.4	Services			
Printing ink	0.3	Manufg.			
Railroads & related services	0.3	Util.			
Accounting, auditing & bookkeeping	0.3	Services			
Automotive rental & leasing, without drivers	0.3	Services			
Detective & protective services	0.3	Services			
Maintenance of nonfarm buildings nec	0.2	Constr.			
Adhesives & sealants	0.2	Manufg.			
Manifold business forms	0.2	Manufg.			
Printing trades machinery	0.2	Manufg.			
Insurance carriers	0.2	Fin/R.E.			
Automotive repair shops & services	0.2	Services			
Business/professional associations	0.2	Services			
Computer & data processing services	0.2	Services			
Photofinishing labs, commercial photography	0.2	Services			
Photographic equipment & supplies	0.1	Manufg.			
Gas production & distribution (utilities)	0.1	Util.			
Transit & bus transportation	0.1	Util.			
Engineering, architectural, & surveying services	0.1	Services			
Personnel supply services	0.1	Services			

Source: Benchmark Input-Output Accounts for the U.S. Economy, 1982, U.S. Department of Commerce, Washington, D.C., July 1991. Data, as reported in the source, are organized by the 1977 SIC structure in use in 1982 but have been matched, as closely as is possible, to the 1987 SIC structure used in this book.

OCCUPATIONS EMPLOYED BY SIC 273 - BOOKS

Occupation	% of Total 1994	Change to 2005	Occupation	% of Total 1994	Change to 2005
Writers & editors, incl technical writers	7.7	14.5	Bookkeeping, accounting, & auditing clerks	2.0	-14.1
Sales & related workers nec	5.8	14.5	Blue collar worker supervisors	2.0	5.5
Bindery machine operators & set-up operators	5.3	14.5	Marketing, advertising, & PR managers	1.9	14.5
Secretaries, ex legal & medical	3.2	4.3	Printing press machine setters, operators	1.9	14.5
Machine feeders & offbearers	3.1	3.1	Order clerks, materials, merchandise, & service	1.8	12.1
General office clerks	3.1	-2.3	Traffic, shipping, & receiving clerks	1.7	10.2
General managers & top executives	3.0	8.7	Assemblers, fabricators, & hand workers nec	1.6	14.6
Offset lithographic press operators	2.7	37.5	Managers & administrators nec	1.5	14.5
Professional workers nec	2.5	37.5	Proofreaders & copy markers	1.4	-25.5
Adjustment clerks	2.4	37.5	Artists & commercial artists	1.4	16.4
Hand packers & packagers	2.3	-1.8	Printing, binding, & related workers nec	1.2	14.5
Helpers, laborers, & material movers nec	2.2	14.5	Systems analysts	1.2	83.2
Strippers, printing	2.1	2.1	Production, planning, & expediting clerks	1.1	37.4
Clerical supervisors & managers	2.0	17.2	Computer programmers	1.1	-7.2
Clerical support workers nec	2.0	-8.4	Management support workers nec	1.0	14.6
Freight, stock, & material movers, hand	2.0	-8.4			

Source: Industry-Occupation Matrix, Bureau of Labor Statistics. These data relate to one or more 3-digit SIC industry groups rather than to a single 4-digit SIC. The change reported for each occupation to the year 2005 is a percent of growth or decline as estimated by the Bureau of Labor Statistics. The abbreviation nec stands for 'not elsewhere classified'.

LOCATION BY STATE AND REGIONAL CONCENTRATION

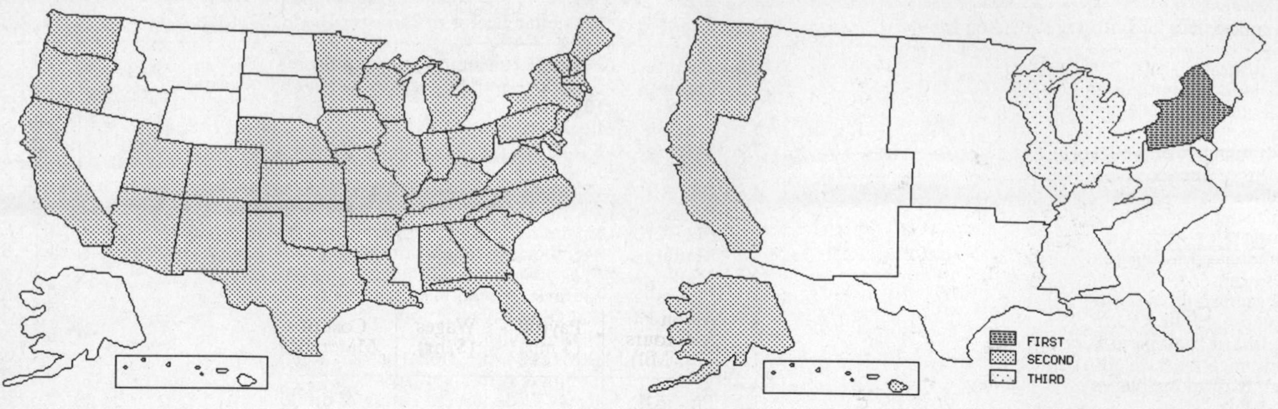

INDUSTRY DATA BY STATE

State	Establish-ments	Shipments			Employment				Cost as % of Shipments	Investment per Employee ($)
		Total ($ mil)	% of U.S.	Per Establ.	Total Number	% of U.S.	Per Establ.	Wages ($/hour)		
New York	383	6,272.3	37.5	16.4	20,400	25.6	53	12.63	33.3	4,711
New Jersey	116	1,350.9	8.1	11.6	6,300	7.9	54	14.19	24.1	2,968
California	405	1,194.9	7.1	3.0	6,800	8.5	17	12.31	27.5	2,794
Massachusetts	103	1,133.4	6.8	11.0	4,800	6.0	47	12.75	36.7	2,396
Illinois	157	1,028.2	6.1	6.5	5,500	6.9	35	11.71	31.1	1,673
Pennsylvania	78	835.8	5.0	10.7	3,300	4.1	42	15.91	27.9	2,242
Minnesota	48	833.9	5.0	17.4	6,200	7.8	129	10.95	38.1	-
Texas	116	517.4	3.1	4.5	3,200	4.0	28	8.00	24.1	2,531
Ohio	64	495.6	3.0	7.7	3,800	4.8	59	16.95	19.1	-
Michigan	58	295.3	1.8	5.1	1,500	1.9	26	12.57	26.1	2,467
Connecticut	63	241.5	1.4	3.8	1,300	1.6	21	16.50	30.8	-
Florida	90	226.2	1.4	2.5	1,400	1.8	16	11.71	18.8	1,143
Tennessee	67	222.6	1.3	3.3	1,500	1.9	22	10.67	40.7	2,400
Wisconsin	39	211.9	1.3	5.4	1,100	1.4	28	16.43	91.2	2,273
Colorado	60	137.0	0.8	2.3	1,300	1.6	22	14.90	12.6	2,692
North Carolina	46	106.3	0.6	2.3	500	0.6	11	7.00	33.5	2,000
Maryland	64	99.3	0.6	1.6	800	1.0	13	9.50	34.0	3,375
Kentucky	20	66.9	0.4	3.3	900	1.1	45	9.60	28.0	778
Oregon	53	56.8	0.3	1.1	400	0.5	8	12.00	40.8	1,750
Georgia	30	32.2	0.2	1.1	300	0.4	10	12.50	24.5	1,333
Oklahoma	22	23.1	0.1	1.0	200	0.3	9	5.00	35.1	-
New Hampshire	11	21.1	0.1	1.9	200	0.3	18	7.00	19.9	-
Maine	14	15.9	0.1	1.1	100	0.1	7	7.00	23.3	-
Utah	28	12.0	0.1	0.4	100 *	0.1	4	-	39.2	4,000
Kansas	25	9.0	0.1	0.4	100 *	0.1	4	-	36.7	-
Louisiana	15	8.4	0.1	0.6	100	0.1	7	5.00	28.6	-
South Carolina	21	7.7	0.0	0.4	100	0.1	5	8.00	24.7	-
Washington	61	(D)	-	-	375 *	0.5	6	-	-	-
Missouri	53	(D)	-	-	1,750 *	2.2	33	-	-	3,714
Virginia	52	(D)	-	-	1,750 *	2.2	34	-	-	-
Arizona	44	(D)	-	-	375 *	0.5	9	-	-	-
Indiana	36	(D)	-	-	750 *	0.9	21	-	-	-
Alabama	27	(D)	-	-	375 *	0.5	14	-	-	-
Vermont	25	(D)	-	-	375 *	0.5	15	-	-	-
New Mexico	24	(D)	-	-	175 *	0.2	7	-	-	-
Iowa	18	(D)	-	-	750 *	0.9	42	-	-	-
Nebraska	11	(D)	-	-	175 *	0.2	16	-	-	-
Arkansas	10	(D)	-	-	375 *	0.5	38	-	-	-

Source: 1992 *Economic Census*. The states are in descending order of shipments or establishments (if shipment data are missing for the majority). The symbol (D) appears when data are withheld to prevent disclosure of competitive information. States marked with (D) are sorted by number of establishments. A dash (-) indicates that the data element cannot be calculated; * indicates the midpoint of a range.

2732 - BOOK PRINTING

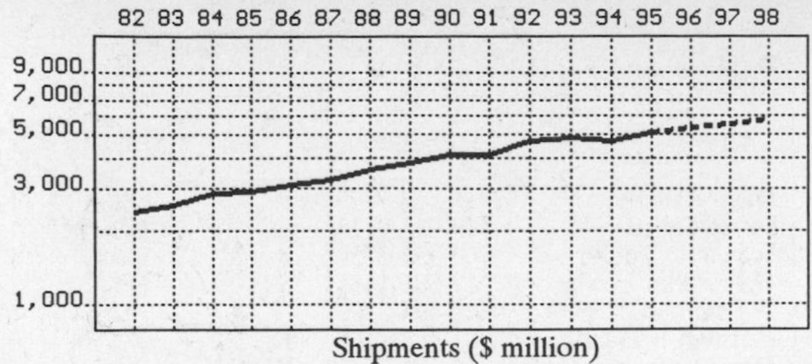

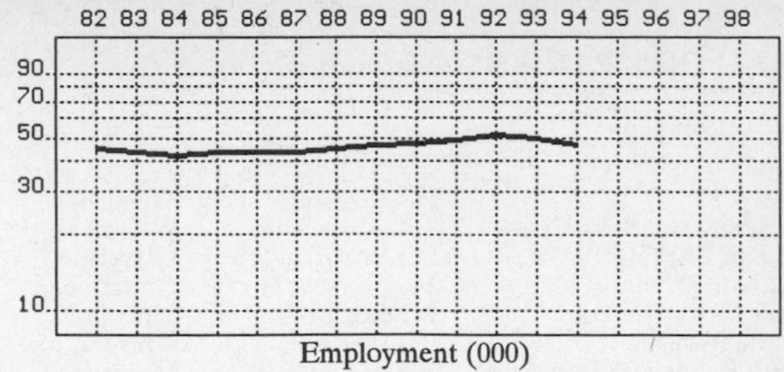

GENERAL STATISTICS

Year	Com-panies	Establishments		Employment			Compensation		Production ($ million)			
		Total	with 20 or more employees	Total (000)	Production Workers (000)	Production Hours (Mil)	Payroll ($ mil)	Wages ($/hr)	Cost of Materials	Value Added by Manufacture	Value of Shipments	Capital Invest.
1982	637	681	309	44.7	34.5	64.7	762.5	8.39	948.1	1,429.9	2,392.4	98.6
1983		658	300	43.6	33.3	64.8	812.1	8.60	1,029.7	1,535.5	2,572.3	100.3
1984		635	291	42.2	32.7	64.8	848.7	9.17	1,169.6	1,671.2	2,828.2	113.3
1985		611	282	43.4	33.9	66.5	886.7	9.29	1,174.9	1,765.3	2,919.4	202.1
1986		566	281	43.5	34.0	68.2	930.4	9.51	1,234.5	1,883.3	3,102.4	181.3
1987	520	561	269	43.5	34.4	67.7	961.4	9.98	1,269.3	1,996.5	3,256.3	154.4
1988		535	266			68.7	1,108.6		1,555.8	2,026.6	3,565.9	
1989		507	261	46.5	37.7	73.0	1,077.5	10.33	1,624.8	2,212.7	3,838.8	179.8
1990		498	255	47.1	37.5	74.7	1,162.7	10.67	1,740.8	2,400.9	4,132.0	211.7
1991		515	244	48.5	37.9	72.6	1,185.8	11.28	1,752.8	2,388.0	4,140.0	163.5
1992	575	623	293	50.9	38.8	76.2	1,360.7	12.12	1,868.4	2,833.6	4,687.9	198.2
1993		632	294	49.8	38.3	78.0	1,378.8	11.77	1,895.7	2,903.7	4,810.1	173.8
1994		529P	262P	46.4	35.6	74.5	1,351.7	12.09	1,869.7	2,840.2	4,698.5	281.2
1995		521P	259P			78.3P	1,444.2P		2,030.3P	3,084.2P	5,102.2P	
1996		512P	256P			79.4P	1,498.6P		2,115.1P	3,213.0P	5,315.2P	
1997		503P	254P			80.6P	1,553.0P		2,199.9P	3,341.7P	5,528.2P	
1998		495P	251P			81.7P	1,607.3P		2,284.6P	3,470.5P	5,741.2P	

Sources: 1982, 1987, 1992 *Economic Census*; *Annual Survey of Manufactures*, 83-86, 88-91, 93-94. Establishment counts for non-Census years are from *County Business Patterns*; establishment values for 83-84 are extrapolations. 'P's show projections by the editors. Industries reclassified in 87 will not have data for prior years.

INDICES OF CHANGE

Year	Com-panies	Establishments		Employment			Compensation		Production ($ million)			
		Total	with 20 or more employees	Total (000)	Production Workers (000)	Production Hours (Mil)	Payroll ($ mil)	Wages ($/hr)	Cost of Materials	Value Added by Manufacture	Value of Shipments	Capital Invest.
1982	111	109	105	88	89	85	56	69	51	50	51	50
1983		106	102	86	86	85	60	71	55	54	55	51
1984		102	99	83	84	85	62	76	63	59	60	57
1985		98	96	85	87	87	65	77	63	62	62	102
1986		91	96	85	88	90	68	78	66	66	66	91
1987	90	90	92	85	89	89	71	82	68	70	69	78
1988		86	91			90	81		83	72	76	
1989		81	89	91	97	96	79	85	87	78	82	91
1990		80	87	93	97	98	85	88	93	85	88	107
1991		83	83	95	98	95	87	93	94	84	88	82
1992	100	100	100	100	100	100	100	100	100	100	100	100
1993		101	100	98	99	102	101	97	101	102	103	88
1994		85P	89P	91	92	98	99	100	100	100	100	142
1995		84P	88P			103P	106P		109P	109P	109P	
1996		82P	87P			104P	110P		113P	113P	113P	
1997		81P	87P			106P	114P		118P	118P	118P	
1998		79P	86P			107P	118P		122P	122P	122P	

Sources: Same as General Statistics. Values reflect change from the base year, 1992. Values above 100 mean greater than 92, values below 100 mean less than 92, and a value of 100 in the 82-91 or 93-98 period means same as 92. 'P's mark projections by the editors.

SELECTED RATIOS

For 1994	Avg. of All Manufact.	Analyzed Industry	Index	For 1994	Avg. of All Manufact.	Analyzed Industry	Index
Employees per Establishment	49	88	179	Value Added per Production Worker	134,084	79,781	60
Payroll per Establishment	1,500,273	2,554,174	170	Cost per Establishment	5,045,178	3,532,988	70
Payroll per Employee	30,620	29,131	95	Cost per Employee	102,970	40,295	39
Production Workers per Establishment	34	67	196	Cost per Production Worker	146,988	52,520	36
Wages per Establishment	853,319	1,701,973	199	Shipments per Establishment	9,576,895	8,878,292	93
Wages per Production Worker	24,861	25,301	102	Shipments per Employee	195,460	101,261	52
Hours per Production Worker	2,056	2,093	102	Shipments per Production Worker	279,017	131,980	47
Wages per Hour	12.09	12.09	100	Investment per Establishment	321,011	531,356	166
Value Added per Establishment	4,602,255	5,366,846	117	Investment per Employee	6,552	6,060	93
Value Added per Employee	93,930	61,211	65	Investment per Production Worker	9,352	7,899	84

Sources: Same as General Statistics. The 'Average of All Manufacturing' column represents the average of all manufacturing industries reported for the most recent complete year available. The Index shows the relationship between the Average and the Analyzed Industry. For example, 100 means that they are equal; 500 that the Analyzed Industry is five times the average; 50 means that the Analyzed Industry is half the national average. The abbreviation 'na' is used to show that data are 'not available'.

LEADING COMPANIES

Number shown: **63** Total sales ($ mil): **2,628** Total employment (000): **25.1**

Company Name	Address				CEO Name	Phone	Co. Type	Sales ($ mil)	Empl. (000)
Banta Corp	PO Box 8003	Menasha	WI	54952	David Belcher	414-722-7777	P	811	4.9
RR Donnelley and Sons Co	1145 Conwell Av	Willard	OH	44888	Bruce Smith	419-935-0111	D	190*	1.8
Bertelsmann Printing	PO Box 272	Berryville	VA	22611	Wayne D Taylor	703-955-2750	S	150	1.5
Times Mirror	2460 Kerper Blv	Dubuque	IA	52001	G Franklin Lewis	319-588-1451	S	111	1.7
Foote and Davies Lincoln	PO Box 81608	Lincoln	NE	68501	D Kozak	402-474-5825	D	92*	1.0
Ringier America Inc	PO Box 110	Dresden	TN	38225	Norman R Hartigan	901-364-4100	D	75	0.8
Walsworth Publishing Company	306 N Kansas Av	Marceline	MO	64658	Don O Walsworth	816-376-3543	R	65	1.3
Edwards Brothers Inc	PO Box 1007	Ann Arbor	MI	48106	Martin H Edwards	313-769-1000	R	56	0.8
John Henry Co	PO Box 17099	Lansing	MI	48901	LJ Brand	517-323-9000	R	52	0.4
Vail Ballou Press Inc	PO Box 1005	Binghamton	NY	13902	James Wisotzkey	607-723-7981	S	52	0.7
BookCrafters USA Inc	140 Buchanan St	Chelsea	MI	48118	WG Nuffer	313-475-9145	S	50	0.6
Offset Paperback Manufacturers	Rte 309	Dallas	PA	18612	Michael J Gallagher	717-675-5261	S	45	0.6
Banta Co	PO Box 60	Menasha	WI	54952	Allan J Williamson	414-722-7771	D	43	0.3
Braceland Brothers Inc	7625 Suffolk Av	Philadelphia	PA	19153	J Braceland	215-492-0200	R	40	0.5
National Computer Print Inc	5200 E Lake Blv	Birmingham	AL	35217	Grady Burrow	205-849-5200	R	40	0.7
Malloy Lithographing Inc	PO Box 1124	Ann Arbor	MI	48106	HH Upton Jr	313-665-6113	R	38	0.4
Graphic Innovators Inc	9600 Manchester	St Louis	MO	63119	Herb M Sayers	314-968-5400	R	38	0.2
Sayers Communications Group	9600 Manchester	St Louis	MO	63119	Herb M Sayers	314-968-5400	S	38	0.2
Worzalla Publishing Co	PO Box 307	Stevens Point	WI	54481	CW Nason	715-344-9600	R	38	0.4
Port City Press Inc	1323 Greenwood	Pikesville	MD	21208	John Broderick	410-486-3000	S	37	0.3
Braun-Brumfield Inc	PO Box 1203	Ann Arbor	MI	48106	Arnold M Ziroli	313-662-3291	S	36	0.5
Delta Lithograph Co	28210 N Stanford	Valencia	CA	91355	Ken Hoffmann	805-257-0584	S	30	0.2
Horowitz-Rae	300 Fairfield Rd	Fairfield	NJ	07006	Raymond Burke	201-575-7070	S	30	0.4
Capital City Press Inc	PO Box 546	Montpelier	VT	05602	Richard E Hearn	802-223-5207	R	24	0.2
McNaughton and Gunn Inc	960 Woodland Dr	Saline	MI	48176	R L McNaughton	313-429-5411	R	23	0.3
Dartmouth Printing Co	69 Lyme Rd	Hanover	NH	03755	SV Smith Jr	603-643-2220	R	22	0.3
CJ Krehbiel Co	3962 Virginia Av	Cincinnati	OH	45227	RC Krehbiel Jr	513-271-6035	R	22	0.2
Dickinson Press Inc	5100 33rd St SE	Grand Rapids	MI	49512	V DeWeerd	616-957-5100	R	20	0.1
DB Hess Co	1530 McConnell	Woodstock	IL	60098	Robert R Duncan	815-338-6900	R	20	0.2
Hunter Publishing Co	PO Box 5867	Winston-Salem	NC	27113	Ron Sisk	910-765-0070	S	20*	0.4
Bushman Press Inc	2600 N Main St	Spanish Fork	UT	84660	Steve Bushman	801-377-6600	S	19	0.3
Stry-Lenkoff Company Inc	PO Box 32120	Louisville	KY	40232	Tom Landis	502-587-6804	R	19*	0.2
Intervisual Books Inc	2850 Ocean Pk Blvd	Santa Monica	CA	90405	Charles E Gates	310-396-8708	P	19	<0.1
Consolidated Printers Inc	2630 8th St	Berkeley	CA	94710	L A Hawkins	510-843-8524	R	19	0.1
Griffin Printing & Lithograph	544 W Colorado St	Glendale	CA	91204	John C Thomas	818-245-3671	R	18	0.1
Rose Printing Company Inc	PO Box 5078	Tallahassee	FL	32314	Charles Rosenberg	904-576-4151	R	18	0.2
Thomson-Shore Inc	7300 W Joy Rd	Dexter	MI	48130	E W Thomson Jr	313-426-3939	R	18	0.2
State Printing Co	PO Box 1388	Columbia	SC	29202	Stephen L Johnson	803-799-9550	S	17	0.2
National Publishing Co	24th & Locust St	Philadelphia	PA	19103	George Q Nichols	215-732-1863	S	16*	0.3
American Printing House	PO Box 6085	Louisville	KY	40206	Tuck Tinsley III	502-895-2405	R	15	0.4
Johnson Publishing Co	1880 S 57th Ct	Boulder	CO	80301	JB Johnson	303-443-1576	R	14	0.1
Adair Printing Company Inc	18544 W 8 Mile Rd	Southfield	MI	48075	RF Adair	313-569-1122	R	14	0.1
Vicks Lithograph and Printing	PO Box 270	Yorkville	NY	13495	Dwight E Vicks Jr	315-736-9346	R	10	0.1
C and M Press Corp	4825 Nome St	Denver	CO	80229	Robert Malkin	303-375-9922	R	9*	0.1
Cushing-Malloy Inc	1350 N Main St	Ann Arbor	MI	48107	JB Cushing	313-663-8554	R	9*	0.1
Phillips Brothers Inc	PO Box 580	Springfield	IL	62705	John L Marinelli	217-787-3014	R	9	<0.1
Whitley Co	PO Box 1564	Austin	TX	78767	JG Jones	512-476-7101	R	9	<0.1
Chicago Press Corp	1112 N Homan Av	Chicago	IL	60651	M Harrison	312-276-1500	R	8	<0.1
Patterson Printing Co	1550 Territorial Rd	Benton Harbor	MI	49022	Leroy Patterson	616-925-2177	R	8*	<0.1
Service Graphics Inc	8350 Allison Av	Indianapolis	IN	46268	Mike Burks	317-471-8246	R	8*	<0.1
United Graphics Inc	PO Box 559	Mattoon	IL	61938	Ralph M Scrimager	217-235-7161	R	8	0.1
Creative Teaching Press Inc	PO Box 6017	Cypress	CA	90630	Luella Connelly	714-995-7888	R	7*	<0.1
CLB Publishers & Lithographers	10580 Metropolitan	Kensington	MD	20895	Paul Fuqua Sr	301-933-5220	R	7	<0.1
KNI Inc	1261 S State College	Anaheim	CA	92806	Jeremy R Bernstein	714-956-7300	R	5	<0.1
Lawton Printing Inc	PO Box 284	Spokane	WA	99210	R W Lawton	509-534-1044	R	5	<0.1
Waterfront Reprographics Ltd	2300 7th Av	Seattle	WA	98121	David Sims	206-467-9889	R	4	<0.1
News Publishing Company Inc	240 Hathaway Dr	Stratford	CT	06497	Evelyn Janello	203-377-3555	R	4	<0.1
Western Newspaper Publishing	537 E Ohio St	Indianapolis	IN	46204	Barbara Gard	317-636-4122	R	3*	<0.1
Roth Publishing Inc	PO Box 406	Great Neck	NY	11022	Harvey Roth	516-466-3676	R	1	<0.1
Smith and Kraus Inc	PO Box 127	Lyme	NH	03768	Marisa Smith	603-795-4331	R	0	<0.1
Touch Books Inc	PO Box 14219	Tampa	FL	33690	Michael J Minardi	813-254-2500	R	0	<0.1
World Tariff Ltd	220 Montgomery St	San Francisco	CA	94104	Scott D Morse	415-391-7501	R	0	<0.1
Automation Printing Co	1230 Long Beach	Los Angeles	CA	90021	David Tobmen	213-488-0450	R	0	<0.1

Source: *Ward's Business Directory of U.S. Private and Public Companies*, Volumes 1 and 2, 1996. The company type code used is as follows: P - Public, R - Private, S - Subsidiary, D - Division, J - Joint Venture, A - Affiliate, G - Group. Sales are in millions of dollars, employees are in thousands. An asterisk (*) indicates an estimated sales volume. The symbol < stands for 'less than'. Company names and addresses are truncated, in some cases, to fit into the available space.

MATERIALS CONSUMED

Material	Quantity	Delivered Cost ($ million)
Materials, ingredients, containers, and supplies	(X)	1,587.6
Newsprint	(X)	35.7
Uncoated paper in sheets	(X)	116.7
Uncoated paper in rolls	(X)	314.5
Coated paper in sheets	(X)	148.1
Coated paper in rolls	(X)	194.9
Pressure-sensitive base stock, self-adhesive, including paper, film, foil, etc.	(X)	14.5
Cloth and nonwoven fabrics for hardbound book covers	(X)	56.1
Glues and adhesives	(X)	29.3
Printing inks (complete formulations)	(X)	64.7
Light sensitive films and papers	(X)	29.7
Unexposed photosensitive printing plates	(X)	23.6
Printing plates, prepared for printing	(X)	33.9
Paperboard containers, boxes, and corrugated paperboard	(X)	60.4
All other materials and components, parts, containers, and supplies	(X)	274.7
Materials, ingredients, containers, and supplies, nsk	(X)	190.7

Source: 1992 *Economic Census*. Explanation of symbols used: (D): Withheld to avoid disclosure of competitive data; na: Not available; (S): Withheld because statistical norms were not met; (X): Not applicable; (Z): Less than half the unit shown; nec: Not elsewhere classified; nsk: Not specified by kind; - : zero; * : 10-19 percent estimated; ** : 20-29 percent estimated.

PRODUCT SHARE DETAILS

Product or Product Class	% Share
Book printing	100.00
Textbooks, printing and binding	14.33
Hardbound elementary and high school (grades K through 12) textbook printing and binding, including teachers' editions	23.91
Paperbound elementary and high school (grades K through 12) textbook printing and binding, including teachers' editions	24.77
Hardbound college (grades 13 and up, for any post high school level courses) textbook printing and binding	20.67
Paperbound college (grades 13 and up, for any post high school level courses) textbook printing and binding	22.20
Workbook and standardized test printing and binding, all grade levels	6.97
Textbooks, printing and binding, nsk	1.47
Technical, scientific, and professional book printing and binding	21.18
Hardbound technical, scientific, and professional book printing and binding	15.23
Paperbound technical, scientific, and professional book printing and binding	79.64
Technical, scientific, and professional books, printing and binding, nsk	5.13
Religious book printing and binding	4.37
Hardbound (including flexible cover) religious book printing and binding	37.10
Paperbound religious book printing and binding	43.04
Religious books, printing and binding, nsk	19.86
General book (trade, etc.) printing and binding	23.78
Hardbound book club and mail order book printing and binding	11.41
Paperbound book club and mail order book printing and binding	7.21
Mass market rack-size paperbound book printing and binding, distributed predominantly to mass market outlets	11.74
Hardbound adult trade book printing and binding, sold primarily through retail or wholesale book sellers	32.39
Paperbound adult trade book printing and binding, sold primarily through retail or wholesale book sellers	24.87
Hardbound juvenile book printing and binding (fiction and nonfiction, including toy and coloring books)	3.97
Paperbound juvenile book printing and binding (fiction and nonfiction, including toy and coloring books)	4.25
General books (trade, etc.), printing and binding, nsk	4.16
Other book printing and binding, nec	15.46
Encyclopedia printing and binding	6.72
Other hardbound reference book printing and binding (including dictionaries, thesauruses, etc.)	6.08
Other paperbound reference book printing and binding (including dictionaries, thesauruses, etc.)	8.78
All other hardbound book printing and binding, nec (including music books, university press books, etc.)	42.77
All other paperbound book printing and binding, nec (including music books, university press books, etc.)	34.83
Other books, nec, printing and binding, nsk	0.82
Books, printing only, not bound	2.90
Pamphlets, printing only or printing and binding (excluding advertising pamphlets)	6.62
Book printing, nsk	11.36

Source: 1992 *Economic Census*. The values shown are percent of total shipments in an industry. Values of indented subcategories are summed in the main heading. The symbol (D) appears when data are withheld to prevent disclosure of competitive information. The abbreviation nsk stands for 'not specified by kind' and nec for 'not elsewhere classified'.

INPUTS AND OUTPUTS FOR BOOK PRINTING

Economic Sector or Industry Providing Inputs	%	Sector	Economic Sector or Industry Buying Outputs	%	Sector
Paper mills, except building paper	34.7	Manufg.	Book publishing	46.5	Manufg.
Typesetting	7.0	Manufg.	Periodicals	18.3	Manufg.
Wholesale trade	6.1	Trade	Business/professional associations	8.5	Services
Miscellaneous plastics products	4.0	Manufg.	Management & consulting services & labs	5.6	Services
Paperboard mills	3.5	Manufg.	Communications, except radio & TV	4.5	Util.
U.S. Postal Service	3.2	Gov't	Libraries, vocation education	2.6	Services
Broadwoven fabric mills	3.0	Manufg.	Computer & data processing services	2.0	Services
Printing ink	2.8	Manufg.	S/L Govt. purch., elem. & secondary education	1.9	S/L Govt
Electric services (utilities)	2.7	Util.	Games, toys, & children's vehicles	1.8	Manufg.
Lithographic platemaking & services	2.6	Manufg.	Social services, nec	1.6	Services
Photographic equipment & supplies	2.3	Manufg.	Federal Government purchases, national defense	1.4	Fed Govt
Motor freight transportation & warehousing	2.1	Util.	Membership organizations nec	1.2	Services

Continued on next page.

INPUTS AND OUTPUTS FOR BOOK PRINTING - Continued

Economic Sector or Industry Providing Inputs	%	Sector	Economic Sector or Industry Buying Outputs	%	Sector
Royalties	1.9	Fin/R.E.	Soap & other detergents	1.1	Manufg.
Advertising	1.8	Services	S/L Govt. purch., higher education	0.8	S/L Govt
Eating & drinking places	1.7	Trade	S/L Govt. purch., other education & libraries	0.7	S/L Govt
Adhesives & sealants	1.5	Manufg.	Federal Government enterprises nec	0.4	Gov't
Printing trades machinery	1.2	Manufg.	Exports	0.4	Foreign
Banking	1.2	Fin/R.E.	U.S. Postal Service	0.3	Gov't
Railroads & related services	1.1	Util.	Miscellaneous publishing	0.2	Manufg.
Chemical preparations, nec	0.9	Manufg.			
Paperboard containers & boxes	0.9	Manufg.			
Communications, except radio & TV	0.9	Util.			
Real estate	0.9	Fin/R.E.			
Equipment rental & leasing services	0.9	Services			
Primary lead	0.8	Manufg.			
Gas production & distribution (utilities)	0.8	Util.			
Mechanical measuring devices	0.7	Manufg.			
Leather tanning & finishing	0.6	Manufg.			
Computer & data processing services	0.6	Services			
Legal services	0.6	Services			
Management & consulting services & labs	0.6	Services			
Maintenance of nonfarm buildings nec	0.5	Constr.			
Metal foil & leaf	0.5	Manufg.			
Air transportation	0.5	Util.			
Automotive repair shops & services	0.5	Services			
Accounting, auditing & bookkeeping	0.4	Services			
Manifold business forms	0.3	Manufg.			
Credit agencies other than banks	0.3	Fin/R.E.			
Book printing	0.2	Manufg.			
Paper coating & glazing	0.2	Manufg.			
Petroleum refining	0.2	Manufg.			
Transit & bus transportation	0.2	Util.			
Detective & protective services	0.2	Services			
Personnel supply services	0.2	Services			
State & local government enterprises, nec	0.2	Gov't			
Engraving & plate printing	0.1	Manufg.			
Insurance carriers	0.1	Fin/R.E.			
Business services nec	0.1	Services			
Electrical repair shops	0.1	Services			
Hotels & lodging places	0.1	Services			

Source: Benchmark Input-Output Accounts for the U.S. Economy, 1982, U.S. Department of Commerce, Washington, D.C., July 1991. Data, as reported in the source, are organized by the 1977 SIC structure in use in 1982 but have been matched, as closely as is possible, to the 1987 SIC structure used in this book.

OCCUPATIONS EMPLOYED BY SIC 273 - BOOKS

Occupation	% of Total 1994	Change to 2005	Occupation	% of Total 1994	Change to 2005
Writers & editors, incl technical writers	7.7	14.5	Bookkeeping, accounting, & auditing clerks	2.0	-14.1
Sales & related workers nec	5.8	14.5	Blue collar worker supervisors	2.0	5.5
Bindery machine operators & set-up operators	5.3	14.5	Marketing, advertising, & PR managers	1.9	14.5
Secretaries, ex legal & medical	3.2	4.3	Printing press machine setters, operators	1.9	14.5
Machine feeders & offbearers	3.1	3.1	Order clerks, materials, merchandise, & service	1.8	12.1
General office clerks	3.1	-2.3	Traffic, shipping, & receiving clerks	1.7	10.2
General managers & top executives	3.0	8.7	Assemblers, fabricators, & hand workers nec	1.6	14.6
Offset lithographic press operators	2.7	37.5	Managers & administrators nec	1.5	14.5
Professional workers nec	2.5	37.5	Proofreaders & copy markers	1.4	-25.5
Adjustment clerks	2.4	37.5	Artists & commercial artists	1.4	16.4
Hand packers & packagers	2.3	-1.8	Printing, binding, & related workers nec	1.2	14.5
Helpers, laborers, & material movers nec	2.2	14.5	Systems analysts	1.2	83.2
Strippers, printing	2.1	2.1	Production, planning, & expediting clerks	1.1	37.4
Clerical supervisors & managers	2.0	17.2	Computer programmers	1.1	-7.2
Clerical support workers nec	2.0	-8.4	Management support workers nec	1.0	14.6
Freight, stock, & material movers, hand	2.0	-8.4			

Source: Industry-Occupation Matrix, Bureau of Labor Statistics. These data relate to one or more 3-digit SIC industry groups rather than to a single 4-digit SIC. The change reported for each occupation to the year 2005 is a percent of growth or decline as estimated by the Bureau of Labor Statistics. The abbreviation nec stands for 'not elsewhere classified'.

LOCATION BY STATE AND REGIONAL CONCENTRATION

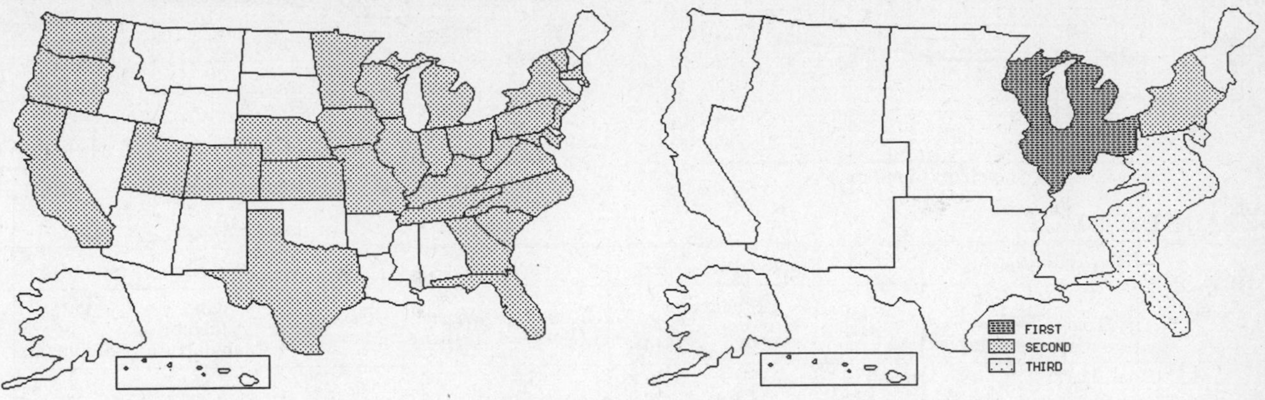

INDUSTRY DATA BY STATE

State	Establish-ments	Shipments			Employment				Cost as % of Shipments	Investment per Employee ($)
		Total ($ mil)	% of U.S.	Per Establ.	Total Number	% of U.S.	Per Establ.	Wages ($/hour)		
Pennsylvania	33	444.3	9.5	13.5	5,200	10.2	158	11.58	35.2	4,519
Tennessee	11	323.8	6.9	29.4	3,900	7.7	355	11.63	34.9	1,000
Wisconsin	18	298.3	6.4	16.6	2,400	4.7	133	13.97	51.8	5,250
Massachusetts	29	285.8	6.1	9.9	3,100	6.1	107	13.67	40.1	3,484
California	79	284.3	6.1	3.6	2,800	5.5	35	12.57	32.6	3,464
New York	53	277.3	5.9	5.2	3,200	6.3	60	14.91	38.9	3,125
Ohio	19	256.5	5.5	13.5	2,400	4.7	126	12.65	37.8	-
Michigan	26	242.1	5.2	9.3	2,900	5.7	112	10.98	37.5	1,793
Illinois	49	186.9	4.0	3.8	2,000	3.9	41	12.00	40.9	2,300
Maryland	25	171.1	3.6	6.8	1,700	3.3	68	11.89	54.0	2,765
Texas	27	167.0	3.6	6.2	2,200	4.3	81	11.77	43.7	4,955
Kentucky	9	128.7	2.7	14.3	1,400	2.8	156	13.60	38.1	2,429
North Carolina	14	98.1	2.1	7.0	1,400	2.8	100	10.23	37.8	1,143
New Jersey	24	82.5	1.8	3.4	700	1.4	29	14.90	23.0	4,286
Utah	10	79.3	1.7	7.9	800	1.6	80	8.58	50.1	6,000
Colorado	13	53.0	1.1	4.1	800	1.6	62	9.60	41.1	5,750
Oregon	6	43.3	0.9	7.2	300	0.6	50	12.75	33.3	15,000
Florida	26	35.8	0.8	1.4	500	1.0	19	12.33	39.1	3,800
Georgia	14	35.3	0.8	2.5	300	0.6	21	14.00	44.5	5,000
Minnesota	8	21.5	0.5	2.7	300	0.6	38	8.00	26.5	-
South Carolina	5	16.1	0.3	3.2	200	0.4	40	11.33	17.4	1,500
Virginia	13	(D)	-	-	1,750 *	3.4	135	-	-	-
Indiana	12	(D)	-	-	3,750 *	7.4	313	-	-	-
Missouri	12	(D)	-	-	1,750 *	3.4	146	-	-	1,771
Iowa	10	(D)	-	-	1,750 *	3.4	175	-	-	-
Washington	8	(D)	-	-	375 *	0.7	47	-	-	-
Nebraska	4	(D)	-	-	175 *	0.3	44	-	-	-
Vermont	4	(D)	-	-	750 *	1.5	188	-	-	-
Kansas	3	(D)	-	-	1,750 *	3.4	583	-	-	-
West Virginia	2	(D)	-	-	375 *	0.7	188	-	-	-

Source: 1992 *Economic Census*. The states are in descending order of shipments or establishments (if shipment data are missing for the majority). The symbol (D) appears when data are withheld to prevent disclosure of competitive information. States marked with (D) are sorted by number of establishments. A dash (-) indicates that the data element cannot be calculated; * indicates the midpoint of a range.

2741 - MISCELLANEOUS PUBLISHING

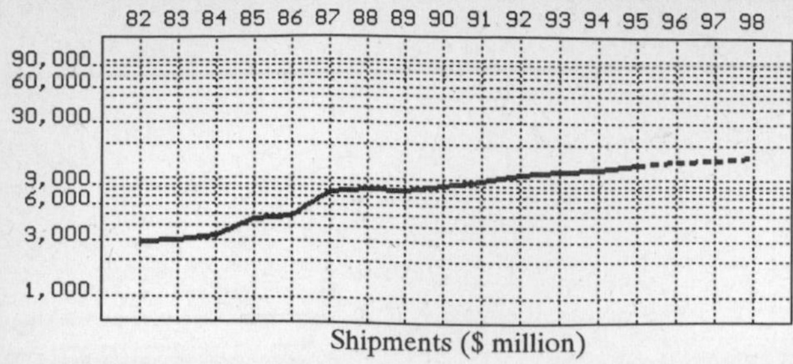

Shipments ($ million)

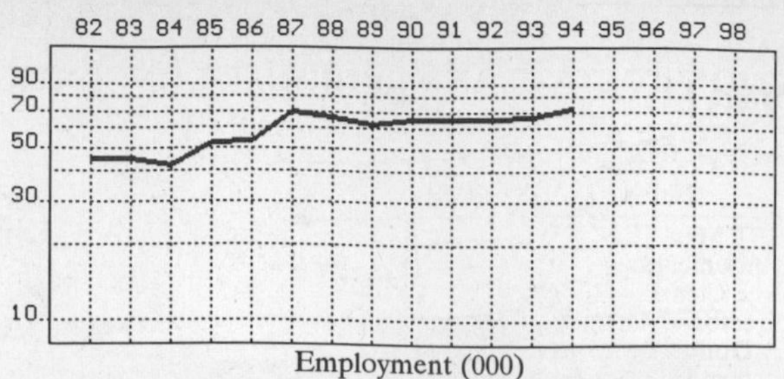

Employment (000)

GENERAL STATISTICS

Year	Com-panies	Establishments: Total	Establishments: with 20 or more employees	Employment: Total (000)	Employment: Production Workers (000)	Employment: Production Hours (Mil)	Compensation: Payroll ($ mil)	Compensation: Wages ($/hr)	Production ($ million): Cost of Materials	Production ($ million): Value Added by Manufacture	Production ($ million): Value of Shipments	Production ($ million): Capital Invest.
1982	1,951	2,057	430	45.3	17.9	29.2	705.9	7.06	909.6	1,958.2	2,871.3	67.1
1983				44.8	18.4	29.9	712.2	7.08	943.4	2,105.4	3,011.7	82.5
1984				42.0	16.6	28.2	775.9	7.48	949.4	2,321.9	3,222.9	69.1
1985				52.0	17.1	29.5	1,047.4	8.11	1,199.5	3,264.6	4,437.0	109.7
1986				53.1	18.4	31.3	1,129.1	8.80	1,246.9	3,631.5	4,887.4	102.6
1987	2,136	2,369	597	69.4	24.1	44.1	1,513.2	8.28	1,791.0	6,022.9	7,809.5	133.0
1988						43.0	1,553.4		1,953.8	6,248.1	8,154.4	
1989		2,131	577	62.4	22.1	40.2	1,594.2	9.24	2,056.3	6,060.0	8,021.2	144.0
1990				65.2	22.3	40.2	1,707.8	9.40	2,266.7	6,656.2	8,874.7	178.6
1991				65.0	22.6	43.4	1,779.7	9.60	2,469.8	7,353.6	9,762.0	165.5
1992	3,159	3,390	570	65.4	23.7	43.3	1,732.9	10.80	2,476.7	8,524.9	10,977.1	190.4
1993				66.6	22.8	42.6	1,896.8	10.41	2,592.1	9,218.1	11,806.6	138.5
1994				71.2	25.3	47.5	1,982.1	10.39	2,802.6	9,522.7	12,332.4	192.8
1995						49.0P	2,196.3P		3,044.0P	10,342.8P	13,394.4P	
1996						50.6P	2,310.9P		3,238.6P	11,004.3P	14,251.1P	
1997						52.2P	2,425.4P		3,433.3P	11,665.8P	15,107.8P	
1998						53.8P	2,539.9P		3,628.0P	12,327.3P	15,964.5P	

Sources: 1982, 1987, 1992 *Economic Census*; *Annual Survey of Manufactures*, 83-86, 88-91, 93-94. Establishment counts for non-Census years are from *County Business Patterns*; establishment values for 83-84 are extrapolations. 'P's show projections by the editors. Industries reclassified in 87 will not have data for prior years.

INDICES OF CHANGE

Year	Com-panies	Establishments: Total	Establishments: with 20 or more employees	Employment: Total (000)	Employment: Production Workers (000)	Employment: Production Hours (Mil)	Compensation: Payroll ($ mil)	Compensation: Wages ($/hr)	Production ($ million): Cost of Materials	Production ($ million): Value Added by Manufacture	Production ($ million): Value of Shipments	Production ($ million): Capital Invest.
1982	62	61	75	69	76	67	41	65	37	23	26	35
1983				69	78	69	41	66	38	25	27	43
1984				64	70	65	45	69	38	27	29	36
1985				80	72	68	60	75	48	38	40	58
1986				81	78	72	65	81	50	43	45	54
1987	68	70	105	106	102	102	87	77	72	71	71	70
1988						99	90		79	73	74	
1989		63	101	95	93	93	92	86	83	71	73	76
1990				100	94	93	99	87	92	78	81	94
1991				99	95	100	103	89	100	86	89	87
1992	100	100	100	100	100	100	100	100	100	100	100	100
1993				102	96	98	109	96	105	108	108	73
1994				109	107	110	114	96	113	112	112	101
1995						113P	127P		123P	121P	122P	
1996						117P	133P		131P	129P	130P	
1997						121P	140P		139P	137P	138P	
1998						124P	147P		146P	145P	145P	

Sources: Same as General Statistics. Values reflect change from the base year, 1992. Values above 100 mean greater than 92, values below 100 mean less than 92, and a value of 100 in the 82-91 or 93-98 period means same as 92. 'P's mark projections by the editors.

SELECTED RATIOS

For 1992	Avg. of All Manufact.	Analyzed Industry	Index
Employees per Establishment	46	19	42
Payroll per Establishment	1,332,320	511,180	38
Payroll per Employee	29,181	26,497	91
Production Workers per Establishment	31	7	22
Wages per Establishment	734,496	137,947	19
Wages per Production Worker	23,390	19,732	84
Hours per Production Worker	2,025	1,827	90
Wages per Hour	11.55	10.80	93
Value Added per Establishment	3,842,210	2,514,720	65
Value Added per Employee	84,153	130,350	155

For 1992	Avg. of All Manufact.	Analyzed Industry	Index
Value Added per Production Worker	122,353	359,700	294
Cost per Establishment	4,239,462	730,590	17
Cost per Employee	92,853	37,870	41
Cost per Production Worker	135,003	104,502	77
Shipments per Establishment	8,100,800	3,238,083	40
Shipments per Employee	177,425	167,846	95
Shipments per Production Worker	257,966	463,169	180
Investment per Establishment	278,244	56,165	20
Investment per Employee	6,094	2,911	48
Investment per Production Worker	8,861	8,034	91

Sources: Same as General Statistics. The 'Average of All Manufacturing' column represents the average of all manufacturing industries reported for the most recent complete year available. The Index shows the relationship between the Average and the Analyzed Industry. For example, 100 means that they are equal; 500 that the Analyzed Industry is five times the average; 50 means that the Analyzed Industry is half the national average. The abbreviation 'na' is used to show that data are 'not available'.

LEADING COMPANIES Number shown: **75** Total sales ($ mil): **6,434** Total employment (000): **49.0**

Company Name	Address				CEO Name	Phone	Co. Type	Sales ($ mil)	Empl. (000)
U S WEST Marketing	198 Invcrncss Dr W	Englewood	CO	80112	Solomon Trujillo	303-667-0652	S	949	2.0
ITT Communications	100 Plaza Dr	Secaucus	NJ	07096	Gerald C Crotty	201-601-4000	S	833	5.0
Commerce Clearing House Inc	2700 Lake Cook Rd	Riverwoods	IL	60015	Edward L Massie	708-940-4600	P	579	5.7
GTE Directories Corp	W Airfield Dr	Dallas-Ft W Apt	TX	75261	Earl Goode	214-453-7000	S	560	4.5
Rubin H Donnelley	711 3rd Av	New York	NY	10017	Frank R Noonan	212-972-8500	S	451	4.2
Southwestern Bell Publications	12800 Publications	St Louis	MO	63131	RM Geschwind	314-957-2261	S	310*	2.5
Reed Reference Publishing	121 Chanlon Rd	New Providence	NJ	07974	Ira T Siegel	908-464-6800	S	189*	1.5
Stevens Graphics Inc	713 R Abernathy	Atlanta	GA	30310	William Davidson	404-753-1121	S	163	0.8
Butterick Company Inc	161 Av Amer	New York	NY	10013	John E Lehmann	212-620-2500	R	130*	1.1
Lawyers Cooperative Publishing	Aqueduct Bldg	Rochester	NY	14694	Kathryn M Downing	716-546-5530	D	110*	0.9
Simplicity Pattern Company Inc	2 Park Av	New York	NY	10016	Louis R Morris	212-372-0500	S	100	1.0
Taylor Publishing Co	PO Box 597	Dallas	TX	75221	Maurice Dake	214-637-2800	S	100	2.0
University Microfilm Inc	300 N Zeeb Rd	Ann Arbor	MI	48106	Joseph Fitzsimmons	313-761-4700	D	100*	1.0
Reed Travel Group Inc	500 Plaza Dr	Secaucus	NJ	07096	Ian Thomas	201-902-2000	S	95*	0.6
Nimbus Manufacturing Inc	PO Box 7427	Charlottesville	VA	22906	Lyndon Faulkner	804-985-1100	R	94	0.8
Value Line Inc	711 3rd Av	New York	NY	10017	J Bernhard Buttner	212-907-1500	P	82	0.4
Sprint Publishing and Advertising	7015 College Blv	Overland Park	KS	66211	Robert J Walsh	913-491-7000	S	78*	0.6
Jeppesen Sanderson Inc	55 Inverness Dr E	Englewood	CO	80112	Horst Bergmann	303-799-9090	S	68	0.5
Institute for Scientific Info	3501 Market St	Philadelphia	PA	19104	Eugene Garfield	215-386-0100	S	60	0.7
Thomas Publishing Co	5 Penn Plz	New York	NY	10001	C T Holst-Knudsen	212-695-0500	R	55	0.5
TransWestern Publishing LP	8328 Claremont	San Diego	CA	92111	Jim Dunning	619-467-2800	R	53	0.5
Media Arts Group Inc	10 Almaden Blv	San Jose	CA	95113	Kenneth E Raasch	408-947-4680	P	53	0.6
Hal Leonard Corp	7777 W Bluemound	Milwaukee	WI	53213	Keith Mardak	414-774-3630	R	52*	0.3
Datapro Information Services	PO Box 7001	Delran	NJ	08075	Steve Thomas	609-764-0100	D	48	0.4
Add Inc	PO Box 609	Waupaca	WI	54981	T M Karavakis	715-258-8450	S	47	1.0
Day Runner Inc	2750 W Moore Av	Fullerton	CA	92633	Mark A Vidovich	714-680-3500	P	43	0.6
Leisure Arts Inc	PO Box 5595	Little Rock	AR	72215	SM Patterson	501-868-8800	R	38*	0.3
NRP Inc	8150 N Central	Dallas	TX	75206	Michael G Santry	214-373-8662	P	37	<0.1
Great Western Directories Inc	2400 Lakeview Dr	Amarillo	TX	79109	Richard O'Neal	806-353-5155	R	37*	0.3
Nystrom Co	3333 Elston Av	Chicago	IL	60618	James Cerza	312-463-1144	D	37*	0.3
White Directory Publishers Inc	1945 Sheridan Dr	Buffalo	NY	14223	Richard D Lewis	716-875-9100	R	37*	0.3
Telecom*USA Publishing Group	PO Box 3162	Cedar Rapids	IA	52401	Art Christoffersen	319-366-1100	R	36*	0.4
Greenwich Workshop Inc	1 Greenwich Pl	Shelton	CT	06484	Peter McEwin	203-925-0131	R	35	0.1
Multi-Local Media Info	100 N Center Av	Rockville Ct	NY	11570	Joseph A Walsh	516-766-1900	R	35	0.5
OneSource Information Services	150 Cambridge Pk	Cambridge	MA	02140	Dan Schimmel	617-441-7000	R	32	0.2
TV Host Inc	3935 Jonestown Rd	Harrisburg	PA	17109	David W Stefanic	717-657-1700	R	30	0.1
Prism Group Inc	15530	Woodinville	WA	98072	KC Aly	206-881-1609	P	27	0.3
Results Media	26 Jericho Tpk	Jericho	NY	11753	Steven R Ferber	516-333-7400	S	27*	0.2
Hadley Cos	11001 Hampshire S	Bloomington	MN	55438	R E Johnson	612-943-8474	R	27	0.2
Geonex Martel Inc	8950 9th St N	St Petersburg	FL	33702	J Gary Reed	813-578-0100	S	25*	0.7
Nazarene Publishing House	PO Box 419527	Kansas City	MO	64141	Robert L Foster	816-931-1900	R	25	0.3
Smith-Edwards-Dunlap Co	2867 Allegheny Av	Philadelphia	PA	19134	Henry K Lobel	215-425-8800	R	25	0.3
Johnson Hill Press Inc	1233 Janesville Av	Fort Atkinson	WI	53538	Richard Moeller	414-563-6388	S	24	0.1
Riverside Publishing Co	8420 W Bryn Mawr	Chicago	IL	60631	John Oswald	312-693-0040	S	22*	0.2
United Communications Group	11300 Rockville Pk	Rockville	MD	20852	Ed Peskowitz	301-816-8950	R	22*	0.2
Warner Press Inc	PO Box 2499	Anderson	IN	46018	Robert G Rist	317-644-7721	R	21	0.3
California Offset Printers Inc	620 W Elk Av	Glendale	CA	91204	JC Hedlund	213-245-6446	R	20	0.1
Carl Fischer Inc	62 Cooper Sq	New York	NY	10003	Walter F Connor	212-777-0900	R	20	0.3
Cobb Group	9420 Bunsen Pkwy	Louisville	KY	40220	Doug Cobb	502-491-1900	D	20	0.2
SRDS Inc	3004 Glenview Rd	Wilmette	IL	60091	James E Meyers	708-256-6067	R	20	0.2
This Week Publications Inc	425 Smith St	Farmingdale	NY	11735	Thomas Rohr	516-753-9009	R	20	0.3
Newsbank Inc	58 Pine St	New Canaan	CT	06840	DS Jones	203-966-1100	R	19*	0.4
American Guidance Service Inc	4201 Woodland Rd	Circle Pines	MN	55014	John G Welshons	612-786-4343	R	18*	0.2
Flashes Publishers Inc	595 Jenner Dr	Allegan	MI	49010	Jack Hendricks	616-673-2141	R	18*	0.1
Sony Tree Music Publishing Inc	8 Music Sq W	Nashville	TN	37212	Donna Hilley	615-726-8300	D	18*	0.2
Flyer Printing Company Inc	201 Kelsey Ln	Tampa	FL	33619	RD Mandt	813-626-9430	R	17	0.2
Optical Data Corp	30 Technology Dr	Warren	NJ	07059	William Clark	908-668-0022	R	16*	0.1
RR Donnelley	1275 Davis Rd	Elgin	IL	60123	John Besch	708-697-8310	D	16*	0.2
DeLorme Publishing Company	PO Box 298	Freeport	ME	04032	David DeLorme	207-865-1234	R	15*	0.1
Geosystems	53 W James St	Lancaster	PA	17603	Barry Glick	717-393-9707	D	15	0.2
KCI Communications Inc	1101 King St	Alexandria	VA	22314	Walter Pearce	703-548-2400	S	15	<0.1
Logistic Services International	6200 Lake Gray	Jacksonville	FL	32244	James McKinney	904-771-2100	R	15	0.3
Rodgers and McDonald Graphics	PO Box 6270	Carson	CA	90749	Doyle McDonald	310-816-0333	R	15	0.1
Economics Press Inc	12 Daniel Rd	Fairfield	NJ	07004	Alan D Yohalem	201-227-1224	R	13	0.2
ADC The Map People	6440 Green	Alexandria	VA	22312	M Turcotte	703-750-0510	D	12	0.1
Centennial Media Corp	5446 N Academy	Co Springs	CO	80918	Earl Mix	719-531-6000	R	12	0.2
Newsfoto Publishing Co	PO Box 1392	San Angelo	TX	76902	Loren Reed	915-949-3776	S	12	0.2
Personal Marketing Co	2 Northpoint Dr	Houston	TX	77060	George R Ditow	713-591-6015	R	12	0.1
TDM Inc	8255 N Central Park	Skokie	IL	60076	Henry J Feinberg	708-329-8100	S	12*	0.1
Wesleyan Church Corp	PO Box 50434	Indianapolis	IN	46250	Lee Haines	317-842-0444	R	12*	0.1
Hammond Inc	515 Valley St	Maplewood	NJ	07040	CD Hammond	201-763-6000	R	11*	<0.1
Cambridge Scientific Abstracts	7200 Wisconsin Av	Bethesda	MD	20814	James P McGinty	301-961-6700	R	10	0.1
ComputerPREP Inc	410 N 44th St	Phoenix	AZ	85008	Michael Holliday	602-275-7700	S	10*	0.1
Law Office Information Systems	PO Box 928	Van Buren	AR	72956	Kyle Parker	501-471-5581	R	10	<0.1
Manufacturers' News Inc	1633 Central St	Evanston	IL	60201	Howard Dubin	708-864-7000	R	10	<0.1

Source: *Ward's Business Directory of U.S. Private and Public Companies*, Volumes 1 and 2, 1996. The company type code used is as follows: P - Public, R - Private, S - Subsidiary, D - Division, J - Joint Venture, A - Affiliate, G - Group. Sales are in millions of dollars, employees are in thousands. An asterisk (*) indicates an estimated sales volume. The symbol < stands for 'less than'. Company names and addresses are truncated, in some cases, to fit into the available space.

MATERIALS CONSUMED

Material	Quantity	Delivered Cost ($ million)
Materials, ingredients, containers, and supplies	(X)	708.6
Newsprint	(X)	43.5
Coated paper	(X)	75.2
Uncoated paper	(X)	103.8
Printing inks (complete formulations)	(X)	4.3
All other materials and components, parts, containers, and supplies	(X)	219.6
Materials, ingredients, containers, and supplies, nsk	(X)	262.2

Source: 1992 *Economic Census*. Explanation of symbols used: (D): Withheld to avoid disclosure of competitive data; na: Not available; (S): Withheld because statistical norms were not met; (X): Not applicable; (Z): Less than half the unit shown; nec: Not elsewhere classified; nsk: Not specified by kind; - : zero; * : 10-19 percent estimated; ** : 20-29 percent estimated.

PRODUCT SHARE DETAILS

Product or Product Class	% Share	Product or Product Class	% Share
Miscellaneous publishing	100.00	Card publishing, other than greeting cards, including picture postcards, souvenir cards, etc.	36.56
Telephone directory publishing	41.56	Sheet music publishing (less than five pages), except music in book or pamphlet form	1.04
Catalog and directory (except telephone directory) publishing	5.30	Calendar publishing	12.94
Directory (except telephone directory) publishing, including business reference services	80.31	Multimedia kit publishing	3.06
Catalog publishing	18.00	Map, hydrographic chart, and globe cover publishing	7.63
Catalogs and directories, except telephone directories, publishing, nsk	1.71	Atlas and gazetteer publishing	3.57
Business service publication publishing	7.76	Micropublishing (publishing in microfilm or microfiche format)	10.49
Business service newsletter publishing, excluding publications which are cumulated in looseleaf index form	45.33	Travel guide publishing, in brochure or pamphlet form	2.69
Other business service publication publishing, looseleaf and hardbound, including tax, credit, regulations, indexes, etc.	49.61	Poster publishing	2.31
Business service publications, publishing, nsk	5.06	Yearbook publishing	3.55
Pattern publishing, including clothing patterns	1.85	Other miscellaneous publication publishing, including almanacs, racing forms, etc.	12.86
Shopping news publishing	8.56	Other miscellaneous publishing, nsk	3.30
Other miscellaneous publishing	19.17	Miscellaneous publishing, nsk	15.79

Source: 1992 *Economic Census*. The values shown are percent of total shipments in an industry. Values of indented subcategories are summed in the main heading. The symbol (D) appears when data are withheld to prevent disclosure of competitive information. The abbreviation nsk stands for 'not specified by kind' and nec for 'not elsewhere classified'.

INPUTS AND OUTPUTS FOR MISCELLANEOUS PUBLISHING

Economic Sector or Industry Providing Inputs	%	Sector	Economic Sector or Industry Buying Outputs	%	Sector
Commercial printing	35.6	Manufg.	Personal consumption expenditures	29.1	
Paper mills, except building paper	11.6	Manufg.	Business/professional associations	15.0	Services
Wholesale trade	7.2	Trade	S/L Govt. purch., elem. & secondary education	5.1	S/L Govt
Miscellaneous plastics products	3.9	Manufg.	Portrait, photographic studios	4.1	Services
Advertising	3.3	Services	Retail trade, except eating & drinking	3.5	Trade
Petroleum refining	3.2	Manufg.	Eating & drinking places	3.3	Trade
Eating & drinking places	2.8	Trade	S/L Govt. purch., other education & libraries	3.2	S/L Govt
Bookbinding & related work	2.6	Manufg.	Federal Government purchases, nondefense	3.0	Fed Govt
Communications, except radio & TV	2.4	Util.	Calculating & accounting machines	2.2	Manufg.
U.S. Postal Service	2.4	Gov't	Wholesale trade	2.2	Trade
Real estate	1.6	Fin/R.E.	Lithographic platemaking & services	1.5	Manufg.
Banking	1.2	Fin/R.E.	S/L Govt. purch., higher education	1.3	S/L Govt
Mechanical measuring devices	1.1	Manufg.	Child day care services	0.9	Services
Air transportation	1.1	Util.	Colleges, universities, & professional schools	0.8	Services
Electric services (utilities)	1.1	Util.	Funeral service & crematories	0.8	Services
Equipment rental & leasing services	1.1	Services	Libraries, vocation education	0.8	Services
Hotels & lodging places	1.1	Services	S/L Govt. purch., other general government	0.8	S/L Govt
Motor freight transportation & warehousing	1.0	Util.	Blankbooks & looseleaf binders	0.7	Manufg.
Legal services	1.0	Services	Elementary & secondary schools	0.7	Services
Management & consulting services & labs	1.0	Services	Hotels & lodging places	0.7	Services
Chemical preparations, nec	0.8	Manufg.	Insurance carriers	0.6	Fin/R.E.
Envelopes	0.8	Manufg.	Engineering, architectural, & surveying services	0.6	Services
Imports	0.8	Foreign	S/L Govt. purch., natural resource & recreation.	0.6	S/L Govt
Automotive rental & leasing, without drivers	0.7	Services	Communications, except radio & TV	0.5	Util.
Lithographic platemaking & services	0.6	Manufg.	Motor freight transportation & warehousing	0.5	Util.
Printing trades machinery	0.6	Manufg.	Banking	0.5	Fin/R.E.
Accounting, auditing & bookkeeping	0.6	Services	Federal Government purchases, national defense	0.5	Fed Govt
Manifold business forms	0.5	Manufg.	Real estate	0.4	Fin/R.E.
Paperboard containers & boxes	0.5	Manufg.	Labor, civic, social, & fraternal associations	0.4	Services
Automotive repair shops & services	0.5	Services	Management & consulting services & labs	0.4	Services
Adhesives & sealants	0.4	Manufg.	Residential 1-unit structures, nonfarm	0.3	Constr.
Broadwoven fabric mills	0.4	Manufg.	Electronic computing equipment	0.3	Manufg.
Gas production & distribution (utilities)	0.4	Util.	Credit agencies other than banks	0.3	Fin/R.E.

Continued on next page.

INPUTS AND OUTPUTS FOR MISCELLANEOUS PUBLISHING - Continued

Economic Sector or Industry Providing Inputs	%	Sector	Economic Sector or Industry Buying Outputs	%	Sector
Maintenance of nonfarm buildings nec	0.3	Constr.	Business services nec	0.3	Services
Book printing	0.3	Manufg.	Computer & data processing services	0.3	Services
Miscellaneous publishing	0.3	Manufg.	Hospitals	0.3	Services
Photographic equipment & supplies	0.3	Manufg.	Laundry, dry cleaning, shoe repair	0.3	Services
Printing ink	0.3	Manufg.	S/L Govt. purch., health & hospitals	0.3	S/L Govt
Railroads & related services	0.3	Util.	Crude petroleum & natural gas	0.2	Mining
Transit & bus transportation	0.3	Util.	Office buildings	0.2	Constr.
Credit agencies other than banks	0.3	Fin/R.E.	Apparel made from purchased materials	0.2	Manufg.
Insurance carriers	0.3	Fin/R.E.	Commercial printing	0.2	Manufg.
Computer & data processing services	0.3	Services	Miscellaneous plastics products	0.2	Manufg.
Personnel supply services	0.3	Services	Miscellaneous publishing	0.2	Manufg.
Engraving & plate printing	0.2	Manufg.	Electric services (utilities)	0.2	Util.
Machinery, except electrical, nec	0.2	Manufg.	Railroads & related services	0.2	Util.
Royalties	0.2	Fin/R.E.	Insurance agents, brokers, & services	0.2	Fin/R.E.
Business services nec	0.2	Services	Security & commodity brokers	0.2	Fin/R.E.
Business/professional associations	0.2	Services	Advertising	0.2	Services
Lubricating oils & greases	0.1	Manufg.	Amusement & recreation services nec	0.2	Services
Motor vehicle parts & accessories	0.1	Manufg.	Automotive repair shops & services	0.2	Services
Tires & inner tubes	0.1	Manufg.	Doctors & dentists	0.2	Services
Retail trade, except eating & drinking	0.1	Trade	Social services, nec	0.2	Services
Security & commodity brokers	0.1	Fin/R.E.	S/L Govt. purch., police	0.2	S/L Govt
			S/L Govt. purch., public assistance & relief	0.2	S/L Govt
			Industrial buildings	0.1	Constr.
			Maintenance of nonfarm buildings nec	0.1	Constr.
			Cold finishing of steel shapes	0.1	Manufg.
			Guided missiles & space vehicles	0.1	Manufg.
			Manufacturing industries, nec	0.1	Manufg.
			Newspapers	0.1	Manufg.
			Radio & TV communication equipment	0.1	Manufg.
			Air transportation	0.1	Util.
			Radio & TV broadcasting	0.1	Util.
			Accounting, auditing & bookkeeping	0.1	Services
			Medical & health services, nec	0.1	Services
			Membership organizations nec	0.1	Services
			Membership sports & recreation clubs	0.1	Services
			Motion pictures	0.1	Services
			Nursing & personal care facilities	0.1	Services
			Religious organizations	0.1	Services
			Services to dwellings & other buildings	0.1	Services
			State & local government enterprises, nec	0.1	Gov't
			U.S. Postal Service	0.1	Gov't
			S/L Govt. purch., correction	0.1	S/L Govt

Source: Benchmark Input-Output Accounts for the U.S. Economy, 1982, U.S. Department of Commerce, Washington, D.C., July 1991. Data, as reported in the source, are organized by the 1977 SIC structure in use in 1982 but have been matched, as closely as is possible, to the 1987 SIC structure used in this book.

OCCUPATIONS EMPLOYED BY SIC 274 - MISCELLANEOUS PUBLISHING

Occupation	% of Total 1994	Change to 2005	Occupation	% of Total 1994	Change to 2005
Sales & related workers nec	16.1	8.0	Paste-up workers	1.6	-29.8
Writers & editors, incl technical writers	5.8	8.0	Printing press machine setters, operators	1.4	-13.5
General office clerks	4.6	-7.9	Truck drivers light & heavy	1.4	11.4
General managers & top executives	4.5	2.5	Typists & word processors	1.4	-46.0
Artists & commercial artists	3.3	9.7	Adjustment clerks	1.3	29.7
Driver/sales workers	2.7	29.6	Data entry keyers, composing	1.2	-73.1
Marketing, advertising, & PR managers	2.7	8.0	Offset lithographic press operators	1.2	8.0
Clerical supervisors & managers	2.6	10.5	Blue collar worker supervisors	1.2	2.8
Secretaries, ex legal & medical	2.4	-1.6	Order clerks, materials, merchandise, & service	1.2	5.7
Bookkeeping, accounting, & auditing clerks	2.2	-19.0	Production, planning, & expediting clerks	1.2	7.9
Proofreaders & copy markers	2.0	-29.8	Professional workers nec	1.2	29.5
Data entry keyers, ex composing	2.0	-20.3	Systems analysts	1.1	72.9
Marketing & sales worker supervisors	2.0	8.0	Bindery machine operators & set-up operators	1.0	8.0
Hand packers & packagers	1.8	-7.4	Managers & administrators nec	1.0	8.0
Receptionists & information clerks	1.7	8.0	Electronic pagination systems workers	1.0	72.8
Advertising clerks	1.7	18.8			

Source: Industry-Occupation Matrix, Bureau of Labor Statistics. These data relate to one or more 3-digit SIC industry groups rather than to a single 4-digit SIC. The change reported for each occupation to the year 2005 is a percent of growth or decline as estimated by the Bureau of Labor Statistics. The abbreviation nec stands for 'not elsewhere classified'.

LOCATION BY STATE AND REGIONAL CONCENTRATION

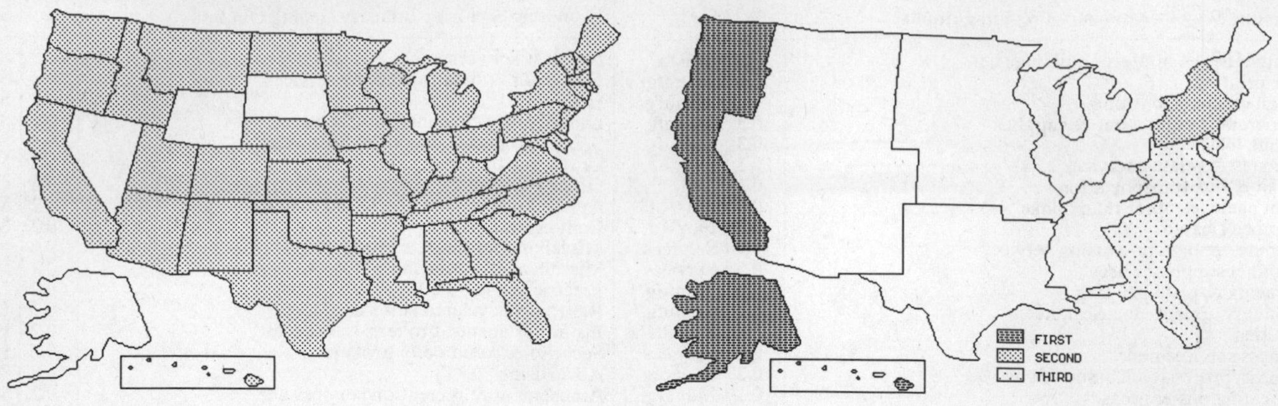

INDUSTRY DATA BY STATE

State	Establish-ments	Shipments			Employment				Cost as % of Shipments	Investment per Employee ($)
		Total ($ mil)	% of U.S.	Per Establ.	Total Number	% of U.S.	Per Establ.	Wages ($/hour)		
California	473	1,965.2	17.9	4.2	8,500	13.0	18	10.75	18.1	4,424
New York	382	1,127.7	10.3	3.0	9,000	13.8	24	13.40	26.3	1,678
Michigan	100	1,112.8	10.1	11.1	3,100	4.7	31	12.38	10.9	3,355
Massachusetts	96	1,018.1	9.3	10.6	2,500	3.8	26	11.10	24.4	-
Pennsylvania	116	779.7	7.1	6.7	3,900	6.0	34	8.91	24.3	2,513
Illinois	136	741.5	6.8	5.5	3,500	5.4	26	16.38	47.5	1,514
Colorado	79	533.4	4.9	6.8	3,400	5.2	43	11.91	17.4	6,059
Kansas	43	443.3	4.0	10.3	2,000	3.1	47	9.91	12.9	2,050
Texas	196	307.5	2.8	1.6	2,400	3.7	12	9.85	26.0	1,208
New Jersey	118	255.5	2.3	2.2	2,500	3.8	21	14.33	21.5	1,480
Florida	199	225.6	2.1	1.1	2,900	4.4	15	9.00	24.2	1,517
Maryland	77	215.3	2.0	2.8	1,700	2.6	22	10.00	19.4	1,824
Washington	88	186.0	1.7	2.1	1,000	1.5	11	10.71	23.0	1,400
Minnesota	75	167.8	1.5	2.2	1,000	1.5	13	10.75	23.2	-
Ohio	103	163.3	1.5	1.6	1,800	2.8	17	8.67	22.0	-
Utah	20	147.3	1.3	7.4	1,600	2.4	80	7.11	36.3	-
Tennessee	106	143.8	1.3	1.4	1,300	2.0	12	9.33	39.8	1,462
Oregon	51	127.9	1.2	2.5	700	1.1	14	13.80	14.5	2,714
Kentucky	33	122.6	1.1	3.7	800	1.2	24	9.14	10.8	750
Connecticut	60	112.6	1.0	1.9	1,100	1.7	18	10.87	24.7	1,545
Virginia	86	109.1	1.0	1.3	1,000	1.5	12	9.29	22.0	1,300
Wisconsin	92	73.8	0.7	0.8	1,600	2.4	17	8.75	28.6	875
Iowa	51	73.2	0.7	1.4	1,000	1.5	20	7.50	21.2	600
Indiana	44	54.8	0.5	1.2	600	0.9	14	10.25	23.7	-
Hawaii	12	41.7	0.4	3.5	200	0.3	17	11.00	28.8	3,000
D.C.	26	33.4	0.3	1.3	300	0.5	12	12.00	17.1	2,000
Oklahoma	26	33.1	0.3	1.3	300	0.5	12	5.00	27.2	667
Alabama	25	30.3	0.3	1.2	400	0.6	16	7.80	27.1	2,250
Maine	19	18.7	0.2	1.0	200	0.3	11	10.00	13.4	2,000
South Carolina	33	18.1	0.2	0.5	200	0.3	6	17.00	25.4	1,000
Louisiana	31	15.5	0.1	0.5	200	0.3	6	9.00	25.8	-
New Hampshire	23	14.9	0.1	0.6	200	0.3	9	10.00	27.5	1,500
Idaho	20	14.1	0.1	0.7	200	0.3	10	8.00	19.1	1,500
Vermont	16	10.3	0.1	0.6	300	0.5	19	7.75	18.4	-
Montana	13	7.7	0.1	0.6	100	0.2	8	4.00	20.8	-
New Mexico	14	4.1	0.0	0.3	100	0.2	7	4.00	24.4	-
Georgia	65	(D)	-	-	375 *	0.6	6	-	-	-
North Carolina	47	(D)	-	-	750 *	1.1	16	-	-	-
Missouri	46	(D)	-	-	750 *	1.1	16	-	-	-
Arizona	41	(D)	-	-	750 *	1.1	18	-	-	-
Arkansas	18	(D)	-	-	175 *	0.3	10	-	-	-
Nebraska	13	(D)	-	-	375 *	0.6	29	-	-	-
North Dakota	5	(D)	-	-	175 *	0.3	35	-	-	-

Source: 1992 *Economic Census*. The states are in descending order of shipments or establishments (if shipment data are missing for the majority). The symbol (D) appears when data are withheld to prevent disclosure of competitive information. States marked with (D) are sorted by number of establishments. A dash (-) indicates that the data element cannot be calculated; * indicates the midpoint of a range.

2752 - COMMERCIAL PRINTING, LITHOGRAPHIC

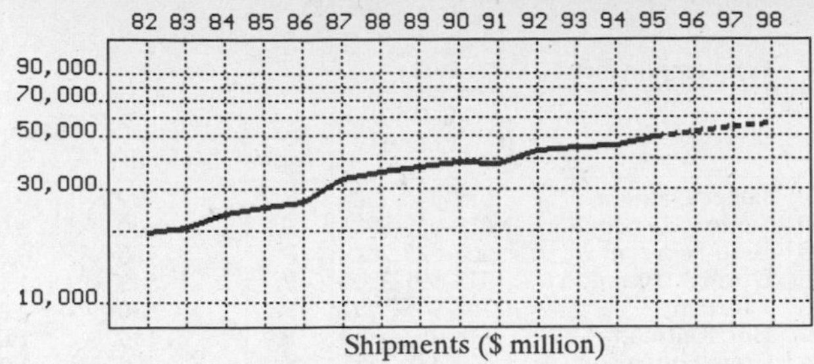

Shipments ($ million)

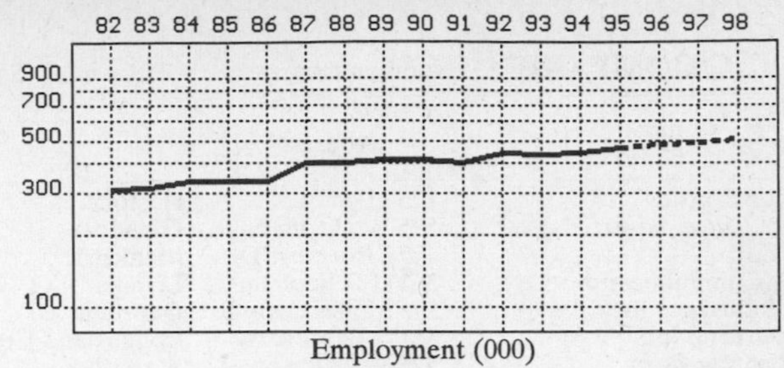

Employment (000)

GENERAL STATISTICS

Year	Companies	Establishments		Employment			Compensation		Production ($ million)			
		Total	with 20 or more employees	Total (000)	Production Workers (000)	Production Hours (Mil)	Payroll ($ mil)	Wages ($/hr)	Cost of Materials	Value Added by Manufacture	Value of Shipments	Capital Invest.
1982	17,332	17,842	3,184	311.9	234.1	434.0	5,746.4	9.06	8,406.4	11,045.1	19,441.6	958.1
1983		17,879	3,299	315.1	236.9	440.1	6,052.1	9.39	9,025.3	11,741.8	20,754.0	962.7
1984		17,916	3,414	334.9	249.0	473.8	6,841.5	9.60	10,485.0	13,271.2	23,646.2	1,279.7
1985		17,952	3,529	335.4	248.2	472.7	7,097.5	10.04	11,079.8	13,949.0	25,024.8	1,410.7
1986		18,031	3,585	337.0	247.9	487.5	7,513.3	10.05	11,598.9	14,819.2	26,371.1	1,335.9
1987	24,328	24,980	4,099	403.0	292.9	580.5	9,132.1	10.14	14,581.7	18,162.1	32,698.2	1,537.3
1988		23,460	4,197	405.2	293.2	586.7	9,524.3	10.36	15,758.3	18,997.0	34,727.0	1,435.4
1989		22,623	4,207	414.7	306.3	615.5	10,149.0	10.57	16,727.9	20,416.1	37,128.0	1,627.6
1990		22,535	4,170	410.1	307.3	631.0	10,606.7	10.72	17,623.2	21,230.3	38,877.4	1,662.4
1991		23,622	4,025	400.1	290.8	594.8	10,386.6	11.04	16,788.0	20,952.4	37,718.9	1,370.0
1992	28,489	29,344	4,251	439.9	317.4	653.0	12,047.5	11.76	18,723.1	24,842.5	43,588.2	1,629.4
1993		27,996	4,265	437.6	319.1	654.7	12,298.9	11.94	19,304.5	25,406.9	44,704.2	1,682.2
1994		28,606P	4,532P	439.8	319.3	664.8	12,618.2	11.94	19,432.4	26,473.9	45,846.8	1,958.8
1995		29,620P	4,636P	466.2P	337.7P	709.3P	13,476.5P	12.18P	20,973.1P	28,572.9P	49,481.8P	1,897.0P
1996		30,634P	4,741P	478.0P	345.7P	730.5P	14,082.8P	12.42P	21,964.0P	29,922.9P	51,819.6P	1,960.9P
1997		31,648P	4,845P	489.9P	353.7P	751.7P	14,689.2P	12.66P	22,954.9P	31,272.8P	54,157.4P	2,024.7P
1998		32,662P	4,950P	501.7P	361.7P	772.9P	15,295.6P	12.90P	23,945.8P	32,622.7P	56,495.2P	2,088.6P

Sources: 1982, 1987, 1992 *Economic Census*; *Annual Survey of Manufactures*, 83-86, 88-91, 93-94. Establishment counts for non-Census years are from *County Business Patterns*; establishment values for 83-84 are extrapolations. 'P's show projections by the editors. Industries reclassified in 87 will not have data for prior years.

INDICES OF CHANGE

Year	Companies	Establishments		Employment			Compensation		Production ($ million)			
		Total	with 20 or more employees	Total (000)	Production Workers (000)	Production Hours (Mil)	Payroll ($ mil)	Wages ($/hr)	Cost of Materials	Value Added by Manufacture	Value of Shipments	Capital Invest.
1982	61	61	75	71	74	66	48	77	45	44	45	59
1983		61	78	72	75	67	50	80	48	47	48	59
1984		61	80	76	78	73	57	82	56	53	54	79
1985		61	83	76	78	72	59	85	59	56	57	87
1986		61	84	77	78	75	62	85	62	60	61	82
1987	85	85	96	92	92	89	76	86	78	73	75	94
1988		80	99	92	92	90	79	88	84	76	80	88
1989		77	99	94	97	94	84	90	89	82	85	100
1990		77	98	93	97	97	88	91	94	85	89	102
1991		81	95	91	92	91	86	94	90	84	87	84
1992	100	100	100	100	100	100	100	100	100	100	100	100
1993		95	100	99	101	100	102	102	103	102	103	103
1994		97P	107P	100	101	102	105	102	104	107	105	120
1995		101P	109P	106P	106P	109P	112P	104P	112P	115P	114P	116P
1996		104P	112P	109P	109P	112P	117P	106P	117P	120P	119P	120P
1997		108P	114P	111P	111P	115P	122P	108P	123P	126P	124P	124P
1998		111P	116P	114P	114P	118P	127P	110P	128P	131P	130P	128P

Sources: Same as General Statistics. Values reflect change from the base year, 1992. Values above 100 mean greater than 92, values below 100 mean less than 92, and a value of 100 in the 82-91 or 93-98 period means same as 92. 'P's mark projections by the editors.

SELECTED RATIOS

For 1994	Avg. of All Manufact.	Analyzed Industry	Index
Employees per Establishment	49	15	31
Payroll per Establishment	1,500,273	441,107	29
Payroll per Employee	30,620	28,691	94
Production Workers per Establishment	34	11	33
Wages per Establishment	853,319	277,487	33
Wages per Production Worker	24,861	24,860	100
Hours per Production Worker	2,056	2,082	101
Wages per Hour	12.09	11.94	99
Value Added per Establishment	4,602,255	925,476	20
Value Added per Employee	93,930	60,195	64

For 1994	Avg. of All Manufact.	Analyzed Industry	Index
Value Added per Production Worker	134,084	82,912	62
Cost per Establishment	5,045,178	679,319	13
Cost per Employee	102,970	44,185	43
Cost per Production Worker	146,988	60,859	41
Shipments per Establishment	9,576,895	1,602,714	17
Shipments per Employee	195,460	104,245	53
Shipments per Production Worker	279,017	143,585	51
Investment per Establishment	321,011	68,476	21
Investment per Employee	6,552	4,454	68
Investment per Production Worker	9,352	6,135	66

Sources: Same as General Statistics. The 'Average of All Manufacturing' column represents the average of all manufacturing industries reported for the most recent complete year available. The Index shows the relationship between the Average and the Analyzed Industry. For example, 100 means that they are equal; 500 that the Analyzed Industry is five times the average; 50 means that the Analyzed Industry is half the national average. The abbreviation 'na' is used to show that data are 'not available'.

LEADING COMPANIES Number shown: 75 Total sales ($ mil): 7,741 Total employment (000): 56.2

Company Name	Address				CEO Name	Phone	Co. Type	Sales ($ mil)	Empl. (000)
Quebecor Printing	125 High St	Boston	MA	02110	James Dawson	617-346-7300	S	999	10.0
Treasure Chest Advertising	511 W Citrus Edge	Glendora	CA	91740	Sanford G Scheller	818-914-3981	R	800	3.0
Taylor Corp	1725 Roecrest Dr	Mankato	MN	56003	Brad Schreier	507-625-2828	R	760•	6.5
Valassis Communications Co	36111 Schoolcraft	Livonia	MI	48150	David A Brandon	313-591-3000	P	543	1.1
Jordan Industries Inc	1751 Lake Cook Rd	Deerfield	IL	60015	J Jordan	708-945-5591	R	330•	2.8
Queens Group Inc	52-35 Barnett Av	Long Island Ct	NY	11104	Eric Kaltman	718-457-7700	R	156	1.0
Perry Printing Corp	575 W Madison St	Waterloo	WI	53594	Craig Hutchison	414-478-3551	S	150	1.2
Moore Data Management	100 Washington S	Minneapolis	MN	55401	Tom Gregorich	612-661-1000	D	125	0.8
Fleming Packaging Corp	1028 SW Adams St	Peoria	IL	61602	William J Mannlein	309-676-2121	R	107	0.8
Continental Graphics Corp	101 S La Brea Av	Los Angeles	CA	90036	Harold Weaver	213-938-2511	D	106	1.5
Judd's Inc	1500 Eckington NE	Washington	DC	20002	John J Broderick	202-635-1200	R	105	1.0
Ivy Hill Corp	375 Hudson St	New York	NY	10014	Ellis Kern	212-741-1404	S	100	1.0
Meehan-Tooker Inc	55 Madison Cir Dr	E Rutherford	NJ	07073	Michael Voss	201-933-9600	R	100	0.6
RR Donnelley Printing LP	5701 SW Park Av	Des Moines	IA	50321	Carl W Zielke	515-283-3900	D	100	0.9
Anderson Lithograph Co	3217 S Garfield Av	Los Angeles	CA	90040	John Fosmire	213-727-7767	R	97	0.4
Arandell-Schmidt Corp	PO Box 405	Menomonee Fls	WI	53051	Don Treis	414-255-4400	R	97•	0.5
Shea Communications Co	2849 Paces Ferry Rd	Atlanta	GA	30339	Michael D Shea	404-431-9077	R	88•	0.5
Dittler Brothers Inc	1375 Seaboard	Atlanta	GA	30318	James J Breen	404-355-3423	S	85	0.6
Sandy-Alexander Inc	200 Entin Rd	Clifton	NJ	07014	Frank Stillo	201-470-8100	S	85	0.4
Brookshore Lithographers Inc	2075 Busse Rd	Elk Grove Vill	IL	60007	James M Cartwright	708-593-1200	S	80•	0.2
Custom Printing Co	1005 Commercial	Owensville	MO	65066	Donald H Lenauer	314-437-4161	R	80	0.6
K/P Corp	2550 Shattuck Av	Berkeley	CA	94704	Kim Wright	510-843-8433	R	80	0.6
Bureau of Engraving Inc	500 S 4th St	Minneapolis	MN	55415	Tom Stuart	612-339-8721	R	78	0.8
McGill-Jensen Inc	655 N Fairview Av	St Paul	MN	55104	James Fogg	612-645-0751	S	76	0.4
MacNaughton Lithography Corp	20-10 Maple Av	Fair Lawn	NJ	07410	Robert C Quain	201-423-1900	R	70	0.3
Segerdahl Corp	1351 S Wheeling Rd	Wheeling	IL	60090	EE Segerdahl	708-541-1080	R	70	0.2
Trend Offset Printing Services	3791 Catalina St	Los Alamitos	CA	90720	Bob Lienau	714-826-2360	R	70	0.4
Continental Web Press Inc	1430 Industrial Dr	Itasca	IL	60143	Kenneth W Field	708-773-1903	R	68	0.4
Graphic Techn Inc	301 Gardner Dr	Indust Apt	KS	66031	Jay Frankenberg	913-764-5550	S	65	0.5
Fort Dearborn Lithograph Co	6035 W Gross Pt Rd	Niles	IL	60714	Thomas Adler	312-774-4321	R	60	0.3
Garber Co	600 Union St	Ashland	OH	44805	JT McMillen	419-289-2666	R	60	0.4
Shepard Poorman	PO Box 68110	Indianapolis	IN	46268	R W Poorman Jr	317-293-1500	R	60	0.5
Print Northwest Company LP	PO Box 1418	Tacoma	WA	98401	Kurt Dammeier	206-922-9393	R	58•	0.5
Consolidated Graphics Inc	2210 W Dallas St	Houston	TX	77019	Joe R Davis	713-529-4200	P	57	0.7
Hennegan Co	1001 Plum St	Cincinnati	OH	45202	RB Ott Jr	513-621-7300	R	57•	0.4
Webcrafters Inc	PO Box 7608	Madison	WI	53707	JJ Frautschi	608-244-3561	R	54	0.6
Pendell Printing Inc	1700 James Savage	Midland	MI	48640	David G Pendell	517-496-3333	S	53•	0.5
Ridgways Inc	5711 Hillcroft Av	Houston	TX	77036	Y Rogers Jr	713-782-8580	S	53	1.0
Colwell Systems	201 Kenyon Rd	Champaign	IL	61820	Tom Bidon	217-351-5400	D	52•	0.6
HM Smyth Co	PO Box 64669	St Paul	MN	55164	Paul Trowbridge	612-646-4544	R	52	0.4
Nielsen Lithographing Co	PO Box 9701	Cincinnati	OH	45209	SC Nielsen	513-321-5200	R	52	0.4
Impulse Designs Inc	PO Box 7454	Van Nuys	CA	90409	Alan Wiener	818-989-7600	R	50•	0.4
Moebius Printing Company Inc	PO Box 302	Milwaukee	WI	53201	Peter Thermensen	414-276-5311	R	50	0.4
Noll Printing Company Inc	100 Noll Plz	Huntington	IN	46750	William E Newell	219-356-2020	S	50	0.4
Colotone Riverside Press Inc	4901 Woodall	Dallas	TX	75247	Robert Rosen	214-631-1150	R	48	0.4
Color Associates Inc	10818 Midwest	St Louis	MO	63132	Charles Bauer	314-423-9300	R	47•	0.4
Japs-Olson Co	30 N 31st Av	Minneapolis	MN	55411	Robert E Murphy	612-522-4461	R	47	0.4
Henry Wurst Inc	1331 Saline	N Kansas City	MO	64116	Mike Wurst	816-842-3113	R	46	0.3
Fleming-Potter Co	1028 SW Adams St	Peoria	IL	61602	William J Mannlein	309-676-2121	S	46	0.4
JII/Sales Promotion Associates	545 Walnut St	Coshocton	OH	43812	James D Jung	614-622-4422	S	45	0.7
Panel Prints Inc	1001 Moosic Rd	Old Forge	PA	18518	Bill Abene	717-457-8334	S	45	0.5
Lithographix Inc	13500 S Figueroa St	Los Angeles	CA	90061	Herb Zebrack	213-770-1000	R	44	0.2
Balmar Printing and Graphics	5130 Wilson Blv	Arlington	VA	22205	James A O'Hare	703-528-9000	R	43	0.5
Penn Lithographic Inc	16221 Arthur St	Cerritos	CA	90703	Robert Howington	310-926-0455	S	43	0.2
Berlin Industries Inc	175 Mercedes Dr	Carol Stream	IL	60188	F Eugene Schmitt	708-682-0600	R	41	0.4
Amsterdam Printing & Litho	55 Wallins Corners	Amsterdam	NY	12010	Robert B Singer	518-842-6000	R	40	0.5
Concord Litho Company Inc	PO Box 2888	Concord	NH	03301	James D Cook	603-225-3328	R	40	0.3
Courier Westford Inc	1 Pleasant St	Westford	MA	01886	Tony Caruso	508-692-6321	S	40	0.4
Dixonweb Printing Co	1226 W 7th St	Dixon	IL	61021	Larry L Dussair	815-284-2211	R	40	0.3
Intelligencer Printing	330 Eden Rd	Lancaster	PA	17601	William L Beckwith	717-291-3100	R	40	0.3
IPD Printing and Distributing	5800 Peachtree Rd	Chamblee	GA	30341	Tom E Jack	404-458-6351	S	40•	0.3
Kukla Press Inc	855 Morse Av	Elk Grove Vill	IL	60007	SJ Kukla Jr	708-593-1090	R	40	0.1
Neenah Printing	PO Box 506	Neenah	WI	54957	Jim Luenenburg	414-751-1700	D	40	0.3
Spear Inc	5510 Courseview Dr	Mason	OH	45040	Rick Spear	513-459-1100	R	40	0.2
Champion Industries Inc	PO Box 2968	Huntington	WV	25728	MT Reynolds	304-528-2791	P	38	0.4
Chapman Printing Company Inc	PO Box 2968	Huntington	WV	25728	MT Reynolds	304-528-2791	S	38	0.2
Lane Press Inc	PO Box 130	Burlington	VT	05402	Phillip Drumheller	802-863-5555	R	38•	0.3
Wessel Company Inc	1201 Kirk St	Elk Grove Vill	IL	60007	Clay Jacobs	708-480-1720	R	38	0.1
Science Press	300 W Chestnut St	Ephrata	PA	17522	P Knox	717-738-9300	D	37	0.4
St Louis Lithographing	6880 Heege Rd	St Louis	MO	63123	Ben Kraft	314-352-1300	S	36	0.3
E and D Web Inc	4633 W 16th St	Cicero	IL	60650	B Love	708-656-6600	R	35	0.2
Nosco Inc	651 S Utica St	Waukegan	IL	60085	Warren F Hall	708-336-4200	R	35	0.3
Printing House Inc	PO Box 310	Quincy	FL	32351	Delbert Archibald	904-875-1500	R	35•	0.4
Bawden Printing Inc	400 S 14th Av	Eldridge	IA	52748	Mark Bawden	319-285-4800	R	34	0.3
Wintor Swan Associates Inc	1614 Clay Av	Detroit	MI	48211	Lyle Whitton	313-874-0015	R	34	0.4

Source: *Ward's Business Directory of U.S. Private and Public Companies*, Volumes 1 and 2, 1996. The company type code used is as follows: P - Public, R - Private, S - Subsidiary, D - Division, J - Joint Venture, A - Affiliate, G - Group. Sales are in millions of dollars, employees are in thousands. An asterisk (•) indicates an estimated sales volume. The symbol < stands for 'less than'. Company names and addresses are truncated, in some cases, to fit into the available space.

MATERIALS CONSUMED

Material	Quantity	Delivered Cost ($ million)
Materials, ingredients, containers, and supplies	(X)	15,389.0
Newsprint	(X)	931.8
Uncoated paper in sheets	(X)	1,064.7
Uncoated paper in rolls	(X)	1,611.6
Coated paper in sheets	(X)	1,347.4
Coated paper in rolls	(X)	2,016.4
Pressure-sensitive base stock, self-adhesive, including paper, film, foil, etc.	(X)	110.4
Cloth and nonwoven fabrics for hardbound book covers	(X)	3.0
Glues and adhesives	(X)	42.9
Printing inks (complete formulations)	(X)	805.2
Light sensitive films and papers	(X)	206.8
Unexposed photosensitive printing plates	(X)	131.1
Printing plates, prepared for printing	(X)	145.0
Engraved printing cylinders for gravure printing	(X)	3.3
Paperboard containers, boxes, and corrugated paperboard	(X)	126.6
All other materials and components, parts, containers, and supplies	(X)	1,310.6
Materials, ingredients, containers, and supplies, nsk	(X)	5,532.4

Source: 1992 *Economic Census*. Explanation of symbols used: (D): Withheld to avoid disclosure of competitive data; na: Not available; (S): Withheld because statistical norms were not met; (X): Not applicable; (Z): Less than half the unit shown; nec: Not elsewhere classified; nsk: Not specified by kind; - : zero; * : 10-19 percent estimated; ** : 20-29 percent estimated.

PRODUCT SHARE DETAILS

Product or Product Class	% Share
Commercial printing, lithographic (offset)	100.00
Magazine and periodical printing, lithographic (offset)	10.99
Magazine and periodical printing (excluding Sunday magazine and comic supplements), (lithographic), sheet-fed	14.88
Magazine and periodical printing (excluding Sunday magazine and comic supplements), (lithographic), web-fed	69.81
Magazine and comic supplement printing (lithographic), for Sunday newspapers	4.26
Magazine and periodical printing (lithographic), nsk	11.05
Label and wrapper printing (lithographic)	3.79
Catalog and directory printing (lithographic)	9.29
Catalog printing (lithographic), including direct mail catalogs, sheet-fed	17.56
Catalog printing (lithographic), including direct mail catalogs, web-fed	47.00
Telephone directory printing (lithographic)	21.46
Financial and legal printing (lithographic), excluding checkbooks	4.21
SEC filing and prospectus printing (lithographic), sheet-fed	5.39
SEC filing and prospectus printing (lithographic), web-fed	14.25
Annual report and other corporate financial printing (lithographic), sheet-fed	18.24
Annual report and other corporate financial printing (lithographic), web-fed	9.19
Bank printing (lithographic), excluding bank forms and checkbooks, web-fed	13.01
Financial and legal printing (lithographic), excluding checkbooks, nsk	16.34
Advertising printing (lithographic)	31.16
Direct mail advertising printing (lithographic), including circulars, letters, pamphlets, cards, etc., sheet-fed	12.55
Direct mail advertising printing (lithographic), including circulars, letters, pamphlets, cards, etc., web-fed	14.19
Preprinted newspaper advertising insert printing (lithographic) (advertising supplements not regularly issued), sections (two pages or more)	11.56
Other advertising printing (lithographic), including brochures, magazine inserts, etc., sheet-fed	20.40
Other advertising printing (lithographic), including brochures, magazine inserts, etc., web-fed	14.47
Advertising printing (lithographic), nsk	15.94
Other general job printing (lithographic)	21.50
Commercial printing, lithographic (offset), nsk	19.05

Source: 1992 *Economic Census*. The values shown are percent of total shipments in an industry. Values of indented subcategories are summed in the main heading. The symbol (D) appears when data are withheld to prevent disclosure of competitive information. The abbreviation nsk stands for 'not specified by kind' and nec for 'not elsewhere classified'.

INPUTS AND OUTPUTS FOR COMMERCIAL PRINTING

Economic Sector or Industry Providing Inputs	%	Sector	Economic Sector or Industry Buying Outputs	%	Sector
Paper mills, except building paper	34.8	Manufg.	Wholesale trade	9.2	Trade
Wholesale trade	7.9	Trade	Periodicals	7.4	Manufg.
Printing ink	5.9	Manufg.	Membership organizations nec	7.2	Services
Miscellaneous plastics products	4.4	Manufg.	Business/professional associations	6.1	Services
Lithographic platemaking & services	3.5	Manufg.	Labor, civic, social, & fraternal associations	4.9	Services
Typesetting	3.3	Manufg.	Insurance carriers	3.6	Fin/R.E.
Cyclic crudes and organics	2.8	Manufg.	Advertising	3.1	Services
Petroleum refining	2.5	Manufg.	Real estate	3.0	Fin/R.E.
Paper coating & glazing	2.4	Manufg.	Hospitals	2.8	Services
Motor freight transportation & warehousing	2.4	Util.	Computer & data processing services	2.6	Services
Electric services (utilities)	2.2	Util.	Miscellaneous publishing	2.4	Manufg.
Eating & drinking places	2.0	Trade	Newspapers	1.9	Manufg.
Photographic equipment & supplies	1.5	Manufg.	Sausages & other prepared meats	1.9	Manufg.
Real estate	1.2	Fin/R.E.	Exports	1.8	Foreign
U.S. Postal Service	1.2	Gov't	Social services, nec	1.6	Services
Railroads & related services	1.1	Util.	Security & commodity brokers	1.5	Fin/R.E.
Advertising	1.0	Services	Business services nec	1.5	Services
Imports	1.0	Foreign	S/L Govt. purch., higher education	1.5	S/L Govt

Continued on next page.

INPUTS AND OUTPUTS FOR COMMERCIAL PRINTING - Continued

Economic Sector or Industry Providing Inputs	%	Sector	Economic Sector or Industry Buying Outputs	%	Sector
Printing trades machinery	0.9	Manufg.	Cigarettes	1.4	Manufg.
Banking	0.9	Fin/R.E.	Banking	1.4	Fin/R.E.
Chemical preparations, nec	0.8	Manufg.	Personal consumption expenditures	1.3	
Mechanical measuring devices	0.8	Manufg.	Metal cans	1.3	Manufg.
Air transportation	0.8	Util.	Federal Government purchases, national defense	1.1	Fed Govt
Equipment rental & leasing services	0.8	Services	S/L Govt. purch., health & hospitals	1.1	S/L Govt
Hotels & lodging places	0.8	Services	Cheese, natural & processed	1.0	Manufg.
Metal foil & leaf	0.7	Manufg.	Food preparations, nec	0.9	Manufg.
Communications, except radio & TV	0.7	Util.	Credit agencies other than banks	0.9	Fin/R.E.
Gas production & distribution (utilities)	0.7	Util.	Federal Government purchases, nondefense	0.9	Fed Govt
Legal services	0.7	Services	Agricultural chemicals, nec	0.8	Manufg.
Management & consulting services & labs	0.7	Services	Malt beverages	0.8	Manufg.
Paperboard mills	0.6	Manufg.	Communications, except radio & TV	0.8	Util.
Photoengraving, electrotyping & stereotyping	0.6	Manufg.	S/L Govt. purch., elem. & secondary education	0.8	S/L Govt
Envelopes	0.5	Manufg.	S/L Govt. purch., natural resource & recreation.	0.8	S/L Govt
Automotive rental & leasing, without drivers	0.5	Services	Pickles, sauces, & salad dressings	0.7	Manufg.
Maintenance of nonfarm buildings nec	0.4	Constr.	Doctors & dentists	0.7	Services
Adhesives & sealants	0.4	Manufg.	Hotels & lodging places	0.7	Services
Accounting, auditing & bookkeeping	0.4	Services	Distilled liquor, except brandy	0.6	Manufg.
Automotive repair shops & services	0.4	Services	Drugs	0.6	Manufg.
Commercial printing	0.3	Manufg.	Insurance agents, brokers, & services	0.6	Fin/R.E.
Industrial inorganic chemicals, nec	0.3	Manufg.	Change in business inventories	0.6	In House
Manifold business forms	0.3	Manufg.	Phonograph records & tapes	0.5	Manufg.
Computer & data processing services	0.3	Services	Roasted coffee	0.5	Manufg.
Engraving & plate printing	0.2	Manufg.	Wines, brandy, & brandy spirits	0.5	Manufg.
Paints & allied products	0.2	Manufg.	Accounting, auditing & bookkeeping	0.5	Services
Paperboard containers & boxes	0.2	Manufg.	Engineering, architectural, & surveying services	0.5	Services
Primary lead	0.2	Manufg.	Legal services	0.5	Services
Transit & bus transportation	0.2	Util.	Management & consulting services & labs	0.5	Services
Water transportation	0.2	Util.	Book publishing	0.4	Manufg.
Insurance carriers	0.2	Fin/R.E.	Motor freight transportation & warehousing	0.4	Util.
Business/professional associations	0.2	Services	Colleges, universities, & professional schools	0.4	Services
Personnel supply services	0.2	Services	Bottled & canned soft drinks	0.3	Manufg.
Lubricating oils & greases	0.1	Manufg.	Canned fruits & vegetables	0.3	Manufg.
Machinery, except electrical, nec	0.1	Manufg.	Dog, cat, & other pet food	0.3	Manufg.
Motor vehicle parts & accessories	0.1	Manufg.	Flavoring extracts & syrups, nec	0.3	Manufg.
Tires & inner tubes	0.1	Manufg.	Greeting card publishing	0.3	Manufg.
Retail trade, except eating & drinking	0.1	Trade	Paints & allied products	0.3	Manufg.
Business services nec	0.1	Services	Shortening & cooking oils	0.3	Manufg.
Photofinishing labs, commercial photography	0.1	Services	Soap & other detergents	0.3	Manufg.
			Libraries, vocation education	0.3	Services
			Nursing & personal care facilities	0.3	Services
			Local government passenger transit	0.3	Gov't
			S/L Govt. purch., other general government	0.3	S/L Govt
			Canned & cured seafoods	0.2	Manufg.
			Canned specialties	0.2	Manufg.
			Commercial printing	0.2	Manufg.
			Condensed & evaporated milk	0.2	Manufg.
			Dehydrated food products	0.2	Manufg.
			Meat packing plants	0.2	Manufg.
			Mechanical measuring devices	0.2	Manufg.
			Polishes & sanitation goods	0.2	Manufg.
			Poultry dressing plants	0.2	Manufg.
			Sugar	0.2	Manufg.
			Toilet preparations	0.2	Manufg.
			Air transportation	0.2	Util.
			Electric services (utilities)	0.2	Util.
			Railroads & related services	0.2	Util.
			Transit & bus transportation	0.2	Util.
			Retail trade, except eating & drinking	0.2	Trade
			Elementary & secondary schools	0.2	Services
			Funeral service & crematories	0.2	Services
			Medical & health services, nec	0.2	Services
			Membership sports & recreation clubs	0.2	Services
			Portrait, photographic studios	0.2	Services
			Religious organizations	0.2	Services
			S/L Govt. purch., police	0.2	S/L Govt
			Confectionery products	0.1	Manufg.
			Frozen fruits, fruit juices & vegetables	0.1	Manufg.
			Frozen specialties	0.1	Manufg.
			Glass containers	0.1	Manufg.
			Hosiery, nec	0.1	Manufg.
			Manifold business forms	0.1	Manufg.
			Wet corn milling	0.1	Manufg.
			Freight forwarders	0.1	Util.

Continued on next page.

INPUTS AND OUTPUTS FOR COMMERCIAL PRINTING - Continued

Economic Sector or Industry Providing Inputs	%	Sector	Economic Sector or Industry Buying Outputs	%	Sector
			Eating & drinking places	0.1	Trade
			Amusement & recreation services nec	0.1	Services
			Miscellaneous repair shops	0.1	Services
			Motion pictures	0.1	Services

Source: Benchmark Input-Output Accounts for the U.S. Economy, 1982, U.S. Department of Commerce, Washington, D.C., July 1991. Data, as reported in the source, are organized by the 1977 SIC structure in use in 1982 but have been matched, as closely as is possible, to the 1987 SIC structure used in this book.

OCCUPATIONS EMPLOYED BY SIC 275 - COMMERCIAL PRINTING AND BUSINESS FORMS

Occupation	% of Total 1994	Change to 2005	Occupation	% of Total 1994	Change to 2005
Offset lithographic press operators	9.2	3.9	Artists & commercial artists	1.5	31.9
Printing press machine setters, operators	8.1	3.9	Typesetting & composing machine operators	1.5	-67.5
Bindery machine operators & set-up operators	6.5	-10.1	Platemakers	1.4	-9.1
Sales & related workers nec	5.9	29.9	Cost estimators	1.3	29.4
General managers & top executives	4.4	23.2	Order clerks, materials, merchandise, & service	1.3	27.1
Strippers, printing	3.4	15.8	Cutting & slicing machine setters, operators	1.3	16.9
Blue collar worker supervisors	3.2	17.8	Production, planning, & expediting clerks	1.3	37.2
Machine feeders & offbearers	3.0	16.9	Camera operators	1.3	3.9
Bookkeeping, accounting, & auditing clerks	2.1	-2.6	Secretaries, ex legal & medical	1.3	18.2
Hand packers & packagers	2.1	22.5	Industrial production managers	1.3	-9.1
General office clerks	1.9	10.8	Screen printing machine setters & set-up operators	1.3	29.9
Printing, binding, & related workers nec	1.8	29.9	Helpers, laborers, & material movers nec	1.2	29.9
Traffic, shipping, & receiving clerks	1.7	25.0	Truck drivers light & heavy	1.2	33.9
Assemblers, fabricators, & hand workers nec	1.7	29.9	Electronic pagination systems workers	1.1	107.8
Job printers	1.6	-22.1	Paste-up workers	1.1	-15.6

Source: Industry-Occupation Matrix, Bureau of Labor Statistics. These data relate to one or more 3-digit SIC industry groups rather than to a single 4-digit SIC. The change reported for each occupation to the year 2005 is a percent of growth or decline as estimated by the Bureau of Labor Statistics. The abbreviation nec stands for 'not elsewhere classified'.

LOCATION BY STATE AND REGIONAL CONCENTRATION

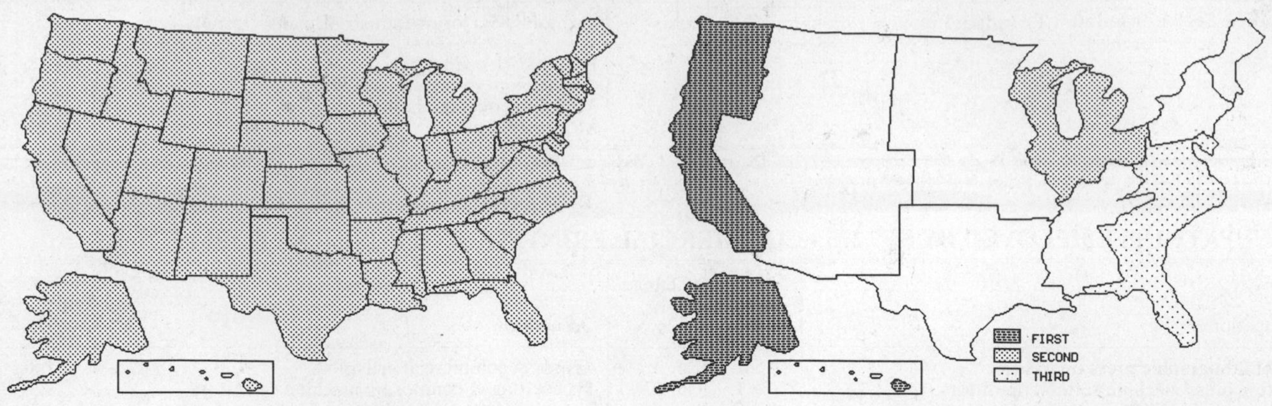

INDUSTRY DATA BY STATE

State	Establish-ments	Shipments			Employment				Cost as % of Shipments	Investment per Employee ($)
		Total ($ mil)	% of U.S.	Per Establ.	Total Number	% of U.S.	Per Establ.	Wages ($/hour)		
California	4,035	4,982.8	11.4	1.2	47,200	10.7	12	12.21	43.2	3,487
Illinois	1,615	3,948.2	9.1	2.4	34,400	7.8	21	12.87	44.4	4,273
New York	2,053	3,168.5	7.3	1.5	30,700	7.0	15	12.60	40.8	3,485
Pennsylvania	1,222	2,400.4	5.5	2.0	24,300	5.5	20	12.11	42.2	3,350
Minnesota	675	2,060.3	4.7	3.1	20,000	4.5	30	11.96	42.2	3,980
Ohio	1,229	1,984.9	4.6	1.6	21,900	5.0	18	11.13	41.6	3,470
New Jersey	1,091	1,916.8	4.4	1.8	17,500	4.0	16	13.27	42.7	4,994
Texas	1,935	1,903.1	4.4	1.0	20,800	4.7	11	10.55	44.6	2,649
Wisconsin	678	1,812.5	4.2	2.7	19,900	4.5	29	12.04	39.0	7,518
Michigan	1,033	1,599.2	3.7	1.5	14,400	3.3	14	11.65	44.1	3,583
Florida	1,730	1,367.7	3.1	0.8	16,300	3.7	9	10.19	45.3	3,190
Massachusetts	760	1,190.0	2.7	1.6	12,000	2.7	16	12.47	42.1	3,483
Georgia	756	1,145.7	2.6	1.5	11,400	2.6	15	11.70	45.6	3,193
Indiana	607	1,100.7	2.5	1.8	10,300	2.3	17	11.21	39.1	3,864
Maryland	539	1,062.1	2.4	2.0	10,300	2.3	19	13.38	43.7	3,068
Missouri	666	1,033.7	2.4	1.6	10,600	2.4	16	11.72	43.9	4,745
Virginia	637	1,012.6	2.3	1.6	11,100	2.5	17	12.51	44.4	2,730
North Carolina	679	869.3	2.0	1.3	9,000	2.0	13	10.95	43.5	3,689
Tennessee	547	861.7	2.0	1.6	9,600	2.2	18	10.49	43.3	2,625
Connecticut	472	737.0	1.7	1.6	7,100	1.6	15	13.13	41.7	4,268
Kentucky	286	725.3	1.7	2.5	7,000	1.6	24	12.18	40.8	3,486
Kansas	321	667.4	1.5	2.1	4,800	1.1	15	11.37	47.2	2,875
Oregon	420	634.3	1.5	1.5	5,300	1.2	13	12.35	47.4	3,604
Washington	599	579.9	1.3	1.0	6,400	1.5	11	11.18	37.9	3,141
Colorado	601	564.6	1.3	0.9	6,000	1.4	10	11.31	45.9	4,217
Iowa	315	521.5	1.2	1.7	5,700	1.3	18	10.07	42.9	2,860
Alabama	332	395.1	0.9	1.2	4,100	0.9	12	10.22	47.4	3,780
Arizona	515	392.4	0.9	0.8	5,000	1.1	10	10.40	41.5	2,780
Oklahoma	302	354.1	0.8	1.2	3,400	0.8	11	10.35	47.6	2,382
Nebraska	194	301.1	0.7	1.6	3,400	0.8	18	11.33	48.5	5,618
South Carolina	304	217.3	0.5	0.7	3,200	0.7	11	9.02	39.4	2,875
Arkansas	175	217.3	0.5	1.2	2,500	0.6	14	10.54	48.3	4,400
Louisiana	273	196.3	0.5	0.7	2,800	0.6	10	8.79	45.8	2,000
Utah	169	167.9	0.4	1.0	2,300	0.5	14	9.42	36.0	2,043
Mississippi	162	156.1	0.4	1.0	2,000	0.5	12	10.56	44.0	2,300
New Hampshire	151	154.9	0.4	1.0	1,800	0.4	12	11.12	43.1	3,556
Rhode Island	125	152.2	0.3	1.2	1,600	0.4	13	12.37	40.1	2,125
Vermont	74	146.0	0.3	2.0	1,700	0.4	23	10.74	40.2	2,529
Maine	124	130.3	0.3	1.1	1,500	0.3	12	9.63	50.0	3,533
Idaho	111	108.5	0.2	1.0	1,700	0.4	15	7.87	40.0	3,235
D.C.	80	97.8	0.2	1.2	1,100	0.3	14	12.56	43.4	1,909
Nevada	103	96.3	0.2	0.9	1,100	0.3	11	11.31	40.3	2,727
Hawaii	78	86.2	0.2	1.1	1,000	0.2	13	13.00	36.7	5,300
West Virginia	94	72.0	0.2	0.8	1,000	0.2	11	10.87	43.5	2,800
New Mexico	125	70.3	0.2	0.6	1,100	0.3	9	9.20	43.1	2,727
Delaware	66	48.2	0.1	0.7	700	0.2	11	10.90	37.8	1,571
Montana	79	43.6	0.1	0.6	700	0.2	9	8.70	37.6	3,571
North Dakota	44	42.5	0.1	1.0	700	0.2	16	8.89	40.2	-
Alaska	39	24.3	0.1	0.6	300	0.1	8	11.80	35.8	3,333
South Dakota	77	(D)	-	-	750 *	0.2	10	-	-	-
Wyoming	47	(D)	-	-	375 *	0.1	8	-	-	-

Source: 1992 *Economic Census*. The states are in descending order of shipments or establishments (if shipment data are missing for the majority). The symbol (D) appears when data are withheld to prevent disclosure of competitive information. States marked with (D) are sorted by number of establishments. A dash (-) indicates that the data element cannot be calculated; * indicates the midpoint of a range.

2754 - COMMERCIAL PRINTING, GRAVURE

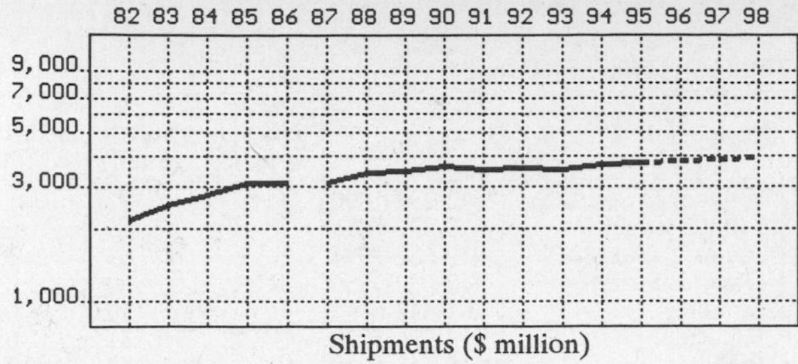

Shipments ($ million)

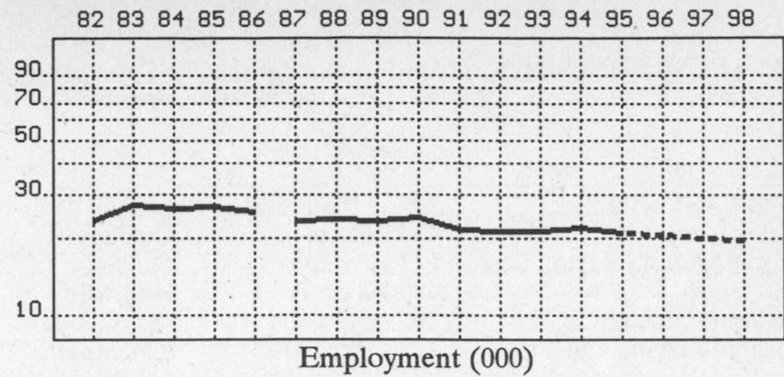

Employment (000)

GENERAL STATISTICS

Year	Com-panies	Establishments: Total	Establishments: with 20 or more employees	Employment: Total (000)	Employment: Production Workers (000)	Employment: Production Hours (Mil)	Compensation: Payroll ($ mil)	Compensation: Wages ($/hr)	Production ($ million): Cost of Materials	Production ($ million): Value Added by Manufacture	Production ($ million): Value of Shipments	Production ($ million): Capital Invest.
1982	612	653	121	23.8	19.5	39.3	545.2	10.61	1,079.1	1,095.5	2,170.0	85.2
1983		633	124	27.3	22.3	45.1	652.4	10.91	1,267.7	1,251.5	2,523.7	194.8
1984		613	127	26.2	20.7	42.1	668.5	11.87	1,376.3	1,430.3	2,785.2	167.5
1985		593	131	27.0	21.4	43.3	687.1	11.72	1,539.9	1,575.3	3,082.3	160.0
1986		581	137	25.7	20.8	42.6	701.5	12.36	1,499.6	1,585.4	3,066.8	172.3
1987*	304	332	91	23.8	19.1	39.6	668.5	12.48	1,545.5	1,534.2	3,059.8	175.5
1988		330	93	24.0	19.4	39.7	693.2	13.13	1,901.8	1,520.1	3,432.1	183.9
1989		338	100	23.7	18.9	39.7	688.2	12.92	1,983.4	1,476.2	3,467.6	178.7
1990		351	103	24.2	19.5	40.5	700.4	12.89	1,883.4	1,742.0	3,635.9	176.1
1991		364	105	22.0	17.9	39.0	693.7	13.52	1,839.9	1,670.0	3,506.0	136.5
1992	401	431	90	21.5	17.9	38.8	726.2	14.48	1,860.9	1,690.9	3,560.5	170.4
1993		440	97	21.5	18.0	39.3	723.5	14.46	1,756.2	1,724.0	3,492.0	176.2
1994		448P	99P	22.1	18.7	39.5	761.2	15.21	1,946.5	1,781.8	3,706.7	260.1
1995		468P	100P	21.1P	17.9P	39.1P	755.5P	15.30P	1,968.8P	1,802.2P	3,749.2P	208.4P
1996		488P	101P	20.7P	17.7P	39.1P	766.3P	15.67P	1,999.9P	1,830.7P	3,808.4P	214.2P
1997		507P	101P	20.3P	17.6P	39.0P	777.1P	16.04P	2,031.0P	1,859.2P	3,867.7P	220.0P
1998		527P	102P	19.9P	17.4P	38.9P	787.9P	16.41P	2,062.1P	1,887.7P	3,926.9P	225.9P

Sources: 1982, 1987, 1992 *Economic Census*; *Annual Survey of Manufactures*, 83-86, 88-91, 93-94. Establishment counts are from *County Business Patterns* for non-Census years; establishment counts for 83-84 are extrapolations. * indicates that industry content changed in 87; earlier years use 77 SICs. 'P's mark projections.

INDICES OF CHANGE

Year	Com-panies	Establishments: Total	Establishments: with 20 or more employees	Employment: Total (000)	Employment: Production Workers (000)	Employment: Production Hours (Mil)	Compensation: Payroll ($ mil)	Compensation: Wages ($/hr)	Production ($ million): Cost of Materials	Production ($ million): Value Added by Manufacture	Production ($ million): Value of Shipments	Production ($ million): Capital Invest.
1982	153	152	134	111	109	101	75	73	58	65	61	50
1983		147	138	127	125	116	90	75	68	74	71	114
1984		142	141	122	116	109	92	82	74	85	78	98
1985		138	146	126	120	112	95	81	83	93	87	94
1986		135	152	120	116	110	97	85	81	94	86	101
1987*	76	77	101	111	107	102	92	86	83	91	86	103
1988		77	103	112	108	102	95	91	102	90	96	108
1989		78	111	110	106	102	95	89	107	87	97	105
1990		81	114	113	109	104	96	89	101	103	102	103
1991		84	117	102	100	101	96	93	99	99	98	80
1992	100	100	100	100	100	100	100	100	100	100	100	100
1993		102	108	100	101	101	100	100	94	102	98	103
1994		104P	110P	103	104	102	105	105	105	105	104	153
1995		109P	111P	98P	100P	101P	104P	106P	106P	107P	105P	122P
1996		113P	112P	96P	99P	101P	106P	108P	107P	108P	107P	126P
1997		118P	113P	94P	98P	100P	107P	111P	109P	110P	109P	129P
1998		122P	113P	92P	97P	100P	108P	113P	111P	112P	110P	133P

Sources: Same as General Statistics. Values reflect change from the base year, 1992. Values above 100 mean greater than 92, values below 100 mean less than 92, and a value of 100 in the 82-91 or 93-98 period means same as 92. * indicates that industry content changed in 87. Data for earlier years are in 77 SIC format.

SELECTED RATIOS

For 1994	Avg. of All Manufact.	Analyzed Industry	Index	For 1994	Avg. of All Manufact.	Analyzed Industry	Index
Employees per Establishment	49	49	101	Value Added per Production Worker	134,084	95,283	71
Payroll per Establishment	1,500,273	1,698,024	113	Cost per Establishment	5,045,178	4,342,097	86
Payroll per Employee	30,620	34,443	112	Cost per Employee	102,970	88,077	86
Production Workers per Establishment	34	42	122	Cost per Production Worker	146,988	104,091	71
Wages per Establishment	853,319	1,340,206	157	Shipments per Establishment	9,576,895	8,268,611	86
Wages per Production Worker	24,861	32,128	129	Shipments per Employee	195,460	167,724	86
Hours per Production Worker	2,056	2,112	103	Shipments per Production Worker	279,017	198,219	71
Wages per Hour	12.09	15.21	126	Investment per Establishment	321,011	580,210	181
Value Added per Establishment	4,602,255	3,974,697	86	Investment per Employee	6,552	11,769	180
Value Added per Employee	93,930	80,624	86	Investment per Production Worker	9,352	13,909	149

Sources: Same as General Statistics. The 'Average of All Manufacturing' column represents the average of all manufacturing industries reported for the most recent complete year available. The Index shows the relationship between the Average and the Analyzed Industry. For example, 100 means that they are equal; 500 that the Analyzed Industry is five times the average; 50 means that the Analyzed Industry is half the national average. The abbreviation 'na' is used to show that data are 'not available'.

LEADING COMPANIES

Number shown: **22** Total sales ($ mil): **620** Total employment (000): **5.7**

Company Name	Address				CEO Name	Phone	Co. Type	Sales ($ mil)	Empl. (000)
Brown and Bigelow Inc	345 E Plato Blv	St Paul	MN	55107	William D Smith Sr	612-293-7000	R	72*	1.2
Multi-Color Corp	4575 Eastern Av	Cincinnati	OH	45226	John C Court	513-321-5381	P	65	0.5
Golden Belt Manufacturing Co	PO Box 2332	Durham	NC	27702	James T Galioto	919-682-9394	S	63	0.3
Sheridan Group	450 Fame Av	Hanover	PA	17331	David L Horst	717-632-3535	R	60	0.6
Myron Manufacturing Co	205 Maywood Av	Maywood	NJ	07607	M Adler	201-843-6464	R	59*	0.6
United States Playing Card Co	4590 Beech St	Cincinnati	OH	45212	RC Rule	513-396-5700	S	55	0.6
Precision Printing and Packaging	801 Alfred Thun Rd	Clarksville	TN	37040	B Miller	615-645-5000	J	52	0.3
JW Fergusson and Sons	4641 International	Richmond	VA	23231	R G Fergusson Jr	804-275-2611	R	39*	0.3
Ringier America Inc	2802 W Palm Ln	Phoenix	AZ	85009	Everett Chamberlain	602-272-3221	D	30*	0.3
Vose-Swain Engraving Co	411 D St	Boston	MA	02210	Donald Cannava	617-542-3711	D	24	0.1
McCleery-Cumming Co	915 E Tyler St	Washington	IA	52353	Jeff Meyer	319-653-2185	R	23	0.3
Quik Print Inc	PO Box 781990	Wichita	KS	67278	Wayne Jenkins	316-636-5666	R	18	0.2
Label America Inc	PO Box 1245	Stone Mt	GA	30086	Joseph Patrick	404-934-8040	R	11	<0.1
Tax Forms Printing	PO Box 1040	Camarillo	CA	93011	Ron Hoffmeyer	805-484-8081	S	10	<0.1
Mutual Engraving Company Inc	511 Hempstead Av	W Hempstead	NY	11552	S Forelli Jr	516-486-2996	R	9	0.1
Heath Printers Inc	1617 Boylston Av	Seattle	WA	98122	Terry Page	206-323-3577	R	8	<0.1
Lorain Printing Company Inc	1310 Colorado Av	Lorain	OH	44052	David M Koethe	216-288-6000	R	6	<0.1
Newco Inc	1 Hicks Av	Newton	NJ	07860	J Berezny	201-383-7777	R	6*	<0.1
Wittco Systems Inc	PO Box 230306	Portland	OR	97223	Bill Witt	503-620-9887	R	5	<0.1
Stationers Engraving Inc	128 E 10th St	St Paul	MN	55101	WE Clevenger	612-222-5883	R	2*	<0.1
Graphic Media Corp	1201 Race St	Philadelphia	PA	19107	Mario Kalman	215-568-1559	R	2	<0.1
Duff Maps	RR 6	E Stroudsburg	PA	18301	Sonya E Rake	717-253-6776	R	0*	<0.1

Source: *Ward's Business Directory of U.S. Private and Public Companies*, Volumes 1 and 2, 1996. The company type code used is as follows: P - Public, R - Private, S - Subsidiary, D - Division, J - Joint Venture, A - Affiliate, G - Group. Sales are in millions of dollars, employees are in thousands. An asterisk (*) indicates an estimated sales volume. The symbol < stands for 'less than'. Company names and addresses are truncated, in some cases, to fit into the available space.

MATERIALS CONSUMED

Material	Quantity	Delivered Cost ($ million)
Materials, ingredients, containers, and supplies	(X)	1,727.7
Uncoated paper in sheets	(X)	2.3
Uncoated paper in rolls	(X)	459.5
Coated paper in sheets	(X)	17.7
Coated paper in rolls	(X)	354.7
Pressure-sensitive base stock, self-adhesive, including paper, film, foil, etc.	(X)	9.0
Glues and adhesives	(X)	9.1
Printing inks (complete formulations)	(X)	458.5
Light sensitive films and papers	(X)	4.3
Unexposed photosensitive printing plates	(X)	0.4
Printing plates, prepared for printing	(X)	1.9
Engraved printing cylinders for gravure printing	(X)	12.4
Paperboard containers, boxes, and corrugated paperboard	(X)	8.7
All other materials and components, parts, containers, and supplies	(X)	260.4
Materials, ingredients, containers, and supplies, nsk	(X)	128.9

Source: 1992 *Economic Census*. Explanation of symbols used: (D): Withheld to avoid disclosure of competitive data; na: Not available; (S): Withheld because statistical norms were not met; (X): Not applicable; (Z): Less than half the unit shown; nec: Not elsewhere classified; nsk: Not specified by kind; - : zero; * : 10-19 percent estimated; ** : 20-29 percent estimated.

PRODUCT SHARE DETAILS

Product or Product Class	% Share
Commercial printing, gravure	100.00
Magazine and periodical printing (gravure)	16.05
Magazine and periodical printing (gravure), excluding magazine and comic supplements for Sunday newspapers	72.26
Magazine and comic supplement printing (gravure) for Sunday newspapers	27.71
Magazine and periodical printing (gravure), nsk	0.04
Label and wrapper printing (gravure)	15.39
Label printing (gravure), custom and stock labels, including bordered, made of paper, flat (except pressure-sensitive)	16.15
Label printing (gravure), custom and stock labels, including bordered, made of paper, rolls (except pressure-sensitive)	37.50
Label printing (gravure), custom and stock labels, including bordered, made of paper, pressure-sensitive (self-adhesive)	1.04
Label printing (gravure), custom and stock labels, including bordered, made of materials other than paper or cloth	11.22
Printed rolls and sheets for packaging purposes (printing only) (gravure), made of paper (single-web)	29.51
Label and wrapper printing (gravure), nsk	4.58
Catalog and directory printing (gravure), including direct mail catalogs and telephone and business reference services directories	25.72
Advertising printing (gravure)	27.11
Other commercial printing (gravure)	9.71
Printed decalcomanias and pressure-sensitives (self-adhesive) (gravure), including bumper stickers, etc., except labels	12.93
All other general commercial gravure printing, nec (including customized stationery and business cards)	84.13
Other commercial printing (gravure), nsk	2.94
Commercial printing, gravure, nsk	6.02

Source: 1992 *Economic Census*. The values shown are percent of total shipments in an industry. Values of indented subcategories are summed in the main heading. The symbol (D) appears when data are withheld to prevent disclosure of competitive information. The abbreviation nsk stands for 'not specified by kind' and nec for 'not elsewhere classified'.

INPUTS AND OUTPUTS FOR COMMERCIAL PRINTING

Economic Sector or Industry Providing Inputs	%	Sector	Economic Sector or Industry Buying Outputs	%	Sector
Paper mills, except building paper	34.8	Manufg.	Wholesale trade	9.2	Trade
Wholesale trade	7.9	Trade	Periodicals	7.4	Manufg.
Printing ink	5.9	Manufg.	Membership organizations nec	7.2	Services
Miscellaneous plastics products	4.4	Manufg.	Business/professional associations	6.1	Services
Lithographic platemaking & services	3.5	Manufg.	Labor, civic, social, & fraternal associations	4.9	Services
Typesetting	3.3	Manufg.	Insurance carriers	3.6	Fin/R.E.
Cyclic crudes and organics	2.8	Manufg.	Advertising	3.1	Services
Petroleum refining	2.5	Manufg.	Real estate	3.0	Fin/R.E.
Paper coating & glazing	2.4	Manufg.	Hospitals	2.8	Services
Motor freight transportation & warehousing	2.4	Util.	Computer & data processing services	2.6	Services
Electric services (utilities)	2.2	Util.	Miscellaneous publishing	2.4	Manufg.
Eating & drinking places	2.0	Trade	Newspapers	1.9	Manufg.
Photographic equipment & supplies	1.5	Manufg.	Sausages & other prepared meats	1.9	Manufg.
Real estate	1.2	Fin/R.E.	Exports	1.8	Foreign
U.S. Postal Service	1.2	Gov't	Social services, nec	1.6	Services
Railroads & related services	1.1	Util.	Security & commodity brokers	1.5	Fin/R.E.
Advertising	1.0	Services	Business services nec	1.5	Services
Imports	1.0	Foreign	S/L Govt. purch., higher education	1.5	S/L Govt
Printing trades machinery	0.9	Manufg.	Cigarettes	1.4	Manufg.
Banking	0.9	Fin/R.E.	Banking	1.4	Fin/R.E.
Chemical preparations, nec	0.8	Manufg.	Personal consumption expenditures	1.3	
Mechanical measuring devices	0.8	Manufg.	Metal cans	1.3	Manufg.
Air transportation	0.8	Util.	Federal Government purchases, national defense	1.1	Fed Govt
Equipment rental & leasing services	0.8	Services	S/L Govt. purch., health & hospitals	1.1	S/L Govt
Hotels & lodging places	0.8	Services	Cheese, natural & processed	1.0	Manufg.
Metal foil & leaf	0.7	Manufg.	Food preparations, nec	0.9	Manufg.
Communications, except radio & TV	0.7	Util.	Credit agencies other than banks	0.9	Fin/R.E.
Gas production & distribution (utilities)	0.7	Util.	Federal Government purchases, nondefense	0.9	Fed Govt
Legal services	0.7	Services	Agricultural chemicals, nec	0.8	Manufg.
Management & consulting services & labs	0.7	Services	Malt beverages	0.8	Manufg.
Paperboard mills	0.6	Manufg.	Communications, except radio & TV	0.8	Util.
Photoengraving, electrotyping & stereotyping	0.6	Manufg.	S/L Govt. purch., elem. & secondary education	0.8	S/L Govt
Envelopes	0.5	Manufg.	S/L Govt. purch., natural resource & recreation.	0.8	S/L Govt
Automotive rental & leasing, without drivers	0.5	Services	Pickles, sauces, & salad dressings	0.7	Manufg.
Maintenance of nonfarm buildings nec	0.4	Constr.	Doctors & dentists	0.7	Services
Adhesives & sealants	0.4	Manufg.	Hotels & lodging places	0.7	Services
Accounting, auditing & bookkeeping	0.4	Services	Distilled liquor, except brandy	0.6	Manufg.
Automotive repair shops & services	0.4	Services	Drugs	0.6	Manufg.
Commercial printing	0.3	Manufg.	Insurance agents, brokers, & services	0.6	Fin/R.E.
Industrial inorganic chemicals, nec	0.3	Manufg.	Change in business inventories	0.6	In House
Manifold business forms	0.3	Manufg.	Phonograph records & tapes	0.5	Manufg.
Computer & data processing services	0.3	Services	Roasted coffee	0.5	Manufg.
Engraving & plate printing	0.2	Manufg.	Wines, brandy, & brandy spirits	0.5	Manufg.
Paints & allied products	0.2	Manufg.	Accounting, auditing & bookkeeping	0.5	Services
Paperboard containers & boxes	0.2	Manufg.	Engineering, architectural, & surveying services	0.5	Services
Primary lead	0.2	Manufg.	Legal services	0.5	Services
Transit & bus transportation	0.2	Util.	Management & consulting services & labs	0.5	Services
Water transportation	0.2	Util.	Book publishing	0.4	Manufg.
Insurance carriers	0.2	Fin/R.E.	Motor freight transportation & warehousing	0.4	Util.
Business/professional associations	0.2	Services	Colleges, universities, & professional schools	0.4	Services
Personnel supply services	0.2	Services	Bottled & canned soft drinks	0.3	Manufg.
Lubricating oils & greases	0.1	Manufg.	Canned fruits & vegetables	0.3	Manufg.
Machinery, except electrical, nec	0.1	Manufg.	Dog, cat, & other pet food	0.3	Manufg.
Motor vehicle parts & accessories	0.1	Manufg.	Flavoring extracts & syrups, nec	0.3	Manufg.
Tires & inner tubes	0.1	Manufg.	Greeting card publishing	0.3	Manufg.
Retail trade, except eating & drinking	0.1	Trade	Paints & allied products	0.3	Manufg.
Business services nec	0.1	Services	Shortening & cooking oils	0.3	Manufg.
Photofinishing labs, commercial photography	0.1	Services	Soap & other detergents	0.3	Manufg.
			Libraries, vocation education	0.3	Services
			Nursing & personal care facilities	0.3	Services
			Local government passenger transit	0.3	Gov't
			S/L Govt. purch., other general government	0.3	S/L Govt
			Canned & cured seafoods	0.2	Manufg.
			Canned specialties	0.2	Manufg.
			Commercial printing	0.2	Manufg.
			Condensed & evaporated milk	0.2	Manufg.
			Dehydrated food products	0.2	Manufg.
			Meat packing plants	0.2	Manufg.
			Mechanical measuring devices	0.2	Manufg.
			Polishes & sanitation goods	0.2	Manufg.
			Poultry dressing plants	0.2	Manufg.
			Sugar	0.2	Manufg.
			Toilet preparations	0.2	Manufg.
			Air transportation	0.2	Util.
			Electric services (utilities)	0.2	Util.
			Railroads & related services	0.2	Util.
			Transit & bus transportation	0.2	Util.
			Retail trade, except eating & drinking	0.2	Trade

Continued on next page.

INPUTS AND OUTPUTS FOR COMMERCIAL PRINTING - Continued

Economic Sector or Industry Providing Inputs	%	Sector	Economic Sector or Industry Buying Outputs	%	Sector
			Elementary & secondary schools	0.2	Services
			Funeral service & crematories	0.2	Services
			Medical & health services, nec	0.2	Services
			Membership sports & recreation clubs	0.2	Services
			Portrait, photographic studios	0.2	Services
			Religious organizations	0.2	Services
			S/L Govt. purch., police	0.2	S/L Govt
			Confectionery products	0.1	Manufg.
			Frozen fruits, fruit juices & vegetables	0.1	Manufg.
			Frozen specialties	0.1	Manufg.
			Glass containers	0.1	Manufg.
			Hosiery, nec	0.1	Manufg.
			Manifold business forms	0.1	Manufg.
			Wet corn milling	0.1	Manufg.
			Freight forwarders	0.1	Util.
			Eating & drinking places	0.1	Trade
			Amusement & recreation services nec	0.1	Services
			Miscellaneous repair shops	0.1	Services
			Motion pictures	0.1	Services

Source: Benchmark Input-Output Accounts for the U.S. Economy, 1982, U.S. Department of Commerce, Washington, D.C., July 1991. Data, as reported in the source, are organized by the 1977 SIC structure in use in 1982 but have been matched, as closely as is possible, to the 1987 SIC structure used in this book.

OCCUPATIONS EMPLOYED BY SIC 275 - COMMERCIAL PRINTING AND BUSINESS FORMS

Occupation	% of Total 1994	Change to 2005	Occupation	% of Total 1994	Change to 2005
Offset lithographic press operators	9.2	3.9	Artists & commercial artists	1.5	31.9
Printing press machine setters, operators	8.1	3.9	Typesetting & composing machine operators	1.5	-67.5
Bindery machine operators & set-up operators	6.5	-10.1	Platemakers	1.4	-9.1
Sales & related workers nec	5.9	29.9	Cost estimators	1.3	29.4
General managers & top executives	4.4	23.2	Order clerks, materials, merchandise, & service	1.3	27.1
Strippers, printing	3.4	15.8	Cutting & slicing machine setters, operators	1.3	16.9
Blue collar worker supervisors	3.2	17.8	Production, planning, & expediting clerks	1.3	37.2
Machine feeders & offbearers	3.0	16.9	Camera operators	1.3	3.9
Bookkeeping, accounting, & auditing clerks	2.1	-2.6	Secretaries, ex legal & medical	1.3	18.2
Hand packers & packagers	2.1	22.5	Industrial production managers	1.3	-9.1
General office clerks	1.9	10.8	Screen printing machine setters & set-up operators	1.3	29.9
Printing, binding, & related workers nec	1.8	29.9	Helpers, laborers, & material movers nec	1.2	29.9
Traffic, shipping, & receiving clerks	1.7	25.0	Truck drivers light & heavy	1.2	33.9
Assemblers, fabricators, & hand workers nec	1.7	29.9	Electronic pagination systems workers	1.1	107.8
Job printers	1.6	-22.1	Paste-up workers	1.1	-15.6

Source: Industry-Occupation Matrix, Bureau of Labor Statistics. These data relate to one or more 3-digit SIC industry groups rather than to a single 4-digit SIC. The change reported for each occupation to the year 2005 is a percent of growth or decline as estimated by the Bureau of Labor Statistics. The abbreviation nec stands for 'not elsewhere classified'.

LOCATION BY STATE AND REGIONAL CONCENTRATION

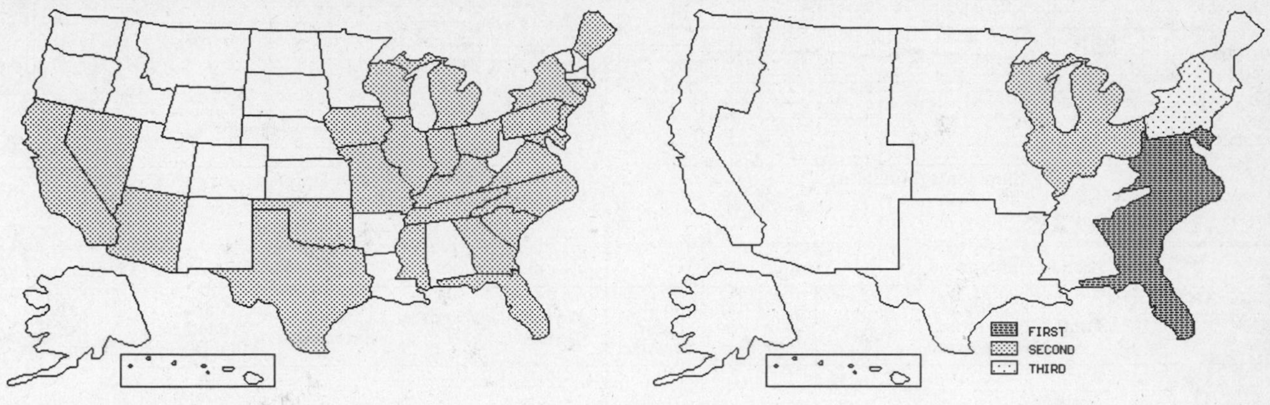

INDUSTRY DATA BY STATE

State	Establish-ments	Shipments			Employment				Cost as % of Shipments	Investment per Employee ($)
		Total ($ mil)	% of U.S.	Per Establ.	Total Number	% of U.S.	Per Establ.	Wages ($/hour)		
Illinois	25	504.8	14.2	20.2	3,600	16.7	144	15.02	45.6	6,444
Tennessee	15	458.1	12.9	30.5	2,200	10.2	147	15.77	59.6	8,273
Virginia	15	308.9	8.7	20.6	1,600	7.4	107	17.00	56.6	6,438
Pennsylvania	13	285.8	8.0	22.0	1,600	7.4	123	15.39	50.2	7,313
Georgia	18	170.7	4.8	9.5	900	4.2	50	13.13	42.6	18,333
California	54	142.2	4.0	2.6	700	3.3	13	16.67	32.7	8,857
New York	36	74.7	2.1	2.1	500	2.3	14	13.29	48.5	4,200
Ohio	15	71.9	2.0	4.8	500	2.3	33	14.38	53.5	2,400
New Jersey	24	44.6	1.3	1.9	400	1.9	17	15.33	30.5	1,500
Michigan	14	23.7	0.7	1.7	200	0.9	14	14.00	66.2	2,500
Connecticut	8	21.0	0.6	2.6	300	1.4	38	13.50	49.0	3,333
Wisconsin	9	12.7	0.4	1.4	100	0.5	11	11.00	48.8	4,000
Florida	21	8.4	0.2	0.4	100	0.5	5	8.00	45.2	4,000
Texas	19	(D)	-	-	750 *	3.5	39	-	-	-
North Carolina	16	(D)	-	-	1,750 *	8.1	109	-	-	3,829
Maryland	15	(D)	-	-	375 *	1.7	25	-	-	3,200
Indiana	10	(D)	-	-	1,750 *	8.1	175	-	-	-
Missouri	7	(D)	-	-	375 *	1.7	54	-	-	-
Nevada	7	(D)	-	-	375 *	1.7	54	-	-	-
Iowa	6	(D)	-	-	750 *	3.5	125	-	-	-
Rhode Island	6	(D)	-	-	175 *	0.8	29	-	-	-
Kentucky	5	(D)	-	-	375 *	1.7	75	-	-	-
Arizona	4	(D)	-	-	375 *	1.7	94	-	-	-
Mississippi	3	(D)	-	-	750 *	3.5	250	-	-	-
South Carolina	3	(D)	-	-	750 *	3.5	250	-	-	-
Maine	2	(D)	-	-	175 *	0.8	88	-	-	-
Oklahoma	1	(D)	-	-	175 *	0.8	175	-	-	-

Source: 1992 *Economic Census*. The states are in descending order of shipments or establishments (if shipment data are missing for the majority). The symbol (D) appears when data are withheld to prevent disclosure of competitive information. States marked with (D) are sorted by number of establishments. A dash (-) indicates that the data element cannot be calculated; * indicates the midpoint of a range.

2759 - COMMERCIAL PRINTING, NEC

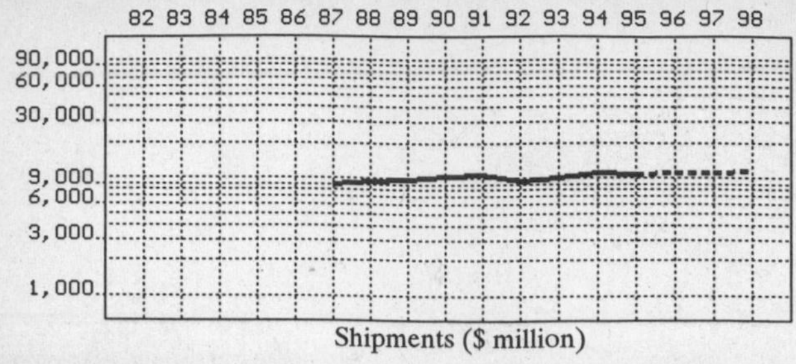

Shipments ($ million)

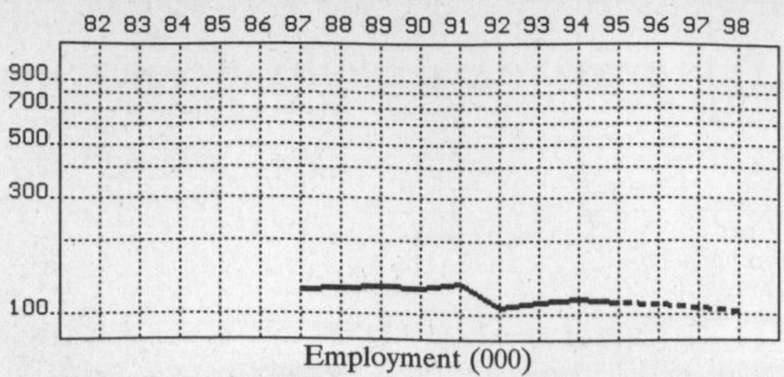

Employment (000)

GENERAL STATISTICS

Year	Companies	Establishments		Employment			Compensation		Production ($ million)			
		Total	with 20 or more employees	Total (000)	Production Workers (000)	Production Hours (Mil)	Payroll ($ mil)	Wages ($/hr)	Cost of Materials	Value Added by Manufacture	Value of Shipments	Capital Invest.
1982												
1983												
1984												
1985												
1986												
1987	10,607	10,796	1,388	126.2	88.7	173.5	2,489.9	8.66	3,707.6	5,298.8	8,973.2	299.4
1988		9,817	1,428	127.7	89.4	189.4	2,602.6	8.27	4,011.9	5,338.8	9,300.4	278.8
1989		9,190	1,451	130.6	89.2	179.8	2,743.2	8.99	4,069.5	5,676.7	9,716.1	329.1
1990		8,754	1,438	128.0	93.8	191.9	2,963.7	9.14	4,347.7	6,029.1	10,390.4	381.8
1991		8,847	1,439	133.8	92.1	191.0	3,055.1	9.31	4,459.2	6,269.9	10,723.2	544.3
1992	8,570	8,690	1,255	107.3	73.9	154.4	2,596.9	9.47	3,790.9	5,441.6	9,290.2	344.5
1993		8,527	1,258	112.7	77.4	159.7	2,790.2	9.99	4,271.6	5,707.5	9,977.0	379.9
1994		7,888P	1,273P	117.1	79.8	167.0	3,051.5	10.13	4,536.6	6,453.6	10,973.3	496.6
1995		7,552P	1,246P	112.1P	76.4P	161.3P	3,028.9P	10.34P	4,464.4P	6,350.9P	10,798.6P	494.0P
1996		7,216P	1,219P	109.6P	74.4P	158.1P	3,082.7P	10.59P	4,545.3P	6,466.0P	10,994.3P	518.9P
1997		6,881P	1,193P	107.2P	72.4P	154.9P	3,136.5P	10.83P	4,626.2P	6,581.1P	11,190.0P	543.9P
1998		6,545P	1,166P	104.8P	70.4P	151.6P	3,190.4P	11.08P	4,707.1P	6,696.2P	11,385.7P	568.8P

Sources: 1982, 1987, 1992 *Economic Census*; *Annual Survey of Manufactures*, 83-86, 88-91, 93-94. Establishment counts for non-Census years are from *County Business Patterns*; establishment values for 83-84 are extrapolations. 'P's show projections by the editors. Industries reclassified in 87 will not have data for prior years.

INDICES OF CHANGE

Year	Companies	Establishments		Employment			Compensation		Production ($ million)			
		Total	with 20 or more employees	Total (000)	Production Workers (000)	Production Hours (Mil)	Payroll ($ mil)	Wages ($/hr)	Cost of Materials	Value Added by Manufacture	Value of Shipments	Capital Invest.
1982												
1983												
1984												
1985												
1986												
1987	124	124	111	118	120	112	96	91	98	97	97	87
1988		113	114	119	121	123	100	87	106	98	100	81
1989		106	116	122	121	116	106	95	107	104	105	96
1990		101	115	119	127	124	114	97	115	111	112	111
1991		102	115	125	125	124	118	98	118	115	115	158
1992	100	100	100	100	100	100	100	100	100	100	100	100
1993		98	100	105	105	103	107	105	113	105	107	110
1994		91P	101P	109	108	108	118	107	120	119	118	144
1995		87P	99P	104P	103P	104P	117P	109P	118P	117P	116P	143P
1996		83P	97P	102P	101P	102P	119P	112P	120P	119P	118P	151P
1997		79P	95P	100P	98P	100P	121P	114P	122P	121P	120P	158P
1998		75P	93P	98P	95P	98P	123P	117P	124P	123P	123P	165P

Sources: Same as General Statistics. Values reflect change from the base year, 1992. Values above 100 mean greater than 92, values below 100 mean less than 92, and a value of 100 in the 82-91 or 93-98 period means same as 92. 'P's mark projections by the editors.

SELECTED RATIOS

For 1994	Avg. of All Manufact.	Analyzed Industry	Index	For 1994	Avg. of All Manufact.	Analyzed Industry	Index
Employees per Establishment	49	15	30	Value Added per Production Worker	134,084	80,872	60
Payroll per Establishment	1,500,273	386,846	26	Cost per Establishment	5,045,178	575,116	11
Payroll per Employee	30,620	26,059	85	Cost per Employee	102,970	38,741	38
Production Workers per Establishment	34	10	29	Cost per Production Worker	146,988	56,850	39
Wages per Establishment	853,319	214,462	25	Shipments per Establishment	9,576,895	1,391,113	15
Wages per Production Worker	24,861	21,199	85	Shipments per Employee	195,460	93,709	48
Hours per Production Worker	2,056	2,093	102	Shipments per Production Worker	279,017	137,510	49
Wages per Hour	12.09	10.13	84	Investment per Establishment	321,011	62,955	20
Value Added per Establishment	4,602,255	818,139	18	Investment per Employee	6,552	4,241	65
Value Added per Employee	93,930	55,112	59	Investment per Production Worker	9,352	6,223	67

Sources: Same as General Statistics. The 'Average of All Manufacturing' column represents the average of all manufacturing industries reported for the most recent complete year available. The Index shows the relationship between the Average and the Analyzed Industry. For example, 100 means that they are equal; 500 that the Analyzed Industry is five times the average; 50 means that the Analyzed Industry is half the national average. The abbreviation 'na' is used to show that data are 'not available'.

LEADING COMPANIES

Number shown: 75 Total sales ($ mil): 9,246 Total employment (000): 82.6

Company Name	Address				CEO Name	Phone	Co. Type	Sales ($ mil)	Empl. (000)
Deluxe Corp	PO Box 64399	St Paul	MN	55126	Harold V Haverty	612-483-7111	P	1,748	18.9
Quad/Graphics Inc	W224 N3322	Pewaukee	WI	53072	Harry V Quadracci	414-691-9200	R	700	6.0
John H Harland Co	PO Box 105250	Atlanta	GA	30348	Robert R Woodson	404-981-9460	P	521	7.0
Bowne and Company Inc	345 Hudson St	New York	NY	10014	Richard H Koontz	212-924-5500	P	381	2.6
Graphic Industries Inc	2155 Monroe NE	Atlanta	GA	30324	Mark C Pope IV	404-874-3327	P	348	3.0
Williamhouse-Regency Inc	28 W 23rd St	New York	NY	10010	Martin R Lewis	212-691-2000	R	300*	3.4
Duplex Products Inc	1947 Bethany Rd	Sycamore	IL	60178	B L McSwiney	815-895-2101	P	266	1.9
Topps Company Inc	1 Whitehall St	New York	NY	10004	Arthur T Shorin	212-514-8190	P	263	1.4
Cadmus Communications Corp	6620 W Broad St	Richmond	VA	23230	CS Gillispie	804-287-5680	P	248	2.4
United States Banknote Corp	51 W 52nd St	New York	NY	10019	Morris Weismann	212-741-8500	P	208	2.3
AmeriSig Inc	777 W Putnam Av	Greenwich	CT	06830	Marc Fors	203-531-1100	S	200	2.1
Curtis 1000 Inc	PO Box 105683	Atlanta	GA	30348	Robert G Baker	404-951-1000	S	200	1.8
Devon Group Inc	281 Tresser Blv	Stamford	CT	06901	M Obernauer Jr	203-964-1444	P	191	1.8
Clarke American Checks Inc	PO Box 460	San Antonio	TX	78292	Charles Korbell	210-697-8888	S	190	2.8
Lehigh Press Inc	51 Haddonfield Rd	Cherry Hill	NJ	08002	John D DePaul	609-665-5200	R	160	0.9
Courier Corp	165 Jackson St	Lowell	MA	01852	James F Conway III	508-458-6351	P	123	1.1
Scientific Games Inc	1500 Bluegrass Lks	Alpharetta	GA	30201	William G Malloy	404-664-3700	S	120	0.6
Scientific Games Holdings Corp	1500 Bluegrass Lks	Alpharetta	GA	30201	William G Malloy	404-664-3700	P	120	0.6
Mickelberry Corp	405 Park Av	New York	NY	10022	James C Marlas	212-832-0303	P	119	0.6
Data Documents Inc	4205 S 96th St	Omaha	NE	68127	Walter Kearns	402-339-0900	R	110*	1.1
Miami Systems Corp	10150 Alliance Rd	Cincinnati	OH	45242	Samuel Peters	513-793-0110	R	100	1.1
Northeast Graphics Inc	291 State St	North Haven	CT	06473	Steven Bortner	203-288-2468	R	94	0.5
Serigraph Inc	760 Indiana Av	West Bend	WI	53095	John Torinus Jr	414-335-7200	R	91	0.9
Keith Clark	101 O'Neil Rd	Sidney	NY	13838	Doug Willies	607-563-9411	D	90*	1.0
Epsen Lithographing Co	2000 California St	Omaha	NE	68102	Gary K Thrasher	402-342-7000	S	86*	0.4
CCL Label Inc	1450 E Amer Ln	Schaumburg	IL	60173	Robert C Broad	708-330-6385	S	85	0.5
Communicolor Inc	PO Box 400	Newark	OH	43058	Michael Spaul	614-928-6110	D	80*	0.4
Decorating Resources Inc	430 Andbro Dr	Pitman	NJ	08071	M A Contreras	609-589-3800	S	80	0.1
International Paper Co	6400 Poplar Av	Memphis	TN	38197	Dennis Colley	901-763-6000	D	80	0.8
RCL Enterprises Inc	1 DLM Park	Allen	TX	75002	F Vern Lahart	214-248-6300	R	75	0.4
Nashua Label Products	3838 S 108th St	Omaha	NE	68144	Bob Geiger	402-397-3600	D	72	0.4
Cello-Foil Products Inc	155 Brook St	Battle Creek	MI	49017	Kenneth M Lesiow	616-964-7137	R	70	0.3
Hippographics Co	1 Forms Ln	Willow Grove	PA	19090	Dick Weissman	215-659-4000	R	70	0.6
Bradley Printing Co	2170 S Mannheim	Des Plaines	IL	60018	Jack Schuh	708-635-8000	S	66*	0.4
Color-Art Inc	10300 Watson Rd	St Louis	MO	63127	Gary P Reim	314-966-2000	R	62	0.3
RR Donnelley and Sons Co	300 Jones Rd	Spartanburg	SC	29302	Tim Weibel	803-579-6000	D	62*	0.6
Oklahoma Graphics	PO Box 26488	Oklahoma City	OK	73126	Mike Shea	405-945-6200	D	60	0.4
Petty Printing Company Inc	PO Box 250	Effingham	IL	62401	R Kronenberger	217-347-7721	R	56	0.6
WinCraft Inc	PO Box 888	Winona	MN	55987	Richard Pope	507-454-5510	R	56	0.6
Sleepeck Printing Co	815 25th Av	Bellwood	IL	60104	Michael W Sleepeck	708-544-8900	R	55	0.4
Cadmus Magazines	2901 Byrdhill Rd	Richmond	VA	23228	David Hajek	804-264-2711	S	52	0.4
Menasha Corp	PO Box 427	Neenah	WI	54957	Robert Bere	414-751-1600	D	50	0.4
Wisconsin Label Corp	1102 Jefferson St	Algoma	WI	54201	Terry Fulwiler	414-487-3424	R	50	0.4
CCL Label	PO Box 5037	Sioux Falls	SD	57117	Craig A Groendyk	605-336-2377	D	45	0.3
John Roberts Co	9687 E River Rd	Minneapolis	MN	55433	Robert A Keene	612-755-5500	R	44	0.3
Banta ISG	7000 Washington S	Eden Prairie	MN	55344	John Colwell	612-941-8780	S	40	0.3
PAXAR Corp	1 Wilcox St	Sayre	PA	18840	A Hershaft	717-888-6641	D	40*	0.3
Perlmuter Printing Co	4437 E 49th St	Cleveland	OH	44125	Richard Perlmuter	216-271-5300	R	40	0.3
Advertising Ltd	1000 Hwy 4 S	Sleepy Eye	MN	56085	Arthur Olsen	507-794-8000	R	39*	0.5
National Print Group Inc	PO Box 1448	Chattanooga	TN	37401	George Diamantis	615-622-1106	R	38	0.4
Hickory Printing Group	PO Box 69	Hickory	NC	28603	Thomas W Reese	704-465-3431	R	37	0.4
American Spirit Graphics Corp	801 SE 9th St	Minneapolis	MN	55414	A Oscar Carlson	612-623-3333	R	36	0.1
Checks in the Mail Inc	PO Box 7802	Irwindale	CA	91706	David Landis	818-962-2500	R	36*	0.4
Allied Printing Service Inc	PO Box 850	Manchester	CT	06045	John G Sommers	203-643-1101	R	35*	0.3
Danbury Printing and Litho Inc	Prindle Ln	Danbury	CT	06810	Melissa Previdi	203-792-5500	S	35	0.3
Gateway Press Inc	4500 Robards Ln	Louisville	KY	40218	C W Georgehead	502-454-0431	R	35*	0.2
Percy Kent Bag Company Inc	5910 Winner Rd	Kansas City	MO	64125	Stephen Barton	816-483-9800	R	35	0.3
Royle Communications Group	112 Market St	Sun Prairie	WI	53590	Richard L Royle	608-837-5161	R	35	0.3
Sells Printing Co	16000 W Rogers Dr	New Berlin	WI	53151	Martin J Krebs	414-784-9500	R	35	0.2
Nahan Printing Inc	PO Box 697	St Cloud	MN	56302	Michael Nahan	612-251-7611	R	34*	0.3
Amer Labelmark Labelmaster	5724 N Pulaski Rd	Chicago	IL	60646	Dwight Curtis	312-478-0900	D	32	0.3
American Labelmark Company	5724 N Pulaski Rd	Chicago	IL	60646	Dwight Curtis	312-478-0900	R	32	0.3
Progress Printing Co	PO Box 4575	Lynchburg	VA	24502	T D Thornton II	804-239-9213	R	32	0.3
Great Western Publishing Inc	1850 E Watkins St	Phoenix	AZ	85034	Nasser Farrokh	602-229-1212	R	31	0.3
Nu-Art	PO Box 2002	Bedford Park	IL	60499	James Motz	708-496-4900	D	31*	0.3
Schwarz Paper Co	8338 N Austin Av	Morton Grove	IL	60053	Andrew McKenna	708-966-2550	R	31	0.3
Continental Datalabel Inc	1855 Fox Ln	Elgin	IL	60123	Timothy Flynn	708-742-1600	R	30	0.1
Envelopes Unlimited Inc	649 N Horners Ln	Rockville	MD	20850	JB Mackey	301-424-3300	R	30*	0.4
Hoyle Products	345 E Plato Blv	St Paul	MN	55107	Rick Farrell	612-293-7500	D	30	0.2
Jefferson Smurfit Corp	Beech & Robertson	Cincinnati	OH	45212	Wayne Gilsdorf	513-396-5600	S	30	0.2
Queens Group New Jersey Inc	180 Talmadge Rd	Edison	NJ	08817	Eric Kaltman	908-287-1300	S	30	0.2
Williams Printing Co	1240 Spring St NW	Atlanta	GA	30309	John R Pope	404-875-6611	S	30*	0.3
Frye and Smith Inc	150 E Baker St	Costa Mesa	CA	92626	Ken Bittner	714-540-7005	S	28	0.2
Bockman Cos	950 S 25th Av	Bellwood	IL	60104	Robert W Perrone	708-544-4090	R	27*	0.3
Lancer Label Inc	PO Box 3637	Omaha	NE	68103	Ric Fisher	402-390-9119	S	26	0.3

Source: *Ward's Business Directory of U.S. Private and Public Companies*, Volumes 1 and 2, 1996. The company type code used is as follows: P - Public, R - Private, S - Subsidiary, D - Division, J - Joint Venture, A - Affiliate, G - Group. Sales are in millions of dollars, employees are in thousands. An asterisk (*) indicates an estimated sales volume. The symbol < stands for 'less than'. Company names and addresses are truncated, in some cases, to fit into the available space.

MATERIALS CONSUMED

Material	Quantity	Delivered Cost ($ million)
Materials, ingredients, containers, and supplies	(X)	3,279.5
Newsprint	(X)	14.3
Uncoated paper in sheets	(X)	85.9
Uncoated paper in rolls	(X)	144.7
Coated paper in sheets	(X)	55.8
Coated paper in rolls	(X)	98.7
Pressure-sensitive base stock, self-adhesive, including paper, film, foil, etc.	(X)	592.6
Cloth and nonwoven fabrics for hardbound book covers	(X)	2.4
Glues and adhesives	(X)	28.7
Printing inks (complete formulations)	(X)	103.5
Light sensitive films and papers	(X)	14.7
Unexposed photosensitive printing plates	(X)	7.7
Printing plates, prepared for printing	(X)	23.1
Engraved printing cylinders for gravure printing	(X)	4.7
Paperboard containers, boxes, and corrugated paperboard	(X)	27.4
All other materials and components, parts, containers, and supplies	(X)	508.6
Materials, ingredients, containers, and supplies, nsk	(X)	1,566.9

Source: 1992 *Economic Census*. Explanation of symbols used: (D): Withheld to avoid disclosure of competitive data; na: Not available; (S): Withheld because statistical norms were not met; (X): Not applicable; (Z): Less than half the unit shown; nec: Not elsewhere classified; nsk: Not specified by kind; - : zero; * : 10-19 percent estimated; ** : 20-29 percent estimated.

PRODUCT SHARE DETAILS

Product or Product Class	% Share
Commercial printing, nec	100.00
Magazine and periodical printing (letterpress)	0.67
Magazine and periodical printing (letterpress), except magazine and comic supplements for Sunday newspapers	56.20
Magazine and periodical printing (letterpress), nsk	43.80
Label and wrapper printing (letterpress)	3.06
Label printing (letterpress), custom and stock labels, including bordered, made of paper, flat (except pressure-sensitive)	9.81
Label printing (letterpress), custom and stock labels, including bordered, made of paper, rolls (except pressure-sensitive)	7.19
Label printing (letterpress), custom and stock labels, including bordered, made of paper, pressure-sensitive (self-adhesive), flat	8.36
Label printing (letterpress), custom and stock labels, including bordered, made of paper, pressure-sensitive (self-adhesive), rolls	42.53
Label printing (letterpress), custom and stock labels, including bordered, made of materials other than paper or cloth	8.36
Printed rolls and sheets for packaging purposes (letterpress), made of paper (single-web)	10.06
Label and wrapper printing (letterpress), nsk	13.67
Catalog and directory printing (letterpress)	0.97
Catalog printing (letterpress), including direct mail catalogs	80.33
Catalog and directory printing (letterpress), nsk	19.56
Financial and legal printing (letterpress)	0.80
SEC filing and prospectus printing (letterpress)	(D)
Annual report and other corporate financial printing (letterpress)	16.51
Other financial and legal printing (letterpress), including insurance forms, security certificates, briefs, etc.	(D)
Bank printing (letterpress), including deposit slips, counter checks, business checks, etc., excluding checkbooks and bank forms	16.91
Bank form printing (letterpress), including passbooks, debit/credit slips, ledger and statement sheets, installment-loan coupons, etc.	11.64
Financial and legal printing (letterpress), nsk	36.81
Advertising printing (letterpress)	3.59
Direct mail advertising printing (letterpress), including circulars, letters, pamphlets, cards, and printed envelopes	35.84
Display advertising poster printing (letterpress), including outdoor advertising, car cards, window, etc.	5.13
Counter, floor display, point-of-purchase, and other display advertising material printing (letterpress)	7.54
Preprinted newspaper advertising insert printing (letterpress) (advertising supplements not regularly issued), rolls, including hi-fi and spectacolor	2.23
Preprinted newspaper advertising insert printing (letterpress) (advertising supplements not regularly issued), sections (two pages or more)	1.93
Shopping news printing (letterpress)	0.33
Other advertising printing (letterpress), including brochures, pamphlets, book jackets, magazine inserts, circular folders, etc.	24.86
Advertising printing (letterpress), nsk	22.17
Other general job printing (letterpress)	9.59
Scientific and technical recording chart and chart paper printing (letterpress) (containing preprinted grids and scale markings)	2.53
Newspaper printing (letterpress)	7.57
Printed decalcomanias and pressure-sensitives (self-adhesive) (letterpress), including bumper stickers, etc., excluding labels	4.36
Business card printing (letterpress)	2.42
Other business form printing, nec (letterpress), excluding blankbooks and looseleaf forms	7.85
Tag printing (letterpress), including embossed	7.52
Ticket, coupon, and food and beverage check printing (letterpress), including transportation and amusement	4.34
Calendar and calendar pad printing (letterpress)	3.30
All other general commercial letterpress printing, nec, including customized stationery	27.09
Other general job printing (letterpress), nsk	33.02
Screen printing, except on textiles	20.68
Screen printed paper labels, custom and stock, including bordered, pressure-sensitive, flat	6.36
Screen printed paper labels, custom and stock, including bordered, pressure-sensitive, rolls	2.98
Other screen printed paper labels, custom and stock, including bordered	0.83
Screen printed labels made of materials other than paper or cloth, custom and stock, including bordered	11.02
Screen printed display advertising posters, including outdoor advertising, car cards, window, etc.	9.24
Screen printed display advertising, including counter, floor display, point-of-purchase, and other printed advertising display material	6.56
Other screen printed advertising materials	4.37
Screen printed decalcomanias and pressure-sensitives (self-adhesive), including bumper stickers, etc., excluding labels	21.22
Screen printing on metal	4.54
Screen printing on glass or plastics containers for others	5.18
All other general commercial screen printing, nec (excluding printing on apparel or fabrics)	10.45
Screen printing, except on textiles, nsk	17.25
Engraving	3.25
Security engraving	39.84
Business card engraving	7.11
Other commercial engraving	32.50
Engraving, nsk	20.59
Nonimpact printing, using laser and ink-jet equipment	1.90
Label and wrapper printing (flexographic)	21.54
Label printing (flexographic), custom and stock labels, including bordered, made of paper, flat (except pressure-sensitive)	1.40

Continued on next page.

PRODUCT SHARE DETAILS - Continued

Product or Product Class	% Share	Product or Product Class	% Share
Label printing (flexographic), custom and stock labels, including bordered, made of paper, rolls (except pressure-sensitive)	6.50	Printed rolls and sheets for packaging purposes (printing only) (flexographic), made of polyethylene (single-web)	7.37
Label printing (flexographic), custom and stock labels, including bordered, made of paper, pressure-sensitive, flat	12.19	Other printed rolls and sheets for packaging purposes (printing only) (flexographic), including multiweb structures	4.96
Label printing (flexographic), custom and stock labels, including bordered, made of paper, pressure-sensitive, rolls	46.81	Label and wrapper printing (flexographic), nsk	9.06
Label printing (flexographic), custom and stock labels, including bordered, made of materials other than paper or cloth	6.13	Flexographic printing, nec (excluding labels and wrappers)	3.38
Printed rolls and sheets for packaging purposes (printing only) (flexographic), made of paper (single-web)	5.58	Magazine and periodical printing (flexographic)	42.99
		Newspaper printing (flexographic), except shopping news	1.51
		All other flexographic printing, nec	42.77
		Flexographic printing, not elsewhere classified (excluding labels and wrappers), nsk	12.76
		Commercial printing, nec, nsk	30.57

Source: 1992 *Economic Census*. The values shown are percent of total shipments in an industry. Values of indented subcategories are summed in the main heading. The symbol (D) appears when data are withheld to prevent disclosure of competitive information. The abbreviation nsk stands for 'not specified by kind' and nec for 'not elsewhere classified'.

INPUTS AND OUTPUTS FOR COMMERCIAL PRINTING

Economic Sector or Industry Providing Inputs	%	Sector	Economic Sector or Industry Buying Outputs	%	Sector
Paper mills, except building paper	34.8	Manufg.	Wholesale trade	9.2	Trade
Wholesale trade	7.9	Trade	Periodicals	7.4	Manufg.
Printing ink	5.9	Manufg.	Membership organizations nec	7.2	Services
Miscellaneous plastics products	4.4	Manufg.	Business/professional associations	6.1	Services
Lithographic platemaking & services	3.5	Manufg.	Labor, civic, social, & fraternal associations	4.9	Services
Typesetting	3.3	Manufg.	Insurance carriers	3.6	Fin/R.E.
Cyclic crudes and organics	2.8	Manufg.	Advertising	3.1	Services
Petroleum refining	2.5	Manufg.	Real estate	3.0	Fin/R.E.
Paper coating & glazing	2.4	Manufg.	Hospitals	2.8	Services
Motor freight transportation & warehousing	2.4	Util.	Computer & data processing services	2.6	Services
Electric services (utilities)	2.2	Util.	Miscellaneous publishing	2.4	Manufg.
Eating & drinking places	2.0	Trade	Newspapers	1.9	Manufg.
Photographic equipment & supplies	1.5	Manufg.	Sausages & other prepared meats	1.9	Manufg.
Real estate	1.2	Fin/R.E.	Exports	1.8	Foreign
U.S. Postal Service	1.2	Gov't	Social services, nec	1.6	Services
Railroads & related services	1.1	Util.	Security & commodity brokers	1.5	Fin/R.E.
Advertising	1.0	Services	Business services nec	1.5	Services
Imports	1.0	Foreign	S/L Govt. purch., higher education	1.5	S/L Govt
Printing trades machinery	0.9	Manufg.	Cigarettes	1.4	Manufg.
Banking	0.9	Fin/R.E.	Banking	1.4	Fin/R.E.
Chemical preparations, nec	0.8	Manufg.	Personal consumption expenditures	1.3	
Mechanical measuring devices	0.8	Manufg.	Metal cans	1.3	Manufg.
Air transportation	0.8	Util.	Federal Government purchases, national defense	1.1	Fed Govt
Equipment rental & leasing services	0.8	Services	S/L Govt. purch., health & hospitals	1.1	S/L Govt
Hotels & lodging places	0.8	Services	Cheese, natural & processed	1.0	Manufg.
Metal foil & leaf	0.7	Manufg.	Food preparations, nec	0.9	Manufg.
Communications, except radio & TV	0.7	Util.	Credit agencies other than banks	0.9	Fin/R.E.
Gas production & distribution (utilities)	0.7	Util.	Federal Government purchases, nondefense	0.9	Fed Govt
Legal services	0.7	Services	Agricultural chemicals, nec	0.8	Manufg.
Management & consulting services & labs	0.7	Services	Malt beverages	0.8	Manufg.
Paperboard mills	0.6	Manufg.	Communications, except radio & TV	0.8	Util.
Photoengraving, electrotyping & stereotyping	0.6	Manufg.	S/L Govt. purch., elem. & secondary education	0.8	S/L Govt
Envelopes	0.5	Manufg.	S/L Govt. purch., natural resource & recreation.	0.8	S/L Govt
Automotive rental & leasing, without drivers	0.5	Services	Pickles, sauces, & salad dressings	0.7	Manufg.
Maintenance of nonfarm buildings nec	0.4	Constr.	Doctors & dentists	0.7	Services
Adhesives & sealants	0.4	Manufg.	Hotels & lodging places	0.7	Services
Accounting, auditing & bookkeeping	0.4	Services	Distilled liquor, except brandy	0.6	Manufg.
Automotive repair shops & services	0.4	Services	Drugs	0.6	Manufg.
Commercial printing	0.3	Manufg.	Insurance agents, brokers, & services	0.6	Fin/R.E.
Industrial inorganic chemicals, nec	0.3	Manufg.	Change in business inventories	0.6	In House
Manifold business forms	0.3	Manufg.	Phonograph records & tapes	0.5	Manufg.
Computer & data processing services	0.3	Services	Roasted coffee	0.5	Manufg.
Engraving & plate printing	0.2	Manufg.	Wines, brandy, & brandy spirits	0.5	Manufg.
Paints & allied products	0.2	Manufg.	Accounting, auditing & bookkeeping	0.5	Services
Paperboard containers & boxes	0.2	Manufg.	Engineering, architectural, & surveying services	0.5	Services
Primary lead	0.2	Manufg.	Legal services	0.5	Services
Transit & bus transportation	0.2	Util.	Management & consulting services & labs	0.5	Services
Water transportation	0.2	Util.	Book publishing	0.4	Manufg.
Insurance carriers	0.2	Fin/R.E.	Motor freight transportation & warehousing	0.4	Util.
Business/professional associations	0.2	Services	Colleges, universities, & professional schools	0.4	Services
Personnel supply services	0.2	Services	Bottled & canned soft drinks	0.3	Manufg.
Lubricating oils & greases	0.1	Manufg.	Canned fruits & vegetables	0.3	Manufg.
Machinery, except electrical, nec	0.1	Manufg.	Dog, cat, & other pet food	0.3	Manufg.
Motor vehicle parts & accessories	0.1	Manufg.	Flavoring extracts & syrups, nec	0.3	Manufg.
Tires & inner tubes	0.1	Manufg.	Greeting card publishing	0.3	Manufg.
Retail trade, except eating & drinking	0.1	Trade	Paints & allied products	0.3	Manufg.
Business services nec	0.1	Services	Shortening & cooking oils	0.3	Manufg.

Continued on next page.

INPUTS AND OUTPUTS FOR COMMERCIAL PRINTING - Continued

Economic Sector or Industry Providing Inputs	%	Sector	Economic Sector or Industry Buying Outputs	%	Sector
Photofinishing labs, commercial photography	0.1	Services	Soap & other detergents	0.3	Manufg.
			Libraries, vocation education	0.3	Services
			Nursing & personal care facilities	0.3	Services
			Local government passenger transit	0.3	Gov't
			S/L Govt. purch., other general government	0.3	S/L Govt
			Canned & cured seafoods	0.2	Manufg.
			Canned specialties	0.2	Manufg.
			Commercial printing	0.2	Manufg.
			Condensed & evaporated milk	0.2	Manufg.
			Dehydrated food products	0.2	Manufg.
			Meat packing plants	0.2	Manufg.
			Mechanical measuring devices	0.2	Manufg.
			Polishes & sanitation goods	0.2	Manufg.
			Poultry dressing plants	0.2	Manufg.
			Sugar	0.2	Manufg.
			Toilet preparations	0.2	Manufg.
			Air transportation	0.2	Util.
			Electric services (utilities)	0.2	Util.
			Railroads & related services	0.2	Util.
			Transit & bus transportation	0.2	Util.
			Retail trade, except eating & drinking	0.2	Trade
			Elementary & secondary schools	0.2	Services
			Funeral service & crematories	0.2	Services
			Medical & health services, nec	0.2	Services
			Membership sports & recreation clubs	0.2	Services
			Portrait, photographic studios	0.2	Services
			Religious organizations	0.2	Services
			S/L Govt. purch., police	0.2	S/L Govt
			Confectionery products	0.1	Manufg.
			Frozen fruits, fruit juices & vegetables	0.1	Manufg.
			Frozen specialties	0.1	Manufg.
			Glass containers	0.1	Manufg.
			Hosiery, nec	0.1	Manufg.
			Manifold business forms	0.1	Manufg.
			Wet corn milling	0.1	Manufg.
			Freight forwarders	0.1	Util.
			Eating & drinking places	0.1	Trade
			Amusement & recreation services nec	0.1	Services
			Miscellaneous repair shops	0.1	Services
			Motion pictures	0.1	Services

Source: Benchmark Input-Output Accounts for the U.S. Economy, 1982, U.S. Department of Commerce, Washington, D.C., July 1991. Data, as reported in the source, are organized by the 1977 SIC structure in use in 1982 but have been matched, as closely as is possible, to the 1987 SIC structure used in this book.

OCCUPATIONS EMPLOYED BY SIC 275 - COMMERCIAL PRINTING AND BUSINESS FORMS

Occupation	% of Total 1994	Change to 2005	Occupation	% of Total 1994	Change to 2005
Offset lithographic press operators	9.2	3.9	Artists & commercial artists	1.5	31.9
Printing press machine setters, operators	8.1	3.9	Typesetting & composing machine operators	1.5	-67.5
Bindery machine operators & set-up operators	6.5	-10.1	Platemakers	1.4	-9.1
Sales & related workers nec	5.9	29.9	Cost estimators	1.3	29.4
General managers & top executives	4.4	23.2	Order clerks, materials, merchandise, & service	1.3	27.1
Strippers, printing	3.4	15.8	Cutting & slicing machine setters, operators	1.3	16.9
Blue collar worker supervisors	3.2	17.8	Production, planning, & expediting clerks	1.3	37.2
Machine feeders & offbearers	3.0	16.9	Camera operators	1.3	3.9
Bookkeeping, accounting, & auditing clerks	2.1	-2.6	Secretaries, ex legal & medical	1.3	18.2
Hand packers & packagers	2.1	22.5	Industrial production managers	1.3	-9.1
General office clerks	1.9	10.8	Screen printing machine setters & set-up operators	1.3	29.9
Printing, binding, & related workers nec	1.8	29.9	Helpers, laborers, & material movers nec	1.2	29.9
Traffic, shipping, & receiving clerks	1.7	25.0	Truck drivers light & heavy	1.2	33.9
Assemblers, fabricators, & hand workers nec	1.7	29.9	Electronic pagination systems workers	1.1	107.8
Job printers	1.6	-22.1	Paste-up workers	1.1	-15.6

Source: Industry-Occupation Matrix, Bureau of Labor Statistics. These data relate to one or more 3-digit SIC industry groups rather than to a single 4-digit SIC. The change reported for each occupation to the year 2005 is a percent of growth or decline as estimated by the Bureau of Labor Statistics. The abbreviation nec stands for 'not elsewhere classified'.

LOCATION BY STATE AND REGIONAL CONCENTRATION

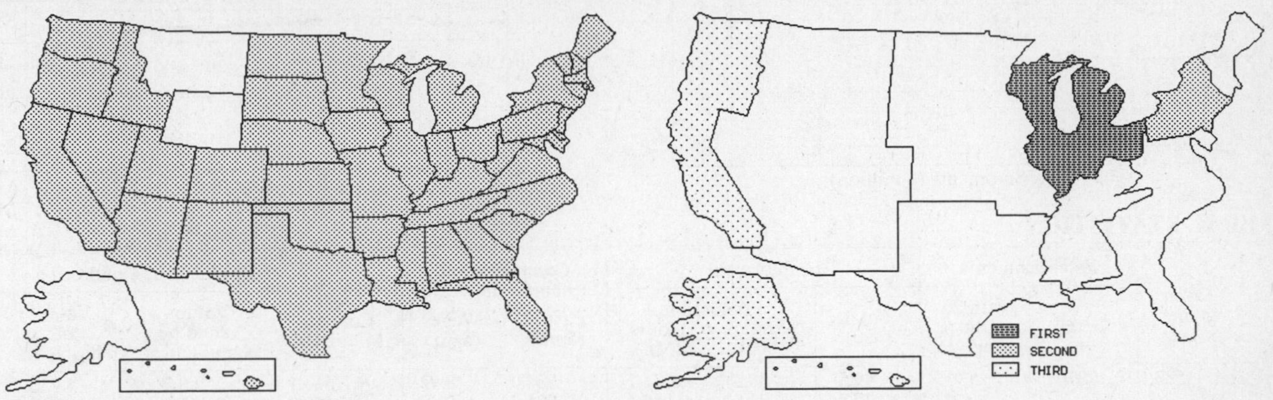

INDUSTRY DATA BY STATE

State	Establish-ments	Shipments			Employment				Cost as % of Shipments	Investment per Employee ($)
		Total ($ mil)	% of U.S.	Per Establ.	Total Number	% of U.S.	Per Establ.	Wages ($/hour)		
Ohio	450	875.5	9.4	1.9	8,600	8.0	19	8.98	42.1	3,430
California	1,130	851.3	9.2	0.8	11,100	10.3	10	9.19	37.1	2,126
New York	670	763.5	8.2	1.1	8,500	7.9	13	10.01	40.0	3,306
Illinois	519	660.4	7.1	1.3	7,600	7.1	15	10.41	38.0	2,737
Wisconsin	190	553.7	6.0	2.9	5,300	4.9	28	10.86	37.1	7,736
Pennsylvania	378	525.7	5.7	1.4	6,100	5.7	16	9.82	41.9	2,016
New Jersey	384	453.0	4.9	1.2	4,900	4.6	13	10.49	39.7	3,816
Michigan	312	335.5	3.6	1.1	3,500	3.3	11	9.60	45.9	3,971
Florida	439	255.7	2.8	0.6	3,600	3.4	8	8.26	41.7	1,806
Georgia	244	239.6	2.6	1.0	2,400	2.2	10	9.68	44.4	4,417
Connecticut	132	225.3	2.4	1.7	2,100	2.0	16	11.77	35.0	3,048
Tennessee	152	190.0	2.0	1.3	2,000	1.9	13	9.77	45.2	2,650
Kansas	76	166.3	1.8	2.2	1,900	1.8	25	8.93	39.7	2,105
Nebraska	58	151.6	1.6	2.6	1,400	1.3	24	10.05	51.2	3,643
Washington	140	133.8	1.4	1.0	1,600	1.5	11	9.55	37.3	2,188
Alabama	101	96.3	1.0	1.0	1,200	1.1	12	8.71	53.4	2,250
Colorado	161	84.2	0.9	0.5	1,200	1.1	7	8.47	42.2	1,833
Virginia	168	76.1	0.8	0.5	900	0.8	5	8.54	45.3	2,333
Oregon	106	71.8	0.8	0.7	800	0.7	8	9.33	43.7	3,375
Louisiana	96	59.4	0.6	0.6	700	0.7	7	7.91	52.4	-
New Hampshire	44	57.4	0.6	1.3	600	0.6	14	9.50	39.2	4,333
D.C.	25	19.9	0.2	0.8	300	0.3	12	8.00	34.7	1,667
Hawaii	27	15.2	0.2	0.6	200	0.2	7	8.67	40.1	2,500
West Virginia	27	8.8	0.1	0.3	100	0.1	4	6.00	40.9	2,000
Texas	543	(D)	-	-	7,500 *	7.0	14	-	-	-
Massachusetts	231	(D)	-	-	3,750 *	3.5	16	-	-	2,933
North Carolina	218	(D)	-	-	1,750 *	1.6	8	-	-	4,914
Missouri	211	(D)	-	-	1,750 *	1.6	8	-	-	-
Minnesota	175	(D)	-	-	3,750 *	3.5	21	-	-	-
Indiana	172	(D)	-	-	1,750 *	1.6	10	-	-	-
Maryland	138	(D)	-	-	1,750 *	1.6	13	-	-	2,171
Arizona	110	(D)	-	-	1,750 *	1.6	16	-	-	-
Oklahoma	107	(D)	-	-	750 *	0.7	7	-	-	-
Kentucky	104	(D)	-	-	1,750 *	1.6	17	-	-	-
South Carolina	88	(D)	-	-	750 *	0.7	9	-	-	-
Iowa	84	(D)	-	-	750 *	0.7	9	-	-	-
Arkansas	63	(D)	-	-	750 *	0.7	12	-	-	-
Rhode Island	56	(D)	-	-	375 *	0.3	7	-	-	-
Utah	55	(D)	-	-	750 *	0.7	14	-	-	-
Mississippi	47	(D)	-	-	375 *	0.3	8	-	-	-
Nevada	41	(D)	-	-	375 *	0.3	9	-	-	-
Maine	39	(D)	-	-	175 *	0.2	4	-	-	-
New Mexico	37	(D)	-	-	175 *	0.2	5	-	-	-
Vermont	29	(D)	-	-	175 *	0.2	6	-	-	-
North Dakota	24	(D)	-	-	175 *	0.2	7	-	-	1,143
Idaho	22	(D)	-	-	175 *	0.2	8	-	-	-
Delaware	14	(D)	-	-	175 *	0.2	13	-	-	-
South Dakota	13	(D)	-	-	375 *	0.3	29	-	-	-

Source: 1992 *Economic Census*. The states are in descending order of shipments or establishments (if shipment data are missing for the majority). The symbol (D) appears when data are withheld to prevent disclosure of competitive information. States marked with (D) are sorted by number of establishments. A dash (-) indicates that the data element cannot be calculated; * indicates the midpoint of a range.

2761 - MANIFOLD BUSINESS FORMS

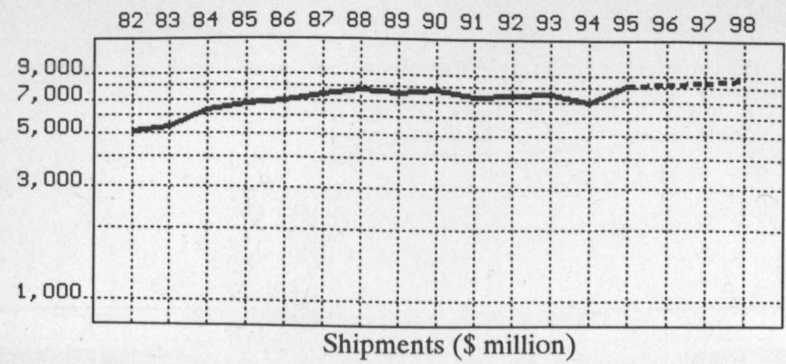

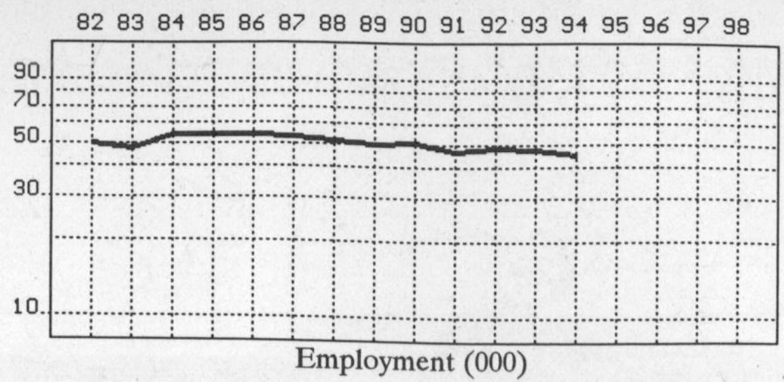

GENERAL STATISTICS

Year	Companies	Establishments: Total	Establishments: with 20 or more employees	Employment: Total (000)	Employment: Production Workers (000)	Employment: Production Hours (Mil)	Compensation: Payroll ($ mil)	Compensation: Wages ($/hr)	Production ($ million): Cost of Materials	Production ($ million): Value Added by Manufacture	Production ($ million): Value of Shipments	Production ($ million): Capital Invest.
1982	583	810	530	49.5	36.2	71.1	934.0	8.92	2,563.1	2,490.7	5,058.7	135.4
1983				47.7	34.5	68.4	981.7	9.60	2,659.2	2,667.5	5,310.7	99.5
1984				53.8	39.1	79.9	1,116.5	9.39	3,132.4	3,203.8	6,297.3	180.9
1985				54.2	38.6	80.1	1,199.6	9.92	3,195.6	3,469.6	6,669.0	218.3
1986				54.2	37.9	80.0	1,272.0	10.34	3,337.1	3,676.1	6,985.1	212.9
1987	601	853	586	53.2	37.2	77.1	1,276.4	10.67	3,478.9	3,882.7	7,397.1	207.5
1988						79.3	1,349.4		3,901.1	3,970.8	7,781.4	
1989		828	569	49.5	34.6	71.9	1,263.4	11.45	3,754.6	3,808.9	7,553.3	213.4
1990				50.3	35.1	71.8	1,326.1	11.74	3,786.7	4,038.1	7,807.5	211.7
1991				46.3	32.2	66.2	1,269.2	12.38	3,381.5	3,839.8	7,233.5	202.1
1992	644	922	540	47.9	33.6	69.3	1,343.2	12.60	3,499.9	3,924.7	7,435.9	160.7
1993				46.9	32.9	67.1	1,329.1	12.86	3,544.9	3,949.2	7,491.3	144.9
1994				45.1	29.6	60.3	1,248.8	12.92	3,292.6	3,706.3	6,981.7	110.6
1995						65.7P	1,409.8P		3,818.1P	4,297.8P	8,096.0P	
1996						64.7P	1,436.4P		3,897.1P	4,386.7P	8,263.5P	
1997						63.7P	1,463.0P		3,976.1P	4,475.7P	8,431.0P	
1998						62.8P	1,489.5P		4,055.1P	4,564.6P	8,598.5P	

Sources: 1982, 1987, 1992 *Economic Census*; *Annual Survey of Manufactures*, 83-86, 88-91, 93-94. Establishment counts for non-Census years are from *County Business Patterns*; establishment values for 83-84 are extrapolations. 'P's show projections by the editors. Industries reclassified in 87 will not have data for prior years.

INDICES OF CHANGE

Year	Companies	Establishments: Total	Establishments: with 20 or more employees	Employment: Total (000)	Employment: Production Workers (000)	Employment: Production Hours (Mil)	Compensation: Payroll ($ mil)	Compensation: Wages ($/hr)	Production ($ million): Cost of Materials	Production ($ million): Value Added by Manufacture	Production ($ million): Value of Shipments	Production ($ million): Capital Invest.
1982	91	88	98	103	108	103	70	71	73	63	68	84
1983				100	103	99	73	76	76	68	71	62
1984				112	116	115	83	75	89	82	85	113
1985				113	115	116	89	79	91	88	90	136
1986				113	113	115	95	82	95	94	94	132
1987	93	93	109	111	111	111	95	85	99	99	99	129
1988						114	100		111	101	105	
1989		90	105	103	103	104	94	91	107	97	102	133
1990				105	104	104	99	93	108	103	105	132
1991				97	96	96	94	98	97	98	97	126
1992	100	100	100	100	100	100	100	100	100	100	100	100
1993				98	98	97	99	102	101	101	101	90
1994				94	88	87	93	103	94	94	94	69
1995						95P	105P		109P	110P	109P	
1996						93P	107P		111P	112P	111P	
1997						92P	109P		114P	114P	113P	
1998						91P	111P		116P	116P	116P	

Sources: Same as General Statistics. Values reflect change from the base year, 1992. Values above 100 mean greater than 92, values below 100 mean less than 92, and a value of 100 in the 82-91 or 93-98 period means same as 92. 'P's mark projections by the editors.

SELECTED RATIOS

For 1992	Avg. of All Manufact.	Analyzed Industry	Index	For 1992	Avg. of All Manufact.	Analyzed Industry	Index
Employees per Establishment	46	52	114	Value Added per Production Worker	122,353	116,807	95
Payroll per Establishment	1,332,320	1,456,833	109	Cost per Establishment	4,239,462	3,795,987	90
Payroll per Employee	29,181	28,042	96	Cost per Employee	92,853	73,067	79
Production Workers per Establishment	31	36	116	Cost per Production Worker	135,003	104,164	77
Wages per Establishment	734,496	947,050	129	Shipments per Establishment	8,100,800	8,064,967	100
Wages per Production Worker	23,390	25,988	111	Shipments per Employee	177,425	155,238	87
Hours per Production Worker	2,025	2,063	102	Shipments per Production Worker	257,966	221,307	86
Wages per Hour	11.55	12.60	109	Investment per Establishment	278,244	174,295	63
Value Added per Establishment	3,842,210	4,256,725	111	Investment per Employee	6,094	3,355	55
Value Added per Employee	84,153	81,935	97	Investment per Production Worker	8,861	4,783	54

Sources: Same as General Statistics. The 'Average of All Manufacturing' column represents the average of all manufacturing industries reported for the most recent complete year available. The Index shows the relationship between the Average and the Analyzed Industry. For example, 100 means that they are equal; 500 that the Analyzed Industry is five times the average; 50 means that the Analyzed Industry is half the national average. The abbreviation 'na' is used to show that data are 'not available'.

LEADING COMPANIES

Number shown: **75** Total sales ($ mil): **2,971** Total employment (000): **23.5**

Company Name	Address				CEO Name	Phone	Co. Type	Sales ($ mil)	Empl. (000)
Standard Register Co	PO Box 1167	Dayton	OH	45401	Peter S Redding	513-443-1506	P	767	6.2
New England Business Service	500 Main St	Groton	MA	01471	William C Love	508-448-6111	P	251	2.1
Shade/Allied Inc	PO Box 19730	Green Bay	WI	54307	Harold L Ellsworth	414-432-6700	R	155	0.6
Vanier Business Forms & Svcs	2140oneridge Mall	Pleasanton	CA	94588	John P Moran	510-416-6100	S	140	1.0
McGregor Printing Corp	2121 K St NW	Washington	DC	20037	Louis M Byron	202-333-4411	R	123	0.4
Bankers Systems Inc	PO Box 1457	St Cloud	MN	56302	JP Weitzel	612-251-3060	R	100	1.0
Transkrit Corp	PO Box 40020	Roanoke	VA	24022	Frank Neubauer	703-853-8000	S	96	1.1
Office Electronics Inc	865 W Irving Pk Rd	Itasca	IL	60143	Robert A Houston	708-773-2270	R	94	0.5
Rapidforms Inc	301 Grove Rd	Thorofare	NJ	08086	James H Bromley	609-257-8354	S	62*	0.5
Paris Business Forms Inc	122 Kissel Rd	Burlington	NJ	08016	D P Toscani Sr	609-387-7300	P	59	0.3
Jordan Graphics	PO Box 668306	Charlotte	NC	28266	Brian F Gallagher	704-394-2121	S	55	0.4
Capital Graphics Inc	PO Box 278	Spring Grove	IL	60081	Ben L McSwiney	815-675-2392	S	45	0.4
General Business Forms Inc	PO Box 457	Skokie	IL	60077	Richard S Kuntz	708-677-1700	R	45	0.4
Adams Business Forms Inc	PO Box 91	Topeka	KS	66601	PE Adams	913-233-4101	R	41	0.5
Ward/Kraft Inc	2401 S Cooper St	Fort Scott	KS	66701	Roger Kraft	316-223-5500	R	41	0.4
Craftsman Press Inc	1155 Valley St	Seattle	WA	98109	George Prue	206-682-8800	R	40	0.3
Holden Business Forms Co	607 Washington N	Minneapolis	MN	55401	George T Holden	612-339-0241	R	37*	0.3
Interform Corp	PO Box A	Bridgeville	PA	15017	G Duncan Fraser Jr	412-221-3300	S	37	0.4
Advance Business Graphics	3810 Wabash Dr	Mira Loma	CA	91752	John Kosta	909-685-7100	R	34	0.3
Miami Systems Corp	40 High School Av	Shelby	OH	44875	Samuel Peters	419-342-3515	S	30	0.3
Wilmer Service Line	PO Box 2237	Dayton	OH	45401	Robert Nevin	513-290-7019	D	28	0.3
Apperson Business Forms Inc	PO Box 60666	Los Angeles	CA	90060	Robert P Apperson	310-927-4718	R	28	0.3
Wise Business Forms Inc	PO Box 1666	Butler	PA	16003	W D Prettyman	412-283-1666	R	28	0.3
TOPS Business Forms	1040 S Milwaukee	Wheeling	IL	60090	Tom Brooker	708-459-4660	D	27*	0.2
Northstar Computer Forms Inc	7130 Nland Cir	Brooklyn Park	MN	55428	Roger T Bredesen	612-531-7340	P	23	0.2
Royal Business Forms Inc	PO Box 5868	Arlington	TX	76005	Alf R Bumgardner	817-640-5248	R	21*	0.2
Adams Investment Co	PO Drawer A	Bartlesville	OK	74005	K Adams	918-335-1010	R	20	0.2
Dataforms Inc	PO Box 51164	New Berlin	WI	53151	Andrew Tully	414-786-2600	R	20*	0.2
Famous Hospitality Inc	3493 Lamar Av	Memphis	TN	38118	John Burkhart	901-365-4742	R	20*	0.2
FCA	PO Box 278	Spring Grove	IL	60081	Doug Friedrich	815-675-2392	D	20	0.2
Rotary Forms Press Inc	835 S High St	Hillsboro	OH	45133	AB Cassner	513-393-3426	R	20	0.1
Wesley's Business Forms	PO Box 7685	Winston-Salem	NC	27109	RN Wesley Jr	910-969-9101	D	20*	0.2
Data Papers Inc	PO Box 149	Muncy	PA	17756	Gene Crawford	717-546-2201	R	18	0.1
Bregg Data Forms Inc	75 Adams Av	Hauppauge	NY	11788	Ron Rothberg	516-273-8383	R	17	0.1
Hygrade Printing Corp	8 Fairfield Crescent	West Caldwell	NJ	07006	Vic Albetta	201-575-7714	R	17	0.1
Datatel Resources Corp	PO Box M	Monaca	PA	15061	Allan J Simon	412-775-5300	R	16	<0.1
Great Lakes Business Forms Inc	PO Box 1157	Grand Rapids	MI	49501	Ken Carpenter	616-791-0100	R	16*	0.2
Performance Computer Forms	21673 Cedar Av	Lakeville	MN	55044	Russel De Fauw	612-469-1400	R	16	<0.1
Specialized Printed Forms Inc	352 Center St	Caledonia	NY	14423	Casey Randall	716-538-2381	R	16	0.2
Kaye-Smith Business Graphics	PO Box 956	Renton	WA	98057	Lester M Smith	206-455-0923	D	15	0.2
Bowater Computer Forms	PO Box 8801	Moline	IL	61265	Shelly Saidman	309-797-1389	D	13	0.1
CB Forms LP	309 Mill Rd	East Prairie	MO	63845	Donald R Sloan	314-649-3557	R	13	<0.1
Forms Manufacturing Inc	312 E Forest St	Girard	KS	66743	James R Orwig	316-724-8225	R	13*	0.1
Kowa Printing Corp	266 Eastgate Dr	Danville	IL	61832	Thomas W Kowa	217-446-6111	R	13	0.2
Liberty Business Forms & Syst	265 Executive Dr	Plainview	NY	11803	William Cosnotti	516-349-1121	R	13	0.1
A-S Hospitality	3493 Lamar Av	Memphis	TN	38118	John W Burkham	901-365-4742	D	13	<0.1
B and D Litho Inc	3820 N 38th Av	Phoenix	AZ	85019	Steven Gaynor	602-269-2526	R	12*	<0.1
International Graphics Inc	PO Box 1680	Little Rock	AR	72203	Sam C Sewell	501-378-2600	R	12	0.2
Vallis Wngroff Business Forms	PO Box 7	Cherryvale	KS	67335	V Neils Agather	316-336-2171	R	12	0.1
Imperial Graphics Inc	PO Box 103	Grand Rapids	MI	49501	MR Bissell	616-784-0100	S	11	<0.1
Eastern Business Forms Inc	PO Box 10	Mauldin	SC	29662	Ralph A Price	803-288-2451	R	11	0.2
Woodbury Business Forms Inc	101 Lukken Indrial	La Grange	GA	30240	Ken Boatwright	706-882-2977	R	11	0.2
Freedom Graphics Systems Inc	PO Box 246	Milton	WI	53563	Marty Liebert	608-868-7007	R	9*	<0.1
Quality Forms	PO Box 1176	Piqua	OH	45356	JT Phillips	513-773-4595	R	9	0.1
Falcon Business Forms Inc	PO Box 326	Corsicana	TX	75151	Maurice Kirkpatrick	903-874-6583	R	9	0.1
Ace Forms Inc	2900 N Rotary Ter	Pittsburg	KS	66762	Leon Bogner	316-232-9290	R	8	0.1
Allen and Company Printers Inc	101 E Bowie St	Fort Worth	TX	76110	James Allen	817-923-7363	R	8	<0.1
Arrow Business Forms & Labels	PO Box 297	Medfield	MA	02052	Michael Hurley	508-359-2344	R	8*	<0.1
Continuous Forms Inc	12238 Woodbine	Detroit	MI	48239	JR Griffith	313-255-7600	R	8*	<0.1
International Business Systems	PO Box 2486	King of Prussia	PA	19406	George Schnyder	215-265-8210	R	8	<0.1
Midwest Rotary Meniforms Inc	PO Box 112	Caro	MI	48723	Daniel S Gale	517-673-2124	R	8	<0.1
NJ Business Forms	55 W Sheffield Av	Englewood	NJ	07631	John Harnett	201-569-4500	R	8	<0.1
Rough Notes Company Inc	PO Box 564	Indianapolis	IN	46204	WJ Gdowski	317-634-1541	R	8	0.1
Graphic Forms and Labels Inc	PO Box 468	Nevada	IA	50201	William Michel	515-382-6561	R	7	<0.1
Diversified Business Systems	PO Box 110	Haverhill	MA	01831	Mary L Gormley	508-373-4748	R	7	<0.1
Eastern Continuous Forms Inc	PO Box 1429	North Wales	PA	19454	Add B Anderson Jr	215-699-7791	R	7*	<0.1
Elgin Business Forms Inc	1779 Fleetwood Dr	Elgin	IL	60123	Thomas Weger	708-695-9480	R	7	<0.1
Perry Printing Company Inc	PO Box 127	Flint	MI	48501	Bruce A Nyland	810-232-6162	R	7	<0.1
System and Methods Inc	4200 Chevy Chase	Los Angeles	CA	90039	LG Shonka	213-245-7331	R	7	<0.1
Automatic Business Products	1531 Airway Cir	N Smyrna Bch	FL	32168	Richard Foote	904-427-3638	R	7	<0.1
Associated Printers Inc	7144 Ambassador	Baltimore	MD	21244	G Curtis Brown Jr	410-944-8560	R	5*	<0.1
Cal Snap and Tab Corp	1210 Fullerton Rd	City of Industry	CA	91748	Frank T Kershner	818-854-1570	R	5	<0.1
Custom Business Forms Inc	210 Edge Pl NE	Minneapolis	MN	55418	FA Miske Jr	612-789-0002	R	5*	<0.1
Edinburgh Press Inc	6575 Chestnut St	Pennsauken	NJ	08109	RL Lipp	609-662-8266	R	5	<0.1
Southern Specialty Printing Inc	PO Box 1968	Gastonia	NC	28053	Albert R Morris	704-864-5484	R	5*	<0.1

Source: *Ward's Business Directory of U.S. Private and Public Companies*, Volumes 1 and 2, 1996. The company type code used is as follows: P - Public, R - Private, S - Subsidiary, D - Division, J - Joint Venture, A - Affiliate, G - Group. Sales are in millions of dollars, employees are in thousands. An asterisk (*) indicates an estimated sales volume. The symbol < stands for 'less than'. Company names and addresses are truncated, in some cases, to fit into the available space.

MATERIALS CONSUMED

Material	Quantity	Delivered Cost ($ million)
Materials, ingredients, containers, and supplies	(X)	3,110.2
Coated paper	(X)	138.8
Uncoated paper	(X)	1,380.8
Carbonless paper	(X)	603.3
Carbonizing tissue stock for conversion into one-time carbon paper	(X)	16.5
One-time carbon paper	(X)	55.1
Pressure-sensitive base stock, self-adhesive, including paper, film, foil, etc.	(X)	73.2
Printing inks (complete formulations)	(X)	32.9
Paperboard containers, boxes, and corrugated paperboard	(X)	77.3
All other materials and components, parts, containers, and supplies	(X)	201.7
Materials, ingredients, containers, and supplies, nsk	(X)	530.5

Source: 1992 *Economic Census*. Explanation of symbols used: (D): Withheld to avoid disclosure of competitive data; na: Not available; (S): Withheld because statistical norms were not met; (X): Not applicable; (Z): Less than half the unit shown; nec: Not elsewhere classified; nsk: Not specified by kind; - : zero; * : 10-19 percent estimated; ** : 20-29 percent estimated.

PRODUCT SHARE DETAILS

Product or Product Class	% Share	Product or Product Class	% Share
Manifold business forms	100.00	Custom continuous insert self-mailer business forms	3.86
Unit set forms, loose or bound	21.83	All other custom continuous self-mailer business forms	1.20
Unit set label/form combination business forms, loose or bound	1.42	Custom continuous business forms, one part, with product affixed	3.19
Unit set business forms, loose or bound, stock (including imprinted), with one-time carbon	9.38	All other custom continuous business forms, nec, one part with no product affixed	20.15
Unit set business forms, loose or bound, stock (including imprinted), carbonless	6.61	All other custom continuous multiple part business forms, with one-time carbon	15.17
Unit set business forms, loose or bound, custom printed, with one-time carbon	25.82	All other custom continuous multiple part business forms, carbonless	35.13
Unit set business forms, loose or bound, custom printed, carbonless	42.38	Custom continuous forms, nsk	11.47
Tabulating card sets	0.63	Stock continuous business forms	22.58
Unit set forms, loose or bound, nsk	13.74	Stock continuous label/form combination business forms	3.03
Manifold books and pegboard accounting systems	4.92	Stock continuous jumbo roll-feed business forms	1.28
Pegboard accounting systems	31.07	All other stock continuous business forms, nec, one part	52.87
Sales and other manifold books	51.12	All other stock continuous business forms, nec, multiple part with one-time carbon	5.81
Manifold books and pegboard accounting systems, nsk	17.81	All other stock continuous business forms, nec, multiple part, carbonless	16.95
Custom continuous business forms	38.17	Stock continuous forms, nsk	20.06
Custom continuous label/form combination business forms	4.07	Manifold business forms, nsk	12.49
Custom continuous jumbo roll-feed business forms	3.40		
Custom continuous peel-back self-mailer business forms	2.36		

Source: 1992 *Economic Census*. The values shown are percent of total shipments in an industry. Values of indented subcategories are summed in the main heading. The symbol (D) appears when data are withheld to prevent disclosure of competitive information. The abbreviation nsk stands for 'not specified by kind' and nec for 'not elsewhere classified'.

INPUTS AND OUTPUTS FOR MANIFOLD BUSINESS FORMS

Economic Sector or Industry Providing Inputs	%	Sector	Economic Sector or Industry Buying Outputs	%	Sector
Paper mills, except building paper	53.7	Manufg.	Hospitals	8.2	Services
Wholesale trade	8.9	Trade	Banking	6.3	Fin/R.E.
Computer & data processing services	6.1	Services	Computer & data processing services	5.8	Services
Carbon paper & inked ribbons	4.4	Manufg.	Insurance carriers	4.9	Fin/R.E.
Typesetting	2.7	Manufg.	S/L Govt. purch., elem. & secondary education	4.4	S/L Govt
Motor freight transportation & warehousing	2.0	Util.	S/L Govt. purch., other general government	4.4	S/L Govt
Electric services (utilities)	1.5	Util.	Federal Government purchases, nondefense	3.2	Fed Govt
Petroleum refining	1.4	Manufg.	S/L Govt. purch., higher education	3.0	S/L Govt
Paperboard containers & boxes	1.3	Manufg.	Communications, except radio & TV	2.7	Util.
Railroads & related services	1.3	Util.	Credit agencies other than banks	2.5	Fin/R.E.
Advertising	1.2	Services	Insurance agents, brokers, & services	2.0	Fin/R.E.
Adhesives & sealants	1.1	Manufg.	Accounting, auditing & bookkeeping	2.0	Services
Eating & drinking places	1.1	Trade	S/L Govt. purch., health & hospitals	1.9	S/L Govt
Commercial printing	0.9	Manufg.	Federal Government purchases, national defense	1.8	Fed Govt
Communications, except radio & TV	0.9	Util.	Engineering, architectural, & surveying services	1.6	Services
Banking	0.9	Fin/R.E.	Social services, nec	1.5	Services
Hotels & lodging places	0.8	Services	Crude petroleum & natural gas	1.4	Mining
Printing ink	0.7	Manufg.	Motor freight transportation & warehousing	1.4	Util.
Air transportation	0.6	Util.	Security & commodity brokers	1.3	Fin/R.E.
Sanitary services, steam supply, irrigation	0.6	Util.	S/L Govt. purch., public assistance & relief	1.3	S/L Govt
Printing trades machinery	0.5	Manufg.	Electric services (utilities)	1.1	Util.
Chemical preparations, nec	0.4	Manufg.	Commercial printing	1.0	Manufg.
Die-cut paper & board	0.4	Manufg.	Electronic computing equipment	0.9	Manufg.
Manifold business forms	0.4	Manufg.	Newspapers	0.9	Manufg.
Mechanical measuring devices	0.4	Manufg.	S/L Govt. purch., police	0.7	S/L Govt

Continued on next page.

INPUTS AND OUTPUTS FOR MANIFOLD BUSINESS FORMS - Continued

Economic Sector or Industry Providing Inputs	%	Sector	Economic Sector or Industry Buying Outputs	%	Sector
Equipment rental & leasing services	0.4	Services	Drugs	0.6	Manufg.
Legal services	0.4	Services	Radio & TV communication equipment	0.6	Manufg.
Management & consulting services & labs	0.4	Services	Colleges, universities, & professional schools	0.6	Services
Maintenance of nonfarm buildings nec	0.3	Constr.	Apparel made from purchased materials	0.5	Manufg.
Gas production & distribution (utilities)	0.3	Util.	Miscellaneous plastics products	0.5	Manufg.
Real estate	0.3	Fin/R.E.	Air transportation	0.5	Util.
Automotive rental & leasing, without drivers	0.3	Services	Radio & TV broadcasting	0.5	Util.
U.S. Postal Service	0.3	Gov't	State & local government enterprises, nec	0.5	Gov't
Paper coating & glazing	0.2	Manufg.	Residential 1-unit structures, nonfarm	0.4	Constr.
Water supply & sewage systems	0.2	Util.	Aircraft	0.4	Manufg.
Insurance carriers	0.2	Fin/R.E.	Electronic components nec	0.4	Manufg.
Accounting, auditing & bookkeeping	0.2	Services	Guided missiles & space vehicles	0.4	Manufg.
Automotive repair shops & services	0.2	Services	Machinery, except electrical, nec	0.4	Manufg.
Lithographic platemaking & services	0.1	Manufg.	Manufacturing industries, nec	0.4	Manufg.
Photographic equipment & supplies	0.1	Manufg.	Motor vehicle parts & accessories	0.4	Manufg.
Transit & bus transportation	0.1	Util.	Motor vehicles & car bodies	0.4	Manufg.
Credit agencies other than banks	0.1	Fin/R.E.	Gas production & distribution (utilities)	0.4	Util.
Royalties	0.1	Fin/R.E.	Railroads & related services	0.4	Util.
Detective & protective services	0.1	Services	Business/professional associations	0.4	Services
Personnel supply services	0.1	Services	Libraries, vocation education	0.4	Services
			Religious organizations	0.4	Services
			Industrial buildings	0.3	Constr.
			Office buildings	0.3	Constr.
			Aircraft & missile engines & engine parts	0.3	Manufg.
			Blast furnaces & steel mills	0.3	Manufg.
			Broadwoven fabric mills	0.3	Manufg.
			Petroleum refining	0.3	Manufg.
			Photographic equipment & supplies	0.3	Manufg.
			Semiconductors & related devices	0.3	Manufg.
			Arrangement of passenger transportation	0.3	Util.
			Elementary & secondary schools	0.3	Services
			Membership organizations nec	0.3	Services
			Exports	0.3	Foreign
			S/L Govt. purch., correction	0.3	S/L Govt
			S/L Govt. purch., natural resource & recreation.	0.3	S/L Govt
			S/L Govt. purch., other education & libraries	0.3	S/L Govt
			Agricultural, forestry, & fishery services	0.2	Agric.
			Coal	0.2	Mining
			Maintenance of nonfarm buildings nec	0.2	Constr.
			Aircraft & missile equipment, nec	0.2	Manufg.
			Book publishing	0.2	Manufg.
			Cyclic crudes and organics	0.2	Manufg.
			Electrical equipment & supplies, nec	0.2	Manufg.
			Industrial inorganic chemicals, nec	0.2	Manufg.
			Manifold business forms	0.2	Manufg.
			Paper mills, except building paper	0.2	Manufg.
			Paperboard containers & boxes	0.2	Manufg.
			Periodicals	0.2	Manufg.
			Refrigeration & heating equipment	0.2	Manufg.
			Special dies & tools & machine tool accessories	0.2	Manufg.
			Surgical & medical instruments	0.2	Manufg.
			Telephone & telegraph apparatus	0.2	Manufg.
			Freight forwarders	0.2	Util.
			Transit & bus transportation	0.2	Util.
			Water transportation	0.2	Util.
			Retail trade, except eating & drinking	0.2	Trade
			Federal Government enterprises nec	0.2	Gov't
			Electric utility facility construction	0.1	Constr.
			Residential additions/alterations, nonfarm	0.1	Constr.
			Bottled & canned soft drinks	0.1	Manufg.
			Construction machinery & equipment	0.1	Manufg.
			Engineering & scientific instruments	0.1	Manufg.
			Fabricated plate work (boiler shops)	0.1	Manufg.
			Farm machinery & equipment	0.1	Manufg.
			Food preparations, nec	0.1	Manufg.
			Glass & glass products, except containers	0.1	Manufg.
			Instruments to measure electricity	0.1	Manufg.
			Iron & steel foundries	0.1	Manufg.
			Mechanical measuring devices	0.1	Manufg.
			Miscellaneous publishing	0.1	Manufg.
			Motors & generators	0.1	Manufg.
			Oil field machinery	0.1	Manufg.
			Organic fibers, noncellulosic	0.1	Manufg.
			Paints & allied products	0.1	Manufg.
			Pipe, valves, & pipe fittings	0.1	Manufg.

Continued on next page.

INPUTS AND OUTPUTS FOR MANIFOLD BUSINESS FORMS - Continued

Economic Sector or Industry Providing Inputs	%	Sector	Economic Sector or Industry Buying Outputs	%	Sector
			Plastics materials & resins	0.1	Manufg.
			Pumps & compressors	0.1	Manufg.
			Radio & TV receiving sets	0.1	Manufg.
			Sheet metal work	0.1	Manufg.
			Ship building & repairing	0.1	Manufg.
			Surgical appliances & supplies	0.1	Manufg.
			Toilet preparations	0.1	Manufg.
			Typewriters & office machines, nec	0.1	Manufg.
			Wiring devices	0.1	Manufg.
			Wood household furniture	0.1	Manufg.
			Yarn mills & finishing of textiles, nec	0.1	Manufg.
			Sanitary services, steam supply, irrigation	0.1	Util.
			Wholesale trade	0.1	Trade
			Child day care services	0.1	Services
			Local government passenger transit	0.1	Gov't
			U.S. Postal Service	0.1	Gov't
			S/L Govt. purch., fire	0.1	S/L Govt

Source: Benchmark Input-Output Accounts for the U.S. Economy, 1982, U.S. Department of Commerce, Washington, D.C., July 1991. Data, as reported in the source, are organized by the 1977 SIC structure in use in 1982 but have been matched, as closely as is possible, to the 1987 SIC structure used in this book.

OCCUPATIONS EMPLOYED BY SIC 276 - COMMERCIAL PRINTING AND BUSINESS FORMS

Occupation	% of Total 1994	Change to 2005	Occupation	% of Total 1994	Change to 2005
Offset lithographic press operators	9.2	3.9	Artists & commercial artists	1.5	31.9
Printing press machine setters, operators	8.1	3.9	Typesetting & composing machine operators	1.5	-67.5
Bindery machine operators & set-up operators	6.5	-10.1	Platemakers	1.4	-9.1
Sales & related workers nec	5.9	29.9	Cost estimators	1.3	29.4
General managers & top executives	4.4	23.2	Order clerks, materials, merchandise, & service	1.3	27.1
Strippers, printing	3.4	15.8	Cutting & slicing machine setters, operators	1.3	16.9
Blue collar worker supervisors	3.2	17.8	Production, planning, & expediting clerks	1.3	37.2
Machine feeders & offbearers	3.0	16.9	Camera operators	1.3	3.9
Bookkeeping, accounting, & auditing clerks	2.1	-2.6	Secretaries, ex legal & medical	1.3	18.2
Hand packers & packagers	2.1	22.5	Industrial production managers	1.3	-9.1
General office clerks	1.9	10.8	Screen printing machine setters & set-up operators	1.3	29.9
Printing, binding, & related workers nec	1.8	29.9	Helpers, laborers, & material movers nec	1.2	29.9
Traffic, shipping, & receiving clerks	1.7	25.0	Truck drivers light & heavy	1.2	33.9
Assemblers, fabricators, & hand workers nec	1.7	29.9	Electronic pagination systems workers	1.1	107.8
Job printers	1.6	-22.1	Paste-up workers	1.1	-15.6

Source: Industry-Occupation Matrix, Bureau of Labor Statistics. These data relate to one or more 3-digit SIC industry groups rather than to a single 4-digit SIC. The change reported for each occupation to the year 2005 is a percent of growth or decline as estimated by the Bureau of Labor Statistics. The abbreviation nec stands for 'not elsewhere classified'.

LOCATION BY STATE AND REGIONAL CONCENTRATION

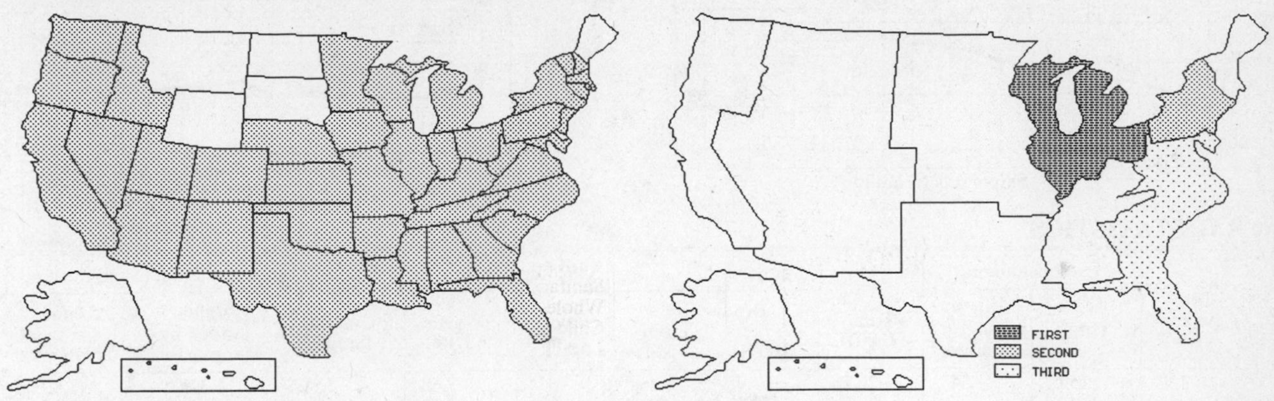

INDUSTRY DATA BY STATE

State	Establish-ments	Shipments			Employment				Cost as % of Shipments	Investment per Employee ($)
		Total ($ mil)	% of U.S.	Per Establ.	Total Number	% of U.S.	Per Establ.	Wages ($/hour)		
Pennsylvania	64	847.1	11.4	13.2	4,500	9.4	70	12.74	52.5	3,756
California	101	639.7	8.6	6.3	4,300	9.0	43	13.46	49.4	2,814
Texas	76	526.6	7.1	6.9	3,400	7.1	45	11.70	49.8	4,147
Illinois	57	519.2	7.0	9.1	3,100	6.5	54	12.47	53.8	5,032
Ohio	36	337.9	4.5	9.4	2,700	5.6	75	12.63	38.1	2,778
Indiana	18	310.9	4.2	17.3	1,500	3.1	83	12.32	53.3	2,867
Missouri	27	289.3	3.9	10.7	1,400	2.9	52	11.18	39.6	1,714
Iowa	17	240.4	3.2	14.1	1,400	2.9	82	12.83	45.2	4,214
Wisconsin	24	225.2	3.0	9.4	1,000	2.1	42	12.27	42.8	1,500
New York	48	208.9	2.8	4.4	2,100	4.4	44	13.23	41.3	1,810
Michigan	33	204.3	2.7	6.2	1,500	3.1	45	13.67	48.1	2,200
New Jersey	29	201.8	2.7	7.0	1,200	2.5	41	14.38	51.4	2,083
Georgia	36	200.4	2.7	5.6	1,400	2.9	39	11.67	45.2	2,500
Kansas	18	173.5	2.3	9.6	1,700	3.5	94	11.28	44.8	3,824
Florida	37	170.2	2.3	4.6	1,200	2.5	32	12.07	55.3	4,583
Tennessee	25	157.2	2.1	6.3	1,100	2.3	44	12.40	42.3	11,364
Minnesota	19	154.2	2.1	8.1	1,200	2.5	63	14.07	44.0	1,750
Oregon	19	145.6	2.0	7.7	1,000	2.1	53	13.67	50.8	1,500
Maryland	9	142.2	1.9	15.8	700	1.5	78	11.33	42.9	3,857
North Carolina	31	139.9	1.9	4.5	1,200	2.5	39	11.11	47.9	3,500
Virginia	17	135.0	1.8	7.9	900	1.9	53	9.67	43.0	3,444
Massachusetts	15	122.8	1.7	8.2	800	1.7	53	13.09	31.4	3,375
Utah	9	119.3	1.6	13.3	700	1.5	78	14.80	30.3	2,000
Vermont	4	115.9	1.6	29.0	500	1.0	125	17.00	46.2	5,600
Oklahoma	8	115.1	1.5	14.4	700	1.5	88	11.60	51.8	2,143
South Carolina	8	111.1	1.5	13.9	600	1.3	75	11.00	48.7	4,667
Kentucky	8	105.1	1.4	13.1	700	1.5	88	12.33	48.6	-
Arizona	20	92.6	1.2	4.6	700	1.5	35	10.82	37.8	1,714
Arkansas	7	91.8	1.2	13.1	600	1.3	86	15.60	35.3	3,167
New Hampshire	6	90.7	1.2	15.1	700	1.5	117	13.82	35.7	-
Connecticut	13	74.3	1.0	5.7	600	1.3	46	12.71	51.7	1,500
Colorado	9	51.3	0.7	5.7	400	0.8	44	12.33	55.9	3,000
Washington	15	39.6	0.5	2.6	400	0.8	27	14.80	47.7	2,250
Louisiana	12	37.0	0.5	3.1	300	0.6	25	9.75	53.0	2,333
Alabama	9	30.4	0.4	3.4	200	0.4	22	11.33	37.5	1,500
Rhode Island	5	26.7	0.4	5.3	200	0.4	40	12.67	47.9	-
Nevada	8	25.8	0.3	3.2	200	0.4	25	14.00	52.3	2,500
Mississippi	7	19.9	0.3	2.8	200	0.4	29	11.50	43.2	2,000
Nebraska	6	(D)	-	-	375 *	0.8	63	-	-	-
West Virginia	3	(D)	-	-	375 *	0.8	125	-	-	-
New Mexico	2	(D)	-	-	175 *	0.4	88	-	-	-
Idaho	1	(D)	-	-	175 *	0.4	175	-	-	-

Source: 1992 *Economic Census*. The states are in descending order of shipments or establishments (if shipment data are missing for the majority). The symbol (D) appears when data are withheld to prevent disclosure of competitive information. States marked with (D) are sorted by number of establishments. A dash (-) indicates that the data element cannot be calculated; * indicates the midpoint of a range.

2771 - GREETING CARDS

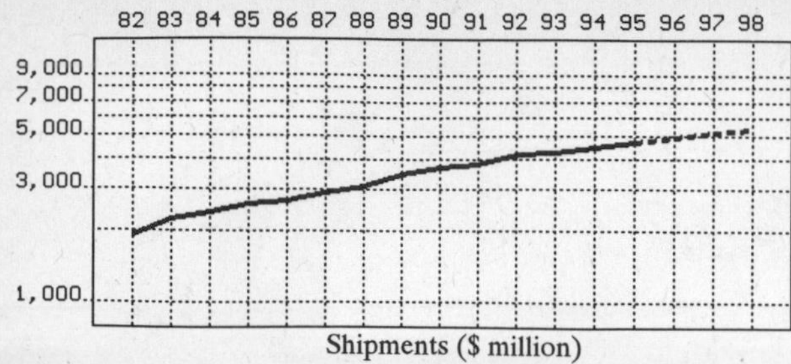

Shipments ($ million)

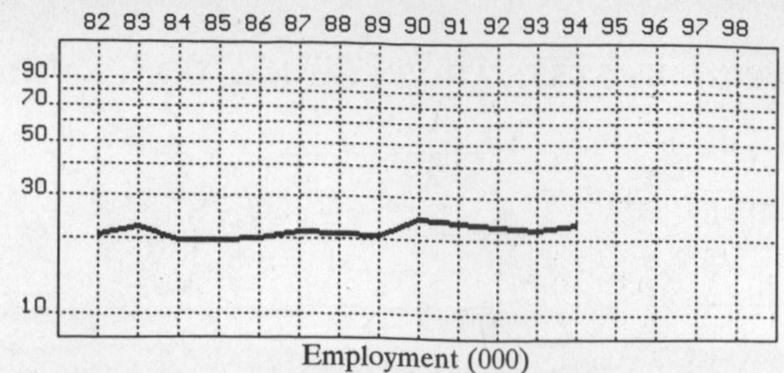

Employment (000)

GENERAL STATISTICS

Year	Companies	Establishments: Total	Establishments: with 20 or more employees	Employment: Total (000)	Employment: Production Workers (000)	Employment: Production Hours (Mil)	Compensation: Payroll ($ mil)	Compensation: Wages ($/hr)	Production ($ million): Cost of Materials	Production ($ million): Value Added by Manufacture	Production ($ million): Value of Shipments	Production ($ million): Capital Invest.
1982	139	154	54	20.8	11.7	20.2	344.2	7.68	554.6	1,348.8	1,893.6	37.2
1983				22.5	13.5	21.0	381.6	8.10	666.4	1,611.2	2,250.6	51.1
1984				19.8	10.8	18.4	386.2	9.20	748.8	1,667.0	2,394.2	91.0
1985				19.9	10.8	17.7	397.5	9.43	672.9	1,894.8	2,598.0	46.5
1986				20.0	10.8	19.3	407.4	9.02	620.2	2,036.2	2,681.4	48.4
1987	147	162	64	21.5	11.9	21.7	471.1	9.54	773.9	2,203.9	2,911.1	65.6
1988						19.0	474.1		810.7	2,279.2	3,081.7	
1989		144	57	20.8	11.2	20.8	537.3	10.15	906.6	2,553.7	3,449.2	107.1
1990				24.6	12.3	23.7	625.2	10.10	938.3	2,827.5	3,720.7	132.0
1991				23.9	12.5	22.8	609.1	10.46	870.2	2,925.4	3,809.9	94.1
1992	157	173	62	22.8	11.8	21.1	585.1	10.76	743.0	3,393.5	4,195.6	85.7
1993				22.2	12.2	20.5	610.4	11.51	825.8	3,481.6	4,274.5	53.8
1994				23.2	13.0	22.2	627.5	11.37	915.0	3,660.0	4,507.2	71.0
1995						22.3P	680.4P		958.8P	3,835.1P	4,722.9P	
1996						22.6P	706.6P		1,002.6P	4,010.3P	4,938.6P	
1997						22.8P	732.8P		1,046.4P	4,185.5P	5,154.3P	
1998						23.0P	759.1P		1,090.2P	4,360.6P	5,370.0P	

Sources: 1982, 1987, 1992 *Economic Census*; *Annual Survey of Manufactures*, 83-86, 88-91, 93-94. Establishment counts for non-Census years are from *County Business Patterns*; establishment values for 83-84 are extrapolations. 'P's show projections by the editors. Industries reclassified in 87 will not have data for prior years.

INDICES OF CHANGE

Year	Companies	Establishments: Total	Establishments: with 20 or more employees	Employment: Total (000)	Employment: Production Workers (000)	Employment: Production Hours (Mil)	Compensation: Payroll ($ mil)	Compensation: Wages ($/hr)	Production ($ million): Cost of Materials	Production ($ million): Value Added by Manufacture	Production ($ million): Value of Shipments	Production ($ million): Capital Invest.
1982	89	89	87	91	99	96	59	71	75	40	45	43
1983				99	114	100	65	75	90	47	54	60
1984				87	92	87	66	86	101	49	57	106
1985				87	92	84	68	88	91	56	62	54
1986				88	92	91	70	84	83	60	64	56
1987	94	94	103	94	101	103	81	89	104	65	69	77
1988						90	81		109	67	73	
1989		83	92	91	95	99	92	94	122	75	82	125
1990				108	104	112	107	94	126	83	89	154
1991				105	106	108	104	97	117	86	91	110
1992	100	100	100	100	100	100	100	100	100	100	100	100
1993				97	103	97	104	107	111	103	102	63
1994				102	110	105	107	106	123	108	107	83
1995						106P	116P		129P	113P	113P	
1996						107P	121P		135P	118P	118P	
1997						108P	125P		141P	123P	123P	
1998						109P	130P		147P	128P	128P	

Sources: Same as General Statistics. Values reflect change from the base year, 1992. Values above 100 mean greater than 92, values below 100 mean less than 92, and a value of 100 in the 82-91 or 93-98 period means same as 92. 'P's mark projections by the editors.

SELECTED RATIOS

For 1992	Avg. of All Manufact.	Analyzed Industry	Index
Employees per Establishment	46	132	289
Payroll per Establishment	1,332,320	3,382,081	254
Payroll per Employee	29,181	25,662	88
Production Workers per Establishment	31	68	217
Wages per Establishment	734,496	1,312,347	179
Wages per Production Worker	23,390	19,240	82
Hours per Production Worker	2,025	1,788	88
Wages per Hour	11.55	10.76	93
Value Added per Establishment	3,842,210	19,615,607	511
Value Added per Employee	84,153	148,838	177

For 1992	Avg. of All Manufact.	Analyzed Industry	Index
Value Added per Production Worker	122,353	287,585	235
Cost per Establishment	4,239,462	4,294,798	101
Cost per Employee	92,853	32,588	35
Cost per Production Worker	135,003	62,966	47
Shipments per Establishment	8,100,800	24,252,023	299
Shipments per Employee	177,425	184,018	104
Shipments per Production Worker	257,966	355,559	138
Investment per Establishment	278,244	495,376	178
Investment per Employee	6,094	3,759	62
Investment per Production Worker	8,861	7,263	82

Sources: Same as General Statistics. The 'Average of All Manufacturing' column represents the average of all manufacturing industries reported for the most recent complete year available. The Index shows the relationship between the Average and the Analyzed Industry. For example, 100 means that they are equal; 500 that the Analyzed Industry is five times the average; 50 means that the Analyzed Industry is half the national average. The abbreviation 'na' is used to show that data are 'not available'.

LEADING COMPANIES

Number shown: **31** Total sales ($ mil): **3,224** Total employment (000): **59.3**

Company Name	Address				CEO Name	Phone	Co. Type	Sales ($ mil)	Empl. (000)
Hallmark Cards Inc	PO Box 419-580	Kansas City	MO	64141	IO Hockaday Jr	816-274-5111	R	280•	22.9
American Greetings Corp	10500 American Rd	Cleveland	OH	44144	Morry Weiss	216-252-7300	P	1,781	21.1
Gibson Greetings Inc	2100 Section Rd	Cincinnati	OH	45237	Benjamin J Sottile	513-841-6600	P	548	10.6
Russ Berrie and Company Inc	111 Bauer Dr	Oakland	NJ	07436	Russell Berrie	201-337-9000	P	278	1.9
Recycled Greetings Inc	3636 N Broadway St	Chicago	IL	60613	Ray Neufeld	312-348-6410	R	104	0.4
Paper Magic Group Inc	PO Box 977	Scranton	PA	18501	Richard Barton	717-961-3863	S	69	0.8
FTD Holdings Inc	29200 Northwestern	Southfield	MI	48034	Ken Coley	313-355-9300	R	36	0.4
Leanin Tree Publishing Co	PO Box 9500	Boulder	CO	80301	Tom Trumble	303-530-1442	R	18•	0.2
Gallant Greetings Corp	2654 W Medill Av	Chicago	IL	60647	Jack McMahon	312-489-2000	R	15	<0.1
Barton-Cotton Inc	1405 Parker Rd	Baltimore	MD	21227	Richard C Riggs Jr	410-247-4800	R	14•	0.2
New England Art Publishers Inc	PO Box 328	Rockland	MA	02370	Richard L Evans	617-878-5151	R	14	0.2
Sunshine Art Studios Inc	45 Warwick St	Springfield	MA	01102	William R Robbins	413-781-5500	R	13	0.2
Marian Heath Greeting Cards	PO Box 3130	Wareham	MA	02571	Marian Heath	508-291-0766	R	8	<0.1
Renaissance Greeting Cards Inc	PO Box 845	Springvale	ME	04083	Randy Kleinrock	207-324-4153	S	8•	<0.1
Perma-Greetings Inc	2470 Schuetz Rd	Maryland H	MO	63043	James W Vaughan	314-567-4606	R	6•	<0.1
Suzy's Zoo	9401 Waples St	San Diego	CA	92121	Suzanne S Robie	619-452-9401	R	6	<0.1
Alfred Mainzer Inc	27-08 40th Av	Long Island Ct	NY	11101	RO Mainzer	718-392-4200	R	6	<0.1
Healthy Planet Products Inc	1129 N McDowell	Petaluma	CA	94954	Bruce A Wilson	707-778-2280	P	5	<0.1
Doty Lithography	PO Box 311	Auburn	IN	46706	R Kadel	219-925-1700	D	4	<0.1
Freedom Greeting Card	PO Box 715	Bristol	PA	19007	Jay Levitt	215-945-3300	R	2•	<0.1
Pet Cards Inc	10389 Lombardi Dr	Ellicott City	MD	21042	Mary Jane Brand	410-465-2922	R	2	<0.1
Nobleworks Inc	108 Clinton St	Hoboken	NJ	07030	Christopher Noble	201-420-0095	R	2	<0.1
Allen and John Inc	528 Sonora Av	Glendale	CA	91201	Edwin Tyler	818-543-0500	R	1•	<0.1
Novo Card Publishers Inc	4513 N Lincoln Av	Chicago	IL	60625	Kristopher Chae	312-769-6000	R	1•	<0.1
Oatmeal Studios Inc	PO Box 138	Rochester	VT	05767	Joe Massimino	802-767-3171	R	1•	<0.1
Kards for Kids Inc	150 Morris Av	Springfield	NJ	07081	Peter Jegou	201-796-8399	S	1•	<0.1
Peaceable Kingdom Press	707-B Heinz Av	Berkeley	CA	94710	Olivia Hurd	510-644-9801	R	1•	<0.1
Elizabeth Lucas Designs	10542 Calle Lee	Los Alamitos	CA	90720	Elizabeth Lucas	714-827-2767	R	1	<0.1
Cardthartic Inc	230 W Superior St	Chicago	IL	60610	Jodee Stevens	312-951-8118	R	0	<0.1
Blue Sky Publishing	6395 Gunpark Dr	Boulder	CO	80301	Bob Marqueen	303-530-4654	R	0•	<0.1
Mother Come Home Inc	80 S Washington St	Seattle	WA	98104	Diane Conway	206-682-2747	R	0	<0.1

Source: *Ward's Business Directory of U.S. Private and Public Companies*, Volumes 1 and 2, 1996. The company type code used is as follows: P - Public, R - Private, S - Subsidiary, D - Division, J - Joint Venture, A - Affiliate, G - Group. Sales are in millions of dollars, employees are in thousands. An asterisk (•) indicates an estimated sales volume. The symbol < stands for 'less than'. Company names and addresses are truncated, in some cases, to fit into the available space.

MATERIALS CONSUMED

Material	Quantity	Delivered Cost ($ million)
Materials, ingredients, containers, and supplies	(X)	473.2
Coated paper	(X)	74.4
Uncoated paper	(X)	92.6
Printing inks (complete formulations)	(X)	4.7
Paperboard containers, boxes, and corrugated paperboard	(X)	17.1
Purchased envelopes	(X)	15.9
All other materials and components, parts, containers, and supplies	(X)	200.9
Materials, ingredients, containers, and supplies, nsk	(X)	67.7

Source: 1992 *Economic Census*. Explanation of symbols used: (D): Withheld to avoid disclosure of competitive data; na: Not available; (S): Withheld because statistical norms were not met; (X): Not applicable; (Z): Less than half the unit shown; nec: Not elsewhere classified; nsk: Not specified by kind; - : zero; * : 10-19 percent estimated; ** : 20-29 percent estimated.

PRODUCT SHARE DETAILS

Product or Product Class	% Share
Greeting cards	100.00
Greeting cards (publishers' sales)	88.57
Christmas counter greeting cards (publishers' sales)	7.98
Packaged Christmas greeting cards, including boxed cards (publishers' sales)	9.34
Valentine counter greeting cards (publishers' sales)	6.83
Packaged Valentine greeting cards, including boxed cards (publishers' sales)	0.86
Mother's Day greeting cards (publishers' sales)	5.42
Easter greeting cards (publishers' sales)	3.84
Seasonal greeting cards other than Christmas, Valentine, Easter, and Mother's Day (publishers' sales)	6.62
Everyday counter greeting cards (publishers' sales)	53.25
Packaged everyday greeting cards, including boxed cards (publishers' sales)	2.23
Greeting cards, publishers' sales, nsk	3.62
Greeting cards, printed for publication by others	2.88
Greeting cards, nsk	8.55

Source: 1992 *Economic Census*. The values shown are percent of total shipments in an industry. Values of indented subcategories are summed in the main heading. The symbol (D) appears when data are withheld to prevent disclosure of competitive information. The abbreviation nsk stands for 'not specified by kind' and nec for 'not elsewhere classified'.

INPUTS AND OUTPUTS FOR GREETING CARD PUBLISHING

Economic Sector or Industry Providing Inputs	%	Sector	Economic Sector or Industry Buying Outputs	%	Sector
Greeting card publishing	22.2	Manufg.	Personal consumption expenditures	84.9	
Paper mills, except building paper	18.7	Manufg.	Greeting card publishing	11.5	Manufg.
Wholesale trade	13.2	Trade	Change in business inventories	2.7	In House
Commercial printing	6.1	Manufg.	Exports	0.9	Foreign
Advertising	4.7	Services			
Miscellaneous plastics products	2.9	Manufg.			
Petroleum refining	2.2	Manufg.			
Eating & drinking places	2.2	Trade			
Banking	1.6	Fin/R.E.			
Electric services (utilities)	1.4	Util.			
Equipment rental & leasing services	1.4	Services			
Envelopes	1.3	Manufg.			
Motor freight transportation & warehousing	1.3	Util.			
Paperboard containers & boxes	1.2	Manufg.			
Chemical preparations, nec	1.1	Manufg.			
Printing trades machinery	1.1	Manufg.			
Hotels & lodging places	1.1	Services			
U.S. Postal Service	1.1	Gov't			
Imports	1.1	Foreign			
Air transportation	0.9	Util.			
Communications, except radio & TV	0.9	Util.			
Mechanical measuring devices	0.8	Manufg.			
Photographic equipment & supplies	0.8	Manufg.			
Printing ink	0.8	Manufg.			
Job training & related services	0.8	Services			
Legal services	0.8	Services			
Management & consulting services & labs	0.8	Services			
Railroads & related services	0.5	Util.			
Real estate	0.5	Fin/R.E.			
Accounting, auditing & bookkeeping	0.5	Services			
Automotive rental & leasing, without drivers	0.5	Services			
Manifold business forms	0.4	Manufg.			
Gas production & distribution (utilities)	0.4	Util.			
Maintenance of nonfarm buildings nec	0.3	Constr.			
Royalties	0.3	Fin/R.E.			
Automotive repair shops & services	0.3	Services			
Computer & data processing services	0.3	Services			
Detective & protective services	0.3	Services			
Bookbinding & related work	0.2	Manufg.			
Paper coating & glazing	0.2	Manufg.			
Sanitary services, steam supply, irrigation	0.2	Util.			
Transit & bus transportation	0.2	Util.			
Insurance carriers	0.2	Fin/R.E.			
Business services nec	0.2	Services			
Personnel supply services	0.2	Services			
Engraving & plate printing	0.1	Manufg.			
Lubricating oils & greases	0.1	Manufg.			
Machinery, except electrical, nec	0.1	Manufg.			
Manufacturing industries, nec	0.1	Manufg.			
Motor vehicle parts & accessories	0.1	Manufg.			
Laundry, dry cleaning, shoe repair	0.1	Services			

Source: Benchmark Input-Output Accounts for the U.S. Economy, 1982, U.S. Department of Commerce, Washington, D.C., July 1991. Data, as reported in the source, are organized by the 1977 SIC structure in use in 1982 but have been matched, as closely as is possible, to the 1987 SIC structure used in this book.

OCCUPATIONS EMPLOYED BY SIC 277 - PRINTING TRADE SERVICES NEC

Occupation	% of Total 1994	Change to 2005	Occupation	% of Total 1994	Change to 2005
Strippers, printing	7.2	-8.6	Adjustment clerks	1.6	34.4
Sales & related workers nec	5.4	6.3	Data entry keyers, composing	1.6	-74.3
Electronic pagination systems workers	4.2	63.7	Secretaries, ex legal & medical	1.6	0.1
Typesetting & composing machine operators	4.2	-74.3	General office clerks	1.6	-8.4
Printing workers, precision nec	3.8	37.9	Freight, stock, & material movers, hand	1.5	-4.4
General managers & top executives	3.8	-1.5	Assemblers, fabricators, & hand workers nec	1.4	15.4
Hand packers & packagers	3.7	3.0	Messengers	1.4	-20.6
Artists & commercial artists	2.6	10.7	Clerical supervisors & managers	1.4	10.7
Proofreaders & copy markers	2.4	-33.2	Management support workers nec	1.4	19.5
Production, planning, & expediting clerks	2.3	22.2	Platemakers	1.3	-27.7
Photoengravers	2.3	-28.4	Offset lithographic press operators	1.3	1.4
Camera operators	2.1	-18.1	Printing, binding, & related workers nec	1.3	14.9
Bookkeeping, accounting, & auditing clerks	2.0	-21.2	Traffic, shipping, & receiving clerks	1.2	7.2
Paste-up workers	1.9	-33.3	Industrial production managers	1.2	5.4
Machine feeders & offbearers	1.8	7.5	Bindery machine operators & set-up operators	1.2	9.9
Printing press machine setters, operators	1.7	-9.0	Data entry keyers, ex composing	1.1	-16.6

Source: Industry-Occupation Matrix, Bureau of Labor Statistics. These data relate to one or more 3-digit SIC industry groups rather than to a single 4-digit SIC. The change reported for each occupation to the year 2005 is a percent of growth or decline as estimated by the Bureau of Labor Statistics. The abbreviation nec stands for 'not elsewhere classified'.

LOCATION BY STATE AND REGIONAL CONCENTRATION

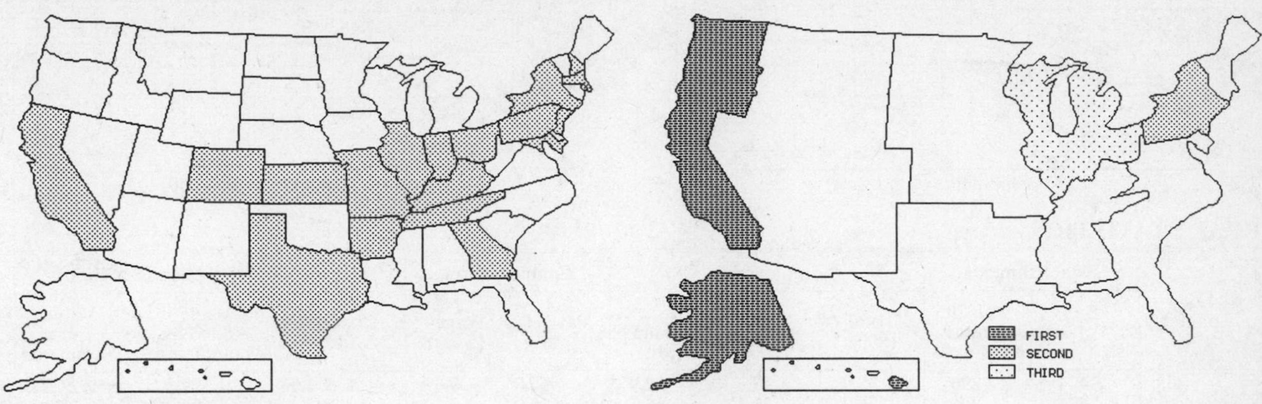

INDUSTRY DATA BY STATE

State	Establish-ments	Shipments			Employment				Cost as % of Shipments	Investment per Employee ($)
		Total ($ mil)	% of U.S.	Per Establ.	Total Number	% of U.S.	Per Establ.	Wages ($/hour)		
Colorado	8	159.9	3.8	20.0	1,600	7.0	200	8.82	23.2	-
Illinois	9	157.7	3.8	17.5	1,500	6.6	167	8.45	27.6	2,400
New York	14	47.7	1.1	3.4	300	1.3	21	8.00	22.9	4,000
New Jersey	5	42.4	1.0	8.5	400	1.8	80	11.25	22.4	1,250
Massachusetts	9	39.7	0.9	4.4	300	1.3	33	7.75	22.2	-
California	29	35.7	0.9	1.2	300	1.3	10	6.50	35.3	2,667
Kentucky	7	(D)	-	-	3,750 *	16.4	536	-	-	-
Missouri	6	(D)	-	-	7,500 *	32.9	1,250	-	-	-
New Hampshire	6	(D)	-	-	175 *	0.8	29	-	-	1,143
Ohio	6	(D)	-	-	1,750 *	7.7	292	-	-	-
Texas	6	(D)	-	-	175 *	0.8	29	-	-	-
Maryland	5	(D)	-	-	175 *	0.8	35	-	-	-
Arkansas	3	(D)	-	-	3,750 *	16.4	1,250	-	-	-
Indiana	3	(D)	-	-	750 *	3.3	250	-	-	-
Kansas	3	(D)	-	-	1,750 *	7.7	583	-	-	-
Pennsylvania	3	(D)	-	-	750 *	3.3	250	-	-	-
Georgia	1	(D)	-	-	375 *	1.6	375	-	-	-
Rhode Island	1	(D)	-	-	375 *	1.6	375	-	-	-
Tennessee	1	(D)	-	-	175 *	0.8	175	-	-	-

Source: 1992 *Economic Census*. The states are in descending order of shipments or establishments (if shipment data are missing for the majority). The symbol (D) appears when data are withheld to prevent disclosure of competitive information. States marked with (D) are sorted by number of establishments. A dash (-) indicates that the data element cannot be calculated; * indicates the midpoint of a range.

2782 - BLANKBOOKS AND LOOSELEAF BINDERS

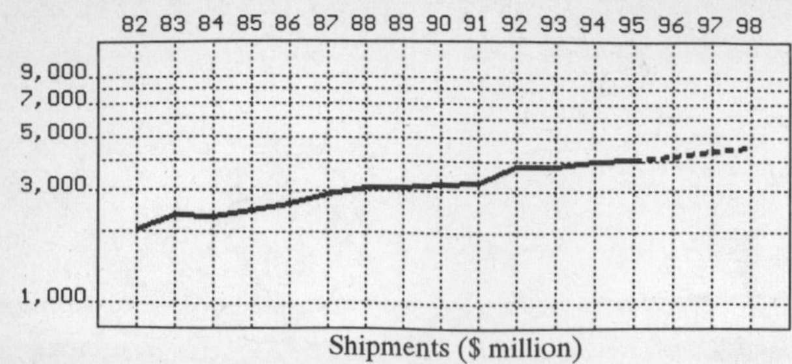

Shipments ($ million)

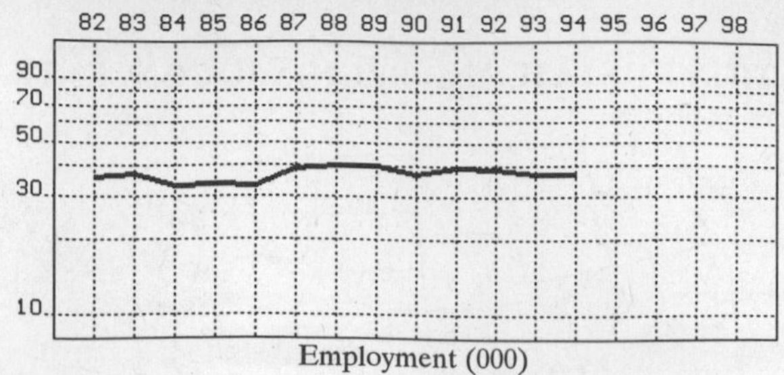

Employment (000)

GENERAL STATISTICS

Year	Companies	Establishments: Total	Establishments: with 20 or more employees	Employment: Total (000)	Employment: Production Workers (000)	Employment: Production Hours (Mil)	Compensation: Payroll ($ mil)	Compensation: Wages ($/hr)	Production ($ million): Cost of Materials	Production ($ million): Value Added by Manufacture	Production ($ million): Value of Shipments	Production ($ million): Capital Invest.
1982	333	474	296	35.9	28.0	52.9	564.8	7.19	671.0	1,379.5	2,039.4	50.5
1983		476	305	36.9	28.8	55.7	635.0	7.63	735.4	1,606.0	2,335.5	60.9
1984		478	314	33.2	24.9	50.0	629.6	8.36	791.3	1,518.7	2,305.3	84.9
1985		479	322	33.3	25.4	51.8	672.1	8.45	819.7	1,642.3	2,463.2	82.4
1986		468	320	33.0	25.4	52.6	708.4	8.74	864.1	1,792.2	2,640.1	79.6
1987	349	511	326	39.1	29.5	57.7	767.9	8.61	897.8	2,021.2	2,903.6	87.5
1988		502	329			58.3	791.8		943.9	2,120.7	3,057.9	
1989		484	330	40.6	28.3	54.4	781.6	9.51	997.6	2,084.2	3,057.8	152.7
1990		488	310	37.5	27.5	53.9	833.1	9.80	1,006.2	2,182.9	3,186.1	108.0
1991		475	308	39.6	28.2	54.2	847.6	9.87	1,005.0	2,207.2	3,243.1	84.1
1992	376	553	354	39.1	29.3	57.1	932.1	10.20	1,123.9	2,658.7	3,788.1	102.0
1993		551	339	37.5	27.0	53.1	876.8	10.28	1,155.4	2,608.8	3,771.2	86.8
1994		531P	340P	37.1	27.3	52.2	899.4	10.60	1,232.6	2,758.6	3,983.5	91.3
1995		537P	343P			54.8P	965.3P		1,260.4P	2,820.9P	4,073.5P	
1996		543P	346P			54.9P	993.9P		1,308.7P	2,928.8P	4,229.3P	
1997		548P	349P			55.0P	1,022.6P		1,356.9P	3,036.7P	4,385.1P	
1998		554P	352P			55.1P	1,051.2P		1,405.1P	3,144.6P	4,540.9P	

Sources: 1982, 1987, 1992 *Economic Census*; *Annual Survey of Manufactures*, 83-86, 88-91, 93-94. Establishment counts for non-Census years are from *County Business Patterns*; establishment values for 83-84 are extrapolations. 'P's show projections by the editors. Industries reclassified in 87 will not have data for prior years.

INDICES OF CHANGE

Year	Companies	Establishments: Total	Establishments: with 20 or more employees	Employment: Total (000)	Employment: Production Workers (000)	Employment: Production Hours (Mil)	Compensation: Payroll ($ mil)	Compensation: Wages ($/hr)	Production ($ million): Cost of Materials	Production ($ million): Value Added by Manufacture	Production ($ million): Value of Shipments	Production ($ million): Capital Invest.
1982	89	86	84	92	96	93	61	70	60	52	54	50
1983		86	86	94	98	98	68	75	65	60	62	60
1984		86	89	85	85	88	68	82	70	57	61	83
1985		87	91	85	87	91	72	83	73	62	65	81
1986		85	90	84	87	92	76	86	77	67	70	78
1987	93	92	92	100	101	101	82	84	80	76	77	86
1988		91	93			102	85		84	80	81	
1989		88	93	104	97	95	84	93	89	78	81	150
1990		88	88	96	94	94	89	96	90	82	84	106
1991		86	87	101	96	95	91	97	89	83	86	82
1992	100	100	100	100	100	100	100	100	100	100	100	100
1993		100	96	96	92	93	94	101	103	98	100	85
1994		96P	96P	95	93	91	96	104	110	104	105	90
1995		97P	97P			96P	104P		112P	106P	108P	
1996		98P	98P			96P	107P		116P	110P	112P	
1997		99P	99P			96P	110P		121P	114P	116P	
1998		100P	99P			97P	113P		125P	118P	120P	

Sources: Same as General Statistics. Values reflect change from the base year, 1992. Values above 100 mean greater than 92, values below 100 mean less than 92, and a value of 100 in the 82-91 or 93-98 period means same as 92. 'P's mark projections by the editors.

SELECTED RATIOS

For 1994	Avg. of All Manufact.	Analyzed Industry	Index
Employees per Establishment	49	70	143
Payroll per Establishment	1,500,273	1,692,674	113
Payroll per Employee	30,620	24,243	79
Production Workers per Establishment	34	51	150
Wages per Establishment	853,319	1,041,350	122
Wages per Production Worker	24,861	20,268	82
Hours per Production Worker	2,056	1,912	93
Wages per Hour	12.09	10.60	88
Value Added per Establishment	4,602,255	5,191,696	113
Value Added per Employee	93,930	74,356	79

For 1994	Avg. of All Manufact.	Analyzed Industry	Index
Value Added per Production Worker	134,084	101,048	75
Cost per Establishment	5,045,178	2,319,758	46
Cost per Employee	102,970	33,224	32
Cost per Production Worker	146,988	45,150	31
Shipments per Establishment	9,576,895	7,496,963	78
Shipments per Employee	195,460	107,372	55
Shipments per Production Worker	279,017	145,916	52
Investment per Establishment	321,011	171,827	54
Investment per Employee	6,552	2,461	38
Investment per Production Worker	9,352	3,344	36

Sources: Same as General Statistics. The 'Average of All Manufacturing' column represents the average of all manufacturing industries reported for the most recent complete year available. The Index shows the relationship between the Average and the Analyzed Industry. For example, 100 means that they are equal; 500 that the Analyzed Industry is five times the average; 50 means that the Analyzed Industry is half the national average. The abbreviation 'na' is used to show that data are 'not available'.

LEADING COMPANIES

Number shown: **60** Total sales ($ mil): **1,000** Total employment (000): **10.9**

Company Name	Address				CEO Name	Phone	Co. Type	Sales ($ mil)	Empl. (000)
Safeguard Business Systems Inc	455 Maryland Dr	Ft Washington	PA	19034	Richard Gommel	215-641-5000	R	220	1.7
ACCO USA Inc	770 S Acco Plz	Wheeling	IL	60090	Bruce A Gescheider	708-541-9500	S	130	2.0
Holson Burnes Group Inc	582 Great Rd	N Smithfield	RI	02896	Charles Gordon	401-769-8000	P	130	0.5
Art Leather Manufacturing	4510 94th	Elmhurst	NY	11373	Mark Roberts	718-699-6300	R	34*	0.5
Samsill Corp	PO Box 15066	Fort Worth	TX	76119	James R Bankes	817-536-1906	R	29*	0.4
Rundel Products Inc	1100 NE 28th Av	Portland	OR	97232	C Dixon Rauch III	503-284-5511	R	25*	0.4
Amer Loose Leaf Business Prod	4015 Papin St	St Louis	MO	63110	Paul Mendelson	314-535-1414	R	24*	0.2
Charles Leonard Inc	79-11 Cooper Av	Glendale	NY	11385	CL Hirsch	718-894-4851	R	24	0.1
Vulcan Binder and Cover Inc	PO Box 29	Vincent	AL	35178	Denson Parker	205-672-2241	D	24	0.2
Graphic Looseleaf Products	900 Oakmont Ln	Westmont	IL	60559	Dennis K Beardall	708-654-2520	D	21*	0.3
Kleer-Vu Industries Inc	PO Box 449	Brownsville	TN	38012	Daniel Dror	901-772-2500	P	18	0.2
Vinyweld	2011 W Hastings St	Chicago	IL	60608	M H Greenberg	312-243-0606	D	18	0.3
Avery Dennison Specialty Prod	1601 Rohlwing Rd	Rolling Mdws	IL	60008	J Lee	708-253-1010	D	15*	0.2
HC Miller Co	PO Box 83347	Milwaukee	WI	53223	JG Lotter	414-357-8111	R	15	0.1
Deluxe Craft Manufacturing Co	1945 N Fairfeld Av	Chicago	IL	60647	S T Mandeltort	312-276-6004	R	14	0.1
Daret Inc	33 Daret Dr	Ringwood	NJ	07456	B Cowan	201-962-6001	R	13*	0.2
BOK Industries Inc	8741 Lake Rd	Le Roy	NY	14482	J Quincey	716-768-8174	R	12	0.3
Forbes Products Corp	PO Box 110	Rochester	NY	14543	R Frame	716-334-4800	R	12	0.2
Heritage Springfield Inc	475 Canal St	Holyoke	MA	01040	Lee Morgan	413-534-3371	S	11	0.1
ABZ Inc	1 Penaljo Dr	De Soto	MO	63020	Gary Eakins	314-337-1002	R	10	0.2
Acme Brief Case Company Inc	440 Nepperhan Av	Yonkers	NY	10701	AI Klotz	914-963-3700	R	10	0.1
Corporate Image	PO Box 1413	Des Moines	IA	50305	Fritz James	515-262-3191	S	10	<0.1
General Loose Leaf Bindery Co	3811 Hawthorne Ct	Waukegan	IL	60087	H Nickow	708-244-9700	R	10	0.1
US Sample Corporation	1840 N Marcey St	Chicago	IL	60614	Morton Kader	312-528-4200	S	10	0.2
Fey Industries Inc	200 4th Av W	Edgerton	MN	56128	Norman E Fey	507-442-4311	R	9	0.2
Formflex	1 N Main	Bloomingdale	IN	47832	Harold Hooe	317-498-8900	D	9*	<0.1
TMC Group Inc	PO Box 346	Derry	NH	03038	Omar Peroza	603-434-4161	R	9	<0.1
Inter City Manufacturing	7401 Alabama Av	St Louis	MO	63111	William Mitchell	314-351-3100	R	9	0.1
General Binding Corp	21039 N 27th Av	Phoenix	AZ	85027	Rudolph Grua	602-869-8100	D	8	<0.1
Heinn Trend Corp	3801 W Green Tree	Milwaukee	WI	53209	Charles C Tuff	414-351-0200	R	8	0.1
American Thermoplastic Co	106 Gamma Dr	Pittsburgh	PA	15219	Steven Silberman	412-967-0900	R	7	0.1
Admiral Binder Corp	2020 Lindell Av	Nashville	TN	37203	DG Adams	615-383-6990	R	7	0.1
Moore American Graphics Inc	8904 S Harlem Av	Bridgeview	IL	60455	Albert F Moore Jr	708-599-2200	R	6	<0.1
D Davis Kenny Co	PO Box 18205	San Antonio	TX	78218	Doug D Kenny	210-662-9882	R	6	<0.1
Eckhart and Company Inc	PO Box 421103	Indianapolis	IN	46242	Brent Eckhart	317-243-3791	R	6	<0.1
Univex International Inc	2635 S Santa Fe Dr	Denver	CO	80223	Doug Miller	303-733-2400	R	6	0.1
Dayton Legal Blank Inc	PO Box 188	Dayton	OH	45401	DR Keeler	513-435-4405	R	5	<0.1
First Health Care Products	PO Box 98120	Tacoma	WA	98498	Larry Smith	206-984-6767	R	5	<0.1
Holum and Sons Company Inc	740 N Burr Oak Dr	Westmont	IL	60559	Stephen Maier	708-654-8222	R	5*	<0.1
Compton Presentation Syst Co	PO Box 1125	Elk Grove Vill	IL	60007	Stephen R Welch	708-364-4940	R	4*	<0.1
JB Kunz Co	1600 Penn St	Huntingdon	PA	16652	JB Kunz	814-643-4320	R	4	<0.1
William Exline Inc	12301 Bennington	Cleveland	OH	44135	William B Exline	216-941-0800	R	4*	<0.1
Buchan Industries Inc	145 S Penn St	Clifton Heights	PA	19018	R S Rothermel	215-622-3500	R	4	<0.1
Integrated Filing	357 E Arrow Hwy	San Dimas	CA	91773	Phil L Knight	818-914-2853	R	4	<0.1
Blue Star Leather Inc	PO Box 6538	Utica	NY	13504	Joseph E Mele	315-733-4600	S	3	<0.1
Bear Graphics Inc	PO Box 3290	Sioux City	IA	51102	Robert L Barron	712-252-0169	R	3	<0.1
Continental Loose Leaf Inc	1316 Yale Pl	Minneapolis	MN	55403	Dick Stigman	612-333-2245	R	3	<0.1
Don Schreiber and Company Inc	PO Box 1009	Laurence Hbr	NJ	08879	Don Schreiber	908-583-6400	R	3	<0.1
Loose Leaf House	5413 S Downey Rd	Vernon	CA	90058	Michelle Lewis	213-749-9291	D	3	<0.1
Trendex Inc	240 Maryland Av E	St Paul	MN	55117	Jeff Polacek	612-489-4655	R	3*	<0.1
Webway Inc	PO Box 767	St Cloud	MN	56302	Lee Morgan	612-251-3822	S	3	0.1
Lessco Products Inc	529 Railroad Av	S San Francisco	CA	94080	Richard Koss	415-873-8700	R	3	<0.1
Rogers Loose Leaf Company Inc	1555 W Fulton	Chicago	IL	60607	John Sturecke	312-226-1947	R	3	<0.1
ST Products Inc	601 S La Salle St	Chicago	IL	60605	Ken Neiman	312-663-4530	R	2	<0.1
Curb Records Inc	47 Music Sq E	Nashville	TN	37203	Mike Curb	615-321-5080	R	2*	<0.1
Data Management Inc	PO Box 789	Farmington	CT	06034	Daniel A Hincks	203-677-8586	R	2	<0.1
National Plastic Co	15505 Cornet Av	Santa Fe Sprgs	CA	90670	John B Mitchell	310-926-4511	R	2	<0.1
Brewer-Cantelmo Company Inc	116 E 27th St	New York	NY	10016	John R Cantelmo	212-685-1200	R	1	<0.1
Columbia Loose Leaf Corp	50-02 5th St	Long Island Ct	NY	11101	Edith J Pelletier	718-937-8585	R	1	<0.1
Colwell Industries Inc	2901 Pullman St	Santa Ana	CA	92705	Sean Gaafar	818-282-5111	D	1	<0.1

Source: *Ward's Business Directory of U.S. Private and Public Companies*, Volumes 1 and 2, 1996. The company type code used is as follows: P - Public, R - Private, S - Subsidiary, D - Division, J - Joint Venture, A - Affiliate, G - Group. Sales are in millions of dollars, employees are in thousands. An asterisk (*) indicates an estimated sales volume. The symbol < stands for 'less than'. Company names and addresses are truncated, in some cases, to fit into the available space.

MATERIALS CONSUMED

Material	Quantity	Delivered Cost ($ million)
Materials, ingredients, containers, and supplies	(X)	983.7
Coated paper	(X)	86.1
Uncoated paper	(X)	185.4
Paperboard (including news, chip, pasted, tablet, check, binders' board), except for shipping	(X)	55.1
Paperboard containers, boxes, and corrugated paperboard	(X)	48.1
Coated or impregnated woven and nonwoven fabrics, except rubberized	(X)	13.7
Metal and plastic looseleaf components, including ring type	(X)	119.1
Plastics film and sheet	(X)	104.3
All other plastics consumed, except looseleaf devices and components	(X)	14.2
Steel, strip and wire	(X)	16.6
All other materials and components, parts, containers, and supplies	(X)	179.3
Materials, ingredients, containers, and supplies, nsk	(X)	161.8

Source: 1992 *Economic Census*. Explanation of symbols used: (D): Withheld to avoid disclosure of competitive data; na: Not available; (S): Withheld because statistical norms were not met; (X): Not applicable; (Z): Less than half the unit shown; nec: Not elsewhere classified; nsk: Not specified by kind; - : zero; * : 10-19 percent estimated; ** : 20-29 percent estimated.

PRODUCT SHARE DETAILS

Product or Product Class	% Share	Product or Product Class	% Share
Blankbooks and looseleaf binders	100.00	Custom (including decorated) three-ring looseleaf binders	29.26
Checkbooks (including inserts and refills, but excluding those in continuous form and die-cut)	48.83	Flexible prong, plastics channel, presentation, report, and brief cover binders	8.87
Blankbook making, except checkbooks	12.08	Post binders	1.10
Albums and scrapbooks, including photograph, stamp, and all other bound books used for storage	57.18	All other binders, including rigid prong, post-and-sleeve, and ring other than three-ring	5.00
Diaries and appointment books, excluding looseleaf	25.06	Looseleaf devices and forms, including indexes, sheet protectors, metals, and looseleaf binder components and devices	16.00
All other blankbooks, including ledger and account books, columnar books, memo books, and address books	11.53	Looseleaf binders, devices, and forms, nsk	8.39
Blankbook making, except checkbooks, nsk	6.23	Blankbooks and looseleaf binders, nsk	6.65
Looseleaf binders, devices, and forms	32.44		
Stock (cataloged) three-ring looseleaf binders	31.38		

Source: 1992 *Economic Census*. The values shown are percent of total shipments in an industry. Values of indented subcategories are summed in the main heading. The symbol (D) appears when data are withheld to prevent disclosure of competitive information. The abbreviation nsk stands for 'not specified by kind' and nec for 'not elsewhere classified'.

INPUTS AND OUTPUTS FOR BLANKBOOKS & LOOSELEAF BINDERS

Economic Sector or Industry Providing Inputs	%	Sector	Economic Sector or Industry Buying Outputs	%	Sector
Paper mills, except building paper	17.5	Manufg.	Banking	41.3	Fin/R.E.
Bookbinding & related work	10.8	Manufg.	Personal consumption expenditures	12.5	
Wholesale trade	7.3	Trade	Phonograph records & tapes	3.9	Manufg.
Die-cut paper & board	5.2	Manufg.	Retail trade, except eating & drinking	2.6	Trade
Miscellaneous plastics products	5.0	Manufg.	Legal services	2.3	Services
Imports	4.6	Foreign	Blankbooks & looseleaf binders	2.1	Manufg.
Blankbooks & looseleaf binders	4.0	Manufg.	Wholesale trade	2.1	Trade
Advertising	4.0	Services	Insurance carriers	1.9	Fin/R.E.
Paperboard mills	3.8	Manufg.	Hospitals	1.8	Services
Miscellaneous fabricated wire products	2.9	Manufg.	Change in business inventories	1.7	In House
Petroleum refining	2.6	Manufg.	S/L Govt. purch., elem. & secondary education	1.7	S/L Govt
Fabricated metal products, nec	2.5	Manufg.	S/L Govt. purch., other general government	1.7	S/L Govt
Eating & drinking places	2.5	Trade	Doctors & dentists	1.2	Services
Electric services (utilities)	1.9	Util.	Federal Government purchases, nondefense	1.2	Fed Govt
Motor freight transportation & warehousing	1.8	Util.	S/L Govt. purch., higher education	1.2	S/L Govt
Coated fabrics, not rubberized	1.3	Manufg.	Exports	1.1	Foreign
Miscellaneous publishing	1.3	Manufg.	Religious organizations	0.9	Services
Printing trades machinery	1.2	Manufg.	Insurance agents, brokers, & services	0.8	Fin/R.E.
Narrow fabric mills	1.1	Manufg.	Colleges, universities, & professional schools	0.8	Services
Real estate	1.1	Fin/R.E.	Real estate	0.7	Fin/R.E.
Communications, except radio & TV	1.0	Util.	Federal Government purchases, national defense	0.7	Fed Govt
Banking	1.0	Fin/R.E.	S/L Govt. purch., health & hospitals	0.7	S/L Govt
Mechanical measuring devices	0.9	Manufg.	Communications, except radio & TV	0.6	Util.
Legal services	0.9	Services	Labor, civic, social, & fraternal associations	0.6	Services
Management & consulting services & labs	0.9	Services	Credit agencies other than banks	0.5	Fin/R.E.
Chemical preparations, nec	0.8	Manufg.	S/L Govt. purch., public assistance & relief	0.5	S/L Govt
Paperboard containers & boxes	0.8	Manufg.	Business services nec	0.4	Services
Insurance carriers	0.8	Fin/R.E.	Elementary & secondary schools	0.4	Services
Equipment rental & leasing services	0.8	Services	Management & consulting services & labs	0.4	Services
Hotels & lodging places	0.8	Services	Motor freight transportation & warehousing	0.3	Util.
Air transportation	0.7	Util.	Eating & drinking places	0.3	Trade
Railroads & related services	0.7	Util.	Security & commodity brokers	0.3	Fin/R.E.
Accounting, auditing & bookkeeping	0.6	Services	Computer & data processing services	0.3	Services
Automotive rental & leasing, without drivers	0.6	Services	Engineering, architectural, & surveying services	0.3	Services

Continued on next page.

INPUTS AND OUTPUTS FOR BLANKBOOKS & LOOSELEAF BINDERS - Continued

Economic Sector or Industry Providing Inputs	%	Sector	Economic Sector or Industry Buying Outputs	%	Sector
Maintenance of nonfarm buildings nec	0.5	Constr.	Medical & health services, nec	0.3	Services
Manifold business forms	0.4	Manufg.	S/L Govt. purch., police	0.3	S/L Govt
Gas production & distribution (utilities)	0.4	Util.	Crude petroleum & natural gas	0.2	Mining
Royalties	0.4	Fin/R.E.	Bookbinding & related work	0.2	Manufg.
Automotive repair shops & services	0.4	Services	Commercial printing	0.2	Manufg.
U.S. Postal Service	0.4	Gov't	Electronic computing equipment	0.2	Manufg.
Photographic equipment & supplies	0.3	Manufg.	Newspapers	0.2	Manufg.
Computer & data processing services	0.3	Services	Electric services (utilities)	0.2	Util.
Engraving & plate printing	0.2	Manufg.	Accounting, auditing & bookkeeping	0.2	Services
Paper coating & glazing	0.2	Manufg.	Advertising	0.2	Services
Transit & bus transportation	0.2	Util.	Personnel supply services	0.2	Services
Business services nec	0.2	Services	Social services, nec	0.2	Services
Personnel supply services	0.2	Services	Miscellaneous plastics products	0.1	Manufg.
Lubricating oils & greases	0.1	Manufg.	Radio & TV communication equipment	0.1	Manufg.
Machinery, except electrical, nec	0.1	Manufg.	Air transportation	0.1	Util.
Motor vehicle parts & accessories	0.1	Manufg.	Radio & TV broadcasting	0.1	Util.
Screw machine and related products	0.1	Manufg.	Hotels & lodging places	0.1	Services
Tires & inner tubes	0.1	Manufg.	Membership organizations nec	0.1	Services
Retail trade, except eating & drinking	0.1	Trade	Nursing & personal care facilities	0.1	Services
Laundry, dry cleaning, shoe repair	0.1	Services	Photofinishing labs, commercial photography	0.1	Services
			S/L Govt. purch., correction	0.1	S/L Govt
			S/L Govt. purch., fire	0.1	S/L Govt
			S/L Govt. purch., natural resource & recreation.	0.1	S/L Govt
			S/L Govt. purch., other education & libraries	0.1	S/L Govt

Source: Benchmark Input-Output Accounts for the U.S. Economy, 1982, U.S. Department of Commerce, Washington, D.C., July 1991. Data, as reported in the source, are organized by the 1977 SIC structure in use in 1982 but have been matched, as closely as is possible, to the 1987 SIC structure used in this book.

OCCUPATIONS EMPLOYED BY SIC 278 - BLANKBOOKS AND BOOKBINDING

Occupation	% of Total 1994	Change to 2005	Occupation	% of Total 1994	Change to 2005
Bindery machine operators & set-up operators	15.6	16.9	Freight, stock, & material movers, hand	2.3	-6.5
Assemblers, fabricators, & hand workers nec	10.7	16.9	Cutting & slicing machine setters, operators	2.3	28.7
Hand packers & packagers	4.3	0.2	Adjustment clerks	2.0	40.3
Bookbinders	4.1	-6.5	Traffic, shipping, & receiving clerks	2.0	12.6
Blue collar worker supervisors	3.9	8.3	Offset lithographic press operators	1.7	40.3
Machine feeders & offbearers	3.5	5.3	General office clerks	1.4	-0.3
Sales & related workers nec	3.1	17.0	Order clerks, materials, merchandise, & service	1.4	14.5
Printing, binding, & related workers nec	2.9	16.9	Bookkeeping, accounting, & auditing clerks	1.3	-12.4
General managers & top executives	2.7	10.9	Industrial production managers	1.2	16.9
Helpers, laborers, & material movers nec	2.6	17.0	Printing press machine setters, operators	1.1	-6.5
Machine operators nec	2.4	3.1	Inspectors, testers, & graders, precision	1.1	17.0

Source: Industry-Occupation Matrix, Bureau of Labor Statistics. These data relate to one or more 3-digit SIC industry groups rather than to a single 4-digit SIC. The change reported for each occupation to the year 2005 is a percent of growth or decline as estimated by the Bureau of Labor Statistics. The abbreviation nec stands for 'not elsewhere classified'.

LOCATION BY STATE AND REGIONAL CONCENTRATION

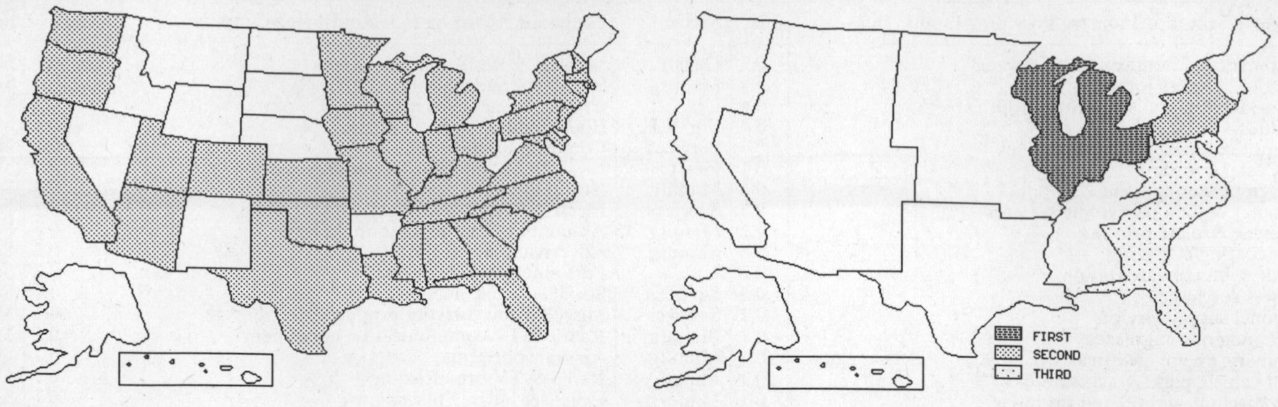

INDUSTRY DATA BY STATE

State	Establish-ments	Shipments			Employment				Cost as % of Shipments	Investment per Employee ($)
		Total ($ mil)	% of U.S.	Per Establ.	Total Number	% of U.S.	Per Establ.	Wages ($/hour)		
California	65	595.8	15.7	9.2	5,300	13.6	82	10.83	35.6	4,396
New York	54	316.7	8.4	5.9	3,200	8.2	59	8.15	37.5	1,969
Illinois	39	311.3	8.2	8.0	3,200	8.2	82	10.76	46.4	3,375
Pennsylvania	18	248.4	6.6	13.8	2,600	6.6	144	11.19	24.3	2,308
Texas	40	239.2	6.3	6.0	2,500	6.4	63	9.73	27.1	2,960
Massachusetts	13	170.5	4.5	13.1	1,600	4.1	123	9.96	33.2	1,938
Tennessee	16	136.4	3.6	8.5	1,500	3.8	94	9.80	31.7	1,533
Michigan	18	121.2	3.2	6.7	1,000	2.6	56	12.79	26.2	2,300
Florida	28	120.0	3.2	4.3	1,300	3.3	46	10.21	21.0	1,077
Connecticut	7	103.8	2.7	14.8	600	1.5	86	10.57	16.6	-
New Jersey	15	101.3	2.7	6.8	1,400	3.6	93	12.50	23.3	-
Ohio	27	101.1	2.7	3.7	1,100	2.8	41	10.75	24.5	-
Missouri	20	101.1	2.7	5.1	1,300	3.3	65	9.32	29.4	1,154
Minnesota	14	99.7	2.6	7.1	1,000	2.6	71	11.07	22.3	1,900
Indiana	12	79.0	2.1	6.6	800	2.0	67	12.08	30.6	2,125
Maryland	12	73.2	1.9	6.1	900	2.3	75	9.58	29.4	-
Georgia	20	64.1	1.7	3.2	800	2.0	40	8.62	18.6	1,125
North Carolina	11	56.0	1.5	5.1	500	1.3	45	11.12	19.1	2,000
Oregon	9	52.9	1.4	5.9	700	1.8	78	10.36	34.2	3,429
Washington	8	52.9	1.4	6.6	600	1.5	75	12.89	23.1	4,000
Virginia	10	51.9	1.4	5.2	600	1.5	60	10.63	22.5	1,667
Arizona	12	40.1	1.1	3.3	500	1.3	42	7.60	32.4	-
Louisiana	7	25.6	0.7	3.7	300	0.8	43	10.20	16.0	-
South Carolina	4	22.8	0.6	5.7	300	0.8	75	7.80	26.8	-
Utah	5	19.2	0.5	3.8	300	0.8	60	7.20	19.3	667
Colorado	9	(D)	-	-	1,750 *	4.5	194	-	-	-
Wisconsin	9	(D)	-	-	750 *	1.9	83	-	-	400
Alabama	7	(D)	-	-	750 *	1.9	107	-	-	-
Kansas	7	(D)	-	-	750 *	1.9	107	-	-	-
Kentucky	5	(D)	-	-	175 *	0.4	35	-	-	571
Mississippi	5	(D)	-	-	375 *	1.0	75	-	-	-
Oklahoma	4	(D)	-	-	375 *	1.0	94	-	-	-
Iowa	3	(D)	-	-	175 *	0.4	58	-	-	571
New Hampshire	3	(D)	-	-	375 *	1.0	125	-	-	-
Rhode Island	1	(D)	-	-	175 *	0.4	175	-	-	-

Source: 1992 *Economic Census*. The states are in descending order of shipments or establishments (if shipment data are missing for the majority). The symbol (D) appears when data are withheld to prevent disclosure of competitive information. States marked with (D) are sorted by number of establishments. A dash (-) indicates that the data element cannot be calculated; * indicates the midpoint of a range.

2789 - BOOKBINDING & RELATED WORK

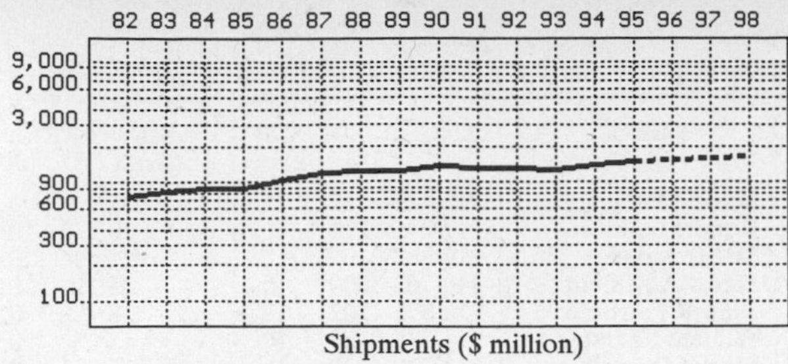

Shipments ($ million)

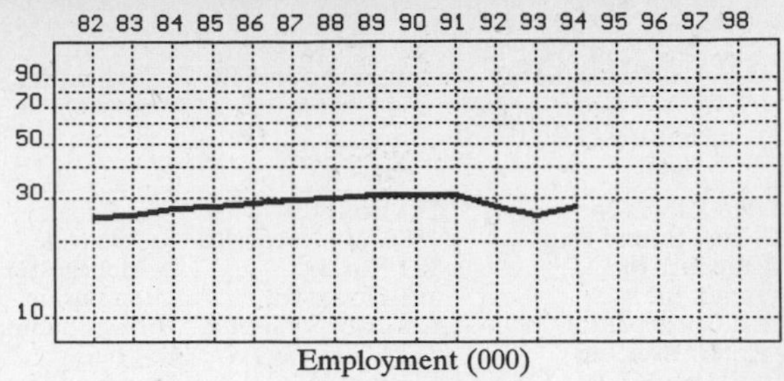

Employment (000)

GENERAL STATISTICS

Year	Companies	Establishments: Total	Establishments: with 20 or more employees	Employment: Total (000)	Production Workers (000)	Production Hours (Mil)	Compensation: Payroll ($ mil)	Wages ($/hr)	Production ($ million): Cost of Materials	Value Added by Manufacture	Value of Shipments	Capital Invest.
1982	994	1,013	335	25.4	21.7	39.7	338.3	6.43	183.3	584.0	763.5	27.3
1983		994	342	25.8	22.2	41.6	365.5	6.61	207.1	647.6	845.6	30.8
1984		975	349	27.5	22.5	42.7	404.4	6.91	215.3	659.8	876.8	28.3
1985		955	357	27.9	23.2	39.3	402.0	7.56	216.2	670.5	890.4	36.2
1986		970	348	28.5	23.2	44.6	458.5	7.57	249.1	803.7	1,048.2	39.5
1987	1,009	1,035	368	29.6	24.6	48.1	496.5	7.46	275.2	905.2	1,176.3	48.3
1988		1,009	364			48.6	507.5		282.7	939.3	1,218.2	
1989		1,000	380	31.2	24.0	48.1	519.4	7.83	294.2	941.8	1,240.2	33.6
1990		1,033	373	30.8	26.4	52.2	563.3	7.76	333.2	1,035.8	1,363.4	44.6
1991		1,052	360	30.8	25.7	50.2	547.0	7.93	314.5	1,009.7	1,328.3	28.5
1992	1,071	1,098	350	27.7	22.7	44.9	548.9	8.71	309.3	1,017.3	1,321.3	41.8
1993		1,104	344	25.6	21.5	43.2	525.2	8.54	302.0	957.6	1,258.0	24.9
1994		1,086P	365P	27.9	23.5	47.3	596.6	8.98	300.4	1,087.3	1,378.5	46.1
1995		1,097P	367P			49.7P	620.8P		326.5P	1,181.8P	1,498.3P	
1996		1,107P	368P			50.3P	640.5P		337.9P	1,223.1P	1,550.7P	
1997		1,117P	370P			50.9P	660.3P		349.3P	1,264.5P	1,603.1P	
1998		1,127P	371P			51.5P	680.0P		360.8P	1,305.8P	1,655.5P	

Sources: 1982, 1987, 1992 *Economic Census*; *Annual Survey of Manufactures*, 83-86, 88-91, 93-94. Establishment counts for non-Census years are from *County Business Patterns*; establishment values for 83-84 are extrapolations. 'P's show projections by the editors. Industries reclassified in 87 will not have data for prior years.

INDICES OF CHANGE

Year	Companies	Establishments: Total	Establishments: with 20 or more employees	Employment: Total (000)	Production Workers (000)	Production Hours (Mil)	Compensation: Payroll ($ mil)	Wages ($/hr)	Production ($ million): Cost of Materials	Value Added by Manufacture	Value of Shipments	Capital Invest.
1982	93	92	96	92	96	88	62	74	59	57	58	65
1983		91	98	93	98	93	67	76	67	64	64	74
1984		89	100	99	99	95	74	79	70	65	66	68
1985		87	102	101	102	88	73	87	70	66	67	87
1986		88	99	103	102	99	84	87	81	79	79	94
1987	94	94	105	107	108	107	90	86	89	89	89	116
1988		92	104			108	92		91	92	92	
1989		91	109	113	106	107	95	90	95	93	94	80
1990		94	107	111	116	116	103	89	108	102	103	107
1991		96	103	111	113	112	100	91	102	99	101	68
1992	100	100	100	100	100	100	100	100	100	100	100	100
1993		101	98	92	95	96	96	98	98	94	95	60
1994		99P	104P	101	104	105	109	103	97	107	104	110
1995		100P	105P			111P	113P		106P	116P	113P	
1996		101P	105P			112P	117P		109P	120P	117P	
1997		102P	106P			113P	120P		113P	124P	121P	
1998		103P	106P			115P	124P		117P	128P	125P	

Sources: Same as General Statistics. Values reflect change from the base year, 1992. Values above 100 mean greater than 92, values below 100 mean less than 92, and a value of 100 in the 82-91 or 93-98 period means same as 92. 'P's mark projections by the editors.

SELECTED RATIOS

For 1994	Avg. of All Manufact.	Analyzed Industry	Index
Employees per Establishment	49	26	52
Payroll per Establishment	1,500,273	549,141	37
Payroll per Employee	30,620	21,384	70
Production Workers per Establishment	34	22	63
Wages per Establishment	853,319	390,965	46
Wages per Production Worker	24,861	18,075	73
Hours per Production Worker	2,056	2,013	98
Wages per Hour	12.09	8.98	74
Value Added per Establishment	4,602,255	1,000,806	22
Value Added per Employee	93,930	38,971	41

For 1994	Avg. of All Manufact.	Analyzed Industry	Index
Value Added per Production Worker	134,084	46,268	35
Cost per Establishment	5,045,178	276,503	5
Cost per Employee	102,970	10,767	10
Cost per Production Worker	146,988	12,783	9
Shipments per Establishment	9,576,895	1,268,841	13
Shipments per Employee	195,460	49,409	25
Shipments per Production Worker	279,017	58,660	21
Investment per Establishment	321,011	42,433	13
Investment per Employee	6,552	1,652	25
Investment per Production Worker	9,352	1,962	21

Sources: Same as General Statistics. The 'Average of All Manufacturing' column represents the average of all manufacturing industries reported for the most recent complete year available. The Index shows the relationship between the Average and the Analyzed Industry. For example, 100 means that they are equal; 500 that the Analyzed Industry is five times the average; 50 means that the Analyzed Industry is half the national average. The abbreviation 'na' is used to show that data are 'not available'.

LEADING COMPANIES

Number shown: **49** Total sales ($ mil): **312** Total employment (000): **5.0**

Company Name	Address				CEO Name	Phone	Co. Type	Sales ($ mil)	Empl. (000)
Consolidated Papers Inc	PO Box 8050	Wis Rapids	WI	54495	David Mancusi	715-422-3111	D	38*	0.5
Bound To Stay Bound Book	1880 W Morton Rd	Jacksonville	IL	62650	Robert L Sibert	217-245-5191	R	30	0.3
Heckman Bindery Inc	PO Box 89	N Manchester	IN	46962	SP Heckman	219-982-2107	R	26	0.4
Optic Graphics Inc	101 Dover Rd	Glen Burnie	MD	21060	David A Kinlein	410-768-3000	R	23	0.3
Information Conservation Inc	6204 Corporate Pk	Browns Summit	NC	27214	John R Fairfield	910-375-1202	R	18	0.3
Foerster Enterprises Inc	2419 Glasgow Av	St Louis	MO	63106	William Foerster	314-535-9700	R	12*	0.1
Southwest Plastic Binding Co	PO Box 150	Maryland H	MO	63043	Mark Mercer	314-739-4400	R	11	0.1
Bindagraphics Inc	2701 Wilmarco Av	Baltimore	MD	21223	FM Anson	410-362-7200	R	10	0.2
California Sample Co	1611 S Hope St	Los Angeles	CA	90015	Donald Oken	213-748-6333	R	10*	0.1
General Bindery Company Inc	300 W Hunting Park	Philadelphia	PA	19140	J Shea	215-457-2515	S	8	0.2
Mazer Corp	2501 Neff Rd	Dayton	OH	45414	William Franklin	513-276-6181	R	7	0.2
Muscle Bound Bindery	701 Plymouth Av N	Minneapolis	MN	55411	Gerald L Hanson	612-522-4406	R	7	<0.1
Samplemasters Inc	43-02 22nd St	Long Island Ct	NY	11101	Vincent Scandura	212-594-9238	R	7	0.1
Bayless Bindery Inc	501 SW 7th St	Renton	WA	98055	GA Bayless Jr	206-226-6395	R	6*	<0.1
Bee Bindery Inc	15 S Throop St	Chicago	IL	60607	Peter Broustis	312-666-6210	R	6	0.1
John H Dekker and Sons	2941 Clydon SW	Grand Rapids	MI	49509	John Dekker	616-538-5160	R	6*	0.1
Professional Binding Co	935 Lively Blv	Wood Dale	IL	60191	Don Heeman	708-616-2990	R	6*	0.1
Southern Binders	PO Box 847	Dalton	GA	30720	Erwin Mitchell	706-277-2227	S	6*	0.1
Automated Binding Company	100 W Manville St	R Dominguez	CA	90220	Emeric M Rodick	213-589-6481	R	5	<0.1
Finishing Plus Inc	4546 W 47th St	Chicago	IL	60632	James Pace	312-523-5510	R	5*	0.1
Printers Bindery Inc	345 Hudson St	New York	NY	10014	David N Russell	212-924-4200	R	5	<0.1
Rickard Circular Folding Co	325 N Ashland Av	Chicago	IL	60607	Jack Rickard	312-243-6300	R	5*	<0.1
National Library Bindery	PO Box 428	Roswell	GA	30077	JT Tolbert	404-442-5490	R	5	<0.1
Bay State Bindery Inc	23 Dry Dock Av	Boston	MA	02110	HT MacDonald	617-426-3282	R	4	<0.1
Hart Bindery Co	3290 E 26th St	Los Angeles	CA	90023	Dan Fulton	213-268-9250	R	4*	<0.1
Hiller Industries Inc	631 N 400 W	Salt Lake City	UT	84103	Mel J Hiller	801-521-2411	R	4	<0.1
Modern Marketing Aids Inc	PO Box 2231	Dalton	GA	30722	Jack Posten	706-277-3845	R	4*	<0.1
Cooke Embossing	1157 W Fullerton	Chicago	IL	60614	Mack J Meyers	312-549-1277	R	3	<0.1
Lander Bookbinding Corp	1630 Macklind Av	St Louis	MO	63110	Arthur Lander	314-773-0210	R	3	<0.1
Paperfold/Graphic Finishers Inc	951 Sampler Way	East Point	GA	30344	Raymond M Friend	404-767-4890	R	3*	<0.1
Ruzicka Library Bindery	6204 Corporate Pk	Browns Summit	NC	27214	Robert J Coyle	919-375-1202	S	3*	<0.1
Zonne Bookbinders Inc	900 S Clinton	Chicago	IL	60607	Robert Goodman	312-427-0504	R	3	<0.1
Frey Bindery Inc	2621 N Ashland Av	Chicago	IL	60614	J Frey	312-525-6030	R	3	<0.1
Bookbinders Co	1240 S Hope St	Los Angeles	CA	90015	Roy Samson	213-748-6261	R	2*	<0.1
Graphic Finishers Inc	3925 Oakcliff	Doraville	GA	30340	Ray Friend	404-449-7260	R	2*	<0.1
Space Age Laminating & Bindery	3400 White Oak	Houston	TX	77007	Shelly Nesleney	713-868-1471	R	2*	<0.1
Steffen Bookbinders Inc	PO Box 187	Macedonia	OH	44056	Bill Turoczy	216-963-0300	R	2*	<0.1
Midwest Editions Inc	1060 33rd Av SE	Minneapolis	MN	55414	Lance Johnson	612-378-2620	R	2	<0.1
Bindery Inc	1216 S Vandeventer	St Louis	MO	63110	David Haffner	314-535-4200	R	1	<0.1
Denver Bookbinding Company	2715 17th St	Denver	CO	80211	Rita Lundquist	303-455-5521	R	1	<0.1
Dunn Bindery Inc	33 Temple St	Detroit	MI	48201	Timothy C Mellish	313-831-5133	R	1*	<0.1
Kater-Crafts Bookbinders Inc	4860 Gregg Rd	Pico Rivera	CA	90660	Melvin Kavin	310-692-0665	R	1*	0.1
Mountain States Bindery	1818 W 2300 S	Salt Lake City	UT	84119	Gary Cox	801-972-2300	R	1	0.1
Stauffer Edition Binding	PO Box 747	Monterey Park	CA	91754	Robert S Stauffer	213-263-9434	R	1*	<0.1
Universal Bindery Co	200 Skipjack Rd	Pr Frederick	MD	20678	D Maccherone	301-855-1370	R	1	<0.1
Capital Binding Co	PO Box 19509	Austin	TX	78760	Gerald D Bogar	512-385-5590	R	1	<0.1
AF Brosius and Company Inc	1702 S 7th St	San Jose	CA	95112	Ward Brosius	408-294-1171	R	1*	<0.1
Nadel Bookbindery Corp	176 Johnson St	Brooklyn	NY	11201	Louis Goldstein	718-624-6569	R	1	<0.1
Golden Ruling and Binding Co	1808 Washington	St Louis	MO	63103	Jim Black	314-241-4069	R	0*	<0.1

Source: *Ward's Business Directory of U.S. Private and Public Companies*, Volumes 1 and 2, 1996. The company type code used is as follows: P - Public, R - Private, S - Subsidiary, D - Division, J - Joint Venture, A - Affiliate, G - Group. Sales are in millions of dollars, employees are in thousands. An asterisk (*) indicates an estimated sales volume. The symbol < stands for 'less than'. Company names and addresses are truncated, in some cases, to fit into the available space.

MATERIALS CONSUMED

Material	Quantity	Delivered Cost ($ million)
Materials, ingredients, containers, and supplies	(X)	245.2
Coated paper	(X)	21.2
Uncoated paper	(X)	17.6
Paperboard (including news, chip, pasted, tablet, check, binders' board), except for shipping	(X)	13.9
Paperboard containers, boxes, and corrugated paperboard	(X)	11.8
Coated or impregnated woven and nonwoven fabrics, except rubberized	(X)	10.5
Metal and plastic looseleaf components, including ring type	(X)	5.3
Plastics film and sheet	(X)	6.4
All other plastics consumed, except looseleaf devices and components	(X)	2.7
Steel, strip and wire	(X)	3.7
All other materials and components, parts, containers, and supplies	(X)	65.8
Materials, ingredients, containers, and supplies, nsk	(X)	86.4

Source: 1992 *Economic Census*. Explanation of symbols used: (D): Withheld to avoid disclosure of competitive data; na: Not available; (S): Withheld because statistical norms were not met; (X): Not applicable; (Z): Less than half the unit shown; nec: Not elsewhere classified; nsk: Not specified by kind; - : zero; * : 10-19 percent estimated; ** : 20-29 percent estimated.

PRODUCT SHARE DETAILS

Product or Product Class	% Share
Bookbinding and related work	100.00
Edition, library, and other hardcover bookbinding	18.89
Hardbound edition binding of elementary, high school, and college textbooks, and technical, scientific, business, and professional books (all grades)	10.42
Hardbound edition binding of general consumer and trade books (including adult and juvenile trade books, book club, and direct mail books)	19.99
Hardbound edition binding of all other books, nec, including religious and reference books	14.38
Library binding, hard cover binding of periodicals and records, and other hard cover binding (except edition)	54.53
Edition, library, and other hardcover bookbinding, nsk	0.68
Other book and pamphlet binding, and related binding work	57.50
Soft cover adhesive binding of books (49 pages or more, exclusive of the covers)	11.40
Soft cover mechanical binding of books (49 pages or more, exclusive of the covers)	10.00
Pamphlet and other soft cover adhesive binding	4.51
Pamphlet and other soft cover mechanical binding	14.82
Sample books, swatches, and cards (color, carpet, upholstery, drapery, etc.)	30.64
Receipts for miscellaneous bookbinding work and service operations related to bookbinding	19.15
Other book and pamphlet binding, and related binding work, nsk	9.49
Bookbinding and related work, nsk	23.61

Source: 1992 *Economic Census*. The values shown are percent of total shipments in an industry. Values of indented subcategories are summed in the main heading. The symbol (D) appears when data are withheld to prevent disclosure of competitive information. The abbreviation nsk stands for 'not specified by kind' and nec for 'not elsewhere classified'.

INPUTS AND OUTPUTS FOR BOOKBINDING & RELATED WORK

Economic Sector or Industry Providing Inputs	%	Sector	Economic Sector or Industry Buying Outputs	%	Sector
Bookbinding & related work	11.6	Manufg.	Book publishing	37.8	Manufg.
Adhesives & sealants	10.8	Manufg.	S/L Govt. purch., elem. & secondary education	18.4	S/L Govt
Paperboard mills	7.8	Manufg.	Blankbooks & looseleaf binders	14.0	Manufg.
Coated fabrics, not rubberized	5.0	Manufg.	S/L Govt. purch., higher education	6.4	S/L Govt
Paper mills, except building paper	5.0	Manufg.	Bookbinding & related work	4.5	Manufg.
Eating & drinking places	4.9	Trade	Miscellaneous publishing	4.1	Manufg.
Wholesale trade	4.3	Trade	Membership organizations nec	3.7	Services
Real estate	3.9	Fin/R.E.	Periodicals	3.1	Manufg.
Electric services (utilities)	3.4	Util.	Libraries, vocation education	2.5	Services
Advertising	3.0	Services	Labor, civic, social, & fraternal associations	1.3	Services
Motor freight transportation & warehousing	2.7	Util.	S/L Govt. purch., other general government	1.1	S/L Govt
Printing trades machinery	2.6	Manufg.	Elementary & secondary schools	0.9	Services
Chemical preparations, nec	2.0	Manufg.	Commercial printing	0.5	Manufg.
Equipment rental & leasing services	2.0	Services	Change in business inventories	0.5	In House
Petroleum refining	1.9	Manufg.	S/L Govt. purch., other education & libraries	0.4	S/L Govt
Mechanical measuring devices	1.8	Manufg.	Federal Government purchases, nondefense	0.3	Fed Govt
Legal services	1.8	Services	Greeting card publishing	0.2	Manufg.
Management & consulting services & labs	1.8	Services	Colleges, universities, & professional schools	0.1	Services
Miscellaneous plastics products	1.5	Manufg.			
Communications, except radio & TV	1.4	Util.			
Blankbooks & looseleaf binders	1.3	Manufg.			
Gas production & distribution (utilities)	1.3	Util.			
Banking	1.3	Fin/R.E.			
Hotels & lodging places	1.3	Services			
Maintenance of nonfarm buildings nec	1.2	Constr.			
Air transportation	1.1	Util.			
Accounting, auditing & bookkeeping	1.1	Services			
Computer & data processing services	1.0	Services			
Manifold business forms	0.9	Manufg.			
Miscellaneous fabricated wire products	0.9	Manufg.			
Railroads & related services	0.9	Util.			
U.S. Postal Service	0.9	Gov't			
Paperboard containers & boxes	0.7	Manufg.			
Photographic equipment & supplies	0.6	Manufg.			
Transit & bus transportation	0.5	Util.			
Detective & protective services	0.5	Services			
Personnel supply services	0.5	Services			
Engraving & plate printing	0.3	Manufg.			
Lubricating oils & greases	0.3	Manufg.			
Machinery, except electrical, nec	0.3	Manufg.			
Insurance carriers	0.3	Fin/R.E.			
Royalties	0.3	Fin/R.E.			
Automotive rental & leasing, without drivers	0.3	Services			
Automotive repair shops & services	0.3	Services			
Business services nec	0.3	Services			
Business/professional associations	0.3	Services			
Manufacturing industries, nec	0.2	Manufg.			
Electrical repair shops	0.2	Services			
Laundry, dry cleaning, shoe repair	0.2	Services			
Envelopes	0.1	Manufg.			
Periodicals	0.1	Manufg.			
Special dies & tools & machine tool accessories	0.1	Manufg.			
Services to dwellings & other buildings	0.1	Services			

Source: Benchmark Input-Output Accounts for the U.S. Economy, 1982, U.S. Department of Commerce, Washington, D.C., July 1991. Data, as reported in the source, are organized by the 1977 SIC structure in use in 1982 but have been matched, as closely as is possible, to the 1987 SIC structure used in this book.

OCCUPATIONS EMPLOYED BY SIC 278 - BLANKBOOKS AND BOOKBINDING

Occupation	% of Total 1994	Change to 2005	Occupation	% of Total 1994	Change to 2005
Bindery machine operators & set-up operators	15.6	16.9	Freight, stock, & material movers, hand	2.3	-6.5
Assemblers, fabricators, & hand workers nec	10.7	16.9	Cutting & slicing machine setters, operators	2.3	28.7
Hand packers & packagers	4.3	0.2	Adjustment clerks	2.0	40.3
Bookbinders	4.1	-6.5	Traffic, shipping, & receiving clerks	2.0	12.6
Blue collar worker supervisors	3.9	8.3	Offset lithographic press operators	1.7	40.3
Machine feeders & offbearers	3.5	5.3	General office clerks	1.4	-0.3
Sales & related workers nec	3.1	17.0	Order clerks, materials, merchandise, & service	1.4	14.5
Printing, binding, & related workers nec	2.9	16.9	Bookkeeping, accounting, & auditing clerks	1.3	-12.4
General managers & top executives	2.7	10.9	Industrial production managers	1.2	16.9
Helpers, laborers, & material movers nec	2.6	17.0	Printing press machine setters, operators	1.1	-6.5
Machine operators nec	2.4	3.1	Inspectors, testers, & graders, precision	1.1	17.0

Source: *Industry-Occupation Matrix*, Bureau of Labor Statistics. These data relate to one or more 3-digit SIC industry groups rather than to a single 4-digit SIC. The change reported for each occupation to the year 2005 is a percent of growth or decline as estimated by the Bureau of Labor Statistics. The abbreviation nec stands for 'not elsewhere classified'.

LOCATION BY STATE AND REGIONAL CONCENTRATION

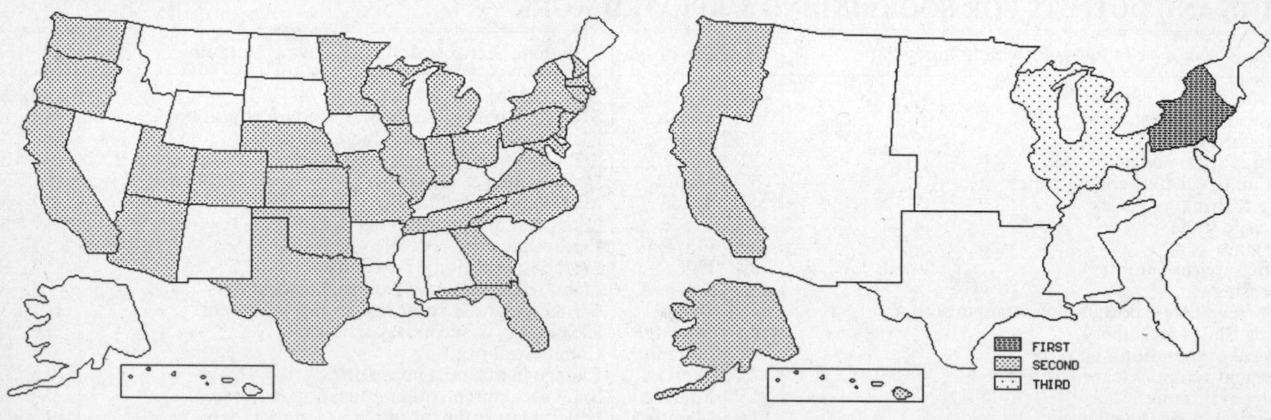

INDUSTRY DATA BY STATE

State	Establish-ments	Shipments			Employment				Cost as % of Shipments	Investment per Employee ($)
		Total ($ mil)	% of U.S.	Per Establ.	Total Number	% of U.S.	Per Establ.	Wages ($/hour)		
Illinois	71	181.6	13.7	2.6	3,300	11.9	46	8.16	27.8	1,121
New York	122	134.8	10.2	1.1	2,700	9.7	22	9.23	22.1	1,519
New Jersey	65	124.8	9.4	1.9	2,300	8.3	35	10.41	22.1	-
California	150	120.7	9.1	0.8	3,000	10.8	20	8.58	15.0	1,567
Georgia	51	94.5	7.2	1.9	2,400	8.7	47	7.74	34.3	1,208
Texas	51	66.7	5.0	1.3	1,500	5.4	29	7.88	22.6	1,000
Indiana	29	65.1	4.9	2.2	1,300	4.7	45	7.95	31.3	1,308
Maryland	26	52.9	4.0	2.0	900	3.2	35	10.86	24.0	2,556
Massachusetts	33	48.8	3.7	1.5	1,000	3.6	30	9.53	19.5	1,100
Wisconsin	19	47.1	3.6	2.5	600	2.2	32	9.88	30.8	2,000
North Carolina	27	26.2	2.0	1.0	600	2.2	22	8.33	22.9	1,500
Oregon	21	18.4	1.4	0.9	300	1.1	14	12.60	14.1	6,667
Washington	24	16.6	1.3	0.7	400	1.4	17	9.50	12.0	1,000
Arizona	14	11.7	0.9	0.8	300	1.1	21	8.40	17.1	1,000
Tennessee	23	10.7	0.8	0.5	300	1.1	13	6.40	25.2	1,000
Utah	7	10.3	0.8	1.5	200	0.7	29	10.33	15.5	-
Pennsylvania	44	(D)	-	-	1,750 *	6.3	40	-	-	-
Ohio	38	(D)	-	-	750 *	2.7	20	-	-	-
Florida	34	(D)	-	-	375 *	1.4	11	-	-	-
Missouri	34	(D)	-	-	375 *	1.4	11	-	-	-
Minnesota	30	(D)	-	-	750 *	2.7	25	-	-	-
Michigan	25	(D)	-	-	375 *	1.4	15	-	-	-
Colorado	23	(D)	-	-	175 *	0.6	8	-	-	-
Connecticut	16	(D)	-	-	375 *	1.4	23	-	-	1,067
Virginia	14	(D)	-	-	175 *	0.6	13	-	-	-
Kansas	10	(D)	-	-	375 *	1.4	38	-	-	1,333
New Hampshire	9	(D)	-	-	375 *	1.4	42	-	-	-
Oklahoma	9	(D)	-	-	175 *	0.6	19	-	-	-
Nebraska	8	(D)	-	-	175 *	0.6	22	-	-	571

Source: 1992 *Economic Census*. The states are in descending order of shipments or establishments (if shipment data are missing for the majority). The symbol (D) appears when data are withheld to prevent disclosure of competitive information. States marked with (D) are sorted by number of establishments. A dash (-) indicates that the data element cannot be calculated; * indicates the midpoint of a range.

2791 - TYPESETTING

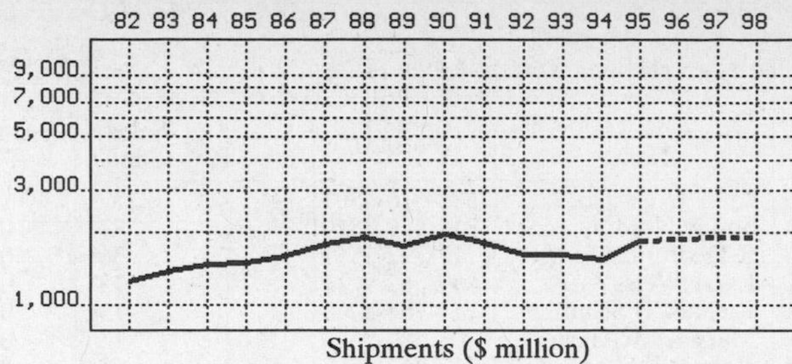

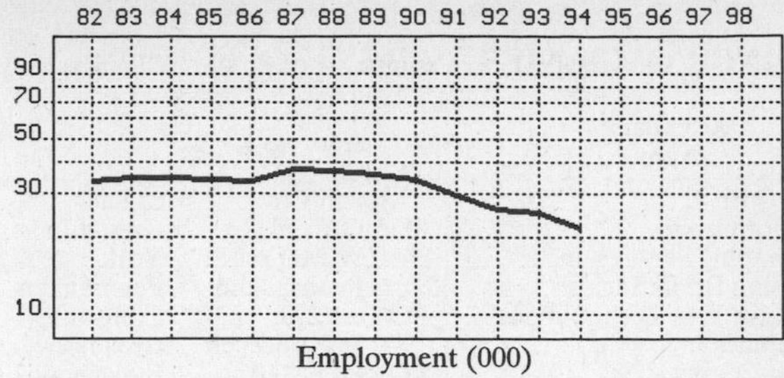

GENERAL STATISTICS

Year	Com-panies	Establishments		Employment			Compensation		Production ($ million)			
		Total	with 20 or more employees	Total (000)	Production Workers (000)	Production Hours (Mil)	Payroll ($ mil)	Wages ($/hr)	Cost of Materials	Value Added by Manufacture	Value of Shipments	Capital Invest.
1982	3,045	3,075	416	33.7	26.5	49.0	570.6	8.54	210.0	1,040.2	1,242.9	64.3
1983		3,057	424	34.7	27.9	51.7	588.4	8.35	248.2	1,138.5	1,384.2	65.6
1984		3,039	432	34.7	27.6	50.7	636.3	9.21	266.3	1,205.3	1,462.3	57.2
1985		3,020	439	34.5	27.1	48.9	665.9	9.81	277.9	1,223.5	1,503.9	67.2
1986		3,014	434	33.6	26.0	49.5	686.6	9.65	311.8	1,282.5	1,593.1	72.1
1987	3,317	3,364	437	37.6	29.5	58.4	809.2	9.67	309.7	1,471.1	1,783.7	73.9
1988		3,157	418			58.8	866.2		333.2	1,587.1	1,919.8	
1989		2,920	405	36.1	25.0	54.3	796.8	9.80	294.0	1,483.0	1,775.7	83.3
1990		2,843	390	34.2	25.1	53.0	826.9	10.36	351.2	1,605.7	1,957.4	72.7
1991		2,727	345	29.6	22.1	46.3	743.6	10.77	320.3	1,487.8	1,812.5	49.8
1992	2,481	2,517	275	26.1	19.7	39.4	687.6	11.76	286.3	1,323.6	1,611.9	60.9
1993		2,297	258	25.4	19.2	37.8	678.8	11.99	316.9	1,320.9	1,635.4	50.6
1994		2,533P	298P	21.9	17.7	35.2	631.0	12.78	291.4	1,250.1	1,546.8	57.6
1995		2,474P	283P			40.9P	765.3P		346.2P	1,485.3P	1,837.8P	
1996		2,415P	269P			39.8P	773.6P		351.7P	1,508.9P	1,867.1P	
1997		2,355P	255P			38.7P	782.0P		357.2P	1,532.6P	1,896.3P	
1998		2,296P	241P			37.6P	790.3P		362.8P	1,556.2P	1,925.6P	

Sources: 1982, 1987, 1992 *Economic Census*; *Annual Survey of Manufactures*, 83-86, 88-91, 93-94. Establishment counts for non-Census years are from *County Business Patterns*; establishment values for 83-84 are extrapolations. 'P's show projections by the editors. Industries reclassified in 87 will not have data for prior years.

INDICES OF CHANGE

Year	Com-panies	Establishments		Employment			Compensation		Production ($ million)			
		Total	with 20 or more employees	Total (000)	Production Workers (000)	Production Hours (Mil)	Payroll ($ mil)	Wages ($/hr)	Cost of Materials	Value Added by Manufacture	Value of Shipments	Capital Invest.
1982	123	122	151	129	135	124	83	73	73	79	77	106
1983		121	154	133	142	131	86	71	87	86	86	108
1984		121	157	133	140	129	93	78	93	91	91	94
1985		120	160	132	138	124	97	83	97	92	93	110
1986		120	158	129	132	126	100	82	109	97	99	118
1987	134	134	159	144	150	148	118	82	108	111	111	121
1988		125	152			149	126		116	120	119	
1989		116	147	138	127	138	116	83	103	112	110	137
1990		113	142	131	127	135	120	88	123	121	121	119
1991		108	125	113	112	118	108	92	112	112	112	82
1992	100	100	100	100	100	100	100	100	100	100	100	100
1993		91	94	97	97	96	99	102	111	100	101	83
1994		101P	108P	84	90	89	92	109	102	94	96	95
1995		98P	103P			104P	111P		121P	112P	114P	
1996		96P	98P			101P	113P		123P	114P	116P	
1997		94P	93P			98P	114P		125P	116P	118P	
1998		91P	88P			95P	115P		127P	118P	119P	

Sources: Same as General Statistics. Values reflect change from the base year, 1992. Values above 100 mean greater than 92, values below 100 mean less than 92, and a value of 100 in the 82-91 or 93-98 period means same as 92. 'P's mark projections by the editors.

SELECTED RATIOS

For 1994	Avg. of All Manufact.	Analyzed Industry	Index	For 1994	Avg. of All Manufact.	Analyzed Industry	Index
Employees per Establishment	49	9	18	Value Added per Production Worker	134,084	70,627	53
Payroll per Establishment	1,500,273	249,077	17	Cost per Establishment	5,045,178	115,026	2
Payroll per Employee	30,620	28,813	94	Cost per Employee	102,970	13,306	13
Production Workers per Establishment	34	7	20	Cost per Production Worker	146,988	16,463	11
Wages per Establishment	853,319	177,574	21	Shipments per Establishment	9,576,895	610,575	6
Wages per Production Worker	24,861	25,416	102	Shipments per Employee	195,460	70,630	36
Hours per Production Worker	2,056	1,989	97	Shipments per Production Worker	279,017	87,390	31
Wages per Hour	12.09	12.78	106	Investment per Establishment	321,011	22,737	7
Value Added per Establishment	4,602,255	493,458	11	Investment per Employee	6,552	2,630	40
Value Added per Employee	93,930	57,082	61	Investment per Production Worker	9,352	3,254	35

Sources: Same as General Statistics. The 'Average of All Manufacturing' column represents the average of all manufacturing industries reported for the most recent complete year available. The Index shows the relationship between the Average and the Analyzed Industry. For example, 100 means that they are equal; 500 that the Analyzed Industry is five times the average; 50 means that the Analyzed Industry is half the national average. The abbreviation 'na' is used to show that data are 'not available'.

LEADING COMPANIES

Number shown: **45** Total sales ($ mil): **480** Total employment (000): **4.8**

Company Name	Address				CEO Name	Phone	Co. Type	Sales ($ mil)	Empl. (000)
Merrill Corp	1 Merrill Cir	St Paul	MN	55108	John W Castro	612-646-4501	P	237	1.7
Black Dot Group	6115 Official Rd	Crystal Lake	IL	60014	Sonny Nardulls	815-459-8520	S	77	0.8
York Graphic Services Inc	3600 W Market St	York	PA	17404	R Dean Poff	717-792-3551	R	36	0.4
Composing Room Inc	9100 Pennsauken	Pennsauken	NJ	08110	Larry Weiss	609-662-9111	S	15	0.2
Progressive Info Technologies	PO Box 278	Emigsville	PA	17318	Richard B Schiding	717-764-5908	R	13*	0.2
Pal Graphics Inc	1940 W Roosevelt	Broadview	IL	60153	Mary K McAllister	708-344-8500	R	12	<0.1
Weimer Graphics	PO Box 68110	Indianapolis	IN	46268	Robert E Shepard	317-267-0565	S	8*	0.1
Media Graphics Corp	427 S La Salle St	Chicago	IL	60605	John Matyasik	312-922-6800	S	7	<0.1
Michael C Berg and Associates	108 Washington N	Minneapolis	MN	55401	Michael C Berg	612-339-2795	R	6	<0.1
Composing Room of Michigan	PO Box 2048	Grand Rapids	MI	49501	Robert C Bartleson	616-452-2171	R	5*	<0.1
TPH Graphics Inc	1177 W Baltimore	Detroit	MI	48202	Ken Cox	313-875-1950	R	5	<0.1
University Graphics Inc	21 W Lincoln Av	Atlantic Hghlds	NJ	07716	Jeffrey M Barrie	908-872-0800	P	5	0.1
University Graphics Incorporated	1940-A Carlisle Rd	York	PA	17404	Jeffrey M Marrie	717-846-9673	S	5	0.1
G and S Typesetters Inc	410 Baylor St	Austin	TX	78703	Bill M Grosskopf	512-478-5341	R	4	0.1
Hunter Graphics Inc	1622 Deere Av	Irvine	CA	92714	David Behrnann	714-975-1899	R	4*	<0.1
Maryland Composition Company	6711 Dover Rd	Glen Burnie	MD	21060	Calvin Cox	410-760-7900	R	4	<0.1
Master Typographers Inc	57 W Grand Av	Chicago	IL	60610	Alan Spoerlein	312-661-1733	R	4	<0.1
New England Typographic	206 W Newberry Rd	Bloomfield	CT	06002	Mike Kern	203-242-2251	R	3*	<0.1
Science Typographers Inc	15 Industrial Blv	Medford	NY	11763	James R Roesser	516-924-4747	R	3	<0.1
Printing Prep Inc	12 E Tupper Rd	Buffalo	NY	14203	Harold Leader	716-852-5011	R	2	<0.1
American Stratford Graphic Svcs	PO Box 8128	Brattleboro	VT	05304	Hank Burr	802-254-6073	R	2	<0.1
Central Graphics Inc	725 13th St	San Diego	CA	92101	Charles Surprise	619-234-6633	R	2*	<0.1
S New England Typographic	PO Box 1881	New Haven	CT	06508	R E Fennelly Sr	203-288-1611	R	2*	<0.1
Trade Press Typography	PO Box 694	Milwaukee	WI	53201	Robert J Wisnewski	414-228-7701	D	2	<0.1
Typography Plus Inc	1601 Prudential Dr	Dallas	TX	75235	J Cangelose	214-630-2800	R	2	<0.1
Production Typographers Inc	239 Mill St	Greenwich	CT	06830	Harvey Eckstein	203-531-4600	R	2	<0.1
Richards Graphic Commun	2700 Van Buren St	Bellwood	IL	60104	Kevin R Richards	708-547-6000	R	2	<0.1
Kettell Enterprises Inc	1005 W Fayette St	Syracuse	NY	13204	Leedom Kettell	315-478-4700	R	1	<0.1
PTC Electronics Prepress Corp	1098 Greenleaf Av	Elk Grove Vill	IL	60007	John Pearson	312-944-0010	R	1	<0.1
Holmes Typography	19 N 2nd St	San Jose	CA	95113	Tom Holmes	408-292-8546	R	1*	<0.1
Jackson Typesetting Co	PO Box 509	Jackson	MI	49204	Lloyd A Foust	517-784-0576	R	1*	<0.1
Monotype Typography Inc	150 S Wacker Dr	Chicago	IL	60606	Ira Mirochnick	312-855-1440	S	1	<0.1
Porter Graphics Inc	1228-A Village Way	Santa Ana	CA	92705	W Porter	714-558-1947	R	1	<0.1
Raven Type Inc	PO Box 36549	Charlotte	NC	28236	Michael T Aldridge	704-376-0064	R	1	<0.1
Techna Type Inc	1805 Loucks Rd	York	PA	17404	Joe Bugelli	717-764-5880	D	1*	<0.1
TeleTypesetting Co	311 Harvard St	Brookline	MA	02146	Edward Friedman	617-734-9700	R	1*	<0.1
Typesetting Inc	1144 S Robertson	Los Angeles	CA	90035	WJ Burns	310-273-3330	R	1	<0.1
Lettergraphics Inc	180 Racine St	Memphis	TN	38111	Dale Somers	901-458-4584	R	1*	<0.1
Orange County Typesetting Inc	1121 E Santa Ana	Santa Ana	CA	92701	Don L McKee	714-541-2288	R	1	<0.1
J and W Typesetting Co	600 W Van Buren	Chicago	IL	60607	George Slifka	312-648-1661	R	1	<0.1
Design Concepts	4427 N Bank Rd	Millersport	OH	43046	Dwight Joseph	614-929-2701	R	0	<0.1
MonoLith	54 Granby St	Bloomfield	CT	06002	Hugh R Brown	203-242-3006	R	0*	<0.1
Tech-Interactive Inc	92 Montvale Av	Stoneham	MA	02180	Jeffrey M Barrie	617-438-5880	S	0*	<0.1
University Graphics	92 Montvale Av	Stoneham	MA	02180	Jeffrey M Barrie	617-438-5880	S	0*	<0.1
Colortricity Inc	1005 N B St	Sacramento	CA	95814	Ted Greene	916-325-9699	R	0	<0.1

Source: *Ward's Business Directory of U.S. Private and Public Companies*, Volumes 1 and 2, 1996. The company type code used is as follows: P - Public, R - Private, S - Subsidiary, D - Division, J - Joint Venture, A - Affiliate, G - Group. Sales are in millions of dollars, employees are in thousands. An asterisk (*) indicates an estimated sales volume. The symbol < stands for 'less than'. Company names and addresses are truncated, in some cases, to fit into the available space.

MATERIALS CONSUMED

Material	Quantity	Delivered Cost ($ million)
Materials, ingredients, containers, and supplies	(X)	167.9
Unexposed photosensitive printing plates	(X)	0.7
Light sensitive films	(X)	21.2
Light sensitive papers (including photographic paper and diffusion transfer paper)	(X)	9.2
Color proofing materials	(X)	3.6
Paper, all types except light sensitive (including newsprint, book, bond, cover, and coated)	(X)	18.4
All other materials and components, parts, containers, and supplies	(X)	17.2
Materials, ingredients, containers, and supplies, nsk	(X)	97.6

Source: 1992 *Economic Census*. Explanation of symbols used: (D): Withheld to avoid disclosure of competitive data; na: Not available; (S): Withheld because statistical norms were not met; (X): Not applicable; (Z): Less than half the unit shown; nec: Not elsewhere classified; nsk: Not specified by kind; - : zero; * : 10-19 percent estimated; ** : 20-29 percent estimated.

PRODUCT SHARE DETAILS

Product or Product Class	% Share	Product or Product Class	% Share
Typesetting	100.00	All other photographic typesetting	6.88
Photographic typesetting, with capability to integrate text and graphics	60.31	Hot metal and related typesetting	0.48
		Direct-impression typesetting	0.60

Source: 1992 *Economic Census*. The values shown are percent of total shipments in an industry. Values of indented subcategories are summed in the main heading. The symbol (D) appears when data are withheld to prevent disclosure of competitive information. The abbreviation nsk stands for 'not specified by kind' and nec for 'not elsewhere classified'.

INPUTS AND OUTPUTS FOR TYPESETTING

Economic Sector or Industry Providing Inputs	%	Sector	Economic Sector or Industry Buying Outputs	%	Sector
Primary lead	16.1	Manufg.	Commercial printing	50.6	Manufg.
Photographic equipment & supplies	13.5	Manufg.	Periodicals	12.1	Manufg.
Printing trades machinery	7.6	Manufg.	Manifold business forms	8.7	Manufg.
Wholesale trade	5.9	Trade	Book printing	8.6	Manufg.
Typesetting	5.2	Manufg.	Book publishing	7.9	Manufg.
Paper mills, except building paper	4.7	Manufg.	Advertising	5.7	Services
Advertising	4.2	Services	Typesetting	2.8	Manufg.
Eating & drinking places	4.0	Trade	Lithographic platemaking & services	0.8	Manufg.
Petroleum refining	3.6	Manufg.	Change in business inventories	0.7	In House
Electric services (utilities)	3.3	Util.	Converted paper products, nec	0.6	Manufg.
Real estate	2.6	Fin/R.E.	S/L Govt. purch., elem. & secondary education	0.5	S/L Govt
Communications, except radio & TV	2.3	Util.	Engraving & plate printing	0.4	Manufg.
Equipment rental & leasing services	2.3	Services	S/L Govt. purch., higher education	0.4	S/L Govt
Chemical preparations, nec	1.6	Manufg.	Federal Government purchases, nondefense	0.2	Fed Govt
Mechanical measuring devices	1.5	Manufg.			
Legal services	1.5	Services			
Management & consulting services & labs	1.4	Services			
Lithographic platemaking & services	1.3	Manufg.			
Banking	1.3	Fin/R.E.			
Hotels & lodging places	1.2	Services			
Air transportation	1.0	Util.			
Motor freight transportation & warehousing	1.0	Util.			
Maintenance of nonfarm buildings nec	0.9	Constr.			
Accounting, auditing & bookkeeping	0.9	Services			
Automotive rental & leasing, without drivers	0.8	Services			
U.S. Postal Service	0.8	Gov't			
Manifold business forms	0.7	Manufg.			
Business/professional associations	0.6	Services			
Computer & data processing services	0.6	Services			
Gas production & distribution (utilities)	0.5	Util.			
Railroads & related services	0.5	Util.			
Automotive repair shops & services	0.5	Services			
Transit & bus transportation	0.4	Util.			
Royalties	0.4	Fin/R.E.			
Personnel supply services	0.4	Services			
Insurance carriers	0.3	Fin/R.E.			
Business services nec	0.3	Services			
Detective & protective services	0.3	Services			
Commercial printing	0.2	Manufg.			
Engraving & plate printing	0.2	Manufg.			
Lubricating oils & greases	0.2	Manufg.			
Machinery, except electrical, nec	0.2	Manufg.			
Motor vehicle parts & accessories	0.2	Manufg.			
Printing ink	0.2	Manufg.			
Tires & inner tubes	0.2	Manufg.			
Laundry, dry cleaning, shoe repair	0.2	Services			
Aluminum rolling & drawing	0.1	Manufg.			
Envelopes	0.1	Manufg.			
Manufacturing industries, nec	0.1	Manufg.			
Paper coating & glazing	0.1	Manufg.			
Paperboard containers & boxes	0.1	Manufg.			
Periodicals	0.1	Manufg.			
Special dies & tools & machine tool accessories	0.1	Manufg.			
Retail trade, except eating & drinking	0.1	Trade			

Source: Benchmark Input-Output Accounts for the U.S. Economy, 1982, U.S. Department of Commerce, Washington, D.C., July 1991. Data, as reported in the source, are organized by the 1977 SIC structure in use in 1982 but have been matched, as closely as is possible, to the 1987 SIC structure used in this book.

OCCUPATIONS EMPLOYED BY SIC 279 - PRINTING TRADE SERVICES NEC

Occupation	% of Total 1994	Change to 2005	Occupation	% of Total 1994	Change to 2005
Strippers, printing	7.2	-8.6	Adjustment clerks	1.6	34.4
Sales & related workers nec	5.4	6.3	Data entry keyers, composing	1.6	-74.3
Electronic pagination systems workers	4.2	63.7	Secretaries, ex legal & medical	1.6	0.1
Typesetting & composing machine operators	4.2	-74.3	General office clerks	1.6	-8.4
Printing workers, precision nec	3.8	37.9	Freight, stock, & material movers, hand	1.5	-4.4
General managers & top executives	3.8	-1.5	Assemblers, fabricators, & hand workers nec	1.4	15.4
Hand packers & packagers	3.7	3.0	Messengers	1.4	-20.6
Artists & commercial artists	2.6	10.7	Clerical supervisors & managers	1.4	10.7
Proofreaders & copy markers	2.4	-33.2	Management support workers nec	1.4	19.5
Production, planning, & expediting clerks	2.3	22.2	Platemakers	1.3	-27.7
Photoengravers	2.3	-28.4	Offset lithographic press operators	1.3	1.4
Camera operators	2.1	-18.1	Printing, binding, & related workers nec	1.3	14.9
Bookkeeping, accounting, & auditing clerks	2.0	-21.2	Traffic, shipping, & receiving clerks	1.2	7.2
Paste-up workers	1.9	-33.3	Industrial production managers	1.2	5.4
Machine feeders & offbearers	1.8	7.5	Bindery machine operators & set-up operators	1.2	9.9
Printing press machine setters, operators	1.7	-9.0	Data entry keyers, ex composing	1.1	-16.6

Source: *Industry-Occupation Matrix*, Bureau of Labor Statistics. These data relate to one or more 3-digit SIC industry groups rather than to a single 4-digit SIC. The change reported for each occupation to the year 2005 is a percent of growth or decline as estimated by the Bureau of Labor Statistics. The abbreviation nec stands for 'not elsewhere classified'.

LOCATION BY STATE AND REGIONAL CONCENTRATION

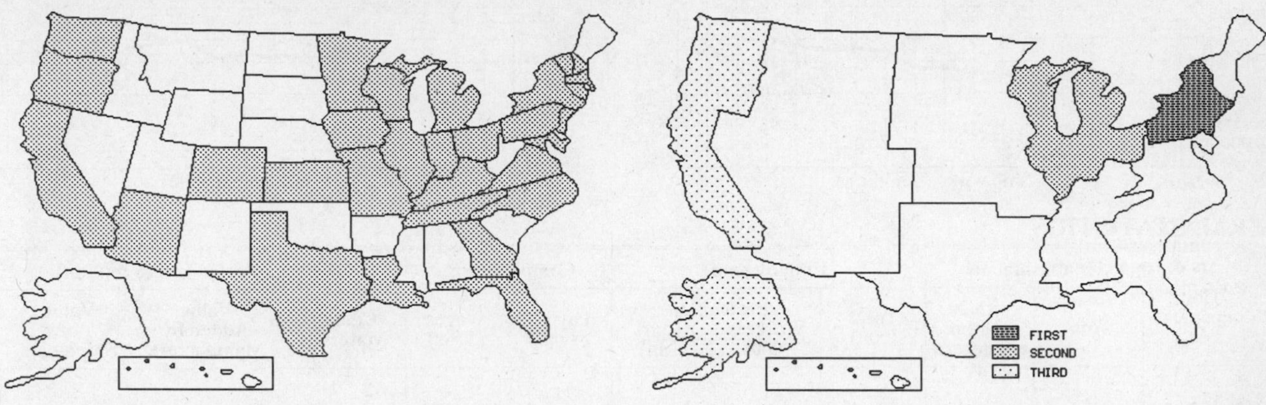

INDUSTRY DATA BY STATE

State	Establish-ments	Shipments			Employment				Cost as % of Shipments	Investment per Employee ($)
		Total ($ mil)	% of U.S.	Per Establ.	Total Number	% of U.S.	Per Establ.	Wages ($/hour)		
New York	278	243.3	15.1	0.9	3,300	12.6	12	13.60	19.6	1,636
Pennsylvania	105	200.0	12.4	1.9	3,500	13.4	33	11.25	13.3	2,686
Illinois	187	196.5	12.2	1.1	2,600	10.0	14	12.84	19.2	2,231
California	333	178.7	11.1	0.5	2,700	10.3	8	11.53	15.8	2,037
New Jersey	120	85.3	5.3	0.7	1,400	5.4	12	14.42	17.0	1,714
Minnesota	43	65.2	4.0	1.5	900	3.4	21	13.85	18.6	5,222
Michigan	103	57.4	3.6	0.6	800	3.1	8	10.75	19.5	2,000
Missouri	67	47.7	3.0	0.7	900	3.4	13	11.00	25.6	1,889
Massachusetts	82	46.8	2.9	0.6	700	2.7	9	11.80	20.7	2,714
Georgia	63	46.7	2.9	0.7	800	3.1	13	11.82	12.0	1,875
Ohio	98	39.7	2.5	0.4	800	3.1	8	10.64	14.4	1,875
Florida	129	36.8	2.3	0.3	700	2.7	5	9.60	19.8	2,143
Connecticut	52	27.0	1.7	0.5	500	1.9	10	12.29	15.6	1,600
Wisconsin	44	25.2	1.6	0.6	500	1.9	11	10.83	22.6	3,000
Virginia	37	20.2	1.3	0.5	400	1.5	11	11.67	12.4	2,750
Iowa	22	16.4	1.0	0.7	400	1.5	18	9.17	14.0	3,000
North Carolina	51	13.8	0.9	0.3	300	1.1	6	10.50	22.5	3,333
Colorado	56	12.1	0.8	0.2	200	0.8	4	10.00	24.8	-
Washington	31	8.7	0.5	0.3	100	0.4	3	9.50	16.1	5,000
Arizona	42	7.6	0.5	0.2	200	0.8	5	9.33	19.7	1,000
Oregon	34	6.7	0.4	0.2	100	0.4	3	10.00	14.9	3,000
Louisiana	18	6.0	0.4	0.3	100	0.4	6	8.00	20.0	1,000
Vermont	10	5.2	0.3	0.5	100	0.4	10	9.50	13.5	1,000
Texas	144	(D)	-	-	1,750 *	6.7	12	-	-	1,543
Maryland	71	(D)	-	-	750 *	2.9	11	-	-	2,267
Indiana	52	(D)	-	-	750 *	2.9	14	-	-	2,133
Tennessee	33	(D)	-	-	175 *	0.7	5	-	-	1,714
Kansas	23	(D)	-	-	375 *	1.4	16	-	-	6,667
Kentucky	19	(D)	-	-	175 *	0.7	9	-	-	1,714
D.C.	18	(D)	-	-	175 *	0.7	10	-	-	1,714
New Hampshire	16	(D)	-	-	175 *	0.7	11	-	-	3,429

Source: 1992 *Economic Census*. The states are in descending order of shipments or establishments (if shipment data are missing for the majority). The symbol (D) appears when data are withheld to prevent disclosure of competitive information. States marked with (D) are sorted by number of establishments. A dash (-) indicates that the data element cannot be calculated; * indicates the midpoint of a range.

2796 - PLATEMAKING SERVICES

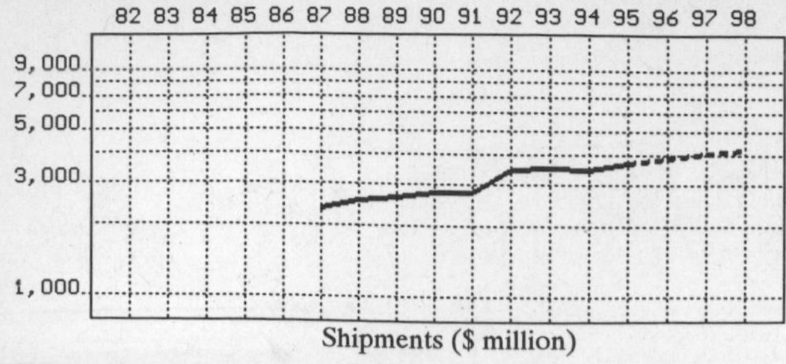

Shipments ($ million)

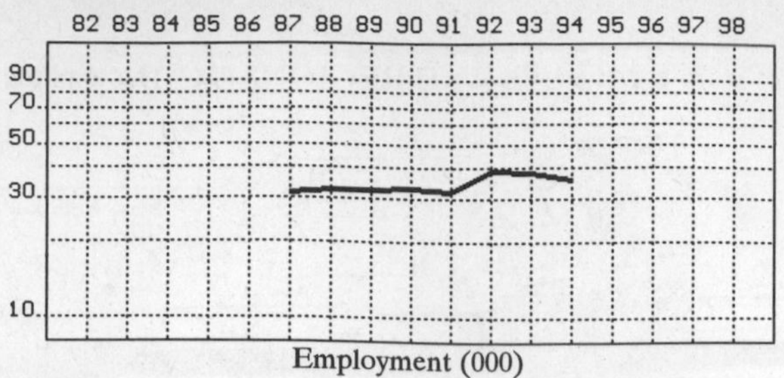

Employment (000)

GENERAL STATISTICS

Year	Com-panies	Establishments		Employment			Compensation		Production ($ million)			
		Total	with 20 or more employees	Total (000)	Production Workers (000)	Production Hours (Mil)	Payroll ($ mil)	Wages ($/hr)	Cost of Materials	Value Added by Manufacture	Value of Shipments	Capital Invest.
1982												
1983												
1984												
1985												
1986												
1987	1,328	1,414	463	31.8	22.1	45.4	974.9	13.93	612.3	1,755.7	2,373.1	116.2
1988		1,392	470			47.7	1,051.7		668.3	1,897.6	2,558.7	
1989		1,344	483	32.8	23.5	46.3	1,095.9	14.71	652.2	2,008.8	2,656.6	135.9
1990		1,348	480	33.2	22.8	44.0	1,125.4	15.43	653.7	2,103.7	2,757.8	143.0
1991		1,343	449	32.0	22.4	42.9	1,140.6	16.11	668.3	2,096.6	2,764.0	111.9
1992	1,558	1,673	590	38.7	26.4	56.5	1,445.4	15.64	789.6	2,657.5	3,451.5	166.3
1993		1,649	571	38.3	26.1	55.1	1,450.5	15.92	766.6	2,729.4	3,493.8	128.6
1994		1,633P	577P	36.2	23.8	51.9	1,426.5	16.39	766.1	2,679.3	3,447.3	170.1
1995		1,678P	596P			54.7P	1,547.0P		826.5P	2,890.7P	3,719.2P	
1996		1,723P	614P			56.1P	1,621.1P		865.1P	3,025.6P	3,892.9P	
1997		1,768P	633P			57.4P	1,695.1P		903.7P	3,160.6P	4,066.5P	
1998		1,814P	652P			58.7P	1,769.1P		942.3P	3,295.5P	4,240.2P	

Sources: 1982, 1987, 1992 *Economic Census*; *Annual Survey of Manufactures*, 83-86, 88-91, 93-94. Establishment counts for non-Census years are from *County Business Patterns*; establishment values for 83-84 are extrapolations. 'P's show projections by the editors. Industries reclassified in 87 will not have data for prior years.

INDICES OF CHANGE

Year	Com-panies	Establishments		Employment			Compensation		Production ($ million)			
		Total	with 20 or more employees	Total (000)	Production Workers (000)	Production Hours (Mil)	Payroll ($ mil)	Wages ($/hr)	Cost of Materials	Value Added by Manufacture	Value of Shipments	Capital Invest.
1982												
1983												
1984												
1985												
1986												
1987	85	85	78	82	84	80	67	89	78	66	69	70
1988		83	80			84	73		85	71	74	
1989		80	82	85	89	82	76	94	83	76	77	82
1990		81	81	86	86	78	78	99	83	79	80	86
1991		80	76	83	85	76	79	103	85	79	80	67
1992	100	100	100	100	100	100	100	100	100	100	100	100
1993		99	97	99	99	98	100	102	97	103	101	77
1994		98P	98P	94	90	92	99	105	97	101	100	102
1995		100P	101P			97P	107P		105P	109P	108P	
1996		103P	104P			99P	112P		110P	114P	113P	
1997		106P	107P			102P	117P		114P	119P	118P	
1998		108P	111P			104P	122P		119P	124P	123P	

Sources: Same as General Statistics. Values reflect change from the base year, 1992. Values above 100 mean greater than 92, values below 100 mean less than 92, and a value of 100 in the 82-91 or 93-98 period means same as 92. 'P's mark projections by the editors.

SELECTED RATIOS

For 1994	Avg. of All Manufact.	Analyzed Industry	Index
Employees per Establishment	49	22	45
Payroll per Establishment	1,500,273	873,698	58
Payroll per Employee	30,620	39,406	129
Production Workers per Establishment	34	15	42
Wages per Establishment	853,319	520,998	61
Wages per Production Worker	24,861	35,741	144
Hours per Production Worker	2,056	2,181	106
Wages per Hour	12.09	16.39	136
Value Added per Establishment	4,602,255	1,641,010	36
Value Added per Employee	93,930	74,014	79

For 1994	Avg. of All Manufact.	Analyzed Industry	Index
Value Added per Production Worker	134,084	112,576	84
Cost per Establishment	5,045,178	469,219	9
Cost per Employee	102,970	21,163	21
Cost per Production Worker	146,988	32,189	22
Shipments per Establishment	9,576,895	2,111,392	22
Shipments per Employee	195,460	95,229	49
Shipments per Production Worker	279,017	144,845	52
Investment per Establishment	321,011	104,182	32
Investment per Employee	6,552	4,699	72
Investment per Production Worker	9,352	7,147	76

Sources: Same as General Statistics. The 'Average of All Manufacturing' column represents the average of all manufacturing industries reported for the most recent complete year available. The Index shows the relationship between the Average and the Analyzed Industry. For example, 100 means that they are equal; 500 that the Analyzed Industry is five times the average; 50 means that the Analyzed Industry is half the national average. The abbreviation 'na' is used to show that data are 'not available'.

LEADING COMPANIES

Number shown: 75 Total sales ($ mil): 1,947 Total employment (000): 15.7

Company Name	Address				CEO Name	Phone	Co. Type	Sales ($ mil)	Empl. (000)
Polychrome Corp	222 Bridge Plaza S	Fort Lee	NJ	07024	Thomas Bittner	201-346-8800	S	500	1.7
Eastman Kodak Co	9952 Eastman Pk	Windsor	CO	80551	David Nelander	303-686-7611	D	260	2.5
Matthews International Corp	2 NorthShore Ctr	Pittsburgh	PA	15212	William M Hauber	412-442-8200	R	151	1.3
Techtron Graphic Arts Inc	2 N Riverside Plz	Chicago	IL	60606	John J Collins	312-876-0533	S	100	1.0
NAPP Systems Inc	360 S Pacific St	San Marcos	CA	92069	John Van Strydonck	619-744-4387	S	62	0.3
Schawk Inc	1600 E Sherwin Av	Des Plaines	IL	60018	Clarence W Schawk	708-694-9080	R	61	0.8
Enteron Group Ltd	815 S Jefferson St	Chicago	IL	60607	John Reilly	312-922-8816	R	59	0.4
Container Graphics Corp	PO Box 5489	Cary	NC	27512	Philip G Saunders	919-481-4200	R	57	0.6
Western Lithotech	3433 Tree Ct	St Louis	MO	63122	C Dan Sells	314-225-5031	S	55	0.3
Lanman Companies Inc	120 Q St NE	Washington	DC	20002	T Cunningham	202-269-5400	R	41	0.4
Matthews International Corp	PO Box 318	Pittsburgh	PA	15230	G Barefoot	412-788-2111	D	37	0.5
Blanks Color Imaging Inc	2343 N Beckley Av	Dallas	TX	75208	Leron Blanks	214-741-3905	R	23	0.2
Printing Developments Inc	2010 Indiana St	Racine	WI	53405	Jeffrey P Green	414-554-1030	S	23	0.1
Misomex North America Inc	9590 Berwyn Av	Rosemont	IL	60018	Howard LeVine	708-671-6170	S	20	<0.1
Mark Trece Inc	806 Race Rd W	Baltimore	MD	21221	Richard A Godfrey	410-879-0060	R	19*	0.2
Ohio Electronic Engravers Inc	4105 Executive Dr	Dayton	OH	45430	Don Muckerheide	513-427-1022	R	19*	0.2
Wilson Engraving Company Inc	PO Box 655591	Dallas	TX	75265	Eugene L Green	214-565-9000	R	19	0.2
NEC Inc	1504 Elm Hill Pike	Nashville	TN	37210	RW Luckett	615-367-9110	R	17*	0.2
Anocoil Corp	PO Box 1318	Vernon	CT	06066	HA Fromson	203-871-1200	R	15*	0.2
Color Control Inc	3820 150th Av NE	Redmond	WA	98052	Thomas L Courtney	206-881-5454	R	15	0.2
Master Eagle Graphic Services	40 W 25th St	New York	NY	10010	Jeffery Brager	212-924-8277	R	15	0.2
MS Chambers and Sons Inc	PO Box 719	Baltic	CT	06330	Samson P Levine	203-822-8213	S	14	0.2
Phototype Color Graphics Inc	7890 Airport Hwy	Pennsauken	NJ	08109	Joel Rubin	609-663-4100	R	14	0.1
Colorhouse Inc	13010 CR 6	Minneapolis	MN	55441	Jeff Borneman	612-553-0100	R	12*	0.1
IR International Inc	PO Box 38130	Richmond	VA	23231	Willi Fenske	804-222-2821	R	12	0.1
Miller Dial Corp	4400 N Temple City	El Monte	CA	91731	L Kranser	818-444-4555	R	12	0.3
American E-Z Type Inc	PO Box 1056	Lilburn	GA	30226	CE Zacharias	404-925-4040	R	10	0.2
Armotek Industries Inc	701 Public Rd	Palmyra	NJ	08065	Dennis Anderson	609-829-4585	R	10	0.1
Chicago Litho-Plate Cies Ltd	450 Windy Point Dr	Glendale H	IL	60139	R E Ludford III	708-858-8900	R	10	0.1
Dixie Graphics	636 Grassmere Park	Nashville	TN	37211	James R Meadows	615-832-7000	R	10*	0.1
Fashion Engravers Inc	373 Huntington Dr	Gaffney	SC	29340	Jesse Leskanic	803-487-5162	R	10*	0.1
Graphic Color Plate Inc	1069 E Main St	Stamford	CT	06902	Martin J Keefe	203-327-1500	R	10	<0.1
Laser Tech Color Inc	2010 Westridge Dr	Irving	TX	75038	Brian Mason	214-242-5700	R	10*	0.1
National Engraving Co	PO Box 2311	Birmingham	AL	35201	Mike Carlson	205-942-2809	R	10*	0.1
Polytype America Corp	3333 Park Av	Union City	NJ	07087	P Van Dergriendt	201-867-1908	S	10*	<0.1
Progress Graphics Inc	418 Summit Av	Jersey City	NJ	07306	Mario DeVita	201-653-0717	R	10*	0.1
Oakland National Engraving Co	PO Box 8277	Emeryville	CA	94662	Kim Fogarty	510-652-9005	R	9*	<0.1
PMSI Photo Mechanical Service	333 W 78th St	Minneapolis	MN	55420	C Thomas Austin	612-881-3200	R	9	0.1
Weston Engraving Company Inc	2626 2nd St NE	Minneapolis	MN	55418	Jim Moen	612-789-8514	S	9	0.1
IPP Lithoplate Corp	1313 W Randolph	Chicago	IL	60607	Robert Lowitz	312-243-0465	R	8	<0.1
Memphis Engraving Co	5120 Elmore Rd	Memphis	TN	38134	Dee Cole	901-388-8200	R	8	<0.1
Northwestern Colorgraphics Inc	PO Box 390	Menasha	WI	54952	R Calder	414-722-3375	S	8*	0.1
Pacific Color Connection Inc	6352 Abeto	Carlsbad	CA	92009	Emory Brazell	619-438-8933	R	8*	<0.1
Infinity USA Inc	6801 Jericho Tpk	Syosset	NY	11791	Harvey Gelber	516-496-3900	R	8	<0.1
Kreber Graphic Inc	PO Box 236010	Columbus	OH	43223	Frank Kreber	614-228-3501	R	8	0.1
Hanson Graphics of Memphis	3086 Bellbrook Dr	Memphis	TN	38116	Paul M Hanson	901-396-4350	R	7	<0.1
Kieffer-Nolde Inc	160 E Illinois St	Chicago	IL	60611	Donald E Kieffer	312-337-5500	S	7*	<0.1
Studio Image Inc	3110 N Clybourn	Burbank	CA	91505	Robert Hutchinson	818-848-1300	R	7	<0.1
Colour Graphics Corp	3355 Republic Av	Minneapolis	MN	55426	Robert McCrea	612-929-0357	R	7	<0.1
All Systems Color Inc	7333 Paragon Rd	Dayton	OH	45459	Geeter Kyrazis	513-433-5054	R	6	<0.1
Capitol Engraving Co	PO Box 22337	Nashville	TN	37202	William E Mullins	615-244-6603	R	6	0.1
Colour Image	2343 Miramar Av	Long Beach	CA	90815	Roy Spiegel	310-498-3731	R	6	<0.1
Graphic Color Systems Inc	1166 W Garvey Av	Monterey Park	CA	91754	Niels Christiansen	213-283-7621	R	6	<0.1
Graphics Atlanta Inc	1555 Oakbrook Dr	Norcross	GA	30093	Rick Davis	404-448-4091	R	6	0.1
Polypore Inc	4601 S 3rd Av	Tucson	AZ	85714	JA Clark	602-889-3306	R	6	<0.1
Ropkey Graphics Inc	117 N East St	Indianapolis	IN	46204	Fred N Ropkey	317-632-5446	R	6	<0.1
ABC Industries Inc	PO Box 30215	Charlotte	NC	28230	Albert Scala	704-394-4161	R	5*	<0.1
KC Photo Engraving Co	2666 E Nina St	Pasadena	CA	91107	Mike Curley	818-795-4127	R	5	<0.1
Rawal Engravers	621 E Wildwood St	Villa Park	IL	60181	Paul G Zieske	708-832-6400	D	5	<0.1
Screaming Color Inc	125 N Prospect Av	Itasca	IL	60143	Mike Sutich	708-250-9500	R	5	<0.1
T and R Engraving Inc	2535 17th St	Denver	CO	80211	Tom P Tucker	303-458-0626	R	5	<0.1
Wescor Graphics Corp	7373 N Scottsdale	Scottsdale	AZ	85253	Randy Stober	602-991-5632	R	5	<0.1
Lake Shore Litho Inc	2101 W Rice St	Chicago	IL	60622	JG Vartan	312-252-8216	R	4	<0.1
Flexcraft Inc	7664 N 81st St	Milwaukee	WI	53223	Dale Betzhold	414-354-8855	R	4	<0.1
Photo Sciences Inc	2542 W 237th St	Torrance	CA	90505	LJ Stogsdill	310-539-9040	R	4	<0.1
Rochester Empire	PO Box 22804	Rochester	NY	14692	William Bachman	716-272-1100	R	4	<0.1
Laserscan Inc	10220 S 51st St	Phoenix	AZ	85044	Tom Bonneville	602-893-7777	R	4	<0.1
Colortronix Corp	8025 S Willow St	Manchester	NH	03103	John Higgins	603-647-4620	R	3	<0.1
Creative Color Service Corp	294 Martin Av	Santa Clara	CA	95050	EJ Winter	408-727-0674	R	3	<0.1
GB Products International Corp	1024 Shary Ct	Concord	CA	94518	Gary Munyon	510-825-3040	R	3	<0.1
Matrix Unlimited Inc	PO Box 1130	Rochester	NY	14603	Michael Curran	716-473-1440	R	3*	<0.1
World Color Inc	PO Box 1327	Ormond Beach	FL	32175	Robert C Elston	904-677-1332	R	3	<0.1
Cal-Litho Color	544 N Oak St	Inglewood	CA	90302	Jerry Waxman	213-749-7821	S	2	<0.1
Grace Engineering Corp	PO Box 202	Memphis	MI	48041	Louis Grace	313-392-2181	R	2	<0.1
Kedie Image Systems	744 San Aleso Av	Sunnyvale	CA	94086	Dave Kedie	408-734-9005	R	2*	<0.1

Source: *Ward's Business Directory of U.S. Private and Public Companies*, Volumes 1 and 2, 1996. The company type code used is as follows: P - Public, R - Private, S - Subsidiary, D - Division, J - Joint Venture, A - Affiliate, G - Group. Sales are in millions of dollars, employees are in thousands. An asterisk (*) indicates an estimated sales volume. The symbol < stands for 'less than'. Company names and addresses are truncated, in some cases, to fit into the available space.

MATERIALS CONSUMED

Material	Quantity	Delivered Cost ($ million)
Materials, ingredients, containers, and supplies	(X)	638.5
Metal for printing plates	(X)	36.1
Unexposed photosensitive printing plates	(X)	19.5
Light sensitive films	(X)	99.9
Light sensitive papers (including photographic paper and diffusion transfer paper)	(X)	8.3
Color proofing materials	(X)	67.0
Paper, all types except light sensitive (including newsprint, book, bond, cover, and coated)	(X)	22.2
All other materials and components, parts, containers, and supplies	(X)	152.8
Materials, ingredients, containers, and supplies, nsk	(X)	232.7

Source: 1992 *Economic Census*. Explanation of symbols used: (D): Withheld to avoid disclosure of competitive data; na: Not available; (S): Withheld because statistical norms were not met; (X): Not applicable; (Z): Less than half the unit shown; nec: Not elsewhere classified; nsk: Not specified by kind; - : zero; * : 10-19 percent estimated; ** : 20-29 percent estimated.

PRODUCT SHARE DETAILS

Product or Product Class	% Share	Product or Product Class	% Share
Platemaking services	100.00	Platemaking services, except lithographic	20.73
Lithographic plates, prepared for printing	5.50	Photopolymer (plastics) duplicate plates for letterpress printing	7.50
Presensitized lithographic plates, exposed, prepared for printing	55.65	Other duplicate plates for letterpress printing	0.84
Wipe-on lithographic plates, prepared for printing	7.59	Natural and synthetic rubber flexographic plates, prepared for printing	10.33
All other lithographic plates, including deep-etch and multimetal (excluding unexposed plates), prepared for printing	16.55	Photopolymer flexographic plates, prepared for printing	17.99
Lithographic plates, prepared for printing, nsk	20.16	Preparation of film for gravure cylindermaking	11.03
Lithographic platemaking services	59.25	Gravure plates and cylinders made for others	25.60
Color corrected process positives or negatives on film, including color separations, for lithographic printing	72.30	Photoengraving plates made for others	6.12
All other lithographic film	8.76	Other printing plates prepared for printing, nec.	2.07
Assembled flats for lithographic platemaking	9.50	Other platemaking services, except lithographic, nec	9.07
Lithographic platemaking services, nsk.	9.45	Platemaking services, except lithographic, nsk	9.43
		Platemaking services, nsk	14.52

Source: 1992 *Economic Census*. The values shown are percent of total shipments in an industry. Values of indented subcategories are summed in the main heading. The symbol (D) appears when data are withheld to prevent disclosure of competitive information. The abbreviation nsk stands for 'not specified by kind' and nec for 'not elsewhere classified'.

INPUTS AND OUTPUTS FOR LITHOGRAPHIC PLATEMAKING & SERVICES

Economic Sector or Industry Providing Inputs	%	Sector	Economic Sector or Industry Buying Outputs	%	Sector
Periodicals	18.5	Manufg.	Commercial printing	73.1	Manufg.
Photographic equipment & supplies	14.2	Manufg.	Newspapers	8.0	Manufg.
Primary lead	9.4	Manufg.	Lithographic platemaking & services	6.2	Manufg.
Wholesale trade	6.7	Trade	Book printing	4.3	Manufg.
Lithographic platemaking & services	6.1	Manufg.	Book publishing	2.7	Manufg.
Printing trades machinery	6.1	Manufg.	Exports	1.5	Foreign
Cyclic crudes and organics	4.6	Manufg.	Miscellaneous publishing	1.2	Manufg.
Miscellaneous publishing	3.9	Manufg.	Periodicals	1.0	Manufg.
Advertising	2.4	Services	Typesetting	0.9	Manufg.
Real estate	2.2	Fin/R.E.	Engraving & plate printing	0.5	Manufg.
Paper mills, except building paper	2.1	Manufg.	Manifold business forms	0.5	Manufg.
Industrial gases	1.9	Manufg.	Photoengraving, electrotyping & stereotyping	0.3	Manufg.
Petroleum refining	1.8	Manufg.			
Electric services (utilities)	1.8	Util.			
Manufacturing industries, nec	1.7	Manufg.			
Motor freight transportation & warehousing	1.7	Util.			
Communications, except radio & TV	1.2	Util.			
Typesetting	1.0	Manufg.			
Air transportation	1.0	Util.			
Sanitary services, steam supply, irrigation	0.8	Util.			
Eating & drinking places	0.8	Trade			
Banking	0.8	Fin/R.E.			
Hotels & lodging places	0.7	Services			
Equipment rental & leasing services	0.6	Services			
Industrial inorganic chemicals, nec	0.5	Manufg.			
Railroads & related services	0.5	Util.			
Abrasive products	0.4	Manufg.			
Chemical preparations, nec	0.4	Manufg.			
Paperboard containers & boxes	0.4	Manufg.			
Automotive rental & leasing, without drivers	0.4	Services			
Computer & data processing services	0.4	Services			
Noncomparable imports	0.4	Foreign			
Maintenance of nonfarm buildings nec	0.3	Constr.			
Mechanical measuring devices	0.3	Manufg.			

Continued on next page.

INPUTS AND OUTPUTS FOR LITHOGRAPHIC PLATEMAKING & SERVICES - Continued

Economic Sector or Industry Providing Inputs	%	Sector	Economic Sector or Industry Buying Outputs	%	Sector
Printing ink	0.3	Manufg.			
Automotive repair shops & services	0.3	Services			
Legal services	0.3	Services			
Management & consulting services & labs	0.3	Services			
Water transportation	0.2	Util.			
Insurance carriers	0.2	Fin/R.E.			
Royalties	0.2	Fin/R.E.			
Accounting, auditing & bookkeeping	0.2	Services			
Imports	0.2	Foreign			
Manifold business forms	0.1	Manufg.			
Nonferrous rolling & drawing, nec	0.1	Manufg.			
Business/professional associations	0.1	Services			

Source: Benchmark Input-Output Accounts for the U.S. Economy, 1982, U.S. Department of Commerce, Washington, D.C., July 1991. Data, as reported in the source, are organized by the 1977 SIC structure in use in 1982 but have been matched, as closely as is possible, to the 1987 SIC structure used in this book.

OCCUPATIONS EMPLOYED BY SIC 279 - PRINTING TRADE SERVICES NEC

Occupation	% of Total 1994	Change to 2005	Occupation	% of Total 1994	Change to 2005
Strippers, printing	7.2	-8.6	Adjustment clerks	1.6	34.4
Sales & related workers nec	5.4	6.3	Data entry keyers, composing	1.6	-74.3
Electronic pagination systems workers	4.2	63.7	Secretaries, ex legal & medical	1.6	0.1
Typesetting & composing machine operators	4.2	-74.3	General office clerks	1.6	-8.4
Printing workers, precision nec	3.8	37.9	Freight, stock, & material movers, hand	1.5	-4.4
General managers & top executives	3.8	-1.5	Assemblers, fabricators, & hand workers nec	1.4	15.4
Hand packers & packagers	3.7	3.0	Messengers	1.4	-20.6
Artists & commercial artists	2.6	10.7	Clerical supervisors & managers	1.4	10.7
Proofreaders & copy markers	2.4	-33.2	Management support workers nec	1.4	19.5
Production, planning, & expediting clerks	2.3	22.2	Platemakers	1.3	-27.7
Photoengravers	2.3	-28.4	Offset lithographic press operators	1.3	1.4
Camera operators	2.1	-18.1	Printing, binding, & related workers nec	1.3	14.9
Bookkeeping, accounting, & auditing clerks	2.0	-21.2	Traffic, shipping, & receiving clerks	1.2	7.2
Paste-up workers	1.9	-33.3	Industrial production managers	1.2	5.4
Machine feeders & offbearers	1.8	7.5	Bindery machine operators & set-up operators	1.2	9.9
Printing press machine setters, operators	1.7	-9.0	Data entry keyers, ex composing	1.1	-16.6

Source: Industry-Occupation Matrix, Bureau of Labor Statistics. These data relate to one or more 3-digit SIC industry groups rather than to a single 4-digit SIC. The change reported for each occupation to the year 2005 is a percent of growth or decline as estimated by the Bureau of Labor Statistics. The abbreviation nec stands for 'not elsewhere classified'.

LOCATION BY STATE AND REGIONAL CONCENTRATION

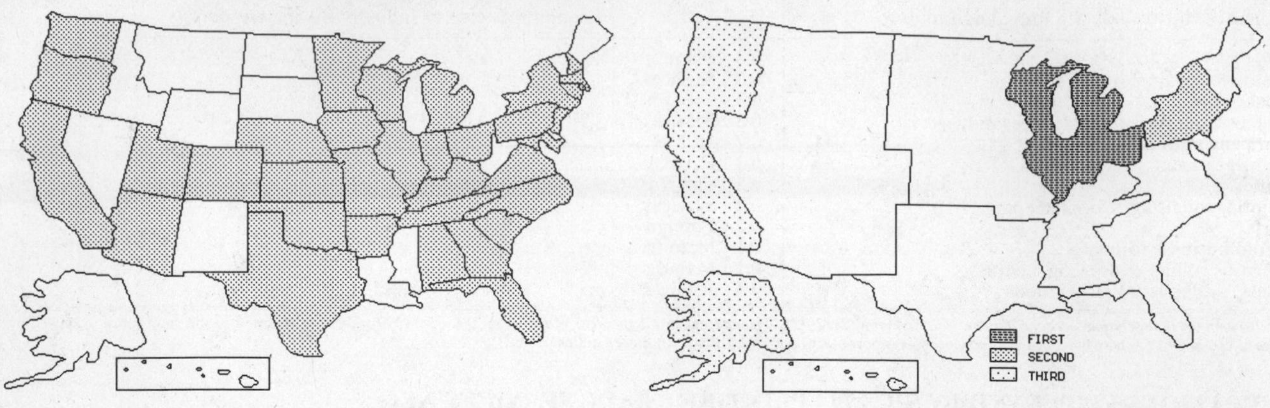

INDUSTRY DATA BY STATE

State	Establish-ments	Shipments Total ($ mil)	Shipments % of U.S.	Shipments Per Establ.	Employment Total Number	Employment % of U.S.	Employment Per Establ.	Employment Wages ($/hour)	Cost as % of Shipments	Investment per Employee ($)
California	236	452.8	13.1	1.9	4,800	12.4	20	15.82	23.2	3,583
Illinois	122	364.1	10.5	3.0	3,600	9.3	30	17.65	22.7	5,056
New York	187	309.8	9.0	1.7	3,100	8.0	17	16.87	22.8	4,677
New Jersey	80	199.0	5.8	2.5	2,200	5.7	28	16.19	22.4	2,955
Ohio	86	185.3	5.4	2.2	2,100	5.4	24	16.63	22.3	4,524
Texas	77	163.7	4.7	2.1	1,900	4.9	25	14.90	20.5	6,316
Wisconsin	62	153.9	4.5	2.5	1,900	4.9	31	14.93	23.5	5,211
Missouri	53	141.6	4.1	2.7	1,800	4.7	34	14.92	24.8	2,833
Pennsylvania	77	130.7	3.8	1.7	1,600	4.1	21	14.41	28.6	2,625
Michigan	55	124.6	3.6	2.3	1,300	3.4	24	15.11	18.4	5,154
Florida	71	115.3	3.3	1.6	1,400	3.6	20	13.55	25.7	3,714
Connecticut	36	109.6	3.2	3.0	1,200	3.1	33	16.94	24.7	2,917
Minnesota	40	106.7	3.1	2.7	1,200	3.1	30	15.72	19.4	5,750
Tennessee	38	98.2	2.8	2.6	1,300	3.4	34	15.24	20.7	2,769
North Carolina	41	89.5	2.6	2.2	1,100	2.8	27	13.22	24.2	4,182
Georgia	40	79.0	2.3	2.0	800	2.1	20	13.85	23.3	6,125
Kentucky	19	70.6	2.0	3.7	800	2.1	42	15.92	21.7	6,250
Massachusetts	49	66.7	1.9	1.4	800	2.1	16	13.83	28.3	4,250
Indiana	28	56.1	1.6	2.0	600	1.6	21	13.67	27.8	3,333
Washington	21	49.2	1.4	2.3	500	1.3	24	16.22	18.5	6,800
Oregon	22	47.6	1.4	2.2	600	1.6	27	15.87	21.6	3,833
Arizona	17	44.1	1.3	2.6	500	1.3	29	19.17	26.1	4,200
Maryland	27	38.5	1.1	1.4	500	1.3	19	16.43	21.6	3,600
Virginia	23	34.8	1.0	1.5	400	1.0	17	14.71	21.6	4,750
Colorado	24	28.6	0.8	1.2	400	1.0	17	14.20	17.8	2,750
South Carolina	12	18.1	0.5	1.5	300	0.8	25	11.25	27.6	2,000
Nebraska	6	17.1	0.5	2.8	200	0.5	33	13.00	23.4	8,500
New Hampshire	6	14.9	0.4	2.5	200	0.5	33	15.33	20.1	4,500
Utah	12	14.3	0.4	1.2	200	0.5	17	12.33	22.4	7,500
Iowa	16	11.3	0.3	0.7	200	0.5	13	9.33	22.1	2,500
Oklahoma	13	11.1	0.3	0.9	100	0.3	8	14.00	18.0	8,000
Alabama	11	11.0	0.3	1.0	100	0.3	9	10.50	26.4	4,000
Kansas	12	(D)	-	-	175 *	0.5	15	-	-	4,571
Rhode Island	9	(D)	-	-	175 *	0.5	19	-	-	-
D.C.	6	(D)	-	-	175 *	0.5	29	-	-	-
Arkansas	5	(D)	-	-	175 *	0.5	35	-	-	-

Source: 1992 *Economic Census*. The states are in descending order of shipments or establishments (if shipment data are missing for the majority). The symbol (D) appears when data are withheld to prevent disclosure of competitive information. States marked with (D) are sorted by number of establishments. A dash (-) indicates that the data element cannot be calculated; * indicates the midpoint of a range.

2812 - ALKALIES AND CHLORINE

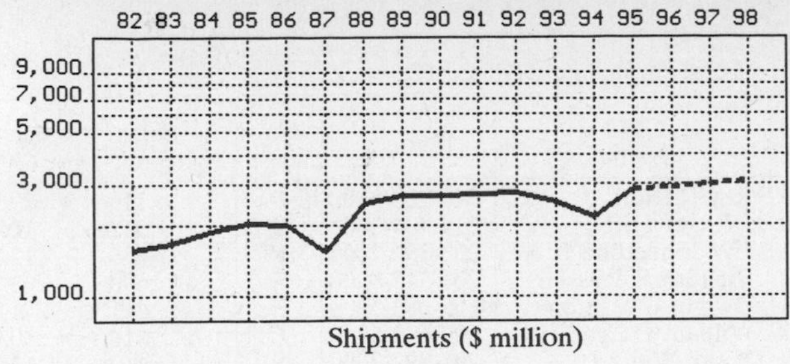

Shipments ($ million)

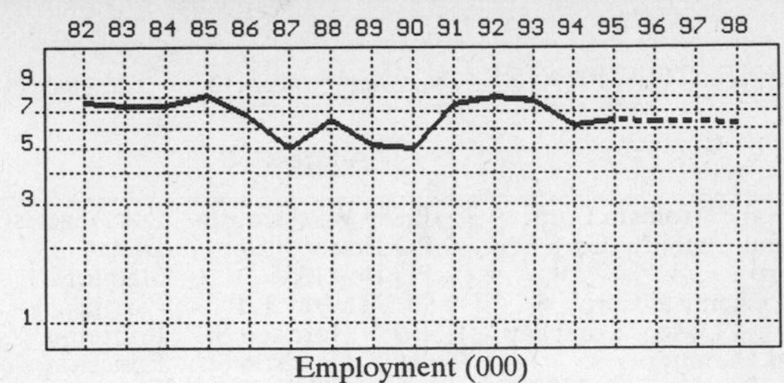

Employment (000)

GENERAL STATISTICS

Year	Companies	Establishments: Total	Establishments: with 20 or more employees	Employment: Total (000)	Employment: Production Workers (000)	Employment: Production Hours (Mil)	Compensation: Payroll ($ mil)	Compensation: Wages ($/hr)	Production ($ million): Cost of Materials	Production ($ million): Value Added by Manufacture	Production ($ million): Value of Shipments	Production ($ million): Capital Invest.
1982	35	51	34	7.6	5.0	9.8	215.7	13.77	856.3	728.8	1,570.5	134.4
1983		50	33	7.3	4.8	9.8	217.9	13.96	898.6	765.0	1,666.8	200.3
1984		49	32	7.4	5.1	10.6	239.7	15.26	984.0	869.6	1,872.4	149.5
1985		48	32	8.2	5.6	11.2	263.2	15.00	978.4	1,073.7	2,042.4	175.2
1986		51	33	6.7	4.5	9.0	218.3	15.24	957.9	1,028.0	2,010.9	122.1
1987	27	45	31	5.0	3.5	7.3	165.3	15.07	809.0	732.1	1,547.9	68.4
1988		50	32	6.5	4.4	9.4	237.5	16.90	1,159.9	1,324.1	2,469.3	104.2
1989		47	33	5.2	4.6	10.0	248.7	16.67	1,309.9	1,383.6	2,699.0	155.6
1990		46	32	5.0	4.7	10.1	263.3	17.40	1,265.8	1,449.9	2,709.8	127.0
1991		52	35	7.5	5.2	11.0	303.5	18.15	1,347.6	1,394.1	2,728.9	144.6
1992	34	51	33	8.0	5.4	11.3	353.3	20.53	1,393.4	1,408.1	2,786.9	176.2
1993		51	33	7.7	5.3	11.1	351.6	20.95	1,425.2	1,093.6	2,480.9	181.5
1994		50P	33P	6.2	4.2	8.9	287.2	21.70	1,121.8	1,015.6	2,171.1	126.5
1995		50P	33P	6.4P	4.8P	10.3P	329.9P	21.55P	1,459.7P	1,321.6P	2,825.2P	142.4P
1996		50P	33P	6.4P	4.8P	10.3P	340.0P	22.20P	1,505.0P	1,362.5P	2,912.7P	142.2P
1997		50P	33P	6.3P	4.8P	10.4P	350.2P	22.85P	1,550.3P	1,403.5P	3,000.3P	142.0P
1998		50P	33P	6.3P	4.7P	10.4P	360.3P	23.51P	1,595.5P	1,444.5P	3,087.9P	141.9P

Sources: 1982, 1987, 1992 *Economic Census*; *Annual Survey of Manufactures*, 83-86, 88-91, 93-94. Establishment counts for non-Census years are from *County Business Patterns*; establishment values for 83-84 are extrapolations. 'P's show projections by the editors. Industries reclassified in 87 will not have data for prior years.

INDICES OF CHANGE

Year	Companies	Establishments: Total	Establishments: with 20 or more employees	Employment: Total (000)	Employment: Production Workers (000)	Employment: Production Hours (Mil)	Compensation: Payroll ($ mil)	Compensation: Wages ($/hr)	Production ($ million): Cost of Materials	Production ($ million): Value Added by Manufacture	Production ($ million): Value of Shipments	Production ($ million): Capital Invest.
1982	103	100	103	95	93	87	61	67	61	52	56	76
1983		98	100	91	89	87	62	68	64	54	60	114
1984		96	97	93	94	94	68	74	71	62	67	85
1985		94	97	102	104	99	74	73	70	76	73	99
1986		100	100	84	83	80	62	74	69	73	72	69
1987	79	88	94	63	65	65	47	73	58	52	56	39
1988		98	97	81	81	83	67	82	83	94	89	59
1989		92	100	65	85	88	70	81	94	98	97	88
1990		90	97	63	87	89	75	85	91	103	97	72
1991		102	106	94	96	97	86	88	97	99	98	82
1992	100	100	100	100	100	100	100	100	100	100	100	100
1993		100	100	96	98	98	100	102	102	78	89	103
1994		97P	100P	78	78	79	81	106	81	72	78	72
1995		97P	100P	80P	88P	91P	93P	105P	105P	94P	101P	81P
1996		97P	100P	80P	88P	91P	96P	108P	108P	97P	105P	81P
1997		97P	100P	79P	88P	92P	99P	111P	111P	100P	108P	81P
1998		98P	100P	79P	88P	92P	102P	114P	115P	103P	111P	81P

Sources: Same as General Statistics. Values reflect change from the base year, 1992. Values above 100 mean greater than 92, values below 100 mean less than 92, and a value of 100 in the 82-91 or 93-98 period means same as 92. 'P's mark projections by the editors.

SELECTED RATIOS

For 1994	Avg. of All Manufact.	Analyzed Industry	Index
Employees per Establishment	49	125	255
Payroll per Establishment	1,500,273	5,796,697	386
Payroll per Employee	30,620	46,323	151
Production Workers per Establishment	34	85	247
Wages per Establishment	853,319	3,898,037	457
Wages per Production Worker	24,861	45,983	185
Hours per Production Worker	2,056	2,119	103
Wages per Hour	12.09	21.70	179
Value Added per Establishment	4,602,255	20,498,349	445
Value Added per Employee	93,930	163,806	174

For 1994	Avg. of All Manufact.	Analyzed Industry	Index
Value Added per Production Worker	134,084	241,810	180
Cost per Establishment	5,045,178	22,641,835	449
Cost per Employee	102,970	180,935	176
Cost per Production Worker	146,988	267,095	182
Shipments per Establishment	9,576,895	43,820,367	458
Shipments per Employee	195,460	350,177	179
Shipments per Production Worker	279,017	516,929	185
Investment per Establishment	321,011	2,553,211	795
Investment per Employee	6,552	20,403	311
Investment per Production Worker	9,352	30,119	322

Sources: Same as General Statistics. The 'Average of All Manufacturing' column represents the average of all manufacturing industries reported for the most recent complete year available. The Index shows the relationship between the Average and the Analyzed Industry. For example, 100 means that they are equal; 500 that the Analyzed Industry is five times the average; 50 means that the Analyzed Industry is half the national average. The abbreviation 'na' is used to show that data are 'not available'.

LEADING COMPANIES Number shown: 13 Total sales ($ mil): 17,395 Total employment (000): 52.9

Company Name	Address				CEO Name	Phone	Co. Type	Sales ($ mil)	Empl. (000)
Occidental Petroleum Corp	10889 Wilshire Blv	Los Angeles	CA	90024	Ray R Irani	310-208-8800	P	8,116	19.9
Occidental Chemical Corp	PO Box 809050	Dallas	TX	75380	J Roger Hirl	214-404-3800	S	4,042	10.4
Olin Corp	PO Box 1355	Stamford	CT	06904	J W Johnstone Jr	203-356-2000	P	2,658	12.8
General Chemical Corp	90 E Halsey Rd	Parsippany	NJ	07054	Richard R Russell	201-515-0900	S	690	3.7
Church and Dwight Company	469 N Harrison St	Princeton	NJ	08543	Dwight C Minton	609-683-5900	P	491	1.0
Arm and Hammer	469 N Harrison St	Princeton	NJ	08543	William C Egan III	609-683-5900	D	410	0.9
Formosa Plastics Corp USA	9 Peach Tree Hill	Livingston	NJ	07039	Susan Wang	201-992-2090	S	410*	2.2
Bio-Lab Inc	PO Box 1489	Decatur	GA	30031	Larry Bloom	404-378-1753	S	400	1.5
Church and Dwight Company	469 N Harrison St	Princeton	NJ	08543	Michael J Kenny	609-683-5900	D	120	0.3
Ashta Chemicals Inc	3509 Middle Rd	Ashtabula	OH	44004	Reginald R Baxter	216-997-5221	R	46	<0.1
Metro Group Inc	PO Box 1070	Long Island Ct	NY	11101	Samuel Levinger	718-729-7200	R	8	0.2
Continental Chemical Co	2175 Acoma St	Sacramento	CA	95815	AB Cord	916-929-4440	S	3	<0.1
Ameralia Inc	2153 Roundtop Ct	Co Springs	CO	80918	Bill H Gunn	719-260-6011	P	1	<0.1

Source: *Ward's Business Directory of U.S. Private and Public Companies*, Volumes 1 and 2, 1996. The company type code used is as follows: P - Public, R - Private, S - Subsidiary, D - Division, J - Joint Venture, A - Affiliate, G - Group. Sales are in millions of dollars, employees are in thousands. An asterisk (*) indicates an estimated sales volume. The symbol < stands for 'less than'. Company names and addresses are truncated, in some cases, to fit into the available space.

MATERIALS CONSUMED

Material		Quantity	Delivered Cost ($ million)
Materials, ingredients, containers, and supplies		(X)	696.7
Sulfuric acid (100 percent H2SO4), except spent	1,000 s tons	85.3*	5.2
Sodium carbonate (soda ash) (58 percent Na2O)		347.7	29.4
Sodium hydroxide (caustic soda)(100 percent NaOH)	1,000 s tons	17.2**	1.7
Salt in brine	1,000 s tons	7,039.9*	121.0
Other industrial inorganic chemicals		(X)	9.6
Synthetic organic chemicals		(X)	(D)
All other crude chemical nonmetallic minerals, including barite, borate, potash, fluorspar, rock salt, etc.		(X)	4.2
Parts and attachments for machinery and equipment		(X)	(D)
Paperboard containers, boxes, and corrugated paperboard		(X)	(D)
Metal containers		(X)	5.3
All other materials and components, parts, containers, and supplies		(X)	369.7
Materials, ingredients, containers, and supplies, nsk		(X)	49.8

Source: 1992 *Economic Census*. Explanation of symbols used: (D): Withheld to avoid disclosure of competitive data; na: Not available; (S): Withheld because statistical norms were not met; (X): Not applicable; (Z): Less than half the unit shown; nec: Not elsewhere classified; nsk: Not specified by kind; - : zero; * : 10-19 percent estimated; ** : 20-29 percent estimated.

PRODUCT SHARE DETAILS

Product or Product Class	% Share	Product or Product Class	% Share
Alkalies and chlorine	100.00	Other alkalies	13.10
Chlorine, compressed or liquefied	7.11	Alkalies and chlorine, nsk	0.70
Sodium hydroxide (caustic soda)	79.10		

Source: 1992 *Economic Census*. The values shown are percent of total shipments in an industry. Values of indented subcategories are summed in the main heading. The symbol (D) appears when data are withheld to prevent disclosure of competitive information. The abbreviation nsk stands for 'not specified by kind' and nec for 'not elsewhere classified'.

INPUTS AND OUTPUTS FOR ALKALIES & CHLORINE

Economic Sector or Industry Providing Inputs	%	Sector	Economic Sector or Industry Buying Outputs	%	Sector
Electric services (utilities)	30.4	Util.	Glass containers	10.4	Manufg.
Gas production & distribution (utilities)	10.7	Util.	Exports	9.3	Foreign
Imports	9.9	Foreign	Cyclic crudes and organics	9.2	Manufg.
Wholesale trade	7.6	Trade	Paper mills, except building paper	7.9	Manufg.
Alkalies & chlorine	3.9	Manufg.	Industrial inorganic chemicals, nec	6.1	Manufg.
Special industry machinery, nec	3.7	Manufg.	Soap & other detergents	5.4	Manufg.
Petroleum refining	3.2	Manufg.	Paperboard mills	4.7	Manufg.
Engineering, architectural, & surveying services	3.0	Services	Pulp mills	4.3	Manufg.
Miscellaneous repair shops	2.2	Services	Hospitals	4.3	Services
Chemical preparations, nec	2.0	Manufg.	Plastics materials & resins	4.1	Manufg.
Advertising	1.9	Services	Chemical preparations, nec	3.2	Manufg.
Chemical & fertilizer mineral	1.8	Mining	Glass & glass products, except containers	3.2	Manufg.
Equipment rental & leasing services	1.8	Services	Polishes & sanitation goods	2.4	Manufg.
Water supply & sewage systems	1.6	Util.	Petroleum refining	2.2	Manufg.
Maintenance of nonfarm buildings nec	1.5	Constr.	Paints & allied products	1.4	Manufg.

Continued on next page.

INPUTS AND OUTPUTS FOR ALKALIES & CHLORINE - Continued

Economic Sector or Industry Providing Inputs	%	Sector	Economic Sector or Industry Buying Outputs	%	Sector
Motor freight transportation & warehousing	1.5	Util.	Alkalies & chlorine	1.3	Manufg.
Coal	1.4	Mining	Personal consumption expenditures	1.2	
Eating & drinking places	1.2	Trade	Inorganic pigments	1.2	Manufg.
Noncomparable imports	0.9	Foreign	Gum & wood chemicals	1.1	Manufg.
Paperboard containers & boxes	0.8	Manufg.	Miscellaneous plastics products	1.1	Manufg.
Pipe, valves, & pipe fittings	0.8	Manufg.	Primary aluminum	1.0	Manufg.
Railroads & related services	0.8	Util.	Synthetic rubber	1.0	Manufg.
Industrial inorganic chemicals, nec	0.7	Manufg.	Chemical & fertilizer mineral	0.9	Mining
Communications, except radio & TV	0.7	Util.	Photographic equipment & supplies	0.9	Manufg.
Legal services	0.6	Services	Drugs	0.8	Manufg.
Metal barrels, drums, & pails	0.5	Manufg.	Agricultural chemicals, nec	0.7	Manufg.
Management & consulting services & labs	0.5	Services	Medical & health services, nec	0.7	Services
Crude petroleum & natural gas	0.4	Mining	Blast furnaces & steel mills	0.5	Manufg.
Air transportation	0.4	Util.	Crude petroleum & natural gas	0.4	Mining
Machinery, except electrical, nec	0.3	Manufg.	Broadwoven fabric mills	0.4	Manufg.
Accounting, auditing & bookkeeping	0.3	Services	Nitrogenous & phosphatic fertilizers	0.4	Manufg.
Computer & data processing services	0.3	Services	Semiconductors & related devices	0.4	Manufg.
Dimension, crushed & broken stone	0.2	Mining	Adhesives & sealants	0.3	Manufg.
Nitrogenous & phosphatic fertilizers	0.2	Manufg.	Food preparations, nec	0.3	Manufg.
Royalties	0.2	Fin/R.E.	Organic fibers, noncellulosic	0.3	Manufg.
U.S. Postal Service	0.2	Gov't	Printing ink	0.3	Manufg.
Glass & glass products, except containers	0.1	Manufg.	Steel pipe & tubes	0.3	Manufg.
Industrial gases	0.1	Manufg.	Toilet preparations	0.3	Manufg.
Lubricating oils & greases	0.1	Manufg.	State & local government enterprises, nec	0.3	Gov't
Manifold business forms	0.1	Manufg.	Commercial printing	0.2	Manufg.
Special dies & tools & machine tool accessories	0.1	Manufg.	Fabricated rubber products, nec	0.2	Manufg.
Water transportation	0.1	Util.	Fertilizers, mixing only	0.2	Manufg.
Retail trade, except eating & drinking	0.1	Trade	Manufacturing industries, nec	0.2	Manufg.
Insurance carriers	0.1	Fin/R.E.	Prepared feeds, nec	0.2	Manufg.
Real estate	0.1	Fin/R.E.	Storage batteries	0.2	Manufg.
			Surface active agents	0.2	Manufg.
			Tires & inner tubes	0.2	Manufg.
			Management & consulting services & labs	0.2	Services
			Cellulosic manmade fibers	0.1	Manufg.
			Paper coating & glazing	0.1	Manufg.
			Special industry machinery, nec	0.1	Manufg.
			Wood preserving	0.1	Manufg.
			Sanitary services, steam supply, irrigation	0.1	Util.

Source: Benchmark Input-Output Accounts for the U.S. Economy, 1982, U.S. Department of Commerce, Washington, D.C., July 1991. Data, as reported in the source, are organized by the 1977 SIC structure in use in 1982 but have been matched, as closely as is possible, to the 1987 SIC structure used in this book.

OCCUPATIONS EMPLOYED BY SIC 281 - INDUSTRIAL INORGANIC CHEMICALS

Occupation	% of Total 1994	Change to 2005	Occupation	% of Total 1994	Change to 2005
Chemical equipment controllers, operators	7.8	-15.9	General managers & top executives	1.9	-11.4
Blue collar worker supervisors	5.4	-5.3	Inspectors, testers, & graders, precision	1.9	-6.6
Management support workers nec	5.3	-6.6	Managers & administrators nec	1.8	-6.6
Chemical plant & system operators	4.7	-6.6	Industrial production managers	1.7	-6.6
Science & mathematics technicians	3.8	-6.6	Engineering, mathematical, & science managers	1.7	6.1
Secretaries, ex legal & medical	3.3	-15.0	Packaging & filling machine operators	1.6	-6.6
Chemical engineers	3.3	2.8	Crushing & mixing machine operators	1.5	-6.6
Maintenance repairers, general utility	3.0	-15.9	Mechanical engineers	1.3	2.8
Industrial machinery mechanics	3.0	2.7	Helpers, laborers, & material movers nec	1.3	-6.6
Truck drivers light & heavy	2.8	-3.7	Electricians	1.2	-12.3
Engineers nec	2.3	40.1	Machine operators nec	1.1	-17.7
Sales & related workers nec	2.3	-6.6	Plant & system operators nec	1.1	-17.5
General office clerks	2.0	-20.3	Precision instrument repairers	1.0	-6.6
Chemists	2.0	-6.6	Accountants & auditors	1.0	-6.6

Source: *Industry-Occupation Matrix*, Bureau of Labor Statistics. These data relate to one or more 3-digit SIC industry groups rather than to a single 4-digit SIC. The change reported for each occupation to the year 2005 is a percent of growth or decline as estimated by the Bureau of Labor Statistics. The abbreviation nec stands for 'not elsewhere classified'.

LOCATION BY STATE AND REGIONAL CONCENTRATION

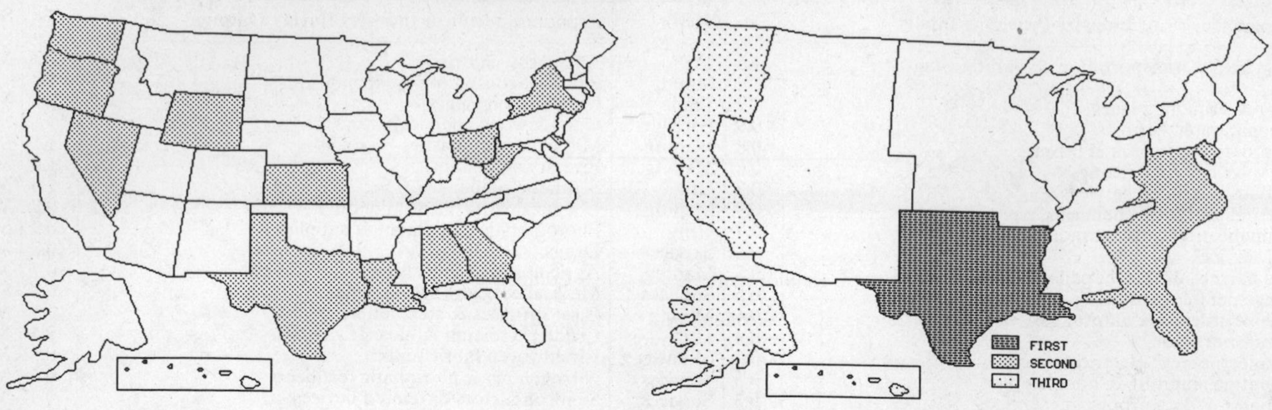

INDUSTRY DATA BY STATE

State	Establish-ments	Shipments			Employment				Cost as % of Shipments	Investment per Employee ($)
		Total ($ mil)	% of U.S.	Per Establ.	Total Number	% of U.S.	Per Establ.	Wages ($/hour)		
Louisiana	6	924.0	33.2	154.0	2,400	30.0	400	20.51	49.5	-
Washington	3	128.6	4.6	42.9	400	5.0	133	17.50	51.8	-
Georgia	6	110.1	4.0	18.4	300	3.8	50	20.20	54.7	20,667
Texas	8	(D)	-	-	750 *	9.4	94	-	-	-
New York	4	(D)	-	-	750 *	9.4	188	-	-	-
Alabama	3	(D)	-	-	750 *	9.4	250	-	-	-
Ohio	2	(D)	-	-	175 *	2.2	88	-	-	-
Wyoming	2	(D)	-	-	375 *	4.7	188	-	-	-
Delaware	1	(D)	-	-	175 *	2.2	175	-	-	-
Kansas	1	(D)	-	-	750 *	9.4	750	-	-	-
Nevada	1	(D)	-	-	175 *	2.2	175	-	-	-
Oregon	1	(D)	-	-	175 *	2.2	175	-	-	-
West Virginia	1	(D)	-	-	750 *	9.4	750	-	-	-

Source: 1992 *Economic Census*. The states are in descending order of shipments or establishments (if shipment data are missing for the majority). The symbol (D) appears when data are withheld to prevent disclosure of competitive information. States marked with (D) are sorted by number of establishments. A dash (-) indicates that the data element cannot be calculated; * indicates the midpoint of a range.

2813 - INDUSTRIAL GASES

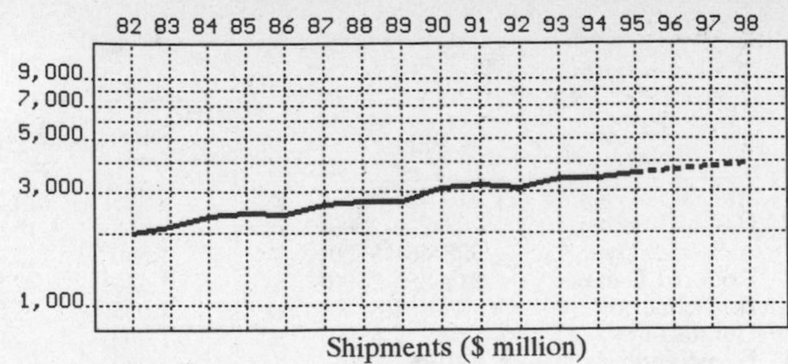

Shipments ($ million)

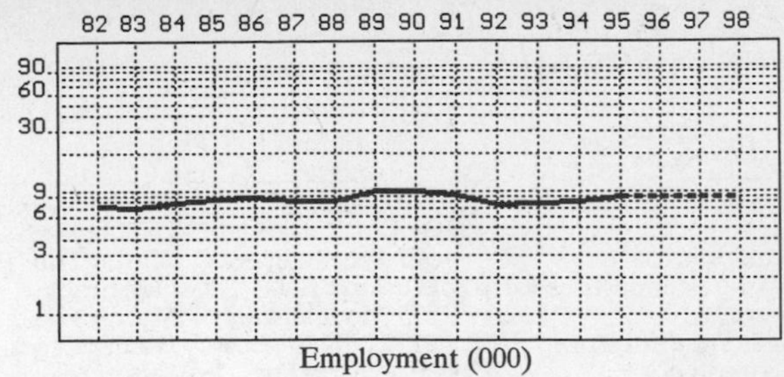

Employment (000)

GENERAL STATISTICS

		Establishments		Employment			Compensation		Production ($ million)			
Year	Com-panies	Total	with 20 or more employees	Total (000)	Production Workers (000)	Production Hours (Mil)	Payroll ($ mil)	Wages ($/hr)	Cost of Materials	Value Added by Manufacture	Value of Shipments	Capital Invest.
1982	107	563	105	7.3	4.3	9.9	174.0	10.18	967.2	1,055.3	2,019.3	223.7
1983		561	116	7.2	3.9	8.8	168.1	10.25	959.9	1,169.6	2,111.9	107.5
1984		559	127	7.9	4.4	9.7	197.2	10.73	1,073.0	1,290.3	2,363.5	263.9
1985		557	139	8.5	4.5	10.5	223.3	10.95	949.1	1,466.7	2,416.0	212.5
1986		566	145	8.6	4.0	8.8	248.4	12.73	1,002.6	1,386.7	2,401.9	122.1
1987	103	594	135	8.1	4.0	8.5	241.4	13.56	1,052.9	1,572.5	2,617.8	104.3
1988		573	126	8.1	4.4	9.4	245.3	13.51	1,134.4	1,589.1	2,721.2	73.0
1989		576	143	9.9	4.7	10.0	261.4	14.00	1,087.2	1,686.2	2,731.5	121.0
1990		587	149	9.9	4.8	9.7	282.8	14.56	1,154.2	1,919.2	3,058.1	177.8
1991		650	144	9.2	4.9	10.4	300.2	14.33	1,148.9	2,047.0	3,193.9	289.7
1992	112	592	122	7.7	4.2	9.1	261.8	14.65	1,012.2	2,076.2	3,095.7	146.3
1993		616	129	7.8	4.1	8.9	275.2	15.02	1,092.7	2,353.2	3,435.7	163.7
1994		621P	142P	8.0	4.2	9.2	289.3	15.72	1,013.2	2,388.9	3,415.7	174.5
1995		626P	144P	8.8P	4.5P	9.3P	313.2P	16.44P	1,059.3P	2,497.6P	3,571.2P	162.9P
1996		632P	146P	8.9P	4.5P	9.3P	323.1P	16.92P	1,094.7P	2,581.0P	3,690.3P	162.2P
1997		638P	147P	9.0P	4.5P	9.3P	333.0P	17.39P	1,130.0P	2,664.3P	3,809.5P	161.5P
1998		644P	149P	9.0P	4.5P	9.3P	342.9P	17.87P	1,165.4P	2,747.6P	3,928.6P	160.8P

Sources: 1982, 1987, 1992 *Economic Census*; *Annual Survey of Manufactures*, 83-86, 88-91, 93-94. Establishment counts for non-Census years are from *County Business Patterns*; establishment values for 83-84 are extrapolations. 'P's show projections by the editors. Industries reclassified in 87 will not have data for prior years.

INDICES OF CHANGE

		Establishments		Employment			Compensation		Production ($ million)			
Year	Com-panies	Total	with 20 or more employees	Total (000)	Production Workers (000)	Production Hours (Mil)	Payroll ($ mil)	Wages ($/hr)	Cost of Materials	Value Added by Manufacture	Value of Shipments	Capital Invest.
1982	96	95	86	95	102	109	66	69	96	51	65	153
1983		95	95	94	93	97	64	70	95	56	68	73
1984		94	104	103	105	107	75	73	106	62	76	180
1985		94	114	110	107	115	85	75	94	71	78	145
1986		96	119	112	95	97	95	87	99	67	78	83
1987	92	100	111	105	95	93	92	93	104	76	85	71
1988		97	103	105	105	103	94	92	112	77	88	50
1989		97	117	129	112	110	100	96	107	81	88	83
1990		99	122	129	114	107	108	99	114	92	99	122
1991		110	118	119	117	114	115	98	114	99	103	198
1992	100	100	100	100	100	100	100	100	100	100	100	100
1993		104	106	101	98	98	105	103	108	113	111	112
1994		105P	117P	104	100	101	111	107	100	115	110	119
1995		106P	118P	115P	106P	103P	120P	112P	105P	120P	115P	111P
1996		107P	119P	115P	107P	102P	123P	115P	108P	124P	119P	111P
1997		108P	121P	116P	107P	102P	127P	119P	112P	128P	123P	110P
1998		109P	122P	117P	107P	102P	131P	122P	115P	132P	127P	110P

Sources: Same as General Statistics. Values reflect change from the base year, 1992. Values above 100 mean greater than 92, values below 100 mean less than 92, and a value of 100 in the 82-91 or 93-98 period means same as 92. 'P's mark projections by the editors.

SELECTED RATIOS

For 1994	Avg. of All Manufact.	Analyzed Industry	Index
Employees per Establishment	49	13	26
Payroll per Establishment	1,500,273	466,226	31
Payroll per Employee	30,620	36,162	118
Production Workers per Establishment	34	7	20
Wages per Establishment	853,319	233,071	27
Wages per Production Worker	24,861	34,434	139
Hours per Production Worker	2,056	2,190	107
Wages per Hour	12.09	15.72	130
Value Added per Establishment	4,602,255	3,849,866	84
Value Added per Employee	93,930	298,612	318

For 1994	Avg. of All Manufact.	Analyzed Industry	Index
Value Added per Production Worker	134,084	568,786	424
Cost per Establishment	5,045,178	1,632,837	32
Cost per Employee	102,970	126,650	123
Cost per Production Worker	146,988	241,238	164
Shipments per Establishment	9,576,895	5,504,620	57
Shipments per Employee	195,460	426,963	218
Shipments per Production Worker	279,017	813,262	291
Investment per Establishment	321,011	281,218	88
Investment per Employee	6,552	21,813	333
Investment per Production Worker	9,352	41,548	444

Sources: Same as General Statistics. The 'Average of All Manufacturing' column represents the average of all manufacturing industries reported for the most recent complete year available. The Index shows the relationship between the Average and the Analyzed Industry. For example, 100 means that they are equal; 500 that the Analyzed Industry is five times the average; 50 means that the Analyzed Industry is half the national average. The abbreviation 'na' is used to show that data are 'not available'.

LEADING COMPANIES

Number shown: **30** Total sales ($ mil): **12,376** Total employment (000): **63.3**

Company Name	Address				CEO Name	Phone	Co. Type	Sales ($ mil)	Empl. (000)
Air Products and Chemicals Inc	PO Box 538	Allentown	PA	18195	Harold A Wagner	610-481-4911	P	3,485	14.0
Praxair Inc	39 Old Ridgebury	Danbury	CT	06810	HW Lichtenberger	203-794-2000	P	2,438	16.8
BOC Group Inc	575 Mountain Av	Murray Hill	NJ	07974	A Patrick Dyer	908-464-8100	S	1,650	9.0
Liquid Carbonic Industries Corp	810 Jorie Blv	Oak Brook	IL	60521	Robert J Daniels	312-855-2500	S	1,540*	7.5
Airco Gases	575 Mountain Av	Murray Hill	NJ	07974	Seifi Ghasemi	908-464-8100	D	1,038	5.0
Air Liquide America Corp	2121 N California	Walnut Creek	CA	94596	Gerald Levy	510-977-6500	S	1,000	4.0
Nippon Sanso USA	30 Seaview Dr	Secaucus	NJ	07096	Don Ramlow	201-867-4100	S	230	1.0
MG Industries	3 Great Valley Pkwy	Malvern	PA	19355	Herb Rudolf	610-695-7400	S	200	1.0
AGA Gas Inc	PO Box 94737	Cleveland	OH	44101	Patrick Murphy	216-642-6600	S	145	1.2
Matheson Gas Products	30 Seaview Dr	Secaucus	NJ	07096	D Ramlow	201-867-4100	S	125	0.8
Scott Specialty Gases Inc	6141 Easton Rd	Plumsteadville	PA	18949	JF Merz Jr	215-766-8861	R	115	0.6
National Welders Supply	PO Box 31007	Charlotte	NC	28231	Erroll C Sult	704-333-5475	R	85	0.7
Specialty Chemical Resources	9100 Val View Rd	Macedonia	OH	44056	Edwin M Roth	216-468-1380	P	45	0.2
Gaspro	2305 Kam Hwy	Honolulu	HI	96819	E MacNaughton	808-842-2222	D	35	0.1
Roberts Oxygen Company Inc	PO Box 5507	Rockville	MD	20855	Bob Roberts	301-948-8100	R	35	0.2
Lincoln Big Three Inc	PO Box 3274	Baton Rouge	LA	70821	C Hodges	504-357-4331	S	33*	0.2
Carbonic Industries Corp	3700 Crestwood	Duluth	GA	30136	JV Hinely	404-979-0250	R	30	0.2
Gulf State Airgas Inc	PO Box 190969	Mobile	AL	36619	Henry B Coker III	205-653-2500	D	30*	0.2
Acetylene Gas Co	PO Box 14858	St Louis	MO	63178	R Curtman Bird	314-533-3100	R	23*	0.1
Holston Gases Inc	PO Box 27248	Knoxville	TN	37927	William W Baxter	615-573-1917	R	18*	<0.1
Beard Co	5600 N May Av	Oklahoma City	OK	73112	WM Beard	405-842-2333	P	18	0.1
Kansas Oxygen Inc	PO Box 3007	Hutchinson	KS	67504	Richard Hollowell	316-665-5551	R	14	0.1
US Medical Inc	600 S Santa Fe Dr	Denver	CO	80223	Rick Lofgren	303-778-1313	D	10	<0.1
Carbonic Reserves Inc	10110 Huebner Rd	San Antonio	TX	78240	Clifford H Collen	210-690-1911	S	9	0.1
De Lille Oxygen Co	772 Marion Rd	Columbus	OH	43207	Jim O'Conner	614-444-1177	R	9	<0.1
Nitrous Oxide Systems Inc	5930 Lakeshore Dr	Cypress	CA	90630	Mike Thermos	714-821-0580	R	5	<0.1
Great Western Airgas Inc	2584 US 6 & 50	Grand Junction	CO	81505	Dennis Schafer	303-243-1944	S	3	<0.1
Gas Arc Supply Inc	5100 Umbria St	Philadelphia	PA	19128	Donald R Griffith	215-482-5100	R	3	<0.1
Osair Inc	PO Box 1020	Mentor	OH	44061	R Osborne	216-951-1111	R	3	<0.1
Gano Welding Supplies Inc	320 Railroad St	Charleston	IL	61920	Kenneth Gano	217-345-3777	R	2	<0.1

Source: *Ward's Business Directory of U.S. Private and Public Companies*, Volumes 1 and 2, 1996. The company type code used is as follows: P - Public, R - Private, S - Subsidiary, D - Division, J - Joint Venture, A - Affiliate, G - Group. Sales are in millions of dollars, employees are in thousands. An asterisk (*) indicates an estimated sales volume. The symbol < stands for 'less than'. Company names and addresses are truncated, in some cases, to fit into the available space.

MATERIALS CONSUMED

Material	Quantity	Delivered Cost ($ million)
No Materials Consumed data available for this industry.		

Source: 1992 *Economic Census*. Explanation of symbols used: (D): Withheld to avoid disclosure of competitive data; na: Not available; (S): Withheld because statistical norms were not met; (X): Not applicable; (Z): Less than half the unit shown; nec: Not elsewhere classified; nsk: Not specified by kind; - : zero; * : 10-19 percent estimated; ** : 20-29 percent estimated.

PRODUCT SHARE DETAILS

Product or Product Class	% Share	Product or Product Class	% Share
Industrial gases	100.00	Oxygen	24.74
Acetylene	4.08	Other industrial gases, including argon, hydrogen, helium, and carbon monoxide	26.10
Carbon dioxide	10.18	Industrial gases, nsk	4.51
Nitrogen	30.40		

Source: 1992 *Economic Census*. The values shown are percent of total shipments in an industry. Values of indented subcategories are summed in the main heading. The symbol (D) appears when data are withheld to prevent disclosure of competitive information. The abbreviation nsk stands for 'not specified by kind' and nec for 'not elsewhere classified'.

INPUTS AND OUTPUTS FOR INDUSTRIAL GASES

Economic Sector or Industry Providing Inputs	%	Sector	Economic Sector or Industry Buying Outputs	%	Sector
Electric services (utilities)	54.6	Util.	Hospitals	21.3	Services
Metal barrels, drums, & pails	10.8	Manufg.	Blast furnaces & steel mills	8.5	Manufg.
Wholesale trade	5.6	Trade	S/L Govt. purch., health & hospitals	7.3	S/L Govt
Gas production & distribution (utilities)	5.5	Util.	Surface active agents	5.5	Manufg.
Advertising	4.3	Services	Cyclic crudes and organics	4.8	Manufg.
Engineering, architectural, & surveying services	3.5	Services	Federal Government purchases, national defense	3.0	Fed Govt
Miscellaneous repair shops	1.5	Services	Personal consumption expenditures	2.8	
Petroleum refining	1.4	Manufg.	Federal Government purchases, nondefense	2.7	Fed Govt
Eating & drinking places	1.4	Trade	Leather tanning & finishing	2.5	Manufg.
Pipe, valves, & pipe fittings	1.2	Manufg.	Exports	2.4	Foreign

Continued on next page.

INPUTS AND OUTPUTS FOR INDUSTRIAL GASES - Continued

Economic Sector or Industry Providing Inputs	%	Sector	Economic Sector or Industry Buying Outputs	%	Sector
Industrial inorganic chemicals, nec	1.0	Manufg.	Miscellaneous repair shops	2.1	Services
Pumps & compressors	1.0	Manufg.	Nonwoven fabrics	1.8	Manufg.
Maintenance of nonfarm buildings nec	0.9	Constr.	Coated fabrics, not rubberized	1.3	Manufg.
Equipment rental & leasing services	0.7	Services	Ship building & repairing	1.1	Manufg.
Legal services	0.7	Services	Knit fabric mills	1.0	Manufg.
Royalties	0.5	Fin/R.E.	Cookies & crackers	0.9	Manufg.
Management & consulting services & labs	0.5	Services	Motor vehicle parts & accessories	0.8	Manufg.
Air transportation	0.4	Util.	Motor vehicles & car bodies	0.8	Manufg.
Machinery, except electrical, nec	0.3	Manufg.	Flavoring extracts & syrups, nec	0.7	Manufg.
Communications, except radio & TV	0.3	Util.	Vitreous plumbing fixtures	0.7	Manufg.
Motor freight transportation & warehousing	0.3	Util.	Wholesale trade	0.7	Trade
Water supply & sewage systems	0.3	Util.	Nursing & personal care facilities	0.7	Services
Accounting, auditing & bookkeeping	0.3	Services	Industrial buildings	0.6	Constr.
Industrial gases	0.2	Manufg.	Fabricated plate work (boiler shops)	0.6	Manufg.
Lubricating oils & greases	0.2	Manufg.	Lithographic platemaking & services	0.6	Manufg.
Manifold business forms	0.2	Manufg.	Office buildings	0.5	Constr.
Insurance carriers	0.2	Fin/R.E.	Knit underwear mills	0.5	Manufg.
Computer & data processing services	0.2	Services	Machinery, except electrical, nec	0.5	Manufg.
U.S. Postal Service	0.2	Gov't	Metal heat treating	0.5	Manufg.
Glass & glass products, except containers	0.1	Manufg.	Sheet metal work	0.5	Manufg.
Photographic equipment & supplies	0.1	Manufg.	Toilet preparations	0.5	Manufg.
Special dies & tools & machine tool accessories	0.1	Manufg.	Railroads & related services	0.5	Util.
Automotive rental & leasing, without drivers	0.1	Services	Crude petroleum & natural gas	0.4	Mining
Automotive repair shops & services	0.1	Services	Residential high-rise apartments	0.4	Constr.
Personnel supply services	0.1	Services	Construction machinery & equipment	0.4	Manufg.
			Fabricated structural metal	0.4	Manufg.
			Farm machinery & equipment	0.4	Manufg.
			Industrial inorganic chemicals, nec	0.4	Manufg.
			Oil field machinery	0.4	Manufg.
			Roasted coffee	0.4	Manufg.
			Electric services (utilities)	0.4	Util.
			Funeral service & crematories	0.4	Services
			Watch, clock, jewelry, & furniture repair	0.4	Services
			Coal	0.3	Mining
			Electric utility facility construction	0.3	Constr.
			Inorganic pigments	0.3	Manufg.
			Iron & steel foundries	0.3	Manufg.
			Manufacturing industries, nec	0.3	Manufg.
			Metal doors, sash, & trim	0.3	Manufg.
			Railroad equipment	0.3	Manufg.
			Tire cord & fabric	0.3	Manufg.
			Highway & street construction	0.2	Constr.
			Aircraft	0.2	Manufg.
			Blended & prepared flour	0.2	Manufg.
			Boat building & repairing	0.2	Manufg.
			Electronic components nec	0.2	Manufg.
			Fabricated metal products, nec	0.2	Manufg.
			Felt goods, nec	0.2	Manufg.
			Ice cream & frozen desserts	0.2	Manufg.
			Petroleum refining	0.2	Manufg.
			Pipe, valves, & pipe fittings	0.2	Manufg.
			Pumps & compressors	0.2	Manufg.
			Refrigeration & heating equipment	0.2	Manufg.
			Shoes, except rubber	0.2	Manufg.
			Shortening & cooking oils	0.2	Manufg.
			Soybean oil mills	0.2	Manufg.
			Thread mills	0.2	Manufg.
			Women's hosiery, except socks	0.2	Manufg.
			Retail trade, except eating & drinking	0.2	Trade
			Automotive repair shops & services	0.2	Services
			S/L Govt. purch., other general government	0.2	S/L Govt
			Forestry products	0.1	Agric.
			Construction of educational buildings	0.1	Constr.
			Construction of hospitals	0.1	Constr.
			Construction of stores & restaurants	0.1	Constr.
			Maintenance of electric utility facilities	0.1	Constr.
			Maintenance of highways & streets	0.1	Constr.
			Telephone & telegraph facility construction	0.1	Constr.
			Architectural metal work	0.1	Manufg.
			Boot & shoe cutstock & findings	0.1	Manufg.
			Chewing & smoking tobacco	0.1	Manufg.
			Conveyors & conveying equipment	0.1	Manufg.
			Industrial trucks & tractors	0.1	Manufg.
			Leather goods, nec	0.1	Manufg.
			Metal stampings, nec	0.1	Manufg.

Continued on next page.

INPUTS AND OUTPUTS FOR INDUSTRIAL GASES - Continued

Economic Sector or Industry Providing Inputs	%	Sector	Economic Sector or Industry Buying Outputs	%	Sector
			Mining machinery, except oil field	0.1	Manufg.
			Padding & upholstery filling	0.1	Manufg.
			Prefabricated metal buildings	0.1	Manufg.
			Semiconductors & related devices	0.1	Manufg.
			Special dies & tools & machine tool accessories	0.1	Manufg.
			Textile goods, nec	0.1	Manufg.
			Gas production & distribution (utilities)	0.1	Util.
			Motor freight transportation & warehousing	0.1	Util.
			S/L Govt. purch., fire	0.1	S/L Govt

Source: Benchmark Input-Output Accounts for the U.S. Economy, 1982, U.S. Department of Commerce, Washington, D.C., July 1991. Data, as reported in the source, are organized by the 1977 SIC structure in use in 1982 but have been matched, as closely as is possible, to the 1987 SIC structure used in this book.

OCCUPATIONS EMPLOYED BY SIC 281 - INDUSTRIAL INORGANIC CHEMICALS

Occupation	% of Total 1994	Change to 2005	Occupation	% of Total 1994	Change to 2005
Chemical equipment controllers, operators	7.8	-15.9	General managers & top executives	1.9	-11.4
Blue collar worker supervisors	5.4	-5.3	Inspectors, testers, & graders, precision	1.9	-6.6
Management support workers nec	5.3	-6.6	Managers & administrators nec	1.8	-6.6
Chemical plant & system operators	4.7	-6.6	Industrial production managers	1.7	-6.6
Science & mathematics technicians	3.8	-6.6	Engineering, mathematical, & science managers	1.7	6.1
Secretaries, ex legal & medical	3.3	-15.0	Packaging & filling machine operators	1.6	-6.6
Chemical engineers	3.3	2.8	Crushing & mixing machine operators	1.5	-6.6
Maintenance repairers, general utility	3.0	-15.9	Mechanical engineers	1.3	2.8
Industrial machinery mechanics	3.0	2.7	Helpers, laborers, & material movers nec	1.3	-6.6
Truck drivers light & heavy	2.8	-3.7	Electricians	1.2	-12.3
Engineers nec	2.3	40.1	Machine operators nec	1.1	-17.7
Sales & related workers nec	2.3	-6.6	Plant & system operators nec	1.1	-17.5
General office clerks	2.0	-20.3	Precision instrument repairers	1.0	-6.6
Chemists	2.0	-6.6	Accountants & auditors	1.0	-6.6

Source: Industry-Occupation Matrix, Bureau of Labor Statistics. These data relate to one or more 3-digit SIC industry groups rather than to a single 4-digit SIC. The change reported for each occupation to the year 2005 is a percent of growth or decline as estimated by the Bureau of Labor Statistics. The abbreviation nec stands for 'not elsewhere classified'.

LOCATION BY STATE AND REGIONAL CONCENTRATION

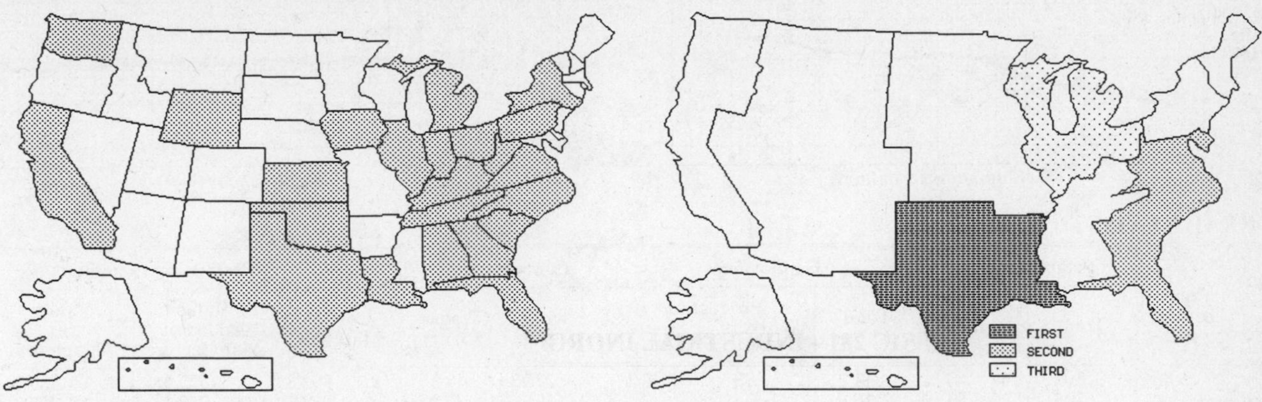

INDUSTRY DATA BY STATE

State	Establish-ments	Shipments			Employment				Cost as % of Shipments	Investment per Employee ($)
		Total ($ mil)	% of U.S.	Per Establ.	Total Number	% of U.S.	Per Establ.	Wages ($/hour)		
Indiana	19	262.1	8.5	13.8	400	5.2	21	17.20	31.7	-
Ohio	31	230.2	7.4	7.4	600	7.8	19	14.00	37.3	16,167
California	52	214.3	6.9	4.1	900	11.7	17	15.00	41.2	-
Pennsylvania	37	139.0	4.5	3.8	400	5.2	11	16.60	34.3	25,500
Illinois	25	106.8	3.4	4.3	200	2.6	8	14.00	34.8	15,000
Kansas	9	90.3	2.9	10.0	200	2.6	22	12.00	10.0	-
New York	12	63.7	2.1	5.3	200	2.6	17	14.00	24.8	3,000
Kentucky	13	51.7	1.7	4.0	200	2.6	15	14.67	69.8	2,500
Michigan	12	50.4	1.6	4.2	100	1.3	8	11.00	31.2	11,000
Washington	15	46.5	1.5	3.1	200	2.6	13	13.00	29.7	15,500
Florida	19	46.3	1.5	2.4	200	2.6	11	14.00	38.9	5,500
Virginia	15	34.2	1.1	2.3	100	1.3	7	19.00	38.0	-
Iowa	10	15.8	0.5	1.6	100	1.3	10	12.00	37.3	-
Texas	63	(D)	-	-	750 *	9.7	12	-	-	-
Louisiana	30	(D)	-	-	375 *	4.9	13	-	-	-
Alabama	19	(D)	-	-	175 *	2.3	9	-	-	-
Georgia	16	(D)	-	-	175 *	2.3	11	-	-	7,429
North Carolina	15	(D)	-	-	175 *	2.3	12	-	-	-
West Virginia	15	(D)	-	-	175 *	2.3	12	-	-	6,286
Tennessee	14	(D)	-	-	175 *	2.3	13	-	-	-
Oklahoma	12	(D)	-	-	175 *	2.3	15	-	-	-
South Carolina	9	(D)	-	-	175 *	2.3	19	-	-	-
Wyoming	7	(D)	-	-	175 *	2.3	25	-	-	-

Source: 1992 *Economic Census*. The states are in descending order of shipments or establishments (if shipment data are missing for the majority). The symbol (D) appears when data are withheld to prevent disclosure of competitive information. States marked with (D) are sorted by number of establishments. A dash (-) indicates that the data element cannot be calculated; * indicates the midpoint of a range.

2816 - INORGANIC PIGMENTS

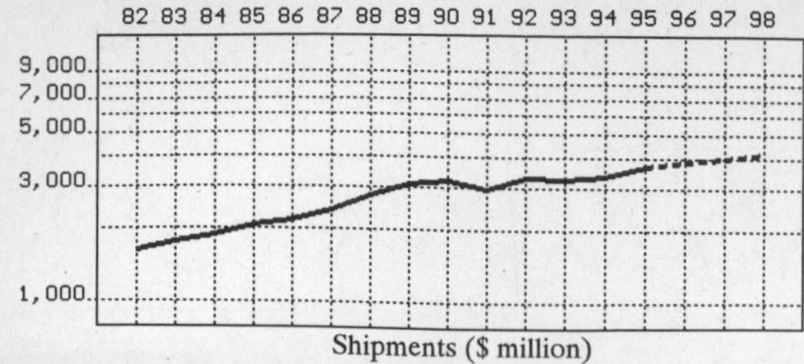

Shipments ($ million)

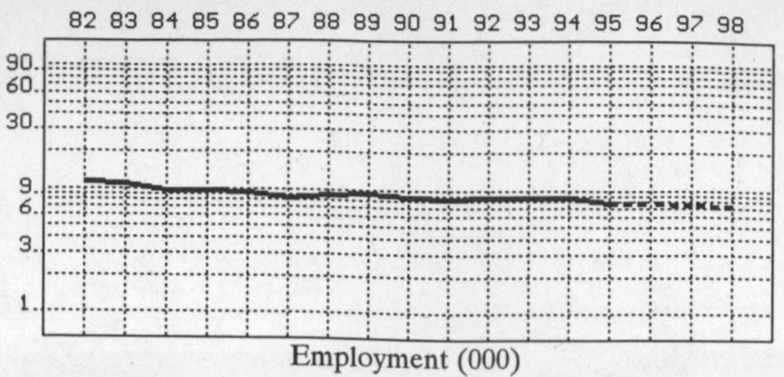

Employment (000)

GENERAL STATISTICS

Year	Com-panies	Establishments		Employment			Compensation		Production ($ million)			
		Total	with 20 or more employees	Total (000)	Production Workers (000)	Production Hours (Mil)	Payroll ($ mil)	Wages ($/hr)	Cost of Materials	Value Added by Manufacture	Value of Shipments	Capital Invest.
1982	86	106	63	11.2	6.8	13.3	271.3	11.17	892.8	723.0	1,630.0	128.9
1983		105	63	10.8	6.6	13.4	291.6	12.07	1,014.1	758.1	1,779.8	93.6
1984		104	63	9.5	6.0	11.9	257.7	12.09	1,030.3	864.6	1,890.4	94.4
1985		103	64	9.7	6.0	12.0	275.2	12.97	1,017.8	1,044.0	2,077.1	100.8
1986		103	63	9.1	5.6	11.5	277.5	13.53	1,036.5	1,152.9	2,192.5	80.3
1987	70	92	55	8.3	5.1	10.5	266.8	14.18	1,001.6	1,398.1	2,388.3	115.3
1988		91	57	8.9	5.3	11.4	295.2	14.12	1,189.6	1,642.4	2,764.3	145.4
1989		95	55	9.2	5.1	10.0	287.2	15.03	1,247.5	1,848.0	3,072.8	357.0
1990		97	56	8.8	5.3	11.3	298.9	14.65	1,282.6	1,930.8	3,203.9	353.5
1991		95	59	8.4	5.1	11.0	324.1	16.06	1,285.1	1,671.1	2,939.0	223.2
1992	73	89	53	8.6	5.6	12.4	347.7	17.03	1,326.0	2,017.6	3,305.6	508.9
1993		90	54	8.7	5.6	12.1	336.2	17.13	1,323.2	1,960.6	3,275.7	149.1
1994		88P	52P	8.6	5.7	12.0	340.4	18.13	1,437.0	1,887.5	3,320.9	156.9
1995		86P	51P	7.9P	5.0P	11.1P	344.1P	18.29P	1,602.0P	2,104.3P	3,702.3P	318.2P
1996		84P	50P	7.8P	5.0P	11.0P	350.8P	18.83P	1,670.0P	2,193.5P	3,859.3P	336.1P
1997		83P	49P	7.6P	4.9P	11.0P	357.4P	19.38P	1,737.9P	2,282.8P	4,016.3P	354.0P
1998		81P	49P	7.4P	4.8P	10.9P	364.0P	19.92P	1,805.9P	2,372.0P	4,173.4P	371.9P

Sources: 1982, 1987, 1992 *Economic Census*; *Annual Survey of Manufactures*, 83-86, 88-91, 93-94. Establishment counts for non-Census years are from *County Business Patterns*; establishment values for 83-84 are extrapolations. 'P's show projections by the editors. Industries reclassified in 87 will not have data for prior years.

INDICES OF CHANGE

Year	Com-panies	Establishments		Employment			Compensation		Production ($ million)			
		Total	with 20 or more employees	Total (000)	Production Workers (000)	Production Hours (Mil)	Payroll ($ mil)	Wages ($/hr)	Cost of Materials	Value Added by Manufacture	Value of Shipments	Capital Invest.
1982	118	119	119	130	121	107	78	66	67	36	49	25
1983		118	119	126	118	108	84	71	76	38	54	18
1984		117	119	110	107	96	74	71	78	43	57	19
1985		116	121	113	107	97	79	76	77	52	63	20
1986		116	119	106	100	93	80	79	78	57	66	16
1987	96	103	104	97	91	85	77	83	76	69	72	23
1988		102	108	103	95	92	85	83	90	81	84	29
1989		107	104	107	91	81	83	88	94	92	93	70
1990		109	106	102	95	91	86	86	97	96	97	69
1991		107	111	98	91	89	93	94	97	83	89	44
1992	100	100	100	100	100	100	100	100	100	100	100	100
1993		101	102	101	100	98	97	101	100	97	99	29
1994		98P	99P	100	102	97	98	106	108	94	100	31
1995		97P	97P	92P	90P	90P	99P	107P	121P	104P	112P	63P
1996		95P	95P	90P	88P	89P	101P	111P	126P	109P	117P	66P
1997		93P	93P	88P	87P	88P	103P	114P	131P	113P	122P	70P
1998		91P	92P	86P	85P	88P	105P	117P	136P	118P	126P	73P

Sources: Same as General Statistics. Values reflect change from the base year, 1992. Values above 100 mean greater than 92, values below 100 mean less than 92, and a value of 100 in the 82-91 or 93-98 period means same as 92. 'P's mark projections by the editors.

SELECTED RATIOS

For 1994	Avg. of All Manufact.	Analyzed Industry	Index
Employees per Establishment	49	98	200
Payroll per Establishment	1,500,273	3,888,266	259
Payroll per Employee	30,620	39,581	129
Production Workers per Establishment	34	65	190
Wages per Establishment	853,319	2,485,109	291
Wages per Production Worker	24,861	38,168	154
Hours per Production Worker	2,056	2,105	102
Wages per Hour	12.09	18.13	150
Value Added per Establishment	4,602,255	21,560,228	468
Value Added per Employee	93,930	219,477	234

For 1994	Avg. of All Manufact.	Analyzed Industry	Index
Value Added per Production Worker	134,084	331,140	247
Cost per Establishment	5,045,178	16,414,330	325
Cost per Employee	102,970	167,093	162
Cost per Production Worker	146,988	252,105	172
Shipments per Establishment	9,576,895	37,933,437	396
Shipments per Employee	195,460	386,151	198
Shipments per Production Worker	279,017	582,614	209
Investment per Establishment	321,011	1,792,212	558
Investment per Employee	6,552	18,244	278
Investment per Production Worker	9,352	27,526	294

Sources: Same as General Statistics. The 'Average of All Manufacturing' column represents the average of all manufacturing industries reported for the most recent complete year available. The Index shows the relationship between the Average and the Analyzed Industry. For example, 100 means that they are equal; 500 that the Analyzed Industry is five times the average; 50 means that the Analyzed Industry is half the national average. The abbreviation 'na' is used to show that data are 'not available'.

LEADING COMPANIES

Number shown: **32** Total sales ($ mil): **5,306** Total employment (000): **21.4**

Company Name	Address				CEO Name	Phone	Co. Type	Sales ($ mil)	Empl. (000)
Ferro Corp	1000 Lakeside Av	Cleveland	OH	44114	Albert C Bersticker	216-641-8580	P	1,194	6.8
SCM Chemicals Inc	7 St Paul St	Baltimore	MD	21202	Donald V Borst	410-783-1120	S	1,040*	2.5
NL Industries Inc	PO Box 4272	Houston	TX	77060	J Landis Martin	713-423-3300	P	888	3.1
Kronos	PO Box 60887	Houston	TX	77032	Lawrence A Wigdor	713-987-6000	D	785	2.7
Zinc Corporation of America	300 Frankfort Rd	Monaca	PA	15061	William A Smells	412-774-1020	S	250	1.2
Ampacet Corp	660 White Plains Rd	Tarrytown	NY	10591	David S Weil	914-631-6600	R	200	0.5
EM Industries Inc	5 Skyline Dr	Hawthorne	NY	10532	Adolf Haasen	914-592-4660	S	170	0.8
Mearl Corp	217 N Highland Av	Ossining	NY	10562	Dominic A Pinciaro	914-941-7450	R	110	0.7
Allied Color Industries Inc	800 Ken Mar Indrial	Broadview H	OH	44147	George Chase	216-526-0230	D	98*	0.5
Penn Color	400 Old Dublin Pike	Doylestown	PA	18901	Edgar Putman	215-345-6550	R	82*	0.4
American Chrome and Chemical	PO Box 9912	Corpus Christi	TX	78469	Jon Moon	512-883-6421	S	70	0.2
Silberline Manufacturing	PO Box B	Tamaqua	PA	18252	Joseph B Scheller	717-668-6050	R	60	0.3
CDR Pigment and Dispersion	410 G Milford	Cincinnati	OH	45215	Lee Burgess	513-771-1900	D	54*	0.3
Cookson Pigments Inc	256 Vanderpool St	Newark	NJ	07114	David Dinsmore	201-242-1800	S	49*	0.2
Boehme Filatex Inc	209 Watlington	Reidsville	NC	27320	Rene Eckert	919-342-6631	S	37	0.1
EM Industries Inc	PO Box 1206	Savannah	GA	31402	H Reichel	912-964-9050	D	27*	0.1
Pea Ridge Iron Ore Co	HC 65	Sullivan	MO	63080	ER Koebbe	314-468-7211	D	20*	<0.1
Plasticolors Inc	2600 Michigan Av	Ashtabula	OH	44004	Steve Walling	216-997-5137	R	19	0.1
Silberline Manufacturing	PO Box 267	Decatur	IN	46733	Tom Anderson	219-728-2111	D	17*	<0.1
Davis Colors	PO Box 23100	Los Angeles	CA	90023	Nick Paris	213-269-7311	S	15	<0.1
RFS Corp	PO Box 5360	Fall River	MA	02723	Stuart I Booth	508-676-3481	R	15	<0.1
Roma Color Inc	PO Box 5360	Fall River	MA	02723	Stuart E Booth	508-676-3481	S	15	<0.1
Reed Spectrum	Holden Indrial Pk	Holden	MA	01520	Mike Smith	508-829-6321	D	13	0.2
Hoover Color Corp	PO Box 218	Hiwassee	VA	24347	CE Hoover	703-980-7233	R	12	<0.1
Radiant Color	PO Box 4019	Richmond	CA	94804	John Mone	510-233-9119	D	12	0.1
Hitox Corporation of America	PO Box 2544	Corpus Christi	TX	78403	Thomas A Landshof	512-882-5175	P	12	<0.1
National Industrial Chemical Co	600 W 52nd St	Chicago	IL	60609	WG Lerch	312-924-3700	R	10	<0.1
Thermocolor Corp	2229 Superior St	Sandusky	OH	44870	Larry Finley	419-626-5677	R	10	<0.1
LM Scofield Co	6533 Bandini Blv	Los Angeles	CA	90040	David R Arnold	213-723-5285	R	9*	<0.1
New Riverside Ochre Company	PO Box 460	Cartersville	GA	30120	Raymond G Morris	404-382-4568	R	6	<0.1
Luster-on Products Inc	PO Box 90247	Springfield	MA	01139	Paul R Lane	413-739-2543	R	5	<0.1
R and A Specialty Chemical	812 E 43rd St	Brooklyn	NY	11210	JB Harrison	718-859-2800	R	4	<0.1

Source: *Ward's Business Directory of U.S. Private and Public Companies*, Volumes 1 and 2, 1996. The company type code used is as follows: P - Public, R - Private, S - Subsidiary, D - Division, J - Joint Venture, A - Affiliate, G - Group. Sales are in millions of dollars, employees are in thousands. An asterisk (*) indicates an estimated sales volume. The symbol < stands for 'less than'. Company names and addresses are truncated, in some cases, to fit into the available space.

MATERIALS CONSUMED

Material		Quantity	Delivered Cost ($ million)
Materials, ingredients, containers, and supplies		(X)	1,107.0
Phosphoric acid, except spent (100 percent P2O5)	1,000 s tons	(S)	1.8
Sulfuric acid (100 percent H2SO4), except spent	1,000 s tons	266.1*	15.2
Chlorine (100 percent Cl basis)	1,000 s tons	250.3	15.6
Phosphorus, elemental (technical)	1,000 s tons	(D)	(D)
Sodium carbonate (soda ash) (58 percent Na2O)	1,000 s tons	16.8	2.0
Sodium hydroxide (caustic soda)(100 percent NaOH)	1,000 s tons	(S)	27.3
Salt in brine	1,000 s tons	(D)	(D)
Other industrial inorganic chemicals		(X)	102.3
Synthetic organic chemicals		(X)	25.4
Sulfur	1,000 l tons	(D)	(D)
Iron and ferroalloy ores, including tungsten, chromite, manganese, molybdenum, and cobalt		(X)	40.4
Nonferrous metal ores, including copper, mercury, vanadium, titanium, platinum, etc.		(X)	408.2
All other crude chemical nonmetallic minerals, including barite, borate, potash, fluorspar, rock salt, etc.		(X)	9.3
Coke including breeze, used as a raw material	1,000 s tons	323.0	40.1
Parts and attachments for machinery and equipment		(X)	63.2
Paperboard containers, boxes, and corrugated paperboard		(X)	10.6
Metal containers		(X)	2.7
All other materials and components, parts, containers, and supplies		(X)	272.4
Materials, ingredients, containers, and supplies, nsk		(X)	60.6

Source: 1992 *Economic Census*. Explanation of symbols used: (D): Withheld to avoid disclosure of competitive data; na: Not available; (S): Withheld because statistical norms were not met; (X): Not applicable; (Z): Less than half the unit shown; nec: Not elsewhere classified; nsk: Not specified by kind; - : zero; * : 10-19 percent estimated; ** : 20-29 percent estimated.

PRODUCT SHARE DETAILS

Product or Product Class	% Share	Product or Product Class	% Share
Inorganic pigments	100.00	Chrome colors	14.09
Titanium dioxide, composite and pure	66.78	White extender pigments, including barytes, blanc fixe, and whiting	15.61
Other white opaque pigments	8.75	Iron oxide pigments	35.53
Zinc oxide pigments	48.19	Ceramic color pigments	12.62
Titanium pigment preparations	14.23	All other inorganic pigments, nec	22.15
All other inorganic white opaque pigments	37.55	Inorganic pigments, nsk	1.83
Other white opaque pigments, nsk	0.03		
Chrome colors and other inorganic pigments	22.63		

Source: 1992 *Economic Census*. The values shown are percent of total shipments in an industry. Values of indented subcategories are summed in the main heading. The symbol (D) appears when data are withheld to prevent disclosure of competitive information. The abbreviation nsk stands for 'not specified by kind' and nec for 'not elsewhere classified'.

INPUTS AND OUTPUTS FOR INORGANIC PIGMENTS

Economic Sector or Industry Providing Inputs	%	Sector	Economic Sector or Industry Buying Outputs	%	Sector
Imports	24.3	Foreign	Paints & allied products	29.6	Manufg.
Nonferrous metal ores, except copper	12.8	Mining	Adhesives & sealants	15.1	Manufg.
Gas production & distribution (utilities)	6.5	Util.	Printing ink	12.4	Manufg.
Electric services (utilities)	6.1	Util.	Paper mills, except building paper	8.5	Manufg.
Wholesale trade	5.6	Trade	Storage batteries	7.6	Manufg.
Cyclic crudes and organics	4.5	Manufg.	Exports	6.6	Foreign
Alkalies & chlorine	3.6	Manufg.	Miscellaneous plastics products	6.4	Manufg.
Noncomparable imports	3.1	Foreign	Tires & inner tubes	4.3	Manufg.
Petroleum refining	3.0	Manufg.	Plastics materials & resins	1.9	Manufg.
Special industry machinery, nec	2.7	Manufg.	Paperboard mills	1.7	Manufg.
Blast furnaces & steel mills	2.6	Manufg.	Fabricated rubber products, nec	1.6	Manufg.
Copper ore	2.2	Mining	Personal consumption expenditures	1.1	
Advertising	1.9	Services	Chemical preparations, nec	0.9	Manufg.
Industrial inorganic chemicals, nec	1.8	Manufg.	Rubber & plastics hose & belting	0.7	Manufg.
Miscellaneous repair shops	1.6	Services	Asbestos products	0.2	Manufg.
Paperboard containers & boxes	1.5	Manufg.	Lead pencils & art goods	0.2	Manufg.
Engineering, architectural, & surveying services	1.5	Services	Hard surface floor coverings	0.1	Manufg.
Motor freight transportation & warehousing	1.1	Util.	Inorganic pigments	0.1	Manufg.
Chemical & fertilizer mineral	1.0	Mining	Petroleum refining	0.1	Manufg.
Coal	1.0	Mining	S/L Govt. purch., elem. & secondary education	0.1	S/L Govt
Railroads & related services	1.0	Util.			
Primary zinc	0.9	Manufg.			
Plastics materials & resins	0.8	Manufg.			
Pipe, valves, & pipe fittings	0.7	Manufg.			
Maintenance of nonfarm buildings nec	0.6	Constr.			
Industrial gases	0.6	Manufg.			
Eating & drinking places	0.6	Trade			
Equipment rental & leasing services	0.6	Services			
Communications, except radio & TV	0.5	Util.			
Water supply & sewage systems	0.5	Util.			
Iron & ferroalloy ores	0.4	Mining			
Chemical preparations, nec	0.4	Manufg.			
Crude petroleum & natural gas	0.3	Mining			
Metal barrels, drums, & pails	0.3	Manufg.			
Air transportation	0.3	Util.			
Legal services	0.3	Services			
Inorganic pigments	0.2	Manufg.			
Nitrogenous & phosphatic fertilizers	0.2	Manufg.			
Water transportation	0.2	Util.			
Royalties	0.2	Fin/R.E.			
Computer & data processing services	0.2	Services			
Management & consulting services & labs	0.2	Services			
U.S. Postal Service	0.2	Gov't			
Dimension, crushed & broken stone	0.1	Mining			
Machinery, except electrical, nec	0.1	Manufg.			
Insurance carriers	0.1	Fin/R.E.			
Real estate	0.1	Fin/R.E.			
Accounting, auditing & bookkeeping	0.1	Services			

Source: Benchmark Input-Output Accounts for the U.S. Economy, 1982, U.S. Department of Commerce, Washington, D.C., July 1991. Data, as reported in the source, are organized by the 1977 SIC structure in use in 1982 but have been matched, as closely as is possible, to the 1987 SIC structure used in this book.

OCCUPATIONS EMPLOYED BY SIC 281 - INDUSTRIAL INORGANIC CHEMICALS

Occupation	% of Total 1994	Change to 2005	Occupation	% of Total 1994	Change to 2005
Chemical equipment controllers, operators	7.8	-15.9	General managers & top executives	1.9	-11.4
Blue collar worker supervisors	5.4	-5.3	Inspectors, testers, & graders, precision	1.9	-6.6
Management support workers nec	5.3	-6.6	Managers & administrators nec	1.8	-6.6
Chemical plant & system operators	4.7	-6.6	Industrial production managers	1.7	-6.6
Science & mathematics technicians	3.8	-6.6	Engineering, mathematical, & science managers	1.7	6.1
Secretaries, ex legal & medical	3.3	-15.0	Packaging & filling machine operators	1.6	-6.6
Chemical engineers	3.3	2.8	Crushing & mixing machine operators	1.5	-6.6
Maintenance repairers, general utility	3.0	-15.9	Mechanical engineers	1.3	2.8
Industrial machinery mechanics	3.0	2.7	Helpers, laborers, & material movers nec	1.3	-6.6
Truck drivers light & heavy	2.8	-3.7	Electricians	1.2	-12.3
Engineers nec	2.3	40.1	Machine operators nec	1.1	-17.7
Sales & related workers nec	2.3	-6.6	Plant & system operators nec	1.1	-17.5
General office clerks	2.0	-20.3	Precision instrument repairers	1.0	-6.6
Chemists	2.0	-6.6	Accountants & auditors	1.0	-6.6

Source: Industry-Occupation Matrix, Bureau of Labor Statistics. These data relate to one or more 3-digit SIC industry groups rather than to a single 4-digit SIC. The change reported for each occupation to the year 2005 is a percent of growth or decline as estimated by the Bureau of Labor Statistics. The abbreviation nec stands for 'not elsewhere classified'.

LOCATION BY STATE AND REGIONAL CONCENTRATION

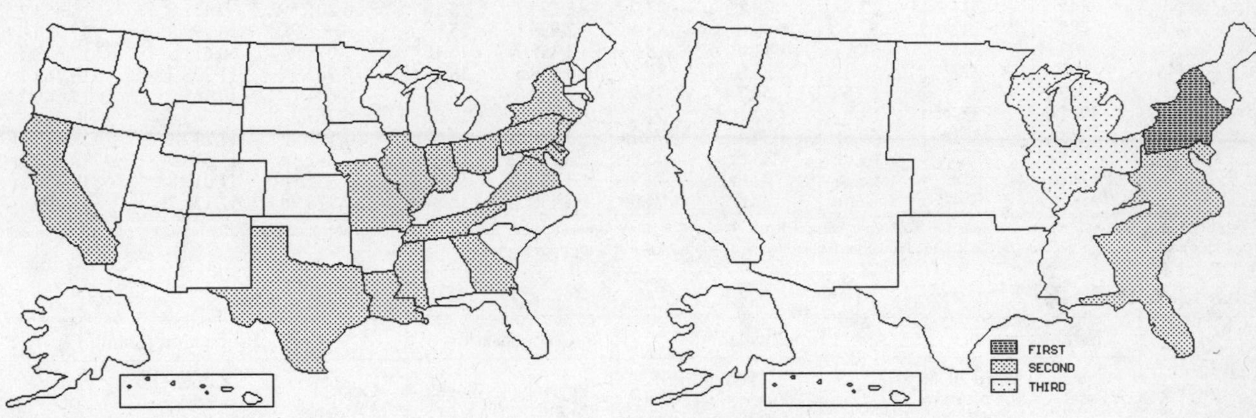

INDUSTRY DATA BY STATE

State	Establish-ments	Shipments			Employment				Cost as % of Shipments	Investment per Employee ($)
		Total ($ mil)	% of U.S.	Per Establ.	Total Number	% of U.S.	Per Establ.	Wages ($/hour)		
Maryland	6	310.7	9.4	51.8	1,000	11.6	167	14.75	50.0	-
Pennsylvania	9	160.6	4.9	17.8	800	9.3	89	15.64	51.7	9,375
New Jersey	10	87.0	2.6	8.7	400	4.7	40	18.60	42.8	10,250
Illinois	6	82.5	2.5	13.8	400	4.7	67	17.43	50.8	8,500
Georgia	7	(D)	-	-	750 *	8.7	107	-	-	31,333
California	6	(D)	-	-	375 *	4.4	63	-	-	-
Ohio	5	(D)	-	-	750 *	8.7	150	-	-	-
New York	4	(D)	-	-	375 *	4.4	94	-	-	-
Tennessee	4	(D)	-	-	750 *	8.7	188	-	-	-
Missouri	3	(D)	-	-	175 *	2.0	58	-	-	-
Texas	3	(D)	-	-	175 *	2.0	58	-	-	-
Indiana	2	(D)	-	-	175 *	2.0	88	-	-	-
Mississippi	2	(D)	-	-	1,750 *	20.3	875	-	-	-
Virginia	2	(D)	-	-	175 *	2.0	88	-	-	-
Delaware	1	(D)	-	-	375 *	4.4	375	-	-	-
Louisiana	1	(D)	-	-	375 *	4.4	375	-	-	-

Source: 1992 *Economic Census*. The states are in descending order of shipments or establishments (if shipment data are missing for the majority). The symbol (D) appears when data are withheld to prevent disclosure of competitive information. States marked with (D) are sorted by number of establishments. A dash (-) indicates that the data element cannot be calculated; * indicates the midpoint of a range.

2819 - INDUSTRIAL INORGANIC CHEMICALS, NEC

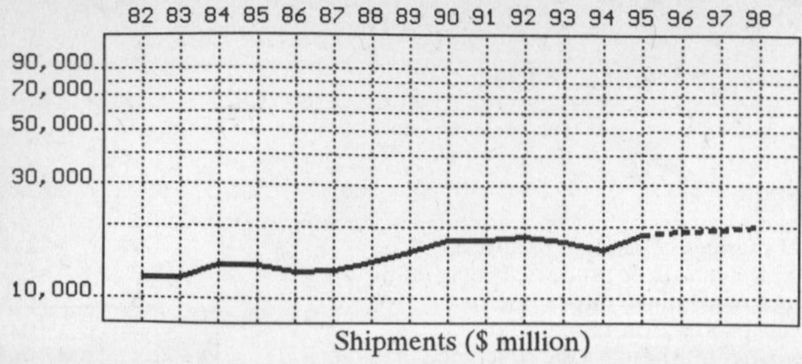

Shipments ($ million)

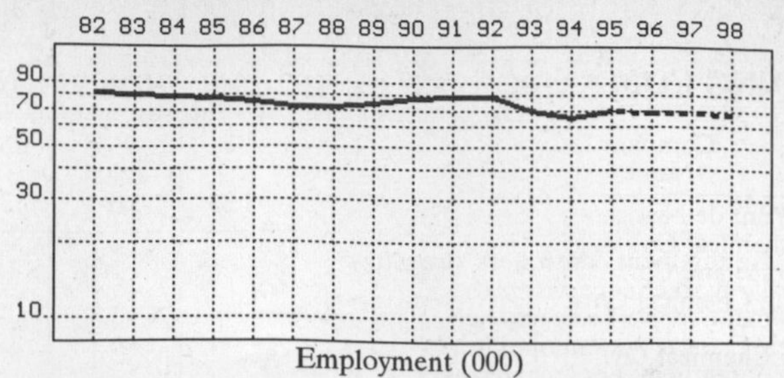

Employment (000)

GENERAL STATISTICS

Year	Companies	Establishments		Employment			Compensation		Production ($ million)			
		Total	with 20 or more employees	Total (000)	Production Workers (000)	Production Hours (Mil)	Payroll ($ mil)	Wages ($/hr)	Cost of Materials	Value Added by Manufacture	Value of Shipments	Capital Invest.
1982	425	645	319	81.7	45.7	91.0	2,134.2	11.84	5,837.1	6,321.4	12,060.4	512.5
1983		641	321	80.3	44.8	87.5	2,184.2	12.46	5,717.8	6,511.9	12,199.6	418.7
1984		637	323	78.8	43.0	87.0	2,344.5	13.34	6,374.4	7,391.8	13,771.6	477.6
1985		634	324	78.6	42.3	86.4	2,451.9	13.69	6,074.5	7,500.5	13,724.6	550.8
1986		627	306	75.0	39.8	82.2	2,398.8	14.10	5,504.0	7,405.3	12,885.4	487.3
1987	428	662	308	72.2	37.5	75.2	2,425.2	15.14	5,639.5	7,529.5	13,211.6	506.1
1988		659	303	72.2	38.0	83.3	2,485.8	13.40	5,920.7	8,285.6	14,154.8	515.8
1989		645	314	73.4	39.1	78.7	2,694.4	15.18	6,201.1	9,481.8	15,654.2	703.9
1990		685	342	77.5	40.0	83.4	2,998.1	15.69	6,955.7	10,799.8	17,719.0	670.6
1991		705	342	78.9	41.0	88.5	3,156.7	16.10	7,078.9	10,611.5	17,648.9	718.9
1992	446	697	327	79.1	39.8	87.5	3,270.5	16.28	6,962.9	11,208.2	18,169.1	722.5
1993		719	325	69.5	34.7	75.9	2,920.6	16.53	6,634.1	10,465.2	17,146.7	684.9
1994		711P	329P	64.6	32.7	71.2	2,751.9	17.38	6,267.2	9,765.6	16,032.2	844.7
1995		718P	331P	69.8P	34.4P	76.7P	3,196.5P	17.62P	7,198.7P	11,217.1P	18,415.2P	807.7P
1996		725P	332P	69.0P	33.6P	75.8P	3,277.1P	18.03P	7,392.1P	11,518.5P	18,909.9P	837.3P
1997		733P	333P	68.2P	32.8P	74.9P	3,357.7P	18.45P	7,585.5P	11,819.8P	19,404.6P	866.8P
1998		740P	334P	67.4P	32.0P	74.0P	3,438.3P	18.87P	7,778.9P	12,121.2P	19,899.4P	896.3P

Sources: 1982, 1987, 1992 *Economic Census*; *Annual Survey of Manufactures*, 83-86, 88-91, 93-94. Establishment counts for non-Census years are from *County Business Patterns*; establishment values for 83-84 are extrapolations. 'P's show projections by the editors. Industries reclassified in 87 will not have data for prior years.

INDICES OF CHANGE

Year	Companies	Establishments		Employment			Compensation		Production ($ million)			
		Total	with 20 or more employees	Total (000)	Production Workers (000)	Production Hours (Mil)	Payroll ($ mil)	Wages ($/hr)	Cost of Materials	Value Added by Manufacture	Value of Shipments	Capital Invest.
1982	95	93	98	103	115	104	65	73	84	56	66	71
1983		92	98	102	113	100	67	77	82	58	67	58
1984		91	99	100	108	99	72	82	92	66	76	66
1985		91	99	99	106	99	75	84	87	67	76	76
1986		90	94	95	100	94	73	87	79	66	71	67
1987	96	95	94	91	94	86	74	93	81	67	73	70
1988		95	93	91	95	95	76	82	85	74	78	71
1989		93	96	93	98	90	82	93	89	85	86	97
1990		98	105	98	101	95	92	96	100	96	98	93
1991		101	105	100	103	101	97	99	102	95	97	100
1992	100	100	100	100	100	100	100	100	100	100	100	100
1993		103	99	88	87	87	89	102	95	93	94	95
1994		102P	101P	82	82	81	84	107	90	87	88	117
1995		103P	101P	88P	86P	88P	98P	108P	103P	100P	101P	112P
1996		104P	102P	87P	84P	87P	100P	111P	106P	103P	104P	116P
1997		105P	102P	86P	82P	86P	103P	113P	109P	105P	107P	120P
1998		106P	102P	85P	80P	85P	105P	116P	112P	108P	110P	124P

Sources: Same as General Statistics. Values reflect change from the base year, 1992. Values above 100 mean greater than 92, values below 100 mean less than 92, and a value of 100 in the 82-91 or 93-98 period means same as 92. 'P's mark projections by the editors.

SELECTED RATIOS

For 1994	Avg. of All Manufact.	Analyzed Industry	Index
Employees per Establishment	49	91	186
Payroll per Establishment	1,500,273	3,871,949	258
Payroll per Employee	30,620	42,599	139
Production Workers per Establishment	34	46	134
Wages per Establishment	853,319	1,741,112	204
Wages per Production Worker	24,861	37,843	152
Hours per Production Worker	2,056	2,177	106
Wages per Hour	12.09	17.38	144
Value Added per Establishment	4,602,255	13,740,292	299
Value Added per Employee	93,930	151,170	161

For 1994	Avg. of All Manufact.	Analyzed Industry	Index
Value Added per Production Worker	134,084	298,642	223
Cost per Establishment	5,045,178	8,818,010	175
Cost per Employee	102,970	97,015	94
Cost per Production Worker	146,988	191,657	130
Shipments per Establishment	9,576,895	22,557,457	236
Shipments per Employee	195,460	248,176	127
Shipments per Production Worker	279,017	490,281	176
Investment per Establishment	321,011	1,188,501	370
Investment per Employee	6,552	13,076	200
Investment per Production Worker	9,352	25,832	276

Sources: Same as General Statistics. The 'Average of All Manufacturing' column represents the average of all manufacturing industries reported for the most recent complete year available. The Index shows the relationship between the Average and the Analyzed Industry. For example, 100 means that they are equal; 500 that the Analyzed Industry is five times the average; 50 means that the Analyzed Industry is half the national average. The abbreviation 'na' is used to show that data are 'not available'.

LEADING COMPANIES

Number shown: 75 Total sales ($ mil): **97,600** Total employment (000): **317.6**

Company Name	Address				CEO Name	Phone	Co. Type	Sales ($ mil)	Empl. (000)
EI du Pont de Nemours	1007 Market St	Wilmington	DE	19898	Edgar S Woolard Jr	302-774-1000	P	39,333	107.0
Dow Chemical Co	2030 WH Dow	Midland	MI	48674	Frank P Popoff	517-636-1000	P	20,015	53.7
WR Grace and Co	1 Town Center Rd	Boca Raton	FL	33486	Thomas A Holmes	407-362-2000	P	5,093	38.0
Eastman Chemical Co	PO Box 511	Kingsport	TN	37662	EW Deavenport	615-229-2000	P	4,329	17.5
FMC Corp	200 E Randolph Dr	Chicago	IL	60601	Robert N Burt	312-861-6000	P	4,011	21.3
ARCO Chemical Co	3801 W Chester Pk	Newtown Sq	PA	19073	Alan R Hirsig	215-359-2000	P	3,423	4.4
Engelhard Corp	101 Wood Av	Iselin	NJ	08830	Orin R Smith	908-205-6000	P	2,386	5.8
Great Lakes Chemical Corp	PO Box 2200	West Lafayette	IN	47906	R B McDonald	317-497-6100	P	2,111	7.0
Ethyl Corp	PO Box 2189	Richmond	VA	23217	F D Gottwald Jr	804-788-5000	P	1,735	5.5
Elf Atochem North America Inc	2000 Market St	Philadelphia	PA	19103	Bernard Azoulay	215-587-7000	S	1,700	5.0
IMC Fertilizer Group Inc	2100 Sanders Rd	Northbrook	IL	60062	Wendell F Bueche	708-272-9200	P	1,442	5.2
Cytec Industries Inc	5 Garret Mountainz	West Paterson	NJ	07424	Darryl D Fry	201-357-3100	P	1,101	5.0
Transelco	1789 Transelco Dr	Penn Yan	NY	14527	GA Braun	315-536-3357	D	1,000	5.0
UOP	25 E Algonquin Rd	Des Plaines	IL	60017	Michael D Winfield	708-391-2000	J	890*	4.0
Harrisons and Crosfield	900 Market St	Wilmington	DE	19801	Mark L Barocas	302-888-1748	S	800	3.0
Vigoro Corp	225 N Michigan Av	Chicago	IL	60601	Robert E Fowler Jr	312-819-2020	P	727	1.4
International Specialty Products	1361 Alps Rd	Wayne	NJ	07470	Samuel J Heyman	201-628-4000	P	571	2.4
Engelhard Corp	Menlo Park	Edison	NJ	08818	W R Gustafson	201-632-6000	D	541	1.9
Kao Corporation of America Inc	2711 Centerville Rd	Wilmington	DE	19808	Ken Wattman	302-992-0188	S	507	1.4
Minerals Technologies Inc	The Chrysler Bldg	New York	NY	10174	Jean-Paul Valles	212-878-1800	P	473	2.2
PQ Corp	PO Box 840	Valley Forge	PA	19482	Richard W Kelso	215-293-7200	R	450	1.4
Vigoro Industries Inc	PO Box 4139	Fairview Hts	IL	62208	R M Van Patten	618-624-5522	S	450	1.0
Calgon Carbon Corp	PO Box 717	Pittsburgh	PA	15230	T A McConomy	412-787-6700	P	274	1.3
OM Group Inc	3800 Terminal Twr	Cleveland	OH	44113	James P Mooney	216-781-0083	P	251	0.3
LaRoche Holdings Inc	1100 Johnson Ferry	Atlanta	GA	30342	Grant Reed	404-851-0300	R	250*	1.0
La Roche Chemicals Inc	PO Box 1031	Baton Rouge	LA	70821	Robert L Jeansonne	504-355-3341	S	200	0.4
Siemens Power Corp	PO Box 90777	Bellevue	WA	98009	David G McAlees	206-453-4300	S	200	1.0
Atotech USA Inc	PO Box 6768	Somerset	NJ	07765	Dennis R Hanlon	908-302-3500	S	180	0.7
FMC Corp	1735 Market St	Philadelphia	PA	19103	Jerry Sibley	215-299-6000	D	180	1.1
Engelhard Corp	9800 Kellner Rd	Huntsville	AL	35824	Joe Steinreich Jr	205-772-9373	D	155*	0.8
American Norit Company Inc	1050 Crown Pte	Atlanta	GA	30338	Hans Kaufmann	404-512-4610	S	150	0.3
FMC Corp	1735 Market St	Philadelphia	PA	19103	William J Harvey	215-299-6000	D	147	0.6
Aldrich Chemical Company Inc	1001 W St Paul Av	Milwaukee	WI	53233	Jai Nagarkatti	414-273-3850	S	139	0.8
Ausimont USA Inc	44 Whippany Rd	Morristown	NJ	07962	Vittorio Cianchini	201-292-6250	S	120	0.3
Solvay Interox	PO Box 27328	Houston	TX	77227	Foster E Brown	713-525-6500	D	112	0.2
Detrex Corp	PO Box 5111	Southfield	MI	48086	Joseph L Wenzler	313-358-5800	P	100	0.4
Lithium	PO Box 3925	Gastonia	NC	28053	PL Schroeder	704-868-5300	D	100	0.7
High Street Associates Inc	160 Federal St	Boston	MA	02110	Walter F Greeley	617-951-1355	R	94	0.6
Phibro-Tech Inc	1 Parker Plz	Fort Lee	NJ	07024	I David Paley	201-944-6000	S	80	0.2
Amax Metals Recovery Inc	3607 Englishturn	Braithwaite	LA	70040	T La Rue	504-682-2341	S	78*	0.3
Texas United Corp	4800 San Felipe	Houston	TX	77056	R W Verhoeve	713-877-1778	R	77*	0.4
United Catalysts Inc	PO Box 32370	Louisville	KY	40232	CB Knight	502-634-7200	R	75	0.7
Amspec Chemical Co	Foot of Water St	Gloucester City	NJ	08030	J Gustavsen	609-456-3930	R	70	<0.1
Chemetals Inc	610 Pittman Rd	Baltimore	MD	21226	RL Mulholland	410-789-8800	S	70*	0.3
Metropolis Works	PO Box 430	Metropolis	IL	62960	Matthew Kosmider	618-524-2111	D	67*	0.4
Hawkins Chemical Inc	3100 E Hennepin	Minneapolis	MN	55413	Howard J Hawkins	612-331-6910	P	66	0.1
Talley Defense Systems Inc	PO Box 849	Mesa	AZ	85211	Ted Ryan	602-898-2200	S	65	0.3
Carus Corp	315 5th St	Peru	IL	61354	MB Carus	815-223-1500	R	62	0.4
JT Baker Inc	222 Red School Ln	Phillipsburg	NJ	08865	D B Mulholland	908-859-2151	S	60*	0.6
Phibro-Tech Inc	8851 Dice Rd	Santa Fe Sprgs	CA	90670	David Paley	310-698-8036	S	60	<0.1
Shepherd Chemical Co	4900 Beech St	Cincinnati	OH	45212	Bernie Darre	513-731-1110	R	60	0.1
American Pacific Corp	3770 H Hughes	Las Vegas	NV	89109	Fred D Gibson Jr	702-735-2200	P	57	0.2
Day-Glo Color Corp	4515 St Clair Av	Cleveland	OH	44103	RL Furry	216-391-7070	S	56	0.3
Cab-O-Sil	75 State St	Boston	MA	02109	William P Noglows	617-345-0100	D	50	0.3
ChemRex Inc	889 Valley Park Dr	Shakopee	MN	55379	Reinhard Rutz	612-496-6000	S	50	0.3
Fluoro Chemicals	PO Box 187	Calvert City	KY	42029	Dave Edwards	502-395-7121	D	50*	0.4
McGean-Rohco Inc	1250 Term Twr	Cleveland	OH	44113	KR Romer	216-441-4900	R	50	0.3
Peridot Chemicals	1680 Rte 23 N	Wayne	NJ	07470	Peter J Fass	201-696-9000	S	50	0.2
Vinings Industries Inc	3950 Cumberland	Atlanta	GA	30339	Seth Spurlock	404-436-1542	S	50	0.2
Anzon Inc	2545 Aramingo Av	Philadelphia	PA	19125	John W Little	215-427-3000	S	45	0.2
Peridot Holdings Inc	1680 Rte 23 N	Wayne	NJ	07470	Peter J Fass	201-696-9000	R	45	0.2
Western Electrochemical Co	PO Box 629	Cedar City	UT	84720	Fred D Gibson Jr	801-865-5000	S	44	0.2
Reheis Inc	PO Box 609	Berkeley H	NJ	07922	P White	908-464-1500	R	39*	0.3
Crosfield Co	101 Ingalls Av	Joliet	IL	60435	DS Bilicki	815-727-3651	S	36	0.2
Mona Industries Inc	PO Box 425	Paterson	NJ	07544	John J McAndrews	201-345-8220	R	36	0.1
McLaughlin Gormley King Co	8810 10th Av N	Minneapolis	MN	55427	WD Gullickson Jr	612-544-0341	R	35	<0.1
Oxide Services Corp	PO Box 681380	Indianapolis	IN	46268	Greg Stevens	317-290-5000	S	35	<0.1
Inolex Chemical Co	Jackson & Swanson	Philadelphia	PA	19148	Robert E Paganelli	215-271-0800	R	34	0.2
AluChem Inc	1 Landy Ln	Cincinnati	OH	45215	RP Zapletal	513-733-8519	R	30*	0.1
American Chemet Corp	400 Lake Cook Rd	Deerfield	IL	60015	WW Shropshire Jr	708-948-0800	R	30	0.1
Intercat Inc	PO Box 412	Sea Girt	NJ	08750	Regis B Lippert	908-223-4644	R	30	<0.1
Kuehne Chemical Co	86 Hackensack Av	South Kearny	NJ	07032	PR Kuehne	201-589-0700	R	30	<0.1
Magnesium Elektron Inc	500 Pt Breeze Rd	Flemington	NJ	08822	William B Fee	908-782-5800	S	30	0.1
Ozark-Mahoning Company Inc	PO Box 2057	Rosiclare	IL	62982	Dan Pilcher	618-285-6232	S	29*	0.2
Powerlab Inc	PO Box 913	Terrell	TX	75160	Lee Swain	214-563-1477	R	29	0.1

Source: *Ward's Business Directory of U.S. Private and Public Companies*, Volumes 1 and 2, 1996. The company type code used is as follows: P - Public, R - Private, S - Subsidiary, D - Division, J - Joint Venture, A - Affiliate, G - Group. Sales are in millions of dollars, employees are in thousands. An asterisk (*) indicates an estimated sales volume. The symbol < stands for 'less than'. Company names and addresses are truncated, in some cases, to fit into the available space.

MATERIALS CONSUMED

Material		Quantity	Delivered Cost ($ million)
Materials, ingredients, containers, and supplies		(X)	5,018.1
Phosphoric acid, except spent (100 percent P2O5)	1,000 s tons	412.8	148.7
Sulfuric acid (100 percent H2SO4), except spent	1,000 s tons	2,357.5	86.6
Chlorine (100 percent Cl basis)	1,000 s tons	178.4*	9.1
Phosphorus, elemental (technical)	1,000 s tons	117.1	216.9
Sodium carbonate (soda ash) (58 percent Na2O)	1,000 s tons	977.8	91.4
Sodium hydroxide (caustic soda)(100 percent NaOH)	1,000 s tons	884.9	188.9
Salt in brine	1,000 s tons	227.1*	4.7
Other industrial inorganic chemicals		(X)	553.6
Synthetic organic chemicals		(X)	192.4
Bauxite	1,000 s tons	11,265.7	348.3
Phosphate rock	1,000 s tons	(D)	(D)
Sulfur	1,000 l tons	1,164.7	65.9
Iron and ferroalloy ores, including tungsten, chromite, manganese, molybdenum, and cobalt		(X)	68.8
Nonferrous metal ores, including copper, mercury, vanadium, titanium, platinum, etc.		(X)	227.5
All other crude chemical nonmetallic minerals, including barite, borate, potash, fluorspar, rock salt, etc.		(X)	112.1
Coke including breeze, used as a raw material	1,000 s tons	(D)	(D)
Parts and attachments for machinery and equipment		(X)	145.7
Paperboard containers, boxes, and corrugated paperboard		(X)	37.6
Metal containers		(X)	23.1
All other materials and components, parts, containers, and supplies		(X)	1,690.9
Materials, ingredients, containers, and supplies, nsk		(X)	748.7

Source: 1992 *Economic Census*. Explanation of symbols used: (D): Withheld to avoid disclosure of competitive data; na: Not available; (S): Withheld because statistical norms were not met; (X): Not applicable; (Z): Less than half the unit shown; nec: Not elsewhere classified; nsk: Not specified by kind; - : zero; * : 10-19 percent estimated; ** : 20-29 percent estimated.

PRODUCT SHARE DETAILS

Product or Product Class	% Share	Product or Product Class	% Share
Industrial inorganic chemicals, nec	100.00	Inorganic potassium and sodium compounds, except alkalies, alums, and bleaches	15.11
Sulfuric acid	4.29	Chemical catalytic preparations	10.63
Inorganic acids, except nitric, sulfuric, and phosphoric	4.22	Other inorganic chemicals, nec	49.73
Aluminum oxide, except natural alumina	7.51	Industrial inorganic chemicals, nec, nsk	3.77
Other inorganic aluminum compounds	4.73		

Source: 1992 *Economic Census*. The values shown are percent of total shipments in an industry. Values of indented subcategories are summed in the main heading. The symbol (D) appears when data are withheld to prevent disclosure of competitive information. The abbreviation nsk stands for 'not specified by kind' and nec for 'not elsewhere classified'.

INPUTS AND OUTPUTS FOR INDUSTRIAL INORGANIC CHEMICALS, NEC

Economic Sector or Industry Providing Inputs	%	Sector	Economic Sector or Industry Buying Outputs	%	Sector
Imports	29.5	Foreign	Exports	14.3	Foreign
Electric services (utilities)	12.6	Util.	Gross private fixed investment	10.4	Cap Inv
Industrial inorganic chemicals, nec	8.0	Manufg.	Federal Government purchases, national defense	5.9	Fed Govt
Gas production & distribution (utilities)	4.5	Util.	Petroleum refining	4.9	Manufg.
Wholesale trade	3.6	Trade	Cyclic crudes and organics	4.5	Manufg.
Advertising	3.4	Services	Hospitals	4.1	Services
Chemical & fertilizer mineral	3.2	Mining	Soap & other detergents	3.9	Manufg.
Iron & ferroalloy ores	3.0	Mining	S/L Govt. purch., health & hospitals	3.9	S/L Govt
Alkalies & chlorine	2.8	Manufg.	Industrial inorganic chemicals, nec	3.8	Manufg.
Engineering, architectural, & surveying services	2.7	Services	Photographic equipment & supplies	3.5	Manufg.
Motor freight transportation & warehousing	2.3	Util.	Feed grains	2.8	Agric.
Railroads & related services	1.8	Util.	Chemical preparations, nec	2.6	Manufg.
Special industry machinery, nec	1.6	Manufg.	Petroleum & natural gas well drilling	2.1	Constr.
Nonferrous metal ores, except copper	1.5	Mining	Fertilizers, mixing only	1.5	Manufg.
Products of petroleum & coal, nec	1.5	Manufg.	Miscellaneous plastics products	1.5	Manufg.
Cyclic crudes and organics	1.4	Manufg.	Drugs	1.2	Manufg.
Noncomparable imports	1.3	Foreign	S/L Govt. purch., elem. & secondary education	1.2	S/L Govt
Blast furnaces & steel mills	1.1	Manufg.	S/L Govt. purch., higher education	1.2	S/L Govt
Eating & drinking places	1.1	Trade	Glass & glass products, except containers	1.0	Manufg.
Nitrogenous & phosphatic fertilizers	1.0	Manufg.	Nitrogenous & phosphatic fertilizers	1.0	Manufg.
Water supply & sewage systems	1.0	Util.	Medical & health services, nec	1.0	Services
Miscellaneous repair shops	1.0	Services	Maintenance of petroleum & natural gas wells	0.9	Constr.
Maintenance of nonfarm buildings nec	0.9	Constr.	Agricultural chemicals, nec	0.9	Manufg.
Petroleum refining	0.8	Manufg.	Semiconductors & related devices	0.9	Manufg.
Paperboard containers & boxes	0.6	Manufg.	Paper mills, except building paper	0.8	Manufg.
Pipe, valves, & pipe fittings	0.5	Manufg.	Abrasive products	0.7	Manufg.
Communications, except radio & TV	0.5	Util.	Organic fibers, noncellulosic	0.7	Manufg.
Water transportation	0.5	Util.	Paperboard mills	0.7	Manufg.
Equipment rental & leasing services	0.5	Services	Plastics materials & resins	0.7	Manufg.
Legal services	0.5	Services	Blast furnaces & steel mills	0.6	Manufg.
Coal	0.4	Mining	Synthetic rubber	0.6	Manufg.

Continued on next page.

INPUTS AND OUTPUTS FOR INDUSTRIAL INORGANIC CHEMICALS, NEC - Continued

Economic Sector or Industry Providing Inputs	%	Sector	Economic Sector or Industry Buying Outputs	%	Sector
Air transportation	0.4	Util.	Oil bearing crops	0.5	Agric.
Royalties	0.4	Fin/R.E.	Crude petroleum & natural gas	0.5	Mining
Management & consulting services & labs	0.4	Services	Nonferrous metal ores, except copper	0.5	Mining
Nonmetallic mineral services	0.3	Mining	Broadwoven fabric mills	0.5	Manufg.
Metal barrels, drums, & pails	0.3	Manufg.	Primary aluminum	0.5	Manufg.
Accounting, auditing & bookkeeping	0.3	Services	Ready-mixed concrete	0.5	Manufg.
Machinery, except electrical, nec	0.2	Manufg.	Adhesives & sealants	0.4	Manufg.
Computer & data processing services	0.2	Services	Food preparations, nec	0.4	Manufg.
U.S. Postal Service	0.2	Gov't	Mineral wool	0.4	Manufg.
Chemical preparations, nec	0.1	Manufg.	Printing ink	0.4	Manufg.
Industrial gases	0.1	Manufg.	S/L Govt. purch., other education & libraries	0.4	S/L Govt
Lubricating oils & greases	0.1	Manufg.	Copper ore	0.3	Mining
Manifold business forms	0.1	Manufg.	Commercial printing	0.3	Manufg.
Special dies & tools & machine tool accessories	0.1	Manufg.	Glass containers	0.3	Manufg.
Insurance carriers	0.1	Fin/R.E.	Prepared feeds, nec	0.3	Manufg.
Real estate	0.1	Fin/R.E.	Primary batteries, dry & wet	0.3	Manufg.
			Pulp mills	0.3	Manufg.
			Tires & inner tubes	0.3	Manufg.
			Welding apparatus, electric	0.3	Manufg.
			Food grains	0.2	Agric.
			Cellulosic manmade fibers	0.2	Manufg.
			Electric lamps	0.2	Manufg.
			Fabricated rubber products, nec	0.2	Manufg.
			Manufacturing industries, nec	0.2	Manufg.
			Minerals, ground or treated	0.2	Manufg.
			Polishes & sanitation goods	0.2	Manufg.
			Storage batteries	0.2	Manufg.
			Toilet preparations	0.2	Manufg.
			Wood preserving	0.2	Manufg.
			Sanitary services, steam supply, irrigation	0.2	Util.
			Colleges, universities, & professional schools	0.2	Services
			Management & consulting services & labs	0.2	Services
			S/L Govt. purch., other general government	0.2	S/L Govt
			Cotton	0.1	Agric.
			Fruits	0.1	Agric.
			Tobacco	0.1	Agric.
			Vegetables	0.1	Agric.
			Iron & ferroalloy ores	0.1	Mining
			Aluminum rolling & drawing	0.1	Manufg.
			Cold finishing of steel shapes	0.1	Manufg.
			Electronic components nec	0.1	Manufg.
			Floor coverings	0.1	Manufg.
			Inorganic pigments	0.1	Manufg.
			Leather tanning & finishing	0.1	Manufg.
			Metal coating & allied services	0.1	Manufg.
			Nonferrous wire drawing & insulating	0.1	Manufg.
			Paper coating & glazing	0.1	Manufg.
			Special industry machinery, nec	0.1	Manufg.
			Yarn mills & finishing of textiles, nec	0.1	Manufg.
			S/L Govt. purch., fire	0.1	S/L Govt

Source: Benchmark Input-Output Accounts for the U.S. Economy, 1982, U.S. Department of Commerce, Washington, D.C., July 1991. Data, as reported in the source, are organized by the 1977 SIC structure in use in 1982 but have been matched, as closely as is possible, to the 1987 SIC structure used in this book.

OCCUPATIONS EMPLOYED BY SIC 281 - INDUSTRIAL INORGANIC CHEMICALS

Occupation	% of Total 1994	Change to 2005	Occupation	% of Total 1994	Change to 2005
Chemical equipment controllers, operators	7.8	-15.9	General managers & top executives	1.9	-11.4
Blue collar worker supervisors	5.4	-5.3	Inspectors, testers, & graders, precision	1.9	-6.6
Management support workers nec	5.3	-6.6	Managers & administrators nec	1.8	-6.6
Chemical plant & system operators	4.7	-6.6	Industrial production managers	1.7	-6.6
Science & mathematics technicians	3.8	-6.6	Engineering, mathematical, & science managers	1.7	6.1
Secretaries, ex legal & medical	3.3	-15.0	Packaging & filling machine operators	1.6	-6.6
Chemical engineers	3.3	2.8	Crushing & mixing machine operators	1.5	-6.6
Maintenance repairers, general utility	3.0	-15.9	Mechanical engineers	1.3	2.8
Industrial machinery mechanics	3.0	2.7	Helpers, laborers, & material movers nec	1.3	-6.6
Truck drivers light & heavy	2.8	-3.7	Electricians	1.2	-12.3
Engineers nec	2.3	40.1	Machine operators nec	1.1	-17.7
Sales & related workers nec	2.3	-6.6	Plant & system operators nec	1.1	-17.5
General office clerks	2.0	-20.3	Precision instrument repairers	1.0	-6.6
Chemists	2.0	-6.6	Accountants & auditors	1.0	-6.6

Source: Industry-Occupation Matrix, Bureau of Labor Statistics. These data relate to one or more 3-digit SIC industry groups rather than to a single 4-digit SIC. The change reported for each occupation to the year 2005 is a percent of growth or decline as estimated by the Bureau of Labor Statistics. The abbreviation nec stands for 'not elsewhere classified'.

LOCATION BY STATE AND REGIONAL CONCENTRATION

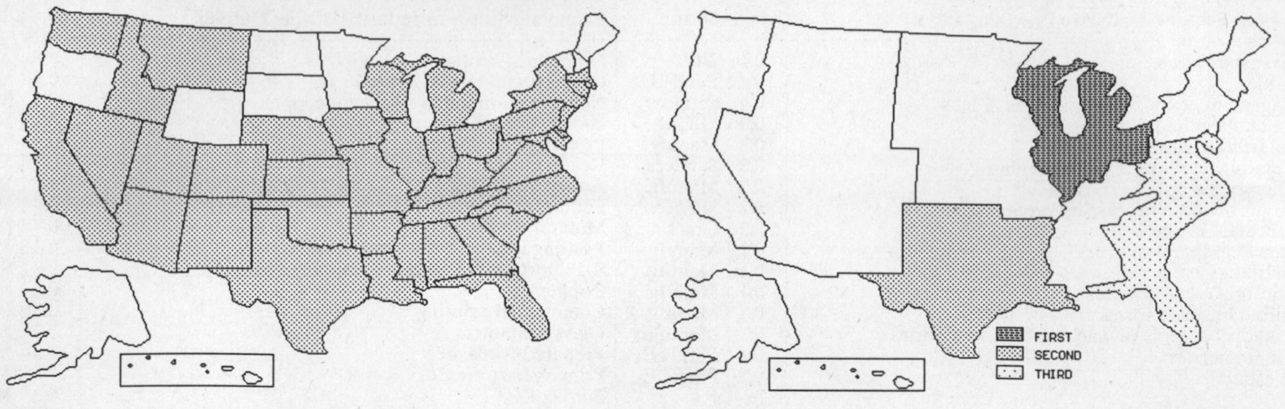

INDUSTRY DATA BY STATE

State	Establish-ments	Shipments Total ($ mil)	Shipments % of U.S.	Shipments Per Establ.	Employment Total Number	Employment % of U.S.	Employment Per Establ.	Employment Wages ($/hour)	Cost as % of Shipments	Investment per Employee ($)
Tennessee	20	1,909.2	10.5	95.5	10,600	13.4	530	15.53	23.5	-
Texas	53	1,348.5	7.4	25.4	4,100	5.2	77	17.90	62.6	20,732
New Jersey	34	1,033.8	5.7	30.4	2,400	3.0	71	15.11	59.2	8,833
California	64	958.7	5.3	15.0	2,700	3.4	42	15.09	40.8	12,593
Ohio	38	957.8	5.3	25.2	3,400	4.3	89	16.91	52.0	4,176
Louisiana	27	924.9	5.1	34.3	2,200	2.8	81	16.44	56.2	59,000
Kentucky	10	756.1	4.2	75.6	2,900	3.7	290	16.89	46.5	1,414
Illinois	32	631.6	3.5	19.7	2,100	2.7	66	15.03	47.5	18,048
North Carolina	18	542.8	3.0	30.2	2,400	3.0	133	18.44	34.0	18,667
Alabama	20	502.2	2.8	25.1	1,700	2.1	85	16.35	54.1	16,059
Georgia	29	367.4	2.0	12.7	1,100	1.4	38	13.80	52.3	5,545
Pennsylvania	45	299.9	1.7	6.7	1,300	1.6	29	14.60	46.2	11,385
New York	23	216.8	1.2	9.4	800	1.0	35	13.90	58.1	8,125
Maryland	12	201.3	1.1	16.8	1,100	1.4	92	17.85	60.1	-
Missouri	18	148.0	0.8	8.2	400	0.5	22	17.17	56.6	7,750
Michigan	17	139.9	0.8	8.2	700	0.9	41	17.00	35.7	13,286
Delaware	3	125.8	0.7	41.9	500	0.6	167	13.29	32.9	9,600
Oklahoma	18	115.6	0.6	6.4	700	0.9	39	13.92	49.5	8,286
Massachusetts	14	94.1	0.5	6.7	500	0.6	36	18.17	45.4	12,000
West Virginia	5	86.1	0.5	17.2	200	0.3	40	17.00	33.8	-
Utah	7	56.4	0.3	8.1	400	0.5	57	12.20	37.6	-
Wisconsin	10	41.2	0.2	4.1	200	0.3	20	11.67	47.8	4,500
Florida	19	39.5	0.2	2.1	200	0.3	11	11.00	68.9	7,000
Colorado	13	32.9	0.2	2.5	200	0.3	15	11.00	48.3	-
Arizona	5	30.4	0.2	6.1	200	0.3	40	15.50	79.6	-
Nevada	5	25.7	0.1	5.1	100	0.1	20	9.00	42.0	6,000
Indiana	24	(D)	-	-	750 *	0.9	31	-	-	19,067
Washington	24	(D)	-	-	17,500 *	22.1	729	-	-	800
South Carolina	10	(D)	-	-	17,500 *	22.1	1,750	-	-	771
Mississippi	9	(D)	-	-	375 *	0.5	42	-	-	-
Virginia	8	(D)	-	-	1,750 *	2.2	219	-	-	-
Arkansas	7	(D)	-	-	750 *	0.9	107	-	-	-
Connecticut	6	(D)	-	-	175 *	0.2	29	-	-	-
Kansas	6	(D)	-	-	375 *	0.5	63	-	-	-
Idaho	5	(D)	-	-	3,750 *	4.7	750	-	-	-
Nebraska	5	(D)	-	-	175 *	0.2	35	-	-	-
Iowa	4	(D)	-	-	175 *	0.2	44	-	-	10,857
Montana	4	(D)	-	-	375 *	0.5	94	-	-	-
New Mexico	3	(D)	-	-	375 *	0.5	125	-	-	-

Source: 1992 *Economic Census*. The states are in descending order of shipments or establishments (if shipment data are missing for the majority). The symbol (D) appears when data are withheld to prevent disclosure of competitive information. States marked with (D) are sorted by number of establishments. A dash (-) indicates that the data element cannot be calculated; * indicates the midpoint of a range.

2821 - PLASTICS MATERIALS & RESINS

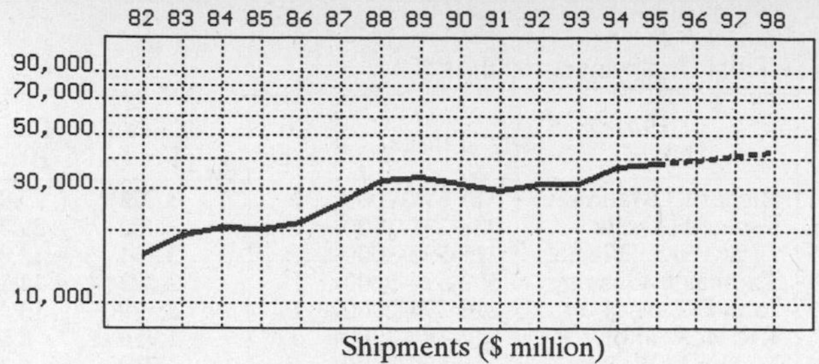

Shipments ($ million)

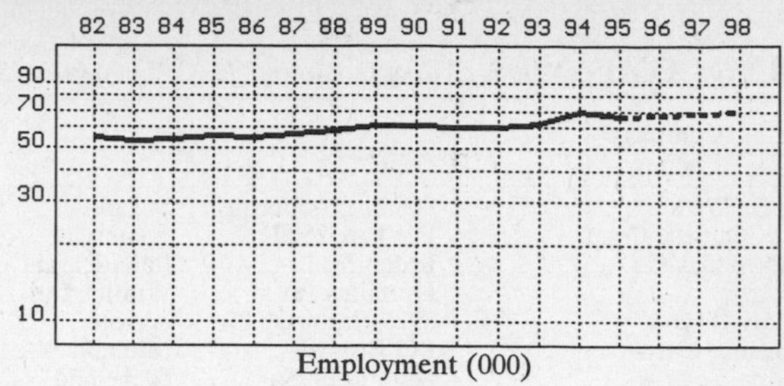

Employment (000)

GENERAL STATISTICS

Year	Com-panies	Establishments		Employment			Compensation		Production ($ million)			
		Total	with 20 or more employees	Total (000)	Production Workers (000)	Production Hours (Mil)	Payroll ($ mil)	Wages ($/hr)	Cost of Materials	Value Added by Manufacture	Value of Shipments	Capital Invest.
1982	264	441	310	54.7	32.8	67.4	1,435.3	11.73	10,812.0	4,785.6	15,813.7	899.2
1983		451	320	53.2	32.7	67.3	1,505.6	12.84	12,298.4	6,716.7	18,935.8	756.4
1984		461	330	54.2	33.2	69.8	1,650.9	13.33	13,298.9	7,653.9	20,776.3	925.3
1985		470	340	55.4	34.4	71.1	1,818.6	14.33	13,201.3	7,036.3	20,261.8	1,115.1
1986		477	350	54.7	34.1	72.2	1,893.6	15.06	13,233.7	8,149.4	21,483.7	1,264.2
1987	288	480	320	56.3	34.9	75.6	2,005.8	15.24	15,410.4	10,872.9	26,245.5	1,247.2
1988		487	331	58.3	36.0	79.8	2,169.9	15.37	19,333.8	13,196.7	32,109.9	1,605.8
1989		498	346	61.4	37.8	83.7	2,383.2	15.92	20,292.9	12,991.2	33,256.7	1,966.2
1990		510	343	61.8	37.9	82.5	2,485.7	16.88	19,390.9	12,195.3	31,325.8	2,436.6
1991		519	341	60.5	36.7	80.8	2,479.9	17.25	18,593.4	11,012.2	29,565.8	2,251.7
1992	240	449	340	60.4	35.9	78.5	2,671.6	18.71	18,839.8	12,494.7	31,303.9	1,707.3
1993		501	352	62.2	36.6	80.9	2,799.3	18.75	19,500.6	11,953.5	31,545.6	1,925.9
1994		509P	352P	69.2	40.6	90.0	3,150.0	19.37	21,937.8	15,116.8	36,964.6	2,554.9
1995		513P	354P	66.0P	39.3P	88.3P	3,126.3P	19.98P	22,503.2P	15,506.4P	37,917.3P	2,565.2P
1996		518P	357P	67.1P	39.8P	89.9P	3,260.3P	20.59P	23,438.0P	16,150.6P	39,492.4P	2,704.7P
1997		522P	360P	68.1P	40.3P	91.5P	3,394.3P	21.19P	24,372.8P	16,794.7P	41,067.6P	2,844.1P
1998		527P	362P	69.2P	40.9P	93.2P	3,528.3P	21.80P	25,307.6P	17,438.9P	42,642.7P	2,983.6P

Sources: 1982, 1987, 1992 *Economic Census*; *Annual Survey of Manufactures*, 83-86, 88-91, 93-94. Establishment counts for non-Census years are from *County Business Patterns*; establishment values for 83-84 are extrapolations. 'P's show projections by the editors. Industries reclassified in 87 will not have data for prior years.

INDICES OF CHANGE

Year	Com-panies	Establishments		Employment			Compensation		Production ($ million)			
		Total	with 20 or more employees	Total (000)	Production Workers (000)	Production Hours (Mil)	Payroll ($ mil)	Wages ($/hr)	Cost of Materials	Value Added by Manufacture	Value of Shipments	Capital Invest.
1982	110	98	91	91	91	86	54	63	57	38	51	53
1983		100	94	88	91	86	56	69	65	54	60	44
1984		103	97	90	92	89	62	71	71	61	66	54
1985		105	100	92	96	91	68	77	70	56	65	65
1986		106	103	91	95	92	71	80	70	65	69	74
1987	120	107	94	93	97	96	75	81	82	87	84	73
1988		108	97	97	100	102	81	82	103	106	103	94
1989		111	102	102	105	107	89	85	108	104	106	115
1990		114	101	102	106	105	93	90	103	98	100	143
1991		116	100	100	102	103	93	92	99	88	94	132
1992	100	100	100	100	100	100	100	100	100	100	100	100
1993		112	104	103	102	103	105	100	104	96	101	113
1994		113P	104P	115	113	115	118	104	116	121	118	150
1995		114P	104P	109P	109P	112P	117P	107P	119P	124P	121P	150P
1996		115P	105P	111P	111P	115P	122P	110P	124P	129P	126P	158P
1997		116P	106P	113P	112P	117P	127P	113P	129P	134P	131P	167P
1998		117P	107P	114P	114P	119P	132P	116P	134P	140P	136P	175P

Sources: Same as General Statistics. Values reflect change from the base year, 1992. Values above 100 mean greater than 92, values below 100 mean less than 92, and a value of 100 in the 82-91 or 93-98 period means same as 92. 'P's mark projections by the editors.

SELECTED RATIOS

For 1994	Avg. of All Manufact.	Analyzed Industry	Index	For 1994	Avg. of All Manufact.	Analyzed Industry	Index
Employees per Establishment	49	136	278	Value Added per Production Worker	134,084	372,335	278
Payroll per Establishment	1,500,273	6,193,214	413	Cost per Establishment	5,045,178	43,131,901	855
Payroll per Employee	30,620	45,520	149	Cost per Employee	102,970	317,020	308
Production Workers per Establishment	34	80	233	Cost per Production Worker	146,988	540,340	368
Wages per Establishment	853,319	3,427,502	402	Shipments per Establishment	9,576,895	72,676,088	759
Wages per Production Worker	24,861	42,938	173	Shipments per Employee	195,460	534,171	273
Hours per Production Worker	2,056	2,217	108	Shipments per Production Worker	279,017	910,458	326
Wages per Hour	12.09	19.37	160	Investment per Establishment	321,011	5,023,188	1,565
Value Added per Establishment	4,602,255	29,721,136	646	Investment per Employee	6,552	36,921	564
Value Added per Employee	93,930	218,451	233	Investment per Production Worker	9,352	62,929	673

Sources: Same as General Statistics. The 'Average of All Manufacturing' column represents the average of all manufacturing industries reported for the most recent complete year available. The Index shows the relationship between the Average and the Analyzed Industry. For example, 100 means that they are equal; 500 that the Analyzed Industry is five times the average; 50 means that the Analyzed Industry is half the national average. The abbreviation 'na' is used to show that data are 'not available'.

LEADING COMPANIES

Number shown: **75** Total sales ($ mil): **47,585** Total employment (000): **174.0**

Company Name	Address				CEO Name	Phone	Co. Type	Sales ($ mil)	Empl. (000)
Monsanto Co	800 N Lindbergh	St Louis	MO	63167	Richard J Mahoney	314-694-1000	P	8,272	29.0
Hoechst Celanese Corp	PO Box 2500	Somerville	NJ	08876	Ernest H Drew	908-231-2000	S	7,800	29.2
Rohm and Haas Co	Indep Mall	Philadelphia	PA	19105	J Lawrence Wilson	215-592-3000	P	3,534	12.0
Hercules Inc	Hercules Plz	Wilmington	DE	19894	Thomas L Gossage	302-594-5000	P	2,773	14.1
BF Goodrich Co	3925 Embassy Pkwy	Akron	OH	44313	John D Ong	216-374-2000	P	2,199	13.4
Dow Corning Corp	PO Box 994	Midland	MI	48686	KR McKennon	517-496-4000	J	1,956	8.6
MA Hanna Co	200 Public Sq	Cleveland	OH	44114	Martin D Walker	216-589-4000	P	1,719	6.2
Himont Inc	2801 Centerville Rd	Wilmington	DE	19850	Paolo Morrione	302-996-6000	S	1,600*	4.0
Union Carbide Corp	PO Box 450	Somerset	NJ	08875	FD Ryan	201-271-2000	D	1,525	1.4
Hoechst Celanese Corp	PO Box 2500	Somerville	NJ	08876	Thomas Bohrer	908-231-2000	D	1,469	5.0
Solvay America Inc	PO Box 27328	Houston	TX	77227	M Whitson Sadler	713-525-6000	S	1,450	4.8
Geon Co	6100 Oak Tree Blv	Independence	OH	44131	William F Patient	216-447-6000	P	1,209	1.8
Phillips Chemical Co	2625 Bay Area Blv	Houston	TX	77058	D W Casselberry	713-244-3100	D	1,000	2.0
Georgia Gulf Corp	400 Perimeter Ctr	Atlanta	GA	30346	Jerry R Satrum	404-395-4500	P	955	1.1
Reichhold Chemicals Inc	PO Box 13582	Res Tri Pk	NC	27709	Phillip D Ashkettle	919-990-7500	S	800	2.2
A Schulman Inc	3550 W Market St	Akron	OH	44333	Terry L Haines	216-666-3751	P	749	1.8
Sterling Chemicals Inc	PO Box 1311	Texas City	TX	77592	J Virgil Waggoner	713-650-3700	P	701	1.2
Foamex International Inc	823 Waterman Av	E Providence	RI	02914	Marshall S Cogan	401-438-0900	P	698	5.4
Solvay Polymers Inc	3333 Richmond Av	Houston	TX	77098	David G Birney	713-525-4000	S	600	1.1
GenCorp Polymer Products	350 Springside Dr	Akron	OH	44333	William E Bachman	216-668-7000	S	569	2.8
Rexene Corp	5005 LBJ	Dallas	TX	75244	Lavon N Anderson	214-450-9000	P	538	1.3
Foamex LP	823 Waterman Av	E Providence	RI	02914	Marshall S Cogan	401-438-0900	S	502	5.3
Huls America Inc	PO Box 456	Piscataway	NJ	08855	Klaus Burzin	908-980-6800	S	500	1.1
Perstorp Inc	238 Nonotuck St	Florence	MA	01060	Mils Lindeblad	413-584-9522	S	440*	1.8
Aristech Chemical Corp	600 Grant St	Pittsburgh	PA	15219	Thomas Marshall	412-433-2747	R	420*	1.7
Budd Co	32055 Edward Av	Madison H	MI	48071	Rick Urso	313-588-3200	D	300	1.2
Crain Industries Inc	PO Drawer 6478	Fort Smith	AR	72906	HC Crain Jr	501-648-3230	R	240	2.0
ICI Composites Inc	2055 E Techn Cir	Tempe	AZ	85284	Carl Smith	602-730-2010	S	240	1.0
Neste Chemicals Holding Inc	5 Post Oak Park St	Houston	TX	77027	Ilkka Pohjanheimo	713-622-7459	R	200	0.4
Rogers Corp Molding Material	PO Box 550	Manchester	CT	06045	Dirk M Baars	203-646-5500	D	135	0.1
K-Bin Inc	5616 Hwy 332 E	Freeport	TX	77541	Todd C Walker	409-233-6610	S	120*	<0.1
Neville Chemical Co	2800 Neville Rd	Pittsburgh	PA	15225	L Van V Dauler Jr	412-331-4200	R	120*	0.5
Novacor Chemical Inc	690 Mechanic St	Leominster	MA	01453	David Clarke	508-537-1111	S	120*	0.2
McWhorter Technologies Inc	400 E Cottage Pl	Carpentersville	IL	60110	John R Stevenson	708-428-2657	P	106	0.6
Alpha Corporation of Tennessee	PO Box 670	Collierville	TN	38027	Jerry Griffith	901-853-2450	R	100	0.6
Hermann Companies Inc	1400 N Price Rd	St Louis	MO	63132	R R Hermann Jr	314-432-2800	R	100	1.0
Neste Resins Corp	1600 Val River Dr	Eugene	OR	97401	Jorma Rinta	503-687-8840	S	100	0.3
Wacker Silicones Corp	3301 Sutton Rd	Adrian	MI	49221	G F Lengnick	517-264-8500	S	100	0.5
Alpha/Owens-Corning	PO Box 610	Collierville	TN	38027	Gerald P Griffith	901-854-2800	R	99*	0.4
Tuscarora Inc	1479 Parker Rd	Conyers	GA	30207	Mike Grunnet	404-922-3513	D	86*	0.4
Acme/Borden	10330 W Roosevelt	Westchester	IL	60154	Edward Krainer	708-343-1900	S	80	0.4
Dash Multi-Corp	2500 Adie Rd	Maryland H	MO	63043	MS Wool	314-432-3200	R	75	0.2
Para-Chem Southern Inc	PO Box 127	Simpsonville	SC	29681	John W Jordan III	803-967-7691	R	75	0.3
Plastics Engineering Co	PO Box 758	Sheboygan	WI	53082	Ralph T Brotz	414-458-2121	R	75	0.5
Washington Penn Plastics	2080 N Main St	Washington	PA	15301	Robert Andy	412-228-1260	R	75	0.3
Shields Bag and Printing Co	PO Box 9848	Yakima	WA	98909	William Shields	509-248-7500	R	67	0.5
BTL Specialty Resins Corp	PO Box 2570	Toledo	OH	43606	Wilfred Kimball	419-244-5856	S	65	0.2
Chemdal International	1530 E Dundee Rd	Palatine	IL	60067	Larry Wasbow	708-705-5600	S	59	0.3
Anchor Packaging	737 Rudder Rd	Fenton	MO	63026	Dennis J Nemura	314-349-2900	S	50	0.3
Rhe Tech Inc	1500 EN Territorial	Whitmore Lake	MI	48189	Richard Gall	313-769-0585	R	50	<0.1
Rodel Inc	Diamond State	Newark	DE	19713	WD Budinger	302-366-0500	R	50*	0.3
MA Industries Inc	PO Box 2322	Peachtree City	GA	30269	Bob Peacock	404-487-7761	R	49*	0.2
Westlake Monomers Corp	2801 Post Oak Blv	Houston	TX	77056	James Chao	713-960-9111	R	43*	0.2
Chemdal Corp	1530 E Dundee Rd	Palatine	IL	60067	John Hughes	708-705-5600	S	40	0.1
Melamine Chemicals Inc	PO Box 748	Donaldsonville	LA	70346	Fred Huber	504-473-3121	P	39	0.1
MPI Inc	PO Box 158	Mount Holly	NJ	08060	Francis C Faulseit	609-267-5900	D	39*	0.2
Delta Resins and Refractories	6263 N Teutonia	Milwaukee	WI	53209	DW Hansen	414-462-1200	R	35	0.1
Dynaric Inc	500 Frank W Burr	Teaneck	NJ	07666	Joseph Martinez	201-692-7700	R	35	0.2
American Shower and Bath	693 S Court St	Lapeer	MI	48446	J Ruberstein	810-664-8501	D	34*	0.1
Pacific Western Resin Co	PO Box 10049	Eugene	OR	97401	N Michael Stickel	503-343-0200	D	32*	0.1
Conap Inc	1405 Buffalo St	Olean	NY	14760	Allen M Hodges	716-372-9650	S	31*	0.1
Tom Smith Industries Inc	PO Box 128	Englewood	OH	45322	Thomas R Smith Sr	513-832-1555	R	31*	0.1
Anderson Development Co	1415 E Michigan	Adrian	MI	49221	JP Rupert	517-263-2121	S	30	0.1
Neste Polyester Inc	5106 Wheeler Av	Fort Smith	AR	72901	Gary Loop	501-646-7865	S	30	0.1
NVF Co	PO Box 516	Kennett Square	PA	19348	Mark Hall	215-444-2800	D	30	0.3
Regalite Plastics Inc	300 Needham St	Newton	MA	02164	Raymond Jarvis	617-969-6000	S	25	0.1
Clark Foam	25887 Crown	South Laguna	CA	92677	G Clark	714-582-1431	R	24*	0.1
Interpak Terminals Inc	4200 Produce Row	Houston	TX	77023	John Tinkle	713-921-3974	R	24*	0.1
Norac Company Inc	PO Box 577	Azusa	CA	91702	C M McCloskey	818-334-2908	R	24	0.1
Rutland Plastic Technologies Inc	PO Box 339	Pineville	NC	28134	James F Beahan	704-553-0046	S	24	0.1
Spartech Compounding	113 Passaic Av	Kearny	NJ	07032	Steve Byron	201-998-8002	S	22	<0.1
American Thermoplastics Corp	1235 Kress St	Houston	TX	77020	Luther W Brenek	713-675-6605	S	20*	<0.1
Chem Polymer Corp	PO Box 6927	Fort Myers	FL	33911	Michael Clifton	813-337-0400	S	20	<0.1
Desalination Systems Inc	1238 Simpson Way	Escondido	CA	92029	Bjarne Nicolaisen	619-746-8141	R	20*	0.2
Epoxylite Corp	PO Box 19671	Irvine	CA	92713	P Dorsa	714-951-3026	R	20*	0.1

Source: Ward's Business Directory of U.S. Private and Public Companies, Volumes 1 and 2, 1996. The company type code used is as follows: P - Public, R - Private, S - Subsidiary, D - Division, J - Joint Venture, A - Affiliate, G - Group. Sales are in millions of dollars, employees are in thousands. An asterisk (*) indicates an estimated sales volume. The symbol < stands for 'less than'. Company names and addresses are truncated, in some cases, to fit into the available space.

MATERIALS CONSUMED

Material		Quantity	Delivered Cost ($ million)
Materials, ingredients, containers, and supplies		(X)	16,946.8
Styrene (100 percent basis)	mil lb	6,219.8*	1,345.6
Phenol (100 percent basis)	mil lb	1,350.4	365.7
Other cyclic crudes and intermediates (including melamine, phthalic anhydride, and benzene)		(X)	554.3
Synthetic organic dyes, pigments, lakes, and toners (100 percent basis)	mil lb	11.3**	22.8
Acrylates and methacrylates, monomers (100 percent basis)	mil lb	1,388.0	774.8
Alcohols, except ethyl (100 percent basis)	mil lb	1,032.9	188.3
Formaldehyde (100 percent HCHO)	mil lb	2,507.9	115.1
Rubber processing chemicals (accelerators, antioxidants, blowing agents, inhibitors, peptizers, etc.)		(X)	194.5
Vinyl acetate, monomer (100 percent basis)	mil lb	1,170.5	278.8
Vinyl chloride, monomer (100 percent basis)	mil lb	7,612.3	1,017.6
Other synthetic organic chemicals (includes acrylonitrile and cellulose acetate)		(X)	1,871.2
Ethylene used as a raw material or feedstock	mil lb	16,426.7	2,899.1
Propylene used as a raw material or feedstock	mil lb	5,263.9*	746.1
Butadiene used as a raw material or feedstock	mil lb	1,406.8	235.6
Other refined petroleum products used as a raw material or feedstock		4,992.7**	747.2
Other hydrocarbons used as raw materials or feedstocks (including crude oil, natural gas and still gas)		(X)	239.5
Plastics resins consumed in the form of granules, pellets, powders, liquids, etc.	mil lb	1,212.1	620.1
Inorganic chemicals		(X)	412.6
Carbon black	mil lb	31.1*	14.5
Paper and paperboard containers, including shipping sacks and other paper packaging supplies		(X)	167.4
All other materials and components, parts, containers, and supplies		(X)	3,352.4
Materials, ingredients, containers, and supplies, nsk		(X)	783.6

Source: 1992 *Economic Census*. Explanation of symbols used: (D): Withheld to avoid disclosure of competitive data; na: Not available; (S): Withheld because statistical norms were not met; (X): Not applicable; (Z): Less than half the unit shown; nec: Not elsewhere classified; nsk: Not specified by kind; - : zero; * : 10-19 percent estimated; ** : 20-29 percent estimated.

PRODUCT SHARE DETAILS

Product or Product Class	% Share	Product or Product Class	% Share
Plastics materials and resins	100.00	Thermosetting resins and plastics materials	16.72
Thermoplastic resins and plastics materials	82.47	Plastics materials and resins, nsk	0.81

Source: 1992 *Economic Census*. The values shown are percent of total shipments in an industry. Values of indented subcategories are summed in the main heading. The symbol (D) appears when data are withheld to prevent disclosure of competitive information. The abbreviation nsk stands for 'not specified by kind' and nec for 'not elsewhere classified'.

INPUTS AND OUTPUTS FOR PLASTICS MATERIALS & RESINS

Economic Sector or Industry Providing Inputs	%	Sector	Economic Sector or Industry Buying Outputs	%	Sector
Cyclic crudes and organics	51.4	Manufg.	Miscellaneous plastics products	44.1	Manufg.
Miscellaneous plastics products	6.6	Manufg.	Exports	13.1	Foreign
Wholesale trade	6.1	Trade	Paints & allied products	5.2	Manufg.
Electric services (utilities)	4.2	Util.	Bags, except textile	3.7	Manufg.
Accounting, auditing & bookkeeping	3.2	Services	Nonferrous wire drawing & insulating	3.3	Manufg.
Gas production & distribution (utilities)	3.1	Util.	Organic fibers, noncellulosic	2.0	Manufg.
Imports	2.5	Foreign	Plastics materials & resins	1.6	Manufg.
Plastics materials & resins	2.3	Manufg.	Adhesives & sealants	1.5	Manufg.
Petroleum refining	1.4	Manufg.	Games, toys, & children's vehicles	1.3	Manufg.
Advertising	1.3	Services	Motor vehicle parts & accessories	1.2	Manufg.
Motor freight transportation & warehousing	1.2	Util.	Paper coating & glazing	1.2	Manufg.
Alkalies & chlorine	1.0	Manufg.	Paperboard containers & boxes	1.0	Manufg.
Chemical preparations, nec	1.0	Manufg.	Photographic equipment & supplies	1.0	Manufg.
Railroads & related services	1.0	Util.	Wiring devices	1.0	Manufg.
Industrial inorganic chemicals, nec	0.8	Manufg.	Chemical preparations, nec	0.9	Manufg.
Paper coating & glazing	0.8	Manufg.	Cyclic crudes and organics	0.7	Manufg.
Paperboard containers & boxes	0.8	Manufg.	Coated fabrics, not rubberized	0.6	Manufg.
Water transportation	0.7	Util.	Electronic components nec	0.6	Manufg.
Miscellaneous repair shops	0.7	Services	Fluid milk	0.6	Manufg.
Gum & wood chemicals	0.6	Manufg.	Soap & other detergents	0.6	Manufg.
Paints & allied products	0.5	Manufg.	Electric housewares & fans	0.5	Manufg.
Engineering, architectural, & surveying services	0.5	Services	Hardware, nec	0.5	Manufg.
Crude petroleum & natural gas	0.4	Mining	Motor vehicles & car bodies	0.5	Manufg.
Pumps & compressors	0.4	Manufg.	Phonograph records & tapes	0.5	Manufg.
Communications, except radio & TV	0.4	Util.	Printing ink	0.5	Manufg.
Automotive repair shops & services	0.4	Services	Asbestos products	0.4	Manufg.
Noncomparable imports	0.4	Foreign	Fabricated rubber products, nec	0.4	Manufg.
Maintenance of nonfarm buildings nec	0.3	Constr.	Lighting fixtures & equipment	0.4	Manufg.
Inorganic pigments	0.3	Manufg.	Sporting & athletic goods, nec	0.4	Manufg.
Surface active agents	0.3	Manufg.	Surgical & medical instruments	0.4	Manufg.
Synthetic rubber	0.3	Manufg.	Telephone & telegraph apparatus	0.4	Manufg.
Banking	0.3	Fin/R.E.	Boat building & repairing	0.3	Manufg.
Electrical repair shops	0.3	Services	Brooms & brushes	0.3	Manufg.

Continued on next page.

INPUTS AND OUTPUTS FOR PLASTICS MATERIALS & RESINS - Continued

Economic Sector or Industry Providing Inputs	%	Sector	Economic Sector or Industry Buying Outputs	%	Sector
Equipment rental & leasing services	0.3	Services	Hard surface floor coverings	0.3	Manufg.
Lubricating oils & greases	0.2	Manufg.	Household refrigerators & freezers	0.3	Manufg.
Metal barrels, drums, & pails	0.2	Manufg.	Paper mills, except building paper	0.3	Manufg.
Nitrogenous & phosphatic fertilizers	0.2	Manufg.	Shoes, except rubber	0.3	Manufg.
Soap & other detergents	0.2	Manufg.	Surgical appliances & supplies	0.3	Manufg.
Soybean oil mills	0.2	Manufg.	Typewriters & office machines, nec	0.3	Manufg.
Air transportation	0.2	Util.	Artificial trees & flowers	0.2	Manufg.
Sanitary services, steam supply, irrigation	0.2	Util.	Converted paper products, nec	0.2	Manufg.
Eating & drinking places	0.2	Trade	Household furniture, nec	0.2	Manufg.
Royalties	0.2	Fin/R.E.	Manufacturing industries, nec	0.2	Manufg.
Colleges, universities, & professional schools	0.2	Services	Mineral wool	0.2	Manufg.
Carbon black	0.1	Manufg.	Nonwoven fabrics	0.2	Manufg.
General industrial machinery, nec	0.1	Manufg.	Paperboard mills	0.2	Manufg.
Glass & glass products, except containers	0.1	Manufg.	Petroleum refining	0.2	Manufg.
Machinery, except electrical, nec	0.1	Manufg.	Refrigeration & heating equipment	0.2	Manufg.
Water supply & sewage systems	0.1	Util.	Semiconductors & related devices	0.2	Manufg.
Insurance carriers	0.1	Fin/R.E.	Service industry machines, nec	0.2	Manufg.
Security & commodity brokers	0.1	Fin/R.E.	Switchgear & switchboard apparatus	0.2	Manufg.
			Aircraft & missile equipment, nec	0.1	Manufg.
			Automotive & apparel trimmings	0.1	Manufg.
			Buttons	0.1	Manufg.
			Crowns & closures	0.1	Manufg.
			Cutlery	0.1	Manufg.
			Engine electrical equipment	0.1	Manufg.
			Gaskets, packing & sealing devices	0.1	Manufg.
			Household vacuum cleaners	0.1	Manufg.
			Ophthalmic goods	0.1	Manufg.
			Rubber & plastics hose & belting	0.1	Manufg.
			Scales & balances	0.1	Manufg.
			Tires & inner tubes	0.1	Manufg.
			Transportation equipment, nec	0.1	Manufg.
			X-ray apparatus & tubes	0.1	Manufg.

Source: Benchmark Input-Output Accounts for the U.S. Economy, 1982, U.S. Department of Commerce, Washington, D.C., July 1991. Data, as reported in the source, are organized by the 1977 SIC structure in use in 1982 but have been matched, as closely as is possible, to the 1987 SIC structure used in this book.

OCCUPATIONS EMPLOYED BY SIC 282 - PLASTICS MATERIALS AND SYNTHETICS

Occupation	% of Total 1994	Change to 2005	Occupation	% of Total 1994	Change to 2005
Chemical equipment controllers, operators	8.7	-16.4	Machine operators nec	1.8	-26.3
Extruding & forming machine workers	7.9	46.3	Helpers, laborers, & material movers nec	1.4	-16.4
Textile draw-out & winding machine operators	5.6	12.8	Packaging & filling machine operators	1.4	-16.4
Blue collar worker supervisors	5.4	-19.5	General office clerks	1.3	-28.7
Science & mathematics technicians	4.2	-16.4	Chemists	1.3	-16.4
Chemical plant & system operators	3.7	-16.4	General managers & top executives	1.2	-20.7
Secretaries, ex legal & medical	2.9	-23.9	Electricians	1.2	-21.5
Industrial machinery mechanics	2.8	-8.1	Management support workers nec	1.2	-16.4
Chemical engineers	2.7	-16.4	Mechanical engineers	1.2	-8.0
Inspectors, testers, & graders, precision	2.7	-16.4	Crushing & mixing machine operators	1.2	-16.4
Maintenance repairers, general utility	2.6	-24.8	Managers & administrators nec	1.1	-16.5
Sales & related workers nec	2.4	-16.4	Industrial production managers	1.1	-16.4
Textile machine setters & set-up operators	1.9	-58.2	Engineering technicians & technologists nec	1.0	-16.4

Source: Industry-Occupation Matrix, Bureau of Labor Statistics. These data relate to one or more 3-digit SIC industry groups rather than to a single 4-digit SIC. The change reported for each occupation to the year 2005 is a percent of growth or decline as estimated by the Bureau of Labor Statistics. The abbreviation nec stands for 'not elsewhere classified'.

LOCATION BY STATE AND REGIONAL CONCENTRATION

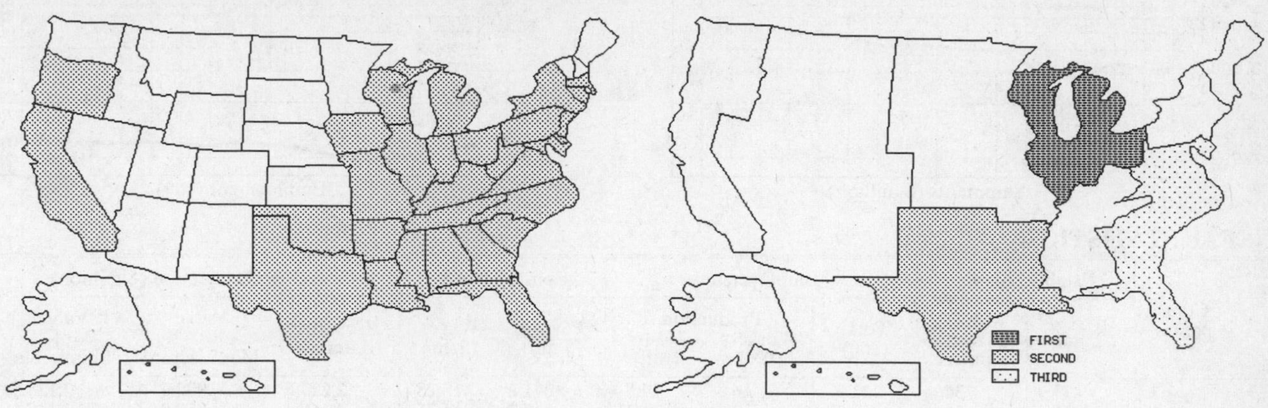

INDUSTRY DATA BY STATE

State	Establish-ments	Shipments			Employment				Cost as % of Shipments	Investment per Employee ($)
		Total ($ mil)	% of U.S.	Per Establ.	Total Number	% of U.S.	Per Establ.	Wages ($/hour)		
Texas	57	9,861.9	31.5	173.0	12,900	21.4	226	21.74	62.7	59,690
Louisiana	20	2,832.6	9.0	141.6	3,400	5.6	170	19.38	68.5	30,676
Michigan	15	1,628.1	5.2	108.5	4,100	6.8	273	17.72	37.8	-
Pennsylvania	22	1,436.5	4.6	65.3	4,100	6.8	186	18.89	64.3	-
California	42	861.7	2.8	20.5	1,900	3.1	45	14.62	67.3	13,105
Tennessee	9	842.1	2.7	93.6	3,300	5.5	367	16.93	72.5	-
Georgia	16	514.3	1.6	32.1	1,700	2.8	106	14.86	63.3	-
Massachusetts	14	384.1	1.2	27.4	1,200	2.0	86	15.27	56.5	-
Arkansas	5	129.4	0.4	25.9	300	0.5	60	14.67	69.9	-
Illinois	36	(D)	-	-	3,750 *	6.2	104	-	-	-
New Jersey	32	(D)	-	-	3,750 *	6.2	117	-	-	-
Ohio	26	(D)	-	-	3,750 *	6.2	144	-	-	-
North Carolina	19	(D)	-	-	1,750 *	2.9	92	-	-	-
Kentucky	12	(D)	-	-	3,750 *	6.2	313	-	-	-
Florida	11	(D)	-	-	375 *	0.6	34	-	-	-
Indiana	11	(D)	-	-	1,750 *	2.9	159	-	-	-
Oregon	10	(D)	-	-	175 *	0.3	18	-	-	-
New York	9	(D)	-	-	1,750 *	2.9	194	-	-	6,571
South Carolina	9	(D)	-	-	1,750 *	2.9	194	-	-	-
Mississippi	8	(D)	-	-	750 *	1.2	94	-	-	-
Alabama	7	(D)	-	-	750 *	1.2	107	-	-	20,133
Maryland	7	(D)	-	-	175 *	0.3	25	-	-	-
Connecticut	6	(D)	-	-	375 *	0.6	63	-	-	25,333
Missouri	6	(D)	-	-	375 *	0.6	63	-	-	-
Iowa	4	(D)	-	-	750 *	1.2	188	-	-	-
West Virginia	4	(D)	-	-	3,750 *	6.2	938	-	-	-
Oklahoma	3	(D)	-	-	175 *	0.3	58	-	-	6,286
Virginia	3	(D)	-	-	175 *	0.3	58	-	-	-
Wisconsin	3	(D)	-	-	375 *	0.6	125	-	-	-
Delaware	2	(D)	-	-	175 *	0.3	88	-	-	-

Source: 1992 *Economic Census*. The states are in descending order of shipments or establishments (if shipment data are missing for the majority). The symbol (D) appears when data are withheld to prevent disclosure of competitive information. States marked with (D) are sorted by number of establishments. A dash (-) indicates that the data element cannot be calculated; * indicates the midpoint of a range.

2822 - SYNTHETIC RUBBER

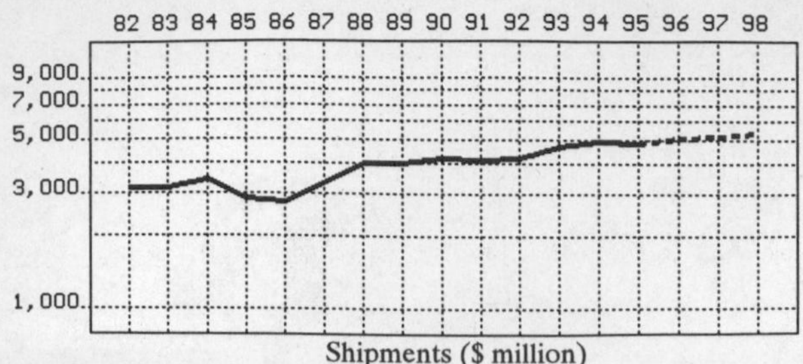

Shipments ($ million)

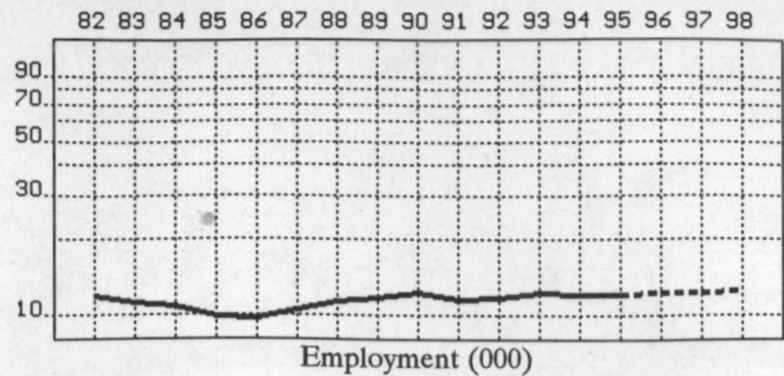

Employment (000)

GENERAL STATISTICS

Year	Companies	Establishments		Employment			Compensation		Production ($ million)			
		Total	with 20 or more employees	Total (000)	Production Workers (000)	Production Hours (Mil)	Payroll ($ mil)	Wages ($/hr)	Cost of Materials	Value Added by Manufacture	Value of Shipments	Capital Invest.
1982	63	77	34	11.8	7.6	14.8	341.2	13.28	2,217.6	900.4	3,138.5	246.0
1983		77	34	11.1	7.1	14.1	343.3	14.35	2,160.1	959.0	3,148.6	101.5
1984		77	34	10.7	7.0	13.9	357.1	15.36	2,279.6	1,167.6	3,408.6	
1985		78	35	9.8	6.3	12.6	323.1	15.18	1,906.3	920.0	2,840.6	117.5
1986		87	39	9.6	6.3	12.9	336.5	15.48	1,594.1	1,099.2	2,739.8	116.6
1987	58	68	31	10.4	6.7	14.4	394.6	15.88	2,082.5	1,248.7	3,283.0	170.5
1988		115	46	11.3	7.1	14.8	428.8	16.36	2,508.9	1,540.6	3,995.5	216.4
1989		76	39	11.7	7.1	15.1	443.6	16.78	2,403.1	1,593.8	4,007.8	265.5
1990		86	43	12.3	7.2	15.0	474.9	17.91	2,533.7	1,706.7	4,210.3	378.6
1991		92	44	11.5	7.4	15.6	491.2	17.79	2,234.6	1,844.8	4,088.3	360.0
1992	76	92	45	11.7	7.5	15.9	513.1	18.74	2,342.6	1,865.4	4,184.1	318.2
1993		109	49	12.2	7.7	16.4	551.0	19.27	2,592.1	2,133.5	4,738.6	255.8
1994		101P	48P	11.9	7.7	16.6	552.5	19.62	2,759.8	2,225.6	4,983.6	230.0
1995		103P	50P	12.1P	7.6P	16.5P	571.6P	20.07P	2,706.4P	2,182.5P	4,887.2P	
1996		105P	51P	12.2P	7.6P	16.7P	592.3P	20.56P	2,796.2P	2,255.0P	5,049.4P	
1997		108P	52P	12.3P	7.7P	17.0P	612.9P	21.05P	2,886.1P	2,327.5P	5,211.7P	
1998		110P	54P	12.4P	7.7P	17.2P	633.6P	21.55P	2,976.0P	2,399.9P	5,373.9P	

Sources: 1982, 1987, 1992 *Economic Census*; *Annual Survey of Manufactures*, 83-86, 88-91, 93-94. Establishment counts for non-Census years are from *County Business Patterns*; establishment values for 83-84 are extrapolations. 'P's show projections by the editors. Industries reclassified in 87 will not have data for prior years.

INDICES OF CHANGE

Year	Companies	Establishments		Employment			Compensation		Production ($ million)			
		Total	with 20 or more employees	Total (000)	Production Workers (000)	Production Hours (Mil)	Payroll ($ mil)	Wages ($/hr)	Cost of Materials	Value Added by Manufacture	Value of Shipments	Capital Invest.
1982	83	84	76	101	101	93	66	71	95	48	75	77
1983		84	76	95	95	89	67	77	92	51	75	32
1984		84	76	91	93	87	70	82	97	63	81	
1985		85	78	84	84	79	63	81	81	49	68	37
1986		95	87	82	84	81	66	83	68	59	65	37
1987	76	74	69	89	89	91	77	85	89	67	78	54
1988		125	102	97	95	93	84	87	107	83	95	68
1989		83	87	100	95	95	86	90	103	85	96	83
1990		93	96	105	96	94	93	96	108	91	101	119
1991		100	98	98	99	98	96	95	95	99	98	113
1992	100	100	100	100	100	100	100	100	100	100	100	100
1993		118	109	104	103	103	107	103	111	114	113	80
1994		110P	107P	102	103	104	108	105	118	119	119	72
1995		112P	110P	103P	101P	104P	111P	107P	116P	117P	117P	
1996		115P	113P	104P	102P	105P	115P	110P	119P	121P	121P	
1997		117P	116P	105P	102P	107P	119P	112P	123P	125P	125P	
1998		119P	119P	106P	103P	108P	123P	115P	127P	129P	128P	

Sources: Same as General Statistics. Values reflect change from the base year, 1992. Values above 100 mean greater than 92, values below 100 mean less than 92, and a value of 100 in the 82-91 or 93-98 period means same as 92. 'P's mark projections by the editors.

SELECTED RATIOS

For 1994	Avg. of All Manufact.	Analyzed Industry	Index	For 1994	Avg. of All Manufact.	Analyzed Industry	Index
Employees per Establishment	49	118	241	Value Added per Production Worker	134,084	289,039	216
Payroll per Establishment	1,500,273	5,478,516	365	Cost per Establishment	5,045,178	27,365,805	542
Payroll per Employee	30,620	46,429	152	Cost per Employee	102,970	231,916	225
Production Workers per Establishment	34	76	222	Cost per Production Worker	146,988	358,416	244
Wages per Establishment	853,319	3,229,518	378	Shipments per Establishment	9,576,895	49,416,707	516
Wages per Production Worker	24,861	42,298	170	Shipments per Employee	195,460	418,790	214
Hours per Production Worker	2,056	2,156	105	Shipments per Production Worker	279,017	647,221	232
Wages per Hour	12.09	19.62	162	Investment per Establishment	321,011	2,280,649	710
Value Added per Establishment	4,602,255	22,068,750	480	Investment per Employee	6,552	19,328	295
Value Added per Employee	93,930	187,025	199	Investment per Production Worker	9,352	29,870	319

Sources: Same as General Statistics. The 'Average of All Manufacturing' column represents the average of all manufacturing industries reported for the most recent complete year available. The Index shows the relationship between the Average and the Analyzed Industry. For example, 100 means that they are equal; 500 that the Analyzed Industry is five times the average; 50 means that the Analyzed Industry is half the national average. The abbreviation 'na' is used to show that data are 'not available'.

LEADING COMPANIES

Number shown: **24** Total sales ($ mil): **1,027** Total employment (000): **6.0**

Company Name	Address				CEO Name	Phone	Co. Type	Sales ($ mil)	Empl. (000)
DSM Copolymer Inc	PO Box 2591	Baton Rouge	LA	70821	Larry Powell	504-355-5655	S	260	0.7
Uniroyal Technology Corp	2 N Tamiami Trail	Sarasota	FL	34236	Howard R Curd	813-361-2220	P	198	1.3
Ameripol Synpol Co	PO Box 667	Port Neches	TX	77651	William D Spence	409-722-8321	R	130*	0.9
JPS Elastomerics Corp	9 Sullivan Rd	Holyoke	MA	01040	Bruce Wilby	413-533-8100	R	120*	0.5
Texas Petrochemicals Corp	8600 Park Pl Blv	Houston	TX	77017	Bill W Waycaster	713-477-9211	S	60*	0.4
JMK International Inc	4800 Bryant Irvin Ct	Fort Worth	TX	76107	AM Micallef	817-737-3703	R	56	0.5
Foamseal Inc	PO Box 455	Oxford	MI	48371	A Marra	810-628-2587	R	50	<0.1
VitaFoam Inc	PO Box 2024	High Point	NC	27261	Brian Aldridge	919-431-1171	S	40	0.5
Firestone Synthetic Rubber	PO Box 26611	Akron	OH	44319	John E Schremp	216-379-7000	D	20	0.1
Custom Coating Inc	204 W Indrial Blvd	Dalton	GA	30720	William C Poteet	706-277-3778	R	15	0.1
Chase Elastomer Corp	635 Tower Dr	Kennedale	TX	76060	Tom Chase	817-483-9797	R	12*	<0.1
Bandag Licensing Corp	2500 Thompson St	Long Beach	CA	90801	Wade Gaitlin	310-531-3880	S	11*	<0.1
Durex Products Inc	PO Box 354	Luck	WI	54853	R Martin	715-472-2111	R	10	0.1
Groendyk Manufacturing	PO Box 278	Buchanan	VA	24066	Steve Schaeffer	703-254-1010	S	10	0.1
Marsh Industries Inc	49680 Leona Dr	Chesterfield	MI	48051	Curtis H Marsh	810-949-9300	R	8	<0.1
Shurclose Seal Rubber & Plastic	PO Box 305	Lake Orion	MI	48361	Suzanne S Blake	810-969-0500	R	7	<0.1
Cri-Tech Inc	85 Winter St	Hanover	MA	02339	R Mastromatteo	617-826-5600	R	6*	<0.1
Specialty Silicone Products Inc	Rte 67 Curtis	Ballston Spa	NY	12020	Daniel S Naterelli	518-885-8826	R	5	<0.1
Cetryco	PO Box 250	Burlington	NJ	08016	AA Gordon	609-386-6448	R	4*	<0.1
Trilogy Plastics Inc	PO Box 130	Louisville	OH	44641	Stephen A Osborn	216-875-5522	R	3	<0.1
Ames Industrial Supply Co	4516 Brazil St	Los Angeles	CA	90039	LH Brown	818-240-9313	R	2	<0.1
Hawkins Indust Resource Corp	PO Box 2631	Muncie	IN	47032	Darryal E Hawkins	317-288-2489	R	0	<0.1
Technic Equipment Corp	540 Rte 10	Randolph	NJ	07869	Bradford C Smith	201-882-0633	R	0*	<0.1
Dow Corning STI	47799 Halyard Dr	Plymouth	MI	48170	Joel A Hickey	313-459-7792	D	0*	0.2

Source: *Ward's Business Directory of U.S. Private and Public Companies*, Volumes 1 and 2, 1996. The company type code used is as follows: P - Public, R - Private, S - Subsidiary, D - Division, J - Joint Venture, A - Affiliate, G - Group. Sales are in millions of dollars, employees are in thousands. An asterisk (*) indicates an estimated sales volume. The symbol < stands for 'less than'. Company names and addresses are truncated, in some cases, to fit into the available space.

MATERIALS CONSUMED

Material		Quantity	Delivered Cost ($ million)
Materials, ingredients, containers, and supplies		(X)	2,003.0
Styrene (100 percent basis)	mil lb	700.8	174.7
Phenol (100 percent basis)	mil lb	(D)	(D)
Other cyclic crudes and intermediates (including melamine, phthalic anhydride, and benzene)		(X)	(D)
Synthetic organic dyes, pigments, lakes, and toners (100 percent basis)	mil lb	(D)	(D)
Acrylates and methacrylates, monomers (100 percent basis)	mil lb	22.5	13.7
Alcohols, except ethyl (100 percent basis)	mil lb	(S)	0.6
Formaldehyde (100 percent HCHO)	mil lb	(D)	(D)
Rubber processing chemicals (accelerators, antioxidants, blowing agents, inhibitors, peptizers, etc.)		(X)	82.4
Vinyl acetate, monomer (100 percent basis)	mil lb	(D)	(D)
Other synthetic organic chemicals (includes acrylonitrile and cellulose acetate)		(X)	134.4
Ethylene used as a raw material or feedstock	mil lb	321.3	58.8
Propylene used as a raw material or feedstock	mil lb	640.2	93.3
Butadiene used as a raw material or feedstock	mil lb	2,690.0	446.6
Other refined petroleum products used as a raw material or feedstock	mil lb	311.7	65.2
Other hydrocarbons used as raw materials or feedstocks (including crude oil, natural gas and still gas)		(X)	(D)
Plastics resins consumed in the form of granules, pellets, powders, liquids, etc.	mil lb	62.2	26.6
Inorganic chemicals		(X)	89.1
Carbon black	mil lb	179.2	29.4
Paper and paperboard containers, including shipping sacks and other paper packaging supplies		(X)	58.0
All other materials and components, parts, containers, and supplies		(X)	524.4
Materials, ingredients, containers, and supplies, nsk		(X)	19.8

Source: 1992 *Economic Census*. Explanation of symbols used: (D): Withheld to avoid disclosure of competitive data; na: Not available; (S): Withheld because statistical norms were not met; (X): Not applicable; (Z): Less than half the unit shown; nec: Not elsewhere classified; nsk: Not specified by kind; - : zero; * : 10-19 percent estimated; ** : 20-29 percent estimated.

PRODUCT SHARE DETAILS

Product or Product Class	% Share	Product or Product Class	% Share
Synthetic rubber (vulcanizable elastomers)	100.00	Stereo polybutadiene elastomers, including latex	9.15
Styrene-butadiene rubber (SBR), except latex	16.89	Ethylene-propylene elastomers, including latex	14.11
Styrene-butadiene rubber (SBR), latex	8.72	Silicone elastomers	10.44
Nitrile rubber, including latex	4.22	Other synthetic rubber (vulcanizable elastomers), except thermoplastic elastomers, including latex	7.07
Butyl, polychloroprene, and stereo polyisoprene elastomers, including latex	14.81	Thermoplastic elastomers	13.43

Source: 1992 *Economic Census*. The values shown are percent of total shipments in an industry. Values of indented subcategories are summed in the main heading. The symbol (D) appears when data are withheld to prevent disclosure of competitive information. The abbreviation nsk stands for 'not specified by kind' and nec for 'not elsewhere classified'.

INPUTS AND OUTPUTS FOR SYNTHETIC RUBBER

Economic Sector or Industry Providing Inputs	%	Sector	Economic Sector or Industry Buying Outputs	%	Sector
Cyclic crudes and organics	54.0	Manufg.	Tires & inner tubes	29.7	Manufg.
Imports	8.8	Foreign	Fabricated rubber products, nec	16.8	Manufg.
Gas production & distribution (utilities)	4.4	Util.	Exports	15.3	Foreign
Wholesale trade	4.2	Trade	Miscellaneous plastics products	9.3	Manufg.
Industrial inorganic chemicals, nec	3.4	Manufg.	Paper mills, except building paper	5.7	Manufg.
Electric services (utilities)	2.7	Util.	Floor coverings	5.2	Manufg.
Lubricating oils & greases	2.5	Manufg.	Rubber & plastics hose & belting	3.8	Manufg.
Carbon black	1.8	Manufg.	Adhesives & sealants	2.3	Manufg.
Surface active agents	1.8	Manufg.	Gaskets, packing & sealing devices	2.3	Manufg.
Petroleum refining	1.5	Manufg.	Nonferrous wire drawing & insulating	1.8	Manufg.
Alkalies & chlorine	1.1	Manufg.	Paperboard mills	1.3	Manufg.
Railroads & related services	1.1	Util.	Plastics materials & resins	1.0	Manufg.
Motor freight transportation & warehousing	0.9	Util.	Sporting & athletic goods, nec	0.9	Manufg.
Water transportation	0.9	Util.	Rubber & plastics footwear	0.7	Manufg.
Advertising	0.9	Services	Paints & allied products	0.6	Manufg.
Pumps & compressors	0.8	Manufg.	Printing ink	0.6	Manufg.
Plastics materials & resins	0.7	Manufg.	Engraving & plate printing	0.5	Manufg.
Gum & wood chemicals	0.6	Manufg.	Chemical preparations, nec	0.4	Manufg.
Paperboard containers & boxes	0.6	Manufg.	Radio & TV communication equipment	0.4	Manufg.
Vegetable oil mills, nec	0.6	Manufg.	Storage batteries	0.4	Manufg.
Noncomparable imports	0.6	Foreign	Mineral wool	0.3	Manufg.
Paints & allied products	0.5	Manufg.	Narrow fabric mills	0.3	Manufg.
Soap & other detergents	0.5	Manufg.	Tire cord & fabric	0.3	Manufg.
Engineering, architectural, & surveying services	0.5	Services			
Maintenance of nonfarm buildings nec	0.4	Constr.			
Miscellaneous repair shops	0.4	Services			
Chemical preparations, nec	0.3	Manufg.			
Communications, except radio & TV	0.3	Util.			
Equipment rental & leasing services	0.3	Services			
Coal	0.2	Mining			
Metal cans	0.2	Manufg.			
Air transportation	0.2	Util.			
Water supply & sewage systems	0.2	Util.			
Eating & drinking places	0.2	Trade			
Banking	0.2	Fin/R.E.			
Automotive repair shops & services	0.2	Services			
Sanitary services, steam supply, irrigation	0.1	Util.			
Real estate	0.1	Fin/R.E.			
Royalties	0.1	Fin/R.E.			
U.S. Postal Service	0.1	Gov't			

Source: Benchmark Input-Output Accounts for the U.S. Economy, 1982, U.S. Department of Commerce, Washington, D.C., July 1991. Data, as reported in the source, are organized by the 1977 SIC structure in use in 1982 but have been matched, as closely as is possible, to the 1987 SIC structure used in this book.

OCCUPATIONS EMPLOYED BY SIC 282 - PLASTICS MATERIALS AND SYNTHETICS

Occupation	% of Total 1994	Change to 2005	Occupation	% of Total 1994	Change to 2005
Chemical equipment controllers, operators	8.7	-16.4	Machine operators nec	1.8	-26.3
Extruding & forming machine workers	7.9	46.3	Helpers, laborers, & material movers nec	1.4	-16.4
Textile draw-out & winding machine operators	5.6	12.8	Packaging & filling machine operators	1.4	-16.4
Blue collar worker supervisors	5.4	-19.5	General office clerks	1.3	-28.7
Science & mathematics technicians	4.2	-16.4	Chemists	1.3	-16.4
Chemical plant & system operators	3.7	-16.4	General managers & top executives	1.2	-20.7
Secretaries, ex legal & medical	2.9	-23.9	Electricians	1.2	-21.5
Industrial machinery mechanics	2.8	-8.1	Management support workers nec	1.2	-16.4
Chemical engineers	2.7	-16.4	Mechanical engineers	1.2	-8.0
Inspectors, testers, & graders, precision	2.7	-16.4	Crushing & mixing machine operators	1.2	-16.4
Maintenance repairers, general utility	2.6	-24.8	Managers & administrators nec	1.1	-16.5
Sales & related workers nec	2.4	-16.4	Industrial production managers	1.1	-16.4
Textile machine setters & set-up operators	1.9	-58.2	Engineering technicians & technologists nec	1.0	-16.4

Source: Industry-Occupation Matrix, Bureau of Labor Statistics. These data relate to one or more 3-digit SIC industry groups rather than to a single 4-digit SIC. The change reported for each occupation to the year 2005 is a percent of growth or decline as estimated by the Bureau of Labor Statistics. The abbreviation nec stands for 'not elsewhere classified'.

LOCATION BY STATE AND REGIONAL CONCENTRATION

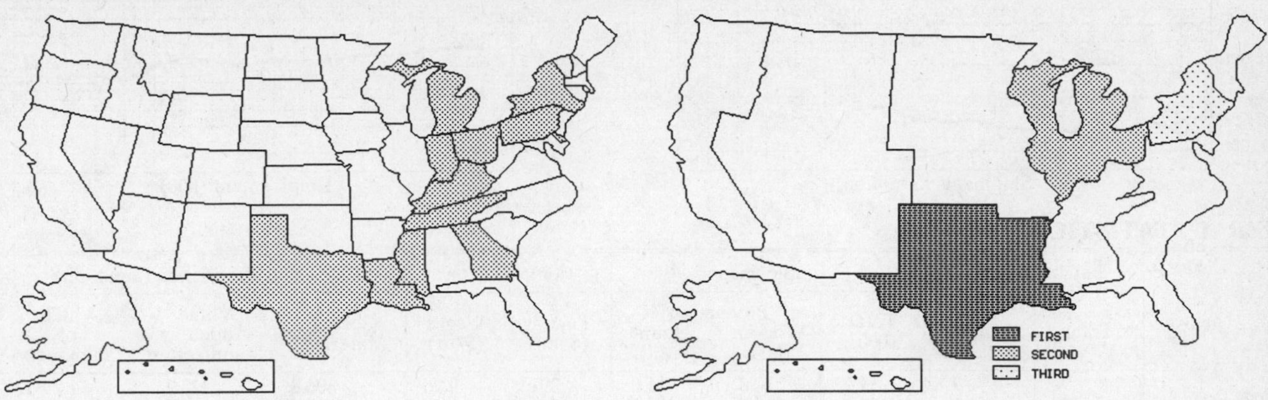

INDUSTRY DATA BY STATE

State	Establish-ments	Shipments			Employment				Cost as % of Shipments	Investment per Employee ($)
		Total ($ mil)	% of U.S.	Per Establ.	Total Number	% of U.S.	Per Establ.	Wages ($/hour)		
Louisiana	5	781.6	18.7	156.3	1,900	16.2	380	21.33	52.7	21,684
Michigan	6	134.2	3.2	22.4	500	4.3	83	15.00	42.2	-
Texas	14	(D)	-	-	3,750 *	32.1	268	-	-	-
New York	5	(D)	-	-	1,750 *	15.0	350	-	-	-
Ohio	5	(D)	-	-	750 *	6.4	150	-	-	-
Pennsylvania	4	(D)	-	-	375 *	3.2	94	-	-	-
Georgia	3	(D)	-	-	175 *	1.5	58	-	-	-
Indiana	3	(D)	-	-	175 *	1.5	58	-	-	1,714
Delaware	2	(D)	-	-	375 *	3.2	188	-	-	-
Kentucky	2	(D)	-	-	750 *	6.4	375	-	-	-
Mississippi	2	(D)	-	-	375 *	3.2	188	-	-	-
Tennessee	2	(D)	-	-	175 *	1.5	88	-	-	-

Source: 1992 *Economic Census.* The states are in descending order of shipments or establishments (if shipment data are missing for the majority). The symbol (D) appears when data are withheld to prevent disclosure of competitive information. States marked with (D) are sorted by number of establishments. A dash (-) indicates that the data element cannot be calculated; * indicates the midpoint of a range.

2823 - CELLULOSIC MANMADE FIBERS

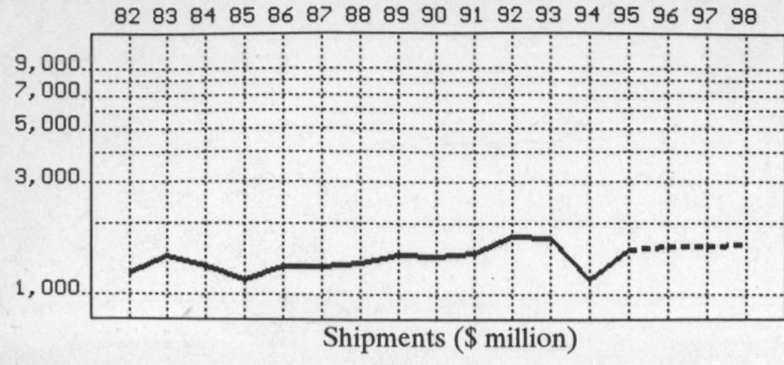

Shipments ($ million)

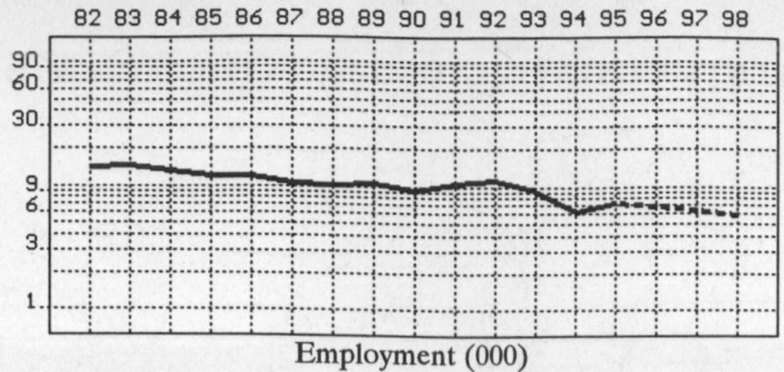

Employment (000)

GENERAL STATISTICS

Year	Com-panies	Establishments		Employment			Compensation		Production ($ million)			
		Total	with 20 or more employees	Total (000)	Production Workers (000)	Production Hours (Mil)	Payroll ($ mil)	Wages ($/hr)	Cost of Materials	Value Added by Manufacture	Value of Shipments	Capital Invest.
1982	5	9	9	14.2	10.8	21.0	291.0	9.26	806.8	428.7	1,239.9	88.4
1983		12	9	14.4	10.7	21.1	311.0	9.38	934.1	522.7	1,445.0	44.4
1984		15	9	13.3	10.0	19.7	320.9	10.77	813.1	489.3	1,307.2	
1985		18	9	12.1	9.0	18.4	311.3	10.84	744.7	390.2	1,148.1	43.3
1986		18	9	12.0	9.0	18.3	314.4	10.95	713.2	615.7	1,321.8	54.9
1987	6	7	7	10.5	7.9	16.5	280.7	10.95	669.7	636.7	1,319.7	23.8
1988		10	7	10.2	7.7	16.9	287.1	10.74	737.4	614.9	1,352.4	113.2
1989		9	7	10.5	7.6	15.8	297.2	11.63	786.0	690.0	1,469.4	104.9
1990		10	9	9.3	7.2	15.0	302.4	12.28	786.3	679.0	1,456.7	71.5
1991		13	10	10.5	7.7	15.6	349.1	13.50	818.3	696.6	1,496.7	105.3
1992	5	7	7	11.0	7.8	16.7	372.8	13.11	950.3	820.9	1,748.1	92.8
1993		10	7	9.3	7.2	15.4	301.2	13.23	800.8	944.7	1,744.6	207.5
1994		9P	7P	6.2	5.0	10.7	181.7	11.91	426.9	718.1	1,153.5	137.5
1995		9P	7P	7.5P	5.6P	12.5P	286.6P	13.57P	578.1P	972.5P	1,562.1P	
1996		8P	7P	7.0P	5.2P	11.8P	284.4P	13.88P	586.7P	986.9P	1,585.2P	
1997		8P	7P	6.4P	4.9P	11.2P	282.2P	14.19P	595.2P	1,001.3P	1,608.4P	
1998		7P	7P	5.9P	4.5P	10.5P	280.1P	14.49P	603.8P	1,015.7P	1,631.5P	

Sources: 1982, 1987, 1992 *Economic Census*; *Annual Survey of Manufactures*, 83-86, 88-91, 93-94. Establishment counts for non-Census years are from *County Business Patterns*; establishment values for 83-84 are extrapolations. 'P's show projections by the editors. Industries reclassified in 87 will not have data for prior years.

INDICES OF CHANGE

Year	Com-panies	Establishments		Employment			Compensation		Production ($ million)			
		Total	with 20 or more employees	Total (000)	Production Workers (000)	Production Hours (Mil)	Payroll ($ mil)	Wages ($/hr)	Cost of Materials	Value Added by Manufacture	Value of Shipments	Capital Invest.
1982	100	129	129	129	138	126	78	71	85	52	71	95
1983		171	129	131	137	126	83	72	98	64	83	48
1984		214	129	121	128	118	86	82	86	60	75	
1985		257	129	110	115	110	84	83	78	48	66	47
1986		257	129	109	115	110	84	84	75	75	76	59
1987	120	100	100	95	101	99	75	84	70	78	75	26
1988		143	100	93	99	101	77	82	78	75	77	122
1989		129	100	95	97	95	80	89	83	84	84	113
1990		143	129	85	92	90	81	94	83	83	83	77
1991		186	143	95	99	93	94	103	86	85	86	113
1992	100	100	100	100	100	100	100	100	100	100	100	100
1993		143	100	85	92	92	81	101	84	115	100	224
1994		128P	105P	56	64	64	49	91	45	87	66	148
1995		122P	103P	68P	72P	75P	77P	104P	61P	118P	89P	
1996		117P	101P	63P	67P	71P	76P	106P	62P	120P	91P	
1997		111P	99P	59P	62P	67P	76P	108P	63P	122P	92P	
1998		106P	97P	54P	58P	63P	75P	111P	64P	124P	93P	

Sources: Same as General Statistics. Values reflect change from the base year, 1992. Values above 100 mean greater than 92, values below 100 mean less than 92, and a value of 100 in the 82-91 or 93-98 period means same as 92. 'P's mark projections by the editors.

SELECTED RATIOS

For 1994	Avg. of All Manufact.	Analyzed Industry	Index	For 1994	Avg. of All Manufact.	Analyzed Industry	Index
Employees per Establishment	49	692	1,413	Value Added per Production Worker	134,084	143,620	107
Payroll per Establishment	1,500,273	20,291,371	1,353	Cost per Establishment	5,045,178	47,674,112	945
Payroll per Employee	30,620	29,306	96	Cost per Employee	102,970	68,855	67
Production Workers per Establishment	34	558	1,627	Cost per Production Worker	146,988	85,380	58
Wages per Establishment	853,319	14,231,543	1,668	Shipments per Establishment	9,576,895	128,817,259	1,345
Wages per Production Worker	24,861	25,487	103	Shipments per Employee	195,460	186,048	95
Hours per Production Worker	2,056	2,140	104	Shipments per Production Worker	279,017	230,700	83
Wages per Hour	12.09	11.91	98	Investment per Establishment	321,011	15,355,330	4,783
Value Added per Establishment	4,602,255	80,193,909	1,742	Investment per Employee	6,552	22,177	338
Value Added per Employee	93,930	115,823	123	Investment per Production Worker	9,352	27,500	294

Sources: Same as General Statistics. The 'Average of All Manufacturing' column represents the average of all manufacturing industries reported for the most recent complete year available. The Index shows the relationship between the Average and the Analyzed Industry. For example, 100 means that they are equal; 500 that the Analyzed Industry is five times the average; 50 means that the Analyzed Industry is half the national average. The abbreviation 'na' is used to show that data are 'not available'.

LEADING COMPANIES

Number shown: **8** Total sales ($ mil): **461** Total employment (000): **4.2**

Company Name	Address				CEO Name	Phone	Co. Type	Sales ($ mil)	Empl. (000)
American Filtrona Corp	PO Box 31640	Richmond	VA	23233	John L Morgan	804-346-2400	P	149	1.1
Lenzing Fibers Corp	6100 Fairview #300	Charlotte	NC	28210	Mikel Dodd	704-551-1400	S	120	0.6
North American Rayon Corp	W Elk Av	Elizabethton	TN	37643	CK Green	615-542-2141	R	80	1.4
Janesville Products	156 S Norwalk Rd	Norwalk	OH	44857	MM Gubesch	419-668-4474	D	49	0.6
Mann Industries Inc	PO Box 919	Williamsburg	VA	23187	Joe Mann	804-888-8000	R	27*	0.3
Spontex Inc	PO Box 561	Columbia	TN	38402	HH Leavitt	615-388-5632	S	20	0.1
Cellusede Products Inc	500 N Madison St	Rockford	IL	61107	H Anaszenicz	815-964-8619	R	9	<0.1
WC Redmon Company Inc	PO Box 7	Peru	IN	46970	Peter Redmon	317-473-6683	R	7	0.1

Source: *Ward's Business Directory of U.S. Private and Public Companies*, Volumes 1 and 2, 1996. The company type code used is as follows: P - Public, R - Private, S - Subsidiary, D - Division, J - Joint Venture, A - Affiliate, G - Group. Sales are in millions of dollars, employees are in thousands. An asterisk (*) indicates an estimated sales volume. The symbol < stands for 'less than'. Company names and addresses are truncated, in some cases, to fit into the available space.

MATERIALS CONSUMED

Material		Quantity	Delivered Cost ($ million)
Materials, ingredients, containers, and supplies		(X)	842.9
Glycols (ethylene, propylene, etc.) (100 percent basis)	mil lb	(D)	(D)
Dimethyl terephthalate (DMT) (100 percent basis)	mil lb	(D)	(D)
Terephthalic acid (TPA) (100 percent basis)	mil lb	(D)	(D)
All other synthetic organic chemicals		(X)	(D)
Polypropylene resins (dry basis)	mil lb	(D)	(D)
Nylon resins (dry basis)	mil lb	(D)	(D)
All other plastics resins (dry basis)	mil lb	(D)	(D)
Woodpulp (air dry basis)	1,000 s tons	(D)	(D)
Paper and paperboard containers, including shipping sacks and other paper packaging supplies		(X)	(D)
All other materials and components, parts, containers, and supplies		(X)	(D)

Source: 1992 *Economic Census*. Explanation of symbols used: (D): Withheld to avoid disclosure of competitive data; na: Not available; (S): Withheld because statistical norms were not met; (X): Not applicable; (Z): Less than half the unit shown; nec: Not elsewhere classified; nsk: Not specified by kind; - : zero; * : 10-19 percent estimated; ** : 20-29 percent estimated.

PRODUCT SHARE DETAILS

Product or Product Class	% Share	Product or Product Class	% Share
Cellulosic manmade fibers	100.00		

Source: 1992 *Economic Census*. The values shown are percent of total shipments in an industry. Values of indented subcategories are summed in the main heading. The symbol (D) appears when data are withheld to prevent disclosure of competitive information. The abbreviation nsk stands for 'not specified by kind' and nec for 'not elsewhere classified'.

INPUTS AND OUTPUTS FOR CELLULOSIC MANMADE FIBERS

Economic Sector or Industry Providing Inputs	%	Sector	Economic Sector or Industry Buying Outputs	%	Sector
Pulp mills	40.7	Manufg.	Broadwoven fabric mills	40.5	Manufg.
Coal	6.5	Mining	Knit fabric mills	19.4	Manufg.
Wholesale trade	5.3	Trade	Nonwoven fabrics	9.3	Manufg.
Industrial inorganic chemicals, nec	4.5	Manufg.	Yarn mills & finishing of textiles, nec	8.8	Manufg.
Railroads & related services	4.1	Util.	Narrow fabric mills	7.9	Manufg.
Gas production & distribution (utilities)	4.0	Util.	Exports	3.5	Foreign
Yarn mills & finishing of textiles, nec	3.7	Manufg.	Organic fibers, noncellulosic	2.7	Manufg.
Cyclic crudes and organics	3.5	Manufg.	Thread mills	2.2	Manufg.
Imports	3.5	Foreign	Knit underwear mills	1.8	Manufg.
Electric services (utilities)	2.8	Util.	Floor coverings	1.1	Manufg.
Engineering, architectural, & surveying services	2.2	Services	Housefurnishings, nec	0.7	Manufg.
Miscellaneous repair shops	2.0	Services	Miscellaneous plastics products	0.7	Manufg.
Petroleum refining	1.5	Manufg.	Tire cord & fabric	0.7	Manufg.
Motor freight transportation & warehousing	1.5	Util.	Fabricated textile products, nec	0.3	Manufg.
Paperboard containers & boxes	1.2	Manufg.	Knit outerwear mills	0.2	Manufg.
Maintenance of nonfarm buildings nec	1.1	Constr.	Cellulosic manmade fibers	0.1	Manufg.
Water supply & sewage systems	1.1	Util.	Federal Government purchases, national defense	0.1	Fed Govt
Communications, except radio & TV	1.0	Util.			
Eating & drinking places	0.9	Trade			
Equipment rental & leasing services	0.7	Services			
Soap & other detergents	0.6	Manufg.			
Alkalies & chlorine	0.5	Manufg.			
Machinery, except electrical, nec	0.5	Manufg.			
Water transportation	0.5	Util.			

Continued on next page.

INPUTS AND OUTPUTS FOR CELLULOSIC MANMADE FIBERS - Continued

Economic Sector or Industry Providing Inputs	%	Sector	Economic Sector or Industry Buying Outputs	%	Sector
Hotels & lodging places	0.4	Services			
Legal services	0.4	Services			
Management & consulting services & labs	0.4	Services			
Lubricating oils & greases	0.3	Manufg.			
Banking	0.3	Fin/R.E.			
Automotive repair shops & services	0.3	Services			
Computer & data processing services	0.3	Services			
U.S. Postal Service	0.3	Gov't			
Broadwoven fabric mills	0.2	Manufg.			
Cellulosic manmade fibers	0.2	Manufg.			
Manifold business forms	0.2	Manufg.			
Plastics materials & resins	0.2	Manufg.			
Special dies & tools & machine tool accessories	0.2	Manufg.			
Insurance carriers	0.2	Fin/R.E.			
Accounting, auditing & bookkeeping	0.2	Services			
Automotive rental & leasing, without drivers	0.2	Services			
Noncomparable imports	0.2	Foreign			
Abrasive products	0.1	Manufg.			
Real estate	0.1	Fin/R.E.			
State & local government enterprises, nec	0.1	Gov't			

Source: Benchmark Input-Output Accounts for the U.S. Economy, 1982, U.S. Department of Commerce, Washington, D.C., July 1991. Data, as reported in the source, are organized by the 1977 SIC structure in use in 1982 but have been matched, as closely as is possible, to the 1987 SIC structure used in this book.

OCCUPATIONS EMPLOYED BY SIC 282 - PLASTICS MATERIALS AND SYNTHETICS

Occupation	% of Total 1994	Change to 2005	Occupation	% of Total 1994	Change to 2005
Chemical equipment controllers, operators	8.7	-16.4	Machine operators nec	1.8	-26.3
Extruding & forming machine workers	7.9	46.3	Helpers, laborers, & material movers nec	1.4	-16.4
Textile draw-out & winding machine operators	5.6	12.8	Packaging & filling machine operators	1.4	-16.4
Blue collar worker supervisors	5.4	-19.5	General office clerks	1.3	-28.7
Science & mathematics technicians	4.2	-16.4	Chemists	1.3	-16.4
Chemical plant & system operators	3.7	-16.4	General managers & top executives	1.2	-20.7
Secretaries, ex legal & medical	2.9	-23.9	Electricians	1.2	-21.5
Industrial machinery mechanics	2.8	-8.1	Management support workers nec	1.2	-16.4
Chemical engineers	2.7	-16.4	Mechanical engineers	1.2	-8.0
Inspectors, testers, & graders, precision	2.7	-16.4	Crushing & mixing machine operators	1.2	-16.4
Maintenance repairers, general utility	2.6	-24.8	Managers & administrators nec	1.1	-16.5
Sales & related workers nec	2.4	-16.4	Industrial production managers	1.1	-16.4
Textile machine setters & set-up operators	1.9	-58.2	Engineering technicians & technologists nec	1.0	-16.4

Source: Industry-Occupation Matrix, Bureau of Labor Statistics. These data relate to one or more 3-digit SIC industry groups rather than to a single 4-digit SIC. The change reported for each occupation to the year 2005 is a percent of growth or decline as estimated by the Bureau of Labor Statistics. The abbreviation nec stands for 'not elsewhere classified'.

LOCATION BY STATE AND REGIONAL CONCENTRATION

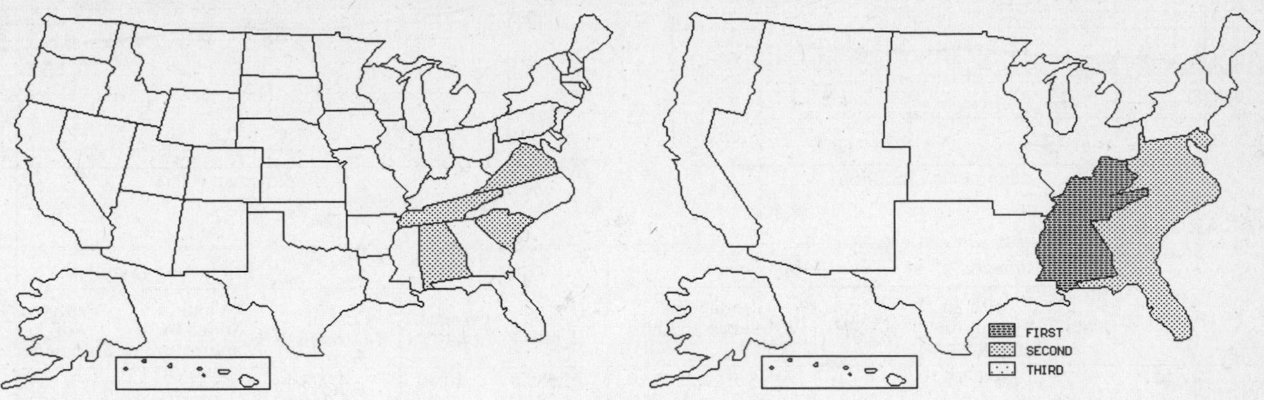

INDUSTRY DATA BY STATE

State	Establish-ments	Shipments			Employment				Cost as % of Shipments	Investment per Employee ($)
		Total ($ mil)	% of U.S.	Per Establ.	Total Number	% of U.S.	Per Establ.	Wages ($/hour)		
Tennessee	3	(D)	-	-	7,500 *	68.2	2,500	-	-	-
Alabama	2	(D)	-	-	750 *	6.8	375	-	-	-
South Carolina	1	(D)	-	-	1,750 *	15.9	1,750	-	-	-
Virginia	1	(D)	-	-	1,750 *	15.9	1,750	-	-	-

Source: 1992 *Economic Census*. The states are in descending order of shipments or establishments (if shipment data are missing for the majority). The symbol (D) appears when data are withheld to prevent disclosure of competitive information. States marked with (D) are sorted by number of establishments. A dash (-) indicates that the data element cannot be calculated; * indicates the midpoint of a range.

2824 - SYNTHETIC ORGANIC FIBERS

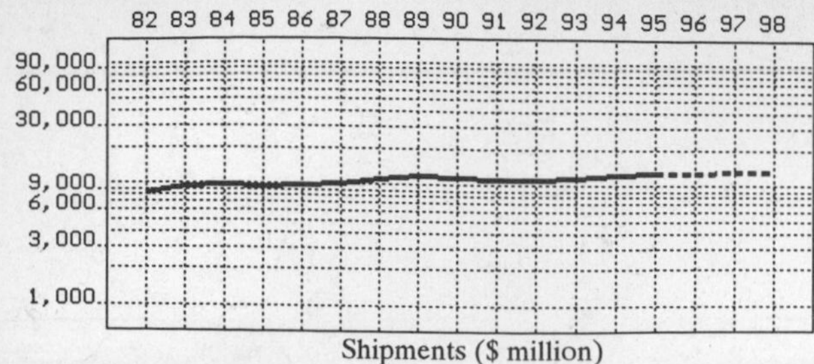

Shipments ($ million)

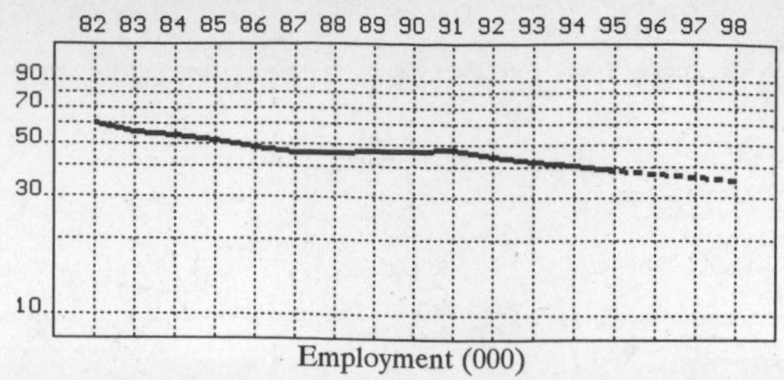

Employment (000)

GENERAL STATISTICS

Year	Com-panies	Establishments		Employment			Compensation		Production ($ million)			
		Total	with 20 or more employees	Total (000)	Production Workers (000)	Production Hours (Mil)	Payroll ($ mil)	Wages ($/hr)	Cost of Materials	Value Added by Manufacture	Value of Shipments	Capital Invest.
1982	44	71	58	60.4	43.3	80.0	1,385.5	10.90	4,973.4	3,329.7	8,287.5	443.2
1983		73	60	55.3	40.6	76.9	1,381.9	11.47	5,261.8	4,196.8	9,463.1	257.4
1984		75	62	54.1	39.8	78.0	1,438.0	11.84	5,633.6	4,367.0	9,919.9	334.9
1985		77	65	50.9	37.0	72.2	1,408.7	12.60	5,349.1	3,851.0	9,283.7	354.3
1986		76	67	48.0	35.7	70.3	1,397.8	13.14	5,371.1	4,287.4	9,676.7	461.9
1987	47	72	63	45.7	34.4	70.5	1,347.4	12.70	5,154.1	5,062.2	10,111.6	460.0
1988		81	68	45.8	34.6	69.5	1,399.2	13.34	5,514.4	5,402.9	10,930.3	632.6
1989		71	59	46.7	36.3	72.5	1,500.7	13.84	5,881.2	6,014.4	11,796.3	690.6
1990		74	62	46.3	36.1	72.7	1,539.3	13.90	5,486.6	5,930.2	11,427.1	814.7
1991		78	65	46.9	35.0	70.4	1,568.7	14.67	4,915.9	6,119.2	11,083.8	810.1
1992	42	71	68	44.4	33.9	71.1	1,545.2	14.48	5,337.1	5,662.0	11,113.7	721.3
1993		88	68	42.3	32.6	67.2	1,474.9	14.95	5,548.0	6,020.2	11,548.4	921.4
1994		79P	68P	40.7	31.6	68.3	1,417.2	14.37	5,778.9	6,436.6	12,212.6	563.9
1995		80P	68P	39.2P	31.0P	66.7P	1,523.4P	15.46P	5,879.4P	6,548.5P	12,424.9P	877.9P
1996		81P	69P	37.9P	30.2P	65.9P	1,534.4P	15.78P	6,007.6P	6,691.4P	12,696.0P	921.3P
1997		81P	69P	36.6P	29.4P	65.1P	1,545.4P	16.10P	6,135.9P	6,834.2P	12,967.1P	964.7P
1998		82P	70P	35.3P	28.7P	64.3P	1,556.4P	16.41P	6,264.2P	6,977.1P	13,238.2P	1,008.0P

Sources: 1982, 1987, 1992 *Economic Census*; *Annual Survey of Manufactures*, 83-86, 88-91, 93-94. Establishment counts for non-Census years are from *County Business Patterns*; establishment values for 83-84 are extrapolations. 'P's show projections by the editors. Industries reclassified in 87 will not have data for prior years.

INDICES OF CHANGE

Year	Com-panies	Establishments		Employment			Compensation		Production ($ million)			
		Total	with 20 or more employees	Total (000)	Production Workers (000)	Production Hours (Mil)	Payroll ($ mil)	Wages ($/hr)	Cost of Materials	Value Added by Manufacture	Value of Shipments	Capital Invest.
1982	105	100	85	136	128	113	90	75	93	59	75	61
1983		103	88	125	120	108	89	79	99	74	85	36
1984		106	91	122	117	110	93	82	106	77	89	46
1985		108	96	115	109	102	91	87	100	68	84	49
1986		107	99	108	105	99	90	91	101	76	87	64
1987	112	101	93	103	101	99	87	88	97	89	91	64
1988		114	100	103	102	98	91	92	103	95	98	88
1989		100	87	105	107	102	97	96	110	106	106	96
1990		104	91	104	106	102	100	96	103	105	103	113
1991		110	96	106	103	99	102	101	92	108	100	112
1992	100	100	100	100	100	100	100	100	100	100	100	100
1993		124	100	95	96	95	95	103	104	106	104	128
1994		112P	99P	92	93	96	92	99	108	114	110	78
1995		113P	100P	88P	91P	94P	99P	107P	110P	116P	112P	122P
1996		114P	101P	85P	89P	93P	99P	109P	113P	118P	114P	128P
1997		114P	102P	82P	87P	92P	100P	111P	115P	121P	117P	134P
1998		115P	103P	79P	85P	90P	101P	113P	117P	123P	119P	140P

Sources: Same as General Statistics. Values reflect change from the base year, 1992. Values above 100 mean greater than 92, values below 100 mean less than 92, and a value of 100 in the 82-91 or 93-98 period means same as 92. 'P's mark projections by the editors.

SELECTED RATIOS

For 1994	Avg. of All Manufact.	Analyzed Industry	Index
Employees per Establishment	49	512	1,046
Payroll per Establishment	1,500,273	17,843,419	1,189
Payroll per Employee	30,620	34,821	114
Production Workers per Establishment	34	398	1,159
Wages per Establishment	853,319	12,357,323	1,448
Wages per Production Worker	24,861	31,059	125
Hours per Production Worker	2,056	2,161	105
Wages per Hour	12.09	14.37	119
Value Added per Establishment	4,602,255	81,040,748	1,761
Value Added per Employee	93,930	158,147	168

For 1994	Avg. of All Manufact.	Analyzed Industry	Index
Value Added per Production Worker	134,084	203,690	152
Cost per Establishment	5,045,178	72,759,901	1,442
Cost per Employee	102,970	141,988	138
Cost per Production Worker	146,988	182,877	124
Shipments per Establishment	9,576,895	153,764,136	1,606
Shipments per Employee	195,460	300,064	154
Shipments per Production Worker	279,017	386,475	139
Investment per Establishment	321,011	7,099,847	2,212
Investment per Employee	6,552	13,855	211
Investment per Production Worker	9,352	17,845	191

Sources: Same as General Statistics. The 'Average of All Manufacturing' column represents the average of all manufacturing industries reported for the most recent complete year available. The Index shows the relationship between the Average and the Analyzed Industry. For example, 100 means that they are equal; 500 that the Analyzed Industry is five times the average; 50 means that the Analyzed Industry is half the national average. The abbreviation 'na' is used to show that data are 'not available'.

LEADING COMPANIES Number shown: 20 Total sales ($ mil): 7,744 Total employment (000): 29.4

Company Name	Address				CEO Name	Phone	Co. Type	Sales ($ mil)	Empl. (000)
Hoechst Celanese Corp	PO Box 32414	Charlotte	NC	28232	Joseph Patterson	704-554-2000	D	3,104	11.2
AlliedSignal Inc	PO Box 31	Petersburg	VA	23804	David C Hill	804-520-3000	D	1,750	5.0
Hoechst Celanese Corp	3 Park Av	New York	NY	10016	Don Lehman	212-251-8000	D	1,210*	5.4
Wellman Inc	1040 Broad St	Shrewsbury	NJ	07702	Thomas M Duff	908-542-7300	P	842	3.6
Alice Manufacturing Company	PO Box 369	Easley	SC	29641	ES McKissick	803-859-6323	R	420	1.8
William Barnet and Son Inc	PO Box 131	Arcadia	SC	29320	William Barnet III	803-576-7154	D	100	0.6
Camac Corp	14401 Industrial Pk	Bristol	VA	24203	Art Roth	703-669-1161	S	76	0.4
Georgia Bonded Fibers Inc	15 Nuttman St	Newark	NJ	07103	Hugo N Surmonte	201-642-3547	P	48	0.2
Textileather Corp	PO Box 875	Toledo	OH	43696	Stephen P Walko	419-729-3731	R	40	0.3
Zeeland Chemicals Inc	215 N Centennial St	Zeeland	MI	49464	Robert M Parlman	616-772-2193	S	30	0.1
Clean Rite Products Co	PO Box 43526	Atlanta	GA	30336	Jeff Rittenbaum	404-691-7133	R	27	0.1
Dianal America Inc	9675 Bayport Blv	Pasadena	TX	77507	Hideki Ando	713-474-7777	S	20	<0.1
Hobbs Industries	PO Box 640	Groesbeck	TX	76642	Ray Varner	817-729-3223	D	18	0.1
Carter Moore and Company Inc	275 Madison Av	New York	NY	10016	AA Shasha	212-736-8879	R	12	0.1
Fibres South Inc	PO Box 189	Trussville	AL	35173	Enrico Merli	205-655-8817	R	12	<0.1
Interplast Universal Industries	PO Box 40	Lodi	NJ	07644	D Goldman	201-471-4100	R	11*	<0.1
American Micrell Inc	PO Box 369	Blacksburg	SC	29702	Franco Tajana	803-839-3042	S	10	<0.1
Western Synthetic Felt Co	PO Box 6248	Carson	CA	90749	David Linder	310-767-1000	D	10	0.1
Remington Group	5413 S Downey Rd	Vernon	CA	90058	Michelle Lewis	213-749-9291	R	3	<0.1
Fibre Fabricators Inc	PO Box 40	Spring Grove	IL	60081	Robert F Schuehle	815-675-6464	R	1	<0.1

Source: *Ward's Business Directory of U.S. Private and Public Companies*, Volumes 1 and 2, 1996. The company type code used is as follows: P - Public, R - Private, S - Subsidiary, D - Division, J - Joint Venture, A - Affiliate, G - Group. Sales are in millions of dollars, employees are in thousands. An asterisk (*) indicates an estimated sales volume. The symbol < stands for 'less than'. Company names and addresses are truncated, in some cases, to fit into the available space.

MATERIALS CONSUMED

Material		Quantity	Delivered Cost ($ million)
Materials, ingredients, containers, and supplies		(X)	4,754.2
Acrylonitrile (100 percent basis)	mil lb	(D)	(D)
Caprolactam (100 percent basis)	mil lb	(D)	(D)
Glycols (ethylene, propylene, etc.) (100 percent basis)	mil lb	1,845.5	413.4
Dimethyl terephthalate (DMT) (100 percent basis)	mil lb	1,148.9	273.0
Terephthalic acid (TPA) (100 percent basis)	mil lb	1,901.9	478.2
All other synthetic organic chemicals		(X)	1,300.5
Polypropylene resins (dry basis)	mil lb	804.9**	278.6
Nylon resins (dry basis)	mil lb	322.9	166.9
All other plastics resins (dry basis)	mil lb	(S)	141.2
Woodpulp (air dry basis)	1,000 s tons	(D)	(D)
Paper and paperboard containers, including shipping sacks and other paper packaging supplies		(X)	92.0
All other materials and components, parts, containers, and supplies		(X)	960.0
Materials, ingredients, containers, and supplies, nsk		(X)	15.5

Source: 1992 *Economic Census*. Explanation of symbols used: (D): Withheld to avoid disclosure of competitive data; na: Not available; (S): Withheld because statistical norms were not met; (X): Not applicable; (Z): Less than half the unit shown; nec: Not elsewhere classified; nsk: Not specified by kind; - : zero; * : 10-19 percent estimated; ** : 20-29 percent estimated.

PRODUCT SHARE DETAILS

Product or Product Class	% Share	Product or Product Class	% Share
Manmade organic fibers, noncellulosic	100.00	Other noncellulosic manmade fibers (except glass, carbon, and graphite)	12.71
Nylon and other polyamide fibers	24.44	Producer textured noncellulosic manmade fibers	27.12
Polyolefin fibers	2.45	Nylon and other polyamide producer textured fibers	78.10
Polyester fibers	33.22	Polyester producer textured fibers	(D)
Industrial polyester yarn, including strip	22.11	Polyolefin producer textured fibers	18.15
Polyester textile yarn, including strip	29.44	Other noncellulosic manmade producer textured fibers	(D)
Polyester fiberfill staple and tow	24.92	Manmade organic fibers, noncellulosic, nsk	0.06
Other polyester staple and tow	22.77		
Polyester fiber salable waste	0.76		

Source: 1992 *Economic Census*. The values shown are percent of total shipments in an industry. Values of indented subcategories are summed in the main heading. The symbol (D) appears when data are withheld to prevent disclosure of competitive information. The abbreviation nsk stands for 'not specified by kind' and nec for 'not elsewhere classified'.

INPUTS AND OUTPUTS FOR ORGANIC FIBERS, NONCELLULOSIC

Economic Sector or Industry Providing Inputs	%	Sector	Economic Sector or Industry Buying Outputs	%	Sector
Cyclic crudes and organics	53.3	Manufg.	Yarn mills & finishing of textiles, nec	29.2	Manufg.
Plastics materials & resins	6.4	Manufg.	Broadwoven fabric mills	18.2	Manufg.
Wholesale trade	6.0	Trade	Floor coverings	15.4	Manufg.
Electric services (utilities)	5.1	Util.	Exports	12.8	Foreign
Imports	2.3	Foreign	Knit fabric mills	7.7	Manufg.
Miscellaneous plastics products	2.2	Manufg.	Tire cord & fabric	5.6	Manufg.
Paperboard containers & boxes	2.0	Manufg.	Women's hosiery, except socks	3.0	Manufg.
Gas production & distribution (utilities)	2.0	Util.	Nonwoven fabrics	2.5	Manufg.
Industrial inorganic chemicals, nec	1.7	Manufg.	Hosiery, nec	1.0	Manufg.
Petroleum refining	1.4	Manufg.	Cordage & twine	0.8	Manufg.
Railroads & related services	1.3	Util.	Thread mills	0.8	Manufg.
Advertising	1.3	Services	Knit underwear mills	0.7	Manufg.
Motor freight transportation & warehousing	1.2	Util.	Narrow fabric mills	0.7	Manufg.
Engineering, architectural, & surveying services	1.2	Services	Housefurnishings, nec	0.6	Manufg.
Coal	1.1	Mining	Knit outerwear mills	0.6	Manufg.
Miscellaneous repair shops	0.8	Services	Fabricated textile products, nec	0.1	Manufg.
Nitrogenous & phosphatic fertilizers	0.7	Manufg.			
Cellulosic manmade fibers	0.6	Manufg.			
Yarn mills & finishing of textiles, nec	0.6	Manufg.			
Communications, except radio & TV	0.6	Util.			
Maintenance of nonfarm buildings nec	0.5	Constr.			
Chemical preparations, nec	0.5	Manufg.			
Water transportation	0.5	Util.			
Eating & drinking places	0.5	Trade			
Pulp mills	0.4	Manufg.			
Surface active agents	0.4	Manufg.			
Equipment rental & leasing services	0.4	Services			
Crude petroleum & natural gas	0.3	Mining			
Machinery, except electrical, nec	0.3	Manufg.			
Soap & other detergents	0.3	Manufg.			
Sanitary services, steam supply, irrigation	0.3	Util.			
Water supply & sewage systems	0.3	Util.			
Banking	0.3	Fin/R.E.			
Hotels & lodging places	0.3	Services			
Noncomparable imports	0.3	Foreign			
Alkalies & chlorine	0.2	Manufg.			
Broadwoven fabric mills	0.2	Manufg.			
Lubricating oils & greases	0.2	Manufg.			
Royalties	0.2	Fin/R.E.			
Computer & data processing services	0.2	Services			
Legal services	0.2	Services			
Management & consulting services & labs	0.2	Services			
Organic fibers, noncellulosic	0.1	Manufg.			
Special dies & tools & machine tool accessories	0.1	Manufg.			
Insurance carriers	0.1	Fin/R.E.			
Accounting, auditing & bookkeeping	0.1	Services			

Source: Benchmark Input-Output Accounts for the U.S. Economy, 1982, U.S. Department of Commerce, Washington, D.C., July 1991. Data, as reported in the source, are organized by the 1977 SIC structure in use in 1982 but have been matched, as closely as is possible, to the 1987 SIC structure used in this book.

OCCUPATIONS EMPLOYED BY SIC 282 - PLASTICS MATERIALS AND SYNTHETICS

Occupation	% of Total 1994	Change to 2005	Occupation	% of Total 1994	Change to 2005
Chemical equipment controllers, operators	8.7	-16.4	Machine operators nec	1.8	-26.3
Extruding & forming machine workers	7.9	46.3	Helpers, laborers, & material movers nec	1.4	-16.4
Textile draw-out & winding machine operators	5.6	12.8	Packaging & filling machine operators	1.4	-16.4
Blue collar worker supervisors	5.4	-19.5	General office clerks	1.3	-28.7
Science & mathematics technicians	4.2	-16.4	Chemists	1.3	-16.4
Chemical plant & system operators	3.7	-16.4	General managers & top executives	1.2	-20.7
Secretaries, ex legal & medical	2.9	-23.9	Electricians	1.2	-21.5
Industrial machinery mechanics	2.8	-8.1	Management support workers nec	1.2	-16.4
Chemical engineers	2.7	-16.4	Mechanical engineers	1.2	-8.0
Inspectors, testers, & graders, precision	2.7	-16.4	Crushing & mixing machine operators	1.2	-16.4
Maintenance repairers, general utility	2.6	-24.8	Managers & administrators nec	1.1	-16.5
Sales & related workers nec	2.4	-16.4	Industrial production managers	1.1	-16.4
Textile machine setters & set-up operators	1.9	-58.2	Engineering technicians & technologists nec	1.0	-16.4

Source: Industry-Occupation Matrix, Bureau of Labor Statistics. These data relate to one or more 3-digit SIC industry groups rather than to a single 4-digit SIC. The change reported for each occupation to the year 2005 is a percent of growth or decline as estimated by the Bureau of Labor Statistics. The abbreviation nec stands for 'not elsewhere classified'.

LOCATION BY STATE AND REGIONAL CONCENTRATION

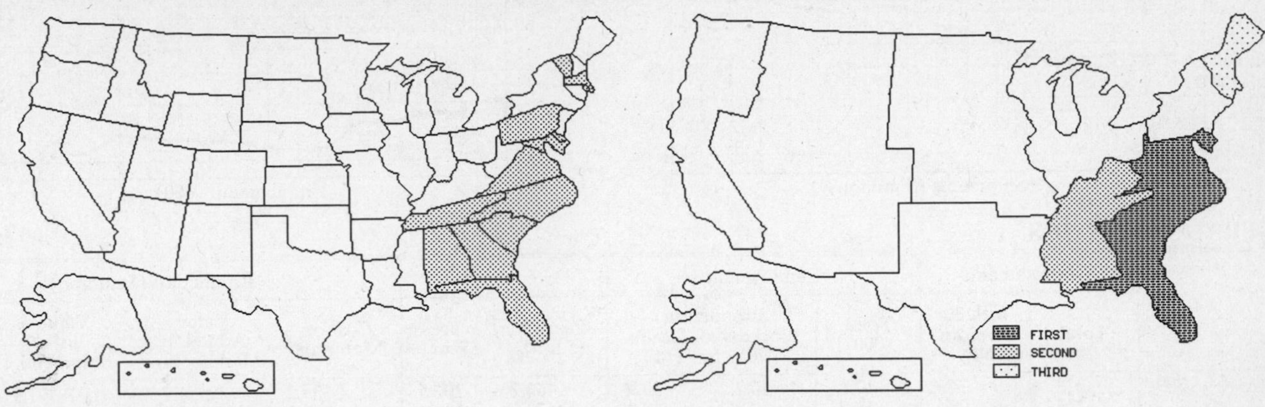

INDUSTRY DATA BY STATE

State	Establish-ments	Shipments			Employment				Cost as % of Shipments	Investment per Employee ($)
		Total ($ mil)	% of U.S.	Per Establ.	Total Number	% of U.S.	Per Establ.	Wages ($/hour)		
South Carolina	18	3,161.7	28.4	175.6	11,900	26.8	661	13.67	50.5	15,782
North Carolina	14	2,550.7	23.0	182.2	9,200	20.7	657	13.90	46.6	19,087
Alabama	5	730.0	6.6	146.0	3,000	6.8	600	10.36	56.4	-
Virginia	9	(D)	-	-	7,500 *	16.9	833	-	-	-
Georgia	6	(D)	-	-	1,750 *	3.9	292	-	-	11,543
Tennessee	6	(D)	-	-	3,750 *	8.4	625	-	-	-
Florida	2	(D)	-	-	1,750 *	3.9	875	-	-	-
Massachusetts	2	(D)	-	-	750 *	1.7	375	-	-	-
Delaware	1	(D)	-	-	1,750 *	3.9	1,750	-	-	-
Maryland	1	(D)	-	-	175 *	0.4	175	-	-	-
Pennsylvania	1	(D)	-	-	375 *	0.8	375	-	-	-
Rhode Island	1	(D)	-	-	175 *	0.4	175	-	-	-
Vermont	1	(D)	-	-	175 *	0.4	175	-	-	-

Source: 1992 *Economic Census.* The states are in descending order of shipments or establishments (if shipment data are missing for the majority). The symbol (D) appears when data are withheld to prevent disclosure of competitive information. States marked with (D) are sorted by number of establishments. A dash (-) indicates that the data element cannot be calculated; * indicates the midpoint of a range.

2833 - MEDICINALS AND BOTANICALS

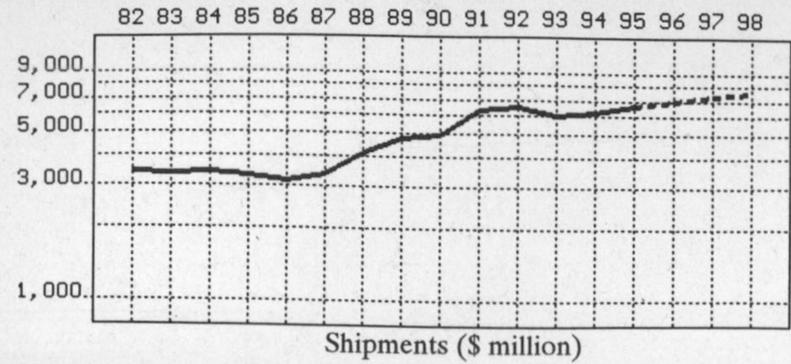

Shipments ($ million)

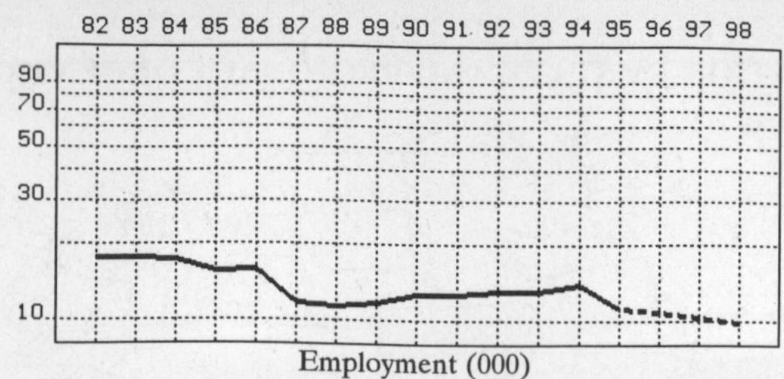

Employment (000)

GENERAL STATISTICS

Year	Companies	Establishments: Total	Establishments: with 20 or more employees	Employment: Total (000)	Production Workers (000)	Production Hours (Mil)	Compensation: Payroll ($ mil)	Compensation: Wages ($/hr)	Cost of Materials	Value Added by Manufacture	Value of Shipments	Capital Invest.
1982	209	228	94	17.8	10.2	20.9	463.2	10.95	1,335.2	2,054.7	3,397.9	283.6
1983		227	98	17.7	9.8	19.0	472.0	12.14	1,287.2	2,057.5	3,370.6	273.9
1984		226	102	17.3	9.5	18.0	497.5	12.50	1,446.8	1,992.4	3,410.3	260.8
1985		224	105	15.7	8.6	17.5	497.5	13.61	1,298.4	1,970.8	3,282.9	170.0
1986		223	107	15.8	8.3	16.6	497.6	14.15	1,285.0	1,854.9	3,153.1	147.2
1987	208	225	84	11.6	6.1	12.0	376.5	15.32	1,613.4	1,780.7	3,350.2	114.5
1988		223	93	11.3	6.2	11.7	381.4	16.09	2,052.9	2,086.2	4,150.4	150.5
1989		221	92	11.7	6.6	13.3	420.3	16.29	2,596.0	2,225.7	4,752.5	219.3
1990		226	93	12.7	6.5	13.1	423.4	17.35	2,579.2	2,392.2	4,919.4	194.5
1991		226	103	12.5	7.2	14.3	540.2	20.06	3,200.0	3,166.4	6,308.2	487.3
1992	208	225	74	13.0	7.4	15.1	587.1	18.91	3,245.9	3,365.7	6,438.5	550.5
1993		248	88	13.0	7.7	16.3	610.8	19.62	2,757.8	3,191.2	5,925.8	482.4
1994		231P	86P	13.9	7.8	15.6	613.7	19.71	2,953.0	3,163.7	6,189.3	504.7
1995		232P	85P	11.1P	6.3P	12.9P	567.0P	21.37P	3,173.7P	3,400.1P	6,651.8P	475.3P
1996		233P	83P	10.6P	6.1P	12.5P	577.8P	22.16P	3,319.5P	3,556.4P	6,957.5P	501.0P
1997		234P	82P	10.2P	5.8P	12.1P	588.7P	22.94P	3,465.4P	3,712.7P	7,263.3P	526.7P
1998		234P	81P	9.8P	5.6P	11.7P	599.6P	23.72P	3,611.3P	3,869.0P	7,569.1P	552.4P

Sources: 1982, 1987, 1992 *Economic Census*; *Annual Survey of Manufactures*, 83-86, 88-91, 93-94. Establishment counts for non-Census years are from *County Business Patterns*; establishment values for 83-84 are extrapolations. 'P's show projections by the editors. Industries reclassified in 87 will not have data for prior years.

INDICES OF CHANGE

Year	Companies	Establishments: Total	Establishments: with 20 or more employees	Employment: Total (000)	Production Workers (000)	Production Hours (Mil)	Compensation: Payroll ($ mil)	Compensation: Wages ($/hr)	Cost of Materials	Value Added by Manufacture	Value of Shipments	Capital Invest.
1982	100	101	127	137	138	138	79	58	41	61	53	52
1983		101	132	136	132	126	80	64	40	61	52	50
1984		100	138	133	128	119	85	66	45	59	53	47
1985		100	142	121	116	116	85	72	40	59	51	31
1986		99	145	122	112	110	85	75	40	55	49	27
1987	100	100	114	89	82	79	64	81	50	53	52	21
1988		99	126	87	84	77	65	85	63	62	64	27
1989		98	124	90	89	88	72	86	80	66	74	40
1990		100	126	98	88	87	72	92	79	71	76	35
1991		100	139	96	97	95	92	106	99	94	98	89
1992	100	100	100	100	100	100	100	100	100	100	100	100
1993		110	119	100	104	108	104	104	85	95	92	88
1994		103P	116P	107	105	103	105	104	91	94	96	92
1995		103P	114P	85P	85P	85P	97P	113P	98P	101P	103P	86P
1996		104P	113P	82P	82P	83P	98P	117P	102P	106P	108P	91P
1997		104P	111P	79P	79P	80P	100P	121P	107P	110P	113P	96P
1998		104P	109P	75P	76P	77P	102P	125P	111P	115P	118P	100P

Sources: Same as General Statistics. Values reflect change from the base year, 1992. Values above 100 mean greater than 92, values below 100 mean less than 92, and a value of 100 in the 82-91 or 93-98 period means same as 92. 'P's mark projections by the editors.

SELECTED RATIOS

For 1994	Avg. of All Manufact.	Analyzed Industry	Index
Employees per Establishment	49	60	123
Payroll per Establishment	1,500,273	2,651,319	177
Payroll per Employee	30,620	44,151	144
Production Workers per Establishment	34	34	98
Wages per Establishment	853,319	1,328,364	156
Wages per Production Worker	24,861	39,420	159
Hours per Production Worker	2,056	2,000	97
Wages per Hour	12.09	19.71	163
Value Added per Establishment	4,602,255	13,667,880	297
Value Added per Employee	93,930	227,604	242

For 1994	Avg. of All Manufact.	Analyzed Industry	Index
Value Added per Production Worker	134,084	405,603	302
Cost per Establishment	5,045,178	12,757,609	253
Cost per Employee	102,970	212,446	206
Cost per Production Worker	146,988	378,590	258
Shipments per Establishment	9,576,895	26,739,137	279
Shipments per Employee	195,460	445,273	228
Shipments per Production Worker	279,017	793,500	284
Investment per Establishment	321,011	2,180,415	679
Investment per Employee	6,552	36,309	554
Investment per Production Worker	9,352	64,705	692

Sources: Same as General Statistics. The 'Average of All Manufacturing' column represents the average of all manufacturing industries reported for the most recent complete year available. The Index shows the relationship between the Average and the Analyzed Industry. For example, 100 means that they are equal; 500 that the Analyzed Industry is five times the average; 50 means that the Analyzed Industry is half the national average. The abbreviation 'na' is used to show that data are 'not available'.

LEADING COMPANIES

Number shown: **48** Total sales ($ mil): **2,861** Total employment (000): **15.8**

Company Name	Address				CEO Name	Phone	Co. Type	Sales ($ mil)	Empl. (000)
Sigma-Aldrich Corp	3050 Spruce St	St Louis	MO	63103	Tom Cori	314-771-5765	P	851	5.5
Pfizer Animal Health Group	235 E 42nd St	New York	NY	10017	Brower A Merriam	212-573-7203	D	578	3.0
Sandoz Nutrition Corp	PO Box 370	Minneapolis	MN	55440	David Pyott	612-925-2100	S	250*	0.8
Stur-Dee Health Products Inc	105 Oroville Dr	Bohemia	NY	11216	Leo Kerpen	516-889-6400	R	190*	1.2
Nature's Sunshine Products Inc	PO Box 19005	Provo	UT	84605	Alan D Kennedy	801-342-4300	P	161	0.8
Sybron Chemicals Inc	PO Box 66	Birmingham	NJ	08011	Richard M Klein	609-893-1100	P	146	0.7
Hydrite Chemical Co	PO Drawer 0948	Brookfield	WI	53008	John Honkamp	414-792-1450	R	140	0.5
Pharmavite Corp	PO Box 9606	Mission Hills	CA	91346	Henry Burdick	818-837-3633	S	88*	0.5
Ganes Chemicals Inc	630 Broad St	Carlstadt	NJ	07072	E Gunthardt	201-507-4300	S	50	0.2
Banner Pharmacaps Inc	PO Box 2157	Chatsworth	CA	91313	Wim Van Pelt	818-341-3060	S	40*	0.3
Natural Alternatives Intern	1185 Linda Vista Dr	San Marcos	CA	92069	Mark A Le Doux	619-744-7340	P	34	0.1
Tishcon Corp	30 New York Av	Westbury	NY	11590	Raj Chopra	516-333-3050	R	32*	0.2
Botanicals International	2550 El Presidio St	Long Beach	CA	90810	Volker Wypyszyk	310-637-9566	S	30	<0.1
Perrigo of South Carolina	PO Box 1968	Greenville	SC	29602	Andrew Morgan	803-288-5521	S	29	0.2
Dover Chemical Corp	PO Box 40	Dover	OH	44622	CJ Fette	216-343-7711	S	25	0.1
Country Life Inc	180 Oser Av	Hauppauge	NY	11788	Halbert Drexler	516-231-1031	R	20	0.1
Bio-Technology General Corp	70 Wood Av S	Iselin	NJ	08830	Sim Fass	908-632-8800	P	17	0.2
Enzymatic Therapy Inc	PO Box 22310	Green Bay	WI	54305	Terry Lemerond	414-469-1313	R	16*	0.1
Lonza Los Angeles Inc	PO Box 01557	Los Angeles	CA	90001	George Lockyer	213-584-5600	S	15*	<0.1
Qualis Inc	4600 Park Av	Des Moines	IA	50321	Roxi Downing	515-243-3000	R	15	0.2
Pep Products Inc	PO Box 715	Castle Rock	CO	80104	Mark Owens	303-688-6633	R	12*	<0.1
Pfanstiehl Laboratories Inc	1219 Glen Rock Av	Waukegan	IL	60085	A George Holstein	708-623-0370	R	11*	<0.1
FoodScience Corp	20 New England Dr	Essex Junction	VT	05452	Lou R Drudi	802-863-1111	R	10	<0.1
Naturade Inc	7110 E Jackson St	Paramount	CA	90723	Allan Schulman	310-531-8120	R	10	<0.1
Naturade Products Inc	7110 E Jackson St	Paramount	CA	90723	Allan Schulman	310-531-8120	S	10	<0.1
Powerfood Inc	2448 6th St	Berkeley	CA	94710	Brian Maxwell	510-843-1330	R	10*	<0.1
Vitamins Inc	200 E Randolph Dr	Chicago	IL	60601	LE Kovacs	312-861-0700	R	10	<0.1
Michael's Arturo Pathic Program	7040 Alamo Downs	San Antonio	TX	78238	Michael Schwartz	210-647-4700	R	8*	<0.1
Polysciences Inc	400 Valley Rd	Warrington	PA	18976	Michael Ott	215-343-6484	R	8	<0.1
Ash Stevens Inc	5861 J C Lodge Fwy	Detroit	MI	48202	Arthur B Ash	313-872-6400	R	8	<0.1
Accurate Chemical	300 Shames Dr	Westbury	NY	11590	R Rosenberg	516-333-2221	R	5	<0.1
Applied Science Laboratories	2701 Carolean	State College	PA	16801	Richard Kurtz	814-238-2406	D	4	<0.1
Edward Mendell Company Inc	2981 Rte 22	Patterson	NY	12563	John V Talley	914-878-3414	S	4*	<0.1
Quality Formulation Labs	204 Lackawanna	West Paterson	NJ	07424	Mohamad Desoky	201-785-8760	R	4	<0.1
Metabolic Nutrition Inc	PO Box 60-0866	Miami	FL	33160	Murray Cohen	305-940-0962	R	4	<0.1
Weider Food Co	1960 S 4250 W	Salt Lake City	UT	84104	Richard Bizarro	801-975-5000	S	3*	<0.1
Wachter Organic Sea Products	360 Shaw Rd	S San Francisco	CA	94080	Earl A Wachter	415-588-9567	R	3	<0.1
Arizona Sun Products Inc	PO Box 1786	Scottsdale	AZ	85252	Robert Wallace	602-998-8861	R	2	<0.1
Pharmachem Corp	PO Box 1035	Bethlehem	PA	18016		610-867-4654	R	2*	<0.1
Test Laboratories Inc	PO Box 306	Reseda	CA	91335	Gregory L Brewster	818-881-4268	R	1	<0.1
Edom Laboratories Inc	860 Grand Blv	Deer Park	NY	11729	A Pollack	516-586-2266	R	1*	<0.1
Nature's Apothecary Inc	6350 Gunpark Dr	Boulder	CO	80302	Lee Weldon	303-581-0288	R	1	<0.1
Nutritional Life Support Syst Co	3745 7th Av	San Diego	CA	92103	J Minogue	619-294-3954	R	1*	<0.1
Ribi ImmunoChem Research Inc	PO Box 1409	Hamilton	MT	59840	Robert E Ivy	406-363-6214	P	1	<0.1
Lichtwer Pharma US Inc	680 Andersen Dr	Pittsburgh	PA	15220	Michael C Moore	412-928-9334	S	1*	<0.1
Sensus Drug Development Corp	98 San Jacinto Blv	Austin	TX	78701	Richard Hawkins	512-476-0270	R	1*	<0.1
Turtle Island Herbs Inc	1705 14th St	Boulder	CO	80302	Feather Jones	303-442-2215	R	0	<0.1
Mt Clemens Mineral Prod Co	10824 W 9 Mile Rd	Oak Park	MI	48237	Max Simon	313-541-7050	R	0	<0.1

Source: *Ward's Business Directory of U.S. Private and Public Companies*, Volumes 1 and 2, 1996. The company type code used is as follows: P - Public, R - Private, S - Subsidiary, D - Division, J - Joint Venture, A - Affiliate, G - Group. Sales are in millions of dollars, employees are in thousands. An asterisk (*) indicates an estimated sales volume. The symbol < stands for 'less than'. Company names and addresses are truncated, in some cases, to fit into the available space.

MATERIALS CONSUMED

Material	Quantity	Delivered Cost ($ million)
Materials, ingredients, containers, and supplies	(X)	2,947.2
Antibiotics, in bulk, for human and veterinary use	(X)	(D)
Antibiotics, in bulk, for animal feeds	(X)	(D)
Vitamins, natural and synthetic, in bulk, for human and veterinary use	(X)	52.9
Vitamins, natural and synthetic, in bulk, for animal feeds	(X)	84.6
Agricultural products (crude), including flowers, grains, seeds, herbs, etc.	(X)	63.6
Processed food and kindred products including lactose, meat packing plant products, yeast, etc.	(X)	7.8
Blood derivatives and extenders	(X)	(D)
All other bulk medicinal and botanical uncompounded drugs, except antibiotics and vitamins	(X)	661.0
Gelatin (pharmaceutical grade) and gelatin capsules	(X)	2.4
Industrial inorganic chemicals	(X)	58.2
Cyclic crudes and intermediates including organic colors	(X)	39.7
Other synthetic organic chemicals including halogenated hydrocarbons	(X)	223.7
Fabricated plastics products, including plastics closures, film, and packaging items, except containers	(X)	1.9
Metal closures and crowns for containers	(X)	(D)
Labels, coupons, instructions, and other printed material	(X)	1.2
Plastics containers	(X)	5.8
Glass containers	(X)	1.9
Metal containers	(X)	4.2
Paperboard containers, boxes, and corrugated paperboard	(X)	12.4
All other materials and components, parts, containers, and supplies	(X)	304.8
Materials, ingredients, containers, and supplies, nsk	(X)	121.5

Source: 1992 *Economic Census*. Explanation of symbols used: (D): Withheld to avoid disclosure of competitive data; na: Not available; (S): Withheld because statistical norms were not met; (X): Not applicable; (Z): Less than half the unit shown; nec: Not elsewhere classified; nsk: Not specified by kind; - : zero; * : 10-19 percent estimated; ** : 20-29 percent estimated.

PRODUCT SHARE DETAILS

Product or Product Class	% Share	Product or Product Class	% Share
Medicinals and botanicals	100.00	Naturally occurring vitamin C.	5.93
Synthetic organic medicinal chemicals, in bulk	83.10	Naturally occurring vitamin E.	13.60
Synthetic organic antibiotics, including all uses such as veterinary, food supplements, food preservation, etc., except preparations	54.89	Other naturally occurring vitamins (from yeast, fish, liver, etc.)	6.25
Other synthetic organic medicinal chemicals, except antibiotics	43.70	Drugs of animal origin, including hormones, dried glands, organs, and tissues and extractions thereof.	3.41
Synthetic organic medicinal chemicals, in bulk, nsk.	1.41	Artificial mixtures of two medicinal or botanical substances or more for therapeutic or prophylactic uses	23.76
Other medicinal chemicals and botanical products, in bulk, nec	15.40	Other organic and inorganic medicinal chemicals, except diagnostics	38.64
Botanical alkaloid drugs, including opium and nicotine.	1.76	Other medicinal chemicals and botanical products, in bulk, nec, nsk	2.30
Other botanical drugs, including glycosides and ginseng extract	4.36	Medicinals and botanicals, nsk	1.50

Source: 1992 *Economic Census*. The values shown are percent of total shipments in an industry. Values of indented subcategories are summed in the main heading. The symbol (D) appears when data are withheld to prevent disclosure of competitive information. The abbreviation nsk stands for 'not specified by kind' and nec for 'not elsewhere classified'.

INPUTS AND OUTPUTS FOR DRUGS

Economic Sector or Industry Providing Inputs	%	Sector	Economic Sector or Industry Buying Outputs	%	Sector
Drugs	19.2	Manufg.	Personal consumption expenditures	47.5	
Imports	14.7	Foreign	Drugs	12.3	Manufg.
Accounting, auditing & bookkeeping	12.9	Services	Hospitals	9.9	Services
Wholesale trade	8.4	Trade	S/L Govt. purch., health & hospitals	8.4	S/L Govt
Management & consulting services & labs	7.2	Services	Exports	7.8	Foreign
Advertising	2.9	Services	Prepared feeds, nec	4.3	Manufg.
Electric services (utilities)	1.9	Util.	Medical & health services, nec	2.5	Services
Banking	1.8	Fin/R.E.	Federal Government purchases, national defense	1.5	Fed Govt
Glass containers	1.7	Manufg.	Change in business inventories	1.2	In House
Miscellaneous plastics products	1.7	Manufg.	Nursing & personal care facilities	1.0	Services
Petroleum refining	1.7	Manufg.	Doctors & dentists	0.8	Services
Paperboard containers & boxes	1.5	Manufg.	Federal Government purchases, nondefense	0.7	Fed Govt
Noncomparable imports	1.4	Foreign	Meat animals	0.5	Agric.
Business services nec	1.2	Services	Cyclic crudes and organics	0.3	Manufg.
Colleges, universities, & professional schools	1.1	Services	Dog, cat, & other pet food	0.3	Manufg.
Cyclic crudes and organics	1.0	Manufg.	Residential care	0.2	Services
Industrial inorganic chemicals, nec	1.0	Manufg.	S/L Govt. purch., other education & libraries	0.2	S/L Govt
Chemical preparations, nec	0.9	Manufg.	Poultry & eggs	0.1	Agric.
Metal cans	0.8	Manufg.			
Communications, except radio & TV	0.8	Util.			
Gas production & distribution (utilities)	0.8	Util.			
Eating & drinking places	0.8	Trade			
Royalties	0.8	Fin/R.E.			

Continued on next page.

INPUTS AND OUTPUTS FOR DRUGS - Continued

Economic Sector or Industry Providing Inputs	%	Sector	Economic Sector or Industry Buying Outputs	%	Sector
Commercial printing	0.7	Manufg.			
Equipment rental & leasing services	0.7	Services			
Motor freight transportation & warehousing	0.6	Util.			
Miscellaneous repair shops	0.6	Services			
Paper coating & glazing	0.5	Manufg.			
Air transportation	0.5	Util.			
Engineering, architectural, & surveying services	0.5	Services			
Maintenance of nonfarm buildings nec	0.4	Constr.			
Meat packing plants	0.4	Manufg.			
Prepared feeds, nec	0.4	Manufg.			
Electrical repair shops	0.4	Services			
Legal services	0.4	Services			
U.S. Postal Service	0.4	Gov't			
Poultry & eggs	0.3	Agric.			
Agricultural chemicals, nec	0.3	Manufg.			
Crowns & closures	0.3	Manufg.			
Fabricated metal products, nec	0.3	Manufg.			
Metal barrels, drums, & pails	0.3	Manufg.			
Pumps & compressors	0.3	Manufg.			
Real estate	0.3	Fin/R.E.			
Greenhouse & nursery products	0.2	Agric.			
Manifold business forms	0.2	Manufg.			
Metal foil & leaf	0.2	Manufg.			
Soap & other detergents	0.2	Manufg.			
Railroads & related services	0.2	Util.			
Water transportation	0.2	Util.			
Insurance carriers	0.2	Fin/R.E.			
Security & commodity brokers	0.2	Fin/R.E.			
Automotive rental & leasing, without drivers	0.2	Services			
Automotive repair shops & services	0.2	Services			
Photofinishing labs, commercial photography	0.2	Services			
Alkalies & chlorine	0.1	Manufg.			
Fabricated rubber products, nec	0.1	Manufg.			
Surgical & medical instruments	0.1	Manufg.			
Wet corn milling	0.1	Manufg.			
Sanitary services, steam supply, irrigation	0.1	Util.			
Credit agencies other than banks	0.1	Fin/R.E.			
Computer & data processing services	0.1	Services			
Hotels & lodging places	0.1	Services			
State & local government enterprises, nec	0.1	Gov't			

Source: Benchmark Input-Output Accounts for the U.S. Economy, 1982, U.S. Department of Commerce, Washington, D.C., July 1991. Data, as reported in the source, are organized by the 1977 SIC structure in use in 1982 but have been matched, as closely as is possible, to the 1987 SIC structure used in this book.

OCCUPATIONS EMPLOYED BY SIC 283 - DRUGS

Occupation	% of Total 1994	Change to 2005	Occupation	% of Total 1994	Change to 2005
Packaging & filling machine operators	7.8	11.2	Medical scientists	1.7	48.3
Science & mathematics technicians	5.7	36.0	Hand packers & packagers	1.7	5.9
Biological scientists	5.5	49.6	Systems analysts	1.6	97.7
Secretaries, ex legal & medical	5.3	12.5	Assemblers, fabricators, & hand workers nec	1.5	23.6
Chemists	4.9	23.6	Freight, stock, & material movers, hand	1.5	-1.1
Sales & related workers nec	4.4	23.6	Janitors & cleaners, incl maids	1.5	-1.1
Chemical equipment controllers, operators	3.1	11.2	Industrial production managers	1.5	23.6
Inspectors, testers, & graders, precision	2.7	23.6	Machine operators nec	1.4	8.9
Engineering, mathematical, & science managers	2.2	40.4	General office clerks	1.2	5.4
Management support workers nec	2.0	23.6	Traffic, shipping, & receiving clerks	1.2	18.9
Industrial machinery mechanics	1.8	36.0	Professional workers nec	1.2	48.3
Managers & administrators nec	1.8	23.5	Helpers, laborers, & material movers nec	1.1	23.6
General managers & top executives	1.8	17.3	Marketing & sales worker supervisors	1.1	23.6
Crushing & mixing machine operators	1.7	23.6	Extruding & forming machine workers	1.1	36.0
Marketing, advertising, & PR managers	1.7	23.6	Bookkeeping, accounting, & auditing clerks	1.0	-7.3

Source: Industry-Occupation Matrix, Bureau of Labor Statistics. These data relate to one or more 3-digit SIC industry groups rather than to a single 4-digit SIC. The change reported for each occupation to the year 2005 is a percent of growth or decline as estimated by the Bureau of Labor Statistics. The abbreviation nec stands for 'not elsewhere classified'.

LOCATION BY STATE AND REGIONAL CONCENTRATION

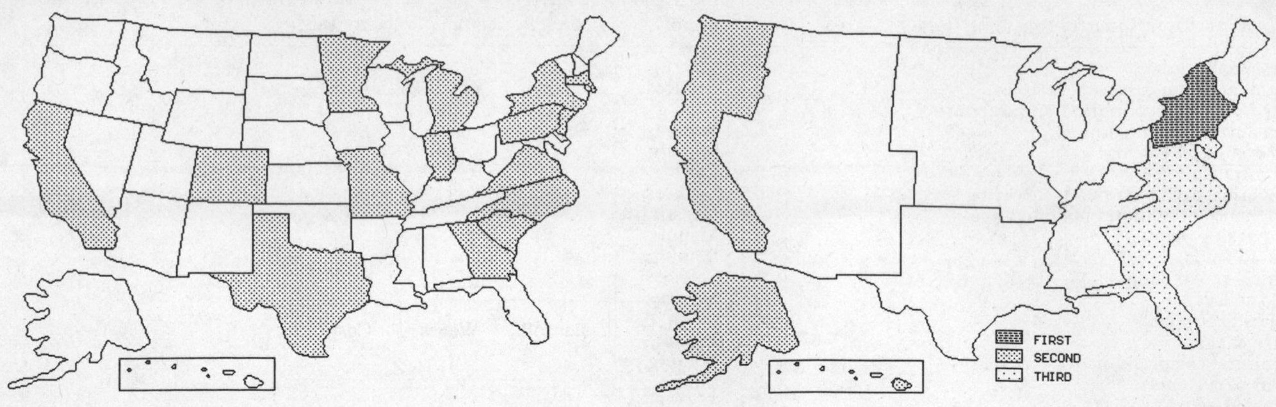

INDUSTRY DATA BY STATE

State	Establish-ments	Shipments			Employment				Cost as % of Shipments	Investment per Employee ($)
		Total ($ mil)	% of U.S.	Per Establ.	Total Number	% of U.S.	Per Establ.	Wages ($/hour)		
New Jersey	23	1,573.8	24.4	68.4	3,000	23.1	130	23.76	45.0	23,567
Georgia	6	275.6	4.3	45.9	800	6.2	133	19.33	84.4	-
North Carolina	8	214.9	3.3	26.9	500	3.8	63	17.71	35.5	-
California	38	171.2	2.7	4.5	900	6.9	24	11.60	38.2	6,333
Texas	11	81.3	1.3	7.4	100	0.8	9	11.50	29.9	9,000
Minnesota	6	36.2	0.6	6.0	200	1.5	33	17.00	70.7	3,000
New York	16	(D)	-	-	375 *	2.9	23	-	-	13,867
Massachusetts	10	(D)	-	-	175 *	1.3	18	-	-	-
Colorado	7	(D)	-	-	375 *	2.9	54	-	-	-
Missouri	6	(D)	-	-	375 *	2.9	63	-	-	-
South Carolina	5	(D)	-	-	175 *	1.3	35	-	-	-
Michigan	4	(D)	-	-	375 *	2.9	94	-	-	-
Pennsylvania	4	(D)	-	-	750 *	5.8	188	-	-	-
Indiana	3	(D)	-	-	3,750 *	28.8	1,250	-	-	-
Virginia	2	(D)	-	-	1,750 *	13.5	875	-	-	-

Source: 1992 *Economic Census*. The states are in descending order of shipments or establishments (if shipment data are missing for the majority). The symbol (D) appears when data are withheld to prevent disclosure of competitive information. States marked with (D) are sorted by number of establishments. A dash (-) indicates that the data element cannot be calculated; * indicates the midpoint of a range.

2834 - PHARMACEUTICAL PREPARATIONS

Shipments ($ million)

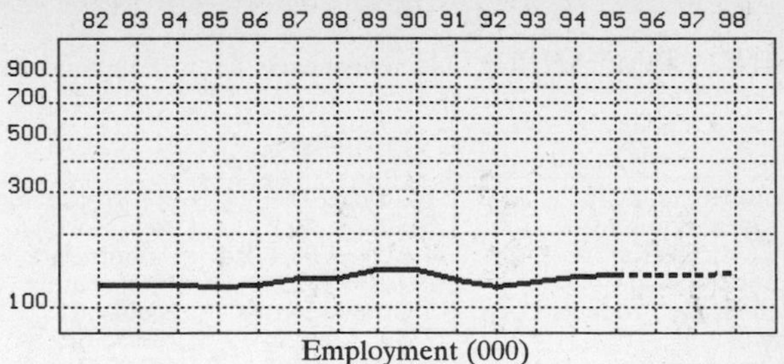

Employment (000)

GENERAL STATISTICS

Year	Companies	Establishments: Total	Establishments: with 20 or more employees	Employment: Total (000)	Production Workers (000)	Production Hours (Mil)	Compensation: Payroll ($ mil)	Compensation: Wages ($/hr)	Production: Cost of Materials	Production: Value Added by Manufacture	Production: Value of Shipments	Production: Capital Invest.
1982	584	683	332	124.4	62.2	120.0	3,052.5	9.69	5,529.8	13,484.0	18,997.6	861.2
1983		685	339	123.7	61.9	117.6	3,173.7	10.22	5,898.8	15,476.4	21,222.0	833.9
1984		687	346	123.8	59.7	111.0	3,367.1	10.96	6,169.9	16,922.6	22,887.6	1,060.0
1985		688	353	123.0	58.4	111.8	3,595.4	11.60	6,417.8	19,094.7	25,335.3	1,171.1
1986		678	354	124.2	58.7	113.5	3,780.3	12.00	7,661.4	20,597.9	28,179.3	1,057.8
1987	640	732	364	131.6	59.9	117.5	4,168.1	12.42	8,463.0	23,883.6	32,094.1	1,471.1
1988		718	376	133.4	60.8	119.0	4,458.3	12.93	9,755.5	26,327.4	35,825.4	1,724.9
1989		699	388	143.9	62.4	121.5	5,142.6	13.83	10,717.3	29,449.8	40,028.0	1,932.5
1990		680	392	144.0	61.5	121.5	5,530.9	14.71	11,763.7	32,744.7	44,182.3	1,808.7
1991		703	388	129.1	59.2	117.0	5,012.3	14.77	12,869.8	34,978.0	47,375.6	1,771.6
1992	585	691	365	122.8	62.5	126.9	4,949.4	14.71	13,542.5	37,229.3	50,417.9	2,450.0
1993		765	408	128.2	62.8	126.5	5,418.9	15.81	14,120.2	39,415.3	53,280.8	2,493.2
1994		725P	405P	134.2	68.6	133.3	5,753.8	16.04	14,497.3	42,614.8	56,960.5	2,713.7
1995		729P	411P	135.4P	63.9P	128.4P	6,049.8P	16.80P	15,249.6P	44,826.2P	59,916.4P	2,747.5P
1996		733P	417P	136.2P	64.3P	129.6P	6,283.3P	17.33P	16,094.6P	47,310.1P	63,236.5P	2,905.4P
1997		737P	423P	137.0P	64.6P	130.8P	6,516.8P	17.87P	16,939.6P	49,794.0P	66,556.5P	3,063.3P
1998		740P	429P	137.8P	65.0P	132.1P	6,750.2P	18.40P	17,784.6P	52,277.9P	69,876.6P	3,221.2P

Sources: 1982, 1987, 1992 *Economic Census*; *Annual Survey of Manufactures*, 83-86, 88-91, 93-94. Establishment counts for non-Census years are from *County Business Patterns*; establishment values for 83-84 are extrapolations. 'P's show projections by the editors. Industries reclassified in 87 will not have data for prior years.

INDICES OF CHANGE

Year	Companies	Establishments: Total	Establishments: with 20 or more employees	Employment: Total (000)	Production Workers (000)	Production Hours (Mil)	Compensation: Payroll ($ mil)	Compensation: Wages ($/hr)	Production: Cost of Materials	Production: Value Added by Manufacture	Production: Value of Shipments	Production: Capital Invest.
1982	100	99	91	101	100	95	62	66	41	36	38	35
1983		99	93	101	99	93	64	69	44	42	42	34
1984		99	95	101	96	87	68	75	46	45	45	43
1985		100	97	100	93	88	73	79	47	51	50	48
1986		98	97	101	94	89	76	82	57	55	56	43
1987	109	106	100	107	96	93	84	84	62	64	64	60
1988		104	103	109	97	94	90	88	72	71	71	70
1989		101	106	117	100	96	104	94	79	79	79	79
1990		98	107	117	98	96	112	100	87	88	88	74
1991		102	106	105	95	92	101	100	95	94	94	72
1992	100	100	100	100	100	100	100	100	100	100	100	100
1993		111	112	104	100	100	109	107	104	106	106	102
1994		105P	111P	109	110	105	116	109	107	114	113	111
1995		105P	113P	110P	102P	101P	122P	114P	113P	120P	119P	112P
1996		106P	114P	111P	103P	102P	127P	118P	119P	127P	125P	119P
1997		107P	116P	112P	103P	103P	132P	121P	125P	134P	132P	125P
1998		107P	117P	112P	104P	104P	136P	125P	131P	140P	139P	131P

Sources: Same as General Statistics. Values reflect change from the base year, 1992. Values above 100 mean greater than 92, values below 100 mean less than 92, and a value of 100 in the 82-91 or 93-98 period means same as 92. 'P's mark projections by the editors.

SELECTED RATIOS

For 1994	Avg. of All Manufact.	Analyzed Industry	Index
Employees per Establishment	49	185	378
Payroll per Establishment	1,500,273	7,933,789	529
Payroll per Employee	30,620	42,875	140
Production Workers per Establishment	34	95	276
Wages per Establishment	853,319	2,948,223	346
Wages per Production Worker	24,861	31,168	125
Hours per Production Worker	2,056	1,943	95
Wages per Hour	12.09	16.04	133
Value Added per Establishment	4,602,255	58,760,614	1,277
Value Added per Employee	93,930	317,547	338

For 1994	Avg. of All Manufact.	Analyzed Industry	Index
Value Added per Production Worker	134,084	621,207	463
Cost per Establishment	5,045,178	19,990,009	396
Cost per Employee	102,970	108,028	105
Cost per Production Worker	146,988	211,331	144
Shipments per Establishment	9,576,895	78,541,586	820
Shipments per Employee	195,460	424,445	217
Shipments per Production Worker	279,017	830,328	298
Investment per Establishment	321,011	3,741,861	1,166
Investment per Employee	6,552	20,221	309
Investment per Production Worker	9,352	39,558	423

Sources: Same as General Statistics. The 'Average of All Manufacturing' column represents the average of all manufacturing industries reported for the most recent complete year available. The Index shows the relationship between the Average and the Analyzed Industry. For example, 100 means that they are equal; 500 that the Analyzed Industry is five times the average; 50 means that the Analyzed Industry is half the national average. The abbreviation 'na' is used to show that data are 'not available'.

LEADING COMPANIES

Number shown: **75** Total sales ($ mil): **122,984** Total employment (000): **598.6**

Company Name	Address				CEO Name	Phone	Co. Type	Sales ($ mil)	Empl. (000)
Merck and Company Inc	PO Box 100	Wh House Stat	NJ	08889	Richard J Markham	908-423-1000	P	14,969	47.5
Bristol-Myers Squibb Co	345 Park Av	New York	NY	10154	C A Heimbold Jr	212-546-4000	P	11,984	47.0
Abbott Laboratories	1 Abbott Park Rd	Abbott Park	IL	60064	Duane L Burnham	708-937-6100	P	9,156	49.5
SmithKline Beecham	PO Box 7929	Philadelphia	PA	19101	Robert P Bauman	215-751-4000	S	9,060	53.0
American Home Products Corp	5 Giralda Farms	Madison	NJ	07940	John R Stafford	201-660-5000	P	8,966	74.0
Pfizer Inc	235 E 42nd St	New York	NY	10017	William C Steere Jr	212-573-2323	P	8,281	40.8
Warner-Lambert Co	201 Tabor Rd	Morris Plains	NJ	07950	Melvin R Goodes	201-540-2000	P	6,417	36.0
Eli Lilly and Co	Lilly Corporate Ctr	Indianapolis	IN	46285	Randall L Tobias	317-276-2000	P	5,712	24.9
Pfizer Pharmaceutical	235 E 42nd St	New York	NY	10017	Edward C Bessey	212-573-2323	D	5,128	27.0
Schering-Plough Corp	1 Giralda Farms	Madison	NJ	07940	Robert P Luciano	201-822-7000	P	4,657	21.2
American Cyanamid Co	1 Cyanamid Plz	Wayne	NJ	07470	Albert J Costello	201-831-2000	P	4,277	26.5
Rhone-Poulenc Rorer Inc	500 Arcola Rd	Collegeville	PA	19426	Robert E Cawthorn	610-454-8000	P	4,175	22.1
Glaxo Inc	5 Moore Dr	Res Tri Pk	NC	27709	Charles A Sanders	919-248-2100	S	3,681	6.0
Upjohn Co	7000 Portage Rd	Kalamazoo	MI	49001	John L Zabriskie	616-323-4000	P	3,344	16.9
Marion Merrell Dow Inc	PO Box 8480	Kansas City	MO	64114	Fred W Lyons Jr	816-966-4000	P	3,060	9.4
Sandoz Corp	608 5th Av	New York	NY	10020	Heinz P Imhof	212-307-1122	S	3,000	10.5
Syntex Corp	3401 Hillview Av	Palo Alto	CA	94304	Paul E Freiman	415-855-5050	S	2,123	10.3
Amgen Inc	1840 DeHavilland	Thousand Oaks	CA	91320	Gordon M Binder	805-447-1000	P	1,648	3.4
GD Searle and Co	5200 Old Orchard	Skokie	IL	60077	Sheldon G Gilgore	708-982-7000	S	1,600*	10.5
Burroughs Wellcome Co	3030 Cornwallis Rd	Res Tri Pk	NC	27709	Philip R Tracy	919-248-3000	S	1,424*	8.0
Hoechst Celanese Corp	PO Box 2500	Somerville	NJ	08876	Hubert E Huckel	908-231-2000	D	757	2.0
Carter-Wallace Inc	1345 Av Amer	New York	NY	10105	Henry H Hoyt Jr	212-339-5000	P	665	4.1
Sanofi Inc	101 Park Av	New York	NY	10178	BG Crouch	212-682-8580	S	600	3.0
Mallinckrodt Veterinary Inc	421 E Hawley St	Mundelein	IL	60060	William J Mercer	708-949-3300	S	592	2.0
AL Pharma Inc	PO Box 1399	Fort Lee	NJ	07024	EW Sissener	201-947-7774	P	469	2.8
Mallinckrodt Spec Chemicals Co	16305 Swingley	Chesterfield	MO	63017	Mack G Nichols	314-530-2000	S	437	2.3
Mylan Laboratories Inc	130 7th St	Pittsburgh	PA	15222	Milan Puskar	412-232-0100	P	396	1.3
Pfizer Consumer Health Care	235 E 42nd St	New York	NY	10017	JF Harmon	212-573-3131	D	374	2.0
ICN Pharmaceuticals Inc	3300 Hyland Av	Costa Mesa	CA	92626	Milan Panic	714-545-0100	P	367	5.8
Forest Laboratories Inc	150 E 58th St	New York	NY	10155	Howard Solomon	212-421-7850	P	361	1.2
Tippecanoe Laboratories	PO Box 685	Lafayette	IN	47902	James Kleck	317-477-4300	D	290	1.3
Alza Corp	PO Box 10950	Palo Alto	CA	94303	Ernest Mario	415-494-5000	P	279	1.2
Merck	Sumneytown Pike	West Point	PA	19486	R V Gilmartin	215-661-5000	D	270*	4.5
Fisons Corp	PO Box 1710	Rochester	NY	14603	William Poole	716-475-9000	S	260	1.0
Lemmon Co	PO Box 630	Sellersville	PA	18960	William A Fletcher	215-723-5544	S	225	0.5
Procter & Gamble	17 Eaton Av	Norwich	NY	13815	G Gilbert Cloyd	607-335-2111	S	220*	1.2
Circa Pharmaceuticals Inc	33 Ralph Av	Copiague	NY	11726	Melvin Sharoky	516-842-8383	P	209	0.1
Melaleuca Inc	3910 S Yellowstone	Idaho Falls	ID	83402	Frank Vander Sloot	208-522-0700	R	200	1.0
PF Labs Inc	700 Union Blv	Totowa	NJ	07512	Edward W Albright	201-256-3100	S	200	0.2
Banner Pharmacaps Inc	1085 Morris Av	Union	NJ	07083	Stephen Fischer	908-354-1122	S	175	1.2
Biogen Inc	14 Cambridge Ctr	Cambridge	MA	02142	James L Vincent	617-252-9200	P	156	0.4
Steris Laboratories Inc	620 N 51st Av	Phoenix	AZ	85043	James Plaza	602-278-1400	S	150*	0.6
Biocraft Laboratories Inc	PO Box 948	Fair Lawn	NJ	07410	Harold Snyder	201-703-0400	P	144	0.8
Solopak Pharmaceuticals Inc	1845 Tonne Rd	Elk Grove Vill	IL	60007	Otto Nonnenmann	708-806-0080	R	120*	0.7
Stiefel Laboratories Inc	255 Alhambra Cir	Coral Gables	FL	33134	WK Stiefel	305-443-3807	R	120	1.2
Copley Pharmaceutical Inc	25 John Rd	Canton	MA	02021	Jane CI Hirsh	617-575-7310	P	114	0.5
Roberts Pharmaceutical Corp	6 Industrial Way W	Eatontown	NJ	07724	Robert A Vukovich	908-389-1182	P	112	0.3
Nutrilite Products Inc	PO Box 5940	Buena Park	CA	90622	Carl S Rehnborg	714-562-6200	S	110*	0.9
BARR Laboratories Inc	2 Quaker Rd	Pomona	NY	10970	Bruce L Downey	914-362-1100	P	109	0.3
Chattem Inc	1715 W 38th St	Chattanooga	TN	37409	Zan Guerry	615-821-4571	P	106	0.3
Hybritech Inc	PO Box 269006	San Diego	CA	92126	Terry Shepherd	619-455-6700	S	100	0.8
Altana Inc	60 Baylis Rd	Melville	NY	11747	George Cole	516-454-7677	S	95	0.4
Farnam Companies Inc	PO Box 34820	Phoenix	AZ	85067	Charles B Duff	602-285-1660	R	94	0.2
Ortho Biotech Inc	700 US Hwy 202	Raritan	NJ	08869		908-704-5000	S	89	0.5
Sidmak Laboratories Inc	17 West St	East Hanover	NJ	07936	Satish Patel	201-386-5566	R	89*	0.5
Galderma Laboratories Inc	PO Box 3313299	Fort Worth	TX	76163	Stephen W Clark	817-263-2600	J	80	0.2
Intern Medication Systems Ltd	17890 Castleton St	City of Industry	CA	91748	J F Bozman Jr	818-442-6757	S	79*	0.6
Baker Cummins Dermatologicals	8800 NW 36th St	Miami	FL	33178	Barry Strumwasser	305-590-2200	S	71*	0.4
Baker Norton Pharmaceuticals	8800 NW 36th St	Miami	FL	33178	Barry Strumwasser	305-590-2200	S	71*	0.4
Medi-Physics Inc	2636 S Clearbrook	Arlington H	IL	60005	Allen Herbert	708-593-6300	S	71*	0.4
Watson Laboratories Inc	311 Bonnie Cir	Corona	CA	91720	Alan Chao	909-270-1400	S	70	0.3
Watson Pharmaceuticals Inc	311 Bonnie Cir	Corona	CA	91720	Allen Y Chao	909-736-8444	P	70	0.3
Paco Pharmaceutical Services Inc	1200 Paco Way	Lakewood	NJ	08701	Russell R Haines	908-367-9000	P	68	1.3
Collagen Corp	2500 Faber Pl	Palo Alto	CA	94303	Howard D Palefsky	415-856-0200	P	65	0.3
Syntex Agribusiness Inc	3401 Hillview Av	Palo Alto	CA	94304	George Holder	415-855-5911	S	65	0.2
Boehringer Mannheim	15204 Omega Dr	Rockville	MD	20850	Ted Wood	301-216-3900	R	62*	0.4
Ben Venue Laboratories Inc	PO Box 46568	Bedford	OH	44146	Thomas Russillo	216-232-3320	R	60	0.4
Fermenta Animal Health Co	10150 N Exec Hills	Kansas City	MO	64153	Henry D Bobe	816-891-5500	S	60	0.3
Vi-Jon Laboratories Inc	8515 Page Av	St Louis	MO	63114	John G Brunner	314-423-8000	R	60	0.3
Pharmaceutical Formulations Inc	460 Plainfield Av	Edison	NJ	08818	Max A Tesler	908-985-7100	P	57	0.3
Hall Laboratories Inc	3580 NE Broadway	Portland	OR	97232	Andy Pinkowski	503-280-9625	R	55	0.3
Miles Inc	PO Box 390	Shawnee Msn	KS	66201	Heinz Wehner	913-631-4800	D	53*	0.3
NeXstar Pharmaceuticals Inc	2860 Wilderness Pl	Boulder	CO	80301	Patrick Mahaffy	303-444-5893	P	50	0.3
Agri Labs Ltd	PO Box 3103	St Joseph	MO	64503	Dennis Feary	816-233-9533	R	50	<0.1
Nepera Inc	Rte 17	Harriman	NY	10926	Roger Noack	914-782-1200	S	50	0.2

Source: *Ward's Business Directory of U.S. Private and Public Companies*, Volumes 1 and 2, 1996. The company type code used is as follows: P - Public, R - Private, S - Subsidiary, D - Division, J - Joint Venture, A - Affiliate, G - Group. Sales are in millions of dollars, employees are in thousands. An asterisk (*) indicates an estimated sales volume. The symbol < stands for 'less than'. Company names and addresses are truncated, in some cases, to fit into the available space.

MATERIALS CONSUMED

Material	Quantity	Delivered Cost ($ million)
Materials, ingredients, containers, and supplies	(X)	10,750.8
Antibiotics, in bulk, for human and veterinary use	(X)	1,805.3
Antibiotics, in bulk, for animal feeds	(X)	77.9
Vitamins, natural and synthetic, in bulk, for human and veterinary use	(X)	427.8
Vitamins, natural and synthetic, in bulk, for animal feeds	(X)	19.6
Agricultural products (crude), including flowers, grains, seeds, herbs, etc.	(X)	74.7
Processed food and kindred products including lactose, meat packing plant products, yeast, etc.	(X)	89.4
Blood derivatives and extenders	(X)	8.4
All other bulk medicinal and botanical uncompounded drugs, except antibiotics and vitamins	(X)	3,687.9
Gelatin (pharmaceutical grade) and gelatin capsules	(X)	48.8
Industrial inorganic chemicals	(X)	281.9
Cyclic crudes and intermediates including organic colors	(X)	218.4
Other synthetic organic chemicals including halogenated hydrocarbons	(X)	183.2
Fabricated plastics products, including plastics closures, film, and packaging items, except containers	(X)	347.5
Metal closures and crowns for containers	(X)	43.5
Labels, coupons, instructions, and other printed material	(X)	276.0
Plastics containers	(X)	349.3
Glass containers	(X)	189.9
Metal containers	(X)	65.3
Paperboard containers, boxes, and corrugated paperboard	(X)	513.1
All other materials and components, parts, containers, and supplies	(X)	1,541.1
Materials, ingredients, containers, and supplies, nsk	(X)	501.8

Source: 1992 *Economic Census*. Explanation of symbols used: (D): Withheld to avoid disclosure of competitive data; na: Not available; (S): Withheld because statistical norms were not met; (X): Not applicable; (Z): Less than half the unit shown; nec: Not elsewhere classified; nsk: Not specified by kind; - : zero; * : 10-19 percent estimated; ** : 20-29 percent estimated.

PRODUCT SHARE DETAILS

Product or Product Class	% Share
Pharmaceutical preparations	100.00
Pharmaceutical preparations affecting neoplasms, the endocrine system, and metabolic diseases, for human use	8.14
Pharmaceutical preparations acting on the central nervous system and the sense organs, for human use	19.53
Pharmaceutical preparations acting on the cardiovascular system, for human use	11.78
Pharmaceutical preparations acting on the respiratory system, for human use	11.69
Pharmaceutical preparations acting on the digestive or the genito-urinary systems, for human use	16.30
Pharmaceutical preparations acting on the skin, for human use	4.05
Vitamin, nutrient, and hematinic preparations, for human use	7.27
Pharmaceutical preparations affecting parasitic and infective diseases, for human use	16.54
Pharmaceutical preparations, for veterinary use	3.03
Pharmaceutical preparations, nsk	1.67

Source: 1992 *Economic Census*. The values shown are percent of total shipments in an industry. Values of indented subcategories are summed in the main heading. The symbol (D) appears when data are withheld to prevent disclosure of competitive information. The abbreviation nsk stands for 'not specified by kind' and nec for 'not elsewhere classified'.

INPUTS AND OUTPUTS FOR DRUGS

Economic Sector or Industry Providing Inputs	%	Sector	Economic Sector or Industry Buying Outputs	%	Sector
Drugs	19.2	Manufg.	Personal consumption expenditures	47.5	
Imports	14.7	Foreign	Drugs	12.3	Manufg.
Accounting, auditing & bookkeeping	12.9	Services	Hospitals	9.9	Services
Wholesale trade	8.4	Trade	S/L Govt. purch., health & hospitals	8.4	S/L Govt
Management & consulting services & labs	7.2	Services	Exports	7.8	Foreign
Advertising	2.9	Services	Prepared feeds, nec	4.3	Manufg.
Electric services (utilities)	1.9	Util.	Medical & health services, nec	2.5	Services
Banking	1.8	Fin/R.E.	Federal Government purchases, national defense	1.5	Fed Govt
Glass containers	1.7	Manufg.	Change in business inventories	1.2	In House
Miscellaneous plastics products	1.7	Manufg.	Nursing & personal care facilities	1.0	Services
Petroleum refining	1.7	Manufg.	Doctors & dentists	0.8	Services
Paperboard containers & boxes	1.5	Manufg.	Federal Government purchases, nondefense	0.7	Fed Govt
Noncomparable imports	1.4	Foreign	Meat animals	0.5	Agric.
Business services nec	1.2	Services	Cyclic crudes and organics	0.3	Manufg.
Colleges, universities, & professional schools	1.1	Services	Dog, cat, & other pet food	0.3	Manufg.
Cyclic crudes and organics	1.0	Manufg.	Residential care	0.2	Services
Industrial inorganic chemicals, nec	1.0	Manufg.	S/L Govt. purch., other education & libraries	0.2	S/L Govt
Chemical preparations, nec	0.9	Manufg.	Poultry & eggs	0.1	Agric.
Metal cans	0.8	Manufg.			
Communications, except radio & TV	0.8	Util.			
Gas production & distribution (utilities)	0.8	Util.			
Eating & drinking places	0.8	Trade			
Royalties	0.8	Fin/R.E.			
Commercial printing	0.7	Manufg.			
Equipment rental & leasing services	0.7	Services			
Motor freight transportation & warehousing	0.6	Util.			

Continued on next page.

INPUTS AND OUTPUTS FOR DRUGS - Continued

Economic Sector or Industry Providing Inputs	%	Sector	Economic Sector or Industry Buying Outputs	%	Sector
Miscellaneous repair shops	0.6	Services			
Paper coating & glazing	0.5	Manufg.			
Air transportation	0.5	Util.			
Engineering, architectural, & surveying services	0.5	Services			
Maintenance of nonfarm buildings nec	0.4	Constr.			
Meat packing plants	0.4	Manufg.			
Prepared feeds, nec	0.4	Manufg.			
Electrical repair shops	0.4	Services			
Legal services	0.4	Services			
U.S. Postal Service	0.4	Gov't			
Poultry & eggs	0.3	Agric.			
Agricultural chemicals, nec	0.3	Manufg.			
Crowns & closures	0.3	Manufg.			
Fabricated metal products, nec	0.3	Manufg.			
Metal barrels, drums, & pails	0.3	Manufg.			
Pumps & compressors	0.3	Manufg.			
Real estate	0.3	Fin/R.E.			
Greenhouse & nursery products	0.2	Agric.			
Manifold business forms	0.2	Manufg.			
Metal foil & leaf	0.2	Manufg.			
Soap & other detergents	0.2	Manufg.			
Railroads & related services	0.2	Util.			
Water transportation	0.2	Util.			
Insurance carriers	0.2	Fin/R.E.			
Security & commodity brokers	0.2	Fin/R.E.			
Automotive rental & leasing, without drivers	0.2	Services			
Automotive repair shops & services	0.2	Services			
Photofinishing labs, commercial photography	0.2	Services			
Alkalies & chlorine	0.1	Manufg.			
Fabricated rubber products, nec	0.1	Manufg.			
Surgical & medical instruments	0.1	Manufg.			
Wet corn milling	0.1	Manufg.			
Sanitary services, steam supply, irrigation	0.1	Util.			
Credit agencies other than banks	0.1	Fin/R.E.			
Computer & data processing services	0.1	Services			
Hotels & lodging places	0.1	Services			
State & local government enterprises, nec	0.1	Gov't			

Source: Benchmark Input-Output Accounts for the U.S. Economy, 1982, U.S. Department of Commerce, Washington, D.C., July 1991. Data, as reported in the source, are organized by the 1977 SIC structure in use in 1982 but have been matched, as closely as is possible, to the 1987 SIC structure used in this book.

OCCUPATIONS EMPLOYED BY SIC 283 - DRUGS

Occupation	% of Total 1994	Change to 2005	Occupation	% of Total 1994	Change to 2005
Packaging & filling machine operators	7.8	11.2	Medical scientists	1.7	48.3
Science & mathematics technicians	5.7	36.0	Hand packers & packagers	1.7	5.9
Biological scientists	5.5	49.6	Systems analysts	1.6	97.7
Secretaries, ex legal & medical	5.3	12.5	Assemblers, fabricators, & hand workers nec	1.5	23.6
Chemists	4.9	23.6	Freight, stock, & material movers, hand	1.5	-1.1
Sales & related workers nec	4.4	23.6	Janitors & cleaners, incl maids	1.5	-1.1
Chemical equipment controllers, operators	3.1	11.2	Industrial production managers	1.5	23.6
Inspectors, testers, & graders, precision	2.7	23.6	Machine operators nec	1.4	8.9
Engineering, mathematical, & science managers	2.2	40.4	General office clerks	1.2	5.4
Management support workers nec	2.0	23.6	Traffic, shipping, & receiving clerks	1.2	18.9
Industrial machinery mechanics	1.8	36.0	Professional workers nec	1.2	48.3
Managers & administrators nec	1.8	23.5	Helpers, laborers, & material movers nec	1.1	23.6
General managers & top executives	1.8	17.3	Marketing & sales worker supervisors	1.1	23.6
Crushing & mixing machine operators	1.7	23.6	Extruding & forming machine workers	1.1	36.0
Marketing, advertising, & PR managers	1.7	23.6	Bookkeeping, accounting, & auditing clerks	1.0	-7.3

Source: Industry-Occupation Matrix, Bureau of Labor Statistics. These data relate to one or more 3-digit SIC industry groups rather than to a single 4-digit SIC. The change reported for each occupation to the year 2005 is a percent of growth or decline as estimated by the Bureau of Labor Statistics. The abbreviation nec stands for 'not elsewhere classified'.

LOCATION BY STATE AND REGIONAL CONCENTRATION

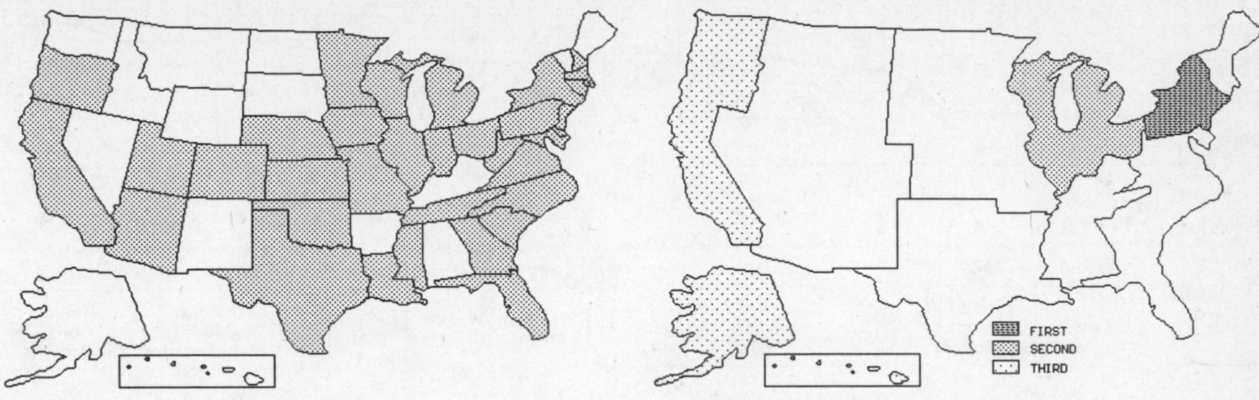

INDUSTRY DATA BY STATE

State	Establish-ments	Shipments			Employment				Cost as % of Shipments	Investment per Employee ($)
		Total ($ mil)	% of U.S.	Per Establ.	Total Number	% of U.S.	Per Establ.	Wages ($/hour)		
New Jersey	79	9,166.9	18.2	116.0	24,100	19.6	305	15.60	24.1	20,311
Pennsylvania	44	7,625.3	15.1	173.3	11,400	9.3	259	17.72	30.4	-
North Carolina	25	6,097.0	12.1	243.9	9,300	7.6	372	13.26	22.0	26,538
New York	75	4,532.6	9.0	60.4	13,500	11.0	180	15.60	25.5	11,119
California	85	3,402.6	6.7	40.0	10,600	8.6	125	13.22	37.0	15,906
Connecticut	11	1,544.8	3.1	140.4	8,000	6.5	727	19.17	26.3	18,725
Missouri	29	1,482.9	2.9	51.1	2,100	1.7	72	13.86	22.6	22,190
Ohio	24	1,463.9	2.9	61.0	2,200	1.8	92	14.72	17.3	15,318
Tennessee	9	1,279.2	2.5	142.1	3,400	2.8	378	9.97	24.0	11,853
Texas	31	1,101.2	2.2	35.5	5,000	4.1	161	15.66	35.5	2,960
South Carolina	8	633.5	1.3	79.2	1,500	1.2	188	12.65	23.7	6,733
Massachusetts	19	439.4	0.9	23.1	1,800	1.5	95	12.65	26.9	31,056
Arizona	7	258.4	0.5	36.9	900	0.7	129	11.93	31.3	13,889
Kansas	7	255.4	0.5	36.5	1,200	1.0	171	11.11	34.7	4,583
Florida	27	202.9	0.4	7.5	1,400	1.1	52	11.07	36.8	4,857
Nebraska	6	180.9	0.4	30.1	600	0.5	100	13.50	41.1	-
Utah	9	144.1	0.3	16.0	700	0.6	78	9.43	29.0	9,429
Minnesota	11	136.3	0.3	12.4	500	0.4	45	12.20	32.6	11,800
Maryland	11	106.6	0.2	9.7	800	0.7	73	13.45	41.9	4,625
Wisconsin	6	94.2	0.2	15.7	500	0.4	83	12.20	35.2	-
Georgia	12	92.4	0.2	7.7	700	0.6	58	9.00	35.7	11,571
Oregon	10	46.1	0.1	4.6	300	0.2	30	10.00	53.1	-
New Hampshire	5	13.2	0.0	2.6	100	0.1	20	8.00	25.0	12,000
Illinois	32	(D)	-	-	1,750 *	1.4	55	-	-	-
Michigan	20	(D)	-	-	7,500 *	6.1	375	-	-	-
Indiana	15	(D)	-	-	7,500 *	6.1	500	-	-	-
Colorado	14	(D)	-	-	750 *	0.6	54	-	-	-
Iowa	11	(D)	-	-	750 *	0.6	68	-	-	10,000
Louisiana	8	(D)	-	-	750 *	0.6	94	-	-	3,067
Mississippi	4	(D)	-	-	1,750 *	1.4	438	-	-	-
Rhode Island	3	(D)	-	-	175 *	0.1	58	-	-	-
Virginia	3	(D)	-	-	1,750 *	1.4	583	-	-	-
Oklahoma	2	(D)	-	-	175 *	0.1	88	-	-	-
West Virginia	2	(D)	-	-	750 *	0.6	375	-	-	-
Delaware	1	(D)	-	-	375 *	0.3	375	-	-	-

Source: 1992 *Economic Census*. The states are in descending order of shipments or establishments (if shipment data are missing for the majority). The symbol (D) appears when data are withheld to prevent disclosure of competitive information. States marked with (D) are sorted by number of establishments. A dash (-) indicates that the data element cannot be calculated; * indicates the midpoint of a range.

2835 - DIAGNOSTIC SUBSTANCES

Shipments ($ million)

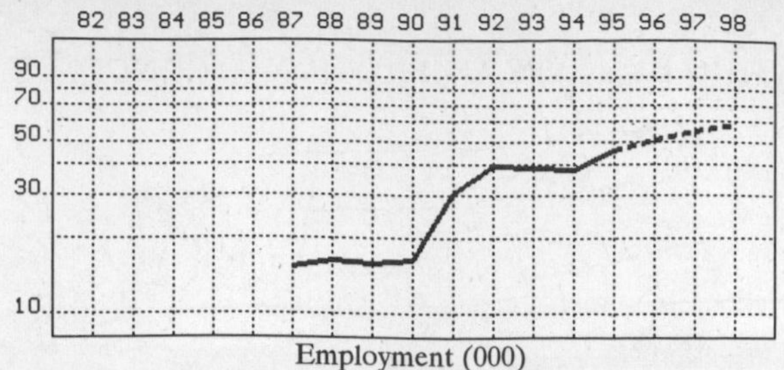

Employment (000)

GENERAL STATISTICS

Year	Companies	Establishments: Total	Establishments: with 20 or more employees	Employment: Total (000)	Employment: Production Workers (000)	Employment: Production Hours (Mil)	Compensation: Payroll ($ mil)	Compensation: Wages ($/hr)	Production ($ million): Cost of Materials	Production ($ million): Value Added by Manufacture	Production ($ million): Value of Shipments	Production ($ million): Capital Invest.
1982												
1983												
1984												
1985												
1986												
1987	137	158	98	15.4	6.8	13.6	437.1	10.74	657.4	1,553.3	2,205.0	93.5
1988		161	100	16.2	7.5	15.3	476.4	10.93	752.4	1,572.4	2,261.3	93.3
1989		159	99	15.8	6.8	13.5	526.8	11.54	754.3	1,560.7	2,325.1	116.8
1990		161	101	16.4	6.6	13.1	499.0	11.80	686.8	1,790.1	2,462.2	147.1
1991		171	98	30.5	9.9	19.4	1,253.5	18.17	1,165.9	3,616.9	4,746.1	302.0
1992	205	234	144	39.8	14.6	29.5	1,658.3	14.03	1,701.2	5,196.1	6,837.8	587.3
1993		236	140	39.3	14.9	30.8	1,759.1	15.64	1,623.3	5,256.1	6,864.4	666.5
1994		239P	142P	38.4	15.6	30.0	1,778.9	16.90	1,951.9	5,920.0	7,777.7	561.1
1995		253P	149P	45.9P	17.0P	33.9P	2,117.7P	18.03P	2,159.6P	6,549.9P	8,605.3P	733.8P
1996		267P	157P	50.2P	18.5P	36.8P	2,355.2P	18.99P	2,392.2P	7,255.3P	9,532.0P	825.5P
1997		281P	165P	54.5P	20.0P	39.7P	2,592.8P	19.95P	2,624.7P	7,960.7P	10,458.8P	917.2P
1998		295P	172P	58.8P	21.5P	42.7P	2,830.3P	20.91P	2,857.3P	8,666.1P	11,385.5P	1,009.0P

Sources: 1982, 1987, 1992 *Economic Census*; *Annual Survey of Manufactures*, 83-86, 88-91, 93-94. Establishment counts for non-Census years are from *County Business Patterns*; establishment values for 83-84 are extrapolations. 'P's show projections by the editors. Industries reclassified in 87 will not have data for prior years.

INDICES OF CHANGE

Year	Companies	Establishments: Total	Establishments: with 20 or more employees	Employment: Total (000)	Employment: Production Workers (000)	Employment: Production Hours (Mil)	Compensation: Payroll ($ mil)	Compensation: Wages ($/hr)	Production ($ million): Cost of Materials	Production ($ million): Value Added by Manufacture	Production ($ million): Value of Shipments	Production ($ million): Capital Invest.
1982												
1983												
1984												
1985												
1986												
1987	67	68	68	39	47	46	26	77	39	30	32	16
1988		69	69	41	51	52	29	78	44	30	33	16
1989		68	69	40	47	46	32	82	44	30	34	20
1990		69	70	41	45	44	30	84	40	34	36	25
1991		73	68	77	68	66	76	130	69	70	69	51
1992	100	100	100	100	100	100	100	100	100	100	100	100
1993		101	97	99	102	104	106	111	95	101	100	113
1994		102P	99P	96	107	102	107	120	115	114	114	96
1995		108P	104P	115P	117P	115P	128P	129P	127P	126P	126P	125P
1996		114P	109P	126P	127P	125P	142P	135P	141P	140P	139P	141P
1997		120P	114P	137P	137P	135P	156P	142P	154P	153P	153P	156P
1998		126P	120P	148P	147P	145P	171P	149P	168P	167P	167P	172P

Sources: Same as General Statistics. Values reflect change from the base year, 1992. Values above 100 mean greater than 92, values below 100 mean less than 92, and a value of 100 in the 82-91 or 93-98 period means same as 92. 'P's mark projections by the editors.

SELECTED RATIOS

For 1994	Avg. of All Manufact.	Analyzed Industry	Index	For 1994	Avg. of All Manufact.	Analyzed Industry	Index
Employees per Establishment	49	161	328	Value Added per Production Worker	134,084	379,487	283
Payroll per Establishment	1,500,273	7,447,548	496	Cost per Establishment	5,045,178	8,171,830	162
Payroll per Employee	30,620	46,326	151	Cost per Employee	102,970	50,831	49
Production Workers per Establishment	34	65	190	Cost per Production Worker	146,988	125,122	85
Wages per Establishment	853,319	2,122,608	249	Shipments per Establishment	9,576,895	32,562,141	340
Wages per Production Worker	24,861	32,500	131	Shipments per Employee	195,460	202,544	104
Hours per Production Worker	2,056	1,923	94	Shipments per Production Worker	279,017	498,571	179
Wages per Hour	12.09	16.90	140	Investment per Establishment	321,011	2,349,103	732
Value Added per Establishment	4,602,255	24,784,689	539	Investment per Employee	6,552	14,612	223
Value Added per Employee	93,930	154,167	164	Investment per Production Worker	9,352	35,968	385

Sources: Same as General Statistics. The 'Average of All Manufacturing' column represents the average of all manufacturing industries reported for the most recent complete year available. The Index shows the relationship between the Average and the Analyzed Industry. For example, 100 means that they are equal; 500 that the Analyzed Industry is five times the average; 50 means that the Analyzed Industry is half the national average. The abbreviation 'na' is used to show that data are 'not available'.

LEADING COMPANIES

Number shown: **51** Total sales ($ mil): **2,819** Total employment (000): **19.7**

Company Name	Address				CEO Name	Phone	Co. Type	Sales ($ mil)	Empl. (000)
Miles Inc	511 Benedict Av	Tarrytown	NY	10591	Hans Lauterbach	914-631-8000	D	780	4.2
Bio-Rad Laboratories Inc	1000 Alfred Nobel	Hercules	CA	94547	David Schwartz	510-724-7000	P	355	2.3
Nichols Institute	33608 Ortega Hwy	S J Capistrano	CA	92690	Albert L Nichols	714-728-4000	P	236	3.4
Life Technologies Inc	8717 Grovemont Cir	Gaithersburg	MD	20877	J Stark Thompson	301-840-8000	P	235	1.3
Bio Merieux Vitek Inc	595 Anglum Dr	Hazelwood	MO	63042	Philippe Archinard	314-731-8500	R	140	0.7
Ortho Diagnostic Systems Inc	1001 US Hwy 202	Raritan	NJ	08869	Jack Goldstein	908-218-1300	S	120	1.0
MediSense Inc	266 2nd Av	Waltham	MA	02154	Robert L Coleman	617-895-6000	P	110	0.8
Genencor International Inc	1870 S Winton Rd	Rochester	NY	14618	W Thomas Mitchell	716-256-5222	J	110*	0.6
Diagnostic Products Corp	5700 W 96th St	Los Angeles	CA	90045	Sigi Ziering	213-776-0180	P	107	0.9
Intern Murex Techn Corp	3075 Northwood Cir	Norcross	GA	30071	C Robert Cusick	404-662-0660	P	102	0.6
IDEXX Laboratories Inc	1 IDEXX Dr	Westbrook	ME	04092	David E Shaw	207-856-0300	P	93	0.4
Coulter Diagnostics	740 W 83rd St	Hialeah	FL	33014	Harold Crews	305-822-8250	D	67*	0.3
Promega Corp	2800 Woods Hollow	Madison	WI	53711	William A Linton	608-274-4330	R	50	0.4
Miles Inc	400 Morgan Ln	West Haven	CT	06516	Ralph M Galustian	203-498-6566	D	42	0.3
Immucor Inc	PO Box 5625	Norcross	GA	30091	Edward L Gallup	404-441-2051	P	30	0.1
Quidel Corp	10165 McKellar Ct	San Diego	CA	92121	Steven T Frankel	619-452-1556	P	28	0.3
MEDA Inc	PO Box 459	Tualatin	OR	97062	Ron Torland	503-692-1030	R	22*	0.1
Meridian Diagnostics Inc	3471 River Hills Dr	Cincinnati	OH	45244	John A Kraeutler	513-271-3700	P	22	0.1
Gamma Biologicals Inc	3700 Mangum Rd	Houston	TX	77092	David E Hatcher	713-681-8481	P	17	0.1
Gull Laboratories Inc	1011 E 4800 S	Salt Lake City	UT	84117	Milton G Adair	801-263-3524	P	15	0.1
MAST Immunosystems Inc	630 Clyde Ct	Mountain View	CA	94043	Clint Severson	415-961-5501	R	15	<0.1
Pel-Freez Inc	PO Box 68	Rogers	AR	72757	D Dubbell	501-636-4361	R	15*	0.1
Oncor Inc	209 Perry Pkwy	Gaithersburg	MD	20877	Stephen Turner	301-963-3500	P	13	0.2
IGEN Inc	1530 E Jefferson St	Rockville	MD	20852	S J Wohlstadter	301-984-8000	P	11	<0.1
Invitrogen Corp	3985-B Sorrento	San Diego	CA	92121	Lyle C Turner	619-597-6200	R	11	<0.1
Advanced Magnetics Inc	61 Mooney St	Cambridge	MA	02138	Jerome Goldstein	617-497-2070	P	8	<0.1
Reagents Applications Inc	8225 Mercury Ct	San Diego	CA	92111	Craig M Jackson	619-569-8009	S	8	<0.1
INOVA Diagnostics Inc	10451 Roselle St	San Diego	CA	92121	Walter L Binder	619-455-9495	R	7*	<0.1
EDITEK Inc	1238 Anthony Rd	Burlington	NC	27215	James D Skinner	919-226-6311	P	7	0.1
TSI Center for Diagnostic Prod	25 Birch St	Milford	MA	01757		508-478-5510	D	6	<0.1
Viral Antigens Inc	5171 Wilfong Rd	Memphis	TN	38134	Preston H Dorsett	901-382-8716	R	5	<0.1
New Horizons Diagnostics Corp	9110 Red Branch	Columbia	MD	21045	Larry Loomis	410-992-9357	R	4	<0.1
Endogen Inc	640 Memorial Dr	Cambridge	MA	02139	Owen A Dempsey	617-225-0055	P	3	<0.1
Epitope Inc	8505 SW Creekside	Beaverton	OR	97005	Aldolph J Ferro	503-641-6115	P	3	0.2
In Vitro International	16632 Millikan Av	Irvine	CA	92714	William Fisher	714-851-8356	R	3*	<0.1
Hemagen Diagnostics Inc	34-40 Bear Hill Rd	Waltham	MA	02154	Carl Franzblau	617-890-3766	P	2	<0.1
Ostex International Inc	2203 Airport Way S	Seattle	WA	98134	HR Cairncross	206-292-8082	P	2	<0.1
Technical Chemicals & Products	PO Box 8726	Ft Lauderdale	FL	33310	Jack L Aronowitz	305-979-0400	P	2	<0.1
XOMA Corp	2910 7th St	Berkeley	CA	94710	John L Castello	510-644-1170	P	2	0.1
Drug Screening Systems Inc	1001 Lower Landing	Blackwood	NJ	08012	Patrick J Brennan	609-228-8500	P	2	<0.1
NeoRx Corp	410 W Harrison St	Seattle	WA	98119	Paul G Abrams	206-281-7001	P	2	<0.1
Advanced Clinical Technologies	117 Broadway	Norwood	MA	02062	Robert Zahradnik	617-762-9801	R	1	<0.1
Bioserv Corp	11211 Sorrento Val	San Diego	CA	92121	Jeanne Dunham	619-450-3123	R	1	<0.1
International Canine Genetics	271 Great Val Pkwy	Malvern	PA	19355	Paul A Rosinack	215-640-1244	P	1	<0.1
MeDiCa Inc	2382 Roble	Carlsbad	CA	92009	Jarka Bartl	619-438-1886	R	1	<0.1
Vicam Ltd	PO Box 726	Somerville	MA	02143	Jack Radlo	617-623-0030	R	1*	<0.1
Diagnostic Technology Inc	240 Vanderbilt	Hauppauge	NY	11788	Imre Pinter	516-582-4949	R	1	<0.1
FHC Corp	5000 E Spring St	Long Beach	CA	90815	G Dale Garlow	310-982-0076	R	0*	<0.1
Saliva Diagnostic Systems Inc	11719 NE 95th St	Vancouver	WA	98682	Ronald Lealos	206-696-4800	P	0	<0.1
Volu-Sol	700 WSunset Rd	Henderson	NV	89015	James Dalton	702-565-1383	S	0	<0.1
Creative Medical Development	870 Gold Flat Rd	Nevada City	CA	95959	Ron Gangemi	916-265-8222	P	0	<0.1

Source: *Ward's Business Directory of U.S. Private and Public Companies*, Volumes 1 and 2, 1996. The company type code used is as follows: P - Public, R - Private, S - Subsidiary, D - Division, J - Joint Venture, A - Affiliate, G - Group. Sales are in millions of dollars, employees are in thousands. An asterisk (*) indicates an estimated sales volume. The symbol < stands for 'less than'. Company names and addresses are truncated, in some cases, to fit into the available space.

MATERIALS CONSUMED

Material	Quantity	Delivered Cost ($ million)
Materials, ingredients, containers, and supplies	(X)	1,344.7
Antibiotics, in bulk, for human and veterinary use	(X)	(D)
Vitamins, natural and synthetic, in bulk, for human and veterinary use	(X)	(D)
Agricultural products (crude), including flowers, grains, seeds, herbs, etc.	(X)	(D)
Processed food and kindred products including lactose, meat packing plant products, yeast, etc.	(X)	20.7
Blood derivatives and extenders	(X)	71.5
All other bulk medicinal and botanical uncompounded drugs, except antibiotics and vitamins	(X)	113.5
Gelatin (pharmaceutical grade) and gelatin capsules	(X)	(D)
Industrial inorganic chemicals	(X)	109.0
Cyclic crudes and intermediates including organic colors	(X)	(D)
Other synthetic organic chemicals including halogenated hydrocarbons	(X)	156.9
Fabricated plastics products, including plastics closures, film, and packaging items, except containers	(X)	276.7
Metal closures and crowns for containers	(X)	10.6
Labels, coupons, instructions, and other printed material	(X)	24.7
Plastics containers	(X)	27.8
Glass containers	(X)	28.8
Metal containers	(X)	6.0
Paperboard containers, boxes, and corrugated paperboard	(X)	21.3
All other materials and components, parts, containers, and supplies	(X)	317.9
Materials, ingredients, containers, and supplies, nsk	(X)	101.4

Source: 1992 *Economic Census*. Explanation of symbols used: (D): Withheld to avoid disclosure of competitive data; na: Not available; (S): Withheld because statistical norms were not met; (X): Not applicable; (Z): Less than half the unit shown; nec: Not elsewhere classified; nsk: Not specified by kind; - : zero; * : 10-19 percent estimated; ** : 20-29 percent estimated.

PRODUCT SHARE DETAILS

Product or Product Class	% Share	Product or Product Class	% Share
Diagnostic substances	100.00	Culture media	5.97
Diagnostic substances, in vitro	82.04	Other in vitro diagnostic products	13.78
In vitro diagnostic (clinical chemistry) reagents, including toxicology	56.78	Diagnostic substances, in vitro, nsk	(D)
In vitro diagnostic (clinical chemistry) standards and controls, including toxicology	4.71	Diagnostic substances, in vivo	17.03
In vitro diagnostic blood bank products	4.93	In vivo diagnostic contrast media products (both iodinated and barium products), including angiourographic agents	(D)
In vitro diagnostic hematology products	1.19	In vivo radioactive reagents (both diagnostic and therapeutic)	30.73
In vitro diagnostic coagulation products	(D)	Other in vivo diagnostic substances	(D)
In vitro diagnostic microbiology, virology, serology, cytology, and histology products	7.01	Diagnostic substances, nsk	0.93

Source: 1992 *Economic Census*. The values shown are percent of total shipments in an industry. Values of indented subcategories are summed in the main heading. The symbol (D) appears when data are withheld to prevent disclosure of competitive information. The abbreviation nsk stands for 'not specified by kind' and nec for 'not elsewhere classified'.

INPUTS AND OUTPUTS FOR DRUGS

Economic Sector or Industry Providing Inputs	%	Sector
Drugs	19.2	Manufg.
Imports	14.7	Foreign
Accounting, auditing & bookkeeping	12.9	Services
Wholesale trade	8.4	Trade
Management & consulting services & labs	7.2	Services
Advertising	2.9	Services
Electric services (utilities)	1.9	Util.
Banking	1.8	Fin/R.E.
Glass containers	1.7	Manufg.
Miscellaneous plastics products	1.7	Manufg.
Petroleum refining	1.7	Manufg.
Paperboard containers & boxes	1.5	Manufg.
Noncomparable imports	1.4	Foreign
Business services nec	1.2	Services
Colleges, universities, & professional schools	1.1	Services
Cyclic crudes and organics	1.0	Manufg.
Industrial inorganic chemicals, nec	1.0	Manufg.
Chemical preparations, nec	0.9	Manufg.
Metal cans	0.8	Manufg.
Communications, except radio & TV	0.8	Util.
Gas production & distribution (utilities)	0.8	Util.
Eating & drinking places	0.8	Trade
Royalties	0.8	Fin/R.E.
Commercial printing	0.7	Manufg.
Equipment rental & leasing services	0.7	Services
Motor freight transportation & warehousing	0.6	Util.
Miscellaneous repair shops	0.6	Services

Economic Sector or Industry Buying Outputs	%	Sector
Personal consumption expenditures	47.5	
Drugs	12.3	Manufg.
Hospitals	9.9	Services
S/L Govt. purch., health & hospitals	8.4	S/L Govt
Exports	7.8	Foreign
Prepared feeds, nec	4.3	Manufg.
Medical & health services, nec	2.5	Services
Federal Government purchases, national defense	1.5	Fed Govt
Change in business inventories	1.2	In House
Nursing & personal care facilities	1.0	Services
Doctors & dentists	0.8	Services
Federal Government purchases, nondefense	0.7	Fed Govt
Meat animals	0.5	Agric.
Cyclic crudes and organics	0.3	Manufg.
Dog, cat, & other pet food	0.3	Manufg.
Residential care	0.2	Services
S/L Govt. purch., other education & libraries	0.2	S/L Govt
Poultry & eggs	0.1	Agric.

Continued on next page.

INPUTS AND OUTPUTS FOR DRUGS - Continued

Economic Sector or Industry Providing Inputs	%	Sector	Economic Sector or Industry Buying Outputs	%	Sector
Paper coating & glazing	0.5	Manufg.			
Air transportation	0.5	Util.			
Engineering, architectural, & surveying services	0.5	Services			
Maintenance of nonfarm buildings nec	0.4	Constr.			
Meat packing plants	0.4	Manufg.			
Prepared feeds, nec	0.4	Manufg.			
Electrical repair shops	0.4	Services			
Legal services	0.4	Services			
U.S. Postal Service	0.4	Gov't			
Poultry & eggs	0.3	Agric.			
Agricultural chemicals, nec	0.3	Manufg.			
Crowns & closures	0.3	Manufg.			
Fabricated metal products, nec	0.3	Manufg.			
Metal barrels, drums, & pails	0.3	Manufg.			
Pumps & compressors	0.3	Manufg.			
Real estate	0.3	Fin/R.E.			
Greenhouse & nursery products	0.2	Agric.			
Manifold business forms	0.2	Manufg.			
Metal foil & leaf	0.2	Manufg.			
Soap & other detergents	0.2	Manufg.			
Railroads & related services	0.2	Util.			
Water transportation	0.2	Util.			
Insurance carriers	0.2	Fin/R.E.			
Security & commodity brokers	0.2	Fin/R.E.			
Automotive rental & leasing, without drivers	0.2	Services			
Automotive repair shops & services	0.2	Services			
Photofinishing labs, commercial photography	0.2	Services			
Alkalies & chlorine	0.1	Manufg.			
Fabricated rubber products, nec	0.1	Manufg.			
Surgical & medical instruments	0.1	Manufg.			
Wet corn milling	0.1	Manufg.			
Sanitary services, steam supply, irrigation	0.1	Util.			
Credit agencies other than banks	0.1	Fin/R.E.			
Computer & data processing services	0.1	Services			
Hotels & lodging places	0.1	Services			
State & local government enterprises, nec	0.1	Gov't			

Source: Benchmark Input-Output Accounts for the U.S. Economy, 1982, U.S. Department of Commerce, Washington, D.C., July 1991. Data, as reported in the source, are organized by the 1977 SIC structure in use in 1982 but have been matched, as closely as is possible, to the 1987 SIC structure used in this book.

OCCUPATIONS EMPLOYED BY SIC 283 - DRUGS

Occupation	% of Total 1994	Change to 2005	Occupation	% of Total 1994	Change to 2005
Packaging & filling machine operators	7.8	11.2	Medical scientists	1.7	48.3
Science & mathematics technicians	5.7	36.0	Hand packers & packagers	1.7	5.9
Biological scientists	5.5	49.6	Systems analysts	1.6	97.7
Secretaries, ex legal & medical	5.3	12.5	Assemblers, fabricators, & hand workers nec	1.5	23.6
Chemists	4.9	23.6	Freight, stock, & material movers, hand	1.5	-1.1
Sales & related workers nec	4.4	23.6	Janitors & cleaners, incl maids	1.5	-1.1
Chemical equipment controllers, operators	3.1	11.2	Industrial production managers	1.5	23.6
Inspectors, testers, & graders, precision	2.7	23.6	Machine operators nec	1.4	8.9
Engineering, mathematical, & science managers	2.2	40.4	General office clerks	1.2	5.4
Management support workers nec	2.0	23.6	Traffic, shipping, & receiving clerks	1.2	18.9
Industrial machinery mechanics	1.8	36.0	Professional workers nec	1.2	48.3
Managers & administrators nec	1.8	23.5	Helpers, laborers, & material movers nec	1.1	23.6
General managers & top executives	1.8	17.3	Marketing & sales worker supervisors	1.1	23.6
Crushing & mixing machine operators	1.7	23.6	Extruding & forming machine workers	1.1	36.0
Marketing, advertising, & PR managers	1.7	23.6	Bookkeeping, accounting, & auditing clerks	1.0	-7.3

Source: Industry-Occupation Matrix, Bureau of Labor Statistics. These data relate to one or more 3-digit SIC industry groups rather than to a single 4-digit SIC. The change reported for each occupation to the year 2005 is a percent of growth or decline as estimated by the Bureau of Labor Statistics. The abbreviation nec stands for 'not elsewhere classified'.

LOCATION BY STATE AND REGIONAL CONCENTRATION

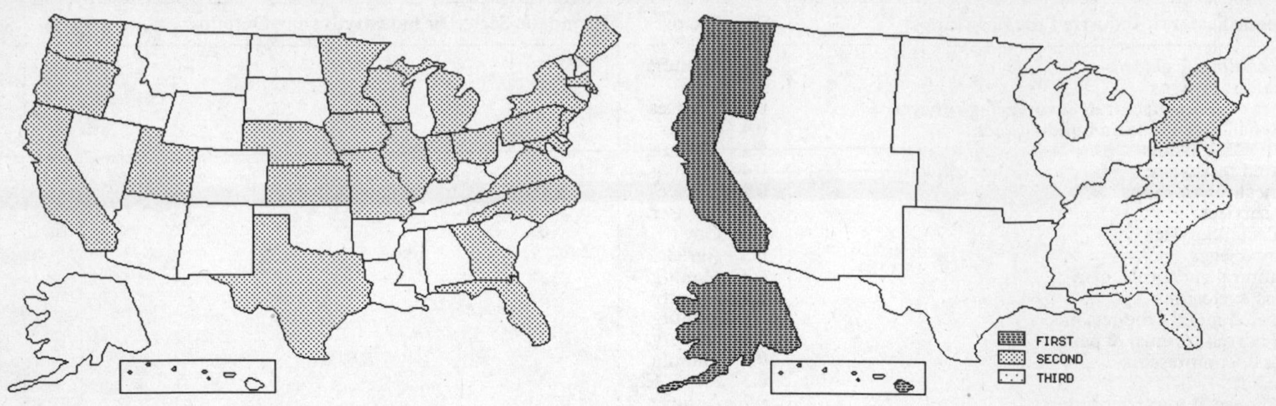

INDUSTRY DATA BY STATE

State	Establish-ments	Shipments			Employment				Cost as % of Shipments	Investment per Employee ($)
		Total ($ mil)	% of U.S.	Per Establ.	Total Number	% of U.S.	Per Establ.	Wages ($/hour)		
California	61	989.8	14.5	16.2	6,400	16.1	105	11.89	21.3	8,781
Massachusetts	18	394.3	5.8	21.9	2,300	5.8	128	15.52	20.1	10,348
Minnesota	7	58.3	0.9	8.3	600	1.5	86	11.67	29.8	
Texas	12	39.5	0.6	3.3	300	0.8	25	9.33	36.5	3,000
Georgia	6	27.5	0.4	4.6	300	0.8	50	9.25	30.2	3,667
Oregon	3	10.2	0.1	3.4	200	0.5	67	9.00	24.5	1,500
New Jersey	15	(D)	-	-	1,750 *	4.4	117	-	-	-
New York	15	(D)	-	-	1,750 *	4.4	117	-	-	6,114
Maryland	11	(D)	-	-	1,750 *	4.4	159	-	-	-
Florida	8	(D)	-	-	1,750 *	4.4	219	-	-	-
Illinois	7	(D)	-	-	17,500 *	44.0	2,500	-	-	-
Pennsylvania	7	(D)	-	-	375 *	0.9	54	-	-	2,133
Maine	6	(D)	-	-	375 *	0.9	63	-	-	-
Wisconsin	6	(D)	-	-	175 *	0.4	29	-	-	5,143
Michigan	5	(D)	-	-	375 *	0.9	75	-	-	-
Missouri	5	(D)	-	-	1,750 *	4.4	350	-	-	-
Washington	5	(D)	-	-	375 *	0.9	75	-	-	-
Indiana	4	(D)	-	-	750 *	1.9	188	-	-	-
North Carolina	4	(D)	-	-	750 *	1.9	188	-	-	-
Iowa	3	(D)	-	-	375 *	0.9	125	-	-	-
Ohio	3	(D)	-	-	175 *	0.4	58	-	-	-
Rhode Island	2	(D)	-	-	175 *	0.4	88	-	-	-
Utah	2	(D)	-	-	175 *	0.4	88	-	-	-
Virginia	2	(D)	-	-	175 *	0.4	88	-	-	-
Kansas	1	(D)	-	-	375 *	0.9	375	-	-	-
Nebraska	1	(D)	-	-	175 *	0.4	175	-	-	-

Source: 1992 *Economic Census*. The states are in descending order of shipments or establishments (if shipment data are missing for the majority). The symbol (D) appears when data are withheld to prevent disclosure of competitive information. States marked with (D) are sorted by number of establishments. A dash (-) indicates that the data element cannot be calculated; * indicates the midpoint of a range.

2836 - BIOLOGICAL PRODUCTS EX DIAGNOSTIC

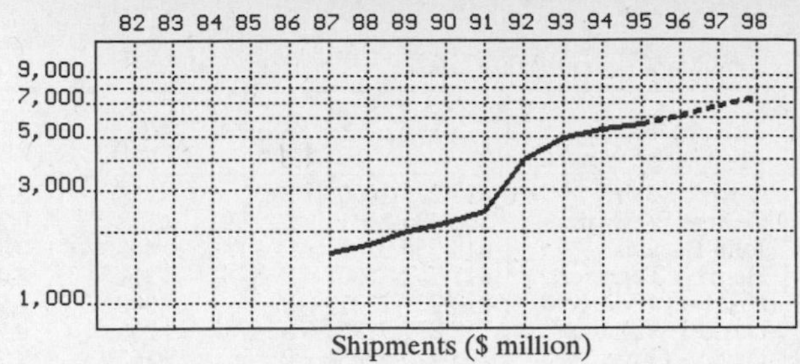

Shipments ($ million)

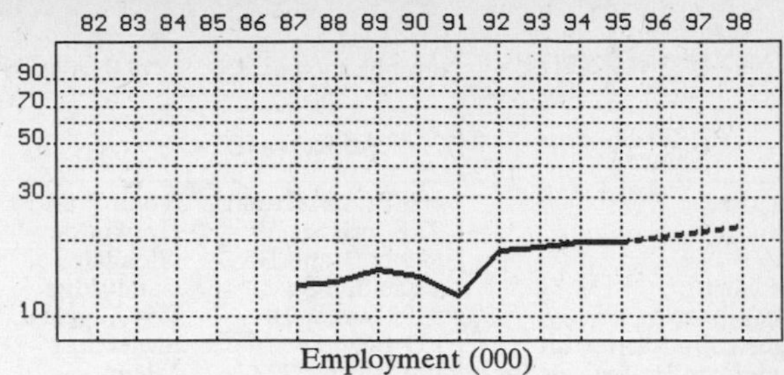

Employment (000)

GENERAL STATISTICS

Year	Companies	Establishments		Employment			Compensation		Production ($ million)			
		Total	with 20 or more employees	Total (000)	Production Workers (000)	Production Hours (Mil)	Payroll ($ mil)	Wages ($/hr)	Cost of Materials	Value Added by Manufacture	Value of Shipments	Capital Invest.
1982												
1983												
1984												
1985												
1986												
1987	174	241	114	13.3	6.8	12.1	322.1	8.87	676.1	943.0	1,614.1	69.9
1988		231	133	13.7	6.5	12.3	340.9	9.13	742.0	1,039.7	1,749.5	89.1
1989		231	132	15.3	7.0	12.7	384.0	9.30	895.6	1,121.5	2,008.3	123.6
1990		220	123	14.4	6.8	13.4	397.4	9.15	901.9	1,317.4	2,155.8	129.9
1991		248	127	12.1	6.4	12.1	391.5	11.00	962.4	1,483.3	2,405.6	108.3
1992	193	275	140	18.4	8.0	15.1	627.2	12.48	1,313.5	2,754.6	3,974.0	294.3
1993		296	137	19.0	9.2	18.1	732.5	12.57	1,483.2	3,479.3	4,914.0	405.1
1994		287P	141P	19.8	9.9	18.6	788.3	13.81	1,570.3	3,829.9	5,310.2	360.6
1995		297P	143P	20.0P	9.6P	18.6P	816.5P	14.17P	1,649.9P	4,024.1P	5,579.4P	417.5P
1996		307P	146P	20.9P	10.1P	19.6P	887.2P	14.92P	1,818.3P	4,434.8P	6,149.0P	466.4P
1997		316P	149P	21.9P	10.5P	20.5P	958.0P	15.68P	1,986.8P	4,845.6P	6,718.5P	515.3P
1998		326P	152P	22.8P	11.0P	21.5P	1,028.8P	16.43P	2,155.2P	5,256.4P	7,288.1P	564.2P

Sources: 1982, 1987, 1992 *Economic Census*; *Annual Survey of Manufactures*, 83-86, 88-91, 93-94. Establishment counts for non-Census years are from *County Business Patterns*; establishment values for 83-84 are extrapolations. 'P's show projections by the editors. Industries reclassified in 87 will not have data for prior years.

INDICES OF CHANGE

Year	Companies	Establishments		Employment			Compensation		Production ($ million)			
		Total	with 20 or more employees	Total (000)	Production Workers (000)	Production Hours (Mil)	Payroll ($ mil)	Wages ($/hr)	Cost of Materials	Value Added by Manufacture	Value of Shipments	Capital Invest.
1982												
1983												
1984												
1985												
1986												
1987	90	88	81	72	85	80	51	71	51	34	41	24
1988		84	95	74	81	81	54	73	56	38	44	30
1989		84	94	83	88	84	61	75	68	41	51	42
1990		80	88	78	85	89	63	73	69	48	54	44
1991		90	91	66	80	80	62	88	73	54	61	37
1992	100	100	100	100	100	100	100	100	100	100	100	100
1993		108	98	103	115	120	117	101	113	126	124	138
1994		105P	100P	108	124	123	126	111	120	139	134	123
1995		108P	102P	109P	120P	123P	130P	114P	126P	146P	140P	142P
1996		112P	104P	114P	126P	130P	141P	120P	138P	161P	155P	158P
1997		115P	106P	119P	131P	136P	153P	126P	151P	176P	169P	175P
1998		119P	108P	124P	137P	142P	164P	132P	164P	191P	183P	192P

Sources: Same as General Statistics. Values reflect change from the base year, 1992. Values above 100 mean greater than 92, values below 100 mean less than 92, and a value of 100 in the 82-91 or 93-98 period means same as 92. 'P's mark projections by the editors.

SELECTED RATIOS

For 1994	Avg. of All Manufact.	Analyzed Industry	Index	For 1994	Avg. of All Manufact.	Analyzed Industry	Index
Employees per Establishment	49	69	141	Value Added per Production Worker	134,084	386,859	289
Payroll per Establishment	1,500,273	2,742,594	183	Cost per Establishment	5,045,178	5,463,270	108
Payroll per Employee	30,620	39,813	130	Cost per Employee	102,970	79,308	77
Production Workers per Establishment	34	34	100	Cost per Production Worker	146,988	158,616	108
Wages per Establishment	853,319	893,669	105	Shipments per Establishment	9,576,895	18,474,851	193
Wages per Production Worker	24,861	25,946	104	Shipments per Employee	195,460	268,192	137
Hours per Production Worker	2,056	1,879	91	Shipments per Production Worker	279,017	536,384	192
Wages per Hour	12.09	13.81	114	Investment per Establishment	321,011	1,254,573	391
Value Added per Establishment	4,602,255	13,324,702	290	Investment per Employee	6,552	18,212	278
Value Added per Employee	93,930	193,429	206	Investment per Production Worker	9,352	36,424	389

Sources: Same as General Statistics. The 'Average of All Manufacturing' column represents the average of all manufacturing industries reported for the most recent complete year available. The Index shows the relationship between the Average and the Analyzed Industry. For example, 100 means that they are equal; 500 that the Analyzed Industry is five times the average; 50 means that the Analyzed Industry is half the national average. The abbreviation 'na' is used to show that data are 'not available'.

LEADING COMPANIES

Number shown: **55** Total sales ($ mil): **3,657** Total employment (000): **16.2**

Company Name	Address				CEO Name	Phone	Co. Type	Sales ($ mil)	Empl. (000)
Genentech Inc	460 Pt San Bruno	S San Francisco	CA	94080	G Kirk Raab	415-225-1000	P	795	2.7
Seragen Inc	97 South St	Hopkinton	MA	01748	George W Masters	508-435-2331	P	588	0.2
Hyland	550 N Brand Blv	Glendale	CA	91203	John Bacich	818-956-3200	D	400	0.9
Genzyme Corp	1 Kendall Sq	Cambridge	MA	02139	Henri A Termeer	617-252-7500	P	311	2.0
Alpha Therapeutic Corp	5555 Valley Blv	Los Angeles	CA	90032	H Edward Matveld	213-225-2221	S	300	1.9
Connaught Laboratories Inc	PO Box 187	Swiftwater	PA	18370	David J Williams	717-839-7187	S	200	0.7
North American Biologicals Inc	PO Box 692222	Miami	FL	33269	David J Gury	305-625-5303	P	165	1.7
Immunex Corp	51 University St	Seattle	WA	98101	Edward V Fritzky	206-587-0430	P	144	0.8
Genetics Institute Inc	87 Cambridge Pk	Cambridge	MA	02140	Gabriel Schmergel	617-876-1170	P	131	0.9
Solvay Animal Health Inc	1201 Northland Dr	Mendota H	MN	55120	Miles Freitag	612-681-9555	S	112	0.7
LifeCell Corp	3606 R Forest	The Woodlands	TX	77381	Paul M Frison	713-367-5368	P	94	<0.1
Food Ingredients	620 Progress Av	Waukesha	WI	53186	David Carpenter	414-547-5531	D	60	0.2
BioWhittaker Inc	8830 Biggs Ford Rd	Walkersville	MD	21793	Noel L Buterbaugh	301-898-7025	P	55	0.5
Centocor Inc	244 Great Val Pkwy	Malvern	PA	19355	David P Holveck	215-651-6000	P	40	0.9
MedChem Products Inc	232 W Cummings	Woburn	MA	01801	Edward J Quilty	617-932-5900	P	29	0.1
Oxford Veterinary Laboratories	PO Box 775	Worthington	MN	56187	CB Schmidt	507-372-7726	S	27*	0.1
PML Microbiologicals Inc	PO Box 459	Tualatin	OR	97062	Ron Torland	503-639-1500	S	22*	0.1
Colorado Serum Co	4950 York St	Denver	CO	80216	JN Huff	303-295-7527	R	13*	0.1
National Diagnostics Inc	305 Patton Dr	Atlanta	GA	30336	Jeffrey Mirsky	404-699-2121	R	13	<0.1
United Biomedical Inc	25 Davids Dr	Hauppauge	NY	11788	Z Jerry Kuliga	516-273-2828	R	13	<0.1
International Biochemicals Inc	10201 Mayfair Dr	Baton Rouge	LA	70809	J Peter Perez	504-291-4459	R	12	<0.1
Standard Homeopathic Company	PO Box 61067	Los Angeles	CA	90061	JE Craig	213-321-4284	R	10*	0.1
Applied Microbiology Inc	170 53rd St	Brooklyn	NY	11232	Frederic D Price	718-492-8100	P	10	<0.1
Biomatrix Inc	65 Railroad Av	Ridgefield	NJ	07657	Endre A Balazs	201-945-9550	P	9	0.1
BioNebraska Inc	3820 NW 46th St	Lincoln	NE	68524	Fred Wagner	402-470-2100	R	8*	<0.1
Tri-Bio Laboratories Inc	1400 Fox Hill Rd	State College	PA	16803	Dennis C Winkler	814-355-1541	R	7	<0.1
American Laboratories Inc	4410 S 102nd St	Omaha	NE	68127	JE Jackson	402-339-2494	R	7	<0.1
Syntro Corp	9669 Lackman Rd	Lenexa	KS	66219	J Donald Todd	913-888-8876	P	7	<0.1
Genosys Biotechnologies Inc	1442 Lake Front Cir	The Woodlands	TX	77380	Tim McGrath	713-363-3693	R	7	<0.1
OraVax Inc	230 Albany St	Cambridge	MA	02139	Lance K Gordon	617-494-1339	R	7*	<0.1
American Biorganics Inc	2236 Liberty Dr	Niagara Falls	NY	14304	Fayyaz Hussain	716-283-1434	R	6	<0.1
BioSurface Technology Inc	64 Sidney St	Cambridge	MA	02139	David L Castaldi	617-494-8484	P	6	0.1
AQUA-10 Laboratories	PO Box 818	Beaufort	NC	28516	W Campbell III	919-728-2270	R	5	<0.1
Biomune Co	8906 Rosehill Rd	Lenexa	KS	66215	Ron Plyar	913-894-0230	R	5*	<0.1
Cryopharm Corp	2585 Nina St	Pasadena	CA	91107	Carl E Brooks	818-793-1040	R	5	<0.1
Landec Corp	3603 Haven Av	Menlo Park	CA	94025	Gary Steele	415-306-1650	R	5*	<0.1
Metra Biosystems Inc	265 N Whisman Rd	Mountain View	CA	94304	George Dunbar	415-903-9100	R	5*	<0.1
SIBIA Inc	505 Coast Blv S	La Jolla	CA	92037	William T Comer	619-452-5892	R	5	<0.1
ExOxEmis Inc	111 Center St	Little Rock	AR	72201	J T Stephens Jr	501-375-0940	R	4	<0.1
Avigen Inc	1201 Harbor Bay	Alameda	CA	94501	John Monahan	510-748-7150	R	2*	<0.1
Microbe Masters Inc	10201 Mayfair Dr	Baton Rouge	LA	70809	Peter Perez	504-293-2033	S	2*	<0.1
PanVera Corp	565 Science Dr	Madison	WI	53711	Terry Sivesind	608-233-9450	R	2	<0.1
Synthetic Genetics Inc	3347 Industrial Ct	San Diego	CA	92121	Richard Tullis	619-793-2661	D	2*	<0.1
Antibodies Inc	PO Box 1560	Davis	CA	95617	Mike Smith	916-758-4400	R	1	<0.1
neoMecs Inc	4832 Park Glen Rd	St Louis Park	MN	55416	Hiroshi Nomura	612-927-7223	R	1	<0.1
SeaLite Sciences Inc	187 Ben Burton Cir	Bogart	GA	30622	Lee Herring	706-546-4960	R	1*	<0.1
Serex International Inc	14435 Sherman Way	Van Nuys	CA	91405	Gino Iovine	818-989-0611	R	1*	<0.1
Maine Biotechnology Services	383 Presumpscot St	Portland	ME	04103	Joseph P Chandler	207-773-1993	R	1*	<0.1
Parasitix Corp	4980 Carroll	San Diego	CA	92121	Charles J Dumbrell	619-453-8030	S	1	<0.1
Viragen Inc	2343 W 76th St	Hialeah	FL	33016	Charles F Fistel	305-557-6000	P	1	<0.1
Vitro Diagnostics Inc	8100 Southpark	Littleton	CO	80120	Roger D Hurst	303-794-2000	P	1	<0.1
Molecular Genetic Resources	6201 Johns Rd	Tampa	FL	33634	G Edwin Houts	813-886-5338	R	1	<0.1
Cistron Biotechnology Inc	10 Bloomfield Av	Pine Brook	NJ	07058	Henry Grausz	201-575-1700	P	0*	<0.1
Devaron Inc	2235 Rte 130	Dayton	NJ	08810	Yair Devash	908-274-0080	S	0*	<0.1
TargeTech Inc	5935 Darwin Ct	Carlsbad	CA	92008	Henry Nordhoff	619-431-7080	S	0*	<0.1

Source: *Ward's Business Directory of U.S. Private and Public Companies*, Volumes 1 and 2, 1996. The company type code used is as follows: P - Public, R - Private, S - Subsidiary, D - Division, J - Joint Venture, A - Affiliate, G - Group. Sales are in millions of dollars, employees are in thousands. An asterisk (*) indicates an estimated sales volume. The symbol < stands for 'less than'. Company names and addresses are truncated, in some cases, to fit into the available space.

MATERIALS CONSUMED

Material	Quantity	Delivered Cost ($ million)
Materials, ingredients, containers, and supplies	(X)	1,111.8
Antibiotics, in bulk, for human and veterinary use	(X)	51.1
Vitamins, natural and synthetic, in bulk, for human and veterinary use	(X)	2.0
Vitamins, natural and synthetic, in bulk, for animal feeds	(X)	(D)
Agricultural products (crude), including flowers, grains, seeds, herbs, etc.	(X)	23.0
Processed food and kindred products including lactose, meat packing plant products, yeast, etc.	(X)	28.4
Blood derivatives and extenders	(X)	486.7
All other bulk medicinal and botanical uncompounded drugs, except antibiotics and vitamins	(X)	25.7
Gelatin (pharmaceutical grade) and gelatin capsules	(X)	(D)
Industrial inorganic chemicals	(X)	31.5
Cyclic crudes and intermediates including organic colors	(X)	(D)
Other synthetic organic chemicals including halogenated hydrocarbons	(X)	1.8
Fabricated plastics products, including plastics closures, film, and packaging items, except containers	(X)	33.5
Metal closures and crowns for containers	(X)	3.3
Labels, coupons, instructions, and other printed material	(X)	5.9
Plastics containers	(X)	14.2
Glass containers	(X)	13.0
Metal containers	(X)	(D)
Paperboard containers, boxes, and corrugated paperboard	(X)	18.4
All other materials and components, parts, containers, and supplies	(X)	228.0
Materials, ingredients, containers, and supplies, nsk	(X)	142.8

Source: 1992 *Economic Census*. Explanation of symbols used: (D): Withheld to avoid disclosure of competitive data; na: Not available; (S): Withheld because statistical norms were not met; (X): Not applicable; (Z): Less than half the unit shown; nec: Not elsewhere classified; nsk: Not specified by kind; - : zero; * : 10-19 percent estimated; ** : 20-29 percent estimated.

PRODUCT SHARE DETAILS

Product or Product Class	% Share
Biological products, except diagnostic	100.00
Blood and blood derivatives, except diagnostics, for human use	23.41
Vaccines, toxoids, and antigens, except allergens, for human use	21.88
Other biologics for human use	31.57
Antitoxins, antivenoms, immune globulins, therapeutic immune serums, etc., for therapeutic use and passive immunization	97.33
Allergenic extracts and other biologics for human use, including poison ivy and oak extracts, except diagnostic allergens	2.68
Biological products for veterinary, industrial, and other uses, nec, except diagnostics	17.71
Biological veterinary vaccines, including vaccines against foot-and-mouth disease	39.00
Biological bacterins, toxoids, and other antigens, except allergens, for active immunization	12.49
Other biological products, including veterinary blood derivatives, antitoxins, immune serums, and allergens, except diagnostics	8.95
Biological products for industrial and other uses, except culture media	31.58
Biological products for veterinary, industrial, and other uses, nec, except diagnostics, nsk	7.98
Biological products, except diagnostic, nsk	5.44

Source: 1992 *Economic Census*. The values shown are percent of total shipments in an industry. Values of indented subcategories are summed in the main heading. The symbol (D) appears when data are withheld to prevent disclosure of competitive information. The abbreviation nsk stands for 'not specified by kind' and nec for 'not elsewhere classified'.

INPUTS AND OUTPUTS FOR DRUGS

Economic Sector or Industry Providing Inputs	%	Sector	Economic Sector or Industry Buying Outputs	%	Sector
Drugs	19.2	Manufg.	Personal consumption expenditures	47.5	
Imports	14.7	Foreign	Drugs	12.3	Manufg.
Accounting, auditing & bookkeeping	12.9	Services	Hospitals	9.9	Services
Wholesale trade	8.4	Trade	S/L Govt. purch., health & hospitals	8.4	S/L Govt
Management & consulting services & labs	7.2	Services	Exports	7.8	Foreign
Advertising	2.9	Services	Prepared feeds, nec	4.3	Manufg.
Electric services (utilities)	1.9	Util.	Medical & health services, nec	2.5	Services
Banking	1.8	Fin/R.E.	Federal Government purchases, national defense	1.5	Fed Govt
Glass containers	1.7	Manufg.	Change in business inventories	1.2	In House
Miscellaneous plastics products	1.7	Manufg.	Nursing & personal care facilities	1.0	Services
Petroleum refining	1.7	Manufg.	Doctors & dentists	0.8	Services
Paperboard containers & boxes	1.5	Manufg.	Federal Government purchases, nondefense	0.7	Fed Govt
Noncomparable imports	1.4	Foreign	Meat animals	0.5	Agric.
Business services nec	1.2	Services	Cyclic crudes and organics	0.3	Manufg.
Colleges, universities, & professional schools	1.1	Services	Dog, cat, & other pet food	0.3	Manufg.
Cyclic crudes and organics	1.0	Manufg.	Residential care	0.2	Services
Industrial inorganic chemicals, nec	1.0	Manufg.	S/L Govt. purch., other education & libraries	0.2	S/L Govt
Chemical preparations, nec	0.9	Manufg.	Poultry & eggs	0.1	Agric.
Metal cans	0.8	Manufg.			
Communications, except radio & TV	0.8	Util.			
Gas production & distribution (utilities)	0.8	Util.			
Eating & drinking places	0.8	Trade			
Royalties	0.8	Fin/R.E.			
Commercial printing	0.7	Manufg.			

Continued on next page.

INPUTS AND OUTPUTS FOR DRUGS - Continued

Economic Sector or Industry Providing Inputs	%	Sector	Economic Sector or Industry Buying Outputs	%	Sector
Equipment rental & leasing services	0.7	Services			
Motor freight transportation & warehousing	0.6	Util.			
Miscellaneous repair shops	0.6	Services			
Paper coating & glazing	0.5	Manufg.			
Air transportation	0.5	Util.			
Engineering, architectural, & surveying services	0.5	Services			
Maintenance of nonfarm buildings nec	0.4	Constr.			
Meat packing plants	0.4	Manufg.			
Prepared feeds, nec	0.4	Manufg.			
Electrical repair shops	0.4	Services			
Legal services	0.4	Services			
U.S. Postal Service	0.4	Gov't			
Poultry & eggs	0.3	Agric.			
Agricultural chemicals, nec	0.3	Manufg.			
Crowns & closures	0.3	Manufg.			
Fabricated metal products, nec	0.3	Manufg.			
Metal barrels, drums, & pails	0.3	Manufg.			
Pumps & compressors	0.3	Manufg.			
Real estate	0.3	Fin/R.E.			
Greenhouse & nursery products	0.2	Agric.			
Manifold business forms	0.2	Manufg.			
Metal foil & leaf	0.2	Manufg.			
Soap & other detergents	0.2	Manufg.			
Railroads & related services	0.2	Util.			
Water transportation	0.2	Util.			
Insurance carriers	0.2	Fin/R.E.			
Security & commodity brokers	0.2	Fin/R.E.			
Automotive rental & leasing, without drivers	0.2	Services			
Automotive repair shops & services	0.2	Services			
Photofinishing labs, commercial photography	0.2	Services			
Alkalies & chlorine	0.1	Manufg.			
Fabricated rubber products, nec	0.1	Manufg.			
Surgical & medical instruments	0.1	Manufg.			
Wet corn milling	0.1	Manufg.			
Sanitary services, steam supply, irrigation	0.1	Util.			
Credit agencies other than banks	0.1	Fin/R.E.			
Computer & data processing services	0.1	Services			
Hotels & lodging places	0.1	Services			
State & local government enterprises, nec	0.1	Gov't			

Source: Benchmark Input-Output Accounts for the U.S. Economy, 1982, U.S. Department of Commerce, Washington, D.C., July 1991. Data, as reported in the source, are organized by the 1977 SIC structure in use in 1982 but have been matched, as closely as is possible, to the 1987 SIC structure used in this book.

OCCUPATIONS EMPLOYED BY SIC 283 - DRUGS

Occupation	% of Total 1994	Change to 2005	Occupation	% of Total 1994	Change to 2005
Packaging & filling machine operators	7.8	11.2	Medical scientists	1.7	48.3
Science & mathematics technicians	5.7	36.0	Hand packers & packagers	1.7	5.9
Biological scientists	5.5	49.6	Systems analysts	1.6	97.7
Secretaries, ex legal & medical	5.3	12.5	Assemblers, fabricators, & hand workers nec	1.5	23.6
Chemists	4.9	23.6	Freight, stock, & material movers, hand	1.5	-1.1
Sales & related workers nec	4.4	23.6	Janitors & cleaners, incl maids	1.5	-1.1
Chemical equipment controllers, operators	3.1	11.2	Industrial production managers	1.5	23.6
Inspectors, testers, & graders, precision	2.7	23.6	Machine operators nec	1.4	8.9
Engineering, mathematical, & science managers	2.2	40.4	General office clerks	1.2	5.4
Management support workers nec	2.0	23.6	Traffic, shipping, & receiving clerks	1.2	18.9
Industrial machinery mechanics	1.8	36.0	Professional workers nec	1.2	48.3
Managers & administrators nec	1.8	23.5	Helpers, laborers, & material movers nec	1.1	23.6
General managers & top executives	1.8	17.3	Marketing & sales worker supervisors	1.1	23.6
Crushing & mixing machine operators	1.7	23.6	Extruding & forming machine workers	1.1	36.0
Marketing, advertising, & PR managers	1.7	23.6	Bookkeeping, accounting, & auditing clerks	1.0	-7.3

Source: Industry-Occupation Matrix, Bureau of Labor Statistics. These data relate to one or more 3-digit SIC industry groups rather than to a single 4-digit SIC. The change reported for each occupation to the year 2005 is a percent of growth or decline as estimated by the Bureau of Labor Statistics. The abbreviation nec stands for 'not elsewhere classified'.

LOCATION BY STATE AND REGIONAL CONCENTRATION

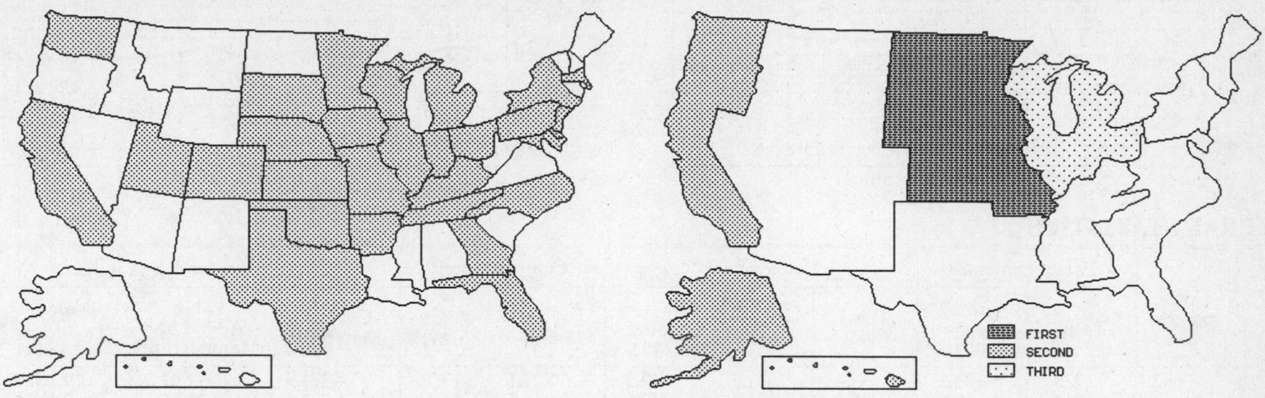

INDUSTRY DATA BY STATE

State	Establish-ments	Shipments			Employment				Cost as % of Shipments	Investment per Employee ($)
		Total ($ mil)	% of U.S.	Per Establ.	Total Number	% of U.S.	Per Establ.	Wages ($/hour)		
California	32	1,571.9	39.6	49.1	5,600	30.4	175	17.91	25.9	30,429
New York	11	220.1	5.5	20.0	1,100	6.0	100	14.56	48.8	8,364
Iowa	10	191.4	4.8	19.1	800	4.3	80	11.75	33.9	-
Maryland	10	80.3	2.0	8.0	600	3.3	60	15.17	30.5	4,500
Wisconsin	8	79.1	2.0	9.9	600	3.3	75	12.60	28.1	7,333
Missouri	12	60.3	1.5	5.0	500	2.7	42	13.25	37.5	4,600
Ohio	12	34.3	0.9	2.9	400	2.2	33	8.60	48.4	1,500
Georgia	6	30.1	0.8	5.0	200	1.1	33	9.00	27.9	-
Texas	22	29.7	0.7	1.4	300	1.6	14	8.75	38.4	3,333
Minnesota	6	29.0	0.7	4.8	300	1.6	50	7.50	31.7	-
Tennessee	7	20.3	0.5	2.9	400	2.2	57	8.75	51.2	1,000
Pennsylvania	21	(D)	-	-	750 *	4.1	36	-	-	-
Kansas	10	(D)	-	-	375 *	2.0	38	-	-	-
Florida	9	(D)	-	-	375 *	2.0	42	-	-	2,933
Massachusetts	8	(D)	-	-	750 *	4.1	94	-	-	-
Michigan	8	(D)	-	-	375 *	2.0	47	-	-	-
Illinois	7	(D)	-	-	750 *	4.1	107	-	-	-
North Carolina	7	(D)	-	-	750 *	4.1	107	-	-	17,200
Washington	7	(D)	-	-	375 *	2.0	54	-	-	-
Kentucky	6	(D)	-	-	175 *	1.0	29	-	-	-
Nebraska	6	(D)	-	-	750 *	4.1	125	-	-	-
Arkansas	5	(D)	-	-	175 *	1.0	35	-	-	-
Indiana	4	(D)	-	-	175 *	1.0	44	-	-	-
New Jersey	4	(D)	-	-	175 *	1.0	44	-	-	-
Oklahoma	4	(D)	-	-	175 *	1.0	44	-	-	-
Colorado	2	(D)	-	-	175 *	1.0	88	-	-	-
Delaware	2	(D)	-	-	375 *	2.0	188	-	-	-
South Dakota	2	(D)	-	-	175 *	1.0	88	-	-	-
Utah	2	(D)	-	-	175 *	1.0	88	-	-	-

Source: 1992 *Economic Census*. The states are in descending order of shipments or establishments (if shipment data are missing for the majority). The symbol (D) appears when data are withheld to prevent disclosure of competitive information. States marked with (D) are sorted by number of establishments. A dash (-) indicates that the data element cannot be calculated; * indicates the midpoint of a range.

2841 - SOAP & DETERGENT

Shipments ($ million)

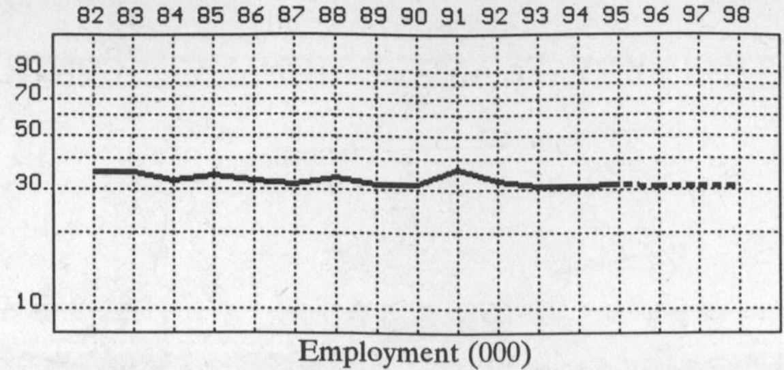

Employment (000)

GENERAL STATISTICS

Year	Com-panies	Establishments: Total	Establishments: with 20 or more employees	Employment: Total (000)	Production Workers (000)	Production Hours (Mil)	Compensation: Payroll ($ mil)	Compensation: Wages ($/hr)	Cost of Materials	Value Added by Manufacture	Value of Shipments	Capital Invest.
1982	642	723	232	35.4	21.2	42.5	827.1	10.76	4,371.9	4,777.1	9,167.3	273.2
1983		717	229	35.5	21.3	42.9	860.5	11.44	4,780.6	4,282.5	9,116.6	240.9
1984		711	226	32.8	19.2	40.8	896.7	12.11	5,184.4	4,366.8	9,468.4	318.9
1985		705	223	34.1	20.0	40.0	946.0	13.20	5,529.7	4,481.8	10,052.7	317.0
1986		725	238	32.3	19.4	40.4	974.5	13.44	5,703.2	4,639.1	10,346.1	287.7
1987	683	764	230	31.7	19.3	39.2	955.7	13.81	5,673.4	5,892.1	11,558.5	338.7
1988		749	226	33.3	21.0	41.4	1,011.8	13.85	5,995.9	6,393.4	12,306.3	368.3
1989		731	229	31.6	22.0	39.8	1,093.1	14.36	6,790.8	6,548.2	13,280.7	396.0
1990		715	228	31.5	22.8	42.7	1,197.7	14.65	7,509.8	7,971.2	15,373.4	475.8
1991		686	222	36.6	23.1	44.1	1,220.7	14.67	7,158.9	8,164.6	15,298.5	630.8
1992	635	710	228	32.9	20.0	41.0	1,175.9	14.85	6,960.1	7,723.3	14,760.9	571.4
1993		704	222	31.2	17.9	38.1	1,144.3	15.06	7,174.4	8,225.1	15,457.7	513.8
1994		711P	224P	31.3	18.5	38.8	1,166.9	14.92	7,077.0	7,376.9	14,527.7	454.4
1995		710P	224P	31.6P	20.0P	39.8P	1,266.3P	15.99P	8,131.1P	8,475.7P	16,691.6P	585.0P
1996		708P	223P	31.3P	19.9P	39.7P	1,299.2P	16.32P	8,432.4P	8,789.7P	17,310.0P	611.6P
1997		707P	223P	31.1P	19.9P	39.5P	1,332.1P	16.66P	8,733.6P	9,103.7P	17,928.4P	638.2P
1998		706P	222P	30.9P	19.8P	39.4P	1,364.9P	17.00P	9,034.9P	9,417.8P	18,546.9P	664.7P

Sources: 1982, 1987, 1992 *Economic Census*; *Annual Survey of Manufactures*, 83-86, 88-91, 93-94. Establishment counts for non-Census years are from *County Business Patterns*; establishment values for 83-84 are extrapolations. 'P's show projections by the editors. Industries reclassified in 87 will not have data for prior years.

INDICES OF CHANGE

Year	Com-panies	Establishments: Total	Establishments: with 20 or more employees	Employment: Total (000)	Production Workers (000)	Production Hours (Mil)	Compensation: Payroll ($ mil)	Compensation: Wages ($/hr)	Cost of Materials	Value Added by Manufacture	Value of Shipments	Capital Invest.
1982	101	102	102	108	106	104	70	72	63	62	62	48
1983		101	100	108	106	105	73	77	69	55	62	42
1984		100	99	100	96	100	76	82	74	57	64	56
1985		99	98	104	100	98	80	89	79	58	68	55
1986		102	104	98	97	99	83	91	82	60	70	50
1987	108	108	101	96	96	96	81	93	82	76	78	59
1988		105	99	101	105	101	86	93	86	83	83	64
1989		103	100	96	110	97	93	97	98	85	90	69
1990		101	100	96	114	104	102	99	108	103	104	83
1991		97	97	111	116	108	104	99	103	106	104	110
1992	100	100	100	100	100	100	100	100	100	100	100	100
1993		99	97	95	90	93	97	101	103	106	105	90
1994		100P	98P	95	93	95	99	100	102	96	98	80
1995		100P	98P	96P	100P	97P	108P	108P	117P	110P	113P	102P
1996		100P	98P	95P	100P	97P	110P	110P	121P	114P	117P	107P
1997		100P	98P	95P	99P	96P	113P	112P	125P	118P	121P	112P
1998		99P	97P	94P	99P	96P	116P	114P	130P	122P	126P	116P

Sources: Same as General Statistics. Values reflect change from the base year, 1992. Values above 100 mean greater than 92, values below 100 mean less than 92, and a value of 100 in the 82-91 or 93-98 period means same as 92. 'P's mark projections by the editors.

SELECTED RATIOS

For 1994	Avg. of All Manufact.	Analyzed Industry	Index
Employees per Establishment	49	44	90
Payroll per Establishment	1,500,273	1,641,105	109
Payroll per Employee	30,620	37,281	122
Production Workers per Establishment	34	26	76
Wages per Establishment	853,319	814,148	95
Wages per Production Worker	24,861	31,292	126
Hours per Production Worker	2,056	2,097	102
Wages per Hour	12.09	14.92	123
Value Added per Establishment	4,602,255	10,374,724	225
Value Added per Employee	93,930	235,684	251

For 1994	Avg. of All Manufact.	Analyzed Industry	Index
Value Added per Production Worker	134,084	398,751	297
Cost per Establishment	5,045,178	9,952,950	197
Cost per Employee	102,970	226,102	220
Cost per Production Worker	146,988	382,541	260
Shipments per Establishment	9,576,895	20,431,465	213
Shipments per Employee	195,460	464,144	237
Shipments per Production Worker	279,017	785,281	281
Investment per Establishment	321,011	639,059	199
Investment per Employee	6,552	14,518	222
Investment per Production Worker	9,352	24,562	263

Sources: Same as General Statistics. The 'Average of All Manufacturing' column represents the average of all manufacturing industries reported for the most recent complete year available. The Index shows the relationship between the Average and the Analyzed Industry. For example, 100 means that they are equal; 500 that the Analyzed Industry is five times the average; 50 means that the Analyzed Industry is half the national average. The abbreviation 'na' is used to show that data are 'not available'.

LEADING COMPANIES

Number shown: **66** Total sales ($ mil): **36,069** Total employment (000): **143.5**

Company Name	Address				CEO Name	Phone	Co. Type	Sales ($ mil)	Empl. (000)
Procter and Gamble Co	1 P & G	Cincinnati	OH	45202	Edwin L Artzt	513-983-1100	P	30,296	96.5
Dial Corp	Dial Twr	Phoenix	AZ	85077	John W Teets	602-207-4000	P	3,547	32.5
Ecolab Inc	Ecolab Ctr	St Paul	MN	55102	Allan L Schuman	612-293-2233	P	1,208	8.2
Allied Colloids Inc	2301 Wilroy Rd	Suffolk	VA	23439	David Farrar	804-538-3700	R	160	0.5
Beiersdorf Inc	PO Box 5529	Norwalk	CT	06856	Peter Metzger	203-853-8008	S	94*	0.4
DeSoto Inc	16750 S Vincennes	South Holland	IL	60473	John R Phillips	708-331-8800	P	87	0.4
State Chemical Mfg Co	3100 Hamilton Av	Cleveland	OH	44114	Malcom Zucker	216-861-7114	R	70*	1.0
Korex Co	PO Box 175	Wixom	MI	48393	Robert J Belanger	810-624-0000	S	60	0.2
Thatcher Co	PO Box 27407	Salt Lake City	UT	84127	L Thatcher	801-972-4587	R	47*	0.2
Scott/Sani-Fresh International	4702 Goldfield	San Antonio	TX	78218	Mary A Bogie	210-661-5374	S	40	0.3
Softsoap Enterprises Inc	134 Colombia Ct S	Chaska	MN	55318	Joe Witkewich	612-448-1700	S	31*	0.2
Hewitt Soap Company Inc	333 Linden Av	Dayton	OH	45403	BL Stichter	513-253-1151	S	28	0.3
T-Chem Products Inc	9028 Dice Rd	Santa Fe Sprgs	CA	90670	Don Thurmond	310-946-6427	R	24	<0.1
James Austin Co	PO Box 827	Mars	PA	16046	JT Austin	412-625-1535	R	23	0.2
Diamond Chemical Co	Union and DuBois	E Rutherford	NJ	07073	AL Diamond	201-935-4300	R	22	0.2
Caswell-Massey Company Ltd	121 Fieldcrest Av	Edison	NJ	08837	Jacquelyn Hadley	908-225-2181	R	20	0.1
Pilot Chemical of California	11756 Burke St	Santa Fe Sprgs	CA	90670	Paul Morrisroe	310-698-6778	R	20*	0.1
Fremont Industries Inc	4400 Val Industrial	Shakopee	MN	55379	M Gruss	612-445-4121	R	18*	0.1
Williamsburg Soap & Candle Co	7521 Richmond Rd	Williamsburg	VA	23188	John B Barnett	804-564-3354	R	16	0.2
Glissen Chemical Company Inc	1321 58th St	Brooklyn	NY	11219	JW Lehr	718-436-4200	R	15	0.1
Crystal Inc	PO Box 950	Lansdale	PA	19446	Thomas Dunn III	215-368-1661	S	14	<0.1
Madison Chemical Company Inc	PO Box 1599	Madison	IN	47250	David R Goodman	812-273-6000	R	14*	<0.1
Norman, Fox and Co	PO Box 58727	Vernon	CA	90058	Keith Johnson	213-583-0016	R	14*	<0.1
Zip-Chem Products Co	1860 Dobbin Dr	San Jose	CA	95133	Chuck Pottier	408-729-0291	R	14*	<0.1
Alex C Fergusson Inc	Spring Mill Dr	Frazer	PA	19355	Robert Sistowicz	215-647-3300	S	13	<0.1
Winfield Brooks Company Inc	70 Conn St	Woburn	MA	01801	KE Perry	617-933-5300	R	13	0.1
Namico Inc	PO Box 4684	Philadelphia	PA	19127	RM McAlaine	215-482-6600	R	12	<0.1
Concord Chemical Co	17th & Federal St	Camden	NJ	08105	JO Cram Jr	609-966-1526	R	12*	<0.1
Grace-Lee Products Inc	2540 2nd St NE	Minneapolis	MN	55418	BJ Graceman	612-379-2711	R	10	0.1
Pecks Products Co	1220 Switzer Av	St Louis	MO	63147	John F Daley	314-385-5454	D	10*	<0.1
Midland Chicago Corp	5300 W 127th St	Alsip	IL	60658	Peter Roth	708-389-6600	R	9	<0.1
Washington Chemical Sales	2498 American Av	Hayward	CA	94545	KW Knapp	510-782-8727	R	8	<0.1
Candy and Co	2515 W 35th St	Chicago	IL	60632	JF Daley	312-523-8320	D	7*	<0.1
Haag Laboratories Inc	1415 W 37th St	Chicago	IL	60609	James B Flanagan	312-247-2000	S	7*	<0.1
National Purity Inc	434 Lakeside Av	Minneapolis	MN	55405	Jack J Spillane	612-378-1465	R	7	<0.1
Time Products Inc	3780 Brownmill SE	Atlanta	GA	30354	Chris Callas	404-767-7526	R	7	<0.1
A and L Laboratories Inc	1001 Glenwood Av	Minneapolis	MN	55405	Guy P Pochard	612-374-9141	R	6*	<0.1
Luseaux Laboratories Inc	4625 Santa Fe Dr	Kingman	AZ	86401	WB Edwards	602-692-0192	R	5	<0.1
Sanolite Corp	26 Papetti Plz	Elizabeth	NJ	07207	Norman E Lubin	908-353-8500	R	5*	<0.1
America's Finest Products	1639 9th St	Santa Monica	CA	90404	Jack N Rothaus	310-450-6555	R	4*	<0.1
Benchmark Inc	PO Box 156	Wyandotte	MI	48192	WF Cook	313-285-0900	R	4*	<0.1
Sani-Co Products	9709 Lurline Av	Chatsworth	CA	91311	Joanne R Medved	818-886-8001	R	4	0.1
Chaska Chemical Company Inc	12502 Xenwood S	Savage	MN	55378	H Poppitz	612-890-1820	R	3	<0.1
Crown Chemical Inc	13740 S Kenton Av	Crestwood	IL	60445	James Spain	708-371-6990	R	3	<0.1
Klix Corp	551 Railroad Av	S San Francisco	CA	94080	Marcel R Takata	415-761-0622	R	3	<0.1
Tronex Chemical Corp	1401 Woodland St	Detroit	MI	48211	R Sarlund	313-865-4600	R	3	<0.1
Warco Laboratories Company	24020 Frampton	Harbor City	CA	90710	David Kanies	213-775-7547	S	3*	<0.1
Eden Sales and Marketing Inc	2009 W Mtn View	Phoenix	AZ	85021	James R Eden	602-371-0069	R	3	<0.1
C and H Chemical Inc	222 Starkey St	St Paul	MN	55107	W R Cammack Jr	612-227-4343	R	3	<0.1
Harvey Universal Inc	1805 W 208 St	Torrance	CA	90501	Larry B Harvey	310-328-9000	P	3	<0.1
Lubar Chemical Co	PO Box 410588	Kansas City	MO	64141	Skip Jackson	816-471-2560	R	3	<0.1
Red Oak Hill Inc	5303 W 33rd St	Little Rock	AR	72204	William G Ellis	501-565-2900	R	3	<0.1
Alconox Inc	9 40th St	New York	NY	10016	F Zizman	212-532-4040	R	2	<0.1
California Soda Co	355 Mandela Pkwy	Oakland	CA	94607	N Hinck	510-444-6217	R	2	<0.1
Glo-Mold Inc	520 S Main St	Akron	OH	44311	Jim Berresford	216-434-4442	R	2	<0.1
Sanitek Product Inc	3959 Goodwin Av	Los Angeles	CA	90039	RL Moseley	213-245-6781	R	2	<0.1
Nelson Products Co	12345 Schaefer Hwy	Detroit	MI	48227	Charlotte Nelson	313-933-1500	R	2	<0.1
Creative Aerosol Corp	PO Box 118	Adelphia	NJ	07710	James Mulligan	908-431-7500	R	1	<0.1
Burge Chemical Products Inc	72 Grandville SW	Grand Rapids	MI	49503	Terry L Wisner	616-458-1135	R	1	<0.1
Fabric Chemical Corp	61 Cornelison Av	Jersey City	NJ	07304	P Jacobson	201-432-0440	R	1*	<0.1
National Chemicals Inc	PO Box 32	Winona	MN	55987	LC Landman Jr	507-454-5640	R	1	<0.1
Superklean Products Inc	6372 Miller Rd	Detroit	MI	48211	Tony Nofsar	313-925-0100	R	1	<0.1
Zoe Chemical Company Inc	PO Box L	New Hyde Park	NY	11040	Edward Axelrod	516-354-1043	R	1*	0.1
Sanitized Inc	PO Box 2211	New Preston	CT	06777	Stewart E Klein	203-868-2173	R	1*	<0.1
Southern Mfg Chemists	PO Box 11643	Richmond	VA	23230	William Wingfield	804-353-6464	R	1	<0.1
Sanford Chemical Company Inc	1945 Touhy Av	Elk Grove Vill	IL	60007	Sanford Arenberg	708-437-3530	R	1	<0.1

Source: *Ward's Business Directory of U.S. Private and Public Companies*, Volumes 1 and 2, 1996. The company type code used is as follows: P - Public, R - Private, S - Subsidiary, D - Division, J - Joint Venture, A - Affiliate, G - Group. Sales are in millions of dollars, employees are in thousands. An asterisk (*) indicates an estimated sales volume. The symbol < stands for 'less than'. Company names and addresses are truncated, in some cases, to fit into the available space.

MATERIALS CONSUMED

Material		Quantity	Delivered Cost ($ million)
Materials, ingredients, containers, and supplies		(X)	5,731.1
Bulk surface active intermediates (active wt.)	mil lb	490.7	257.0
Bulk surface active agents primarily for detergent purposes (active wt.), except intermediates	mil lb	499.1	266.7
Other bulk surface active agents	mil lb	85.3	42.8
Perfume oil mixtures and blends	mil lb	37.4*	219.2
Fatty acids	mil lb	299.9	102.1
Grease and inedible tallow	mil lb	765.3	130.2
Chlorine (100 percent Cl basis)	1,000 s tons	(S)	9.3
Sodium carbonate (soda ash) (58 percent Na2O)	1,000 s tons	713.3	96.2
Sodium hydroxide (caustic soda)(100 percent NaOH)	1,000 s tons	470.3	104.2
Sodium tripolyphosphate (STPP) (100 percent NaP0)	1,000 s tons	259.8	153.7
All other potassium and sodium compounds		(X)	281.3
Refined petroleum products, including mineral oil, naphtha solvents, petrolatum, waxes, etc.		(X)	32.1
All other organic and inorganic chemicals		(X)	1,685.8
Labels, coupons, instructions, and other printed material		(X)	70.2
Paperboard containers, boxes, and corrugated paperboard		(X)	563.8
Metal containers		(X)	25.5
Plastics containers		(X)	499.6
Fabricated plastics products, including dispensing pumps and sprayers		(X)	38.7
All other materials and components, parts, containers, and supplies		(X)	602.1
Materials, ingredients, containers, and supplies, nsk		(X)	550.7

Source: 1992 *Economic Census*. Explanation of symbols used: (D): Withheld to avoid disclosure of competitive data; na: Not available; (S): Withheld because statistical norms were not met; (X): Not applicable; (Z): Less than half the unit shown; nec: Not elsewhere classified; nsk: Not specified by kind; - : zero; * : 10-19 percent estimated; ** : 20-29 percent estimated.

PRODUCT SHARE DETAILS

Product or Product Class	% Share
Soap and other detergents	100.00
Soaps and detergents, commercial, industrial, and institutional	19.44
Soap chips, flakes, granules, powders, and sprays, including washing powders, except specialty cleaners (commercial, industrial, and institutional)	3.92
Liquid (potash and other) commercial, industrial, and institutional soaps, excluding shampoos and specialty cleaners	8.73
Other commercial, industrial, and institutional soaps, including mechanics' hand soap, except specialty cleaners	3.46
Commercial, industrial, and institutional liquid alkaline dishwashing compounds	7.03
Commercial, industrial, and institutional dry alkaline dishwashing compounds	4.95
Commercial, industrial, and institutional alkaline scouring cleaners	0.94
Other liquid alkaline commercial, industrial, and institutional detergents	18.28
Dry hard surface alkaline commercial, industrial, and institutional cleaners	3.96
Other dry alkaline commercial, industrial, and institutional cleaners	3.72
Commercial, industrial, and institutional dry synthetic organic detergents, anionic base	1.40
Commercial, industrial, and institutional dry synthetic organic detergents, nonionic base or other base	2.50
Commercial, industrial, and institutional liquid synthetic organic detergents, anionic base	9.15
Commercial, industrial, and institutional liquid synthetic organic detergents, cationic or amphoteric base	2.98
Commercial, industrial, and institutional liquid synthetic organic detergents, nonionic base or other base	6.16
Liquid dairy, farm, and food plant acid-type halogenated cleaners, sanitizers, etc.	1.37
Liquid dairy, farm, and food plant acid-type nonhalogenated cleaners, sanitizers, etc.	4.87
Commercial, industrial, and institutional acid-type liquid metal cleaners	4.27
All other commercial, industrial, and institutional acid-type cleaners, including dry cleaners	3.53
Soaps and detergents, commercial, industrial, and institutional, nsk	8.78
Household detergents	54.55
Household liquid alkaline automatic dishwashing detergents	0.89
Household dry alkaline automatic dishwashing detergents	4.75
Household liquid alkaline hard surface cleaners, including general-purpose cleaners and degreasers	8.35
Household liquid alkaline scouring cleaners	3.55
All other household alkaline detergents	0.07
Household dry laundry detergents, light-duty	0.12
Household dry laundry detergents, heavy-duty, phosphate based	15.27
Household dry laundry detergents, heavy-duty, phosphate free	30.99
Household liquid laundry detergents, light-duty	12.10
Household liquid laundry detergents, heavy-duty	21.71
Household laundry presoaks	1.21
Household detergents, nsk	0.99
Household soaps, except specialty cleaners	17.78
Household deodorant bar soaps (except novelty), excluding medicated	50.20
Household nondeodorant bar soaps (except novelty), excluding medicated	30.67
Household novelty bar soaps, excluding medicated	3.84
Household liquid toilet soaps, excluding medicated	11.10
Other household soaps, including mechanics' hand soaps (except waterless), and medicated soaps	4.09
Soaps, except specialty cleaners, household, nsk	0.11
Glycerin, natural	1.25
Crude glycerin, natural, 100-percent basis	25.02
High-gravity, dynamite, and yellow distilled natural glycerin, 100-percent basis	74.98
Soap and other detergents, nsk	6.98

Source: 1992 *Economic Census*. The values shown are percent of total shipments in an industry. Values of indented subcategories are summed in the main heading. The symbol (D) appears when data are withheld to prevent disclosure of competitive information. The abbreviation nsk stands for 'not specified by kind' and nec for 'not elsewhere classified'.

INPUTS AND OUTPUTS FOR SOAP & OTHER DETERGENTS

Economic Sector or Industry Providing Inputs	%	Sector	Economic Sector or Industry Buying Outputs	%	Sector
Industrial inorganic chemicals, nec	14.1	Manufg.	Personal consumption expenditures	75.2	
Wholesale trade	13.1	Trade	Hospitals	3.6	Services
Surface active agents	9.2	Manufg.	Eating & drinking places	2.1	Trade
Paperboard containers & boxes	7.0	Manufg.	Exports	2.1	Foreign
Miscellaneous plastics products	6.3	Manufg.	Hotels & lodging places	2.0	Services
Advertising	4.3	Services	Services to dwellings & other buildings	1.7	Services
Alkalies & chlorine	4.2	Manufg.	Laundry, dry cleaning, shoe repair	1.2	Services
Petroleum refining	3.3	Manufg.	Soap & other detergents	0.9	Manufg.
Plastics materials & resins	2.6	Manufg.	Nursing & personal care facilities	0.8	Services
Pumps & compressors	2.5	Manufg.	S/L Govt. purch., higher education	0.7	S/L Govt
Soap & other detergents	1.9	Manufg.	Meat packing plants	0.6	Manufg.
Commercial printing	1.7	Manufg.	Toilet preparations	0.5	Manufg.
Toilet preparations	1.6	Manufg.	Dairy farm products	0.4	Agric.
Motor freight transportation & warehousing	1.6	Util.	S/L Govt. purch., natural resource & recreation.	0.4	S/L Govt
Railroads & related services	1.6	Util.	Drugs	0.3	Manufg.
Electric services (utilities)	1.5	Util.	Miscellaneous plastics products	0.3	Manufg.
Gas production & distribution (utilities)	1.5	Util.	Plastics materials & resins	0.3	Manufg.
Animal & marine fats & oils	1.4	Manufg.	Federal Government purchases, national defense	0.3	Fed Govt
Chemical preparations, nec	1.3	Manufg.	S/L Govt. purch., sanitation	0.3	S/L Govt
Metal barrels, drums, & pails	1.3	Manufg.	Bottled & canned soft drinks	0.2	Manufg.
Vegetable oil mills, nec	1.3	Manufg.	Cheese, natural & processed	0.2	Manufg.
Imports	1.2	Foreign	Cigarettes	0.2	Manufg.
Cyclic crudes and organics	1.1	Manufg.	Fluid milk	0.2	Manufg.
Vitreous china food utensils	1.0	Manufg.	Malt beverages	0.2	Manufg.
Metal foil & leaf	0.9	Manufg.	Organic fibers, noncellulosic	0.2	Manufg.
Metal cans	0.8	Manufg.	Paints & allied products	0.2	Manufg.
Book printing	0.7	Manufg.	Polishes & sanitation goods	0.2	Manufg.
Communications, except radio & TV	0.7	Util.	Poultry dressing plants	0.2	Manufg.
Water transportation	0.7	Util.	Synthetic rubber	0.2	Manufg.
Eating & drinking places	0.6	Trade	Federal Government purchases, nondefense	0.2	Fed Govt
Noncomparable imports	0.6	Foreign	S/L Govt. purch., elem. & secondary education	0.2	S/L Govt
Air transportation	0.5	Util.	S/L Govt. purch., health & hospitals	0.2	S/L Govt
Banking	0.5	Fin/R.E.	Canned specialties	0.1	Manufg.
Miscellaneous repair shops	0.5	Services	Metal cans	0.1	Manufg.
U.S. Postal Service	0.5	Gov't	Prepared feeds, nec	0.1	Manufg.
Maintenance of nonfarm buildings nec	0.4	Constr.	Sausages & other prepared meats	0.1	Manufg.
Glass containers	0.4	Manufg.	Surface active agents	0.1	Manufg.
Real estate	0.4	Fin/R.E.	Colleges, universities, & professional schools	0.1	Services
Engineering, architectural, & surveying services	0.4	Services	Elementary & secondary schools	0.1	Services
Gum & wood chemicals	0.3	Manufg.	Social services, nec	0.1	Services
Pipe, valves, & pipe fittings	0.3	Manufg.	S/L Govt. purch., correction	0.1	S/L Govt
Royalties	0.3	Fin/R.E.			
Equipment rental & leasing services	0.3	Services			
Glass & glass products, except containers	0.2	Manufg.			
Pens & mechanical pencils	0.2	Manufg.			
Insurance carriers	0.2	Fin/R.E.			
Colleges, universities, & professional schools	0.2	Services			
Hotels & lodging places	0.2	Services			
Legal services	0.2	Services			
Management & consulting services & labs	0.2	Services			
State & local government enterprises, nec	0.2	Gov't			
Manifold business forms	0.1	Manufg.			
Wet corn milling	0.1	Manufg.			
Sanitary services, steam supply, irrigation	0.1	Util.			
Security & commodity brokers	0.1	Fin/R.E.			
Accounting, auditing & bookkeeping	0.1	Services			
Computer & data processing services	0.1	Services			

Source: Benchmark Input-Output Accounts for the U.S. Economy, 1982, U.S. Department of Commerce, Washington, D.C., July 1991. Data, as reported in the source, are organized by the 1977 SIC structure in use in 1982 but have been matched, as closely as is possible, to the 1987 SIC structure used in this book.

OCCUPATIONS EMPLOYED BY SIC 284 - SOAP, CLEANERS, AND TOILET GOODS

Occupation	% of Total 1994	Change to 2005	Occupation	% of Total 1994	Change to 2005
Packaging & filling machine operators	8.5	-30.1	Bookkeeping, accounting, & auditing clerks	1.8	-12.6
Hand packers & packagers	6.3	-20.1	Maintenance repairers, general utility	1.7	4.8
Assemblers, fabricators, & hand workers nec	5.7	16.5	Inspectors, testers, & graders, precision	1.6	16.5
Sales & related workers nec	4.9	16.5	General office clerks	1.6	-0.7
Freight, stock, & material movers, hand	3.6	-6.8	Order clerks, materials, merchandise, & service	1.5	13.9
Secretaries, ex legal & medical	3.5	6.0	Machine feeders & offbearers	1.5	4.8
Chemical equipment controllers, operators	3.0	4.8	Clerical supervisors & managers	1.5	19.1
Industrial machinery mechanics	2.7	28.1	Professional workers nec	1.4	39.7
Machine operators nec	2.6	2.6	Industrial production managers	1.4	16.4
Industrial truck & tractor operators	2.6	16.5	Stock clerks	1.4	-5.3
Chemists	2.5	28.1	Managers & administrators nec	1.3	16.4
Crushing & mixing machine operators	2.5	16.4	Adjustment clerks	1.2	39.8
General managers & top executives	2.5	10.5	Accountants & auditors	1.2	16.5
Traffic, shipping, & receiving clerks	2.2	12.1	Management support workers nec	1.1	16.4
Marketing, advertising, & PR managers	2.0	16.5	Engineering, mathematical, & science managers	1.1	32.2
Science & mathematics technicians	1.8	16.5	Truck drivers light & heavy	1.0	20.1

Source: *Industry-Occupation Matrix*, Bureau of Labor Statistics. These data relate to one or more 3-digit SIC industry groups rather than to a single 4-digit SIC. The change reported for each occupation to the year 2005 is a percent of growth or decline as estimated by the Bureau of Labor Statistics. The abbreviation nec stands for 'not elsewhere classified'.

LOCATION BY STATE AND REGIONAL CONCENTRATION

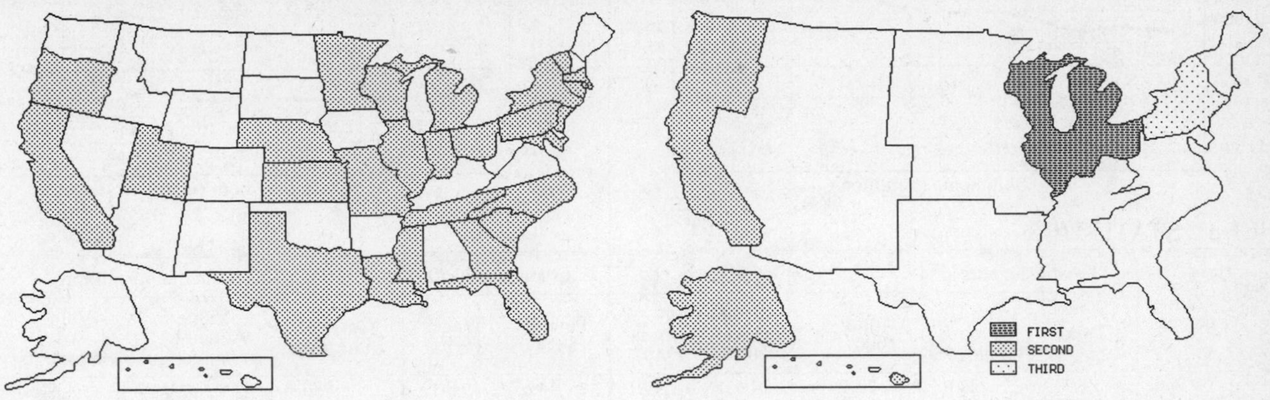

INDUSTRY DATA BY STATE

State	Establish-ments	Shipments			Employment				Cost as % of Shipments	Investment per Employee ($)
		Total ($ mil)	% of U.S.	Per Establ.	Total Number	% of U.S.	Per Establ.	Wages ($/hour)		
Ohio	43	2,823.8	19.1	65.7	4,000	12.2	93	15.61	47.8	54,900
Michigan	42	1,657.3	11.2	39.5	5,000	15.2	119	14.05	41.7	-
California	99	1,384.9	9.4	14.0	3,000	9.1	30	14.44	60.9	10,067
Georgia	29	1,028.4	7.0	35.5	2,200	6.7	76	15.43	48.3	11,955
Missouri	26	1,022.0	6.9	39.3	1,800	5.5	69	17.29	47.1	-
Illinois	48	864.8	5.9	18.0	2,400	7.3	50	14.73	38.9	6,875
New Jersey	42	515.8	3.5	12.3	1,400	4.3	33	12.82	43.9	5,500
Texas	53	460.1	3.1	8.7	1,300	4.0	25	13.94	41.6	4,154
Pennsylvania	33	293.2	2.0	8.9	900	2.7	27	10.00	37.6	-
New York	31	206.1	1.4	6.6	1,000	3.0	32	11.00	45.5	6,300
Minnesota	16	176.1	1.2	11.0	600	1.8	38	13.40	51.9	5,167
Tennessee	14	158.2	1.1	11.3	600	1.8	43	10.57	33.1	6,000
Wisconsin	22	93.6	0.6	4.3	500	1.5	23	8.83	65.3	-
North Carolina	14	92.6	0.6	6.6	500	1.5	36	10.67	46.9	-
Oregon	11	19.5	0.1	1.8	100	0.3	9	9.00	45.1	3,000
Florida	29	(D)	-	-	375 *	1.1	13	-	-	-
Massachusetts	16	(D)	-	-	750 *	2.3	47	-	-	-
South Carolina	13	(D)	-	-	375 *	1.1	29	-	-	1,867
Indiana	11	(D)	-	-	1,750 *	5.3	159	-	-	-
Connecticut	9	(D)	-	-	175 *	0.5	19	-	-	1,714
Kansas	8	(D)	-	-	1,750 *	5.3	219	-	-	-
Louisiana	8	(D)	-	-	375 *	1.1	47	-	-	-
Mississippi	8	(D)	-	-	175 *	0.5	22	-	-	-
Utah	7	(D)	-	-	750 *	2.3	107	-	-	-
Maryland	6	(D)	-	-	1,750 *	5.3	292	-	-	-
Rhode Island	3	(D)	-	-	375 *	1.1	125	-	-	-
Nebraska	1	(D)	-	-	175 *	0.5	175	-	-	-
Vermont	1	(D)	-	-	175 *	0.5	175	-	-	-

Source: 1992 *Economic Census*. The states are in descending order of shipments or establishments (if shipment data are missing for the majority). The symbol (D) appears when data are withheld to prevent disclosure of competitive information. States marked with (D) are sorted by number of establishments. A dash (-) indicates that the data element cannot be calculated; * indicates the midpoint of a range.

2842 - POLISHES & SANITATION GOODS

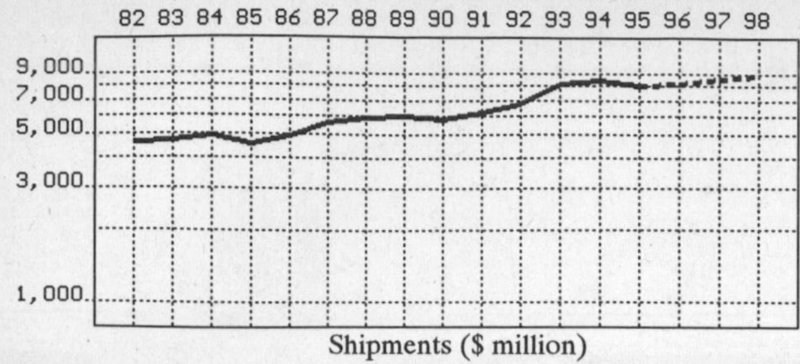

Shipments ($ million)

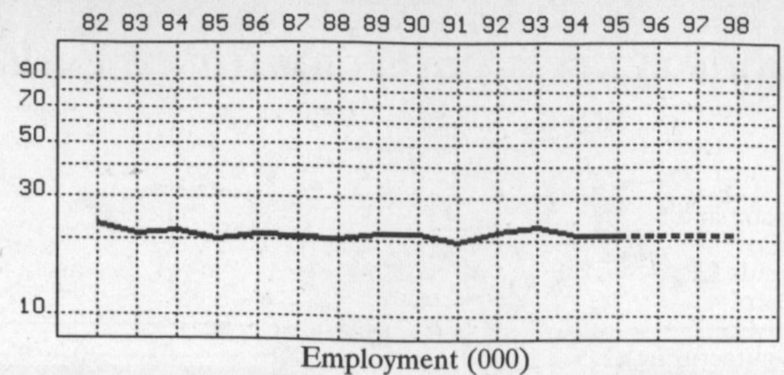

Employment (000)

GENERAL STATISTICS

Year	Com-panies	Establishments		Employment			Compensation		Production ($ million)			
		Total	with 20 or more employees	Total (000)	Production Workers (000)	Production Hours (Mil)	Payroll ($ mil)	Wages ($/hr)	Cost of Materials	Value Added by Manufacture	Value of Shipments	Capital Invest.
1982	748	808	220	23.0	14.6	29.1	444.7	8.13	1,980.1	2,632.9	4,626.1	80.9
1983		782	222	21.2	13.4	27.4	432.0	8.69	1,942.5	2,781.4	4,717.0	55.9
1984		756	224	21.9	13.8	28.2	459.8	8.94	2,144.9	2,794.4	4,902.1	87.3
1985		731	227	20.2	12.8	26.4	443.2	9.04	1,758.0	2,792.6	4,540.7	78.0
1986		702	225	21.1	13.2	27.9	478.5	9.29	1,854.4	3,080.1	4,927.7	105.7
1987	669	726	213	20.6	13.2	26.5	500.4	9.89	1,943.8	3,654.1	5,593.9	117.7
1988		683	226	20.5	13.4	27.0	502.2	10.06	2,109.8	3,764.2	5,857.7	71.7
1989		643	223	21.3	13.4	26.7	555.6	10.24	2,299.5	3,733.8	5,987.4	141.1
1990		636	224	21.4	12.3	24.4	532.2	10.63	2,167.9	3,691.4	5,847.9	95.0
1991		656	214	19.6	12.2	24.4	573.4	11.09	2,283.9	3,894.6	6,171.5	137.2
1992	694	749	225	22.0	13.4	27.2	662.4	11.84	2,463.4	4,214.9	6,676.2	121.5
1993		732	222	22.8	13.8	27.2	707.7	11.94	2,963.8	5,134.8	8,078.6	130.4
1994		660P	221P	21.2	12.9	25.6	649.0	11.17	2,912.2	5,467.6	8,371.7	123.5
1995		651P	221P	21.2P	12.8P	25.3P	686.5P	12.20P	2,757.5P	5,177.1P	7,927.0P	139.9P
1996		642P	221P	21.2P	12.7P	25.1P	708.3P	12.50P	2,859.8P	5,369.1P	8,221.0P	145.0P
1997		633P	221P	21.1P	12.6P	24.9P	730.1P	12.81P	2,962.0P	5,561.1P	8,514.9P	150.2P
1998		624P	221P	21.1P	12.5P	24.6P	751.9P	13.11P	3,064.3P	5,753.1P	8,808.9P	155.4P

Sources: 1982, 1987, 1992 *Economic Census*; *Annual Survey of Manufactures*, 83-86, 88-91, 93-94. Establishment counts for non-Census years are from *County Business Patterns*; establishment values for 83-84 are extrapolations. 'P's show projections by the editors. Industries reclassified in 87 will not have data for prior years.

INDICES OF CHANGE

Year	Com-panies	Establishments		Employment			Compensation		Production ($ million)			
		Total	with 20 or more employees	Total (000)	Production Workers (000)	Production Hours (Mil)	Payroll ($ mil)	Wages ($/hr)	Cost of Materials	Value Added by Manufacture	Value of Shipments	Capital Invest.
1982	108	108	98	105	109	107	67	69	80	62	69	67
1983		104	99	96	100	101	65	73	79	66	71	46
1984		101	100	100	103	104	69	76	87	66	73	72
1985		98	101	92	96	97	67	76	71	66	68	64
1986		94	100	96	99	103	72	78	75	73	74	87
1987	96	97	95	94	99	97	76	84	79	87	84	97
1988		91	100	93	100	99	76	85	86	89	88	59
1989		86	99	97	100	98	84	86	93	89	90	116
1990		85	100	97	92	90	80	90	88	88	88	78
1991		88	95	89	91	90	87	94	93	92	92	113
1992	100	100	100	100	100	100	100	100	100	100	100	100
1993		98	99	104	103	100	107	101	120	122	121	107
1994		88P	98P	96	96	94	98	94	118	130	125	102
1995		87P	98P	96P	95P	93P	104P	103P	112P	123P	119P	115P
1996		86P	98P	96P	95P	92P	107P	106P	116P	127P	123P	119P
1997		85P	98P	96P	94P	91P	110P	108P	120P	132P	128P	124P
1998		83P	98P	96P	94P	91P	114P	111P	124P	136P	132P	128P

Sources: Same as General Statistics. Values reflect change from the base year, 1992. Values above 100 mean greater than 92, values below 100 mean less than 92, and a value of 100 in the 82-91 or 93-98 period means same as 92. 'P's mark projections by the editors.

SELECTED RATIOS

For 1994	Avg. of All Manufact.	Analyzed Industry	Index
Employees per Establishment	49	32	66
Payroll per Establishment	1,500,273	984,011	66
Payroll per Employee	30,620	30,613	100
Production Workers per Establishment	34	20	57
Wages per Establishment	853,319	433,559	51
Wages per Production Worker	24,861	22,167	89
Hours per Production Worker	2,056	1,984	97
Wages per Hour	12.09	11.17	92
Value Added per Establishment	4,602,255	8,289,952	180
Value Added per Employee	93,930	257,906	275

For 1994	Avg. of All Manufact.	Analyzed Industry	Index
Value Added per Production Worker	134,084	423,845	316
Cost per Establishment	5,045,178	4,415,465	88
Cost per Employee	102,970	137,368	133
Cost per Production Worker	146,988	225,752	154
Shipments per Establishment	9,576,895	12,693,136	133
Shipments per Employee	195,460	394,892	202
Shipments per Production Worker	279,017	648,969	233
Investment per Establishment	321,011	187,250	58
Investment per Employee	6,552	5,825	89
Investment per Production Worker	9,352	9,574	102

Sources: Same as General Statistics. The 'Average of All Manufacturing' column represents the average of all manufacturing industries reported for the most recent complete year available. The Index shows the relationship between the Average and the Analyzed Industry. For example, 100 means that they are equal; 500 that the Analyzed Industry is five times the average; 50 means that the Analyzed Industry is half the national average. The abbreviation 'na' is used to show that data are 'not available'.

LEADING COMPANIES Number shown: **75** Total sales ($ mil): **9,557** Total employment (000): **48.1**

Company Name	Address				CEO Name	Phone	Co. Type	Sales ($ mil)	Empl. (000)
SC Johnson and Son Inc	1525 Howe St	Racine	WI	53403	W F Geroge Jr	414-631-2000	R	3,000	13.6
Clorox Co	1221 Broadway	Oakland	CA	94612	G Craig Sullivan	510-271-7000	P	1,837	4.8
DowBrands LP	PO Box 68511	Indianapolis	IN	46268	Lee Shobe	317-873-7000	S	930	3.2
NCH Corp	PO Box 152170	Irving	TX	75015	Irwin L Levy	214-438-0211	P	680	9.9
Drackett Co	8600 Governors Hill	Cincinnati	OH	45249	James M Shephard	513-677-3200	S	570*	1.5
Zep Manufacturing Co	PO Box 2015	Atlanta	GA	30301	Harry Maziar	404-352-1680	S	306	2.0
Reckitt and Colman Inc	1655 Valley Rd	Wayne	NJ	07474	Michael Turrell	201-633-3600	S	180	1.0
Occidental Chemical Corp	PO Box 809050	Dallas	TX	75380	Richard Maglisceau	214-404-3800	D	160	0.7
Kiwi Brands Inc	447 Old Swede Rd	Douglassville	PA	19518	Edward L Collier	610-385-3041	S	150	0.5
Blue Coral Inc	1215 Valley Belt Rd	Cleveland	OH	44131	Sheldon Adlemon	216-351-3000	R	95	0.1
BS and CP	PO Box 318	Prairie du Chien	WI	53821	M Schultz	608-326-2466	D	83	0.5
Rochester Midland Corp	PO Box 1515	Rochester	NY	14603	Harlan D Calkins	716-336-2200	R	68	1.1
Huntington Laboratories Inc	970 E Tipton St	Huntington	IN	46750	Gary A Mullennix	219-356-8100	R	60	0.5
Willert Home Products Inc	4044 Park Av	St Louis	MO	63110	WD Willert	314-772-2822	R	57	0.4
Scott's Liquid Gold Inc	4880 Havana St	Denver	CO	80239	Mark E Goldstein	303-373-4860	P	53	0.2
Chemidyne Corp	PO Box 171	Macedonia	OH	44056	David M Trombley	216-467-1400	R	53	1.3
Man Gill Chemical Co	23000 St Clair Av	Cleveland	OH	44117	AJ Reid	216-486-5300	R	53*	0.3
Airosol Company Inc	PO Box 120	Neodesha	KS	66757	Carl Stratemeier	316-325-2666	R	50	<0.1
Oil-Dri Corp	PO Box 200-A	Ochlocknee	GA	31773	Richard M Jaffee	912-574-5131	S	50	0.3
Spartan Chemical Co	PO Box 3457	Toledo	OH	43607	TJ Swigart	419-531-5551	R	50	0.2
Cello Corp	1354 Old Post Rd	Havre De Grace	MD	21078	William Rogers	410-939-1234	S	44	0.2
Sunshine Makers Inc	15922 Pacific Coast	Huntington Bch	CA	92649	Bruce Fabrizio	714-840-1319	R	44*	<0.1
Turtle Wax Inc	5655 W 73rd St	Chicago	IL	60638	Denis J Healy	708-563-3600	R	44	0.3
Stahl USA Inc	26 Howley St	Peabody	MA	01960	John Bouchard	508-531-0371	S	40*	0.2
Amrep Inc	990 Industrial Pk Dr	Marietta	GA	30062	Kevin Gallagher	404-422-2071	R	39	0.3
Texo Corp	2801 Highland Av	Cincinnati	OH	45212	Robert Fisher	513-731-3400	R	35	0.2
Blue Coral Systems	4775 S Butterfield	Tucson	AZ	85714	Richard Iverson	602-571-0909	D	33*	<0.1
Hillyard Industry Inc	PO Box 909	St Joseph	MO	64502	James P Carolus	816-233-1321	R	32*	0.2
Penn Champ Inc	PO Box 55	East Butler	PA	16029	EF Ivnik	412-287-8771	S	32	0.2
HB Fuller Co	3900 Jackson NE	Minneapolis	MN	55421	Bill McNellis	612-781-8071	D	30	0.1
Starr National Mfg Corp	PO Box 12470	Memphis	TN	38112	William L Starr	901-452-2440	R	28	<0.1
Texwipe Company Inc	PO Box 575	U Saddle Rvr	NJ	07458	E Paley	201-327-9100	R	28	0.2
Chem Lab Products Inc	300 E 2nd St	Reno	NV	89501	Jeffrey R Cornett	702-329-7595	R	26*	0.2
Selig Chemical Industries	PO Box 43106	Atlanta	GA	30378	Lyons B Joel	404-691-9220	D	25	0.2
National Chemical Laboratories	401 N 10th St	Philadelphia	PA	19123	Alfred Pollack	215-922-1200	R	23*	0.1
Copper Brite Inc	PO Box 50610	Santa Barbara	CA	93150	AD Brite	805-565-1566	R	21*	0.1
N Jonas and Company Inc	4520 Adams Cir	Bensalem	PA	19020	Sheila Wexler	215-639-8071	R	21*	0.1
Talsol Corp	4677 Devitt Dr	Cincinnati	OH	45246	Terry Merrill	513-874-5151	S	21*	0.1
Betco Corp	1001 Brown Av	Toledo	OH	43607	Paul C Betz	419-241-2156	R	20	0.1
Brulin and Company Inc	PO Box 270	Indianapolis	IN	46206	Charles Pollnow	317-923-3211	R	20	0.3
Car Brite Inc	1910 S State Av	Indianapolis	IN	46203	John W Campbell	317-788-9925	R	20	<0.1
Carroll Co	2900 W Kingsley Rd	Garland	TX	75041	KW Ogden	214-278-1304	R	20	0.2
Claire Manufacturing Company	500 Vista Av	Addison	IL	60101	Greg Ledford	708-543-7600	R	20	0.1
Frederick Gumm Chemical	538 Forest St	Kearny	NJ	07032	F Gumm	201-991-4171	R	20	0.1
Manhattan Products Inc	333 Starke Rd	Carlstadt	NJ	07072	RA Yaffa	201-933-3500	R	20	0.1
Wilen Manufacturing Company	PO Box 161129	Atlanta	GA	30321	J Wilen	404-366-2111	R	20	0.3
Blue Cross Laboratories Inc	PO Box 50	Saugus	CA	91350	Darrell Mahler	805-255-0955	R	18	0.2
Chemtronics Inc	8125 Cobb Ctr Dr	Kennesaw	GA	30144	Joseph Wise	404-424-4888	S	17*	0.1
Bullen Companies Inc	PO Box 37	Folcroft	PA	19032	Fred S Jarden	215-724-8100	R	16*	<0.1
Momar Inc	PO Box 19567	Atlanta	GA	30325	Julian B Mohr	404-355-4580	R	15*	<0.1
BAF Industries	1910 S Yale St	Santa Ana	CA	92704	OF Bell	714-540-3852	R	15	0.1
Mission Kleensweep Inc	2433 Birk Dale St	Los Angeles	CA	90031	Robert Rosenbaum	213-223-1405	R	14*	<0.1
Whink Products Co	PO Box 230	Eldora	IA	50627	S Throssel	515-858-2353	R	13	0.1
Steccone Products Company Inc	8469 Pardee Dr	Oakland	CA	94621	Michael Smahlik	510-638-4870	R	13	<0.1
Bullen Midwest Inc	1415 W 37th St	Chicago	IL	60609	James B Flanagan	312-247-2000	R	12	<0.1
Camco Chemical Co	8150 Holton Dr	Florence	KY	41042	Steve Hancox	606-727-3200	R	12	0.1
Chemical Packaging Corp	PO Box 9947	Ft Lauderdale	FL	33310	Terry M Colker	305-974-5440	R	12	0.1
MD Stetson Co	92 York Av	Randolph	MA	02368	L Glass	617-986-6161	R	12	<0.1
Schaffner Manufacturing	21 Herron Av	Pittsburgh	PA	15202	Gus J Schaffner III	412-761-9902	R	12*	<0.1
Spectrowax Corp	70 Hichborn St	Brighton	MA	02135	Arnold Rosenberg	617-254-2800	R	12*	<0.1
TWS Industries Inc	PO Box 10226	Bakersfield	CA	93389	Jess R Winters	805-397-5274	R	12*	<0.1
US Chemical and Plastics Inc	1446 Tuscarawas W	Canton	OH	44702	A Lesko	216-455-4311	S	12*	0.1
Warsaw Chemical Company Inc	PO Box 858	Warsaw	IN	46580	Robert F Steele	219-267-3251	R	12*	<0.1
Prime Leather Finishes Co	205 S 2nd St	Milwaukee	WI	53204	Robert Welch	414-276-1668	R	11*	<0.1
Garland Floor Co	4500 Willow Pkwy	Cleveland	OH	44125	Jon Wise	216-883-4100	R	10	<0.1
Granitize Products Inc	PO Box 2306	South Gate	CA	90280	T Raymondo	310-923-5438	R	10*	<0.1
Guardian Chemical Co	PO Box 93667	Atlanta	GA	30377	WK Fawcett Jr	404-873-1692	R	10*	<0.1
Rite-Off Inc	105 Park Av	Seaford	DE	19973	Terence Cunniffe	302-628-2100	R	10	<0.1
SecondWind Products Inc	PO Box 2300	Paso Robles	CA	93447	Gus Blythe	805-239-2555	R	10	<0.1
William H Harvey Co	4334 S 67th St	Omaha	NE	68117	Richard Harvey	402-331-1175	R	10	0.1
Patterson Laboratories Inc	11930 Pleasant Av	Detroit	MI	48217	J Moon	313-843-4500	R	10*	<0.1
Ocean Bio-Chem Inc	4041 SW 47th Av	Ft Lauderdale	FL	33314	Peter G Dornau	305-587-6280	P	10	<0.1
Chemstar Inc	5111 Southwest Av	St Louis	MO	63110	J Scott Westberg	314-865-5500	R	9	<0.1
Crest Products Inc	PO Box 1739	Oldsmar	FL	34677	WL Parker	813-855-6688	R	9	<0.1
Empire Chemical Company Inc	715 Lamar St	Los Angeles	CA	90031	Robert Cronyn	213-225-4186	R	9	<0.1

Source: *Ward's Business Directory of U.S. Private and Public Companies*, Volumes 1 and 2, 1996. The company type code used is as follows: P - Public, R - Private, S - Subsidiary, D - Division, J - Joint Venture, A - Affiliate, G - Group. Sales are in millions of dollars, employees are in thousands. An asterisk (*) indicates an estimated sales volume. The symbol < stands for 'less than'. Company names and addresses are truncated, in some cases, to fit into the available space.

MATERIALS CONSUMED

Material		Quantity	Delivered Cost ($ million)
Materials, ingredients, containers, and supplies		(X)	2,054.2
Bulk surface active intermediates (active wt.)	mil lb	48.2	23.8
Bulk surface active agents primarily for detergent purposes (active wt.), except intermediates	mil lb	32.8*	20.7
Other bulk surface active agents	mil lb	39.1	28.7
Vegetable oil	mil lb	(S)	1.1
Perfume oil mixtures and blends	mil lb	10.4**	67.0
Fatty acids	mil lb	13.0**	5.3
Grease and inedible tallow	mil lb	5.0*	3.4
Chlorine (100 percent Cl basis)	1,000 s tons	129.4*	15.5
Sodium carbonate (soda ash) (58 percent Na2O)	1,000 s tons	55.6	8.3
Sodium hydroxide (caustic soda)(100 percent NaOH)	1,000 s tons	155.1	31.6
Sodium tripolyphosphate (STPP) (100 percent NaP0)	1,000 s tons	3.5**	2.7
All other potassium and sodium compounds		(X)	22.4
Refined petroleum products, including mineral oil, naphtha solvents, petrolatum, waxes, etc.		(X)	72.1
All other organic and inorganic chemicals		(X)	234.3
Labels, coupons, instructions, and other printed material		(X)	46.1
Paperboard containers, boxes, and corrugated paperboard		(X)	147.0
Metal containers		(X)	143.8
Plastics containers		(X)	250.8
Fabricated plastics products, including dispensing pumps and sprayers		(X)	99.6
All other materials and components, parts, containers, and supplies		(X)	359.4
Materials, ingredients, containers, and supplies, nsk		(X)	470.3

Source: 1992 *Economic Census*. Explanation of symbols used: (D): Withheld to avoid disclosure of competitive data; na: Not available; (S): Withheld because statistical norms were not met; (X): Not applicable; (Z): Less than half the unit shown; nec: Not elsewhere classified; nsk: Not specified by kind; - : zero; * : 10-19 percent estimated; ** : 20-29 percent estimated.

PRODUCT SHARE DETAILS

Product or Product Class	% Share
Polishes and sanitation goods	100.00
Household bleaches (chlorine and nonchlorine)	14.49
Household liquid bleaches (sodium hypochlorite, etc.) (chlorine and nonchlorine)	79.00
Household dry bleaches (calcium hypochlorite, etc.) (chlorine and nonchlorine)	20.04
Household bleaches (chlorine and nonchlorine), nsk	0.97
Specialty cleaning and sanitation products	55.41
Glass window cleaning preparations, except automotive windshield washer fluid	4.77
Automotive windshield washer fluid	0.82
Oven cleaners	1.79
Toilet bowl cleaners	6.70
Drain pipe solvents	3.64
Bathroom, tub, and tile cleaners	3.47
Disinfectants, nonagricultural	14.37
Household liquid laundry fabric softeners and rinses	14.95
Household dry laundry fabric softeners and rinses (except dryer sheets)	(D)
Household laundry dryer sheets	4.10
Household laundry starch preparations, including permanent types	1.37
Other household laundry aids, including ironing aids and drycleaning spotting preparations	2.84
Rug and upholstery cleaners, consumer-type preparations	4.14
Rug and upholstery cleaners, industrial- and institutional-type preparations	0.65
Household ammonia	0.48
Air and room fresheners, aerosol-type	6.10
Other air and room fresheners (except potpourri)	7.35
Cat litter, except natural and untreated materials	(D)
Other specialty detergents, including sweeping compounds, waterless hand cleaners, wallpaper cleaners, etc.	9.20
Specialty cleaning and sanitation products, nsk	3.81
Polishing preparations and related products	16.28
Automobile body polish and cleaners	26.91
Furniture polish and cleaners	17.51
Floor polish, water emulsion	23.88
Floor polish, liquid (nonemulsion)	3.32
Floor polish other than liquid form, including paste and cake	0.36
Shoe polishes and cleaners	9.45
Leather dressings and finishes, excluding shoe polish	4.82
Other polishing preparations and related products, including metal polish and polishing cloths and papers	12.90
Polishing preparations and related products, nsk	0.85
Polishes and sanitation goods, nsk	13.83

Source: 1992 *Economic Census*. The values shown are percent of total shipments in an industry. Values of indented subcategories are summed in the main heading. The symbol (D) appears when data are withheld to prevent disclosure of competitive information. The abbreviation nsk stands for 'not specified by kind' and nec for 'not elsewhere classified'.

INPUTS AND OUTPUTS FOR POLISHES & SANITATION GOODS

Economic Sector or Industry Providing Inputs	%	Sector	Economic Sector or Industry Buying Outputs	%	Sector
Miscellaneous plastics products	12.2	Manufg.	Personal consumption expenditures	66.8	
Wholesale trade	9.5	Trade	Services to dwellings & other buildings	4.5	Services
Paperboard containers & boxes	8.4	Manufg.	Polishes & sanitation goods	3.9	Manufg.
Polishes & sanitation goods	7.3	Manufg.	Hospitals	3.1	Services
Surface active agents	5.9	Manufg.	Exports	3.0	Foreign
Advertising	4.3	Services	Surface active agents	2.2	Manufg.
Metal cans	4.0	Manufg.	Retail trade, except eating & drinking	2.0	Trade
Metal stampings, nec	3.6	Manufg.	Nursing & personal care facilities	1.7	Services
Alkalies & chlorine	3.4	Manufg.	Wholesale trade	1.4	Trade
Paints & allied products	3.4	Manufg.	Leather tanning & finishing	0.9	Manufg.
Petroleum refining	3.2	Manufg.	Membership organizations nec	0.8	Services
Motor freight transportation & warehousing	3.1	Util.	Doctors & dentists	0.7	Services

Continued on next page.

INPUTS AND OUTPUTS FOR POLISHES & SANITATION GOODS - Continued

Economic Sector or Industry Providing Inputs	%	Sector	Economic Sector or Industry Buying Outputs	%	Sector
Pipe, valves, & pipe fittings	1.9	Manufg.	Real estate	0.6	Fin/R.E.
Toilet preparations	1.9	Manufg.	Laundry, dry cleaning, shoe repair	0.6	Services
Metal barrels, drums, & pails	1.7	Manufg.	Legal services	0.5	Services
Commercial printing	1.4	Manufg.	Labor, civic, social, & fraternal associations	0.4	Services
Crowns & closures	1.4	Manufg.	Federal Government purchases, national defense	0.4	Fed Govt
Electric services (utilities)	1.2	Util.	Change in business inventories	0.4	In House
Glass containers	1.1	Manufg.	Banking	0.3	Fin/R.E.
Industrial inorganic chemicals, nec	1.1	Manufg.	Computer & data processing services	0.3	Services
Imports	1.1	Foreign	Management & consulting services & labs	0.3	Services
Clay, ceramic, & refractory minerals	1.0	Mining	S/L Govt. purch., natural resource & recreation.	0.3	S/L Govt
Communications, except radio & TV	0.9	Util.	Motor vehicle parts & accessories	0.2	Manufg.
Fabricated metal products, nec	0.8	Manufg.	Eating & drinking places	0.2	Trade
Plastics materials & resins	0.8	Manufg.	Business services nec	0.2	Services
Eating & drinking places	0.8	Trade	Colleges, universities, & professional schools	0.2	Services
Noncomparable imports	0.7	Foreign	Hotels & lodging places	0.2	Services
Cyclic crudes and organics	0.6	Manufg.	Residential care	0.2	Services
Nonwoven fabrics	0.6	Manufg.	Federal Government purchases, nondefense	0.2	Fed Govt
Soap & other detergents	0.6	Manufg.	S/L Govt. purch., correction	0.2	S/L Govt
Gas production & distribution (utilities)	0.6	Util.	S/L Govt. purch., higher education	0.2	S/L Govt
Equipment rental & leasing services	0.6	Services	Shoes, except rubber	0.1	Manufg.
Miscellaneous livestock	0.5	Agric.	Beauty & barber shops	0.1	Services
Paper coating & glazing	0.5	Manufg.	Medical & health services, nec	0.1	Services
Air transportation	0.5	Util.	Social services, nec	0.1	Services
Banking	0.5	Fin/R.E.	U.S. Postal Service	0.1	Gov't
Real estate	0.5	Fin/R.E.	S/L Govt. purch., police	0.1	S/L Govt
Electrical repair shops	0.5	Services			
Engineering, architectural, & surveying services	0.5	Services			
Miscellaneous repair shops	0.5	Services			
U.S. Postal Service	0.5	Gov't			
Maintenance of nonfarm buildings nec	0.4	Constr.			
Railroads & related services	0.4	Util.			
Chemical preparations, nec	0.3	Manufg.			
Sawmills & planning mills, general	0.3	Manufg.			
Water transportation	0.3	Util.			
Royalties	0.3	Fin/R.E.			
Legal services	0.3	Services			
Management & consulting services & labs	0.3	Services			
Manifold business forms	0.2	Manufg.			
Vegetable oil mills, nec	0.2	Manufg.			
Credit agencies other than banks	0.2	Fin/R.E.			
Insurance carriers	0.2	Fin/R.E.			
Accounting, auditing & bookkeeping	0.2	Services			
Business/professional associations	0.2	Services			
Colleges, universities, & professional schools	0.2	Services			
Hotels & lodging places	0.2	Services			
Services to dwellings & other buildings	0.2	Services			
Lubricating oils & greases	0.1	Manufg.			
Machinery, except electrical, nec	0.1	Manufg.			
Sanitary services, steam supply, irrigation	0.1	Util.			
Automotive rental & leasing, without drivers	0.1	Services			
Computer & data processing services	0.1	Services			
State & local government enterprises, nec	0.1	Gov't			

Source: Benchmark Input-Output Accounts for the U.S. Economy, 1982, U.S. Department of Commerce, Washington, D.C., July 1991. Data, as reported in the source, are organized by the 1977 SIC structure in use in 1982 but have been matched, as closely as is possible, to the 1987 SIC structure used in this book.

OCCUPATIONS EMPLOYED BY SIC 284 - SOAP, CLEANERS, AND TOILET GOODS

Occupation	% of Total 1994	Change to 2005	Occupation	% of Total 1994	Change to 2005
Packaging & filling machine operators	8.5	-30.1	Bookkeeping, accounting, & auditing clerks	1.8	-12.6
Hand packers & packagers	6.3	-20.1	Maintenance repairers, general utility	1.7	4.8
Assemblers, fabricators, & hand workers nec	5.7	16.5	Inspectors, testers, & graders, precision	1.6	16.5
Sales & related workers nec	4.9	16.5	General office clerks	1.6	-0.7
Freight, stock, & material movers, hand	3.6	-6.8	Order clerks, materials, merchandise, & service	1.5	13.9
Secretaries, ex legal & medical	3.5	6.0	Machine feeders & offbearers	1.5	4.8
Chemical equipment controllers, operators	3.0	4.8	Clerical supervisors & managers	1.5	19.1
Industrial machinery mechanics	2.7	28.1	Professional workers nec	1.4	39.7
Machine operators nec	2.6	2.6	Industrial production managers	1.4	16.4
Industrial truck & tractor operators	2.6	16.5	Stock clerks	1.4	-5.3
Chemists	2.5	28.1	Managers & administrators nec	1.3	16.4
Crushing & mixing machine operators	2.5	16.4	Adjustment clerks	1.2	39.8
General managers & top executives	2.5	10.5	Accountants & auditors	1.2	16.5
Traffic, shipping, & receiving clerks	2.2	12.1	Management support workers nec	1.1	16.4
Marketing, advertising, & PR managers	2.0	16.5	Engineering, mathematical, & science managers	1.1	32.2
Science & mathematics technicians	1.8	16.5	Truck drivers light & heavy	1.0	20.1

Source: Industry-Occupation Matrix, Bureau of Labor Statistics. These data relate to one or more 3-digit SIC industry groups rather than to a single 4-digit SIC. The change reported for each occupation to the year 2005 is a percent of growth or decline as estimated by the Bureau of Labor Statistics. The abbreviation nec stands for 'not elsewhere classified'.

LOCATION BY STATE AND REGIONAL CONCENTRATION

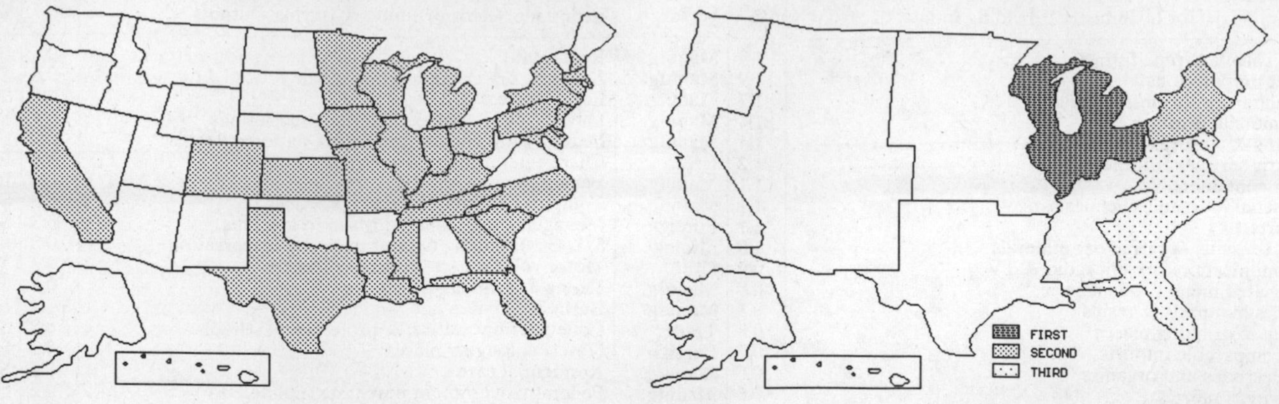

INDUSTRY DATA BY STATE

State	Establish-ments	Shipments			Employment				Cost as % of Shipments	Investment per Employee ($)
		Total ($ mil)	% of U.S.	Per Establ.	Total Number	% of U.S.	Per Establ.	Wages ($/hour)		
Illinois	53	748.7	11.2	14.1	2,200	10.0	42	13.00	35.1	5,273
New Jersey	35	579.1	8.7	16.5	1,300	5.9	37	13.44	32.6	5,308
Ohio	34	529.7	7.9	15.6	1,900	8.6	56	11.85	35.0	4,316
Georgia	28	484.4	7.3	17.3	1,300	5.9	46	11.58	36.0	3,846
Missouri	24	445.1	6.7	18.5	1,100	5.0	46	11.13	40.1	2,818
California	89	431.1	6.5	4.8	1,600	7.3	18	14.00	37.4	3,188
Pennsylvania	33	255.8	3.8	7.8	1,200	5.5	36	11.60	44.8	2,750
New York	57	203.2	3.0	3.6	1,200	5.5	21	8.73	39.2	3,500
Texas	43	191.1	2.9	4.4	900	4.1	21	8.70	32.5	4,667
Florida	44	172.1	2.6	3.9	700	3.2	16	10.00	39.6	4,857
Indiana	19	136.2	2.0	7.2	900	4.1	47	7.29	44.3	2,000
Michigan	23	63.7	1.0	2.8	200	0.9	9	10.00	55.9	-
North Carolina	20	52.6	0.8	2.6	400	1.8	20	8.50	50.4	4,000
Mississippi	10	36.6	0.5	3.7	400	1.8	40	8.83	66.9	-
Connecticut	9	33.6	0.5	3.7	200	0.9	22	23.00	52.1	-
Colorado	10	32.2	0.5	3.2	200	0.9	20	9.00	43.2	2,000
Kansas	8	23.9	0.4	3.0	200	0.9	25	8.50	41.8	2,500
Louisiana	19	21.8	0.3	1.1	200	0.9	11	12.00	42.7	2,500
Massachusetts	21	(D)	-	-	375 *	1.7	18	-	-	2,400
Tennessee	21	(D)	-	-	175 *	0.8	8	-	-	-
Wisconsin	20	(D)	-	-	1,750 *	8.0	88	-	-	-
Minnesota	19	(D)	-	-	750 *	3.4	39	-	-	-
Maryland	14	(D)	-	-	375 *	1.7	27	-	-	-
Iowa	7	(D)	-	-	175 *	0.8	25	-	-	-
Kentucky	7	(D)	-	-	375 *	1.7	54	-	-	-
South Carolina	6	(D)	-	-	375 *	1.7	63	-	-	-
New Hampshire	4	(D)	-	-	175 *	0.8	44	-	-	-
Delaware	2	(D)	-	-	175 *	0.8	88	-	-	-

Source: 1992 *Economic Census*. The states are in descending order of shipments or establishments (if shipment data are missing for the majority). The symbol (D) appears when data are withheld to prevent disclosure of competitive information. States marked with (D) are sorted by number of establishments. A dash (-) indicates that the data element cannot be calculated; * indicates the midpoint of a range.

2843 - SURFACE ACTIVE AGENTS

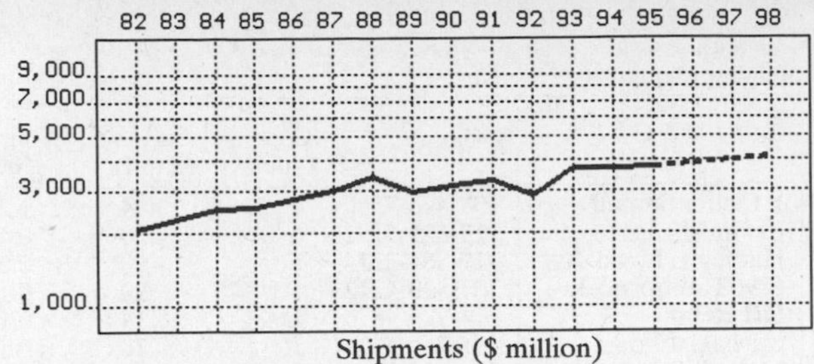

Shipments ($ million)

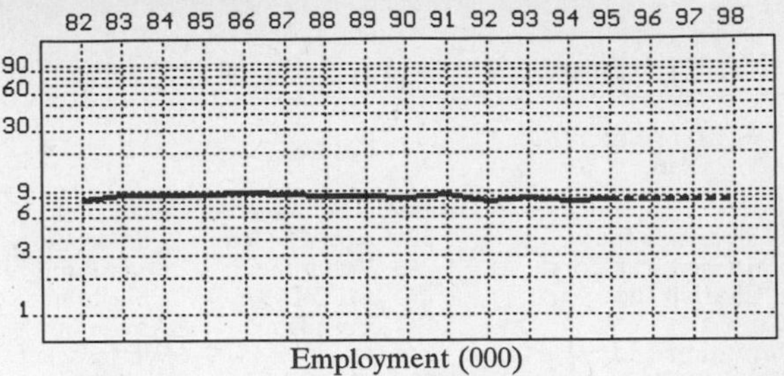

Employment (000)

GENERAL STATISTICS

Year	Com-panies	Establishments		Employment			Compensation		Production ($ million)			
		Total	with 20 or more employees	Total (000)	Production Workers (000)	Production Hours (Mil)	Payroll ($ mil)	Wages ($/hr)	Cost of Materials	Value Added by Manufacture	Value of Shipments	Capital Invest.
1982	180	209	95	8.5	3.8	7.8	207.5	9.87	1,309.5	745.8	2,060.3	86.6
1983		209	95	9.3	4.3	8.9	238.8	10.52	1,426.8	836.0	2,275.8	88.8
1984		209	95	9.3	4.5	9.4	253.4	11.03	1,494.2	1,013.2	2,481.9	76.7
1985		208	95	9.3	4.4	9.2	261.9	11.55	1,449.5	1,095.9	2,534.4	76.4
1986		199	91	9.5	4.4	9.5	286.9	10.94	1,590.2	1,182.8	2,779.5	71.4
1987	184	217	99	9.1	4.7	10.0	289.8	13.37	1,683.7	1,318.0	3,002.2	103.4
1988		204	98	9.0	4.8	10.2	296.5	13.70	2,045.4	1,391.3	3,398.5	191.7
1989		196	94	9.0	4.6	10.3	311.8	13.32	1,771.8	1,193.2	2,959.2	129.3
1990		197	95	8.8	4.6	10.2	332.1	13.71	1,945.7	1,241.0	3,168.3	165.0
1991		200	92	9.3	4.8	10.7	339.5	14.28	2,024.8	1,267.8	3,298.8	157.4
1992	176	205	90	8.2	4.2	9.0	320.3	14.94	1,689.5	1,171.5	2,864.0	92.4
1993		199	92	8.6	4.3	9.4	358.0	15.95	2,087.8	1,572.4	3,660.5	203.4
1994		198P	92P	8.0	3.9	8.8	347.1	16.57	2,080.6	1,594.8	3,678.3	204.5
1995		197P	92P	8.4P	4.4P	10.0P	374.4P	16.78P	2,121.4P	1,626.1P	3,750.4P	195.9P
1996		196P	92P	8.4P	4.4P	10.1P	385.6P	17.31P	2,187.2P	1,676.5P	3,866.8P	205.8P
1997		195P	91P	8.3P	4.5P	10.1P	396.9P	17.84P	2,253.1P	1,727.0P	3,983.3P	215.7P
1998		194P	91P	8.2P	4.5P	10.2P	408.1P	18.37P	2,318.9P	1,777.5P	4,099.7P	225.6P

Sources: 1982, 1987, 1992 *Economic Census*; *Annual Survey of Manufactures*, 83-86, 88-91, 93-94. Establishment counts for non-Census years are from *County Business Patterns*; establishment values for 83-84 are extrapolations. 'P's show projections by the editors. Industries reclassified in 87 will not have data for prior years.

INDICES OF CHANGE

Year	Com-panies	Establishments		Employment			Compensation		Production ($ million)			
		Total	with 20 or more employees	Total (000)	Production Workers (000)	Production Hours (Mil)	Payroll ($ mil)	Wages ($/hr)	Cost of Materials	Value Added by Manufacture	Value of Shipments	Capital Invest.
1982	102	102	106	104	90	87	65	66	78	64	72	94
1983		102	106	113	102	99	75	70	84	71	79	96
1984		102	106	113	107	104	79	74	88	86	87	83
1985		101	106	113	105	102	82	77	86	94	88	83
1986		97	101	116	105	106	90	73	94	101	97	77
1987	105	106	110	111	112	111	90	89	100	113	105	112
1988		100	109	110	114	113	93	92	121	119	119	207
1989		96	104	110	110	114	97	89	105	102	103	140
1990		96	106	107	110	113	104	92	115	106	111	179
1991		98	102	113	114	119	106	96	120	108	115	170
1992	100	100	100	100	100	100	100	100	100	100	100	100
1993		97	102	105	102	104	112	107	124	134	128	220
1994		97P	102P	98	93	98	108	111	123	136	128	221
1995		96P	102P	103P	106P	111P	117P	112P	126P	139P	131P	212P
1996		96P	102P	102P	106P	112P	120P	116P	129P	143P	135P	223P
1997		95P	101P	101P	106P	113P	124P	119P	133P	147P	139P	233P
1998		95P	101P	100P	106P	113P	127P	123P	137P	152P	143P	244P

Sources: Same as General Statistics. Values reflect change from the base year, 1992. Values above 100 mean greater than 92, values below 100 mean less than 92, and a value of 100 in the 82-91 or 93-98 period means same as 92. 'P's mark projections by the editors.

SELECTED RATIOS

For 1994	Avg. of All Manufact.	Analyzed Industry	Index	For 1994	Avg. of All Manufact.	Analyzed Industry	Index
Employees per Establishment	49	40	83	Value Added per Production Worker	134,084	408,923	305
Payroll per Establishment	1,500,273	1,754,507	117	Cost per Establishment	5,045,178	10,516,933	208
Payroll per Employee	30,620	43,388	142	Cost per Employee	102,970	260,075	253
Production Workers per Establishment	34	20	57	Cost per Production Worker	146,988	533,487	363
Wages per Establishment	853,319	737,065	86	Shipments per Establishment	9,576,895	18,592,923	194
Wages per Production Worker	24,861	37,389	150	Shipments per Employee	195,460	459,787	235
Hours per Production Worker	2,056	2,256	110	Shipments per Production Worker	279,017	943,154	338
Wages per Hour	12.09	16.57	137	Investment per Establishment	321,011	1,033,698	322
Value Added per Establishment	4,602,255	8,061,331	175	Investment per Employee	6,552	25,563	390
Value Added per Employee	93,930	199,350	212	Investment per Production Worker	9,352	52,436	561

Sources: Same as General Statistics. The 'Average of All Manufacturing' column represents the average of all manufacturing industries reported for the most recent complete year available. The Index shows the relationship between the Average and the Analyzed Industry. For example, 100 means that they are equal; 500 that the Analyzed Industry is five times the average; 50 means that the Analyzed Industry is half the national average. The abbreviation 'na' is used to show that data are 'not available'.

LEADING COMPANIES Number shown: 9 Total sales ($ mil): 787 Total employment (000): 2.2

Company Name	Address				CEO Name	Phone	Co. Type	Sales ($ mil)	Empl. (000)
Stepan Co	Edens & Winnetka	Northfield	IL	60093	F Quinn Stepan	708-446-7500	P	444	1.3
Harcros Chemicals Inc	5200 Speaker Rd	Kansas City	KS	66106	Kevin Mirner	913-321-3131	S	220*	0.4
High Point Chemical Corp	243 Woodbine St	High Point	NC	27260	Harvey L Lowd	919-884-2214	S	70	0.2
Catawba-Charlab Inc	PO Box 240497	Charlotte	NC	28224	HM Thompson Jr	704-523-4242	R	20	0.1
Stepan Co	PO Box 4060	Anaheim	CA	92803	DC Rehms	714-776-9870	D	14	<0.1
CNC International LP	PO Box 3000	Woonsocket	RI	02895	Michael J Fox	401-769-6100	R	10	<0.1
Lloyd Laboratories Inc	23 Caller St	Peabody	MA	01960	M Castelman	508-531-0053	R	4	<0.1
Louis Marsch Inc	PO Box 42	Morrisonville	IL	62546	Paul L Vocks	217-526-4423	R	3*	<0.1
CORPEX Technologies Inc	PO Box 13486	Res Tri Pk	NC	27709	John K Pirotte	919-941-0847	R	2	<0.1

Source: *Ward's Business Directory of U.S. Private and Public Companies*, Volumes 1 and 2, 1996. The company type code used is as follows: P - Public, R - Private, S - Subsidiary, D - Division, J - Joint Venture, A - Affiliate, G - Group. Sales are in millions of dollars, employees are in thousands. An asterisk (*) indicates an estimated sales volume. The symbol < stands for 'less than'. Company names and addresses are truncated, in some cases, to fit into the available space.

MATERIALS CONSUMED

Material		Quantity	Delivered Cost ($ million)
Materials, ingredients, containers, and supplies		(X)	1,510.8
Bulk surface active intermediates (active wt.)	mil lb	187.7	58.7
Bulk surface active agents primarily for detergent purposes (active wt.), except intermediates	mil lb	150.7	54.1
Other bulk surface active agents	mil lb	29.0*	26.8
Glycerin (100 percent)	mil lb	14.8	8.4
Vegetable oil	mil lb	235.9	65.9
Perfume oil mixtures and blends	mil lb	(S)	0.2
Fatty acids	mil lb	224.6	109.7
Grease and inedible tallow	mil lb	88.2	30.6
Sodium carbonate (soda ash) (58 percent Na2O)	1,000 s tons	5.1**	0.7
Sodium hydroxide (caustic soda)(100 percent NaOH)	1,000 s tons	20.0	3.5
Sodium tripolyphosphate (STPP) (100 percent NaP0)	1,000 s tons	0.2**	0.1
All other potassium and sodium compounds		(X)	4.2
Refined petroleum products, including mineral oil, naphtha solvents, petrolatum, waxes, etc.		(X)	93.0
All other organic and inorganic chemicals		(X)	353.4
Labels, coupons, instructions, and other printed material		(X)	0.6
Paperboard containers, boxes, and corrugated paperboard		(X)	13.3
Metal containers		(X)	24.9
Plastics containers		(X)	6.7
All other materials and components, parts, containers, and supplies		(X)	419.6
Materials, ingredients, containers, and supplies, nsk		(X)	236.4

Source: 1992 *Economic Census*. Explanation of symbols used: (D): Withheld to avoid disclosure of competitive data; na: Not available; (S): Withheld because statistical norms were not met; (X): Not applicable; (Z): Less than half the unit shown; nec: Not elsewhere classified; nsk: Not specified by kind; - : zero; * : 10-19 percent estimated; ** : 20-29 percent estimated.

PRODUCT SHARE DETAILS

Product or Product Class	% Share	Product or Product Class	% Share
Surfactants, finishing agents, and assistants	100.00	Leather assistants and finishes	1.40
Textile assistants	4.33	Surfactants (bulk surface active agents)	79.07
Textile finishes	7.28		

Source: 1992 *Economic Census*. The values shown are percent of total shipments in an industry. Values of indented subcategories are summed in the main heading. The symbol (D) appears when data are withheld to prevent disclosure of competitive information. The abbreviation nsk stands for 'not specified by kind' and nec for 'not elsewhere classified'.

INPUTS AND OUTPUTS FOR SURFACE ACTIVE AGENTS

Economic Sector or Industry Providing Inputs	%	Sector	Economic Sector or Industry Buying Outputs	%	Sector
Surface active agents	18.4	Manufg.	Soap & other detergents	13.9	Manufg.
Industrial gases	10.4	Manufg.	Petroleum refining	8.6	Manufg.
Wholesale trade	8.9	Trade	Surface active agents	7.9	Manufg.
Miscellaneous plastics products	8.7	Manufg.	Exports	6.5	Foreign
Polishes & sanitation goods	8.2	Manufg.	Toilet preparations	5.0	Manufg.
Imports	6.0	Foreign	Polishes & sanitation goods	4.9	Manufg.
Gas production & distribution (utilities)	5.0	Util.	Knit fabric mills	4.7	Manufg.
Petroleum refining	4.9	Manufg.	Broadwoven fabric mills	4.1	Manufg.
Electric services (utilities)	2.5	Util.	Lubricating oils & greases	4.1	Manufg.
Chemical preparations, nec	2.0	Manufg.	Paper mills, except building paper	3.6	Manufg.
Motor freight transportation & warehousing	2.0	Util.	Chemical preparations, nec	3.5	Manufg.

Continued on next page.

INPUTS AND OUTPUTS FOR SURFACE ACTIVE AGENTS - Continued

Economic Sector or Industry Providing Inputs	%	Sector	Economic Sector or Industry Buying Outputs	%	Sector
Advertising	1.7	Services	Paperboard mills	3.4	Manufg.
Miscellaneous repair shops	1.7	Services	Knit outerwear mills	2.3	Manufg.
Metal cans	1.4	Manufg.	Agricultural chemicals, nec	1.8	Manufg.
Metal barrels, drums, & pails	1.2	Manufg.	Synthetic rubber	1.8	Manufg.
Plastics materials & resins	1.2	Manufg.	S/L Govt. purch., health & hospitals	1.7	S/L Govt
Fabricated plate work (boiler shops)	1.1	Manufg.	Paints & allied products	1.6	Manufg.
Animal & marine fats & oils	1.0	Manufg.	Plastics materials & resins	1.6	Manufg.
Industrial inorganic chemicals, nec	1.0	Manufg.	Women's hosiery, except socks	1.5	Manufg.
Soap & other detergents	0.9	Manufg.	Hosiery, nec	1.4	Manufg.
Vegetable oil mills, nec	0.9	Manufg.	Ready-mixed concrete	1.3	Manufg.
Paperboard containers & boxes	0.8	Manufg.	Yarn mills & finishing of textiles, nec	1.2	Manufg.
Railroads & related services	0.8	Util.	Management & consulting services & labs	1.2	Services
Noncomparable imports	0.8	Foreign	Leather tanning & finishing	1.0	Manufg.
Communications, except radio & TV	0.7	Util.	Knit underwear mills	0.8	Manufg.
Alkalies & chlorine	0.6	Manufg.	Organic fibers, noncellulosic	0.8	Manufg.
Banking	0.5	Fin/R.E.	Paving mixtures & blocks	0.8	Manufg.
U.S. Postal Service	0.5	Gov't	Floor coverings	0.7	Manufg.
Air transportation	0.4	Util.	Leather goods, nec	0.7	Manufg.
Pipelines, except natural gas	0.4	Util.	S/L Govt. purch., other education & libraries	0.7	S/L Govt
Commercial printing	0.3	Manufg.	S/L Govt. purch., other general government	0.6	S/L Govt
Water supply & sewage systems	0.3	Util.	Gypsum products	0.5	Manufg.
Water transportation	0.3	Util.	Laundry, dry cleaning, shoe repair	0.5	Services
Eating & drinking places	0.3	Trade	Crude petroleum & natural gas	0.4	Mining
Real estate	0.3	Fin/R.E.	Maintenance of petroleum & natural gas wells	0.4	Constr.
Equipment rental & leasing services	0.3	Services	Nonwoven fabrics	0.4	Manufg.
Coal	0.2	Mining	Pulp mills	0.4	Manufg.
Maintenance of nonfarm buildings nec	0.2	Constr.	Hospitals	0.4	Services
Mechanical measuring devices	0.2	Manufg.	State & local electric utilities	0.4	Gov't
Sanitary services, steam supply, irrigation	0.2	Util.	S/L Govt. purch., public assistance & relief	0.4	S/L Govt
Insurance carriers	0.2	Fin/R.E.	U.S. Postal Service	0.3	Gov't
Security & commodity brokers	0.2	Fin/R.E.	S/L Govt. purch., natural resource & recreation.	0.3	S/L Govt
Computer & data processing services	0.2	Services	Knitting mills, nec	0.2	Manufg.
Detective & protective services	0.2	Services	Gas production & distribution (utilities)	0.2	Util.
Engineering, architectural, & surveying services	0.2	Services	Real estate	0.2	Fin/R.E.
State & local government enterprises, nec	0.2	Gov't	Local government passenger transit	0.2	Gov't
Bags, except textile	0.1	Manufg.	State & local government enterprises, nec	0.2	Gov't
Cyclic crudes and organics	0.1	Manufg.	S/L Govt. purch., correction	0.2	S/L Govt
Royalties	0.1	Fin/R.E.	S/L Govt. purch., police	0.2	S/L Govt
Hotels & lodging places	0.1	Services			
Legal services	0.1	Services			

Source: Benchmark Input-Output Accounts for the U.S. Economy, 1982, U.S. Department of Commerce, Washington, D.C., July 1991. Data, as reported in the source, are organized by the 1977 SIC structure in use in 1982 but have been matched, as closely as is possible, to the 1987 SIC structure used in this book.

OCCUPATIONS EMPLOYED BY SIC 284 - SOAP, CLEANERS, AND TOILET GOODS

Occupation	% of Total 1994	Change to 2005	Occupation	% of Total 1994	Change to 2005
Packaging & filling machine operators	8.5	-30.1	Bookkeeping, accounting, & auditing clerks	1.8	-12.6
Hand packers & packagers	6.3	-20.1	Maintenance repairers, general utility	1.7	4.8
Assemblers, fabricators, & hand workers nec	5.7	16.5	Inspectors, testers, & graders, precision	1.6	16.5
Sales & related workers nec	4.9	16.5	General office clerks	1.6	-0.7
Freight, stock, & material movers, hand	3.6	-6.8	Order clerks, materials, merchandise, & service	1.5	13.9
Secretaries, ex legal & medical	3.5	6.0	Machine feeders & offbearers	1.5	4.8
Chemical equipment controllers, operators	3.0	4.8	Clerical supervisors & managers	1.5	19.1
Industrial machinery mechanics	2.7	28.1	Professional workers nec	1.4	39.7
Machine operators nec	2.6	2.6	Industrial production managers	1.4	16.4
Industrial truck & tractor operators	2.6	16.5	Stock clerks	1.4	-5.3
Chemists	2.5	28.1	Managers & administrators nec	1.3	16.4
Crushing & mixing machine operators	2.5	16.4	Adjustment clerks	1.2	39.8
General managers & top executives	2.5	10.5	Accountants & auditors	1.2	16.5
Traffic, shipping, & receiving clerks	2.2	12.1	Management support workers nec	1.1	16.4
Marketing, advertising, & PR managers	2.0	16.5	Engineering, mathematical, & science managers	1.1	32.2
Science & mathematics technicians	1.8	16.5	Truck drivers light & heavy	1.0	20.1

Source: Industry-Occupation Matrix, Bureau of Labor Statistics. These data relate to one or more 3-digit SIC industry groups rather than to a single 4-digit SIC. The change reported for each occupation to the year 2005 is a percent of growth or decline as estimated by the Bureau of Labor Statistics. The abbreviation nec stands for 'not elsewhere classified'.

LOCATION BY STATE AND REGIONAL CONCENTRATION

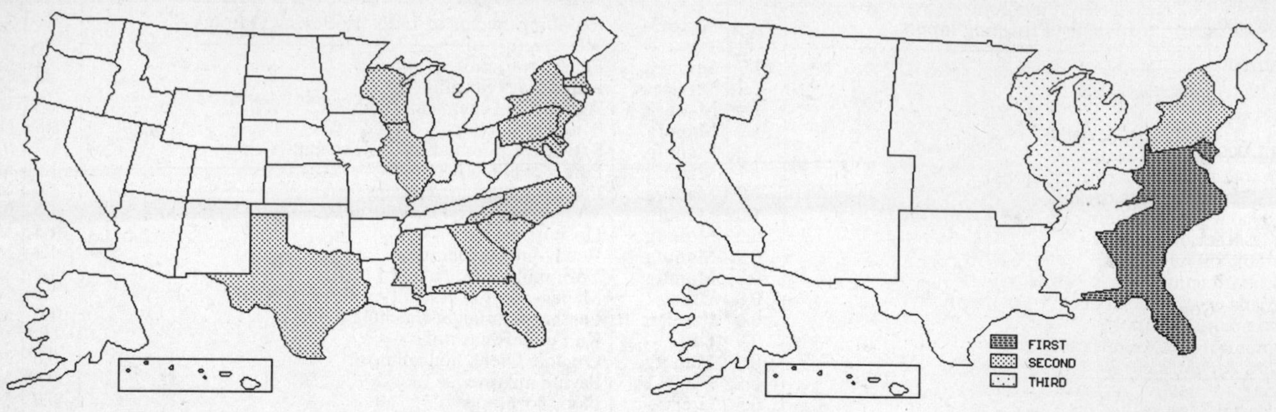

INDUSTRY DATA BY STATE

State	Establish-ments	Shipments			Employment				Cost as % of Shipments	Investment per Employee ($)
		Total ($ mil)	% of U.S.	Per Establ.	Total Number	% of U.S.	Per Establ.	Wages ($/hour)		
Illinois	16	629.6	22.0	39.3	1,500	18.3	94	16.17	57.1	13,200
South Carolina	20	275.4	9.6	13.8	800	9.8	40	12.88	64.7	7,625
Texas	12	264.0	9.2	22.0	600	7.3	50	15.43	60.2	14,667
North Carolina	25	245.0	8.6	9.8	900	11.0	36	10.78	62.1	14,333
New Jersey	23	244.4	8.5	10.6	800	9.8	35	16.78	65.8	10,250
Georgia	11	173.5	6.1	15.8	600	7.3	55	12.33	56.4	11,167
Wisconsin	5	150.1	5.2	30.0	200	2.4	40	25.50	64.2	19,000
Massachusetts	13	93.1	3.3	7.2	400	4.9	31	13.33	54.2	5,500
Pennsylvania	10	89.8	3.1	9.0	200	2.4	20	11.00	55.7	10,000
New York	8	79.9	2.8	10.0	300	3.7	38	18.33	44.4	8,333
Florida	4	(D)	-	-	175 *	2.1	44	-	-	-
Maryland	2	(D)	-	-	175 *	2.1	88	-	-	-
Mississippi	2	(D)	-	-	375 *	4.6	188	-	-	-
Delaware	1	(D)	-	-	375 *	4.6	375	-	-	-

Source: 1992 *Economic Census*. The states are in descending order of shipments or establishments (if shipment data are missing for the majority). The symbol (D) appears when data are withheld to prevent disclosure of competitive information. States marked with (D) are sorted by number of establishments. A dash (-) indicates that the data element cannot be calculated; * indicates the midpoint of a range.

2844 - TOILET PREPARATIONS

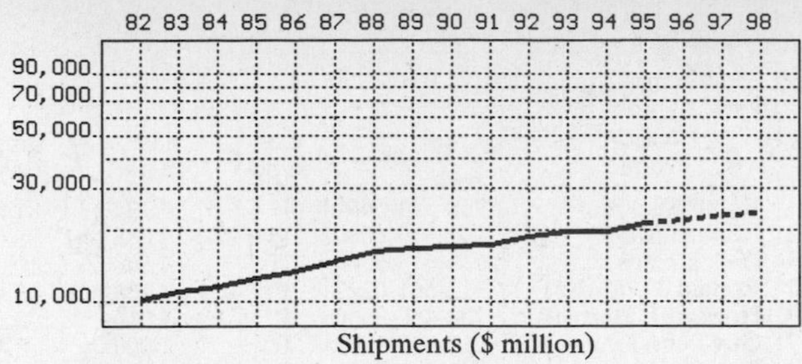

Shipments ($ million)

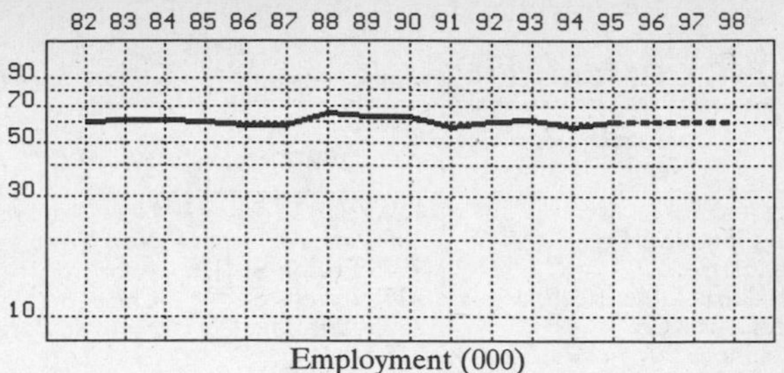

Employment (000)

GENERAL STATISTICS

Year	Companies	Establishments		Employment			Compensation		Production ($ million)			
		Total	with 20 or more employees	Total (000)	Production Workers (000)	Production Hours (Mil)	Payroll ($ mil)	Wages ($/hr)	Cost of Materials	Value Added by Manufacture	Value of Shipments	Capital Invest.
1982	596	639	257	60.4	35.8	68.6	1,102.1	7.59	3,026.3	7,124.4	10,183.2	220.7
1983		641	257	60.9	36.3	69.9	1,142.5	7.68	3,338.8	7,603.0	10,925.1	254.4
1984		643	257	60.9	35.9	67.6	1,208.4	8.38	3,450.2	8,310.0	11,664.9	231.3
1985		645	258	59.8	34.7	66.0	1,250.4	8.83	3,527.1	8,975.6	12,426.9	291.0
1986		654	266	58.8	33.8	66.0	1,388.1	9.32	3,647.0	9,725.1	13,332.9	276.9
1987	649	694	272	57.9	35.1	69.9	1,352.8	9.22	3,881.6	10,801.1	14,592.9	225.5
1988		687	277	64.9	40.5	78.1	1,551.3	9.08	4,445.1	12,053.2	16,293.6	292.6
1989		676	282	63.6	39.4	75.4	1,615.5	9.69	4,758.2	11,979.2	16,641.9	313.7
1990		682	284	63.6	38.1	74.3	1,620.6	10.14	4,904.6	12,104.2	17,048.4	280.4
1991		674	271	57.4	35.6	69.8	1,616.3	10.81	5,046.3	12,047.4	17,085.4	299.5
1992	707	756	305	60.1	37.2	75.6	1,783.3	10.82	5,611.3	13,167.2	18,753.5	507.3
1993		778	299	61.7	38.6	79.7	1,857.8	10.59	6,152.6	13,588.8	19,706.4	472.6
1994		750P	300P	57.6	35.3	72.8	1,796.6	10.93	6,482.1	13,327.2	19,736.0	490.6
1995		760P	305P	60.3P	37.8P	77.2P	1,940.0P	11.48P	6,945.4P	14,279.8P	21,146.7P	471.1P
1996		771P	309P	60.2P	37.9P	78.0P	2,005.2P	11.77P	7,221.6P	14,847.6P	21,987.6P	492.7P
1997		781P	313P	60.2P	38.1P	78.7P	2,070.4P	12.06P	7,497.8P	15,415.4P	22,828.4P	514.3P
1998		792P	317P	60.2P	38.2P	79.5P	2,135.6P	12.35P	7,773.9P	15,983.2P	23,669.3P	535.9P

Sources: 1982, 1987, 1992 *Economic Census; Annual Survey of Manufactures*, 83-86, 88-91, 93-94. Establishment counts for non-Census years are from *County Business Patterns*; establishment values for 83-84 are extrapolations. 'P's show projections by the editors. Industries reclassified in 87 will not have data for prior years.

INDICES OF CHANGE

Year	Companies	Establishments		Employment			Compensation		Production ($ million)			
		Total	with 20 or more employees	Total (000)	Production Workers (000)	Production Hours (Mil)	Payroll ($ mil)	Wages ($/hr)	Cost of Materials	Value Added by Manufacture	Value of Shipments	Capital Invest.
1982	84	85	84	100	96	91	62	70	54	54	54	44
1983		85	84	101	98	92	64	71	60	58	58	50
1984		85	84	101	97	89	68	77	61	63	62	46
1985		85	85	100	93	87	70	82	63	68	66	57
1986		87	87	98	91	87	78	86	65	74	71	55
1987	92	92	89	96	94	92	76	85	69	82	78	44
1988		91	91	108	109	103	87	84	79	92	87	58
1989		89	92	106	106	100	91	90	85	91	89	62
1990		90	93	106	102	98	91	94	87	92	91	55
1991		89	89	96	96	92	91	100	90	91	91	59
1992	100	100	100	100	100	100	100	100	100	100	100	100
1993		103	98	103	104	105	104	98	110	103	105	93
1994		99P	99P	96	95	96	101	101	116	101	105	97
1995		101P	100P	100P	102P	102P	109P	106P	124P	108P	113P	93P
1996		102P	101P	100P	102P	103P	112P	109P	129P	113P	117P	97P
1997		103P	103P	100P	102P	104P	116P	111P	134P	117P	122P	101P
1998		105P	104P	100P	103P	105P	120P	114P	139P	121P	126P	106P

Sources: Same as General Statistics. Values reflect change from the base year, 1992. Values above 100 mean greater than 92, values below 100 mean less than 92, and a value of 100 in the 82-91 or 93-98 period means same as 92. 'P's mark projections by the editors.

SELECTED RATIOS

For 1994	Avg. of All Manufact.	Analyzed Industry	Index	For 1994	Avg. of All Manufact.	Analyzed Industry	Index
Employees per Establishment	49	77	157	Value Added per Production Worker	134,084	377,541	282
Payroll per Establishment	1,500,273	2,397,065	160	Cost per Establishment	5,045,178	8,648,566	171
Payroll per Employee	30,620	31,191	102	Cost per Employee	102,970	112,536	109
Production Workers per Establishment	34	47	137	Cost per Production Worker	146,988	183,629	125
Wages per Establishment	853,319	1,061,646	124	Shipments per Establishment	9,576,895	26,332,221	275
Wages per Production Worker	24,861	22,541	91	Shipments per Employee	195,460	342,639	175
Hours per Production Worker	2,056	2,062	100	Shipments per Production Worker	279,017	559,093	200
Wages per Hour	12.09	10.93	90	Investment per Establishment	321,011	654,570	204
Value Added per Establishment	4,602,255	17,781,454	386	Investment per Employee	6,552	8,517	130
Value Added per Employee	93,930	231,375	246	Investment per Production Worker	9,352	13,898	149

Sources: Same as General Statistics. The 'Average of All Manufacturing' column represents the average of all manufacturing industries reported for the most recent complete year available. The Index shows the relationship between the Average and the Analyzed Industry. For example, 100 means that they are equal; 500 that the Analyzed Industry is five times the average; 50 means that the Analyzed Industry is half the national average. The abbreviation 'na' is used to show that data are 'not available'.

LEADING COMPANIES

Number shown: 75 Total sales ($ mil): **37,426** Total employment (000): **160.3**

Company Name	Address				CEO Name	Phone	Co. Type	Sales ($ mil)	Empl. (000)
Johnson and Johnson	1 J & J	New Brunswick	NJ	08933	Ralph S Larsen	908-524-0400	P	15,734	81.5
Colgate-Palmolive Co	300 Park Av	New York	NY	10022	Reuben Mark	212-310-2000	P	7,588	28.0
Amway Corp	7575 Fulton St E	Ada	MI	49355	Dick DeVos	616-676-6000	R	4,500	10.0
Helene Curtis Industries Inc	325 N Wells St	Chicago	IL	60610	Ronald J Gidwitz	312-661-0222	P	1,266	3.4
Alberto-Culver Co	2525 Armitage Av	Melrose Park	IL	60160	Howard B Bernick	708-450-3000	P	1,216	8.5
Cosmair Inc	575 5th Av	New York	NY	10017	Guy Peyrelongue	212-818-1500	R	1,000	0.4
Forever Living Products Intern	PO Box 29041	Phoenix	AZ	85038	Rex Maughan	602-968-3999	R	939	0.9
Perrigo Co	117 Water St	Allegan	MI	49010	Michael J Jandernoa	616-673-8451	P	669	3.9
Clairol Inc	345 Park Av	New York	NY	10154	Stephen Sadove	212-546-5000	S	350*	2.0
Freedom Chemical Co	1735 Market St	Philadelphia	PA	19103	Fred P Rullo	215-979-3100	R	300	1.0
Neutrogena Corp	PO Box 45036	Los Angeles	CA	90045	Lloyd E Cotsen	310-642-1150	P	282	0.8
Benckiser Consumer Products	55 Federal Rd	Danbury	CT	06810	Albert Dechellis	203-731-5000	S	230	1.5
John Paul Mitchell Systems	PO Box 10597	Beverly Hills	CA	90213	JP Jones Dejoria	310-276-7957	R	190*	<0.1
Del Laboratories Inc	565 Broad Hollow	Farmingdale	NY	11735	Dan K Wassong	516-293-7070	P	167	1.1
Johnson & Johnson	199 Grandview Rd	Skillman	NJ	08558	JC Nugent	908-874-1000	S	140	0.9
Dep Corp	2101 E Via Arado	R Dominguez	CA	90220	Robert Berglass	310-604-0777	P	138	0.4
Kolmar Laboratories Inc	PO Box 1111	Port Jervis	NY	12771	Chris Denney	914-856-5311	S	130	0.8
Guest Supply Inc	720 US Hwy 1	New Brunswick	NJ	08902	Clifford W Stanley	908-246-3011	P	116	0.7
Redmond Products Inc	18930 W 78th St	Chanhassen	MN	55317	Tom Redmond	612-934-4868	R	115	0.2
Cosmolab Inc	1100 Garrett Rd	Lewisburg	TN	37091	Wista Crawford	615-359-6253	R	110	0.7
Accra Pac Group Inc	PO Box 878	Elkhart	IN	46515	Satish Shah	219-295-0000	R	100	0.8
Sebastian International Inc	6109 DeSoto Av	Woodland Hills	CA	91367	John Sebastian	818-999-5112	R	100	0.4
Andrew Jergens Co	PO Box 145444	Cincinnati	OH	45250	Roger Reed	513-421-1400	S	97*	0.6
Houbigant Inc	PO Box 299	Ridgefield	NJ	07657	Enrico Donati	201-941-3400	R	97*	0.6
Cumberland-Swan Inc	1 Swan Dr	Smyrna	TN	37167	Lonnie L Smith	615-459-8900	S	80	0.8
Combe Inc	1101 Westchester	White Plains	NY	10604	P Chapin Nolen	914-694-5454	R	70*	0.4
BeautiControl Cosmetics Inc	PO Box 815189	Dallas	TX	75381	Richard W Heath	214-458-0601	P	64	0.3
Shiseido Cosmetics	178 Bauer Dr	Oakland	NJ	07436	Yuji Kishida	201-337-3750	S	60	0.2
Jean Philippe Fragrances Inc	551 5th Av	New York	NY	10176	Jean Madar	212-983-2640	P	59	<0.1
NutraMax Products Inc	9 Blackburn Dr	Gloucester	MA	01930	Donald E Lepone	508-283-1800	P	56	0.5
Arthur Matney Company Inc	4014 1st Av	Brooklyn	NY	11232	Arthur Matney	718-788-3200	R	55	0.5
Aramis Inc	767 5th Av	New York	NY	10153	Leonard Lauder	212-572-3700	S	53*	0.3
Luster Products Co	1104 W 43rd	Chicago	IL	60609	Jori Luster	312-431-1150	R	53*	0.3
Ranir Corp	PO Box 8547	Grand Rapids	MI	49518	Barry Silverman	616-698-8880	R	53*	0.3
Aveda Corp	4000 Pheasant	Blaine	MN	55449	Horst Rechelbacher	612-783-4000	R	50*	0.3
DeMert and Dougherty Inc	5 Westbrook Corp	Westchester	IL	60154	Sidney Kulek	708-409-9000	R	50	0.2
Russ Kalvin Inc	25655 Springbrook	Saugus	CA	91350	Russ Kalvin	805-253-2723	R	49*	0.3
Scott Chemical Co	106 Grand Av	Englewood	NJ	07631	Herbert Paer	201-568-9700	R	48	0.3
CCA Industries Inc	200 Murray Hill	E Rutherford	NJ	07073	David Edell	201-330-1400	P	48	0.1
Image Laboratories Inc	2340 Eastman	Oxnard	CA	93030	Michael Blair	805-988-1767	R	47*	0.3
Cosmyl Inc	4401 Ponce de Leon	Coral Gabies	FL	33146	Jordie Dalmau	305-446-5666	R	44*	0.3
Pavion Ltd	60 Cedar Hill Av	Nyack	NY	10960	Stanley Acker	914-353-3000	R	40	0.5
MEM Company Inc	PO Box 928	Northvale	NJ	07647	Gay A Mayer	201-767-0100	P	38	0.3
Pro-Line Corp	2121 Panoramic Cir	Dallas	TX	75212	CJ Cottrell	214-631-4247	R	38	0.3
Belcam Inc	4 Montgomery St	Rouses Point	NY	12979	M Bellm	518-297-6641	R	35	0.3
Penthouse Manufacturing	225 Buffalo Av	Freeport	NY	11520	W Ostrower	516-379-1300	R	35*	0.2
Cosmar Corp	7432 Prince Dr	Huntington Bch	CA	92647	Tom Bonoma	714-848-0411	D	33	<0.1
Megas Beauty Care Inc	15501 Indrial Pkwy	Cleveland	OH	44135	John Kostantaras	216-676-6400	S	32	0.3
American Intern Industries	2220 Gaspar Av	City of Com	CA	90040	Zvi Ryzman	213-728-2999	R	31	0.2
Aminco Inc	PO Box 22309	Savannah	GA	31403	M De La Guardia	912-651-3400	R	31*	0.2
Coty Inc	237 Park Av	New York	NY	10017	Jerry Abernathy	212-850-2300	S	31*	0.2
Marianna-Imports Inc	11222 I St	Omaha	NE	68137	Michael Cosentino	402-593-0211	R	31*	0.2
Tri Tech Laboratories Inc	1000 Robins Rd	Lynchburg	VA	24506	Ronald W Rodgers	804-845-7073	R	31	0.2
Belmay Inc	200 Corporate S	Yonkers	NY	10701	A Kesten	914-376-1515	R	30*	0.1
Brooks Industries Inc	70 Tyler Pl	South Plainfield	NJ	07080	Ivar Malmstrom	908-561-5200	R	30	<0.1
Freeman Cosmetics Corp	PO Box 4074	Beverly Hills	CA	90213	Larry Freeman	310-470-6840	R	30*	0.1
HydroTech Labs LP	845 W Madison St	Chicago	IL	60607	Joe Parzale	708-296-9545	R	30	0.1
JM Products Inc	PO Box 4025	Little Rock	AR	72204	Michael W Joshua	501-371-0040	R	30	0.2
Alfin Inc	720 5th Av	New York	NY	10019	Mayer D Moyal	212-333-7700	P	29	0.1
Carson Products Co	PO Box 22309	Savannah	GA	31403	David Young	912-651-3400	S	26*	0.2
Parlux Fragrances Inc	650 SW 16th Ter	Pompano Bch	FL	33069	Robert J Kaufman	305-946-7700	P	25	<0.1
Joico Laboratories Inc	345 Baldwin Pk	City of Industry	CA	91746	Steve Stefano	818-968-6111	R	24*	0.1
Waterbury Companies Inc	PO Box 1812	Waterbury	CT	06722	Michael J Tragakiss	203-597-1812	S	24	0.4
Dana Perfumes Corp	635 Madison Av	New York	NY	10022	William Quinn	212-751-3700	S	23	0.3
Les Parfums de Dana Inc	635 Madison Av	New York	NY	10022	William E Quinn	212-751-3700	R	23	0.3
Tiro Industries Inc	2700 E 28th St	Minneapolis	MN	55406	Robert Vaa	612-721-6591	R	23	0.3
Perfumer's Workshop Ltd	18 E 48th St	New York	NY	10017	Donald Bauchner	212-759-9491	R	20	<0.1
CBI Laboratories Inc	2055-C Luna Rd	Carrollton	TX	75006	Paul Cain	214-241-7546	S	19	0.2
Framesi USA/Roffler Indust	400 Chess St	Coraopolis	PA	15108	Kevin Weir	412-269-2950	S	18	0.1
ALOECORP	PO Box 2624	Harlingen	TX	78551	B William Lee	210-425-7597	R	18	0.3
Aloette Cosmetics Inc	1301 Wrights Ln E	West Chester	PA	19380	Patricia J Defibaugh	610-692-0600	P	17	<0.1
Bijan Fragrances Inc	421 N Rodeo Dr	Beverly Hills	CA	90210	Sally Yeh	310-271-1122	S	17*	0.1
Guerlain Inc	444 Madison 17th	New York	NY	10022	Patrick Waterfield	212-751-1870	R	17	0.1
Noevir Inc	1095 SE Main St	Irvine	CA	92714	Hiro Shoda	714-660-1111	S	17*	0.1
Para Laboratories Inc	100 Rose Av	Hempstead	NY	11550	Alan Estrin	516-538-4600	R	16	0.1

Source: Ward's Business Directory of U.S. Private and Public Companies, Volumes 1 and 2, 1996. The company type code used is as follows: P - Public, R - Private, S - Subsidiary, D - Division, J - Joint Venture, A - Affiliate, G - Group. Sales are in millions of dollars, employees are in thousands. An asterisk (*) indicates an estimated sales volume. The symbol < stands for 'less than'. Company names and addresses are truncated, in some cases, to fit into the available space.

MATERIALS CONSUMED

Material	Quantity	Delivered Cost ($ million)
Materials, ingredients, containers, and supplies	(X)	4,799.5
Perfume oil mixtures and blends	(X)	323.8
Perfume materials (synthetic organic)	(X)	92.7
Essential oils, natural	(X)	95.3
Bulk surface active agents other than sulfonated oils and fats	(X)	170.6
Fats, oils, greases, and tallow	(X)	107.3
Refined petroleum products, including mineral oil, naphtha solvents, petrolatum, waxes, etc.	(X)	119.2
Alcohols	(X)	101.4
Other synthetic organic chemicals including halogenated hydrocarbons	(X)	215.2
Silicates	(X)	96.4
Fabricated plastics products, including dispensing pumps and sprayers	(X)	190.4
Plastics containers	(X)	993.4
Glass containers	(X)	206.3
Paper and paperboard containers including shipping containers, setup and folding cartons, etc.	(X)	566.6
Metal containers	(X)	194.2
All other materials and components, parts, containers, and supplies	(X)	618.6
Materials, ingredients, containers, and supplies, nsk	(X)	708.0

Source: 1992 *Economic Census*. Explanation of symbols used: (D): Withheld to avoid disclosure of competitive data; na: Not available; (S): Withheld because statistical norms were not met; (X): Not applicable; (Z): Less than half the unit shown; nec: Not elsewhere classified; nsk: Not specified by kind; - : zero; * : 10-19 percent estimated; ** : 20-29 percent estimated.

PRODUCT SHARE DETAILS

Product or Product Class	% Share
Toilet preparations	100.00
Shaving preparations	2.65
Shaving soap and cream	54.19
Aftershave preparations (all forms)	43.65
Other shaving preparations, including preshave preparations and styptics	2.16
Perfumes, toilet waters, and colognes	11.71
Perfume oil mixtures and blends	23.71
Perfumes	16.89
Toilet waters	9.35
Colognes	44.70
Perfumes, toilet waters, and colognes, nsk	5.35
Hair preparations (including shampoos)	24.45
Professional hair shampoos containing soap, including products with additives for coloring, dandruff removal, etc.	1.24
Consumer use hair shampoos containing soap, including products with additives for coloring, dandruff removal, etc.	12.21
Professional liquid hair shampoos containing synthetic organic detergents, including products with additives for coloring, dandruff removal, etc.	2.22
Consumer use liquid hair shampoos containing synthetic organic detergents, including products with additives for coloring, dandruff removal, etc.	19.06
Cream and gel hair shampoos (professional and consumer use) containing synthetic organic detergents, including products with additives for coloring, dandruff removal, etc.	0.46
Professional hair tonics, including hair and scalp conditioners	2.33
Consumer use hair tonics, including hair and scalp conditioners	11.31
Hair mousse (professional and consumer use)	3.03
Home use hair perms (complete and refill)	2.43
Professional hair perms	4.56
Hair dressings, including brilliantines, creams, and pomades	2.89
Hair coloring preparations (bleaches, dyes, rinses, tints, etc.), except combination shampoo/coloring preparations	16.41
Aerosol hair spray	7.25
Nonaerosol hair spray	9.60
Hair rinses, except color rinses	0.46
Other hair preparations, including heat setting wave solutions	1.93
Hair preparations (including shampoos), nsk	2.63
Dentifrices, mouthwashes, gargles, and rinses	9.06
Toothpaste, including gels and toothpowder	67.56
Denture cleaners	32.44
Creams, lotions, and oils, excluding shaving, hair, deodorant, eye, manicuring, and bath	16.32
Cleansing creams	12.29
Foundation creams	11.69
Lubricating creams, including hormone creams	9.35
Moisturizing creams	17.33
Other creams, excluding shaving, hair, deodorant, eye, and manicuring creams	1.75
Suntan lotions and oils	4.11
Sunscreens and sunblocks (lotions and oils)	6.12
Cleansing lotions (except hair, shaving, and bath)	4.10
Cosmetic oils, including baby oils but excluding suntan oils	1.39
Hand lotions	17.25
Body lotions, except bath lotions	5.55
Other lotions and oils, excluding hair, shaving, and bath	2.41
Creams, lotions and oils, excluding shaving, hair, and deodorant, nsk	6.67
Other cosmetics and toilet preparations, nec	30.15
Lip cosmetics and toilet preparations (lipstick, lip gloss, lip conditioners, etc.)	13.26
Blushers	3.95
Eye cosmetics and toilet preparations (mascara, eye shadow, eye liners, eye creams, etc.)	13.75
Feminine hygiene douches and deodorants (except medicated)	1.43
Underarm deodorants, aerosol and spray type	3.10
Underarm deodorants, roll-on, solid, and other types	18.01
Nail enamels and polishes	6.26
Nail enamel and polish removers	0.83
Other manicuring preparations (including nail and cuticle conditioners and creams)	0.87
Talcum and toilet powder	4.27
Face powder (pressed and loose)	7.65
Other powder, including foot powder, etc.	0.18
Bath salts, tablets, oils, and bubble baths	4.85
Premoistened towelettes, including wipes for babies	7.96
Facial scrubs and masks	1.30
Depilatories	0.52
Other cosmetics and toilet preparations	7.20
Other cosmetics and toilet preparations, nsk	4.62
Toilet preparations, nsk	5.66

Source: 1992 *Economic Census*. The values shown are percent of total shipments in an industry. Values of indented subcategories are summed in the main heading. The symbol (D) appears when data are withheld to prevent disclosure of competitive information. The abbreviation nsk stands for 'not specified by kind' and nec for 'not elsewhere classified'.

INPUTS AND OUTPUTS FOR TOILET PREPARATIONS

Economic Sector or Industry Providing Inputs	%	Sector	Economic Sector or Industry Buying Outputs	%	Sector
Miscellaneous plastics products	10.6	Manufg.	Personal consumption expenditures	87.3	
Wholesale trade	10.3	Trade	Beauty & barber shops	4.1	Services
Cyclic crudes and organics	9.7	Manufg.	Exports	3.5	Foreign
Imports	9.3	Foreign	Toilet preparations	1.8	Manufg.
Paperboard containers & boxes	7.3	Manufg.	Change in business inventories	1.1	In House
Advertising	6.0	Services	Federal Government purchases, national defense	0.8	Fed Govt
Glass containers	4.5	Manufg.	Soap & other detergents	0.6	Manufg.
Toilet preparations	4.3	Manufg.	Polishes & sanitation goods	0.4	Manufg.
Metal cans	3.0	Manufg.	Chemical preparations, nec	0.1	Manufg.
Surface active agents	2.9	Manufg.	Drugs	0.1	Manufg.
Fabricated metal products, nec	2.7	Manufg.	S/L Govt. purch., public assistance & relief	0.1	S/L Govt
Business services nec	2.7	Services			
Petroleum refining	2.3	Manufg.			
Motor freight transportation & warehousing	1.6	Util.			
Shortening & cooking oils	1.5	Manufg.			
Electric services (utilities)	1.2	Util.			
Animal & marine fats & oils	1.1	Manufg.			
Noncomparable imports	1.1	Foreign			
Communications, except radio & TV	0.9	Util.			
Chemical preparations, nec	0.8	Manufg.			
Metal stampings, nec	0.8	Manufg.			
Soap & other detergents	0.8	Manufg.			
Eating & drinking places	0.8	Trade			
Banking	0.8	Fin/R.E.			
Commercial printing	0.7	Manufg.			
Industrial inorganic chemicals, nec	0.7	Manufg.			
Pipe, valves, & pipe fittings	0.7	Manufg.			
Metal foil & leaf	0.6	Manufg.			
Vegetable oil mills, nec	0.6	Manufg.			
Air transportation	0.6	Util.			
Equipment rental & leasing services	0.6	Services			
Engineering, architectural, & surveying services	0.5	Services			
U.S. Postal Service	0.5	Gov't			
Gas production & distribution (utilities)	0.4	Util.			
Railroads & related services	0.4	Util.			
Real estate	0.4	Fin/R.E.			
Royalties	0.4	Fin/R.E.			
Maintenance of nonfarm buildings nec	0.3	Constr.			
Crowns & closures	0.3	Manufg.			
Sanitary services, steam supply, irrigation	0.3	Util.			
Legal services	0.3	Services			
Management & consulting services & labs	0.3	Services			
Miscellaneous repair shops	0.3	Services			
Alkalies & chlorine	0.2	Manufg.			
Glass & glass products, except containers	0.2	Manufg.			
Industrial gases	0.2	Manufg.			
Manifold business forms	0.2	Manufg.			
Paints & allied products	0.2	Manufg.			
Insurance carriers	0.2	Fin/R.E.			
Accounting, auditing & bookkeeping	0.2	Services			
Colleges, universities, & professional schools	0.2	Services			
Hotels & lodging places	0.2	Services			
Lubricating oils & greases	0.1	Manufg.			
Machinery, except electrical, nec	0.1	Manufg.			
Nonwoven fabrics	0.1	Manufg.			
Paper coating & glazing	0.1	Manufg.			
Paper mills, except building paper	0.1	Manufg.			
Plastics materials & resins	0.1	Manufg.			
Water transportation	0.1	Util.			
Automotive rental & leasing, without drivers	0.1	Services			
Business/professional associations	0.1	Services			
Computer & data processing services	0.1	Services			

Source: Benchmark Input-Output Accounts for the U.S. Economy, 1982, U.S. Department of Commerce, Washington, D.C., July 1991. Data, as reported in the source, are organized by the 1977 SIC structure in use in 1982 but have been matched, as closely as is possible, to the 1987 SIC structure used in this book.

OCCUPATIONS EMPLOYED BY SIC 284 - SOAP, CLEANERS, AND TOILET GOODS

Occupation	% of Total 1994	Change to 2005	Occupation	% of Total 1994	Change to 2005
Packaging & filling machine operators	8.5	-30.1	Bookkeeping, accounting, & auditing clerks	1.8	-12.6
Hand packers & packagers	6.3	-20.1	Maintenance repairers, general utility	1.7	4.8
Assemblers, fabricators, & hand workers nec	5.7	16.5	Inspectors, testers, & graders, precision	1.6	16.5
Sales & related workers nec	4.9	16.5	General office clerks	1.6	-0.7
Freight, stock, & material movers, hand	3.6	-6.8	Order clerks, materials, merchandise, & service	1.5	13.9
Secretaries, ex legal & medical	3.5	6.0	Machine feeders & offbearers	1.5	4.8
Chemical equipment controllers, operators	3.0	4.8	Clerical supervisors & managers	1.5	19.1
Industrial machinery mechanics	2.7	28.1	Professional workers nec	1.4	39.7
Machine operators nec	2.6	2.6	Industrial production managers	1.4	16.4
Industrial truck & tractor operators	2.6	16.5	Stock clerks	1.4	-5.3
Chemists	2.5	28.1	Managers & administrators nec	1.3	16.4
Crushing & mixing machine operators	2.5	16.4	Adjustment clerks	1.2	39.8
General managers & top executives	2.5	10.5	Accountants & auditors	1.2	16.5
Traffic, shipping, & receiving clerks	2.2	12.1	Management support workers nec	1.1	16.4
Marketing, advertising, & PR managers	2.0	16.5	Engineering, mathematical, & science managers	1.1	32.2
Science & mathematics technicians	1.8	16.5	Truck drivers light & heavy	1.0	20.1

Source: *Industry-Occupation Matrix*, Bureau of Labor Statistics. These data relate to one or more 3-digit SIC industry groups rather than to a single 4-digit SIC. The change reported for each occupation to the year 2005 is a percent of growth or decline as estimated by the Bureau of Labor Statistics. The abbreviation nec stands for 'not elsewhere classified'.

LOCATION BY STATE AND REGIONAL CONCENTRATION

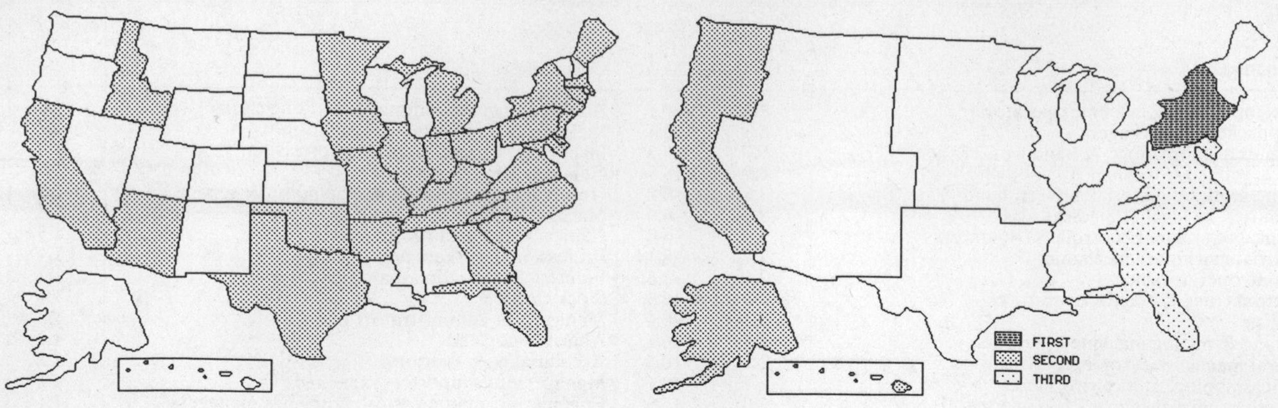

INDUSTRY DATA BY STATE

State	Establish-ments	Shipments			Employment				Cost as % of Shipments	Investment per Employee ($)
		Total ($ mil)	% of U.S.	Per Establ.	Total Number	% of U.S.	Per Establ.	Wages ($/hour)		
New Jersey	103	3,456.1	18.4	33.6	10,900	18.1	106	11.91	29.4	11,917
New York	92	2,126.3	11.3	23.1	8,600	14.3	93	8.44	21.5	2,733
Illinois	39	1,744.7	9.3	44.7	4,500	7.5	115	11.62	33.3	7,867
California	141	1,583.4	8.4	11.2	8,000	13.3	57	8.82	38.0	5,625
North Carolina	10	1,129.0	6.0	112.9	3,100	5.2	310	10.60	24.5	-
Connecticut	21	1,105.1	5.9	52.6	2,600	4.3	124	12.67	25.0	3,192
Texas	58	748.0	4.0	12.9	2,000	3.3	34	10.13	21.8	6,350
Ohio	24	705.8	3.8	29.4	1,900	3.2	79	12.52	32.8	6,526
Virginia	7	604.5	3.2	86.4	1,300	2.2	186	12.63	28.2	-
Minnesota	13	511.4	2.7	39.3	1,900	3.2	146	12.95	40.3	8,316
Pennsylvania	20	394.5	2.1	19.7	1,000	1.7	50	11.86	20.5	-
Tennessee	9	352.3	1.9	39.1	1,500	2.5	167	8.63	29.8	3,867
Massachusetts	10	283.1	1.5	28.3	900	1.5	90	21.91	43.9	-
Florida	43	258.7	1.4	6.0	1,000	1.7	23	8.00	34.7	6,300
Georgia	19	236.2	1.3	12.4	800	1.3	42	9.90	32.0	10,625
Arkansas	7	210.1	1.1	30.0	1,200	2.0	171	11.53	65.3	-
South Carolina	5	48.3	0.3	9.7	200	0.3	40	7.33	30.4	-
Michigan	15	33.9	0.2	2.3	300	0.5	20	6.20	34.5	-
Oklahoma	5	14.9	0.1	3.0	200	0.3	40	5.50	32.2	1,000
Missouri	12	(D)	-	-	1,750 *	2.9	146	-	-	-
Arizona	9	(D)	-	-	1,750 *	2.9	194	-	-	-
Indiana	7	(D)	-	-	750 *	1.2	107	-	-	-
Maine	4	(D)	-	-	175 *	0.3	44	-	-	-
Maryland	4	(D)	-	-	1,750 *	2.9	438	-	-	-
Iowa	3	(D)	-	-	750 *	1.2	250	-	-	-
Kentucky	3	(D)	-	-	175 *	0.3	58	-	-	-
Idaho	2	(D)	-	-	375 *	0.6	188	-	-	-
Delaware	1	(D)	-	-	375 *	0.6	375	-	-	-

Source: 1992 *Economic Census*. The states are in descending order of shipments or establishments (if shipment data are missing for the majority). The symbol (D) appears when data are withheld to prevent disclosure of competitive information. States marked with (D) are sorted by number of establishments. A dash (-) indicates that the data element cannot be calculated; * indicates the midpoint of a range.

2851 - PAINTS VARNISHES LACQUERS ENAMELS

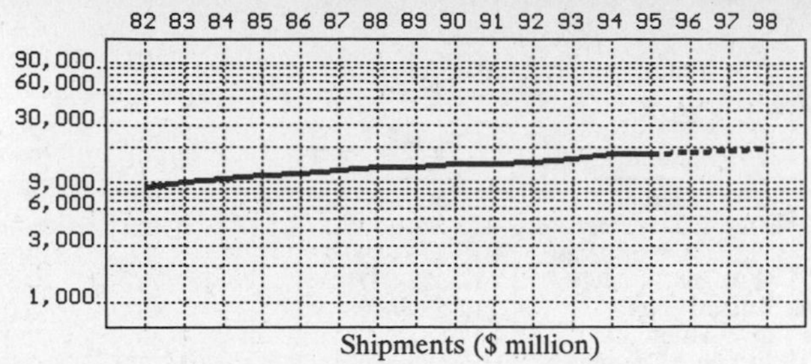

Shipments ($ million)

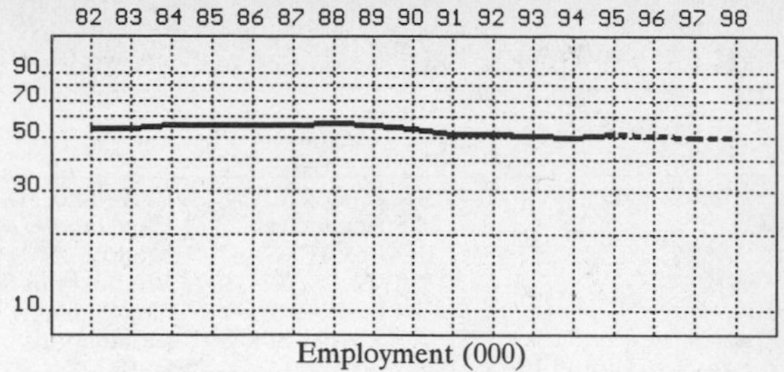

Employment (000)

GENERAL STATISTICS

Year	Companies	Establishments		Employment			Compensation		Production ($ million)			
		Total	with 20 or more employees	Total (000)	Production Workers (000)	Production Hours (Mil)	Payroll ($ mil)	Wages ($/hr)	Cost of Materials	Value Added by Manufacture	Value of Shipments	Capital Invest.
1982	1,170	1,441	622	54.1	27.6	53.6	1,157.7	8.98	5,167.6	3,952.5	9,162.1	264.2
1983				53.6	27.5	54.1	1,207.7	9.32	5,577.3	4,706.3	10,194.6	280.1
1984				55.3	29.1	56.9	1,286.8	9.92	6,011.3	4,932.1	10,848.4	283.6
1985				55.5	29.0	56.9	1,359.5	10.48	6,396.8	5,169.3	11,562.4	336.3
1986				55.8	28.8	57.0	1,416.3	10.73	6,302.6	5,407.2	11,724.9	254.2
1987	1,123	1,426	626	55.2	28.3	56.3	1,491.3	11.16	6,508.9	6,220.5	12,702.4	275.1
1988				56.9	28.3	57.0	1,564.7	11.20	7,088.6	6,488.9	13,531.7	252.7
1989		1,409	641	55.0	27.7	55.8	1,607.5	11.69	7,291.5	6,453.0	13,656.3	240.8
1990				53.9	27.2	55.6	1,627.6	11.89	7,461.2	6,765.7	14,238.7	271.3
1991				51.1	25.2	52.1	1,568.2	12.09	7,434.7	6,784.1	14,254.9	255.7
1992	1,130	1,418	578	51.2	25.7	53.2	1,711.4	12.72	7,806.2	7,158.7	14,973.7	290.2
1993				50.3	25.9	53.4	1,697.7	13.00	8,293.3	7,722.7	16,030.3	256.3
1994				50.1	27.0	55.7	1,911.1	13.98	9,125.4	8,501.0	17,544.4	279.5
1995				50.8P	25.9P	54.3P	1,886.5P	13.91P	9,019.9P	8,402.7P	17,341.6P	263.0P
1996				50.4P	25.7P	54.2P	1,940.5P	14.28P	9,334.4P	8,695.7P	17,946.2P	261.6P
1997				50.0P	25.5P	54.0P	1,994.6P	14.65P	9,648.8P	8,988.6P	18,550.8P	260.3P
1998				49.6P	25.3P	53.9P	2,048.6P	15.02P	9,963.3P	9,281.6P	19,155.3P	259.0P

Sources: 1982, 1987, 1992 *Economic Census*; *Annual Survey of Manufactures*, 83-86, 88-91, 93-94. Establishment counts for non-Census years are from *County Business Patterns*; establishment values for 83-84 are extrapolations. 'P's show projections by the editors. Industries reclassified in 87 will not have data for prior years.

INDICES OF CHANGE

Year	Companies	Establishments		Employment			Compensation		Production ($ million)			
		Total	with 20 or more employees	Total (000)	Production Workers (000)	Production Hours (Mil)	Payroll ($ mil)	Wages ($/hr)	Cost of Materials	Value Added by Manufacture	Value of Shipments	Capital Invest.
1982	104	102	108	106	107	101	68	71	66	55	61	91
1983				105	107	102	71	73	71	66	68	97
1984				108	113	107	75	78	77	69	72	98
1985				108	113	107	79	82	82	72	77	116
1986				109	112	107	83	84	81	76	78	88
1987	99	101	108	108	110	106	87	88	83	87	85	95
1988				111	110	107	91	88	91	91	90	87
1989		99	111	107	108	105	94	92	93	90	91	83
1990				105	106	105	95	93	96	95	95	93
1991				100	98	98	92	95	95	95	95	88
1992	100	100	100	100	100	100	100	100	100	100	100	100
1993				98	101	100	99	102	106	108	107	88
1994				98	105	105	112	110	117	119	117	96
1995				99P	101P	102P	110P	109P	116P	117P	116P	91P
1996				99P	100P	102P	113P	112P	120P	121P	120P	90P
1997				98P	99P	102P	117P	115P	124P	126P	124P	90P
1998				97P	98P	101P	120P	118P	128P	130P	128P	89P

Sources: Same as General Statistics. Values reflect change from the base year, 1992. Values above 100 mean greater than 92, values below 100 mean less than 92, and a value of 100 in the 82-91 or 93-98 period means same as 92. 'P's mark projections by the editors.

SELECTED RATIOS

For 1992	Avg. of All Manufact.	Analyzed Industry	Index	For 1992	Avg. of All Manufact.	Analyzed Industry	Index
Employees per Establishment	46	36	79	Value Added per Production Worker	122,353	278,549	228
Payroll per Establishment	1,332,320	1,206,911	91	Cost per Establishment	4,239,462	5,505,078	130
Payroll per Employee	29,181	33,426	115	Cost per Employee	92,853	152,465	164
Production Workers per Establishment	31	18	58	Cost per Production Worker	135,003	303,743	225
Wages per Establishment	734,496	477,224	65	Shipments per Establishment	8,100,800	10,559,732	130
Wages per Production Worker	23,390	26,331	113	Shipments per Employee	177,425	292,455	165
Hours per Production Worker	2,025	2,070	102	Shipments per Production Worker	257,966	582,634	226
Wages per Hour	11.55	12.72	110	Investment per Establishment	278,244	204,654	74
Value Added per Establishment	3,842,210	5,048,449	131	Investment per Employee	6,094	5,668	93
Value Added per Employee	84,153	139,818	166	Investment per Production Worker	8,861	11,292	127

Sources: Same as General Statistics. The 'Average of All Manufacturing' column represents the average of all manufacturing industries reported for the most recent complete year available. The Index shows the relationship between the Average and the Analyzed Industry. For example, 100 means that they are equal; 500 that the Analyzed Industry is five times the average; 50 means that the Analyzed Industry is half the national average. The abbreviation 'na' is used to show that data are 'not available'.

LEADING COMPANIES

Number shown: **74** Total sales ($ mil): **12,063** Total employment (000): **62.1**

Company Name	Address				CEO Name	Phone	Co. Type	Sales ($ mil)	Empl. (000)
Sherwin-Williams Co	101 Prospect NW	Cleveland	OH	44115	John G Breen	216-566-2000	P	3,100	17.9
Glidden Co	925 Euclid Av	Cleveland	OH	44115	John R Danzeisen	216-344-8216	S	1,400	5.0
RPM Inc	PO Box 777	Medina	OH	44258	Thomas C Sullivan	216-273-5090	P	816	4.5
Valspar Corp	1101 3rd St S	Minneapolis	MN	55415	C Angus Wurtele	612-332-7371	P	787	2.5
Grow Group Inc	200 Park Av	New York	NY	10166	Russell Banks	212-599-4400	P	402	2.0
Lilly Industries Inc	733 S West St	Indianapolis	IN	46225	D W Huemme	317-687-6700	P	331	1.2
Pratt and Lambert United Inc	PO Box 22	Buffalo	NY	14240	Joseph J Castigila	716-873-6000	P	329	2.0
Lord Corp	PO Box 10038	Erie	PA	16514	Charles J Hora	814-868-0924	R	270	1.7
Sherwin-Williams Co	101 Prospect NW	Cleveland	OH	44115	Joe Scaminace	216-566-2000	D	250	1.7
Devoe and Raynolds Co	PO Box 7600	Louisville	KY	40257	Gary W Miller	502-897-9861	S	210	1.2
Guardsman Products Inc	PO Box 1521	Grand Rapids	MI	49501	Charles E Bennett	616-957-2600	P	202	1.0
Duron Inc	10406 Tucker St	Beltsville	MD	20705	Robert Feinberg	301-937-4600	R	200	1.2
PPG Industries	1148 NW Larry Way	Seattle	WA	98107	Susan Chabot	206-781-5366	S	200*	0.5
HB Fuller Co Specialty Group	1210 County EW	Arden Hills	MN	55112	Sarah Coffin	612-481-9739	D	170	0.8
MA Bruder and Sons Inc	PO Box 600	Broomall	PA	19008	T A Bruder Jr	215-353-5100	R	170	1.2
Dunn Edwards Corp	PO Box 30389	Los Angeles	CA	90039	George Matthew	213-771-3330	R	160	1.2
Sinclair Paint Co	6100 S Garfield Av	Los Angeles	CA	90040	Robert Wilkinson	213-888-8888	D	150	0.9
WM Barr and Company Inc	PO Box 1879	Memphis	TN	38113	A V Richmond	901-775-0100	R	150	0.4
Morton Automotive Coating Inc	2700 E 170th St	Lansing	IL	60438	John Harigan	708-474-7000	S	140	0.6
Frazee Industries Inc	6625 Miramar Rd	San Diego	CA	92121	Hobart L Overocker	619-276-9500	S	100	0.7
Fuller-O'Brien Paints Inc	395 Oyster Pt Blvd	S San Francisco	CA	94080	J J Crowley Jr	415-871-6060	R	90	0.6
Penn Color Inc	400 Old Dublin Pike	Doylestown	PA	18901	K Putman	215-345-6550	R	90	0.4
Behr Process Corp	PO Box 1287	Santa Ana	CA	92702	JV Croul	714-545-7101	R	88*	0.4
Ferro Corp	PO Box 6550	Cleveland	OH	44101	Al Bersticker	216-641-8580	D	87*	0.5
Sherwin-Williams Co	101 Prospect NW	Cleveland	OH	44115	T Scott King	216-566-2000	D	86*	0.5
Jones Blair Co	PO Box 35286	Dallas	TX	75235	PD Dague	214-353-1600	R	84	0.5
Yenkin Majestic Paint Corp	PO Box 369004	Columbus	OH	43236	BK Yenkin	614-253-8511	R	80	0.6
Red Spot Paint Varnish Co	PO Box 418	Evansville	IN	47703	CD Storms	812-428-9100	R	79	0.5
Deposition Technologies Inc	4540 Viewridge Av	San Diego	CA	92123	John R Robinson	619-576-0200	S	74	0.1
Rust-Oleum Corp	11 Hawthorne Pkwy	Vernon Hills	IL	60061	Michael D Tellor	708-367-7700	S	74*	0.5
Glidden Co Southcentral Region	1900 Josey Ln	Carrollton	TX	75006	Phillip Baldwin	214-416-1420	D	67	0.4
United Coatings Inc	2850 Festival Dr	Kankakee	IL	60901	Jules F Knapp	815-935-1200	S	65	0.5
Hirshfield's Inc	725 2nd Av N	Minneapolis	MN	55405	Frank Hirshfield	612-377-3910	R	62	0.2
Klean-Strip	PO Box 1879	Memphis	TN	38113	AV Richmond	901-775-0100	D	60	0.4
Willamette Valley Co	PO Box 2280	Eugene	OR	97402	John R Harrison	503-484-9621	R	60	0.1
Martin-Senour Paints	101 Prospect NW	Cleveland	OH	44115	Scott King	216-566-2316	S	55	0.4
Mobile Paint Manufacturing Co	4775 Hamilton Blv	Theodore	AL	36582	Robert A Williams	334-443-6110	R	55	0.4
Mautz Paint Co	PO Box 7068	Madison	WI	53707	BF Mautz Jr	608-255-1661	R	52	0.3
Thompson and Formby	825 Crossover Ln	Memphis	TN	38117	Bill Stewart	901-685-7555	S	52	0.3
Ameritone Paint Corp	PO Box 190	Long Beach	CA	90801	JJ Espelage	310-639-6791	S	50	0.3
Plasti-Kote Company Inc	PO Box 708	Medina	OH	44258	PW McKenna	216-725-4511	R	50	0.2
Tnemec Company Inc	PO Box 411749	Kansas City	MO	64141	PC Cortelyou	816-483-3400	R	50	0.2
ECP Inc	1 Westbrook	Westchester	IL	60154	Larry Bettendorf	708-409-5015	S	48	<0.1
Southern Coatings Inc	PO Box 160	Sumter	SC	29151	Austin E Floyd	803-775-6351	S	45	0.3
Testor Corp	620 Buckbee St	Rockford	IL	61104	David Miller	815-962-6654	S	43	0.3
Muralo Company Inc	PO Box 455	Bayonne	NJ	07002	James S Norton	201-437-0770	R	42	0.4
Lilly Industries High Point	PO Box 2358	High Point	NC	27261	Robert Taylor	910-889-2157	D	40*	0.2
O'Brien Powder Products Inc	9800 Genard Rd	Houston	TX	77041	John R Brvenik	713-939-4000	R	39*	0.2
Mohawk Finishing Products Inc	4715 State Hwy 30	Amsterdam	NY	12010	Glenn Hornberger	518-843-1380	S	37*	0.3
Monarch Paint Co	PO Box 55604	Houston	TX	77255	James Awalt	713-680-2799	R	36*	0.3
Kurfees Coatings Inc	201 E Market St	Louisville	KY	40202	J D Wittenberg	502-584-0151	R	35	<0.1
Watson-Standard Co	PO Box 11250	Pittsburgh	PA	15238	HK Watson III	412-362-8300	R	35*	0.2
California Products Corp	PO Box 569	Cambridge	MA	02139	JS Junkin	617-547-5300	R	34*	0.3
Columbia Paint and Coating Inc	PO Box 4569	Spokane	WA	99202	HH Larison	509-535-9741	R	32	0.3
Decratrend Paints Corp	13530 E Nelson Av	City of Industry	CA	91746	Scott Holt	818-333-4592	S	32*	0.2
Moline Paint Manufacturing Co	5400 23rd Av	Moline	IL	61265	John H Sadler	309-762-7546	S	32	0.2
Old Quaker Paint Co	1958 E Edinger Av	Santa Ana	CA	92707	Ron Goodman	714-258-3410	R	31*	0.2
Bruning Paint Co	601 S Haven	Baltimore	MD	21224	Douglas Ramer	410-342-3636	R	30	0.2
Color Wheel Paint Mfg	2814 Silver Star Rd	Orlando	FL	32808	Steve Strube	407-293-6810	R	30	0.2
Iowa Paint Manufacturing	PO Box 1417	Des Moines	IA	50305	Thomas Goldman	515-283-1501	R	30	0.2
Linear Dynamics Inc	400 Lanidex Plz	Parsippany	NJ	07054	W Henry III	201-884-0300	R	30*	0.2
Samuel Cabot Inc	100 Hale St	Newburyport	MA	01950	Samuel Cabot III	508-465-1900	R	30	0.1
Diamond Products Co	POBox 8001	Marshalltown	IA	50158	Blair Vogel	515-753-6617	D	28	0.1
MAB Paints	630 N 3rd St	Terre Haute	IN	47808	Lee Roads	812-234-6621	S	28*	0.2
Olympic Home Care Prod Co	6804 Enterprise Dr	Louisville	KY	40214	Lou Komis	502-361-2681	D	28*	<0.1
Southwestern Petroleum Corp	PO Box 961005	Fort Worth	TX	76161	AJ Dickerson	817-332-2336	R	26	0.1
Cardinal Industrial Finish Inc	1329 Potrero Av	S El Monte	CA	91733	Stan Ekstrom	818-444-9274	R	25	0.1
Con-Lux Coatings Inc	PO Box 847	Edison	NJ	08818	S Biedron	908-287-4000	R	25	0.2
Daniel Products Company Inc	400 Claremont Av	Jersey City	NJ	07304	R Himics	201-432-0800	R	25	<0.1
Perry and Derrick Co	2510 Highland Av	Cincinnati	OH	45212	Mark E Derrick	513-351-5800	R	25	0.1
US Paint Corp	831 S 21st St	St Louis	MO	63103	C von der Heyde	314-621-0525	S	25	0.1
Zynolyte Products Co	PO Box 6244	Carson	CA	90749	Craig Gioia	310-513-0700	S	25	0.1
Gilman Paint	PO Box 1257	Chattanooga	TN	37401	RA Nayes	615-752-3000	D	23*	0.1
Kelly-Moore Paint Company Inc	301 W Hurst Blv	Hurst	TX	76053	Benny Puckett	817-268-3131	D	23	0.1

Source: *Ward's Business Directory of U.S. Private and Public Companies*, Volumes 1 and 2, 1996. The company type code used is as follows: P - Public, R - Private, S - Subsidiary, D - Division, J - Joint Venture, A - Affiliate, G - Group. Sales are in millions of dollars, employees are in thousands. An asterisk (*) indicates an estimated sales volume. The symbol < stands for 'less than'. Company names and addresses are truncated, in some cases, to fit into the available space.

MATERIALS CONSUMED

Material		Quantity	Delivered Cost ($ million)
Materials, ingredients, containers, and supplies		(X)	7,122.1
Vegetable oils	mil lb	125.4	50.9
Titanium dioxide pigments, composite and pure (100 percent TiO2)	mil lb	904.5	763.8
Other inorganic pigments (chrome colors, whiting, white and red lead, litharge, lithopane, etc.)		(X)	254.5
Organic color pigments, lakes, and toners		(X)	333.5
Hydrocarbon solvents (toluene, xylene, etc.)	mil lb	893.0*	163.7
Alcohol solvents (butyl, ethyl, isopropyl, etc.)	mil lb	314.7	99.2
Ketone and ester solvents (methyl ethyl ketone, ethyl acetate, etc.)	mil lb	398.6	176.4
Other solvents	mil lb	420.9	149.5
Alkyd plastics resins	mil lb	763.3	414.4
Acrylic plastics resins	mil lb	802.8	495.6
Vinyl plastics resins	mil lb	603.7	217.9
Other plastics resins	mil lb	678.7	585.7
Petroleum thinners (naphtha)		(X)	110.7
Minerals and earths, ground or otherwise treated		(X)	210.4
All other organic and inorganic chemicals, nec		(X)	686.9
Metal containers		(X)	393.7
All other materials and components, parts, containers, and supplies		(X)	725.1
Materials, ingredients, containers, and supplies, nsk		(X)	1,290.2

Source: 1992 *Economic Census*. Explanation of symbols used: (D): Withheld to avoid disclosure of competitive data; na: Not available; (S): Withheld because statistical norms were not met; (X): Not applicable; (Z): Less than half the unit shown; nec: Not elsewhere classified; nsk: Not specified by kind; - : zero; * : 10-19 percent estimated; ** : 20-29 percent estimated.

PRODUCT SHARE DETAILS

Product or Product Class	% Share	Product or Product Class	% Share
Paints and allied products	100.00	marking paints, etc.	20.10
Architectural coatings	37.30	Miscellaneous allied paint products (including paint and varnish removers, thinners, pigment dispersions, glazing compounds, etc.)	8.59
Product finishes for original equipment manufacturers (OEM), excluding marine coatings	29.57	Paints and allied products, nsk	4.44
Special-purpose coatings, including all marine coatings, industrial, construction and maintenance coatings, traffic			

Source: 1992 *Economic Census*. The values shown are percent of total shipments in an industry. Values of indented subcategories are summed in the main heading. The symbol (D) appears when data are withheld to prevent disclosure of competitive information. The abbreviation nsk stands for 'not specified by kind' and nec for 'not elsewhere classified'.

INPUTS AND OUTPUTS FOR PAINTS & ALLIED PRODUCTS

Economic Sector or Industry Providing Inputs	%	Sector	Economic Sector or Industry Buying Outputs	%	Sector
Cyclic crudes and organics	17.5	Manufg.	Nonfarm residential structure maintenance	10.9	Constr.
Plastics materials & resins	16.7	Manufg.	Residential additions/alterations, nonfarm	9.2	Constr.
Inorganic pigments	9.8	Manufg.	Maintenance of nonfarm buildings nec	7.0	Constr.
Wholesale trade	6.9	Trade	Automotive repair shops & services	6.2	Services
Metal cans	5.4	Manufg.	Motor vehicles & car bodies	4.5	Manufg.
Metal barrels, drums, & pails	3.0	Manufg.	Residential 1-unit structures, nonfarm	4.3	Constr.
Petroleum refining	2.5	Manufg.	Personal consumption expenditures	3.7	
Motor freight transportation & warehousing	2.5	Util.	Exports	3.0	Foreign
Crude petroleum & natural gas	2.0	Mining	Metal cans	2.3	Manufg.
Advertising	1.8	Services	Metal coating & allied services	2.1	Manufg.
Paints & allied products	1.6	Manufg.	S/L Govt. purch., elem. & secondary education	1.9	S/L Govt
Railroads & related services	1.6	Util.	Highway & street construction	1.7	Constr.
Chemical preparations, nec	1.4	Manufg.	Cyclic crudes and organics	1.6	Manufg.
Minerals, ground or treated	1.2	Manufg.	Wood household furniture	1.4	Manufg.
Noncomparable imports	1.2	Foreign	Printing ink	1.3	Manufg.
Electric services (utilities)	1.1	Util.	Paints & allied products	1.0	Manufg.
Commercial printing	0.9	Manufg.	Office buildings	0.9	Constr.
Shortening & cooking oils	0.9	Manufg.	Ship building & repairing	0.9	Manufg.
Paperboard containers & boxes	0.8	Manufg.	Communications, except radio & TV	0.9	Util.
Surface active agents	0.8	Manufg.	Motor vehicle parts & accessories	0.8	Manufg.
Water transportation	0.8	Util.	Plastics materials & resins	0.8	Manufg.
Eating & drinking places	0.8	Trade	Polishes & sanitation goods	0.8	Manufg.
Forestry products	0.7	Agric.	Typewriters & office machines, nec	0.8	Manufg.
Alkalies & chlorine	0.7	Manufg.	Miscellaneous repair shops	0.8	Services
Cottonseed oil mills	0.7	Manufg.	Industrial buildings	0.6	Constr.
Primary lead	0.7	Manufg.	Residential garden apartments	0.6	Constr.
Communications, except radio & TV	0.7	Util.	Manufacturing industries, nec	0.6	Manufg.
Banking	0.7	Fin/R.E.	Sheet metal work	0.6	Manufg.
Nonmetallic mineral services	0.6	Mining	Wood products, nec	0.6	Manufg.
Vegetable oil mills, nec	0.6	Manufg.	Maintenance of farm service facilities	0.5	Constr.
Gas production & distribution (utilities)	0.6	Util.	Maintenance of water supply facilities	0.5	Constr.
Maintenance of nonfarm buildings nec	0.5	Constr.	Lighting fixtures & equipment	0.5	Manufg.
Pipe, valves, & pipe fittings	0.5	Manufg.	Metal office furniture	0.5	Manufg.

Continued on next page.

INPUTS AND OUTPUTS FOR PAINTS & ALLIED PRODUCTS - Continued

Economic Sector or Industry Providing Inputs	%	Sector	Economic Sector or Industry Buying Outputs	%	Sector
Primary metal products, nec	0.5	Manufg.	Millwork	0.5	Manufg.
Soybean oil mills	0.5	Manufg.	Miscellaneous plastics products	0.5	Manufg.
Engineering, architectural, & surveying services	0.5	Services	Telephone & telegraph apparatus	0.5	Manufg.
Equipment rental & leasing services	0.5	Services	Wood kitchen cabinets	0.5	Manufg.
U.S. Postal Service	0.5	Gov't	Automotive rental & leasing, without drivers	0.5	Services
Imports	0.5	Foreign	Construction of stores & restaurants	0.4	Constr.
Nonferrous metal ores, except copper	0.4	Mining	Maintenance of highways & streets	0.4	Constr.
Agricultural chemicals, nec	0.4	Manufg.	Residential 2-4 unit structures, nonfarm	0.4	Constr.
Fabricated metal products, nec	0.4	Manufg.	Aircraft	0.4	Manufg.
Synthetic rubber	0.4	Manufg.	Commercial printing	0.4	Manufg.
Miscellaneous repair shops	0.4	Services	Farm machinery & equipment	0.4	Manufg.
Copper ore	0.3	Mining	Metal stampings, nec	0.4	Manufg.
Miscellaneous plastics products	0.3	Manufg.	Paperboard containers & boxes	0.4	Manufg.
Primary nonferrous metals, nec	0.3	Manufg.	Wood preserving	0.4	Manufg.
Primary zinc	0.3	Manufg.	Water transportation	0.4	Util.
Soap & other detergents	0.3	Manufg.	Electric utility facility construction	0.3	Constr.
Air transportation	0.3	Util.	Maintenance of electric utility facilities	0.3	Constr.
Real estate	0.3	Fin/R.E.	Maintenance of sewer facilities	0.3	Constr.
Automotive repair shops & services	0.3	Services	Boat building & repairing	0.3	Manufg.
Hotels & lodging places	0.3	Services	Concrete products, nec	0.3	Manufg.
Legal services	0.3	Services	Construction machinery & equipment	0.3	Manufg.
Management & consulting services & labs	0.3	Services	Fabricated structural metal	0.3	Manufg.
Clay, ceramic, & refractory minerals	0.2	Mining	Games, toys, & children's vehicles	0.3	Manufg.
Carbon black	0.2	Manufg.	Glass & glass products, except containers	0.3	Manufg.
Glass containers	0.2	Manufg.	Household cooking equipment	0.3	Manufg.
Gum & wood chemicals	0.2	Manufg.	Metal barrels, drums, & pails	0.3	Manufg.
Industrial inorganic chemicals, nec	0.2	Manufg.	Metal partitions & fixtures	0.3	Manufg.
Screw machine and related products	0.2	Manufg.	Mobile homes	0.3	Manufg.
Sanitary services, steam supply, irrigation	0.2	Util.	Refrigeration & heating equipment	0.3	Manufg.
Accounting, auditing & bookkeeping	0.2	Services	Signs & advertising displays	0.3	Manufg.
Business/professional associations	0.2	Services	Special dies & tools & machine tool accessories	0.3	Manufg.
Chemical & fertilizer mineral	0.1	Mining	Structural wood members, nec	0.3	Manufg.
Manifold business forms	0.1	Manufg.	Truck & bus bodies	0.3	Manufg.
Insurance carriers	0.1	Fin/R.E.	Veneer & plywood	0.3	Manufg.
Royalties	0.1	Fin/R.E.	X-ray apparatus & tubes	0.3	Manufg.
Computer & data processing services	0.1	Services	Crude petroleum & natural gas	0.2	Mining
			Construction of educational buildings	0.2	Constr.
			Construction of hospitals	0.2	Constr.
			Farm housing units & additions & alterations	0.2	Constr.
			Farm service facilities	0.2	Constr.
			Maintenance of farm residential buildings	0.2	Constr.
			Maintenance of nonbuilding facilities nec	0.2	Constr.
			Aircraft & missile equipment, nec	0.2	Manufg.
			Aluminum rolling & drawing	0.2	Manufg.
			Automotive stampings	0.2	Manufg.
			Crowns & closures	0.2	Manufg.
			Dolls	0.2	Manufg.
			Fabricated metal products, nec	0.2	Manufg.
			Fabricated plate work (boiler shops)	0.2	Manufg.
			Household appliances, nec	0.2	Manufg.
			Household laundry equipment	0.2	Manufg.
			Household refrigerators & freezers	0.2	Manufg.
			Metal household furniture	0.2	Manufg.
			Motors & generators	0.2	Manufg.
			Plating & polishing	0.2	Manufg.
			Service industry machines, nec	0.2	Manufg.
			Sporting & athletic goods, nec	0.2	Manufg.
			Surgical & medical instruments	0.2	Manufg.
			Wood partitions & fixtures	0.2	Manufg.
			Motor freight transportation & warehousing	0.2	Util.
			Management & consulting services & labs	0.2	Services
			S/L Govt. purch., correction	0.2	S/L Govt
			S/L Govt. purch., health & hospitals	0.2	S/L Govt
			Hotels & motels	0.1	Constr.
			Maintenance of local transit facilities	0.1	Constr.
			Maintenance of military facilities	0.1	Constr.
			Maintenance of telephone & telegraph facilities	0.1	Constr.
			Residential high-rise apartments	0.1	Constr.
			Sewer system facility construction	0.1	Constr.
			Aircraft & missile engines & engine parts	0.1	Manufg.
			Blast furnaces & steel mills	0.1	Manufg.
			Burial caskets & vaults	0.1	Manufg.
			Electric housewares & fans	0.1	Manufg.
			Furniture & fixtures, nec	0.1	Manufg.
			Gypsum products	0.1	Manufg.

Continued on next page.

INPUTS AND OUTPUTS FOR PAINTS & ALLIED PRODUCTS - Continued

Economic Sector or Industry Providing Inputs	%	Sector	Economic Sector or Industry Buying Outputs	%	Sector
			Hardware, nec	0.1	Manufg.
			Industrial controls	0.1	Manufg.
			Logging camps & logging contractors	0.1	Manufg.
			Metal heat treating	0.1	Manufg.
			Miscellaneous metal work	0.1	Manufg.
			Musical instruments	0.1	Manufg.
			Nonferrous wire drawing & insulating	0.1	Manufg.
			Nonmetallic mineral products, nec	0.1	Manufg.
			Prefabricated metal buildings	0.1	Manufg.
			Railroad equipment	0.1	Manufg.
			Switchgear & switchboard apparatus	0.1	Manufg.
			Synthetic rubber	0.1	Manufg.
			Transformers	0.1	Manufg.
			Truck trailers	0.1	Manufg.
			Upholstered household furniture	0.1	Manufg.
			Wood office furniture	0.1	Manufg.

Source: Benchmark Input-Output Accounts for the U.S. Economy, 1982, U.S. Department of Commerce, Washington, D.C., July 1991. Data, as reported in the source, are organized by the 1977 SIC structure in use in 1982 but have been matched, as closely as is possible, to the 1987 SIC structure used in this book.

OCCUPATIONS EMPLOYED BY SIC 285 - PAINTS AND ALLIED PRODUCTS

Occupation	% of Total 1994	Change to 2005	Occupation	% of Total 1994	Change to 2005
Crushing & mixing machine operators	10.8	-21.3	Truck drivers light & heavy	2.0	-9.9
Sales & related workers nec	9.5	-12.6	Marketing, advertising, & PR managers	1.9	-12.6
Packaging & filling machine operators	6.8	-12.6	Helpers, laborers, & material movers nec	1.8	-12.6
Blue collar worker supervisors	4.4	-19.0	Industrial truck & tractor operators	1.8	-12.5
Science & mathematics technicians	4.1	-12.6	Hand packers & packagers	1.7	-25.1
Chemists	3.7	-12.6	Order clerks, materials, merchandise, & service	1.7	-14.4
Chemical equipment controllers, operators	3.7	-21.3	Machine operators nec	1.7	-22.9
General managers & top executives	3.0	-17.0	Maintenance repairers, general utility	1.5	-21.3
Traffic, shipping, & receiving clerks	2.8	-15.8	Clerical supervisors & managers	1.4	-10.6
Freight, stock, & material movers, hand	2.5	-30.1	General office clerks	1.4	-25.4
Secretaries, ex legal & medical	2.3	-20.4	Marketing & sales worker supervisors	1.4	-12.5
Bookkeeping, accounting, & auditing clerks	2.2	-34.4	Industrial machinery mechanics	1.3	-3.9
Industrial production managers	2.1	-12.5	Coating, painting, & spraying machine workers	1.2	-12.5
Inspectors, testers, & graders, precision	2.0	-12.6	Managers & administrators nec	1.0	-12.6

Source: Industry-Occupation Matrix, Bureau of Labor Statistics. These data relate to one or more 3-digit SIC industry groups rather than to a single 4-digit SIC. The change reported for each occupation to the year 2005 is a percent of growth or decline as estimated by the Bureau of Labor Statistics. The abbreviation nec stands for 'not elsewhere classified'.

LOCATION BY STATE AND REGIONAL CONCENTRATION

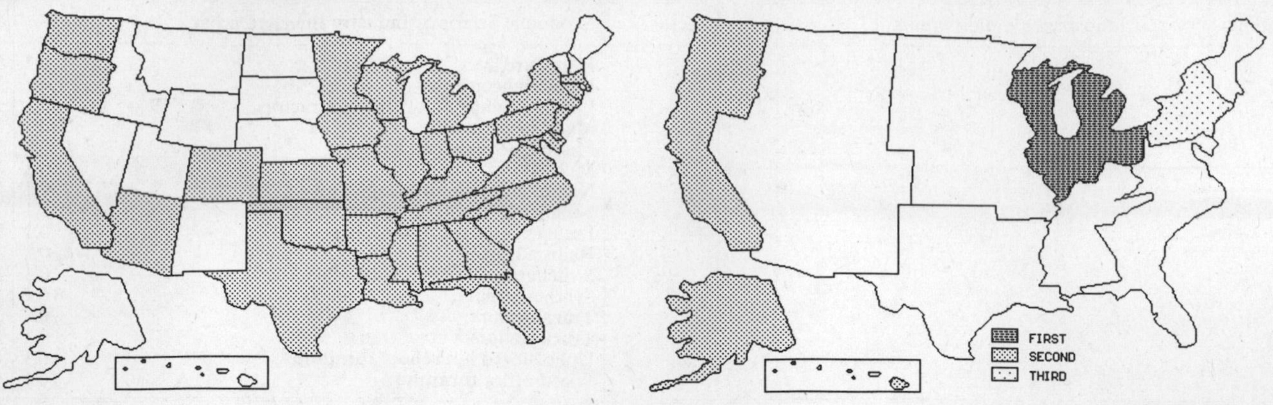

INDUSTRY DATA BY STATE

State	Establish-ments	Shipments			Employment				Cost as % of Shipments	Investment per Employee ($)
		Total ($ mil)	% of U.S.	Per Establ.	Total Number	% of U.S.	Per Establ.	Wages ($/hour)		
Ohio	79	1,852.8	12.4	23.5	6,000	11.7	76	14.94	49.4	10,933
California	189	1,758.6	11.7	9.3	5,400	10.5	29	13.02	51.4	4,352
Illinois	125	1,675.5	11.2	13.4	5,500	10.7	44	12.73	52.2	-
Michigan	76	931.5	6.2	12.3	3,200	6.3	42	13.59	60.7	7,563
Texas	84	917.4	6.1	10.9	2,500	4.9	30	11.24	55.0	10,040
Pennsylvania	65	875.9	5.8	13.5	3,000	5.9	46	13.65	49.2	3,967
New Jersey	91	761.4	5.1	8.4	2,800	5.5	31	12.33	48.6	5,179
Georgia	45	637.3	4.3	14.2	1,500	2.9	33	11.41	58.4	3,667
Kentucky	26	588.1	3.9	22.6	1,200	2.3	46	10.94	36.4	4,417
Maryland	20	463.7	3.1	23.2	1,200	2.3	60	12.90	56.9	5,833
Wisconsin	38	444.5	3.0	11.7	1,800	3.5	47	13.22	50.1	5,667
Indiana	34	398.8	2.7	11.7	1,700	3.3	50	13.71	48.3	-
Missouri	57	374.3	2.5	6.6	1,400	2.7	25	11.71	54.6	5,071
North Carolina	28	369.8	2.5	13.2	1,500	2.9	54	12.64	52.7	3,667
Virginia	18	359.0	2.4	19.9	800	1.6	44	15.90	69.8	-
Massachusetts	41	336.2	2.2	8.2	1,600	3.1	39	14.88	45.3	4,500
Florida	83	297.8	2.0	3.6	1,300	2.5	16	10.08	49.0	3,462
New York	62	268.4	1.8	4.3	1,600	3.1	26	10.16	44.6	-
Iowa	12	266.1	1.8	22.2	700	1.4	58	10.67	51.3	-
Tennessee	31	190.1	1.3	6.1	800	1.6	26	10.00	66.6	6,000
Alabama	21	186.3	1.2	8.9	900	1.8	43	14.00	60.8	-
Washington	25	109.6	0.7	4.4	500	1.0	20	11.00	52.7	4,800
Oregon	22	99.5	0.7	4.5	400	0.8	18	13.50	56.1	3,000
Minnesota	17	81.3	0.5	4.8	500	1.0	29	11.00	55.6	7,000
Connecticut	14	80.3	0.5	5.7	300	0.6	21	12.67	51.2	-
Louisiana	11	64.9	0.4	5.9	200	0.4	18	8.67	53.9	2,500
Arkansas	9	57.6	0.4	6.4	400	0.8	44	10.75	64.8	-
Colorado	7	50.6	0.3	7.2	200	0.4	29	17.00	60.3	2,000
Oklahoma	12	50.4	0.3	4.2	300	0.6	25	12.00	48.8	1,000
Kansas	8	50.1	0.3	6.3	300	0.6	38	11.67	58.5	-
Arizona	18	48.3	0.3	2.7	200	0.4	11	9.50	42.2	3,000
Mississippi	6	38.9	0.3	6.5	200	0.4	33	6.50	59.4	1,000
South Carolina	8	(D)	-	-	375 *	0.7	47	-	-	1,600
Delaware	2	(D)	-	-	175 *	0.3	88	-	-	-

Source: 1992 *Economic Census*. The states are in descending order of shipments or establishments (if shipment data are missing for the majority). The symbol (D) appears when data are withheld to prevent disclosure of competitive information. States marked with (D) are sorted by number of establishments. A dash (-) indicates that the data element cannot be calculated; * indicates the midpoint of a range.

2861 - GUM & WOOD CHEMICALS

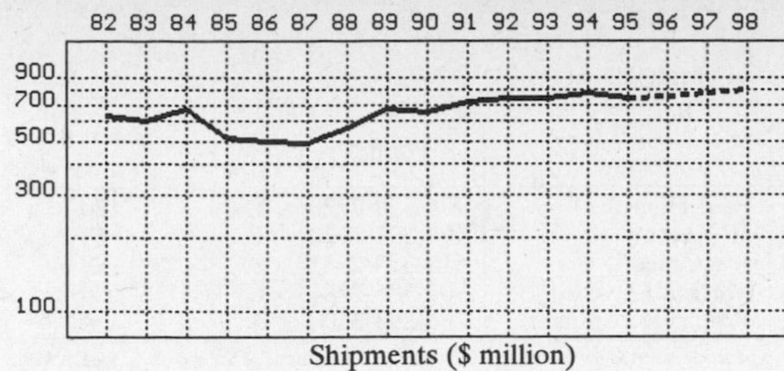

Shipments ($ million)

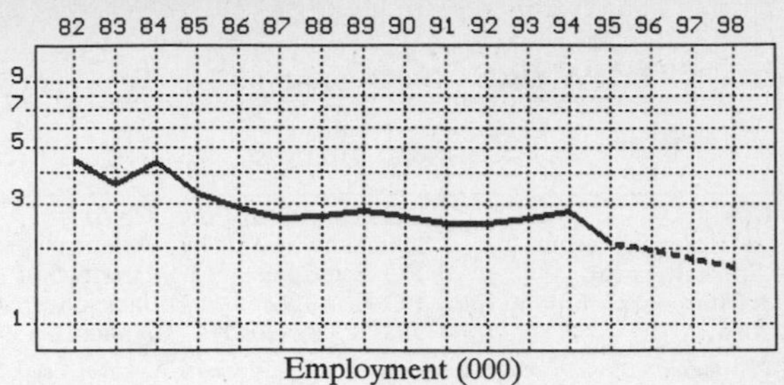

Employment (000)

GENERAL STATISTICS

Year	Companies	Establishments: Total	Establishments: with 20 or more employees	Employment: Total (000)	Employment: Production Workers (000)	Employment: Hours (Mil)	Compensation: Payroll ($ mil)	Compensation: Wages ($/hr)	Production ($ million): Cost of Materials	Production ($ million): Value Added by Manufacture	Production ($ million): Value of Shipments	Production ($ million): Capital Invest.
1982	67	92	40	4.5	3.5	7.5	82.5	7.56	409.2	215.5	624.2	40.2
1983		94	41	3.6	2.6	5.2	86.6	11.29	438.3	161.3	603.7	26.3
1984		96	42	4.4	3.3	7.1	88.6	8.69	431.0	256.3	669.0	26.6
1985		97	42	3.3	2.6	5.5	64.9	8.53	340.8	172.1	514.2	25.0
1986		94	42	2.9	2.3	4.9	63.7	9.14	287.8	205.5	493.1	19.5
1987	52	77	29	2.6	2.1	4.1	57.4	10.24	275.4	212.6	486.5	35.2
1988		75	31	2.7	2.2	4.3	61.1	10.37	299.8	284.7	566.2	19.8
1989		75	31	2.8	2.1	4.3	65.9	10.79	345.9	327.3	668.9	24.7
1990		76	32	2.7	2.0	3.8	59.9	10.89	304.9	340.5	642.9	40.2
1991		79	31	2.5	2.0	4.0	63.6	11.02	360.9	363.0	711.4	19.8
1992	47	76	28	2.5	1.9	4.0	67.8	11.75	352.1	379.0	734.6	42.8
1993		73	27	2.6	2.0	4.2	72.1	11.36	373.7	362.1	738.8	33.4
1994		69P	25P	2.8	2.2	4.5	76.5	11.69	367.2	407.2	774.1	42.1
1995		67P	24P	2.1P	1.6P	3.3P	62.6P	12.14P	353.3P	391.8P	744.8P	35.3P
1996		64P	22P	2.0P	1.5P	3.0P	61.5P	12.40P	360.9P	400.2P	760.8P	36.0P
1997		62P	21P	1.8P	1.4P	2.8P	60.4P	12.67P	368.5P	408.6P	776.8P	36.7P
1998		60P	19P	1.7P	1.3P	2.6P	59.3P	12.94P	376.1P	417.1P	792.8P	37.4P

Sources: 1982, 1987, 1992 *Economic Census*; *Annual Survey of Manufactures*, 83-86, 88-91, 93-94. Establishment counts for non-Census years are from *County Business Patterns*; establishment values for 83-84 are extrapolations. 'P's show projections by the editors. Industries reclassified in 87 will not have data for prior years.

INDICES OF CHANGE

Year	Companies	Establishments: Total	Establishments: with 20 or more employees	Employment: Total (000)	Employment: Production Workers (000)	Employment: Hours (Mil)	Compensation: Payroll ($ mil)	Compensation: Wages ($/hr)	Production ($ million): Cost of Materials	Production ($ million): Value Added by Manufacture	Production ($ million): Value of Shipments	Production ($ million): Capital Invest.
1982	143	121	143	180	184	188	122	64	116	57	85	94
1983		124	146	144	137	130	128	96	124	43	82	61
1984		126	150	176	174	177	131	74	122	68	91	62
1985		128	150	132	137	138	96	73	97	45	70	58
1986		124	150	116	121	123	94	78	82	54	67	46
1987	111	101	104	104	111	102	85	87	78	56	66	82
1988		99	111	108	116	108	90	88	85	75	77	46
1989		99	111	112	111	108	97	92	98	86	91	58
1990		100	114	108	105	95	88	93	87	90	88	94
1991		104	111	100	105	100	94	94	102	96	97	46
1992	100	100	100	100	100	100	100	100	100	100	100	100
1993		96	96	104	105	105	106	97	106	96	101	78
1994		91P	90P	112	116	113	113	99	104	107	105	98
1995		88P	85P	84P	87P	82P	92P	103P	100P	103P	101P	83P
1996		85P	79P	78P	81P	76P	91P	106P	103P	106P	104P	84P
1997		82P	74P	73P	76P	70P	89P	108P	105P	108P	106P	86P
1998		78P	69P	67P	70P	64P	88P	110P	107P	110P	108P	87P

Sources: Same as General Statistics. Values reflect change from the base year, 1992. Values above 100 mean greater than 92, values below 100 mean less than 92, and a value of 100 in the 82-91 or 93-98 period means same as 92. 'P's mark projections by the editors.

SELECTED RATIOS

For 1994	Avg. of All Manufact.	Analyzed Industry	Index
Employees per Establishment	49	41	83
Payroll per Establishment	1,500,273	1,111,870	74
Payroll per Employee	30,620	27,321	89
Production Workers per Establishment	34	32	93
Wages per Establishment	853,319	764,574	90
Wages per Production Worker	24,861	23,911	96
Hours per Production Worker	2,056	2,045	99
Wages per Hour	12.09	11.69	97
Value Added per Establishment	4,602,255	5,918,344	129
Value Added per Employee	93,930	145,429	155

For 1994	Avg. of All Manufact.	Analyzed Industry	Index
Value Added per Production Worker	134,084	185,091	138
Cost per Establishment	5,045,178	5,336,974	106
Cost per Employee	102,970	131,143	127
Cost per Production Worker	146,988	166,909	114
Shipments per Establishment	9,576,895	11,250,958	117
Shipments per Employee	195,460	276,464	141
Shipments per Production Worker	279,017	351,864	126
Investment per Establishment	321,011	611,892	191
Investment per Employee	6,552	15,036	229
Investment per Production Worker	9,352	19,136	205

Sources: Same as General Statistics. The 'Average of All Manufacturing' column represents the average of all manufacturing industries reported for the most recent complete year available. The Index shows the relationship between the Average and the Analyzed Industry. For example, 100 means that they are equal; 500 that the Analyzed Industry is five times the average; 50 means that the Analyzed Industry is half the national average. The abbreviation 'na' is used to show that data are 'not available'.

LEADING COMPANIES

Number shown: 5 Total sales ($ mil): **234** Total employment (000): **0.7**

Company Name	Address				CEO Name	Phone	Co. Type	Sales ($ mil)	Empl. (000)
Zeneca Colours	9129 Southern Pine	Charlotte	NC	28241	Paul Davies	704-559-7720	D	120	<0.1
Royal Oak Enterprises Inc	900 Ashwood Pkwy	Atlanta	GA	30338	JP Keeter	404-393-1430	R	61	0.4
Hickory Specialties Inc	PO Box 1669	Brentwood	TN	37024	Joe Crace	615-373-2581	S	29	0.2
Campfire Charcoal Company Inc	PO Box 1389	Jacksonville	TX	75766	Marion Lewis	903-586-2484	D	20*	<0.1
Tecnal Corp	708 N Texas Rd	Anacortes	WA	98221	Rauno Luttinen	206-293-3200	S	4	<0.1

Source: *Ward's Business Directory of U.S. Private and Public Companies*, Volumes 1 and 2, 1996. The company type code is used as follows: P - Public, R - Private, S - Subsidiary, D - Division, J - Joint Venture, A - Affiliate, G - Group. Sales are in millions of dollars, employees are in thousands. An asterisk (*) indicates an estimated sales volume. The symbol < stands for 'less than'. Company names and addresses are truncated, in some cases, to fit into the available space.

MATERIALS CONSUMED

Material		Quantity	Delivered Cost ($ million)
Materials, ingredients, containers, and supplies		(X)	318.2
Tall oil and rosin	mil lb	794.4	72.8
Industrial organic and inorganic chemicals, including acids and alcohols, but excluding fatty acids		(X)	14.5
Chips, slabs, edgings, shavings, sawdust, and other wood waste		(X)	(D)
Lignite, raw or prepared, used as a raw material		(X)	(D)
Paper and paperboard containers, including shipping sacks and other paper packaging supplies		(X)	10.7
Metal containers		(X)	4.1
All other materials and components, parts, containers, and supplies		(X)	121.3
Materials, ingredients, containers, and supplies, nsk		(X)	34.7

Source: 1992 *Economic Census*. Explanation of symbols used: (D): Withheld to avoid disclosure of competitive data; na: Not available; (S): Withheld because statistical norms were not met; (X): Not applicable; (Z): Less than half the unit shown; nec: Not elsewhere classified; nsk: Not specified by kind; - : zero; * : 10-19 percent estimated; ** : 20-29 percent estimated.

PRODUCT SHARE DETAILS

Product or Product Class	% Share
Gum and wood chemicals	100.00
Hardwood charcoal and charcoal briquets, including blends with lignite or other materials	51.21
Softwood distillation products, including wood rosin, charcoal and charcoal briquets, vegetable pitches, etc.	(D)
Crude tall oil	14.58
Refined tall oil (containing less than 90 percent free fatty acids, including tall oil resins, other than tall oil rosin)	1.87
Tall oil rosin	8.64
Other tall oil derivatives, including rosin acid salts (except tall oil fatty acids)	(D)
Other gum and wood chemicals, including gum naval stores, natural tanning and dying materials, tannic acid, etc.	10.18

Source: 1992 *Economic Census*. The values shown are percent of total shipments in an industry. Values of indented subcategories are summed in the main heading. The symbol (D) appears when data are withheld to prevent disclosure of competitive information. The abbreviation nsk stands for 'not specified by kind' and nec for 'not elsewhere classified'.

INPUTS AND OUTPUTS FOR GUM & WOOD CHEMICALS

Economic Sector or Industry Providing Inputs	%	Sector	Economic Sector or Industry Buying Outputs	%	Sector
Gum & wood chemicals	17.2	Manufg.	Personal consumption expenditures	23.9	
Imports	6.2	Foreign	Gum & wood chemicals	14.4	Manufg.
Forestry products	6.0	Agric.	Exports	11.7	Foreign
Sanitary services, steam supply, irrigation	5.9	Util.	Plastics materials & resins	10.8	Manufg.
Alkalies & chlorine	5.8	Manufg.	Chemical preparations, nec	8.6	Manufg.
Wholesale trade	5.1	Trade	Lubricating oils & greases	4.2	Manufg.
Paperboard containers & boxes	5.0	Manufg.	Eating & drinking places	4.2	Trade
Logging camps & logging contractors	4.2	Manufg.	Adhesives & sealants	3.8	Manufg.
Petroleum refining	3.9	Manufg.	Printing ink	3.8	Manufg.
Miscellaneous plastics products	3.3	Manufg.	Synthetic rubber	2.2	Manufg.
Pumps & compressors	3.3	Manufg.	Federal Government purchases, nondefense	1.9	Fed Govt
Cyclic crudes and organics	3.1	Manufg.	Drugs	1.7	Manufg.
Sawmills & planning mills, general	2.6	Manufg.	Paints & allied products	1.7	Manufg.
Coal	2.3	Mining	Soap & other detergents	1.5	Manufg.
Electric services (utilities)	2.1	Util.	Secondary nonferrous metals	1.2	Manufg.
Gas production & distribution (utilities)	2.1	Util.	Leather tanning & finishing	0.9	Manufg.
Railroads & related services	1.9	Util.	Federal Government purchases, national defense	0.7	Fed Govt
Metal cans	1.8	Manufg.	Reclaimed rubber	0.6	Manufg.
Engineering, architectural, & surveying services	1.7	Services	Paper mills, except building paper	0.3	Manufg.
Security & commodity brokers	1.5	Fin/R.E.	Paperboard mills	0.3	Manufg.
Motor freight transportation & warehousing	1.4	Util.	Ready-mixed concrete	0.2	Manufg.
Miscellaneous repair shops	0.9	Services			
Eating & drinking places	0.7	Trade			

Continued on next page.

INPUTS AND OUTPUTS FOR GUM & WOOD CHEMICALS - Continued

Economic Sector or Industry Providing Inputs	%	Sector	Economic Sector or Industry Buying Outputs	%	Sector
State & local government enterprises, nec	0.7	Gov't			
Noncomparable imports	0.7	Foreign			
Pipe, valves, & pipe fittings	0.6	Manufg.			
Banking	0.6	Fin/R.E.			
Advertising	0.6	Services			
Detective & protective services	0.6	Services			
Maintenance of nonfarm buildings nec	0.5	Constr.			
Chemical preparations, nec	0.5	Manufg.			
Communications, except radio & TV	0.5	Util.			
Equipment rental & leasing services	0.5	Services			
Industrial inorganic chemicals, nec	0.4	Manufg.			
Soap & other detergents	0.4	Manufg.			
Air transportation	0.4	Util.			
Water transportation	0.4	Util.			
Bags, except textile	0.3	Manufg.			
General industrial machinery, nec	0.3	Manufg.			
Mechanical measuring devices	0.3	Manufg.			
Credit agencies other than banks	0.3	Fin/R.E.			
Real estate	0.3	Fin/R.E.			
Electrical repair shops	0.3	Services			
Legal services	0.3	Services			
Management & consulting services & labs	0.3	Services			
Machinery, except electrical, nec	0.2	Manufg.			
Insurance carriers	0.2	Fin/R.E.			
Royalties	0.2	Fin/R.E.			
Accounting, auditing & bookkeeping	0.2	Services			
U.S. Postal Service	0.2	Gov't			
Lubricating oils & greases	0.1	Manufg.			
Manifold business forms	0.1	Manufg.			
Metal barrels, drums, & pails	0.1	Manufg.			
Retail trade, except eating & drinking	0.1	Trade			
Computer & data processing services	0.1	Services			

Source: Benchmark Input-Output Accounts for the U.S. Economy, 1982, U.S. Department of Commerce, Washington, D.C., July 1991. Data, as reported in the source, are organized by the 1977 SIC structure in use in 1982 but have been matched, as closely as is possible, to the 1987 SIC structure used in this book.

OCCUPATIONS EMPLOYED BY SIC 286 - INDUSTRIAL ORGANIC CHEMICALS

Occupation	% of Total 1994	Change to 2005	Occupation	% of Total 1994	Change to 2005
Chemical equipment controllers, operators	10.6	-5.2	Crushing & mixing machine operators	1.7	-5.2
Chemical plant & system operators	8.9	-5.2	Engineering technicians & technologists nec	1.6	-5.2
Blue collar worker supervisors	7.4	-5.7	General managers & top executives	1.3	-10.0
Science & mathematics technicians	7.0	-5.2	Industrial production managers	1.3	-5.2
Maintenance repairers, general utility	4.3	-14.7	Mechanical engineers	1.2	4.3
Chemists	3.8	-5.2	Electricians	1.2	-11.0
Chemical engineers	3.7	13.8	Engineering, mathematical, & science managers	1.1	7.7
Secretaries, ex legal & medical	2.7	-13.7	Electrical & electronic technicians,technologists	1.1	-5.2
Industrial machinery mechanics	2.3	4.3	Managers & administrators nec	1.1	-5.2
Sales & related workers nec	1.9	-5.2	Freight, stock, & material movers, hand	1.1	-24.2
Helpers, laborers, & material movers nec	1.8	-5.2	Bookkeeping, accounting, & auditing clerks	1.0	-28.9
General office clerks	1.8	-19.2	Plumbers, pipefitters, & steamfitters	1.0	-5.1
Precision instrument repairers	1.7	28.0			

Source: Industry-Occupation Matrix, Bureau of Labor Statistics. These data relate to one or more 3-digit SIC industry groups rather than to a single 4-digit SIC. The change reported for each occupation to the year 2005 is a percent of growth or decline as estimated by the Bureau of Labor Statistics. The abbreviation nec stands for 'not elsewhere classified'.

LOCATION BY STATE AND REGIONAL CONCENTRATION

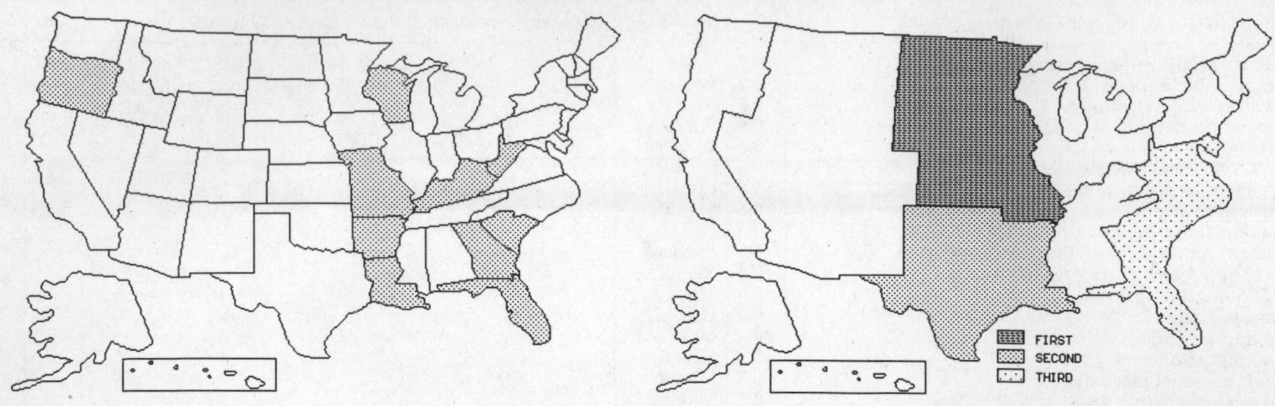

INDUSTRY DATA BY STATE

State	Establish-ments	Shipments			Employment				Cost as % of Shipments	Investment per Employee ($)
		Total ($ mil)	% of U.S.	Per Establ.	Total Number	% of U.S.	Per Establ.	Wages ($/hour)		
Missouri	16	(D)	-	-	750 *	30.0	47	-	-	-
Arkansas	10	(D)	-	-	175 *	7.0	18	-	-	4,000
Louisiana	4	(D)	-	-	175 *	7.0	44	-	-	-
Florida	2	(D)	-	-	375 *	15.0	188	-	-	-
Georgia	2	(D)	-	-	175 *	7.0	88	-	-	-
Kentucky	2	(D)	-	-	175 *	7.0	88	-	-	-
Oregon	2	(D)	-	-	175 *	7.0	88	-	-	-
South Carolina	2	(D)	-	-	175 *	7.0	88	-	-	-
Wisconsin	2	(D)	-	-	175 *	7.0	88	-	-	-
West Virginia	1	(D)	-	-	175 *	7.0	175	-	-	-

Source: 1992 *Economic Census*. The states are in descending order of shipments or establishments (if shipment data are missing for the majority). The symbol (D) appears when data are withheld to prevent disclosure of competitive information. States marked with (D) are sorted by number of establishments. A dash (-) indicates that the data element cannot be calculated; * indicates the midpoint of a range.

2865 - CYCLIC CRUDES AND INTERMEDIATES

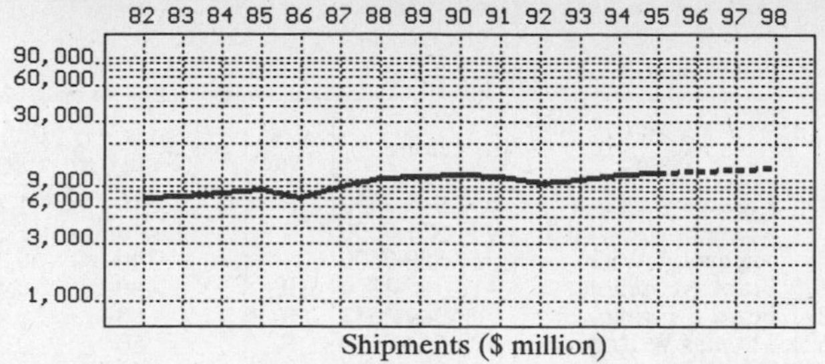

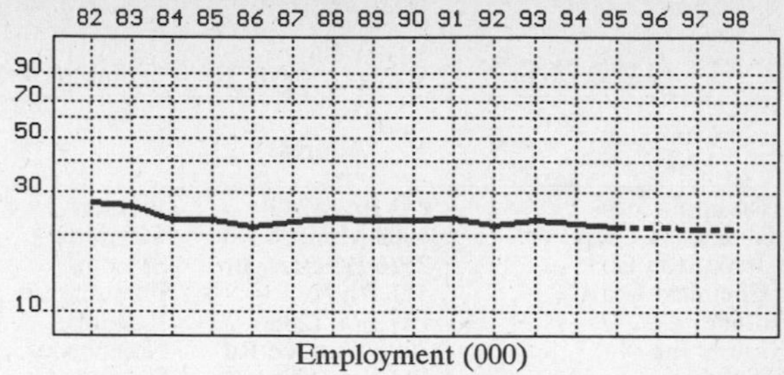

GENERAL STATISTICS

Year	Companies	Establishments: Total	Establishments: with 20 or more employees	Employment: Total (000)	Production Workers (000)	Production Hours (Mil)	Compensation: Payroll ($ mil)	Compensation: Wages ($/hr)	Production ($ million): Cost of Materials	Value Added by Manufacture	Value of Shipments	Capital Invest.
1982	143	189	134	27.3	16.0	32.3	731.0	12.30	5,007.8	2,031.5	7,138.2	454.7
1983		187	132	26.4	15.6	31.2	749.5	13.12	5,036.9	2,333.8	7,398.0	532.4
1984		185	130	23.3	14.0	28.5	699.1	13.83	5,172.1	2,679.7	7,762.0	261.9
1985		182	128	23.4	13.7	27.5	728.9	14.31	5,328.9	2,824.2	8,209.8	383.4
1986		183	123	22.0	12.7	26.3	735.1	15.04	4,242.3	2,687.9	7,013.4	332.6
1987	131	186	121	22.8	13.4	27.6	786.6	15.76	5,502.7	3,414.2	8,859.4	378.8
1988		186	123	23.9	13.9	29.5	877.8	16.01	6,121.7	4,252.5	10,301.9	428.3
1989		181	126	23.3	13.9	29.5	873.6	16.34	7,020.7	3,794.2	10,812.0	584.9
1990		185	130	23.4	13.9	29.6	910.9	16.84	7,027.7	3,980.1	10,892.6	954.9
1991		190	132	23.5	14.1	30.9	962.0	16.96	6,796.4	3,830.3	10,651.8	713.9
1992	150	206	143	22.2	13.2	29.1	934.6	17.10	6,311.4	3,333.0	9,572.8	540.7
1993		213	137	23.3	13.4	28.9	1,028.1	18.27	6,457.2	3,710.6	10,177.0	669.5
1994		200P	134P	22.7	13.1	28.9	1,017.6	18.17	6,954.1	4,205.8	11,151.5	564.6
1995		202P	134P	22.0P	12.9P	28.8P	1,048.5P	19.01P	7,246.6P	4,382.7P	11,620.6P	711.7P
1996		204P	135P	21.7P	12.7P	28.7P	1,077.1P	19.48P	7,459.9P	4,511.7P	11,962.7P	738.6P
1997		205P	135P	21.5P	12.6P	28.7P	1,105.6P	19.96P	7,673.3P	4,640.7P	12,304.7P	765.5P
1998		207P	136P	21.2P	12.4P	28.6P	1,134.1P	20.43P	7,886.6P	4,769.7P	12,646.8P	792.5P

Sources: 1982, 1987, 1992 *Economic Census*; *Annual Survey of Manufactures*, 83-86, 88-91, 93-94. Establishment counts for non-Census years are from *County Business Patterns*; establishment values for 83-84 are extrapolations. 'P's show projections by the editors. Industries reclassified in 87 will not have data for prior years.

INDICES OF CHANGE

Year	Companies	Establishments: Total	Establishments: with 20 or more employees	Employment: Total (000)	Production Workers (000)	Production Hours (Mil)	Compensation: Payroll ($ mil)	Compensation: Wages ($/hr)	Production ($ million): Cost of Materials	Value Added by Manufacture	Value of Shipments	Capital Invest.
1982	95	92	94	123	121	111	78	72	79	61	75	84
1983		91	92	119	118	107	80	77	80	70	77	98
1984		90	91	105	106	98	75	81	82	80	81	48
1985		88	90	105	104	95	78	84	84	85	86	71
1986		89	86	99	96	90	79	88	67	81	73	62
1987	87	90	85	103	102	95	84	92	87	102	93	70
1988		90	86	108	105	101	94	94	97	128	108	79
1989		88	88	105	105	101	93	96	111	114	113	108
1990		90	91	105	105	102	97	98	111	119	114	177
1991		92	92	106	107	106	103	99	108	115	111	132
1992	100	100	100	100	100	100	100	100	100	100	100	100
1993		103	96	105	102	99	110	107	102	111	106	124
1994		97P	94P	102	99	99	109	106	110	126	116	104
1995		98P	94P	99P	97P	99P	112P	111P	115P	131P	121P	132P
1996		99P	94P	98P	96P	99P	115P	114P	118P	135P	125P	137P
1997		100P	95P	97P	95P	99P	118P	117P	122P	139P	129P	142P
1998		100P	95P	96P	94P	98P	121P	119P	125P	143P	132P	147P

Sources: Same as General Statistics. Values reflect change from the base year, 1992. Values above 100 mean greater than 92, values below 100 mean less than 92, and a value of 100 in the 82-91 or 93-98 period means same as 92. 'P's mark projections by the editors.

SELECTED RATIOS

For 1994	Avg. of All Manufact.	Analyzed Industry	Index	For 1994	Avg. of All Manufact.	Analyzed Industry	Index
Employees per Establishment	49	113	231	Value Added per Production Worker	134,084	321,053	239
Payroll per Establishment	1,500,273	5,080,303	339	Cost per Establishment	5,045,178	34,717,897	688
Payroll per Employee	30,620	44,828	146	Cost per Employee	102,970	306,348	298
Production Workers per Establishment	34	65	191	Cost per Production Worker	146,988	530,847	361
Wages per Establishment	853,319	2,621,593	307	Shipments per Establishment	9,576,895	55,673,147	581
Wages per Production Worker	24,861	40,085	161	Shipments per Employee	195,460	491,256	251
Hours per Production Worker	2,056	2,206	107	Shipments per Production Worker	279,017	851,260	305
Wages per Hour	12.09	18.17	150	Investment per Establishment	321,011	2,818,729	878
Value Added per Establishment	4,602,255	20,997,186	456	Investment per Employee	6,552	24,872	380
Value Added per Employee	93,930	185,278	197	Investment per Production Worker	9,352	43,099	461

Sources: Same as General Statistics. The 'Average of All Manufacturing' column represents the average of all manufacturing industries reported for the most recent complete year available. The Index shows the relationship between the Average and the Analyzed Industry. For example, 100 means that they are equal; 500 that the Analyzed Industry is five times the average; 50 means that the Analyzed Industry is half the national average. The abbreviation 'na' is used to show that data are 'not available'.

LEADING COMPANIES

Number shown: 25   Total sales ($ mil): 1,630   Total employment (000): 5.2

Company Name	Address				CEO Name	Phone	Co. Type	Sales ($ mil)	Empl. (000)
First Mississippi Corp	PO Box 1249	Jackson	MS	39215	J Kelley Williams	601-948-7550	P	510	1.2
Sandoz Chemicals Corp	4000 Monroe Rd	Charlotte	NC	28205	Kenneth Brewton Jr	704-331-7000	S	410	1.3
Warner-Jenkinson Co	2526 Baldwin St	St Louis	MO	63106	Michael A Wick	314-889-7600	S	140	0.3
Indspec Chemical Corp	411 7th Av	Pittsburgh	PA	15219	Frank M Spinola	412-765-1200	R	130	0.4
Fred Whitaker Co	PO Box 12886	Roanoke	VA	24029	Floyd L Firing	703-344-4343	R	90	0.4
Apollo Colors Inc	3000 Dundee Rd	Northbrook	IL	60062	Thomas W Rogers	708-564-9190	R	50	0.2
Allied Color Inc	PO Box 278	Vonore	TN	37885	George Chase	615-884-6625	S	40	0.2
Pfister Chemicals Inc	Linden Av	Ridgefield	NJ	07657	Alan Bendelius	201-945-5400	R	40	0.2
Ruetgers-Nease Corp	201 Struble Rd	State College	PA	16801	Thomas W Buettner	814-238-2424	S	38	0.2
Western Tar Products Corp	PO Box 270	Terre Haute	IN	47808	JB Card	812-232-2384	R	35*	0.1
Triangle Dies and Supplies Inc	1040 S 25th Av	Bellwood	IL	60104	Joseph Marovich	708-544-7901	R	29*	0.1
RBH Dispersions Inc	L-5 Factory	Bound Brook	NJ	08805	John Gaither	908-356-1800	S	20	<0.1
Carey Industries Inc	PO Box 620	Danbury	CT	06813	Raymond J Carey	203-744-7280	R	14	<0.1
ABC Compounding Company	PO Drawer 585	Morrow	GA	30260	Stephen R Walker	404-968-3630	R	13	0.1
Natural Gas Odorizing Inc	PO Box 1429	Baytown	TX	77522	Tim Johnson	713-424-5568	S	12	<0.1
Allco Chemical Corp	17304 N Preston Rd	Dallas	TX	75252	W H Chambless	214-733-6831	S	10	<0.1
Industrial Color Inc	50 Industry Av	Joliet	IL	60435	Atillio P Nonnie	815-722-7402	R	10*	<0.1
Accurate Color Inc	PO Box 120	Lodi	OH	44254	Bruce Muller	216-948-2035	R	9	<0.1
R-M Industries Inc	PO Box 997	Fort Mill	SC	29715	John Dickson	803-548-3210	R	8	<0.1
Max Marx Color Co	1200 Grove St	Irvington	NJ	07111	Walter Sichel	201-373-7801	R	6*	<0.1
American Diagnostica Inc	PO Box 1165	Greenwich	CT	06836	Richard Hart	203-661-0000	R	5*	<0.1
Alliance Chemical Inc	33 Avnue P	Newark	NJ	07105	Albert R Bendelius	201-344-2344	S	4	<0.1
Dye Specialties Inc	PO Box 1447	Secaucus	NJ	07096	Robert W Lindley	201-866-9504	R	4	<0.1
Custom Colorants Inc	PO Box 1242	Dalton	GA	30722	James Martin	706-226-8409	S	2*	<0.1
Custom Polymer Inc	2728 N Pace Blv	Pensacola	FL	32505	Sean O'Mahoney	904-436-4990	S	1*	<0.1

Source: *Ward's Business Directory of U.S. Private and Public Companies*, Volumes 1 and 2, 1996. The company type code used is as follows: P - Public, R - Private, S - Subsidiary, D - Division, J - Joint Venture, A - Affiliate, G - Group. Sales are in millions of dollars, employees are in thousands. An asterisk (*) indicates an estimated sales volume. The symbol < stands for 'less than'. Company names and addresses are truncated, in some cases, to fit into the available space.

MATERIALS CONSUMED

Material		Quantity	Delivered Cost ($ million)
Materials, ingredients, containers, and supplies		(X)	5,604.1
Hydrochloric acid (100 percent HCl)	1,000 s tons	59.8*	5.9
Nitric acid (100 percent HNO3)	1,000 s tons	220.8	24.4
Sulfuric acid (100 percent H2SO4), except spent	1,000 s tons	249.5*	24.8
Ammonia, synthetic anhydrous (100 percent NH3)	1,000 s tons	171.1	29.2
Chlorine (100 percent Cl basis)	1,000 s tons	342.8	25.2
Sodium hydroxide (caustic soda)(100 percent NaOH)	1,000 s tons	214.1	52.7
All other industrial inorganic chemicals		(X)	241.4
Acetylene and other industrial gases		(X)	20.6
Alcohol, ethyl (pure and denatured)		(X)	2.6
Other alcohols, including amyl, butyl, methyl, and propyl		(X)	51.6
Toluene and xylene (100 percent basis)	mil lb	(D)	(D)
Phenol (100 percent basis)	mil lb	(D)	(D)
Ortho and para-xylene (100 percent basis)	mil lb	(D)	(D)
Benzol (benzene) (100 percent C6H6)	mil lb	2,855.6	436.5
Tar, crude	1,000 s tons	1,276.5	131.3
Other cyclic crudes and intermediates	mil lb	496.5**	517.0
Acetone (natural and synthetic)	mil lb	1.4	0.4
Other synthetic organic chemicals, nec		(X)	760.4
Natural gas used as a raw material	bil cu ft	60.4	156.0
Ethane used as a raw material or feedstock	mil lb	(D)	(D)
Ethylene used as a raw material or feedstock	mil lb	651.1	117.6
Propane used as a raw material or feedstock	mil lb	787.7	61.2
Propylene used as a raw material or feedstock	mil lb	650.8**	123.6
Butane and iso-butane used as a raw material or feedstock	mil lb	(D)	(D)
Butylene and iso-butylene used as a raw material or feedstock	mil lb	(D)	(D)
Other hydrocarbons used as raw materials or feedstocks		(X)	215.1
Sulfur	1,000 l tons	(D)	(D)
Plastics resins consumed in the form of granules, pellets, powders, liquids, etc.	mil lb	14.8	7.7
Agricultural products (crude), including flowers, grains, seeds, herbs, etc.	mil lb	(D)	(D)
Parts and attachments for machinery and equipment		(X)	39.4
Paperboard containers, boxes, and corrugated paperboard		(X)	14.6
Metal containers		(X)	27.5
All other materials and components, parts, containers, and supplies		(X)	1,339.5
Materials, ingredients, containers, and supplies, nsk		(X)	123.1

Source: 1992 *Economic Census*. Explanation of symbols used: (D): Withheld to avoid disclosure of competitive data; na: Not available; (S): Withheld because statistical norms were not met; (X): Not applicable; (Z): Less than half the unit shown; nec: Not elsewhere classified; nsk: Not specified by kind; - : zero; * : 10-19 percent estimated; ** : 20-29 percent estimated.

PRODUCT SHARE DETAILS

Product or Product Class	% Share	Product or Product Class	% Share
Cyclic crudes and intermediates	100.00	made in a refinery	15.33
Cyclic (coal tar) intermediates	59.73	Aromatics (including benzene, toluene, and xylene) not made in a refinery, for use as a chemical raw material	87.69
Synthetic organic dyes	10.46	Aromatics (including benzene, toluene, and xylene) not made in a refinery, for other uses	12.31
Synthetic organic pigments, lakes, and toners	9.62	Cyclic crudes and intermediates, nsk	1.01
Tar, tar crudes, and tar pitches	3.85		
Aromatics (including benzene, toluene, and xylene) not			

Source: 1992 *Economic Census*. The values shown are percent of total shipments in an industry. Values of indented subcategories are summed in the main heading. The symbol (D) appears when data are withheld to prevent disclosure of competitive information. The abbreviation nsk stands for 'not specified by kind' and nec for 'not elsewhere classified'.

INPUTS AND OUTPUTS FOR CYCLIC CRUDES AND ORGANICS

Economic Sector or Industry Providing Inputs	%	Sector	Economic Sector or Industry Buying Outputs	%	Sector
Cyclic crudes and organics	36.9	Manufg.	Cyclic crudes and organics	20.1	Manufg.
Imports	12.4	Foreign	Plastics materials & resins	12.7	Manufg.
Gas production & distribution (utilities)	6.3	Util.	Exports	12.6	Foreign
Wholesale trade	4.9	Trade	Organic fibers, noncellulosic	6.1	Manufg.
Petroleum refining	4.4	Manufg.	Synthetic rubber	2.8	Manufg.
Electric services (utilities)	4.1	Util.	Petroleum refining	2.7	Manufg.
Crude petroleum & natural gas	3.5	Mining	Medical & health services, nec	2.3	Services
Industrial inorganic chemicals, nec	2.3	Manufg.	Paints & allied products	2.0	Manufg.
Miscellaneous plastics products	2.2	Manufg.	Miscellaneous plastics products	1.9	Manufg.
Pipe, valves, & pipe fittings	1.9	Manufg.	Hospitals	1.9	Services
Motor freight transportation & warehousing	1.7	Util.	Agricultural chemicals, nec	1.6	Manufg.
Miscellaneous repair shops	1.2	Services	Blast furnaces & steel mills	1.6	Manufg.
Alkalies & chlorine	1.0	Manufg.	Paper mills, except building paper	1.4	Manufg.
Railroads & related services	1.0	Util.	Nitrogenous & phosphatic fertilizers	1.2	Manufg.
Special industry machinery, nec	0.9	Manufg.	Semiconductors & related devices	1.2	Manufg.
Engineering, architectural, & surveying services	0.9	Services	Crude petroleum & natural gas	1.1	Mining
Noncomparable imports	0.9	Foreign	Broadwoven fabric mills	1.1	Manufg.
Maintenance of nonfarm buildings nec	0.8	Constr.	Primary aluminum	1.1	Manufg.
Pulp mills	0.7	Manufg.	Steel pipe & tubes	1.1	Manufg.
Advertising	0.7	Services	State & local government enterprises, nec	1.0	Gov't
Nitrogenous & phosphatic fertilizers	0.6	Manufg.	Food preparations, nec	0.9	Manufg.
Chemical & fertilizer mineral	0.5	Mining	Toilet preparations	0.9	Manufg.
Coal	0.5	Mining	Adhesives & sealants	0.8	Manufg.
Nonferrous metal ores, except copper	0.5	Mining	Commercial printing	0.8	Manufg.
Paints & allied products	0.5	Manufg.	Prepared feeds, nec	0.8	Manufg.
Plastics materials & resins	0.5	Manufg.	Chemical preparations, nec	0.7	Manufg.
Water supply & sewage systems	0.5	Util.	Paperboard mills	0.7	Manufg.
Equipment rental & leasing services	0.5	Services	Storage batteries	0.7	Manufg.
Blast furnaces & steel mills	0.4	Manufg.	Glass containers	0.6	Manufg.
Industrial gases	0.4	Manufg.	Tires & inner tubes	0.6	Manufg.
Metal barrels, drums, & pails	0.4	Manufg.	Glass & glass products, except containers	0.5	Manufg.
Paperboard containers & boxes	0.4	Manufg.	Manufacturing industries, nec	0.5	Manufg.
Primary zinc	0.4	Manufg.	Management & consulting services & labs	0.5	Services
Eating & drinking places	0.4	Trade	Fabricated rubber products, nec	0.4	Manufg.
Banking	0.4	Fin/R.E.	Pulp mills	0.4	Manufg.
Drugs	0.3	Manufg.	Sanitary services, steam supply, irrigation	0.4	Util.
Paper mills, except building paper	0.3	Manufg.	S/L Govt. purch., health & hospitals	0.4	S/L Govt
Air transportation	0.3	Util.	Aluminum rolling & drawing	0.3	Manufg.
Communications, except radio & TV	0.3	Util.	Cold finishing of steel shapes	0.3	Manufg.
Water transportation	0.3	Util.	Drugs	0.3	Manufg.
Accounting, auditing & bookkeeping	0.3	Services	Floor coverings	0.3	Manufg.
Chemical preparations, nec	0.2	Manufg.	Leather tanning & finishing	0.3	Manufg.
Mechanical measuring devices	0.2	Manufg.	Lubricating oils & greases	0.3	Manufg.
Royalties	0.2	Fin/R.E.	Metal coating & allied services	0.3	Manufg.
Legal services	0.2	Services	Nonferrous wire drawing & insulating	0.3	Manufg.
U.S. Postal Service	0.2	Gov't	Paper coating & glazing	0.3	Manufg.
Carbon & graphite products	0.1	Manufg.	Special industry machinery, nec	0.3	Manufg.
Refrigeration & heating equipment	0.1	Manufg.	Wood preserving	0.3	Manufg.
Real estate	0.1	Fin/R.E.	Chemical & fertilizer mineral	0.2	Mining
Computer & data processing services	0.1	Services	Copper rolling & drawing	0.2	Manufg.
Management & consulting services & labs	0.1	Services	Environmental controls	0.2	Manufg.
State & local government enterprises, nec	0.1	Gov't	Frozen fruits, fruit juices & vegetables	0.2	Manufg.
			Frozen specialties	0.2	Manufg.
			Industrial inorganic chemicals, nec	0.2	Manufg.
			Mineral wool	0.2	Manufg.
			Nonferrous rolling & drawing, nec	0.2	Manufg.
			Nonwoven fabrics	0.2	Manufg.
			Photographic equipment & supplies	0.2	Manufg.
			Primary batteries, dry & wet	0.2	Manufg.
			Printing ink	0.2	Manufg.
			Electric services (utilities)	0.2	Util.
			Coal	0.1	Mining
			Electronic components nec	0.1	Manufg.
			Knit fabric mills	0.1	Manufg.

Continued on next page.

INPUTS AND OUTPUTS FOR CYCLIC CRUDES AND ORGANICS - Continued

Economic Sector or Industry Providing Inputs	%	Sector	Economic Sector or Industry Buying Outputs	%	Sector
			Meat packing plants	0.1	Manufg.
			Paperboard containers & boxes	0.1	Manufg.
			Pipe, valves, & pipe fittings	0.1	Manufg.
			Plating & polishing	0.1	Manufg.
			Primary metal products, nec	0.1	Manufg.
			Ready-mixed concrete	0.1	Manufg.
			Special dies & tools & machine tool accessories	0.1	Manufg.
			Yarn mills & finishing of textiles, nec	0.1	Manufg.
			Elementary & secondary schools	0.1	Services
			Laundry, dry cleaning, shoe repair	0.1	Services

Source: Benchmark Input-Output Accounts for the U.S. Economy, 1982, U.S. Department of Commerce, Washington, D.C., July 1991. Data, as reported in the source, are organized by the 1977 SIC structure in use in 1982 but have been matched, as closely as is possible, to the 1987 SIC structure used in this book.

OCCUPATIONS EMPLOYED BY SIC 286 - INDUSTRIAL ORGANIC CHEMICALS

Occupation	% of Total 1994	Change to 2005	Occupation	% of Total 1994	Change to 2005
Chemical equipment controllers, operators	10.6	-5.2	Crushing & mixing machine operators	1.7	-5.2
Chemical plant & system operators	8.9	-5.2	Engineering technicians & technologists nec	1.6	-5.2
Blue collar worker supervisors	7.4	-5.7	General managers & top executives	1.3	-10.0
Science & mathematics technicians	7.0	-5.2	Industrial production managers	1.3	-5.2
Maintenance repairers, general utility	4.3	-14.7	Mechanical engineers	1.2	4.3
Chemists	3.8	-5.2	Electricians	1.2	-11.0
Chemical engineers	3.7	13.8	Engineering, mathematical, & science managers	1.1	7.7
Secretaries, ex legal & medical	2.7	-13.7	Electrical & electronic technicians,technologists	1.1	-5.2
Industrial machinery mechanics	2.3	4.3	Managers & administrators nec	1.1	-5.2
Sales & related workers nec	1.9	-5.2	Freight, stock, & material movers, hand	1.1	-24.2
Helpers, laborers, & material movers nec	1.8	-5.2	Bookkeeping, accounting, & auditing clerks	1.0	-28.9
General office clerks	1.8	-19.2	Plumbers, pipefitters, & steamfitters	1.0	-5.1
Precision instrument repairers	1.7	28.0			

Source: Industry-Occupation Matrix, Bureau of Labor Statistics. These data relate to one or more 3-digit SIC industry groups rather than to a single 4-digit SIC. The change reported for each occupation to the year 2005 is a percent of growth or decline as estimated by the Bureau of Labor Statistics. The abbreviation nec stands for 'not elsewhere classified'.

LOCATION BY STATE AND REGIONAL CONCENTRATION

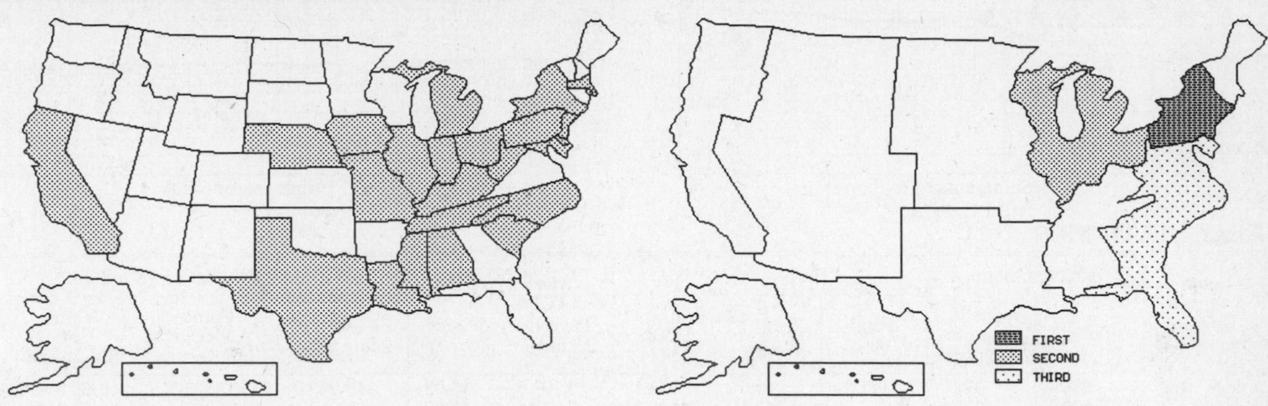

INDUSTRY DATA BY STATE

State	Establish-ments	Shipments			Employment				Cost as % of Shipments	Investment per Employee ($)
		Total ($ mil)	% of U.S.	Per Establ.	Total Number	% of U.S.	Per Establ.	Wages ($/hour)		
South Carolina	10	794.9	8.3	79.5	1,500	6.8	150	16.25	58.7	-
New Jersey	39	779.8	8.1	20.0	2,400	10.8	62	15.69	57.4	-
New York	11	616.7	6.4	56.1	1,900	8.6	173	16.08	48.7	-
Pennsylvania	17	581.2	6.1	34.2	1,700	7.7	100	17.83	67.2	-
Illinois	11	453.5	4.7	41.2	1,300	5.9	118	18.85	54.5	15,923
Michigan	8	254.2	2.7	31.8	900	4.1	113	14.92	57.6	-
California	13	55.0	0.6	4.2	200	0.9	15	10.75	51.1	10,500
Ohio	19	(D)	-	-	1,750 *	7.9	92	-	-	-
Texas	15	(D)	-	-	1,750 *	7.9	117	-	-	-
North Carolina	9	(D)	-	-	1,750 *	7.9	194	-	-	-
Louisiana	5	(D)	-	-	750 *	3.4	150	-	-	-
Alabama	4	(D)	-	-	750 *	3.4	188	-	-	-
Kentucky	4	(D)	-	-	375 *	1.7	94	-	-	-
Massachusetts	4	(D)	-	-	175 *	0.8	44	-	-	-
Tennessee	4	(D)	-	-	375 *	1.7	94	-	-	-
West Virginia	3	(D)	-	-	1,750 *	7.9	583	-	-	-
Delaware	2	(D)	-	-	375 *	1.7	188	-	-	-
Indiana	2	(D)	-	-	375 *	1.7	188	-	-	-
Missouri	2	(D)	-	-	375 *	1.7	188	-	-	-
Rhode Island	2	(D)	-	-	750 *	3.4	375	-	-	-
Iowa	1	(D)	-	-	175 *	0.8	175	-	-	-
Maryland	1	(D)	-	-	175 *	0.8	175	-	-	-
Mississippi	1	(D)	-	-	175 *	0.8	175	-	-	-
Nebraska	1	(D)	-	-	175 *	0.8	175	-	-	-

Source: 1992 *Economic Census*. The states are in descending order of shipments or establishments (if shipment data are missing for the majority). The symbol (D) appears when data are withheld to prevent disclosure of competitive information. States marked with (D) are sorted by number of establishments. A dash (-) indicates that the data element cannot be calculated; * indicates the midpoint of a range.

2869 - INDUSTRIAL ORGANIC CHEMICALS, NEC

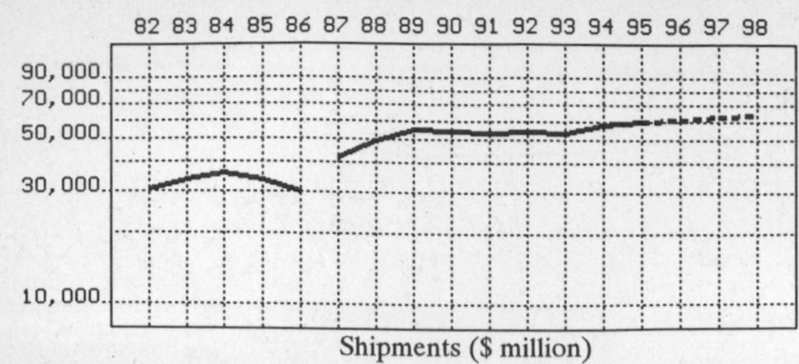

Shipments ($ million)

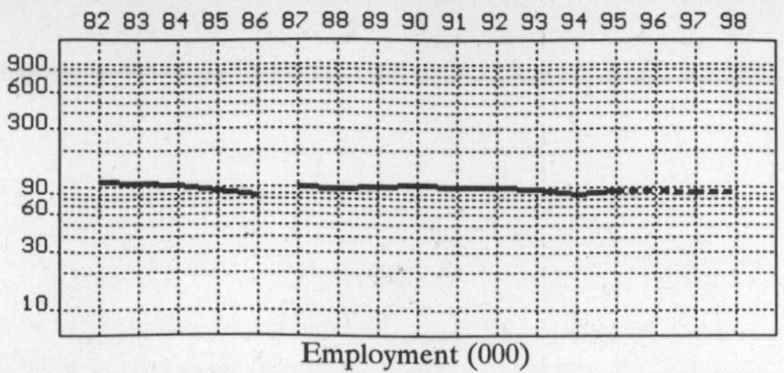

Employment (000)

GENERAL STATISTICS

Year	Com-panies	Establishments		Employment			Compensation		Production ($ million)			
		Total	with 20 or more employees	Total (000)	Production Workers (000)	Production Hours (Mil)	Payroll ($ mil)	Wages ($/hr)	Cost of Materials	Value Added by Manufacture	Value of Shipments	Capital Invest.
1982	488	688	376	111.8	65.0	131.1	3,191.3	13.08	19,989.0	10,093.5	30,394.4	2,580.5
1983		670	379	106.7	62.9	128.1	3,237.1	13.87	21,210.5	12,017.4	33,262.0	1,821.6
1984		652	382	103.4	60.7	124.3	3,395.6	14.73	23,112.9	13,054.8	35,777.0	1,617.7
1985		635	384	96.5	56.3	115.6	3,293.3	15.31	20,948.8	11,875.9	33,061.7	1,613.5
1986		619	383	86.7	51.3	106.6	3,097.2	15.88	17,778.7	11,822.2	29,759.7	1,491.0
1987*	491	699	431	100.3	57.9	122.4	3,696.4	16.03	24,226.0	17,902.1	42,189.1	1,986.9
1988		685	432	97.1	56.9	122.3	3,717.2	16.62	27,102.2	22,448.1	49,103.6	2,753.6
1989		651	419	100.0	58.3	125.1	3,944.8	17.17	29,433.1	25,299.1	54,512.4	3,484.2
1990		648	424	103.2	58.8	126.2	4,216.3	17.93	30,091.0	24,492.4	54,160.0	4,156.2
1991		661	421	101.0	58.4	125.0	4,403.0	18.61	30,671.3	22,248.0	53,069.3	4,537.6
1992	489	705	428	100.1	57.4	126.3	4,504.8	19.07	31,860.6	22,511.7	54,254.2	4,216.6
1993		695	429	97.5	57.5	127.0	4,503.0	19.01	30,666.7	22,674.8	53,364.2	3,358.3
1994		683P	425P	89.3	52.6	116.2	4,501.0	20.74	33,449.2	24,328.6	57,670.5	2,958.9
1995		684P	424P	94.4P	55.2P	122.9P	4,798.0P	20.90P	34,299.9P	24,947.4P	59,137.2P	4,096.2P
1996		686P	424P	93.5P	54.8P	122.7P	4,934.1P	21.51P	35,182.4P	25,589.2P	60,658.8P	4,243.8P
1997		687P	423P	92.6P	54.3P	122.5P	5,070.1P	22.12P	36,064.9P	26,231.1P	62,180.3P	4,391.5P
1998		689P	423P	91.7P	53.9P	122.3P	5,206.2P	22.73P	36,947.4P	26,872.9P	63,701.8P	4,539.2P

Sources: 1982, 1987, 1992 *Economic Census*; *Annual Survey of Manufactures*, 83-86, 88-91, 93-94. Establishment counts are from *County Business Patterns* for non-Census years; establishment counts for 83-84 are extrapolations. * indicates that industry content changed in 87; earlier years use 77 SICs. 'P's mark projections.

INDICES OF CHANGE

Year	Com-panies	Establishments		Employment			Compensation		Production ($ million)			
		Total	with 20 or more employees	Total (000)	Production Workers (000)	Production Hours (Mil)	Payroll ($ mil)	Wages ($/hr)	Cost of Materials	Value Added by Manufacture	Value of Shipments	Capital Invest.
1982	100	98	88	112	113	104	71	69	63	45	56	61
1983		95	89	107	110	101	72	73	67	53	61	43
1984		92	89	103	106	98	75	77	73	58	66	38
1985		90	90	96	98	92	73	80	66	53	61	38
1986		88	89	87	89	84	69	83	56	53	55	35
1987*	100	99	101	100	101	97	82	84	76	80	78	47
1988		97	101	97	99	97	83	87	85	100	91	65
1989		92	98	100	102	99	88	90	92	112	100	83
1990		92	99	103	102	100	94	94	94	109	100	99
1991		94	98	101	102	99	98	98	96	99	98	108
1992	100	100	100	100	100	100	100	100	100	100	100	100
1993		99	100	97	100	101	100	100	96	101	98	80
1994		97P	99P	89	92	92	100	109	105	108	106	70
1995		97P	99P	94P	96P	97P	107P	110P	108P	111P	109P	97P
1996		97P	99P	93P	95P	97P	110P	113P	110P	114P	112P	101P
1997		97P	99P	93P	95P	97P	113P	116P	113P	117P	115P	104P
1998		98P	99P	92P	94P	97P	116P	119P	116P	119P	117P	108P

Sources: Same as General Statistics. Values reflect change from the base year, 1992. Values above 100 mean greater than 92, values below 100 mean less than 92, and a value of 100 in the 82-91 or 93-98 period means same as 92. * indicates that industry content changed in 87. Data for earlier years are in 77 SIC format.

SELECTED RATIOS

For 1994	Avg. of All Manufact.	Analyzed Industry	Index
Employees per Establishment	49	131	267
Payroll per Establishment	1,500,273	6,588,666	439
Payroll per Employee	30,620	50,403	165
Production Workers per Establishment	34	77	224
Wages per Establishment	853,319	3,527,795	413
Wages per Production Worker	24,861	45,817	184
Hours per Production Worker	2,056	2,209	107
Wages per Hour	12.09	20.74	172
Value Added per Establishment	4,602,255	35,612,756	774
Value Added per Employee	93,930	272,437	290

For 1994	Avg. of All Manufact.	Analyzed Industry	Index
Value Added per Production Worker	134,084	462,521	345
Cost per Establishment	5,045,178	48,963,697	971
Cost per Employee	102,970	374,571	364
Cost per Production Worker	146,988	635,916	433
Shipments per Establishment	9,576,895	84,419,385	881
Shipments per Employee	195,460	645,806	330
Shipments per Production Worker	279,017	1,096,397	393
Investment per Establishment	321,011	4,331,305	1,349
Investment per Employee	6,552	33,134	506
Investment per Production Worker	9,352	56,253	601

Sources: Same as General Statistics. The 'Average of All Manufacturing' column represents the average of all manufacturing industries reported for the most recent complete year available. The Index shows the relationship between the Average and the Analyzed Industry. For example, 100 means that they are equal; 500 that the Analyzed Industry is five times the average; 50 means that the Analyzed Industry is half the national average. The abbreviation 'na' is used to show that data are 'not available'.

LEADING COMPANIES Number shown: **75** Total sales ($ mil): **42,321** Total employment (000): **125.0**

Company Name	Address				CEO Name	Phone	Co. Type	Sales ($ mil)	Empl. (000)
Exxon Chemical Co	580 Westlake Pk	Houston	TX	77079	RB Nesbitt	713-584-7600	D	8,641	15.9
Bayer Corp	500 Grant St	Pittsburgh	PA	15219	Helge H Wehmeier	412-394-5500	S	6,500	23.0
Union Carbide Corp	39 Old Ridgebury	Danbury	CT	06817	Robert D Kennedy	203-794-2000	P	4,865	12.0
Amoco Chemical Co	200 E Randolph Dr	Chicago	IL	60601	James E Fligg	312-856-3200	S	3,773	18.0
Witco Corp	1 America Ln	Greenwich	CT	06831	William R Toller	203-552-2000	P	2,225	8.0
Hoechst Celanese Corp	1601 LBJ Fwy	Dallas	TX	75234	Thomas Kennedy	214-689-4000	D	1,774	2.0
Lubrizol Corp	29400 Lakeland	Wickliffe	OH	44092	LE Coleman	216-943-4200	P	1,599	4.5
Quantum Chemical Co	PO Box 429549	Cincinnati	OH	45249	Ronald H Yocum	513-530-6500	S	1,510*	3.5
Intern Flavors and Fragrances	521 W 57th St	New York	NY	10019	Eugene P Grisanti	212-765-5500	P	1,315	4.6
Albemarle Corp	PO Box 1335	Richmond	VA	23219	F D Gottwald Jr	804-788-6000	P	1,081	3.7
Albright and Wilson Americas	100 Lakeridge Pkwy	Ashland	VA	23005	Paul S Rocheleau	804-550-4300	S	914	4.3
NutraSweet Co	1751 Lake Cook Rd	Deerfield	IL	60015	Robert E Flynn	708-940-9800	S	843	1.4
Vista Chemical Co	PO Box 19029	Houston	TX	77224	JR Ball	713-588-3000	S	700	1.8
IVAX Corp	8800 NW 36th St	Miami	FL	33178	Phillip Frost	305-590-2200	P	645	2.9
Borden Chemicals & Plastics LP	PO Box 427	Geismar	LA	70734	Joseph Sagesse	504-387-5101	R	433	0.5
Amoco Performance Products	4500 McGinnis	Alpharetta	GA	30202	Rick McNeel	404-772-8200	S	370*	1.2
Rohm and Haas Texas Inc	PO Box 672	Deer Park	TX	77536	Robert Brinley	713-476-8100	S	370*	1.2
Emery Group	PO Box 429557	Cincinnati	OH	45249	Robert Betz	513-530-7300	D	300	1.3
Florasynth Inc	300 North St	Teterboro	NJ	07608	Jack N Friedman	201-288-3200	R	270	0.9
Cambrex Corp	1 Meadowlands Plz	E Rutherford	NJ	07073	Cyril C Baldwin Jr	201-804-3000	P	242	1.3
ICC Industries Inc	720 5th Av	New York	NY	10019	John Oran	212-903-1700	R	220	1.0
Buckman Laboratories Intern	1256 N McLean	Memphis	TN	38108	Robert H Buckman	901-278-0330	S	200	1.0
Grant Chemical	111 W Irene Rd	Zachary	LA	70791	EB Wroten	504-654-6801	D	200*	0.1
RT Vanderbilt Company Inc	PO Box 5150	Norwalk	CT	06856	GL Fiederlein	203-853-1400	R	170	0.6
Millmaster Onyx Group Inc	500 Post Rd E	Westport	CT	06880	Ronald Baker	203-454-1800	R	160*	0.6
CPS Chemical Company Inc	123 White Oak Ln	Old Bridge	NJ	08857	Phillip L Meisel	908-607-2700	R	150	0.4
LaRoche Industries Inc	1100 Johnson Ferry	Atlanta	GA	30342	Grant Reed	404-851-0300	S	150*	0.5
Petrolite Corp	369 Marshall Av	St Louis	MO	63119	Dave Winflett	314-961-3500	D	131*	0.4
Mace Security International Inc	PO Box 679	Bennington	VT	05201	Jon E Goodrich	802-447-1503	P	123*	0.4
Union Texas Petroleum	PO Box 2120	Houston	TX	77252	A Clark Johnson	713-968-2816	S	117	0.1
Hilton Davis Co	2235 Langdon Farm	Cincinnati	OH	45237	Nick Lynam	513-841-4000	S	110	0.5
Intermediates&Fine Chemicals	PO Box 2500	West Lafayette	IN	47906	L Donald Simpson	317-497-6300	S	110	0.5
South Point Ethanol	PO Box 1004	South Point	OH	45680	William C Hopkins	614-377-2765	J	110*	0.2
Rheox Inc	PO Box 700	Hightstown	NJ	08520	Lawrence A Wigdor	609-443-2000	S	109	0.4
ANGUS Chemical Co	1500 E Lake Cook	Buffalo Grove	IL	60089	Gary Granzow	708-498-6700	S	100	0.4
CP Hall Co	311 S Wacker Dr	Chicago	IL	60606	George A Vincent	312-554-7400	R	100	0.2
Synthetic Products Co	1000 Wayside Rd	Cleveland	OH	44110	Thomas C Jennings	216-531-6010	D	100	0.2
Unichema North America	4650 S Racine Av	Chicago	IL	60609	Robert Drennan	312-376-9000	S	100	0.1
Cape Industries	PO Box 327	Wilmington	NC	28402	EB Hackman	910-341-5500	S	85	0.4
Hall Chemical Co	28960 Lakeland	Wickliffe	OH	44092	JB Mueller	216-944-8500	R	75	0.2
SCM Glidco Organics Corp	PO Box 389	Jacksonville	FL	32201	GW Robbins	904-768-5800	S	61*	0.2
Hauser Chemical Research Inc	5555 Airport Blv	Boulder	CO	80301	Dean P Stull	303-443-4662	P	60	0.2
Pharmacia P-L Biochemicals Inc	2202 N Bartlett Av	Milwaukee	WI	53202	Micheal Woehler	414-227-3600	S	60	0.2
Freedom Textile Chemicals Co	8309 Wilkinson Blv	Charlotte	NC	28214	Robert G Kitchen	704-393-0089	S	55	0.1
Witco Corp	1000 Convery Blv	Perth Amboy	NJ	08862	Robert Serretti	908-826-6600	D	55*	0.2
ABCO Industries Ltd	PO Box 1089	Roebuck	SC	29376	A B Bullington Jr	803-576-6821	R	50	0.1
Amerchol Corp	PO Box 4051	Edison	NJ	08817	Linda Koffenberger	908-287-1600	S	50*	0.2
Bell Flavors and Fragrances Inc	500 Academy Dr	Northbrook	IL	60062	James H Heinz	708-291-8300	R	50	0.5
Haarmann and Reimer Corp	70 Diamond Rd	Springfield	NJ	07081	JM Adams	201-467-5600	S	50	0.2
Hardwicke Chemical Co	2114 Larry Jeffers	Elgin	SC	29045	Charles E Marble	803-438-3471	S	50*	0.2
Quality Chemicals Inc	PO Box 216	Tyrone	PA	16686	Bob Barker	814-684-4310	S	47*	0.1
CPS Chemical of Arkansas	PO Box 2107	West Memphis	AR	72303	Phillip Meisel	501-735-8750	S	46*	0.2
J Manheimer Inc	47-22 Pearson Pl	Long Island Ct	NY	11101	S R Manheimer	718-392-7800	R	46	0.2
Lomac Inc	5025 Evanston	Muskegon	MI	49442	Arthur Hopmeier	616-788-2341	S	44*	0.1
Bedford Chemical	7050 Krick Rd	Walton Hills	OH	44146	LS Milazzo	216-641-8580	D	40	0.2
Buffalo Color Corp	959 Rte 46 E	Parsippany	NJ	07054	KW McCourt	201-316-5600	R	40	0.3
EniChem Elastomers Americas	2000 W Loop	Houston	TX	77027	Luciano Topi	713-940-0700	S	40*	0.1
Burdick and Jackson Inc	1953 S Harvey St	Muskegon	MI	49442	Russell L Bromley	616-726-3171	D	36*	0.1
Michelman Inc	9080 Shell Rd	Cincinnati	OH	45236	John Michelman	513-793-7766	R	36*	0.2
Gage Products Co	821 Wanda Av	Ferndale	MI	48220	Donald Dixon	313-541-3824	S	35	0.1
High Plains Corp	OW Garvey Bldg	Wichita	KS	67202	Stanley E Larson	316-269-4310	P	33	0.1
Detrex Corp	26000 Capitol Av	Redford	MI	48239	Mark T Rohde	313-937-0600	D	33*	0.1
Morflex Inc	2110 High Point Rd	Greensboro	NC	27403	GF Taft	910-292-1781	S	30	<0.1
PCR Inc	8570 Phillips Hwy	Jacksonville	FL	32256	Arthur C Wotiz	904-730-7511	R	30	0.1
Penray Companies Inc	440 Denniston Ct	Wheeling	IL	60090	Rodney Mckenzie	708-459-5000	R	29*	0.1
Henkel Corp	PO Box 628	Mauldin	SC	29662	Bernard E Korte	803-963-4031	D	27	<0.1
Chemical Exchange Industries	3813 Buffalo	Houston	TX	77098	David Smith	713-526-8291	R	25	<0.1
King Industries Inc	Science Rd	Norwalk	CT	06852	Richard S King	203-866-5551	R	25	0.1
PMP Fermentation Products Inc	9525 Bryn Mawr	Rosemont	IL	60018	K Takahashi	708-928-0050	S	25	<0.1
ESCO Company LP	PO Box 448	Muskegon	MI	49443	Robert D Hovey	616-726-3106	R	24*	<0.1
Ardrox Inc	921 Sherwood Dr	Lake Bluff	IL	60044	Sam Currie	708-295-1660	S	20	0.1
Dexter Chemical Corp	845 Edgewater Rd	Bronx	NY	10474	SM Edelstein	212-542-7700	R	20	<0.1
Perstorp Polyols Inc	600 Matzinger Rd	Toledo	OH	43612	David Wolf	419-729-5448	S	20*	<0.1
Environmental Techn Corp	550 James St	Lakewood	NJ	08701	George Cannan Sr	908-370-3400	P	20	<0.1
Sutton Laboratories	116 Summit Av	Chatham	NJ	07928	William E Rosen	201-635-1551	D	18	<0.1

Source: *Ward's Business Directory of U.S. Private and Public Companies*, Volumes 1 and 2, 1996. The company type code used is as follows: P - Public, R - Private, S - Subsidiary, D - Division, J - Joint Venture, A - Affiliate, G - Group. Sales are in millions of dollars, employees are in thousands. An asterisk (*) indicates an estimated sales volume. The symbol < stands for 'less than'. Company names and addresses are truncated, in some cases, to fit into the available space.

MATERIALS CONSUMED

Material		Quantity	Delivered Cost ($ million)
Materials, ingredients, containers, and supplies		(X)	26,535.5
Hydrochloric acid (100 percent HCl)	1,000 s tons	(S)	18.9
Hydrofluoric acid (100 percent HF)	1,000 s tons	125.9	101.6
Nitric acid (100 percent HNO3)	1,000 s tons	73.5	9.3
Sulfuric acid (100 percent H2SO4), except spent	1,000 s tons	1,158.8	79.5
Ammonia, synthetic anhydrous (100 percent NH3)	1,000 s tons	1,742.8	172.6
Chlorine (100 percent Cl basis)	1,000 s tons	791.6*	50.0
Sodium hydroxide (caustic soda)(100 percent NaOH)	1,000 s tons	1,398.9*	300.1
All other industrial inorganic chemicals		(X)	975.8
Acetylene and other industrial gases		(X)	162.1
Alcohol, ethyl (pure and denatured)		(X)	270.1
Other alcohols, including amyl, butyl, methyl, and propyl		(X)	913.7
Toluene and xylene (100 percent basis)	mil lb	2,449.5	310.6
Phenol (100 percent basis)	mil lb	2,569.8	481.8
Ortho and para-xylene (100 percent basis)	mil lb	2,418.4	347.3
Benzol (benzene) (100 percent C6H6)	mil lb	3,852.6	573.8
Other cyclic crudes and intermediates	mil lb	2,846.2**	698.2
Acetone (natural and synthetic)	mil lb	931.8	175.1
Other synthetic organic chemicals, nec		(X)	2,382.3
Natural gas used as a raw material	bil cu ft	171.6	326.0
Ethane used as a raw material or feedstock	mil lb	17,708.9	1,330.1
Ethylene used as a raw material or feedstock	mil lb	8,827.1	1,432.9
Propane used as a raw material or feedstock	mil lb	17,587.6	1,338.8
Propylene used as a raw material or feedstock	mil lb	14,977.2	1,539.4
Butane and iso-butane used as a raw material or feedstock	mil lb	4,281.1	686.1
Butylene and iso-butylene used as a raw material or feedstock	mil lb	2,430.8	469.6
Other hydrocarbons used as raw materials or feedstocks		(X)	2,619.8
Sulfur	1,000 l tons	983.2	72.6
Plastics resins consumed in the form of granules, pellets, powders, liquids, etc.	mil lb	37.7	16.6
Agricultural products (crude), including flowers, grains, seeds, herbs, etc.	mil lb	10,940.7	544.2
Parts and attachments for machinery and equipment		(X)	248.7
Paperboard containers, boxes, and corrugated paperboard		(X)	168.6
Metal containers		(X)	148.6
All other materials and components, parts, containers, and supplies		(X)	6,562.6
Materials, ingredients, containers, and supplies, nsk		(X)	1,008.0

Source: 1992 *Economic Census*. Explanation of symbols used: (D): Withheld to avoid disclosure of competitive data; na: Not available; (S): Withheld because statistical norms were not met; (X): Not applicable; (Z): Less than half the unit shown; nec: Not elsewhere classified; nsk: Not specified by kind; - : zero; * : 10-19 percent estimated; ** : 20-29 percent estimated.

PRODUCT SHARE DETAILS

Product or Product Class	% Share
Industrial organic chemicals, nec	100.00
Liquefied refinery gases (aliphatics) not made in a refinery	18.02
Liquefied refinery gases (aliphatics) not made in a refinery, for use as a chemical raw material	80.83
Liquefied refinery gases (aliphatics) not made in a refinery, for other uses	19.17
Ethyl alcohol	3.11
Pure (natural) ethyl alcohol, manufactured by the wet mill process (proof gal basis)	4.37
Fuel ethanol (fuel-grade ethyl alcohol), manufactured by the wet mill process	60.00
Other denatured (special or complete) ethyl alcohol, including natural and synthetic, for uses other than rubbing, manufactured by the wet mill process	7.35
Pure (natural) ethyl alcohol, manufactured by other processes (dry mill/distillation) (proof gal basis)	7.26
Fuel ethanol (fuel-grade ethyl alcohol), manufactured by other processes (dry mill/distillation)	15.08
Other denatured (special or complete) ethyl alcohol, including natural and synthetic, for uses other than rubbing, manufactured by other processes (dry mill/distillation)	5.94
Synthetic organic chemicals, nec	7.69
Synthetic organic chemical compounds for use as flavor and perfume materials, unmixed	45.60
Synthetic organic chemical compounds for use as flavor and perfume materials, mixed	7.64
Synthetic organic rubber-processing chemicals	17.58
Synthetic organic plasticizers	25.81
Synthetic organic chemicals, nec, nsk	3.38
Bulk synthetic organic pesticides and other bulk synthetic organic agricultural chemicals, except preparations	2.64
Miscellaneous synthetic organic end-use chemicals and chemical products, excluding urea	13.70
Miscellaneous cyclic and acyclic chemicals and chemical products	46.51
Other industrial organic chemicals (data which are not reported to the International Trade Commission)	6.76
Industrial organic flavor oil chemical mixtures and blends	6.58
Reagent and high purity grades of organic chemicals refined from purchased technical grades	11.04
Natural organic chemical derivatives of fatty substances, including salts, alcohols, and esters, except plasticizers and surface active agents	9.69
Other natural organic chemicals, nec	11.41
Other industrial organic chemicals, nec	61.27
Other industrial organic chemicals (data which are not reported to the international trade commission), nsk	0.01
Industrial organic chemicals, nec, nsk	1.57

Source: 1992 *Economic Census*. The values shown are percent of total shipments in an industry. Values of indented subcategories are summed in the main heading. The symbol (D) appears when data are withheld to prevent disclosure of competitive information. The abbreviation nsk stands for 'not specified by kind' and nec for 'not elsewhere classified'.

INPUTS AND OUTPUTS FOR CYCLIC CRUDES AND ORGANICS

Economic Sector or Industry Providing Inputs	%	Sector	Economic Sector or Industry Buying Outputs	%	Sector
Cyclic crudes and organics	36.9	Manufg.	Cyclic crudes and organics	20.1	Manufg.
Imports	12.4	Foreign	Plastics materials & resins	12.7	Manufg.
Gas production & distribution (utilities)	6.3	Util.	Exports	12.6	Foreign
Wholesale trade	4.9	Trade	Organic fibers, noncellulosic	6.1	Manufg.
Petroleum refining	4.4	Manufg.	Synthetic rubber	2.8	Manufg.
Electric services (utilities)	4.1	Util.	Petroleum refining	2.7	Manufg.
Crude petroleum & natural gas	3.5	Mining	Medical & health services, nec	2.3	Services
Industrial inorganic chemicals, nec	2.3	Manufg.	Paints & allied products	2.0	Manufg.
Miscellaneous plastics products	2.2	Manufg.	Miscellaneous plastics products	1.9	Manufg.
Pipe, valves, & pipe fittings	1.9	Manufg.	Hospitals	1.9	Services
Motor freight transportation & warehousing	1.7	Util.	Agricultural chemicals, nec	1.6	Manufg.
Miscellaneous repair shops	1.2	Services	Blast furnaces & steel mills	1.6	Manufg.
Alkalies & chlorine	1.0	Manufg.	Paper mills, except building paper	1.4	Manufg.
Railroads & related services	1.0	Util.	Nitrogenous & phosphatic fertilizers	1.2	Manufg.
Special industry machinery, nec	0.9	Manufg.	Semiconductors & related devices	1.2	Manufg.
Engineering, architectural, & surveying services	0.9	Services	Crude petroleum & natural gas	1.1	Mining
Noncomparable imports	0.9	Foreign	Broadwoven fabric mills	1.1	Manufg.
Maintenance of nonfarm buildings nec	0.8	Constr.	Primary aluminum	1.1	Manufg.
Pulp mills	0.7	Manufg.	Steel pipe & tubes	1.1	Manufg.
Advertising	0.7	Services	State & local government enterprises, nec	1.0	Gov't
Nitrogenous & phosphatic fertilizers	0.6	Manufg.	Food preparations, nec	0.9	Manufg.
Chemical & fertilizer mineral	0.5	Mining	Toilet preparations	0.9	Manufg.
Coal	0.5	Mining	Adhesives & sealants	0.8	Manufg.
Nonferrous metal ores, except copper	0.5	Mining	Commercial printing	0.8	Manufg.
Paints & allied products	0.5	Manufg.	Prepared feeds, nec	0.8	Manufg.
Plastics materials & resins	0.5	Manufg.	Chemical preparations, nec	0.7	Manufg.
Water supply & sewage systems	0.5	Util.	Paperboard mills	0.7	Manufg.
Equipment rental & leasing services	0.5	Services	Storage batteries	0.7	Manufg.
Blast furnaces & steel mills	0.4	Manufg.	Glass containers	0.6	Manufg.
Industrial gases	0.4	Manufg.	Tires & inner tubes	0.6	Manufg.
Metal barrels, drums, & pails	0.4	Manufg.	Glass & glass products, except containers	0.5	Manufg.
Paperboard containers & boxes	0.4	Manufg.	Manufacturing industries, nec	0.5	Manufg.
Primary zinc	0.4	Manufg.	Management & consulting services & labs	0.5	Services
Eating & drinking places	0.4	Trade	Fabricated rubber products, nec	0.4	Manufg.
Banking	0.4	Fin/R.E.	Pulp mills	0.4	Manufg.
Drugs	0.3	Manufg.	Sanitary services, steam supply, irrigation	0.4	Util.
Paper mills, except building paper	0.3	Manufg.	S/L Govt. purch., health & hospitals	0.4	S/L Govt
Air transportation	0.3	Util.	Aluminum rolling & drawing	0.3	Manufg.
Communications, except radio & TV	0.3	Util.	Cold finishing of steel shapes	0.3	Manufg.
Water transportation	0.3	Util.	Drugs	0.3	Manufg.
Accounting, auditing & bookkeeping	0.3	Services	Floor coverings	0.3	Manufg.
Chemical preparations, nec	0.2	Manufg.	Leather tanning & finishing	0.3	Manufg.
Mechanical measuring devices	0.2	Manufg.	Lubricating oils & greases	0.3	Manufg.
Royalties	0.2	Fin/R.E.	Metal coating & allied services	0.3	Manufg.
Legal services	0.2	Services	Nonferrous wire drawing & insulating	0.3	Manufg.
U.S. Postal Service	0.2	Gov't	Paper coating & glazing	0.3	Manufg.
Carbon & graphite products	0.1	Manufg.	Special industry machinery, nec	0.3	Manufg.
Refrigeration & heating equipment	0.1	Manufg.	Wood preserving	0.3	Manufg.
Real estate	0.1	Fin/R.E.	Chemical & fertilizer mineral	0.2	Mining
Computer & data processing services	0.1	Services	Copper rolling & drawing	0.2	Manufg.
Management & consulting services & labs	0.1	Services	Environmental controls	0.2	Manufg.
State & local government enterprises, nec	0.1	Gov't	Frozen fruits, fruit juices & vegetables	0.2	Manufg.
			Frozen specialties	0.2	Manufg.
			Industrial inorganic chemicals, nec	0.2	Manufg.
			Mineral wool	0.2	Manufg.
			Nonferrous rolling & drawing, nec	0.2	Manufg.
			Nonwoven fabrics	0.2	Manufg.
			Photographic equipment & supplies	0.2	Manufg.
			Primary batteries, dry & wet	0.2	Manufg.
			Printing ink	0.2	Manufg.
			Electric services (utilities)	0.2	Util.
			Coal	0.1	Mining
			Electronic components nec	0.1	Manufg.
			Knit fabric mills	0.1	Manufg.
			Meat packing plants	0.1	Manufg.
			Paperboard containers & boxes	0.1	Manufg.
			Pipe, valves, & pipe fittings	0.1	Manufg.
			Plating & polishing	0.1	Manufg.
			Primary metal products, nec	0.1	Manufg.
			Ready-mixed concrete	0.1	Manufg.
			Special dies & tools & machine tool accessories	0.1	Manufg.
			Yarn mills & finishing of textiles, nec	0.1	Manufg.
			Elementary & secondary schools	0.1	Services
			Laundry, dry cleaning, shoe repair	0.1	Services

Source: Benchmark Input-Output Accounts for the U.S. Economy, 1982, U.S. Department of Commerce, Washington, D.C., July 1991. Data, as reported in the source, are organized by the 1977 SIC structure in use in 1982 but have been matched, as closely as is possible, to the 1987 SIC structure used in this book.

OCCUPATIONS EMPLOYED BY SIC 286 - INDUSTRIAL ORGANIC CHEMICALS

Occupation	% of Total 1994	Change to 2005	Occupation	% of Total 1994	Change to 2005
Chemical equipment controllers, operators	10.6	-5.2	Crushing & mixing machine operators	1.7	-5.2
Chemical plant & system operators	8.9	-5.2	Engineering technicians & technologists nec	1.6	-5.2
Blue collar worker supervisors	7.4	-5.7	General managers & top executives	1.3	-10.0
Science & mathematics technicians	7.0	-5.2	Industrial production managers	1.3	-5.2
Maintenance repairers, general utility	4.3	-14.7	Mechanical engineers	1.2	4.3
Chemists	3.8	-5.2	Electricians	1.2	-11.0
Chemical engineers	3.7	13.8	Engineering, mathematical, & science managers	1.1	7.7
Secretaries, ex legal & medical	2.7	-13.7	Electrical & electronic technicians,technologists	1.1	-5.2
Industrial machinery mechanics	2.3	4.3	Managers & administrators nec	1.1	-5.2
Sales & related workers nec	1.9	-5.2	Freight, stock, & material movers, hand	1.1	-24.2
Helpers, laborers, & material movers nec	1.8	-5.2	Bookkeeping, accounting, & auditing clerks	1.0	-28.9
General office clerks	1.8	-19.2	Plumbers, pipefitters, & steamfitters	1.0	-5.1
Precision instrument repairers	1.7	28.0			

Source: *Industry-Occupation Matrix*, Bureau of Labor Statistics. These data relate to one or more 3-digit SIC industry groups rather than to a single 4-digit SIC. The change reported for each occupation to the year 2005 is a percent of growth or decline as estimated by the Bureau of Labor Statistics. The abbreviation nec stands for 'not elsewhere classified'.

LOCATION BY STATE AND REGIONAL CONCENTRATION

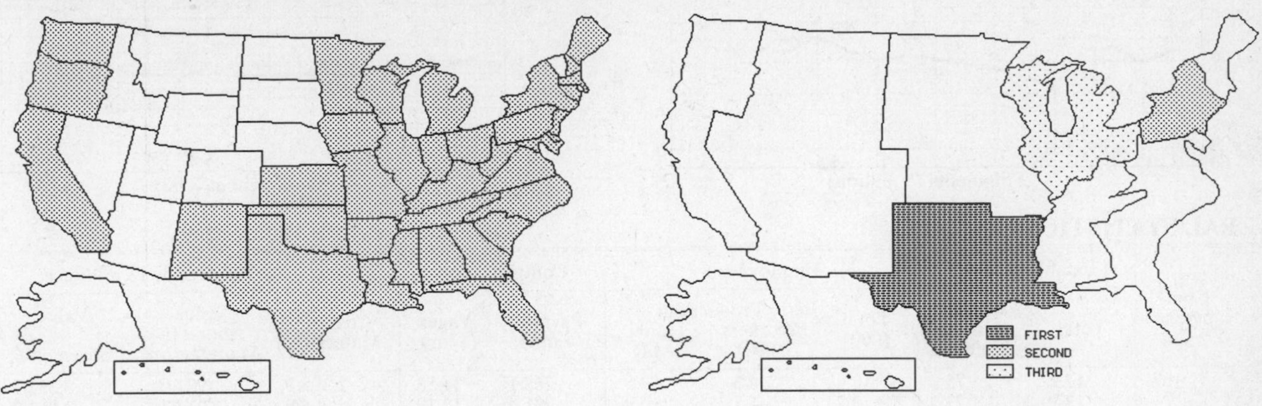

INDUSTRY DATA BY STATE

State	Establish-ments	Shipments			Employment				Cost as % of Shipments	Investment per Employee ($)
		Total ($ mil)	% of U.S.	Per Establ.	Total Number	% of U.S.	Per Establ.	Wages ($/hour)		
Texas	97	24,476.8	45.1	252.3	30,700	30.7	316	23.04	65.4	55,668
Louisiana	31	7,679.1	14.2	247.7	11,100	11.1	358	17.47	63.3	91,730
New Jersey	69	2,816.2	5.2	40.8	8,300	8.3	120	17.69	47.2	16,133
Illinois	37	2,453.3	4.5	66.3	3,300	3.3	89	18.80	51.9	30,818
West Virginia	13	1,688.4	3.1	129.9	4,600	4.6	354	19.71	45.2	27,435
Kentucky	11	1,583.0	2.9	143.9	3,100	3.1	282	18.94	47.6	60,774
Michigan	15	1,351.0	2.5	90.1	5,200	5.2	347	18.80	46.7	-
Ohio	44	1,322.9	2.4	30.1	3,100	3.1	70	17.37	61.8	15,419
New York	39	926.9	1.7	23.8	2,800	2.8	72	16.37	45.7	13,643
Georgia	14	784.9	1.4	56.1	1,200	1.2	86	17.14	33.6	27,833
California	48	587.4	1.1	12.2	1,400	1.4	29	15.79	42.8	29,571
North Carolina	25	561.3	1.0	22.5	1,300	1.3	52	14.93	51.3	-
Alabama	17	532.7	1.0	31.3	1,600	1.6	94	17.17	39.0	-
Florida	21	438.3	0.8	20.9	1,300	1.3	62	14.24	54.6	-
Missouri	18	409.7	0.8	22.8	1,800	1.8	100	17.18	53.5	8,556
Connecticut	15	282.2	0.5	18.8	600	0.6	40	17.44	65.7	6,833
Massachusetts	9	197.5	0.4	21.9	700	0.7	78	21.56	31.6	-
Iowa	4	63.1	0.1	15.8	300	0.3	75	9.25	64.5	-
New Mexico	4	36.0	0.1	9.0	400	0.4	100	11.00	31.7	-
Pennsylvania	24	(D)	-	-	1,750 *	1.7	73	-	-	12,114
South Carolina	18	(D)	-	-	1,750 *	1.7	97	-	-	11,257
Virginia	14	(D)	-	-	1,750 *	1.7	125	-	-	-
Wisconsin	14	(D)	-	-	1,750 *	1.7	125	-	-	-
Kansas	11	(D)	-	-	375 *	0.4	34	-	-	-
Tennessee	11	(D)	-	-	7,500 *	7.5	682	-	-	-
Washington	11	(D)	-	-	375 *	0.4	34	-	-	-
Minnesota	9	(D)	-	-	175 *	0.2	19	-	-	9,714
Arkansas	8	(D)	-	-	1,750 *	1.7	219	-	-	49,829
Indiana	8	(D)	-	-	750 *	0.7	94	-	-	-
Delaware	5	(D)	-	-	175 *	0.2	35	-	-	-
Mississippi	5	(D)	-	-	175 *	0.2	35	-	-	9,714
Oregon	3	(D)	-	-	175 *	0.2	58	-	-	-
Maryland	2	(D)	-	-	375 *	0.4	188	-	-	-
New Hampshire	2	(D)	-	-	375 *	0.4	188	-	-	-
Oklahoma	2	(D)	-	-	175 *	0.2	88	-	-	-
Maine	1	(D)	-	-	175 *	0.2	175	-	-	-

Source: 1992 *Economic Census*. The states are in descending order of shipments or establishments (if shipment data are missing for the majority). The symbol (D) appears when data are withheld to prevent disclosure of competitive information. States marked with (D) are sorted by number of establishments. A dash (-) indicates that the data element cannot be calculated; * indicates the midpoint of a range.

2873 - NITROGENOUS FERTILIZERS

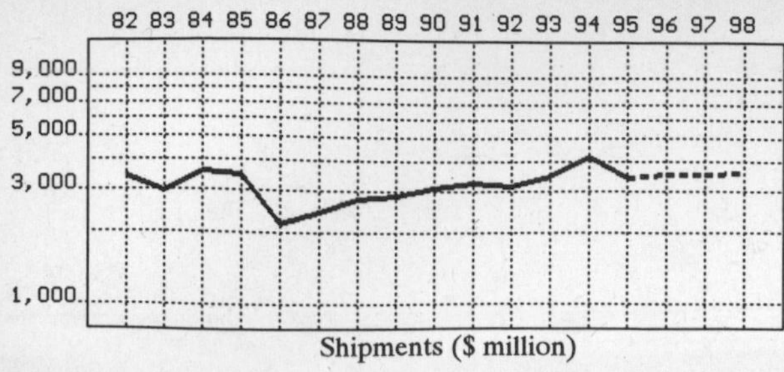

Shipments ($ million)

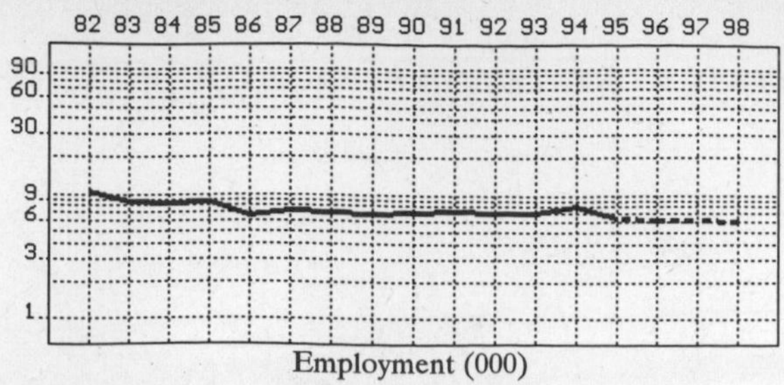

Employment (000)

GENERAL STATISTICS

Year	Com- panies	Establishments		Employment			Compensation		Production ($ million)			
		Total	with 20 or more employees	Total (000)	Production Workers (000)	Production Hours (Mil)	Payroll ($ mil)	Wages ($/hr)	Cost of Materials	Value Added by Manufacture	Value of Shipments	Capital Invest.
1982	109	143	75	10.4	6.3	13.5	268.1	11.58	2,395.3	981.0	3,391.1	145.3
1983		137	73	8.7	5.1	10.8	231.0	12.18	2,006.8	913.2	2,950.2	55.3
1984		131	71	8.5	5.2	10.8	244.0	12.67	2,346.3	1,307.1	3,574.8	77.9
1985		124	70	8.7	5.4	11.0	259.5	13.62	2,393.9	1,086.3	3,469.6	112.5
1986		128	72	6.6	4.0	8.8	202.4	12.97	1,433.6	626.6	2,177.6	84.9
1987	117	164	72	7.4	4.5	9.6	222.8	13.04	1,503.5	874.7	2,447.2	36.9
1988		159	81	7.2	4.4	9.6	222.0	12.96	1,626.4	1,173.2	2,761.1	48.1
1989		157	80	6.8	4.4	9.7	231.6	14.03	1,724.4	1,156.8	2,866.0	122.7
1990		151	81	7.2	4.8	10.4	253.6	13.80	1,905.3	1,213.3	3,113.4	99.4
1991		155	85	7.3	4.7	10.3	260.2	14.77	1,982.1	1,290.5	3,238.1	220.1
1992	103	152	77	7.0	4.7	10.1	257.6	15.65	1,871.7	1,262.5	3,174.6	208.8
1993		166	82	7.0	4.7	10.3	270.4	16.11	2,118.8	1,341.6	3,467.1	186.0
1994		165P	83P	8.0	5.4	11.8	308.1	16.69	2,251.2	1,965.6	4,246.1	174.6
1995		168P	84P	6.5P	4.5P	10.0P	271.8P	16.48P	1,824.3P	1,592.9P	3,440.9P	189.8P
1996		170P	85P	6.3P	4.5P	9.9P	275.1P	16.86P	1,846.8P	1,612.5P	3,483.3P	199.7P
1997		173P	87P	6.1P	4.4P	9.8P	278.5P	17.23P	1,869.2P	1,632.1P	3,525.6P	209.5P
1998		176P	88P	6.0P	4.3P	9.7P	281.8P	17.61P	1,891.7P	1,651.7P	3,568.0P	219.3P

Sources: 1982, 1987, 1992 *Economic Census*; *Annual Survey of Manufactures*, 83-86, 88-91, 93-94. Establishment counts for non-Census years are from *County Business Patterns*; establishment values for 83-84 are extrapolations. 'P's show projections by the editors. Industries reclassified in 87 will not have data for prior years.

INDICES OF CHANGE

Year	Com- panies	Establishments		Employment			Compensation		Production ($ million)			
		Total	with 20 or more employees	Total (000)	Production Workers (000)	Production Hours (Mil)	Payroll ($ mil)	Wages ($/hr)	Cost of Materials	Value Added by Manufacture	Value of Shipments	Capital Invest.
1982	106	94	97	149	134	134	104	74	128	78	107	70
1983		90	95	124	109	107	90	78	107	72	93	26
1984		86	92	121	111	107	95	81	125	104	113	37
1985		82	91	124	115	109	101	87	128	86	109	54
1986		84	94	94	85	87	79	83	77	50	69	41
1987	114	108	94	106	96	95	86	83	80	69	77	18
1988		105	105	103	94	95	86	83	87	93	87	23
1989		103	104	97	94	96	90	90	92	92	90	59
1990		99	105	103	102	103	98	88	102	96	98	48
1991		102	110	104	100	102	101	94	106	102	102	105
1992	100	100	100	100	100	100	100	100	100	100	100	100
1993		109	106	100	100	102	105	103	113	106	109	89
1994		108P	108P	114	115	117	120	107	120	156	134	84
1995		110P	110P	93P	96P	99P	106P	105P	97P	126P	108P	91P
1996		112P	111P	90P	95P	98P	107P	108P	99P	128P	110P	96P
1997		114P	112P	88P	94P	97P	108P	110P	100P	129P	111P	100P
1998		116P	114P	85P	92P	96P	109P	112P	101P	131P	112P	105P

Sources: Same as General Statistics. Values reflect change from the base year, 1992. Values above 100 mean greater than 92, values below 100 mean less than 92, and a value of 100 in the 82-91 or 93-98 period means same as 92. 'P's mark projections by the editors.

SELECTED RATIOS

For 1994	Avg. of All Manufact.	Analyzed Industry	Index	For 1994	Avg. of All Manufact.	Analyzed Industry	Index
Employees per Establishment	49	49	99	Value Added per Production Worker	134,084	364,000	271
Payroll per Establishment	1,500,273	1,869,333	125	Cost per Establishment	5,045,178	13,658,687	271
Payroll per Employee	30,620	38,512	126	Cost per Employee	102,970	281,400	273
Production Workers per Establishment	34	33	95	Cost per Production Worker	146,988	416,889	284
Wages per Establishment	853,319	1,194,905	140	Shipments per Establishment	9,576,895	25,762,328	269
Wages per Production Worker	24,861	36,471	147	Shipments per Employee	195,460	530,762	272
Hours per Production Worker	2,056	2,185	106	Shipments per Production Worker	279,017	786,315	282
Wages per Hour	12.09	16.69	138	Investment per Establishment	321,011	1,059,349	330
Value Added per Establishment	4,602,255	11,925,869	259	Investment per Employee	6,552	21,825	333
Value Added per Employee	93,930	245,700	262	Investment per Production Worker	9,352	32,333	346

Sources: Same as General Statistics. The 'Average of All Manufacturing' column represents the average of all manufacturing industries reported for the most recent complete year available. The Index shows the relationship between the Average and the Analyzed Industry. For example, 100 means that they are equal; 500 that the Analyzed Industry is five times the average; 50 means that the Analyzed Industry is half the national average. The abbreviation 'na' is used to show that data are 'not available'.

LEADING COMPANIES Number shown: 37 Total sales ($ mil): 7,517 Total employment (000): 25.0

Company Name	Address				CEO Name	Phone	Co. Type	Sales ($ mil)	Empl. (000)
Terra Industries Inc	600 4th St	Sioux City	IA	51101	Burton M Joyce	712-277-1340	P	1,082	3.5
CF Industries Inc	Salem Lake Dr	Long Grove	IL	60049	Robert C Liuzzi	708-438-9500	R	905	1.6
Arcadian Corp	6750 Poplar Av	Memphis	TN	38138	JD Campbell	901-758-5200	R	800	1.3
Cominco Fertilizer	601 W Riverside	Spokane	WA	99201	John Van Brunt	509-747-6111	D	800*	3.0
JR Simplot Co	PO Box 912	Pocatello	ID	83204	Larry Hinderager	208-238-2830	D	750	4.5
Scotts Co	14111 Scottslawn	Marysville	OH	43041	Tadd C Seitz	513-644-0011	P	606	2.5
OM Scott and Sons Co	14111 Scottslawn	Marysville	OH	43041	Tadd C Seitz	513-644-0011	S	466	2.0
Unocal Chemicals & Minerals	PO Box 60455	Los Angeles	CA	90060	Neal E Schmale	213-977-7600	D	460	1.0
Mississippi Chemical Corp	PO Box 388	Yazoo City	MS	39194	Charles O Dunn	601-746-4131	P	309	1.0
Terra Nitrogen Company LP	5100 E Skelly Dr	Tulsa	OK	74135	W Mark Rosenbury	918-660-0050	P	300	0.3
Texasgulf Phosphate Operations	PO Box 48	Aurora	NC	27806	WT Cooper	919-322-4111	D	300	1.2
Lebanon Chemical Corp	PO Box 180	Lebanon	PA	17042	Katherine J Bishop	717-273-1685	R	180	0.7
Hyponex Corp	14111 Scottslawn	Marysville	OH	43041	Ted Host	513-644-0011	S	120	0.8
Sun Gro Horticulture Inc	110 110th Av NE	Bellevue	WA	98004	Mike Crowe	206-450-9379	R	120	0.5
Coastal Chem Inc	PO Box 1287	Cheyenne	WY	82003	Michael F Ray	307-637-2700	S	50	0.2
Stern's Miracle-Gro Products Inc	PO Box 888	Pt Washington	NY	11050	Robert Morea	516-883-6550	R	40*	<0.1
Willard Grain and Feed Inc	Rte 2	Celina	TX	75009	Jane Willard	214-382-2367	R	28	0.1
Dexol Industries Inc	1450 W 228th St	Torrance	CA	90501	Jane Donaldson	310-326-8373	R	27	0.1
Miller Chemical & Fertilizer	PO Box 333	Hanover	PA	17331	Donald E Fiery	717-632-8921	S	19	<0.1
Poag Grain Inc	PO Box 2037	Chickasha	OK	73023	Stephen A Poag	405-224-6350	R	16	<0.1
Growers Fertilizer Corp	PO Box 1407	Lake Alfred	FL	33850	Don K Webb	813-956-1101	R	15	<0.1
Kellogg Supply Co	350 W Sepulveda	Carson	CA	90745	H Clay Kellogg IV	310-830-2200	R	15	0.1
Lebanon Chemical Corp	PO Box 686	Danville	IL	61834	Dennis Faith	217-446-0983	D	15	<0.1
Ringer Corp	9959 Val View Rd	Eden Prairie	MN	55344	Stanley Goldberg	612-941-4180	P	15	<0.1
Associated Tagline Inc	PO Box 1330	Salinas	CA	93902	Norman E Dickens	408-422-6452	R	13*	<0.1
Vigoro Industries Inc	4060 E 26th St	Los Angeles	CA	90023	Don Hanson	213-264-5800	D	12*	<0.1
John Pryor Company Inc	PO Box 59	Salinas	CA	93902	Les Breschini	408-422-5307	R	11	<0.1
Allerton Supply Company Inc	PO Box 200	Allerton	IL	61810	HT Allen	217-834-3301	R	10	<0.1
Cooperative Country	Railroad Av	Renville	MN	56284	Dana Persson	612-329-8371	D	7	<0.1
K & C Organic Soil Prod Corp	1514 Airport Blv	Santa Rosa	CA	95403	RS Kolodge	707-525-8584	R	6*	<0.1
Nu Life Fertilizers	PO Box 883	Tacoma	WA	98401	Brooke VanWyck	206-272-5171	D	6*	<0.1
Chamberlin and Barclay Inc	PO Box 416	Cranbury	NJ	08512	WS Barclay	609-655-0700	R	5	<0.1
Sierra Ag Chemical	2749 E Malaga Av	Fresno	CA	93725	Rick Hunt	209-233-0585	R	3*	<0.1
Hynite Corp	4301 E Depot Rd	Oak Creek	WI	53154	Tom Squire	414-762-1068	R	2	<0.1
Liquinox Co	221 W Meats Av	Orange	CA	92665	HC Garner	714-637-6300	R	1	<0.1
Phoenix Zinc	4599 Big Creek	Millington	TN	38053	RH Odabashian	901-872-2295	R	1	<0.1
Spray-N-Grow Inc	20 Hwy 35 S	Rockport	TX	78382	Bill Muskopf	512-790-9033	R	1*	<0.1

Source: *Ward's Business Directory of U.S. Private and Public Companies*, Volumes 1 and 2, 1996. The company type code used is as follows: P - Public, R - Private, S - Subsidiary, D - Division, J - Joint Venture, A - Affiliate, G - Group. Sales are in millions of dollars, employees are in thousands. An asterisk (*) indicates an estimated sales volume. The symbol < stands for 'less than'. Company names and addresses are truncated, in some cases, to fit into the available space.

MATERIALS CONSUMED

Material		Quantity	Delivered Cost ($ million)
Materials, ingredients, containers, and supplies		(X)	1,300.7
Ammonia, synthetic anhydrous (100 percent NH3)	1,000 s tons	2,162.7	248.1
Ammoniating or nitrogen solutions	1,000 s tons	(S)	12.2
Ammonium nitrate (solid only) (100 percent NH4NO3)	1,000 s tons	(D)	(D)
Ammonium sulfate (100 percent (NH4)2SO4)	1,000 s tons	(D)	(D)
Urea (solid only) (100 percent CO(NH2)2)	1,000 s tons	171.4	24.0
Other nitrogenous materials including calcium cyanamide and limestone mixtures	1,000 s tons	30.5*	2.7
Superphosphate - total used in mixed goods (100 percent P2O5)	1,000 s tons	(D)	(D)
Phosphoric acid, except spent (100 percent P2O5)	1,000 s tons	1.9	0.4
Other phosphatic materials	1,000 s tons	(D)	(D)
Muriate of potash (all grades) (60-62 percent K2O)	1,000 s tons	(D)	(D)
Other potassic materials, including potassium nitrate and sulfate	1,000 s tons	2.4	0.7
Inert fillers, secondary plant food, soil conditioners, sand, limestone, peat, nut hulls, etc.	1,000 s tons	(S)	6.5
Sulfuric acid (new and spent) (100 percent H2SO4)	1,000 s tons	40.6**	1.8
Phosphate rock	1,000 s tons	(D)	(D)
Sulfur	1,000 l tons	(D)	(D)
Natural gas used as a raw material	bil cu ft	342.7**	625.5
Bags, except textile, including shipping sacks, multiwall bags, and polyethylene liners		(X)	2.9
All other materials and components, parts, containers, and supplies		(X)	216.0
Materials, ingredients, containers, and supplies, nsk		(X)	109.5

Source: 1992 *Economic Census*. Explanation of symbols used: (D): Withheld to avoid disclosure of competitive data; na: Not available; (S): Withheld because statistical norms were not met; (X): Not applicable; (Z): Less than half the unit shown; nec: Not elsewhere classified; nsk: Not specified by kind; - : zero; * : 10-19 percent estimated; ** : 20-29 percent estimated.

PRODUCT SHARE DETAILS

Product or Product Class	% Share	Product or Product Class	% Share
Nitrogenous fertilizers	100.00	Nitrogenous fertilizer materials of organic origin, including activated sewage sludge, processed tankage, etc.	4.09
Synthetic ammonia, nitric acid, and ammonium compounds	74.96	Nitrogenous fertilizers, nsk	1.19
Urea	19.75		

Source: 1992 *Economic Census*. The values shown are percent of total shipments in an industry. Values of indented subcategories are summed in the main heading. The symbol (D) appears when data are withheld to prevent disclosure of competitive information. The abbreviation nsk stands for 'not specified by kind' and nec for 'not elsewhere classified'.

INPUTS AND OUTPUTS FOR NITROGENOUS & PHOSPHATIC FERTILIZERS

Economic Sector or Industry Providing Inputs	%	Sector	Economic Sector or Industry Buying Outputs	%	Sector
Chemical & fertilizer mineral	16.0	Mining	Feed grains	28.8	Agric.
Nitrogenous & phosphatic fertilizers	13.3	Manufg.	Exports	16.7	Foreign
Imports	11.4	Foreign	Agricultural, forestry, & fishery services	12.2	Agric.
Crude petroleum & natural gas	11.2	Mining	Nitrogenous & phosphatic fertilizers	9.2	Manufg.
Cyclic crudes and organics	9.4	Manufg.	Food grains	5.9	Agric.
Gas production & distribution (utilities)	9.1	Util.	Fertilizers, mixing only	5.0	Manufg.
Electric services (utilities)	5.1	Util.	Landscape & horticultural services	2.7	Agric.
Motor freight transportation & warehousing	4.8	Util.	Owner-occupied dwellings	1.9	Fin/R.E.
Wholesale trade	4.0	Trade	Cyclic crudes and organics	1.8	Manufg.
Railroads & related services	2.9	Util.	Fruits	1.2	Agric.
Industrial inorganic chemicals, nec	2.1	Manufg.	Cotton	1.1	Agric.
Miscellaneous plastics products	1.2	Manufg.	Oil bearing crops	1.1	Agric.
Miscellaneous repair shops	1.1	Services	Vegetables	1.1	Agric.
Water transportation	0.9	Util.	Personal consumption expenditures	1.0	
Petroleum refining	0.7	Manufg.	Coal	1.0	Mining
Sanitary services, steam supply, irrigation	0.5	Util.	State & local government enterprises, nec	0.9	Gov't
Noncomparable imports	0.5	Foreign	Greenhouse & nursery products	0.8	Agric.
Maintenance of nonfarm buildings nec	0.4	Constr.	S/L Govt. purch., natural resource & recreation.	0.8	S/L Govt
Water supply & sewage systems	0.4	Util.	Industrial inorganic chemicals, nec	0.7	Manufg.
Banking	0.4	Fin/R.E.	Real estate	0.7	Fin/R.E.
Equipment rental & leasing services	0.4	Services	Explosives	0.6	Manufg.
Pipe, valves, & pipe fittings	0.3	Manufg.	Paper mills, except building paper	0.6	Manufg.
Communications, except radio & TV	0.3	Util.	Tobacco	0.5	Agric.
Advertising	0.3	Services	Prepared feeds, nec	0.5	Manufg.
Engineering, architectural, & surveying services	0.3	Services	Sugar crops	0.4	Agric.
Alkalies & chlorine	0.2	Manufg.	Organic fibers, noncellulosic	0.4	Manufg.
Bags, except textile	0.2	Manufg.	Hotels & lodging places	0.4	Services
Pumps & compressors	0.2	Manufg.	Miscellaneous crops	0.3	Agric.
Air transportation	0.2	Util.	Logging camps & logging contractors	0.3	Manufg.
Eating & drinking places	0.2	Trade	Tree nuts	0.2	Agric.
Mechanical measuring devices	0.1	Manufg.	Plastics materials & resins	0.2	Manufg.
Insurance carriers	0.1	Fin/R.E.	Elementary & secondary schools	0.2	Services
Security & commodity brokers	0.1	Fin/R.E.	S/L Govt. purch., higher education	0.2	S/L Govt
Computer & data processing services	0.1	Services	Forestry products	0.1	Agric.
Scrap	0.1	Scrap	Adhesives & sealants	0.1	Manufg.

Source: Benchmark Input-Output Accounts for the U.S. Economy, 1982, U.S. Department of Commerce, Washington, D.C., July 1991. Data, as reported in the source, are organized by the 1977 SIC structure in use in 1982 but have been matched, as closely as is possible, to the 1987 SIC structure used in this book.

OCCUPATIONS EMPLOYED BY SIC 287 - AGRICULTURAL CHEMICALS

Occupation	% of Total 1994	Change to 2005	Occupation	% of Total 1994	Change to 2005
Chemical plant & system operators	9.4	-5.2	Material moving equipment operators nec	2.1	-21.0
Blue collar worker supervisors	6.8	-24.7	Freight, stock, & material movers, hand	2.0	-36.8
Industrial machinery mechanics	5.3	-13.1	Bookkeeping, accounting, & auditing clerks	1.9	-40.8
Chemical equipment controllers, operators	5.2	-36.8	Chemists	1.7	-21.0
Sales & related workers nec	4.4	-21.0	General office clerks	1.7	-32.6
Crushing & mixing machine operators	3.4	-21.0	Hand packers & packagers	1.6	-32.2
Packaging & filling machine operators	3.4	-21.0	Industrial production managers	1.3	-21.1
Truck drivers light & heavy	3.4	-18.5	Electricians	1.3	-25.8
Helpers, laborers, & material movers nec	3.2	-21.0	Chemical engineers	1.3	-21.0
Science & mathematics technicians	2.9	-21.0	Marketing, advertising, & PR managers	1.2	-21.0
Maintenance repairers, general utility	2.8	-28.9	Clerical supervisors & managers	1.1	-19.1
General managers & top executives	2.8	-25.1	Machine feeders & offbearers	1.1	-28.8
Industrial truck & tractor operators	2.6	-21.0	Managers & administrators nec	1.0	-21.1
Secretaries, ex legal & medical	2.2	-28.1			

Source: *Industry-Occupation Matrix*, Bureau of Labor Statistics. These data relate to one or more 3-digit SIC industry groups rather than to a single 4-digit SIC. The change reported for each occupation to the year 2005 is a percent of growth or decline as estimated by the Bureau of Labor Statistics. The abbreviation nec stands for 'not elsewhere classified'.

LOCATION BY STATE AND REGIONAL CONCENTRATION

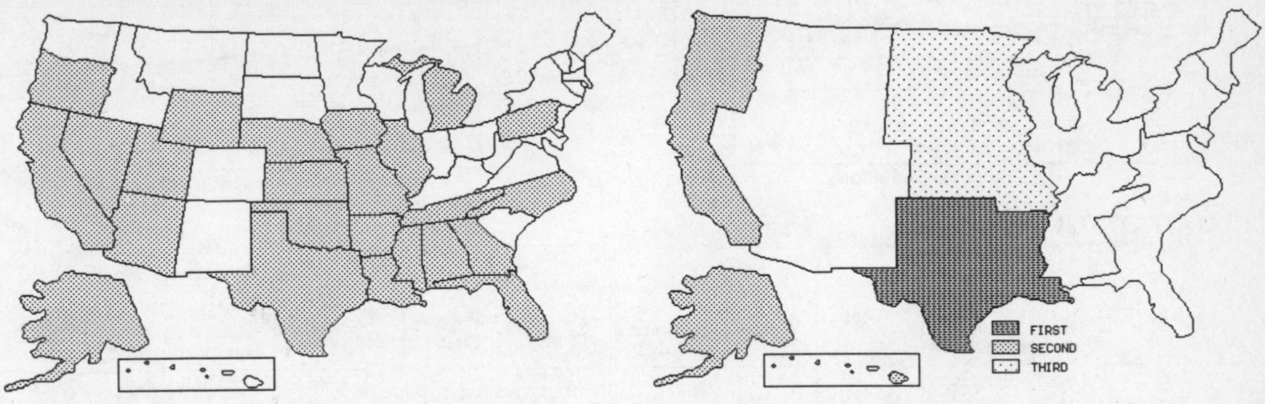

INDUSTRY DATA BY STATE

State	Establish-ments	Shipments			Employment				Cost as % of Shipments	Investment per Employee ($)
		Total ($ mil)	% of U.S.	Per Establ.	Total Number	% of U.S.	Per Establ.	Wages ($/hour)		
Louisiana	8	721.8	22.7	90.2	900	12.9	113	20.45	65.6	-
Iowa	5	132.2	4.2	26.4	300	4.3	60	14.80	60.7	-
Nebraska	3	96.9	3.1	32.3	200	2.9	67	17.00	65.5	-
Illinois	7	83.5	2.6	11.9	200	2.9	29	14.75	58.3	-
Florida	5	65.3	2.1	13.1	200	2.9	40	13.00	64.5	-
Pennsylvania	6	39.4	1.2	6.6	200	2.9	33	9.67	49.7	4,500
Michigan	3	18.0	0.6	6.0	100	1.4	33	8.33	47.8	-
California	17	(D)	-	-	375 *	5.4	22	-	-	-
Texas	12	(D)	-	-	375 *	5.4	31	-	-	9,067
Oklahoma	6	(D)	-	-	375 *	5.4	63	-	-	-
Georgia	5	(D)	-	-	375 *	5.4	75	-	-	-
Alabama	4	(D)	-	-	175 *	2.5	44	-	-	-
Arizona	4	(D)	-	-	175 *	2.5	44	-	-	-
Utah	4	(D)	-	-	175 *	2.5	44	-	-	-
Arkansas	3	(D)	-	-	175 *	2.5	58	-	-	-
Kansas	3	(D)	-	-	375 *	5.4	125	-	-	-
Missouri	3	(D)	-	-	175 *	2.5	58	-	-	-
Oregon	3	(D)	-	-	175 *	2.5	58	-	-	-
Alaska	2	(D)	-	-	375 *	5.4	188	-	-	-
Nevada	2	(D)	-	-	375 *	5.4	188	-	-	-
North Carolina	2	(D)	-	-	175 *	2.5	88	-	-	-
Wyoming	2	(D)	-	-	175 *	2.5	88	-	-	-
Mississippi	1	(D)	-	-	750 *	10.7	750	-	-	-
Tennessee	1	(D)	-	-	175 *	2.5	175	-	-	-

Source: 1992 *Economic Census*. The states are in descending order of shipments or establishments (if shipment data are missing for the majority). The symbol (D) appears when data are withheld to prevent disclosure of competitive information. States marked with (D) are sorted by number of establishments. A dash (-) indicates that the data element cannot be calculated; * indicates the midpoint of a range.

2874 - PHOSPHATIC FERTILIZERS

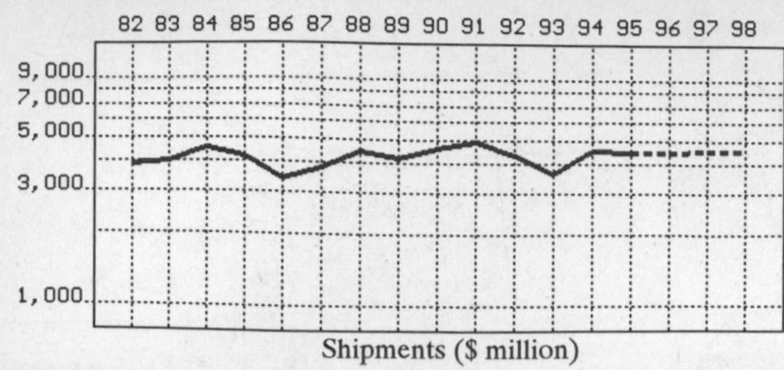

Shipments ($ million)

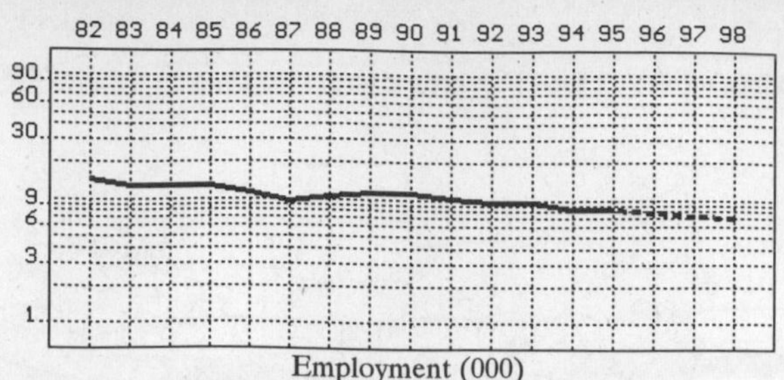

Employment (000)

GENERAL STATISTICS

Year	Com-panies	Establishments: Total	Establishments: with 20 or more employees	Employment: Total (000)	Production Workers (000)	Production Hours (Mil)	Compensation: Payroll ($ mil)	Compensation: Wages ($/hr)	Production ($ million): Cost of Materials	Value Added by Manufacture	Value of Shipments	Capital Invest.
1982	69	110	76	14.3	9.7	20.0	328.2	10.34	3,055.8	760.5	3,921.9	229.6
1983		109	73	12.9	9.1	19.0	308.0	10.85	2,981.4	965.5	3,969.4	99.2
1984		108	70	13.0	8.9	18.8	337.2	11.54	3,576.6	1,065.0	4,541.1	139.8
1985		108	68	13.0	8.7	18.0	350.5	12.12	3,392.1	771.4	4,184.2	178.7
1986		97	63	11.3	7.3	15.1	321.9	12.66	2,709.6	612.4	3,396.4	218.2
1987	55	77	42	9.4	6.2	13.2	286.2	12.94	2,612.4	1,167.2	3,819.3	63.6
1988		75	40	10.4	7.1	15.8	324.7	13.10	2,882.2	1,619.5	4,474.2	133.7
1989		77	38	11.2	7.4	16.1	348.5	13.55	3,035.7	1,167.0	4,187.3	132.2
1990		75	37	11.0	7.5	17.0	364.0	13.70	3,462.4	1,151.1	4,636.2	137.5
1991		71	38	10.3	7.3	16.4	368.4	14.65	3,619.4	1,372.6	4,983.9	197.1
1992	54	75	41	9.5	6.7	15.8	342.1	13.82	3,076.4	1,245.5	4,332.8	307.7
1993		84	41	9.4	6.6	14.5	332.6	14.70	2,625.9	975.4	3,648.0	149.9
1994		64P	27P	8.5	6.2	13.7	339.0	16.69	3,006.8	1,632.0	4,596.5	159.3
1995		61P	23P	8.3P	5.9P	13.7P	350.4P	16.08P	2,924.5P	1,587.3P	4,470.6P	183.0P
1996		57P	19P	7.9P	5.6P	13.3P	352.6P	16.50P	2,949.1P	1,600.7P	4,508.3P	185.6P
1997		53P	15P	7.5P	5.4P	12.9P	354.9P	16.92P	2,973.7P	1,614.1P	4,546.0P	188.1P
1998		49P	11P	7.1P	5.1P	12.5P	357.1P	17.34P	2,998.4P	1,627.4P	4,583.6P	190.7P

Sources: 1982, 1987, 1992 *Economic Census*; *Annual Survey of Manufactures*, 83-86, 88-91, 93-94. Establishment counts for non-Census years are from *County Business Patterns*; establishment values for 83-84 are extrapolations. 'P's show projections by the editors. Industries reclassified in 87 will not have data for prior years.

INDICES OF CHANGE

Year	Com-panies	Establishments: Total	Establishments: with 20 or more employees	Employment: Total (000)	Production Workers (000)	Production Hours (Mil)	Compensation: Payroll ($ mil)	Compensation: Wages ($/hr)	Production ($ million): Cost of Materials	Value Added by Manufacture	Value of Shipments	Capital Invest.
1982	128	147	185	151	145	127	96	75	99	61	91	75
1983		145	178	136	136	120	90	79	97	78	92	32
1984		144	171	137	133	119	99	84	116	86	105	45
1985		144	166	137	130	114	102	88	110	62	97	58
1986		129	154	119	109	96	94	92	88	49	78	71
1987	102	103	102	99	93	84	84	94	85	94	88	21
1988		100	98	109	106	100	95	95	94	130	103	43
1989		103	93	118	110	102	102	98	99	94	97	43
1990		100	90	116	112	108	106	99	113	92	107	45
1991		95	93	108	109	104	108	106	118	110	115	64
1992	100	100	100	100	100	100	100	100	100	100	100	100
1993		112	100	99	99	92	97	106	85	78	84	49
1994		86P	65P	89	93	87	99	121	98	131	106	52
1995		81P	55P	87P	88P	87P	102P	116P	95P	127P	103P	59P
1996		76P	46P	83P	84P	84P	103P	119P	96P	129P	104P	60P
1997		71P	36P	79P	80P	82P	104P	122P	97P	130P	105P	61P
1998		66P	26P	74P	76P	79P	104P	126P	97P	131P	106P	62P

Sources: Same as General Statistics. Values reflect change from the base year, 1992. Values above 100 mean greater than 92, values below 100 mean less than 92, and a value of 100 in the 82-91 or 93-98 period means same as 92. 'P's mark projections by the editors.

SELECTED RATIOS

For 1994	Avg. of All Manufact.	Analyzed Industry	Index	For 1994	Avg. of All Manufact.	Analyzed Industry	Index
Employees per Establishment	49	132	270	Value Added per Production Worker	134,084	263,226	196
Payroll per Establishment	1,500,273	5,269,430	351	Cost per Establishment	5,045,178	46,737,824	926
Payroll per Employee	30,620	39,882	130	Cost per Employee	102,970	353,741	344
Production Workers per Establishment	34	96	281	Cost per Production Worker	146,988	484,968	330
Wages per Establishment	853,319	3,554,192	417	Shipments per Establishment	9,576,895	71,448,187	746
Wages per Production Worker	24,861	36,880	148	Shipments per Employee	195,460	540,765	277
Hours per Production Worker	2,056	2,210	107	Shipments per Production Worker	279,017	741,371	266
Wages per Hour	12.09	16.69	138	Investment per Establishment	321,011	2,476,166	771
Value Added per Establishment	4,602,255	25,367,876	551	Investment per Employee	6,552	18,741	286
Value Added per Employee	93,930	192,000	204	Investment per Production Worker	9,352	25,694	275

Sources: Same as General Statistics. The 'Average of All Manufacturing' column represents the average of all manufacturing industries reported for the most recent complete year available. The Index shows the relationship between the Average and the Analyzed Industry. For example, 100 means that they are equal; 500 that the Analyzed Industry is five times the average; 50 means that the Analyzed Industry is half the national average. The abbreviation 'na' is used to show that data are 'not available'.

LEADING COMPANIES

Number shown: **13** Total sales ($ mil): **1,497** Total employment (000): **3.4**

Company Name	Address				CEO Name	Phone	Co. Type	Sales ($ mil)	Empl. (000)
Freeport-McMoRan	1615 Poydras St	New Orleans	LA	70112	Rene L Latiolais	504-582-4000	P	765	1.0
LESCO Inc	20005 Lake Rd	Rocky River	OH	44116	William A Foley	216-333-9250	P	204	1.0
Mobil Mining and Minerals Co	PO Box 3447	Pasadena	TX	77501	Steve E Pierce	713-920-5300	D	160	0.2
Cargill Fertilizer Inc	8813 Hwy 41 S	Riverview	FL	33569	Hank Mathot	813-677-9111	S	150*	0.5
Nu-West Industries Inc	8400 E Prentice Av	Englewood	CO	80111	Craig D Harlen	303-721-1396	P	94	0.2
Sunniland Corp	PO Box 8001	Sanford	FL	32772	Tomas W Moore	407-322-2424	R	50*	0.2
Conklin Company Inc	PO Box 155	Shakopee	MN	55379	Charles Herbster	612-445-6010	R	30	0.1
Milford Fertilizer Co	PO Box 243	Milford	DE	19963	Robert A Fischer Jr	302-422-3001	S	30	0.2
HD Campbell Mfg Co	238 N Main St	Rochelle	IL	61068	HD Campbell	815-562-2322	R	4	<0.1
Agro-Culture Liquid Fertilizers	PO Box 150	St Johns	MI	48879	Douglas Cook	517-224-4117	S	3	<0.1
COG Marketers Ltd	PO Box 150	St Johns	MI	48879	Douglas Cook	517-224-4117	R	3	<0.1
Gulf Coast Fertilizer Inc	PO Box 8	Cottondale	FL	32431	JA Gibbs	904-352-4251	R	3	<0.1
National Liquid Fertilizer Corp	3724 W 38th St	Chicago	IL	60632	Joan Nutt	312-254-3115	R	0	<0.1

Source: *Ward's Business Directory of U.S. Private and Public Companies*, Volumes 1 and 2, 1996. The company type code used is as follows: P - Public, R - Private, S - Subsidiary, D - Division, J - Joint Venture, A - Affiliate, G - Group. Sales are in millions of dollars, employees are in thousands. An asterisk (*) indicates an estimated sales volume. The symbol < stands for 'less than'. Company names and addresses are truncated, in some cases, to fit into the available space.

MATERIALS CONSUMED

Material		Quantity	Delivered Cost ($ million)
Materials, ingredients, containers, and supplies		(X)	2,696.4
Ammonia, synthetic anhydrous (100 percent NH3)	1,000 s tons	3,120.8	334.2
Ammoniating or nitrogen solutions	1,000 s tons	38.9*	6.1
Ammonium nitrate (solid only) (100 percent NH4NO3)	1,000 s tons	(D)	(D)
Ammonium sulfate (100 percent (NH4)2SO4)	1,000 s tons	51.4**	3.9
Urea (solid only) (100 percent CO(NH2)2)	1,000 s tons	74.5	11.3
Other nitrogenous materials including calcium cyanamide and limestone mixtures	1,000 s tons	(D)	(D)
Superphosphate - total used in mixed goods (100 percent P2O5)	1,000 s tons	37.7	6.6
Phosphoric acid, except spent (100 percent P2O5)	1,000 s tons	1,949.3	424.3
Other phosphatic materials	1,000 s tons	249.9	36.4
Muriate of potash (all grades) (60-62 percent K2O)	1,000 s tons	157.8	15.1
Other potassic materials, including potassium nitrate and sulfate	1,000 s tons	48.8	10.0
Inert fillers, secondary plant food, soil conditioners, sand, limestone, peat, nut hulls, etc.	1,000 s tons	255.4*	6.9
Sulfuric acid (new and spent) (100 percent H2SO4)	1,000 s tons	3,402.1	115.7
Phosphate rock	1,000 s tons	33,960.4	753.7
Sulfur	1,000 l tons	8,473.9	709.6
Natural gas used as a raw material	bil cu ft	(D)	(D)
Bags, except textile, including shipping sacks, multiwall bags, and polyethylene liners		(X)	4.6
All other materials and components, parts, containers, and supplies		(X)	219.0
Materials, ingredients, containers, and supplies, nsk		(X)	29.4

Source: 1992 *Economic Census*. Explanation of symbols used: (D): Withheld to avoid disclosure of competitive data; na: Not available; (S): Withheld because statistical norms were not met; (X): Not applicable; (Z): Less than half the unit shown; nec: Not elsewhere classified; nsk: Not specified by kind; - : zero; * : 10-19 percent estimated; ** : 20-29 percent estimated.

PRODUCT SHARE DETAILS

Product or Product Class	% Share
Phosphatic fertilizers	100.00
Phosphoric acid	28.43
Superphosphate and other phosphatic fertilizer materials	62.58
Mixed fertilizers, made by plants which manufacture fertilizer materials	8.43
Mixed fertilizers, shipped in packages, tablets, and similar forms of a gross weight not exceeding 10 kg (22 lb), made by plants which manufacture fertilizer materials	(D)
Mixed fertilizers, dry, shipped in bulk, made by plants which manufacture fertilizer materials	(D)
Mixed fertilizers, dry, shipped in bags of a gross weight of 10 kg (22 lb) or more, made by plants which manufacture fertilizer materials	25.75
Mixed fertilizers, liquid, shipped in bulk or in packages of a gross weight of 10 kg (22 lb) or more, made by plants which manufacture fertilizer materials	12.51
Mixed fertilizers, nsk	4.42
Phosphatic fertilizers, nsk	0.56

Source: 1992 *Economic Census*. The values shown are percent of total shipments in an industry. Values of indented subcategories are summed in the main heading. The symbol (D) appears when data are withheld to prevent disclosure of competitive information. The abbreviation nsk stands for 'not specified by kind' and nec for 'not elsewhere classified'.

INPUTS AND OUTPUTS FOR NITROGENOUS & PHOSPHATIC FERTILIZERS

Economic Sector or Industry Providing Inputs	%	Sector	Economic Sector or Industry Buying Outputs	%	Sector
Chemical & fertilizer mineral	16.0	Mining	Feed grains	28.8	Agric.
Nitrogenous & phosphatic fertilizers	13.3	Manufg.	Exports	16.7	Foreign
Imports	11.4	Foreign	Agricultural, forestry, & fishery services	12.2	Agric.
Crude petroleum & natural gas	11.2	Mining	Nitrogenous & phosphatic fertilizers	9.2	Manufg.
Cyclic crudes and organics	9.4	Manufg.	Food grains	5.9	Agric.
Gas production & distribution (utilities)	9.1	Util.	Fertilizers, mixing only	5.0	Manufg.
Electric services (utilities)	5.1	Util.	Landscape & horticultural services	2.7	Agric.
Motor freight transportation & warehousing	4.8	Util.	Owner-occupied dwellings	1.9	Fin/R.E.
Wholesale trade	4.0	Trade	Cyclic crudes and organics	1.8	Manufg.
Railroads & related services	2.9	Util.	Fruits	1.2	Agric.
Industrial inorganic chemicals, nec	2.1	Manufg.	Cotton	1.1	Agric.
Miscellaneous plastics products	1.2	Manufg.	Oil bearing crops	1.1	Agric.
Miscellaneous repair shops	1.1	Services	Vegetables	1.1	Agric.
Water transportation	0.9	Util.	Personal consumption expenditures	1.0	
Petroleum refining	0.7	Manufg.	Coal	1.0	Mining
Sanitary services, steam supply, irrigation	0.5	Util.	State & local government enterprises, nec	0.9	Gov't
Noncomparable imports	0.5	Foreign	Greenhouse & nursery products	0.8	Agric.
Maintenance of nonfarm buildings nec	0.4	Constr.	S/L Govt. purch., natural resource & recreation.	0.8	S/L Govt
Water supply & sewage systems	0.4	Util.	Industrial inorganic chemicals, nec	0.7	Manufg.
Banking	0.4	Fin/R.E.	Real estate	0.7	Fin/R.E.
Equipment rental & leasing services	0.4	Services	Explosives	0.6	Manufg.
Pipe, valves, & pipe fittings	0.3	Manufg.	Paper mills, except building paper	0.6	Manufg.
Communications, except radio & TV	0.3	Util.	Tobacco	0.5	Agric.
Advertising	0.3	Services	Prepared feeds, nec	0.5	Manufg.
Engineering, architectural, & surveying services	0.3	Services	Sugar crops	0.4	Agric.
Alkalies & chlorine	0.2	Manufg.	Organic fibers, noncellulosic	0.4	Manufg.
Bags, except textile	0.2	Manufg.	Hotels & lodging places	0.4	Services
Pumps & compressors	0.2	Manufg.	Miscellaneous crops	0.3	Agric.
Air transportation	0.2	Util.	Logging camps & logging contractors	0.3	Manufg.
Eating & drinking places	0.2	Trade	Tree nuts	0.2	Agric.
Mechanical measuring devices	0.1	Manufg.	Plastics materials & resins	0.2	Manufg.
Insurance carriers	0.1	Fin/R.E.	Elementary & secondary schools	0.2	Services
Security & commodity brokers	0.1	Fin/R.E.	S/L Govt. purch., higher education	0.2	S/L Govt
Computer & data processing services	0.1	Services	Forestry products	0.1	Agric.
Scrap	0.1	Scrap	Adhesives & sealants	0.1	Manufg.

Source: Benchmark Input-Output Accounts for the U.S. Economy, 1982, U.S. Department of Commerce, Washington, D.C., July 1991. Data, as reported in the source, are organized by the 1977 SIC structure in use in 1982 but have been matched, as closely as is possible, to the 1987 SIC structure used in this book.

OCCUPATIONS EMPLOYED BY SIC 287 - AGRICULTURAL CHEMICALS

Occupation	% of Total 1994	Change to 2005	Occupation	% of Total 1994	Change to 2005
Chemical plant & system operators	9.4	-5.2	Material moving equipment operators nec	2.1	-21.0
Blue collar worker supervisors	6.8	-24.7	Freight, stock, & material movers, hand	2.0	-36.8
Industrial machinery mechanics	5.3	-13.1	Bookkeeping, accounting, & auditing clerks	1.9	-40.8
Chemical equipment controllers, operators	5.2	-36.8	Chemists	1.7	-21.0
Sales & related workers nec	4.4	-21.0	General office clerks	1.7	-32.6
Crushing & mixing machine operators	3.4	-21.0	Hand packers & packagers	1.6	-32.2
Packaging & filling machine operators	3.4	-21.0	Industrial production managers	1.3	-21.1
Truck drivers light & heavy	3.4	-18.5	Electricians	1.3	-25.8
Helpers, laborers, & material movers nec	3.2	-21.0	Chemical engineers	1.3	-21.0
Science & mathematics technicians	2.9	-21.0	Marketing, advertising, & PR managers	1.2	-21.0
Maintenance repairers, general utility	2.8	-28.9	Clerical supervisors & managers	1.1	-19.1
General managers & top executives	2.8	-25.1	Machine feeders & offbearers	1.1	-28.8
Industrial truck & tractor operators	2.6	-21.0	Managers & administrators nec	1.0	-21.1
Secretaries, ex legal & medical	2.2	-28.1			

Source: Industry-Occupation Matrix, Bureau of Labor Statistics. These data relate to one or more 3-digit SIC industry groups rather than to a single 4-digit SIC. The change reported for each occupation to the year 2005 is a percent of growth or decline as estimated by the Bureau of Labor Statistics. The abbreviation nec stands for 'not elsewhere classified'.

LOCATION BY STATE AND REGIONAL CONCENTRATION

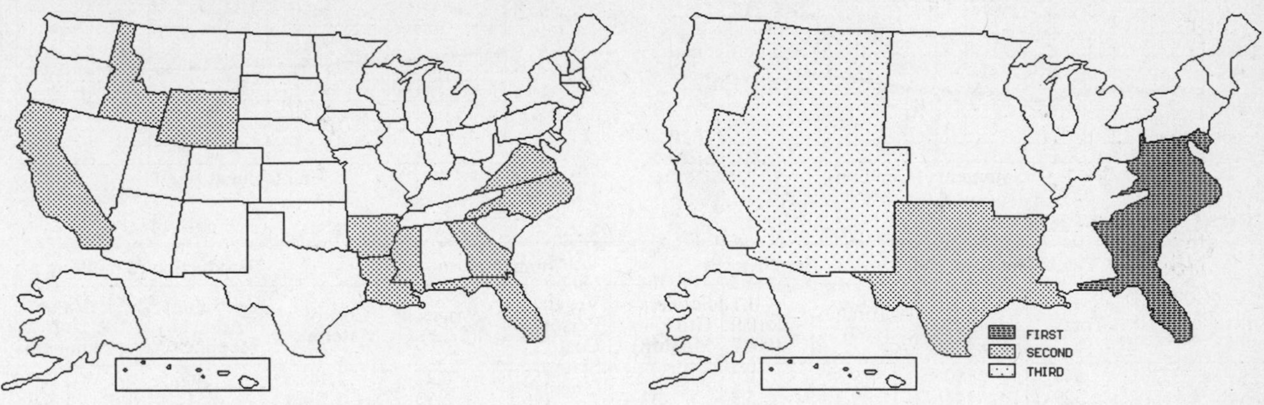

INDUSTRY DATA BY STATE

State	Establish-ments	Shipments Total ($ mil)	Shipments % of U.S.	Shipments Per Establ.	Employment Total Number	Employment % of U.S.	Employment Per Establ.	Employment Wages ($/hour)	Cost as % of Shipments	Investment per Employee ($)
Florida	15	2,527.9	58.3	168.5	5,900	62.1	393	13.04	73.6	37,102
Georgia	5	62.2	1.4	12.4	200	2.1	40	9.67	59.5	2,000
North Carolina	9	(D)	-	-	750 *	7.9	83	-	-	-
Louisiana	4	(D)	-	-	750 *	7.9	188	-	-	-
Virginia	4	(D)	-	-	175 *	1.8	44	-	-	-
Idaho	3	(D)	-	-	750 *	7.9	250	-	-	-
Arkansas	2	(D)	-	-	175 *	1.8	88	-	-	-
California	2	(D)	-	-	175 *	1.8	88	-	-	-
Mississippi	1	(D)	-	-	175 *	1.8	175	-	-	-
Wyoming	1	(D)	-	-	175 *	1.8	175	-	-	-

Source: 1992 *Economic Census*. The states are in descending order of shipments or establishments (if shipment data are missing for the majority). The symbol (D) appears when data are withheld to prevent disclosure of competitive information. States marked with (D) are sorted by number of establishments. A dash (-) indicates that the data element cannot be calculated; * indicates the midpoint of a range.

2875 - FERTILIZERS, MIXING ONLY

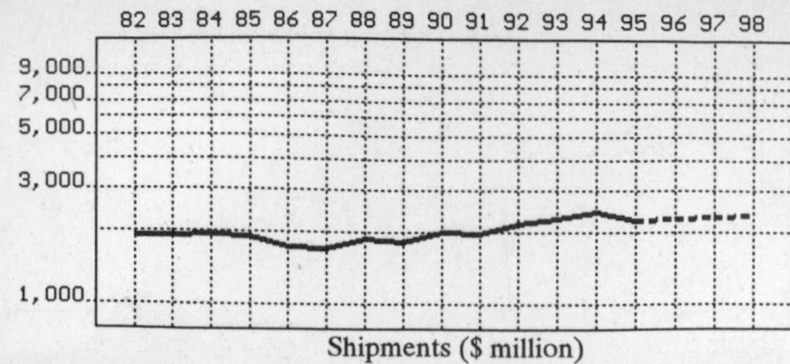

Shipments ($ million)

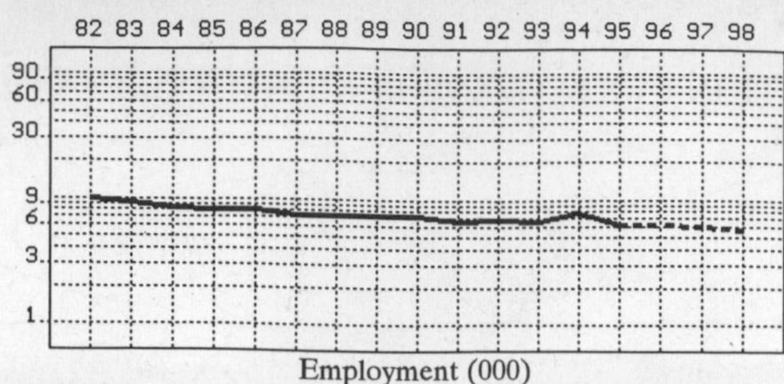

Employment (000)

GENERAL STATISTICS

Year	Companies	Establishments: Total	Establishments: with 20 or more employees	Employment: Total (000)	Employment: Production Workers (000)	Employment: Production Hours (Mil)	Compensation: Payroll ($ mil)	Compensation: Wages ($/hr)	Production ($ million): Cost of Materials	Production ($ million): Value Added by Manufacture	Production ($ million): Value of Shipments	Production ($ million): Capital Invest.
1982	372	544	150	9.8	6.0	12.2	155.7	6.27	1,445.5	406.5	1,903.4	35.4
1983		529	144	9.3	5.8	11.4	146.1	6.53	1,386.1	516.4	1,902.9	34.3
1984		514	138	8.5	5.5	10.8	147.1	6.90	1,450.5	487.3	1,947.2	30.4
1985		500	133	8.2	5.2	10.3	149.7	7.42	1,369.4	515.8	1,894.2	22.0
1986		496	129	8.2	5.1	10.4	150.0	7.37	1,242.7	492.3	1,738.9	19.3
1987	307	452	115	7.5	4.7	9.6	145.2	7.48	1,240.4	464.3	1,701.1	26.3
1988		415	119	7.5	4.7	9.5	145.9	7.72	1,375.2	526.3	1,864.2	16.2
1989		397	118	7.4	4.1	8.6	138.0	8.01	1,373.2	457.9	1,831.7	26.6
1990		400	108	7.3	4.3	9.5	163.6	7.86	1,465.3	552.9	2,018.8	31.2
1991		394	103	6.7	4.1	9.1	157.4	7.96	1,443.8	506.7	1,954.3	26.4
1992	313	401	99	6.9	4.2	9.4	181.9	8.90	1,562.7	634.1	2,188.8	43.7
1993		413	112	6.7	4.3	9.5	179.2	9.26	1,574.5	721.2	2,272.9	33.9
1994		358P	95P	7.8	5.1	11.0	202.7	9.42	1,592.3	806.6	2,420.7	38.1
1995		343P	90P	6.4P	3.9P	9.0P	182.9P	9.46P	1,469.1P	744.2P	2,233.4P	33.5P
1996		328P	86P	6.2P	3.8P	8.8P	186.3P	9.70P	1,493.7P	756.6P	2,270.7P	34.1P
1997		313P	82P	6.0P	3.7P	8.7P	189.8P	9.94P	1,518.2P	769.1P	2,308.1P	34.7P
1998		298P	77P	5.8P	3.6P	8.5P	193.3P	10.18P	1,542.7P	781.5P	2,345.4P	35.3P

Sources: 1982, 1987, 1992 *Economic Census*; *Annual Survey of Manufactures*, 83-86, 88-91, 93-94. Establishment counts for non-Census years are from *County Business Patterns*; establishment values for 83-84 are extrapolations. 'P's show projections by the editors. Industries reclassified in 87 will not have data for prior years.

INDICES OF CHANGE

Year	Companies	Establishments: Total	Establishments: with 20 or more employees	Employment: Total (000)	Employment: Production Workers (000)	Employment: Production Hours (Mil)	Compensation: Payroll ($ mil)	Compensation: Wages ($/hr)	Production ($ million): Cost of Materials	Production ($ million): Value Added by Manufacture	Production ($ million): Value of Shipments	Production ($ million): Capital Invest.
1982	119	136	152	142	143	130	86	70	93	64	87	81
1983		132	145	135	138	121	80	73	89	81	87	78
1984		128	139	123	131	115	81	78	93	77	89	70
1985		125	134	119	124	110	82	83	88	81	87	50
1986		124	130	119	121	111	82	83	80	78	79	44
1987	98	113	116	109	112	102	80	84	79	73	78	60
1988		103	120	109	112	101	80	87	88	83	85	37
1989		99	119	107	98	91	76	90	88	72	84	61
1990		100	109	106	102	101	90	88	94	87	92	71
1991		98	104	97	98	97	87	89	92	80	89	60
1992	100	100	100	100	100	100	100	100	100	100	100	100
1993		103	113	97	102	101	99	104	101	114	104	78
1994		89P	96P	113	121	117	111	106	102	127	111	87
1995		85P	91P	92P	94P	96P	101P	106P	94P	117P	102P	77P
1996		82P	87P	89P	91P	94P	102P	109P	96P	119P	104P	78P
1997		78P	83P	86P	88P	92P	104P	112P	97P	121P	105P	79P
1998		74P	78P	83P	85P	91P	106P	114P	99P	123P	107P	81P

Sources: Same as General Statistics. Values reflect change from the base year, 1992. Values above 100 mean greater than 92, values below 100 mean less than 92, and a value of 100 in the 82-91 or 93-98 period means same as 92. 'P's mark projections by the editors.

SELECTED RATIOS

For 1994	Avg. of All Manufact.	Analyzed Industry	Index
Employees per Establishment	49	22	45
Payroll per Establishment	1,500,273	566,825	38
Payroll per Employee	30,620	25,987	85
Production Workers per Establishment	34	14	42
Wages per Establishment	853,319	289,760	34
Wages per Production Worker	24,861	20,318	82
Hours per Production Worker	2,056	2,157	105
Wages per Hour	12.09	9.42	78
Value Added per Establishment	4,602,255	2,255,555	49
Value Added per Employee	93,930	103,410	110

For 1994	Avg. of All Manufact.	Analyzed Industry	Index
Value Added per Production Worker	134,084	158,157	118
Cost per Establishment	5,045,178	4,452,665	88
Cost per Employee	102,970	204,141	198
Cost per Production Worker	146,988	312,216	212
Shipments per Establishment	9,576,895	6,769,181	71
Shipments per Employee	195,460	310,346	159
Shipments per Production Worker	279,017	474,647	170
Investment per Establishment	321,011	106,542	33
Investment per Employee	6,552	4,885	75
Investment per Production Worker	9,352	7,471	80

Sources: Same as General Statistics. The 'Average of All Manufacturing' column represents the average of all manufacturing industries reported for the most recent complete year available. The Index shows the relationship between the Average and the Analyzed Industry. For example, 100 means that they are equal; 500 that the Analyzed Industry is five times the average; 50 means that the Analyzed Industry is half the national average. The abbreviation 'na' is used to show that data are 'not available'.

LEADING COMPANIES Number shown: **60** Total sales ($ mil): **3,728** Total employment (000): **7.3**

Company Name	Address				CEO Name	Phone	Co. Type	Sales ($ mil)	Empl. (000)
Cenex/Land O'Lakes Ag Services	PO Box 64089	St Paul	MN	55164	Noel Estenson	612-451-5151	J	2,200	3.0
Tennessee Farmers Cooperative	PO Box 3003	La Vergne	TN	37086	Philip Walker	615-793-8011	R	300	0.6
Royster-Clark Inc	PO Box 250	Tarboro	NC	27886	S Clark Jenkins	919-823-2101	R	209	0.5
Earthgro Inc	PO Box 143	Lebanon	CT	06249	Paul Sellew	203-642-7591	R	83*	0.2
Florida Favorite Fertilizers Inc	PO Box 8000	Lakeland	FL	33802	Carlos Smith	813-688-2442	R	69*	0.2
PCS Joint Ventures	PO Box 8000	Lakeland	FL	33802	Carlos Smith	813-688-2442	R	69*	0.2
HJ Baker and Brother Inc	595 Summer St	Stamford	CT	06901	John M Smith	203-328-9200	R	67*	0.2
Brewer Environmental Industries	PO Box 48	Honolulu	HI	96810	Willibrord Tallett	808-532-7400	S	64	0.2
Kugler Oil Co	PO Box 1748	McCook	NE	69001	John Kugler	308-345-2280	R	62*	0.2
Diamond R Fertilizer Company	PO Box 771137	Winter Garden	FL	34777	Edward H Sullivan	407-656-3007	R	60	0.1
Frit Inc	PO Box 1589	Ozark	AL	36361	SE Allred	205-774-2515	R	60	0.4
Chester Inc	PO Box 2237	Valparaiso	IN	46384	CF Bowman	219-462-1131	R	30*	0.1
Weatherly Consumer Products	651 Perimeter Dr	Lexington	KY	40517	James R Hills	606-268-1962	R	26*	0.1
Wolfkill Feed&Fertilizer Corp	PO Box 578	Monroe	WA	98272	RV Wolfkill	206-794-7065	R	25	0.1
All-American Cooperative	PO Box 125	Stewartville	MN	55976	Ron Nelson	507-533-4222	R	24	<0.1
Farmers Cooperative	Hwy 257	Hanska	MN	56041	Randall M Rieke	507-439-6222	R	23	<0.1
Wheaton Dumont Coop Elevator	1115 Broadway Av	Wheaton	MN	56296	Orval Kohls	612-563-8152	R	23	<0.1
South Central Co-op	PO Box E	Fairfax	MN	55332	Richard Graufman	507-426-8263	R	22	<0.1
AH Hoffman Inc	77 Cooper Av	Landisville	PA	17538	G Ewing Jr	717-898-2461	R	22	0.1
Culpeper Farmers Cooperative	PO Box 2002	Culpeper	VA	22701	Taylor E Gore	703-825-2200	R	22	0.1
Guthrie Corp	PO Box 429	Guthrie	OK	73044	John C Pearson	405-282-4400	R	20*	<0.1
Producers Supply Cooperative	PO Drawer J	Nampa	ID	83653	Clinton Pline	208-466-7841	R	19	<0.1
Farmers Union Coop Oil Assoc	425 Clinton St	South St Paul	MN	55075	Kevin Sexton	612-451-6200	R	18*	<0.1
Atlantic Fertilizer & Chemical	PO Box 1488	Homestead	FL	33090	R F Wysemann	305-247-8800	R	16*	<0.1
Frit Industries Inc	PO Box 1589	Ozark	AL	36361	SE Allred	205-774-2515	S	16	0.1
Bandini Fertilizer Co	4139 Bandini Blv	Los Angeles	CA	90023	James Joseph	213-263-7391	R	14*	<0.1
Farm Services Inc	PO Box 360	Vinton	IA	52349	John Swift	319-472-2394	S	13	<0.1
Farmers Cooperative Oil Co	PO Box 315	Wanamingo	MN	55983	Lester Greseth	507-824-2251	R	13*	<0.1
Senesac Inc	PO Box 592	Fowler	IN	47944	RJ Puetz Sr	317-884-1300	R	12*	<0.1
Carol Service Co	PO Box 25	Lanark	IL	61046	Clarence Hasz	815-493-2181	R	10	<0.1
Cargill Inc	PO Box 218	Elmore	MN	56027	Mike Schiltz	507-943-3111	D	9	<0.1
Eckroat Seed Co	PO Box 17610	Oklahoma City	OK	73136	Arthur V Eckroat	405-427-2484	R	8	<0.1
Clunette Elevator Company Inc	4316 W 600 N	Leesburg	IN	46538	J Anglin Sr	219-858-2281	R	6	<0.1
Cedar Grove Composting Inc	54 S Dawson St	Seattle	WA	98134	Richard Ramsey	206-763-2700	S	6*	<0.1
Farmers Cooperative Association	PO Box 187	Okarche	OK	73762	Dean Anderson	405-263-7289	R	6	<0.1
Starbuck Creamery Co	101 W 5th St	Starbuck	MN	56381	Chuck Valek	612-239-2226	R	6	<0.1
Texas Liquid Fertilizer	PO Box 947	Hempstead	TX	77445	Kim Cohen	409-826-8063	S	6*	<0.1
Black Magic Products Ltd	10291 Iron Rock	Elk Grove	CA	95624	Edith Halsey	916-686-8585	R	5	<0.1
Klein Fertilizers Inc	PO Box 335	Fowlerville	MI	48836	Darrell Klein	517-223-9148	R	5	<0.1
Polk County Fertilizer Co	PO Box 366	Haines City	FL	33845	Wykliffe C Tunno	813-422-1186	R	5*	<0.1
Applegate Insulation Mfg	PO Box 292	Okemos	MI	48805	Aaron Applegate	517-349-0466	R	4	<0.1
Four County Agricultural Svcs	PO Box 486	Faribault	MN	55021	Vernon Pommeranz	507-334-3943	R	4	<0.1
Graco Fertilizer Co	PO Box 89	Cairo	GA	31728	Ken Legette	912-377-1602	R	4*	<0.1
Millburn Peat Company Inc	PO Box 236	La Porte	IN	46350	LE Holder	219-362-7025	R	4	<0.1
Valley Fertilizer and Chemical	PO Box 816	Mount Jackson	VA	22842	Orville L Smoot	703-477-3121	R	4	<0.1
WW Gregory Co	PO Box 400	Dothan	AL	36302	WW Gregory	205-794-9222	R	4	<0.1
Agri Mark Farmers Co-op	PO Box 215	Smithville	OH	44677	Al Holdren	216-669-2711	R	3	<0.1
Chokio Equity Exchange Inc	PO Box 126	Chokio	MN	56221	Steve Negen	612-324-2477	R	3*	<0.1
Farmers Union Oil Co	PO Box 70	Climax	MN	56523	Robert Burner	218-857-2165	R	3	<0.1
Fieldcrest Fertilizer Inc	Rte 3	Madison	MN	56256	Kevin Tollefson	612-598-7567	R	3*	<0.1
Webb Super-Gro Product Inc	PO Box C	Mill Hall	PA	17751	James P Webb Jr	717-726-4525	R	3	<0.1
Sun-Vue Fertilizer Inc	PO Box 56	Plainview	TX	79072	Edwin L Vadder	806-293-2527	R	3	<0.1
Dawson AG Service Inc	PO Box 351	Dawson	MN	56232	Dale Breberg	612-769-4396	R	3	<0.1
Fosston Cooperative Association	104 S Mark Av	Fosston	MN	56542	O Nyhus	218-435-1221	R	3	<0.1
Agronomy	PO Box 267	Madelia	MN	56062	John Graff	507-642-3275	D	2	<0.1
Oregon Hydrocarbon Inc	9333 N Harborgate	Portland	OR	97203	Jim Loufararian	503-735-9525	S	2*	<0.1
Canton Mills Inc	PO Box 97	Minnesota City	MN	55959	David C Bunke	507-689-2131	R	2	<0.1
Bird Island Soil Service Center	511 Oak Av	Bird Island	MN	55310	Brad Asteh	612-365-3655	R	1	<0.1
Amos Eby Co	PO Box 26	Paradise	PA	17562	Robert C Ranck Sr	717-687-6091	R	1*	<0.1
American Soil Inc	PO Box 295	Ramsey	NJ	07446	Robert F Young	201-327-2312	R	1	<0.1

Source: *Ward's Business Directory of U.S. Private and Public Companies*, Volumes 1 and 2, 1996. The company type code used is as follows: P - Public, R - Private, S - Subsidiary, D - Division, J - Joint Venture, A - Affiliate, G - Group. Sales are in millions of dollars, employees are in thousands. An asterisk (*) indicates an estimated sales volume. The symbol < stands for 'less than'. Company names and addresses are truncated, in some cases, to fit into the available space.

MATERIALS CONSUMED

Material		Quantity	Delivered Cost ($ million)
Materials, ingredients, containers, and supplies		(X)	1,173.1
Ammonia, synthetic anhydrous (100 percent NH3)	1,000 s tons	339.4	39.6
Ammoniating or nitrogen solutions	1,000 s tons	574.5*	61.5
Ammonium nitrate (solid only) (100 percent NH4NO3)	1,000 s tons	232.0	30.0
Ammonium sulfate (100 percent (NH4)2SO4)	1,000 s tons	334.6*	30.4
Urea (solid only) (100 percent CO(NH2)2)	1,000 s tons	376.4	60.0
Other nitrogenous materials including calcium cyanamide and limestone mixtures	1,000 s tons	95.9	16.8
Superphosphate - total used in mixed goods (100 percent P2O5)	1,000 s tons	171.2*	18.9
Phosphoric acid, except spent (100 percent P2O5)	1,000 s tons	171.2	49.4
Other phosphatic materials	1,000 s tons	345.4*	59.3
Muriate of potash (all grades) (60-62 percent K2O)	1,000 s tons	659.0*	72.0
Other potassic materials, including potassium nitrate and sulfate	1,000 s tons	193.8	34.4
Inert fillers, secondary plant food, soil conditioners, sand, limestone, peat, nut hulls, etc.	1,000 s tons	(S)	34.9
Sulfuric acid (new and spent) (100 percent H2SO4)	1,000 s tons	150.5*	5.9
Phosphate rock	1,000 s tons	(D)	(D)
Sulfur	1,000 l tons	(D)	(D)
Natural gas used as a raw material	bil cu ft	(D)	(D)
Bags, except textile, including shipping sacks, multiwall bags, and polyethylene liners		(X)	23.0
All other materials and components, parts, containers, and supplies		(X)	302.9
Materials, ingredients, containers, and supplies, nsk		(X)	286.3

Source: 1992 *Economic Census*. Explanation of symbols used: (D): Withheld to avoid disclosure of competitive data; na: Not available; (S): Withheld because statistical norms were not met; (X): Not applicable; (Z): Less than half the unit shown; nec: Not elsewhere classified; nsk: Not specified by kind; - : zero; * : 10-19 percent estimated; ** : 20-29 percent estimated.

PRODUCT SHARE DETAILS

Product or Product Class	% Share	Product or Product Class	% Share
Fertilizers, mixing only	100.00	Mixed fertilizers, dry, shipped in bags of a gross weight of 10 kg (22 lb) or more, made by plants which do not manufacture fertilizer materials	29.82
Mixed fertilizers, shipped in packages, tablets, and similar forms of a gross weight not exceeding 10 kg (22 lb), made by plants which do not manufacture fertilizer materials	(D)	Mixed fertilizers, liquid, shipped in bulk or in packages of a gross weight of 10 kg (22 lb) or more, made by plants which do not manufacture fertilizer materials	15.60
Mixed fertilizers, dry, shipped in bulk, made by plants which do not manufacture fertilizer materials	(D)		

Source: 1992 *Economic Census*. The values shown are percent of total shipments in an industry. Values of indented subcategories are summed in the main heading. The symbol (D) appears when data are withheld to prevent disclosure of competitive information. The abbreviation nsk stands for 'not specified by kind' and nec for 'not elsewhere classified'.

INPUTS AND OUTPUTS FOR FERTILIZERS, MIXING ONLY

Economic Sector or Industry Providing Inputs	%	Sector	Economic Sector or Industry Buying Outputs	%	Sector
Nitrogenous & phosphatic fertilizers	33.6	Manufg.	Paints & allied products	29.6	Manufg.
Industrial inorganic chemicals, nec	14.5	Manufg.	Adhesives & sealants	15.1	Manufg.
Wholesale trade	7.3	Trade	Printing ink	12.4	Manufg.
Accounting, auditing & bookkeeping	7.1	Services	Paper mills, except building paper	8.5	Manufg.
Motor freight transportation & warehousing	5.9	Util.	Storage batteries	7.6	Manufg.
Clay, ceramic, & refractory minerals	3.2	Mining	Exports	6.6	Foreign
Cyclic crudes and organics	2.9	Manufg.	Miscellaneous plastics products	6.4	Manufg.
Railroads & related services	2.8	Util.	Tires & inner tubes	4.3	Manufg.
Miscellaneous plastics products	2.0	Manufg.	Plastics materials & resins	1.9	Manufg.
Business services nec	1.7	Services	Paperboard mills	1.7	Manufg.
Bags, except textile	1.6	Manufg.	Fabricated rubber products, nec	1.6	Manufg.
Pumps & compressors	1.6	Manufg.	Personal consumption expenditures	1.1	
Scrap	1.2	Scrap	Chemical preparations, nec	0.9	Manufg.
Electric services (utilities)	1.0	Util.	Rubber & plastics hose & belting	0.7	Manufg.
Nonmetallic mineral services	0.8	Mining	Asbestos products	0.2	Manufg.
Gas production & distribution (utilities)	0.8	Util.	Lead pencils & art goods	0.2	Manufg.
Petroleum refining	0.7	Manufg.	Hard surface floor coverings	0.1	Manufg.
Water transportation	0.7	Util.	Inorganic pigments	0.1	Manufg.
Equipment rental & leasing services	0.7	Services	Petroleum refining	0.1	Manufg.
Agricultural chemicals, nec	0.6	Manufg.	S/L Govt. purch., elem. & secondary education	0.1	S/L Govt
Animal & marine fats & oils	0.6	Manufg.			
Textile bags	0.6	Manufg.			
Banking	0.6	Fin/R.E.			
Advertising	0.6	Services			
Engineering, architectural, & surveying services	0.6	Services			
Miscellaneous repair shops	0.5	Services			
Alkalies & chlorine	0.4	Manufg.			
Communications, except radio & TV	0.4	Util.			
Eating & drinking places	0.4	Trade			
Maintenance of nonfarm buildings nec	0.3	Constr.			
Mechanical measuring devices	0.3	Manufg.			
Air transportation	0.3	Util.			

Continued on next page.

INPUTS AND OUTPUTS FOR FERTILIZERS, MIXING ONLY - Continued

Economic Sector or Industry Providing Inputs	%	Sector	Economic Sector or Industry Buying Outputs	%	Sector
Sanitary services, steam supply, irrigation	0.3	Util.			
Credit agencies other than banks	0.3	Fin/R.E.			
Business/professional associations	0.3	Services			
U.S. Postal Service	0.3	Gov't			
Chemical & fertilizer mineral	0.2	Mining			
General industrial machinery, nec	0.2	Manufg.			
Real estate	0.2	Fin/R.E.			
Legal services	0.2	Services			
Management & consulting services & labs	0.2	Services			
Metal barrels, drums, & pails	0.1	Manufg.			
Paper coating & glazing	0.1	Manufg.			
Insurance carriers	0.1	Fin/R.E.			
Automotive rental & leasing, without drivers	0.1	Services			
Computer & data processing services	0.1	Services			

Source: Benchmark Input-Output Accounts for the U.S. Economy, 1982, U.S. Department of Commerce, Washington, D.C., July 1991. Data, as reported in the source, are organized by the 1977 SIC structure in use in 1982 but have been matched, as closely as is possible, to the 1987 SIC structure used in this book.

OCCUPATIONS EMPLOYED BY SIC 287 - AGRICULTURAL CHEMICALS

Occupation	% of Total 1994	Change to 2005	Occupation	% of Total 1994	Change to 2005
Chemical plant & system operators	9.4	-5.2	Material moving equipment operators nec	2.1	-21.0
Blue collar worker supervisors	6.8	-24.7	Freight, stock, & material movers, hand	2.0	-36.8
Industrial machinery mechanics	5.3	-13.1	Bookkeeping, accounting, & auditing clerks	1.9	-40.8
Chemical equipment controllers, operators	5.2	-36.8	Chemists	1.7	-21.0
Sales & related workers nec	4.4	-21.0	General office clerks	1.7	-32.6
Crushing & mixing machine operators	3.4	-21.0	Hand packers & packagers	1.6	-32.2
Packaging & filling machine operators	3.4	-21.0	Industrial production managers	1.3	-21.1
Truck drivers light & heavy	3.4	-18.5	Electricians	1.3	-25.8
Helpers, laborers, & material movers nec	3.2	-21.0	Chemical engineers	1.3	-21.0
Science & mathematics technicians	2.9	-21.0	Marketing, advertising, & PR managers	1.2	-21.0
Maintenance repairers, general utility	2.8	-28.9	Clerical supervisors & managers	1.1	-19.1
General managers & top executives	2.8	-25.1	Machine feeders & offbearers	1.1	-28.8
Industrial truck & tractor operators	2.6	-21.0	Managers & administrators nec	1.0	-21.1
Secretaries, ex legal & medical	2.2	-28.1			

Source: Industry-Occupation Matrix, Bureau of Labor Statistics. These data relate to one or more 3-digit SIC industry groups rather than to a single 4-digit SIC. The change reported for each occupation to the year 2005 is a percent of growth or decline as estimated by the Bureau of Labor Statistics. The abbreviation nec stands for 'not elsewhere classified'.

LOCATION BY STATE AND REGIONAL CONCENTRATION

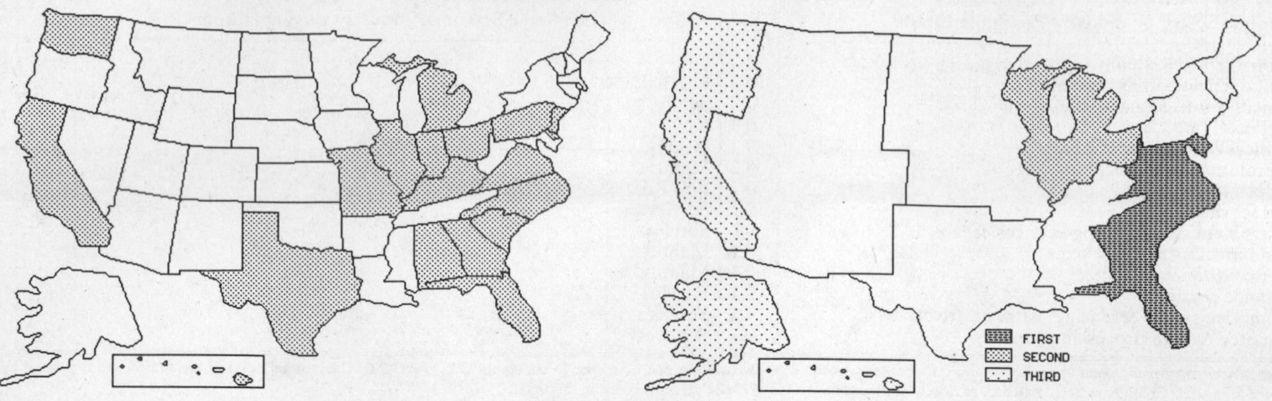

INDUSTRY DATA BY STATE

State	Establish-ments	Shipments			Employment				Cost as % of Shipments	Investment per Employee ($)
		Total ($ mil)	% of U.S.	Per Establ.	Total Number	% of U.S.	Per Establ.	Wages ($/hour)		
Florida	42	384.9	17.6	9.2	1,000	14.5	24	8.00	74.6	6,300
Ohio	31	233.8	10.7	7.5	900	13.0	29	8.69	70.6	7,333
Texas	26	215.9	9.9	8.3	500	7.2	19	11.00	84.9	-
Washington	15	127.1	5.8	8.5	300	4.3	20	13.00	95.6	8,000
California	25	99.0	4.5	4.0	500	7.2	20	10.00	61.3	3,800
South Carolina	13	75.0	3.4	5.8	300	4.3	23	9.50	60.0	-
Pennsylvania	13	62.9	2.9	4.8	300	4.3	23	12.33	71.1	-
Michigan	10	47.8	2.2	4.8	200	2.9	20	7.33	68.8	3,000
Kentucky	7	42.8	2.0	6.1	200	2.9	29	11.00	57.7	5,500
Illinois	14	42.4	1.9	3.0	200	2.9	14	11.00	79.2	-
Indiana	10	42.1	1.9	4.2	200	2.9	20	8.00	66.5	3,000
New Jersey	10	39.0	1.8	3.9	100	1.4	10	9.00	74.4	5,000
Virginia	9	27.3	1.2	3.0	200	2.9	22	8.50	75.5	2,000
North Carolina	19	(D)	-	-	175 *	2.5	9	-	-	-
Georgia	17	(D)	-	-	175 *	2.5	10	-	-	-
Alabama	15	(D)	-	-	375 *	5.4	25	-	-	-
Missouri	13	(D)	-	-	175 *	2.5	13	-	-	2,286
Hawaii	2	(D)	-	-	175 *	2.5	88	-	-	-
Delaware	1	(D)	-	-	175 *	2.5	175	-	-	-

Source: 1992 *Economic Census*. The states are in descending order of shipments or establishments (if shipment data are missing for the majority). The symbol (D) appears when data are withheld to prevent disclosure of competitive information. States marked with (D) are sorted by number of establishments. A dash (-) indicates that the data element cannot be calculated; * indicates the midpoint of a range.

2879 - AGRICULTURAL CHEMICALS, NEC

Shipments ($ million)

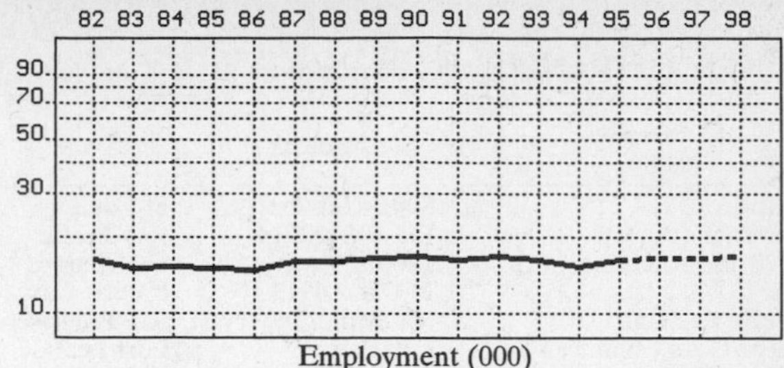

Employment (000)

GENERAL STATISTICS

Year	Companies	Establishments: Total	Establishments: with 20 or more employees	Employment: Total (000)	Employment: Production Workers (000)	Employment: Production Hours (Mil)	Compensation: Payroll ($ mil)	Compensation: Wages ($/hr)	Production ($ million): Cost of Materials	Production ($ million): Value Added by Manufacture	Production ($ million): Value of Shipments	Production ($ million): Capital Invest.
1982	286	330	119	16.5	9.7	18.7	403.8	10.93	2,449.2	2,948.9	5,436.1	288.5
1983		317	116	15.0	8.7	16.6	389.3	11.77	2,180.7	2,713.1	4,903.6	141.7
1984		304	113	15.3	9.2	18.4	433.4	12.07	2,599.2	3,051.4	5,694.6	200.4
1985		290	110	15.0	8.9	17.7	436.8	12.51	2,490.2	2,754.5	5,217.1	194.8
1986		273	110	14.8	8.8	18.0	477.6	13.40	2,396.7	2,976.2	5,357.0	200.6
1987	233	277	105	16.1	9.1	18.5	518.3	13.69	2,442.9	3,831.5	6,299.7	234.1
1988		254	105	15.9	8.9	18.5	531.7	13.98	2,761.6	4,285.8	6,977.6	331.6
1989		243	104	16.6	9.8	20.1	621.3	15.08	3,451.5	4,914.3	8,327.2	503.0
1990		237	106	17.0	10.2	21.1	664.1	16.27	3,414.9	5,142.7	8,538.9	557.7
1991		249	106	16.4	9.1	20.1	619.6	15.15	3,399.3	4,950.9	8,345.5	481.0
1992	224	263	111	16.9	9.6	20.2	670.2	15.59	3,645.8	5,519.5	9,151.4	428.4
1993		258	107	16.3	9.2	19.8	665.5	16.41	3,515.8	6,042.4	9,553.8	356.1
1994		228P	103P	15.3	8.8	18.4	700.2	18.40	3,695.2	5,897.8	9,636.1	299.3
1995		221P	102P	16.5P	9.3P	20.3P	745.9P	17.99P	3,937.0P	6,283.7P	10,266.6P	474.0P
1996		214P	101P	16.6P	9.4P	20.5P	774.1P	18.52P	4,105.7P	6,552.9P	10,706.5P	495.4P
1997		207P	101P	16.7P	9.4P	20.7P	802.3P	19.05P	4,274.3P	6,822.1P	11,146.3P	516.8P
1998		200P	100P	16.7P	9.4P	20.9P	830.5P	19.59P	4,443.0P	7,091.4P	11,586.2P	538.2P

Sources: 1982, 1987, 1992 *Economic Census*; *Annual Survey of Manufactures*, 83-86, 88-91, 93-94. Establishment counts for non-Census years are from *County Business Patterns*; establishment values for 83-84 are extrapolations. 'P's show projections by the editors. Industries reclassified in 87 will not have data for prior years.

INDICES OF CHANGE

Year	Companies	Establishments: Total	Establishments: with 20 or more employees	Employment: Total (000)	Employment: Production Workers (000)	Employment: Production Hours (Mil)	Compensation: Payroll ($ mil)	Compensation: Wages ($/hr)	Production ($ million): Cost of Materials	Production ($ million): Value Added by Manufacture	Production ($ million): Value of Shipments	Production ($ million): Capital Invest.
1982	128	125	107	98	101	93	60	70	67	53	59	67
1983		121	105	89	91	82	58	75	60	49	54	33
1984		116	102	91	96	91	65	77	71	55	62	47
1985		110	99	89	93	88	65	80	68	50	57	45
1986		104	99	88	92	89	71	86	66	54	59	47
1987	104	105	95	95	95	92	77	88	67	69	69	55
1988		97	95	94	93	92	79	90	76	78	76	77
1989		92	94	98	102	100	93	97	95	89	91	117
1990		90	95	101	106	104	99	104	94	93	93	130
1991		95	95	97	95	100	92	97	93	90	91	112
1992	100	100	100	100	100	100	100	100	100	100	100	100
1993		98	96	96	96	98	99	105	96	109	104	83
1994		87P	93P	91	92	91	104	118	101	107	105	70
1995		84P	92P	98P	97P	101P	111P	115P	108P	114P	112P	111P
1996		81P	91P	98P	97P	102P	116P	119P	113P	119P	117P	116P
1997		79P	91P	99P	98P	103P	120P	122P	117P	124P	122P	121P
1998		76P	90P	99P	98P	104P	124P	126P	122P	128P	127P	126P

Sources: Same as General Statistics. Values reflect change from the base year, 1992. Values above 100 mean greater than 92, values below 100 mean less than 92, and a value of 100 in the 82-91 or 93-98 period means same as 92. 'P's mark projections by the editors.

SELECTED RATIOS

For 1994	Avg. of All Manufact.	Analyzed Industry	Index	For 1994	Avg. of All Manufact.	Analyzed Industry	Index
Employees per Establishment	49	67	137	Value Added per Production Worker	134,084	670,205	500
Payroll per Establishment	1,500,273	3,068,402	205	Cost per Establishment	5,045,178	16,193,028	321
Payroll per Employee	30,620	45,765	149	Cost per Employee	102,970	241,516	235
Production Workers per Establishment	34	39	112	Cost per Production Worker	146,988	419,909	286
Wages per Establishment	853,319	1,483,631	174	Shipments per Establishment	9,576,895	42,227,116	441
Wages per Production Worker	24,861	38,473	155	Shipments per Employee	195,460	629,810	322
Hours per Production Worker	2,056	2,091	102	Shipments per Production Worker	279,017	1,095,011	392
Wages per Hour	12.09	18.40	152	Investment per Establishment	321,011	1,311,586	409
Value Added per Establishment	4,602,255	25,845,216	562	Investment per Employee	6,552	19,562	299
Value Added per Employee	93,930	385,477	410	Investment per Production Worker	9,352	34,011	364

Sources: Same as General Statistics. The 'Average of All Manufacturing' column represents the average of all manufacturing industries reported for the most recent complete year available. The Index shows the relationship between the Average and the Analyzed Industry. For example, 100 means that they are equal; 500 that the Analyzed Industry is five times the average; 50 means that the Analyzed Industry is half the national average. The abbreviation 'na' is used to show that data are 'not available'.

LEADING COMPANIES

Number shown: **53** Total sales ($ mil): **4,601** Total employment (000): **14.7**

Company Name	Address				CEO Name	Phone	Co. Type	Sales ($ mil)	Empl. (000)
Monsanto Co	800 N Lindbergh	St Louis	MO	63167	Hendrik Verfaillie	314-694-1000	D	1,676	3.3
Rhone-Poulenc Ag Co	PO Box 12014	Res Tri Pk	NC	27709	Charles Jongeward	919-549-2000	D	500	2.2
Sandoz Crop Protection Corp	1300 E Touhy Av	Des Plaines	IL	60018	Dale A Miller	708-699-1616	S	410*	1.2
Miles Inc	PO Box 4913	Kansas City	MO	64120	Hermann Werner	816-242-2000	D	300	1.2
ISK Enterprises Corp	600 Montgomery St	San Francisco	CA	94111	S Sekiguchi	415-249-4747	R	220*	1.1
Philipp Brothers Chemicals Inc	1 Parker Plz	Fort Lee	NJ	07024	Jack Bendheim	201-944-6020	R	160	0.5
Roussel Bio Corp	400 Sylvan Av	Englewood Clfs	NJ	07632	Larry Nouvel	201-871-0771	R	150	0.5
Aceto Corp	1 Hollow Ln	Lake Success	NY	11042	Arnold Frankel	516-627-6000	P	150	0.1
Mycogen Corp	4980 Carroll	San Diego	CA	92121	Jerry D Caulder	619-453-8030	P	115	0.8
Griffin Corp	PO Box 1847	Valdosta	GA	31603	George C Thornton	912-242-8635	R	100	0.3
Valent USA Corp	1333 N California	Walnut Creek	CA	94596		510-256-2700	S	83*	0.3
NOR-AM Chemical Co	2711 Centerville Rd	Wilmington	DE	19808	W Leo Ekins	302-892-3000	S	81*	0.3
Elf Atochem North America Inc	2000 Market St 21st	Philadelphia	PA	19103	PT Bromley	215-419-7885	D	70	<0.1
Enforcer Products Inc	PO Box 1068	Cartersville	GA	30120	Wayne Biasetti	404-386-0801	R	67*	0.2
Drexel Chemical Co	2487 Pennsylvania	Memphis	TN	38190	Robert D Shockey	901-774-4370	R	60	0.1
Fritz Industries Inc	PO Drawer 17040	Dallas	TX	75217	CF Weisend	214-285-5471	R	58	0.3
Troy Corp	PO Box 366	East Hanover	NJ	07936	Daryl D Smith	201-884-4300	R	55	0.2
American Vanguard Corp	2110 Davie Av	Commerce	CA	90040	Eric G Wintemute	213-264-3910	P	45	0.1
AMVAC Chemical Corp	4100 E Washington	Los Angeles	CA	90023	Eric G Wintemute	213-264-3910	S	45	0.1
LiphaTech Inc	3101 W Custer	Milwaukee	WI	53209	TH Winkofske	414-462-7600	S	30	<0.1
Consep Inc	213 SW Columbia	Bend	OR	97702	Volker G Oakey	503-388-3688	P	25	0.1
Bengal Chemical Co	PO Box 40487	Baton Rouge	LA	70835	Bob Leblanc	504-753-1313	R	23	<0.1
Riverdale Chemical Co	425 W 194th St	Glenwood	IL	60425	James R Champion	708-754-3330	R	20	<0.1
Ecogen Inc	PO Box 3023	Langhorne	PA	19047	James P Reilly Jr	215-757-1590	P	20	0.1
Prentiss Inc	21 Vernon St	Floral Park	NY	11001	Richard A Miller	516-326-1919	R	17	<0.1
Red Panther Chemical Co	PO Box 550	Clarksdale	MS	38614	Ross Davis	601-627-4731	R	15*	0.1
EcoScience Corp	377 Plantation St	Worcester	MA	01605	Haim B Gunner	508-754-0300	P	11	0.1
Pro-Serve Inc	400 E Brooks Rd	Memphis	TN	38109	WJ Roche	901-332-7052	S	7	0.1
Trece Corp	PO Box 6278	Salinas	CA	93912	Bill Lingren	408-758-0204	R	7*	<0.1
IBG Corp	PO Box 769	Clifton	NJ	07015	William L Burge	201-471-1070	R	7	<0.1
Walco Linck Co	PO Box 769	Clifton	NJ	07015	William L Burge	201-471-1070	S	7	<0.1
Athea Laboratories Inc	PO Box 23926	Milwaukee	WI	53223	Robert C Wellman	414-354-6417	S	6	<0.1
Research Products Company Inc	PO Box 1460	Salina	KS	67402	Jim R Allen	913-825-2181	D	6*	<0.1
International Sulphur Inc	I-30 W	Mount Pleasant	TX	75455	Robert H Acock	903-577-5500	R	6	0.3
Bay Zinc Co	PO Box 167	Moxee	WA	98936	Richard J Camp	509-248-4911	R	5*	<0.1
Summit Chemical Co	7657 Canton Ctr Dr	Baltimore	MD	21224	Lawrence Case	410-282-5200	R	5	<0.1
Curtis Dyna-Fog Ltd	PO Box 297	Westfield	IN	46074	C McGinnis	317-896-2561	R	4	<0.1
Soilserv Inc	PO Box 3650	Salinas	CA	93912	Dennis Sites	408-422-6473	S	4*	0.1
Huge Company Inc	PO Box 24198	St Louis	MO	63133	Tom Huge	314-725-2555	R	4	<0.1
Biofac Inc	PO Box 87	Mathis	TX	78368	Malcom Maedgen	512-547-3259	R	3*	<0.1
Burlington Scientific Corp	222 Sherwood Av	Farmingdale	NY	11735	M Blum	516-694-9000	R	3	<0.1
CH Products	PO Box 1000	Braddock	PA	15104	AH Zlotnik	412-351-2100	D	3	<0.1
JT Eaton and Co	1392 E Highland Rd	Twinsburg	OH	44087	Stanley Baker	216-425-7801	R	3*	<0.1
LittlePoint Corp	25th First St	Cambridge	MA	02141	Joe Knowles	617-621-1460	R	3	<0.1
Plato Industries Inc	2020 Holmes Rd	Houston	TX	77045	Thomas A Plato	713-797-0406	R	3*	<0.1
Agroline Inc	6525 Quail Hollow	Memphis	TN	38119		901-756-4422	S	2*	<0.1
Bacon Products Company Inc	PO Box 22187	Chattanooga	TN	37422	RL Bacon Jr	615-892-0414	R	2*	<0.1
Mycotech Corp	630 Utah Av	Butte	MT	59701	Robert Kearns	406-782-2386	R	2	<0.1
SAFFETA INC	PO Box 188	Safety Harbor	FL	34695	Kurt Avery	813-725-1177	R	2	<0.1
Westbridge Research Group	2776 Loker Av W	Carlsbad	CA	92008	Tina Koenemann	619-438-8639	P	1	<0.1
Nu-Method Pest Control Prod	8719 Linwood Av	Detroit	MI	48206	Albert Scott	313-898-1543	R	1*	<0.1
Stop-Shock Inc	5015 Sharp St	Dallas	TX	75247	Fred J Nayfa	214-630-2280	R	1	<0.1
EcoHealth Inc	110 Broad St	Boston	MA	02110	Fred DeFinis	617-742-2400	R	1	<0.1

Source: *Ward's Business Directory of U.S. Private and Public Companies*, Volumes 1 and 2, 1996. The company type code used is as follows: P - Public, R - Private, S - Subsidiary, D - Division, J - Joint Venture, A - Affiliate, G - Group. Sales are in millions of dollars, employees are in thousands. An asterisk (*) indicates an estimated sales volume. The symbol < stands for 'less than'. Company names and addresses are truncated, in some cases, to fit into the available space.

MATERIALS CONSUMED

Material		Quantity	Delivered Cost ($ million)
Materials, ingredients, containers, and supplies		(X)	3,167.8
Petroleum distillates used as solvents	mil lb	286.1	75.2
Other synthetic organic chemical solvents	mil lb	(S)	78.0
Synthetic organic pesticides and related synthetic organic agricultural chemical toxicants	mil lb	350.9*	758.3
Inorganic chemical toxicants	mil lb	479.9	192.5
Surfactants		(X)	62.6
All other organic and inorganic chemicals, nec		(X)	831.6
Plastics containers		(X)	87.6
Paperboard containers, boxes, and corrugated paperboard		(X)	72.4
Metal containers		(X)	43.8
All other materials and components, parts, containers, and supplies		(X)	772.0
Materials, ingredients, containers, and supplies, nsk		(X)	193.8

Source: 1992 *Economic Census*. Explanation of symbols used: (D): Withheld to avoid disclosure of competitive data; na: Not available; (S): Withheld because statistical norms were not met; (X): Not applicable; (Z): Less than half the unit shown; nec: Not elsewhere classified; nsk: Not specified by kind; - : zero; * : 10-19 percent estimated; ** : 20-29 percent estimated.

PRODUCT SHARE DETAILS

Product or Product Class	% Share
Agricultural chemicals, nec	100.00
Insecticidal preparations primarily for agricultural, garden, and health service use	19.03
Carbamate insecticidal preparations primarily for agricultural, garden, and health service use	32.67
Organo-phosphate insecticidal preparations primarily for agricultural, garden, and health service use	31.04
Biological (botanical, bacterial, etc.) insecticidal preparations primarily for agricultural, garden, and health service use	4.22
All other insecticidal preparations primarily for agricultural, garden, and health service use	19.41
Insecticidal preparations primarily for agricultural, garden, and health service use, nsk	12.67
Herbicidal preparations primarily for agricultural, garden, and health service use	51.04
Phenoxy compound herbicidal preparations primarily for agricultural, garden, and health service use	6.41
Urea herbicidal preparations primarily for agricultural, garden, and health service use	(D)
Triazine herbicidal preparations primarily for agricultural, garden, and health service use	24.78
Benzoic herbicidal preparations primarily for agricultural, garden, and health service use	1.64
All other herbicidal preparations primarily for agricultural, garden, and health service use	59.61
Herbicidal preparations primarily for agricultural, garden, and health service use, nsk	(D)
Fungicidal preparations primarily for agricultural, garden, and health service use	8.50
Fungicidal preparations containing inorganic compounds, primarily for agricultural, garden, and health service use	20.78
Fungicidal preparations containing organic compounds, primarily for agricultural, garden, and health service use	76.80
Fungicidal preparations primarily for agricultural, garden, and health service use, nsk	2.40
Other pesticidal preparations and agricultural chemicals, nec, primarily for agricultural use	7.22
Soil fumigants primarily for agricultural use	7.35
All other fumigants, including space, excluding household, primarily for agricultural use	(D)
Defoliants and desiccants primarily for agricultural use	(D)
All other pesticidal preparations and agricultural chemicals, nec, primarily for agricultural and health service use	83.59
Other pesticidal preparations and agricultural chemicals, nec, primarily for agricultural use, nsk	3.43
Household pesticidal preparations, including industrial exterminants	10.62
Household aerosol insecticides for crawling insects, except fumigants	30.74
Household nonaerosol insecticides for crawling insects, except fumigants	16.78
Household aerosol insecticides for flying insects, except fumigants	9.65
Household nonaerosol insecticides for flying insects, except fumigants	(D)
Household repellents and attractants for insects, birds, fish, and other animals, except for human and pet use	2.54
Insect repellents for human use	(D)
Household pet flea and tick products, including collars	15.32
Household rodenticides	5.83
Other household pesticidal preparations, nec, including fumigants	9.36
Household pesticidal preparations, including industrial exterminants, nsk	1.29
Agricultural chemicals, nec, nsk	3.60

Source: 1992 *Economic Census*. The values shown are percent of total shipments in an industry. Values of indented subcategories are summed in the main heading. The symbol (D) appears when data are withheld to prevent disclosure of competitive information. The abbreviation nsk stands for 'not specified by kind' and nec for 'not elsewhere classified'.

INPUTS AND OUTPUTS FOR AGRICULTURAL CHEMICALS, NEC

Economic Sector or Industry Providing Inputs	%	Sector	Economic Sector or Industry Buying Outputs	%	Sector
Cyclic crudes and organics	26.1	Manufg.	Feed grains	25.1	Agric.
Wholesale trade	8.8	Trade	Agricultural, forestry, & fishery services	11.6	Agric.
Banking	6.4	Fin/R.E.	Personal consumption expenditures	10.0	
Commercial printing	4.8	Manufg.	Oil bearing crops	9.6	Agric.
Business services nec	4.4	Services	Exports	8.7	Foreign
Industrial inorganic chemicals, nec	4.2	Manufg.	Fruits	6.4	Agric.
Advertising	3.6	Services	Cotton	4.5	Agric.
Motor freight transportation & warehousing	3.4	Util.	Food grains	4.4	Agric.
Petroleum refining	2.5	Manufg.	Vegetables	3.4	Agric.
Chemical & fertilizer mineral	2.4	Mining	Meat animals	1.8	Agric.
Agricultural chemicals, nec	2.4	Manufg.	Agricultural chemicals, nec	1.5	Manufg.
Electric services (utilities)	2.3	Util.	Sugar crops	1.2	Agric.
Wet corn milling	2.2	Manufg.	Tobacco	1.2	Agric.
Imports	2.2	Foreign	Poultry & eggs	0.9	Agric.
Gas production & distribution (utilities)	2.1	Util.	Drugs	0.9	Manufg.
Railroads & related services	2.0	Util.	Services to dwellings & other buildings	0.9	Services
Metal cans	1.7	Manufg.	S/L Govt. purch., elem. & secondary education	0.9	S/L Govt
Surface active agents	1.5	Manufg.	S/L Govt. purch., natural resource & recreation.	0.8	S/L Govt
Minerals, ground or treated	1.1	Manufg.	Landscape & horticultural services	0.6	Agric.
Sanitary services, steam supply, irrigation	1.1	Util.	Owner-occupied dwellings	0.6	Fin/R.E.
Miscellaneous repair shops	1.1	Services	Paints & allied products	0.5	Manufg.
Glass containers	1.0	Manufg.	S/L Govt. purch., higher education	0.5	S/L Govt
Paperboard containers & boxes	1.0	Manufg.	Greenhouse & nursery products	0.4	Agric.
Miscellaneous plastics products	0.8	Manufg.	Tree nuts	0.4	Agric.
Nonmetallic mineral services	0.7	Mining	Forest products	0.3	Agric.
Alkalies & chlorine	0.7	Manufg.	Railroads & related services	0.3	Util.
Metal barrels, drums, & pails	0.7	Manufg.	Management & consulting services & labs	0.3	Services
Noncomparable imports	0.7	Foreign	S/L Govt. purch., health & hospitals	0.3	S/L Govt
Pipe, valves, & pipe fittings	0.6	Manufg.	Dairy farm products	0.2	Agric.
Water transportation	0.6	Util.	Grass seeds	0.2	Agric.
Bags, except textile	0.5	Manufg.	Miscellaneous crops	0.2	Agric.
Engineering, architectural, & surveying services	0.5	Services	Fertilizers, mixing only	0.2	Manufg.
Clay, ceramic, & refractory minerals	0.4	Mining	Hotels & lodging places	0.2	Services
Maintenance of nonfarm buildings nec	0.4	Constr.	S/L Govt. purch., other general government	0.2	S/L Govt
Communications, except radio & TV	0.4	Util.	Water transportation	0.1	Util.
Eating & drinking places	0.4	Trade			
Equipment rental & leasing services	0.4	Services			

Continued on next page.

INPUTS AND OUTPUTS FOR AGRICULTURAL CHEMICALS, NEC - Continued

Economic Sector or Industry Providing Inputs	%	Sector	Economic Sector or Industry Buying Outputs	%	Sector
Fabricated metal products, nec	0.2	Manufg.			
Air transportation	0.2	Util.			
Credit agencies other than banks	0.2	Fin/R.E.			
Insurance carriers	0.2	Fin/R.E.			
Real estate	0.2	Fin/R.E.			
Royalties	0.2	Fin/R.E.			
Legal services	0.2	Services			
Management & consulting services & labs	0.2	Services			
General industrial machinery, nec	0.1	Manufg.			
Wood pallets & skids	0.1	Manufg.			
Security & commodity brokers	0.1	Fin/R.E.			
Accounting, auditing & bookkeeping	0.1	Services			
Automotive rental & leasing, without drivers	0.1	Services			
Colleges, universities, & professional schools	0.1	Services			
Computer & data processing services	0.1	Services			
State & local government enterprises, nec	0.1	Gov't			
U.S. Postal Service	0.1	Gov't			

Source: Benchmark Input-Output Accounts for the U.S. Economy, 1982, U.S. Department of Commerce, Washington, D.C., July 1991. Data, as reported in the source, are organized by the 1977 SIC structure in use in 1982 but have been matched, as closely as is possible, to the 1987 SIC structure used in this book.

OCCUPATIONS EMPLOYED BY SIC 287 - AGRICULTURAL CHEMICALS

Occupation	% of Total 1994	Change to 2005	Occupation	% of Total 1994	Change to 2005
Chemical plant & system operators	9.4	-5.2	Material moving equipment operators nec	2.1	-21.0
Blue collar worker supervisors	6.8	-24.7	Freight, stock, & material movers, hand	2.0	-36.8
Industrial machinery mechanics	5.3	-13.1	Bookkeeping, accounting, & auditing clerks	1.9	-40.8
Chemical equipment controllers, operators	5.2	-36.8	Chemists	1.7	-21.0
Sales & related workers nec	4.4	-21.0	General office clerks	1.7	-32.6
Crushing & mixing machine operators	3.4	-21.0	Hand packers & packagers	1.6	-32.2
Packaging & filling machine operators	3.4	-21.0	Industrial production managers	1.3	-21.1
Truck drivers light & heavy	3.4	-18.5	Electricians	1.3	-25.8
Helpers, laborers, & material movers nec	3.2	-21.0	Chemical engineers	1.3	-21.0
Science & mathematics technicians	2.9	-21.0	Marketing, advertising, & PR managers	1.2	-21.0
Maintenance repairers, general utility	2.8	-28.9	Clerical supervisors & managers	1.1	-19.1
General managers & top executives	2.8	-25.1	Machine feeders & offbearers	1.1	-28.8
Industrial truck & tractor operators	2.6	-21.0	Managers & administrators nec	1.0	-21.1
Secretaries, ex legal & medical	2.2	-28.1			

Source: Industry-Occupation Matrix, Bureau of Labor Statistics. These data relate to one or more 3-digit SIC industry groups rather than to a single 4-digit SIC. The change reported for each occupation to the year 2005 is a percent of growth or decline as estimated by the Bureau of Labor Statistics. The abbreviation nec stands for 'not elsewhere classified'.

LOCATION BY STATE AND REGIONAL CONCENTRATION

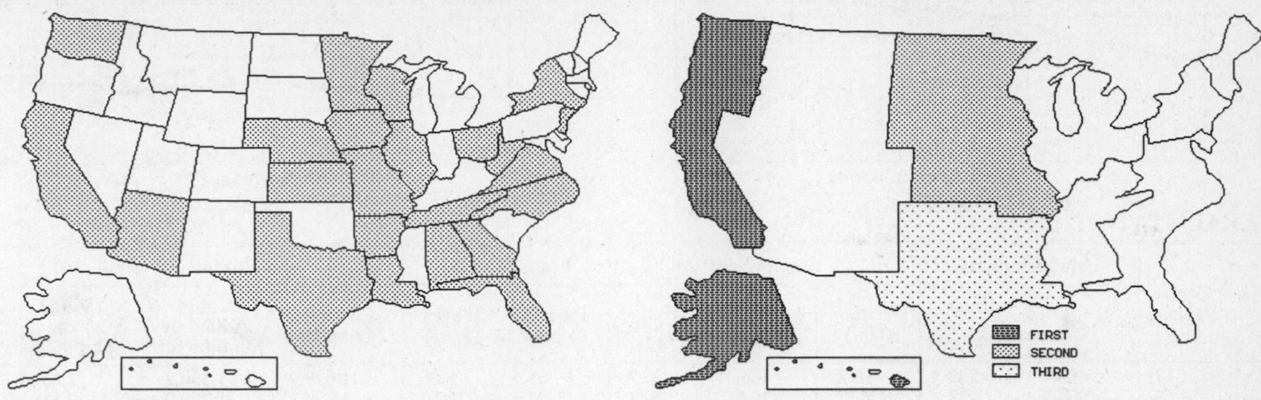

INDUSTRY DATA BY STATE

State	Establish-ments	Shipments			Employment				Cost as % of Shipments	Investment per Employee ($)
		Total ($ mil)	% of U.S.	Per Establ.	Total Number	% of U.S.	Per Establ.	Wages ($/hour)		
Missouri	18	1,634.4	17.9	90.8	2,700	16.0	150	12.93	31.8	-
Texas	25	1,157.0	12.6	46.3	2,200	13.0	88	17.57	41.5	25,409
California	36	636.6	7.0	17.7	1,800	10.7	50	18.24	44.9	19,778
Ohio	8	324.4	3.5	40.6	500	3.0	63	15.17	43.4	-
Illinois	11	240.1	2.6	21.8	400	2.4	36	13.17	61.1	-
Arkansas	4	167.1	1.8	41.8	400	2.4	100	10.20	40.8	9,250
North Carolina	8	159.8	1.7	20.0	200	1.2	25	17.50	46.7	10,000
Georgia	15	155.9	1.7	10.4	600	3.6	40	11.00	80.8	25,667
Florida	8	130.1	1.4	16.3	200	1.2	25	10.50	52.7	-
Minnesota	9	62.3	0.7	6.9	100	0.6	11	9.50	62.4	10,000
Washington	9	53.4	0.6	5.9	200	1.2	22	11.50	51.3	4,000
Wisconsin	6	39.8	0.4	6.6	300	1.8	50	8.00	42.5	6,000
Virginia	3	32.3	0.4	10.8	100	0.6	33	14.00	38.1	-
Louisiana	12	(D)	-	-	1,750 *	10.4	146	-	-	-
Iowa	8	(D)	-	-	750 *	4.4	94	-	-	-
New York	8	(D)	-	-	175 *	1.0	22	-	-	-
Tennessee	8	(D)	-	-	375 *	2.2	47	-	-	-
New Jersey	6	(D)	-	-	750 *	4.4	125	-	-	1,600
Arizona	5	(D)	-	-	175 *	1.0	35	-	-	5,143
Kansas	4	(D)	-	-	175 *	1.0	44	-	-	-
Alabama	3	(D)	-	-	1,750 *	10.4	583	-	-	-
Nebraska	2	(D)	-	-	175 *	1.0	88	-	-	-
West Virginia	2	(D)	-	-	1,750 *	10.4	875	-	-	-

Source: 1992 *Economic Census*. The states are in descending order of shipments or establishments (if shipment data are missing for the majority). The symbol (D) appears when data are withheld to prevent disclosure of competitive information. States marked with (D) are sorted by number of establishments. A dash (-) indicates that the data element cannot be calculated; * indicates the midpoint of a range.

2891 - ADHESIVES & SEALANTS

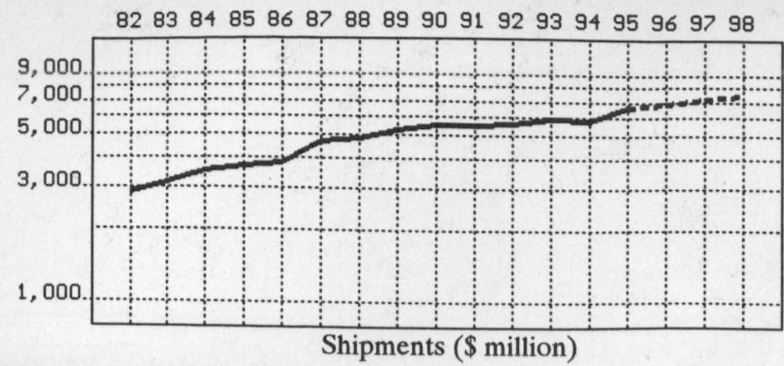

Shipments ($ million)

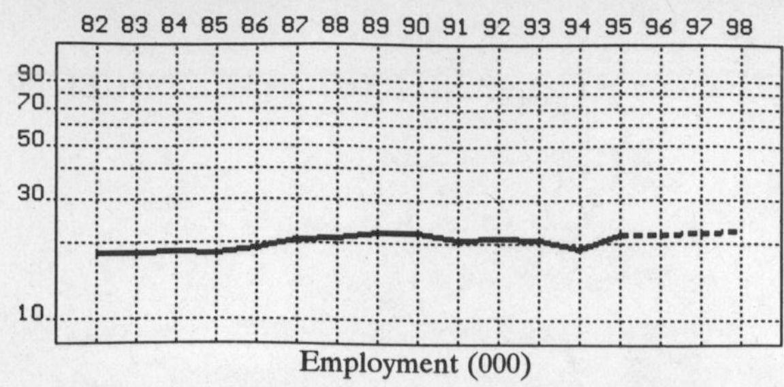

Employment (000)

GENERAL STATISTICS

Year	Companies	Establishments: Total	Establishments: with 20 or more employees	Employment: Total (000)	Employment: Production Workers (000)	Employment: Production Hours (Mil)	Compensation: Payroll ($ mil)	Compensation: Wages ($/hr)	Production ($ million): Cost of Materials	Production ($ million): Value Added by Manufacture	Production ($ million): Value of Shipments	Production ($ million): Capital Invest.
1982	517	683	233	18.2	10.9	20.7	365.5	8.36	1,699.9	1,150.2	2,856.7	72.4
1983		676	238	18.2	10.8	20.9	384.5	8.84	1,909.8	1,209.0	3,118.5	42.0
1984		669	243	18.5	11.4	22.3	415.8	8.94	2,075.0	1,428.5	3,488.2	55.8
1985		662	248	18.4	11.4	22.1	420.6	9.26	2,147.4	1,528.7	3,672.0	74.3
1986		664	259	19.3	11.6	22.4	441.8	9.45	2,233.3	1,596.4	3,838.3	82.8
1987	537	714	274	20.9	11.8	24.2	552.8	10.59	2,694.8	1,996.1	4,678.1	111.7
1988		722	295	21.2	11.8	23.9	579.0	11.05	2,875.6	1,994.8	4,859.9	118.4
1989		729	290	22.1	12.3	25.6	612.7	11.02	3,128.8	2,169.1	5,285.7	136.2
1990		710	294	22.1	11.9	24.6	633.3	11.50	3,167.9	2,333.2	5,485.1	127.1
1991		706	283	20.9	11.7	25.1	645.5	11.43	3,181.3	2,297.5	5,483.4	139.4
1992	517	685	271	21.1	11.6	24.5	677.8	12.41	3,016.9	2,643.0	5,659.0	189.6
1993		680	276	20.9	11.5	24.6	684.0	12.57	3,131.2	2,746.0	5,859.3	182.8
1994		709P	299P	19.2	11.3	23.7	687.1	13.41	3,338.5	2,503.2	5,848.9	204.2
1995		711P	304P	21.8P	11.9P	25.7P	761.3P	13.52P	3,730.8P	2,797.4P	6,536.2P	208.1P
1996		714P	308P	22.0P	11.9P	26.1P	792.0P	13.93P	3,886.6P	2,914.2P	6,809.2P	221.0P
1997		717P	313P	22.3P	12.0P	26.4P	822.7P	14.33P	4,042.4P	3,031.0P	7,082.1P	233.8P
1998		719P	318P	22.5P	12.0P	26.7P	853.5P	14.74P	4,198.2P	3,147.8P	7,355.1P	246.7P

Sources: 1982, 1987, 1992 *Economic Census*; *Annual Survey of Manufactures*, 83-86, 88-91, 93-94. Establishment counts for non-Census years are from *County Business Patterns*; establishment values for 83-84 are extrapolations. 'P's show projections by the editors. Industries reclassified in 87 will not have data for prior years.

INDICES OF CHANGE

Year	Companies	Establishments: Total	Establishments: with 20 or more employees	Employment: Total (000)	Employment: Production Workers (000)	Employment: Production Hours (Mil)	Compensation: Payroll ($ mil)	Compensation: Wages ($/hr)	Production ($ million): Cost of Materials	Production ($ million): Value Added by Manufacture	Production ($ million): Value of Shipments	Production ($ million): Capital Invest.
1982	100	100	86	86	94	84	54	67	56	44	50	38
1983		99	88	86	93	85	57	71	63	46	55	22
1984		98	90	88	98	91	61	72	69	54	62	29
1985		97	92	87	98	90	62	75	71	58	65	39
1986		97	96	91	100	91	65	76	74	60	68	44
1987	104	104	101	99	102	99	82	85	89	76	83	59
1988		105	109	100	102	98	85	89	95	75	86	62
1989		106	107	105	106	104	90	89	104	82	93	72
1990		104	108	105	103	100	93	93	105	88	97	67
1991		103	104	99	101	102	95	92	105	87	97	74
1992	100	100	100	100	100	100	100	100	100	100	100	100
1993		99	102	99	99	100	101	101	104	104	104	96
1994		103P	110P	91	97	97	101	108	111	95	103	108
1995		104P	112P	103P	102P	105P	112P	109P	124P	106P	116P	110P
1996		104P	114P	104P	103P	106P	117P	112P	129P	110P	120P	117P
1997		105P	116P	106P	103P	108P	121P	115P	134P	115P	125P	123P
1998		105P	117P	107P	104P	109P	126P	119P	139P	119P	130P	130P

Sources: Same as General Statistics. Values reflect change from the base year, 1992. Values above 100 mean greater than 92, values below 100 mean less than 92, and a value of 100 in the 82-91 or 93-98 period means same as 92. 'P's mark projections by the editors.

SELECTED RATIOS

For 1994	Avg. of All Manufact.	Analyzed Industry	Index
Employees per Establishment	49	27	55
Payroll per Establishment	1,500,273	969,505	65
Payroll per Employee	30,620	35,786	117
Production Workers per Establishment	34	16	46
Wages per Establishment	853,319	448,443	53
Wages per Production Worker	24,861	28,125	113
Hours per Production Worker	2,056	2,097	102
Wages per Hour	12.09	13.41	111
Value Added per Establishment	4,602,255	3,532,041	77
Value Added per Employee	93,930	130,375	139

For 1994	Avg. of All Manufact.	Analyzed Industry	Index
Value Added per Production Worker	134,084	221,522	165
Cost per Establishment	5,045,178	4,710,657	93
Cost per Employee	102,970	173,880	169
Cost per Production Worker	146,988	295,442	201
Shipments per Establishment	9,576,895	8,252,857	86
Shipments per Employee	195,460	304,630	156
Shipments per Production Worker	279,017	517,602	186
Investment per Establishment	321,011	288,128	90
Investment per Employee	6,552	10,635	162
Investment per Production Worker	9,352	18,071	193

Sources: Same as General Statistics. The 'Average of All Manufacturing' column represents the average of all manufacturing industries reported for the most recent complete year available. The Index shows the relationship between the Average and the Analyzed Industry. For example, 100 means that they are equal; 500 that the Analyzed Industry is five times the average; 50 means that the Analyzed Industry is half the national average. The abbreviation 'na' is used to show that data are 'not available'.

LEADING COMPANIES Number shown: **75** Total sales ($ mil): **13,954** Total employment (000): **71.8**

Company Name	Address				CEO Name	Phone	Co. Type	Sales ($ mil)	Empl. (000)
Avery Dennison Corp	150 N Orange	Pasadena	CA	91103	Charles D Miller	818-304-2000	P	2,857	15.4
Morton International Inc	100 N Riverside Plz	Chicago	IL	60606	S Jay Stewart	312-807-2000	P	2,850	13.1
National Starch&Chemical Co	10 Finderne Av	Bridgewater	NJ	08807	JA Kennedy	908-685-5000	S	1,809	8.0
HB Fuller Co	2400 Energy Pk Dr	St Paul	MN	55108	A L Andersen	612-645-3401	P	1,097	6.4
Dexter Corp	1 Elm St	Windsor Locks	CT	06096	K Grahame Walker	203-627-9051	P	975	4.7
Loctite Corp	10 Columbus Blv	Hartford	CT	06106	David Freeman	203-520-5000	P	613	4.0
Freudenberg-NOK	47690 E Anchor Ct	Plymouth	MI	48170	Joseph C Day	313-451-0020	R	500	3.6
LePage's Inc	120 Delta Dr	Pittsburgh	PA	15238	William L Baggett	412-967-0250	S	300*	0.3
WH Brady Co	PO Box 571	Milwaukee	WI	53201	K M Hudson	414-332-8100	P	256	1.9
Loctite Corp	705 North Mountain	Newington	CT	06111	Gerry Briels	203-278-1280	D	230*	1.4
Armor All Products Corp	6 Liberty Dr	Aliso Viejo	CA	92656	Kenneth M Evans	714-362-0600	P	217	0.1
Master Builders Inc	23700 Chagrin Blv	Cleveland	OH	44122	Truman Koehler	216-831-5500	S	210*	1.2
DAP Products Inc	PO Box 277	Dayton	OH	45401	John J McLaughlin	513-667-4461	S	180	0.8
Brady USA Inc	PO Box 2131	Milwaukee	WI	53201	Katherine Hudson	414-351-6600	S	130*	1.0
Lord Corp	PO Box 10038	Erie	PA	16514	Charles J Hora	814-868-3611	D	110*	0.7
Bostik Inc	211 Boston St	Middleton	MA	01949	John Fox	508-777-0100	S	100	0.5
Essex Specialty Products Inc	1250 Harmon Rd	Auburn Hills	MI	48326	George Braendle	810-391-6300	S	100	0.4
Dexter Automotive Mat	1 Dexter Dr	Seabrook	NH	03874	C Call	603-474-5541	D	90	0.5
Swift Adhesives	PO Box 13582	Res Tri Pk	NC	27709	Thomas A Walsh	919-990-7500	D	60*	0.4
Rohm Tech Inc	119 Authority Dr	Fitchburg	MA	01420	Ekkehard Grampp	508-342-5831	D	59	0.2
Gibson-Homans Co	1755 Enterprise	Twinsburg	OH	44087	G Golenberg	216-425-3255	R	50	0.3
Lord Corp	2000 W Grandview	Erie	PA	16514	CH Hora	814-868-3611	D	50	0.5
Sealmaster Inc	PO Box 2277	Sandusky	OH	44870	Duke Thorson	419-626-5470	R	44*	0.3
HB Fuller Automotive Products	31601 Research Pk	Madison H	MI	48071	Jim Conaty	313-585-2200	S	42*	0.3
Ohio Sealants Inc	7405 Production Dr	Mentor	OH	44060	Pete Longo	216-951-5678	S	40	0.1
TEC Inc	315 S Hicks Rd	Palatine	IL	60067	Frank A Devlin	708-358-9500	S	36*	0.2
Adhesive Research Inc	PO Box 100	Glen Rock	PA	17327	Erwin W Huber	717-235-7979	R	35	0.2
Fosroc Inc	150 Carley Ct	Georgetown	KY	40324	Andy Rodgers	502-863-6800	S	35	0.2
Mameco International Inc	4475 E 175th St	Cleveland	OH	44128	Jim Chessin	216-752-4400	S	35	0.1
Imperial Adhesives Inc	6315 Wiehe Rd	Cincinnati	OH	45237	Robert D Johnson	513-351-1300	S	33	0.2
Adco Products Inc	4401 Page Av	Michigan Ctr	MI	49254	Charles E Sax	517-764-0334	S	31	0.2
Adco Technologies Inc	4401 Page Av	Michigan Ctr	MI	49254	Charles E Sax	517-764-0334	P	31	0.2
Pratt and Lambert United Inc	PO Box 1505	Buffalo	NY	14240	Norm Doucet	716-873-2770	D	31	<0.1
Daubert Chemical Company Inc	4700 S Central Av	Chicago	IL	60638	Michael A Dwyer	708-496-7350	S	30	<0.1
L and L Products Inc	74100 Van Dyke	Romeo	MI	48065	Larry R Schmidt	313-752-3591	R	30	0.4
Uniseal Inc	1800 W Maryland St	Evansville	IN	47712	Randy Zahn	812-425-1361	S	29*	0.2
Coating Sciences Inc	111 Great Pond Dr	Windsor	CT	06002	Curtiss Rutsky	203-688-8000	R	25	0.1
Ensolite Inc	PO Box 2000	Mishawaka	IN	46544	Philip Foster	219-255-2181	S	25	0.2
Evode Tanner Industries	PO Box 1967	Greenville	SC	29602	Mike Prude	803-232-3893	D	25	<0.1
ITW Devcon	30 Endicott St	Danvers	MA	01923	David Perry	508-777-1100	D	25	0.1
TACC International Corp	Air Sta Indrial Pk	Rockland	MA	02370	MA Damelio	617-878-7015	R	25	0.1
Brady USA Inc	PO Box 298	Milwaukee	WI	53201	Mike Cherbeny	414-332-8100	D	22*	0.1
Columbia Cement Company Inc	159 Hanse Av	Freeport	NY	11520	Howard M Maisel	516-623-6000	S	22	<0.1
Harcros Chemicals Inc	600 Cortlandt St	Belleville	NJ	07109	Pinakin Patel	201-751-3000	S	20	<0.1
IPS Corp	PO Box 379	Gardena	CA	90248	Patel Naresh	310-366-3300	R	20	0.2
National Casein Co	601 W 80th St	Chicago	IL	60620	HT Cook	312-846-7300	R	20	0.2
Pacer Technology	9420 Santa Anita	R Cucamonga	CA	91730	James T Munn	909-987-0550	P	20	0.2
Beadex Manufacturing Company	401 C St NW	Auburn	WA	98001	Jim Ritchie	206-228-6600	S	19*	<0.1
Bemis Associates Inc	1 Bemis Way	Shirley	MA	01464	Steve Howard	508-425-6761	R	18	0.1
Aabitt Adhesives Inc	2403 N Oakley Av	Chicago	IL	60647	Benjamin Sarmas	312-227-2700	R	17	0.1
Ajax Adhesive Industries Inc	1314 W 21st St	Chicago	IL	60608	Murray Stempel	312-829-2990	R	17	<0.1
Schnee-Morehead Inc	PO Box 2465	Santa Fe Sprgs	CA	90670	RA Schnee	310-698-9735	R	17	0.2
Norwood Coated Products	57 Morehall Rd	Frazer	PA	19355	Charles Grandi	610-647-3500	S	16	<0.1
Chicago Adhesive Products Co	4658 W 60th St	Chicago	IL	60629	Ray W Kline Jr	312-581-1300	R	15	<0.1
Darworth Co	PO Box 639	Simsbury	CT	06070	Richard F Tripodi	203-843-1200	D	15*	0.1
Furane Aerospace Products	5121 San Fernando	Los Angeles	CA	90039	Kenneth D Cressy	818-247-6210	D	15	0.1
Grow Group Inc	PO Box 7026	Troy	MI	48007	Chuck Eisenstein	313-643-4600	D	15	0.1
Loctite Vsi Inc	405 Jordan Rd	Troy	NY	12180	William Gelinas	518-285-6300	S	15	0.1
Western Adhesives	1221 W 12th St	Kansas City	MO	64101	T Newman	816-421-3000	R	15	<0.1
Newport Adhesives	1822 Reynolds Av	Irvine	CA	92714	Terry Nogami	714-979-5250	S	14	<0.1
Sun Process Converting Inc	505 Bonnie Ln	Elk Grove Vill	IL	60007	M Moore	708-593-0447	R	14	0.2
UPACO Adhesives	3 E Spit Brook Rd	Nashua	NH	03060	Robert Bragole	603-888-5443	D	14	<0.1
Welco Manufacturing Company	1225 Ozark St	N Kansas City	MO	64116	Milton Strader	816-471-1788	R	14	<0.1
Ruvan Inc	1175 Diamond Av	Evansville	IN	47711	George Lutz	812-464-2488	R	13	0.2
White Lightning Products Corp	2375 130th Av NE	Bellevue	WA	98005	Roger Victor	206-881-5770	R	13	<0.1
Gaco Western Inc	PO Box 88698	Seattle	WA	98138	Peter Davis	206-575-0450	R	12	<0.1
Label Systems/OSI Corp	56 Cherry St	Bridgeport	CT	06605		203-333-5503	S	12*	<0.1
Permabond International	480 S Dean St	Englewood	NJ	07631	Harold Ruchlin	201-567-9494	D	12	<0.1
Evans Adhesive Corp	925 Old Henderson	Columbus	OH	43220	Ralph Kowaluk	614-451-2665	R	10	<0.1
Henkel Adhesives Corp	25817 Clawiter Rd	Hayward	CA	94545	JD Russo	510-786-3700	S	10*	0.1
Key Tech Corp	12420 Evergreen Dr	Mukilteo	WA	98275	Ron Carstens	206-347-3600	R	10*	<0.1
La-Co Industries Inc	250 N Washtenaw	Chicago	IL	60612	Donald Lytton	312-826-1700	R	10	0.1
Markal Co	250 N Washtenaw	Chicago	IL	60612	Daniel J Kleiman	312-826-1700	R	10	0.1
Roman Adhesives Inc	824 State St	Calumet City	IL	60409	Rick Bessette	708-891-0188	R	10	<0.1
Brady Coated Products Co	N144 Pioneer	Cedarburg	WI	53012	Matt Williamson	414-961-6073	S	9*	<0.1

Source: *Ward's Business Directory of U.S. Private and Public Companies*, Volumes 1 and 2, 1996. The company type code used is as follows: P - Public, R - Private, S - Subsidiary, D - Division, J - Joint Venture, A - Affiliate, G - Group. Sales are in millions of dollars, employees are in thousands. An asterisk (*) indicates an estimated sales volume. The symbol < stands for 'less than'. Company names and addresses are truncated, in some cases, to fit into the available space.

MATERIALS CONSUMED

Material		Quantity	Delivered Cost ($ million)
Materials, ingredients, containers, and supplies		(X)	2,715.8
Polyvinyl acetate resins purchased from other establishments	mil lb	360.8	112.1
All other plastics resins purchased from other establishments	mil lb	569.6	251.3
Synthetic rubber	mil lb	202.6	171.3
Starch and dextrin	mil lb	104.2	23.9
Industrial organic chemicals, nec, including synthetic organic		(X)	653.0
Industrial inorganic chemicals		(X)	115.0
Refined petroleum products, including mineral oil, naphtha solvents, petrolatum, waxes, etc.		(X)	226.6
Nonmetalic minerals and earths, ground or otherwise treated, used as extenders and fillers		(X)	204.7
Plastics containers		(X)	60.0
Metal containers		(X)	77.6
Paper and paperboard boxes and fiber cans, tubes and drums		(X)	87.4
All other materials and components, parts, containers, and supplies		(X)	359.6
Materials, ingredients, containers, and supplies, nsk		(X)	373.2

Source: 1992 *Economic Census*. Explanation of symbols used: (D): Withheld to avoid disclosure of competitive data; na: Not available; (S): Withheld because statistical norms were not met; (X): Not applicable; (Z): Less than half the unit shown; nec: Not elsewhere classified; nsk: Not specified by kind; - : zero; * : 10-19 percent estimated; ** : 20-29 percent estimated.

PRODUCT SHARE DETAILS

Product or Product Class	% Share
Adhesives and sealants	100.00
Natural base glues and adhesives	3.51
Hide (dry form) animal glues	8.44
Flexible, nonwarp, and liquid animal glues (not glue stock)	14.25
Protein adhesives, including casein, blood, fish, soybean, albumen, etc.	13.83
Dextrine adhesives	29.71
Starch adhesives	17.52
Other natural base glues and adhesives made from natural gums, shellac, silicates, lacquers, and oleoresinous varnishes	13.19
Natural base glues and adhesives, nsk	3.06
Synthetic resin and rubber adhesives, including all types of bonding and laminating adhesives	65.85
Epoxy adhesives	7.01
Phenolics and phenolic derivative adhesives, including resorcinol	5.97
Urea and modified urea adhesives	(D)
Polyvinyl acetate adhesives, latex-type	14.47
Polyvinyl acetate adhesives, solvent-type	(D)
Polyvinyl chloride and copolymer adhesives	1.27
Other vinyl polymer type adhesives	1.04
Acrylic adhesives	5.31
Cyanoacrylate adhesives	2.90
Polyester adhesives	2.03
Urethane adhesives	1.92
Styrenic adhesives	3.67
Hot melt adhesives, including polyamide, polyolefin, and other hot melts	10.24
Adhesive films, all types, including pressure-sensitive structural and nonstructural adhesive films	7.56
Rubber and synthetic resin combinations	13.53
Latex-type rubber cement, for sale as such	2.79
Solvent-type rubber cement, for sale as such	3.74
Other synthetic resin and rubber adhesives, including cellulose, nitrocellulose, polyamide, anaerobic, etc.	6.03
Synthetic resin and rubber adhesives, including all types of bonding and laminating adhesives, nsk	6.07
Structural sealants (load-bearing)	6.36
Synthetic base general-performance structural (load-bearing) sealants (PVAC, butyl, vinyl, acrylic, neoprene, etc.)	14.76
Synthetic base special-performance structural (load-bearing) sealants, including polysulfide, silicone, epoxy, urethane, etc.	76.83
Synthetic base structural (load-bearing) sealant preformed tapes (butyl, polybutene, polyisobutylene, etc.)	(D)
Structural sealants (load bearing), nsk	(D)
Nonstructural caulking compounds and sealants	15.03
Natural base nonstructural (nonload-bearing) caulks, modified and unmodified oil base	4.62
Natural bituminous base (coal tar or asphalt) nonstructural (nonload-bearing) caulking compounds and sealants	3.67
Synthetic base nonstructural (nonload-bearing) general performance sealants (PVAC, butyl, vinyl, acrylic, neoprene, etc.)	41.84
Synthetic base nonstructural (nonload-bearing) special performance sealants, including polysulfide, silcone, epoxy, urethane, etc.	34.87
Synthetic base nonstructural (nonload-bearing) sealant preformed tapes (butyl, polybutene, polyisobutylene, etc.)	15.00
Adhesives and sealants, nsk	9.25

Source: 1992 *Economic Census*. The values shown are percent of total shipments in an industry. Values of indented subcategories are summed in the main heading. The symbol (D) appears when data are withheld to prevent disclosure of competitive information. The abbreviation nsk stands for 'not specified by kind' and nec for 'not elsewhere classified'.

INPUTS AND OUTPUTS FOR ADHESIVES & SEALANTS

Economic Sector or Industry Providing Inputs	%	Sector	Economic Sector or Industry Buying Outputs	%	Sector
Cyclic crudes and organics	18.3	Manufg.	Personal consumption expenditures	5.4	
Inorganic pigments	12.3	Manufg.	Maintenance of nonfarm buildings nec	5.1	Constr.
Plastics materials & resins	11.6	Manufg.	Paperboard containers & boxes	5.0	Manufg.
Wholesale trade	6.1	Trade	Nonfarm residential structure maintenance	4.9	Constr.
Petroleum refining	6.0	Manufg.	Residential additions/alterations, nonfarm	4.6	Constr.
Motor freight transportation & warehousing	3.8	Util.	Paper coating & glazing	4.4	Manufg.
Synthetic rubber	3.5	Manufg.	Veneer & plywood	4.4	Manufg.
Metal cans	2.6	Manufg.	Wood products, nec	3.2	Manufg.
Adhesives & sealants	2.3	Manufg.	Glass & glass products, except containers	3.1	Manufg.
Industrial inorganic chemicals, nec	2.1	Manufg.	Motor vehicles & car bodies	3.0	Manufg.
Primary lead	2.1	Manufg.	Particleboard	2.8	Manufg.
Imports	1.9	Foreign	Miscellaneous plastics products	2.7	Manufg.
Paperboard containers & boxes	1.6	Manufg.	Exports	2.7	Foreign

Continued on next page.

INPUTS AND OUTPUTS FOR ADHESIVES & SEALANTS - Continued

Economic Sector or Industry Providing Inputs	%	Sector	Economic Sector or Industry Buying Outputs	%	Sector
Electric services (utilities)	1.6	Util.	Abrasive products	2.2	Manufg.
Nonmetallic mineral services	1.4	Mining	Nonwoven fabrics	2.1	Manufg.
Railroads & related services	1.4	Util.	Sanitary paper products	2.0	Manufg.
Wet corn milling	1.3	Manufg.	Electronic components nec	1.9	Manufg.
Engineering, architectural, & surveying services	1.3	Services	Adhesives & sealants	1.8	Manufg.
Gum & wood chemicals	1.2	Manufg.	Telephone & telegraph apparatus	1.8	Manufg.
Fabricated metal products, nec	1.1	Manufg.	Commercial printing	1.7	Manufg.
Fabricated rubber products, nec	1.1	Manufg.	Wood kitchen cabinets	1.4	Manufg.
Advertising	1.1	Services	Industrial buildings	1.3	Constr.
Miscellaneous plastics products	1.0	Manufg.	Asbestos products	1.3	Manufg.
Gas production & distribution (utilities)	0.9	Util.	Bookbinding & related work	1.2	Manufg.
Forestry products	0.8	Agric.	Surgical appliances & supplies	1.2	Manufg.
Clay, ceramic, & refractory minerals	0.8	Mining	Residential 1-unit structures, nonfarm	1.1	Constr.
Metal barrels, drums, & pails	0.7	Manufg.	Manifold business forms	1.1	Manufg.
Communications, except radio & TV	0.7	Util.	Metal stampings, nec	1.1	Manufg.
Water transportation	0.7	Util.	Communications, except radio & TV	1.1	Util.
Chemical preparations, nec	0.6	Manufg.	Bags, except textile	0.9	Manufg.
Maintenance of nonfarm buildings nec	0.5	Constr.	Envelopes	0.9	Manufg.
Air transportation	0.5	Util.	Fabricated structural metal	0.8	Manufg.
Eating & drinking places	0.5	Trade	Games, toys, & children's vehicles	0.8	Manufg.
Alkalies & chlorine	0.4	Manufg.	Millwork	0.7	Manufg.
Converted paper products, nec	0.4	Manufg.	Mineral wool	0.7	Manufg.
Nitrogenous & phosphatic fertilizers	0.4	Manufg.	Book printing	0.6	Manufg.
Banking	0.4	Fin/R.E.	Maintenance of farm residential buildings	0.5	Constr.
Equipment rental & leasing services	0.4	Services	Automotive stampings	0.5	Manufg.
Miscellaneous repair shops	0.4	Services	Fabricated rubber products, nec	0.5	Manufg.
Noncomparable imports	0.4	Foreign	Motor vehicle parts & accessories	0.5	Manufg.
Animal & marine fats & oils	0.3	Manufg.	Optical instruments & lenses	0.5	Manufg.
Pumps & compressors	0.3	Manufg.	Upholstered household furniture	0.5	Manufg.
Sanitary services, steam supply, irrigation	0.3	Util.	Wood household furniture	0.5	Manufg.
Real estate	0.3	Fin/R.E.	Motor freight transportation & warehousing	0.5	Util.
Legal services	0.3	Services	Maintenance of water supply facilities	0.4	Constr.
Management & consulting services & labs	0.2	Services	Boat building & repairing	0.4	Manufg.
Machinery, except electrical, nec	0.1	Manufg.	Cigarettes	0.4	Manufg.
Manifold business forms	0.1	Manufg.	Crowns & closures	0.4	Manufg.
Meat packing plants	0.1	Manufg.	Paper mills, except building paper	0.4	Manufg.
Pipe, valves, & pipe fittings	0.1	Manufg.	Sawmills & planning mills, general	0.4	Manufg.
Accounting, auditing & bookkeeping	0.1	Services	Shoes, except rubber	0.4	Manufg.
Computer & data processing services	0.1	Services	Wood pallets & skids	0.4	Manufg.
U.S. Postal Service	0.1	Gov't	Maintenance of farm service facilities	0.3	Constr.
			Maintenance of sewer facilities	0.3	Constr.
			Book publishing	0.3	Manufg.
			Converted paper products, nec	0.3	Manufg.
			Die-cut paper & board	0.3	Manufg.
			Fresh or frozen packaged fish	0.3	Manufg.
			House slippers	0.3	Manufg.
			Household furniture, nec	0.3	Manufg.
			Leather goods, nec	0.3	Manufg.
			Metal office furniture	0.3	Manufg.
			Paperboard mills	0.3	Manufg.
			Personal leather goods	0.3	Manufg.
			Women's handbags & purses	0.3	Manufg.
			Social services, nec	0.3	Services
			S/L Govt. purch., public assistance & relief	0.3	S/L Govt
			Farm service facilities	0.2	Constr.
			Maintenance of telephone & telegraph facilities	0.2	Constr.
			Metal household furniture	0.2	Manufg.
			Metal partitions & fixtures	0.2	Manufg.
			Miscellaneous publishing	0.2	Manufg.
			Mobile homes	0.2	Manufg.
			Motor homes (made on purchased chassis)	0.2	Manufg.
			Structural wood members, nec	0.2	Manufg.
			Truck trailers	0.2	Manufg.
			Wood partitions & fixtures	0.2	Manufg.
			Electric services (utilities)	0.2	Util.
			Federal Government purchases, national defense	0.2	Fed Govt
			S/L Govt. purch., higher education	0.2	S/L Govt
			Farm housing units & additions & alterations	0.1	Constr.
			Maintenance of local transit facilities	0.1	Constr.
			Maintenance of petroleum pipelines	0.1	Constr.
			Office buildings	0.1	Constr.
			Residential garden apartments	0.1	Constr.
			Warehouses	0.1	Constr.
			Gaskets, packing & sealing devices	0.1	Manufg.
			Hardwood dimension & flooring mills	0.1	Manufg.

Continued on next page.

INPUTS AND OUTPUTS FOR ADHESIVES & SEALANTS - Continued

Economic Sector or Industry Providing Inputs	%	Sector	Economic Sector or Industry Buying Outputs	%	Sector
			Manufacturing industries, nec	0.1	Manufg.
			Public building furniture	0.1	Manufg.
			Radio & TV receiving sets	0.1	Manufg.
			Refrigeration & heating equipment	0.1	Manufg.
			Sporting & athletic goods, nec	0.1	Manufg.
			Surgical & medical instruments	0.1	Manufg.
			Wood office furniture	0.1	Manufg.
			Air transportation	0.1	Util.
			Colleges, universities, & professional schools	0.1	Services
			Elementary & secondary schools	0.1	Services
			Religious organizations	0.1	Services
			Federal Government purchases, nondefense	0.1	Fed Govt

Source: Benchmark Input-Output Accounts for the U.S. Economy, 1982, U.S. Department of Commerce, Washington, D.C., July 1991. Data, as reported in the source, are organized by the 1977 SIC structure in use in 1982 but have been matched, as closely as is possible, to the 1987 SIC structure used in this book.

OCCUPATIONS EMPLOYED BY SIC 289 - MISCELLANEOUS CHEMICAL PRODUCTS

Occupation	% of Total 1994	Change to 2005	Occupation	% of Total 1994	Change to 2005
Crushing & mixing machine operators	7.9	-42.7	Maintenance repairers, general utility	2.0	-14.1
Sales & related workers nec	5.0	-4.6	Truck drivers light & heavy	1.9	-1.6
Chemical equipment controllers, operators	4.8	-14.1	Industrial production managers	1.9	-4.5
Science & mathematics technicians	4.6	-4.5	Hand packers & packagers	1.8	-18.2
Packaging & filling machine operators	3.8	-4.6	Bookkeeping, accounting, & auditing clerks	1.7	-28.4
General managers & top executives	3.6	-9.5	General office clerks	1.7	-18.6
Secretaries, ex legal & medical	3.5	-13.1	Extruding & forming machine workers	1.5	5.0
Assemblers, fabricators, & hand workers nec	3.3	-4.6	Clerical supervisors & managers	1.4	-2.4
Chemists	3.1	-4.6	Freight, stock, & material movers, hand	1.3	-23.6
Chemical plant & system operators	2.7	43.1	Industrial truck & tractor operators	1.2	-4.5
Machine operators nec	2.6	-15.9	Managers & administrators nec	1.2	-4.6
Traffic, shipping, & receiving clerks	2.3	-8.2	Chemical engineers	1.2	-4.6
Industrial machinery mechanics	2.2	5.0	Machinists	1.1	-4.6
Inspectors, testers, & graders, precision	2.1	-4.6	Order clerks, materials, merchandise, & service	1.0	-6.7
Marketing, advertising, & PR managers	2.0	-4.6			

Source: Industry-Occupation Matrix, Bureau of Labor Statistics. These data relate to one or more 3-digit SIC industry groups rather than to a single 4-digit SIC. The change reported for each occupation to the year 2005 is a percent of growth or decline as estimated by the Bureau of Labor Statistics. The abbreviation nec stands for 'not elsewhere classified'.

LOCATION BY STATE AND REGIONAL CONCENTRATION

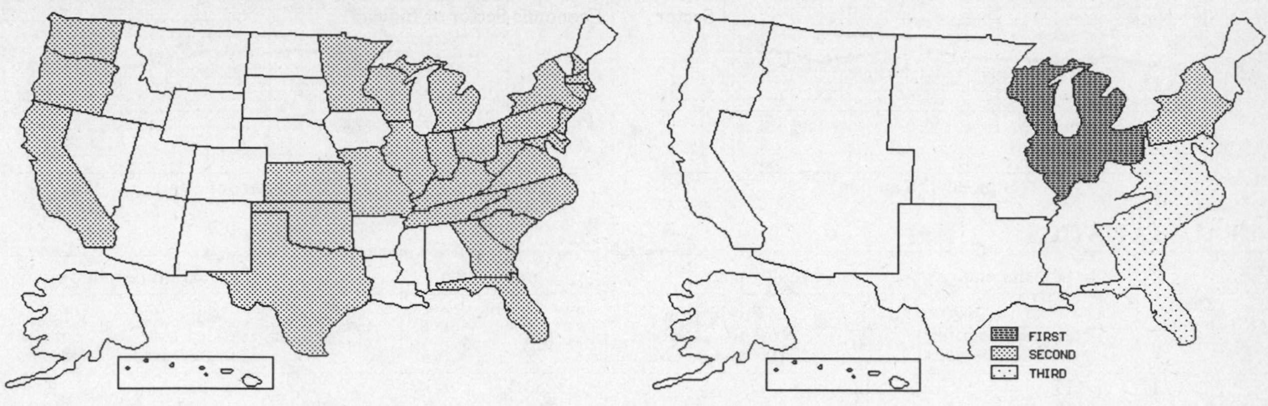

INDUSTRY DATA BY STATE

State	Establish-ments	Shipments			Employment				Cost as % of Shipments	Investment per Employee ($)
		Total ($ mil)	% of U.S.	Per Establ.	Total Number	% of U.S.	Per Establ.	Wages ($/hour)		
Ohio	53	817.2	14.4	15.4	3,100	14.7	58	12.94	50.0	5,419
Illinois	48	598.9	10.6	12.5	1,700	8.1	35	12.41	55.0	6,294
New Jersey	53	457.0	8.1	8.6	1,500	7.1	28	12.89	56.5	7,467
California	75	400.9	7.1	5.3	2,100	10.0	28	13.91	49.1	4,238
Kentucky	9	400.7	7.1	44.5	800	3.8	89	14.25	65.3	34,000
Michigan	36	337.1	6.0	9.4	1,300	6.2	36	13.69	51.0	5,154
Missouri	22	285.0	5.0	13.0	1,200	5.7	55	10.67	47.5	15,333
Georgia	38	262.9	4.6	6.9	700	3.3	18	13.13	52.8	7,143
Pennsylvania	40	231.0	4.1	5.8	700	3.3	18	14.50	52.8	7,000
Texas	38	207.8	3.7	5.5	700	3.3	18	10.13	52.5	7,714
New York	29	173.9	3.1	6.0	800	3.8	28	9.67	49.3	4,250
North Carolina	20	164.3	2.9	8.2	400	1.9	20	13.40	58.5	12,000
Connecticut	13	155.8	2.8	12.0	1,500	7.1	115	8.83	46.7	-
Massachusetts	24	114.1	2.0	4.8	600	2.8	25	13.00	52.7	3,000
Maryland	8	109.7	1.9	13.7	600	2.8	75	15.14	35.0	-
Oregon	11	99.6	1.8	9.1	200	0.9	18	12.67	65.2	7,000
Wisconsin	19	94.7	1.7	5.0	300	1.4	16	10.25	59.6	-
Minnesota	10	74.5	1.3	7.4	200	0.9	20	14.00	51.0	3,000
Washington	14	62.5	1.1	4.5	200	0.9	14	15.50	45.4	-
Oklahoma	6	59.7	1.1	9.9	200	0.9	33	15.00	54.1	-
New Hampshire	6	46.7	0.8	7.8	300	1.4	50	15.00	49.3	-
South Carolina	4	39.6	0.7	9.9	100	0.5	25	21.00	58.1	-
Kansas	9	25.3	0.4	2.8	100	0.5	11	18.00	60.1	3,000
Florida	20	(D)	-	-	175 *	0.8	9	-	-	-
Indiana	19	(D)	-	-	375 *	1.8	20	-	-	3,200
Tennessee	9	(D)	-	-	175 *	0.8	19	-	-	11,429
Virginia	7	(D)	-	-	175 *	0.8	25	-	-	-
West Virginia	4	(D)	-	-	375 *	1.8	94	-	-	-

Source: 1992 *Economic Census*. The states are in descending order of shipments or establishments (if shipment data are missing for the majority). The symbol (D) appears when data are withheld to prevent disclosure of competitive information. States marked with (D) are sorted by number of establishments. A dash (-) indicates that the data element cannot be calculated; * indicates the midpoint of a range.

2892 - EXPLOSIVES

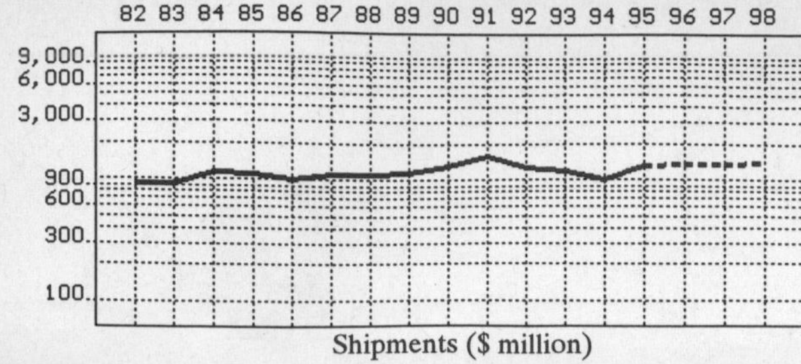

Shipments ($ million)

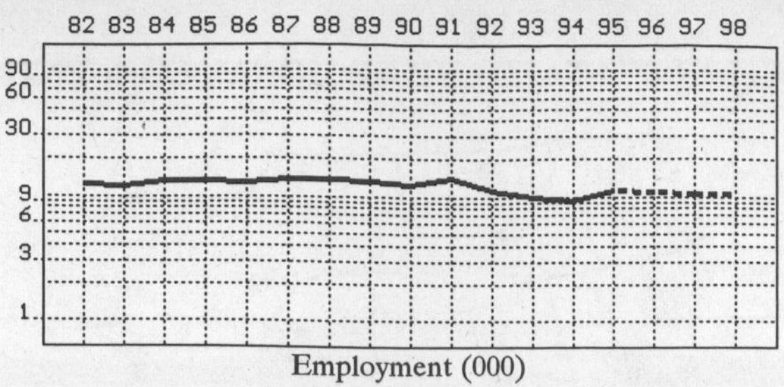

Employment (000)

GENERAL STATISTICS

Year	Companies	Establishments		Employment			Compensation		Production ($ million)			
		Total	with 20 or more employees	Total (000)	Production Workers (000)	Production Hours (Mil)	Payroll ($ mil)	Wages ($/hr)	Cost of Materials	Value Added by Manufacture	Value of Shipments	Capital Invest.
1982	73	114	45	12.3	7.9	15.1	253.3	9.54	340.8	580.7	922.7	32.9
1983		116	46	12.0	7.9	14.9	266.9	10.47	308.9	612.7	919.7	22.0
1984		118	47	13.3	8.9	17.5	307.3	10.46	392.9	756.1	1,135.7	34.9
1985		120	47	13.2	8.8	16.6	325.4	11.13	379.5	740.8	1,110.7	48.4
1986		116	49	13.0	8.5	16.0	331.8	11.58	351.7	667.7	1,020.3	32.2
1987	77	132	45	13.8	9.2	17.9	349.2	11.45	362.6	758.4	1,117.8	22.6
1988		126	45	13.6	9.1	17.8	359.1	11.83	361.6	764.3	1,128.4	26.8
1989		116	45	13.1	8.9	17.3	342.8	11.85	383.4	775.6	1,151.0	49.3
1990		129	46	12.3	9.4	17.6	380.2	13.10	454.1	874.4	1,324.6	43.6
1991		135	52	14.0	9.2	16.9	401.2	13.70	573.7	1,020.8	1,592.4	84.3
1992	65	123	50	11.4	7.5	13.4	338.6	14.83	402.1	851.7	1,252.0	31.7
1993		119	52	10.0	6.8	13.2	314.7	13.78	385.2	793.6	1,172.6	49.1
1994		128P	50P	9.1	6.4	12.6	303.1	14.49	421.0	613.1	1,023.4	52.6
1995		129P	51P	11.0P	7.7P	14.5P	366.5P	15.05P	540.5P	787.2P	1,314.0P	56.1P
1996		130P	51P	10.8P	7.6P	14.3P	371.9P	15.46P	550.5P	801.7P	1,338.3P	58.3P
1997		131P	52P	10.6P	7.5P	14.1P	377.2P	15.87P	560.5P	816.3P	1,362.6P	60.5P
1998		132P	52P	10.4P	7.4P	13.9P	382.6P	16.28P	570.5P	830.8P	1,386.8P	62.7P

Sources: 1982, 1987, 1992 *Economic Census*; *Annual Survey of Manufactures*, 83-86, 88-91, 93-94. Establishment counts for non-Census years are from *County Business Patterns*; establishment values for 83-84 are extrapolations. 'P's show projections by the editors. Industries reclassified in 87 will not have data for prior years.

INDICES OF CHANGE

Year	Companies	Establishments		Employment			Compensation		Production ($ million)			
		Total	with 20 or more employees	Total (000)	Production Workers (000)	Production Hours (Mil)	Payroll ($ mil)	Wages ($/hr)	Cost of Materials	Value Added by Manufacture	Value of Shipments	Capital Invest.
1982	112	93	90	108	105	113	75	64	85	68	74	104
1983		94	92	105	105	111	79	71	77	72	73	69
1984		96	94	117	119	131	91	71	98	89	91	110
1985		98	94	116	117	124	96	75	94	87	89	153
1986		94	98	114	113	119	98	78	87	78	81	102
1987	118	107	90	121	123	134	103	77	90	89	89	71
1988		102	90	119	121	133	106	80	90	90	90	85
1989		94	90	115	119	129	101	80	95	91	92	156
1990		105	92	108	125	131	112	88	113	103	106	138
1991		110	104	123	123	126	118	92	143	120	127	266
1992	100	100	100	100	100	100	100	100	100	100	100	100
1993		97	104	88	91	99	93	93	96	93	94	155
1994		104P	101P	80	85	94	90	98	105	72	82	166
1995		105P	102P	96P	102P	108P	108P	101P	134P	92P	105P	177P
1996		106P	103P	95P	101P	107P	110P	104P	137P	94P	107P	184P
1997		107P	104P	93P	100P	105P	111P	107P	139P	96P	109P	191P
1998		107P	104P	91P	99P	104P	113P	110P	142P	98P	111P	198P

Sources: Same as General Statistics. Values reflect change from the base year, 1992. Values above 100 mean greater than 92, values below 100 mean less than 92, and a value of 100 in the 82-91 or 93-98 period means same as 92. 'P's mark projections by the editors.

SELECTED RATIOS

For 1994	Avg. of All Manufact.	Analyzed Industry	Index
Employees per Establishment	49	71	145
Payroll per Establishment	1,500,273	2,362,934	158
Payroll per Employee	30,620	33,308	109
Production Workers per Establishment	34	50	145
Wages per Establishment	853,319	1,423,327	167
Wages per Production Worker	24,861	28,527	115
Hours per Production Worker	2,056	1,969	96
Wages per Hour	12.09	14.49	120
Value Added per Establishment	4,602,255	4,779,660	104
Value Added per Employee	93,930	67,374	72

For 1994	Avg. of All Manufact.	Analyzed Industry	Index
Value Added per Production Worker	134,084	95,797	71
Cost per Establishment	5,045,178	3,282,069	65
Cost per Employee	102,970	46,264	45
Cost per Production Worker	146,988	65,781	45
Shipments per Establishment	9,576,895	7,978,313	83
Shipments per Employee	195,460	112,462	58
Shipments per Production Worker	279,017	159,906	57
Investment per Establishment	321,011	410,064	128
Investment per Employee	6,552	5,780	88
Investment per Production Worker	9,352	8,219	88

Sources: Same as General Statistics. The 'Average of All Manufacturing' column represents the average of all manufacturing industries reported for the most recent complete year available. The Index shows the relationship between the Average and the Analyzed Industry. For example, 100 means that they are equal; 500 that the Analyzed Industry is five times the average; 50 means that the Analyzed Industry is half the national average. The abbreviation 'na' is used to show that data are 'not available'.

LEADING COMPANIES

Number shown: **22** Total sales ($ mil): **1,842** Total employment (000): **9.8**

Company Name	Address				CEO Name	Phone	Co. Type	Sales ($ mil)	Empl. (000)
ETI Explosives Techn Intern	3511 Silverside Rd	Wilmington	DE	19810	Darryl Dillenback	302-477-3500	R	400	0.4
Dyno Nobel Inc	50 S Main St	Salt Lake City	UT	84144	Gary R Lindsay	801-364-4800	S	280	2.0
LSB Industries Inc	16 S Pennsylvania	Oklahoma City	OK	73107	Jack E Golsen	405-235-4546	P	250	1.4
ICI Explosives USA Inc	15301 Dallas St	Dallas	TX	75248	D W Waugaman	214-387-2400	S	240*	1.6
Ensign-Bickford Industries Inc	PO Box 7	Simsbury	CT	06070	Herman J Fonteyne	203-658-4411	R	190	1.2
Austin Powder Co	25800 Science Pk Dr	Cleveland	OH	44122	David Gleason	216-464-2400	R	145	0.9
Holston Defense Corp	PO Box 1483	Kingsport	TN	37662	JW Hoard	615-247-6099	S	75	0.6
Apache Nitrogen Products Inc	PO Box 700	Benson	AZ	85602	RD Willis	602-720-2217	R	30	0.1
Hitech Holding Inc	PO Box 3112	East Camden	AR	71701	Gene Hill	501-798-4171	S	30	0.1
Buckley Powder Co	42 Inverness Dr E	Englewood	CO	80112	Daniel J Buckley	303-790-7007	S	28	<0.1
OEA Aerospace Inc	PO Box KK	Fairfield	CA	94533	GB Huber	707-422-1880	S	28	0.3
Trojan Corp	PO Box 310	Spanish Fork	UT	84660	John Feasler	801-798-8613	S	26	0.1
Pacific Scientific Co	7403 W Boston St	Chandler	AZ	85226	Robert L Day	602-961-0023	D	20*	0.2
HITECH Inc	PO Box 3112	East Camden	AR	71701	Gene Hill	501-798-4171	S	20	0.1
Mining Services Intern Corp	5284 S Com Dr	Salt Lake City	UT	84107	John T Day	801-261-5666	P	19	<0.1
Hodgdon Powder Company Inc	PO Box 2932	Shawnee Msn	KS	66202	RE Hodgdon	913-362-9455	R	16	<0.1
Propellex Corp	PO Box 387	Edwardsville	IL	62025	RG Jones	618-656-3400	R	11*	0.1
Accurate Arms Company Inc	5891 Hwy 230 W	McEwen	TN	37101	John Sonday	615-729-4207	D	10	<0.1
Accurate Arms Company Inc	5891 Hwy 230 W	McEwen	TN	37101	John Sonday	615-729-4207	R	10	<0.1
Technical Ordnance Inc	PO Box 800	St Bonifacius	MN	55375	NH Hoffman	612-446-1526	R	8	0.1
Cartridge Actuated Devices Inc	123 Clinton Rd	Fairfield	NJ	07004	Ralph Dodd	201-575-1312	R	4	<0.1
Ladshaw Explosives Inc	393 Landa St	New Braunfels	TX	78130	John Ladshaw	210-625-4789	R	4	<0.1

Source: *Ward's Business Directory of U.S. Private and Public Companies*, Volumes 1 and 2, 1996. The company type code used is as follows: P - Public, R - Private, S - Subsidiary, D - Division, J - Joint Venture, A - Affiliate, G - Group. Sales are in millions of dollars, employees are in thousands. An asterisk (*) indicates an estimated sales volume. The symbol < stands for 'less than'. Company names and addresses are truncated, in some cases, to fit into the available space.

MATERIALS CONSUMED

Material		Quantity	Delivered Cost ($ million)
Materials, ingredients, containers, and supplies		(X)	303.2
Ammonia, synthetic anhydrous (100 percent NH3)	1,000 s tons	(D)	(D)
Ammonium nitrate (100 percent NH4NO3)	1,000 s tons	394.0	44.2
Nitric acid (100 percent HNO3)	1,000 s tons	37.4	5.9
Sulfuric acid (100 percent H2SO4), except spent	1,000 s tons	48.5*	3.4
High explosives, including PETN, TNT, azides, and fulminates		(X)	14.0
Paper and paperboard containers, including shipping sacks and other paper packaging supplies		(X)	14.0
All other materials and components, parts, containers, and supplies		(X)	179.1
Materials, ingredients, containers, and supplies, nsk		(X)	(D)

Source: 1992 *Economic Census*. Explanation of symbols used: (D): Withheld to avoid disclosure of competitive data; na: Not available; (S): Withheld because statistical norms were not met; (X): Not applicable; (Z): Less than half the unit shown; nec: Not elsewhere classified; nsk: Not specified by kind; - : zero; * : 10-19 percent estimated; ** : 20-29 percent estimated.

PRODUCT SHARE DETAILS

Product or Product Class	% Share	Product or Product Class	% Share
Explosives	100.00	dynamites, black blasting powder, nitroglycerin, etc.	(D)
Industrial ammonium nitrate explosives, fuel sensitized, except slurry	13.54	Propellants, including smokeless and black powder	(D)
Industrial water gel and slurry explosives, cap and noncap sensitive, except permissible slurries	5.60	Blasting accessories, including blasting caps, squibs, ignitors, detonating primers, fuses, detonating cord, etc.	31.93
Other industrial explosives, including permissibles,		Other explosives, including military detonators, jet starters, fuse and explosive assemblies, etc.	12.35

Source: 1992 *Economic Census*. The values shown are percent of total shipments in an industry. Values of indented subcategories are summed in the main heading. The symbol (D) appears when data are withheld to prevent disclosure of competitive information. The abbreviation nsk stands for 'not specified by kind' and nec for 'not elsewhere classified'.

INPUTS AND OUTPUTS FOR EXPLOSIVES

Economic Sector or Industry Providing Inputs	%	Sector	Economic Sector or Industry Buying Outputs	%	Sector
Pumps & compressors	13.5	Manufg.	Federal Government purchases, national defense	33.5	Fed Govt
Nitrogenous & phosphatic fertilizers	10.5	Manufg.	Coal	13.4	Mining
Explosives	8.7	Manufg.	Exports	5.9	Foreign
Wholesale trade	7.8	Trade	Explosives	5.5	Manufg.
Cyclic crudes and organics	6.5	Manufg.	Chemical preparations, nec	4.8	Manufg.
Miscellaneous plastics products	5.5	Manufg.	Logging camps & logging contractors	4.0	Manufg.
Electric services (utilities)	4.7	Util.	Cement, hydraulic	3.7	Manufg.
Imports	4.7	Foreign	Small arms	3.7	Manufg.
Engineering, architectural, & surveying services	4.4	Services	Dimension, crushed & broken stone	3.5	Mining
Gas production & distribution (utilities)	2.9	Util.	Ordnance & accessories nec	3.5	Manufg.
Petroleum refining	2.7	Manufg.	Small arms ammunition	3.0	Manufg.
Crude petroleum & natural gas	2.0	Mining	Motion pictures	2.4	Services
Motor freight transportation & warehousing	1.7	Util.	Highway & street construction	1.4	Constr.
Eating & drinking places	1.7	Trade	Nonferrous metal ores, except copper	1.3	Mining
Advertising	1.7	Services	Ready-mixed concrete	1.3	Manufg.
Maintenance of nonfarm buildings nec	1.6	Constr.	Iron & ferroalloy ores	1.2	Mining
Paperboard containers & boxes	1.6	Manufg.	Lime	1.2	Manufg.
Communications, except radio & TV	1.2	Util.	Copper ore	1.1	Mining
Wood products, nec	1.1	Manufg.	Change in business inventories	0.8	In House
Sanitary services, steam supply, irrigation	1.0	Util.	Sewer system facility construction	0.6	Constr.
Miscellaneous repair shops	1.0	Services	Chemical & fertilizer mineral	0.5	Mining
Noncomparable imports	1.0	Foreign	Office buildings	0.3	Constr.
Copper rolling & drawing	0.9	Manufg.	Petroleum, gas, & solid mineral exploration	0.3	Constr.
Railroads & related services	0.8	Util.	Sand & gravel	0.2	Mining
Legal services	0.8	Services	Industrial buildings	0.2	Constr.
Air transportation	0.7	Util.	Ammunition, except for small arms, nec	0.2	Manufg.
Management & consulting services & labs	0.7	Services	Brick & structural clay tile	0.2	Manufg.
Equipment rental & leasing services	0.6	Services	Clay refractories	0.2	Manufg.
Coal	0.5	Mining	Gypsum products	0.2	Manufg.
Banking	0.5	Fin/R.E.	Structural clay products, nec	0.2	Manufg.
U.S. Postal Service	0.5	Gov't	Clay, ceramic, & refractory minerals	0.1	Mining
Machinery, except electrical, nec	0.4	Manufg.	Nonmetallic mineral services	0.1	Mining
Soap & other detergents	0.4	Manufg.	Access structures for mineral development	0.1	Constr.
Water transportation	0.4	Util.	Maintenance of petroleum & natural gas wells	0.1	Constr.
Accounting, auditing & bookkeeping	0.4	Services	Railroads & related services	0.1	Util.
Manifold business forms	0.3	Manufg.			
Metal barrels, drums, & pails	0.3	Manufg.			
Paper coating & glazing	0.3	Manufg.			
Computer & data processing services	0.3	Services			
Glass & glass products, except containers	0.2	Manufg.			
Industrial inorganic chemicals, nec	0.2	Manufg.			
Lubricating oils & greases	0.2	Manufg.			
Special dies & tools & machine tool accessories	0.2	Manufg.			
Real estate	0.2	Fin/R.E.			
Automotive repair shops & services	0.2	Services			
Alkalies & chlorine	0.1	Manufg.			
Photographic equipment & supplies	0.1	Manufg.			
Transit & bus transportation	0.1	Util.			
Insurance carriers	0.1	Fin/R.E.			
Royalties	0.1	Fin/R.E.			
Security & commodity brokers	0.1	Fin/R.E.			
Automotive rental & leasing, without drivers	0.1	Services			
Hotels & lodging places	0.1	Services			
Personnel supply services	0.1	Services			

Source: Benchmark Input-Output Accounts for the U.S. Economy, 1982, U.S. Department of Commerce, Washington, D.C., July 1991. Data, as reported in the source, are organized by the 1977 SIC structure in use in 1982 but have been matched, as closely as is possible, to the 1987 SIC structure used in this book.

OCCUPATIONS EMPLOYED BY SIC 289 - MISCELLANEOUS CHEMICAL PRODUCTS

Occupation	% of Total 1994	Change to 2005	Occupation	% of Total 1994	Change to 2005
Crushing & mixing machine operators	7.9	-42.7	Maintenance repairers, general utility	2.0	-14.1
Sales & related workers nec	5.0	-4.6	Truck drivers light & heavy	1.9	-1.6
Chemical equipment controllers, operators	4.8	-14.1	Industrial production managers	1.9	-4.5
Science & mathematics technicians	4.6	-4.5	Hand packers & packagers	1.8	-18.2
Packaging & filling machine operators	3.8	-4.6	Bookkeeping, accounting, & auditing clerks	1.7	-28.4
General managers & top executives	3.6	-9.5	General office clerks	1.7	-18.6
Secretaries, ex legal & medical	3.5	-13.1	Extruding & forming machine workers	1.5	5.0
Assemblers, fabricators, & hand workers nec	3.3	-4.6	Clerical supervisors & managers	1.4	-2.4
Chemists	3.1	-4.6	Freight, stock, & material movers, hand	1.3	-23.6
Chemical plant & system operators	2.7	43.1	Industrial truck & tractor operators	1.2	-4.5
Machine operators nec	2.6	-15.9	Managers & administrators nec	1.2	-4.6
Traffic, shipping, & receiving clerks	2.3	-8.2	Chemical engineers	1.2	-4.6
Industrial machinery mechanics	2.2	5.0	Machinists	1.1	-4.6
Inspectors, testers, & graders, precision	2.1	-4.6	Order clerks, materials, merchandise, & service	1.0	-6.7
Marketing, advertising, & PR managers	2.0	-4.6			

Source: Industry-Occupation Matrix, Bureau of Labor Statistics. These data relate to one or more 3-digit SIC industry groups rather than to a single 4-digit SIC. The change reported for each occupation to the year 2005 is a percent of growth or decline as estimated by the Bureau of Labor Statistics. The abbreviation nec stands for 'not elsewhere classified'.

LOCATION BY STATE AND REGIONAL CONCENTRATION

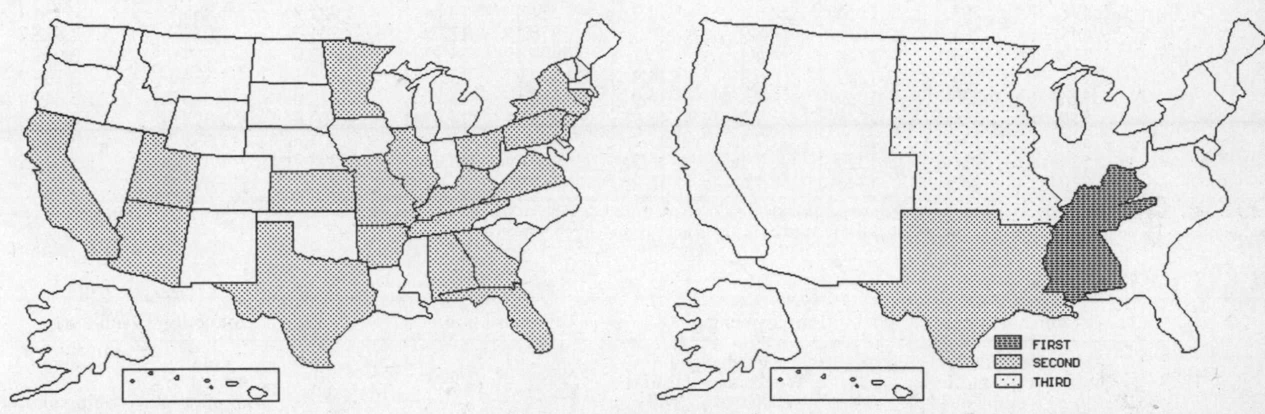

INDUSTRY DATA BY STATE

State	Establish-ments	Shipments			Employment				Cost as % of Shipments	Investment per Employee ($)
		Total ($ mil)	% of U.S.	Per Establ.	Total Number	% of U.S.	Per Establ.	Wages ($/hour)		
California	11	87.2	7.0	7.9	1,000	8.8	91	12.25	44.3	-
Kentucky	12	76.4	6.1	6.4	300	2.6	25	13.25	45.0	-
Texas	14	58.3	4.7	4.2	400	3.5	29	13.25	50.8	6,750
Pennsylvania	5	50.2	4.0	10.0	400	3.5	80	11.67	45.2	4,750
Illinois	7	50.2	4.0	7.2	300	2.6	43	9.20	30.1	-
Missouri	7	(D)	-	-	750 *	6.6	107	-	-	-
Florida	6	(D)	-	-	375 *	3.3	63	-	-	-
Alabama	4	(D)	-	-	175 *	1.5	44	-	-	-
Arizona	4	(D)	-	-	175 *	1.5	44	-	-	-
Arkansas	4	(D)	-	-	175 *	1.5	44	-	-	-
Minnesota	4	(D)	-	-	175 *	1.5	44	-	-	-
Ohio	4	(D)	-	-	375 *	3.3	94	-	-	-
Utah	4	(D)	-	-	175 *	1.5	44	-	-	-
New York	3	(D)	-	-	750 *	6.6	250	-	-	-
Tennessee	3	(D)	-	-	1,750 *	15.4	583	-	-	-
Georgia	2	(D)	-	-	175 *	1.5	88	-	-	-
Kansas	2	(D)	-	-	750 *	6.6	375	-	-	-
Virginia	2	(D)	-	-	3,750 *	32.9	1,875	-	-	-
Connecticut	1	(D)	-	-	750 *	6.6	750	-	-	-
New Jersey	1	(D)	-	-	375 *	3.3	375	-	-	-

Source: 1992 *Economic Census.* The states are in descending order of shipments or establishments (if shipment data are missing for the majority). The symbol (D) appears when data are withheld to prevent disclosure of competitive information. States marked with (D) are sorted by number of establishments. A dash (-) indicates that the data element cannot be calculated; * indicates the midpoint of a range.

2893 - PRINTING INK

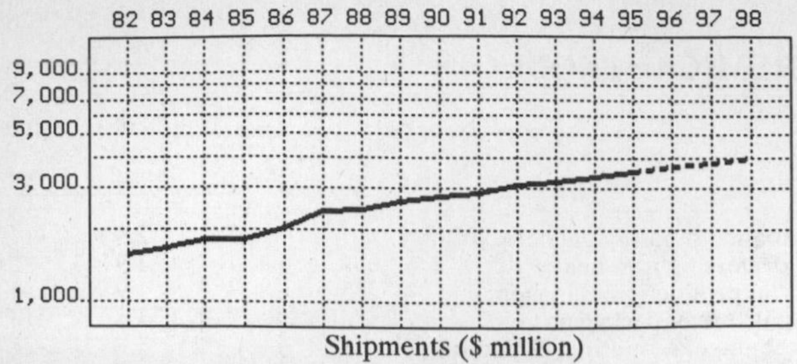

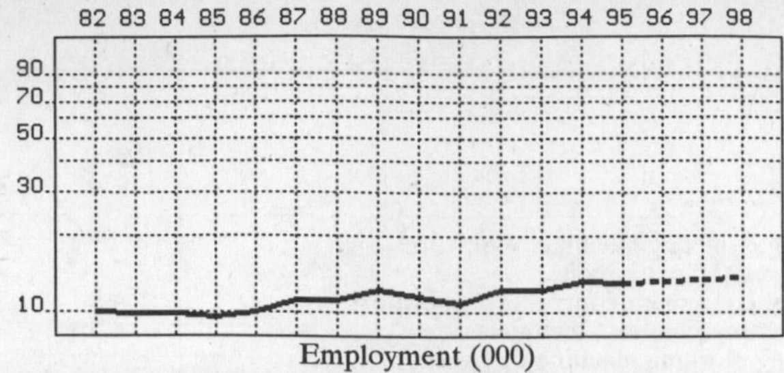

GENERAL STATISTICS

Year	Companies	Establishments: Total	Establishments: with 20 or more employees	Employment: Total (000)	Production Workers (000)	Production Hours (Mil)	Compensation: Payroll ($ mil)	Compensation: Wages ($/hr)	Production ($ million): Cost of Materials	Value Added by Manufacture	Value of Shipments	Capital Invest.
1982	228	467	153	9.9	5.5	11.0	214.1	9.26	1,016.2	556.4	1,571.5	25.5
1983		477	159	9.8	5.4	11.4	222.5	9.25	1,064.3	602.9	1,665.8	24.0
1984		487	165	9.8	5.8	11.8	239.2	10.24	1,185.5	643.4	1,821.4	33.3
1985		498	171	9.5	5.4	11.2	250.2	11.26	1,163.6	664.3	1,827.5	38.2
1986		501	163	9.9	5.7	12.0	271.7	11.33	1,293.3	753.0	2,036.0	39.7
1987	224	504	185	11.1	6.2	13.0	310.9	11.76	1,410.5	985.1	2,391.7	37.8
1988		484	183	11.1	6.4	13.5	336.7	12.91	1,511.8	947.9	2,447.2	32.7
1989		498	196	12.2	6.3	13.1	356.8	12.61	1,602.5	1,038.5	2,637.2	46.6
1990		491	203	11.5	6.2	12.9	354.4	12.64	1,727.2	1,035.7	2,754.4	44.3
1991		495	204	10.8	5.9	12.5	358.1	12.92	1,761.7	1,032.9	2,825.7	29.2
1992	220	519	214	12.3	6.5	13.1	407.4	14.12	1,973.0	1,114.0	3,075.1	46.0
1993		517	205	12.2	6.8	14.2	404.9	13.85	2,084.1	1,134.5	3,209.9	55.8
1994		516P	220P	13.2	7.8	16.0	458.5	13.92	2,110.0	1,266.2	3,366.0	55.4
1995		519P	225P	12.9P	7.2P	14.9P	459.9P	14.89P	2,204.6P	1,322.9P	3,516.8P	53.7P
1996		522P	231P	13.2P	7.3P	15.2P	479.6P	15.30P	2,301.6P	1,381.2P	3,671.7P	55.8P
1997		525P	236P	13.5P	7.4P	15.5P	499.3P	15.71P	2,398.7P	1,439.4P	3,826.5P	57.9P
1998		529P	242P	13.8P	7.6P	15.8P	519.0P	16.12P	2,495.7P	1,497.7P	3,981.3P	60.0P

Sources: 1982, 1987, 1992 *Economic Census*; *Annual Survey of Manufactures*, 83-86, 88-91, 93-94. Establishment counts for non-Census years are from *County Business Patterns*; establishment values for 83-84 are extrapolations. 'P's show projections by the editors. Industries reclassified in 87 will not have data for prior years.

INDICES OF CHANGE

Year	Companies	Establishments: Total	Establishments: with 20 or more employees	Employment: Total (000)	Production Workers (000)	Production Hours (Mil)	Compensation: Payroll ($ mil)	Compensation: Wages ($/hr)	Production ($ million): Cost of Materials	Value Added by Manufacture	Value of Shipments	Capital Invest.
1982	104	90	71	80	85	84	53	66	52	50	51	55
1983		92	74	80	83	87	55	66	54	54	54	52
1984		94	77	80	89	90	59	73	60	58	59	72
1985		96	80	77	83	85	61	80	59	60	59	83
1986		97	76	80	88	92	67	80	66	68	66	86
1987	102	97	86	90	95	99	76	83	71	88	78	82
1988		93	86	90	98	103	83	91	77	85	80	71
1989		96	92	99	97	100	88	89	81	93	86	101
1990		95	95	93	95	98	87	90	88	93	90	96
1991		95	95	88	91	95	88	92	89	93	92	63
1992	100	100	100	100	100	100	100	100	100	100	100	100
1993		100	96	99	105	108	99	98	106	102	104	121
1994		99P	103P	107	120	122	113	99	107	114	109	120
1995		100P	105P	105P	110P	113P	113P	105P	112P	119P	114P	117P
1996		101P	108P	107P	112P	116P	118P	108P	117P	124P	119P	121P
1997		101P	110P	110P	114P	118P	123P	111P	122P	129P	124P	126P
1998		102P	113P	112P	117P	120P	127P	114P	126P	134P	129P	130P

Sources: Same as General Statistics. Values reflect change from the base year, 1992. Values above 100 mean greater than 92, values below 100 mean less than 92, and a value of 100 in the 82-91 or 93-98 period means same as 92. 'P's mark projections by the editors.

SELECTED RATIOS

For 1994	Avg. of All Manufact.	Analyzed Industry	Index
Employees per Establishment	49	26	52
Payroll per Establishment	1,500,273	889,010	59
Payroll per Employee	30,620	34,735	113
Production Workers per Establishment	34	15	44
Wages per Establishment	853,319	431,843	51
Wages per Production Worker	24,861	28,554	115
Hours per Production Worker	2,056	2,051	100
Wages per Hour	12.09	13.92	115
Value Added per Establishment	4,602,255	2,455,102	53
Value Added per Employee	93,930	95,924	102

For 1994	Avg. of All Manufact.	Analyzed Industry	Index
Value Added per Production Worker	134,084	162,333	121
Cost per Establishment	5,045,178	4,091,190	81
Cost per Employee	102,970	159,848	155
Cost per Production Worker	146,988	270,513	184
Shipments per Establishment	9,576,895	6,526,514	68
Shipments per Employee	195,460	255,000	130
Shipments per Production Worker	279,017	431,538	155
Investment per Establishment	321,011	107,418	33
Investment per Employee	6,552	4,197	64
Investment per Production Worker	9,352	7,103	76

Sources: Same as General Statistics. The 'Average of All Manufacturing' column represents the average of all manufacturing industries reported for the most recent complete year available. The Index shows the relationship between the Average and the Analyzed Industry. For example, 100 means that they are equal; 500 that the Analyzed Industry is five times the average; 50 means that the Analyzed Industry is half the national average. The abbreviation 'na' is used to show that data are 'not available'.

LEADING COMPANIES

Number shown: **40** Total sales ($ mil): **4,067** Total employment (000): **19.2**

Company Name	Address				CEO Name	Phone	Co. Type	Sales ($ mil)	Empl. (000)
Sun Chemical Corp	222 Bridge Plaza S	Fort Lee	NJ	07024	Edward E Barr	201-224-4600	S	2,500	10.0
Flint Ink Corp	25111 Glendale Av	Detroit	MI	48239	H Howard Flint II	313-538-6800	R	500	2.6
Inx International Ink Co	651 Bonnie Ln	Elk Grove Vill	IL	60007	Gerald Braznell	708-981-9399	R	210	1.6
Lawter International Inc	990 Skokie Blv	Northbrook	IL	60062	Daniel J Terra	708-498-4700	P	191	0.6
Wikoff Color Corp	PO Box W	Fort Mill	SC	29715	Phil Lambert	803-548-2210	R	77*	0.4
CZ Inks	4150 Carr Ln	St Louis	MO	63119	J Reinhardt	314-645-3333	D	70	0.2
Ink Co	1115 Shore St	Sacramento	CA	95691	George Tohlke	916-372-6868	R	58*	0.3
Van Son Holland Corporation	92 Union St	Mineola	NY	11501	Joseph Bendowski	516-294-8811	R	42	0.1
Braden Sutphin Ink Co	3650 E 93rd St	Cleveland	OH	44105	T Zelek	216-271-2300	R	37	0.2
Custom Chemical Corp	30 Paul Kohner Pl	Elmwood Park	NJ	07407	Robert C Vielee	201-791-5100	S	33	0.1
Central Ink Corp	1100 N Harvester	West Chicago	IL	60185	Richard E Breen	708-231-6500	R	30	<0.1
Croda Inks Corp	7777 N Merrimac	Niles	IL	60714	T D Hentschel	708-967-7575	S	29*	0.2
Morrison Group	4801 W 160th St	Cleveland	OH	44135	D Scott Morrison	216-267-8820	R	25	<0.1
North American Printing Ink	1524 Davis Rd	Elgin	IL	60123	Larry L Yoder	708-695-0800	R	25	<0.1
Akzo Nobel Resins and Vehicles	21625 Oak St	Matteson	IL	60443	Lan Maycock	708-481-8900	D	24	<0.1
Color Converting Industries Co	11229 Aurora Av	Des Moines	IA	50322	Ronald Barry	515-263-6500	R	22	1.4
Gans Ink and Supply Company	1441 Boyd St	Los Angeles	CA	90033	RJ Gans	213-264-2200	R	20	0.2
Colonial Printing Ink Corp	180 E Union Av	E Rutherford	NJ	07073	Barry Marshall	201-933-6100	S	18	0.1
Nor-Cote International Inc	PO Box 668	Crawfordsville	IN	47933	NG Wolcott Jr	317-362-9180	R	18	<0.1
Borden Coatings	630 Glendale	Cincinnati	OH	45215	W Gerson	513-782-6200	D	17	0.2
American Inks & Coatings Corp	PO Box 803	Valley Forge	PA	19482	WP Rimmel	215-272-8866	R	15	0.1
AJ Daw Printing Ink Co	3559 S Greenwood	Los Angeles	CA	90040	James C Daw	213-723-3253	R	13	<0.1
Colonial Converting Corp	2020 S Mannheim	Des Plaines	IL	60018	Dan Masson	708-299-0111	R	10	<0.1
Hurst Graphics Inc	2500 San Fernando	Los Angeles	CA	90065	Joanne Hirsh	213-223-4121	R	10	<0.1
Polytex Environmental Inks Ltd	820 E 140th St	Bronx	NY	10454	Steve Landau	718-402-2000	R	10	<0.1
Ink Co	8360 10th Av N	Minneapolis	MN	55427	Harvey Luxford	612-546-8333	R	9	<0.1
Gotham Ink and Color Company	19 Kay Fries Dr	Stony Point	NY	10980	N Rosen	914-947-4000	S	8	<0.1
Arcar Graphics Inc	450 Wegner Dr	West Chicago	IL	60185	Scott Billings	708-231-7313	R	7	<0.1
Ron Ink Company Inc	61 Halstead St	Rochester	NY	14610	RG Saunders Jr	716-482-7050	S	7	<0.1
US Ink	PO Box 88700	Seattle	WA	98138	Joe Suplee	206-251-8700	D	6*	<0.1
International Blending Corp	1173 Osborne NE	Minneapolis	MN	55432	Wayne E Densmore	612-780-5377	R	5	<0.1
Miller-Cooper Co	1601 Prospect Av	Kansas City	MO	64127	Larry Nylund	816-483-5020	S	5	<0.1
Rogersol Inc	5538 Northwest N	Chicago	IL	60630	Norman Nichol	312-735-5100	S	5*	<0.1
Cudner and O'Connor Co	4035 W Kinzie St	Chicago	IL	60624	David Knoll	312-826-0200	R	3*	<0.1
Patriot Printing Ink Co	2842 S 17th Av	Broadview	IL	60153		708-345-7272	R	3	<0.1
Bomark Inc	601 S 6th Av	City of Industry	CA	91746	RT Schowe	818-968-1666	R	3	<0.1
Laser-Pro Inc	675 E Irving Pk Rd	Roselle	IL	60172	Larry Olson	708-893-1888	R	1	<0.1
Walter W Lawrence Inc	9715 Alpaca St	S El Monte	CA	91733	Carlos J Carbajal	213-629-2595	R	1	<0.1
Easy Transfer Cartridges Inc	230 California St	San Francisco	CA	94111	Jamie Morse	415-433-5780	R	1	<0.1
Regents Ltd	PO Box 920129	Norcross	GA	30092	Oscar Hasan	404-447-5555	R	0*	<0.1

Source: *Ward's Business Directory of U.S. Private and Public Companies*, Volumes 1 and 2, 1996. The company type code used is as follows: P - Public, R - Private, S - Subsidiary, D - Division, J - Joint Venture, A - Affiliate, G - Group. Sales are in millions of dollars, employees are in thousands. An asterisk (*) indicates an estimated sales volume. The symbol < stands for 'less than'. Company names and addresses are truncated, in some cases, to fit into the available space.

MATERIALS CONSUMED

Material		Quantity	Delivered Cost ($ million)
Materials, ingredients, containers, and supplies		(X)	1,901.5
Pigments, organic and inorganic	mil lb	310.6	563.7
Carbon black	mil lb	193.9	61.0
Plastics resins consumed in the form of granules, pellets, powders, liquids, etc.	mil lb	135.8	119.4
Paints, varnishes, stains, lacquers, shellacs, japans, enamels, and allied products	mil lb	530.8	318.2
Wood rosin, turpentine, and other wood chemicals	mil lb	38.7	28.1
Hydrocarbon oils and solvents	mil gal	102.4*	102.2
Oxygenated solvents	mil gal	43.4	58.5
Metal containers		(X)	27.4
All other materials and components, parts, containers, and supplies		(X)	168.7
Materials, ingredients, containers, and supplies, nsk		(X)	454.3

Source: 1992 *Economic Census*. Explanation of symbols used: (D): Withheld to avoid disclosure of competitive data; na: Not available; (S): Withheld because statistical norms were not met; (X): Not applicable; (Z): Less than half the unit shown; nec: Not elsewhere classified; nsk: Not specified by kind; - : zero; * : 10-19 percent estimated; ** : 20-29 percent estimated.

PRODUCT SHARE DETAILS

Product or Product Class	% Share	Product or Product Class	% Share
Printing ink	100.00	Gravure packaging printing inks, water-type	12.34
Letterpress printing inks	4.57	Gravure publication printing inks, solvent-type	51.09
Letterpress news printing inks	41.32	Gravure publication printing inks, water-type	(D)
Letterpress packaging printing inks	51.18	Other gravure printing inks	1.98
Other letterpress printing inks, including publication inks	7.43	Gravure inks, nsk	(D)
Lithographic and offset printing inks	44.98	Flexographic printing inks	19.22
Lithographic and offset news and nonheat web offset printing inks	24.74	Flexographic packaging printing inks, solvent-type	39.51
Lithographic and offset publication and commercial web printing inks	35.24	Flexographic packaging printing inks, water-type	45.34
Lithographic and offset sheet-fed packaging printing inks	11.53	Flexographic news and commercial printing inks	4.36
Lithographic and offset sheet-fed general printing inks	19.30	Other flexographic printing inks	5.50
Other lithographic and offset printing inks	6.48	Flexographic inks, nsk	5.26
Lithographic and offset inks, nsk	2.71	Printing inks, nec	6.89
Gravure printing inks	15.16	Textile printing inks	26.74
Gravure packaging printing inks, solvent-type	26.31	Screen printing inks	41.46
		Other printing inks, including stencil inks	31.80
		Printing ink, nsk	9.19

Source: 1992 *Economic Census*. The values shown are percent of total shipments in an industry. Values of indented subcategories are summed in the main heading. The symbol (D) appears when data are withheld to prevent disclosure of competitive information. The abbreviation nsk stands for 'not specified by kind' and nec for 'not elsewhere classified'.

INPUTS AND OUTPUTS FOR PRINTING INK

Economic Sector or Industry Providing Inputs	%	Sector	Economic Sector or Industry Buying Outputs	%	Sector
Inorganic pigments	20.3	Manufg.	Commercial printing	53.1	Manufg.
Cyclic crudes and organics	10.1	Manufg.	Paperboard containers & boxes	11.2	Manufg.
Paints & allied products	9.6	Manufg.	Newspapers	7.7	Manufg.
Petroleum refining	9.3	Manufg.	Bags, except textile	4.1	Manufg.
Plastics materials & resins	8.4	Manufg.	Paper coating & glazing	2.9	Manufg.
Wholesale trade	6.4	Trade	Pleating & stitching	2.9	Manufg.
Industrial inorganic chemicals, nec	4.4	Manufg.	Periodicals	2.6	Manufg.
Carbon black	2.4	Manufg.	Book printing	2.0	Manufg.
Gum & wood chemicals	2.3	Manufg.	Converted paper products, nec	1.9	Manufg.
Metal cans	2.2	Manufg.	Metal cans	1.9	Manufg.
Printing ink	2.0	Manufg.	Exports	1.9	Foreign
Motor freight transportation & warehousing	1.9	Util.	Printing ink	1.4	Manufg.
Imports	1.9	Foreign	Manifold business forms	1.3	Manufg.
Synthetic rubber	1.7	Manufg.	Book publishing	0.7	Manufg.
Engineering, architectural, & surveying services	1.6	Services	Miscellaneous plastics products	0.7	Manufg.
Railroads & related services	1.4	Util.	Carbon paper & inked ribbons	0.6	Manufg.
Electric services (utilities)	1.2	Util.	S/L Govt. purch., elem. & secondary education	0.6	S/L Govt
Advertising	1.0	Services	Sanitary paper products	0.5	Manufg.
Maintenance of nonfarm buildings nec	0.9	Constr.	S/L Govt. purch., higher education	0.5	S/L Govt
Animal & marine fats & oils	0.9	Manufg.	Greeting card publishing	0.4	Manufg.
Alkalies & chlorine	0.7	Manufg.	Engraving & plate printing	0.2	Manufg.
Miscellaneous plastics products	0.6	Manufg.	Miscellaneous publishing	0.2	Manufg.
Communications, except radio & TV	0.6	Util.	Lithographic platemaking & services	0.1	Manufg.
Gas production & distribution (utilities)	0.6	Util.	Stationery products	0.1	Manufg.
Eating & drinking places	0.6	Trade	Labor, civic, social, & fraternal associations	0.1	Services
Air transportation	0.5	Util.			
Water transportation	0.5	Util.			
Metal barrels, drums, & pails	0.4	Manufg.			
Banking	0.4	Fin/R.E.			
Miscellaneous repair shops	0.4	Services			
Noncomparable imports	0.4	Foreign			
Nonmetallic mineral services	0.3	Mining			
Polishes & sanitation goods	0.3	Manufg.			
Equipment rental & leasing services	0.3	Services			
Legal services	0.3	Services			
Mechanical measuring devices	0.2	Manufg.			
Accounting, auditing & bookkeeping	0.2	Services			
Management & consulting services & labs	0.2	Services			
U.S. Postal Service	0.2	Gov't			
Machinery, except electrical, nec	0.1	Manufg.			
Manifold business forms	0.1	Manufg.			
Paperboard containers & boxes	0.1	Manufg.			
Sanitary services, steam supply, irrigation	0.1	Util.			
Real estate	0.1	Fin/R.E.			
Computer & data processing services	0.1	Services			

Source: Benchmark Input-Output Accounts for the U.S. Economy, 1982, U.S. Department of Commerce, Washington, D.C., July 1991. Data, as reported in the source, are organized by the 1977 SIC structure in use in 1982 but have been matched, as closely as is possible, to the 1987 SIC structure used in this book.

OCCUPATIONS EMPLOYED BY SIC 289 - MISCELLANEOUS CHEMICAL PRODUCTS

Occupation	% of Total 1994	Change to 2005	Occupation	% of Total 1994	Change to 2005
Crushing & mixing machine operators	7.9	-42.7	Maintenance repairers, general utility	2.0	-14.1
Sales & related workers nec	5.0	-4.6	Truck drivers light & heavy	1.9	-1.6
Chemical equipment controllers, operators	4.8	-14.1	Industrial production managers	1.9	-4.5
Science & mathematics technicians	4.6	-4.5	Hand packers & packagers	1.8	-18.2
Packaging & filling machine operators	3.8	-4.6	Bookkeeping, accounting, & auditing clerks	1.7	-28.4
General managers & top executives	3.6	-9.5	General office clerks	1.7	-18.6
Secretaries, ex legal & medical	3.5	-13.1	Extruding & forming machine workers	1.5	5.0
Assemblers, fabricators, & hand workers nec	3.3	-4.6	Clerical supervisors & managers	1.4	-2.4
Chemists	3.1	-4.6	Freight, stock, & material movers, hand	1.3	-23.6
Chemical plant & system operators	2.7	43.1	Industrial truck & tractor operators	1.2	-4.5
Machine operators nec	2.6	-15.9	Managers & administrators nec	1.2	-4.6
Traffic, shipping, & receiving clerks	2.3	-8.2	Chemical engineers	1.2	-4.6
Industrial machinery mechanics	2.2	5.0	Machinists	1.1	-4.6
Inspectors, testers, & graders, precision	2.1	-4.6	Order clerks, materials, merchandise, & service	1.0	-6.7
Marketing, advertising, & PR managers	2.0	-4.6			

Source: *Industry-Occupation Matrix*, Bureau of Labor Statistics. These data relate to one or more 3-digit SIC industry groups rather than to a single 4-digit SIC. The change reported for each occupation to the year 2005 is a percent of growth or decline as estimated by the Bureau of Labor Statistics. The abbreviation nec stands for 'not elsewhere classified'.

LOCATION BY STATE AND REGIONAL CONCENTRATION

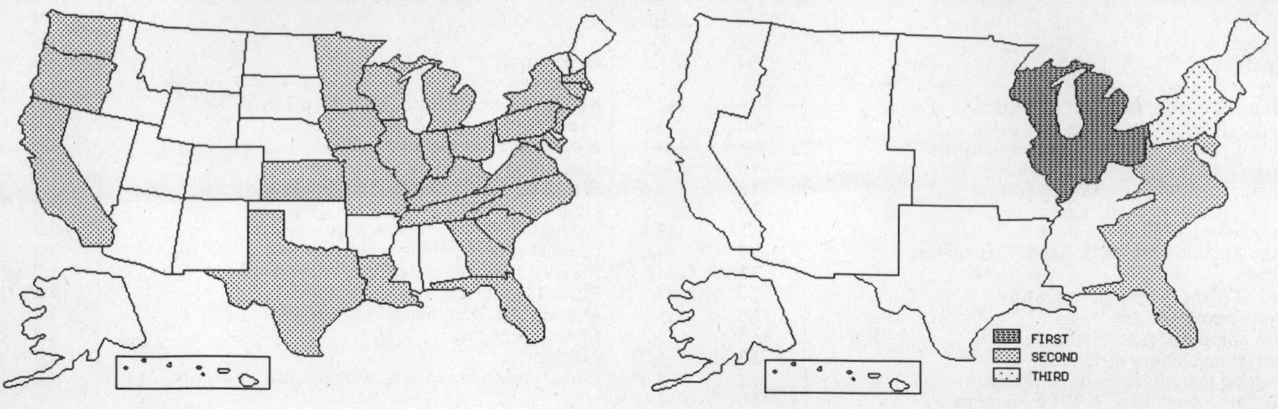

INDUSTRY DATA BY STATE

State	Establish-ments	Shipments			Employment				Cost as % of Shipments	Investment per Employee ($)
		Total ($ mil)	% of U.S.	Per Establ.	Total Number	% of U.S.	Per Establ.	Wages ($/hour)		
Illinois	47	377.9	12.3	8.0	1,500	12.2	32	16.07	62.2	-
California	50	268.6	8.7	5.4	1,300	10.6	26	15.31	64.5	-
Indiana	7	208.2	6.8	29.7	300	2.4	43	14.00	98.5	-
Ohio	42	197.8	6.4	4.7	900	7.3	21	13.89	52.4	-
Texas	26	126.1	4.1	4.8	400	3.3	15	12.80	61.1	5,250
North Carolina	21	120.8	3.9	5.8	600	4.9	29	12.14	54.2	3,000
Virginia	16	110.9	3.6	6.9	400	3.3	25	13.00	63.5	5,000
Wisconsin	24	110.9	3.6	4.6	400	3.3	17	14.40	58.9	-
Minnesota	10	95.1	3.1	9.5	400	3.3	40	16.80	59.8	3,500
Pennsylvania	21	89.5	2.9	4.3	400	3.3	19	15.75	65.9	2,250
Tennessee	21	79.5	2.6	3.8	300	2.4	14	13.00	68.8	-
South Carolina	7	65.8	2.1	9.4	200	1.6	29	9.00	81.5	-
Kentucky	7	62.8	2.0	9.0	100	0.8	14	12.50	65.1	-
Michigan	11	61.4	2.0	5.6	200	1.6	18	14.00	66.1	5,000
Maryland	12	61.2	2.0	5.1	300	2.4	25	12.33	67.8	-
Florida	19	57.1	1.9	3.0	200	1.6	11	14.50	68.3	3,000
Massachusetts	15	43.8	1.4	2.9	300	2.4	20	13.00	67.1	2,000
Oregon	8	37.0	1.2	4.6	200	1.6	25	13.50	55.9	3,500
Washington	5	22.7	0.7	4.5	100	0.8	20	19.00	57.3	-
Louisiana	8	22.2	0.7	2.8	100	0.8	13	14.00	62.2	5,000
New Jersey	39	(D)	-	-	1,750 *	14.2	45	-	-	-
Georgia	22	(D)	-	-	375 *	3.0	17	-	-	-
Missouri	19	(D)	-	-	750 *	6.1	39	-	-	-
New York	15	(D)	-	-	750 *	6.1	50	-	-	-
Connecticut	4	(D)	-	-	175 *	1.4	44	-	-	1,714
Iowa	3	(D)	-	-	175 *	1.4	58	-	-	-
Kansas	3	(D)	-	-	175 *	1.4	58	-	-	-

Source: 1992 *Economic Census*. The states are in descending order of shipments or establishments (if shipment data are missing for the majority). The symbol (D) appears when data are withheld to prevent disclosure of competitive information. States marked with (D) are sorted by number of establishments. A dash (-) indicates that the data element cannot be calculated; * indicates the midpoint of a range.

2895 - CARBON BLACK

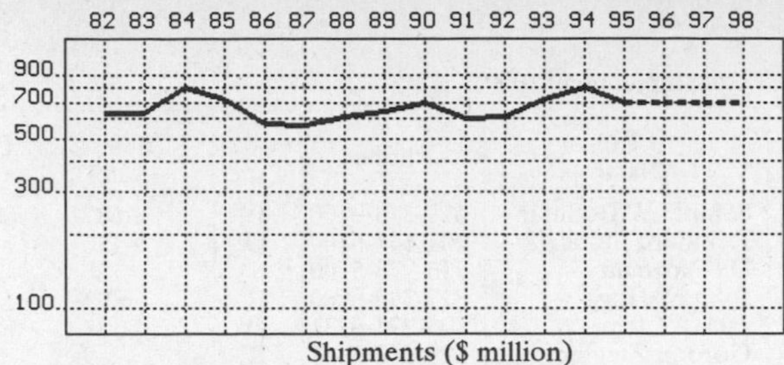

Shipments ($ million)

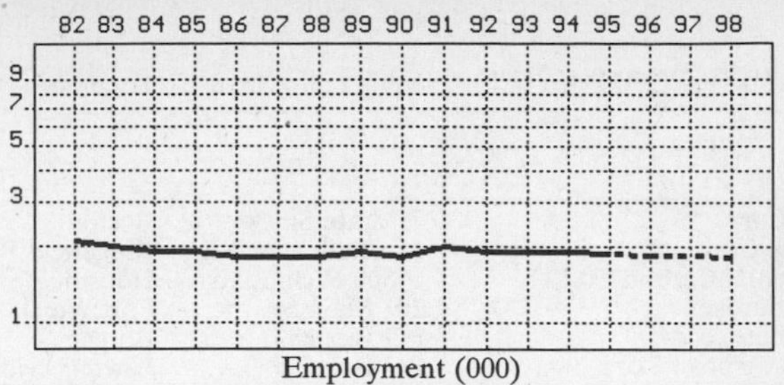

Employment (000)

GENERAL STATISTICS

Year	Com-panies	Establishments		Employment			Compensation		Production ($ million)			
		Total	with 20 or more employees	Total (000)	Production Workers (000)	Hours (Mil)	Payroll ($ mil)	Wages ($/hr)	Cost of Materials	Value Added by Manufacture	Value of Shipments	Capital Invest.
1982	8	25	24	2.1	1.6	3.0	54.9	13.03	433.7	190.8	632.9	39.4
1983		25	24	2.0	1.4	3.1	57.1	13.35	440.8	170.3	623.9	27.3
1984		25	24	1.9	1.5	3.2	63.1	14.25	505.6	312.4	804.5	46.2
1985		25	23	1.9	1.4	3.1	60.8	14.19	425.3	288.8	715.0	40.3
1986		24	23	1.8	1.3	3.0	63.1	14.93	315.3	243.9	570.2	23.2
1987	7	22	21	1.8	1.4	3.0	64.7	15.40	306.8	272.6	569.6	39.2
1988		26	21	1.8	1.3	3.0	67.4	16.03	284.0	330.8	615.7	49.0
1989		23	21	1.9	1.3	2.7	71.1	17.33	325.8	318.7	640.3	50.6
1990		22	20	1.8	1.2	2.7	70.1	17.33	316.3	380.0	691.9	60.1
1991		23	20	2.0	1.2	2.8	72.0	17.18	282.7	315.0	604.3	53.3
1992	9	23	20	1.9	1.2	2.7	73.7	17.07	286.8	320.4	606.8	28.7
1993		22	20	1.9	1.3	2.8	76.4	18.57	312.6	412.8	723.8	33.3
1994		22P	19P	1.9	1.2	2.8	77.0	17.50	311.2	489.0	804.7	45.7
1995		22P	18P	1.9P	1.1P	2.7P	79.5P	18.93P	266.7P	419.0P	689.6P	45.9P
1996		21P	18P	1.8P	1.1P	2.6P	81.3P	19.37P	268.2P	421.4P	693.5P	46.6P
1997		21P	17P	1.8P	1.1P	2.6P	83.1P	19.81P	269.7P	423.9P	697.5P	47.3P
1998		21P	17P	1.8P	1.1P	2.6P	84.9P	20.25P	271.3P	426.3P	701.5P	48.0P

Sources: 1982, 1987, 1992 *Economic Census*; *Annual Survey of Manufactures*, 83-86, 88-91, 93-94. Establishment counts for non-Census years are from *County Business Patterns*; establishment values for 83-84 are extrapolations. 'P's show projections by the editors. Industries reclassified in 87 will not have data for prior years.

INDICES OF CHANGE

Year	Com-panies	Establishments		Employment			Compensation		Production ($ million)			
		Total	with 20 or more employees	Total (000)	Production Workers (000)	Hours (Mil)	Payroll ($ mil)	Wages ($/hr)	Cost of Materials	Value Added by Manufacture	Value of Shipments	Capital Invest.
1982	89	109	120	111	133	111	74	76	151	60	104	137
1983		109	120	105	117	115	77	78	154	53	103	95
1984		109	120	100	125	119	86	83	176	98	133	161
1985		109	115	100	117	115	82	83	148	90	118	140
1986		104	115	95	108	111	86	87	110	76	94	81
1987	78	96	105	95	117	111	88	90	107	85	94	137
1988		113	105	95	108	111	91	94	99	103	101	171
1989		100	105	100	108	100	96	102	114	99	106	176
1990		96	100	95	100	100	95	102	110	119	114	209
1991		100	100	105	100	104	98	101	99	98	100	186
1992	100	100	100	100	100	100	100	100	100	100	100	100
1993		96	100	100	108	104	104	109	109	129	119	116
1994		95P	94P	100	100	104	104	103	109	153	133	159
1995		94P	92P	97P	95P	99P	108P	111P	93P	131P	114P	160P
1996		93P	90P	97P	93P	97P	110P	113P	94P	132P	114P	162P
1997		92P	87P	97P	90P	96P	113P	116P	94P	132P	115P	165P
1998		91P	85P	96P	88P	95P	115P	119P	95P	133P	116P	167P

Sources: Same as General Statistics. Values reflect change from the base year, 1992. Values above 100 mean greater than 92, values below 100 mean less than 92, and a value of 100 in the 82-91 or 93-98 period means same as 92. 'P's mark projections by the editors.

SELECTED RATIOS

For 1994	Avg. of All Manufact.	Analyzed Industry	Index
Employees per Establishment	49	87	177
Payroll per Establishment	1,500,273	3,507,246	234
Payroll per Employee	30,620	40,526	132
Production Workers per Establishment	34	55	159
Wages per Establishment	853,319	2,231,884	262
Wages per Production Worker	24,861	40,833	164
Hours per Production Worker	2,056	2,333	113
Wages per Hour	12.09	17.50	145
Value Added per Establishment	4,602,255	22,273,292	484
Value Added per Employee	93,930	257,368	274

For 1994	Avg. of All Manufact.	Analyzed Industry	Index
Value Added per Production Worker	134,084	407,500	304
Cost per Establishment	5,045,178	14,174,741	281
Cost per Employee	102,970	163,789	159
Cost per Production Worker	146,988	259,333	176
Shipments per Establishment	9,576,895	36,653,002	383
Shipments per Employee	195,460	423,526	217
Shipments per Production Worker	279,017	670,583	240
Investment per Establishment	321,011	2,081,573	648
Investment per Employee	6,552	24,053	367
Investment per Production Worker	9,352	38,083	407

Sources: Same as General Statistics. The 'Average of All Manufacturing' column represents the average of all manufacturing industries reported for the most recent complete year available. The Index shows the relationship between the Average and the Analyzed Industry. For example, 100 means that they are equal; 500 that the Analyzed Industry is five times the average; 50 means that the Analyzed Industry is half the national average. The abbreviation 'na' is used to show that data are 'not available'.

LEADING COMPANIES

Number shown: **6** Total sales ($ mil): **2,148** Total employment (000): **6.8**

Company Name	Address				CEO Name	Phone	Co. Type	Sales ($ mil)	Empl. (000)
Cabot Corp	75 State St	Boston	MA	02109	Samuel W Bodman	617-345-0100	P	1,687	5.4
Degussa Corp	65 Challenger Rd	Ridgefield Park	NJ	07660	Reinhard Stober	201-641-6100	D	150	0.3
Continental Carbon Co	10500 Richmond	Houston	TX	77042	DT Norman	713-978-5700	S	126	0.3
Sid Richardson	201 Main St	Fort Worth	TX	76102	John M Hogg	817-390-8600	R	93*	0.5
JM Huber Corp	PO Box 2831	Borger	TX	79008	Jack L Clem	806-274-6331	D	84	0.3
Pioneer Asphalt Corp	PO Box 535	Lawrenceville	IL	62439	Gordon Ziegler	618-943-3341	R	9*	<0.1

Source: Ward's Business Directory of U.S. Private and Public Companies, Volumes 1 and 2, 1996. The company type code used is as follows: P - Public, R - Private, S - Subsidiary, D - Division, J - Joint Venture, A - Affiliate, G - Group. Sales are in millions of dollars, employees are in thousands. An asterisk (*) indicates an estimated sales volume. The symbol < stands for 'less than'. Company names and addresses are truncated, in some cases, to fit into the available space.

MATERIALS CONSUMED

Material		Quantity	Delivered Cost ($ million)
Materials, ingredients, containers, and supplies		(X)	244.4
Carbon black feedstock	mil bbl	13.5	179.8
Natural gas used as a raw material	bil cu ft	16.4	34.2
Paper and paperboard containers, including shipping sacks and other paper packaging supplies		(X)	7.3
All other materials and components, parts, containers, and supplies		(X)	23.1

Source: 1992 Economic Census. Explanation of symbols used: (D): Withheld to avoid disclosure of competitive data; na: Not available; (S): Withheld because statistical norms were not met; (X): Not applicable; (Z): Less than half the unit shown; nec: Not elsewhere classified; nsk: Not specified by kind; - : zero; * : 10-19 percent estimated; ** : 20-29 percent estimated.

PRODUCT SHARE DETAILS

Product or Product Class	% Share	Product or Product Class	% Share
Carbon black	100.00		

Source: 1992 Economic Census. The values shown are percent of total shipments in an industry. Values of indented subcategories are summed in the main heading. The symbol (D) appears when data are withheld to prevent disclosure of competitive information. The abbreviation nsk stands for 'not specified by kind' and nec for 'not elsewhere classified'.

INPUTS AND OUTPUTS FOR CARBON BLACK

Economic Sector or Industry Providing Inputs	%	Sector	Economic Sector or Industry Buying Outputs	%	Sector
Petroleum refining	54.8	Manufg.	Tires & inner tubes	51.8	Manufg.
Crude petroleum & natural gas	8.6	Mining	Fabricated rubber products, nec	13.5	Manufg.
Gas production & distribution (utilities)	6.9	Util.	Chemical preparations, nec	8.2	Manufg.
Electric services (utilities)	5.2	Util.	Synthetic rubber	6.7	Manufg.
Wholesale trade	4.3	Trade	Exports	4.5	Foreign
Pumps & compressors	3.9	Manufg.	Printing ink	4.0	Manufg.
Imports	3.2	Foreign	Rubber & plastics hose & belting	3.9	Manufg.
Miscellaneous repair shops	2.5	Services	Carbon paper & inked ribbons	2.2	Manufg.
Engineering, architectural, & surveying services	1.1	Services	Paints & allied products	2.0	Manufg.
Water transportation	1.0	Util.	Plastics materials & resins	1.9	Manufg.
Motor freight transportation & warehousing	0.9	Util.	Converted paper products, nec	1.0	Manufg.
Paperboard containers & boxes	0.7	Manufg.	Reclaimed rubber	0.2	Manufg.
Advertising	0.7	Services			
Maintenance of nonfarm buildings nec	0.6	Constr.			
Air transportation	0.6	Util.			
Noncomparable imports	0.6	Foreign			
Pipelines, except natural gas	0.5	Util.			
Eating & drinking places	0.5	Trade			
Banking	0.4	Fin/R.E.			
Communications, except radio & TV	0.3	Util.			
Equipment rental & leasing services	0.3	Services			
Railroads & related services	0.2	Util.			
Sanitary services, steam supply, irrigation	0.2	Util.			
Computer & data processing services	0.2	Services			
Legal services	0.2	Services			
Management & consulting services & labs	0.2	Services			
Bags, except textile	0.1	Manufg.			
Mechanical measuring devices	0.1	Manufg.			
U.S. Postal Service	0.1	Gov't			

Source: Benchmark Input-Output Accounts for the U.S. Economy, 1982, U.S. Department of Commerce, Washington, D.C., July 1991. Data, as reported in the source, are organized by the 1977 SIC structure in use in 1982 but have been matched, as closely as is possible, to the 1987 SIC structure used in this book.

OCCUPATIONS EMPLOYED BY SIC 289 - MISCELLANEOUS CHEMICAL PRODUCTS

Occupation	% of Total 1994	Change to 2005	Occupation	% of Total 1994	Change to 2005
Crushing & mixing machine operators	7.9	-42.7	Maintenance repairers, general utility	2.0	-14.1
Sales & related workers nec	5.0	-4.6	Truck drivers light & heavy	1.9	-1.6
Chemical equipment controllers, operators	4.8	-14.1	Industrial production managers	1.9	-4.5
Science & mathematics technicians	4.6	-4.5	Hand packers & packagers	1.8	-18.2
Packaging & filling machine operators	3.8	-4.6	Bookkeeping, accounting, & auditing clerks	1.7	-28.4
General managers & top executives	3.6	-9.5	General office clerks	1.7	-18.6
Secretaries, ex legal & medical	3.5	-13.1	Extruding & forming machine workers	1.5	5.0
Assemblers, fabricators, & hand workers nec	3.3	-4.6	Clerical supervisors & managers	1.4	-2.4
Chemists	3.1	-4.6	Freight, stock, & material movers, hand	1.3	-23.6
Chemical plant & system operators	2.7	43.1	Industrial truck & tractor operators	1.2	-4.5
Machine operators nec	2.6	-15.9	Managers & administrators nec	1.2	-4.6
Traffic, shipping, & receiving clerks	2.3	-8.2	Chemical engineers	1.2	-4.6
Industrial machinery mechanics	2.2	5.0	Machinists	1.1	-4.6
Inspectors, testers, & graders, precision	2.1	-4.6	Order clerks, materials, merchandise, & service	1.0	-6.7
Marketing, advertising, & PR managers	2.0	-4.6			

Source: Industry-Occupation Matrix, Bureau of Labor Statistics. These data relate to one or more 3-digit SIC industry groups rather than to a single 4-digit SIC. The change reported for each occupation to the year 2005 is a percent of growth or decline as estimated by the Bureau of Labor Statistics. The abbreviation nec stands for 'not elsewhere classified'.

LOCATION BY STATE AND REGIONAL CONCENTRATION

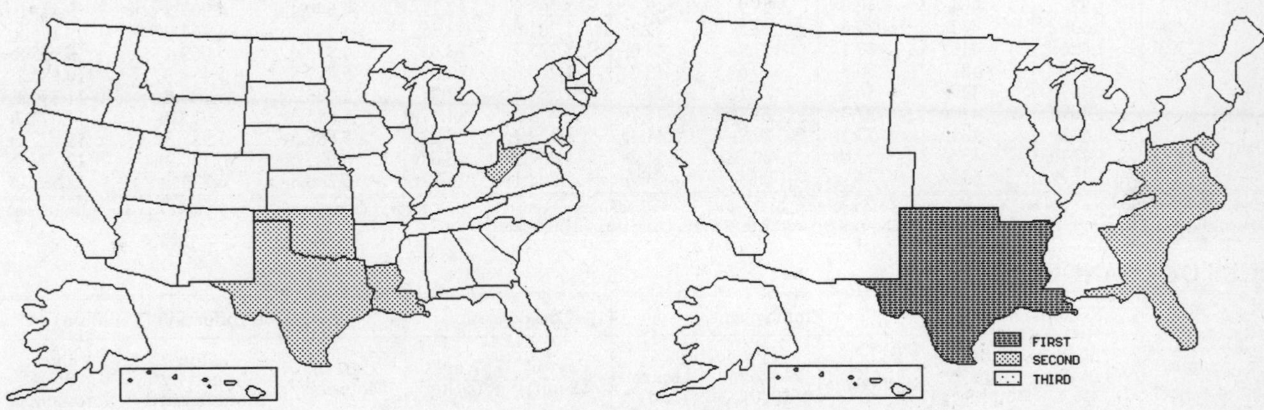

INDUSTRY DATA BY STATE

State	Establish-ments	Shipments Total ($ mil)	Shipments % of U.S.	Shipments Per Establ.	Employment Total Number	Employment % of U.S.	Employment Per Establ.	Wages ($/hour)	Cost as % of Shipments	Investment per Employee ($)
Texas	8	223.3	36.8	27.9	800	42.1	100	15.83	49.2	9,750
Louisiana	5	206.1	34.0	41.2	700	36.8	140	18.33	48.0	-
West Virginia	2	(D)	-	-	175 *	9.2	88	-	-	-
Oklahoma	1	(D)	-	-	175 *	9.2	175	-	-	-

Source: 1992 *Economic Census*. The states are in descending order of shipments or establishments (if shipment data are missing for the majority). The symbol (D) appears when data are withheld to prevent disclosure of competitive information. States marked with (D) are sorted by number of establishments. A dash (-) indicates that the data element cannot be calculated; * indicates the midpoint of a range.

2899 - CHEMICAL PREPARATIONS, NEC

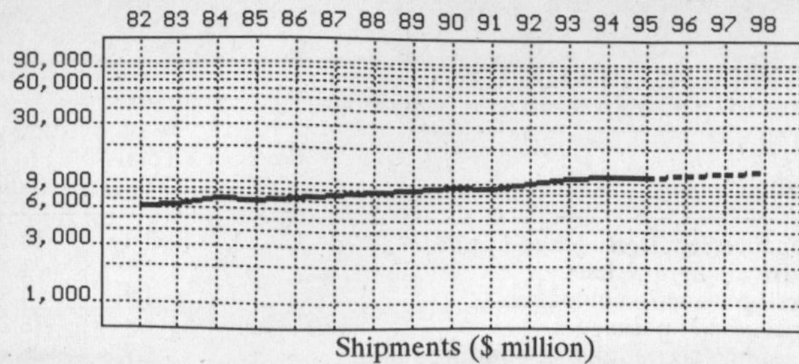

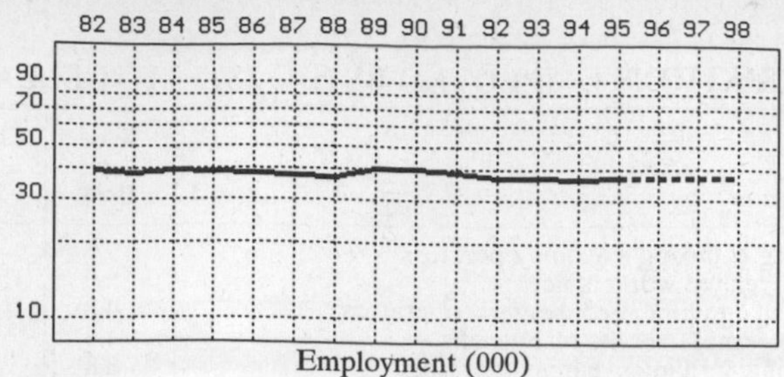

GENERAL STATISTICS

Year	Com-panies	Establishments		Employment			Compensation		Production ($ million)			
		Total	with 20 or more employees	Total (000)	Production Workers (000)	Production Hours (Mil)	Payroll ($ mil)	Wages ($/hr)	Cost of Materials	Value Added by Manufacture	Value of Shipments	Capital Invest.
1982	1,242	1,439	409	39.6	23.0	46.6	834.2	9.20	3,350.8	2,942.9	6,329.5	350.4
1983		1,397	417	38.3	22.5	45.9	817.5	9.23	3,408.6	3,080.3	6,498.5	174.7
1984		1,355	425	39.6	23.3	48.7	911.7	9.86	3,827.2	3,605.0	7,375.0	273.8
1985		1,312	432	39.3	23.4	48.6	955.4	10.20	3,685.7	3,521.0	7,192.4	303.2
1986		1,267	400	38.0	22.5	47.4	963.5	10.68	3,662.8	3,777.3	7,448.4	327.0
1987	1,365	1,529	407	37.9	22.4	46.2	1,020.7	11.30	3,767.6	4,261.0	8,023.9	234.3
1988		1,462	438	37.0	21.8	44.6	1,040.7	12.11	4,248.6	4,537.9	8,726.7	258.6
1989		1,371	426	40.1	23.2	48.5	1,094.5	11.39	4,376.7	4,548.7	8,838.3	341.3
1990		1,329	434	40.3	23.9	49.3	1,205.0	12.11	4,540.4	4,907.2	9,418.0	352.2
1991		1,338	433	39.4	22.5	46.8	1,201.6	12.35	4,418.4	4,764.9	9,175.9	453.4
1992	1,303	1,486	419	37.1	21.4	44.0	1,227.7	13.62	4,933.0	5,063.4	9,965.8	441.1
1993		1,410	421	36.8	20.6	43.3	1,265.8	14.09	5,419.8	5,484.3	10,885.1	468.6
1994		1,407P	429P	36.5	20.1	44.1	1,364.6	14.77	5,683.2	5,723.6	11,370.4	378.7
1995		1,409P	430P	37.3P	21.1P	44.7P	1,376.5P	14.77P	5,685.3P	5,725.8P	11,374.7P	447.3P
1996		1,412P	431P	37.2P	20.9P	44.4P	1,420.4P	15.22P	5,886.5P	5,928.3P	11,777.1P	463.4P
1997		1,414P	433P	37.0P	20.7P	44.2P	1,464.2P	15.67P	6,087.6P	6,130.9P	12,179.6P	479.4P
1998		1,417P	434P	36.9P	20.5P	43.9P	1,508.1P	16.12P	6,288.8P	6,333.5P	12,582.0P	495.4P

Sources: 1982, 1987, 1992 *Economic Census*; *Annual Survey of Manufactures*, 83-86, 88-91, 93-94. Establishment counts for non-Census years are from *County Business Patterns*; establishment values for 83-84 are extrapolations. 'P's show projections by the editors. Industries reclassified in 87 will not have data for prior years.

INDICES OF CHANGE

Year	Com-panies	Establishments		Employment			Compensation		Production ($ million)			
		Total	with 20 or more employees	Total (000)	Production Workers (000)	Production Hours (Mil)	Payroll ($ mil)	Wages ($/hr)	Cost of Materials	Value Added by Manufacture	Value of Shipments	Capital Invest.
1982	95	97	98	107	107	106	68	68	68	58	64	79
1983		94	100	103	105	104	67	68	69	61	65	40
1984		91	101	107	109	111	74	72	78	71	74	62
1985		88	103	106	109	110	78	75	75	70	72	69
1986		85	95	102	105	108	78	78	74	75	75	74
1987	105	103	97	102	105	105	83	83	76	84	81	53
1988		98	105	100	102	101	85	89	86	90	88	59
1989		92	102	108	108	110	89	84	89	90	89	77
1990		89	104	109	112	112	98	89	92	97	95	80
1991		90	103	106	105	106	98	91	90	94	92	103
1992	100	100	100	100	100	100	100	100	100	100	100	100
1993		95	100	99	96	98	103	103	110	108	109	106
1994		95P	102P	98	94	100	111	108	115	113	114	86
1995		95P	103P	101P	98P	102P	112P	108P	115P	113P	114P	101P
1996		95P	103P	100P	98P	101P	116P	112P	119P	117P	118P	105P
1997		95P	103P	100P	97P	100P	119P	115P	123P	121P	122P	109P
1998		95P	104P	99P	96P	100P	123P	118P	127P	125P	126P	112P

Sources: Same as General Statistics. Values reflect change from the base year, 1992. Values above 100 mean greater than 92, values below 100 mean less than 92, and a value of 100 in the 82-91 or 93-98 period means same as 92. 'P's mark projections by the editors.

SELECTED RATIOS

For 1994	Avg. of All Manufact.	Analyzed Industry	Index
Employees per Establishment	49	26	53
Payroll per Establishment	1,500,273	969,865	65
Payroll per Employee	30,620	37,386	122
Production Workers per Establishment	34	14	42
Wages per Establishment	853,319	462,940	54
Wages per Production Worker	24,861	32,406	130
Hours per Production Worker	2,056	2,194	107
Wages per Hour	12.09	14.77	122
Value Added per Establishment	4,602,255	4,067,946	88
Value Added per Employee	93,930	156,811	167

For 1994	Avg. of All Manufact.	Analyzed Industry	Index
Value Added per Production Worker	134,084	284,756	212
Cost per Establishment	5,045,178	4,039,232	80
Cost per Employee	102,970	155,704	151
Cost per Production Worker	146,988	282,746	192
Shipments per Establishment	9,576,895	8,081,308	84
Shipments per Employee	195,460	311,518	159
Shipments per Production Worker	279,017	565,692	203
Investment per Establishment	321,011	269,154	84
Investment per Employee	6,552	10,375	158
Investment per Production Worker	9,352	18,841	201

Sources: Same as General Statistics. The 'Average of All Manufacturing' column represents the average of all manufacturing industries reported for the most recent complete year available. The Index shows the relationship between the Average and the Analyzed Industry. For example, 100 means that they are equal; 500 that the Analyzed Industry is five times the average; 50 means that the Analyzed Industry is half the national average. The abbreviation 'na' is used to show that data are 'not available'.

LEADING COMPANIES Number shown: **75** Total sales ($ mil): **9,492** Total employment (000): **41.5**

Company Name	Address				CEO Name	Phone	Co. Type	Sales ($ mil)	Empl. (000)
Nalco Chemical Co	1 Nalco Ctr	Naperville	IL	60563	Edward J Mooney	708-305-1000	P	1,346	5.6
GAF Corp	1361 Alps Rd	Wayne	NJ	07470	Samuel J Heyman	201-628-3000	R	1,043	4.3
Uniroyal Chemical Company Inc	Benson Rd	Middlebury	CT	06749	Robert J Mazaika	203-573-2000	S	947	2.7
Betz Laboratories Inc	4636 Somerton Rd	Trevose	PA	19053	William R Cook	215-355-3300	P	708	4.0
Morton Salt	100 N Riverside Plz	Chicago	IL	60606	W E Johnston Jr	312-807-2000	D	511	2.0
RP Scherer Corp	PO Box 7060	Troy	MI	48007	Aleksandar Erdeljan	313-649-0900	P	449	3.1
RP Scherer International Corp	PO Box 7060	Troy	MI	48007	Aleksandar Erdeljan	313-649-0900	S	449	3.1
Petrolite Corp	369 Marshall Av	St Louis	MO	63119	William E Nasser	314-961-3500	P	368	1.8
Norton Chemical	3855 Fishcreek Rd	Stow	OH	44224	Robert Ayotte	216-673-5860	S	280	0.4
Calgon Corp	PO Box 1346	Pittsburgh	PA	15230	A Fred Kerst	412-777-8000	S	231	1.5
Morton Electronic Materials	2631 Michelle Dr	Tustin	CA	92680	Daniel Feinberg	714-730-4200	D	200	0.7
LeaRonal Inc	272 Buffalo Av	Freeport	NY	11520	Ronald Ostrow	516-868-8800	P	177	0.6
Velsicol Chemical Corp	10400 WHiggins Rd	Rosemont	IL	60018	Arthur R Sigel	708-698-9700	R	170	0.6
MacDermid Inc	245 Freight St	Waterbury	CT	06702	Daniel H Leever	203-575-5700	P	150	0.8
Aqualon	PO Box 271	Hopewell	VA	23860	JH Doud	804-541-4505	D	144	0.5
Betz PaperChem Inc	7510 Baymead	Jacksonville	FL	32256	John L Holland	904-733-7110	S	140*	0.5
PENWEST Ltd	777 108th Av NE	Bellevue	WA	98004	Tod R Hamachek	206-462-6000	P	135	0.5
Cincinnati Milacron Inc	PO Box 9013	Cincinnati	OH	45209	William J Gruber	513-841-8121	D	100	0.5
Eltech Systems Corp	6100 Glades Rd	Boca Raton	FL	33434	Kevin O'Leary	407-487-3600	R	100*	0.4
General Latex & Chemical Corp	675 Massachusetts	Cambridge	MA	02139	R W MacPherson	617-576-8000	R	100	0.3
Pace International LP	PO Box	Kirkland	WA	98083	Brooke Van Wyk	206-827-8711	R	100*	0.4
Radiator Specialty Co	PO Box 34689	Charlotte	NC	28234	Herman Blumenthal	704-377-6555	R	100	0.6
Parker+Amchem	32100ephenson Hwy	Madison H	MI	48071	Robert Lurcott	313-583-9300	S	87	0.6
Henkel Corp Textile Chemicals	PO Box 411729	Charlotte	NC	28241	JC Porterfield	704-587-3800	D	85	<0.1
DA Stuart Co	7575 Plaza Ct	Willowbrook	IL	60521	J Castle	708-655-4595	R	80	0.3
Technical Chemical Co	PO Box 540095	Dallas	TX	75354	NH Dudley	214-556-1421	R	80	<0.1
Monsanto Co	260 Springside Dr	Akron	OH	44334	Ian Kirkwood	216-666-4111	D	64	0.4
Kester Solder	515 E Touhy Av	Des Plaines	IL	60018	LD Kramer	708-297-1600	D	60	0.5
Turco Products Inc	PO Box 195	Marion	OH	43302	AL Hiller	614-382-5172	S	60	0.1
Westco Chemicals Inc	11312 Hartland St	N Hollywood	CA	91605	Alan Zwillinger	818-980-1152	R	52	<0.1
CRC Industries Inc	885 Louis Dr	Warminster	PA	18974	Eugene Fleishman	215-674-4300	S	50	0.1
DGF Stoess Inc	PO Box 3286	Sioux City	IA	51102	Jorg Siebert	712-943-1670	S	50	0.2
Eastman Gelatine Corp	227 Washington St	Peabody	MA	01960	Wayne Jones	508-531-1700	S	50*	0.3
Kind and Knox Gelatine Inc	PO Box 927	Sioux City	IA	51102	Charles P Markham	712-943-5516	S	50*	0.2
Varn Products Company Inc	8 Allerman Rd	Oakland	NJ	07436	Joseph Von Zwehl	201-337-3600	R	47	0.3
Chemonics Industries Inc	PO Box 21568	Phoenix	AZ	85036	Frank M Feffer Jr	602-262-5401	S	40*	0.3
Isolatek International	41 Furnace St	Stanhope	NJ	07874	James P Verhalen	201-347-1200	S	38*	0.2
United Laboratories Inc	955 Hawthorne Dr	Itasca	IL	60143	NJ Savaiano	708-773-0252	R	37*	0.3
Koch Chemical Co	PO Box 2256	Wichita	KS	67201	William G Spence	316-832-5500	D	28	0.2
Colorcon	Moyer Blv	West Point	PA	19486	TD Boehning	215-699-7733	S	25*	0.2
Laticrete International Inc	1 Laticrete Park N	Bethany	CT	06525	David Rothberg	203-393-0010	R	25	0.1
US Packaging Corp	440 Denniston Ct	Wheeling	IL	60090	Dennis D Swick	708-459-5030	S	25	0.1
Auric Corp	470 Frelinghuysen	Newark	NJ	07114	Maurice Bick	201-242-4110	P	23	<0.1
Hill Brothers Chemical Co	1675 N Main St	Orange	CA	92667	B Douglas Hill	714-998-8800	R	22	0.1
JM Huber Corp	4940 Peachtree	Norcross	GA	30071	Charles Snyder	404-441-1301	D	21*	0.1
Lion Industries Inc	2801 SE Columbia	Vancouver	WA	98661	Charles McQueeney	206-694-9780	R	20	<0.1
Pelikan Inc	1 Imaging Ln	Derry	PA	15627	Don Polak	412-694-9600	D	20	0.1
Tanner Industries	5811 Tacony St	Philadelphia	PA	19135	Steven B Tanner	215-535-7530	R	20	0.1
Euclid Chemical Co	19218 Redwood Rd	Cleveland	OH	44110	JL Korach	216-531-9222	D	19	0.1
Heatbath Corp	PO Box 2978	Springfield	MA	01102	EA Walen	413-543-3381	R	19*	0.1
Hydrolabs Inc	PO Box 610	Albemarle	NC	28002	David Farrar	704-983-4136	S	17	<0.1
Berryman Products Inc	3800 E Randol Mill	Arlington	TX	76011	R T Blankenship	817-640-2376	R	16	<0.1
Fiber Materials Inc	5 Morin St	Biddeford	ME	04005	M Subilia	207-282-5911	R	16*	0.2
Standard Fusee Corp	PO Box 1047	Easton	MD	21601	Charles H O'Reilly	410-822-0318	R	16	0.1
Advanced Polymer Systems Inc	3696 Haven Av	Redwood City	CA	94063	John J Meakem Jr	415-366-2626	P	16	<0.1
Apollo of the Ozarks Inc	PO Box 25	Stanton	MO	63079	T Scaman	314-927-5271	R	15*	<0.1
Blue Magic Products Inc	PO Box 4175	Stockton	CA	95204	Anthony Bova	209-948-8075	R	15	0.1
Browning Chemical Corp	707 Westchester	White Plains	NY	10604	F M Browning	914-686-0300	R	15*	0.1
Elco Corp	PO Box 609168	Cleveland	OH	44109	RD Wyvill	216-749-2605	S	15	<0.1
Enthone-OMI Inc	PO Box 1900	New Haven	CT	06508	Richard G Ferretti	203-799-4907	S	15*	0.1
Industrial Terminal Systems Inc	PO Box 4127	N Kensington	PA	15068	Mike Steimer	412-335-9837	R	15*	<0.1
Niacet Corp	PO Box 258	Niagara Falls	NY	14304	Michael R Brannen	716-285-1474	R	15	<0.1
Unelko Corp	7428 E Karen Dr	Scottsdale	AZ	85260	Howard Ohlhausen	602-991-7272	R	15	<0.1
Wheatland Waters Inc	PO Box 2170	Olathe	KS	66061	Al Cerne	913-782-4141	R	15*	<0.1
Balchem Corp	PO Box 175	Slate Hill	NY	10973	Herb Weiss	914-355-2861	P	15	0.1
Tempo Shain Corp	23 Upton St	Peabody	MA	01960	Robin Delaney	508-532-2421	R	13	<0.1
Koos Inc	4500 13th Ct	Kenosha	WI	53140	PP Lederer	414-654-5301	S	12	0.1
Mitco Inc	1601 Steele Av	Grand Rapids	MI	49507	Bernard D Mitchell	616-241-4684	R	12	<0.1
SKW Chemicals Inc	1509 Johnson Ferry	Marietta	GA	30062	Alan R Mick	404-971-1317	S	12*	<0.1
SKW Holding Inc	PO Box 368	Niagara Falls	NY	14302	Herbert Knahl	716-285-1252	R	12	<0.1
Symons Corp	Glenridge Industrial	Centralia	IL	62801	Bill Miller	618-533-2761	D	12	<0.1
Tech Spray Inc	PO Box 949	Amarillo	TX	79105	RG Russell	806-372-8523	R	12	<0.1
American Polywater Corp	PO Box 53	Stillwater	MN	55082	John M Fee	612-430-2270	R	10	<0.1
Anderson Chemical Company	Box 1041	Litchfield	MN	55355	J Terry Anderson	612-693-2477	R	10	<0.1
Betz MetChem	508 Prudential Rd	Horsham	PA	19044	William A Milsky	215-957-2460	D	10*	0.1

Source: *Ward's Business Directory of U.S. Private and Public Companies*, Volumes 1 and 2, 1996. The company type code used is as follows: P - Public, R - Private, S - Subsidiary, D - Division, J - Joint Venture, A - Affiliate, G - Group. Sales are in millions of dollars, employees are in thousands. An asterisk (*) indicates an estimated sales volume. The symbol < stands for 'less than'. Company names and addresses are truncated, in some cases, to fit into the available space.

MATERIALS CONSUMED

Material	Quantity	Delivered Cost ($ million)
Materials, ingredients, containers, and supplies	(X)	4,379.5
Crude nonmetallic minerals, including limestone, clay, gypsum, talc, etc.	(X)	80.9
Fats, oils, greases, and tallow	(X)	323.3
Alkalies and chlorine	(X)	168.4
Industrial inorganic chemicals	(X)	528.8
Wood rosin, turpentine, and other wood chemicals, including tall oil	(X)	71.5
Synthetic organic chemicals, not elsewhere classified	(X)	868.9
Refined petroleum products, including naphtha solvents, petrolatum, waxes, etc.	(X)	283.9
Plastics and resin materials (synthetic)	(X)	89.4
Paperboard containers, boxes, and corrugated paperboard	(X)	106.9
Plastics containers	(X)	59.4
Metal containers	(X)	104.3
All other materials and components, parts, containers, and supplies	(X)	920.6
Materials, ingredients, containers, and supplies, nsk	(X)	773.2

Source: 1992 *Economic Census*. Explanation of symbols used: (D): Withheld to avoid disclosure of competitive data; na: Not available; (S): Withheld because statistical norms were not met; (X): Not applicable; (Z): Less than half the unit shown; nec: Not elsewhere classified; nsk: Not specified by kind; - : zero; * : 10-19 percent estimated; ** : 20-29 percent estimated.

PRODUCT SHARE DETAILS

Product or Product Class	% Share
Chemical preparations, nec	100.00
Evaporated salt (bulk, pressed blocks, and packaged)	5.65
Fatty acids (produced for sale as such)	5.30
Saturated stearic fatty acids (40 to 50 percent stearic content)	21.85
Saturated hydrogenated animal and vegetable fatty acids.	9.43
Other saturated fatty acids, including hydrogenated fish and marine mammal fatty acids	34.18
Unsaturated oleic fatty acids, including white oleic acid and red oil	11.79
Other unsaturated fatty acids	(D)
Tall oil fatty acids containing less than 2 percent rosin acids and more than 95 percent fatty acids	11.99
Tall oil fatty acids containing 2 percent or more rosin acids	(D)
Fatty acids (produced for sale as such), nsk	1.35
Gelatin, except ready-to-eat desserts	3.30
Food grade gelatin, excluding ready-to-eat desserts and pharmaceutical grade	27.98
Pharmaceutical grade gelatin, except unfilled capsules	17.22
Other gelatin products (unfilled capsules, gelatin sheets for theatrical use, photographic, or technical grade gelatin)	(D)
Gelatin, except ready-to-eat desserts, nsk	(D)
Chemical preparations, nec, including essential oils, automotive chemicals, and water treating compounds	74.77
Citrus fruit essential oils (unblended, natural), including orange, lemon, and lime	1.48
Other essential oils (unblended, natural), including spearmint, peppermint, cedar wood, clove, and nutmeg oils	2.11
Fireworks	0.32
Pyrotechnics (including flares, jet fuel igniters, railroad torpedoes, toy pistol caps, etc.)	1.71
Rubber processing preparations, including red lead and 2-mercaptoimidazoline rubber accelerator composition	0.69
Automotive antifreeze preparations	5.21
Other automotive chemicals (antiknock compounds, additives for lubrication oils, battery acid, de-icing fluid, etc.)	5.79
Concrete curing and floor hardening materials	1.84
Drilling mud materials, mud thinners, thickeners, and purifiers	0.77
Chemical foundry supplies, including binders, core oils, core wash, etc.	3.38
Household tints and dyes	(D)
Metal-treating compounds (nonoil-base) for nitriding, pickling, drawing, and cutting	3.89
Oil-treating compounds (nonoil-base)	0.98
Sizes (textile, paper, and other)	3.26
Inks, writing and stamp pad ink, including indelible ink and marking fluid, excluding drawing and printing inks	1.11
Boiler water treating compounds	3.00
Swimming pool chemical preparations	4.57
Cooling tower water treating compounds	4.71
Other water treating compounds	14.52
Waterproofing compounds (textile, paper, electrical, leather, masonry, etc.)	2.64
Vitrifiable enamels and glass frit	0.70
Plating compounds	2.55
Lighter fluids (cigarette, charcoal, etc.)	0.86
Waxes (animal, vegetable, mineral, including blends), except petroleum waxes and polishing preparations	(D)
Distilled water	0.68
Other industrial chemical specialties, including fluxes, plastics wood preparations, embalming prepartions, etc.	28.03
Chemical preparations, nec, including essential oils, automotive chemicals, and water treating compounds, nsk	3.87
Chemical preparations, nec, nsk	10.98

Source: 1992 *Economic Census*. The values shown are percent of total shipments in an industry. Values of indented subcategories are summed in the main heading. The symbol (D) appears when data are withheld to prevent disclosure of competitive information. The abbreviation nsk stands for 'not specified by kind' and nec for 'not elsewhere classified'.

INPUTS AND OUTPUTS FOR CHEMICAL PREPARATIONS, NEC

Economic Sector or Industry Providing Inputs	%	Sector	Economic Sector or Industry Buying Outputs	%	Sector
Wholesale trade	9.9	Trade	Petroleum & natural gas well drilling	10.6	Constr.
Industrial inorganic chemicals, nec	7.5	Manufg.	Exports	8.6	Foreign
Cyclic crudes and organics	7.1	Manufg.	Petroleum refining	6.1	Manufg.
Petroleum refining	6.4	Manufg.	Personal consumption expenditures	4.6	
Imports	6.3	Foreign	Plating & polishing	4.5	Manufg.
Chemical & fertilizer mineral	5.3	Mining	State & local government enterprises, nec	4.3	Gov't
Motor freight transportation & warehousing	5.2	Util.	Electric services (utilities)	2.8	Util.
Plastics materials & resins	3.6	Manufg.	Metal coating & allied services	2.3	Manufg.
Nonferrous rolling & drawing, nec	2.7	Manufg.	Drugs	2.2	Manufg.
Paperboard containers & boxes	2.4	Manufg.	Medical & health services, nec	2.2	Services

Continued on next page.

INPUTS AND OUTPUTS FOR CHEMICAL PREPARATIONS, NEC - Continued

Economic Sector or Industry Providing Inputs	%	Sector	Economic Sector or Industry Buying Outputs	%	Sector
Railroads & related services	2.4	Util.	Semiconductors & related devices	2.1	Manufg.
Animal & marine fats & oils	2.1	Manufg.	Plastics materials & resins	1.9	Manufg.
Alkalies & chlorine	2.0	Manufg.	Commercial printing	1.7	Manufg.
Gas production & distribution (utilities)	2.0	Util.	Flavoring extracts & syrups, nec	1.6	Manufg.
Surface active agents	1.9	Manufg.	Chemical preparations, nec	1.3	Manufg.
Chemical preparations, nec	1.8	Manufg.	Electronic components nec	1.3	Manufg.
Metal cans	1.7	Manufg.	Paints & allied products	1.2	Manufg.
Electric services (utilities)	1.7	Util.	Ready-mixed concrete	1.1	Manufg.
Primary nonferrous metals, nec	1.5	Manufg.	Motor vehicle parts & accessories	1.0	Manufg.
Advertising	1.5	Services	Steel wire & related products	1.0	Manufg.
Glass containers	1.4	Manufg.	Welding apparatus, electric	1.0	Manufg.
Miscellaneous plastics products	1.3	Manufg.	Meat animals	0.9	Agric.
Engineering, architectural, & surveying services	1.3	Services	Cyclic crudes and organics	0.9	Manufg.
Carbon black	1.2	Manufg.	Water supply & sewage systems	0.9	Util.
Gum & wood chemicals	1.2	Manufg.	Federal Government purchases, national defense	0.9	Fed Govt
Banking	1.2	Fin/R.E.	Food preparations, nec	0.8	Manufg.
Miscellaneous crops	1.0	Agric.	Metal heat treating	0.8	Manufg.
Water transportation	1.0	Util.	Soap & other detergents	0.8	Manufg.
Nonferrous metal ores, except copper	0.9	Mining	Blast furnaces & steel mills	0.7	Manufg.
Explosives	0.9	Manufg.	Manufacturing industries, nec	0.7	Manufg.
Noncomparable imports	0.9	Foreign	Radio & TV communication equipment	0.7	Manufg.
Chewing gum	0.7	Manufg.	Sanitary services, steam supply, irrigation	0.7	Util.
Clay, ceramic, & refractory minerals	0.6	Mining	Hospitals	0.7	Services
Maintenance of nonfarm buildings nec	0.6	Constr.	Paper mills, except building paper	0.6	Manufg.
Air transportation	0.5	Util.	Sporting & athletic goods, nec	0.6	Manufg.
Communications, except radio & TV	0.5	Util.	Tires & inner tubes	0.6	Manufg.
Eating & drinking places	0.5	Trade	Paperboard mills	0.5	Manufg.
Miscellaneous repair shops	0.5	Services	Toilet preparations	0.5	Manufg.
Commercial printing	0.4	Manufg.	Feed grains	0.4	Agric.
Pipe, valves, & pipe fittings	0.4	Manufg.	Fabricated rubber products, nec	0.4	Manufg.
Vegetable oil mills, nec	0.4	Manufg.	Organic fibers, noncellulosic	0.4	Manufg.
Equipment rental & leasing services	0.4	Services	Prepared feeds, nec	0.4	Manufg.
Inorganic pigments	0.3	Manufg.	Steel pipe & tubes	0.4	Manufg.
Metal stampings, nec	0.3	Manufg.	Transit & bus transportation	0.4	Util.
Synthetic rubber	0.3	Manufg.	Wholesale trade	0.4	Trade
Toilet preparations	0.3	Manufg.	Nursing & personal care facilities	0.4	Services
Wood products, nec	0.3	Manufg.	Federal Government purchases, nondefense	0.4	Fed Govt
Real estate	0.3	Fin/R.E.	S/L Govt. purch., natural resource & recreation.	0.4	S/L Govt
Legal services	0.3	Services	Alkalies & chlorine	0.3	Manufg.
Forestry products	0.2	Agric.	Aluminum rolling & drawing	0.3	Manufg.
Coal	0.2	Mining	Cold finishing of steel shapes	0.3	Manufg.
Bags, except textile	0.2	Manufg.	Household cooking equipment	0.3	Manufg.
Fabricated metal products, nec	0.2	Manufg.	Iron & steel foundries	0.3	Manufg.
Fabricated textile products, nec	0.2	Manufg.	Mineral wool	0.3	Manufg.
Meat packing plants	0.2	Manufg.	Nonferrous wire drawing & insulating	0.3	Manufg.
Metal barrels, drums, & pails	0.2	Manufg.	Periodicals	0.3	Manufg.
Metal foil & leaf	0.2	Manufg.	Photographic equipment & supplies	0.3	Manufg.
Sanitary services, steam supply, irrigation	0.2	Util.	Pipe, valves, & pipe fittings	0.3	Manufg.
Management & consulting services & labs	0.2	Services	Secondary nonferrous metals	0.3	Manufg.
U.S. Postal Service	0.2	Gov't	Surface active agents	0.3	Manufg.
Machinery, except electrical, nec	0.1	Manufg.	Telephone & telegraph apparatus	0.3	Manufg.
Rubber & plastics hose & belting	0.1	Manufg.	Eating & drinking places	0.3	Trade
Wet corn milling	0.1	Manufg.	Retail trade, except eating & drinking	0.3	Trade
Water supply & sewage systems	0.1	Util.	S/L Govt. purch., other general government	0.3	S/L Govt
Insurance carriers	0.1	Fin/R.E.	Dairy farm products	0.2	Agric.
Accounting, auditing & bookkeeping	0.1	Services	Poultry & eggs	0.2	Agric.
Business/professional associations	0.1	Services	Industrial buildings	0.2	Constr.
Computer & data processing services	0.1	Services	Residential 1-unit structures, nonfarm	0.2	Constr.
Scrap	0.1	Scrap	Adhesives & sealants	0.2	Manufg.
			Aircraft & missile equipment, nec	0.2	Manufg.
			Book publishing	0.2	Manufg.
			Concrete products, nec	0.2	Manufg.
			Confectionery products	0.2	Manufg.
			Fabricated textile products, nec	0.2	Manufg.
			Hardware, nec	0.2	Manufg.
			Household appliances, nec	0.2	Manufg.
			Manifold business forms	0.2	Manufg.
			Meat packing plants	0.2	Manufg.
			Metal stampings, nec	0.2	Manufg.
			Miscellaneous publishing	0.2	Manufg.
			Nonferrous rolling & drawing, nec	0.2	Manufg.
			Pottery products, nec	0.2	Manufg.
			Shoes, except rubber	0.2	Manufg.
			Surgical appliances & supplies	0.2	Manufg.
			Radio & TV broadcasting	0.2	Util.

Continued on next page.

INPUTS AND OUTPUTS FOR CHEMICAL PREPARATIONS, NEC - Continued

Economic Sector or Industry Providing Inputs	%	Sector	Economic Sector or Industry Buying Outputs	%	Sector
			Railroads & related services	0.2	Util.
			Real estate	0.2	Fin/R.E.
			Amusement & recreation services nec	0.2	Services
			Funeral service & crematories	0.2	Services
			Labor, civic, social, & fraternal associations	0.2	Services
			S/L Govt. purch., police	0.2	S/L Govt
			Oil bearing crops	0.1	Agric.
			Crude petroleum & natural gas	0.1	Mining
			Electric utility facility construction	0.1	Constr.
			Maintenance of nonfarm buildings nec	0.1	Constr.
			Nonfarm residential structure maintenance	0.1	Constr.
			Office buildings	0.1	Constr.
			Residential additions/alterations, nonfarm	0.1	Constr.
			Automotive stampings	0.1	Manufg.
			Blankbooks & looseleaf binders	0.1	Manufg.
			Book printing	0.1	Manufg.
			Broadwoven fabric mills	0.1	Manufg.
			Canvas & related products	0.1	Manufg.
			Coated fabrics, not rubberized	0.1	Manufg.
			Electric housewares & fans	0.1	Manufg.
			Fabricated plate work (boiler shops)	0.1	Manufg.
			Frozen fruits, fruit juices & vegetables	0.1	Manufg.
			Games, toys, & children's vehicles	0.1	Manufg.
			Greeting card publishing	0.1	Manufg.
			Gypsum products	0.1	Manufg.
			Household refrigerators & freezers	0.1	Manufg.
			Ice cream & frozen desserts	0.1	Manufg.
			Industrial inorganic chemicals, nec	0.1	Manufg.
			Lubricating oils & greases	0.1	Manufg.
			Metal sanitary ware	0.1	Manufg.
			Miscellaneous plastics products	0.1	Manufg.
			Optical instruments & lenses	0.1	Manufg.
			Pickles, sauces, & salad dressings	0.1	Manufg.
			Polishes & sanitation goods	0.1	Manufg.
			Primary aluminum	0.1	Manufg.
			Synthetic rubber	0.1	Manufg.
			Typesetting	0.1	Manufg.
			Water transportation	0.1	Util.
			Business services nec	0.1	Services
			Membership sports & recreation clubs	0.1	Services
			Motion pictures	0.1	Services
			Theatrical producers, bands, entertainers	0.1	Services
			S/L Govt. purch., health & hospitals	0.1	S/L Govt
			S/L Govt. purch., higher education	0.1	S/L Govt

Source: Benchmark Input-Output Accounts for the U.S. Economy, 1982, U.S. Department of Commerce, Washington, D.C., July 1991. Data, as reported in the source, are organized by the 1977 SIC structure in use in 1982 but have been matched, as closely as is possible, to the 1987 SIC structure used in this book.

OCCUPATIONS EMPLOYED BY SIC 289 - MISCELLANEOUS CHEMICAL PRODUCTS

Occupation	% of Total 1994	Change to 2005	Occupation	% of Total 1994	Change to 2005
Crushing & mixing machine operators	7.9	-42.7	Maintenance repairers, general utility	2.0	-14.1
Sales & related workers nec	5.0	-4.6	Truck drivers light & heavy	1.9	-1.6
Chemical equipment controllers, operators	4.8	-14.1	Industrial production managers	1.9	-4.5
Science & mathematics technicians	4.6	-4.5	Hand packers & packagers	1.8	-18.2
Packaging & filling machine operators	3.8	-4.6	Bookkeeping, accounting, & auditing clerks	1.7	-28.4
General managers & top executives	3.6	-9.5	General office clerks	1.7	-18.6
Secretaries, ex legal & medical	3.5	-13.1	Extruding & forming machine workers	1.5	5.0
Assemblers, fabricators, & hand workers nec	3.3	-4.6	Clerical supervisors & managers	1.4	-2.4
Chemists	3.1	-4.6	Freight, stock, & material movers, hand	1.3	-23.6
Chemical plant & system operators	2.7	43.1	Industrial truck & tractor operators	1.2	-4.5
Machine operators nec	2.6	-15.9	Managers & administrators nec	1.2	-4.6
Traffic, shipping, & receiving clerks	2.3	-8.2	Chemical engineers	1.2	-4.6
Industrial machinery mechanics	2.2	5.0	Machinists	1.1	-4.6
Inspectors, testers, & graders, precision	2.1	-4.6	Order clerks, materials, merchandise, & service	1.0	-6.7
Marketing, advertising, & PR managers	2.0	-4.6			

Source: Industry-Occupation Matrix, Bureau of Labor Statistics. These data relate to one or more 3-digit SIC industry groups rather than to a single 4-digit SIC. The change reported for each occupation to the year 2005 is a percent of growth or decline as estimated by the Bureau of Labor Statistics. The abbreviation nec stands for 'not elsewhere classified'.

LOCATION BY STATE AND REGIONAL CONCENTRATION

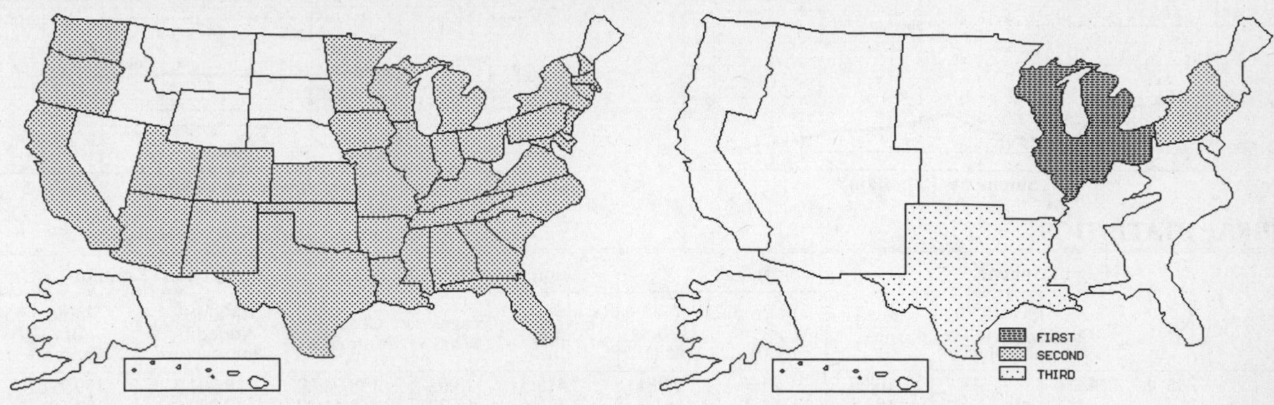

INDUSTRY DATA BY STATE

State	Establish-ments	Shipments			Employment				Cost as % of Shipments	Investment per Employee ($)
		Total ($ mil)	% of U.S.	Per Establ.	Total Number	% of U.S.	Per Establ.	Wages ($/hour)		
Illinois	97	1,209.1	12.1	12.5	2,700	7.3	28	16.17	48.6	13,296
Texas	157	1,149.3	11.5	7.3	3,300	8.9	21	12.00	43.2	7,485
Ohio	101	932.6	9.4	9.2	3,700	10.0	37	14.83	51.5	19,595
California	167	654.0	6.6	3.9	2,900	7.8	17	12.54	43.9	7,517
Michigan	60	605.4	6.1	10.1	2,300	6.2	38	15.11	48.1	7,391
New Jersey	85	504.2	5.1	5.9	2,000	5.4	24	12.04	46.9	3,000
Georgia	42	373.3	3.7	8.9	1,000	2.7	24	12.93	55.8	6,400
New York	67	369.7	3.7	5.5	1,900	5.1	28	14.30	50.9	8,316
Pennsylvania	81	365.2	3.7	4.5	1,400	3.8	17	14.00	61.0	12,071
Massachusetts	28	326.7	3.3	11.7	1,700	4.6	61	14.20	48.4	10,647
South Carolina	19	237.1	2.4	12.5	1,000	2.7	53	14.64	41.2	10,900
Tennessee	24	216.4	2.2	9.0	1,300	3.5	54	13.43	56.1	6,692
Missouri	29	169.6	1.7	5.8	600	1.6	21	12.33	36.0	6,333
Wisconsin	35	163.5	1.6	4.7	700	1.9	20	11.00	56.5	5,000
Florida	54	161.0	1.6	3.0	800	2.2	15	11.00	52.1	5,250
Kansas	13	160.2	1.6	12.3	700	1.9	54	11.70	46.6	9,000
Indiana	41	156.4	1.6	3.8	600	1.6	15	10.33	50.8	9,333
Louisiana	22	147.4	1.5	6.7	600	1.6	27	14.67	71.9	-
North Carolina	48	146.5	1.5	3.1	600	1.6	13	12.80	53.7	9,000
Connecticut	21	103.8	1.0	4.9	600	1.6	29	12.20	50.0	5,167
Virginia	16	99.8	1.0	6.2	500	1.3	31	10.43	63.8	4,800
Washington	23	88.5	0.9	3.8	300	0.8	13	10.33	69.4	4,333
Utah	16	59.2	0.6	3.7	300	0.8	19	10.40	44.3	12,333
Arkansas	8	57.5	0.6	7.2	200	0.5	25	12.33	48.5	10,000
Arizona	17	56.0	0.6	3.3	200	0.5	12	11.50	31.1	5,000
Oregon	16	49.8	0.5	3.1	100	0.3	6	13.50	53.0	10,000
Maryland	18	46.0	0.5	2.6	400	1.1	22	11.20	42.2	5,000
Kentucky	10	42.5	0.4	4.3	300	0.8	30	10.00	48.2	2,667
Rhode Island	13	41.9	0.4	3.2	200	0.5	15	10.50	69.0	-
Colorado	17	14.5	0.1	0.9	200	0.5	12	18.50	49.0	4,500
Minnesota	28	(D)	-	-	175 *	0.5	6	-	-	-
Oklahoma	20	(D)	-	-	175 *	0.5	9	-	-	9,143
Alabama	18	(D)	-	-	1,750 *	4.7	97	-	-	1,086
Mississippi	12	(D)	-	-	375 *	1.0	31	-	-	-
Iowa	11	(D)	-	-	375 *	1.0	34	-	-	-
New Hampshire	8	(D)	-	-	175 *	0.5	22	-	-	4,571
New Mexico	8	(D)	-	-	175 *	0.5	22	-	-	-

Source: 1992 *Economic Census*. The states are in descending order of shipments or establishments (if shipment data are missing for the majority). The symbol (D) appears when data are withheld to prevent disclosure of competitive information. States marked with (D) are sorted by number of establishments. A dash (-) indicates that the data element cannot be calculated; * indicates the midpoint of a range.

2911 - PETROLEUM REFINING

Shipments ($ million)

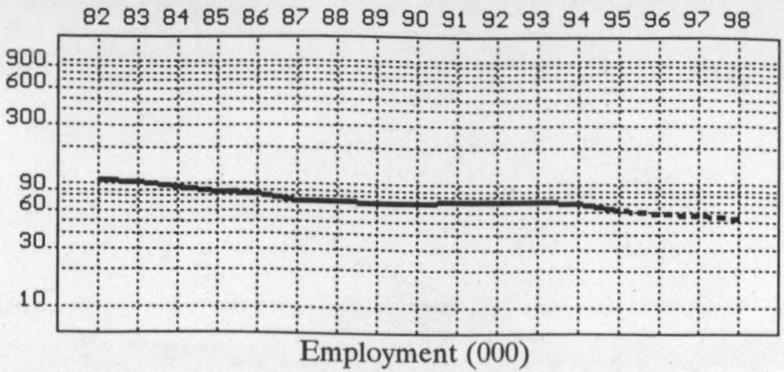

Employment (000)

GENERAL STATISTICS

Year	Companies	Establishments Total	Establishments with 20 or more employees	Employment Total (000)	Production Workers (000)	Production Hours (Mil)	Compensation Payroll ($ mil)	Compensation Wages ($/hr)	Cost of Materials	Value Added by Manufacture	Value of Shipments	Capital Invest.
1982	283	434	313	108.7	71.3	148.4	3,410.3	13.92	178,947.0	19,204.3	199,722.8	6,412.3
1983				103.5	66.7	141.3	3,440.4	15.20	163,416.7	17,880.8	182,591.8	4,319.1
1984				94.6	61.3	131.9	3,326.3	15.40	164,812.7	12,743.3	177,692.3	3,494.4
1985				85.7	56.1	119.9	3,073.0	16.05	153,095.1	13,659.5	167,501.8	3,037.5
1986				84.2	55.2	112.8	3,131.1	17.44	95,995.2	13,761.7	113,286.4	2,273.0
1987	201	309	221	74.6	50.0	103.3	2,845.5	17.39	104,826.4	14,223.3	118,186.2	2,035.0
1988				73.2	49.5	102.9	2,928.9	17.80	97,320.7	20,687.6	118,829.5	2,326.7
1989		326	219	72.4	47.9	104.6	2,984.1	17.77	110,521.6	21,580.0	131,192.3	2,986.9
1990				71.9	47.3	105.8	3,195.6	18.56	138,537.0	22,822.0	159,411.1	3,818.7
1991				73.9	47.6	106.5	3,448.4	19.46	123,916.8	19,795.7	145,391.5	5,600.8
1992	132	232	197	74.8	47.9	109.3	3,636.3	19.74	116,908.0	19,100.6	136,239.0	6,139.7
1993				73.1	47.3	106.5	3,735.3	21.04	110,279.0	18,710.3	129,961.1	5,985.8
1994				71.7	46.3	107.1	3,796.0	21.64	105,722.7	23,231.6	128,235.6	5,215.2
1995				61.9P	40.2P	93.7P	3,551.0P	21.87P	95,049.1P	20,886.2P	115,289.1P	5,029.1P
1996				59.1P	38.3P	90.6P	3,586.2P	22.45P	91,339.3P	20,071.0P	110,789.3P	5,158.0P
1997				56.2P	36.4P	87.5P	3,621.5P	23.03P	87,629.4P	19,255.8P	106,289.5P	5,286.9P
1998				53.4P	34.5P	84.4P	3,656.8P	23.61P	83,919.6P	18,440.6P	101,789.7P	5,415.8P

Sources: 1982, 1987, 1992 *Economic Census*; *Annual Survey of Manufactures*, 83-86, 88-91, 93-94. Establishment counts for non-Census years are from *County Business Patterns*; establishment values for 83-84 are extrapolations. 'P's show projections by the editors. Industries reclassified in 87 will not have data for prior years.

INDICES OF CHANGE

Year	Companies	Establishments Total	Establishments with 20 or more employees	Employment Total (000)	Production Workers (000)	Production Hours (Mil)	Compensation Payroll ($ mil)	Compensation Wages ($/hr)	Cost of Materials	Value Added by Manufacture	Value of Shipments	Capital Invest.
1982	214	187	159	145	149	136	94	71	153	101	147	104
1983				138	139	129	95	77	140	94	134	70
1984				126	128	121	91	78	141	67	130	57
1985				115	117	110	85	81	131	72	123	49
1986				113	115	103	86	88	82	72	83	37
1987	152	133	112	100	104	95	78	88	90	74	87	33
1988				98	103	94	81	90	83	108	87	38
1989		141	111	97	100	96	82	90	95	113	96	49
1990				96	99	97	88	94	119	119	117	62
1991				99	99	97	95	99	106	104	107	91
1992	100	100	100	100	100	100	100	100	100	100	100	100
1993				98	99	97	103	107	94	98	95	97
1994				96	97	98	104	110	90	122	94	85
1995				83P	84P	86P	98P	111P	81P	109P	85P	82P
1996				79P	80P	83P	99P	114P	78P	105P	81P	84P
1997				75P	76P	80P	100P	117P	75P	101P	78P	86P
1998				71P	72P	77P	101P	120P	72P	97P	75P	88P

Sources: Same as General Statistics. Values reflect change from the base year, 1992. Values above 100 mean greater than 92, values below 100 mean less than 92, and a value of 100 in the 82-91 or 93-98 period means same as 92. 'P's mark projections by the editors.

SELECTED RATIOS

For 1992	Avg. of All Manufact.	Analyzed Industry	Index	For 1992	Avg. of All Manufact.	Analyzed Industry	Index
Employees per Establishment	46	322	706	Value Added per Production Worker	122,353	398,760	326
Payroll per Establishment	1,332,320	15,673,707	1,176	Cost per Establishment	4,239,462	503,913,793	11,886
Payroll per Employee	29,181	48,614	167	Cost per Employee	92,853	1,562,941	1,683
Production Workers per Establishment	31	206	657	Cost per Production Worker	135,003	2,440,668	1,808
Wages per Establishment	734,496	9,299,922	1,266	Shipments per Establishment	8,100,800	587,237,069	7,249
Wages per Production Worker	23,390	45,043	193	Shipments per Employee	177,425	1,821,377	1,027
Hours per Production Worker	2,025	2,282	113	Shipments per Production Worker	257,966	2,844,238	1,103
Wages per Hour	11.55	19.74	171	Investment per Establishment	278,244	26,464,224	9,511
Value Added per Establishment	3,842,210	82,330,172	2,143	Investment per Employee	6,094	82,082	1,347
Value Added per Employee	84,153	255,356	303	Investment per Production Worker	8,861	128,177	1,447

Sources: Same as General Statistics. The 'Average of All Manufacturing' column represents the average of all manufacturing industries reported for the most recent complete year available. The Index shows the relationship between the Average and the Analyzed Industry. For example, 100 means that they are equal; 500 that the Analyzed Industry is five times the average; 50 means that the Analyzed Industry is half the national average. The abbreviation 'na' is used to show that data are 'not available'.

LEADING COMPANIES

Number shown: 75 Total sales ($ mil): **471,263** Total employment (000): **470.4**

Company Name	Address				CEO Name	Phone	Co. Type	Sales ($ mil)	Empl. (000)
Exxon Corp	225 E John W	Irving	TX	75062	LG Rawl	214-444-1000	P	108,851	91.0
Mobil Corp	3225 Gallows Rd	Fairfax	VA	22037	Allen E Murray	703-849-3000	P	53,363	55.5
Mobil Oil Corp	3225 Gallows Rd	Fairfax	VA	22037	Allen E Murray	703-849-3000	S	51,736	39.1
Chevron Corp	225 Bush St	San Francisco	CA	94104	Kenneth T Derr	415-894-7700	P	35,854	45.8
Texaco Inc	2000 Westchester	White Plains	NY	10650	A C DeCrane Jr	914-253-4000	P	32,540	32.5
Shell Oil Co	PO Box 2463	Houston	TX	77252	Philip J Carroll	713-241-6161	S	21,600	21.5
Chevron USA Products	575 Market St	San Francisco	CA	94105	David R Hoyer	415-894-7700	S	17,500	10.6
Atlantic Richfield Co	515 S Flower St	Los Angeles	CA	90071	Mike R Bowlin	213-486-3511	P	17,199	23.2
Conoco Inc	600 N Dairy	Houston	TX	77079	Robert E McKee II	713-293-1000	S	15,800	15.2
Mobil Oil Corp US	3225 Gallows Rd	Fairfax	VA	22037	JL Cooper	703-849-3000	D	14,041	11.1
Caltex Petroleum Corp	PO Box 619500	Dallas	TX	75261	Patrick J Ward	214-830-1000	J	14,000	8.0
Ashland Inc	PO Box 391	Ashland	KY	41114	John R Hall	606-329-3333	P	10,256	30.1
CITGO Petroleum Corp	PO Box 3758	Tulsa	OK	74102	Ron E Hall	918-495-4000	S	9,134	0.4
Star Enterprise	12700 Northbo	Houston	TX	77067	Lester Wilkes	713-874-7000	J	8,000*	5.0
Amerada Hess Corp	1185 Av Amer	New York	NY	10036	Leon Hess	212-997-8500	P	6,699	9.9
Tosco Corp	72 Cummings Pt Rd	Stamford	CT	06902	Thomas D O'Malley	203-977-1000	P	6,366	3.6
Unocal Refining & Marketing	PO Box 7600	Los Angeles	CA	90051	Neal E Schmale	213-977-7600	D	6,118	4.1
Farmland Industries Inc	PO Box 7305	Kansas City	MO	64116	HD Cleberg	816-459-6000	R	4,723	6.9
Lyondell Petrochemical Co	PO Box 3646	Houston	TX	77253	Bob G Gower	713-652-7200	P	3,857	2.3
Lyondell-CITGO Refining Ltd	PO Box 2451	Houston	TX	77252	Bob G Gower	713-652-7200	S	2,761	1.6
Diamond Shamrock Inc	PO Box 696000	San Antonio	TX	78269	R R Hemminghaus	210-641-6800	P	2,606	6.4
Ultramar Corp	2 Pickwick Plz	Greenwich	CT	06830	Jean Gaulin	203-622-7000	P	2,438	3.1
UNO-VEN Co	3850 N Wilke Rd	Arlington H	IL	60004	Edward T DiCorcia	708-818-1800	R	2,421	1.1
Clark Refining & Marketing Co	8182 Maryland Av	St Louis	MO	63105	Paul Melnuk	314-854-9696	S	2,258	5.5
Total Petroleum	900 19th St	Denver	CO	80202	Daniel L Valot	303-291-2000	P	2,205	6.4
Tosco Refining Co	2300 Clayton Rd	Concord	CA	94520	James M Cleary	510-602-4000	D	2,200*	1.0
United Refining Co	PO Box 780	Warren	PA	16365	John A Catsimatidis	814-723-1500	R	1,990	2.8
Crown Central Petroleum Corp	PO Box 1168	Baltimore	MD	21203	H A Rosenberg Jr	410-539-7400	P	1,699	3.0
Koch Refining Co	PO Box 2302	Wichita	KS	67201	Cy Nobles	316-832-5119	S	1,350	2.0
Valero Energy Corp	PO Box 500	San Antonio	TX	78292	William E Greehey	210-246-2000	P	1,222	1.7
Ultramar Inc	111 W Ocean Blv	Long Beach	CA	90802	John G Drosdick	310-495-5300	S	1,102	2.0
Tesoro Petroleum Corp	PO Box 17536	San Antonio	TX	78217	Michael D Burke	210-828-8484	P	877	0.9
Quaker State Corp	PO Box 989	Oil City	PA	16301	Herbert M Baum	814-676-7676	P	755	5.4
Thrifty Oil Co	10000 Lakewood	Downey	CA	90240	Ted Orden	310-923-9876	R	750	1.0
Pride Refining LP	500 Chestnut St	Abilene	TX	79602	Brad Stephens	915-677-2223	R	660	0.6
Holly Corp	100 Crescent Ct	Dallas	TX	75201	Lamar Norsworthy	214-871-3555	P	552	0.5
Navajo Refining Co	501 E Main St	Artesia	NM	88210	Jack Reid	505-748-3311	S	550*	0.4
Witco Corp	One American Ln	Greenwich	CT	06831	ER Myers	203-552-3211	D	400	1.0
National Coop Refinery Assoc	PO Box 1404	McPherson	KS	67460	Larry E Williams	316-241-2340	R	380*	0.5
Valero Refining Co	PO Box 9370	Corpus Christi	TX	78469	George Kain	512-282-6000	S	370*	0.6
Giant Industries Inc	23733 N Scottsdale	Scottsdale	AZ	85255	James E Acridge	602-585-8888	P	294	1.4
Lion Oil Co	PO Box 7005	El Dorado	AR	71731	Leslie B Lampton	501-862-8111	R	280	0.4
Indian Refining Ltd	PO Box 519	Lawrenceville	IL	62439	William Fedhaus	618-943-5555	S	250*	0.4
Frontier Oil Corp	1700 Lincoln St	Denver	CO	80203	Clark Johnson	303-860-6100	S	240	0.4
US Oil and Refining Co	PO Box 2255	Tacoma	WA	98401	Thomas C Temple	206-383-1651	S	236	0.2
Westland Oil Co	2740 Val View Dr	Shreveport	LA	71108	David Myatt	318-688-1300	R	210*	0.3
Chevron USA Products	1200 State St	Perth Amboy	NJ	08861	Charlie Lucas	908-738-2000	D	170*	0.1
Hunt Refining Co	PO Box 038995	Tuscaloosa	AL	35403	John Matson	205-758-6006	S	170*	0.3
La Gloria Oil and Gas Co	PO Box 840	Tyler	TX	75710	Charles L Dunlap	903-535-2200	S	170*	0.3
Locot Corp	4747 Bellaire Blv	Bellaire	TX	77401	Charles L Dunlap	713-660-4573	S	170*	0.3
Marathon Oil Co	PO Box 1191	Texas City	TX	77592	LJ Nordhousen	409-945-2331	D	170	0.3
Gary-Williams Energy Corp	370 17th St	Denver	CO	80202	RW Williams	303-628-3800	S	160	0.2
Placid Refining Co	1940 LA Hwy 1 N	Port Allen	LA	70767	Jerry Wright	504-387-0278	S	140	0.2
International Group Inc	PO Box 383	Wayne	PA	19087	W Ross Reucassel	610-687-9030	R	110	0.3
Calcasieu Refining Co	654 N Belt Dr E	Houston	TX	77060	FM Doughty	713-847-0846	S	107	<0.1
Huntway Partners LP	23822 W Valencia	Valencia	CA	91355	Juan Y Foster	805-253-1799	P	101	0.1
Cibro Petroleum Inc	1066 Zerega Av	Bronx	NY	10462	Nicholas Cirillo	718-824-5000	R	100*	0.2
Mapco Alaska Petroleum Inc	1076 Ocean Dock	Anchorage	AK	99501	Jeff Cook	907-276-4100	S	92*	0.1
DeMenno-Kerdoon	2000 N Alameda St	Compton	CA	90222	Bruce DeMenno	310-537-7100	R	82	0.2
Galaxie Corp	PO Box 338	Jackson	MS	39205	Mathew Holleman	601-961-6879	R	81*	0.1
Chemoil Corp	750 Battery St	San Francisco	CA	94111	Robert V Chandran	415-956-3834	R	71*	0.1
Barrett Refining Corp	23 E 9th St	Shawnee	OK	74801	John A Barrett Jr	405-275-3051	R	67*	<0.1
Somerset Refinery Inc	PO Box 1547	Somerset	KY	42501	WT Walker	606-679-6301	R	63	0.1
Anchor Gasoline Corp	114 E 5th St	Tulsa	OK	74103	Michael E Mockley	918-584-5291	R	60	<0.1
VGS Corp	PO Box 13609	Jackson	MS	39236	RG McGrath III	601-981-4151	S	58	0.1
San Joaquin Refining Company	PO Box 5576	Bakersfield	CA	93388	M Mojibi	805-327-4257	R	55	<0.1
Little America Refining Co	PO Box 510	Evansville	WY	82636	R Earl Holding	307-265-2800	S	53*	0.1
Montana Refining Co	1900 10th St	Great Falls	MT	59404	John Knorr	406-761-4100	S	51*	<0.1
CITGO Asphalt Refining Co	PO Box 3000	Blue Bell	PA	19422	Bruce Beck	215-542-4020	S	50	0.2
Moore and Munger Marketing	2 Corporate Dr	Shelton	CT	06484	Malcolm Orloff	203-925-4300	R	50	<0.1
Big West Oil Co	PO Box 678	Brigham City	UT	84302	Richard E Germer	801-734-6400	S	45	0.1
Ziegler Chemical & Mineral	100 Jericho	Jericho	NY	11753	G Ziegler Jr	516-681-9600	R	35	0.1
Tesoro Alaska Petroleum Co	PO Box 196272	Anchorage	AK	99519	Michael Burke	907-561-5521	S	30	0.2
TPA Inc	9101 LBJ Fwy LB-2	Dallas	TX	75243	Charles D Jinks	214-669-2908	R	30	0.2
Dyson Oil Inc	PO Box 266	Durant	OK	74702	Mike Dyson	405-924-8834	R	28*	<0.1

Source: *Ward's Business Directory of U.S. Private and Public Companies*, Volumes 1 and 2, 1996. The company type code used is as follows: P - Public, R - Private, S - Subsidiary, D - Division, J - Joint Venture, A - Affiliate, G - Group. Sales are in millions of dollars, employees are in thousands. An asterisk (*) indicates an estimated sales volume. The symbol < stands for 'less than'. Company names and addresses are truncated, in some cases, to fit into the available space.

MATERIALS CONSUMED

Material		Quantity	Delivered Cost ($ million)
Materials, ingredients, containers, and supplies		(X)	107,872.2
Domestic crude petroleum, including lease condensate	mil bbl	2,745.8	51,203.6
Foreign crude petroleum, including lease condensate	mil bbl	2,209.6	39,235.4
Foreign unfinished oils (received from foreign countries for further processing)	mil bbl	81.7	1,477.3
Ethane (C2), at least 80 percent purity	mil bbl	(D)	(D)
Propane (C3), at least 80 percent purity	mil bbl	24.2	285.1
Butane (C4), at least 80 percent purity	mil bbl	105.8	1,815.3
Gas mixtures (C2, C3, C4)	mil bbl	41.7	773.2
Isopentane and natural gasoline	mil bbl	63.1	1,212.2
Other natural gas liquids, including plant condensate	mil bbl	30.6	564.3
Benzol (benzene) (100 percent C6H6)	mil bbl	3.8	141.6
Toluene and xylene (100 percent basis)	mil lb	3,010.4	312.9
Antioxidant, antiknock compound, and inhibitor additives	mil lb	447.4	348.9
Other additives, including soaps and detergents	mil lb	246.7*	170.4
Animal and vegetable oils	mil lb	(D)	(D)
Chemical catalytic preparations		(X)	543.6
Sodium hydroxide (caustic soda)(100 percent NaOH)	1,000 s tons	343.6	62.0
Sulfuric acid (100 percent H2SO4), except spent	1,000 s tons	1,725.0	115.6
Metal containers		(X)	16.5
Plastics containers		(X)	31.9
Paper and paperboard containers		(X)	7.3
Fiber cans, bodies with combinations of fiber and other materials (foil, plastics, etc.) with metal ends		(X)	(D)
Cost of materials received from petroleum refineries and lube manufacturers	mil bbl	263.5	4,692.8
All other materials and components, parts, containers, and supplies		(X)	4,374.6
Materials, ingredients, containers, and supplies, nsk		(X)	274.4

Source: 1992 *Economic Census*. Explanation of symbols used: (D): Withheld to avoid disclosure of competitive data; na: Not available; (S): Withheld because statistical norms were not met; (X): Not applicable; (Z): Less than half the unit shown; nec: Not elsewhere classified; nsk: Not specified by kind; - : zero; * : 10-19 percent estimated; ** : 20-29 percent estimated.

PRODUCT SHARE DETAILS

Product or Product Class	% Share
Petroleum refining	100.00
Gasoline, including finished base stocks and blending agents	53.38
Aviation gasoline (except jet fuel), including finished base stocks and blending agents	1.24
Motor gasoline, including finished base stocks and blending agents	98.76
Jet fuel	9.39
Jet fuel, naphtha-type	14.32
Jet fuel, kerosene-type	85.68
Kerosene, except jet fuel	0.41
Light fuel oils	20.11
Distillate light fuel oil, including grades No. 1, 2, light diesel-type, light gas-enrichment oils, etc.	98.05
No. 4 type light fuel oil	1.95
Heavy fuel oils, including grades No. 5, 6, heavy diesel-type, heavy gas-enrichment oils, etc.	3.60
Lubricating oils and greases, made in a refinery	1.40
Lubricating oils (including hydraulic fluids, quenching and cutting oils, transformer oils, liquid rust preventives, etc.), made in a refinery	96.10
Lubricating greases, made in a refinery	3.90
Unfinished oils and lubricating oil base stock	3.61
Unfinished oils, naphthenic and paraffinic	31.27
Naphtha and other unfinished oils for use as petrochemical feedstocks, excluding carbon black	24.99
Carbon black feedstock (unfinshed oils)	4.73
Lubricating oil petroleum-base bright stock	3.93
Lubricating oil petroleum-base neutral stock	20.91
Lubricating oil petroleum-base red and pale oils	1.77
Other lubricating oil petroleum-base stocks	12.38
Unfinished oils and lubricating oil base stock, nsk	0.01
Asphalt	1.40
Paving grade asphalts	77.43
Roofing grade asphalts	13.40
Miscellaneous asphalts, nec	9.18
Liquefied refinery gases, including other aliphatics (feed stock and other uses), made in a refinery	3.72
Liquefied refinery gases (including other aliphatics), for use as a chemical raw material (including synthetic rubber components), made in a refinery	59.84
Liquefied refinery gases (including other aliphatics), produced for other uses, made in a refinery	40.16
Other finished petroleum products, including waxes	2.90
Petrolatum	4.82
Petroleum coke	6.72
Calcined petroleum coke, made in a refinery	3.96
Road oil, made in a refinery	0.39
Still gas (refinery gas)	2.32
Special petroleum naphthas	4.82
Aromatics (benzene, toluene, xylene, etc.), made in a refinery, for use as a chemical raw material	46.83
Aromatics (benzene, toluene, xylene, etc.), made in a refinery, for other uses	10.70
Microcrystalline petroleum waxes, made in a refinery	2.39
Fully-refined crystalline petroleum waxes, made in a refinery	4.77
Other crystalline petroleum waxes, made in a refinery	1.00
Other finished petroleum products made in a refinery	11.26
Petroleum refining, nsk	0.08

Source: 1992 *Economic Census*. The values shown are percent of total shipments in an industry. Values of indented subcategories are summed in the main heading. The symbol (D) appears when data are withheld to prevent disclosure of competitive information. The abbreviation nsk stands for 'not specified by kind' and nec for 'not elsewhere classified'.

INPUTS AND OUTPUTS FOR PETROLEUM REFINING

Economic Sector or Industry Providing Inputs	%	Sector	Economic Sector or Industry Buying Outputs	%	Sector
Crude petroleum & natural gas	69.0	Mining	Personal consumption expenditures	36.4	
Imports	10.1	Foreign	Petroleum refining	6.8	Manufg.
Petroleum refining	7.5	Manufg.	Air transportation	5.1	Util.
Pipelines, except natural gas	3.0	Util.	Exports	4.1	Foreign
Wholesale trade	2.2	Trade	Motor freight transportation & warehousing	3.5	Util.
Gas production & distribution (utilities)	1.8	Util.	Federal Government purchases, national defense	3.3	Fed Govt
Electric services (utilities)	0.9	Util.	Electric services (utilities)	3.0	Util.
Cyclic crudes and organics	0.7	Manufg.	Retail trade, except eating & drinking	2.9	Trade
Water transportation	0.7	Util.	Wholesale trade	2.5	Trade
Banking	0.6	Fin/R.E.	Railroads & related services	1.9	Util.
Industrial inorganic chemicals, nec	0.4	Manufg.	Feed grains	1.4	Agric.
Management & consulting services & labs	0.3	Services	S/L Govt. purch., other general government	1.2	S/L Govt
Maintenance of nonfarm buildings nec	0.2	Constr.	Water transportation	1.1	Util.
Chemical preparations, nec	0.2	Manufg.	S/L Govt. purch., elem. & secondary education	0.9	S/L Govt
Motor freight transportation & warehousing	0.2	Util.	Transit & bus transportation	0.8	Util.
Royalties	0.2	Fin/R.E.	Highway & street construction	0.7	Constr.
Miscellaneous repair shops	0.2	Services	State & local electric utilities	0.7	Gov't
Noncomparable imports	0.2	Foreign	S/L Govt. purch., higher education	0.7	S/L Govt
Miscellaneous plastics products	0.1	Manufg.	Cyclic crudes and organics	0.6	Manufg.
Surface active agents	0.1	Manufg.	Food grains	0.5	Agric.
Railroads & related services	0.1	Util.	Paving mixtures & blocks	0.5	Manufg.
Security & commodity brokers	0.1	Fin/R.E.	Crude petroleum & natural gas	0.4	Mining
			Industrial buildings	0.4	Constr.
			Maintenance of nonfarm buildings nec	0.4	Constr.
			Asphalt felts & coatings	0.4	Manufg.
			Lubricating oils & greases	0.4	Manufg.
			Paper mills, except building paper	0.4	Manufg.
			Real estate	0.4	Fin/R.E.
			Automotive rental & leasing, without drivers	0.4	Services
			Local government passenger transit	0.4	Gov't
			Landscape & horticultural services	0.3	Agric.
			Meat animals	0.3	Agric.
			Oil bearing crops	0.3	Agric.
			Coal	0.3	Mining
			Electric utility facility construction	0.3	Constr.
			Nonfarm residential structure maintenance	0.3	Constr.
			Petroleum & natural gas well drilling	0.3	Constr.
			Residential additions/alterations, nonfarm	0.3	Constr.
			Paperboard mills	0.3	Manufg.
			Doctors & dentists	0.3	Services
			Hospitals	0.3	Services
			Federal electric utilities	0.3	Gov't
			Fruits	0.2	Agric.
			Maintenance of highways & streets	0.2	Constr.
			Residential 1-unit structures, nonfarm	0.2	Constr.
			Apparel made from purchased materials	0.2	Manufg.
			Blast furnaces & steel mills	0.2	Manufg.
			Commercial printing	0.2	Manufg.
			Newspapers	0.2	Manufg.
			Paperboard containers & boxes	0.2	Manufg.
			Gas production & distribution (utilities)	0.2	Util.
			Sanitary services, steam supply, irrigation	0.2	Util.
			Eating & drinking places	0.2	Trade
			Banking	0.2	Fin/R.E.
			Hotels & lodging places	0.2	Services
			Legal services	0.2	Services
			Management & consulting services & labs	0.2	Services
			State & local government enterprises, nec	0.2	Gov't
			S/L Govt. purch., police	0.2	S/L Govt
			S/L Govt. purch., sanitation	0.2	S/L Govt
			Commercial fishing	0.1	Agric.
			Greenhouse & nursery products	0.1	Agric.
			Poultry & eggs	0.1	Agric.
			Farm service facilities	0.1	Constr.
			Office buildings	0.1	Constr.
			Carbon black	0.1	Manufg.
			Chemical preparations, nec	0.1	Manufg.
			Drugs	0.1	Manufg.
			Electronic computing equipment	0.1	Manufg.
			Logging camps & logging contractors	0.1	Manufg.
			Motor vehicle parts & accessories	0.1	Manufg.
			Motor vehicles & car bodies	0.1	Manufg.
			Communications, except radio & TV	0.1	Util.

Continued on next page.

INPUTS AND OUTPUTS FOR PETROLEUM REFINING - Continued

Economic Sector or Industry Providing Inputs	%	Sector	Economic Sector or Industry Buying Outputs	%	Sector
			Insurance carriers	0.1	Fin/R.E.
			Automotive repair shops & services	0.1	Services
			Laundry, dry cleaning, shoe repair	0.1	Services
			Libraries, vocation education	0.1	Services
			Membership organizations nec	0.1	Services
			Nursing & personal care facilities	0.1	Services
			Religious organizations	0.1	Services
			S/L Govt. purch., natural resource & recreation.	0.1	S/L Govt

Source: Benchmark Input-Output Accounts for the U.S. Economy, 1982, U.S. Department of Commerce, Washington, D.C., July 1991. Data, as reported in the source, are organized by the 1977 SIC structure in use in 1982 but have been matched, as closely as is possible, to the 1987 SIC structure used in this book.

OCCUPATIONS EMPLOYED BY SIC 291 - PETROLEUM REFINING

Occupation	% of Total 1994	Change to 2005	Occupation	% of Total 1994	Change to 2005
Gas & petroleum plant & system occupations	16.7	-6.1	Engineers nec	1.8	40.8
Chemical equipment controllers, operators	6.1	-15.5	Chemists	1.7	-6.1
Chemical engineers	4.0	-6.1	Engineering technicians & technologists nec	1.6	-6.1
Science & mathematics technicians	3.7	-6.1	Bookkeeping, accounting, & auditing clerks	1.6	-29.6
Plumbers, pipefitters, & steamfitters	3.3	-6.1	Accountants & auditors	1.6	-6.1
Industrial machinery mechanics	3.1	3.3	General office clerks	1.5	-20.0
Plant & system operators nec	2.7	24.4	Mechanical engineers	1.4	3.3
Secretaries, ex legal & medical	2.3	-14.5	Truck drivers light & heavy	1.4	-3.2
Management support workers nec	2.2	-6.1	General managers & top executives	1.2	-11.0
Helpers, laborers, & material movers nec	2.1	-6.1	Managers & administrators nec	1.1	-6.1
Precision instrument repairers	2.1	12.6	Mechanics, installers, & repairers nec	1.1	-6.1
Chemical plant & system operators	2.0	-6.1	Engineering, mathematical, & science managers	1.1	6.6
Material moving equipment operators nec	2.0	-6.1	Furnace, kiln, or kettle operators	1.0	12.6
Maintenance repairers, general utility	1.9	-15.5	Welders & cutters	1.0	-6.2
Electricians	1.9	-11.9	Crushing & mixing machine operators	1.0	-6.2

Source: Industry-Occupation Matrix, Bureau of Labor Statistics. These data relate to one or more 3-digit SIC industry groups rather than to a single 4-digit SIC. The change reported for each occupation to the year 2005 is a percent of growth or decline as estimated by the Bureau of Labor Statistics. The abbreviation nec stands for 'not elsewhere classified'.

LOCATION BY STATE AND REGIONAL CONCENTRATION

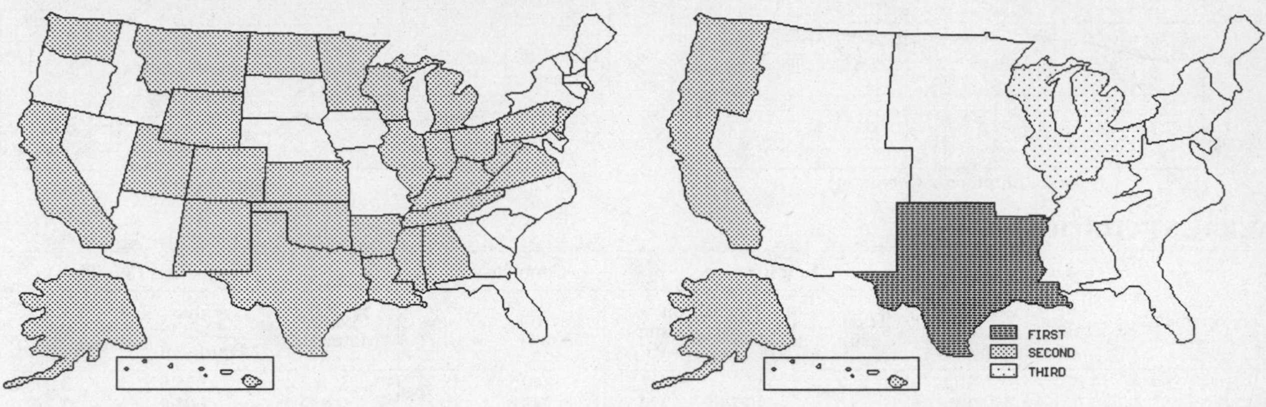

INDUSTRY DATA BY STATE

State	Establish-ments	Shipments			Employment				Cost as % of Shipments	Investment per Employee ($)
		Total ($ mil)	% of U.S.	Per Establ.	Total Number	% of U.S.	Per Establ.	Wages ($/hour)		
Texas	44	38,372.0	28.2	872.1	20,600	27.5	468	19.50	88.7	107,068
Louisiana	20	20,450.0	15.0	1,022.5	9,000	12.0	450	20.94	87.4	92,122
California	32	17,224.9	12.6	538.3	11,600	15.5	363	20.67	81.1	84,379
Illinois	7	8,265.3	6.1	1,180.8	4,600	6.1	657	20.95	87.8	86,804
Pennsylvania	14	7,994.7	5.9	571.0	4,400	5.9	314	17.79	73.3	28,750
New Jersey	6	4,843.4	3.6	807.2	2,600	3.5	433	21.08	94.7	23,462
Washington	7	4,062.9	3.0	580.4	1,800	2.4	257	21.00	93.4	76,222
Ohio	7	3,955.6	2.9	565.1	2,000	2.7	286	17.34	90.3	44,300
Oklahoma	7	3,504.8	2.6	500.7	2,000	2.7	286	17.81	89.0	32,450
Kansas	6	2,903.0	2.1	483.8	1,800	2.4	300	19.08	84.9	105,389
Utah	8	1,458.2	1.1	182.3	800	1.1	100	19.00	77.1	93,375
Wyoming	4	932.9	0.7	233.2	700	0.9	175	18.09	88.0	-
New Mexico	3	880.4	0.6	293.5	600	0.8	200	17.63	81.8	-
Indiana	7	(D)	-	-	1,750 *	2.3	250	-	-	-
Alaska	6	(D)	-	-	375 *	0.5	63	-	-	-
Mississippi	6	(D)	-	-	1,750 *	2.3	292	-	-	-
Michigan	4	(D)	-	-	750 *	1.0	188	-	-	-
Montana	4	(D)	-	-	750 *	1.0	188	-	-	-
Alabama	3	(D)	-	-	375 *	0.5	125	-	-	-
Arkansas	3	(D)	-	-	750 *	1.0	250	-	-	-
Colorado	3	(D)	-	-	375 *	0.5	125	-	-	-
Delaware	2	(D)	-	-	750 *	1.0	375	-	-	-
Hawaii	2	(D)	-	-	375 *	0.5	188	-	-	-
Kentucky	2	(D)	-	-	1,750 *	2.3	875	-	-	-
Minnesota	2	(D)	-	-	1,750 *	2.3	875	-	-	-
Virginia	2	(D)	-	-	375 *	0.5	188	-	-	-
West Virginia	2	(D)	-	-	375 *	0.5	188	-	-	-
Wisconsin	2	(D)	-	-	175 *	0.2	88	-	-	-
North Dakota	1	(D)	-	-	175 *	0.2	175	-	-	-
Tennessee	1	(D)	-	-	375 *	0.5	375	-	-	-

Source: 1992 *Economic Census*. The states are in descending order of shipments or establishments (if shipment data are missing for the majority). The symbol (D) appears when data are withheld to prevent disclosure of competitive information. States marked with (D) are sorted by number of establishments. A dash (-) indicates that the data element cannot be calculated; * indicates the midpoint of a range.

2951 - ASPHALT PAVING MIXTURES & BLOCKS

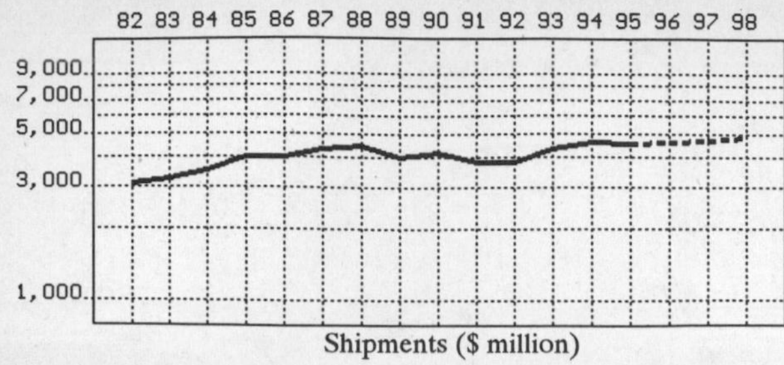

Shipments ($ million)

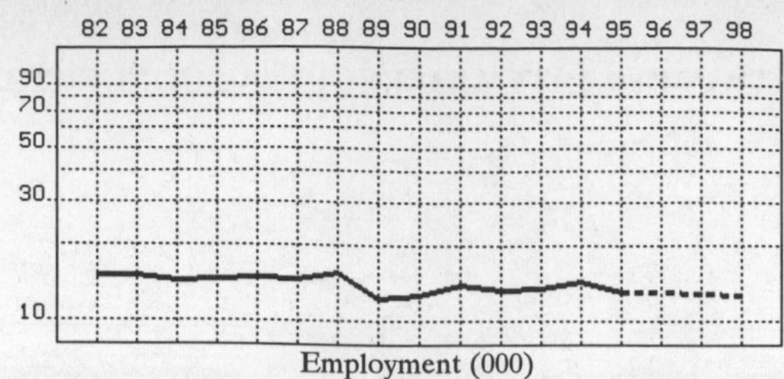

Employment (000)

GENERAL STATISTICS

Year	Companies	Establishments Total	Establishments with 20 or more employees	Employment Total (000)	Production Workers (000)	Production Hours (Mil)	Compensation Payroll ($ mil)	Compensation Wages ($/hr)	Cost of Materials	Value Added by Manufacture	Value of Shipments	Capital Invest.
1982	569	1,034	202	15.2	11.1	22.2	340.5	10.32	2,162.4	925.9	3,098.6	76.1
1983		1,032	188	15.0	10.7	22.1	343.4	10.43	2,242.1	1,005.2	3,237.4	48.1
1984		1,030	174	14.4	10.3	22.6	358.3	10.19	2,445.9	1,072.5	3,515.9	111.2
1985		1,027	161	14.6	10.6	23.7	375.4	10.07	2,811.9	1,164.9	3,971.8	144.1
1986		1,032	169	14.7	10.6	22.1	404.7	11.56	2,644.0	1,330.9	4,024.1	102.9
1987	542	1,101	199	14.6	10.0	20.9	430.1	12.76	2,758.2	1,602.9	4,346.2	123.4
1988		1,068	146	15.5	10.6	21.8	475.2	13.24	2,730.1	1,771.3	4,509.2	108.5
1989		1,061	149	12.2	9.7	21.1	430.4	12.53	2,535.9	1,469.1	4,001.1	178.6
1990		1,063	154	12.6	10.4	22.9	466.9	13.34	2,784.0	1,449.8	4,213.8	128.0
1991		1,085	153	13.9	10.0	21.0	461.0	13.43	2,524.5	1,306.1	3,794.4	105.8
1992	539	1,150	168	13.2	9.3	20.0	433.8	14.24	2,405.2	1,416.1	3,835.8	111.4
1993		1,105	162	13.4	9.7	20.9	451.0	14.57	2,802.2	1,568.2	4,362.6	130.5
1994		1,122P	148P	14.4	10.4	20.3	500.7	16.37	2,852.4	1,763.8	4,617.6	199.9
1995		1,130P	145P	13.1P	9.7P	20.4P	504.8P	15.87P	2,817.3P	1,742.1P	4,560.7P	164.7P
1996		1,139P	142P	13.0P	9.6P	20.2P	516.8P	16.35P	2,869.9P	1,774.6P	4,646.0P	171.0P
1997		1,147P	138P	12.8P	9.5P	20.0P	528.8P	16.83P	2,922.6P	1,807.2P	4,731.3P	177.3P
1998		1,156P	135P	12.7P	9.4P	19.8P	540.8P	17.30P	2,975.3P	1,839.8P	4,816.6P	183.6P

Sources: 1982, 1987, 1992 *Economic Census*; *Annual Survey of Manufactures*, 83-86, 88-91, 93-94. Establishment counts for non-Census years are from *County Business Patterns*; establishment values for 83-84 are extrapolations. 'P's show projections by the editors. Industries reclassified in 87 will not have data for prior years.

INDICES OF CHANGE

Year	Companies	Establishments Total	Establishments with 20 or more employees	Employment Total (000)	Production Workers (000)	Production Hours (Mil)	Compensation Payroll ($ mil)	Compensation Wages ($/hr)	Cost of Materials	Value Added by Manufacture	Value of Shipments	Capital Invest.
1982	106	90	120	115	119	111	78	72	90	65	81	68
1983		90	112	114	115	110	79	73	93	71	84	43
1984		90	104	109	111	113	83	72	102	76	92	100
1985		89	96	111	114	119	87	71	117	82	104	129
1986		90	101	111	114	110	93	81	110	94	105	92
1987	101	96	118	111	108	105	99	90	115	113	113	111
1988		93	87	117	114	109	110	93	114	125	118	97
1989		92	89	92	104	106	99	88	105	104	104	160
1990		92	92	95	112	115	108	94	116	102	110	115
1991		94	91	105	108	105	106	94	105	92	99	95
1992	100	100	100	100	100	100	100	100	100	100	100	100
1993		96	96	102	104	105	104	102	117	111	114	117
1994		98P	88P	109	112	101	115	115	119	125	120	179
1995		98P	86P	99P	104P	102P	116P	111P	117P	123P	119P	148P
1996		99P	84P	98P	103P	101P	119P	115P	119P	125P	121P	154P
1997		100P	82P	97P	102P	100P	122P	118P	122P	128P	123P	159P
1998		101P	80P	96P	101P	99P	125P	121P	124P	130P	126P	165P

Sources: Same as General Statistics. Values reflect change from the base year, 1992. Values above 100 mean greater than 92, values below 100 mean less than 92, and a value of 100 in the 82-91 or 93-98 period means same as 92. 'P's mark projections by the editors.

SELECTED RATIOS

For 1994	Avg. of All Manufact.	Analyzed Industry	Index
Employees per Establishment	49	13	26
Payroll per Establishment	1,500,273	446,407	30
Payroll per Employee	30,620	34,771	114
Production Workers per Establishment	34	9	27
Wages per Establishment	853,319	296,277	35
Wages per Production Worker	24,861	31,953	129
Hours per Production Worker	2,056	1,952	95
Wages per Hour	12.09	16.37	135
Value Added per Establishment	4,602,255	1,572,545	34
Value Added per Employee	93,930	122,486	130

For 1994	Avg. of All Manufact.	Analyzed Industry	Index
Value Added per Production Worker	134,084	169,596	126
Cost per Establishment	5,045,178	2,543,105	50
Cost per Employee	102,970	198,083	192
Cost per Production Worker	146,988	274,269	187
Shipments per Establishment	9,576,895	4,116,898	43
Shipments per Employee	195,460	320,667	164
Shipments per Production Worker	279,017	444,000	159
Investment per Establishment	321,011	178,224	56
Investment per Employee	6,552	13,882	212
Investment per Production Worker	9,352	19,221	206

Sources: Same as General Statistics. The 'Average of All Manufacturing' column represents the average of all manufacturing industries reported for the most recent complete year available. The Index shows the relationship between the Average and the Analyzed Industry. For example, 100 means that they are equal; 500 that the Analyzed Industry is five times the average; 50 means that the Analyzed Industry is half the national average. The abbreviation 'na' is used to show that data are 'not available'.

LEADING COMPANIES

Number shown: **75** Total sales ($ mil): **6,322** Total employment (000): **18.1**

Company Name	Address				CEO Name	Phone	Co. Type	Sales ($ mil)	Empl. (000)
Spectrum Construction Group	809 S Military Hwy	Virginia Beach	VA	23464	DJ Eastwood	804-420-4140	R	4,000	4.0
CalMat Co	3200 San Fernando	Los Angeles	CA	90065	AF Gerstell	213-258-2777	P	377	1.7
Bardon Trimount Inc	PO Box 39	Burlington	MA	01803	Paul Bartley	617-221-8400	R	200*	1.4
Reilly Industries Inc	1510 Mkt Sq Ctr	Indianapolis	IN	46204	Robert D McNeeley	317-638-7531	R	160	0.9
Pike Industries Inc	RFD 2	Tilton	NH	03276	Randy Pike	603-286-4324	S	86	0.7
Shelly and Sands Inc	PO Box 1585	Zanesville	OH	43702	Richard McClelland	614-453-0721	R	84*	0.5
Couch Inc	381 Twichell Rd	Dothan	AL	36303	Charles Owens	205-794-2631	S	75	0.5
Sloan Construction Company Inc	PO Box 2008	Greenville	SC	29602	RD Reeves	803-271-9090	S	68	0.3
Southern States Asphalt Co	PO Box 78217	Nashville	TN	37207	Robert L Langdon	615-226-6000	S	60	0.1
Hardrives Inc	9724 10th Av N	Minneapolis	MN	55441	Steven K Hall	612-542-9060	R	50*	0.3
McClinton-Anchor	PO Box 1367	Fayetteville	AR	72702	David McClinton	501-521-3550	D	50*	0.3
Richard F Kline Inc	PO Box 665	Frederick	MD	21701		301-662-8211	R	46*	0.3
All-Amer Asphalt & Aggregates	PO Box 2229	Corona	CA	91718	Dan Sisemore	909-736-7600	R	42*	0.3
Glenn O Hawbaker Inc	PO Box 135	State College	PA	16804	Daniel R Hawbaker	814-237-1444	R	41	0.4
APAC Carolina Inc	PO Box 521	Darlington	SC	29532	David Kilpatrick	803-393-2837	S	40	0.2
Atlantic Coast Asphalt Co	PO Box 40949	Jacksonville	FL	32203	Larry Pruitt	904-786-1020	D	40*	<0.1
Kaiser Sand and Gravel Co	PO Box 580	Pleasanton	CA	94566	MJ Bishop	510-846-8800	S	39	0.2
Cessford Construction Co	PO Box 160	Le Grand	IA	50142	Stephen Krabbe	515-479-2695	R	37*	0.2
Harper Bros Inc	14860 6 Mile	Fort Myers	FL	33912	DR Harper	813-481-2350	R	35	0.4
Arkhola Sand and Gravel Co	PO Box 1627	Fort Smith	AR	72902	John C Sulcor	501-785-4271	S	34	0.3
A Barletta and Sons Inc	PO Box 40	Hazleton	PA	18201	F Barletta	717-455-1511	R	33*	0.2
Brannan Sand and Gravel Co	4800 Brighton Blv	Denver	CO	80216	JC Marvel	303-534-1231	R	33	0.2
Tilcon Maine Inc	PO Box 209	Fairfield	ME	04937	David Boston	207-453-9381	S	33*	0.2
WR Meadows Inc	PO Box 338	Hampshire	IL	60140	James F Dwyer	708-683-4500	R	33*	0.2
LP Cavett Co	600 Shepherd Av	Cincinnati	OH	45215	Don Mill	513-554-0400	S	29*	0.2
Arrow Road Construction Co	PO Box 334	Mt Prospect	IL	60056	Wayne E Healy	708-437-0700	R	25	0.2
EM Chadbourne Inc	4375 McCoy Dr	Pensacola	FL	32503	EM Chadbourne Jr	904-433-3001	R	25	0.2
J Lee Milligan Inc	PO Box 30188	Amarillo	TX	79120	Ruth Wall	806-373-4386	R	25*	0.2
Peter Baker and Son Co	1349 Rockland Rd	Lake Bluff	IL	60044	Peter A Baker	708-362-3663	R	24*	0.2
Asphalt Paving Co	14802 W 44th Av	Golden	CO	80403	William J Keller	303-279-6611	R	22	0.2
Bankhead Asphalt Paving	PO Box 93006	Atlanta	GA	30377	Glenn Taylor	404-894-7992	D	20	0.2
Gulf Asphalt Corp	PO Box 2462	Panama City	FL	32402	Richard Bodd	904-785-4675	R	20*	0.1
Thompson-McCully Co	5905 Belleville Rd	Belleville	MI	48111	Robert Thompson	313-397-2050	R	19*	0.3
W Hodgman and Sons Inc	PO Box 1100	Fairmont	MN	56031	L Maschoff	507-235-3321	R	19*	0.2
Bank Construction Company Inc	PO Box 71505	Charleston H	SC	29415	Ronald S Banks	803-744-8261	R	18	0.1
Midwest Asphalt Corp	PO Box 5477	Hopkins	MN	55343	Blaine Johnson	612-937-8033	R	17	0.1
Dalrymple Gravel & Contracting	2105 S Broadway	Pine City	NY	14871	E C Dalrymple Sr	607-737-6200	R	16*	0.1
Mansfield Asphalt Paving Co	1300 W 4th St	Mansfield	OH	44906	Richard McClelland	419-529-8455	S	16*	0.1
Mid-State Constr & Materials	PO Box 339	Malvern	AR	72104	RJ Cumberworth	501-844-4232	R	16*	0.1
Tennessee Asphalt Co	PO Box 1111	Knoxville	TN	37901	WT Ratliff Jr	615-579-2000	R	16	0.1
Peavy and Son Construction	Rte 4	Havana	FL	32333	MD Peavy III	904-539-5019	R	15	<0.1
General Asphalt Company Inc	PO Box 522306	Miami	FL	33152	Robert A Lopez	305-592-3480	R	14*	0.1
Allied Inc	PO Box 190	Hays	KS	67601	GA Stannard	913-625-3459	R	13	0.1
Walter R Earle Corp	PO Drawer 757	Farmingdale	NJ	07727	Walter R Earle	908-657-8551	R	13	<0.1
Grady Brothers Inc	PO Box 421519	Indianapolis	IN	46242	TF Grady	317-244-3343	R	12	<0.1
Central Oil Asphalt Corp	8 E Long St	Columbus	OH	43215	Charles H Knowlton	614-224-8111	R	11*	<0.1
Grannas Brothers	PO Box 488	Hollidaysburg	PA	16648	Samuel Paul	814-695-5021	R	11*	<0.1
Okaloosa Asphalt Inc	PO Box 893	Shalimar	FL	32579	Cloyce Darnell	904-651-1821	R	11*	<0.1
Highway Materials Inc	1750 Walton Rd	Blue Bell	PA	19422	Peter DePaul	610-832-8000	R	10	<0.1
Bituminous Roadways Inc	9050 Jefferson Trail	Inver Grove H	MN	55077	PG Peterson	612-686-7001	R	10	<0.1
Halifax Paving Inc	PO Box 11349	Daytona Beach	FL	32120	Thomas Durrance	904-676-0200	R	10	0.1
Joseph McCormick Construction	PO Box 176	Erie	PA	16512	J J McCormick Jr	814-899-3111	R	10	<0.1
Midland Asphalt Corp	PO Box 388	Tonawanda	NY	14151	Bradford H Banks	716-692-0730	R	10*	<0.1
Taylor Ready Mix Inc	PO Box 1628	Elizabethton	TN	37643	Robert T Summers	615-926-8881	S	10*	<0.1
Thompson-McCully Co	4751 White Lake Rd	Clarkston	MI	48346	R Thompson	313-625-5891	D	10	<0.1
Tower Asphalt Inc	15001 Hudson Blv	Lakeland	MN	55043	Ron Hocken	612-436-8444	R	10	<0.1
Ashbach Construction Co	PO Box 65738	St Paul	MN	55165	Bernard Ashbach	612-224-7611	R	9	<0.1
Hot-Mix Asphalt Inc	PO Box 8327	Laurel	MS	39441	Harry H Bush	601-649-4111	S	9	<0.1
Baxters Asphalt and Concrete	PO Box 938	Marianna	FL	32446	William D Baxter	904-482-4621	R	8	<0.1
Eaton Asphalt Paving Company	1075 Eaton Dr	Covington	KY	41017	Charles Bucklew	606-331-2303	R	8	<0.1
Greer Limestone Co	Greer Bldg	Morgantown	WV	26505	John R Raese	304-296-1751	S	8	<0.1
Jet Asphalt and Rock Company	PO Box 1567	El Dorado	AR	71731	Alan K Alderson	501-863-7801	R	8*	<0.1
Rochester Sand and Gravel Inc	4105 E River NE	Rochester	MN	55906	Mark J Hindermann	507-288-7447	R	8	<0.1
Quapaw Company Inc	PO Box 609	Stillwater	OK	74076	Robert L Childress	405-377-9240	R	8	<0.1
Gator Asphalt Co	PO Box 20309	Bradenton	FL	34203	T Downs	813-355-9306	R	7	<0.1
Detroit Concrete Products Corp	4900 McCarthy Dr	Milford	MI	48381	John R MacInnis	313-685-9590	R	6	<0.1
Northwood Asphalt Products	PO Box 938	Lima	OH	45802	Dan Montgomery	419-229-2736	S	6	<0.1
Worlock Paving Corp	PO Box 488	Canastota	NY	13032	James K Johnson	315-697-9633	R	6	<0.1
Chicago Paving	12701 S Doty Av	Chicago	IL	60633	Robert Arquilla	312-646-2525	R	5	<0.1
Flint Asphalt and Paving Co	PO Box 765	Flint	MI	48501	A Keith Kerr	313-742-6680	R	5	<0.1
West Houston Asphalt Inc	PO Box 654	Galena Park	TX	77547	Omri R Meek	713-673-0023	R	5	<0.1
Concrete Coring Co	4024 Jason St	Denver	CO	80211	Margaret Hainey	303-433-8818	R	4*	<0.1
Paul Rohe Company Inc	PO Box 67	Aurora	IN	47001	KS Mosier	812-926-1471	R	4	<0.1
Ararat Rock Products Inc	PO Box 988	Mount Airy	NC	27030	Jim C Crossingham	910-786-4693	R	3*	<0.1
Dunn Blacktop Company Inc	PO Box 208	Winona	MN	55987	R Kramer	507-452-4394	S	3	<0.1

Source: *Ward's Business Directory of U.S. Private and Public Companies*, Volumes 1 and 2, 1996. The company type code used is as follows: P - Public, R - Private, S - Subsidiary, D - Division, J - Joint Venture, A - Affiliate, G - Group. Sales are in millions of dollars, employees are in thousands. An asterisk (*) indicates an estimated sales volume. The symbol < stands for 'less than'. Company names and addresses are truncated, in some cases, to fit into the available space.

MATERIALS CONSUMED

Material		Quantity	Delivered Cost ($ million)
Materials, ingredients, containers, and supplies		(X)	2,090.3
Paving grade asphalts	mil bbl	48.1	737.0
Roofing grade asphalts	mil bbl	0.3**	4.0
Asphalts other than paving and roofing grade	mil bbl	3.0	54.4
Sand and gravel	1,000 s tons	69,298.3	389.7
All other materials and components, parts, containers, and supplies		(X)	320.0
Materials, ingredients, containers, and supplies, nsk		(X)	585.1

Source: 1992 *Economic Census*. Explanation of symbols used: (D): Withheld to avoid disclosure of competitive data; na: Not available; (S): Withheld because statistical norms were not met; (X): Not applicable; (Z): Less than half the unit shown; nec: Not elsewhere classified; nsk: Not specified by kind; - : zero; * : 10-19 percent estimated; ** : 20-29 percent estimated.

PRODUCT SHARE DETAILS

Product or Product Class	% Share	Product or Product Class	% Share
Asphalt paving mixtures and blocks	100.00	Asphalt and tar paving mixtures (except liquid), including bituminous or asphaltic concrete, and asphaltic paving cements	59.69
Emulsified asphalt, including liquid additives	13.36	Other asphalt paving mixtures	1.31
Other liquid asphalt and tar paving materials, including cut-backs	8.13		

Source: 1992 *Economic Census*. The values shown are percent of total shipments in an industry. Values of indented subcategories are summed in the main heading. The symbol (D) appears when data are withheld to prevent disclosure of competitive information. The abbreviation nsk stands for 'not specified by kind' and nec for 'not elsewhere classified'.

INPUTS AND OUTPUTS FOR PAVING MIXTURES & BLOCKS

Economic Sector or Industry Providing Inputs	%	Sector	Economic Sector or Industry Buying Outputs	%	Sector
Petroleum refining	53.5	Manufg.	Highway & street construction	30.6	Constr.
Sand & gravel	9.9	Mining	Maintenance of highways & streets	15.0	Constr.
Wholesale trade	5.0	Trade	Office buildings	10.8	Constr.
Motor freight transportation & warehousing	4.2	Util.	Nonfarm residential structure maintenance	4.3	Constr.
Electric services (utilities)	2.7	Util.	Maintenance of water supply facilities	2.8	Constr.
Paving mixtures & blocks	2.6	Manufg.	Electric utility facility construction	2.7	Constr.
Gas production & distribution (utilities)	2.6	Util.	Construction of educational buildings	2.4	Constr.
Miscellaneous plastics products	2.4	Manufg.	Construction of stores & restaurants	2.4	Constr.
Cyclic crudes and organics	2.3	Manufg.	Sewer system facility construction	2.4	Constr.
Paperboard containers & boxes	1.4	Manufg.	Maintenance of nonbuilding facilities nec	2.2	Constr.
Wood products, nec	1.4	Manufg.	Construction of hospitals	2.1	Constr.
Advertising	1.3	Services	Industrial buildings	2.1	Constr.
Water transportation	1.2	Util.	Telephone & telegraph facility construction	2.0	Constr.
Surface active agents	1.0	Manufg.	Residential garden apartments	1.7	Constr.
Equipment rental & leasing services	1.0	Services	Paving mixtures & blocks	1.7	Manufg.
Communications, except radio & TV	0.8	Util.	Nonbuilding facilities nec	1.5	Constr.
Railroads & related services	0.6	Util.	Maintenance of nonfarm buildings nec	1.2	Constr.
Fabricated metal products, nec	0.5	Manufg.	Residential 1-unit structures, nonfarm	1.1	Constr.
Banking	0.5	Fin/R.E.	Hotels & motels	1.0	Constr.
Miscellaneous repair shops	0.5	Services	Maintenance of sewer facilities	1.0	Constr.
Computer & data processing services	0.4	Services	Construction of nonfarm buildings nec	0.8	Constr.
Coal	0.3	Mining	Local transit facility construction	0.8	Constr.
Maintenance of nonfarm buildings nec	0.3	Constr.	Maintenance of electric utility facilities	0.7	Constr.
Industrial inorganic chemicals, nec	0.3	Manufg.	Maintenance of farm residential buildings	0.7	Constr.
Automotive repair shops & services	0.3	Services	Maintenance of farm service facilities	0.6	Constr.
Chemical preparations, nec	0.2	Manufg.	Maintenance of gas utility facilities	0.6	Constr.
Paints & allied products	0.2	Manufg.	Maintenance of military facilities	0.6	Constr.
Air transportation	0.2	Util.	Resid. & other health facility construction	0.3	Constr.
Eating & drinking places	0.2	Trade	Residential 2-4 unit structures, nonfarm	0.3	Constr.
Business/professional associations	0.2	Services	Water supply facility construction	0.3	Constr.
Mechanical measuring devices	0.1	Manufg.	Exports	0.3	Foreign
Metal barrels, drums, & pails	0.1	Manufg.	Change in business inventories	0.3	In House
Pipelines, except natural gas	0.1	Util.	Farm service facilities	0.2	Constr.
Retail trade, except eating & drinking	0.1	Trade	Maintenance of local transit facilities	0.2	Constr.
Credit agencies other than banks	0.1	Fin/R.E.	Maintenance of railroads	0.2	Constr.
Detective & protective services	0.1	Services	Maintenance, conservation & development facilities	0.2	Constr.
U.S. Postal Service	0.1	Gov't	Residential high-rise apartments	0.2	Constr.
			Warehouses	0.2	Constr.
			Cement, hydraulic	0.2	Manufg.
			Amusement & recreation building construction	0.1	Constr.
			Construction of religious buildings	0.1	Constr.
			Maintenance of petroleum & natural gas wells	0.1	Constr.
			Residential additions/alterations, nonfarm	0.1	Constr.
			Concrete products, nec	0.1	Manufg.

Source: Benchmark Input-Output Accounts for the U.S. Economy, 1982, U.S. Department of Commerce, Washington, D.C., July 1991. Data, as reported in the source, are organized by the 1977 SIC structure in use in 1982 but have been matched, as closely as is possible, to the 1987 SIC structure used in this book.

OCCUPATIONS EMPLOYED BY SIC 295 - MISCELLANEOUS PETROLEUM AND COAL PRODUCTS

Occupation	% of Total 1994	Change to 2005	Occupation	% of Total 1994	Change to 2005
Helpers, laborers, & material movers nec	8.1	-3.3	Assemblers, fabricators, & hand workers nec	2.3	-3.3
Crushing & mixing machine operators	7.7	-3.3	Machine feeders & offbearers	2.2	-12.9
Truck drivers light & heavy	7.4	-0.3	Bookkeeping, accounting, & auditing clerks	2.2	-27.5
Sales & related workers nec	5.5	-3.3	Coating, painting, & spraying machine workers	1.9	-3.3
Industrial truck & tractor operators	4.7	-3.3	Freight, stock, & material movers, hand	1.9	-22.5
General managers & top executives	4.5	-8.3	Industrial production managers	1.8	-3.3
Packaging & filling machine operators	4.5	-3.4	Science & mathematics technicians	1.8	-3.2
Material moving equipment operators nec	3.8	-3.3	Construction trades workers nec	1.6	-22.6
Industrial machinery mechanics	3.5	6.4	Clerical supervisors & managers	1.5	-1.2
Plant & system operators nec	2.6	28.1	Order clerks, materials, merchandise, & service	1.3	-5.2
Maintenance repairers, general utility	2.6	-13.0	Furnace, kiln, or kettle operators	1.2	-3.2
Secretaries, ex legal & medical	2.5	-12.0	Chemists	1.1	-3.3
General office clerks	2.4	-17.6			

Source: *Industry-Occupation Matrix*, Bureau of Labor Statistics. These data relate to one or more 3-digit SIC industry groups rather than to a single 4-digit SIC. The change reported for each occupation to the year 2005 is a percent of growth or decline as estimated by the Bureau of Labor Statistics. The abbreviation nec stands for 'not elsewhere classified'.

LOCATION BY STATE AND REGIONAL CONCENTRATION

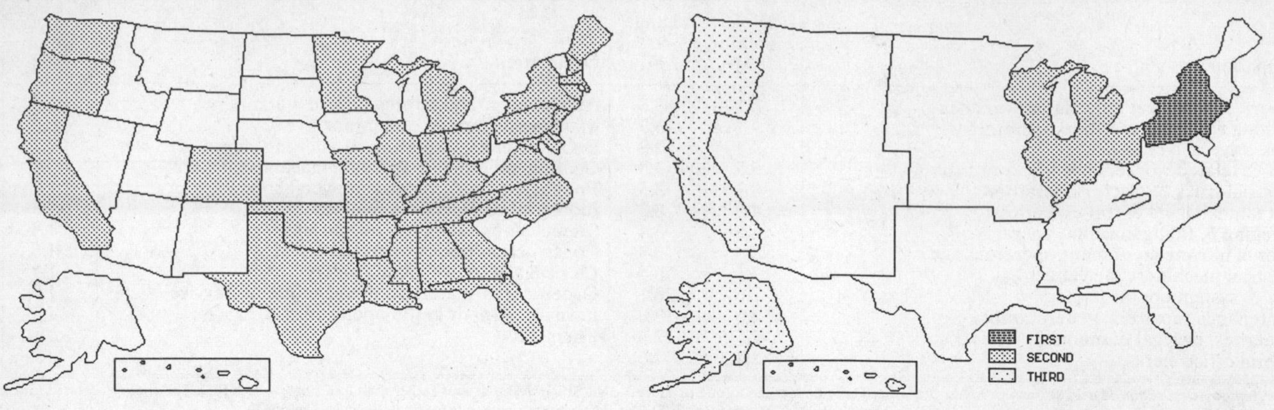

INDUSTRY DATA BY STATE

State	Establish-ments	Shipments			Employment				Cost as % of Shipments	Investment per Employee ($)
		Total ($ mil)	% of U.S.	Per Establ.	Total Number	% of U.S.	Per Establ.	Wages ($/hour)		
Ohio	127	425.4	11.1	3.3	1,100	8.3	9	13.72	69.7	9,091
California	115	419.1	10.9	3.6	1,000	7.6	9	20.46	63.8	9,500
New York	130	408.4	10.6	3.1	1,500	11.4	12	15.83	57.5	10,600
Pennsylvania	95	249.3	6.5	2.6	800	6.1	8	12.85	62.1	3,875
Texas	57	246.3	6.4	4.3	1,000	7.6	18	9.89	65.3	16,500
Connecticut	27	155.8	4.1	5.8	600	4.5	22	19.44	51.1	3,833
Massachusetts	45	143.7	3.7	3.2	500	3.8	11	17.50	55.5	-
New Jersey	36	127.5	3.3	3.5	500	3.8	14	17.00	65.8	4,400
Illinois	29	115.5	3.0	4.0	300	2.3	10	18.00	65.0	7,000
Florida	27	102.6	2.7	3.8	600	4.5	22	10.00	55.9	3,333
Georgia	31	89.4	2.3	2.9	300	2.3	10	10.83	70.9	9,000
Maryland	26	63.9	1.7	2.5	200	1.5	8	16.00	69.2	6,000
Alabama	19	62.0	1.6	3.3	300	2.3	16	10.50	71.0	3,667
Indiana	28	59.9	1.6	2.1	200	1.5	7	12.67	63.3	-
Oklahoma	20	39.7	1.0	2.0	300	2.3	15	12.00	57.4	-
Oregon	10	37.3	1.0	3.7	300	2.3	30	14.00	57.6	-
Arkansas	11	33.1	0.9	3.0	200	1.5	18	9.33	65.9	-
Virginia	14	33.1	0.9	2.4	100	0.8	7	9.00	66.8	-
Maine	8	32.5	0.8	4.1	200	1.5	25	12.60	61.2	5,000
Tennessee	35	(D)	-	-	375 *	2.8	11	-	-	-
Missouri	29	(D)	-	-	375 *	2.8	13	-	-	-
Kentucky	28	(D)	-	-	175 *	1.3	6	-	-	-
Michigan	27	(D)	-	-	375 *	2.8	14	-	-	-
North Carolina	21	(D)	-	-	175 *	1.3	8	-	-	-
Minnesota	13	(D)	-	-	375 *	2.8	29	-	-	5,600
Louisiana	12	(D)	-	-	175 *	1.3	15	-	-	-
Colorado	11	(D)	-	-	175 *	1.3	16	-	-	-
Mississippi	11	(D)	-	-	175 *	1.3	16	-	-	-
Washington	10	(D)	-	-	375 *	2.8	38	-	-	-
New Hampshire	5	(D)	-	-	175 *	1.3	35	-	-	-

Source: 1992 *Economic Census*. The states are in descending order of shipments or establishments (if shipment data are missing for the majority). The symbol (D) appears when data are withheld to prevent disclosure of competitive information. States marked with (D) are sorted by number of establishments. A dash (-) indicates that the data element cannot be calculated; * indicates the midpoint of a range.

2952 - ASPHALT FELTS & COATINGS

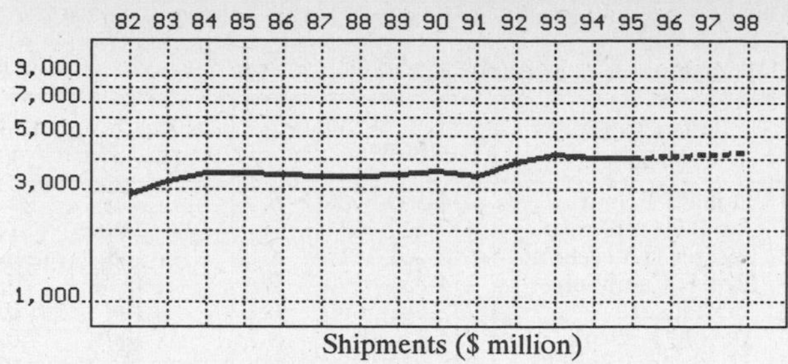

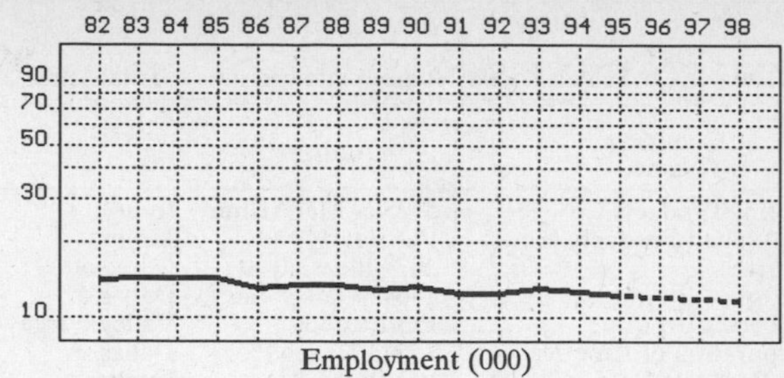

GENERAL STATISTICS

Year	Com-panies	Establishments		Employment			Compensation		Production ($ million)			
		Total	with 20 or more employees	Total (000)	Production Workers (000)	Production Hours (Mil)	Payroll ($ mil)	Wages ($/hr)	Cost of Materials	Value Added by Manufacture	Value of Shipments	Capital Invest.
1982	147	273	155	14.2	10.4	21.0	288.7	9.29	1,993.7	816.9	2,849.5	57.1
1983		270	154	14.5	10.6	22.7	312.9	9.36	2,373.6	892.6	3,256.6	56.0
1984		267	153	14.5	10.5	21.6	329.7	10.25	2,402.8	1,083.6	3,487.7	69.4
1985		264	151	14.4	10.1	20.6	331.7	10.83	2,506.7	1,015.7	3,515.5	101.4
1986		276	152	13.1	9.3	19.4	340.1	11.38	2,279.4	1,164.5	3,474.9	89.0
1987	162	266	145	13.5	9.7	20.2	354.9	11.75	2,147.2	1,284.1	3,402.9	89.8
1988		269	142	13.4	9.6	20.0	361.0	11.86	2,137.9	1,287.9	3,420.5	74.8
1989		260	135	12.8	9.0	19.7	363.8	12.06	2,223.2	1,248.0	3,475.6	65.7
1990		249	140	13.2	8.9	18.9	381.2	12.69	2,311.5	1,284.9	3,584.9	66.1
1991		262	142	12.4	8.8	18.5	382.0	13.02	2,196.9	1,237.2	3,438.2	62.9
1992	151	245	123	12.4	9.0	20.3	412.5	13.16	2,358.7	1,550.6	3,913.0	69.1
1993		246	126	12.9	9.3	21.0	441.0	13.56	2,539.1	1,634.0	4,173.0	73.6
1994		247P	125P	12.6	9.3	20.5	434.7	13.61	2,570.3	1,481.5	4,050.8	96.6
1995		244P	123P	12.1P	8.6P	19.4P	444.5P	14.37P	2,578.0P	1,486.0P	4,063.0P	80.1P
1996		242P	120P	11.9P	8.5P	19.3P	456.0P	14.75P	2,625.3P	1,513.2P	4,137.5P	80.8P
1997		240P	117P	11.8P	8.4P	19.1P	467.5P	15.12P	2,672.5P	1,540.4P	4,211.9P	81.6P
1998		237P	114P	11.6P	8.2P	19.0P	479.0P	15.49P	2,719.8P	1,567.7P	4,286.4P	82.3P

Sources: 1982, 1987, 1992 *Economic Census*; *Annual Survey of Manufactures*, 83-86, 88-91, 93-94. Establishment counts for non-Census years are from *County Business Patterns*; establishment values for 83-84 are extrapolations. 'P's show projections by the editors. Industries reclassified in 87 will not have data for prior years.

INDICES OF CHANGE

Year	Com-panies	Establishments		Employment			Compensation		Production ($ million)			
		Total	with 20 or more employees	Total (000)	Production Workers (000)	Production Hours (Mil)	Payroll ($ mil)	Wages ($/hr)	Cost of Materials	Value Added by Manufacture	Value of Shipments	Capital Invest.
1982	97	111	126	115	116	103	70	71	85	53	73	83
1983		110	125	117	118	112	76	71	101	58	83	81
1984		109	124	117	117	106	80	78	102	70	89	100
1985		108	123	116	112	101	80	82	106	66	90	147
1986		113	124	106	103	96	82	86	97	75	89	129
1987	107	109	118	109	108	100	86	89	91	83	87	130
1988		110	115	108	107	99	88	90	91	83	87	108
1989		106	110	103	100	97	88	92	94	80	89	95
1990		102	114	106	99	93	92	96	98	83	92	96
1991		107	115	100	98	91	93	99	93	80	88	91
1992	100	100	100	100	100	100	100	100	100	100	100	100
1993		100	102	104	103	103	107	103	108	105	107	107
1994		101P	102P	102	103	101	105	103	109	96	104	140
1995		100P	100P	98P	96P	96P	108P	109P	109P	96P	104P	116P
1996		99P	97P	96P	94P	95P	111P	112P	111P	98P	106P	117P
1997		98P	95P	95P	93P	94P	113P	115P	113P	99P	108P	118P
1998		97P	93P	93P	91P	94P	116P	118P	115P	101P	110P	119P

Sources: Same as General Statistics. Values reflect change from the base year, 1992. Values above 100 mean greater than 92, values below 100 mean less than 92, and a value of 100 in the 82-91 or 93-98 period means same as 92. 'P's mark projections by the editors.

SELECTED RATIOS

For 1994	Avg. of All Manufact.	Analyzed Industry	Index	For 1994	Avg. of All Manufact.	Analyzed Industry	Index
Employees per Establishment	49	51	104	Value Added per Production Worker	134,084	159,301	119
Payroll per Establishment	1,500,273	1,760,891	117	Cost per Establishment	5,045,178	10,411,821	206
Payroll per Employee	30,620	34,500	113	Cost per Employee	102,970	203,992	198
Production Workers per Establishment	34	38	110	Cost per Production Worker	146,988	276,376	188
Wages per Establishment	853,319	1,130,199	132	Shipments per Establishment	9,576,895	16,409,059	171
Wages per Production Worker	24,861	30,001	121	Shipments per Employee	195,460	321,492	164
Hours per Production Worker	2,056	2,204	107	Shipments per Production Worker	279,017	435,570	156
Wages per Hour	12.09	13.61	113	Investment per Establishment	321,011	391,309	122
Value Added per Establishment	4,602,255	6,001,289	130	Investment per Employee	6,552	7,667	117
Value Added per Employee	93,930	117,579	125	Investment per Production Worker	9,352	10,387	111

Sources: Same as General Statistics. The 'Average of All Manufacturing' column represents the average of all manufacturing industries reported for the most recent complete year available. The Index shows the relationship between the Average and the Analyzed Industry. For example, 100 means that they are equal; 500 that the Analyzed Industry is five times the average; 50 means that the Analyzed Industry is half the national average. The abbreviation 'na' is used to show that data are 'not available'.

LEADING COMPANIES

Number shown: **29** Total sales ($ mil): **1,403** Total employment (000): **6.7**

Company Name	Address				CEO Name	Phone	Co. Type	Sales ($ mil)	Empl. (000)
GS Roofing Products Co	5525 N MacArthur	Irving	TX	75038	Donald F Smith	214-580-5600	R	275	1.2
Tamko Asphalt Products Inc	PO Box 1404	Joplin	MO	64802	Jay P Humphreys	417-624-6644	R	240*	1.3
Bird Corp	1077 Pleasant St	Norwood	MA	02062	Joseph D Vecchiolla	617-461-1414	P	168	0.5
Elcor Corp	14643 Dallas Pkwy	Dallas	TX	75240	Roy E Campbell	214-851-0500	P	157	0.6
CertainTeed Corp	PO Box 860	Valley Forge	PA	19482	Jim Hilyard	215-341-7000	D	100	0.6
Elk Corporation of America	14643 Dallas Pkwy	Dallas	TX	75240	Harold K Work	214-851-0400	S	100*	0.5
Monsey Products Co	PO Box 368	Kimberton	PA	19442	JT Mooney Jr	215-933-8888	R	50	0.4
Lunday-Thagard Co	PO Box 1519	South Gate	CA	90280	Robert S Roth	310-928-7000	R	41	0.1
Gulf States Asphalt Company	300 Christy Pl	South Houston	TX	77587	Louis Pena	713-941-4410	R	40*	0.1
Consolidated Fiber	PO Box 5248	Bakersfield	CA	93388	William L Thomas	805-323-6026	R	30	0.2
Gardner Asphalt Corp	PO Box 5449	Tampa	FL	33675	Ed Plemons	813-248-2101	R	30	0.2
Fields Corp	2240 Taylor Way	Tacoma	WA	98421	John Fields	206-627-4098	R	24	0.1
Herbert Melarky Roofing Co	PO Box 17217	Portland	OR	97217	Griffith Marshall	503-283-1191	R	24	0.1
Allied Asphalt Paving Co	1100 Brandt Dr	Elgin	IL	60120	Victor Verdico	708-695-9300	R	18*	0.1
Russell Standard Corp	PO Box 479	Bridgeville	PA	15017	James R Johnson	412-563-4500	R	16	0.1
Pabco Roofing Products	1014 Chesley Av	Richmond	CA	94801	Dave Luchetti	510-234-2130	D	15*	0.1
Consolidated Coatings Corp	1801 E 9th St	Cleveland	OH	44114	RD Deitz	216-771-3258	S	10*	0.1
Fred A Wilson Co	4533 Indrial Pkwy	Cleveland	OH	44135	James Schattinger	216-671-6896	D	10*	0.1
Seal-Dry USA Inc	3300 S Woodrow St	Little Rock	AR	72204	Jack Givens	501-663-3063	R	9*	<0.1
Armor Cote Corp	PO Box 3226	Odessa	TX	79760	RN Conley	915-332-0558	R	8	<0.1
Striker Industries Inc	1 River Way	Houston	TX	77056	David Collins	713-622-4092	P	8	0.2
DeWitt Products Co	5860 Plumer	Detroit	MI	48209	Jack D McClellan	313-554-0575	R	6	<0.1
Ondura Corp	4994 Ondura Dr	Fredericksburg	VA	22407	John D Adair	703-898-7000	R	6	<0.1
Palmer Asphalt Co	PO Box 58	Bayonne	NJ	07002	Lewis S Ripps	201-339-0855	R	6	<0.1
Truco Inc	4301 Train Av	Cleveland	OH	44113	Christopher Hoskins	216-631-1000	R	6	<0.1
American Tar Co	3405 Lincoln Av	Tacoma	WA	98459	John Fields	206-627-1368	S	5	<0.1
Asphalt Cutbacks Inc	3000 Gary Rd	East Chicago	IN	46312	G Bizoukas	219-398-4230	R	2*	<0.1
Emulsicoat Inc	705 E University	Urbana	IL	61801	Fred Fehsenfeld	217-344-7775	S	1*	<0.1
San Antonio Developers Inc	5536 Business Park	San Antonio	TX	78218	Howard C Hansen	210-666-2777	R	0*	<0.1

Source: *Ward's Business Directory of U.S. Private and Public Companies*, Volumes 1 and 2, 1996. The company type code used is as follows: P - Public, R - Private, S - Subsidiary, D - Division, J - Joint Venture, A - Affiliate, G - Group. Sales are in millions of dollars, employees are in thousands. An asterisk (*) indicates an estimated sales volume. The symbol < stands for 'less than'. Company names and addresses are truncated, in some cases, to fit into the available space.

MATERIALS CONSUMED

Material		Quantity	Delivered Cost ($ million)
Materials, ingredients, containers, and supplies		(X)	2,131.0
Paving grade asphalts	mil bbl	4.5	74.1
Roofing grade asphalts	mil bbl	29.4	514.6
Asphalts other than paving and roofing grade	mil bbl	136.2	39.7
Roofing felts, unsaturated	1,000 s tons	563.3	104.8
Glass fiber, textile type, bonded mat type, etc.	mil lb	322.3	347.3
Roofing granules	1,000 s tons	5,530.2	358.6
Sand and gravel	1,000 s tons	2,394.5	48.5
All other materials and components, parts, containers, and supplies		(X)	511.5
Materials, ingredients, containers, and supplies, nsk		(X)	132.0

Source: 1992 *Economic Census*. Explanation of symbols used: (D): Withheld to avoid disclosure of competitive data; na: Not available; (S): Withheld because statistical norms were not met; (X): Not applicable; (Z): Less than half the unit shown; nec: Not elsewhere classified; nsk: Not specified by kind; - : zero; * : 10-19 percent estimated; ** : 20-29 percent estimated.

PRODUCT SHARE DETAILS

Product or Product Class	% Share
Asphalt felts and coatings	100.00
Roofing asphalts and pitches, coatings, and cements	14.65
Roofing asphalt	36.30
Fibrated asphaltic roofing coatings	20.27
Nonfibrated asphaltic roofing coatings	17.34
Asphaltic roofing cements	7.87
Other roofing asphalts and pitches, coatings, and cements, including coal-tar base coatings, cements, and roofing pitch	18.22
Prepared asphalt and tar roofing and siding products, including saturated felts and boards for nonbuilding use	80.35
Asphalt and tar saturated felts and boards for nonbuilding use	0.66
Asphalt smooth-surfaced roll roofing and cap sheets, organic base	3.26
Asphalt smooth-surfaced roll roofing and cap sheets, fiberglass base	8.80
Asphalt mineral-surfaced roll roofing and cap sheets, organic base	2.52
Asphalt mineral-surfaced roll roofing and cap sheets, fiberglass base	4.29
Asphalt strip shingles, organic base (excluding laminated), 235 to 240 lb/sales sq	4.27
Asphalt strip shingles, organic base (excluding laminated), all other weights	4.76
Asphalt strip shingles, inorganic base (excluding laminated), 215 to 235 lb/sales sq	16.07
Asphalt strip shingles, inorganic base (excluding laminated), all other weights	25.47
Laminated or multilayered asphalt strip shingles, organic and/or inorganic base	17.11
Asphalt and tar individual shingles, organic or inorganic base, all styles	1.31
Saturated asphalt and tar building ply felts, organic base	2.65
Saturated asphalt and tar building ply felts, fiberglass base	1.73
Other saturated asphalt and tar building felts, organic base	2.48
Other saturated asphalt and tar building felts, fiberglass base	0.41
Other prepared asphalt and tar products for roofing and siding	4.20
Asphalt felts and coatings, nsk	5.00

Source: 1992 *Economic Census*. The values shown are percent of total shipments in an industry. Values of indented subcategories are summed in the main heading. The symbol (D) appears when data are withheld to prevent disclosure of competitive information. The abbreviation nsk stands for 'not specified by kind' and nec for 'not elsewhere classified'.

INPUTS AND OUTPUTS FOR ASPHALT FELTS & COATINGS

Economic Sector or Industry Providing Inputs	%	Sector	Economic Sector or Industry Buying Outputs	%	Sector
Petroleum refining	41.8	Manufg.	Nonfarm residential structure maintenance	24.4	Constr.
Glass & glass products, except containers	9.7	Manufg.	Maintenance of nonfarm buildings nec	22.0	Constr.
Wholesale trade	7.6	Trade	Residential 1-unit structures, nonfarm	13.4	Constr.
Minerals, ground or treated	6.4	Manufg.	Office buildings	7.1	Constr.
Building paper & board mills	4.9	Manufg.	Residential additions/alterations, nonfarm	4.7	Constr.
Railroads & related services	3.5	Util.	Construction of educational buildings	3.1	Constr.
Gas production & distribution (utilities)	3.1	Util.	Industrial buildings	3.1	Constr.
Motor freight transportation & warehousing	3.0	Util.	Residential garden apartments	2.9	Constr.
Miscellaneous plastics products	1.9	Manufg.	Construction of hospitals	2.5	Constr.
Electric services (utilities)	1.8	Util.	Construction of stores & restaurants	2.1	Constr.
Imports	1.7	Foreign	Farm service facilities	1.5	Constr.
Felt goods, nec	1.6	Manufg.	Electric utility facility construction	1.3	Constr.
Paperboard containers & boxes	1.3	Manufg.	Residential 2-4 unit structures, nonfarm	1.3	Constr.
Advertising	1.3	Services	Motor vehicles & car bodies	1.3	Manufg.
Water transportation	1.0	Util.	Amusement & recreation building construction	0.7	Constr.
Communications, except radio & TV	0.9	Util.	Construction of nonfarm buildings nec	0.7	Constr.
Sand & gravel	0.8	Mining	Mobile homes	0.7	Manufg.
Cyclic crudes and organics	0.6	Manufg.	Exports	0.7	Foreign
Banking	0.6	Fin/R.E.	Maintenance of farm service facilities	0.5	Constr.
Equipment rental & leasing services	0.6	Services	Prefabricated wood buildings	0.5	Manufg.
Maintenance of nonfarm buildings nec	0.4	Constr.	Construction of religious buildings	0.4	Constr.
Metal cans	0.4	Manufg.	Hotels & motels	0.4	Constr.
Sanitary services, steam supply, irrigation	0.4	Util.	Maintenance of telephone & telegraph facilities	0.4	Constr.
Automotive repair shops & services	0.4	Services	Resid. & other health facility construction	0.4	Constr.
Nonmetallic mineral services	0.3	Mining	Warehouses	0.4	Constr.
Business services nec	0.3	Services	Farm housing units & additions & alterations	0.3	Constr.
Computer & data processing services	0.3	Services	Garage & service station construction	0.3	Constr.
Miscellaneous repair shops	0.3	Services	Maintenance of farm residential buildings	0.3	Constr.
Asphalt felts & coatings	0.2	Manufg.	Maintenance of nonbuilding facilities nec	0.3	Constr.
Lime	0.2	Manufg.	Maintenance of electric utility facilities	0.2	Constr.
Paints & allied products	0.2	Manufg.	Nonbuilding facilities nec	0.2	Constr.
Air transportation	0.2	Util.	Residential high-rise apartments	0.2	Constr.
Eating & drinking places	0.2	Trade	Asphalt felts & coatings	0.2	Manufg.
Real estate	0.2	Fin/R.E.	Construction of conservation facilities	0.1	Constr.
Business/professional associations	0.2	Services	Maintenance of local transit facilities	0.1	Constr.
U.S. Postal Service	0.2	Gov't	Maintenance of military facilities	0.1	Constr.
Mechanical measuring devices	0.1	Manufg.	Telephone & telegraph facility construction	0.1	Constr.
Plastics materials & resins	0.1	Manufg.	Household refrigerators & freezers	0.1	Manufg.
Credit agencies other than banks	0.1	Fin/R.E.			
Detective & protective services	0.1	Services			
Hotels & lodging places	0.1	Services			

Source: Benchmark Input-Output Accounts for the U.S. Economy, 1982, U.S. Department of Commerce, Washington, D.C., July 1991. Data, as reported in the source, are organized by the 1977 SIC structure in use in 1982 but have been matched, as closely as is possible, to the 1987 SIC structure used in this book.

OCCUPATIONS EMPLOYED BY SIC 295 - MISCELLANEOUS PETROLEUM AND COAL PRODUCTS

Occupation	% of Total 1994	Change to 2005	Occupation	% of Total 1994	Change to 2005
Helpers, laborers, & material movers nec	8.1	-3.3	Assemblers, fabricators, & hand workers nec	2.3	-3.3
Crushing & mixing machine operators	7.7	-3.3	Machine feeders & offbearers	2.2	-12.9
Truck drivers light & heavy	7.4	-0.3	Bookkeeping, accounting, & auditing clerks	2.2	-27.5
Sales & related workers nec	5.5	-3.3	Coating, painting, & spraying machine workers	1.9	-3.3
Industrial truck & tractor operators	4.7	-3.3	Freight, stock, & material movers, hand	1.9	-22.5
General managers & top executives	4.5	-8.3	Industrial production managers	1.8	-3.3
Packaging & filling machine operators	4.5	-3.4	Science & mathematics technicians	1.8	-3.2
Material moving equipment operators nec	3.8	-3.3	Construction trades workers nec	1.6	-22.6
Industrial machinery mechanics	3.5	6.4	Clerical supervisors & managers	1.5	-1.2
Plant & system operators nec	2.6	28.1	Order clerks, materials, merchandise, & service	1.3	-5.2
Maintenance repairers, general utility	2.6	-13.0	Furnace, kiln, or kettle operators	1.2	-3.2
Secretaries, ex legal & medical	2.5	-12.0	Chemists	1.1	-3.3
General office clerks	2.4	-17.6			

Source: Industry-Occupation Matrix, Bureau of Labor Statistics. These data relate to one or more 3-digit SIC industry groups rather than to a single 4-digit SIC. The change reported for each occupation to the year 2005 is a percent of growth or decline as estimated by the Bureau of Labor Statistics. The abbreviation nec stands for 'not elsewhere classified'.

LOCATION BY STATE AND REGIONAL CONCENTRATION

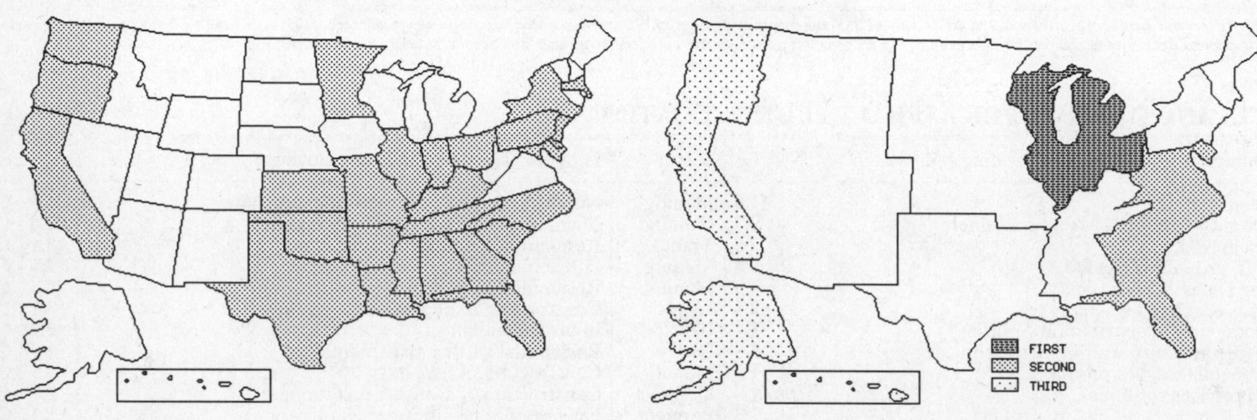

INDUSTRY DATA BY STATE

State	Establish-ments	Shipments Total ($ mil)	Shipments % of U.S.	Shipments Per Establ.	Employment Total Number	Employment % of U.S.	Employment Per Establ.	Wages ($/hour)	Cost as % of Shipments	Investment per Employee ($)
Texas	24	493.2	12.6	20.6	1,400	11.3	58	12.92	60.5	4,571
California	28	436.4	11.2	15.6	1,200	9.7	43	15.42	59.9	9,667
Ohio	23	348.8	8.9	15.2	1,200	9.7	52	13.56	52.8	3,667
Illinois	16	237.3	6.1	14.8	800	6.5	50	12.15	62.3	7,000
Alabama	8	227.3	5.8	28.4	700	5.6	88	13.00	58.0	5,000
Georgia	10	218.3	5.6	21.8	600	4.8	60	14.00	72.8	4,167
Florida	16	190.7	4.9	11.9	400	3.2	25	13.00	57.4	8,250
Indiana	8	174.4	4.5	21.8	500	4.0	63	15.38	64.8	3,800
Maryland	5	172.1	4.4	34.4	400	3.2	80	15.43	58.2	4,000
Pennsylvania	12	116.1	3.0	9.7	500	4.0	42	12.29	64.2	6,600
New Jersey	9	107.0	2.7	11.9	400	3.2	44	13.80	65.4	-
Massachusetts	5	85.0	2.2	17.0	300	2.4	60	12.80	53.6	-
North Carolina	7	82.2	2.1	11.7	400	3.2	57	11.43	68.5	-
Oregon	4	80.3	2.1	20.1	300	2.4	75	13.50	71.0	-
Arkansas	4	63.6	1.6	15.9	200	1.6	50	11.00	67.9	-
Oklahoma	3	57.6	1.5	19.2	200	1.6	67	13.00	76.7	-
New York	8	29.9	0.8	3.7	100	0.8	13	9.50	61.5	4,000
Minnesota	6	(D)	-	-	750 *	6.0	125	-	-	3,867
Kansas	5	(D)	-	-	375 *	3.0	75	-	-	-
Missouri	4	(D)	-	-	750 *	6.0	188	-	-	-
Tennessee	4	(D)	-	-	175 *	1.4	44	-	-	-
Washington	4	(D)	-	-	175 *	1.4	44	-	-	-
Delaware	3	(D)	-	-	175 *	1.4	58	-	-	-
Louisiana	3	(D)	-	-	175 *	1.4	58	-	-	-
South Carolina	2	(D)	-	-	175 *	1.4	88	-	-	-
Kentucky	1	(D)	-	-	175 *	1.4	175	-	-	-
Mississippi	1	(D)	-	-	175 *	1.4	175	-	-	-

Source: 1992 *Economic Census*. The states are in descending order of shipments or establishments (if shipment data are missing for the majority). The symbol (D) appears when data are withheld to prevent disclosure of competitive information. States marked with (D) are sorted by number of establishments. A dash (-) indicates that the data element cannot be calculated; * indicates the midpoint of a range.

2992 - LUBRICATING OILS & GREASES

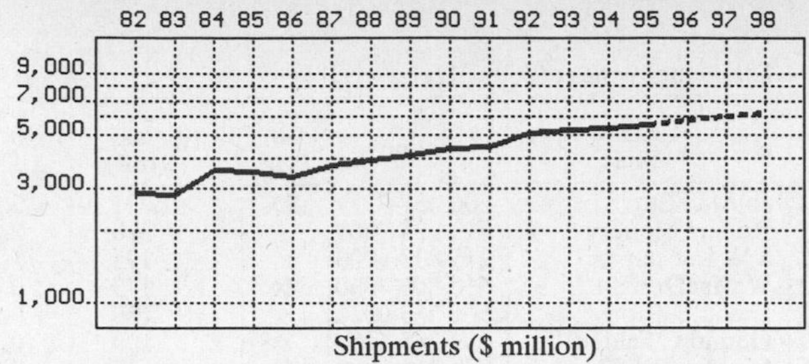

Shipments ($ million)

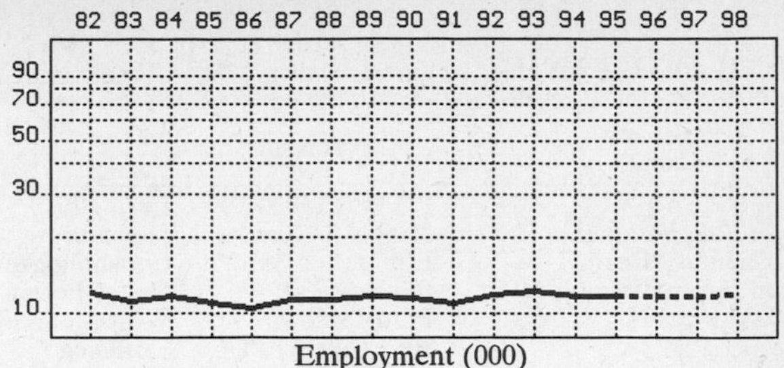

Employment (000)

GENERAL STATISTICS

Year	Companies	Establishments: Total	Establishments: with 20 or more employees	Employment: Total (000)	Employment: Production Workers (000)	Employment: Production Hours (Mil)	Compensation: Payroll ($ mil)	Compensation: Wages ($/hr)	Production ($ million): Cost of Materials	Production ($ million): Value Added by Manufacture	Production ($ million): Value of Shipments	Production ($ million): Capital Invest.
1982	401	473	153	11.9	5.6	11.3	266.2	9.05	1,949.5	902.6	2,875.3	67.8
1983		445	154	11.1	5.5	11.1	261.6	9.11	1,744.2	1,116.9	2,821.2	44.6
1984		417	155	11.7	6.1	12.1	309.8	10.79	2,561.9	1,072.8	3,595.1	71.1
1985		388	157	10.9	5.4	10.5	298.8	10.97	2,433.9	1,046.2	3,483.3	79.6
1986		391	152	10.4	5.3	10.7	283.0	11.16	2,339.0	991.4	3,355.6	101.1
1987	372	451	163	11.2	5.5	11.1	311.8	11.19	2,629.8	1,143.2	3,765.6	79.5
1988		414	158	11.3	5.5	11.3	323.5	11.80	2,649.4	1,284.0	3,936.1	91.5
1989		405	169	11.7	5.7	11.4	349.0	12.99	2,836.1	1,387.2	4,129.0	79.4
1990		391	164	11.5	5.6	10.9	372.8	13.74	3,165.3	1,280.3	4,398.5	131.0
1991		382	149	10.9	5.5	11.4	374.2	13.32	3,162.7	1,303.2	4,478.6	95.7
1992	332	419	173	11.8	6.0	12.5	413.9	13.62	3,691.8	1,388.2	5,103.5	197.2
1993		405	167	12.2	6.2	13.1	434.7	13.52	3,617.7	1,703.2	5,294.6	90.8
1994		388P	168P	11.6	6.0	12.8	422.1	13.34	3,639.5	1,744.5	5,381.6	86.3
1995		383P	169P	11.7P	5.9P	12.5P	442.4P	14.70P	3,748.4P	1,796.7P	5,542.7P	130.2P
1996		379P	170P	11.7P	6.0P	12.6P	457.0P	15.11P	3,892.9P	1,866.0P	5,756.3P	135.5P
1997		375P	172P	11.7P	6.0P	12.7P	471.7P	15.51P	4,037.3P	1,935.2P	5,969.9P	140.7P
1998		371P	173P	11.8P	6.0P	12.9P	486.3P	15.91P	4,181.8P	2,004.4P	6,183.4P	145.9P

Sources: 1982, 1987, 1992 *Economic Census*; *Annual Survey of Manufactures*, 83-86, 88-91, 93-94. Establishment counts for non-Census years are from *County Business Patterns*; establishment values for 83-84 are extrapolations. 'P's show projections by the editors. Industries reclassified in 87 will not have data for prior years.

INDICES OF CHANGE

Year	Companies	Establishments: Total	Establishments: with 20 or more employees	Employment: Total (000)	Employment: Production Workers (000)	Employment: Production Hours (Mil)	Compensation: Payroll ($ mil)	Compensation: Wages ($/hr)	Production ($ million): Cost of Materials	Production ($ million): Value Added by Manufacture	Production ($ million): Value of Shipments	Production ($ million): Capital Invest.
1982	121	113	88	101	93	90	64	66	53	65	56	34
1983		106	89	94	92	89	63	67	47	80	55	23
1984		100	90	99	102	97	75	79	69	77	70	36
1985		93	91	92	90	84	72	81	66	75	68	40
1986		93	88	88	88	86	68	82	63	71	66	51
1987	112	108	94	95	92	89	75	82	71	82	74	40
1988		99	91	96	92	90	78	87	72	92	77	46
1989		97	98	99	95	91	84	95	77	100	81	40
1990		93	95	97	93	87	90	101	86	92	86	66
1991		91	86	92	92	91	90	98	86	94	88	49
1992	100	100	100	100	100	100	100	100	100	100	100	100
1993		97	97	103	103	105	105	99	98	123	104	46
1994		93P	97P	98	100	102	102	98	99	126	105	44
1995		92P	98P	99P	99P	100P	107P	108P	102P	129P	109P	66P
1996		91P	98P	99P	100P	101P	110P	111P	105P	134P	113P	69P
1997		89P	99P	99P	100P	102P	114P	114P	109P	139P	117P	71P
1998		88P	100P	100P	101P	103P	117P	117P	113P	144P	121P	74P

Sources: Same as General Statistics. Values reflect change from the base year, 1992. Values above 100 mean greater than 92, values below 100 mean less than 92, and a value of 100 in the 82-91 or 93-98 period means same as 92. 'P's mark projections by the editors.

SELECTED RATIOS

For 1994	Avg. of All Manufact.	Analyzed Industry	Index
Employees per Establishment	49	30	61
Payroll per Establishment	1,500,273	1,088,865	73
Payroll per Employee	30,620	36,388	119
Production Workers per Establishment	34	15	45
Wages per Establishment	853,319	440,478	52
Wages per Production Worker	24,861	28,459	114
Hours per Production Worker	2,056	2,133	104
Wages per Hour	12.09	13.34	110
Value Added per Establishment	4,602,255	4,500,176	98
Value Added per Employee	93,930	150,388	160

For 1994	Avg. of All Manufact.	Analyzed Industry	Index
Value Added per Production Worker	134,084	290,750	217
Cost per Establishment	5,045,178	9,388,587	186
Cost per Employee	102,970	313,750	305
Cost per Production Worker	146,988	606,583	413
Shipments per Establishment	9,576,895	13,882,572	145
Shipments per Employee	195,460	463,931	237
Shipments per Production Worker	279,017	896,933	321
Investment per Establishment	321,011	222,623	69
Investment per Employee	6,552	7,440	114
Investment per Production Worker	9,352	14,383	154

Sources: Same as General Statistics. The 'Average of All Manufacturing' column represents the average of all manufacturing industries reported for the most recent complete year available. The Index shows the relationship between the Average and the Analyzed Industry. For example, 100 means that they are equal; 500 that the Analyzed Industry is five times the average; 50 means that the Analyzed Industry is half the national average. The abbreviation 'na' is used to show that data are 'not available'.

LEADING COMPANIES

Number shown: **75** Total sales ($ mil): **3,108** Total employment (000): **12.6**

Company Name	Address				CEO Name	Phone	Co. Type	Sales ($ mil)	Empl. (000)
Valvoline Oil Co	PO Box 14000	Lexington	KY	40512	John D Barr	606-357-7777	D	1,001	3.5
Baroid Drilling Fluids Inc	3000 N S Houston	Houston	TX	77032	Robert Menery	713-987-5900	S	310*	2.1
Quaker Chemical Corp	Elm & Lee Sts	Conshohocken	PA	19428	S W Lubsen	215-832-4000	P	195	1.0
Houghton International Inc	PO Box 930	Valley Forge	PA	19482	W MacDonald Jr	610-666-4000	R	175	0.4
Coastal Unilube Inc	PO Box 2048	West Memphis	AR	72303	David C Rippy	501-735-0020	S	130	0.5
WD-40 Co	1061 Cudahy Pl	San Diego	CA	92110	Gerald C Schleif	619-275-1400	P	109	0.1
Castrol Industrial North America	1001 31st St	Downers Grove	IL	60515	Charles H Gaiser	708-241-4000	D	77*	0.3
Cato Oil and Grease Co	PO Box 26868	Oklahoma City	OK	73126	Richard S Pereles	405-270-6200	S	63	0.2
Lubricating Specialties Co	8015 Paramount	Pico Rivera	CA	90660	MA Delaney	310-928-3311	R	50	0.1
Tribol Inc	21031 Ventura Blv	Woodland Hills	CA	91364	William Purosky	818-888-0808	S	50	0.4
Viscosity Oil Co	600-H Joliet Rd	Willowbrook	IL	60521	Jeffrey A Hoch	708-850-4000	S	50	<0.1
Gold Eagle Co	4400 S Kildare Av	Chicago	IL	60632	Robert Hirsch	312-376-4400	R	46	0.2
Cooks Industrial Lubricants Inc	5 N Stiles St	Linden	NJ	07036	Tony Soriano	908-862-2500	D	36	<0.1
Texas Refinery Corp	PO Box 711	Fort Worth	TX	76101	Sebert L Pate	817-332-1161	R	34	0.3
Battenfeld Grease and Oil Corp	PO Box 728	N Tonawanda	NY	14120	JA Bellanti	716-695-2100	S	30	0.2
Battenfeld-American Inc	1575 Clinton St	Buffalo	NY	14206	John A Bellanti	716-822-8410	S	30	0.2
Century Lubricants Co	2140 S 88th St	Kansas City	KS	66111	Michael K Ryan	913-422-4022	S	30	0.1
Master Chemical Corp	PO Box 10001	Perrysburg	OH	43552	William A Sluhan	419-874-7902	R	30	0.1
Royal Lubricants Company Inc	PO Box 518	East Hanover	NJ	07936	Edward Dent Jr	201-887-7410	S	30	<0.1
LPS Laboratories Inc	PO 105052	Tucker	GA	30084	Peter W Muldowney	404-934-7800	S	26	0.1
Southwest Lubricants	1031 Middlesex St	Gibsonia	PA	15044	Dan Green	412-443-5971	D	25	0.1
Eppert Oil Co	9100 Freeland St	Detroit	MI	48228	VR Eppert	313-273-7374	R	22	<0.1
Benz Oil Inc	2724 W Hampton	Milwaukee	WI	53209	DW Benz	414-442-2900	R	20	<0.1
Castrol Inc	16715 Von Karman	Irvine	CA	92714	J Gallina	714-660-9414	D	20	<0.1
Lubrication Engineers Inc	3851 Airport Fwy	Fort Worth	TX	76111	Joe Valentine	817-834-6321	R	20	0.1
Mayco Oil	PO Box 2809	Warminster	PA	18974	CL Hermann	215-672-6600	R	20	<0.1
Schaeffer Manufacturing Co	102 Barton St	St Louis	MO	63104	Tom Herrmann	314-865-4100	R	20	<0.1
Wolfs Head Oil Co	PO Box 393	Reno	PA	16343	Ronald L Wickwire	814-677-1333	S	20	0.1
Lowe Oil Co	510 Price Ln	Clinton	MO	64735	Ralph Lowe Jr	816-885-8151	R	18	<0.1
Magie Brother Oil Co	9101 Fullerton Av	Franklin Park	IL	60131	Richard Hoster	708-455-4500	D	18*	<0.1
Darmex Industrial Corp	71 Jane St	Roslyn Heights	NY	11577	MJ Rozenblum	516-621-3000	R	18	0.1
RW Eaken Inc	PO Box 171	Leesport	PA	19533	William G Mills	610-926-2136	S	16	<0.1
United Oil Co	1800 N Franklin St	Pittsburgh	PA	15233	William R Powers	412-231-1269	R	16	0.1
BG Products Inc	PO Box 1282	Wichita	KS	67201	Galen R Myers	316-265-2686	R	15	<0.1
Franklin Oil Corp	PO Box 46030	Cleveland	OH	44146	J Bortak	216-232-3000	S	15	0.1
Rock Valley Oil and Chemical	1911 Windsor Rd	Rockford	IL	61111	RL Schramm	815-654-2400	R	13	<0.1
K and W Products	239 W Grimes Ln	Bloomington	IN	47403	John M Goode	812-336-3083	D	12	<0.1
Jesco Resources Inc	PO Box 12337	N Kansas City	MO	64116	RS Howell	816-471-4590	R	12	<0.1
Jet-Lube Inc	PO Box 21258	Houston	TX	77228	Cliff Strozier	713-674-7617	R	12	<0.1
Petro-Lube Inc	PO Box 639	Whitmore Lake	MI	48189	Richard Gallagher	313-449-2091	R	12	<0.1
Sun Drilling Products Corp	PO Box 129	Belle Chasse	LA	70037	Jerry Rayburn	504-393-2778	R	12*	<0.1
Wallover Enterprises Inc	21845 Drake Rd	Strongsville	OH	44136	George Marquis	216-238-9250	R	12	<0.1
Castrol Industrial West Inc	5511 District Blv	Los Angeles	CA	90040	Lawrence Tomback	213-771-7000	S	11*	<0.1
Oil Center Research Inc	PO Box 91510	Lafayette	LA	70509	Robert Ahrabi	318-232-2496	R	11	<0.1
McCollister and Co	PO Box 587	Council Bluffs	IA	51502	John S McCollister	712-322-4038	R	11	<0.1
Bodie-Hoover Petroleum Corp	PO Box 698	Lemont	IL	60439	Richard L Hoover	708-257-7781	R	10	<0.1
Fiske Brothers Refining Co	129 Lockwood St	Newark	NJ	07105	F J Snyder Jr	201-589-9150	R	10	0.2
LubeCon Systems Inc	PO Box 589	Fremont	MI	49412	Lyle G Myers	616-924-0653	R	10	<0.1
Lubricating Specialties Co	3365 E Slauson Av	Vernon	CA	90058	MA Delaney	213-727-7792	D	10	<0.1
Novamax Technologies Inc	12801 Newburgh Rd	Livonia	MI	48150	Donald Evans	313-464-4555	D	10*	<0.1
Oil Chem Inc	711 W 12th St	Flint	MI	48503	R Massey	313-235-3040	R	10*	<0.1
Wallover Oil Company Inc	21845 Drake Rd	Strongsville	OH	44136	George Marquis	216-238-9250	S	10	<0.1
American Grease Stick Co	PO Box 729	Muskegon	MI	49443	Kurt Rosen	616-733-2101	R	9*	<0.1
GC Quality Lubricants Inc	PO Box 4304	Macon	GA	31208	John P Jones Jr	912-738-3900	R	9*	<0.1
Elf Atochem North America Inc	2375 State Rd	Cornwells H	PA	19020	James Conmstock	215-245-3113	D	8	<0.1
Mich-I-Penn Oil and Grease Co	9100 Freeland St	Detroit	MI	48208	VR Eppert	313-838-8000	S	8	<0.1
Non-Fluid Oil Corp	298 Delancy St	Newark	NJ	07105	Bruce Kirschenbaum	201-344-3451	R	8*	<0.1
Dylon Industries Inc	7700 Clinton Rd	Cleveland	OH	44144	Bill Manrodt	216-651-1300	R	7*	<0.1
Haynes Manufacturing Co	24142 Detroit Rd	Cleveland	OH	44145	Beth A Kloos	216-631-2166	R	7	<0.1
Break-Free Inc	1035 S Linwood Av	Santa Ana	CA	92705	Dwight B Woodruff	714-953-1900	S	6	<0.1
Epp-Tech Oil Co	9100 Freeland Av	Detroit	MI	48228	RA Eppert	313-272-5580	R	6	<0.1
JTM Products Inc	PO Box 22747	Beachwood	OH	44122	Henry M Vavrik	216-831-0404	R	6	<0.1
Monroe Fluid Technology Inc	36 Draffin Rd	Hilton	NY	14468	JE Silloway	716-392-3434	R	6	<0.1
Blachford Corp	401 Center Rd	Frankfort	IL	60423	William Russell	815-464-2100	S	6	<0.1
Apex Alkali Products Co	4212-24 Main St	Philadelphia	PA	19127	JH Richards III	215-483-3939	R	5	<0.1
Hangsterfers Laboratories Inc	Box 128	Mantua	NJ	08051	Anna Jones	609-468-0216	R	5	<0.1
Illinois Oil Products Inc	321 24th St	Rock Island	IL	61201	RA Jackson	309-786-4474	R	5	<0.1
Intercontinental Lubricants Corp	PO Box 208	Brookfield	CT	06804	Barbara Wehman	203-775-1291	R	5	<0.1
International Refining	2117 Greenleaf St	Evanston	IL	60202	W Jeff Jeffery	708-864-0255	R	5	<0.1
Phoenix Oil Co	PO Box 1777	Augusta	GA	30913	EL Douglass Jr	706-722-5321	R	5	<0.1
Northcoast Oil Inc	2121 University W	St Paul	MN	55114	K Anderson Jr	612-645-4130	R	5	<0.1
Spectro Oils of America	PO Box 208	Brookfield	CT	06804	Barbara Wehman	203-775-1291	D	5	<0.1
Behnke Lubricants Inc	PO Box 25281	Milwaukee	WI	53225	Eric Peter	414-781-8850	R	4	<0.1
Cadillac Oil Co	13650 Helen Av	Detroit	MI	48212	Roger B Piceu	313-365-6200	R	4	<0.1
Famous Lubricants Inc	124 W 47th St	Chicago	IL	60609	VW Hapeman II	312-268-2555	R	4	<0.1

Source: *Ward's Business Directory of U.S. Private and Public Companies*, Volumes 1 and 2, 1996. The company type code used is as follows: P - Public, R - Private, S - Subsidiary, D - Division, J - Joint Venture, A - Affiliate, G - Group. Sales are in millions of dollars, employees are in thousands. An asterisk (*) indicates an estimated sales volume. The symbol < stands for 'less than'. Company names and addresses are truncated, in some cases, to fit into the available space.

MATERIALS CONSUMED

Material		Quantity	Delivered Cost ($ million)
Materials, ingredients, containers, and supplies		(X)	3,460.7
Antioxidant, antiknock compound, and inhibitor additives	mil lb	170.1	114.2
Other additives, including soaps and detergents	mil lb	529.6	420.0
Animal and vegetable oils	mil lb	208.9	80.3
Sodium hydroxide (caustic soda)(100 percent NaOH)	1,000 s tons	19.7	3.4
Sulfuric acid (100 percent H2SO4), except spent	1,000 s tons	25.0	2.8
Metal containers		(X)	97.0
Plastics containers		(X)	210.2
Paper and paperboard containers		(X)	55.6
Fiber cans, bodies with combinations of fiber and other materials (foil, plastics, etc.) with metal ends		(X)	16.5
Cost of materials received from petroleum refineries and lube manufacturers	mil bbl	60.2	1,642.6
All other materials and components, parts, containers, and supplies		(X)	456.4
Materials, ingredients, containers, and supplies, nsk		(X)	361.7

Source: 1992 *Economic Census*. Explanation of symbols used: (D): Withheld to avoid disclosure of competitive data; na: Not available; (S): Withheld because statistical norms were not met; (X): Not applicable; (Z): Less than half the unit shown; nec: Not elsewhere classified; nsk: Not specified by kind; - : zero; * : 10-19 percent estimated; ** : 20-29 percent estimated.

PRODUCT SHARE DETAILS

Product or Product Class	% Share	Product or Product Class	% Share
Lubricating oils and greases	100.00	not made in a refinery	83.15
Lubricating oils (including hydraulic fluids, quenching and cutting oils, transformer oils, liquid rust preventives, etc.),		Lubricating greases, not made in a refinery	7.72

Source: 1992 *Economic Census*. The values shown are percent of total shipments in an industry. Values of indented subcategories are summed in the main heading. The symbol (D) appears when data are withheld to prevent disclosure of competitive information. The abbreviation nsk stands for 'not specified by kind' and nec for 'not elsewhere classified'.

INPUTS AND OUTPUTS FOR LUBRICATING OILS & GREASES

Economic Sector or Industry Providing Inputs	%	Sector	Economic Sector or Industry Buying Outputs	%	Sector
Petroleum refining	42.0	Manufg.	Personal consumption expenditures	25.8	
Imports	12.1	Foreign	Exports	8.3	Foreign
Cyclic crudes and organics	6.6	Manufg.	Crude petroleum & natural gas	3.7	Mining
Surface active agents	5.0	Manufg.	Coal	3.2	Mining
Wholesale trade	4.9	Trade	Commercial fishing	2.9	Agric.
Paperboard containers & boxes	3.8	Manufg.	Wholesale trade	2.8	Trade
Fabricated metal products, nec	3.0	Manufg.	Retail trade, except eating & drinking	2.4	Trade
Metal cans	2.0	Manufg.	Blast furnaces & steel mills	2.2	Manufg.
Lubricating oils & greases	1.8	Manufg.	Automotive repair shops & services	2.2	Services
Metal barrels, drums, & pails	1.8	Manufg.	Petroleum & natural gas well drilling	2.0	Constr.
Advertising	1.7	Services	Broadwoven fabric mills	1.4	Manufg.
Motor freight transportation & warehousing	1.6	Util.	Transformers	1.2	Manufg.
Gum & wood chemicals	1.4	Manufg.	Synthetic rubber	1.1	Manufg.
Motor vehicle parts & accessories	1.4	Manufg.	Motor freight transportation & warehousing	1.1	Util.
Banking	0.9	Fin/R.E.	Miscellaneous plastics products	1.0	Manufg.
Animal & marine fats & oils	0.8	Manufg.	Air transportation	0.8	Util.
Communications, except radio & TV	0.8	Util.	Electric services (utilities)	0.8	Util.
Electric services (utilities)	0.8	Util.	Federal Government purchases, nondefense	0.7	Fed Govt
Gas production & distribution (utilities)	0.8	Util.	S/L Govt. purch., other general government	0.7	S/L Govt
Water transportation	0.8	Util.	Apparel made from purchased materials	0.6	Manufg.
Plastics materials & resins	0.6	Manufg.	Lubricating oils & greases	0.6	Manufg.
Industrial inorganic chemicals, nec	0.5	Manufg.	Motor vehicle parts & accessories	0.6	Manufg.
Chemical preparations, nec	0.4	Manufg.	Motor vehicles & car bodies	0.6	Manufg.
Pipelines, except natural gas	0.4	Util.	Yarn mills & finishing of textiles, nec	0.6	Manufg.
Railroads & related services	0.4	Util.	Federal Government purchases, national defense	0.6	Fed Govt
Maintenance of nonfarm buildings nec	0.3	Constr.	S/L Govt. purch., elem. & secondary education	0.6	S/L Govt
Miscellaneous plastics products	0.3	Manufg.	S/L Govt. purch., police	0.6	S/L Govt
Real estate	0.3	Fin/R.E.	Hospitals	0.5	Services
Equipment rental & leasing services	0.3	Services	Machinery, except electrical, nec	0.4	Manufg.
Mechanical measuring devices	0.2	Manufg.	Paper mills, except building paper	0.4	Manufg.
Air transportation	0.2	Util.	Paperboard containers & boxes	0.4	Manufg.
Sanitary services, steam supply, irrigation	0.2	Util.	Plastics materials & resins	0.4	Manufg.
Eating & drinking places	0.2	Trade	Automotive rental & leasing, without drivers	0.4	Services
Security & commodity brokers	0.2	Fin/R.E.	Miscellaneous repair shops	0.4	Services
Computer & data processing services	0.2	Services	S/L Govt. purch., higher education	0.4	S/L Govt
Miscellaneous repair shops	0.2	Services	Feed grains	0.3	Agric.
Alkalies & chlorine	0.1	Manufg.	Industrial buildings	0.3	Constr.
			Maintenance of nonfarm buildings nec	0.3	Constr.
			Maintenance of petroleum & natural gas wells	0.3	Constr.
			Office buildings	0.3	Constr.
			Residential 1-unit structures, nonfarm	0.3	Constr.
			Commercial printing	0.3	Manufg.

Continued on next page.

INPUTS AND OUTPUTS FOR LUBRICATING OILS & GREASES - Continued

Economic Sector or Industry Providing Inputs	%	Sector	Economic Sector or Industry Buying Outputs	%	Sector
			Ship building & repairing	0.3	Manufg.
			Transit & bus transportation	0.3	Util.
			Real estate	0.3	Fin/R.E.
			Local government passenger transit	0.3	Gov't
			State & local government enterprises, nec	0.3	Gov't
			S/L Govt. purch., health & hospitals	0.3	S/L Govt
			Agricultural, forestry, & fishery services	0.2	Agric.
			Landscape & horticultural services	0.2	Agric.
			Meat animals	0.2	Agric.
			Iron & ferroalloy ores	0.2	Mining
			Nonferrous metal ores, except copper	0.2	Mining
			Electric utility facility construction	0.2	Constr.
			Nonfarm residential structure maintenance	0.2	Constr.
			Residential additions/alterations, nonfarm	0.2	Constr.
			Aircraft	0.2	Manufg.
			Bottled & canned soft drinks	0.2	Manufg.
			Bread, cake, & related products	0.2	Manufg.
			Cigarettes	0.2	Manufg.
			Cyclic crudes and organics	0.2	Manufg.
			Drugs	0.2	Manufg.
			Electronic components nec	0.2	Manufg.
			Electronic computing equipment	0.2	Manufg.
			Glass & glass products, except containers	0.2	Manufg.
			Industrial inorganic chemicals, nec	0.2	Manufg.
			Iron & steel foundries	0.2	Manufg.
			Knit outerwear mills	0.2	Manufg.
			Manufacturing industries, nec	0.2	Manufg.
			Newspapers	0.2	Manufg.
			Paperboard mills	0.2	Manufg.
			Petroleum refining	0.2	Manufg.
			Photographic equipment & supplies	0.2	Manufg.
			Pipe, valves, & pipe fittings	0.2	Manufg.
			Semiconductors & related devices	0.2	Manufg.
			Special dies & tools & machine tool accessories	0.2	Manufg.
			Communications, except radio & TV	0.2	Util.
			Gas production & distribution (utilities)	0.2	Util.
			Railroads & related services	0.2	Util.
			Eating & drinking places	0.2	Trade
			Business services nec	0.2	Services
			Hotels & lodging places	0.2	Services
			Laundry, dry cleaning, shoe repair	0.2	Services
			Legal services	0.2	Services
			Management & consulting services & labs	0.2	Services
			U.S. Postal Service	0.2	Gov't
			S/L Govt. purch., highways	0.2	S/L Govt
			Dairy farm products	0.1	Agric.
			Oil bearing crops	0.1	Agric.
			Copper ore	0.1	Mining
			Aluminum rolling & drawing	0.1	Manufg.
			Bags, except textile	0.1	Manufg.
			Canned fruits & vegetables	0.1	Manufg.
			Fabricated rubber products, nec	0.1	Manufg.
			Farm machinery & equipment	0.1	Manufg.
			Floor coverings	0.1	Manufg.
			Food preparations, nec	0.1	Manufg.
			Glass containers	0.1	Manufg.
			Knit fabric mills	0.1	Manufg.
			Meat packing plants	0.1	Manufg.
			Narrow fabric mills	0.1	Manufg.
			Nonferrous wire drawing & insulating	0.1	Manufg.
			Oil field machinery	0.1	Manufg.
			Organic fibers, noncellulosic	0.1	Manufg.
			Paper coating & glazing	0.1	Manufg.
			Pumps & compressors	0.1	Manufg.
			Radio & TV communication equipment	0.1	Manufg.
			Refrigeration & heating equipment	0.1	Manufg.
			Sawmills & planning mills, general	0.1	Manufg.
			Banking	0.1	Fin/R.E.
			Insurance carriers	0.1	Fin/R.E.
			Advertising	0.1	Services
			Colleges, universities, & professional schools	0.1	Services
			Computer & data processing services	0.1	Services
			Doctors & dentists	0.1	Services
			Electrical repair shops	0.1	Services
			Nursing & personal care facilities	0.1	Services

Continued on next page.

INPUTS AND OUTPUTS FOR LUBRICATING OILS & GREASES - Continued

Economic Sector or Industry Providing Inputs	%	Sector	Economic Sector or Industry Buying Outputs	%	Sector
			S/L Govt. purch., natural resource & recreation.	0.1	S/L Govt
			S/L Govt. purch., public assistance & relief	0.1	S/L Govt

Source: Benchmark Input-Output Accounts for the U.S. Economy, 1982, U.S. Department of Commerce, Washington, D.C., July 1991. Data, as reported in the source, are organized by the 1977 SIC structure in use in 1982 but have been matched, as closely as is possible, to the 1987 SIC structure used in this book.

OCCUPATIONS EMPLOYED BY SIC 299 - MISCELLANEOUS PETROLEUM AND COAL PRODUCTS

Occupation	% of Total 1994	Change to 2005	Occupation	% of Total 1994	Change to 2005
Helpers, laborers, & material movers nec	8.1	-3.3	Assemblers, fabricators, & hand workers nec	2.3	-3.3
Crushing & mixing machine operators	7.7	-3.3	Machine feeders & offbearers	2.2	-12.9
Truck drivers light & heavy	7.4	-0.3	Bookkeeping, accounting, & auditing clerks	2.2	-27.5
Sales & related workers nec	5.5	-3.3	Coating, painting, & spraying machine workers	1.9	-3.3
Industrial truck & tractor operators	4.7	-3.3	Freight, stock, & material movers, hand	1.9	-22.5
General managers & top executives	4.5	-8.3	Industrial production managers	1.8	-3.3
Packaging & filling machine operators	4.5	-3.4	Science & mathematics technicians	1.8	-3.2
Material moving equipment operators nec	3.8	-3.3	Construction trades workers nec	1.6	-22.6
Industrial machinery mechanics	3.5	6.4	Clerical supervisors & managers	1.5	-1.2
Plant & system operators nec	2.6	28.1	Order clerks, materials, merchandise, & service	1.3	-5.2
Maintenance repairers, general utility	2.6	-13.0	Furnace, kiln, or kettle operators	1.2	-3.2
Secretaries, ex legal & medical	2.5	-12.0	Chemists	1.1	-3.3
General office clerks	2.4	-17.6			

Source: Industry-Occupation Matrix, Bureau of Labor Statistics. These data relate to one or more 3-digit SIC industry groups rather than to a single 4-digit SIC. The change reported for each occupation to the year 2005 is a percent of growth or decline as estimated by the Bureau of Labor Statistics. The abbreviation nec stands for 'not elsewhere classified'.

LOCATION BY STATE AND REGIONAL CONCENTRATION

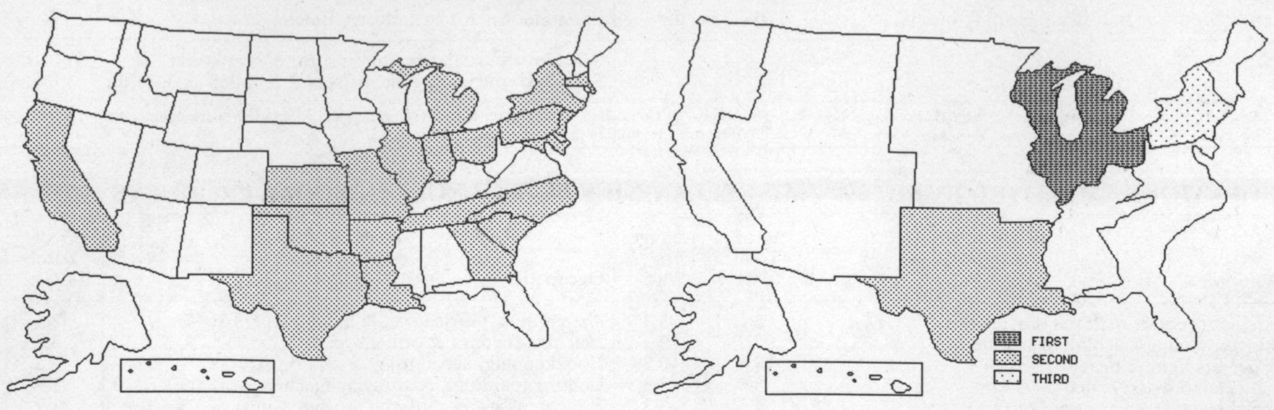

INDUSTRY DATA BY STATE

State	Establish-ments	Shipments			Employment				Cost as % of Shipments	Investment per Employee ($)
		Total ($ mil)	% of U.S.	Per Establ.	Total Number	% of U.S.	Per Establ.	Wages ($/hour)		
Louisiana	18	604.2	11.8	33.6	900	7.6	50	14.55	88.8	-
Illinois	34	558.5	10.9	16.4	1,100	9.3	32	15.82	73.3	13,182
Pennsylvania	28	549.2	10.8	19.6	1,100	9.3	39	13.71	77.0	6,273
California	37	509.2	10.0	13.8	900	7.6	24	14.09	64.0	9,111
Texas	48	298.4	5.8	6.2	900	7.6	19	16.50	93.8	22,111
Missouri	12	147.3	2.9	12.3	300	2.5	25	16.50	76.8	1,667
Kansas	8	108.4	2.1	13.5	400	3.4	50	12.33	61.5	12,500
New York	10	73.2	1.4	7.3	300	2.5	30	13.00	64.5	667
Ohio	34	(D)	-	-	750 *	6.4	22	-	-	5,467
Michigan	33	(D)	-	-	750 *	6.4	23	-	-	-
New Jersey	17	(D)	-	-	1,750 *	14.8	103	-	-	-
Indiana	14	(D)	-	-	375 *	3.2	27	-	-	-
Massachusetts	10	(D)	-	-	175 *	1.5	18	-	-	-
Tennessee	10	(D)	-	-	375 *	3.2	38	-	-	-
North Carolina	8	(D)	-	-	375 *	3.2	47	-	-	2,667
Oklahoma	8	(D)	-	-	375 *	3.2	47	-	-	-
Georgia	7	(D)	-	-	175 *	1.5	25	-	-	-
Arkansas	4	(D)	-	-	175 *	1.5	44	-	-	-
Maryland	4	(D)	-	-	375 *	3.2	94	-	-	-
South Carolina	3	(D)	-	-	175 *	1.5	58	-	-	-

Source: 1992 *Economic Census*. The states are in descending order of shipments or establishments (if shipment data are missing for the majority). The symbol (D) appears when data are withheld to prevent disclosure of competitive information. States marked with (D) are sorted by number of establishments. A dash (-) indicates that the data element cannot be calculated; * indicates the midpoint of a range.

2999 - PETROLEUM & COAL PRODUCTS, NEC

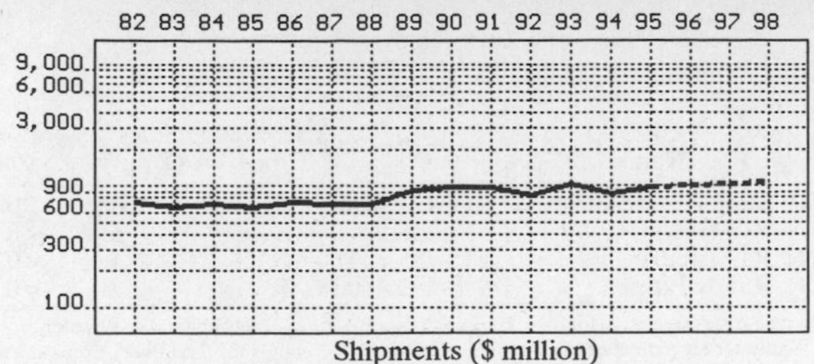

Shipments ($ million)

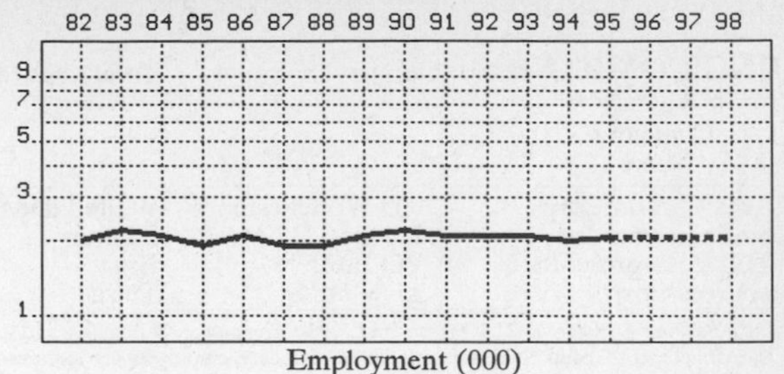

Employment (000)

GENERAL STATISTICS

Year	Com-panies	Establishments		Employment			Compensation		Production ($ million)			
		Total	with 20 or more employees	Total (000)	Production Workers (000)	Production Hours (Mil)	Payroll ($ mil)	Wages ($/hr)	Cost of Materials	Value Added by Manufacture	Value of Shipments	Capital Invest.
1982	100	109	27	2.0	1.4	2.8	45.5	10.25	561.1	176.4	738.8	55.6
1983		100	27	2.2	1.5	3.1	50.9	10.32	532.4	148.0	663.4	115.2
1984		91	27	2.1	1.5	3.3	56.3	10.70	532.5	191.3	719.9	28.5
1985		82	27	1.9	1.3	2.8	52.9	11.82	443.6	225.5	662.4	75.4
1986		62	25	2.1	1.4	3.0	55.8	11.73	483.3	247.3	737.3	11.5
1987	92	106	24	1.9	1.2	2.6	53.6	13.04	440.6	269.3	713.1	12.9
1988		95	22	1.9	1.3	2.6	53.6	13.04	467.7	249.0	719.5	12.6
1989		98	27	2.1	1.3	2.6	54.2	13.46	552.9	363.3	904.0	20.6
1990	-	98	30	2.2	1.3	2.8	57.8	13.54	605.3	377.1	980.2	14.4
1991		96	30	2.1	1.4	3.1	63.8	13.35	588.1	381.4	973.7	30.7
1992	71	82	27	2.1	1.4	3.3	69.3	13.06	504.3	344.1	849.7	21.6
1993		81	31	2.1	1.5	2.9	75.7	16.38	609.3	436.3	1,042.1	21.8
1994		86P	29P	2.0	1.3	2.8	70.9	15.64	494.9	372.9	864.2	26.0
1995		85P	29P	2.1P	1.3P	2.9P	72.6P	15.90P	570.7P	430.0P	996.6P	3.9P
1996		84P	29P	2.1P	1.3P	2.9P	74.6P	16.34P	585.8P	441.4P	1,022.9P	
1997		83P	30P	2.1P	1.3P	2.9P	76.6P	16.79P	600.8P	452.7P	1,049.1P	
1998		82P	30P	2.1P	1.3P	2.9P	78.6P	17.23P	615.8P	464.0P	1,075.3P	

Sources: 1982, 1987, 1992 *Economic Census*; *Annual Survey of Manufactures*, 83-86, 88-91, 93-94. Establishment counts for non-Census years are from *County Business Patterns*; establishment values for 83-84 are extrapolations. 'P's show projections by the editors. Industries reclassified in 87 will not have data for prior years.

INDICES OF CHANGE

Year	Com-panies	Establishments		Employment			Compensation		Production ($ million)			
		Total	with 20 or more employees	Total (000)	Production Workers (000)	Production Hours (Mil)	Payroll ($ mil)	Wages ($/hr)	Cost of Materials	Value Added by Manufacture	Value of Shipments	Capital Invest.
1982	141	133	100	95	100	85	66	78	111	51	87	257
1983		122	100	105	107	94	73	79	106	43	78	533
1984		111	100	100	107	100	81	82	106	56	85	132
1985		100	100	90	93	85	76	91	88	66	78	349
1986		76	93	100	100	91	81	90	96	72	87	53
1987	130	129	89	90	86	79	77	100	87	78	84	60
1988		116	81	90	93	79	77	100	93	72	85	58
1989		120	100	100	93	79	78	103	110	106	106	95
1990		120	111	105	93	85	83	104	120	110	115	67
1991		117	111	100	100	94	92	102	117	111	115	142
1992	100	100	100	100	100	100	100	100	100	100	100	100
1993		99	115	100	107	88	109	125	121	127	123	101
1994		105P	107P	95	93	85	102	120	98	108	102	120
1995		104P	108P	99P	96P	87P	105P	122P	113P	125P	117P	18P
1996		102P	109P	99P	95P	87P	108P	125P	116P	128P	120P	
1997		101P	110P	99P	95P	87P	110P	129P	119P	132P	123P	
1998		100P	111P	99P	95P	87P	113P	132P	122P	135P	127P	

Sources: Same as General Statistics. Values reflect change from the base year, 1992. Values above 100 mean greater than 92, values below 100 mean less than 92, and a value of 100 in the 82-91 or 93-98 period means same as 92. 'P's mark projections by the editors.

SELECTED RATIOS

For 1994	Avg. of All Manufact.	Analyzed Industry	Index
Employees per Establishment	49	23	48
Payroll per Establishment	1,500,273	826,311	55
Payroll per Employee	30,620	35,450	116
Production Workers per Establishment	34	15	44
Wages per Establishment	853,319	510,378	60
Wages per Production Worker	24,861	33,686	135
Hours per Production Worker	2,056	2,154	105
Wages per Hour	12.09	15.64	129
Value Added per Establishment	4,602,255	4,346,000	94
Value Added per Employee	93,930	186,450	198

For 1994	Avg. of All Manufact.	Analyzed Industry	Index
Value Added per Production Worker	134,084	286,846	214
Cost per Establishment	5,045,178	5,767,862	114
Cost per Employee	102,970	247,450	240
Cost per Production Worker	146,988	380,692	259
Shipments per Establishment	9,576,895	10,071,905	105
Shipments per Employee	195,460	432,100	221
Shipments per Production Worker	279,017	664,769	238
Investment per Establishment	321,011	303,020	94
Investment per Employee	6,552	13,000	198
Investment per Production Worker	9,352	20,000	214

Sources: Same as General Statistics. The 'Average of All Manufacturing' column represents the average of all manufacturing industries reported for the most recent complete year available. The Index shows the relationship between the Average and the Analyzed Industry. For example, 100 means that they are equal; 500 that the Analyzed Industry is five times the average; 50 means that the Analyzed Industry is half the national average. The abbreviation 'na' is used to show that data are 'not available'.

LEADING COMPANIES

Number shown: **4** Total sales ($ mil): **63** Total employment (000): **0.3**

Company Name	Address				CEO Name	Phone	Co. Type	Sales ($ mil)	Empl. (000)
Great Lakes Carbon Corp	709 Westchester	White Plains	NY	10604	James D McKenzie	914-421-4600	S	51*	0.2
Anthracite Industries Inc	PO Box 112	Sunbury	PA	17801	RG Gilson	717-286-2176	S	5	<0.1
Walnut Hill Enterprises Inc	PO Box 599	Bristol	PA	19007	RJ Scuderi	215-785-6511	R	5	<0.1
Colt Resources Corp	15 W 6th St	Tulsa	OK	74119	Randy Foutch	918-583-1600	R	2	<0.1

Source: *Ward's Business Directory of U.S. Private and Public Companies*, Volumes 1 and 2, 1996. The company type code used is as follows: P - Public, R - Private, S - Subsidiary, D - Division, J - Joint Venture, A - Affiliate, G - Group. Sales are in millions of dollars, employees are in thousands. An asterisk (*) indicates an estimated sales volume. The symbol < stands for 'less than'. Company names and addresses are truncated, in some cases, to fit into the available space.

MATERIALS CONSUMED

Material	Quantity	Delivered Cost ($ million)
No Materials Consumed data available for this industry.		

Source: 1992 *Economic Census*. Explanation of symbols used: (D): Withheld to avoid disclosure of competitive data; na: Not available; (S): Withheld because statistical norms were not met; (X): Not applicable; (Z): Less than half the unit shown; nec: Not elsewhere classified; nsk: Not specified by kind; - : zero; * : 10-19 percent estimated; ** : 20-29 percent estimated.

PRODUCT SHARE DETAILS

Product or Product Class	% Share	Product or Product Class	% Share
Petroleum and coal products, nec	100.00	Other petroleum and coal products, nec, including packaged fuel and fuel briquettes, and petroleum pitches, not made in a refinery	18.85
Microcrystalline petroleum waxes, not made in a refinery	12.47		
Crystalline petroleum waxes, not made in a refinery	6.81		
Calcined petroleum coke, not made in a refinery	54.81		

Source: 1992 *Economic Census*. The values shown are percent of total shipments in an industry. Values of indented subcategories are summed in the main heading. The symbol (D) appears when data are withheld to prevent disclosure of competitive information. The abbreviation nsk stands for 'not specified by kind' and nec for 'not elsewhere classified'.

INPUTS AND OUTPUTS FOR PRODUCTS OF PETROLEUM & COAL, NEC

Economic Sector or Industry Providing Inputs	%	Sector	Economic Sector or Industry Buying Outputs	%	Sector
Petroleum refining	47.8	Manufg.	Primary aluminum	42.1	Manufg.
Crude petroleum & natural gas	14.5	Mining	Exports	32.9	Foreign
Gas production & distribution (utilities)	6.3	Util.	Industrial inorganic chemicals, nec	12.8	Manufg.
Motor freight transportation & warehousing	5.2	Util.	Carbon & graphite products	7.3	Manufg.
Imports	5.2	Foreign	Personal consumption expenditures	3.7	
Wholesale trade	3.3	Trade	Cyclic crudes and organics	0.7	Manufg.
Water transportation	3.2	Util.	Federal Government purchases, national defense	0.4	Fed Govt
Electric services (utilities)	2.4	Util.			
Sanitary services, steam supply, irrigation	1.4	Util.			
Advertising	1.4	Services			
Libraries, vocation education	1.2	Services			
Miscellaneous repair shops	1.0	Services			
Banking	0.8	Fin/R.E.			
Security & commodity brokers	0.7	Fin/R.E.			
Paperboard containers & boxes	0.6	Manufg.			
Automotive repair shops & services	0.6	Services			
Arrangement of passenger transportation	0.5	Util.			
Communications, except radio & TV	0.5	Util.			
Computer & data processing services	0.5	Services			
Equipment rental & leasing services	0.5	Services			
Maintenance of nonfarm buildings nec	0.3	Constr.			
Mechanical measuring devices	0.2	Manufg.			
Air transportation	0.2	Util.			
Pipelines, except natural gas	0.2	Util.			
Railroads & related services	0.2	Util.			
Credit agencies other than banks	0.2	Fin/R.E.			
Real estate	0.2	Fin/R.E.			
Business/professional associations	0.2	Services			
Eating & drinking places	0.1	Trade			
Insurance carriers	0.1	Fin/R.E.			

Source: Benchmark Input-Output Accounts for the U.S. Economy, 1982, U.S. Department of Commerce, Washington, D.C., July 1991. Data, as reported in the source, are organized by the 1977 SIC structure in use in 1982 but have been matched, as closely as is possible, to the 1987 SIC structure used in this book.

OCCUPATIONS EMPLOYED BY SIC 299 - MISCELLANEOUS PETROLEUM AND COAL PRODUCTS

Occupation	% of Total 1994	Change to 2005	Occupation	% of Total 1994	Change to 2005
Helpers, laborers, & material movers nec	8.1	-3.3	Assemblers, fabricators, & hand workers nec	2.3	-3.3
Crushing & mixing machine operators	7.7	-3.3	Machine feeders & offbearers	2.2	-12.9
Truck drivers light & heavy	7.4	-0.3	Bookkeeping, accounting, & auditing clerks	2.2	-27.5
Sales & related workers nec	5.5	-3.3	Coating, painting, & spraying machine workers	1.9	-3.3
Industrial truck & tractor operators	4.7	-3.3	Freight, stock, & material movers, hand	1.9	-22.5
General managers & top executives	4.5	-8.3	Industrial production managers	1.8	-3.3
Packaging & filling machine operators	4.5	-3.4	Science & mathematics technicians	1.8	-3.2
Material moving equipment operators nec	3.8	-3.3	Construction trades workers nec	1.6	-22.6
Industrial machinery mechanics	3.5	6.4	Clerical supervisors & managers	1.5	-1.2
Plant & system operators nec	2.6	28.1	Order clerks, materials, merchandise, & service	1.3	-5.2
Maintenance repairers, general utility	2.6	-13.0	Furnace, kiln, or kettle operators	1.2	-3.2
Secretaries, ex legal & medical	2.5	-12.0	Chemists	1.1	-3.3
General office clerks	2.4	-17.6			

Source: Industry-Occupation Matrix, Bureau of Labor Statistics. These data relate to one or more 3-digit SIC industry groups rather than to a single 4-digit SIC. The change reported for each occupation to the year 2005 is a percent of growth or decline as estimated by the Bureau of Labor Statistics. The abbreviation nec stands for 'not elsewhere classified'.

LOCATION BY STATE AND REGIONAL CONCENTRATION

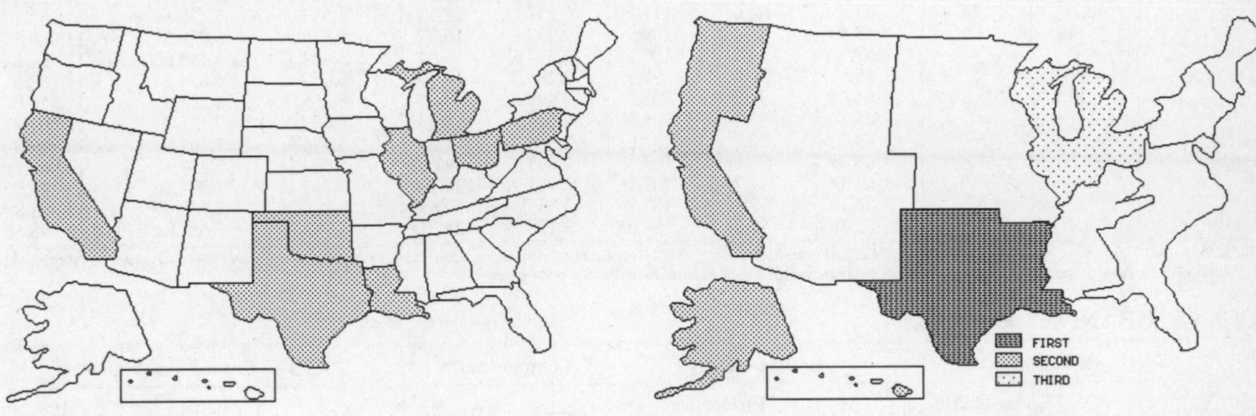

INDUSTRY DATA BY STATE

State	Establish-ments	Shipments: Total ($ mil)	Shipments: % of U.S.	Shipments: Per Establ.	Employment: Total Number	Employment: % of U.S.	Employment: Per Establ.	Employment: Wages ($/hour)	Cost as % of Shipments	Investment per Employee ($)
Louisiana	5	146.7	17.3	29.3	200	9.5	40	19.25	55.7	-
Texas	8	140.9	16.6	17.6	200	9.5	25	20.25	62.5	5,000
California	10	129.9	15.3	13.0	200	9.5	20	16.33	52.5	10,500
Pennsylvania	8	82.4	9.7	10.3	300	14.3	38	14.25	62.0	4,333
Illinois	4	64.7	7.6	16.2	200	9.5	50	11.00	65.1	5,500
Oklahoma	5	(D)	-	-	175 *	8.3	35	-	-	-
Ohio	3	(D)	-	-	175 *	8.3	58	-	-	571
Michigan	2	(D)	-	-	175 *	8.3	88	-	-	-

Source: 1992 *Economic Census*. The states are in descending order of shipments or establishments (if shipment data are missing for the majority). The symbol (D) appears when data are withheld to prevent disclosure of competitive information. States marked with (D) are sorted by number of establishments. A dash (-) indicates that the data element cannot be calculated; * indicates the midpoint of a range.

3011 - TIRES & INNER TUBES

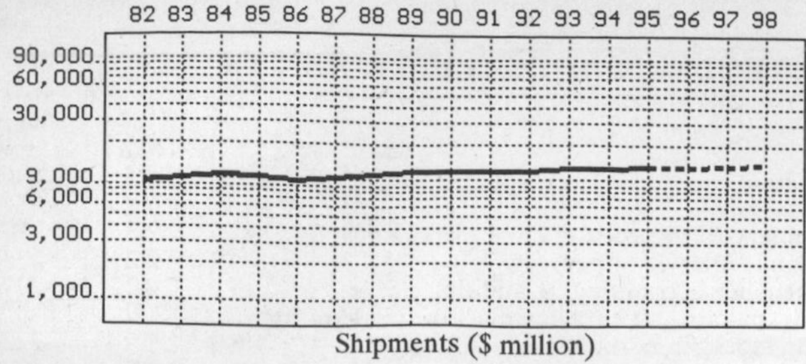

Shipments ($ million)

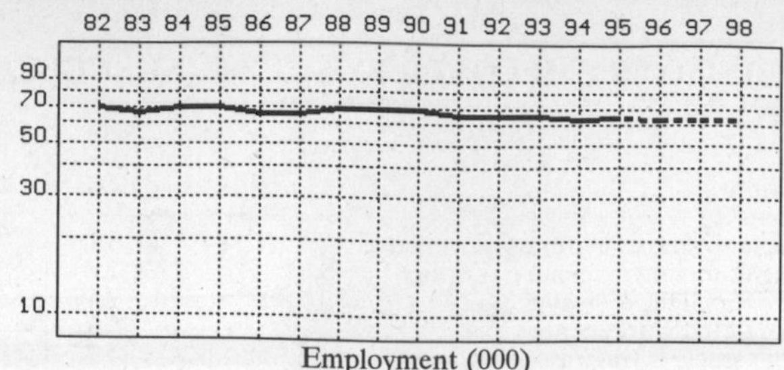

Employment (000)

GENERAL STATISTICS

Year	Companies	Establishments: Total	Establishments: with 20 or more employees	Employment: Total (000)	Employment: Production Workers (000)	Employment: Production Hours (Mil)	Compensation: Payroll ($ mil)	Compensation: Wages ($/hr)	Production ($ million): Cost of Materials	Production ($ million): Value Added by Manufacture	Production ($ million): Value of Shipments	Production ($ million): Capital Invest.
1982	108	164	99	70.3	54.6	101.1	1,733.9	12.72	4,594.6	4,660.4	9,340.1	227.0
1983				66.9	52.2	103.5	185.7	13.50	4,731.6	5,263.8	10,165.4	243.5
1984				70.4	56.3	112.3	2,088.6	14.18	5,541.9	5,312.0	10,722.8	310.1
1985				70.3	55.9	105.2	2,045.8	14.70	5,182.2	5,300.4	10,434.0	496.7
1986				65.2	51.7	98.8	2,020.4	15.50	4,517.1	5,249.9	9,909.5	389.9
1987	115	163	97	65.4	52.6	103.7	2,069.9	15.39	4,864.9	5,559.4	10,427.4	336.7
1988				67.8	54.6	111.1	2,237.6	15.52	5,517.7	5,778.6	11,240.1	417.8
1989		147	95	68.0	54.6	108.5	2,339.6	16.57	5,617.9	6,089.3	11,680.3	784.7
1990				67.7	54.7	106.1	2,314.5	16.84	5,434.7	6,488.6	11,860.8	652.4
1991				65.5	52.4	99.5	2,286.2	17.70	5,057.6	6,654.2	11,882.5	505.9
1992	104	152	86	64.6	52.8	105.7	2,498.5	18.56	5,368.6	6,502.3	11,810.0	506.1
1993				65.1	53.3	109.4	2,595.9	18.63	5,492.0	7,125.2	12,601.2	489.6
1994				63.7	52.7	107.5	2,588.6	18.99	5,596.7	7,201.8	12,882.8	514.6
1995				64.0P	52.9P	107.3P	2,861.9P	19.66P	5,634.2P	7,250.1P	12,969.2P	634.3P
1996				63.5P	52.7P	107.5P	2,973.9P	20.18P	5,747.1P	7,395.3P	13,229.0P	660.3P
1997				63.1P	52.6P	107.7P	3,086.0P	20.69P	5,860.0P	7,540.6P	13,488.8P	686.4P
1998				62.7P	52.5P	108.0P	3,198.1P	21.21P	5,972.8P	7,685.8P	13,748.6P	712.4P

Sources: 1982, 1987, 1992 *Economic Census*; *Annual Survey of Manufactures*, 83-86, 88-91, 93-94. Establishment counts for non-Census years are from *County Business Patterns*; establishment values for 83-84 are extrapolations. 'P's show projections by the editors. Industries reclassified in 87 will not have data for prior years.

INDICES OF CHANGE

Year	Companies	Establishments: Total	Establishments: with 20 or more employees	Employment: Total (000)	Employment: Production Workers (000)	Employment: Production Hours (Mil)	Compensation: Payroll ($ mil)	Compensation: Wages ($/hr)	Production ($ million): Cost of Materials	Production ($ million): Value Added by Manufacture	Production ($ million): Value of Shipments	Production ($ million): Capital Invest.
1982	104	108	115	109	103	96	69	69	86	72	79	45
1983				104	99	98	7	73	88	81	86	48
1984				109	107	106	84	76	103	82	91	61
1985				109	106	100	82	79	97	82	88	98
1986				101	98	93	81	84	84	81	84	77
1987	111	107	113	101	100	98	83	83	91	85	88	67
1988				105	103	105	90	84	103	89	95	83
1989		97	110	105	103	103	94	89	105	94	99	155
1990				105	104	100	93	91	101	100	100	129
1991				101	99	94	92	95	94	102	101	100
1992	100	100	100	100	100	100	100	100	100	100	100	100
1993				101	101	104	104	100	102	110	107	97
1994				99	100	102	104	102	104	111	109	102
1995				99P	100P	101P	115P	106P	105P	112P	110P	125P
1996				98P	100P	102P	119P	109P	107P	114P	112P	130P
1997				98P	100P	102P	124P	111P	109P	116P	114P	136P
1998				97P	99P	102P	128P	114P	111P	118P	116P	141P

Sources: Same as General Statistics. Values reflect change from the base year, 1992. Values above 100 mean greater than 92, values below 100 mean less than 92, and a value of 100 in the 82-91 or 93-98 period means same as 92. 'P's mark projections by the editors.

SELECTED RATIOS

For 1992	Avg. of All Manufact.	Analyzed Industry	Index
Employees per Establishment	46	425	931
Payroll per Establishment	1,332,320	16,437,500	1,234
Payroll per Employee	29,181	38,676	133
Production Workers per Establishment	31	347	1,106
Wages per Establishment	734,496	12,906,526	1,757
Wages per Production Worker	23,390	37,155	159
Hours per Production Worker	2,025	2,002	99
Wages per Hour	11.55	18.56	161
Value Added per Establishment	3,842,210	42,778,289	1,113
Value Added per Employee	84,153	100,655	120

For 1992	Avg. of All Manufact.	Analyzed Industry	Index
Value Added per Production Worker	122,353	123,150	101
Cost per Establishment	4,239,462	35,319,737	833
Cost per Employee	92,853	83,105	90
Cost per Production Worker	135,003	101,678	75
Shipments per Establishment	8,100,800	77,697,368	959
Shipments per Employee	177,425	182,817	103
Shipments per Production Worker	257,966	223,674	87
Investment per Establishment	278,244	3,329,605	1,197
Investment per Employee	6,094	7,834	129
Investment per Production Worker	8,861	9,585	108

Sources: Same as General Statistics. The 'Average of All Manufacturing' column represents the average of all manufacturing industries reported for the most recent complete year available. The Index shows the relationship between the Average and the Analyzed Industry. For example, 100 means that they are equal; 500 that the Analyzed Industry is five times the average; 50 means that the Analyzed Industry is half the national average. The abbreviation 'na' is used to show that data are 'not available'.

LEADING COMPANIES

Number shown: **29** Total sales ($ mil): **25,516** Total employment (000): **167.9**

Company Name	Address				CEO Name	Phone	Co. Type	Sales ($ mil)	Empl. (000)
Goodyear Tire and Rubber Co	1144 E Market St	Akron	OH	44316	Stanley C Gault	216-796-2121	P	11,643	90.4
Bridgestone/Firestone Inc	1 Bridgestone Park	Nashville	TN	37214	Masatoshi Oho	615-391-0088	S	6,000	30.0
Michelin Tire Corp	PO Box 19001	Greenville	SC	29602	Edouard Michelin	803-458-5000	S	1,840*	11.5
General Tire Inc	1 General St	Akron	OH	44329	Alan L Ockene	216-798-3000	S	1,400	8.0
Cooper Tire and Rubber Co	701 Lima Av	Findlay	OH	45840	Ivan W Gorr	419-423-1321	P	1,194	7.6
Kelly-Springfield Tire Co	12501 Willow Brook	Cumberland	MD	21502	Lee Fiedler	301-777-6000	S	1,000	7.0
Bandag Inc	2905 N Hwy 61	Muscatine	IA	52761	Martin G Carver	319-262-1400	P	666	2.5
Dunlop Tire Corp	PO Box 1109	Buffalo	NY	14240	Peter K Fujita	716-639-5200	S	410	3.2
Pirelli Armstrong Tire Corp	PO Box 2001	New Haven	CT	06536	Paul Calvi	203-784-2200	S	410	1.5
Dayton Tire Co	2500 S Council Rd	Oklahoma City	OK	73124	John T Lampe	405-745-3421	D	320*	1.6
Condere Corp	2750 Dixwell Av	Hamden	CT	06518	Dennis Terwilliger	203-287-2200	R	97*	0.8
Michelin Aircraft Tire Corp	9700 Research Dr	Charlotte	NC	28262	Viktor Hanuska	704-548-2400	S	90	0.7
Dico Tire Inc	520 JD Yarnell	Clinton	TN	37716		615-463-3600	S	65	0.4
Gans Tire Company Inc	730 Eastern Av	Malden	MA	02148	David Gans	617-321-3910	R	60	<0.1
Polymer Enterprises Inc	401 Berkshire Ctr	Greensburg	PA	15601	DD Mateer	412-838-2340	R	57*	0.4
Specialty Tires of America Inc	1600 Washington St	Indiana	PA	15701	Donald D Mateer	412-349-9010	S	51*	0.4
Cupples Rubber Co	9430 Page Av	St Louis	MO	63132	HM Stuhl	314-426-7750	R	45*	0.4
Edwards Warren Tire	PO Box 640	Bloomington	IL	61702	LD Duckett	309-452-4411	D	35	0.3
Monarch Industrial Tire Corp	61 State Rte 43 N	Hartville	OH	44632	Timothy Ryan	216-877-1211	S	26*	0.2
Pirelli Armstrong Tire Corp	5701 Murray St	Little Rock	AR	72209	Sergio Rossi	501-562-5410	D	25	0.2
Trintex Corp	PO Box 309	Bowdon	GA	30108	Kirk Dortch	404-258-5551	R	25	0.3
Camel Products	PO Box 769	Muskogee	OK	74402	Randy Garvin	918-687-5427	D	21	0.2
Mitchell Industrial Tire Co	PO Box 71839	Chattanooga	TN	37407	Benton Hood	615-698-4442	R	11	<0.1
Darnell Corp	PO Box 7009	City of Industry	CA	91744	Sal Aziotta	818-912-1688	S	7	0.1
Topflite	PO Box 89	Guntersville	AL	35976	John W Price	205-582-3134	D	6	<0.1
Western States Mfg Co	PO Box 3655	Sioux City	IA	51102	M Kline	712-252-4248	R	4	<0.1
R and K Industrial Products Co	1945 N 7th St	Richmond	CA	94801	Bruce Gultin	510-234-7212	R	3*	<0.1
World Trade Industries Inc	PO Box 421	Chester	PA	19016	Anthony Kuc	215-876-6600	R	3	<0.1
Davis Rubber Co	PO Box 3774	Little Rock	AR	72203	Phillip Davis	501-374-1473	R	2	<0.1

Source: *Ward's Business Directory of U.S. Private and Public Companies*, Volumes 1 and 2, 1996. The company type code used is as follows: P - Public, R - Private, S - Subsidiary, D - Division, J - Joint Venture, A - Affiliate, G - Group. Sales are in millions of dollars, employees are in thousands. An asterisk (*) indicates an estimated sales volume. The symbol < stands for 'less than'. Company names and addresses are truncated, in some cases, to fit into the available space.

MATERIALS CONSUMED

Material		Quantity	Delivered Cost ($ million)
Materials, ingredients, containers, and supplies		(X)	4,784.3
Natural latex rubber (dry solids content)	mil lb	317.4	166.4
Natural dry rubber	mil lb	1,395.6	494.2
Inorganic pigments	mil lb	172.1	80.0
Plastics resins consumed in the form of granules, pellets, powders, liquids, etc.	mil lb	63.5	31.8
Synthetic rubber, including vulcanizable elastomers		(X)	1,142.8
Rubber processing chemicals (accelerators, antioxidants, blowing agents, inhibitors, peptizers, etc.)		(X)	319.4
Plasticizers	mil lb	111.3	28.1
Carbon black	mil lb	1,765.2	401.7
All other chemical and allied products		(X)	272.9
Reclaimed rubber, excluding mud and crumb or ground scrap	mil lb	36.3*	12.4
Rubber compounds and mixtures purchased (dry rubber solids content)	mil lb	133.7*	90.3
All other fabricated rubber products		(X)	18.7
Nylon tire cord	mil lb	87.8	203.4
Polyester tire cord	mil lb	149.0	322.3
Metallic tire cord	mil lb	570.4	621.0
All tire fabrics, and rayon, fiberglass, chafer, and other tire cord		(X)	121.7
Fabricated metal products (except castings and forgings)		(X)	36.0
Castings (rough and semifinished)		(X)	(D)
Steel wire	1,000 s tons	71.7*	63.8
All other steel shapes and forms (except castings, forgings, and fabricated metal products)		(X)	10.0
Nonferrous shapes and forms (except castings, forgings, and fabricated metal products)		(X)	(D)
Paper and paperboard containers, including shipping sacks and other paper packaging supplies		(X)	(D)
All other materials and components, parts, containers, and supplies		(X)	253.3
Materials, ingredients, containers, and supplies, nsk		(X)	81.3

Source: 1992 *Economic Census*. Explanation of symbols used: (D): Withheld to avoid disclosure of competitive data; na: Not available; (S): Withheld because statistical norms were not met; (X): Not applicable; (Z): Less than half the unit shown; nec: Not elsewhere classified; nsk: Not specified by kind; - : zero; * : 10-19 percent estimated; ** : 20-29 percent estimated.

PRODUCT SHARE DETAILS

Product or Product Class	% Share
Tires and inner tubes	100.00
Passenger car pneumatic tires (casings)	52.40
Radial passenger car pneumatic tires (casings)	98.74
Other passenger car pneumatic tires (casings)	1.26
Truck and bus (including off-the-highway) pneumatic tires	31.89
Light truck (including off-the-highway) radial pneumatic tires	58.63
Other light truck (including off-the-highway) pneumatic tires	8.96
Large off-the-highway (sizes 16.00 in. and larger) radial pneumatic tires	7.65
Other large off-the-highway (sizes 16.00 in. and larger) pneumatic tires	(D)
Other truck and bus radial pneumatic tires	(D)
Other truck and bus pneumatic tires	(D)
Tractor and implement (farm and industrial) pneumatic tires	3.83
Industrial and utility pneumatic tires (including garden)	1.59
Other pneumatic tires	1.39
Motorcycle, motorbike, and moped pneumatic tires (casings)	(D)
Aircraft pneumatic tires	(D)
Other pneumatic tires and casings (including bicycle and mobile home)	20.43
Other pneumatic tires, nsk	7.64
Solid and semipneumatic tires	0.98
Solid tires (industrial, highway, bogie, idler, and support rollers)	41.95
Other solid and semipneumatic tires (including hand lawnmower, baby carriage, tricycle, juvenile, etc.)	58.05
Inner tubes	1.03
Passenger car and motorcycle inner tubes	19.90
Truck and bus inner tubes (including off-the-highway)	45.99
Tractor and implement (farm and industrial) inner tubes	34.11
Tread rubber, tire sundries, and repair materials	6.38
Tread rubber (camelback) (including slab rubber for use in automatic tread rubber extruding machines)	83.35
Tire flaps	2.65
Other tire sundries, repair materials, and tiring	11.41
Tread rubber, tire sundries, and repair materials, nsk	2.59
Tires and inner tubes, nsk	0.53

Source: 1992 *Economic Census*. The values shown are percent of total shipments in an industry. Values of indented subcategories are summed in the main heading. The symbol (D) appears when data are withheld to prevent disclosure of competitive information. The abbreviation nsk stands for 'not specified by kind' and nec for 'not elsewhere classified'.

INPUTS AND OUTPUTS FOR TIRES & INNER TUBES

Economic Sector or Industry Providing Inputs	%	Sector
Imports	19.7	Foreign
Synthetic rubber	15.3	Manufg.
Tire cord & fabric	12.3	Manufg.
Wholesale trade	6.8	Trade
Carbon black	5.2	Manufg.
Noncomparable imports	5.2	Foreign
Cyclic crudes and organics	4.2	Manufg.
Motor freight transportation & warehousing	3.7	Util.
Miscellaneous fabricated wire products	2.5	Manufg.
Electric services (utilities)	2.5	Util.
Advertising	2.4	Services
Fabricated rubber products, nec	2.3	Manufg.
Accounting, auditing & bookkeeping	2.1	Services
Railroads & related services	1.7	Util.
Petroleum refining	1.6	Manufg.
Gas production & distribution (utilities)	1.5	Util.
Inorganic pigments	1.2	Manufg.
Banking	1.1	Fin/R.E.
Chemical preparations, nec	0.6	Manufg.
Industrial inorganic chemicals, nec	0.6	Manufg.
Water transportation	0.6	Util.
Reclaimed rubber	0.4	Manufg.
Sanitary services, steam supply, irrigation	0.4	Util.
Royalties	0.4	Fin/R.E.
Plastics materials & resins	0.3	Manufg.
Automotive rental & leasing, without drivers	0.3	Services
Business services nec	0.3	Services
U.S. Postal Service	0.3	Gov't
Chemical & fertilizer mineral	0.2	Mining
Maintenance of nonfarm buildings nec	0.2	Constr.
Broadwoven fabric mills	0.2	Manufg.
Paperboard containers & boxes	0.2	Manufg.
Pumps & compressors	0.2	Manufg.
Air transportation	0.2	Util.
Communications, except radio & TV	0.2	Util.
Eating & drinking places	0.2	Trade
Insurance carriers	0.2	Fin/R.E.
Automotive repair shops & services	0.2	Services
Equipment rental & leasing services	0.2	Services
Alkalies & chlorine	0.1	Manufg.
Tires & inner tubes	0.1	Manufg.
Security & commodity brokers	0.1	Fin/R.E.
Computer & data processing services	0.1	Services
Engineering, architectural, & surveying services	0.1	Services

Economic Sector or Industry Buying Outputs	%	Sector
Personal consumption expenditures	40.4	
Motor vehicles & car bodies	13.0	Manufg.
Motor freight transportation & warehousing	7.2	Util.
Exports	3.6	Foreign
Retail trade, except eating & drinking	3.4	Trade
Wholesale trade	2.8	Trade
Farm machinery & equipment	2.5	Manufg.
Construction machinery & equipment	1.6	Manufg.
Federal Government purchases, national defense	1.6	Fed Govt
Truck trailers	1.2	Manufg.
Coal	1.0	Mining
Transit & bus transportation	0.9	Util.
Feed grains	0.7	Agric.
Motorcycles, bicycles, & parts	0.7	Manufg.
Automotive rental & leasing, without drivers	0.7	Services
Change in business inventories	0.7	In House
Local government passenger transit	0.6	Gov't
Lawn & garden equipment	0.5	Manufg.
Mobile homes	0.5	Manufg.
Legal services	0.5	Services
Meat animals	0.4	Agric.
Residential 1-unit structures, nonfarm	0.4	Constr.
Real estate	0.4	Fin/R.E.
Landscape & horticultural services	0.3	Agric.
Copper ore	0.3	Mining
Industrial buildings	0.3	Constr.
Maintenance of nonfarm buildings nec	0.3	Constr.
Nonfarm residential structure maintenance	0.3	Constr.
Office buildings	0.3	Constr.
Hospitals	0.3	Services
Management & consulting services & labs	0.3	Services
S/L Govt. purch., police	0.3	S/L Govt
Agricultural, forestry, & fishery services	0.2	Agric.
Oil bearing crops	0.2	Agric.
Electric utility facility construction	0.2	Constr.
Residential additions/alterations, nonfarm	0.2	Constr.
Newspapers	0.2	Manufg.
Transportation equipment, nec	0.2	Manufg.
Travel trailers & campers	0.2	Manufg.
Electric services (utilities)	0.2	Util.
Railroads & related services	0.2	Util.
Eating & drinking places	0.2	Trade
Banking	0.2	Fin/R.E.
Insurance carriers	0.2	Fin/R.E.
Advertising	0.2	Services
Automotive repair shops & services	0.2	Services
Doctors & dentists	0.2	Services
Federal Government purchases, nondefense	0.2	Fed Govt
Food grains	0.1	Agric.

Continued on next page.

INPUTS AND OUTPUTS FOR TIRES & INNER TUBES - Continued

Economic Sector or Industry Providing Inputs	%	Sector	Economic Sector or Industry Buying Outputs	%	Sector
			Tobacco	0.1	Agric.
			Dimension, crushed & broken stone	0.1	Mining
			Nonferrous metal ores, except copper	0.1	Mining
			Highway & street construction	0.1	Constr.
			Apparel made from purchased materials	0.1	Manufg.
			Commercial printing	0.1	Manufg.
			Industrial trucks & tractors	0.1	Manufg.
			Logging camps & logging contractors	0.1	Manufg.
			Mining machinery, except oil field	0.1	Manufg.
			Communications, except radio & TV	0.1	Util.
			Gas production & distribution (utilities)	0.1	Util.
			Hotels & lodging places	0.1	Services
			Laundry, dry cleaning, shoe repair	0.1	Services
			Miscellaneous repair shops	0.1	Services
			Nursing & personal care facilities	0.1	Services
			Services to dwellings & other buildings	0.1	Services
			State & local government enterprises, nec	0.1	Gov't
			S/L Govt. purch., elem. & secondary education	0.1	S/L Govt
			S/L Govt. purch., other general government	0.1	S/L Govt

Source: Benchmark Input-Output Accounts for the U.S. Economy, 1982, U.S. Department of Commerce, Washington, D.C., July 1991. Data, as reported in the source, are organized by the 1977 SIC structure in use in 1982 but have been matched, as closely as is possible, to the 1987 SIC structure used in this book.

OCCUPATIONS EMPLOYED BY SIC 301 - TIRES AND INNER TUBES

Occupation	% of Total 1994	Change to 2005	Occupation	% of Total 1994	Change to 2005
Tire building machine operators	18.0	-6.5	Furnace, kiln, or kettle operators	2.7	-5.1
Machine operators nec	10.8	-2.5	Helpers, laborers, & material movers nec	2.6	-36.8
Extruding & forming machine workers	7.6	10.7	Machine feeders & offbearers	2.1	-43.1
Blue collar worker supervisors	5.9	-41.9	Cutting & slicing machine setters, operators	2.1	-30.4
Inspectors, testers, & graders, precision	5.6	-36.8	Maintenance repairers, general utility	1.9	-43.1
Industrial truck & tractor operators	4.7	-36.8	Material moving equipment operators nec	1.7	-36.8
Assemblers, fabricators, & hand workers nec	4.0	-36.8	Electricians	1.2	-40.6
Industrial machinery mechanics	3.7	-30.4	Coating, painting, & spraying machine workers	1.1	-36.8
Crushing & mixing machine operators	3.2	-36.8			

Source: Industry-Occupation Matrix, Bureau of Labor Statistics. These data relate to one or more 3-digit SIC industry groups rather than to a single 4-digit SIC. The change reported for each occupation to the year 2005 is a percent of growth or decline as estimated by the Bureau of Labor Statistics. The abbreviation nec stands for 'not elsewhere classified'.

LOCATION BY STATE AND REGIONAL CONCENTRATION

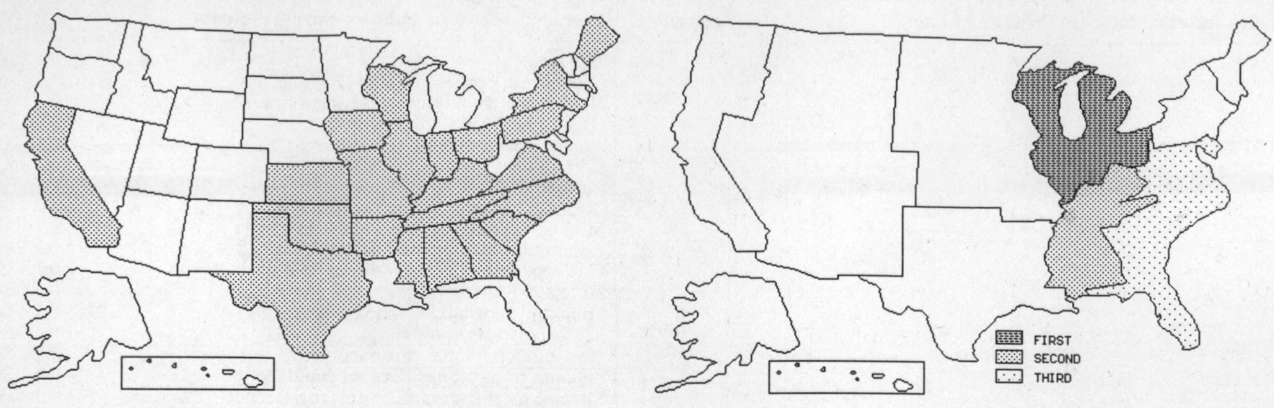

INDUSTRY DATA BY STATE

State	Establish-ments	Shipments			Employment				Cost as % of Shipments	Investment per Employee ($)
		Total ($ mil)	% of U.S.	Per Establ.	Total Number	% of U.S.	Per Establ.	Wages ($/hour)		
Alabama	9	1,446.4	12.2	160.7	9,600	14.9	1,067	18.18	47.6	7,542
North Carolina	9	1,405.7	11.9	156.2	7,300	11.3	811	20.03	44.3	5,356
Oklahoma	5	1,356.0	11.5	271.2	6,100	9.4	1,220	16.60	35.0	14,131
Illinois	8	1,043.2	8.8	130.4	5,000	7.7	625	18.81	51.8	-
Tennessee	9	961.4	8.1	106.8	6,000	9.3	667	18.76	51.2	3,833
Ohio	14	443.5	3.8	31.7	2,900	4.5	207	21.14	40.1	-
Iowa	5	427.4	3.6	85.5	2,900	4.5	580	19.15	52.2	7,207
Texas	11	401.9	3.4	36.5	1,800	2.8	164	20.37	40.1	-
Georgia	5	180.6	1.5	36.1	800	1.2	160	12.14	58.9	12,000
Pennsylvania	9	147.0	1.2	16.3	1,100	1.7	122	10.67	39.0	3,273
California	11	(D)	-	-	750 *	1.2	68	-	-	-
Indiana	6	(D)	-	-	1,750 *	2.7	292	-	-	-
New York	5	(D)	-	-	1,750 *	2.7	350	-	-	-
Virginia	5	(D)	-	-	3,750 *	5.8	750	-	-	-
South Carolina	4	(D)	-	-	3,750 *	5.8	938	-	-	-
Arkansas	3	(D)	-	-	1,750 *	2.7	583	-	-	-
Kentucky	3	(D)	-	-	1,750 *	2.7	583	-	-	-
Mississippi	3	(D)	-	-	1,750 *	2.7	583	-	-	-
Missouri	3	(D)	-	-	375 *	0.6	125	-	-	-
Kansas	2	(D)	-	-	1,750 *	2.7	875	-	-	-
Wisconsin	2	(D)	-	-	375 *	0.6	188	-	-	-
Maine	1	(D)	-	-	175 *	0.3	175	-	-	-

Source: 1992 *Economic Census*. The states are in descending order of shipments or establishments (if shipment data are missing for the majority). The symbol (D) appears when data are withheld to prevent disclosure of competitive information. States marked with (D) are sorted by number of establishments. A dash (-) indicates that the data element cannot be calculated; * indicates the midpoint of a range.

3021 - RUBBER & PLASTICS FOOTWEAR

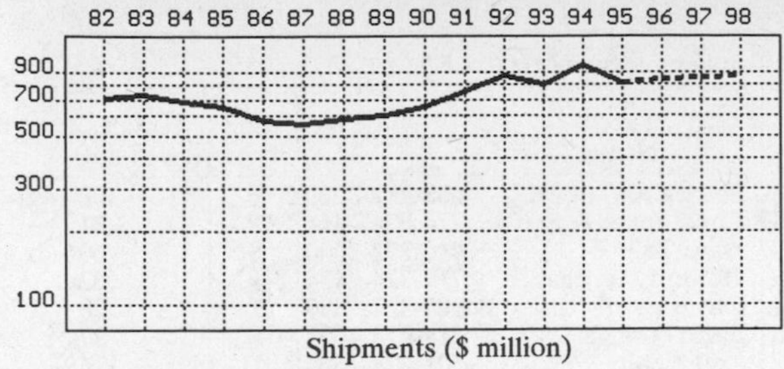

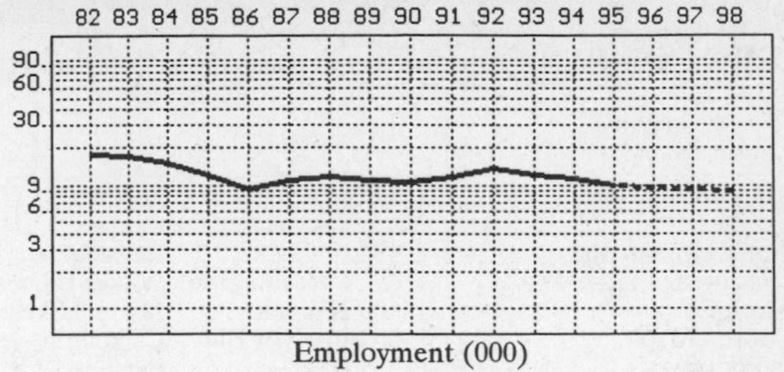

GENERAL STATISTICS

Year	Companies	Establishments: Total	Establishments: with 20 or more employees	Employment: Total (000)	Production Workers (000)	Production Hours (Mil)	Compensation: Payroll ($ mil)	Compensation: Wages ($/hr)	Production ($ million): Cost of Materials	Value Added by Manufacture	Value of Shipments	Capital Invest.
1982	53	65	40	17.6	15.0	27.8	196.5	5.36	333.8	360.1	706.2	12.4
1983				17.3	14.9	27.1	200.0	5.49	339.2	425.9	728.0	12.7
1984				15.0	12.4	22.5	181.8	5.70	330.8	340.9	681.3	23.0
1985				12.0	9.7	18.3	161.1	6.30	322.6	318.0	647.2	8.4
1986				9.2	7.5	13.9	136.8	6.41	283.8	286.5	573.3	6.3
1987	55	65	38	10.9	9.1	16.6	153.3	6.23	252.4	315.8	557.2	9.4
1988				11.7	9.9	18.7	160.2	6.18	278.7	315.8	582.7	11.7
1989		65	38	10.9	9.2	18.9	151.7	5.83	305.0	288.6	604.6	9.0
1990				10.5	8.8	18.1	158.9	6.18	323.2	338.7	650.0	6.4
1991				11.7	9.7	21.1	181.9	6.27	373.3	384.0	756.9	12.3
1992	53	67	39	13.6	11.2	22.3	215.5	6.74	410.8	463.7	867.5	12.9
1993				12.0	10.0	20.7	201.4	6.80	377.2	409.5	796.4	13.5
1994				11.4	9.2	18.3	198.0	7.24	498.0	476.3	961.2	12.6
1995				10.0P	8.1P	17.6P	186.5P	7.02P	425.9P	407.3P	822.0P	10.7P
1996				9.6P	7.8P	17.2P	187.9P	7.13P	434.8P	415.9P	839.3P	10.5P
1997				9.3P	7.5P	16.8P	189.3P	7.25P	443.8P	424.5P	856.6P	10.4P
1998				8.9P	7.1P	16.4P	190.8P	7.37P	452.7P	433.0P	873.9P	10.3P

Sources: 1982, 1987, 1992 *Economic Census*; *Annual Survey of Manufactures*, 83-86, 88-91, 93-94. Establishment counts for non-Census years are from *County Business Patterns*; establishment values for 83-84 are extrapolations. 'P's show projections by the editors. Industries reclassified in 87 will not have data for prior years.

INDICES OF CHANGE

Year	Companies	Establishments: Total	Establishments: with 20 or more employees	Employment: Total (000)	Production Workers (000)	Production Hours (Mil)	Compensation: Payroll ($ mil)	Compensation: Wages ($/hr)	Production ($ million): Cost of Materials	Value Added by Manufacture	Value of Shipments	Capital Invest.
1982	100	97	103	129	134	125	91	80	81	78	81	96
1983				127	133	122	93	81	83	92	84	98
1984				110	111	101	84	85	81	74	79	178
1985				88	87	82	75	93	79	69	75	65
1986				68	67	62	63	95	69	62	66	49
1987	104	97	97	80	81	74	71	92	61	68	64	73
1988				86	88	84	74	92	68	68	67	91
1989		97	97	80	82	85	70	86	74	62	70	70
1990				77	79	81	74	92	79	73	75	50
1991				86	87	95	84	93	91	83	87	95
1992	100	100	100	100	100	100	100	100	100	100	100	100
1993				88	89	93	93	101	92	88	92	105
1994				84	82	82	92	107	121	103	111	98
1995				74P	73P	79P	87P	104P	104P	88P	95P	83P
1996				71P	70P	77P	87P	106P	106P	90P	97P	82P
1997				68P	67P	75P	88P	108P	108P	92P	99P	81P
1998				65P	64P	74P	89P	109P	110P	93P	101P	80P

Sources: Same as General Statistics. Values reflect change from the base year, 1992. Values above 100 mean greater than 92, values below 100 mean less than 92, and a value of 100 in the 82-91 or 93-98 period means same as 92. 'P's mark projections by the editors.

SELECTED RATIOS

For 1992	Avg. of All Manufact.	Analyzed Industry	Index	For 1992	Avg. of All Manufact.	Analyzed Industry	Index
Employees per Establishment	46	203	445	Value Added per Production Worker	122,353	41,402	34
Payroll per Establishment	1,332,320	3,216,418	241	Cost per Establishment	4,239,462	6,131,343	145
Payroll per Employee	29,181	15,846	54	Cost per Employee	92,853	30,206	33
Production Workers per Establishment	31	167	532	Cost per Production Worker	135,003	36,679	27
Wages per Establishment	734,496	2,243,313	305	Shipments per Establishment	8,100,800	12,947,761	160
Wages per Production Worker	23,390	13,420	57	Shipments per Employee	177,425	63,787	36
Hours per Production Worker	2,025	1,991	98	Shipments per Production Worker	257,966	77,455	30
Wages per Hour	11.55	6.74	58	Investment per Establishment	278,244	192,537	69
Value Added per Establishment	3,842,210	6,920,896	180	Investment per Employee	6,094	949	16
Value Added per Employee	84,153	34,096	41	Investment per Production Worker	8,861	1,152	13

Sources: Same as General Statistics. The 'Average of All Manufacturing' column represents the average of all manufacturing industries reported for the most recent complete year available. The Index shows the relationship between the Average and the Analyzed Industry. For example, 100 means that they are equal; 500 that the Analyzed Industry is five times the average; 50 means that the Analyzed Industry is half the national average. The abbreviation 'na' is used to show that data are 'not available'.

LEADING COMPANIES

Number shown: **12** Total sales ($ mil): **368** Total employment (000): **5.9**

Company Name	Address				CEO Name	Phone	Co. Type	Sales ($ mil)	Empl. (000)
LaCrosse Footwear Inc	1319 St Andrew St	La Crosse	WI	54602	Patrick K Gantert	608-782-3020	P	108	1.6
Vans Inc	2095 Batavia St	Orange	CA	92665	Christopher G Staff	714-974-7414	P	81	2.6
Bata Shoe Company Inc	US Hwy 40	Belcamp	MD	21017	Dave Talbot	410-272-2000	S	60	0.3
Carter Footwear Inc	1167 N Washington	Wilkes-Barre	PA	18705	Howard Gonchar	717-824-2434	R	32*	0.5
Suave Shoe Corp	14100 NW 60th Av	Miami Lakes	FL	33014	David Egozi	305-822-7880	P	28	0.4
Lotto Sport USA	1900 Surveyor Blv	Carrollton	TX	75006	Ilario Sfoggia	214-416-4003	S	27	<0.1
Parsons Footwear	PO Box 345	Parsons	WV	26287	Neil Aubil	304-478-2864	D	14*	0.2
Tingley Rubber Corp	200 South Av	South Plainfield	NJ	07080	David D Rand	908-757-7474	R	12*	0.2
In Step Promotions Inc	10821 Lakeview	Lenexa	KS	66219	Steve Robertson	913-599-5995	R	5*	<0.1
Ewing Athletics USA Inc	560 White Plains Rd	Tarrytown	NY	10591	Jonathan Bobbett	914-332-5252	R	1*	<0.1
Island Slipper Factory Inc	1733 Dillingham	Honolulu	HI	96819	John Carpenter	808-847-2621	R	1*	<0.1
Puddleduckers Inc	59 Waters Av	Boston	MA	02149	Steve Drongowski	617-394-0330	R	0	<0.1

Source: *Ward's Business Directory of U.S. Private and Public Companies*, Volumes 1 and 2, 1996. The company type code used is as follows: P - Public, R - Private, S - Subsidiary, D - Division, J - Joint Venture, A - Affiliate, G - Group. Sales are in millions of dollars, employees are in thousands. An asterisk (*) indicates an estimated sales volume. The symbol < stands for 'less than'. Company names and addresses are truncated, in some cases, to fit into the available space.

MATERIALS CONSUMED

Material	Quantity	Delivered Cost ($ million)
Materials, ingredients, containers, and supplies	(X)	355.5
Natural rubber	(X)	18.7
Plastics resins consumed in the form of granules, pellets, powders, liquids, etc.	(X)	19.0
Synthetic rubber, including vulcanizable elastomers	(X)	20.0
Rubber processing chemicals (accelerators, antioxidants, blowing agents, inhibitors, peptizers, etc.)	(X)	13.4
Plasticizers	(X)	6.7
All other industrial organic chemicals	(X)	4.1
Glues and adhesives	(X)	2.3
All other chemical and allied products	(X)	(D)
Rubber compounds and mixtures purchased (dry rubber solids content)	(X)	(D)
Textile fabrics	(X)	81.7
Paper and paperboard containers, including shipping sacks and other paper packaging supplies	(X)	15.1
All other materials and components, parts, containers, and supplies	(X)	110.6
Materials, ingredients, containers, and supplies, nsk	(X)	61.6

Source: 1992 *Economic Census*. Explanation of symbols used: (D): Withheld to avoid disclosure of competitive data; na: Not available; (S): Withheld because statistical norms were not met; (X): Not applicable; (Z): Less than half the unit shown; nec: Not elsewhere classified; nsk: Not specified by kind; - : zero; * : 10-19 percent estimated; ** : 20-29 percent estimated.

PRODUCT SHARE DETAILS

Product or Product Class	% Share	Product or Product Class	% Share
Rubber and plastics footwear	100.00	uppers, excluding sandals and slippers	67.71
Protective footwear	29.24	Rubber and plastics footwear, nsk	3.06
Shoes with soles vulcanized, molded, or cemented to fabric			

Source: 1992 *Economic Census*. The values shown are percent of total shipments in an industry. Values of indented subcategories are summed in the main heading. The symbol (D) appears when data are withheld to prevent disclosure of competitive information. The abbreviation nsk stands for 'not specified by kind' and nec for 'not elsewhere classified'.

INPUTS AND OUTPUTS FOR RUBBER & PLASTICS FOOTWEAR

Economic Sector or Industry Providing Inputs	%	Sector	Economic Sector or Industry Buying Outputs	%	Sector
Imports	76.1	Foreign	Personal consumption expenditures	96.9	
Broadwoven fabric mills	5.1	Manufg.	Change in business inventories	1.8	In House
Fabricated rubber products, nec	3.0	Manufg.	Exports	0.8	Foreign
Wholesale trade	2.9	Trade	Rubber & plastics footwear	0.1	Manufg.
Synthetic rubber	1.5	Manufg.			
Noncomparable imports	1.1	Foreign			
Plastics materials & resins	0.9	Manufg.			
Thread mills	0.9	Manufg.			
Paperboard containers & boxes	0.7	Manufg.			
Electric services (utilities)	0.7	Util.			
Motor freight transportation & warehousing	0.5	Util.			
Advertising	0.5	Services			
Cyclic crudes and organics	0.4	Manufg.			
Narrow fabric mills	0.4	Manufg.			
Nonwoven fabrics	0.4	Manufg.			

Continued on next page.

INPUTS AND OUTPUTS FOR RUBBER & PLASTICS FOOTWEAR - Continued

Economic Sector or Industry Providing Inputs	%	Sector	Economic Sector or Industry Buying Outputs	%	Sector
Eating & drinking places	0.3	Trade			
Banking	0.3	Fin/R.E.			
Real estate	0.3	Fin/R.E.			
Engineering, architectural, & surveying services	0.3	Services			
Maintenance of nonfarm buildings nec	0.2	Constr.			
Machinery, except electrical, nec	0.2	Manufg.			
Miscellaneous plastics products	0.2	Manufg.			
Communications, except radio & TV	0.2	Util.			
Gas production & distribution (utilities)	0.2	Util.			
Equipment rental & leasing services	0.2	Services			
U.S. Postal Service	0.2	Gov't			
Chemical preparations, nec	0.1	Manufg.			
Industrial inorganic chemicals, nec	0.1	Manufg.			
Petroleum refining	0.1	Manufg.			
Rubber & plastics footwear	0.1	Manufg.			
Railroads & related services	0.1	Util.			
Laundry, dry cleaning, shoe repair	0.1	Services			
Legal services	0.1	Services			
Management & consulting services & labs	0.1	Services			

Source: Benchmark Input-Output Accounts for the U.S. Economy, 1982, U.S. Department of Commerce, Washington, D.C., July 1991. Data, as reported in the source, are organized by the 1977 SIC structure in use in 1982 but have been matched, as closely as is possible, to the 1987 SIC structure used in this book.

OCCUPATIONS EMPLOYED BY SIC 302 - RUBBER PRODUCTS AND PLASTIC HOSE AND FOOTWEAR

Occupation	% of Total 1994	Change to 2005	Occupation	% of Total 1994	Change to 2005
Assemblers, fabricators, & hand workers nec	11.9	0.3	Machine forming operators, metal & plastic	1.9	0.3
Extruding & forming machine workers	11.1	-29.8	Freight, stock, & material movers, hand	1.8	-19.8
Inspectors, testers, & graders, precision	5.1	0.3	Traffic, shipping, & receiving clerks	1.8	-3.5
Machine operators nec	4.9	-11.6	Industrial machinery mechanics	1.8	10.3
Blue collar worker supervisors	4.8	-5.6	Metal & plastic machine workers nec	1.6	-11.1
Cutters & trimmers, hand	3.7	10.3	Maintenance repairers, general utility	1.5	-9.7
Plastic molding machine workers	3.5	0.3	Industrial production managers	1.4	0.3
Hand packers & packagers	2.9	-14.1	Machinists	1.4	0.3
Cutting & slicing machine setters, operators	2.8	-9.8	Secretaries, ex legal & medical	1.3	-8.7
Helpers, laborers, & material movers nec	2.7	0.3	Machine feeders & offbearers	1.2	-9.8
Crushing & mixing machine operators	2.6	-9.8	Industrial truck & tractor operators	1.1	0.3
General managers & top executives	2.2	-4.9	Bookkeeping, accounting, & auditing clerks	1.0	-24.8

Source: Industry-Occupation Matrix, Bureau of Labor Statistics. These data relate to one or more 3-digit SIC industry groups rather than to a single 4-digit SIC. The change reported for each occupation to the year 2005 is a percent of growth or decline as estimated by the Bureau of Labor Statistics. The abbreviation nec stands for 'not elsewhere classified'.

LOCATION BY STATE AND REGIONAL CONCENTRATION

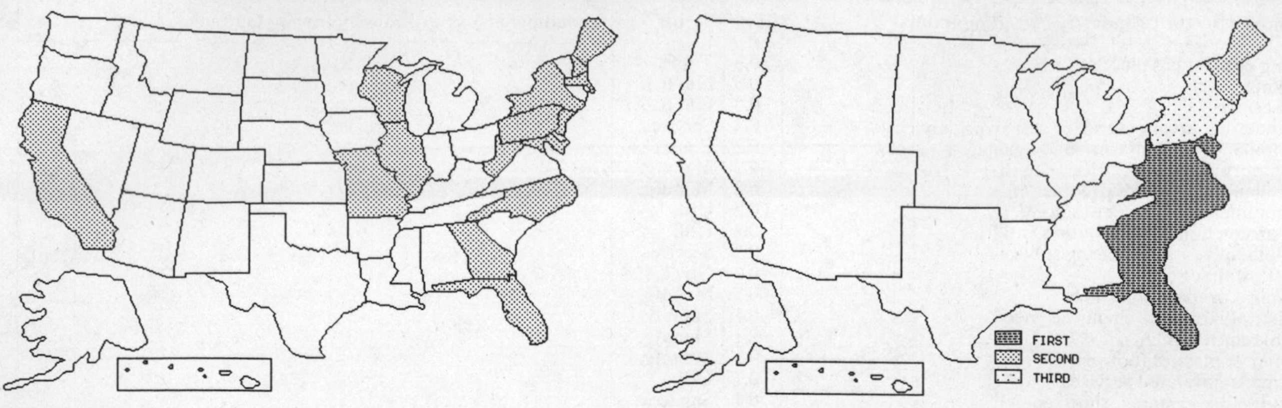

INDUSTRY DATA BY STATE

State	Establish-ments	Shipments Total ($ mil)	Shipments % of U.S.	Shipments Per Establ.	Employment Total Number	Employment % of U.S.	Employment Per Establ.	Employment Wages ($/hour)	Cost as % of Shipments	Investment per Employee ($)
Florida	8	180.5	20.8	22.6	2,800	20.6	350	5.94	50.9	714
California	7	(D)	-	-	1,750 *	12.9	250	-	-	-
Pennsylvania	6	(D)	-	-	750 *	5.5	125	-	-	-
Massachusetts	5	(D)	-	-	375 *	2.8	75	-	-	-
Georgia	4	(D)	-	-	750 *	5.5	188	-	-	-
Maine	4	(D)	-	-	750 *	5.5	188	-	-	-
Wisconsin	4	(D)	-	-	750 *	5.5	188	-	-	-
Missouri	3	(D)	-	-	750 *	5.5	250	-	-	-
New Hampshire	3	(D)	-	-	175 *	1.3	58	-	-	-
New Jersey	3	(D)	-	-	750 *	5.5	250	-	-	-
New York	3	(D)	-	-	375 *	2.8	125	-	-	-
Illinois	2	(D)	-	-	750 *	5.5	375	-	-	-
Maryland	1	(D)	-	-	175 *	1.3	175	-	-	-
North Carolina	1	(D)	-	-	1,750 *	12.9	1,750	-	-	-
West Virginia	1	(D)	-	-	175 *	1.3	175	-	-	-

Source: 1992 *Economic Census*. The states are in descending order of shipments or establishments (if shipment data are missing for the majority). The symbol (D) appears when data are withheld to prevent disclosure of competitive information. States marked with (D) are sorted by number of establishments. A dash (-) indicates that the data element cannot be calculated; * indicates the midpoint of a range.

3052 - RUBBER & PLASTICS HOSE & BELTING

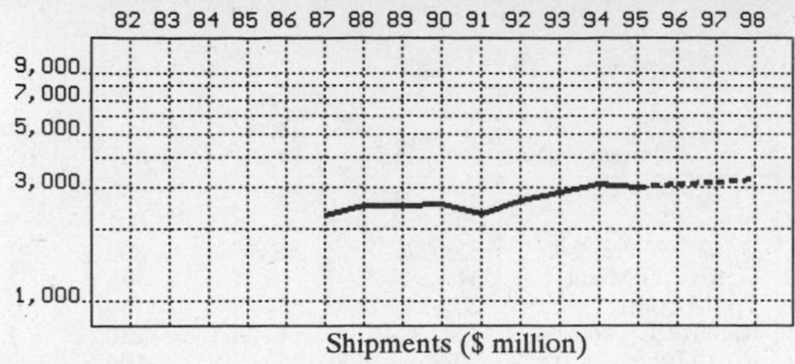

Shipments ($ million)

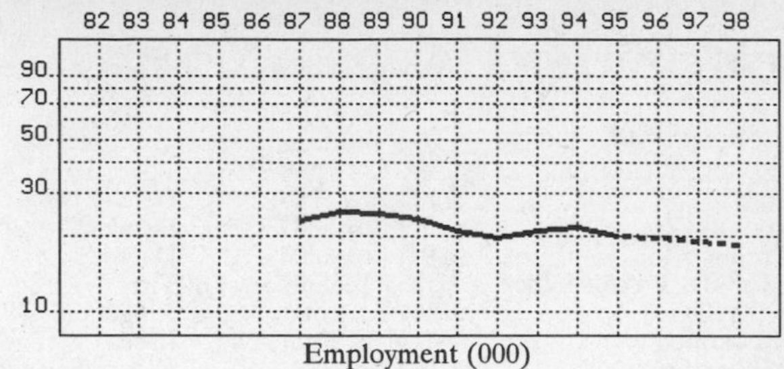

Employment (000)

GENERAL STATISTICS

Year	Companies	Establishments: Total	Establishments: with 20 or more employees	Employment: Total (000)	Production Workers (000)	Production Hours (Mil)	Compensation: Payroll ($ mil)	Compensation: Wages ($/hr)	Production: Cost of Materials	Production: Value Added by Manufacture	Production: Value of Shipments	Production: Capital Invest.
1982												
1983												
1984												
1985												
1986												
1987	127	188	122	23.2	16.6	33.3	531.4	10.28	1,028.2	1,240.8	2,268.2	74.5
1988		184	121	25.0	18.0	36.8	624.5	10.62	1,224.9	1,323.0	2,522.9	148.0
1989		189	122	24.9	18.5	36.8	599.3	10.75	1,184.6	1,307.2	2,504.4	82.6
1990		195	126	23.8	17.7	37.5	547.7	10.11	1,225.4	1,380.1	2,574.8	92.8
1991		197	127	21.1	16.2	32.4	522.9	10.92	1,148.3	1,177.4	2,330.2	62.6
1992	146	204	117	19.9	15.2	31.3	533.4	11.56	1,284.1	1,334.4	2,612.9	74.1
1993		197	115	21.1	16.0	32.9	559.2	11.66	1,390.4	1,517.3	2,872.6	82.6
1994		204P	118P	22.0	17.5	36.5	624.0	12.00	1,555.9	1,517.7	3,070.0	127.2
1995		207P	117P	20.2P	16.2P	33.7P	573.1P	12.08P	1,517.0P	1,479.7P	2,993.2P	92.3P
1996		210P	116P	19.6P	16.0P	33.5P	574.3P	12.33P	1,561.9P	1,523.5P	3,081.8P	92.1P
1997		212P	115P	19.1P	15.8P	33.2P	575.5P	12.57P	1,606.8P	1,567.3P	3,170.4P	92.0P
1998		215P	115P	18.6P	15.6P	33.0P	576.7P	12.82P	1,651.7P	1,611.1P	3,259.0P	91.8P

Sources: 1982, 1987, 1992 *Economic Census*; *Annual Survey of Manufactures*, 83-86, 88-91, 93-94. Establishment counts for non-Census years are from *County Business Patterns*; establishment values for 83-84 are extrapolations. 'P's show projections by the editors. Industries reclassified in 87 will not have data for prior years.

INDICES OF CHANGE

Year	Companies	Establishments: Total	Establishments: with 20 or more employees	Employment: Total (000)	Production Workers (000)	Production Hours (Mil)	Compensation: Payroll ($ mil)	Compensation: Wages ($/hr)	Production: Cost of Materials	Production: Value Added by Manufacture	Production: Value of Shipments	Production: Capital Invest.
1982												
1983												
1984												
1985												
1986												
1987	87	92	104	117	109	106	100	89	80	93	87	101
1988		90	103	126	118	118	117	92	95	99	97	200
1989		93	104	125	122	118	112	93	92	98	96	111
1990		96	108	120	116	120	103	87	95	103	99	125
1991		97	109	106	107	104	98	94	89	88	89	84
1992	100	100	100	100	100	100	100	100	100	100	100	100
1993		97	98	106	105	105	105	101	108	114	110	111
1994		100P	101P	111	115	117	117	104	121	114	117	172
1995		101P	100P	101P	106P	108P	107P	105P	118P	111P	115P	125P
1996		103P	99P	99P	105P	107P	108P	107P	122P	114P	118P	124P
1997		104P	99P	96P	104P	106P	108P	109P	125P	117P	121P	124P
1998		105P	98P	93P	103P	105P	108P	111P	129P	121P	125P	124P

Sources: Same as General Statistics. Values reflect change from the base year, 1992. Values above 100 mean greater than 92, values below 100 mean less than 92, and a value of 100 in the 82-91 or 93-98 period means same as 92. 'P's mark projections by the editors.

SELECTED RATIOS

For 1994	Avg. of All Manufact.	Analyzed Industry	Index
Employees per Establishment	49	108	220
Payroll per Establishment	1,500,273	3,056,683	204
Payroll per Employee	30,620	28,364	93
Production Workers per Establishment	34	86	250
Wages per Establishment	853,319	2,145,556	251
Wages per Production Worker	24,861	25,029	101
Hours per Production Worker	2,056	2,086	101
Wages per Hour	12.09	12.00	99
Value Added per Establishment	4,602,255	7,434,500	162
Value Added per Employee	93,930	68,986	73

For 1994	Avg. of All Manufact.	Analyzed Industry	Index
Value Added per Production Worker	134,084	86,726	65
Cost per Establishment	5,045,178	7,621,624	151
Cost per Employee	102,970	70,723	69
Cost per Production Worker	146,988	88,909	60
Shipments per Establishment	9,576,895	15,038,488	157
Shipments per Employee	195,460	139,545	71
Shipments per Production Worker	279,017	175,429	63
Investment per Establishment	321,011	623,093	194
Investment per Employee	6,552	5,782	88
Investment per Production Worker	9,352	7,269	78

Sources: Same as General Statistics. The 'Average of All Manufacturing' column represents the average of all manufacturing industries reported for the most recent complete year available. The Index shows the relationship between the Average and the Analyzed Industry. For example, 100 means that they are equal; 500 that the Analyzed Industry is five times the average; 50 means that the Analyzed Industry is half the national average. The abbreviation 'na' is used to show that data are 'not available'.

LEADING COMPANIES Number shown: **54** Total sales ($ mil): **4,485** Total employment (000): **42.8**

Company Name	Address				CEO Name	Phone	Co. Type	Sales ($ mil)	Empl. (000)
Gates Corp	PO Box 5887	Denver	CO	80217	Charles C Gates	303-744-1911	R	1,300	17.0
Gates Rubber Co	PO Box 5887	Denver	CO	80217	John Riess	303-744-1911	S	1,002	7.0
Dayco Products Inc	PO Box 1004	Dayton	OH	45401	Bruce McNeil	513-226-7000	S	800	7.3
Fayette Tubular Products Inc	1835 Technology Dr	Troy	MI	48083	George D Mach	313-589-7710	S	175	1.5
Colorite Plastic Co	101 Railroad Av	Ridgefield	NJ	07657	Fred Broling	201-941-2900	D	150	0.5
Imperial Eastman	1151 W Bryn Av	Itasca	IL	60143	Richard Locsmondy	708-285-6100	D	130	1.0
Gates Rubber Co	PO Box 888	Siloam Springs	AR	72761	Burt Hoefs	501-524-8164	D	100	0.7
HBD Industries Inc	1301 W Sandusky St	Bellefontaine	OH	43311	Robert Lyons	513-593-5010	R	100	1.4
ATCO Rubber Products Inc	7101 Gumm Ln	Fort Worth	TX	76118	Ramesh Bhatia	817-595-2894	R	85*	0.9
Gates Export Corp	PO Box 5887	Denver	CO	80217	John M Riess	303-744-5042	S	40	<0.1
Lawrence Industries	PO Box 1838	Burlington	NC	27216	M Fuller	910-578-2161	D	40	0.3
Scandura Inc	PO Box 30606	Charlotte	NC	28230	Robert Haley	704-334-5353	S	39	0.5
Flexfab Inc	1843 W Gun Lake	Hastings	MI	49058	Doug Decamp	616-945-2433	R	38*	0.4
Handy & Harman	400 S Tuscarawas	Dover	OH	44622	Henry C Dade	216-364-7551	D	36	0.4
Burrell Leder Beltech Inc	7501 N Saint Louis	Skokie	IL	60076	KH Kraft	708-673-6720	S	34	0.2
Fenner Inc	311 W Stiegel St	Manheim	PA	17545	John Mullineaux	717-665-2421	S	33	0.4
Aquapore Moisture Systems Inc	610 S 80th Av	Phoenix	AZ	85043	Shannon Bard	602-936-8083	R	30	0.1
Davidson-Textron	750evephson Hwy	Troy	MI	48083	Fred Hubacher	810-616-5100	D	30*	0.3
Goodyear Tire	13601 Indrial Pkwy	Marysville	OH	43040	RM Tinker	513-644-8900	D	30*	0.3
Globe International Inc	PO Box 1062	Buffalo	NY	14240	Harry M Cardillo	716-824-8484	R	25	0.2
GT Sales and Manufacturing Inc	PO Box 9408	Wichita	KS	67277	Nick M Onofrio Jr	316-943-2171	R	20	<0.1
MBL USA Corp	601 Dayton Rd	Ottawa	IL	61350	Keiji Murata	815-434-1282	S	20	0.3
WH Salisbury and Co	7520 N Long Av	Skokie	IL	60077	Paul Dittmer	708-679-6700	S	20	0.2
Mason Industries Inc	350 Rabro Dr	Hauppauge	NY	11787	NJ Mason	516-348-0282	R	16	0.2
Fenner Manheim	311 W Stiegel St	Manheim	PA	17545	John Mullineaux	717-665-2421	D	15*	0.2
Coilhose Pneumatics Inc	200 Clay Av	Middlesex	NJ	08846	Gabor Farkas	908-752-5000	R	13	0.1
RE Darling Co	3749 N Romero Rd	Tucson	AZ	85705	Ralph E Darling Jr	602-887-2400	D	13	0.1
Anchor Rubber Co	PO Box 832	Dayton	OH	45401	CL Woods	513-223-5191	R	12	<0.1
Gilmour Hose Co	140 Corum Rd	Excelsior Sprgs	MO	64024	Richard Sager	816-637-2114	S	12*	0.1
Nephi Rubber Products Inc	255 W 1100 N	Nephi	UT	84648	Terry Jones	801-623-1740	R	12*	0.1
Chapin Watermatics Inc	PO Box 490	Watertown	NY	13601	William Chapin	315-782-1170	R	10*	0.1
HB Sherman Manufacturing	1450 Rowe Pkwy	Poplar Bluff	MO	63901	Shirley Douglas	314-785-5754	R	10	<0.1
Price Rubber Corp	PO Box 210489	Montgomery	AL	36121	John W Price	205-277-5470	R	9*	0.1
Legg Company Inc	325 E 10th St	Halstead	KS	67056	Steven C Chartier	316-835-2256	R	8	<0.1
Briggs Co	3 Bellecor Dr	New Castle	DE	19720	Richard A Hartman	302-328-9471	R	8	<0.1
Unaflex Inc	2056 N Dixie Hwy	Ft Lauderdale	FL	33305	HD White	305-561-0500	R	8	0.1
Avon Plastics Inc	PO Box 662	Albany	MN	56301	Donald J Reum Sr	612-845-2111	R	7*	<0.1
NewAge Industries Inc	2300 Maryland Rd	Willow Grove	PA	19090	Ken Baker	215-657-3151	D	6*	<0.1
Salem-Republic Rubber Co	PO Box 389	Sebring	OH	44672	Andrew V Ney	216-938-9801	R	6	<0.1
Atcoflex Inc	PO Box 118	Grand Haven	MI	49417	W H Tuggle Jr	616-842-4661	R	5	<0.1
Mercer Rubber Co	PO Box 410	Smithtown	NY	11787	Norm J Mason	516-582-1524	S	5*	<0.1
Copper State Rubber of Arizona	750 S 59th Av	Phoenix	AZ	85043	Joyce Grimes	602-269-5927	S	4*	<0.1
Insulated Duct and Cable Co	PO Box 850	Trenton	NJ	08605	Charles A Logue	609-883-3030	R	4	<0.1
KVP Systems Inc	11300 Trade Ctr Dr	R Cordova	CA	95742	KV Palmaer	916-635-5151	S	4	<0.1
Couse and Bolten Co	42 Lafayette St	Newark	NJ	07102	Michael F Nelson	201-624-4200	R	3*	<0.1
Hi-Tech Hose Inc	2111 Standard Av	Santa Ana	CA	92707	William P Liebegott	714-540-7622	R	3*	<0.1
Mesa Industries Inc	1726 S Magnolia	Monrovia	CA	91016	JR Sexton	818-359-9361	R	3	<0.1
Mesa Rubber Co	1726 S Magnolia	Monrovia	CA	91016	JR Sexton	818-359-9361	D	3	<0.1
Ton-Tex Corp	5346 36th St SE	Grand Rapids	MI	49512	Robert H Beaman	616-957-3200	R	3*	<0.1
Ace Hose and Rubber Co	1516 S Wabash Av	Chicago	IL	60605	Bruce Behrstock	312-663-9000	R	2	<0.1
York Rubber Co	3530 W Fort St	Detroit	MI	48216	Craig Pilkington	313-496-0400	R	2*	<0.1
Lockwood Products Inc	5615 SW Willow Ln	Lake Oswego	OR	97035	Rick Holmboe	503-635-8113	R	1*	<0.1
Godman Hi-Performance	5255 Elmore Rd	Memphis	TN	38134	Raymond Godman	901-761-5949	R	1	<0.1
GT Industries of Texas	2919 Blystone Ln	Dallas	TX	75220	Gordon Pendergraft	214-243-4251	R	1*	<0.1

Source: *Ward's Business Directory of U.S. Private and Public Companies*, Volumes 1 and 2, 1996. The company type code used is as follows: P - Public, R - Private, S - Subsidiary, D - Division, J - Joint Venture, A - Affiliate, G - Group. Sales are in millions of dollars, employees are in thousands. An asterisk (*) indicates an estimated sales volume. The symbol < stands for 'less than'. Company names and addresses are truncated, in some cases, to fit into the available space.

MATERIALS CONSUMED

Material	Quantity	Delivered Cost ($ million)
Materials, ingredients, containers, and supplies	(X)	1,202.3
Natural latex rubber (dry solids content)	(X)	(D)
Natural dry rubber	(X)	1.7
Plastics resins consumed in the form of granules, pellets, powders, liquids, etc.	(X)	87.2
Synthetic rubber, including vulcanizable elastomers	(X)	155.5
Rubber processing chemicals (accelerators, antioxidants, blowing agents, inhibitors, peptizers, etc.)	(X)	17.3
Plasticizers	(X)	21.9
All other industrial organic chemicals	(X)	(D)
Carbon black	(X)	35.7
All other chemicals and allied products	(X)	36.0
Rubber compounds and mixtures purchased (dry rubber solids content)	(X)	143.2
Metal hose fittings and couplings	(X)	55.1
Other fabricated metal products (including forgings)	(X)	4.1
Steel wire	(X)	70.0
Other shapes and forms (including castings)	(X)	5.6
Textile fabrics	(X)	256.7
Paper and paperboard containers, including shipping sacks and other paper packaging supplies	(X)	43.9
All other materials and components, parts, containers, and supplies	(X)	172.7
Materials, ingredients, containers, and supplies, nsk	(X)	78.1

Source: 1992 *Economic Census*. Explanation of symbols used: (D): Withheld to avoid disclosure of competitive data; na: Not available; (S): Withheld because statistical norms were not met; (X): Not applicable; (Z): Less than half the unit shown; nec: Not elsewhere classified; nsk: Not specified by kind; - : zero; * : 10-19 percent estimated; ** : 20-29 percent estimated.

PRODUCT SHARE DETAILS

Product or Product Class	% Share
Rubber and plastics hose and belting	100.00
Flat rubber and plastics belts and belting	16.70
Lightweight flat rubber and plastics belts and belting	35.79
Heavy-duty flat rubber and plastics belts and belting	39.95
Flat rubber and plastics transmission belts and belting	3.20
Other flat rubber and plastics belts and belting	16.95
Rubber and plastics belts and belting, flat, nsk	4.09
Rubber and plastics transmission belts and belting other than flat	21.08
Motor vehicle rubber and plastics transmission belts and belting other than flat	49.97
Industrial (except fractional horsepower) rubber and plastics transmission belts and belting other than flat	35.39
Agricultural (except fractional horsepower) rubber and plastics transmission belts and belting other than flat	2.83
Fractional horsepower rubber and plastics transmission belts and belting other than flat	(D)
All other rubber and plastics belts and belting, other than flat	(D)
Rubber and plastics transmission belts and belting other than flat, nsk	1.37
Hose for on- and off-highway motor vehicles (made of rubber and other materials, including plastics and nylon)	21.65
High-pressure rubber and plastics hose (greater than 300 p.s.i. working pressure), including air-conditioning, brake line, etc., for on-and off-highway motor vehicles	27.30
Low-pressure rubber and plastics hose (less than 300 p.s.i. working pressure), including value of pre-positioned sleeves, clamps, etc., for on-and off-highway motor vehicles	72.70
Industrial rubber and plastics hose without fittings (chemical handling, food and beverage, petroleum curb pump, dock, transfer, etc.)	7.64
Rubber and plastics water hose without fittings (including fire, irrigation, water suction/discharge, and other water hose, nec)	4.93
Rubber and plastics garden hose (with or without fittings)	7.97
Plastics garden hose, with or without fittings, including perforated sprinkler	86.71
Rubber garden hose, with or without fittings	13.29
Rubber and plastics inner tube type airhose (other than pneumatic power transfer)	4.52
Rubber inner tube type airhose, including rubber and plastics combinations (other than pneumatic power transfer), wire reinforced (including wire/textile reinforced combinations)	23.78
Rubber inner tube type airhose, including rubber and plastics combinations (other than pneumatic power transfer), textile reinforced (except wire/textile reinforced combinations)	17.14
Nonrubber inner tube type airhose (other than pneumatic power transfer), wire reinforced (including wire/textile combinations)	40.34
Nonrubber inner tube type airhose (other than pneumatic power transfer), textile reinforced (except wire/textile combinations)	13.87
Air hose (other than pneumatic power transfer), nsk	4.87
Pneumatic and hydraulic inner tube type hose, nec, without fittings (made of rubber and other materials, including plastics and nylon)	12.30
Rubber inner tube type pneumatic and hydraulic hose, nec, (including rubber and plastics combinations), without fittings, wire reinforced (including wire/textile combinations)	71.14
Rubber inner tube type pneumatic and hydraulic hose, nec, (including rubber and plastics combinations), without fittings, textile reinforced (except wire/textile combinations)	21.67
Nonrubber inner tube type pneumatic and hydraulic hose, nec, without fittings, wire reinforced (including wire/textile combinations)	0.43
Nonrubber inner tube type pneumatic and hydraulic hose, nec, without fittings, textile reinforced (except wire/textile combinations)	5.80
Pneumatic and hydraulic hose, nec, without fittings (made of rubber and other materials -e.g., plastics, nylon)	0.93
Rubber and plastics hose and belting, nsk	3.23

Source: 1992 *Economic Census*. The values shown are percent of total shipments in an industry. Values of indented subcategories are summed in the main heading. The symbol (D) appears when data are withheld to prevent disclosure of competitive information. The abbreviation nsk stands for 'not specified by kind' and nec for 'not elsewhere classified'.

INPUTS AND OUTPUTS FOR RUBBER & PLASTICS HOSE & BELTING

Economic Sector or Industry Providing Inputs	%	Sector	Economic Sector or Industry Buying Outputs	%	Sector
Broadwoven fabric mills	14.3	Manufg.	Exports	8.9	Foreign
Synthetic rubber	13.4	Manufg.	Coal	7.4	Mining
Imports	12.0	Foreign	Personal consumption expenditures	6.5	
Fabricated rubber products, nec	7.1	Manufg.	Electric services (utilities)	4.2	Util.
Wholesale trade	6.7	Trade	Wholesale trade	4.2	Trade
Cyclic crudes and organics	4.3	Manufg.	Motor vehicles & car bodies	3.3	Manufg.
Electric services (utilities)	4.0	Util.	Owner-occupied dwellings	2.9	Fin/R.E.
Blast furnaces & steel mills	3.2	Manufg.	Construction machinery & equipment	2.5	Manufg.
Carbon black	2.7	Manufg.	Motor vehicle parts & accessories	2.3	Manufg.
Plastics materials & resins	2.7	Manufg.	Pipe, valves, & pipe fittings	1.9	Manufg.
Gas production & distribution (utilities)	2.0	Util.	Printing trades machinery	1.9	Manufg.
Motor freight transportation & warehousing	1.9	Util.	Internal combustion engines, nec	1.8	Manufg.
Noncomparable imports	1.9	Foreign	Farm machinery & equipment	1.7	Manufg.
Advertising	1.8	Services	Real estate	1.6	Fin/R.E.
Nonwoven fabrics	1.7	Manufg.	Pumps & compressors	1.5	Manufg.
Paperboard containers & boxes	1.7	Manufg.	Transit & bus transportation	1.5	Util.
Inorganic pigments	1.3	Manufg.	Oil field machinery	1.4	Manufg.
Hardware, nec	1.2	Manufg.	Household laundry equipment	1.3	Manufg.
Railroads & related services	1.2	Util.	Logging camps & logging contractors	1.2	Manufg.
Banking	1.2	Fin/R.E.	Freight forwarders	1.2	Util.
Petroleum refining	1.0	Manufg.	Federal Government purchases, national defense	1.2	Fed Govt
Communications, except radio & TV	1.0	Util.	S/L Govt. purch., other general government	1.2	S/L Govt
Narrow fabric mills	0.8	Manufg.	Feed grains	1.1	Agric.
Chemical preparations, nec	0.7	Manufg.	Aluminum rolling & drawing	1.1	Manufg.
Industrial inorganic chemicals, nec	0.7	Manufg.	Motors & generators	1.1	Manufg.
Equipment rental & leasing services	0.7	Services	Conveyors & conveying equipment	1.0	Manufg.
Maintenance of nonfarm buildings nec	0.6	Constr.	Refrigeration & heating equipment	1.0	Manufg.
Eating & drinking places	0.6	Trade	Copper ore	0.9	Mining
U.S. Postal Service	0.6	Gov't	Prepared feeds, nec	0.9	Manufg.
Computer & data processing services	0.5	Services	Roasted coffee	0.9	Manufg.
Engineering, architectural, & surveying services	0.5	Services	Special industry machinery, nec	0.9	Manufg.
Coal	0.3	Mining	Surgical & medical instruments	0.9	Manufg.
Machinery, except electrical, nec	0.3	Manufg.	Iron & ferroalloy ores	0.8	Mining
Miscellaneous plastics products	0.3	Manufg.	Bottled & canned soft drinks	0.8	Manufg.
Reclaimed rubber	0.3	Manufg.	Sporting & athletic goods, nec	0.8	Manufg.
Rubber & plastics hose & belting	0.3	Manufg.	Blowers & fans	0.7	Manufg.
Real estate	0.3	Fin/R.E.	Electronic computing equipment	0.7	Manufg.
Royalties	0.3	Fin/R.E.	Small arms ammunition	0.7	Manufg.
Lubricating oils & greases	0.2	Manufg.	S/L Govt. purch., fire	0.7	S/L Govt
Special dies & tools & machine tool accessories	0.2	Manufg.	Meat animals	0.6	Agric.
Air transportation	0.2	Util.	Chemical & fertilizer mineral	0.6	Mining
Sanitary services, steam supply, irrigation	0.2	Util.	Dimension, crushed & broken stone	0.6	Mining
Water transportation	0.2	Util.	Nonferrous metal ores, except copper	0.6	Mining
Insurance carriers	0.2	Fin/R.E.	Distilled liquor, except brandy	0.6	Manufg.
Legal services	0.2	Services	Railroads & related services	0.6	Util.
Management & consulting services & labs	0.2	Services	Glass & glass products, except containers	0.5	Manufg.
Alkalies & chlorine	0.1	Manufg.	Meat packing plants	0.5	Manufg.
Manifold business forms	0.1	Manufg.	Motorcycles, bicycles, & parts	0.5	Manufg.
Water supply & sewage systems	0.1	Util.	Radio & TV communication equipment	0.5	Manufg.
Accounting, auditing & bookkeeping	0.1	Services	Textile machinery	0.5	Manufg.
Automotive rental & leasing, without drivers	0.1	Services	Crude petroleum & natural gas	0.4	Mining
Automotive repair shops & services	0.1	Services	Chemical preparations, nec	0.4	Manufg.
Electrical repair shops	0.1	Services	Electric housewares & fans	0.4	Manufg.
State & local government enterprises, nec	0.1	Gov't	Food products machinery	0.4	Manufg.
			Lawn & garden equipment	0.4	Manufg.
			Nonferrous rolling & drawing, nec	0.4	Manufg.
			Credit agencies other than banks	0.4	Fin/R.E.
			S/L Govt. purch., natural resource & recreation.	0.4	S/L Govt
			Oil bearing crops	0.3	Agric.
			Blast furnaces & steel mills	0.3	Manufg.
			Copper rolling & drawing	0.3	Manufg.
			Fresh or frozen packaged fish	0.3	Manufg.
			Frozen fruits, fruit juices & vegetables	0.3	Manufg.
			Frozen specialties	0.3	Manufg.
			Industrial trucks & tractors	0.3	Manufg.
			Iron & steel foundries	0.3	Manufg.
			Nonferrous wire drawing & insulating	0.3	Manufg.
			Railroad equipment	0.3	Manufg.
			Service industry machines, nec	0.3	Manufg.
			Sewing machines	0.3	Manufg.
			Ship building & repairing	0.3	Manufg.
			Tire cord & fabric	0.3	Manufg.
			Doctors & dentists	0.3	Services
			S/L Govt. purch., correction	0.3	S/L Govt
			S/L Govt. purch., elem. & secondary education	0.3	S/L Govt
			Food grains	0.2	Agric.
			Tobacco	0.2	Agric.
			Clay, ceramic, & refractory minerals	0.2	Mining

Continued on next page.

INPUTS AND OUTPUTS FOR RUBBER & PLASTICS HOSE & BELTING - Continued

Economic Sector or Industry Providing Inputs	%	Sector	Economic Sector or Industry Buying Outputs	%	Sector
			Bread, cake, & related products	0.2	Manufg.
			Cement, hydraulic	0.2	Manufg.
			Fluid milk	0.2	Manufg.
			Household cooking equipment	0.2	Manufg.
			Household refrigerators & freezers	0.2	Manufg.
			Household vacuum cleaners	0.2	Manufg.
			Measuring & dispensing pumps	0.2	Manufg.
			Mining machinery, except oil field	0.2	Manufg.
			Paper industries machinery	0.2	Manufg.
			Rubber & plastics hose & belting	0.2	Manufg.
			Sawmills & planning mills, general	0.2	Manufg.
			Retail trade, except eating & drinking	0.2	Trade
			Dairy farm products	0.1	Agric.
			Fruits	0.1	Agric.
			Vegetables	0.1	Agric.
			Sand & gravel	0.1	Mining
			Boat building & repairing	0.1	Manufg.
			Carburetors, pistons, rings, & valves	0.1	Manufg.
			Cheese, natural & processed	0.1	Manufg.
			Electronic components nec	0.1	Manufg.
			Food preparations, nec	0.1	Manufg.
			Machine tools, metal cutting types	0.1	Manufg.
			Malt beverages	0.1	Manufg.
			Mechanical measuring devices	0.1	Manufg.
			Metalworking machinery, nec	0.1	Manufg.
			Poultry dressing plants	0.1	Manufg.
			Radio & TV receiving sets	0.1	Manufg.
			Sausages & other prepared meats	0.1	Manufg.
			Soybean oil mills	0.1	Manufg.
			Welding apparatus, electric	0.1	Manufg.
			Woodworking machinery	0.1	Manufg.
			Motor freight transportation & warehousing	0.1	Util.
			S/L Govt. purch., health & hospitals	0.1	S/L Govt

Source: Benchmark Input-Output Accounts for the U.S. Economy, 1982, U.S. Department of Commerce, Washington, D.C., July 1991. Data, as reported in the source, are organized by the 1977 SIC structure in use in 1982 but have been matched, as closely as is possible, to the 1987 SIC structure used in this book.

OCCUPATIONS EMPLOYED BY SIC 305 - RUBBER PRODUCTS AND PLASTIC HOSE AND FOOTWEAR

Occupation	% of Total 1994	Change to 2005	Occupation	% of Total 1994	Change to 2005
Assemblers, fabricators, & hand workers nec	11.9	0.3	Machine forming operators, metal & plastic	1.9	0.3
Extruding & forming machine workers	11.1	-29.8	Freight, stock, & material movers, hand	1.8	-19.8
Inspectors, testers, & graders, precision	5.1	0.3	Traffic, shipping, & receiving clerks	1.8	-3.5
Machine operators nec	4.9	-11.6	Industrial machinery mechanics	1.8	10.3
Blue collar worker supervisors	4.8	-5.6	Metal & plastic machine workers nec	1.6	-11.1
Cutters & trimmers, hand	3.7	10.3	Maintenance repairers, general utility	1.5	-9.7
Plastic molding machine workers	3.5	0.3	Industrial production managers	1.4	0.3
Hand packers & packagers	2.9	-14.1	Machinists	1.4	0.3
Cutting & slicing machine setters, operators	2.8	-9.8	Secretaries, ex legal & medical	1.3	-8.7
Helpers, laborers, & material movers nec	2.7	0.3	Machine feeders & offbearers	1.2	-9.8
Crushing & mixing machine operators	2.6	-9.8	Industrial truck & tractor operators	1.1	0.3
General managers & top executives	2.2	-4.9	Bookkeeping, accounting, & auditing clerks	1.0	-24.8

Source: Industry-Occupation Matrix, Bureau of Labor Statistics. These data relate to one or more 3-digit SIC industry groups rather than to a single 4-digit SIC. The change reported for each occupation to the year 2005 is a percent of growth or decline as estimated by the Bureau of Labor Statistics. The abbreviation nec stands for 'not elsewhere classified'.

LOCATION BY STATE AND REGIONAL CONCENTRATION

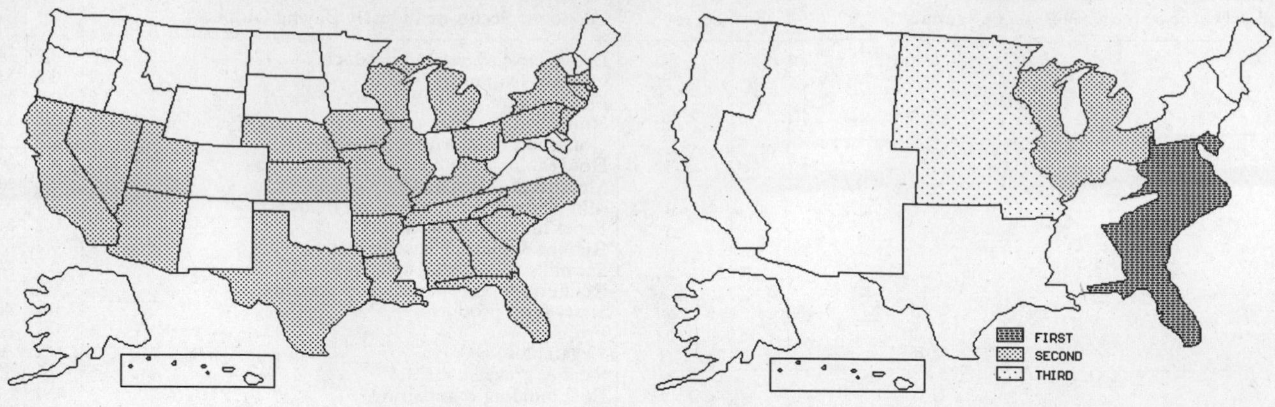

INDUSTRY DATA BY STATE

State	Establish-ments	Shipments Total ($ mil)	Shipments % of U.S.	Shipments Per Establ.	Employment Total Number	Employment % of U.S.	Employment Per Establ.	Wages ($/hour)	Cost as % of Shipments	Investment per Employee ($)
Ohio	16	384.4	14.7	24.0	2,400	12.1	150	12.82	55.3	2,958
North Carolina	19	265.9	10.2	14.0	2,400	12.1	126	11.59	50.5	2,500
Tennessee	6	141.5	5.4	23.6	1,200	6.0	200	9.32	61.8	1,417
South Carolina	10	126.6	4.8	12.7	1,200	6.0	120	10.89	48.0	-
Illinois	11	113.5	4.3	10.3	900	4.5	82	12.14	43.6	5,222
Kansas	8	100.2	3.8	12.5	800	4.0	100	9.62	42.5	1,375
Missouri	6	91.7	3.5	15.3	700	3.5	117	10.55	41.0	5,286
California	22	78.2	3.0	3.6	600	3.0	27	8.40	53.3	10,167
Florida	7	64.8	2.5	9.3	500	2.5	71	9.11	53.9	-
New Jersey	9	(D)	-	-	375 *	1.9	42	-	-	-
Pennsylvania	9	(D)	-	-	375 *	1.9	42	-	-	-
Michigan	8	(D)	-	-	750 *	3.8	94	-	-	-
Nebraska	6	(D)	-	-	1,750 *	8.8	292	-	-	-
Massachusetts	5	(D)	-	-	175 *	0.9	35	-	-	-
New York	5	(D)	-	-	375 *	1.9	75	-	-	-
Texas	5	(D)	-	-	175 *	0.9	35	-	-	-
Alabama	4	(D)	-	-	175 *	0.9	44	-	-	-
Arizona	4	(D)	-	-	175 *	0.9	44	-	-	-
Iowa	4	(D)	-	-	375 *	1.9	94	-	-	2,400
Georgia	3	(D)	-	-	375 *	1.9	125	-	-	-
Kentucky	3	(D)	-	-	750 *	3.8	250	-	-	-
Arkansas	2	(D)	-	-	750 *	3.8	375	-	-	-
Connecticut	2	(D)	-	-	175 *	0.9	88	-	-	-
Nevada	2	(D)	-	-	175 *	0.9	88	-	-	-
Louisiana	1	(D)	-	-	375 *	1.9	375	-	-	-
Utah	1	(D)	-	-	175 *	0.9	175	-	-	-
Wisconsin	1	(D)	-	-	175 *	0.9	175	-	-	-

Source: 1992 *Economic Census*. The states are in descending order of shipments or establishments (if shipment data are missing for the majority). The symbol (D) appears when data are withheld to prevent disclosure of competitive information. States marked with (D) are sorted by number of establishments. A dash (-) indicates that the data element cannot be calculated; * indicates the midpoint of a range.

3053 - GASKETS PACKING & SEALING DEVICES

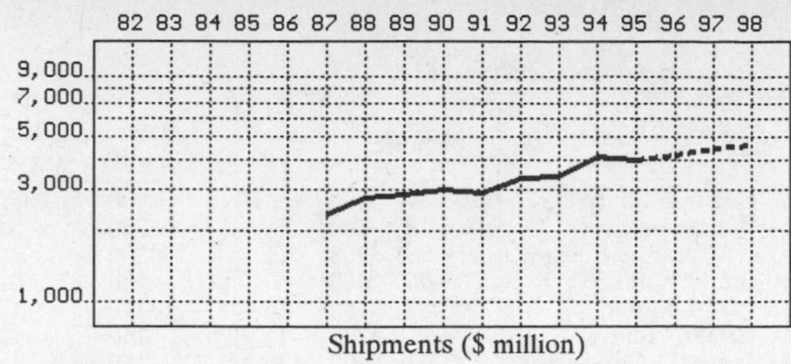

Shipments ($ million)

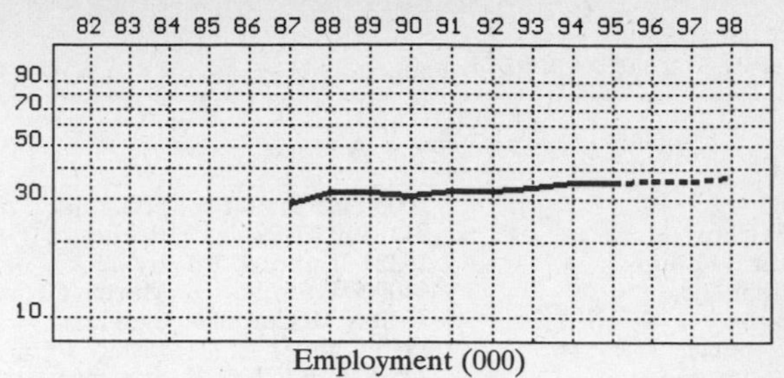

Employment (000)

GENERAL STATISTICS

Year	Com-panies	Establishments		Employment			Compensation		Production ($ million)			
		Total	with 20 or more employees	Total (000)	Production Workers (000)	Production Hours (Mil)	Payroll ($ mil)	Wages ($/hr)	Cost of Materials	Value Added by Manufacture	Value of Shipments	Capital Invest.
1982												
1983												
1984												
1985												
1986												
1987	439	496	258	28.4	19.9	40.7	627.1	9.23	980.8	1,416.2	2,379.3	83.4
1988		494	278	32.2	23.1	47.7	732.1	9.55	1,140.2	1,633.5	2,745.1	97.0
1989		480	276	32.1	23.5	46.2	779.2	9.92	1,212.8	1,619.1	2,843.1	144.4
1990		484	279	31.3	23.9	47.9	826.9	10.06	1,237.9	1,763.3	2,995.4	93.9
1991		503	271	32.3	23.2	46.8	809.3	10.23	1,246.3	1,665.8	2,911.1	72.0
1992	473	550	281	32.4	22.8	47.2	879.3	10.24	1,365.8	1,962.0	3,344.5	90.3
1993		551	278	33.4	23.6	48.6	912.1	10.50	1,421.2	2,009.1	3,433.8	77.6
1994		551P	283P	35.1	25.0	52.3	1,025.9	11.68	1,627.4	2,554.1	4,151.9	151.7
1995		562P	285P	35.1P	25.0P	51.9P	1,036.9P	11.41P	1,578.0P	2,476.5P	4,025.8P	111.8P
1996		573P	288P	35.7P	25.4P	52.9P	1,084.2P	11.68P	1,658.6P	2,603.0P	4,231.4P	114.2P
1997		583P	290P	36.4P	25.9P	54.0P	1,131.5P	11.96P	1,739.2P	2,729.5P	4,437.0P	116.5P
1998		594P	292P	37.0P	26.3P	55.0P	1,178.8P	12.23P	1,819.7P	2,856.0P	4,642.6P	118.9P

Sources: 1982, 1987, 1992 *Economic Census*; *Annual Survey of Manufactures*, 83-86, 88-91, 93-94. Establishment counts for non-Census years are from *County Business Patterns*; establishment values for 83-84 are extrapolations. 'P's show projections by the editors. Industries reclassified in 87 will not have data for prior years.

INDICES OF CHANGE

Year	Com-panies	Establishments		Employment			Compensation		Production ($ million)			
		Total	with 20 or more employees	Total (000)	Production Workers (000)	Production Hours (Mil)	Payroll ($ mil)	Wages ($/hr)	Cost of Materials	Value Added by Manufacture	Value of Shipments	Capital Invest.
1982												
1983												
1984												
1985												
1986												
1987	93	90	92	88	87	86	71	90	72	72	71	92
1988		90	99	99	101	101	83	93	83	83	82	107
1989		87	98	99	103	98	89	97	89	83	85	160
1990		88	99	97	105	101	94	98	91	90	90	104
1991		91	96	100	102	99	92	100	91	85	87	80
1992	100	100	100	100	100	100	100	100	100	100	100	100
1993		100	99	103	104	103	104	103	104	102	103	86
1994		100P	101P	108	110	111	117	114	119	130	124	168
1995		102P	102P	108P	110P	110P	118P	111P	116P	126P	120P	124P
1996		104P	102P	110P	112P	112P	123P	114P	121P	133P	127P	126P
1997		106P	103P	112P	113P	114P	129P	117P	127P	139P	133P	129P
1998		108P	104P	111P	115P	117P	134P	119P	133P	146P	139P	132P

Sources: Same as General Statistics. Values reflect change from the base year, 1992. Values above 100 mean greater than 92, values below 100 mean less than 92, and a value of 100 in the 82-91 or 93-98 period means same as 92. 'P's mark projections by the editors.

SELECTED RATIOS

For 1994	Avg. of All Manufact.	Analyzed Industry	Index
Employees per Establishment	49	64	130
Payroll per Establishment	1,500,273	1,861,405	124
Payroll per Employee	30,620	29,228	95
Production Workers per Establishment	34	45	132
Wages per Establishment	853,319	1,108,359	130
Wages per Production Worker	24,861	24,435	98
Hours per Production Worker	2,056	2,092	102
Wages per Hour	12.09	11.68	97
Value Added per Establishment	4,602,255	4,634,189	101
Value Added per Employee	93,930	72,766	77

For 1994	Avg. of All Manufact.	Analyzed Industry	Index
Value Added per Production Worker	134,084	102,164	76
Cost per Establishment	5,045,178	2,952,773	59
Cost per Employee	102,970	46,365	45
Cost per Production Worker	146,988	65,096	44
Shipments per Establishment	9,576,895	7,533,256	79
Shipments per Employee	195,460	118,288	61
Shipments per Production Worker	279,017	166,076	60
Investment per Establishment	321,011	275,246	86
Investment per Employee	6,552	4,322	66
Investment per Production Worker	9,352	6,068	65

Sources: Same as General Statistics. The 'Average of All Manufacturing' column represents the average of all manufacturing industries reported for the most recent complete year available. The Index shows the relationship between the Average and the Analyzed Industry. For example, 100 means that they are equal; 500 that the Analyzed Industry is five times the average; 50 means that the Analyzed Industry is half the national average. The abbreviation 'na' is used to show that data are 'not available'.

LEADING COMPANIES Number shown: 75 Total sales ($ mil): 4,426 Total employment (000): 163.1

Company Name	Address				CEO Name	Phone	Co. Type	Sales ($ mil)	Empl. (000)
BTR Inc	1000 One Main Pl	Stamford	CT	06902	Edgar E Sharp	203-324-3600	S	1,700	135.1
Schlegel Corp	PO Box 23197	Rochester	NY	14692	Wayne Bowser	716-427-7200	S	370	3.0
Parker Seal Group	18321 Jamboree Rd	Irvine	CA	92715	N W Vande Steeg	714-851-3763	D	200	2.3
John Crane Inc	6400 Oakton St	Morton Grove	IL	60053	James Fluharty	708-967-2400	S	190	2.1
Fel-Pro Inc	7450 N McCormick	Skokie	IL	60076	Paul Lehman	708-674-7700	R	170*	1.8
Victor Products	1945 Ohio St	Lisle	IL	60532	CJ McNamara	708-960-4200	D	150	1.0
AW Chesterton Co	225 Fallon Rd	Stoneham	MA	02180	James D Chesterton	617-438-7000	R	140	1.5
Durametallic Corp	2100 Factory St	Kalamazoo	MI	49001	JS Ware	616-381-2650	R	120	1.1
American United Global Inc	11634 Patton Rd	Downey	CA	90241	John Shahid	310-862-8163	P	102	0.8
Goshen Rubber Company Inc	PO Box 517	Goshen	IN	46526	WP Johnson	219-533-1111	R	95	1.5
Rubatex Corp	5221 Valley Park Dr	Roanoke	VA	24019	Steven W Schaefer	703-586-2611	S	77	1.0
Stemco Inc	PO Box 1989	Longview	TX	75606	Paul Norton	903-758-9981	D	75	0.5
Chomerics Inc	77 Dragon Ct	Woburn	MA	01888	R Schnyer	617-935-4850	S	70	0.7
Power Packing Company Inc	PO Box 52915	Baton Rouge	LA	70892	Marshall Vass	504-356-4333	R	70	<0.1
Garlock Mechanical Packing	1666 Division St	Palmyra	NY	14522	Michael J Burdulis	315-597-4811	D	65	1.1
Greene, Tweed and Co	Detwiler Rd	Kulpsville	PA	19443	FA Paino	215-256-9521	R	45	0.5
Johnson Rubber Co	PO Box 67	Middlefield	OH	44062	PC Miller Jr	216-632-1611	S	41*	0.5
Southland Industries Inc	PO Box 868	Norfolk	VA	23501	John Dannenhoffer	804-543-5701	R	41	0.4
Farnam Sealing Systems	650ephenson Hwy	Troy	MI	48083	FL Zernhelt	313-588-0044	D	40	0.4
Unique Fabricating Inc	1601 Hamlin Rd	Rochester Hills	MI	48309	GC Wilms	313-853-2333	R	39	0.5
Crotty Corp	PO Box 37	Quincy	MI	49082	Willard E Crotty Jr	517-639-8787	R	35	0.8
John Crane Inc	Rte 51 & Payne Dr	Vandalia	IL	62471	Bob Ingram	618-283-4700	D	32	0.4
Macrotech Polyseal Inc	1754 W 500 S	Salt Lake City	UT	84104	Gordon Zitting	801-973-9171	R	27	0.4
American United Products Inc	11634 Patton Rd	Downey	CA	90241	John Shahid	310-862-8163	S	25	0.4
Argent Automotive Systems Inc	41131 Vincenti Ct	Novi	MI	48375	F Perenic	810-473-0500	R	25	0.1
Moxness Products Inc	1914 Indiana St	Racine	WI	53405	HW Plimpton	414-554-5050	S	24	0.2
JM Clipper Corp	7333 W Jefferson St	Denver	CO	80235	Brian Collier	303-985-1133	R	22*	0.3
American Rubber Products Corp	PO Box 190	La Porte	IN	46352	JA Bernel	219-326-1315	R	20	0.5
Forest City Technologies Inc	PO Box 86	Wellington	OH	44090	John D Cloud	216-647-2115	R	20	0.4
O Seal	10567 Jefferson	Culver City	CA	90232	Steven D Barnes	310-204-3000	D	20	0.2
UCAR Carbon Company Inc	PO Box 94637	Cleveland	OH	44101	WD Cate	216-529-3777	S	19*	0.3
Sealing Devices Inc	4400 Walden Av	Lancaster	NY	14086	TS Galanis Sr	716-684-7600	R	18	<0.1
Amesbury Group Inc	57 Hunt Rd	Amesbury	MA	01913	Martin Barnes	508-388-0581	S	17	0.2
Parco Inc	2150 Parco Av	Ontario	CA	91761	LW Burgener	909-947-2200	R	16*	0.2
Bal Seal Engineering Company	620 W Warner Av	Santa Ana	CA	92707	Jon Stillman	714-557-5192	R	14*	0.2
Advanced Products Co	33 Defco Park Rd	North Haven	CT	06473	Nancy S Nicholson	203-239-3341	R	12	0.1
Standco Industries Inc	PO Box 87	Houston	TX	77001	Minor Peeples Jr	713-224-6311	R	12	0.2
American Gasket&Rubber Co	9509 Winona Av	Schiller Park	IL	60176	N Weiner	708-678-3550	S	11*	0.1
Rockford International	2501 9th St	Rockford	IL	60125	Richard L Goff	815-397-6000	D	11*	0.1
Sur-Seal Gasket and Packing Inc	PO Box 11010	Cincinnati	OH	45211	Edward Wilz	513-574-8500	R	11	0.1
Chicago-Allis Mfg Corp	113 N Green St	Chicago	IL	60607	John W Ball	312-666-5050	R	10	0.1
Cooper Manufacturing Co	PO Box 220	Marshalltown	IA	50158	Ron Kelling	515-752-6736	R	10	<0.1
Industrial Custom Prod LLC	5200 Quincy St	Mounds View	MN	55112	Doug Stearley	612-785-2266	S	10	<0.1
International Seal Company Inc	2041 E Wilshire Av	Santa Ana	CA	92705	O A Marvick Jr	714-834-0602	R	10	0.1
Pac-Seal Incorporated Intern	211 Frontage Rd	Burr Ridge	IL	60521	Edward E Euwer	708-986-0430	R	10	0.1
Sierracin Corp	3020 Empire Av	Burbank	CA	91504	Chris Tribull	818-842-2131	D	10	<0.1
Vanguard Products Corp	144 Old Brookfield	Danbury	CT	06811	Robert C Benn	203-744-7265	R	10	<0.1
Gasket Engineering Co	4500 E 75th Ter	Kansas City	MO	64132	JJ Fitzgerald	816-363-8333	R	9	<0.1
Hoosier Gasket Corp	3333 Massachusetts	Indianapolis	IN	46218	Argyle G Jackson	317-545-2000	R	9*	0.1
Industrial Gasket and Shim	PO Box 368	Meadow Lands	PA	15347	KR Desch	412-222-5800	R	9	0.1
American United Seal Inc	6020nida Encinas	Carlsbad	CA	92009	John Shahid	619-438-1011	S	9	0.2
GNP Operations	41 W 195 Railroad	Hampshire	IL	60140	Jim Miserendino	708-464-5202	D	8*	<0.1
Presray Corp	159 Coleman	Pawling	NY	12564	TC Hollander Jr	914-855-1220	S	8	<0.1
Higbee Gaskets & Sealing Prod	PO Box 6449	Syracuse	NY	13217	Lawrence E Higbee	315-432-8021	R	8	<0.1
Press-Seal Gasket Corp	PO Box 10482	Fort Wayne	IN	46852	JW Skinner	219-436-0521	R	8	<0.1
Coast Industrial Supply Company	15959 Piuma Av	Cerritos	CA	90703	Arnold R Dasaro	310-865-4466	R	7*	<0.1
Five Star Seal Corp	PO Box 5656	Florence	SC	29502	Robert J Russell	803-662-2100	R	7	<0.1
Quigley Industries Inc	21547 Telegraph Rd	Southfield	MI	48034	Carol Quigley	313-352-8500	R	7*	<0.1
Cincinnati Gasket Packing Mfg	40 Illinois Av	Cincinnati	OH	45215	LJ Uhlenbrock	513-761-3458	R	6	<0.1
Melrath Gasket Inc	PO Box 3099	Philadelphia	PA	19129	Bruce C Duffy	215-223-6000	R	6	<0.1
Seal Methods Inc	10230 Freeman Av	Santa Fe Sprgs	CA	90670	GT Welter	310-944-0291	R	6	<0.1
Stockwell Rubber Company Inc	4749 Tolbut St	Philadelphia	PA	19136	WB Stockwell	215-355-3005	R	6	<0.1
Chambers Gasket & Mfg Co	4701 W Rice St	Chicago	IL	60651	M E Holmberg	312-626-8800	R	5	<0.1
EG and G Sealol Inc	455 W Fullerton	Elmhurst	IL	60126	Mike Galucio	708-941-1888	S	5	<0.1
Industrial Gasket Inc	8100 SW 15th St	Oklahoma City	OK	73128	L Renth	405-745-2361	R	5	<0.1
Punch Prod Manufacturing Co	500 S Kolmar Av	Chicago	IL	60624	M Shaikh	312-533-2800	R	5	<0.1
Chicago Gasket Co	1701 Lake Av	Glenview	IL	60025	Eberhard Kohl	708-657-9510	R	4	<0.1
Chicago Wilcox Mfg Co	16928 State St	South Holland	IL	60473	SC Anthony	708-339-5000	R	4	<0.1
Excelsior Inc	PO Box 970	Rockford	IL	61105	WE Duclon	815-987-2940	R	4	<0.1
Precision Gasket Co	5625 W 78th St	Minneapolis	MN	55439	TA Jamieson	612-942-6711	R	4	<0.1
Presscut Industries Inc	2828 Nagel St	Dallas	TX	75220	James Swanson	214-956-9100	R	4*	<0.1
Rhopac Fabricators Inc	3425 Cleveland St	Skokie	IL	60076	Daniel Rebecca	708-673-8020	R	4	<0.1
Bentley Manufacturing Company	15123 Colorado Av	Paramount	CA	90723	Kevin Crampton	310-634-4051	R	3	<0.1
United Seal and Rubber Co	7025-C Amwiler	Atlanta	GA	30360	Virgil Alonso	404-729-8880	R	3	<0.1
Akron Gasket	1244 Home Av	Akron	OH	44310	Carter Ray	216-633-3742	R	3	<0.1

Source: *Ward's Business Directory of U.S. Private and Public Companies*, Volumes 1 and 2, 1996. The company type code is used as follows: P - Public, R - Private, S - Subsidiary, D - Division, J - Joint Venture, A - Affiliate, G - Group. Sales are in millions of dollars, employees are in thousands. An asterisk (*) indicates an estimated sales volume. The symbol < stands for 'less than'. Company names and addresses are truncated, in some cases, to fit into the available space.

MATERIALS CONSUMED

Material	Quantity	Delivered Cost ($ million)
Materials, ingredients, containers, and supplies	(X)	1,166.3
Asbestos, crude (including fiber)	(X)	5.2
Cork products	(X)	53.9
Building paper and board	(X)	59.7
Plastics resins consumed in the form of granules, pellets, powders, liquids, etc.	(X)	53.2
Synthetic rubber	(X)	140.9
Other plastics materials and synthetic resins	(X)	93.7
Natural rubber	(X)	10.7
Fabricated rubber products, except tires, tubes, hose, belting, and gaskets	(X)	47.0
Fabricated metal wire products (including wire rope, cable, springs, etc.)	(X)	25.0
All other fabricated metal products (including forgings)	(X)	116.9
Steel tinplate, tin free steel, terneplate, and blackplate	(X)	13.8
All other steel shapes and forms (except forgings and fabricated metal products)	(X)	118.4
All other nonferrous shapes and forms (except castings, forgings, and fabricated metal products)	(X)	4.9
All other materials and components, parts, containers, and supplies	(X)	300.0
Materials, ingredients, containers, and supplies, nsk	(X)	122.9

Source: 1992 *Economic Census*. Explanation of symbols used: (D): Withheld to avoid disclosure of competitive data; na: Not available; (S): Withheld because statistical norms were not met; (X): Not applicable; (Z): Less than half the unit shown; nec: Not elsewhere classified; nsk: Not specified by kind; - : zero; * : 10-19 percent estimated; ** : 20-29 percent estimated.

PRODUCT SHARE DETAILS

Product or Product Class	% Share
Gaskets, packing, and sealing devices	100.00
Compression packings	3.26
Plant fiber compression packings	5.75
Synthetic fiber, plastics composition compression packings	28.65
All other compression packings, nec	65.59
Nonmetallic gaskets and gasketing	27.97
Asbestos gaskets and gasketing, compressed	1.37
Asbestos gaskets and gasketing, beater saturated	0.30
Elastomeric gaskets and gasketing, all materials	22.27
Paper, felt base, and plant fiber gaskets and gasketing	8.71
Cork and cork composition gaskets and gasketing	9.20
Fluorocarbon (including envelope-type) gaskets and gasketing	1.01
Other nonmetallic gaskets and gasketing, nec	56.51
Nonmetallic gaskets and gasketing, nsk	0.62
Molded packings and seals	21.77
Molded O-rings (including spliced, excluding metal)	30.27
Molded squeeze-type, solid section ring seals (including rectangular, quad, Delta, D, and Tee) (excluding O-rings)	3.66
Molded flexible seals, dual component-cushioned rings, backed, constrained, or loaded by an elastomeric ring	4.29
Molded flexible seals, single and multiple component lip type, both symmetrical and nonsymmetrical, V-rings, V-ring sets, U-cup	7.96
Molded diaphragm seal-flat, rolling	3.47
All other molded packings and seals, including nonmetallic exclusion devices and nonmetallic piston rings	49.23
Molded packings and seals, nsk	1.12
Metallic gaskets and machined seals	16.35
Metallic spiral wound filler type gaskets and machined seals	9.12
Other metallic gaskets and machined seals (exclusion devices, heavy cross-section API type, nonautomotive piston rings)	90.36
Metallic gaskets and machined seals, nsk	0.54
Axial mechanical face seals	6.83
Complete axial mechanical seals with single coil springs	30.71
Complete axial mechanical seals with multiple coil springs	19.64
Complete axial mechanical seals with bellows	14.38
Parts for all axial mechanical face seals	22.06
Clearance, labyrinth, and other axial mechanical face seals, nec	12.42
Axial mechanical face seals, nsk	0.79
Rotary oil seals	15.68
Bonded, sprung (spring-loaded) rotary oil seals	51.67
Bonded, unsprung (nonspring-loaded) rotary oil seals	(D)
Unitized rotary oil seals	(D)
Nonmetallic rotary oil seals	1.93
Nonbonded assembled rotary oil seals	(D)
Other rotary oil seals (labyrinth, proximity, all metallic, inflatable, displacement, or boundary lubrication seals)	7.78
Rotary oil seals, nsk	0.08
Gaskets, packing, and sealing devices, nsk	8.13

Source: 1992 *Economic Census*. The values shown are percent of total shipments in an industry. Values of indented subcategories are summed in the main heading. The symbol (D) appears when data are withheld to prevent disclosure of competitive information. The abbreviation nsk stands for 'not specified by kind' and nec for 'not elsewhere classified'.

INPUTS AND OUTPUTS FOR GASKETS, PACKING & SEALING DEVICES

Economic Sector or Industry Providing Inputs	%	Sector	Economic Sector or Industry Buying Outputs	%	Sector
Imports	12.0	Foreign	Automotive repair shops & services	14.4	Services
Synthetic rubber	11.6	Manufg.	Electronic computing equipment	6.2	Manufg.
Wholesale trade	10.6	Trade	Motor vehicles & car bodies	5.5	Manufg.
Metal coating & allied services	4.9	Manufg.	Motor vehicle parts & accessories	4.9	Manufg.
Electric services (utilities)	4.2	Util.	Exports	3.7	Foreign
Nonferrous rolling & drawing, nec	4.1	Manufg.	Internal combustion engines, nec	2.9	Manufg.
Motor freight transportation & warehousing	3.4	Util.	Photographic equipment & supplies	2.6	Manufg.
Plastics materials & resins	3.2	Manufg.	Retail trade, except eating & drinking	2.5	Trade
Gaskets, packing & sealing devices	3.0	Manufg.	Personal consumption expenditures	2.4	
Reclaimed rubber	2.7	Manufg.	Wholesale trade	2.3	Trade
Miscellaneous plastics products	2.3	Manufg.	Pumps & compressors	2.1	Manufg.
Wood products, nec	2.0	Manufg.	Machinery, except electrical, nec	2.0	Manufg.
Advertising	1.9	Services	Oil field machinery	1.7	Manufg.
Building paper & board mills	1.8	Manufg.	Crude petroleum & natural gas	1.5	Mining
Communications, except radio & TV	1.6	Util.	Construction machinery & equipment	1.2	Manufg.
Asbestos products	1.4	Manufg.	Gaskets, packing & sealing devices	1.2	Manufg.

Continued on next page.

INPUTS AND OUTPUTS FOR GASKETS, PACKING & SEALING DEVICES - Continued

Economic Sector or Industry Providing Inputs	%	Sector	Economic Sector or Industry Buying Outputs	%	Sector
Paperboard containers & boxes	1.4	Manufg.	Motors & generators	1.2	Manufg.
Water transportation	1.4	Util.	Instruments to measure electricity	1.0	Manufg.
Eating & drinking places	1.4	Trade	Automotive rental & leasing, without drivers	1.0	Services
Petroleum refining	1.3	Manufg.	Federal Government purchases, national defense	1.0	Fed Govt
Gas production & distribution (utilities)	1.3	Util.	Household refrigerators & freezers	0.9	Manufg.
Maintenance of nonfarm buildings nec	1.2	Constr.	Special industry machinery, nec	0.9	Manufg.
Real estate	1.2	Fin/R.E.	Surgical appliances & supplies	0.9	Manufg.
Equipment rental & leasing services	1.2	Services	Industrial controls	0.8	Manufg.
Nonmetallic mineral services	1.1	Mining	Petroleum refining	0.8	Manufg.
Fabricated rubber products, nec	1.1	Manufg.	Switchgear & switchboard apparatus	0.8	Manufg.
Miscellaneous fabricated wire products	1.1	Manufg.	Fabricated metal products, nec	0.7	Manufg.
Railroads & related services	1.0	Util.	General industrial machinery, nec	0.7	Manufg.
Banking	1.0	Fin/R.E.	Pipe, valves, & pipe fittings	0.7	Manufg.
Machinery, except electrical, nec	0.7	Manufg.	Surgical & medical instruments	0.7	Manufg.
Air transportation	0.7	Util.	Business services nec	0.7	Services
U.S. Postal Service	0.7	Gov't	Cyclic crudes and organics	0.6	Manufg.
Adhesives & sealants	0.6	Manufg.	Mobile homes	0.6	Manufg.
Metal stampings, nec	0.6	Manufg.	Optical instruments & lenses	0.6	Manufg.
Management & consulting services & labs	0.6	Services	Refrigeration & heating equipment	0.6	Manufg.
Noncomparable imports	0.6	Foreign	Typewriters & office machines, nec	0.6	Manufg.
Computer & data processing services	0.5	Services	Coal	0.5	Mining
Legal services	0.5	Services	Engineering & scientific instruments	0.5	Manufg.
Abrasive products	0.4	Manufg.	Lighting fixtures & equipment	0.5	Manufg.
Converted paper products, nec	0.4	Manufg.	Power transmission equipment	0.5	Manufg.
Die-cut paper & board	0.4	Manufg.	Motor freight transportation & warehousing	0.5	Util.
Mineral wool	0.4	Manufg.	Aircraft & missile engines & engine parts	0.4	Manufg.
Paints & allied products	0.4	Manufg.	Blast furnaces & steel mills	0.4	Manufg.
Sawmills & planning mills, general	0.4	Manufg.	Boat building & repairing	0.4	Manufg.
Special dies & tools & machine tool accessories	0.4	Manufg.	Conveyors & conveying equipment	0.4	Manufg.
Royalties	0.4	Fin/R.E.	Food products machinery	0.4	Manufg.
General industrial machinery, nec	0.3	Manufg.	Lawn & garden equipment	0.4	Manufg.
Lubricating oils & greases	0.3	Manufg.	Mechanical measuring devices	0.4	Manufg.
Accounting, auditing & bookkeeping	0.3	Services	Paper mills, except building paper	0.4	Manufg.
Cyclic crudes and organics	0.2	Manufg.	Plumbing fixture fittings & trim	0.4	Manufg.
Hand & edge tools, nec	0.2	Manufg.	Prefabricated metal buildings	0.4	Manufg.
Industrial inorganic chemicals, nec	0.2	Manufg.	Printing trades machinery	0.4	Manufg.
Inorganic pigments	0.2	Manufg.	Service industry machines, nec	0.4	Manufg.
Manifold business forms	0.2	Manufg.	Computer & data processing services	0.4	Services
Sanitary services, steam supply, irrigation	0.2	Util.	Management & consulting services & labs	0.4	Services
Insurance carriers	0.2	Fin/R.E.	Office buildings	0.3	Constr.
Automotive rental & leasing, without drivers	0.2	Services	Aircraft	0.3	Manufg.
Automotive repair shops & services	0.2	Services	Aircraft & missile equipment, nec	0.3	Manufg.
Coal	0.1	Mining	Blowers & fans	0.3	Manufg.
Hotels & lodging places	0.1	Services	Carburetors, pistons, rings, & valves	0.3	Manufg.
Personnel supply services	0.1	Services	Environmental controls	0.3	Manufg.
			Farm machinery & equipment	0.3	Manufg.
			Guided missiles & space vehicles	0.3	Manufg.
			Heating equipment, except electric	0.3	Manufg.
			Industrial trucks & tractors	0.3	Manufg.
			Paperboard mills	0.3	Manufg.
			Semiconductors & related devices	0.3	Manufg.
			Equipment rental & leasing services	0.3	Services
			Hotels & lodging places	0.3	Services
			Feed grains	0.2	Agric.
			Electric utility facility construction	0.2	Constr.
			Industrial buildings	0.2	Constr.
			Broadwoven fabric mills	0.2	Manufg.
			Calculating & accounting machines	0.2	Manufg.
			Commercial printing	0.2	Manufg.
			Dental equipment & supplies	0.2	Manufg.
			Drugs	0.2	Manufg.
			Electrical industrial apparatus, nec	0.2	Manufg.
			Electronic components nec	0.2	Manufg.
			Elevators & moving stairways	0.2	Manufg.
			Hoists, cranes, & monorails	0.2	Manufg.
			Household cooking equipment	0.2	Manufg.
			Household laundry equipment	0.2	Manufg.
			Motorcycles, bicycles, & parts	0.2	Manufg.
			Newspapers	0.2	Manufg.
			Ophthalmic goods	0.2	Manufg.
			Paper industries machinery	0.2	Manufg.
			Radio & TV communication equipment	0.2	Manufg.
			Textile machinery	0.2	Manufg.
			Transformers	0.2	Manufg.
			Transportation equipment, nec	0.2	Manufg.

Continued on next page.

INPUTS AND OUTPUTS FOR GASKETS, PACKING & SEALING DEVICES - Continued

Economic Sector or Industry Providing Inputs	%	Sector	Economic Sector or Industry Buying Outputs	%	Sector
			Travel trailers & campers	0.2	Manufg.
			Amusement & recreation services nec	0.2	Services
			Construction of stores & restaurants	0.1	Constr.
			Maintenance of farm service facilities	0.1	Constr.
			Maintenance of nonfarm buildings nec	0.1	Constr.
			Bottled & canned soft drinks	0.1	Manufg.
			Electric housewares & fans	0.1	Manufg.
			Industrial furnaces & ovens	0.1	Manufg.
			Plastics materials & resins	0.1	Manufg.
			Primary aluminum	0.1	Manufg.
			Pulp mills	0.1	Manufg.
			Sporting & athletic goods, nec	0.1	Manufg.
			Woodworking machinery	0.1	Manufg.
			Transit & bus transportation	0.1	Util.
			Laundry, dry cleaning, shoe repair	0.1	Services
			S/L Govt. purch., elem. & secondary education	0.1	S/L Govt

Source: Benchmark Input-Output Accounts for the U.S. Economy, 1982, U.S. Department of Commerce, Washington, D.C., July 1991. Data, as reported in the source, are organized by the 1977 SIC structure in use in 1982 but have been matched, as closely as is possible, to the 1987 SIC structure used in this book.

OCCUPATIONS EMPLOYED BY SIC 305 - RUBBER PRODUCTS AND PLASTIC HOSE AND FOOTWEAR

Occupation	% of Total 1994	Change to 2005	Occupation	% of Total 1994	Change to 2005
Assemblers, fabricators, & hand workers nec	11.9	0.3	Machine forming operators, metal & plastic	1.9	0.3
Extruding & forming machine workers	11.1	-29.8	Freight, stock, & material movers, hand	1.8	-19.8
Inspectors, testers, & graders, precision	5.1	0.3	Traffic, shipping, & receiving clerks	1.8	-3.5
Machine operators nec	4.9	-11.6	Industrial machinery mechanics	1.8	10.3
Blue collar worker supervisors	4.8	-5.6	Metal & plastic machine workers nec	1.6	-11.1
Cutters & trimmers, hand	3.7	10.3	Maintenance repairers, general utility	1.5	-9.7
Plastic molding machine workers	3.5	0.3	Industrial production managers	1.4	0.3
Hand packers & packagers	2.9	-14.1	Machinists	1.4	0.3
Cutting & slicing machine setters, operators	2.8	-9.8	Secretaries, ex legal & medical	1.3	-8.7
Helpers, laborers, & material movers nec	2.7	0.3	Machine feeders & offbearers	1.2	-9.8
Crushing & mixing machine operators	2.6	-9.8	Industrial truck & tractor operators	1.1	0.3
General managers & top executives	2.2	-4.9	Bookkeeping, accounting, & auditing clerks	1.0	-24.8

Source: Industry-Occupation Matrix, Bureau of Labor Statistics. These data relate to one or more 3-digit SIC industry groups rather than to a single 4-digit SIC. The change reported for each occupation to the year 2005 is a percent of growth or decline as estimated by the Bureau of Labor Statistics. The abbreviation nec stands for 'not elsewhere classified'.

LOCATION BY STATE AND REGIONAL CONCENTRATION

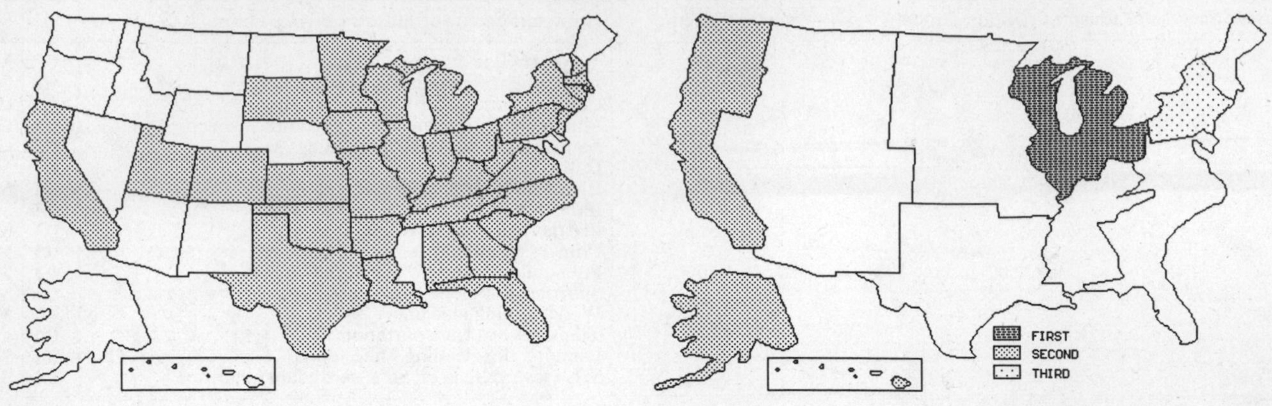

INDUSTRY DATA BY STATE

State	Establish-ments	Shipments			Employment				Cost as % of Shipments	Investment per Employee ($)
		Total ($ mil)	% of U.S.	Per Establ.	Total Number	% of U.S.	Per Establ.	Wages ($/hour)		
Illinois	50	616.6	18.4	12.3	5,900	18.2	118	11.89	53.5	2,508
California	80	285.2	8.5	3.6	3,500	10.8	44	9.59	35.7	2,000
Texas	50	200.3	6.0	4.0	2,300	7.1	46	9.29	32.4	1,739
Ohio	42	190.2	5.7	4.5	1,900	5.9	45	10.75	32.4	-
Massachusetts	20	175.4	5.2	8.8	1,300	4.0	65	12.85	32.4	3,077
New York	25	148.8	4.4	6.0	1,300	4.0	52	11.83	33.2	-
Wisconsin	14	144.1	4.3	10.3	1,200	3.7	86	10.59	52.4	-
Michigan	28	126.9	3.8	4.5	1,200	3.7	43	8.53	47.7	1,667
New Jersey	26	109.4	3.3	4.2	900	2.8	35	15.18	40.7	3,000
Tennessee	8	91.7	2.7	11.5	900	2.8	113	9.63	39.9	2,667
Oklahoma	9	70.8	2.1	7.9	400	1.2	44	7.86	28.2	-
Pennsylvania	25	69.5	2.1	2.8	800	2.5	32	10.64	43.6	2,250
Missouri	10	17.4	0.5	1.7	200	0.6	20	8.33	47.1	1,500
Colorado	11	10.9	0.3	1.0	100	0.3	9	11.00	29.4	3,000
Indiana	16	(D)	-	-	1,750 *	5.4	109	-	-	-
Minnesota	15	(D)	-	-	750 *	2.3	50	-	-	-
Connecticut	13	(D)	-	-	175 *	0.5	13	-	-	-
Georgia	10	(D)	-	-	750 *	2.3	75	-	-	-
North Carolina	10	(D)	-	-	750 *	2.3	75	-	-	-
New Hampshire	7	(D)	-	-	1,750 *	5.4	250	-	-	-
Virginia	7	(D)	-	-	750 *	2.3	107	-	-	-
Florida	6	(D)	-	-	375 *	1.2	63	-	-	4,000
Alabama	5	(D)	-	-	375 *	1.2	75	-	-	-
Kansas	5	(D)	-	-	375 *	1.2	75	-	-	-
Louisiana	5	(D)	-	-	175 *	0.5	35	-	-	-
South Carolina	5	(D)	-	-	750 *	2.3	150	-	-	1,067
Utah	5	(D)	-	-	375 *	1.2	75	-	-	-
Iowa	4	(D)	-	-	175 *	0.5	44	-	-	-
Kentucky	3	(D)	-	-	750 *	2.3	250	-	-	-
Rhode Island	3	(D)	-	-	375 *	1.2	125	-	-	-
Arkansas	2	(D)	-	-	175 *	0.5	88	-	-	-
South Dakota	1	(D)	-	-	175 *	0.5	175	-	-	-
West Virginia	1	(D)	-	-	175 *	0.5	175	-	-	-

Source: 1992 *Economic Census*. The states are in descending order of shipments or establishments (if shipment data are missing for the majority). The symbol (D) appears when data are withheld to prevent disclosure of competitive information. States marked with (D) are sorted by number of establishments. A dash (-) indicates that the data element cannot be calculated; * indicates the midpoint of a range.

3061 - MECHANICAL RUBBER GOODS

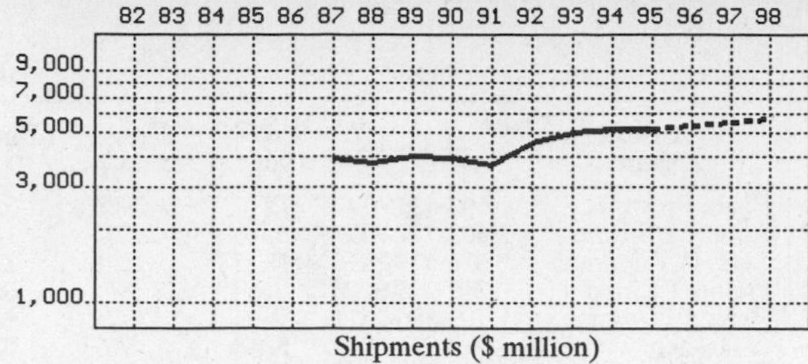

Shipments ($ million)

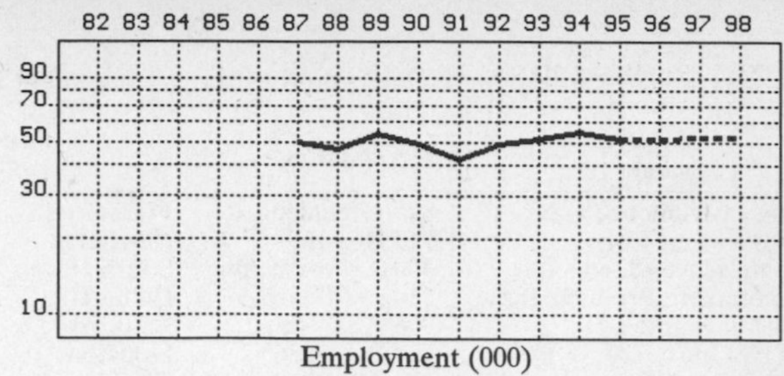

Employment (000)

GENERAL STATISTICS

Year	Companies	Establishments: Total	Establishments: with 20 or more employees	Employment: Total (000)	Production Workers (000)	Production Hours (Mil)	Compensation: Payroll ($ mil)	Compensation: Wages ($/hr)	Production ($ million): Cost of Materials	Value Added by Manufacture	Value of Shipments	Capital Invest.
1982												
1983												
1984												
1985												
1986												
1987	537	624	328	49.8	37.9	77.6	1,092.2	9.35	1,755.6	2,208.5	3,963.2	148.6
1988		618	315	46.6	36.5	73.9	987.9	9.11	1,655.1	2,101.0	3,743.4	104.3
1989		626	345	53.4	37.3	78.9	1,170.5	9.82	1,874.8	2,133.4	3,997.6	152.3
1990		613	348	48.4	36.5	74.2	1,083.4	9.89	1,850.5	2,086.3	3,930.2	116.6
1991		610	342	42.4	32.5	67.5	1,044.4	10.27	1,729.9	1,995.6	3,726.1	108.4
1992	560	649	378	48.5	37.1	76.3	1,196.3	10.16	1,991.9	2,554.9	4,545.0	154.0
1993		643	370	50.7	38.6	78.6	1,278.5	10.51	2,123.6	2,885.2	4,996.3	254.0
1994		641P	382P	54.5	43.7	87.8	1,308.8	10.07	2,271.5	2,958.8	5,219.9	160.3
1995		645P	391P	51.0P	40.0P	81.2P	1,306.4P	10.62P	2,240.7P	2,918.7P	5,149.1P	194.1P
1996		648P	400P	51.4P	40.6P	82.1P	1,342.2P	10.78P	2,326.2P	3,030.0P	5,345.5P	204.0P
1997		652P	409P	51.8P	41.1P	83.1P	1,378.0P	10.94P	2,411.6P	3,141.4P	5,542.0P	213.8P
1998		656P	418P	52.2P	41.7P	84.0P	1,413.8P	11.10P	2,497.1P	3,252.7P	5,738.4P	223.7P

Sources: 1982, 1987, 1992 *Economic Census*; *Annual Survey of Manufactures*, 83-86, 88-91, 93-94. Establishment counts for non-Census years are from *County Business Patterns*; establishment values for 83-84 are extrapolations. 'P's show projections by the editors. Industries reclassified in 87 will not have data for prior years.

INDICES OF CHANGE

Year	Companies	Establishments: Total	Establishments: with 20 or more employees	Employment: Total (000)	Production Workers (000)	Production Hours (Mil)	Compensation: Payroll ($ mil)	Compensation: Wages ($/hr)	Production ($ million): Cost of Materials	Value Added by Manufacture	Value of Shipments	Capital Invest.
1982												
1983												
1984												
1985												
1986												
1987	96	96	87	103	102	102	91	92	88	86	87	96
1988		95	83	96	98	97	83	90	83	82	82	68
1989		96	91	110	101	103	98	97	94	84	88	99
1990		94	92	100	98	97	91	97	93	82	86	76
1991		94	90	87	88	88	87	101	87	78	82	70
1992	100	100	100	100	100	100	100	100	100	100	100	100
1993		99	98	105	104	103	107	103	107	113	110	165
1994		99P	101P	112	118	115	109	99	114	116	115	104
1995		99P	103P	105P	108P	106P	109P	105P	112P	114P	113P	126P
1996		100P	106P	106P	109P	108P	112P	106P	117P	119P	118P	132P
1997		100P	108P	107P	111P	109P	115P	108P	121P	123P	122P	139P
1998		101P	111P	108P	112P	110P	118P	109P	125P	127P	126P	145P

Sources: Same as General Statistics. Values reflect change from the base year, 1992. Values above 100 mean greater than 92, values below 100 mean less than 92, and a value of 100 in the 82-91 or 93-98 period means same as 92. 'P's mark projections by the editors.

SELECTED RATIOS

For 1994	Avg. of All Manufact.	Analyzed Industry	Index
Employees per Establishment	49	85	174
Payroll per Establishment	1,500,273	2,042,265	136
Payroll per Employee	30,620	24,015	78
Production Workers per Establishment	34	68	199
Wages per Establishment	853,319	1,379,630	162
Wages per Production Worker	24,861	20,232	81
Hours per Production Worker	2,056	2,009	98
Wages per Hour	12.09	10.07	83
Value Added per Establishment	4,602,255	4,616,942	100
Value Added per Employee	93,930	54,290	58

For 1994	Avg. of All Manufact.	Analyzed Industry	Index
Value Added per Production Worker	134,084	67,707	50
Cost per Establishment	5,045,178	3,544,472	70
Cost per Employee	102,970	41,679	40
Cost per Production Worker	146,988	51,979	35
Shipments per Establishment	9,576,895	8,145,185	85
Shipments per Employee	195,460	95,778	49
Shipments per Production Worker	279,017	119,449	43
Investment per Establishment	321,011	250,134	78
Investment per Employee	6,552	2,941	45
Investment per Production Worker	9,352	3,668	39

Sources: Same as General Statistics. The 'Average of All Manufacturing' column represents the average of all manufacturing industries reported for the most recent complete year available. The Index shows the relationship between the Average and the Analyzed Industry. For example, 100 means that they are equal; 500 that the Analyzed Industry is five times the average; 50 means that the Analyzed Industry is half the national average. The abbreviation 'na' is used to show that data are 'not available'.

LEADING COMPANIES

Number shown: **58** Total sales ($ mil): **1,674** Total employment (000): **19.8**

Company Name	Address				CEO Name	Phone	Co. Type	Sales ($ mil)	Empl. (000)
Davidson Instrument Panel	875 Greenland Rd	Portsmouth	NH	03801	Frank Preston	603-433-4142	D	390*	5.0
Kingston-Warren Corp	PO Box 169	Newfields	NH	03056	Robert L Snyder	603-772-3771	S	150	1.5
Yale-South Haven Inc	400 Aylworth Av	South Haven	MI	49090	Terry A Friedman	616-637-2116	R	120*	1.1
CTS Automotive Products Inc	1142 W Beardsley	Elkhart	IN	46514	Phillip T Christ	219-295-3575	S	87	0.7
RBX Holdings Inc	906 Adams St	Bedford	VA	24523	Ronald L Adams	703-586-2611	R	77*	1.0
Grant TFW Inc	PO Box 60865	Houston	TX	77205	G Hashem	713-931-0040	S	70	0.6
Chardon Rubber Co	373 Washington St	Chardon	OH	44024	Tom Judy	216-285-2161	R	65	0.6
Acushnet Rubber Company Inc	PO Box 6916	New Bedford	MA	02742	James G DeMello	508-998-4000	R	64	1.1
Vernay Laboratories Inc	PO Box 310	Yellow Springs	OH	45387	Tom Allen	513-767-7261	R	63	0.8
Cadillac Rubber and Plastics Inc	805 W 13th St	Cadillac	MI	49601	Don Samardich	616-775-1345	R	55	0.7
BRC Rubber Group Inc	PO Box 227	Churubusco	IN	46723	Charles V Chaffee	219-693-2171	R	50	0.9
Burke Industries Inc	PO Box 190	San Jose	CA	95103	Rocky Genovese	408-297-3500	R	50	0.5
CKR Industries Inc	590 Baxter Ln	Winchester	TN	37398	John Thoman	615-967-5189	S	46	0.6
Thunderline Corp	8707 Samuel Barton	Belleville	MI	48112	Curtis Peterson	313-397-5000	R	30	0.3
MCP Industries Inc	1660 Leeson Ln	Corona	CA	91719	Walter Garrett	909-736-1881	R	25	0.3
Western Consolidated Techn	620 E Douglas	Goshen	IN	46526	Kevin G Kelly	219-533-4126	S	25	0.5
Paulstra CRC Corp	PO Box 209	Cadillac	MI	49601	Phil Wood	616-775-9737	D	22*	0.1
Beebe Rubber Co	20 Marshall St	Nashua	NH	03060	Maurice Grasso	603-883-5576	S	16*	0.1
Buckhorn Rubber Products Inc	PO Box 998	Hannibal	MO	63401	Dennis D Roberts	314-221-8933	S	15	0.2
Dowty Palmer-Chenard Inc	366 Rte 108	Somersworth	NH	03878	D Roy	603-692-7400	S	15	0.2
DS Brown Company Inc	PO Box 158	N Baltimore	OH	45872	Daniel H Brown	419-257-3561	R	15*	0.2
Delta Rubber Co	PO Box 300	Danielson	CT	06239	David Harrington	203-779-0300	R	14	0.2
Sperry Rubber and Plastics	9146 US Rte 52	Brookville	IN	47012	JM Boyd	317-647-4141	S	14	0.2
Mantaline Corp	PO Box M	Mantua	OH	44255	Terry Green	216-274-2264	R	13	0.2
Burke Rubber Co	107 S Riverside Dr	Modesto	CA	95354	Rocky Genovese	209-571-6400	S	12*	0.1
Holz Rubber Company Inc	PO Box 241002	Lodi	CA	95241	Edward Marchese	209-368-7171	R	12	0.2
BRC Rubber Group Inc	PO Box 255	Bluffton	IN	46714	Charles V Chaffee	219-824-4501	D	11	0.2
Acro Products Inc	2701 Dwenger Av	Fort Wayne	IN	46803	Charles A Wilson	219-424-1601	R	10	0.1
Allied Baltic Rubber Inc	PO Box 6329	Akron	OH	44312	Allen R Myers	216-699-2216	R	9*	0.1
Ottawa Rubber Co	PO Box 553	Holland	OH	43528	James H Bugert	419-865-1378	R	9	0.1
Specification Rubber Products	PO Box 568	Alabaster	AL	35007	PL Robertson	205-663-2521	S	9	0.1
Regal International Inc	PO Box 1237	Corsicana	TX	75151	Janak N Desai	903-872-3091	P	9	<0.1
Carmi Molded Rubber Products	1720 W Main St	Carmi	IL	62821	Terrance Friedman	618-382-2318	S	8*	0.1
Vernay Manufacturing Inc	PO Box 759	Griffin	GA	30224	Thomas W Allen	404-228-6291	S	8	<0.1
Kismet Products Inc	PO Box 306	Painesville	OH	44077	Dennis W Lawrance	216-352-3119	R	7	<0.1
Plas-Tec Corp	601 W Indiana St	Edon	OH	43518	PA Jones	419-272-2731	R	7	0.1
Imco Inc	PO Box 444	Huntington	IN	46750	Raymond N Meyers	219-356-4810	R	7	0.1
Airex Rubber Products Corp	PO Box 247	Portland	CT	06480	James O Hetrick Jr	203-342-0850	R	6	<0.1
Ro-Lab American Rubber	PO Box 450	Tracy	CA	95378	Henry P Wright	209-836-0965	R	6	<0.1
Rubber Rolls Inc	PO Box 398	Meadow Lands	PA	15347	Frank J Kelly Jr	412-225-9240	S	6*	<0.1
Santa Fe Rubber Products Inc	12306 Washington	Whittier	CA	90606	William Krames	310-693-2779	R	5	<0.1
Scully Rubber Manufacturing Co	4501 E Lombard St	Baltimore	MD	21224	Gail Schulhoff	410-342-6190	R	5	<0.1
Cardwell International Ltd	PO Box 1105	El Dorado	KS	67042	Art Teichgraeber	316-321-2770	R	4*	<0.1
Harper Rubber Products	PO Box 46	Bethany	CT	06524	David A Harper	203-393-2815	R	4	<0.1
Superior Mold and Die Co	449 N Main St	Munroe Falls	OH	44262	Richard Yamokoski	216-688-8251	R	3*	<0.1
Associated Rubber Inc	PO Box 520	Quakertown	PA	18951	BR Henderson	215-536-2800	R	3	<0.1
Axil Corp	PO Box 98	South Plainfield	NJ	07080	Marc Sanders	908-754-8100	R	3	<0.1
California Gasket & Rubber	PO Box 1037	Gardena	CA	90249	S Franklin	310-323-4250	R	3	<0.1
Cycletech Inc	PO Box 428	Hudson	NY	12534	David M Guido	518-822-0436	R	3*	<0.1
Minisink Rubber Company Inc	PO Box 359	Unionville	NY	10988	Peter Pappas	914-726-3311	R	3	<0.1
Lehigh Rubber Works Inc	32 W Bridge St	Morrisville	PA	19067	HP Moran	215-295-5059	R	2	<0.1
Bell Petroleum Services Inc	2047 Commerce Dr	Midland	TX	79702	Jack Thompson	915-694-9653	S	2*	<0.1
Bobber Products Company Inc	PO Box 3175	Fullerton	CA	92631	MR McCollum	714-879-9988	R	2	<0.1
Gordon Rubber and Packing	PO Box 298	Derby	CT	06418	SR Nichols	203-735-7441	R	2*	<0.1
ARC Rubber Inc	100 Water St	Geneva	OH	44041	Robert Johnson Sr	216-466-4555	R	1	<0.1
National Cycle Inc	2200 Maywood Dr	Maywood	IL	60153	Barry Willey	708-343-0400	D	1*	<0.1
Wefco Rubber Mfg Corp	1655 Euclid St	Santa Monica	CA	90404	Peter Stigers	310-393-0303	R	1	<0.1
Thona Corp	3915 Research Pk	Ann Arbor	MI	48108	Sam Jyawook	313-668-6900	R	1*	<0.1

Source: *Ward's Business Directory of U.S. Private and Public Companies*, Volumes 1 and 2, 1996. The company type code used is as follows: P - Public, R - Private, S - Subsidiary, D - Division, J - Joint Venture, A - Affiliate, G - Group. Sales are in millions of dollars, employees are in thousands. An asterisk (*) indicates an estimated sales volume. The symbol < stands for 'less than'. Company names and addresses are truncated, in some cases, to fit into the available space.

MATERIALS CONSUMED

Material	Quantity	Delivered Cost ($ million)
Materials, ingredients, containers, and supplies	(X)	1,775.7
Natural latex rubber (dry solids content)	(X)	11.1
Natural dry rubber	(X)	23.1
Plastics resins consumed in the form of granules, pellets, powders, liquids, etc.	(X)	17.4
Polyurethane elastomers and plastics (except thermoplastics)	(X)	4.4
Thermoplastic polyurethane elastomers	(X)	13.6
SBR-type synthetic rubber	(X)	48.7
Polychloroprene-type synthetic rubber	(X)	12.3
Nitrile type (butadiene-acrylonitrile) synthetic rubber	(X)	11.4
Ethylene-propylene type plastics and synthetic rubber	(X)	25.1

Continued on next page.

MATERIALS CONSUMED - Continued

Material	Quantity	Delivered Cost ($ million)
Other plastics materials and synthetic resins	(X)	75.6
Reclaimed rubber, excluding mud and crumb or ground scrap	(X)	4.3
Rubber compounds and mixtures purchased (dry rubber solids content)	(X)	240.2
All other fabricated rubber products	(X)	80.5
Rubber processing chemicals (accelerators, antioxidants, blowing agents, inhibitors, peptizers, etc.)	(X)	45.8
Plasticizers	(X)	6.1
All other industrial organic chemicals	(X)	13.4
Carbon black	(X)	34.0
Inorganic pigments	(X)	3.0
Plastics products consumed in the form of sheets, rods, tubes, film, and other shapes	(X)	56.2
Fabricated metal products (except castings and forgings)	(X)	179.6
Iron and steel castings	(X)	18.0
Forgings	(X)	6.8
Steel wire	(X)	23.2
All other steel shapes and forms (except castings, forgings, and fabricated metal products)	(X)	67.2
Nonferrous shapes and forms (except castings, forgings, and fabricated metal products)	(X)	6.4
Fabrics, except tire fabrics (including cotton, nylon, polyester, and rayon)	(X)	17.8
Paper and paperboard containers, including shipping sacks and other paper packaging supplies	(X)	22.6
All other materials and components, parts, containers, and supplies	(X)	383.3
Materials, ingredients, containers, and supplies, nsk	(X)	324.7

Source: 1992 *Economic Census*. Explanation of symbols used: (D): Withheld to avoid disclosure of competitive data; na: Not available; (S): Withheld because statistical norms were not met; (X): Not applicable; (Z): Less than half the unit shown; nec: Not elsewhere classified; nsk: Not specified by kind; - : zero; * : 10-19 percent estimated; ** : 20-29 percent estimated.

PRODUCT SHARE DETAILS

Product or Product Class	% Share
Mechanical rubber goods	100.00
Molded rubber mechanical goods, automotive	37.65
Molded rubber mechanical goods, transportation (except automotive) and off-highway machinery and equipment	6.32
Other molded rubber mechanical goods	21.73
Extruded rubber mechanical goods, automotive (except tubing)	16.13
Other extruded rubber mechanical goods, except automotive	9.59
Lathe-cut rubber mechanical goods, automotive and transportation (including on-and off-the-road, and gasoline and diesel equipment)	1.51
Other lathe-cut rubber mechanical goods, except automotive	1.12
Mechanical rubber goods, nsk	5.95

Source: 1992 *Economic Census*. The values shown are percent of total shipments in an industry. Values of indented subcategories are summed in the main heading. The symbol (D) appears when data are withheld to prevent disclosure of competitive information. The abbreviation nsk stands for 'not specified by kind' and nec for 'not elsewhere classified'.

INPUTS AND OUTPUTS FOR FABRICATED RUBBER PRODUCTS, NEC

Economic Sector or Industry Providing Inputs	%	Sector	Economic Sector or Industry Buying Outputs	%	Sector
Synthetic rubber	16.9	Manufg.	Motor vehicles & car bodies	14.3	Manufg.
Noncomparable imports	7.4	Foreign	Personal consumption expenditures	8.0	
Wholesale trade	6.4	Trade	Hospitals	5.7	Services
Cyclic crudes and organics	6.0	Manufg.	Federal Government purchases, national defense	5.5	Fed Govt
Imports	5.2	Foreign	S/L Govt. purch., public assistance & relief	4.6	S/L Govt
Electric services (utilities)	3.8	Util.	Exports	4.0	Foreign
Fabricated rubber products, nec	3.6	Manufg.	Oil field machinery	2.9	Manufg.
Broadwoven fabric mills	3.5	Manufg.	Motor vehicle parts & accessories	2.6	Manufg.
Motor freight transportation & warehousing	3.5	Util.	Tires & inner tubes	2.5	Manufg.
Miscellaneous fabricated wire products	3.3	Manufg.	Shoes, except rubber	2.4	Manufg.
Carbon black	2.6	Manufg.	Fabricated rubber products, nec	2.1	Manufg.
Petroleum refining	2.5	Manufg.	Floor coverings	2.1	Manufg.
Metal stampings, nec	2.3	Manufg.	Pens & mechanical pencils	1.5	Manufg.
Advertising	2.2	Services	S/L Govt. purch., health & hospitals	1.5	S/L Govt
Plastics materials & resins	2.1	Manufg.	Miscellaneous plastics products	1.3	Manufg.
Gas production & distribution (utilities)	1.9	Util.	Paper mills, except building paper	1.3	Manufg.
Nonmetallic mineral products, nec	1.6	Manufg.	Coal	1.1	Mining
Screw machine and related products	1.6	Manufg.	Rubber & plastics hose & belting	1.1	Manufg.
Railroads & related services	1.4	Util.	Surgical & medical instruments	1.1	Manufg.
Miscellaneous plastics products	1.2	Manufg.	Mattresses & bedsprings	0.9	Manufg.
Paperboard containers & boxes	1.1	Manufg.	Rubber & plastics footwear	0.8	Manufg.
Banking	1.1	Fin/R.E.	Federal Government purchases, nondefense	0.8	Fed Govt
Blast furnaces & steel mills	0.9	Manufg.	Pumps & compressors	0.7	Manufg.
Industrial inorganic chemicals, nec	0.9	Manufg.	Aircraft & missile engines & engine parts	0.6	Manufg.
Inorganic pigments	0.9	Manufg.	Aircraft & missile equipment, nec	0.6	Manufg.
Iron & steel foundries	0.9	Manufg.	Electronic components nec	0.6	Manufg.
Maintenance of nonfarm buildings nec	0.8	Constr.	Radio & TV communication equipment	0.6	Manufg.
Communications, except radio & TV	0.8	Util.	Sporting & athletic goods, nec	0.6	Manufg.
Eating & drinking places	0.8	Trade	Upholstered household furniture	0.6	Manufg.
Chemical preparations, nec	0.7	Manufg.	Water transportation	0.6	Util.

Continued on next page.

INPUTS AND OUTPUTS FOR FABRICATED RUBBER PRODUCTS, NEC - Continued

Economic Sector or Industry Providing Inputs	%	Sector	Economic Sector or Industry Buying Outputs	%	Sector
Engineering, architectural, & surveying services	0.7	Services	Residential additions/alterations, nonfarm	0.5	Constr.
Equipment rental & leasing services	0.7	Services	Farm machinery & equipment	0.5	Manufg.
Sanitary services, steam supply, irrigation	0.6	Util.	Narrow fabric mills	0.5	Manufg.
Water transportation	0.6	Util.	Paperboard mills	0.5	Manufg.
Real estate	0.6	Fin/R.E.	Semiconductors & related devices	0.5	Manufg.
Business services nec	0.6	Services	Storage batteries	0.5	Manufg.
U.S. Postal Service	0.6	Gov't	Surgical appliances & supplies	0.5	Manufg.
Machinery, except electrical, nec	0.5	Manufg.	Tanks & tank components	0.5	Manufg.
Adhesives & sealants	0.4	Manufg.	Automotive rental & leasing, without drivers	0.5	Services
Royalties	0.4	Fin/R.E.	Engineering, architectural, & surveying services	0.5	Services
Automotive rental & leasing, without drivers	0.4	Services	Medical & health services, nec	0.5	Services
Commercial printing	0.3	Manufg.	Residential 1-unit structures, nonfarm	0.4	Constr.
Lubricating oils & greases	0.3	Manufg.	Adhesives & sealants	0.4	Manufg.
Reclaimed rubber	0.3	Manufg.	Apparel made from purchased materials	0.4	Manufg.
Air transportation	0.3	Util.	Drugs	0.4	Manufg.
Automotive repair shops & services	0.3	Services	Mechanical measuring devices	0.4	Manufg.
Computer & data processing services	0.3	Services	Photographic equipment & supplies	0.4	Manufg.
Legal services	0.3	Services	Pipe, valves, & pipe fittings	0.4	Manufg.
Management & consulting services & labs	0.3	Services	Primary batteries, dry & wet	0.4	Manufg.
Alkalies & chlorine	0.2	Manufg.	Communications, except radio & TV	0.4	Util.
Nonwoven fabrics	0.2	Manufg.	Maintenance of nonfarm buildings nec	0.3	Constr.
Paper coating & glazing	0.2	Manufg.	Nonfarm residential structure maintenance	0.3	Constr.
Special dies & tools & machine tool accessories	0.2	Manufg.	Aircraft	0.3	Manufg.
Insurance carriers	0.2	Fin/R.E.	Electronic computing equipment	0.3	Manufg.
Accounting, auditing & bookkeeping	0.2	Services	Engineering & scientific instruments	0.3	Manufg.
Clay, ceramic, & refractory minerals	0.1	Mining	Glass & glass products, except containers	0.3	Manufg.
Die-cut paper & board	0.1	Manufg.	Logging camps & logging contractors	0.3	Manufg.
Manifold business forms	0.1	Manufg.	Metal household furniture	0.3	Manufg.
Retail trade, except eating & drinking	0.1	Trade	Miscellaneous fabricated wire products	0.3	Manufg.
Business/professional associations	0.1	Services	Nonferrous wire drawing & insulating	0.3	Manufg.
State & local government enterprises, nec	0.1	Gov't	Paper coating & glazing	0.3	Manufg.
			Printing trades machinery	0.3	Manufg.
			Pulp mills	0.3	Manufg.
			Refrigeration & heating equipment	0.3	Manufg.
			Truck trailers	0.3	Manufg.
			Wiring devices	0.3	Manufg.
			Retail trade, except eating & drinking	0.3	Trade
			Colleges, universities, & professional schools	0.3	Services
			Gross private fixed investment	0.3	Cap Inv
			S/L Govt. purch., fire	0.3	S/L Govt
			Asbestos products	0.2	Manufg.
			Automotive stampings	0.2	Manufg.
			Construction machinery & equipment	0.2	Manufg.
			Environmental controls	0.2	Manufg.
			General industrial machinery, nec	0.2	Manufg.
			Hardware, nec	0.2	Manufg.
			House slippers	0.2	Manufg.
			Household appliances, nec	0.2	Manufg.
			Industrial controls	0.2	Manufg.
			Manufacturing industries, nec	0.2	Manufg.
			Metal cans	0.2	Manufg.
			Metal office furniture	0.2	Manufg.
			Motors & generators	0.2	Manufg.
			Power transmission equipment	0.2	Manufg.
			Special industry machinery, nec	0.2	Manufg.
			Wholesale trade	0.2	Trade
			Beauty & barber shops	0.2	Services
			Nursing & personal care facilities	0.2	Services
			S/L Govt. purch., police	0.2	S/L Govt
			Office buildings	0.1	Constr.
			Residential garden apartments	0.1	Constr.
			Cold finishing of steel shapes	0.1	Manufg.
			Engine electrical equipment	0.1	Manufg.
			Felt goods, nec	0.1	Manufg.
			Gaskets, packing & sealing devices	0.1	Manufg.
			Household cooking equipment	0.1	Manufg.
			Household laundry equipment	0.1	Manufg.
			Industrial furnaces & ovens	0.1	Manufg.
			Lawn & garden equipment	0.1	Manufg.
			Marking devices	0.1	Manufg.
			Plumbing fixture fittings & trim	0.1	Manufg.
			Radio & TV receiving sets	0.1	Manufg.
			Railroad equipment	0.1	Manufg.
			Service industry machines, nec	0.1	Manufg.
			Switchgear & switchboard apparatus	0.1	Manufg.

Continued on next page.

INPUTS AND OUTPUTS FOR FABRICATED RUBBER PRODUCTS, NEC - Continued

Economic Sector or Industry Providing Inputs	%	Sector	Economic Sector or Industry Buying Outputs	%	Sector
			Telephone & telegraph apparatus	0.1	Manufg.
			Textile machinery	0.1	Manufg.
			Electrical repair shops	0.1	Services
			Elementary & secondary schools	0.1	Services
			S/L Govt. purch., higher education	0.1	S/L Govt

Source: Benchmark Input-Output Accounts for the U.S. Economy, 1982, U.S. Department of Commerce, Washington, D.C., July 1991. Data, as reported in the source, are organized by the 1977 SIC structure in use in 1982 but have been matched, as closely as is possible, to the 1987 SIC structure used in this book.

OCCUPATIONS EMPLOYED BY SIC 306 - RUBBER PRODUCTS AND PLASTIC HOSE AND FOOTWEAR

Occupation	% of Total 1994	Change to 2005	Occupation	% of Total 1994	Change to 2005
Assemblers, fabricators, & hand workers nec	11.9	0.3	Machine forming operators, metal & plastic	1.9	0.3
Extruding & forming machine workers	11.1	-29.8	Freight, stock, & material movers, hand	1.8	-19.8
Inspectors, testers, & graders, precision	5.1	0.3	Traffic, shipping, & receiving clerks	1.8	-3.5
Machine operators nec	4.9	-11.6	Industrial machinery mechanics	1.8	10.3
Blue collar worker supervisors	4.8	-5.6	Metal & plastic machine workers nec	1.6	-11.1
Cutters & trimmers, hand	3.7	10.3	Maintenance repairers, general utility	1.5	-9.7
Plastic molding machine workers	3.5	0.3	Industrial production managers	1.4	0.3
Hand packers & packagers	2.9	-14.1	Machinists	1.4	0.3
Cutting & slicing machine setters, operators	2.8	-9.8	Secretaries, ex legal & medical	1.3	-8.7
Helpers, laborers, & material movers nec	2.7	0.3	Machine feeders & offbearers	1.2	-9.8
Crushing & mixing machine operators	2.6	-9.8	Industrial truck & tractor operators	1.1	0.3
General managers & top executives	2.2	-4.9	Bookkeeping, accounting, & auditing clerks	1.0	-24.8

Source: Industry-Occupation Matrix, Bureau of Labor Statistics. These data relate to one or more 3-digit SIC industry groups rather than to a single 4-digit SIC. The change reported for each occupation to the year 2005 is a percent of growth or decline as estimated by the Bureau of Labor Statistics. The abbreviation nec stands for 'not elsewhere classified'.

LOCATION BY STATE AND REGIONAL CONCENTRATION

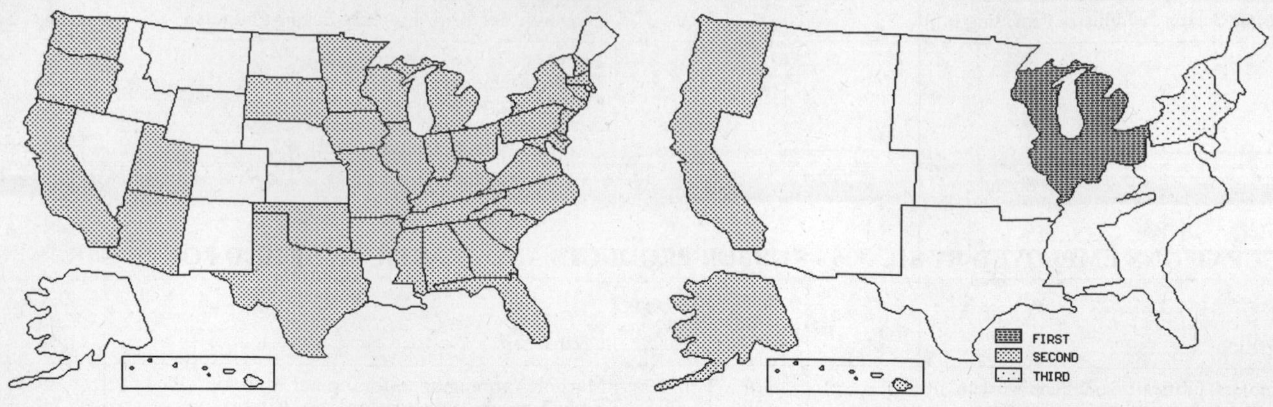

INDUSTRY DATA BY STATE

State	Establish-ments	Shipments			Employment				Cost as % of Shipments	Investment per Employee ($)
		Total ($ mil)	% of U.S.	Per Establ.	Total Number	% of U.S.	Per Establ.	Wages ($/hour)		
Ohio	99	1,040.8	22.9	10.5	9,300	19.2	94	11.78	50.8	2,591
Indiana	52	670.8	14.8	12.9	7,300	15.1	140	9.98	41.4	4,671
Michigan	41	309.9	6.8	7.6	2,700	5.6	66	8.88	47.0	3,037
Tennessee	17	294.5	6.5	17.3	3,300	6.8	194	8.27	45.3	5,364
California	62	204.2	4.5	3.3	2,700	5.6	44	9.84	42.2	2,481
North Carolina	19	174.6	3.8	9.2	2,000	4.1	105	9.41	47.4	2,700
Pennsylvania	28	163.7	3.6	5.8	1,800	3.7	64	15.52	30.7	2,833
Texas	46	134.9	3.0	2.9	1,700	3.5	37	9.07	50.5	2,706
Arkansas	8	122.2	2.7	15.3	1,300	2.7	163	9.63	39.8	2,769
Wisconsin	13	101.7	2.2	7.8	1,400	2.9	108	8.39	29.4	2,857
New Jersey	26	97.2	2.1	3.7	1,100	2.3	42	10.06	36.8	2,545
Minnesota	15	92.4	2.0	6.2	1,100	2.3	73	12.40	39.3	3,273
Virginia	7	88.7	2.0	12.7	1,200	2.5	171	9.56	46.6	2,000
Massachusetts	14	85.9	1.9	6.1	1,000	2.1	71	10.00	51.1	3,500
Connecticut	16	83.1	1.8	5.2	1,000	2.1	63	10.53	36.3	2,700
New York	17	60.0	1.3	3.5	600	1.2	35	9.89	39.2	5,333
Georgia	11	59.4	1.3	5.4	700	1.4	64	7.83	47.3	3,143
Alabama	14	50.7	1.1	3.6	500	1.0	36	9.50	39.4	-
Oklahoma	10	49.6	1.1	5.0	700	1.4	70	8.22	31.7	-
Florida	11	45.6	1.0	4.1	600	1.2	55	8.10	42.3	500
South Carolina	8	33.6	0.7	4.2	200	0.4	25	11.33	42.3	3,000
Oregon	12	24.7	0.5	2.1	300	0.6	25	7.80	32.4	1,000
Maryland	6	24.1	0.5	4.0	300	0.6	50	8.60	42.7	-
Mississippi	8	20.6	0.5	2.6	300	0.6	38	6.25	51.9	-
Arizona	5	12.7	0.3	2.5	200	0.4	40	8.33	26.8	2,500
Missouri	7	11.3	0.2	1.6	100	0.2	14	8.50	34.5	1,000
Washington	5	7.4	0.2	1.5	100	0.2	20	8.00	41.9	1,000
Illinois	35	(D)	-	-	1,750 *	3.6	50	-	-	3,257
Iowa	6	(D)	-	-	1,750 *	3.6	292	-	-	-
Kentucky	4	(D)	-	-	375 *	0.8	94	-	-	2,667
New Hampshire	4	(D)	-	-	375 *	0.8	94	-	-	-
Delaware	2	(D)	-	-	750 *	1.5	375	-	-	-
Utah	2	(D)	-	-	175 *	0.4	88	-	-	-
South Dakota	1	(D)	-	-	375 *	0.8	375	-	-	-

Source: 1992 *Economic Census*. The states are in descending order of shipments or establishments (if shipment data are missing for the majority). The symbol (D) appears when data are withheld to prevent disclosure of competitive information. States marked with (D) are sorted by number of establishments. A dash (-) indicates that the data element cannot be calculated; * indicates the midpoint of a range.

3069 - FABRICATED RUBBER PRODUCTS, NEC

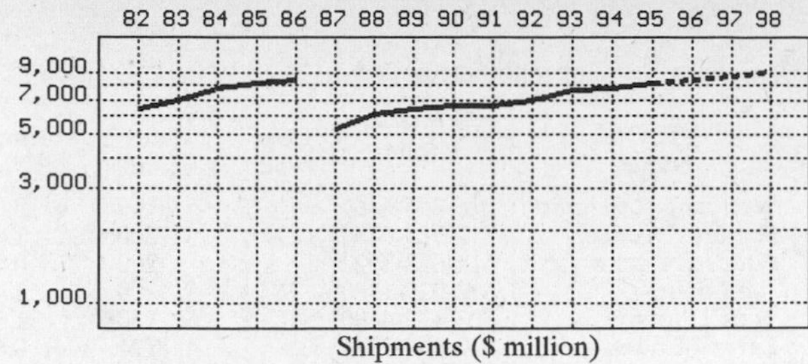

Shipments ($ million)

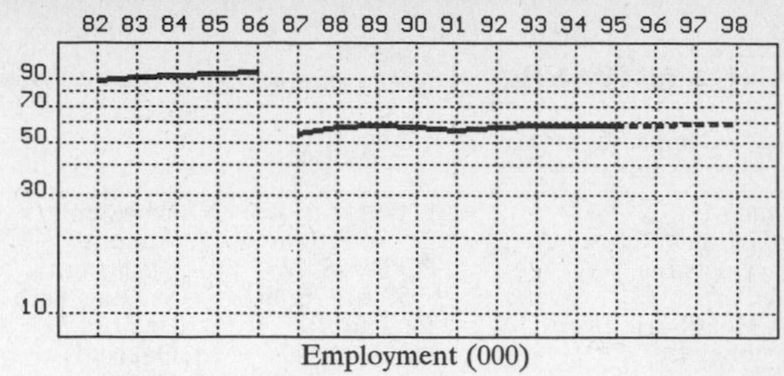

Employment (000)

GENERAL STATISTICS

Year	Com-panies	Establishments: Total	Establishments: with 20 or more employees	Employment: Total (000)	Production Workers (000)	Production Hours (Mil)	Compensation: Payroll ($ mil)	Compensation: Wages ($/hr)	Production ($ million): Cost of Materials	Value Added by Manufacture	Value of Shipments	Capital Invest.
1982	1,213	1,380	686	89.4	66.3	128.8	1,561.1	7.69	3,132.0	3,212.6	6,365.7	219.3
1983				91.2	68.2	135.5	1,685.0	7.93	3,453.0	3,584.3	7,002.7	172.5
1984				92.4	70.0	141.9	1,836.9	8.45	3,941.3	3,905.4	7,804.4	238.0
1985				94.3	70.7	143.2	1,975.1	8.76	4,095.5	4,067.7	8,119.2	256.0
1986				95.7	71.3	143.2	2,057.0	9.05	4,104.3	4,211.6	8,325.7	240.2
1987*	869	1,007	458	54.3	40.6	83.1	1,149.8	8.68	2,668.1	2,600.1	5,263.7	139.6
1988		1,024	501	57.2	43.2	88.4	1,301.9	9.28	3,145.4	3,010.3	6,123.8	167.2
1989		1,008	498	58.7	44.0	88.7	1,244.9	9.15	3,365.7	3,037.9	6,343.1	212.1
1990		998	509	57.3	43.6	87.4	1,252.8	9.30	3,495.6	3,139.1	6,629.0	181.9
1991		1,035	521	55.8	42.6	82.9	1,278.1	9.84	3,334.0	3,296.9	6,644.1	160.3
1992	984	1,131	523	57.3	42.1	85.1	1,413.9	10.08	3,460.0	3,464.6	6,934.0	204.2
1993		1,139	516	58.4	43.4	89.5	1,483.5	10.33	3,874.1	3,727.6	7,608.2	222.1
1994		1,140P	538P	57.8	43.2	89.7	1,489.8	10.30	3,622.0	4,173.3	7,729.0	226.6
1995		1,163P	547P	58.4P	43.5P	88.8P	1,531.5P	10.69P	3,785.2P	4,361.3P	8,077.2P	234.2P
1996		1,185P	555P	58.7P	43.7P	89.2P	1,577.0P	10.92P	3,932.8P	4,531.5P	8,392.3P	244.1P
1997		1,208P	564P	59.0P	43.8P	89.7P	1,622.5P	11.16P	4,080.5P	4,701.6P	8,707.4P	254.1P
1998		1,231P	573P	59.3P	44.0P	90.1P	1,667.9P	11.40P	4,228.2P	4,871.7P	9,022.5P	264.1P

Sources: 1982, 1987, 1992 *Economic Census*; *Annual Survey of Manufactures*, 83-86, 88-91, 93-94. Establishment counts are from *County Business Patterns* for non-Census years; establishment counts for 83-84 are extrapolations. * indicates that industry content changed in 87; earlier years use 77 SICs. 'P's mark projections.

INDICES OF CHANGE

Year	Com-panies	Establishments: Total	Establishments: with 20 or more employees	Employment: Total (000)	Production Workers (000)	Production Hours (Mil)	Compensation: Payroll ($ mil)	Compensation: Wages ($/hr)	Production ($ million): Cost of Materials	Value Added by Manufacture	Value of Shipments	Capital Invest.
1982	123	122	131	156	157	151	110	76	91	93	92	107
1983				159	162	159	119	79	100	103	101	84
1984				161	166	167	130	84	114	113	113	117
1985				165	168	168	140	87	118	117	117	125
1986				167	169	168	145	90	119	122	120	118
1987*	88	89	88	95	96	98	81	86	77	75	76	68
1988		91	96	100	103	104	92	92	91	87	88	82
1989		89	95	102	105	104	88	91	97	88	91	104
1990		88	97	100	104	103	89	92	101	91	96	89
1991		92	100	97	101	97	90	98	96	95	96	79
1992	100	100	100	100	100	100	100	100	100	100	100	100
1993		101	99	102	103	105	105	102	112	108	110	109
1994		101P	103P	101	103	105	105	102	105	120	111	111
1995		103P	105P	102P	103P	104P	108P	106P	109P	126P	116P	115P
1996		105P	106P	102P	104P	105P	112P	108P	114P	131P	121P	120P
1997		107P	108P	103P	104P	105P	115P	111P	118P	136P	126P	124P
1998		109P	109P	104P	104P	106P	118P	113P	122P	141P	130P	129P

Sources: Same as General Statistics. Values reflect change from the base year, 1992. Values above 100 mean greater than 92, values below 100 mean less than 92, and a value of 100 in the 82-91 or 93-98 period means same as 92. * indicates that industry content changed in 87. Data for earlier years are in 77 SIC format.

SELECTED RATIOS

For 1994	Avg. of All Manufact.	Analyzed Industry	Index	For 1994	Avg. of All Manufact.	Analyzed Industry	Index
Employees per Establishment	49	51	103	Value Added per Production Worker	134,084	96,604	72
Payroll per Establishment	1,500,273	1,307,006	87	Cost per Establishment	5,045,178	3,177,591	63
Payroll per Employee	30,620	25,775	84	Cost per Employee	102,970	62,664	61
Production Workers per Establishment	34	38	110	Cost per Production Worker	146,988	83,843	57
Wages per Establishment	853,319	810,549	95	Shipments per Establishment	9,576,895	6,780,674	71
Wages per Production Worker	24,861	21,387	86	Shipments per Employee	195,460	133,720	68
Hours per Production Worker	2,056	2,076	101	Shipments per Production Worker	279,017	178,912	64
Wages per Hour	12.09	10.30	85	Investment per Establishment	321,011	198,797	62
Value Added per Establishment	4,602,255	3,661,248	80	Investment per Employee	6,552	3,920	60
Value Added per Employee	93,930	72,202	77	Investment per Production Worker	9,352	5,245	56

Sources: Same as General Statistics. The 'Average of All Manufacturing' column represents the average of all manufacturing industries reported for the most recent complete year available. The Index shows the relationship between the Average and the Analyzed Industry. For example, 100 means that they are equal; 500 that the Analyzed Industry is five times the average; 50 means that the Analyzed Industry is half the national average. The abbreviation 'na' is used to show that data are 'not available'.

LEADING COMPANIES Number shown: **75** Total sales ($ mil): **5,471** Total employment (000): **47.0**

Company Name	Address				CEO Name	Phone	Co. Type	Sales ($ mil)	Empl. (000)
Rubbermaid Inc	1147 Akron Rd	Wooster	OH	44691	Wolfgang R Schmitt	216-264-6464	P	2,169	13.0
Cooper Tire and Rubber Co	725 W 11th St	Auburn	IN	46706	Robert C Gasser	219-925-0700	D	200	1.9
Pretty Products Inc	PO Box 6002	Coshocton	OH	43812	James R Lockwood	614-622-3522	S	200	0.7
Quadion Corp	5957 W 37th St	St Louis Park	MN	55416	Jim Lande	612-927-1400	R	200	2.4
Tillotson Healthcare Corp	360 Rte 101	Bedford	NH	03110	Tom Tillotson	603-472-6600	R	130*	1.3
Oliver Rubber Co	PO Box 8447	Oakland	CA	94662	Larry J Enders	510-654-7711	S	124	0.6
Carlisle SynTec Systems	PO Box 7000	Carlisle	PA	17013	Kem Scott	717-245-7000	S	110	1.0
Minnesota Rubber Co	3630 Woodale Av	Minneapolis	MN	55416	R W Carlson Jr	612-927-1400	S	100*	1.3
Schlegel Tennessee Inc	1713 Henry G Lane	Maryville	TN	37801	Leo Fuchs	615-984-7600	S	94*	0.9
Safeskin Corp	5100 Town Ctr Cir	Boca Raton	FL	33486	Neil K Braverman	407-395-9988	P	84	2.5
Aladan Corp	PO Box 921548	Norcross	GA	30092	Julian Danielly	404-840-9665	R	77*	0.6
Gleason Corp	10474 Santa Monica	Los Angeles	CA	90025	A Kotler	310-470-6001	R	70*	0.8
Wynn's Precision Inc	Hartmann Dr	Lebanon	TN	37087	John W Huber	615-444-0191	S	70	0.6
General Foam Plastics Corp	3321 E Pr Anne	Norfolk	VA	23502	Burke Zanft	804-857-0153	R	67	0.8
Duramax Inc	16025 Johnson St	Middlefield	OH	44062	Charles Miller Jr	216-632-1611	R	60*	0.7
Thermwell Products Company	150 E 7th St	Paterson	NJ	07524	David B Gerstein	201-684-5000	R	60	0.6
Acadia Polymers Inc	1420 Coulter NW	Roanoke	VA	24012	Pat Malone	703-265-2700	D	55	0.6
Paulstra CRC Corp	460 Fuller NE	Grand Rapids	MI	49501	Yves Huet	616-459-4541	S	55	0.5
Jasper Rubber Products Inc	1010 1st Av	Jasper	IN	47546	AW Place Jr	812-482-3242	R	51	0.6
Stearns Manufacturing Co	PO Box 1498	St Cloud	MN	56302	David G Cook	612-252-1642	S	50	0.8
Vinyl Plastics Inc	PO Box 451	Sheboygan	WI	53082	R Bruce Grover	414-458-4664	R	50	0.3
Utex Industries Inc	10810 Old Katy Rd	Houston	TX	77043	Joel J Pippert	713-467-1000	R	47*	0.5
Rotation Dynamics Corp	15 Salt Creek Ln	Hinsdale	IL	60521	Steve Melgard	708-325-1460	R	45	0.6
Ames Rubber Corp	2347 Ames Blv	Hamburg	NJ	07419	JD Marvil	201-827-9101	S	44	0.4
Eaton Corp	PO Box 1848	Laurinburg	NC	28353	ES Hill	910-276-6901	D	42*	0.4
G and T Industries Inc	3413 Eastern Av SE	Grand Rapids	MI	49508	RH Wood	616-452-8611	R	42*	0.4
American Roller Co	2223 Lakeside Dr	Bannockburn	IL	60015	RL Ditzler	708-295-6750	R	40	0.5
CTI Industries Corp	22160 N Pepper Rd	Barrington	IL	60010	John C Davis	708-382-1000	R	40	0.4
Engineered Fabrics Corp	669 Goodyear St	Rockmart	GA	30153	RC Martin	404-684-7855	S	40	0.5
RM Engineered Products Inc	4854 O'Hear Av	N Charleston	SC	29406	John Halberda	803-744-6261	S	40	0.5
Roppe Corp	PO Box X	Fostoria	OH	44830	Donald P Miller	419-435-8546	R	40	0.3
Air Cruisers Co	PO Box 180	Belmar	NJ	07719	Jose Redento	908-681-3527	S	36*	0.4
Bingham Co	1555 Mittel Dr	Wood Dale	IL	60191	Larry Ekstrom	708-238-4000	R	36	0.4
Rondy and Company Inc	255 Wooster Rd N	Barberton	OH	44203	Donald R Rondy	216-745-9016	R	35	0.3
West American Holding Inc	750 N Main St	Orange	CA	92668	HC Blackerby	714-532-3355	R	34	0.4
West American Rubber	750 N Main St	Orange	CA	92668	Steven R Hemstreet	714-532-3355	S	34	0.4
Plastomer Corp	37819 Schoolcraft	Livonia	MI	48150	Bill Baughman	313-464-0700	R	33	0.3
Bio Clinic Corp	4083 E Airport Dr	Ontario	CA	91761	Brad Nutter	909-391-0041	S	31	0.3
Reeves International	PO Box 1531	Spartanburg	SC	29304	William Lenoci	803-576-9210	D	31	0.2
Mapa Professional	512 E Tiffin St	Willard	OH	44890	Mike Breton	419-933-2211	S	30	0.3
OddzOn Products Inc	PO Box 1590	Campbell	CA	95009	John Banboun	408-379-3906	R	30	<0.1
Koneta Rubber-LRV	PO Box 150	Wapakoneta	OH	45895	Kenneth E Leffel	419-739-4200	D	29	0.3
Mitchell Rubber Products Inc	491 Wilson Way	City of Industry	CA	91744	J Mitchell	818-961-9711	R	26*	0.3
Balsam Corp	727 Goddard Av	Chesterfield	MO	63005	Michael G McGraw	314-530-8200	R	25	0.2
Royal Rubber & Mfg Co	5951 E Firestone	South Gate	CA	90280	Bruce Crenshaw	310-928-3381	R	25	0.2
Waycross Molded Products Inc	PO Box 58	Waycross	GA	31502	Keith Bryant	912-285-1234	S	25*	0.3
Crossville Rubber Products Inc	PO Box 729	Crossville	TN	38557	William Schaffer	615-484-5187	R	24	0.3
Chardon Rubber Co	1776 Hilltop Rd	St Joseph	MI	49085	Jeff W Keener Jr	616-983-7741	D	21*	0.2
Rice Chadwick Rubber Co	PO Box 405	Killbuck	OH	44637	JF Bell	216-276-2801	D	21	0.2
Kitco Inc	PO Box 456	Bluffton	IN	46714	Rhett Burgess	219-824-2700	R	20	0.3
Mid-States Rubber Products Inc	PO Box 370	Princeton	IN	47670	G Richard Eykamp	812-385-3473	R	20	0.3
Rex-Hide Inc	PO Box 4726	Tyler	TX	75712	Warren E Hoeffner	903-593-7387	R	20	0.3
RCA Rubber Co	PO Box 9240	Akron	OH	44305	RT Reiss	216-784-1291	R	20	0.3
Siebe North	PO Box 70729	Charleston	SC	29415	JK Hane	803-745-5900	D	20*	0.7
Wearwell/Tennessee Mat	1414 4th Av S	Nashville	TN	37210	C Gross	615-254-8381	R	20	0.1
Lavelle Industries Inc	665 McHenry St	Burlington	WI	53105	Rhonda Sullivan	414-763-2434	R	19	0.2
Neff-Perkins Co	3715 Parmly Rd	Perry	OH	44081	Robert A Elly	216-259-5051	R	19	0.3
Vulcan International Corp	300 Delaware Av	Wilmington	DE	19801	Benjamin Gettler	302-427-5804	P	18	0.2
Buckeye Rubber Products Inc	PO Box 389	Lima	OH	45802	Norma Rakowsky	419-228-4441	R	18	0.2
Sponge-Cushion Inc	PO Box 709	Morris	IL	60450	Frank Raus	815-942-2300	R	18	0.1
Syracuse Rubber Products	501 Sycamore St	Syracuse	IN	46567	Larry Smith	219-457-3141	S	18*	0.3
Vulcan Corp	PO Box 709	Clarksville	TN	37041	Edward Ritter	615-645-6431	D	17	0.3
Wisconsin Pharmacal Company	1 Repel Rd	Jackson	WI	53037	John A Wundrock	414-677-4121	P	16	<0.1
Kirkhill Inc	12021 S Woodruff	Downey	CA	90241	Robert E Harold	310-803-3421	R	16	0.2
Monarch Rubber Company Inc	3500 Pulaski Hwy	Baltimore	MD	21224	David M Schwaber	410-342-8510	R	16	0.2
Ronsil Rubber	PO Box 72	Blackstone	VA	23824	Harry Newton	804-292-1600	D	16	0.2
Roxanne of New Jersey Inc	1109 9th Av	Neptune	NJ	07753	Irving Engel	908-775-7137	S	16*	0.2
Superior Manufacturing Group	7171 W 65th St	Chicago	IL	60638	John V Wood	708-458-4600	R	16	0.2
Aldan Rubber Co	2701 E Tioga St	Philadelphia	PA	19134	Barry Fleischer	215-739-6500	R	15	0.2
Ashtabula Rubber Co	2751 West Av	Ashtabula	OH	44004	JN Jammal	216-992-2195	R	15	0.2
Dynex Inc	101 Expansion Joint	Savannah	GA	31405	Thomas R Brown	912-944-0100	R	15	<0.1
Foamex LP	PO Box 1210	Cape Girardeau	MO	63702	Gary Morningstar	314-334-5236	D	15*	<0.1
Ludlow Composites Corp	2100 Commerce Dr	Fremont	OH	43420	RJ Moran	419-332-5531	R	15	0.1
Mold Ex Rubber Co	8052 Armstrong Rd	Milton	FL	32583	Tom W Henry	904-626-7211	R	15*	0.2
Parker Hannifin Corp	PO Box 15009	Spartanburg	SC	29302	Dale Burnett	803-573-7332	D	15	0.2

Source: *Ward's Business Directory of U.S. Private and Public Companies*, Volumes 1 and 2, 1996. The company type code used is as follows: P - Public, R - Private, S - Subsidiary, D - Division, J - Joint Venture, A - Affiliate, G - Group. Sales are in millions of dollars, employees are in thousands. An asterisk (*) indicates an estimated sales volume. The symbol < stands for 'less than'. Company names and addresses are truncated, in some cases, to fit into the available space.

MATERIALS CONSUMED

Material	Quantity	Delivered Cost ($ million)
Materials, ingredients, containers, and supplies	(X)	3,060.5
Natural latex rubber (dry solids content)	(X)	135.6
Natural dry rubber	(X)	89.9
Plastics resins consumed in the form of granules, pellets, powders, liquids, etc.	(X)	82.7
Polyurethane elastomers and plastics (except thermoplastics)	(X)	66.0
Thermoplastic polyurethane elastomers	(X)	23.5
SBR-type synthetic rubber	(X)	85.3
Polychloroprene-type synthetic rubber	(X)	49.3
Nitrile type (butadiene-acrylonitrile) synthetic rubber	(X)	62.7
Ethylene-propylene type plastics and synthetic rubber	(X)	125.9
Other plastics materials and synthetic resins	(X)	256.4
Reclaimed rubber, excluding mud and crumb or ground scrap	(X)	15.4
Rubber compounds and mixtures purchased (dry rubber solids content)	(X)	135.6
All other fabricated rubber products	(X)	59.1
Rubber processing chemicals (accelerators, antioxidants, blowing agents, inhibitors, peptizers, etc.)	(X)	172.0
Plasticizers	(X)	46.4
All other industrial organic chemicals	(X)	123.2
Carbon black	(X)	85.7
Inorganic pigments	(X)	20.3
Plastics products consumed in the form of sheets, rods, tubes, film, and other shapes	(X)	28.0
Fabricated metal products (except castings and forgings)	(X)	123.9
Iron and steel castings	(X)	(D)
Forgings	(X)	(D)
Steel wire	(X)	1.2
All other steel shapes and forms (except castings, forgings, and fabricated metal products)	(X)	(D)
Nonferrous shapes and forms (except castings, forgings, and fabricated metal products)	(X)	0.9
Fabrics, except tire fabrics (including cotton, nylon, polyester, and rayon)	(X)	163.9
Paper and paperboard containers, including shipping sacks and other paper packaging supplies	(X)	51.3
All other materials and components, parts, containers, and supplies	(X)	499.5
Materials, ingredients, containers, and supplies, nsk	(X)	524.2

Source: 1992 *Economic Census*. Explanation of symbols used: (D): Withheld to avoid disclosure of competitive data; na: Not available; (S): Withheld because statistical norms were not met; (X): Not applicable; (Z): Less than half the unit shown; nec: Not elsewhere classified; nsk: Not specified by kind; - : zero; * : 10-19 percent estimated; ** : 20-29 percent estimated.

PRODUCT SHARE DETAILS

Product or Product Class	% Share
Fabricated rubber products, nec	100.00
Rubber sponge, expanded and foam rubber products	14.86
Latex foam, for automotive applications	6.78
Latex foam, for upholstery (sheet and slab stock)	3.53
Latex foam, for carpet and rug cushions	6.39
Other latex foam products (including clothing, insulation and padding, hospital padding, and topper pads)	17.75
Chemically blown open cell rubber sponge for carpet and rug cushions	6.19
Chemically blown open cell rubber sponge for automotive applications	3.27
Chemically blown open cell rubber sponge for other uses	16.81
Chemically blown closed cell rubber sponge for automotive applications	13.33
Chemically blown closed cell rubber sponge for appliances, air-conditioning, and refrigeration	6.58
Chemically blown closed cell rubber sponge for construction applications	2.06
Chemically blown closed cell rubber sponge for other uses	12.11
Sponge, expanded and foam rubber products, nsk	5.21
Rubber floor and wall coverings	6.63
Rubber floor mats, matting, and stair treads, in rolls	13.93
Individual rubber automotive floor mats and matting	71.16
Other rubber floor and wall coverings (including cove base, wainscotting, etc.)	14.88
Prophylactics	3.12
Rubber shoe products, elastomer resin	2.12
Rubber shoe heels and soles	36.79
Rubber shoe soling slabs and top lift sheets	36.71
Rubber shoe unit soles (sole and heel combinations)	25.86
Shoe products, rubber, elastomer resin, nsk	0.71
Rubber druggist and medical sundries, including household gloves	7.94
Rubber nipples and pacifiers	(D)
Rubber household gloves (including rubberized)	(D)
Rubber surgical gloves (including rubberized)	43.99
Other rubber druggist and medical sundries (including diaphragms, ice bags, caps, water bottles, fountain syringes, and combinations)	36.55
Rubber druggist and medical sundries, including household gloves, nsk	4.39
Rubber compounds or mixtures for sale or interplant transfer	18.28
Industrial rubber products, nec	18.59
Graphics arts roll coverings, rubber and plastics (printing trade)	8.88
Paper mill roll coverings, rubber	10.78
Industrial roll coverings, rubber (excluding steel mills and plastics)	4.24
Other roll coverings (including steel mills and plastics)	5.84
Pressure-sensitive tape, rubber-backed (including friction)	4.24
Single-ply rubber membrane roofing	25.11
Vulcanized film and sheet rubber	16.43
Vulcanizable elastomeric linings	2.12
Printers' rubber blankets	10.87
Other industrial rubber products (including jar rings and fuel cells)	7.66
Industrial rubber products, nec, nsk	3.85
Rubber coated fabrics and rubber clothing	5.52
Rubber coated garment and footwear fabrics	6.79
Rubber coated inflatable fabrics	6.29
Other rubber coated fabrics (automotive and furniture upholstery, hospital and crib sheeting, and protective covering fabrics)	26.77
Industrial rubber gloves	24.85
Other rubber clothing (including wet suits, rainwear, aprons, dress shields, baby pants, bathing and shower caps)	18.25
Rubber coated fabrics and rubber clothing, nsk	17.05
Other rubber goods	13.64
Hard rubber battery jars, boxes, and parts	0.58
Other hard rubber mechanical goods	4.40
Reclaimed rubber	2.92
Rubber thread, bare	(D)
Rubber boats, pontoons, and life rafts	6.25
Rubber balloons (toy, advertising, meteorological, etc.)	16.31
Rubber stationer's sundries (including bands, finger cots, and erasers, but excluding pencil plugs)	2.50
Rubber toys (including balls, except balloons and dolls)	4.66
Rubber tank blocks, treads, and band tracks	(D)
Other rubber goods	34.56
Other rubber goods, nsk	1.40
Fabricated rubber products, nec, nsk	9.29

Source: 1992 *Economic Census*. The values shown are percent of total shipments in an industry. Values of indented subcategories are summed in the main heading. The symbol (D) appears when data are withheld to prevent disclosure of competitive information. The abbreviation nsk stands for 'not specified by kind' and nec for 'not elsewhere classified'.

INPUTS AND OUTPUTS FOR FABRICATED RUBBER PRODUCTS, NEC

Economic Sector or Industry Providing Inputs	%	Sector	Economic Sector or Industry Buying Outputs	%	Sector
Synthetic rubber	16.9	Manufg.	Motor vehicles & car bodies	14.3	Manufg.
Noncomparable imports	7.4	Foreign	Personal consumption expenditures	8.0	
Wholesale trade	6.4	Trade	Hospitals	5.7	Services
Cyclic crudes and organics	6.0	Manufg.	Federal Government purchases, national defense	5.5	Fed Govt
Imports	5.2	Foreign	S/L Govt. purch., public assistance & relief	4.6	S/L Govt
Electric services (utilities)	3.8	Util.	Exports	4.0	Foreign
Fabricated rubber products, nec	3.6	Manufg.	Oil field machinery	2.9	Manufg.
Broadwoven fabric mills	3.5	Manufg.	Motor vehicle parts & accessories	2.6	Manufg.
Motor freight transportation & warehousing	3.5	Util.	Tires & inner tubes	2.5	Manufg.
Miscellaneous fabricated wire products	3.3	Manufg.	Shoes, except rubber	2.4	Manufg.
Carbon black	2.6	Manufg.	Fabricated rubber products, nec	2.1	Manufg.
Petroleum refining	2.5	Manufg.	Floor coverings	2.1	Manufg.
Metal stampings, nec	2.3	Manufg.	Pens & mechanical pencils	1.5	Manufg.
Advertising	2.2	Services	S/L Govt. purch., health & hospitals	1.5	S/L Govt
Plastics materials & resins	2.1	Manufg.	Miscellaneous plastics products	1.3	Manufg.
Gas production & distribution (utilities)	1.9	Util.	Paper mills, except building paper	1.3	Manufg.
Nonmetallic mineral products, nec	1.6	Manufg.	Coal	1.1	Mining
Screw machine and related products	1.6	Manufg.	Rubber & plastics hose & belting	1.1	Manufg.
Railroads & related services	1.4	Util.	Surgical & medical instruments	1.1	Manufg.
Miscellaneous plastics products	1.2	Manufg.	Mattresses & bedsprings	0.9	Manufg.
Paperboard containers & boxes	1.1	Manufg.	Rubber & plastics footwear	0.8	Manufg.
Banking	1.1	Fin/R.E.	Federal Government purchases, nondefense	0.8	Fed Govt
Blast furnaces & steel mills	0.9	Manufg.	Pumps & compressors	0.7	Manufg.
Industrial inorganic chemicals, nec	0.9	Manufg.	Aircraft & missile engines & engine parts	0.6	Manufg.
Inorganic pigments	0.9	Manufg.	Aircraft & missile equipment, nec	0.6	Manufg.
Iron & steel foundries	0.9	Manufg.	Electronic components nec	0.6	Manufg.
Maintenance of nonfarm buildings nec	0.8	Constr.	Radio & TV communication equipment	0.6	Manufg.
Communications, except radio & TV	0.8	Util.	Sporting & athletic goods, nec	0.6	Manufg.

Continued on next page.

INPUTS AND OUTPUTS FOR FABRICATED RUBBER PRODUCTS, NEC - Continued

Economic Sector or Industry Providing Inputs	%	Sector	Economic Sector or Industry Buying Outputs	%	Sector
Eating & drinking places	0.8	Trade	Upholstered household furniture	0.6	Manufg.
Chemical preparations, nec	0.7	Manufg.	Water transportation	0.6	Util.
Engineering, architectural, & surveying services	0.7	Services	Residential additions/alterations, nonfarm	0.5	Constr.
Equipment rental & leasing services	0.7	Services	Farm machinery & equipment	0.5	Manufg.
Sanitary services, steam supply, irrigation	0.6	Util.	Narrow fabric mills	0.5	Manufg.
Water transportation	0.6	Util.	Paperboard mills	0.5	Manufg.
Real estate	0.6	Fin/R.E.	Semiconductors & related devices	0.5	Manufg.
Business services nec	0.6	Services	Storage batteries	0.5	Manufg.
U.S. Postal Service	0.6	Gov't	Surgical appliances & supplies	0.5	Manufg.
Machinery, except electrical, nec	0.5	Manufg.	Tanks & tank components	0.5	Manufg.
Adhesives & sealants	0.4	Manufg.	Automotive rental & leasing, without drivers	0.5	Services
Royalties	0.4	Fin/R.E.	Engineering, architectural, & surveying services	0.5	Services
Automotive rental & leasing, without drivers	0.4	Services	Medical & health services, nec	0.5	Services
Commercial printing	0.3	Manufg.	Residential 1-unit structures, nonfarm	0.4	Constr.
Lubricating oils & greases	0.3	Manufg.	Adhesives & sealants	0.4	Manufg.
Reclaimed rubber	0.3	Manufg.	Apparel made from purchased materials	0.4	Manufg.
Air transportation	0.3	Util.	Drugs	0.4	Manufg.
Automotive repair shops & services	0.3	Services	Mechanical measuring devices	0.4	Manufg.
Computer & data processing services	0.3	Services	Photographic equipment & supplies	0.4	Manufg.
Legal services	0.3	Services	Pipe, valves, & pipe fittings	0.4	Manufg.
Management & consulting services & labs	0.3	Services	Primary batteries, dry & wet	0.4	Manufg.
Alkalies & chlorine	0.2	Manufg.	Communications, except radio & TV	0.4	Util.
Nonwoven fabrics	0.2	Manufg.	Maintenance of nonfarm buildings nec	0.3	Constr.
Paper coating & glazing	0.2	Manufg.	Nonfarm residential structure maintenance	0.3	Constr.
Special dies & tools & machine tool accessories	0.2	Manufg.	Aircraft	0.3	Manufg.
Insurance carriers	0.2	Fin/R.E.	Electronic computing equipment	0.3	Manufg.
Accounting, auditing & bookkeeping	0.2	Services	Engineering & scientific instruments	0.3	Manufg.
Clay, ceramic, & refractory minerals	0.1	Mining	Glass & glass products, except containers	0.3	Manufg.
Die-cut paper & board	0.1	Manufg.	Logging camps & logging contractors	0.3	Manufg.
Manifold business forms	0.1	Manufg.	Metal household furniture	0.3	Manufg.
Retail trade, except eating & drinking	0.1	Trade	Miscellaneous fabricated wire products	0.3	Manufg.
Business/professional associations	0.1	Services	Nonferrous wire drawing & insulating	0.3	Manufg.
State & local government enterprises, nec	0.1	Gov't	Paper coating & glazing	0.3	Manufg.
			Printing trades machinery	0.3	Manufg.
			Pulp mills	0.3	Manufg.
			Refrigeration & heating equipment	0.3	Manufg.
			Truck trailers	0.3	Manufg.
			Wiring devices	0.3	Manufg.
			Retail trade, except eating & drinking	0.3	Trade
			Colleges, universities, & professional schools	0.3	Services
			Gross private fixed investment	0.3	Cap Inv
			S/L Govt. purch., fire	0.3	S/L Govt
			Asbestos products	0.2	Manufg.
			Automotive stampings	0.2	Manufg.
			Construction machinery & equipment	0.2	Manufg.
			Environmental controls	0.2	Manufg.
			General industrial machinery, nec	0.2	Manufg.
			Hardware, nec	0.2	Manufg.
			House slippers	0.2	Manufg.
			Household appliances, nec	0.2	Manufg.
			Industrial controls	0.2	Manufg.
			Manufacturing industries, nec	0.2	Manufg.
			Metal cans	0.2	Manufg.
			Metal office furniture	0.2	Manufg.
			Motors & generators	0.2	Manufg.
			Power transmission equipment	0.2	Manufg.
			Special industry machinery, nec	0.2	Manufg.
			Wholesale trade	0.2	Trade
			Beauty & barber shops	0.2	Services
			Nursing & personal care facilities	0.2	Services
			S/L Govt. purch., police	0.2	S/L Govt
			Office buildings	0.1	Constr.
			Residential garden apartments	0.1	Constr.
			Cold finishing of steel shapes	0.1	Manufg.
			Engine electrical equipment	0.1	Manufg.
			Felt goods, nec	0.1	Manufg.
			Gaskets, packing & sealing devices	0.1	Manufg.
			Household cooking equipment	0.1	Manufg.
			Household laundry equipment	0.1	Manufg.
			Industrial furnaces & ovens	0.1	Manufg.
			Lawn & garden equipment	0.1	Manufg.
			Marking devices	0.1	Manufg.
			Plumbing fixture fittings & trim	0.1	Manufg.
			Radio & TV receiving sets	0.1	Manufg.
			Railroad equipment	0.1	Manufg.

Continued on next page.

INPUTS AND OUTPUTS FOR FABRICATED RUBBER PRODUCTS, NEC - Continued

Economic Sector or Industry Providing Inputs	%	Sector	Economic Sector or Industry Buying Outputs	%	Sector
			Service industry machines, nec	0.1	Manufg.
			Switchgear & switchboard apparatus	0.1	Manufg.
			Telephone & telegraph apparatus	0.1	Manufg.
			Textile machinery	0.1	Manufg.
			Electrical repair shops	0.1	Services
			Elementary & secondary schools	0.1	Services
			S/L Govt. purch., higher education	0.1	S/L Govt

Source: Benchmark Input-Output Accounts for the U.S. Economy, 1982, U.S. Department of Commerce, Washington, D.C., July 1991. Data, as reported in the source, are organized by the 1977 SIC structure in use in 1982 but have been matched, as closely as is possible, to the 1987 SIC structure used in this book.

OCCUPATIONS EMPLOYED BY SIC 306 - RUBBER PRODUCTS AND PLASTIC HOSE AND FOOTWEAR

Occupation	% of Total 1994	Change to 2005	Occupation	% of Total 1994	Change to 2005
Assemblers, fabricators, & hand workers nec	11.9	0.3	Machine forming operators, metal & plastic	1.9	0.3
Extruding & forming machine workers	11.1	-29.8	Freight, stock, & material movers, hand	1.8	-19.8
Inspectors, testers, & graders, precision	5.1	0.3	Traffic, shipping, & receiving clerks	1.8	-3.5
Machine operators nec	4.9	-11.6	Industrial machinery mechanics	1.8	10.3
Blue collar worker supervisors	4.8	-5.6	Metal & plastic machine workers nec	1.6	-11.1
Cutters & trimmers, hand	3.7	10.3	Maintenance repairers, general utility	1.5	-9.7
Plastic molding machine workers	3.5	0.3	Industrial production managers	1.4	0.3
Hand packers & packagers	2.9	-14.1	Machinists	1.4	0.3
Cutting & slicing machine setters, operators	2.8	-9.8	Secretaries, ex legal & medical	1.3	-8.7
Helpers, laborers, & material movers nec	2.7	0.3	Machine feeders & offbearers	1.2	-9.8
Crushing & mixing machine operators	2.6	-9.8	Industrial truck & tractor operators	1.1	0.3
General managers & top executives	2.2	-4.9	Bookkeeping, accounting, & auditing clerks	1.0	-24.8

Source: Industry-Occupation Matrix, Bureau of Labor Statistics. These data relate to one or more 3-digit SIC industry groups rather than to a single 4-digit SIC. The change reported for each occupation to the year 2005 is a percent of growth or decline as estimated by the Bureau of Labor Statistics. The abbreviation nec stands for 'not elsewhere classified'.

LOCATION BY STATE AND REGIONAL CONCENTRATION

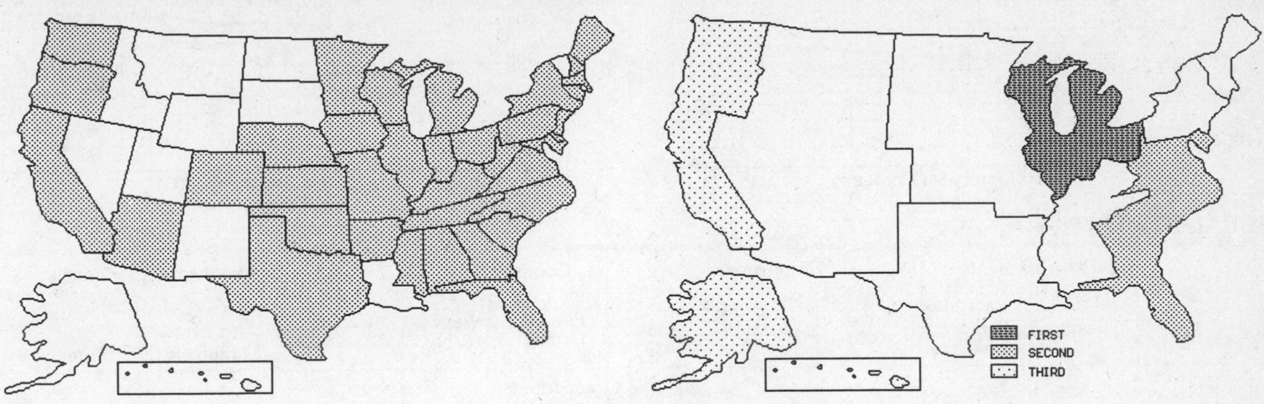

INDUSTRY DATA BY STATE

State	Establish-ments	Shipments			Employment				Cost as % of Shipments	Investment per Employee ($)
		Total ($ mil)	% of U.S.	Per Establ.	Total Number	% of U.S.	Per Establ.	Wages ($/hour)		
Ohio	110	1,155.9	16.7	10.5	8,500	14.8	77	11.25	54.7	3,024
South Carolina	21	614.6	8.9	29.3	3,300	5.8	157	12.64	65.3	5,273
California	134	492.3	7.1	3.7	5,600	9.8	42	9.01	45.0	2,750
North Carolina	40	467.7	6.7	11.7	3,400	5.9	85	9.18	49.6	5,265
Tennessee	31	399.6	5.8	12.9	2,600	4.5	84	10.65	55.6	2,885
Georgia	41	325.6	4.7	7.9	1,800	3.1	44	9.00	57.8	3,556
Pennsylvania	40	304.4	4.4	7.6	2,100	3.7	53	10.72	49.6	3,095
New Jersey	52	240.8	3.5	4.6	2,000	3.5	38	11.04	33.7	2,800
Massachusetts	40	240.2	3.5	6.0	1,700	3.0	43	12.69	51.0	2,824
Arkansas	17	219.1	3.2	12.9	1,400	2.4	82	9.19	50.6	3,571
Illinois	56	218.2	3.1	3.9	1,800	3.1	32	11.44	45.8	3,278
Texas	74	208.8	3.0	2.8	3,100	5.4	42	9.37	35.7	3,871
Missouri	25	179.2	2.6	7.2	1,900	3.3	76	8.63	55.2	1,263
Minnesota	22	165.6	2.4	7.5	1,100	1.9	50	12.13	42.6	8,545
Michigan	47	164.6	2.4	3.5	1,500	2.6	32	9.13	46.7	3,600
Indiana	38	157.5	2.3	4.1	2,000	3.5	53	8.78	45.7	4,900
Virginia	12	157.0	2.3	13.1	1,500	2.6	125	11.32	40.3	4,533
Alabama	10	131.7	1.9	13.2	1,600	2.8	160	8.48	47.6	-
Florida	44	128.9	1.9	2.9	1,300	2.3	30	9.50	37.8	5,846
Wisconsin	24	116.1	1.7	4.8	1,000	1.7	42	10.87	44.8	5,300
New York	37	114.9	1.7	3.1	1,200	2.1	32	8.83	50.4	2,917
Connecticut	16	85.4	1.2	5.3	800	1.4	50	9.33	43.3	2,750
West Virginia	12	75.0	1.1	6.3	600	1.0	50	8.11	52.4	-
Maryland	11	37.7	0.5	3.4	500	0.9	45	8.57	39.3	2,200
Arizona	14	36.5	0.5	2.6	400	0.7	29	10.20	37.8	2,500
Washington	21	34.5	0.5	1.6	400	0.7	19	10.80	32.2	4,750
Kentucky	7	30.3	0.4	4.3	300	0.5	43	8.50	60.1	2,000
Oregon	24	29.4	0.4	1.2	300	0.5	13	9.00	41.8	3,333
Maine	6	13.4	0.2	2.2	200	0.3	33	6.67	59.7	1,000
Mississippi	20	(D)	-	-	1,750 *	3.1	88	-	-	-
Colorado	11	(D)	-	-	175 *	0.3	16	-	-	1,714
New Hampshire	10	(D)	-	-	375 *	0.7	38	-	-	-
Oklahoma	10	(D)	-	-	175 *	0.3	18	-	-	-
Delaware	6	(D)	-	-	175 *	0.3	29	-	-	-
Iowa	5	(D)	-	-	175 *	0.3	35	-	-	-
Kansas	4	(D)	-	-	175 *	0.3	44	-	-	-
Nebraska	3	(D)	-	-	375 *	0.7	125	-	-	-

Source: 1992 *Economic Census*. The states are in descending order of shipments or establishments (if shipment data are missing for the majority). The symbol (D) appears when data are withheld to prevent disclosure of competitive information. States marked with (D) are sorted by number of establishments. A dash (-) indicates that the data element cannot be calculated; * indicates the midpoint of a range.

3081 - UNSUPPORTED PLASTICS FILM & SHEET

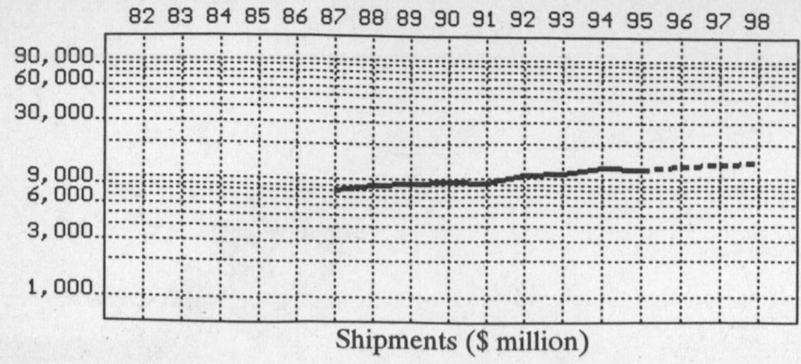

Shipments ($ million)

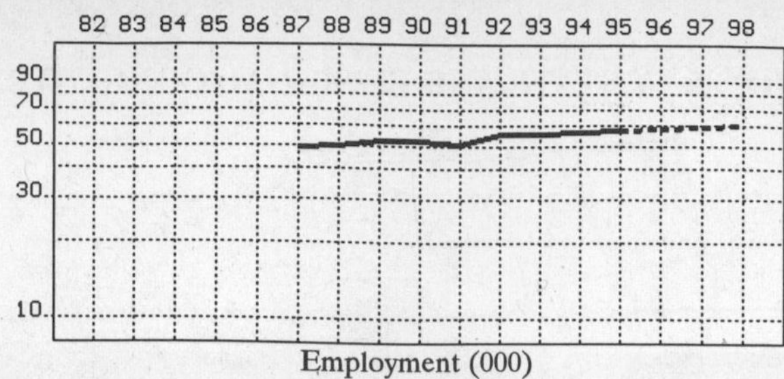

Employment (000)

GENERAL STATISTICS

Year	Companies	Establishments: Total	Establishments: with 20 or more employees	Employment: Total (000)	Employment: Production Workers (000)	Employment: Production Hours (Mil)	Compensation: Payroll ($ mil)	Compensation: Wages ($/hr)	Production ($ million): Cost of Materials	Production ($ million): Value Added by Manufacture	Production ($ million): Value of Shipments	Production ($ million): Capital Invest.
1982												
1983												
1984												
1985												
1986												
1987	474	594	385	48.4	35.2	74.3	1,256.0	10.66	4,137.3	4,041.6	8,139.9	418.7
1988		604	384	49.6	36.6	77.8	1,344.1	10.75	4,937.3	4,097.7	8,946.2	482.5
1989		575	379	52.2	37.0	78.2	1,407.3	11.04	5,152.4	4,067.4	9,196.6	435.8
1990		581	386	52.1	36.8	77.9	1,431.1	11.25	4,954.0	4,294.3	9,284.7	514.0
1991		606	390	50.5	36.0	77.0	1,488.8	11.77	4,901.6	4,245.9	9,169.2	520.4
1992	634	756	456	54.9	39.1	84.0	1,680.9	12.07	5,358.2	5,263.2	10,613.4	592.3
1993		760	476	55.3	40.2	86.3	1,714.5	12.23	5,666.1	5,524.5	11,173.3	407.1
1994		758P	469P	56.3	41.7	92.2	1,821.8	12.61	6,520.2	6,102.5	12,562.3	465.4
1995		788P	484P	57.3P	41.5P	90.8P	1,876.5P	12.87P	6,416.3P	6,005.3P	12,362.2P	502.3P
1996		818P	500P	58.3P	42.3P	93.0P	1,956.2P	13.16P	6,702.0P	6,272.6P	12,912.5P	507.4P
1997		848P	515P	59.4P	43.2P	95.2P	2,035.8P	13.46P	6,987.6P	6,539.9P	13,462.8P	512.5P
1998		877P	530P	60.5P	44.0P	97.4P	2,115.5P	13.75P	7,273.2P	6,807.3P	14,013.1P	517.5P

Sources: 1982, 1987, 1992 *Economic Census*; *Annual Survey of Manufactures*, 83-86, 88-91, 93-94. Establishment counts for non-Census years are from *County Business Patterns*; establishment values for 83-84 are extrapolations. 'P's show projections by the editors. Industries reclassified in 87 will not have data for prior years.

INDICES OF CHANGE

Year	Companies	Establishments: Total	Establishments: with 20 or more employees	Employment: Total (000)	Employment: Production Workers (000)	Employment: Production Hours (Mil)	Compensation: Payroll ($ mil)	Compensation: Wages ($/hr)	Production ($ million): Cost of Materials	Production ($ million): Value Added by Manufacture	Production ($ million): Value of Shipments	Production ($ million): Capital Invest.
1982												
1983												
1984												
1985												
1986												
1987	75	79	84	88	90	88	75	88	77	77	77	71
1988		80	84	90	94	93	80	89	92	78	84	81
1989		76	83	95	95	93	84	91	96	77	87	74
1990		77	85	95	94	93	85	93	92	82	87	87
1991		80	86	92	92	92	89	98	91	81	86	88
1992	100	100	100	100	100	100	100	100	100	100	100	100
1993		101	104	101	103	103	102	101	106	105	105	69
1994		100P	103P	103	107	110	108	104	122	116	118	79
1995		104P	106P	104P	106P	108P	112P	107P	120P	114P	116P	85P
1996		108P	110P	106P	108P	111P	116P	109P	125P	119P	122P	86P
1997		112P	113P	108P	110P	113P	121P	111P	130P	124P	127P	87P
1998		116P	116P	110P	112P	116P	126P	114P	136P	129P	132P	87P

Sources: Same as General Statistics. Values reflect change from the base year, 1992. Values above 100 mean greater than 92, values below 100 mean less than 92, and a value of 100 in the 82-91 or 93-98 period means same as 92. 'P's mark projections by the editors.

SELECTED RATIOS

For 1994	Avg. of All Manufact.	Analyzed Industry	Index
Employees per Establishment	49	74	152
Payroll per Establishment	1,500,273	2,402,072	160
Payroll per Employee	30,620	32,359	106
Production Workers per Establishment	34	55	160
Wages per Establishment	853,319	1,532,962	180
Wages per Production Worker	24,861	27,881	112
Hours per Production Worker	2,056	2,211	108
Wages per Hour	12.09	12.61	104
Value Added per Establishment	4,602,255	8,046,242	175
Value Added per Employee	93,930	108,393	115

For 1994	Avg. of All Manufact.	Analyzed Industry	Index
Value Added per Production Worker	134,084	146,343	109
Cost per Establishment	5,045,178	8,596,986	170
Cost per Employee	102,970	115,812	112
Cost per Production Worker	146,988	156,360	106
Shipments per Establishment	9,576,895	16,563,590	173
Shipments per Employee	195,460	223,131	114
Shipments per Production Worker	279,017	301,254	108
Investment per Establishment	321,011	613,637	191
Investment per Employee	6,552	8,266	126
Investment per Production Worker	9,352	11,161	119

Sources: Same as General Statistics. The 'Average of All Manufacturing' column represents the average of all manufacturing industries reported for the most recent complete year available. The Index shows the relationship between the Average and the Analyzed Industry. For example, 100 means that they are equal; 500 that the Analyzed Industry is five times the average; 50 means that the Analyzed Industry is half the national average. The abbreviation 'na' is used to show that data are 'not available'.

LEADING COMPANIES Number shown: **75** Total sales ($ mil): **5,222** Total employment (000): **29.8**

Company Name	Address				CEO Name	Phone	Co. Type	Sales ($ mil)	Empl. (000)
First Brands Corp	PO Box 1911	Danbury	CT	06813	Thomas Rowland	203-731-2300	D	607	2.0
Envirodyne Industries Inc	701 Harger Rd	Oak Brook	IL	60521	Donald P Kelly	708-571-8800	P	599	4.9
ICI Films Group	PO Box 15391	Wilmington	DE	19850	James A Alles	302-887-3000	D	300	1.0
Atlantis Plastics Inc	2665 S Bayshore Dr	Miami	FL	33133	Anthony F Bova	305-858-2200	P	260	1.3
Atlantis Plastic Films Inc	1870 The Exchange	Atlanta	GA	30339	Randell Litten	404-953-4567	S	240	0.8
CYRO Industries	PO Box 950	Mt Arlington	NJ	07856	Matthew A Taylor	201-770-3000	J	194	1.0
AEP Industries Inc	125 Phillips Av	S Hackensack	NJ	07606	J Brendan Barba	201-641-6600	P	185	1.0
Consolidated Thermoplastics Co	5005 LBJ Fwy	Dallas	TX	75244	Jim Ruberto	214-448-9200	D	180	0.5
Hoechst Diafoil Co	PO Box 1400	Greer	SC	29652	Joseph Ritchie	803-879-5000	J	175	0.9
Blessings Corp	1 Crossroads Dr	Bedminster	NJ	07921	Elwood M Miller	908-719-2300	P	151	1.4
Flexcon Company Inc	Flexcon Industrial	Spencer	MA	01562	Neil McDonough	508-885-3973	R	150	1.0
Gundle Environmental Systems	19103 Gundle Rd	Houston	TX	77073	Thomas L Caltrider	713-443-8564	P	133	0.5
Transilwrap Company Inc	2828 N Paulina St	Chicago	IL	60657	Herb Drower	312-296-1000	R	120	0.7
Edison Plastics	230 Enterprise Dr	Newport News	VA	23603	RL Swenson	804-888-1700	D	115	0.4
Bagcraft Corporation of America	3900 W 43rd St	Chicago	IL	60632	Mark Santacrose	312-254-8000	S	114	1.0
Deerfield Plastics Company Inc	PO Box 97	Deerfield	MA	01373	William A Tychsen	413-665-2145	R	100	0.3
National Seal Co	1245 Corporate	Aurora	IL	60504	John Hardison	708-898-1161	R	100	0.5
Polycast Technology Corp	70 Carlisle Pl	Stamford	CT	06902	Joseph F Matrange	203-327-6010	D	100	0.8
Polymer Corp	PO Box 14235	Reading	PA	19612	Jerry L Thurston	215-320-6600	S	100	1.0
Klockner-Pentaplast of America	PO Box 500	Gordonsville	VA	22942	Harry J Van Beek	703-832-3600	S	99*	0.7
Courtaulds Performance Films	PO Box 5068	Martinsville	VA	24115	Tom Boyle	703-629-1711	D	70*	0.5
Industrial Coatings Group Inc	2141 S Jefferson	Chicago	IL	60616	John P Clark	312-421-4030	R	60	0.4
CMS Gilbreth Packaging Systems	8 Neshaminy Inter	Trevose	PA	19047	Edward Polite	215-244-2400	D	40	0.2
Madico Inc	PO Box 4023	Woburn	MA	01888	C Ian Dodd	617-935-7850	S	40	0.2
Reflexite Corp	120 Darling Dr	Avon	CT	06001	Cecil Upsprung	203-676-7100	R	40	0.3
Associated Bag Co	400 W Boden St	Milwaukee	WI	53207	Herb Rubenstein	414-769-1000	R	35	0.2
Master Shield Building Prod LP	1202 N Bowie Dr	Weatherford	TX	76086	Vernon Weber	817-594-8791	S	35*	0.3
Poly-Hi Solidur	PO Box 9086	Fort Wayne	IN	46899	Dale Mosier	219-479-4100	D	35*	0.3
Serrot Corp	5401 Argosy Av	Huntington Bch	CA	92648	GM Torres	714-895-3010	R	35	0.1
Vernon Plastics Corp	PO Box 8248	Ward Hill	MA	01835	Norman Lee	508-373-1551	S	35*	0.3
Portage Industries Corp	1325 Adams St	Portage	WI	53901	Anthony J Lisauskas	608-742-7123	P	32	0.2
Deerfield Plastics Company Inc	PO Box 97	Deerfield	MA	01373	Charles Barker	413-665-2145	D	30	0.2
Dunmore Corp	207 Penns Trail	Newtown	PA	18940	Richard M Segel	215-968-0442	R	30	0.2
Lustro Plastics Co	PO Box 3011	Evanston	IL	60204	EN Scully	708-864-4050	R	30	0.1
Sheffield Plastics Inc	119 Salisbury Rd	Sheffield	MA	01257	R F Hartmayer	413-229-8711	S	30	0.1
Southern Film Extruders Inc	PO Box 2104	High Point	NC	27261	Joseph Martinez	919-885-8091	R	30	0.1
Plastofilm Industries Inc	935 W Union Av	Wheaton	IL	60187	Robert W George	708-668-2838	S	29	0.3
Web Technologies Inc	27 Main St	Oakville	CT	06779	John Jaran	203-274-9657	R	28	0.1
Simpro Inc	4949 Windfern Dr	Houston	TX	77041	Danny Demaris	713-460-7600	R	26	0.2
American Mirrex Corp	PO Box 728	New Castle	DE	19720	William Bullard	302-836-5950	R	25	0.3
Chris-Craft Industrial Products	450 W 169th St	South Holland	IL	60473	James M Rossman	708-339-6000	S	25	0.1
Watersaver Company Inc	PO Box 16465	Denver	CO	80216	Bill Slifer	303-289-1818	R	25	<0.1
Southwall Technologies Inc	1029 Cor Way	Palo Alto	CA	94303	Martin M Schwartz	415-962-9111	P	23	0.2
Tetra Plastics Inc	13878 Pks Steed Dr	Earth City	MO	63045	Paul H Mitchell	314-770-9822	S	23*	0.2
Allen Extruders Inc	1305 Lincoln	Holland	MI	49423	AD Angell	616-392-9004	R	20	<0.1
Gage Industries Inc	PO Box 1318	Lake Oswego	OR	97035	Jeff Gage	503-639-2177	R	20	0.3
GOEX Corp	2532 Foster Av	Janesville	WI	53545	Joe Pregont	608-754-3303	R	20	<0.1
Coast Converters Inc	1601 Perrino Pl	Los Angeles	CA	90023	Leonard Greif	213-269-0662	R	19	0.2
Futurex Industries Inc	PO Box 158	Bloomingdale	IN	47832	Richard Kramer	317-498-3900	R	18*	0.2
AEP Industries Inc Chino	14000 S M Vista	Chino	CA	91710	Brendon Barba	909-465-9055	D	17*	0.1
Midwest Film Corp	4848 S Hoyne Av	Chicago	IL	60609	Knowell Korey	312-254-5959	R	17	0.2
Huntsman Film Products Corp	3575 Forest Lake	Uniontown	OH	44685	Brian Stevenson	216-896-6700	S	16	0.2
Kama Corp	666 Dietrich Av	Hazleton	PA	18201	Eugene Whitacre	717-455-2021	S	16	0.2
Ellay Inc	6900 Elm St	City of Com	CA	90040	S Edmond	213-725-0050	R	15	<0.1
Newcastle Packaging	PO Box 3026	Santa Fe Sprgs	CA	90670	Lance Rosenzweig	310-921-9705	R	15	<0.1
Petoskey Plastics Inc	4226 US 31 S	Petoskey	MI	49770	Paul C Keiswetter	616-347-2602	R	15*	0.1
Exmark Corp	PO Box 726	Monroe	WA	98272	Chuck Egner	206-794-6246	R	14*	0.1
Polymask Corp	PO Box 309	Conover	NC	28613	Jerry W Akins	704-465-3053	J	14*	0.1
Profile Plastics Inc	1840 Janke Dr	Northbrook	IL	60062	Steve Murrill	708-272-4280	R	14*	0.1
Pak-Sak Industries Inc	122 S Aspen St	Sparta	MI	49345	Jay L Doelder	616-887-8837	S	13	0.2
SI Jacobson Manufacturing Co	1414 Jacobson Dr	Waukegan	IL	60085	AF Jacobson	708-623-1414	R	13	0.2
Fabrico Manufacturing Corp	4222 S Pulaski Rd	Chicago	IL	60632	AM Ross	312-890-5350	R	10	0.1
Flexwrap Corp	40 Meta Ln	Lodi	NJ	07644	Mark Loeffelman	201-777-5877	R	10	<0.1
General Films Inc	645 S High St	Covington	OH	45318	RJ Weikert	513-473-2051	R	10*	<0.1
Ellehammer Packaging Inc	3139 Ferguson	Olympia	WA	98502	R Pineda	206-754-4602	S	9	0.1
Kimoto Tech Inc	PO Box 1783	Cedartown	GA	30125	Yutaka Arita	404-748-2643	S	9*	<0.1
VCF Films Inc	1100 Sutton Av	Howell	MI	48843	William Plahta	517-546-2300	S	9*	<0.1
Lake Zurich Film	351 N Oakwood Rd	Lake Zurich	IL	60047	DG Beard	708-438-2111	D	8*	0.2
Quality Films Inc	PO Box 65	Schoolcraft	MI	49087	BA Rabbers	616-679-5263	R	8	<0.1
Blako Industries Inc	PO Box 179	Dunbridge	OH	43414	JR Kretzschmar	419-833-4491	R	8	<0.1
Ex-Tech Plastics Inc	9703 US 12 S	Richmond	IL	60071	Bill Field	815-678-2131	R	7	<0.1
Mohawk Western Plastics Inc	PO Box 493	La Verne	CA	91750	JR Mordoff	909-593-7547	R	7*	<0.1
Rayven Inc	431 N Griggs St	St Paul	MN	55104	G Ingalls	612-642-1112	R	7	<0.1
Crystal-X Corp	100 Pine St	Darby	PA	19023	EF Westlake Sr	610-586-3200	R	6	<0.1
Impact Plastics Inc	PO Box 306	Kensington	CT	06037	Steven M Ryan	203-828-6396	R	6*	<0.1

Source: *Ward's Business Directory of U.S. Private and Public Companies*, Volumes 1 and 2, 1996. The company type code used is as follows: P - Public, R - Private, S - Subsidiary, D - Division, J - Joint Venture, A - Affiliate, G - Group. Sales are in millions of dollars, employees are in thousands. An asterisk (*) indicates an estimated sales volume. The symbol < stands for 'less than'. Company names and addresses are truncated, in some cases, to fit into the available space.

MATERIALS CONSUMED

Material	Quantity	Delivered Cost ($ million)
Materials, ingredients, containers, and supplies	(X)	4,825.6
Hardboard (wood fiberboard)	(X)	11.1
Industrial inorganic chemicals	(X)	160.1
Inorganic pigments	(X)	49.8
Plastics resins consumed in the form of granules, pellets, powders, liquids, etc.	(X)	2,450.3
Industrial organic and synthetic organic chemicals, including plasticizers	(X)	378.0
Synthetic dyes, pigments, lakes, and toners	(X)	44.1
All other chemical and allied products	(X)	113.2
Plastics products consumed in the form of sheets, rods, tubes, film, and other shapes	(X)	303.7
Custom compounded plastics resins (purchased)	(X)	44.3
Broadwoven fabrics	(X)	9.7
Paper and paperboard products except packaging, photographic	(X)	149.0
Paperboard containers, boxes, and corrugated paperboard	(X)	106.2
Parts and attachments specially designed for plastics working machinery	(X)	24.6
All other materials and components, parts, containers, and supplies	(X)	480.2
Materials, ingredients, containers, and supplies, nsk	(X)	501.2

Source: 1992 *Economic Census*. Explanation of symbols used: (D): Withheld to avoid disclosure of competitive data; na: Not available; (S): Withheld because statistical norms were not met; (X): Not applicable; (Z): Less than half the unit shown; nec: Not elsewhere classified; nsk: Not specified by kind; - : zero; * : 10-19 percent estimated; ** : 20-29 percent estimated.

PRODUCT SHARE DETAILS

Product or Product Class	% Share	Product or Product Class	% Share
Unsupported plastics film and sheet	100.00	Unsupported polypropylene film and sheet	9.13
Unsupported cellulosic film and sheet	1.95	Unsupported vinyl and vinyl copolymer film and sheet	18.86
Unsupported polyethylene film and sheet	29.06	Other unsupported plastics film and sheet	32.24

Source: 1992 *Economic Census*. The values shown are percent of total shipments in an industry. Values of indented subcategories are summed in the main heading. The symbol (D) appears when data are withheld to prevent disclosure of competitive information. The abbreviation nsk stands for 'not specified by kind' and nec for 'not elsewhere classified'.

INPUTS AND OUTPUTS FOR MISCELLANEOUS PLASTICS PRODUCTS

Economic Sector or Industry Providing Inputs	%	Sector	Economic Sector or Industry Buying Outputs	%	Sector
Plastics materials & resins	36.2	Manufg.	Hospitals	5.6	Services
Wholesale trade	8.5	Trade	Electronic components nec	5.2	Manufg.
Miscellaneous plastics products	7.2	Manufg.	Personal consumption expenditures	4.3	
Imports	5.8	Foreign	Miscellaneous plastics products	4.0	Manufg.
Cyclic crudes and organics	4.4	Manufg.	Exports	4.0	Foreign
Electric services (utilities)	4.4	Util.	Telephone & telegraph apparatus	3.0	Manufg.
Paperboard containers & boxes	2.6	Manufg.	Motor vehicles & car bodies	2.8	Manufg.
Communications, except radio & TV	2.3	Util.	Eating & drinking places	2.8	Trade
Motor freight transportation & warehousing	2.0	Util.	Maintenance of nonfarm buildings nec	2.4	Constr.
Paperboard mills	1.5	Manufg.	Food preparations, nec	2.3	Manufg.
Synthetic rubber	1.5	Manufg.	Plastics materials & resins	2.1	Manufg.
Railroads & related services	1.3	Util.	Typewriters & office machines, nec	1.7	Manufg.
Glass & glass products, except containers	1.2	Manufg.	Commercial printing	1.6	Manufg.
Gas production & distribution (utilities)	1.0	Util.	Cyclic crudes and organics	1.5	Manufg.
Noncomparable imports	1.0	Foreign	Electronic computing equipment	1.5	Manufg.
Industrial inorganic chemicals, nec	0.9	Manufg.	Motor vehicle parts & accessories	1.3	Manufg.
Crude petroleum & natural gas	0.7	Mining	Paper mills, except building paper	1.3	Manufg.
Maintenance of nonfarm buildings nec	0.7	Constr.	Bottled & canned soft drinks	1.2	Manufg.
Eating & drinking places	0.7	Trade	Toilet preparations	1.2	Manufg.
Real estate	0.7	Fin/R.E.	Aircraft	1.1	Manufg.
Computer & data processing services	0.7	Services	Medical & health services, nec	1.1	Services
Broadwoven fabric mills	0.6	Manufg.	Nonfarm residential structure maintenance	1.0	Constr.
Machinery, except electrical, nec	0.6	Manufg.	Optical instruments & lenses	0.9	Manufg.
Petroleum refining	0.6	Manufg.	Wholesale trade	0.9	Trade
Banking	0.6	Fin/R.E.	Office buildings	0.8	Constr.
Inorganic pigments	0.5	Manufg.	Computer & data processing services	0.8	Services
Wood products, nec	0.5	Manufg.	Hotels & lodging places	0.8	Services
Advertising	0.5	Services	S/L Govt. purch., health & hospitals	0.8	S/L Govt
Equipment rental & leasing services	0.5	Services	Residential additions/alterations, nonfarm	0.7	Constr.
Adhesives & sealants	0.4	Manufg.	Animal & marine fats & oils	0.7	Manufg.
Fabricated rubber products, nec	0.4	Manufg.	Drugs	0.7	Manufg.
Special industry machinery, nec	0.4	Manufg.	Fluid milk	0.7	Manufg.
Job training & related services	0.4	Services	Paper coating & glazing	0.7	Manufg.
Fabricated metal products, nec	0.3	Manufg.	Polishes & sanitation goods	0.7	Manufg.
Lighting fixtures & equipment	0.3	Manufg.	Automotive & apparel trimmings	0.6	Manufg.
Lubricating oils & greases	0.3	Manufg.	Broadwoven fabric mills	0.6	Manufg.
Metal stampings, nec	0.3	Manufg.	Frozen fruits, fruit juices & vegetables	0.6	Manufg.
Primary metal products, nec	0.3	Manufg.	Frozen specialties	0.6	Manufg.
Special dies & tools & machine tool accessories	0.3	Manufg.	Knit outerwear mills	0.6	Manufg.

Continued on next page.

INPUTS AND OUTPUTS FOR MISCELLANEOUS PLASTICS PRODUCTS - Continued

Economic Sector or Industry Providing Inputs	%	Sector	Economic Sector or Industry Buying Outputs	%	Sector
Water transportation	0.3	Util.	Miscellaneous fabricated wire products	0.6	Manufg.
Royalties	0.3	Fin/R.E.	Photographic equipment & supplies	0.6	Manufg.
Management & consulting services & labs	0.3	Services	Pickles, sauces, & salad dressings	0.6	Manufg.
Metal foil & leaf	0.2	Manufg.	Soap & other detergents	0.6	Manufg.
Narrow fabric mills	0.2	Manufg.	Residential garden apartments	0.5	Constr.
Paints & allied products	0.2	Manufg.	Bags, except textile	0.5	Manufg.
Primary copper	0.2	Manufg.	Petroleum refining	0.5	Manufg.
Sanitary services, steam supply, irrigation	0.2	Util.	Semiconductors & related devices	0.5	Manufg.
Accounting, auditing & bookkeeping	0.2	Services	Real estate	0.5	Fin/R.E.
Electrical repair shops	0.2	Services	Beauty & barber shops	0.5	Services
Engineering, architectural, & surveying services	0.2	Services	Residential 1-unit structures, nonfarm	0.4	Constr.
Legal services	0.2	Services	Carbon paper & inked ribbons	0.4	Manufg.
Alkalies & chlorine	0.1	Manufg.	Roasted coffee	0.4	Manufg.
Building paper & board mills	0.1	Manufg.	Storage batteries	0.4	Manufg.
Manifold business forms	0.1	Manufg.	Upholstered household furniture	0.4	Manufg.
Mineral wool	0.1	Manufg.	Communications, except radio & TV	0.4	Util.
Pipe, valves, & pipe fittings	0.1	Manufg.	Water supply & sewage systems	0.4	Util.
Screw machine and related products	0.1	Manufg.	Business services nec	0.4	Services
Air transportation	0.1	Util.	Doctors & dentists	0.4	Services
Insurance carriers	0.1	Fin/R.E.	Miscellaneous repair shops	0.4	Services
Business/professional associations	0.1	Services	Construction of hospitals	0.3	Constr.
U.S. Postal Service	0.1	Gov't	Industrial buildings	0.3	Constr.
			Maintenance of highways & streets	0.3	Constr.
			Games, toys, & children's vehicles	0.3	Manufg.
			Logging camps & logging contractors	0.3	Manufg.
			Mattresses & bedsprings	0.3	Manufg.
			Nonferrous wire drawing & insulating	0.3	Manufg.
			Organic fibers, noncellulosic	0.3	Manufg.
			Sanitary paper products	0.3	Manufg.
			Sausages & other prepared meats	0.3	Manufg.
			Signs & advertising displays	0.3	Manufg.
			Surgical & medical instruments	0.3	Manufg.
			Retail trade, except eating & drinking	0.3	Trade
			Amusement & recreation services nec	0.3	Services
			Child day care services	0.3	Services
			Management & consulting services & labs	0.3	Services
			Nursing & personal care facilities	0.3	Services
			Construction of educational buildings	0.2	Constr.
			Construction of stores & restaurants	0.2	Constr.
			Electric utility facility construction	0.2	Constr.
			Warehouses	0.2	Constr.
			Aluminum rolling & drawing	0.2	Manufg.
			Bread, cake, & related products	0.2	Manufg.
			Carbon & graphite products	0.2	Manufg.
			Chemical preparations, nec	0.2	Manufg.
			Cigarettes	0.2	Manufg.
			Cookies & crackers	0.2	Manufg.
			Dog, cat, & other pet food	0.2	Manufg.
			Electric housewares & fans	0.2	Manufg.
			Fabricated plate work (boiler shops)	0.2	Manufg.
			Fabricated structural metal	0.2	Manufg.
			General industrial machinery, nec	0.2	Manufg.
			Glass & glass products, except containers	0.2	Manufg.
			Hard surface floor coverings	0.2	Manufg.
			Household refrigerators & freezers	0.2	Manufg.
			Knit fabric mills	0.2	Manufg.
			Lighting fixtures & equipment	0.2	Manufg.
			Macaroni & spaghetti	0.2	Manufg.
			Meat packing plants	0.2	Manufg.
			Nitrogenous & phosphatic fertilizers	0.2	Manufg.
			Radio & TV communication equipment	0.2	Manufg.
			Radio & TV receiving sets	0.2	Manufg.
			Refrigeration & heating equipment	0.2	Manufg.
			Shoes, except rubber	0.2	Manufg.
			Shortening & cooking oils	0.2	Manufg.
			Sporting & athletic goods, nec	0.2	Manufg.
			Surface active agents	0.2	Manufg.
			Surgical appliances & supplies	0.2	Manufg.
			Wood partitions & fixtures	0.2	Manufg.
			Job training & related services	0.2	Services
			Laundry, dry cleaning, shoe repair	0.2	Services
			Social services, nec	0.2	Services
			Federal Government purchases, national defense	0.2	Fed Govt
			Greenhouse & nursery products	0.1	Agric.
			Farm service facilities	0.1	Constr.

Continued on next page.

INPUTS AND OUTPUTS FOR MISCELLANEOUS PLASTICS PRODUCTS - Continued

Economic Sector or Industry Providing Inputs	%	Sector	Economic Sector or Industry Buying Outputs	%	Sector
			Hotels & motels	0.1	Constr.
			Maintenance of nonbuilding facilities nec	0.1	Constr.
			Maintenance of water supply facilities	0.1	Constr.
			Aircraft & missile equipment, nec	0.1	Manufg.
			Architectural metal work	0.1	Manufg.
			Blankbooks & looseleaf binders	0.1	Manufg.
			Book printing	0.1	Manufg.
			Cheese, natural & processed	0.1	Manufg.
			Chocolate & cocoa products	0.1	Manufg.
			Condensed & evaporated milk	0.1	Manufg.
			Confectionery products	0.1	Manufg.
			Distilled liquor, except brandy	0.1	Manufg.
			Drapery hardware & blinds & shades	0.1	Manufg.
			Engine electrical equipment	0.1	Manufg.
			Fabricated rubber products, nec	0.1	Manufg.
			Guided missiles & space vehicles	0.1	Manufg.
			Metal foil & leaf	0.1	Manufg.
			Metal household furniture	0.1	Manufg.
			Metal office furniture	0.1	Manufg.
			Miscellaneous publishing	0.1	Manufg.
			Motors & generators	0.1	Manufg.
			Paperboard containers & boxes	0.1	Manufg.
			Paving mixtures & blocks	0.1	Manufg.
			Phonograph records & tapes	0.1	Manufg.
			Pumps & compressors	0.1	Manufg.
			Secondary nonferrous metals	0.1	Manufg.
			Sheet metal work	0.1	Manufg.
			Special dies & tools & machine tool accessories	0.1	Manufg.
			Sugar	0.1	Manufg.
			Watches, clocks, & parts	0.1	Manufg.
			Women's hosiery, except socks	0.1	Manufg.
			Wood household furniture	0.1	Manufg.
			Wood products, nec	0.1	Manufg.
			Engineering, architectural, & surveying services	0.1	Services
			Local government passenger transit	0.1	Gov't

Source: Benchmark Input-Output Accounts for the U.S. Economy, 1982, U.S. Department of Commerce, Washington, D.C., July 1991. Data, as reported in the source, are organized by the 1977 SIC structure in use in 1982 but have been matched, as closely as is possible, to the 1987 SIC structure used in this book.

OCCUPATIONS EMPLOYED BY SIC 308 - MISCELLANEOUS PLASTICS PRODUCTS

Occupation	% of Total 1994	Change to 2005	Occupation	% of Total 1994	Change to 2005
Plastic molding machine workers	18.3	6.7	Maintenance repairers, general utility	1.6	6.7
Assemblers, fabricators, & hand workers nec	9.5	18.5	Industrial truck & tractor operators	1.5	18.5
Blue collar worker supervisors	5.2	10.7	Tool & die makers	1.4	77.8
Hand packers & packagers	4.7	-8.6	Extruding & forming machine workers	1.4	-40.7
Machine tool cutting & forming etc. nec	3.4	50.5	Industrial production managers	1.4	18.5
Inspectors, testers, & graders, precision	3.4	6.7	Machine feeders & offbearers	1.4	6.7
Helpers, laborers, & material movers nec	2.6	18.5	Packaging & filling machine operators	1.3	18.5
Machine forming operators, metal & plastic	2.5	30.4	Cutters & trimmers, hand	1.2	18.5
Metal & plastic machine workers nec	2.4	89.0	Bookkeeping, accounting, & auditing clerks	1.1	-11.1
General managers & top executives	2.3	12.4	Secretaries, ex legal & medical	1.1	7.9
Industrial machinery mechanics	2.2	30.4	Coating, painting, & spraying machine workers	1.1	6.7
Sales & related workers nec	1.9	18.5	Crushing & mixing machine operators	1.1	77.8
Traffic, shipping, & receiving clerks	1.8	14.0	Machine operators nec	1.1	-32.1
Freight, stock, & material movers, hand	1.7	-5.2			

Source: Industry-Occupation Matrix, Bureau of Labor Statistics. These data relate to one or more 3-digit SIC industry groups rather than to a single 4-digit SIC. The change reported for each occupation to the year 2005 is a percent of growth or decline as estimated by the Bureau of Labor Statistics. The abbreviation nec stands for 'not elsewhere classified'.

LOCATION BY STATE AND REGIONAL CONCENTRATION

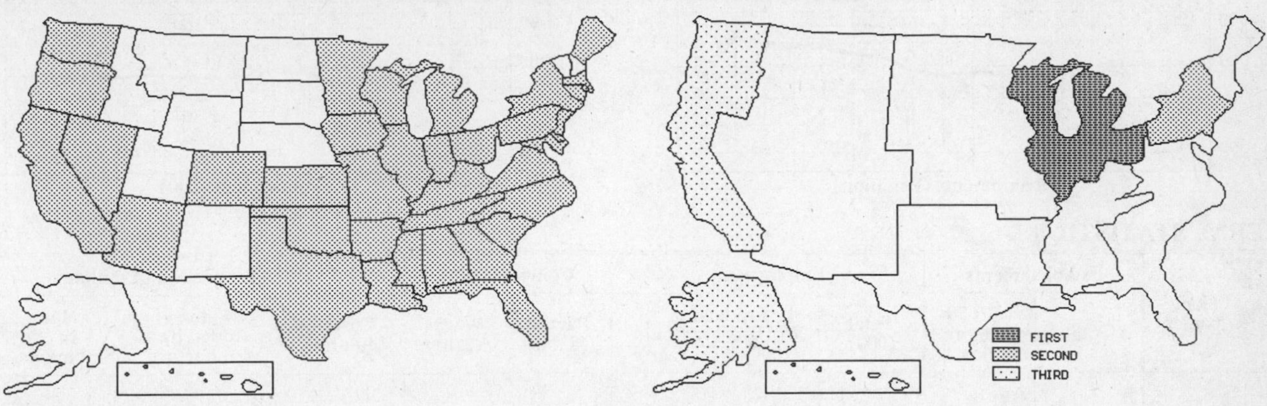

INDUSTRY DATA BY STATE

State	Establish-ments	Shipments			Employment				Cost as % of Shipments	Investment per Employee ($)
		Total ($ mil)	% of U.S.	Per Establ.	Total Number	% of U.S.	Per Establ.	Wages ($/hour)		
Massachusetts	37	822.4	7.7	22.2	3,900	7.1	105	15.25	57.7	9,821
Texas	33	784.3	7.4	23.8	3,400	6.2	103	12.68	49.4	48,059
South Carolina	8	716.3	6.7	89.5	3,300	6.0	413	15.06	39.8	-
Ohio	41	647.7	6.1	15.8	3,300	6.0	80	12.54	45.5	18,515
Virginia	14	586.4	5.5	41.9	2,600	4.7	186	14.94	36.5	6,192
New Jersey	64	578.7	5.5	9.0	3,300	6.0	52	11.65	57.9	3,394
California	98	571.5	5.4	5.8	3,900	7.1	40	10.00	49.9	6,436
Illinois	46	517.7	4.9	11.3	3,100	5.6	67	12.13	45.3	8,387
Indiana	21	495.0	4.7	23.6	2,500	4.6	119	12.00	44.6	5,400
North Carolina	23	425.6	4.0	18.5	1,900	3.5	83	12.10	50.5	9,789
Pennsylvania	43	419.5	4.0	9.8	2,500	4.6	58	11.59	56.5	6,800
Georgia	26	379.4	3.6	14.6	1,900	3.5	73	9.75	56.8	5,105
New York	39	378.7	3.6	9.7	2,200	4.0	56	10.66	55.2	5,045
Missouri	14	287.0	2.7	20.5	1,100	2.0	79	12.83	44.2	18,364
Michigan	31	281.2	2.6	9.1	1,500	2.7	48	13.10	67.9	14,533
Oklahoma	11	276.1	2.6	25.1	1,000	1.8	91	11.29	47.3	-
Delaware	8	238.0	2.2	29.7	900	1.6	113	10.59	49.9	7,222
Kentucky	11	221.6	2.1	20.1	900	1.6	82	11.64	54.2	10,111
Alabama	6	211.4	2.0	35.2	700	1.3	117	13.00	34.5	-
Connecticut	20	206.2	1.9	10.3	1,100	2.0	55	12.71	53.4	6,636
Minnesota	24	191.5	1.8	8.0	1,400	2.6	58	9.48	58.2	-
Wisconsin	24	179.4	1.7	7.5	1,000	1.8	42	10.80	60.4	9,100
Iowa	8	142.6	1.3	17.8	800	1.5	100	13.75	41.7	-
Rhode Island	6	112.0	1.1	18.7	500	0.9	83	13.83	58.6	-
Louisiana	5	110.1	1.0	22.0	600	1.1	120	8.27	62.8	5,167
Tennessee	8	97.3	0.9	12.2	600	1.1	75	14.87	46.4	7,000
Kansas	6	94.1	0.9	15.7	1,200	2.2	200	8.28	57.6	-
Washington	9	88.9	0.8	9.9	500	0.9	56	14.13	51.4	5,400
Arkansas	5	83.9	0.8	16.8	700	1.3	140	9.33	54.1	3,143
Oregon	9	60.8	0.6	6.8	500	0.9	56	11.38	47.0	6,000
Maryland	4	50.4	0.5	12.6	300	0.5	75	10.00	64.7	11,333
Colorado	9	49.8	0.5	5.5	300	0.5	33	10.33	71.9	1,667
Florida	16	23.9	0.2	1.5	200	0.4	13	8.67	53.1	6,000
Arizona	4	(D)	-	-	750 *	1.4	188	-	-	-
Nevada	4	(D)	-	-	175 *	0.3	44	-	-	1,714
Maine	1	(D)	-	-	375 *	0.7	375	-	-	-
Mississippi	1	(D)	-	-	175 *	0.3	175	-	-	-

Source: 1992 *Economic Census*. The states are in descending order of shipments or establishments (if shipment data are missing for the majority). The symbol (D) appears when data are withheld to prevent disclosure of competitive information. States marked with (D) are sorted by number of establishments. A dash (-) indicates that the data element cannot be calculated; * indicates the midpoint of a range.

3082 - UNSUPPORTED PLASTICS PROFILE SHAPES

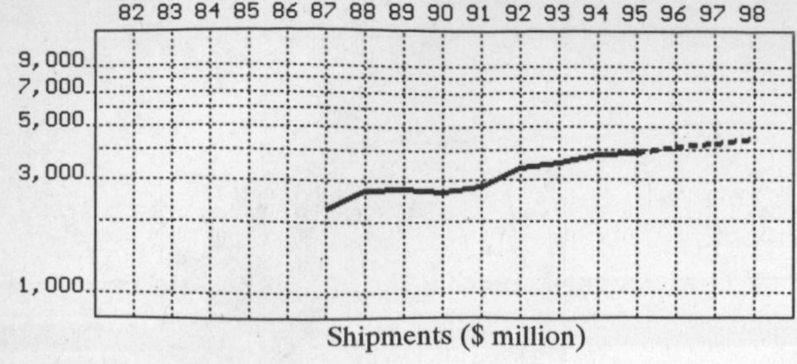

Shipments ($ million)

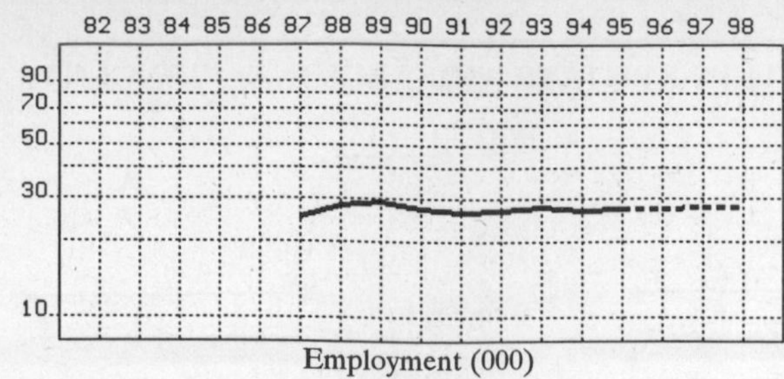

Employment (000)

GENERAL STATISTICS

Year	Companies	Establishments: Total	Establishments: with 20 or more employees	Employment: Total (000)	Employment: Production Workers (000)	Employment: Production Hours (Mil)	Compensation: Payroll ($ mil)	Compensation: Wages ($/hr)	Production ($ million): Cost of Materials	Production ($ million): Value Added by Manufacture	Production ($ million): Value of Shipments	Production ($ million): Capital Invest.
1982												
1983												
1984												
1985												
1986												
1987	551	581	298	25.2	19.1	37.8	512.2	8.31	1,116.3	1,192.1	2,280.8	133.7
1988		594	323	28.1	21.2	43.3	587.1	8.32	1,459.1	1,288.3	2,726.8	146.6
1989		557	311	29.4	21.3	44.3	601.9	8.37	1,462.9	1,322.0	2,775.8	137.1
1990		531	296	27.5	20.3	41.4	637.0	9.63	1,392.8	1,285.7	2,688.8	135.9
1991		547	293	26.4	20.1	41.1	646.0	9.74	1,460.3	1,343.2	2,801.9	120.6
1992	632	673	327	27.0	20.1	41.3	706.3	10.01	1,571.4	1,775.5	3,332.8	198.4
1993		705	365	28.0	21.4	42.7	722.6	10.41	1,698.3	1,815.5	3,517.3	179.9
1994		673P	343P	26.9	20.6	42.8	779.3	11.09	1,898.0	1,968.1	3,842.7	173.7
1995		691P	350P	27.5P	20.9P	43.1P	802.8P	11.36P	1,920.8P	1,991.8P	3,888.9P	186.2P
1996		710P	357P	27.5P	21.0P	43.3P	836.9P	11.77P	2,018.8P	2,093.4P	4,087.3P	193.5P
1997		728P	364P	27.6P	21.1P	43.6P	871.1P	12.19P	2,116.9P	2,195.0P	4,285.8P	200.8P
1998		747P	371P	27.6P	21.2P	43.9P	905.2P	12.60P	2,214.9P	2,296.7P	4,484.2P	208.2P

Sources: 1982, 1987, 1992 *Economic Census*; *Annual Survey of Manufactures*, 83-86, 88-91, 93-94. Establishment counts for non-Census years are from *County Business Patterns*; establishment values for 83-84 are extrapolations. 'P's show projections by the editors. Industries reclassified in 87 will not have data for prior years.

INDICES OF CHANGE

Year	Companies	Establishments: Total	Establishments: with 20 or more employees	Employment: Total (000)	Employment: Production Workers (000)	Employment: Production Hours (Mil)	Compensation: Payroll ($ mil)	Compensation: Wages ($/hr)	Production ($ million): Cost of Materials	Production ($ million): Value Added by Manufacture	Production ($ million): Value of Shipments	Production ($ million): Capital Invest.
1982												
1983												
1984												
1985												
1986												
1987	87	86	91	93	95	92	73	83	71	67	68	67
1988		88	99	104	105	105	83	83	93	73	82	74
1989		83	95	109	106	107	85	84	93	74	83	69
1990		79	91	102	101	100	90	96	89	72	81	68
1991		81	90	98	100	100	91	97	93	76	84	61
1992	100	100	100	100	100	100	100	100	100	100	100	100
1993		105	112	104	106	103	102	104	108	102	106	91
1994		100P	105P	100	102	104	110	111	121	111	115	88
1995		103P	107P	102P	104P	104P	114P	113P	122P	112P	117P	94P
1996		105P	109P	102P	105P	105P	118P	118P	128P	118P	123P	98P
1997		108P	111P	102P	105P	106P	123P	122P	135P	124P	129P	101P
1998		111P	113P	102P	105P	106P	128P	126P	141P	129P	135P	105P

Sources: Same as General Statistics. Values reflect change from the base year, 1992. Values above 100 mean greater than 92, values below 100 mean less than 92, and a value of 100 in the 82-91 or 93-98 period means same as 92. 'P's mark projections by the editors.

SELECTED RATIOS

For 1994	Avg. of All Manufact.	Analyzed Industry	Index
Employees per Establishment	49	40	82
Payroll per Establishment	1,500,273	1,158,687	77
Payroll per Employee	30,620	28,970	95
Production Workers per Establishment	34	31	89
Wages per Establishment	853,319	705,727	83
Wages per Production Worker	24,861	23,041	93
Hours per Production Worker	2,056	2,078	101
Wages per Hour	12.09	11.09	92
Value Added per Establishment	4,602,255	2,926,232	64
Value Added per Employee	93,930	73,164	78

For 1994	Avg. of All Manufact.	Analyzed Industry	Index
Value Added per Production Worker	134,084	95,539	71
Cost per Establishment	5,045,178	2,822,005	56
Cost per Employee	102,970	70,558	69
Cost per Production Worker	146,988	92,136	63
Shipments per Establishment	9,576,895	5,713,445	60
Shipments per Employee	195,460	142,851	73
Shipments per Production Worker	279,017	186,539	67
Investment per Establishment	321,011	258,263	80
Investment per Employee	6,552	6,457	99
Investment per Production Worker	9,352	8,432	90

Sources: Same as General Statistics. The 'Average of All Manufacturing' column represents the average of all manufacturing industries reported for the most recent complete year available. The Index shows the relationship between the Average and the Analyzed Industry. For example, 100 means that they are equal; 500 that the Analyzed Industry is five times the average; 50 means that the Analyzed Industry is half the national average. The abbreviation 'na' is used to show that data are 'not available'.

LEADING COMPANIES

Number shown: **16** Total sales ($ mil): **529** Total employment (000): **5.0**

Company Name	Address				CEO Name	Phone	Co. Type	Sales ($ mil)	Empl. (000)
AutoStyle Plastics Inc	5015 52nd St SE	Grand Rapids	MI	49512	R Dale Herman	616-940-9500	S	107	1.0
Crane Plastics Co	2141 Fairwood Av	Columbus	OH	43207	Jameson Crane	614-443-4891	R	100	0.6
Autostyle Inc	5015 52nd St SE	Grand Rapids	MI	49512	RD Herman	616-940-9500	R	74*	0.7
Laird Plastics Inc	1400 Centrepark	W Palm Beach	FL	33401	John W Perdiue	407-689-2200	S	57*	0.5
Tubed Products Inc	PO Box 471	Easthampton	MA	01027	R W Schroeder	413-527-1250	S	38	0.8
Prent Corp	PO Box 471	Janesville	WI	53547	JT Pregont	608-754-0276	R	30	0.4
Nebraska Plastics Inc	PO Box 45	Cozad	NE	69130	Rex German	308-784-2500	R	25	0.1
Lavanture Products Co	PO Box 2088	Elkhart	IN	46515	R A Lavanture	219-264-0658	R	23	0.2
Plastron	19555 E Arenth Av	City of Industry	CA	91748	Lawrence Szyz	909-594-3660	D	16	0.1
Thermoplastic Processes Inc	1268 Valley Rd	Stirling	NJ	07980	JR Dupont	908-561-3000	R	15	0.1
Fiberglass Specialties Inc	PO Box 1340	Henderson	TX	75653	Rocky Hall	903-657-6522	R	15*	0.1
Hastings Fiber Glass Products	PO Box 218	Hastings	MI	49058	LR Baum	616-945-9541	R	12	<0.1
Allied Resinous Products Inc	PO Box 620	Conneaut	OH	44030	Luis R Vizurraga	216-599-8175	R	8*	<0.1
Cole-Flex Corp	91 Cabot St	West Babylon	NY	11704	A Rosenblum	516-249-6150	R	4*	<0.1
Anaheim Custom Extruders Inc	4640 E La Palma	Anaheim	CA	92807	William A Czapar	714-693-8508	R	3	<0.1
Rextrude Co	230 Elliot St	Brockton	MA	02402	Morton Oppenheim	508-587-2290	R	2	<0.1

Source: *Ward's Business Directory of U.S. Private and Public Companies*, Volumes 1 and 2, 1996. The company type code used is as follows: P - Public, R - Private, S - Subsidiary, D - Division, J - Joint Venture, A - Affiliate, G - Group. Sales are in millions of dollars, employees are in thousands. An asterisk (*) indicates an estimated sales volume. The symbol < stands for 'less than'. Company names and addresses are truncated, in some cases, to fit into the available space.

MATERIALS CONSUMED

Material	Quantity	Delivered Cost ($ million)
Materials, ingredients, containers, and supplies	(X)	1,426.5
Hardboard (wood fiberboard)	(X)	2.3
Inorganic pigments	(X)	33.3
Plastics resins consumed in the form of granules, pellets, powders, liquids, etc.	(X)	802.5
Industrial organic and synthetic organic chemicals, including plasticizers	(X)	58.6
Synthetic dyes, pigments, lakes, and toners	(X)	15.9
All other chemical and allied products	(X)	20.2
Plastics products consumed in the form of sheets, rods, tubes, film, and other shapes	(X)	56.3
Custom compounded plastics resins (purchased)	(X)	23.6
Textile-type glass fiber	(X)	1.6
Paper and paperboard products except packaging, photographic	(X)	14.7
Paperboard containers, boxes, and corrugated paperboard	(X)	43.3
Parts and attachments specially designed for plastics working machinery	(X)	7.2
All other materials and components, parts, containers, and supplies	(X)	183.3
Materials, ingredients, containers, and supplies, nsk	(X)	163.8

Source: 1992 *Economic Census*. Explanation of symbols used: (D): Withheld to avoid disclosure of competitive data; na: Not available; (S): Withheld because statistical norms were not met; (X): Not applicable; (Z): Less than half the unit shown; nec: Not elsewhere classified; nsk: Not specified by kind; - : zero; * : 10-19 percent estimated; ** : 20-29 percent estimated.

PRODUCT SHARE DETAILS

Product or Product Class	% Share
Unsupported plastics profile shapes	100.00
Unsupported acrylate and methacrylate rods, tubes, profiles, and other shapes	6.34
Unsupported cellulosic rods, tubes, profiles, and other shapes	(D)
Unsupported polyamide (nylon) rods, tubes, profiles, and other shapes	5.04
Unsupported polyethylene rods, tubes, profiles, and other shapes	17.29
Unsupported polypropylene rods, tubes, profiles, and other shapes	7.86
Unsupported polystyrene rods, tubes, profiles, and other shapes	11.87
Unsupported styrene copolymer rods, tubes, profiles, and other shapes	(D)
Unsupported vinyl and vinyl copolymer rods, tubes, profiles, and other shapes	17.74
Other unsupported plastics rods, tubes, profiles, and other shapes	17.77

Source: 1992 *Economic Census*. The values shown are percent of total shipments in an industry. Values of indented subcategories are summed in the main heading. The symbol (D) appears when data are withheld to prevent disclosure of competitive information. The abbreviation nsk stands for 'not specified by kind' and nec for 'not elsewhere classified'.

INPUTS AND OUTPUTS FOR MISCELLANEOUS PLASTICS PRODUCTS

Economic Sector or Industry Providing Inputs	%	Sector	Economic Sector or Industry Buying Outputs	%	Sector
Plastics materials & resins	36.2	Manufg.	Hospitals	5.6	Services
Wholesale trade	8.5	Trade	Electronic components nec	5.2	Manufg.
Miscellaneous plastics products	7.2	Manufg.	Personal consumption expenditures	4.3	
Imports	5.8	Foreign	Miscellaneous plastics products	4.0	Manufg.
Cyclic crudes and organics	4.4	Manufg.	Exports	4.0	Foreign
Electric services (utilities)	4.4	Util.	Telephone & telegraph apparatus	3.0	Manufg.
Paperboard containers & boxes	2.6	Manufg.	Motor vehicles & car bodies	2.8	Manufg.
Communications, except radio & TV	2.3	Util.	Eating & drinking places	2.8	Trade
Motor freight transportation & warehousing	2.0	Util.	Maintenance of nonfarm buildings nec	2.4	Constr.
Paperboard mills	1.5	Manufg.	Food preparations, nec	2.3	Manufg.
Synthetic rubber	1.5	Manufg.	Plastics materials & resins	2.1	Manufg.
Railroads & related services	1.3	Util.	Typewriters & office machines, nec	1.7	Manufg.
Glass & glass products, except containers	1.2	Manufg.	Commercial printing	1.6	Manufg.
Gas production & distribution (utilities)	1.0	Util.	Cyclic crudes and organics	1.5	Manufg.
Noncomparable imports	1.0	Foreign	Electronic computing equipment	1.5	Manufg.
Industrial inorganic chemicals, nec	0.9	Manufg.	Motor vehicle parts & accessories	1.3	Manufg.
Crude petroleum & natural gas	0.7	Mining	Paper mills, except building paper	1.3	Manufg.
Maintenance of nonfarm buildings nec	0.7	Constr.	Bottled & canned soft drinks	1.2	Manufg.
Eating & drinking places	0.7	Trade	Toilet preparations	1.2	Manufg.
Real estate	0.7	Fin/R.E.	Aircraft	1.1	Manufg.
Computer & data processing services	0.7	Services	Medical & health services, nec	1.1	Services
Broadwoven fabric mills	0.6	Manufg.	Nonfarm residential structure maintenance	1.0	Constr.
Machinery, except electrical, nec	0.6	Manufg.	Optical instruments & lenses	0.9	Manufg.
Petroleum refining	0.6	Manufg.	Wholesale trade	0.9	Trade
Banking	0.6	Fin/R.E.	Office buildings	0.8	Constr.
Inorganic pigments	0.5	Manufg.	Computer & data processing services	0.8	Services
Wood products, nec	0.5	Manufg.	Hotels & lodging places	0.8	Services
Advertising	0.5	Services	S/L Govt. purch., health & hospitals	0.8	S/L Govt
Equipment rental & leasing services	0.5	Services	Residential additions/alterations, nonfarm	0.7	Constr.
Adhesives & sealants	0.4	Manufg.	Animal & marine fats & oils	0.7	Manufg.
Fabricated rubber products, nec	0.4	Manufg.	Drugs	0.7	Manufg.
Special industry machinery, nec	0.4	Manufg.	Fluid milk	0.7	Manufg.
Job training & related services	0.4	Services	Paper coating & glazing	0.7	Manufg.
Fabricated metal products, nec	0.3	Manufg.	Polishes & sanitation goods	0.7	Manufg.
Lighting fixtures & equipment	0.3	Manufg.	Automotive & apparel trimmings	0.6	Manufg.
Lubricating oils & greases	0.3	Manufg.	Broadwoven fabric mills	0.6	Manufg.
Metal stampings, nec	0.3	Manufg.	Frozen fruits, fruit juices & vegetables	0.6	Manufg.
Primary metal products, nec	0.3	Manufg.	Frozen specialties	0.6	Manufg.
Special dies & tools & machine tool accessories	0.3	Manufg.	Knit outerwear mills	0.6	Manufg.
Water transportation	0.3	Util.	Miscellaneous fabricated wire products	0.6	Manufg.
Royalties	0.3	Fin/R.E.	Photographic equipment & supplies	0.6	Manufg.
Management & consulting services & labs	0.3	Services	Pickles, sauces, & salad dressings	0.6	Manufg.
Metal foil & leaf	0.2	Manufg.	Soap & other detergents	0.6	Manufg.
Narrow fabric mills	0.2	Manufg.	Residential garden apartments	0.5	Constr.
Paints & allied products	0.2	Manufg.	Bags, except textile	0.5	Manufg.
Primary copper	0.2	Manufg.	Petroleum refining	0.5	Manufg.
Sanitary services, steam supply, irrigation	0.2	Util.	Semiconductors & related devices	0.5	Manufg.
Accounting, auditing & bookkeeping	0.2	Services	Real estate	0.5	Fin/R.E.
Electrical repair shops	0.2	Services	Beauty & barber shops	0.5	Services
Engineering, architectural, & surveying services	0.2	Services	Residential 1-unit structures, nonfarm	0.4	Constr.
Legal services	0.2	Services	Carbon paper & inked ribbons	0.4	Manufg.
Alkalies & chlorine	0.1	Manufg.	Roasted coffee	0.4	Manufg.
Building paper & board mills	0.1	Manufg.	Storage batteries	0.4	Manufg.
Manifold business forms	0.1	Manufg.	Upholstered household furniture	0.4	Manufg.
Mineral wool	0.1	Manufg.	Communications, except radio & TV	0.4	Util.
Pipe, valves, & pipe fittings	0.1	Manufg.	Water supply & sewage systems	0.4	Util.
Screw machine and related products	0.1	Manufg.	Business services nec	0.4	Services
Air transportation	0.1	Util.	Doctors & dentists	0.4	Services
Insurance carriers	0.1	Fin/R.E.	Miscellaneous repair shops	0.4	Services
Business/professional associations	0.1	Services	Construction of hospitals	0.3	Constr.
U.S. Postal Service	0.1	Gov't	Industrial buildings	0.3	Constr.
			Maintenance of highways & streets	0.3	Constr.
			Games, toys, & children's vehicles	0.3	Manufg.
			Logging camps & logging contractors	0.3	Manufg.
			Mattresses & bedsprings	0.3	Manufg.
			Nonferrous wire drawing & insulating	0.3	Manufg.
			Organic fibers, noncellulosic	0.3	Manufg.
			Sanitary paper products	0.3	Manufg.
			Sausages & other prepared meats	0.3	Manufg.
			Signs & advertising displays	0.3	Manufg.
			Surgical & medical instruments	0.3	Manufg.
			Retail trade, except eating & drinking	0.3	Trade
			Amusement & recreation services nec	0.3	Services
			Child day care services	0.3	Services
			Management & consulting services & labs	0.3	Services
			Nursing & personal care facilities	0.3	Services
			Construction of educational buildings	0.2	Constr.
			Construction of stores & restaurants	0.2	Constr.

Continued on next page.

INPUTS AND OUTPUTS FOR MISCELLANEOUS PLASTICS PRODUCTS - Continued

Economic Sector or Industry Providing Inputs	%	Sector	Economic Sector or Industry Buying Outputs	%	Sector
			Electric utility facility construction	0.2	Constr.
			Warehouses	0.2	Constr.
			Aluminum rolling & drawing	0.2	Manufg.
			Bread, cake, & related products	0.2	Manufg.
			Carbon & graphite products	0.2	Manufg.
			Chemical preparations, nec	0.2	Manufg.
			Cigarettes	0.2	Manufg.
			Cookies & crackers	0.2	Manufg.
			Dog, cat, & other pet food	0.2	Manufg.
			Electric housewares & fans	0.2	Manufg.
			Fabricated plate work (boiler shops)	0.2	Manufg.
			Fabricated structural metal	0.2	Manufg.
			General industrial machinery, nec	0.2	Manufg.
			Glass & glass products, except containers	0.2	Manufg.
			Hard surface floor coverings	0.2	Manufg.
			Household refrigerators & freezers	0.2	Manufg.
			Knit fabric mills	0.2	Manufg.
			Lighting fixtures & equipment	0.2	Manufg.
			Macaroni & spaghetti	0.2	Manufg.
			Meat packing plants	0.2	Manufg.
			Nitrogenous & phosphatic fertilizers	0.2	Manufg.
			Radio & TV communication equipment	0.2	Manufg.
			Radio & TV receiving sets	0.2	Manufg.
			Refrigeration & heating equipment	0.2	Manufg.
			Shoes, except rubber	0.2	Manufg.
			Shortening & cooking oils	0.2	Manufg.
			Sporting & athletic goods, nec	0.2	Manufg.
			Surface active agents	0.2	Manufg.
			Surgical appliances & supplies	0.2	Manufg.
			Wood partitions & fixtures	0.2	Manufg.
			Job training & related services	0.2	Services
			Laundry, dry cleaning, shoe repair	0.2	Services
			Social services, nec	0.2	Services
			Federal Government purchases, national defense	0.2	Fed Govt
			Greenhouse & nursery products	0.1	Agric.
			Farm service facilities	0.1	Constr.
			Hotels & motels	0.1	Constr.
			Maintenance of nonbuilding facilities nec	0.1	Constr.
			Maintenance of water supply facilities	0.1	Constr.
			Aircraft & missile equipment, nec	0.1	Manufg.
			Architectural metal work	0.1	Manufg.
			Blankbooks & looseleaf binders	0.1	Manufg.
			Book printing	0.1	Manufg.
			Cheese, natural & processed	0.1	Manufg.
			Chocolate & cocoa products	0.1	Manufg.
			Condensed & evaporated milk	0.1	Manufg.
			Confectionery products	0.1	Manufg.
			Distilled liquor, except brandy	0.1	Manufg.
			Drapery hardware & blinds & shades	0.1	Manufg.
			Engine electrical equipment	0.1	Manufg.
			Fabricated rubber products, nec	0.1	Manufg.
			Guided missiles & space vehicles	0.1	Manufg.
			Metal foil & leaf	0.1	Manufg.
			Metal household furniture	0.1	Manufg.
			Metal office furniture	0.1	Manufg.
			Miscellaneous publishing	0.1	Manufg.
			Motors & generators	0.1	Manufg.
			Paperboard containers & boxes	0.1	Manufg.
			Paving mixtures & blocks	0.1	Manufg.
			Phonograph records & tapes	0.1	Manufg.
			Pumps & compressors	0.1	Manufg.
			Secondary nonferrous metals	0.1	Manufg.
			Sheet metal work	0.1	Manufg.
			Special dies & tools & machine tool accessories	0.1	Manufg.
			Sugar	0.1	Manufg.
			Watches, clocks, & parts	0.1	Manufg.
			Women's hosiery, except socks	0.1	Manufg.
			Wood household furniture	0.1	Manufg.
			Wood products, nec	0.1	Manufg.
			Engineering, architectural, & surveying services	0.1	Services
			Local government passenger transit	0.1	Gov't

Source: Benchmark Input-Output Accounts for the U.S. Economy, 1982, U.S. Department of Commerce, Washington, D.C., July 1991. Data, as reported in the source, are organized by the 1977 SIC structure in use in 1982 but have been matched, as closely as is possible, to the 1987 SIC structure used in this book.

OCCUPATIONS EMPLOYED BY SIC 308 - MISCELLANEOUS PLASTICS PRODUCTS

Occupation	% of Total 1994	Change to 2005	Occupation	% of Total 1994	Change to 2005
Plastic molding machine workers	18.3	6.7	Maintenance repairers, general utility	1.6	6.7
Assemblers, fabricators, & hand workers nec	9.5	18.5	Industrial truck & tractor operators	1.5	18.5
Blue collar worker supervisors	5.2	10.7	Tool & die makers	1.4	77.8
Hand packers & packagers	4.7	-8.6	Extruding & forming machine workers	1.4	-40.7
Machine tool cutting & forming etc. nec	3.4	50.5	Industrial production managers	1.4	18.5
Inspectors, testers, & graders, precision	3.4	6.7	Machine feeders & offbearers	1.4	6.7
Helpers, laborers, & material movers nec	2.6	18.5	Packaging & filling machine operators	1.3	18.5
Machine forming operators, metal & plastic	2.5	30.4	Cutters & trimmers, hand	1.2	18.5
Metal & plastic machine workers nec	2.4	89.0	Bookkeeping, accounting, & auditing clerks	1.1	-11.1
General managers & top executives	2.3	12.4	Secretaries, ex legal & medical	1.1	7.9
Industrial machinery mechanics	2.2	30.4	Coating, painting, & spraying machine workers	1.1	6.7
Sales & related workers nec	1.9	18.5	Crushing & mixing machine operators	1.1	77.8
Traffic, shipping, & receiving clerks	1.8	14.0	Machine operators nec	1.1	-32.1
Freight, stock, & material movers, hand	1.7	-5.2			

Source: Industry-Occupation Matrix, Bureau of Labor Statistics. These data relate to one or more 3-digit SIC industry groups rather than to a single 4-digit SIC. The change reported for each occupation to the year 2005 is a percent of growth or decline as estimated by the Bureau of Labor Statistics. The abbreviation nec stands for 'not elsewhere classified'.

LOCATION BY STATE AND REGIONAL CONCENTRATION

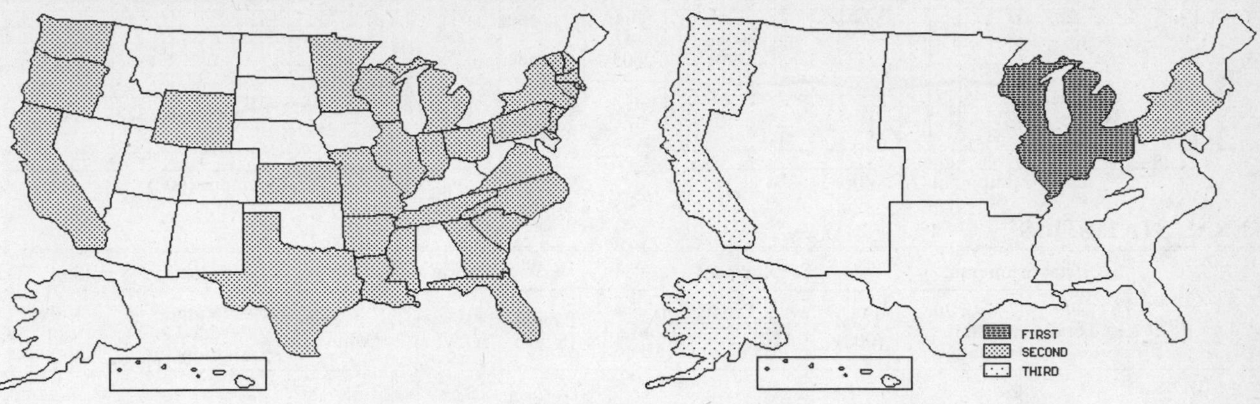

INDUSTRY DATA BY STATE

State	Establish-ments	Shipments			Employment				Cost as % of Shipments	Investment per Employee ($)
		Total ($ mil)	% of U.S.	Per Establ.	Total Number	% of U.S.	Per Establ.	Wages ($/hour)		
Illinois	39	312.8	9.4	8.0	2,300	8.5	59	11.88	27.4	6,000
New York	45	303.2	9.1	6.7	1,600	5.9	36	12.08	29.6	9,000
Ohio	60	239.1	7.2	4.0	2,300	8.5	38	10.83	49.7	5,130
New Jersey	45	224.9	6.7	5.0	1,800	6.7	40	10.87	49.0	4,833
California	84	218.6	6.6	2.6	2,300	8.5	27	9.29	43.9	4,304
Pennsylvania	41	203.0	6.1	5.0	1,900	7.0	46	10.08	50.2	3,632
Indiana	28	142.5	4.3	5.1	1,500	5.6	54	9.65	45.5	2,867
Massachusetts	21	131.6	3.9	6.3	1,100	4.1	52	10.32	37.5	4,909
Virginia	8	118.2	3.5	14.8	1,100	4.1	138	8.30	59.9	2,545
South Carolina	11	117.0	3.5	10.6	1,000	3.7	91	8.41	66.6	2,600
Texas	39	109.6	3.3	2.8	1,100	4.1	28	9.27	45.3	3,727
Michigan	27	96.9	2.9	3.6	1,100	4.1	41	9.07	42.0	2,818
Missouri	12	94.4	2.8	7.9	600	2.2	50	8.78	46.2	4,500
Georgia	17	94.1	2.8	5.5	900	3.3	53	8.86	43.4	5,111
Minnesota	13	65.6	2.0	5.0	700	2.6	54	12.44	43.8	3,000
New Hampshire	7	63.9	1.9	9.1	500	1.9	71	9.14	46.5	2,600
Florida	29	61.4	1.8	2.1	600	2.2	21	9.22	55.2	4,333
Washington	11	59.2	1.8	5.4	600	2.2	55	12.22	44.4	8,333
Connecticut	12	42.0	1.3	3.5	300	1.1	25	10.40	26.2	-
Wisconsin	10	36.9	1.1	3.7	500	1.9	50	8.50	39.8	3,000
North Carolina	14	24.5	0.7	1.8	200	0.7	14	10.00	69.4	-
Rhode Island	3	9.9	0.3	3.3	100	0.4	33	8.00	48.5	-
Oregon	10	8.7	0.3	0.9	100	0.4	10	7.50	40.2	3,000
Tennessee	13	(D)	-	-	375 *	1.4	29	-	-	3,733
Kansas	6	(D)	-	-	750 *	2.8	125	-	-	-
Arkansas	4	(D)	-	-	175 *	0.6	44	-	-	-
Delaware	4	(D)	-	-	750 *	2.8	188	-	-	-
Louisiana	3	(D)	-	-	175 *	0.6	58	-	-	-
Vermont	3	(D)	-	-	175 *	0.6	58	-	-	-
Mississippi	2	(D)	-	-	175 *	0.6	88	-	-	-
Wyoming	1	(D)	-	-	175 *	0.6	175	-	-	-

Source: 1992 *Economic Census*. The states are in descending order of shipments or establishments (if shipment data are missing for the majority). The symbol (D) appears when data are withheld to prevent disclosure of competitive information. States marked with (D) are sorted by number of establishments. A dash (-) indicates that the data element cannot be calculated; * indicates the midpoint of a range.

3083 - LAMINATED PLASTICS PLATE & SHEET

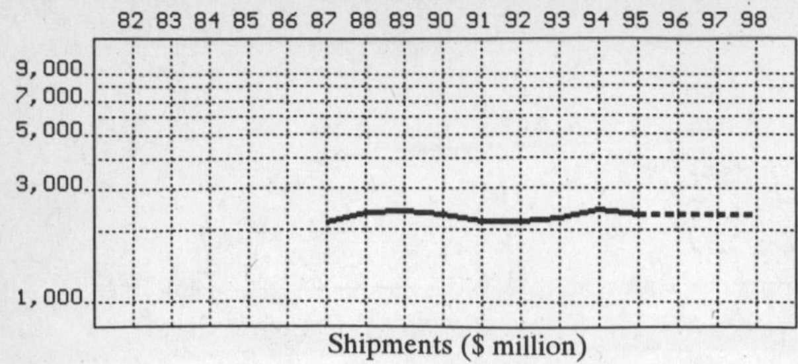

Shipments ($ million)

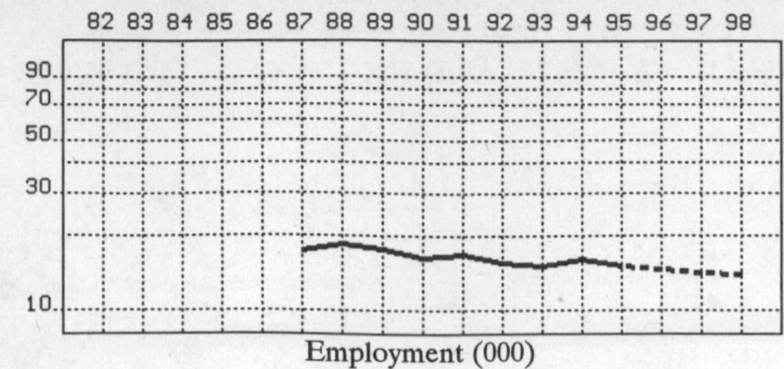

Employment (000)

GENERAL STATISTICS

Year	Companies	Establishments: Total	Establishments: with 20 or more employees	Employment: Total (000)	Employment: Production Workers (000)	Employment: Production Hours (Mil)	Compensation: Payroll ($ mil)	Compensation: Wages ($/hr)	Production ($ million): Cost of Materials	Production ($ million): Value Added by Manufacture	Production ($ million): Value of Shipments	Production ($ million): Capital Invest.
1982												
1983												
1984												
1985												
1986												
1987	214	234	104	17.3	12.9	27.6	412.9	9.98	1,025.7	1,122.6	2,143.9	53.8
1988		225	104	18.6	14.0	28.3	438.8	10.23	1,145.7	1,208.7	2,352.0	81.9
1989		224	101	17.6	14.1	30.3	460.3	10.15	1,147.9	1,238.8	2,389.4	77.3
1990		234	104	16.4	13.4	28.1	448.5	10.97	1,139.3	1,159.6	2,293.0	83.3
1991		252	107	16.9	12.6	26.1	455.0	11.62	1,046.7	1,093.3	2,157.3	77.5
1992	283	302	112	15.6	11.4	25.2	435.2	11.25	1,072.9	1,093.6	2,183.7	57.7
1993		292	115	15.1	11.2	24.5	438.9	11.49	1,102.8	1,162.6	2,261.4	60.4
1994		303P	115P	16.0	12.0	25.7	453.9	12.11	1,147.4	1,271.1	2,405.7	64.2
1995		315P	117P	15.0P	11.1P	24.3P	454.7P	12.32P	1,100.3P	1,218.9P	2,306.9P	64.2P
1996		328P	118P	14.6P	10.8P	23.7P	457.3P	12.62P	1,103.8P	1,222.8P	2,314.3P	63.0P
1997		341P	120P	14.2P	10.4P	23.1P	459.9P	12.92P	1,107.4P	1,226.8P	2,321.8P	61.8P
1998		354P	122P	13.8P	10.1P	22.5P	462.5P	13.22P	1,110.9P	1,230.7P	2,329.3P	60.6P

Sources: 1982, 1987, 1992 *Economic Census*; *Annual Survey of Manufactures*, 83-86, 88-91, 93-94. Establishment counts for non-Census years are from *County Business Patterns*; establishment values for 83-84 are extrapolations. 'P's show projections by the editors. Industries reclassified in 87 will not have data for prior years.

INDICES OF CHANGE

Year	Companies	Establishments: Total	Establishments: with 20 or more employees	Employment: Total (000)	Employment: Production Workers (000)	Employment: Production Hours (Mil)	Compensation: Payroll ($ mil)	Compensation: Wages ($/hr)	Production ($ million): Cost of Materials	Production ($ million): Value Added by Manufacture	Production ($ million): Value of Shipments	Production ($ million): Capital Invest.
1982												
1983												
1984												
1985												
1986												
1987	76	77	93	111	113	110	95	89	96	103	98	93
1988		75	93	119	123	112	101	91	107	111	108	142
1989		74	90	113	124	120	106	90	107	113	109	134
1990		77	93	105	118	112	103	98	106	106	105	144
1991		83	96	108	111	104	105	103	98	100	99	134
1992	100	100	100	100	100	100	100	100	100	100	100	100
1993		97	103	97	98	97	101	102	103	106	104	105
1994		100P	102P	103	105	102	104	108	107	116	110	111
1995		104P	104P	96P	98P	96P	104P	110P	103P	111P	106P	111P
1996		109P	106P	93P	95P	94P	105P	112P	103P	112P	106P	109P
1997		113P	108P	91P	92P	92P	106P	115P	103P	112P	106P	107P
1998		117P	109P	89P	89P	89P	106P	118P	104P	113P	107P	105P

Sources: Same as General Statistics. Values reflect change from the base year, 1992. Values above 100 mean greater than 92, values below 100 mean less than 92, and a value of 100 in the 82-91 or 93-98 period means same as 92. 'P's mark projections by the editors.

SELECTED RATIOS

For 1994	Avg. of All Manufact.	Analyzed Industry	Index	For 1994	Avg. of All Manufact.	Analyzed Industry	Index
Employees per Establishment	49	53	108	Value Added per Production Worker	134,084	105,925	79
Payroll per Establishment	1,500,273	1,499,434	100	Cost per Establishment	5,045,178	3,790,373	75
Payroll per Employee	30,620	28,369	93	Cost per Employee	102,970	71,712	70
Production Workers per Establishment	34	40	115	Cost per Production Worker	146,988	95,617	65
Wages per Establishment	853,319	1,028,121	120	Shipments per Establishment	9,576,895	7,947,098	83
Wages per Production Worker	24,861	25,936	104	Shipments per Employee	195,460	150,356	77
Hours per Production Worker	2,056	2,142	104	Shipments per Production Worker	279,017	200,475	72
Wages per Hour	12.09	12.11	100	Investment per Establishment	321,011	212,081	66
Value Added per Establishment	4,602,255	4,199,009	91	Investment per Employee	6,552	4,012	61
Value Added per Employee	93,930	79,444	85	Investment per Production Worker	9,352	5,350	57

Sources: Same as General Statistics. The 'Average of All Manufacturing' column represents the average of all manufacturing industries reported for the most recent complete year available. The Index shows the relationship between the Average and the Analyzed Industry. For example, 100 means that they are equal; 500 that the Analyzed Industry is five times the average; 50 means that the Analyzed Industry is half the national average. The abbreviation 'na' is used to show that data are 'not available'.

LEADING COMPANIES

Number shown: **52** Total sales ($ mil): **2,554** Total employment (000): **16.9**

Company Name	Address				CEO Name	Phone	Co. Type	Sales ($ mil)	Empl. (000)
Klockner Capital Corp	PO Box 750	Gordonsville	VA	22942	HJG van Beek	703-832-3400	S	400	2.0
AlliedSignal	PO Box 1448	La Crosse	WI	54602	Mark Bulriff	608-784-6070	S	350	2.3
Ralph Wilson Plastics Co	PO Box 6110	Temple	TX	76503	Bill Reeb	817-778-2711	S	350	2.9
Spartech Corp	7733 Forsyth Blv	Clayton	MO	63105	Bradley B Buechler	314-721-4242	P	257	1.2
Sekisui America Corp	666 5th Av	New York	NY	10103	Y Tamaki	212-489-3500	S	168	0.6
Primex Plastics Corp	1235 N F St	Richmond	IN	47434	Paul J Bertsch	317-966-7774	S	135	0.7
Wolverine Technologies	17199 Laurel Pk Dr	Livonia	MI	48152	Peter Dachowski	313-953-1100	S	130	0.6
Nevamar	8339 Telegraph Rd	Odenton	MD	21113	Evans Heath	410-551-5000	D	100	1.0
Formica Corp US	10155 Reading Rd	Cincinnati	OH	45241	Vince Langone	513-786-3400	D	72	0.8
Eslon Thermoplastics	PO Box 240696	Charlotte	NC	28224	T Tamura	704-889-2431	D	60	0.2
Evans Industries Inc	200 Renaissance Ctr	Detroit	MI	48243		313-259-2266	R	60	0.4
GBC Film Products	712 W Winthrop	Addison	IL	60101	Govi Reddy	708-543-7100	D	52	0.3
Spaulding Composites Company	One Morgan Pl	Rochester	NH	03866	R M Kirkpatrick	603-332-0555	R	40	0.5
Plastic Fabricating Company Inc	PO Box 9410	Wichita	KS	67277	Roy Best	316-942-1241	S	32	0.3
Resinoid Engineering Corp	7557 N Saint Louis	Skokie	IL	60076	Allen Olson	708-673-1050	R	30*	0.4
Macristy Industries Inc	206 Newington Av	New Britain	CT	06050	JB Barlow	203-225-4637	R	24	0.3
Glassmaster Co	PO Box 788	Lexington	SC	29072	R M Trewhella	803-359-2594	P	20	0.2
Anatomical Chart Co	8221 Kimball Av	Skokie	IL	60076	Marshall Cordell	708-679-4700	R	18	0.1
Rogers Corp	100 S Roosevelt Av	Chandler	AZ	85226	Bob Hodges	602-961-1382	D	18	0.1
Haysite Reinforced Plastics	5599 New Perry	Erie	PA	16509	Joseph A Schneider	814-868-3691	D	15	0.1
Lamart Corp	16 Richmond St	Clifton	NJ	07015	Steven B Hirsh	201-772-6262	R	15	<0.1
OMEGA Pultrusions Inc	1331 S Chillicothe	Aurora	OH	44202	Tom Deller	216-562-5201	R	15	0.2
J-Von LP	25 Litchfield St	Leominster	MA	01453	Daniel Hunter	508-537-4721	R	14	<0.1
Mar-Bal Inc	16930 Munn Rd	Chagrin Falls	OH	44023	J Balogh	216-543-7526	R	14	0.2
American Sheet Extrusion Corp	1618 Lynch Rd	Evansville	IN	47711	Ken Hedges	812-423-7376	R	13*	0.1
Landmark Plastic Corp	1183 Home Av	Akron	OH	44310	Bob Merzweiler	216-630-9334	R	13*	0.1
Polyplastex International Inc	6200 49th St N	Pinellas Park	FL	34665	Dennis Peskin	813-525-2173	S	13	0.2
Crescent Plastics Inc	955 Diamond Av	Evansville	IN	47711	JH Schroeder	812-428-9300	R	10	0.1
Ethylene Corp	PO Box 918	Murray Hill	NJ	07974	JA Jaffe	908-464-2600	R	9*	<0.1
Recto Molded Products Inc	4425 Appleton St	Cincinnati	OH	45209	FA Backscheider	513-871-5544	R	9	0.2
Sani-Top Inc	PO Box 130	Gardena	CA	90247	Allan F Snyder	213-321-5531	R	9	<0.1
Connecticut Laminating	162 James St	New Haven	CT	06513	Henry Snow	203-787-2184	R	8	0.1
Glasflex	PO Box 197	Stirling	NJ	07980	Joseph Matrange	908-647-4100	D	8	<0.1
ABC Industries Inc	PO Box 77	Warsaw	IN	46581	S B Rufenbarger	219-267-5166	R	7	<0.1
Jayar Manufacturing Co	3700 Cypress Av	El Monte	CA	91731	Norman L Jackson	818-579-5300	R	7*	<0.1
Sigmaform	5695 Hwy 61 S	Vicksburg	MS	39180	JD Hobbs	601-638-8209	D	7	<0.1
American Commodities Inc	2945 Davison Rd	Flint	MI	48506	Mark Lieberman	810-767-3800	R	7*	<0.1
Ly-Line Products Inc	PO Box 38	Enumclaw	WA	98022	Hugh Lyman Jr	360-825-1611	R	7	<0.1
Lamination Services Inc	PO Box 750365	Memphis	TN	38175	Mason Ezzell	901-794-3032	R	4	<0.1
Arcy Plastic Laminates Inc	100 N Mohawk St	Cohoes	NY	12047	Roy R Ceccucci	518-235-0753	R	4*	<0.1
Rauschert Industries Inc	351 Indrial Pk Rd	Madisonville	TN	37354	Tom Rauschert	615-442-4471	R	4*	<0.1
Streamline Plastics Company Inc	1112 Brook Av	Bronx	NY	10456	Joe Bartner	718-588-1211	R	4	<0.1
California Combining Corp	5607 S Santa Fe Av	Los Angeles	CA	90058	Maurice L Heller	213-589-5727	R	4	<0.1
Cast-All Corp	PO Box 0271	Mineola	NY	11501	Jack H Mandell	516-741-4025	R	3	<0.1
Engineering Plastics Inc	PO Box 1440	Westborough	MA	01581	John Morse	508-366-4425	R	3	<0.1
Mesa Fiberglass Inc	6471 E 49th Dr	Commerce City	CO	80022	EM Ardelt	303-287-2576	R	3	<0.1
Precision Laminates Corp	7 E Franklin St	Danbury	CT	06810	L Owen III	203-744-7880	R	3	<0.1
ST Laminating Corp	PO Box 1371	Elkhart	IN	46515	Ron Spain	219-262-4199	R	3	<0.1
Leed Plastics Corp	793 E Pico Blv	Los Angeles	CA	90021	I Sankey	213-746-5984	R	2	<0.1
Top Manufacturing Company	5825 Ordway St	Riverside	CA	92504	Tracy Barber	909-688-4141	R	2*	<0.1
Maplewood Inc	PO Box 540	Ashburnham	MA	01430	Mark P Drouin	508-827-6064	R	1	<0.1
Temp Tronix Inc	PO Box 1618	La Jolla	CA	92038	Jim Mize	619-578-4530	R	1	<0.1

Source: *Ward's Business Directory of U.S. Private and Public Companies*, Volumes 1 and 2, 1996. The company type code used is as follows: P - Public, R - Private, S - Subsidiary, D - Division, J - Joint Venture, A - Affiliate, G - Group. Sales are in millions of dollars, employees are in thousands. An asterisk (*) indicates an estimated sales volume. The symbol < stands for 'less than'. Company names and addresses are truncated, in some cases, to fit into the available space.

MATERIALS CONSUMED

Material	Quantity	Delivered Cost ($ million)
Materials, ingredients, containers, and supplies	(X)	993.6
Hardboard (wood fiberboard)	(X)	4.0
Industrial inorganic chemicals	(X)	6.8
Inorganic pigments	(X)	5.0
Plastics resins consumed in the form of granules, pellets, powders, liquids, etc.	(X)	131.3
Industrial organic and synthetic organic chemicals, including plasticizers	(X)	23.4
Synthetic dyes, pigments, lakes, and toners	(X)	1.9
All other chemical and allied products	(X)	9.8
Plastics products consumed in the form of sheets, rods, tubes, film, and other shapes	(X)	138.7
Custom compounded plastics resins (purchased)	(X)	18.1
Textile-type glass fiber	(X)	61.5
Broadwoven fabrics	(X)	11.8
Paper and paperboard products except paperboard boxes, containers, and corrugated paperboard	(X)	233.4
Paperboard containers, boxes, and corrugated paperboard	(X)	11.2
Parts and attachments specially designed for plastics working machinery	(X)	1.5
All other materials and components, parts, containers, and supplies	(X)	166.8
Materials, ingredients, containers, and supplies, nsk	(X)	168.5

Source: 1992 *Economic Census*. Explanation of symbols used: (D): Withheld to avoid disclosure of competitive data; na: Not available; (S): Withheld because statistical norms were not met; (X): Not applicable; (Z): Less than half the unit shown; nec: Not elsewhere classified; nsk: Not specified by kind; - : zero; * : 10-19 percent estimated; ** : 20-29 percent estimated.

PRODUCT SHARE DETAILS

Product or Product Class	% Share	Product or Product Class	% Share
Laminated plastics plate and sheet	100.00	Thermoplastic plastics laminates (excluding flexible packaging)	12.96
Thermosetting plastics laminates (excluding flexible packaging)	42.87	Other plastics laminates (excluding flexible packaging)	36.43

Source: 1992 *Economic Census*. The values shown are percent of total shipments in an industry. Values of indented subcategories are summed in the main heading. The symbol (D) appears when data are withheld to prevent disclosure of competitive information. The abbreviation nsk stands for 'not specified by kind' and nec for 'not elsewhere classified'.

INPUTS AND OUTPUTS FOR MISCELLANEOUS PLASTICS PRODUCTS

Economic Sector or Industry Providing Inputs	%	Sector	Economic Sector or Industry Buying Outputs	%	Sector
Plastics materials & resins	36.2	Manufg.	Hospitals	5.6	Services
Wholesale trade	8.5	Trade	Electronic components nec	5.2	Manufg.
Miscellaneous plastics products	7.2	Manufg.	Personal consumption expenditures	4.3	
Imports	5.8	Foreign	Miscellaneous plastics products	4.0	Manufg.
Cyclic crudes and organics	4.4	Manufg.	Exports	4.0	Foreign
Electric services (utilities)	4.4	Util.	Telephone & telegraph apparatus	3.0	Manufg.
Paperboard containers & boxes	2.6	Manufg.	Motor vehicles & car bodies	2.8	Manufg.
Communications, except radio & TV	2.3	Util.	Eating & drinking places	2.8	Trade
Motor freight transportation & warehousing	2.0	Util.	Maintenance of nonfarm buildings nec	2.4	Constr.
Paperboard mills	1.5	Manufg.	Food preparations, nec	2.3	Manufg.
Synthetic rubber	1.5	Manufg.	Plastics materials & resins	2.1	Manufg.
Railroads & related services	1.3	Util.	Typewriters & office machines, nec	1.7	Manufg.
Glass & glass products, except containers	1.2	Manufg.	Commercial printing	1.6	Manufg.
Gas production & distribution (utilities)	1.0	Util.	Cyclic crudes and organics	1.5	Manufg.
Noncomparable imports	1.0	Foreign	Electronic computing equipment	1.5	Manufg.
Industrial inorganic chemicals, nec	0.9	Manufg.	Motor vehicle parts & accessories	1.3	Manufg.
Crude petroleum & natural gas	0.7	Mining	Paper mills, except building paper	1.3	Manufg.
Maintenance of nonfarm buildings nec	0.7	Constr.	Bottled & canned soft drinks	1.2	Manufg.
Eating & drinking places	0.7	Trade	Toilet preparations	1.2	Manufg.
Real estate	0.7	Fin/R.E.	Aircraft	1.1	Manufg.
Computer & data processing services	0.7	Services	Medical & health services, nec	1.1	Services
Broadwoven fabric mills	0.6	Manufg.	Nonfarm residential structure maintenance	1.0	Constr.
Machinery, except electrical, nec	0.6	Manufg.	Optical instruments & lenses	0.9	Manufg.
Petroleum refining	0.6	Manufg.	Wholesale trade	0.9	Trade
Banking	0.6	Fin/R.E.	Office buildings	0.8	Constr.
Inorganic pigments	0.5	Manufg.	Computer & data processing services	0.8	Services
Wood products, nec	0.5	Manufg.	Hotels & lodging places	0.8	Services
Advertising	0.5	Services	S/L Govt. purch., health & hospitals	0.8	S/L Govt
Equipment rental & leasing services	0.5	Services	Residential additions/alterations, nonfarm	0.7	Constr.
Adhesives & sealants	0.4	Manufg.	Animal & marine fats & oils	0.7	Manufg.
Fabricated rubber products, nec	0.4	Manufg.	Drugs	0.7	Manufg.
Special industry machinery, nec	0.4	Manufg.	Fluid milk	0.7	Manufg.
Job training & related services	0.4	Services	Paper coating & glazing	0.7	Manufg.
Fabricated metal products, nec	0.3	Manufg.	Polishes & sanitation goods	0.7	Manufg.
Lighting fixtures & equipment	0.3	Manufg.	Automotive & apparel trimmings	0.6	Manufg.
Lubricating oils & greases	0.3	Manufg.	Broadwoven fabric mills	0.6	Manufg.
Metal stampings, nec	0.3	Manufg.	Frozen fruits, fruit juices & vegetables	0.6	Manufg.
Primary metal products, nec	0.3	Manufg.	Frozen specialties	0.6	Manufg.

Continued on next page.

INPUTS AND OUTPUTS FOR MISCELLANEOUS PLASTICS PRODUCTS - Continued

Economic Sector or Industry Providing Inputs	%	Sector	Economic Sector or Industry Buying Outputs	%	Sector
Special dies & tools & machine tool accessories	0.3	Manufg.	Knit outerwear mills	0.6	Manufg.
Water transportation	0.3	Util.	Miscellaneous fabricated wire products	0.6	Manufg.
Royalties	0.3	Fin/R.E.	Photographic equipment & supplies	0.6	Manufg.
Management & consulting services & labs	0.3	Services	Pickles, sauces, & salad dressings	0.6	Manufg.
Metal foil & leaf	0.2	Manufg.	Soap & other detergents	0.6	Manufg.
Narrow fabric mills	0.2	Manufg.	Residential garden apartments	0.5	Constr.
Paints & allied products	0.2	Manufg.	Bags, except textile	0.5	Manufg.
Primary copper	0.2	Manufg.	Petroleum refining	0.5	Manufg.
Sanitary services, steam supply, irrigation	0.2	Util.	Semiconductors & related devices	0.5	Manufg.
Accounting, auditing & bookkeeping	0.2	Services	Real estate	0.5	Fin/R.E.
Electrical repair shops	0.2	Services	Beauty & barber shops	0.5	Services
Engineering, architectural, & surveying services	0.2	Services	Residential 1-unit structures, nonfarm	0.4	Constr.
Legal services	0.2	Services	Carbon paper & inked ribbons	0.4	Manufg.
Alkalies & chlorine	0.1	Manufg.	Roasted coffee	0.4	Manufg.
Building paper & board mills	0.1	Manufg.	Storage batteries	0.4	Manufg.
Manifold business forms	0.1	Manufg.	Upholstered household furniture	0.4	Manufg.
Mineral wool	0.1	Manufg.	Communications, except radio & TV	0.4	Util.
Pipe, valves, & pipe fittings	0.1	Manufg.	Water supply & sewage systems	0.4	Util.
Screw machine and related products	0.1	Manufg.	Business services nec	0.4	Services
Air transportation	0.1	Util.	Doctors & dentists	0.4	Services
Insurance carriers	0.1	Fin/R.E.	Miscellaneous repair shops	0.4	Services
Business/professional associations	0.1	Services	Construction of hospitals	0.3	Constr.
U.S. Postal Service	0.1	Gov't	Industrial buildings	0.3	Constr.
			Maintenance of highways & streets	0.3	Constr.
			Games, toys, & children's vehicles	0.3	Manufg.
			Logging camps & logging contractors	0.3	Manufg.
			Mattresses & bedsprings	0.3	Manufg.
			Nonferrous wire drawing & insulating	0.3	Manufg.
			Organic fibers, noncellulosic	0.3	Manufg.
			Sanitary paper products	0.3	Manufg.
			Sausages & other prepared meats	0.3	Manufg.
			Signs & advertising displays	0.3	Manufg.
			Surgical & medical instruments	0.3	Manufg.
			Retail trade, except eating & drinking	0.3	Trade
			Amusement & recreation services nec	0.3	Services
			Child day care services	0.3	Services
			Management & consulting services & labs	0.3	Services
			Nursing & personal care facilities	0.3	Services
			Construction of educational buildings	0.2	Constr.
			Construction of stores & restaurants	0.2	Constr.
			Electric utility facility construction	0.2	Constr.
			Warehouses	0.2	Constr.
			Aluminum rolling & drawing	0.2	Manufg.
			Bread, cake, & related products	0.2	Manufg.
			Carbon & graphite products	0.2	Manufg.
			Chemical preparations, nec	0.2	Manufg.
			Cigarettes	0.2	Manufg.
			Cookies & crackers	0.2	Manufg.
			Dog, cat, & other pet food	0.2	Manufg.
			Electric housewares & fans	0.2	Manufg.
			Fabricated plate work (boiler shops)	0.2	Manufg.
			Fabricated structural metal	0.2	Manufg.
			General industrial machinery, nec	0.2	Manufg.
			Glass & glass products, except containers	0.2	Manufg.
			Hard surface floor coverings	0.2	Manufg.
			Household refrigerators & freezers	0.2	Manufg.
			Knit fabric mills	0.2	Manufg.
			Lighting fixtures & equipment	0.2	Manufg.
			Macaroni & spaghetti	0.2	Manufg.
			Meat packing plants	0.2	Manufg.
			Nitrogenous & phosphatic fertilizers	0.2	Manufg.
			Radio & TV communication equipment	0.2	Manufg.
			Radio & TV receiving sets	0.2	Manufg.
			Refrigeration & heating equipment	0.2	Manufg.
			Shoes, except rubber	0.2	Manufg.
			Shortening & cooking oils	0.2	Manufg.
			Sporting & athletic goods, nec	0.2	Manufg.
			Surface active agents	0.2	Manufg.
			Surgical appliances & supplies	0.2	Manufg.
			Wood partitions & fixtures	0.2	Manufg.
			Job training & related services	0.2	Services
			Laundry, dry cleaning, shoe repair	0.2	Services
			Social services, nec	0.2	Services
			Federal Government purchases, national defense	0.2	Fed Govt
			Greenhouse & nursery products	0.1	Agric.

Continued on next page.

INPUTS AND OUTPUTS FOR MISCELLANEOUS PLASTICS PRODUCTS - Continued

Economic Sector or Industry Providing Inputs	%	Sector	Economic Sector or Industry Buying Outputs	%	Sector
			Farm service facilities	0.1	Constr.
			Hotels & motels	0.1	Constr.
			Maintenance of nonbuilding facilities nec	0.1	Constr.
			Maintenance of water supply facilities	0.1	Constr.
			Aircraft & missile equipment, nec	0.1	Manufg.
			Architectural metal work	0.1	Manufg.
			Blankbooks & looseleaf binders	0.1	Manufg.
			Book printing	0.1	Manufg.
			Cheese, natural & processed	0.1	Manufg.
			Chocolate & cocoa products	0.1	Manufg.
			Condensed & evaporated milk	0.1	Manufg.
			Confectionery products	0.1	Manufg.
			Distilled liquor, except brandy	0.1	Manufg.
			Drapery hardware & blinds & shades	0.1	Manufg.
			Engine electrical equipment	0.1	Manufg.
			Fabricated rubber products, nec	0.1	Manufg.
			Guided missiles & space vehicles	0.1	Manufg.
			Metal foil & leaf	0.1	Manufg.
			Metal household furniture	0.1	Manufg.
			Metal office furniture	0.1	Manufg.
			Miscellaneous publishing	0.1	Manufg.
			Motors & generators	0.1	Manufg.
			Paperboard containers & boxes	0.1	Manufg.
			Paving mixtures & blocks	0.1	Manufg.
			Phonograph records & tapes	0.1	Manufg.
			Pumps & compressors	0.1	Manufg.
			Secondary nonferrous metals	0.1	Manufg.
			Sheet metal work	0.1	Manufg.
			Special dies & tools & machine tool accessories	0.1	Manufg.
			Sugar	0.1	Manufg.
			Watches, clocks, & parts	0.1	Manufg.
			Women's hosiery, except socks	0.1	Manufg.
			Wood household furniture	0.1	Manufg.
			Wood products, nec	0.1	Manufg.
			Engineering, architectural, & surveying services	0.1	Services
			Local government passenger transit	0.1	Gov't

Source: Benchmark Input-Output Accounts for the U.S. Economy, 1982, U.S. Department of Commerce, Washington, D.C., July 1991. Data, as reported in the source, are organized by the 1977 SIC structure in use in 1982 but have been matched, as closely as is possible, to the 1987 SIC structure used in this book.

OCCUPATIONS EMPLOYED BY SIC 308 - MISCELLANEOUS PLASTICS PRODUCTS

Occupation	% of Total 1994	Change to 2005	Occupation	% of Total 1994	Change to 2005
Plastic molding machine workers	18.3	6.7	Maintenance repairers, general utility	1.6	6.7
Assemblers, fabricators, & hand workers nec	9.5	18.5	Industrial truck & tractor operators	1.5	18.5
Blue collar worker supervisors	5.2	10.7	Tool & die makers	1.4	77.8
Hand packers & packagers	4.7	-8.6	Extruding & forming machine workers	1.4	-40.7
Machine tool cutting & forming etc. nec	3.4	50.5	Industrial production managers	1.4	18.5
Inspectors, testers, & graders, precision	3.4	6.7	Machine feeders & offbearers	1.4	6.7
Helpers, laborers, & material movers nec	2.6	18.5	Packaging & filling machine operators	1.3	18.5
Machine forming operators, metal & plastic	2.5	30.4	Cutters & trimmers, hand	1.2	18.5
Metal & plastic machine workers nec	2.4	89.0	Bookkeeping, accounting, & auditing clerks	1.1	-11.1
General managers & top executives	2.3	12.4	Secretaries, ex legal & medical	1.1	7.9
Industrial machinery mechanics	2.2	30.4	Coating, painting, & spraying machine workers	1.1	6.7
Sales & related workers nec	1.9	18.5	Crushing & mixing machine operators	1.1	77.8
Traffic, shipping, & receiving clerks	1.8	14.0	Machine operators nec	1.1	-32.1
Freight, stock, & material movers, hand	1.7	-5.2			

Source: Industry-Occupation Matrix, Bureau of Labor Statistics. These data relate to one or more 3-digit SIC industry groups rather than to a single 4-digit SIC. The change reported for each occupation to the year 2005 is a percent of growth or decline as estimated by the Bureau of Labor Statistics. The abbreviation nec stands for 'not elsewhere classified'.

LOCATION BY STATE AND REGIONAL CONCENTRATION

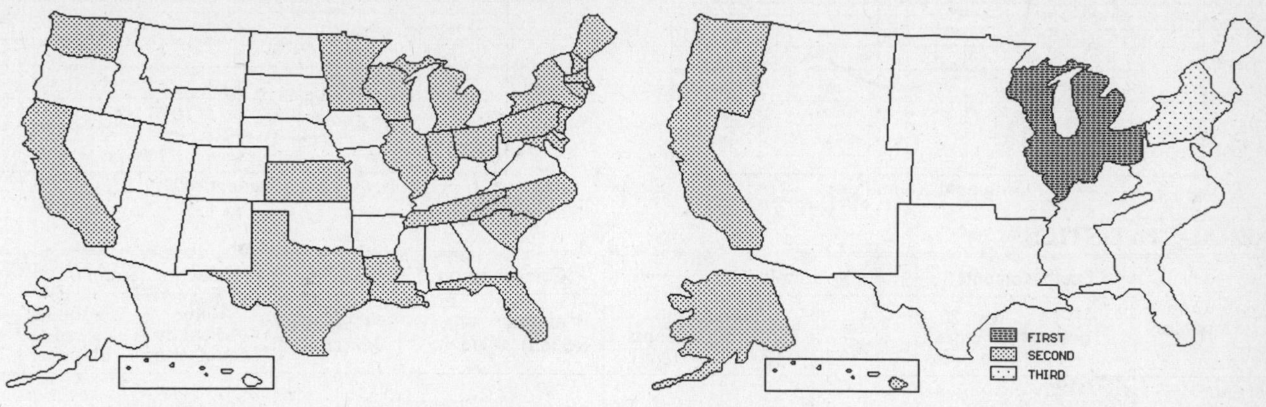

INDUSTRY DATA BY STATE

State	Establish-ments	Shipments Total ($ mil)	Shipments % of U.S.	Shipments Per Establ.	Employment Total Number	Employment % of U.S.	Employment Per Establ.	Wages ($/hour)	Cost as % of Shipments	Investment per Employee ($)
Ohio	28	307.5	14.1	11.0	2,200	14.1	79	13.39	50.0	2,773
California	44	223.9	10.3	5.1	1,600	10.3	36	9.23	47.2	2,500
Illinois	20	150.1	6.9	7.5	1,100	7.1	55	10.72	51.4	5,455
Pennsylvania	17	102.3	4.7	6.0	900	5.8	53	13.00	45.6	4,556
Massachusetts	12	77.6	3.6	6.5	400	2.6	33	11.80	51.5	2,000
Indiana	9	34.8	1.6	3.9	400	2.6	44	7.40	46.6	750
Michigan	7	26.9	1.2	3.8	100	0.6	14	10.00	59.1	-
New York	15	26.7	1.2	1.8	400	2.6	27	9.40	40.1	500
New Jersey	11	23.5	1.1	2.1	300	1.9	27	13.00	37.4	-
Florida	7	20.9	1.0	3.0	200	1.3	29	9.33	49.3	-
Washington	10	8.6	0.4	0.9	100	0.6	10	13.00	47.7	-
Texas	15	(D)	-	-	1,750 *	11.2	117	-	-	-
North Carolina	10	(D)	-	-	1,750 *	11.2	175	-	-	2,286
Minnesota	8	(D)	-	-	175 *	1.1	22	-	-	-
South Carolina	7	(D)	-	-	1,750 *	11.2	250	-	-	-
Connecticut	5	(D)	-	-	175 *	1.1	35	-	-	1,143
Louisiana	5	(D)	-	-	175 *	1.1	35	-	-	571
New Hampshire	5	(D)	-	-	375 *	2.4	75	-	-	-
Wisconsin	5	(D)	-	-	175 *	1.1	35	-	-	-
Maryland	4	(D)	-	-	750 *	4.8	188	-	-	-
Kansas	3	(D)	-	-	175 *	1.1	58	-	-	-
Tennessee	3	(D)	-	-	750 *	4.8	250	-	-	-
Maine	1	(D)	-	-	750 *	4.8	750	-	-	-

Source: 1992 *Economic Census*. The states are in descending order of shipments or establishments (if shipment data are missing for the majority). The symbol (D) appears when data are withheld to prevent disclosure of competitive information. States marked with (D) are sorted by number of establishments. A dash (-) indicates that the data element cannot be calculated; * indicates the midpoint of a range.

3084 - PLASTICS PIPE

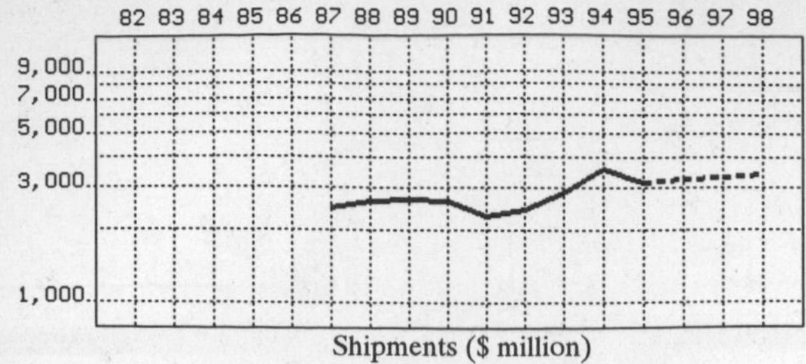

Shipments ($ million)

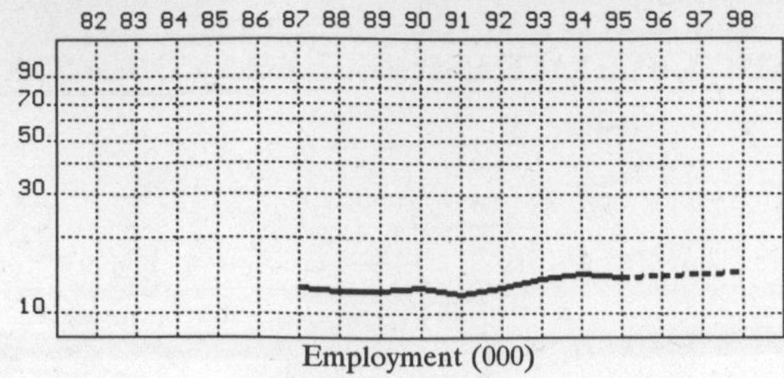

Employment (000)

GENERAL STATISTICS

Year	Com-panies	Establishments: Total	Establishments: with 20 or more employees	Employment: Total (000)	Employment: Production Workers (000)	Employment: Production Hours (Mil)	Compensation: Payroll ($ mil)	Compensation: Wages ($/hr)	Production ($ million): Cost of Materials	Production ($ million): Value Added by Manufacture	Production ($ million): Value of Shipments	Production ($ million): Capital Invest.
1982												
1983												
1984												
1985												
1986												
1987	184	251	177	12.5	9.5	19.1	263.1	9.14	1,476.7	980.7	2,455.8	56.4
1988		246	181	12.3	9.4	18.5	276.0	9.48	1,781.5	951.5	2,657.1	68.9
1989		242	177	12.3	10.0	19.6	287.6	9.47	1,848.7	801.9	2,696.5	79.2
1990		236	179	12.7	9.8	20.1	295.3	9.74	1,849.6	807.7	2,616.0	100.3
1991		234	176	11.8	8.8	18.4	291.8	10.24	1,522.3	717.3	2,285.6	76.0
1992	198	280	192	12.6	9.7	20.3	314.1	10.28	1,599.9	859.6	2,446.1	105.2
1993		273	173	13.8	10.5	22.0	344.3	10.37	1,851.5	1,021.1	2,846.0	77.3
1994		270P	181P	14.4	11.2	23.0	363.0	10.59	2,328.8	1,336.5	3,600.7	118.7
1995		274P	181P	13.9P	10.7P	22.5P	364.2P	10.85P	2,019.5P	1,159.0P	3,122.5P	113.7P
1996		279P	181P	14.2P	10.9P	23.1P	377.5P	11.06P	2,080.1P	1,193.8P	3,216.2P	120.1P
1997		283P	182P	14.4P	11.1P	23.6P	390.8P	11.27P	2,140.8P	1,228.6P	3,310.0P	126.4P
1998		288P	182P	14.7P	11.2P	24.2P	404.1P	11.48P	2,201.5P	1,263.4P	3,403.8P	132.7P

Sources: 1982, 1987, 1992 *Economic Census*; *Annual Survey of Manufactures*, 83-86, 88-91, 93-94. Establishment counts for non-Census years are from *County Business Patterns*; establishment values for 83-84 are extrapolations. 'P's show projections by the editors. Industries reclassified in 87 will not have data for prior years.

INDICES OF CHANGE

Year	Com-panies	Establishments: Total	Establishments: with 20 or more employees	Employment: Total (000)	Employment: Production Workers (000)	Employment: Production Hours (Mil)	Compensation: Payroll ($ mil)	Compensation: Wages ($/hr)	Production ($ million): Cost of Materials	Production ($ million): Value Added by Manufacture	Production ($ million): Value of Shipments	Production ($ million): Capital Invest.
1982												
1983												
1984												
1985												
1986												
1987	93	90	92	99	98	94	84	89	92	114	100	54
1988		88	94	98	97	91	88	92	111	111	109	65
1989		86	92	98	103	97	92	92	116	93	110	75
1990		84	93	101	101	99	94	95	116	94	107	95
1991		84	92	94	91	91	93	100	95	83	93	72
1992	100	100	100	100	100	100	100	100	100	100	100	100
1993		98	90	110	108	108	110	101	116	119	116	73
1994		96P	94P	114	115	113	116	103	146	155	147	113
1995		98P	94P	110P	110P	111P	116P	106P	126P	135P	128P	108P
1996		100P	94P	112P	112P	114P	120P	108P	130P	139P	131P	114P
1997		101P	95P	114P	114P	116P	124P	110P	134P	143P	135P	120P
1998		103P	95P	116P	116P	119P	129P	112P	138P	147P	139P	126P

Sources: Same as General Statistics. Values reflect change from the base year, 1992. Values above 100 mean greater than 92, values below 100 mean less than 92, and a value of 100 in the 82-91 or 93-98 period means same as 92. 'P's mark projections by the editors.

SELECTED RATIOS

For 1994	Avg. of All Manufact.	Analyzed Industry	Index
Employees per Establishment	49	53	109
Payroll per Establishment	1,500,273	1,345,869	90
Payroll per Employee	30,620	25,208	82
Production Workers per Establishment	34	42	121
Wages per Establishment	853,319	903,067	106
Wages per Production Worker	24,861	21,747	87
Hours per Production Worker	2,056	2,054	100
Wages per Hour	12.09	10.59	88
Value Added per Establishment	4,602,255	4,955,244	108
Value Added per Employee	93,930	92,813	99

For 1994	Avg. of All Manufact.	Analyzed Industry	Index
Value Added per Production Worker	134,084	119,330	89
Cost per Establishment	5,045,178	8,634,322	171
Cost per Employee	102,970	161,722	157
Cost per Production Worker	146,988	207,929	141
Shipments per Establishment	9,576,895	13,350,053	139
Shipments per Employee	195,460	250,049	128
Shipments per Production Worker	279,017	321,491	115
Investment per Establishment	321,011	440,095	137
Investment per Employee	6,552	8,243	126
Investment per Production Worker	9,352	10,598	113

Sources: Same as General Statistics. The 'Average of All Manufacturing' column represents the average of all manufacturing industries reported for the most recent complete year available. The Index shows the relationship between the Average and the Analyzed Industry. For example, 100 means that they are equal; 500 that the Analyzed Industry is five times the average; 50 means that the Analyzed Industry is half the national average. The abbreviation 'na' is used to show that data are 'not available'.

LEADING COMPANIES

Number shown: **36** Total sales ($ mil): **1,086** Total employment (000): **6.9**

Company Name	Address				CEO Name	Phone	Co. Type	Sales ($ mil)	Empl. (000)
Advanced Drainage Systems Inc	3300 Riverside Dr	Columbus	OH	43221	Frank E Eck	614-457-3051	R	160*	1.0
Phillips Driscopipe Inc	PO Box 83-3866	Richardson	TX	75083	Jeff Dancer	214-783-2666	S	120	0.4
LCP National Pipe Inc	3421 Old Vestal Rd	Vestal	NY	13850	J Allen McLean	607-729-9381	R	100	0.5
Pacific Western Extruded Plastics	PO Box 10049	Eugene	OR	97440	J Rash	503-343-0200	R	81*	0.5
Cantex Inc	PO Box 340	Mineral Wells	TX	76067	George Levine	817-325-3344	S	67*	0.4
Genova Products Inc	PO Box 309	Davison	MI	48423	D Van Steenkiste	810-744-4500	R	67*	0.4
Smith Fiberglass Products Inc	2700 W 65th St	Little Rock	AR	72209	WV Waters	501-568-4010	S	59	0.5
Ameron Inc	1004 Ameron Rd	Burkburnett	TX	76354	ML Herrian	817-569-1471	D	55	0.3
Charlotte Pipe and Foundry Co	PO Box 1339	Monroe	NC	28111	Charles Cobb	704-289-2531	D	48*	0.5
Lamson Home Products	25701 Science Pk Dr	Beachwood	OH	44122	John B Schulze	216-831-4000	D	41	0.2
Total Containment Inc	PO Box 939	Oaks	PA	19456	Marc Guindon	610-666-7777	P	40	<0.1
Diamond Plastics Corp	PO Box 1608	Grand Island	NE	68802	John Britton	308-384-4400	R	35*	0.2
Apache Plastics LP	PO Box 5127	Stockton	CA	95205	Lawrence Beasley	209-466-4356	R	30	0.1
Resistoflex Co	PO Box 1449	Marion	NC	28752	William C Hayes	704-724-4000	S	23	0.2
Freedom Plastics Inc	PO Box 1488	Janesville	WI	53547	JM Borden	608-754-2710	R	20	0.1
Tomkins Industries Inc	PO Box 116	Brownsville	TN	38012	Jack McDonald	901-772-3180	D	17	0.3
Orion Fittings Inc	PO Box 17-1580	Kansas City	KS	66117	JB McCoy	913-342-1653	R	13*	<0.1
PW Pipe Co	PO Box 10049	Eugene	OR	97440	Jim Rush	503-343-0200	S	11*	<0.1
ENDOT Industries Inc	60 Green Pond Rd	Rockaway	NJ	07866	Gary F Wellmann	201-625-8500	R	10	<0.1
Beetle Plastics Inc	PO Box 1569	Ardmore	OK	73402	Dan Barney	405-389-5421	R	8*	<0.1
George Fischer Inc	2882 Dow Av	Tustin	CA	92680	Peter Georgi	714-731-8800	S	8*	<0.1
RW Fowler and Associates Inc	PO Box 508	Atlantic Beach	FL	32233	Robert W Fowler	904-246-4886	R	8	0.1
Winrock Enterprises Inc	PO Box 8080	Little Rock	AR	72203	RB McDonough Jr	501-663-5340	R	8	0.1
Jet Stream Plastic Pipe Co	PO Box 190	Siloam Springs	AR	72761	Joe T Baty	501-524-5151	D	7	<0.1
Perma-Cote Plastics Inc	PO Box 1103	Uniontown	PA	15401	Joe Gearing	412-439-9300	R	6*	<0.1
Normandy Industries	1001 South Av	Pittsburgh	PA	15221	Robert Americus	412-731-7130	R	6	<0.1
Diller Tile Company Inc	PO Box 727	Chatsworth	IL	60921	James E Diller	815-635-3131	R	5*	<0.1
Plastinetics Inc	439 Rt 202	Towaco	NJ	07082	Edward J Batta	201-316-6600	R	5	<0.1
Rehau Inc	PO Box 1706	Leesburg	VA	22075	H Wagner	703-777-5255	R	5*	0.1
Southern Plastics of Louisiana	PO Box 5095	Slidell	LA	70469	Roy Viola	504-641-5660	R	5	<0.1
Excalibur Extrusions Inc	110 E Crowther	Placentia	CA	92670	Glenn Baldwin	714-528-8834	R	4*	<0.1
Fusibond Piping Systems Inc	2615 Curtis St	Downers Grove	IL	60515	R Krause	708-969-4488	R	4	<0.1
Wesflex Inc	1255 Rec Trail	Redding	CA	96003	Austin Morris	916-244-9366	R	4	<0.1
Georges Enterprises Inc	1528 S West Hwy 17	Arcadia	FL	33821	Richard P Georges	813-494-4489	R	3	<0.1
Mermade Filter	PO Box 306	Denmark	SC	29042	David Painter	803-793-4263	R	3	<0.1
Bristol Pipe	PO Box 609	Bristol	IN	46507	J Minelli	219-848-7681	D	1*	0.1

Source: *Ward's Business Directory of U.S. Private and Public Companies*, Volumes 1 and 2, 1996. The company type code used is as follows: P - Public, R - Private, S - Subsidiary, D - Division, J - Joint Venture, A - Affiliate, G - Group. Sales are in millions of dollars, employees are in thousands. An asterisk (*) indicates an estimated sales volume. The symbol < stands for 'less than'. Company names and addresses are truncated, in some cases, to fit into the available space.

MATERIALS CONSUMED

Material	Quantity	Delivered Cost ($ million)
Materials, ingredients, containers, and supplies	(X)	1,469.1
Hardboard (wood fiberboard)	(X)	1.8
Industrial inorganic chemicals	(X)	7.6
Inorganic pigments	(X)	5.3
Plastics resins consumed in the form of granules, pellets, powders, liquids, etc.	(X)	1,111.5
Industrial organic and synthetic organic chemicals, including plasticizers	(X)	25.8
Synthetic dyes, pigments, lakes, and toners	(X)	3.2
All other chemical and allied products	(X)	16.0
Plastics products consumed in the form of sheets, rods, tubes, film, and other shapes	(X)	19.3
Custom compounded plastics resins (purchased)	(X)	31.9
Textile-type glass fiber	(X)	5.4
Broadwoven fabrics	(X)	0.2
Paper and paperboard products except paperboard boxes, containers, and corrugated paperboard	(X)	1.1
Paperboard containers, boxes, and corrugated paperboard	(X)	3.7
Parts and attachments specially designed for plastics working machinery	(X)	2.8
All other materials and components, parts, containers, and supplies	(X)	90.6
Materials, ingredients, containers, and supplies, nsk	(X)	143.1

Source: 1992 *Economic Census*. Explanation of symbols used: (D): Withheld to avoid disclosure of competitive data; na: Not available; (S): Withheld because statistical norms were not met; (X): Not applicable; (Z): Less than half the unit shown; nec: Not elsewhere classified; nsk: Not specified by kind; - : zero; * : 10-19 percent estimated; ** : 20-29 percent estimated.

PRODUCT SHARE DETAILS

Product or Product Class	% Share	Product or Product Class	% Share
Plastics pipe	100.00	Plastics water pipe	28.53
Plastics drain, waste, and vent pipe	21.32	Plastics industrial and mining pipe (including chemical processing, food processing)	6.49
Plastics sewer pipe	11.60	Other plastics pipe	12.62
Plastics oil and gas pipe	11.73		

Source: 1992 *Economic Census*. The values shown are percent of total shipments in an industry. Values of indented subcategories are summed in the main heading. The symbol (D) appears when data are withheld to prevent disclosure of competitive information. The abbreviation nsk stands for 'not specified by kind' and nec for 'not elsewhere classified'.

INPUTS AND OUTPUTS FOR MISCELLANEOUS PLASTICS PRODUCTS

Economic Sector or Industry Providing Inputs	%	Sector	Economic Sector or Industry Buying Outputs	%	Sector
Plastics materials & resins	36.2	Manufg.	Hospitals	5.6	Services
Wholesale trade	8.5	Trade	Electronic components nec	5.2	Manufg.
Miscellaneous plastics products	7.2	Manufg.	Personal consumption expenditures	4.3	
Imports	5.8	Foreign	Miscellaneous plastics products	4.0	Manufg.
Cyclic crudes and organics	4.4	Manufg.	Exports	4.0	Foreign
Electric services (utilities)	4.4	Util.	Telephone & telegraph apparatus	3.0	Manufg.
Paperboard containers & boxes	2.6	Manufg.	Motor vehicles & car bodies	2.8	Manufg.
Communications, except radio & TV	2.3	Util.	Eating & drinking places	2.8	Trade
Motor freight transportation & warehousing	2.0	Util.	Maintenance of nonfarm buildings nec	2.4	Constr.
Paperboard mills	1.5	Manufg.	Food preparations, nec	2.3	Manufg.
Synthetic rubber	1.5	Manufg.	Plastics materials & resins	2.1	Manufg.
Railroads & related services	1.3	Util.	Typewriters & office machines, nec	1.7	Manufg.
Glass & glass products, except containers	1.2	Manufg.	Commercial printing	1.6	Manufg.
Gas production & distribution (utilities)	1.0	Util.	Cyclic crudes and organics	1.5	Manufg.
Noncomparable imports	1.0	Foreign	Electronic computing equipment	1.5	Manufg.
Industrial inorganic chemicals, nec	0.9	Manufg.	Motor vehicle parts & accessories	1.3	Manufg.
Crude petroleum & natural gas	0.7	Mining	Paper mills, except building paper	1.3	Manufg.
Maintenance of nonfarm buildings nec	0.7	Constr.	Bottled & canned soft drinks	1.2	Manufg.
Eating & drinking places	0.7	Trade	Toilet preparations	1.2	Manufg.
Real estate	0.7	Fin/R.E.	Aircraft	1.1	Manufg.
Computer & data processing services	0.7	Services	Medical & health services, nec	1.1	Services
Broadwoven fabric mills	0.6	Manufg.	Nonfarm residential structure maintenance	1.0	Constr.
Machinery, except electrical, nec	0.6	Manufg.	Optical instruments & lenses	0.9	Manufg.
Petroleum refining	0.6	Manufg.	Wholesale trade	0.9	Trade
Banking	0.6	Fin/R.E.	Office buildings	0.8	Constr.
Inorganic pigments	0.5	Manufg.	Computer & data processing services	0.8	Services
Wood products, nec	0.5	Manufg.	Hotels & lodging places	0.8	Services
Advertising	0.5	Services	S/L Govt. purch., health & hospitals	0.8	S/L Govt
Equipment rental & leasing services	0.5	Services	Residential additions/alterations, nonfarm	0.7	Constr.
Adhesives & sealants	0.4	Manufg.	Animal & marine fats & oils	0.7	Manufg.
Fabricated rubber products, nec	0.4	Manufg.	Drugs	0.7	Manufg.
Special industry machinery, nec	0.4	Manufg.	Fluid milk	0.7	Manufg.
Job training & related services	0.4	Services	Paper coating & glazing	0.7	Manufg.
Fabricated metal products, nec	0.3	Manufg.	Polishes & sanitation goods	0.7	Manufg.
Lighting fixtures & equipment	0.3	Manufg.	Automotive & apparel trimmings	0.6	Manufg.
Lubricating oils & greases	0.3	Manufg.	Broadwoven fabric mills	0.6	Manufg.
Metal stampings, nec	0.3	Manufg.	Frozen fruits, fruit juices & vegetables	0.6	Manufg.
Primary metal products, nec	0.3	Manufg.	Frozen specialties	0.6	Manufg.
Special dies & tools & machine tool accessories	0.3	Manufg.	Knit outerwear mills	0.6	Manufg.
Water transportation	0.3	Util.	Miscellaneous fabricated wire products	0.6	Manufg.
Royalties	0.3	Fin/R.E.	Photographic equipment & supplies	0.6	Manufg.
Management & consulting services & labs	0.3	Services	Pickles, sauces, & salad dressings	0.6	Manufg.
Metal foil & leaf	0.2	Manufg.	Soap & other detergents	0.6	Manufg.
Narrow fabric mills	0.2	Manufg.	Residential garden apartments	0.5	Constr.
Paints & allied products	0.2	Manufg.	Bags, except textile	0.5	Manufg.
Primary copper	0.2	Manufg.	Petroleum refining	0.5	Manufg.
Sanitary services, steam supply, irrigation	0.2	Util.	Semiconductors & related devices	0.5	Manufg.
Accounting, auditing & bookkeeping	0.2	Services	Real estate	0.5	Fin/R.E.
Electrical repair shops	0.2	Services	Beauty & barber shops	0.5	Services
Engineering, architectural, & surveying services	0.2	Services	Residential 1-unit structures, nonfarm	0.4	Constr.
Legal services	0.2	Services	Carbon paper & inked ribbons	0.4	Manufg.
Alkalies & chlorine	0.1	Manufg.	Roasted coffee	0.4	Manufg.
Building paper & board mills	0.1	Manufg.	Storage batteries	0.4	Manufg.
Manifold business forms	0.1	Manufg.	Upholstered household furniture	0.4	Manufg.
Mineral wool	0.1	Manufg.	Communications, except radio & TV	0.4	Util.
Pipe, valves, & pipe fittings	0.1	Manufg.	Water supply & sewage systems	0.4	Util.
Screw machine and related products	0.1	Manufg.	Business services nec	0.4	Services
Air transportation	0.1	Util.	Doctors & dentists	0.4	Services
Insurance carriers	0.1	Fin/R.E.	Miscellaneous repair shops	0.4	Services
Business/professional associations	0.1	Services	Construction of hospitals	0.3	Constr.
U.S. Postal Service	0.1	Gov't	Industrial buildings	0.3	Constr.
			Maintenance of highways & streets	0.3	Constr.
			Games, toys, & children's vehicles	0.3	Manufg.
			Logging camps & logging contractors	0.3	Manufg.
			Mattresses & bedsprings	0.3	Manufg.
			Nonferrous wire drawing & insulating	0.3	Manufg.

Continued on next page.

INPUTS AND OUTPUTS FOR MISCELLANEOUS PLASTICS PRODUCTS - Continued

Economic Sector or Industry Providing Inputs	%	Sector	Economic Sector or Industry Buying Outputs	%	Sector
			Organic fibers, noncellulosic	0.3	Manufg.
			Sanitary paper products	0.3	Manufg.
			Sausages & other prepared meats	0.3	Manufg.
			Signs & advertising displays	0.3	Manufg.
			Surgical & medical instruments	0.3	Manufg.
			Retail trade, except eating & drinking	0.3	Trade
			Amusement & recreation services nec	0.3	Services
			Child day care services	0.3	Services
			Management & consulting services & labs	0.3	Services
			Nursing & personal care facilities	0.3	Services
			Construction of educational buildings	0.2	Constr.
			Construction of stores & restaurants	0.2	Constr.
			Electric utility facility construction	0.2	Constr.
			Warehouses	0.2	Constr.
			Aluminum rolling & drawing	0.2	Manufg.
			Bread, cake, & related products	0.2	Manufg.
			Carbon & graphite products	0.2	Manufg.
			Chemical preparations, nec	0.2	Manufg.
			Cigarettes	0.2	Manufg.
			Cookies & crackers	0.2	Manufg.
			Dog, cat, & other pet food	0.2	Manufg.
			Electric housewares & fans	0.2	Manufg.
			Fabricated plate work (boiler shops)	0.2	Manufg.
			Fabricated structural metal	0.2	Manufg.
			General industrial machinery, nec	0.2	Manufg.
			Glass & glass products, except containers	0.2	Manufg.
			Hard surface floor coverings	0.2	Manufg.
			Household refrigerators & freezers	0.2	Manufg.
			Knit fabric mills	0.2	Manufg.
			Lighting fixtures & equipment	0.2	Manufg.
			Macaroni & spaghetti	0.2	Manufg.
			Meat packing plants	0.2	Manufg.
			Nitrogenous & phosphatic fertilizers	0.2	Manufg.
			Radio & TV communication equipment	0.2	Manufg.
			Radio & TV receiving sets	0.2	Manufg.
			Refrigeration & heating equipment	0.2	Manufg.
			Shoes, except rubber	0.2	Manufg.
			Shortening & cooking oils	0.2	Manufg.
			Sporting & athletic goods, nec	0.2	Manufg.
			Surface active agents	0.2	Manufg.
			Surgical appliances & supplies	0.2	Manufg.
			Wood partitions & fixtures	0.2	Manufg.
			Job training & related services	0.2	Services
			Laundry, dry cleaning, shoe repair	0.2	Services
			Social services, nec	0.2	Services
			Federal Government purchases, national defense	0.2	Fed Govt
			Greenhouse & nursery products	0.1	Agric.
			Farm service facilities	0.1	Constr.
			Hotels & motels	0.1	Constr.
			Maintenance of nonbuilding facilities nec	0.1	Constr.
			Maintenance of water supply facilities	0.1	Constr.
			Aircraft & missile equipment, nec	0.1	Manufg.
			Architectural metal work	0.1	Manufg.
			Blankbooks & looseleaf binders	0.1	Manufg.
			Book printing	0.1	Manufg.
			Cheese, natural & processed	0.1	Manufg.
			Chocolate & cocoa products	0.1	Manufg.
			Condensed & evaporated milk	0.1	Manufg.
			Confectionery products	0.1	Manufg.
			Distilled liquor, except brandy	0.1	Manufg.
			Drapery hardware & blinds & shades	0.1	Manufg.
			Engine electrical equipment	0.1	Manufg.
			Fabricated rubber products, nec	0.1	Manufg.
			Guided missiles & space vehicles	0.1	Manufg.
			Metal foil & leaf	0.1	Manufg.
			Metal household furniture	0.1	Manufg.
			Metal office furniture	0.1	Manufg.
			Miscellaneous publishing	0.1	Manufg.
			Motors & generators	0.1	Manufg.
			Paperboard containers & boxes	0.1	Manufg.
			Paving mixtures & blocks	0.1	Manufg.
			Phonograph records & tapes	0.1	Manufg.
			Pumps & compressors	0.1	Manufg.
			Secondary nonferrous metals	0.1	Manufg.
			Sheet metal work	0.1	Manufg.

Continued on next page.

INPUTS AND OUTPUTS FOR MISCELLANEOUS PLASTICS PRODUCTS - Continued

Economic Sector or Industry Providing Inputs	%	Sector	Economic Sector or Industry Buying Outputs	%	Sector
			Special dies & tools & machine tool accessories	0.1	Manufg.
			Sugar	0.1	Manufg.
			Watches, clocks, & parts	0.1	Manufg.
			Women's hosiery, except socks	0.1	Manufg.
			Wood household furniture	0.1	Manufg.
			Wood products, nec	0.1	Manufg.
			Engineering, architectural, & surveying services	0.1	Services
			Local government passenger transit	0.1	Gov't

Source: Benchmark Input-Output Accounts for the U.S. Economy, 1982, U.S. Department of Commerce, Washington, D.C., July 1991. Data, as reported in the source, are organized by the 1977 SIC structure in use in 1982 but have been matched, as closely as is possible, to the 1987 SIC structure used in this book.

OCCUPATIONS EMPLOYED BY SIC 308 - MISCELLANEOUS PLASTICS PRODUCTS

Occupation	% of Total 1994	Change to 2005	Occupation	% of Total 1994	Change to 2005
Plastic molding machine workers	18.3	6.7	Maintenance repairers, general utility	1.6	6.7
Assemblers, fabricators, & hand workers nec	9.5	18.5	Industrial truck & tractor operators	1.5	18.5
Blue collar worker supervisors	5.2	10.7	Tool & die makers	1.4	77.8
Hand packers & packagers	4.7	-8.6	Extruding & forming machine workers	1.4	-40.7
Machine tool cutting & forming etc. nec	3.4	50.5	Industrial production managers	1.4	18.5
Inspectors, testers, & graders, precision	3.4	6.7	Machine feeders & offbearers	1.4	6.7
Helpers, laborers, & material movers nec	2.6	18.5	Packaging & filling machine operators	1.3	18.5
Machine forming operators, metal & plastic	2.5	30.4	Cutters & trimmers, hand	1.2	18.5
Metal & plastic machine workers nec	2.4	89.0	Bookkeeping, accounting, & auditing clerks	1.1	-11.1
General managers & top executives	2.3	12.4	Secretaries, ex legal & medical	1.1	7.9
Industrial machinery mechanics	2.2	30.4	Coating, painting, & spraying machine workers	1.1	6.7
Sales & related workers nec	1.9	18.5	Crushing & mixing machine operators	1.1	77.8
Traffic, shipping, & receiving clerks	1.8	14.0	Machine operators nec	1.1	-32.1
Freight, stock, & material movers, hand	1.7	-5.2			

Source: Industry-Occupation Matrix, Bureau of Labor Statistics. These data relate to one or more 3-digit SIC industry groups rather than to a single 4-digit SIC. The change reported for each occupation to the year 2005 is a percent of growth or decline as estimated by the Bureau of Labor Statistics. The abbreviation nec stands for 'not elsewhere classified'.

LOCATION BY STATE AND REGIONAL CONCENTRATION

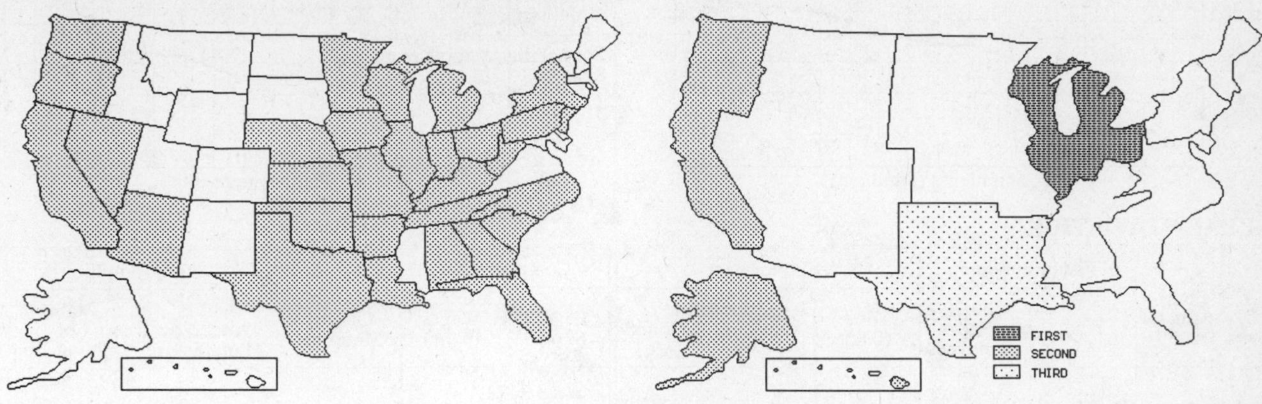

INDUSTRY DATA BY STATE

State	Establish-ments	Shipments			Employment				Cost as % of Shipments	Investment per Employee ($)
		Total ($ mil)	% of U.S.	Per Establ.	Total Number	% of U.S.	Per Establ.	Wages ($/hour)		
California	37	282.9	11.6	7.6	1,500	11.9	41	10.29	67.9	7,733
Texas	28	271.4	11.1	9.7	1,300	10.3	46	9.19	64.9	15,615
North Carolina	11	193.9	7.9	17.6	1,100	8.7	100	11.11	71.8	12,909
Indiana	12	132.3	5.4	11.0	700	5.6	58	9.09	65.8	2,000
Florida	14	128.5	5.3	9.2	700	5.6	50	8.58	67.9	-
Georgia	12	121.7	5.0	10.1	500	4.0	42	10.63	69.8	9,800
Oklahoma	6	105.1	4.3	17.5	700	5.6	117	13.36	60.2	-
Ohio	19	98.4	4.0	5.2	700	5.6	37	11.00	48.5	5,714
Pennsylvania	8	96.4	3.9	12.0	400	3.2	50	11.50	66.9	6,000
Kentucky	5	93.3	3.8	18.7	400	3.2	80	11.50	67.3	4,250
Oregon	6	72.9	3.0	12.2	200	1.6	33	15.67	63.4	7,000
Iowa	10	72.6	3.0	7.3	300	2.4	30	11.60	61.3	3,667
Kansas	6	63.4	2.6	10.6	300	2.4	50	11.00	68.8	4,000
New York	7	59.7	2.4	8.5	600	4.8	86	6.42	52.3	8,000
Nebraska	5	57.4	2.3	11.5	300	2.4	60	10.25	70.6	2,333
Tennessee	4	45.4	1.9	11.4	200	1.6	50	10.33	56.6	-
Arkansas	4	44.9	1.8	11.2	200	1.6	50	8.67	70.2	-
Minnesota	5	43.4	1.8	8.7	200	1.6	40	7.67	64.3	-
Alabama	9	40.7	1.7	4.5	200	1.6	22	10.33	53.3	7,500
South Carolina	3	40.4	1.7	13.5	100	0.8	33	12.00	80.0	-
Washington	7	39.6	1.6	5.7	200	1.6	29	10.33	54.5	1,000
Illinois	8	38.9	1.6	4.9	200	1.6	25	10.00	73.0	-
Michigan	9	37.1	1.5	4.1	300	2.4	33	13.00	51.2	-
Wisconsin	4	31.5	1.3	7.9	200	1.6	50	9.00	55.9	6,500
West Virginia	4	30.9	1.3	7.7	200	1.6	50	7.00	66.3	7,500
New Jersey	4	18.8	0.8	4.7	200	1.6	50	13.00	55.9	-
Louisiana	6	18.2	0.7	3.0	200	1.6	33	9.00	42.3	-
Arizona	4	(D)	-	-	175 *	1.4	44	-	-	-
Missouri	3	(D)	-	-	175 *	1.4	58	-	-	-
Nevada	2	(D)	-	-	175 *	1.4	88	-	-	-

Source: 1992 *Economic Census*. The states are in descending order of shipments or establishments (if shipment data are missing for the majority). The symbol (D) appears when data are withheld to prevent disclosure of competitive information. States marked with (D) are sorted by number of establishments. A dash (-) indicates that the data element cannot be calculated; * indicates the midpoint of a range.

3085 - PLASTICS BOTTLES

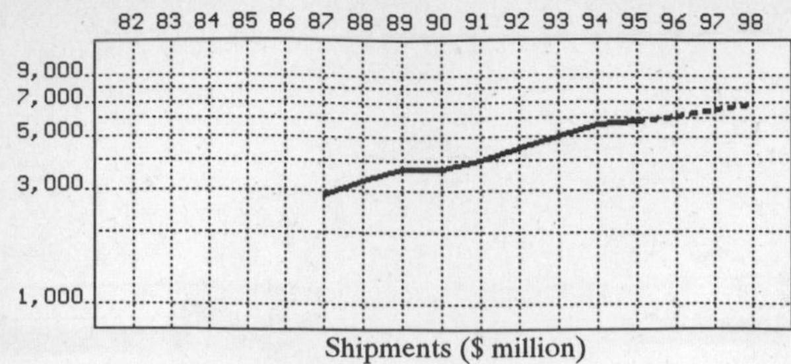

Shipments ($ million)

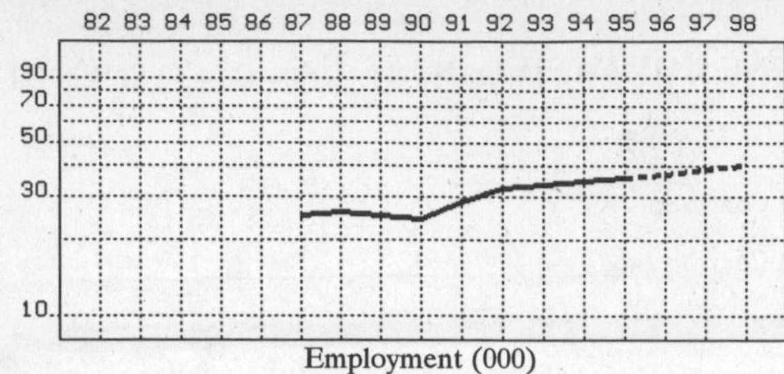

Employment (000)

GENERAL STATISTICS

Year	Com-panies	Establishments		Employment			Compensation		Production ($ million)			
		Total	with 20 or more employees	Total (000)	Production Workers (000)	Production Hours (Mil)	Payroll ($ mil)	Wages ($/hr)	Cost of Materials	Value Added by Manufacture	Value of Shipments	Capital Invest.
1982												
1983												
1984												
1985												
1986												
1987	155	286	227	25.1	21.5	44.0	501.6	8.74	1,480.6	1,351.9	2,835.3	172.1
1988		280	223	26.0	22.0	45.5	536.2	9.07	1,855.2	1,451.6	3,296.5	142.2
1989		288	227	25.1	24.5	51.0	610.2	9.46	2,142.4	1,524.6	3,674.9	190.1
1990		284	232	24.4	25.2	52.1	645.1	9.83	2,088.1	1,626.4	3,728.9	200.2
1991		298	228	28.6	25.0	51.8	646.7	9.72	2,028.8	1,953.1	3,992.6	190.2
1992	224	410	306	32.7	27.8	58.6	781.4	10.02	2,305.7	2,173.9	4,458.2	263.2
1993		398	287	33.5	28.3	60.0	846.0	10.44	2,709.1	2,360.6	5,036.3	365.3
1994		407P	297P	34.7	29.5	61.8	894.5	11.08	3,013.3	2,717.4	5,654.6	510.1
1995		429P	309P	35.8P	30.7P	64.9P	940.6P	11.12P	3,063.0P	2,762.3P	5,747.9P	451.9P
1996		450P	322P	37.4P	31.8P	67.5P	997.9P	11.42P	3,260.0P	2,939.9P	6,117.5P	495.8P
1997		472P	334P	39.0P	33.0P	70.1P	1,055.3P	11.71P	3,457.0P	3,117.5P	6,487.2P	539.8P
1998		494P	346P	40.5P	34.2P	72.7P	1,112.6P	12.01P	3,653.9P	3,295.1P	6,856.8P	583.7P

Sources: 1982, 1987, 1992 *Economic Census*; *Annual Survey of Manufactures*, 83-86, 88-91, 93-94. Establishment counts for non-Census years are from *County Business Patterns*; establishment values for 83-84 are extrapolations. 'P's show projections by the editors. Industries reclassified in 87 will not have data for prior years.

INDICES OF CHANGE

Year	Com-panies	Establishments		Employment			Compensation		Production ($ million)			
		Total	with 20 or more employees	Total (000)	Production Workers (000)	Production Hours (Mil)	Payroll ($ mil)	Wages ($/hr)	Cost of Materials	Value Added by Manufacture	Value of Shipments	Capital Invest.
1982												
1983												
1984												
1985												
1986												
1987	69	70	74	77	77	75	64	87	64	62	64	65
1988		68	73	80	79	78	69	91	80	67	74	54
1989		70	74	77	88	87	78	94	93	70	82	72
1990		69	76	75	91	89	83	98	91	75	84	76
1991		73	75	87	90	88	83	97	88	90	90	72
1992	100	100	100	100	100	100	100	100	100	100	100	100
1993		97	94	102	102	102	108	104	117	109	113	139
1994		99P	97P	106	106	105	114	111	131	125	127	194
1995		105P	101P	110P	110P	111P	120P	111P	133P	127P	129P	172P
1996		110P	105P	114P	115P	115P	128P	114P	141P	135P	137P	188P
1997		115P	109P	119P	119P	120P	135P	117P	150P	143P	146P	205P
1998		120P	113P	124P	123P	124P	142P	120P	158P	152P	154P	222P

Sources: Same as General Statistics. Values reflect change from the base year, 1992. Values above 100 mean greater than 92, values below 100 mean less than 92, and a value of 100 in the 82-91 or 93-98 period means same as 92. 'P's mark projections by the editors.

SELECTED RATIOS

For 1994	Avg. of All Manufact.	Analyzed Industry	Index	For 1994	Avg. of All Manufact.	Analyzed Industry	Index
Employees per Establishment	49	85	174	Value Added per Production Worker	134,084	92,115	69
Payroll per Establishment	1,500,273	2,197,018	146	Cost per Establishment	5,045,178	7,401,088	147
Payroll per Employee	30,620	25,778	84	Cost per Employee	102,970	86,839	84
Production Workers per Establishment	34	72	211	Cost per Production Worker	146,988	102,146	69
Wages per Establishment	853,319	1,681,827	197	Shipments per Establishment	9,576,895	13,888,491	145
Wages per Production Worker	24,861	23,212	93	Shipments per Employee	195,460	162,957	83
Hours per Production Worker	2,056	2,095	102	Shipments per Production Worker	279,017	191,681	69
Wages per Hour	12.09	11.08	92	Investment per Establishment	321,011	1,252,877	390
Value Added per Establishment	4,602,255	6,674,316	145	Investment per Employee	6,552	14,700	224
Value Added per Employee	93,930	78,311	83	Investment per Production Worker	9,352	17,292	185

Sources: Same as General Statistics. The 'Average of All Manufacturing' column represents the average of all manufacturing industries reported for the most recent complete year available. The Index shows the relationship between the Average and the Analyzed Industry. For example, 100 means that they are equal; 500 that the Analyzed Industry is five times the average; 50 means that the Analyzed Industry is half the national average. The abbreviation 'na' is used to show that data are 'not available'.

LEADING COMPANIES

Number shown: **25** Total sales ($ mil): **2,407** Total employment (000): **11.7**

Company Name	Address				CEO Name	Phone	Co. Type	Sales ($ mil)	Empl. (000)
Johnson Controls	912 City Rd	Manchester	MI	48158	John Fiori	313-428-9741	D	818	2.2
CONSTAR Plastics Inc	PO Box 43325	Atlanta	GA	30336	Robert E Nickels	404-691-4256	S	540	3.5
Johnson Controls Inc	912 City Rd	Manchester	MI	48158	James King	313-428-9741	D	400	1.7
Ring Can Corp	35 Industrial Pkwy	Oakland	TN	38060	Carl Ring	901-465-3607	R	140*	0.6
Empak Inc	950 Lake Dr	Chanhassen	MN	55317	Chuck Eitel	612-949-9311	R	75	0.7
American National Can Co	8770 W Bryn Mawr	Chicago	IL	60631	Robert Valle	312-399-3000	D	65	0.3
Evenflo Products Company Inc	PO Box 709	Canton	GA	30114	Paul Whiting	404-704-2000	D	60	0.4
Southeastern Container Inc	PO Box 909	Enka	NC	28728	Richard Roswech	704-667-0101	R	59*	0.3
Polycon Industries Inc	1001 E 99th St	Chicago	IL	60628	RS Arvans	312-374-5500	R	47*	0.2
Blanke Plastic Company Inc	PO Box 296	Hermann	MO	65041	Keith Harbison	314-486-2811	R	33*	0.1
Drug Plastic and Glass Co	1 Bottle Dr	Boyertown	PA	19512	Fred N Biesecker	610-367-5000	R	30*	0.3
Progressive Plastics Inc	14801 Emery Av	Cleveland	OH	44135	AJ Busa	216-252-5595	R	30	0.4
Pluto Corp	812 Larry Bird Blv	French Lick	IN	47432	Alan Friedman	812-936-9988	R	29*	0.1
Charter Supply Company Inc	4562 Martindale Rd	Philmont	NY	12565	Ken Janowitz	518-672-7721	S	16	0.2
Colts Plastics Co	PO Box 429	Dayville	CT	06241	C W Bentley Jr	203-774-2277	R	12	0.2
Cardwell Containers Inc	835 Herbert Rd	Cordova	TN	38018	Robert H Cardwell	901-756-1474	R	11	<0.1
Owens-Illinois Plastic Products	4034 Mint Way	Dallas	TX	75237	TE Eaton	214-339-5211	D	9	0.1
Hub Plastics Inc	725 Reyn	Blacklick	OH	43004	Terry Trego	614-861-1791	R	6	<0.1
Plastic Industries Inc	12400 Industry St	Garden Grove	CA	92641	Ron Brown	714-897-2111	R	6*	<0.1
Kinpak Inc	2780 Gunter Pk E	Montgomery	AL	36109	Harry Jones	205-279-6550	S	5	0.2
Contour Packaging Corp	637 W Rockland St	Philadelphia	PA	19120	SF Moat	215-457-1600	R	5	<0.1
Suscon Inc	600 Railway St	Williamsport	PA	17701	Anthony Cenimo	717-326-2003	R	5	<0.1
Quality Plastics of Prescott Inc	PO Box 2509	Prescott	AZ	86302	CF Bagby	602-445-2592	R	3*	<0.1
PLASNETICS USA Inc	PO Box 1387	Great Falls	MT	59403	William McPhail	406-727-0553	R	2	<0.1
Septipack Inc	2313 Benson Mill	Sparks	MD	21152	Herve Franceschi	410-472-2575	R	0	<0.1

Source: *Ward's Business Directory of U.S. Private and Public Companies*, Volumes 1 and 2, 1996. The company type code used is as follows: P - Public, R - Private, S - Subsidiary, D - Division, J - Joint Venture, A - Affiliate, G - Group. Sales are in millions of dollars, employees are in thousands. An asterisk (*) indicates an estimated sales volume. The symbol < stands for 'less than'. Company names and addresses are truncated, in some cases, to fit into the available space.

MATERIALS CONSUMED

Material	Quantity	Delivered Cost ($ million)
Materials, ingredients, containers, and supplies	(X)	2,084.1
Hardboard (wood fiberboard)	(X)	(D)
Industrial inorganic chemicals	(X)	(D)
Inorganic pigments	(X)	3.4
Plastics resins consumed in the form of granules, pellets, powders, liquids, etc.	(X)	1,348.1
Industrial organic and synthetic organic chemicals, including plasticizers	(X)	(D)
Synthetic dyes, pigments, lakes, and toners	(X)	10.7
All other chemical and allied products	(X)	0.3
Plastics products consumed in the form of sheets, rods, tubes, film, and other shapes	(X)	157.5
Custom compounded plastics resins (purchased)	(X)	29.0
Textile-type glass fiber	(X)	(D)
Broadwoven fabrics	(X)	(D)
Paper and paperboard products except paperboard boxes, containers, and corrugated paperboard	(X)	13.7
Paperboard containers, boxes, and corrugated paperboard	(X)	174.3
Parts and attachments specially designed for plastics working machinery	(X)	23.7
All other materials and components, parts, containers, and supplies	(X)	175.7
Materials, ingredients, containers, and supplies, nsk	(X)	134.6

Source: 1992 *Economic Census*. Explanation of symbols used: (D): Withheld to avoid disclosure of competitive data; na: Not available; (S): Withheld because statistical norms were not met; (X): Not applicable; (Z): Less than half the unit shown; nec: Not elsewhere classified; nsk: Not specified by kind; - : zero; * : 10-19 percent estimated; ** : 20-29 percent estimated.

PRODUCT SHARE DETAILS

Product or Product Class	% Share	Product or Product Class	% Share
Plastics bottles	100.00		

Source: 1992 *Economic Census*. The values shown are percent of total shipments in an industry. Values of indented subcategories are summed in the main heading. The symbol (D) appears when data are withheld to prevent disclosure of competitive information. The abbreviation nsk stands for 'not specified by kind' and nec for 'not elsewhere classified'.

INPUTS AND OUTPUTS FOR MISCELLANEOUS PLASTICS PRODUCTS

Economic Sector or Industry Providing Inputs	%	Sector	Economic Sector or Industry Buying Outputs	%	Sector
Plastics materials & resins	36.2	Manufg.	Hospitals	5.6	Services
Wholesale trade	8.5	Trade	Electronic components nec	5.2	Manufg.
Miscellaneous plastics products	7.2	Manufg.	Personal consumption expenditures	4.3	
Imports	5.8	Foreign	Miscellaneous plastics products	4.0	Manufg.
Cyclic crudes and organics	4.4	Manufg.	Exports	4.0	Foreign
Electric services (utilities)	4.4	Util.	Telephone & telegraph apparatus	3.0	Manufg.
Paperboard containers & boxes	2.6	Manufg.	Motor vehicles & car bodies	2.8	Manufg.
Communications, except radio & TV	2.3	Util.	Eating & drinking places	2.8	Trade
Motor freight transportation & warehousing	2.0	Util.	Maintenance of nonfarm buildings nec	2.4	Constr.
Paperboard mills	1.5	Manufg.	Food preparations, nec	2.3	Manufg.
Synthetic rubber	1.5	Manufg.	Plastics materials & resins	2.1	Manufg.
Railroads & related services	1.3	Util.	Typewriters & office machines, nec	1.7	Manufg.
Glass & glass products, except containers	1.2	Manufg.	Commercial printing	1.6	Manufg.
Gas production & distribution (utilities)	1.0	Util.	Cyclic crudes and organics	1.5	Manufg.
Noncomparable imports	1.0	Foreign	Electronic computing equipment	1.5	Manufg.
Industrial inorganic chemicals, nec	0.9	Manufg.	Motor vehicle parts & accessories	1.3	Manufg.
Crude petroleum & natural gas	0.7	Mining	Paper mills, except building paper	1.3	Manufg.
Maintenance of nonfarm buildings nec	0.7	Constr.	Bottled & canned soft drinks	1.2	Manufg.
Eating & drinking places	0.7	Trade	Toilet preparations	1.2	Manufg.
Real estate	0.7	Fin/R.E.	Aircraft	1.1	Manufg.
Computer & data processing services	0.7	Services	Medical & health services, nec	1.1	Services
Broadwoven fabric mills	0.6	Manufg.	Nonfarm residential structure maintenance	1.0	Constr.
Machinery, except electrical, nec	0.6	Manufg.	Optical instruments & lenses	0.9	Manufg.
Petroleum refining	0.6	Manufg.	Wholesale trade	0.9	Trade
Banking	0.6	Fin/R.E.	Office buildings	0.8	Constr.
Inorganic pigments	0.5	Manufg.	Computer & data processing services	0.8	Services
Wood products, nec	0.5	Manufg.	Hotels & lodging places	0.8	Services
Advertising	0.5	Services	S/L Govt. purch., health & hospitals	0.8	S/L Govt
Equipment rental & leasing services	0.5	Services	Residential additions/alterations, nonfarm	0.7	Constr.
Adhesives & sealants	0.4	Manufg.	Animal & marine fats & oils	0.7	Manufg.
Fabricated rubber products, nec	0.4	Manufg.	Drugs	0.7	Manufg.
Special industry machinery, nec	0.4	Manufg.	Fluid milk	0.7	Manufg.
Job training & related services	0.4	Services	Paper coating & glazing	0.7	Manufg.
Fabricated metal products, nec	0.3	Manufg.	Polishes & sanitation goods	0.7	Manufg.
Lighting fixtures & equipment	0.3	Manufg.	Automotive & apparel trimmings	0.6	Manufg.
Lubricating oils & greases	0.3	Manufg.	Broadwoven fabric mills	0.6	Manufg.
Metal stampings, nec	0.3	Manufg.	Frozen fruits, fruit juices & vegetables	0.6	Manufg.
Primary metal products, nec	0.3	Manufg.	Frozen specialties	0.6	Manufg.
Special dies & tools & machine tool accessories	0.3	Manufg.	Knit outerwear mills	0.6	Manufg.
Water transportation	0.3	Util.	Miscellaneous fabricated wire products	0.6	Manufg.
Royalties	0.3	Fin/R.E.	Photographic equipment & supplies	0.6	Manufg.
Management & consulting services & labs	0.3	Services	Pickles, sauces, & salad dressings	0.6	Manufg.
Metal foil & leaf	0.2	Manufg.	Soap & other detergents	0.6	Manufg.
Narrow fabric mills	0.2	Manufg.	Residential garden apartments	0.5	Constr.
Paints & allied products	0.2	Manufg.	Bags, except textile	0.5	Manufg.
Primary copper	0.2	Manufg.	Petroleum refining	0.5	Manufg.
Sanitary services, steam supply, irrigation	0.2	Util.	Semiconductors & related devices	0.5	Manufg.
Accounting, auditing & bookkeeping	0.2	Services	Real estate	0.5	Fin/R.E.
Electrical repair shops	0.2	Services	Beauty & barber shops	0.5	Services
Engineering, architectural, & surveying services	0.2	Services	Residential 1-unit structures, nonfarm	0.4	Constr.
Legal services	0.2	Services	Carbon paper & inked ribbons	0.4	Manufg.
Alkalies & chlorine	0.1	Manufg.	Roasted coffee	0.4	Manufg.
Building paper & board mills	0.1	Manufg.	Storage batteries	0.4	Manufg.
Manifold business forms	0.1	Manufg.	Upholstered household furniture	0.4	Manufg.
Mineral wool	0.1	Manufg.	Communications, except radio & TV	0.4	Util.
Pipe, valves, & pipe fittings	0.1	Manufg.	Water supply & sewage systems	0.4	Util.
Screw machine and related products	0.1	Manufg.	Business services nec	0.4	Services
Air transportation	0.1	Util.	Doctors & dentists	0.4	Services
Insurance carriers	0.1	Fin/R.E.	Miscellaneous repair shops	0.4	Services
Business/professional associations	0.1	Services	Construction of hospitals	0.3	Constr.
U.S. Postal Service	0.1	Gov't	Industrial buildings	0.3	Constr.
			Maintenance of highways & streets	0.3	Constr.
			Games, toys, & children's vehicles	0.3	Manufg.
			Logging camps & logging contractors	0.3	Manufg.
			Mattresses & bedsprings	0.3	Manufg.
			Nonferrous wire drawing & insulating	0.3	Manufg.
			Organic fibers, noncellulosic	0.3	Manufg.
			Sanitary paper products	0.3	Manufg.
			Sausages & other prepared meats	0.3	Manufg.
			Signs & advertising displays	0.3	Manufg.
			Surgical & medical instruments	0.3	Manufg.
			Retail trade, except eating & drinking	0.3	Trade
			Amusement & recreation services nec	0.3	Services
			Child day care services	0.3	Services
			Management & consulting services & labs	0.3	Services
			Nursing & personal care facilities	0.3	Services
			Construction of educational buildings	0.2	Constr.
			Construction of stores & restaurants	0.2	Constr.

Continued on next page.

INPUTS AND OUTPUTS FOR MISCELLANEOUS PLASTICS PRODUCTS - Continued

Economic Sector or Industry Providing Inputs	%	Sector	Economic Sector or Industry Buying Outputs	%	Sector
			Electric utility facility construction	0.2	Constr.
			Warehouses	0.2	Constr.
			Aluminum rolling & drawing	0.2	Manufg.
			Bread, cake, & related products	0.2	Manufg.
			Carbon & graphite products	0.2	Manufg.
			Chemical preparations, nec	0.2	Manufg.
			Cigarettes	0.2	Manufg.
			Cookies & crackers	0.2	Manufg.
			Dog, cat, & other pet food	0.2	Manufg.
			Electric housewares & fans	0.2	Manufg.
			Fabricated plate work (boiler shops)	0.2	Manufg.
			Fabricated structural metal	0.2	Manufg.
			General industrial machinery, nec	0.2	Manufg.
			Glass & glass products, except containers	0.2	Manufg.
			Hard surface floor coverings	0.2	Manufg.
			Household refrigerators & freezers	0.2	Manufg.
			Knit fabric mills	0.2	Manufg.
			Lighting fixtures & equipment	0.2	Manufg.
			Macaroni & spaghetti	0.2	Manufg.
			Meat packing plants	0.2	Manufg.
			Nitrogenous & phosphatic fertilizers	0.2	Manufg.
			Radio & TV communication equipment	0.2	Manufg.
			Radio & TV receiving sets	0.2	Manufg.
			Refrigeration & heating equipment	0.2	Manufg.
			Shoes, except rubber	0.2	Manufg.
			Shortening & cooking oils	0.2	Manufg.
			Sporting & athletic goods, nec	0.2	Manufg.
			Surface active agents	0.2	Manufg.
			Surgical appliances & supplies	0.2	Manufg.
			Wood partitions & fixtures	0.2	Manufg.
			Job training & related services	0.2	Services
			Laundry, dry cleaning, shoe repair	0.2	Services
			Social services, nec	0.2	Services
			Federal Government purchases, national defense	0.2	Fed Govt
			Greenhouse & nursery products	0.1	Agric.
			Farm service facilities	0.1	Constr.
			Hotels & motels	0.1	Constr.
			Maintenance of nonbuilding facilities nec	0.1	Constr.
			Maintenance of water supply facilities	0.1	Constr.
			Aircraft & missile equipment, nec	0.1	Manufg.
			Architectural metal work	0.1	Manufg.
			Blankbooks & looseleaf binders	0.1	Manufg.
			Book printing	0.1	Manufg.
			Cheese, natural & processed	0.1	Manufg.
			Chocolate & cocoa products	0.1	Manufg.
			Condensed & evaporated milk	0.1	Manufg.
			Confectionery products	0.1	Manufg.
			Distilled liquor, except brandy	0.1	Manufg.
			Drapery hardware & blinds & shades	0.1	Manufg.
			Engine electrical equipment	0.1	Manufg.
			Fabricated rubber products, nec	0.1	Manufg.
			Guided missiles & space vehicles	0.1	Manufg.
			Metal foil & leaf	0.1	Manufg.
			Metal household furniture	0.1	Manufg.
			Metal office furniture	0.1	Manufg.
			Miscellaneous publishing	0.1	Manufg.
			Motors & generators	0.1	Manufg.
			Paperboard containers & boxes	0.1	Manufg.
			Paving mixtures & blocks	0.1	Manufg.
			Phonograph records & tapes	0.1	Manufg.
			Pumps & compressors	0.1	Manufg.
			Secondary nonferrous metals	0.1	Manufg.
			Sheet metal work	0.1	Manufg.
			Special dies & tools & machine tool accessories	0.1	Manufg.
			Sugar	0.1	Manufg.
			Watches, clocks, & parts	0.1	Manufg.
			Women's hosiery, except socks	0.1	Manufg.
			Wood household furniture	0.1	Manufg.
			Wood products, nec	0.1	Manufg.
			Engineering, architectural, & surveying services	0.1	Services
			Local government passenger transit	0.1	Gov't

Source: Benchmark Input-Output Accounts for the U.S. Economy, 1982, U.S. Department of Commerce, Washington, D.C., July 1991. Data, as reported in the source, are organized by the 1977 SIC structure in use in 1982 but have been matched, as closely as is possible, to the 1987 SIC structure used in this book.

OCCUPATIONS EMPLOYED BY SIC 308 - MISCELLANEOUS PLASTICS PRODUCTS

Occupation	% of Total 1994	Change to 2005	Occupation	% of Total 1994	Change to 2005
Plastic molding machine workers	18.3	6.7	Maintenance repairers, general utility	1.6	6.7
Assemblers, fabricators, & hand workers nec	9.5	18.5	Industrial truck & tractor operators	1.5	18.5
Blue collar worker supervisors	5.2	10.7	Tool & die makers	1.4	77.8
Hand packers & packagers	4.7	-8.6	Extruding & forming machine workers	1.4	-40.7
Machine tool cutting & forming etc. nec	3.4	50.5	Industrial production managers	1.4	18.5
Inspectors, testers, & graders, precision	3.4	6.7	Machine feeders & offbearers	1.4	6.7
Helpers, laborers, & material movers nec	2.6	18.5	Packaging & filling machine operators	1.3	18.5
Machine forming operators, metal & plastic	2.5	30.4	Cutters & trimmers, hand	1.2	18.5
Metal & plastic machine workers nec	2.4	89.0	Bookkeeping, accounting, & auditing clerks	1.1	-11.1
General managers & top executives	2.3	12.4	Secretaries, ex legal & medical	1.1	7.9
Industrial machinery mechanics	2.2	30.4	Coating, painting, & spraying machine workers	1.1	6.7
Sales & related workers nec	1.9	18.5	Crushing & mixing machine operators	1.1	77.8
Traffic, shipping, & receiving clerks	1.8	14.0	Machine operators nec	1.1	-32.1
Freight, stock, & material movers, hand	1.7	-5.2			

Source: *Industry-Occupation Matrix*, Bureau of Labor Statistics. These data relate to one or more 3-digit SIC industry groups rather than to a single 4-digit SIC. The change reported for each occupation to the year 2005 is a percent of growth or decline as estimated by the Bureau of Labor Statistics. The abbreviation nec stands for 'not elsewhere classified'.

LOCATION BY STATE AND REGIONAL CONCENTRATION

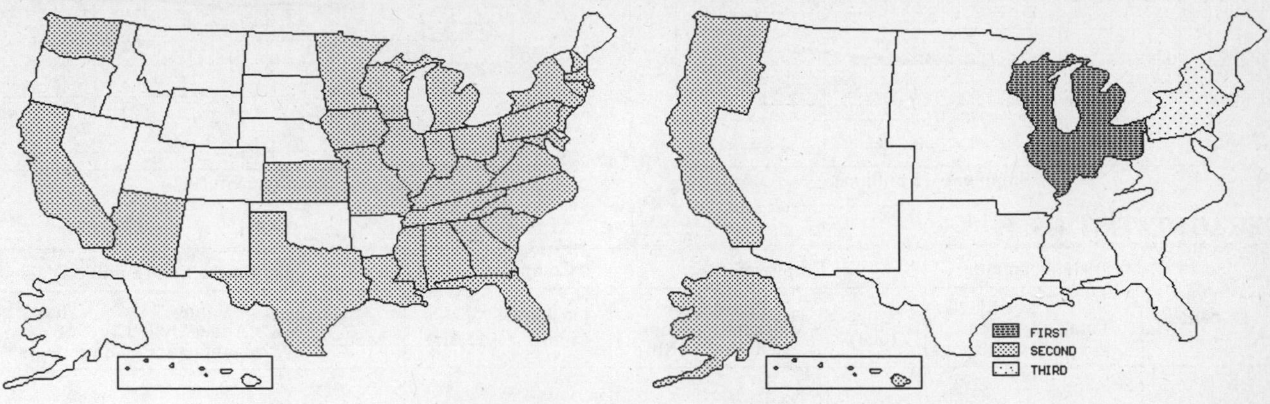

INDUSTRY DATA BY STATE

State	Establish-ments	Shipments			Employment				Cost as % of Shipments	Investment per Employee ($)
		Total ($ mil)	% of U.S.	Per Establ.	Total Number	% of U.S.	Per Establ.	Wages ($/hour)		
Ohio	32	518.7	11.6	16.2	3,800	11.6	119	10.41	46.5	4,947
California	56	505.7	11.3	9.0	4,100	12.5	73	9.59	51.6	9,098
Illinois	33	439.3	9.9	13.3	2,900	8.9	88	10.94	47.0	9,138
New Jersey	26	365.3	8.2	14.1	2,900	8.9	112	11.66	52.4	6,241
Texas	27	296.6	6.7	11.0	2,000	6.1	74	9.56	60.9	9,900
Pennsylvania	28	213.0	4.8	7.6	1,900	5.8	68	9.77	50.2	4,684
Kentucky	11	157.8	3.5	14.3	1,100	3.4	100	9.47	48.6	12,273
Missouri	16	147.5	3.3	9.2	1,500	4.6	94	8.89	45.3	7,867
Florida	17	144.5	3.2	8.5	900	2.8	53	9.88	59.8	2,444
North Carolina	7	139.8	3.1	20.0	700	2.1	100	9.38	61.8	-
Georgia	12	124.2	2.8	10.3	1,000	3.1	83	9.75	49.9	6,600
Indiana	9	118.9	2.7	13.2	900	2.8	100	11.27	44.5	5,556
Michigan	8	115.4	2.6	14.4	700	2.1	88	8.82	60.1	5,000
Maryland	6	105.4	2.4	17.6	800	2.4	133	10.25	54.5	6,875
Massachusetts	11	93.7	2.1	8.5	500	1.5	45	9.36	56.9	2,400
Louisiana	6	87.7	2.0	14.6	900	2.8	150	6.81	55.6	2,778
Tennessee	6	85.8	1.9	14.3	500	1.5	83	8.92	47.6	7,800
South Carolina	5	84.1	1.9	16.8	400	1.2	80	11.57	59.9	28,250
Alabama	7	75.7	1.7	10.8	500	1.5	71	9.78	54.7	3,800
New Hampshire	7	64.0	1.4	9.1	600	1.8	86	11.20	55.0	4,333
Washington	9	60.0	1.3	6.7	400	1.2	44	11.33	56.0	-
New York	7	41.9	0.9	6.0	400	1.2	57	8.86	59.4	8,000
Iowa	5	30.9	0.7	6.2	300	0.9	60	9.00	57.6	-
Connecticut	6	30.4	0.7	5.1	300	0.9	50	11.60	37.8	3,000
Arizona	7	25.9	0.6	3.7	300	0.9	43	9.25	62.2	1,000
Minnesota	5	(D)	-	-	175 *	0.5	35	-	-	2,286
Mississippi	5	(D)	-	-	175 *	0.5	35	-	-	-
Virginia	5	(D)	-	-	375 *	1.1	75	-	-	-
Kansas	4	(D)	-	-	375 *	1.1	94	-	-	-
Wisconsin	4	(D)	-	-	750 *	2.3	188	-	-	-
West Virginia	2	(D)	-	-	175 *	0.5	88	-	-	-

Source: 1992 *Economic Census*. The states are in descending order of shipments or establishments (if shipment data are missing for the majority). The symbol (D) appears when data are withheld to prevent disclosure of competitive information. States marked with (D) are sorted by number of establishments. A dash (-) indicates that the data element cannot be calculated; * indicates the midpoint of a range.

3086 - PLASTICS FOAM PRODUCTS

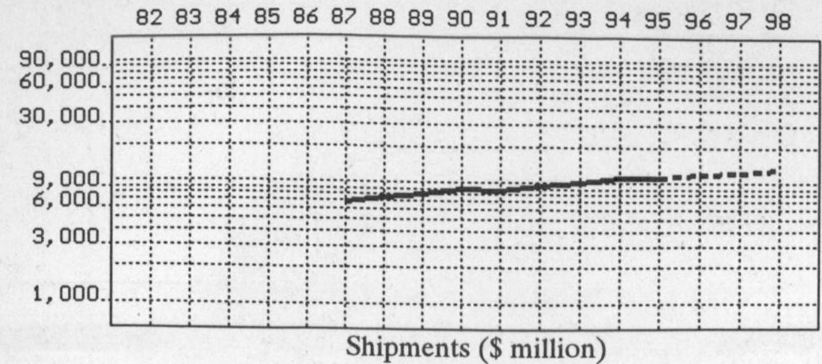

Shipments ($ million)

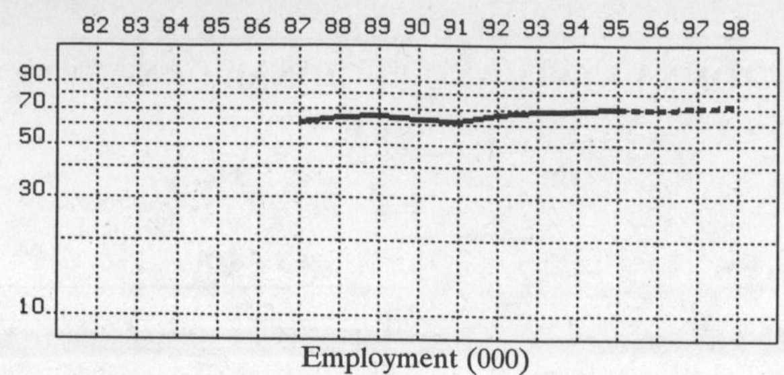

Employment (000)

GENERAL STATISTICS

Year	Companies	Establishments: Total	Establishments: with 20 or more employees	Employment: Total (000)	Employment: Production Workers (000)	Employment: Production Hours (Mil)	Compensation: Payroll ($ mil)	Compensation: Wages ($/hr)	Production ($ million): Cost of Materials	Production ($ million): Value Added by Manufacture	Production ($ million): Value of Shipments	Production ($ million): Capital Invest.
1982												
1983												
1984												
1985												
1986												
1987	656	946	587	61.3	47.7	91.8	1,184.0	8.53	3,874.4	3,045.6	6,912.8	334.8
1988		971	582	63.9	50.0	97.5	1,271.1	8.77	4,243.3	3,290.3	7,506.5	328.1
1989		956	612	64.4	48.8	92.4	1,308.3	9.29	4,832.8	3,271.0	8,108.9	322.0
1990		968	608	63.6	49.6	95.6	1,395.7	9.75	5,153.9	3,788.3	8,988.2	353.2
1991		1,007	601	62.0	47.8	92.1	1,431.6	10.03	4,766.6	3,790.5	8,578.0	335.9
1992	850	1,217	678	66.9	52.3	100.5	1,587.9	10.49	5,179.1	4,335.8	9,488.4	368.6
1993		1,179	675	69.0	54.8	105.4	1,653.9	10.57	5,475.8	4,630.9	10,095.2	399.0
1994		1,212P	684P	68.2	54.3	110.6	1,759.2	10.73	6,091.1	4,978.0	11,065.2	485.4
1995		1,257P	700P	69.2P	54.9P	108.5P	1,814.1P	11.29P	6,216.6P	5,080.6P	11,293.2P	447.9P
1996		1,301P	716P	70.1P	55.8P	110.8P	1,895.2P	11.62P	6,516.3P	5,325.5P	11,837.7P	466.1P
1997		1,345P	732P	71.1P	56.8P	113.1P	1,976.3P	11.96P	6,816.1P	5,570.5P	12,382.2P	484.4P
1998		1,390P	748P	72.0P	57.7P	115.4P	2,057.5P	12.29P	7,115.8P	5,815.5P	12,926.7P	502.6P

Sources: 1982, 1987, 1992 *Economic Census*; *Annual Survey of Manufactures*, 83-86, 88-91, 93-94. Establishment counts for non-Census years are from *County Business Patterns*; establishment values for 83-84 are extrapolations. 'P's show projections by the editors. Industries reclassified in 87 will not have data for prior years.

INDICES OF CHANGE

Year	Companies	Establishments: Total	Establishments: with 20 or more employees	Employment: Total (000)	Employment: Production Workers (000)	Employment: Production Hours (Mil)	Compensation: Payroll ($ mil)	Compensation: Wages ($/hr)	Production ($ million): Cost of Materials	Production ($ million): Value Added by Manufacture	Production ($ million): Value of Shipments	Production ($ million): Capital Invest.
1982												
1983												
1984												
1985												
1986												
1987	77	78	87	92	91	91	75	81	75	70	73	91
1988		80	86	96	96	97	80	84	82	76	79	89
1989		79	90	96	93	92	82	89	93	75	85	87
1990		80	90	95	95	95	88	93	100	87	95	96
1991		83	89	93	91	92	90	96	92	87	90	91
1992	100	100	100	100	100	100	100	100	100	100	100	100
1993		97	100	103	105	105	104	101	106	107	106	108
1994		100P	101P	102	104	110	111	102	118	115	117	132
1995		103P	103P	103P	105P	108P	114P	108P	120P	117P	119P	122P
1996		107P	106P	105P	107P	110P	119P	111P	126P	123P	125P	126P
1997		111P	108P	106P	109P	113P	124P	114P	132P	128P	130P	131P
1998		114P	110P	108P	110P	115P	130P	117P	137P	134P	136P	136P

Sources: Same as General Statistics. Values reflect change from the base year, 1992. Values above 100 mean greater than 92, values below 100 mean less than 92, and a value of 100 in the 82-91 or 93-98 period means same as 92. 'P's mark projections by the editors.

SELECTED RATIOS

For 1994	Avg. of All Manufact.	Analyzed Industry	Index
Employees per Establishment	49	56	115
Payroll per Establishment	1,500,273	1,451,143	97
Payroll per Employee	30,620	25,795	84
Production Workers per Establishment	34	45	130
Wages per Establishment	853,319	978,926	115
Wages per Production Worker	24,861	21,855	88
Hours per Production Worker	2,056	2,037	99
Wages per Hour	12.09	10.73	89
Value Added per Establishment	4,602,255	4,106,293	89
Value Added per Employee	93,930	72,991	78

For 1994	Avg. of All Manufact.	Analyzed Industry	Index
Value Added per Production Worker	134,084	91,676	68
Cost per Establishment	5,045,178	5,024,476	100
Cost per Employee	102,970	89,312	87
Cost per Production Worker	146,988	112,175	76
Shipments per Establishment	9,576,895	9,127,551	95
Shipments per Employee	195,460	162,246	83
Shipments per Production Worker	279,017	203,779	73
Investment per Establishment	321,011	400,401	125
Investment per Employee	6,552	7,117	109
Investment per Production Worker	9,352	8,939	96

Sources: Same as General Statistics. The 'Average of All Manufacturing' column represents the average of all manufacturing industries reported for the most recent complete year available. The Index shows the relationship between the Average and the Analyzed Industry. For example, 100 means that they are equal; 500 that the Analyzed Industry is five times the average; 50 means that the Analyzed Industry is half the national average. The abbreviation 'na' is used to show that data are 'not available'.

LEADING COMPANIES Number shown: **75** Total sales ($ mil): **3,976** Total employment (000): **40.3**

Company Name	Address				CEO Name	Phone	Co. Type	Sales ($ mil)	Empl. (000)
Carpenter Co	PO Box 27205	Richmond	VA	23261	William Easterling	804-359-0800	R	600	6.8
Sealed Air Corp	Park 80 E	Saddle Brook	NJ	07662	TJ Dermot Dunphy	201-791-7600	P	452	2.8
Dart Container Corp	500 Hogsback Rd	Mason	MI	48854	Ken Dart	517-676-3800	R	370*	3.0
Amoco Foam Products Co	375 Northridge Rd	Atlanta	GA	30350	Joe Strickland	404-901-5252	S	170	1.9
Rexham Inc	PO Box 472528	Charlotte	NC	28226	Eric Priestly	704-551-1500	S	150	7.5
Standard Industries Inc	52 Courtland St	Paterson	NJ	07503	Cary Wellington	201-278-6300	R	150	2.0
Kerr Group Inc	1840 Century Pk E	Los Angeles	CA	90067	Roger W Norian	310-556-2200	P	139	1.1
Ropak Corp	660 S State College	Fullerton	CA	92631	William H Roper	714-870-9757	P	128	0.9
Textile Rubber and Chemical	1400 SW Tiarco Dr	Dalton	GA	30720	Harvey Howalt Jr	706-277-1300	R	125	0.4
Tuscarora Inc	PO Box 448	New Brighton	PA	15066	John P O'Leary Jr	412-843-8200	P	120	1.2
Genpak Corp	PO Box 727	Glens Falls	NY	12801	James J Reilly	518-798-9511	S	100	0.5
James River Corporation	240 Tamal Vista Dr	Corte Madera	CA	94925	Mike Lutz	415-927-0800	D	100*	0.7
London Plastics Inc	787 Waterv	Latham	NY	12110	Dom DeMichele	518-783-7776	S	100	0.3
Perstorp Components Inc	47785 Anchor Ct	Plymouth	MI	48170	Tore Claesson	313-332-0267	S	80*	0.7
Future Foam Inc	400 N 10th St	Council Bluffs	IA	51501	W Grassman	712-323-9122	R	70*	0.4
Premier Industries Inc	1019 Pacific Av	Tacoma	WA	98402	Michael Wall	206-572-5111	R	70	0.6
Wellington Home Products	52 Courtland St	Paterson	NJ	07503	John Vidovich	201-278-6300	S	61	0.5
CelloFoam North America Inc	PO Box 406	Conyers	GA	30207	Greg Bontrager	404-483-4491	R	50	0.3
Creative Foam Corp	300 N Alloy	Fenton	MI	48430	David A Duthie	313-629-4149	R	50	0.4
CLS Industries Inc	4699 Nautilus Ct S	Boulder	CO	80301	Paul Kingsbury	303-530-2435	R	40*	0.3
Tech Industries Inc	85 Fairmount St	Woonsocket	RI	02895	David M Wang	401-765-0600	R	38	0.5
Free-Flow Packaging Corp	1093 Charter St	Redwood City	CA	94063	A Graham	415-364-1145	R	35	0.3
UFP Technologies Inc	172 E Main St	Georgetown	MA	01833	R Jeffrey Bailly	508-352-2200	P	32	0.3
EFP Corp	PO Box 2368	Elkhart	IN	46515	James Chandler	219-295-4690	R	30	0.5
Kenkor Molding	Mount Vernon Rd	Englishtown	NJ	07726	Ted Reiss	908-446-6100	D	30	0.3
Polyfoam Packers Corp	2320 Foster Av	Wheeling	IL	60090	Mort Rosen	708-398-0110	R	30	0.3
Renosol Corp	PO Box 1424	Ann Arbor	MI	48106	WE Wright	313-429-5418	R	30	0.2
Sentinel Products Corp	70 Airport Rd	Hyannis	MA	02601	John D Bambara	508-775-5220	R	30*	0.2
HL Blachford Inc	1855ephenson Hwy	Troy	MI	48083	Kurt Straube	313-689-7800	S	28	0.2
Federal Foam Technologies	3558 N 2nd St	Minneapolis	MN	55412	Jim Van Hooser	612-522-3643	S	25	0.3
Hopple Plastics Inc	7430 Empire Dr	Florence	KY	41042	James McCarty	606-283-1570	S	25	0.3
Boyd Corp	6630 Owens Dr	Pleasanton	CA	94588	Richard Andrews	510-463-2760	R	24*	0.2
Hickory Springs Manufacturing	4542 E Dunham St	Los Angeles	CA	90023	Don Simpson	213-266-0422	S	23	<0.1
Storopack Inc	12007 S Woodruff	Downey	CA	90241	J Mellott	310-803-1584	R	23	0.2
Great Western Carpet Cushion	2060 N Batavia St	Orange	CA	92665	John Rallis	714-637-0110	S	22*	0.3
Burkart Foam Inc	36th & Sycamore St	Cairo	IL	62914	Louie Moller	618-734-3911	S	21*	0.2
Robinson Industries Inc	3051 W Curtice	Coleman	MI	48618	AV Robinson	517-465-6111	R	21*	0.2
Rogers Foam Corp	20 Vernon St	Somerville	MA	02145	James H Rogers Jr	617-623-3010	R	21	0.4
Foamade Industries	PO Box 215110	Auburn Hills	MI	48321	Michael Egren	810-852-6010	R	20	0.3
Instapak	10 O Sherman	Danbury	CT	06810	Warren McCandless	203-791-3550	D	18	0.2
Diversifoam Products	9091 County Rd	Rockford	MN	55373	Ben Sachs	612-477-5854	R	17	0.1
Parade Packaging Materials	2907 Huron St	Denver	CO	80202	R Hopkins	303-297-3711	R	17	0.1
Horn Packaging Corp	PO Box 190	Ayer	MA	01432	Robert Lang	508-772-0290	R	16	0.2
No-Sag Foam	1750 W Downs Dr	West Chicago	IL	60185	Joe Proger	708-293-0780	D	15*	0.1
Stephenson and Lawyer Inc	PO Box 8834	Grand Rapids	MI	49518	John Barrows	616-949-8100	R	15	0.2
Soundcoat Company Inc	1 Burt Dr	Deer Park	NY	11729	Phillipe LaCarriere	516-242-2200	S	14	<0.1
Foam Rubber Products Inc	PO Box 525	New Castle	IN	47362	Frank Nold	317-521-2000	R	13	0.1
Gaska-Tape Inc	PO Box 1968	Elkhart	IN	46516	JB Smith Jr	219-294-5431	R	12*	0.1
Life-Like Products Inc	1600 Union Av	Baltimore	MD	21211	GJ Kandel	410-889-1023	R	12	0.2
Unico Inc	1740 S Sacramento	Ontario	CA	91761		909-947-3993	R	12*	0.1
Buckley Industries Inc	PO Box 574	Wichita	KS	67201	DJ Buckley	316-262-0425	R	11	<0.1
Foam Plastics of New England	PO Box 7075	Prospect	CT	06712	David Lewis	203-758-6651	R	10	<0.1
General Packaging Corp	PO Box 832630	Richardson	TX	75083	James W Brown	214-234-5499	R	10	0.1
General Plastics Mfg Co	PO Box 9097	Tacoma	WA	98409	Henry T Schatz	206-473-5000	R	10	<0.1
M and D Flexographic Printers	837 Redwood Av	Manteno	IL	60950	Scott W Harris	815-468-8900	R	10	<0.1
Polycel Corp	60 Readington Rd	Somerville	NJ	08876	John Marshall	908-725-4600	R	10	0.1
George Carroll Inc	PO Box 144	Northwood	IA	50459	G George	515-324-2231	R	10	0.2
Styro-Molders Corp	PO Box 577	Co Springs	CO	80901	William Watkins	719-598-0602	R	9	<0.1
Poly Foam Inc	116 Pine St S	Lester Prairie	MN	55354	RE Humboldt	612-395-2551	R	8	<0.1
EFP South Corp	PO Box 1844	Decatur	AL	35602	Matt Mckinney	205-353-0476	D	8	0.1
Klegecell-Polimex Inc	204 N Dooley	Grapevine	TX	76051	JP Morgan	817-481-3547	R	8*	<0.1
Edge-Sweets Co	2887 3 Mile Rd NW	Grand Rapids	MI	49504	Dieter Misch	616-453-5458	R	7	<0.1
Milcut Inc	PO Box 229	Butler	WI	53007	Carl Strohmaier Jr	414-783-7690	R	7	<0.1
Foam Pack Inc	PO Box 363633	San Juan	PR	00936	Arturo Barreiro	809-731-9000	R	7	<0.1
Custom Pack Inc	3 Bacton Hill Rd	Malvern	PA	19355	Frank A Menichini	610-644-7000	R	7	<0.1
Drew Foam Company Inc	PO Box 420	Monticello	AR	71655	Zach McClendon	501-367-6245	R	7	<0.1
Beacon Converters Inc	PO Box 8208	Saddle Brook	NJ	07663	Willaim P Daly	201-797-2600	R	6	<0.1
Elm Packaging Co	1261 Brukner Dr	Troy	OH	45373	Donald C McCann	513-339-2655	R	6	<0.1
EO Wood Company Inc	PO Box 7416	Fort Worth	TX	76111	MU Kaastad	817-834-8811	R	6	<0.1
Donray Co	8200 Tyler Blv	Mentor	OH	44060	GE Studen	216-974-6444	R	5	<0.1
Gilman Brothers Co	Gilman Rd	Gilman	CT	06336	Charles M Gilman	203-889-8444	R	5	0.1
Modern Milltex Corp	PO Box 217	Springf Grdns	NY	11413	R Marks	718-525-6000	R	5	<0.1
Convenience Products Inc	866 Horan Dr	Fenton	MO	63026	BR Lapin	314-349-5333	S	4*	<0.1
Perma-Foam Inc	605-609 S 21st St	Irvington	NJ	07111	William Finkle	201-373-5626	R	4	<0.1
Packaging Enterprises Inc	1405 N Lilac Dr	Minneapolis	MN	55422	L Sanford	612-544-1216	R	4	<0.1

Source: *Ward's Business Directory of U.S. Private and Public Companies*, Volumes 1 and 2, 1996. The company type code used is as follows: P - Public, R - Private, S - Subsidiary, D - Division, J - Joint Venture, A - Affiliate, G - Group. Sales are in millions of dollars, employees are in thousands. An asterisk (*) indicates an estimated sales volume. The symbol < stands for 'less than'. Company names and addresses are truncated, in some cases, to fit into the available space.

MATERIALS CONSUMED

Material	Quantity	Delivered Cost ($ million)
Materials, ingredients, containers, and supplies	(X)	4,780.3
Hardboard (wood fiberboard)	(X)	8.1
Industrial inorganic chemicals	(X)	135.9
Inorganic pigments	(X)	8.3
Plastics resins consumed in the form of granules, pellets, powders, liquids, etc.	(X)	1,191.2
Industrial organic and synthetic organic chemicals, including plasticizers	(X)	841.5
Synthetic dyes, pigments, lakes, and toners	(X)	14.3
All other chemical and allied products	(X)	102.8
Plastics products consumed in the form of sheets, rods, tubes, film, and other shapes	(X)	288.2
Custom compounded plastics resins (purchased)	(X)	315.6
Textile-type glass fiber	(X)	20.9
Broadwoven fabrics	(X)	83.3
Paper and paperboard products except paperboard boxes, containers, and corrugated paperboard	(X)	49.0
Paperboard containers, boxes, and corrugated paperboard	(X)	89.8
Parts and attachments specially designed for plastics working machinery	(X)	11.5
All other materials and components, parts, containers, and supplies	(X)	892.8
Materials, ingredients, containers, and supplies, nsk	(X)	727.1

Source: 1992 *Economic Census*. Explanation of symbols used: (D): Withheld to avoid disclosure of competitive data; na: Not available; (S): Withheld because statistical norms were not met; (X): Not applicable; (Z): Less than half the unit shown; nec: Not elsewhere classified; nsk: Not specified by kind; - : zero; * : 10-19 percent estimated; ** : 20-29 percent estimated.

PRODUCT SHARE DETAILS

Product or Product Class	% Share
Plastics foam products	100.00
Transportation plastics foam products (including seating, dash, and other interior/exterior components)	16.47
Packaging plastics foam products	17.44
Plastics foam protective shipping pads and shaped cushioning (peanuts, disks, etc.)	36.08
Plastics foam food containers	43.79
Other plastics foam packaging products	18.76
Packaging, nsk	1.37
Building and construction plastics foam products	12.64
Plastics foam building and construction insulation (including pipe and block)	77.63
Other plastics foam building and construction products	15.59
Building and construction, nsk	6.78
Furniture and furnishings plastics foam products	20.99
Plastics foam carpet underlay, carpet and rug cushions	32.86
Plastics foam formed and slab stock for pillows, seating, and cushioning	52.50
Plastics foam mattress cores (uncovered only)	4.46
Other plastics foam furniture and furnishings products	8.92
Furniture and furnishings, nsk	1.27
Consumer and institutional plastics foam products	17.24
Plastics foam cups, consumer and institutional	45.82
Plastics foam plates and bowls, consumer and institutional	24.59
Plastics foam cooler chests, consumer and institutional	5.17
Plastics foam trays, consumer and institutional	2.74
Other consumer and institutional plastics foam products	17.83
Consumer and institutional, nsk	3.85
Other plastics foam products	6.91
Electrical and electronic plastics foam products	10.06
Other plastics foam products	87.60
Other, nsk	2.34
Plastics foam products, nsk	8.31

Source: 1992 *Economic Census*. The values shown are percent of total shipments in an industry. Values of indented subcategories are summed in the main heading. The symbol (D) appears when data are withheld to prevent disclosure of competitive information. The abbreviation nsk stands for 'not specified by kind' and nec for 'not elsewhere classified'.

INPUTS AND OUTPUTS FOR MISCELLANEOUS PLASTICS PRODUCTS

Economic Sector or Industry Providing Inputs	%	Sector	Economic Sector or Industry Buying Outputs	%	Sector
Plastics materials & resins	36.2	Manufg.	Hospitals	5.6	Services
Wholesale trade	8.5	Trade	Electronic components nec	5.2	Manufg.
Miscellaneous plastics products	7.2	Manufg.	Personal consumption expenditures	4.3	
Imports	5.8	Foreign	Miscellaneous plastics products	4.0	Manufg.
Cyclic crudes and organics	4.4	Manufg.	Exports	4.0	Foreign
Electric services (utilities)	4.4	Util.	Telephone & telegraph apparatus	3.0	Manufg.
Paperboard containers & boxes	2.6	Manufg.	Motor vehicles & car bodies	2.8	Manufg.
Communications, except radio & TV	2.3	Util.	Eating & drinking places	2.8	Trade
Motor freight transportation & warehousing	2.0	Util.	Maintenance of nonfarm buildings nec	2.4	Constr.
Paperboard mills	1.5	Manufg.	Food preparations, nec	2.3	Manufg.
Synthetic rubber	1.5	Manufg.	Plastics materials & resins	2.1	Manufg.
Railroads & related services	1.3	Util.	Typewriters & office machines, nec	1.7	Manufg.
Glass & glass products, except containers	1.2	Manufg.	Commercial printing	1.6	Manufg.
Gas production & distribution (utilities)	1.0	Util.	Cyclic crudes and organics	1.5	Manufg.
Noncomparable imports	1.0	Foreign	Electronic computing equipment	1.5	Manufg.
Industrial inorganic chemicals, nec	0.9	Manufg.	Motor vehicle parts & accessories	1.3	Manufg.
Crude petroleum & natural gas	0.7	Mining	Paper mills, except building paper	1.3	Manufg.
Maintenance of nonfarm buildings nec	0.7	Constr.	Bottled & canned soft drinks	1.2	Manufg.
Eating & drinking places	0.7	Trade	Toilet preparations	1.2	Manufg.
Real estate	0.7	Fin/R.E.	Aircraft	1.1	Manufg.
Computer & data processing services	0.7	Services	Medical & health services, nec	1.1	Services
Broadwoven fabric mills	0.6	Manufg.	Nonfarm residential structure maintenance	1.0	Constr.
Machinery, except electrical, nec	0.6	Manufg.	Optical instruments & lenses	0.9	Manufg.
Petroleum refining	0.6	Manufg.	Wholesale trade	0.9	Trade

Continued on next page.

INPUTS AND OUTPUTS FOR MISCELLANEOUS PLASTICS PRODUCTS - Continued

Economic Sector or Industry Providing Inputs	%	Sector	Economic Sector or Industry Buying Outputs	%	Sector
Banking	0.6	Fin/R.E.	Office buildings	0.8	Constr.
Inorganic pigments	0.5	Manufg.	Computer & data processing services	0.8	Services
Wood products, nec	0.5	Manufg.	Hotels & lodging places	0.8	Services
Advertising	0.5	Services	S/L Govt. purch., health & hospitals	0.8	S/L Govt
Equipment rental & leasing services	0.5	Services	Residential additions/alterations, nonfarm	0.7	Constr.
Adhesives & sealants	0.4	Manufg.	Animal & marine fats & oils	0.7	Manufg.
Fabricated rubber products, nec	0.4	Manufg.	Drugs	0.7	Manufg.
Special industry machinery, nec	0.4	Manufg.	Fluid milk	0.7	Manufg.
Job training & related services	0.4	Services	Paper coating & glazing	0.7	Manufg.
Fabricated metal products, nec	0.3	Manufg.	Polishes & sanitation goods	0.7	Manufg.
Lighting fixtures & equipment	0.3	Manufg.	Automotive & apparel trimmings	0.6	Manufg.
Lubricating oils & greases	0.3	Manufg.	Broadwoven fabric mills	0.6	Manufg.
Metal stampings, nec	0.3	Manufg.	Frozen fruits, fruit juices & vegetables	0.6	Manufg.
Primary metal products, nec	0.3	Manufg.	Frozen specialties	0.6	Manufg.
Special dies & tools & machine tool accessories	0.3	Manufg.	Knit outerwear mills	0.6	Manufg.
Water transportation	0.3	Util.	Miscellaneous fabricated wire products	0.6	Manufg.
Royalties	0.3	Fin/R.E.	Photographic equipment & supplies	0.6	Manufg.
Management & consulting services & labs	0.3	Services	Pickles, sauces, & salad dressings	0.6	Manufg.
Metal foil & leaf	0.2	Manufg.	Soap & other detergents	0.6	Manufg.
Narrow fabric mills	0.2	Manufg.	Residential garden apartments	0.5	Constr.
Paints & allied products	0.2	Manufg.	Bags, except textile	0.5	Manufg.
Primary copper	0.2	Manufg.	Petroleum refining	0.5	Manufg.
Sanitary services, steam supply, irrigation	0.2	Util.	Semiconductors & related devices	0.5	Manufg.
Accounting, auditing & bookkeeping	0.2	Services	Real estate	0.5	Fin/R.E.
Electrical repair shops	0.2	Services	Beauty & barber shops	0.5	Services
Engineering, architectural, & surveying services	0.2	Services	Residential 1-unit structures, nonfarm	0.4	Constr.
Legal services	0.2	Services	Carbon paper & inked ribbons	0.4	Manufg.
Alkalies & chlorine	0.1	Manufg.	Roasted coffee	0.4	Manufg.
Building paper & board mills	0.1	Manufg.	Storage batteries	0.4	Manufg.
Manifold business forms	0.1	Manufg.	Upholstered household furniture	0.4	Manufg.
Mineral wool	0.1	Manufg.	Communications, except radio & TV	0.4	Util.
Pipe, valves, & pipe fittings	0.1	Manufg.	Water supply & sewage systems	0.4	Util.
Screw machine and related products	0.1	Manufg.	Business services nec	0.4	Services
Air transportation	0.1	Util.	Doctors & dentists	0.4	Services
Insurance carriers	0.1	Fin/R.E.	Miscellaneous repair shops	0.4	Services
Business/professional associations	0.1	Services	Construction of hospitals	0.3	Constr.
U.S. Postal Service	0.1	Gov't	Industrial buildings	0.3	Constr.
			Maintenance of highways & streets	0.3	Constr.
			Games, toys, & children's vehicles	0.3	Manufg.
			Logging camps & logging contractors	0.3	Manufg.
			Mattresses & bedsprings	0.3	Manufg.
			Nonferrous wire drawing & insulating	0.3	Manufg.
			Organic fibers, noncellulosic	0.3	Manufg.
			Sanitary paper products	0.3	Manufg.
			Sausages & other prepared meats	0.3	Manufg.
			Signs & advertising displays	0.3	Manufg.
			Surgical & medical instruments	0.3	Manufg.
			Retail trade, except eating & drinking	0.3	Trade
			Amusement & recreation services nec	0.3	Services
			Child day care services	0.3	Services
			Management & consulting services & labs	0.3	Services
			Nursing & personal care facilities	0.3	Services
			Construction of educational buildings	0.2	Constr.
			Construction of stores & restaurants	0.2	Constr.
			Electric utility facility construction	0.2	Constr.
			Warehouses	0.2	Constr.
			Aluminum rolling & drawing	0.2	Manufg.
			Bread, cake, & related products	0.2	Manufg.
			Carbon & graphite products	0.2	Manufg.
			Chemical preparations, nec	0.2	Manufg.
			Cigarettes	0.2	Manufg.
			Cookies & crackers	0.2	Manufg.
			Dog, cat, & other pet food	0.2	Manufg.
			Electric housewares & fans	0.2	Manufg.
			Fabricated plate work (boiler shops)	0.2	Manufg.
			Fabricated structural metal	0.2	Manufg.
			General industrial machinery, nec	0.2	Manufg.
			Glass & glass products, except containers	0.2	Manufg.
			Hard surface floor coverings	0.2	Manufg.
			Household refrigerators & freezers	0.2	Manufg.
			Knit fabric mills	0.2	Manufg.
			Lighting fixtures & equipment	0.2	Manufg.
			Macaroni & spaghetti	0.2	Manufg.
			Meat packing plants	0.2	Manufg.
			Nitrogenous & phosphatic fertilizers	0.2	Manufg.

Continued on next page.

INPUTS AND OUTPUTS FOR MISCELLANEOUS PLASTICS PRODUCTS - Continued

Economic Sector or Industry Providing Inputs	%	Sector	Economic Sector or Industry Buying Outputs	%	Sector
			Radio & TV communication equipment	0.2	Manufg.
			Radio & TV receiving sets	0.2	Manufg.
			Refrigeration & heating equipment	0.2	Manufg.
			Shoes, except rubber	0.2	Manufg.
			Shortening & cooking oils	0.2	Manufg.
			Sporting & athletic goods, nec	0.2	Manufg.
			Surface active agents	0.2	Manufg.
			Surgical appliances & supplies	0.2	Manufg.
			Wood partitions & fixtures	0.2	Manufg.
			Job training & related services	0.2	Services
			Laundry, dry cleaning, shoe repair	0.2	Services
			Social services, nec	0.2	Services
			Federal Government purchases, national defense	0.2	Fed Govt
			Greenhouse & nursery products	0.1	Agric.
			Farm service facilities	0.1	Constr.
			Hotels & motels	0.1	Constr.
			Maintenance of nonbuilding facilities nec	0.1	Constr.
			Maintenance of water supply facilities	0.1	Constr.
			Aircraft & missile equipment, nec	0.1	Manufg.
			Architectural metal work	0.1	Manufg.
			Blankbooks & looseleaf binders	0.1	Manufg.
			Book printing	0.1	Manufg.
			Cheese, natural & processed	0.1	Manufg.
			Chocolate & cocoa products	0.1	Manufg.
			Condensed & evaporated milk	0.1	Manufg.
			Confectionery products	0.1	Manufg.
			Distilled liquor, except brandy	0.1	Manufg.
			Drapery hardware & blinds & shades	0.1	Manufg.
			Engine electrical equipment	0.1	Manufg.
			Fabricated rubber products, nec	0.1	Manufg.
			Guided missiles & space vehicles	0.1	Manufg.
			Metal foil & leaf	0.1	Manufg.
			Metal household furniture	0.1	Manufg.
			Metal office furniture	0.1	Manufg.
			Miscellaneous publishing	0.1	Manufg.
			Motors & generators	0.1	Manufg.
			Paperboard containers & boxes	0.1	Manufg.
			Paving mixtures & blocks	0.1	Manufg.
			Phonograph records & tapes	0.1	Manufg.
			Pumps & compressors	0.1	Manufg.
			Secondary nonferrous metals	0.1	Manufg.
			Sheet metal work	0.1	Manufg.
			Special dies & tools & machine tool accessories	0.1	Manufg.
			Sugar	0.1	Manufg.
			Watches, clocks, & parts	0.1	Manufg.
			Women's hosiery, except socks	0.1	Manufg.
			Wood household furniture	0.1	Manufg.
			Wood products, nec	0.1	Manufg.
			Engineering, architectural, & surveying services	0.1	Services
			Local government passenger transit	0.1	Gov't

Source: Benchmark Input-Output Accounts for the U.S. Economy, 1982, U.S. Department of Commerce, Washington, D.C., July 1991. Data, as reported in the source, are organized by the 1977 SIC structure in use in 1982 but have been matched, as closely as is possible, to the 1987 SIC structure used in this book.

OCCUPATIONS EMPLOYED BY SIC 308 - MISCELLANEOUS PLASTICS PRODUCTS

Occupation	% of Total 1994	Change to 2005	Occupation	% of Total 1994	Change to 2005
Plastic molding machine workers	18.3	6.7	Maintenance repairers, general utility	1.6	6.7
Assemblers, fabricators, & hand workers nec	9.5	18.5	Industrial truck & tractor operators	1.5	18.5
Blue collar worker supervisors	5.2	10.7	Tool & die makers	1.4	77.8
Hand packers & packagers	4.7	-8.6	Extruding & forming machine workers	1.4	-40.7
Machine tool cutting & forming etc. nec	3.4	50.5	Industrial production managers	1.4	18.5
Inspectors, testers, & graders, precision	3.4	6.7	Machine feeders & offbearers	1.4	6.7
Helpers, laborers, & material movers nec	2.6	18.5	Packaging & filling machine operators	1.3	18.5
Machine forming operators, metal & plastic	2.5	30.4	Cutters & trimmers, hand	1.2	18.5
Metal & plastic machine workers nec	2.4	89.0	Bookkeeping, accounting, & auditing clerks	1.1	-11.1
General managers & top executives	2.3	12.4	Secretaries, ex legal & medical	1.1	7.9
Industrial machinery mechanics	2.2	30.4	Coating, painting, & spraying machine workers	1.1	6.7
Sales & related workers nec	1.9	18.5	Crushing & mixing machine operators	1.1	77.8
Traffic, shipping, & receiving clerks	1.8	14.0	Machine operators nec	1.1	-32.1
Freight, stock, & material movers, hand	1.7	-5.2			

Source: Industry-Occupation Matrix, Bureau of Labor Statistics. These data relate to one or more 3-digit SIC industry groups rather than to a single 4-digit SIC. The change reported for each occupation to the year 2005 is a percent of growth or decline as estimated by the Bureau of Labor Statistics. The abbreviation nec stands for 'not elsewhere classified'.

LOCATION BY STATE AND REGIONAL CONCENTRATION

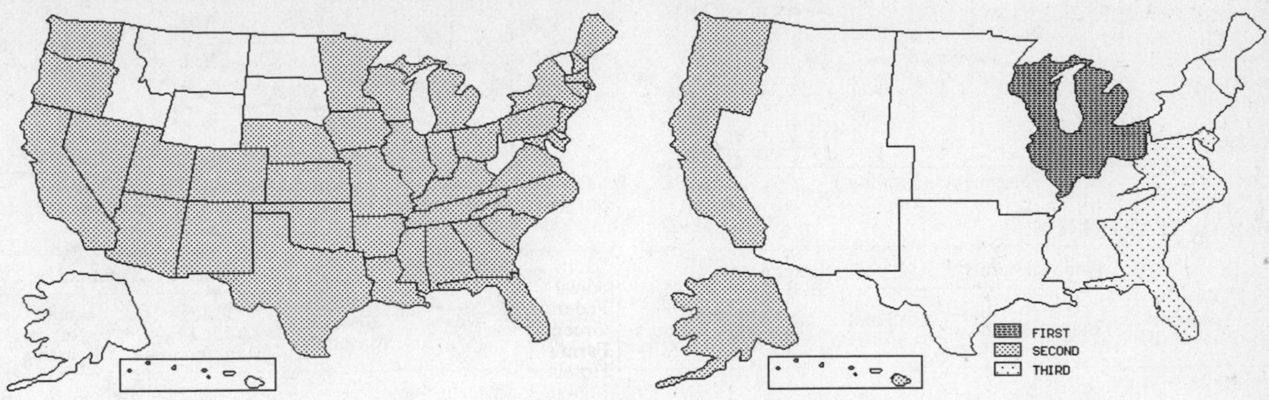

INDUSTRY DATA BY STATE

State	Establish-ments	Shipments			Employment				Cost as % of Shipments	Investment per Employee ($)
		Total ($ mil)	% of U.S.	Per Establ.	Total Number	% of U.S.	Per Establ.	Wages ($/hour)		
California	171	996.8	10.5	5.8	7,100	10.6	42	10.02	53.4	4,239
Texas	83	652.8	6.9	7.9	4,100	6.1	49	9.75	51.9	5,707
Pennsylvania	60	610.5	6.4	10.2	3,800	5.7	63	11.00	61.3	14,000
North Carolina	70	585.0	6.2	8.4	4,200	6.3	60	9.95	56.6	4,238
Illinois	47	525.2	5.5	11.2	3,000	4.5	64	11.78	52.9	3,867
Ohio	62	516.7	5.4	8.3	3,400	5.1	55	10.41	61.5	2,824
Indiana	41	477.3	5.0	11.6	3,500	5.2	85	9.90	56.2	3,086
Michigan	59	473.9	5.0	8.0	3,800	5.7	64	10.67	59.9	10,895
Tennessee	48	464.8	4.9	9.7	3,500	5.2	73	10.37	59.3	2,657
Georgia	39	449.2	4.7	11.5	3,200	4.8	82	10.12	50.8	8,250
Kentucky	23	415.6	4.4	18.1	2,500	3.7	109	11.14	47.8	12,840
Mississippi	30	306.9	3.2	10.2	2,200	3.3	73	9.09	61.3	3,000
New York	38	290.2	3.1	7.6	2,400	3.6	63	11.24	46.2	6,000
Missouri	29	281.6	3.0	9.7	1,500	2.2	52	11.70	54.5	4,733
New Jersey	39	274.0	2.9	7.0	1,800	2.7	46	11.46	53.3	3,222
Wisconsin	23	207.3	2.2	9.0	1,700	2.5	74	9.48	55.2	4,000
Kansas	12	179.5	1.9	15.0	1,300	1.9	108	9.73	37.2	-
Massachusetts	27	177.7	1.9	6.6	1,600	2.4	59	11.53	49.3	3,125
Florida	52	164.0	1.7	3.2	1,300	1.9	25	8.85	58.2	3,231
Virginia	15	161.7	1.7	10.8	1,000	1.5	67	13.57	42.3	3,400
Maryland	12	133.2	1.4	11.1	800	1.2	67	10.54	63.7	-
Iowa	14	128.3	1.4	9.2	1,200	1.8	86	12.25	51.3	417
South Carolina	15	113.0	1.2	7.5	900	1.3	60	10.43	54.3	7,556
Arkansas	20	108.5	1.1	5.4	600	0.9	30	9.70	53.8	2,000
Minnesota	24	85.1	0.9	3.5	600	0.9	25	10.11	53.9	3,667
Connecticut	12	74.0	0.8	6.2	500	0.7	42	9.63	53.6	6,200
Colorado	21	68.8	0.7	3.3	500	0.7	24	8.63	53.1	7,600
Washington	18	59.6	0.6	3.3	500	0.7	28	11.57	50.7	3,600
Alabama	13	44.7	0.5	3.4	400	0.6	31	8.17	48.1	2,500
New Mexico	6	37.4	0.4	6.2	100	0.1	17	7.50	56.1	-
Oregon	17	37.0	0.4	2.2	300	0.4	18	8.50	57.6	2,000
Nevada	4	25.3	0.3	6.3	200	0.3	50	12.33	49.8	3,500
Utah	11	24.6	0.3	2.2	200	0.3	18	10.50	57.7	2,500
Oklahoma	10	17.4	0.2	1.7	100	0.1	10	9.00	51.1	5,000
Rhode Island	7	13.8	0.1	2.0	100	0.1	14	9.00	44.9	2,000
Arizona	12	13.2	0.1	1.1	100	0.1	8	8.50	50.0	1,000
Nebraska	5	12.6	0.1	2.5	200	0.3	40	9.50	54.0	1,500
New Hampshire	5	(D)	-	-	1,750 *	2.6	350	-	-	-
Maine	4	(D)	-	-	175 *	0.3	44	-	-	-
Louisiana	2	(D)	-	-	175 *	0.3	88	-	-	-

Source: 1992 *Economic Census*. The states are in descending order of shipments or establishments (if shipment data are missing for the majority). The symbol (D) appears when data are withheld to prevent disclosure of competitive information. States marked with (D) are sorted by number of establishments. A dash (-) indicates that the data element cannot be calculated; * indicates the midpoint of a range.

3087 - CUSTOM COMPOUND PURCHASED RESINS

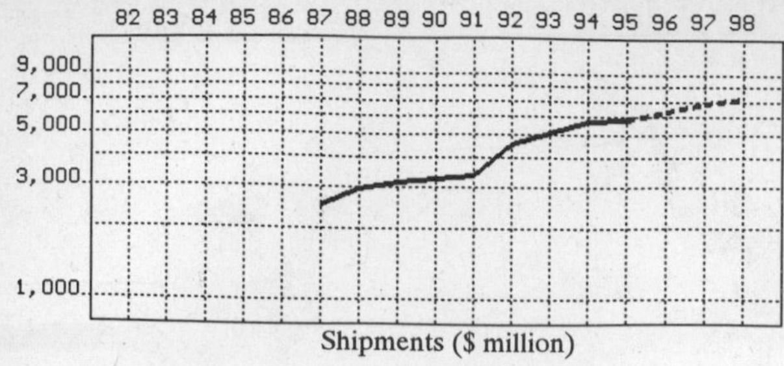

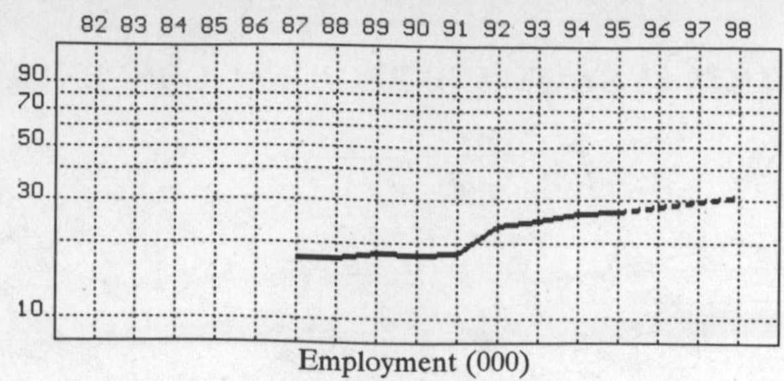

GENERAL STATISTICS

Year	Companies	Establishments: Total	Establishments: with 20 or more employees	Employment: Total (000)	Employment: Production Workers (000)	Employment: Production Hours (Mil)	Compensation: Payroll ($ mil)	Compensation: Wages ($/hr)	Production ($ million): Cost of Materials	Production ($ million): Value Added by Manufacture	Production ($ million): Value of Shipments	Production ($ million): Capital Invest.
1982												
1983												
1984												
1985												
1986												
1987	357	405	201	17.3	12.1	25.1	398.3	8.92	1,509.5	1,011.1	2,503.1	94.2
1988		403	209	17.3	12.1	25.0	406.5	9.18	1,768.6	1,195.6	2,948.7	53.5
1989		388	210	18.1	12.7	26.7	460.6	9.53	1,947.0	1,229.8	3,179.4	101.1
1990		382	204	18.0	13.0	27.3	473.6	9.79	1,954.3	1,297.8	3,246.9	94.8
1991		374	197	18.1	12.4	26.2	508.0	10.52	2,045.0	1,314.9	3,365.3	78.7
1992	576	662	314	23.6	15.7	33.5	684.3	10.96	2,723.6	1,870.2	4,581.7	146.8
1993		642	312	24.8	17.5	36.6	738.0	11.34	3,110.4	1,975.8	5,080.1	121.2
1994		639P	311P	26.5	18.2	37.7	805.6	11.43	3,450.2	2,306.3	5,731.1	164.5
1995		682P	330P	26.8P	18.4P	38.6P	838.7P	12.00P	3,517.4P	2,351.2P	5,842.7P	157.8P
1996		725P	349P	28.2P	19.3P	40.6P	900.8P	12.40P	3,786.7P	2,531.2P	6,290.0P	169.2P
1997		769P	368P	29.6P	20.3P	42.6P	962.8P	12.79P	4,056.0P	2,711.2P	6,737.4P	180.5P
1998		812P	387P	31.0P	21.2P	44.5P	1,024.9P	13.19P	4,325.3P	2,891.3P	7,184.7P	191.8P

Sources: 1982, 1987, 1992 *Economic Census*; *Annual Survey of Manufactures*, 83-86, 88-91, 93-94. Establishment counts for non-Census years are from *County Business Patterns*; establishment values for 83-84 are extrapolations. 'P's show projections by the editors. Industries reclassified in 87 will not have data for prior years.

INDICES OF CHANGE

Year	Companies	Establishments: Total	Establishments: with 20 or more employees	Employment: Total (000)	Employment: Production Workers (000)	Employment: Production Hours (Mil)	Compensation: Payroll ($ mil)	Compensation: Wages ($/hr)	Production ($ million): Cost of Materials	Production ($ million): Value Added by Manufacture	Production ($ million): Value of Shipments	Production ($ million): Capital Invest.
1982												
1983												
1984												
1985												
1986												
1987	62	61	64	73	77	75	58	81	55	54	55	64
1988		61	67	73	77	75	59	84	65	64	64	36
1989		59	67	77	81	80	67	87	71	66	69	69
1990		58	65	76	83	81	69	89	72	69	71	65
1991		56	63	77	79	78	74	96	75	70	73	54
1992	100	100	100	100	100	100	100	100	100	100	100	100
1993		97	99	105	111	109	108	103	114	106	111	83
1994		96P	99P	112	116	113	118	104	127	123	125	112
1995		103P	105P	114P	117P	115P	123P	109P	129P	126P	128P	108P
1996		110P	111P	120P	123P	121P	132P	113P	139P	135P	137P	115P
1997		116P	117P	126P	129P	127P	141P	117P	149P	145P	147P	123P
1998		123P	123P	132P	135P	133P	150P	120P	159P	155P	157P	131P

Sources: Same as General Statistics. Values reflect change from the base year, 1992. Values above 100 mean greater than 92, values below 100 mean less than 92, and a value of 100 in the 82-91 or 93-98 period means same as 92. 'P's mark projections by the editors.

SELECTED RATIOS

For 1994	Avg. of All Manufact.	Analyzed Industry	Index
Employees per Establishment	49	41	85
Payroll per Establishment	1,500,273	1,261,284	84
Payroll per Employee	30,620	30,400	99
Production Workers per Establishment	34	28	83
Wages per Establishment	853,319	674,654	79
Wages per Production Worker	24,861	23,676	95
Hours per Production Worker	2,056	2,071	101
Wages per Hour	12.09	11.43	95
Value Added per Establishment	4,602,255	3,610,848	78
Value Added per Employee	93,930	87,030	93

For 1994	Avg. of All Manufact.	Analyzed Industry	Index
Value Added per Production Worker	134,084	126,720	95
Cost per Establishment	5,045,178	5,401,789	107
Cost per Employee	102,970	130,196	126
Cost per Production Worker	146,988	189,571	129
Shipments per Establishment	9,576,895	8,972,870	94
Shipments per Employee	195,460	216,268	111
Shipments per Production Worker	279,017	314,896	113
Investment per Establishment	321,011	257,549	80
Investment per Employee	6,552	6,208	95
Investment per Production Worker	9,352	9,038	97

Sources: Same as General Statistics. The 'Average of All Manufacturing' column represents the average of all manufacturing industries reported for the most recent complete year available. The Index shows the relationship between the Average and the Analyzed Industry. For example, 100 means that they are equal; 500 that the Analyzed Industry is five times the average; 50 means that the Analyzed Industry is half the national average. The abbreviation 'na' is used to show that data are 'not available'.

LEADING COMPANIES

Number shown: **14** Total sales ($ mil): **182** Total employment (000): **0.9**

Company Name	Address				CEO Name	Phone	Co. Type	Sales ($ mil)	Empl. (000)
Fibre Glass-Evercoat Company	6600 Cornell Rd	Cincinnati	OH	45242	Ronald Shibich	513-489-7600	R	40	0.1
Lynn Plastics Corp	92 Brookline St	Lynn	MA	01902	Sidney Goldstein	617-598-5900	R	30	<0.1
Insta-Foam Products Inc	1500 Cedarwood Dr	Joliet	IL	60435	Randy Peterson	815-741-6800	S	28	0.1
Dennis Chemical Co	2700 Papin St	St Louis	MO	63103	AS Dennis	314-771-1800	R	25	0.1
Thermoset Plastics Inc	PO Box 20902	Indianapolis	IN	46220	Robert R Meyer	317-259-4161	R	20	<0.1
Premiere Polymers	PO Box 99571	Jeffersontown	KY	40269	Phillip Foote	502-267-1011	D	15*	<0.1
Crown-Snyder	PO Box 577	Marked Tree	AR	72365	Wes Manuel	501-358-3400	D	7*	0.1
Dynepco Inc	80 N Main St	Wharton	NJ	07885	CS Schmaltz	201-361-8900	S	5	<0.1
Cosmic Plastics Inc	27939 Beale Ct	Valencia	CA	91355	Lillian Luh	805-257-3274	R	4	<0.1
Advanced Polymer	PO Box 729	Carpentersville	IL	60110	Stan Jakopin	708-426-3350	R	3*	<0.1
Custom Compounding Inc	50 Milton Dr	Aston	PA	19014	James V Sullivan	610-497-8899	S	3	<0.1
Engineered Plastics Inc	PO Box 227	Gibsonville	NC	27249	D M Davidson III	910-449-4121	R	1*	<0.1
Premier Plastics Co	1225 Pearl St	Waukesha	WI	53186	Jack Hill	414-383-1038	R	1	<0.1
Armstrong Brands Inc	227 Thorn Av	Orchard Park	NY	14127	S Roger Sverson	716-662-6913	R	0*	<0.1

Source: *Ward's Business Directory of U.S. Private and Public Companies*, Volumes 1 and 2, 1996. The company type code used is as follows: P - Public, R - Private, S - Subsidiary, D - Division, J - Joint Venture, A - Affiliate, G - Group. Sales are in millions of dollars, employees are in thousands. An asterisk (*) indicates an estimated sales volume. The symbol < stands for 'less than'. Company names and addresses are truncated, in some cases, to fit into the available space.

MATERIALS CONSUMED

Material	Quantity	Delivered Cost ($ million)
Materials, ingredients, containers, and supplies	(X)	2,531.1
Hardboard (wood fiberboard)	(X)	1.4
Industrial inorganic chemicals	(X)	96.0
Inorganic pigments	(X)	188.2
Plastics resins consumed in the form of granules, pellets, powders, liquids, etc.	(X)	1,031.7
Industrial organic and synthetic organic chemicals, including plasticizers	(X)	189.4
Synthetic dyes, pigments, lakes, and toners	(X)	144.1
All other chemical and allied products	(X)	149.8
Plastics products consumed in the form of sheets, rods, tubes, film, and other shapes	(X)	12.2
Custom compounded plastics resins (purchased)	(X)	84.8
Textile-type glass fiber	(X)	18.4
Paper and paperboard products except paperboard boxes, containers, and corrugated paperboard	(X)	1.2
Paperboard containers, boxes, and corrugated paperboard	(X)	36.2
Parts and attachments specially designed for plastics working machinery	(X)	8.2
All other materials and components, parts, containers, and supplies	(X)	250.8
Materials, ingredients, containers, and supplies, nsk	(X)	318.6

Source: 1992 *Economic Census*. Explanation of symbols used: (D): Withheld to avoid disclosure of competitive data; na: Not available; (S): Withheld because statistical norms were not met; (X): Not applicable; (Z): Less than half the unit shown; nec: Not elsewhere classified; nsk: Not specified by kind; - : zero; * : 10-19 percent estimated; ** : 20-29 percent estimated.

PRODUCT SHARE DETAILS

Product or Product Class	% Share	Product or Product Class	% Share
Custom compound purchased resins	100.00	Plastics color concentrates	18.27
Custom compounding of purchased resins	72.64		

Source: 1992 *Economic Census*. The values shown are percent of total shipments in an industry. Values of indented subcategories are summed in the main heading. The symbol (D) appears when data are withheld to prevent disclosure of competitive information. The abbreviation nsk stands for 'not specified by kind' and nec for 'not elsewhere classified'.

INPUTS AND OUTPUTS FOR PLASTICS MATERIALS & RESINS

Economic Sector or Industry Providing Inputs	%	Sector	Economic Sector or Industry Buying Outputs	%	Sector
Cyclic crudes and organics	51.4	Manufg.	Miscellaneous plastics products	44.1	Manufg.
Miscellaneous plastics products	6.6	Manufg.	Exports	13.1	Foreign
Wholesale trade	6.1	Trade	Paints & allied products	5.2	Manufg.
Electric services (utilities)	4.2	Util.	Bags, except textile	3.7	Manufg.
Accounting, auditing & bookkeeping	3.2	Services	Nonferrous wire drawing & insulating	3.3	Manufg.
Gas production & distribution (utilities)	3.1	Util.	Organic fibers, noncellulosic	2.0	Manufg.
Imports	2.5	Foreign	Plastics materials & resins	1.6	Manufg.
Plastics materials & resins	2.3	Manufg.	Adhesives & sealants	1.5	Manufg.
Petroleum refining	1.4	Manufg.	Games, toys, & children's vehicles	1.3	Manufg.
Advertising	1.3	Services	Motor vehicle parts & accessories	1.2	Manufg.
Motor freight transportation & warehousing	1.2	Util.	Paper coating & glazing	1.2	Manufg.
Alkalies & chlorine	1.0	Manufg.	Paperboard containers & boxes	1.0	Manufg.

Continued on next page.

INPUTS AND OUTPUTS FOR PLASTICS MATERIALS & RESINS - Continued

Economic Sector or Industry Providing Inputs	%	Sector	Economic Sector or Industry Buying Outputs	%	Sector
Chemical preparations, nec	1.0	Manufg.	Photographic equipment & supplies	1.0	Manufg.
Railroads & related services	1.0	Util.	Wiring devices	1.0	Manufg.
Industrial inorganic chemicals, nec	0.8	Manufg.	Chemical preparations, nec	0.9	Manufg.
Paper coating & glazing	0.8	Manufg.	Cyclic crudes and organics	0.7	Manufg.
Paperboard containers & boxes	0.8	Manufg.	Coated fabrics, not rubberized	0.6	Manufg.
Water transportation	0.7	Util.	Electronic components nec	0.6	Manufg.
Miscellaneous repair shops	0.7	Services	Fluid milk	0.6	Manufg.
Gum & wood chemicals	0.6	Manufg.	Soap & other detergents	0.6	Manufg.
Paints & allied products	0.5	Manufg.	Electric housewares & fans	0.5	Manufg.
Engineering, architectural, & surveying services	0.5	Services	Hardware, nec	0.5	Manufg.
Crude petroleum & natural gas	0.4	Mining	Motor vehicles & car bodies	0.5	Manufg.
Pumps & compressors	0.4	Manufg.	Phonograph records & tapes	0.5	Manufg.
Communications, except radio & TV	0.4	Util.	Printing ink	0.5	Manufg.
Automotive repair shops & services	0.4	Services	Asbestos products	0.4	Manufg.
Noncomparable imports	0.4	Foreign	Fabricated rubber products, nec	0.4	Manufg.
Maintenance of nonfarm buildings nec	0.3	Constr.	Lighting fixtures & equipment	0.4	Manufg.
Inorganic pigments	0.3	Manufg.	Sporting & athletic goods, nec	0.4	Manufg.
Surface active agents	0.3	Manufg.	Surgical & medical instruments	0.4	Manufg.
Synthetic rubber	0.3	Manufg.	Telephone & telegraph apparatus	0.4	Manufg.
Banking	0.3	Fin/R.E.	Boat building & repairing	0.3	Manufg.
Electrical repair shops	0.3	Services	Brooms & brushes	0.3	Manufg.
Equipment rental & leasing services	0.3	Services	Hard surface floor coverings	0.3	Manufg.
Lubricating oils & greases	0.2	Manufg.	Household refrigerators & freezers	0.3	Manufg.
Metal barrels, drums, & pails	0.2	Manufg.	Paper mills, except building paper	0.3	Manufg.
Nitrogenous & phosphatic fertilizers	0.2	Manufg.	Shoes, except rubber	0.3	Manufg.
Soap & other detergents	0.2	Manufg.	Surgical appliances & supplies	0.3	Manufg.
Soybean oil mills	0.2	Manufg.	Typewriters & office machines, nec	0.3	Manufg.
Air transportation	0.2	Util.	Artificial trees & flowers	0.2	Manufg.
Sanitary services, steam supply, irrigation	0.2	Util.	Converted paper products, nec	0.2	Manufg.
Eating & drinking places	0.2	Trade	Household furniture, nec	0.2	Manufg.
Royalties	0.2	Fin/R.E.	Manufacturing industries, nec	0.2	Manufg.
Colleges, universities, & professional schools	0.2	Services	Mineral wool	0.2	Manufg.
Carbon black	0.1	Manufg.	Nonwoven fabrics	0.2	Manufg.
General industrial machinery, nec	0.1	Manufg.	Paperboard mills	0.2	Manufg.
Glass & glass products, except containers	0.1	Manufg.	Petroleum refining	0.2	Manufg.
Machinery, except electrical, nec	0.1	Manufg.	Refrigeration & heating equipment	0.2	Manufg.
Water supply & sewage systems	0.1	Util.	Semiconductors & related devices	0.2	Manufg.
Insurance carriers	0.1	Fin/R.E.	Service industry machines, nec	0.2	Manufg.
Security & commodity brokers	0.1	Fin/R.E.	Switchgear & switchboard apparatus	0.2	Manufg.
			Aircraft & missile equipment, nec	0.1	Manufg.
			Automotive & apparel trimmings	0.1	Manufg.
			Buttons	0.1	Manufg.
			Crowns & closures	0.1	Manufg.
			Cutlery	0.1	Manufg.
			Engine electrical equipment	0.1	Manufg.
			Gaskets, packing & sealing devices	0.1	Manufg.
			Household vacuum cleaners	0.1	Manufg.
			Ophthalmic goods	0.1	Manufg.
			Rubber & plastics hose & belting	0.1	Manufg.
			Scales & balances	0.1	Manufg.
			Tires & inner tubes	0.1	Manufg.
			Transportation equipment, nec	0.1	Manufg.
			X-ray apparatus & tubes	0.1	Manufg.

Source: Benchmark Input-Output Accounts for the U.S. Economy, 1982, U.S. Department of Commerce, Washington, D.C., July 1991. Data, as reported in the source, are organized by the 1977 SIC structure in use in 1982 but have been matched, as closely as is possible, to the 1987 SIC structure used in this book.

OCCUPATIONS EMPLOYED BY SIC 308 - MISCELLANEOUS PLASTICS PRODUCTS

Occupation	% of Total 1994	Change to 2005	Occupation	% of Total 1994	Change to 2005
Plastic molding machine workers	18.3	6.7	Maintenance repairers, general utility	1.6	6.7
Assemblers, fabricators, & hand workers nec	9.5	18.5	Industrial truck & tractor operators	1.5	18.5
Blue collar worker supervisors	5.2	10.7	Tool & die makers	1.4	77.8
Hand packers & packagers	4.7	-8.6	Extruding & forming machine workers	1.4	-40.7
Machine tool cutting & forming etc. nec	3.4	50.5	Industrial production managers	1.4	18.5
Inspectors, testers, & graders, precision	3.4	6.7	Machine feeders & offbearers	1.4	6.7
Helpers, laborers, & material movers nec	2.6	18.5	Packaging & filling machine operators	1.3	18.5
Machine forming operators, metal & plastic	2.5	30.4	Cutters & trimmers, hand	1.2	18.5
Metal & plastic machine workers nec	2.4	89.0	Bookkeeping, accounting, & auditing clerks	1.1	-11.1
General managers & top executives	2.3	12.4	Secretaries, ex legal & medical	1.1	7.9
Industrial machinery mechanics	2.2	30.4	Coating, painting, & spraying machine workers	1.1	6.7
Sales & related workers nec	1.9	18.5	Crushing & mixing machine operators	1.1	77.8
Traffic, shipping, & receiving clerks	1.8	14.0	Machine operators nec	1.1	-32.1
Freight, stock, & material movers, hand	1.7	-5.2			

Source: Industry-Occupation Matrix, Bureau of Labor Statistics. These data relate to one or more 3-digit SIC industry groups rather than to a single 4-digit SIC. The change reported for each occupation to the year 2005 is a percent of growth or decline as estimated by the Bureau of Labor Statistics. The abbreviation nec stands for 'not elsewhere classified'.

LOCATION BY STATE AND REGIONAL CONCENTRATION

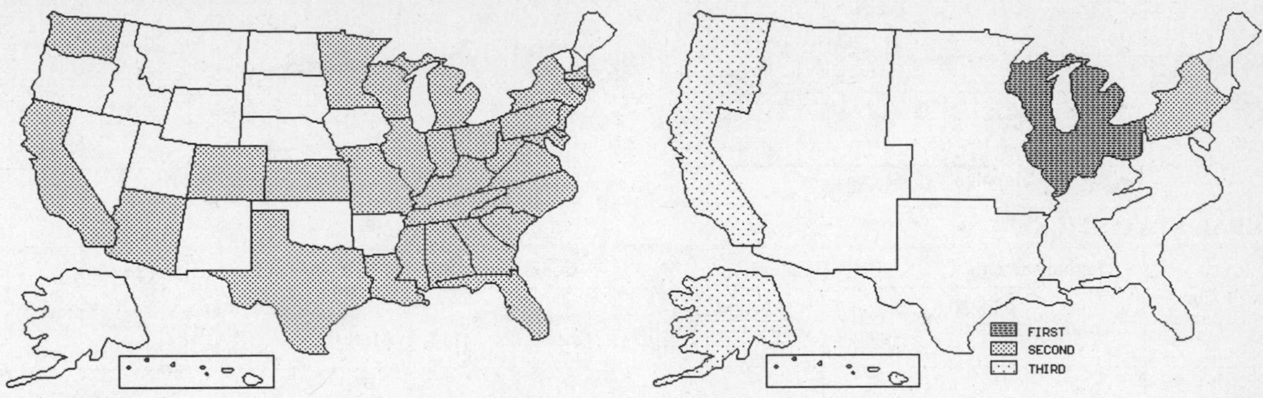

INDUSTRY DATA BY STATE

State	Establish-ments	Shipments			Employment				Cost as % of Shipments	Investment per Employee ($)
		Total ($ mil)	% of U.S.	Per Establ.	Total Number	% of U.S.	Per Establ.	Wages ($/hour)		
Ohio	48	610.2	13.3	12.7	3,100	13.1	65	11.81	62.6	6,387
New Jersey	44	434.4	9.5	9.9	2,000	8.5	45	11.63	62.1	8,050
Texas	52	356.2	7.8	6.8	1,700	7.2	33	12.30	60.0	7,118
Indiana	22	318.1	6.9	14.5	1,000	4.2	45	11.31	62.8	7,200
California	81	313.4	6.8	3.9	2,000	8.5	25	10.64	55.2	3,450
Massachusetts	41	309.9	6.8	7.6	1,500	6.4	37	11.10	59.4	5,867
Tennessee	21	303.2	6.6	14.4	1,500	6.4	71	9.84	63.9	10,200
Pennsylvania	36	240.0	5.2	6.7	1,200	5.1	33	11.29	59.3	9,667
Illinois	36	178.2	3.9	4.9	1,400	5.9	39	10.16	54.8	4,000
Michigan	29	151.6	3.3	5.2	900	3.8	31	11.89	61.0	4,222
New York	17	134.0	2.9	7.9	700	3.0	41	10.50	51.1	3,714
Georgia	11	110.5	2.4	10.0	400	1.7	36	12.43	69.3	8,750
Mississippi	6	110.3	2.4	18.4	200	0.8	33	10.67	70.1	-
North Carolina	15	106.1	2.3	7.1	700	3.0	47	11.36	60.7	5,429
Connecticut	12	104.4	2.3	8.7	300	1.3	25	13.67	47.3	9,667
Minnesota	13	85.6	1.9	6.6	500	2.1	38	11.29	52.3	8,600
Delaware	4	77.5	1.7	19.4	300	1.3	75	12.20	71.6	667
Louisiana	6	75.1	1.6	12.5	200	0.8	33	14.67	56.3	8,000
Missouri	9	67.6	1.5	7.5	400	1.7	44	9.83	59.8	1,500
Wisconsin	19	49.9	1.1	2.6	300	1.3	16	9.00	65.1	4,000
Florida	21	41.2	0.9	2.0	300	1.3	14	10.50	54.9	4,667
Virginia	9	40.2	0.9	4.5	300	1.3	33	11.25	38.6	5,333
Arizona	10	37.0	0.8	3.7	200	0.8	20	10.00	63.8	13,500
South Carolina	6	36.0	0.8	6.0	200	0.8	33	10.00	52.5	3,000
Kentucky	7	27.4	0.6	3.9	200	0.8	29	9.33	47.8	-
West Virginia	4	21.5	0.5	5.4	300	1.3	75	7.67	35.3	-
Alabama	6	15.7	0.3	2.6	100	0.4	17	8.00	47.8	8,000
Washington	15	12.5	0.3	0.8	100	0.4	7	9.50	48.8	7,000
Colorado	7	12.1	0.3	1.7	100	0.4	14	8.50	51.2	3,000
Rhode Island	10	(D)	-	-	750 *	3.2	75	-	-	1,467
Kansas	5	(D)	-	-	175 *	0.7	35	-	-	-
Maryland	2	(D)	-	-	175 *	0.7	88	-	-	-

Source: 1992 *Economic Census*. The states are in descending order of shipments or establishments (if shipment data are missing for the majority). The symbol (D) appears when data are withheld to prevent disclosure of competitive information. States marked with (D) are sorted by number of establishments. A dash (-) indicates that the data element cannot be calculated; * indicates the midpoint of a range.

3088 - PLASTICS PLUMBING FIXTURES

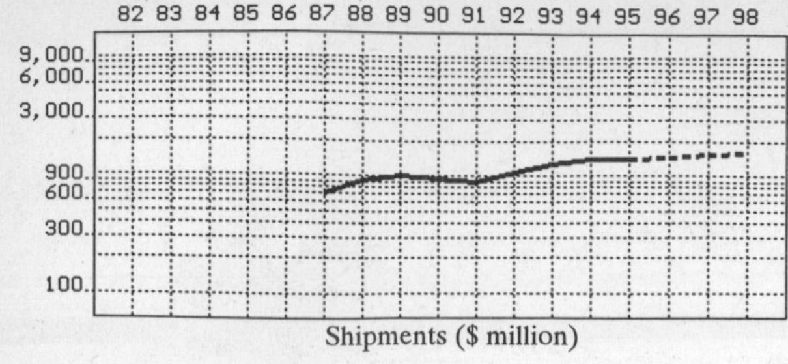

Shipments ($ million)

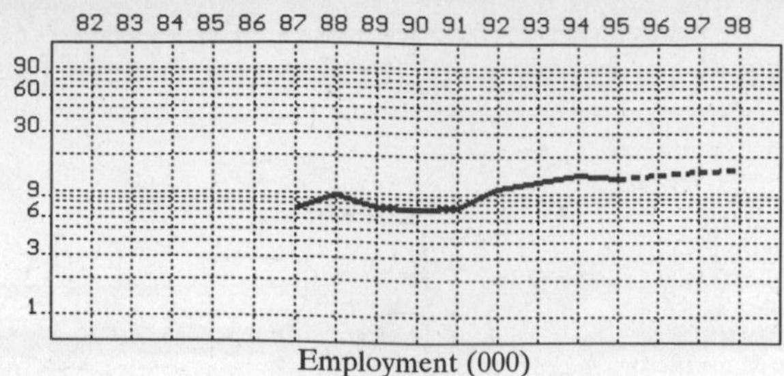

Employment (000)

GENERAL STATISTICS

Year	Com-panies	Establishments		Employment			Compensation		Production ($ million)			
		Total	with 20 or more employees	Total (000)	Production Workers (000)	Production Hours (Mil)	Payroll ($ mil)	Wages ($/hr)	Cost of Materials	Value Added by Manufacture	Value of Shipments	Capital Invest.
1982												
1983												
1984												
1985												
1986												
1987	162	176	81	7.5	5.6	10.8	138.0	7.82	302.1	411.8	708.8	14.5
1988		171	80	9.4	7.1	14.6	184.4	8.15	389.9	542.3	926.6	18.9
1989		168	82	7.7	7.0	13.4	185.9	8.16	414.5	614.3	1,022.5	68.5
1990		177	75	7.4	6.8	12.9	189.8	8.53	385.6	577.2	965.2	109.9
1991		202	75	7.7	5.9	11.4	167.5	8.98	346.1	542.5	879.3	91.1
1992	322	340	117	10.7	8.1	15.9	228.2	8.95	456.7	626.2	1,081.8	30.9
1993		354	125	12.2	8.9	17.4	255.4	8.91	533.8	731.8	1,272.2	31.2
1994		356P	119P	14.0	10.4	20.7	295.6	9.08	596.1	802.8	1,379.4	56.8
1995		389P	126P	13.3P	9.9P	19.4P	289.3P	9.40P	595.7P	802.2P	1,378.4P	64.8P
1996		421P	133P	14.1P	10.4P	20.5P	307.9P	9.58P	629.2P	847.4P	1,456.0P	67.5P
1997		453P	140P	14.9P	11.0P	21.5P	326.5P	9.77P	662.7P	892.5P	1,533.5P	70.2P
1998		486P	148P	15.7P	11.5P	22.6P	345.1P	9.95P	696.2P	937.6P	1,611.1P	72.9P

Sources: 1982, 1987, 1992 *Economic Census*; *Annual Survey of Manufactures*, 83-86, 88-91, 93-94. Establishment counts for non-Census years are from *County Business Patterns*; establishment values for 83-84 are extrapolations. 'P's show projections by the editors. Industries reclassified in 87 will not have data for prior years.

INDICES OF CHANGE

Year	Com-panies	Establishments		Employment			Compensation		Production ($ million)			
		Total	with 20 or more employees	Total (000)	Production Workers (000)	Production Hours (Mil)	Payroll ($ mil)	Wages ($/hr)	Cost of Materials	Value Added by Manufacture	Value of Shipments	Capital Invest.
1982												
1983												
1984												
1985												
1986												
1987	50	52	69	70	69	68	60	87	66	66	66	47
1988		50	68	88	88	92	81	91	85	87	86	61
1989		49	70	72	86	84	81	91	91	98	95	222
1990		52	64	69	84	81	83	95	84	92	89	356
1991		59	64	72	73	72	73	100	76	87	81	295
1992	100	100	100	100	100	100	100	100	100	100	100	100
1993		104	107	114	110	109	112	100	117	117	118	101
1994		105P	102P	131	128	130	130	101	131	128	128	184
1995		114P	108P	124P	122P	122P	127P	105P	130P	128P	127P	210P
1996		124P	114P	132P	129P	129P	135P	107P	138P	135P	135P	219P
1997		133P	120P	139P	135P	136P	143P	109P	145P	143P	142P	227P
1998		143P	126P	147P	142P	142P	151P	111P	152P	150P	149P	236P

Sources: Same as General Statistics. Values reflect change from the base year, 1992. Values above 100 mean greater than 92, values below 100 mean less than 92, and a value of 100 in the 82-91 or 93-98 period means same as 92. 'P's mark projections by the editors.

SELECTED RATIOS

For 1994	Avg. of All Manufact.	Analyzed Industry	Index	For 1994	Avg. of All Manufact.	Analyzed Industry	Index
Employees per Establishment	49	39	80	Value Added per Production Worker	134,084	77,192	58
Payroll per Establishment	1,500,273	829,671	55	Cost per Establishment	5,045,178	1,673,095	33
Payroll per Employee	30,620	21,114	69	Cost per Employee	102,970	42,579	41
Production Workers per Establishment	34	29	85	Cost per Production Worker	146,988	57,317	39
Wages per Establishment	853,319	527,543	62	Shipments per Establishment	9,576,895	3,871,612	40
Wages per Production Worker	24,861	18,073	73	Shipments per Employee	195,460	98,529	50
Hours per Production Worker	2,056	1,990	97	Shipments per Production Worker	279,017	132,635	48
Wages per Hour	12.09	9.08	75	Investment per Establishment	321,011	159,423	50
Value Added per Establishment	4,602,255	2,253,248	49	Investment per Employee	6,552	4,057	62
Value Added per Employee	93,930	57,343	61	Investment per Production Worker	9,352	5,462	58

Sources: Same as General Statistics. The 'Average of All Manufacturing' column represents the average of all manufacturing industries reported for the most recent complete year available. The Index shows the relationship between the Average and the Analyzed Industry. For example, 100 means that they are equal; 500 that the Analyzed Industry is five times the average; 50 means that the Analyzed Industry is half the national average. The abbreviation 'na' is used to show that data are 'not available'.

LEADING COMPANIES

Number shown: **31** Total sales ($ mil): **1,099** Total employment (000): **9.5**

Company Name	Address				CEO Name	Phone	Co. Type	Sales ($ mil)	Empl. (000)
Lasco Bathware	3255 E Miraloma	Anaheim	CA	92806	David Bienek	714-993-1220	D	160	1.5
Lasco Products Group	3255 E Miraloma	Anaheim	CA	92806	David Bienek	714-993-1220	D	160	1.2
California Acrylic Industries Inc	1462 E 9th St	Pomona	CA	91766	Charles Hewitt	909-623-8781	R	140*	1.3
Aqua Glass Corp	Industrial Park	Adamsville	TN	38310	Harry A Boosey	901-632-0911	S	135	1.2
Bristol Corp	1203 State Rd 15 S	Bristol	IN	46507	William Schmuhl	219-848-7681	R	110*	0.5
Watkins Manufacturing Corp	1280 Park Ctr Dr	Vista	CA	92083	Jeff Watkins	619-598-6464	S	80*	0.7
Hancor Co	PO Box 1047	Findlay	OH	45840	Wayne Gulley	419-422-6521	R	54	0.6
Aker Plastics Company Inc	PO Box 484	Plymouth	IN	46563	Donald Aker	219-936-3838	R	36	0.4
Clark Manufacturing Inc	13951 Monte Vista	Chino	CA	91710	Ron Clark	909-627-7670	R	35	0.3
Novi American Inc	PO Box 44649	Atlanta	GA	30336	P Douglas Daniels	404-344-5600	R	25	0.2
SWC Industries Inc	PO Box 210	Henderson	TX	75653	Glen Alexander	903-657-1436	R	24*	0.2
Swan Corp	1 City Ctr	St Louis	MO	63101	JW Moore	314-231-8148	R	22	0.2
Hessco Industries Inc	160 E Foundation	La Habra	CA	90631	Stephen W Hess	714-871-7448	R	18	0.2
Aquatic Industries Inc	Route 6	Leander	TX	78641	Brad Roten	512-259-2255	R	17	0.2
Eagle Plastics Inc	1530 Commerce Dr	Stow	OH	44224	Jerry E Brighton	216-688-9330	R	13*	0.1
Bremen Glas Inc	PO Box 209	Bremen	IN	46506	Pat Flynn	219-546-3298	R	11*	0.1
Koral Industries Inc	PO Box 1270	Ennis	TX	75120	R C Christopher	214-875-6555	R	11*	0.1
BPC Manufacturing	1755 N Oak Rd	Plymouth	IN	46563	Bill DeHaven	219-936-9894	D	9*	0.2
EL Mustee and Sons Inc	5431 W 164th St	Cleveland	OH	44142	Frank A Mustee	216-267-3100	R	7*	0.1
Lippert Corp	PO Box 1030	Menomonee Fls	WI	53052	Daniel Lippert	414-255-2350	R	7	0.1
Midgard Inc	1255 Nursery Rd	Green Lane	PA	18054	Robert Brown	215-536-3174	R	7*	<0.1
Duracraft Plastics Inc	PO Box 11159	Newington	CT	06111	Stuart Holden Jr	203-666-3342	R	3	<0.1
Royal Spa Manufacturing Corp	2041 W Epler St	Indianapolis	IN	46217	Richard Bartlett	317-848-7615	R	3	<0.1
SeaLand Technology Corp	PO Box 38	Big Prairie	OH	44611	Ed McKiernan	216-496-3211	S	3	<0.1
Con-Tech Industries Inc	145 de Oro	San Marcos	CA	92069	Jay J Martin	619-471-9597	S	3	<0.1
Century Marble Company Inc	4347 W 96th St	Indianapolis	IN	46268	Ronald L Maurer	317-876-9771	R	3	<0.1
Re-Bath Corp	1055 S Country C	Mesa	AZ	85210	D Highly Falkner	602-844-1575	S	2	<0.1
Fabcor Inc	PO Box 444	Rindge	NH	03461	David Lamoureux	603-899-6111	R	1	<0.1
National Fiberglass Corp	PO Box 876	Gilroy	CA	95020	John E Hermann	408-842-3115	R	0*	<0.1
Unique Bathing Supplies Inc	7 Monroe St	Troy	NY	12180	Gary Hull	518-274-2284	R	0	<0.1
Urinette Inc	7012 Pine Forest Rd	Pensacola	FL	32526	Kathie Jones	904-944-9779	R	0	<0.1

Source: *Ward's Business Directory of U.S. Private and Public Companies*, Volumes 1 and 2, 1996. The company type code used is as follows: P - Public, R - Private, S - Subsidiary, D - Division, J - Joint Venture, A - Affiliate, G - Group. Sales are in millions of dollars, employees are in thousands. An asterisk (*) indicates an estimated sales volume. The symbol < stands for 'less than'. Company names and addresses are truncated, in some cases, to fit into the available space.

MATERIALS CONSUMED

Material	Quantity	Delivered Cost ($ million)
Materials, ingredients, containers, and supplies	(X)	411.8
Hardboard (wood fiberboard)	(X)	6.2
Industrial inorganic chemicals	(X)	8.3
Inorganic pigments	(X)	1.2
Plastics resins consumed in the form of granules, pellets, powders, liquids, etc.	(X)	91.3
Industrial organic and synthetic organic chemicals, including plasticizers	(X)	1.5
Synthetic dyes, pigments, lakes, and toners	(X)	0.9
All other chemical and allied products	(X)	12.4
Plastics products consumed in the form of sheets, rods, tubes, film, and other shapes	(X)	50.3
Custom compounded plastics resins (purchased)	(X)	1.2
Textile-type glass fiber	(X)	14.4
Broadwoven fabrics	(X)	(D)
Paper and paperboard products except paperboard boxes, containers, and corrugated paperboard	(X)	(D)
Paperboard containers, boxes, and corrugated paperboard	(X)	15.0
Parts and attachments specially designed for plastics working machinery	(X)	(D)
All other materials and components, parts, containers, and supplies	(X)	140.8
Materials, ingredients, containers, and supplies, nsk	(X)	62.7

Source: 1992 *Economic Census*. Explanation of symbols used: (D): Withheld to avoid disclosure of competitive data; na: Not available; (S): Withheld because statistical norms were not met; (X): Not applicable; (Z): Less than half the unit shown; nec: Not elsewhere classified; nsk: Not specified by kind; - : zero; * : 10-19 percent estimated; ** : 20-29 percent estimated.

PRODUCT SHARE DETAILS

Product or Product Class	% Share	Product or Product Class	% Share
Plastics plumbing fixtures	100.00		

Source: 1992 *Economic Census*. The values shown are percent of total shipments in an industry. Values of indented subcategories are summed in the main heading. The symbol (D) appears when data are withheld to prevent disclosure of competitive information. The abbreviation nsk stands for 'not specified by kind' and nec for 'not elsewhere classified'.

INPUTS AND OUTPUTS FOR MISCELLANEOUS PLASTICS PRODUCTS

Economic Sector or Industry Providing Inputs	%	Sector	Economic Sector or Industry Buying Outputs	%	Sector
Plastics materials & resins	36.2	Manufg.	Hospitals	5.6	Services
Wholesale trade	8.5	Trade	Electronic components nec	5.2	Manufg.
Miscellaneous plastics products	7.2	Manufg.	Personal consumption expenditures	4.3	
Imports	5.8	Foreign	Miscellaneous plastics products	4.0	Manufg.
Cyclic crudes and organics	4.4	Manufg.	Exports	4.0	Foreign
Electric services (utilities)	4.4	Util.	Telephone & telegraph apparatus	3.0	Manufg.
Paperboard containers & boxes	2.6	Manufg.	Motor vehicles & car bodies	2.8	Manufg.
Communications, except radio & TV	2.3	Util.	Eating & drinking places	2.8	Trade
Motor freight transportation & warehousing	2.0	Util.	Maintenance of nonfarm buildings nec	2.4	Constr.
Paperboard mills	1.5	Manufg.	Food preparations, nec	2.3	Manufg.
Synthetic rubber	1.5	Manufg.	Plastics materials & resins	2.1	Manufg.
Railroads & related services	1.3	Util.	Typewriters & office machines, nec	1.7	Manufg.
Glass & glass products, except containers	1.2	Manufg.	Commercial printing	1.6	Manufg.
Gas production & distribution (utilities)	1.0	Util.	Cyclic crudes and organics	1.5	Manufg.
Noncomparable imports	1.0	Foreign	Electronic computing equipment	1.5	Manufg.
Industrial inorganic chemicals, nec	0.9	Manufg.	Motor vehicle parts & accessories	1.3	Manufg.
Crude petroleum & natural gas	0.7	Mining	Paper mills, except building paper	1.3	Manufg.
Maintenance of nonfarm buildings nec	0.7	Constr.	Bottled & canned soft drinks	1.2	Manufg.
Eating & drinking places	0.7	Trade	Toilet preparations	1.2	Manufg.
Real estate	0.7	Fin/R.E.	Aircraft	1.1	Manufg.
Computer & data processing services	0.7	Services	Medical & health services, nec	1.1	Services
Broadwoven fabric mills	0.6	Manufg.	Nonfarm residential structure maintenance	1.0	Constr.
Machinery, except electrical, nec	0.6	Manufg.	Optical instruments & lenses	0.9	Manufg.
Petroleum refining	0.6	Manufg.	Wholesale trade	0.9	Trade
Banking	0.6	Fin/R.E.	Office buildings	0.8	Constr.
Inorganic pigments	0.5	Manufg.	Computer & data processing services	0.8	Services
Wood products, nec	0.5	Manufg.	Hotels & lodging places	0.8	Services
Advertising	0.5	Services	S/L Govt. purch., health & hospitals	0.8	S/L Govt
Equipment rental & leasing services	0.5	Services	Residential additions/alterations, nonfarm	0.7	Constr.
Adhesives & sealants	0.4	Manufg.	Animal & marine fats & oils	0.7	Manufg.
Fabricated rubber products, nec	0.4	Manufg.	Drugs	0.7	Manufg.
Special industry machinery, nec	0.4	Manufg.	Fluid milk	0.7	Manufg.
Job training & related services	0.4	Services	Paper coating & glazing	0.7	Manufg.
Fabricated metal products, nec	0.3	Manufg.	Polishes & sanitation goods	0.7	Manufg.
Lighting fixtures & equipment	0.3	Manufg.	Automotive & apparel trimmings	0.6	Manufg.
Lubricating oils & greases	0.3	Manufg.	Broadwoven fabric mills	0.6	Manufg.
Metal stampings, nec	0.3	Manufg.	Frozen fruits, fruit juices & vegetables	0.6	Manufg.
Primary metal products, nec	0.3	Manufg.	Frozen specialties	0.6	Manufg.
Special dies & tools & machine tool accessories	0.3	Manufg.	Knit outerwear mills	0.6	Manufg.
Water transportation	0.3	Util.	Miscellaneous fabricated wire products	0.6	Manufg.
Royalties	0.3	Fin/R.E.	Photographic equipment & supplies	0.6	Manufg.
Management & consulting services & labs	0.3	Services	Pickles, sauces, & salad dressings	0.6	Manufg.
Metal foil & leaf	0.2	Manufg.	Soap & other detergents	0.6	Manufg.
Narrow fabric mills	0.2	Manufg.	Residential garden apartments	0.5	Constr.
Paints & allied products	0.2	Manufg.	Bags, except textile	0.5	Manufg.
Primary copper	0.2	Manufg.	Petroleum refining	0.5	Manufg.
Sanitary services, steam supply, irrigation	0.2	Util.	Semiconductors & related devices	0.5	Manufg.
Accounting, auditing & bookkeeping	0.2	Services	Real estate	0.5	Fin/R.E.
Electrical repair shops	0.2	Services	Beauty & barber shops	0.5	Services
Engineering, architectural, & surveying services	0.2	Services	Residential 1-unit structures, nonfarm	0.4	Constr.
Legal services	0.2	Services	Carbon paper & inked ribbons	0.4	Manufg.
Alkalies & chlorine	0.1	Manufg.	Roasted coffee	0.4	Manufg.
Building paper & board mills	0.1	Manufg.	Storage batteries	0.4	Manufg.
Manifold business forms	0.1	Manufg.	Upholstered household furniture	0.4	Manufg.
Mineral wool	0.1	Manufg.	Communications, except radio & TV	0.4	Util.
Pipe, valves, & pipe fittings	0.1	Manufg.	Water supply & sewage systems	0.4	Util.
Screw machine and related products	0.1	Manufg.	Business services nec	0.4	Services
Air transportation	0.1	Util.	Doctors & dentists	0.4	Services
Insurance carriers	0.1	Fin/R.E.	Miscellaneous repair shops	0.4	Services
Business/professional associations	0.1	Services	Construction of hospitals	0.3	Constr.
U.S. Postal Service	0.1	Gov't	Industrial buildings	0.3	Constr.
			Maintenance of highways & streets	0.3	Constr.
			Games, toys, & children's vehicles	0.3	Manufg.
			Logging camps & logging contractors	0.3	Manufg.
			Mattresses & bedsprings	0.3	Manufg.
			Nonferrous wire drawing & insulating	0.3	Manufg.
			Organic fibers, noncellulosic	0.3	Manufg.
			Sanitary paper products	0.3	Manufg.
			Sausages & other prepared meats	0.3	Manufg.
			Signs & advertising displays	0.3	Manufg.
			Surgical & medical instruments	0.3	Manufg.
			Retail trade, except eating & drinking	0.3	Trade
			Amusement & recreation services nec	0.3	Services
			Child day care services	0.3	Services
			Management & consulting services & labs	0.3	Services
			Nursing & personal care facilities	0.3	Services
			Construction of educational buildings	0.2	Constr.
			Construction of stores & restaurants	0.2	Constr.

Continued on next page.

INPUTS AND OUTPUTS FOR MISCELLANEOUS PLASTICS PRODUCTS - Continued

Economic Sector or Industry Providing Inputs	%	Sector	Economic Sector or Industry Buying Outputs	%	Sector
			Electric utility facility construction	0.2	Constr.
			Warehouses	0.2	Constr.
			Aluminum rolling & drawing	0.2	Manufg.
			Bread, cake, & related products	0.2	Manufg.
			Carbon & graphite products	0.2	Manufg.
			Chemical preparations, nec	0.2	Manufg.
			Cigarettes	0.2	Manufg.
			Cookies & crackers	0.2	Manufg.
			Dog, cat, & other pet food	0.2	Manufg.
			Electric housewares & fans	0.2	Manufg.
			Fabricated plate work (boiler shops)	0.2	Manufg.
			Fabricated structural metal	0.2	Manufg.
			General industrial machinery, nec	0.2	Manufg.
			Glass & glass products, except containers	0.2	Manufg.
			Hard surface floor coverings	0.2	Manufg.
			Household refrigerators & freezers	0.2	Manufg.
			Knit fabric mills	0.2	Manufg.
			Lighting fixtures & equipment	0.2	Manufg.
			Macaroni & spaghetti	0.2	Manufg.
			Meat packing plants	0.2	Manufg.
			Nitrogenous & phosphatic fertilizers	0.2	Manufg.
			Radio & TV communication equipment	0.2	Manufg.
			Radio & TV receiving sets	0.2	Manufg.
			Refrigeration & heating equipment	0.2	Manufg.
			Shoes, except rubber	0.2	Manufg.
			Shortening & cooking oils	0.2	Manufg.
			Sporting & athletic goods, nec	0.2	Manufg.
			Surface active agents	0.2	Manufg.
			Surgical appliances & supplies	0.2	Manufg.
			Wood partitions & fixtures	0.2	Manufg.
			Job training & related services	0.2	Services
			Laundry, dry cleaning, shoe repair	0.2	Services
			Social services, nec	0.2	Services
			Federal Government purchases, national defense	0.2	Fed Govt
			Greenhouse & nursery products	0.1	Agric.
			Farm service facilities	0.1	Constr.
			Hotels & motels	0.1	Constr.
			Maintenance of nonbuilding facilities nec	0.1	Constr.
			Maintenance of water supply facilities	0.1	Constr.
			Aircraft & missile equipment, nec	0.1	Manufg.
			Architectural metal work	0.1	Manufg.
			Blankbooks & looseleaf binders	0.1	Manufg.
			Book printing	0.1	Manufg.
			Cheese, natural & processed	0.1	Manufg.
			Chocolate & cocoa products	0.1	Manufg.
			Condensed & evaporated milk	0.1	Manufg.
			Confectionery products	0.1	Manufg.
			Distilled liquor, except brandy	0.1	Manufg.
			Drapery hardware & blinds & shades	0.1	Manufg.
			Engine electrical equipment	0.1	Manufg.
			Fabricated rubber products, nec	0.1	Manufg.
			Guided missiles & space vehicles	0.1	Manufg.
			Metal foil & leaf	0.1	Manufg.
			Metal household furniture	0.1	Manufg.
			Metal office furniture	0.1	Manufg.
			Miscellaneous publishing	0.1	Manufg.
			Motors & generators	0.1	Manufg.
			Paperboard containers & boxes	0.1	Manufg.
			Paving mixtures & blocks	0.1	Manufg.
			Phonograph records & tapes	0.1	Manufg.
			Pumps & compressors	0.1	Manufg.
			Secondary nonferrous metals	0.1	Manufg.
			Sheet metal work	0.1	Manufg.
			Special dies & tools & machine tool accessories	0.1	Manufg.
			Sugar	0.1	Manufg.
			Watches, clocks, & parts	0.1	Manufg.
			Women's hosiery, except socks	0.1	Manufg.
			Wood household furniture	0.1	Manufg.
			Wood products, nec	0.1	Manufg.
			Engineering, architectural, & surveying services	0.1	Services
			Local government passenger transit	0.1	Gov't

Source: Benchmark Input-Output Accounts for the U.S. Economy, 1982, U.S. Department of Commerce, Washington, D.C., July 1991. Data, as reported in the source, are organized by the 1977 SIC structure in use in 1982 but have been matched, as closely as is possible, to the 1987 SIC structure used in this book.

OCCUPATIONS EMPLOYED BY SIC 308 - MISCELLANEOUS PLASTICS PRODUCTS

Occupation	% of Total 1994	Change to 2005	Occupation	% of Total 1994	Change to 2005
Plastic molding machine workers	18.3	6.7	Maintenance repairers, general utility	1.6	6.7
Assemblers, fabricators, & hand workers nec	9.5	18.5	Industrial truck & tractor operators	1.5	18.5
Blue collar worker supervisors	5.2	10.7	Tool & die makers	1.4	77.8
Hand packers & packagers	4.7	-8.6	Extruding & forming machine workers	1.4	-40.7
Machine tool cutting & forming etc. nec	3.4	50.5	Industrial production managers	1.4	18.5
Inspectors, testers, & graders, precision	3.4	6.7	Machine feeders & offbearers	1.4	6.7
Helpers, laborers, & material movers nec	2.6	18.5	Packaging & filling machine operators	1.3	18.5
Machine forming operators, metal & plastic	2.5	30.4	Cutters & trimmers, hand	1.2	18.5
Metal & plastic machine workers nec	2.4	89.0	Bookkeeping, accounting, & auditing clerks	1.1	-11.1
General managers & top executives	2.3	12.4	Secretaries, ex legal & medical	1.1	7.9
Industrial machinery mechanics	2.2	30.4	Coating, painting, & spraying machine workers	1.1	6.7
Sales & related workers nec	1.9	18.5	Crushing & mixing machine operators	1.1	77.8
Traffic, shipping, & receiving clerks	1.8	14.0	Machine operators nec	1.1	-32.1
Freight, stock, & material movers, hand	1.7	-5.2			

Source: *Industry-Occupation Matrix*, Bureau of Labor Statistics. These data relate to one or more 3-digit SIC industry groups rather than to a single 4-digit SIC. The change reported for each occupation to the year 2005 is a percent of growth or decline as estimated by the Bureau of Labor Statistics. The abbreviation nec stands for 'not elsewhere classified'.

LOCATION BY STATE AND REGIONAL CONCENTRATION

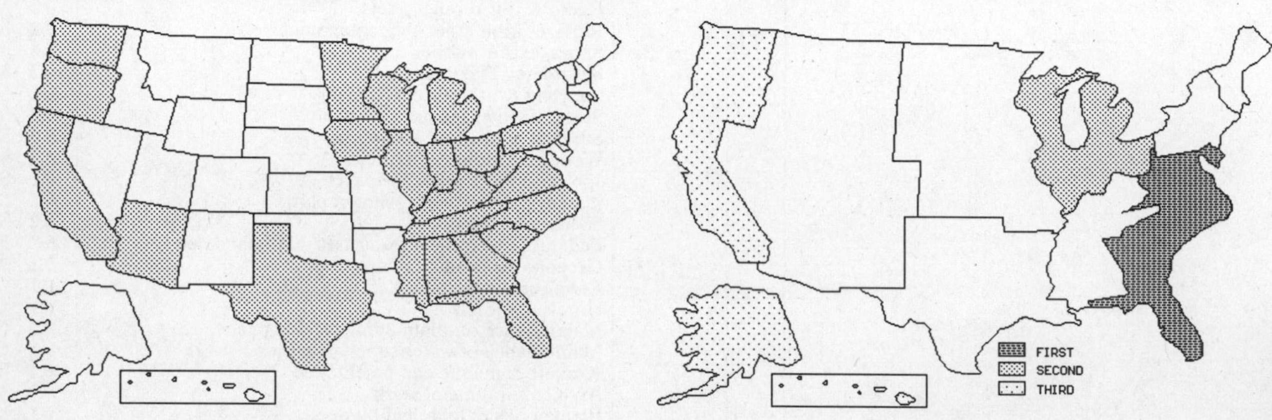

INDUSTRY DATA BY STATE

State	Establish-ments	Shipments Total ($ mil)	Shipments % of U.S.	Shipments Per Establ.	Employment Total Number	Employment % of U.S.	Employment Per Establ.	Wages ($/hour)	Cost as % of Shipments	Investment per Employee ($)
California	43	239.0	22.1	5.6	2,100	19.6	49	7.66	47.4	2,333
Michigan	13	75.7	7.0	5.8	500	4.7	38	12.43	38.6	3,200
Ohio	15	69.1	6.4	4.6	400	3.7	27	10.80	50.9	2,250
Pennsylvania	11	44.7	4.1	4.1	400	3.7	36	11.00	39.6	2,500
Florida	31	39.8	3.7	1.3	500	4.7	16	7.25	41.5	3,000
Virginia	7	34.1	3.2	4.9	500	4.7	71	9.22	41.6	1,600
Washington	11	31.6	2.9	2.9	300	2.8	27	10.80	37.0	3,000
Indiana	16	28.6	2.6	1.8	400	3.7	25	8.83	37.4	4,250
Illinois	14	26.8	2.5	1.9	300	2.8	21	9.83	36.9	-
Kentucky	9	24.9	2.3	2.8	300	2.8	33	8.80	45.4	6,000
Arizona	8	24.2	2.2	3.0	300	2.8	38	7.50	38.4	7,000
Minnesota	9	17.1	1.6	1.9	200	1.9	22	8.50	65.5	4,000
Oregon	5	9.8	0.9	2.0	100	0.9	20	18.00	56.1	5,000
Mississippi	4	4.9	0.5	1.2	100	0.9	25	5.00	38.8	3,000
Texas	29	(D)	-	-	750 *	7.0	26	-	-	-
Georgia	17	(D)	-	-	750 *	7.0	44	-	-	-
Tennessee	9	(D)	-	-	750 *	7.0	83	-	-	-
North Carolina	8	(D)	-	-	175 *	1.6	22	-	-	1,714
South Carolina	8	(D)	-	-	175 *	1.6	22	-	-	3,429
Alabama	7	(D)	-	-	375 *	3.5	54	-	-	2,400
Wisconsin	4	(D)	-	-	175 *	1.6	44	-	-	-
West Virginia	3	(D)	-	-	175 *	1.6	58	-	-	2,857
Iowa	1	(D)	-	-	175 *	1.6	175	-	-	-

Source: 1992 *Economic Census*. The states are in descending order of shipments or establishments (if shipment data are missing for the majority). The symbol (D) appears when data are withheld to prevent disclosure of competitive information. States marked with (D) are sorted by number of establishments. A dash (-) indicates that the data element cannot be calculated; * indicates the midpoint of a range.

3089 - PLASTICS PRODUCTS, NEC

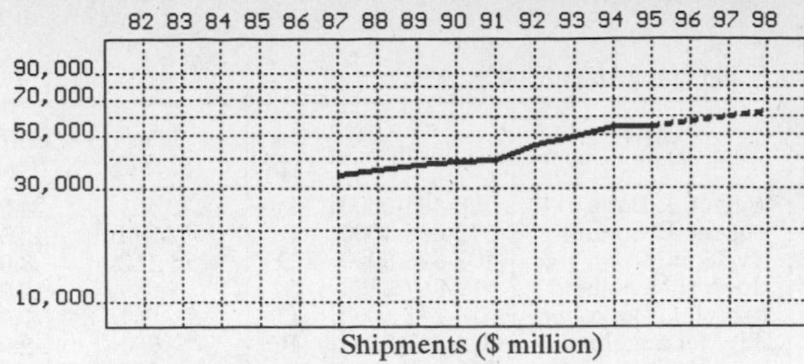

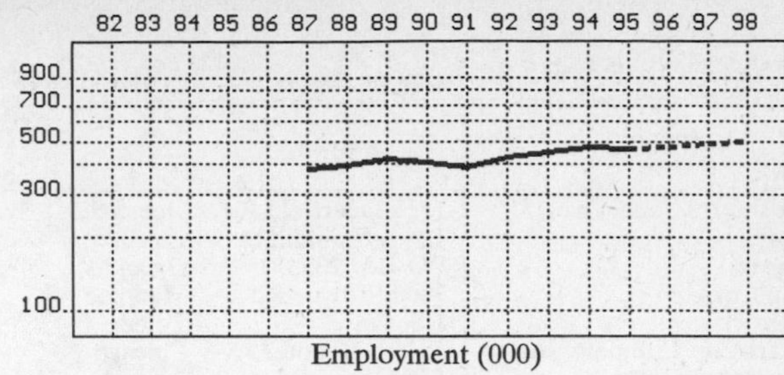

GENERAL STATISTICS

Year	Companies	Establishments: Total	Establishments: with 20 or more employees	Employment: Total (000)	Employment: Production Workers (000)	Employment: Production Hours (Mil)	Compensation: Payroll ($ mil)	Compensation: Wages ($/hr)	Production ($ million): Cost of Materials	Production ($ million): Value Added by Manufacture	Production ($ million): Value of Shipments	Production ($ million): Capital Invest.
1982												
1983												
1984												
1985												
1986												
1987	7,770	8,571	3,939	384.7	303.0	597.5	7,285.5	8.03	16,031.9	17,919.8	33,773.8	1,339.7
1988		8,563	4,107	394.3	308.6	610.8	7,661.9	8.13	17,666.6	18,396.7	35,881.9	1,290.0
1989		7,991	4,057	420.2	316.0	628.7	8,052.7	8.27	19,341.0	19,220.2	37,399.6	1,776.9
1990		8,045	4,038	408.0	313.8	625.6	8,535.7	8.73	19,094.2	19,855.8	38,946.3	1,609.2
1991		8,390	3,976	388.9	301.9	607.0	8,540.0	9.01	19,075.9	20,120.6	39,187.9	1,803.2
1992	7,600	8,455	4,047	426.4	331.1	665.0	9,965.4	9.50	21,026.6	24,378.5	45,311.3	1,985.3
1993		8,335	4,057	443.9	348.0	701.3	10,722.8	9.81	22,979.5	26,306.8	49,187.1	2,220.2
1994		8,261P	4,053P	470.7	372.8	752.5	11,442.9	9.85	25,375.8	29,247.8	54,296.5	2,542.4
1995		8,242P	4,059P	462.6P	362.9P	735.8P	11,712.4P	10.26P	25,373.9P	29,245.6P	54,292.4P	2,564.9P
1996		8,223P	4,064P	472.8P	371.5P	755.1P	12,309.4P	10.56P	26,676.7P	30,747.2P	57,080.1P	2,730.3P
1997		8,204P	4,070P	482.9P	380.0P	774.5P	12,906.4P	10.86P	27,979.5P	32,248.8P	59,867.7P	2,895.6P
1998		8,186P	4,075P	493.0P	388.6P	793.9P	13,503.4P	11.16P	29,282.4P	33,750.4P	62,655.3P	3,061.0P

Sources: 1982, 1987, 1992 *Economic Census*; *Annual Survey of Manufactures*, 83-86, 88-91, 93-94. Establishment counts for non-Census years are from *County Business Patterns*; establishment values for 83-84 are extrapolations. 'P's show projections by the editors. Industries reclassified in 87 will not have data for prior years.

INDICES OF CHANGE

Year	Companies	Establishments: Total	Establishments: with 20 or more employees	Employment: Total (000)	Employment: Production Workers (000)	Employment: Production Hours (Mil)	Compensation: Payroll ($ mil)	Compensation: Wages ($/hr)	Production ($ million): Cost of Materials	Production ($ million): Value Added by Manufacture	Production ($ million): Value of Shipments	Production ($ million): Capital Invest.
1982												
1983												
1984												
1985												
1986												
1987	102	101	97	90	92	90	73	85	76	74	75	67
1988		101	101	92	93	92	77	86	84	75	79	65
1989		95	100	99	95	95	81	87	92	79	83	90
1990		95	100	96	95	94	86	92	91	81	86	81
1991		99	98	91	91	91	86	95	91	83	86	91
1992	100	100	100	100	100	100	100	100	100	100	100	100
1993		99	100	104	105	105	108	103	109	108	109	112
1994		98P	100P	110	113	113	115	104	121	120	120	128
1995		97P	100P	109P	110P	111P	118P	108P	121P	120P	120P	129P
1996		97P	100P	111P	112P	114P	124P	111P	127P	126P	126P	138P
1997		97P	101P	113P	115P	116P	130P	114P	133P	132P	132P	146P
1998		97P	101P	116P	117P	119P	136P	117P	139P	138P	138P	154P

Sources: Same as General Statistics. Values reflect change from the base year, 1992. Values above 100 mean greater than 92, values below 100 mean less than 92, and a value of 100 in the 82-91 or 93-98 period means same as 92. 'P's mark projections by the editors.

SELECTED RATIOS

For 1994	Avg. of All Manufact.	Analyzed Industry	Index
Employees per Establishment	49	57	116
Payroll per Establishment	1,500,273	1,385,219	92
Payroll per Employee	30,620	24,310	79
Production Workers per Establishment	34	45	131
Wages per Establishment	853,319	897,274	105
Wages per Production Worker	24,861	19,882	80
Hours per Production Worker	2,056	2,019	98
Wages per Hour	12.09	9.85	81
Value Added per Establishment	4,602,255	3,540,590	77
Value Added per Employee	93,930	62,137	66

For 1994	Avg. of All Manufact.	Analyzed Industry	Index
Value Added per Production Worker	134,084	78,454	59
Cost per Establishment	5,045,178	3,071,865	61
Cost per Employee	102,970	53,911	52
Cost per Production Worker	146,988	68,068	46
Shipments per Establishment	9,576,895	6,572,858	69
Shipments per Employee	195,460	115,353	59
Shipments per Production Worker	279,017	145,645	52
Investment per Establishment	321,011	307,770	96
Investment per Employee	6,552	5,401	82
Investment per Production Worker	9,352	6,820	73

Sources: Same as General Statistics. The 'Average of All Manufacturing' column represents the average of all manufacturing industries reported for the most recent complete year available. The Index shows the relationship between the Average and the Analyzed Industry. For example, 100 means that they are equal; 500 that the Analyzed Industry is five times the average; 50 means that the Analyzed Industry is half the national average. The abbreviation 'na' is used to show that data are 'not available'.

LEADING COMPANIES Number shown: **75** Total sales ($ mil): **22,552** Total employment (000): **176.1**

Company Name	Address				CEO Name	Phone	Co. Type	Sales ($ mil)	Empl. (000)
Premark International Inc	1717 Deerfield Rd	Deerfield	IL	60015	Warren L Batts	708-405-6000	P	3,451	24.0
USG Corp	125 S Franklin St	Chicago	IL	60606	Eugene B Connolly	312-606-4000	P	2,290	12.3
Tupperware	PO Box 2353	Orlando	FL	32802	EV Goings	407-826-5050	D	1,112	8.0
Aeroquip Corp	3000 Strayer Rd	Maumee	OH	43537	Howard M Selland	419-867-2200	S	1,080	10.0
Owens-Brockway	1 Seagate	Toledo	OH	43666	Russell C Berkoben	419-247-5000	D	909	7.0
Sweetheart Cup Company Inc	7575 S Kostner Av	Chicago	IL	60652	Bill McLaughlin	312-767-3300	R	900	8.0
GenCorp Automotive	175 Ghent Rd	Akron	OH	44333	John Yasinsky	216-869-4200	S	577	6.3
Silgan Holdings Inc	4 Landmark Sq	Stamford	CT	06901	Phil Silver	203-975-7110	R	470	5.2
American Western	1401 W 9th St	Minneapolis	MN	55431	Dennis Shafer	612-884-7281	D	388	0.5
Carlisle Plastics Inc	1401 W 9th St	Minneapolis	MN	55431	William H Binnie	612-884-7281	P	388	2.9
West Company Inc	PO Box 645	Lionville	PA	19341	William G Little	610-594-2900	P	365	3.6
Plastipak Packaging Inc	9135 General Ct	Plymouth	MI	48170	William C Young	313-455-3600	R	360	1.5
Aeroquip Corp	300 S East Av	Jackson	MI	49203	Steve Schwab	517-787-8121	D	327	2.8
Furon Co	29982 Ivy Glenn Dr	Laguna Niguel	CA	92677	J Michael Hagan	714-831-5350	P	312	2.1
Hillside Capital Inc	405 Park Av	New York	NY	10022	John N Irwin III	212-935-6090	R	310*	3.0
Hillside Industries Inc	405 Park Av	New York	NY	10022	John N Irwin III	212-935-6090	S	310*	3.0
DataCard Corp	PO Box 9355	Minneapolis	MN	55440	Glenn Highland	612-933-1223	R	300	3.0
Worthington Custom Plastics Inc	1055 Dearborn Dr	Columbus	OH	43085	John R Halula	614-438-3011	S	290*	2.8
Contico International Inc	1101 Warson Rd	St Louis	MO	63132	Bill Miller	314-997-5900	R	270	2.5
Congoleum Corp	PO Box 3127	Mercerville	NJ	08619	Roger S Marcus	609-584-3000	P	266	1.3
Eagle Plastics Corp	45-31 Court Sq	Long Island Ct	NY	11101	N Kluger	718-937-8000	R	260*	2.5
Nordic Group	522 South Blv	Baraboo	WI	53913	WR Sauey	608-356-5551	R	250	1.8
Continental Plastic Containers	PO Box 5410	Norwalk	CT	06856	C F DiGiovanna	203-855-5000	S	231	1.7
Nypro Inc	101 Union St	Clinton	MA	01510	Gordon B Lankton	508-365-9721	R	225	2.0
Silgan Plastics Corp	PO Box 1080	Chesterfield	MO	63006	Russell Gervais	314-537-3223	S	225	1.8
Teepak Inc	3 Westbrook Corp	Westchester	IL	60154	J E Hermesdorf	708-409-3000	S	210	3.0
White Cap Inc	1140 31st St	Downers Grove	IL	60515	John Scales	708-515-8383	S	210*	2.0
Key Plastics Inc	39325 Plymouth Rd	Livonia	MI	48150	George Mars	313-462-6116	R	195	1.8
O'Sullivan Corp	1944 Valley Av	Winchester	VA	22601	Arthur H Bryant II	703-667-6666	P	195	2.0
Letica Corp	PO Box 5005	Rochester	MI	48308	I Letica	810-652-0577	R	190	1.5
Plastek Industries Inc	2425 W 23rd St	Erie	PA	16506	J Prischak	814-838-9667	R	185*	1.8
International Plastic Co	1950 3rd Av	New York	NY	10029	Morton M Ross	212-534-3982	R	182	<0.1
Quixote Corp	1 E Wacker Dr	Chicago	IL	60601	P E Rollhaus Jr	312-467-6755	P	177	1.6
Zero Corp	444 S Flower St	Los Angeles	CA	90071	W D Godbold Jr	213-629-7000	P	171	1.6
Larizza Industries Inc	201 W Big Beaver	Troy	MI	48084	Ronald T Larizza	810-689-5800	P	169	1.9
Manchester Plastics	201 W Big Beaver	Troy	MI	48084	Ronald T Larizza	810-524-9650	D	169	1.5
Packaging Resources Inc	1 Conway Park	Lake Forest	IL	60045	Howard Hoeper	708-295-6100	S	160	1.2
Astro-Valcour Inc	PO Box 148	Glens Falls	NY	12801	Christopher Angus	518-793-2524	S	150	0.7
GenCorp Automotive	PO Box 9067	Farmington Hls	MI	48333	HB Thompson	313-553-5180	D	150	0.7
Liberty Diversified Industries	5600 N Hwy 169	New Hope	MN	55428	Michael Fiterman	612-536-6600	R	150*	1.3
LNP Engineering Plastics Inc	475 Creamery Way	Exton	PA	19341	RE Schulz	610-363-4500	S	150	0.5
Norton Performance	150 Dey Rd	Wayne	NJ	07470	Louis F Laucirica	201-696-4700	S	150	1.5
Teknor Apex Co	505 Central Av	Pawtucket	RI	02861	Norman M Fain	401-725-8000	R	150	1.5
Variform Inc	PO Box 559	Kearney	MO	64060		816-635-6400	S	150	0.6
Wheaton Plastic Products	6115 Old Harding	Mays Landing	NJ	08330	John F Glowacki	609-625-4811	D	150*	1.5
Park-Ohio Industries Inc	20600 Chagrin Blv	Cleveland	OH	44122	Edward F Crawford	216-991-9700	P	147	1.7
Igloo Holdings Inc	1001 Houston	Houston	TX	77043	J H Godshall	713-461-5955	R	135	1.5
Flambeau Corp	801 Lynn Av	Baraboo	WI	53913	CL Sauey	608-356-5551	S	133	1.2
A and E Products Group	1460 Rte9 N	Woodbridge	NJ	07095	Cliff Dupree	908-855-9110	D	130*	1.0
Automotive Plastic Technologies	6600 E 15 Mile Rd	Sterling Hts	MI	48312	Cheuck Becker	313-979-5000	S	130	1.1
Robroy Industries Inc	River Rd	Verona	PA	15147	Peter McIlroy II	412-828-2100	R	130*	1.0
Batts Inc	200 Franklin St	Zeeland	MI	49464	Russel A Magel	616-772-4635	R	125	1.0
Premix Inc	PO Box 281	North Kingsville	OH	44068	John Maimone	216-224-2181	R	124	0.5
Igloo Products Corp	PO Box 19322	Houston	TX	77224	J H Godshall	713-461-5955	S	120	1.0
Johnson Controls Inc	47912 Halyard Dr	Plymouth	MI	48170	Conrad Zumhagen	313-454-5307	D	110	<0.1
Sterilite Corp	198 Main St	Townsend	MA	01469	Albert Stone	508-597-8702	R	110*	0.7
Bailey Corp	PO Box 307	Seabrook	NH	03874	Roger R Phillips	603-474-3011	P	108	1.8
Kerr Group Inc	1840 Century Pk E	Los Angeles	CA	90067	Roger W Norian	310-556-2200	D	107	0.9
ESSEF Corp	220 Park Dr	Chardon	OH	44024	Thomas B Waldin	216-286-2200	P	104	0.7
Carlisle Geauga Co	100 7th Av	Chardon	OH	44024	Allen J Hofmann	216-286-1059	S	100	0.9
Comar Inc	PO Box 608	Buena	NJ	08310	Henry Tamagni	609-692-6100	R	100	1.0
Landis Plastics Inc	10800 S Central Av	Chicago Ridge	IL	60415	HR Landis	312-239-2390	R	100	1.0
Morrison Molded Fiber	400 Commonwealth	Bristol	VA	24201	John D Tickle	703-645-8000	R	100	0.9
Mulay Plastics	10 Laura Dr	Addison	IL	60101	Douglas T Mulay	708-628-3639	R	100*	1.0
Rapid Industrial Plastics Co	13 Linden Av E	Jersey City	NJ	07305	Martin Sirotkin	201-433-5500	R	100	0.2
Reiss Corp	Mt Vernon Rd	Englishtown	NJ	07726	TJ Reiss	908-446-6100	R	100	0.6
Shape Inc	PO Box 366	Biddeford	ME	04005	Michael Thomas	207-282-6155	R	100	1.0
Tech Group Inc	7975 N Hayden Rd	Scottsdale	AZ	85258	Steve Uhlmann	602-951-3000	R	100	1.0
Fluoroware Inc	102 Jonathan N	Chaska	MN	55318	Dan Quernemoen	612-448-3131	R	97	0.6
J-M Manufacturing Company	9 Peach Tree Hill	Livingston	NJ	07039	Walter Wang	201-992-2090	S	95*	0.9
Plastics Inc	PO Box 2830	St Paul	MN	55102	Frederic Contino	612-227-7371	S	95*	0.8
Summit Polymers Inc	6715 Sprinkle Rd	Kalamazoo	MI	49001	JH Haas	616-323-1301	R	95	2.0
United Screw and Bolt Corp	20325 Ctr Ridge Rd	Rocky River	OH	44116	John J Tanis	216-331-7317	P	95	0.9
NVF Co	1166 Yorklyn Rd	Yorklyn	DE	19736	Victor Posner	302-239-5281	P	94	0.8
Cadillac Products Inc	1650 Research Dr	Troy	MI	48083	Robert J Williams	810-740-4000	R	90*	0.9

Source: Ward's Business Directory of U.S. Private and Public Companies, Volumes 1 and 2, 1996. The company type code used is as follows: P - Public, R - Private, S - Subsidiary, D - Division, J - Joint Venture, A - Affiliate, G - Group. Sales are in millions of dollars, employees are in thousands. An asterisk (*) indicates an estimated sales volume. The symbol < stands for 'less than'. Company names and addresses are truncated, in some cases, to fit into the available space.

MATERIALS CONSUMED

Material	Quantity	Delivered Cost ($ million)
Materials, ingredients, containers, and supplies	(X)	18,300.4
Hardboard (wood fiberboard)	(X)	55.6
Industrial inorganic chemicals	(X)	89.0
Inorganic pigments	(X)	94.7
Plastics resins consumed in the form of granules, pellets, powders, liquids, etc.	(X)	6,103.0
Industrial organic and synthetic organic chemicals, including plasticizers	(X)	171.8
Synthetic dyes, pigments, lakes, and toners	(X)	120.2
All other chemical and allied products	(X)	175.8
Plastics products consumed in the form of sheets, rods, tubes, film, and other shapes	(X)	1,616.0
Custom compounded plastics resins (purchased)	(X)	384.5
Textile-type glass fiber	(X)	338.7
Broadwoven fabrics	(X)	182.8
Paper and paperboard products except paperboard boxes, containers, and corrugated paperboard	(X)	182.4
Paperboard containers, boxes, and corrugated paperboard	(X)	527.9
Parts and attachments specially designed for plastics working machinery	(X)	175.0
All other materials and components, parts, containers, and supplies	(X)	3,909.6
Materials, ingredients, containers, and supplies, nsk	(X)	4,174.2

Source: 1992 *Economic Census.* Explanation of symbols used: (D): Withheld to avoid disclosure of competitive data; na: Not available; (S): Withheld because statistical norms were not met; (X): Not applicable; (Z): Less than half the unit shown; nec: Not elsewhere classified; nsk: Not specified by kind; - : zero; * : 10-19 percent estimated; ** : 20-29 percent estimated.

PRODUCT SHARE DETAILS

Product or Product Class	% Share
Plastics products, nec	100.00
Transportation fabricated plastics products (except foam and reinforced plastics)	18.42
Fabricated plastics components, housings, accessories, and parts for motor vehicles (except foam and reinforced plastics)	88.42
Fabricated plastics components, housings, accessories, and parts for aircraft, space equipment and missiles (except foam and reinforced plastics)	5.54
Fabricated plastics components, housings, accessories, and parts for other transportation equipment (except foam and reinforced plastics)	3.19
Transportation fabricated plastics products (except foam and reinforced plastics), nsk	2.85
Electrical and electronic fabricated plastics products (except foam and reinforced plastics)	7.39
Electrical and electronic fabricated plastics products for office, computing and accounting machines, cash registers, and data processing machines (except foam and reinforced plastics)	24.36
Electrical and electronic fabricated plastics products for household and commercial appliances (except foam and reinforced plastics)	25.76
Electrical and electronic fabricated plastics products for communications equipment (except foam and reinforced plastics)	10.60
Other electrical and electronic fabricated plastics products, including wiring devices and parts (except foam and reinforced plastics)	32.74
Electrical and electronic fabricated plastics (except foam and reinforced plastics), nsk	6.53
Industrial machinery plastics products, except foam (including gears, bearings, bushings, cams, and other components)	2.14
Plastics packaging (except film and sheet, foam, and bottles)	13.99
Plastics pails and drums, more than 3 gallons	10.34
Plastics tubs (for food products)	11.52
Plastics jars (for toilet goods, cosmetics, and food products)	6.40
Plastics blister and bubble formed packaging	4.48
Plastics shipping boxes and cases	4.53
Plastics food trays (baskets, shipping boxes, and cases) (except foam)	6.76
Plastics pallets	0.65
Plastics nonpressure child-resistant closures, for prescription products	1.07
Plastics nonpressure child-resistant closures, for all other products, including nonprescription products	1.62
Plastics nonpressure, nonchild-resistant closures, including dispensing and nondispensing	14.62
Plastics closures for glass, metal, or plastics pressure containers	9.19
Other plastics packaging	26.33
Plastics packaging (except film and sheet, foam, and bottles), nsk	2.50
Plastics dinnerware, tableware, kitchenware and oven/microwave ware (except foam and cups)	3.00
Plastics dinnerware and tableware (except foam)	50.91
Plastics kitchenware (except foam and cups)	36.89
Plastics oven/microwave ware (for use in conventional and microwave ovens) (except foam and cups)	10.36
Plastics dinnerware, tableware, kitchenware, and oven/microwave ware (except foam and cups), nsk	1.83
Plastics consumer, institutional, and commercial fabricated plastics products (except foam and wire coated), nec	21.05
Plastics cups (except foam, including vending machines, over-the-counter, carryout, etc.)	5.36
Plastics sinkware (flatware or dish drainers, drainer trays and mats, sink mats, sink strainers, dustpans, soapdishes, etc.) (except foam and wire coated)	0.88
Plastics bathware (shower and bath caddies, shower and bath mats, tissue holders, toothbrush holders, toilet bowl brush, etc.) (except foam and wire coated)	1.74
Plastics utility containers (including buckets, pails, laundry baskets, vegetable bins, dishpans, etc.) (except foam)	3.60
Plastics organizers and holders for closets, drawers, and shelves including paper towel holders, dust mop and broom holders, etc. (except foam and wire coated)	3.02
Plastics wastebaskets (except foam)	0.90
Plastics garbage and trash containers (excluding trash bags) (except foam)	2.99
Plastics grower flowerpots and accessories (except foam and wire coated)	1.45
Plastics decorative flowerpots, flower boxes, planters, and accessories (except foam and wire coated)	1.45
Plastics picnic jugs, cooler chests, and ice buckets (except foam)	3.36
Plastics hardware (including clamps, handles, hinges, locks, casters, knobs, nails, etc.) (except foam and wire coated)	2.39
Plastics hospitalware (including pitchers, wash basins, trays, bedpans, etc.) (except foam and wire coated)	3.28
Plastics laboratory ware (including petri dishes, flasks, funnels, etc.) (except foam and wire coated)	3.78
Plastics individual packing boxes and cases for consumer products (except foam)	4.61
Plastics sponges and scrubbing pads (except foam)	1.23
Other consumer, institutional, and commercial plastics products (except foam and wire coated)	55.44
Consumer, institutional, and commercial fabricated plastics products (except foam and wire coated), nec, nsk	4.53
Plastics furniture components and furnishings (excluding foam and reinforced plastics)	1.72
Plastics furniture components, accessories, and parts (except foam and reinforced plastics)	60.97
Other plastics furniture components and furnishings (including fixtures, lamp shades, mirror and picture frames, etc.) (except foam and reinforced plastics)	29.54

Continued on next page.

PRODUCT SHARE DETAILS - Continued

Product or Product Class	% Share	Product or Product Class	% Share
foam and reinforced plastics), nsk	9.50	wall and ceiling tile) (except foam and reinforced plastics)	1.24
Building and construction fabricated plastics products (except foam, plumbing fixtures, hardware or reinforced plastics)	9.76	Plastics swimming pool liners and covers (except foam and reinforced plastics)	1.39
Plastics corrugated and flat panels (except foam and reinforced plastics)	4.15	Other building and construction plastics products (except foam and reinforced plastics)	20.78
Plastics glazing panels (except foam and reinforced plastics)	0.23	Building and construction fabricated plastics products, nsk	2.04
Plastics doors, partitions, moldings, windows and frames, and decorative trim (except foam, hardware, and reinforced plastics)	32.97	Plastics shoe products, including taps, soling slabs, and quarterlinings	0.27
Plastics siding and accessories (including soffit, fascia, and skirts) (except foam, plumbing fixtures, hardware, and reinforced plastics)	23.98	Reinforced and fiberglass plastics products, nec	8.75
Building and construction plastics fittings and unions (except foam, plumbing fixtures, hardware, and reinforced plastics)	12.71	Reinforced and fiberglass plastics transportation products, nec	37.66
Plastics supported wall and counter coverings (except foam and reinforced plastics)	0.51	Reinforced and fiberglass plastics electrical and electronic products, nec	15.27
Plastics unsupported wall and counter coverings (including		Reinforced and fiberglass plastics building and construction products, nec	17.96
		Other fabricated fiberglass and reinforced plastics products (except furniture)	27.23
		Reinforced and fiberglass plastics products, nec, nsk	1.87
		Plastics products, nec, nsk	13.51

Source: 1992 *Economic Census*. The values shown are percent of total shipments in an industry. Values of indented subcategories are summed in the main heading. The symbol (D) appears when data are withheld to prevent disclosure of competitive information. The abbreviation nsk stands for 'not specified by kind' and nec for 'not elsewhere classified'.

INPUTS AND OUTPUTS FOR MISCELLANEOUS PLASTICS PRODUCTS

Economic Sector or Industry Providing Inputs	%	Sector	Economic Sector or Industry Buying Outputs	%	Sector
Plastics materials & resins	36.2	Manufg.	Hospitals	5.6	Services
Wholesale trade	8.5	Trade	Electronic components nec	5.2	Manufg.
Miscellaneous plastics products	7.2	Manufg.	Personal consumption expenditures	4.3	
Imports	5.8	Foreign	Miscellaneous plastics products	4.0	Manufg.
Cyclic crudes and organics	4.4	Manufg.	Exports	4.0	Foreign
Electric services (utilities)	4.4	Util.	Telephone & telegraph apparatus	3.0	Manufg.
Paperboard containers & boxes	2.6	Manufg.	Motor vehicles & car bodies	2.8	Manufg.
Communications, except radio & TV	2.3	Util.	Eating & drinking places	2.8	Trade
Motor freight transportation & warehousing	2.0	Util.	Maintenance of nonfarm buildings nec	2.4	Constr.
Paperboard mills	1.5	Manufg.	Food preparations, nec	2.3	Manufg.
Synthetic rubber	1.5	Manufg.	Plastics materials & resins	2.1	Manufg.
Railroads & related services	1.3	Util.	Typewriters & office machines, nec	1.7	Manufg.
Glass & glass products, except containers	1.2	Manufg.	Commercial printing	1.6	Manufg.
Gas production & distribution (utilities)	1.0	Util.	Cyclic crudes and organics	1.5	Manufg.
Noncomparable imports	1.0	Foreign	Electronic computing equipment	1.5	Manufg.
Industrial inorganic chemicals, nec	0.9	Manufg.	Motor vehicle parts & accessories	1.3	Manufg.
Crude petroleum & natural gas	0.7	Mining	Paper mills, except building paper	1.3	Manufg.
Maintenance of nonfarm buildings nec	0.7	Constr.	Bottled & canned soft drinks	1.2	Manufg.
Eating & drinking places	0.7	Trade	Toilet preparations	1.2	Manufg.
Real estate	0.7	Fin/R.E.	Aircraft	1.1	Manufg.
Computer & data processing services	0.7	Services	Medical & health services, nec	1.1	Services
Broadwoven fabric mills	0.6	Manufg.	Nonfarm residential structure maintenance	1.0	Constr.
Machinery, except electrical, nec	0.6	Manufg.	Optical instruments & lenses	0.9	Manufg.
Petroleum refining	0.6	Manufg.	Wholesale trade	0.9	Trade
Banking	0.6	Fin/R.E.	Office buildings	0.8	Constr.
Inorganic pigments	0.5	Manufg.	Computer & data processing services	0.8	Services
Wood products, nec	0.5	Manufg.	Hotels & lodging places	0.8	Services
Advertising	0.5	Services	S/L Govt. purch., health & hospitals	0.8	S/L Govt
Equipment rental & leasing services	0.5	Services	Residential additions/alterations, nonfarm	0.7	Constr.
Adhesives & sealants	0.4	Manufg.	Animal & marine fats & oils	0.7	Manufg.
Fabricated rubber products, nec	0.4	Manufg.	Drugs	0.7	Manufg.
Special industry machinery, nec	0.4	Manufg.	Fluid milk	0.7	Manufg.
Job training & related services	0.4	Services	Paper coating & glazing	0.7	Manufg.
Fabricated metal products, nec	0.3	Manufg.	Polishes & sanitation goods	0.7	Manufg.
Lighting fixtures & equipment	0.3	Manufg.	Automotive & apparel trimmings	0.6	Manufg.
Lubricating oils & greases	0.3	Manufg.	Broadwoven fabric mills	0.6	Manufg.
Metal stampings, nec	0.3	Manufg.	Frozen fruits, fruit juices & vegetables	0.6	Manufg.
Primary metal products, nec	0.3	Manufg.	Frozen specialties	0.6	Manufg.
Special dies & tools & machine tool accessories	0.3	Manufg.	Knit outerwear mills	0.6	Manufg.
Water transportation	0.3	Util.	Miscellaneous fabricated wire products	0.6	Manufg.
Royalties	0.3	Fin/R.E.	Photographic equipment & supplies	0.6	Manufg.
Management & consulting services & labs	0.3	Services	Pickles, sauces, & salad dressings	0.6	Manufg.
Metal foil & leaf	0.2	Manufg.	Soap & other detergents	0.6	Manufg.
Narrow fabric mills	0.2	Manufg.	Residential garden apartments	0.5	Constr.
Paints & allied products	0.2	Manufg.	Bags, except textile	0.5	Manufg.
Primary copper	0.2	Manufg.	Petroleum refining	0.5	Manufg.
Sanitary services, steam supply, irrigation	0.2	Util.	Semiconductors & related devices	0.5	Manufg.
Accounting, auditing & bookkeeping	0.2	Services	Real estate	0.5	Fin/R.E.
Electrical repair shops	0.2	Services	Beauty & barber shops	0.5	Services
Engineering, architectural, & surveying services	0.2	Services	Residential 1-unit structures, nonfarm	0.4	Constr.
Legal services	0.2	Services	Carbon paper & inked ribbons	0.4	Manufg.

Continued on next page.

INPUTS AND OUTPUTS FOR MISCELLANEOUS PLASTICS PRODUCTS - Continued

Economic Sector or Industry Providing Inputs	%	Sector	Economic Sector or Industry Buying Outputs	%	Sector
Alkalies & chlorine	0.1	Manufg.	Roasted coffee	0.4	Manufg.
Building paper & board mills	0.1	Manufg.	Storage batteries	0.4	Manufg.
Manifold business forms	0.1	Manufg.	Upholstered household furniture	0.4	Manufg.
Mineral wool	0.1	Manufg.	Communications, except radio & TV	0.4	Util.
Pipe, valves, & pipe fittings	0.1	Manufg.	Water supply & sewage systems	0.4	Util.
Screw machine and related products	0.1	Manufg.	Business services nec	0.4	Services
Air transportation	0.1	Util.	Doctors & dentists	0.4	Services
Insurance carriers	0.1	Fin/R.E.	Miscellaneous repair shops	0.4	Services
Business/professional associations	0.1	Services	Construction of hospitals	0.3	Constr.
U.S. Postal Service	0.1	Gov't	Industrial buildings	0.3	Constr.
			Maintenance of highways & streets	0.3	Constr.
			Games, toys, & children's vehicles	0.3	Manufg.
			Logging camps & logging contractors	0.3	Manufg.
			Mattresses & bedsprings	0.3	Manufg.
			Nonferrous wire drawing & insulating	0.3	Manufg.
			Organic fibers, noncellulosic	0.3	Manufg.
			Sanitary paper products	0.3	Manufg.
			Sausages & other prepared meats	0.3	Manufg.
			Signs & advertising displays	0.3	Manufg.
			Surgical & medical instruments	0.3	Manufg.
			Retail trade, except eating & drinking	0.3	Trade
			Amusement & recreation services nec	0.3	Services
			Child day care services	0.3	Services
			Management & consulting services & labs	0.3	Services
			Nursing & personal care facilities	0.3	Services
			Construction of educational buildings	0.2	Constr.
			Construction of stores & restaurants	0.2	Constr.
			Electric utility facility construction	0.2	Constr.
			Warehouses	0.2	Constr.
			Aluminum rolling & drawing	0.2	Manufg.
			Bread, cake, & related products	0.2	Manufg.
			Carbon & graphite products	0.2	Manufg.
			Chemical preparations, nec	0.2	Manufg.
			Cigarettes	0.2	Manufg.
			Cookies & crackers	0.2	Manufg.
			Dog, cat, & other pet food	0.2	Manufg.
			Electric housewares & fans	0.2	Manufg.
			Fabricated plate work (boiler shops)	0.2	Manufg.
			Fabricated structural metal	0.2	Manufg.
			General industrial machinery, nec	0.2	Manufg.
			Glass & glass products, except containers	0.2	Manufg.
			Hard surface floor coverings	0.2	Manufg.
			Household refrigerators & freezers	0.2	Manufg.
			Knit fabric mills	0.2	Manufg.
			Lighting fixtures & equipment	0.2	Manufg.
			Macaroni & spaghetti	0.2	Manufg.
			Meat packing plants	0.2	Manufg.
			Nitrogenous & phosphatic fertilizers	0.2	Manufg.
			Radio & TV communication equipment	0.2	Manufg.
			Radio & TV receiving sets	0.2	Manufg.
			Refrigeration & heating equipment	0.2	Manufg.
			Shoes, except rubber	0.2	Manufg.
			Shortening & cooking oils	0.2	Manufg.
			Sporting & athletic goods, nec	0.2	Manufg.
			Surface active agents	0.2	Manufg.
			Surgical appliances & supplies	0.2	Manufg.
			Wood partitions & fixtures	0.2	Manufg.
			Job training & related services	0.2	Services
			Laundry, dry cleaning, shoe repair	0.2	Services
			Social services, nec	0.2	Services
			Federal Government purchases, national defense	0.2	Fed Govt
			Greenhouse & nursery products	0.1	Agric.
			Farm service facilities	0.1	Constr.
			Hotels & motels	0.1	Constr.
			Maintenance of nonbuilding facilities nec	0.1	Constr.
			Maintenance of water supply facilities	0.1	Constr.
			Aircraft & missile equipment, nec	0.1	Manufg.
			Architectural metal work	0.1	Manufg.
			Blankbooks & looseleaf binders	0.1	Manufg.
			Book printing	0.1	Manufg.
			Cheese, natural & processed	0.1	Manufg.
			Chocolate & cocoa products	0.1	Manufg.
			Condensed & evaporated milk	0.1	Manufg.
			Confectionery products	0.1	Manufg.
			Distilled liquor, except brandy	0.1	Manufg.

Continued on next page.

INPUTS AND OUTPUTS FOR MISCELLANEOUS PLASTICS PRODUCTS - Continued

Economic Sector or Industry Providing Inputs	%	Sector	Economic Sector or Industry Buying Outputs	%	Sector
			Drapery hardware & blinds & shades	0.1	Manufg.
			Engine electrical equipment	0.1	Manufg.
			Fabricated rubber products, nec	0.1	Manufg.
			Guided missiles & space vehicles	0.1	Manufg.
			Metal foil & leaf	0.1	Manufg.
			Metal household furniture	0.1	Manufg.
			Metal office furniture	0.1	Manufg.
			Miscellaneous publishing	0.1	Manufg.
			Motors & generators	0.1	Manufg.
			Paperboard containers & boxes	0.1	Manufg.
			Paving mixtures & blocks	0.1	Manufg.
			Phonograph records & tapes	0.1	Manufg.
			Pumps & compressors	0.1	Manufg.
			Secondary nonferrous metals	0.1	Manufg.
			Sheet metal work	0.1	Manufg.
			Special dies & tools & machine tool accessories	0.1	Manufg.
			Sugar	0.1	Manufg.
			Watches, clocks, & parts	0.1	Manufg.
			Women's hosiery, except socks	0.1	Manufg.
			Wood household furniture	0.1	Manufg.
			Wood products, nec	0.1	Manufg.
			Engineering, architectural, & surveying services	0.1	Services
			Local government passenger transit	0.1	Gov't

Source: Benchmark Input-Output Accounts for the U.S. Economy, 1982, U.S. Department of Commerce, Washington, D.C., July 1991. Data, as reported in the source, are organized by the 1977 SIC structure in use in 1982 but have been matched, as closely as is possible, to the 1987 SIC structure used in this book.

OCCUPATIONS EMPLOYED BY SIC 308 - MISCELLANEOUS PLASTICS PRODUCTS

Occupation	% of Total 1994	Change to 2005	Occupation	% of Total 1994	Change to 2005
Plastic molding machine workers	18.3	6.7	Maintenance repairers, general utility	1.6	6.7
Assemblers, fabricators, & hand workers nec	9.5	18.5	Industrial truck & tractor operators	1.5	18.5
Blue collar worker supervisors	5.2	10.7	Tool & die makers	1.4	77.8
Hand packers & packagers	4.7	-8.6	Extruding & forming machine workers	1.4	-40.7
Machine tool cutting & forming etc. nec	3.4	50.5	Industrial production managers	1.4	18.5
Inspectors, testers, & graders, precision	3.4	6.7	Machine feeders & offbearers	1.4	6.7
Helpers, laborers, & material movers nec	2.6	18.5	Packaging & filling machine operators	1.3	18.5
Machine forming operators, metal & plastic	2.5	30.4	Cutters & trimmers, hand	1.2	18.5
Metal & plastic machine workers nec	2.4	89.0	Bookkeeping, accounting, & auditing clerks	1.1	-11.1
General managers & top executives	2.3	12.4	Secretaries, ex legal & medical	1.1	7.9
Industrial machinery mechanics	2.2	30.4	Coating, painting, & spraying machine workers	1.1	6.7
Sales & related workers nec	1.9	18.5	Crushing & mixing machine operators	1.1	77.8
Traffic, shipping, & receiving clerks	1.8	14.0	Machine operators nec	1.1	-32.1
Freight, stock, & material movers, hand	1.7	-5.2			

Source: Industry-Occupation Matrix, Bureau of Labor Statistics. These data relate to one or more 3-digit SIC industry groups rather than to a single 4-digit SIC. The change reported for each occupation to the year 2005 is a percent of growth or decline as estimated by the Bureau of Labor Statistics. The abbreviation nec stands for 'not elsewhere classified'.

LOCATION BY STATE AND REGIONAL CONCENTRATION

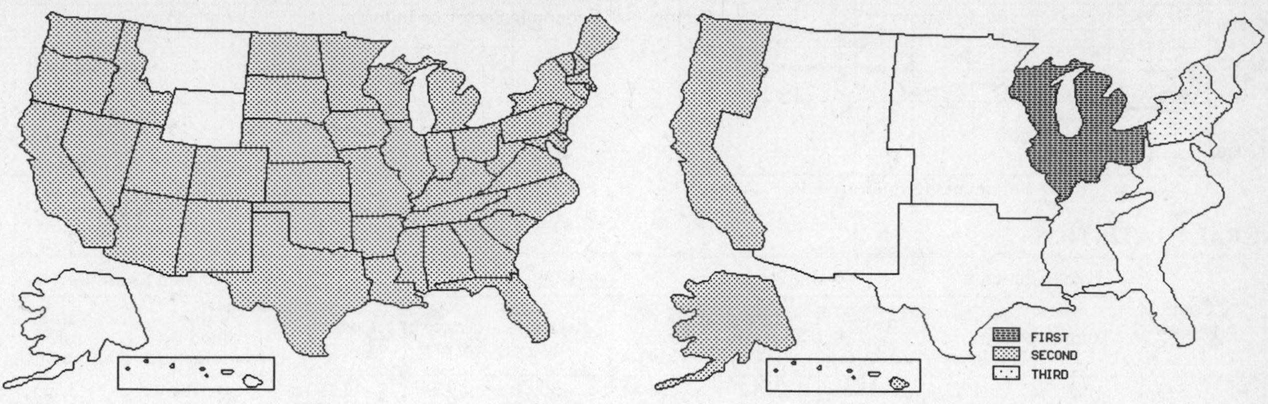

INDUSTRY DATA BY STATE

State	Establish-ments	Shipments Total ($ mil)	Shipments % of U.S.	Shipments Per Establ.	Employment Total Number	Employment % of U.S.	Employment Per Establ.	Employment Wages ($/hour)	Cost as % of Shipments	Investment per Employee ($)
Michigan	609	4,835.4	10.7	7.9	39,700	9.3	65	9.62	48.9	3,942
California	1,141	4,551.7	10.0	4.0	45,500	10.7	40	10.36	40.6	3,936
Ohio	615	4,346.0	9.6	7.1	41,000	9.6	67	9.39	47.3	5,134
Illinois	512	3,512.1	7.8	6.9	31,900	7.5	62	9.97	47.0	5,016
Indiana	326	2,421.2	5.3	7.4	23,000	5.4	71	9.06	50.0	4,609
Pennsylvania	385	2,359.5	5.2	6.1	21,900	5.1	57	9.96	45.6	5,119
Texas	451	2,077.0	4.6	4.6	18,900	4.4	42	8.68	45.4	5,106
New York	447	1,843.6	4.1	4.1	20,300	4.8	45	9.20	46.6	4,197
Wisconsin	270	1,660.0	3.7	6.1	15,500	3.6	57	10.15	45.5	5,497
New Jersey	334	1,511.3	3.3	4.5	15,500	3.6	46	9.47	45.1	4,303
Massachusetts	270	1,302.0	2.9	4.8	11,300	2.7	42	10.36	44.2	4,929
North Carolina	196	1,231.6	2.7	6.3	11,800	2.8	60	8.93	47.6	4,263
Tennessee	149	1,144.7	2.5	7.7	9,300	2.2	62	8.19	47.4	4,796
Minnesota	215	984.5	2.2	4.6	9,500	2.2	44	10.07	43.2	5,695
Florida	369	859.9	1.9	2.3	8,900	2.1	24	8.67	48.1	3,528
Missouri	154	810.7	1.8	5.3	8,200	1.9	53	8.13	49.1	5,598
Kentucky	87	757.0	1.7	8.7	7,600	1.8	87	9.45	53.7	3,868
Georgia	149	719.3	1.6	4.8	5,900	1.4	40	9.67	53.1	9,068
South Carolina	90	676.1	1.5	7.5	6,100	1.4	68	8.87	40.5	6,131
Iowa	98	640.6	1.4	6.5	6,000	1.4	61	8.96	46.4	4,933
Virginia	71	639.3	1.4	9.0	5,600	1.3	79	8.80	53.8	3,607
Kansas	82	630.0	1.4	7.7	5,200	1.2	63	10.44	46.6	4,712
Connecticut	159	626.3	1.4	3.9	6,200	1.5	39	10.53	43.3	4,274
Washington	126	476.6	1.1	3.8	5,200	1.2	41	9.76	42.9	3,750
Colorado	118	460.2	1.0	3.9	4,300	1.0	36	9.08	40.3	4,070
Mississippi	63	443.5	1.0	7.0	3,200	0.8	51	8.65	54.3	6,094
Alabama	71	427.5	0.9	6.0	4,700	1.1	66	9.28	54.9	4,277
Arizona	109	423.8	0.9	3.9	3,700	0.9	34	9.45	41.0	7,081
Maryland	73	418.8	0.9	5.7	4,100	1.0	56	10.14	41.2	3,927
Arkansas	64	329.9	0.7	5.2	3,400	0.8	53	8.25	47.3	4,500
Oregon	104	302.7	0.7	2.9	2,900	0.7	28	9.56	48.6	3,690
Oklahoma	79	292.5	0.6	3.7	2,600	0.6	33	8.54	53.7	2,885
Rhode Island	64	236.4	0.5	3.7	3,000	0.7	47	9.43	40.2	2,033
New Hampshire	54	204.1	0.5	3.8	2,300	0.5	43	9.76	45.4	2,652
Nebraska	33	168.9	0.4	5.1	2,000	0.5	61	8.54	51.0	6,100
Maine	25	155.5	0.3	6.2	1,500	0.4	60	7.48	38.6	8,133
Nevada	40	140.3	0.3	3.5	1,400	0.3	35	8.08	42.8	4,286
Vermont	21	133.6	0.3	6.4	1,300	0.3	62	11.26	43.0	5,077
West Virginia	13	108.9	0.2	8.4	1,200	0.3	92	8.53	44.9	3,000
Louisiana	38	104.4	0.2	2.7	1,100	0.3	29	9.76	47.7	3,364
Delaware	27	101.4	0.2	3.8	900	0.2	33	8.60	43.9	8,333
Utah	60	92.2	0.2	1.5	1,000	0.2	17	9.56	42.3	2,900
Idaho	23	43.6	0.1	1.9	500	0.1	22	8.29	40.8	3,200
South Dakota	16	37.4	0.1	2.3	600	0.1	38	8.60	39.6	2,500
New Mexico	16	26.5	0.1	1.7	300	0.1	19	8.00	46.8	2,000
North Dakota	11	(D)	-	-	375 *	0.1	34	-	-	-

Source: 1992 *Economic Census*. The states are in descending order of shipments or establishments (if shipment data are missing for the majority). The symbol (D) appears when data are withheld to prevent disclosure of competitive information. States marked with (D) are sorted by number of establishments. A dash (-) indicates that the data element cannot be calculated; * indicates the midpoint of a range.

3111 - LEATHER TANNING & FINISHING

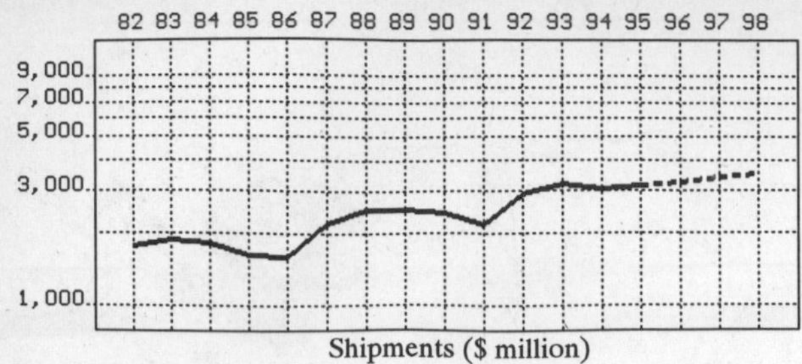

Shipments ($ million)

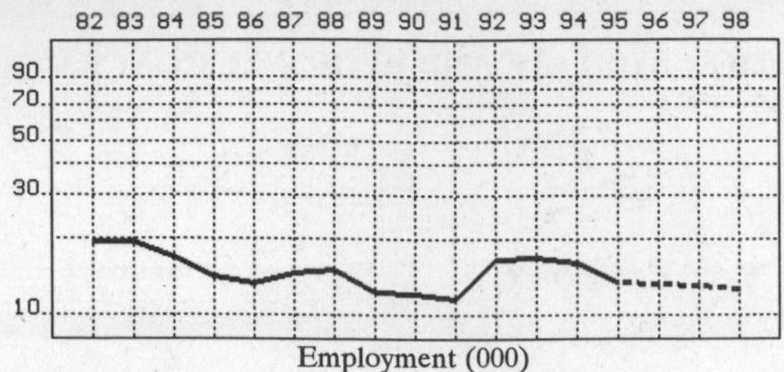

Employment (000)

GENERAL STATISTICS

Year	Companies	Establishments		Employment			Compensation		Production ($ million)			
		Total	with 20 or more employees	Total (000)	Production Workers (000)	Production Hours (Mil)	Payroll ($ mil)	Wages ($/hr)	Cost of Materials	Value Added by Manufacture	Value of Shipments	Capital Invest.
1982	342	384	172	19.5	16.2	31.4	309.1	7.14	1,164.8	578.5	1,751.5	33.2
1983				19.5	16.2	31.8	332.0	7.63	1,271.3	649.5	1,881.7	41.0
1984				16.7	14.0	26.7	291.5	7.94	1,220.3	573.7	1,813.6	21.8
1985				14.2	11.7	23.6	262.5	8.03	1,128.0	508.6	1,643.0	23.5
1986				13.2	10.9	22.1	249.1	8.22	1,114.8	474.9	1,589.1	20.7
1987	311	344	139	14.6	12.1	24.6	291.6	8.61	1,496.5	747.4	2,218.6	27.7
1988				15.1	12.5	25.5	314.4	8.89	1,661.8	839.5	2,487.8	34.6
1989		332	140	12.3	10.6	21.4	281.5	9.67	1,715.8	875.6	2,501.4	47.9
1990				12.1	10.3	21.2	282.2	9.58	1,638.5	779.9	2,410.9	39.0
1991				11.5	9.8	19.1	278.3	10.62	1,485.8	710.1	2,183.1	41.4
1992	297	332	126	16.6	13.3	27.9	420.3	10.52	2,035.9	895.9	2,910.4	48.5
1993				16.9	13.8	28.9	428.9	10.65	2,238.0	1,016.7	3,198.0	52.2
1994				15.9	13.4	28.6	416.4	10.61	2,076.5	985.3	3,037.8	45.5
1995				13.4P	11.1P	23.9P	387.0P	11.31P	2,142.3P	1,016.5P	3,134.1P	50.0P
1996				13.1P	10.9P	23.6P	396.6P	11.63P	2,225.8P	1,056.2P	3,256.3P	51.9P
1997				12.9P	10.7P	23.4P	406.2P	11.94P	2,309.3P	1,095.8P	3,378.4P	53.9P
1998				12.6P	10.5P	23.1P	415.8P	12.26P	2,392.8P	1,135.4P	3,500.6P	55.8P

Sources: 1982, 1987, 1992 *Economic Census*; *Annual Survey of Manufactures*, 83-86, 88-91, 93-94. Establishment counts for non-Census years are from *County Business Patterns*; establishment values for 83-84 are extrapolations. 'P's show projections by the editors. Industries reclassified in 87 will not have data for prior years.

INDICES OF CHANGE

Year	Companies	Establishments		Employment			Compensation		Production ($ million)			
		Total	with 20 or more employees	Total (000)	Production Workers (000)	Production Hours (Mil)	Payroll ($ mil)	Wages ($/hr)	Cost of Materials	Value Added by Manufacture	Value of Shipments	Capital Invest.
1982	115	116	137	117	122	113	74	68	57	65	60	68
1983				117	122	114	79	73	62	72	65	85
1984				101	105	96	69	75	60	64	62	45
1985				86	88	85	62	76	55	57	56	48
1986				80	82	79	59	78	55	53	55	43
1987	105	104	110	88	91	88	69	82	74	83	76	57
1988				91	94	91	75	85	82	94	85	71
1989		100	111	74	80	77	67	92	84	98	86	99
1990				73	77	76	67	91	80	87	83	80
1991				69	74	68	66	101	73	79	75	85
1992	100	100	100	100	100	100	100	100	100	100	100	100
1993				102	104	104	102	101	110	113	110	108
1994				96	101	103	99	101	102	110	104	94
1995				81P	84P	86P	92P	107P	105P	113P	108P	103P
1996				79P	82P	85P	94P	111P	109P	118P	112P	107P
1997				78P	80P	84P	97P	114P	113P	122P	116P	111P
1998				76P	79P	83P	99P	117P	118P	127P	120P	115P

Sources: Same as General Statistics. Values reflect change from the base year, 1992. Values above 100 mean greater than 92, values below 100 mean less than 92, and a value of 100 in the 82-91 or 93-98 period means same as 92. 'P's mark projections by the editors.

SELECTED RATIOS

For 1992	Avg. of All Manufact.	Analyzed Industry	Index	For 1992	Avg. of All Manufact.	Analyzed Industry	Index
Employees per Establishment	46	50	110	Value Added per Production Worker	122,353	67,361	55
Payroll per Establishment	1,332,320	1,265,964	95	Cost per Establishment	4,239,462	6,132,229	145
Payroll per Employee	29,181	25,319	87	Cost per Employee	92,853	122,645	132
Production Workers per Establishment	31	40	128	Cost per Production Worker	135,003	153,075	113
Wages per Establishment	734,496	884,060	120	Shipments per Establishment	8,100,800	8,766,265	108
Wages per Production Worker	23,390	22,068	94	Shipments per Employee	177,425	175,325	99
Hours per Production Worker	2,025	2,098	104	Shipments per Production Worker	257,966	218,827	85
Wages per Hour	11.55	10.52	91	Investment per Establishment	278,244	146,084	53
Value Added per Establishment	3,842,210	2,698,494	70	Investment per Employee	6,094	2,922	48
Value Added per Employee	84,153	53,970	64	Investment per Production Worker	8,861	3,647	41

Sources: Same as General Statistics. The 'Average of All Manufacturing' column represents the average of all manufacturing industries reported for the most recent complete year available. The Index shows the relationship between the Average and the Analyzed Industry. For example, 100 means that they are equal; 500 that the Analyzed Industry is five times the average; 50 means that the Analyzed Industry is half the national average. The abbreviation 'na' is used to show that data are 'not available'.

LEADING COMPANIES

Number shown: **53** Total sales ($ mil): **3,114** Total employment (000): **15.7**

Company Name	Address				CEO Name	Phone	Co. Type	Sales ($ mil)	Empl. (000)
United States Leather Holdings	1110 Old World	Milwaukee	WI	53203	Robert E Koe	414-765-1040	P	372	1.6
US Leather Inc	1110 Old World	Milwaukee	WI	53203	Robert Koe	414-765-1040	R	350	1.5
Albert Trostel and Sons Co	PO Box 743	Milwaukee	WI	53201	Anders Sederbahl	414-327-4870	R	300	1.5
Eagle Ottawa Leather Co	200 N Beechtree St	Grand Haven	MI	49417	Anders Segerdahl	616-842-4000	D	300	0.9
Seton Co	50 W Big Beaver	Troy	MI	48084	P D Kaltenbacher	810-689-0990	R	250	1.4
Garden State Tanning	630 Freedom	King of Prussia	PA	19406	Sean G Traynor	610-265-3400	S	190*	1.6
Vista Resources Inc	1201 W Peachtree	Atlanta	GA	30309	S W Norwood III	404-815-2000	P	167	0.7
Lackawanna Leather Company	PO Box 939	Conover	NC	28613	Anton Mayer	704-322-2015	S	153	0.6
Pfister and Vogel Leather Co	PO Box 745	Milwaukee	WI	53201	Ernst Hagen	414-273-7160	D	137	0.6
Irving Tanning Co	Main St	Hartland	ME	04943	Richard Larochelle	207-938-4491	S	120	0.5
Prime Tanning Company Inc	Sullivan St	Berwick	ME	03901	Kenneth R Purdy	207-698-1100	R	93*	0.8
LB International Inc	30 Hub Dr	Melville	NY	11747	David Finkelstein	516-420-8844	R	75	0.2
AL Gebhardt Company Inc	PO Box 1164	Milwaukee	WI	53201	Gordon V Little	414-383-6030	D	72	0.4
Etienne Aigner Inc	712 5th Av	New York	NY	10019	Trevor Brenthall	212-246-8660	S	49*	0.4
Blueside Company Inc	PO Box 383	St Joseph	MO	64502	Gary Gagnon	816-279-7468	S	47*	0.3
Salz Leathers Inc	PO Box 1840	Santa Cruz	CA	95061	Norman S Lezin	408-423-4470	R	40	0.2
Cudahy Tanning Company Inc	5043 S Packard Av	Cudahy	WI	53110	William R Law	414-483-8100	R	38	0.2
SB Foot Tanning Co	805 Bench St	Red Wing	MN	55066	Silas B Foot III	612-388-4731	R	37*	0.3
Delta Tanning Corp	1615 51st St	North Bergen	NJ	07047	David Kaufman	201-865-3700	R	30*	<0.1
Midwest Tanning Co	PO Box 189	S Milwaukee	WI	53172	AJ Glubka	414-768-7000	S	23	<0.1
Horween Leather Co	2015 N Elston Av	Chicago	IL	60614	Arnold Horween Jr	312-772-2026	R	21*	0.2
Cromwell Leather Company Inc	715 Mamaroneck	Mamaroneck	NY	10543	HM Fleisch	914-381-0100	R	20	<0.1
Travel Leather Company Inc	PO Box 747	Peabody	MA	01960	Steven N Orgettas	508-531-4456	R	19	<0.1
Dart Manufacturing Company	4012 Bronze Way	Dallas	TX	75237	Sam M Kogutt	214-333-4221	R	18*	0.2
George Newman and Co	1100 W Hutchinson	Madison	IN	47250	George Newman	812-273-4183	R	18	0.1
Blackhawk Leather Ltd	1000 W Bruce St	Milwaukee	WI	53204	TJ Hauske	414-671-2690	S	14*	0.1
Wood and Hyde Leather	PO Box 786	Gloversville	NY	12078	Randall Doerter	518-725-7105	R	13	<0.1
Caldwell-Moser Leather	PO Box 1177	New Albany	IN	47150	Tom Brown	812-944-6761	R	10*	0.1
Gutmann Leather Company Inc	1511 W Webster	Chicago	IL	60614	Adolph Meyer Jr	312-348-5300	R	10	<0.1
Hermann Oak Leather Company	4050 N 1st St	St Louis	MO	63147	Shepley Hermann	314-421-1173	R	10	<0.1
Pan American Tanning Corp	318 W Fulton St	Gloversville	NY	12078	Erwin Feuer	518-773-7565	R	9*	<0.1
Tennessee Tanning Co	PO Box 967	Tullahoma	TN	37388	M R Cunningham	615-455-3441	D	9	<0.1
Coey Tanning Company Inc	441 Bug Scuffle Rd	Wartrace	TN	37183	John M Lane	615-389-6423	R	8*	<0.1
Seagrave Leather Corp	PO Box 204	East Wilton	ME	04234	Geoffery Thorne	207-645-2559	S	8	<0.1
WB Place LLC	PO Box 160	Hartford	WI	53027	Thomas R Packee	414-673-3130	R	8*	<0.1
Calnap Tanning Co	PO Box 2190	Napa	CA	94558	Sal Espinoza	707-252-8000	R	8	<0.1
SB Foot Tanning Co	PO Box 845	Dumas	TX	79029	SB Foot III	806-966-5121	D	7	0.1
Berlin Leather	PO Box 306	Berlin	WI	54923	Patrick M Howard	414-361-5020	D	6	<0.1
M Lyon and Co	800 N Atlantic St	Kansas City	MO	64116	Dean Carlson	816-842-0815	R	6*	<0.1
AF Gallun and Sons Co	1818 N Water St	Milwaukee	WI	53201	Edwin B Gallun	414-271-4400	R	5	<0.1
Carville-National Leather Corp	Knox Av	Johnstown	NY	12095	Hugh Carville	518-762-1634	R	5	<0.1
Oshkosh Tanning Company Inc	Industrial Park Rd	Boone	IA	50036	Richard M Odell	515-432-8500	R	5	<0.1
Simco Leather Corp	PO Box 509	Johnstown	NY	12095	David Simek	518-762-7100	R	5*	<0.1
Walter L Johnson Co	932 N Montello St	Brockton	MA	02401	Richard Hynes	508-583-8200	S	5	<0.1
Brauer Brothers Mfg Co	2020 Delmar Blv	St Louis	MO	63103	Teresa E Downs	314-231-2864	R	4	<0.1
Gunnison Brothers Inc	PO Box 327	Girard	PA	16417	Michael Giles	814-774-5616	R	4	<0.1
Slip-Not Belting Corp	PO Box 89	Kingsport	TN	37662	David B Shivell	615-246-8141	R	4	<0.1
Nelson and Sons Inc	625 Humble Av	San Antonio	TX	78225	Marvin Threapleton	210-923-4331	R	3*	<0.1
Robert Lee Morris Inc	161 6th Av	New York	NY	10013	Robert L Morris	212-645-5252	R	3*	<0.1
Southern Tier Hide and Tallow	3385 Lower Maple	Elmira	NY	14901	Roy E Slusser	607-734-3661	R	3	<0.1
Richard Leather Company Inc	PO Box 868	Salem	MA	01970	James Meniates	508-745-5440	R	3	<0.1
Uber Glove Co	308 Adams Av	Owatonna	MN	55060	H Uber Jr	507-451-1990	R	1	<0.1
Front Range Saddlery Inc	7476 Maple St	Longmont	CO	80504	Ron Vallejos	303-659-3333	R	0	<0.1

Source: *Ward's Business Directory of U.S. Private and Public Companies*, Volumes 1 and 2, 1996. The company type code used is as follows: P - Public, R - Private, S - Subsidiary, D - Division, J - Joint Venture, A - Affiliate, G - Group. Sales are in millions of dollars, employees are in thousands. An asterisk (*) indicates an estimated sales volume. The symbol < stands for 'less than'. Company names and addresses are truncated, in some cases, to fit into the available space.

MATERIALS CONSUMED

Material	Quantity	Delivered Cost ($ million)
Materials, ingredients, containers, and supplies	(X)	1,817.5
Hides, skins, and pelts	(X)	1,217.5
Tanning materials, dressings, dyes, and finishing agents	(X)	281.5
Finished upper leather	(X)	129.2
Finished soling leather	(X)	33.1
All other finished leather	(X)	16.9
All other materials and components, parts, containers, and supplies	(X)	67.5
Materials, ingredients, containers, and supplies, nsk	(X)	71.7

Source: 1992 *Economic Census*. Explanation of symbols used: (D): Withheld to avoid disclosure of competitive data; na: Not available; (S): Withheld because statistical norms were not met; (X): Not applicable; (Z): Less than half the unit shown; nec: Not elsewhere classified; nsk: Not specified by kind; - : zero; * : 10-19 percent estimated; ** : 20-29 percent estimated.

PRODUCT SHARE DETAILS

Product or Product Class	% Share	Product or Product Class	% Share
Leather tanning and finishing	100.00	etc.) and welting leather, finished	1.45
Finished and unfinished leather	89.09	Finished cattle hide and kip side leather splits, including shoulder splits, deep buffs, buffing, and fleshers	2.36
Sole leather, full grain and grain split (except offal and welting), cattle hide and kip side	8.59	Wet blues, cattle hide and kip side leathers, unfinished	12.76
Bag, case, and strap leather (sides), full grain and grain split (except offal and welting), cattle hide and kip side	2.62	Other cattle hide and kip side leathers, unfinished	6.85
Upholstery leather (top grains and machine buffs), full grain and grain split (except offal and welting), cattle hide and kip side	26.17	All calf and whole kip leathers, finished and unfinished	1.37
Upper leather (including patent (sides)), full grain and grain split (except offal and welting), cattle hide and kip side	24.84	Sheep and lamb garment leathers, finished and unfinished	0.71
Garment leather (sides), full grain and grain split (except offal and welting), cattle hide and kip side	1.99	Other sheep and lamb leathers, finished and unfinished (including glove, shoe, fleshers, skivers, and shearlings)	1.31
Other leather grains, including flat and handbag leather, lining leather (sides), and belting and mechanical leather, cattle hide and kip side	7.93	Goat and kid leathers, finished and unfinished	(D)
Cattle hide and kip side offal (heads, shoulders, bellies,		Pig skin leathers, finished and unfinished	(D)
		Other animal leathers, finished and unfinished (including horse, colt, mule, ass, and pony leathers)	0.63
		Finished and unfinished leather, nsk	0.27
		Contract and commission receipts for tanning or finishing leather owned by others	6.36
		Leather tanning and finishing, nsk	4.54

Source: 1992 *Economic Census*. The values shown are percent of total shipments in an industry. Values of indented subcategories are summed in the main heading. The symbol (D) appears when data are withheld to prevent disclosure of competitive information. The abbreviation nsk stands for 'not specified by kind' and nec for 'not elsewhere classified'.

INPUTS AND OUTPUTS FOR LEATHER TANNING & FINISHING

Economic Sector or Industry Providing Inputs	%	Sector	Economic Sector or Industry Buying Outputs	%	Sector
Meat packing plants	34.8	Manufg.	Shoes, except rubber	40.0	Manufg.
Imports	19.6	Foreign	Exports	14.0	Foreign
Cyclic crudes and organics	9.6	Manufg.	Apparel made from purchased materials	9.4	Manufg.
Wholesale trade	7.3	Trade	Automotive & apparel trimmings	7.2	Manufg.
Leather tanning & finishing	5.6	Manufg.	Women's handbags & purses	4.9	Manufg.
Industrial gases	3.1	Manufg.	Leather tanning & finishing	4.6	Manufg.
Polishes & sanitation goods	2.1	Manufg.	Boot & shoe cutstock & findings	4.3	Manufg.
Motor freight transportation & warehousing	1.7	Util.	Leather goods, nec	4.2	Manufg.
Surface active agents	1.5	Manufg.	Upholstered household furniture	3.3	Manufg.
Petroleum refining	1.4	Manufg.	Leather gloves & mittens	2.4	Manufg.
Hotels & lodging places	1.4	Services	Personal leather goods	2.2	Manufg.
Electric services (utilities)	1.3	Util.	Sporting & athletic goods, nec	1.7	Manufg.
Gas production & distribution (utilities)	1.1	Util.	Luggage	0.7	Manufg.
Animal & marine fats & oils	0.9	Manufg.	Book printing	0.3	Manufg.
Industrial inorganic chemicals, nec	0.9	Manufg.	Games, toys, & children's vehicles	0.3	Manufg.
Paperboard containers & boxes	0.6	Manufg.	Wood office furniture	0.3	Manufg.
Advertising	0.5	Services	House slippers	0.2	Manufg.
State & local government enterprises, nec	0.5	Gov't			
Gum & wood chemicals	0.4	Manufg.			
Railroads & related services	0.4	Util.			
Banking	0.4	Fin/R.E.			
Maintenance of nonfarm buildings nec	0.3	Constr.			
Chemical preparations, nec	0.3	Manufg.			
Lime	0.3	Manufg.			
Communications, except radio & TV	0.3	Util.			
Eating & drinking places	0.3	Trade			
Business services nec	0.3	Services			
Equipment rental & leasing services	0.3	Services			
Laundry, dry cleaning, shoe repair	0.3	Services			
U.S. Postal Service	0.3	Gov't			
Chemical & fertilizer mineral	0.2	Mining			
Sanitary services, steam supply, irrigation	0.2	Util.			
Real estate	0.2	Fin/R.E.			
Computer & data processing services	0.2	Services			
Alkalies & chlorine	0.1	Manufg.			
Pipelines, except natural gas	0.1	Util.			
Water transportation	0.1	Util.			
Management & consulting services & labs	0.1	Services			

Source: Benchmark Input-Output Accounts for the U.S. Economy, 1982, U.S. Department of Commerce, Washington, D.C., July 1991. Data, as reported in the source, are organized by the 1977 SIC structure in use in 1982 but have been matched, as closely as is possible, to the 1987 SIC structure used in this book.

OCCUPATIONS EMPLOYED BY SIC 311 - LUGGAGE, HANDBAGS, AND LEATHER PRODUCTS, NEC

Occupation	% of Total 1994	Change to 2005	Occupation	% of Total 1994	Change to 2005
Assemblers, fabricators, & hand workers nec	11.7	-22.1	Freight, stock, & material movers, hand	2.5	-37.7
Sewing machine operators, non-garment	9.7	-68.8	Sales & related workers nec	2.3	-22.1
Shoe & leather workers & repairers, precision	7.1	-29.9	Cement & gluing machine operators	2.3	-49.4
Sewing machine operators, garment	5.4	-29.9	Crushing & mixing machine operators	1.7	-22.1
Helpers, laborers, & material movers nec	4.9	-22.1	Bookkeeping, accounting, & auditing clerks	1.3	-41.6
Blue collar worker supervisors	4.4	-26.2	General office clerks	1.3	-33.6
Cutting & slicing machine setters, operators	4.1	-14.3	Coating, painting, & spraying machine workers	1.3	-22.1
Machine operators nec	3.9	-31.3	Hand packers & packagers	1.2	-33.3
Inspectors, testers, & graders, precision	2.9	-22.1	Secretaries, ex legal & medical	1.2	-29.0
Cutters & trimmers, hand	2.7	-29.9	Shoe sewing machine operators	1.1	-37.6
General managers & top executives	2.7	-26.1	Industrial production managers	1.1	-22.1
Traffic, shipping, & receiving clerks	2.6	-25.0	Sewers, hand	1.0	-50.0
Machine feeders & offbearers	2.5	-29.9			

Source: *Industry-Occupation Matrix*, Bureau of Labor Statistics. These data relate to one or more 3-digit SIC industry groups rather than to a single 4-digit SIC. The change reported for each occupation to the year 2005 is a percent of growth or decline as estimated by the Bureau of Labor Statistics. The abbreviation nec stands for 'not elsewhere classified'.

LOCATION BY STATE AND REGIONAL CONCENTRATION

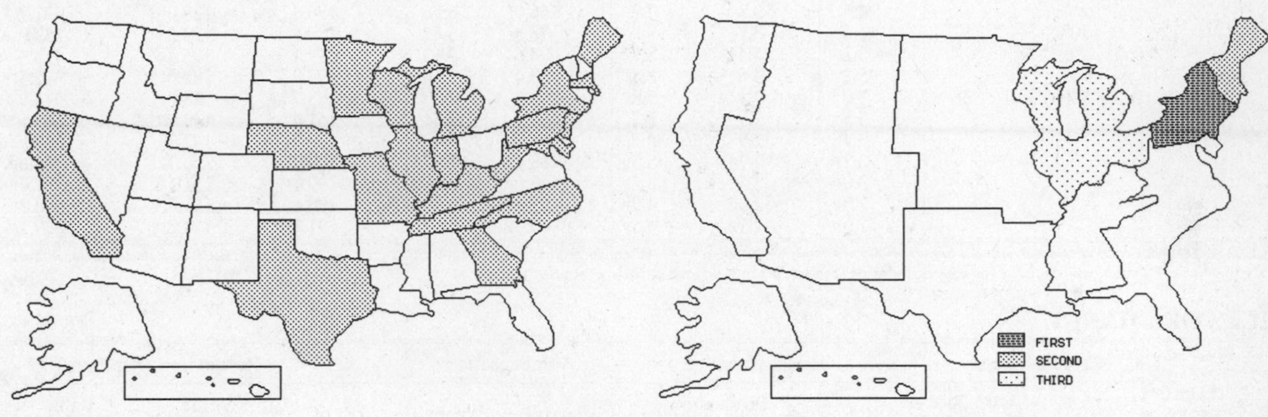

INDUSTRY DATA BY STATE

State	Establish-ments	Shipments: Total ($ mil)	Shipments: % of U.S.	Shipments: Per Establ.	Employment: Total Number	Employment: % of U.S.	Employment: Per Establ.	Employment: Wages ($/hour)	Cost as % of Shipments	Investment per Employee ($)
Pennsylvania	17	473.5	16.3	27.9	2,100	12.7	124	10.61	81.7	2,714
Wisconsin	16	336.9	11.6	21.1	1,800	10.8	113	10.03	66.8	6,167
Michigan	11	312.2	10.7	28.4	2,000	12.0	182	11.03	56.5	-
North Carolina	10	170.4	5.9	17.0	700	4.2	70	10.55	73.1	3,000
Massachusetts	45	153.6	5.3	3.4	1,000	6.0	22	10.76	66.0	2,000
New York	67	148.9	5.1	2.2	1,500	9.0	22	9.52	55.4	733
New Jersey	11	127.0	4.4	11.5	600	3.6	55	13.50	47.9	2,833
California	24	95.6	3.3	4.0	700	4.2	29	10.92	73.7	3,429
Missouri	8	58.8	2.0	7.3	600	3.6	75	9.44	60.0	-
Tennessee	7	50.7	1.7	7.2	200	1.2	29	5.75	62.7	1,500
Texas	20	34.1	1.2	1.7	500	3.0	25	7.43	55.7	2,000
Georgia	6	14.3	0.5	2.4	100	0.6	17	8.00	45.5	1,000
Illinois	7	(D)	-	-	375 *	2.3	54	-	-	-
Maine	6	(D)	-	-	1,750 *	10.5	292	-	-	-
Kentucky	5	(D)	-	-	175 *	1.1	35	-	-	-
Minnesota	5	(D)	-	-	375 *	2.3	75	-	-	-
Nebraska	5	(D)	-	-	375 *	2.3	75	-	-	-
Indiana	3	(D)	-	-	175 *	1.1	58	-	-	-
Maryland	2	(D)	-	-	1,750 *	10.5	875	-	-	-
West Virginia	1	(D)	-	-	175 *	1.1	175	-	-	-

Source: 1992 *Economic Census*. The states are in descending order of shipments or establishments (if shipment data are missing for the majority). The symbol (D) appears when data are withheld to prevent disclosure of competitive information. States marked with (D) are sorted by number of establishments. A dash (-) indicates that the data element cannot be calculated; * indicates the midpoint of a range.

3131 - FOOTWEAR CUT STOCK

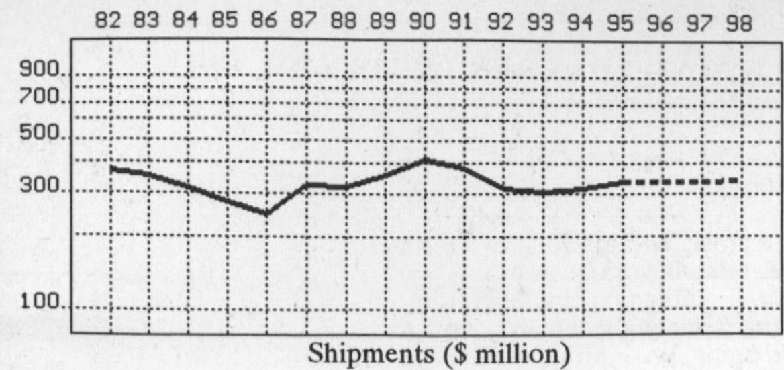

Shipments ($ million)

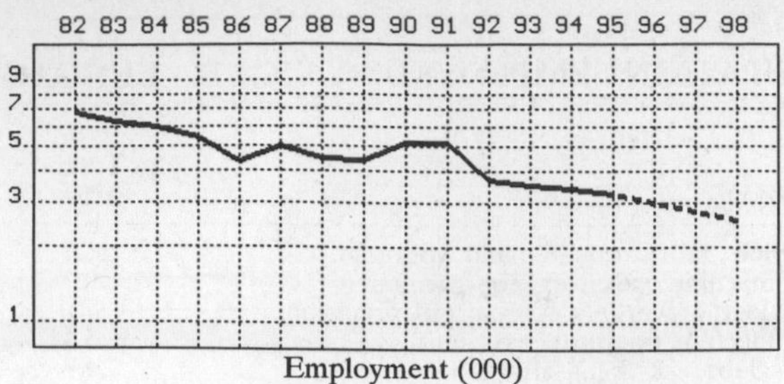

Employment (000)

GENERAL STATISTICS

Year	Com-panies	Establishments		Employment			Compensation		Production ($ million)			
		Total	with 20 or more employees	Total (000)	Production Workers (000)	Production Hours (Mil)	Payroll ($ mil)	Wages ($/hr)	Cost of Materials	Value Added by Manufacture	Value of Shipments	Capital Invest.
1982	149	161	80	6.8	5.7	10.4	80.8	5.23	212.8	154.7	367.8	6.0
1983				6.3	5.7	10.6	75.7	5.41	206.7	142.0	353.1	4.5
1984				6.0	5.1	9.3	73.8	5.66	186.5	128.3	313.8	2.8
1985				5.4	4.7	8.2	64.5	5.55	168.8	111.1	277.3	2.9
1986				4.3	3.8	6.8	56.3	6.06	149.4	97.2	246.5	2.1
1987	113	127	57	5.0	4.3	8.5	69.6	5.86	182.9	141.4	324.1	3.3
1988				4.5	3.8	7.2	66.0	6.56	196.4	128.0	321.7	2.5
1989		108	52	4.4	3.7	8.0	73.5	6.72	187.5	173.5	359.0	2.1
1990				5.2	4.4	8.7	93.6	7.13	217.1	196.4	413.3	3.6
1991				5.2	4.6	8.5	83.4	7.56	199.8	182.0	382.5	1.9
1992	94	100	38	3.7	3.1	5.8	63.3	7.29	163.7	148.6	316.9	3.3
1993				3.5	2.9	5.7	64.7	7.54	161.4	143.0	303.5	2.0
1994				3.4	2.9	5.7	61.9	7.40	179.6	142.7	318.7	0.4
1995				3.2P	2.7P	5.5P	68.4P	7.97P	189.7P	150.7P	336.6P	1.1P
1996				3.0P	2.5P	5.2P	68.0P	8.18P	190.1P	151.1P	337.4P	0.9P
1997				2.8P	2.3P	4.9P	67.6P	8.40P	190.6P	151.4P	338.2P	0.6P
1998				2.5P	2.1P	4.5P	67.2P	8.61P	191.1P	151.8P	339.1P	0.4P

Sources: 1982, 1987, 1992 *Economic Census*; *Annual Survey of Manufactures*, 83-86, 88-91, 93-94. Establishment counts for non-Census years are from *County Business Patterns*; establishment values for 83-84 are extrapolations. 'P's show projections by the editors. Industries reclassified in 87 will not have data for prior years.

INDICES OF CHANGE

Year	Com-panies	Establishments		Employment			Compensation		Production ($ million)			
		Total	with 20 or more employees	Total (000)	Production Workers (000)	Production Hours (Mil)	Payroll ($ mil)	Wages ($/hr)	Cost of Materials	Value Added by Manufacture	Value of Shipments	Capital Invest.
1982	159	161	211	184	184	179	128	72	130	104	116	182
1983				170	184	183	120	74	126	96	111	136
1984				162	165	160	117	78	114	86	99	85
1985				146	152	141	102	76	103	75	88	88
1986				116	123	117	89	83	91	65	78	64
1987	120	127	150	135	139	147	110	80	112	95	102	100
1988				122	123	124	104	90	120	86	102	76
1989		108	137	119	119	138	116	92	115	117	113	64
1990				141	142	150	148	98	133	132	130	109
1991				141	148	147	132	104	122	122	121	58
1992	100	100	100	100	100	100	100	100	100	100	100	100
1993				95	94	98	102	103	99	96	96	61
1994				92	94	98	98	102	110	96	101	12
1995				88P	88P	96P	108P	109P	116P	101P	106P	34P
1996				81P	81P	90P	107P	112P	116P	102P	106P	27P
1997				75P	74P	84P	107P	115P	116P	102P	107P	19P
1998				69P	67P	78P	106P	118P	117P	102P	107P	12P

Sources: Same as General Statistics. Values reflect change from the base year, 1992. Values above 100 mean greater than 92, values below 100 mean less than 92, and a value of 100 in the 82-91 or 93-98 period means same as 92. 'P's mark projections by the editors.

SELECTED RATIOS

For 1992	Avg. of All Manufact.	Analyzed Industry	Index	For 1992	Avg. of All Manufact.	Analyzed Industry	Index
Employees per Establishment	46	37	81	Value Added per Production Worker	122,353	47,935	39
Payroll per Establishment	1,332,320	633,000	48	Cost per Establishment	4,239,462	1,637,000	39
Payroll per Employee	29,181	17,108	59	Cost per Employee	92,853	44,243	48
Production Workers per Establishment	31	31	99	Cost per Production Worker	135,003	52,806	39
Wages per Establishment	734,496	422,820	58	Shipments per Establishment	8,100,800	3,169,000	39
Wages per Production Worker	23,390	13,639	58	Shipments per Employee	177,425	85,649	48
Hours per Production Worker	2,025	1,871	92	Shipments per Production Worker	257,966	102,226	40
Wages per Hour	11.55	7.29	63	Investment per Establishment	278,244	33,000	12
Value Added per Establishment	3,842,210	1,486,000	39	Investment per Employee	6,094	892	15
Value Added per Employee	84,153	40,162	48	Investment per Production Worker	8,861	1,065	12

Sources: Same as General Statistics. The 'Average of All Manufacturing' column represents the average of all manufacturing industries reported for the most recent complete year available. The Index shows the relationship between the Average and the Analyzed Industry. For example, 100 means that they are equal; 500 that the Analyzed Industry is five times the average; 50 means that the Analyzed Industry is half the national average. The abbreviation 'na' is used to show that data are 'not available'.

LEADING COMPANIES

Number shown: **22** Total sales ($ mil): **117** Total employment (000): **1.7**

Company Name	Address				CEO Name	Phone	Co. Type	Sales ($ mil)	Empl. (000)
United States Shoe Corp	PO Box 253	Vanceburg	KY	41179	Clayton Goodman	606-796-3036	D	20*	0.4
Barbour Corporation Inc	PO Box 2158	Brockton	MA	02405	Richard Hynes	508-583-8200	R	14	0.2
Der-Tex Corp	360 Merrimack St	Lawrence	MA	01843	Jerome Lunder	508-686-0154	R	11*	0.2
L Farber Company Inc	160 Fremont St	Worcester	MA	01603	Paul O'Conor	508-752-1945	R	9	<0.1
Lyn-Flex West Inc	PO Box 570	Owensville	MO	65066	Wayne R Dieckhaus	314-437-4125	R	8	<0.1
Eastern Tool and Stamping Co	109 Ballard St	Saugus	MA	01906	Roger H Howland	617-233-3800	R	7*	0.1
Consolidated Counter Inc	1130 Minot Av	Auburn	ME	04210	Norm Farrar	207-784-6933	R	6*	<0.1
National Stay Company Inc	680 Lynnway	Lynn	MA	01905	E Madow	617-593-5880	R	6*	<0.1
Heel Rite Co	PO Box 560	Wright City	MO	63390	Ned Stanley	314-745-8628	S	5*	<0.1
Rite Sole Corp	PO Box 398	Wright City	MO	63390	Ned Stanley	314-745-3335	R	5*	<0.1
West Coast Shoe Co	PO Box 607	Scappoose	OR	97056	R W Shoemaker	503-543-7114	R	4	<0.1
Allens Manufacturing Company	89 Shipyard St	Providence	RI	02905	Richard Squizzero	401-461-1223	R	4	<0.1
Davco Industries Inc	PO Box 369	Haverhill	MA	01831	K Kolizeras	508-373-5693	R	3*	<0.1
Proctor Products Inc	160 Chesterfield	Chesterfield	MO	63005	John C Proctor	314-532-8444	R	3	<0.1
American Shoe Shank Company	PO Box 1423	Brockton	MA	02403	H Shuman	508-584-8273	R	2	<0.1
Bowcraft Trimming Company	100 8th St	Passaic	NJ	07055	Sid Kowal	201-472-7920	R	2*	<0.1
Montello Heel Manufacturing	PO Box 2116	Brockton	MA	02405	JR Pearson	508-586-0603	R	2	<0.1
Alger Inc	PO Box 2002	Abington	MA	02351	JD Hopkins	617-878-8320	R	2	<0.1
Central Counter Co	6260 N Broadway	St Louis	MO	63147	Roger E Stahlhuth	314-385-6322	R	1	<0.1
Maynard H Moore Jr Inc	PO Box 80152	Stoneham	MA	02180	CB Moore	617-438-1300	R	1*	<0.1
Pedorthic Center Inc	7283 W Appleton	Milwaukee	WI	53216	Dennis Janisse	414-438-1211	R	1*	<0.1
North American Chemical Co	19 S Canal St	Lawrence	MA	01843	Lance E Macomber	508-686-2907	R	1*	<0.1

Source: Ward's Business Directory of U.S. Private and Public Companies, Volumes 1 and 2, 1996. The company type code used is as follows: P - Public, R - Private, S - Subsidiary, D - Division, J - Joint Venture, A - Affiliate, G - Group. Sales are in millions of dollars, employees are in thousands. An asterisk (*) indicates an estimated sales volume. The symbol < stands for 'less than'. Company names and addresses are truncated, in some cases, to fit into the available space.

MATERIALS CONSUMED

Material	Quantity	Delivered Cost ($ million)
Materials, ingredients, containers, and supplies	(X)	154.3
Hides, skins, and pelts	(X)	18.5
Tanning materials, dressings, dyes, and finishing agents	(X)	(D)
Finished upper leather	(X)	13.2
Finished soling leather	(X)	49.2
All other finished leather	(X)	(D)
All other materials and components, parts, containers, and supplies	(X)	54.3
Materials, ingredients, containers, and supplies, nsk	(X)	11.8

Source: 1992 *Economic Census*. Explanation of symbols used: (D): Withheld to avoid disclosure of competitive data; na: Not available; (S): Withheld because statistical norms were not met; (X): Not applicable; (Z): Less than half the unit shown; nec: Not elsewhere classified; nsk: Not specified by kind; - : zero; * : 10-19 percent estimated; ** : 20-29 percent estimated.

PRODUCT SHARE DETAILS

Product or Product Class	% Share
Boot and shoe cut stock and findings	100.00
Boot and shoe outer soles and innersoles of leather	30.78
Other boot and shoe leather cut stock (heels, counters, box toes, taps, etc.)	24.53
Other boot and shoe findings (wood heel blocks made for sale as such, finished wood heels, shanks, welting, etc.)	42.46

Source: 1992 *Economic Census*. The values shown are percent of total shipments in an industry. Values of indented subcategories are summed in the main heading. The symbol (D) appears when data are withheld to prevent disclosure of competitive information. The abbreviation nsk stands for 'not specified by kind' and nec for 'not elsewhere classified'.

INPUTS AND OUTPUTS FOR BOOT & SHOE CUTSTOCK & FINDINGS

Economic Sector or Industry Providing Inputs	%	Sector	Economic Sector or Industry Buying Outputs	%	Sector
Imports	29.2	Foreign	Laundry, dry cleaning, shoe repair	46.6	Services
Leather tanning & finishing	24.3	Manufg.	Shoes, except rubber	29.2	Manufg.
Boot & shoe cutstock & findings	14.8	Manufg.	Boot & shoe cutstock & findings	11.8	Manufg.
Wholesale trade	3.5	Trade	House slippers	5.3	Manufg.
Broadwoven fabric mills	3.1	Manufg.	S/L Govt. purch., correction	3.6	S/L Govt
Nonwoven fabrics	2.8	Manufg.	Exports	3.3	Foreign
U.S. Postal Service	1.7	Gov't	Personal consumption expenditures	0.2	
Textile goods, nec	1.5	Manufg.			
Hardwood dimension & flooring mills	1.2	Manufg.			
Meat packing plants	1.1	Manufg.			
Electric services (utilities)	1.1	Util.			

Continued on next page.

INPUTS AND OUTPUTS FOR BOOT & SHOE CUTSTOCK & FINDINGS - Continued

Economic Sector or Industry Providing Inputs	%	Sector	Economic Sector or Industry Buying Outputs	%	Sector
Motor freight transportation & warehousing	1.1	Util.			
Felt goods, nec	1.0	Manufg.			
Paperboard containers & boxes	0.9	Manufg.			
Synthetic rubber	0.8	Manufg.			
Chemical preparations, nec	0.7	Manufg.			
Eating & drinking places	0.7	Trade			
Advertising	0.7	Services			
Cyclic crudes and organics	0.6	Manufg.			
Industrial gases	0.6	Manufg.			
Miscellaneous plastics products	0.6	Manufg.			
Plastics materials & resins	0.6	Manufg.			
Reclaimed rubber	0.6	Manufg.			
Sawmills & planning mills, general	0.5	Manufg.			
Real estate	0.5	Fin/R.E.			
Air transportation	0.3	Util.			
Gas production & distribution (utilities)	0.3	Util.			
Banking	0.3	Fin/R.E.			
Maintenance of nonfarm buildings nec	0.2	Constr.			
Industrial inorganic chemicals, nec	0.2	Manufg.			
Machinery, except electrical, nec	0.2	Manufg.			
Petroleum refining	0.2	Manufg.			
Polishes & sanitation goods	0.2	Manufg.			
Veneer & plywood	0.2	Manufg.			
Communications, except radio & TV	0.2	Util.			
Railroads & related services	0.2	Util.			
Sanitary services, steam supply, irrigation	0.2	Util.			
Water supply & sewage systems	0.2	Util.			
Legal services	0.2	Services			
Management & consulting services & labs	0.2	Services			
Manifold business forms	0.1	Manufg.			
Paperboard mills	0.1	Manufg.			
Special dies & tools & machine tool accessories	0.1	Manufg.			
Accounting, auditing & bookkeeping	0.1	Services			
Automotive repair shops & services	0.1	Services			
Equipment rental & leasing services	0.1	Services			
Hotels & lodging places	0.1	Services			

Source: Benchmark Input-Output Accounts for the U.S. Economy, 1982, U.S. Department of Commerce, Washington, D.C., July 1991. Data, as reported in the source, are organized by the 1977 SIC structure in use in 1982 but have been matched, as closely as is possible, to the 1987 SIC structure used in this book.

OCCUPATIONS EMPLOYED BY SIC 313 - FOOTWEAR, EX RUBBER AND PLASTIC

Occupation	% of Total 1994	Change to 2005	Occupation	% of Total 1994	Change to 2005
Shoe sewing machine operators	18.8	-72.1	Sewers, hand	2.4	-64.2
Shoe & leather workers & repairers, precision	13.7	-49.7	Inspectors, testers, & graders, precision	2.1	-44.2
Assemblers, fabricators, & hand workers nec	8.7	-44.1	Freight, stock, & material movers, hand	1.6	-55.3
Helpers, laborers, & material movers nec	4.9	-44.2	Sales & related workers nec	1.4	-44.1
Cutting & slicing machine setters, operators	4.7	-38.5	General managers & top executives	1.3	-47.1
Hand packers & packagers	4.6	-52.1	Traffic, shipping, & receiving clerks	1.3	-46.2
Blue collar worker supervisors	3.4	-47.2	Coating, painting, & spraying machine workers	1.2	-44.1
Cement & gluing machine operators	3.3	-83.2	Cutters & trimmers, hand	1.1	-49.8
Machine operators nec	3.2	-50.8	Industrial machinery mechanics	1.1	-38.6

Source: Industry-Occupation Matrix, Bureau of Labor Statistics. These data relate to one or more 3-digit SIC industry groups rather than to a single 4-digit SIC. The change reported for each occupation to the year 2005 is a percent of growth or decline as estimated by the Bureau of Labor Statistics. The abbreviation nec stands for 'not elsewhere classified'.

LOCATION BY STATE AND REGIONAL CONCENTRATION

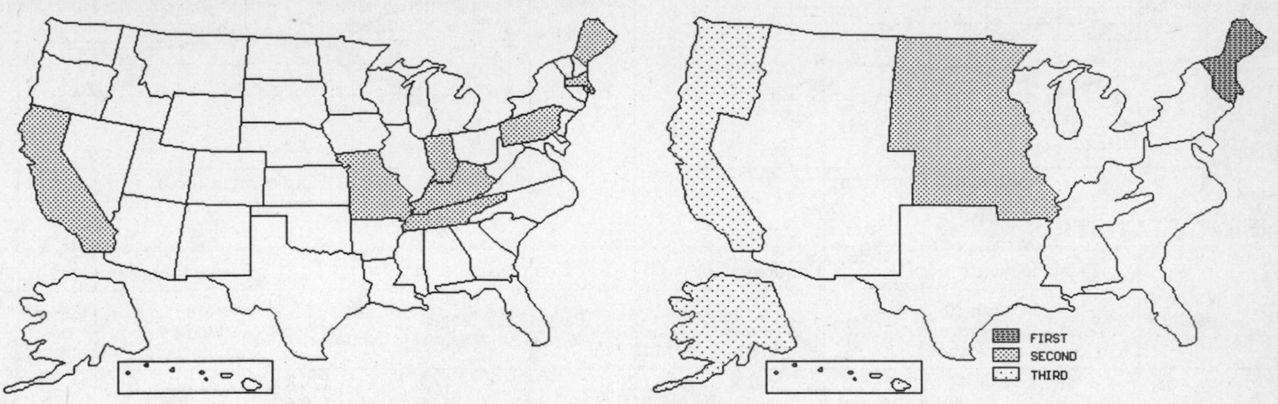

INDUSTRY DATA BY STATE

State	Establish-ments	Shipments			Employment				Cost as % of Shipments	Investment per Employee ($)
		Total ($ mil)	% of U.S.	Per Establ.	Total Number	% of U.S.	Per Establ.	Wages ($/hour)		
Missouri	19	78.4	24.7	4.1	1,300	35.1	68	6.79	51.3	385
Massachusetts	26	54.8	17.3	2.1	600	16.2	23	9.33	59.9	833
Pennsylvania	5	21.7	6.8	4.3	100	2.7	20	9.00	78.3	1,000
Rhode Island	5	8.3	2.6	1.7	100	2.7	20	12.00	53.0	-
California	6	6.5	2.1	1.1	100	2.7	17	5.50	49.2	-
Tennessee	5	(D)	-	-	375 *	10.1	75	-	-	-
Maine	3	(D)	-	-	175 *	4.7	58	-	-	-
Indiana	1	(D)	-	-	375 *	10.1	375	-	-	-
Kentucky	1	(D)	-	-	175 *	4.7	175	-	-	-

Source: 1992 *Economic Census*. The states are in descending order of shipments or establishments (if shipment data are missing for the majority). The symbol (D) appears when data are withheld to prevent disclosure of competitive information. States marked with (D) are sorted by number of establishments. A dash (-) indicates that the data element cannot be calculated; * indicates the midpoint of a range.

3142 - HOUSE SLIPPERS

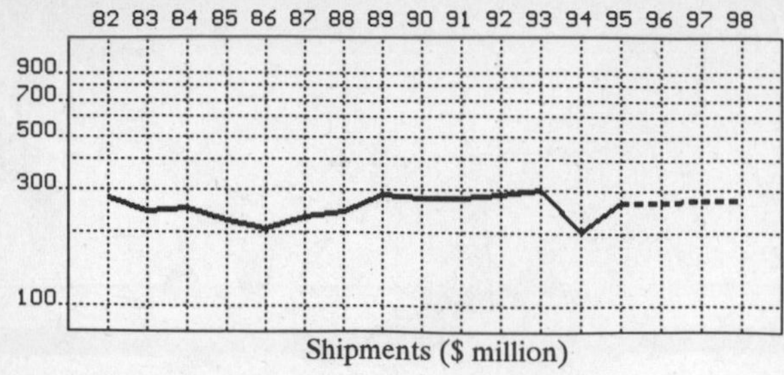

Shipments ($ million)

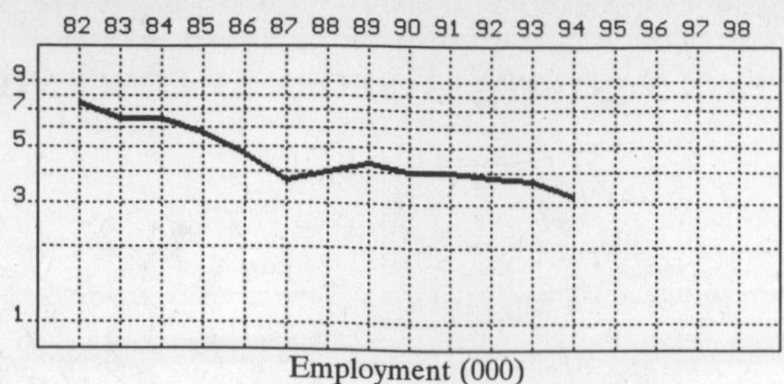

Employment (000)

GENERAL STATISTICS

Year	Companies	Establishments: Total	Establishments: with 20 or more employees	Employment: Total (000)	Employment: Production Workers (000)	Employment: Production Hours (Mil)	Compensation: Payroll ($ mil)	Compensation: Wages ($/hr)	Production ($ million): Cost of Materials	Production ($ million): Value Added by Manufacture	Production ($ million): Value of Shipments	Production ($ million): Capital Invest.
1982	53	62	44	7.5	6.4	11.2	71.3	4.62	128.8	149.7	275.8	3.1
1983		58	39	6.4	5.4	9.8	64.2	4.67	108.6	128.9	241.9	2.6
1984		54	34	6.5	5.4	9.3	66.8	5.31	118.5	133.6	248.4	4.1
1985		49	29	5.7	4.9	8.7	62.5	5.29	110.6	112.3	223.2	4.2
1986		43	26	4.7	3.9	6.6	57.3	5.48	104.3	103.4	208.7	6.0
1987	34	37	23	3.7	3.0	5.6	50.3	5.38	99.6	132.9	232.5	2.7
1988		37	20			6.3	52.6		114.3	133.1	244.3	4.1
1989		36	23	4.3	3.9	6.9	63.3	6.39	139.0	160.9	286.8	3.8
1990		33	23	4.0	3.4	6.5	58.9	6.09	113.1	160.7	276.0	3.3
1991		36	23	4.0	3.2	6.1	61.3	6.79	116.6	158.0	277.3	2.4
1992	28	31	21	3.8	3.0	5.5	59.2	6.47	109.6	176.3	285.1	2.1
1993		34	19	3.7	2.9	5.2	61.8	6.88	117.3	189.2	301.8	2.5
1994		25P	14P	3.2	2.4	4.6	48.2	6.72	79.3	126.9	203.5	4.8
1995		22P	12P			3.8P	53.3P		104.5P	167.3P	268.2P	3.2P
1996		19P	10P			3.4P	52.4P		105.3P	168.5P	270.2P	3.2P
1997		17P	9P			2.9P	51.5P		106.1P	169.8P	272.2P	3.1P
1998		14P	7P			2.5P	50.6P		106.9P	171.0P	274.2P	3.1P

Sources: 1982, 1987, 1992 *Economic Census*; *Annual Survey of Manufactures*, 83-86, 88-91, 93-94. Establishment counts for non-Census years are from *County Business Patterns*; establishment values for 83-84 are extrapolations. 'P's show projections by the editors. Industries reclassified in 87 will not have data for prior years.

INDICES OF CHANGE

Year	Companies	Establishments: Total	Establishments: with 20 or more employees	Employment: Total (000)	Employment: Production Workers (000)	Employment: Production Hours (Mil)	Compensation: Payroll ($ mil)	Compensation: Wages ($/hr)	Production ($ million): Cost of Materials	Production ($ million): Value Added by Manufacture	Production ($ million): Value of Shipments	Production ($ million): Capital Invest.
1982	189	200	210	197	213	204	120	71	118	85	97	148
1983		187	186	168	180	178	108	72	99	73	85	124
1984		174	162	171	180	169	113	82	108	76	87	195
1985		158	138	150	163	158	106	82	101	64	78	200
1986		139	124	124	130	120	97	85	95	59	73	286
1987	121	119	110	97	100	102	85	83	91	75	82	129
1988		119	95			115	89		104	75	86	195
1989		116	110	113	130	125	107	99	127	91	101	181
1990		106	110	105	113	118	99	94	103	91	97	157
1991		116	110	105	107	111	104	105	106	90	97	114
1992	100	100	100	100	100	100	100	100	100	100	100	100
1993		110	90	97	97	95	104	106	107	107	106	119
1994		80P	68P	84	80	84	81	104	72	72	71	229
1995		71P	59P			70P	90P		95P	95P	94P	153P
1996		63P	50P			62P	89P		96P	96P	95P	151P
1997		54P	41P			53P	87P		97P	96P	95P	149P
1998		45P	31P			45P	85P		98P	97P	96P	146P

Sources: Same as General Statistics. Values reflect change from the base year, 1992. Values above 100 mean greater than 92, values below 100 mean less than 92, and a value of 100 in the 82-91 or 93-98 period means same as 92. 'P's mark projections by the editors.

SELECTED RATIOS

For 1994	Avg. of All Manufact.	Analyzed Industry	Index
Employees per Establishment	49	129	263
Payroll per Establishment	1,500,273	1,942,125	129
Payroll per Employee	30,620	15,063	49
Production Workers per Establishment	34	97	282
Wages per Establishment	853,319	1,245,538	146
Wages per Production Worker	24,861	12,880	52
Hours per Production Worker	2,056	1,917	93
Wages per Hour	12.09	6.72	56
Value Added per Establishment	4,602,255	5,113,187	111
Value Added per Employee	93,930	39,656	42

For 1994	Avg. of All Manufact.	Analyzed Industry	Index
Value Added per Production Worker	134,084	52,875	39
Cost per Establishment	5,045,178	3,195,238	63
Cost per Employee	102,970	24,781	24
Cost per Production Worker	146,988	33,042	22
Shipments per Establishment	9,576,895	8,199,634	86
Shipments per Employee	195,460	63,594	33
Shipments per Production Worker	279,017	84,792	30
Investment per Establishment	321,011	193,407	60
Investment per Employee	6,552	1,500	23
Investment per Production Worker	9,352	2,000	21

Sources: Same as General Statistics. The 'Average of All Manufacturing' column represents the average of all manufacturing industries reported for the most recent complete year available. The Index shows the relationship between the Average and the Analyzed Industry. For example, 100 means that they are equal; 500 that the Analyzed Industry is five times the average; 50 means that the Analyzed Industry is half the national average. The abbreviation 'na' is used to show that data are 'not available'.

LEADING COMPANIES

Number shown: **4** Total sales ($ mil): **189** Total employment (000): **3.6**

Company Name	Address				CEO Name	Phone	Co. Type	Sales ($ mil)	Empl. (000)
RG Barry Corp	PO Box 129	Columbus	OH	43216	Gordon Zacks	614-864-6400	P	117	2.5
Supreme Slipper Mfg Corp	PO Box 1376	Lewiston	ME	04240	Samuel Z Smith	207-784-2921	R	48*	0.5
Daniel Green Co	1 Main St	Dolgeville	NY	13329	W J Reardon III	315-429-3131	P	23	0.6
E and W Moccasin Company Inc	PO Box 23	Moira	NY	12957	FB Elliott	518-529-8923	R	2	<0.1

Source: *Ward's Business Directory of U.S. Private and Public Companies*, Volumes 1 and 2, 1996. The company type code used is as follows: P - Public, R - Private, S - Subsidiary, D - Division, J - Joint Venture, A - Affiliate, G - Group. Sales are in millions of dollars, employees are in thousands. An asterisk (*) indicates an estimated sales volume. The symbol < stands for 'less than'. Company names and addresses are truncated, in some cases, to fit into the available space.

MATERIALS CONSUMED

Material		Quantity	Delivered Cost ($ million)
Materials, ingredients, containers, and supplies		(X)	93.3
Plastics coated, impregnated, or laminated fabrics	mil sq yd	9.7	27.1
Plastics and natural or synthetic rubber cut stock and findings		(X)	4.5
Composition cut stock and findings		(X)	(D)
Leather and other material cut stock and findings		(X)	0.8
Plastics products consumed in the form of sheets, rods, tubes, film, and other shapes		(X)	(D)
Finished upper leather	mil sq ft	11.6	16.5
Finished soling leather	mil pairs	0.6	2.7
Other finished leather		(X)	(D)
Paper and paperboard containers, including shipping sacks and other paper packaging supplies		(X)	4.9
All other materials and components, parts, containers, and supplies		(X)	34.9
Materials, ingredients, containers, and supplies, nsk		(X)	0.8

Source: 1992 *Economic Census*. Explanation of symbols used: (D): Withheld to avoid disclosure of competitive data; na: Not available; (S): Withheld because statistical norms were not met; (X): Not applicable; (Z): Less than half the unit shown; nec: Not elsewhere classified; nsk: Not specified by kind; - : zero; * : 10-19 percent estimated; ** : 20-29 percent estimated.

PRODUCT SHARE DETAILS

Product or Product Class	% Share	Product or Product Class	% Share
House slippers	100.00	Slipper socks made from purchased socks	4.60
House slippers, all types, except slipper socks	95.02		

Source: 1992 *Economic Census*. The values shown are percent of total shipments in an industry. Values of indented subcategories are summed in the main heading. The symbol (D) appears when data are withheld to prevent disclosure of competitive information. The abbreviation nsk stands for 'not specified by kind' and nec for 'not elsewhere classified'.

INPUTS AND OUTPUTS FOR HOUSE SLIPPERS

Economic Sector or Industry Providing Inputs	%	Sector	Economic Sector or Industry Buying Outputs	%	Sector
Coated fabrics, not rubberized	18.9	Manufg.	Personal consumption expenditures	92.6	
Boot & shoe cutstock & findings	10.6	Manufg.	S/L Govt. purch., health & hospitals	2.9	S/L Govt
Imports	8.6	Foreign	Change in business inventories	2.7	In House
Banking	6.7	Fin/R.E.	Exports	1.3	Foreign
Wholesale trade	6.3	Trade	House slippers	0.5	Manufg.
Fabricated rubber products, nec	6.0	Manufg.			
Adhesives & sealants	4.3	Manufg.			
Textile goods, nec	4.1	Manufg.			
Broadwoven fabric mills	4.0	Manufg.			
Advertising	3.7	Services			
Narrow fabric mills	3.6	Manufg.			
Textile machinery	2.5	Manufg.			
Paperboard containers & boxes	2.4	Manufg.			
U.S. Postal Service	2.4	Gov't			
Automotive repair shops & services	1.9	Services			
Leather tanning & finishing	1.4	Manufg.			
Thread mills	1.3	Manufg.			
Motor freight transportation & warehousing	1.3	Util.			
Eating & drinking places	1.0	Trade			
Miscellaneous plastics products	0.9	Manufg.			
Electric services (utilities)	0.8	Util.			
House slippers	0.6	Manufg.			
Machinery, except electrical, nec	0.4	Manufg.			
Air transportation	0.4	Util.			
Communications, except radio & TV	0.4	Util.			
Gas production & distribution (utilities)	0.4	Util.			

Continued on next page.

INPUTS AND OUTPUTS FOR HOUSE SLIPPERS - Continued

Economic Sector or Industry Providing Inputs	%	Sector	Economic Sector or Industry Buying Outputs	%	Sector
Real estate	0.4	Fin/R.E.			
Plastics materials & resins	0.3	Manufg.			
Yarn mills & finishing of textiles, nec	0.3	Manufg.			
Credit agencies other than banks	0.3	Fin/R.E.			
Royalties	0.3	Fin/R.E.			
Legal services	0.3	Services			
Management & consulting services & labs	0.3	Services			
Maintenance of nonfarm buildings nec	0.2	Constr.			
Distilled liquor, except brandy	0.2	Manufg.			
Manifold business forms	0.2	Manufg.			
Accounting, auditing & bookkeeping	0.2	Services			
Equipment rental & leasing services	0.2	Services			
Laundry, dry cleaning, shoe repair	0.2	Services			
Lubricating oils & greases	0.1	Manufg.			
Special dies & tools & machine tool accessories	0.1	Manufg.			
Railroads & related services	0.1	Util.			
Electrical repair shops	0.1	Services			
Hotels & lodging places	0.1	Services			

Source: Benchmark Input-Output Accounts for the U.S. Economy, 1982, U.S. Department of Commerce, Washington, D.C., July 1991. Data, as reported in the source, are organized by the 1977 SIC structure in use in 1982 but have been matched, as closely as is possible, to the 1987 SIC structure used in this book.

OCCUPATIONS EMPLOYED BY SIC 314 - FOOTWEAR, EX RUBBER AND PLASTIC

Occupation	% of Total 1994	Change to 2005	Occupation	% of Total 1994	Change to 2005
Shoe sewing machine operators	18.8	-72.1	Sewers, hand	2.4	-64.2
Shoe & leather workers & repairers, precision	13.7	-49.7	Inspectors, testers, & graders, precision	2.1	-44.2
Assemblers, fabricators, & hand workers nec	8.7	-44.1	Freight, stock, & material movers, hand	1.6	-55.3
Helpers, laborers, & material movers nec	4.9	-44.2	Sales & related workers nec	1.4	-44.1
Cutting & slicing machine setters, operators	4.7	-38.5	General managers & top executives	1.3	-47.1
Hand packers & packagers	4.6	-52.1	Traffic, shipping, & receiving clerks	1.3	-46.2
Blue collar worker supervisors	3.4	-47.2	Coating, painting, & spraying machine workers	1.2	-44.1
Cement & gluing machine operators	3.3	-83.2	Cutters & trimmers, hand	1.1	-49.8
Machine operators nec	3.2	-50.8	Industrial machinery mechanics	1.1	-38.6

Source: Industry-Occupation Matrix, Bureau of Labor Statistics. These data relate to one or more 3-digit SIC industry groups rather than to a single 4-digit SIC. The change reported for each occupation to the year 2005 is a percent of growth or decline as estimated by the Bureau of Labor Statistics. The abbreviation nec stands for 'not elsewhere classified'.

LOCATION BY STATE AND REGIONAL CONCENTRATION

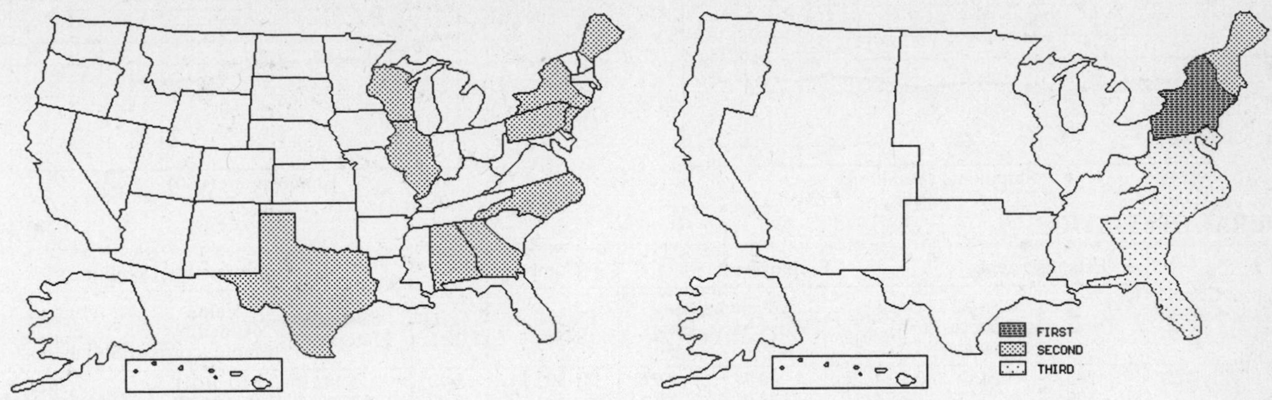

INDUSTRY DATA BY STATE

State	Establish-ments	Shipments			Employment				Cost as % of Shipments	Investment per Employee ($)
		Total ($ mil)	% of U.S.	Per Establ.	Total Number	% of U.S.	Per Establ.	Wages ($/hour)		
Maine	4	(D)	-	-	750 *	19.7	188	-	-	-
New Jersey	4	(D)	-	-	375 *	9.9	94	-	-	-
New York	4	(D)	-	-	1,750 *	46.1	438	-	-	-
Pennsylvania	3	(D)	-	-	375 *	9.9	125	-	-	-
Georgia	2	(D)	-	-	175 *	4.6	88	-	-	-
North Carolina	2	(D)	-	-	175 *	4.6	88	-	-	-
Texas	2	(D)	-	-	375 *	9.9	188	-	-	-
Wisconsin	2	(D)	-	-	175 *	4.6	88	-	-	-
Alabama	1	(D)	-	-	175 *	4.6	175	-	-	-
Illinois	1	(D)	-	-	175 *	4.6	175	-	-	-

Source: 1992 *Economic Census*. The states are in descending order of shipments or establishments (if shipment data are missing for the majority). The symbol (D) appears when data are withheld to prevent disclosure of competitive information. States marked with (D) are sorted by number of establishments. A dash (-) indicates that the data element cannot be calculated; * indicates the midpoint of a range.

3143 - MEN'S FOOTWEAR, EXCEPT ATHLETIC

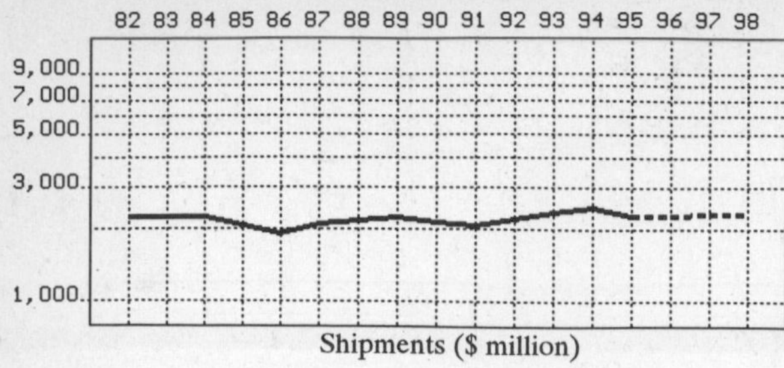

Shipments ($ million)

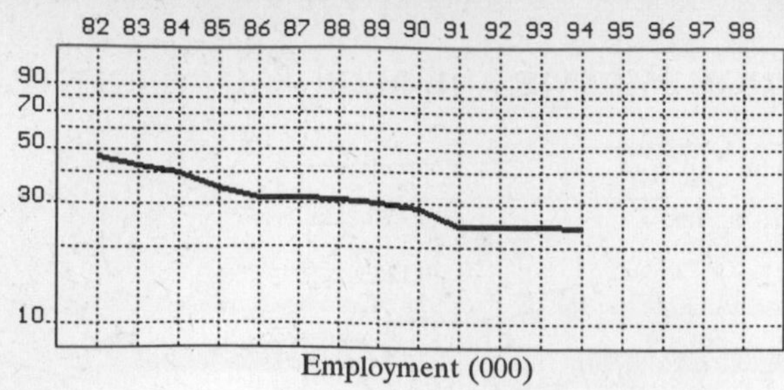

Employment (000)

GENERAL STATISTICS

Year	Com-panies	Establishments		Employment			Compensation		Production ($ million)			
		Total	with 20 or more employees	Total (000)	Production Workers (000)	Production Hours (Mil)	Payroll ($ mil)	Wages ($/hr)	Cost of Materials	Value Added by Manufacture	Value of Shipments	Capital Invest.
1982	129	203	159	46.5	40.7	69.6	503.1	5.49	1,141.3	1,101.1	2,261.4	28.3
1983		190	147	43.0	38.0	67.1	494.1	5.68	1,120.5	1,138.7	2,264.0	18.8
1984		177	135	40.1	35.3	61.5	472.7	5.99	1,104.0	1,118.9	2,230.6	28.0
1985		165	124	34.9	30.8	53.8	435.9	6.26	1,031.8	1,051.4	2,070.5	28.9
1986		147	110	31.8	28.0	49.3	416.6	6.41	968.8	913.1	1,891.4	16.2
1987	110	154	111	31.6	27.5	51.3	434.1	6.36	1,056.6	1,046.7	2,104.8	17.4
1988		154	115			49.0	438.0		1,095.8	1,093.6	2,168.0	17.4
1989		141	106	30.3	26.6	47.4	462.1	7.22	1,157.8	1,083.1	2,228.4	21.2
1990		129	96	28.4	24.6	44.0	444.9	7.11	1,080.3	1,058.6	2,148.8	22.8
1991		135	89	24.5	21.0	35.4	387.0	7.74	1,054.5	997.9	2,064.0	18.1
1992	108	140	88	24.2	20.0	36.6	398.9	7.72	1,135.6	1,087.7	2,209.5	32.8
1993		143	89	24.6	20.8	40.9	430.3	7.56	1,183.8	1,196.5	2,351.1	26.1
1994		120P	74P	24.0	20.5	39.7	421.6	7.80	1,177.5	1,353.3	2,461.0	43.3
1995		114P	68P			31.2P	396.7P		1,087.1P	1,249.4P	2,272.1P	29.6P
1996		109P	61P			28.6P	390.3P		1,092.8P	1,256.0P	2,284.0P	30.3P
1997		103P	55P			25.9P	383.9P		1,098.5P	1,262.5P	2,295.9P	31.0P
1998		98P	49P			23.3P	377.5P		1,104.2P	1,269.1P	2,307.8P	31.7P

Sources: 1982, 1987, 1992 *Economic Census*; *Annual Survey of Manufactures*, 83-86, 88-91, 93-94. Establishment counts for non-Census years are from *County Business Patterns*; establishment values for 83-84 are extrapolations. 'P's show projections by the editors. Industries reclassified in 87 will not have data for prior years.

INDICES OF CHANGE

Year	Com-panies	Establishments		Employment			Compensation		Production ($ million)			
		Total	with 20 or more employees	Total (000)	Production Workers (000)	Production Hours (Mil)	Payroll ($ mil)	Wages ($/hr)	Cost of Materials	Value Added by Manufacture	Value of Shipments	Capital Invest.
1982	119	145	181	192	203	190	126	71	101	101	102	86
1983		136	167	178	190	183	124	74	99	105	102	57
1984		126	153	166	176	168	119	78	97	103	101	85
1985		118	141	144	154	147	109	81	91	97	94	88
1986		105	125	131	140	135	104	83	85	84	86	49
1987	102	110	126	131	138	140	109	82	93	96	95	53
1988		110	131			134	110		96	101	98	53
1989		101	120	125	133	130	116	94	102	100	101	65
1990		92	109	117	123	120	112	92	95	97	97	70
1991		96	101	101	105	97	97	100	93	92	93	55
1992	100	100	100	100	100	100	100	100	100	100	100	100
1993		102	101	102	104	112	108	98	104	110	106	80
1994		86P	84P	99	102	108	106	101	104	124	111	132
1995		82P	77P			85P	99P		96P	115P	103P	90P
1996		78P	70P			78P	98P		96P	115P	103P	92P
1997		74P	63P			71P	96P		97P	116P	104P	95P
1998		70P	56P			64P	95P		97P	117P	104P	97P

Sources: Same as General Statistics. Values reflect change from the base year, 1992. Values above 100 mean greater than 92, values below 100 mean less than 92, and a value of 100 in the 82-91 or 93-98 period means same as 92. 'P's mark projections by the editors.

SELECTED RATIOS

For 1994	Avg. of All Manufact.	Analyzed Industry	Index
Employees per Establishment	49	200	408
Payroll per Establishment	1,500,273	3,510,674	234
Payroll per Employee	30,620	17,567	57
Production Workers per Establishment	34	171	497
Wages per Establishment	853,319	2,578,547	302
Wages per Production Worker	24,861	15,105	61
Hours per Production Worker	2,056	1,937	94
Wages per Hour	12.09	7.80	65
Value Added per Establishment	4,602,255	11,268,963	245
Value Added per Employee	93,930	56,387	60

For 1994	Avg. of All Manufact.	Analyzed Industry	Index
Value Added per Production Worker	134,084	66,015	49
Cost per Establishment	5,045,178	9,805,072	194
Cost per Employee	102,970	49,063	48
Cost per Production Worker	146,988	57,439	39
Shipments per Establishment	9,576,895	20,492,808	214
Shipments per Employee	195,460	102,542	52
Shipments per Production Worker	279,017	120,049	43
Investment per Establishment	321,011	360,560	112
Investment per Employee	6,552	1,804	28
Investment per Production Worker	9,352	2,112	23

Sources: Same as General Statistics. The 'Average of All Manufacturing' column represents the average of all manufacturing industries reported for the most recent complete year available. The Index shows the relationship between the Average and the Analyzed Industry. For example, 100 means that they are equal; 500 that the Analyzed Industry is five times the average; 50 means that the Analyzed Industry is half the national average. The abbreviation 'na' is used to show that data are 'not available'.

LEADING COMPANIES

Number shown: **53** Total sales ($ mil): **5,192** Total employment (000): **63.0**

Company Name	Address				CEO Name	Phone	Co. Type	Sales ($ mil)	Empl. (000)
Brown Group Inc	PO Box 29	St Louis	MO	63166	BA Bridgewater Jr	314-854-4000	P	1,462	14.5
Timberland Co	PO Box 5050	Hampton	NH	03842	Sidney W Swartz	603-772-9500	P	638	6.7
Genesco Inc	PO Box 731	Nashville	TN	37202	D M Chamberlain	615-967-7000	P	463	5.4
Wolverine World Wide Inc	9341 Courtland Dr	Rockford	MI	49341	Geoffrey B Bloom	616-866-5500	P	378	5.2
Florsheim Shoe Co	130 S Canal St	Chicago	IL	60606	Ronald J Mueller	312-559-2500	P	302	3.2
Red Wing Shoe Company Inc	314 Main St	Red Wing	MN	55066	Joe Goggin	612-388-8211	R	186	1.3
Munro and Co	PO Box 1157	Hot Springs	AR	71902	M J Hennessy Jr	501-262-1440	R	160	2.5
Dexter Shoe Co	114 Railroad Av	Dexter	ME	04930	Peter Lunder	207-924-7341	R	140*	2.0
Endicott Johnson Corp	1100 E Main St	Endicott	NY	13760	David Pasquale	607-757-4000	S	130*	1.9
WEYCO Group Inc	PO Box 1188	Milwaukee	WI	53201	T W Florsheim	414-263-8800	P	115	0.5
HH Brown Shoe Company Inc	124 W Putnam Av	Greenwich	CT	06830	James E Issler	203-661-2424	S	100	2.0
Justin Boot Co	610 W Daggett Av	Fort Worth	TX	76104	Gary Liggett	817-332-4385	S	100	1.8
Texas Boot Co	127 E Forest Av	Lebanon	TN	37087	Harry Vise	615-444-5440	D	77	1.4
Kinney Shoe Corp	PO Box 370	Carlisle	PA	17013	Philip Suraci	717-249-2011	D	70	1.7
Wrangler Boot Co	127 E Forrest Av	Lebanon	TN	37087	Harry Vise	615-444-5440	D	61	1.2
Georgia Boot Inc	1810 Columbia Av	Franklin	TN	37064	Sam McConnell	615-794-1556	S	60	1.2
Tony Lama Co	PO Box 9518	El Paso	TX	79985	Rudolph E Lama	915-778-8311	S	60	0.9
Sebago Inc	Bridge St	Westbrook	ME	04092	John Marshall	207-854-8474	R	55*	0.9
Charles David of California Inc	5731 Bucking	Culver City	CA	90230	Charles Malka	310-348-5050	R	50	<0.1
Carolina Shoe Co	PO Box 1079	Morganton	NC	28655	W C Keaton Jr	704-437-7755	D	45	0.5
Rocky Shoes and Boots Inc	294 S Harper St	Nelsonville	OH	45764	Mike Brooks	614-753-1951	P	41	1.2
Lehigh Safety Shoe Co	1100 E Main St	Endicott	NY	13760	Alan R Hutson	607-754-7980	S	40	0.2
Norcross Footwear Inc	PO Box 23569	Louisville	KY	40223		502-327-6100	R	40	1.2
Wolverine World Wide Inc	9341 Courtland Dr	Rockford	MI	49341	Dean Estes	616-866-5500	D	40	<0.1
Mason Shoe Manufacturing Inc	1251 1st Av	Chippewa Falls	WI	54729	John Lubs	715-723-1871	R	35	0.7
Allen-Edmonds Shoe Corp	PO Box 998	Pt Washington	WI	53074	John Stollenwerk	414-284-3461	R	32*	0.5
Cowtown Boot Company Inc	PO Box 26428	El Paso	TX	79926	Paul Calcaterra	915-593-2565	R	30*	0.4
Nocona Boot Co	E Hwy 82	Nocona	TX	76255	SA Pickens	817-825-3321	S	30	0.4
Weinbrenner Shoe Company Inc	108 S Polk St	Merrill	WI	54452	Lance Nienow	715-536-5521	R	30	0.5
Bates Shoe Co	9341 Courtland Dr	Rockford	MI	49351	Martin P Neslusan	616-866-5500	D	25	0.3
Altama Combat Boots	2330 DeFoor Hills	Atlanta	GA	30318	W Whitlow Wyatt	404-355-6400	R	20	0.3
Wellco Enterprises Inc	PO Box 188	Waynesville	NC	28786	Rolf Kaufman	704-456-3545	P	18	0.2
George E Keith Co	31 Perkins St	Bridgewater	MA	02324	Jeffrey Weber	508-697-6104	R	18	0.3
Walk-Over Shoes	31 Perkins St	Bridgewater	MA	02324	Jeffrey Weber	508-697-6104	D	18	0.3
Falcon Shoe Manufacturing Co	PO Box 1286	Lewiston	ME	04241	Theodore Johanson	207-784-9186	R	16*	0.2
Frye Co	160 Great Neck Rd	Great Neck	NY	11021	David T DiPasquale	516-829-1717	D	15	<0.1
Vasque Outdoor Footwear	314 Main St	Red Wing	MN	55066	George Pugh	612-388-8211	D	15	<0.1
Thurmont Shoe Co	148 W Franklin St	Hagerstown	MD	21740	Bennett S Rubin	301-739-1664	R	14*	0.2
McRae Industries Inc	402 N Main St	Mount Gilead	NC	27306	Branson J McRae	919-439-6147	P	12	0.4
McRae Footwear	PO Box 726	Mount Gilead	NC	27306	Branson J McRae	910-439-6149	D	11	0.2
Danner Shoe Manufacturing Co	PO Box 30148	Portland	OR	97230	Eric Merk	503-251-1100	S	9	0.1
Miller Industries Inc	11333 Rojas St	El Paso	TX	79936	JD Ward	915-591-1024	R	9	0.1
Custom Stitchers Inc	PO Box 1178	Auburn	ME	04211	Jane Theberge	207-786-2973	R	5	0.2
Olathe Boot Co	PO Box 190	Olathe	KS	66061	Chris D'Adamo	913-764-5110	R	5	<0.1
Franklin-Leddy Corp	2200 W Beauregard	San Angelo	TX	76901	WD Franklin	915-942-7655	R	3	<0.1
Deja Inc	7165 SW Fir Loop	Tigard	OR	97223	Bruce MacGreger	503-624-7443	R	2	<0.1
Swedish Clogs Inc	320 State Rd 16	St Augustine	FL	32095	Peter Johansson	904-824-8844	R	2	<0.1
Stewart Boot Company Inc	30 W 28th St	South Tucson	AZ	85713	Victor Borg	602-622-2706	R	1	<0.1
Alden Shoe Co	Taunton St	Middleboro	MA	02346	Arthur S Tarlow Jr	508-947-3926	R	1	0.2
Friedson Corp	153 Post Rd E	Westport	CT	06880	Ronald Friedson	203-227-6272	R	1	<0.1
TO Dey Service Corp	9 E 38th St	New York	NY	10016	TO Dey	212-683-6300	R	1	<0.1
Warson Group Inc	121 Hunter Av	St Louis	MO	63124	James Maritz III	314-721-8500	R	1	<0.1
Amark Inc	PO Box 1467	Merrimack	NH	03054	Francis Mahoney	603-424-0449	R	0	<0.1

Source: *Ward's Business Directory of U.S. Private and Public Companies*, Volumes 1 and 2, 1996. The company type code used is as follows: P - Public, R - Private, S - Subsidiary, D - Division, J - Joint Venture, A - Affiliate, G - Group. Sales are in millions of dollars, employees are in thousands. An asterisk (*) indicates an estimated sales volume. The symbol < stands for 'less than'. Company names and addresses are truncated, in some cases, to fit into the available space.

MATERIALS CONSUMED

Material		Quantity	Delivered Cost ($ million)
Materials, ingredients, containers, and supplies		(X)	927.6
Plastics coated, impregnated, or laminated fabrics	mil sq yd	13.6	34.1
Plastics and natural or synthetic rubber cut stock and findings		(X)	24.0
Composition cut stock and findings		(X)	32.7
Leather and other material cut stock and findings		(X)	67.1
Plastics products consumed in the form of sheets, rods, tubes, film, and other shapes		(X)	(D)
Finished upper leather	mil sq ft	195.8*	485.2
Finished soling leather	mil pairs	25.2	61.4
Other finished leather		(X)	38.8
Paper and paperboard containers, including shipping sacks and other paper packaging supplies		(X)	(D)
All other materials and components, parts, containers, and supplies		(X)	120.9
Materials, ingredients, containers, and supplies, nsk		(X)	15.5

Source: 1992 *Economic Census*. Explanation of symbols used: (D): Withheld to avoid disclosure of competitive data; na: Not available; (S): Withheld because statistical norms were not met; (X): Not applicable; (Z): Less than half the unit shown; nec: Not elsewhere classified; nsk: Not specified by kind; - : zero; * : 10-19 percent estimated; ** : 20-29 percent estimated.

PRODUCT SHARE DETAILS

Product or Product Class	% Share	Product or Product Class	% Share
Men's footwear, except athletic	100.00		

Source: 1992 *Economic Census*. The values shown are percent of total shipments in an industry. Values of indented subcategories are summed in the main heading. The symbol (D) appears when data are withheld to prevent disclosure of competitive information. The abbreviation nsk stands for 'not specified by kind' and nec for 'not elsewhere classified'.

INPUTS AND OUTPUTS FOR SHOES, EXCEPT RUBBER

Economic Sector or Industry Providing Inputs	%	Sector	Economic Sector or Industry Buying Outputs	%	Sector
Imports	53.7	Foreign	Personal consumption expenditures	96.0	
Leather tanning & finishing	15.5	Manufg.	Change in business inventories	1.7	In House
Wholesale trade	3.7	Trade	Exports	1.4	Foreign
Advertising	2.9	Services	Shoes, except rubber	0.4	Manufg.
Fabricated rubber products, nec	2.8	Manufg.	S/L Govt. purch., correction	0.2	S/L Govt
Boot & shoe cutstock & findings	2.5	Manufg.	Federal Government purchases, national defense	0.1	Fed Govt
Miscellaneous plastics products	1.5	Manufg.			
Coated fabrics, not rubberized	1.4	Manufg.			
Banking	1.4	Fin/R.E.			
Paperboard containers & boxes	1.3	Manufg.			
Needles, pins, & fasteners	1.1	Manufg.			
Plastics materials & resins	1.0	Manufg.			
U.S. Postal Service	0.9	Gov't			
Electric services (utilities)	0.7	Util.			
Shoes, except rubber	0.6	Manufg.			
Eating & drinking places	0.6	Trade			
Equipment rental & leasing services	0.6	Services			
Thread mills	0.5	Manufg.			
Motor freight transportation & warehousing	0.5	Util.			
Narrow fabric mills	0.4	Manufg.			
Chemical preparations, nec	0.3	Manufg.			
Communications, except radio & TV	0.3	Util.			
Detective & protective services	0.3	Services			
Maintenance of nonfarm buildings nec	0.2	Constr.			
Adhesives & sealants	0.2	Manufg.			
Broadwoven fabric mills	0.2	Manufg.			
Cyclic crudes and organics	0.2	Manufg.			
Machinery, except electrical, nec	0.2	Manufg.			
Nonwoven fabrics	0.2	Manufg.			
Textile goods, nec	0.2	Manufg.			
Air transportation	0.2	Util.			
Real estate	0.2	Fin/R.E.			
Royalties	0.2	Fin/R.E.			
Computer & data processing services	0.2	Services			
Legal services	0.2	Services			
Management & consulting services & labs	0.2	Services			
Polishes & sanitation goods	0.1	Manufg.			
Wood products, nec	0.1	Manufg.			
Yarn mills & finishing of textiles, nec	0.1	Manufg.			
Water transportation	0.1	Util.			
Accounting, auditing & bookkeeping	0.1	Services			
Automotive repair shops & services	0.1	Services			
Hotels & lodging places	0.1	Services			
Laundry, dry cleaning, shoe repair	0.1	Services			

Source: Benchmark Input-Output Accounts for the U.S. Economy, 1982, U.S. Department of Commerce, Washington, D.C., July 1991. Data, as reported in the source, are organized by the 1977 SIC structure in use in 1982 but have been matched, as closely as is possible, to the 1987 SIC structure used in this book.

OCCUPATIONS EMPLOYED BY SIC 314 - FOOTWEAR, EX RUBBER AND PLASTIC

Occupation	% of Total 1994	Change to 2005	Occupation	% of Total 1994	Change to 2005
Shoe sewing machine operators	18.8	-72.1	Sewers, hand	2.4	-64.2
Shoe & leather workers & repairers, precision	13.7	-49.7	Inspectors, testers, & graders, precision	2.1	-44.2
Assemblers, fabricators, & hand workers nec	8.7	-44.1	Freight, stock, & material movers, hand	1.6	-55.3
Helpers, laborers, & material movers nec	4.9	-44.2	Sales & related workers nec	1.4	-44.1
Cutting & slicing machine setters, operators	4.7	-38.5	General managers & top executives	1.3	-47.1
Hand packers & packagers	4.6	-52.1	Traffic, shipping, & receiving clerks	1.3	-46.2
Blue collar worker supervisors	3.4	-47.2	Coating, painting, & spraying machine workers	1.2	-44.1
Cement & gluing machine operators	3.3	-83.2	Cutters & trimmers, hand	1.1	-49.8
Machine operators nec	3.2	-50.8	Industrial machinery mechanics	1.1	-38.6

Source: *Industry-Occupation Matrix*, Bureau of Labor Statistics. These data relate to one or more 3-digit SIC industry groups rather than to a single 4-digit SIC. The change reported for each occupation to the year 2005 is a percent of growth or decline as estimated by the Bureau of Labor Statistics. The abbreviation nec stands for 'not elsewhere classified'.

LOCATION BY STATE AND REGIONAL CONCENTRATION

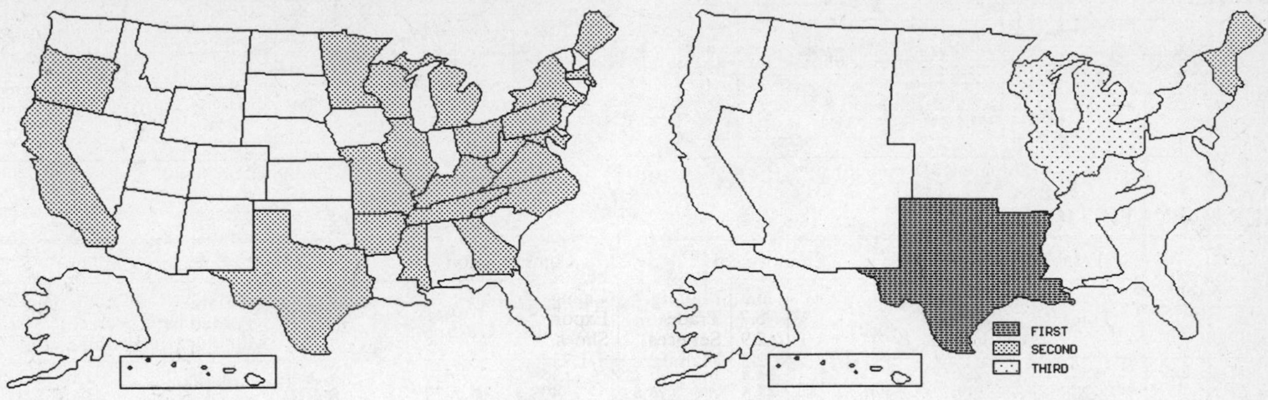

INDUSTRY DATA BY STATE

State	Establish-ments	Shipments			Employment				Cost as % of Shipments	Investment per Employee ($)
		Total ($ mil)	% of U.S.	Per Establ.	Total Number	% of U.S.	Per Establ.	Wages ($/hour)		
Maine	11	382.8	17.3	34.8	4,300	17.8	391	8.69	48.3	-
Texas	25	312.0	14.1	12.5	2,600	10.7	104	7.16	62.4	2,654
Tennessee	7	274.6	12.4	39.2	2,900	12.0	414	6.95	47.8	1,310
Wisconsin	11	198.4	9.0	18.0	2,000	8.3	182	8.37	56.6	1,000
Pennsylvania	12	143.6	6.5	12.0	1,900	7.9	158	7.59	51.1	789
Massachusetts	8	47.0	2.1	5.9	700	2.9	88	8.00	59.1	857
California	11	(D)	-	-	375 *	1.5	34	-	-	-
North Carolina	6	(D)	-	-	1,750 *	7.2	292	-	-	914
Missouri	5	(D)	-	-	1,750 *	7.2	350	-	-	-
Arkansas	4	(D)	-	-	750 *	3.1	188	-	-	-
Minnesota	4	(D)	-	-	1,750 *	7.2	438	-	-	-
New York	4	(D)	-	-	375 *	1.5	94	-	-	-
Virginia	4	(D)	-	-	750 *	3.1	188	-	-	-
Michigan	3	(D)	-	-	375 *	1.5	125	-	-	-
Oregon	3	(D)	-	-	175 *	0.7	58	-	-	1,143
Maryland	2	(D)	-	-	175 *	0.7	88	-	-	-
Mississippi	2	(D)	-	-	375 *	1.5	188	-	-	-
Georgia	1	(D)	-	-	375 *	1.5	375	-	-	-
Illinois	1	(D)	-	-	375 *	1.5	375	-	-	-
Kentucky	1	(D)	-	-	175 *	0.7	175	-	-	-
Ohio	1	(D)	-	-	375 *	1.5	375	-	-	-
West Virginia	1	(D)	-	-	750 *	3.1	750	-	-	-

Source: 1992 *Economic Census*. The states are in descending order of shipments or establishments (if shipment data are missing for the majority). The symbol (D) appears when data are withheld to prevent disclosure of competitive information. States marked with (D) are sorted by number of establishments. A dash (-) indicates that the data element cannot be calculated; * indicates the midpoint of a range.

3144 - WOMEN'S FOOTWEAR EXCEPT ATHLETIC

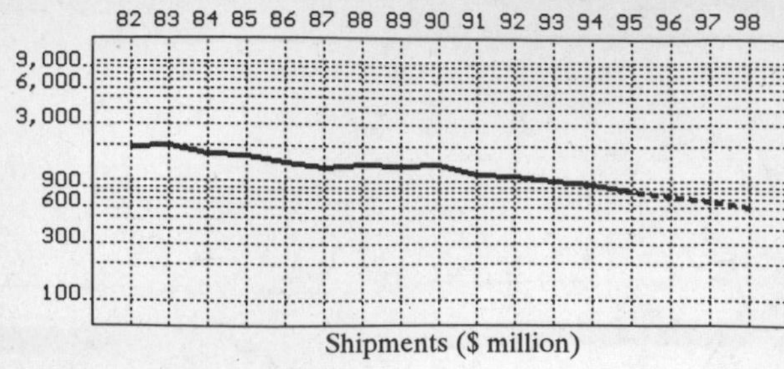

Shipments ($ million)

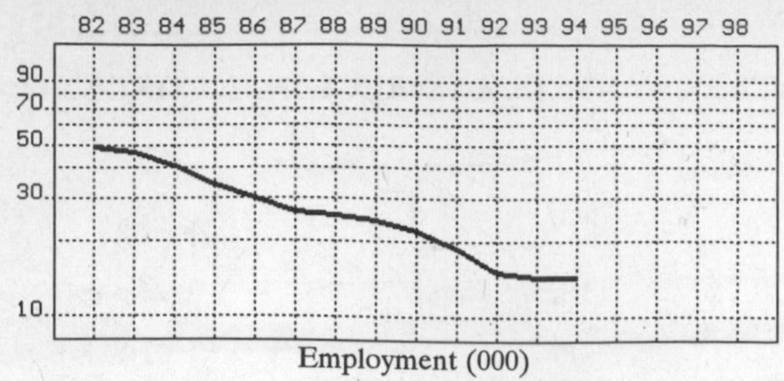

Employment (000)

GENERAL STATISTICS

Year	Com-panies	Establishments		Employment			Compensation		Production ($ million)			
		Total	with 20 or more employees	Total (000)	Production Workers (000)	Production Hours (Mil)	Payroll ($ mil)	Wages ($/hr)	Cost of Materials	Value Added by Manufacture	Value of Shipments	Capital Invest.
1982	209	293	226	48.4	43.4	77.1	483.1	5.10	821.9	1,107.0	1,933.2	20.2
1983		268	208	46.5	41.5	74.4	495.4	5.29	809.9	1,156.2	1,957.7	22.8
1984		243	190	40.7	36.1	63.7	431.2	5.32	737.1	987.1	1,728.1	23.2
1985		219	172	34.3	30.3	54.9	378.8	5.39	684.1	919.6	1,613.0	12.3
1986		192	148	30.2	26.3	46.5	341.9	5.80	597.8	812.3	1,425.9	13.8
1987	122	163	123	26.6	23.7	45.5	320.0	5.56	572.4	755.8	1,316.0	11.3
1988		156	113			44.7	320.2		655.4	716.2	1,373.5	12.4
1989		137	104	24.5	20.5	40.5	290.3	5.57	645.7	703.0	1,351.3	11.1
1990		128	99	22.2	19.1	35.8	292.8	5.96	727.9	682.7	1,393.2	13.4
1991		126	95	19.0	17.0	31.0	247.9	6.10	505.5	633.7	1,153.7	9.1
1992	99	127	77	15.0	13.2	23.7	219.5	7.01	479.6	636.9	1,095.1	10.5
1993		124	77	14.4	12.7	22.5	219.8	7.50	449.1	569.4	1,010.3	6.8
1994		77P	45P	14.4	12.8	22.5	211.8	7.31	403.4	550.2	949.9	7.6
1995		61P	31P			12.3P	158.9P		359.7P	490.7P	847.1P	5.1P
1996		45P	17P			7.7P	134.9P		325.7P	444.3P	767.0P	3.9P
1997		29P	3P			3.0P	110.9P		291.7P	397.9P	686.9P	2.7P
1998		13P					86.8P		257.7P	351.5P	606.8P	1.5P

Sources: 1982, 1987, 1992 *Economic Census*; *Annual Survey of Manufactures*, 83-86, 88-91, 93-94. Establishment counts for non-Census years are from *County Business Patterns*; establishment values for 83-84 are extrapolations. 'P's show projections by the editors. Industries reclassified in 87 will not have data for prior years.

INDICES OF CHANGE

Year	Com-panies	Establishments		Employment			Compensation		Production ($ million)			
		Total	with 20 or more employees	Total (000)	Production Workers (000)	Production Hours (Mil)	Payroll ($ mil)	Wages ($/hr)	Cost of Materials	Value Added by Manufacture	Value of Shipments	Capital Invest.
1982	211	231	294	323	329	325	220	73	171	174	177	192
1983		211	270	310	314	314	226	75	169	182	179	217
1984		191	247	271	273	269	196	76	154	155	158	221
1985		172	223	229	230	232	173	77	143	144	147	117
1986		151	192	201	199	196	156	83	125	128	130	131
1987	123	128	160	177	180	192	146	79	119	119	120	108
1988		123	147			189	146		137	112	125	118
1989		108	135	163	155	171	132	79	135	110	123	106
1990		101	129	148	145	151	133	85	152	107	127	128
1991		99	123	127	129	131	113	87	105	99	105	87
1992	100	100	100	100	100	100	100	100	100	100	100	100
1993		98	100	96	96	95	100	107	94	89	92	65
1994		61P	59P	96	97	95	96	104	84	86	87	72
1995		48P	41P			52P	72P		75P	77P	77P	48P
1996		36P	23P			32P	61P		68P	70P	70P	37P
1997		23P	5P			13P	51P		61P	62P	63P	26P
1998		11P					40P		54P	55P	55P	14P

Sources: Same as General Statistics. Values reflect change from the base year, 1992. Values above 100 mean greater than 92, values below 100 mean less than 92, and a value of 100 in the 82-91 or 93-98 period means same as 92. 'P's mark projections by the editors.

SELECTED RATIOS

For 1994	Avg. of All Manufact.	Analyzed Industry	Index	For 1994	Avg. of All Manufact.	Analyzed Industry	Index
Employees per Establishment	49	186	380	Value Added per Production Worker	134,084	42,984	32
Payroll per Establishment	1,500,273	2,737,184	182	Cost per Establishment	5,045,178	5,213,315	103
Payroll per Employee	30,620	14,708	48	Cost per Employee	102,970	28,014	27
Production Workers per Establishment	34	165	482	Cost per Production Worker	146,988	31,516	21
Wages per Establishment	853,319	2,125,583	249	Shipments per Establishment	9,576,895	12,275,974	128
Wages per Production Worker	24,861	12,850	52	Shipments per Employee	195,460	65,965	34
Hours per Production Worker	2,056	1,758	85	Shipments per Production Worker	279,017	74,211	27
Wages per Hour	12.09	7.31	60	Investment per Establishment	321,011	98,218	31
Value Added per Establishment	4,602,255	7,110,476	154	Investment per Employee	6,552	528	8
Value Added per Employee	93,930	38,208	41	Investment per Production Worker	9,352	594	6

Sources: Same as General Statistics. The 'Average of All Manufacturing' column represents the average of all manufacturing industries reported for the most recent complete year available. The Index shows the relationship between the Average and the Analyzed Industry. For example, 100 means that they are equal; 500 that the Analyzed Industry is five times the average; 50 means that the Analyzed Industry is half the national average. The abbreviation 'na' is used to show that data are 'not available'.

LEADING COMPANIES Number shown: 25 Total sales ($ mil): 767 Total employment (000): 7.3

Company Name	Address				CEO Name	Phone	Co. Type	Sales ($ mil)	Empl. (000)
Brown Shoe Co	PO Box 354	St Louis	MO	63166	Thomas A Williams	314-854-4000	S	210•	2.9
Cherokee Shoe Co	2985 E Hillcrest Dr	Westlake Vil	CA	91362		805-496-1777	D	114	0.3
Bally Inc	1 Bally Pl	New Rochelle	NY	10801	John Heinn	914-632-4444	S	100	0.3
Kenneth Cole Productions Inc	152 W 57th St	New York	NY	10019	Kenneth D Cole	212-265-1500	P	85	0.3
Maxwell Shoe Company Inc	101 Sprague St	Boston	MA	02136	Maxwell V Blum	617-364-5090	P	50	<0.1
Eastland Shoe Mfg Corp	5 Park St	Freeport	ME	04032	James B Klein	207-865-6314	R	39•	0.6
Shaer Shoe Corp	PO Box 10600	Bedford	NH	03102	Milton Shaer	603-625-8566	R	21•	0.6
Beaver Shoe Co	Snyder Av	Beaver Springs	PA	17812	Harold Rowen	717-658-2473	S	17•	0.3
Cardinal Shoe Corp	PO Box 1349	Lawrence	MA	01842	Alan C Ornsteen	508-686-9706	R	15	0.3
Pleasant Mountain	Halifax St	Bridgton	ME	04009	Dan Wellehan	207-854-8474	D	15	0.3
Penobscot Shoe Co	PO Box 545	Old Town	ME	04468	Paul Hansen	207-827-4431	P	15	0.1
Penn Footwear Co	PO Box 87	Nanticoke	PA	18634	William Davidowitz	717-735-3200	R	11•	0.2
Northland Shoe Corp	58 Main St	Fryeburg	ME	04037	Joyce Taylor	207-935-2540	D	10•	0.2
Johansen Brothers Shoe Co	710 N Tucker Blv	St Louis	MO	63101	Paul E Johansen Jr	314-231-0700	R	9	0.2
Clinic Shoe Co	Carnation Dr	Aurora	MO	65605	Garry Neilson	417-678-2181	S	9	0.1
Steven Madden Ltd	52-16 Barnett Av	Long Island Ct	NY	11104	Steven Madden	718-446-1800	P	9	<0.1
Cels Enterprises Inc	3485 S La Cienega	Los Angeles	CA	90016	Bob Goldman	310-838-2103	R	8•	0.2
Marx and Newman	1 Eastwood Dr	Cincinnati	OH	45227	Peter Berunelle	513-527-7000	D	7•	0.1
Easy Spirit Shoes	1 Eastwood Dr	Cincinnati	OH	45227	Joe Dzialo	513-527-7707	D	6	0.1
Ugg Holdings Inc	2221 Las Palmas Dr	Carlsbad	CA	92009	Ron Cunningham	619-431-8090	R	5	<0.1
Intershoe Inc	57 Seaview Blv	Pt Washington	NY	11005	Arnold Dunn	516-484-9595	R	4•	<0.1
Dyeables Inc	Robin Hill	Patterson	NY	12563	Jim Botti	914-878-8000	R	3•	<0.1
Sbicca of California	PO Box 3807	S El Monte	CA	91733	Arthur Sbicca Sr	818-443-2281	R	3	<0.1
Prima Royale Enterprises Ltd	2119 S Myrtle Av	Monrovia	CA	91016	Harry Chow	818-303-0898	R	2	<0.1
Stuart Weitzman Inc	50 W 57th St	New York	NY	10019	Stuart Weitzman	212-582-9500	R	1	<0.1

Source: *Ward's Business Directory of U.S. Private and Public Companies*, Volumes 1 and 2, 1996. The company type code used is as follows: P - Public, R - Private, S - Subsidiary, D - Division, J - Joint Venture, A - Affiliate, G - Group. Sales are in millions of dollars, employees are in thousands. An asterisk (*) indicates an estimated sales volume. The symbol < stands for 'less than'. Company names and addresses are truncated, in some cases, to fit into the available space.

MATERIALS CONSUMED

Material		Quantity	Delivered Cost ($ million)
Materials, ingredients, containers, and supplies		(X)	452.2
Plastics coated, impregnated, or laminated fabrics	mil sq yd	6.8*	32.1
Plastics and natural or synthetic rubber cut stock and findings		(X)	16.9
Composition cut stock and findings		(X)	(D)
Leather and other material cut stock and findings		(X)	22.5
Plastics products consumed in the form of sheets, rods, tubes, film, and other shapes		(X)	(D)
Finished upper leather	mil sq ft	68.7	184.9
Finished soling leather	mil pairs	31.5*	36.2
Other finished leather		(X)	(D)
Paper and paperboard containers, including shipping sacks and other paper packaging supplies		(X)	14.7
All other materials and components, parts, containers, and supplies		(X)	76.8
Materials, ingredients, containers, and supplies, nsk		(X)	35.7

Source: 1992 *Economic Census*. Explanation of symbols used: (D): Withheld to avoid disclosure of competitive data; na: Not available; (S): Withheld because statistical norms were not met; (X): Not applicable; (Z): Less than half the unit shown; nec: Not elsewhere classified; nsk: Not specified by kind; - : zero; * : 10-19 percent estimated; ** : 20-29 percent estimated.

PRODUCT SHARE DETAILS

Product or Product Class	% Share	Product or Product Class	% Share
Women's footwear, except athletic	100.00		

Source: 1992 *Economic Census*. The values shown are percent of total shipments in an industry. Values of indented subcategories are summed in the main heading. The symbol (D) appears when data are withheld to prevent disclosure of competitive information. The abbreviation nsk stands for 'not specified by kind' and nec for 'not elsewhere classified'.

INPUTS AND OUTPUTS FOR SHOES, EXCEPT RUBBER

Economic Sector or Industry Providing Inputs	%	Sector	Economic Sector or Industry Buying Outputs	%	Sector
Imports	53.7	Foreign	Personal consumption expenditures	96.0	
Leather tanning & finishing	15.5	Manufg.	Change in business inventories	1.7	In House
Wholesale trade	3.7	Trade	Exports	1.4	Foreign
Advertising	2.9	Services	Shoes, except rubber	0.4	Manufg.
Fabricated rubber products, nec	2.8	Manufg.	S/L Govt. purch., correction	0.2	S/L Govt
Boot & shoe cutstock & findings	2.5	Manufg.	Federal Government purchases, national defense	0.1	Fed Govt
Miscellaneous plastics products	1.5	Manufg.			
Coated fabrics, not rubberized	1.4	Manufg.			
Banking	1.4	Fin/R.E.			
Paperboard containers & boxes	1.3	Manufg.			
Needles, pins, & fasteners	1.1	Manufg.			
Plastics materials & resins	1.0	Manufg.			
U.S. Postal Service	0.9	Gov't			
Electric services (utilities)	0.7	Util.			
Shoes, except rubber	0.6	Manufg.			
Eating & drinking places	0.6	Trade			
Equipment rental & leasing services	0.6	Services			
Thread mills	0.5	Manufg.			
Motor freight transportation & warehousing	0.5	Util.			
Narrow fabric mills	0.4	Manufg.			
Chemical preparations, nec	0.3	Manufg.			
Communications, except radio & TV	0.3	Util.			
Detective & protective services	0.3	Services			
Maintenance of nonfarm buildings nec	0.2	Constr.			
Adhesives & sealants	0.2	Manufg.			
Broadwoven fabric mills	0.2	Manufg.			
Cyclic crudes and organics	0.2	Manufg.			
Machinery, except electrical, nec	0.2	Manufg.			
Nonwoven fabrics	0.2	Manufg.			
Textile goods, nec	0.2	Manufg.			
Air transportation	0.2	Util.			
Real estate	0.2	Fin/R.E.			
Royalties	0.2	Fin/R.E.			
Computer & data processing services	0.2	Services			
Legal services	0.2	Services			
Management & consulting services & labs	0.2	Services			
Polishes & sanitation goods	0.1	Manufg.			
Wood products, nec	0.1	Manufg.			
Yarn mills & finishing of textiles, nec	0.1	Manufg.			
Water transportation	0.1	Util.			
Accounting, auditing & bookkeeping	0.1	Services			
Automotive repair shops & services	0.1	Services			
Hotels & lodging places	0.1	Services			
Laundry, dry cleaning, shoe repair	0.1	Services			

Source: Benchmark Input-Output Accounts for the U.S. Economy, 1982, U.S. Department of Commerce, Washington, D.C., July 1991. Data, as reported in the source, are organized by the 1977 SIC structure in use in 1982 but have been matched, as closely as is possible, to the 1987 SIC structure used in this book.

OCCUPATIONS EMPLOYED BY SIC 314 - FOOTWEAR, EX RUBBER AND PLASTIC

Occupation	% of Total 1994	Change to 2005	Occupation	% of Total 1994	Change to 2005
Shoe sewing machine operators	18.8	-72.1	Sewers, hand	2.4	-64.2
Shoe & leather workers & repairers, precision	13.7	-49.7	Inspectors, testers, & graders, precision	2.1	-44.2
Assemblers, fabricators, & hand workers nec	8.7	-44.1	Freight, stock, & material movers, hand	1.6	-55.3
Helpers, laborers, & material movers nec	4.9	-44.2	Sales & related workers nec	1.4	-44.1
Cutting & slicing machine setters, operators	4.7	-38.5	General managers & top executives	1.3	-47.1
Hand packers & packagers	4.6	-52.1	Traffic, shipping, & receiving clerks	1.3	-46.2
Blue collar worker supervisors	3.4	-47.2	Coating, painting, & spraying machine workers	1.2	-44.1
Cement & gluing machine operators	3.3	-83.2	Cutters & trimmers, hand	1.1	-49.8
Machine operators nec	3.2	-50.8	Industrial machinery mechanics	1.1	-38.6

Source: Industry-Occupation Matrix, Bureau of Labor Statistics. These data relate to one or more 3-digit SIC industry groups rather than to a single 4-digit SIC. The change reported for each occupation to the year 2005 is a percent of growth or decline as estimated by the Bureau of Labor Statistics. The abbreviation nec stands for 'not elsewhere classified'.

LOCATION BY STATE AND REGIONAL CONCENTRATION

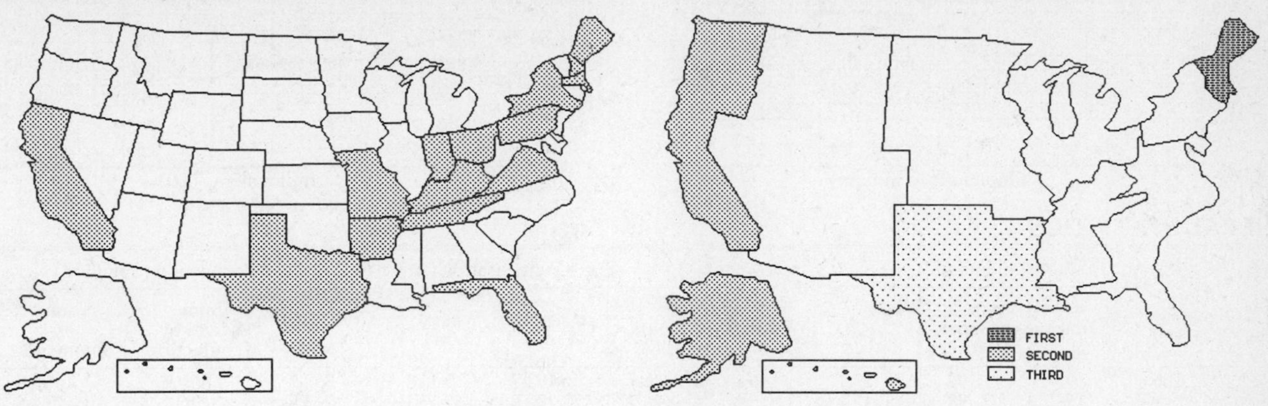

INDUSTRY DATA BY STATE

State	Establish-ments	Shipments			Employment				Cost as % of Shipments	Investment per Employee ($)
		Total ($ mil)	% of U.S.	Per Establ.	Total Number	% of U.S.	Per Establ.	Wages ($/hour)		
Maine	11	112.2	10.2	10.2	1,600	10.7	145	7.36	54.2	-
California	20	53.4	4.9	2.7	900	6.0	45	8.20	34.1	444
New York	17	35.6	3.3	2.1	500	3.3	29	6.71	29.8	800
Massachusetts	5	34.6	3.2	6.9	600	4.0	120	7.18	61.6	-
Arkansas	10	(D)	-	-	1,750 *	11.7	175	-	-	-
Missouri	10	(D)	-	-	1,750 *	11.7	175	-	-	-
Tennessee	10	(D)	-	-	1,750 *	11.7	175	-	-	-
Texas	9	(D)	-	-	750 *	5.0	83	-	-	-
New Hampshire	6	(D)	-	-	750 *	5.0	125	-	-	-
Florida	5	(D)	-	-	175 *	1.2	35	-	-	571
Indiana	3	(D)	-	-	750 *	5.0	250	-	-	-
Ohio	3	(D)	-	-	750 *	5.0	250	-	-	-
Kentucky	2	(D)	-	-	750 *	5.0	375	-	-	-
Pennsylvania	2	(D)	-	-	175 *	1.2	88	-	-	-
Virginia	2	(D)	-	-	375 *	2.5	188	-	-	-

Source: 1992 *Economic Census*. The states are in descending order of shipments or establishments (if shipment data are missing for the majority). The symbol (D) appears when data are withheld to prevent disclosure of competitive information. States marked with (D) are sorted by number of establishments. A dash (-) indicates that the data element cannot be calculated; * indicates the midpoint of a range.

3149 - FOOTWEAR, EXCEPT RUBBER, NEC

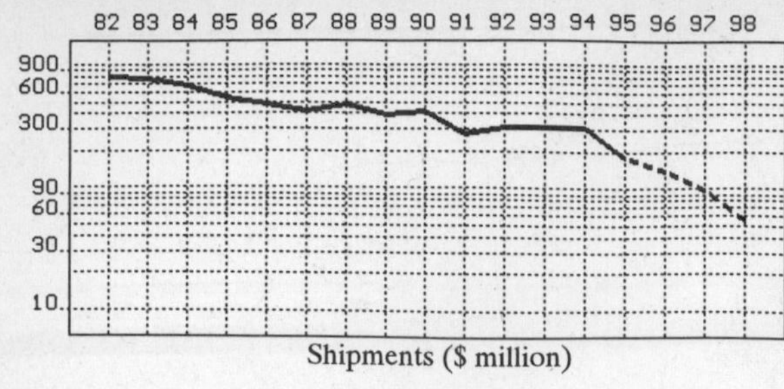

Shipments ($ million)

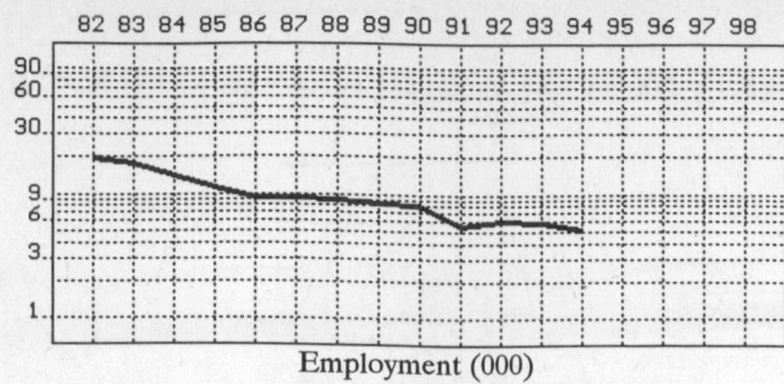

Employment (000)

GENERAL STATISTICS

Year	Companies	Establishments		Employment			Compensation		Production ($ million)			
		Total	with 20 or more employees	Total (000)	Production Workers (000)	Production Hours (Mil)	Payroll ($ mil)	Wages ($/hr)	Cost of Materials	Value Added by Manufacture	Value of Shipments	Capital Invest.
1982	166	193	107	19.1	16.8	28.7	192.7	5.11	352.8	450.9	798.9	14.0
1983		178	98	17.4	15.2	26.7	182.9	5.13	333.8	426.0	764.5	7.7
1984		163	89	14.0	12.1	21.1	155.2	5.22	311.2	363.2	676.2	8.6
1985		147	81	11.2	9.7	17.2	125.6	5.35	272.2	274.0	541.4	7.9
1986		128	75	9.2	7.9	13.8	111.4	5.75	254.3	232.5	481.7	5.7
1987	120	129	61	9.2	8.0	14.5	108.6	5.61	202.2	217.2	419.3	6.6
1988		115	58			14.9	113.4		252.7	228.8	472.3	5.1
1989		109	50	8.5	6.5	12.6	98.6	5.83	192.3	206.7	395.5	4.6
1990		102	48	8.0	6.4	11.8	99.5	6.13	197.9	218.2	414.1	2.6
1991		100	46	5.6	4.8	9.0	73.4	5.80	133.3	152.1	279.7	1.9
1992	84	94	41	6.0	5.2	9.1	84.4	6.77	149.4	159.0	308.6	5.8
1993		92	42	5.8	4.9	8.7	83.4	7.03	154.0	156.7	310.3	4.9
1994		70P	26P	5.2	4.6	8.6	77.1	6.53	147.8	160.2	308.9	3.1
1995		61P	20P			4.0P	51.8P		86.8P	94.1P	181.4P	1.5P
1996		52P	14P			2.4P	42.7P		66.8P	72.4P	139.5P	0.9P
1997		43P	7P			0.8P	33.5P		46.7P	50.6P	97.6P	0.3P
1998		34P	1P				24.4P		26.7P	28.9P	55.7P	

Sources: 1982, 1987, 1992 *Economic Census*; *Annual Survey of Manufactures*, 83-86, 88-91, 93-94. Establishment counts for non-Census years are from *County Business Patterns*; establishment values for 83-84 are extrapolations. 'P's show projections by the editors. Industries reclassified in 87 will not have data for prior years.

INDICES OF CHANGE

Year	Companies	Establishments		Employment			Compensation		Production ($ million)			
		Total	with 20 or more employees	Total (000)	Production Workers (000)	Production Hours (Mil)	Payroll ($ mil)	Wages ($/hr)	Cost of Materials	Value Added by Manufacture	Value of Shipments	Capital Invest.
1982	198	205	261	318	323	315	228	75	236	284	259	241
1983		189	239	290	292	293	217	76	223	268	248	133
1984		173	217	233	233	232	184	77	208	228	219	148
1985		156	198	187	187	189	149	79	182	172	175	136
1986		136	183	153	152	152	132	85	170	146	156	98
1987	143	137	149	153	154	159	129	83	135	137	136	114
1988		122	141			164	134		169	144	153	88
1989		116	122	142	125	138	117	86	129	130	128	79
1990		109	117	133	123	130	118	91	132	137	134	45
1991		106	112	93	92	99	87	86	89	96	91	33
1992	100	100	100	100	100	100	100	100	100	100	100	100
1993		98	102	97	94	96	99	104	103	99	101	84
1994		74P	64P	87	88	95	91	96	99	101	100	53
1995		65P	48P			44P	61P		58P	59P	59P	27P
1996		55P	33P			27P	51P		45P	46P	45P	16P
1997		45P	18P			9P	40P		31P	32P	32P	5P
1998		36P	3P				29P		18P	18P	18P	

Sources: Same as General Statistics. Values reflect change from the base year, 1992. Values above 100 mean greater than 92, values below 100 mean less than 92, and a value of 100 in the 82-91 or 93-98 period means same as 92. 'P's mark projections by the editors.

SELECTED RATIOS

For 1994	Avg. of All Manufact.	Analyzed Industry	Index
Employees per Establishment	49	74	152
Payroll per Establishment	1,500,273	1,101,667	73
Payroll per Employee	30,620	14,827	48
Production Workers per Establishment	34	66	191
Wages per Establishment	853,319	802,431	94
Wages per Production Worker	24,861	12,208	49
Hours per Production Worker	2,056	1,870	91
Wages per Hour	12.09	6.53	54
Value Added per Establishment	4,602,255	2,289,067	50
Value Added per Employee	93,930	30,808	33

For 1994	Avg. of All Manufact.	Analyzed Industry	Index
Value Added per Production Worker	134,084	34,826	26
Cost per Establishment	5,045,178	2,111,886	42
Cost per Employee	102,970	28,423	28
Cost per Production Worker	146,988	32,130	22
Shipments per Establishment	9,576,895	4,413,813	46
Shipments per Employee	195,460	59,404	30
Shipments per Production Worker	279,017	67,152	24
Investment per Establishment	321,011	44,295	14
Investment per Employee	6,552	596	9
Investment per Production Worker	9,352	674	7

Sources: Same as General Statistics. The 'Average of All Manufacturing' column represents the average of all manufacturing industries reported for the most recent complete year available. The Index shows the relationship between the Average and the Analyzed Industry. For example, 100 means that they are equal; 500 that the Analyzed Industry is five times the average; 50 means that the Analyzed Industry is half the national average. The abbreviation 'na' is used to show that data are 'not available'.

LEADING COMPANIES

Number shown: **31** Total sales ($ mil): **5,996** Total employment (000): **21.7**

Company Name	Address				CEO Name	Phone	Co. Type	Sales ($ mil)	Empl. (000)
Nike Inc	1 Bowerman Dr	Beaverton	OR	97005	Philip H Knight	503-671-6453	P	3,790	9.6
Stride Rite Corp	5 Cambridge Ctr	Cambridge	MA	02142	Robert C Siegel	617-491-8800	P	524	3.7
LA Gear Inc	2850 Ocean Pk Blvd	Santa Monica	CA	90405	Stanley P Gold	310-452-4327	P	416	0.7
Converse Inc	1 Fordham Rd	North Reading	MA	01864	Gilbert Ford	508-664-1100	P	380	3.1
K-Swiss Inc	20664 Bahama St	Chatsworth	CA	91331	Steven Nickols	818-998-3388	P	155	0.3
Etonic Inc	147 Centre St	Brockton	MA	02402	William Kirkendall	508-583-9100	S	149	0.3
Hyde Athletic Industries Inc	13 Centennial Dr	Peabody	MA	01960	John H Fisher	508-532-9000	P	108	0.4
Barry Manufacturing Company	Bubier St	Lynn	MA	01901	Richard Rothbard	617-598-1055	R	79*	0.2
Brooks Sports Inc	11720 N Creek N	Bothell	WA	98011	Helen Rockey	206-488-3131	R	70	<0.1
Gator Industries Inc	1000 SE 8th St	Hialeah	FL	33010	G Miranda Jr	305-888-5000	R	60	0.8
Ballet Makers Inc	1 Campus Rd	Totowa	NJ	07512	A Terlizzi	201-595-9000	R	50	0.6
Fancy Feet Inc	1850 W 11 Mile Rd	Berkley	MI	48072	Mary Ann Fontana	313-585-8460	R	39*	0.1
Badorf Shoe Company Inc	101 W Lincoln Av	Lititz	PA	17543	Duane Gingerich	717-626-8521	R	31*	<0.1
Jumping Jacks	PO Box 6048	Hot Springs	AR	71901	Jim Shumacher	501-262-6000	D	27	0.4
Tobin-Hamilton Company Inc	PO Box 227	Mansfield	MO	65704	Edward Tognoni	417-924-3223	R	25*	0.3
Trimfoot Co	115 Trimfoot Ter	Farmington	MO	63640	Tim Corbet	314-756-6616	S	18*	0.4
Spot-Bilt Inc	99 Farm Rd	Bangor	ME	04401	Douglas Later	207-942-5222	S	16*	0.1
QF and C Foot Apparel Ltd	803 Westover St	Oconomowoc	WI	53066	Dan Dooley	414-567-4416	R	15*	<0.1
Newville Shoe	14-16 S Washington	Newville	PA	17241	Ron Laurett	717-776-3141	D	10	0.1
Tanel Corp	1818 N Water St	Milwaukee	WI	53201	Michael Tanel	414-271-7005	R	9*	<0.1
Brookside Enterprises Inc	7 E Fredrick Pl	Cedar Knolls	NJ	07927	Mario Lubrani	201-993-9020	S	5	<0.1
Lind Shoe Co	501 Laser Dr	Somerset	WI	54025	Jeffrey R Lind	715-247-5463	R	4*	<0.1
Ephrata Shoe Company Inc	PO Box 29	Ephrata	PA	17522	J Daniel Mentzer	717-733-2215	R	4	<0.1
Saddlecraft Inc	PO Box 308	Cherokee	NC	28719	Paul T Brown	704-497-4051	R	4	0.1
Walkin Shoe Company Inc	PO Box 30	Schuylkill H	PA	17972	S Ngan	717-385-0100	R	3*	<0.1
Conaway-Winter Inc	PO Box 280	Willow Springs	MO	65793	Truman Wiles	417-469-3125	R	2*	0.1
Kepner-Scott Shoe Company Inc	209 N Liberty St	Orwigsburg	PA	17961	H Clair Zimmerman	717-366-0229	R	2	<0.1
StoneMark Inc	27 Congress St	Salem	MA	01970	Stephen Encarnacao	508-744-9600	R	1	<0.1
Maytown Shoe Manufacturing	1820 8th Av	Altoona	PA	16602	V Lombardo	814-943-5343	R	1*	<0.1
Bear Feet	PO Box 549	Brownwood	TX	76804	Mary Stanley	915-646-0141	R	0	<0.1
NaturalSport	8300 Maryland Av	St Louis	MO	63105	Tom Williams	314-854-4000	D	0*	<0.1

Source: *Ward's Business Directory of U.S. Private and Public Companies*, Volumes 1 and 2, 1996. The company type code used is as follows: P - Public, R - Private, S - Subsidiary, D - Division, J - Joint Venture, A - Affiliate, G - Group. Sales are in millions of dollars, employees are in thousands. An asterisk (*) indicates an estimated sales volume. The symbol < stands for 'less than'. Company names and addresses are truncated, in some cases, to fit into the available space.

MATERIALS CONSUMED

Material		Quantity	Delivered Cost ($ million)
Materials, ingredients, containers, and supplies		(X)	132.9
Plastics coated, impregnated, or laminated fabrics	mil sq yd	5.9*	21.9
Plastics and natural or synthetic rubber cut stock and findings		(X)	12.9
Composition cut stock and findings		(X)	(D)
Leather and other material cut stock and findings		(X)	16.6
Plastics products consumed in the form of sheets, rods, tubes, film, and other shapes		(X)	(D)
Finished upper leather	mil sq ft	19.2	38.2
Finished soling leather	mil pairs	10.9*	7.3
Other finished leather		(X)	0.4
Paper and paperboard containers, including shipping sacks and other paper packaging supplies		(X)	7.7
All other materials and components, parts, containers, and supplies		(X)	19.3
Materials, ingredients, containers, and supplies, nsk		(X)	5.5

Source: 1992 *Economic Census*. Explanation of symbols used: (D): Withheld to avoid disclosure of competitive data; na: Not available; (S): Withheld because statistical norms were not met; (X): Not applicable; (Z): Less than half the unit shown; nec: Not elsewhere classified; nsk: Not specified by kind; - : zero; * : 10-19 percent estimated; ** : 20-29 percent estimated.

PRODUCT SHARE DETAILS

Product or Product Class	% Share	Product or Product Class	% Share
Footwear, except rubber, nec	100.00	All other footwear, including youths' and boys', misses', children's, and infants' (excluding rubber and slippers)	63.97
Athletic shoes, except rubber sole/fabric upper	33.29		

Source: 1992 *Economic Census*. The values shown are percent of total shipments in an industry. Values of indented subcategories are summed in the main heading. The symbol (D) appears when data are withheld to prevent disclosure of competitive information. The abbreviation nsk stands for 'not specified by kind' and nec for 'not elsewhere classified'.

INPUTS AND OUTPUTS FOR SHOES, EXCEPT RUBBER

Economic Sector or Industry Providing Inputs	%	Sector	Economic Sector or Industry Buying Outputs	%	Sector
Imports	53.7	Foreign	Personal consumption expenditures	96.0	
Leather tanning & finishing	15.5	Manufg.	Change in business inventories	1.7	In House
Wholesale trade	3.7	Trade	Exports	1.4	Foreign
Advertising	2.9	Services	Shoes, except rubber	0.4	Manufg.
Fabricated rubber products, nec	2.8	Manufg.	S/L Govt. purch., correction	0.2	S/L Govt
Boot & shoe cutstock & findings	2.5	Manufg.	Federal Government purchases, national defense	0.1	Fed Govt
Miscellaneous plastics products	1.5	Manufg.			
Coated fabrics, not rubberized	1.4	Manufg.			
Banking	1.4	Fin/R.E.			
Paperboard containers & boxes	1.3	Manufg.			
Needles, pins, & fasteners	1.1	Manufg.			
Plastics materials & resins	1.0	Manufg.			
U.S. Postal Service	0.9	Gov't			
Electric services (utilities)	0.7	Util.			
Shoes, except rubber	0.6	Manufg.			
Eating & drinking places	0.6	Trade			
Equipment rental & leasing services	0.6	Services			
Thread mills	0.5	Manufg.			
Motor freight transportation & warehousing	0.5	Util.			
Narrow fabric mills	0.4	Manufg.			
Chemical preparations, nec	0.3	Manufg.			
Communications, except radio & TV	0.3	Util.			
Detective & protective services	0.3	Services			
Maintenance of nonfarm buildings nec	0.2	Constr.			
Adhesives & sealants	0.2	Manufg.			
Broadwoven fabric mills	0.2	Manufg.			
Cyclic crudes and organics	0.2	Manufg.			
Machinery, except electrical, nec	0.2	Manufg.			
Nonwoven fabrics	0.2	Manufg.			
Textile goods, nec	0.2	Manufg.			
Air transportation	0.2	Util.			
Real estate	0.2	Fin/R.E.			
Royalties	0.2	Fin/R.E.			
Computer & data processing services	0.2	Services			
Legal services	0.2	Services			
Management & consulting services & labs	0.2	Services			
Polishes & sanitation goods	0.1	Manufg.			
Wood products, nec	0.1	Manufg.			
Yarn mills & finishing of textiles, nec	0.1	Manufg.			
Water transportation	0.1	Util.			
Accounting, auditing & bookkeeping	0.1	Services			
Automotive repair shops & services	0.1	Services			
Hotels & lodging places	0.1	Services			
Laundry, dry cleaning, shoe repair	0.1	Services			

Source: Benchmark Input-Output Accounts for the U.S. Economy, 1982, U.S. Department of Commerce, Washington, D.C., July 1991. Data, as reported in the source, are organized by the 1977 SIC structure in use in 1982 but have been matched, as closely as is possible, to the 1987 SIC structure used in this book.

OCCUPATIONS EMPLOYED BY SIC 314 - FOOTWEAR, EX RUBBER AND PLASTIC

Occupation	% of Total 1994	Change to 2005	Occupation	% of Total 1994	Change to 2005
Shoe sewing machine operators	18.8	-72.1	Sewers, hand	2.4	-64.2
Shoe & leather workers & repairers, precision	13.7	-49.7	Inspectors, testers, & graders, precision	2.1	-44.2
Assemblers, fabricators, & hand workers nec	8.7	-44.1	Freight, stock, & material movers, hand	1.6	-55.3
Helpers, laborers, & material movers nec	4.9	-44.2	Sales & related workers nec	1.4	-44.1
Cutting & slicing machine setters, operators	4.7	-38.5	General managers & top executives	1.3	-47.1
Hand packers & packagers	4.6	-52.1	Traffic, shipping, & receiving clerks	1.3	-46.2
Blue collar worker supervisors	3.4	-47.2	Coating, painting, & spraying machine workers	1.2	-44.1
Cement & gluing machine operators	3.3	-83.2	Cutters & trimmers, hand	1.1	-49.8
Machine operators nec	3.2	-50.8	Industrial machinery mechanics	1.1	-38.6

Source: Industry-Occupation Matrix, Bureau of Labor Statistics. These data relate to one or more 3-digit SIC industry groups rather than to a single 4-digit SIC. The change reported for each occupation to the year 2005 is a percent of growth or decline as estimated by the Bureau of Labor Statistics. The abbreviation nec stands for 'not elsewhere classified'.

LOCATION BY STATE AND REGIONAL CONCENTRATION

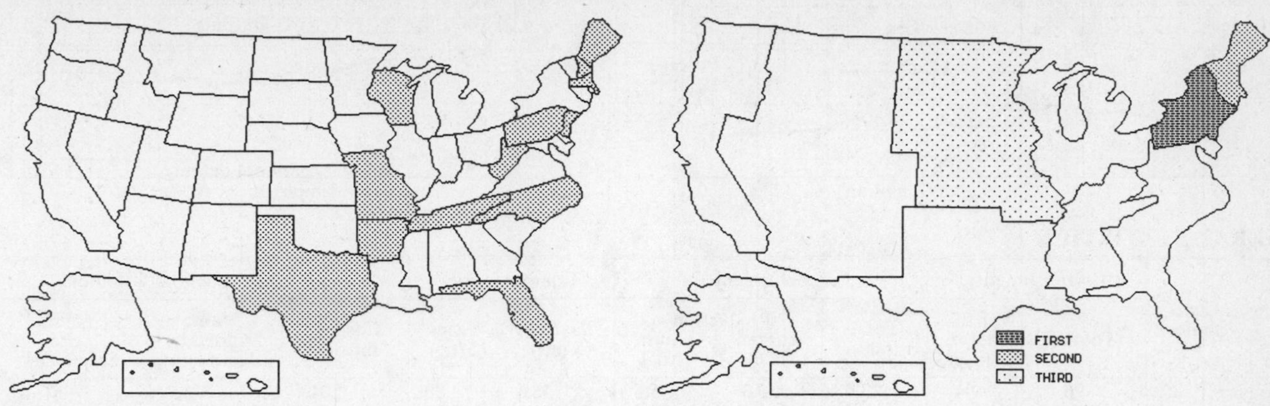

INDUSTRY DATA BY STATE

State	Establish-ments	Shipments			Employment				Cost as % of Shipments	Investment per Employee ($)
		Total ($ mil)	% of U.S.	Per Establ.	Total Number	% of U.S.	Per Establ.	Wages ($/hour)		
Missouri	11	76.0	24.6	6.9	1,500	25.0	136	7.14	44.5	867
Pennsylvania	12	47.7	15.5	4.0	1,000	16.7	83	6.80	46.1	-
Massachusetts	6	31.2	10.1	5.2	500	8.3	83	7.86	44.2	-
Florida	7	(D)	-	-	375 *	6.3	54	-	-	-
Wisconsin	6	(D)	-	-	175 *	2.9	29	-	-	-
Maine	5	(D)	-	-	375 *	6.3	75	-	-	-
Texas	4	(D)	-	-	375 *	6.3	94	-	-	-
Arkansas	2	(D)	-	-	750 *	12.5	375	-	-	-
New Hampshire	2	(D)	-	-	175 *	2.9	88	-	-	-
New Jersey	2	(D)	-	-	175 *	2.9	88	-	-	-
North Carolina	2	(D)	-	-	175 *	2.9	88	-	-	-
Tennessee	2	(D)	-	-	750 *	12.5	375	-	-	-
West Virginia	1	(D)	-	-	175 *	2.9	175	-	-	-

Source: 1992 *Economic Census*. The states are in descending order of shipments or establishments (if shipment data are missing for the majority). The symbol (D) appears when data are withheld to prevent disclosure of competitive information. States marked with (D) are sorted by number of establishments. A dash (-) indicates that the data element cannot be calculated; * indicates the midpoint of a range.

3151 - LEATHER GLOVES & MITTENS

Shipments ($ million)

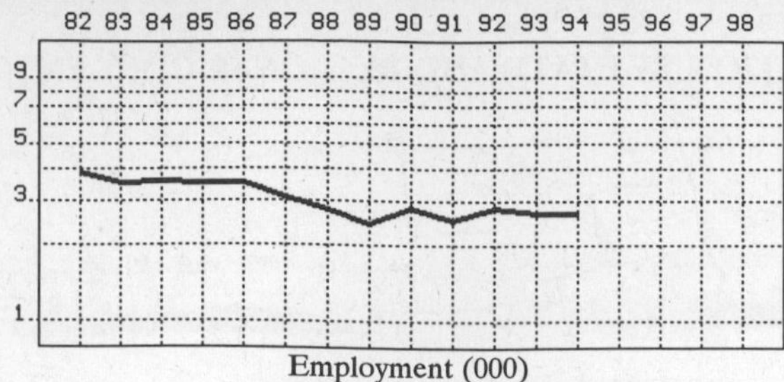

Employment (000)

GENERAL STATISTICS

Year	Com-panies	Establishments Total	Establishments with 20 or more employees	Employment Total (000)	Production Workers (000)	Production Hours (Mil)	Compensation Payroll ($ mil)	Compensation Wages ($/hr)	Cost of Materials	Value Added by Manufacture	Value of Shipments	Capital Invest.
1982	80	96	54	3.9	3.3	5.6	36.6	4.80	104.4	72.5	177.6	0.7
1983				3.5	3.0	4.5	31.8	5.38	99.7	69.1	167.4	0.8
1984				3.6	3.2	5.6	34.4	4.70	109.2	72.4	180.8	0.9
1985				3.5	3.1	5.3	32.3	4.62	112.1	65.5	177.6	1.0
1986				3.5	3.1	5.4	33.7	4.76	131.0	63.4	202.9	0.8
1987	67	77	45	3.1	2.7	4.9	33.6	5.33	112.3	74.6	184.8	0.7
1988						4.5	32.4		118.0	73.3	191.5	0.6
1989		75	41	2.4	2.1	3.8	26.6	5.47	69.4	51.4	148.7	0.5
1990				2.8	2.4	4.2	33.6	6.33	99.3	59.2	154.8	0.5
1991				2.5	2.1	4.1	33.3	6.22	84.4	58.1	141.1	0.2
1992	56	71	39	2.8	2.4	4.4	36.2	6.16	69.6	65.9	136.9	0.5
1993				2.7	2.4	4.3	33.6	6.33	84.8	82.0	169.2	0.3
1994				2.7	2.4	4.2	34.9	6.71	86.2	63.4	142.5	12.2
1995						3.9P	33.4P		86.8P	63.9P	143.6P	3.9P
1996						3.7P	33.4P		84.8P	62.4P	140.2P	4.2P
1997						3.6P	33.4P		82.7P	60.8P	136.8P	4.6P
1998						3.5P	33.4P		80.7P	59.3P	133.4P	4.9P

Sources: 1982, 1987, 1992 *Economic Census*; *Annual Survey of Manufactures*, 83-86, 88-91, 93-94. Establishment counts for non-Census years are from *County Business Patterns*; establishment values for 83-84 are extrapolations. 'P's show projections by the editors. Industries reclassified in 87 will not have data for prior years.

INDICES OF CHANGE

Year	Com-panies	Establishments Total	Establishments with 20 or more employees	Employment Total (000)	Production Workers (000)	Production Hours (Mil)	Compensation Payroll ($ mil)	Compensation Wages ($/hr)	Cost of Materials	Value Added by Manufacture	Value of Shipments	Capital Invest.
1982	143	135	138	139	137	127	101	78	150	110	130	140
1983				125	125	102	88	87	143	105	122	160
1984				129	133	127	95	76	157	110	132	180
1985				125	129	120	89	75	161	99	130	200
1986				125	129	123	93	77	188	96	148	160
1987	120	108	115	111	113	111	93	87	161	113	135	140
1988						102	90		170	111	140	120
1989		106	105	86	87	86	73	89	100	78	109	100
1990				100	100	95	93	103	143	90	113	100
1991				89	87	93	92	101	121	88	103	40
1992	100	100	100	100	100	100	100	100	100	100	100	100
1993				96	100	98	93	103	122	124	124	60
1994				96	100	95	96	109	124	96	104	2,440
1995						88P	92P		125P	97P	105P	778P
1996						85P	92P		122P	95P	102P	845P
1997						82P	92P		119P	92P	100P	913P
1998						80P	92P		116P	90P	97P	981P

Sources: Same as General Statistics. Values reflect change from the base year, 1992. Values above 100 mean greater than 92, values below 100 mean less than 92, and a value of 100 in the 82-91 or 93-98 period means same as 92. 'P's mark projections by the editors.

SELECTED RATIOS

For 1992	Avg. of All Manufact.	Analyzed Industry	Index	For 1992	Avg. of All Manufact.	Analyzed Industry	Index
Employees per Establishment	46	39	86	Value Added per Production Worker	122,353	27,458	22
Payroll per Establishment	1,332,320	509,859	38	Cost per Establishment	4,239,462	980,282	23
Payroll per Employee	29,181	12,929	44	Cost per Employee	92,853	24,857	27
Production Workers per Establishment	31	34	108	Cost per Production Worker	135,003	29,000	21
Wages per Establishment	734,496	381,746	52	Shipments per Establishment	8,100,800	1,928,169	24
Wages per Production Worker	23,390	11,293	48	Shipments per Employee	177,425	48,893	28
Hours per Production Worker	2,025	1,833	91	Shipments per Production Worker	257,966	57,042	22
Wages per Hour	11.55	6.16	53	Investment per Establishment	278,244	7,042	3
Value Added per Establishment	3,842,210	928,169	24	Investment per Employee	6,094	179	3
Value Added per Employee	84,153	23,536	28	Investment per Production Worker	8,861	208	2

Sources: Same as General Statistics. The 'Average of All Manufacturing' column represents the average of all manufacturing industries reported for the most recent complete year available. The Index shows the relationship between the Average and the Analyzed Industry. For example, 100 means that they are equal; 500 that the Analyzed Industry is five times the average; 50 means that the Analyzed Industry is half the national average. The abbreviation 'na' is used to show that data are 'not available'.

LEADING COMPANIES

Number shown: **17** Total sales ($ mil): **399** Total employment (000): **1.7**

Company Name	Address				CEO Name	Phone	Co. Type	Sales ($ mil)	Empl. (000)
Aris Isotoner Inc	417 5th Av	New York	NY	10016	Lari Stanton	212-532-8627	D	250*	0.2
Fownes Brothers and Company	411 5th Av	New York	NY	10016	Thomas Gluckman	212-683-0150	R	38	0.2
Pacific Great Lakes Corp	1375 E 9th St #950	Cleveland	OH	44114	Thomas Coakley	216-623-6300	R	32	0.3
Gates Mills Inc	Harrison St	Johnstown	NY	12095	William B Gates	518-762-4526	R	20	0.2
North Star Glove Co	PO Box 1214	Tacoma	WA	98401	Robert G Wekell	206-627-7107	R	10*	0.1
Guard-Line Inc	PO Box 1030	Atlanta	TX	75551	Dennis Stanley	903-796-4111	R	8	0.2
Genco Corp	PO Box 231	Chattanooga	TN	37401		615-265-4513	S	6	0.1
Ross Glove Co	PO Box 209	Sheboygan	WI	53082	Carl Ross	414-457-4331	R	6	<0.1
Elliott Corp	PO Box 410	Oconto	WI	54153	Thomas Coakley	414-834-5622	S	5	<0.1
Elmer Little and Sons Inc	PO Box 867	Gloversville	NY	12078	Ichiro Kuwahara	518-725-2000	S	5	<0.1
Montpelier Glove Company Inc	PO Box 187	Hartford	KY	42347	Hugh M Smaltz II	502-298-3622	R	5	0.1
Joseph P Conroy Inc	PO Box 505	Johnstown	NY	12095	Joseph P Conroy	518-762-9444	R	4	<0.1
Glove Corp Heber Springs	PO Box 151	Heber Springs	AR	72543	Roger Rew	501-362-2437	D	3	<0.1
Napa Glove Company Inc	PO Box 509	Napa	CA	94559	EE Deits	707-226-1888	R	3	<0.1
Leisure Leather Ltd	86 E Fulton St	Gloversville	NY	12078	EP Fritts	518-773-7373	R	2	<0.1
Carolina Amato Inc	389 5th Av	New York	NY	10016	Carolina Amato	212-532-8413	R	1	<0.1
Modern Gloves Inc	16 Mill St	Gloversville	NY	12078	Frank L Vertucci	518-725-3725	R	0	<0.1

Source: *Ward's Business Directory of U.S. Private and Public Companies*, Volumes 1 and 2, 1996. The company type code is used as follows: P - Public, R - Private, S - Subsidiary, D - Division, J - Joint Venture, A - Affiliate, G - Group. Sales are in millions of dollars, employees are in thousands. An asterisk (*) indicates an estimated sales volume. The symbol < stands for 'less than'. Company names and addresses are truncated, in some cases, to fit into the available space.

MATERIALS CONSUMED

Material		Quantity	Delivered Cost ($ million)
Materials, ingredients, containers, and supplies		(X)	56.0
Broadwoven fabrics (piece goods)	mil lin yd	(S)	3.6
Knit fabrics	mil lb	1.5*	3.6
Finished leather	mil sq ft	37.8*	33.9
All other materials and components, parts, containers, and supplies		(X)	7.3
Materials, ingredients, containers, and supplies, nsk		(X)	7.6

Source: 1992 *Economic Census*. Explanation of symbols used: (D): Withheld to avoid disclosure of competitive data; na: Not available; (S): Withheld because statistical norms were not met; (X): Not applicable; (Z): Less than half the unit shown; nec: Not elsewhere classified; nsk: Not specified by kind; - : zero; * : 10-19 percent estimated; ** : 20-29 percent estimated.

PRODUCT SHARE DETAILS

Product or Product Class	% Share	Product or Product Class	% Share
Leather gloves and mittens	100.00		

Source: 1992 *Economic Census*. The values shown are percent of total shipments in an industry. Values of indented subcategories are summed in the main heading. The symbol (D) appears when data are withheld to prevent disclosure of competitive information. The abbreviation nsk stands for 'not specified by kind' and nec for 'not elsewhere classified'.

INPUTS AND OUTPUTS FOR LEATHER GLOVES & MITTENS

Economic Sector or Industry Providing Inputs	%	Sector	Economic Sector or Industry Buying Outputs	%	Sector
Imports	39.1	Foreign	Personal consumption expenditures	95.0	
Leather tanning & finishing	24.0	Manufg.	Exports	3.2	Foreign
Air transportation	14.9	Util.	Leather gloves & mittens	0.8	Manufg.
Broadwoven fabric mills	2.8	Manufg.	Motion pictures	0.8	Services
Wholesale trade	2.8	Trade	Federal Government purchases, national defense	0.2	Fed Govt
Knit fabric mills	2.5	Manufg.			
Thread mills	1.7	Manufg.			
Hotels & lodging places	1.4	Services			
Paperboard containers & boxes	1.1	Manufg.			
Electric services (utilities)	1.1	Util.			
Leather gloves & mittens	0.8	Manufg.			
Gas production & distribution (utilities)	0.8	Util.			
Eating & drinking places	0.7	Trade			
Advertising	0.7	Services			
Communications, except radio & TV	0.6	Util.			
Plastics materials & resins	0.5	Manufg.			
Motor freight transportation & warehousing	0.5	Util.			
Real estate	0.4	Fin/R.E.			
Coated fabrics, not rubberized	0.3	Manufg.			
Banking	0.3	Fin/R.E.			

Continued on next page.

INPUTS AND OUTPUTS FOR LEATHER GLOVES & MITTENS - Continued

Economic Sector or Industry Providing Inputs	%	Sector	Economic Sector or Industry Buying Outputs	%	Sector
Commercial printing	0.2	Manufg.			
Automotive repair shops & services	0.2	Services			
Detective & protective services	0.2	Services			
Equipment rental & leasing services	0.2	Services			
Management & consulting services & labs	0.2	Services			
Distilled liquor, except brandy	0.1	Manufg.			
Accounting, auditing & bookkeeping	0.1	Services			
Electrical repair shops	0.1	Services			
Legal services	0.1	Services			

Source: Benchmark Input-Output Accounts for the U.S. Economy, 1982, U.S. Department of Commerce, Washington, D.C., July 1991. Data, as reported in the source, are organized by the 1977 SIC structure in use in 1982 but have been matched, as closely as is possible, to the 1987 SIC structure used in this book.

OCCUPATIONS EMPLOYED BY SIC 315 - LUGGAGE, HANDBAGS, AND LEATHER PRODUCTS, NEC

Occupation	% of Total 1994	Change to 2005	Occupation	% of Total 1994	Change to 2005
Assemblers, fabricators, & hand workers nec	11.7	-22.1	Freight, stock, & material movers, hand	2.5	-37.7
Sewing machine operators, non-garment	9.7	-68.8	Sales & related workers nec	2.3	-22.1
Shoe & leather workers & repairers, precision	7.1	-29.9	Cement & gluing machine operators	2.3	-49.4
Sewing machine operators, garment	5.4	-29.9	Crushing & mixing machine operators	1.7	-22.1
Helpers, laborers, & material movers nec	4.9	-22.1	Bookkeeping, accounting, & auditing clerks	1.3	-41.6
Blue collar worker supervisors	4.4	-26.2	General office clerks	1.3	-33.6
Cutting & slicing machine setters, operators	4.1	-14.3	Coating, painting, & spraying machine workers	1.3	-22.1
Machine operators nec	3.9	-31.3	Hand packers & packagers	1.2	-33.3
Inspectors, testers, & graders, precision	2.9	-22.1	Secretaries, ex legal & medical	1.2	-29.0
Cutters & trimmers, hand	2.7	-29.9	Shoe sewing machine operators	1.1	-37.6
General managers & top executives	2.7	-26.1	Industrial production managers	1.1	-22.1
Traffic, shipping, & receiving clerks	2.6	-25.0	Sewers, hand	1.0	-50.0
Machine feeders & offbearers	2.5	-29.9			

Source: Industry-Occupation Matrix, Bureau of Labor Statistics. These data relate to one or more 3-digit SIC industry groups rather than to a single 4-digit SIC. The change reported for each occupation to the year 2005 is a percent of growth or decline as estimated by the Bureau of Labor Statistics. The abbreviation nec stands for 'not elsewhere classified'.

LOCATION BY STATE AND REGIONAL CONCENTRATION

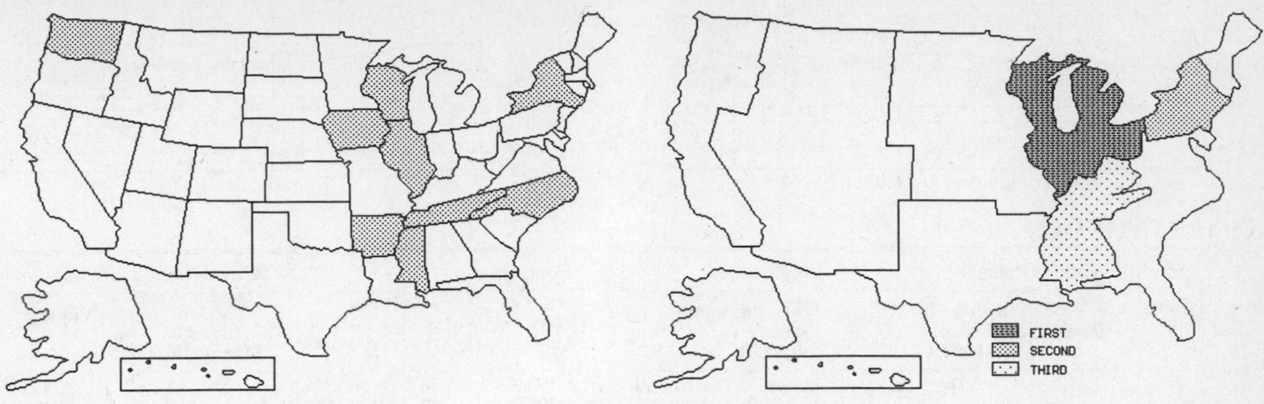

INDUSTRY DATA BY STATE

State	Establish-ments	Shipments			Employment				Cost as % of Shipments	Investment per Employee ($)
		Total ($ mil)	% of U.S.	Per Establ.	Total Number	% of U.S.	Per Establ.	Wages ($/hour)		
Wisconsin	12	26.4	19.3	2.2	400	14.3	33	6.43	56.1	250
Arkansas	4	18.7	13.7	4.7	300	10.7	75	6.40	42.2	333
Mississippi	6	16.8	12.3	2.8	400	14.3	67	5.29	47.6	-
Illinois	5	9.7	7.1	1.9	300	10.7	60	5.60	55.7	-
Washington	5	2.3	1.7	0.5	100	3.6	20	11.00	43.5	-
New York	11	(D)	-	-	175 *	6.3	16	-	-	-
Iowa	3	(D)	-	-	175 *	6.3	58	-	-	-
Tennessee	2	(D)	-	-	175 *	6.3	88	-	-	-
North Carolina	1	(D)	-	-	175 *	6.3	175	-	-	-

Source: 1992 *Economic Census*. The states are in descending order of shipments or establishments (if shipment data are missing for the majority). The symbol (D) appears when data are withheld to prevent disclosure of competitive information. States marked with (D) are sorted by number of establishments. A dash (-) indicates that the data element cannot be calculated; * indicates the midpoint of a range.

3161 - LUGGAGE

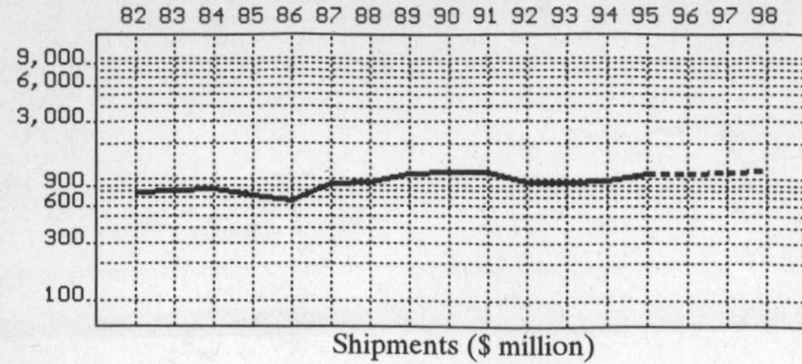

Shipments ($ million)

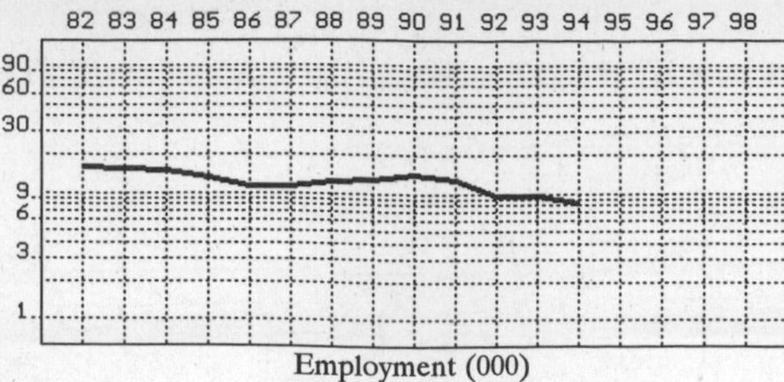

Employment (000)

GENERAL STATISTICS

Year	Companies	Establishments: Total	Establishments: with 20 or more employees	Employment: Total (000)	Production Workers (000)	Production Hours (Mil)	Compensation: Payroll ($ mil)	Compensation: Wages ($/hr)	Production ($ million): Cost of Materials	Value Added by Manufacture	Value of Shipments	Capital Invest.
1982	287	292	131	16.0	12.5	21.0	193.8	5.36	355.5	432.8	789.0	12.0
1983				15.3	11.8	20.2	206.8	5.57	362.8	442.9	813.5	8.4
1984				14.7	11.4	20.9	207.2	5.71	388.9	467.8	827.1	10.3
1985				13.1	9.8	17.1	189.5	6.16	349.8	371.9	724.6	10.6
1986				11.4	8.3	14.6	165.7	6.24	318.2	338.8	665.8	9.5
1987	231	241	109	11.4	8.3	15.1	195.7	6.89	430.0	505.9	928.9	11.8
1988						14.9	192.1		447.1	504.5	956.7	9.2
1989		216	110	12.9	9.7	17.3	216.7	7.12	520.9	604.8	1,121.2	15.0
1990				14.0	10.8	16.9	244.0	8.36	544.3	618.0	1,169.4	11.5
1991				12.5	9.4	14.3	230.3	8.80	541.9	598.3	1,147.5	9.6
1992	284	292	110	9.7	7.6	14.2	181.8	7.50	448.9	494.9	944.0	14.5
1993				9.6	7.4	14.7	189.7	7.50	464.7	490.7	930.4	16.4
1994				8.5	6.6	12.7	174.3	7.83	450.3	548.7	991.4	9.5
1995						12.4P	198.9P		502.3P	612.1P	1,105.9P	13.2P
1996						11.8P	198.9P		514.1P	626.5P	1,131.9P	13.4P
1997						11.2P	198.8P		525.9P	640.9P	1,157.9P	13.7P
1998						10.6P	198.8P		537.8P	655.3P	1,184.0P	13.9P

Sources: 1982, 1987, 1992 *Economic Census*; *Annual Survey of Manufactures*, 83-86, 88-91, 93-94. Establishment counts for non-Census years are from *County Business Patterns*; establishment values for 83-84 are extrapolations. 'P's show projections by the editors. Industries reclassified in 87 will not have data for prior years.

INDICES OF CHANGE

Year	Companies	Establishments: Total	Establishments: with 20 or more employees	Employment: Total (000)	Production Workers (000)	Production Hours (Mil)	Compensation: Payroll ($ mil)	Compensation: Wages ($/hr)	Production ($ million): Cost of Materials	Value Added by Manufacture	Value of Shipments	Capital Invest.
1982	101	100	119	165	164	148	107	71	79	87	84	83
1983				158	155	142	114	74	81	89	86	58
1984				152	150	147	114	76	87	95	88	71
1985				135	129	120	104	82	78	75	77	73
1986				118	109	103	91	83	71	68	71	66
1987	81	83	99	118	109	106	108	92	96	102	98	81
1988						105	106		100	102	101	63
1989		74	100	133	128	122	119	95	116	122	119	103
1990				144	142	119	134	111	121	125	124	79
1991				129	124	101	127	117	121	121	122	66
1992	100	100	100	100	100	100	100	100	100	100	100	100
1993				99	97	104	104	100	104	99	99	113
1994				88	87	89	96	104	100	111	105	66
1995						87P	109P		112P	124P	117P	91P
1996						83P	109P		115P	127P	120P	93P
1997						79P	109P		117P	129P	123P	94P
1998						75P	109P		120P	132P	125P	96P

Sources: Same as General Statistics. Values reflect change from the base year, 1992. Values above 100 mean greater than 92, values below 100 mean less than 92, and a value of 100 in the 82-91 or 93-98 period means same as 92. 'P's mark projections by the editors.

SELECTED RATIOS

For 1992	Avg. of All Manufact.	Analyzed Industry	Index
Employees per Establishment	46	33	73
Payroll per Establishment	1,332,320	622,603	47
Payroll per Employee	29,181	18,742	64
Production Workers per Establishment	31	26	83
Wages per Establishment	734,496	364,726	50
Wages per Production Worker	23,390	14,013	60
Hours per Production Worker	2,025	1,868	92
Wages per Hour	11.55	7.50	65
Value Added per Establishment	3,842,210	1,694,863	44
Value Added per Employee	84,153	51,021	61

For 1992	Avg. of All Manufact.	Analyzed Industry	Index
Value Added per Production Worker	122,353	65,118	53
Cost per Establishment	4,239,462	1,537,329	36
Cost per Employee	92,853	46,278	50
Cost per Production Worker	135,003	59,066	44
Shipments per Establishment	8,100,800	3,232,877	40
Shipments per Employee	177,425	97,320	55
Shipments per Production Worker	257,966	124,211	48
Investment per Establishment	278,244	49,658	18
Investment per Employee	6,094	1,495	25
Investment per Production Worker	8,861	1,908	22

Sources: Same as General Statistics. The 'Average of All Manufacturing' column represents the average of all manufacturing industries reported for the most recent complete year available. The Index shows the relationship between the Average and the Analyzed Industry. For example, 100 means that they are equal; 500 that the Analyzed Industry is five times the average; 50 means that the Analyzed Industry is half the national average. The abbreviation 'na' is used to show that data are 'not available'.

LEADING COMPANIES

Number shown: **32** Total sales ($ mil): **2,209** Total employment (000): **16.3**

Company Name	Address				CEO Name	Phone	Co. Type	Sales ($ mil)	Empl. (000)
Hillenbrand Industries Inc	1069 State Rte 46 E	Batesville	IN	47006	WA Hillenbrand	812-934-7000	P	1,577	10.0
American Tourister Inc	91 Main St	Warren	RI	02885	John Pulichino	401-245-2100	S	140*	1.0
Samsonite Corp	11200 E 45th Av	Denver	CO	80239	Steve Green	303-373-2000	S	120	1.2
Humphrey's Inc	2009 W Hastings St	Chicago	IL	60608	Sheldon Young	312-997-2358	R	95	0.7
York Luggage Co	1422 Rte 179	Lambertville	NJ	08530	Jerome Popkin	609-397-2044	R	50	0.2
Hartmann Luggage Co	PO Box 550	Lebanon	TN	37087	Peter Lathrop	615-444-5000	S	46	0.6
Caseworks International Inc	1133 N Kilbourn	Chicago	IL	60651	Sukie Rapavi	312-772-1331	R	20	0.2
French Co	753 Arrow Grand	Covina	CA	91722	Tom Johnston	818-967-1511	R	20	0.2
Seward Co	434 High St	Petersburg	VA	23803	Nathan Hamner	804-733-5111	R	18*	0.2
Leather Specialty Co	10570 Chester Rd	Cincinnati	OH	45215	Michael Korchmar	513-771-0200	R	15*	0.2
Zero Enclosures	200 N 500 W	North Salt Lake	UT	84054	Jay Manwaring	801-298-5900	D	14*	0.3
Bob Allen Companies Inc	PO Box 477	Des Moines	IA	50302	Matthew R Allen	515-283-2191	R	11	0.2
Tannenbaum and Sons Inc	1045 43rd St	Brooklyn	NY	11219	H Tannenbaum	718-435-5986	R	10	0.2
Jameslee Corp	4619 N Ravenswood	Chicago	IL	60640	Chong H Lee	312-271-6000	R	9*	0.1
Mercury Luggage Mfg Co	PO Box 47558	Jacksonville	FL	32247	Andrew Pradella	904-733-9595	R	9	0.1
Neely Manufacturing Company	PO Box 338	Corydon	IA	50060	Tom Baranowski	515-872-1100	R	8	0.1
Fiberbilt Cases Inc	601 W 26th St	New York	NY	10001	AR Ernst	212-675-5820	R	6	0.1
Bel Aire Products Inc	PO Box 189	Akron	OH	44309	John Beringer	216-253-3116	R	5	<0.1
Dana Designs Ltd	1950 N 19th St	Bozeman	MT	59715	Dana Gleason	406-587-4188	R	5	0.1
Universal Trav-ler Inc	359 Wales Av	Bronx	NY	10454	J Ross	718-993-7100	R	5	<0.1
Lion Leather Products Inc	1831 Starr St	Ridgewood	NY	11385	Leo Mintzer	718-366-9133	R	4	<0.1
Tumi Luggage Inc	250 Lackland Dr	Middlesex	NJ	08846	Charles J Clifford	908-271-9500	R	4*	<0.1
Berman Leather Company Inc	25 WBD Melcher St	Boston	MA	02210	Robert S Berman	617-426-0870	R	3	<0.1
Savaage	PO Box 969	Smithtown	NY	11787	Lawrence Krulik	516-434-3777	R	3*	<0.1
Robert Manufacturing Company	1055 E 35th St	Hialeah	FL	33013	Peter Levine	305-691-5311	R	3	<0.1
Action USA Inc	PO Box 12689	St Petersburg	FL	33733	Naswa k Hahn	813-821-5000	R	2	<0.1
Delsey Luggage Inc	6735 Business Pkwy	Baltimore	MD	21227	Marc Ducloz	410-796-5655	S	2	<0.1
Savannah Luggage Works Inc	PO Box 447	Vidalia	GA	30474	Allen Rice	912-537-3016	R	2	0.2
S and S Leather Goods	11747 Darlington	Los Angeles	CA	90049	George Rapoport	310-207-2040	R	1	<0.1
Trimco Mfg & Eng	11142 Addison Av	Franklin Park	IL	60131	Robert L McKillop	708-288-0020	R	1	<0.1
Diversified Case Company Inc	50 Harbor Point	Utica	NY	13502	David Kerr	315-797-2725	R	1	<0.1
Madson Line	PO Box 338	Corte Madera	CA	94925	Michael Madson	415-927-3600	R	0	<0.1

Source: *Ward's Business Directory of U.S. Private and Public Companies*, Volumes 1 and 2, 1996. The company type code used is as follows: P - Public, R - Private, S - Subsidiary, D - Division, J - Joint Venture, A - Affiliate, G - Group. Sales are in millions of dollars, employees are in thousands. An asterisk (*) indicates an estimated sales volume. The symbol < stands for 'less than'. Company names and addresses are truncated, in some cases, to fit into the available space.

MATERIALS CONSUMED

Material	Quantity	Delivered Cost ($ million)
Materials, ingredients, containers, and supplies	(X)	376.0
Broadwoven fabrics (piece goods)	(X)	66.1
Plastics coated, impregnated, or laminated fabrics	(X)	85.2
Plastics resins consumed in the form of granules, pellets, powders, liquids, etc.	(X)	9.5
Plastics products consumed in the form of sheets, rods, tubes, film, and other shapes	(X)	19.4
Finished leather	(X)	38.5
Trunk and luggage hardware, including locks	(X)	37.9
All other materials and components, parts, containers, and supplies	(X)	78.5
Materials, ingredients, containers, and supplies, nsk	(X)	42.1

Source: 1992 *Economic Census*. Explanation of symbols used: (D): Withheld to avoid disclosure of competitive data; na: Not available; (S): Withheld because statistical norms were not met; (X): Not applicable; (Z): Less than half the unit shown; nec: Not elsewhere classified; nsk: Not specified by kind; - : zero; * : 10-19 percent estimated; ** : 20-29 percent estimated.

PRODUCT SHARE DETAILS

Product or Product Class	% Share	Product or Product Class	% Share
Luggage	100.00	Luggage tote bags, open, without closures	1.61
Hand luggage (including zippered), outer surface of all leather or mostly leather	7.73	Occupational luggage cases, sample cases, binocular, and camera cases	7.91
Hand luggage (including zippered), outer surface of all textile or mostly textile materials	22.70	Luggage trunks, hand trunks, and lockers	2.19
Hand luggage (including zippered), outer surface of supported vinyl or plastics	17.33	Briefcases, briefbags, school bags, envelopes, catalog cases, and zippered ring binders	9.16
Hand luggage (including zippered), molded and semimolded	(D)	Musical instrument cases	2.45
Hand luggage (including zippered), all other materials	(D)	Attache cases	5.36
		Other luggage	5.56

Source: 1992 *Economic Census*. The values shown are percent of total shipments in an industry. Values of indented subcategories are summed in the main heading. The symbol (D) appears when data are withheld to prevent disclosure of competitive information. The abbreviation nsk stands for 'not specified by kind' and nec for 'not elsewhere classified'.

INPUTS AND OUTPUTS FOR LUGGAGE

Economic Sector or Industry Providing Inputs	%	Sector	Economic Sector or Industry Buying Outputs	%	Sector
Imports	54.0	Foreign	Personal consumption expenditures	86.2	
Coated fabrics, not rubberized	6.0	Manufg.	Exports	3.5	Foreign
Wholesale trade	4.9	Trade	Eating & drinking places	2.0	Trade
Veneer & plywood	4.3	Manufg.	Retail trade, except eating & drinking	1.0	Trade
Hardware, nec	3.5	Manufg.	Musical instruments	0.7	Manufg.
Broadwoven fabric mills	3.3	Manufg.	Wholesale trade	0.7	Trade
Miscellaneous plastics products	2.2	Manufg.	Change in business inventories	0.6	In House
Leather tanning & finishing	1.7	Manufg.	Luggage	0.2	Manufg.
Narrow fabric mills	1.5	Manufg.	Motor freight transportation & warehousing	0.2	Util.
Nonwoven fabrics	1.5	Manufg.	Insurance carriers	0.2	Fin/R.E.
Plastics materials & resins	1.5	Manufg.	Hotels & lodging places	0.2	Services
Banking	1.4	Fin/R.E.	Communications, except radio & TV	0.1	Util.
Hotels & lodging places	1.2	Services	Banking	0.1	Fin/R.E.
Advertising	1.1	Services	Real estate	0.1	Fin/R.E.
Needles, pins, & fasteners	0.8	Manufg.	Labor, civic, social, & fraternal associations	0.1	Services
Thread mills	0.8	Manufg.	Management & consulting services & labs	0.1	Services
Business services nec	0.8	Services	S/L Govt. purch., other general government	0.1	S/L Govt
Electric services (utilities)	0.7	Util.			
Paperboard containers & boxes	0.6	Manufg.			
Eating & drinking places	0.6	Trade			
U.S. Postal Service	0.6	Gov't			
Felt goods, nec	0.4	Manufg.			
Communications, except radio & TV	0.4	Util.			
Motor freight transportation & warehousing	0.4	Util.			
Hardwood dimension & flooring mills	0.3	Manufg.			
Luggage	0.3	Manufg.			
Manufacturing industries, nec	0.3	Manufg.			
Sawmills & planning mills, general	0.3	Manufg.			
Yarn mills & finishing of textiles, nec	0.3	Manufg.			
Gas production & distribution (utilities)	0.3	Util.			
Railroads & related services	0.3	Util.			
Credit agencies other than banks	0.3	Fin/R.E.			
Real estate	0.3	Fin/R.E.			
Security & commodity brokers	0.3	Fin/R.E.			
Management & consulting services & labs	0.2	Services			
Services to dwellings & other buildings	0.2	Services			
Maintenance of nonfarm buildings nec	0.1	Constr.			
Wood products, nec	0.1	Manufg.			
Royalties	0.1	Fin/R.E.			
Accounting, auditing & bookkeeping	0.1	Services			
Computer & data processing services	0.1	Services			
Equipment rental & leasing services	0.1	Services			
Legal services	0.1	Services			

Source: Benchmark Input-Output Accounts for the U.S. Economy, 1982, U.S. Department of Commerce, Washington, D.C., July 1991. Data, as reported in the source, are organized by the 1977 SIC structure in use in 1982 but have been matched, as closely as is possible, to the 1987 SIC structure used in this book.

OCCUPATIONS EMPLOYED BY SIC 316 - LUGGAGE, HANDBAGS, AND LEATHER PRODUCTS, NEC

Occupation	% of Total 1994	Change to 2005	Occupation	% of Total 1994	Change to 2005
Assemblers, fabricators, & hand workers nec	11.7	-22.1	Freight, stock, & material movers, hand	2.5	-37.7
Sewing machine operators, non-garment	9.7	-68.8	Sales & related workers nec	2.3	-22.1
Shoe & leather workers & repairers, precision	7.1	-29.9	Cement & gluing machine operators	2.3	-49.4
Sewing machine operators, garment	5.4	-29.9	Crushing & mixing machine operators	1.7	-22.1
Helpers, laborers, & material movers nec	4.9	-22.1	Bookkeeping, accounting, & auditing clerks	1.3	-41.6
Blue collar worker supervisors	4.4	-26.2	General office clerks	1.3	-33.6
Cutting & slicing machine setters, operators	4.1	-14.3	Coating, painting, & spraying machine workers	1.3	-22.1
Machine operators nec	3.9	-31.3	Hand packers & packagers	1.2	-33.3
Inspectors, testers, & graders, precision	2.9	-22.1	Secretaries, ex legal & medical	1.2	-29.0
Cutters & trimmers, hand	2.7	-29.9	Shoe sewing machine operators	1.1	-37.6
General managers & top executives	2.7	-26.1	Industrial production managers	1.1	-22.1
Traffic, shipping, & receiving clerks	2.6	-25.0	Sewers, hand	1.0	-50.0
Machine feeders & offbearers	2.5	-29.9			

Source: Industry-Occupation Matrix, Bureau of Labor Statistics. These data relate to one or more 3-digit SIC industry groups rather than to a single 4-digit SIC. The change reported for each occupation to the year 2005 is a percent of growth or decline as estimated by the Bureau of Labor Statistics. The abbreviation nec stands for 'not elsewhere classified'.

LOCATION BY STATE AND REGIONAL CONCENTRATION

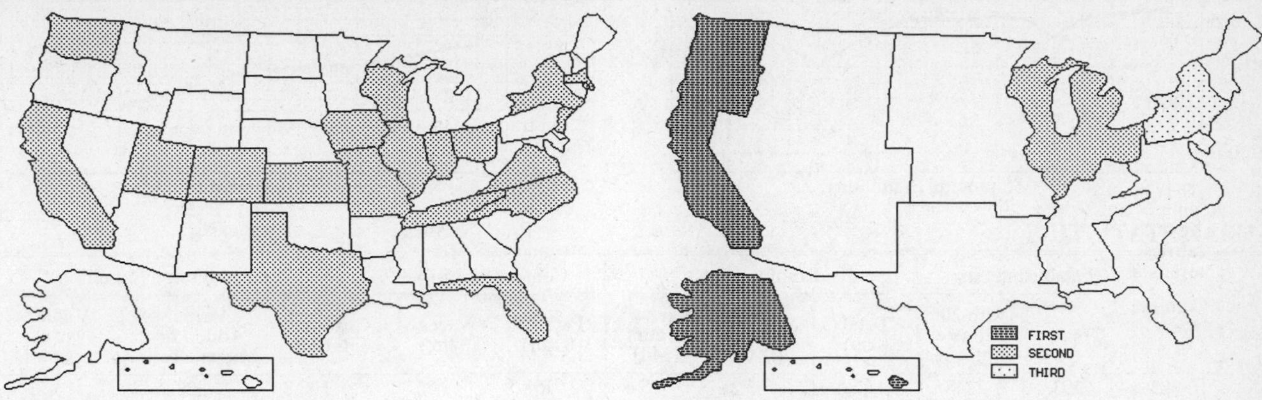

INDUSTRY DATA BY STATE

State	Establish-ments	Shipments			Employment				Cost as % of Shipments	Investment per Employee ($)
		Total ($ mil)	% of U.S.	Per Establ.	Total Number	% of U.S.	Per Establ.	Wages ($/hour)		
California	46	117.4	12.4	2.6	1,500	15.5	33	7.71	40.4	667
New York	42	96.6	10.2	2.3	1,100	11.3	26	7.53	46.0	1,000
Illinois	20	33.6	3.6	1.7	500	5.2	25	7.13	45.8	400
Indiana	12	28.3	3.0	2.4	700	7.2	58	6.33	39.9	429
Missouri	14	22.6	2.4	1.6	500	5.2	36	5.50	45.6	-
Florida	10	21.1	2.2	2.1	400	4.1	40	6.17	63.0	250
Ohio	11	15.4	1.6	1.4	200	2.1	18	9.67	40.3	500
North Carolina	7	9.0	1.0	1.3	100	1.0	14	6.50	42.2	-
Wisconsin	11	8.1	0.9	0.7	200	2.1	18	6.67	40.7	-
Texas	9	7.2	0.8	0.8	200	2.1	22	6.33	43.1	-
Utah	8	5.9	0.6	0.7	200	2.1	25	5.33	40.7	-
Colorado	15	(D)	-	-	1,750 *	18.0	117	-	-	-
Washington	11	(D)	-	-	375 *	3.9	34	-	-	533
Massachusetts	10	(D)	-	-	175 *	1.8	18	-	-	571
New Jersey	9	(D)	-	-	175 *	1.8	19	-	-	-
Iowa	5	(D)	-	-	375 *	3.9	75	-	-	-
Tennessee	4	(D)	-	-	375 *	3.9	94	-	-	-
Rhode Island	3	(D)	-	-	375 *	3.9	125	-	-	-
Virginia	3	(D)	-	-	175 *	1.8	58	-	-	-
Kansas	2	(D)	-	-	175 *	1.8	88	-	-	-

Source: 1992 *Economic Census*. The states are in descending order of shipments or establishments (if shipment data are missing for the majority). The symbol (D) appears when data are withheld to prevent disclosure of competitive information. States marked with (D) are sorted by number of establishments. A dash (-) indicates that the data element cannot be calculated; * indicates the midpoint of a range.

3171 - WOMEN'S HANDBAGS & PURSES

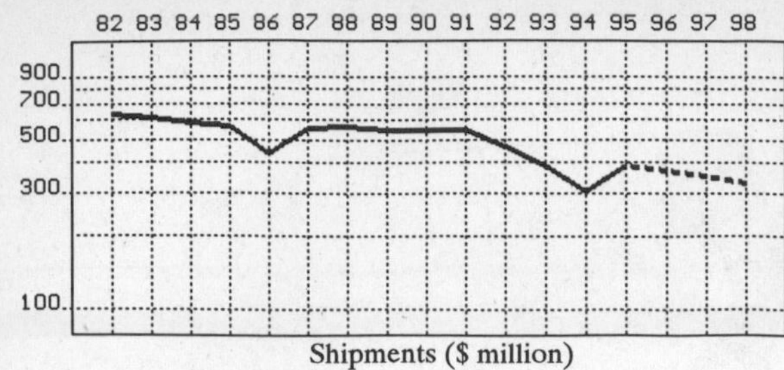

Shipments ($ million)

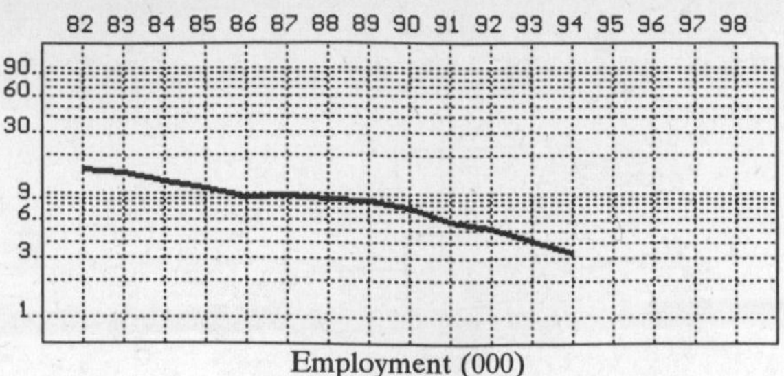

Employment (000)

GENERAL STATISTICS

Year	Com-panies	Establishments: Total	Establishments: with 20 or more employees	Employment: Total (000)	Employment: Production Workers (000)	Employment: Production Hours (Mil)	Compensation: Payroll ($ mil)	Compensation: Wages ($/hr)	Production ($ million): Cost of Materials	Production ($ million): Value Added by Manufacture	Production ($ million): Value of Shipments	Production ($ million): Capital Invest.
1982	383	393	148	15.4	13.2	25.6	158.5	4.36	302.2	320.4	623.7	5.6
1983		364	131	14.5	12.3	21.7	149.2	4.62	340.9	275.5	613.1	6.3
1984		335	114	12.4	10.3	19.2	128.3	4.43	305.6	261.3	585.1	7.8
1985		307	98	10.8	8.6	15.9	124.6	5.35	272.4	278.2	559.7	4.6
1986		279	94	9.2	7.3	13.0	100.7	5.44	219.9	215.2	438.4	3.5
1987	315	321	88	9.5	7.9	14.9	130.7	6.16	236.0	317.6	548.8	10.2
1988		284	92			14.1	139.8		238.6	326.3	563.3	8.1
1989		261	80	8.6	6.0	11.1	122.6	6.81	235.7	317.6	543.8	6.3
1990		235	66	7.6	5.1	9.6	110.8	6.83	227.7	319.7	546.9	6.8
1991		209	65	5.8	4.6	9.1	112.0	7.18	223.1	314.7	544.5	3.1
1992	205	213	62	5.1	4.1	7.3	94.7	8.29	189.2	274.3	462.8	3.4
1993		204	52	4.1	3.2	5.7	69.7	7.82	170.7	213.9	387.3	4.2
1994		175P	40P	3.3	2.8	5.8	49.0	6.79	145.9	161.4	303.9	3.1
1995		159P	33P			2.6P	67.9P		186.0P	205.7P	387.4P	3.9P
1996		142P	25P			1.1P	61.3P		177.1P	195.9P	368.9P	3.6P
1997		125P	17P				54.6P		168.2P	186.1P	350.3P	3.4P
1998		109P	9P				47.9P		159.3P	176.2P	331.8P	3.1P

Sources: 1982, 1987, 1992 *Economic Census*; *Annual Survey of Manufactures*, 83-86, 88-91, 93-94. Establishment counts for non-Census years are from *County Business Patterns*; establishment values for 83-84 are extrapolations. 'P's show projections by the editors. Industries reclassified in 87 will not have data for prior years.

INDICES OF CHANGE

Year	Com-panies	Establishments: Total	Establishments: with 20 or more employees	Employment: Total (000)	Employment: Production Workers (000)	Employment: Production Hours (Mil)	Compensation: Payroll ($ mil)	Compensation: Wages ($/hr)	Production ($ million): Cost of Materials	Production ($ million): Value Added by Manufacture	Production ($ million): Value of Shipments	Production ($ million): Capital Invest.
1982	187	185	239	302	322	351	167	53	160	117	135	165
1983		171	211	284	300	297	158	56	180	100	132	185
1984		157	184	243	251	263	135	53	162	95	126	229
1985		144	158	212	210	218	132	65	144	101	121	135
1986		131	152	180	178	178	106	66	116	78	95	103
1987	154	151	142	186	193	204	138	74	125	116	119	300
1988		133	148			193	148		126	119	122	238
1989		123	129	169	146	152	129	82	125	116	118	185
1990		110	106	149	124	132	117	82	120	117	118	200
1991		98	105	114	112	125	118	87	118	115	118	91
1992	100	100	100	100	100	100	100	100	100	100	100	100
1993		96	84	80	78	78	74	94	90	78	84	124
1994		82P	65P	65	68	79	52	82	77	59	66	91
1995		74P	53P			36P	72P		98P	75P	84P	114P
1996		67P	40P			15P	65P		94P	71P	80P	107P
1997		59P	28P				58P		89P	68P	76P	100P
1998		51P	15P				51P		84P	64P	72P	93P

Sources: Same as General Statistics. Values reflect change from the base year, 1992. Values above 100 mean greater than 92, values below 100 mean less than 92, and a value of 100 in the 82-91 or 93-98 period means same as 92. 'P's mark projections by the editors.

SELECTED RATIOS

For 1994	Avg. of All Manufact.	Analyzed Industry	Index
Employees per Establishment	49	19	38
Payroll per Establishment	1,500,273	279,492	19
Payroll per Employee	30,620	14,848	48
Production Workers per Establishment	34	16	47
Wages per Establishment	853,319	224,632	26
Wages per Production Worker	24,861	14,065	57
Hours per Production Worker	2,056	2,071	101
Wages per Hour	12.09	6.79	56
Value Added per Establishment	4,602,255	920,612	20
Value Added per Employee	93,930	48,909	52

For 1994	Avg. of All Manufact.	Analyzed Industry	Index
Value Added per Production Worker	134,084	57,643	43
Cost per Establishment	5,045,178	832,201	16
Cost per Employee	102,970	44,212	43
Cost per Production Worker	146,988	52,107	35
Shipments per Establishment	9,576,895	1,733,420	18
Shipments per Employee	195,460	92,091	47
Shipments per Production Worker	279,017	108,536	39
Investment per Establishment	321,011	17,682	6
Investment per Employee	6,552	939	14
Investment per Production Worker	9,352	1,107	12

Sources: Same as General Statistics. The 'Average of All Manufacturing' column represents the average of all manufacturing industries reported for the most recent complete year available. The Index shows the relationship between the Average and the Analyzed Industry. For example, 100 means that they are equal; 500 that the Analyzed Industry is five times the average; 50 means that the Analyzed Industry is half the national average. The abbreviation 'na' is used to show that data are 'not available'.

LEADING COMPANIES

Number shown: **18** Total sales ($ mil): **686** Total employment (000): **5.3**

Company Name	Address				CEO Name	Phone	Co. Type	Sales ($ mil)	Empl. (000)
Coach Leatherware Company	516 W 34th St	New York	NY	10001	Laurence Franklin	212-594-1850	S	460*	3.5
Erez Fashions Inc	525 7th Av	New York	NY	10018	Erez Levy	212-869-2980	R	40*	0.1
AD Sutton and Sons Inc	10 W 33rd St	New York	NY	10001	R Shalom	212-695-7070	R	35	0.2
Trina Inc	PO Box 1431	Fall River	MA	02722	David Manasco	508-678-7601	R	33*	0.3
LeSportsac Inc	320 5th Av	New York	NY	10001	Timothy W Schifter	212-736-6262	R	30	0.2
Pyramid Handbags Inc	100 W 33rd St	New York	NY	10001	Henry Fisher	212-714-2211	R	30	0.5
Koret Inc	136 Madison Av	New York	NY	10016	Michael Gordon	212-683-8544	R	20	0.2
Marilyn USA	111 N Main St	Ferris	TX	75125	Joe Allan	214-544-2271	R	16*	0.1
Melbourne Manufacturing	1708 Delmar Blv	St Louis	MO	63103	Don Fendelman	314-231-7123	R	10	0.2
Lisette Handbags Ltd	1 E 33rd St	New York	NY	10016	Gary Katz	212-684-6272	R	3*	<0.1
IMT Accessories Inc	15 W 36th St	New York	NY	10018	Ike Tawil	212-695-6878	R	2*	<0.1
Ourse	2801 SW 31th Av	Coconut Grove	FL	33133	David Sharples	305-446-2275	R	2	<0.1
IMA Fashions Phillippe	10 W 33rd St	New York	NY	10001	Bob Zeinonu	212-564-9191	D	1	<0.1
Linea Pelle Inc	850 S Broadway	Los Angeles	CA	90014	Wynn Katz	213-622-9116	R	1*	<0.1
Ohio Bag Corp	7020 Kennedy Blv	North Bergen	NJ	07047	Ralph Berger	201-869-9600	R	1	<0.1
Original Collins of Texas Inc	PO Drawer 1000	Medina	TX	78055	Sia Parstabarp	210-589-2877	R	1	<0.1
Maxx Inc	385 5th Av	New York	NY	10016	Cherie Christmas	212-679-3220	R	0*	<0.1
Avante Handbag Company Inc	330 5th Av	New York	NY	10001	Ron Rand	212-695-6725	R	0*	<0.1

Source: *Ward's Business Directory of U.S. Private and Public Companies*, Volumes 1 and 2, 1996. The company type code used is as follows: P - Public, R - Private, S - Subsidiary, D - Division, J - Joint Venture, A - Affiliate, G - Group. Sales are in millions of dollars, employees are in thousands. An asterisk (*) indicates an estimated sales volume. The symbol < stands for 'less than'. Company names and addresses are truncated, in some cases, to fit into the available space.

MATERIALS CONSUMED

Material	Quantity	Delivered Cost ($ million)
Materials, ingredients, containers, and supplies	(X)	146.5
Broadwoven fabrics (piece goods)	(X)	7.6
Plastics coated, impregnated, or laminated fabrics	(X)	8.8
Plastics products consumed in the form of sheets, rods, tubes, film, and other shapes	(X)	6.3
Finished leather	(X)	82.0
Trunk and luggage hardware, including locks	(X)	(D)
All other materials and components, parts, containers, and supplies	(X)	(D)
Materials, ingredients, containers, and supplies, nsk	(X)	22.0

Source: 1992 *Economic Census*. Explanation of symbols used: (D): Withheld to avoid disclosure of competitive data; na: Not available; (S): Withheld because statistical norms were not met; (X): Not applicable; (Z): Less than half the unit shown; nec: Not elsewhere classified; nsk: Not specified by kind; - : zero; * : 10-19 percent estimated; ** : 20-29 percent estimated.

PRODUCT SHARE DETAILS

Product or Product Class	% Share
Women's and children's handbags and purses	100.00
Women's and children's handbags and purses, outer surface of all leather or mostly leather	63.62
Women's and children's handbags and purses, outer surface of all plastics or mostly plastics (including vinyl)	15.36
Women's and children's handbags and purses, outer surface of all other materials, except precious metals	8.13

Source: 1992 *Economic Census*. The values shown are percent of total shipments in an industry. Values of indented subcategories are summed in the main heading. The symbol (D) appears when data are withheld to prevent disclosure of competitive information. The abbreviation nsk stands for 'not specified by kind' and nec for 'not elsewhere classified'.

INPUTS AND OUTPUTS FOR WOMEN'S HANDBAGS & PURSES

Economic Sector or Industry Providing Inputs	%	Sector	Economic Sector or Industry Buying Outputs	%	Sector
Imports	62.1	Foreign	Personal consumption expenditures	95.4	
Leather tanning & finishing	12.0	Manufg.	Women's handbags & purses	3.0	Manufg.
Women's handbags & purses	3.9	Manufg.	Exports	1.5	Foreign
Coated fabrics, not rubberized	3.2	Manufg.			
Wholesale trade	3.0	Trade			
Needles, pins, & fasteners	2.0	Manufg.			
Broadwoven fabric mills	1.8	Manufg.			
Adhesives & sealants	1.0	Manufg.			
Miscellaneous plastics products	1.0	Manufg.			
Hotels & lodging places	1.0	Services			
Thread mills	0.8	Manufg.			
Advertising	0.8	Services			
Hardware, nec	0.7	Manufg.			
Eating & drinking places	0.7	Trade			

Continued on next page.

INPUTS AND OUTPUTS FOR WOMEN'S HANDBAGS & PURSES - Continued

Economic Sector or Industry Providing Inputs	%	Sector	Economic Sector or Industry Buying Outputs	%	Sector
U.S. Postal Service	0.7	Gov't			
Electric services (utilities)	0.5	Util.			
Real estate	0.5	Fin/R.E.			
Motor freight transportation & warehousing	0.4	Util.			
Narrow fabric mills	0.3	Manufg.			
Banking	0.3	Fin/R.E.			
Paperboard containers & boxes	0.2	Manufg.			
Communications, except radio & TV	0.2	Util.			
Accounting, auditing & bookkeeping	0.2	Services			
Equipment rental & leasing services	0.2	Services			
Legal services	0.2	Services			
Management & consulting services & labs	0.2	Services			
Maintenance of nonfarm buildings nec	0.1	Constr.			
Machinery, except electrical, nec	0.1	Manufg.			

Source: Benchmark Input-Output Accounts for the U.S. Economy, 1982, U.S. Department of Commerce, Washington, D.C., July 1991. Data, as reported in the source, are organized by the 1977 SIC structure in use in 1982 but have been matched, as closely as is possible, to the 1987 SIC structure used in this book.

OCCUPATIONS EMPLOYED BY SIC 317 - LUGGAGE, HANDBAGS, AND LEATHER PRODUCTS, NEC

Occupation	% of Total 1994	Change to 2005	Occupation	% of Total 1994	Change to 2005
Assemblers, fabricators, & hand workers nec	11.7	-22.1	Freight, stock, & material movers, hand	2.5	-37.7
Sewing machine operators, non-garment	9.7	-68.8	Sales & related workers nec	2.3	-22.1
Shoe & leather workers & repairers, precision	7.1	-29.9	Cement & gluing machine operators	2.3	-49.4
Sewing machine operators, garment	5.4	-29.9	Crushing & mixing machine operators	1.7	-22.1
Helpers, laborers, & material movers nec	4.9	-22.1	Bookkeeping, accounting, & auditing clerks	1.3	-41.6
Blue collar worker supervisors	4.4	-26.2	General office clerks	1.3	-33.6
Cutting & slicing machine setters, operators	4.1	-14.3	Coating, painting, & spraying machine workers	1.3	-22.1
Machine operators nec	3.9	-31.3	Hand packers & packagers	1.2	-33.3
Inspectors, testers, & graders, precision	2.9	-22.1	Secretaries, ex legal & medical	1.2	-29.0
Cutters & trimmers, hand	2.7	-29.9	Shoe sewing machine operators	1.1	-37.6
General managers & top executives	2.7	-26.1	Industrial production managers	1.1	-22.1
Traffic, shipping, & receiving clerks	2.6	-25.0	Sewers, hand	1.0	-50.0
Machine feeders & offbearers	2.5	-29.9			

Source: Industry-Occupation Matrix, Bureau of Labor Statistics. These data relate to one or more 3-digit SIC industry groups rather than to a single 4-digit SIC. The change reported for each occupation to the year 2005 is a percent of growth or decline as estimated by the Bureau of Labor Statistics. The abbreviation nec stands for 'not elsewhere classified'.

LOCATION BY STATE AND REGIONAL CONCENTRATION

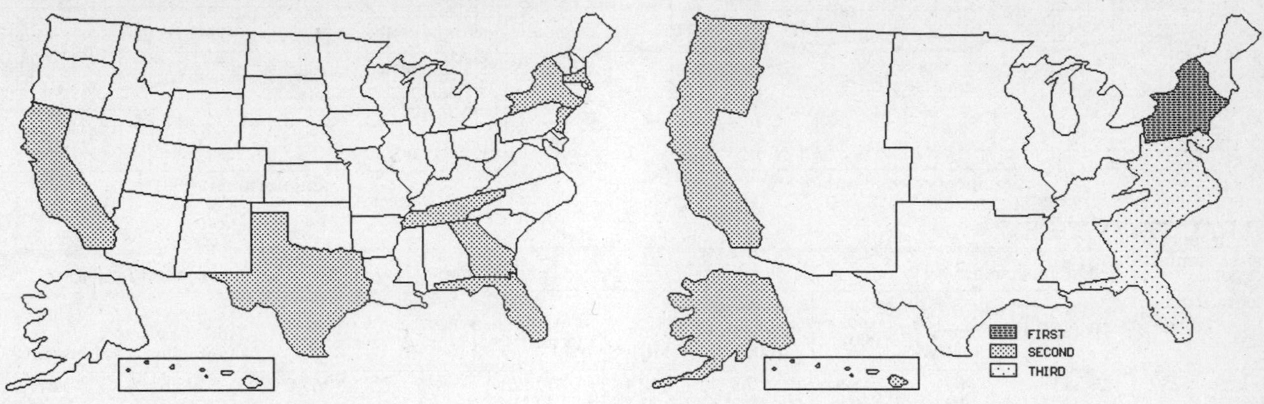

INDUSTRY DATA BY STATE

State	Establish-ments	Shipments			Employment				Cost as % of Shipments	Investment per Employee ($)
		Total ($ mil)	% of U.S.	Per Establ.	Total Number	% of U.S.	Per Establ.	Wages ($/hour)		
New York	85	213.5	46.1	2.5	1,700	33.3	20	8.61	43.3	1,118
Massachusetts	14	38.3	8.3	2.7	400	7.8	29	11.83	43.6	-
California	19	13.5	2.9	0.7	300	5.9	16	6.50	45.2	333
Texas	12	10.5	2.3	0.9	300	5.9	25	7.25	48.6	333
New Jersey	14	(D)	-	-	750 *	14.7	54	-	-	267
Florida	12	(D)	-	-	750 *	14.7	63	-	-	-
Georgia	5	(D)	-	-	375 *	7.4	75	-	-	-
Tennessee	2	(D)	-	-	175 *	3.4	88	-	-	-

Source: 1992 *Economic Census*. The states are in descending order of shipments or establishments (if shipment data are missing for the majority). The symbol (D) appears when data are withheld to prevent disclosure of competitive information. States marked with (D) are sorted by number of establishments. A dash (-) indicates that the data element cannot be calculated; * indicates the midpoint of a range.

3172 - PERSONAL LEATHER GOODS, NEC

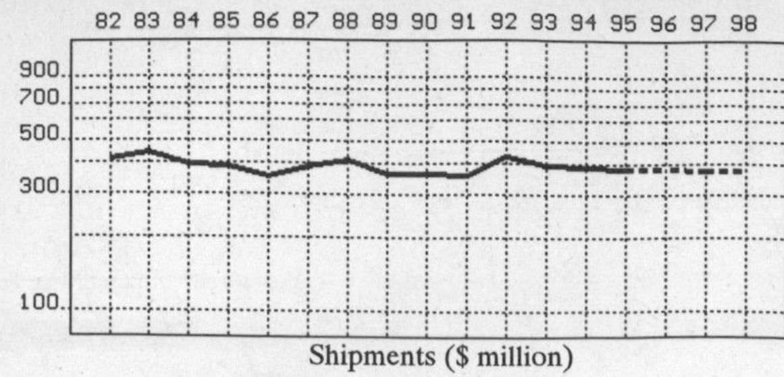

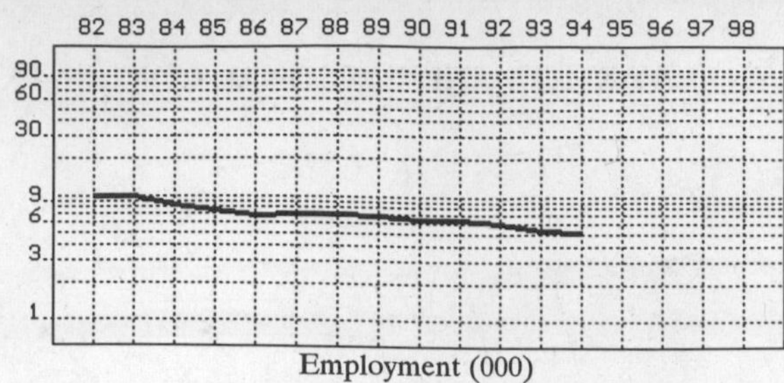

GENERAL STATISTICS

Year	Com-panies	Establishments		Employment			Compensation		Production ($ million)			
		Total	with 20 or more employees	Total (000)	Production Workers (000)	Production Hours (Mil)	Payroll ($ mil)	Wages ($/hr)	Cost of Materials	Value Added by Manufacture	Value of Shipments	Capital Invest.
1982	239	243	87	9.9	7.3	13.4	112.6	4.95	167.0	243.6	411.4	3.2
1983		232	83	9.8	7.2	13.2	117.2	5.14	184.1	260.0	441.9	2.2
1984		221	79	8.4	6.9	11.5	111.0	5.92	169.3	231.7	397.2	3.9
1985		209	75	7.6	6.2	10.2	109.9	6.65	149.5	231.2	388.1	5.4
1986		192	68	6.8	5.7	8.9	88.1	6.06	163.4	193.6	353.1	2.7
1987	205	209	62	7.2	5.7	10.6	101.3	5.98	175.8	212.6	393.3	3.5
1988		193	67			11.1	108.1		192.3	224.5	415.5	2.9
1989		183	66	6.9	5.4	10.6	104.7	5.84	167.3	197.3	363.4	5.6
1990		189	61	6.4	5.2	9.6	96.2	6.18	185.1	189.9	365.2	5.2
1991		181	60	6.4	5.1	9.6	97.6	6.07	176.9	180.4	361.9	5.0
1992	190	196	60	6.1	4.6	8.4	106.4	6.92	159.1	271.8	427.5	6.8
1993		183	60	5.3	3.9	7.2	99.0	7.44	146.4	249.3	394.5	5.7
1994		171P	53P	5.2	3.8	6.0	93.0	8.18	136.5	254.9	392.9	1.9
1995		166P	50P			6.7P	94.1P		132.3P	247.0P	380.8P	5.2P
1996		161P	48P			6.2P	92.7P		131.7P	245.9P	379.1P	5.3P
1997		156P	45P			5.7P	91.4P		131.1P	244.8P	377.4P	5.5P
1998		151P	43P			5.2P	90.0P		130.5P	243.7P	375.7P	5.6P

Sources: 1982, 1987, 1992 *Economic Census*; *Annual Survey of Manufactures*, 83-86, 88-91, 93-94. Establishment counts for non-Census years are from *County Business Patterns*; establishment values for 83-84 are extrapolations. 'P's show projections by the editors. Industries reclassified in 87 will not have data for prior years.

INDICES OF CHANGE

Year	Com-panies	Establishments		Employment			Compensation		Production ($ million)			
		Total	with 20 or more employees	Total (000)	Production Workers (000)	Production Hours (Mil)	Payroll ($ mil)	Wages ($/hr)	Cost of Materials	Value Added by Manufacture	Value of Shipments	Capital Invest.
1982	126	124	145	162	159	160	106	72	105	90	96	47
1983		118	138	161	157	157	110	74	116	96	103	32
1984		113	132	138	150	137	104	86	106	85	93	57
1985		107	125	125	135	121	103	96	94	85	91	79
1986		98	113	111	124	106	83	88	103	71	83	40
1987	108	107	103	118	124	126	95	86	110	78	92	51
1988		98	112			132	102		121	83	97	43
1989		93	110	113	117	126	98	84	105	73	85	82
1990		96	102	105	113	114	90	89	116	70	85	76
1991		92	100	105	111	114	92	88	111	66	85	74
1992	100	100	100	100	100	100	100	100	100	100	100	100
1993		93	100	87	85	86	93	108	92	92	92	84
1994		87P	88P	85	83	71	87	118	86	94	92	28
1995		85P	84P			79P	88P		83P	91P	89P	76P
1996		82P	80P			74P	87P		83P	90P	89P	79P
1997		80P	76P			68P	86P		82P	90P	88P	81P
1998		77P	72P			62P	85P		82P	90P	88P	83P

Sources: Same as General Statistics. Values reflect change from the base year, 1992. Values above 100 mean greater than 92, values below 100 mean less than 92, and a value of 100 in the 82-91 or 93-98 period means same as 92. 'P's mark projections by the editors.

SELECTED RATIOS

For 1994	Avg. of All Manufact.	Analyzed Industry	Index
Employees per Establishment	49	30	62
Payroll per Establishment	1,500,273	545,115	36
Payroll per Employee	30,620	17,885	58
Production Workers per Establishment	34	22	65
Wages per Establishment	853,319	287,680	34
Wages per Production Worker	24,861	12,916	52
Hours per Production Worker	2,056	1,579	77
Wages per Hour	12.09	8.18	68
Value Added per Establishment	4,602,255	1,494,085	32
Value Added per Employee	93,930	49,019	52

For 1994	Avg. of All Manufact.	Analyzed Industry	Index
Value Added per Production Worker	134,084	67,079	50
Cost per Establishment	5,045,178	800,089	16
Cost per Employee	102,970	26,250	25
Cost per Production Worker	146,988	35,921	24
Shipments per Establishment	9,576,895	2,302,966	24
Shipments per Employee	195,460	75,558	39
Shipments per Production Worker	279,017	103,395	37
Investment per Establishment	321,011	11,137	3
Investment per Employee	6,552	365	6
Investment per Production Worker	9,352	500	5

Sources: Same as General Statistics. The 'Average of All Manufacturing' column represents the average of all manufacturing industries reported for the most recent complete year available. The Index shows the relationship between the Average and the Analyzed Industry. For example, 100 means that they are equal; 500 that the Analyzed Industry is five times the average; 50 means that the Analyzed Industry is half the national average. The abbreviation 'na' is used to show that data are 'not available'.

LEADING COMPANIES

Number shown: **23** Total sales ($ mil): **416** Total employment (000): **6.5**

Company Name	Address				CEO Name	Phone	Co. Type	Sales ($ mil)	Empl. (000)
Prince Gardner Inc	6245 Lemay Ferry	St Louis	MO	63129	Dennis Barron	314-487-3100	R	77*	1.0
Amity Leather Products Co	735 S Main St	West Bend	WI	53095	John F Rozek	414-335-1000	R	64*	1.5
Tandy Leather Co	PO Box 791	Fort Worth	TX	76101	Jim Whitmire	817-551-9770	S	50	1.0
Leegin Creative Leather Products	PO Box 406	City of Industry	CA	91746	Jerry Kohl	818-961-9381	R	43*	0.6
Buxton Co	PO Box 1650	Springfield	MA	01102	Russell Whiteford	413-734-5900	S	35	0.4
Sharif Designs Ltd	34-12 36th Av	Long Island Ct	NY	11106	Sharif El Fouly	718-472-1100	R	20	<0.1
Circle Y of Yoakum Inc	PO Box 797	Yoakum	TX	77995	Anton J Stary	512-293-3501	R	18	0.4
Bridgeport Metal Goods Mfg Co	PO Box 3155	Bridgeport	CT	06605	Herman Beach III	203-366-4701	R	17	0.3
Harper Leather Goods Mfg Co	1050 W 40th St	Chicago	IL	60609	Louis Lauch Jr	312-376-2662	R	16	0.3
Hugo Bosca Company Inc	1905 W Jefferson St	Springfield	OH	45506	C B Bosca	513-323-5523	R	16*	0.2
California Optical Leather Inc	14447 Griffith St	San Leandro	CA	94577	Larry B Nathanson	510-352-4774	R	15	0.2
Enger-Kress Co	151 Wisconsin St	West Bend	WI	53095	William A Bauman	414-334-3455	R	11	0.2
Bond Street	385 5th Av	New York	NY	10016	Michael Schwartz	212-481-0205	R	5	<0.1
Rico Industries Inc	1712 S Michigan	Chicago	IL	60616	Cary Schack	312-427-0313	R	5	<0.1
DEO Enterprises Inc	5235 Whitby Av	Philadelphia	PA	19143	DE Orlowski	215-747-9300	R	4	<0.1
Genal Strap Company Inc	31-00 47th Av	Long Island Ct	NY	11101	Aaron Greenwald	718-706-8700	R	4	<0.1
Chums Ltd	PO Box 950	Hurricane	UT	84737	Mike Taggett	801-635-9831	R	3	<0.1
Leather Goods Inc	PO Box 5130	Bridgeport	CT	06610	Ralph Mazel	203-373-1174	R	3	<0.1
Penmar Inc	37 W Broad St	Haverstraw	NY	10927	MR Langer	914-429-2600	R	3	<0.1
Dimensional Graphics Corp	PO Box 1893	Mason City	IA	50402	Paul Gold	515-423-8931	R	3	<0.1
Bren Corp	35 Carlsbad St	Cranston	RI	02920	Ed Cianciarulo	401-943-8200	R	2*	<0.1
Kapak Corp	5305 Parkdale Dr	Minneapolis	MN	55416	Gary M Bell	612-541-0730	R	2	<0.1
Magnum Importers Inc	PO Box 2704	Huntington St	NY	11746	Peter Carlin	516-547-6905	R	1	<0.1

Source: *Ward's Business Directory of U.S. Private and Public Companies*, Volumes 1 and 2, 1996. The company type code used is as follows: P - Public, R - Private, S - Subsidiary, D - Division, J - Joint Venture, A - Affiliate, G - Group. Sales are in millions of dollars, employees are in thousands. An asterisk (*) indicates an estimated sales volume. The symbol < stands for 'less than'. Company names and addresses are truncated, in some cases, to fit into the available space.

MATERIALS CONSUMED

Material	Quantity	Delivered Cost ($ million)
Materials, ingredients, containers, and supplies	(X)	131.6
Broadwoven fabrics (piece goods)	(X)	13.3
Plastics coated, impregnated, or laminated fabrics	(X)	10.9
Plastics resins consumed in the form of granules, pellets, powders, liquids, etc.	(X)	0.2
Plastics products consumed in the form of sheets, rods, tubes, film, and other shapes	(X)	2.1
Finished leather	(X)	42.6
Trunk and luggage hardware, including locks	(X)	2.1
All other materials and components, parts, containers, and supplies	(X)	52.2
Materials, ingredients, containers, and supplies, nsk	(X)	8.6

Source: 1992 *Economic Census*. Explanation of symbols used: (D): Withheld to avoid disclosure of competitive data; na: Not available; (S): Withheld because statistical norms were not met; (X): Not applicable; (Z): Less than half the unit shown; nec: Not elsewhere classified; nsk: Not specified by kind; - : zero; * : 10-19 percent estimated; ** : 20-29 percent estimated.

PRODUCT SHARE DETAILS

Product or Product Class	% Share
Personal leather goods, nec.	100.00
Leather or mostly leather billfolds, wallets, french purses, and clutches	44.42
Billfolds, wallets, french purses, and clutches other than leather (plastics, fiber, etc.)	2.62
Personal leather travel kits (fitted and unfitted)	6.47
Personal leather jewelry boxes and cases (except precious metal), pocket size	5.15
Other personal goods (including key, cigarette, eyeglass, and pass card cases), all leather or mostly leather	20.52
Other personal goods (including key, cigarette, eyeglass, and pass card cases), other than leather (plastics, fiber, etc.)	15.14

Source: 1992 *Economic Census*. The values shown are percent of total shipments in an industry. Values of indented subcategories are summed in the main heading. The symbol (D) appears when data are withheld to prevent disclosure of competitive information. The abbreviation nsk stands for 'not specified by kind' and nec for 'not elsewhere classified'.

INPUTS AND OUTPUTS FOR PERSONAL LEATHER GOODS

Economic Sector or Industry Providing Inputs	%	Sector	Economic Sector or Industry Buying Outputs	%	Sector
Imports	41.0	Foreign	Personal consumption expenditures	72.9	
Leather tanning & finishing	15.0	Manufg.	Wholesale trade	6.8	Trade
Broadwoven fabric mills	4.7	Manufg.	Jewelry, precious metal	4.0	Manufg.
Wholesale trade	3.6	Trade	Costume jewelry	3.8	Manufg.
Coated fabrics, not rubberized	3.2	Manufg.	Business/professional associations	2.3	Services
Adhesives & sealants	2.9	Manufg.	Insurance carriers	1.8	Fin/R.E.
Narrow fabric mills	2.4	Manufg.	Exports	1.3	Foreign
Business services nec	2.3	Services	Watches, clocks, & parts	1.1	Manufg.
Miscellaneous plastics products	2.1	Manufg.	Labor, civic, social, & fraternal associations	0.5	Services
Hotels & lodging places	2.0	Services	Real estate	0.4	Fin/R.E.
U.S. Postal Service	1.8	Gov't	Freight forwarders	0.3	Util.
Advertising	1.7	Services	Retail trade, except eating & drinking	0.3	Trade
Eating & drinking places	1.4	Trade	Elementary & secondary schools	0.3	Services
Banking	1.2	Fin/R.E.	Legal services	0.3	Services
Fabricated metal products, nec	1.1	Manufg.	Personal leather goods	0.2	Manufg.
Personnel supply services	1.1	Services	Arrangement of passenger transportation	0.2	Util.
Thread mills	0.9	Manufg.	Eating & drinking places	0.2	Trade
Electric services (utilities)	0.9	Util.	Banking	0.2	Fin/R.E.
Motor freight transportation & warehousing	0.9	Util.	Credit agencies other than banks	0.1	Fin/R.E.
Hardware, nec	0.8	Manufg.	Insurance agents, brokers, & services	0.1	Fin/R.E.
Real estate	0.6	Fin/R.E.	Accounting, auditing & bookkeeping	0.1	Services
Equipment rental & leasing services	0.6	Services	State & local government enterprises, nec	0.1	Gov't
Plastics materials & resins	0.5	Manufg.			
Communications, except radio & TV	0.5	Util.			
Management & consulting services & labs	0.5	Services			
Gas production & distribution (utilities)	0.4	Util.			
Legal services	0.4	Services			
Maintenance of nonfarm buildings nec	0.3	Constr.			
Metal stampings, nec	0.3	Manufg.			
Personal leather goods	0.3	Manufg.			
Accounting, auditing & bookkeeping	0.3	Services			
Machinery, except electrical, nec	0.2	Manufg.			
Manifold business forms	0.2	Manufg.			
Miscellaneous fabricated wire products	0.2	Manufg.			
Needles, pins, & fasteners	0.2	Manufg.			
Screw machine and related products	0.2	Manufg.			
Sanitary services, steam supply, irrigation	0.2	Util.			
Credit agencies other than banks	0.2	Fin/R.E.			
Royalties	0.2	Fin/R.E.			
Automotive repair shops & services	0.2	Services			
Photofinishing labs, commercial photography	0.2	Services			
Leather goods, nec	0.1	Manufg.			
Paperboard containers & boxes	0.1	Manufg.			
Sawmills & planning mills, general	0.1	Manufg.			
Special dies & tools & machine tool accessories	0.1	Manufg.			
Computer & data processing services	0.1	Services			
Detective & protective services	0.1	Services			

Source: Benchmark Input-Output Accounts for the U.S. Economy, 1982, U.S. Department of Commerce, Washington, D.C., July 1991. Data, as reported in the source, are organized by the 1977 SIC structure in use in 1982 but have been matched, as closely as is possible, to the 1987 SIC structure used in this book.

OCCUPATIONS EMPLOYED BY SIC 317 - LUGGAGE, HANDBAGS, AND LEATHER PRODUCTS, NEC

Occupation	% of Total 1994	Change to 2005	Occupation	% of Total 1994	Change to 2005
Assemblers, fabricators, & hand workers nec	11.7	-22.1	Freight, stock, & material movers, hand	2.5	-37.7
Sewing machine operators, non-garment	9.7	-68.8	Sales & related workers nec	2.3	-22.1
Shoe & leather workers & repairers, precision	7.1	-29.9	Cement & gluing machine operators	2.3	-49.4
Sewing machine operators, garment	5.4	-29.9	Crushing & mixing machine operators	1.7	-22.1
Helpers, laborers, & material movers nec	4.9	-22.1	Bookkeeping, accounting, & auditing clerks	1.3	-41.6
Blue collar worker supervisors	4.4	-26.2	General office clerks	1.3	-33.6
Cutting & slicing machine setters, operators	4.1	-14.3	Coating, painting, & spraying machine workers	1.3	-22.1
Machine operators nec	3.9	-31.3	Hand packers & packagers	1.2	-33.3
Inspectors, testers, & graders, precision	2.9	-22.1	Secretaries, ex legal & medical	1.2	-29.0
Cutters & trimmers, hand	2.7	-29.9	Shoe sewing machine operators	1.1	-37.6
General managers & top executives	2.7	-26.1	Industrial production managers	1.1	-22.1
Traffic, shipping, & receiving clerks	2.6	-25.0	Sewers, hand	1.0	-50.0
Machine feeders & offbearers	2.5	-29.9			

Source: Industry-Occupation Matrix, Bureau of Labor Statistics. These data relate to one or more 3-digit SIC industry groups rather than to a single 4-digit SIC. The change reported for each occupation to the year 2005 is a percent of growth or decline as estimated by the Bureau of Labor Statistics. The abbreviation nec stands for 'not elsewhere classified'.

LOCATION BY STATE AND REGIONAL CONCENTRATION

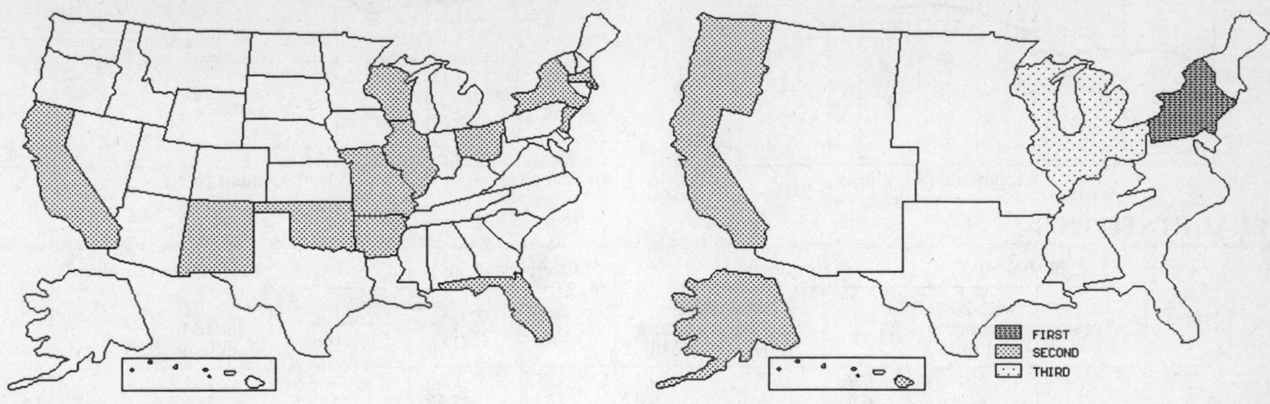

INDUSTRY DATA BY STATE

State	Establish-ments	Shipments Total ($ mil)	Shipments % of U.S.	Shipments Per Establ.	Employment Total Number	Employment % of U.S.	Employment Per Establ.	Wages ($/hour)	Cost as % of Shipments	Investment per Employee ($)
Massachusetts	9	74.0	17.3	8.2	800	13.1	89	8.30	45.8	-
New York	39	64.0	15.0	1.6	1,100	18.0	28	7.12	42.8	455
California	29	43.6	10.2	1.5	700	11.5	24	6.22	38.1	286
Rhode Island	8	17.4	4.1	2.2	300	4.9	38	6.67	42.0	-
Oklahoma	4	5.3	1.2	1.3	200	3.3	50	6.00	45.3	500
New Jersey	12	(D)	-	-	375 *	6.1	31	-	-	267
Florida	9	(D)	-	-	175 *	2.9	19	-	-	-
Illinois	8	(D)	-	-	175 *	2.9	22	-	-	-
Missouri	7	(D)	-	-	175 *	2.9	25	-	-	-
Wisconsin	6	(D)	-	-	750 *	12.3	125	-	-	-
Ohio	5	(D)	-	-	175 *	2.9	35	-	-	-
Arkansas	3	(D)	-	-	375 *	6.1	125	-	-	-
New Mexico	2	(D)	-	-	375 *	6.1	188	-	-	-

Source: 1992 *Economic Census*. The states are in descending order of shipments or establishments (if shipment data are missing for the majority). The symbol (D) appears when data are withheld to prevent disclosure of competitive information. States marked with (D) are sorted by number of establishments. A dash (-) indicates that the data element cannot be calculated; * indicates the midpoint of a range.

3199 - LEATHER GOODS, NEC

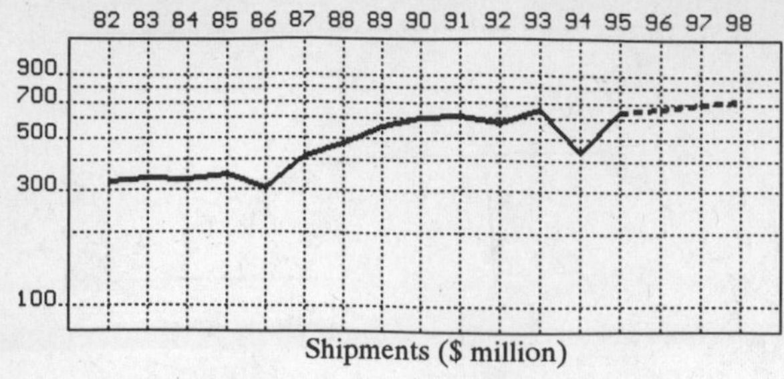

Shipments ($ million)

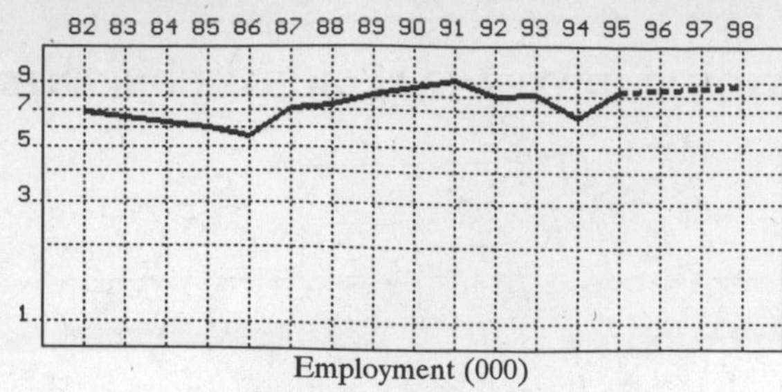

Employment (000)

GENERAL STATISTICS

Year	Companies	Establishments		Employment			Compensation		Production ($ million)			
		Total	with 20 or more employees	Total (000)	Production Workers (000)	Production Hours (Mil)	Payroll ($ mil)	Wages ($/hr)	Cost of Materials	Value Added by Manufacture	Value of Shipments	Capital Invest.
1982	399	414	104	6.9	5.7	10.3	75.0	5.06	163.8	159.4	325.1	5.7
1983				6.6	5.5	9.8	75.9	5.18	167.5	163.7	332.1	6.5
1984				6.3	5.3	10.8	73.8	4.85	158.6	172.8	330.5	2.5
1985				6.0	5.0	9.9	77.1	5.42	164.8	183.8	348.8	2.1
1986				5.5	4.5	9.2	69.5	5.22	134.5	167.0	305.2	2.2
1987	380	396	97	7.1	5.8	10.4	95.0	6.09	190.6	225.8	411.3	5.6
1988				7.3	5.9	10.6	103.5	6.15	211.8	260.3	469.1	3.1
1989		349	94	8.1	6.5	12.6	120.8	6.15	277.6	276.2	552.5	3.9
1990				8.6	6.8	13.1	131.7	6.49	289.6	303.2	594.7	5.8
1991				9.2	7.3	14.3	148.6	6.53	295.9	307.6	607.0	6.8
1992	428	441	95	7.9	6.3	12.0	132.3	7.02	275.0	300.3	571.0	4.9
1993				8.1	6.7	12.1	136.5	8.18	326.0	334.7	650.5	9.7
1994				6.6	6.0	11.2	123.4	8.16	158.6	275.5	434.1	3.7
1995				8.4P	6.9P	13.0P	150.7P	8.05P	232.8P	404.4P	637.2P	6.1P
1996				8.5P	7.0P	13.2P	157.3P	8.31P	242.2P	420.8P	663.0P	6.3P
1997				8.7P	7.1P	13.5P	163.8P	8.58P	251.7P	437.2P	688.9P	6.4P
1998				8.8P	7.3P	13.7P	170.4P	8.84P	261.1P	453.6P	714.7P	6.6P

Sources: 1982, 1987, 1992 *Economic Census*; *Annual Survey of Manufactures*, 83-86, 88-91, 93-94. Establishment counts for non-Census years are from *County Business Patterns*; establishment values for 83-84 are extrapolations. 'P's show projections by the editors. Industries reclassified in 87 will not have data for prior years.

INDICES OF CHANGE

Year	Companies	Establishments		Employment			Compensation		Production ($ million)			
		Total	with 20 or more employees	Total (000)	Production Workers (000)	Production Hours (Mil)	Payroll ($ mil)	Wages ($/hr)	Cost of Materials	Value Added by Manufacture	Value of Shipments	Capital Invest.
1982	93	94	109	87	90	86	57	72	60	53	57	116
1983				84	87	82	57	74	61	55	58	133
1984				80	84	90	56	69	58	58	58	51
1985				76	79	83	58	77	60	61	61	43
1986				70	71	77	53	74	49	56	53	45
1987	89	90	102	90	92	87	72	87	69	75	72	114
1988				92	94	88	78	88	77	87	82	63
1989		79	99	103	103	105	91	88	101	92	97	80
1990				109	108	109	100	92	105	101	104	118
1991				116	116	119	112	93	108	102	106	139
1992	100	100	100	100	100	100	100	100	100	100	100	100
1993				103	106	101	103	117	119	111	114	198
1994				84	95	93	93	116	58	92	76	76
1995				106P	109P	108P	114P	115P	85P	135P	112P	124P
1996				108P	111P	110P	119P	118P	88P	140P	116P	128P
1997				110P	113P	112P	124P	122P	92P	146P	121P	132P
1998				112P	115P	114P	129P	126P	95P	151P	125P	135P

Sources: Same as General Statistics. Values reflect change from the base year, 1992. Values above 100 mean greater than 92, values below 100 mean less than 92, and a value of 100 in the 82-91 or 93-98 period means same as 92. 'P's mark projections by the editors.

SELECTED RATIOS

For 1992	Avg. of All Manufact.	Analyzed Industry	Index	For 1992	Avg. of All Manufact.	Analyzed Industry	Index
Employees per Establishment	46	18	39	Value Added per Production Worker	122,353	47,667	39
Payroll per Establishment	1,332,320	300,000	23	Cost per Establishment	4,239,462	623,583	15
Payroll per Employee	29,181	16,747	57	Cost per Employee	92,853	34,810	37
Production Workers per Establishment	31	14	45	Cost per Production Worker	135,003	43,651	32
Wages per Establishment	734,496	191,020	26	Shipments per Establishment	8,100,800	1,294,785	16
Wages per Production Worker	23,390	13,371	57	Shipments per Employee	177,425	72,278	41
Hours per Production Worker	2,025	1,905	94	Shipments per Production Worker	257,966	90,635	35
Wages per Hour	11.55	7.02	61	Investment per Establishment	278,244	11,111	4
Value Added per Establishment	3,842,210	680,952	18	Investment per Employee	6,094	620	10
Value Added per Employee	84,153	38,013	45	Investment per Production Worker	8,861	778	9

Sources: Same as General Statistics. The 'Average of All Manufacturing' column represents the average of all manufacturing industries reported for the most recent complete year available. The Index shows the relationship between the Average and the Analyzed Industry. For example, 100 means that they are equal; 500 that the Analyzed Industry is five times the average; 50 means that the Analyzed Industry is half the national average. The abbreviation 'na' is used to show that data are 'not available'.

LEADING COMPANIES

Number shown: **36** Total sales ($ mil): **225** Total employment (000): **3.1**

Company Name	Address				CEO Name	Phone	Co. Type	Sales ($ mil)	Empl. (000)
McGuire-Nicholas Company Inc	2331 Tubeway Av	City of Com	CA	90040	Ed Donegan	213-722-6961	R	40*	0.5
Bianchi International	100 Calle Cortez	Temecula	CA	92590	Gary French	909-676-5621	R	20	0.2
Chase Companies Inc	507 Alden St	Fall River	MA	02723	Leonard S Chase III	508-678-7556	R	16	0.2
Klein Tools Inc	PO Box 10103	Fort Smith	AR	72917	Paul W Stiegler Jr	501-646-7347	D	13	0.1
Safariland Limited Inc	PO Box 51478	Ontario	CA	91761	Scott O'Brien	909-923-7300	R	12*	0.5
Big Horn Inc	PO Box 72965	Chattanooga	TN	37407	Mike Stocker	615-867-9901	R	11	0.2
Stebco Products Corp	3950 S Morgan St	Chicago	IL	60609	EB Stein	312-254-3800	R	11	<0.1
Tex Shoemaker and Sons Inc	714 W Cienega Av	San Dimas	CA	91773	Sharon Shoemaker	909-592-2071	R	9	<0.1
Oklahoma Leather Products Inc	500 26th St NW	Miami	OK	74354	Richard G Platt	918-542-6651	R	8	0.2
Gould and Goodrich Leather Inc	PO Box 1479	Lillington	NC	27546	Bob Gould	910-893-2071	R	7*	0.1
Simco Leather Co	1800 Daisy St	Chattanooga	TN	37406	John Sands	615-624-3331	R	7*	0.1
Bloom Brothers Co	5050 W 78th St	Minneapolis	MN	55435	ED Willette	612-832-3250	S	6	<0.1
Gary's Leather Creations	2850 E Vernon Av	Vernon	CA	90058	Gary Matzdorff	213-588-5500	R	6*	0.1
John Tillman and Co	2735 Signal Pkwy	Signal Hill	CA	90806	B Brown	310-426-2573	R	6*	0.1
Biological Engineering Inc	2476 Palma Dr	Ventura	CA	93003	Nick Bonge	805-644-1797	R	6	<0.1
Atchison Products Inc	PO Box 248	Atchison	KS	66002	Daniel L Fangman	913-367-6431	R	5	0.1
Bashlin Industries Inc	PO Box 867	Grove City	PA	16127	RE Schell	412-458-8340	R	5*	<0.1
Champion Turf Equipment Inc	330 S Mission Rd	Los Angeles	CA	90033	Norman Berliner	213-264-0746	R	5	<0.1
Colorado Saddlery Co	1631 15th St	Denver	CO	80202	PR Vanscoyk	303-572-8350	R	4	<0.1
Auburn Leather Co	One Caldwell St	Auburn	KY	42206	LJ Howlett	502-542-4116	R	4	<0.1
JC Decker Company Inc	PO Box 127	Montgomery	PA	17752	James Knouse	717-547-6601	R	3*	<0.1
Merzon Leather Company Inc	85 N 3rd St	Brooklyn	NY	11211	Richard Merzon	718-782-6260	R	3	<0.1
AE Burgess Leather Inc	Brigham Hill Rd	Grafton	MA	01519	Russel S Lesniewsri	508-839-6553	R	3	<0.1
Joe Sharp Manufacturing Inc	8740 Flower Rd	R Cucamonga	CA	91730	Joseph T Sharp	909-944-9964	R	3	<0.1
Eller Manufacturing Company	738 Livonia Av	Brooklyn	NY	11207	Dennis Stiler	718-345-3200	R	2	<0.1
Benjamin T Crump Company	PO Box 1597	Richmond	VA	23213	Samuel E Monroe	804-649-3601	R	2*	<0.1
Gaudette Leather Goods Inc	PO Box 1109	N Attleboro	MA	02761	John K Arabian	508-695-5632	R	1	<0.1
A and M Leatherlines Inc	85 F Hoffman Ln	Islandia	NY	11722	Richard Jonas	516-232-3876	R	1	<0.1
California Stay Company Inc	8525 Higuera St	Culver City	CA	90232	L Saltsman	310-839-4355	R	1	<0.1
EL Heacock Company Inc	110 N Arlington	Gloversville	NY	12078	David C Heacock	518-725-5423	R	1	<0.1
Indiana Harness and Saddlery	E 3030 Sprague Av	Spokane	WA	99202	Elaine Edwards	509-535-3400	R	1	<0.1
Kangaroos Inc	1 Bridge Plz	Fort Lee	NJ	07024	Ruth Bodden	201-224-6101	R	1	<0.1
Robert F Lewis Inc	64 Rte 4 W	Woodstock	VT	05091	RF Lewis	802-457-1205	R	1	<0.1
Capitol Saddlery	PO Box 216	Austin	TX	78707	TC Steiner	512-478-9309	R	1	<0.1
Smith-Worthington Saddlery	275 Homestead Av	Hartford	CT	06112	Curtis Hanks	203-527-9117	R	1	<0.1
Texas Saddlery Co	PO Box 850	Clarendon	TX	79226	Gary Skinner	806-874-3566	R	1	<0.1

Source: *Ward's Business Directory of U.S. Private and Public Companies*, Volumes 1 and 2, 1996. The company type code used is as follows: P - Public, R - Private, S - Subsidiary, D - Division, J - Joint Venture, A - Affiliate, G - Group. Sales are in millions of dollars, employees are in thousands. An asterisk (*) indicates an estimated sales volume. The symbol < stands for 'less than'. Company names and addresses are truncated, in some cases, to fit into the available space.

MATERIALS CONSUMED

Material	Quantity	Delivered Cost ($ million)
Materials, ingredients, containers, and supplies	(X)	229.7
Broadwoven fabrics (piece goods)	(X)	12.7
Plastics coated, impregnated, or laminated fabrics	(X)	4.4
Plastics resins consumed in the form of granules, pellets, powders, liquids, etc.	(X)	0.2
Plastics products consumed in the form of sheets, rods, tubes, film, and other shapes	(X)	5.5
Finished leather	(X)	63.5
Trunk and luggage hardware, including locks	(X)	1.2
All other materials and components, parts, containers, and supplies	(X)	79.9
Materials, ingredients, containers, and supplies, nsk	(X)	62.4

Source: 1992 *Economic Census*. Explanation of symbols used: (D): Withheld to avoid disclosure of competitive data; na: Not available; (S): Withheld because statistical norms were not met; (X): Not applicable; (Z): Less than half the unit shown; nec: Not elsewhere classified; nsk: Not specified by kind; - : zero; * : 10-19 percent estimated; ** : 20-29 percent estimated.

PRODUCT SHARE DETAILS

Product or Product Class	% Share
Leather goods, nec	100.00
Leather novelties	12.29
Leather saddlery, harness, and accouterments	18.07
Industrial leather belting and other industrial leather products made wholly or mostly of leather	8.95
Dog collars, leashes, and other household pet accessories made of leather	17.24
Other leather goods (desk sets, holsters, etc.)	28.80

Source: 1992 *Economic Census*. The values shown are percent of total shipments in an industry. Values of indented subcategories are summed in the main heading. The symbol (D) appears when data are withheld to prevent disclosure of competitive information. The abbreviation nsk stands for 'not specified by kind' and nec for 'not elsewhere classified'.

INPUTS AND OUTPUTS FOR LEATHER GOODS, NEC

Economic Sector or Industry Providing Inputs	%	Sector	Economic Sector or Industry Buying Outputs	%	Sector
Leather tanning & finishing	24.5	Manufg.	Personal consumption expenditures	58.5	
Imports	20.6	Foreign	Federal Government purchases, national defense	7.4	Fed Govt
Wholesale trade	7.4	Trade	Miscellaneous livestock	6.3	Agric.
Miscellaneous plastics products	6.4	Manufg.	Exports	5.8	Foreign
Surface active agents	5.3	Manufg.	Racing (including track operations)	2.7	Services
Needles, pins, & fasteners	3.9	Manufg.	S/L Govt. purch., correction	2.3	S/L Govt
Screw machine and related products	3.4	Manufg.	Logging camps & logging contractors	1.7	Manufg.
Hardware, nec	2.9	Manufg.	Legal services	1.4	Services
Adhesives & sealants	2.5	Manufg.	Leather goods, nec	1.3	Manufg.
Hardwood dimension & flooring mills	2.0	Manufg.	Membership sports & recreation clubs	1.2	Services
Metal stampings, nec	1.7	Manufg.	U.S. Postal Service	1.2	Gov't
Cyclic crudes and organics	1.6	Manufg.	Petroleum refining	0.8	Manufg.
Leather goods, nec	1.4	Manufg.	Apparel made from purchased materials	0.6	Manufg.
Hotels & lodging places	1.3	Services	Broadwoven fabric mills	0.6	Manufg.
Motor freight transportation & warehousing	1.2	Util.	Glass & glass products, except containers	0.6	Manufg.
Equipment rental & leasing services	1.0	Services	Blast furnaces & steel mills	0.5	Manufg.
Thread mills	0.9	Manufg.	Chemical preparations, nec	0.5	Manufg.
Electric services (utilities)	0.9	Util.	Motor vehicles & car bodies	0.5	Manufg.
Eating & drinking places	0.9	Trade	Shoes, except rubber	0.5	Manufg.
Advertising	0.9	Services	Yarn mills & finishing of textiles, nec	0.5	Manufg.
Paperboard containers & boxes	0.8	Manufg.	Real estate	0.4	Fin/R.E.
Industrial gases	0.7	Manufg.	Agricultural, forestry, & fishery services	0.3	Agric.
Gas production & distribution (utilities)	0.5	Util.	Retail trade, except eating & drinking	0.3	Trade
Real estate	0.5	Fin/R.E.	Wholesale trade	0.3	Trade
U.S. Postal Service	0.4	Gov't	Insurance carriers	0.3	Fin/R.E.
Maintenance of nonfarm buildings nec	0.3	Constr.	S/L Govt. purch., fire	0.3	S/L Govt
Nonwoven fabrics	0.3	Manufg.	Eating & drinking places	0.2	Trade
Communications, except radio & TV	0.3	Util.	Banking	0.2	Fin/R.E.
Banking	0.3	Fin/R.E.	Paper mills, except building paper	0.1	Manufg.
Management & consulting services & labs	0.3	Services	Personal leather goods	0.1	Manufg.
Chemical preparations, nec	0.2	Manufg.	Credit agencies other than banks	0.1	Fin/R.E.
Fabricated rubber products, nec	0.2	Manufg.	Accounting, auditing & bookkeeping	0.1	Services
Industrial inorganic chemicals, nec	0.2	Manufg.	Doctors & dentists	0.1	Services
Miscellaneous fabricated wire products	0.2	Manufg.	Hospitals	0.1	Services
Narrow fabric mills	0.2	Manufg.	Management & consulting services & labs	0.1	Services
Power driven hand tools	0.2	Manufg.	Federal Government purchases, nondefense	0.1	Fed Govt
Sawmills & planning mills, general	0.2	Manufg.			
Railroads & related services	0.2	Util.			
Credit agencies other than banks	0.2	Fin/R.E.			
Accounting, auditing & bookkeeping	0.2	Services			
Legal services	0.2	Services			
Distilled liquor, except brandy	0.1	Manufg.			
Fabricated metal products, nec	0.1	Manufg.			
Machinery, except electrical, nec	0.1	Manufg.			
Manifold business forms	0.1	Manufg.			
Petroleum refining	0.1	Manufg.			
Polishes & sanitation goods	0.1	Manufg.			
Air transportation	0.1	Util.			
Royalties	0.1	Fin/R.E.			
Business/professional associations	0.1	Services			
Computer & data processing services	0.1	Services			
Detective & protective services	0.1	Services			
Services to dwellings & other buildings	0.1	Services			

Source: Benchmark Input-Output Accounts for the U.S. Economy, 1982, U.S. Department of Commerce, Washington, D.C., July 1991. Data, as reported in the source, are organized by the 1977 SIC structure in use in 1982 but have been matched, as closely as is possible, to the 1987 SIC structure used in this book.

OCCUPATIONS EMPLOYED BY SIC 319 - LUGGAGE, HANDBAGS, AND LEATHER PRODUCTS, NEC

Occupation	% of Total 1994	Change to 2005	Occupation	% of Total 1994	Change to 2005
Assemblers, fabricators, & hand workers nec	11.7	-22.1	Freight, stock, & material movers, hand	2.5	-37.7
Sewing machine operators, non-garment	9.7	-68.8	Sales & related workers nec	2.3	-22.1
Shoe & leather workers & repairers, precision	7.1	-29.9	Cement & gluing machine operators	2.3	-49.4
Sewing machine operators, garment	5.4	-29.9	Crushing & mixing machine operators	1.7	-22.1
Helpers, laborers, & material movers nec	4.9	-22.1	Bookkeeping, accounting, & auditing clerks	1.3	-41.6
Blue collar worker supervisors	4.4	-26.2	General office clerks	1.3	-33.6
Cutting & slicing machine setters, operators	4.1	-14.3	Coating, painting, & spraying machine workers	1.3	-22.1
Machine operators nec	3.9	-31.3	Hand packers & packagers	1.2	-33.3
Inspectors, testers, & graders, precision	2.9	-22.1	Secretaries, ex legal & medical	1.2	-29.0
Cutters & trimmers, hand	2.7	-29.9	Shoe sewing machine operators	1.1	-37.6
General managers & top executives	2.7	-26.1	Industrial production managers	1.1	-22.1
Traffic, shipping, & receiving clerks	2.6	-25.0	Sewers, hand	1.0	-50.0
Machine feeders & offbearers	2.5	-29.9			

Source: Industry-Occupation Matrix, Bureau of Labor Statistics. These data relate to one or more 3-digit SIC industry groups rather than to a single 4-digit SIC. The change reported for each occupation to the year 2005 is a percent of growth or decline as estimated by the Bureau of Labor Statistics. The abbreviation nec stands for 'not elsewhere classified'.

LOCATION BY STATE AND REGIONAL CONCENTRATION

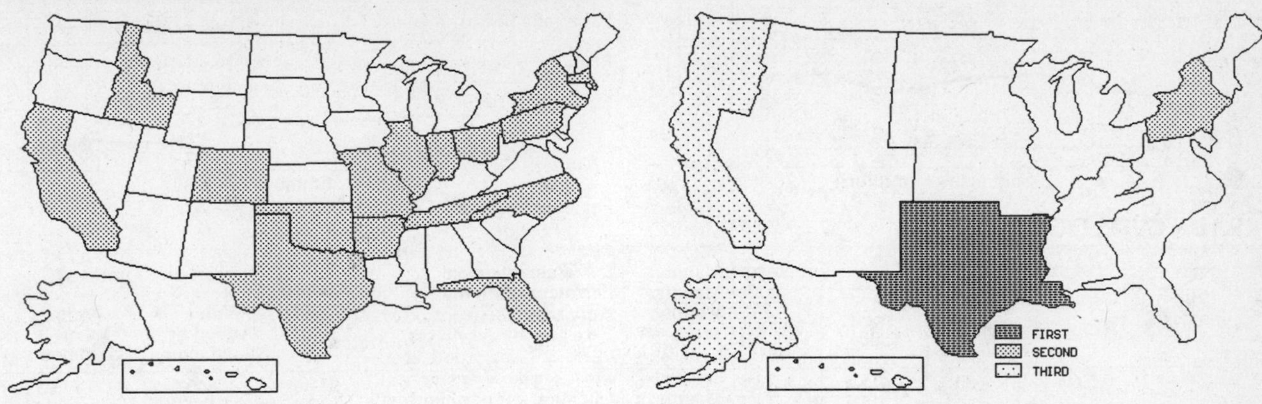

INDUSTRY DATA BY STATE

State	Establish-ments	Shipments			Employment				Cost as % of Shipments	Investment per Employee ($)
		Total ($ mil)	% of U.S.	Per Establ.	Total Number	% of U.S.	Per Establ.	Wages ($/hour)		
California	51	105.4	18.5	2.1	1,500	19.0	29	7.61	44.5	533
Texas	67	67.0	11.7	1.0	1,000	12.7	15	6.80	51.3	400
New York	40	53.2	9.3	1.3	700	8.9	18	8.10	48.9	-
Illinois	13	50.6	8.9	3.9	700	8.9	54	6.38	53.0	714
Ohio	10	43.5	7.6	4.3	500	6.3	50	7.00	50.1	600
Massachusetts	15	36.1	6.3	2.4	300	3.8	20	8.60	47.4	667
Tennessee	20	30.5	5.3	1.5	400	5.1	20	6.33	56.7	1,000
Pennsylvania	15	22.4	3.9	1.5	200	2.5	13	6.67	49.1	-
Oklahoma	14	16.4	2.9	1.2	400	5.1	29	6.00	51.2	500
Arkansas	6	12.4	2.2	2.1	200	2.5	33	5.33	49.2	500
North Carolina	6	11.2	2.0	1.9	200	2.5	33	5.33	42.9	-
Indiana	10	9.3	1.6	0.9	200	2.5	20	5.50	38.7	-
Colorado	10	9.1	1.6	0.9	100	1.3	10	9.00	56.0	-
Missouri	12	7.2	1.3	0.6	100	1.3	8	6.00	33.3	-
Florida	13	(D)	-	-	175 *	2.2	13	-	-	-
Idaho	6	(D)	-	-	175 *	2.2	29	-	-	-

Source: 1992 *Economic Census*. The states are in descending order of shipments or establishments (if shipment data are missing for the majority). The symbol (D) appears when data are withheld to prevent disclosure of competitive information. States marked with (D) are sorted by number of establishments. A dash (-) indicates that the data element cannot be calculated; * indicates the midpoint of a range.

3211 - FLAT GLASS

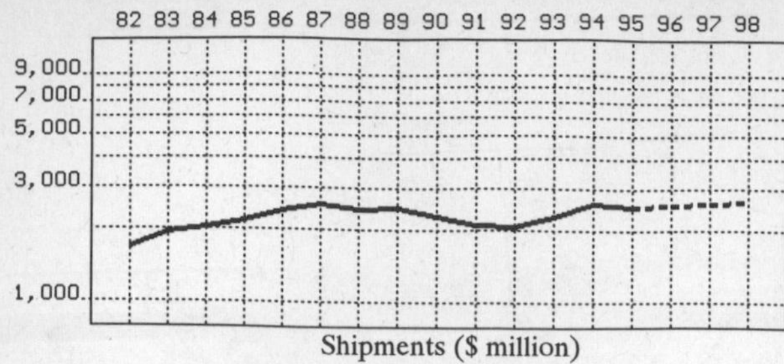

Shipments ($ million)

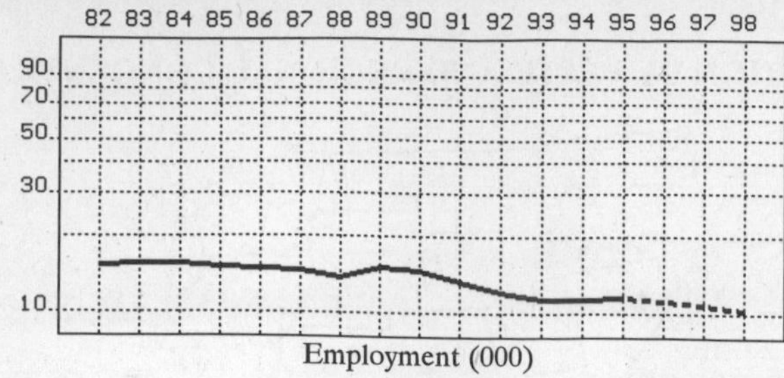

Employment (000)

GENERAL STATISTICS

Year	Com-panies	Establishments		Employment			Compensation		Production ($ million)			
		Total	with 20 or more employees	Total (000)	Production Workers (000)	Production Hours (Mil)	Payroll ($ mil)	Wages ($/hr)	Cost of Materials	Value Added by Manufacture	Value of Shipments	Capital Invest.
1982	49	69	33	15.3	12.0	24.6	413.8	13.09	827.0	846.5	1,665.5	97.6
1983				15.7	12.7	26.5	448.6	13.49	837.8	1,124.2	1,930.3	108.4
1984				15.6	12.7	27.1	477.5	14.12	921.2	1,119.9	2,043.3	100.8
1985				15.2	12.3	26.7	501.4	15.10	925.9	1,239.9	2,155.4	260.1
1986				14.9	12.1	25.4	493.7	15.45	957.1	1,409.7	2,397.6	85.7
1987	66	84	38	14.6	11.8	24.9	506.7	15.90	915.3	1,618.4	2,549.3	151.3
1988				13.8	11.2	25.0	513.3	16.18	944.7	1,516.6	2,442.2	150.9
1989		101	51	15.0	12.1	25.4	534.1	16.47	963.6	1,538.4	2,477.1	144.0
1990				14.6	11.9	24.7	508.5	16.19	902.9	1,394.8	2,279.0	127.4
1991				13.2	10.7	22.9	486.0	16.77	827.7	1,254.1	2,104.1	112.1
1992	16	36	33	11.9	9.7	20.5	452.1	17.39	770.5	1,313.0	2,078.3	148.0
1993				11.3	9.2	20.3	466.4	18.03	844.1	1,413.9	2,283.0	158.5
1994				11.2	9.2	20.9	503.3	19.01	913.3	1,651.2	2,599.6	137.1
1995				11.4P	9.4P	20.7P	505.6P	18.95P	879.0P	1,589.3P	2,502.1P	148.9P
1996				11.1P	9.1P	20.2P	508.6P	19.38P	892.6P	1,613.8P	2,540.8P	150.6P
1997				10.7P	8.8P	19.7P	511.5P	19.81P	906.2P	1,638.4P	2,579.5P	152.3P
1998				10.3P	8.5P	19.2P	514.4P	20.24P	919.8P	1,663.0P	2,618.2P	154.0P

Sources: 1982, 1987, 1992 *Economic Census*; *Annual Survey of Manufactures*, 83-86, 88-91, 93-94. Establishment counts for non-Census years are from *County Business Patterns*; establishment values for 83-84 are extrapolations. 'P's show projections by the editors. Industries reclassified in 87 will not have data for prior years.

INDICES OF CHANGE

Year	Com-panies	Establishments		Employment			Compensation		Production ($ million)			
		Total	with 20 or more employees	Total (000)	Production Workers (000)	Production Hours (Mil)	Payroll ($ mil)	Wages ($/hr)	Cost of Materials	Value Added by Manufacture	Value of Shipments	Capital Invest.
1982	306	192	100	129	124	120	92	75	107	64	80	66
1983				132	131	129	99	78	109	86	93	73
1984				131	131	132	106	81	120	85	98	68
1985				128	127	130	111	87	120	94	104	176
1986				125	125	124	109	89	124	107	115	58
1987	413	233	115	123	122	121	112	91	119	123	123	102
1988				116	115	122	114	93	123	116	118	102
1989		281	155	126	125	124	118	95	125	117	119	97
1990				123	123	120	112	93	117	106	110	86
1991				111	110	112	107	96	107	96	101	76
1992	100	100	100	100	100	100	100	100	100	100	100	100
1993				95	95	99	103	104	110	108	110	107
1994				94	95	102	111	109	119	126	125	93
1995				96P	97P	101P	112P	109P	114P	121P	120P	101P
1996				93P	94P	98P	112P	111P	116P	123P	122P	102P
1997				90P	91P	96P	113P	114P	118P	125P	124P	103P
1998				87P	88P	94P	114P	116P	119P	127P	126P	104P

Sources: Same as General Statistics. Values reflect change from the base year, 1992. Values above 100 mean greater than 92, values below 100 mean less than 92, and a value of 100 in the 82-91 or 93-98 period means same as 92. 'P's mark projections by the editors.

SELECTED RATIOS

For 1992	Avg. of All Manufact.	Analyzed Industry	Index
Employees per Establishment	46	331	724
Payroll per Establishment	1,332,320	12,558,333	943
Payroll per Employee	29,181	37,992	130
Production Workers per Establishment	31	269	858
Wages per Establishment	734,496	9,902,639	1,348
Wages per Production Worker	23,390	36,752	157
Hours per Production Worker	2,025	2,113	104
Wages per Hour	11.55	17.39	151
Value Added per Establishment	3,842,210	36,472,222	949
Value Added per Employee	84,153	110,336	131

For 1992	Avg. of All Manufact.	Analyzed Industry	Index
Value Added per Production Worker	122,353	135,361	111
Cost per Establishment	4,239,462	21,402,778	505
Cost per Employee	92,853	64,748	70
Cost per Production Worker	135,003	79,433	59
Shipments per Establishment	8,100,800	57,730,556	713
Shipments per Employee	177,425	174,647	98
Shipments per Production Worker	257,966	214,258	83
Investment per Establishment	278,244	4,111,111	1,478
Investment per Employee	6,094	12,437	204
Investment per Production Worker	8,861	15,258	172

Sources: Same as General Statistics. The 'Average of All Manufacturing' column represents the average of all manufacturing industries reported for the most recent complete year available. The Index shows the relationship between the Average and the Analyzed Industry. For example, 100 means that they are equal; 500 that the Analyzed Industry is five times the average; 50 means that the Analyzed Industry is half the national average. The abbreviation 'na' is used to show that data are 'not available'.

LEADING COMPANIES

Number shown: **35** Total sales ($ mil): **11,457** Total employment (000): **71.6**

Company Name	Address				CEO Name	Phone	Co. Type	Sales ($ mil)	Empl. (000)
PPG Industries Inc	1 PPG Pl	Pittsburgh	PA	15272	Jerry E Dempsey	412-434-3131	P	6,331	30.8
PPG Industries Inc	1 PPG Pl	Pittsburgh	PA	15272	Robert D Duncan	412-434-3131	D	2,168	17.0
Libbey-Owens-Ford Co	PO Box 799	Toledo	OH	43697	Rodney Stansfield	419-247-3731	S	850	7.0
Apogee Enterprises Inc	7900 Xerxes Av S	Minneapolis	MN	55431	Donald W Goldfus	612-835-1874	P	757	5.8
Safelite Glass Corp	PO Box 2000	Columbus	OH	43216	Garen Staglin	614-842-3000	R	400*	3.6
AP Techno Glass Co	PO Box 819	Bellefontaine	OH	43311	Makoto Sakabe	513-599-3131	S	150	1.1
Asahi Glass America Inc	450 Lexington Av	New York	NY	10017	Tadao Horikoshi	212-687-4600	S	150	1.1
HGP Industries Inc	3811 Turtle Creek	Dallas	TX	75219	John Wittstock	214-663-3800	S	110	0.8
Gemtron Corp	615 Hwy 68	Sweetwater	TN	37874	Gary K Kimsey	615-337-3522	S	80	0.8
Hoffers Inc	PO Box 777	Wausau	WI	54401	Otto Seidenberg	715-359-2432	S	70	0.5
ODL Inc	215 E Roosevelt	Zeeland	MI	49464	Larry Mulder	616-772-9111	R	60	0.3
Erie Scientific Co	Portsmouth Ind Pk	Portsmouth	NH	03801	FH Jellinek	603-431-8410	S	57	0.3
Hamilton Glass Products Inc	PO Box 317	Vincennes	IN	47591	Bruce Crockett	812-882-2680	S	40	0.4
Hartung Agalite Glass Co	17830 W Val Hwy	Tukwila	WA	98188	Nick Sciola	206-656-2626	R	30	0.2
US Precision Glass Inc	4307 US Rt 40 E	Lewisburg	OH	45338	Robert Jaynes	513-962-2696	D	25*	0.2
Vinyl Air Window Corp	1441 Chestnut Av	Hillside	NJ	07205	Harold Kaye	201-926-1010	S	17*	0.1
Viratec Tru Vue Inc	1315 N NBranch	Chicago	IL	60622	Tom Graham	312-943-4200	S	17	<0.1
D and A Technology Inc	PO Box 691	Mount Pleasant	TN	38474	Charles E Nyhus	615-379-4994	J	16	0.3
Wallside Window Factory Inc	27000 Trolley	Taylor	MI	48180	Martin Blanck	313-292-4400	R	16	0.1
O'Keeffe's Inc	75 Williams Av	San Francisco	CA	94124	W F O'Keeffe Jr	415-822-4222	R	15	0.1
Wasco Products Inc	PO Box 351	Sanford	ME	04073	MA Taylor	207-324-8060	R	13*	0.1
Oregon Glass Co	PO Box 649	Wilsonville	OR	97070	Wayne Metcalfe	503-682-3846	R	13	0.1
Brin-Northwestern Glass Co	2300 N 2nd St	Minneapolis	MN	55411	Douglas Nelson	612-529-9671	R	12	0.1
Cardinal Glass Co	PO Box 707	Rockford	IL	61105	WH Williams	815-394-1400	R	10	0.2
Century Mfg & Equity Concepts	1513 N A St	Las Vegas	NV	89106	Mark Powers	702-385-2447	P	10	<0.1
Spectrum Glass Co	PO Box 646	Woodinville	WA	98072	Don Hansen	206-483-6699	R	8	0.1
Standard Glass and Screen Co	1304 University N	Minneapolis	MN	55413	Robert Wones	612-331-6674	R	7*	0.1
Hillsdale Industries Inc	5049 S National Dr	Knoxville	TN	37914	Gary D O'Neal	615-637-1711	S	5	<0.1
Louisville Plate Glass Company	1401 W Broadway	Louisville	KY	40201	William Stone	502-584-6145	R	5*	<0.1
Fiberlux Inc	1634 S Frankin St	South Bend	IN	46613	Ralph J Vasami	219-233-6603	S	4	<0.1
Amcoa Glass Company Inc	6301 NE 4th Av	Miami	FL	33138	Steven Goldsmith	305-751-2202	R	3	<0.1
Royal Glass Corp	500 Nordhoff Pl	Englewood	NJ	07631	David Ulrich	201-567-1000	R	3	<0.1
Torstenson Glass Co	3233 N Sheffield	Chicago	IL	60657	Douglas Studt	312-525-0435	R	3*	<0.1
Indepane IG Inc	7447 S Sayre Av	Bedford Park	IL	60638	Peter Pappas	708-458-7300	R	2*	<0.1
Cemcel Corp	3040 Giant Rd	San Pablo	CA	94806	Charles Marsh Jr	510-235-9911	R	1*	<0.1

Source: *Ward's Business Directory of U.S. Private and Public Companies*, Volumes 1 and 2, 1996. The company type code is used is as follows: P - Public, R - Private, S - Subsidiary, D - Division, J - Joint Venture, A - Affiliate, G - Group. Sales are in millions of dollars, employees are in thousands. An asterisk (*) indicates an estimated sales volume. The symbol < stands for 'less than'. Company names and addresses are truncated, in some cases, to fit into the available space.

MATERIALS CONSUMED

Material	Quantity	Delivered Cost ($ million)
Materials, ingredients, containers, and supplies	(X)	502.2
Glass sand, all types	(X)	61.6
Sodium carbonate (soda ash) (58 percent Na2O)	(X)	112.2
Industrial inorganic chemicals, except sodium carbonate	(X)	35.8
Other chemicals and allied products	(X)	9.5
Glass (float, sheet and plate)	(X)	(D)
Minerals and earths, ground or otherwise treated	(X)	(D)
Other stone, clay, and concrete products	(X)	1.2
Paperboard containers, boxes, and corrugated paperboard	(X)	22.8
Rough and dressed lumber	(X)	6.3
Wood boxes, pallets, skids, and containers	(X)	36.0
Other lumber and wood products, except furniture	(X)	2.0
Plastics film and sheet, unsupported	(X)	(D)
Cullet (glass scrap)	(X)	32.3
All other materials and components, parts, containers, and supplies	(X)	99.9
Materials, ingredients, containers, and supplies, nsk	(X)	3.1

Source: 1992 *Economic Census*. Explanation of symbols used: (D): Withheld to avoid disclosure of competitive data; na: Not available; (S): Withheld because statistical norms were not met; (X): Not applicable; (Z): Less than half the unit shown; nec: Not elsewhere classified; nsk: Not specified by kind; - : zero; * : 10-19 percent estimated; ** : 20-29 percent estimated.

PRODUCT SHARE DETAILS

Product or Product Class	% Share	Product or Product Class	% Share
Flat glass	100.00	Multiple-glazed, sealed insulating units, made by flat glass producers	(D)
Laminated glass, made by flat glass producers	(D)	Other glass products (including such items as bent, enameled, stained, leaded, faceted, and colored glass slabs), made by flat glass producers	4.73
Laminated glass, made by flat glass producers	(D)	Flat glass (float, sheet, and plate), made by flat glass producers	70.08
Other glass products, made by flat glass producers	(D)	Flat glass, nsk	0.03
Tempered glass for construction, architectural, and automotive purposes, made by flat glass producers	14.61		
Tempered glass for other uses, such as for appliances, made by flat glass producers	(D)		

Source: 1992 *Economic Census*. The values shown are percent of total shipments in an industry. Values of indented subcategories are summed in the main heading. The symbol (D) appears when data are withheld to prevent disclosure of competitive information. The abbreviation nsk stands for 'not specified by kind' and nec for 'not elsewhere classified'.

INPUTS AND OUTPUTS FOR GLASS & GLASS PRODUCTS, EXCEPT CONTAINERS

Economic Sector or Industry Providing Inputs	%	Sector	Economic Sector or Industry Buying Outputs	%	Sector
Glass & glass products, except containers	15.5	Manufg.	Personal consumption expenditures	15.2	
Imports	14.6	Foreign	Glass & glass products, except containers	9.7	Manufg.
Wholesale trade	8.2	Trade	Exports	7.8	Foreign
Gas production & distribution (utilities)	7.8	Util.	Motor vehicles & car bodies	5.6	Manufg.
Cyclic crudes and organics	5.4	Manufg.	Eating & drinking places	4.5	Trade
Communications, except radio & TV	4.9	Util.	Automotive repair shops & services	4.4	Services
Electric services (utilities)	4.4	Util.	Electron tubes	3.3	Manufg.
Advertising	3.4	Services	Lighting fixtures & equipment	3.3	Manufg.
Industrial inorganic chemicals, nec	2.7	Manufg.	Miscellaneous plastics products	3.3	Manufg.
Paperboard containers & boxes	2.0	Manufg.	Hotels & lodging places	2.8	Services
Wood products, nec	2.0	Manufg.	Electric lamps	2.6	Manufg.
Alkalies & chlorine	1.9	Manufg.	Metal doors, sash, & trim	2.6	Manufg.
Adhesives & sealants	1.8	Manufg.	Asphalt felts & coatings	2.5	Manufg.
Motor freight transportation & warehousing	1.8	Util.	Hospitals	2.4	Services
Railroads & related services	1.5	Util.	Maintenance of nonfarm buildings nec	1.6	Constr.
Miscellaneous plastics products	1.4	Manufg.	Office buildings	1.1	Constr.
Maintenance of nonfarm buildings nec	1.3	Constr.	Broadwoven fabric mills	1.1	Manufg.
Petroleum refining	1.3	Manufg.	Ophthalmic goods	1.1	Manufg.
Sand & gravel	1.2	Mining	Tire cord & fabric	1.1	Manufg.
Wood containers	1.2	Manufg.	S/L Govt. purch., public assistance & relief	1.1	S/L Govt
Noncomparable imports	1.2	Foreign	Boat building & repairing	0.8	Manufg.
Banking	0.9	Fin/R.E.	Millwork	0.8	Manufg.
Air transportation	0.8	Util.	Medical & health services, nec	0.8	Services
Scrap	0.8	Scrap	Household cooking equipment	0.7	Manufg.
Machinery, except electrical, nec	0.7	Manufg.	Optical instruments & lenses	0.7	Manufg.
Automotive repair shops & services	0.7	Services	Industrial buildings	0.6	Constr.
Eating & drinking places	0.6	Trade	Electric housewares & fans	0.6	Manufg.
Carbon & graphite products	0.5	Manufg.	Wood household furniture	0.6	Manufg.
Metal stampings, nec	0.5	Manufg.	S/L Govt. purch., higher education	0.6	S/L Govt
Minerals, ground or treated	0.5	Manufg.	Nonfarm residential structure maintenance	0.5	Constr.
Computer & data processing services	0.5	Services	Mineral wool	0.5	Manufg.
Fabricated rubber products, nec	0.4	Manufg.	Automotive rental & leasing, without drivers	0.5	Services
Paints & allied products	0.4	Manufg.	Elementary & secondary schools	0.5	Services
Real estate	0.4	Fin/R.E.	Construction of stores & restaurants	0.4	Constr.
Equipment rental & leasing services	0.4	Services	Metal stampings, nec	0.4	Manufg.
U.S. Postal Service	0.4	Gov't	Semiconductors & related devices	0.4	Manufg.
Lubricating oils & greases	0.3	Manufg.	Travel trailers & campers	0.4	Manufg.
Sawmills & planning mills, general	0.3	Manufg.	Federal Government purchases, nondefense	0.4	Fed Govt
Special dies & tools & machine tool accessories	0.3	Manufg.	Metal household furniture	0.3	Manufg.
Chemical & fertilizer mineral	0.2	Mining	Nonferrous wire drawing & insulating	0.3	Manufg.
Mechanical measuring devices	0.2	Manufg.	Special industry machinery, nec	0.3	Manufg.
Rubber & plastics hose & belting	0.2	Manufg.	Doctors & dentists	0.3	Services
Textile machinery	0.2	Manufg.	Federal Government purchases, national defense	0.3	Fed Govt
Sanitary services, steam supply, irrigation	0.2	Util.	S/L Govt. purch., health & hospitals	0.3	S/L Govt
Water transportation	0.2	Util.	S/L Govt. purch., police	0.3	S/L Govt
Credit agencies other than banks	0.2	Fin/R.E.	Crude petroleum & natural gas	0.2	Mining
Insurance carriers	0.2	Fin/R.E.	Construction of hospitals	0.2	Constr.
Royalties	0.2	Fin/R.E.	Residential 1-unit structures, nonfarm	0.2	Constr.
Accounting, auditing & bookkeeping	0.2	Services	Residential additions/alterations, nonfarm	0.2	Constr.
Automotive rental & leasing, without drivers	0.2	Services	Warehouses	0.2	Constr.
Hotels & lodging places	0.2	Services	Drugs	0.2	Manufg.
Legal services	0.2	Services	Electronic components nec	0.2	Manufg.
Management & consulting services & labs	0.2	Services	Fabricated metal products, nec	0.2	Manufg.
Abrasive products	0.1	Manufg.	Fabricated plate work (boiler shops)	0.2	Manufg.
Manifold business forms	0.1	Manufg.	Hardware, nec	0.2	Manufg.
Paper coating & glazing	0.1	Manufg.	Instruments to measure electricity	0.2	Manufg.
Pumps & compressors	0.1	Manufg.	Mechanical measuring devices	0.2	Manufg.
Electrical repair shops	0.1	Services	Motor homes (made on purchased chassis)	0.2	Manufg.
			Plastics materials & resins	0.2	Manufg.
			Plating & polishing	0.2	Manufg.
			Radio & TV communication equipment	0.2	Manufg.
			Railroad equipment	0.2	Manufg.

Continued on next page.

INPUTS AND OUTPUTS FOR GLASS & GLASS PRODUCTS, EXCEPT CONTAINERS - Continued

Economic Sector or Industry Providing Inputs	%	Sector	Economic Sector or Industry Buying Outputs	%	Sector
			Refrigeration & heating equipment	0.2	Manufg.
			Telephone & telegraph apparatus	0.2	Manufg.
			Wiring devices	0.2	Manufg.
			Transit & bus transportation	0.2	Util.
			Colleges, universities, & professional schools	0.2	Services
			Libraries, vocation education	0.2	Services
			Management & consulting services & labs	0.2	Services
			S/L Govt. purch., correction	0.2	S/L Govt
			Construction of educational buildings	0.1	Constr.
			Construction of religious buildings	0.1	Constr.
			Aircraft	0.1	Manufg.
			Cyclic crudes and organics	0.1	Manufg.
			Engineering & scientific instruments	0.1	Manufg.
			Household appliances, nec	0.1	Manufg.
			Motor vehicle parts & accessories	0.1	Manufg.
			Radio & TV receiving sets	0.1	Manufg.
			Surgical & medical instruments	0.1	Manufg.
			Surgical appliances & supplies	0.1	Manufg.
			Toilet preparations	0.1	Manufg.
			Truck & bus bodies	0.1	Manufg.
			Wood partitions & fixtures	0.1	Manufg.
			Wood products, nec	0.1	Manufg.
			Railroads & related services	0.1	Util.
			Banking	0.1	Fin/R.E.
			S/L Govt. purch., other general government	0.1	S/L Govt

Source: Benchmark Input-Output Accounts for the U.S. Economy, 1982, U.S. Department of Commerce, Washington, D.C., July 1991. Data, as reported in the source, are organized by the 1977 SIC structure in use in 1982 but have been matched, as closely as is possible, to the 1987 SIC structure used in this book.

OCCUPATIONS EMPLOYED BY SIC 321 - FLAT GLASS AND PRODUCTS OF PURCHASED GLASS

Occupation	% of Total 1994	Change to 2005	Occupation	% of Total 1994	Change to 2005
Assemblers, fabricators, & hand workers nec	14.1	4.4	Precision workers nec	1.9	-6.0
Helpers, laborers, & material movers nec	8.4	4.4	Cutters & trimmers, hand	1.9	-6.0
Machine operators nec	5.2	-7.9	Industrial machinery mechanics	1.7	14.9
Cutting & slicing machine setters, operators	4.7	14.9	Grinders & polishers, hand	1.7	4.5
Machine feeders & offbearers	4.4	-6.0	Truck drivers light & heavy	1.5	7.7
Hand packers & packagers	3.8	-10.5	Traffic, shipping, & receiving clerks	1.5	0.5
Inspectors, testers, & graders, precision	3.5	4.4	Maintenance repairers, general utility	1.4	-6.0
Furnace, kiln, or kettle operators	2.7	-6.0	Coating, painting, & spraying machine workers	1.2	4.5
Freight, stock, & material movers, hand	2.5	-16.5	Industrial production managers	1.1	4.5
Industrial truck & tractor operators	2.2	4.4	Extruding & forming machine workers	1.1	14.9
Sales & related workers nec	2.2	4.4	Secretaries, ex legal & medical	1.1	-4.9
General managers & top executives	2.1	-0.9	General office clerks	1.1	-10.9
Combination machine tool operators	1.9	14.9	Screen printing machine setters & set-up operators	1.1	4.5

Source: Industry-Occupation Matrix, Bureau of Labor Statistics. These data relate to one or more 3-digit SIC industry groups rather than to a single 4-digit SIC. The change reported for each occupation to the year 2005 is a percent of growth or decline as estimated by the Bureau of Labor Statistics. The abbreviation nec stands for 'not elsewhere classified'.

LOCATION BY STATE AND REGIONAL CONCENTRATION

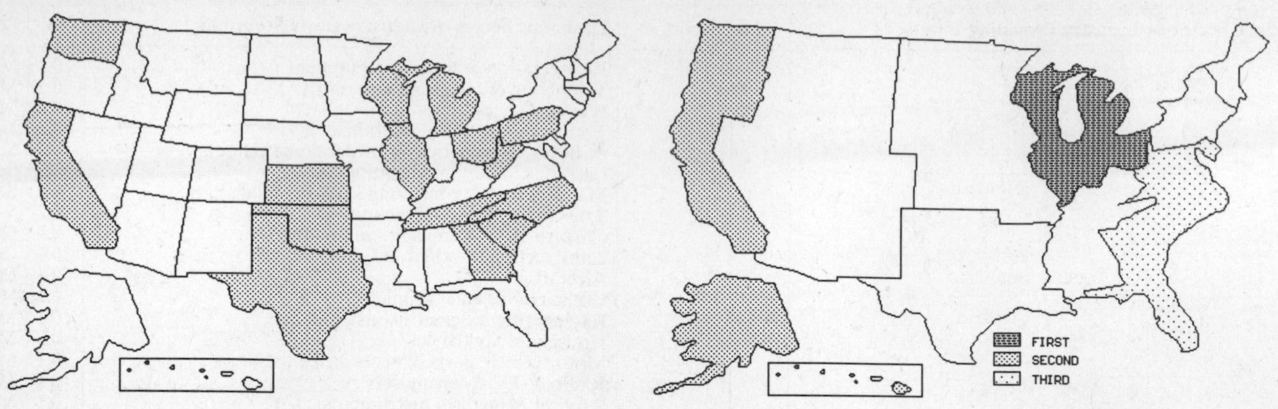

INDUSTRY DATA BY STATE

State	Establish-ments	Shipments Total ($ mil)	Shipments % of U.S.	Shipments Per Establ.	Employment Total Number	Employment % of U.S.	Employment Per Establ.	Employment Wages ($/hour)	Cost as % of Shipments	Investment per Employee ($)
California	5	230.0	11.1	46.0	1,300	10.9	260	15.41	36.0	1,000
Pennsylvania	4	(D)	-	-	1,750 *	14.7	438	-	-	1,657
Tennessee	4	(D)	-	-	3,750 *	31.5	938	-	-	-
Georgia	2	(D)	-	-	175 *	1.5	88	-	-	-
Illinois	2	(D)	-	-	750 *	6.3	375	-	-	-
Michigan	2	(D)	-	-	1,750 *	14.7	875	-	-	-
Texas	2	(D)	-	-	750 *	6.3	375	-	-	-
West Virginia	2	(D)	-	-	375 *	3.2	188	-	-	-
Wisconsin	2	(D)	-	-	175 *	1.5	88	-	-	-
Kansas	1	(D)	-	-	375 *	3.2	375	-	-	-
North Carolina	1	(D)	-	-	750 *	6.3	750	-	-	-
Ohio	1	(D)	-	-	375 *	3.2	375	-	-	-
Oklahoma	1	(D)	-	-	750 *	6.3	750	-	-	-
South Carolina	1	(D)	-	-	375 *	3.2	375	-	-	-
Washington	1	(D)	-	-	175 *	1.5	175	-	-	-

Source: 1992 *Economic Census*. The states are in descending order of shipments or establishments (if shipment data are missing for the majority). The symbol (D) appears when data are withheld to prevent disclosure of competitive information. States marked with (D) are sorted by number of establishments. A dash (-) indicates that the data element cannot be calculated; * indicates the midpoint of a range.

3221 - GLASS CONTAINERS

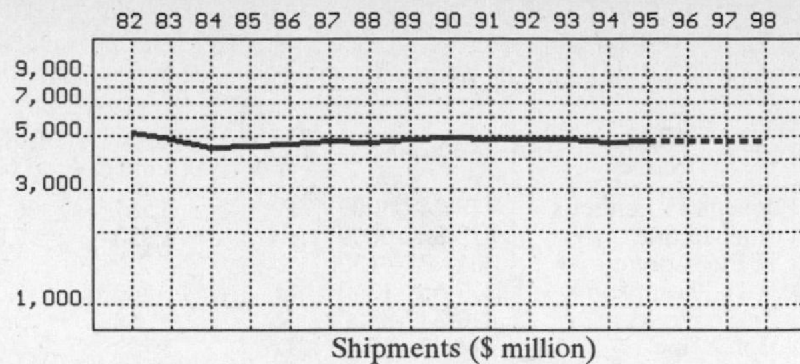

Shipments ($ million)

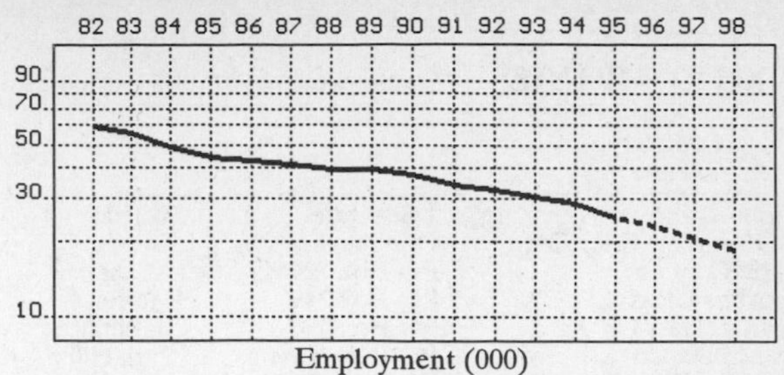

Employment (000)

GENERAL STATISTICS

Year	Com-panies	Establishments		Employment			Compensation		Production ($ million)			
		Total	with 20 or more employees	Total (000)	Production Workers (000)	Production Hours (Mil)	Payroll ($ mil)	Wages ($/hr)	Cost of Materials	Value Added by Manufacture	Value of Shipments	Capital Invest.
1982	41	128	113	59.0	51.7	101.0	1,306.4	10.81	2,521.8	2,739.1	5,216.8	297.4
1983		124	109	55.0	48.1	94.3	1,295.0	11.52	2,402.9	2,492.5	4,860.2	187.0
1984		120	105	48.5	42.3	79.8	1,191.7	12.39	2,187.2	2,246.2	4,478.5	185.3
1985		117	102	44.1	38.5	76.9	1,144.4	12.53	2,143.2	2,406.4	4,600.3	182.9
1986		107	93	42.8	37.8	75.8	1,083.4	12.10	1,997.3	2,649.5	4,627.4	211.4
1987	35	106	93	41.1	36.0	70.8	1,065.2	12.60	2,037.9	2,766.2	4,777.9	226.6
1988		104	94	39.7	34.5	71.0	1,083.5	12.68	2,090.8	2,697.3	4,704.4	239.8
1989		102	92	39.5	34.5	65.0	1,073.3	13.63	2,256.9	2,599.4	4,812.2	214.4
1990		99	88	37.6	32.1	62.2	1,076.1	14.38	2,287.2	2,751.4	4,946.1	258.0
1991		99	84	34.5	30.1	59.7	1,068.9	14.84	2,213.7	2,635.4	4,888.3	285.6
1992	16	76	76	32.3	28.1	57.3	1,052.4	15.28	1,903.7	3,038.4	4,859.6	233.0
1993		78	74	30.6	26.4	53.0	999.1	15.87	1,879.9	2,750.3	4,824.8	218.4
1994		77P	72P	28.8	25.0	49.9	962.8	16.00	1,778.0	2,903.3	4,681.3	238.2
1995		73P	69P	25.3P	21.8P	44.1P	941.3P	16.39P	1,814.7P	2,963.2P	4,777.9P	243.8P
1996		68P	65P	23.1P	19.8P	40.3P	917.5P	16.82P	1,814.0P	2,962.1P	4,776.1P	245.9P
1997		64P	62P	20.8P	17.8P	36.5P	893.7P	17.24P	1,813.3P	2,961.0P	4,774.3P	248.0P
1998		60P	59P	18.6P	15.8P	32.7P	869.9P	17.66P	1,812.6P	2,959.8P	4,772.5P	250.0P

Sources: 1982, 1987, 1992 *Economic Census*; *Annual Survey of Manufactures*, 83-86, 88-91, 93-94. Establishment counts for non-Census years are from *County Business Patterns*; establishment values for 83-84 are extrapolations. 'P's show projections by the editors. Industries reclassified in 87 will not have data for prior years.

INDICES OF CHANGE

Year	Com-panies	Establishments		Employment			Compensation		Production ($ million)			
		Total	with 20 or more employees	Total (000)	Production Workers (000)	Production Hours (Mil)	Payroll ($ mil)	Wages ($/hr)	Cost of Materials	Value Added by Manufacture	Value of Shipments	Capital Invest.
1982	256	168	149	183	184	176	124	71	132	90	107	128
1983		163	143	170	171	165	123	75	126	82	100	80
1984		158	138	150	151	139	113	81	115	74	92	80
1985		154	134	137	137	134	109	82	113	79	95	78
1986		141	122	133	135	132	103	79	105	87	95	91
1987	219	139	122	127	128	124	101	82	107	91	98	97
1988		137	124	123	123	124	103	83	110	89	97	103
1989		134	121	122	123	113	102	89	119	86	99	92
1990		130	116	116	114	109	102	94	120	91	102	111
1991		130	111	107	107	104	102	97	116	87	101	123
1992	100	100	100	100	100	100	100	100	100	100	100	100
1993		103	97	95	94	92	95	104	99	91	99	94
1994		101P	95P	89	89	87	91	105	93	96	96	102
1995		96P	91P	78P	78P	77P	89P	107P	95P	98P	98P	105P
1996		90P	86P	71P	70P	70P	87P	110P	95P	97P	98P	106P
1997		84P	82P	64P	63P	64P	85P	113P	95P	97P	98P	106P
1998		78P	77P	58P	56P	57P	83P	116P	95P	97P	98P	107P

Sources: Same as General Statistics. Values reflect change from the base year, 1992. Values above 100 mean greater than 92, values below 100 mean less than 92, and a value of 100 in the 82-91 or 93-98 period means same as 92. 'P's mark projections by the editors.

SELECTED RATIOS

For 1994	Avg. of All Manufact.	Analyzed Industry	Index	For 1994	Avg. of All Manufact.	Analyzed Industry	Index
Employees per Establishment	49	374	764	Value Added per Production Worker	134,084	116,132	87
Payroll per Establishment	1,500,273	12,518,676	834	Cost per Establishment	5,045,178	23,118,203	458
Payroll per Employee	30,620	33,431	109	Cost per Employee	102,970	61,736	60
Production Workers per Establishment	34	325	947	Cost per Production Worker	146,988	71,120	48
Wages per Establishment	853,319	10,381,087	1,217	Shipments per Establishment	9,576,895	60,867,967	636
Wages per Production Worker	24,861	31,936	128	Shipments per Employee	195,460	162,545	83
Hours per Production Worker	2,056	1,996	97	Shipments per Production Worker	279,017	187,252	67
Wages per Hour	12.09	16.00	132	Investment per Establishment	321,011	3,097,163	965
Value Added per Establishment	4,602,255	37,749,764	820	Investment per Employee	6,552	8,271	126
Value Added per Employee	93,930	100,809	107	Investment per Production Worker	9,352	9,528	102

Sources: Same as General Statistics. The 'Average of All Manufacturing' column represents the average of all manufacturing industries reported for the most recent complete year available. The Index shows the relationship between the Average and the Analyzed Industry. For example, 100 means that they are equal; 500 that the Analyzed Industry is five times the average; 50 means that the Analyzed Industry is half the national average. The abbreviation 'na' is used to show that data are 'not available'.

LEADING COMPANIES

Number shown: **14** Total sales ($ mil): **6,384** Total employment (000): **46.0**

Company Name	Address				CEO Name	Phone	Co. Type	Sales ($ mil)	Empl. (000)
Owens-Illinois Inc	1 SeaGate	Toledo	OH	43666	Joseph H Lemieux	419-247-5000	P	3,567	26.7
Anchor Glass Container Corp	One Anchor Plz	Tampa	FL	33634	Jim Malone	813-884-0000	S	1,250	7.0
Ball Plastic Container	PO Box 724447	Atlanta	GA	31139	H Ray Looney	404-437-7130	S	790	7.0
Foster Forbes Glass	PO Box 249	Marion	IN	46952	H H Thompson	317-668-1200	D	560	3.3
Carr Lowrey Glass Co	PO Box 356	Baltimore	MD	21203	Peter Wodtke	410-347-8800	R	53	0.6
Flat River Glass Co	PO Box G	Park Hills	MO	63601	Bob Peine	314-431-5743	D	53	0.6
Consumer Products Co	PO Box 2729	Muncie	IN	47307	Michael D Patrick	317-281-5019	S	44	0.1
Wheaton Science Products Inc	1000 N 10th St	Millville	NJ	08332	E Scott Wheaton	609-825-1100	S	22*	0.2
Hillsboro Glass Co	PO Box 430	Hillsboro	IL	62049	Al Fleming	217-532-3976	S	20	0.2
Munchkin Bottling Inc	7535 Woodman Pl	Van Nuys	CA	91405	Steve Dunn	818-786-2229	R	11*	0.1
Meteor Glass Company Inc	538 Northeast Av	Vineland	NJ	08360	William Bozarth	609-691-8251	R	6	<0.1
Pennsylvania Glass Products Co	430 N Craig St	Pittsburgh	PA	15213	LC Dykema	412-621-2853	R	4	<0.1
Acme Vial and Glass Company	1601 Com Way	Paso Robles	CA	93446	CT Knowles	805-239-2666	R	2	<0.1
Bergin and Thomas Ltd	986 Kaiser Rd	Napa	CA	94558	Michael Bergin	707-224-0111	R	2*	<0.1

Source: *Ward's Business Directory of U.S. Private and Public Companies*, Volumes 1 and 2, 1996. The company type code used is as follows: P - Public, R - Private, S - Subsidiary, D - Division, J - Joint Venture, A - Affiliate, G - Group. Sales are in millions of dollars, employees are in thousands. An asterisk (*) indicates an estimated sales volume. The symbol < stands for 'less than'. Company names and addresses are truncated, in some cases, to fit into the available space.

MATERIALS CONSUMED

Material		Quantity	Delivered Cost ($ million)
Materials, ingredients, containers, and supplies		(X)	1,495.5
Sodium carbonate (soda ash) (58 percent Na2O)	1,000 s tons	1,821.9	214.2
Glass sand, all types	1,000 s tons	5,521.3	126.3
Lime (including quicklime and dead-burned dolomite)	1,000 s tons	1,560.7	36.4
Nonmetallic minerals and earths, ground or otherwise treated	1,000 s tons	678.6*	30.7
Other stone, clay, glass, and concrete products	1,000 s tons	(S)	18.0
Paperboard containers, boxes, and corrugated paperboard	1,000 s tons	(S)	551.5
Cullet (glass scrap)	mil lb	4,590.2	152.8
Plastics film and sheet, unsupported		(X)	82.6
Industrial dies, molds, jigs, and fixtures		(X)	66.9
All other materials and components, parts, containers, and supplies		(X)	156.0
Materials, ingredients, containers, and supplies, nsk		(X)	60.1

Source: 1992 *Economic Census*. Explanation of symbols used: (D): Withheld to avoid disclosure of competitive data; na: Not available; (S): Withheld because statistical norms were not met; (X): Not applicable; (Z): Less than half the unit shown; nec: Not elsewhere classified; nsk: Not specified by kind; - : zero; * : 10-19 percent estimated; ** : 20-29 percent estimated.

PRODUCT SHARE DETAILS

Product or Product Class	% Share	Product or Product Class	% Share
Glass containers	100.00		

Source: 1992 *Economic Census*. The values shown are percent of total shipments in an industry. Values of indented subcategories are summed in the main heading. The symbol (D) appears when data are withheld to prevent disclosure of competitive information. The abbreviation nsk stands for 'not specified by kind' and nec for 'not elsewhere classified'.

INPUTS AND OUTPUTS FOR GLASS CONTAINERS

Economic Sector or Industry Providing Inputs	%	Sector	Economic Sector or Industry Buying Outputs	%	Sector
Paperboard containers & boxes	18.1	Manufg.	Malt beverages	24.4	Manufg.
Gas production & distribution (utilities)	13.4	Util.	Bottled & canned soft drinks	14.3	Manufg.
Alkalies & chlorine	9.4	Manufg.	Canned fruits & vegetables	7.7	Manufg.
Cyclic crudes and organics	8.9	Manufg.	Distilled liquor, except brandy	7.6	Manufg.
Electric services (utilities)	7.2	Util.	Pickles, sauces, & salad dressings	6.5	Manufg.
Wholesale trade	4.8	Trade	Wines, brandy, & brandy spirits	6.1	Manufg.
Advertising	3.8	Services	Drugs	5.1	Manufg.
Railroads & related services	3.3	Util.	Canned specialties	3.8	Manufg.
Sand & gravel	3.1	Mining	Food preparations, nec	3.8	Manufg.
Motor freight transportation & warehousing	2.4	Util.	Toilet preparations	3.8	Manufg.
Imports	2.4	Foreign	Wholesale trade	2.3	Trade
Glass containers	2.2	Manufg.	Shortening & cooking oils	1.8	Manufg.
Special dies & tools & machine tool accessories	2.2	Manufg.	Glass containers	1.4	Manufg.
Scrap	1.7	Scrap	Exports	1.4	Foreign
Minerals, ground or treated	1.6	Manufg.	Chemical preparations, nec	1.3	Manufg.
Petroleum refining	1.3	Manufg.	Roasted coffee	1.0	Manufg.
Maintenance of nonfarm buildings nec	1.0	Constr.	Water supply & sewage systems	0.9	Util.

Continued on next page.

INPUTS AND OUTPUTS FOR GLASS CONTAINERS - Continued

Economic Sector or Industry Providing Inputs	%	Sector	Economic Sector or Industry Buying Outputs	%	Sector
Industrial inorganic chemicals, nec	1.0	Manufg.	Personal consumption expenditures	0.7	
Lime	0.9	Manufg.	Confectionery products	0.7	Manufg.
Miscellaneous plastics products	0.9	Manufg.	Hardware, nec	0.7	Manufg.
Air transportation	0.8	Util.	Agricultural chemicals, nec	0.6	Manufg.
Commercial printing	0.7	Manufg.	Condensed & evaporated milk	0.6	Manufg.
Banking	0.7	Fin/R.E.	Household laundry equipment	0.6	Manufg.
Machinery, except electrical, nec	0.6	Manufg.	Polishes & sanitation goods	0.5	Manufg.
Communications, except radio & TV	0.6	Util.	Change in business inventories	0.4	In House
Eating & drinking places	0.6	Trade	Soap & other detergents	0.3	Manufg.
Water transportation	0.5	Util.	Paints & allied products	0.2	Manufg.
Sanitary services, steam supply, irrigation	0.4	Util.	Nursing & personal care facilities	0.2	Services
Real estate	0.4	Fin/R.E.	Cheese, natural & processed	0.1	Manufg.
Equipment rental & leasing services	0.4	Services	Flavoring extracts & syrups, nec	0.1	Manufg.
Lubricating oils & greases	0.3	Manufg.	Colleges, universities, & professional schools	0.1	Services
Computer & data processing services	0.3	Services	Elementary & secondary schools	0.1	Services
U.S. Postal Service	0.3	Gov't	Hospitals	0.1	Services
Crowns & closures	0.2	Manufg.	Medical & health services, nec	0.1	Services
Wood pallets & skids	0.2	Manufg.			
Insurance carriers	0.2	Fin/R.E.			
Royalties	0.2	Fin/R.E.			
Accounting, auditing & bookkeeping	0.2	Services			
Automotive rental & leasing, without drivers	0.2	Services			
Automotive repair shops & services	0.2	Services			
Hotels & lodging places	0.2	Services			
Legal services	0.2	Services			
Management & consulting services & labs	0.2	Services			
Clay, ceramic, & refractory minerals	0.1	Mining			
Abrasive products	0.1	Manufg.			
Manifold business forms	0.1	Manufg.			
Mechanical measuring devices	0.1	Manufg.			

Source: Benchmark Input-Output Accounts for the U.S. Economy, 1982, U.S. Department of Commerce, Washington, D.C., July 1991. Data, as reported in the source, are organized by the 1977 SIC structure in use in 1982 but have been matched, as closely as is possible, to the 1987 SIC structure used in this book.

OCCUPATIONS EMPLOYED BY SIC 322 - GLASS AND GLASSWARE, PRESSED OR BLOWN

Occupation	% of Total 1994	Change to 2005	Occupation	% of Total 1994	Change to 2005
Inspectors, testers, & graders, precision	13.6	-39.1	Maintenance repairers, general utility	2.4	-45.1
Hand packers & packagers	7.9	-47.8	Furnace, kiln, or kettle operators	2.1	-63.5
Helpers, laborers, & material movers nec	7.4	-39.1	Precision workers nec	2.0	-45.2
Extruding & forming machine workers	7.1	-33.0	Freight, stock, & material movers, hand	1.9	-51.2
Extruding & forming machine workers	5.9	21.9	Crushing & mixing machine operators	1.5	-39.1
Industrial machinery mechanics	4.9	-33.0	Machine forming operators, metal & plastic	1.5	-39.1
Blue collar worker supervisors	4.9	-41.9	Machinists	1.2	-39.1
Industrial truck & tractor operators	3.9	-39.1	Grinders & polishers, hand	1.1	-39.1
Assemblers, fabricators, & hand workers nec	3.3	-39.1	Electricians	1.1	-42.8
Packaging & filling machine operators	3.2	-39.1	Industrial production managers	1.1	-39.1
Machine feeders & offbearers	3.2	-45.2	Engineering technicians & technologists nec	1.0	-39.1

Source: Industry-Occupation Matrix, Bureau of Labor Statistics. These data relate to one or more 3-digit SIC industry groups rather than to a single 4-digit SIC. The change reported for each occupation to the year 2005 is a percent of growth or decline as estimated by the Bureau of Labor Statistics. The abbreviation nec stands for 'not elsewhere classified'.

LOCATION BY STATE AND REGIONAL CONCENTRATION

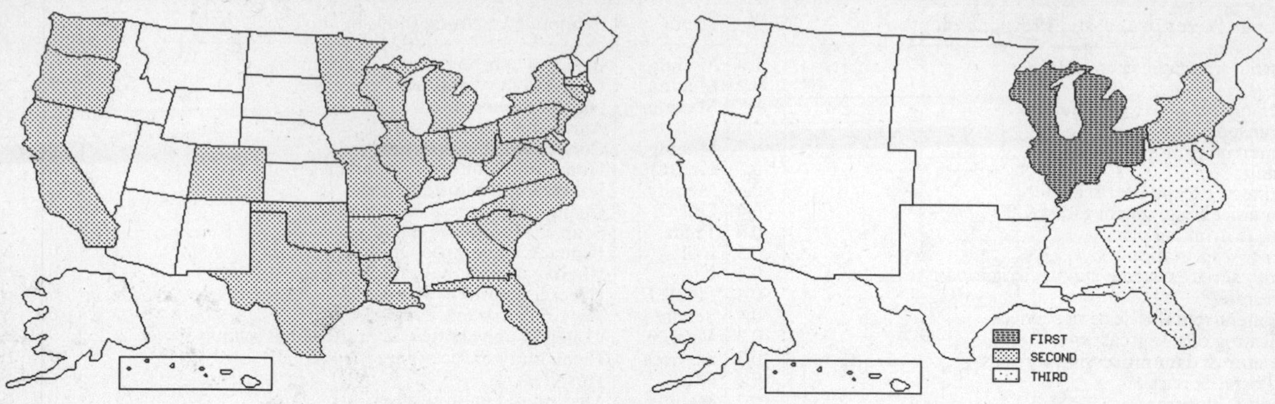

INDUSTRY DATA BY STATE

State	Establish-ments	Shipments			Employment				Cost as % of Shipments	Investment per Employee ($)
		Total ($ mil)	% of U.S.	Per Establ.	Total Number	% of U.S.	Per Establ.	Wages ($/hour)		
California	12	893.7	18.4	74.5	5,400	16.7	450	15.86	41.9	5,019
Pennsylvania	5	444.7	9.2	88.9	3,400	10.5	680	15.54	34.7	6,324
New Jersey	8	385.6	7.9	48.2	3,400	10.5	425	12.93	43.8	5,000
Illinois	8	372.5	7.7	46.6	3,100	9.6	388	14.89	40.2	-
New York	3	249.7	5.1	83.2	1,100	3.4	367	17.11	42.7	-
Florida	3	157.6	3.2	52.5	1,100	3.4	367	15.40	48.4	-
Indiana	5	(D)	-	-	1,750 *	5.4	350	-	-	-
Oklahoma	5	(D)	-	-	1,750 *	5.4	350	-	-	-
North Carolina	4	(D)	-	-	1,750 *	5.4	438	-	-	-
Texas	3	(D)	-	-	1,750 *	5.4	583	-	-	-
Georgia	2	(D)	-	-	1,750 *	5.4	875	-	-	-
Virginia	2	(D)	-	-	750 *	2.3	375	-	-	-
West Virginia	2	(D)	-	-	750 *	2.3	375	-	-	-
Arkansas	1	(D)	-	-	375 *	1.2	375	-	-	-
Colorado	1	(D)	-	-	375 *	1.2	375	-	-	-
Connecticut	1	(D)	-	-	375 *	1.2	375	-	-	-
Louisiana	1	(D)	-	-	375 *	1.2	375	-	-	-
Maryland	1	(D)	-	-	750 *	2.3	750	-	-	-
Massachusetts	1	(D)	-	-	175 *	0.5	175	-	-	-
Michigan	1	(D)	-	-	375 *	1.2	375	-	-	-
Minnesota	1	(D)	-	-	375 *	1.2	375	-	-	-
Missouri	1	(D)	-	-	175 *	0.5	175	-	-	-
Ohio	1	(D)	-	-	750 *	2.3	750	-	-	-
Oregon	1	(D)	-	-	375 *	1.2	375	-	-	-
South Carolina	1	(D)	-	-	375 *	1.2	375	-	-	-
Washington	1	(D)	-	-	750 *	2.3	750	-	-	-
Wisconsin	1	(D)	-	-	375 *	1.2	375	-	-	-

Source: 1992 *Economic Census*. The states are in descending order of shipments or establishments (if shipment data are missing for the majority). The symbol (D) appears when data are withheld to prevent disclosure of competitive information. States marked with (D) are sorted by number of establishments. A dash (-) indicates that the data element cannot be calculated; * indicates the midpoint of a range.

3229 - PRESSED & BLOWN GLASS, NEC

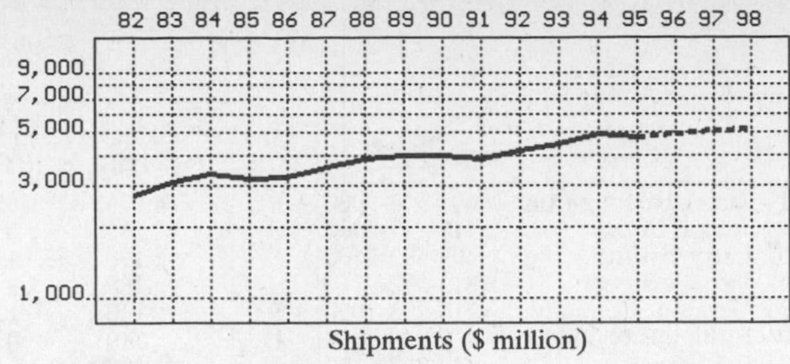

Shipments ($ million)

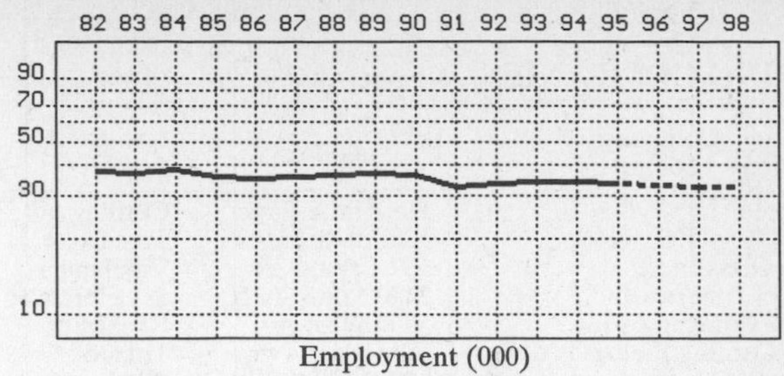

Employment (000)

GENERAL STATISTICS

Year	Companies	Establishments: Total	Establishments: with 20 or more employees	Employment: Total (000)	Employment: Production Workers (000)	Employment: Production Hours (Mil)	Compensation: Payroll ($ mil)	Compensation: Wages ($/hr)	Production ($ million): Cost of Materials	Production ($ million): Value Added by Manufacture	Production ($ million): Value of Shipments	Production ($ million): Capital Invest.
1982	276	331	116	37.6	29.5	56.8	726.0	9.41	984.0	1,743.1	2,724.0	233.3
1983		328	115	37.4	29.9	59.4	785.9	9.94	1,075.0	2,022.8	3,106.1	173.7
1984		325	114	38.2	31.5	61.3	834.8	10.53	1,234.8	2,160.8	3,338.7	181.4
1985		322	113	36.0	29.2	55.6	815.0	11.15	1,176.5	2,017.1	3,207.7	247.7
1986		328	109	35.0	29.0	56.5	843.6	11.41	1,163.8	2,039.4	3,241.9	228.5
1987	363	417	119	36.4	29.9	58.8	896.5	11.66	1,221.2	2,304.5	3,568.0	195.8
1988		403	133	36.6	30.5	58.8	927.6	12.23	1,312.3	2,542.1	3,858.1	238.6
1989		393	138	36.9	29.2	59.8	951.3	12.26	1,411.0	2,636.7	4,016.7	431.7
1990		404	142	36.7	29.5	60.4	983.1	12.53	1,435.8	2,591.4	3,971.9	297.3
1991		437	145	32.9	26.9	54.4	946.0	13.04	1,337.3	2,493.9	3,866.3	296.4
1992	411	450	98	33.9	27.8	57.2	1,024.6	13.69	1,351.0	2,867.3	4,182.2	343.8
1993		471	113	34.1	28.0	57.9	1,052.3	14.01	1,509.6	2,950.5	4,464.5	252.8
1994		475P	128P	34.2	28.6	59.2	1,087.8	14.45	1,648.6	3,294.6	4,946.5	345.2
1995		489P	129P	33.6P	27.8P	58.0P	1,105.3P	14.78P	1,594.3P	3,186.0P	4,783.5P	352.6P
1996		503P	129P	33.2P	27.6P	58.0P	1,132.7P	15.18P	1,644.4P	3,286.2P	4,934.0P	364.9P
1997		517P	130P	32.9P	27.4P	57.9P	1,160.1P	15.57P	1,694.6P	3,386.5P	5,084.4P	377.2P
1998		531P	131P	32.6P	27.2P	57.9P	1,187.5P	15.97P	1,744.7P	3,486.7P	5,234.9P	389.5P

Sources: 1982, 1987, 1992 *Economic Census*; *Annual Survey of Manufactures*, 83-86, 88-91, 93-94. Establishment counts for non-Census years are from *County Business Patterns*; establishment values for 83-84 are extrapolations. 'P's show projections by the editors. Industries reclassified in 87 will not have data for prior years.

INDICES OF CHANGE

Year	Companies	Establishments: Total	Establishments: with 20 or more employees	Employment: Total (000)	Employment: Production Workers (000)	Employment: Production Hours (Mil)	Compensation: Payroll ($ mil)	Compensation: Wages ($/hr)	Production ($ million): Cost of Materials	Production ($ million): Value Added by Manufacture	Production ($ million): Value of Shipments	Production ($ million): Capital Invest.
1982	67	74	118	111	106	99	71	69	73	61	65	68
1983		73	117	110	108	104	77	73	80	71	74	51
1984		72	116	113	113	107	81	77	91	75	80	53
1985		72	115	106	105	97	80	81	87	70	77	72
1986		73	111	103	104	99	82	83	86	71	78	66
1987	88	93	121	107	108	103	87	85	90	80	85	57
1988		90	136	108	110	103	91	89	97	89	92	69
1989		87	141	109	105	105	93	90	104	92	96	126
1990		90	145	108	106	106	96	92	106	90	95	86
1991		97	148	97	97	95	92	95	99	87	92	86
1992	100	100	100	100	100	100	100	100	100	100	100	100
1993		105	115	101	101	101	103	102	112	103	107	74
1994		106P	130P	101	103	103	106	106	122	115	118	100
1995		109P	131P	99P	100P	101P	108P	108P	118P	111P	114P	103P
1996		112P	132P	98P	99P	101P	111P	111P	122P	115P	118P	106P
1997		115P	133P	97P	99P	101P	113P	114P	125P	118P	122P	110P
1998		118P	134P	96P	98P	101P	116P	117P	129P	122P	125P	113P

Sources: Same as General Statistics. Values reflect change from the base year, 1992. Values above 100 mean greater than 92, values below 100 mean less than 92, and a value of 100 in the 82-91 or 93-98 period means same as 92. 'P's mark projections by the editors.

SELECTED RATIOS

For 1994	Avg. of All Manufact.	Analyzed Industry	Index	For 1994	Avg. of All Manufact.	Analyzed Industry	Index
Employees per Establishment	49	72	147	Value Added per Production Worker	134,084	115,196	86
Payroll per Establishment	1,500,273	2,288,718	153	Cost per Establishment	5,045,178	3,468,635	69
Payroll per Employee	30,620	31,807	104	Cost per Employee	102,970	48,205	47
Production Workers per Establishment	34	60	175	Cost per Production Worker	146,988	57,643	39
Wages per Establishment	853,319	1,799,836	211	Shipments per Establishment	9,576,895	10,407,377	109
Wages per Production Worker	24,861	29,910	120	Shipments per Employee	195,460	144,635	74
Hours per Production Worker	2,056	2,070	101	Shipments per Production Worker	279,017	172,955	62
Wages per Hour	12.09	14.45	120	Investment per Establishment	321,011	726,297	226
Value Added per Establishment	4,602,255	6,931,799	151	Investment per Employee	6,552	10,094	154
Value Added per Employee	93,930	96,333	103	Investment per Production Worker	9,352	12,070	129

Sources: Same as General Statistics. The 'Average of All Manufacturing' column represents the average of all manufacturing industries reported for the most recent complete year available. The Index shows the relationship between the Average and the Analyzed Industry. For example, 100 means that they are equal; 500 that the Analyzed Industry is five times the average; 50 means that the Analyzed Industry is half the national average. The abbreviation 'na' is used to show that data are 'not available'.

LEADING COMPANIES Number shown: **75** Total sales ($ mil): **6,768** Total employment (000): **58.0**

Company Name	Address				CEO Name	Phone	Co. Type	Sales ($ mil)	Empl. (000)
Corning Inc	Houghton Park	Corning	NY	14831	James R Houghton	607-974-9000	P	4,770	40.0
Libbey Glass Inc	420 Madison Av	Toledo	OH	43699	John F Meier	419-727-2100	S	281	2.9
Kimble Glass Inc	537 Crystal Av	Vineland	NJ	08360	Larry Griffith	609-692-3600	J	198	1.0
Essilor of America Inc	2400 118th Av N	St Petersburg	FL	33716	Jacques Stoerr	813-572-0844	S	180	1.7
Pfaudler Companies Inc	1000 West Av	Rochester	NY	14692	Gerald L Connelly	716-235-1000	S	140	1.4
Owens-Corning Fiberglas Corp	Fiberglass Twr	Toledo	OH	43659	Efthimios O Vidalis	419-248-7898	D	110*	0.7
Pittsburgh Corning Corp	800 Presque Isle Dr	Pittsburgh	PA	15239	CA Francik	412-327-6100	J	100	1.1
Crystal Clear Industries Inc	2 Bergen Tpk	Ridgefield Park	NJ	07660	Abraham Lefkowitz	201-440-4200	R	90	0.3
Photronics Inc	PO Box 5226	Brookfield	CT	06804	C S Macricostas	203-775-9000	P	81	0.4
Creation Windows Inc	PO Box 1046	Elkhart	IN	46515	Robert Hotovy	219-264-3131	S	55	0.6
Forsch Corp	1000 Abernathy NE	Atlanta	GA	30328	K V Madreh Jr	404-668-8800	R	54	0.6
Reliable Power Products	11411 Addison St	Franklin Park	IL	60131	Barry MacLean	708-455-0014	S	50	0.3
Schott Glass Technologies Inc	400 York Av	Duryea	PA	18642	John G Gulbin	717-457-7485	R	50	0.5
Rauch Industries Inc	PO Box 609	Gastonia	NC	28053	Marshall A Rauch	704-867-5333	P	45	0.6
Fenton Art Glass Co	700 Elizabeth St	Williamstown	WV	26187	George W Fenton	304-375-6122	R	42*	0.4
Pitman-Dreitzer	4460 Lake Forest	Cincinnati	OH	45242	Anton Katrus	513-563-7767	D	41*	<0.1
Gemco-Ware Inc	PO Box 0813	Freeport	NY	11520		516-623-9300	S	40	0.3
Steuben	717 5th Av	New York	NY	10022	Donald Rorke	212-752-1441	D	34	0.3
Ortel Corp	2015 W Chestnut St	Alhambra	CA	91803	Wim HJ Selders	818-281-3636	R	28	0.3
SpecTran Corp	50 Hall Rd	Sturbridge	MA	01566	Raymond E Jaeger	508-347-2261	P	27	0.2
Crane Cor Tec	2351 Kenskill Av	Wash Ct House	OH	43160	FS Prior	614-335-9400	S	25	<0.1
Lenox Crystal Inc	Lenox & Rte 31 E	Mount Pleasant	PA	15666	Richard Stearns	412-547-4541	S	25	0.2
Schott Corp	3 Odell Plz	Yonkers	NY	10701	Guy De Coninck	914-968-8900	D	23	0.3
Southwestern Glass Company	PO Drawer Z	Van Buren	AR	72956	Dwight Morland	501-474-5293	R	21*	0.2
Harmonic Lightwaves Inc	3005 Bunker Hill Ln	Santa Clara	CA	95054	Tony Ley	408-970-9880	P	18	0.1
Louie Glass Company Inc	PO Box 1028	Weston	WV	26452	Jeffrey F Smith	304-269-4700	S	16	0.3
Schott Process Systems Inc	PO Box T	Vineland	NJ	08360	Erich Stolz	609-692-4700	S	12	0.1
Superior Glass Fibers Inc	PO Box 89	Bremen	OH	43107	Richard L Frazier	614-569-4175	R	11	0.2
Blenko Glass Company Inc	PO Box 67	Milton	WV	25541	WH Blenko Jr	304-743-9081	R	10	0.1
Dlubak Corp	PO Box 397	Freeport	PA	16229	Frank Dlubak	412-295-5167	R	10	0.1
Fibair	PO Box 478	Reedsville	WV	26547	William Daniel	304-864-3321	S	10*	<0.1
Kopp Glass Inc	2108 Palmer St	Pittsburgh	PA	15218	JD Stephens	412-271-0190	R	10	0.1
Emerson & Cuming	59 Walpole St	Canton	MA	02021	Michael Small	617-821-4250	R	9*	<0.1
LE Smith Glass Co	PO Box 963	Mount Pleasant	PA	15666	Michael Miller	412-547-3544	S	9	0.2
LE Smith Holding Co	PO Box 963	Mount Pleasant	PA	15666	Micheal Miller	412-547-3544	R	9	0.2
Elan Technology	140 Little St	Belleville	NJ	07109	PA Argentinis	201-759-8600	D	8	0.1
Lumitex Inc	8443 Dow Cir	Cleveland	OH	44136	Peter W Broer	216-243-8401	R	8*	<0.1
Mansol Industries Inc	140 Little St	Belleville	NJ	07109	PA Argentinis	201-759-8600	R	8	0.1
Simon Pearce Inc	The Mill	Quechee	VT	05059	Simon Pearce	802-295-2711	R	8	0.1
Mid-Atlantic of West Virginia	Lamberton Rte 50	Ellenboro	WV	26346	R Spencer	304-869-3351	R	7	0.2
Precision Electronic Glass Inc	1013 Hendee Rd	Vineland	NJ	08360	Philip Rossi	609-691-2234	R	6	<0.1
Amalga Composites Inc	10600 W Mitchell St	West Allis	WI	53214	James L Dorman	414-453-9555	R	6	<0.1
Pilgrim Glass Corp	PO Box 395	Ceredo	WV	25507	Alfred Knobler	304-453-3553	R	6	0.1
ACCU-GLASS	10765 Trenton Av	St Louis	MO	63132	Robert P Weathers	314-423-0300	D	5	0.1
In Vitro Scientific Products Inc	823 Hanley Indrial	St Louis	MO	63144	Rick St Pierre	314-963-1993	R	5	<0.1
Jeannette Shade and Novelty	PO Box 99	Jeannette	PA	15644	Theodore Sarniak III	412-523-5567	R	5	<0.1
Kraftware Corp	675 Garfield Av	Jersey City	NJ	07305	Donald Grant	201-434-4200	R	5	<0.1
Polymicro Technologies Inc	18019 N 25th Av	Phoenix	AZ	85023	Gary Nelson	602-375-4100	S	4*	<0.1
Raylan Corp	2525 E Bayshore Dr	Palo Alto	CA	94303	N D'Arcy Roche	415-813-0400	R	4	<0.1
Richland Glass Company Inc	Tuckahoe Rd	Richland	NJ	08350	G Evey	609-691-1697	R	4	<0.1
Annieglass Inc	PO Box 8445	Santa Cruz	CA	95061	Ann Morhauser	408-426-5086	R	3	<0.1
Dalzell Corp	PO Box 459	N Martinsvl	WV	26155	Kenneth B Dalzell	304-455-2900	R	3	<0.1
Davis-Lynch Glass Co	PO Box 4268	Star City	WV	26504	R Emmett Lynch	304-599-2244	R	3	<0.1
Gillinder Brothers Inc	PO Box 1007	Port Jervis	NY	12771	C Gillinder	914-856-5375	R	3	<0.1
Iris Arc Crystal Inc	114 E Haley St	Santa Barbara	CA	93101	Jonathon Wygant	805-963-3661	R	3	<0.1
Peltier Glass Co	PO Box 490	Ottawa	IL	61350	J Jankowski	815-433-0026	R	3	<0.1
Specialty Plastics Inc	PO Box 77011	Baton Rouge	LA	70879	Richard H Lea Sr	504-752-2705	R	3	<0.1
Susquehanna Glass Co	731 Avnue H	Columbia	PA	17512	Nancy L Roye	717-684-2155	R	2	<0.1
Brooke Glass Company Inc	PO Box 109	Wellsburg	WV	26070	HA Rithner	304-737-3461	R	2	<0.1
DiCon Fiberoptics Inc	1331 8th St	Berkeley	CA	94710	Ho Lee	510-528-0427	R	2	<0.1
Fiberguide Industries Inc	1 Bay St	Stirling	NJ	07980	Theodore Rich	908-647-6601	R	2*	<0.1
Garner Glass Co	177 S Indian Hill	Claremont	CA	91711	TH Garner	909-626-3526	R	2	<0.1
Hartford Prospect Industries Inc	PO Box 667	Manchester	CT	06045	Peter Dengenis	203-645-4070	R	2*	<0.1
Neolens Inc	18963 NE 4th Ct	Miami	FL	33179	Daniel J Kunst	305-651-0003	P	2	<0.1
Aurora Optics Inc	1777 Sentry Pkwy W	Blue Bell	PA	19422	Larry Wesson	215-646-0690	R	1*	<0.1
Fiber and Sensor Technologies	PO Box 11704	Blacksburg	VA	24062	Kent Murphy	703-382-7556	R	1*	<0.1
GC Technologies Inc	1897 Providence Ct	Atlanta	GA	30337	Walter Pelletier	404-991-9200	D	1	<0.1
General Fiber Optics Inc	1 Washington Av	Fairfield	NJ	07004	Tim Bhule	201-239-3400	R	1	<0.1
IGS Inc	916 E California	Sunnyvale	CA	94086	Juan Gracia	408-733-4621	R	1	<0.1
Hal Reed Co	12004 NE 172nd St	Kearney	MO	64060	Hal E Reed	816-628-6722	R	1*	<0.1
Leucos USA Inc	70 Campus Plz	Edison	NJ	08037	Josie Anthony	908-225-0010	S	1*	<0.1
Canyon Materials Inc	6665 Nancy Ridge	San Diego	CA	92121	Chuck Wu	619-552-1188	R	1*	<0.1
Sloan Glass Inc	PO Box 182	Culloden	WV	25510	Charles T Sloan	304-743-9101	R	1	<0.1
Lighthouse Digital Systems Inc	PO Box 1802	Grass Valley	CA	95945	Bob Grant	916-272-8240	R	1*	<0.1
Port City Fiberglass Inc	418 Hermitage Rd	Castle Hayne	NC	28429	Chuck Bower	910-675-3599	R	1	<0.1

Source: *Ward's Business Directory of U.S. Private and Public Companies*, Volumes 1 and 2, 1996. The company type code used is as follows: P - Public, R - Private, S - Subsidiary, D - Division, J - Joint Venture, A - Affiliate, G - Group. Sales are in millions of dollars, employees are in thousands. An asterisk (*) indicates an estimated sales volume. The symbol < stands for 'less than'. Company names and addresses are truncated, in some cases, to fit into the available space.

MATERIALS CONSUMED

Material	Quantity	Delivered Cost ($ million)
Materials, ingredients, containers, and supplies	(X)	929.8
Glass sand, all types	(X)	123.8
Sodium carbonate (soda ash) (58 percent Na2O)	(X)	31.4
Industrial inorganic chemicals, except sodium carbonate	(X)	147.0
Other chemicals and allied products	(X)	97.7
Glass (float, sheet and plate)	(X)	(D)
Other glass products (including glass tumblers, stemware, and tableware, excluding scrap)	(X)	14.8
Minerals and earths, ground or otherwise treated	(X)	22.3
Other stone, clay, and concrete products	(X)	12.6
Paperboard containers, boxes, and corrugated paperboard	(X)	86.9
Rough and dressed lumber	(X)	(D)
Wood boxes, pallets, skids, and containers	(X)	19.7
Other lumber and wood products, except furniture	(X)	0.1
Plastics film and sheet, unsupported	(X)	3.8
Cullet (glass scrap)	(X)	14.2
All other materials and components, parts, containers, and supplies	(X)	297.8
Materials, ingredients, containers, and supplies, nsk	(X)	57.0

Source: 1992 *Economic Census*. Explanation of symbols used: (D): Withheld to avoid disclosure of competitive data; na: Not available; (S): Withheld because statistical norms were not met; (X): Not applicable; (Z): Less than half the unit shown; nec: Not elsewhere classified; nsk: Not specified by kind; - : zero; * : 10-19 percent estimated; ** : 20-29 percent estimated.

PRODUCT SHARE DETAILS

Product or Product Class	% Share
Pressed and blown glass, nec	100.00
Glass fiber, textile-type, pressed and blown glassware made by establishments producing glass	30.82
Mat, pressed and blown glassware made by establishments producing glass	18.31
Other textile-type fiber (including yarn, strand, staple yarn, sliver, roving, chopped strand, and milled fiber), pressed and blown glassware made by establishments producing glass	81.68
Glass fiber, textile-type, nsk	0.01
Machine-made table, kitchen, art, and novelty glassware, pressed and blown glassware made by establishments producing glass	19.13
Machine-made lighting, automotive, and electronic glassware, pressed and blown glassware made by establishments producing glass	28.27
All other machine-made glassware (including technical and scientific glassware, glass blocks, and lens blanks), pressed and blown glassware made by establishments producing glass	15.79
Handmade pressed and blown glassware, made by establishments producing glass	2.89
Pressed and blown glass, nec, nsk	3.10

Source: 1992 *Economic Census*. The values shown are percent of total shipments in an industry. Values of indented subcategories are summed in the main heading. The symbol (D) appears when data are withheld to prevent disclosure of competitive information. The abbreviation nsk stands for 'not specified by kind' and nec for 'not elsewhere classified'.

INPUTS AND OUTPUTS FOR GLASS & GLASS PRODUCTS, EXCEPT CONTAINERS

Economic Sector or Industry Providing Inputs	%	Sector	Economic Sector or Industry Buying Outputs	%	Sector
Glass & glass products, except containers	15.5	Manufg.	Personal consumption expenditures	15.2	
Imports	14.6	Foreign	Glass & glass products, except containers	9.7	Manufg.
Wholesale trade	8.2	Trade	Exports	7.8	Foreign
Gas production & distribution (utilities)	7.8	Util.	Motor vehicles & car bodies	5.6	Manufg.
Cyclic crudes and organics	5.4	Manufg.	Eating & drinking places	4.5	Trade
Communications, except radio & TV	4.9	Util.	Automotive repair shops & services	4.4	Services
Electric services (utilities)	4.4	Util.	Electron tubes	3.3	Manufg.
Advertising	3.4	Services	Lighting fixtures & equipment	3.3	Manufg.
Industrial inorganic chemicals, nec	2.7	Manufg.	Miscellaneous plastics products	3.3	Manufg.
Paperboard containers & boxes	2.0	Manufg.	Hotels & lodging places	2.8	Services
Wood products, nec	2.0	Manufg.	Electric lamps	2.6	Manufg.
Alkalies & chlorine	1.9	Manufg.	Metal doors, sash, & trim	2.6	Manufg.
Adhesives & sealants	1.8	Manufg.	Asphalt felts & coatings	2.5	Manufg.
Motor freight transportation & warehousing	1.8	Util.	Hospitals	2.4	Services
Railroads & related services	1.5	Util.	Maintenance of nonfarm buildings nec	1.6	Constr.
Miscellaneous plastics products	1.4	Manufg.	Office buildings	1.1	Constr.
Maintenance of nonfarm buildings nec	1.3	Constr.	Broadwoven fabric mills	1.1	Manufg.
Petroleum refining	1.3	Manufg.	Ophthalmic goods	1.1	Manufg.
Sand & gravel	1.2	Mining	Tire cord & fabric	1.1	Manufg.
Wood containers	1.2	Manufg.	S/L Govt. purch., public assistance & relief	1.1	S/L Govt
Noncomparable imports	1.2	Foreign	Boat building & repairing	0.8	Manufg.
Banking	0.9	Fin/R.E.	Millwork	0.8	Manufg.
Air transportation	0.8	Util.	Medical & health services, nec	0.8	Services
Scrap	0.8	Scrap	Household cooking equipment	0.7	Manufg.
Machinery, except electrical, nec	0.7	Manufg.	Optical instruments & lenses	0.7	Manufg.
Automotive repair shops & services	0.7	Services	Industrial buildings	0.6	Constr.
Eating & drinking places	0.6	Trade	Electric housewares & fans	0.6	Manufg.
Carbon & graphite products	0.5	Manufg.	Wood household furniture	0.6	Manufg.
Metal stampings, nec	0.5	Manufg.	S/L Govt. purch., higher education	0.6	S/L Govt

Continued on next page.

INPUTS AND OUTPUTS FOR GLASS & GLASS PRODUCTS, EXCEPT CONTAINERS - Continued

Economic Sector or Industry Providing Inputs	%	Sector	Economic Sector or Industry Buying Outputs	%	Sector
Minerals, ground or treated	0.5	Manufg.	Nonfarm residential structure maintenance	0.5	Constr.
Computer & data processing services	0.5	Services	Mineral wool	0.5	Manufg.
Fabricated rubber products, nec	0.4	Manufg.	Automotive rental & leasing, without drivers	0.5	Services
Paints & allied products	0.4	Manufg.	Elementary & secondary schools	0.5	Services
Real estate	0.4	Fin/R.E.	Construction of stores & restaurants	0.4	Constr.
Equipment rental & leasing services	0.4	Services	Metal stampings, nec	0.4	Manufg.
U.S. Postal Service	0.4	Gov't	Semiconductors & related devices	0.4	Manufg.
Lubricating oils & greases	0.3	Manufg.	Travel trailers & campers	0.4	Manufg.
Sawmills & planning mills, general	0.3	Manufg.	Federal Government purchases, nondefense	0.4	Fed Govt
Special dies & tools & machine tool accessories	0.3	Manufg.	Metal household furniture	0.3	Manufg.
Chemical & fertilizer mineral	0.2	Mining	Nonferrous wire drawing & insulating	0.3	Manufg.
Mechanical measuring devices	0.2	Manufg.	Special industry machinery, nec	0.3	Manufg.
Rubber & plastics hose & belting	0.2	Manufg.	Doctors & dentists	0.3	Services
Textile machinery	0.2	Manufg.	Federal Government purchases, national defense	0.3	Fed Govt
Sanitary services, steam supply, irrigation	0.2	Util.	S/L Govt. purch., health & hospitals	0.3	S/L Govt
Water transportation	0.2	Util.	S/L Govt. purch., police	0.3	S/L Govt
Credit agencies other than banks	0.2	Fin/R.E.	Crude petroleum & natural gas	0.2	Mining
Insurance carriers	0.2	Fin/R.E.	Construction of hospitals	0.2	Constr.
Royalties	0.2	Fin/R.E.	Residential 1-unit structures, nonfarm	0.2	Constr.
Accounting, auditing & bookkeeping	0.2	Services	Residential additions/alterations, nonfarm	0.2	Constr.
Automotive rental & leasing, without drivers	0.2	Services	Warehouses	0.2	Constr.
Hotels & lodging places	0.2	Services	Drugs	0.2	Manufg.
Legal services	0.2	Services	Electronic components nec	0.2	Manufg.
Management & consulting services & labs	0.2	Services	Fabricated metal products, nec	0.2	Manufg.
Abrasive products	0.1	Manufg.	Fabricated plate work (boiler shops)	0.2	Manufg.
Manifold business forms	0.1	Manufg.	Hardware, nec	0.2	Manufg.
Paper coating & glazing	0.1	Manufg.	Instruments to measure electricity	0.2	Manufg.
Pumps & compressors	0.1	Manufg.	Mechanical measuring devices	0.2	Manufg.
Electrical repair shops	0.1	Services	Motor homes (made on purchased chassis)	0.2	Manufg.
			Plastics materials & resins	0.2	Manufg.
			Plating & polishing	0.2	Manufg.
			Radio & TV communication equipment	0.2	Manufg.
			Railroad equipment	0.2	Manufg.
			Refrigeration & heating equipment	0.2	Manufg.
			Telephone & telegraph apparatus	0.2	Manufg.
			Wiring devices	0.2	Manufg.
			Transit & bus transportation	0.2	Util.
			Colleges, universities, & professional schools	0.2	Services
			Libraries, vocation education	0.2	Services
			Management & consulting services & labs	0.2	Services
			S/L Govt. purch., correction	0.2	S/L Govt
			Construction of educational buildings	0.1	Constr.
			Construction of religious buildings	0.1	Constr.
			Aircraft	0.1	Manufg.
			Cyclic crudes and organics	0.1	Manufg.
			Engineering & scientific instruments	0.1	Manufg.
			Household appliances, nec	0.1	Manufg.
			Motor vehicle parts & accessories	0.1	Manufg.
			Radio & TV receiving sets	0.1	Manufg.
			Surgical & medical instruments	0.1	Manufg.
			Surgical appliances & supplies	0.1	Manufg.
			Toilet preparations	0.1	Manufg.
			Truck & bus bodies	0.1	Manufg.
			Wood partitions & fixtures	0.1	Manufg.
			Wood products, nec	0.1	Manufg.
			Railroads & related services	0.1	Util.
			Banking	0.1	Fin/R.E.
			S/L Govt. purch., other general government	0.1	S/L Govt

Source: Benchmark Input-Output Accounts for the U.S. Economy, 1982, U.S. Department of Commerce, Washington, D.C., July 1991. Data, as reported in the source, are organized by the 1977 SIC structure in use in 1982 but have been matched, as closely as is possible, to the 1987 SIC structure used in this book.

OCCUPATIONS EMPLOYED BY SIC 322 - GLASS AND GLASSWARE, PRESSED OR BLOWN

Occupation	% of Total 1994	Change to 2005	Occupation	% of Total 1994	Change to 2005
Inspectors, testers, & graders, precision	13.6	-39.1	Maintenance repairers, general utility	2.4	-45.1
Hand packers & packagers	7.9	-47.8	Furnace, kiln, or kettle operators	2.1	-63.5
Helpers, laborers, & material movers nec	7.4	-39.1	Precision workers nec	2.0	-45.2
Extruding & forming machine workers	7.1	-33.0	Freight, stock, & material movers, hand	1.9	-51.2
Extruding & forming machine workers	5.9	21.9	Crushing & mixing machine operators	1.5	-39.1
Industrial machinery mechanics	4.9	-33.0	Machine forming operators, metal & plastic	1.5	-39.1
Blue collar worker supervisors	4.9	-41.9	Machinists	1.2	-39.1
Industrial truck & tractor operators	3.9	-39.1	Grinders & polishers, hand	1.1	-39.1
Assemblers, fabricators, & hand workers nec	3.3	-39.1	Electricians	1.1	-42.8
Packaging & filling machine operators	3.2	-39.1	Industrial production managers	1.1	-39.1
Machine feeders & offbearers	3.2	-45.2	Engineering technicians & technologists nec	1.0	-39.1

Source: Industry-Occupation Matrix, Bureau of Labor Statistics. These data relate to one or more 3-digit SIC industry groups rather than to a single 4-digit SIC. The change reported for each occupation to the year 2005 is a percent of growth or decline as estimated by the Bureau of Labor Statistics. The abbreviation nec stands for 'not elsewhere classified'.

LOCATION BY STATE AND REGIONAL CONCENTRATION

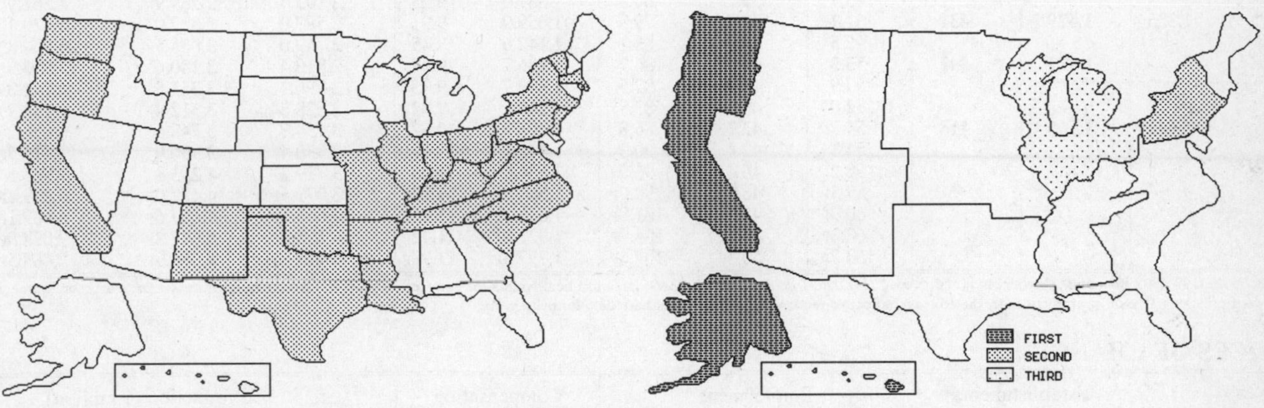

INDUSTRY DATA BY STATE

State	Establish-ments	Shipments			Employment				Cost as % of Shipments	Investment per Employee ($)
		Total ($ mil)	% of U.S.	Per Establ.	Total Number	% of U.S.	Per Establ.	Wages ($/hour)		
Pennsylvania	32	782.8	18.7	24.5	5,900	17.4	184	13.35	38.0	10,610
Kentucky	9	213.0	5.1	23.7	1,400	4.1	156	13.84	24.1	9,714
New Jersey	21	210.1	5.0	10.0	1,900	5.6	90	14.80	27.0	6,316
New York	41	170.8	4.1	4.2	1,800	5.3	44	13.62	27.5	-
California	76	88.1	2.1	1.2	800	2.4	11	12.23	25.1	2,750
Illinois	10	16.2	0.4	1.6	200	0.6	20	9.67	34.6	-
Arkansas	8	10.8	0.3	1.4	200	0.6	25	7.75	41.7	500
Washington	13	9.2	0.2	0.7	100	0.3	8	15.00	19.6	-
Ohio	41	(D)	-	-	7,500 *	22.1	183	-	-	-
West Virginia	20	(D)	-	-	1,750 *	5.2	88	-	-	-
Texas	17	(D)	-	-	1,750 *	5.2	103	-	-	-
Massachusetts	15	(D)	-	-	175 *	0.5	12	-	-	-
Oregon	12	(D)	-	-	175 *	0.5	15	-	-	2,857
North Carolina	11	(D)	-	-	3,750 *	11.1	341	-	-	-
Virginia	7	(D)	-	-	375 *	1.1	54	-	-	-
Missouri	6	(D)	-	-	750 *	2.2	125	-	-	-
New Mexico	5	(D)	-	-	175 *	0.5	35	-	-	-
Vermont	5	(D)	-	-	175 *	0.5	35	-	-	-
South Carolina	4	(D)	-	-	1,750 *	5.2	438	-	-	-
Tennessee	4	(D)	-	-	375 *	1.1	94	-	-	-
Indiana	3	(D)	-	-	750 *	2.2	250	-	-	-
Oklahoma	3	(D)	-	-	375 *	1.1	125	-	-	-
Rhode Island	2	(D)	-	-	750 *	2.2	375	-	-	-
Louisiana	1	(D)	-	-	1,750 *	5.2	1,750	-	-	-

Source: 1992 *Economic Census*. The states are in descending order of shipments or establishments (if shipment data are missing for the majority). The symbol (D) appears when data are withheld to prevent disclosure of competitive information. States marked with (D) are sorted by number of establishments. A dash (-) indicates that the data element cannot be calculated; * indicates the midpoint of a range.

3231 - PRODUCTS OF PURCHASED GLASS

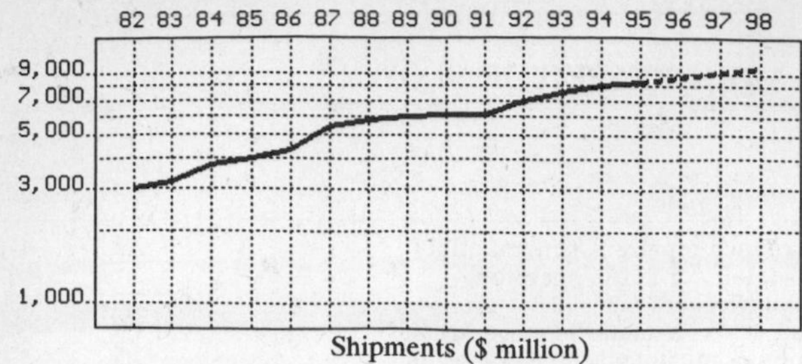

Shipments ($ million)

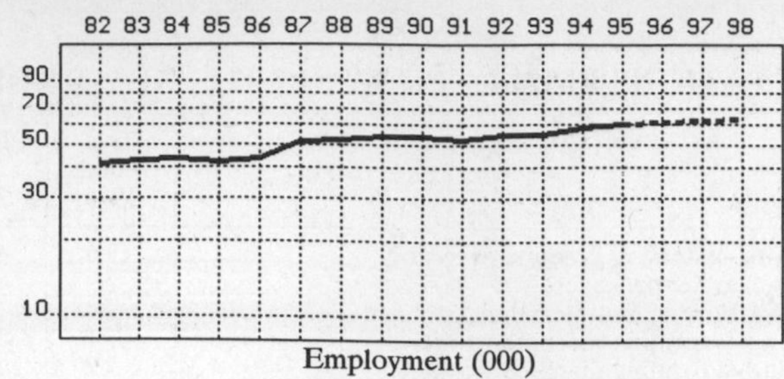

Employment (000)

GENERAL STATISTICS

Year	Companies	Establishments		Employment			Compensation		Production ($ million)			
		Total	with 20 or more employees	Total (000)	Production Workers (000)	Production Hours (Mil)	Payroll ($ mil)	Wages ($/hr)	Cost of Materials	Value Added by Manufacture	Value of Shipments	Capital Invest.
1982	1,228	1,337	387	41.3	31.5	60.8	696.3	7.68	1,480.2	1,483.7	2,976.5	119.1
1983				42.8	33.1	64.0	741.1	7.87	1,595.0	1,644.4	3,204.0	72.2
1984				43.2	33.8	66.2	816.9	8.58	1,942.7	1,816.0	3,734.3	110.0
1985				42.7	33.3	66.1	843.6	8.94	1,974.0	1,995.1	3,964.3	148.6
1986				43.7	33.7	66.3	887.0	9.25	2,105.4	2,269.9	4,361.9	219.3
1987	1,325	1,429	431	51.1	39.5	79.9	1,059.9	9.01	2,587.0	2,837.0	5,429.1	204.3
1988				52.5	41.0	83.1	1,142.6	9.45	2,769.0	3,035.5	5,800.8	195.1
1989		1,421	442	53.3	42.4	86.7	1,206.7	9.44	2,810.4	3,180.6	5,992.9	277.1
1990				53.9	42.4	87.5	1,249.7	9.75	2,796.1	3,341.5	6,141.3	234.0
1991				52.0	40.6	83.9	1,243.1	9.92	2,828.8	3,312.4	6,154.7	297.4
1992	1,441	1,566	418	54.7	42.2	86.8	1,363.8	10.52	3,154.7	3,748.6	6,876.7	275.3
1993				54.8	42.4	90.3	1,442.1	10.79	3,530.4	3,950.0	7,515.7	250.5
1994				58.2	46.4	96.9	1,534.6	11.03	3,719.2	4,253.8	7,934.5	268.3
1995				59.5P	46.8P	98.9P	1,586.5P	11.20P	3,871.5P	4,428.0P	8,259.4P	320.7P
1996				60.9P	47.9P	101.8P	1,656.7P	11.46P	4,063.5P	4,647.6P	8,669.1P	337.2P
1997				62.3P	49.1P	104.7P	1,727.0P	11.72P	4,255.6P	4,867.3P	9,078.8P	353.7P
1998				63.7P	50.3P	107.6P	1,797.3P	11.98P	4,447.6P	5,086.9P	9,488.5P	370.1P

Sources: 1982, 1987, 1992 *Economic Census*; *Annual Survey of Manufactures*, 83-86, 88-91, 93-94. Establishment counts for non-Census years are from *County Business Patterns*; establishment values for 83-84 are extrapolations. 'P's show projections by the editors. Industries reclassified in 87 will not have data for prior years.

INDICES OF CHANGE

Year	Companies	Establishments		Employment			Compensation		Production ($ million)			
		Total	with 20 or more employees	Total (000)	Production Workers (000)	Production Hours (Mil)	Payroll ($ mil)	Wages ($/hr)	Cost of Materials	Value Added by Manufacture	Value of Shipments	Capital Invest.
1982	85	85	93	76	75	70	51	73	47	40	43	43
1983				78	78	74	54	75	51	44	47	26
1984				79	80	76	60	82	62	48	54	40
1985				78	79	76	62	85	63	53	58	54
1986				80	80	76	65	88	67	61	63	80
1987	92	91	103	93	94	92	78	86	82	76	79	74
1988				96	97	96	84	90	88	81	84	71
1989		91	106	97	100	100	88	90	89	85	87	101
1990				99	100	101	92	93	89	89	89	85
1991				95	96	97	91	94	90	88	90	108
1992	100	100	100	100	100	100	100	100	100	100	100	100
1993				100	100	104	106	103	112	105	109	91
1994				106	110	112	113	105	118	113	115	97
1995				109P	111P	114P	116P	106P	123P	118P	120P	117P
1996				111P	114P	117P	121P	109P	129P	124P	126P	122P
1997				114P	116P	121P	127P	111P	135P	130P	132P	128P
1998				116P	119P	124P	132P	114P	141P	136P	138P	134P

Sources: Same as General Statistics. Values reflect change from the base year, 1992. Values above 100 mean greater than 92, values below 100 mean less than 92, and a value of 100 in the 82-91 or 93-98 period means same as 92. 'P's mark projections by the editors.

SELECTED RATIOS

For 1992	Avg. of All Manufact.	Analyzed Industry	Index
Employees per Establishment	46	35	77
Payroll per Establishment	1,332,320	870,881	65
Payroll per Employee	29,181	24,932	85
Production Workers per Establishment	31	27	86
Wages per Establishment	734,496	583,101	79
Wages per Production Worker	23,390	21,638	93
Hours per Production Worker	2,025	2,057	102
Wages per Hour	11.55	10.52	91
Value Added per Establishment	3,842,210	2,393,742	62
Value Added per Employee	84,153	68,530	81

For 1992	Avg. of All Manufact.	Analyzed Industry	Index
Value Added per Production Worker	122,353	88,829	73
Cost per Establishment	4,239,462	2,014,496	48
Cost per Employee	92,853	57,673	62
Cost per Production Worker	135,003	74,756	55
Shipments per Establishment	8,100,800	4,391,252	54
Shipments per Employee	177,425	125,717	71
Shipments per Production Worker	257,966	162,955	63
Investment per Establishment	278,244	175,798	63
Investment per Employee	6,094	5,033	83
Investment per Production Worker	8,861	6,524	74

Sources: Same as General Statistics. The 'Average of All Manufacturing' column represents the average of all manufacturing industries reported for the most recent complete year available. The Index shows the relationship between the Average and the Analyzed Industry. For example, 100 means that they are equal; 500 that the Analyzed Industry is five times the average; 50 means that the Analyzed Industry is half the national average. The abbreviation 'na' is used to show that data are 'not available'.

LEADING COMPANIES

Number shown: **75** Total sales ($ mil): **4,589** Total employment (000): **38.5**

Company Name	Address				CEO Name	Phone	Co. Type	Sales ($ mil)	Empl. (000)
Guardian Industries Corp	2300 Harmon Rd	Auburn Hills	MI	48326	William Davidson	810-340-1800	R	1,070*	8.0
Harvard Industries Inc	2502 N Rocky Pt Dr	Tampa	FL	33607	Vincent Naimoli	813-288-5000	P	615	5.6
Ford Motor Co	300 Renaissance Ctr	Detroit	MI	48243	Robert R Reilly	313-446-5945	D	375	3.5
Donnelly Corp	414 E 40th St	Holland	MI	49423	JD Baumgardner	616-786-7000	P	337	2.7
Schott Corp	3 Odell Plz	Yonkers	NY	10701	Guy De Coninck	914-968-1400	S	325	2.5
Weather Shield Manufacturing	PO Box 309	Medford	WI	54451	EL Schield	715-748-2100	R	260*	2.0
Cardinal IG Co	12301 Whitewater	Minnetonka	MN	55343	R O'Shaughnessey	612-935-1722	R	200*	1.5
Viracon Inc	800 Park Dr	Owatonna	MN	55060	James L Martineau	507-451-9555	S	120	0.9
Ardco Inc	12400 S Laramie	Chicago	IL	60658	Henry Buchbinder	708-388-4300	R	100	0.7
Durand Glass Manufacturing Co	PO Box 805	Millville	NJ	08332	Jean-Rene Gougelet	609-327-4800	S	93*	0.7
Gentex Corp	600 N Centennial St	Zeeland	MI	49464	Fred Bauer	616-772-1800	P	90	0.7
Allwaste Recycling Inc	5151 San Felipe	Houston	TX	77056	Steven B Bowles	713-623-8777	S	70	0.1
Bartlett-Collins Co	PO Box 1288	Sapulpa	OK	74067	Fred Givens	918-224-1860	S	67*	0.5
Sierracin/Sylmar Corp	12780 San Fernando	Sylmar	CA	91342	William Brewer	818-362-6711	D	53	0.4
Consolidated Glass	PO Box 389	Galax	VA	24333	Bobby N Frost	703-236-5196	S	50	0.8
Modular and Plastic Products	6300 Hughes Dr	Sterling Hts	MI	48312	James Carino	810-939-3030	S	50	0.3
Carolina Mirror Co	PO Box 548	N Wilkesboro	NC	28659	Tommy Huskey	919-838-2151	R	48*	0.6
US Precision Glass Inc	1900 Holmes Rd	Elgin	IL	60123	W Glenn Gies	708-931-1200	R	42	0.5
Marsel Mirror & Glass Products	10101 Foster Av	Brooklyn	NY	11236	Michael Barlow	718-272-9700	R	35*	0.5
Allwaste Glass Recycling Inc	35325 Fircrest St	Newark	CA	94560	RL Nelson	510-791-6985	S	29	0.2
Kinkead	PO Box 769	Union City	TN	38261	Ken Ussery	901-885-1200	D	29*	0.3
Penn Bottle and Supply Co	7150 Lindbergh	Philadelphia	PA	19153	Daniel Probinsky	215-365-5700	R	26*	0.1
Durand International	PO Box 5001	Millville	NJ	08332	Jean-Rene Gougelet	609-825-5620	S	24*	0.2
Northwestern Industries Inc	2500 W Jameson St	Seattle	WA	98199	Tim McQuade	206-285-3140	S	23	0.2
Ace Glass Inc	PO Box 688	Vineland	NJ	08360	PE Kramme Jr	609-692-3333	R	20*	0.2
Cataphote Inc	PO Box 2369	Jackson	MS	39225	Constance M Fason	601-939-4612	S	20	0.1
Gilkey Window Company Inc	3625 Hauk Rd	Cincinnati	OH	45241	Mike Gilkey	513-769-4527	R	18*	0.2
Kasson and Keller Inc	PO Box 545	Fonda	NY	12068	William Keller III	518-853-3421	S	15	0.1
Lancaster Glass Corp	PO Box 70	Lancaster	OH	43130	David Gallimore	614-653-0311	S	15	0.3
Binswanger Mirror Products	PO Box 1400	Grenada	MS	38901	Barry Williams	601-226-5551	D	13	0.1
Howard Industries Inc	8130 NW 74th Av	Miami	FL	33166	MJ Zuckerman	305-888-1521	R	13	0.2
Mechanical Mirror Works Inc	27-02 1st St	Long Island Ct	NY	11102	Joseph Bezborodko	718-204-0200	R	13	0.2
Western Shower Door Inc	4140 Business Ctr	Fremont	CA	94538	DC Geery	510-438-0340	R	13	<0.1
Sharon Concepts Inc	1831 Burnet Av	Union	NJ	07083	Sharon Bezak	908-964-1900	R	13	0.2
Wilmad Glass	US Rte 40 & Oak	Buena	NJ	08310	Jack Partridge	609-697-3000	D	12	0.2
Maran-Wurzell	2300 E Slauson Av	Huntington Pk	CA	90255	Jesse Weiser	213-233-4256	R	11	<0.1
Marsco Manufacturing Co	2857 S Halsted St	Chicago	IL	60608	Terry Long	312-326-4710	R	11*	<0.1
Silverwood Products Inc	PO Box 4038	Little Rock	AR	72214	Jeff Pool	501-664-7416	S	11	0.2
Quartz Scientific Inc	819 East St	Fairport Harbor	OH	44077	James R Atwell Jr	216-354-2186	R	10	<0.1
Basco Co	7201 Snider	Mason	OH	45040	George W Rohde	513-573-1900	R	10	0.1
Keystone Shower Door Company	Keystone Rd	Southampton	PA	18966	R Frieder	215-464-2700	R	10	<0.1
Laminated Glass Corp	PO Box 1003	Telford	PA	18969	Martin Lerner	215-721-0400	R	10	<0.1
Samuels Glass Co	PO Box 1769	San Antonio	TX	78296	Perry Samuels	210-227-2481	R	10	<0.1
Aluma-Glass Industries Inc	16265 Star Rd	Nampa	ID	83687	Rick M Atkinson	208-467-4491	R	9*	0.2
Artistic Glass Products Co	PO Box 70	Trumbauersville	PA	18970	Nelson P Bolton	215-536-0333	R	9	0.1
Beach Manufacturing Company	PO Box 129	Donnelsville	OH	45319	Ted Beach	513-882-6372	R	9*	0.1
Capitol Glass & Aluminum Corp	3515 S 300 W	Salt Lake City	UT	84115	DH Brown II	801-268-2521	R	9*	0.1
Holly Decorations Inc	PO Box 62519	Los Angeles	CA	90062	Edward H Scott	213-233-5272	R	9*	<0.1
Settles Glass Company Inc	196 Washington St	Quincy	MA	02169	RC Settles	617-479-4400	R	9	0.1
Stroupe Mirror Company Inc	PO Box 728	Thomasville	NC	27360	RE Stroupe	919-475-2181	R	9	0.1
Swift Glass Company Inc	PO Box 879	Elmira	NY	14902	Daniel J Burke	607-733-7166	R	9	<0.1
Glass Dynamics Inc	PO Box 938	Stoneville	NC	27048	Robert M Lankford	919-573-2393	R	8	0.1
Slocomb Industries Inc	PO Box 9410	Wilmington	DE	19809	Leon F Slocomb Jr	302-762-4445	R	8	0.1
SWIBCO Inc	4810 Venture Rd	Lisle	IL	60532	John Pouleson	708-968-8900	R	8*	<0.1
Thermoseal Glass Corp	400 Water St	Gloucester City	NJ	08030	Irvin Newman	609-456-3109	R	8	<0.1
Eagle Convex Glass Co	PO Box 1340	Clarksburg	WV	26302	JF Aucremanne	304-624-7461	R	7	0.1
Lab Glass	PO Box 610	Vineland	NJ	08360	Jack Partridge	609-697-3000	D	7	<0.1
Lewcott Corp	86 Providence Rd	Millbury	MA	01527	Thomas Ronay	508-865-1791	R	7	0.1
MC Decorating Co	PO Box 201	Rio Grande	NJ	08242	Joe Majowicz	609-886-6700	R	7	<0.1
Bay Mirror Inc	6792 Central Av	Newark	CA	94560	Eugene Jaffe	510-796-5432	R	6*	<0.1
O'Dell Industries Inc	PO Box 248	Surgoinsville	TN	37873	Ralph Armstron	615-345-3265	R	6*	<0.1
Summerhill Crystal	PO Box 1479	Fairfield	IA	52556	Imal Wagner	515-472-8279	D	6*	<0.1
Virginia Glass Products Corp	PO Box 5431	Martinsville	VA	24115	WC Beeler	703-956-3131	S	6*	<0.1
Keane Monroe Corp	PO Box 5016	Monroe	NC	28110	TL Doerr	704-289-5581	R	6	<0.1
Marlock Inc	200 Raccoon Val	Maynardville	TN	37807	Stephen A Goldman	615-992-8552	R	6	0.1
Acme Specialty Mfg Co	PO Box 2510	Toledo	OH	43606	R T Skilliter Jr	419-243-8109	D	5	<0.1
Capri Industries Inc	PO Box 8040	Morganton	NC	28680	Louis Scalise	704-437-4243	R	5	0.2
Dacra Glass Inc	7126 N State Rd 3 N	Montpelier	IN	47359	David Heavenridge	317-348-2190	R	5	<0.1
Viox Corp	6701 6th Av S	Seattle	WA	98108	William E Coats	206-763-2170	R	5*	<0.1
Allen Co	712 E Main St	Blanchester	OH	45107	SA Dohan	513-783-2491	R	4	<0.1
Andrews Glass Company Inc	410 S 4th St	Vineland	NJ	08360	Dennis Courtney	609-692-4435	R	4	<0.1
Bullseye Glass Co	3722 SE 21st Av	Portland	OR	97202	Daniel Schowerer	503-232-8887	R	4	<0.1
Diston Industries Inc	3293 E 11th Av	Hialeah	FL	33013	John J Murphy	305-691-4141	S	4*	<0.1
Fireguard Inc	PO Box 413	North Haven	CT	06473	Christopher Adamo	203-248-9308	R	4*	<0.1
Fred Silver and Company Inc	145 Sussex Av	Newark	NJ	07103	Martin Schlossberg	201-621-8848	R	4	<0.1

Source: *Ward's Business Directory of U.S. Private and Public Companies*, Volumes 1 and 2, 1996. The company type code used is as follows: P - Public, R - Private, S - Subsidiary, D - Division, J - Joint Venture, A - Affiliate, G - Group. Sales are in millions of dollars, employees are in thousands. An asterisk (*) indicates an estimated sales volume. The symbol < stands for 'less than'. Company names and addresses are truncated, in some cases, to fit into the available space.

MATERIALS CONSUMED

Material	Quantity	Delivered Cost ($ million)
Materials, ingredients, containers, and supplies	(X)	2,863.7
Glass sand, all types	(X)	(D)
Sodium carbonate (soda ash) (58 percent Na2O)	(X)	(Z)
Industrial inorganic chemicals, except sodium carbonate	(X)	15.9
Other chemicals and allied products	(X)	47.3
Glass (float, sheet and plate)	(X)	1,117.9
Other glass products (including glass tumblers, stemware, and tableware, excluding scrap)	(X)	486.4
Minerals and earths, ground or otherwise treated	(X)	0.2
Other stone, clay, and concrete products	(X)	(D)
Paperboard containers, boxes, and corrugated paperboard	(X)	75.4
Rough and dressed lumber	(X)	8.8
Wood boxes, pallets, skids, and containers	(X)	19.9
Other lumber and wood products, except furniture	(X)	4.0
Plastics film and sheet, unsupported	(X)	96.1
Cullet (glass scrap)	(X)	12.3
All other materials and components, parts, containers, and supplies	(X)	658.6
Materials, ingredients, containers, and supplies, nsk	(X)	318.1

Source: 1992 *Economic Census*. Explanation of symbols used: (D): Withheld to avoid disclosure of competitive data; na: Not available; (S): Withheld because statistical norms were not met; (X): Not applicable; (Z): Less than half the unit shown; nec: Not elsewhere classified; nsk: Not specified by kind; - : zero; * : 10-19 percent estimated; ** : 20-29 percent estimated.

PRODUCT SHARE DETAILS

Product or Product Class	% Share
Products of purchased glass	100.00
Machine-made pressed and blown glassware (table, kitchen, novelty, lighting, electronic, scientific, industrial, etc.) made in establishments not producing glass	16.36
Handmade pressed and blown glassware, made in establishments not producing glass	2.20
Laminated glass, made in establishments not producing glass	(D)
Laminated glass, made in establishments not producing glass	(D)
Mirrors (decorated or undecorated), made in establishments not producing glass	11.65
Framed mirrors (decorated or undecorated), made in establishments not producing glass	33.08
Unframed mirrors (decorated or undecorated), made in establishments not producing glass	31.43
Automotive mirrors (decorated or undecorated), made in establishments not producing glass	33.90
Mirrors (decorated or undecorated), nsk	1.59
Other glass products, made in establishments not producing glass	(D)
Stained, leaded, and faceted glass and colored glass slabs, made in establishments not producing glass	6.59
Multiple-glazed, sealed insulating glass units, made in establishments not producing glass	(D)
Tempered glass for construction, architectural, and automotive purposes, made in establishments not producing glass	192.78
Tempered glass for other uses, such as for appliances, made in establishments not producing glass	(D)
Optical glass fiber, data and nondata transmission, made in establishments not producing glass	69.49
Glass and glass fiber optical components, made in establishments not producing glass	1.84
Other glass products not listed above, made in establishments not producing glass	62.60
Other glass products, nsk	12.73
Products of purchased glass, nsk	5.85

Source: 1992 *Economic Census*. The values shown are percent of total shipments in an industry. Values of indented subcategories are summed in the main heading. The symbol (D) appears when data are withheld to prevent disclosure of competitive information. The abbreviation nsk stands for 'not specified by kind' and nec for 'not elsewhere classified'.

INPUTS AND OUTPUTS FOR GLASS & GLASS PRODUCTS, EXCEPT CONTAINERS

Economic Sector or Industry Providing Inputs	%	Sector	Economic Sector or Industry Buying Outputs	%	Sector
Glass & glass products, except containers	15.5	Manufg.	Personal consumption expenditures	15.2	
Imports	14.6	Foreign	Glass & glass products, except containers	9.7	Manufg.
Wholesale trade	8.2	Trade	Exports	7.8	Foreign
Gas production & distribution (utilities)	7.8	Util.	Motor vehicles & car bodies	5.6	Manufg.
Cyclic crudes and organics	5.4	Manufg.	Eating & drinking places	4.5	Trade
Communications, except radio & TV	4.9	Util.	Automotive repair shops & services	4.4	Services
Electric services (utilities)	4.4	Util.	Electron tubes	3.3	Manufg.
Advertising	3.4	Services	Lighting fixtures & equipment	3.3	Manufg.
Industrial inorganic chemicals, nec	2.7	Manufg.	Miscellaneous plastics products	3.3	Manufg.
Paperboard containers & boxes	2.0	Manufg.	Hotels & lodging places	2.8	Services
Wood products, nec	2.0	Manufg.	Electric lamps	2.6	Manufg.
Alkalies & chlorine	1.9	Manufg.	Metal doors, sash, & trim	2.6	Manufg.
Adhesives & sealants	1.8	Manufg.	Asphalt felts & coatings	2.5	Manufg.
Motor freight transportation & warehousing	1.8	Util.	Hospitals	2.4	Services
Railroads & related services	1.5	Util.	Maintenance of nonfarm buildings nec	1.6	Constr.
Miscellaneous plastics products	1.4	Manufg.	Office buildings	1.1	Constr.
Maintenance of nonfarm buildings nec	1.3	Constr.	Broadwoven fabric mills	1.1	Manufg.
Petroleum refining	1.3	Manufg.	Ophthalmic goods	1.1	Manufg.
Sand & gravel	1.2	Mining	Tire cord & fabric	1.1	Manufg.
Wood containers	1.2	Manufg.	S/L Govt. purch., public assistance & relief	1.1	S/L Govt
Noncomparable imports	1.2	Foreign	Boat building & repairing	0.8	Manufg.
Banking	0.9	Fin/R.E.	Millwork	0.8	Manufg.

Continued on next page.

INPUTS AND OUTPUTS FOR GLASS & GLASS PRODUCTS, EXCEPT CONTAINERS - Continued

Economic Sector or Industry Providing Inputs	%	Sector	Economic Sector or Industry Buying Outputs	%	Sector
Air transportation	0.8	Util.	Medical & health services, nec	0.8	Services
Scrap	0.8	Scrap	Household cooking equipment	0.7	Manufg.
Machinery, except electrical, nec	0.7	Manufg.	Optical instruments & lenses	0.7	Manufg.
Automotive repair shops & services	0.7	Services	Industrial buildings	0.6	Constr.
Eating & drinking places	0.6	Trade	Electric housewares & fans	0.6	Manufg.
Carbon & graphite products	0.5	Manufg.	Wood household furniture	0.6	Manufg.
Metal stampings, nec	0.5	Manufg.	S/L Govt. purch., higher education	0.6	S/L Govt
Minerals, ground or treated	0.5	Manufg.	Nonfarm residential structure maintenance	0.5	Constr.
Computer & data processing services	0.5	Services	Mineral wool	0.5	Manufg.
Fabricated rubber products, nec	0.4	Manufg.	Automotive rental & leasing, without drivers	0.5	Services
Paints & allied products	0.4	Manufg.	Elementary & secondary schools	0.5	Services
Real estate	0.4	Fin/R.E.	Construction of stores & restaurants	0.4	Constr.
Equipment rental & leasing services	0.4	Services	Metal stampings, nec	0.4	Manufg.
U.S. Postal Service	0.4	Gov't	Semiconductors & related devices	0.4	Manufg.
Lubricating oils & greases	0.3	Manufg.	Travel trailers & campers	0.4	Manufg.
Sawmills & planning mills, general	0.3	Manufg.	Federal Government purchases, nondefense	0.4	Fed Govt
Special dies & tools & machine tool accessories	0.3	Manufg.	Metal household furniture	0.3	Manufg.
Chemical & fertilizer mineral	0.2	Mining	Nonferrous wire drawing & insulating	0.3	Manufg.
Mechanical measuring devices	0.2	Manufg.	Special industry machinery, nec	0.3	Manufg.
Rubber & plastics hose & belting	0.2	Manufg.	Doctors & dentists	0.3	Services
Textile machinery	0.2	Manufg.	Federal Government purchases, national defense	0.3	Fed Govt
Sanitary services, steam supply, irrigation	0.2	Util.	S/L Govt. purch., health & hospitals	0.3	S/L Govt
Water transportation	0.2	Util.	S/L Govt. purch., police	0.3	S/L Govt
Credit agencies other than banks	0.2	Fin/R.E.	Crude petroleum & natural gas	0.2	Mining
Insurance carriers	0.2	Fin/R.E.	Construction of hospitals	0.2	Constr.
Royalties	0.2	Fin/R.E.	Residential 1-unit structures, nonfarm	0.2	Constr.
Accounting, auditing & bookkeeping	0.2	Services	Residential additions/alterations, nonfarm	0.2	Constr.
Automotive rental & leasing, without drivers	0.2	Services	Warehouses	0.2	Constr.
Hotels & lodging places	0.2	Services	Drugs	0.2	Manufg.
Legal services	0.2	Services	Electronic components nec	0.2	Manufg.
Management & consulting services & labs	0.2	Services	Fabricated metal products, nec	0.2	Manufg.
Abrasive products	0.1	Manufg.	Fabricated plate work (boiler shops)	0.2	Manufg.
Manifold business forms	0.1	Manufg.	Hardware, nec	0.2	Manufg.
Paper coating & glazing	0.1	Manufg.	Instruments to measure electricity	0.2	Manufg.
Pumps & compressors	0.1	Manufg.	Mechanical measuring devices	0.2	Manufg.
Electrical repair shops	0.1	Services	Motor homes (made on purchased chassis)	0.2	Manufg.
			Plastics materials & resins	0.2	Manufg.
			Plating & polishing	0.2	Manufg.
			Radio & TV communication equipment	0.2	Manufg.
			Railroad equipment	0.2	Manufg.
			Refrigeration & heating equipment	0.2	Manufg.
			Telephone & telegraph apparatus	0.2	Manufg.
			Wiring devices	0.2	Manufg.
			Transit & bus transportation	0.2	Util.
			Colleges, universities, & professional schools	0.2	Services
			Libraries, vocation education	0.2	Services
			Management & consulting services & labs	0.2	Services
			S/L Govt. purch., correction	0.2	S/L Govt
			Construction of educational buildings	0.1	Constr.
			Construction of religious buildings	0.1	Constr.
			Aircraft	0.1	Manufg.
			Cyclic crudes and organics	0.1	Manufg.
			Engineering & scientific instruments	0.1	Manufg.
			Household appliances, nec	0.1	Manufg.
			Motor vehicle parts & accessories	0.1	Manufg.
			Radio & TV receiving sets	0.1	Manufg.
			Surgical & medical instruments	0.1	Manufg.
			Surgical appliances & supplies	0.1	Manufg.
			Toilet preparations	0.1	Manufg.
			Truck & bus bodies	0.1	Manufg.
			Wood partitions & fixtures	0.1	Manufg.
			Wood products, nec	0.1	Manufg.
			Railroads & related services	0.1	Util.
			Banking	0.1	Fin/R.E.
			S/L Govt. purch., other general government	0.1	S/L Govt

Source: Benchmark Input-Output Accounts for the U.S. Economy, 1982, U.S. Department of Commerce, Washington, D.C., July 1991. Data, as reported in the source, are organized by the 1977 SIC structure in use in 1982 but have been matched, as closely as is possible, to the 1987 SIC structure used in this book.

OCCUPATIONS EMPLOYED BY SIC 323 - FLAT GLASS AND PRODUCTS OF PURCHASED GLASS

Occupation	% of Total 1994	Change to 2005	Occupation	% of Total 1994	Change to 2005
Assemblers, fabricators, & hand workers nec	14.1	4.4	Precision workers nec	1.9	-6.0
Helpers, laborers, & material movers nec	8.4	4.4	Cutters & trimmers, hand	1.9	-6.0
Machine operators nec	5.2	-7.9	Industrial machinery mechanics	1.7	14.9
Cutting & slicing machine setters, operators	4.7	14.9	Grinders & polishers, hand	1.7	4.5
Machine feeders & offbearers	4.4	-6.0	Truck drivers light & heavy	1.5	7.7
Hand packers & packagers	3.8	-10.5	Traffic, shipping, & receiving clerks	1.5	0.5
Inspectors, testers, & graders, precision	3.5	4.4	Maintenance repairers, general utility	1.4	-6.0
Furnace, kiln, or kettle operators	2.7	-6.0	Coating, painting, & spraying machine workers	1.2	4.5
Freight, stock, & material movers, hand	2.5	-16.5	Industrial production managers	1.1	4.5
Industrial truck & tractor operators	2.2	4.4	Extruding & forming machine workers	1.1	14.9
Sales & related workers nec	2.2	4.4	Secretaries, ex legal & medical	1.1	-4.9
General managers & top executives	2.1	-0.9	General office clerks	1.1	-10.9
Combination machine tool operators	1.9	14.9	Screen printing machine setters & set-up operators	1.1	4.5

Source: *Industry-Occupation Matrix*, Bureau of Labor Statistics. These data relate to one or more 3-digit SIC industry groups rather than to a single 4-digit SIC. The change reported for each occupation to the year 2005 is a percent of growth or decline as estimated by the Bureau of Labor Statistics. The abbreviation nec stands for 'not elsewhere classified'.

LOCATION BY STATE AND REGIONAL CONCENTRATION

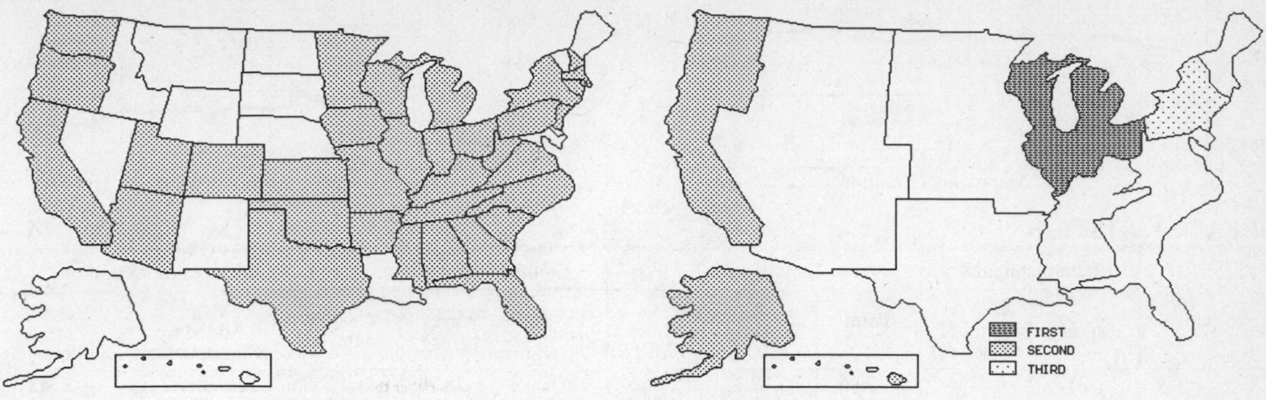

INDUSTRY DATA BY STATE

State	Establish-ments	Shipments			Employment				Cost as % of Shipments	Investment per Employee ($)
		Total ($ mil)	% of U.S.	Per Establ.	Total Number	% of U.S.	Per Establ.	Wages ($/hour)		
Pennsylvania	77	793.3	11.5	10.3	3,700	6.8	48	12.71	46.8	2,324
Michigan	70	687.4	10.0	9.8	5,100	9.3	73	13.75	43.8	5,118
North Carolina	46	627.8	9.1	13.6	4,300	7.9	93	9.49	25.9	-
Ohio	87	562.8	8.2	6.5	4,200	7.7	48	10.79	49.2	2,976
California	235	434.0	6.3	1.8	4,200	7.7	18	10.35	43.2	2,048
Indiana	53	410.5	6.0	7.7	3,200	5.9	60	10.96	46.3	4,313
Tennessee	33	398.8	5.8	12.1	2,800	5.1	85	9.29	64.3	5,857
New Jersey	86	280.0	4.1	3.3	3,100	5.7	36	10.28	37.8	3,194
Kentucky	19	270.8	3.9	14.3	1,900	3.5	100	10.76	51.8	4,053
Wisconsin	41	265.8	3.9	6.5	1,700	3.1	41	10.14	62.0	9,471
Texas	81	253.9	3.7	3.1	1,900	3.5	23	10.74	47.7	4,316
New York	114	252.6	3.7	2.2	2,800	5.1	25	9.37	46.0	1,964
Florida	104	176.7	2.6	1.7	2,000	3.7	19	9.16	47.2	2,800
Virginia	34	151.8	2.2	4.5	2,300	4.2	68	7.30	49.2	1,870
South Carolina	13	145.5	2.1	11.2	1,000	1.8	77	11.24	33.9	-
Georgia	25	113.7	1.7	4.5	700	1.3	28	10.08	61.7	4,429
Illinois	48	96.5	1.4	2.0	1,100	2.0	23	10.44	41.6	2,545
Mississippi	9	91.3	1.3	10.1	800	1.5	89	7.93	51.3	1,500
Washington	38	85.0	1.2	2.2	1,000	1.8	26	9.86	43.4	3,600
Massachusetts	27	60.3	0.9	2.2	500	0.9	19	11.71	43.0	3,600
Rhode Island	11	45.4	0.7	4.1	300	0.5	27	8.33	48.0	667
Colorado	37	43.0	0.6	1.2	500	0.9	14	8.25	39.1	-
Connecticut	24	41.7	0.6	1.7	600	1.1	25	8.63	45.6	-
Kansas	18	33.2	0.5	1.8	300	0.5	17	9.75	60.5	4,667
Missouri	26	30.9	0.4	1.2	400	0.7	15	11.00	43.0	3,250
Arizona	24	29.9	0.4	1.2	300	0.5	13	9.60	43.5	2,333
Arkansas	13	23.8	0.3	1.8	200	0.4	15	8.00	60.1	-
Oregon	21	23.5	0.3	1.1	300	0.5	14	12.25	37.4	2,000
Utah	9	12.3	0.2	1.4	100	0.2	11	9.00	62.6	1,000
West Virginia	13	11.5	0.2	0.9	200	0.4	15	9.67	44.3	2,000
Minnesota	25	(D)	-	-	1,750 *	3.2	70	-	-	-
Alabama	14	(D)	-	-	750 *	1.4	54	-	-	267
Oklahoma	14	(D)	-	-	375 *	0.7	27	-	-	-
Iowa	9	(D)	-	-	375 *	0.7	42	-	-	-
New Hampshire	3	(D)	-	-	375 *	0.7	125	-	-	-

Source: 1992 *Economic Census*. The states are in descending order of shipments or establishments (if shipment data are missing for the majority). The symbol (D) appears when data are withheld to prevent disclosure of competitive information. States marked with (D) are sorted by number of establishments. A dash (-) indicates that the data element cannot be calculated; * indicates the midpoint of a range.

3241 - CEMENT, HYDRAULIC

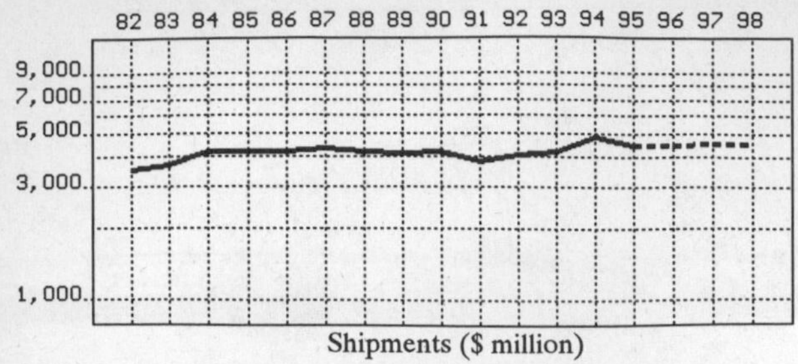

Shipments ($ million)

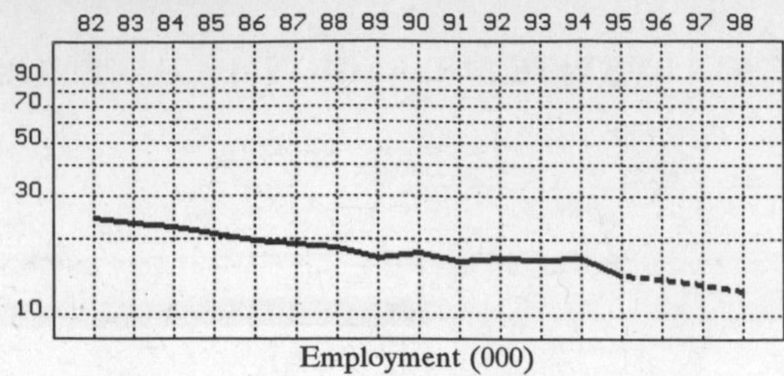

Employment (000)

GENERAL STATISTICS

Year	Com-panies	Establishments		Employment			Compensation		Production ($ million)			
		Total	with 20 or more employees	Total (000)	Production Workers (000)	Production Hours (Mil)	Payroll ($ mil)	Wages ($/hr)	Cost of Materials	Value Added by Manufacture	Value of Shipments	Capital Invest.
1982	119	237	160	24.6	19.1	36.5	636.4	12.98	1,752.6	1,815.7	3,542.0	421.9
1983				23.1	17.8	35.2	639.6	13.50	1,761.8	1,914.6	3,683.1	201.3
1984				22.6	17.4	33.4	658.0	14.32	1,966.5	2,218.1	4,182.9	346.7
1985				21.2	15.9	32.2	645.4	14.20	2,031.5	2,220.8	4,222.1	196.3
1986				19.7	14.9	31.2	622.6	14.29	2,017.1	2,153.1	4,220.1	169.3
1987	122	215	140	19.1	14.5	30.2	601.7	14.05	1,999.8	2,286.3	4,335.4	166.2
1988				18.6	14.2	29.7	584.2	13.97	2,042.9	2,184.7	4,234.3	193.0
1989		214	141	16.9	13.0	27.6	558.2	14.53	2,014.4	2,139.0	4,129.4	262.6
1990				17.6	13.4	27.8	598.6	15.16	2,079.2	2,196.8	4,250.7	264.9
1991				16.4	12.2	25.6	559.8	14.86	1,883.5	1,936.9	3,777.7	225.3
1992	122	218	138	17.0	12.8	26.8	594.9	15.15	1,869.2	2,149.3	4,050.8	226.2
1993				16.6	12.5	26.1	589.7	15.48	1,948.5	2,146.2	4,186.8	227.2
1994				16.7	12.4	27.0	628.9	15.83	2,000.3	2,799.6	4,808.2	279.6
1995				14.5P	10.8P	23.9P	574.6P	15.81P	1,845.8P	2,583.3P	4,436.8P	212.7P
1996				13.8P	10.2P	23.0P	569.7P	16.00P	1,864.3P	2,609.3P	4,481.3P	208.1P
1997				13.2P	9.6P	22.1P	564.8P	16.19P	1,882.9P	2,635.2P	4,525.9P	203.5P
1998				12.5P	9.1P	21.3P	559.9P	16.38P	1,901.4P	2,661.2P	4,570.5P	199.0P

Sources: 1982, 1987, 1992 *Economic Census*; *Annual Survey of Manufactures*, 83-86, 88-91, 93-94. Establishment counts for non-Census years are from *County Business Patterns*; establishment values for 83-84 are extrapolations. 'P's show projections by the editors. Industries reclassified in 87 will not have data for prior years.

INDICES OF CHANGE

Year	Com-panies	Establishments		Employment			Compensation		Production ($ million)			
		Total	with 20 or more employees	Total (000)	Production Workers (000)	Production Hours (Mil)	Payroll ($ mil)	Wages ($/hr)	Cost of Materials	Value Added by Manufacture	Value of Shipments	Capital Invest.
1982	98	109	116	145	149	136	107	86	94	84	87	187
1983				136	139	131	108	89	94	89	91	89
1984				133	136	125	111	95	105	103	103	153
1985				125	124	120	108	94	109	103	104	87
1986				116	116	116	105	94	108	100	104	75
1987	100	99	101	112	113	113	101	93	107	106	107	73
1988				109	111	111	98	92	109	102	105	85
1989		98	102	99	102	103	94	96	108	100	102	116
1990				104	105	104	101	100	111	102	105	117
1991				96	95	96	94	98	101	90	93	100
1992	100	100	100	100	100	100	100	100	100	100	100	100
1993				98	98	97	99	102	104	100	103	100
1994				98	97	101	106	104	107	130	119	124
1995				85P	84P	89P	97P	104P	99P	120P	110P	94P
1996				81P	80P	86P	96P	106P	100P	121P	111P	92P
1997				77P	75P	83P	95P	107P	101P	123P	112P	90P
1998				73P	71P	79P	94P	108P	102P	124P	113P	88P

Sources: Same as General Statistics. Values reflect change from the base year, 1992. Values above 100 mean greater than 92, values below 100 mean less than 92, and a value of 100 in the 82-91 or 93-98 period means same as 92. 'P's mark projections by the editors.

SELECTED RATIOS

For 1992	Avg. of All Manufact.	Analyzed Industry	Index	For 1992	Avg. of All Manufact.	Analyzed Industry	Index
Employees per Establishment	46	78	171	Value Added per Production Worker	122,353	167,914	137
Payroll per Establishment	1,332,320	2,728,899	205	Cost per Establishment	4,239,462	8,574,312	202
Payroll per Employee	29,181	34,994	120	Cost per Employee	92,853	109,953	118
Production Workers per Establishment	31	59	187	Cost per Production Worker	135,003	146,031	108
Wages per Establishment	734,496	1,862,477	254	Shipments per Establishment	8,100,800	18,581,651	229
Wages per Production Worker	23,390	31,720	136	Shipments per Employee	177,425	238,282	134
Hours per Production Worker	2,025	2,094	103	Shipments per Production Worker	257,966	316,469	123
Wages per Hour	11.55	15.15	131	Investment per Establishment	278,244	1,037,615	373
Value Added per Establishment	3,842,210	9,859,174	257	Investment per Employee	6,094	13,306	218
Value Added per Employee	84,153	126,429	150	Investment per Production Worker	8,861	17,672	199

Sources: Same as General Statistics. The 'Average of All Manufacturing' column represents the average of all manufacturing industries reported for the most recent complete year available. The Index shows the relationship between the Average and the Analyzed Industry. For example, 100 means that they are equal; 500 that the Analyzed Industry is five times the average; 50 means that the Analyzed Industry is half the national average. The abbreviation 'na' is used to show that data are 'not available'.

LEADING COMPANIES

Number shown: **32** Total sales ($ mil): **4,575** Total employment (000): **23.0**

Company Name	Address				CEO Name	Phone	Co. Type	Sales ($ mil)	Empl. (000)
Lafarge Corp	PO Box 4600	Reston	VA	22090	Michael Rose	703-264-3600	P	1,563	6.5
CBR Cement Corp	1875 S Grant St	San Mateo	CA	94402	Richard D Kline	415-572-8900	S	660*	3.3
Ash Grove Cement Co	PO Box 25900	Overland Park	KS	66225	George M Wells	913-451-8900	R	330*	1.7
Lone Star Industries Inc	PO Box 120014	Stamford	CT	06912	David W Wallace	203-969-8600	P	262	1.5
Medusa Corp	3008 Monticello	Cleveland H	OH	44118	Robert S Evans	216-371-4000	P	248	1.1
Lehigh Portland Cement Co	7660 Imperial Way	Allentown	PA	18195	Russell M Memmer	610-366-4600	S	240	1.8
Centex Construction Products	3710 Rawlins	Dallas	TX	75219	Greg Dagnan	214-559-6500	P	194	1.0
ESSROC Materials Inc	430 Mountain Av	Murray Hill	NJ	07974	Claude Grinfeder	908-771-0024	S	150*	1.1
Giant Cement Holding Inc	Hwy 453 & I-26	Harleyville	SC	29448	Gary L Pechota	803-496-7880	P	90	0.4
Independent Cement Corp	PO Box 12-310	Albany	NY	12212	Dennis W Skidmore	518-459-3211	S	71*	0.4
Riverside Cement Co	PO Box 4904	Diamond Bar	CA	91765	W R McCormick	909-861-2174	J	68	0.5
RC Cement Company Inc	PO Box 69	Stockertown	PA	18083	David Nepereny	215-759-6300	S	52*	0.3
River Cement Co	PO Box 69	Stockertown	PA	18083	David Nepereny	215-759-6300	S	52*	0.3
Capitol Cement Corp	PO Box 885	Martinsburg	WV	25401	CL Duncan	304-267-8966	S	50	0.3
Dragon Products Company Inc	PO Box 1521	Portland	ME	04104	Joseph M Koch III	207-774-6355	S	50	0.3
Blue Circle Cement	PO Box 3	Ravena	NY	12143	Gary Gentles	518-756-5000	S	48*	0.2
Blue Circle Raia Inc	PO Box 505	Hackensack	NJ	07602	Jeffrey Pope	201-488-0500	R	44	0.3
Kaiser Cement Corp	PO Box 309	Pleasanton	CA	94566	MJ Bishop	510-846-8800	S	44	0.3
Giant Cement Co	PO Box 218	Harleyville	SC	29448	Gary Pechota	803-496-7880	S	44	0.2
Texas-Lehigh Cement Co	PO Box 610	Buda	TX	78610	Gerry J Essl	512-295-6111	J	40	0.2
Continental Cement Company	PO Box 71	Hannibal	MO	63401	Ronald Powell	314-221-1740	R	33*	0.2
Arizona Portland Cement Co	2400 N Central Av	Phoenix	AZ	85004	Vaughn S Corley	602-271-0069	S	30	0.2
Glens Falls Cement Company	PO Box 440	Glens Falls	NY	12801	MB Clarke	518-792-1137	S	30	0.1
Illinois Cement Co	PO Box 442	La Salle	IL	61301	Joseph Baker	815-224-2112	S	30	0.1
Phoenix Cement Co	PO Box 43740	Phoenix	AZ	85080	JE Carmichael	602-264-0511	S	30	0.1
Sunbelt Cement Inc	2625 S 19th Av	Phoenix	AZ	85009	William Hopper	602-220-0025	S	26	<0.1
Dixon-Marquette Cement	E River Rd	Dixon	IL	61021	Charles Broneck	815-284-3357	D	24	0.1
Hercules Cement Co	PO Box 69	Stockertown	PA	18083	David Nepereny	215-759-6300	S	22	0.2
Alamo Cement Co	PO Box 34807	San Antonio	TX	78265	Bill Manning	210-651-6624	R	20*	0.1
Riverton Corp	100 Riverton Rd	Front Royal	VA	22630	Toby G Mercuro	703-635-4131	S	15	0.2
Signal Mountain Cement Co	1201 Suck Creek Rd	Chattanooga	TN	37405	David Nepereny	615-886-0800	R	13	0.2
Lindsay Concrete Products Inc	1485 S Waterman	San Bernardino	CA	92408	Lindsay Barto	909-885-6055	R	2	<0.1

Source: *Ward's Business Directory of U.S. Private and Public Companies*, Volumes 1 and 2, 1996. The company type code used is as follows: P - Public, R - Private, S - Subsidiary, D - Division, J - Joint Venture, A - Affiliate, G - Group. Sales are in millions of dollars, employees are in thousands. An asterisk (*) indicates an estimated sales volume. The symbol < stands for 'less than'. Company names and addresses are truncated, in some cases, to fit into the available space.

MATERIALS CONSUMED

Material	Quantity	Delivered Cost ($ million)
Materials, ingredients, containers, and supplies	(X)	873.8
Paperboard liners	(X)	0.8
Paper shipping sacks and multiwall bags	(X)	35.6
Other paper and paperboard products	(X)	0.9
Refractories, clay or nonclay	(X)	43.3
Cement clinker	(X)	160.5
Minerals and earths, ground or otherwise treated	(X)	128.0
Other stone, clay, glass, and concrete products	(X)	34.2
Crushed and broken stone (including cement rock, limestone, etc.)	(X)	72.3
All other materials and components, parts, containers, and supplies	(X)	374.9
Materials, ingredients, containers, and supplies, nsk	(X)	23.2

Source: 1992 *Economic Census*. Explanation of symbols used: (D): Withheld to avoid disclosure of competitive data; na: Not available; (S): Withheld because statistical norms were not met; (X): Not applicable; (Z): Less than half the unit shown; nec: Not elsewhere classified; nsk: Not specified by kind; - : zero; * : 10-19 percent estimated; ** : 20-29 percent estimated.

PRODUCT SHARE DETAILS

Product or Product Class	% Share
Cement, hydraulic	100.00
Normal portland cement ASTM type I, hydraulic (including cost of shipping containers)	61.74
Portland cement, moderate heat of hydration (moderate sulfate resistance) ASTM type II, hydraulic (including cost of shipping containers)	18.32
Portland cement, high early strength ASTM type III, hydraulic (including cost of shipping containers)	3.43
Portland cement, high sulfate resistance ASTM type V, hydraulic (including cost of shipping containers)	2.18
Other portland hydraulic cements (oil well, white cement, blended cements, etc.) including low heat of hydration ASTM type IV (including cost of shipping containers)	3.61
Masonry cement, hydraulic (including cost of shipping containers)	5.34
Other cements (e.g., natural, hydraulic lime, etc.) (including cost of shipping containers)	1.39
Cement clinker, for sale separately, hydraulic (including cost of shipping containers)	0.72

Source: 1992 *Economic Census*. The values shown are percent of total shipments in an industry. Values of indented subcategories are summed in the main heading. The symbol (D) appears when data are withheld to prevent disclosure of competitive information. The abbreviation nsk stands for 'not specified by kind' and nec for 'not elsewhere classified'.

INPUTS AND OUTPUTS FOR CEMENT, HYDRAULIC

Economic Sector or Industry Providing Inputs	%	Sector	Economic Sector or Industry Buying Outputs	%	Sector
Electric services (utilities)	20.0	Util.	Ready-mixed concrete	53.8	Manufg.
Coal	13.9	Mining	Petroleum & natural gas well drilling	14.6	Constr.
Gas production & distribution (utilities)	7.8	Util.	Concrete products, nec	6.4	Manufg.
Railroads & related services	5.9	Util.	Concrete block & brick	4.3	Manufg.
Imports	5.8	Foreign	Highway & street construction	3.2	Constr.
Motor freight transportation & warehousing	4.8	Util.	Maintenance of petroleum & natural gas wells	3.0	Constr.
Minerals, ground or treated	4.3	Manufg.	Maintenance of nonfarm buildings nec	2.4	Constr.
Wholesale trade	4.3	Trade	Office buildings	1.4	Constr.
Dimension, crushed & broken stone	4.2	Mining	Exports	1.1	Foreign
Small arms ammunition	2.9	Manufg.	Change in business inventories	1.0	In House
Maintenance of nonfarm buildings nec	2.8	Constr.	Maintenance of highways & streets	0.9	Constr.
Banking	2.7	Fin/R.E.	Residential 1-unit structures, nonfarm	0.8	Constr.
Petroleum refining	2.4	Manufg.	Maintenance of water supply facilities	0.6	Constr.
Explosives	1.6	Manufg.	Construction of stores & restaurants	0.5	Constr.
Clay, ceramic, & refractory minerals	1.4	Mining	Nonfarm residential structure maintenance	0.4	Constr.
Advertising	1.4	Services	Residential additions/alterations, nonfarm	0.4	Constr.
Bags, except textile	1.2	Manufg.	Residential high-rise apartments	0.4	Constr.
Water transportation	0.8	Util.	Construction of conservation facilities	0.3	Constr.
Cyclic crudes and organics	0.7	Manufg.	Construction of hospitals	0.3	Constr.
Pipe, valves, & pipe fittings	0.7	Manufg.	Industrial buildings	0.3	Constr.
Communications, except radio & TV	0.7	Util.	Maintenance of nonbuilding facilities nec	0.3	Constr.
Computer & data processing services	0.7	Services	Residential garden apartments	0.3	Constr.
Equipment rental & leasing services	0.6	Services	Water supply facility construction	0.3	Constr.
Nonmetallic mineral services	0.5	Mining	Asbestos products	0.3	Manufg.
Engineering, architectural, & surveying services	0.5	Services	Construction of educational buildings	0.2	Constr.
Sanitary services, steam supply, irrigation	0.4	Util.	Electric utility facility construction	0.2	Constr.
Water supply & sewage systems	0.4	Util.	Hotels & motels	0.2	Constr.
Eating & drinking places	0.4	Trade	Maintenance of sewer facilities	0.2	Constr.
Paving mixtures & blocks	0.3	Manufg.	Maintenance of telephone & telegraph facilities	0.2	Constr.
Plastics materials & resins	0.3	Manufg.	Sewer system facility construction	0.2	Constr.
Pumps & compressors	0.3	Manufg.	Construction of religious buildings	0.1	Constr.
Sawmills & planning mills, general	0.3	Manufg.	Maintenance of local transit facilities	0.1	Constr.
Royalties	0.3	Fin/R.E.	Nonbuilding facilities nec	0.1	Constr.
Automotive rental & leasing, without drivers	0.3	Services	Residential 2-4 unit structures, nonfarm	0.1	Constr.
Fabricated structural metal	0.2	Manufg.	Warehouses	0.1	Constr.
Rubber & plastics hose & belting	0.2	Manufg.			
Wood pallets & skids	0.2	Manufg.			
Insurance carriers	0.2	Fin/R.E.			
Automotive repair shops & services	0.2	Services			
Detective & protective services	0.2	Services			
Electrical repair shops	0.2	Services			
Management & consulting services & labs	0.2	Services			
Blast furnaces & steel mills	0.1	Manufg.			
Cement, hydraulic	0.1	Manufg.			
Distilled liquor, except brandy	0.1	Manufg.			
Manufacturing industries, nec	0.1	Manufg.			
Miscellaneous fabricated wire products	0.1	Manufg.			
Air transportation	0.1	Util.			
Real estate	0.1	Fin/R.E.			
Security & commodity brokers	0.1	Fin/R.E.			
Accounting, auditing & bookkeeping	0.1	Services			
Legal services	0.1	Services			
U.S. Postal Service	0.1	Gov't			

Source: Benchmark Input-Output Accounts for the U.S. Economy, 1982, U.S. Department of Commerce, Washington, D.C., July 1991. Data, as reported in the source, are organized by the 1977 SIC structure in use in 1982 but have been matched, as closely as is possible, to the 1987 SIC structure used in this book.

OCCUPATIONS EMPLOYED BY SIC 324 - STONE, CLAY, AND MISC MINING PRODUCTS NEC

Occupation	% of Total 1994	Change to 2005	Occupation	% of Total 1994	Change to 2005
Helpers, laborers, & material movers nec	6.7	-23.3	Machine feeders & offbearers	2.3	-31.4
Assemblers, fabricators, & hand workers nec	6.4	-23.9	Painting, coating, & decorating workers, hand	2.0	52.3
Furnace, kiln, or kettle operators	4.2	-16.7	Freight, stock, & material movers, hand	1.9	-38.8
Crushing & mixing machine operators	3.9	-9.5	Truck drivers light & heavy	1.9	-20.6
Industrial machinery mechanics	3.9	-15.2	Coating, painting, & spraying machine workers	1.8	-23.8
Hand packers & packagers	3.6	-34.7	Secretaries, ex legal & medical	1.8	-30.4
Extruding & forming machine workers	3.4	-80.6	Cutting & slicing machine setters, operators	1.6	-16.2
Sales & related workers nec	3.2	-23.6	Grinders & polishers, hand	1.6	-16.2
Packaging & filling machine operators	3.2	-23.7	Industrial production managers	1.5	-23.5
Precision workers nec	3.0	-8.7	Traffic, shipping, & receiving clerks	1.5	-26.6
Industrial truck & tractor operators	2.8	-23.7	General office clerks	1.5	-34.9
General managers & top executives	2.8	-27.5	Bookkeeping, accounting, & auditing clerks	1.3	-42.7
Inspectors, testers, & graders, precision	2.8	-23.6	Electricians	1.1	-27.3
Maintenance repairers, general utility	2.6	-30.8	Machinists	1.0	-23.6

Source: Industry-Occupation Matrix, Bureau of Labor Statistics. These data relate to one or more 3-digit SIC industry groups rather than to a single 4-digit SIC. The change reported for each occupation to the year 2005 is a percent of growth or decline as estimated by the Bureau of Labor Statistics. The abbreviation nec stands for 'not elsewhere classified'.

LOCATION BY STATE AND REGIONAL CONCENTRATION

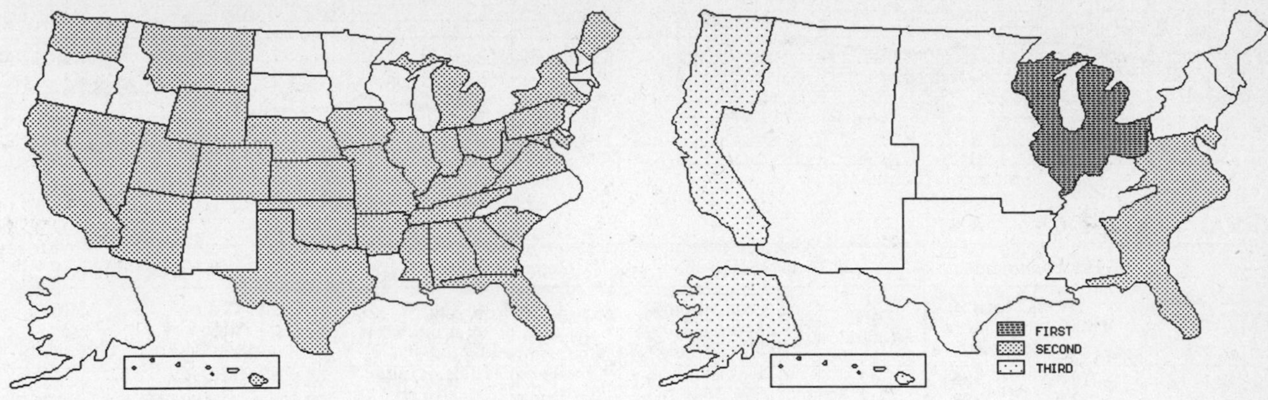

INDUSTRY DATA BY STATE

State	Establish-ments	Shipments			Employment				Cost as % of Shipments	Investment per Employee ($)
		Total ($ mil)	% of U.S.	Per Establ.	Total Number	% of U.S.	Per Establ.	Wages ($/hour)		
California	22	524.2	12.9	23.8	2,000	11.8	91	17.35	45.7	14,650
Texas	17	370.6	9.1	21.8	1,500	8.8	88	13.58	47.2	8,467
Pennsylvania	19	315.8	7.8	16.6	1,800	10.6	95	14.88	49.7	25,667
Michigan	11	246.0	6.1	22.4	700	4.1	64	16.21	46.4	18,857
Missouri	7	222.3	5.5	31.8	900	5.3	129	14.38	32.1	14,111
Florida	13	211.5	5.2	16.3	600	3.5	46	15.00	57.1	8,833
Indiana	6	155.8	3.8	26.0	600	3.5	100	14.30	43.2	8,333
Alabama	6	147.6	3.6	24.6	600	3.5	100	15.20	46.6	21,500
Illinois	10	137.0	3.4	13.7	500	2.9	50	13.30	46.1	9,000
Iowa	4	135.1	3.3	33.8	500	2.9	125	14.62	46.0	9,000
New York	9	130.5	3.2	14.5	700	4.1	78	16.50	49.0	10,143
Virginia	7	121.6	3.0	17.4	500	2.9	71	12.37	48.5	6,800
South Carolina	4	119.3	2.9	29.8	500	2.9	125	18.75	39.1	12,600
Ohio	9	118.0	2.9	13.1	600	3.5	67	12.27	42.3	9,500
Maryland	5	94.1	2.3	18.8	400	2.4	80	16.14	47.8	13,500
Washington	7	88.0	2.2	12.6	200	1.2	29	12.25	47.5	-
Kansas	4	76.0	1.9	19.0	600	3.5	150	16.25	41.3	9,500
Oklahoma	4	62.5	1.5	15.6	400	2.4	100	18.00	47.0	9,500
Georgia	4	(D)	-	-	375 *	2.2	94	-	-	-
Tennessee	4	(D)	-	-	375 *	2.2	94	-	-	1,067
Arizona	3	(D)	-	-	375 *	2.2	125	-	-	-
Arkansas	3	(D)	-	-	375 *	2.2	125	-	-	-
Colorado	3	(D)	-	-	375 *	2.2	125	-	-	-
Maine	3	(D)	-	-	175 *	1.0	58	-	-	-
Utah	3	(D)	-	-	175 *	1.0	58	-	-	-
Kentucky	2	(D)	-	-	175 *	1.0	88	-	-	-
Montana	2	(D)	-	-	175 *	1.0	88	-	-	-
Hawaii	1	(D)	-	-	175 *	1.0	175	-	-	-
Mississippi	1	(D)	-	-	175 *	1.0	175	-	-	-
Nebraska	1	(D)	-	-	175 *	1.0	175	-	-	-
Nevada	1	(D)	-	-	175 *	1.0	175	-	-	-
West Virginia	1	(D)	-	-	175 *	1.0	175	-	-	-
Wyoming	1	(D)	-	-	175 *	1.0	175	-	-	-

Source: 1992 *Economic Census*. The states are in descending order of shipments or establishments (if shipment data are missing for the majority). The symbol (D) appears when data are withheld to prevent disclosure of competitive information. States marked with (D) are sorted by number of establishments. A dash (-) indicates that the data element cannot be calculated; * indicates the midpoint of a range.

3251 - BRICK & STRUCTURAL CLAY TILE

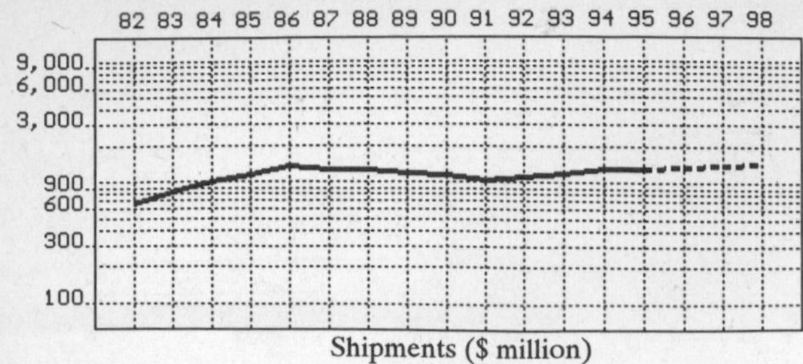

Shipments ($ million)

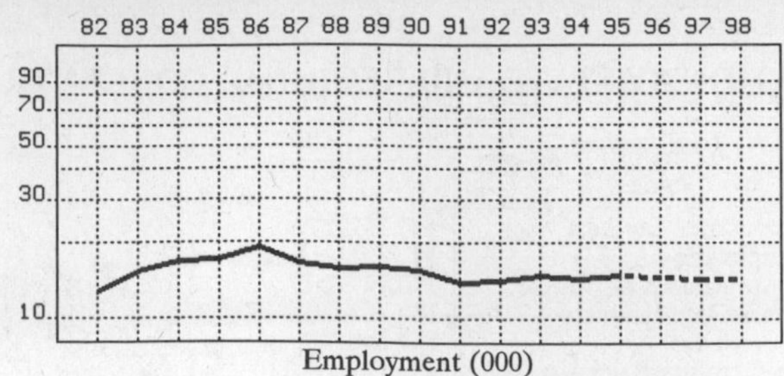

Employment (000)

GENERAL STATISTICS

Year	Companies	Establishments		Employment			Compensation		Production ($ million)			
		Total	with 20 or more employees	Total (000)	Production Workers (000)	Production Hours (Mil)	Payroll ($ mil)	Wages ($/hr)	Cost of Materials	Value Added by Manufacture	Value of Shipments	Capital Invest.
1982	195	294	185	12.5	9.9	19.7	185.4	6.60	295.7	338.6	657.3	25.7
1983		287	188	15.4	11.7	24.5	229.9	6.64	378.5	456.6	836.7	49.7
1984		280	191	16.9	13.9	28.2	272.5	7.28	473.5	534.2	1,015.4	60.6
1985		273	193	17.2	14.1	28.9	305.5	7.71	511.6	622.6	1,139.6	77.9
1986		255	187	19.1	15.4	31.9	348.5	7.83	533.4	796.1	1,347.7	43.8
1987	167	266	204	16.6	13.4	27.8	311.5	8.07	480.2	771.9	1,254.0	56.4
1988		261	195	15.8	12.7	26.2	307.9	8.27	516.9	744.0	1,242.9	65.8
1989		267	193	15.9	13.0	27.1	335.2	8.67	481.6	741.5	1,191.6	62.3
1990		265	196	15.5	12.5	26.0	334.5	8.83	429.4	753.5	1,168.7	30.0
1991		268	182	14.0	11.2	22.6	306.4	9.30	386.3	663.1	1,044.6	47.2
1992	117	220	186	14.2	11.1	22.3	316.3	9.59	372.2	727.7	1,116.0	42.9
1993		258	172	14.7	11.2	23.4	335.5	9.80	437.3	759.8	1,199.1	56.1
1994		241P	185P	14.3	11.0	23.3	336.4	10.04	463.4	829.1	1,319.1	63.8
1995		238P	184P	14.7P	11.5P	24.0P	363.8P	10.40P	466.8P	835.1P	1,328.7P	55.4P
1996		234P	183P	14.6P	11.4P	23.8P	372.6P	10.69P	477.3P	854.0P	1,358.8P	55.8P
1997		230P	183P	14.5P	11.3P	23.6P	381.5P	10.98P	487.9P	873.0P	1,388.9P	56.2P
1998		226P	182P	14.4P	11.2P	23.4P	390.3P	11.27P	498.5P	891.9P	1,419.0P	56.7P

Sources: 1982, 1987, 1992 *Economic Census*; *Annual Survey of Manufactures*, 83-86, 88-91, 93-94. Establishment counts for non-Census years are from *County Business Patterns*; establishment values for 83-84 are extrapolations. 'P's show projections by the editors. Industries reclassified in 87 will not have data for prior years.

INDICES OF CHANGE

Year	Companies	Establishments		Employment			Compensation		Production ($ million)			
		Total	with 20 or more employees	Total (000)	Production Workers (000)	Production Hours (Mil)	Payroll ($ mil)	Wages ($/hr)	Cost of Materials	Value Added by Manufacture	Value of Shipments	Capital Invest.
1982	167	134	99	88	89	88	59	69	79	47	59	60
1983		130	101	108	105	110	73	69	102	63	75	116
1984		127	103	119	125	126	86	76	127	73	91	141
1985		124	104	121	127	130	97	80	137	86	102	182
1986		116	101	135	139	143	110	82	143	109	121	102
1987	143	121	110	117	121	125	98	84	129	106	112	131
1988		119	105	111	114	117	97	86	139	102	111	153
1989		121	104	112	117	122	106	90	129	102	107	145
1990		120	105	109	113	117	106	92	115	104	105	70
1991		122	98	99	101	101	97	97	104	91	94	110
1992	100	100	100	100	100	100	100	100	100	100	100	100
1993		117	92	104	101	105	106	102	117	104	107	131
1994		110P	99P	101	99	104	106	105	125	114	118	149
1995		108P	99P	104P	104P	108P	115P	108P	125P	115P	119P	129P
1996		106P	99P	103P	103P	107P	118P	111P	128P	117P	122P	130P
1997		104P	98P	102P	102P	106P	121P	114P	131P	120P	124P	131P
1998		103P	98P	101P	101P	105P	123P	118P	134P	123P	127P	132P

Sources: Same as General Statistics. Values reflect change from the base year, 1992. Values above 100 mean greater than 92, values below 100 mean less than 92, and a value of 100 in the 82-91 or 93-98 period means same as 92. 'P's mark projections by the editors.

SELECTED RATIOS

For 1994	Avg. of All Manufact.	Analyzed Industry	Index	For 1994	Avg. of All Manufact.	Analyzed Industry	Index
Employees per Establishment	49	59	121	Value Added per Production Worker	134,084	75,373	56
Payroll per Establishment	1,500,273	1,393,835	93	Cost per Establishment	5,045,178	1,920,045	38
Payroll per Employee	30,620	23,524	77	Cost per Employee	102,970	32,406	31
Production Workers per Establishment	34	46	133	Cost per Production Worker	146,988	42,127	29
Wages per Establishment	853,319	969,271	114	Shipments per Establishment	9,576,895	5,465,541	57
Wages per Production Worker	24,861	21,267	86	Shipments per Employee	195,460	92,245	47
Hours per Production Worker	2,056	2,118	103	Shipments per Production Worker	279,017	119,918	43
Wages per Hour	12.09	10.04	83	Investment per Establishment	321,011	264,348	82
Value Added per Establishment	4,602,255	3,435,282	75	Investment per Employee	6,552	4,462	68
Value Added per Employee	93,930	57,979	62	Investment per Production Worker	9,352	5,800	62

Sources: Same as General Statistics. The 'Average of All Manufacturing' column represents the average of all manufacturing industries reported for the most recent complete year available. The Index shows the relationship between the Average and the Analyzed Industry. For example, 100 means that they are equal; 500 that the Analyzed Industry is five times the average; 50 means that the Analyzed Industry is half the national average. The abbreviation 'na' is used to show that data are 'not available'.

LEADING COMPANIES Number shown: **67** Total sales ($ mil): **1,263** Total employment (000): **15.6**

Company Name	Address				CEO Name	Phone	Co. Type	Sales ($ mil)	Empl. (000)
Justin Industries Inc	PO Box 425	Fort Worth	TX	76101	John Justin	817-336-5125	P	483	5.0
Boral Bricks Inc	PO Box 1957	Augusta	GA	30903	Timothy Tuff	706-722-6831	S	130	1.9
Mutual Materials Co	PO Box 2009	Bellevue	WA	98009	R C Houlahan	206-455-2869	R	45	0.5
Bickerstaff Clay Products	PO Box 1178	Columbus	GA	31902	R H Bickerstaff	706-322-9360	R	44	0.5
Belden Brick Co	PO Box 20910	Canton	OH	44701	W H Belden Jr	216-456-0031	R	38	0.5
Georgia-Carolina Brick Co	PO Box 1957	Augusta	GA	30913	Woods W Burnett	706-722-6831	D	30	0.5
Pine Hall Brick Company Inc	PO Box 11044	Winston-Salem	NC	27116	WF Steele	910-721-7500	R	30	0.3
Richtex Corp	PO Box 3307	Columbia	SC	29230	SB Beuchler	803-786-1260	S	30	0.3
Henderson Brick	PO Box 2110	Henderson	TX	75653	Gene Mitchell	903-657-3505	D	23*	0.4
Pacific Clay Brick Products Inc	PO Box 549	Lake Elsinore	CA	92531	David Hollingsworth	909-674-2131	D	20	0.2
Sioux City Brick and Tile Co	310 S Floyd Blv	Sioux City	IA	51102	John D Hill	712-258-6571	R	18	0.3
Freeport Brick Co	PO Drawer F	Freeport	PA	16229	Edward L Straughn	412-295-2111	S	16	<0.1
Robinson Brick Co	1845 W Dartmouth	Denver	CO	80110	FG Robinson Jr	303-783-3000	R	14	<0.1
Southern Brick Co	PO Box 208	Ninety Six	SC	29666	Joseph H Patrick Jr	803-543-3211	R	14*	0.2
Interstate Brick Co	9780 S 5200 W	West Jordan	UT	84088	David Lucchetti	801-561-1471	S	13	0.1
Endicott Clay Products Co	PO Box 17	Fairbury	NE	68352	Roger D Judd	402-729-3315	R	12	0.2
JL Anderson Company Inc	PO Box 430	Cheraw	SC	29520	RS Rogers III	803-537-7861	R	12	0.1
Richards Brick Co	234 Springer Av	Edwardsville	IL	62025	John Motley	618-656-0230	R	12	0.1
Stark Ceramics Inc	PO Box 8880	Canton	OH	44711	Mark A Rojek	216-488-1211	R	12	0.2
Cherokee Brick and Tile Co	PO Box 4567	Macon	GA	31213	Kenneth D Sams	912-781-6800	R	11*	0.2
Advanced Ceramics Corp	PO Box 94924	Cleveland	OH	44101	Gerry Weimann	216-529-3900	R	10*	0.1
Glen-Gery Corp	PO Box 68	Summerville	PA	15864	Charles Cockrell	814-856-2181	D	10*	0.2
Ludowici-Celadon Inc	4757 Tile Plant Rd	New Lexington	OH	43764	J Hilyard	614-342-1995	S	10	0.1
Ochs Brick Co	PO Box 106	Springfield	MN	56087	P Van Hoomissen	507-723-4221	R	10*	<0.1
Palmetto Brick Co	PO Box 430	Cheraw	SC	29520	RS Rogers III	803-537-7861	S	10	0.1
Triangle Brick Co	6523 Apex Rd	Durham	NC	27713	William A Howie	919-544-1796	R	10	0.1
Castaic Clay Manufacturing Co	PO Box 8	Castaic	CA	91310	Mike Malow	818-365-5112	R	9	0.1
Kentwood Brick & Tile Mfg	PO Drawer F	Kentwood	LA	70444	Don Clemons	504-229-7112	R	9	<0.1
Brick and Tile Corp	PO Box 45	Lawrenceville	VA	23868	J Reid Wrenn	804-848-3151	R	8*	0.1
Delta Brick	Rte 4	Macon	MS	39341	Ron Polen	601-726-4236	D	8*	0.1
Elgin-Butler Brick Co	PO Box 1947	Austin	TX	78767	John R Butler	512-453-7366	R	8	1.2
Insaco Inc	PO Box 9006	Quakertown	PA	18951	David M Haines	215-536-3500	R	8*	<0.1
Riverside Brick and Supply Co	PO Box 24096	Richmond	VA	23224	Bill McNeer	804-232-6786	S	8*	<0.1
Irvins Interstate Brick & Block	PO Box 19783	Indianapolis	IN	46219	G Irvin	317-547-9511	R	7	<0.1
Taylor Clay Products Company	PO Box 2128	Salisbury	NC	28144	Charlie D Taylor Jr	704-636-2411	R	7	0.1
Ashe Brick	PO Box 99	Van Wyck	SC	29744	Greg Butler	803-286-5566	D	6	0.1
Eureka Brick and Tile Company	PO Box 379	Clarksville	AR	72830	Earl K Johnson	501-754-3040	R	6	<0.1
Henry Brick Company Inc	PO Box 857	Selma	AL	36702	Art Gleason Jr	205-875-2600	R	6	0.1
Lee Brick and Tile Co	PO Box 1027	Sanford	NC	27330	Frank Perry	919-774-4800	R	6*	<0.1
Marseilles Brick Venture LP	PO Box 306	Marseilles	IL	61341	Jim Johnson	815-795-6911	R	6	<0.1
Statesville Brick Company Inc	PO Box 28687	Statesville	NC	28677	HB Foster	704-872-4123	R	6	<0.1
Summit Brick and Tile	PO Box 533	Pueblo	CO	81002	Joseph C Welte	719-542-8278	R	6	<0.1
Burns Brick	PO Box 4787	Macon	GA	31208	William V Argo	912-743-8621	D	5*	<0.1
Columbus Brick Company Inc	PO Box 9630	Columbus	MS	39705	Allen Puckett III	601-328-4931	R	5	<0.1
Kansas Brick and Tile Company	PO Box 450	Hoisington	KS	67544	LR Smith	316-653-2157	R	5	<0.1
LP McNear Brick Company Inc	PO Box 1380	San Rafael	CA	94915	John McNear	415-454-6811	R	5	<0.1
United Brick and Tile Co	PO Box 35	Adel	IA	50003	Norman Mahoney	515-993-4549	D	5*	0.1
Yankee Hill Brick Mfg Co	3705 S Soddington	Lincoln	NE	68522	Roger L Meints	402-477-6663	S	5*	<0.1
Stone Creek Brick Co	PO Box 116	Stone Creek	OH	43840	Chester Tarulli Jr	216-339-5511	R	5	<0.1
Baltimore Brick Co	9009 Yellow Brick	Baltimore	MD	21237	Charles Stein	410-682-6700	D	4	<0.1
Bowerston Shale Co	PO Box 199	Bowerston	OH	44695	WU Milliken	614-269-2921	S	4	<0.1
Cunningham Brick Company Inc	1437 CB	Thomasville	NC	27360	NS Cunningham	919-472-6181	R	4	0.1
Orbco Inc	PO Box 907	Owensboro	KY	42302	William J Richard	502-926-3330	R	4	<0.1
Streator Brick Systems Inc	PO Box E	Streator	IL	61364	B Mallonee	815-672-2106	R	4	<0.1
Nash Brick Co	PO Box 962	Rocky Mount	NC	27802	Tom Fisher	919-446-3804	R	3	<0.1
Blasch Precision Ceramics Inc	580 Broadway	Albany	NY	12204	David Bobrick	518-436-1263	R	3	<0.1
Continental Brick Co	1441 Charles Town	Martinsburg	WV	25401	Lynch Christian	304-263-6974	R	3*	<0.1
Hanford Brick Company Inc	PO Box 1215	Burlington	NC	27216	James E Hanford	910-229-5811	R	3*	<0.1
Athens Brick Co	PO Box 70	Athens	TX	75751	Roy Martin	903-675-2256	S	3	<0.1
Deleo Clay Tile Inc	600 Chaney St	Lake Elsinore	CA	92530	Joe Deleo	909-674-1578	R	3	<0.1
Kinney Brick Co	PO Box 1804	Albuquerque	NM	87103	WR Jurgena	505-877-4550	R	3	<0.1
Gloria Ent Inc	PO Box 57825	Sherman Oaks	CA	91413	Stanley May	818-783-6311	R	2	<0.1
Klamath Falls Brick and Title Co	PO Box 242	Klamath Falls	OR	97601	Philip A Partington	503-884-5419	D	2	<0.1
Southern Brick and Tile	PO Box 328	Byhalia	MS	38611	Fred Spence	601-838-2141	R	2	<0.1
Galena Brick Products Inc	PO Box 368	Galena	OH	43021	FT Hopper	614-965-1010	R	1	<0.1
Monroe Brick and Tile	PO Box 1912	Monroe	OR	97456	Roger Lucas	503-847-6300	D	1	<0.1
ORPAC Inc	PO Box 5436	Oak Ridge	TN	37831	Cres Holcombe	615-482-4635	R	0*	<0.1

Source: *Ward's Business Directory of U.S. Private and Public Companies*, Volumes 1 and 2, 1996. The company type code used is as follows: P - Public, R - Private, S - Subsidiary, D - Division, J - Joint Venture, A - Affiliate, G - Group. Sales are in millions of dollars, employees are in thousands. An asterisk (*) indicates an estimated sales volume. The symbol < stands for 'less than'. Company names and addresses are truncated, in some cases, to fit into the available space.

MATERIALS CONSUMED

Material	Quantity	Delivered Cost ($ million)
Materials, ingredients, containers, and supplies	(X)	191.1
Clay, ceramic, and refractory minerals	(X)	57.6
Industrial chemicals	(X)	6.5
All other materials and components, parts, containers, and supplies	(X)	97.6
Materials, ingredients, containers, and supplies, nsk	(X)	29.4

Source: 1992 *Economic Census*. Explanation of symbols used: (D): Withheld to avoid disclosure of competitive data; na: Not available; (S): Withheld because statistical norms were not met; (X): Not applicable; (Z): Less than half the unit shown; nec: Not elsewhere classified; nsk: Not specified by kind; - : zero; * : 10-19 percent estimated; ** : 20-29 percent estimated.

PRODUCT SHARE DETAILS

Product or Product Class	% Share	Product or Product Class	% Share
Brick and structural clay tile	100.00	Other brick (paving, floor, and sewer)	2.31
Building or common brick	91.18	Glazed brick and structural hollow tile	2.71

Source: 1992 *Economic Census*. The values shown are percent of total shipments in an industry. Values of indented subcategories are summed in the main heading. The symbol (D) appears when data are withheld to prevent disclosure of competitive information. The abbreviation nsk stands for 'not specified by kind' and nec for 'not elsewhere classified'.

INPUTS AND OUTPUTS FOR BRICK & STRUCTURAL CLAY TILE

Economic Sector or Industry Providing Inputs	%	Sector	Economic Sector or Industry Buying Outputs	%	Sector
Gas production & distribution (utilities)	27.4	Util.	Office buildings	18.7	Constr.
Motor freight transportation & warehousing	11.5	Util.	Residential 1-unit structures, nonfarm	16.0	Constr.
Electric services (utilities)	9.3	Util.	Residential garden apartments	11.0	Constr.
Nonmetallic mineral services	5.6	Mining	Industrial buildings	8.2	Constr.
Clay, ceramic, & refractory minerals	5.1	Mining	Residential additions/alterations, nonfarm	5.7	Constr.
Petroleum refining	4.4	Manufg.	Construction of educational buildings	5.2	Constr.
Imports	3.3	Foreign	Residential high-rise apartments	4.9	Constr.
Maintenance of nonfarm buildings nec	2.6	Constr.	Maintenance of nonfarm buildings nec	4.3	Constr.
Wholesale trade	2.4	Trade	Construction of stores & restaurants	4.0	Constr.
Industrial inorganic chemicals, nec	1.8	Manufg.	Nonfarm residential structure maintenance	2.8	Constr.
Paints & allied products	1.7	Manufg.	Residential 2-4 unit structures, nonfarm	2.8	Constr.
Railroads & related services	1.7	Util.	Construction of hospitals	2.6	Constr.
Eating & drinking places	1.7	Trade	Hotels & motels	1.9	Constr.
Fabricated metal products, nec	1.6	Manufg.	Construction of religious buildings	1.6	Constr.
Water transportation	1.6	Util.	Construction of nonfarm buildings nec	1.1	Constr.
Veneer & plywood	1.4	Manufg.	Warehouses	1.1	Constr.
Coal	1.3	Mining	Maintenance of nonbuilding facilities nec	1.0	Constr.
Communications, except radio & TV	1.1	Util.	Exports	0.8	Foreign
Banking	1.0	Fin/R.E.	Sewer system facility construction	0.7	Constr.
Brick & structural clay tile	0.9	Manufg.	Telephone & telegraph facility construction	0.7	Constr.
Computer & data processing services	0.8	Services	Brick & structural clay tile	0.6	Manufg.
U.S. Postal Service	0.8	Gov't	Dormitories & other group housing	0.5	Constr.
Cyclic crudes and organics	0.7	Manufg.	Resid. & other health facility construction	0.5	Constr.
Machinery, except electrical, nec	0.7	Manufg.	Amusement & recreation building construction	0.4	Constr.
Management & consulting services & labs	0.7	Services	Electric utility facility construction	0.4	Constr.
Legal services	0.6	Services	Farm housing units & additions & alterations	0.3	Constr.
Paving mixtures & blocks	0.5	Manufg.	Farm service facilities	0.3	Constr.
Automotive rental & leasing, without drivers	0.5	Services	Maintenance of sewer facilities	0.3	Constr.
Automotive repair shops & services	0.5	Services	Highway & street construction	0.2	Constr.
Conveyors & conveying equipment	0.4	Manufg.	Water supply facility construction	0.2	Constr.
Explosives	0.4	Manufg.	Local transit facility construction	0.1	Constr.
Lubricating oils & greases	0.4	Manufg.	Maintenance of electric utility facilities	0.1	Constr.
Abrasive products	0.3	Manufg.	Maintenance of military facilities	0.1	Constr.
Special dies & tools & machine tool accessories	0.3	Manufg.	Maintenance of railroads	0.1	Constr.
Accounting, auditing & bookkeeping	0.3	Services			
Engineering, architectural, & surveying services	0.3	Services			
Equipment rental & leasing services	0.3	Services			
Laundry, dry cleaning, shoe repair	0.3	Services			
Manifold business forms	0.2	Manufg.			
Paperboard containers & boxes	0.2	Manufg.			
Tires & inner tubes	0.2	Manufg.			
Retail trade, except eating & drinking	0.2	Trade			
Insurance carriers	0.2	Fin/R.E.			
Advertising	0.2	Services			
Electrical repair shops	0.2	Services			
Motor vehicle parts & accessories	0.1	Manufg.			
Transit & bus transportation	0.1	Util.			
Real estate	0.1	Fin/R.E.			
Security & commodity brokers	0.1	Fin/R.E.			
Personnel supply services	0.1	Services			
Services to dwellings & other buildings	0.1	Services			

Source: Benchmark Input-Output Accounts for the U.S. Economy, 1982, U.S. Department of Commerce, Washington, D.C., July 1991. Data, as reported in the source, are organized by the 1977 SIC structure in use in 1982 but have been matched, as closely as is possible, to the 1987 SIC structure used in this book.

OCCUPATIONS EMPLOYED BY SIC 325 - STONE, CLAY, AND MISC MINING PRODUCTS NEC

Occupation	% of Total 1994	Change to 2005	Occupation	% of Total 1994	Change to 2005
Helpers, laborers, & material movers nec	6.7	-23.3	Machine feeders & offbearers	2.3	-31.4
Assemblers, fabricators, & hand workers nec	6.4	-23.9	Painting, coating, & decorating workers, hand	2.0	52.3
Furnace, kiln, or kettle operators	4.2	-16.7	Freight, stock, & material movers, hand	1.9	-38.8
Crushing & mixing machine operators	3.9	-9.5	Truck drivers light & heavy	1.9	-20.6
Industrial machinery mechanics	3.9	-15.2	Coating, painting, & spraying machine workers	1.8	-23.8
Hand packers & packagers	3.6	-34.7	Secretaries, ex legal & medical	1.8	-30.4
Extruding & forming machine workers	3.4	-80.6	Cutting & slicing machine setters, operators	1.6	-16.2
Sales & related workers nec	3.2	-23.6	Grinders & polishers, hand	1.6	-16.2
Packaging & filling machine operators	3.2	-23.7	Industrial production managers	1.5	-23.5
Precision workers nec	3.0	-8.7	Traffic, shipping, & receiving clerks	1.5	-26.6
Industrial truck & tractor operators	2.8	-23.7	General office clerks	1.5	-34.9
General managers & top executives	2.8	-27.5	Bookkeeping, accounting, & auditing clerks	1.3	-42.7
Inspectors, testers, & graders, precision	2.8	-23.6	Electricians	1.1	-27.3
Maintenance repairers, general utility	2.6	-30.8	Machinists	1.0	-23.6

Source: Industry-Occupation Matrix, Bureau of Labor Statistics. These data relate to one or more 3-digit SIC industry groups rather than to a single 4-digit SIC. The change reported for each occupation to the year 2005 is a percent of growth or decline as estimated by the Bureau of Labor Statistics. The abbreviation nec stands for 'not elsewhere classified'.

LOCATION BY STATE AND REGIONAL CONCENTRATION

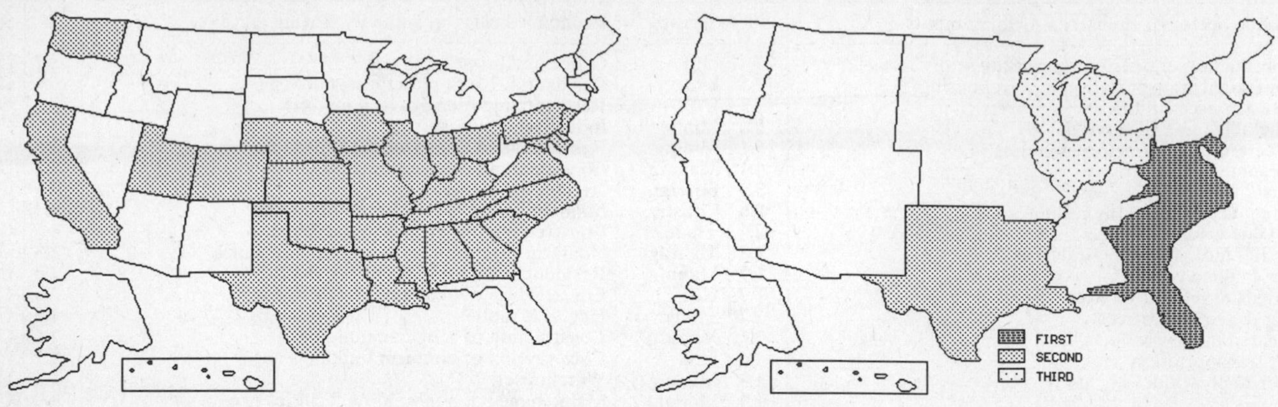

INDUSTRY DATA BY STATE

State	Establish-ments	Shipments			Employment				Cost as % of Shipments	Investment per Employee ($)
		Total ($ mil)	% of U.S.	Per Establ.	Total Number	% of U.S.	Per Establ.	Wages ($/hour)		
Texas	17	117.2	10.5	6.9	1,400	9.9	82	7.92	21.8	4,286
Ohio	24	109.5	9.8	4.6	1,600	11.3	67	10.27	36.1	-
Alabama	12	70.0	6.3	5.8	700	4.9	58	8.17	33.7	2,571
Georgia	5	57.3	5.1	11.5	800	5.6	160	8.15	48.2	5,250
California	11	49.7	4.5	4.5	600	4.2	55	10.44	28.6	2,500
Mississippi	6	31.9	2.9	5.3	500	3.5	83	7.43	41.4	-
Colorado	4	28.4	2.5	7.1	300	2.1	75	10.75	33.1	-
Iowa	5	21.2	1.9	4.2	300	2.1	60	9.40	36.8	-
New Jersey	4	10.5	0.9	2.6	200	1.4	50	10.50	31.4	2,500
North Carolina	23	(D)	-	-	1,750 *	12.3	76	-	-	4,686
Pennsylvania	15	(D)	-	-	750 *	5.3	50	-	-	3,067
South Carolina	10	(D)	-	-	750 *	5.3	75	-	-	-
Virginia	9	(D)	-	-	750 *	5.3	83	-	-	-
Arkansas	7	(D)	-	-	375 *	2.6	54	-	-	-
Kentucky	6	(D)	-	-	375 *	2.6	63	-	-	-
Oklahoma	6	(D)	-	-	375 *	2.6	63	-	-	-
Kansas	4	(D)	-	-	175 *	1.2	44	-	-	-
Louisiana	4	(D)	-	-	175 *	1.2	44	-	-	-
Maryland	4	(D)	-	-	175 *	1.2	44	-	-	-
Tennessee	4	(D)	-	-	375 *	2.6	94	-	-	-
Illinois	3	(D)	-	-	175 *	1.2	58	-	-	-
Missouri	3	(D)	-	-	175 *	1.2	58	-	-	-
Nebraska	3	(D)	-	-	175 *	1.2	58	-	-	-
Washington	3	(D)	-	-	175 *	1.2	58	-	-	-
Indiana	2	(D)	-	-	175 *	1.2	88	-	-	-
Utah	2	(D)	-	-	175 *	1.2	88	-	-	-

Source: 1992 *Economic Census*. The states are in descending order of shipments or establishments (if shipment data are missing for the majority). The symbol (D) appears when data are withheld to prevent disclosure of competitive information. States marked with (D) are sorted by number of establishments. A dash (-) indicates that the data element cannot be calculated; * indicates the midpoint of a range.

3253 - CERAMIC WALL & FLOOR TILE

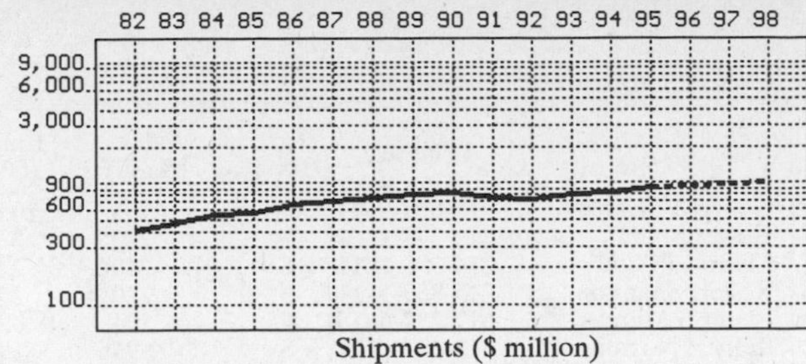

Shipments ($ million)

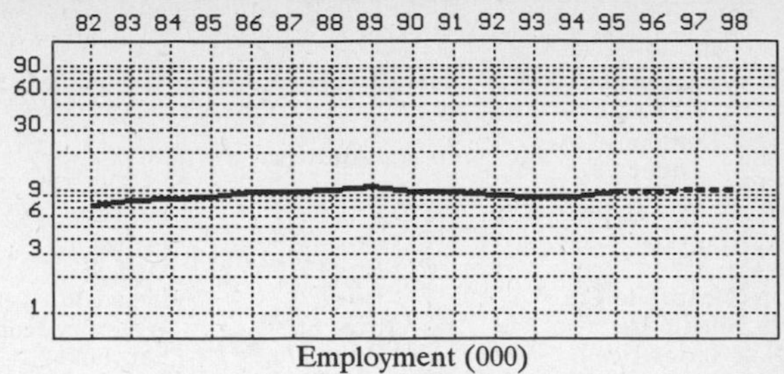

Employment (000)

GENERAL STATISTICS

Year	Companies	Establishments: Total	Establishments: with 20 or more employees	Employment: Total (000)	Employment: Production Workers (000)	Employment: Production Hours (Mil)	Compensation: Payroll ($ mil)	Compensation: Wages ($/hr)	Production ($ million): Cost of Materials	Production ($ million): Value Added by Manufacture	Production ($ million): Value of Shipments	Production ($ million): Capital Invest.
1982	77	97	52	7.5	6.1	12.3	114.2	6.52	149.7	256.1	406.9	7.7
1983		99	52	8.2	6.8	14.4	127.2	6.73	169.0	302.9	470.8	13.0
1984		101	52	8.5	7.1	14.7	144.4	7.59	190.8	373.7	553.5	84.2
1985		104	52	8.7	7.2	15.1	153.6	7.79	204.7	354.4	568.8	28.2
1986		104	48	9.6	7.8	16.0	175.2	8.06	239.4	442.1	665.9	51.3
1987	95	114	51	9.5	7.7	15.6	182.8	8.63	261.9	463.1	717.4	33.2
1988		112	53	9.8	8.1	15.7	196.4	9.50	281.1	489.6	756.0	71.9
1989		111	51	10.4	8.4	17.3	203.6	8.98	299.1	501.9	792.6	32.3
1990		113	51	9.6	8.1	16.4	208.6	9.57	303.5	556.6	845.0	68.8
1991		123	54	9.5	7.7	15.7	192.8	8.94	264.3	465.1	750.8	22.1
1992	102	118	55	8.9	7.3	15.3	196.9	9.50	261.3	458.1	731.3	48.9
1993		129	53	8.7	7.3	15.0	206.3	10.41	260.9	567.8	810.9	68.0
1994		127P	53P	8.6	7.1	15.6	220.1	9.85	294.0	576.4	847.3	73.1
1995		130P	54P	9.6P	7.9P	16.4P	234.2P	10.65P	318.5P	624.5P	918.0P	67.2P
1996		132P	54P	9.7P	8.0P	16.6P	242.2P	10.94P	330.0P	647.0P	951.1P	70.2P
1997		135P	54P	9.7P	8.0P	16.8P	250.1P	11.23P	341.5P	669.6P	984.3P	73.2P
1998		138P	54P	9.8P	8.1P	16.9P	258.1P	11.52P	353.0P	692.1P	1,017.4P	76.1P

Sources: 1982, 1987, 1992 *Economic Census*; *Annual Survey of Manufactures*, 83-86, 88-91, 93-94. Establishment counts for non-Census years are from *County Business Patterns*; establishment values for 83-84 are extrapolations. 'P's show projections by the editors. Industries reclassified in 87 will not have data for prior years.

INDICES OF CHANGE

Year	Companies	Establishments: Total	Establishments: with 20 or more employees	Employment: Total (000)	Employment: Production Workers (000)	Employment: Production Hours (Mil)	Compensation: Payroll ($ mil)	Compensation: Wages ($/hr)	Production ($ million): Cost of Materials	Production ($ million): Value Added by Manufacture	Production ($ million): Value of Shipments	Production ($ million): Capital Invest.
1982	75	82	95	84	84	80	58	69	57	56	56	16
1983		84	95	92	93	94	65	71	65	66	64	27
1984		86	95	96	97	96	73	80	73	82	76	172
1985		88	95	98	99	99	78	82	78	77	78	58
1986		88	87	108	107	105	89	85	92	97	91	105
1987	93	97	93	107	105	102	93	91	100	101	98	68
1988		95	96	110	111	103	100	100	108	107	103	147
1989		94	93	117	115	113	103	95	114	110	108	66
1990		96	93	108	111	107	106	101	116	122	116	141
1991		104	98	107	105	103	98	94	101	102	103	45
1992	100	100	100	100	100	100	100	100	100	100	100	100
1993		109	96	98	100	98	105	110	100	124	111	139
1994		108P	97P	97	97	102	112	104	113	126	116	149
1995		110P	97P	108P	108P	108P	119P	112P	122P	136P	126P	137P
1996		112P	98P	108P	109P	109P	123P	115P	126P	141P	130P	144P
1997		114P	98P	109P	110P	110P	127P	118P	131P	146P	135P	150P
1998		117P	98P	110P	111P	111P	131P	121P	135P	151P	139P	156P

Sources: Same as General Statistics. Values reflect change from the base year, 1992. Values above 100 mean greater than 92, values below 100 mean less than 92, and a value of 100 in the 82-91 or 93-98 period means same as 92. 'P's mark projections by the editors.

SELECTED RATIOS

For 1994	Avg. of All Manufact.	Analyzed Industry	Index
Employees per Establishment	49	68	138
Payroll per Establishment	1,500,273	1,729,563	115
Payroll per Employee	30,620	25,593	84
Production Workers per Establishment	34	56	163
Wages per Establishment	853,319	1,207,472	142
Wages per Production Worker	24,861	21,642	87
Hours per Production Worker	2,056	2,197	107
Wages per Hour	12.09	9.85	81
Value Added per Establishment	4,602,255	4,529,396	98
Value Added per Employee	93,930	67,023	71

For 1994	Avg. of All Manufact.	Analyzed Industry	Index
Value Added per Production Worker	134,084	81,183	61
Cost per Establishment	5,045,178	2,310,275	46
Cost per Employee	102,970	34,186	33
Cost per Production Worker	146,988	41,408	28
Shipments per Establishment	9,576,895	6,658,150	70
Shipments per Employee	195,460	98,523	50
Shipments per Production Worker	279,017	119,338	43
Investment per Establishment	321,011	574,426	179
Investment per Employee	6,552	8,500	130
Investment per Production Worker	9,352	10,296	110

Sources: Same as General Statistics. The 'Average of All Manufacturing' column represents the average of all manufacturing industries reported for the most recent complete year available. The Index shows the relationship between the Average and the Analyzed Industry. For example, 100 means that they are equal; 500 that the Analyzed Industry is five times the average; 50 means that the Analyzed Industry is half the national average. The abbreviation 'na' is used to show that data are 'not available'.

LEADING COMPANIES

Number shown: **34** Total sales ($ mil): **4,083** Total employment (000): **34.1**

Company Name	Address				CEO Name	Phone	Co. Type	Sales ($ mil)	Empl. (000)
Armstrong World Industries Inc	PO Box 3001	Lancaster	PA	17604	George A Lorch	717-397-0611	P	2,753	20.6
Dal-Tile Group Inc	PO Box 17130	Dallas	TX	75217	Howard Hull	214-398-1411	R	280	3.2
Dal-Tile Corp	PO Box 17130	Dallas	TX	75217	Charles Pilliod	214-398-1411	S	240*	2.5
American Olean Tile Co	PO Box 271	Lansdale	PA	19446	Robert Shannon	215-855-1111	S	220	2.3
American Biltrite Inc	57 River St	Wellesley Hills	MA	02181	Roger S Marcus	617-237-6655	P	104	0.6
Florida Tile Industries Inc	PO Box 477	Lakeland	FL	33802	Kelly E Norton	813-687-7171	S	96*	1.0
American Marazzi Tile Inc	359 Clay Rd	Sunnyvale	TX	75182	Filippo Marazzi	214-226-0110	S	50	0.2
Monarch Tile Inc	PO Box 999	Florence	AL	35631	Thomas S White III	205-764-6181	R	47*	0.6
P and M Tile Inc	PO Box 1777	Lexington	NC	27293	Al Cox	704-249-3931	S	40	0.5
Ceramicus Inc	19 Minnekoning Rd	Flemington	NJ	08822	Robert Schlemmer	908-788-8969	R	39	0.5
United States Ceramic Tile Co	PO Box 338	East Sparta	OH	44626	R E Schlemmer	216-866-5531	S	32	0.5
Romany Ceramics Inc	PO Box 338	East Sparta	OH	44626	Richard Falbo	216-866-5531	S	30	0.3
TileCera Inc	300 Arcata Blv	Clarksville	TN	37040	Wongbuddhapitak	615-647-9974	S	30	0.3
MK Diamond Products Inc	PO Box 2803	Torrance	CA	90509	Robert J Delahaut	310-539-5221	R	29*	0.1
Magneco/Metrel Inc	223 Interstate Rd	Addison	IL	60101	Chester Connors	708-543-6660	R	19*	0.2
Harris Potteries	800 N Wells St	Chicago	IL	60610	Robert Harris	312-951-0186	R	14*	0.2
KPT Inc	PO Box 468	Bloomfield	IN	47424	Matthew Lo	812-384-3563	R	10	0.1
Metropolitan Industries Inc	PO Box 9240	Canton	OH	44711	John S Renkert	216-484-4887	R	10	<0.1
Ann Sacks Tile and Stone	8120 NE 33rd Dr	Portland	OR	97211	Ann Sacks	503-281-7751	S	8*	0.1
St Henry Tile Inc	PO Box 318	St Henry	OH	45883	Bob Homan	419-678-4841	R	8*	<0.1
Epro Inc	156 E Broadway St	Westerville	OH	43081	Susan Edgar	614-882-6990	R	4	<0.1
Marion Ceramics Inc	PO Box 1134	Marion	SC	29571	D Cabeza	803-423-1311	R	4	<0.1
B and W Tile Company Inc	14600 S Western	Gardena	CA	90249	R Logan	310-538-9579	R	4	<0.1
Quarry Tile Co	12 Spokane Indrial	Spokane	WA	99216	RE Baiter	509-924-1466	R	3*	<0.1
Paris Ceramics Inc	31 E Elm St	Greenwich	CT	06830	Christopher Peacock	203-862-9538	R	2	<0.1
Universal Ceramics Inc	PO Box 469	Adairsville	GA	30103	Don Dewberry	404-773-7726	P	2	<0.1
Stonelight Tile Inc	1651 Pomona Av	San Jose	CA	95110	DG Anson	408-292-7424	R	2	<0.1
Kraftile Co	800 Kraftile Rd	Fremont	CA	94536	James F Kraft	510-793-4432	R	1*	<0.1
McIntyre Tile Company Inc	PO Box 14	Healdsburg	CA	95448	RL McIntyre	707-433-8866	R	1	<0.1
Handcraft Tile Inc	1696 S Main St	Milpitas	CA	95035	Clay J Scott	408-262-1140	R	1	<0.1
Tile Helper Inc	3110 N River Rd	River Grove	IL	60171	Theodore Izewski	708-453-6900	R	1	<0.1
Payne Creations Tile	4829 N Antioch Rd	Kansas City	MO	64119	Carolyn L Payne	816-452-0070	R	0	<0.1
Deer Creek Pottery	305 Richardson St	Grass Valley	CA	95945	Rob Kellenbeck	916-272-3373	R	0	<0.1
Kepcor Inc	PO Box 119	Minerva	OH	44657	R B Keplinger Jr	216-868-6434	R	0	<0.1

Source: *Ward's Business Directory of U.S. Private and Public Companies*, Volumes 1 and 2, 1996. The company type code used is as follows: P - Public, R - Private, S - Subsidiary, D - Division, J - Joint Venture, A - Affiliate, G - Group. Sales are in millions of dollars, employees are in thousands. An asterisk (*) indicates an estimated sales volume. The symbol < stands for 'less than'. Company names and addresses are truncated, in some cases, to fit into the available space.

MATERIALS CONSUMED

Material	Quantity	Delivered Cost ($ million)
Materials, ingredients, containers, and supplies	(X)	165.0
Clay, ceramic, and refractory minerals	(X)	78.0
Industrial chemicals	(X)	5.4
All other materials and components, parts, containers, and supplies	(X)	55.3
Materials, ingredients, containers, and supplies, nsk	(X)	26.3

Source: 1992 *Economic Census*. Explanation of symbols used: (D): Withheld to avoid disclosure of competitive data; na: Not available; (S): Withheld because statistical norms were not met; (X): Not applicable; (Z): Less than half the unit shown; nec: Not elsewhere classified; nsk: Not specified by kind; - : zero; * : 10-19 percent estimated; ** : 20-29 percent estimated.

PRODUCT SHARE DETAILS

Product or Product Class	% Share	Product or Product Class	% Share
Ceramic wall and floor tile	100.00		

Source: 1992 *Economic Census*. The values shown are percent of total shipments in an industry. Values of indented subcategories are summed in the main heading. The symbol (D) appears when data are withheld to prevent disclosure of competitive information. The abbreviation nsk stands for 'not specified by kind' and nec for 'not elsewhere classified'.

INPUTS AND OUTPUTS FOR CERAMIC WALL & FLOOR TILE

Economic Sector or Industry Providing Inputs	%	Sector	Economic Sector or Industry Buying Outputs	%	Sector
Imports	47.3	Foreign	Residential additions/alterations, nonfarm	11.8	Constr.
Motor freight transportation & warehousing	7.0	Util.	Maintenance of nonfarm buildings nec	10.3	Constr.
Cyclic crudes and organics	6.7	Manufg.	Office buildings	10.3	Constr.
Gas production & distribution (utilities)	6.4	Util.	Residential 1-unit structures, nonfarm	9.7	Constr.
Clay, ceramic, & refractory minerals	5.5	Mining	Construction of hospitals	7.4	Constr.
Ceramic wall & floor tile	3.3	Manufg.	Nonfarm residential structure maintenance	6.8	Constr.
Wholesale trade	3.2	Trade	Residential garden apartments	5.5	Constr.
Electric services (utilities)	2.5	Util.	Hotels & motels	4.1	Constr.
Maintenance of nonfarm buildings nec	2.0	Constr.	Resid. & other health facility construction	3.6	Constr.
Industrial inorganic chemicals, nec	1.6	Manufg.	Construction of educational buildings	3.2	Constr.
Paints & allied products	1.4	Manufg.	Industrial buildings	3.2	Constr.
Petroleum refining	1.1	Manufg.	Residential 2-4 unit structures, nonfarm	3.2	Constr.
Eating & drinking places	1.0	Trade	Mobile homes	2.4	Manufg.
Paperboard containers & boxes	0.7	Manufg.	Ceramic wall & floor tile	2.3	Manufg.
Banking	0.7	Fin/R.E.	Exports	2.1	Foreign
Real estate	0.7	Fin/R.E.	Construction of stores & restaurants	1.8	Constr.
Communications, except radio & TV	0.6	Util.	Amusement & recreation building construction	1.7	Constr.
Advertising	0.5	Services	Farm housing units & additions & alterations	1.7	Constr.
U.S. Postal Service	0.5	Gov't	Dormitories & other group housing	1.6	Constr.
Machinery, except electrical, nec	0.4	Manufg.	Residential high-rise apartments	1.4	Constr.
Railroads & related services	0.4	Util.	Construction of nonfarm buildings nec	0.9	Constr.
Water supply & sewage systems	0.4	Util.	Telephone & telegraph facility construction	0.8	Constr.
Detective & protective services	0.4	Services	Construction of religious buildings	0.7	Constr.
Management & consulting services & labs	0.4	Services	Ship building & repairing	0.6	Manufg.
Minerals, ground or treated	0.3	Manufg.	Local transit facility construction	0.5	Constr.
Water transportation	0.3	Util.	Maintenance of farm residential buildings	0.5	Constr.
Automotive rental & leasing, without drivers	0.3	Services	Change in business inventories	0.5	In House
Equipment rental & leasing services	0.3	Services	Maintenance of local transit facilities	0.4	Constr.
Legal services	0.3	Services	Electric utility facility construction	0.2	Constr.
Noncomparable imports	0.3	Foreign	Maintenance, conservation & development facilities	0.2	Constr.
Abrasive products	0.2	Manufg.	Maintenance of military facilities	0.1	Constr.
Lubricating oils & greases	0.2	Manufg.			
Special dies & tools & machine tool accessories	0.2	Manufg.			
Accounting, auditing & bookkeeping	0.2	Services			
Automotive repair shops & services	0.2	Services			
Computer & data processing services	0.2	Services			
Laundry, dry cleaning, shoe repair	0.2	Services			
Alkalies & chlorine	0.1	Manufg.			
Fabricated rubber products, nec	0.1	Manufg.			
Manifold business forms	0.1	Manufg.			
Nonclay refractories	0.1	Manufg.			
Insurance carriers	0.1	Fin/R.E.			
Royalties	0.1	Fin/R.E.			

Source: Benchmark Input-Output Accounts for the U.S. Economy, 1982, U.S. Department of Commerce, Washington, D.C., July 1991. Data, as reported in the source, are organized by the 1977 SIC structure in use in 1982 but have been matched, as closely as is possible, to the 1987 SIC structure used in this book.

OCCUPATIONS EMPLOYED BY SIC 325 - STONE, CLAY, AND MISC MINING PRODUCTS NEC

Occupation	% of Total 1994	Change to 2005	Occupation	% of Total 1994	Change to 2005
Helpers, laborers, & material movers nec	6.7	-23.3	Machine feeders & offbearers	2.3	-31.4
Assemblers, fabricators, & hand workers nec	6.4	-23.9	Painting, coating, & decorating workers, hand	2.0	52.3
Furnace, kiln, or kettle operators	4.2	-16.7	Freight, stock, & material movers, hand	1.9	-38.8
Crushing & mixing machine operators	3.9	-9.5	Truck drivers light & heavy	1.9	-20.6
Industrial machinery mechanics	3.9	-15.2	Coating, painting, & spraying machine workers	1.8	-23.8
Hand packers & packagers	3.6	-34.7	Secretaries, ex legal & medical	1.8	-30.4
Extruding & forming machine workers	3.4	-80.6	Cutting & slicing machine setters, operators	1.6	-16.2
Sales & related workers nec	3.2	-23.6	Grinders & polishers, hand	1.6	-16.2
Packaging & filling machine operators	3.2	-23.7	Industrial production managers	1.5	-23.5
Precision workers nec	3.0	-8.7	Traffic, shipping, & receiving clerks	1.5	-26.6
Industrial truck & tractor operators	2.8	-23.7	General office clerks	1.5	-34.9
General managers & top executives	2.8	-27.5	Bookkeeping, accounting, & auditing clerks	1.3	-42.7
Inspectors, testers, & graders, precision	2.8	-23.6	Electricians	1.1	-27.3
Maintenance repairers, general utility	2.6	-30.8	Machinists	1.0	-23.6

Source: Industry-Occupation Matrix, Bureau of Labor Statistics. These data relate to one or more 3-digit SIC industry groups rather than to a single 4-digit SIC. The change reported for each occupation to the year 2005 is a percent of growth or decline as estimated by the Bureau of Labor Statistics. The abbreviation nec stands for 'not elsewhere classified'.

LOCATION BY STATE AND REGIONAL CONCENTRATION

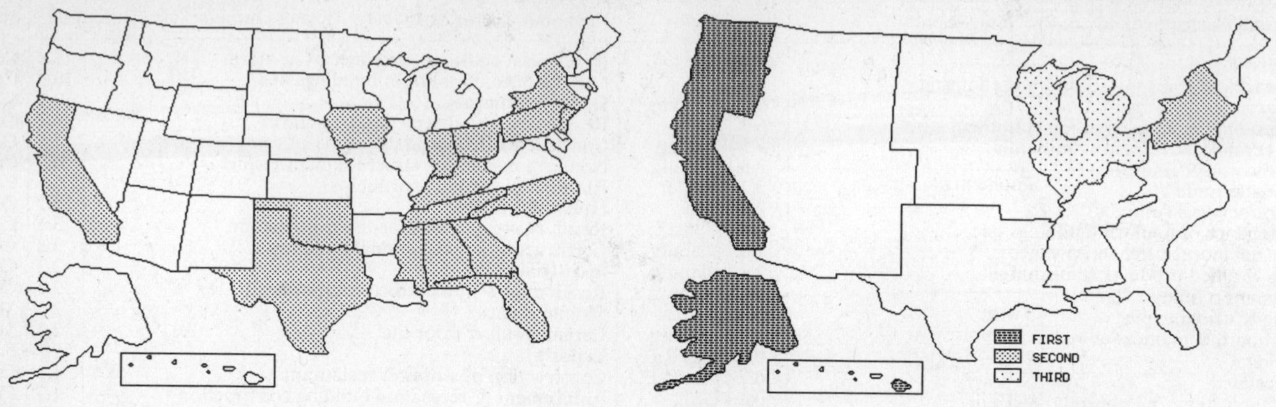

INDUSTRY DATA BY STATE

State	Establish-ments	Shipments			Employment				Cost as % of Shipments	Investment per Employee ($)
		Total ($ mil)	% of U.S.	Per Establ.	Total Number	% of U.S.	Per Establ.	Wages ($/hour)		
Ohio	10	64.1	8.8	6.4	900	10.1	90	9.40	36.7	7,333
Florida	5	33.2	4.5	6.6	600	6.7	120	11.11	42.2	7,500
New Jersey	8	21.7	3.0	2.7	300	3.4	38	7.80	38.7	1,000
California	17	16.9	2.3	1.0	300	3.4	18	8.25	36.7	1,333
Texas	10	(D)	-	-	1,750 *	19.7	175	-	-	2,686
Georgia	5	(D)	-	-	375 *	4.2	75	-	-	-
New York	5	(D)	-	-	375 *	4.2	75	-	-	-
Tennessee	5	(D)	-	-	750 *	8.4	150	-	-	-
Indiana	4	(D)	-	-	175 *	2.0	44	-	-	-
Alabama	3	(D)	-	-	375 *	4.2	125	-	-	-
Iowa	3	(D)	-	-	175 *	2.0	58	-	-	-
Pennsylvania	3	(D)	-	-	1,750 *	19.7	583	-	-	-
Kentucky	2	(D)	-	-	375 *	4.2	188	-	-	-
Mississippi	2	(D)	-	-	375 *	4.2	188	-	-	-
North Carolina	2	(D)	-	-	375 *	4.2	188	-	-	-
Oklahoma	1	(D)	-	-	175 *	2.0	175	-	-	-

Source: 1992 *Economic Census*. The states are in descending order of shipments or establishments (if shipment data are missing for the majority). The symbol (D) appears when data are withheld to prevent disclosure of competitive information. States marked with (D) are sorted by number of establishments. A dash (-) indicates that the data element cannot be calculated; * indicates the midpoint of a range.

3255 - CLAY REFRACTORIES

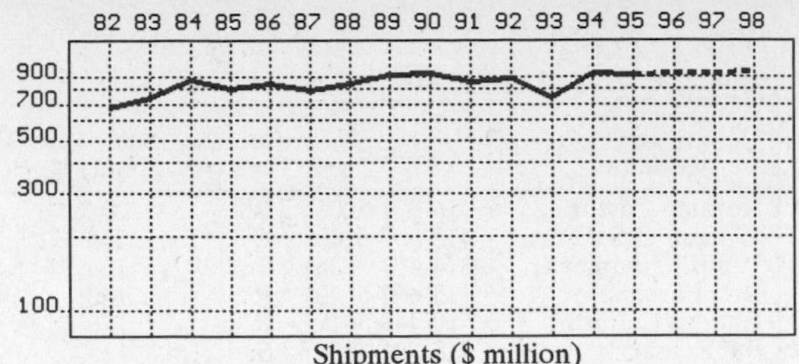

Shipments ($ million)

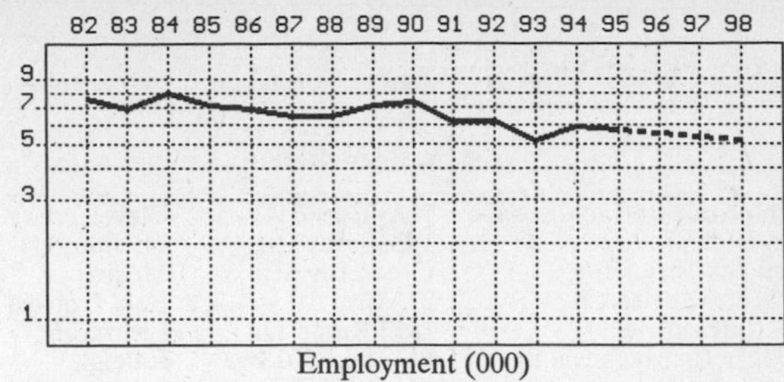

Employment (000)

GENERAL STATISTICS

Year	Companies	Establishments: Total	Establishments: with 20 or more employees	Employment: Total (000)	Employment: Production Workers (000)	Employment: Production Hours (Mil)	Compensation: Payroll ($ mil)	Compensation: Wages ($/hr)	Production ($ million): Cost of Materials	Production ($ million): Value Added by Manufacture	Production ($ million): Value of Shipments	Production ($ million): Capital Invest.
1982	106	159	103	7.6	5.6	10.4	155.2	10.51	339.0	316.5	670.3	21.2
1983		159	101	6.9	5.1	10.0	147.1	10.39	358.5	398.0	745.5	12.0
1984		159	99	7.9	6.1	12.0	176.6	10.83	438.2	421.0	868.6	22.0
1985		158	96	7.1	5.3	10.4	166.8	11.42	397.5	400.8	803.0	22.7
1986		147	87	6.9	5.0	9.7	160.4	11.21	412.6	425.9	843.5	15.8
1987	111	153	82	6.4	4.7	9.3	150.2	10.69	387.5	405.1	788.2	11.7
1988		158	91	6.4	4.8	9.3	160.0	11.65	401.7	437.6	836.7	14.0
1989		146	84	7.1	5.2	10.6	176.7	11.55	451.3	470.2	906.3	11.9
1990		152	87	7.3	4.8	9.6	168.8	12.31	475.3	451.4	922.9	15.2
1991		150	86	6.2	4.5	9.0	166.0	12.43	464.8	391.2	850.4	18.5
1992	95	145	84	6.2	4.4	8.8	183.8	12.84	452.8	435.7	886.8	24.6
1993		145	80	5.2	3.8	7.8	162.2	13.73	367.6	374.7	742.4	7.2
1994		144P	78P	5.9	4.4	9.2	179.0	13.20	494.0	453.8	938.8	16.5
1995		143P	76P	5.7P	4.0P	8.4P	176.7P	13.56P	479.5P	440.5P	911.3P	14.3P
1996		142P	74P	5.5P	3.9P	8.2P	178.3P	13.82P	485.6P	446.1P	922.8P	14.0P
1997		140P	72P	5.4P	3.8P	8.0P	179.8P	14.07P	491.6P	451.6P	934.3P	13.7P
1998		139P	70P	5.2P	3.6P	7.8P	181.4P	14.33P	497.6P	457.1P	945.7P	13.4P

Sources: 1982, 1987, 1992 *Economic Census*; *Annual Survey of Manufactures*, 83-86, 88-91, 93-94. Establishment counts for non-Census years are from *County Business Patterns*; establishment values for 83-84 are extrapolations. 'P's show projections by the editors. Industries reclassified in 87 will not have data for prior years.

INDICES OF CHANGE

Year	Companies	Establishments: Total	Establishments: with 20 or more employees	Employment: Total (000)	Employment: Production Workers (000)	Employment: Production Hours (Mil)	Compensation: Payroll ($ mil)	Compensation: Wages ($/hr)	Production ($ million): Cost of Materials	Production ($ million): Value Added by Manufacture	Production ($ million): Value of Shipments	Production ($ million): Capital Invest.
1982	112	110	123	123	127	118	84	82	75	73	76	86
1983		110	120	111	116	114	80	81	79	91	84	49
1984		110	118	127	139	136	96	84	97	97	98	89
1985		109	114	115	120	118	91	89	88	92	91	92
1986		101	104	111	114	110	87	87	91	98	95	64
1987	117	106	98	103	107	106	82	83	86	93	89	48
1988		109	108	103	109	106	87	91	89	100	94	57
1989		101	100	115	118	120	96	90	100	108	102	48
1990		105	104	118	109	109	92	96	105	104	104	62
1991		103	102	100	102	102	90	97	103	90	96	75
1992	100	100	100	100	100	100	100	100	100	100	100	100
1993		100	95	84	86	89	88	107	81	86	84	29
1994		99P	92P	95	100	105	97	103	109	104	106	67
1995		99P	90P	92P	91P	95P	96P	106P	106P	101P	103P	58P
1996		98P	88P	89P	89P	93P	97P	108P	107P	102P	104P	57P
1997		97P	86P	87P	86P	91P	98P	110P	109P	104P	105P	56P
1998		96P	83P	84P	83P	89P	99P	112P	110P	105P	107P	54P

Sources: Same as General Statistics. Values reflect change from the base year, 1992. Values above 100 mean greater than 92, values below 100 mean less than 92, and a value of 100 in the 82-91 or 93-98 period means same as 92. 'P's mark projections by the editors.

SELECTED RATIOS

For 1994	Avg. of All Manufact.	Analyzed Industry	Index
Employees per Establishment	49	41	84
Payroll per Establishment	1,500,273	1,241,749	83
Payroll per Employee	30,620	30,339	99
Production Workers per Establishment	34	31	89
Wages per Establishment	853,319	842,447	99
Wages per Production Worker	24,861	27,600	111
Hours per Production Worker	2,056	2,091	102
Wages per Hour	12.09	13.20	109
Value Added per Establishment	4,602,255	3,148,077	68
Value Added per Employee	93,930	76,915	82

For 1994	Avg. of All Manufact.	Analyzed Industry	Index
Value Added per Production Worker	134,084	103,136	77
Cost per Establishment	5,045,178	3,426,950	68
Cost per Employee	102,970	83,729	81
Cost per Production Worker	146,988	112,273	76
Shipments per Establishment	9,576,895	6,512,592	68
Shipments per Employee	195,460	159,119	81
Shipments per Production Worker	279,017	213,364	76
Investment per Establishment	321,011	114,463	36
Investment per Employee	6,552	2,797	43
Investment per Production Worker	9,352	3,750	40

Sources: Same as General Statistics. The 'Average of All Manufacturing' column represents the average of all manufacturing industries reported for the most recent complete year available. The Index shows the relationship between the Average and the Analyzed Industry. For example, 100 means that they are equal; 500 that the Analyzed Industry is five times the average; 50 means that the Analyzed Industry is half the national average. The abbreviation 'na' is used to show that data are 'not available'.

LEADING COMPANIES

Number shown: **28** Total sales ($ mil): **1,434** Total employment (000): **11.0**

Company Name	Address				CEO Name	Phone	Co. Type	Sales ($ mil)	Empl. (000)
North American Refractories Co	1228 Euclid Av	Cleveland	OH	44115	Norman Taylor	216-621-5200	R	290	2.0
Harbison-Walker	1 Gateway Ctr	Pittsburgh	PA	15222	William G Sekeras	412-562-6200	D	243	1.8
AP Green Industries Inc	Green Blv	Mexico	MO	65265	Paul F Hummer II	314-473-3626	P	196	1.7
General Refractories Co	225 City Av	Bala Cynwyd	PA	19004	R G Perelman	215-667-6640	R	160*	1.1
National Refractories	1852 Rutan Dr	Livermore	CA	94550	Charles C Smith	510-449-5010	R	120	0.9
Martin Marietta Magnesia Spec	PO Box 30013	Raleigh	NC	27622	S P Zelnak Jr	919-781-4550	S	115	0.7
General Shale Products Corp	PO Box 3547	Johnson City	TN	37602	Richard L Green	615-282-4661	S	110	1.5
Plibrico Co	1800 N Kingsbury St	Chicago	IL	60614	Scott Schaefer	312-549-7014	R	27	0.2
CFB Industries Inc	1467 N Elston Av	Chicago	IL	60622	George H Taylor	312-278-8000	R	25	0.2
Chicago Fire Brick Co	1467 N Elston Av	Chicago	IL	60622	George H Taylor	312-278-8000	S	18	<0.1
Pryor-Giggey Co	PO Box 739	Whittier	CA	90608	Charles N Sparks	310-945-3781	R	18	<0.1
Wellsville Fire Brick Co	PO Box 71	Wellsville	MO	63384	George H Taylor	314-684-2222	S	17	0.1
New Castle Refractory Co	915 Industrial St	New Castle	PA	16102	Tom Maskell	412-654-7711	D	14	0.1
North State Pyrophyllite	PO Box 7247	Greensboro	NC	27417	Ruben B Arthur	919-299-1441	D	14*	0.1
Riverside Refractories Inc	PO Box 1770	Pell City	AL	35125	JC Morris	205-338-3366	R	12	0.1
Wahl Refractories Inc	PO Box 530	Fremont	OH	43420	Daniel Wahl	419-334-2658	R	12	<0.1
Western Industrial Ceramics Inc	10725 SW Taulatin	Tualatin	OR	97062	J Houston	503-692-3770	R	10*	<0.1
Findlay Refractories Co	PO Box 517	Washington	PA	15301	Will Bellows	412-225-4400	S	7	<0.1
Whitacre-Greer Fireproofing Co	1400 S Mahoning	Alliance	OH	44601	LA Morrison	216-823-1610	R	7	<0.1
Petrillo Brothers Inc	PO Box 628	New Castle	DE	19720	C A Petrillo Jr	302-654-5232	R	4*	<0.1
Ipsen Ceramics	PO Box 420	Pecatonica	IL	61063	Mario Ciampini	815-239-2385	D	4	<0.1
Louisville Fire Brick Works	4500 Louisville Av	Louisville	KY	40209	Bill Shuck	606-286-4436	R	3	<0.1
D'Hanis Brick and Tile Co	11931 Radium Dr	San Antonio	TX	78216	John A Oberman	210-525-8142	R	2	<0.1
Industrial Minerals Co	7268 Frasinetti Rd	Sacramento	CA	95828	Robert Smith	916-383-2811	S	2	<0.1
Rutland Fire Clay Co	PO Box 340	Rutland	VT	05702	Tom Martin	802-775-5519	R	2	<0.1
Maryland Refractories Co	267 Salisbury Rd	Irondale	OH	43932	Robert T Oxnard	216-532-9845	R	1	<0.1
Fels Refractories Inc	1133 Inman Av	Edison	NJ	08820	J C Younghans	908-757-0767	R	1	<0.1
AFC Co	5183 W W Res	Canfield	OH	44406	AD Powers	216-533-5581	R	0	<0.1

Source: *Ward's Business Directory of U.S. Private and Public Companies*, Volumes 1 and 2, 1996. The company type code used is as follows: P - Public, R - Private, S - Subsidiary, D - Division, J - Joint Venture, A - Affiliate, G - Group. Sales are in millions of dollars, employees are in thousands. An asterisk (*) indicates an estimated sales volume. The symbol < stands for 'less than'. Company names and addresses are truncated, in some cases, to fit into the available space.

MATERIALS CONSUMED

Material	Quantity	Delivered Cost ($ million)
Materials, ingredients, containers, and supplies	(X)	375.7
Clay, ceramic, and refractory minerals	(X)	192.5
Dead-burned magnesia or magnesite	(X)	7.7
Refractories, clay or nonclay	(X)	73.3
Other stone, clay, glass, and concrete products	(X)	4.8
Industrial chemicals	(X)	2.0
All other materials and components, parts, containers, and supplies	(X)	70.8
Materials, ingredients, containers, and supplies, nsk	(X)	24.7

Source: 1992 *Economic Census*. Explanation of symbols used: (D): Withheld to avoid disclosure of competitive data; na: Not available; (S): Withheld because statistical norms were not met; (X): Not applicable; (Z): Less than half the unit shown; nec: Not elsewhere classified; nsk: Not specified by kind; - : zero; * : 10-19 percent estimated; ** : 20-29 percent estimated.

PRODUCT SHARE DETAILS

Product or Product Class	% Share	Product or Product Class	% Share
Clay refractories	100.00		

Source: 1992 *Economic Census*. The values shown are percent of total shipments in an industry. Values of indented subcategories are summed in the main heading. The symbol (D) appears when data are withheld to prevent disclosure of competitive information. The abbreviation nsk stands for 'not specified by kind' and nec for 'not elsewhere classified'.

INPUTS AND OUTPUTS FOR CLAY REFRACTORIES

Economic Sector or Industry Providing Inputs	%	Sector	Economic Sector or Industry Buying Outputs	%	Sector
Motor freight transportation & warehousing	19.2	Util.	Industrial buildings	37.3	Constr.
Nonclay refractories	18.0	Manufg.	Maintenance of nonfarm buildings nec	19.5	Constr.
Clay, ceramic, & refractory minerals	14.6	Mining	Exports	13.6	Foreign
Gas production & distribution (utilities)	11.6	Util.	Clay refractories	4.2	Manufg.
Clay refractories	6.9	Manufg.	Electric utility facility construction	3.3	Constr.
Petroleum refining	5.6	Manufg.	Nonclay refractories	3.0	Manufg.
Electric services (utilities)	4.1	Util.	Sewer system facility construction	2.5	Constr.
Wood pallets & skids	1.3	Manufg.	Residential additions/alterations, nonfarm	1.8	Constr.
Wholesale trade	1.3	Trade	Maintenance of electric utility facilities	1.7	Constr.
Imports	1.3	Foreign	Residential 1-unit structures, nonfarm	1.5	Constr.
Water transportation	1.2	Util.	Construction of stores & restaurants	1.3	Constr.
Automotive rental & leasing, without drivers	1.1	Services	Construction of hospitals	1.2	Constr.
Maintenance of nonfarm buildings nec	1.0	Constr.	Office buildings	1.1	Constr.
Eating & drinking places	1.0	Trade	Water supply facility construction	0.7	Constr.
Communications, except radio & TV	0.9	Util.	Iron & steel foundries	0.7	Manufg.
Railroads & related services	0.8	Util.	Farm service facilities	0.6	Constr.
Banking	0.8	Fin/R.E.	Residential garden apartments	0.6	Constr.
Automotive repair shops & services	0.8	Services	Blast furnaces & steel mills	0.6	Manufg.
Advertising	0.5	Services	Amusement & recreation building construction	0.5	Constr.
U.S. Postal Service	0.5	Gov't	Warehouses	0.5	Constr.
Nonferrous metal ores, except copper	0.4	Mining	Hotels & motels	0.4	Constr.
Explosives	0.4	Manufg.	Nonfarm residential structure maintenance	0.4	Constr.
Machinery, except electrical, nec	0.4	Manufg.	Construction of nonfarm buildings nec	0.3	Constr.
Paperboard containers & boxes	0.4	Manufg.	Maintenance of water supply facilities	0.3	Constr.
Legal services	0.4	Services	Construction of educational buildings	0.2	Constr.
Management & consulting services & labs	0.4	Services	Construction of religious buildings	0.2	Constr.
Industrial inorganic chemicals, nec	0.3	Manufg.	Maintenance of sewer facilities	0.2	Constr.
Lubricating oils & greases	0.3	Manufg.	Resid. & other health facility construction	0.2	Constr.
Motor vehicle parts & accessories	0.3	Manufg.	Residential 2-4 unit structures, nonfarm	0.2	Constr.
Insurance carriers	0.3	Fin/R.E.	Farm housing units & additions & alterations	0.1	Constr.
Computer & data processing services	0.3	Services	Maintenance of farm residential buildings	0.1	Constr.
Equipment rental & leasing services	0.3	Services	Residential high-rise apartments	0.1	Constr.
Noncomparable imports	0.3	Foreign			
Abrasive products	0.2	Manufg.			
Manifold business forms	0.2	Manufg.			
Special dies & tools & machine tool accessories	0.2	Manufg.			
Tires & inner tubes	0.2	Manufg.			
Sanitary services, steam supply, irrigation	0.2	Util.			
Retail trade, except eating & drinking	0.2	Trade			
Accounting, auditing & bookkeeping	0.2	Services			
Laundry, dry cleaning, shoe repair	0.2	Services			
Coal	0.1	Mining			
Metal barrels, drums, & pails	0.1	Manufg.			
Real estate	0.1	Fin/R.E.			
Royalties	0.1	Fin/R.E.			
Personnel supply services	0.1	Services			
State & local government enterprises, nec	0.1	Gov't			

Source: Benchmark Input-Output Accounts for the U.S. Economy, 1982, U.S. Department of Commerce, Washington, D.C., July 1991. Data, as reported in the source, are organized by the 1977 SIC structure in use in 1982 but have been matched, as closely as is possible, to the 1987 SIC structure used in this book.

OCCUPATIONS EMPLOYED BY SIC 325 - STONE, CLAY, AND MISC MINING PRODUCTS NEC

Occupation	% of Total 1994	Change to 2005	Occupation	% of Total 1994	Change to 2005
Helpers, laborers, & material movers nec	6.7	-23.3	Machine feeders & offbearers	2.3	-31.4
Assemblers, fabricators, & hand workers nec	6.4	-23.9	Painting, coating, & decorating workers, hand	2.0	52.3
Furnace, kiln, or kettle operators	4.2	-16.7	Freight, stock, & material movers, hand	1.9	-38.8
Crushing & mixing machine operators	3.9	-9.5	Truck drivers light & heavy	1.9	-20.6
Industrial machinery mechanics	3.9	-15.2	Coating, painting, & spraying machine workers	1.8	-23.8
Hand packers & packagers	3.6	-34.7	Secretaries, ex legal & medical	1.8	-30.4
Extruding & forming machine workers	3.4	-80.6	Cutting & slicing machine setters, operators	1.6	-16.2
Sales & related workers nec	3.2	-23.6	Grinders & polishers, hand	1.6	-16.2
Packaging & filling machine operators	3.2	-23.7	Industrial production managers	1.5	-23.5
Precision workers nec	3.0	-8.7	Traffic, shipping, & receiving clerks	1.5	-26.6
Industrial truck & tractor operators	2.8	-23.7	General office clerks	1.5	-34.9
General managers & top executives	2.8	-27.5	Bookkeeping, accounting, & auditing clerks	1.3	-42.7
Inspectors, testers, & graders, precision	2.8	-23.6	Electricians	1.1	-27.3
Maintenance repairers, general utility	2.6	-30.8	Machinists	1.0	-23.6

Source: Industry-Occupation Matrix, Bureau of Labor Statistics. These data relate to one or more 3-digit SIC industry groups rather than to a single 4-digit SIC. The change reported for each occupation to the year 2005 is a percent of growth or decline as estimated by the Bureau of Labor Statistics. The abbreviation nec stands for 'not elsewhere classified'.

LOCATION BY STATE AND REGIONAL CONCENTRATION

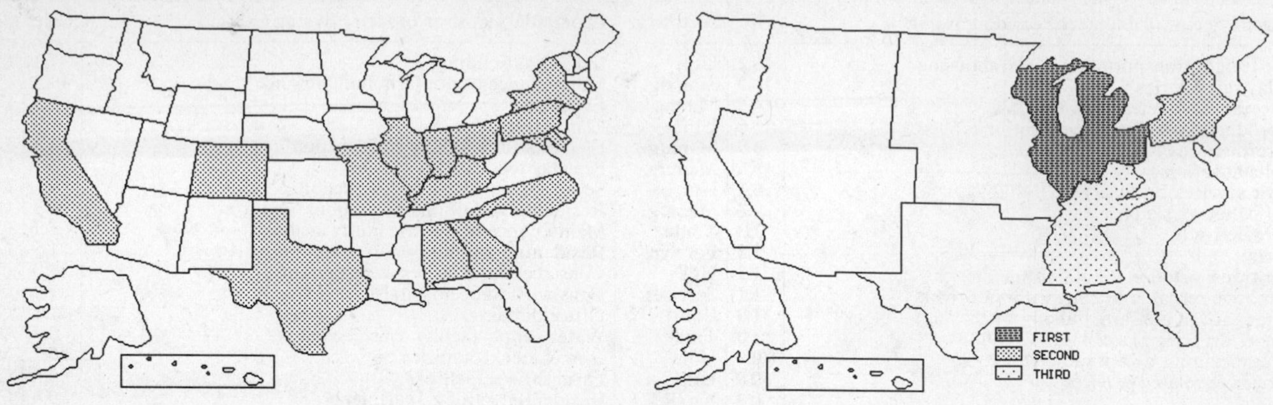

INDUSTRY DATA BY STATE

State	Establish-ments	Shipments			Employment				Cost as % of Shipments	Investment per Employee ($)
		Total ($ mil)	% of U.S.	Per Establ.	Total Number	% of U.S.	Per Establ.	Wages ($/hour)		
Ohio	29	127.2	14.3	4.4	800	12.9	28	12.92	56.1	5,750
Pennsylvania	25	126.0	14.2	5.0	1,000	16.1	40	12.17	55.0	-
Illinois	6	94.1	10.6	15.7	300	4.8	50	11.50	48.1	4,000
Alabama	9	57.1	6.4	6.3	400	6.5	44	13.50	54.6	-
Texas	5	48.0	5.4	9.6	300	4.8	60	10.40	56.9	-
California	10	23.9	2.7	2.4	200	3.2	20	14.00	50.2	2,000
Kentucky	3	15.3	1.7	5.1	100	1.6	33	14.50	55.6	-
Indiana	7	14.9	1.7	2.1	200	3.2	29	14.50	43.0	2,000
Colorado	4	10.2	1.2	2.5	100	1.6	25	7.50	41.2	-
Missouri	11	(D)	-	-	1,750 *	28.2	159	-	-	-
Georgia	3	(D)	-	-	750 *	12.1	250	-	-	-
Maryland	3	(D)	-	-	175 *	2.8	58	-	-	-
North Carolina	2	(D)	-	-	175 *	2.8	88	-	-	-
New York	1	(D)	-	-	175 *	2.8	175	-	-	-

Source: 1992 *Economic Census*. The states are in descending order of shipments or establishments (if shipment data are missing for the majority). The symbol (D) appears when data are withheld to prevent disclosure of competitive information. States marked with (D) are sorted by number of establishments. A dash (-) indicates that the data element cannot be calculated; * indicates the midpoint of a range.

3259 - STRUCTURAL CLAY PRODUCTS, NEC

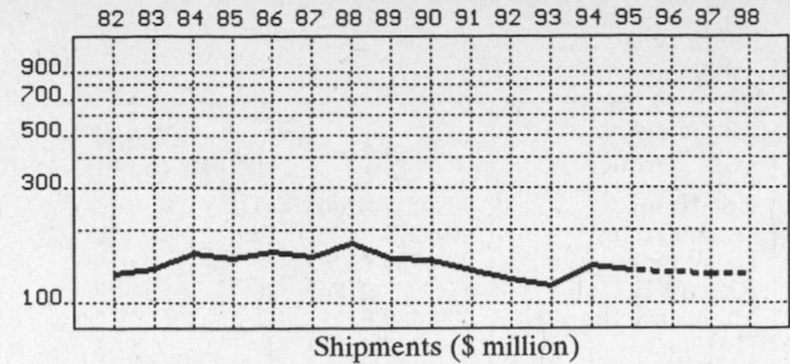

Shipments ($ million)

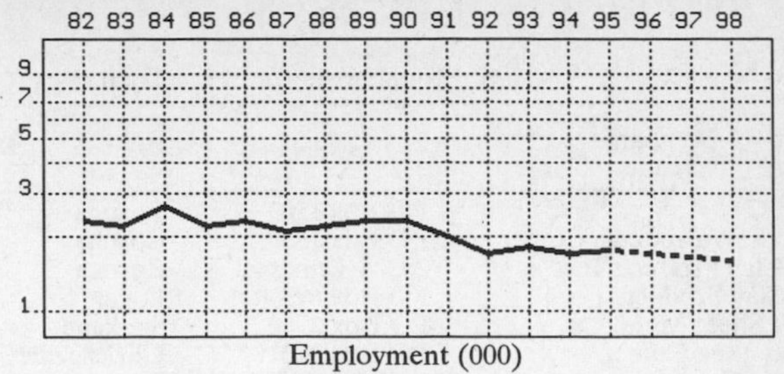

Employment (000)

GENERAL STATISTICS

Year	Com-panies	Establishments Total	Establishments with 20 or more employees	Employment Total (000)	Production Workers (000)	Production Hours (Mil)	Compensation Payroll ($ mil)	Compensation Wages ($/hr)	Production ($ million) Cost of Materials	Value Added by Manufacture	Value of Shipments	Capital Invest.
1982	67	78	31	2.3	1.8	3.6	35.7	7.61	53.8	77.9	133.6	2.3
1983		76	30	2.2	1.7	3.6	36.2	8.06	54.7	87.8	139.7	0.9
1984		74	29	2.7	2.2	4.5	47.0	8.09	70.6	91.6	158.4	2.3
1985		72	29	2.2	1.7	3.7	42.4	8.19	60.2	87.6	152.5	4.7
1986		73	31	2.3	1.8	3.7	45.4	8.65	66.2	97.5	163.8	3.0
1987	58	67	29	2.1	1.7	3.6	44.9	8.94	53.5	99.9	155.2	3.9
1988		68	24	2.2	1.7	3.5	47.8	9.49	64.2	108.7	175.4	4.2
1989		63	24	2.3	1.7	3.5	45.6	9.14	68.5	82.5	153.3	4.1
1990		61	28	2.3	1.7	3.1	43.6	9.61	57.4	91.3	149.8	4.8
1991		65	23	2.0	1.5	2.8	39.4	9.21	47.8	85.0	136.1	12.3
1992	59	65	22	1.7	1.2	2.3	37.8	10.22	49.3	74.6	125.8	5.4
1993		63	27	1.8	1.3	2.5	41.2	10.08	47.6	71.4	118.3	6.8
1994		59P	23P	1.7	1.4	2.6	42.1	11.04	57.0	84.7	142.1	4.0
1995		58P	22P	1.8P	1.3P	2.4P	42.8P	10.81P	54.7P	81.2P	136.2P	7.5P
1996		57P	22P	1.7P	1.2P	2.2P	42.9P	11.05P	54.1P	80.3P	134.8P	8.0P
1997		55P	21P	1.6P	1.2P	2.1P	43.0P	11.30P	53.5P	79.5P	133.3P	8.4P
1998		54P	20P	1.6P	1.1P	2.0P	43.0P	11.54P	52.9P	78.6P	131.9P	8.8P

Sources: 1982, 1987, 1992 *Economic Census*; *Annual Survey of Manufactures*, 83-86, 88-91, 93-94. Establishment counts for non-Census years are from *County Business Patterns*; establishment values for 83-84 are extrapolations. 'P's show projections by the editors. Industries reclassified in 87 will not have data for prior years.

INDICES OF CHANGE

Year	Com-panies	Establishments Total	Establishments with 20 or more employees	Employment Total (000)	Production Workers (000)	Production Hours (Mil)	Compensation Payroll ($ mil)	Compensation Wages ($/hr)	Production ($ million) Cost of Materials	Value Added by Manufacture	Value of Shipments	Capital Invest.
1982	114	120	141	135	150	157	94	74	109	104	106	43
1983		117	136	129	142	157	96	79	111	118	111	17
1984		114	132	159	183	196	124	79	143	123	126	43
1985		111	132	129	142	161	112	80	122	117	121	87
1986		112	141	135	150	161	120	85	134	131	130	56
1987	98	103	132	124	142	157	119	87	109	134	123	72
1988		105	109	129	142	152	126	93	130	146	139	78
1989		97	109	135	142	152	121	89	139	111	122	76
1990		94	127	135	142	135	115	94	116	122	119	89
1991		100	105	118	125	122	104	90	97	114	108	228
1992	100	100	100	100	100	100	100	100	100	100	100	100
1993		97	123	106	108	109	109	99	97	96	94	126
1994		91P	104P	100	117	113	111	108	116	114	113	74
1995		89P	101P	103P	108P	103P	113P	106P	111P	109P	108P	140P
1996		87P	98P	100P	103P	97P	113P	108P	110P	108P	107P	148P
1997		85P	95P	97P	99P	92P	114P	111P	108P	107P	106P	156P
1998		83P	92P	93P	95P	86P	114P	113P	107P	105P	105P	164P

Sources: Same as General Statistics. Values reflect change from the base year, 1992. Values above 100 mean greater than 92, values below 100 mean less than 92, and a value of 100 in the 82-91 or 93-98 period means same as 92. 'P's mark projections by the editors.

SELECTED RATIOS

For 1994	Avg. of All Manufact.	Analyzed Industry	Index
Employees per Establishment	49	29	58
Payroll per Establishment	1,500,273	708,646	47
Payroll per Employee	30,620	24,765	81
Production Workers per Establishment	34	24	69
Wages per Establishment	853,319	483,158	57
Wages per Production Worker	24,861	20,503	82
Hours per Production Worker	2,056	1,857	90
Wages per Hour	12.09	11.04	91
Value Added per Establishment	4,602,255	1,425,708	31
Value Added per Employee	93,930	49,824	53

For 1994	Avg. of All Manufact.	Analyzed Industry	Index
Value Added per Production Worker	134,084	60,500	45
Cost per Establishment	5,045,178	959,449	19
Cost per Employee	102,970	33,529	33
Cost per Production Worker	146,988	40,714	28
Shipments per Establishment	9,576,895	2,391,890	25
Shipments per Employee	195,460	83,588	43
Shipments per Production Worker	279,017	101,500	36
Investment per Establishment	321,011	67,330	21
Investment per Employee	6,552	2,353	36
Investment per Production Worker	9,352	2,857	31

Sources: Same as General Statistics. The 'Average of All Manufacturing' column represents the average of all manufacturing industries reported for the most recent complete year available. The Index shows the relationship between the Average and the Analyzed Industry. For example, 100 means that they are equal; 500 that the Analyzed Industry is five times the average; 50 means that the Analyzed Industry is half the national average. The abbreviation 'na' is used to show that data are 'not available'.

LEADING COMPANIES

Number shown: **9** Total sales ($ mil): **59** Total employment (000): **0.7**

Company Name	Address				CEO Name	Phone	Co. Type	Sales ($ mil)	Empl. (000)
US Tile Co	PO Box 1509	Corona	CA	91720	Eric Hahn	909-737-0200	D	15	0.1
Mission Clay Products Corp	PO Box 1839	Corona	CA	91718	Owen Garrett	909-277-4600	D	10	0.1
Pacific Clay Products Inc	20325 Temescal	Corona	CA	91719	David Hollingsworth	909-735-6020	S	9	0.1
Logan Clay Products Co	PO Box 698	Logan	OH	43138	Richard H Holl	614-385-2184	R	8	0.1
Krueger Sheet Metal Co	PO Box 2963	Spokane	WA	99220	Thomas H Brandt	509-489-0221	R	7	<0.1
Clay City Pipe Co	PO Box 272	Uhrichsville	OH	44683	H Hillyer	614-922-2611	R	6	<0.1
Durawear Corp	2598 Alton Rd	Birmingham	AL	35210	Jay Wadekar	205-833-1210	R	2*	<0.1
Brockway Clay Co	PO Box C	Brockway	PA	15824	EL Kilgus	814-268-3715	R	1	<0.1
Hans Sumpf Company Inc	40101 Avnue 10	Madera	CA	93638	Tom Bryan	209-439-3214	R	1	<0.1

Source: *Ward's Business Directory of U.S. Private and Public Companies*, Volumes 1 and 2, 1996. The company type code used is as follows: P - Public, R - Private, S - Subsidiary, D - Division, J - Joint Venture, A - Affiliate, G - Group. Sales are in millions of dollars, employees are in thousands. An asterisk (*) indicates an estimated sales volume. The symbol < stands for 'less than'. Company names and addresses are truncated, in some cases, to fit into the available space.

MATERIALS CONSUMED

Material	Quantity	Delivered Cost ($ million)
Materials, ingredients, containers, and supplies	(X)	31.0
Clay, ceramic, and refractory minerals	(X)	4.9
Industrial chemicals	(X)	0.8
All other materials and components, parts, containers, and supplies	(X)	15.7
Materials, ingredients, containers, and supplies, nsk	(X)	9.5

Source: 1992 *Economic Census*. Explanation of symbols used: (D): Withheld to avoid disclosure of competitive data; na: Not available; (S): Withheld because statistical norms were not met; (X): Not applicable; (Z): Less than half the unit shown; nec: Not elsewhere classified; nsk: Not specified by kind; - : zero; * : 10-19 percent estimated; ** : 20-29 percent estimated.

PRODUCT SHARE DETAILS

Product or Product Class	% Share	Product or Product Class	% Share
Structural clay products, nec	100.00	cotta, drain tile, flue tile, roofing tile, conduit, etc.), except clay refractories	52.69
Vitrified clay sewer pipe and fittings	34.40	Structural clay products, nec, nsk	12.99
Other structural clay products, nec (architectural terra			

Source: 1992 *Economic Census*. The values shown are percent of total shipments in an industry. Values of indented subcategories are summed in the main heading. The symbol (D) appears when data are withheld to prevent disclosure of competitive information. The abbreviation nsk stands for 'not specified by kind' and nec for 'not elsewhere classified'.

INPUTS AND OUTPUTS FOR STRUCTURAL CLAY PRODUCTS, NEC

Economic Sector or Industry Providing Inputs	%	Sector	Economic Sector or Industry Buying Outputs	%	Sector
Motor freight transportation & warehousing	28.1	Util.	Sewer system facility construction	20.3	Constr.
Gas production & distribution (utilities)	19.1	Util.	Residential 1-unit structures, nonfarm	11.3	Constr.
Petroleum refining	7.4	Manufg.	Office buildings	7.7	Constr.
Nonmetallic mineral services	6.0	Mining	Residential additions/alterations, nonfarm	7.3	Constr.
Electric services (utilities)	4.3	Util.	Highway & street construction	7.1	Constr.
Imports	4.2	Foreign	Industrial buildings	5.4	Constr.
Clay, ceramic, & refractory minerals	2.9	Mining	Exports	4.9	Foreign
Maintenance of nonfarm buildings nec	2.0	Constr.	Electric utility facility construction	4.4	Constr.
Wholesale trade	2.0	Trade	Nonfarm residential structure maintenance	4.4	Constr.
Automotive rental & leasing, without drivers	2.0	Services	Construction of stores & restaurants	4.0	Constr.
Gypsum products	1.9	Manufg.	Residential garden apartments	3.2	Constr.
Water transportation	1.8	Util.	Telephone & telegraph facility construction	3.0	Constr.
Automotive repair shops & services	1.6	Services	Construction of educational buildings	2.1	Constr.
Explosives	1.4	Manufg.	Local transit facility construction	1.7	Constr.
Railroads & related services	1.4	Util.	Maintenance of nonfarm buildings nec	1.2	Constr.
Industrial inorganic chemicals, nec	1.1	Manufg.	Maintenance of sewer facilities	1.1	Constr.
Eating & drinking places	1.1	Trade	Residential 2-4 unit structures, nonfarm	1.1	Constr.
U.S. Postal Service	1.0	Gov't	Maintenance, conservation & development facilities	1.0	Constr.
Banking	0.8	Fin/R.E.	Construction of conservation facilities	0.8	Constr.
Structural clay products, nec	0.7	Manufg.	Construction of hospitals	0.8	Constr.
Internal combustion engines, nec	0.5	Manufg.	Residential high-rise apartments	0.6	Constr.
Water supply & sewage systems	0.5	Util.	Structural clay products, nec	0.6	Manufg.
Insurance carriers	0.5	Fin/R.E.	Construction of nonfarm buildings nec	0.5	Constr.
Advertising	0.5	Services	Construction of religious buildings	0.5	Constr.
Detective & protective services	0.5	Services	Farm housing units & additions & alterations	0.5	Constr.
Machinery, except electrical, nec	0.4	Manufg.	Hotels & motels	0.5	Constr.
Communications, except radio & TV	0.4	Util.	Maintenance of local transit facilities	0.5	Constr.

Continued on next page.

INPUTS AND OUTPUTS FOR STRUCTURAL CLAY PRODUCTS, NEC - Continued

Economic Sector or Industry Providing Inputs	%	Sector	Economic Sector or Industry Buying Outputs	%	Sector
Electrical repair shops	0.4	Services	Nonbuilding facilities nec	0.5	Constr.
Legal services	0.4	Services	Water supply facility construction	0.5	Constr.
Management & consulting services & labs	0.4	Services	Maintenance of nonbuilding facilities nec	0.4	Constr.
Abrasive products	0.3	Manufg.	Amusement & recreation building construction	0.2	Constr.
Conveyors & conveying equipment	0.3	Manufg.	Construction of dams & reservoirs	0.2	Constr.
Lubricating oils & greases	0.3	Manufg.	Maintenance of farm residential buildings	0.2	Constr.
Miscellaneous fabricated wire products	0.3	Manufg.	Maintenance of farm service facilities	0.2	Constr.
Motor vehicle parts & accessories	0.3	Manufg.	Maintenance of gas utility facilities	0.2	Constr.
Tires & inner tubes	0.3	Manufg.	Maintenance of highways & streets	0.2	Constr.
Retail trade, except eating & drinking	0.3	Trade	Maintenance of military facilities	0.2	Constr.
Equipment rental & leasing services	0.3	Services	Maintenance of water supply facilities	0.2	Constr.
Coal	0.2	Mining	Resid. & other health facility construction	0.2	Constr.
Manifold business forms	0.2	Manufg.			
Nonclay refractories	0.2	Manufg.			
Special dies & tools & machine tool accessories	0.2	Manufg.			
Wood pallets & skids	0.2	Manufg.			
Royalties	0.2	Fin/R.E.			
Accounting, auditing & bookkeeping	0.2	Services			
Computer & data processing services	0.2	Services			
Engineering, architectural, & surveying services	0.2	Services			
Laundry, dry cleaning, shoe repair	0.2	Services			
State & local government enterprises, nec	0.2	Gov't			
Noncomparable imports	0.2	Foreign			

Source: Benchmark Input-Output Accounts for the U.S. Economy, 1982, U.S. Department of Commerce, Washington, D.C., July 1991. Data, as reported in the source, are organized by the 1977 SIC structure in use in 1982 but have been matched, as closely as is possible, to the 1987 SIC structure used in this book.

OCCUPATIONS EMPLOYED BY SIC 325 - STONE, CLAY, AND MISC MINING PRODUCTS NEC

Occupation	% of Total 1994	Change to 2005	Occupation	% of Total 1994	Change to 2005
Helpers, laborers, & material movers nec	6.7	-23.3	Machine feeders & offbearers	2.3	-31.4
Assemblers, fabricators, & hand workers nec	6.4	-23.9	Painting, coating, & decorating workers, hand	2.0	52.3
Furnace, kiln, or kettle operators	4.2	-16.7	Freight, stock, & material movers, hand	1.9	-38.8
Crushing & mixing machine operators	3.9	-9.5	Truck drivers light & heavy	1.9	-20.6
Industrial machinery mechanics	3.9	-15.2	Coating, painting, & spraying machine workers	1.8	-23.8
Hand packers & packagers	3.6	-34.7	Secretaries, ex legal & medical	1.8	-30.4
Extruding & forming machine workers	3.4	-80.6	Cutting & slicing machine setters, operators	1.6	-16.2
Sales & related workers nec	3.2	-23.6	Grinders & polishers, hand	1.6	-16.2
Packaging & filling machine operators	3.2	-23.7	Industrial production managers	1.5	-23.5
Precision workers nec	3.0	-8.7	Traffic, shipping, & receiving clerks	1.5	-26.6
Industrial truck & tractor operators	2.8	-23.7	General office clerks	1.5	-34.9
General managers & top executives	2.8	-27.5	Bookkeeping, accounting, & auditing clerks	1.3	-42.7
Inspectors, testers, & graders, precision	2.8	-23.6	Electricians	1.1	-27.3
Maintenance repairers, general utility	2.6	-30.8	Machinists	1.0	-23.6

Source: Industry-Occupation Matrix, Bureau of Labor Statistics. These data relate to one or more 3-digit SIC industry groups rather than to a single 4-digit SIC. The change reported for each occupation to the year 2005 is a percent of growth or decline as estimated by the Bureau of Labor Statistics. The abbreviation nec stands for 'not elsewhere classified'.

LOCATION BY STATE AND REGIONAL CONCENTRATION

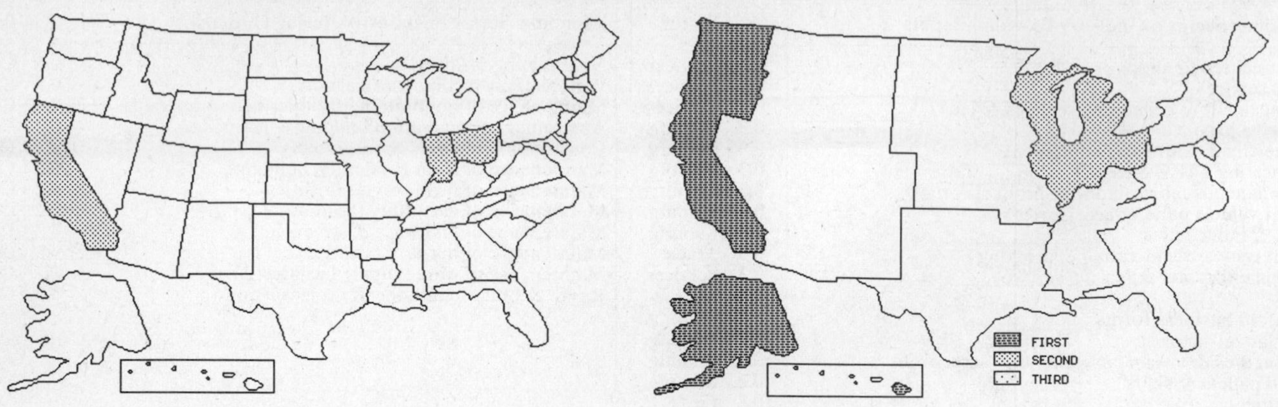

INDUSTRY DATA BY STATE

State	Establish-ments	Shipments			Employment				Cost as % of Shipments	Investment per Employee ($)
		Total ($ mil)	% of U.S.	Per Establ.	Total Number	% of U.S.	Per Establ.	Wages ($/hour)		
California	15	49.5	39.3	3.3	700	41.2	47	9.00	42.0	2,143
Ohio	8	30.8	24.5	3.8	400	23.5	50	11.67	32.5	-
Indiana	3	(D)	-	-	175 *	10.3	58	-	-	-

Source: 1992 *Economic Census*. The states are in descending order of shipments or establishments (if shipment data are missing for the majority). The symbol (D) appears when data are withheld to prevent disclosure of competitive information. States marked with (D) are sorted by number of establishments. A dash (-) indicates that the data element cannot be calculated; * indicates the midpoint of a range.

3261 - VITREOUS PLUMBING FIXTURES

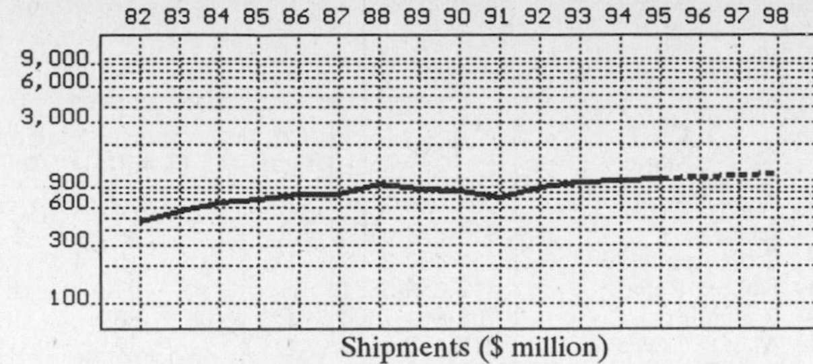

Shipments ($ million)

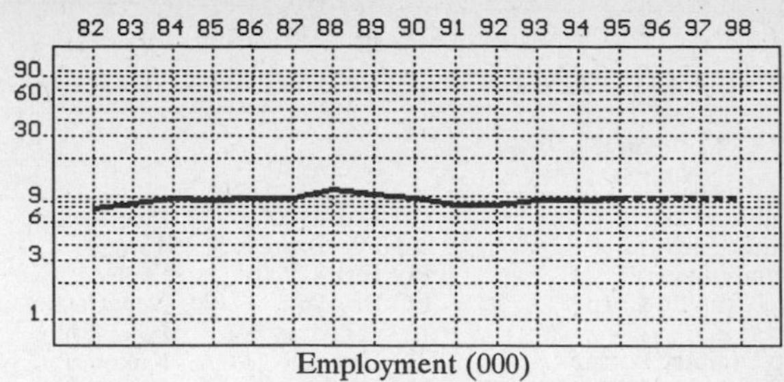

Employment (000)

GENERAL STATISTICS

Year	Companies	Establishments		Employment			Compensation		Production ($ million)			
		Total	with 20 or more employees	Total (000)	Production Workers (000)	Production Hours (Mil)	Payroll ($ mil)	Wages ($/hr)	Cost of Materials	Value Added by Manufacture	Value of Shipments	Capital Invest.
1982	41	56	35	7.9	6.6	12.6	142.9	9.09	162.5	313.9	474.0	28.8
1983		56	36	8.7	7.4	14.4	165.1	9.27	197.3	380.1	570.6	15.0
1984		56	37	9.4	8.0	15.5	184.4	9.61	216.4	440.4	657.2	15.0
1985		57	37	9.3	7.9	15.8	196.1	10.13	232.3	471.5	706.7	
1986		55	38	9.6	8.1	16.9	212.6	10.28	257.0	525.2	772.3	
1987	49	65	40	9.7	8.2	17.2	217.0	10.26	262.5	536.9	790.6	30.9
1988		63	38	11.1	9.4	19.7	259.4	10.42	302.9	648.6	940.8	17.3
1989		63	37	10.1	7.9	15.7	243.5	12.10	290.7	580.2	871.1	22.8
1990		61	39	9.6	7.8	15.1	236.1	11.96	251.3	578.0	825.1	16.3
1991		60	36	8.4	7.0	13.3	213.8	12.44	230.2	511.5	741.5	17.9
1992	48	61	30	8.4	7.1	13.6	216.8	12.77	236.4	658.5	902.1	14.3
1993		60	32	9.1	7.9	15.3	240.4	12.73	278.5	697.5	982.3	12.8
1994		63P	34P	9.2	7.9	16.3	251.9	12.75	284.3	740.1	1,020.0	25.3
1995		64P	34P	9.4P	7.9P	15.7P	263.3P	13.53P	290.7P	756.7P	1,042.8P	
1996		64P	34P	9.4P	7.9P	15.8P	270.4P	13.88P	300.8P	783.0P	1,079.1P	
1997		65P	33P	9.4P	7.9P	15.8P	277.5P	14.23P	310.9P	809.3P	1,115.4P	
1998		65P	33P	9.5P	8.0P	15.8P	284.5P	14.58P	321.0P	835.6P	1,151.7P	

Sources: 1982, 1987, 1992 *Economic Census*; *Annual Survey of Manufactures*, 83-86, 88-91, 93-94. Establishment counts for non-Census years are from *County Business Patterns*; establishment values for 83-84 are extrapolations. 'P's show projections by the editors. Industries reclassified in 87 will not have data for prior years.

INDICES OF CHANGE

Year	Companies	Establishments		Employment			Compensation		Production ($ million)			
		Total	with 20 or more employees	Total (000)	Production Workers (000)	Production Hours (Mil)	Payroll ($ mil)	Wages ($/hr)	Cost of Materials	Value Added by Manufacture	Value of Shipments	Capital Invest.
1982	85	92	117	94	93	93	66	71	69	48	53	201
1983		92	120	104	104	106	76	73	83	58	63	105
1984		92	123	112	113	114	85	75	92	67	73	105
1985		93	123	111	111	116	90	79	98	72	78	
1986		90	127	114	114	124	98	81	109	80	86	
1987	102	107	133	115	115	126	100	80	111	82	88	216
1988		103	127	132	132	145	120	82	128	98	104	121
1989		103	123	120	111	115	112	95	123	88	97	159
1990		100	130	114	110	111	109	94	106	88	91	114
1991		98	120	100	99	98	99	97	97	78	82	125
1992	100	100	100	100	100	100	100	100	100	100	100	100
1993		98	107	108	111	113	111	100	118	106	109	90
1994		103P	114P	110	111	120	116	100	120	112	113	177
1995		104P	113P	112P	111P	116P	121P	106P	123P	115P	116P	
1996		105P	112P	112P	112P	116P	125P	109P	127P	119P	120P	
1997		106P	111P	112P	112P	116P	128P	111P	132P	123P	124P	
1998		107P	110P	113P	112P	117P	131P	114P	136P	127P	128P	

Sources: Same as General Statistics. Values reflect change from the base year, 1992. Values above 100 mean greater than 92, values below 100 mean less than 92, and a value of 100 in the 82-91 or 93-98 period means same as 92. 'P's mark projections by the editors.

SELECTED RATIOS

For 1994	Avg. of All Manufact.	Analyzed Industry	Index	For 1994	Avg. of All Manufact.	Analyzed Industry	Index
Employees per Establishment	49	146	298	Value Added per Production Worker	134,084	93,684	70
Payroll per Establishment	1,500,273	3,996,490	266	Cost per Establishment	5,045,178	4,510,529	89
Payroll per Employee	30,620	27,380	89	Cost per Employee	102,970	30,902	30
Production Workers per Establishment	34	125	365	Cost per Production Worker	146,988	35,987	24
Wages per Establishment	853,319	3,297,224	386	Shipments per Establishment	9,576,895	16,182,692	169
Wages per Production Worker	24,861	26,307	106	Shipments per Employee	195,460	110,870	57
Hours per Production Worker	2,056	2,063	100	Shipments per Production Worker	279,017	129,114	46
Wages per Hour	12.09	12.75	105	Investment per Establishment	321,011	401,394	125
Value Added per Establishment	4,602,255	11,741,971	255	Investment per Employee	6,552	2,750	42
Value Added per Employee	93,930	80,446	86	Investment per Production Worker	9,352	3,203	34

Sources: Same as General Statistics. The 'Average of All Manufacturing' column represents the average of all manufacturing industries reported for the most recent complete year available. The Index shows the relationship between the Average and the Analyzed Industry. For example, 100 means that they are equal; 500 that the Analyzed Industry is five times the average; 50 means that the Analyzed Industry is half the national average. The abbreviation 'na' is used to show that data are 'not available'.

LEADING COMPANIES

Number shown: **13** Total sales ($ mil): **4,133** Total employment (000): **20.9**

Company Name	Address				CEO Name	Phone	Co. Type	Sales ($ mil)	Empl. (000)
US Plumbing Co	PO Box 6820	Piscataway	NJ	08855	Wade Smith	908-980-3000	D	3,500	13.0
Briggs Industries Inc	4350 W Cypress St	Tampa	FL	33607	Jack Huss	813-878-0178	R	130	1.2
Eljer Plumbingware	PO Box 879001	Dallas	TX	75287	Scott Arbuckle	214-407-2600	D	110	1.6
Universal-Rundle Corp	PO Box 960	New Castle	PA	16103	Robert Regal	412-658-6631	S	97	1.3
CR/PL LP	1235 Hartrey Av	Evanston	IL	60202	R Beidler	708-864-7600	R	86	1.2
Kokomo Sanitary Pottery	PO Box 829	Kokomo	IN	46903	Alan G Lewis	317-459-5113	D	72	0.9
Mansfield Plumbing Products	150 1st St	Perrysville	OH	44864	Paul Fischer	419-938-5211	S	46	0.6
Mansfield Plumbing Products	PO Box 472	Kilgore	TX	75662	Paul Fischer	903-984-3525	S	30*	0.4
Norris Plumbing Fixtures	PO Box 370	Walnut	CA	91788	Paul Fischer	909-595-1271	D	28	0.3
Peerless Pottery Inc	PO Box 145	Rockport	IN	47635	C Weaver	812-649-2261	R	20	0.3
AAA Plumbing Pottery Corp	PO Box 1340	Gadsden	AL	35999	Alan G Lewis	205-538-7804	D	11	0.2
Taylor Industries Inc	Anderson Rd	Parker Ford	PA	19457	William W Taylor	215-495-5261	R	2	<0.1
Schumacher Architectural	3257-C Monier Cir	R Cordova	CA	95742	R J Schumacher	916-635-3350	R	0	<0.1

Source: *Ward's Business Directory of U.S. Private and Public Companies*, Volumes 1 and 2, 1996. The company type code used is as follows: P - Public, R - Private, S - Subsidiary, D - Division, J - Joint Venture, A - Affiliate, G - Group. Sales are in millions of dollars, employees are in thousands. An asterisk (*) indicates an estimated sales volume. The symbol < stands for 'less than'. Company names and addresses are truncated, in some cases, to fit into the available space.

MATERIALS CONSUMED

Material	Quantity	Delivered Cost ($ million)
Materials, ingredients, containers, and supplies	(X)	170.0
Clay, ceramic, and refractory minerals	(X)	58.2
Paperboard containers, boxes, and corrugated paperboard	(X)	23.4
All other materials and components, parts, containers, and supplies	(X)	84.9
Materials, ingredients, containers, and supplies, nsk	(X)	3.6

Source: 1992 *Economic Census*. Explanation of symbols used: (D): Withheld to avoid disclosure of competitive data; na: Not available; (S): Withheld because statistical norms were not met; (X): Not applicable; (Z): Less than half the unit shown; nec: Not elsewhere classified; nsk: Not specified by kind; - : zero; * : 10-19 percent estimated; ** : 20-29 percent estimated.

PRODUCT SHARE DETAILS

Product or Product Class	% Share	Product or Product Class	% Share
Vitreous plumbing fixtures	100.00	towel racks, soap cups, earthenware plumbing fixtures, etc.)	(D)
China plumbing fixtures	95.54	Earthenware plumbing fixtures, accessories, and fittings	(D)
China plumbing fixtures, accessories, and fittings (including			

Source: 1992 *Economic Census*. The values shown are percent of total shipments in an industry. Values of indented subcategories are summed in the main heading. The symbol (D) appears when data are withheld to prevent disclosure of competitive information. The abbreviation nsk stands for 'not specified by kind' and nec for 'not elsewhere classified'.

INPUTS AND OUTPUTS FOR VITREOUS PLUMBING FIXTURES

Economic Sector or Industry Providing Inputs	%	Sector	Economic Sector or Industry Buying Outputs	%	Sector
Cyclic crudes and organics	14.8	Manufg.	Office buildings	18.7	Constr.
Gas production & distribution (utilities)	11.9	Util.	Maintenance of nonfarm buildings nec	14.1	Constr.
Motor freight transportation & warehousing	9.7	Util.	Nonfarm residential structure maintenance	9.5	Constr.
Clay, ceramic, & refractory minerals	6.6	Mining	Residential 1-unit structures, nonfarm	8.2	Constr.
Paperboard containers & boxes	6.4	Manufg.	Residential garden apartments	7.6	Constr.
Industrial gases	6.1	Manufg.	Residential additions/alterations, nonfarm	6.4	Constr.
Imports	5.1	Foreign	Industrial buildings	6.0	Constr.
Wholesale trade	4.7	Trade	Exports	5.4	Foreign
Gypsum products	4.5	Manufg.	Construction of educational buildings	3.8	Constr.
Electric services (utilities)	4.2	Util.	Construction of hospitals	3.6	Constr.
Wiring devices	2.7	Manufg.	Construction of stores & restaurants	3.1	Constr.
Advertising	2.4	Services	Warehouses	2.3	Constr.
Metal stampings, nec	1.7	Manufg.	Residential 2-4 unit structures, nonfarm	1.9	Constr.
Lime	1.3	Manufg.	Residential high-rise apartments	1.6	Constr.
Banking	1.2	Fin/R.E.	Hotels & motels	1.5	Constr.
Machinery, except electrical, nec	1.0	Manufg.	Sewer system facility construction	1.1	Constr.
Railroads & related services	1.0	Util.	Construction of religious buildings	0.8	Constr.
Photographic equipment & supplies	0.9	Manufg.	Resid. & other health facility construction	0.6	Constr.
Eating & drinking places	0.9	Trade	Electric utility facility construction	0.4	Constr.
Maintenance of nonfarm buildings nec	0.8	Constr.	Construction of nonfarm buildings nec	0.3	Constr.
Petroleum refining	0.8	Manufg.	Farm housing units & additions & alterations	0.3	Constr.
Communications, except radio & TV	0.8	Util.	Maintenance of farm residential buildings	0.3	Constr.
Water transportation	0.8	Util.	Maintenance of military facilities	0.3	Constr.

Continued on next page.

INPUTS AND OUTPUTS FOR VITREOUS PLUMBING FIXTURES - Continued

Economic Sector or Industry Providing Inputs	%	Sector	Economic Sector or Industry Buying Outputs	%	Sector
Equipment rental & leasing services	0.6	Services	Telephone & telegraph facility construction	0.3	Constr.
Personnel supply services	0.6	Services	Dormitories & other group housing	0.2	Constr.
Minerals, ground or treated	0.5	Manufg.	Maintenance of local transit facilities	0.2	Constr.
Special dies & tools & machine tool accessories	0.5	Manufg.	Water supply facility construction	0.2	Constr.
Royalties	0.5	Fin/R.E.	Amusement & recreation building construction	0.1	Constr.
Engineering, architectural, & surveying services	0.5	Services	Maintenance of electric utility facilities	0.1	Constr.
U.S. Postal Service	0.5	Gov't	Maintenance of railroads	0.1	Constr.
Industrial inorganic chemicals, nec	0.4	Manufg.	Maintenance of sewer facilities	0.1	Constr.
Sanitary services, steam supply, irrigation	0.4	Util.	Maintenance of telephone & telegraph facilities	0.1	Constr.
Automotive repair shops & services	0.4	Services			
Computer & data processing services	0.4	Services			
Abrasive products	0.3	Manufg.			
Alkalies & chlorine	0.3	Manufg.			
Lubricating oils & greases	0.3	Manufg.			
Real estate	0.3	Fin/R.E.			
Laundry, dry cleaning, shoe repair	0.3	Services			
Legal services	0.3	Services			
Management & consulting services & labs	0.3	Services			
Noncomparable imports	0.3	Foreign			
Chemical preparations, nec	0.2	Manufg.			
Manifold business forms	0.2	Manufg.			
Pipelines, except natural gas	0.2	Util.			
Accounting, auditing & bookkeeping	0.2	Services			
Sawmills & planning mills, general	0.1	Manufg.			
Insurance carriers	0.1	Fin/R.E.			
Business services nec	0.1	Services			
Hotels & lodging places	0.1	Services			
Photofinishing labs, commercial photography	0.1	Services			

Source: Benchmark Input-Output Accounts for the U.S. Economy, 1982, U.S. Department of Commerce, Washington, D.C., July 1991. Data, as reported in the source, are organized by the 1977 SIC structure in use in 1982 but have been matched, as closely as is possible, to the 1987 SIC structure used in this book.

OCCUPATIONS EMPLOYED BY SIC 326 - STONE, CLAY, AND MISC MINING PRODUCTS NEC

Occupation	% of Total 1994	Change to 2005	Occupation	% of Total 1994	Change to 2005
Helpers, laborers, & material movers nec	6.7	-23.3	Machine feeders & offbearers	2.3	-31.4
Assemblers, fabricators, & hand workers nec	6.4	-23.9	Painting, coating, & decorating workers, hand	2.0	52.3
Furnace, kiln, or kettle operators	4.2	-16.7	Freight, stock, & material movers, hand	1.9	-38.8
Crushing & mixing machine operators	3.9	-9.5	Truck drivers light & heavy	1.9	-20.6
Industrial machinery mechanics	3.9	-15.2	Coating, painting, & spraying machine workers	1.8	-23.8
Hand packers & packagers	3.6	-34.7	Secretaries, ex legal & medical	1.8	-30.4
Extruding & forming machine workers	3.4	-80.6	Cutting & slicing machine setters, operators	1.6	-16.2
Sales & related workers nec	3.2	-23.6	Grinders & polishers, hand	1.6	-16.2
Packaging & filling machine operators	3.2	-23.7	Industrial production managers	1.5	-23.5
Precision workers nec	3.0	-8.7	Traffic, shipping, & receiving clerks	1.5	-26.6
Industrial truck & tractor operators	2.8	-23.7	General office clerks	1.5	-34.9
General managers & top executives	2.8	-27.5	Bookkeeping, accounting, & auditing clerks	1.3	-42.7
Inspectors, testers, & graders, precision	2.8	-23.6	Electricians	1.1	-27.3
Maintenance repairers, general utility	2.6	-30.8	Machinists	1.0	-23.6

Source: Industry-Occupation Matrix, Bureau of Labor Statistics. These data relate to one or more 3-digit SIC industry groups rather than to a single 4-digit SIC. The change reported for each occupation to the year 2005 is a percent of growth or decline as estimated by the Bureau of Labor Statistics. The abbreviation nec stands for 'not elsewhere classified'.

LOCATION BY STATE AND REGIONAL CONCENTRATION

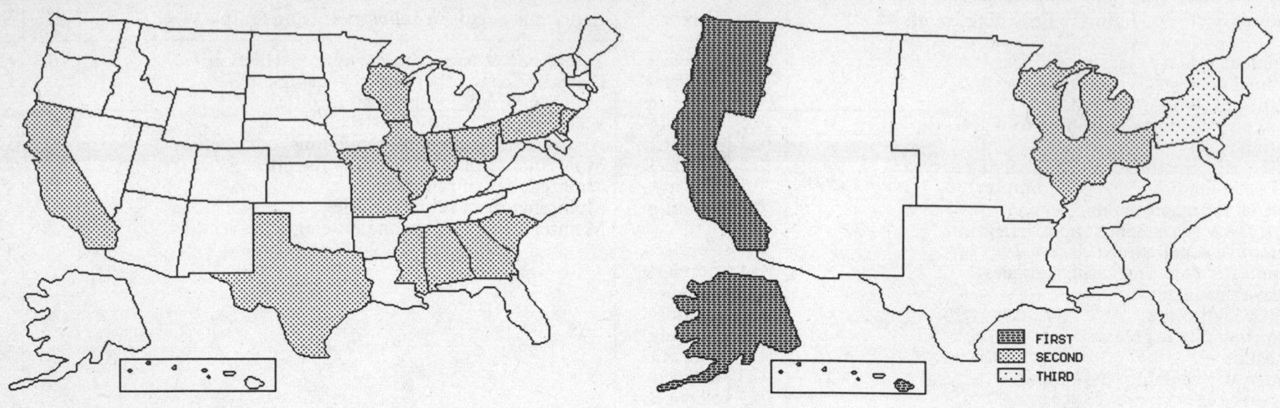

INDUSTRY DATA BY STATE

State	Establish-ments	Shipments			Employment				Cost as % of Shipments	Investment per Employee ($)
		Total ($ mil)	% of U.S.	Per Establ.	Total Number	% of U.S.	Per Establ.	Wages ($/hour)		
Texas	7	217.7	24.1	31.1	1,700	20.2	243	11.30	21.1	-
Ohio	5	124.8	13.8	25.0	1,600	19.0	320	13.88	40.1	-
California	15	36.5	4.0	2.4	500	6.0	33	10.29	44.4	-
New Jersey	5	(D)	-	-	750 *	8.9	150	-	-	-
Pennsylvania	5	(D)	-	-	750 *	8.9	150	-	-	-
Georgia	3	(D)	-	-	375 *	4.5	125	-	-	-
Alabama	2	(D)	-	-	175 *	2.1	88	-	-	-
Illinois	2	(D)	-	-	750 *	8.9	375	-	-	-
Indiana	2	(D)	-	-	375 *	4.5	188	-	-	-
Mississippi	1	(D)	-	-	175 *	2.1	175	-	-	-
Missouri	1	(D)	-	-	175 *	2.1	175	-	-	-
South Carolina	1	(D)	-	-	750 *	8.9	750	-	-	-
Wisconsin	1	(D)	-	-	375 *	4.5	375	-	-	-

Source: 1992 *Economic Census*. The states are in descending order of shipments or establishments (if shipment data are missing for the majority). The symbol (D) appears when data are withheld to prevent disclosure of competitive information. States marked with (D) are sorted by number of establishments. A dash (-) indicates that the data element cannot be calculated; * indicates the midpoint of a range.

3262 - VITREOUS CHINA FOOD UTENSILS

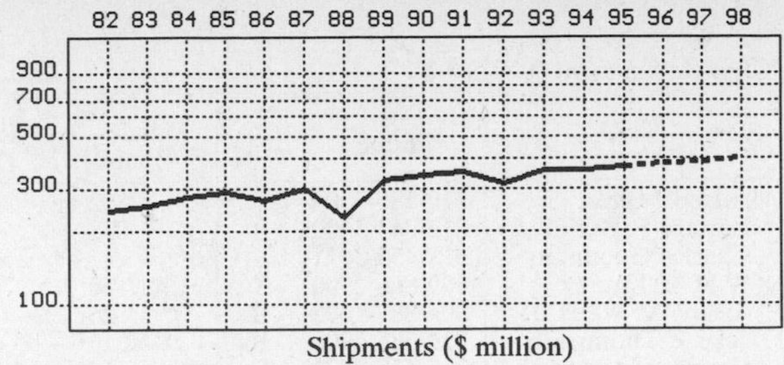

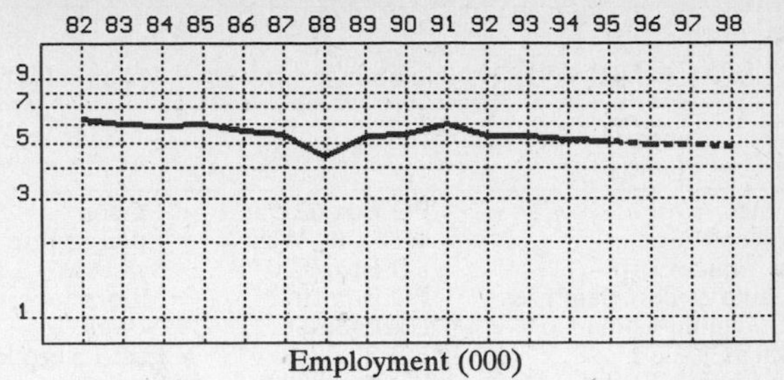

GENERAL STATISTICS

Year	Com-panies	Establishments		Employment			Compensation		Production ($ million)			
		Total	with 20 or more employees	Total (000)	Production Workers (000)	Production Hours (Mil)	Payroll ($ mil)	Wages ($/hr)	Cost of Materials	Value Added by Manufacture	Value of Shipments	Capital Invest.
1982	31	32	20	6.3	5.1	9.1	98.0	8.15	49.2	196.3	241.6	5.2
1983		35	19	6.0	4.7	8.5	96.8	8.16	61.8	218.3	256.9	7.3
1984		38	18	5.9	4.7	9.0	108.0	8.59	69.2	208.6	274.8	5.9
1985		40	18	6.0	4.7	8.9	112.8	8.88	72.0	219.6	289.9	
1986		38	18	5.6	4.6	8.7	102.0	8.79	50.1	222.7	268.3	
1987	32	34	14	5.4	4.4	8.3	104.6	9.51	53.4	247.6	298.4	7.0
1988		34	16	4.4	3.6	7.3	82.9	8.08	58.4	169.0	227.4	
1989		33	16	5.3	4.5	9.0	131.5	9.56	91.2	242.2	324.3	
1990		34	16	5.4	4.8	9.5	136.4	11.27	68.9	278.1	342.0	23.1
1991		34	16	6.0	4.8	9.7	141.8	11.19	69.9	282.2	355.6	30.0
1992	35	39	24	5.3	4.3	8.4	118.2	9.82	81.2	239.1	315.6	15.8
1993		40	23	5.3	4.4	7.8	121.2	10.90	82.6	270.4	357.6	31.4
1994		37P	19P	5.2	4.2	8.1	122.3	10.81	81.0	283.4	361.7	5.1
1995		37P	19P	5.0P	4.2P	8.4P	132.5P	11.31P	82.6P	288.9P	368.7P	
1996		37P	20P	5.0P	4.2P	8.3P	135.2P	11.56P	84.7P	296.4P	378.3P	
1997		38P	20P	4.9P	4.1P	8.3P	137.9P	11.82P	86.9P	304.0P	388.0P	
1998		38P	20P	4.8P	4.1P	8.2P	140.6P	12.07P	89.1P	311.6P	397.7P	

Sources: 1982, 1987, 1992 *Economic Census*; *Annual Survey of Manufactures*, 83-86, 88-91, 93-94. Establishment counts for non-Census years are from *County Business Patterns*; establishment values for 83-84 are extrapolations. 'P's show projections by the editors. Industries reclassified in 87 will not have data for prior years.

INDICES OF CHANGE

Year	Com-panies	Establishments		Employment			Compensation		Production ($ million)			
		Total	with 20 or more employees	Total (000)	Production Workers (000)	Production Hours (Mil)	Payroll ($ mil)	Wages ($/hr)	Cost of Materials	Value Added by Manufacture	Value of Shipments	Capital Invest.
1982	89	82	83	119	119	108	83	83	61	82	77	33
1983		90	79	113	109	101	82	83	76	91	81	46
1984		97	75	111	109	107	91	87	85	87	87	37
1985		103	75	113	109	106	95	90	89	92	92	
1986		97	75	106	107	104	86	90	62	93	85	
1987	91	87	58	102	102	99	88	97	66	104	95	44
1988		87	67	83	84	87	70	82	72	71	72	
1989		85	67	100	105	107	111	97	112	101	103	
1990		87	67	102	112	113	115	115	85	116	108	146
1991		87	67	113	112	115	120	114	86	118	113	190
1992	100	100	100	100	100	100	100	100	100	100	100	100
1993		103	96	100	102	93	103	111	102	113	113	199
1994		95P	80P	98	98	96	103	110	100	119	115	32
1995		96P	81P	95P	98P	100P	112P	115P	102P	121P	117P	
1996		96P	82P	94P	97P	99P	114P	118P	104P	124P	120P	
1997		96P	83P	93P	96P	99P	117P	120P	107P	127P	123P	
1998		97P	83P	91P	95P	98P	119P	123P	110P	130P	126P	

Sources: Same as General Statistics. Values reflect change from the base year, 1992. Values above 100 mean greater than 92, values below 100 mean less than 92, and a value of 100 in the 82-91 or 93-98 period means same as 92. 'P's mark projections by the editors.

SELECTED RATIOS

For 1994	Avg. of All Manufact.	Analyzed Industry	Index	For 1994	Avg. of All Manufact.	Analyzed Industry	Index
Employees per Establishment	49	140	286	Value Added per Production Worker	134,084	67,476	50
Payroll per Establishment	1,500,273	3,298,651	220	Cost per Establishment	5,045,178	2,184,716	43
Payroll per Employee	30,620	23,519	77	Cost per Employee	102,970	15,577	15
Production Workers per Establishment	34	113	330	Cost per Production Worker	146,988	19,286	13
Wages per Establishment	853,319	2,361,678	277	Shipments per Establishment	9,576,895	9,755,701	102
Wages per Production Worker	24,861	20,848	84	Shipments per Employee	195,460	69,558	36
Hours per Production Worker	2,056	1,929	94	Shipments per Production Worker	279,017	86,119	31
Wages per Hour	12.09	10.81	89	Investment per Establishment	321,011	137,556	43
Value Added per Establishment	4,602,255	7,643,809	166	Investment per Employee	6,552	981	15
Value Added per Employee	93,930	54,500	58	Investment per Production Worker	9,352	1,214	13

Sources: Same as General Statistics. The 'Average of All Manufacturing' column represents the average of all manufacturing industries reported for the most recent complete year available. The Index shows the relationship between the Average and the Analyzed Industry. For example, 100 means that they are equal; 500 that the Analyzed Industry is five times the average; 50 means that the Analyzed Industry is half the national average. The abbreviation 'na' is used to show that data are 'not available'.

LEADING COMPANIES

Number shown: **18** Total sales ($ mil): **725** Total employment (000): **3.2**

Company Name	Address				CEO Name	Phone	Co. Type	Sales ($ mil)	Empl. (000)
Mikasa Inc	PO Box 6239	Carson	CA	90749	Alfred J Blake	310-886-3700	P	332	0.2
Department 56 Inc	6436 City West	Eden Prairie	MN	55344	Edward R Bazinet	612-944-5600	P	218	0.2
Syracuse China Corp	PO Box 4820	Syracuse	NY	13221	Charles Goodman	315-455-5671	S	41	0.5
Royal China & Porcelain Cies	PO Box 1012	Moorestown	NJ	08057	W H McKinney	609-866-2900	S	30*	0.1
Homer Laughlin China Co	Harrison St	Newell	WV	26050	Joseph M Wells III	304-387-1300	R	26	0.8
Hall China Co	PO Box 989	East Liverpool	OH	43920	John C Thompson	216-385-2900	R	16*	0.4
Shenago China	PO Box 4820	Syracuse	NY	13221	Charles Goodman	315-455-5671	D	14	0.2
Sterling China Company Inc	PO Box 756	East Liverpool	OH	43920	JW Aldrich	216-532-1544	R	14	0.3
Mayer China	PO Box 4820	Syracuse	NY	13221	Charles Goodman	315-455-5671	D	12	0.1
Americana Art China Co	356 E Maryland Av	Sebring	OH	44672	Joan R Mercer	216-938-6133	R	7	<0.1
HF Coors China Co	8729 Aviation Blv	Inglewood	CA	90301	Robert S Gasbarro	310-338-8921	D	5	<0.1
Burden China Company Inc	PO Box 208	San Gabriel	CA	91778	B Burden	818-350-0612	R	3	<0.1
Heritage Home Inc	41 Madison Av	New York	NY	10010	Louis Federico	212-685-1660	R	3	<0.1
Queens China Company Inc	465 W Virginia Av	Sebring	OH	44672	JR Mercer	216-938-9298	S	2	<0.1
Racket Merchandise Co	713 Walnut St	Kansas City	MO	64106	Joseph Hoagland	816-842-8986	R	1	<0.1
Chase Ltd	38C Grove St	Ridgefield	CT	06877	Richard R Gillespie	203-438-9655	R	1*	<0.1
Ranmaru-Sakura Inc	41 Madison Av	New York	NY	10010	Nick Nishuwaki	212-683-4000	R	1*	<0.1
International 21 Inc	6324 Variel Av	Woodland Hills	CA	91367	John Jeramaz	818-883-3886	R	1*	<0.1

Source: *Ward's Business Directory of U.S. Private and Public Companies*, Volumes 1 and 2, 1996. The company type code used is as follows: P - Public, R - Private, S - Subsidiary, D - Division, J - Joint Venture, A - Affiliate, G - Group. Sales are in millions of dollars, employees are in thousands. An asterisk (*) indicates an estimated sales volume. The symbol < stands for 'less than'. Company names and addresses are truncated, in some cases, to fit into the available space.

MATERIALS CONSUMED

Material	Quantity	Delivered Cost ($ million)
Materials, ingredients, containers, and supplies	(X)	56.8
Clay, ceramic, and refractory minerals	(X)	24.6
Paperboard containers, boxes, and corrugated paperboard	(X)	4.5
All other materials and components, parts, containers, and supplies	(X)	26.6
Materials, ingredients, containers, and supplies, nsk	(X)	1.1

Source: 1992 *Economic Census*. Explanation of symbols used: (D): Withheld to avoid disclosure of competitive data; na: Not available; (S): Withheld because statistical norms were not met; (X): Not applicable; (Z): Less than half the unit shown; nec: Not elsewhere classified; nsk: Not specified by kind; - : zero; * : 10-19 percent estimated; ** : 20-29 percent estimated.

PRODUCT SHARE DETAILS

Product or Product Class	% Share	Product or Product Class	% Share
Vitreous china table and kitchenware	100.00		

Source: 1992 *Economic Census*. The values shown are percent of total shipments in an industry. Values of indented subcategories are summed in the main heading. The symbol (D) appears when data are withheld to prevent disclosure of competitive information. The abbreviation nsk stands for 'not specified by kind' and nec for 'not elsewhere classified'.

INPUTS AND OUTPUTS FOR VITREOUS CHINA FOOD UTENSILS

Economic Sector or Industry Providing Inputs	%	Sector	Economic Sector or Industry Buying Outputs	%	Sector
Imports	71.2	Foreign	Personal consumption expenditures	50.8	
Motor freight transportation & warehousing	7.7	Util.	Nursing & personal care facilities	23.3	Services
Noncomparable imports	4.0	Foreign	Soap & other detergents	9.0	Manufg.
Gas production & distribution (utilities)	3.6	Util.	Eating & drinking places	7.6	Trade
Wholesale trade	1.9	Trade	Exports	4.0	Foreign
Clay, ceramic, & refractory minerals	1.8	Mining	S/L Govt. purch., elem. & secondary education	2.2	S/L Govt
Electric services (utilities)	1.3	Util.	S/L Govt. purch., higher education	1.4	S/L Govt
Advertising	0.9	Services	Water transportation	0.8	Util.
Maintenance of nonfarm buildings nec	0.7	Constr.	Hospitals	0.3	Services
Cyclic crudes and organics	0.6	Manufg.	S/L Govt. purch., correction	0.3	S/L Govt
Gypsum products	0.6	Manufg.	Change in business inventories	0.2	In House
Communications, except radio & TV	0.6	Util.	S/L Govt. purch., health & hospitals	0.2	S/L Govt
Paperboard containers & boxes	0.5	Manufg.			
Machinery, except electrical, nec	0.4	Manufg.			
Eating & drinking places	0.4	Trade			
Banking	0.3	Fin/R.E.			
Computer & data processing services	0.3	Services			
Industrial gases	0.2	Manufg.			
Special dies & tools & machine tool accessories	0.2	Manufg.			
Sanitary services, steam supply, irrigation	0.2	Util.			
Royalties	0.2	Fin/R.E.			
Equipment rental & leasing services	0.2	Services			
Laundry, dry cleaning, shoe repair	0.2	Services			
U.S. Postal Service	0.2	Gov't			
Water transportation	0.1	Util.			
Legal services	0.1	Services			
Management & consulting services & labs	0.1	Services			

Source: Benchmark Input-Output Accounts for the U.S. Economy, 1982, U.S. Department of Commerce, Washington, D.C., July 1991. Data, as reported in the source, are organized by the 1977 SIC structure in use in 1982 but have been matched, as closely as is possible, to the 1987 SIC structure used in this book.

OCCUPATIONS EMPLOYED BY SIC 326 - STONE, CLAY, AND MISC MINING PRODUCTS NEC

Occupation	% of Total 1994	Change to 2005	Occupation	% of Total 1994	Change to 2005
Helpers, laborers, & material movers nec	6.7	-23.3	Machine feeders & offbearers	2.3	-31.4
Assemblers, fabricators, & hand workers nec	6.4	-23.9	Painting, coating, & decorating workers, hand	2.0	52.3
Furnace, kiln, or kettle operators	4.2	-16.7	Freight, stock, & material movers, hand	1.9	-38.8
Crushing & mixing machine operators	3.9	-9.5	Truck drivers light & heavy	1.9	-20.6
Industrial machinery mechanics	3.9	-15.2	Coating, painting, & spraying machine workers	1.8	-23.8
Hand packers & packagers	3.6	-34.7	Secretaries, ex legal & medical	1.8	-30.4
Extruding & forming machine workers	3.4	-80.6	Cutting & slicing machine setters, operators	1.6	-16.2
Sales & related workers nec	3.2	-23.6	Grinders & polishers, hand	1.6	-16.2
Packaging & filling machine operators	3.2	-23.7	Industrial production managers	1.5	-23.5
Precision workers nec	3.0	-8.7	Traffic, shipping, & receiving clerks	1.5	-26.6
Industrial truck & tractor operators	2.8	-23.7	General office clerks	1.5	-34.9
General managers & top executives	2.8	-27.5	Bookkeeping, accounting, & auditing clerks	1.3	-42.7
Inspectors, testers, & graders, precision	2.8	-23.6	Electricians	1.1	-27.3
Maintenance repairers, general utility	2.6	-30.8	Machinists	1.0	-23.6

Source: Industry-Occupation Matrix, Bureau of Labor Statistics. These data relate to one or more 3-digit SIC industry groups rather than to a single 4-digit SIC. The change reported for each occupation to the year 2005 is a percent of growth or decline as estimated by the Bureau of Labor Statistics. The abbreviation nec stands for 'not elsewhere classified'.

LOCATION BY STATE AND REGIONAL CONCENTRATION

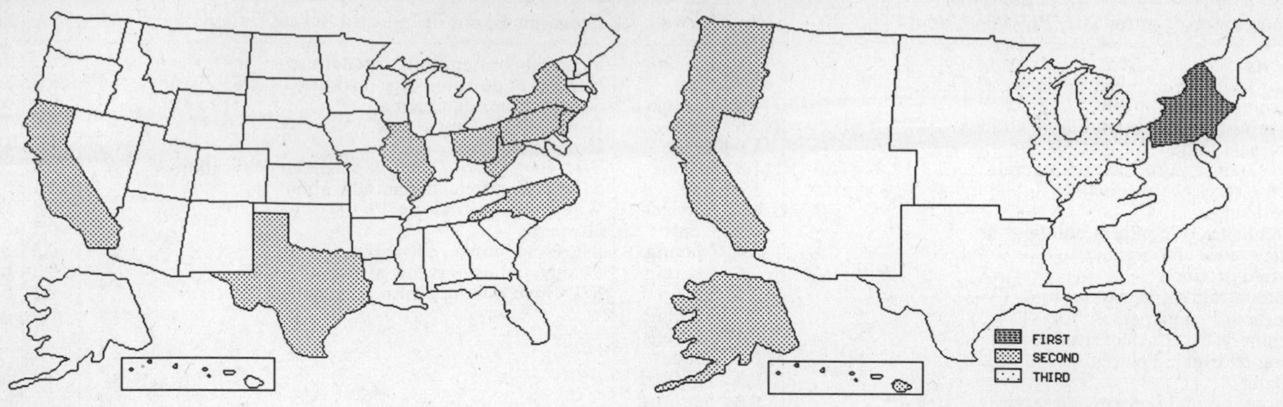

INDUSTRY DATA BY STATE

State	Establish-ments	Shipments Total ($ mil)	Shipments % of U.S.	Shipments Per Establ.	Employment Total Number	Employment % of U.S.	Employment Per Establ.	Wages ($/hour)	Cost as % of Shipments	Investment per Employee ($)
California	7	9.6	3.0	1.4	200	3.8	29	6.75	26.0	-
Ohio	5	(D)	-	-	750 *	14.2	150	-	-	2,400
New York	4	(D)	-	-	1,750 *	33.0	438	-	-	-
Pennsylvania	4	(D)	-	-	375 *	7.1	94	-	-	-
North Carolina	3	(D)	-	-	750 *	14.2	250	-	-	-
Illinois	2	(D)	-	-	175 *	3.3	88	-	-	-
New Jersey	2	(D)	-	-	1,750 *	33.0	875	-	-	-
Texas	2	(D)	-	-	175 *	3.3	88	-	-	-
West Virginia	1	(D)	-	-	750 *	14.2	750	-	-	-

Source: 1992 *Economic Census*. The states are in descending order of shipments or establishments (if shipment data are missing for the majority). The symbol (D) appears when data are withheld to prevent disclosure of competitive information. States marked with (D) are sorted by number of establishments. A dash (-) indicates that the data element cannot be calculated; * indicates the midpoint of a range.

3263 - FINE EARTHENWARE, WHITEWARE

Shipments ($ million)

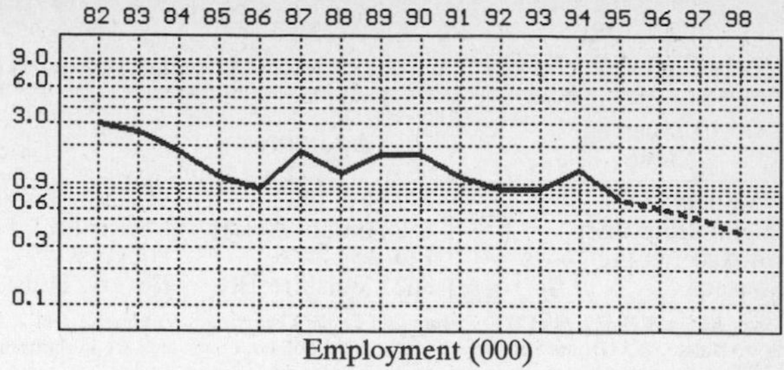

Employment (000)

GENERAL STATISTICS

Year	Companies	Establishments: Total	Establishments: with 20 or more employees	Employment: Total (000)	Employment: Production Workers (000)	Employment: Production Hours (Mil)	Compensation: Payroll ($ mil)	Compensation: Wages ($/hr)	Production: Cost of Materials	Production: Value Added by Manufacture	Production: Value of Shipments	Production: Capital Invest.
1982	38	38	18	3.0	2.5	4.5	37.1	6.53	23.7	61.6	87.6	1.7
1983		39	17	2.6	2.1	3.9	32.5	6.62	22.6	52.3	73.1	1.6
1984		40	16	1.8	1.5	2.9	16.5	3.97	14.8	27.5	49.5	0.5
1985		41	14	1.1	0.9	1.5	13.9	6.07	12.2	20.3	34.1	0.3
1986		41	13	0.9	0.7	1.4	10.6	5.86	7.0	13.9	22.5	0.3
1987	43	44	18	1.8	1.5	3.3	25.6	5.79	18.9	74.2	93.0	1.2
1988		35	13	1.2	1.0	2.0	14.9	5.50	10.4	27.7	38.2	
1989		37	14	1.7	1.0	1.9	16.4	6.37	11.2	37.1	47.0	
1990		29	13	1.7	1.0	2.2	17.0	5.59	10.7	34.2	44.5	0.6
1991		30	10	1.1	0.9	2.1	16.9	5.52	16.9	25.7	42.0	1.1
1992	28	29	8	0.9	0.8	1.8	17.0	7.11	16.7	28.6	45.2	1.5
1993		31	8	0.9	0.8	1.7	18.5	8.29	17.1	34.2	51.2	1.4
1994		29P	8P	1.3	1.2	2.5	26.3	10.04	23.0	34.6	57.0	5.2
1995		28P	7P	0.7P	0.6P	1.5P	15.6P	7.96P	16.8P	25.2P	41.6P	
1996		27P	6P	0.6P	0.5P	1.3P	15.0P	8.18P	16.1P	24.3P	40.0P	
1997		26P	6P	0.5P	0.4P	1.2P	14.3P	8.40P	15.5P	23.3P	38.4P	
1998		24P	5P	0.4P	0.3P	1.0P	13.6P	8.62P	14.9P	22.4P	36.8P	

Sources: 1982, 1987, 1992 *Economic Census*; *Annual Survey of Manufactures*, 83-86, 88-91, 93-94. Establishment counts for non-Census years are from *County Business Patterns*; establishment values for 83-84 are extrapolations. 'P's show projections by the editors. Industries reclassified in 87 will not have data for prior years.

INDICES OF CHANGE

Year	Companies	Establishments: Total	Establishments: with 20 or more employees	Employment: Total (000)	Employment: Production Workers (000)	Employment: Production Hours (Mil)	Compensation: Payroll ($ mil)	Compensation: Wages ($/hr)	Production: Cost of Materials	Production: Value Added by Manufacture	Production: Value of Shipments	Production: Capital Invest.
1982	136	131	225	333	313	250	218	92	142	215	194	113
1983		134	213	289	262	217	191	93	135	183	162	107
1984		138	200	200	188	161	97	56	89	96	110	33
1985		141	175	122	113	83	82	85	73	71	75	20
1986		141	163	100	88	78	62	82	42	49	50	20
1987	154	152	225	200	188	183	151	81	113	259	206	80
1988		121	163	133	125	111	88	77	62	97	85	
1989		128	175	189	125	106	96	90	67	130	104	
1990		100	163	189	125	122	100	79	64	120	98	40
1991		103	125	122	113	117	99	78	101	90	93	73
1992	100	100	100	100	100	100	100	100	100	100	100	100
1993		107	100	100	100	94	109	117	102	120	113	93
1994		100P	101P	144	150	139	155	141	138	121	126	347
1995		96P	90P	82P	71P	81P	92P	112P	100P	88P	92P	
1996		92P	80P	69P	59P	73P	88P	115P	97P	85P	88P	
1997		88P	69P	57P	48P	66P	84P	118P	93P	82P	85P	
1998		84P	59P	44P	36P	58P	80P	121P	89P	78P	81P	

Sources: Same as General Statistics. Values reflect change from the base year, 1992. Values above 100 mean greater than 92, values below 100 mean less than 92, and a value of 100 in the 82-91 or 93-98 period means same as 92. 'P's mark projections by the editors.

SELECTED RATIOS

For 1994	Avg. of All Manufact.	Analyzed Industry	Index	For 1994	Avg. of All Manufact.	Analyzed Industry	Index
Employees per Establishment	49	45	92	Value Added per Production Worker	134,084	28,833	22
Payroll per Establishment	1,500,273	908,796	61	Cost per Establishment	5,045,178	794,764	16
Payroll per Employee	30,620	20,231	66	Cost per Employee	102,970	17,692	17
Production Workers per Establishment	34	41	121	Cost per Production Worker	146,988	19,167	13
Wages per Establishment	853,319	867,330	102	Shipments per Establishment	9,576,895	1,969,634	21
Wages per Production Worker	24,861	20,917	84	Shipments per Employee	195,460	43,846	22
Hours per Production Worker	2,056	2,083	101	Shipments per Production Worker	279,017	47,500	17
Wages per Hour	12.09	10.04	83	Investment per Establishment	321,011	179,686	56
Value Added per Establishment	4,602,255	1,195,602	26	Investment per Employee	6,552	4,000	61
Value Added per Employee	93,930	26,615	28	Investment per Production Worker	9,352	4,333	46

Sources: Same as General Statistics. The 'Average of All Manufacturing' column represents the average of all manufacturing industries reported for the most recent complete year available. The Index shows the relationship between the Average and the Analyzed Industry. For example, 100 means that they are equal; 500 that the Analyzed Industry is five times the average; 50 means that the Analyzed Industry is half the national average. The abbreviation 'na' is used to show that data are 'not available'.

LEADING COMPANIES

Number shown: **4** Total sales ($ mil): **22** Total employment (000): **0.3**

Company Name	Address				CEO Name	Phone	Co. Type	Sales ($ mil)	Empl. (000)
Bonny Products Inc	PO Box 1908	Washington	NC	27889	Robert E Furer	919-975-6669	S	10	0.2
Leeds Engineering Corp	881 Avnida Acaso	Camarillo	CA	90312	D M Shumway	805-482-7477	R	7*	<0.1
Vanguard Accents Inc	PO Box 2068	Hickory	NC	28603	T Corpening	704-322-3400	S	3	<0.1
Direct Sources	8621 Wilshire Blv	Beverly Hills	CA	90211	Dan Hanasab	310-289-8663	R	2*	<0.1

Source: *Ward's Business Directory of U.S. Private and Public Companies*, Volumes 1 and 2, 1996. The company type code used is as follows: P - Public, R - Private, S - Subsidiary, D - Division, J - Joint Venture, A - Affiliate, G - Group. Sales are in millions of dollars, employees are in thousands. An asterisk (*) indicates an estimated sales volume. The symbol < stands for 'less than'. Company names and addresses are truncated, in some cases, to fit into the available space.

MATERIALS CONSUMED

Material	Quantity	Delivered Cost ($ million)
Materials, ingredients, containers, and supplies	(X)	14.0
Paperboard containers, boxes, and corrugated paperboard	(X)	0.7
All other materials and components, parts, containers, and supplies	(X)	12.6
Materials, ingredients, containers, and supplies, nsk	(X)	0.7

Source: 1992 *Economic Census*. Explanation of symbols used: (D): Withheld to avoid disclosure of competitive data; na: Not available; (S): Withheld because statistical norms were not met; (X): Not applicable; (Z): Less than half the unit shown; nec: Not elsewhere classified; nsk: Not specified by kind; - : zero; * : 10-19 percent estimated; ** : 20-29 percent estimated.

PRODUCT SHARE DETAILS

Product or Product Class	% Share	Product or Product Class	% Share
Semivitreous table and kitchenware	100.00		

Source: 1992 *Economic Census*. The values shown are percent of total shipments in an industry. Values of indented subcategories are summed in the main heading. The symbol (D) appears when data are withheld to prevent disclosure of competitive information. The abbreviation nsk stands for 'not specified by kind' and nec for 'not elsewhere classified'.

INPUTS AND OUTPUTS FOR FINE EARTHENWARE FOOD UTENSILS

Economic Sector or Industry Providing Inputs	%	Sector	Economic Sector or Industry Buying Outputs	%	Sector
Imports	82.7	Foreign	Personal consumption expenditures	96.2	
Motor freight transportation & warehousing	4.5	Util.	Eating & drinking places	2.0	Trade
Wholesale trade	1.7	Trade	Exports	1.5	Foreign
Gas production & distribution (utilities)	1.4	Util.	S/L Govt. purch., elem. & secondary education	0.3	S/L Govt
Clay, ceramic, & refractory minerals	1.3	Mining			
Cyclic crudes and organics	0.8	Manufg.			
Gypsum products	0.8	Manufg.			
Electric services (utilities)	0.6	Util.			
Noncomparable imports	0.5	Foreign			
Industrial gases	0.3	Manufg.			
Industrial inorganic chemicals, nec	0.3	Manufg.			
Machinery, except electrical, nec	0.3	Manufg.			
Metal stampings, nec	0.3	Manufg.			
Communications, except radio & TV	0.3	Util.			
Eating & drinking places	0.3	Trade			
Maintenance of nonfarm buildings nec	0.2	Constr.			
Paperboard containers & boxes	0.2	Manufg.			
Special dies & tools & machine tool accessories	0.2	Manufg.			
Sanitary services, steam supply, irrigation	0.2	Util.			
Advertising	0.2	Services			
Detective & protective services	0.2	Services			
Equipment rental & leasing services	0.2	Services			
Laundry, dry cleaning, shoe repair	0.2	Services			
U.S. Postal Service	0.2	Gov't			
Coal	0.1	Mining			
Abrasive products	0.1	Manufg.			
Chemical preparations, nec	0.1	Manufg.			
Petroleum refining	0.1	Manufg.			
Railroads & related services	0.1	Util.			
Water transportation	0.1	Util.			
Banking	0.1	Fin/R.E.			
Electrical repair shops	0.1	Services			
Legal services	0.1	Services			
Management & consulting services & labs	0.1	Services			

Source: Benchmark Input-Output Accounts for the U.S. Economy, 1982, U.S. Department of Commerce, Washington, D.C., July 1991. Data, as reported in the source, are organized by the 1977 SIC structure in use in 1982 but have been matched, as closely as is possible, to the 1987 SIC structure used in this book.

OCCUPATIONS EMPLOYED BY SIC 326 - STONE, CLAY, AND MISC MINING PRODUCTS NEC

Occupation	% of Total 1994	Change to 2005	Occupation	% of Total 1994	Change to 2005
Helpers, laborers, & material movers nec	6.7	-23.3	Machine feeders & offbearers	2.3	-31.4
Assemblers, fabricators, & hand workers nec	6.4	-23.9	Painting, coating, & decorating workers, hand	2.0	52.3
Furnace, kiln, or kettle operators	4.2	-16.7	Freight, stock, & material movers, hand	1.9	-38.8
Crushing & mixing machine operators	3.9	-9.5	Truck drivers light & heavy	1.9	-20.6
Industrial machinery mechanics	3.9	-15.2	Coating, painting, & spraying machine workers	1.8	-23.8
Hand packers & packagers	3.6	-34.7	Secretaries, ex legal & medical	1.8	-30.4
Extruding & forming machine workers	3.4	-80.6	Cutting & slicing machine setters, operators	1.6	-16.2
Sales & related workers nec	3.2	-23.6	Grinders & polishers, hand	1.6	-16.2
Packaging & filling machine operators	3.2	-23.7	Industrial production managers	1.5	-23.5
Precision workers nec	3.0	-8.7	Traffic, shipping, & receiving clerks	1.5	-26.6
Industrial truck & tractor operators	2.8	-23.7	General office clerks	1.5	-34.9
General managers & top executives	2.8	-27.5	Bookkeeping, accounting, & auditing clerks	1.3	-42.7
Inspectors, testers, & graders, precision	2.8	-23.6	Electricians	1.1	-27.3
Maintenance repairers, general utility	2.6	-30.8	Machinists	1.0	-23.6

Source: *Industry-Occupation Matrix*, Bureau of Labor Statistics. These data relate to one or more 3-digit SIC industry groups rather than to a single 4-digit SIC. The change reported for each occupation to the year 2005 is a percent of growth or decline as estimated by the Bureau of Labor Statistics. The abbreviation nec stands for 'not elsewhere classified'.

LOCATION BY STATE AND REGIONAL CONCENTRATION

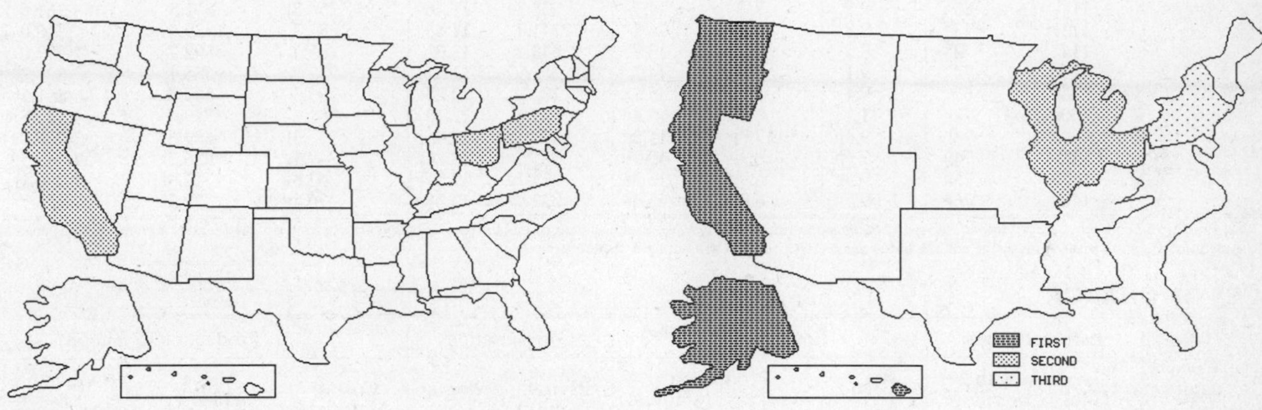

INDUSTRY DATA BY STATE

State	Establish-ments	Shipments			Employment				Cost as % of Shipments	Investment per Employee ($)
		Total ($ mil)	% of U.S.	Per Establ.	Total Number	% of U.S.	Per Establ.	Wages ($/hour)		
California	6	4.1	9.1	0.7	100	11.1	17	4.50	26.8	1,000
Ohio	5	(D)	-	-	175 *	19.4	35	-	-	-
Pennsylvania	2	(D)	-	-	375 *	41.7	188	-	-	-

Source: 1992 *Economic Census*. The states are in descending order of shipments or establishments (if shipment data are missing for the majority). The symbol (D) appears when data are withheld to prevent disclosure of competitive information. States marked with (D) are sorted by number of establishments. A dash (-) indicates that the data element cannot be calculated; * indicates the midpoint of a range.

3264 - PORCELAIN ELECTRICAL SUPPLIES

82 83 84 85 86 87 88 89 90 91 92 93 94 95 96 97 98

9,000. 6,000. 3,000. 900. 600. 300. 100.

Shipments ($ million)

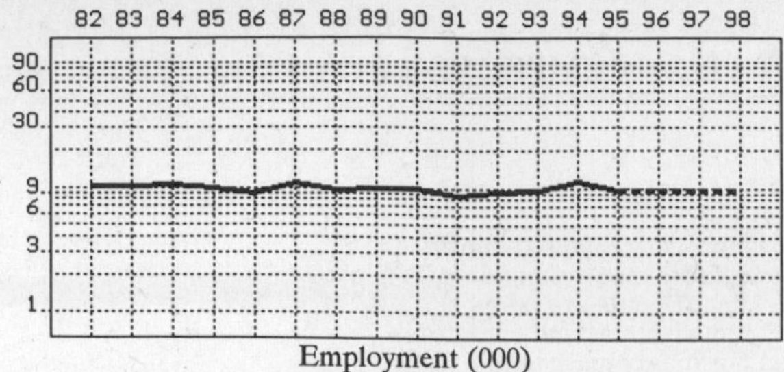

Employment (000)

GENERAL STATISTICS

Year	Companies	Establishments Total	Establishments with 20 or more employees	Employment Total (000)	Production Workers (000)	Production Hours (Mil)	Compensation Payroll ($ mil)	Compensation Wages ($/hr)	Cost of Materials	Value Added by Manufacture	Value of Shipments	Capital Invest.
1982	79	90	62	10.1	8.0	14.8	197.1	8.94	183.4	350.0	528.0	25.9
1983		89	63	10.1	8.1	14.6	197.0	9.27	186.4	357.3	542.8	36.7
1984		88	64	10.4	7.9	15.5	221.2	9.30	231.9	392.9	620.8	26.3
1985		86	66	10.0	7.6	15.0	219.3	9.56	227.7	359.1	585.8	46.0
1986		85	61	9.0	6.8	12.7	197.6	10.04	189.7	287.6	479.3	22.6
1987	103	116	66	10.7	8.2	16.2	248.2	10.25	247.9	474.7	714.2	26.4
1988		107	62	9.5	7.4	14.8	234.5	10.96	241.1	469.3	717.5	29.6
1989		112	66	9.9	7.2	14.7	238.3	11.46	256.8	502.5	761.6	48.1
1990		113	73	9.8	6.9	14.1	241.8	11.88	282.7	539.4	810.0	50.9
1991		114	72	8.7	6.7	13.7	238.2	12.01	285.4	502.7	793.0	57.1
1992	112	127	74	9.1	6.8	14.2	261.1	11.87	272.7	565.1	827.2	31.0
1993		126	67	9.4	7.1	15.1	280.9	12.23	289.5	565.9	851.5	42.6
1994		130P	72P	11.1	8.2	17.4	331.2	12.18	381.2	749.4	1,141.8	62.1
1995		134P	73P	9.6P	7.0P	15.2P	297.4P	12.95P	335.5P	659.6P	1,005.0P	53.4P
1996		138P	74P	9.6P	6.9P	15.3P	305.7P	13.26P	349.1P	686.2P	1,045.5P	55.4P
1997		142P	75P	9.5P	6.9P	15.3P	314.1P	13.57P	362.6P	712.8P	1,086.1P	57.5P
1998		146P	76P	9.5P	6.8P	15.4P	322.4P	13.88P	376.1P	739.5P	1,126.7P	59.6P

Sources: 1982, 1987, 1992 *Economic Census*; *Annual Survey of Manufactures*, 83-86, 88-91, 93-94. Establishment counts for non-Census years are from *County Business Patterns*; establishment values for 83-84 are extrapolations. 'P's show projections by the editors. Industries reclassified in 87 will not have data for prior years.

INDICES OF CHANGE

Year	Companies	Establishments Total	Establishments with 20 or more employees	Employment Total (000)	Production Workers (000)	Production Hours (Mil)	Compensation Payroll ($ mil)	Compensation Wages ($/hr)	Cost of Materials	Value Added by Manufacture	Value of Shipments	Capital Invest.
1982	71	71	84	111	118	104	75	75	67	62	64	84
1983		70	85	111	119	103	75	78	68	63	66	118
1984		69	86	114	116	109	85	78	85	70	75	85
1985		68	89	110	112	106	84	81	83	64	71	148
1986		67	82	99	100	89	76	85	70	51	58	73
1987	92	91	89	118	121	114	95	86	91	84	86	85
1988		84	84	104	109	104	90	92	88	83	87	95
1989		88	89	109	106	104	91	97	94	89	92	155
1990		89	99	108	101	99	93	100	104	95	98	164
1991		90	97	96	99	96	91	101	105	89	96	184
1992	100	100	100	100	100	100	100	100	100	100	100	100
1993		99	91	103	104	106	108	103	106	100	103	137
1994		102P	98P	122	121	123	127	103	140	133	138	200
1995		105P	99P	106P	103P	107P	114P	109P	123P	117P	121P	172P
1996		109P	100P	105P	102P	108P	117P	112P	128P	121P	126P	179P
1997		112P	101P	105P	101P	108P	120P	114P	133P	126P	131P	186P
1998		115P	102P	105P	100P	108P	123P	117P	138P	131P	136P	192P

Sources: Same as General Statistics. Values reflect change from the base year, 1992. Values above 100 mean greater than 92, values below 100 mean less than 92, and a value of 100 in the 82-91 or 93-98 period means same as 92. 'P's mark projections by the editors.

SELECTED RATIOS

For 1994	Avg. of All Manufact.	Analyzed Industry	Index
Employees per Establishment	49	85	174
Payroll per Establishment	1,500,273	2,547,099	170
Payroll per Employee	30,620	29,838	97
Production Workers per Establishment	34	63	184
Wages per Establishment	853,319	1,629,866	191
Wages per Production Worker	24,861	25,845	104
Hours per Production Worker	2,056	2,122	103
Wages per Hour	12.09	12.18	101
Value Added per Establishment	4,602,255	5,763,272	125
Value Added per Employee	93,930	67,514	72

For 1994	Avg. of All Manufact.	Analyzed Industry	Index
Value Added per Production Worker	134,084	91,390	68
Cost per Establishment	5,045,178	2,931,624	58
Cost per Employee	102,970	34,342	33
Cost per Production Worker	146,988	46,488	32
Shipments per Establishment	9,576,895	8,781,030	92
Shipments per Employee	195,460	102,865	53
Shipments per Production Worker	279,017	139,244	50
Investment per Establishment	321,011	477,581	149
Investment per Employee	6,552	5,595	85
Investment per Production Worker	9,352	7,573	81

Sources: Same as General Statistics. The 'Average of All Manufacturing' column represents the average of all manufacturing industries reported for the most recent complete year available. The Index shows the relationship between the Average and the Analyzed Industry. For example, 100 means that they are equal; 500 that the Analyzed Industry is five times the average; 50 means that the Analyzed Industry is half the national average. The abbreviation 'na' is used to show that data are 'not available'.

LEADING COMPANIES

Number shown: **25** Total sales ($ mil): **1,271** Total employment (000): **10.5**

Company Name	Address				CEO Name	Phone	Co. Type	Sales ($ mil)	Empl. (000)
ACX Technologies Inc	16000 T Mtn	Golden	CO	80403	Harold R Smethills	303-271-7000	P	642	4.2
Coors Porcelain Co	600 9th St	Golden	CO	80401	Jim Wade	303-278-4000	S	200	2.1
Lapp Insulator Co	130 Gilbert St	Le Roy	NY	14482	H David Culley	716-768-6221	S	90	0.8
TDK Ferrites Corp	5900 N Harrison St	Shawnee	OK	74801	James B Gollhardt	405-275-2100	S	63*	0.8
Intermagnetics General Corp	PO Box 566	Guilderland	NY	12084	Carl H Rosner	518-456-5456	P	51	0.5
Stackpole Magnet	700 Elk Av	Kane	PA	16735	Delbert Williams	814-837-7000	D	35	0.4
Porcelain Products Co	225 N Patterson St	Carey	OH	43316	Haywood Bower	419-396-7621	S	25	0.2
Active Industries Inc	20 Solar Dr	Clifton Park	NY	12065	Norman Hayes Jr	518-371-2020	R	24	0.1
General Magnetic Co	5252 Investment Dr	Dallas	TX	75236	Arthur M Dennis	214-296-4711	S	20	0.2
Victor Insulators Inc	280 Maple Av	Victor	NY	14564	R Graczyk	716-924-2127	R	17	0.2
Du-Co Ceramics Company Inc	PO Box 568	Saxonburg	PA	16056	Reldon Cooper	412-352-1511	R	16*	0.2
Cookson Magnet Sales	272 Titus Av	Warrington	PA	18976	Michael Miller	215-343-5518	R	15	<0.1
Alberox Corp	Industrial Park	New Bedford	MA	02745	David W Carter	508-995-1725	S	12*	0.1
New Jersey Porcelain Co	PO Box 5103	Trenton	NJ	08638	S M Bielawski	609-394-5376	R	11	0.1
Ceramaseal	PO Box 260	New Lebanon	NY	12125	Gary L Balfour	518-794-7800	D	8	<0.1
Maryland Lava Company Inc	PO Box 527	Bel Air	MD	21014	E L Dinning IV	410-838-4114	R	8*	0.1
Superior Technical	PO Box 1028	St Albans	VT	05478	Theodore H Church	802-527-7726	R	7	<0.1
National Magnetics Group Inc	1210 Win Dr	Bethlehem	PA	18017	Paul B Oberbeck	215-867-7600	R	5	<0.1
National Magnetics Company	222 J Rowen Blvd	Bardstown	KY	40004	Masaru Yokokura	502-348-3765	S	5	<0.1
Ohio Magnetics Inc	5400 Dunham Rd	Maple Heights	OH	44137	Robert T Growner	216-662-8484	S	5*	<0.1
Metsch Refractories Inc	PO Box 268	Chester	WV	26034	Patricia B Hays	304-387-1067	R	5	<0.1
AZ Industries Inc	PO Box 250	Ash Flat	AR	72513	Les Adam	501-856-3041	R	4	<0.1
Star Porcelain Co	101 Muirhead Av	Trenton	NJ	08638	AH Weigold	609-392-3154	R	2	<0.1
Universal Clay Products Co	PO Box 438	Sandusky	OH	44870	David E Dunlay	419-626-4912	R	2	<0.1
MAGNETCARDS	PO Box 300230	Fern Park	FL	32730	Larry Furlong	407-260-6993	R	0	<0.1

Source: *Ward's Business Directory of U.S. Private and Public Companies*, Volumes 1 and 2, 1996. The company type code used is as follows: P - Public, R - Private, S - Subsidiary, D - Division, J - Joint Venture, A - Affiliate, G - Group. Sales are in millions of dollars, employees are in thousands. An asterisk (*) indicates an estimated sales volume. The symbol < stands for 'less than'. Company names and addresses are truncated, in some cases, to fit into the available space.

MATERIALS CONSUMED

Material	Quantity	Delivered Cost ($ million)
Materials, ingredients, containers, and supplies	(X)	219.1
Clay, ceramic, and refractory minerals	(X)	84.1
Paperboard containers, boxes, and corrugated paperboard	(X)	10.2
Metal stampings	(X)	30.4
All other materials and components, parts, containers, and supplies	(X)	70.0
Materials, ingredients, containers, and supplies, nsk	(X)	24.5

Source: 1992 *Economic Census*. Explanation of symbols used: (D): Withheld to avoid disclosure of competitive data; na: Not available; (S): Withheld because statistical norms were not met; (X): Not applicable; (Z): Less than half the unit shown; nec: Not elsewhere classified; nsk: Not specified by kind; - : zero; * : 10-19 percent estimated; ** : 20-29 percent estimated.

PRODUCT SHARE DETAILS

Product or Product Class	% Share
Porcelain electrical supplies	100.00
Pin-type porcelain electrical insulators and line posts, wet process voltage products shipped as complete	2.85
Suspension-type porcelain electrical insulators, 7 1/2 inch disc and smaller, wet process voltage products shipped as complete	1.55
Suspension-type porcelain electrical insulators, larger than 7 1/2 inch disc, wet process voltage products shipped as complete	3.28
Switch and bus porcelain electrical insulators (including cap-and-pin, and post types), wet process voltage products shipped as complete	6.23
All other porcelain electrical insulators (including guy strain insulators and spools), wet process voltage products shipped as complete	8.92
Wet process voltage products shipped as porcelain pieces only for component parts of other electrical equipment	7.69
All dry process electrical porcelain (including porcelain parts for wiring devices, fuses, circuit breakers, etc.)	17.60
Steatite electrical products	2.67
Ceramic permanent magnets	12.46
Other ferrites	5.61
Alumina materials for electronic application	5.13
Beryllia, titanate, and other ceramic electrical products and components for electronic applications not included above	20.33

Source: 1992 *Economic Census*. The values shown are percent of total shipments in an industry. Values of indented subcategories are summed in the main heading. The symbol (D) appears when data are withheld to prevent disclosure of competitive information. The abbreviation nsk stands for 'not specified by kind' and nec for 'not elsewhere classified'.

INPUTS AND OUTPUTS FOR PORCELAIN ELECTRICAL SUPPLIES

Economic Sector or Industry Providing Inputs	%	Sector	Economic Sector or Industry Buying Outputs	%	Sector
Imports	22.4	Foreign	Electric utility facility construction	46.3	Constr.
Motor freight transportation & warehousing	12.2	Util.	Exports	16.6	Foreign
Clay, ceramic, & refractory minerals	9.7	Mining	Switchgear & switchboard apparatus	7.0	Manufg.
Metal stampings, nec	7.6	Manufg.	Maintenance of electric utility facilities	6.3	Constr.
Lighting fixtures & equipment	6.8	Manufg.	Transformers	5.2	Manufg.
Gas production & distribution (utilities)	6.8	Util.	Nonfarm residential structure maintenance	4.5	Constr.
Electric services (utilities)	5.2	Util.	Office buildings	3.7	Constr.
Wholesale trade	3.6	Trade	Motors & generators	3.1	Manufg.
Mechanical measuring devices	2.6	Manufg.	Construction of hospitals	1.1	Constr.
Paperboard containers & boxes	2.1	Manufg.	Industrial buildings	1.0	Constr.
Communications, except radio & TV	1.5	Util.	Residential 2-4 unit structures, nonfarm	1.0	Constr.
Advertising	1.4	Services	Residential garden apartments	0.6	Constr.
Maintenance of nonfarm buildings nec	1.1	Constr.	Hotels & motels	0.5	Constr.
Minerals, ground or treated	1.1	Manufg.	Carbon & graphite products	0.4	Manufg.
Machinery, except electrical, nec	1.0	Manufg.	Electrical industrial apparatus, nec	0.4	Manufg.
Eating & drinking places	1.0	Trade	Porcelain electrical supplies	0.4	Manufg.
Porcelain electrical supplies	0.9	Manufg.	Construction of educational buildings	0.3	Constr.
Banking	0.9	Fin/R.E.	Industrial controls	0.2	Manufg.
Real estate	0.9	Fin/R.E.	Federal Government purchases, national defense	0.2	Fed Govt
Automotive repair shops & services	0.9	Services	Change in business inventories	0.2	In House
Railroads & related services	0.7	Util.	Farm service facilities	0.1	Constr.
Water transportation	0.7	Util.	Maintenance of telephone & telegraph facilities	0.1	Constr.
U.S. Postal Service	0.7	Gov't	Telephone & telegraph facility construction	0.1	Constr.
Noncomparable imports	0.6	Foreign	Warehouses	0.1	Constr.
Cyclic crudes and organics	0.5	Manufg.			
Special dies & tools & machine tool accessories	0.5	Manufg.			
Computer & data processing services	0.5	Services			
Sanitary services, steam supply, irrigation	0.4	Util.			
Equipment rental & leasing services	0.4	Services			
Legal services	0.4	Services			
Management & consulting services & labs	0.4	Services			
Abrasive products	0.3	Manufg.			
Lubricating oils & greases	0.3	Manufg.			
Petroleum refining	0.3	Manufg.			
Royalties	0.3	Fin/R.E.			
Laundry, dry cleaning, shoe repair	0.3	Services			
General industrial machinery, nec	0.2	Manufg.			
Industrial gases	0.2	Manufg.			
Manifold business forms	0.2	Manufg.			
Security & commodity brokers	0.2	Fin/R.E.			
Accounting, auditing & bookkeeping	0.2	Services			
Gaskets, packing & sealing devices	0.1	Manufg.			
Insurance carriers	0.1	Fin/R.E.			
Business services nec	0.1	Services			
Electrical repair shops	0.1	Services			
Hotels & lodging places	0.1	Services			

Source: Benchmark Input-Output Accounts for the U.S. Economy, 1982, U.S. Department of Commerce, Washington, D.C., July 1991. Data, as reported in the source, are organized by the 1977 SIC structure in use in 1982 but have been matched, as closely as is possible, to the 1987 SIC structure used in this book.

OCCUPATIONS EMPLOYED BY SIC 326 - STONE, CLAY, AND MISC MINING PRODUCTS NEC

Occupation	% of Total 1994	Change to 2005	Occupation	% of Total 1994	Change to 2005
Helpers, laborers, & material movers nec	6.7	-23.3	Machine feeders & offbearers	2.3	-31.4
Assemblers, fabricators, & hand workers nec	6.4	-23.9	Painting, coating, & decorating workers, hand	2.0	52.3
Furnace, kiln, or kettle operators	4.2	-16.7	Freight, stock, & material movers, hand	1.9	-38.8
Crushing & mixing machine operators	3.9	-9.5	Truck drivers light & heavy	1.9	-20.6
Industrial machinery mechanics	3.9	-15.2	Coating, painting, & spraying machine workers	1.8	-23.8
Hand packers & packagers	3.6	-34.7	Secretaries, ex legal & medical	1.8	-30.4
Extruding & forming machine workers	3.4	-80.6	Cutting & slicing machine setters, operators	1.6	-16.2
Sales & related workers nec	3.2	-23.6	Grinders & polishers, hand	1.6	-16.2
Packaging & filling machine operators	3.2	-23.7	Industrial production managers	1.5	-23.5
Precision workers nec	3.0	-8.7	Traffic, shipping, & receiving clerks	1.5	-26.6
Industrial truck & tractor operators	2.8	-23.7	General office clerks	1.5	-34.9
General managers & top executives	2.8	-27.5	Bookkeeping, accounting, & auditing clerks	1.3	-42.7
Inspectors, testers, & graders, precision	2.8	-23.6	Electricians	1.1	-27.3
Maintenance repairers, general utility	2.6	-30.8	Machinists	1.0	-23.6

Source: Industry-Occupation Matrix, Bureau of Labor Statistics. These data relate to one or more 3-digit SIC industry groups rather than to a single 4-digit SIC. The change reported for each occupation to the year 2005 is a percent of growth or decline as estimated by the Bureau of Labor Statistics. The abbreviation nec stands for 'not elsewhere classified'.

LOCATION BY STATE AND REGIONAL CONCENTRATION

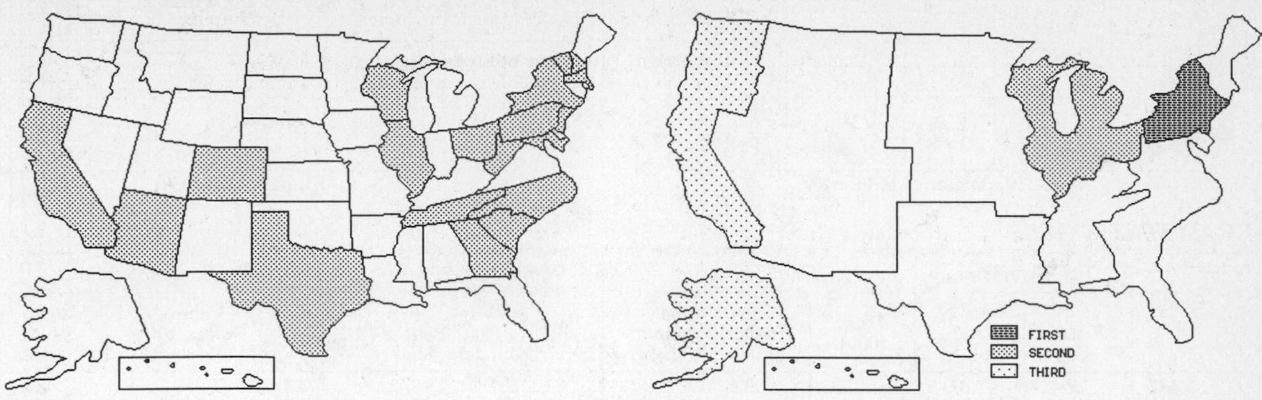

INDUSTRY DATA BY STATE

State	Establish-ments	Shipments			Employment				Cost as % of Shipments	Investment per Employee ($)
		Total ($ mil)	% of U.S.	Per Establ.	Total Number	% of U.S.	Per Establ.	Wages ($/hour)		
New York	11	247.2	29.9	22.5	2,300	25.3	209	13.24	29.0	4,130
Ohio	10	83.6	10.1	8.4	700	7.7	70	13.10	37.1	1,714
Pennsylvania	10	62.5	7.6	6.3	800	8.8	80	12.54	26.4	1,500
Tennessee	5	48.1	5.8	9.6	600	6.6	120	10.20	25.6	3,833
California	19	42.8	5.2	2.3	500	5.5	26	11.29	33.4	2,200
New Jersey	9	25.9	3.1	2.9	400	4.4	44	11.60	29.0	500
Texas	7	22.6	2.7	3.2	200	2.2	29	9.75	39.8	3,500
Massachusetts	6	18.9	2.3	3.2	200	2.2	33	15.00	32.8	3,000
Illinois	8	(D)	-	-	375 *	4.1	47	-	-	1,067
Colorado	4	(D)	-	-	375 *	4.1	94	-	-	-
Georgia	3	(D)	-	-	175 *	1.9	58	-	-	-
Maryland	3	(D)	-	-	375 *	4.1	125	-	-	-
North Carolina	3	(D)	-	-	175 *	1.9	58	-	-	-
South Carolina	3	(D)	-	-	750 *	8.2	250	-	-	-
Vermont	3	(D)	-	-	175 *	1.9	58	-	-	-
West Virginia	3	(D)	-	-	375 *	4.1	125	-	-	-
Wisconsin	2	(D)	-	-	175 *	1.9	88	-	-	-
Arizona	1	(D)	-	-	175 *	1.9	175	-	-	-
New Hampshire	1	(D)	-	-	175 *	1.9	175	-	-	-

Source: 1992 *Economic Census*. The states are in descending order of shipments or establishments (if shipment data are missing for the majority). The symbol (D) appears when data are withheld to prevent disclosure of competitive information. States marked with (D) are sorted by number of establishments. A dash (-) indicates that the data element cannot be calculated; * indicates the midpoint of a range.

3269 - POTTERY PRODUCTS, NEC

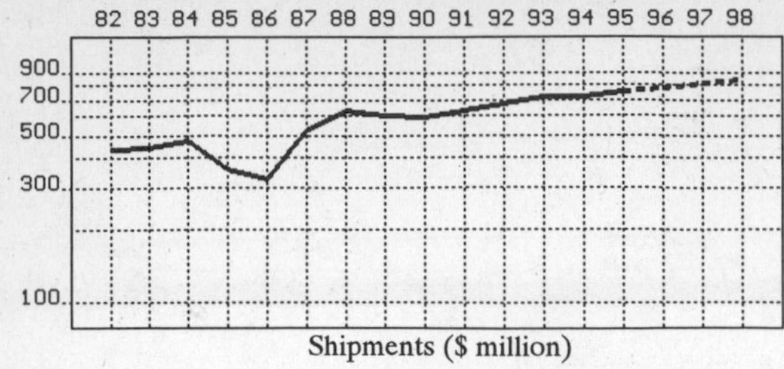

Shipments ($ million)

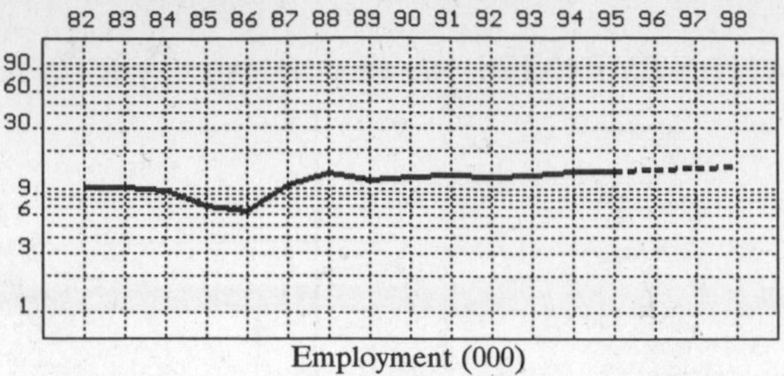

Employment (000)

GENERAL STATISTICS

Year	Com-panies	Establishments		Employment			Compensation		Production ($ million)			
		Total	with 20 or more employees	Total (000)	Production Workers (000)	Production Hours (Mil)	Payroll ($ mil)	Wages ($/hr)	Cost of Materials	Value Added by Manufacture	Value of Shipments	Capital Invest.
1982	682	694	103	10.1	8.6	15.4	122.9	5.96	178.3	251.7	430.6	18.0
1983		693	106	10.1	8.5	15.6	128.7	6.15	150.9	292.6	442.4	7.3
1984		692	109	9.5	7.9	15.5	124.8	5.77	165.5	302.3	468.1	10.6
1985		690	113	7.1	5.7	11.1	108.6	6.79	126.4	229.1	358.3	17.6
1986		661	107	6.5	5.2	11.2	98.5	5.85	113.4	214.5	326.7	9.4
1987	742	754	115	10.5	8.1	15.3	166.8	7.06	170.5	352.8	519.7	17.0
1988		673	121	13.1	9.8	18.8	209.0	7.18	197.1	437.3	626.6	26.2
1989		701	121	11.6	9.2	18.4	192.5	6.69	194.1	419.3	602.7	23.1
1990		762	131	12.2	9.6	18.9	201.0	6.76	183.8	409.1	591.7	16.8
1991		765	127	12.5	9.9	19.8	209.4	6.65	191.6	435.9	626.3	31.9
1992	829	834	121	12.2	9.3	17.5	231.7	7.78	205.2	467.4	669.4	21.9
1993		877	138	12.9	10.1	18.7	229.5	8.34	207.9	512.4	718.0	24.1
1994		828P	135P	13.6	10.9	19.6	242.2	7.77	197.9	514.2	720.0	22.4
1995		843P	138P	13.8P	10.6P	20.2P	258.1P	8.01P	206.5P	536.7P	751.4P	27.4P
1996		858P	141P	14.2P	10.9P	20.7P	270.1P	8.18P	214.6P	557.6P	780.8P	28.6P
1997		872P	144P	14.6P	11.1P	21.2P	282.1P	8.35P	222.7P	578.5P	810.1P	29.8P
1998		887P	146P	15.0P	11.4P	21.7P	294.1P	8.52P	230.7P	599.5P	839.4P	31.0P

Sources: 1982, 1987, 1992 *Economic Census*; *Annual Survey of Manufactures*, 83-86, 88-91, 93-94. Establishment counts for non-Census years are from *County Business Patterns*; establishment values for 83-84 are extrapolations. 'P's show projections by the editors. Industries reclassified in 87 will not have data for prior years.

INDICES OF CHANGE

Year	Com-panies	Establishments		Employment			Compensation		Production ($ million)			
		Total	with 20 or more employees	Total (000)	Production Workers (000)	Production Hours (Mil)	Payroll ($ mil)	Wages ($/hr)	Cost of Materials	Value Added by Manufacture	Value of Shipments	Capital Invest.
1982	82	83	85	83	92	88	53	77	87	54	64	82
1983		83	88	83	91	89	56	79	74	63	66	33
1984		83	90	78	85	89	54	74	81	65	70	48
1985		83	93	58	61	63	47	87	62	49	54	80
1986		79	88	53	56	64	43	75	55	46	49	43
1987	90	90	95	86	87	87	72	91	83	75	78	78
1988		81	100	107	105	107	90	92	96	94	94	120
1989		84	100	95	99	105	83	86	95	90	90	105
1990		91	108	100	103	108	87	87	90	88	88	77
1991		92	105	102	106	113	90	85	93	93	94	146
1992	100	100	100	100	100	100	100	100	100	100	100	100
1993		105	114	106	109	107	99	107	101	110	107	110
1994		99P	112P	111	117	112	105	100	96	110	108	102
1995		101P	114P	113P	114P	115P	111P	103P	101P	115P	112P	125P
1996		103P	117P	116P	117P	118P	117P	105P	105P	119P	117P	131P
1997		105P	119P	120P	120P	121P	122P	107P	109P	124P	121P	136P
1998		106P	121P	123P	123P	124P	127P	110P	112P	128P	125P	142P

Sources: Same as General Statistics. Values reflect change from the base year, 1992. Values above 100 mean greater than 92, values below 100 mean less than 92, and a value of 100 in the 82-91 or 93-98 period means same as 92. 'P's mark projections by the editors.

SELECTED RATIOS

For 1994	Avg. of All Manufact.	Analyzed Industry	Index	For 1994	Avg. of All Manufact.	Analyzed Industry	Index
Employees per Establishment	49	16	34	Value Added per Production Worker	134,084	47,174	35
Payroll per Establishment	1,500,273	292,416	19	Cost per Establishment	5,045,178	238,931	5
Payroll per Employee	30,620	17,809	58	Cost per Employee	102,970	14,551	14
Production Workers per Establishment	34	13	38	Cost per Production Worker	146,988	18,156	12
Wages per Establishment	853,319	183,867	22	Shipments per Establishment	9,576,895	869,279	9
Wages per Production Worker	24,861	13,972	56	Shipments per Employee	195,460	52,941	27
Hours per Production Worker	2,056	1,798	87	Shipments per Production Worker	279,017	66,055	24
Wages per Hour	12.09	7.77	64	Investment per Establishment	321,011	27,044	8
Value Added per Establishment	4,602,255	620,810	13	Investment per Employee	6,552	1,647	25
Value Added per Employee	93,930	37,809	40	Investment per Production Worker	9,352	2,055	22

Sources: Same as General Statistics. The 'Average of All Manufacturing' column represents the average of all manufacturing industries reported for the most recent complete year available. The Index shows the relationship between the Average and the Analyzed Industry. For example, 100 means that they are equal; 500 that the Analyzed Industry is five times the average; 50 means that the Analyzed Industry is half the national average. The abbreviation 'na' is used to show that data are 'not available'.

LEADING COMPANIES

Number shown: **30** Total sales ($ mil): **282** Total employment (000): **3.4**

Company Name	Address				CEO Name	Phone	Co. Type	Sales ($ mil)	Empl. (000)
Duncan Enterprises	PO Box 7827	Fresno	CA	93727	L Duncan	209-291-4444	R	50	0.4
Treasure Craft Co	2320 N Alameda St	Compton	CA	90222	Paul Helgesen	213-636-9777	S	33	0.5
Haeger Industries Inc	7 Maiden Ln	Dundee	IL	60118	AH Estes	708-426-3441	R	26	0.3
Ceradyne Inc	3169 Redhill Av	Costa Mesa	CA	92626	Joel P Moskowitz	714-549-0421	P	18	0.2
Austin Productions Inc	815 Grundy Av	Holbrook	NY	11741	Peter Strugatz	516-981-7300	R	15	0.2
Haeger Potteries	7 Maiden Ln	Dundee	IL	60118	Alexandra H Estes	708-426-3441	D	14	0.2
Vesuvius McDanel Co	PO Box 560	Beaver Falls	PA	15010	Del E Goedeker	412-843-8300	S	13	0.2
Edward Marshall Boehm Inc	25 Fairfacts St	Trenton	NJ	08638	Helen F Boehm	609-392-2207	R	10	0.1
Haeger Potteries of Macomb	7 Maiden Ln	Dundee	IL	60118	A Haeger-Estes	708-426-3441	S	10	0.1
Marshall Pottery	PO Box 1839	Marshall	TX	75671	CH Iles	903-938-9203	R	10	0.2
Willitts Design International Inc	1129 Industrial Av	Petaluma	CA	94952	Joseph E Walswith	707-778-7211	R	9*	<0.1
Ceramo Company Inc	PO Drawer 485	Jackson	MO	63755	V Kasten	314-243-3138	R	9	0.1
Robinson-Ransbottom	Rte 1	Roseville	OH	43777	Peter P Petratsas	614-697-7355	R	9	0.2
ICI Advanced Ceramics Inc	13395 New Airport	Auburn	CA	95603	David Small	916-823-3401	S	7*	0.1
Louisville Stoneware Co	731 Brent St	Louisville	KY	40204	John Robertson	502-582-1900	R	7*	<0.1
Hartstone Inc	PO Box 2626	Zanesville	OH	43702	Patrick Hart	614-452-9000	R	6	<0.1
Art Line Inc	600 N Kilbourn Av	Chicago	IL	60624	Steven Pahos	312-722-8100	R	5	<0.1
Gare Inc	165 Rosemont St	Haverhill	MA	01830	TL Alaimo	508-373-9131	R	5*	<0.1
Metrokane Inc	964 3rd Av	New York	NY	10022	Riki Kane	212-759-6262	R	5	<0.1
Woodmere China Inc	PO Box 5305	New Castle	PA	16105	Alan J Polansky	412-658-1630	R	5	<0.1
FW Ritter Sons Co	12670 N Dixie	S Rockwood	MI	48179	Fred W Ritter	313-379-9622	R	3	<0.1
General Porcelain Mfg Co	951 Pennsylvania	Trenton	NJ	08638	FW Przechacki	609-396-7588	R	3	<0.1
Western Stoneware	PO Box 710	Monmouth	IL	61462	James C Hutchins	309-734-2161	R	3*	0.1
Scio Pottery Associates Inc	PO Box 566	Scio	OH	43988	Chris Reese	614-945-3111	R	2	<0.1
US Pottery Manufacturing Inc	PO Box 167	Paramount	CA	90723	Robert D Diulio	310-630-2982	R	2*	<0.1
Heath Ceramics Inc	400 Gate 5 Rd	Sausalito	CA	94965	Brian Heath	415-332-3732	R	2	<0.1
Van Briggle Art Pottery	PO Box 96	Co Springs	CO	80901	Bertha Stevenson	719-633-7729	R	1	<0.1
Swid Powell Designs Inc	55 W 13th St	New York	NY	10011	Nan Swid	212-633-6699	R	1*	<0.1
Portland Pottery Inc	118 Washington Av	Portland	ME	04101	Chris Bruni	207-772-4334	R	1*	<0.1
Brinker Pots	1521 Minnesota Av	Kansas City	KS	66102	Linda Brinkerhoff	913-371-0250	R	0*	<0.1

Source: *Ward's Business Directory of U.S. Private and Public Companies*, Volumes 1 and 2, 1996. The company type code used is as follows: P - Public, R - Private, S - Subsidiary, D - Division, J - Joint Venture, A - Affiliate, G - Group. Sales are in millions of dollars, employees are in thousands. An asterisk (*) indicates an estimated sales volume. The symbol < stands for 'less than'. Company names and addresses are truncated, in some cases, to fit into the available space.

MATERIALS CONSUMED

Material	Quantity	Delivered Cost ($ million)
Materials, ingredients, containers, and supplies	(X)	155.3
Clay, ceramic, and refractory minerals	(X)	48.7
Paperboard containers, boxes, and corrugated paperboard	(X)	11.8
All other materials and components, parts, containers, and supplies	(X)	59.0
Materials, ingredients, containers, and supplies, nsk	(X)	35.8

Source: 1992 *Economic Census*. Explanation of symbols used: (D): Withheld to avoid disclosure of competitive data; na: Not available; (S): Withheld because statistical norms were not met; (X): Not applicable; (Z): Less than half the unit shown; nec: Not elsewhere classified; nsk: Not specified by kind; - : zero; * : 10-19 percent estimated; ** : 20-29 percent estimated.

PRODUCT SHARE DETAILS

Product or Product Class	% Share
Pottery products, nec	100.00
China and porcelain pottery products (including china decorating for the trade), art, decorative, and novelty pottery ware (including vases, lamp bases, figures)	18.32
Earthenware and stoneware pottery products (including china decorating for the trade)	25.39
Stoneware table and kitchen articles, household and commercial (for serving, cooking, and storing food and drink), pottery products (including china decorating for the trade)	12.84
Other pottery products, nec, chemical, technical, and industrial pottery ware (including chemical stoneware and porcelain, pyrometric tubes, etc.)	17.94
Other pottery products, nec, red unglazed earthenware (flowerpots, etc.)	3.48
All other pottery products, nec, (including pyrometric cones, veritas rings, etc.)	7.96

Source: 1992 *Economic Census*. The values shown are percent of total shipments in an industry. Values of indented subcategories are summed in the main heading. The symbol (D) appears when data are withheld to prevent disclosure of competitive information. The abbreviation nsk stands for 'not specified by kind' and nec for 'not elsewhere classified'.

INPUTS AND OUTPUTS FOR POTTERY PRODUCTS, NEC

Economic Sector or Industry Providing Inputs	%	Sector	Economic Sector or Industry Buying Outputs	%	Sector
Imports	60.5	Foreign	Personal consumption expenditures	77.7	
Motor freight transportation & warehousing	8.7	Util.	Exports	4.1	Foreign
Clay, ceramic, & refractory minerals	6.9	Mining	Hospitals	3.2	Services
Sanitary services, steam supply, irrigation	5.9	Util.	Hotels & lodging places	2.1	Services
Wholesale trade	3.3	Trade	Wholesale trade	1.8	Trade
Chemical preparations, nec	2.5	Manufg.	Greenhouse & nursery products	1.5	Agric.
Gas production & distribution (utilities)	1.9	Util.	Lighting fixtures & equipment	1.2	Manufg.
Electric services (utilities)	1.0	Util.	Mining machinery, except oil field	0.8	Manufg.
Advertising	0.7	Services	Nursing & personal care facilities	0.8	Services
Pottery products, nec	0.6	Manufg.	S/L Govt. purch., public assistance & relief	0.7	S/L Govt
Paperboard containers & boxes	0.5	Manufg.	Glass & glass products, except containers	0.6	Manufg.
Maintenance of nonfarm buildings nec	0.4	Constr.	S/L Govt. purch., other general government	0.6	S/L Govt
Machinery, except electrical, nec	0.4	Manufg.	Retail trade, except eating & drinking	0.5	Trade
Water transportation	0.4	Util.	Real estate	0.5	Fin/R.E.
Eating & drinking places	0.4	Trade	Pottery products, nec	0.4	Manufg.
Real estate	0.4	Fin/R.E.	Change in business inventories	0.4	In House
Noncomparable imports	0.4	Foreign	S/L Govt. purch., health & hospitals	0.4	S/L Govt
Cyclic crudes and organics	0.3	Manufg.	Federal Government purchases, national defense	0.3	Fed Govt
Communications, except radio & TV	0.3	Util.	Commercial printing	0.2	Manufg.
Railroads & related services	0.3	Util.	Drugs	0.2	Manufg.
Banking	0.3	Fin/R.E.	Eating & drinking places	0.2	Trade
Detective & protective services	0.3	Services	Banking	0.2	Fin/R.E.
General industrial machinery, nec	0.2	Manufg.	Credit agencies other than banks	0.2	Fin/R.E.
Industrial inorganic chemicals, nec	0.2	Manufg.	Security & commodity brokers	0.2	Fin/R.E.
Minerals, ground or treated	0.2	Manufg.	Elementary & secondary schools	0.2	Services
Petroleum refining	0.2	Manufg.	Miscellaneous repair shops	0.2	Services
Special dies & tools & machine tool accessories	0.2	Manufg.	S/L Govt. purch., elem. & secondary education	0.2	S/L Govt
Business/professional associations	0.2	Services	Business/professional associations	0.1	Services
Management & consulting services & labs	0.2	Services			
U.S. Postal Service	0.2	Gov't			
Abrasive products	0.1	Manufg.			
Industrial gases	0.1	Manufg.			
Lubricating oils & greases	0.1	Manufg.			
Metal heat treating	0.1	Manufg.			
Metal stampings, nec	0.1	Manufg.			
Royalties	0.1	Fin/R.E.			
Automotive repair shops & services	0.1	Services			
Equipment rental & leasing services	0.1	Services			
Laundry, dry cleaning, shoe repair	0.1	Services			
Legal services	0.1	Services			

Source: Benchmark Input-Output Accounts for the U.S. Economy, 1982, U.S. Department of Commerce, Washington, D.C., July 1991. Data, as reported in the source, are organized by the 1977 SIC structure in use in 1982 but have been matched, as closely as is possible, to the 1987 SIC structure used in this book.

OCCUPATIONS EMPLOYED BY SIC 326 - STONE, CLAY, AND MISC MINING PRODUCTS NEC

Occupation	% of Total 1994	Change to 2005	Occupation	% of Total 1994	Change to 2005
Helpers, laborers, & material movers nec	6.7	-23.3	Machine feeders & offbearers	2.3	-31.4
Assemblers, fabricators, & hand workers nec	6.4	-23.9	Painting, coating, & decorating workers, hand	2.0	52.3
Furnace, kiln, or kettle operators	4.2	-16.7	Freight, stock, & material movers, hand	1.9	-38.8
Crushing & mixing machine operators	3.9	-9.5	Truck drivers light & heavy	1.9	-20.6
Industrial machinery mechanics	3.9	-15.2	Coating, painting, & spraying machine workers	1.8	-23.8
Hand packers & packagers	3.6	-34.7	Secretaries, ex legal & medical	1.8	-30.4
Extruding & forming machine workers	3.4	-80.6	Cutting & slicing machine setters, operators	1.6	-16.2
Sales & related workers nec	3.2	-23.6	Grinders & polishers, hand	1.6	-16.2
Packaging & filling machine operators	3.2	-23.7	Industrial production managers	1.5	-23.5
Precision workers nec	3.0	-8.7	Traffic, shipping, & receiving clerks	1.5	-26.6
Industrial truck & tractor operators	2.8	-23.7	General office clerks	1.5	-34.9
General managers & top executives	2.8	-27.5	Bookkeeping, accounting, & auditing clerks	1.3	-42.7
Inspectors, testers, & graders, precision	2.8	-23.6	Electricians	1.1	-27.3
Maintenance repairers, general utility	2.6	-30.8	Machinists	1.0	-23.6

Source: Industry-Occupation Matrix, Bureau of Labor Statistics. These data relate to one or more 3-digit SIC industry groups rather than to a single 4-digit SIC. The change reported for each occupation to the year 2005 is a percent of growth or decline as estimated by the Bureau of Labor Statistics. The abbreviation nec stands for 'not elsewhere classified'.

LOCATION BY STATE AND REGIONAL CONCENTRATION

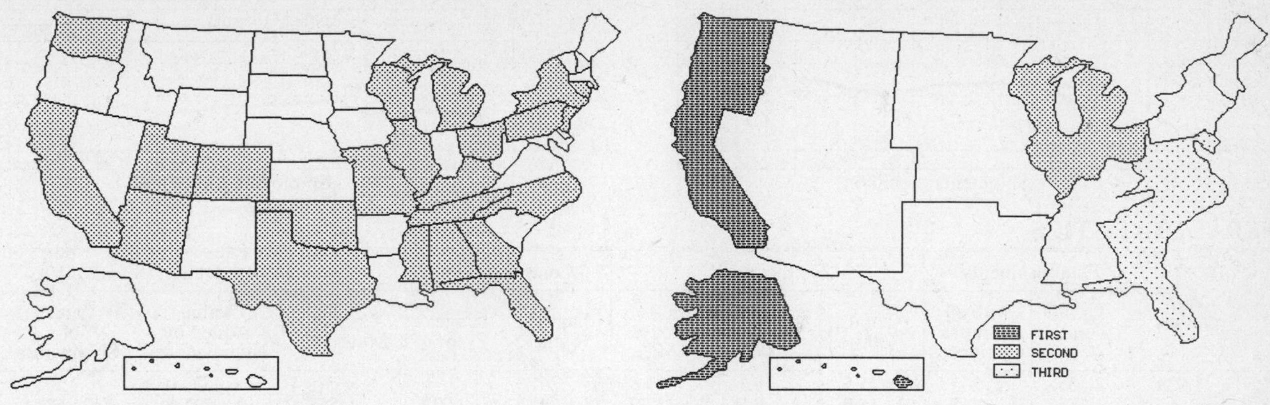

INDUSTRY DATA BY STATE

State	Establish-ments	Shipments			Employment				Cost as % of Shipments	Investment per Employee ($)
		Total ($ mil)	% of U.S.	Per Establ.	Total Number	% of U.S.	Per Establ.	Wages ($/hour)		
California	143	148.0	22.1	1.0	2,800	23.0	20	7.29	36.9	964
Ohio	43	60.3	9.0	1.4	1,200	9.8	28	6.81	21.7	1,667
Pennsylvania	33	39.8	5.9	1.2	700	5.7	21	7.92	22.4	-
Tennessee	26	37.3	5.6	1.4	500	4.1	19	8.00	30.6	1,800
Illinois	19	32.1	4.8	1.7	700	5.7	37	8.80	27.1	714
Kentucky	16	21.5	3.2	1.3	300	2.5	19	7.00	31.6	-
New York	26	19.3	2.9	0.7	300	2.5	12	8.67	30.6	1,333
New Jersey	14	13.7	2.0	1.0	200	1.6	14	8.50	19.0	500
Michigan	14	10.2	1.5	0.7	100	0.8	7	10.00	29.4	-
Florida	43	9.3	1.4	0.2	200	1.6	5	7.50	31.2	1,000
Wisconsin	20	8.0	1.2	0.4	200	1.6	10	12.50	16.3	500
Arizona	35	5.9	0.9	0.2	200	1.6	6	7.50	23.7	500
Alabama	8	3.3	0.5	0.4	100	0.8	13	11.00	42.4	-
Texas	48	(D)	-	-	375 *	3.1	8	-	-	1,333
North Carolina	33	(D)	-	-	375 *	3.1	11	-	-	-
Washington	29	(D)	-	-	175 *	1.4	6	-	-	-
Colorado	20	(D)	-	-	1,750 *	14.3	88	-	-	-
Georgia	12	(D)	-	-	175 *	1.4	15	-	-	571
Utah	10	(D)	-	-	175 *	1.4	18	-	-	-
Missouri	9	(D)	-	-	175 *	1.4	19	-	-	-
Connecticut	5	(D)	-	-	175 *	1.4	35	-	-	-
Mississippi	5	(D)	-	-	375 *	3.1	75	-	-	-
Oklahoma	5	(D)	-	-	750 *	6.1	150	-	-	-

Source: 1992 *Economic Census*. The states are in descending order of shipments or establishments (if shipment data are missing for the majority). The symbol (D) appears when data are withheld to prevent disclosure of competitive information. States marked with (D) are sorted by number of establishments. A dash (-) indicates that the data element cannot be calculated; * indicates the midpoint of a range.

3271 - CONCRETE BLOCK & BRICK

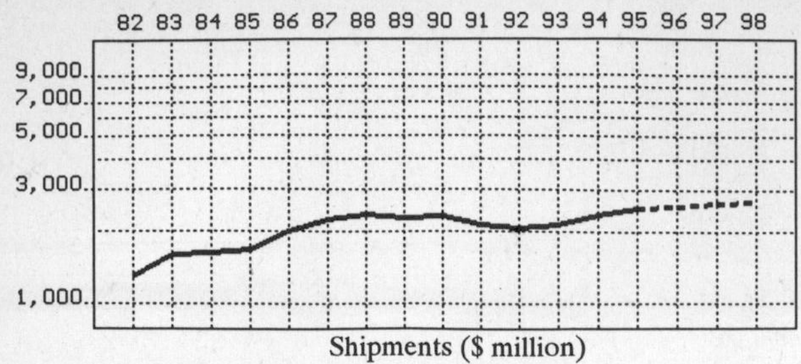

Shipments ($ million)

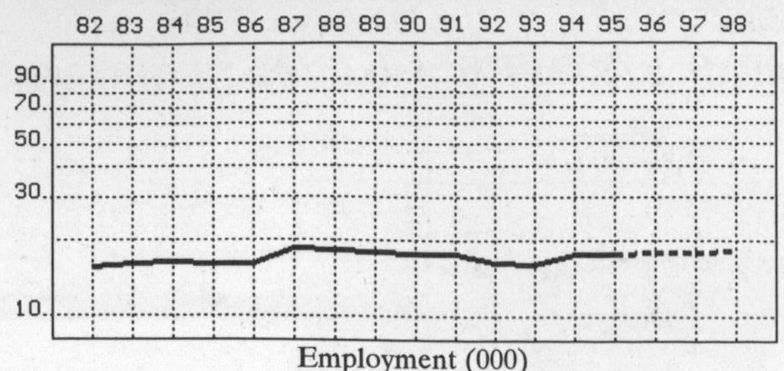

Employment (000)

GENERAL STATISTICS

Year	Com-panies	Establishments		Employment			Compensation		Production ($ million)			
		Total	with 20 or more employees	Total (000)	Production Workers (000)	Production Hours (Mil)	Payroll ($ mil)	Wages ($/hr)	Cost of Materials	Value Added by Manufacture	Value of Shipments	Capital Invest.
1982	1,039	1,155	251	15.5	9.1	17.8	261.9	7.51	718.4	577.8	1,301.8	37.6
1983		1,114	265	15.9	9.5	17.9	282.4	7.92	858.5	731.1	1,581.9	107.9
1984		1,073	279	16.2	9.7	18.9	297.2	7.87	894.5	746.1	1,632.2	56.4
1985		1,031	292	16.0	9.5	18.8	311.0	8.41	936.9	771.9	1,689.7	72.5
1986		1,000	313	16.1	9.4	20.0	337.1	8.65	1,080.1	922.0	1,989.4	70.6
1987	976	1,129	339	18.6	10.8	23.5	411.8	9.20	1,185.6	1,071.7	2,245.8	72.0
1988		1,043	322	18.3	10.4	22.9	433.2	9.71	1,207.3	1,125.3	2,338.8	39.5
1989		998	316	18.0	10.4	22.2	432.0	9.51	1,194.5	1,087.9	2,282.1	75.1
1990		977	309	17.8	10.5	22.0	438.9	9.73	1,162.5	1,134.3	2,304.0	65.9
1991		948	265	17.8	9.9	22.4	461.8	10.07	1,072.6	1,064.2	2,143.8	48.8
1992	887	1,071	290	16.4	9.2	20.3	429.9	10.27	1,025.1	1,030.8	2,051.1	57.3
1993		963	276	16.0	9.1	19.7	411.3	10.47	1,104.5	1,019.4	2,125.2	50.5
1994		957P	304P	17.6	10.0	21.8	471.5	10.93	1,225.0	1,137.4	2,350.2	74.9
1995		944P	306P	17.8P	10.0P	22.6P	502.7P	11.19P	1,298.7P	1,205.8P	2,491.6P	58.5P
1996		931P	307P	17.9P	10.0P	22.9P	519.7P	11.46P	1,335.1P	1,239.6P	2,561.5P	57.7P
1997		918P	309P	18.0P	10.0P	23.2P	536.8P	11.74P	1,371.5P	1,273.4P	2,631.3P	57.0P
1998		905P	311P	18.2P	10.0P	23.5P	553.9P	12.01P	1,407.9P	1,307.2P	2,701.1P	56.2P

Sources: 1982, 1987, 1992 *Economic Census*; *Annual Survey of Manufactures*, 83-86, 88-91, 93-94. Establishment counts for non-Census years are from *County Business Patterns*; establishment values for 83-84 are extrapolations. 'P's show projections by the editors. Industries reclassified in 87 will not have data for prior years.

INDICES OF CHANGE

Year	Com-panies	Establishments		Employment			Compensation		Production ($ million)			
		Total	with 20 or more employees	Total (000)	Production Workers (000)	Production Hours (Mil)	Payroll ($ mil)	Wages ($/hr)	Cost of Materials	Value Added by Manufacture	Value of Shipments	Capital Invest.
1982	117	108	87	95	99	88	61	73	70	56	63	66
1983		104	91	97	103	88	66	77	84	71	77	188
1984		100	96	99	105	93	69	77	87	72	80	98
1985		96	101	98	103	93	72	82	91	75	82	127
1986		93	108	98	102	99	78	84	105	89	97	123
1987	110	105	117	113	117	116	96	90	116	104	109	126
1988		97	111	112	113	113	101	95	118	109	114	69
1989		93	109	110	113	109	100	93	117	106	111	131
1990		91	107	109	114	108	102	95	113	110	112	115
1991		89	91	109	108	110	107	98	105	103	105	85
1992	100	100	100	100	100	100	100	100	100	100	100	100
1993		90	95	98	99	97	96	102	108	99	104	88
1994		89P	105P	107	109	107	110	106	120	110	115	131
1995		88P	105P	108P	108P	112P	117P	109P	127P	117P	121P	102P
1996		87P	106P	109P	109P	113P	121P	112P	130P	120P	125P	101P
1997		86P	107P	110P	109P	114P	125P	114P	134P	124P	128P	99P
1998		84P	107P	111P	109P	116P	129P	117P	137P	127P	132P	98P

Sources: Same as General Statistics. Values reflect change from the base year, 1992. Values above 100 mean greater than 92, values below 100 mean less than 92, and a value of 100 in the 82-91 or 93-98 period means same as 92. 'P's mark projections by the editors.

SELECTED RATIOS

For 1994	Avg. of All Manufact.	Analyzed Industry	Index	For 1994	Avg. of All Manufact.	Analyzed Industry	Index
Employees per Establishment	49	18	38	Value Added per Production Worker	134,084	113,740	85
Payroll per Establishment	1,500,273	492,724	33	Cost per Establishment	5,045,178	1,280,143	25
Payroll per Employee	30,620	26,790	87	Cost per Employee	102,970	69,602	68
Production Workers per Establishment	34	10	30	Cost per Production Worker	146,988	122,500	83
Wages per Establishment	853,319	249,000	29	Shipments per Establishment	9,576,895	2,455,994	26
Wages per Production Worker	24,861	23,827	96	Shipments per Employee	195,460	133,534	68
Hours per Production Worker	2,056	2,180	106	Shipments per Production Worker	279,017	235,020	84
Wages per Hour	12.09	10.93	90	Investment per Establishment	321,011	78,272	24
Value Added per Establishment	4,602,255	1,188,600	26	Investment per Employee	6,552	4,256	65
Value Added per Employee	93,930	64,625	69	Investment per Production Worker	9,352	7,490	80

Sources: Same as General Statistics. The 'Average of All Manufacturing' column represents the average of all manufacturing industries reported for the most recent complete year available. The Index shows the relationship between the Average and the Analyzed Industry. For example, 100 means that they are equal; 500 that the Analyzed Industry is five times the average; 50 means that the Analyzed Industry is half the national average. The abbreviation 'na' is used to show that data are 'not available'.

LEADING COMPANIES Number shown: **75** Total sales ($ mil): **788** Total employment (000): **6.7**

Company Name	Address				CEO Name	Phone	Co. Type	Sales ($ mil)	Empl. (000)
Glen-Gery Corp	PO Box 7001	Wyomissing	PA	19610	Philip Mengel	215-374-4011	S	150	1.4
Featherlite Building Prod Corp	PO Box 1029	Austin	TX	78767	HV Moss	512-472-2424	S	45	0.4
Chaney Enterprises LP	PO Box 548	Waldorf	MD	20604	Francis H Chaney II	301-843-6101	R	40	0.4
Clayton Block Co	PO Box 3015	Lakewood	NJ	08701	William Clayton Sr	908-363-1800	R	21	0.2
Orco Block Company Inc	PO Box E	Stanton	CA	90680	Rick Muth	714-527-2239	R	21	0.2
Anchor Block and Concrete Co	2300 McKnight Rd	North St Paul	MN	55109	Glenn Bolles	612-777-8321	R	20	0.2
RCP Block and Brick Inc	PO Box 579	Lemon Grove	CA	91946	Marvin H Finch	619-460-7250	R	19	0.2
Betco Block and Products Inc	7920 Notes Dr	Manassas	VA	22110	Peter Hoyt	703-591-2770	R	17*	0.2
Terre Hill Concrete Products	PO Box 10	Terre Hill	PA	17581	Robert Lazarchick	215-445-6736	R	17	0.2
Theut Products Inc	73408 Van Dyke St	Romeo	MI	48065	EC Theut	810-752-4541	R	16	<0.1
Aman Brothers Inc	PO Box 4233	Covina	CA	91723	Rhonda Gnecco	818-966-8471	R	15*	0.1
Fankhauser Inc	PO Box 579	Garden City	KS	67846	Dick Fankhauser	316-276-8294	R	15	<0.1
Lee Masonry Products Inc	PO Box 646	Hopkinsville	KY	42240	Carol T Lee	502-886-6696	R	15	0.1
Higgins Brick Co	PO Box 7000-167	Redondo Beach	CA	90277	R Higgins	310-540-1126	R	14	<0.1
RI Lampus Co	816 RR Lampus	Springdale	PA	15144	DL Lampus	412-274-5035	R	14	<0.1
Shiely Masonry Products	2915 Waters Rd	Eagan	MN	55121	Pat Groff	612-686-7100	D	14	<0.1
Western Materials Inc	PO Box 430	Yakima	WA	98907	Stan Martinkus	509-575-3000	R	14	<0.1
Cranesville Block Company Inc	774 State Hwy 5S	Amsterdam	NY	12010	John A Tesiero Jr	518-887-5560	R	13	0.1
Basalite	355 Greg St	Sparks	NV	89431	Gordon Hinkel	702-358-1200	D	12	0.1
EP Henry Corp	PO Box 615	Woodbury	NJ	08096	JC Henry Jr	609-845-6200	R	12	0.1
Carolina Quality Block Co	PO Box 16026	Greensboro	NC	27416	D L Cockerham	910-272-0119	S	11*	<0.1
Trenwyth Industries Inc	PO Box 438	Emigsville	PA	17318	AC Kingston	717-767-6868	R	11	0.1
Binkley and Ober Inc	PO Box 7	E Petersburg	PA	17520	Donald Emich	717-569-0441	R	10	<0.1
Crego Block Co	PO Box 6466	Albuquerque	NM	87197	Rob Lewis	505-345-4451	R	9*	<0.1
North Florida Concrete Inc	PO Box 1388	Lake City	FL	32055	Ernest A Rose	904-752-5161	R	9*	<0.1
Beavertown Block Company Inc	PO Box 337	Middleburg	PA	17842	David L Kline	717-837-1744	R	8	<0.1
A Duchini Inc	PO Box 10005	Erie	PA	16514	James A Duchini	814-456-7027	R	8	<0.1
Ernest Maier Inc	4700 Annapolis Rd	Bladensburg	MD	20710	Alvin Maier	301-927-8300	R	8	<0.1
Illinois Concrete Company Inc	PO Box 3096	Champaign	IL	61826	Lee W Johnston	217-352-4181	R	8	<0.1
Layrite Products Co	PO Box 2585	Spokane	WA	99220	Robert Bakie	509-535-1737	R	8	<0.1
Superior Block and Supply Co	1403 Meriden	Milldale	CT	06467	Ralph Crispino Jr	203-239-4216	R	8*	<0.1
Grand Blanc Cement Products	PO Box 585	Grand Blanc	MI	48439	Norman A Nelson	810-694-7500	R	8	<0.1
Nattinger Materials Co	PO Box 4007	Springfield	MO	65808	CW Nattinger	417-869-2595	R	8	<0.1
Cinder and Concrete Block Corp	PO Box 9	Cockeysville	MD	21030	Frank W Keeney Jr	410-666-2350	R	7	<0.1
Cumberland Concrete Corp	PO Box 3369	Lavale	MD	21504	Fred Baker	301-724-2000	R	7*	<0.1
King's Material Inc	650 12th Av SW	Cedar Rapids	IA	52405	Charles A Rohde	319-363-0233	R	7	0.1
Willamette Graystone Inc	PO Box 7816	Eugene	OR	97401	DW Jones	503-726-7666	R	7*	<0.1
Mathis-Akins Concrete Block	PO Box 45	Macon	GA	31202	Donald C Sheffield	912-746-5154	R	6	<0.1
Waukesha Block Co	10919 Bluem	Milwaukee	WI	53226	Robert H Nagy	414-453-7980	S	6	0.1
Westbrook Concrete Block	PO Drawer J	Westbrook	CT	06498	PJ Orsina	203-399-6201	R	6	<0.1
Best's Blocks Inc	4751 Power Inn Rd	Sacramento	CA	95826	F Roodenburg	916-452-5233	R	5*	<0.1
Cement Products and Supply	PO Box 12	Lakeland	FL	33802	C Zimmerman	813-686-5141	R	5	<0.1
Chandler Materials Co	5805 E 15th St	Tulsa	OK	74112	Jim M Chandler	918-836-9151	R	5	<0.1
Domine Builders Supply Inc	PO Box 10310	Rochester	NY	14610	Lawrence W Green	716-271-6330	R	5	<0.1
E DeVecchis and Sons Inc	11 N Depot St	Mount Union	PA	17066	Arthur P DeVecchis	814-542-2549	R	5	<0.1
E-Quality Concrete Inc	9304 D'Arcy Rd	U Marlboro	MD	20772	DH Bowling	301-336-6400	R	5*	<0.1
Flower City Builders Supply	1275 Mount Read	Rochester	NY	14606	Andrew Colaruotolo	716-254-8100	R	5*	<0.1
Greensburg Concrete Block Co	PO Box 729	Greensburg	PA	15601	Joseph Repasky	412-834-5210	R	5*	<0.1
L Thorn Company Inc	PO Box 198	New Albany	IN	47150	MS Ludden	812-246-4461	R	5	<0.1
Salina Concrete Products Inc	PO Box 136	Salina	KS	67402	Flavel Simcox	913-827-7281	R	5	<0.1
Bristol Concrete Products Corp	PO Box 517	Bristol	VA	24201	FW Hayter	703-669-7112	S	4	<0.1
Clalite Concrete Products Inc	5050 Race St	Denver	CO	80216	Ryan Clark	303-292-2345	S	4	<0.1
Flittie, Marshall Concrete Prod	2610 Marshall NE	Minneapolis	MN	55418	John H Miller	612-789-4303	R	4*	<0.1
Marble Cliff	4033 Alum Creek	Columbus	OH	43207	Richard Roberts	614-491-7643	S	4	<0.1
San Joaquin Blocklite Inc	PO Box AE	Selma	CA	93662	WA Grindle	209-896-0753	R	4	<0.1
Concrete Products Co	39 Folly Rd	Charleston	SC	29407	FW Stevenson Jr	803-556-7234	R	4	<0.1
Fairview Block and Supply Corp	68 Violet Av	Poughkeepsie	NY	12601	Arthur Ackert	914-452-0210	R	4*	<0.1
C and S Block Inc	PO Box 1605	Dalton	GA	30722	Stephen T Swift	706-278-5123	R	3	<0.1
Cook Block and Brick Co	PO Box 2513	Anderson	IN	46018	Virgil E Cook	317-644-4464	R	3	<0.1
Darnall Concrete Products Co	705 Pine St	Normal	IL	61761	R Leman	309-452-4469	R	3	<0.1
Federal Block Corp	129 Walsh Av	New Windsor	NY	12553	John Montfort	914-561-4108	R	3	<0.1
Ferguson Block Co	10052 E Coldwater	Davison	MI	48423	Lilian Deal	810-653-2812	R	3*	<0.1
Gomoljak Block	1841 McGuckian St	Annapolis	MD	21401	Kurt Pfaff	410-263-6744	D	3	<0.1
Greystone Concrete Products	PO Box 680	Henderson	NC	27536	John F Cannady III	919-438-5144	R	3	<0.1
Zenith Products Co	PO Box 35	Osseo	MN	55369	T M Dougherty	612-425-4111	R	3*	<0.1
Balcon Inc	PO Box 3388	Crofton	MD	21114	Christopher C Ross	410-721-1900	S	3*	<0.1
Anchor Concrete Products	975 Burnt Tavern	Brick	NJ	08724	M O'Neill	908-458-9440	R	3	<0.1
Calstone Company Inc	PO Box 70960	Sunnyvale	CA	94086	Tom J Morey	408-984-8800	R	3	<0.1
Atlas Concrete Products Co	2500 Peerless Mine	Springfield	IL	62702	C William Bennett	217-528-7368	R	3	<0.1
Capitol Concrete Products Co	PO Box 8159	Topeka	KS	66608	Ray A Browning	913-233-3271	R	3	<0.1
Phelps Cement Products Inc	PO Box 40	Phelps	NY	14532	Phillip Haers	315-548-2221	R	3	<0.1
Sesser Concrete Products Co	PO Box 100	Sesser	IL	62884	Juanita Cook	618-625-2811	R	3	<0.1
Superior Concrete Block Co	401 McKinzie St	Mankato	MN	56001	Paul Bailey	507-387-7068	R	2	<0.1
Bomanite Corp	232 S Schnoor Av	Madera	CA	93637	L Russell Ingersoll	209-673-2411	R	2*	<0.1
Fankhauser Inc	PO Box 579	Garden City	KS	67846	Dick Fankhauser	316-276-8294	D	2	<0.1

Source: *Ward's Business Directory of U.S. Private and Public Companies*, Volumes 1 and 2, 1996. The company type code used is as follows: P - Public, R - Private, S - Subsidiary, D - Division, J - Joint Venture, A - Affiliate, G - Group. Sales are in millions of dollars, employees are in thousands. An asterisk (*) indicates an estimated sales volume. The symbol < stands for 'less than'. Company names and addresses are truncated, in some cases, to fit into the available space.

MATERIALS CONSUMED

Material	Quantity	Delivered Cost ($ million)
Materials, ingredients, containers, and supplies	(X)	634.9
Portland cement	(X)	137.3
Ready-mixed concrete	(X)	5.1
Other stone, clay, glass, and concrete products	(X)	36.1
Crushed and broken stone (including cement rock, limestone, etc.)	(X)	34.6
Sand and gravel	(X)	78.1
Other mining and quarrying of nonmetallic minerals, except fuels	(X)	20.1
Steel wire strand and bars or rods, high strength, stress relieved	(X)	0.8
Welded steel wire concrete reinforcing mesh	(X)	1.0
Steel concrete reinforcing bars	(X)	1.6
Other steel shapes and forms (except castings, forgings, and fabricated metal products)	(X)	0.6
Nonferrous shapes and forms (except castings, forgings, and fabricated metal products)	(X)	1.3
All other materials and components, parts, containers, and supplies	(X)	109.9
Materials, ingredients, containers, and supplies, nsk	(X)	208.3

Source: 1992 *Economic Census*. Explanation of symbols used: (D): Withheld to avoid disclosure of competitive data; na: Not available; (S): Withheld because statistical norms were not met; (X): Not applicable; (Z): Less than half the unit shown; nec: Not elsewhere classified; nsk: Not specified by kind; - : zero; * : 10-19 percent estimated; ** : 20-29 percent estimated.

PRODUCT SHARE DETAILS

Product or Product Class	% Share	Product or Product Class	% Share
Concrete block and brick	100.00	Structural block, normal weight units (units made with concrete weighing at least 125 lb per cubic foot) (dry weight)	29.06
Structural block, lightweight units (units made with concrete weighing less than 105 lb per cubic foot) (dry weight)	29.02	Decorative block (such as screen block, split block, slump block, shadowal block, etc.)	7.68
Structural block, mediumweight units (units made with concrete weighing at least 105 lb but less than 125 lb per cubic foot) (dry weight)	8.91	Concrete pavers (including grid, interlocking, etc.)	6.27
		Concrete brick	3.16

Source: 1992 *Economic Census*. The values shown are percent of total shipments in an industry. Values of indented subcategories are summed in the main heading. The symbol (D) appears when data are withheld to prevent disclosure of competitive information. The abbreviation nsk stands for 'not specified by kind' and nec for 'not elsewhere classified'.

INPUTS AND OUTPUTS FOR CONCRETE BLOCK & BRICK

Economic Sector or Industry Providing Inputs	%	Sector	Economic Sector or Industry Buying Outputs	%	Sector
Cement, hydraulic	26.4	Manufg.	Residential 1-unit structures, nonfarm	15.6	Constr.
Motor freight transportation & warehousing	11.5	Util.	Office buildings	12.8	Constr.
Sand & gravel	11.1	Mining	Industrial buildings	7.7	Constr.
Dimension, crushed & broken stone	9.5	Mining	Construction of stores & restaurants	6.9	Constr.
Advertising	3.8	Services	Maintenance of nonfarm buildings nec	6.8	Constr.
Petroleum refining	3.3	Manufg.	Construction of hospitals	4.5	Constr.
Electric services (utilities)	3.0	Util.	Construction of educational buildings	4.1	Constr.
Wholesale trade	2.8	Trade	Residential additions/alterations, nonfarm	3.9	Constr.
Railroads & related services	2.6	Util.	Nonfarm residential structure maintenance	3.6	Constr.
Banking	2.5	Fin/R.E.	Residential garden apartments	3.5	Constr.
Gas production & distribution (utilities)	2.3	Util.	Hotels & motels	2.8	Constr.
Concrete block & brick	1.9	Manufg.	Construction of religious buildings	2.6	Constr.
Maintenance of nonfarm buildings nec	1.7	Constr.	Construction of nonfarm buildings nec	2.2	Constr.
Minerals, ground or treated	1.3	Manufg.	Electric utility facility construction	2.2	Constr.
Computer & data processing services	1.3	Services	Sewer system facility construction	1.8	Constr.
Communications, except radio & TV	1.1	Util.	Residential 2-4 unit structures, nonfarm	1.7	Constr.
Small arms ammunition	0.9	Manufg.	Warehouses	1.6	Constr.
Water transportation	0.9	Util.	Water supply facility construction	1.6	Constr.
Eating & drinking places	0.9	Trade	Telephone & telegraph facility construction	1.5	Constr.
Paints & allied products	0.7	Manufg.	Dormitories & other group housing	1.0	Constr.
Photographic equipment & supplies	0.6	Manufg.	Maintenance of farm service facilities	1.0	Constr.
Clay, ceramic, & refractory minerals	0.5	Mining	Residential high-rise apartments	1.0	Constr.
Blast furnaces & steel mills	0.5	Manufg.	Concrete block & brick	1.0	Manufg.
Miscellaneous fabricated wire products	0.5	Manufg.	Resid. & other health facility construction	0.9	Constr.
Sawmills & planning mills, general	0.5	Manufg.	Amusement & recreation building construction	0.8	Constr.
U.S. Postal Service	0.5	Gov't	Construction of conservation facilities	0.7	Constr.
Ready-mixed concrete	0.4	Manufg.	Local transit facility construction	0.7	Constr.
Real estate	0.4	Fin/R.E.	Maintenance of electric utility facilities	0.6	Constr.
Management & consulting services & labs	0.4	Services	Coal	0.4	Mining
Surface active agents	0.3	Manufg.	Farm housing units & additions & alterations	0.4	Constr.
Sanitary services, steam supply, irrigation	0.3	Util.	Maintenance of nonbuilding facilities nec	0.4	Constr.
Accounting, auditing & bookkeeping	0.3	Services	Maintenance of railroads	0.4	Constr.
Automotive rental & leasing, without drivers	0.3	Services	Construction of dams & reservoirs	0.3	Constr.
Electrical repair shops	0.3	Services	Farm service facilities	0.3	Constr.
Engineering, architectural, & surveying services	0.3	Services	Garage & service station construction	0.3	Constr.
Equipment rental & leasing services	0.3	Services	Maintenance of farm residential buildings	0.3	Constr.
Legal services	0.3	Services	Maintenance of sewer facilities	0.3	Constr.

Continued on next page.

INPUTS AND OUTPUTS FOR CONCRETE BLOCK & BRICK - Continued

Economic Sector or Industry Providing Inputs	%	Sector	Economic Sector or Industry Buying Outputs	%	Sector
Coal	0.2	Mining	Maintenance of telephone & telegraph facilities	0.3	Constr.
Lubricating oils & greases	0.2	Manufg.	Maintenance of water supply facilities	0.3	Constr.
Air transportation	0.2	Util.	Nonbuilding facilities nec	0.3	Constr.
Retail trade, except eating & drinking	0.2	Trade	Gas utility facility construction	0.2	Constr.
Insurance carriers	0.2	Fin/R.E.	Exports	0.2	Foreign
Automotive repair shops & services	0.2	Services	Maintenance of gas utility facilities	0.1	Constr.
Business/professional associations	0.2	Services	Maintenance of military facilities	0.1	Constr.
Glass & glass products, except containers	0.1	Manufg.	Maintenance, conservation & development facilities	0.1	Constr.
Machinery, except electrical, nec	0.1	Manufg.			
Manifold business forms	0.1	Manufg.			
Security & commodity brokers	0.1	Fin/R.E.			
Laundry, dry cleaning, shoe repair	0.1	Services			
Miscellaneous repair shops	0.1	Services			
Personnel supply services	0.1	Services			
Imports	0.1	Foreign			

Source: Benchmark Input-Output Accounts for the U.S. Economy, 1982, U.S. Department of Commerce, Washington, D.C., July 1991. Data, as reported in the source, are organized by the 1977 SIC structure in use in 1982 but have been matched, as closely as is possible, to the 1987 SIC structure used in this book.

OCCUPATIONS EMPLOYED BY SIC 327 - CONCRETE, GYPSUM, AND PLASTER PRODUCTS

Occupation	% of Total 1994	Change to 2005	Occupation	% of Total 1994	Change to 2005
Truck drivers light & heavy	31.4	-10.5	Concrete & terrazzo finishers	2.2	-13.2
Helpers, laborers, & material movers nec	4.6	-13.2	Crushing & mixing machine operators	2.1	-13.2
General managers & top executives	4.3	-17.6	General office clerks	1.8	-26.0
Blue collar worker supervisors	4.2	-19.9	Helpers, construction trades	1.8	-13.2
Sales & related workers nec	3.2	-13.2	Industrial machinery mechanics	1.7	-4.5
Bookkeeping, accounting, & auditing clerks	2.5	-34.9	Industrial production managers	1.5	-13.1
Industrial truck & tractor operators	2.5	-13.2	Secretaries, ex legal & medical	1.4	-20.9
Bus & truck mechanics & diesel engine specialists	2.4	-13.2	Maintenance repairers, general utility	1.4	-21.9
Dispatchers, ex police, fire, & ambulance	2.4	-13.2	Welders & cutters	1.3	-13.1
Extruding & forming machine workers	2.3	21.6	Freight, stock, & material movers, hand	1.2	-30.5
Assemblers, fabricators, & hand workers nec	2.2	-13.2	Machine feeders & offbearers	1.1	-21.9
Precision workers nec	2.2	4.2			

Source: Industry-Occupation Matrix, Bureau of Labor Statistics. These data relate to one or more 3-digit SIC industry groups rather than to a single 4-digit SIC. The change reported for each occupation to the year 2005 is a percent of growth or decline as estimated by the Bureau of Labor Statistics. The abbreviation nec stands for 'not elsewhere classified'.

LOCATION BY STATE AND REGIONAL CONCENTRATION

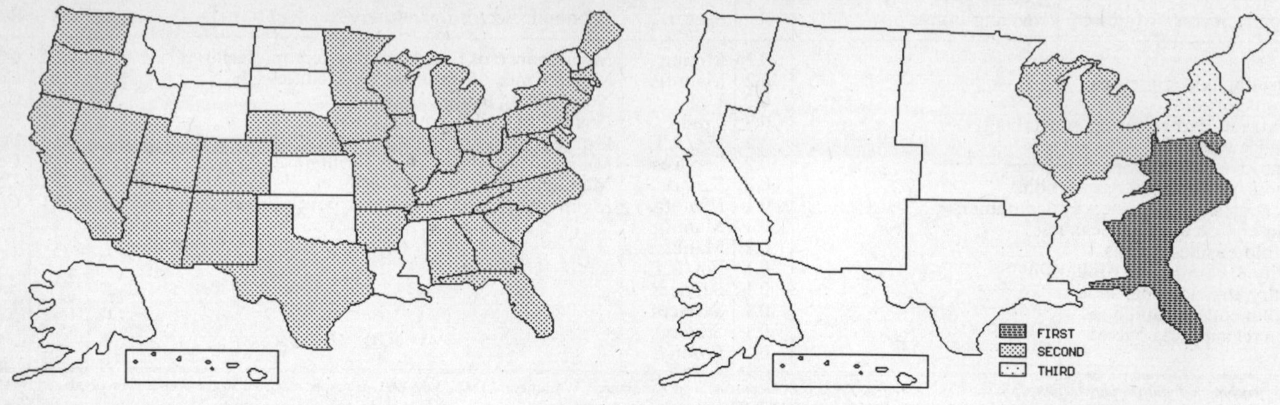

INDUSTRY DATA BY STATE

State	Establish-ments	Shipments			Employment				Cost as % of Shipments	Investment per Employee ($)
		Total ($ mil)	% of U.S.	Per Establ.	Total Number	% of U.S.	Per Establ.	Wages ($/hour)		
Pennsylvania	91	173.3	8.4	1.9	1,500	9.1	16	9.90	46.0	2,667
Ohio	49	102.1	5.0	2.1	700	4.3	14	11.50	52.9	-
Texas	44	96.9	4.7	2.2	800	4.9	18	8.50	55.2	3,125
Michigan	56	94.0	4.6	1.7	800	4.9	14	10.14	49.9	-
Minnesota	34	78.4	3.8	2.3	500	3.0	15	13.00	42.0	4,200
Virginia	32	72.3	3.5	2.3	500	3.0	16	9.43	54.5	-
North Carolina	37	72.1	3.5	1.9	600	3.7	16	9.29	68.5	-
Wisconsin	26	65.4	3.2	2.5	400	2.4	15	10.50	47.9	6,500
Illinois	33	62.0	3.0	1.9	500	3.0	15	10.71	48.2	2,200
Georgia	28	45.5	2.2	1.6	400	2.4	14	7.83	47.9	1,500
Oregon	12	24.4	1.2	2.0	100	0.6	8	10.00	50.0	4,000
Washington	11	24.3	1.2	2.2	200	1.2	18	13.50	40.3	-
West Virginia	16	22.4	1.1	1.4	200	1.2	13	7.00	54.0	2,500
Utah	9	21.4	1.0	2.4	200	1.2	22	9.67	65.0	-
Colorado	12	19.5	1.0	1.6	200	1.2	17	10.00	46.2	-
Arkansas	17	15.3	0.7	0.9	200	1.2	12	7.00	47.7	1,500
Maine	6	14.2	0.7	2.4	100	0.6	17	11.00	53.5	-
California	74	(D)	-	-	1,750 *	10.7	24	-	-	-
Florida	71	(D)	-	-	750 *	4.6	11	-	-	-
New York	58	(D)	-	-	750 *	4.6	13	-	-	-
Tennessee	38	(D)	-	-	750 *	4.6	20	-	-	-
New Jersey	28	(D)	-	-	750 *	4.6	27	-	-	2,133
Arizona	27	(D)	-	-	375 *	2.3	14	-	-	7,200
Indiana	26	(D)	-	-	750 *	4.6	29	-	-	-
Alabama	23	(D)	-	-	375 *	2.3	16	-	-	3,200
Kentucky	23	(D)	-	-	375 *	2.3	16	-	-	6,400
Massachusetts	23	(D)	-	-	175 *	1.1	8	-	-	-
Missouri	20	(D)	-	-	375 *	2.3	19	-	-	-
Maryland	19	(D)	-	-	375 *	2.3	20	-	-	-
South Carolina	16	(D)	-	-	375 *	2.3	23	-	-	-
Iowa	14	(D)	-	-	175 *	1.1	13	-	-	4,000
Connecticut	11	(D)	-	-	175 *	1.1	16	-	-	-
New Mexico	8	(D)	-	-	175 *	1.1	22	-	-	-
Nebraska	6	(D)	-	-	175 *	1.1	29	-	-	-
Nevada	6	(D)	-	-	175 *	1.1	29	-	-	5,143

Source: 1992 *Economic Census*. The states are in descending order of shipments or establishments (if shipment data are missing for the majority). The symbol (D) appears when data are withheld to prevent disclosure of competitive information. States marked with (D) are sorted by number of establishments. A dash (-) indicates that the data element cannot be calculated; * indicates the midpoint of a range.

3272 - CONCRETE PRODUCTS, NEC

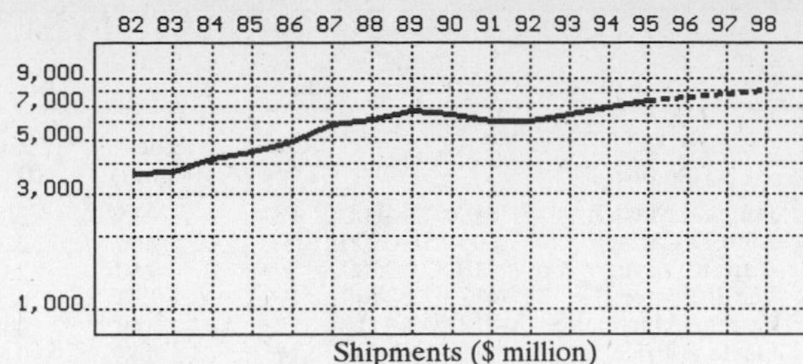

Shipments ($ million)

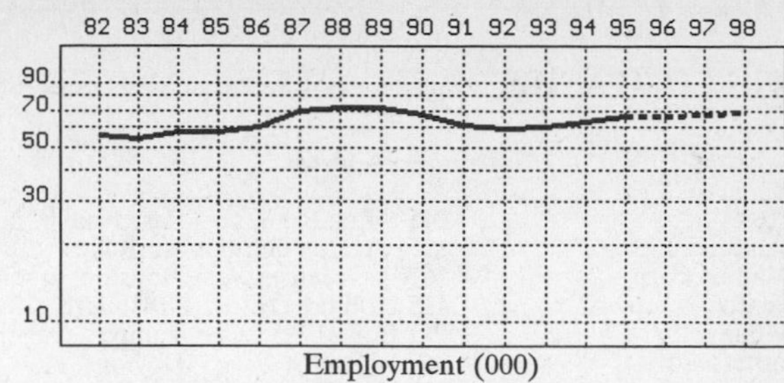

Employment (000)

GENERAL STATISTICS

Year	Companies	Establishments: Total	Establishments: with 20 or more employees	Employment: Total (000)	Employment: Production Workers (000)	Employment: Production Hours (Mil)	Compensation: Payroll ($ mil)	Compensation: Wages ($/hr)	Production ($ million): Cost of Materials	Production ($ million): Value Added by Manufacture	Production ($ million): Value of Shipments	Production ($ million): Capital Invest.
1982	2,749	3,173	730	55.7	42.5	84.8	961.7	7.66	1,627.7	2,006.4	3,649.2	127.7
1983		3,115	775	54.2	41.3	83.8	960.0	7.61	1,666.9	2,099.9	3,719.2	112.9
1984		3,057	820	57.4	43.2	87.9	1,061.1	8.02	1,991.4	2,276.8	4,194.2	145.1
1985		2,999	866	57.4	43.9	89.9	1,109.6	8.40	1,990.5	2,540.7	4,509.8	212.2
1986		2,977	890	59.7	46.1	93.9	1,181.3	8.51	2,227.6	2,736.7	4,931.2	137.4
1987	2,687	3,154	922	70.0	53.1	112.7	1,467.2	8.81	2,540.9	3,313.1	5,828.4	194.1
1988		3,046	923	71.5	53.4	115.0	1,550.3	9.12	2,736.1	3,453.3	6,144.8	131.5
1989		2,984	943	71.3	54.9	114.1	1,572.9	9.23	2,921.4	3,687.7	6,554.6	260.3
1990		2,991	950	67.6	51.5	107.6	1,524.4	9.47	2,876.1	3,504.2	6,366.5	219.9
1991		3,029	872	61.0	45.0	95.4	1,406.8	9.58	2,676.7	3,226.5	5,917.1	153.4
1992	2,606	3,113	888	58.9	42.7	90.9	1,513.3	10.43	2,581.7	3,353.5	5,934.2	171.9
1993		3,083	888	59.9	44.2	93.8	1,569.4	10.76	2,780.7	3,625.8	6,389.0	164.2
1994		3,030P	956P	62.7	44.9	95.8	1,631.6	10.50	3,007.7	3,785.1	6,784.3	196.4
1995		3,025P	969P	66.1P	48.3P	104.0P	1,753.0P	10.94P	3,219.0P	4,051.0P	7,260.9P	203.3P
1996		3,021P	982P	66.7P	48.6P	105.0P	1,811.0P	11.21P	3,333.3P	4,194.9P	7,518.8P	207.8P
1997		3,016P	995P	67.3P	48.8P	105.9P	1,869.0P	11.47P	3,447.7P	4,338.8P	7,776.7P	212.4P
1998		3,011P	1,008P	67.8P	49.0P	106.9P	1,927.0P	11.74P	3,562.0P	4,482.7P	8,034.6P	217.0P

Sources: 1982, 1987, 1992 *Economic Census*; *Annual Survey of Manufactures*, 83-86, 88-91, 93-94. Establishment counts for non-Census years are from *County Business Patterns*; establishment values for 83-84 are extrapolations. 'P's show projections by the editors. Industries reclassified in 87 will not have data for prior years.

INDICES OF CHANGE

Year	Companies	Establishments: Total	Establishments: with 20 or more employees	Employment: Total (000)	Employment: Production Workers (000)	Employment: Production Hours (Mil)	Compensation: Payroll ($ mil)	Compensation: Wages ($/hr)	Production ($ million): Cost of Materials	Production ($ million): Value Added by Manufacture	Production ($ million): Value of Shipments	Production ($ million): Capital Invest.
1982	105	102	82	95	100	93	64	73	63	60	61	74
1983		100	87	92	97	92	63	73	65	63	63	66
1984		98	92	97	101	97	70	77	77	68	71	84
1985		96	98	97	103	99	73	81	77	76	76	123
1986		96	100	101	108	103	78	82	86	82	83	80
1987	103	101	104	119	124	124	97	84	98	99	98	113
1988		98	104	121	125	127	102	87	106	103	104	76
1989		96	106	121	129	126	104	88	113	110	110	151
1990		96	107	115	121	118	101	91	111	104	107	128
1991		97	98	104	105	105	93	92	104	96	100	89
1992	100	100	100	100	100	100	100	100	100	100	100	100
1993		99	100	102	104	103	104	103	108	108	108	96
1994		97P	108P	106	105	105	108	101	117	113	114	114
1995		97P	109P	112P	113P	114P	116P	105P	125P	121P	122P	118P
1996		97P	111P	113P	114P	115P	120P	107P	129P	125P	127P	121P
1997		97P	112P	114P	114P	117P	124P	110P	134P	129P	131P	124P
1998		97P	114P	115P	115P	118P	127P	113P	138P	134P	135P	126P

Sources: Same as General Statistics. Values reflect change from the base year, 1992. Values above 100 mean greater than 92, values below 100 mean less than 92, and a value of 100 in the 82-91 or 93-98 period means same as 92. 'P's mark projections by the editors.

SELECTED RATIOS

For 1994	Avg. of All Manufact.	Analyzed Industry	Index	For 1994	Avg. of All Manufact.	Analyzed Industry	Index
Employees per Establishment	49	21	42	Value Added per Production Worker	134,084	84,301	63
Payroll per Establishment	1,500,273	538,511	36	Cost per Establishment	5,045,178	992,695	20
Payroll per Employee	30,620	26,022	85	Cost per Employee	102,970	47,970	47
Production Workers per Establishment	34	15	43	Cost per Production Worker	146,988	66,987	46
Wages per Establishment	853,319	331,998	39	Shipments per Establishment	9,576,895	2,239,166	23
Wages per Production Worker	24,861	22,403	90	Shipments per Employee	195,460	108,203	55
Hours per Production Worker	2,056	2,134	104	Shipments per Production Worker	279,017	151,098	54
Wages per Hour	12.09	10.50	87	Investment per Establishment	321,011	64,822	20
Value Added per Establishment	4,602,255	1,249,277	27	Investment per Employee	6,552	3,132	48
Value Added per Employee	93,930	60,368	64	Investment per Production Worker	9,352	4,374	47

Sources: Same as General Statistics. The 'Average of All Manufacturing' column represents the average of all manufacturing industries reported for the most recent complete year available. The Index shows the relationship between the Average and the Analyzed Industry. For example, 100 means that they are equal; 500 that the Analyzed Industry is five times the average; 50 means that the Analyzed Industry is half the national average. The abbreviation 'na' is used to show that data are 'not available'.

LEADING COMPANIES Number shown: 75 Total sales ($ mil): 3,708 Total employment (000): 26.6

Company Name	Address				CEO Name	Phone	Co. Type	Sales ($ mil)	Empl. (000)
Ameron Inc	245 S Los Robles	Pasadena	CA	91101	James S Marlen	818-683-4000	P	418	2.2
Tarmac America Inc	1151 Azalea Garden	Norfolk	VA	23502	John D Carr	804-858-6500	S	400	2.3
Hydro Conduit Corp	16701 Greenspt	Houston	TX	77060	Adrian Driver	713-872-3500	S	250	2.0
LB Foster Co	415 Holiday Dr	Pittsburgh	PA	15220	Lee B Foster II	412-928-3400	P	234	0.5
Florida Mining	PO Box 31965	Tampa	FL	33631	Eugene Martineau	813-933-6711	D	150	0.9
Price Brothers Co	367 W 2nd St	Dayton	OH	45402	Gayle B Price Jr	513-226-8700	R	142	0.8
Cretex Company Inc	311 Lowell Av	Elk River	MN	55330	John H Bailey	612-441-2121	R	120*	1.0
North Star Concrete Co	PO Box 240599	Apple Valley	MN	55124	WD Radichel	612-432-6050	R	100	1.0
Concrete Pipe and Products	PO Box 1223	Richmond	VA	23209	Stanley R Navas	804-233-5471	R	97	0.8
Phelps-Tointon Inc	PO Box 1518	Greeley	CO	80632	Robert G Tointon	303-353-7000	R	80	0.6
Monier Roof Tile Inc	PO Box 5567	Orange	CA	92668	John W Clarke	714-750-5366	S	65	0.5
Barrango Inc	360 Swift Av	S San Francisco	CA	94080	E Barrango	415-871-1931	R	61*	0.5
Gifford-Hill-American Inc	PO Box 569470	Dallas	TX	75356	A Leroy Burch	214-262-3600	J	60	0.5
Dayton Superior Corp	721 Richard St	Miamisburg	OH	45342	John Ciccarelli	513-866-0711	S	58*	0.5
Oldcastle Precast East Inc	151 Old Farm Rd	Avon	CT	06001	James Schack	203-673-3291	R	56	0.5
Heatilator Inc	1915 W Saunders St	Mount Pleasant	IA	52641	Robert Burns	319-385-9211	S	50	0.4
Spancrete Northeast Inc	South St	S Bethlehem	NY	12161	Tom Conroy	518-767-2269	S	50*	0.1
Caterpillar Paving Products Inc	PO Box 1362	Minneapolis	MN	55440	Richard Cooper	612-425-4100	S	48*	0.4
Choctaw Inc	PO Box 2057	Memphis	TN	38101	WL Quinlen III	901-458-4481	R	48*	0.4
Fabcon Inc	6111 W Hwy 13	Savage	MN	55378	David W Hanson	612-890-4444	R	45	0.2
Shockey Brothers Inc	PO Box 2530	Winchester	VA	22601	J Donald Shockey	703-667-7700	R	45	0.5
Premarc Corp	7505 Hwy M-71	Durand	MI	48429	Daniel C Marsh	517-288-2661	R	40	0.3
Wilbert Inc	PO Box 147	Forest Park	IL	60130	Joseph P Maladra	708-865-1600	R	40	0.2
Petricca Industries Inc	PO Box 1145	Pittsfield	MA	01202	Robert W Petricca	413-442-6926	R	36*	0.3
Precast Masonry of America Inc	40485D Murrieta	Murrieta	CA	92563	Adrian T Morrisette	909-698-6431	R	36	0.3
Amcor Inc	PO Box 868	Bountiful	UT	84010	RH Paul	801-298-7628	S	35*	0.3
Pennsy Supply Inc	PO Box 3331	Harrisburg	PA	17105	Donald E Eshleman	717-233-4511	R	33*	0.3
Clawson Concrete Co	PO Box 768	Novi	MI	48376	Steven R Simpson	313-349-6000	S	31	0.2
Strescon Industries Inc	3501 Sinclair Ln	Baltimore	MD	21213	William Dausch	410-327-7703	R	30*	0.3
Ameron Pole Products	1020 B St	Fillmore	CA	93016	John Reynolds	805-524-0223	S	30	0.2
JW Peters and Son Inc	PO Box 160	Burlington	WI	53105	John Nanna	414-763-2401	S	30	0.3
T-PAC	PO Box 20128	Phoenix	AZ	85036	Thoburn E Blizzard	602-262-1360	D	30	0.4
Florida Engineered Constr	PO Box 24567	Tampa	FL	33623	John Stanton	813-621-4641	R	28	0.3
Richmond Screw Anchor Co	7214 Burns St	Fort Worth	TX	76118	Merrill Nash	817-284-4981	S	27	0.2
Pacific International	755 NE Columbia	Portland	OR	97211	Lloyd Babler Jr	503-285-8391	R	26*	0.3
Exposaic Industries Incorporated	PO Box 5445	Charlotte	NC	28225	John J McLeod	704-372-1080	S	25*	0.1
Pomeroy Corp	PO Box 411	Petaluma	CA	94953	RI Roberts	707-763-1918	S	25	0.1
James Hardie Building Products	10901 Elm Av	Fontana	CA	92335	Louis Gries	909-356-6300	S	24	0.2
Bend Industries Inc	PO Box 178	West Bend	WI	53095	James Weber	414-334-5557	R	23	0.2
J and J Mill and Lumber Co	180 N 300 East	St George	UT	84770	ML Jennings	801-634-2200	R	23	0.2
Nitterhouse Concrete Product	PO Box N	Chambersburg	PA	17201	W K Nitterhouse	717-264-6154	R	22	0.3
Varmicon Industries Inc	PO Box 531808	Harlingen	TX	78550	John C Waples	210-423-6380	D	22	0.2
Chandler-Wilbert Vault Co	2280 N Hamline	St Paul	MN	55113	Lucy Chandler-Lake	612-631-1234	R	20*	0.2
Dura-Stress Inc	PO Box 490779	Leesburg	FL	34749	G Kent Fuller	904-787-1422	R	20	0.3
Gary Concrete Products Inc	PO Box 204600	Augusta	GA	30917	Pete S Seley	706-733-2263	S	20*	0.3
Sherman Concrete Pipe	PO Box 1926	Birmingham	AL	35201	J Thomas Holton	205-252-6900	D	20	0.2
Wilson Concrete Company Inc	200 Commerce Dr	Red Oak	IA	51566	Charles W Wilson	712-623-4978	R	20	0.5
Arban and Carosi Inc	13800 Dawson	Woodbridge	VA	22191	Nicholas Carosi III	703-491-5121	R	19	0.1
Buehner Corp	5200 S Main St	Murray	UT	84107	Scott Waldron	801-262-5511	R	19	0.2
Supradur Companies Inc	PO Box 908	Rye	NY	10580	Alfred E Netter	914-967-8230	P	18	0.3
Coreslab Structures	10501 NW 121	Medley	FL	33178	William Witcher	305-823-8950	R	18	0.2
Schuylkill Products Inc	121 River St	Cressona	PA	17929	G Nagle	717-385-2352	R	18	0.2
Sherman Prestressed Concrete	PO Box 845	Pelham	AL	35124	Harold Bush	205-663-4681	D	18	0.1
Spancrete Midwest Co	PO Box 1360	Maple Grove	MN	55311	Pat Meservey	612-425-5555	R	18	0.2
Independent Concrete Pipe Corp	PO Box 21007	Indianapolis	IN	46221	Barry Bundrant	317-632-5535	R	17	0.1
WR White Co	1625 Wall Av	Ogden	UT	84404	Rick Fairbanks	801-394-6621	R	17	0.1
Amer Building Components Co	6975 Danville Rd	Nicholasville	KY	40356	John Holmes	606-887-4406	S	15*	0.1
Blakeslee Prestress Inc	PO Box 510	Branford	CT	06405	Mario J Bertolini	203-481-5306	R	15*	0.1
Concrete Technology Corp	PO Box 2259	Tacoma	WA	98401	James R Anderson	206-383-3545	R	15	0.2
Package Pavement Company Inc	PO Box 408	Stormville	NY	12582	Frank J Doherty	914-221-2224	R	15	0.1
PBM Concrete Inc	PO Box 460	Rochelle	IL	61068	Craig Wagenbach	815-562-4136	R	15	0.2
Stresscon Corp	PO Box 15129	Co Springs	CO	80935	Donald R Logan	719-390-5041	R	15*	0.1
Goria Enterprises	PO Box 14489	Greensboro	NC	27415	Pete Hoyt	919-375-5656	D	14	<0.1
WG Block Co	PO Box 3010	Davenport	IA	52808	Harold Rayburn	319-322-6010	R	14	0.1
Exposaic Industries	4717 Massap	Fredericksburg	VA	22408	John C Graube	703-898-1221	S	13	0.1
Gulf Coast Pre-Stress	PO Drawer D	Pass Christian	MS	39571	Quilla D Spruill Jr	601-452-9486	R	13	0.1
Quinn Concrete Company Inc	PO Box 996	Marshall	MO	65340	Richard E Quinn	816-886-3306	R	13	0.1
Gulf Coast Pre-Stress Inc	PO Drawer D	Pass Christian	MS	39571	QD Spruill Jr	601-452-9486	S	13	0.1
Amis Materials Co	PO Box 1871	Oklahoma City	OK	73101	WD Amis Jr	405-235-3555	R	12*	0.1
ASI RCC Inc	PO Box 3127	Buena Vista	CO	81211	Jeff Allen	719-395-8625	R	12	0.1
Cast Crete Tampa	PO Box 24567	Tampa	FL	33623	RW Hughes	813-621-4641	D	12*	0.2
Concrete Tie and Anchor Corp	PO Box 5406	Compton	CA	90224	C E Schoendiest	310-886-1000	R	12	<0.1
Material Supply Inc	510 Century Blv	Wilmington	DE	19808	Blaise Saienni	302-633-5600	R	12*	0.1
NC Products Corp	PO Box 27077	Raleigh	NC	27611	William Eakes	919-834-2557	S	12*	0.1
Texas Concrete Co	PO Drawer 1070	Victoria	TX	77902	PM Guthrie	512-573-9145	R	12	0.2

Source: Ward's Business Directory of U.S. Private and Public Companies, Volumes 1 and 2, 1996. The company type code used is as follows: P - Public, R - Private, S - Subsidiary, D - Division, J - Joint Venture, A - Affiliate, G - Group. Sales are in millions of dollars, employees are in thousands. An asterisk (*) indicates an estimated sales volume. The symbol < stands for 'less than'. Company names and addresses are truncated, in some cases, to fit into the available space.

MATERIALS CONSUMED

Material	Quantity	Delivered Cost ($ million)
Materials, ingredients, containers, and supplies	(X)	2,036.2
Portland cement	(X)	327.8
Ready-mixed concrete	(X)	66.8
Other stone, clay, glass, and concrete products	(X)	27.7
Crushed and broken stone (including cement rock, limestone, etc.)	(X)	43.9
Sand and gravel	(X)	165.4
Other mining and quarrying of nonmetallic minerals, except fuels	(X)	3.7
Steel wire strand and bars or rods, high strength, stress relieved	(X)	121.1
Welded steel wire concrete reinforcing mesh	(X)	94.5
Steel concrete reinforcing bars	(X)	69.8
Other steel shapes and forms (except castings, forgings, and fabricated metal products)	(X)	44.1
Nonferrous shapes and forms (except castings, forgings, and fabricated metal products)	(X)	33.1
All other materials and components, parts, containers, and supplies	(X)	478.9
Materials, ingredients, containers, and supplies, nsk	(X)	559.3

Source: 1992 *Economic Census*. Explanation of symbols used: (D): Withheld to avoid disclosure of competitive data; na: Not available; (S): Withheld because statistical norms were not met; (X): Not applicable; (Z): Less than half the unit shown; nec: Not elsewhere classified; nsk: Not specified by kind; - : zero; * : 10-19 percent estimated; ** : 20-29 percent estimated.

PRODUCT SHARE DETAILS

Product or Product Class	% Share
Concrete products, nec	100.00
Concrete pipe	22.13
Concrete reinforced culvert pipe, 36 inches or more	12.42
Concrete reinforced culvert pipe, less than 36 inches	7.12
Concrete nonreinforced culvert pipe	0.70
Concrete reinforced storm sewer pipe, 36 inches or more	15.16
Concrete reinforced storm sewer pipe, less than 36 inches	13.66
Concrete nonreinforced storm sewer pipe	0.67
Concrete reinforced sanitary sewer pipe, 24 inches or more	6.67
Concrete reinforced sanitary sewer pipe, less than 24 inches	1.40
Concrete nonreinforced sanitary sewer pipe	0.35
Reinforced concrete pressure pipe	1.48
Prestressed concrete cylinder pressure pipe	7.36
Concrete irrigation pipe and drain tile	1.82
Other concrete pipe (such as manholes and conduits)	25.79
Concrete pipe, nsk	5.38
Precast concrete products	47.43
Precast concrete slabs and tile, roof and floor units	11.53
Precast concrete joists and beams, roof and floor units	0.48
Precast concrete architectural wall panels	10.99
Precast concrete piling, posts, and poles	1.04
Precast concrete stone products for architectural purposes (except architectural wall panels, such as window sills, ashlar, etc.)	2.34
Precast concrete, prefabricated building systems, primarily concrete, sold as complete units, and shipped in panel or modular form	5.03
Other precast concrete construction or building products (including prefabricated housing components)	15.29
Burial vaults, precast concrete	8.82
Burial boxes, precast concrete	2.20
Septic tanks, precast concrete	5.72
Precast concrete, dry-mixed concrete materials (including prepackaged sand, gravel and cement, mortar and cement premixes)	17.84
Other precast concrete products (except construction or building products)	10.83
Precast concrete products, nsk	7.87
Prestressed concrete products	16.30
Prestressed concrete single tees, double tees, and channels	16.28
Prestressed concrete piling, bearing piles, and sheet piles	9.22
Prestressed concrete bridge beams	25.39
Prestressed concrete joists, girders, and beams (other than bridge beams)	5.56
Prestressed concrete solid and hollow cored slabs and panels	22.25
Other prestressed concrete products (such as arches, columns, etc.)	15.43
Prestressed concrete products, nsk	5.84
Concrete products, nec, nsk	14.14

Source: 1992 *Economic Census*. The values shown are percent of total shipments in an industry. Values of indented subcategories are summed in the main heading. The symbol (D) appears when data are withheld to prevent disclosure of competitive information. The abbreviation nsk stands for 'not specified by kind' and nec for 'not elsewhere classified'.

INPUTS AND OUTPUTS FOR CONCRETE PRODUCTS, NEC

Economic Sector or Industry Providing Inputs	%	Sector	Economic Sector or Industry Buying Outputs	%	Sector
Cement, hydraulic	14.7	Manufg.	Highway & street construction	13.2	Constr.
Miscellaneous fabricated wire products	13.3	Manufg.	Sewer system facility construction	11.4	Constr.
Motor freight transportation & warehousing	5.8	Util.	Electric utility facility construction	7.6	Constr.
Advertising	5.7	Services	Office buildings	5.1	Constr.
Sand & gravel	5.5	Mining	Industrial buildings	4.7	Constr.
Wholesale trade	5.3	Trade	Maintenance of nonfarm buildings nec	4.5	Constr.
Concrete products, nec	4.4	Manufg.	Funeral service & crematories	4.2	Services
Blast furnaces & steel mills	3.7	Manufg.	Construction of hospitals	3.6	Constr.
Petroleum refining	3.3	Manufg.	Water supply facility construction	3.6	Constr.
Ready-mixed concrete	2.7	Manufg.	Construction of educational buildings	2.7	Constr.
Banking	2.7	Fin/R.E.	Warehouses	2.7	Constr.
Mining machinery, except oil field	2.5	Manufg.	Nonfarm residential structure maintenance	2.6	Constr.
Electric services (utilities)	2.2	Util.	Maintenance of highways & streets	2.4	Constr.
Dimension, crushed & broken stone	1.9	Mining	Local transit facility construction	2.1	Constr.
Maintenance of nonfarm buildings nec	1.7	Constr.	Construction of stores & restaurants	1.9	Constr.
Paints & allied products	1.7	Manufg.	Maintenance of water supply facilities	1.8	Constr.
Communications, except radio & TV	1.7	Util.	Residential additions/alterations, nonfarm	1.8	Constr.
Gas production & distribution (utilities)	1.4	Util.	Concrete products, nec	1.8	Manufg.
Railroads & related services	1.3	Util.	Residential 1-unit structures, nonfarm	1.7	Constr.

Continued on next page.

INPUTS AND OUTPUTS FOR CONCRETE PRODUCTS, NEC - Continued

Economic Sector or Industry Providing Inputs	%	Sector	Economic Sector or Industry Buying Outputs	%	Sector
Eating & drinking places	1.3	Trade	Residential garden apartments	1.5	Constr.
Imports	1.3	Foreign	Amusement & recreation building construction	1.2	Constr.
Equipment rental & leasing services	1.0	Services	Hotels & motels	1.2	Constr.
Water transportation	0.7	Util.	Maintenance of electric utility facilities	1.1	Constr.
Real estate	0.7	Fin/R.E.	Construction of religious buildings	1.0	Constr.
Business services nec	0.7	Services	Maintenance of farm service facilities	1.0	Constr.
Detective & protective services	0.7	Services	Maintenance of nonbuilding facilities nec	1.0	Constr.
Chemical preparations, nec	0.6	Manufg.	Maintenance of sewer facilities	1.0	Constr.
Sawmills & planning mills, general	0.6	Manufg.	Construction of conservation facilities	0.9	Constr.
Veneer & plywood	0.6	Manufg.	Farm service facilities	0.9	Constr.
Computer & data processing services	0.6	Services	Coal	0.8	Mining
Engineering, architectural, & surveying services	0.6	Services	Telephone & telegraph facility construction	0.8	Constr.
Business/professional associations	0.5	Services	Construction of nonfarm buildings nec	0.7	Constr.
Management & consulting services & labs	0.5	Services	Nonbuilding facilities nec	0.7	Constr.
Jewelry, precious metal	0.4	Manufg.	Resid. & other health facility construction	0.7	Constr.
Accounting, auditing & bookkeeping	0.4	Services	Residential high-rise apartments	0.6	Constr.
Legal services	0.4	Services	Garage & service station construction	0.5	Constr.
Clay, ceramic, & refractory minerals	0.3	Mining	Real estate	0.5	Fin/R.E.
Nonmetallic mineral services	0.3	Mining	Exports	0.5	Foreign
Cutstone & stone products	0.3	Manufg.	S/L Govt. purch., natural resource & recreation.	0.5	S/L Govt
Lubricating oils & greases	0.3	Manufg.	Construction of dams & reservoirs	0.4	Constr.
Automotive rental & leasing, without drivers	0.3	Services	Maintenance, conservation & development facilities	0.4	Constr.
Automotive repair shops & services	0.3	Services	Residential 2-4 unit structures, nonfarm	0.4	Constr.
U.S. Postal Service	0.3	Gov't	Maintenance of military facilities	0.3	Constr.
Coal	0.2	Mining	Maintenance of railroads	0.3	Constr.
Fabricated rubber products, nec	0.2	Manufg.	Maintenance of telephone & telegraph facilities	0.3	Constr.
General industrial machinery, nec	0.2	Manufg.	Dormitories & other group housing	0.2	Constr.
Hardwood dimension & flooring mills	0.2	Manufg.	Maintenance of farm residential buildings	0.2	Constr.
Machinery, except electrical, nec	0.2	Manufg.	Maintenance of gas utility facilities	0.2	Constr.
Minerals, ground or treated	0.2	Manufg.	Maintenance of petroleum & natural gas wells	0.2	Constr.
Paperboard containers & boxes	0.2	Manufg.	Change in business inventories	0.2	In House
Paving mixtures & blocks	0.2	Manufg.	Gas utility facility construction	0.1	Constr.
Small arms ammunition	0.2	Manufg.	Maintenance of local transit facilities	0.1	Constr.
Air transportation	0.2	Util.	Railroad construction	0.1	Constr.
Retail trade, except eating & drinking	0.2	Trade	Water supply & sewage systems	0.1	Util.
Insurance carriers	0.2	Fin/R.E.			
Laundry, dry cleaning, shoe repair	0.2	Services			
Manifold business forms	0.1	Manufg.			
Surface active agents	0.1	Manufg.			
Royalties	0.1	Fin/R.E.			
Electrical repair shops	0.1	Services			
Personnel supply services	0.1	Services			

Source: Benchmark Input-Output Accounts for the U.S. Economy, 1982, U.S. Department of Commerce, Washington, D.C., July 1991. Data, as reported in the source, are organized by the 1977 SIC structure in use in 1982 but have been matched, as closely as is possible, to the 1987 SIC structure used in this book.

OCCUPATIONS EMPLOYED BY SIC 327 - CONCRETE, GYPSUM, AND PLASTER PRODUCTS

Occupation	% of Total 1994	Change to 2005	Occupation	% of Total 1994	Change to 2005
Truck drivers light & heavy	31.4	-10.5	Concrete & terrazzo finishers	2.2	-13.2
Helpers, laborers, & material movers nec	4.6	-13.2	Crushing & mixing machine operators	2.1	-13.2
General managers & top executives	4.3	-17.6	General office clerks	1.8	-26.0
Blue collar worker supervisors	4.2	-19.9	Helpers, construction trades	1.8	-13.2
Sales & related workers nec	3.2	-13.2	Industrial machinery mechanics	1.7	-4.5
Bookkeeping, accounting, & auditing clerks	2.5	-34.9	Industrial production managers	1.5	-13.1
Industrial truck & tractor operators	2.5	-13.2	Secretaries, ex legal & medical	1.4	-20.9
Bus & truck mechanics & diesel engine specialists	2.4	-13.2	Maintenance repairers, general utility	1.4	-21.9
Dispatchers, ex police, fire, & ambulance	2.4	-13.2	Welders & cutters	1.3	-13.1
Extruding & forming machine workers	2.3	21.6	Freight, stock, & material movers, hand	1.2	-30.5
Assemblers, fabricators, & hand workers nec	2.2	-13.2	Machine feeders & offbearers	1.1	-21.9
Precision workers nec	2.2	4.2			

Source: Industry-Occupation Matrix, Bureau of Labor Statistics. These data relate to one or more 3-digit SIC industry groups rather than to a single 4-digit SIC. The change reported for each occupation to the year 2005 is a percent of growth or decline as estimated by the Bureau of Labor Statistics. The abbreviation nec stands for 'not elsewhere classified'.

LOCATION BY STATE AND REGIONAL CONCENTRATION

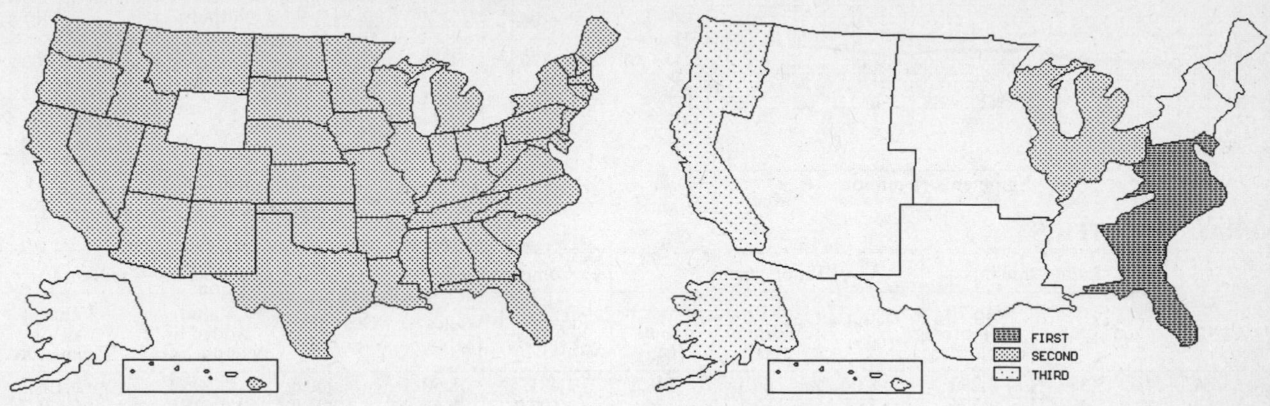

INDUSTRY DATA BY STATE

State	Establish-ments	Shipments			Employment				Cost as % of Shipments	Investment per Employee ($)
		Total ($ mil)	% of U.S.	Per Establ.	Total Number	% of U.S.	Per Establ.	Wages ($/hour)		
California	244	736.1	12.4	3.0	5,800	9.8	24	12.15	50.1	4,190
Florida	234	459.2	7.7	2.0	5,100	8.7	22	9.34	44.4	2,569
Texas	194	364.3	6.1	1.9	4,100	7.0	21	8.94	42.8	2,585
Pennsylvania	164	296.0	5.0	1.8	3,100	5.3	19	10.60	46.3	2,839
Illinois	120	246.0	4.1	2.0	2,300	3.9	19	12.56	45.0	3,783
Ohio	125	223.4	3.8	1.8	2,400	4.1	19	10.19	39.8	1,958
Virginia	86	207.3	3.5	2.4	2,400	4.1	28	10.09	40.5	2,042
Georgia	118	201.5	3.4	1.7	2,300	3.9	19	9.26	40.8	2,261
Minnesota	79	178.7	3.0	2.3	1,600	2.7	20	12.22	37.5	3,375
Colorado	50	175.5	3.0	3.5	1,400	2.4	28	9.70	41.8	2,857
Michigan	100	168.1	2.8	1.7	1,400	2.4	14	11.71	49.9	3,643
New York	114	167.2	2.8	1.5	1,700	2.9	15	10.56	39.8	2,882
Wisconsin	89	147.2	2.5	1.7	1,300	2.2	15	11.15	38.7	3,769
New Jersey	64	139.1	2.3	2.2	1,300	2.2	20	12.29	43.5	2,154
Washington	65	136.3	2.3	2.1	1,200	2.0	18	12.11	41.5	3,417
Arizona	47	135.2	2.3	2.9	1,100	1.9	23	11.65	44.9	-
North Carolina	87	127.9	2.2	1.5	1,600	2.7	18	8.91	40.0	1,438
Indiana	108	127.1	2.1	1.2	1,400	2.4	13	11.38	42.0	3,071
Massachusetts	57	106.5	1.8	1.9	1,000	1.7	18	11.67	40.6	3,800
Missouri	82	106.2	1.8	1.3	1,200	2.0	15	10.50	40.2	3,167
Connecticut	45	97.0	1.6	2.2	800	1.4	18	14.38	40.7	3,250
Alabama	81	96.8	1.6	1.2	1,100	1.9	14	7.80	49.9	1,636
South Carolina	37	96.7	1.6	2.6	1,100	1.9	30	9.13	48.3	1,455
Maryland	45	93.0	1.6	2.1	1,000	1.7	22	11.64	46.1	2,700
Louisiana	48	88.4	1.5	1.8	1,000	1.7	21	7.87	40.5	6,100
Iowa	63	87.1	1.5	1.4	900	1.5	14	9.80	39.2	2,444
Tennessee	70	86.0	1.4	1.2	1,100	1.9	16	8.63	38.0	2,000
Mississippi	29	83.2	1.4	2.9	800	1.4	28	8.21	42.5	-
Kentucky	56	74.3	1.3	1.3	800	1.4	14	9.33	44.1	-
Oregon	40	72.1	1.2	1.8	600	1.0	15	11.11	40.6	3,667
Nebraska	26	64.4	1.1	2.5	700	1.2	27	8.86	43.9	2,000
Nevada	17	64.1	1.1	3.8	400	0.7	24	12.50	49.3	3,750
Hawaii	16	56.9	1.0	3.6	300	0.5	19	15.20	42.5	-
Kansas	34	56.5	1.0	1.7	600	1.0	18	9.70	39.8	5,667
Utah	22	50.8	0.9	2.3	600	1.0	27	10.33	48.6	2,833
Oklahoma	43	39.9	0.7	0.9	400	0.7	9	9.14	40.4	-
Arkansas	39	38.4	0.6	1.0	500	0.8	13	8.00	35.2	2,400
Maine	17	32.6	0.5	1.9	300	0.5	18	9.00	32.2	-
New Mexico	20	27.7	0.5	1.4	200	0.3	10	9.50	47.3	5,000
North Dakota	16	20.3	0.3	1.3	300	0.5	19	11.00	35.0	-
Montana	18	12.2	0.2	0.7	100	0.2	6	10.00	48.4	2,000
Idaho	14	11.4	0.2	0.8	100	0.2	7	9.50	47.4	5,000
New Hampshire	24	(D)	-	-	375 *	0.6	16	-	-	3,733
West Virginia	17	(D)	-	-	375 *	0.6	22	-	-	-
Vermont	11	(D)	-	-	175 *	0.3	16	-	-	-
South Dakota	10	(D)	-	-	175 *	0.3	18	-	-	-
Delaware	9	(D)	-	-	175 *	0.3	19	-	-	4,000

Source: 1992 *Economic Census*. The states are in descending order of shipments or establishments (if shipment data are missing for the majority). The symbol (D) appears when data are withheld to prevent disclosure of competitive information. States marked with (D) are sorted by number of establishments. A dash (-) indicates that the data element cannot be calculated; * indicates the midpoint of a range.

3273 - READY-MIXED CONCRETE

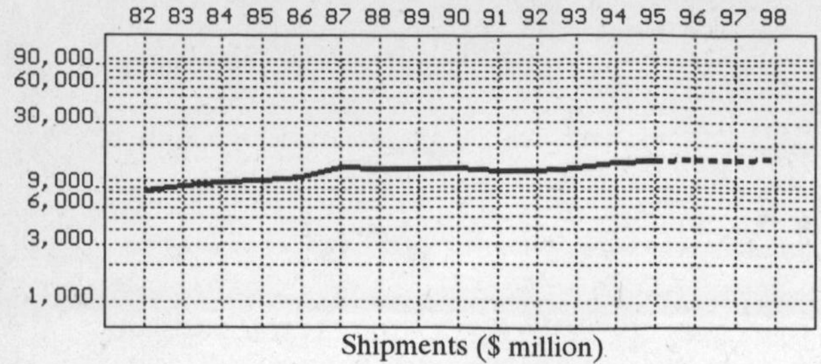

Shipments ($ million)

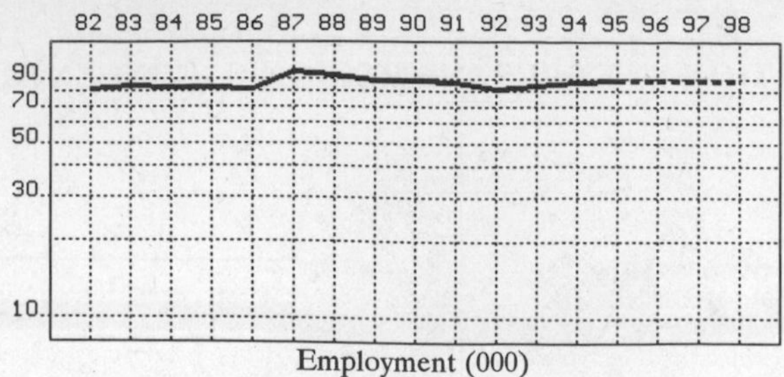

Employment (000)

GENERAL STATISTICS

Year	Companies	Establishments		Employment			Compensation		Production ($ million)			
		Total	with 20 or more employees	Total (000)	Production Workers (000)	Production Hours (Mil)	Payroll ($ mil)	Wages ($/hr)	Cost of Materials	Value Added by Manufacture	Value of Shipments	Capital Invest.
1982	4,161	5,379	1,239	81.6	60.5	118.8	1,481.7	8.50	4,900.6	3,295.1	8,199.3	284.3
1983		5,283	1,276	83.8	63.1	126.6	1,602.0	8.63	5,394.0	3,635.0	9,025.7	284.5
1984		5,187	1,313	83.3	65.2	133.8	1,728.8	9.27	5,658.6	4,041.8	9,675.6	398.5
1985		5,092	1,349	83.5	66.2	135.0	1,785.7	9.57	5,843.2	4,249.0	10,087.9	465.4
1986		5,059	1,359	81.6	62.9	133.3	1,874.0	10.08	6,058.0	4,553.0	10,614.3	378.0
1987	3,749	5,321	1,532	96.9	73.9	154.9	2,288.7	10.59	7,259.7	5,732.9	12,975.4	479.3
1988		5,201	1,450	93.2	68.8	135.2	2,280.3	11.91	7,179.0	5,715.2	12,884.0	338.0
1989		5,090	1,387	89.5	70.9	148.2	2,279.7	11.00	7,057.6	5,792.8	12,860.3	491.3
1990		5,007	1,418	89.4	70.4	152.7	2,353.2	11.04	7,197.9	5,633.5	12,829.6	470.8
1991		5,123	1,271	86.1	62.8	138.3	2,243.1	11.18	6,520.7	5,169.7	11,681.2	263.6
1992	3,248	5,254	1,362	82.4	60.9	129.2	2,291.5	12.21	6,662.4	5,342.5	12,009.9	313.0
1993		5,095	1,289	83.8	62.7	133.5	2,397.2	12.58	7,046.6	5,668.6	12,708.1	330.3
1994		5,077P	1,385P	87.2	67.6	147.4	2,551.0	12.44	7,655.7	6,167.7	13,830.9	458.9
1995		5,062P	1,390P	88.1P	66.8P	146.3P	2,664.5P	13.09P	7,864.2P	6,335.7P	14,207.6P	401.5P
1996		5,047P	1,395P	88.4P	66.9P	147.6P	2,746.8P	13.43P	8,079.1P	6,508.8P	14,595.7P	404.4P
1997		5,032P	1,399P	88.6P	67.1P	148.8P	2,829.0P	13.77P	8,293.9P	6,681.8P	14,983.8P	407.3P
1998		5,017P	1,404P	88.9P	67.2P	150.1P	2,911.2P	14.12P	8,508.7P	6,854.9P	15,371.9P	410.2P

Sources: 1982, 1987, 1992 *Economic Census*; *Annual Survey of Manufactures*, 83-86, 88-91, 93-94. Establishment counts for non-Census years are from *County Business Patterns*; establishment values for 83-84 are extrapolations. 'P's show projections by the editors. Industries reclassified in 87 will not have data for prior years.

INDICES OF CHANGE

Year	Companies	Establishments		Employment			Compensation		Production ($ million)			
		Total	with 20 or more employees	Total (000)	Production Workers (000)	Production Hours (Mil)	Payroll ($ mil)	Wages ($/hr)	Cost of Materials	Value Added by Manufacture	Value of Shipments	Capital Invest.
1982	128	102	91	99	99	92	65	70	74	62	68	91
1983		101	94	102	104	98	70	71	81	68	75	91
1984		99	96	101	107	104	75	76	85	76	81	127
1985		97	99	101	109	104	78	78	88	80	84	149
1986		96	100	99	103	103	82	83	91	85	88	121
1987	115	101	112	118	121	120	100	87	109	107	108	153
1988		99	106	113	113	105	100	98	108	107	107	108
1989		97	102	109	116	115	99	90	106	108	107	157
1990		95	104	108	116	118	103	90	108	105	107	150
1991		98	93	104	103	107	98	92	98	97	97	84
1992	100	100	100	100	100	100	100	100	100	100	100	100
1993		97	95	102	103	103	105	103	106	106	106	106
1994		97P	102P	106	111	114	111	102	115	115	115	147
1995		96P	102P	107P	110P	113P	116P	107P	118P	119P	118P	128P
1996		96P	102P	107P	110P	114P	120P	110P	121P	122P	122P	129P
1997		96P	103P	108P	110P	115P	123P	113P	124P	125P	125P	130P
1998		95P	103P	108P	110P	116P	127P	116P	128P	128P	128P	131P

Sources: Same as General Statistics. Values reflect change from the base year, 1992. Values above 100 mean greater than 92, values below 100 mean less than 92, and a value of 100 in the 82-91 or 93-98 period means same as 92. 'P's mark projections by the editors.

SELECTED RATIOS

For 1994	Avg. of All Manufact.	Analyzed Industry	Index
Employees per Establishment	49	17	35
Payroll per Establishment	1,500,273	502,476	33
Payroll per Employee	30,620	29,255	96
Production Workers per Establishment	34	13	39
Wages per Establishment	853,319	361,179	42
Wages per Production Worker	24,861	27,125	109
Hours per Production Worker	2,056	2,180	106
Wages per Hour	12.09	12.44	103
Value Added per Establishment	4,602,255	1,214,864	26
Value Added per Employee	93,930	70,731	75

For 1994	Avg. of All Manufact.	Analyzed Industry	Index
Value Added per Production Worker	134,084	91,238	68
Cost per Establishment	5,045,178	1,507,959	30
Cost per Employee	102,970	87,795	85
Cost per Production Worker	146,988	113,250	77
Shipments per Establishment	9,576,895	2,724,300	28
Shipments per Employee	195,460	158,611	81
Shipments per Production Worker	279,017	204,599	73
Investment per Establishment	321,011	90,390	28
Investment per Employee	6,552	5,263	80
Investment per Production Worker	9,352	6,788	73

Sources: Same as General Statistics. The 'Average of All Manufacturing' column represents the average of all manufacturing industries reported for the most recent complete year available. The Index shows the relationship between the Average and the Analyzed Industry. For example, 100 means that they are equal; 500 that the Analyzed Industry is five times the average; 50 means that the Analyzed Industry is half the national average. The abbreviation 'na' is used to show that data are 'not available'.

LEADING COMPANIES

Number shown: **75** Total sales ($ mil): **5,853** Total employment (000): **38.9**

Company Name	Address				CEO Name	Phone	Co. Type	Sales ($ mil)	Empl. (000)
CSR America Inc	945 E Paces Ferry	Atlanta	GA	30326	David Clarke	404-237-8811	S	1,200	9.0
Southdown Inc	1200 Smith St	Houston	TX	77002	Clarence C Comer	713-650-6200	P	562	2.6
Rinker Materials Corp	PO Box 24635	W Palm Beach	FL	33416	Bill Snyder	407-833-5555	S	400	2.2
Florida Rock Industries Inc	155 E 21st St	Jacksonville	FL	32206	Edward L Baker	904-355-1781	P	337	2.2
Pioneer Concrete of Texas Inc	800 Gessner St	Houston	TX	77024	Gary Bullock	713-468-6868	S	260	1.3
Pioneer Concrete of America Inc	800 Gessner St	Houston	TX	77024	Gary Bullock	713-468-6868	S	260	1.6
DW Dickey and Son Inc	7896 Dickey Dr	Lisbon	OH	44432	G Allen Dickey	216-424-1441	R	250	0.2
Material Service Corp	222 N La Salle St	Chicago	IL	60601	Gerald Nagel	312-372-3600	S	240	2.2
Sunbelt Corp	5111 Woodway Dr	Houston	TX	77056	Ignacio Murguia	713-621-8510	R	130	1.0
Irving Materials Inc	8032 N State Rd 9	Greenfield	IN	46140	Fred R Irving	317-326-3101	R	120	0.6
RMC Lone Star	PO Box 5252	Pleasanton	CA	94566	Ron L Blick	510-426-8787	R	120*	0.9
Arundel Corp	PO Box 5000	Sparks	MD	21152	T S Baker II	410-329-5000	S	100	0.6
Prairie Material Sales Inc	7601 W 79th St	Bridgeview	IL	60455	John Oremus	708-458-0400	R	80*	0.8
Central Reddi-Mix Inc	305 E Summa	Centralia	WA	98531	Larry Granger	206-736-1131	R	70	<0.1
Devcon International Corp	1350 E Newport Ctr	Deerfield Bch	FL	33442	Donald L Smith Jr	305-429-1500	P	66	0.6
Mississippi Materials Co	PO Box 23070	Jackson	MS	39205	Elton Cook	601-355-5038	S	65	0.5
Gibbons and Reed Co	1111 Brickyard Rd	Salt Lake City	UT	84130	PM Gibbons	801-486-2411	S	58	0.7
Associated Sand and Gravel	PO Box 2037	Everett	WA	98203	M Donohoe	206-355-2111	S	50	0.5
Cemstone Products Company	2025 Centre Pointe	Mendota H	MN	55120	HT Becken	612-688-9292	R	50	0.4
Ready Mix Concrete Inc	PO Box 27326	Raleigh	NC	27611	George C Turner	919-828-0668	R	49	0.5
Mid-Continent Concrete Co	PO Box 3878	Tulsa	OK	74102	Floyd R Hardesty	918-582-8111	R	46*	0.4
Western Mobile New Mexico Inc	PO Box 91570	Albuquerque	NM	87199	Al Vaio	505-343-7800	R	46	0.2
MCC Inc	1911 W Wisconsin	Appleton	WI	54914	William D Murphy	414-734-9295	R	42	0.4
Tews Co	6200 W Center St	Milwaukee	WI	53210	William Tews	414-442-8000	R	40	<0.1
Concrete Supply Co	3823 Raleigh St	Charlotte	NC	28206	James T Haney	704-372-2930	R	38	0.3
Suzio L Concrete Company Inc	PO Box 748	Meriden	CT	06450	Leonardo H Suzio	203-237-8421	R	38	<0.1
Superior Ready Mix	1508 W Mission Rd	Escondido	CA	92025	Jack Browwer	619-745-0556	R	38	0.4
BR De Witt Inc	6895 Ellicott St	Pavilion	NY	14525	Byron R De Witt	716-584-3132	R	36	0.3
Nova Materials Inc	843 Quince Orchard	Gaithersburg	MD	20878	James Topper	301-869-9863	R	34	0.3
Monroc Inc	PO Box 537	Salt Lake City	UT	84110	Robert A Parry	801-359-3701	P	33	0.4
Quikrete Cos	PO Box 29097	Atlanta	GA	30359	James Winchester	404-634-9100	R	33*	0.3
Unicorn Concrete Inc	100 Meredith Dr	Durham	NC	27713	Chet Miller	919-544-4350	S	33	0.3
AVR Inc	6801 W 150th St	Apple Valley	MN	55124	M Fischer	612-432-7132	R	32	0.2
Unicon Concrete Inc	PO Box 62289	Charleston	SC	29419	Chet Miller	803-744-3535	R	32*	0.2
Acme Materials	PO Box 2503	Spokane	WA	99218	Steve Robinson	509-535-3081	S	30	0.5
Southern Ready-Mix Inc	4200 Colonnade	Birmingham	AL	35243	CF Greene	205-970-2400	S	30	0.3
United Premix Concrete	16282 Constr	Irvine	CA	92714	Joe S Tedesco	714-552-5566	D	30*	0.2
Thomas Concrete Inc	2700 Cumberland	Atlanta	GA	30339	Jan Meijer	404-431-3300	R	29*	0.3
Nelson and Sloan Co	PO Box 488	Chula Vista	CA	91912	James R Nelson	619-476-8340	R	28	0.2
Hunterdon Concrete Co	PO Box 2050	Flemington	NJ	08822	Frank Lentine	908-782-3619	R	26	0.2
Model Stone and Ready Mix Co	400 W 61st St	Minneapolis	MN	55419	Gary Reiersen	612-861-6041	R	26*	0.2
Pre-Mix Industries Inc	932 Professional Pl	Chesapeake	VA	23320	Charles Jett	804-547-9411	R	26*	0.2
Bonanza Materials Inc	PO Box 92170	Henderson	NV	89009	Richard Norman	702-565-1313	S	25	0.1
LYCON Inc	PO Box 427	Janesville	WI	53547	G R Lyons Jr	608-754-7701	R	25	0.1
Silvi Concrete Products Inc	355 Newbold Rd	Fairless Hills	PA	19030	John L Silvi	215-295-0777	R	25*	0.2
Delta Industries Inc	100 W Wilson	Jackson	MS	39213	TR Slough Jr	601-354-3801	R	24	0.2
Phoenix Redi-Mix Company Inc	3635 S 43rd Av	Phoenix	AZ	85009	Thomas Valentie	602-272-2637	R	24*	0.2
American Materials Corp	PO Box 388	Eau Claire	WI	54702	John Ayres	715-835-2251	R	23	0.2
EL Gardner Inc	1914 Forest Dr	Annapolis	MD	21401	EL Gardner Jr	410-721-2550	R	23*	0.2
Kuhlman Corp	PO Box 714	Toledo	OH	43697	TL Goligoski	419-243-2121	R	22	0.1
Varmicon Industries Inc	PO Box 531808	Harlingen	TX	78553	John C Waples	210-423-6380	R	22	0.2
Concrete Materials Co	PO Box 84140	Sioux Falls	SD	57118	Merle Davis	605-336-2928	R	21	0.2
Joe Brown Company Inc	PO Box 1669	Ardmore	OK	73402	JD Brown	405-223-4555	R	21	0.3
Jackson Ready Mix Inc	PO Drawer 1292	Jackson	MS	39215	David Robison	601-354-3801	S	21	0.2
Allied Readymix Inc	PO Box 728	Decatur	GA	30031	Don Williams	404-378-3671	S	20	0.2
Central Concrete Supply	610 McKendrie St	San Jose	CA	95110	William Albanese	408-293-6272	R	20*	0.2
Dixie Readymix	1104 M St	Waycross	GA	31501	Bob Hopkins	912-283-6645	R	20*	0.2
Hardway Concrete Co	PO Box 4128	Columbia	SC	29240	GM Tate III	803-254-4350	R	20	0.1
Hoover Inc	PO Box 1700	La Vergne	TN	37086	Thomas Hoover	615-793-2600	R	20*	0.2
Michigan Foundation Co	1 W Jefferson Av	Trenton	MI	48183	WJ Foley	313-282-9100	R	20	0.1
Fidler Inc	PO Box 99	Goshen	IN	46526	Douglas Anderson	219-533-0415	S	20	0.2
Lentine Management Inc	PO Box 2050	Flemington	NJ	08822	Frank Lentine	908-782-8545	R	19	0.1
Plainville Concrete Services Inc	1978 Clark Ln	Batavia	OH	45103	Jack Clark	513-724-7000	R	18	0.3
Wingra Stone Co	PO Box 44284	Madison	WI	53744	RF Shea	608-271-5555	R	18*	0.1
Grand Rapids Gravel Co	PO Box 9160	Grand Rapids	MI	49509	Andrew Dykema	616-538-9000	R	17*	0.1
Braswell Industries Inc	PO Box 6617	Shreveport	LA	71136	Oren Bailess	318-868-3694	S	16	<0.1
Chapman Grading and Concrete	2180 Chesnee Hwy	Spartanburg	SC	29303	Robert Chapman	803-585-8133	R	16*	0.1
Ingram Enterprises Inc	PO Box 1166	Brownwood	TX	76804	Jerry Roberts	915-646-6518	R	16*	0.1
James River Limestone Co	PO Box 617	Buchanan	VA	24066	MJ O'Brien	703-254-1241	R	16*	0.2
Louisiana Industries-Bossier City	PO Box 5396	Bossier City	LA	71171	Robert H Hable	318-742-3111	D	16	<0.1
Central Ready Mixed LP	PO Box 08281	Milwaukee	WI	53208	John C Madderom	414-258-7000	R	15	0.1
Elsinore Ready-Mix Co	PO Box 959	Lake Elsinore	CA	92530	RL Cartier	909-674-2127	R	15	<0.1
Standard Concrete Products	PO Box 15326	Santa Ana	CA	92705	Clayton Higuhi	714-566-0400	D	15	0.2
Stoneway Concrete Inc	1915 Maple Val	Renton	WA	98055	Don Merlino	206-226-1000	S	15	0.1
JE Simon Co	PO Box 347	Cheyenne	WY	82003	JE Simon	307-634-0137	R	14*	0.1

Source: *Ward's Business Directory of U.S. Private and Public Companies*, Volumes 1 and 2, 1996. The company type code used is as follows: P - Public, R - Private, S - Subsidiary, D - Division, J - Joint Venture, A - Affiliate, G - Group. Sales are in millions of dollars, employees are in thousands. An asterisk (*) indicates an estimated sales volume. The symbol < stands for 'less than'. Company names and addresses are truncated, in some cases, to fit into the available space.

MATERIALS CONSUMED

Material	Quantity	Delivered Cost ($ million)
Materials, ingredients, containers, and supplies	(X)	5,964.8
Sand and gravel	(X)	974.6
Mining and quarrying of crushed and broken limestone (including dolomite, cement rock, marl, etc.)	(X)	225.5
Mining and quarrying of crushed and broken granite (including gneiss, syenite, and diorite)	(X)	47.4
Mining and quarrying of other crushed and broken stone	(X)	74.2
Mining and quarrying of other nonmetallic minerals, except fuels	(X)	4.1
Fly ash	(X)	0.8
Ready-mixed concrete chemical processing preparations and materials	(X)	230.2
Portland and blended cements	(X)	1,576.5
Lightweight aggregate (including vermiculite, perlite, expanded clays, shale, and slag)	(X)	1.6
Other stone, clay, glass, and concrete products	(X)	73.9
All other materials and components, parts, containers, and supplies	(X)	398.0
Materials, ingredients, containers, and supplies, nsk	(X)	2,358.0

Source: 1992 *Economic Census*. Explanation of symbols used: (D): Withheld to avoid disclosure of competitive data; na: Not available; (S): Withheld because statistical norms were not met; (X): Not applicable; (Z): Less than half the unit shown; nec: Not elsewhere classified; nsk: Not specified by kind; - : zero; * : 10-19 percent estimated; ** : 20-29 percent estimated.

PRODUCT SHARE DETAILS

Product or Product Class	% Share	Product or Product Class	% Share
Ready-mixed concrete	100.00		

Source: 1992 *Economic Census*. The values shown are percent of total shipments in an industry. Values of indented subcategories are summed in the main heading. The symbol (D) appears when data are withheld to prevent disclosure of competitive information. The abbreviation nsk stands for 'not specified by kind' and nec for 'not elsewhere classified'.

INPUTS AND OUTPUTS FOR READY-MIXED CONCRETE

Economic Sector or Industry Providing Inputs	%	Sector	Economic Sector or Industry Buying Outputs	%	Sector
Cement, hydraulic	35.8	Manufg.	Residential 1-unit structures, nonfarm	19.5	Constr.
Sand & gravel	15.8	Mining	Highway & street construction	8.2	Constr.
Motor freight transportation & warehousing	12.3	Util.	Residential additions/alterations, nonfarm	8.2	Constr.
Dimension, crushed & broken stone	4.8	Mining	Office buildings	8.0	Constr.
Wholesale trade	3.8	Trade	Electric utility facility construction	7.6	Constr.
Railroads & related services	3.1	Util.	Maintenance of nonfarm buildings nec	6.5	Constr.
Petroleum refining	2.8	Manufg.	Industrial buildings	5.5	Constr.
Advertising	2.6	Services	Nonfarm residential structure maintenance	3.9	Constr.
Ready-mixed concrete	1.8	Manufg.	Maintenance of highways & streets	2.6	Constr.
Minerals, ground or treated	1.4	Manufg.	Construction of hospitals	2.2	Constr.
Chemical preparations, nec	1.3	Manufg.	Residential garden apartments	2.2	Constr.
Cyclic crudes and organics	1.3	Manufg.	Construction of educational buildings	2.1	Constr.
Industrial inorganic chemicals, nec	1.3	Manufg.	Construction of stores & restaurants	1.8	Constr.
Water transportation	1.2	Util.	Warehouses	1.7	Constr.
Electric services (utilities)	1.1	Util.	Sewer system facility construction	1.6	Constr.
Maintenance of nonfarm buildings nec	0.7	Constr.	Hotels & motels	1.4	Constr.
Mining machinery, except oil field	0.7	Manufg.	Farm service facilities	1.2	Constr.
Surface active agents	0.6	Manufg.	Ready-mixed concrete	1.2	Manufg.
Communications, except radio & TV	0.5	Util.	Maintenance of sewer facilities	1.0	Constr.
Eating & drinking places	0.5	Trade	Residential 2-4 unit structures, nonfarm	0.9	Constr.
Banking	0.5	Fin/R.E.	Telephone & telegraph facility construction	0.9	Constr.
Equipment rental & leasing services	0.5	Services	Amusement & recreation building construction	0.8	Constr.
Small arms ammunition	0.4	Manufg.	Local transit facility construction	0.8	Constr.
Computer & data processing services	0.4	Services	Maintenance of nonbuilding facilities nec	0.8	Constr.
Sawmills & planning mills, general	0.3	Manufg.	Maintenance of electric utility facilities	0.7	Constr.
Explosives	0.2	Manufg.	Maintenance of farm service facilities	0.7	Constr.
Gas production & distribution (utilities)	0.2	Util.	Nonbuilding facilities nec	0.7	Constr.
Insurance carriers	0.2	Fin/R.E.	Resid. & other health facility construction	0.7	Constr.
Royalties	0.2	Fin/R.E.	Water supply facility construction	0.7	Constr.
Accounting, auditing & bookkeeping	0.2	Services	Construction of nonfarm buildings nec	0.6	Constr.
Automotive rental & leasing, without drivers	0.2	Services	Maintenance of water supply facilities	0.5	Constr.
Detective & protective services	0.2	Services	Residential high-rise apartments	0.5	Constr.
Engineering, architectural, & surveying services	0.2	Services	Concrete products, nec	0.5	Manufg.
Legal services	0.2	Services	Construction of conservation facilities	0.4	Constr.
Management & consulting services & labs	0.2	Services	Construction of religious buildings	0.4	Constr.
U.S. Postal Service	0.2	Gov't	Farm housing units & additions & alterations	0.4	Constr.
Clay, ceramic, & refractory minerals	0.1	Mining	Garage & service station construction	0.4	Constr.
Lubricating oils & greases	0.1	Manufg.	Maintenance of military facilities	0.3	Constr.
Miscellaneous fabricated wire products	0.1	Manufg.	Maintenance of petroleum pipelines	0.3	Constr.
Air transportation	0.1	Util.	Maintenance of railroads	0.3	Constr.
Retail trade, except eating & drinking	0.1	Trade	Maintenance, conservation & development facilities	0.3	Constr.
Real estate	0.1	Fin/R.E.	Gas utility facility construction	0.2	Constr.
Automotive repair shops & services	0.1	Services	Maintenance of farm residential buildings	0.2	Constr.
Electrical repair shops	0.1	Services	Maintenance of telephone & telegraph facilities	0.2	Constr.
			Construction of dams & reservoirs	0.1	Constr.
			Maintenance of gas utility facilities	0.1	Constr.
			Maintenance of local transit facilities	0.1	Constr.

Source: Benchmark Input-Output Accounts for the U.S. Economy, 1982, U.S. Department of Commerce, Washington, D.C., July 1991. Data, as reported in the source, are organized by the 1977 SIC structure in use in 1982 but have been matched, as closely as is possible, to the 1987 SIC structure used in this book.

OCCUPATIONS EMPLOYED BY SIC 327 - CONCRETE, GYPSUM, AND PLASTER PRODUCTS

Occupation	% of Total 1994	Change to 2005	Occupation	% of Total 1994	Change to 2005
Truck drivers light & heavy	31.4	-10.5	Concrete & terrazzo finishers	2.2	-13.2
Helpers, laborers, & material movers nec	4.6	-13.2	Crushing & mixing machine operators	2.1	-13.2
General managers & top executives	4.3	-17.6	General office clerks	1.8	-26.0
Blue collar worker supervisors	4.2	-19.9	Helpers, construction trades	1.8	-13.2
Sales & related workers nec	3.2	-13.2	Industrial machinery mechanics	1.7	-4.5
Bookkeeping, accounting, & auditing clerks	2.5	-34.9	Industrial production managers	1.5	-13.1
Industrial truck & tractor operators	2.5	-13.2	Secretaries, ex legal & medical	1.4	-20.9
Bus & truck mechanics & diesel engine specialists	2.4	-13.2	Maintenance repairers, general utility	1.4	-21.9
Dispatchers, ex police, fire, & ambulance	2.4	-13.2	Welders & cutters	1.3	-13.1
Extruding & forming machine workers	2.3	21.6	Freight, stock, & material movers, hand	1.2	-30.5
Assemblers, fabricators, & hand workers nec	2.2	-13.2	Machine feeders & offbearers	1.1	-21.9
Precision workers nec	2.2	4.2			

Source: Industry-Occupation Matrix, Bureau of Labor Statistics. These data relate to one or more 3-digit SIC industry groups rather than to a single 4-digit SIC. The change reported for each occupation to the year 2005 is a percent of growth or decline as estimated by the Bureau of Labor Statistics. The abbreviation nec stands for 'not elsewhere classified'.

LOCATION BY STATE AND REGIONAL CONCENTRATION

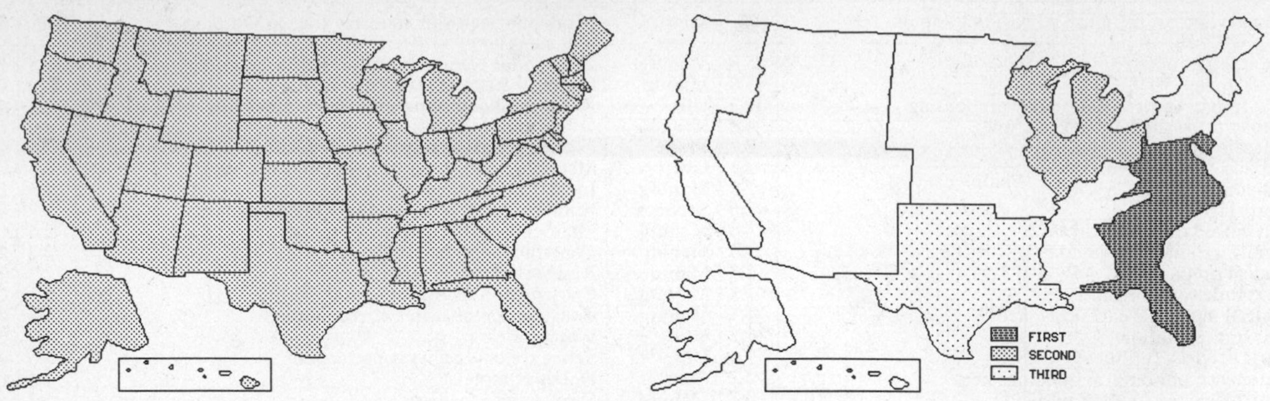

INDUSTRY DATA BY STATE

State	Establish-ments	Shipments: Total ($ mil)	Shipments: % of U.S.	Shipments: Per Establ.	Employment: Total Number	Employment: % of U.S.	Employment: Per Establ.	Employment: Wages ($/hour)	Cost as % of Shipments	Investment per Employee ($)
California	436	1,420.9	11.8	3.3	8,500	10.3	19	15.81	57.7	2,506
Texas	430	914.2	7.6	2.1	6,200	7.5	14	9.67	57.9	3,694
Florida	313	762.3	6.3	2.4	4,700	5.7	15	10.40	61.0	1,979
Illinois	215	558.9	4.7	2.6	3,400	4.1	16	15.69	55.6	4,382
Ohio	238	546.7	4.6	2.3	3,500	4.2	15	12.12	55.4	5,714
New York	185	491.1	4.1	2.7	3,000	3.6	16	14.77	51.9	3,267
Pennsylvania	188	410.8	3.4	2.2	2,900	3.5	15	12.48	56.3	3,655
Michigan	206	380.7	3.2	1.8	2,400	2.9	12	14.14	51.2	4,458
Georgia	160	366.7	3.1	2.3	2,500	3.0	16	10.55	56.4	2,960
Indiana	140	323.6	2.7	2.3	2,000	2.4	14	13.03	52.2	6,750
North Carolina	166	312.0	2.6	1.9	2,600	3.2	16	9.73	56.5	4,385
Wisconsin	137	310.7	2.6	2.3	2,000	2.4	15	12.63	52.7	5,050
Washington	98	304.5	2.5	3.1	2,100	2.5	21	15.53	46.8	5,381
Virginia	118	276.0	2.3	2.3	1,900	2.3	16	11.20	52.5	5,316
Colorado	70	267.6	2.2	3.8	1,700	2.1	24	12.46	54.8	4,059
Missouri	186	263.1	2.2	1.4	2,200	2.7	12	10.94	56.3	3,864
New Jersey	74	259.9	2.2	3.5	1,400	1.7	19	17.10	56.1	4,214
Iowa	157	236.4	2.0	1.5	1,700	2.1	11	10.96	56.4	4,412
Arizona	75	224.6	1.9	3.0	1,800	2.2	24	11.04	54.4	3,056
Kentucky	105	211.1	1.8	2.0	1,700	2.1	16	9.40	55.7	2,882
Maryland	63	202.3	1.7	3.2	1,300	1.6	21	12.96	56.5	3,462
Minnesota	110	198.5	1.7	1.8	1,500	1.8	14	12.36	52.9	3,467
Tennessee	103	196.9	1.6	1.9	1,600	1.9	16	9.96	55.2	3,875
Massachusetts	53	180.0	1.5	3.4	1,200	1.5	23	15.00	51.6	4,500
Louisiana	71	178.8	1.5	2.5	1,600	1.9	23	9.04	59.3	3,313
Alabama	89	170.1	1.4	1.9	1,300	1.6	15	9.67	51.4	5,462
Utah	31	168.4	1.4	5.4	1,100	1.3	35	12.00	52.9	3,455
South Carolina	83	152.9	1.3	1.8	1,200	1.5	14	10.45	57.0	3,417
Kansas	102	143.9	1.2	1.4	1,200	1.5	12	9.65	55.4	4,000
Nevada	29	141.7	1.2	4.9	1,000	1.2	34	15.35	54.1	5,000
Oklahoma	124	140.5	1.2	1.1	1,400	1.7	11	9.50	54.3	2,357
Oregon	55	126.3	1.1	2.3	1,100	1.3	20	13.80	57.0	3,909
Mississippi	79	117.1	1.0	1.5	1,000	1.2	13	9.38	52.9	3,400
Nebraska	75	116.3	1.0	1.6	800	1.0	11	10.46	59.2	3,500
Arkansas	80	109.9	0.9	1.4	900	1.1	11	8.87	55.2	5,667
New Mexico	36	95.9	0.8	2.7	800	1.0	22	9.82	51.1	2,500
Connecticut	33	94.9	0.8	2.9	500	0.6	15	14.44	56.4	4,000
West Virginia	41	70.1	0.6	1.7	500	0.6	12	10.87	51.9	3,200
Montana	41	60.8	0.5	1.5	500	0.6	12	10.71	52.6	3,800
Idaho	40	59.1	0.5	1.5	500	0.6	13	11.44	55.3	2,800
Maine	29	46.7	0.4	1.6	300	0.4	10	9.57	52.0	2,667
Delaware	13	43.2	0.4	3.3	400	0.5	31	10.50	46.3	1,250
New Hampshire	19	42.2	0.4	2.2	300	0.4	16	11.20	52.8	-
Wyoming	26	36.7	0.3	1.4	300	0.4	12	12.00	44.1	4,667
Alaska	17	35.0	0.3	2.1	200	0.2	12	14.33	51.7	-
South Dakota	34	29.5	0.2	0.9	200	0.2	6	9.00	60.7	4,000
North Dakota	37	29.1	0.2	0.8	300	0.4	8	12.00	53.3	2,000
Vermont	13	26.3	0.2	2.0	200	0.2	15	14.00	48.7	-
Rhode Island	11	24.1	0.2	2.2	100	0.1	9	12.00	55.6	7,000
Hawaii	15	(D)	-	-	375 *	0.5	25	-	-	8,267
D.C.	5	(D)	-	-	175 *	0.2	35	-	-	-

Source: 1992 *Economic Census*. The states are in descending order of shipments or establishments (if shipment data are missing for the majority). The symbol (D) appears when data are withheld to prevent disclosure of competitive information. States marked with (D) are sorted by number of establishments. A dash (-) indicates that the data element cannot be calculated; * indicates the midpoint of a range.

3274 - LIME

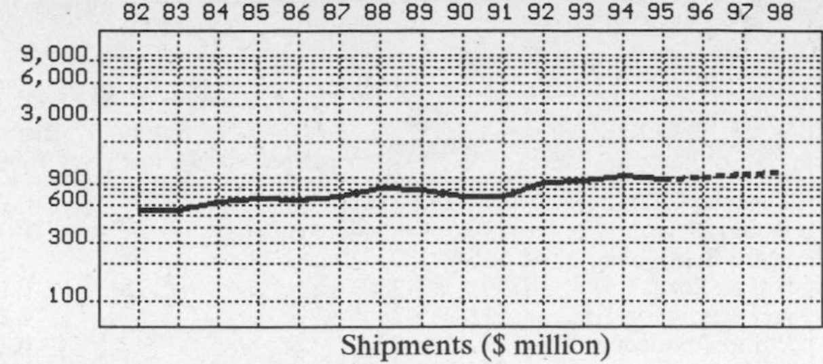

Shipments ($ million)

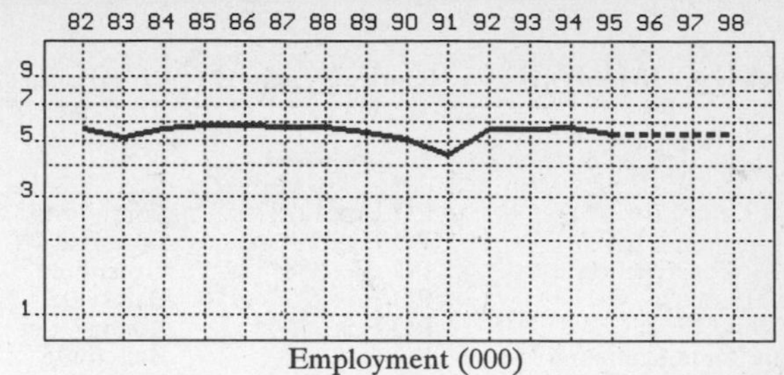

Employment (000)

GENERAL STATISTICS

Year	Companies	Establishments: Total	Establishments: with 20 or more employees	Employment: Total (000)	Production Workers (000)	Production Hours (Mil)	Compensation: Payroll ($ mil)	Compensation: Wages ($/hr)	Cost of Materials	Value Added by Manufacture	Value of Shipments	Capital Invest.
1982	59	87	59	5.6	4.4	8.5	108.6	9.34	298.2	245.0	543.2	36.0
1983		85	57	5.2	4.1	8.4	109.9	9.65	305.6	250.6	557.7	20.9
1984		83	55	5.6	4.5	9.2	121.1	9.89	347.6	295.1	642.3	72.9
1985		80	54	5.8	4.6	9.6	133.2	10.46	359.2	316.5	675.8	70.1
1986		81	57	5.8	4.6	9.3	136.5	10.94	351.8	318.0	670.9	38.8
1987	56	82	56	5.7	4.5	9.4	141.9	11.02	364.5	350.4	715.5	33.0
1988		75	50	5.7	4.6	9.6	150.7	11.86	413.9	418.0	830.6	28.0
1989		71	49	5.4	5.0	10.3	168.6	11.25	385.0	430.9	812.2	41.7
1990		76	49	5.1	3.7	8.7	148.4	12.84	300.6	422.5	719.8	43.7
1991		74	49	4.4	3.3	7.4	148.0	13.97	299.8	411.5	715.4	66.4
1992	57	88	59	5.6	4.3	9.6	171.4	12.64	446.2	461.1	903.7	47.9
1993		86	57	5.6	4.3	9.4	180.1	13.32	480.0	464.4	946.2	35.5
1994		78P	52P	5.7	4.5	8.9	175.0	14.10	529.9	511.5	1,037.8	21.6
1995		78P	52P	5.3P	4.2P	9.2P	185.9P	14.42P	506.9P	489.3P	992.7P	38.7P
1996		78P	51P	5.3P	4.1P	9.2P	191.6P	14.82P	524.5P	506.3P	1,027.2P	38.1P
1997		77P	51P	5.3P	4.1P	9.2P	197.3P	15.22P	542.1P	523.2P	1,061.6P	37.6P
1998		77P	51P	5.3P	4.1P	9.2P	203.1P	15.62P	559.7P	540.2P	1,096.1P	37.0P

Sources: 1982, 1987, 1992 *Economic Census*; *Annual Survey of Manufactures*, 83-86, 88-91, 93-94. Establishment counts for non-Census years are from *County Business Patterns*; establishment values for 83-84 are extrapolations. 'P's show projections by the editors. Industries reclassified in 87 will not have data for prior years.

INDICES OF CHANGE

Year	Companies	Establishments: Total	Establishments: with 20 or more employees	Employment: Total (000)	Production Workers (000)	Production Hours (Mil)	Compensation: Payroll ($ mil)	Compensation: Wages ($/hr)	Cost of Materials	Value Added by Manufacture	Value of Shipments	Capital Invest.
1982	104	99	100	100	102	89	63	74	67	53	60	75
1983		97	97	93	95	87	64	76	68	54	62	44
1984		94	93	100	105	96	71	78	78	64	71	152
1985		91	92	104	107	100	78	83	81	69	75	146
1986		92	97	104	107	97	80	87	79	69	74	81
1987	98	93	95	102	105	98	83	87	82	76	79	69
1988		85	85	102	107	100	88	94	93	91	92	58
1989		81	83	96	116	107	98	89	86	93	90	87
1990		86	83	91	86	91	87	102	67	92	80	91
1991		84	83	79	77	77	86	111	67	89	79	139
1992	100	100	100	100	100	100	100	100	100	100	100	100
1993		98	97	100	100	98	105	105	108	101	105	74
1994		89P	88P	102	105	93	102	112	119	111	115	45
1995		89P	87P	96P	97P	96P	108P	114P	114P	106P	110P	81P
1996		88P	87P	95P	96P	96P	112P	117P	118P	110P	114P	80P
1997		88P	86P	95P	96P	96P	115P	120P	121P	113P	117P	78P
1998		87P	86P	95P	95P	96P	118P	124P	125P	117P	121P	77P

Sources: Same as General Statistics. Values reflect change from the base year, 1992. Values above 100 mean greater than 92, values below 100 mean less than 92, and a value of 100 in the 82-91 or 93-98 period means same as 92. 'P's mark projections by the editors.

SELECTED RATIOS

For 1994	Avg. of All Manufact.	Analyzed Industry	Index
Employees per Establishment	49	73	149
Payroll per Establishment	1,500,273	2,234,907	149
Payroll per Employee	30,620	30,702	100
Production Workers per Establishment	34	57	167
Wages per Establishment	853,319	1,602,620	188
Wages per Production Worker	24,861	27,887	112
Hours per Production Worker	2,056	1,978	96
Wages per Hour	12.09	14.10	117
Value Added per Establishment	4,602,255	6,532,314	142
Value Added per Employee	93,930	89,737	96

For 1994	Avg. of All Manufact.	Analyzed Industry	Index
Value Added per Production Worker	134,084	113,667	85
Cost per Establishment	5,045,178	6,767,299	134
Cost per Employee	102,970	92,965	90
Cost per Production Worker	146,988	117,756	80
Shipments per Establishment	9,576,895	13,253,638	138
Shipments per Employee	195,460	182,070	93
Shipments per Production Worker	279,017	230,622	83
Investment per Establishment	321,011	275,851	86
Investment per Employee	6,552	3,789	58
Investment per Production Worker	9,352	4,800	51

Sources: Same as General Statistics. The 'Average of All Manufacturing' column represents the average of all manufacturing industries reported for the most recent complete year available. The Index shows the relationship between the Average and the Analyzed Industry. For example, 100 means that they are equal; 500 that the Analyzed Industry is five times the average; 50 means that the Analyzed Industry is half the national average. The abbreviation 'na' is used to show that data are 'not available'.

LEADING COMPANIES

Number shown: **17** Total sales ($ mil): **347** Total employment (000): **2.4**

Company Name	Address				CEO Name	Phone	Co. Type	Sales ($ mil)	Empl. (000)
Chemical Lime Co	PO Box 121874	Fort Worth	TX	76121	Thomas Chambers	817-732-8164	R	175	0.9
Martin Limestone Inc	PO Box 550	Blue Ball	PA	17506	Robert L Spotts	717-354-8544	S	36	0.3
Schildberg Construction	PO Box 358	Greenfield	IA	50849	Mark Schildberg	515-743-2131	R	34*	0.3
Arkansas Lime Co	PO Box 2356	Batesville	AR	72503	Bill Keller	501-793-2301	S	15*	0.1
Austin White Lime Co	PO Box 9556	Austin	TX	78766	AH Robinson III	512-255-3646	R	12	0.2
Bellefonte Lime Company Inc	PO Box 448	Bellefonte	PA	16823	Philip J Senechal	814-355-4761	R	12	0.1
Western Lime and Cement Co	PO Box 57	West Bend	WI	53095	VF Nast III	414-334-3005	R	10	0.1
Adams Corp	PO Box 2320	Pikeville	KY	41502	Stuart Adams	606-432-2584	R	9	<0.1
CLM Corp	PO Box 16807	Duluth	MN	55816	CE Laliberte	218-722-3981	R	9*	<0.1
Con-Lime Inc	PO Box 118	Bellefonte	PA	16823	Irvin L Confer	814-355-4744	R	7*	<0.1
Rockwell Lime Company Inc	4110 Rockwood Rd	Manitowoc	WI	54220	Donald R Brisch	414-682-7771	R	6	<0.1
Germany Valley Limestone Co	PO Box 302	Riverton	WV	26814	John R Raese	304-567-2141	D	5	<0.1
Chesterhill Stone Co	PO Box 599	McConnelsville	OH	43756	Fred R Price	614-962-5621	R	4*	<0.1
WS Frey Company Inc	257 E Market St	York	PA	17403	William S Frey	717-848-2369	R	4*	<0.1
Chemlime NJ Inc	32 Com Dr CN-1148	Cranford	NJ	07016	JJ Fitzpatrick	908-272-0330	R	4	<0.1
Tacoma Lime	1220 Alexander Av	Tacoma	WA	98421	WE Dodge	206-272-7231	D	3	<0.1
Spreckels Limestone	PO Box 280	Cool	CA	95614	Ron Friedman	916-885-4244	S	2*	<0.1

Source: *Ward's Business Directory of U.S. Private and Public Companies*, Volumes 1 and 2, 1996. The company type code used is as follows: P - Public, R - Private, S - Subsidiary, D - Division, J - Joint Venture, A - Affiliate, G - Group. Sales are in millions of dollars, employees are in thousands. An asterisk (*) indicates an estimated sales volume. The symbol < stands for 'less than'. Company names and addresses are truncated, in some cases, to fit into the available space.

MATERIALS CONSUMED

Material	Quantity	Delivered Cost ($ million)
Materials, ingredients, containers, and supplies	(X)	194.7
Paperboard liners	(X)	(D)
Paper shipping sacks and multiwall bags	(X)	8.4
Other paper and paperboard products	(X)	0.8
Refractories, clay or nonclay	(X)	20.6
Minerals and earths, ground or otherwise treated	(X)	2.0
Other stone, clay, glass, and concrete products	(X)	(D)
Crushed and broken stone (including cement rock, limestone, etc.)	(X)	62.7
All other materials and components, parts, containers, and supplies	(X)	89.4
Materials, ingredients, containers, and supplies, nsk	(X)	8.1

Source: 1992 *Economic Census*. Explanation of symbols used: (D): Withheld to avoid disclosure of competitive data; na: Not available; (S): Withheld because statistical norms were not met; (X): Not applicable; (Z): Less than half the unit shown; nec: Not elsewhere classified; nsk: Not specified by kind; - : zero; * : 10-19 percent estimated; ** : 20-29 percent estimated.

PRODUCT SHARE DETAILS

Product or Product Class	% Share	Product or Product Class	% Share
Lime	100.00	Dead-burned dolomite, lime, including cost of containers	3.33
Quicklime, including cost of containers	72.16	Other lime, including cost of containers	4.37
Hydrated lime, including cost of containers	14.63		

Source: 1992 *Economic Census*. The values shown are percent of total shipments in an industry. Values of indented subcategories are summed in the main heading. The symbol (D) appears when data are withheld to prevent disclosure of competitive information. The abbreviation nsk stands for 'not specified by kind' and nec for 'not elsewhere classified'.

INPUTS AND OUTPUTS FOR LIME

Economic Sector or Industry Providing Inputs	%	Sector	Economic Sector or Industry Buying Outputs	%	Sector
Coal	15.5	Mining	Blast furnaces & steel mills	25.8	Manufg.
Gas production & distribution (utilities)	13.7	Util.	State & local government enterprises, nec	18.0	Gov't
Electric services (utilities)	10.1	Util.	Nonmetallic mineral products, nec	7.5	Manufg.
Dimension, crushed & broken stone	5.5	Mining	Glass containers	5.6	Manufg.
Wholesale trade	5.5	Trade	Paper mills, except building paper	5.1	Manufg.
Railroads & related services	4.9	Util.	Primary aluminum	4.4	Manufg.
Imports	4.8	Foreign	Paperboard mills	3.1	Manufg.
Motor freight transportation & warehousing	4.5	Util.	Copper ore	2.4	Mining
Petroleum refining	4.1	Manufg.	Sewer system facility construction	2.3	Constr.
Banking	3.0	Fin/R.E.	Pulp mills	2.3	Manufg.
Maintenance of nonfarm buildings nec	2.9	Constr.	Cyclic crudes and organics	1.6	Manufg.
Explosives	2.7	Manufg.	Exports	1.4	Foreign
Machinery, except electrical, nec	2.7	Manufg.	Nonferrous metal ores, except copper	1.3	Mining
Advertising	2.0	Services	Nonclay refractories	1.2	Manufg.

Continued on next page.

INPUTS AND OUTPUTS FOR LIME - Continued

Economic Sector or Industry Providing Inputs	%	Sector	Economic Sector or Industry Buying Outputs	%	Sector
Bags, except textile	1.5	Manufg.	Industrial buildings	1.1	Constr.
Mining machinery, except oil field	1.5	Manufg.	Residential additions/alterations, nonfarm	1.0	Constr.
Cyclic crudes and organics	1.2	Manufg.	Office buildings	0.9	Constr.
Paperboard containers & boxes	1.2	Manufg.	Residential 1-unit structures, nonfarm	0.9	Constr.
Small arms ammunition	1.2	Manufg.	Leather tanning & finishing	0.8	Manufg.
Lime	0.9	Manufg.	Agricultural, forestry, & fishery services	0.7	Agric.
Communications, except radio & TV	0.9	Util.	Asphalt felts & coatings	0.7	Manufg.
Nonmetallic mineral services	0.8	Mining	Lime	0.7	Manufg.
Sawmills & planning mills, general	0.7	Manufg.	Coal	0.6	Mining
Water transportation	0.7	Util.	Maintenance of nonfarm buildings nec	0.6	Constr.
Minerals, ground or treated	0.5	Manufg.	Nonfarm residential structure maintenance	0.6	Constr.
Sanitary services, steam supply, irrigation	0.5	Util.	Electric services (utilities)	0.6	Util.
Eating & drinking places	0.5	Trade	Construction of stores & restaurants	0.5	Constr.
Automotive rental & leasing, without drivers	0.5	Services	Agricultural chemicals, nec	0.5	Manufg.
Automotive repair shops & services	0.5	Services	Vitreous plumbing fixtures	0.5	Manufg.
Internal combustion engines, nec	0.3	Manufg.	Minerals, ground or treated	0.4	Manufg.
Computer & data processing services	0.3	Services	Plastics materials & resins	0.4	Manufg.
Equipment rental & leasing services	0.3	Services	Construction of educational buildings	0.3	Constr.
Blast furnaces & steel mills	0.2	Manufg.	Petroleum & natural gas well drilling	0.3	Constr.
Paints & allied products	0.2	Manufg.	Residential garden apartments	0.3	Constr.
Retail trade, except eating & drinking	0.2	Trade	Glass & glass products, except containers	0.3	Manufg.
Insurance carriers	0.2	Fin/R.E.	Mineral wool	0.3	Manufg.
Legal services	0.2	Services	Prepared feeds, nec	0.3	Manufg.
Management & consulting services & labs	0.2	Services	Primary nonferrous metals, nec	0.3	Manufg.
U.S. Postal Service	0.2	Gov't	Steel wire & related products	0.3	Manufg.
Fabricated structural metal	0.1	Manufg.	Sugar	0.3	Manufg.
Industrial inorganic chemicals, nec	0.1	Manufg.	Construction of hospitals	0.2	Constr.
Lubricating oils & greases	0.1	Manufg.	Highway & street construction	0.2	Constr.
Miscellaneous fabricated wire products	0.1	Manufg.	Maintenance of sewer facilities	0.2	Constr.
Tires & inner tubes	0.1	Manufg.	Water supply facility construction	0.2	Constr.
Air transportation	0.1	Util.	Petroleum refining	0.2	Manufg.
Accounting, auditing & bookkeeping	0.1	Services	Federal Government purchases, nondefense	0.2	Fed Govt
			Construction of religious buildings	0.1	Constr.
			Hotels & motels	0.1	Constr.
			Maintenance of highways & streets	0.1	Constr.
			Maintenance of water supply facilities	0.1	Constr.
			Residential 2-4 unit structures, nonfarm	0.1	Constr.
			Residential high-rise apartments	0.1	Constr.
			Electrometallurgical products	0.1	Manufg.
			Federal Government purchases, national defense	0.1	Fed Govt

Source: Benchmark Input-Output Accounts for the U.S. Economy, 1982, U.S. Department of Commerce, Washington, D.C., July 1991. Data, as reported in the source, are organized by the 1977 SIC structure in use in 1982 but have been matched, as closely as is possible, to the 1987 SIC structure used in this book.

OCCUPATIONS EMPLOYED BY SIC 327 - CONCRETE, GYPSUM, AND PLASTER PRODUCTS

Occupation	% of Total 1994	Change to 2005	Occupation	% of Total 1994	Change to 2005
Truck drivers light & heavy	31.4	-10.5	Concrete & terrazzo finishers	2.2	-13.2
Helpers, laborers, & material movers nec	4.6	-13.2	Crushing & mixing machine operators	2.1	-13.2
General managers & top executives	4.3	-17.6	General office clerks	1.8	-26.0
Blue collar worker supervisors	4.2	-19.9	Helpers, construction trades	1.8	-13.2
Sales & related workers nec	3.2	-13.2	Industrial machinery mechanics	1.7	-4.5
Bookkeeping, accounting, & auditing clerks	2.5	-34.9	Industrial production managers	1.5	-13.1
Industrial truck & tractor operators	2.5	-13.2	Secretaries, ex legal & medical	1.4	-20.9
Bus & truck mechanics & diesel engine specialists	2.4	-13.2	Maintenance repairers, general utility	1.4	-21.9
Dispatchers, ex police, fire, & ambulance	2.4	-13.2	Welders & cutters	1.3	-13.1
Extruding & forming machine workers	2.3	21.6	Freight, stock, & material movers, hand	1.2	-30.5
Assemblers, fabricators, & hand workers nec	2.2	-13.2	Machine feeders & offbearers	1.1	-21.9
Precision workers nec	2.2	4.2			

Source: Industry-Occupation Matrix, Bureau of Labor Statistics. These data relate to one or more 3-digit SIC industry groups rather than to a single 4-digit SIC. The change reported for each occupation to the year 2005 is a percent of growth or decline as estimated by the Bureau of Labor Statistics. The abbreviation nec stands for 'not elsewhere classified'.

LOCATION BY STATE AND REGIONAL CONCENTRATION

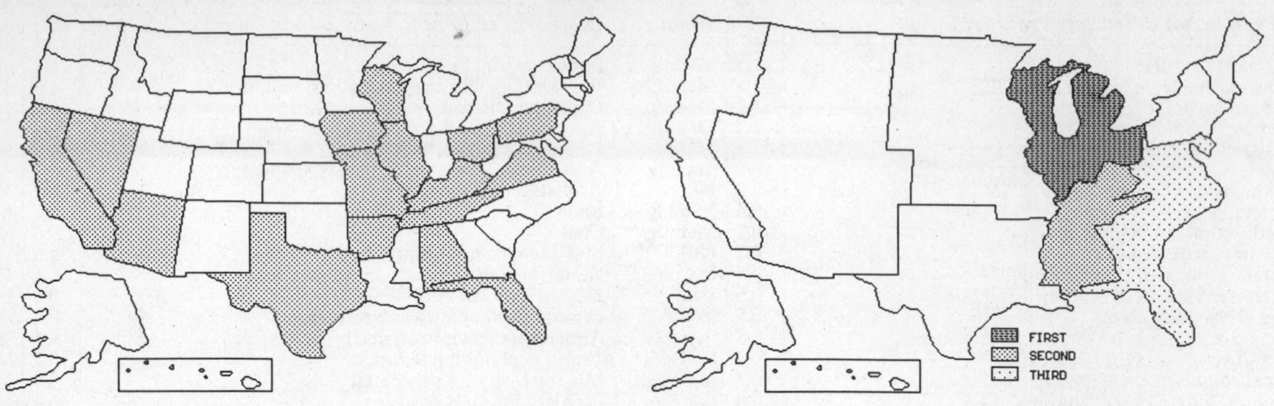

INDUSTRY DATA BY STATE

State	Establish-ments	Shipments			Employment				Cost as % of Shipments	Investment per Employee ($)
		Total ($ mil)	% of U.S.	Per Establ.	Total Number	% of U.S.	Per Establ.	Wages ($/hour)		
Ohio	9	110.5	12.2	12.3	600	10.7	67	13.89	51.6	8,167
Pennsylvania	8	88.5	9.8	11.1	600	10.7	75	14.18	59.9	-
Alabama	7	80.1	8.9	11.4	400	7.1	57	12.71	57.6	-
Texas	6	77.0	8.5	12.8	500	8.9	83	10.00	39.5	6,400
Virginia	7	(D)	-	-	375 *	6.7	54	-	-	6,933
Wisconsin	5	(D)	-	-	175 *	3.1	35	-	-	-
Illinois	4	(D)	-	-	175 *	3.1	44	-	-	-
Tennessee	4	(D)	-	-	175 *	3.1	44	-	-	-
California	3	(D)	-	-	175 *	3.1	58	-	-	-
Iowa	3	(D)	-	-	175 *	3.1	58	-	-	-
Kentucky	3	(D)	-	-	375 *	6.7	125	-	-	-
Arizona	2	(D)	-	-	175 *	3.1	88	-	-	-
Florida	2	(D)	-	-	175 *	3.1	88	-	-	-
Missouri	2	(D)	-	-	750 *	13.4	375	-	-	-
Nevada	2	(D)	-	-	175 *	3.1	88	-	-	-
Arkansas	1	(D)	-	-	175 *	3.1	175	-	-	-

Source: 1992 *Economic Census*. The states are in descending order of shipments or establishments (if shipment data are missing for the majority). The symbol (D) appears when data are withheld to prevent disclosure of competitive information. States marked with (D) are sorted by number of establishments. A dash (-) indicates that the data element cannot be calculated; * indicates the midpoint of a range.

3275 - GYPSUM PRODUCTS

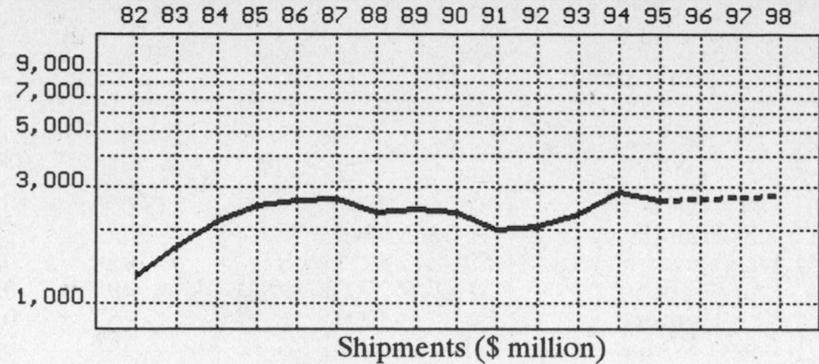

Shipments ($ million)

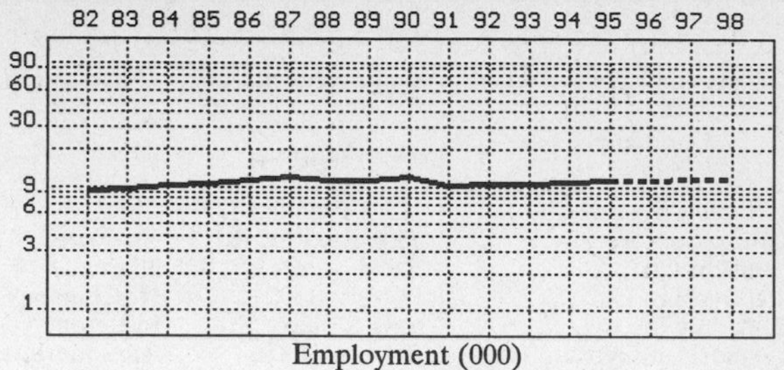

Employment (000)

GENERAL STATISTICS

Year	Com-panies	Establishments		Employment			Compensation		Production ($ million)			
		Total	with 20 or more employees	Total (000)	Production Workers (000)	Production Hours (Mil)	Payroll ($ mil)	Wages ($/hr)	Cost of Materials	Value Added by Manufacture	Value of Shipments	Capital Invest.
1982	70	139	84	9.1	7.1	15.5	186.9	8.96	809.2	492.1	1,289.2	85.5
1983		134	85	9.4	7.5	16.8	211.5	9.78	974.5	722.2	1,709.7	34.5
1984		129	86	10.3	8.2	18.5	241.0	10.02	1,173.5	1,009.3	2,176.4	59.4
1985		124	86	10.6	8.4	19.2	262.6	10.38	1,263.0	1,249.5	2,511.7	101.8
1986		134	91	11.1	8.8	20.6	290.6	10.64	1,221.8	1,392.4	2,619.0	139.3
1987	80	152	97	12.1	9.6	22.3	322.7	10.78	1,347.5	1,331.4	2,670.9	88.1
1988		144	94	11.4	9.2	21.4	313.4	11.00	1,300.9	1,076.9	2,378.5	57.0
1989		146	95	11.4	9.0	20.7	332.9	12.00	1,332.1	1,075.3	2,408.0	53.6
1990		165	103	11.8	9.1	20.5	341.0	12.27	1,404.9	967.0	2,375.1	68.1
1991		152	102	10.3	8.1	17.8	311.6	12.83	1,232.6	759.8	2,008.3	34.2
1992	80	152	95	10.5	8.3	19.0	329.0	12.74	1,283.9	793.3	2,075.9	43.8
1993		161	109	10.4	8.3	18.9	336.4	13.06	1,358.7	929.1	2,290.4	39.8
1994		162P	107P	10.7	8.6	20.1	364.9	13.53	1,667.9	1,181.0	2,849.4	74.2
1995		165P	109P	11.3P	9.0P	20.6P	384.3P	13.94P	1,538.3P	1,089.2P	2,628.0P	49.0P
1996		168P	111P	11.4P	9.0P	20.8P	396.9P	14.31P	1,569.2P	1,111.1P	2,680.7P	46.4P
1997		171P	113P	11.5P	9.1P	21.0P	409.6P	14.67P	1,600.0P	1,132.9P	2,733.5P	43.7P
1998		174P	115P	11.5P	9.2P	21.2P	422.2P	15.04P	1,630.9P	1,154.8P	2,786.2P	41.1P

Sources: 1982, 1987, 1992 *Economic Census*; *Annual Survey of Manufactures*, 83-86, 88-91, 93-94. Establishment counts for non-Census years are from *County Business Patterns*; establishment values for 83-84 are extrapolations. 'P's show projections by the editors. Industries reclassified in 87 will not have data for prior years.

INDICES OF CHANGE

Year	Com-panies	Establishments		Employment			Compensation		Production ($ million)			
		Total	with 20 or more employees	Total (000)	Production Workers (000)	Production Hours (Mil)	Payroll ($ mil)	Wages ($/hr)	Cost of Materials	Value Added by Manufacture	Value of Shipments	Capital Invest.
1982	88	91	88	87	86	82	57	70	63	62	62	195
1983		88	89	90	90	88	64	77	76	91	82	79
1984		85	91	98	99	97	73	79	91	127	105	136
1985		82	91	101	101	101	80	81	98	158	121	232
1986		88	96	106	106	108	88	84	95	176	126	318
1987	100	100	102	115	116	117	98	85	105	168	129	201
1988		95	99	109	111	113	95	86	101	136	115	130
1989		96	100	109	108	109	101	94	104	136	116	122
1990		109	108	112	110	108	104	96	109	122	114	155
1991		100	107	98	98	94	95	101	96	96	97	78
1992	100	100	100	100	100	100	100	100	100	100	100	100
1993		106	115	99	100	99	102	103	106	117	110	91
1994		107P	113P	102	104	106	111	106	130	149	137	169
1995		109P	115P	107P	108P	109P	117P	109P	120P	137P	127P	112P
1996		111P	117P	108P	109P	110P	121P	112P	122P	140P	129P	106P
1997		112P	119P	109P	110P	111P	124P	115P	125P	143P	132P	100P
1998		114P	121P	110P	110P	112P	128P	118P	127P	146P	134P	94P

Sources: Same as General Statistics. Values reflect change from the base year, 1992. Values above 100 mean greater than 92, values below 100 mean less than 92, and a value of 100 in the 82-91 or 93-98 period means same as 92. 'P's mark projections by the editors.

SELECTED RATIOS

For 1994	Avg. of All Manufact.	Analyzed Industry	Index	For 1994	Avg. of All Manufact.	Analyzed Industry	Index
Employees per Establishment	49	66	134	Value Added per Production Worker	134,084	137,326	102
Payroll per Establishment	1,500,273	2,245,957	150	Cost per Establishment	5,045,178	10,265,914	203
Payroll per Employee	30,620	34,103	111	Cost per Employee	102,970	155,879	151
Production Workers per Establishment	34	53	154	Cost per Production Worker	146,988	193,942	132
Wages per Establishment	853,319	1,673,869	196	Shipments per Establishment	9,576,895	17,538,040	183
Wages per Production Worker	24,861	31,622	127	Shipments per Employee	195,460	266,299	136
Hours per Production Worker	2,056	2,337	114	Shipments per Production Worker	279,017	331,326	119
Wages per Hour	12.09	13.53	112	Investment per Establishment	321,011	456,701	142
Value Added per Establishment	4,602,255	7,269,048	158	Investment per Employee	6,552	6,935	106
Value Added per Employee	93,930	110,374	118	Investment per Production Worker	9,352	8,628	92

Sources: Same as General Statistics. The 'Average of All Manufacturing' column represents the average of all manufacturing industries reported for the most recent complete year available. The Index shows the relationship between the Average and the Analyzed Industry. For example, 100 means that they are equal; 500 that the Analyzed Industry is five times the average; 50 means that the Analyzed Industry is half the national average. The abbreviation 'na' is used to show that data are 'not available'.

LEADING COMPANIES

Number shown: **11** Total sales ($ mil): **1,868** Total employment (000): **13.6**

Company Name	Address				CEO Name	Phone	Co. Type	Sales ($ mil)	Empl. (000)
United States Gypsum Co	125 S Franklin Dr	Chicago	IL	60606	DE Roller	312-606-4000	S	1,400	10.0
National Gypsum Co	2001 Rexford Rd	Charlotte	NC	28211	S M Humphrey	704-365-7300	P	273	2.6
Briar Gypsum Co	Rte 4	Nashville	AR	71852	Ivan Kovarik	501-845-4951	S	75	0.2
Republic Gypsum Co	PO Box 1307	Hutchinson	KS	67504	Phil Simpson	316-727-2700	P	49	0.4
BNZ Materials Inc	6901 S Pierce St	Littleton	CO	80123	Ken Hunter	303-978-1199	R	15	0.1
Centex American Gypsum Co	PO Box 90820	Albuquerque	NM	87199	Roger Wallace	505-823-2022	S	15*	0.1
Gyp-Crete Corp	920 Hamel Rd	Hamel	MN	55340		612-478-6072	R	12	<0.1
Hamilton Materials Inc	345 W Meats Av	Orange	CA	92665	W Hamilton	714-637-2770	R	12*	0.1
Capaul Corp	1300 N Division St	Plainfield	IL	60544	Dave Sactise	815-436-8500	R	10	<0.1
Pittcon Industries	6409 Rhode Island	Riverdale	MD	20737	Rubin Goldklang	301-927-1000	R	4*	<0.1
Snap Wall Inc	2835 Sisson St	Baltimore	MD	21211	William J Wilson	410-467-8900	R	2	<0.1

Source: *Ward's Business Directory of U.S. Private and Public Companies*, Volumes 1 and 2, 1996. The company type code used is as follows: P - Public, R - Private, S - Subsidiary, D - Division, J - Joint Venture, A - Affiliate, G - Group. Sales are in millions of dollars, employees are in thousands. An asterisk (*) indicates an estimated sales volume. The symbol < stands for 'less than'. Company names and addresses are truncated, in some cases, to fit into the available space.

MATERIALS CONSUMED

Material	Quantity	Delivered Cost ($ million)
Materials, ingredients, containers, and supplies	(X)	1,001.1
Paperboard liners	(X)	108.2
Paper shipping sacks and multiwall bags	(X)	(D)
Other paper and paperboard products	(X)	208.6
Refractories, clay or nonclay	(X)	0.6
Cement clinker	(X)	(D)
Minerals and earths, ground or otherwise treated	(X)	93.3
Other stone, clay, glass, and concrete products	(X)	29.8
Crushed and broken stone (including cement rock, limestone, etc.)	(X)	122.2
All other materials and components, parts, containers, and supplies	(X)	401.5
Materials, ingredients, containers, and supplies, nsk	(X)	27.5

Source: 1992 *Economic Census*. Explanation of symbols used: (D): Withheld to avoid disclosure of competitive data; na: Not available; (S): Withheld because statistical norms were not met; (X): Not applicable; (Z): Less than half the unit shown; nec: Not elsewhere classified; nsk: Not specified by kind; - : zero; * : 10-19 percent estimated; ** : 20-29 percent estimated.

PRODUCT SHARE DETAILS

Product or Product Class	% Share	Product or Product Class	% Share
Gypsum products	100.00	Other gypsum products	14.74
Gypsum building materials	82.08	Industrial plasters, gypsum	22.75
Gypsum plaster building boards and lath	86.99	Other calcined gypsum products	73.59
Gypsum building plasters	12.76	Other gypsum products, nsk	3.66
Gypsum building materials, nsk	0.26	Gypsum products, nsk	3.18

Source: 1992 *Economic Census*. The values shown are percent of total shipments in an industry. Values of indented subcategories are summed in the main heading. The symbol (D) appears when data are withheld to prevent disclosure of competitive information. The abbreviation nsk stands for 'not specified by kind' and nec for 'not elsewhere classified'.

INPUTS AND OUTPUTS FOR GYPSUM PRODUCTS

Economic Sector or Industry Providing Inputs	%	Sector	Economic Sector or Industry Buying Outputs	%	Sector
Gas production & distribution (utilities)	15.1	Util.	Residential additions/alterations, nonfarm	20.0	Constr.
Nonmetallic mineral services	11.8	Mining	Residential 1-unit structures, nonfarm	14.8	Constr.
Minerals, ground or treated	10.9	Manufg.	Nonfarm residential structure maintenance	14.2	Constr.
Paperboard mills	10.9	Manufg.	Maintenance of nonfarm buildings nec	6.8	Constr.
Railroads & related services	5.6	Util.	Residential garden apartments	6.5	Constr.
Electric services (utilities)	5.3	Util.	Office buildings	5.8	Constr.
Motor freight transportation & warehousing	4.8	Util.	Construction of hospitals	3.3	Constr.
Advertising	3.4	Services	Construction of stores & restaurants	2.7	Constr.
Wholesale trade	3.3	Trade	Industrial buildings	2.2	Constr.
Petroleum refining	2.6	Manufg.	Residential 2-4 unit structures, nonfarm	2.0	Constr.
Imports	1.8	Foreign	Exports	2.0	Foreign
Cyclic crudes and organics	1.6	Manufg.	Change in business inventories	2.0	In House
Dimension, crushed & broken stone	1.4	Mining	Residential high-rise apartments	1.8	Constr.
Bags, except textile	1.4	Manufg.	Hotels & motels	1.6	Constr.
Paints & allied products	1.4	Manufg.	Mobile homes	1.2	Manufg.
Surface active agents	1.4	Manufg.	Prefabricated wood buildings	1.2	Manufg.
Water transportation	1.4	Util.	Lead pencils & art goods	1.0	Manufg.

Continued on next page.

INPUTS AND OUTPUTS FOR GYPSUM PRODUCTS - Continued

Economic Sector or Industry Providing Inputs	%	Sector	Economic Sector or Industry Buying Outputs	%	Sector
Chemical preparations, nec	1.1	Manufg.	Resid. & other health facility construction	0.9	Constr.
Miscellaneous plastics products	1.0	Manufg.	Sewer system facility construction	0.9	Constr.
Mining machinery, except oil field	0.9	Manufg.	Nonmetallic mineral products, nec	0.9	Manufg.
Air transportation	0.9	Util.	Vitreous plumbing fixtures	0.9	Manufg.
Maintenance of nonfarm buildings nec	0.8	Constr.	Construction of nonfarm buildings nec	0.8	Constr.
Sanitary services, steam supply, irrigation	0.7	Util.	Warehouses	0.8	Constr.
Banking	0.7	Fin/R.E.	Construction of educational buildings	0.6	Constr.
Coal	0.6	Mining	Amusement & recreation building construction	0.5	Constr.
Power transmission equipment	0.6	Manufg.	Federal Government purchases, nondefense	0.5	Fed Govt
Communications, except radio & TV	0.6	Util.	Farm housing units & additions & alterations	0.4	Constr.
Paper coating & glazing	0.5	Manufg.	Dental equipment & supplies	0.4	Manufg.
Equipment rental & leasing services	0.5	Services	Farm service facilities	0.3	Constr.
Miscellaneous fabricated wire products	0.4	Manufg.	Glass & glass products, except containers	0.3	Manufg.
Motors & generators	0.4	Manufg.	Dormitories & other group housing	0.2	Constr.
Small arms ammunition	0.4	Manufg.	Electric utility facility construction	0.2	Constr.
Eating & drinking places	0.4	Trade	Maintenance of farm residential buildings	0.2	Constr.
Paperboard containers & boxes	0.3	Manufg.	Water supply facility construction	0.2	Constr.
Computer & data processing services	0.3	Services	Fine earthenware food utensils	0.2	Manufg.
Ball & roller bearings	0.2	Manufg.	Structural clay products, nec	0.2	Manufg.
Explosives	0.2	Manufg.	S/L Govt. purch., health & hospitals	0.2	S/L Govt
Hand & edge tools, nec	0.2	Manufg.	Maintenance of water supply facilities	0.1	Constr.
Industrial inorganic chemicals, nec	0.2	Manufg.	Telephone & telegraph facility construction	0.1	Constr.
Internal combustion engines, nec	0.2	Manufg.	Surgical appliances & supplies	0.1	Manufg.
Security & commodity brokers	0.2	Fin/R.E.	Vitreous china food utensils	0.1	Manufg.
Automotive rental & leasing, without drivers	0.2	Services			
Detective & protective services	0.2	Services			
Hotels & lodging places	0.2	Services			
Management & consulting services & labs	0.2	Services			
Lubricating oils & greases	0.1	Manufg.			
Nonferrous wire drawing & insulating	0.1	Manufg.			
Ready-mixed concrete	0.1	Manufg.			
Screw machine and related products	0.1	Manufg.			
Insurance carriers	0.1	Fin/R.E.			
Real estate	0.1	Fin/R.E.			
Accounting, auditing & bookkeeping	0.1	Services			
Automotive repair shops & services	0.1	Services			
Legal services	0.1	Services			
U.S. Postal Service	0.1	Gov't			

Source: Benchmark Input-Output Accounts for the U.S. Economy, 1982, U.S. Department of Commerce, Washington, D.C., July 1991. Data, as reported in the source, are organized by the 1977 SIC structure in use in 1982 but have been matched, as closely as is possible, to the 1987 SIC structure used in this book.

OCCUPATIONS EMPLOYED BY SIC 327 - CONCRETE, GYPSUM, AND PLASTER PRODUCTS

Occupation	% of Total 1994	Change to 2005	Occupation	% of Total 1994	Change to 2005
Truck drivers light & heavy	31.4	-10.5	Concrete & terrazzo finishers	2.2	-13.2
Helpers, laborers, & material movers nec	4.6	-13.2	Crushing & mixing machine operators	2.1	-13.2
General managers & top executives	4.3	-17.6	General office clerks	1.8	-26.0
Blue collar worker supervisors	4.2	-19.9	Helpers, construction trades	1.8	-13.2
Sales & related workers nec	3.2	-13.2	Industrial machinery mechanics	1.7	-4.5
Bookkeeping, accounting, & auditing clerks	2.5	-34.9	Industrial production managers	1.5	-13.1
Industrial truck & tractor operators	2.5	-13.2	Secretaries, ex legal & medical	1.4	-20.9
Bus & truck mechanics & diesel engine specialists	2.4	-13.2	Maintenance repairers, general utility	1.4	-21.9
Dispatchers, ex police, fire, & ambulance	2.4	-13.2	Welders & cutters	1.3	-13.1
Extruding & forming machine workers	2.3	21.6	Freight, stock, & material movers, hand	1.2	-30.5
Assemblers, fabricators, & hand workers nec	2.2	-13.2	Machine feeders & offbearers	1.1	-21.9
Precision workers nec	2.2	4.2			

Source: Industry-Occupation Matrix, Bureau of Labor Statistics. These data relate to one or more 3-digit SIC industry groups rather than to a single 4-digit SIC. The change reported for each occupation to the year 2005 is a percent of growth or decline as estimated by the Bureau of Labor Statistics. The abbreviation nec stands for 'not elsewhere classified'.

LOCATION BY STATE AND REGIONAL CONCENTRATION

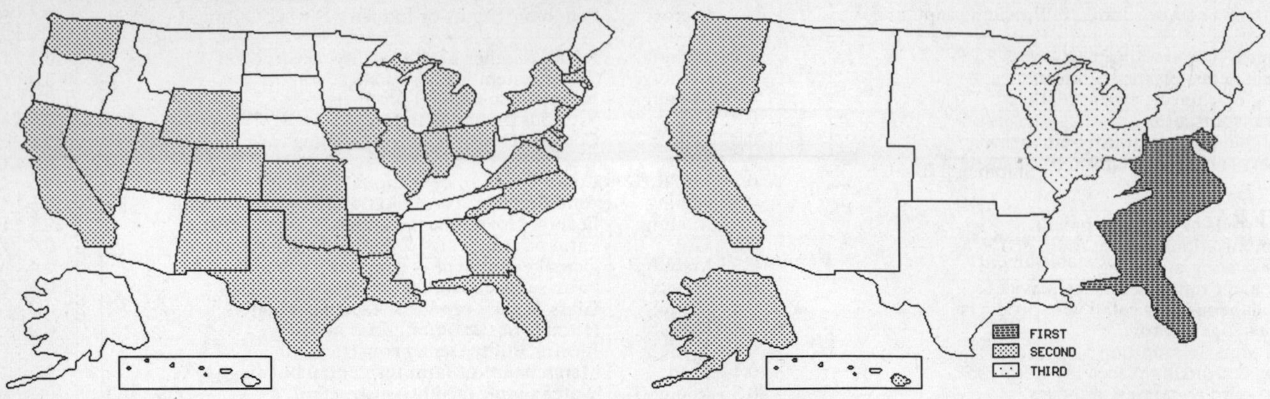

INDUSTRY DATA BY STATE

State	Establish-ments	Shipments			Employment				Cost as % of Shipments	Investment per Employee ($)
		Total ($ mil)	% of U.S.	Per Establ.	Total Number	% of U.S.	Per Establ.	Wages ($/hour)		
California	21	252.1	12.1	12.0	1,200	11.4	57	12.96	69.4	5,583
Florida	11	156.0	7.5	14.2	700	6.7	64	12.36	63.8	6,286
Iowa	6	148.8	7.2	24.8	800	7.6	133	12.73	57.5	-
Indiana	5	146.9	7.1	29.4	600	5.7	120	12.83	49.7	3,667
Texas	9	128.3	6.2	14.3	700	6.7	78	12.31	62.0	2,714
New York	7	117.9	5.7	16.8	600	5.7	86	15.30	55.3	-
Georgia	8	109.6	5.3	13.7	500	4.8	63	13.88	61.7	1,600
Ohio	7	95.7	4.6	13.7	500	4.8	71	12.20	57.8	-
Oklahoma	4	71.7	3.5	17.9	500	4.8	125	11.11	56.5	2,000
Washington	3	70.1	3.4	23.4	300	2.9	100	15.50	61.9	-
Nevada	4	65.9	3.2	16.5	400	3.8	100	14.00	58.1	-
North Carolina	3	39.6	1.9	13.2	100	1.0	33	9.33	62.9	-
Michigan	6	(D)	-	-	375 *	3.6	63	-	-	5,600
Illinois	5	(D)	-	-	175 *	1.7	35	-	-	-
Virginia	4	(D)	-	-	375 *	3.6	94	-	-	-
Arkansas	3	(D)	-	-	375 *	3.6	125	-	-	-
Louisiana	3	(D)	-	-	175 *	1.7	58	-	-	-
Maryland	3	(D)	-	-	375 *	3.6	125	-	-	-
New Jersey	3	(D)	-	-	175 *	1.7	58	-	-	-
Colorado	2	(D)	-	-	175 *	1.7	88	-	-	-
Kansas	2	(D)	-	-	375 *	3.6	188	-	-	-
New Hampshire	2	(D)	-	-	175 *	1.7	88	-	-	-
New Mexico	2	(D)	-	-	175 *	1.7	88	-	-	-
Utah	2	(D)	-	-	175 *	1.7	88	-	-	-
Wyoming	2	(D)	-	-	175 *	1.7	88	-	-	-
Delaware	1	(D)	-	-	175 *	1.7	175	-	-	-
Massachusetts	1	(D)	-	-	175 *	1.7	175	-	-	-

Source: 1992 *Economic Census*. The states are in descending order of shipments or establishments (if shipment data are missing for the majority). The symbol (D) appears when data are withheld to prevent disclosure of competitive information. States marked with (D) are sorted by number of establishments. A dash (-) indicates that the data element cannot be calculated; * indicates the midpoint of a range.

3281 - CUT STONE & STONE PRODUCTS

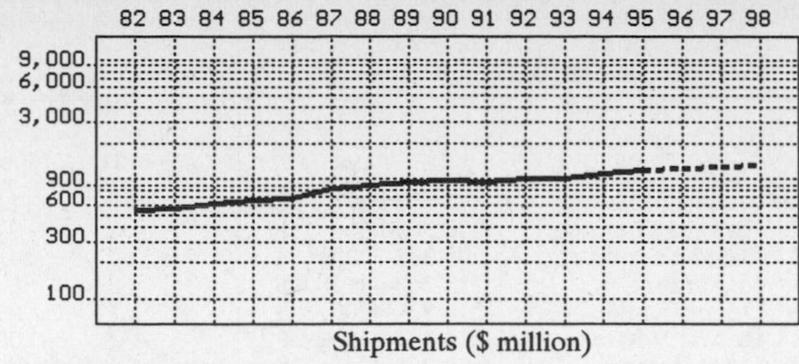

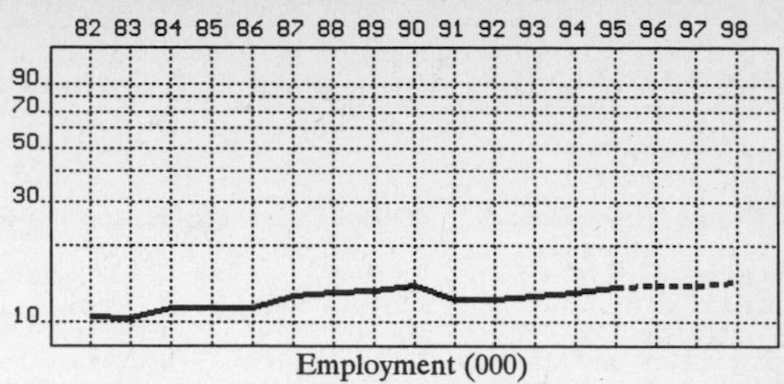

GENERAL STATISTICS

Year	Companies	Establishments		Employment			Compensation		Production ($ million)			
		Total	with 20 or more employees	Total (000)	Production Workers (000)	Production Hours (Mil)	Payroll ($ mil)	Wages ($/hr)	Cost of Materials	Value Added by Manufacture	Value of Shipments	Capital Invest.
1982	698	711	132	10.5	8.5	16.5	155.9	7.18	259.0	295.2	555.4	23.9
1983				10.2	8.5	16.3	158.3	7.40	266.7	302.1	570.0	7.0
1984				11.3	8.9	16.7	187.3	8.35	275.2	344.3	626.3	27.9
1985				11.2	8.9	17.4	199.5	8.56	317.0	352.8	674.3	30.5
1986				11.2	8.8	17.6	198.9	8.38	317.5	375.5	683.0	33.2
1987	731	746	167	12.5	10.0	19.8	243.0	8.77	385.8	450.5	840.8	30.6
1988				13.0	9.9	19.7	257.7	8.68	380.8	518.7	890.1	31.4
1989		740	159	13.3	10.2	20.2	281.0	9.31	395.3	550.0	934.9	40.6
1990				13.9	10.6	20.5	297.0	9.70	430.4	575.3	988.8	38.4
1991				12.2	9.5	18.6	267.1	10.28	371.5	582.0	956.3	27.5
1992	901	921	161	12.3	9.5	19.3	284.4	10.66	407.1	607.4	1,011.3	36.9
1993				12.6	9.7	19.8	292.9	10.71	408.3	614.6	1,025.0	19.8
1994				12.9	10.0	21.4	310.7	10.65	441.1	661.5	1,111.9	36.9
1995				13.6P	10.3P	21.3P	334.4P	11.24P	464.5P	696.6P	1,170.8P	36.9P
1996				13.8P	10.5P	21.7P	347.7P	11.54P	483.5P	725.0P	1,218.7P	37.9P
1997				14.0P	10.6P	22.1P	361.1P	11.84P	502.4P	753.5P	1,266.5P	39.0P
1998				14.3P	10.7P	22.4P	374.4P	12.14P	521.4P	781.9P	1,314.3P	40.0P

Sources: 1982, 1987, 1992 *Economic Census*; *Annual Survey of Manufactures*, 83-86, 88-91, 93-94. Establishment counts for non-Census years are from *County Business Patterns*; establishment values for 83-84 are extrapolations. 'P's show projections by the editors. Industries reclassified in 87 will not have data for prior years.

INDICES OF CHANGE

Year	Companies	Establishments		Employment			Compensation		Production ($ million)			
		Total	with 20 or more employees	Total (000)	Production Workers (000)	Production Hours (Mil)	Payroll ($ mil)	Wages ($/hr)	Cost of Materials	Value Added by Manufacture	Value of Shipments	Capital Invest.
1982	77	77	82	85	89	85	55	67	64	49	55	65
1983				83	89	84	56	69	66	50	56	19
1984				92	94	87	66	78	68	57	62	76
1985				91	94	90	70	80	78	58	67	83
1986				91	93	91	70	79	78	62	68	90
1987	81	81	104	102	105	103	85	82	95	74	83	83
1988				106	104	102	91	81	94	85	88	85
1989		80	99	108	107	105	99	87	97	91	92	110
1990				113	112	106	104	91	106	95	98	104
1991				99	100	96	94	96	91	96	95	75
1992	100	100	100	100	100	100	100	100	100	100	100	100
1993				102	102	103	103	100	100	101	101	54
1994				105	105	111	109	100	108	109	110	100
1995				111P	109P	111P	118P	105P	114P	115P	116P	100P
1996				112P	110P	112P	122P	108P	119P	119P	121P	103P
1997				114P	112P	114P	127P	111P	123P	124P	125P	106P
1998				116P	113P	116P	132P	114P	128P	129P	130P	108P

Sources: Same as General Statistics. Values reflect change from the base year, 1992. Values above 100 mean greater than 92, values below 100 mean less than 92, and a value of 100 in the 82-91 or 93-98 period means same as 92. 'P's mark projections by the editors.

SELECTED RATIOS

For 1992	Avg. of All Manufact.	Analyzed Industry	Index	For 1992	Avg. of All Manufact.	Analyzed Industry	Index
Employees per Establishment	46	13	29	Value Added per Production Worker	122,353	63,937	52
Payroll per Establishment	1,332,320	308,795	23	Cost per Establishment	4,239,462	442,020	10
Payroll per Employee	29,181	23,122	79	Cost per Employee	92,853	33,098	36
Production Workers per Establishment	31	10	33	Cost per Production Worker	135,003	42,853	32
Wages per Establishment	734,496	223,385	30	Shipments per Establishment	8,100,800	1,098,046	14
Wages per Production Worker	23,390	21,657	93	Shipments per Employee	177,425	82,220	46
Hours per Production Worker	2,025	2,032	100	Shipments per Production Worker	257,966	106,453	41
Wages per Hour	11.55	10.66	92	Investment per Establishment	278,244	40,065	14
Value Added per Establishment	3,842,210	659,501	17	Investment per Employee	6,094	3,000	49
Value Added per Employee	84,153	49,382	59	Investment per Production Worker	8,861	3,884	44

Sources: Same as General Statistics. The 'Average of All Manufacturing' column represents the average of all manufacturing industries reported for the most recent complete year available. The Index shows the relationship between the Average and the Analyzed Industry. For example, 100 means that they are equal; 500 that the Analyzed Industry is five times the average; 50 means that the Analyzed Industry is half the national average. The abbreviation 'na' is used to show that data are 'not available'.

LEADING COMPANIES

Number shown: **53** Total sales ($ mil): **657** Total employment (000): **5.5**

Company Name	Address				CEO Name	Phone	Co. Type	Sales ($ mil)	Empl. (000)
General Crushed Stone Co	PO Box 231	Easton	PA	18044	Frederick Moore	215-253-4271	S	160*	1.5
Quartet Manufacturing Co	5700 Old Orchard	Skokie	IL	60077	Howard Green	708-965-0600	R	105	0.8
Alabama Limestone Ltd	Rte 3	Russellville	AL	35653	David Teitelbaum	205-332-3700	S	60	<0.1
Marblehead Lime Co	222 N La Salle St	Chicago	IL	60601	MD Henry	312-263-4490	S	60*	0.5
Medusa Aggregates Co	PO Box 5668	Cleveland	OH	44101	Dennis Knight	216-371-4000	S	37	0.3
United States Lime and Minerals	12221 Merit Dr	Dallas	TX	75251	Robert F Kizer	214-991-8400	P	37	0.3
Fletcher Granite Company Inc	275 Groton Rd	N Chelmsford	MA	01863	Duke Pointer	508-251-4031	S	15	0.2
North Carolina Granite Corp	PO Box 151	Mount Airy	NC	27030	Donald R Shulton	910-786-5141	R	14	0.2
Bybee Stone Company Inc	PO Box 968	Bloomington	IN	47402	Daniel Bybee	812-876-2215	R	11	0.1
Linwood Mining & Minerals	4321 E 60th St	Davenport	IA	52807	Greg Bush	319-359-8251	S	11*	0.1
Delaware Quarries Inc	River Rd	Lumberville	PA	18933	J Kevan Busik	215-297-5647	R	10	0.1
Buckingham-Virginia Slate Corp	PO Box 8	Arvonia	VA	23004	Hugh D Crummette	804-581-1131	R	9*	<0.1
Anthony Dally and Sons Inc	PO Box 27	Pen Argyl	PA	18072	Alfred S Dally	610-863-4172	R	8*	<0.1
Granit Bronz CSG Inc	202 S 3rd St	Cold Spring	MN	56320	Pat Alexander	612-685-3621	S	8*	0.1
Holland Company Inc	PO Box 1947	Decatur	AL	35602	Neil A Holland Jr	205-353-1841	R	8*	<0.1
Columbus Marble Works Inc	PO Box 791	Columbus	MS	39701	William L Jones	601-328-1477	R	7	0.1
Genesee Leroy Stone Corp	6896 Ellicott St	Pavilion	NY	14525	Byron R DeWitt	716-584-8840	S	7	<0.1
Beck and Beck Inc	PO Box 467	Barre	VT	05641	Robert W Zider	802-476-3179	R	5	<0.1
Hindostone Products Inc	6355 Morenci Trail	Indianapolis	IN	46268	Jay Peacock	317-299-2200	R	5	<0.1
Piqua Minerals Inc	1750 W Statler Rd	Piqua	OH	45356	Albert R Donovan	513-773-4824	D	5	<0.1
Vetter Stone Co	PO Box 38	Kasota	MN	56050	Howard J Vetter	507-345-4568	R	5	<0.1
Western States Stone Co	PO Box 668	Santa Clara	CA	95052	CE Webster	408-296-4525	R	5	<0.1
Charles W Barger and Son Inc	PO Box 778	Lexington	VA	24450	C W Barger III	703-463-2106	R	4*	<0.1
Lang Stone Co	PO Box 360747	Columbus	OH	43236	E Dean Coffman	614-228-5489	R	4	<0.1
Tru-Stone Corp	PO Box 430	Waite Park	MN	56387	Ronald S Carlson	612-251-7171	R	4	<0.1
WE Neal Slate Co	7975 Wallace Rd	Eden Prairie	MN	55344	Gene Ziemer	612-937-2404	R	4	<0.1
Hilltop Slate Inc	PO Box 201	Mid Granville	NY	12849	Adrian Curtis	518-642-2270	S	4	<0.1
Texas Architectural Aggregate	PO Box 608	San Saba	TX	76877	JR Williams	915-372-5105	R	4	<0.1
Vermont Structural Slate	PO Box 98	Fair Haven	VT	05743	W E Markcrow	802-265-4933	R	4	<0.1
A Ottavino Corp	80-60 Pitkin Av	Ozone Park	NY	11417	AG Ottavino	718-848-9404	R	3	<0.1
Behm Quartz Industries Inc	131 Janney Rd	Dayton	OH	45404	Thomas Biesel	513-236-3250	R	3*	<0.1
Granse and Associates Inc	21670 Hamburg Av	Lakeville	MN	55044	Gordan Granse	612-488-9708	R	3*	<0.1
Milwaukee Marble and Granite	4535 W Mitchell St	Milwaukee	WI	53214	G O Brueckner	414-645-0305	R	3*	<0.1
Newton County Stone Co	US Hwy 24 E	Kentland	IN	47951	Terry Sosong	219-474-5125	D	3	<0.1
Monumental Sales Inc	PO Box 667	St Cloud	MN	56302	James Schiffler	612-251-6585	D	3	<0.1
Kotecki Monuments Inc	3636 Pearl Rd	Cleveland	OH	44109	E E Kotecki III	216-749-2880	R	2	<0.1
Adam Ross Cut Stone Company	1003 Broadway	Albany	NY	12204	RE Ross	518-463-6674	R	2	<0.1
Biesanz Stone Company Inc	4600 Goodview Rd	Winona	MN	55987	CW Biesanz Jr	507-454-4336	R	2	<0.1
Little Falls Granite Works Inc	S Hwy 10	Little Falls	MN	56345	Ronald Nagle	612-632-9277	R	2	<0.1
Oregon Stone Inc	PO Box 496	Oregon	IL	61061	Arlyn Lawrence	815-732-2154	R	2	<0.1
Sheridan Corp	1212 W Maple St	Lebanon	PA	17046	RJ McMindes	717-273-1608	R	2*	<0.1
Northwestern Tile & Marble Co	6403 Cecelia Cir	Minneapolis	MN	55439	David C Gramling	612-941-8601	R	2	<0.1
Harmony Blue Granite Co	PO Box 958	Elberton	GA	30635	Allan E McGarity	706-283-3111	R	1*	<0.1
Jonny Shower Door Corp	425 N Marshall Av	El Cajon	CA	92020	Inez W Weymiller	619-440-1212	R	1	<0.1
Kollmann Monumental Works	1915 Divison St	St Cloud	MN	56301	Richard Kollmann	612-251-8010	R	1	<0.1
Winona Monument Company	PO Box 529	Winona	MN	55987	Donn Seitz	507-452-4672	R	1	<0.1
Braham Monument Co	PO Box 226	Braham	MN	55006	Thomas Backman	612-396-2938	R	1	<0.1
TA Sullivan and Son	3023 N Washington	Arlington	VA	22201	Joseph Poldiak	703-528-2026	R	1	<0.1
Design 7 Corp	2317 Interstate Av	Grand Junction	CO	81505	Kent Pfleider	303-241-2345	R	1*	<0.1
Mulherin Architectural	94 Algana Ct	St Peters	MO	63376	Harold Mulherin	314-441-3533	R	1	<0.1
Dakota Marble Inc	902 W 19th St	Yankton	SD	57078	Jeb Christensen	605-665-7241	R	0	<0.1
Bentley Marble Corp	671 Wyoming St	Buffalo	NY	14215	Joan Yang	716-834-9851	R	0	<0.1
New Alberene Stone Company	255 Ridge McIntire	Charlottesville	VA	22903	Esko Teerikorpi	804-977-5500	S	0*	<0.1

Source: *Ward's Business Directory of U.S. Private and Public Companies*, Volumes 1 and 2, 1996. The company type code used is as follows: P - Public, R - Private, S - Subsidiary, D - Division, J - Joint Venture, A - Affiliate, G - Group. Sales are in millions of dollars, employees are in thousands. An asterisk (*) indicates an estimated sales volume. The symbol < stands for 'less than'. Company names and addresses are truncated, in some cases, to fit into the available space.

MATERIALS CONSUMED

Material	Quantity	Delivered Cost ($ million)
Materials, ingredients, containers, and supplies	(X)	271.5
Rough blocks used to produce dressed stone	(X)	83.5
Abrasives and abrasive products	(X)	4.8
Stonecutting tools and accessories (including blades)	(X)	12.5
All other materials and components, parts, containers, and supplies	(X)	32.7
Materials, ingredients, containers, and supplies, nsk	(X)	138.0

Source: 1992 *Economic Census*. Explanation of symbols used: (D): Withheld to avoid disclosure of competitive data; na: Not available; (S): Withheld because statistical norms were not met; (X): Not applicable; (Z): Less than half the unit shown; nec: Not elsewhere classified; nsk: Not specified by kind; - : zero; * : 10-19 percent estimated; ** : 20-29 percent estimated.

PRODUCT SHARE DETAILS

Product or Product Class	% Share
Cut stone and stone products	100.00
Dressed dimension granite (including gneiss, syenite, diorite, and cut granite)	47.37
Building stone, dressed dimension granite (including gneiss, syenite, diorite, and cut granite)	39.48
Monumental stone, dressed dimension granite (including gneiss, syenite, diorite, and cut granite)	45.92
Other granite products, such as paving blocks and curbing, dressed dimension granite (including gneiss, syenite, diorite, and cut granite)	12.44
Dressed dimension granite (including gneiss, syenite, diorite, and cut granite), nsk	2.16
Dressed dimension limestone (including dolomite, travertine, calcareous, tufa, and cut limestone)	13.00
Building stone, dressed dimension limestone (including dolomite, travertine, calcareous, tufa, and cut limestone)	55.64
Other limestone products, such as flagging, dressed dimension limestone (including dolomite, travertine, calcareous, tufa, and cut limestone)	25.47
Dressed dimension limestone (including dolomite, travertine, calcareous, tufa, and cut limestone), nsk	18.90
Dressed dimension marble and other stone	16.82
Dressed dimension building stone, monumental stone, and other marble products	59.50
Other dressed dimension stone, such as slate, sandstone, gabbro, basalt, etc., and other dressed dimension stone products	31.22
Dressed dimension marble and other stone, nsk	9.34
Cut stone and stone products, nsk	22.81

Source: 1992 *Economic Census*. The values shown are percent of total shipments in an industry. Values of indented subcategories are summed in the main heading. The symbol (D) appears when data are withheld to prevent disclosure of competitive information. The abbreviation nsk stands for 'not specified by kind' and nec for 'not elsewhere classified'.

INPUTS AND OUTPUTS FOR CUTSTONE & STONE PRODUCTS

Economic Sector or Industry Providing Inputs	%	Sector	Economic Sector or Industry Buying Outputs	%	Sector
Imports	43.3	Foreign	Personal consumption expenditures	42.4	
Dimension, crushed & broken stone	17.9	Mining	Office buildings	26.3	Constr.
Wholesale trade	5.4	Trade	Residential 1-unit structures, nonfarm	3.9	Constr.
Abrasive products	3.6	Manufg.	Construction of hospitals	2.6	Constr.
Cutstone & stone products	3.2	Manufg.	Construction of stores & restaurants	2.5	Constr.
Nonmetallic mineral products, nec	2.9	Manufg.	Construction of educational buildings	2.0	Constr.
Electric services (utilities)	2.6	Util.	Hotels & motels	2.0	Constr.
Hand & edge tools, nec	2.2	Manufg.	Cutstone & stone products	1.9	Manufg.
Mining machinery, except oil field	2.1	Manufg.	Residential additions/alterations, nonfarm	1.7	Constr.
Railroads & related services	1.2	Util.	Construction of nonfarm buildings nec	1.4	Constr.
Paints & allied products	1.0	Manufg.	Change in business inventories	1.4	In House
Gas production & distribution (utilities)	1.0	Util.	Sporting & athletic goods, nec	1.2	Manufg.
Eating & drinking places	1.0	Trade	Exports	1.1	Foreign
Advertising	1.0	Services	Amusement & recreation building construction	0.9	Constr.
Banking	0.8	Fin/R.E.	S/L Govt. purch., elem. & secondary education	0.9	S/L Govt
Paperboard containers & boxes	0.7	Manufg.	Residential garden apartments	0.8	Constr.
Sawmills & planning mills, general	0.7	Manufg.	Industrial buildings	0.7	Constr.
Maintenance of nonfarm buildings nec	0.6	Constr.	Federal Government purchases, national defense	0.7	Fed Govt
Motor freight transportation & warehousing	0.6	Util.	Maintenance of nonfarm buildings nec	0.6	Constr.
Machinery, except electrical, nec	0.5	Manufg.	Asbestos products	0.6	Manufg.
Detective & protective services	0.5	Services	Concrete products, nec	0.6	Manufg.
U.S. Postal Service	0.5	Gov't	Nonfarm residential structure maintenance	0.5	Constr.
Communications, except radio & TV	0.4	Util.	Residential 2-4 unit structures, nonfarm	0.5	Constr.
Legal services	0.4	Services	Construction of religious buildings	0.4	Constr.
Management & consulting services & labs	0.4	Services	Local transit facility construction	0.4	Constr.
Miscellaneous plastics products	0.3	Manufg.	Resid. & other health facility construction	0.4	Constr.
Petroleum refining	0.3	Manufg.	Dormitories & other group housing	0.2	Constr.
Plastics materials & resins	0.3	Manufg.	Farm housing units & additions & alterations	0.2	Constr.
Air transportation	0.3	Util.	Maintenance of local transit facilities	0.2	Constr.
Glass & glass products, except containers	0.2	Manufg.	Telephone & telegraph facility construction	0.2	Constr.
Lubricating oils & greases	0.2	Manufg.	Public building furniture	0.2	Manufg.
Manifold business forms	0.2	Manufg.	S/L Govt. purch., other general government	0.2	S/L Govt
Special dies & tools & machine tool accessories	0.2	Manufg.	Residential high-rise apartments	0.1	Constr.
Real estate	0.2	Fin/R.E.	Sewer system facility construction	0.1	Constr.
Royalties	0.2	Fin/R.E.			
Accounting, auditing & bookkeeping	0.2	Services			
Business/professional associations	0.2	Services			
Computer & data processing services	0.2	Services			
Equipment rental & leasing services	0.2	Services			
Noncomparable imports	0.2	Foreign			
General industrial machinery, nec	0.1	Manufg.			
Credit agencies other than banks	0.1	Fin/R.E.			
Insurance carriers	0.1	Fin/R.E.			
Laundry, dry cleaning, shoe repair	0.1	Services			

Source: Benchmark Input-Output Accounts for the U.S. Economy, 1982, U.S. Department of Commerce, Washington, D.C., July 1991. Data, as reported in the source, are organized by the 1977 SIC structure in use in 1982 but have been matched, as closely as is possible, to the 1987 SIC structure used in this book.

OCCUPATIONS EMPLOYED BY SIC 328 - STONE, CLAY, AND MISC MINING PRODUCTS NEC

Occupation	% of Total 1994	Change to 2005	Occupation	% of Total 1994	Change to 2005
Helpers, laborers, & material movers nec	6.7	-23.3	Machine feeders & offbearers	2.3	-31.4
Assemblers, fabricators, & hand workers nec	6.4	-23.9	Painting, coating, & decorating workers, hand	2.0	52.3
Furnace, kiln, or kettle operators	4.2	-16.7	Freight, stock, & material movers, hand	1.9	-38.8
Crushing & mixing machine operators	3.9	-9.5	Truck drivers light & heavy	1.9	-20.6
Industrial machinery mechanics	3.9	-15.2	Coating, painting, & spraying machine workers	1.8	-23.8
Hand packers & packagers	3.6	-34.7	Secretaries, ex legal & medical	1.8	-30.4
Extruding & forming machine workers	3.4	-80.6	Cutting & slicing machine setters, operators	1.6	-16.2
Sales & related workers nec	3.2	-23.6	Grinders & polishers, hand	1.6	-16.2
Packaging & filling machine operators	3.2	-23.7	Industrial production managers	1.5	-23.5
Precision workers nec	3.0	-8.7	Traffic, shipping, & receiving clerks	1.5	-26.6
Industrial truck & tractor operators	2.8	-23.7	General office clerks	1.5	-34.9
General managers & top executives	2.8	-27.5	Bookkeeping, accounting, & auditing clerks	1.3	-42.7
Inspectors, testers, & graders, precision	2.8	-23.6	Electricians	1.1	-27.3
Maintenance repairers, general utility	2.6	-30.8	Machinists	1.0	-23.6

Source: *Industry-Occupation Matrix*, Bureau of Labor Statistics. These data relate to one or more 3-digit SIC industry groups rather than to a single 4-digit SIC. The change reported for each occupation to the year 2005 is a percent of growth or decline as estimated by the Bureau of Labor Statistics. The abbreviation nec stands for 'not elsewhere classified'.

LOCATION BY STATE AND REGIONAL CONCENTRATION

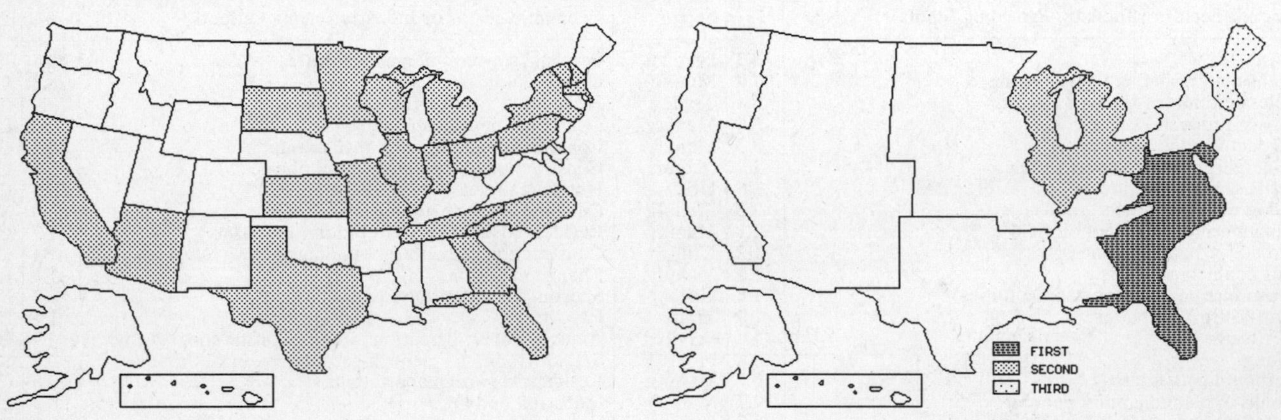

INDUSTRY DATA BY STATE

State	Establish-ments	Shipments: Total ($ mil)	Shipments: % of U.S.	Shipments: Per Establ.	Employment: Total Number	Employment: % of U.S.	Employment: Per Establ.	Employment: Wages ($/hour)	Cost as % of Shipments	Investment per Employee ($)
Minnesota	18	165.6	16.4	9.2	1,700	13.8	94	11.32	28.1	-
Vermont	66	113.9	11.3	1.7	1,100	8.9	17	11.50	48.1	4,273
Georgia	113	107.6	10.6	1.0	1,500	12.2	13	10.09	44.0	2,133
California	86	59.6	5.9	0.7	700	5.7	8	9.92	36.2	2,286
Indiana	26	57.3	5.7	2.2	800	6.5	31	13.50	44.3	1,125
New York	51	41.2	4.1	0.8	500	4.1	10	11.63	36.9	-
Massachusetts	23	27.6	2.7	1.2	200	1.6	9	13.25	54.0	2,000
Florida	51	22.3	2.2	0.4	300	2.4	6	8.80	48.4	2,333
Tennessee	27	17.0	1.7	0.6	200	1.6	7	9.67	45.3	2,000
New Hampshire	5	13.7	1.4	2.7	200	1.6	40	10.50	32.8	-
Wisconsin	16	13.3	1.3	0.8	200	1.6	13	8.00	44.4	1,500
Arizona	13	11.4	1.1	0.9	100	0.8	8	10.00	39.5	-
Michigan	15	10.4	1.0	0.7	200	1.6	13	11.00	41.3	2,000
Missouri	21	8.2	0.8	0.4	100	0.8	5	10.50	45.1	-
Texas	72	(D)	-	-	750 *	6.1	10	-	-	2,400
Ohio	36	(D)	-	-	375 *	3.0	10	-	-	-
Pennsylvania	35	(D)	-	-	375 *	3.0	11	-	-	800
Illinois	31	(D)	-	-	750 *	6.1	24	-	-	-
North Carolina	30	(D)	-	-	750 *	6.1	25	-	-	-
Kansas	9	(D)	-	-	175 *	1.4	19	-	-	571
South Dakota	3	(D)	-	-	175 *	1.4	58	-	-	-

Source: 1992 *Economic Census*. The states are in descending order of shipments or establishments (if shipment data are missing for the majority). The symbol (D) appears when data are withheld to prevent disclosure of competitive information. States marked with (D) are sorted by number of establishments. A dash (-) indicates that the data element cannot be calculated; * indicates the midpoint of a range.

3291 - ABRASIVE PRODUCTS

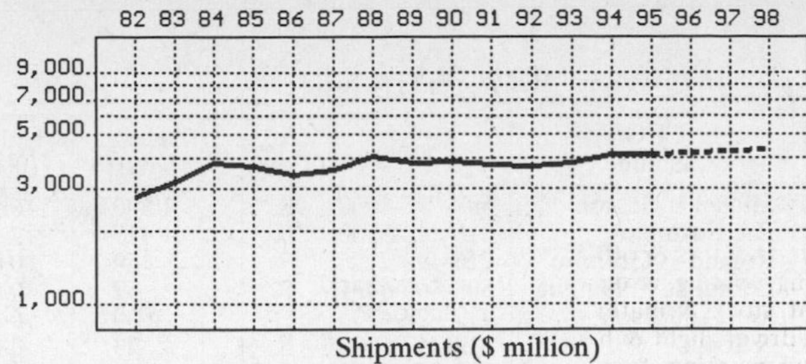

Shipments ($ million)

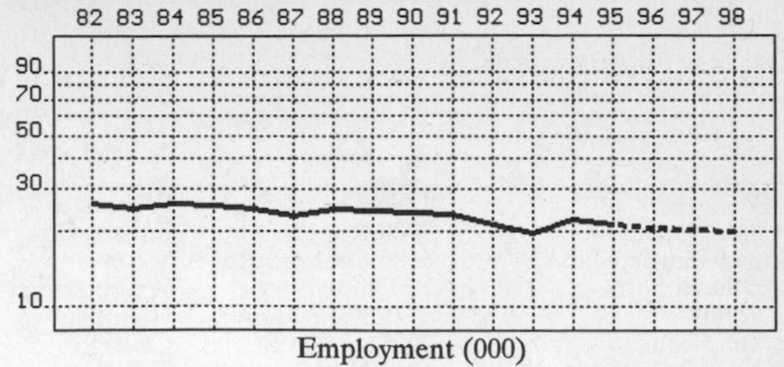

Employment (000)

GENERAL STATISTICS

Year	Com-panies	Establishments		Employment			Compensation		Production ($ million)			
		Total	with 20 or more employees	Total (000)	Production Workers (000)	Production Hours (Mil)	Payroll ($ mil)	Wages ($/hr)	Cost of Materials	Value Added by Manufacture	Value of Shipments	Capital Invest.
1982	326	374	177	26.0	17.0	31.6	531.8	9.66	1,277.2	1,451.8	2,750.7	96.9
1983		374	179	24.8	16.5	31.6	535.4	9.66	1,428.1	1,698.6	3,195.9	78.3
1984		374	181	26.0	17.5	34.8	594.7	9.68	1,879.7	1,943.2	3,781.8	137.8
1985		373	184	25.5	17.1	33.2	604.4	10.17	1,805.0	1,833.0	3,675.3	143.1
1986		370	178	24.8	16.7	33.5	607.6	10.10	1,640.5	1,738.9	3,383.5	95.2
1987	360	405	178	23.4	15.5	31.2	624.2	11.21	1,656.3	2,001.2	3,621.4	113.5
1988		394	186	24.9	16.4	33.5	680.7	11.33	1,834.2	2,250.9	4,050.6	102.2
1989		386	183	24.4	16.4	33.8	700.4	11.71	1,646.8	2,192.9	3,822.7	97.8
1990		386	186	24.1	16.4	33.6	765.9	12.04	1,746.3	2,130.6	3,898.4	135.4
1991		382	177	23.5	16.3	32.4		12.47	1,675.1	2,104.3	3,763.0	119.2
1992	367	414	189	21.5	15.1	31.1	651.7	12.16	1,674.3	2,030.6	3,731.1	121.5
1993		413	185	19.9	13.5	28.0	635.6	12.65	1,589.2	2,197.0	3,783.4	154.1
1994		409P	186P	22.7	15.9	33.3	732.3	11.77	1,732.1	2,425.4	4,124.0	128.6
1995		412P	187P	21.3P	14.9P	31.6P		13.00P	1,738.7P	2,434.6P	4,139.7P	136.3P
1996		415P	187P	20.9P	14.7P	31.5P		13.27P	1,767.5P	2,474.9P	4,208.2P	139.0P
1997		419P	188P	20.6P	14.5P	31.3P		13.54P	1,796.2P	2,515.2P	4,276.7P	141.8P
1998		422P	189P	20.2P	14.3P	31.2P		13.81P	1,825.0P	2,555.5P	4,345.2P	144.5P

Sources: 1982, 1987, 1992 *Economic Census*; *Annual Survey of Manufactures*, 83-86, 88-91, 93-94. Establishment counts for non-Census years are from *County Business Patterns*; establishment values for 83-84 are extrapolations. 'P's show projections by the editors. Industries reclassified in 87 will not have data for prior years.

INDICES OF CHANGE

Year	Com-panies	Establishments		Employment			Compensation		Production ($ million)			
		Total	with 20 or more employees	Total (000)	Production Workers (000)	Production Hours (Mil)	Payroll ($ mil)	Wages ($/hr)	Cost of Materials	Value Added by Manufacture	Value of Shipments	Capital Invest.
1982	89	90	94	121	113	102	82	79	76	71	74	80
1983		90	95	115	109	102	82	79	85	84	86	64
1984		90	96	121	116	112	91	80	112	96	101	113
1985		90	97	119	113	107	93	84	108	90	99	118
1986		89	94	115	111	108	93	83	98	86	91	78
1987	98	98	94	109	103	100	96	92	99	99	97	93
1988		95	98	116	109	108	104	93	110	111	109	84
1989		93	97	113	109	109	107	96	98	108	102	80
1990		93	98	112	109	108	118	99	104	105	104	111
1991		92	94	109	108	104		103	100	104	101	98
1992	100	100	100	100	100	100	100	100	100	100	100	100
1993		100	98	93	89	90	98	104	95	108	101	127
1994		99P	98P	106	105	107	112	97	103	119	111	106
1995		99P	99P	99P	99P	102P		107P	104P	120P	111P	112P
1996		100P	99P	97P	97P	101P		109P	106P	122P	113P	114P
1997		101P	99P	96P	96P	101P		111P	107P	124P	115P	117P
1998		102P	100P	94P	95P	100P		114P	109P	126P	116P	119P

Sources: Same as General Statistics. Values reflect change from the base year, 1992. Values above 100 mean greater than 92, values below 100 mean less than 92, and a value of 100 in the 82-91 or 93-98 period means same as 92. 'P's mark projections by the editors.

SELECTED RATIOS

For 1994	Avg. of All Manufact.	Analyzed Industry	Index	For 1994	Avg. of All Manufact.	Analyzed Industry	Index
Employees per Establishment	49	56	113	Value Added per Production Worker	134,084	152,541	114
Payroll per Establishment	1,500,273	1,792,191	119	Cost per Establishment	5,045,178	4,239,046	84
Payroll per Employee	30,620	32,260	105	Cost per Employee	102,970	76,304	74
Production Workers per Establishment	34	39	113	Cost per Production Worker	146,988	108,937	74
Wages per Establishment	853,319	959,215	112	Shipments per Establishment	9,576,895	10,092,851	105
Wages per Production Worker	24,861	24,650	99	Shipments per Employee	195,460	181,674	93
Hours per Production Worker	2,056	2,094	102	Shipments per Production Worker	279,017	259,371	93
Wages per Hour	12.09	11.77	97	Investment per Establishment	321,011	314,729	98
Value Added per Establishment	4,602,255	5,935,791	129	Investment per Employee	6,552	5,665	86
Value Added per Employee	93,930	106,846	114	Investment per Production Worker	9,352	8,088	86

Sources: Same as General Statistics. The 'Average of All Manufacturing' column represents the average of all manufacturing industries reported for the most recent complete year available. The Index shows the relationship between the Average and the Analyzed Industry. For example, 100 means that they are equal; 500 that the Analyzed Industry is five times the average; 50 means that the Analyzed Industry is half the national average. The abbreviation 'na' is used to show that data are 'not available'.

LEADING COMPANIES

Number shown: **62** Total sales ($ mil): **2,428** Total employment (000): **23.8**

Company Name	Address				CEO Name	Phone	Co. Type	Sales ($ mil)	Empl. (000)
Norton Co	1 New Bond St	Worcester	MA	01606	Michel L Besson	508-795-5000	S	1,500	16.5
GS Technologies Inc	7000 Roberts St	Kansas City	MO	64125	RA Cushman	816-242-5100	R	415	2.4
SK Wellman Limited Inc	6180 Cochran Rd	Solon	OH	44139	Ronald E Grambo	216-492-2275	S	60	0.6
Bay State/Sterling Inc	12 Union St	Westborough	MA	01581	Bernard A Phaneuf	508-366-4431	R	57	0.5
Reed Minerals	8149 Kennedy Av	Highland	IN	46322	Ken Anderson	219-923-4200	D	30	0.3
Rhodes American	2825 W 31st St	Chicago	IL	60623	N Soep	312-247-6000	R	20	0.2
VSM Abrasives Corp	1012 E Wabash St	O'Fallon	MO	63366	Brent S Barton	314-272-7432	S	20	0.1
International Steel Wool Corp	PO Box 1767	Springfield	OH	45501	Neal F Bonn	513-323-4651	S	17	0.2
National Metal Abrasive Inc	142 Auble St	Wadsworth	OH	44281	Robert L Fuller	216-334-1566	R	15	0.1
Clipper Abrasives Inc	PO Box 350	Niagara Falls	NY	14304	Ralph Griffin	716-731-7777	R	15•	0.3
Engis Corp	105 W Hintz Rd	Wheeling	IL	60090	RE Reid	708-808-9400	R	14•	0.1
Amplex Corp	PO Box 335	Bloomfield	CT	06002	Rick Johnson	203-243-1775	D	13	0.1
Cincinnati Milacron	4 Cave Hill Dr	Carlisle	PA	17013	James L Burkepile	717-243-3471	D	11	<0.1
Allison Abrasives Inc	PO Box 192	Lancaster	KY	40444	DA Farmer	606-792-3033	R	10	0.1
Barker Brothers Inc	1666 Summerfield	Ridgewood	NY	11385	EF Doyle	718-456-6400	R	10	0.1
Continental Abrasives Inc	16871 Noyes Av	Irvine	CA	92714	B Taylor	714-474-1101	R	10	<0.1
Furniture Makers Supply Co	PO Box 728	Lexington	NC	27292	Dan E Smith	704-956-2722	R	10	<0.1
Jet Abrasives Inc	4383 Fruitland Av	Vernon	CA	90058	Martin Rothstein	213-588-1245	R	10	<0.1
Moyco Industries Inc	21st & Clearfields	Philadelphia	PA	19132	Marvin E Sternberg	215-229-0470	P	10	0.1
Pacific Grinding Wheel Company	PO Box 468	Marysville	WA	98270	James H Kean	206-659-6201	R	10	<0.1
Pres-On Abrasives	39 Factory Rd	Addison	IL	60101	H Gianatasio	708-543-9466	R	10	0.1
Americo Manufacturing	PO Box 10000	Acworth	GA	30101	James Rones	404-974-7000	R	9	<0.1
Carborundum	PO Box 759	Logan	OH	43138	William Machetti	614-385-2171	R	8•	0.1
Microtron Abrasives Inc	PO Box 745	Pineville	NC	28134	Glenn W Turcotte	704-889-7256	S	8	<0.1
Mount Pulaski Products Inc	PO Box 110	Mount Pulaski	IL	62548	Scott Steinfort	217-792-3211	R	8	<0.1
Avery Abrasives Inc	2225 Reservoir Av	Trumbull	CT	06611	Raymond J Avery	203-372-3513	R	7•	<0.1
Micro Abrasives Corp	PO Box 669	Westfield	MA	01086	A Nesin	413-562-3641	R	7	<0.1
JacksonLea	75 Progress Ln	Waterbury	CT	06705	Nicholas Litwin	203-753-5116	D	6•	<0.1
Rex Cut Products Inc	PO Box 2109	Fall River	MA	02722	Robert C Hurst	508-678-1985	R	6	<0.1
Divine Brothers Co	200 Seward Av	Utica	NY	13502	BL Divine	315-797-0470	R	6	0.1
FL and JC Codman Company	PO Box 388	Rockland	MA	02370	EW Hall Jr	617-878-1000	R	6	<0.1
Agrashell Inc	5934 Keystone Dr	Bath	PA	18014	CS Ayers	215-837-6705	R	5	<0.1
AGSCO Corp	945 Chaddick Dr	Wheeling	IL	60090	Harvey R Plonsker	708-520-4455	R	5	<0.1
Bates Abrasive Products Inc	6230 S Oak Pk Av	Chicago	IL	60638	Mark D Maran	312-586-8700	R	5•	<0.1
Electro Abrasives Corp	701 Willet Rd	Buffalo	NY	14218	Allan D Ramming	716-822-2500	R	5	<0.1
Garfield Industries	PO Box 839	Fairfield	NJ	07006	Steve Gelvan	201-575-8800	R	5	<0.1
Precision Diamond Tool Co	PO Box 274	Elgin	IL	60121	Frederick Taeyaerts	708-888-7100	R	5	<0.1
SPEDETOOL Manufacturing	PO Box 40	Adelanto	CA	92301	Douglas W Myers	619-246-6850	R	5•	<0.1
Bullard Abrasives Inc	50 Hopkinton Rd	Westborough	MA	01581	Richard A White	508-366-4300	R	4•	<0.1
Cratex Manufacturing Company	7754 Arjons Dr	San Diego	CA	92126	Allen R McCasland	619-566-4511	R	4	<0.1
Perry Chemical & Manufacturing	PO Box 6419	Lafayette	IN	47903	WP Thayer Jr	317-474-3404	R	4	<0.1
Mosher Company Inc	PO Box 177	Chicopee	MA	01014	J Templeton	413-598-8341	R	4	<0.1
KC Abrasive Company Inc	3140 Dodge Rd	Kansas City	KS	66115	RJ Bysel	913-342-2900	R	4	<0.1
Bancroft Company Inc	23841 Kean St	Dearborn	MI	48124	Peter J Russ III	313-274-2100	R	3	<0.1
Agrashell Inc	4560 E 26th St	Los Angeles	CA	90040	Caroline Ayres	213-261-8128	R	3•	<0.1
Clemtex Inc	PO Box 15214	Houston	TX	77220	CA Tacker	713-672-8251	R	3	<0.1
Diamonex Inc	7150 Windsor Dr	Allentown	PA	18106	J Wetherington	215-366-7100	S	3	<0.1
Field Abrasive Mfg Co	PO Box 192	Dayton	OH	45404	Karen Hopkins	513-223-7209	R	3•	<0.1
MDC Industries Inc	Collins St	Philadelphia	PA	19134	A Schwab	215-426-5925	R	3	<0.1
Truing Systems Inc	1060 Chicago Rd	Troy	MI	48083	Ronald Stempin	810-588-9060	R	3•	<0.1
Warren Diamond Powder	PO Box 177	Olyphant	PA	18447	Kevin C Kearns	717-383-3261	R	3•	<0.1
Gulf State Abrasive Mfg	PO Box 7927	Houston	TX	77270	Freeman B Dunn	713-869-4841	S	3	<0.1
Ferro Industries Inc	PO Box 86	Mount Clemens	MI	48046	JV Clemente	810-792-6001	R	2	<0.1
DACO Abrasives Inc	PO Box 9523	Houston	TX	77261	Jim Glover	713-923-4664	R	1	<0.1
Abrasive Systems Inc	8770 Val Forge Ln	Maple Grove	MN	55369	Charles Mattson	612-424-7400	R	1	<0.1
Acme Belt Recoating Inc	PO Box 7	Quincy	MI	49082	RE Schield	517-639-8711	R	1	<0.1
Co-Ab-Co Abrasive Products Inc	4343 S Kilpatrick	Chicago	IL	60632	Donald Herbert	312-582-2800	R	1•	<0.1
Diagrind Inc	10491 W 164th Pl	Orland Park	IL	60462	Donald Sommer	708-460-4333	R	1	<0.1
Kalamazoo Industries Inc	PO Box 2558	Kalamazoo	MI	49003	F Allen	616-382-2050	R	1•	<0.1
Sattex Corp	PO Box 2593	White City	OR	97503	Mary Warrick	503-826-8808	R	1•	<0.1
Viets Engineering Co	2101 E 27th St	Long Beach	CA	90806	HG Viets	310-426-2107	R	1	<0.1
Belt Master Inc	936 N Stadem Dr	Tempe	AZ	85281	Larry D Mohr	602-921-3110	R	0	<0.1

Source: *Ward's Business Directory of U.S. Private and Public Companies*, Volumes 1 and 2, 1996. The company type code used is as follows: P - Public, R - Private, S - Subsidiary, D - Division, J - Joint Venture, A - Affiliate, G - Group. Sales are in millions of dollars, employees are in thousands. An asterisk (*) indicates an estimated sales volume. The symbol < stands for 'less than'. Company names and addresses are truncated, in some cases, to fit into the available space.

MATERIALS CONSUMED

Material	Quantity	Delivered Cost ($ million)
Materials, ingredients, containers, and supplies	(X)	1,491.5
Natural abrasive materials, except diamonds	(X)	127.1
Diamonds	(X)	43.0
Cotton and manmade fiber fabrics, broadwoven and narrow woven	(X)	110.0
Paper and paperboard products including paperboard boxes, containers, and corrugated paperboard	(X)	89.0
Synthetic aluminum oxide	(X)	74.0
Alumina zirconia	(X)	(D)
Synthetic silicon carbide	(X)	38.4
Other industrial inorganic chemicals	(X)	(D)
Glues and adhesives	(X)	42.2
Other chemicals and allied products	(X)	54.2
All other materials and components, parts, containers, and supplies	(X)	781.9
Materials, ingredients, containers, and supplies, nsk	(X)	77.5

Source: 1992 *Economic Census*. Explanation of symbols used: (D): Withheld to avoid disclosure of competitive data; na: Not available; (S): Withheld because statistical norms were not met; (X): Not applicable; (Z): Less than half the unit shown; nec: Not elsewhere classified; nsk: Not specified by kind; - : zero; * : 10-19 percent estimated; ** : 20-29 percent estimated.

PRODUCT SHARE DETAILS

Product or Product Class	% Share
Abrasive products	100.00
Nonmetallic sized grains, powders, and flour abrasives (including graded products only)	17.16
Silicon carbide, nonmetallic sized grains, powders, and flour abrasives (including graded products only)	13.27
Aluminum oxide, nonmetallic sized grains, powders, and flour abrasives (including graded products only)	28.21
Other nonmetallic artificial sized grains, powders, and flour abrasives (including combinations thereof)	54.54
Nonmetallic natural sized grains, powders, and flours	3.27
Nonmetallic sized grains, powders, and flour abrasives (including graded products only), nsk	0.73
Nonmetallic abrasive products (including diamond abrasives)	23.74
Nonmetallic vitrified bond, artificial and natural bonded abrasives (including diamond abrasives)	25.08
Nonmetallic resinoid and shellac bond - reinforced, artificial and natural bonded abrasives (including diamond abrasives)	15.58
Nonmetallic resinoid and shellac bond - nonreinforced, artificial and natural bonded abrasives (including diamond abrasives)	17.53
Nonmetallic rubber bond, artificial and natural bonded abrasives (including diamond abrasives)	3.88
Other nonmetallic diamond wheel bonded abrasives, artificial and natural bonded abrasives (including diamond abrasives)	6.07
Nonmetallic metal diamond wheel bond, artificial and natural bonded abrasives (including diamond abrasives)	10.10
Other nonmetallic diamond wheel bond, artificial and natural bonded abrasives (including diamond abrasives)	8.20
Nonmetallic diamond cubic boron nitride wheels, all bonds, artificial and natural bonded abrasives (including diamond abrasives)	3.17
Other artificial and natural nonmetallic abrasive products (except coated abrasives)	8.65
Nonmetallic abrasive products (including diamond abrasives), nsk	1.74
Nonmetallic coated abrasive products and buffing wheels, polishing wheels, and laps	45.73
Nonmetallic belts coated or impregnated with any natural or artificial abrasive material, cloth-glue bond	0.67
Other nonmetallic shapes, coated or impregnated with any natural or artificial abrasive material, cloth-glue bond	9.68
Nonmetallic belts coated or impregnated with any natural or artificial abrasive material, cloth-resin and waterproof bond	21.16
Other nonmetallic shapes, coated or impregnated with any natural or artificial abrasive material, cloth-resin and waterproof bond	26.39
Nonmetallic paper-glue bond, coated or impregnated with any natural or artificial abrasive material	(D)
Other nonmetallic coated or impregnated with any natural or artificial abrasive material, (paper-cloth or vulcanized fiber-cloth combinations, vulcanized fibers, paper-resin, waterproof bond, etc.)	(D)
Buffing and polishing wheels and laps of cloth, leather, felt, etc., but containing no abrasive grains, powders, or flour	3.51
Nonmetallic coated abrasive products and buffing wheels, polishing wheels, and laps, nsk	1.75
Metal abrasives (including scouring pads)	9.13
Steel and iron grit, shot, and sand, metal abrasives (including scouring pads)	43.72
Steel wool, metal abrasives (including scouring pads)	15.02
Other metal abrasives and scouring pads (including metal pads with soaps)	41.26
Abrasive products, nsk	4.24

Source: 1992 *Economic Census*. The values shown are percent of total shipments in an industry. Values of indented subcategories are summed in the main heading. The symbol (D) appears when data are withheld to prevent disclosure of competitive information. The abbreviation nsk stands for 'not specified by kind' and nec for 'not elsewhere classified'.

INPUTS AND OUTPUTS FOR ABRASIVE PRODUCTS

Economic Sector or Industry Providing Inputs	%	Sector	Economic Sector or Industry Buying Outputs	%	Sector
Imports	15.3	Foreign	Personal consumption expenditures	7.0	
Primary aluminum	8.0	Manufg.	Exports	6.6	Foreign
Industrial inorganic chemicals, nec	7.5	Manufg.	Special dies & tools & machine tool accessories	4.5	Manufg.
Paper mills, except building paper	6.0	Manufg.	Machinery, except electrical, nec	3.6	Manufg.
Wholesale trade	5.7	Trade	Iron & steel foundries	3.2	Manufg.
Adhesives & sealants	5.1	Manufg.	Motor vehicle parts & accessories	3.1	Manufg.
Abrasive products	5.0	Manufg.	Motor vehicles & car bodies	2.9	Manufg.
Narrow fabric mills	4.2	Manufg.	Abrasive products	2.7	Manufg.
Motor freight transportation & warehousing	3.4	Util.	Aircraft	2.6	Manufg.
Electric services (utilities)	3.2	Util.	Blast furnaces & steel mills	2.2	Manufg.
Communications, except radio & TV	2.9	Util.	Machine tools, metal cutting types	1.5	Manufg.

Continued on next page.

INPUTS AND OUTPUTS FOR ABRASIVE PRODUCTS - Continued

Economic Sector or Industry Providing Inputs	%	Sector	Economic Sector or Industry Buying Outputs	%	Sector
Broadwoven fabric mills	2.7	Manufg.	Refrigeration & heating equipment	1.5	Manufg.
Advertising	2.3	Services	Aircraft & missile engines & engine parts	1.3	Manufg.
Noncomparable imports	2.2	Foreign	Hardware, nec	1.3	Manufg.
Cyclic crudes and organics	2.1	Manufg.	S/L Govt. purch., other general government	1.2	S/L Govt
Railroads & related services	2.1	Util.	Aircraft & missile equipment, nec	1.1	Manufg.
Gas production & distribution (utilities)	2.0	Util.	Ball & roller bearings	1.1	Manufg.
Paperboard containers & boxes	1.7	Manufg.	Wood household furniture	1.1	Manufg.
Nonmetallic mineral services	1.5	Mining	Miscellaneous repair shops	1.1	Services
Petroleum refining	1.2	Manufg.	Manufacturing industries, nec	1.0	Manufg.
Plastics materials & resins	1.2	Manufg.	Plating & polishing	1.0	Manufg.
Equipment rental & leasing services	1.2	Services	Wholesale trade	1.0	Trade
Nonmetallic mineral products, nec	1.0	Manufg.	Federal Government purchases, nondefense	1.0	Fed Govt
Banking	1.0	Fin/R.E.	Power transmission equipment	0.9	Manufg.
Real estate	1.0	Fin/R.E.	Internal combustion engines, nec	0.8	Manufg.
Jewelers' materials & lapidary work	0.9	Manufg.	Miscellaneous plastics products	0.8	Manufg.
Miscellaneous plastics products	0.8	Manufg.	Pumps & compressors	0.8	Manufg.
Maintenance of nonfarm buildings nec	0.7	Constr.	Cutstone & stone products	0.7	Manufg.
Eating & drinking places	0.7	Trade	Electronic components nec	0.7	Manufg.
U.S. Postal Service	0.6	Gov't	Hand & edge tools, nec	0.7	Manufg.
Air transportation	0.5	Util.	Screw machine and related products	0.7	Manufg.
Water transportation	0.4	Util.	Upholstered household furniture	0.7	Manufg.
Royalties	0.4	Fin/R.E.	Federal Government purchases, national defense	0.7	Fed Govt
Computer & data processing services	0.4	Services	S/L Govt. purch., higher education	0.7	S/L Govt
Detective & protective services	0.4	Services	General industrial machinery, nec	0.6	Manufg.
Carbon & graphite products	0.3	Manufg.	Mineral wool	0.6	Manufg.
Machinery, except electrical, nec	0.3	Manufg.	Pipe, valves, & pipe fittings	0.6	Manufg.
Business/professional associations	0.3	Services	Radio & TV communication equipment	0.6	Manufg.
Legal services	0.3	Services	Construction machinery & equipment	0.5	Manufg.
Management & consulting services & labs	0.3	Services	Fabricated plate work (boiler shops)	0.5	Manufg.
Alkalies & chlorine	0.2	Manufg.	Farm machinery & equipment	0.5	Manufg.
Lubricating oils & greases	0.2	Manufg.	Metal stampings, nec	0.5	Manufg.
Special dies & tools & machine tool accessories	0.2	Manufg.	Oil field machinery	0.5	Manufg.
Insurance carriers	0.2	Fin/R.E.	Semiconductors & related devices	0.5	Manufg.
Accounting, auditing & bookkeeping	0.2	Services	Ship building & repairing	0.5	Manufg.
Nonferrous metal ores, except copper	0.1	Mining	Special industry machinery, nec	0.5	Manufg.
Manifold business forms	0.1	Manufg.	Retail trade, except eating & drinking	0.5	Trade
Automotive rental & leasing, without drivers	0.1	Services	Crude petroleum & natural gas	0.4	Mining
Automotive repair shops & services	0.1	Services	Aluminum castings	0.4	Manufg.
Hotels & lodging places	0.1	Services	Ammunition, except for small arms, nec	0.4	Manufg.
			Automotive stampings	0.4	Manufg.
			Blowers & fans	0.4	Manufg.
			Carburetors, pistons, rings, & valves	0.4	Manufg.
			Electronic computing equipment	0.4	Manufg.
			Food products machinery	0.4	Manufg.
			Guided missiles & space vehicles	0.4	Manufg.
			Machine tools, metal forming types	0.4	Manufg.
			Metal cans	0.4	Manufg.
			Power driven hand tools	0.4	Manufg.
			Sawmills & planning mills, general	0.4	Manufg.
			Service industry machines, nec	0.4	Manufg.
			Sheet metal work	0.4	Manufg.
			Signs & advertising displays	0.4	Manufg.
			Turbines & turbine generator sets	0.4	Manufg.
			Aluminum rolling & drawing	0.3	Manufg.
			Fabricated metal products, nec	0.3	Manufg.
			Fabricated structural metal	0.3	Manufg.
			Glass & glass products, except containers	0.3	Manufg.
			Jewelry, precious metal	0.3	Manufg.
			Mattresses & bedsprings	0.3	Manufg.
			Metal coating & allied services	0.3	Manufg.
			Metal doors, sash, & trim	0.3	Manufg.
			Metal office furniture	0.3	Manufg.
			Miscellaneous fabricated wire products	0.3	Manufg.
			Motors & generators	0.3	Manufg.
			Nonferrous wire drawing & insulating	0.3	Manufg.
			Printing trades machinery	0.3	Manufg.
			Railroad equipment	0.3	Manufg.
			Surgical & medical instruments	0.3	Manufg.
			Surgical appliances & supplies	0.3	Manufg.
			Truck & bus bodies	0.3	Manufg.
			Wood partitions & fixtures	0.3	Manufg.
			Wood products, nec	0.3	Manufg.
			Costume jewelry	0.2	Manufg.
			Cutlery	0.2	Manufg.
			Electric housewares & fans	0.2	Manufg.

Continued on next page.

INPUTS AND OUTPUTS FOR ABRASIVE PRODUCTS - Continued

Economic Sector or Industry Providing Inputs	%	Sector	Economic Sector or Industry Buying Outputs	%	Sector
			Electrical equipment & supplies, nec	0.2	Manufg.
			Games, toys, & children's vehicles	0.2	Manufg.
			Glass containers	0.2	Manufg.
			Heating equipment, except electric	0.2	Manufg.
			Industrial controls	0.2	Manufg.
			Industrial furnaces & ovens	0.2	Manufg.
			Instruments to measure electricity	0.2	Manufg.
			Mechanical measuring devices	0.2	Manufg.
			Metal household furniture	0.2	Manufg.
			Metal partitions & fixtures	0.2	Manufg.
			Metalworking machinery, nec	0.2	Manufg.
			Millwork	0.2	Manufg.
			Mining machinery, except oil field	0.2	Manufg.
			Musical instruments	0.2	Manufg.
			Ophthalmic goods	0.2	Manufg.
			Paper industries machinery	0.2	Manufg.
			Paper mills, except building paper	0.2	Manufg.
			Photographic equipment & supplies	0.2	Manufg.
			Plumbing fixture fittings & trim	0.2	Manufg.
			Public building furniture	0.2	Manufg.
			Small arms	0.2	Manufg.
			Sporting & athletic goods, nec	0.2	Manufg.
			Steel pipe & tubes	0.2	Manufg.
			Telephone & telegraph apparatus	0.2	Manufg.
			Textile machinery	0.2	Manufg.
			Truck trailers	0.2	Manufg.
			Typewriters & office machines, nec	0.2	Manufg.
			Wiring devices	0.2	Manufg.
			Wood office furniture	0.2	Manufg.
			Automotive repair shops & services	0.2	Services
			Hospitals	0.2	Services
			Watch, clock, jewelry, & furniture repair	0.2	Services
			S/L Govt. purch., elem. & secondary education	0.2	S/L Govt
			Nonfarm residential structure maintenance	0.1	Constr.
			Residential 1-unit structures, nonfarm	0.1	Constr.
			Architectural metal work	0.1	Manufg.
			Automatic merchandising machines	0.1	Manufg.
			Boat building & repairing	0.1	Manufg.
			Brass, bronze, & copper castings	0.1	Manufg.
			Broadwoven fabric mills	0.1	Manufg.
			Brooms & brushes	0.1	Manufg.
			Conveyors & conveying equipment	0.1	Manufg.
			Cyclic crudes and organics	0.1	Manufg.
			Drapery hardware & blinds & shades	0.1	Manufg.
			Engine electrical equipment	0.1	Manufg.
			Engineering & scientific instruments	0.1	Manufg.
			Fabricated rubber products, nec	0.1	Manufg.
			Furniture & fixtures, nec	0.1	Manufg.
			Gaskets, packing & sealing devices	0.1	Manufg.
			Hand saws & saw blades	0.1	Manufg.
			Household cooking equipment	0.1	Manufg.
			Household refrigerators & freezers	0.1	Manufg.
			Industrial trucks & tractors	0.1	Manufg.
			Iron & steel forgings	0.1	Manufg.
			Lighting fixtures & equipment	0.1	Manufg.
			Lithographic platemaking & services	0.1	Manufg.
			Optical instruments & lenses	0.1	Manufg.
			Ordnance & accessories nec	0.1	Manufg.
			Primary aluminum	0.1	Manufg.
			Rolling mill machinery	0.1	Manufg.
			Small arms ammunition	0.1	Manufg.
			Steel wire & related products	0.1	Manufg.
			Switchgear & switchboard apparatus	0.1	Manufg.
			Transformers	0.1	Manufg.
			Veneer & plywood	0.1	Manufg.
			Wood kitchen cabinets	0.1	Manufg.
			Wood pallets & skids	0.1	Manufg.

Source: Benchmark Input-Output Accounts for the U.S. Economy, 1982, U.S. Department of Commerce, Washington, D.C., July 1991. Data, as reported in the source, are organized by the 1977 SIC structure in use in 1982 but have been matched, as closely as is possible, to the 1987 SIC structure used in this book.

OCCUPATIONS EMPLOYED BY SIC 329 - STONE, CLAY, AND MISC MINING PRODUCTS NEC

Occupation	% of Total 1994	Change to 2005	Occupation	% of Total 1994	Change to 2005
Helpers, laborers, & material movers nec	6.7	-23.3	Machine feeders & offbearers	2.3	-31.4
Assemblers, fabricators, & hand workers nec	6.4	-23.9	Painting, coating, & decorating workers, hand	2.0	52.3
Furnace, kiln, or kettle operators	4.2	-16.7	Freight, stock, & material movers, hand	1.9	-38.8
Crushing & mixing machine operators	3.9	-9.5	Truck drivers light & heavy	1.9	-20.6
Industrial machinery mechanics	3.9	-15.2	Coating, painting, & spraying machine workers	1.8	-23.8
Hand packers & packagers	3.6	-34.7	Secretaries, ex legal & medical	1.8	-30.4
Extruding & forming machine workers	3.4	-80.6	Cutting & slicing machine setters, operators	1.6	-16.2
Sales & related workers nec	3.2	-23.6	Grinders & polishers, hand	1.6	-16.2
Packaging & filling machine operators	3.2	-23.7	Industrial production managers	1.5	-23.5
Precision workers nec	3.0	-8.7	Traffic, shipping, & receiving clerks	1.5	-26.6
Industrial truck & tractor operators	2.8	-23.7	General office clerks	1.5	-34.9
General managers & top executives	2.8	-27.5	Bookkeeping, accounting, & auditing clerks	1.3	-42.7
Inspectors, testers, & graders, precision	2.8	-23.6	Electricians	1.1	-27.3
Maintenance repairers, general utility	2.6	-30.8	Machinists	1.0	-23.6

Source: Industry-Occupation Matrix, Bureau of Labor Statistics. These data relate to one or more 3-digit SIC industry groups rather than to a single 4-digit SIC. The change reported for each occupation to the year 2005 is a percent of growth or decline as estimated by the Bureau of Labor Statistics. The abbreviation nec stands for 'not elsewhere classified'.

LOCATION BY STATE AND REGIONAL CONCENTRATION

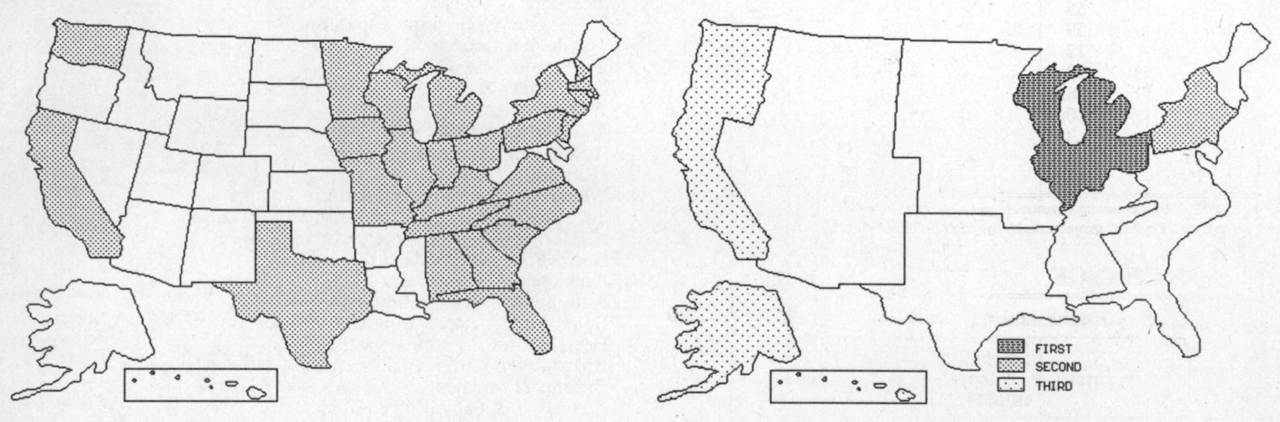

INDUSTRY DATA BY STATE

State	Establish-ments	Shipments Total ($ mil)	Shipments % of U.S.	Shipments Per Establ.	Employment Total Number	Employment % of U.S.	Employment Per Establ.	Employment Wages ($/hour)	Cost as % of Shipments	Investment per Employee ($)
Massachusetts	28	394.6	10.6	14.1	2,900	13.5	104	14.65	41.2	-
New York	34	368.5	9.9	10.8	2,400	11.2	71	13.73	48.7	7,708
Ohio	36	361.2	9.7	10.0	2,500	11.6	69	12.82	47.0	4,800
Illinois	39	260.1	7.0	6.7	2,000	9.3	51	11.66	33.3	2,500
Michigan	47	159.5	4.3	3.4	1,000	4.7	21	12.57	44.8	3,000
Texas	16	128.5	3.4	8.0	1,200	5.6	75	6.61	72.6	1,333
California	43	98.0	2.6	2.3	1,000	4.7	23	9.67	39.2	4,000
Pennsylvania	29	93.8	2.5	3.2	700	3.3	24	11.80	43.7	3,000
North Carolina	18	80.8	2.2	4.5	700	3.3	39	8.88	45.4	2,286
Virginia	5	65.2	1.7	13.0	400	1.9	80	9.00	53.5	4,250
Connecticut	11	59.6	1.6	5.4	400	1.9	36	11.50	45.8	3,750
Georgia	7	50.2	1.3	7.2	400	1.9	57	9.00	47.8	-
New Jersey	16	22.9	0.6	1.4	200	0.9	13	13.67	34.5	-
Indiana	11	21.0	0.6	1.9	200	0.9	18	8.50	34.3	2,500
Florida	7	17.3	0.5	2.5	200	0.9	29	6.33	42.2	-
Washington	6	15.7	0.4	2.6	200	0.9	33	6.67	44.6	2,500
Wisconsin	9	(D)	-	-	1,750 *	8.1	194	-	-	-
Minnesota	6	(D)	-	-	1,750 *	8.1	292	-	-	-
Alabama	5	(D)	-	-	175 *	0.8	35	-	-	-
Missouri	5	(D)	-	-	750 *	3.5	150	-	-	-
Tennessee	4	(D)	-	-	175 *	0.8	44	-	-	-
New Hampshire	3	(D)	-	-	375 *	1.7	125	-	-	-
Iowa	2	(D)	-	-	375 *	1.7	188	-	-	-
South Carolina	2	(D)	-	-	175 *	0.8	88	-	-	-
Kentucky	1	(D)	-	-	175 *	0.8	175	-	-	-

Source: 1992 *Economic Census*. The states are in descending order of shipments or establishments (if shipment data are missing for the majority). The symbol (D) appears when data are withheld to prevent disclosure of competitive information. States marked with (D) are sorted by number of establishments. A dash (-) indicates that the data element cannot be calculated; * indicates the midpoint of a range.

3292 - ASBESTOS PRODUCTS

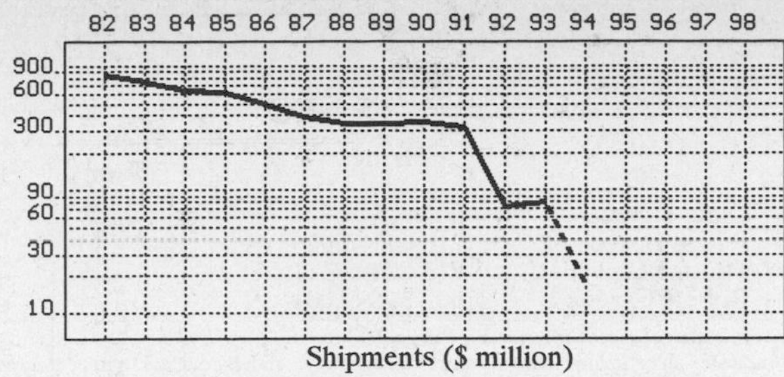

Shipments ($ million)

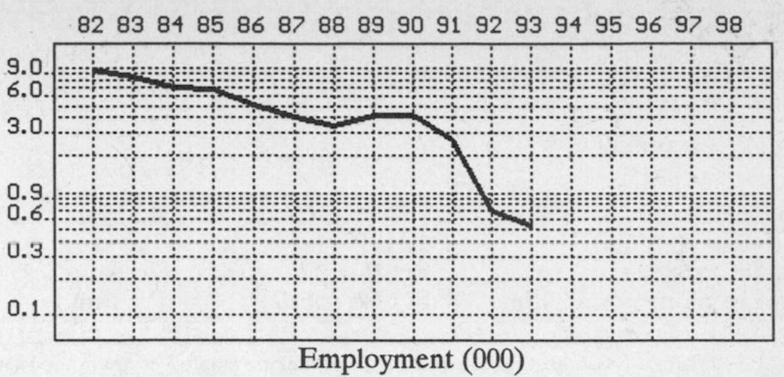

Employment (000)

GENERAL STATISTICS

Year	Companies	Establishments: Total	Establishments: with 20 or more employees	Employment: Total (000)	Employment: Production Workers (000)	Employment: Production Hours (Mil)	Compensation: Payroll ($ mil)	Compensation: Wages ($/hr)	Production ($ million): Cost of Materials	Production ($ million): Value Added by Manufacture	Production ($ million): Value of Shipments	Production ($ million): Capital Invest.
1982	77	96	53	9.7	7.4	14.6	179.8	8.67	429.3	397.4	842.8	31.3
1983		95	54	8.6	6.7	13.5	173.7	8.83	376.0	385.5	750.0	21.2
1984		94	55	7.1	5.5	11.1	156.2	9.93	304.2	345.8	641.8	21.1
1985		92	56	6.8	5.2	10.5	152.9	10.05	280.3	318.4	607.5	24.1
1986		85	57	5.1	3.9	7.6	121.8	10.89	219.5	260.6	485.9	23.6
1987	50	54	22	4.0	3.1	6.3	98.7	11.16	185.2	202.6	386.5	14.9
1988		57	29	3.4	2.5	5.1	84.9	11.55	141.0	210.5	348.2	8.5
1989		57	28	4.2	2.5	5.2	88.6	10.88	143.9	198.2	344.4	14.0
1990		55	28	4.2	2.3	4.5	87.0	12.22	154.2	198.7	352.6	18.9
1991		59	32	2.7	2.0	3.8	75.7	12.32	130.5	187.9	319.8	11.1
1992	12	12	6	0.7	0.5	1.0	21.8	13.70	30.0	43.0	74.0	2.1
1993		22	6	0.5P			28.0P	13.56P			81.4P	4.9P
1994		18P	5P				13.9P	14.00P			16.9P	2.8P
1995		10P	1P					14.44P				0.7P
1996		3P						14.88P				
1997								15.32P				
1998								15.76P				

Sources: 1982, 1987, 1992 *Economic Census*; *Annual Survey of Manufactures*, 83-86, 88-91, 93-94. Establishment counts for non-Census years are from *County Business Patterns*; establishment values for 83-84 are extrapolations. 'P's show projections by the editors. Industries reclassified in 87 will not have data for prior years.

INDICES OF CHANGE

Year	Companies	Establishments: Total	Establishments: with 20 or more employees	Employment: Total (000)	Employment: Production Workers (000)	Employment: Production Hours (Mil)	Compensation: Payroll ($ mil)	Compensation: Wages ($/hr)	Production ($ million): Cost of Materials	Production ($ million): Value Added by Manufacture	Production ($ million): Value of Shipments	Production ($ million): Capital Invest.
1982	642	800	883	1,386	1,480	1,460	825	63	1,431	924	1,139	1,490
1983		792	900	1,229	1,340	1,350	797	64	1,253	897	1,014	1,010
1984		783	917	1,014	1,100	1,110	717	72	1,014	804	867	1,005
1985		767	933	971	1,040	1,050	701	73	934	740	821	1,148
1986		708	950	729	780	760	559	79	732	606	657	1,124
1987	417	450	367	571	620	630	453	81	617	471	522	710
1988		475	483	486	500	510	389	84	470	490	471	405
1989		475	467	600	500	520	406	79	480	461	465	667
1990		458	467	600	460	450	399	89	514	462	476	900
1991		492	533	386	400	380	347	90	435	437	432	529
1992	100	100	100	100	100	100	100	100	100	100	100	100
1993		183	100	78P			128P	99P			110P	233P
1994		148P	88P				64P	102P			23P	134P
1995		87P	10P					105P				35P
1996		27P						109P				
1997								112P				
1998								115P				

Sources: Same as General Statistics. Values reflect change from the base year, 1992. Values above 100 mean greater than 92, values below 100 mean less than 92, and a value of 100 in the 82-91 or 93-98 period means same as 92. 'P's mark projections by the editors.

SELECTED RATIOS

For 1992	Avg. of All Manufact.	Analyzed Industry	Index	For 1992	Avg. of All Manufact.	Analyzed Industry	Index
Employees per Establishment	46	58	128	Value Added per Production Worker	122,353	86,000	70
Payroll per Establishment	1,332,320	1,816,667	136	Cost per Establishment	4,239,462	2,500,000	59
Payroll per Employee	29,181	31,143	107	Cost per Employee	92,853	42,857	46
Production Workers per Establishment	31	42	133	Cost per Production Worker	135,003	60,000	44
Wages per Establishment	734,496	1,141,667	155	Shipments per Establishment	8,100,800	6,166,667	76
Wages per Production Worker	23,390	27,400	117	Shipments per Employee	177,425	105,714	60
Hours per Production Worker	2,025	2,000	99	Shipments per Production Worker	257,966	148,000	57
Wages per Hour	11.55	13.70	119	Investment per Establishment	278,244	175,000	63
Value Added per Establishment	3,842,210	3,583,333	93	Investment per Employee	6,094	3,000	49
Value Added per Employee	84,153	61,429	73	Investment per Production Worker	8,861	4,200	47

Sources: Same as General Statistics. The 'Average of All Manufacturing' column represents the average of all manufacturing industries reported for the most recent complete year available. The Index shows the relationship between the Average and the Analyzed Industry. For example, 100 means that they are equal; 500 that the Analyzed Industry is five times the average; 50 means that the Analyzed Industry is half the national average. The abbreviation 'na' is used to show that data are 'not available'.

LEADING COMPANIES

Number shown: 4 Total sales ($ mil): **217** Total employment (000): **1.5**

Company Name	Address				CEO Name	Phone	Co. Type	Sales ($ mil)	Empl. (000)
Raytech Corp	1 Corporate Dr	Shelton	CT	06484	Craig R Smith	203-925-8023	P	168	1.2
Garland Company Inc	3800 E 91st St	Cleveland	OH	44105	RJ De Bacco	216-641-7500	R	40	0.2
Standco Industries Inc	PO Box 87	Houston	TX	77001	Minor Peeples Jr	713-224-6311	D	5	<0.1
Friction Division Products Inc	PO Box 5627	Trenton	NJ	08638	Robert Carney	609-396-6500	R	4	<0.1

Source: *Ward's Business Directory of U.S. Private and Public Companies*, Volumes 1 and 2, 1996. The company type code used is as follows: P - Public, R - Private, S - Subsidiary, D - Division, J - Joint Venture, A - Affiliate, G - Group. Sales are in millions of dollars, employees are in thousands. An asterisk (*) indicates an estimated sales volume. The symbol < stands for 'less than'. Company names and addresses are truncated, in some cases, to fit into the available space.

MATERIALS CONSUMED

Material	Quantity	Delivered Cost ($ million)
Materials, ingredients, containers, and supplies	(X)	24.8
Asbestos, crude (including fiber)	(X)	4.7
Building paper and board	(X)	(D)
Plastics resins consumed in the form of granules, pellets, powders, liquids, etc.	(X)	(D)
Synthetic rubber	(X)	(D)
Other chemicals and allied products	(X)	(D)
Portland cement	(X)	(D)
All other materials and components, parts, containers, and supplies	(X)	16.4
Materials, ingredients, containers, and supplies, nsk	(X)	1.1

Source: 1992 *Economic Census*. Explanation of symbols used: (D): Withheld to avoid disclosure of competitive data; na: Not available; (S): Withheld because statistical norms were not met; (X): Not applicable; (Z): Less than half the unit shown; nec: Not elsewhere classified; nsk: Not specified by kind; - : zero; * : 10-19 percent estimated; ** : 20-29 percent estimated.

PRODUCT SHARE DETAILS

Product or Product Class	% Share
Asbestos products	100.00
Asbestos friction materials	84.04
Asbestos friction materials, woven brake lining, containing asbestos yarn, tape, or cloth	(D)
Asbestos friction materials, molded brake lining (including all nonwoven types)	51.72
Asbestos friction materials, disc brake pads	41.41
Asbestos friction materials, clutch facings (nonwoven, woven, and molded)	(D)
Other asbestos products	12.93
Other asbestos textiles, all types (yarn, cord, thread, rope, tape, lap, roving, wick, carded fibers, etc.)	(D)
Other asbestos felts, all kinds (roofing, asphalt, tar saturated, etc.)	(D)
Other asbestos-cement products, all kinds, including flat sheet, wallboard, shingles, clapboard, pipe, conduits, ducts, etc.	85.11
Other brake lining asbestos products (vinyl asbestos floor tile, pipe and block insulation, asphalt floor tile, millboard, etc.)	(D)
Asbestos products, nsk	3.03

Source: 1992 *Economic Census*. The values shown are percent of total shipments in an industry. Values of indented subcategories are summed in the main heading. The symbol (D) appears when data are withheld to prevent disclosure of competitive information. The abbreviation nsk stands for 'not specified by kind' and nec for 'not elsewhere classified'.

INPUTS AND OUTPUTS FOR ASBESTOS PRODUCTS

Economic Sector or Industry Providing Inputs	%	Sector	Economic Sector or Industry Buying Outputs	%	Sector
Plastics materials & resins	12.3	Manufg.	Motor vehicle parts & accessories	18.2	Manufg.
Wholesale trade	10.3	Trade	Nonfarm residential structure maintenance	10.9	Constr.
Motor freight transportation & warehousing	8.1	Util.	Exports	9.9	Foreign
Adhesives & sealants	7.3	Manufg.	Residential additions/alterations, nonfarm	7.0	Constr.
Nonmetallic mineral services	6.7	Mining	Maintenance of nonfarm buildings nec	4.6	Constr.
Imports	5.7	Foreign	Industrial buildings	4.1	Constr.
Electric services (utilities)	4.2	Util.	Electric utility facility construction	3.9	Constr.
Miscellaneous plastics products	3.3	Manufg.	Office buildings	3.4	Constr.
Paperboard containers & boxes	2.6	Manufg.	Residential 1-unit structures, nonfarm	3.2	Constr.
Railroads & related services	2.1	Util.	Residential garden apartments	2.6	Constr.
Fabricated rubber products, nec	1.9	Manufg.	Construction of stores & restaurants	2.1	Constr.
Gas production & distribution (utilities)	1.9	Util.	Sewer system facility construction	2.1	Constr.
Water transportation	1.9	Util.	Construction machinery & equipment	1.8	Manufg.
Cement, hydraulic	1.8	Manufg.	Water supply facility construction	1.6	Constr.
Industrial inorganic chemicals, nec	1.5	Manufg.	Maintenance of electric utility facilities	1.4	Constr.
Metal stampings, nec	1.4	Manufg.	Aircraft & missile equipment, nec	1.3	Manufg.
Petroleum refining	1.4	Manufg.	Federal Government purchases, national defense	1.3	Fed Govt
Primary metal products, nec	1.4	Manufg.	Gaskets, packing & sealing devices	1.1	Manufg.
Advertising	1.2	Services	Miscellaneous plastics products	1.1	Manufg.
Nonmetallic mineral products, nec	1.1	Manufg.	Automotive repair shops & services	1.1	Services

Continued on next page.

INPUTS AND OUTPUTS FOR ASBESTOS PRODUCTS - Continued

Economic Sector or Industry Providing Inputs	%	Sector	Economic Sector or Industry Buying Outputs	%	Sector
Maintenance of nonfarm buildings nec	1.0	Constr.	Construction of educational buildings	1.0	Constr.
Eating & drinking places	1.0	Trade	Farm machinery & equipment	1.0	Manufg.
Banking	1.0	Fin/R.E.	Motor freight transportation & warehousing	1.0	Util.
Cutstone & stone products	0.9	Manufg.	Logging camps & logging contractors	0.9	Manufg.
Glass & glass products, except containers	0.9	Manufg.	Nonferrous wire drawing & insulating	0.9	Manufg.
Noncomparable imports	0.9	Foreign	Transit & bus transportation	0.9	Util.
Asbestos products	0.8	Manufg.	Construction of hospitals	0.8	Constr.
Cyclic crudes and organics	0.8	Manufg.	Telephone & telegraph facility construction	0.8	Constr.
Inorganic pigments	0.7	Manufg.	Residential 2-4 unit structures, nonfarm	0.7	Constr.
Communications, except radio & TV	0.7	Util.	Residential high-rise apartments	0.6	Constr.
U.S. Postal Service	0.7	Gov't	Power transmission equipment	0.6	Manufg.
Paving mixtures & blocks	0.6	Manufg.	Surgical appliances & supplies	0.6	Manufg.
Air transportation	0.6	Util.	Maintenance of sewer facilities	0.5	Constr.
Detective & protective services	0.6	Services	Asbestos products	0.5	Manufg.
Coal	0.5	Mining	Metal foil & leaf	0.5	Manufg.
Building paper & board mills	0.5	Manufg.	Farm housing units & additions & alterations	0.4	Constr.
Machinery, except electrical, nec	0.5	Manufg.	Construction of nonfarm buildings nec	0.3	Constr.
Sawmills & planning mills, general	0.5	Manufg.	Maintenance of water supply facilities	0.3	Constr.
Sanitary services, steam supply, irrigation	0.5	Util.	Fabricated plate work (boiler shops)	0.3	Manufg.
Credit agencies other than banks	0.5	Fin/R.E.	Hoists, cranes, & monorails	0.3	Manufg.
Nonferrous rolling & drawing, nec	0.4	Manufg.	Mineral wool	0.3	Manufg.
Synthetic rubber	0.4	Manufg.	Mining machinery, except oil field	0.3	Manufg.
Computer & data processing services	0.4	Services	Motor vehicles & car bodies	0.3	Manufg.
Legal services	0.4	Services	Amusement & recreation building construction	0.2	Constr.
Management & consulting services & labs	0.4	Services	Dormitories & other group housing	0.2	Constr.
Abrasive products	0.3	Manufg.	Hotels & motels	0.2	Constr.
Asphalt felts & coatings	0.3	Manufg.	Local transit facility construction	0.2	Constr.
Miscellaneous fabricated wire products	0.3	Manufg.	Maintenance of farm residential buildings	0.2	Constr.
Real estate	0.3	Fin/R.E.	Maintenance of farm service facilities	0.2	Constr.
Equipment rental & leasing services	0.3	Services	Maintenance of local transit facilities	0.2	Constr.
Alkalies & chlorine	0.2	Manufg.	Maintenance of nonbuilding facilities nec	0.2	Constr.
Lubricating oils & greases	0.2	Manufg.	Maintenance of telephone & telegraph facilities	0.2	Constr.
Manifold business forms	0.2	Manufg.	Nonbuilding facilities nec	0.2	Constr.
Special dies & tools & machine tool accessories	0.2	Manufg.	Resid. & other health facility construction	0.2	Constr.
Vegetable oil mills, nec	0.2	Manufg.	Industrial trucks & tractors	0.2	Manufg.
Wood products, nec	0.2	Manufg.	Maintenance of gas utility facilities	0.1	Constr.
Insurance carriers	0.2	Fin/R.E.	Maintenance of petroleum pipelines	0.1	Constr.
Royalties	0.2	Fin/R.E.	Mobile homes	0.1	Manufg.
Security & commodity brokers	0.2	Fin/R.E.	Railroads & related services	0.1	Util.
Accounting, auditing & bookkeeping	0.2	Services			
Automotive rental & leasing, without drivers	0.2	Services			
Automotive repair shops & services	0.2	Services			
Hotels & lodging places	0.1	Services			
Laundry, dry cleaning, shoe repair	0.1	Services			

Source: Benchmark Input-Output Accounts for the U.S. Economy, 1982, U.S. Department of Commerce, Washington, D.C., July 1991. Data, as reported in the source, are organized by the 1977 SIC structure in use in 1982 but have been matched, as closely as is possible, to the 1987 SIC structure used in this book.

OCCUPATIONS EMPLOYED BY SIC 329 - STONE, CLAY, AND MISC MINING PRODUCTS NEC

Occupation	% of Total 1994	Change to 2005	Occupation	% of Total 1994	Change to 2005
Helpers, laborers, & material movers nec	6.7	-23.3	Machine feeders & offbearers	2.3	-31.4
Assemblers, fabricators, & hand workers nec	6.4	-23.9	Painting, coating, & decorating workers, hand	2.0	52.3
Furnace, kiln, or kettle operators	4.2	-16.7	Freight, stock, & material movers, hand	1.9	-38.8
Crushing & mixing machine operators	3.9	-9.5	Truck drivers light & heavy	1.9	-20.6
Industrial machinery mechanics	3.9	-15.2	Coating, painting, & spraying machine workers	1.8	-23.8
Hand packers & packagers	3.6	-34.7	Secretaries, ex legal & medical	1.8	-30.4
Extruding & forming machine workers	3.4	-80.6	Cutting & slicing machine setters, operators	1.6	-16.2
Sales & related workers nec	3.2	-23.6	Grinders & polishers, hand	1.6	-16.2
Packaging & filling machine operators	3.2	-23.7	Industrial production managers	1.5	-23.5
Precision workers nec	3.0	-8.7	Traffic, shipping, & receiving clerks	1.5	-26.6
Industrial truck & tractor operators	2.8	-23.7	General office clerks	1.5	-34.9
General managers & top executives	2.8	-27.5	Bookkeeping, accounting, & auditing clerks	1.3	-42.7
Inspectors, testers, & graders, precision	2.8	-23.6	Electricians	1.1	-27.3
Maintenance repairers, general utility	2.6	-30.8	Machinists	1.0	-23.6

Source: Industry-Occupation Matrix, Bureau of Labor Statistics. These data relate to one or more 3-digit SIC industry groups rather than to a single 4-digit SIC. The change reported for each occupation to the year 2005 is a percent of growth or decline as estimated by the Bureau of Labor Statistics. The abbreviation nec stands for 'not elsewhere classified'.

LOCATION BY STATE AND REGIONAL CONCENTRATION

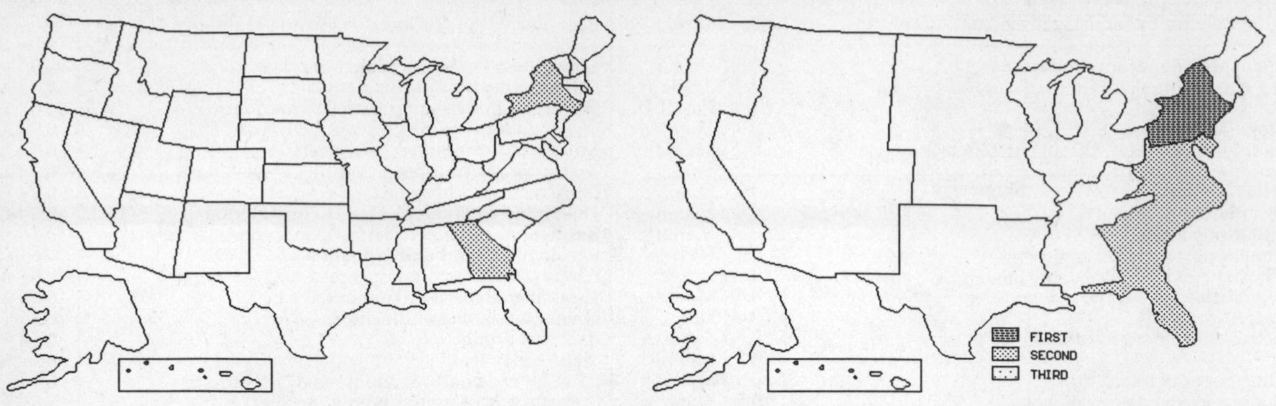

INDUSTRY DATA BY STATE

State	Establish-ments	Shipments			Employment				Cost as % of Shipments	Investment per Employee ($)
		Total ($ mil)	% of U.S.	Per Establ.	Total Number	% of U.S.	Per Establ.	Wages ($/hour)		
Georgia	1	(D)	-	-	175 *	25.0	175	-	-	-
New York	1	(D)	-	-	375 *	53.6	375	-	-	-

Source: 1992 *Economic Census*. The states are in descending order of shipments or establishments (if shipment data are missing for the majority). The symbol (D) appears when data are withheld to prevent disclosure of competitive information. States marked with (D) are sorted by number of establishments. A dash (-) indicates that the data element cannot be calculated; * indicates the midpoint of a range.

3295 - MINERALS & EARTHS GROUND ETC.

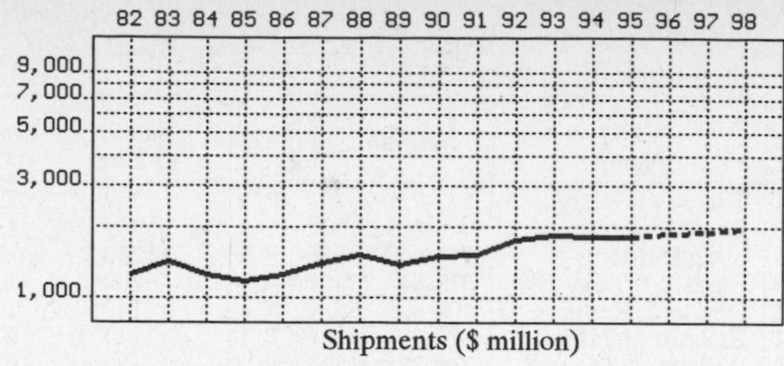

Shipments ($ million)

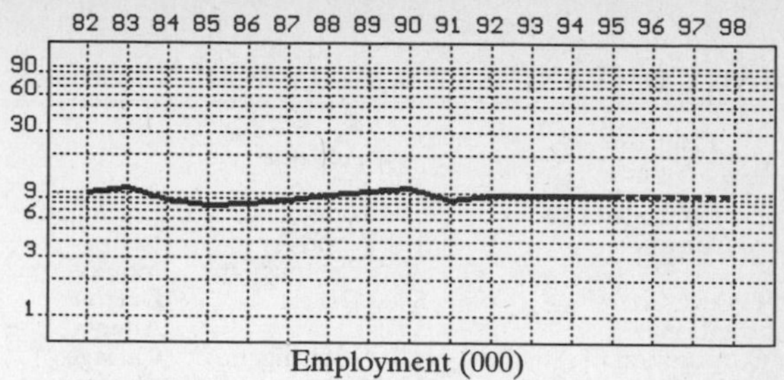

Employment (000)

GENERAL STATISTICS

Year	Com-panies	Establishments		Employment			Compensation		Production ($ million)			
		Total	with 20 or more employees	Total (000)	Production Workers (000)	Production Hours (Mil)	Payroll ($ mil)	Wages ($/hr)	Cost of Materials	Value Added by Manufacture	Value of Shipments	Capital Invest.
1982	279	436	142	9.9	7.4	14.3	188.9	8.99	617.1	637.4	1,256.5	71.7
1983		432	142	10.7	8.0	16.3	225.7	9.51	696.0	723.8	1,423.6	47.9
1984		428	142	8.8	6.4	12.8	187.7	9.29	585.3	680.0	1,259.0	48.9
1985		423	141	7.8	5.6	11.0	183.5	10.46	490.2	676.3	1,170.5	76.3
1986		403	134	8.2	6.0	11.6	201.6	11.10	510.7	731.3	1,261.4	54.3
1987	245	381	108	8.8	6.4	12.9	218.4	11.61	563.9	834.4	1,406.2	53.2
1988		371	113	9.4	7.0	14.8	242.6	10.96	628.1	901.4	1,524.4	38.8
1989		357	124	10.1	6.5	13.2	226.7	11.76	583.8	824.8	1,401.0	53.2
1990		347	130	10.7	6.8	14.0	241.6	11.49	661.7	848.7	1,499.8	50.7
1991		354	129	8.7	6.6	13.6	237.5	11.70	666.2	845.5	1,523.3	53.9
1992	247	368	127	9.5	7.1	15.2	299.1	12.77	690.6	1,081.2	1,774.4	47.1
1993		357	120	9.4	7.0	15.3	297.3	12.65	768.8	1,085.8	1,847.6	64.7
1994		331P	117P	9.4	7.0	14.6	305.2	14.10	757.2	1,072.6	1,830.1	86.5
1995		323P	115P	9.4P	6.8P	14.6P	302.4P	13.76P	756.0P	1,070.9P	1,827.3P	61.0P
1996		314P	113P	9.4P	6.8P	14.7P	312.1P	14.11P	776.8P	1,100.4P	1,877.6P	61.5P
1997		305P	111P	9.5P	6.8P	14.8P	321.7P	14.47P	797.6P	1,129.9P	1,927.8P	62.0P
1998		297P	109P	9.5P	6.8P	14.9P	331.3P	14.83P	818.5P	1,159.4P	1,978.1P	62.5P

Sources: 1982, 1987, 1992 *Economic Census*; *Annual Survey of Manufactures*, 83-86, 88-91, 93-94. Establishment counts for non-Census years are from *County Business Patterns*; establishment values for 83-84 are extrapolations. 'P's show projections by the editors. Industries reclassified in 87 will not have data for prior years.

INDICES OF CHANGE

Year	Com-panies	Establishments		Employment			Compensation		Production ($ million)			
		Total	with 20 or more employees	Total (000)	Production Workers (000)	Production Hours (Mil)	Payroll ($ mil)	Wages ($/hr)	Cost of Materials	Value Added by Manufacture	Value of Shipments	Capital Invest.
1982	113	118	112	104	104	94	63	70	89	59	71	152
1983		117	112	113	113	107	75	74	101	67	80	102
1984		116	112	93	90	84	63	73	85	63	71	104
1985		115	111	82	79	72	61	82	71	63	66	162
1986		110	106	86	85	76	67	87	74	68	71	115
1987	99	104	85	93	90	85	73	91	82	77	79	113
1988		101	89	99	99	97	81	86	91	83	86	82
1989		97	98	106	92	87	76	92	85	76	79	113
1990		94	102	113	96	92	81	90	96	78	85	108
1991		96	102	92	93	89	79	92	96	78	86	114
1992	100	100	100	100	100	100	100	100	100	100	100	100
1993		97	94	99	99	101	99	99	111	100	104	137
1994		90P	92P	99	99	96	102	110	110	99	103	184
1995		88P	91P	99P	95P	96P	101P	108P	109P	99P	103P	129P
1996		85P	89P	99P	95P	96P	104P	111P	112P	102P	106P	131P
1997		83P	88P	99P	95P	97P	108P	113P	115P	105P	109P	132P
1998		81P	86P	100P	95P	98P	111P	116P	119P	107P	111P	133P

Sources: Same as General Statistics. Values reflect change from the base year, 1992. Values above 100 mean greater than 92, values below 100 mean less than 92, and a value of 100 in the 82-91 or 93-98 period means same as 92. 'P's mark projections by the editors.

SELECTED RATIOS

For 1994	Avg. of All Manufact.	Analyzed Industry	Index
Employees per Establishment	49	28	58
Payroll per Establishment	1,500,273	920,748	61
Payroll per Employee	30,620	32,468	106
Production Workers per Establishment	34	21	62
Wages per Establishment	853,319	621,052	73
Wages per Production Worker	24,861	29,409	118
Hours per Production Worker	2,056	2,086	101
Wages per Hour	12.09	14.10	117
Value Added per Establishment	4,602,255	3,235,892	70
Value Added per Employee	93,930	114,106	121

For 1994	Avg. of All Manufact.	Analyzed Industry	Index
Value Added per Production Worker	134,084	153,229	114
Cost per Establishment	5,045,178	2,284,372	45
Cost per Employee	102,970	80,553	78
Cost per Production Worker	146,988	108,171	74
Shipments per Establishment	9,576,895	5,521,168	58
Shipments per Employee	195,460	194,691	100
Shipments per Production Worker	279,017	261,443	94
Investment per Establishment	321,011	260,959	81
Investment per Employee	6,552	9,202	140
Investment per Production Worker	9,352	12,357	132

Sources: Same as General Statistics. The 'Average of All Manufacturing' column represents the average of all manufacturing industries reported for the most recent complete year available. The Index shows the relationship between the Average and the Analyzed Industry. For example, 100 means that they are equal; 500 that the Analyzed Industry is five times the average; 50 means that the Analyzed Industry is half the national average. The abbreviation 'na' is used to show that data are 'not available'.

LEADING COMPANIES

Number shown: **42** Total sales ($ mil): **2,410** Total employment (000): **19.7**

Company Name	Address				CEO Name	Phone	Co. Type	Sales ($ mil)	Empl. (000)
Eagle-Picher Industries Inc	580 Walnut	Cincinnati	OH	45201	Thomas E Petry	513-721-7010	P	757	7.5
Engelhard Corp	101 Wood Av	Iselin	NJ	08830	Barry W Perry	908-205-5000	D	369	1.8
Owl Cos	2465 Campus Dr	Irvine	CA	92715	Greg Burden	714-660-4966	R	250	2.3
Edward C Levy Co	8800 Dix Av	Detroit	MI	48209	Edward C Levy Jr	313-843-7200	R	200	2.0
ECC International	5775	Atlanta	GA	30342	Dennis L Rediker	404-843-1551	S	140	1.4
Oil-Dri Corporation of America	410 N Michigan Av	Chicago	IL	60611	Richard M Jaffee	312-321-1515	P	140	0.7
Fairmont Minerals Ltd	11830 Ravenna Rd	Chardon	OH	44024	William Conway	216-285-3132	R	90	0.3
Zemex Corp	1 W Pack Sq	Asheville	NC	28801	Richard L Lister	704-255-4900	P	55	0.5
Asbury Carbons Inc	41 Main St	Asbury	NJ	08802	HM Riddle III	908-537-2155	R	50	0.4
Superior Graphite Co	120 S Riverside Plz	Chicago	IL	60606	PR Carney	312-559-2999	R	50	0.3
Multiform Desiccants Inc	960 Busti St	Buffalo	NY	14213	John S Cullen	716-883-8900	R	35	0.3
Asbury Graphite Mills Inc	41 Main St	Asbury	NJ	08802	HM Riddle III	908-537-2155	S	25*	0.1
Floridin Co	11011 N Madison St	Quincy	FL	32351	David Ruff	904-562-5005	S	25	0.2
Franklin Industrial Minerals	612 10th Av N	Nashville	TN	37203	Nelson Severinghaus	615-259-4222	D	25	0.2
Levy Company Inc	PO Box 540	Portage	IN	46368	F Lesters	219-787-8666	R	21	0.2
Omya Inc	61 Main St	Proctor	VT	05765	Jeremy C Croggon	802-459-3311	S	15*	0.2
Kaser Corp	PO Box 3569	Des Moines	IA	50322	Peter G Kaser	515-278-0205	R	14	0.2
Silbrico Corp	6300 River Rd	Hodgkins	IL	60525	Tom Mendius	708-354-3350	R	11	<0.1
Eugene Sand and Gravel Inc	3000 N Delta Hwy	Eugene	OR	97401	Michael J Alltucker	503-683-6400	R	11*	0.1
Polar Minerals Inc	5060 R Atlanta	Tucker	GA	30084	Joseph Z Keating	404-934-4411	R	10	<0.1
Meshberger Brothers Stone	PO Box 345	Berne	IN	46711	C Fryback	219-334-5311	R	10	<0.1
Minnesota Mining & Mfg	County Rte 601	Belle Mead	NJ	08502	Gene Pierce	908-874-3200	D	9*	<0.1
Hydraulic Press Brick Co	705 Olive St	St Louis	MO	63101	Warren W Allen Jr	314-621-9306	P	9	<0.1
Chemrock Corp	1101 Kermit Dr	Nashville	TN	37217	Raymond Perlman	615-360-7911	S	8	<0.1
Dixie Clay Co	30 Winfield St	Norwalk	CT	06855	GL Fiederlein	203-853-1400	S	8*	<0.1
Textile Technologies Industries	2800 Turnpike Dr	Hatboro	PA	19040	Andrew Dunn	215-443-5325	R	8	<0.1
ISP Mineral Products Inc	34 Charles St	Hagerstown	MD	21740		301-733-4000	S	7	<0.1
Schundler Co	PO Box 249	Metuchen	NJ	08840	BE Schundler	908-287-2244	R	7	<0.1
Cummings-Moore Graphite Co	1646 Green Av	Detroit	MI	48209	NE Mares	313-841-1615	S	6	<0.1
Arkalite	PO Box 1567	West Memphis	AR	72301	Merle Weaver	501-735-7932	S	5*	<0.1
Fourth Street Rock Crusher	PO Box 6490	San Bernardino	CA	92412	H N Johnson Jr	909-885-6866	R	5*	<0.1
Keystone Filler & Mfg Co	214 Railroad St	Muncy	PA	17756	David Pfleegor	717-546-3148	R	5	<0.1
Lynn Products Company Inc	400 Boston St	Lynn	MA	01905	DC Cullinane Jr	617-593-2500	R	5	<0.1
Redco II	11831 Vose St	N Hollywood	CA	91605	James C Duncan	213-875-0440	R	5	<0.1
TR Metals Corp	1 Pavilion Av	Riverside	NJ	08075	Martin Kraemer	609-461-9000	R	5*	<0.1
Virginia Materials and Supplies	PO Box 7400	Norfolk	VA	23509	John Burns	804-855-0155	R	4	<0.1
Asbury Graphite of California	2855 Franklin	Rodeo	CA	94572	Marvin Riddle	510-799-3636	D	3*	<0.1
Tionesta Sand and Gravel Inc	PO Box 307	Tionesta	PA	16353	J Jack Sherman	814-755-3547	R	3*	<0.1
Aardvark Clay and Supplies Inc	1400 E Pomona St	Santa Ana	CA	92705	Klaus Blume	714-541-4157	R	3	<0.1
Carbonite Filter Corp	PO Box 1	Delano	PA	18220	JA Monaghan	717-467-3350	R	2	<0.1
Advanced Silicon Materials Inc	3322 Road N NE	Moses Lake	WA	98837	S Tamura	509-765-2106	S	1*	<0.1
Paramount Perlite Co	PO Box 48	Paramount	CA	90723	William E Gillean	310-633-1291	R	1	<0.1

Source: *Ward's Business Directory of U.S. Private and Public Companies*, Volumes 1 and 2, 1996. The company type code used is as follows: P - Public, R - Private, S - Subsidiary, D - Division, J - Joint Venture, A - Affiliate, G - Group. Sales are in millions of dollars, employees are in thousands. An asterisk (*) indicates an estimated sales volume. The symbol < stands for 'less than'. Company names and addresses are truncated, in some cases, to fit into the available space.

MATERIALS CONSUMED

Material	Quantity	Delivered Cost ($ million)
No Materials Consumed data available for this industry.		

Source: 1992 *Economic Census*. Explanation of symbols used: (D): Withheld to avoid disclosure of competitive data; na: Not available; (S): Withheld because statistical norms were not met; (X): Not applicable; (Z): Less than half the unit shown; nec: Not elsewhere classified; nsk: Not specified by kind; - : zero; * : 10-19 percent estimated; ** : 20-29 percent estimated.

PRODUCT SHARE DETAILS

Product or Product Class	% Share	Product or Product Class	% Share
Minerals, ground or treated	100.00	and anhydrite), minerals and earths, ground or otherwise treated	1.08
Lightweight aggregate (diatomaceous earth, expanded clay, expanded slag, cinders, perlite, haydite, pumice, etc.), minerals and earths, ground or otherwise treated	13.22	Natural graphite (ground, refined, or blended) minerals and earths, ground or otherwise treated	4.46
Exfoliated vermiculite aggregate, minerals and earths, ground or otherwise treated	3.47	Ground crude fire clay, high alumina clay, and silica fire clay, minerals and earths, ground or otherwise treated	2.09
Other exfoliated vermiculite (such as loose fill insulation, acoustical, etc.), minerals and earths, ground or otherwise treated	1.13	Clays, artificially activated with acid or other materials, minerals and earths, ground or otherwise treated	4.44
Dead-burned magnesia or magnesite, minerals and earths, ground or otherwise treated	5.81	Mica, ground or treated, minerals and earths, ground or otherwise treated	(D)
Crushed slag, minerals and earths, ground or otherwise treated	8.82	Talc, steatite, soapstone, and pyrophyllite, minerals and earths, ground or otherwise treated	(D)
Crushed and ground uncalcined gypsum (including gypsite		Other minerals and earths, ground or otherwise treated (including feldspar, roofing granules, and ground barite)	44.42

Source: 1992 *Economic Census*. The values shown are percent of total shipments in an industry. Values of indented subcategories are summed in the main heading. The symbol (D) appears when data are withheld to prevent disclosure of competitive information. The abbreviation nsk stands for 'not specified by kind' and nec for 'not elsewhere classified'.

INPUTS AND OUTPUTS FOR MINERALS, GROUND OR TREATED

Economic Sector or Industry Providing Inputs	%	Sector	Economic Sector or Industry Buying Outputs	%	Sector
Motor freight transportation & warehousing	20.6	Util.	Petroleum & natural gas well drilling	28.1	Constr.
Minerals, ground or treated	15.4	Manufg.	Asphalt felts & coatings	9.7	Manufg.
Gas production & distribution (utilities)	6.7	Util.	Minerals, ground or treated	8.8	Manufg.
Railroads & related services	6.5	Util.	Gypsum products	7.1	Manufg.
Clay, ceramic, & refractory minerals	5.5	Mining	Cement, hydraulic	6.8	Manufg.
Electric services (utilities)	5.1	Util.	Ready-mixed concrete	5.6	Manufg.
Dimension, crushed & broken stone	3.9	Mining	Paints & allied products	5.2	Manufg.
Chemical & fertilizer mineral	3.5	Mining	Glass containers	4.0	Manufg.
Iron & ferroalloy ores	3.0	Mining	Blast furnaces & steel mills	3.0	Manufg.
Industrial inorganic chemicals, nec	3.0	Manufg.	Personal consumption expenditures	2.9	
Nonmetallic mineral services	2.6	Mining	Agricultural chemicals, nec	2.5	Manufg.
Bags, except textile	2.6	Manufg.	Glass & glass products, except containers	2.0	Manufg.
Advertising	2.0	Services	Exports	2.0	Foreign
Blast furnaces & steel mills	1.6	Manufg.	Carbon & graphite products	1.4	Manufg.
Petroleum refining	1.6	Manufg.	Office buildings	1.2	Constr.
Water transportation	1.6	Util.	Mineral wool	1.0	Manufg.
Business services nec	1.6	Services	Semiconductors & related devices	0.8	Manufg.
Banking	1.5	Fin/R.E.	Coal	0.7	Mining
Wholesale trade	1.1	Trade	Concrete block & brick	0.5	Manufg.
Eating & drinking places	0.7	Trade	Tires & inner tubes	0.4	Manufg.
Noncomparable imports	0.6	Foreign	Industrial buildings	0.3	Constr.
Sand & gravel	0.5	Mining	Nonfarm residential structure maintenance	0.3	Constr.
Maintenance of nonfarm buildings nec	0.5	Constr.	Residential 1-unit structures, nonfarm	0.3	Constr.
Communications, except radio & TV	0.5	Util.	Cyclic crudes and organics	0.3	Manufg.
Cement, hydraulic	0.4	Manufg.	Miscellaneous plastics products	0.3	Manufg.
Cyclic crudes and organics	0.4	Manufg.	Vegetable oil mills, nec	0.3	Manufg.
Air transportation	0.4	Util.	Construction of educational buildings	0.2	Constr.
Royalties	0.4	Fin/R.E.	Construction of hospitals	0.2	Constr.
Coal	0.3	Mining	Electric utility facility construction	0.2	Constr.
General industrial machinery, nec	0.3	Manufg.	Residential additions/alterations, nonfarm	0.2	Constr.
Lime	0.3	Manufg.	Animal & marine fats & oils	0.2	Manufg.
Machinery, except electrical, nec	0.3	Manufg.	Concrete products, nec	0.2	Manufg.
Sawmills & planning mills, general	0.3	Manufg.	Lime	0.2	Manufg.
Sanitary services, steam supply, irrigation	0.3	Util.	Porcelain electrical supplies	0.2	Manufg.
Credit agencies other than banks	0.3	Fin/R.E.	Maintenance of petroleum & natural gas wells	0.1	Constr.
Legal services	0.3	Services	Residential 2-4 unit structures, nonfarm	0.1	Constr.
Management & consulting services & labs	0.3	Services	Optical instruments & lenses	0.1	Manufg.
Imports	0.3	Foreign	Paving mixtures & blocks	0.1	Manufg.
Abrasive products	0.2	Manufg.	Petroleum refining	0.1	Manufg.
Lubricating oils & greases	0.2	Manufg.			
Special dies & tools & machine tool accessories	0.2	Manufg.			
Water supply & sewage systems	0.2	Util.			
Real estate	0.2	Fin/R.E.			
Accounting, auditing & bookkeeping	0.2	Services			
Computer & data processing services	0.2	Services			
Equipment rental & leasing services	0.2	Services			
Services to dwellings & other buildings	0.2	Services			
Manifold business forms	0.1	Manufg.			
Paperboard containers & boxes	0.1	Manufg.			
Insurance carriers	0.1	Fin/R.E.			
Automotive rental & leasing, without drivers	0.1	Services			
Automotive repair shops & services	0.1	Services			
U.S. Postal Service	0.1	Gov't			

Source: Benchmark Input-Output Accounts for the U.S. Economy, 1982, U.S. Department of Commerce, Washington, D.C., July 1991. Data, as reported in the source, are organized by the 1977 SIC structure in use in 1982 but have been matched, as closely as is possible, to the 1987 SIC structure used in this book.

OCCUPATIONS EMPLOYED BY SIC 329 - STONE, CLAY, AND MISC MINING PRODUCTS NEC

Occupation	% of Total 1994	Change to 2005	Occupation	% of Total 1994	Change to 2005
Helpers, laborers, & material movers nec	6.7	-23.3	Machine feeders & offbearers	2.3	-31.4
Assemblers, fabricators, & hand workers nec	6.4	-23.9	Painting, coating, & decorating workers, hand	2.0	52.3
Furnace, kiln, or kettle operators	4.2	-16.7	Freight, stock, & material movers, hand	1.9	-38.8
Crushing & mixing machine operators	3.9	-9.5	Truck drivers light & heavy	1.9	-20.6
Industrial machinery mechanics	3.9	-15.2	Coating, painting, & spraying machine workers	1.8	-23.8
Hand packers & packagers	3.6	-34.7	Secretaries, ex legal & medical	1.8	-30.4
Extruding & forming machine workers	3.4	-80.6	Cutting & slicing machine setters, operators	1.6	-16.2
Sales & related workers nec	3.2	-23.6	Grinders & polishers, hand	1.6	-16.2
Packaging & filling machine operators	3.2	-23.7	Industrial production managers	1.5	-23.5
Precision workers nec	3.0	-8.7	Traffic, shipping, & receiving clerks	1.5	-26.6
Industrial truck & tractor operators	2.8	-23.7	General office clerks	1.5	-34.9
General managers & top executives	2.8	-27.5	Bookkeeping, accounting, & auditing clerks	1.3	-42.7
Inspectors, testers, & graders, precision	2.8	-23.6	Electricians	1.1	-27.3
Maintenance repairers, general utility	2.6	-30.8	Machinists	1.0	-23.6

Source: Industry-Occupation Matrix, Bureau of Labor Statistics. These data relate to one or more 3-digit SIC industry groups rather than to a single 4-digit SIC. The change reported for each occupation to the year 2005 is a percent of growth or decline as estimated by the Bureau of Labor Statistics. The abbreviation nec stands for 'not elsewhere classified'.

LOCATION BY STATE AND REGIONAL CONCENTRATION

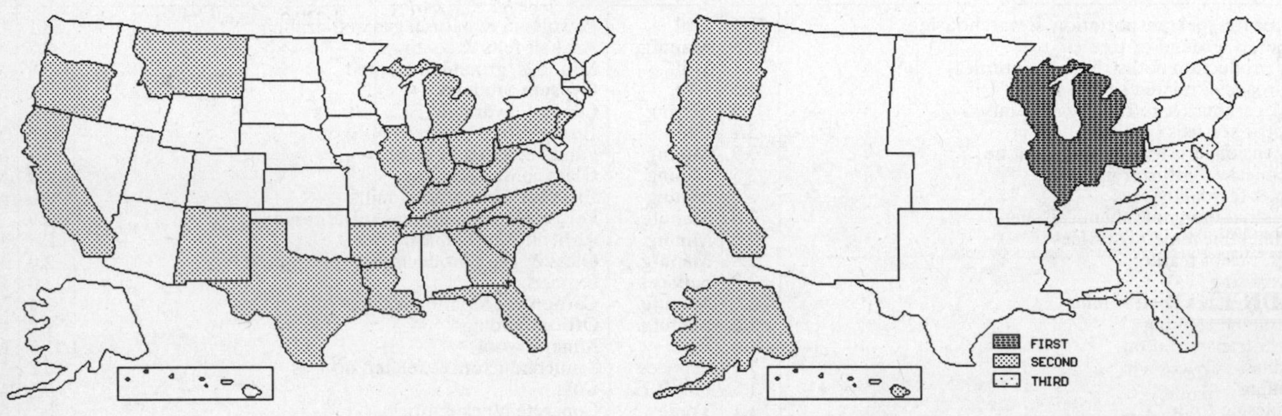

INDUSTRY DATA BY STATE

State	Establish-ments	Shipments Total ($ mil)	Shipments % of U.S.	Shipments Per Establ.	Employment Total Number	Employment % of U.S.	Employment Per Establ.	Wages ($/hour)	Cost as % of Shipments	Investment per Employee ($)
Pennsylvania	28	134.5	7.6	4.8	1,000	10.5	36	11.67	33.6	7,100
Ohio	34	128.9	7.3	3.8	600	6.3	18	11.78	54.7	5,833
California	36	118.0	6.7	3.3	800	8.4	22	12.64	51.3	3,375
Illinois	22	99.5	5.6	4.5	600	6.3	27	11.33	54.4	6,333
Louisiana	11	93.6	5.3	8.5	400	4.2	36	11.00	31.3	-
New Jersey	12	57.9	3.3	4.8	300	3.2	25	12.50	53.2	6,667
Texas	26	52.7	3.0	2.0	300	3.2	12	9.60	49.3	3,667
Florida	12	50.1	2.8	4.2	300	3.2	25	11.20	39.5	3,333
Tennessee	9	46.7	2.6	5.2	200	2.1	22	14.33	27.8	-
Indiana	14	45.5	2.6	3.3	400	4.2	29	18.14	39.1	-
Arkansas	7	40.5	2.3	5.8	200	2.1	29	10.00	34.3	2,000
Oregon	10	34.6	1.9	3.5	200	2.1	20	10.67	33.5	3,000
North Carolina	10	20.0	1.1	2.0	100	1.1	10	10.00	42.0	-
Georgia	12	(D)	-	-	1,750 *	18.4	146	-	-	-
Michigan	9	(D)	-	-	375 *	3.9	42	-	-	4,267
West Virginia	8	(D)	-	-	175 *	1.8	22	-	-	6,286
Kentucky	6	(D)	-	-	175 *	1.8	29	-	-	-
New Mexico	4	(D)	-	-	175 *	1.8	44	-	-	-
South Carolina	4	(D)	-	-	175 *	1.8	44	-	-	2,286
Montana	3	(D)	-	-	175 *	1.8	58	-	-	-

Source: 1992 *Economic Census*. The states are in descending order of shipments or establishments (if shipment data are missing for the majority). The symbol (D) appears when data are withheld to prevent disclosure of competitive information. States marked with (D) are sorted by number of establishments. A dash (-) indicates that the data element cannot be calculated; * indicates the midpoint of a range.

3296 - MINERAL WOOL

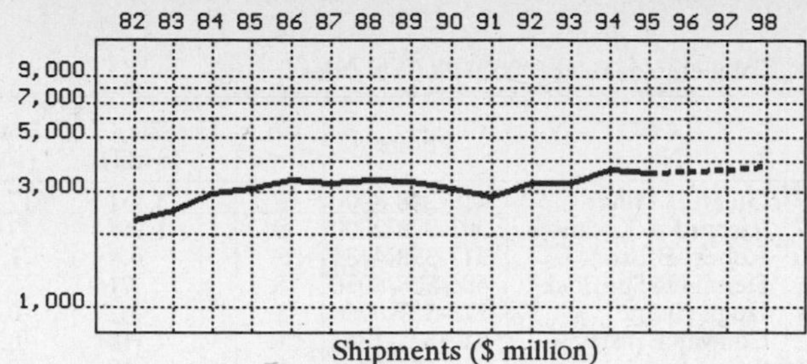

Shipments ($ million)

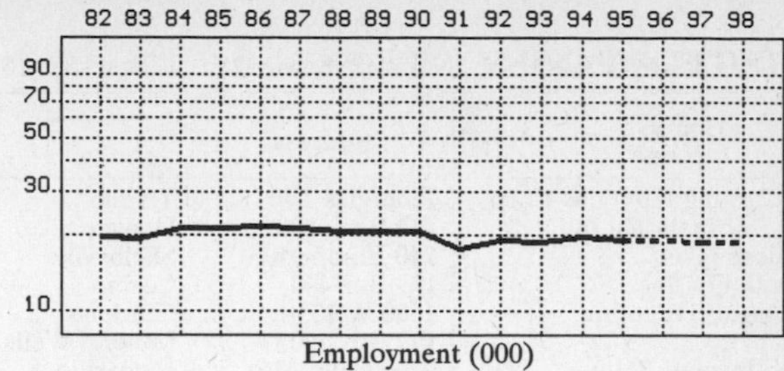

Employment (000)

GENERAL STATISTICS

Year	Com-panies	Establishments		Employment			Compensation		Production ($ million)			
		Total	with 20 or more employees	Total (000)	Production Workers (000)	Production Hours (Mil)	Payroll ($ mil)	Wages ($/hr)	Cost of Materials	Value Added by Manufacture	Value of Shipments	Capital Invest.
1982	132	179	94	19.7	15.5	31.9	438.9	10.48	1,041.5	1,236.7	2,281.1	67.0
1983		178	100	19.5	15.6	32.9	476.2	11.08	1,082.0	1,440.7	2,517.6	56.4
1984		177	106	21.4	17.3	36.5	542.8	11.49	1,241.1	1,733.6	2,964.4	131.1
1985		176	112	21.3	17.0	35.8	583.1	12.49	1,277.9	1,823.0	3,100.6	161.7
1986		172	108	21.9	17.7	36.8	624.2	13.09	1,300.9	2,021.5	3,314.7	160.9
1987	173	231	109	21.5	17.4	36.6	619.4	13.21	1,268.8	1,985.6	3,260.3	177.6
1988		222	117	20.8	16.8	34.4	620.4	14.09	1,312.1	2,065.8	3,376.2	184.9
1989		209	113	20.9	15.9	33.2	595.2	14.10	1,350.8	1,943.8	3,284.5	134.7
1990		207	118	20.9	15.6	31.8	582.5	14.21	1,286.7	1,807.7	3,099.8	130.2
1991		204	116	17.6	14.2	29.2	552.8	14.53	1,177.7	1,666.1	2,852.2	110.1
1992	162	225	119	19.1	15.5	32.2	628.6	14.86	1,311.9	1,915.6	3,231.7	115.1
1993		229	118	18.9	15.5	31.8	629.5	15.21	1,364.8	1,886.9	3,259.4	100.5
1994		233P	124P	19.8	16.2	34.5	689.8	15.28	1,505.8	2,234.8	3,725.1	122.2
1995		238P	125P	19.3P	15.5P	32.1P	676.3P	16.17P	1,443.2P	2,141.9P	3,570.3P	135.9P
1996		243P	127P	19.1P	15.4P	31.9P	689.6P	16.57P	1,470.5P	2,182.4P	3,637.8P	137.2P
1997		248P	129P	19.0P	15.3P	31.7P	702.8P	16.96P	1,497.8P	2,222.9P	3,705.3P	138.4P
1998		253P	131P	18.9P	15.2P	31.4P	716.1P	17.36P	1,525.1P	2,263.5P	3,772.9P	139.7P

Sources: 1982, 1987, 1992 *Economic Census*; *Annual Survey of Manufactures*, 83-86, 88-91, 93-94. Establishment counts for non-Census years are from *County Business Patterns*; establishment values for 83-84 are extrapolations. 'P's show projections by the editors. Industries reclassified in 87 will not have data for prior years.

INDICES OF CHANGE

Year	Com-panies	Establishments		Employment			Compensation		Production ($ million)			
		Total	with 20 or more employees	Total (000)	Production Workers (000)	Production Hours (Mil)	Payroll ($ mil)	Wages ($/hr)	Cost of Materials	Value Added by Manufacture	Value of Shipments	Capital Invest.
1982	81	80	79	103	100	99	70	71	79	65	71	58
1983		79	84	102	101	102	76	75	82	75	78	49
1984		79	89	112	112	113	86	77	95	90	92	114
1985		78	94	112	110	111	93	84	97	95	96	140
1986		76	91	115	114	114	99	88	99	106	103	140
1987	107	103	92	113	112	114	99	89	97	104	101	154
1988		99	98	109	108	107	99	95	100	108	104	161
1989		93	95	109	103	103	95	95	103	101	102	117
1990		92	99	109	101	99	93	96	98	94	96	113
1991		91	97	92	92	91	88	98	90	87	88	96
1992	100	100	100	100	100	100	100	100	100	100	100	100
1993		102	99	99	100	99	100	102	104	99	101	87
1994		104P	104P	104	105	107	110	103	115	117	115	106
1995		106P	105P	101P	100P	100P	108P	109P	110P	112P	110P	118P
1996		108P	107P	100P	99P	99P	110P	111P	112P	114P	113P	119P
1997		110P	109P	99P	99P	98P	112P	114P	114P	116P	115P	120P
1998		112P	110P	99P	98P	98P	114P	117P	116P	118P	117P	121P

Sources: Same as General Statistics. Values reflect change from the base year, 1992. Values above 100 mean greater than 92, values below 100 mean less than 92, and a value of 100 in the 82-91 or 93-98 period means same as 92. 'P's mark projections by the editors.

SELECTED RATIOS

For 1994	Avg. of All Manufact.	Analyzed Industry	Index
Employees per Establishment	49	85	173
Payroll per Establishment	1,500,273	2,960,515	197
Payroll per Employee	30,620	34,838	114
Production Workers per Establishment	34	70	203
Wages per Establishment	853,319	2,262,489	265
Wages per Production Worker	24,861	32,541	131
Hours per Production Worker	2,056	2,130	104
Wages per Hour	12.09	15.28	126
Value Added per Establishment	4,602,255	9,591,416	208
Value Added per Employee	93,930	112,869	120

For 1994	Avg. of All Manufact.	Analyzed Industry	Index
Value Added per Production Worker	134,084	137,951	103
Cost per Establishment	5,045,178	6,462,661	128
Cost per Employee	102,970	76,051	74
Cost per Production Worker	146,988	92,951	63
Shipments per Establishment	9,576,895	15,987,554	167
Shipments per Employee	195,460	188,136	96
Shipments per Production Worker	279,017	229,944	82
Investment per Establishment	321,011	524,464	163
Investment per Employee	6,552	6,172	94
Investment per Production Worker	9,352	7,543	81

Sources: Same as General Statistics. The 'Average of All Manufacturing' column represents the average of all manufacturing industries reported for the most recent complete year available. The Index shows the relationship between the Average and the Analyzed Industry. For example, 100 means that they are equal; 500 that the Analyzed Industry is five times the average; 50 means that the Analyzed Industry is half the national average. The abbreviation 'na' is used to show that data are 'not available'.

LEADING COMPANIES

Number shown: **28** Total sales ($ mil): **5,001** Total employment (000): **28.0**

Company Name	Address				CEO Name	Phone	Co. Type	Sales ($ mil)	Empl. (000)
Owens-Corning Fiberglas Corp	Fiberglas Twr	Toledo	OH	43659	Glenn H Hiner	419-248-8000	P	3,351	17.2
Schuller International Inc	PO Box 5108	Denver	CO	80217	Richard A Kashnow	303-978-2000	S	1,164	7.0
Knauf Fiber Glass	240 Elizabeth St	Shelbyville	IN	46176	Robert Britton	317-398-4434	S	140*	1.0
CTA Insulation Inc	PO Box 448	Corbin	KY	40701	Dennis R Spurlock	606-528-8050	R	71*	0.5
BP Chemicals Hitco Inc	1600 W 135th St	Gardena	CA	90249	Hugh Chare	213-527-0700	S	62	0.4
Centron Corp	PO Box 490	Mineral Wells	TX	76067	Conway Beasley	817-325-1341	R	18*	0.2
Hi-Temp Insulation Inc	4700 Calle Alto	Camarillo	CA	93012	S Borck	805-484-2774	R	18	0.3
Scott Manufacturing Inc	2583 Harrison Rd	Columbus	OH	43204	Scott Miller	614-276-3588	R	18*	0.1
IMCOA	4325 Murray Av	Haltom City	TX	76117	Robert W Simpson	817-485-5290	R	16	<0.1
Molded Acoustical Products	3 Danforth Dr	Easton	PA	18042	JA Damico Sr	215-253-7135	R	15	0.1
Rock Wool Manufacturing Co	PO Box 506	Leeds	AL	35094	GC Cusick	205-699-6121	R	14	<0.1
Eckel Industries Inc	155 Fawcett St	Cambridge	MA	02138	Alan Eckel	617-491-3221	R	13*	0.1
Partek Insulations Inc	908 SE Partek Dr	Phenix City	AL	36869		334-294-6300	S	12*	0.1
Rex Roto Corp	PO Box 980	Fowlerville	MI	48836	JP Rex	517-223-3787	R	10	0.2
Rice Engineering Corp	1020 Hoover St	Great Bend	KS	67530	Loy B Goodheart	316-793-5483	S	10*	0.2
Pres Glas Corp	125 N Blue Rd	Greenfield	IN	46140	WK Cunningham	317-462-9201	R	9*	<0.1
Cogebi Inc	14 Faraday Dr	Dover	NH	03820	W Lehman	603-749-6896	S	8	<0.1
EJ Davis Co	PO Box 326	North Haven	CT	06473	Gregory J Godbout	203-239-5391	R	8	<0.1
American Rockwool Inc	PO Box 880	Spring Hope	NC	27882	O Gould	919-478-5111	R	8	<0.1
Claremont Company Inc	PO Box 952	Meriden	CT	06450	RD Williams	203-238-2384	R	7*	<0.1
Refractory Products Co	770 Tollgate Rd	Elgin	IL	60123	David S Woodruff	708-697-2350	R	7	<0.1
Warminster Fiberglass Co	PO Box 188	Southampton	PA	18966	John J Roley	215-953-1260	R	7	0.1
Tankinetics Inc	PO Box 1195	Harrison	AR	72602	George Christner	501-741-3626	R	5	0.1
Flight Insulation	925 Industrial Pk Dr	Marietta	GA	30062	Jim Potter	404-427-9441	S	5	<0.1
Pamrod Products	PO Box 399	McQueeney	TX	78123	Richard La Pierre	210-557-5322	R	3	<0.1
Conarc Inc	PO Box 24	Terryville	CT	06786	Lynford Dayton	203-589-4075	R	1	<0.1
ICA Inc	PO Box 353	Lehighton	PA	18235	Joe Izzi	610-377-4120	S	1	<0.1
Lamvin Inc	6260 Marindustry	San Diego	CA	92121	Joan Siok	619-452-7480	R	1	<0.1

Source: *Ward's Business Directory of U.S. Private and Public Companies*, Volumes 1 and 2, 1996. The company type code used is as follows: P - Public, R - Private, S - Subsidiary, D - Division, J - Joint Venture, A - Affiliate, G - Group. Sales are in millions of dollars, employees are in thousands. An asterisk (*) indicates an estimated sales volume. The symbol < stands for 'less than'. Company names and addresses are truncated, in some cases, to fit into the available space.

MATERIALS CONSUMED

Material	Quantity	Delivered Cost ($ million)
Materials, ingredients, containers, and supplies	(X)	1,005.1
Kaolin and ball clay	(X)	9.3
Mining, quarrying of chemical and fertilizer minerals	(X)	44.2
Mining and quarrying of other nonmetallic minerals, except fuels	(X)	111.8
Cotton and manmade fiber fabrics, broadwoven and narrow woven	(X)	21.4
Paper shipping sacks and multiwall bags	(X)	13.0
Other converted paper and paperboard products	(X)	37.0
Other paper and paperboard products	(X)	51.6
Industrial inorganic chemicals	(X)	33.6
Plastics materials and resins	(X)	81.1
Glues and adhesives	(X)	24.5
Other chemical and allied products	(X)	35.8
Plastics products consumed in the form of sheets, rods, tubes, film, and other shapes	(X)	48.6
Glass fiber, textile type, bonded mat type, etc.	(X)	81.4
Crude blast furnace slag	(X)	30.3
Aluminum sheet, plate, foil, and welded tubings	(X)	9.9
Converted aluminum foil	(X)	11.0
All other materials and components, parts, containers, and supplies	(X)	279.3
Materials, ingredients, containers, and supplies, nsk	(X)	81.2

Source: 1992 *Economic Census*. Explanation of symbols used: (D): Withheld to avoid disclosure of competitive data; na: Not available; (S): Withheld because statistical norms were not met; (X): Not applicable; (Z): Less than half the unit shown; nec: Not elsewhere classified; nsk: Not specified by kind; - : zero; * : 10-19 percent estimated; ** : 20-29 percent estimated.

PRODUCT SHARE DETAILS

Product or Product Class	% Share
Mineral wool	100.00
Mineral wool for thermal and acoustical envelope insulation (for insulating homes and commercial and industrial buildings)	66.57
Loose fiber (blowing and pouring) (shipped as such) and granulated fiber, mineral wool for thermal and acoustical envelope insulation (for insulating homes and commercial and industrial buildings)	9.86
Building batts, blankets, and rolls (in thermal resistance (R) values, R19 or more, mineral wool for thermal and acoustical envelope insulation (for homes and commercial and industrial buildings)	27.28
Building batts, blankets, and rolls (in thermal resistance (R) values, R11 to R18.9, mineral wool for thermal and acoustical envelope insulation (for homes and commercial and industrial buildings)	18.08
Building batts, blankets, and rolls (in thermal resistance (R) values, R10.9 or less, mineral wool for thermal and acoustical envelope insulation (for homes and commercial and industrial buildings)	3.42

Continued on next page.

PRODUCT SHARE DETAILS - Continued

Product or Product Class	% Share
Board (such as roof insulation), mineral wool for thermal and acoustical envelope insulation (for homes and commercial and industrial buildings)	7.86
Acoustical, such as wall and ceiling (sold as acoustical insulation), mineral wool for thermal and acoustical envelope insulation (for homes and commercial and industrial buildings)	29.95
Other mineral wool for thermal and acoustical envelope insulation (for homes and commercial and industrial buildings)	2.22
Mineral wool for thermal and acoustical envelope insulation (for homes, commercial and industrial buildings), nsk.	1.33
Mineral wool for industrial, equipment, and appliance insulation	28.90
Plain blankets (flexible) (including fabricated pieces, rolls, and batts), mineral wool for industrial, equipment, and appliance insulation.	14.73
Coated blankets (flexible) (including fabricated pieces, rolls, and batts), mineral wool for industrial, equipment, and appliance insulation	8.30
Faced and metal meshed blankets (flexible) (including fabricated pieces, rolls, and batts), mineral wool for industrial, equipment, and appliance insulation	2.78
Special-purpose mineral wool for industrial, equipment, and appliance insulation pieces (special-purpose automotive, appliance, aerospace items and original equipment parts)	24.71
Other mineral wool for industrial, equipment, and appliance insulation, blocks and boards	4.56
Mineral wool for industrial, equipment, and appliance pipe insulation	18.18
Mineral wool for industrial, equipment, and appliance acoustical insulation (including pads, boards, patches, etc.)	2.88
Other mineral wool for industrial, equipment, and appliance insulation (including air duct, loose fiber, granulated fiber, insulating and finishing cements, etc.)	22.43
Mineral wool for industrial, equipment, and appliance insulation, nsk	1.41
Mineral wool, nsk	4.54

Source: 1992 *Economic Census*. The values shown are percent of total shipments in an industry. Values of indented subcategories are summed in the main heading. The symbol (D) appears when data are withheld to prevent disclosure of competitive information. The abbreviation nsk stands for 'not specified by kind' and nec for 'not elsewhere classified'.

INPUTS AND OUTPUTS FOR MINERAL WOOL

Economic Sector or Industry Providing Inputs	%	Sector	Economic Sector or Industry Buying Outputs	%	Sector
Gas production & distribution (utilities)	11.5	Util.	Maintenance of nonfarm buildings nec	16.1	Constr.
Electric services (utilities)	9.7	Util.	Residential 1-unit structures, nonfarm	11.5	Constr.
Wholesale trade	7.7	Trade	Nonfarm residential structure maintenance	7.7	Constr.
Cyclic crudes and organics	6.5	Manufg.	Office buildings	7.6	Constr.
Industrial inorganic chemicals, nec	5.2	Manufg.	Exports	5.8	Foreign
Paper mills, except building paper	4.0	Manufg.	Residential additions/alterations, nonfarm	5.1	Constr.
Plastics materials & resins	3.8	Manufg.	Industrial buildings	4.7	Constr.
Glass & glass products, except containers	3.6	Manufg.	Machinery, except electrical, nec	4.1	Manufg.
Mineral wool	3.6	Manufg.	Mobile homes	4.0	Manufg.
Motor freight transportation & warehousing	3.5	Util.	Construction of hospitals	3.8	Constr.
Imports	2.4	Foreign	Construction of stores & restaurants	3.3	Constr.
Advertising	2.2	Services	Construction of educational buildings	3.0	Constr.
Chemical preparations, nec	2.0	Manufg.	Residential garden apartments	2.5	Constr.
Railroads & related services	2.0	Util.	Ship building & repairing	2.0	Manufg.
Chemical & fertilizer mineral	1.8	Mining	Mineral wool	1.9	Manufg.
Metal foil & leaf	1.8	Manufg.	Hotels & motels	1.3	Constr.
Adhesives & sealants	1.7	Manufg.	Residential 2-4 unit structures, nonfarm	1.1	Constr.
Nonmetallic mineral services	1.4	Mining	Amusement & recreation building construction	1.0	Constr.
Paperboard containers & boxes	1.4	Manufg.	Electric utility facility construction	1.0	Constr.
Abrasive products	1.3	Manufg.	Miscellaneous plastics products	1.0	Manufg.
Minerals, ground or treated	1.2	Manufg.	Warehouses	0.9	Constr.
Miscellaneous fabricated wire products	1.2	Manufg.	Electric housewares & fans	0.9	Manufg.
Miscellaneous plastics products	1.1	Manufg.	Refrigeration & heating equipment	0.9	Manufg.
Petroleum refining	1.0	Manufg.	Resid. & other health facility construction	0.8	Constr.
Synthetic rubber	1.0	Manufg.	Household cooking equipment	0.8	Manufg.
Sanitary services, steam supply, irrigation	1.0	Util.	Prefabricated wood buildings	0.8	Manufg.
Banking	1.0	Fin/R.E.	Construction of nonfarm buildings nec	0.7	Constr.
Bags, except textile	0.9	Manufg.	Household refrigerators & freezers	0.6	Manufg.
Eating & drinking places	0.9	Trade	Change in business inventories	0.6	In House
Maintenance of nonfarm buildings nec	0.8	Constr.	Farm housing units & additions & alterations	0.4	Constr.
Aluminum rolling & drawing	0.7	Manufg.	Highway & street construction	0.4	Constr.
Wet corn milling	0.7	Manufg.	Household laundry equipment	0.4	Manufg.
Business services nec	0.6	Services	Residential high-rise apartments	0.3	Constr.
Broadwoven fabric mills	0.5	Manufg.	Motor vehicles & car bodies	0.3	Manufg.
Air transportation	0.5	Util.	Motors & generators	0.3	Manufg.
Communications, except radio & TV	0.5	Util.	Truck trailers	0.3	Manufg.
Equipment rental & leasing services	0.5	Services	Construction of religious buildings	0.2	Constr.
Machinery, except electrical, nec	0.4	Manufg.	Telephone & telegraph facility construction	0.2	Constr.
Water transportation	0.4	Util.	Household appliances, nec	0.2	Manufg.
Real estate	0.4	Fin/R.E.	Gaskets, packing & sealing devices	0.1	Manufg.
Royalties	0.4	Fin/R.E.	Metal stampings, nec	0.1	Manufg.
Computer & data processing services	0.4	Services	Travel trailers & campers	0.1	Manufg.
Management & consulting services & labs	0.4	Services	Truck & bus bodies	0.1	Manufg.
Coal	0.3	Mining			
Paper coating & glazing	0.3	Manufg.			
Legal services	0.3	Services			
Photofinishing labs, commercial photography	0.3	Services			
Clay, ceramic, & refractory minerals	0.2	Mining			
Asbestos products	0.2	Manufg.			
Blast furnaces & steel mills	0.2	Manufg.			

Continued on next page.

INPUTS AND OUTPUTS FOR MINERAL WOOL - Continued

Economic Sector or Industry Providing Inputs	%	Sector	Economic Sector or Industry Buying Outputs	%	Sector
Lime	0.2	Manufg.			
Lubricating oils & greases	0.2	Manufg.			
Primary nonferrous metals, nec	0.2	Manufg.			
Sawmills & planning mills, general	0.2	Manufg.			
Special dies & tools & machine tool accessories	0.2	Manufg.			
Credit agencies other than banks	0.2	Fin/R.E.			
Insurance carriers	0.2	Fin/R.E.			
Accounting, auditing & bookkeeping	0.2	Services			
State & local government enterprises, nec	0.2	Gov't			
U.S. Postal Service	0.2	Gov't			
Noncomparable imports	0.2	Foreign			
Alkalies & chlorine	0.1	Manufg.			
Building paper & board mills	0.1	Manufg.			
Manifold business forms	0.1	Manufg.			
Security & commodity brokers	0.1	Fin/R.E.			
Automotive rental & leasing, without drivers	0.1	Services			
Automotive repair shops & services	0.1	Services			
Electrical repair shops	0.1	Services			
Hotels & lodging places	0.1	Services			

Source: Benchmark Input-Output Accounts for the U.S. Economy, 1982, U.S. Department of Commerce, Washington, D.C., July 1991. Data, as reported in the source, are organized by the 1977 SIC structure in use in 1982 but have been matched, as closely as is possible, to the 1987 SIC structure used in this book.

OCCUPATIONS EMPLOYED BY SIC 329 - STONE, CLAY, AND MISC MINING PRODUCTS NEC

Occupation	% of Total 1994	Change to 2005	Occupation	% of Total 1994	Change to 2005
Helpers, laborers, & material movers nec	6.7	-23.3	Machine feeders & offbearers	2.3	-31.4
Assemblers, fabricators, & hand workers nec	6.4	-23.9	Painting, coating, & decorating workers, hand	2.0	52.3
Furnace, kiln, or kettle operators	4.2	-16.7	Freight, stock, & material movers, hand	1.9	-38.8
Crushing & mixing machine operators	3.9	-9.5	Truck drivers light & heavy	1.9	-20.6
Industrial machinery mechanics	3.9	-15.2	Coating, painting, & spraying machine workers	1.8	-23.8
Hand packers & packagers	3.6	-34.7	Secretaries, ex legal & medical	1.8	-30.4
Extruding & forming machine workers	3.4	-80.6	Cutting & slicing machine setters, operators	1.6	-16.2
Sales & related workers nec	3.2	-23.6	Grinders & polishers, hand	1.6	-16.2
Packaging & filling machine operators	3.2	-23.7	Industrial production managers	1.5	-23.5
Precision workers nec	3.0	-8.7	Traffic, shipping, & receiving clerks	1.5	-26.6
Industrial truck & tractor operators	2.8	-23.7	General office clerks	1.5	-34.9
General managers & top executives	2.8	-27.5	Bookkeeping, accounting, & auditing clerks	1.3	-42.7
Inspectors, testers, & graders, precision	2.8	-23.6	Electricians	1.1	-27.3
Maintenance repairers, general utility	2.6	-30.8	Machinists	1.0	-23.6

Source: Industry-Occupation Matrix, Bureau of Labor Statistics. These data relate to one or more 3-digit SIC industry groups rather than to a single 4-digit SIC. The change reported for each occupation to the year 2005 is a percent of growth or decline as estimated by the Bureau of Labor Statistics. The abbreviation nec stands for 'not elsewhere classified'.

LOCATION BY STATE AND REGIONAL CONCENTRATION

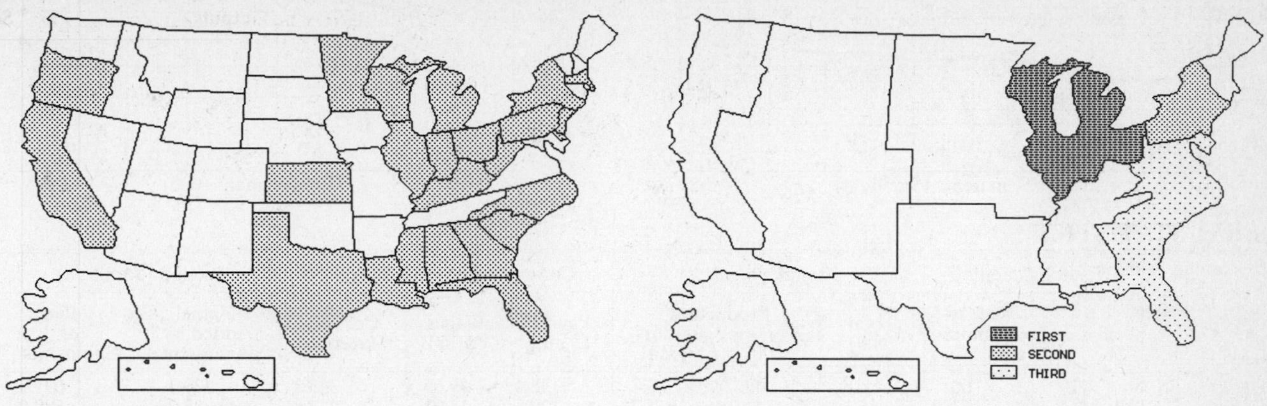

INDUSTRY DATA BY STATE

State	Establish-ments	Shipments Total ($ mil)	Shipments % of U.S.	Shipments Per Establ.	Employment Total Number	Employment % of U.S.	Employment Per Establ.	Employment Wages ($/hour)	Cost as % of Shipments	Investment per Employee ($)
Ohio	23	551.4	17.1	24.0	3,100	16.2	135	15.93	36.7	4,935
Georgia	13	331.9	10.3	25.5	1,800	9.4	138	17.25	37.9	5,944
California	21	311.0	9.6	14.8	1,700	8.9	81	15.61	39.5	6,941
Kansas	4	284.1	8.8	71.0	1,500	7.9	375	18.36	35.2	8,133
Pennsylvania	15	211.4	6.5	14.1	1,500	7.9	100	15.69	41.6	11,267
Indiana	10	192.0	5.9	19.2	1,400	7.3	140	14.95	47.8	5,857
Texas	20	190.6	5.9	9.5	1,100	5.8	55	14.76	42.4	6,091
Mississippi	4	151.3	4.7	37.8	800	4.2	200	11.12	46.3	-
Alabama	8	126.5	3.9	15.8	800	4.2	100	13.77	52.7	5,125
Michigan	5	85.3	2.6	17.1	600	3.1	120	10.80	44.1	7,333
New Jersey	9	58.5	1.8	6.5	500	2.6	56	18.57	51.8	4,600
Illinois	7	48.0	1.5	6.9	300	1.6	43	11.25	36.5	3,667
North Carolina	7	19.8	0.6	2.8	200	1.0	29	7.67	57.1	3,000
Massachusetts	5	14.3	0.4	2.9	100	0.5	20	12.00	35.7	-
New York	9	(D)	-	-	750 *	3.9	83	-	-	-
Florida	8	(D)	-	-	375 *	2.0	47	-	-	-
Kentucky	5	(D)	-	-	750 *	3.9	150	-	-	-
Wisconsin	3	(D)	-	-	175 *	0.9	58	-	-	-
Louisiana	2	(D)	-	-	175 *	0.9	88	-	-	-
Minnesota	2	(D)	-	-	750 *	3.9	375	-	-	-
South Carolina	2	(D)	-	-	175 *	0.9	88	-	-	-
Delaware	1	(D)	-	-	175 *	0.9	175	-	-	-
Oregon	1	(D)	-	-	175 *	0.9	175	-	-	-
West Virginia	1	(D)	-	-	375 *	2.0	375	-	-	-

Source: 1992 *Economic Census*. The states are in descending order of shipments or establishments (if shipment data are missing for the majority). The symbol (D) appears when data are withheld to prevent disclosure of competitive information. States marked with (D) are sorted by number of establishments. A dash (-) indicates that the data element cannot be calculated; * indicates the midpoint of a range.

3297 - NONCLAY REFRACTORIES

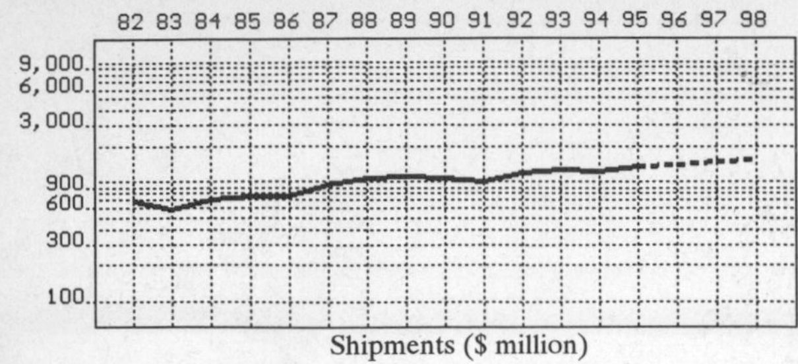

Shipments ($ million)

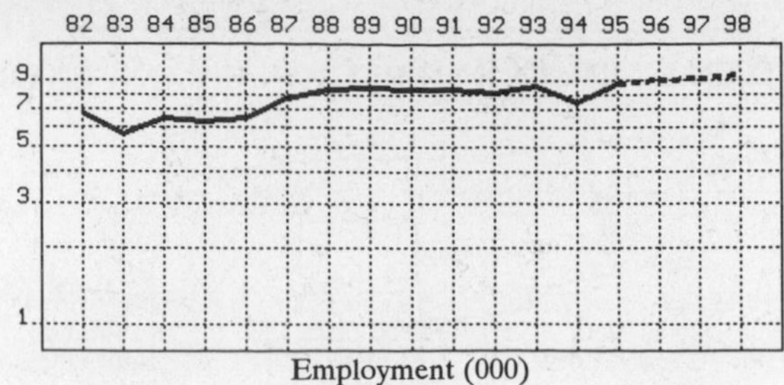

Employment (000)

GENERAL STATISTICS

Year	Companies	Establishments: Total	Establishments: with 20 or more employees	Employment: Total (000)	Production Workers (000)	Production Hours (Mil)	Compensation: Payroll ($ mil)	Compensation: Wages ($/hr)	Production ($ million): Cost of Materials	Value Added by Manufacture	Value of Shipments	Capital Invest.
1982	76	119	66	6.8	4.6	8.7	148.4	10.69	343.3	333.1	691.0	48.5
1983		114	64	5.6	4.1	7.7	129.5	11.01	312.8	288.3	588.9	20.8
1984		109	62	6.5	4.8	9.1	147.5	10.49	347.1	361.3	701.4	24.7
1985		105	60	6.3	4.5	8.8	152.0	11.27	369.2	377.1	755.3	32.5
1986		113	62	6.4	4.6	9.1	162.7	11.29	372.1	399.2	768.5	13.7
1987	99	135	79	7.7	5.6	11.2	201.6	11.63	443.5	510.9	954.5	16.3
1988		136	79	8.3	6.2	11.4	209.6	12.23	470.7	615.8	1,078.1	18.0
1989		139	78	8.5	6.3	12.3	232.6	12.15	480.4	628.1	1,113.3	36.3
1990		133	78	8.3	6.0	12.0	239.9	12.72	499.0	573.4	1,077.6	30.3
1991		133	75	8.3	5.7	11.2	241.3	12.91	500.6	496.8	1,009.2	26.5
1992	101	142	83	8.1	5.7	11.4	249.2	13.56	541.4	650.4	1,203.5	44.9
1993		153	81	8.6	6.0	12.5	279.4	13.78	579.0	709.7	1,282.5	62.5
1994		151P	85P	7.5	5.2	10.5	247.6	14.49	562.5	681.3	1,232.2	41.1
1995		154P	87P	8.8P	6.2P	12.7P	288.0P	14.37P	617.6P	748.0P	1,352.9P	42.8P
1996		158P	89P	9.0P	6.4P	13.0P	300.1P	14.69P	643.3P	779.2P	1,409.2P	44.3P
1997		161P	91P	9.2P	6.5P	13.3P	312.2P	15.00P	669.1P	810.4P	1,465.6P	45.9P
1998		165P	93P	9.4P	6.6P	13.6P	324.3P	15.32P	694.8P	841.5P	1,522.0P	47.4P

Sources: 1982, 1987, 1992 *Economic Census*; *Annual Survey of Manufactures*, 83-86, 88-91, 93-94. Establishment counts for non-Census years are from *County Business Patterns*; establishment values for 83-84 are extrapolations. 'P's show projections by the editors. Industries reclassified in 87 will not have data for prior years.

INDICES OF CHANGE

Year	Companies	Establishments: Total	Establishments: with 20 or more employees	Employment: Total (000)	Production Workers (000)	Production Hours (Mil)	Compensation: Payroll ($ mil)	Compensation: Wages ($/hr)	Production ($ million): Cost of Materials	Value Added by Manufacture	Value of Shipments	Capital Invest.
1982	75	84	80	84	81	76	60	79	63	51	57	108
1983		80	77	69	72	68	52	81	58	44	49	46
1984		77	75	80	84	80	59	77	64	56	58	55
1985		74	72	78	79	77	61	83	68	58	63	72
1986		80	75	79	81	80	65	83	69	61	64	31
1987	98	95	95	95	98	98	81	86	82	79	79	36
1988		96	95	102	109	100	84	90	87	95	90	40
1989		98	94	105	111	108	93	90	89	97	93	81
1990		94	94	102	105	105	96	94	92	88	90	67
1991		94	90	102	100	98	97	95	92	76	84	59
1992	100	100	100	100	100	100	100	100	100	100	100	100
1993		108	98	106	105	110	112	102	107	109	107	139
1994		106P	103P	93	91	92	99	107	104	105	102	92
1995		109P	105P	109P	110P	111P	116P	106P	114P	115P	112P	95P
1996		111P	107P	112P	112P	114P	120P	108P	119P	120P	117P	99P
1997		114P	110P	114P	114P	117P	125P	111P	124P	125P	122P	102P
1998		116P	112P	117P	116P	120P	130P	113P	128P	129P	126P	106P

Sources: Same as General Statistics. Values reflect change from the base year, 1992. Values above 100 mean greater than 92, values below 100 mean less than 92, and a value of 100 in the 82-91 or 93-98 period means same as 92. 'P's mark projections by the editors.

SELECTED RATIOS

For 1994	Avg. of All Manufact.	Analyzed Industry	Index	For 1994	Avg. of All Manufact.	Analyzed Industry	Index
Employees per Establishment	49	50	102	Value Added per Production Worker	134,084	131,019	98
Payroll per Establishment	1,500,273	1,644,024	110	Cost per Establishment	5,045,178	3,734,909	74
Payroll per Employee	30,620	33,013	108	Cost per Employee	102,970	75,000	73
Production Workers per Establishment	34	35	101	Cost per Production Worker	146,988	108,173	74
Wages per Establishment	853,319	1,010,218	118	Shipments per Establishment	9,576,895	8,181,610	85
Wages per Production Worker	24,861	29,259	118	Shipments per Employee	195,460	164,293	84
Hours per Production Worker	2,056	2,019	98	Shipments per Production Worker	279,017	236,962	85
Wages per Hour	12.09	14.49	120	Investment per Establishment	321,011	272,897	85
Value Added per Establishment	4,602,255	4,523,722	98	Investment per Employee	6,552	5,480	84
Value Added per Employee	93,930	90,840	97	Investment per Production Worker	9,352	7,904	85

Sources: Same as General Statistics. The 'Average of All Manufacturing' column represents the average of all manufacturing industries reported for the most recent complete year available. The Index shows the relationship between the Average and the Analyzed Industry. For example, 100 means that they are equal; 500 that the Analyzed Industry is five times the average; 50 means that the Analyzed Industry is half the national average. The abbreviation 'na' is used to show that data are 'not available'.

LEADING COMPANIES

Number shown: 15 Total sales ($ mil): 657 Total employment (000): 4.2

Company Name	Address				CEO Name	Phone	Co. Type	Sales ($ mil)	Empl. (000)
JE Baker Co	PO Box 1189	York	PA	17405	David F Manchester	717-848-1501	R	160	0.6
MINTEQ International Inc	405 Lexington Av	New York	NY	10174	J C O'Donoghue	212-878-1800	S	140*	1.0
C-E Minerals Inc	901 E 8th Av	King of Prussia	PA	19406	TJ McCarthy	215-265-6880	R	70	0.3
Resco Products Inc	PO Box 108	Norristown	PA	19401	WT Tredennick	610-292-3500	R	60	0.4
Allied Mineral Products	2700 Scioto Pkwy	Columbus	OH	43221	J Tabor	614-876-0244	R	42	0.2
Corhart Refractories Corp	PO Box 740009	Louisville	KY	40201	RC Ayotte	502-778-3311	S	40	0.7
Monofrax Refractories	501 New York Av	Falconer	NY	14733	David E Brooks	716-483-7200	D	39	0.3
Wulfrath Refractory Inc	PO Box 28	Tarentum	PA	15084	David Robinson	412-224-8800	S	27	0.2
Zedmark	395 Grove City Rd	Slippery Rock	PA	16057	JC O'Donoghue	412-794-3000	D	22	0.1
Inland Refractories Co	38600 Chester Rd	Avon	OH	44011	EK Chambers	216-934-6600	R	15	0.1
TYK Refractories Co	301 Brick Yard Rd	Clairton	PA	15025	Y Watanabe	412-384-4259	S	14	0.1
Christy Refractories Co	4641 McRee Av	St Louis	MO	63110	FR O'Brien	314-773-7500	R	13	<0.1
AP Green Refractories Inc	1000 N Clark Rd	Gary	IN	46406	Joseph Stein	219-949-1546	S	7*	<0.1
Advanced Refractory Techn	699 Hertel Av	Buffalo	NY	14207	Keith A Blakely	716-875-4091	R	5	<0.1
ER Advanced Ceramics Inc	600 E Clark St	East Palestine	OH	44413	Louis J Layda	216-426-9433	R	4	<0.1

Source: *Ward's Business Directory of U.S. Private and Public Companies*, Volumes 1 and 2, 1996. The company type code used is as follows: P - Public, R - Private, S - Subsidiary, D - Division, J - Joint Venture, A - Affiliate, G - Group. Sales are in millions of dollars, employees are in thousands. An asterisk (*) indicates an estimated sales volume. The symbol < stands for 'less than'. Company names and addresses are truncated, in some cases, to fit into the available space.

MATERIALS CONSUMED

Material	Quantity	Delivered Cost ($ million)
Materials, ingredients, containers, and supplies	(X)	455.6
Clay, ceramic, and refractory minerals	(X)	143.9
Dead-burned magnesia or magnesite	(X)	54.4
Refractories, clay or nonclay	(X)	60.4
Industrial chemicals	(X)	19.4
All other materials and components, parts, containers, and supplies	(X)	113.4
Materials, ingredients, containers, and supplies, nsk	(X)	64.1

Source: 1992 *Economic Census*. Explanation of symbols used: (D): Withheld to avoid disclosure of competitive data; na: Not available; (S): Withheld because statistical norms were not met; (X): Not applicable; (Z): Less than half the unit shown; nec: Not elsewhere classified; nsk: Not specified by kind; - : zero; * : 10-19 percent estimated; ** : 20-29 percent estimated.

PRODUCT SHARE DETAILS

Product or Product Class	% Share	Product or Product Class	% Share
Nonclay refractories	100.00		

Source: 1992 *Economic Census*. The values shown are percent of total shipments in an industry. Values of indented subcategories are summed in the main heading. The symbol (D) appears when data are withheld to prevent disclosure of competitive information. The abbreviation nsk stands for 'not specified by kind' and nec for 'not elsewhere classified'.

INPUTS AND OUTPUTS FOR NONCLAY REFRACTORIES

Economic Sector or Industry Providing Inputs	%	Sector	Economic Sector or Industry Buying Outputs	%	Sector
Nonclay refractories	22.0	Manufg.	Industrial buildings	50.3	Constr.
Imports	13.7	Foreign	Maintenance of nonfarm buildings nec	18.0	Constr.
Motor freight transportation & warehousing	10.1	Util.	Exports	11.9	Foreign
Gas production & distribution (utilities)	6.2	Util.	Nonclay refractories	10.7	Manufg.
Clay, ceramic, & refractory minerals	5.6	Mining	Clay refractories	7.8	Manufg.
Electric services (utilities)	4.9	Util.	Iron & steel foundries	0.6	Manufg.
Clay refractories	4.3	Manufg.	Blast furnaces & steel mills	0.3	Manufg.
Nonferrous metal ores, except copper	4.0	Mining			
Noncomparable imports	3.6	Foreign			
Petroleum refining	2.5	Manufg.			
Nonmetallic mineral services	1.7	Mining			
Cyclic crudes and organics	1.5	Manufg.			
Lime	1.5	Manufg.			
Railroads & related services	1.5	Util.			
Water transportation	1.5	Util.			
Primary aluminum	1.4	Manufg.			
Wholesale trade	1.1	Trade			
Advertising	1.1	Services			
Communications, except radio & TV	0.9	Util.			
Eating & drinking places	0.8	Trade			
Maintenance of nonfarm buildings nec	0.7	Constr.			

Continued on next page.

INPUTS AND OUTPUTS FOR NONCLAY REFRACTORIES - Continued

Economic Sector or Industry Providing Inputs	%	Sector	Economic Sector or Industry Buying Outputs	%	Sector
Wood pallets & skids	0.7	Manufg.			
Banking	0.7	Fin/R.E.			
Coal	0.6	Mining			
Real estate	0.6	Fin/R.E.			
Air transportation	0.5	Util.			
Equipment rental & leasing services	0.5	Services			
Machinery, except electrical, nec	0.4	Manufg.			
Paperboard containers & boxes	0.4	Manufg.			
Plastics materials & resins	0.4	Manufg.			
Blast furnaces & steel mills	0.3	Manufg.			
Computer & data processing services	0.3	Services			
Legal services	0.3	Services			
Management & consulting services & labs	0.3	Services			
Abrasive products	0.2	Manufg.			
Industrial inorganic chemicals, nec	0.2	Manufg.			
Lubricating oils & greases	0.2	Manufg.			
Special dies & tools & machine tool accessories	0.2	Manufg.			
Sanitary services, steam supply, irrigation	0.2	Util.			
Insurance carriers	0.2	Fin/R.E.			
Royalties	0.2	Fin/R.E.			
Accounting, auditing & bookkeeping	0.2	Services			
Automotive rental & leasing, without drivers	0.2	Services			
Automotive repair shops & services	0.2	Services			
U.S. Postal Service	0.2	Gov't			
Manifold business forms	0.1	Manufg.			
State & local government enterprises, nec	0.1	Gov't			

Source: Benchmark Input-Output Accounts for the U.S. Economy, 1982, U.S. Department of Commerce, Washington, D.C., July 1991. Data, as reported in the source, are organized by the 1977 SIC structure in use in 1982 but have been matched, as closely as is possible, to the 1987 SIC structure used in this book.

OCCUPATIONS EMPLOYED BY SIC 329 - STONE, CLAY, AND MISC MINING PRODUCTS NEC

Occupation	% of Total 1994	Change to 2005	Occupation	% of Total 1994	Change to 2005
Helpers, laborers, & material movers nec	6.7	-23.3	Machine feeders & offbearers	2.3	-31.4
Assemblers, fabricators, & hand workers nec	6.4	-23.9	Painting, coating, & decorating workers, hand	2.0	52.3
Furnace, kiln, or kettle operators	4.2	-16.7	Freight, stock, & material movers, hand	1.9	-38.8
Crushing & mixing machine operators	3.9	-9.5	Truck drivers light & heavy	1.9	-20.6
Industrial machinery mechanics	3.9	-15.2	Coating, painting, & spraying machine workers	1.8	-23.8
Hand packers & packagers	3.6	-34.7	Secretaries, ex legal & medical	1.8	-30.4
Extruding & forming machine workers	3.4	-80.6	Cutting & slicing machine setters, operators	1.6	-16.2
Sales & related workers nec	3.2	-23.6	Grinders & polishers, hand	1.6	-16.2
Packaging & filling machine operators	3.2	-23.7	Industrial production managers	1.5	-23.5
Precision workers nec	3.0	-8.7	Traffic, shipping, & receiving clerks	1.5	-26.6
Industrial truck & tractor operators	2.8	-23.7	General office clerks	1.5	-34.9
General managers & top executives	2.8	-27.5	Bookkeeping, accounting, & auditing clerks	1.3	-42.7
Inspectors, testers, & graders, precision	2.8	-23.6	Electricians	1.1	-27.3
Maintenance repairers, general utility	2.6	-30.8	Machinists	1.0	-23.6

Source: Industry-Occupation Matrix, Bureau of Labor Statistics. These data relate to one or more 3-digit SIC industry groups rather than to a single 4-digit SIC. The change reported for each occupation to the year 2005 is a percent of growth or decline as estimated by the Bureau of Labor Statistics. The abbreviation nec stands for 'not elsewhere classified'.

LOCATION BY STATE AND REGIONAL CONCENTRATION

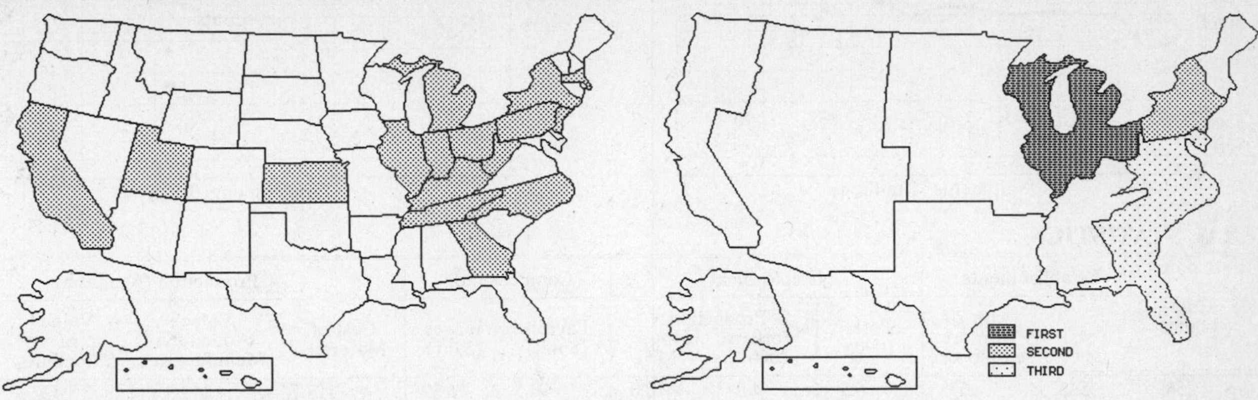

INDUSTRY DATA BY STATE

State	Establish-ments	Shipments			Employment				Cost as % of Shipments	Investment per Employee ($)
		Total ($ mil)	% of U.S.	Per Establ.	Total Number	% of U.S.	Per Establ.	Wages ($/hour)		
Ohio	31	250.9	20.8	8.1	1,600	19.8	52	12.70	48.4	2,688
Pennsylvania	20	250.0	20.8	12.5	1,400	17.3	70	13.18	41.4	10,786
New York	7	98.4	8.2	14.1	700	8.6	100	15.20	37.1	5,000
Illinois	12	88.0	7.3	7.3	600	7.4	50	11.88	46.6	1,833
Michigan	7	80.4	6.7	11.5	600	7.4	86	14.25	39.9	-
Indiana	6	39.3	3.3	6.6	200	2.5	33	14.67	59.3	-
Georgia	5	25.0	2.1	5.0	200	2.5	40	9.25	48.4	3,000
California	7	(D)	-	-	375 *	4.6	54	-	-	-
Kentucky	4	(D)	-	-	375 *	4.6	94	-	-	-
Massachusetts	4	(D)	-	-	375 *	4.6	94	-	-	-
Kansas	3	(D)	-	-	175 *	2.2	58	-	-	-
New Jersey	3	(D)	-	-	175 *	2.2	58	-	-	-
North Carolina	2	(D)	-	-	175 *	2.2	88	-	-	-
Tennessee	2	(D)	-	-	175 *	2.2	88	-	-	-
Utah	2	(D)	-	-	175 *	2.2	88	-	-	-
West Virginia	2	(D)	-	-	175 *	2.2	88	-	-	-

Source: 1992 *Economic Census*. The states are in descending order of shipments or establishments (if shipment data are missing for the majority). The symbol (D) appears when data are withheld to prevent disclosure of competitive information. States marked with (D) are sorted by number of establishments. A dash (-) indicates that the data element cannot be calculated; * indicates the midpoint of a range.

3299 - NONMETALLIC MINERAL PRODUCTS, NEC

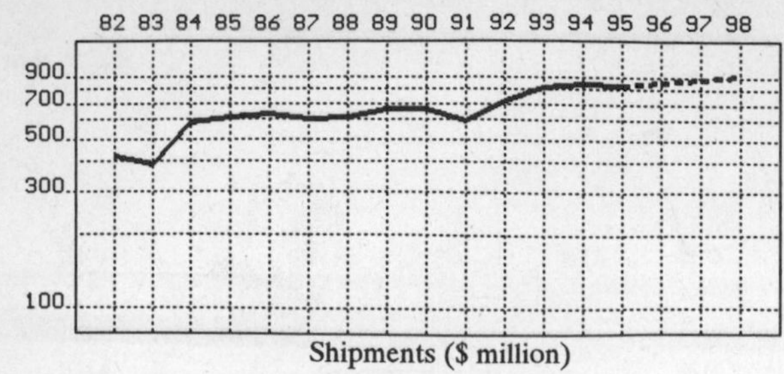

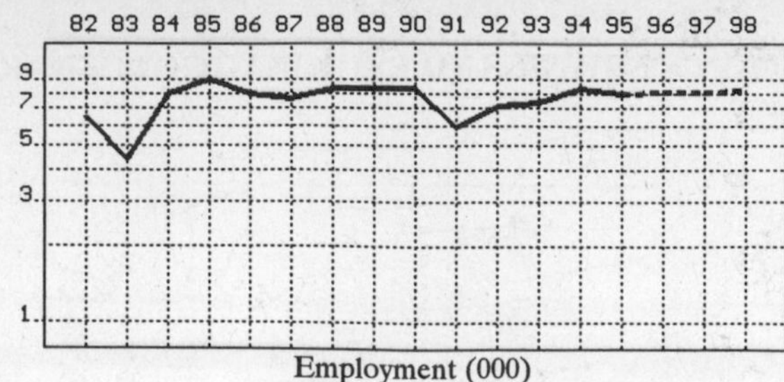

GENERAL STATISTICS

Year	Com-panies	Establishments		Employment			Compensation		Production ($ million)			
		Total	with 20 or more employees	Total (000)	Production Workers (000)	Production Hours (Mil)	Payroll ($ mil)	Wages ($/hr)	Cost of Materials	Value Added by Manufacture	Value of Shipments	Capital Invest.
1982	569	583	67	6.5	4.8	10.0	94.5	6.39	177.7	240.3	422.3	38.3
1983		559	73	4.4	3.7	7.8	84.8	8.19	166.0	232.9	392.3	23.5
1984		535	79	8.0	6.1	12.3	124.0	6.93	217.5	373.5	582.3	28.2
1985		510	86	9.1	7.1	14.0	153.6	7.77	218.2	395.2	606.9	33.0
1986		490	85	8.0	6.1	12.4	152.9	8.61	209.7	420.1	626.2	24.0
1987	534	543	89	7.6	5.7	10.8	134.6	7.86	248.4	351.8	597.1	13.0
1988		508	92	8.3	6.3	12.0	146.9	7.78	235.2	375.2	614.4	11.1
1989		479	100	8.4	5.5	10.8	138.5	8.04	287.0	379.3	659.0	13.6
1990		467	96	8.4	5.5	9.8	145.3	9.20	303.8	376.6	667.2	18.8
1991		460	100	5.9	4.6	8.8	134.7	10.13	255.8	329.7	590.0	11.9
1992	503	510	99	7.1	5.2	10.5	172.8	9.83	257.5	458.3	716.1	20.4
1993		494	94	7.4	5.4	11.0	182.6	10.07	322.4	504.0	821.7	35.2
1994		461P	106P	8.3	6.0	11.9	196.7	9.74	307.9	530.2	833.0	39.4
1995		453P	109P	8.0P	5.7P	10.9P	190.5P	10.41P	305.6P	526.2P	826.8P	22.4P
1996		445P	111P	8.1P	5.7P	10.9P	197.3P	10.68P	316.2P	544.6P	855.6P	22.2P
1997		437P	114P	8.2P	5.7P	10.9P	204.0P	10.95P	326.9P	562.9P	884.4P	21.9P
1998		430P	117P	8.3P	5.7P	10.9P	210.8P	11.23P	337.5P	581.2P	913.2P	21.7P

Sources: 1982, 1987, 1992 *Economic Census*; *Annual Survey of Manufactures*, 83-86, 88-91, 93-94. Establishment counts for non-Census years are from *County Business Patterns*; establishment values for 83-84 are extrapolations. 'P's show projections by the editors. Industries reclassified in 87 will not have data for prior years.

INDICES OF CHANGE

Year	Com-panies	Establishments		Employment			Compensation		Production ($ million)			
		Total	with 20 or more employees	Total (000)	Production Workers (000)	Production Hours (Mil)	Payroll ($ mil)	Wages ($/hr)	Cost of Materials	Value Added by Manufacture	Value of Shipments	Capital Invest.
1982	113	114	68	92	92	95	55	65	69	52	59	188
1983		110	74	62	71	74	49	83	64	51	55	115
1984		105	80	113	117	117	72	70	84	81	81	138
1985		100	87	128	137	133	89	79	85	86	85	162
1986		96	86	113	117	118	88	88	81	92	87	118
1987	106	106	90	107	110	103	78	80	96	77	83	64
1988		100	93	117	121	114	85	79	91	82	86	54
1989		94	101	118	106	103	80	82	111	83	92	67
1990		92	97	118	106	93	84	94	118	82	93	92
1991		90	101	83	88	84	78	103	99	72	82	58
1992	100	100	100	100	100	100	100	100	100	100	100	100
1993		97	95	104	104	105	106	102	125	110	115	173
1994		90P	107P	117	115	113	114	99	120	116	116	193
1995		89P	110P	113P	109P	104P	110P	106P	119P	115P	115P	110P
1996		87P	113P	114P	109P	104P	114P	109P	123P	119P	119P	109P
1997		86P	115P	115P	110P	104P	118P	111P	127P	123P	123P	108P
1998		84P	118P	117P	110P	104P	122P	114P	131P	127P	128P	106P

Sources: Same as General Statistics. Values reflect change from the base year, 1992. Values above 100 mean greater than 92, values below 100 mean less than 92, and a value of 100 in the 82-91 or 93-98 period means same as 92. 'P's mark projections by the editors.

SELECTED RATIOS

For 1994	Avg. of All Manufact.	Analyzed Industry	Index
Employees per Establishment	49	18	37
Payroll per Establishment	1,500,273	426,807	28
Payroll per Employee	30,620	23,699	77
Production Workers per Establishment	34	13	38
Wages per Establishment	853,319	251,497	29
Wages per Production Worker	24,861	19,318	78
Hours per Production Worker	2,056	1,983	96
Wages per Hour	12.09	9.74	81
Value Added per Establishment	4,602,255	1,150,449	25
Value Added per Employee	93,930	63,880	68

For 1994	Avg. of All Manufact.	Analyzed Industry	Index
Value Added per Production Worker	134,084	88,367	66
Cost per Establishment	5,045,178	668,094	13
Cost per Employee	102,970	37,096	36
Cost per Production Worker	146,988	51,317	35
Shipments per Establishment	9,576,895	1,807,476	19
Shipments per Employee	195,460	100,361	51
Shipments per Production Worker	279,017	138,833	50
Investment per Establishment	321,011	85,492	27
Investment per Employee	6,552	4,747	72
Investment per Production Worker	9,352	6,567	70

Sources: Same as General Statistics. The 'Average of All Manufacturing' column represents the average of all manufacturing industries reported for the most recent complete year available. The Index shows the relationship between the Average and the Analyzed Industry. For example, 100 means that they are equal; 500 that the Analyzed Industry is five times the average; 50 means that the Analyzed Industry is half the national average. The abbreviation 'na' is used to show that data are 'not available'.

LEADING COMPANIES

Number shown: **40** Total sales ($ mil): **906** Total employment (000): **8.9**

Company Name	Address				CEO Name	Phone	Co. Type	Sales ($ mil)	Empl. (000)
Carborundum Co	PO Box 337	Niagara Falls	NY	14302	Luiz F Kahl	716-278-2000	S	340	3.2
Hoechst CeramTec	171 Forbes Blv	Mansfield	MA	02048	Rudolf Roell	508-339-1911	S	170	1.8
Channel Technologies Inc	839 Ward Dr	Santa Barbara	CA	93111	RF Carlson	805-967-0171	R	58	0.7
Pabco Insulation	PO Box 1328	Ruston	LA	71270	Herbert Elliott	318-251-2920	D	52	0.5
Tam Ceramics Inc	PO Box 67	Niagara Falls	NY	14305	D Kurtz	716-278-9400	S	52*	0.3
Smithers-Oasis Co	2020 Front St	Cuyahoga Falls	OH	44221	Charles Walton	216-945-5100	R	41*	0.5
Alsimag Technical Ceramics Inc	1 Technology Pl	Laurens	SC	29360	Peter Eichler	803-682-3215	S	24	0.3
Radiation Systems	6200 118th Av N	Largo	FL	34643	Kenneth A Grannan	813-541-6681	D	20	0.1
Wilbanks International Inc	555 NE 53rd Av	Hillsboro	OR	97124	Bill Czaplinski	503-648-3183	S	18*	0.2
Scan-Pac Manufacturing Inc	9950 N Pt Wash	Mequon	WI	53092	Henry A Scandrett	414-241-3890	R	12	0.2
Expo Industries Inc	PO Box 26370	San Diego	CA	92196	Robert Papera	619-566-4343	R	10*	<0.1
Proscotech Industries Inc	1001 W Oak St	Louisville	KY	40210	Rick Fransen	502-585-5866	R	10	<0.1
Smithers-Oasis USA	PO Box 118	Kent	OH	44240	Tom Hession	216-673-5831	S	10*	0.1
Imperial Industries Inc	3009 NW 75th Av	Miami	FL	33122	S Daniel Ponce	305-477-7000	P	8	<0.1
Saxonburg Ceramics Inc	PO Box 688	Saxonburg	PA	16056	Furman South III	412-352-1561	R	8	0.1
La Habra Products Inc	PO Box 3700	Anaheim	CA	92803	Tod Kingsland	714-778-2266	R	7*	<0.1
Boride Products Inc	2879 Aero Park Dr	Traverse City	MI	49684		616-946-2100	S	7	<0.1
Chand Kare Technical Ceramics	2 Coppage Dr	Worcester	MA	01603	Ronald Chand	508-791-9549	R	6*	<0.1
Kaiser Ceramic Composites	880 Doolittle Dr	San Leandro	CA	94577	Brett Able	510-562-2456	J	5	<0.1
Kirkwood Industries	4853 W 130th St	Cleveland	OH	44135	Wayne N Beadnell	216-433-7474	D	5	0.1
Spruce Pine Mica Company Inc	PO Box 219	Spruce Pine	NC	28777	RB Montague	704-765-4241	R	5	<0.1
Cercom Inc	1960 Watson Hwy	Vista	CA	92083	Richard Palicka	619-727-6200	R	4	<0.1
Crystal Systems Inc	27 Congress St	Salem	MA	01970	F Schmid	508-745-0088	R	4	<0.1
Premix Acrocrete Inc	3009 NW 75th Av	Miami	FL	33122	Gary J Hasbach	305-592-5000	S	4*	<0.1
Western Slate Co	PO Box 845	Elmhurst	IL	60126	RC Hanisch	708-279-6660	R	4	<0.1
Acme Limestone Co	PO Drawer 90	Fort Spring	WV	24936	Edwin P Webb	304-647-4443	R	4	<0.1
Merlex Stucco Co	2911 Orange-Olive	Orange	CA	92665	Steve Combs	714-637-1700	R	3*	<0.1
Mykroy-Mycalex	125 Clifton Blv	Clifton	NJ	07011	Donald Seip	201-779-8866	D	3*	<0.1
North American Advanced	120 Sherlake Dr	Knoxville	TN	37922	Samuel C Weaver	615-691-2170	P	3	<0.1
Architectural Reproductions Inc	525 N Tillamook St	Portland	OR	97227	David Talbott	503-284-8007	R	2	<0.1
Bichler Gravel and Concrete	PO Box 263	Escanaba	MI	49829	TL Brayak	906-786-0343	R	2	<0.1
Ceramic Powders Inc	PO Box 2893	Joliet	IL	60434	Herb Toler	815-729-4315	R	2	<0.1
Alberta's Molds Inc	PO Box 2018	Atascadero	CA	93423	James N Gaskell	805-466-9255	R	1*	<0.1
Mission Stucco Company Inc	7751 E 70th St	Paramount	CA	90723	JH Well	310-634-1400	R	1	<0.1
Sacramento Stucco Company Inc	PO Box 1166	W Sacramento	CA	95691	Louis A Winchell Jr	916-372-7442	R	1*	<0.1
California Blended Products	PO Box 628	Canoga Park	CA	91305	Jeff McGinn	818-347-8222	R	1	<0.1
Nanophase Technologies Corp	8205 Cass Av	Darien	IL	60561	Robert W Cross	708-963-0282	R	0	<0.1
Sculptoons Inc	PO Box 91235	Portland	OR	97291	Thomas Gasek	503-292-8001	R	0	<0.1
Architectural Sculpture Ltd	242 Lafayette St	New York	NY	10012	Euclides Pagam	212-431-5873	R	0	<0.1
World Shelter	1545 Wilshire Blv	Los Angeles	CA	90017	Craig Chamberlain	213-483-8300	R	0	<0.1

Source: *Ward's Business Directory of U.S. Private and Public Companies*, Volumes 1 and 2, 1996. The company type code used is as follows: P - Public, R - Private, S - Subsidiary, D - Division, J - Joint Venture, A - Affiliate, G - Group. Sales are in millions of dollars, employees are in thousands. An asterisk (*) indicates an estimated sales volume. The symbol < stands for 'less than'. Company names and addresses are truncated, in some cases, to fit into the available space.

MATERIALS CONSUMED

Material	Quantity	Delivered Cost ($ million)
Materials, ingredients, containers, and supplies	(X)	201.3
Kaolin and ball clay	(X)	(D)
Cotton and manmade fiber fabrics, broadwoven and narrow woven	(X)	0.4
Paper shipping sacks and multiwall bags	(X)	1.4
Other converted paper and paperboard products	(X)	1.8
Other paper and paperboard products	(X)	0.4
Industrial inorganic chemicals	(X)	(D)
Glass fiber, textile type, bonded mat type, etc.	(X)	4.1
Aluminum sheet, plate, foil, and welded tubings	(X)	(D)
All other materials and components, parts, containers, and supplies	(X)	83.1
Materials, ingredients, containers, and supplies, nsk	(X)	85.6

Source: 1992 *Economic Census*. Explanation of symbols used: (D): Withheld to avoid disclosure of competitive data; na: Not available; (S): Withheld because statistical norms were not met; (X): Not applicable; (Z): Less than half the unit shown; nec: Not elsewhere classified; nsk: Not specified by kind; - : zero; * : 10-19 percent estimated; ** : 20-29 percent estimated.

PRODUCT SHARE DETAILS

Product or Product Class	% Share	Product or Product Class	% Share
Nonmetallic mineral products, nec	100.00	production)	17.42
Other nonmetallic mineral built-up sheet mica products	(D)	Other nonmetallic mineral products (magnesite floor composition, stucco, artificial graphite, synthetic stones, etc.)	58.15
Other nonmetallic mineral sheet mica products	(D)		
Other nonmetallic mineral mica products, other than sheet	1.85		
Other nonmetallic mineral statuary and art goods (factory			

Source: 1992 *Economic Census*. The values shown are percent of total shipments in an industry. Values of indented subcategories are summed in the main heading. The symbol (D) appears when data are withheld to prevent disclosure of competitive information. The abbreviation nsk stands for 'not specified by kind' and nec for 'not elsewhere classified'.

INPUTS AND OUTPUTS FOR NONMETALLIC MINERAL PRODUCTS, NEC

Economic Sector or Industry Providing Inputs	%	Sector	Economic Sector or Industry Buying Outputs	%	Sector
Imports	19.9	Foreign	Nonferrous wire drawing & insulating	10.8	Manufg.
Lime	11.1	Manufg.	Fabricated rubber products, nec	10.3	Manufg.
Sand & gravel	8.6	Mining	Exports	9.5	Foreign
Motor freight transportation & warehousing	6.0	Util.	Personal consumption expenditures	8.8	
Railroads & related services	5.9	Util.	Nonferrous castings, nec	7.5	Manufg.
Gas production & distribution (utilities)	5.4	Util.	Motors & generators	4.2	Manufg.
Wholesale trade	4.7	Trade	Industrial buildings	3.7	Constr.
Fabricated metal products, nec	3.9	Manufg.	Coal	3.5	Mining
Nonmetallic mineral products, nec	3.6	Manufg.	Blast furnaces & steel mills	3.1	Manufg.
Cyclic crudes and organics	3.1	Manufg.	Special dies & tools & machine tool accessories	3.0	Manufg.
Electric services (utilities)	2.9	Util.	Wholesale trade	3.0	Trade
Gypsum products	2.8	Manufg.	Jewelers' materials & lapidary work	2.9	Manufg.
Paints & allied products	2.5	Manufg.	Nonmetallic mineral products, nec	2.5	Manufg.
Petroleum refining	2.3	Manufg.	Abrasive products	2.4	Manufg.
Nonmetallic mineral services	1.5	Mining	Cutstone & stone products	2.4	Manufg.
Real estate	1.3	Fin/R.E.	Pens & mechanical pencils	2.3	Manufg.
Advertising	1.3	Services	Motor vehicles & car bodies	1.9	Manufg.
Noncomparable imports	0.9	Foreign	Lead pencils & art goods	1.8	Manufg.
Paperboard containers & boxes	0.7	Manufg.	Oil field machinery	1.8	Manufg.
Communications, except radio & TV	0.7	Util.	Carbon paper & inked ribbons	1.4	Manufg.
Sanitary services, steam supply, irrigation	0.7	Util.	Aircraft	1.3	Manufg.
Eating & drinking places	0.7	Trade	Electrometallurgical products	1.3	Manufg.
Water transportation	0.6	Util.	Asbestos products	1.1	Manufg.
Banking	0.6	Fin/R.E.	Maintenance of nonfarm buildings nec	1.0	Constr.
Maintenance of nonfarm buildings nec	0.5	Constr.	Costume jewelry	0.9	Manufg.
Equipment rental & leasing services	0.5	Services	Dental equipment & supplies	0.9	Manufg.
Industrial inorganic chemicals, nec	0.4	Manufg.	Ball & roller bearings	0.8	Manufg.
Miscellaneous plastics products	0.4	Manufg.	Cyclic crudes and organics	0.8	Manufg.
Adhesives & sealants	0.3	Manufg.	Electron tubes	0.8	Manufg.
Carbon & graphite products	0.3	Manufg.	Metal stampings, nec	0.8	Manufg.
Machinery, except electrical, nec	0.3	Manufg.	Ship building & repairing	0.8	Manufg.
Automotive rental & leasing, without drivers	0.3	Services	Electronic components nec	0.4	Manufg.
Business services nec	0.3	Services	Surgical & medical instruments	0.3	Manufg.
Engineering, architectural, & surveying services	0.3	Services	Farm service facilities	0.2	Constr.
Management & consulting services & labs	0.3	Services	Hand & edge tools, nec	0.2	Manufg.
U.S. Postal Service	0.3	Gov't	Machine tools, metal cutting types	0.2	Manufg.
Abrasive products	0.2	Manufg.	Marking devices	0.2	Manufg.
Glass & glass products, except containers	0.2	Manufg.	Mechanical measuring devices	0.2	Manufg.
Lubricating oils & greases	0.2	Manufg.	Power driven hand tools	0.2	Manufg.
Special dies & tools & machine tool accessories	0.2	Manufg.	Farm housing units & additions & alterations	0.1	Constr.
Air transportation	0.2	Util.	Radio & TV communication equipment	0.1	Manufg.
Insurance carriers	0.2	Fin/R.E.			
Royalties	0.2	Fin/R.E.			
Accounting, auditing & bookkeeping	0.2	Services			
Automotive repair shops & services	0.2	Services			
Business/professional associations	0.2	Services			
Computer & data processing services	0.2	Services			
Legal services	0.2	Services			
Bags, except textile	0.1	Manufg.			
Distilled liquor, except brandy	0.1	Manufg.			
General industrial machinery, nec	0.1	Manufg.			
Manifold business forms	0.1	Manufg.			
Plastics materials & resins	0.1	Manufg.			
Sawmills & planning mills, general	0.1	Manufg.			
Security & commodity brokers	0.1	Fin/R.E.			

Source: Benchmark Input-Output Accounts for the U.S. Economy, 1982, U.S. Department of Commerce, Washington, D.C., July 1991. Data, as reported in the source, are organized by the 1977 SIC structure in use in 1982 but have been matched, as closely as is possible, to the 1987 SIC structure used in this book.

OCCUPATIONS EMPLOYED BY SIC 329 - STONE, CLAY, AND MISC MINING PRODUCTS NEC

Occupation	% of Total 1994	Change to 2005	Occupation	% of Total 1994	Change to 2005
Helpers, laborers, & material movers nec	6.7	-23.3	Machine feeders & offbearers	2.3	-31.4
Assemblers, fabricators, & hand workers nec	6.4	-23.9	Painting, coating, & decorating workers, hand	2.0	52.3
Furnace, kiln, or kettle operators	4.2	-16.7	Freight, stock, & material movers, hand	1.9	-38.8
Crushing & mixing machine operators	3.9	-9.5	Truck drivers light & heavy	1.9	-20.6
Industrial machinery mechanics	3.9	-15.2	Coating, painting, & spraying machine workers	1.8	-23.8
Hand packers & packagers	3.6	-34.7	Secretaries, ex legal & medical	1.8	-30.4
Extruding & forming machine workers	3.4	-80.6	Cutting & slicing machine setters, operators	1.6	-16.2
Sales & related workers nec	3.2	-23.6	Grinders & polishers, hand	1.6	-16.2
Packaging & filling machine operators	3.2	-23.7	Industrial production managers	1.5	-23.5
Precision workers nec	3.0	-8.7	Traffic, shipping, & receiving clerks	1.5	-26.6
Industrial truck & tractor operators	2.8	-23.7	General office clerks	1.5	-34.9
General managers & top executives	2.8	-27.5	Bookkeeping, accounting, & auditing clerks	1.3	-42.7
Inspectors, testers, & graders, precision	2.8	-23.6	Electricians	1.1	-27.3
Maintenance repairers, general utility	2.6	-30.8	Machinists	1.0	-23.6

Source: Industry-Occupation Matrix, Bureau of Labor Statistics. These data relate to one or more 3-digit SIC industry groups rather than to a single 4-digit SIC. The change reported for each occupation to the year 2005 is a percent of growth or decline as estimated by the Bureau of Labor Statistics. The abbreviation nec stands for 'not elsewhere classified'.

LOCATION BY STATE AND REGIONAL CONCENTRATION

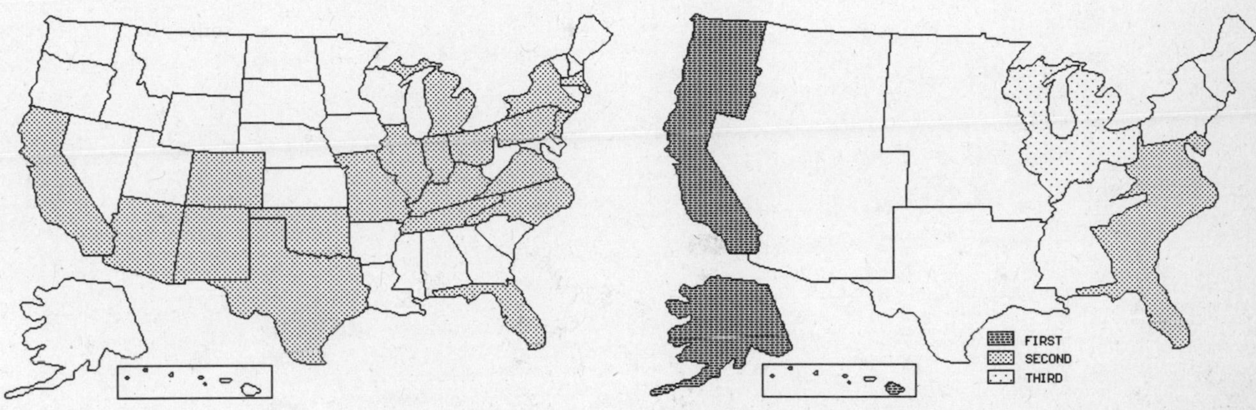

INDUSTRY DATA BY STATE

State	Establish-ments	Shipments			Employment				Cost as % of Shipments	Investment per Employee ($)
		Total ($ mil)	% of U.S.	Per Establ.	Total Number	% of U.S.	Per Establ.	Wages ($/hour)		
California	84	108.4	15.1	1.3	1,200	16.9	14	9.67	37.5	-
New York	20	71.0	9.9	3.5	500	7.0	25	10.87	35.6	1,000
Illinois	22	58.4	8.2	2.7	900	12.7	41	8.64	33.7	1,222
Texas	37	35.8	5.0	1.0	300	4.2	8	8.80	35.5	-
Florida	49	28.5	4.0	0.6	400	5.6	8	7.00	44.6	1,500
Massachusetts	16	25.3	3.5	1.6	200	2.8	13	12.00	28.9	23,000
Oklahoma	11	23.0	3.2	2.1	100	1.4	9	11.50	42.6	3,000
Indiana	5	19.7	2.8	3.9	100	1.4	20	13.00	58.9	7,000
New Mexico	9	15.9	2.2	1.8	200	2.8	22	9.00	44.0	-
Kentucky	12	15.8	2.2	1.3	200	2.8	17	8.50	35.4	1,500
Tennessee	13	11.1	1.6	0.9	200	2.8	15	6.67	45.9	1,000
Arizona	12	10.9	1.5	0.9	100	1.4	8	7.00	46.8	2,000
Missouri	16	8.3	1.2	0.5	200	2.8	13	8.50	39.8	1,000
Colorado	9	6.9	1.0	0.8	100	1.4	11	6.50	50.7	-
Ohio	22	(D)	-	-	375 *	5.3	17	-	-	-
Pennsylvania	22	(D)	-	-	175 *	2.5	8	-	-	-
Michigan	16	(D)	-	-	175 *	2.5	11	-	-	-
New Jersey	16	(D)	-	-	175 *	2.5	11	-	-	2,857
North Carolina	12	(D)	-	-	375 *	5.3	31	-	-	-
Virginia	10	(D)	-	-	375 *	5.3	38	-	-	-

Source: 1992 *Economic Census*. The states are in descending order of shipments or establishments (if shipment data are missing for the majority). The symbol (D) appears when data are withheld to prevent disclosure of competitive information. States marked with (D) are sorted by number of establishments. A dash (-) indicates that the data element cannot be calculated; * indicates the midpoint of a range.